CONTENTS
ÍNDICE

Project Management
Direção da obra
Luzia Araújo　Valerie Grundy

Editors
Redação
Alison Aiken　Maria Inês Alves
Laura Bocco　Shirley Brotherton-Pinniger
Salete Cechin　Karoll Ferreira
José A. Gálvez　Daniel Grassi
Mike Harland　Bill Martin
Viviane Possamai　Julia Rice
Christine Robinson　Sergio Tellaroli

Publishing Manager
Direção Geral
Janice McNeillie

Prepress
Diagramação
David Reid　Sharon McTeir

PREFACE

This CONCISE dictionary is a reliable and user-friendly tool for use in all language situations. It provides accurate and up-to-date information on written and spoken Portuguese and English as they are used today.

Its 90,000 words and phrases and 120,000 translations give you access to Portuguese texts of all types. The dictionary aims to be as comprehensive as possible in a book of this size, and includes many proper names and abbreviations, as well as a selection of the most common terms from computing, business and currents affairs.

Carefully construced entries and a clear page design help you to find the translation that you are looking for fast. Examples (from basic constructions and common phrases to idioms) have been included to help put a word in context and give a clear picture of how it is used.

The dictionary provides extra help for students of Portuguese with the inclusion of boxes on life and culture in Brazil that appear within the dictionary text itself, and a central section which gives fuller background details on political and cultural life in Brazil, as well as a useful communication guide.

A NOSSOS LEITORES

Este Dicionário AVANÇADO é a ferramenta de consulta ideal para toda uma gama de situações que vão da aprendizagem de uma língua estrangeira, em casa ou na escola, até as necessidades cotidianas no trabalho.

O Dicionário AVANÇADO Inglês-Português foi desenvolvido para responder com rapidez e eficiência às dificuldades com que nos defrontamos na leitura do inglês contemporâneo, bem como na redação de trabalhos escolares, cartas e relatórios.

Com suas mais de 90 mil palavras e expressões – e um número de traduções superior a 120 mil –, este dicionário permitirá ao leitor compreender com clareza toda uma variedade de textos, desde obras literárias e artigos jornalísticos até documentos comerciais, folhetos e manuais, possibilitando a realização de resumos e traduções com eficácia e apuro.

A atualidade das siglas e abreviações, bem como dos termos comerciais e de informática aqui incluídos, é outro fator a atestar a abrangência e contemporaneidade deste dicionário.

Valendo-se do tratamento claro e detalhado dado aqui ao vocabulário básico, dos muitos exemplos de construções gramaticais e de uso mais atualizado da língua, bem como dos indicadores de contexto a conduzir à tradução mais adequada, o usuário deste Dicionário AVANÇADO poderá expressar-se em inglês com precisão e segurança.

Especial atenção foi dedicada também à apresentação de cada entrada, tanto do ponto de vista de sua estrutura quanto da tipologia empregada, visando a facilitar a consulta e o entendimento.

Aliando precisão e praticidade, profundidade de conteúdo e facilidade de consulta, o Dicionário AVANÇADO é a obra ideal para todos aqueles que já superaram os níveis iniciais de aprendizagem da língua inglesa, demandando para o seu cotidiano – na escola, em casa ou no trabalho – um dicionário prático, mas abrangente.

ABREVIATURAS		ABBREVIATIONS
abreviatura	*abrev/abbr*	abbreviation
adjetivo	*adj*	adjective
advérbio	*adv*	adverb
antes de substantivo	*antes de subst*	before noun
artigo	*art*	article
auxiliar	*aux*	auxiliary
comparativo	*compar*	comparative
conjunção	*conj*	conjuction
contínuo	*cont*	continuous
definido	*def*	definite
demonstrativo	*dem/demos*	demonstrative
especialmente	*esp*	especially
interjeição	*excl*	exclamation
substantivo feminino	*f*	feminine noun
familiar	*fam*	informal
figurado	*fig*	figurative
formal	*fml*	formal
inseparável	*fus*	inseparable
geralmente	*ger/gen*	generally
humorístico	*hum*	humorous
indefinido	*indef*	indefinite
familiar	*inf*	informal
interjeição	*interj*	exclamation
invariável	*inv*	invariable
irônico	*irôn/iro*	ironic
literal	*lit*	literal
locução	*loc*	phrase
substantivo masculino	*m*	masculine noun
substantivo	*n*	noun
numeral	*num*	numeral
	o.s.	oneself
pejorativo	*pej*	pejorative
pessoal	*pess/pers*	personal
plural	*pl*	plural
possessivo	*poss*	possessive
particípio passado	*pp*	past participle
preposição	*prep*	preposition
pronome	*pron*	pronoun
passado	*pt*	past tense
marca registrada	®	registered trademark
relativo	*relat*	relative
substantivo	*s*	noun
	sb	someone, somebody
separável	*sep*	separable
singular	*sg*	singular
gíria	*sl*	slang
	sthg	something
sujeito	*suj/subj*	subject
superlativo	*superl*	superlative
substantivo incontável	*U*	uncountable noun

ABREVIATURAS		ABBREVIATIONS
inglês britânico	*UK*	British English
inglês americano	*US*	American English
verbo	*v/vb*	verb
verbo intransitivo	*vi*	intransitive verb
verbo impessoal	*v impess/impers*	impersonal verb
verbo pronominal	*vpr*	pronominal verb
verbo transitivo	*vt*	transitive verb
vulgar	*vulg*	vulgar
equivalente cultural	≃	cultural equivalent

CAMPOS SEMÂNTICOS		FIELD LABELS
administração	**ADMIN**	administration
aeronáutica	**AERON**	aeronautics
agricultura	**AGR**	agriculture
anatomia	**ANAT**	anatomy
arqueologia	**ARCHEOL**	archeology
arquitetura	**ARQUIT/ARCHIT**	architecture
astrologia	**ASTROL**	astrology
astronomia	**ASTRON**	astronomy
automóveis	**AUT(O)**	automobiles, cars
biologia	**BIOL**	biology
botânica	**BOT**	botany
química	**CHEM**	chemistry
ciências	**CIÊN/SCIENCE**	science
cinema	**CINE(MA)**	cinema
comércio	**COM(M)**	commerce
informática	**COMPUT**	information technology
construção	**CONSTR**	construction, building
costura	**COST**	sewing
culinária	**CULIN**	culinary, cooking
ecologia	**ECOLOG**	ecology
economia	**ECON**	economy
educação, escola	**EDUC**	education, school
eletricidade, eletrônica	**ELETR/ELEC**	electricity, electronics
esporte	**ESP**	sport
farmacologia	**FARM**	pharmacology
finanças	**FIN**	finance
física	**FÍS**	physics
fotografia	**FOTO**	photography
geografia	**GEOGR**	geography
geologia	**GEOL**	geology
geometria	**GEOM**	geometry
gramática	**GRAM(M)**	grammar
história	**HIST**	history
indústria	**IND**	industry
jornalismo	**JORN**	journalism
jurídico	**JUR**	juridical, legal
lingüística	**LING**	linguistics
literatura	**LITER**	literature
matemática	**MAT(H)**	mathematics
mecânica	**MEC**	mechanical engineering
medicina	**MED**	medicine
metalurgia	**METAL**	metallurgy
meteorologia	**METEOR**	meteorology
militar	**MIL**	military
mineralogia	**MIN**	mineralogy
mitologia	**MITOL/MYTH**	mythology
música	**MÚS/MUS**	music
náutica	**NAUT**	nautical
farmacologia	**PHARM**	pharmacology
fotografia	**PHOT**	photography
física	**PHYS**	physics
política	**POL(ÍT)**	politics
psicologia	**PSICOL/PSYCH**	psychology
química	**QUÍM**	chemistry
ferrovia	**RAIL**	railways
religião	**RELIG**	religion
escola	**SCH**	school
sociologia	**SOCIOL**	sociology

CAMPOS SEMÂNTICOS		FIELD LABELS
bolsa de valores	**ST EX**	stock exchange
teatro	**TEATR/THEAT**	theatre
técnico, tecnologia	**TEC/TECH**	technical, technology
telecomunicações	**TELEC**	telecommunications
tipografia	**TIP/TYP**	printing, typography
televisão	**TV**	television
universidade	**UNIV**	university
veterinária	**VETER**	veterinary science
zoologia	**ZOOL**	zoology

FONÉTICA

Vogais portuguesas

[a] **pá** cada
[ɛ] **sé**, seta, hera
[e] ler mês
[i] **ir**, sino, nave
[ɔ] nota, **pó**
[o] corvo, avô
[u] az**u**l, tribo

Ditongos portugueses

[aj] f**ai**xa, m**ai**s
[ej] l**ei**te, r**ei**
[ɛj] hot**éi**s, past**éi**s
[ɔj] her**ói**, b**ói**a
[oj] c**oi**sa, n**oi**te
[uj] az**ui**s, f**ui**
[aw] n**au**, j**au**la
[ɛw] c**éu**, v**éu**
[ew] d**eu**s, s**eu**
[iw] r**iu**, v**iu**

Vogais nasais

[ã] maç**ã**, s**an**to
[ẽ] l**en**çol, s**em**pre
[ĩ] f**im**, pat**im**
[õ] **on**de, c**om**, h**on**ra
[ũ] jej**um**, n**un**ca

Ditongos nasais

[ãj] c**ãi**bra, m**ãe**
[ãw] camar**ão**, c**ão**
[ẽj] b**em**, qu**em**
[õj] cord**õe**s, le**õe**s

Semivogais portuguesas

[j] elei**t**o, ma**i**o
[w] l**u**ar, q**u**adro

Consoantes

[b] **b**eijo, a**b**rir
[d] **d**ama, pren**d**a

PHONETICS

English vowels

[ɪ] p**i**t, b**i**g, r**i**d
[e] p**e**t, t**e**nd
[æ] p**a**t, b**a**g, m**a**d
[ʌ] r**u**n, c**u**t
[ɒ] p**o**t, l**o**g
[ʊ] p**u**t, f**u**ll
[ə] moth**e**r, s**u**ppose
[iː] b**ea**n, w**ee**d
[aː] b**ar**n, c**ar**
[ɔː] b**or**n, l**aw**n
[uː] l**oo**p, l**oo**se
[ɜː] b**ur**n, l**ear**n, b**ir**d

English dipthongs

[eɪ] b**ay**, l**a**te, gr**ea**t
[aɪ] b**uy**, l**igh**t, **ais**le
[ɔɪ] b**oy**, f**oi**l
[əʊ] n**o**, r**oa**d, bl**ow**
[aʊ] n**ow**, sh**ou**t, t**ow**n
[ɪə] p**ee**r, f**ie**rce, id**ea**
[eə] p**ai**r, b**ea**r, sh**are**
[ʊə] s**ur**e, t**our**

English semi-vowels

[j] **y**ou, spani**e**l
[w] **w**et, **w**hy, t**w**in

English consonants

[p] **p**o**p**, **p**eo**p**le
[b] **b**ottle, **b**i**b**

[dʒ]	**d**ia, bon**d**e
[f]	**f**aca, a**f**inal
[g]	**g**rande, a**g**ora
[ʒ]	**g**elo, ci**s**ne, an**j**o
[l]	**l**ata, fe**l**iz, co**l**a
[ʎ]	ma**lh**a, te**lh**a
[m]	**m**esa, ca**m**a
[n]	**n**ada, ba**n**a**n**a
[ɲ]	li**nh**a, so**nh**o
[ŋ]	a**n**ca, i**n**glês
[p]	**p**ão, gri**p**e
[s]	**c**ima, de**ss**e, ca**ç**a
[ʃ]	no**z**, bi**s**, cai**x**a, **ch**á
[t]	**t**ema, la**t**a, por**t**a
[tʃ]	**t**io, infan**t**il
[v]	**v**ela, a**v**e
[x]	**r**ádio, te**rr**a
[z]	**z**elo, bri**s**a

[t]	**t**rain, **t**ip
[d]	**d**og, **did**
[k]	**c**ome, **k**itchen
[g]	**g**a**g**, **g**reat
[tʃ]	**ch**ain, wre**tch**ed
[dʒ]	**j**et, fri**dge**
[f]	**f**ib, **ph**ysical
[v]	**v**ine, li**v**e
[θ]	**th**ink, fif**th**
[ð]	**th**is, wi**th**
[s]	**s**eal, pea**c**e
[z]	**z**ip, hi**s**
[ʃ]	**sh**eep, ma**ch**ine
[ʒ]	u**s**ual, mea**s**ure
[h]	**h**ow, per**h**aps
[m]	**m**etal, co**mb**
[n]	**n**ight, di**nn**er
[ŋ]	su**ng**, parki**ng**
[l]	**l**ittle, he**l**p
[r]	**r**ight, ca**rr**y

O símbolo fonético [(x)] em português indica que o 'r' final da palavra é apenas levemente pronunciado, exceto quando seguido de uma vogal: nesse caso, pronuncia-se [r].

O símbolo ['] indica que a sílaba subseqüente é a tônica, sobre a qual recai o acento principal; [ˌ] indica que a sílaba subseqüente é a subtônica, sobre a qual recai o acento secundário.

As regras de pronúncia aplicadas ao português refletem a língua falada no Rio de Janeiro.

The symbol [(x)] in Portuguese phonetics indicates that final 'r' is often barely sounded unless it is followed by a word beginning with a vowel, in which case it is pronounced [r].

The symbol ['] indicates that the following syllable carries primary stress and [ˌ] that the following syllable carries secondary stress.

Portuguese phonetics reflect the language as spoken in Rio de Janeiro.

Como encontrar a palavra ou expressão que procuramos?

A primeira coisa a fazer é perguntar:

Trata-se de uma palavra ou de uma abreviatura?
Seria um substantivo composto?
Uma expressão ou locução?
Trata-se de um verbo pronominal ou *phrasal verb*?

Palavras e abreviaturas

Em geral, encontraremos a palavra que procuramos no lugar que lhe corresponde na ordem alfabética. Se desejamos a tradução para o português de uma palavra inglesa, consultamos a parte inglês-português do dicionário; se desconhecemos o sentido de uma palavra do português, procuraremos por sua tradução na parte português-inglês. A palavra em **negrito**, que aparece no início de cada verbete do dicionário, chama-se "entrada".

Se duas palavras são escritas de forma idêntica, mas uma delas começa com **maiúscula**, a palavra em maiúscula aparecerá depois daquela que começa com letra minúscula.

> **ad** (*abbr of* **advertisement**) *n fam* **-1.** [in newspaper] anúncio *m.* **-2.** [on TV] propaganda *f.*
> **AD** (*abbr of* **Anno Domini**) d.C.

Palavras contendo **hífen, apóstrofe** ou **ponto** aparecem depois daquelas de mesma grafia, mas que não apresentam esses sinais gráficos.

> **its** [ɪts] *poss adj* o seu (a sua), dele (dela).
> **it's** [ɪts] = **it is, it has**.

Da mesma forma, uma palavra com **acento** figurará depois de outra de mesma grafia, mas sem acento.

> **do** [du] = **de + o**.
> **dó** ['dɔ] *m* **-1.** [piedade] pity; **ter ~ de alguém** to take pity on sb. **-2.** *MÚS* doh.

Em alguns casos, as entradas são seguidas de um pequeno **número sobrescrito**. Isso quer dizer que, imediatamente antes ou após, haverá outra entrada idêntica, também seguida de um número, mas com significado ou pronúncia diferente. São os chamados homógrafos. Atenção: certifique-se de não estar consultando a entrada errada! É necessário prestar muita atenção à categoria gramatical.

> **bow**[1] [baʊ] <> *n* **-1.** [act of bowing] reverência *f* **-2.** [of ship] proa *f.* <> *vt* [lower] inclinar. <> *vi* **-1.** [make a bow] inclinar-se **-2.** [defer]: **to ~ to sthg** submeter-se a algo.
> ◆ **bow down** *vi* [give in]: **to ~ down (to sb)** render-se(a alguém).
> ◆ **bow out** *vi* afastar-se.
> **bow**[2] [bəʊ] *n* **-1.** [gen & *MUS*] arco *m* **-2.** [knot] laço *m.*

Às vezes, vamos encontrar palavras precedidas de um losango negro (◆), chamadas "sub-entradas". Um exemplo disso são os verbos pronominais do português ou os *phrasal verbs* ingleses. Além disso, se buscamos uma palavra que possui duas formas, maiúscula e minúscula, com significados diferentes, nós encontraremos a forma em maiúscula como sub-entrada daquela em minúscula, precedida de um losango negro.

> **beneficiar** [16] [benefi'sja(x)] *vt* **-1.** [favorecer] to benefit. **-2.** [processar] to process. **-3.** [melhorar] to improve.
> ◆ **beneficiar-se** *vp* [favorecer-se] to profit.

> **ascension** [ə'senʃn] *n* [to throne] ascensão *f.*
> ◆ **Ascension** *n RELIG* Ascensão *f.*

Da mesma forma, se procuramos um substantivo cuja forma plural possui um significado distinto do singular (como **glass/glasses** em inglês; ou **bem/bens**, em português), encontraremos a palavra no plural como sub-entrada da forma singular, precedida do símbolo (◆).

glass [glɑ:s] ◇ *n* **-1.** *(U)* [material] vidro *m* **-2.** [for drinking] copo *m* **-3.** *(U)* [glassware] objetos *mpl* de cristal. ◇ *comp* de vidro.
◆ **glasses** *npl* [spectacles] óculos *m inv*; [binoculars] binóculos *mpl*.

Alguns substantivos aparecem como entradas já no plural, seja porque não existem no singular ou porque a forma singular é pouco freqüente. É o caso, por exemplo, de **scissors**, em inglês, ou **juros**, em português.

Substantivos compostos

O substantivo composto é uma expressão que, como tal, possui um significado próprio, mas que se compõe de mais de uma palavra (**virtual reality**, por exemplo, ou **café com leite**). Os substantivos compostos poderão ser encontrados na entrada correspondente a seu primeiro elemento. Assim sendo, **café com leite** aparecerá em **café**. Os demais compostos com o substantivo **café** como primeiro elemento - **café expresso**, **café pingado** - figuram em ordem alfabética.

café [ka'fɛ] *m* **-1.** [ger] coffee; ~ **(preto)** black coffee; ~ **com leite** white coffee *UK*, coffee with cream *US*; ~ **expresso** espresso; ~ **pingado** *coffee with a tiny drop of milk*; **ser ~ pequeno** *fam* [tarefa] to be small beer; [pessoa] to be small fry. **-2.** [desjejum]: ~ **(da manhã)** breakfast. **-3.** [estabelecimento] café.

blood count *n* contagem *f* de glóbulos sangüíneos.
blood-curdling *adj* de gelar o sangue.
blood donor *n* doador *m*, -ra *f* de sangue.

No caso dos substantivos compostos do inglês, é característica deste dicionário listá-los como entradas, em ordem alfabética. Assim, **blood donor** aparecerá depois de **blood-curdling**, que, por sua vez, sucede a **blood count**.

Se o composto, seja em inglês ou português, se tornou uma unidade autônoma - isto é, se seu significado conjunto já se destacou da soma de seus elementos -, ele é tratado à parte, sendo precedido de um losango negro.

Expressões e locuções

Expressões e locuções devem ser localizadas a partir do primeiro substantivo que as forma. Se a expressão não possui um substantivo, deve-se procurá-la pelo adjetivo ou, na ausência deste, pelo verbo. No interior de cada verbete, as expressões aparecem em **negrito**, com o símbolo ~ representando a entrada correspondente.

time [taɪm] ◇ *n* **-1.** *(U)* [general measurement, spell] tempo *m*; **to get the ~ to do sthg** ter tempo para fazer algo; **to take ~** levar tempo; **to take ~ out to do sthg** tirar tempo para fazer algo; **it's high ~ ...** já é hora de ...; **to get ~ and a half** receber o pagamento combinado mais a metade; **to have no ~ for sb/sthg** não ter tempo a perder com alguém/algo; **to make good ~** fazer uma boa média (de tempo); **to pass the ~** passar o tempo; **to play for ~** tentar ganhar tempo; **to take one's ~ (doing sthg)** dar-se seu tempo(para fazer algo)...

Algumas expressões de significado e valor gramatical próprio (as chamadas locuções), como **in spite of** (inglês) ou **atrás de** (português), figuram vinculadas a seu primeiro elemento importante, precedidas do símbolo (◆).

spite [spaɪt] ◇ *n (U)* rancor *m*; **to do sthg out of** OR **from ~** fazer algo por maldade. ◇ *vt* magoar.
◆ **in spite of** *prep* apesar de; **to do sthg in ~ of o.s.** [unintentionally] fazer algo a contragosto.

Isso possibilita destacar a diferença de sentido e função gramatical entre a locução em si e a entrada à qual ela está vinculada.

atrás [a'trajʃ] *adv* **-1.** [posição] behind; **lá ~** back there. **-2.** [no tempo] ago. **-3.** [em classificação]: **estar/ficar ~ (de)** to be ranked behind; **não ficar ~** *fam fig* not to be far behind.
◆ **atrás de** *loc prep* **-1.** [posição] behind. **-2.** [em seguimento a] after; **logo ~ de** right behind. **-3.** [em busca de - pessoa] after; [- objeto, explicação] looking for.

Verbos pronominais e *phrasal verbs*

A maioria dos verbos pronominais e *phrasal verbs* apresenta-se na entrada correspondente ao verbo em questão, precedida do símbolo (◆).

> **aclarar** [4] [akla'ra(x)] *vt* [questão, mistério] to clarify.
> ◆ **aclarar-se** *vp* to become clear.

Informações culturais

Para entender e falar melhor uma língua estrangeira, é necessário algum conhecimento acerca das especificidades culturais do(s) país(es) onde ela é falada. Contudo, uma entrada de dicionário não é o local apropriado para esse tipo de informação. Assim sendo, na parte inglês-português deste dicionário, o leitor de língua portuguesa encontrará **boxes** informativos dedicados a particularidades culturais dos países de língua inglesa.

> **GUY FAWKES NIGHT**
>
> Festividade britânica celebrada na noite de 5 de novembro, em comemoração ao complô católico encabeçado por Guy Fawkes, em 1605, que tinha por objetivo explodir as casas do Parlamento. Nessa noite, os britânicos acendem fogueiras, nas quais queimam uma efígie de Guy Fawkes, e soltam fogos de artifício, razão pela qual a noite é também conhecida como *Fireworks Night* ou *Bonfire Night*.

O box **Guy Fawkes' Night**, por exemplo, nos informa sobre uma peculiaridade histórico-cultural britânica para a qual não há equivalente no Brasil.

How to find the word or expression you are looking for:

First ask yourself some basic questions:

Is it a single word, a hyphenated word or an abbreviation?
Is it a compound noun?
Is it a phrase?
Is it a reflexive verb?

Single words, hyphenated words and abbreviations

As a rule, you can find the word you are looking for in its alphabetical order. If you want to translate an English word into Portuguese, you should look on the English–Portuguese side of the dictionary, and if you want to know what a Portuguese term means, you should look on the Portuguese–English side. The word in **bold** at the start of each entry is called the 'headword'.

Entries beginning with a **capital** appear after those spelled the same way but with a small letter.

> **ad** (*abbr of* **advertisement**) *n fam* **-1.** [in newspaper] anúncio *m.* **-2.** [on TV] propaganda *f.*
> **AD** (*abbr of* **Anno Domini**) d.C.

Words with a **hyphen**, a **full stop** or an **apostrophe** come after those spelled the same way but without any of these punctuation marks.

> **its** [ɪts] *poss adj* o seu (a sua), dele (dela).
> **it's** [ɪts] = **it is**, **it has**.

In some cases, the entry is followed by a number in **superscript**. This means that just before or just after there is another entry, also followed by a number, which is written the same way but which has a completely different meaning or pronunciation. You must take care not to choose the wrong entry.

> **bow**[1] [baʊ] ◇ *n* **-1.** [act of bowing] reverência *f* **-2.** [of ship] proa *f.* ◇ *vt* [lower] inclinar. ◇ *vi* **-1.** [make a bow] inclinar-se **-2.** [defer]: **to ~ to sthg** submeter-se a algo.
> ◆ **bow down** *vi* [give in]: **to ~ down (to sb)** render-se(a alguém).
> ◆ **bow out** *vi* afastar-se.
> **bow**[2] [bəʊ] *n* **-1.** [gen & MUS] arco *m* **-2.** [knot] laço *m.*

You will sometimes see words followed by a grey lozenge, called sub-entries. English phrasal verbs and Portuguese pronominal verbs fall into this category.

> **beneficiar** [16] [benefi'sja(x)] *vt* **-1.** [favorecer] to benefit. **-2.** [processar] to process. **-3.** [melhorar] to improve.
> ◆ **beneficiar-se** *vp* [favorecer-se] to profit.

If you are looking up a noun which has a form with an initial capital which has a different meaning from the form without a capital, you should look at the form without a capital.

> **ascension** [ə'senʃn] *n* [to throne] ascensão *f.*
> ◆ **Ascension** *n* RELIG Ascensão *f.*

If you are looking up a noun which, in the plural, has a different meaning from the noun in its singular form (like **glass/glasses** in English), you will find it under the singular form; the plural form will be there as a sub-entry, indicated by the symbol ◆.

glass [glɑːs] ◇ *n* **-1.** *(U)* [material] vidro *m* **-2.** [for drinking] copo *m* **-3.** *(U)* [glassware] objetos *mpl* de cristal. ◇ *comp* de vidro.
◆ **glasses** *npl* [spectacles] óculos *m inv*; [binoculars] binóculos *mpl*.

Some plural nouns appear as headwords in their own right when they are never or rarely used in the singular (e.g. **juros** in Portuguese, **scissors** in English).

Compound nouns

A compound is a word or expression which has a single meaning but is made up of more than one word, e.g. **point of order, kiss of life, virtual reality, International Monetary Fund**.

It is a feature of this dictionary that English compounds appear in the A–Z list in strict alphabetical order. The compound **blood donor** will therefore come after **blood-curdling** which itself follows **blood count**.

blood count *n* contagem *f* de glóbulos sangüíneos.
blood-curdling *adj* de gelar o sangue.
blood donor *n* doador *m*, -ra *f* de sangue.

On the Portuguese-English side however you should look under the first element of the compound. So, for example, you will find **café com leite** at the entry **café.** If there is more than one compound within an entry they will appear in their alphabetical order within the entry, regardless of any preposition between the two parts of the compound. So at **café** you will find **café pingado** after **café expresso**.

Phrases

If looking for a phrase, you should look first under the noun that is used in the phrase. If there is no noun, then you should look under the adjective, and if there is no adjective, under the verb. Phrases appear in entries in bold, the symbol ~ standing for the headword.

time [taɪm] ◇ *n* **-1.** *(U)* [general measurement, spell] tempo *m*; **to get the ~ to do sthg** ter tempo para fazer algo; **to take ~** levar tempo; **to take ~ out to do sthg** tirar tempo para fazer algo; **it's high ~ ...** já é hora de ...; **to get ~ and a half** receber o pagamento combinado mais a metade; **to have no ~ for sb/sthg** não ter tempo a perder com alguém/algo; **to make good ~** fazer uma boa média (de tempo); **to pass the ~** passar o tempo; **to play for ~** tentar ganhar tempo; **to take one's ~ (doing sthg)** dar-se seu tempo(para fazer algo)...

Some very fixed phrases like **in spite of** in English or **atrás de** in Portuguese are entered under the first important element and preceded by ◆.

spite [spaɪt] ◇ *n (U)* rancor *m*; **to do sthg out of** *OR* **from ~** fazer algo por maldade. ◇ *vt* magoar.
◆ **in spite of** *prep* apesar de; **to do sthg in ~ of o.s.** [unintentionally] fazer algo a contragosto.

atrás [a'trajʃ] *adv* **-1.** [posição] behind; **lá ~** back there. **-2.** [no tempo] ago. **-3.** [em classificação]**: estar/ficar ~ (de)** to be ranked behind; **não ficar ~** *fam fig* not to be far behind.
◆ **atrás de** *loc prep* **-1.** [posição] behind. **-2.** [em seguimento a] after; **logo ~ de** right behind. **-3.** [em busca de - pessoa] after; [- objeto, explicação] looking for.

Reflexive verbs

Portuguese reflexive verbs are entered under the main form, after the symbol ◆.

aclarar [4] [akla'ra(x)] *vt* [questão, mistério] to clarify.
◆ **aclarar-se** *vp* to become clear.

Cultural information

An appreciation of the culture of a foreign country is key to being able to understand and speak its language well. Cultural information on Brazil is provided in this dictionary in boxes on the Portuguese–English side of the dictionary.

BOSSA NOVA

Musical movement born in Rio de Janeiro in the late 50s; the bossa nova revolutionized the samba, condensing its rhythmic wealth into a syncopated beat with polished jazz chords for piano and guitar. The bossa nova's delicate melody and subtle song were to have a great influence on western popular music through two of the art form's greatest exponents, Tom Jobim and João Gilberto.

TRADEMARKS

Words considered to be trademarks are marked with the symbol ®. However, neither the presence nor the absence of such designation should be regarded as affecting the legal status of any trademark.

MARCAS REGISTRADAS

O símbolo ® indica que a palavra em questão é uma marca registrada. Este símbolo, ou a sua eventual ausência, não afeta, no entanto, a situação legal da marca.

PORTUGUESE VERBS

Portuguese verbs have a number, which refers to the conjugation table given at the back of the dictionary. This number is not repeated for reflexive verbs when they are sub-entries.

VERBOS PORTUGUESES

Os verbos portugueses são seguidos de um número que remete à tabela de conjugação, ao final do dicionário. Esse número não se repete nos verbos pronominais tratados como sub-entrada.

LIST OF BRAZILIAN CULTURAL BOXES
LISTA DE BOXES CULTURAIS BRASILEIROS

AFOXÉS
AMAZÔNIA
BAHIA
BIODIVERSIDADE
BOSSA NOVA
BRASÍLIA
CACHAÇA
CAFÉ
CAIPIRINHA
CANDOMBLÉ
CAPOEIRA
CARNAVAL
CATARATAS DO IGUAÇU
CHORO
CORDEL
DITADURA MILITAR
ESPORTES
FAVELAS
FEIJOADA
FERNANDO DE NORONHA
FESTAS JUNINAS
FUTEBOL
GENOMA
GUARANÁ
ILHAS
JEITINHO BRASILEIRO
LÍNGUA PORTUGUESA
LITERATURA BRASILEIRA
MERCOSUL
MISTURA DE RAÇAS
MOEDA
MÚSICA
OURO PRETO
PANTANAL
PATRIMÔNIOS CULTURAIS
PAU-BRASIL
POROROCA
RIO DE JANEIRO
SAMBA
SANTOS-DUMONT
SÃO FRANCISCO
SECA
TELENOVELAS
TROPICALISMO
TUPI
VESTIBULAR

LISTA DE BOXES CULTURAIS INGLESES
LIST OF ENGLISH CULTURAL BOXES

A-LEVEL
APRIL FOOL'S DAY
BILL OF RIGHTS
BROADSHEET/BROADSIDE
BUILDING SOCIETY
CHURCH OF ENGLAND
THE CITY
CONGRESS
CONSTITUTION
DOWNING STREET
ELECTION
ENGLISH BREAKFAST
FLEET STREET
FOURTH OF JULY
FRATERNITY
-GATE
GREEN CARD
GUY FAWKES' NIGHT
HALLOWEEN
HOUSE OF COMMONS
HOUSE OF LORDS
HOUSE OF REPRESENTIVES
L
LABOR DAY
LICENSING HOURS
MEDICARE/MEDICAID
NATIVE AMERICAN
OXBRIDGE
PENTAGON
PILGRIM FATHERS
POPPY DAY
PRIMARIES
PUB
PUBLIC SCHOOL
SAINT PATRICK'S DAY
SAT
SENATE
SUPREME COURT
TABLOID
THANKSGIVING
WALL STREET
WESTMINSTER
WHITEHALL
WHITE HOUSE
WORLD SERIES
YANKEE

PORTUGUÊS - INGLÊS

PORTUGUESE-ENGLISH

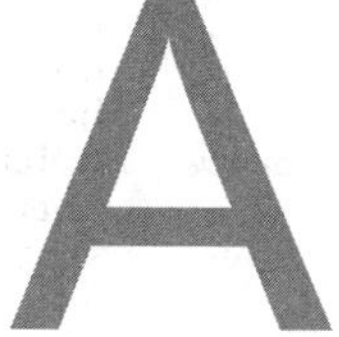

a¹, A [a] *m* [letra] a, A.

a² [a] ◇ *artigo definido* ▷ **o**. ◇ *prep* **-1.** [introduz um complemento indireto] to; **mostrar algo a alguém** to show sthg to sb, to show sb sthg; **diga ao Zé para vir** tell Zé to come; **peça o chapéu ao Paulo** ask Paulo for the hat. **-2.** [relativo a direção] to; **fomos à praia** we went to the beach; **vamos ao cinema** we're going to the movies; **cheguei a Salvador ontem** I arrived in Salvador yesterday; **ele percorreu o país de norte a sul** he travelled the country from north to south. **-3.** [relativo a posição, lugar, distância]: **é à esquerda/direita** it's on the left/right; **fica na saída do teatro** it's on the way out of the theatre. **-4.** [introduz um complemento direto]: **amar a Deus** to love God; **ele criou o menino como a um filho** he raised the boy like his own son. **-5.** [relativo a quantidade, medida, preço]: **aos centos/às dezenas** by the hundred/dozen; **a quanto estão as pêras?** how much are the pears?; **a quilo/metro** by the kilo/metre. **-6.** [indica modo, maneira]: **feito à mão** handmade; **bater à máquina** to type; **ir a pé/cavalo** to go on foot/horseback; **viajar a trabalho/passeio** to go on a business/pleasure trip; **à moda da casa** house style; **sal a gosto** salt to taste; **pagar à vista/a prazo** to pay cash/on time; **a olho nu** with the naked eye. **-7.** [relativo a velocidade]: **dirigir a 60 km/h** to drive at 60 kph; **ela ia a 100km/h** she was doing 100 kph. **-8.** [indica freqüência]: **três vezes ao dia** three times a day; **estou lá às terças e quintas** I'm there on Tuesdays and Thursdays. **-9.** [introduz complemento de tempo]: **as lojas abrem às nove horas** the shops open at nine (o'clock); **eles chegam daqui a 2 horas** they're arriving in two hours' time; **fica a dez minutos daqui** it's ten minutes from here; **à noite** at night. **-10.** [indica série]: **de ... a** from ... to; **façam os exercícios de um a dez** do exercises one to ten. **-11.** [seguido de infinitivo para exprimir momento]: **ele começou a falar** he started speaking; **ele tropeçou ao subir no ônibus** he tripped as he was getting on the bus. **-12.** [seguido de infinitivo indicando duas ações]: **ela saiu a cantar** she went out singing; **ele nunca aprendeu a assobiar** he never learned to whistle; **começou a chover** it started to rain. **-13.** [em locuções]: **a não ser que** unless; **à exceção de** except for; **a partir de** from; **a respeito de** regarding.

à [a] = **a** + **a**.

AA (*abrev de* **Alcoólicos Anônimos**) *m* AA.

AACC (*abrev de* **Associação de Assistência à Criança com Câncer**) *f Brazilian association for assistance to children with cancer.*

AACD (*abrev de* **Associação de Assistência à Criança Defeituosa**) *f Brazilian association for assistance to disabled children.*

aba ['aba] *f* **-1.** [de chapéu] brim. **-2.** [de casaca] tail.

abacate [aba'katʃi] *m* avocado.

abacateiro [abaka'tejru] *m* avocado tree.

abacaxi [abaka'ʃi] *m* **-1.** [fruta] pineapple. **-2.** *fam* [problema, dificuldade] difficulty; **ter ~s para resolver** to have some difficulties to sort out; **descascar um ~** to get out of a fix.

abade, dessa [a'badʒi, desa] *m, f* abbot (*f* abbess).

abadia [aba'dʒia] *f* abbey.

abafado, da [aba'fadu, da] *adj* **-1.** [ar, sala] stuffy. **-2.** [pessoa - sem ar] suffocated. **-3.** [som] muffled.

abafador [abafa'do(x)] *m* **-1.** [de bule de chá] tea cosy. **-2.** [de instrumento] mute.

abafamento [abafa'mẽntu] *m* **-1.** [sufoco] suffocation. **-2.** [de som] muffling.

abafar [4] [aba'fa(x)] ◇ *vt* **-1.** [sufocar] to suffocate. **-2.** [cobrir] to cover. **-3.** [apagar] to smother. **-4.** [amortecer] to muffle. **-5.** [ocultar] to cover up. ◇ *vi* **-1.** [sufocar] to suffocate. **-2.** *fam* [fazer sucesso] to steal the show.

abagunçado, da [abagũn'sadu, da] *adj* messed-up.

abagunçar [abagũn'sa(x)] *vt* to mess sthg up.

abaixado, da [abaj'ʃadu, da] <> *pp* ▷ **abaixar**. <> *adj* **-1.** [pessoa] stooped. **-2.** [persiana] lowered.
abaixar [4] [abaj'ʃa(x)] *vt* to lower; ~ **o volume** to turn down the volume.
◆ **abaixar-se** *vp* [curvar-se] to crouch down.
abaixo [a'bajʃu] <> *adv* **-1.** [posição] down; **mais** ~ lower down. **-2.** [direção] further down; **escada** ~ downstairs; **ladeira** ~ downhill; **rio** ~ downstream. **-3.** [em texto] below. <> *interj* down with; ~ **a opressão!** down with oppression!
◆ **abaixo de** *loc prep* **-1.** [em posição inferior] below. **-2.** [em número inferior etc] under.
abaixo-assinado [a,bajʃuasi'nadu] (*pl* **abaixo-assinados**) *m* petition.
abajur [aba'ʒu(x)] (*pl* **-es**) *m* **-1.** [pantalha] shade. **-2.** [lâmpada] table lamp.
abalado, da [aba'ladu, da] *adj* **-1.** [pessoa] shaken. **-2.** [saúde] impaired.
abalar [4] [aba'la(x)] *vt* **-1.** [prédio, fundações] to rock. **-2.** [pessoa] to shake. **-3.** [saúde] to impair.
◆ **abalar-se** *vp* [comover-se] to be moved.
abalizado, da [abali'zadu, da] *adj* **-1.** [profissional] skilled. **-2.** [opinião] expert.
abalo [a'balu] *m* **-1.** [tremor] tremor; ~ **sísmico** earth tremor. **-2.** [efeito ruim] setback. **-3.** *fig* [comoção] uproar.
abalroar [20] [abawro'a(x)] *vt* to collide with.
abanar [4] [aba'na(x)] *vt* **-1.** [com leque, jornal] to fan. **-2.** [com mão, lenço] to wave. **-3.** [rabo] to wag. **-4.** [cabeça] to shake.
◆ **abanar-se** *vp* [ventilar-se] to fan o.s.
abandonado, da [abãndo'nadu, da] *adj* **-1.** [desamparado] abandoned. **-2.** [descuidado] neglected.
abandonar [4] [abãndo'na(x)] *vt* **-1.** [desamparar] to abandon. **-2.** [negligenciar] to neglect. **-3.** [deixar - estudos, profissão] to give up; [- cônjuge] to leave. **-4.** [renegar] to reject.
◆ **abandonar-se** *vp* **-1.** [desleixar-se] to let o.s. go. **-2.** [entregar-se]: ~**-se a algo** to surrender o.s. to sthg.
abandono [abãn'donu] *m* **-1.** [ato] abandonment. **-2.** [estado] neglect. **-3.** [relaxamento] shabbiness. **-4.** [entrega] surrender.
abarcar [12] [abax'ka(x)] *vt* **-1.** [abranger] to comprise. **-2.** [alcançar] to cover. **-3.** [monopolizar] to monopolize.
abarrotado, da [abaxo'tadu, da] *adj*: ~ **(de)** packed (with).
abarrotar [4] [abaxo'ta(x)] *vt*: ~ **algo (de)** to pack sthg (with).
abastado, da [abaʃ'tadu, da] *adj* well-off.
abastardar [4] [abaʃtax'da(x)] *vt* to bastardize.
abastecer [25] [abaʃte'se(x)] *vt*: ~ **algo (de)** to supply sthg (with).
◆ **abastecer-se** *vp*: ~**-se (de algo)** to stock up (with sthg).
abastecimento [abaʃtesi'mẽntu] *m* supply.
abate [a'batʃi] *m* slaughter.
abatedouro [abate'doru] *m* [matadouro] slaughterhouse.
abater [5] [aba'te(x)] *vt* **-1.** [matar - animais] to slaughter; [- pessoa] to kill. **-2.** [diminuir] to reduce. **-3.** [enfraquecer] to weaken. **-4.** [desanimar] to shatter.
abatido, da [aba'tʃidu, da] *adj* **-1.** [pálido] drawn. **-2.** [enfraquecido] weakened. **-3.** [desanimado] downcast.
abatimento [abatʃi'mẽntu] *m* **-1.** [palidez] paleness. **-2.** [fraqueza] weakness. **-3.** [desânimo] dejection. **-4.** [redução] reduction; **fazer um** ~ to give a discount.
abaulado, da [abaw'ladu, da] *adj* convex.
abdicação [abdʒika'sãw] (*pl* **-ões**) *f* abdication.
abdicar [12] [abdʒi'ka(x)] <> *vt*: ~ **o trono (em favor de alguém)** to abdicate the throne (in favour of sb). <> *vi* to abdicate; ~ **de algo** *fig* to forgo sthg.
abdominal [abdomi'naw] (*pl* **-ais**) *adj* abdominal.
◆ **abdominais** *mpl* sit-ups.
abecê [abe'se] *m* **-1.** [alfabeto] ABC. **-2.** *fig* [rudimentos] fundamentals *(pl)*.
abecedário [abese'darju] *m* alphabet.
abeirar [4] [abej'ra(x)] *vt* to bring near.
◆ **abeirar-se** *vp*: ~**-se de** to draw near to.
abelha [a'beʎa] *f* bee.
abelha-mestra [a,eʎa'mɛʃtra] (*pl* **abelhas-mestras**) *f* queen bee.
abelhudo, da [abe'ʎudu, da] *adj* nosy.
abençoado, da [abẽn'swadu, da] *adj* **-1.** [bento] blessed. **-2.** [bem-sucedido] successful.
abençoar [20] [abẽn'swa(x)] *vt* to bless; **(que) Deus te abençoe!** God bless you!
aberração [abexa'sãw] (*pl* **-ões**) *f* aberration.
aberrante [abe'xãntʃi] *adj* incongruous.
aberto, ta [a'bɛxtu, ta] <> *pp* ▷ **abrir**. <> *adj* **-1.** [ger] open. **-2.** [registro, torneira] turned on. **-3.** [sem cobertura - terraço] open-air; [- carro] convertible. **-4.** [céu] clear. **-5.** [embrulho, pacote etc] unwrapped. **-6.** [camisa etc] undone. **-7.** [sincero] frank. **-8.** [liberal] open-minded.
◆ **aberto** *m* ESP open.
abertura [abex'tura] *f* **-1.** [ger] opening; **cerimônia de** ~ opening ceremony. **-2.** [orifício] gap. **-3.** [início] start. **-4.** [de golfo, enseada] width. **-5.** [em roupa] neckline. **-6.** [em idéias] openness. **-7.** FOT aperture. **-8.** MÚS overture. **-9.** [POL - democrática] liberalization; [- de aeroporto, porto] deregulation.
abestalhado, da [abeʃta'ʎadu, da] *adj* moronic.
ABF (*abrev de* **Associação Brasileira de Franchising**) *f Brazilian franchising association.*
ABI (*abrev de* **Associação Brasileira de Imprensa**) *f Brazilian press association.*
abilolado, da [abilo'ladu, da] *adj* ***fam*** potty, loony.
abismado, da [abiʒ'madu, da] *adj* dismayed.
abismo [a'biʒmu] *m* **-1.** [precipício] abyss. **-2.** *fig* [grande diferença] chasm. **-3.** *fig* [situação difícil]: **estar à beira de um** ~ to be on the brink.
abissal [abi'saw] (*pl* **-ais**) *adj* [região] deep.
abjeto, ta [ab'ʒɛtu, ta] *adj* abject.
ABL (*abrev de* **Academia Brasileira de Letras**) *f*

Brazilian academy of arts.
abnegação [abnega'sãw] *f* self-sacrifice.
abnegado, da [abne'gadu, da] *adj* self-sacrificing.
abnegar [14] [abne'ga(x)] *vi* [renunciar]: ~ **de algo** to renounce sthg.
◆ **abnegar-se** *vp* [sacrificar-se] to sacrifice o.s.
ABNT (*abrev de* **Associação Brasileira de Normas Técnicas**) *f Brazilian body overseeing technical standards,* ≃ BSI *UK*, ≃ ANSI *US*.
abóbada [a'bɔbada] *f* vault.
abóbora [a'bɔbora] *f* pumpkin.
abobrinha [abɔ'briɲa] *f* courgette *UK*, zucchini *US*.
abocanhar [4] [aboka'ɲa(x)] *vt* **-1.** [morder] to bite. **-2.** *fig* [apoderar-se de] to seize.
aboletar-se [abole'ta(x)si] *vp* to install o.s.
abolição [abolisãw] *f* abolition.
abolir [79] [abo'li(x)] *vt* to abolish.
abominação [abomina'sãw] (*pl* **-ões**) *f* abomination.
abominar [4] [abomi'na(x)] *vt* to loathe.
abominável [abomi'navew] (*pl* **-eis**) *adj* abominable.
abonado, da [abo'nadu, da] ◇ *adj* [rico] well-off. ◇ *m, f* [rico] well-off person; **os ~s** the well-off.
abonar [4] [abo'na(x)] *vt* **-1.** [gen] to back up. **-2.** [afiançar] to guarantee. **-3.** [aprovar] to approve. **-4.** [dar] to grant. **-5.** [adiantar] to advance. **-6.** [relevar] to excuse.
abono [a'bonu] *m* **-1.** [aprovação] approval. **-2.** [fiança] collateral. **-3.** [pagamento extra] bonus; ~ **de Natal** Christmas bonus. **-4.** [relevação] pardon.
abordagem [abox'daʒẽ] (*pl* **-ns**) *f* approach.
abordar [4] [abox'da(x)] *vt* **-1.** [ir a bordo de] to board. **-2.** [pessoa] to approach. **-3.** [assunto] to broach.
aborígine [abo'riʒeni] *adj* **-1.** [indígena] native. **-2.** [da Austrália] aboriginal.
◆ **aborígines** *mpl & fpl* **-1.** [população indígena] natives. **-2.** [da Austrália] Aborigines.
aborrecer [25] [aboxe'se(x)] *vt* **-1.** [amolar] to annoy. **-2.** [entediar] to bore.
◆ **aborrecer-se** *vp* **-1.** [amolar-se]: **~-se com alguém** to get annoyed with sb. **-2.** [entediar-se]: **~-se (com alguém/algo)** to get bored (with sb/sthg).
aborrecido, da [aboxe'sidu, da] *adj* **-1.** [amolado] annoyed. **-2.** [enfadonho] boring.
aborrecimento [aboxesi'mẽntu] *m* [amolação] annoyance.
abortar [4] [abox'ta(x)] ◇ *vi* [*MED* - espontaneamente] to have a miscarriage; [- intencionalmente] to have an abortion. ◇ *vt* [plano, greve, etc] to abort.
aborto [a'boxtu] *m* [*MED* - espontâneo] miscarriage; [- intencional] abortion.
abotoadura [abotwa'dura] *f* cuff-link.
abotoar [20] [abo'twa(x)] *vt* [roupa] to button.
abr. (*abrev de* **abril**) Apr.
abraçar [13] [abra'sa(x)] *vt* **-1.** [com os braços] to hug. **-2.** *fig* [seguir] to embrace.
◆ **abraçar-se** *vp* to hug each other.
abraço [a'brasu] *m* hug; **dar um ~ em alguém** to give sb a hug; **um ~** [em cartas] best wishes.
abrandar [4] [abrãn'da(x)] ◇ *vt* **-1.** [dor] to ease. **-2.** [lei, palavreado] to moderate. ◇ *vi* **-1.** [ger] to soften. **-2.** [dor, ira, calor, vento] to die down.
abrangente [abrãn'ʒẽntʃi] *adj* all-embracing.
abranger [26] [abrãn'ʒe(x)] *vt* **-1.** [incluir] to include. **-2.** [entender] to grasp. **-3.** [conter em sua área] to comprise.
abrasar [4] [abra'za(x)] *vt* **-1.** [incendiar] to set alight. **-2.** [esquentar muito] to scorch.
abrasileirar [4] [abrazilej'ra(x)] *vt* to Brazilianize.
◆ **abrasileirar-se** *vp* [pessoa] to become Brazilianized.
abrasivo, va [abra'zivu, va] *adj* abrasive.
abreugrafia [abrewgra'fia] *f* X-ray.
abreviação [abrevja'sãw] (*pl* **-ões**) *f* **-1.** [de palavra] abbreviation. **-2.** [resumo] abridgement. **-3.** [diminuição] curtailment.
abreviar [16] [abre'vja(x)] *vt* **-1.** [pôr em abreviatura] to abbreviate. **-2.** [resumir] to abridge. **-3.** [tornar breve] to shorten.
abreviatura [abrevja'tura] *f* abbreviation.
abridor [abri'do(x)] (*pl* **-es**) *m*: ~ **de garrafa** bottle opener; ~ **de lata** can opener.
abrigar [14] [abri'ga(x)] *vt* **-1.** [albergar] to shelter. **-2.** [proteger]: ~ **alguém de algo** to protect sb from sthg.
◆ **abrigar-se** *vp* [albergar-se] to take shelter.
abrigo [a'brigu] *m* **-1.** [refúgio] shelter; ~ **antiaéreo** bomb shelter. **-2.** [cobertura] cover. **-3.** [asilo] home.
abril [a'briw] *m* April; **primeiro de ~** April Fool's Day; *veja também* **setembro**.
abrilhantar [4] [abriʎãn'ta(x)] *vt fig* enhance.
abrir [6] [a'bri(x)] ◇ *vt* **-1.** [ger] to open. **-2.** [pernas, braços] to stretch out. **-3.** [camisa etc] to undo. **-4.** [mapa] to open out. **-5.** [registro, torneira, água] to turn on. **-6.** [túnel] to bore. **-7.** [estrada] to make. **-8.** [exceção, precedente] to create. **-9.** [apetite] to whet. ◇ *vi* **-1.** [ger] to open. **-2.** [sinal de tráfego] to turn green. **-3.** [tempo] to clear up.
◆ **abrir-se** *vp* [confidenciar]: **~-se com alguém** to confide in sb.
ab-rogação [abxoga'sãw] (*pl* **-ões**) *f* **-1.** [de lei] repeal. **-2.** [de uso, costume] discontinuation.
ab-rogar [14] [abxo'ga(x)] *vt* **-1.** [lei] to repeal. **-2.** [uso, costume] to discontinue.
abrolho [a'broʎu] *m* thorn.
abrupto, ta [a'bruptu, ta] *adj* **-1.** [súbito] sudden. **-2.** [áspero] abrupt.
abrutalhado, da [abruta'ʎadu, da] *adj* brusque.
ABS (*abrev de* **antilock braking system**) *m* ABS; **freios ~** ABS brakes.
absenteísmo [absẽnte'iʒmu] *m* absenteeism.
absolutamente [abso͵luta'mẽntʃi] *adv* **-1.** [completamente] absolutely. **-2.** [de modo nenhum] absolutely not.

absoluto, ta [abso'lutu, ta] *adj* absolute; **em ~** not at all.
absolver [5] [absow've(x)] *vt*: **~ alguém (de algo)** *JUR* to acquit sb (of sthg); *RELIG* to absolve sb (of sthg); [inocentar] to clear sb (of sthg).
absolvição [absowvi'sãw] *f* **-1.** *JUR* acquittal. **-2.** *RELIG* absolution.
absorção [absox'sãw] *f* **-1.** [de água, vapores, gases] absorption. **-2.** [de valores, cultura] absorption.
absorto, ta [ab'soxtu, ta] *adj* [concentrado] absorbed.
absorvente [absox'vẽntʃi] *adj* **-1.** [substância] absorbent. **-2.** [pessoa, leitura, trabalho] absorbing.
◆ **absorvente** *m*: **~ higiênico** sanitary towel.
absorver [5] [absoxve(x)] *vt* to absorb; **~ energia** to use up energy; **~ tempo** to take up time.
◆ **absorver-se** *vp* [concentrar-se]: **~-se em algo** to absorb o.s. in sthg.
abstêmio, mia [abʃ'temju, mja] <> *adj* abstemious. <> *m, f* teetotaller.
abstenção [abʃtẽn'sãw] (*pl* **-ões**) *f* **-1.** [de prazeres, de fumo] abstinence. **-2.** [do voto] abstention.
abster-se [1] [abʃ'texsi] *vp*: **~ (de algo/de fazer algo)** to abstain (from sthg/from doing sthg).
abstinência [abʃtʃi'nẽnsja] *f* abstinence.
abstração [abʃtra'sãw] *f* **-1.** [alheamento] abstraction. **-2.** [isolamento] isolation. **-3.** [concentração] concentration.
abstrair [68] [abʃtra'i(x)] *vt* **-1.** [afastar] to keep away from. **-2.** [isolar] to separate out.
◆ **abstrair-se** *vp* **-1.** [alhear-se]: **~-se de** to distance o.s. from. **-2.** [concentrar-se]: **~-se em** to absorb o.s. in. **-3.** [abster-se]: **~-se de** to abstain from.
abstrato, ta [abʃ'tratu, ta] *adj* abstract.
absurdo, da [ab'suxdu, da] *adj* absurd.
◆ **absurdo** *m* absurdity.
abulia [abu'abu'dabi] *f* apathy.
abundância [abũn'dãnsja] *f* **-1.** [grande quantidade] abundance; **em ~** in abundance. **-2.** [riqueza]: **ele vive com ~** he is a man of means.
abundante [abũn'dãntʃi] *adj*: **~ (em/de)** abundant (in/with).
abundar [4] [abũn'da(x)] *vi* to abound; **~ em** *ou* **de** to abound in *ou* with.
aburguesado, da [abuxge'zadu, da] *adj* bourgeois.
aburguesar [4] [abuxge'za(x)] *vt* to gentrify.
◆ **aburguesar-se** *vp* **-1.** [pessoa] to become bourgeois. **-2.** [área] to become gentrified.
abusado, da [abu'zadu, da] *adj* forward.
abusar [4] [abu'za(x)] *vi* **-1.** [aproveitar-se, exceder-se] to go too far. **-2.** [praticar excessos]: **~ de algo** to abuse sthg. **-3.** [aproveitar-se]: **~ de alguém/algo** to take advantage of sb/sthg. **-4.** [sexualmente]: **~ de alguém** to abuse sb.
abusivo, va [abu'zivu, va] *adj* **-1.** [tratamento] abusive. **-2.** [preço] excessive.
abuso [a'buzu] *m*: **~ (de)** abuse (of); **~ de confiança** breach of trust; **~ sexual** sexual abuse.
abutre [a'butri] *m* vulture.
AC (*abrev de* **Estado do Acre**) *m State of Acre.*
a.C. (*abrev de* **antes de Cristo**) *adj* BC.
acabado, da [aka'badu, da] *adj* **-1.** [terminado] finished. **-2.** [móvel, roupa etc]: **bem/mal ~** well/badly finished. **-3.** [gasto] worn. **-4.** [abatido, exausto] exhausted. **-5.** [envelhecido] aged.
acabamento [akaba'mẽntu] *m* finish.
acabar [4] [aka'ba(x)] <> *vt* **-1.** [terminar] to finish. **-2.** [rematar] to finish off. <> *vi* **-1.** [terminar] to finish, to end; **~ bem/mal** to end well/badly; **~ de fazer algo** to finish doing sthg; [há pouco] to have just done sthg. **-2.** [terminar por]: **~ fazendo algo** to end up doing sthg. **-3.** [ter como conseqüência]: **~ em algo** to end up in sthg. **-4.** [ter como limite]: **~ em algo** to end in sthg. **-5.** [abolir]: **~ com algo** to put an end to sthg. **-6.** [destruir]: **~ com algo** to destroy sthg. **-7.** [tornar-se] to end up.
◆ **acabar-se** *vp* **-1.** [terminar] to finish, to end. **-2.** [desgastar-se] to wear o.s. out.
acabrunhado, da [akabru'ɲadu, da] *adj* **-1.** [desanimado] disheartened. **-2.** [envergonhado] embarrassed.
acabrunhar [4] [akabru'ɲa(x)] *vt* **-1.** [desanimar] to dishearten. **-2.** [envergonhar] to embarrass.
acácia [a'kasja] *f* acacia.
academia [akade'mia] *f* **-1.** [escola] school. **-2.** [sociedade] academy; **Academia Brasileira de Letras** *Brazilian Academy of language and literature.* **-3.** *ESP* school; **~ de ginástica** gym.
acadêmico, ca [aka'demiku, ka] <> *adj* academic. <> *m, f* academic.
açafrão [asa'frãw] *m* saffron.
acalanto [aka'lãntu] *m* lullaby.
acalentar [4] [akalẽn'ta(x)] *vt* **-1.** [ninar] to lull. **-2.** *fig* [nutrir] to cherish. **-3.** [aconchegar] to cuddle.
acalmar [4] [akaw'ma(x)] <> *vt* [pessoa, ânimos] to calm. <> *vi* **-1.** [pessoa] to calm down. **-2.** [ventania] to abate. **-3.** [mar] to become calm.
◆ **acalmar-se** *vp* [pessoa, ânimos] to calm down.
acalorado, da [akalo'radu, da] *adj* [discussão etc] heated.
acamado, da [aka'madu, da] *adj* bedridden.
açambarcar [12] [asãnbax'ka(x)] *vt* **-1.** [apropriar-se de] to appropriate. **-2.** [monopolizar] to corner.
acampamento [akãnpa'mẽntu] *m* **-1.** [atividade] camping; [lugar] campsite. **-2.** *MIL* encampment.
acampar [4] [akãn'pa(x)] <> *vt* to encamp. <> *vi* to camp.
acanhado, da [aka'ɲadu, da] *adj* shy.
acanhamento [akaɲa'mẽntu] *m* shyness.
acanhar-se [4] [aka'ɲaxsi] *vp*: **~ (de fazer algo)** to be shy (about doing sthg).
ação [a'sãw] (*pl* **-ões**) *f* **-1.** [atuação] action. **-2.** [feito] act; **~ de graças** thanksgiving. **-3.** [capacidade de agir]: **sem ~** helpless. **-4.** [efeito] effect. **-5.** [enredo] plot; **filme de ~** action movie. **-6.** *JUR* legal action; **mover uma ~ contra alguém** to bring a legal action against sb; **~ judicial** lawsuit. **-7.** *FIN* share; **~ ordinária** ordinary share; **~ preferencial** preference share. **-8.** *MIL* action.
acarajé [akara'ʒɛ] *m bean fritter.*

acareação [akarja'sãw] (*pl* **-ões**) *f* confrontation.
acarear [15] [aka'rja(x)] *vt* to confront.
acariciar [16] [akari'sja(x)] *vt* to caress.
acarinhar [4] [akari'ɲa(x)] *vt* to caress.
acarretar [4] [akaxe'ta(x)] *vt* to cause.
acasalamento [akazala'mẽntu] *m* mating.
acasalar [4] [akaza'la(x)] *vt* to mate.
acaso [a'kazu] *m* chance; **essa descoberta foi um ~** it was a chance discovery.
◆ **ao acaso** *loc adv* at random.
◆ **por acaso** *loc adv* by chance.
acastanhado, da [akaʃta'ɲadu, da] *adj* brown.
acatamento [akata'mẽntu] *m* **-1.** [respeito]: **~ (a)** respect (for). **-2.** [cumprimento]: **~ (a** *ou* **de)** deference (to).
acatar [4] [aka'ta(x)] *vt* **-1.** [respeitar] to respect. **-2.** [cumprir] to obey.
acautelar [4] [akawte'la(x)] *vt* to caution.
◆ **acautelar-se** *vp*: **~-se (contra)** to guard (against).
acebolado, da [asebo'ladu, da] *adj cooked with onions.*
aceder [5] [ase'de(x)] *vi*: **~ a algo** to accede to sthg; **~ em fazer algo** to agree to do sthg.
aceitação [asejta'sãw] *f* **-1.** [anuência] acceptance. **-2.** [admissão, aprovação] approval. **-3.** [receptividade] acceptability.
aceitar [4] [asej'ta(x)] *vt* **-1.** [anuir a] to accept. **-2.** [admitir, aprovar] to approve.
aceitável [asej'tavew] (*pl* **-eis**) *adj* acceptable.
aceito, ta [a'sejtu, ta] ◇ *pp* ▷ **aceitar**. ◇ *adj* **-1.** [pessoa, produto] well-received. **-2.** [proposta, solução] accepted.
aceleração [aselera'sãw] *f* **-1.** *FÍS* acceleration. **-2.** [de processo etc] progress.
acelerado, da [asele'radu, da] *adj* quick.
acelerador [aselera'do(x)] (*pl* **-es**) *m* accelerator.
acelerar [4] [asele'ra(x)] ◇ *vt* **-1.** *AUTO* to accelerate. **-2.** [apressar] to hurry. ◇ *vi AUTO* to accelerate.
acelga [a'sewga] *f* chard.
acenar [4] [ase'na(x)] ◇ *vt* **-1.** [sinalizar] to indicate. **-2.** [fazer movimento com - cabeça] to nod; [- mãos] to wave. ◇ *vi* **-1.** [sinalizar - com cabeça] to nod; [- com mãos,lenço] to wave. **-2.** [prometer]: **~ algo (a alguém)** to offer (sb) sthg.
acendedor [asẽnde'do(x)] *m* [de bico de gás] lighter.
acender [5] [asẽn'de(x)] ◇ *vt* **-1.** [cigarro, fósforo] to light. **-2.** [lâmpada, luz] to switch on. **-3.** *fig* [ânimo] to excite. ◇ *vp* [lâmpada, luz] to be turned on.
aceno [a'senu] *m* **-1.** [gesto] gesture. **-2.** [com a cabeça] nod. **-3.** [com a mão] wave.
acento [a'sẽntu] *m* **-1.** [gráfico] accent; **~ agudo/circunflexo** acute/circumflex accent. **-2.** [intensidade] stress.
acentuação [asẽntwa'sãw] *f* accentuation.
acentuado, da [asẽn'twadu, da] *adj* **-1.** [palavra, vogal] accented. **-2.** [sílaba] stressed. **-3.** [proeminente] accentuated. **-4.** [marcante] marked.
acentuar [4] [asẽn'twa(x)] *vt* **-1.** [palavra, vogal] to stress. **-2.** [enfatizar] to emphasize. **-3.** [realçar] to accentuate.
acepção [asep'sãw] (*pl* **-ões**) *f* sense.
acerca [a'sexka] ◆ **acerca de** *loc adv* about, concerning.
acercar-se [12] [asex'kaxsi] *vp*: **~ de** [ir] to go towards; [vir] to draw near to.
acerola [ase'rɔla] *f fruit similar to Barbados Cherry, commonly drunk as a fruit juice, rich in vitamins and minerals.*
acertado, da [asex'tadu, da] *adj* **-1.** [relógio] correct. **-2.** [medida, decisão] sensible. **-3.** [combinado] arranged.
acertar [4] [asex'ta(x)] ◇ *vt* **-1.** [relógio] to set. **-2.** [combinar] to arrange. **-3.** [contas] to settle. **-4.** [igualar] to even up. **-5.** [endireitar] to put right. **-6.** [encontrar] to find. **-7.** [fazer atingir]: **~ algo em algo** to land sthg on sthg. **-8.** [aplicar] to strike. ◇ *vi* **-1.** [em adivinhação, jogo] to guess correctly. **-2.** [atingir]: **~ em algo/alguém** to hit sthg/sb.
acerto [a'sextu] *m* **-1.** [em decisão, escolha] right decision. **-2.** [acordo] agreement. **-3.** [de contas] settling. **-4.** [sensatez]: **com ~** with sensitivity.
acervo [a'sexvu] *m* [patrimônio] collection.
aceso, sa [a'sezu, za] ◇ *pp* ▷ **acender**. ◇ *adj* **-1.** [cigarro, fósforo] lit. **-2.** [lâmpada, luz] on. **-3.** *fig* [pessoa] excited.
acessar [4] [ase'sa(x)] *vt COMPUT* to access.
acessível [ase'sivɛw] (*pl* **-eis**) *adj* **-1.** [de acesso fácil] accessible. **-2.** [que se pode obter] available. **-3.** [tratável] approachable. **-4.** [inteligível] comprehensible. **-5.** [módico] affordable.
acesso [a'sɛsu] *m* **-1.** [ger] access. **-2.** [aproximação] approach; **de fácil ~** accessible; **de difícil ~** inaccessible. **-3.** [trato]: **de fácil ~** approachable. **-4.** [ímpeto] fit. **-5.** *MED* attack. **-6.** *COMPUT* access; **~ discado** dial-up access.
acessório, ria [ase'sɔrju] *adj* accessory.
◆ **acessório** *m* accessory.
acetinado, da [aseti'nadu, da] *adj* satiny.
acetona [ase'tona] *f* [removedor de esmalte] nail polish remover.
achacar [12] [aʃa'ka(x)] *vt* **-1.** [tachar]: **~ alguém de algo** to accuse sb of sthg. **-2.** *fam* [extorquir dinheiro de] to extort money from.
achado [a'ʃadu] *m* **-1.** [coisa encontrada] find. **-2.** [descoberta] discovery. **-3.** [pechincha] bargain. **-4.** [coisa providencial] godsend. **-5.** *loc*: **não se dar por ~** to play dumb.
achaque [a'ʃaki] *m* ailment.
achar [4] [a'ʃa(x)] ◇ *vt* **-1.** [encontrar - procurando] to find; [- por acaso] to come across. **-2.** [descobrir, encontrar] to find. **-3.**: **~ graça em algo** to find sthg amusing. **-4.** [supor, opinar] to think; **~ que ...** to think that ...; **acho que sim** I think so. ◇ *vi* [decidir]: **~ de fazer algo** to decide to do sthg.
◆ **achar-se** *vp* **-1.** [estar] to be. **-2.** [considerar-se] to consider o.s.
achatar [4] [aʃa'ta(x)] *vt* **-1.** [aplanar] to flatten. **-2.** [rebaixar] to lower.

achegar-se [14] [aʃe'gaxsi] *vp*: ~ **(a/de)** to get closer (to).

acidentado, da [asidẽn'tadu, da] <> *adj* **-1.** [terreno] rough. **-2.** [viagem, vida] turbulent. **-3.** [pessoa] injured. <> *m, f* [pessoa] injured person.

acidental [asidẽn'taw] (*pl* **-ais**) *adj* **-1.** [fortuito] accidental. **-2.** [secundário] incidental.

acidentar-se [asidẽn'tarsi] *vp* **-1.** [sofrer acidente] to have an accident. **-2.** [vitimar-se] to be injured.

acidente [asi'dẽntʃi] *m* **-1.** [desastre] accident; ~ **de carro** car accident. **-2.** [eventualidade] circumstance; **por** ~ by chance. ~ **geográfico** geographic accident. ~ **de trabalho** accident at work, industrial accident. ~ **vascular cerebral** *MED* stroke.

acidez [asi'deʒ] *f* acidity.

ácido, da ['asidu, da] *adj* **-1.** *QUÍM* acid. **-2.** [bebida, fruta, sabor] acidic.
◆ **ácido** *m* **-1.** *QUÍM* acid; ~ **úrico** uric acid. **-2.** *fam* [droga] acid.

acima [a'sima] *adj* **-1.** [ger] above; **mais** ~ higher up. **-2.** [em direção à parte superior]: **morro** *ou* **ladeira** ~ uphill.
◆ **acima de** *loc prep* **-1.** [em posição superior] above. **-2.** [quantia, quantidade] more than.

acinte [a'sĩntʃi] *m* provocation.

acintosamente [asĩntoza'mẽntʃi] *adv* deliberately.

acintoso, osa [asĩn'tozu, oza] *adj* provocative.

acinzentado, da [da, asĩnzẽ'tadu] *adj* greyish.

acionar [4] [asjo'na(x)] *vt* **-1.** [mecanismo, medidas] to set in motion. **-2.** *JUR* to sue.

acionista [asjo'niʃta] *mf* shareholder; ~ **majoritário/minoritário** majority/minority shareholder.

acirrado, da [asi'xadu, da] *adj* **-1.** [luta, discussão, ânimo] tough. **-2.** [ódio] bitter.

acirrar [4] [asi'xa(x)] *vt* **-1.** [instigar]: ~ **alguém contra algo/alguém** to incite sb against sthg/sb. **-2.** [exacerbar] to stir up.

aclamação [aklama'sãw] *f* **-1.** [ovação] ovation; **por** ~ by acclamation. **-2.** [proclamação] proclamation.

aclamar [4] [akla'ma(x)] *vt* **-1.** [ovacionar] to applaud. **-2.** [proclamar] to proclaim.

aclarado, da [akla'radu, da] *adj* [questão, mistério] clarified.

aclarar [4] [akla'ra(x)] *vt* [questão, mistério] to clarify.
◆ **aclarar-se** *vp* to become clear.

aclimatação [aklimata'sãw] *f* acclimatization.

aclimatar [4] [aklima'ta(x)] *vt*: ~ **algo/alguém a algo** to acclimatize sth/sb to sthg.
◆ **aclimatar-se** *vp*: ~**-se (a algo)** to acclimatize o.s. (to sthg).

aclive [a'klivi] *m* slope; **um caminho em** ~ an uphill slope.

ACM (*abrev de* **Associação Cristã de Moços**) *f* ≃ YMCA.

acne ['akni] *f* acne.

aço ['asu] *m* steel; ~ **inoxidável** stainless steel.

acocorado, da [akoko'radu, da] *adj* squatting.

acocorar-se [4] [akoko'raxsi] *vp* to squat down.

ações [a'sõjʃ] *pl* ▷ **ação**.

açoitar [4] [asoj'ta(x)] *vt* **-1.** [com açoite] to whip. **-2.** [suj: vento, temporal] to lash.

açoite [a'sojtʃi] *m* whip.

acolá [ako'la] *adv* over there.

acolchoado, da [akow'ʃwadu, da] *adj* [forrado] quilted.
◆ **acolchoado** *m* quilt.

acolchoar [20] [akow'ʃwa(x)] *vt* [forrar] to quilt.

acolhedor, ra [akoʎe'do(x), ra] *adj* welcoming.

acolher [5] [ako'ʎe(x)] *vt* **-1.** [ger] to welcome. **-2.** [hospedar] to put sb up. **-3.** [admitir] to receive.

acolhida [ako'ʎida] *f* **-1.** [hospedagem] hospitality. **-2.** [recepção] welcome.

acometer [5] [akome'te(x)] *vt* **-1.** [atacar] to attack. **-2.** [suj: doença, desejo, sentimento] to strike.

acomodação [akomoda'sãw] (*pl* **-ões**) *f* **-1.** [alojamento] accommodation. **-2.** [aposento, instalação] room. **-3.** [arranjo, arrumação] layout. **-4.** [adaptação] adaptation.

acomodado, da [akomo'dadu, da] *adj* **-1.** [alojado, instalado] settled. **-2.** [conformado] reconciled.

acomodar [4] [akomo'da(x)] *vt* **-1.** [alojar, instalar] to accommodate. **-2.** [adaptar]: ~ **algo a** *ou* **com algo** to adapt sthg to sthg.
◆ **acomodar-se** *vp* **-1.** [alojar-se, instalar-se] to settle o.s. **-2.** [conformar-se] to reconcile o.s.

acompanhado, da [akõnpa'ɲadu, da] *adj* accompanied.

acompanhamento [akõnpaɲa'mẽntu] *m* **-1.** [de processo, doença] monitoring. **-2.** *MÚS* accompaniment. **-3.** *CULIN* side order, side dish.

acompanhante [akõnpa'ɲãntʃi] *mf* companion.

acompanhar [4] [akõnpa'ɲa(x)] <> *vt* **-1.** [ger] to accompany. **-2.** [processo, doença] to monitor. **-3.** [suj: problema, preocupações] to stay with. **-4.** [margear] to run parallel to. **-5.** [compreender] to keep up with. **-6.** [combinar]: ~ **algo com algo** to accompany sthg with sthg. **-7.** *CULIN* to go with. <> *vi MÚS* to accompany.

Aconcágua [akon'kagwa] *n*: **o (Monte)** ~ (Mount) Aconcagua.

aconchegado, da [akõnʃe'gadu, da] *adj* snug, cosy.

aconchegante [akõnʃe'gãntʃi] *adj* cosy.

aconchegar [14] [akõnʃe'ga(x)] *vt* **-1.** [nos braços] to cuddle. **-2.** [na cama, nas cobertas] to tuck up *ou* in.
◆ **aconchegar-se** *vp* **-1.** [nos braços] to snuggle. **-2.** [na cama, nas cobertas] to tuck o.s. up *ou* in.

aconchego [akõn'ʃegu] *m* warmth.

acondicionamento [akõndʒisjona'mẽntu] *m* packaging.

acondicionar [4] [akõndʒisjo'na(x)] *vt* **-1.** [embrulhar] to wrap. **-2.** [embalar] to package.

aconselhar [4] [akõnse'ʎa(x)] *vt* **-1.** [dar conselho a]: ~ **alguém (a fazer algo** *ou* **a que faça algo)** to advise sb (to do sthg). **-2.** [recomendar] to recommend.
◆ **aconselhar-se** *vp* to seek advice; ~**-se com**

alguém to seek the advice of sb.
aconselhável [akõnse'ʎavɛw] (*pl* **-eis**) *adj* advisable.
acontecer [25] [akõnte'se(x)] *vi* to happen.
acontecimento [akõntesi'mẽntu] *m* event.
acoplado, da [ako'pladu, da] *adj* [conectado - peças] connected; [- naves espaciais] docked.
acoplar [4] [ako'pla(x)] *vt* to couple.
acordado, da [akox'dadu, da] *adj* **-1.** [desperto] awake; **sonhar ~** to daydream. **-2.** [combinado] agreed.
acordar [4] [akox'da(x)] ◇ *vt* **-1.** [despertar] to wake. **-2.** [combinar]: **~ algo/fazer algo** to arrange sthg/to do sthg; **~ que** to agree that. ◇ *vi* **-1.** [despertar] to wake. **-2.** [concordar]: **~ em algo/fazer algo** to agree to sthg/to do sthg.
acorde [a'kɔxdʒi] *m* *MÚS* chord.
acordeão [akox'dʒjãw] (*pl* **-ões**) *m* accordion.
acordeonista [akoxdʒjo'niʃta] *mf* accordionist.
acordo [a'koxdu] *m* agreement; **chegar a um ~** to arrive at an agreement; **de ~** agreed; **de ~ com** [conforme] according to; **estar de ~ (com alguém/em fazer algo)** to be in agreement (with sb/to do sthg); **de comum ~** by common accord.
Açores [a'soriʃ] *npl*: **os ~** the Azores.
acorrentar [4] [akoxẽn'ta(x)] *vt* to chain.
acossado, da [ako'sadu, da] ◇ *adj* [perseguido] persecuted, hounded. ◇ *m, f* victim.
acossar [4] [ako'sa(x)] *vt* **-1.** [perseguir] to pursue. **-2.** [acuar] to corner.
acostamento [akoʃta'mẽntu] *m* hard shoulder.
acostumado, da [akoʃtu'madu, da] *adj* **-1.** [habitual] usual. **-2.** [habituado]: **estar ~ a** *ou* **com algo** to be used to sthg; **estar ~ a fazer algo** to be in the habit of doing sthg.
acostumar [4] [akoʃtu'ma(x)] ◇ *vt*: **~ alguém/algo a algo** to accustom sb/sthg to sthg; **~ alguém a fazer algo** to accustom sb to doing sthg. ◇ *vi*: **~ com algo** to get used to sthg.
◆ **acostumar-se** *vp* to accustom o.s.; **~-se a algo/a fazer algo** to accustom o.s. to sthg/to doing sthg.
acotovelar [4] [akotove'la(x)] *vt* **-1.** [para chamar a atenção] to nudge. **-2.** [empurrar] to elbow.
◆ **acotovelar-se** *vp* [empurrar-se] to elbow one's way.
açougue [a'sogi] *m* butcher's.
açougueiro, ra [aso'gejru, ra] *m* butcher.
acovardado, da [akovax'dadu, da] *adj* intimidated.
acovardar [4] [akovax'da(x)] *vt* [amedrontar] to intimidate.
◆ **acovardar-se** *vp* **-1.** [amedrontar-se] to be intimidated. **-2.** [perder o ânimo] to become disheartened.
acre ['akri] *adj* **-1.** [ácido, amargo] acrid. **-2.** *fig* [áspero] harsh.
Acre ['akri] *n* Acre.
acreditar [4] [akredʒi'ta(x)] ◇ *vt* **-1.** [crer] to believe. **-2.** [abonar] to confirm. ◇ *vi* **-1.** [crer]: **~ em algo/alguém** to believe in sthg/sb. **-2.** [confiar]: **~ em algo/alguém** to have confidence in sthg/sb.
acrescentar [4] [akresẽn'ta(x)] *vt* to add.
acrescer [25] [akre'se(x)] ◇ *vt* [adicionar]: **~ algo (a algo)** to add sthg (to sthg). ◇ *vi*: **acresce que ...** in addition to which ...
acréscimo [a'krɛsimu] *m* **-1.** [adição] addition. **-2.** [aumento] increase.
acrílico [a'kriliku] *m* acrylic.
acrimônia [akri'monja] *f* acrimony.
acrobacia [akroba'sia] *f* acrobatics *(pl)*.
acrobata [akro'bata] *mf* acrobat.
acuado, da [a'kuadu, da] *adj* [acossado] cornered.
acuar [4] [a'kwa(x)] ◇ *vt* to corner. ◇ *vi* to retreat.
açúcar [a'suka(x)] *m* sugar; **~ mascavo** brown sugar.
açucarado, da [asuka'radu, da] *adj* sugary.
açucareiro [asuka'rejru] *m* sugar bowl.
açude [a'sudʒi] *m* dam.
acudir [61] [aku'dʒi(x)] ◇ *vt* to run to help. ◇ *vi* to rush to sb's aid.
acuidade [akwi'dadʒi] *f* sharpness.
acumulação [akumula'sãw] (*pl* **-ões**) *f* accumulation.
acumulado, da [akumu'ladu, da] *adj* **-1.** [juros] accrued. **-2.** [prêmio] rollover.
acumular [4] [akumu'la(x)] *vt* **-1.** [ajuntar] to accrue. **-2.** [amontoar] to accumulate. **-3.** [reunir] to collate. **-4.** [cargos] to combine.
acúmulo [a'kumulu] *m* accumulation.
acupuntura [akupũn'tura] *f* acupuncture.
acupunturista [akupũntu'riʃta] *mf* acupuncturist.
acusação [akuza'sãw] (*pl* **-ões**) *f* **-1.** [incriminação] accusation. **-2.** [promotoria]: **a ~** the prosecution.
acusado, da [aku'zadu, da] *m, f* [réu] defendant.
acusar [4] [aku'za(x)] *vt* **-1.** [gen]: **~ alguém (de algo)** to accuse sb (of sthg). **-2.** *JUR*: **~ alguém de algo** to charge sb with sthg. **-3.** [recebimento] to acknowledge. **-4.** [mostrar] to reveal.
acústico, ca [a'kuʃtʃiku, ka] *adj* acoustic.
◆ **acústica** *f* *FÍS* acoustics.
AD (*abrev de* **Anno Domini**) AD.
adaga [a'daga] *f* dagger.
adágio [a'daʒu] *m* **-1.** *MÚS* adagio. **-2.** [provérbio] adage.
adaptação [adapta'sãw] (*pl* **-ões**) *f* adaptation.
adaptado, da [adap'tadu, da] *adj* adapted.
adaptador [adapta'do(x)] (*pl* **-res**) *m*: **~ de rede** *COMPUT* network adaptor.
adaptar [4] [adap'ta(x)] *vt* **-1.** [fixar] to fit. **-2.** [peça teatral, música, linguagem] to adapt.
◆ **adaptar-se** *vp* [ambientar-se] to adapt o.s.
adega [a'dɛga] *f* cellar.
ademais [adʒi'majʃ] *adv* [além disso] moreover.
adendo [a'dẽndu] *m* addendum.
adentro [a'dẽntru] *adv*: **casa/noite ~** into the house/night; **mar ~** out to sea.
adepto, ta [a'dɛptu, ta] *m, f*: **~ (de)** follower (of).

adequadamente [adekwada'mẽntʃi] *adv* adequately.
adequado, da [ade'kwadu, da] *adj* appropriate.
adequar [23] [ade'kwa(x)] *vt*: ~ **algo a algo** to adapt sthg to sthg.
adereço [ade'resu] *m* **-1.** [enfeite] decoration. **-2.** [jóia] adornment.
aderência [ade'rẽnsja] *f* **-1.** [de cola] adherence. **-2.** [a partido, campanha etc] support.
aderente [ade'rẽntʃi] <> *adj* [substância] adhesive. <> *mf* [adepto] adherent.
aderir [57] [ade'ri(x)] *vi* **-1.** [colar-se] to stick. **-2.** [a partido, campanha] to adhere. **-3.** [a moda, estilo de vida] to follow.
adesão [ade'zãw] (*pl* **-ões**) *f* [a partido, campanha] adhesion; **jantar de** ~ fund-raising dinner; **documento de** ~ petition.
adesivo, va [ade'zivu, va] *adj* adhesive.
◆ **adesivo** *m* Sellotape® *UK*, Scotch tape® *US*.
adestrador, ra [adeʃ'trado(x), ra] *m, f* [de animais] trainer.
adestramento [adeʃtra'mẽntu] *m* training.
adestrar [4] [adeʃ'tra(x)] *vt* to train.
adeus [a'dewʃ] <> *m* farewell. <> *interj* goodbye!
adiamento [adʒja'mẽntu] *m* [prorrogação] postponement.
adiantado, da [adʒjãn'tadu, da] *adj* **-1.** [trabalho] ahead of schedule. **-2.** [relógio] fast. **-3.** [pagamento] advance *(antes de subst)*. **-4.** [aluno, povo] advanced.
◆ **adiantado** *adv*: **pagar** ~ to pay in advance; **cheguei** ~ **ao encontro** I arrived early for the meeting.
adiantamento [adʒjãnta'mẽntu] *m* **-1.** [progresso] progress. **-2.** [de quantia, salário] advance.
adiantar [4] [adʒjãn'ta(x)] <> *vt* **-1.** [trabalho] to get ahead with. **-2.** [relógio] to put forward. **-3.** [quantia, salário] to advance. **-4.** [dizer antecipadamente] to anticipate. <> *vi* **-1.** [relógio] to be fast. **-2.** [trazer benefício]: ~ **fazer algo** to be worth doing sthg.
◆ **adiantar-se** *vp* **-1.** [em trabalho, estudos] to get ahead. **-2.** [avançar]: **~-se para** to go towards. **-3.** [sobrepujar]: **~-se a alguém** to surpass sb.
adiante [a'dʒjãntʃi] *adv* **-1.** [na frente] ahead; **mais** ~ [no espaço] further on; [no tempo] later on; **logo** ~ just ahead. **-2.** [em explicação, narração]: **ir** ~ to go ahead. **-3.**: **levar algo** ~ [obra, plano] to go ahead with sthg.
adiar [16] [a'dʒja(x)] *vt* to postpone.
adição [adʒi'sãw] (*pl* **-ões**) *f* **-1.** [acréscimo] addition. **-2.** *MAT* sum.
adicionar [4] [adʒisjo'na(x)] *vt* **-1.** [acrescentar] to add. **-2.** *MAT* to add up.
adido, da [a'dʒidu, da] *m,f* [em embaixada] attaché.
adiposo, osa [adʒi'pozu, ɔza] *adj* adipose.
aditivo [adʒi'tʃivu] *m* additive.
adivinhação [adʒiviɲa'sãw] *f* **-1.** [previsão] prediction. **-2.** [conjetura] guess. **-3.** [decifração] solution.
adivinhar [4] [adʒivi'ɲa(x)] *vt* **-1.** [presente, futuro] to predict. **-2.** [resposta, causa, intenção] to guess. **-3.** [enigma, mistério] to solve.
adivinho, nha [adʒi'viɲu, ɲa] *m,f* fortune-teller.
◆ **adivinha** *f* [adivinhação] riddle.
adjacências [adʒa'sẽnsjaʃ] *fpl* neighbourhood.
adjacente [adʒa'sẽntʃi] *adj* adjacent.
adjetivo [adʒɛ'tʃivu] *m* adjective.
adjudicação [adʒudʒika'sãw] (*pl* **-ões**) *f* *JUR* adjudication.
adjudicar [12] [adʒudʒi'ka(x)] *vt JUR*: ~ **algo a alguém** to adjudicate sthg for sb.
adjunto, ta [ad'ʒũntu, ta] <> *adj* [assistente] assistant. <> *m, f* **-1.** [assistente] assistant. **-2.** *GRAM* adjunct.
administração [adʒiminiʃtra'sãw] (*pl* **-ões**) *f* **-1.** [ger] administration; ~ **de empresas** [curso] business studies; ~ **pública** public administration. **-2.** [pessoal] management.
◆ **Administração** *f* [governo] Administration.
administrador, ra [adʒiminiʃtra'do(x), ra] (*mpl* **-es**, *fpl* **-s**) *m, f* administrator.
administrar [4] [adʒiminiʃ'tra(x)] *vt* **-1.** [gerir] to manage. **-2.** [dar] to administer.
administrativo, va [adʒiminiʃtra'tʃivu, va] *adj* administrative.
admiração [adʒimira'sãw] *f* **-1.** [respeito] admiration. **-2.** [surpresa] surprise.
admirado, da [adʒimi'radu, da] *adj* **-1.** [respeitado] admired. **-2.** [surpreso]: ~ **(de)** astonished (at).
admirador, ra [adʒimira'do(x), ra] *m, f* admirer.
admirar [4] [adʒimi'ra(x)] <> *vt* **-1.** [respeitar, contemplar] to admire. **-2.** [surpreender] to surprise. <> *vi* [surpreender] to be astounding; **não é de** ~ **(que ...)** it's no wonder (that ...).
◆ **admirar-se** *vp* **-1.** [mutuamente] to admire each other. **-2.** [surpreender-se]: **~-se (de algo)** to be surprised (at sthg); **não me admiro!** I'm not surprised!
admirável [adʒimi'ravɛw] (*pl* **-eis**) *adj* **-1.** [excelente] admirable. **-2.** [assombroso] amazing.
admissão [adʒimi'sãw] (*pl* **-ões**) *f* **-1.** [ger] admission. **-2.** [contratação] employment.
admissível [adʒimi'sivew] (*pl* **-eis**) *adj* acceptable.
admitir [6] [adʒimi'tʃi(x)] *vt* **-1.** [ger] to admit. **-2.** [aceitar] to tolerate. **-3.** [consentir em] to permit. **-4.** [contratar] to take on. **-5.** [comportar] to allow.
admoestação [adʒmweʃta'sãw] (*pl* **-ões**) *f* **-1.** [advertência] warning. **-2.** [reprimenda] reprimand.
admoestar [4] [adʒmweʃ'ta(x)] *vt* **-1.** [advertir]: ~ **alguém de** *ou* **sobre** to warn sb of *ou* about. **-2.** [repreender]: ~ **alguém (de)** to reprimand sb (for).
ADN (*abrev de* **ácido desoxirribonucleico**) *m* DNA.
adoçante [ado'sãntʃi] *m* sweetener.
adoção [ado'sãw] (*pl* **-ões**) [-õjʃ] *f* adoption.
adoçar [13] [ado'sa(x)] *vt* **-1.** [café, chá] to sweeten. **-2.** *fig* [velhice, vida] to ease.
adocicado, da [adosi'kadu, da] *adj* slightly sweet.
adoecer [25] [adwe'se(x)] <> *vi*: ~ **(de)** to fall ill

(with). <> *vt* to make ill.
adoentado, da [adwẽn'tadu, da] *adj* ill.
adoidado, da [adoj'dadu, da] <> *adj* [amalucado] mad. <> *adv fam* [muito] madly.
adolescência [adole'sẽnsja] *f* adolescence.
adolescente [adole'sẽntʃi] <> *adj* adolescent. <> *mf* adolescent.
adoração [adora'sãw] *f* adoration.
adorar [4] [ado'ra(x)] *vt* **-1.** [divindade] to adore. **-2.** [gostar muito de] to love.
adorável [ado'ravɛw] (*pl* **-eis**) *adj* lovely.
adormecer [25] [adoxme'se(x)] <> *vi* **-1.** [dormir] to fall asleep. **-2.** [ficar dormente] to go numb. <> *vt* [causar sono a] to make sleepy.
adormecido, da [adoxme'sidu, da] *adj* **-1.** [que está dormindo] asleep. **-2.** [dormente] numb.
adornar [4] [adox'na(x)] *vt* to adorn.
adorno [a'doxnu] *m* adornment; **de ~** decorative.
adotar [4] [ado'ta(x)] *vt* to adopt.
adotivo, va [ado'tʃivu, va] *adj* adoptive.
adquirir [6] [adʒiki'ri(x)] *vt* **-1.** [comprar] to buy. **-2.** [conseguir] to acquire.
adrede [a'dredʒi] *adv* on purpose.
adrenalina [adrena'lina] *f* adrenalin.
Adriático [a'drjatʃiku] *n*: **o (mar) ~** the Adriatic (Sea).
adro ['adru] *m* churchyard.
adstringente [adʒiʃtrĩn'ʒẽntʃi] <> *adj* astringent. <> *m* astringent lotion.
aduana [a'dwana] *f* customs *(pl)*.
aduaneiro, ra [adwa'nejru, ra] *adj* customs *(pl)*.
adubar [4] [adu'ba(x)] *vt* to fertilize.
adubo [a'dubu] *m* [fertilizante] fertilizer; **~ orgânico/químico** organic/chemical fertilizer.
adulação [adula'sãw] *f* flattery.
adulador, ra [adula'do(x), ra] <> *adj* flattering. <> *m, f* flatterer.
adular [4] [adu'la(x)] *vt* to flatter.
adulteração [aduwtera'sãw] (*pl* **-ões**) *f* **-1.** [de texto] falsification. **-2.** [de alimento, medicamento] adulteration.
adulterar [4] [aduwte'ra(x)] *vt* **-1.** [texto] to falsify. **-2.** [alimento, medicamento] to adulterate.
adultério [aduw'tɛrju] *m* adultery.
adúltero, ra [a'duwteru, ra] <> *adj* adulterous. <> *m, f* adulterer (*f* adulteress).
adulto, ta [a'duwtu, ta] <> *adj* adult. <> *m, f* adult.
adunco [a'dũnku] *adj* [nariz] hooked.
adventício, cia [adʒvẽn'tʃisju, sja] <> *adj* **-1.** [forasteiro] alien. **-2.** [casual] chance. <> *m, f* [forasteiro] outsider.
advento [adʒ'vẽntu] *m* advent.
advérbio [adʒ'vɛxbju] *m* adverb.
adversário, ria [adʒivex'sarju, rja] *m, f* adversary.
adversidade [adʒivexsi'dadʒi] *f* adversity.
adverso, sa [adʒi'vɛxsu, sa] *adj* **-1.** [difícil] adverse. **-2.** [desfavorável]: **~ a algo** unfavourable to sthg. **-3.** [contrário]: **~ a algo** opposed to sthg.
advertência [adʒivex'tẽnsja] *f* **-1.** [aviso] warning. **-2.** [repreensão] reprimand.
advertir [54] [adʒivex'tʃi(x)] *vt* **-1.** [prevenir, avisar] to warn. **-2.** [repreender] to reprimand.
advindo, da [ad'vĩndu, da] *adj*: **~ de** resulting from.
advir [67] [adʒ'vi(x)] *vi* **-1.** [resultar]: **~ de** to result from. **-2.** [suceder]: **~ (a)** to happen to.
advocacia [adʒivoka'sia] *f* advocacy.
advogado, da [adʒivo'gadu, da] *m, f* lawyer; **~ do diabo** devil's advocate.
advogar [14] [adʒivo'ga(x)] <> *vt* **-1.** JUR to advocate. **-2.** *fig* [defender] to defend. <> *vi* **-1.** [exercer a profissão de advogado] to practise law. **-2.** [interceder]: **~ por algo/alguém** to represent sthg/sb.
aéreo, rea [a'ɛrju, rja] *adj* **-1.** AERON air *(antes de subst)*. **-2.** [pessoa] absent-minded.
aerobarco [aɛro'baxku] *m* hovercraft.
aeróbico, ca [ae'rɔbiku, ka] *adj* aerobic.
◆ **aeróbica** *f* aerobics *(sg)*.
aeroclube [aɛro'klubi] *m* flying club.
aerodinâmico, ca [aɛrodʒi'nãmiku, ka] *adj* aerodynamic.
◆ **aerodinâmica** *f* aerodynamics *(pl)*.
aeródromo [aɛ'rɔdromu] *m* airfield.
aeroespacial [aɛroʃpa'sjaw] (*pl* **-ais**) *adj* aerospace *(antes de subst)*.
aerofoto [aɛro'fɔtu] *f* aerial photograph.
aerograma [aɛro'grama] *m* aerogramme *UK*, aerogram *US*.
aeromoça [aɛro'mosa] *f* air stewardess, flight attendant.
aeromodelismo [a,ɛromode'liʒmu] *m* **-1.** [técnica] model aeroplane making. **-2.** ESP model aeroplane flying.
aeronauta [aɛro'nawta] *m, f* airline pilot.
aeronáutica [aɛro'nawtʃika] *f* **-1.** [ciência] aeronautics *(sg)*. **-2.** MIL air force.
aeronave [aɛro'navi] *f* aircraft.
aeroporto [aɛro'poxtu] *m* airport.
aerossol [aɛro'sɔw] (*pl* **-óis**) *m* aerosol.
afã [a'fã] *m* **-1.** [ânsia - por sucesso] longing; [- de agradar] eagerness; [- para fazer algo] urge. **-2.** [entusiasmo, vontade] enthusiasm.
afabilidade [afabili'dadʒi] *f* affability.
afagar [14] [afa'ga(x)] *vt* **-1.** [person] to caress. **-2.** [animal, hair] to stroke.
afago [a'fagu] *m* stroke, caress.
afamado, da [afa'madu, da] *adj* famous.
afanar [4] [afa'na(x)] *vt fam* [roubar] to nick, to steal.
afasia [afa'zia] *f* aphasia.
afastado, da [afaʃ'tadu, da] *adj* **-1.** [praia, terras] remote. **-2.** [casa] isolated. **-3.** [parente] distant. **-4.** [pernas] apart.
afastamento [afaʃta'mẽntu] *m* **-1.** [distanciamento] withdrawal. **-2.** [de cargo] removal.
afastar [4] [afaʃ'ta(x)] *vt* **-1.** [tirar do caminho] to push out of the way. **-2.** [apartar] to put aside. **-3.** [pôr de lado] to part. **-4.** [distanciar] to keep away

(sep). **-5.** [de cargo] to remove. **-6.** [frustrar] to thwart.

◆ **afastar-se** *vp* **-1.** [distanciar-se - no espaço] to move aside *(sep)*; [- de amigos etc] to part. **-2.** [sair] to leave. **-3.** [de cargo] to take leave from.

afável [a'favɛw] (*pl* **-eis**) *adj* affable.

afazeres [afa'zeriʃ] *mpl* affairs; ~ **domésticos** housework *(sg)*.

Afeganistão [afeganiʃ'tãw] *n* Afghanistan.

afegão, gã [afegiãw, gã] <> *adj* Afghan. <> *m, f* Afghan.

afeição [afej'sãw] *f* affection; **sentir ~ por alguém/algo** to feel affection for sb/sthg.

afeiçoado, da [afej'swadu, da] *adj* attached.

afeiçoar-se [20] [afej'swaxsi] *vp*: ~ **a alguém/algo** to become attached to sb/sthg.

afeito, ta [a'fejtu, ta] *adj*: ~ **a** accustomed to.

aferidor [aferi'do(x)] *m* [instrumento] meter.

aferir [57] [afe'ri(x)] *vt* **-1.** [conferir] to check. **-2.** [avaliar] to estimate. **-3.** [cotejar]: ~ **algo/alguém por algo** to judge sthg/sb by sthg.

aferrado, da [afe'xadu, da] *adj* [apegado] attached.

aferrar-se [4] [afe'xaxsi] *vp* [apegar-se]: ~ **a algo** to cling to sthg.

aferrolhar [4] [afexo'ʎa(x)] *vt* **-1.** [com ferrolho] to bolt. **-2.** *fig* [aprisionar] to lock up *(sep)*.

aferventar [4] [afexvẽn'ta(x)] *vt* to boil.

afetação [afeta'sãw] *f* affectation.

afetado, da [afe'tadu, da] *adj* affected.

afetar [4] [afe'ta(x)] *vt* to affect.

afetividade [afetʃivi'dadʒi] *f* **-1.** affection. **-2.** *PSIC* affectivity.

afetivo, va [afe'tʃivu, va] *adj* **-1.** affectionate, kind. **-2.** *PSIC* affective.

afeto [a'fɛtu] *m* **-1.** affection. **-2.** *PSIC* affect.

afetuoso, osa [afe'tuozu, ɔza] *adj* affectionate.

afiado, da [a'fjadu, da] *adj* sharp.

afiançar [13] [afjãn'sa(x)] *vt* **-1.** [réu] to bail out. **-2.** [dívida, empréstimo] to guarantee.

afiar [16] [a'fja(x)] *vt* [faca, tesoura] to sharpen.

aficionado, da [afisjo'nadu, da] *m, f* enthusiast.

afigurar-se [4] [afigu'raxsi] *vp* to seem, to appear.

afilado, da [afi'ladu, da] *adj* fine.

afilhado, da [afi'ʎadu, da] *m, f* godchild.

afiliação [afilja'sãw] *f* affiliation.

afiliado, da [afi'ljadu, da] *m, f* affiliate.

afiliar [16] [afi'lja(x)] *vt* to affiliate.

◆ **afiliar-se** *vp*: **~-se a algo** to join sthg.

afim [a'fĩ] (*pl* **-ns**) *adj* **-1.** [objetivos] similar. **-2.** [almas] kindred.

afinação [afina'sãw] (*pl* **-ões**) [sõjʃ] *f MÚS* tuning.

afinado, da [afi'nadu, da] *adj* **-1.** [instrumento] tuned. **-2.** [pessoa]: ~ **com** attuned to.

afinal [afi'naw] *adv* **-1.** [por fim] finally, in the end; ~ **, ele vem ou não vem?** so is he coming or not?; ~ **(de contas)** in the end. **-2.** [pensando bem] all things considered.

afinar [4] [afi'na(x)] <> *vt* **-1.** [voz, instrumento] to tune. **-2.** [idéias, sentimentos]: ~ **algo com algo** to attune sthg to sthg. **-3.** [estilo, modos] to refine. <> *vi* **-1.** [emagrecer] to slim down. **-2.** [concordar]: ~ **com alguém em algo** to see eye to eye with sb over sthg. **-3.** [dar-se bem]: ~ **com alguém** to get on with sb.

afinco [a'fĩŋku] *m* perseverance; **com ~** assiduously.

afinidade [afini'dadʒi] *f* **-1.** [semelhança] affinity. **-2.** [parentesco]: **são primas por ~** they look on each other as cousins.

afins [a'fĩʃ] *pl* ▻ **afim**.

afirmação [afixma'sãw] (*pl* **-ões**) *f* **-1.** [declaração] assertion. **-2.** [auto-afirmação] self-assertion.

afirmar [4] [afix'ma(x)] *vt* **-1.** [declarar] to declare. **-2.** [confirmar] to assert.

◆ **afirmar-se** *vp* **-1.** [estabelecer-se] to establish o.s. **-2.** [sentir-se seguro] to assert o.s.

afirmativamente [afixmatʃiva'mẽntʃi] *adv*: **responder ~** to reply in the affirmative.

afirmativo, va [afixma'tʃivu, va] *adj* affirmative.

◆ **afirmativa** *f* assertion.

afivelar [4] [afive'la(x)] *vt* to buckle.

afixar [4] [afik'sa(x)] *vt* [aviso, cartaz] to affix.

aflição [afli'sãw] (*pl* **-ões**) *f* **-1.** [sofrimento] distress *(U)*. **-2.** [ansiedade] anxiety. **-3.** [desconforto]: **dar ~ a alguém** to unsettle sb.

afligir [52] [afli'ʒi(x)] *vt* **-1.** [fazer sofrer] to distress. **-2.** [causar ansiedade a] to trouble. **-3.** [suj: mal] to torment.

◆ **afligir-se** *vp*: **~-se (com)** to worry (about).

aflitivo, va [afli'tʃivu, va] *adj* distressing.

aflito, ta [a'flitu, ta] *adj* distressed; **estar ~ com algo/para fazer algo** to be desperate about sthg/to do sthg.

aflorar [4] [aflo'ra(x)] *vi* **-1.** [vir à tona] to come to the surface. **-2.** [surgir] to surface.

afluência [aflu'ẽnsja] *f* **-1.** [de líquido] flow. **-2.** [de pessoas] flood. **-3.** [riqueza] affluence.

afluente [aflu'ẽntʃi] <> *adj* [rico] affluent. <> *m* [curso de rio] tributary.

afluir [74] [a'flwi(x)] *vt*: ~ **a** *ou* **para/de** to flow into *ou* towards/from; [pessoas] to flock to *ou* towards/from.

afobação [afoba'sãw] *f* **-1.** [agitação, atrapalhação] turmoil. **-2.** [pressa] haste. **-3.** [ansiedade] anxiety.

afobado, da [afo'badu, da] *adj* **-1.** [ger] flustered. **-2.** [ansioso] upset.

afobamento [afoba'mẽntu] *m* = **afobação**.

afobar [4] [afo'ba(x)] *vt* **-1.** [ger] to fluster. **-2.** [deixar ansioso] to perturb.

◆ **afobar-se** *vp* **-1.** [ficar agitado] to get flustered. **-2.** [apressar-se] to fret. **-3.** [ficar ansioso] to worry.

afofar [4] [afo'fa(x)] *vt* **-1.** [almofada] to fluff up. **-2.** [terra] to loosen.

afogado, da [afo'gadu, da] *adj* **-1.** [pessoa] drowned. **-2.** [motor] flooded. **-3.** [em dívidas] weighed down. **-4.** [em trabalho] swamped.

afogador [afoga'do(x)] (*pl* **-es**) *m AUTO* choke.

afogamento [afoga'mẽntu] *m* drowning.

afogar [14] [afo'ga(x)] <> *vt* **-1.** [pessoa] to drown.

-2. [motor] to flood. -3. [pensamentos, sentimento] to quell. ◇ *vi* -1. [pessoa] to drown. -2. [motor] to flood.
◆ **afogar-se** *vp* [pessoa] to drown o.s.
afoito, ta [a'fojtu, ta] *adj* in a hurry *(depois de subst/de verbo)*.
afonia [afo'nia] *f* aphonia.
afônico, ca [a'foniku, ka] *adj* silent.
afora [a'fɔra] ◇ *adv*: **pelo mundo** ~ throughout the world; **mar** ~ across the sea; **pela vida** ~ throughout life; **sair** *ou* **ir por aí** ~ to go off; **porta** ~ out the door. ◇ *prep* apart from.
aforismo [afo'riʒmu] *m* aphorism.
afortunado, da [afoxtu'nadu, da] *adj* fortunate.
Afoxés [a'foʃɛʃ] *mpl traditional groups who parade through the streets during Carnival.*

AFOXÉS

Religious procession related to *candomblé*; *afoxés* were made up of groups of black people, who took to the streets and sang to the sound of percussion instruments such as *atabaques* and *agogôs*. Nowadays, *afoxés* are carnival displays typical of Bahia. The most popular one is known as *Filhos de Gandhi* ('Sons of Gandhi').

afrescalhado, da [afreʃka'ʎadu, da] *adj fam* camp.
afresco [a'freʃku] *m* fresco.
África ['afrika] *n* Africa.
africano, na [afri'kãnu, na] ◇ *adj* African. ◇ *m, f* African.
afro-americano, na [afrwameri'kãnu, na] ◇ *adj* Afro-American. ◇ *m, f* Afro-American.
afro-brasileiro, ra [afrobrazi'lejru, ra] *adj* Afro-Brazilian.
afrodisíaco, ca [afrodʒi'ziaku, ka] *adj* aphrodisiac.
◆ **afrodisíaco** *m* aphrodisiac.
afronta [a'frõnta] *f* affront.
afrontado, da [afrõn'tadu, da] *adj* [ultrajado] outraged.
afrontar [4] [afrõn'ta(x)] *vt* -1. [ultrajar] to outrage. -2. [atacar] to confront.
afrouxar [4] [afro'ʃa(x)] ◇ *vt* -1. [soltar] to loosen. -2. [relaxar] to relax. ◇ *vi* -1. [soltar-se] to come undone. -2. [pessoa] to give up.
afta ['afta] *f* mouth ulcer.
afugentar [4] [afuʒẽn'ta(x)] *vt* to chase away.
afundar [4] [afũn'da(x)] ◇ *vt* -1. [fazer ir ao fundo - pessoa] to force to the ground; [- âncora] to drop. -2. [aprofundar] to deepen. ◇ *vi* to sink.
◆ **afundar-se** *vp* -1. *fam* [em exame] to fail. -2. [embrenhar-se - em afazeres] to become engulfed; [- no matagal] to go deep. -3. [imergir] to sink. -4. [perder-se] to lose o.s.
afunilar [4] [afuni'la(x)] *vt* -1. [dar forma de funil] to shape into a funnel. -2. [estreitar] to narrow.
◆ **afunilar-se** *vp* [estreitar-se - rio] to narrow; [- análise] to be narrowed down.
agá [a'ga] *m* aitch.
agachado, da [aga'ʃadu, da] *adj* squat.
agachar-se [7] [aga'ʃaxsi] *vp* -1. [acocorar-se] to squat. -2. *fig* [aviltar-se] to grovel.
agarrado, da [aga'xadu, da] *adj* -1. [preso com força]: ~ **a** *ou* **em algo** clinging to *ou* onto sthg. -2. [apegado]: ~ **a** *ou* **com alguém** clinging to *ou* onto sb.
agarramento [agaxa'mẽntu] *m* [entre namorados] clinch; **ser pego de** ~ **com alguém** to be caught in a clinch with sb.
agarrar [4] [aga'xa(x)] ◇ *vt* -1. [segurar com força] to grasp. -2. [capturar] to catch. ◇ *vi* -1. [segurar com força]: ~ **em** to hold on to. -2. [goleiro] to defend.
◆ **agarrar-se** *vp* -1. [segurar com força]: ~**-se a** *ou* **em** to hold on to. -2. [abraçar-se fortemente] to cling to each other.
agasalhado, da [agaza'ʎadu, da] *adj* warmly wrapped.
agasalhar [4] [agaza'ʎa(x)] *vt* to wrap up warmly.
◆ **agasalhar-se** *vp* to wrap o.s. up warmly.
agasalho [aga'zaʎu] *m* -1. [casaco, manta] warm clothing. -2. [suéter] jumper.
ágeis ['aʒejʃ] *pl* ▻ **ágil**.
agência [a'ʒẽnsja] *f* -1. [empresa] agency; ~ **de notícias** news agency; ~ **de viagens** travel agency. -2. [sucursal] branch; ~ **de correios** post-office branch.
agenciamento [a'ʒẽsjamẽntu] *m* -1. [negociação] negotiation. -2. [representação] representation. -3. [obtenção, busca] recruitment.
agenciar [16] [a'ʒẽsja(x)] *vt* -1. [ger] to manage. -2. [servir de agente a] to act as agent for.
agenda [a'ʒẽnda] *f* -1. [de compromissos] diary; ~ **eletrônica** electronic organizer. -2. [programação - de reunião] agenda; [- de semana] schedule.
agendar [4] [aʒẽnda(x)] *vt* to schedule.
agente [a'ʒẽntʃi] ◇ *m, f* [pessoa] agent; ~ **secreto** secret agent; ~ **de viagens** travel agent. ◇ *m* -1. [ger] agent. -2. GRAM subject.
agigantado, da [aʒigãn'tadu, da] *adj* gigantic.
agigantar [4] [aʒigãn'ta(x)] *vt* to magnify; **o vento agigantou as ondas** the wind swelled the waves.
ágil ['aʒiw] (*pl* **ágeis**) *adj* agile.
agilidade [aʒili'dadʒi] *f* agility.
agilizar [4] [aʒili'za(x)] *vt* to activate.
ágio ['aʒju] *m* interest.
agiota [a'ʒjɔta] *m, f* [usurário] usurer.
agir [52] [a'ʒi(x)] *vi* to act; ~ **bem/mal** to act properly/wrongly.
agitação [aʒita'sãw] (*pl* **-ões**) *f* -1. [movimento - de garrafa] shaking; [- de líquido] stirring; [- de braços] waving. -2. PSIC [excitação] agitation. -3. [inquietação] restlessness. -4. [rebuliço] agitation. -5. [política, social] unrest.
agitado, da [aʒi'tadu, da] *adj* -1. [excitado] agitated. -2. [inquieto] disturbed. -3. [tumultuado] unsettled. -4. [mar] rough.
agitador, ra [aʒita'do(x), ra] *m, f* agitator.
agitar [4] [aʒi'ta(x)] ◇ *vt* -1. [movimentar - garrafa etc] to shake; [- líquido] to stir; [- braços] to wave.

-2. [excitar] to unnerve. -3. [inquietar] to worry. -4. [sublevar] to agitate. -5. *fam* [fazer, organizar] to organize. ◇ *vi* [movimentar]: **'agite antes de usar'** 'shake before use'.
◆ **agitar-se** *vp* -1. [inquietar-se] to become agitated. -2. [movimentar-se - na cama] to be restless; [- na rua, no trabalho etc] to run around.
agito [a'ʒitu] *m fam* excitement.
aglomeração [aglomera'sãw] (*pl* -ões) *f* -1. [de coisas] stack. -2. [de pessoas] mass; ~ **urbana** built-up area.
aglomerado [aglome'radu] *m* -1. [de coisas] pile. -2. [de pessoas] mass.
aglomerar [4] [aglome'ra(x)] *vt* to mass.
◆ **aglomerar-se** *vp* [pessoas] to swarm.
aglutinação [aglutʃina'sãw] *f* -1. [fusão] agglutination. -2. [combinação] almagamation.
aglutinar [4] [aglutʃi'na(x)] *vt* -1. [com cola] to glue. -2. [palavras, sufixo] to agglutinate.
ago. (*abrev de* **agosto**) Aug.
agonia [ago'nia] *f* -1. [ger] agony; **que** ~**!** *fig* what a pain! -2. [de moribundo] death throes *(pl)*. -3. *fig* [declínio] decline.
agoniado, da [ago'njadu, da] *adj* -1. [aflito] distressed. -2. [irritado] irritated.
agoniar [16] [ago'nja(x)] *vt* -1. [afligir] to distress. -2. [irritar] to irritate.
agonizante [agoni'zãntʃi] *adj* dying.
agonizar [4] [agoni'za(x)] *vi* to be dying.
agora [a'gɔra] ◇ *adv* -1. [neste momento] now; **e** ~**?** now what?; ~ **mesmo** right now; [há pouco] just now; **até** ~ until now; **de** ~ **em diante** from now on. -2. [atualmente] nowadays. -3. [doravante] from now on. ◇ *conj* [mas] now.
agorafobia [ˌagorafo'bia] *f* agoraphobia.
agorinha [agɔ'riɲa] *adv* just now.
agosto [a'goʃtu] *m* August; *veja também* **setembro**.
agourar [4] [ago'ra(x)] ◇ *vt* [pressagiar] to portend. ◇ *vi* [fazer mau agouro] to bode ill.
agourento, ta [ago'rẽntu, ta] *adj* -1. [supersticioso] superstitious. -2. [que anuncia desgraças] ominous; **que mulher mais agourenta!** what a prophet of doom that woman is!
agouro [a'goru] *m* omen; **mau** ~ bad omen.
agraciar [16] [agra'sja(x)] *vt* -1. [condecorar] to decorate. -2. [preso, exilado] to pardon.
agradabilíssimo, ma [agradabi'lisimu, ma] *adj* = *superl de* **agradável**.
agradar [4] [agra'da(x)] ◇ *vt* [causar prazer a] to please. ◇ *vi* -1. [satisfazer]: ~ **(a) alguém** to please sb. -2. [aprazer]: ~ **a** to delight. -3. [ser agradável] to please, to be pleasing.
agradável [agra'davɛw] (*pl* -eis) *adj* pleasant.
agradecer [25] [agrade'se(x)] ◇ *vt*: ~ **algo** to say thank you for sthg. ◇ *vi* -1. [dizer obrigado] to say thank you; ~ **a alguém por algo** to thank sb for sthg. -2. [ficar grato] to be grateful.
agradecido, da [agrade'sidu, da] *adj* grateful.
agradecimento [agradesi'mẽntu] *m* [gratidão] thanks *(pl)*, thank you; **carta de** ~ thank-you letter.
◆ **agradecimentos** *mpl* thanks.
agrado [a'gradu] *m*: **fazer um** ~ **a alguém** [presentear] to give sb a present; [acariciar] to be affectionate with sb.
agrário, ria [a'grarju, rja] *adj* agrarian.
agravamento [agrava'mẽntu] *m* worsening.
agravante [agra'vãntʃi] ◇ *adj* aggravating. ◇ *m* [o que piora a situação]: **o agravante é que ...** the annoying thing is that ...
agravar [4] [agra'va(x)] ◇ *vt* [piorar] to worsen. ◇ *vi JUR*: ~ **de algo** to appeal against sthg.
◆ **agravar-se** *vp* [piorar] to worsen.
agravo [a'gravu] *m JUR* appeal.
agredir [58] [agre'dʒi(x)] *vt* -1. [atacar] to attack. -2. [insultar] to insult. -3. *fig* [afetar] to offend.
agregado, da [agre'gadu, da] ◇ *adj* attached. ◇ *m, f* [hóspede] guest.
◆ **agregado** *m CONSTR* aggregate.
agregar [4] [agre'ga(x)] *vt* to add; ~ **algo a algo** to add sthg to sthg.
◆ **agregar-se** *vp* [associar-se]: ~**-se a algo** to join sthg.
agressão [agre'sãw] (*pl* -ões) *f* aggression.
agressividade [agresivi'dadʒi] *f* aggressiveness.
agressivo, va [agre'sivu, va] *adj* aggressive.
agressor, ra [agre'so(x), ra] *m, f* aggressor.
agreste [a'grɛʃtʃi] ◇ *adj* rural. ◇ *m stony, unfertile area of north-eastern Brazil.*
agrião [agri'ãw] (*pl* -ões) *m* watercress.
agrícola [a'grikola] *adj* agricultural.
agricultor, ra [agrikuw'to(x), ra] *m, f* farmer.
agricultura [agrikuw'tura] *f* agriculture.
agridoce [agri'dosi] *adj* -1. [comida] sweet and sour. -2. [emoções] bitter-sweet.
agroindústria [agrwĩn'duʃtrja] *f* agro-industry.
agronomia [agrono'mia] *f* agronomy.
agrônomo, ma [a'gronomu, ma] *m, f* agronomist.
agropecuário, ria [agrope'kwarju, rja] *adj* mixed-farming *(antes de subst)*.
◆ **agropecuária** *f* mixed farming.
agrotóxico [agro'tɔksiku] *m* pesticide.
agrupamento [agrupa'mẽntu] *m* collection.
agrupar [4] [agru'pa(x)] *vt* to collect.
◆ **agrupar-se** *vp* to be grouped together.
agrura [a'grura] *f* scourge.
água ['agwa] *f* -1. water; ~ **benta** holy water; ~ **boricada** boric acid; ~ **corrente** running water; ~ **doce/salgada** fresh/salt water; **peixe de** ~ **doce** freshwater fish; ~ **mineral/gasosa/sem gás** mineral/sparkling/still water; ~ **oxigenada** hydrogen peroxide; ~ **potável** drinking water; ~ **de rosas** rose water; ~ **sanitária** chemically purified water; **claro como** ~ crystal-clear; **com** ~ **na boca** watering at the mouth; **ir nas** ~**s de alguém** to go with sb's wishes. -2. *fig* [plano]: **ir por** ~ **abaixo** to go down the drain.
◆ **águas** *fpl* -1. [chuvas] rainwater *(sg)*. -2. [minerais, termais] waters, thermal springs.
aguaceiro [agwa'sejru] *m* downpour.

água-com-açúcar [ˌagwakwa'suka(x)] *adj (inv)* sentimental.
água-de-coco [ˌagwadʒi'koku] *f* coconut milk.
água-de-colônia [ˌagwadʒiko'lonja] (*pl* **águas-de-colônia**) *f* eau-de-Cologne.
aguado, da [a'gwadu, da] *adj* watered-down.
água-furtada [ˌagwafux'tada] (*pl* **águas-furtadas**) *f* garret.
água-marinha [ˌagwama'riɲa] (*pl* **águas-marinhas**) *f* aquamarine.
aguar [22] [a'gwa(x)] *vt* **-1.** [diluir] to water down. **-2.** [regar] to water.
aguardar [4] [agwax'da(x)] <> *vt* to await. <> *vi* to wait; ~ **por** to wait for.
aguardente [agwax'dẽntʃi] *f* brandy; ~ **de cana** cachaça.
aguarrás [agwa'xaʃ] *f* turpentine.
água-viva [ˌagwa'viva] (*pl* **águas-vivas**) *f* jellyfish.
aguçado, da [agu'sadu, da] *adj* **-1.** [ger] sharp. **-2.** [apetite] keen; [interesse] lively.
aguçar [13] [agu'sa(x)] *vt* **-1.** [ger] to sharpen. **-2.** [estimular] to stimulate.
agudeza [agu'deza] *f* sharpness.
agudo, da [a'gudu, da] *adj* **-1.** [ger] acute. **-2.** [penetrante] sharp. **-3.** [nota, voz] shrill.
agüentar [4] [agwẽn'ta(x)] <> *vt* **-1.** [ger] to bear; ~ **fazer algo** to be able to bear to do sthg. **-2.** [tolerar] to put up with. <> *vi* **-1.** [resistir] to support; **não** ~ **de algo** to be unable to bear sthg. **-2.** *loc*: ~ **a mão** *fam* [esperar] to hold on; [resistir a situação difícil] to hang on.
◆ **agüentar-se** *vp* [permanecer] to remain.
aguerrido, da [age'xidu, da] *adj* **-1.** [afeito à guerra] warlike. **-2.** [combativo] bellicose.
águia ['agja] *f* **-1.** [ave] eagle. **-2.** *fig* [pessoa] talented person.
agulha [a'guʎa] *f* needle.
ah [a] *interj* ah!
ai [ˌaj] <> *interj* **-1.** [de dor] ouch! **-2.** [de cócegas] eek! **-3.** [suspiro] oh! **-4.** [lamento] oh dear! **-5.** [gemido] oh no! <> *m* [de dor] groan.
◆ **ai de** *loc adj* damn.
aí [a'i] <> *adv* **-1.** [ger] there; **espera** ~! wait there! **-2.** [em lugar indeterminado]: **por** ~ around. **-3.** [para lugar indeterminado]: **sair por** ~ **(afora)** to go off somewhere. **-4.** [junto, em anexo] herewith. **-5.** [nesse caso, então] then. **-6.** [aproximadamente]: **por** ~ around. **-7.** [em data, período]: ~ **pelos anos 60** around the 60s. **-8.** [e assim por diante]: **e por** ~ **afora** and so on and so forth. **-9.** *fam* [saudando]: **e** ~! hi! <> *interj* **-1.** [animando] go on! **-2.** [maliciando]: ~ **... hein?** well, now ...
aiatolá [ajato'la] *m* ayatollah.
aidético, ca [aj'dɛtʃiku, ka] <> *adj* suffering from AIDS. <> *m, f* AIDS sufferer, person with AIDS.
AIDS (*abrev de* **Acquired Immunodeficiency Syndrome**) *f* AIDS.
ainda [a'ĩnda] *adv* **-1.** [ger] still; ~ **não** not yet; ~ **(assim)** still. **-2.** [um dia] one day. **-3.** [ao menos]: **se** ~ ... if at least.
◆ **ainda agora** *loc adv* just now.
◆ **ainda bem** *loc adv* just as well.
◆ **ainda por cima** *loc adv* still; **ele não ajuda, e** ~ **por cima reclama** he's not helping, and on top of that he's complaining.
◆ **ainda que** *loc conj* even if.
aipim [aj'pĩ] (*pl* **-ns**) *m* cassava.
aipo ['ajpu] *m* celery.
airoso, osa [aj'rozu, ɔza] *adj* elegant.
ajardinado, da [aʒaxdʒi'nadu, da] *adj* with garden.
ajardinar [4] [aʒaxdʒi'na(x)] *vt* to turn into a garden.
ajeitar [4] [aʒej'ta(x)] *vt* **-1.** [endireitar] to straighten. **-2.** [arrumar] to tidy up. **-3.** [acomodar] to tuck up.
◆ **ajeitar-se** *vp* **-1.** [arrumar-se] to tidy o.s. up. **-2.** [a emprego] to adapt. **-3.** [acomodar-se] to settle down. **-4.** [adaptar-se]: ~**-se com algo** to get used to sthg.
ajoelhado, da [aʒwe'ʎadu, da] *adj* kneeling.
ajoelhar [4] [aʒwe'ʎa(x)] *vi* to kneel.
◆ **ajoelhar-se** *vp* to kneel down.
ajuda [a'ʒuda] *f* **-1.** [auxílio] help; **dar** ~ **a alguém (em algo)** to help sb (with sthg); **sem** ~ without help; **vir em** ~ **de alguém** to come to sb's aid. **-2.** *ECON & POL* aid; ~ **de custo** financial assistance.
ajudante [aʒu'dãntʃi] *mf* assistant.
ajudar [4] [aʒu'da(x)] <> *vt* **-1.** [auxiliar]: ~ **alguém (em algo)** to help sb (with sthg); ~ **alguém a fazer algo** to help sb do sthg. **-2.** [facilitar] to help. **-3.** [missa] to serve at. <> *vi* **-1.** [auxiliar] to help; ~ **a alguém** to help sb; ~ **em algo** to help with sthg. **-2.** [facilitar] to help.
◆ **ajudar-se** *vp* to help each other.
ajuizado, da [aʒwi'zadu, da] *adj* sensible.
ajuizar [4] [aʒwi'za(x)] *vt* **-1.** *JUR* [levar a juízo] to bring before a court. **-2.** [formar juízo sobre] to form an opinion on.
ajuntamento [aʒũnta'mẽntu] *m* **-1.** [de pessoas] gathering. **-2.** [de objetos] pile.
ajuntar [4] [aʒũn'ta(x)] *vt* **-1.** [reunir] to assemble. **-2.** [amontoar] to pile up. **-3.** [acrescentar] to add.
ajustar [4] [aʒuʃ'ta(x)] *vt* **-1.** [regular] to adjust. **-2.** [adaptar]: ~ **algo a algo** [idéias, procedimento] to adapt sthg to sthg; ~ **algo em algo** [peça] to fit sthg into sthg. **-3.** [apertar] to tighten. **-4.** [acertar] to agree; ~ **contas** to settle accounts.
◆ **ajustar-se** *vp* [adaptar-se] to adapt.
ajustável [aʒuʃ'tavew] (*pl* **-eis**) *adj* adjustable.
ajuste [a'ʒuʃtʃi] *m* **-1.** [acordo] agreement. **-2.** [de peça - encaixe] fitting; [- aperto] tightening. **-3.** [regulagem] adjustment. **-4.** [acerto]: ~ **de contas** settlement of accounts; *fig* settling of scores.
AL (*abrev de* **Estado de Alagoas**) *n State of Alagoas*.
ala ['ala] *f* **-1.** [ger] wing. **-2.** [de escola de samba] group; **a** ~ **das baianas** *the section of the carnival parade made up of women wearing typical Bahia costumes*.
Alá [a'la] *m* Allah.

alagadiço, ça [alaga'dʒisu, sa] *adj* subject to flooding *(depois de verbo)*.
alagado, da [ala'gadu, da] *adj* flooded.
alagamento [alaga'mẽntu] *m* flooding.
alagar [14] [ala'ga(x)] *vt* to flood.
Alagoas [ala'goaʃ] *n* Alagoas.
ALALC (*abrev de* **Associação Latino-Americana de Livre Comércio**) *f Latin-American free trade association.*
alambique [alãn'biki] *m* still *(for making alcohol)*.
alameda [ala'meda] *f* avenue.
alaranjado, da [alarãn'ʒadu, da] *adj* orange-coloured.
alarde [a'laxdʒi] *m* **-1.** [ostentação] ostentation; **fazer ~ de algo** to show off sthg. **-2.** [bazófia] boastfulness; **fazer ~ de algo** to brag about sthg.
alardear [15] [alax'dʒja(x)] *vt* **-1.** [ostentar] to parade. **-2.** [gabar-se de] to brag about.
alargamento [alaxga'mẽntu] *m* [de estrada] widening.
alargar [14] [alax'ga(x)] *vt* **-1.** [estrada] to widen. **-2.** [roupa] to let out.
alarido [ala'ridu] *m* [gritaria, algazarra] uproar.
alarmante [alax'mãntʃi] *adj* alarming.
alarmar [4] [alax'ma(x)] *vt* to alarm.
◆ **alarmar-se** *vp* to become alarmed.
alarme [a'laxmi] *m* alarm; **campainha de ~** alarm bell; **dar o ~** to sound the alarm.
alarmista [alax'miʃta] *adj* alarmist.
Alasca [a'laʃka] *n* Alaska.
alastrar [4] [alaʃ'tra(x)] *vt* [propagar, espalhar] to spread.
◆ **alastrar-se** *vp* to spread.
alavanca [ala'vãŋka] *f* **-1.** [peça] lever; **~ de mudanças** *AUTO* gear lever. **-2.** *fig* [meio de ação] lever.
alavancagem [alavãŋ'kaʒẽ] *f ECON* leverage.
alavancar [alavaɲ'ka(x)] *vt* [promover] to launch; *ECON* to leverage.
albanês, esa [awbã'neʃ] ◇ *adj* Albanian. ◇ *m, f* Albanian.
◆ **albanês** *m* [língua] Albanian.
Albânia [aw'bãnja] *n* Albania.
albergue [aw'bɛxgi] *m* **-1.** [hospedaria] hostel; [para jovens] youth hostel. **-2.** [asilo] refuge.
albino, na [aw'binu, na] ◇ *adj* albino. ◇ *m, f* albino.
álbum ['awbũ] (*pl* **-ns**) *m* album.
albumina [awbu'mina] *f* albumin.
ALCA (*abrev de* **Área de Livre Comércio das Américas**) *f* FTAA.
alça ['awsa] *f* **-1.** [de mala, vestido] strap. **-2.** [em arma]: **~ de mira** sights *(pl)*.
alcachofra [awka'ʃofra] *f* artichoke.
alcaçuz [awka'suʒ] *m* liquorice plant.
alçada [aw'sada] *f* **-1.** [competência] competence; **ser da ~ de alguém** to be sb's responsibility. **-2.** *JUR* jurisdiction.
álcali ['awkali] *m* alkali.
alcalino, na [awka'linu, na] *adj* alkaline.
alcançar [13] [awkãn'sa(x)] *vt* **-1.** [ger] to reach. **-2.** [pegar] to catch. **-3.** [entender] to grasp. **-4.** [conseguir] to attain.
alcançável [awkãn'savew] (*pl* **-eis**) *adj* attainable.
alcance [aw'kãnsi] *m* **-1.** [de arma, míssil] range. **-2.** [de pessoa]: **ao meu/ao teu ~** within my/your reach; **ao ~ da vista** within sight; **fora do ~ de** [objeto, pessoa] out of reach of; [entendimento] beyond the grasp of. **-3.** [importância]: **de pequeno/grande ~** of minor/major importance.
alçapão [awsa'pãw] (*pl* **-ões**) *m* **-1.** [portinhola] trapdoor. **-2.** [armadilha] trap.
alcaparra [awka'paxa] *f* caper.
alçar [13] [aw'sa(x)] *vt* **-1.** [levantar - carga, viga] to lift; [- braço] to raise. **-2.** [voz] to raise. **-3.** [vôo] to rise.
◆ **alçar-se** *vp* [a cargo] to rise.
alcatéia [awka'tɛja] *f* [de lobos] pack.
alcatra [aw'katra] *f* rump steak.
alcatrão [awka'trãw] *m* tar.
álcool ['awkow] (*pl* **-óis**) *m* alcohol.
alcoólatra [aw'kɔlatra] ◇ *adj* alcoholic. ◇ *mf* alcoholic.
alcoólico, ca [aw'kwɔliku, ka] *adj* alcoholic.
alcoolismo [awko'liʒmu] *m* alcoholism.
alcoolizado, da [awkoli'zadu, da] *adj* [pessoa] drunk.
Alcorão [awko'rãw] *m* Koran.
alcova [aw'kova] *f* dressing room.
alcoviteiro, ra [awkovi'tejru, ra] *m, f* gossip.
alcunha [aw'kuɲa] *f* nickname.
aldeão, deã [aw'dʒjãw, dja] (*mpl* **-ões**, **-ãos**, *fpl* **-s**) *m, f* villager.
aldeia [aw'deja] *f* village; **~ de pescadores** fishing village.
aldraba [aw'draba] *f* [de bater] door-knocker.
aleatório, ria [alea'tɔrju, rja] *adj* random.
alecrim [ale'krĩ] *m* rosemary.
alegação [alega'sãw] (*pl* **-ões**) *f* allegation.
alegado, da [ale'gadu, da] *adj* alleged.
◆ **alegado** *m JUR* allegation.
alegar [14] [ale'ga(x)] *vt* to allege; **~ que** to allege that; *JUR* to allege that.
alegoria [alego'ria] *f* allegory.
alegórico, ca [ale'gɔriku] *adj* allegorical; ▻ **carro**.
alegrar [4] [ale'gra(x)] *vt* to cheer up.
◆ **alegrar-se** *vp* to be happy; **alegre-se!** cheer up!
alegre [a'lɛgri] *adj* **-1.** [pessoa] cheerful. **-2.** [festa, bar, voz] lively. **-3.** [cor] bright. **-4.** [embriagado] merry.
alegria [ale'gria] *f* **-1.** [qualidade] cheerfulness. **-2.** [satisfação] contentment. **-3.** [júbilo] joy.
aléia [a'lɛja] *f* **-1.** [alameda] alley. **-2.** [passagem] alley.
aleijado, da [alej'ʒadu, da] ◇ *adj* crippled. ◇ *m, f* cripple.
aleijar [4] [alej'ʒa(x)] *vt* to cripple.
aleitamento [alejtamẽntu] *m* breastfeeding.
além [a'lẽj] ◇ *m* [o outro mundo]: **o ~** the beyond. ◇ *adv* **-1.** [em lugar afastado] over there. **-2.** [mais

adiante] further on; **mais** ~ further.

◆ **além de** *loc prep* **-1.** [mais adiante de] beyond. **-2.** [do outro lado de, acima de] beyond. **-3.** [afora] apart from.

◆ **além disso** *loc conj* besides.

◆ **além do mais** *loc conj* furthermore.

Alemanha [ale'mãɲa] *n* Germany.

alemão, mã [ale'mãw, mã] ◇ *adj* German. ◇ *m, f* German.

◆ **alemão** *m* [língua] German.

alentado, da [alẽntadu, da] *adj* **-1.** [animoso] brave. **-2.** [volumoso] bulky. **-3.** [corpulento] stout.

alentar [4] [alẽnta(x)] *vt* to comfort.

alento [a'lẽntu] *m* **-1.** [ânimo] courage. **-2.** [fôlego] breath.

alergia [alex'ʒia] *f* **-1.** *MED* allergy; **ter** ~ **a algo** to be allergic to sthg. **-2.** *fig* [aversão] allergy; **ter** ~ **a algo/alguém** to be allergic to sthg/sb.

alérgico, ca [a'lɛxʒiku, ka] *adj* **-1.** *MED* **:** ~ **(a)** allergic (to). **-2.** *fig* [averso]**:** ~ **a** allergic to.

alerta [a'lɛxta] ◇ *adj* alert. ◇ *adv* alert. ◇ *m* warning.

alertar [4] [alex'ta(x)] *vt*: ~ **alguém (de/sobre algo)** to alert sb (to sthg).

alfabético, ca [awfa'bɛtʃiku, ka] *adj* alphabetical.

alfabetização [awfabetʃiza'sãw] *f* **-1.** [ato] teaching to read and write. **-2.** [estado] literacy.

alfabetizado, da [awfabetʃi'zadu, da] *adj* literate.

alfabetizar [4] [awfabetʃi'za(x)] *vt* to teach to read and write.

alfabeto [awfa'bɛtu] *m* alphabet.

alface [aw'fasi] *f* lettuce.

alfafa [aw'fafa] *f* alfalfa.

alfaiataria [awfajata'ria] *f* tailor's shop.

alfaiate [awfa'jatʃi] *m* tailor.

alfândega [aw'fãndega] *f* **-1.** [administração] customs *(pl)*. **-2.** [local] customs house.

alfandegário, ria [awfãnde'garju, rja] *adj* customs *(antes de subst)*.

alfazema [awfa'zema] *f* lavender.

alfinetada [awfine'tada] *f* **-1.** [picada de alfinete] pin-prick. **-2.** [dor] sharp pain. **-3.** *fig* [dito] stinging remark; **dar uma** ~ **em alguém** to make a stinging remark to sb.

alfinetar [4] [awfine'ta(x)] *vt* **-1.** *COST* to pin. **-2.** *fig* [criticar] to criticize.

alfinete [awfi'netʃi] *m* **-1.** *COST* pin. **-2.** [prendedor]**:** ~ **de fralda** nappy pin; ~ **de segurança** safety pin. **-3.** [jóia] pin.

alfineteira [awfine'tejra] *f* **-1.** [caixa] pin box. **-2.** [almofadinha] pincushion.

alforje [aw'fɔxʒi] *m* saddlebag.

alga ['awga] *f* seaweed.

algarismo [awga'riʒmu] *m* number.

algazarra [awga'zaxa] *f* shouting; **fazer** ~ to make a racket.

álgebra ['awʒebra] *f* algebra.

algébrico, ca [aw'ʒɛbriku, ka] *adj MAT* algebraic.

algemar [4] [awʒe'ma(x)] *vt* to handcuff.

algemas [aw'ʒemaʃ] *fpl* handcuffs.

algo ['awgu] ◇ *pron* **-1.** *(em frases afirmativas)* something. **-2.** *(em frases interrogativas)* anything. ◇ *adv* somewhat.

algodão [awgo'dãw] *m* cotton; ~ **(hidrófilo)** cotton wool; **uma camisa de** ~ a cotton shirt.

algodão-doce [awgo,dãw'dosi] (*pl* **algodões-doces**) *m* candyfloss.

algodoeiro [awgo'dwejru] *m* cotton plant.

algoritmo [awgo'xitʃimu] *m* algorithm.

algoz [aw'gɔʒ] *m* **-1.** [carrasco] executioner. **-2.** [pessoa cruel] cruel person.

alguém [aw'gẽj] ◇ *pron indef* **-1.** [alguma pessoa] someone; ~ **quebrou este vaso** someone broke this vase; **tem** ~ **lá embaixo** there's someone downstairs **-2.** [em frases interrogativas] anybody, anyone; ~ **me telefonou?** did anybody phone me?; ~ **quer mais café?** does anybody want more coffee?; **tem** ~ **aí?** is anybody there?; ~ **mais** anybody else. **-3.** [determinada pessoa] somebody; **ele sabia que haveria** ~ **à sua espera** he knew there would be somebody waiting for him; **você é** ~ **que admiro muito** you are somebody I admire greatly. **-4.** *fig* [pessoa importante] somebody; **se um dia eu me tornar** ~**, lembrarei dos velhos amigos** if one day I become somebody, I'll remember my old friends; **ele é** ~ **na empresa?** is he somebody in the company?; **ser** ~ **(na vida)** to be somebody in life. ◇ *m* [uma pessoa]**: esse** ~ that person; **um** ~ a person.

algum, ma [aw'gũ, ma] (*mpl* **-ns**, *fpl* **-s**) ◇ *adj* **-1.** [indeterminado] some; **ela morou** ~ **tempo em Londres** she lived for some time in London; **me dê** ~ **dinheiro** give me some money; ~ **dia vamos te visitar** some day we'll come and see you **-2.** [em interrogativas, negativas] any; ~ **problema?** any problems?; **de jeito** *ou* **modo** ~ in no way; **não há problema** ~ there's no problem, there aren't any problems; **em parte alguma do país** nowhere in the country; **coisa alguma** nothing; **não há melhora alguma** there is no improvement, there isn't any improvement. ◇ *pron* **-1.** [indicando pessoa] somebody; **alguns preferem cinema, outros, teatro** some people prefer the cinema, others the theatre **-2.** [indicando coisa] one; **abra a caixa de bombons e prove alguns** open the box of sweets and try some **-3.** [em interrogativas: pessoa] anybody **-4.** [em interrogativas: coisa] any; ~ **dia** one *ou* some day; **alguma coisa** something, anything; **alguma vez** sometime.

◆ **alguns** *pron pl* some.

◆ **alguma** *f* [evento, feito]**: deve ter lhe acontecido alguma** something must have happened to him; **esse menino aprontou alguma** that boy has been up to something.

alheamento [aʎea'mẽntu] *m* [indiferença] indifference.

alhear [15] [aʎeia(x)] *vt* **-1.** [desviar] to turn. **-2.** [bens] to separate.

◆ **alhear-se** *vp* [distanciar-se] to distance o.s.

alheio, alheia [a'ʎeju, a'ʎeja] *adj* **-1.** [de outra

pessoa]: **um problema** ~ somebody else's problem. **-2.** [irrelevante]: ~ **a** irrelevant to. **-3.** [afastado, abstraído]: ~ **(a)** unaware (of).

◆ **alheios** *mpl* [estranhos] outsiders.

alho ['aʎu] *m* garlic; **confundir** ~**s com bugalhos** to confuse two different things.

alho-poró [aʎupo'rɔ] (*pl* **alhos-porós**) *m* leek.

alhures [a'ʎuriʃ] *adv* elsewhere.

ali [a'li] *adv* **-1.** [naquele lugar] there; ~ **dentro/fora** in/out there; **logo** ~ right there; **por** ~ around there. **-2.** [naquele momento] then.

aliado, da [a'ljadu, da] ◇ *adj* allied. ◇ *m, f* ally.

◆ **Aliados** *mpl*: **os Aliados** the Allies.

aliança [a'ljãnsa] *f* **-1.** [pacto] alliance. **-2.** [anel] wedding ring.

aliar [16] [a'lja(x)] *vt* [qualidades] to combine.

◆ **aliar-se** *vp* [nações] to become allied.

aliás [a'ljajʃ] *adv* **-1.** [a propósito] as a matter of fact. **-2.** [diga-se de passagem] incidentally. **-3.** [ou por outra] or rather.

álibi ['alibi] *m* alibi.

alicate [ali'katʃi] *m* pliers *(pl)*; ~ **de unhas** nail clippers *(pl)*.

alicerçado, da [alisex'sadu, da] *adj* based.

alicerce [ali'sɛxsi] *m* CONSTR foundation.

aliciamento [alisia'mẽntu] *m* [sedução] seduction.

aliciar [16] [ali'sja(x)] *vt* **-1.** [atrair, seduzir] to entice. **-2.** [convocar] to recruit. **-3.** [subornar] to bribe.

alienação [aljena'sãw] *f* **-1.** [falta de consciência, participação] lack of awareness. **-2.** PSIC : ~ **mental** mental illness. **-3.** [de bens] assignment.

alienado, da [alje'nadu, da] *adj* **-1.** [não participante] alienated. **-2.** [louco] insane. **-3.** [bens] assigned.

alienar [4] [alje'na(x)] *vt* **-1.** [tornar não participante] to alienate. **-2.** [afastar] to drive away. **-3.** [bens] to assign.

◆ **alienar-se** *vp* [afastar-se] to withdraw.

alienígena [alje'niʒena] *mf* alien.

alijar [4] [ali'ʒa(x)] *vt* **-1.** [carga] to jettison. **-2.** [isentar]: ~ **alguém de algo** to free sb of sthg.

◆ **alijar-se** *vp* [isentar-se]: ~**-se de algo** to be released from sthg.

alimentação [alimẽnta'sãw] *f* **-1.** [ato] feeding. **-2.** [dieta] diet. **-3.** [de máquina, impressora] feeding. **-4.** ELETR supply.

alimentador [alimẽnta'do(x)] *m*: ~ **de papel** paper feed.

alimentar [4] [alimẽn'ta(x)] (*pl* **-es**) ◇ *adj* alimentary. ◇ *vt* **-1.** [ger] to feed. **-2.** [nutrir] to feed. **-3.** [esperança] to feed. ◇ *vi* [nutrir] to provide nourishment.

◆ **alimentar-se** *vp* to feed o.s.; ~**-se de algo** to live on sthg.

alimentício, cia [alimẽn'tʃisju, sja] *adj* **-1.** [qualidades] nutritious; **gêneros** ~**s** foodstuffs. **-2.** [pensão] maintenance.

alimento [ali'mẽntu] *m* **-1.** [comida] food. **-2.** [nutrição] nourishment.

alínea [a'linja] *f* indent.

alinhado, da [ali'ɲadu, da] *adj* **-1.** [posto em linha reta] in a row. **-2.** [elegante] elegant. **-3.** [correto] correct.

alinhamento [aliɲa'mẽntu] *m* **-1.** [enfileiramento] row. **-2.** [de estrada] direction. **-3.** TIP justifying.

alinhar [4] [ali'ɲa(x)] *vt* **-1.** [enfileirar] to line up. **-2.** [estrada] to straighten. **-3.** TIP to justify.

alinhavar [4] [aliɲa'va(x)] *vt* COST to tack *UK*, to baste.

alinhavo [ali'ɲavu] *m* tacking *UK*, basting.

alíquota [a'likwota] *f* tax rate.

alisar [4] [ali'za(x)] *vt* **-1.** [tornar liso - cama, cabelo] to smooth; [- tábua] to plane. **-2.** [acariciar] to caress.

alistamento [aliʃta'mẽntu] *m* **-1.** [em partido] enrolment. **-2.** MIL enlistment.

alistar [4] [aliʃ'ta(x)] *vt* **-1.** [em partido] to enrol. **-2.** MIL to enlist.

◆ **alistar-se** *vp* **-1.** [em partido] to enrol. **-2.** MIL to enlist.

aliteração [alitera'sãw] *f* alliteration.

aliviado, da [ali'vjadu, da] *adj* **-1.** [pessoa - tranqüilizado] relieved; [- folgado] slackened. **-2.** [consciência] relieved. **-3.** [embarcação] lightened.

aliviar [16] [ali'vja(x)] ◇ *vt* **-1.** [gen] to relieve. **-2.** [folgar] to slacken. **-3.** [desafogar]: ~ **alguém de algo** to unburden sb of sthg. **-4.** [embarcação] to lighten. ◇ *vi* **-1.** [diminuir] to ease. **-2.** [confortar] to comfort.

◆ **aliviar-se** *vp* to be relieved; ~**-se de algo** to be relieved of sthg.

alívio [a'livju] *m* relief; **que** ~! what a relief!

alma ['awma] *f* **-1.** [essência humana] soul. **-2.** [espírito desencarnado] spirit; ~ **do outro mundo** ghost. **-3.** [pessoa]: **não ver viva** ~ not to see a living soul. **-4.** [caráter] heart; ~ **gêmea** soulmate. **-5.** [entusiasmo] heart and soul; **com** ~ with enthusiasm. **-6.** [bondade]: **pessoa sem** ~ heartless person. **-7.** *fig* [de negócio, empresa, partido] essence.

almaço [aw'masu] *adj* [papel] foolscap.

almanaque [awma'naki] *m* almanac.

almejar [4] [awme'ʒa(x)] ◇ *vt* to long for; ~ **fazer algo** to long to do sthg. ◇ *vi*: ~ **por algo** to long for sthg.

almirantado [awmirãn'tadu] *m* **-1.** [corporação] admiralty. **-2.** [posto] admiralship.

almirante [awmi'rãntʃi] *m* admiral.

almoçar [13] [awmo'sa(x)] ◇ *vt* to have for lunch. ◇ *vi* to have lunch.

almoço [aw'mosu] *m* lunch; **na hora do** ~ at lunchtime; ~ **americano** buffet lunch; ~ **de negócios** business lunch.

almofada [awmo'fada] *f* cushion.

almofadinha [awmofa'dʒiɲa] *f* [para alfinetes] pincushion.

almôndega [aw'mõndega] *f* meatball.

almoxarifado [awmoʃari'fadu] *m* warehouse.

almoxarife [awmoʃa'rifi] *mf* warehouseperson.

alô [a'lo] ◇ *interj* [ao telefone] hello! ◇ *m* hello.

alocação [aloka'sãw] (*pl* **-ões**) *f* allocation.

alocar [12] [alo'ka(x)] *vt* to allocate.

aloirado, da [aloj'radu, da] *adj* fair-haired.
alojamento [aloʒa'mẽntu] *m* **-1.** [ger] accommodation. **-2.** MIL billet.
alojar [4] [alo'ʒa(x)] *vt* **-1.** [hospedar] to accommodate. **-2.** MIL to billet. **-3.** [armazenar] to store.
◆ **alojar-se** *vp* **-1.** [hospedar-se] to stay. **-2.** [acampar] to camp.
alongamento [alõŋga'mẽntu] *m* **-1.** [ger] lengthening. **-2.** [de prazo] extension. **-3.** [ginástica] stretching.
alongar [14] [alõŋ'ga(x)] *vt* **-1.** [ger] to lengthen. **-2.** [perna, braço] to stretch. **-3.** [conversa] to prolong.
◆ **alongar-se** *vp* **-1.** [corpo] to stretch. **-2.** [conversa] to prolong. **-3.** [sobre assunto] to expand.
alopata [alo'pata] *mf* allopath.
alopatia [alopa'tʃia] *f* allopathy.
aloprado, da [alo'pradu, da] *adj fam* crazy.
alourado, da [alow'radu, da], **aloirado, da** [aloj'radu, da] *adj* fair-haired.
alpaca [aw'paka] *f* alpaca.
alpargata [aw'paxgata] *f* espadrille.
alpendre [aw'pẽndri] *m* [telheiro] porch.
alpercata [awpex'kata] = **alpargata**.
Alpes ['awpiʃ] *npl*: **os** ~ the Alps.
alpinismo [awpi'niʒmu] *m* mountaineering.
alpinista [awpi'niʃta] *mf* mountaineer.
alpino, na [aw'pinu, na] *adj* Alpine.
alpiste [aw'piʃtʃi] *m* [planta] canary grass.
alqueire [aw'kejri] *m measure for land area = 4.84 hectares in Rio de Janeiro, Minas Gerais e Goiás and 2.42 hectares in São Paulo.*
alquimia [awki'mia] *f* alchemy.
alquimista [awki'miʃta] *mf* alchemist.
alta ['awta] *f* ▷ **alto**.
alta-fidelidade [ˌawtafideli'dadʒi] *f* hi-fi.
altaneiro, ra [awta'nejru, ra] *adj* haughty.
altar [aw'ta(x)] (*pl* **-es**) *m* altar.
altar-mor [awˌta(x)'mɔ(x)] (*pl* **altares-mores**) *m* high altar.
alta-roda [ˌawta'xɔda] (*pl* **altas-rodas**) *f* high society.
alta-tensão [ˌawtatẽnsãw] (*pl* **altas-tensões**) *f* high voltage.
altear [15] [awte'a(x)] *vt* **-1.** [construção] to build. **-2.** [preço, voz] to raise. **-3.** [posição]: ~ **sua posição numa firma** to move up within a company.
alteração [awtera'sãw] (*pl* **-ões**) *f* **-1.** [modificação - em gosto, clima, programação] change; [- de texto, roupa] alteration. **-2.** [perturbação] worry. **-3.** [tumulto] commotion.
alterado, da [awte'radu, da] *adj* **-1.** [modificado - gosto, clima, programação] changed; [- texto, roupa] altered. **-2.** [perturbado] worried.
alterar [4] [awte'ra(x)] *vt* **-1.** [modificar] to change. **-2.** [perturbar] to worry.
◆ **alterar-se** *vp* [perturbar-se] to be worried.
altercar [12] [awtex'ka(x)] *vi*: ~ **(com)** to quarrel (with).
alternado, da [awtex'nadu, da] *adj* alternated.
alternância [awtex'nãnsja] *f* alternation.
alternar [4] [awtex'na(x)] ◇ *vt*: ~ **algo (com)** to alternate sthg (with). ◇ *vi*: ~ **com** to alternate with.
◆ **alternar-se** *vp* [revezar-se] to alternate; [pessoas] to take turns.
alternativo, va [awtexna'tʃivu, va] *adj* alternative.
◆ **alternativa** *f* alternative.
alteza [aw'teza] *f*: **Sua Alteza** Your Highness.
altissonante [awtʃiso'nãntʃi] *adj* **-1.** [voz] booming. **-2.** [orquestra] majestic.
altitude [awtʃi'tudʒi] *f* altitude.
altivez [awtʃi'veʒ] *f* **-1.** [arrogância] presumption. **-2.** [dignidade] dignity.
altivo, va [aw'tʃivu, va] *adj* **-1.** [arrogante] presumptuous. **-2.** [digno] dignified.
alto, ta ['awtu, ta] *adj* **-1.** [ger] high; [forte] loud; **ler em voz** ~ to read aloud. **-2.** [em estatura] tall. **-3.** *(antes de subst)* [superior] high; **de** ~ **luxo** of great luxury. **-4.** *(antes de subst)* [importante - cargo] top; [- negócio] big. **-5.** [avançado]: **altas horas (da noite)** late; **altas horas da madrugada** early hours of the morning. **-6.** *(antes de subst)* [grave - risco] high; [- perigo] grave; **alta traição** high treason. **-7.** GEOGR upper. **-8.** HIST high; **alta Antigüidade** early antiquity. **-9.** [MÚS - tom, nota] high; [- voz, saxofone] alto. **-10.** *fam* [embriagado] high.
◆ **alto** ◇ *m* **-1.** [topo] top. **-2.** MÚS [saxofone] alto. **-3.** [mando, poder]: **do** ~ from above. ◇ *adv* **-1.** [falar] aloud. **-2.** [voar] high. ◇ *interj*: **alto!** stop!
◆ **alta** *f* **-1.** MED discharge; **dar/receber** ~ to discharge/to be discharged. **-2.** [de preços] rise. **-3.** [de cotação] rise; **estar em** ~ [cotação] to be rising; *fam* [reputação] to be in favour; *fam* [moda] to be highly fashionable.
◆ **por alto** *loc adv* roughly.
alto-astral [ˌawtwaʃ'traw] (*pl* **-ais**) *fam* ◇ *m* cool; **estar de** ~ to be cool. ◇ *adj* cool.
alto-falante ['awtufa'lãntʃi] (*pl* **-s**) *m* loudspeaker.
alto-mar [ˌawtu'ma(x)] (*pl* **altos-mares**) *m* open sea.
alto-relevo [ˌawture'levu] (*pl* **altos-relevos**) *m* high relief; **em** ~ in relief.
altruísmo [awtru'iʒmu] *m* altruism.
altruísta [awtru'iʃta] ◇ *adj* altruistic. ◇ *mf* [pessoa] altruist.
altruístico, ca [awtru'iʃtʃiku, ka] *adj* altruistic.
altura [aw'tura] *f* **-1.** [ger] height; **a dez mil metros de** ~ at an altitude of ten thousand metres. **-2.** [de som, volume] level. **-3.** [momento] time; **nessa** ~ **do campeonato** *fam fig* at this stage. **-4.** [localização]: **na** ~ **de** close to; **a loja fica na avenida principal, mas em que** ~**?** the shop is on the main road, but how far up? **-5.** [nível]: **à** ~ **de** equal to.
◆ **alturas** *fpl* RELIG [céu]: **as** ~**s** the heavens; **pôr algo/alguém nas** ~**s** *fig* to praise sthg/sb highly.
aluado, da [alu'adu, da] *adj* crazy, lunatic.
alucinação [alusina'sãw] (*pl* **-ões**) *f* hallucination.
alucinado, da [alusi'nadu, da] ◇ *adj* **-1.** PSIC

hallucinated. **-2.** *fig* [apaixonado]: ~ **por** crazy about. **-3.** *fig* [desvairado] frantic. ◇ *m, f* PSIC lunatic.

alucinante [alusi'nãntʃi] *adj fam* **-1.** [enlouquecedor] maddening. **-2.** [ótimo, incrível] amazing.

alucinar [4] [alusi'na(x)] ◇ *vt* **-1.** [enlouquecer] to drive crazy. **-2.** [apaixonar] to drive wild. **-3.** PSIC to cause to hallucinate. ◇ *vi* PSIC to be hallucinogenic.

alucinógeno, na [alusi'nɔʒenu, na] *adj* hallucinogenic.

◆ **alucinógeno** *m* hallucinogen.

aludir [6] [alu'dʒi(x)] *vi*: ~ **a** to allude to.

alugar [14] [alu'ga(x)] *vt* **-1.** [tomar de aluguel - carro, traje] to hire; [- apartamento] to rent. **-2.** [dar em aluguel - carro, traje] to hire out; [- apartamento] to rent out. **-3.** *fam* [incomodar] to annoy.

aluguel [alu'gɛw] (*pl* **-eis**) *m* **-1.** [ato - carro] rental; [- apartamento] renting. **-2.** [pagamento] rent.

alumínio [alu'minju] *m* aluminium *UK*, aluminum *US*.

alunissagem [aluni'saʒẽ] (*pl* **-ns**) *f* lunar landing.

alunissar [4] [aluni'sa(x)] *vi* to land on the moon.

aluno, na [a'lunu, na] *m, f* pupil; ~ **externo** day pupil; ~ **interno** boarder.

alusão [alu'zãw] (*pl* **-ões**) *f* allusion; **fazer uma ~ a** to allude to, to make a reference to.

alusivo, va [alu'zivu, va] *adj* allusive.

alvará [awva'ra] *m* permit.

alvejante [awve'ʒãntʃi] ◇ *adj* bleaching. ◇ *m* bleach.

alvejar [4] [awve'ʒa(x)] *vt* **-1.** [mirar em] to aim at. **-2.** [branquear] to bleach, to whiten.

alvenaria [awvena'ria] *f* masonry; **de ~** stonework.

alvéolo [al'vɛwlu] *f* **-1.** [cavidade] cavity. **-2.** [ANAT - do pulmão]: ~ **pulmonar** alveolus; [- de dente] cavity.

alvo, va ['awvu, 'va] *adj* white.

◆ **alvo** *m* **-1.** [mira] target; **acertar no ~** to hit the target. **-2.** *fig* [objeto]: **ser ~ de** to be the target of.

alvorada [awvo'rada] *f* dawn.

alvorecer [25] [awvore'se(x)] ◇ *m* [alvorada] daybreak. ◇ *vi* [amanhecer] to dawn.

alvoroçar [13] [awvoro'sa(x)] *vt* **-1.** [agitar] to stir up. **-2.** [entusiasmar] to excite.

◆ **alvoroçar-se** *vp* **-1.** [agitar-se] to be startled. **-2.** [entusiasmar-se] to get excited.

alvoroço [awvo'rosu] *m* [agitação] commotion; **fazer ~** to cause a commotion.

alvura [aw'vura] *f* **-1.** [branqueza] whiteness. **-2.** [pureza] innocence.

AM ◇ *f* (*abrev de* **Amplitude Modulation**) AM. ◇ *m* (*abrev de* **Estado do Amazonas**) *State of Amazon*.

ama ['ama] *f* ▷ **amo**.

amabilidade [amabili'dadʒi] *f* **-1.** [delicadeza, cortesia] courtesy. **-2.** [de gesto, palavra] kindness.

amabilíssimo, ma [amabi'lisimu, ma] *superl* ▷ **amável**.

amaciante [ama'sjãntʃi] *m*: ~ **de roupas** fabric conditioner.

amaciar [16] [ama'sja(x)] ◇ *vt* **-1.** [tornar macio] to soften. **-2.** [bife] to tenderize. **-3.** [motor] to run in. ◇ *vi* [motor] to run in.

ama-de-leite [ˌãmadʒi'lejtʃi] (*pl* **amas-de-leite**) *f* wet nurse.

amado, da [a'madu, da] ◇ *adj* **-1.** [ger] favourite. **-2.** [person] beloved. ◇ *m, f* beloved, love.

amador, ra [ama'do(x)] (*mpl* **-es**, *fpl* **-s**) ◇ *adj* amateur. ◇ *m, f* amateur.

amadorismo [amado'riʒmu] *m* **-1.** [diletantismo] dilettantism. **-2.** *pej* [antiprofissionalismo] amateurism.

amadorístico, ca [amado'riʃtʃiku, ka] *adj* amateurish.

amadurecer [25] [amadure'se(x)] ◇ *vt* **-1.** [frutar] to ripen. **-2.** *fig* [pessoa] to mature. ◇ *vi* **-1.** [fruta] to ripen. **-2.** *fig* [pessoa] to mature. **-3.** *fig* [idéia, projeto] to come to fruition.

âmago ['ãmagu] *m* **-1.** [cerne - de madeira] heart; [- de questão] heart. **-2.** [essência] essence. **-3.** [alma, interior] heart.

amainar [4] [amaj'na(x)] *vi* **-1.** [tormenta, tempestade] to die down. **-2.** [ira] to subside. **-3.** [distúrbio, bombardeio] to ease off.

amaldiçoar [20] [amawdi'swa(x)] *vt* to curse.

amálgama [a'mawgama] *m* amalgam.

amalgamar [4] [amawga'ma(x)] *vt* to amalgamate.

amalucado, da [amalu'kadu, da] *adj* crazy.

amamentação [amamẽnta'sãw] (*pl* **-ões**) *f* breastfeeding.

amamentar [4] [amamẽn'ta(x)] *vt* & *vi* to breastfeed.

amanhã [amã'ɲã] ◇ *adv* tomorrow; ~ **de manhã** tomorrow morning; ~ **à noite** tomorrow night; ~ **de tarde** tomorrow afternoon/evening; **depois de ~** the day after tomorrow. ◇ *m* tomorrow.

amanhecer [25] [amãɲe'se(x)] ◇ *m* dawn; **ao ~** at dawn. ◇ *vi* **-1.** [dia] to dawn. **-2.** [pessoa]: **hoje amanheci com dor de cabeça** today I woke up with a headache.

amansar [4] [amãn'sa(x)] ◇ *vt* **-1.** [animal] to break in. **-2.** *fig* [pessoa etc] to calm down. ◇ *vi* **-1.** [animal] to become tame. **-2.** *fig* [pessoa etc] to relent.

amante [a'mãntʃi] *mf* lover.

amanteigado, da [amãntej'gadu, da] *adj* **-1.** [torrada, pão] buttered. **-2.** [biscoito] buttery.

Amapá [ama'pa] *n* Amapá.

amar [4] [a'ma(x)] ◇ *vt* **-1.** [sentir amor por] to love. **-2.** [fazer amor com] to make love to. ◇ *vi* [sentir amor] to be in love.

◆ **amar-se** *vp* **-1.** [mutuamente] to love each other. **-2.** [fazer amor] to make love.

amarelado, da [amare'ladu, da] *adj* yellowish.

amarelar [4] [amare'la(x)] ◇ *vt* [tornar amarelado]

to turn yellow. ◇ *vi fam* [acovardar-se] to pale.
amarelinha [amarɛ'liɲa] *f* hopscotch.
amarelo, la [ama'rɛlu, la] *adj* yellow.
◆ **amarelo** *m* yellow.
amarfanhar [4] [amaxfa'ɲa(x)] *vt* to crumple.
amargar [14] [amax'ga(x)] ◇ *vt* **-1.** [tornar amargo] to make bitter. **-2.** *fig* [fazer sofrer] to embitter. ◇ *vi* **-1.** [tornar-se amargo] to go bitter. **-2.** *loc*: **ser de ~** to be the last straw.
amargo, ga [a'maxgu, ga] *adj* bitter.
amargor [amax'go(x)] *m* **-1.** [sabor amargo] bitter taste. **-2.** [sensação de desgosto] bitterness.
amargura [amax'gura] *f* **-1.** [ger] bitterness. **-2.** *fig* [sofrimento] bitterness.
amargurado, da [amaxgu'radu, da] *adj* **-1.** [pessoa] bitter. **-2.** [expressão, texto] acrimonious.
amargurar [4] [amaxgu'ra(x)] *vt* **-1.** [afligir] to make bitter. **-2.** [tornar sofrido] to sour.
amarra [a'maxa] *f* **-1.** [corrente, cabo - de âncora] moorings *(pl)*; [- de vela] sheet. **-2.** [grilhão] shackle.
amarrado, da [ama'xadu, da] *adj* **-1.** [atado] tied up. **-2.** *fig* [cara] glowering. **-3.** *fam fig* [comprometido] committed.
amarrar [4] [ama'xa(x)] *vt* **-1.** [atar] to tie. **-2.** *NÁUT* to moor. **-3.** *fig*: **~ a cara** to glower.
◆ **amarrar-se** *vp fam* **-1.** [apaixonar-se]: **~-se em alguém** to become attached to sb. **-2.** [gostar muito]: **~-se em algo** to be keen on sthg.
amarronzado, da [amaxõn'zadu, da] *adj* brownish.
amarrotar [4] [amaxo'ta(x)] ◇ *vt* to crumple. ◇ *vi* to be crumpled.
ama-seca [ˌama'seka] *(pl* **amas-secas***)* *f* nanny.
amasiar-se [7] [amazi'axsi] *vp* **dated** to live together; **~ com alguém** to live with sb.
amassado, da [ama'sadu, da] *adj* [tecido, roupa, papel] crumpled; [carro] smashed up.
amassar [4] [ama'sa(x)] *vt* **-1.** [massa] to knead; [bolo, pão] to mix. **-2.** [roupa] to crease. **-3.** [papel] to crumple. **-4.** [carro] to smash up.
amável [a'mavɛw] *(pl* **-eis***)* *adj* friendly.
amazona [ama'zona] *f* **-1.** [mulher que anda a cavalo] horsewoman. **-2.** [mulher guerreira] Amazon.
Amazonas [ama'zonaʃ] *n* **-1.** [rio]: **o ~** the Amazon. **-2.** [estado] Amazonas.
Amazônia [ama'zonja] *n* Amazonia.

AMAZÔNIA

The area of *Amazônia* exceeds 7 million km^2, over half of which is in Brazilian territory. The Amazon basin has the most extensive river network and the greatest flow of freshwater in the world; it is also home to the world's largest tropical forest. Its enormous biodiversity includes over 60,000 species of trees, some of which can reach a height of 100m or more.

amazônico, ca [ama'zoniku, ka] *adj* Amazonian.
Amã [a'mã] *n* Amman.
âmbar ['ãnba(x)] *m* amber.
AmBev *(abrev de* **American Beverage Company***)* *f* ≃ AmBev, *Brazilian drinks manufacturer.*
ambição [ãnbi'sãw] *(pl* **-ões***)* *f* ambition.
ambicionar [4] [ãnbisjo'na(x)] *vt* to set one's sights on.
ambicioso, osa [ãnbi'sjozu, ɔza] ◇ *adj* ambitious. ◇ *m, f* go-getter.
ambidestro, tra [ãnbi'deʃtru, tra] *adj* ambidextrous.
ambiental [ãnbjẽn'taw] *(pl* **-ais***)* *adj* environmental.
ambientalista [ãnbjẽnta'liʃta] ◇ *adj* environmental. ◇ *mf* environmentalist.
ambientar [4] [ãnbjẽn'tar] *vt* **-1.** [filme, enredo] to set. **-2.** [adaptar] to acclimatize.
◆ **ambientar-se** *vp* [adaptar-se] to mingle.
ambiente [ãn'bjẽntʃi] ◇ *adj* ambient. ◇ *m* **-1.** [gen & *COMPUT*] environment. **-2.** [em sala, boate] area. **-3.** *fig* [atmosfera] atmosphere.
ambigüidade [ãnbigwi'dadʒi] *f* ambiguity.
ambíguo, gua [ãn'bigwu, gwa] *adj* ambiguous.
âmbito ['ãnbitu] *m* [campo de ação] field.
ambivalência [ãnbiva'lẽnsja] *f* ambivalence.
ambivalente [ãnbiva'lẽntʃi] *adj* ambivalent.
ambos, bas ['ãnbuʃ, baʃ] ◇ *adj* both. ◇ *pron* both.
ambrosia [ãnbro'zia] *f a sweet dish of eggs and milk.*
ambulância [ãnbu'lãnsja] *f* ambulance.
ambulante [ãnbu'lãntʃi] ◇ *adj* **-1.** [vendedor, pipoqueiro - na calçada] street *(antes de subst)*; [- de porta em porta] door-to-door *(antes de subst)*. **-2.** [biblioteca, posto médico] mobile. **-3.** *fam fig*: **ele é uma enciclopédia ~** he's a walking encyclopedia. ◇ *mf* [vendedor ambulante] street vendor.
ambulatório [ãnbula'tɔrju] *m* outpatient department.
ameaça [a'mjasa] *f* threat; **~ de bomba** bomb scare; **~ de enfarte** risk of heart attack; **~ de morte** death threat.
ameaçador, ra [amjasa'do(x), ra] *adj* threatening, menacing.
ameaçar [13] [amja'sa(x)] *vt* to threaten; **~ fazer algo** to threaten to do sthg; **~ alguém de morte** to threaten sb with death.
amealhar [4] [amja'ʎa(x)] ◇ *vt* [juntar] to amass. ◇ *vi* [poupar] to save up.
ameba [a'mɛba] *f* amoeba ***UK***, ameba ***US***.
amedrontador, ra [amedrõnta'do(x), ra] *adj* frightening.
amedrontar [4] [amedrõn'ta(x)] *vt* to frighten.
◆ **amedrontar-se** *vp* to feel afraid.
ameia [a'meja] *f* battlement.
ameixa [a'mejʃa] *f* **-1.** [fresca] plum. **-2.** [seca] prune.
amém [a'mẽ] ◇ *interj* amen! ◇ *m fig*: **dizer ~ a** to give in to.
amêndoa [a'mẽndwa] *f* almond.
amendoado, da [amẽn'dwadu, da] *adj* [olhos] almond-shaped.
amendoeira [amẽn'dwejra] *f* almond tree.

amendoim [amẽn'dwĩ] (*pl* **-ns**) *m* peanut; ~ **torrado** roasted peanut.

amenidade [ameni'dadʒi] *f* **-1.** [suavidade] mildness. **-2.** [delicadeza] gentleness.
◆ **amenidades** *fpl* [futilidades] trivialities.

amenizar [4] [ameni'za(x)] *vt* **-1.** [abrandar] to reduce. **-2.** [tornar agradável] to make pleasant. **-3.** [briga, conflito] to settle. **-4.** [facilitar] to lighten.

ameno, na [a'menu, na] *adj* **-1.** [brando - sabor] mild; [- repreensão] quiet; [- pena] light. **-2.** [agradável] pleasant.

América [a'mɛrika] *n* America; ~ **Central** Central American; ~ **do Norte** North America; ~ **do Sul** South America; ~ **Hispânica** Spanish America; ~ **Latina** Latin America.

americanizado, da [amerikãni'zadu, da] *adj* Americanized.

americanizar [amerikãni'za(x)] *vt* to Americanize.

americano, na [ameri'kãnu, na] <> *adj* American. <> *m, f* American.

ameríndio, dia [ame'rĩndʒu, dʒa] <> *adj* Amerindian. <> *m, f* Amerindian.

amesquinhar [4] [ameʃki'ɲa(x)] *vt* [tornar mesquinho] to demean.
◆ **amesquinhar-se** *vp* **-1.** [tornar-se avaro] to become mean. **-2.** [humilhar-se] to demean o.s.

ametista [ame'tʃiʃta] *f* amethyst.

amianto [a'mjãntu] *m* asbestos.

amicíssimo, ma [ami'sisimu, ma] *superl* ▷ **amigo**.

amido [a'midu] *m* starch.

amigar-se [14] [ami'gaxsi] *vp* [amancebar-se] to live together; ~ **com alguém** to live with sb.

amigável [ami'gavɛw] (*pl* **-eis**) *adj* friendly.

amígdala [a'migdala] *f* tonsil.

amigdalite [amigda'litʃi] *f* tonsillitis.

amigo, ga [a'migu, ga] <> *adj* friendly. <> *m, f* friend; ~ **do peito** bosom buddy; ~ **secreto** *ou* **oculto** [jogo] *a game of present swapping in which you draw a person's name from a hat and then anonymously give them a present after a certain period of time*; [pessoa] *the person to whom the present is given in this game.*

amigo-da-onça, amiga-da-onça [ˌamiguda'õsa, ˌamigada'õsa] *m, f fam* false friend.

amistoso, osa [amiʃ'tozu, ɔza] *adj* friendly.
◆ **amistoso** *m ESP* friendly.

amiúde [a'mjudʒi] *adv* often.

amizade [ami'zadʒi] *f* **-1.** [relação] friendship; **fazer** ~ **(com alguém)** to make friends (with sb); ~ **colorida** *fam* casual relationship. **-2.** [estima] friendliness; **ela o tratou com** ~ she treated him in a friendly manner.

amnésia [am'nɛzja] *f* amnesia.

amo, ma ['amo, ma] *m, f* master (*f* mistress).
◆ **ama** *f* [governanta] nanny.

amolação [amola'sãw] (*pl* **-ões**) *f* [incômodo, aborrecimento] hassle.

amolado, da [amo'ladu, da] *adj* **-1.** [afiado] sharp. **-2.** [aborrecido] annoyed.

amolador [amola'do(x)] *m* [de facas] knife sharpener.

amolar [4] [amo'la(x)] <> *vt* **-1.** [faca] to sharpen. **-2.** [incomodar, aborrecer] to annoy. <> *vi* [causar incômodo] to be annoying.
◆ **amolar-se** *vp* [aborrecer-se] to get annoyed.

amoldar [4] [amow'da(x)] *vt* [adaptar, ajustar]: ~ **algo (a)** to adapt sthg (to).
◆ **amoldar-se** *vp* [adaptar-se, ajustar-se]: ~**-se (a)** to adapt (to).

amolecer [25] [amole'se(x)] <> *vt* **-1.** [tornar mole] to soften. **-2.** *fig* [abrandar] to mollify. <> *vi* **-1.** [tornar-se mole] to soften. **-2.** *fig* [tornar-se brando] to relent.

amônia [a'monja] *f* ammonia.

amoníaco [amo'niaku] *m* ammonia.

amontoado [amõn'twadu] *m* pile.

amontoar [20] [amõn'twa(x)] *vt* to pile up.
◆ **amontoar-se** *vp* to pile up.

amor [a'mo(x)] (*pl* **-es**) *m* love; ~ **livre** free love; **fazer** ~ to make love; **pelo** ~ **de Deus!** for God's sake!; **ser um** ~ **(de pessoa)** to be a gem (of a person).

amora [a'mɔra] *f* mulberry.

amoral [amo'raw] (*pl* **-ais**) <> *adj* amoral. <> *mf* unscrupulous person.

amora-preta [aˌmɔra'preta] (*pl* **amoras-pretas**) *f* mulberry.

amordaçar [13] [amoxda'sa(x)] *vt* to gag.

amoreco [amo'rɛku] *m*: **um** ~ a darling.

amorenado, da [amore'nadu, da] *adj* swarthy.

amorfo, fa [a'mɔxfu, fa] *adj* **-1.** [sem forma] amorphous. **-2.** *fig* [pessoa] dreary.

amornar [4] [amox'na(x)] <> *vt* to warm up. <> *vi* to cool down.

amoroso, osa [amo'rozu, ɔza] *adj* [pessoa] loving; **um caso** ~ a love affair.

amor-perfeito [aˌmoxpex'fejtu] (*pl* **amores-perfeitos**) *m* heartsease.

amor-próprio [aˌmox'prɔprju] (*pl* **amores-próprios**) *m* **-1.** [auto-estima] self-esteem. **-2.** [orgulho] conceitedness.

amortecedor [amoxtese'do(x)] (*pl* **-es**) *m* shock absorber.

amortização [amoxtiza'sãw] (*pl* **-ões**) *f* **-1.** [pagamento parcial] part payment. **-2.** *FIN* [de ações] amortization.

amortizar [4] [amoxti'za(x)] *vt* **-1.** [pagar parte de] to repay (in part). **-2.** *FIN* [ações] to amortize.

amostra [a'mɔʃtra] *f* sample; ~ **grátis** free sample.

amostragem [amoʃ'traʒẽ] (*pl* **-ns**) *f* **-1.** [coleta, seleção] sampling. **-2.** [amostra] selection. **-3.** [em estatística] cross sample.

amotinado, da [amotʃi'nadu, da] *adj* mutinous.

amotinar [4] [amotʃi'na(x)] *vt* to lead into mutiny.
◆ **amotinar-se** *vp* to mutiny.

amparar [4] [ãnpa'ra(x)] *vt* **-1.** [escorar, segurar] to hold. **-2.** [ajudar] to support.
◆ **amparar-se** *vp* [escorar-se, segurar-se]: ~**-se**

(contra/em) to lean (against/on).
amparo [ãn'paru] *m* **-1.** [apoio] hold. **-2.** [ajuda] support.
amperagem [ãnpe'raʒẽ] *f* [eletr] amperage.
ampère [ãn'pɛri] *m* amp, ampere.
ampliação [ãnplia'sãw] (*pl* **-ões**) *f* **-1.** [aumento - de forma, imagem] enlargement; [- de ângulo] widening. **-2.** [extensão] extension. **-3.** [desenvolvimento - de estudos] broadening; [- de negócio] expansion. **-4.** [*FOT* - processo] blow-up; [- exemplar] enlargement.
ampliar [16] [ãnpli'a(x)] *vt* **-1.** [aumentar - forma, imagem] to enlarge; [- ângulo] to widen. **-2.** [estender] to extend. **-3.** [desenvolver - estudos] to broaden; [- negócio] to expand.
amplificação [anplifika'sãw] (*pl* **-ões**) *f* **-1.** [aumento - de forma, imagem] enlargement; [- de ângulo] widening. **-2.** [de som] amplification.
amplificador [ãnplifika'do(x)] (*pl* **-es**) *m* [de som] amplifier.
amplificar [12] [ãnplifi'ka(x)] *vt* **-1.** [aumentar - forma, imagem] to enlarge; [- ângulo] to widen. **-2.** [som] to amplify.
amplitude [ãnpli'tudʒi] *f* **-1.** [espaço] spaciousness. **-2.** *fig* [abrangência] scope. **-3.** *TEC* amplitude.
amplo, pla ['ãnplu, 'pla] *adj* **-1.** [espaçoso] spacious. **-2.** [abrangente] broad. **-3.** [lato]**: no sentido mais ~ da palavra** in the broadest sense of the word. **-4.** *(antes de subst)* [ilimitado] ample.
ampola [ãn'pola] *f* ampoule ***UK***, ampule ***US***.
ampulheta [ãnpu'ʎeta] *f* hour-glass.
amputação [ãnputa'sãw] (*pl* **-ões**) *f* amputation.
amputar [4] [ãnpu'ta(x)] *vt* to amputate.
Amsterdã [amiʃtex'dã] *n* Amsterdam.
amuado, da [a'mwadu, da] *adj* [aborrecido] sulking.
amuar [4] [a'mwa(x)] *vt* [aborrecer] to annoy.
◆ **amuar-se** *vp* [aborrecer-se]**: ~-se (com** *ou* **contra)** to get annoyed (with).
amulatado, da [amula'tadu, da] *adj* mulatto-looking.
amuleto [amu'letu] *m* amulet.
anã [a'nã] *f* ▷ **anão**.
anacrônico, ca [ana'kroniku, ka] *adj* anachronistic.
anacronismo [anakro'niʒmu] *m* anachronism.
anafilático, ca [anafi'latiku, ka] *adj* ▷ **choque**.
anagrama [ana'grãma] *m* anagram.
anágua [a'nagwa] *f* petticoat.
anais [a'najʃ] *mpl* annals.
anal [a'naw] (*pl* **-ais**) *adj* anal.
analfabetismo [anawfabe'tʃiʒmu] *m* illiteracy.
analfabeto, ta [anawfa'bɛtu, ta] ◇ *adj* illiterate. ◇ *m, f* illiterate.
analgésico, ca [anaw'ʒɛziku, ka] *adj* analgesic.
◆ **analgésico** *m* [remédio] painkiller, analgesic.
analisar [4] [anali'za(x)] *vt* **-1.** [examinar, avaliar] to analyse. **-2.** *PSIC* to put through analysis.
análise [a'nalizi] *f* [ger & *PSIC*] analysis; **~s clínicas** clinical tests.
analista [ana'liʃta] *mf* **-1.** [ger & *PSIC*] analyst; **~ de sistemas** systems analyst.
analítico, ca [ana'litʃiku, ka] *adj* analytical.
analogia [analo'ʒia] *f* analogy; **por ~** by analogy.
análogo, ga [a'nalogu, ga] *adj* analogous.
ananás [ana'naʃ] (*pl* **-ases**) *m* pineapple.
anão, ã [a'nãw, ã] (*mpl* **-ões**, *fpl* **-s**) *m, f* dwarf.
anarquia [anax'kia] *f* **-1.** [ausência de governo] anarchy. **-2.** *fig* [bagunça] shambles.
anárquico, ca [a'naxkiku, ka] *adj* **-1.** [sistema, sociedade] anarchic. **-2.** *fig* [caótico] chaotic.
anarquismo [anax'kizmu] *m* anarchism.
anarquista [anax'kiʃta] ◇ *adj* [partido, sociedade] anarchist. ◇ *mf* **-1.** [militante] anarchist. **-2.** *fig* [bagunceiro, agitador] agitator.
anarquizar [4] [anaxki'za(x)] *vt fig* **-1.** [tornar anárquico] to reduce to anarchy. **-2.** [incitar à desordem] to incite to riot. **-3.** [abagunçar] to make a mess of. **-4.** [desmoralizar, ridicularizar] to satirize.
ANATEL (*abrev de* **Agência Nacional de Telecomunicações**) *f Brazilian state telecommunications regulator,* ≃ Oftel ***UK***, ≃ ODTR ***US***.
anátema [a'natema] *m* [maldição, estigma] anathema.
anatomia [anato'mia] *f* anatomy.
anatômico, ca [ana'tomiku, ka] *adj* anatomical.
anca ['ãŋka] *f* **-1.** [de pessoa] hip. **-2.** [de animal] haunch.
ancestral [ãn'seʃtraw] (*pl* **-ais**) ◇ *adj* ancestral, age-old. ◇ *mf* ancestor.
◆ **ancestrais** *mpl* ancestors.
anchova [ãn'ʃova] *f* anchovy.
ancião, ciã [ã'sjãw, sjã] (*mpl* **-ões**, *fpl* **-s**) ◇ *adj* aged. ◇ *m, f* venerable person.
ancinho [ãn'siɲu] *m* rake.
anciões [ã'sjõjʃ] *pl* ▷ **ancião**.
âncora ['ãŋkora] *f ECON*: **~ cambial** exchange rate pegging.
ancoradouro [ãŋkora'doru] *m* anchorage.
ancorar [4] [ãŋko'ra(x)] ◇ *vt* **-1.** [fundear] to anchor. **-2.** *fig* [basear] to base. ◇ *vi* [fundear] to base.
◆ **ancorar-se** *vp fig* [basear-se] to be based.
andada [ãn'dada] *f* walk; **dar uma ~** to take a walk.
andaime [ãn'dãjmi] *m* scaffolding.
andamento [ãnda'mẽntu] *m* **-1.** [prosseguimento] progress; **dar ~ a algo** to set in motion; **estar em ~** to be under way. **-2.** [direção] direction. **-3.** *MÚS* tempo.
andança [ãn'dãnsaʃ] *f* [viagem] travel.
andar [4] [ãn'da(x)] (*pl* **-es**) ◇ *m* **-1.** [jeito de caminhar] walk. **-2.** [pavimento] storey ***UK***, story ***US***. ◇ *vi* **-1.** [caminhar] to walk. **-2.** [usar como transporte]**: ~ de bicicleta/a cavalo** to ride a bicycle/horse; **~ de avião/carro/trem** to go by plane/car/train. **-3.** [movimentar-se] to go. **-4.** [errar] to wander. **-5.** [progredir, funcionar] to go. **-6.** [passar] to go, to pass. **-7.** [conviver]**: ~ com alguém** to get along with sb. **-8.** [ter caso amoroso]**: ~ com alguém** to be going out with sb. **-9.** [estar] to be; **~ em** *ou* **por** to be

travelling in; ~ **fazendo algo** to be doing sthg. **-10.**: ~ **por** to be around. **-11.** [ir-se]: **ir andando** to be on one's way. **-12.** [apressar-se]: **anda (com isso)!** get a move on! <> *vt* [percorrer] to do; **andamos 50 quilômetros em um dia** we did 50 kms in one day.
andarilho, lha [ãnda'riʎu, ʎa] *m, f* walker.
Andes ['ãndiʃ] *npl*: **os** ~ the Andes.
andino, na [ãn'dinu, na] <> *adj* Andean. <> *m, f* Andean.
andorinha [ãndo'riɲa] *f* swallow.
Andorra [ãn'doxa] *n*: **(o principado de)** ~ (the principality of) Andorra.
andrógino, na [ãn'drɔʒinu, na] *adj* androgynous.
anedota [ane'dɔta] *f* joke.
anel [a'nɛw] (*pl* **-éis**) *m* **-1.** [ger] ring. **-2.** [de corrente] circuit. **-3.** [de cabelo] lock.
anelado, da [ane'ladu, da] *adj* curly.
anemia [ane'mia] *f* anaemia *UK*, anemia *US*.
anêmico, ca [a'nemiku, ka] *adj* anaemic *UK*, anemic *US*.
anestesia [aneʃte'zia] *f* **-1.** [efeito] anaesthesia *UK*, anesthesia *US*. **-2.** [anestésico] anaesthetic *UK*, anesthetic *US*; **tomar** ~ to have an anaesthetic; ~ **geral/local** general/local anaesthetic.
anestesiado, da [aneʃte'zjadu, da] *adj* [paciente] anaesthetized.
anestesiar [16] [aneʃte'zja(x)] *vt* **-1.** [entorpecer] to anaesthetize *UK*, anesthetize *US*. **-2.** [aplicar anestesia] to give an anaesthetic to *UK*, to give an anesthetic to *US*.
anestésico, ca [aneʃ'tɛziku, ka] *adj* anaesthetizing *UK*, anesthetizing *US*.
◆ **anestésico** *m* anaesthetic *UK*, anesthetic *US*.
anexação [aneksa'sãw] (*pl* **-ões**) *f* **-1.** [de cláusulas, documentos] attachment. **-2.** [de terras, país] annexation.
anexado, da [ane'ksadu, da] *adj* COMPUT attached.
anexar [4] [anek'sa(x)] *vt* COMPUT: ~ **um arquivo** to attach a file.
anexo [a'nɛksu] *m* COMPUT attachment.
ANFAVEA (*abrev de* **Associação Nacional dos Fabricantes de Veículos Automotores**) *f Brazilian association of automobile manufacturers.*
anfetamina [ãnfeta'mina] *f* amphetamine.
anfíbio, bia [ãn'fibju, bja] *adj* amphibious.
◆ **anfíbio** *m* amphibian.
anfiteatro [ãnfi'tʃjatru] *m* amphitheatre *UK*, amphitheater *US*.
anfitrião, triã [ãnfi'trjãw, trjã] (*mpl* **-ões**, *fpl* **-s**) *m, f* host (*f* hostess).
angariar [16] [ãŋga'rja(x)] *vt* to attract.
angelical [ãnʒeli'kaw] (*pl* **-ais**) *adj* angelic.
angina [ãn'ʒina] *f*: ~ **(do peito)** angina (pectoris).
anglicano, na [ãŋgli'kanu, na] <> *adj* Anglican. <> *m, f* Anglican.
anglicismo [ãɲgli'siʒmu] *m* Anglicism.
anglófono, na [ãŋ'glɔfonu, na] <> *adj* English-speaking. <> *m, f* English speaker.
anglo-saxão, xã [ˌãŋglosak'sãw, sã] (*mpl* **-ões**, *fpl* **-ãs**) <> *adj* Anglo-Saxon. <> *m, f* Anglo-Saxon.
anglo-saxônico, ca [ˌãŋglosak'soniku, ka] (*mpl* **-s**, *fpl* **-s**) *adj* Anglo-Saxon.
Angola [ãŋ'gɔla] *n* Angola.
angolano, na [ãŋgo'lãnu, na] <> *adj* Angolan. <> *m, f* Angolan.
angorá [ãŋgo'ra] <> *adj* angora. <> *m* [tecido] angora. <> *mf* [gato] angora.
angra ['ãŋgra] *f* bay.
angu [ãŋ'gu] *m* **-1.** [ger] ≃ porridge. **-2.** ***fam fig*** [confusão, problema]: **um** ~**-de-caroço** a tough nut to crack.
angular [ãŋgu'la(x)] *adj* angular.
ângulo ['ãŋgulu] *m* **-1.** [ger] angle; ~ **agudo/obtuso/reto** acute/obtuse/right angle. **-2.** [canto] corner. **-3.** [de mira] angle (of vision).
anguloso, sa [ãŋgu'lozu, lɔza] *adj* angled.
angústia [ãŋ'guʃtʃja] *f* anguish.
angustiado, da [ãŋguʃ'tʃjadu, da] *adj* anguished.
angustiante [ãŋguʃ'tʃjãntʃi] *adj* harrowing.
angustiar [16] [ãŋguʃ'tʃja(x)] *vt* to cause anguish to.
◆ **angustiar-se** *vp* to become distressed; ~**-se com algo** to be distressed by sthg; ~**-se de** *ou* **por** to be distressed about.
anil [a'niw] *m* [cor] blue.
animação [anima'sãw] *f* **-1.** [entusiasmo] enthusiasm. **-2.** [alegria] jollity. **-3.** [movimento] hustle and bustle. **-4.** CINE animation.
animado, da [ani'madu, da] *adj* **-1.** [entusiasmado] spirited. **-2.** [alegre, movimentado] lively.
animador, ra [anima'do(x), ra] (*mpl* **-es**, *fpl* **-s**) <> *adj* encouraging. <> *m, f* animator.
animal [ani'maw] (*pl* **-ais**) <> *adj* **-1.** [ger] animal. **-2.** ***fam pej*** [pessoa] brutal. <> *mf* ***fam pej*** [pessoa - bruto] brute; [- ignorante] ass. <> *m* ZOOL animal; ~ **doméstico** [de estimação] domestic animal; [de criação] livestock.
animalesco, ca [animal'leʃku, ka] *adj* animal.
animar [4] [ani'ma(x)] *vt* **-1.** [ger] to liven up. **-2.** [encorajar]: ~ **alguém (a fazer algo)** to encourage sb (to do sthg). **-3.** [entusiasmar] to enthuse. **-4.** [fomentar, estimular] to stimulate. **-5.** [dar animação] to animate. **-6.** RELIG [dar vida a] to bring to life.
◆ **animar-se** *vp* **-1.** [tomar coragem]: ~**-se (a fazer algo)** to resolve (to do sthg). **-2.** [entusiasmar-se] to become enthusiastic. **-3.** [debate, conversa, festa] to liven up. **-4.** [alegrar-se] to cheer up. **-5.** RELIG [ganhar vida] to come to life.
ânimo ['ãnimu] <> *m* **-1.** [coragem] courage. **-2.** [entusiasmo] enthusiasm; **perder o** ~ to lose courage; **recobrar o** ~ to regain one's resolve. **-3.** [estímulo] life; **representar um novo** ~ **para** to give a new lease of life to. <> *interj*: ~! come on!
animosidade [animozi'dadʒi] *f* animosity.

aninhar [4] [ani'ɲa(x)] ◇ *vt* **-1.** [acolher, aconchegar] to cuddle. **-2.** [abrigar] to shelter. ◇ *vi* [fazer ninho] to nest.
◆ **aninhar-se** *vp* **-1.** [aconchegar-se] to nestle. **-2.** [fazer ninho] to nest.

aniquilação [anikila'sãw] *f* **-1.** [anulação] rescission. **-2.** [esgotamento] exhaustion. **-3.** [destruição] annihilation; ~ **moral** moral decay. **-4.** *fig* [ruína] ruin.

aniquilar [4] [aniki'la(x)] *vt* **-1.** [anular] to rescind. **-2.** [esgotar] to exhaust. **-3.** [destruir] to annihilate. **-4.** *fig* [arruinar] to ruin.
◆ **aniquilar-se** *vp* **-1.** [esgotar-se] to be exhausted. **-2.** *fig* [moralmente] to destroy o.s.

anis [a'niʃ] (*pl* **-es**) *m* aniseed; **licor de** ~ anisette.

anistia [aniʃ'tʃia] *f* amnesty.

anistiado, da [aniʃ'tʃiadu, da] ◇ *adj* amnestied. ◇ *m, f person granted amnesty.*

aniversariante [anivexsa'rjãntʃi] ◇ *adj*: **a cidade** ~ the city that is celebrating its anniversary. ◇ *mf* [pessoa] birthday boy (*f* birthday girl).

aniversariar [16] [anivexsa'rja(x)] *vi* **-1.** [pessoa] *to celebrate one's birthday/anniversary.* **-2.** [cidade] *to celebrate its anniversary.*

aniversário [anivex'sarju] *m* **-1.** [de acontecimento] anniversary. **-2.** [de nascimento] birthday. **-3.** [festa] birthday party.

anjo ['ãnʒu] *m* angel; ~ **da guarda** guardian angel.

Ankara [ãŋ'kara] *n* Ankara.

ano ['ãnu] *m* [período] year; **no** ~ **de 1969, o homem foi à Lua** in 1969, man went to the moon; **os** ~**s 70** the 1970s; ~ **bissexto** leap year; ~ **civil** calendar year; ~ **corrente** current year; ~ **financeiro** financial year; ~ **fiscal** tax year; ~ **letivo** academic year; **este** ~ this year; **há** ~**s** *ou* **faz** ~**s que** it's years since; **faz** ~**s que não o vejo** it's years since I saw him, I haven't seen him for years; **(no)** ~ **passado** last year; **(no)** ~ **que vem** next year; **por** ~ a year, per year.
◆ **anos** *mpl* [idade]: **tenho vinte** ~ **(de idade)** I'm twenty (years old); **quantos** ~**s você tem?** how old are you?; **ela faz nove** ~**s em outubro** she'll be nine in October.

ano-bom [ˌãnu'bõ] (*pl* **anos-bons**) *m* [festa] New Year.

anões [a'nõjʃ] *pl* ▷ **anão**.

anoitecer [25] [anojte'se(x)] ◇ *m* nightfall; **ao** ~ at nightfall. ◇ *vi* **-1.** [cair a noite]: **quando anoiteceu, acendemos as luzes** when it got dark we turned on the lights. **-2.** [estar em algum lugar ao anoitecer] to be somewhere when night falls; **anoitecemos na estrada** night fell while we were on the road.

ano-luz [ˌãnu'luʃ] (*pl* **anos-luz**) *m* light year.

anomalia [anoma'lia] *f* abnormality.

anômalo, la [a'nomalu, la] *adj* abnormal.

anonimato [anoni'matu] *m* anonymity; **ficar no** ~ to remain in anonymity; **viver no** ~ to live in anonymity.

anônimo, ma [a'nonimu, ma] *adj* anonymous.

ano-novo [ˌãnu'novu] (*pl* **anos-novos**) *m* **-1.** [período] new year. **-2.** [festa] New Year.

anoraque [ano'raki] *m* anorak.

anorexia [anorek'sia] *f* anorexia.

anoréxico, ca [ano'reksiku, ka] ◇ *adj* anorexic. ◇ *m, f* anorexic.

anormal [anox'maw] (*pl* **-ais**) ◇ *adj* **-1.** [ger] abnormal. **-2.** [incomum] unusual. **-3.** [extraordinário] extraordinary. **-4.** [deficiente] retarded. ◇ *m* **-1.** [pessoa excepcional] abnormal person. **-2.** *fam pej* [idiota] cretin.

anormalidade [anoxmali'dadʒi] *f* **-1.** [anomalia] abnormality. **-2.** [situação] abnormal situation.

anotação [anota'sãw] (*pl* **-ões**) *f* note.

anotar [4] [ano'ta(x)] *vt* **-1.** [tomar nota de] to note down. **-2.** [apor observações a] to annotate.

anseio [ãn'seju] *m* desire; **no** ~ **de fazer algo** in one's eagerness to do sthg.

ânsia ['ãnsja] *f* **-1.** [desejo]: **ter** ~ **(por algo/de fazer algo)** to be longing for sthg/to do sthg; ~**s de vômito** nausea. **-2.** [ansiedade] anxiety.

ansiar [17] [ãn'sja(x)] *vi*: ~ **por algo/por fazer algo** to long for sthg/to do sth.

ansiedade [ãnsje'dadʒi] *f* **-1.** [ger] anxiety; **com** ~ anxiously. **-2.** [desejo] longing.

ansioso, osa [ãn'sjozu, ɔza] *adj* [angustiado, desejoso] anxious; **o presidente aguarda** ~ **o resultado das eleições** the president is anxiously awaiting the election results.

anta ['ãnta] *f* **-1.** ZOOL tapir. **-2.** *fam pej* [idiota]: **ser uma** ~ to be an ass.

antagônico, ca [ãnta'goniku, ka] *adj* [contrário] antagonistic; **opiniões antagônicas** conflicting opinions.

antagonismo [ãntago'niʒmu] *m* **-1.** [oposição] antagonism; ~ **de idéias** conflict of ideas. **-2.** [rivalidade] competition.

antagonista [ãntago'niʃta] ◇ *adj* **-1.** [candidato, partido] opposing. **-2.** [opinião, idéia] conflicting. ◇ *mf* [rival] opponent.

antártico, ca [ãn'taxtʃiku, ka] *adj* Antarctic.
◆ **Antártico** *n*: **o (oceano)** ~ the Antarctic (Ocean).

Antártida [ãn'taxtʃida] *n*: **a** ~ Antarctica.

ante ['ãntʃi] *prep* **-1.** [diante de] before; **jurar** ~ **a Bíblia** to swear on the Bible; **jurar** ~ **o juiz** to swear before the judge. **-2.** [em conseqüência de] as a result of.

ante- ['ãntʃi-] *prefixo* ante-.

antebraço [ãntʃi'brasu] *m* forearm.

antecedência [ãntese'dênsja] *f*: **com** ~ in advance; **com uma semana de** ~ a week in advance.

antecedente [ãntese'dêntʃi] ◇ *adj* [precedente] preceding. ◇ *m* **-1.** [precedente] predecessor. **-2.** GRAM, MAT antecedent.
◆ **antecedentes** *mpl* [pessoais] track record (*sg*); **ter bons** ~**s** to have a clean record; ~**s criminais** criminal record (*sg*).

anteceder [5] [ãntese'de(x)] ◇ *vt* [preceder, chegar antes de] to precede. ◇ *vi* [preceder]: ~ **a** to precede.

◆ **anteceder-se** *vp* [antecipar-se]: **~ (a)** to be ahead (of).
antecessor, ra [ãntese'so(x), ra] ◇ *adj* preceding. ◇ *m, f* predecessor.
antecipação [ãntesipa'sãw] (*pl* **-ões**) *f* **-1.** [adiantamento]: **a ~ de metas** the early achievement of goals; **a ~ do comunicado provocou uma crise** the bringing forward of the announcement caused a crisis. **-2.** [salarial] advance. **-3.** [antecedência]: **com ~** in advance; **com uma semana/um mês de ~** a week/month in advance.
antecipadamente [ãntesi,pada'mẽntʃi] *adv* in advance.
antecipado, da [ãntesi'padu, da] *adj* **-1.** [pagamento] advance *(antes de subst)*. **-2.** [eleições] early.
antecipar [4] [ãntesi'pa(x)] *vt* **-1.** [fazer ocorrer mais cedo] to bring forward. **-2.** [adiantar-se a] to anticipate.
◆ **antecipar-se** *vp* [adiantar-se]: **~-se a algo/alguém** to pre-empt sthg/sb; **~-se a alguém em algo** to steal a march on sb in sthg.
antegozar [4] [ãntego'za(x)] *vt* to have a foretaste of.
antemão [ãnte'mãw] ◆ **de antemão** *loc adv* beforehand.
antena [ãn'tena] *f* **-1.** [ger] antenna; **de ~s ligadas** with one's antennae out. **-2.** *RÁDIO, TV* aerial; **~ parabólica** satellite dish.
anteontem [ãntʃi'õntẽ] *adv* the day before yesterday.
anteparo [ãnte'paru] *m* [proteção] screen.
antepassado, da [,ãntepa'sadu, da] *m, f* ancestor.
antepenúltimo, ma [ãntepe'nuwtʃimu, ma] *adj* last but two, antepenultimate.
antepor [45] [ãnteẽpo(x)] *vt* **-1.** [contrapor]: **~ algo a algo** to respond to sthg with sthg. **-2.** [preferir]: **~ algo a algo** to prefer sthg to sthg.
◆ **antepor-se** *vp* [contrapor-se]: **~-se a algo** to place o.s. in front of sthg.
anterior [ãnte'rjo(x)] (*pl* **-es**) *adj* **-1.** [prévio]: **~ (a)** before. **-2.** [antigo]: **~ (a)** previous (to). **-3.** [em posição] front; **membro ~** forelimb; **músculo ~** anterior muscle.
anteriormente [ãnterioxẽmẽntʃi] *adv* [previamente] previously; **~ a algo** prior to sthg.
antes ['ãnʃiʃ] *adv* **-1.** [previamente] beforehand; **o quanto ~** as soon as possible; **pouco ~** a little before. **-2.** [antigamente] in the past; **como ~** as ever; **de** *ou* **que ~** as before. **-3.** [de preferência] rather. **-4.** [ao contrário] on the contrary.
◆ **antes de** *loc prep* before; **~ de fazer algo** before doing sthg; **~ da hora/do tempo** early; **~ de tudo** above all.
◆ **antes que** *loc conj* before; **fui embora ~ que chovesse** I left before it rained.
ante-sala [,ãnte'sala] (*pl* **-s**) *f* antechamber.
antever [40] [ãnte've(x)] *vt* to foresee.
antevéspera [,ãnte'vɛʃpera] *f*: **(na) ~** the day before yesterday.
antevisão [,ãnte'vizãw] *f* **-1.** [visão antecipada]: **ter uma ~ de** to foresee. **-2.** [pressentimento] premonition.
anti- ['ãntʃi-] *prefixo* anti-, non-.
antiácido, da [ãn'tʃjasidu, da] *adj* antacid.
◆ **antiácido** *m* antacid.
antiaderente [ãntʃjade'rẽntʃi] (*pl* **-s**) ◇ *adj* non-stick. ◇ *m* non-stick surface.
antiaéreo, rea [ãntʃja'ɛrju, rja] *adj* anti-aircraft; **abrigo ~** bomb shelter.
antialérgico, ca [ãntʃja'lɛxʒiku, ka] *adj* hypoallergenic.
◆ **antialérgico** *m* antihistamine.
antiamericano, na [ãntʃjameri'kãnu, na] *adj* anti-American.
antibiótico, ca [ãntʃi'bjɔtʃiku, ka] *adj* antibiotic.
◆ **antibiótico** *m* antibiotic.
anticaspa [ãntʃi'kaʃpa] *adj* anti-dandruff.
anticlímax [ãntʃi'klimãks] *m inv* anticlimax.
anticoagulante [ãntʃikwagu'lãntʃi] ◇ *adj* anticoagulant. ◇ *m* anticoagulant.
anticomunista [ãntʃikomu'niʃta] ◇ *adj* anticommunist. ◇ *mf* [pessoa] anti-communist.
anticoncepcional [ãntʃikõnsepsjo'naw] (*pl* **-ais**) ◇ *adj* contraceptive. ◇ *m* [pílula, dispositivo] contraceptive.
anticongelante [ãntʃikõnʒe'lãntʃi] ◇ *adj* antifreeze. ◇ *m* antifreeze.
anticorpo [ãntʃi'koxpu] *m* antibody.
anticorrosivo [ãntʃikoxo'zivu] *adj* **-1.** non-corrosive. **-2.** [proteção] anti-corrosive.
antidemocrático, ca [ãntʃidemo'kratʃiku, ka] *adj* anti-democratic.
antidepressivo, va [ãntʃidepre'sivu, va] *adj* antidepressant.
◆ **antidepressivo** *m* antidepressant.
antiderrapante [ãntʃidexa'pãntʃi] *adj* non-skid.
antídoto [ãn'tʃidotu] *m* antidote.
antiestético, ca [ãntʃjeʃ'tɛtʃiku, ka] *adj* tasteless.
antiético, ca [ãn'tʃjɛtʃiku, ka] *adj* unethical.
antigamente [ãntʃiga'mẽntʃi] *adv* in the past; **de ~** old-fashioned.
antigo, ga [ãn'tʃigu, ga] *adj* **-1.** [ger] old. **-2.** [antiquado, remoto] old-fashioned. **-3.** *(antes de subst)* [anterior] former, previous. **-4.** *(antes de subst)* [veterano] longstanding; **ser ~ no clube** to be a longstanding member of the club; **ser ~ na empresa** to be a longstanding member of staff; **ser ~ no cargo** to be an old hand at the job. **-5.** *HIST* [da Antigüidade] ancient.
◆ **antigos** *mpl HIST* [homens] ancients.
antigüidade [ãntʃigwi'dadʒi] *f* **-1.** [idade] age. **-2.** [em cargo, função] seniority. **-3.** [peça, monumento] antique.
◆ **Antigüidade** *f* [época] antiquity.
◆ **antigüidades** *fpl* **-1.** [peças] antiques; **loja de ~s** antique shop. **-2.** [monumentos] ancient monuments.
anti-higiênico, ca [ãntʃji'ʒjeniku, ka] (*mpl* **-s**, *fpl* **-s**) *adj* unhygienic.

anti-histamínico, ca [ãntʃji'iʃta'miniku, ka] *adj* antihistamine.
◆ **anti-histamínico** *m* antihistamine.
anti-horário [ãntʃjo'rarju] *adj*: **sentido/movimento** ~ anticlockwise direction/movement.
antiinflacionário, ria [ãntʃiflasjo'narju, rja] *adj* anti-inflationary.
antiinflamatório, ria [ãntʃiĩnflama'tɔriu, rja] <> *adj* anti-inflammatory. <> *m* anti-inflammatory.
antilhano, na [ãntʃi'ʎanu, na] <> *adj* West Indian. <> *m, f* West Indian.
Antilhas [ãn'tʃiʎas] *npl*: **as** ~ the West Indies.
antílope [ãn'tʃilopi] *m* antelope.
antinatural [ãntʃinatu'raw] (*pl* **-ais**) *adj* unnatural.
antinuclear [ãntʃinukle'a(x)] *adj* anti-nuclear.
antipático, ca [ãntʃi'patʃiku, ka] *adj* unpleasant.
antipatizar [4] [ãntʃipatʃi'za(x)] *vi*: ~ **com alguém** to dislike sb.
antipatriótico, ca [ãntʃipa'trjɔtʃiku, ka] *adj* unpatriotic.
antiperspirante [ãntʃipexʃpi'rantʃi] <> *adj* antiperspirant. <> *mf* antiperspirant.
antipoluente [ãntʃipo'lwẽntʃi] <> *adj* **-1.** [sistema, proteção] anti-pollution. **-2.** [material] non-polluting. <> *m* anti-pollution agent.
antiquado, da [ãntʃi'kwadu, da] *adj* antiquated.
antiquário, ria [ãntʃi'kwarju, rja] *m, f* [comerciante] antique dealer.
◆ **antiquário** *m* [loja] antique shop.
antiqüíssimo, ma [ãntʃi'kisimu, ma] *superl* ▷ **antigo**.
anti-semita [ãntʃise'mita] (*pl* **-s**) <> *adj* anti-Semitic. <> *mf* [pessoa] anti-Semite.
anti-séptico, ca [antʃi'sɛptʃiku, ka] *adj* antiseptic.
◆ **anti-séptico, antisséptico** *m* [desinfetante] antiseptic.
anti-social [ãntʃiso'sjaw] (*pl* **-ais**) *adj* antisocial.
antisséptico [ˌãntʃi'sɛptʃiku] = **anti-séptico**.
antitabagismo [ãntʃitaba'ʒizmu] *m* anti-smoking.
antitabagista [ãntʃitaba'ʒista] <> *adj* anti-smoking. <> *mf* anti-smoker.
antitérmico, ca [ãntʃi'tɛxmiku, ka] *adj* antipyretic.
◆ **antitérmico** *m* [comprimido] antipyretic.
antiterrorismo [ãntʃitexo'riʒmu] *m* anti-terrorism.
antiterrorista [ãntʃitexo'riʃta] <> *adj* anti-terrorist. <> *mf* anti-terrorist.
antítese [ãn'tʃitezi] *f* antithesis.
antivírus [ãntʃi'viruʃ] *m inv* **-1.** BIOL antivirus. **-2.** COMPUT antivirus program.
antolhos [ã'tɔʎuʃ] *mpl* blinkers.
antologia [ãntolo'ʒia] *f* anthology.
antológico, ca [ãnto'lɔʒiko, ka] *adj* outstanding.
antônimo [ãn'tonimu] *m* antonym.
antro ['ãntru] *m* **-1.** [caverna] cave. **-2.** [de animal] lair. **-3.** [de bandidos etc] den.
antropofagia [ãntropofa'ʒia] *f* cannibalism.
antropófago, ga [ãntro'pɔfagu, ga] <> *adj* cannibalistic. <> *m, f* cannibal.
antropologia [ãntropolo'ʒia] *f* anthropology.
antropólogo, ga [ãntro'pɔlogu, ga] *m, f* anthropologist.
anual [a'nwaw] (*pl* **-ais**) *adj* annual, yearly.
anuário [a'nwarju] *m* yearbook.
anuidade [anwi'dadʒi] *f* annuity.
anuir [74] [a'nwi(x)] *vi* to agree; ~ **a** *ou* **em algo** to agree to *ou* on sthg; ~ **a** *ou* **em fazer algo** to agree to do sthg.
anulação [anula'sãw] (*pl* **-ões**) *f* **-1.** [cancelamento, invalidação] cancellation. **-2.** [casamento] annulment. **-3.** [pena] revocation. **-4.** [gol] disallowance.
anular [4] [anu'la(x)] <> *vt* **-1.** [cancelar, invalidar] to cancel. **-2.** [casamento] to annul. **-3.** [pena] to revoke. **-4.** [gol] to disallow. **-5.** [sobrepujar] to cancel out. <> *adj* **-1.** [forma] circular. **-2.** [dedo] ring. <> *m* [dedo] ring finger.
anunciante [anũn'sjãntʃi] *m* COM advertiser.
anunciar [16] [anũn'sja(x)] *vt* **-1.** [ger] to announce. **-2.** COM [produto] to advertise.
anúncio [a'nũnsju] *m* **-1.** [comunicado] announcement. **-2.** [cartaz, aviso] notice. **-3.** [publicitário] advertisement; ~**s classificados** classifieds.
ânus ['ãnuʃ] *m inv* anus.
anuviar [16] [anuvi'a(x)] *vt* to cloud.
◆ **anuviar-se** *vp* **-1.** [o céu] to become cloudy. **-2.** *fig* [rosto] to cloud.
anverso [ãn'vɛxsu] *m* obverse.
anzol [ãn'zɔw] (*pl* **-óis**) *m* hook.
ao [aw] = **a** + **o**.
aonde [a'õndʒi] *adv* where; ~ **quer que ...** wherever ...
aos [awʃ] = **a** + **os**.
AP (*abrev de* **Estado do Amapá**) *n State of Amapá.*
apadrinhar [4] [apadri'ɲa(x)] *vt* **-1.** [criança] to be godfather to. **-2.** [noivo] to be best man to. **-3.** *fig* [proteger] to take under one's wing. **-4.** *fig* [patrocinar] to sponsor.
APAE (*abrev de* **Associação de Pais e Amigos dos Excepcionais**) *f Brazilian association of parents and friends of the disabled.*
apagado, da [apa'gadu, da] *adj* **-1.** [fogo] extinguished. **-2.** [desligado] out *(depois de verbo)*. **-3.** [com borracha] rubbed out *UK*, erased *US*. **-4.** [desvanecido] faded. **-5.** *fig* [sem brilho] lacklustre. **-6.** *fig* [pessoa] dull.
apagador [apaga'do(x)] *m* board eraser.
apagão [apa'gãw] (*pl* **-ões**) *m* [blecaute] power cut.
apagar [14] [apa'ga(x)] <> *vt* **-1.** [fogo] to put out. **-2.** [vela] to blow out. **-3.** [luz, lanterna] to turn out. **-4.** [lustre] to dim. **-5.** [com borracha, apagador] to rub out. **-6.** [fazer desvanecer-se] to fade. **-7.** [abrandar] to dull. **-8.** COMPUT [eliminar] to delete. **-9.** *fam fig* [matar] to wipe out. <> *vi fam fig* [adormecer] to crash out.
◆ **apagar-se** *vp* **-1.** [extingüir-se] to die out. **-2.** [desligar-se] to go out. **-3.** [desvanecer-se] to fade. **-4.** [abrandar-se] to dull.

apaixonado, da [apajʃo'nadu, da] *adj* **-1.** [enamorado] in love; **estar ~ (por alguém)** to be in love (with sb). **-2.** [exaltado] impassioned. **-3.** [aficcionado]: **ser ~ (por algo)** to be passionate about sthg.

apaixonante [apajʃo'nãntʃi] *adj* exciting.

apaixonar-se [4] [apajʃo'naxsi] *vp* **-1.** [enamorar-se]: **~ (por alguém)** to fall in love (with sb). **-2.** [aficcionar-se]: **~ (por algo)** to become passionate (about sthg).

apalermado, da [apalex'madu, da] *adj* idiotic.

apalpar [4] [apaw'pa(x)] *vt* to feel.
◆ **apalpar-se** *vp* [examinar-se] to examine o.s.

apanhado [apã'ɲadu] *m* **-1.** [resumo] summary. **-2.** [de flores] bunch.

apanhar [4] [apã'ɲa(x)] ◇ *vt* **-1.** [ger] to catch. **-2.** [pegar] to pick out. **-3.** [alcançar] to get. **-4.** [pegar do chão] to pick up. **-5.** [agarrar] to grab. **-6.** [colher] to pick. **-7.** [ir buscar] to fetch. **-8.** [tomar condução] to take. ◇ *vi* **-1.** [ser espancado] to be beaten; **~ de alguém** to take a beating from sb; **~ de algo** to be beaten with sthg. **-2.** *ESP* [perder] to lose. **-3.** *fig* [ter dificuldades] to go through a lot.

apara [a'para] *f* **-1.** [madeira] shaving. **-2.** [papel] shred.

aparador [apara'do(x)] (*pl* **-es**) *m* [móvel] sideboard.

aparafusar [4] [aparafu'za(x)] *vt* **-1.** [parafuso] to screw in. **-2.** [prender] to screw.

aparar [4] [apa'ra(x)] *vt* **-1.** [cabelo, barba, unhas] to trim. **-2.** [unhas] to clip. **-3.** [golpe] to fend off. **-4.** [tábua, folhas] to smooth out.

aparato [apa'ratu] *m* **-1.** [pompa] ceremony. **-2.** [conjunto - de ferramentas] collection; [- de armas] apparatus. **-3.** *fig* [de conceitos, análises] structure.

aparecer [25] [apare'se(x)] *vi* **-1.** [ger] to appear. **-2.** [ser perceptível] to be apparent. **-3.** [comparecer] to turn up; *fam* [fazer visita] to drop in. **-4.** *fam pej* [exibir-se] to show off.

aparecimento [aparesi'mẽntu] *m* appearance.

aparelhado, da [apare'ʎadu, da] *adj* **-1.** [preparado] prepared. **-2.** [madeira] planed.

aparelhagem [apare'ʎaʒẽ] (*pl* **-ns**) *f* **-1.** [equipamento] equipment; [de som] sound system. **-2.** [da madeira] planing. **-3.** *NÁUT* rigging.

aparelhar [4] [apare'ʎa(x)] *vt* **-1.** [preparar] to equip. **-2.** *NÁUT* to rig.
◆ **aparelhar-se** *vp* [preparar-se] to equip o.s.

aparelho [apa'reʎu] *m* **-1.** [conjunto] set; **~ de chá** tea set; **~ de jantar** dinner service. **-2.** [equipamento] equipment; **~ de som** sound system. **-3.** [máquina] machine; **~ de barbear** shaving equipment; **~ de rádio/TV** radio/television set; **~ eletrodoméstico** domestic appliance. **-4.** *PESCA* tackle. **-5.** *POL* hideout. **-6.** *ANAT* system; **~ digestivo** digestive system; **~ fonador** voice box.

aparência [apa'rẽnsja] *f* **-1.** [aspecto] appearance; **sob a ~ de** in the guise of; **na ~** by all appearances. **-2.** [ilusão] show.
◆ **aparências** *fpl* [exterioridades] appearances; **as ~s enganam** *prov* one shouldn't judge by appearances; **manter as ~s** to keep up appearances; **salvar as ~s** to save appearances.

aparentado, da [aparẽn'tadu, da] *adj* **-1.** [que tem parentesco] related; **ser ~ de alguém** to be related to sb; **bem ~** well connected. **-2.** [que tem boa aparência]: **bem ~** smart.

aparentar [4] [aparẽn'ta(x)] *vt* **-1.** [parecer] to seem. **-2.** [fingir] to pretend.

aparente [apa'rẽntʃi] *adj* **-1.** [falso] feigned. **-2.** [visível] visible.

aparição [apari'sãw] (*pl* **-ões**) *f* apparition.

apartamento [apaxta'mẽntu] *m* **-1.** [residência] apartment, flat *UK*. **-2.** [de hotel] hotel suite.

apartar [4] [apax'ta(x)] *vt* **-1.** [separar] to split. **-2.** [briga] to break up.
◆ **apartar-se** *vp* [afastar-se] to split from.

aparte [a'paxtʃi] *m* [observação] aside; **fazer um ~** to make an aside.

apartheid [apax'tajdʒi] *m* apartheid.

apartidário, ria [apartʃi'darju, rja] *adj* non-partisan.

aparvalhado, da [apaxva'ʎadu, da] *adj* **-1.** [idiota] idiotic. **-2.** [sem reação]: **ficar ~** to be stunned.

apatetado, da [apate'tadu, da] *adj* [trapalhão] foolish.

apatia [apa'tʃia] *f* indifference.

apático, ca [a'patʃiku, ka] *adj* indifferent.

apátrida [a'patrida] *mf* stateless person.

apavorado, da [apavo'radu, da] *adj* terrified.

apavoramento [apavora'mẽntu] *m* panic, terror.

apavorante [apavo'rãntʃi] *adj* terrifying.

apavorar [4] [apavo'ra(x)] ◇ *vt* to terrify. ◇ *vi* to be terrifying.
◆ **apavorar-se** *vp* to become terrified.

apaziguar [21] [apazi'gwa(x)] *vt* to calm.
◆ **apaziguar-se** *vp* **-1.** to calm down. **-2.** [inimigos] to make peace.

apear [a'pja(x)] *vi* to dismount.

apedrejar [4] [apedre'ʒa(x)] *vt* to stone.

apegado, da [ape'gadu, da] *adj* [afeiçoado]: **~ (a)** attached (to).

apegar-se [14] [ape'gaxsi] *vp* [afeiçoar-se]: **~ a algo/alguém** to become attached to sthg/sb.

apego [a'pegu] *m* [afeição] attachment; **ter ~ por** to be attached to.

apelação [apela'sãw] (*pl* **-ões**) *f* **-1.** [apelo] appeal. **-2.** *JUR* appeal. **-3.** *fam* [vulgarização] solicitation.

apelante [ape'lãntʃi] *mf* appellant.

apelar [4] [ape'la(x)] *vi* **-1.** [recorrer]: **~ a** to appeal to; **~ (para a violência)** to turn nasty. **-2.** [invocar]: **~ a** [compreensão, amizade] to call upon. **-3.** *JUR*: **~ (de)** to appeal (against). **-4.** [vulgarmente] to turn nasty.

apelidar [4] [apeli'da(x)] *vt*: **~ alguém de algo** to nickname sb sthg.

apelido [ape'lidu] *m* [alcunha] nickname; **chato é ~! ele é insuportável!** *fam* boring's an understatement! he's odious!

apelo [a'pelu] *m* appeal; **~ a alguém/algo** appeal to sb/sthg.

apenas [a'penaʃ] ◇ *adv* [só] only. ◇ *conj* [logo que] as soon as.

apêndice [a'pẽndʒisi] *m* appendix.

apendicite [apẽndʒi'sitʃi] *f* appendicitis.

Apeninos [ape'ninuʃ] *npl*: **os ~** the Apennines.

apequenar [4] [apeke'na(x)] *vt* **-1.** [tornar pequeno] to lessen. **-2.** *fig* [rebaixar, humilhar] to belittle.
◆ **apequenar-se** *vp fig* [rebaixar-se, humilhar-se] to belittle o.s.

aperceber-se [5] [apexse'bexsi] *vp*: **~ de** to realise.

aperfeiçoamento [apexfejswa'mẽntu] *m* [aprimoramento] improvement.

aperfeiçoar [20] [apexfej'swa(x)] *vt* to improve.
◆ **aperfeiçoar-se** *vp* [aprimorar-se] to improve; **~-se em algo** to improve in *ou* at sthg.

aperitivo, va [aperi'tʃivu, va] *adj* appetizing.
◆ **aperitivo** *m* **-1.** [bebida] aperitif. **-2.** [petisco] appetizer.

aperreação [apexja'sãw] (*pl* **-ões**) *f* **-1.** [aborrecimento] vexation. **-2.** [situação difícil] hardship.

aperreado, da [ape'xjadu, da] *adj* **-1.** [aborrecido] vexed. **-2.** [em situação difícil] troubled.

aperrear [15] [ape'xja(x)] *vt* **-1.** [aborrecer] to annoy. **-2.** [afligir] to vex.
◆ **aperrear-se** *vp* **-1.** [aborrecer-se] to become vexed. **-2.** [afligir-se] to be anxious.

apertado, da [apex'tadu, da] ◇ *adj* **-1.** [ger] tight. **-2.** [passagem] narrow. **-3.** [poltrona, sala, teatro] cramped. **-4.** [difícil] hard. **-5.** [sem tempo] pressed. **-6.** [sem dinheiro] strapped for cash; **orçamento ~** tight budget. **-7.** *fam* [para ir ao banheiro]: **estar ~** to be desperate to go to the bathroom. **-8.** [coração]: **estar com o coração ~** to be anguished. ◇ *adv* [com dificuldade] only just.

apertar [4] [apex'ta(x)] ◇ *vt* **-1.** [cingir]: **~ algo (contra/entre)** to clasp sthg (against/between); **~ alguém (contra/entre)** to clasp sb (against/between); **~ a mão de alguém** [cumprimentar] to shake sb's hand. **-2.** [espremer] to squeeze. **-3.** [incomodar por ser justo] to constrict. **-4.** [tornar mais justo] to tighten. **-5.** [pressionar - botão] to do up; [- gatilho] to squeeze. **-6.** *fig* [intensificar] to tighten up on. **-7.** [passo, ritmo] to speed up. **-8.** [cortar] to cut. **-9.** [coração] to wring. **-10.** *fig* [pessoa] to put pressure on. ◇ *vi* **-1.** [roupa, sapato] to be tight. **-2.** [chuva, frio, fome] to intensify. **-3.** [prazo] to run out. **-4.** [estrada, rio] to narrow.
◆ **apertar-se** *vp* **-1.** [cortar gastos] to tighten one's belt. **-2.** [ficar sem dinheiro] to be pressed for cash. **-3.** [com a roupa] to squeeze o.s. into.

aperto [a'pextu] *m* **-1.** [em cumprimento]: **~ de mãos** handshake. **-2.** *fig* [apuro] problem; **passar um ~** to have a rough time. **-3.** *fig* [financeiro] hardship.

apesar [ape'za(x)] *prep*: **~ de** in spite of; **~ de que** even though; **~ disso** in spite of this.

apetecer [25] [apete'se(x)] *vi* to be appetizing; **~ a alguém** to appeal to sb.

apetecível [apete'sivew] (*pl* **-eis**) *adj* **-1.** [prato, receita] appetizing. **-2.** *fig* [idéia proposta] attractive.

apetite [ape'tʃitʃi] *m* appetite; **abrir o ~** to whet the appetite; **bom ~!** enjoy your meal!; **ter um ~ de sucesso/riqueza/poder** to have an appetite for success/wealth/power.

apetitoso, osa [apetʃi'tozu, ɔza] *adj* tasty.

apetrechar [4] [apetre'ʃa(x)] *vt*: **~ alguém (com/para algo)** to equip sb (with/for sthg).
◆ **apetrechar-se** *vp*: **~-se (com/para algo)** to equip o.s. (with/for sthg).

apetrechos [ape'treʃuʃ] *mpl* **-1.** [de guerra] equipment *(U)*. **-2.** [de pesca] tackle *(U)*.

ápice ['apisi] *m* **-1.** [cimo] top, summit. **-2.** *fig* [apogeu] peak.

apicultura [apikuw'tura] *f* bee-keeping.

apiedar-se [4] [apje'daxsi] *vp*: **~ (de alguém/algo)** to feel sorry (for sb/sthg).

apimentado, da [apimẽn'tadu, da] *adj* **-1.** [com muita pimenta] peppery. **-2.** *fig* [sensual] spicy.

apimentar [4] [apimẽn'ta(x)] *vt* to pepper.

apinhado, da [api'ɲadu, da] *adj* crowded; **~ de gente** crowded with people.

apinhar [4] [api'ɲa(x)] *vt* [lotar] to crowd.
◆ **apinhar-se** *vp* **-1.** [aglomerar-se] to crowd. **-2.** [lotar]: **~-se (de gente)** to be crowded (with people).

apitar [4] [api'ta(x)] ◇ *vi* **-1.** [com apito] to whistle. **-2.** *fam fig* [ter autoridade] to know a lot; **ele apita muito em medicina** he knows a lot about medicine; **ele não apita nada em casa** he's not the one who wears the trousers. ◇ *vt* [*ESP* - arbitrar] to referee; [- falta, pênalti] to whistle.

apito [a'pitu] *m* [instrumento, silvo] whistle.

aplacar [12] [apla'ka(x)] ◇ *vt* **-1.** [serenar] to subdue. **-2.** [abrandar] to assuage. ◇ *vi* **-1.** [serenar-se] to die down. **-2.** [abrandar-se] to calm down.
◆ **aplacar-se** *vp* to calm down.

aplainar [4] [aplaj'na(x)] *vt* **-1.** [madeira] to plane. **-2.** [nivelar] to level out.

aplanar [4] [apla'na(x)] *vt* **-1.** [nivelar] to level out. **-2.** [alisar] to smooth. **-3.** *fig* [obstáculos] to smooth out.

aplaudir [6] [aplaw'di(x)] ◇ *vt* to applaud; **~ alguém/algo de pé** to give sb/sthg a standing ovation. ◇ *vi* to clap, to applaud.

aplauso [a'plawzu] *m* **-1.** [ger] applause; **o filme recebeu o ~ da crítica** the film received critical acclaim. **-2.** *fig* [aprovação] approval; **as medidas contra o crime contam com meu ~** I applaud the measures against crime.

aplicação [aplika'sãw] (*pl* **-ões**) *f* **-1.** [ger] application. **-2.** [ornato] adornment.

aplicado, da [apli'kadu, da] *adj* **-1.** [esforçado] hard-working. **-2.** [prático] applied.

aplicar [12] [apli'ka(x)] ◇ *vt* **-1.** [ger] to apply. **-2.** [injeção] to give. **-3.** *FIN* to invest. ◇ *vi FIN* to invest.
◆ **aplicar-se** *vp* **-1.** [esforçar-se]: **~-se em/para algo** to work hard at/for sthg. **-2.** [adequar-se]: **~-se a algo** to apply to sthg.

aplicativo, va [aplika'tʃivu, va] *adj COMPUT*: **programa ~** application.

◆ **aplicativo** *m COMPUT* application.
aplicável [apli'kavɛw] (*pl* **-eis**) *adj* **-1.** [ger] applicable. **-2.** [apropriado] appropriate.
aplique [a'pliki] *m* **-1.** [de luz] wall light. **-2.** [peruca] hairpiece.
APM (*abrev de* **Associação de Pais e Mestres**) *f* ≃ PTA.
apocalipse [apoka'lipsi] *m* apocalypse.
apocalíptico, ca [apoka'liptʃiku, ka] *adj* **-1.** [do Apocalipse] apocalyptic. **-2.** [terrível] terrifying. **-3.** [difícil de entender] enigmatic.
apócrifo, fa [a'pɔkrifu, fa] *adj* apocryphal.
◆ **apócrifo** *m* [texto] apocrypha *(pl)*.
apoderar-se [4] [apode'raxsi] *vp*: ~ **de algo** to take over sthg.
apodrecer [25] [apodre'se(x)] <> *vi* **-1.** [comida] to go off. **-2.** [dente] to rot. **-3.** *fam* [pessoa]: ~ **em** to rot in. <> *vt* [tornar podre] to rot.
apodrecimento [apodresi'mẽntu] *m* rot.
apogeu [apo'ʒew] *m* **-1.** [de império, carreira, romance] crowning point. **-2.** *ASTRON* apogee.
apoiar [16] [apo'ja(x)] *vt* **-1.** [ger] to support. **-2.** [firmar]: ~ **algo em** *ou* **sobre algo** to rest sthg on sthg. **-3.** [fundamentar]: ~ **algo em** *ou* **sobre algo** to base sthg on sthg.
◆ **apoiar-se** *vp* **-1.** [amparar-se mutuamente] to support one another. **-2.** [firmar-se] to lean. **-3.** [fundamentar-se] to be based on.
apoio [a'poju] *m* **-1.** [ger] support; ~ **moral** moral support. **-2.** [patrocínio] sponsorship; ~ **cultural** cultural sponsorship. **-3.** [alicerce] foundations *(pl)*. **-4.** *fig* [fundamento] basis.
apólice [a'pɔlisi] *f* policy; ~ **de seguro** insurance policy.
apolítico, ca [apo'litʃiku, ka] *adj* apolitical.
apologia [apolo'ʒia] *f* defence.
apologista [apolo'ʒiʃta] *mf* apologist.
apontador [apõnta'do(x)] (*pl* **-es**) *m* **-1.** [de lápis] pencil sharpener. **-2.** [de jogo] marker.
apontamento [apõnta'mẽntu] *m* [anotação] notes *(pl)*.
apontar [4] [apõn'ta(x)] <> *vt* **-1.** [ger] to point out. **-2.** [arma] to aim. **-3.** [citar] to name. **-4.** [notas] to make notes. **-5.** [jogo] to mark. **-6.** [lápis] to sharpen. <> *vi* **-1.** [com arma]: ~ **para** to aim at; **apontar!** aim! **-2.** [com o dedo]: ~ **para** to point at. **-3.** [aparecer] to appear.
apoplético, ca [apo'plɛtʃiku, ka] *adj* apoplectic.
apoquentar [4] [apokẽnta(x)] *vt* to annoy.
◆ **apoquentar-se** *vp* to get annoyed.
aporrinhação [apoxiɲa'sãw] (*pl* **-ões**) *f mfam* annoyance.
aporrinhar [4] [apoxi'ɲa(x)] *vt mfam* to annoy.
aportar [4] [apox'ta(x)] *vi* [desembarcar, ancorar]: ~ **em** to dock in.
aportuguesar [4] [apoxtuge'za(x)] *vt* to make Portuguese.
◆ **aportuguesar-se** *vp* to become Portuguese.
após [a'pɔjʃ] *prep* after.
aposentado, da [apozẽn'tadu, da] <> *adj* **-1.** [pessoa] retired. **-2.** [sapato] discarded. **-3.** [carro, máquina] disused. <> *m, f* retired person.
aposentadoria [apozẽntado'ria] *f* **-1.** [condição] retirement. **-2.** [vencimentos] pension.
aposentar [4] [apozẽn'ta(x)] *vt* **-1.** [pessoa] to pension off. **-2.** [máquina] to discard.
◆ **aposentar-se** *vp* to retire.
aposento [apo'zẽntu] *m* bedroom.
apossar-se [4] [apo'saxsi] *vp*: ~ **de algo** to take possession of sthg.
aposta [a'pɔʃta] *f* bet.
apostar [4] [apoʃ'ta(x)] <> *vt* to bet; ~ **que** to bet that. <> *vi*: ~ **em** to bet on.
apostila [apoʃ'tʃila] *f* **-1.** [nota marginal] marginal note. **-2.** [matéria de aula] handout.
apóstolo [a'pɔʃtulu] *m* apostle.
apóstrofo [a'pɔʃtrofu] *m* apostrophe.
apoteose [apote'ɔzi] *f* apotheosis.
aprazer [32] [apra'ze(x)] *vi*: ~ **a alguém** to please sb.
aprazível [apra'zivɛw] (*pl* **-eis**) *adj* pleasant.
apreçar [13] [apre'sa(x)] *vt* [dar valor a] to value.
apreciação [apresja'sãw] (*pl* **-ões**) *f* **-1.** [análise] consideration. **-2.** [julgamento] assessment.
apreciador, ra [apresja'do(x), ra] *m, f* aficionado.
apreciar [16] [apre'sja(x)] *vt* **-1.** [ger] to appreciate. **-2.** [gostar de] to enjoy.
apreciativo, va [apresja'tʃivu, va] *adj* appreciative.
apreciável [apre'sjavɛw] (*pl* **-eis**) *adj* **-1.** [estimável] considerable. **-2.** [significativo] notable.
apreço [a'presu] *m* [estima, consideração] consideration.
apreender [5] [aprjẽn'de(x)] *vt* **-1.** [tomar] to seize; ~ **algo a alguém** to seize sthg from sb. **-2.** [compreender] to understand, to comprehend.
apreensão [aprjẽn'sãw] (*pl* **-ões**) *f* **-1.** [tomada] seizure. **-2.** [percepção] understanding, comprehension. **-3.** [preocupação] apprehension.
apreensivo, va [aprjẽn'sivu, va] *adj* apprehensive.
apregoar [20] [apre'gwa(x)] *vt* to proclaim.
aprender [5] [aprẽn'de(x)] <> *vt* to learn. <> *vi* to learn; ~ **a fazer algo** to learn to do sthg; ~ **de cor** to learn by heart.
aprendiz [aprẽn'dʒiʒ] (*pl* **-es**) *mf* learner.
aprendizado [aprendʒi'zadu] (*pl* **-es**) *m*, **aprendizagem** *f* [aprẽndʒi'zaʒẽ] learning.
apresentação [aprezẽnta'sãw] (*pl* **-ões**) *f* [ger] presentation.
apresentador, ra [aprezẽnta'do(x), ra] *m, f* **-1.** [de seminário, painel] speaker. **-2.** *RÁDIO, TV* presenter.
apresentar [4] [aprezẽn'ta(x)] *vt* **-1.** [ger] to present; ~ **uma comunicação** to give a talk. **-2.** [fazer] to make. **-3.** [moção, recurso] to introduce.
◆ **apresentar-se** *vp* **-1.** [dar-se a conhecer] to introduce o.s. **-2.** [comparecer] to present o.s. **-3.** [manifestar-se] to arise. **-4.** [candidatar-se] to put o.s. forward.
apresentável [aprezẽn'tavɛw] (*pl* **-eis**) *adj* presentable.

apressado, da [apre'sadu, da] *adj* hurried; **estar ~** to be in a hurry.

apressar [4] [apre'sa(x)] *vt* to hurry.

◆ **apressar-se** *vp* to hurry.

aprimorado, da [aprimo'radu, da] *adj* improved.

aprimoramento [aprimora'mẽntu] *m* improvement.

aprimorar [4] [aprimo'ra(x)] *vt* to improve.

◆ **aprimorar-se** *vp*: **~-se (em algo)** to try hard (at sthg).

aprisionamento [aprizjona'mẽntu] *m* **-1.** [de pessoa] imprisonment. **-2.** [de passarinho] captivity.

aprisionar [4] [aprizjo'na(x)] *vt* **-1.** [prender] to imprison. **-2.** [meter em prisão] to put in prison. **-3.** [capturar] to keep in captivity.

aprofundamento [aprofũnda'mẽntu] *m* in-depth examination.

aprofundar [4] [aprofũn'da(x)] *vt* **-1.** [ger] to deepen. **-2.** [investigação] to intensify. **-3.** [conhecimentos] to improve. **-4.** [divergências] to increase.

◆ **aprofundar-se** *vp* **-1.** [no solo, no mar] to go down. **-2.** [em investigações, análise] to intensify. **-3.** [em área de conhecimento] to immerse o.s. **-4.** [em selva, mato] to penetrate deeper.

aprontar [4] [aprõnta(x)] ◇ *vt* **-1.** [preparar] to prepare. **-2.** [terminar] to complete. **-3.** *fam* [briga, confusão] to cause. ◇ *vi fam* [criar confusão] to play up.

◆ **aprontar-se** *vp* **-1.** [vestir-se, arrumar-se] to get ready. **-2.** [preparar-se] to prepare o.s.

apropriação [aproprja'sãw] (*pl* **-ões**) *f* **-1.** [assenhoramento] takeover. **-2.** [tomada] seizure. **-3.** *COM* [adequação]: **~ de custos** cost adjustment.

apropriado, da [apro'prjadu, da] *adj* **-1.** [adequado] appropriate. **-2.** [tomado] seized.

apropriar [16] [apro'prja(x)] *vt* [adequar] to adapt.

◆ **apropriar-se** *vp*: **~-se de algo** to take possession of sthg.

aprovação [aprova'sãw] (*pl* **-ões**) *f* **-1.** [ger] approval. **-2.** [em exame] pass.

aprovar [4] [apro'va(x)] *vt* **-1.** [apoiar] to approve. **-2.** [sancionar] to approve. **-3.** [em exame] to pass.

aproveitador, ra [aprovejta'do(x), ra] (*mpl* **-es**, *fpl* **-s**) ◇ *adj* opportunistic. ◇ *m, f* opportunist.

aproveitamento [aprovejta'mẽntu] *m* **-1.** [uso] good use. **-2.** [nos estudos] improvement; **ter um bom ~** to do well.

aproveitar [4] [aprovej'ta(x)] ◇ *vt* **-1.** [tirar proveito de]: **aproveitei que chovia para descansar** I took advantage of the rainy weather to have a rest. **-2.** [não desperdiçar] to make the most of, to put to good use. **-3.** [usar] to use. ◇ *vi* [tirar proveito]: **~ para fazer algo** to take opportunity to do sthg; **aproveite!** make the most of it!; **aproveite enquanto é tempo!** make the most of it while you can!, make hay while the sun shines!

◆ **aproveitar-se** *vp*: **~-se de algo/alguém** to take advantage of sthg/sb.

aproveitável [aprovej'tavew] (*pl* **-eis**) *adj* reusable.

aprovisionamento [aprovizjona'mẽntu] *m* supply.

aprovisionar [4] [aprovizjo'na(x)] *vt* [abastecer] to supply.

aprox. (*abrev de* **aproximadamente**) *adv* approx.

aproximação [aprosima'sãw] (*pl* **-ões**) *f* **-1.** [chegada] approach. **-2.** [estimativa] approximation. **-3.** [de países] coming together. **-4.** [de pontos de vista] similarity.

aproximado, da [aprosi'madu, da] *adj* approximate.

aproximar [4] [aprosi'ma(x)] *vt* **-1.** [precipitar] to bring forward. **-2.** [cálculo] to approximate. **-3.** [pessoas, países] to bring together. **-4.** [levar para perto] to draw up. **-5.** [fazer parecer perto] to bring closer.

◆ **aproximar-se** *vp* **-1.** [achegar-se] to approach. **-2.** [pessoas, países] to draw closer. **-3.** [assemelhar-se] to be similar.

aprumado, da [apru'madu, da] *adj* **-1.** [vertical] straight. **-2.** *fig* [altivo] upright. **-3.** [elegante] elegant.

aprumo [a'prumu] *m* **-1.** [posição vertical] straightness. **-2.** [altivez] rectitude. **-3.** [elegância] elegance.

aptidão [aptʃi'dãw] (*pl* **-ões**) *f* **-1.** [ger] aptitude. **-2.** [jeito]: **ter ~ para** to have an aptitude for.

apto, ta ['aptu, ta] *adj* suitable; **~ para** fit for.

Apto. (*abrev de* **apartamento**) *m* Flat no. *UK*, Apt. *US*.

apunhalar [4] [apuɲa'la(x)] *vt* **-1.** [esfaquear] to stab. **-2.** *fig* [trair] to stab in the back.

apuração [apura'sãw] (*pl* **-ões**) *f* **-1.** [de votos] counting. **-2.** [de fatos, informações] examination. **-3.** [de conta] checking.

apurado, da [apu'radu, da] *adj* **-1.** [ger] refined. **-2.** [aguçado] sharp.

apurar [4] [apu'ra(x)] *vt* **-1.** [tornar puro] to purify. **-2.** [refinar] to refine. **-3.** [aprimorar] to perfect. **-4.** [aguçar] to sharpen. **-5.** [averiguar] to verify. **-6.** [votos] to count. **-7.** [conta] to check.

◆ **apurar-se** *vp* **-1.** [tornar-se puro] to become pure. **-2.** [no trajar] to smarten o.s. up. **-3.** [aprimorar-se] to become perfect.

apuro [a'puru] *m* **-1.** [esmero] care. **-2.** [dificuldade] fix; **estar em ~s** to be in a fix. **-3.** [aperto financeiro] hardship.

aquarela [akwa'rɛla] *f* water colour.

aquariano, na [akwa'rjãnu, na] *m, f* *ASTROL* Aquarian.

aquário [a'kwarju] *m* [para peixes] aquarium.

◆ **Aquário** *m* *ASTROL* Aquarius.

aquático, ca [a'kwatʃiku, ka] *adj* aquatic; **pólo/massagem ~** water polo/massage; **ginástica ~** aquarobics; **esportes ~s** aquatics.

aquecedor [akese'do(x)] (*pl* **-es**) *adj* heating.

◆ **aquecedor** *m* heater.

aquecer [25] [ake'se(x)] ◇ *vt* **-1.** [ger] to warm up. **-2.** [esquentar] to heat. ◇ *vi* **-1.** [esquentar] to become hot. **-2.** [dar calor] to give warmth.

◆ **aquecer-se** *vp* **-1.** [ger] to warm up. **-2.**

[esquentar-se] to warm o.s. **-3.** *fig* [debate] to become heated.

aquecimento [akesi'mẽntu] *m* **-1.** [ger] heating; ~ **central** central heating. **-2.** [econômico] warming. **-3.** *ESP* [muscular] warm up; **ir para o** ~ to go for a warm-up.

àquela [a'kɛla] = **a + aquela.**

aquele, aquela [a'keli, a'kɛla] <> *adj* that, those *pl.* <> *pron* that one; ~ **ali** that one there; ~ **que** [relativo a pessoa] the one who, those who *pl*; [relativo a objeto] the one which; **peça àquele homem/àquela mulher** ask that man/woman.

àquele [a'keli] = **a + aquele.**

aquém [a'kẽj] *adv* **-1.** [deste lado] this side; ~ **de** on this side of. **-2.** [abaixo]: ~ **de** below.

aqui [a'ki] *adv* **-1.** [neste lugar] here; ~ **dentro/fora** in/out here; ~ **e agora** here and now; ~ **mesmo** right here; **eis** ~ here is; **por** ~ round here; **estar por** ~ **(com algo/alguém)** to be up to here (with sthg/sb). **-2.** [neste momento] at that point; **até** ~ up to now. **-3.** [nisto] on this point.

aquiescência [akje'sẽnsja] *f* acquiescence.

aquiescer [25] [akje'se(x)] *vi*: ~ **a** to accede to; ~ **em** to agree to.

aquietar [4] [akje'ta(x)] *vt* to quieten.

◆ **aquietar-se** *vp* to quieten down.

aquilatar [4] [akila'ta(x)] *vt* **-1.** [metais] to assay. **-2.** [estimar] to weigh up.

aquilino, na [aki'linu, na] *adj* [nariz] aquiline.

aquilo [a'kilu] *pron* that; **você chama aquilo de carro!** you call that a car!

àquilo [a'kilu] = **a + aquilo.**

aquinhoar [20] [akiɲo'a(x)] *vt* to endow.

aquisição [akizi'sãw] (*pl* **-ões**) *f* acquisition.

aquisitivo, va [akizi'tʃivu, va] *adj* [poder] acquisitive.

ar [a(x)] (*pl* **-ares**) *m* **-1.** [ger] air; **o avião está no** ~ the plane is in the sky; **ao** ~ **livre** in the open air; **tomar** ~ **(fresco)** to get some (fresh) air; ~ **condicionado** [atmosfera] air conditioning; **ir pelos ares** to be blown sky-high; **corrente de** ~ draught. **-2.** *RÁDIO, TV*: **no** ~ on the air; **ir ao** ~ to be broadcast, to go on the air; **sair do** ~ to come off the air. **-3.** *fig* [aspecto] appearance. **-4.** *loc*: **apanhar as coisas no** ~ to pick things up quickly; **dar o** ~ **de sua** *ou* **da graça** to show up; **estar no** ~ to be up in the air; **ficar no** ~ to be confused.

◆ **ares** *mpl* **-1.** [clima] air; **mudar de ares** to get a change of air. **-2.** [pose] airs *(pl)*.

árabe ['arabi] <> *adj* Arab. <> *m, f* Arab. <> *m* [língua] Arabic.

arabesco [ara'beʃku] *m* arabesque.

Arábia Saudita [a,rabjasaw'dʒita] *n* Saudi Arabia.

arábico, ca [a'rabiku, ka] *adj* **-1.** [da Arábia] Arabian. **-2.** [algarismo] Arabic. **-3.** [goma]: **goma arábica** gum arabic.

Aracajú [araka'ʒu] *n* Aracajú.

arado [a'radu] *m* plough.

aragem [a'raʒẽ] (*pl* **-ns** [a'raʒẽʃ]) *f* breeze.

Aral [a'raw] *n*: **o mar de** ~ the Aral Sea.

aramado, da [ara'madu, da] *adj* [estádio] fenced in.

◆ **aramado** *m* **-1.** [cerca] wire fencing. **-2.** [porta-objetos] wire basket/rack.

arame [a'rãmi] *m* [cabo] wire; ~ **farpado** barbed wire.

aranha [a'rãɲa] *f* spider.

aranha-caranguejeira [a,rãɲakarãŋge'ʒejra] (*pl* **aranhas-caranguejeiras**) *f* bird-eating spider.

arapuca [ara'puka] *f* **-1.** [armadilha, cilada] trap; **cair numa** ~ to fall into a trap. **-2.** *fam fig* [estabelecimento] shady company.

araque [a'raki] *m*: **de** ~ *fam* rubbish.

arar [4] [a'ra(x)] *vt* to plough.

arara [a'rara] *f* macaw; **estar/ficar uma** ~ to be hopping mad.

araruta [ara'ruta] *f* arrowroot.

arbitragem [axbi'traʒẽ] (*pl* **-ns**) *f* **-1.** [julgamento] arbitration. **-2.** [*ESP* - ato] adjudication; [- decisão] decision; [- os juízes] referees *(pl)*.

arbitrar [4] [axbi'tra(x)] *vt* **-1.** [questão, litígio] to arbitrate. **-2.** *ESP* [partida, campeonato] to referee. **-3.** [adjudicar]: ~ **algo a alguém** to award sb sthg.

arbitrariedade [axbitrarje'dadʒi] *f* arbitrariness.

arbitrário, ria [axbi'trarju, rja] *adj* arbitrary.

arbítrio [ax'bitrju] *m* **-1.** [resolução] judgment; **deixar algo ao** ~ **de alguém** to leave sthg to the discretion of sb. **-2.** [faculdade] free will.

árbitro ['axbitru] *m* **-1.** [de questão, litígio] mediator. **-2.** [juiz] judge. **-3.** [*ESP* - em futebol, box] referee; [- em tênis] umpire.

arborizado, da [axbori'zadu, da] *adj* **-1.** [bairro, terreno] wooded. **-2.** [rua] tree-lined.

arborizar [4] [axbori'za(x)] *vt* to plant with trees.

arbusto [ax'buʃtu] *m* bush.

arca ['axka] *f* **-1.** [caixa] chest. **-2.** [barca]: **Arca de Noé** Noah's Ark.

arcabouço [axka'bosu] *m* **-1.** [linhas gerais] outline. **-2.** *ARQUIT* [estrutura] framework.

arcada [ax'kada] *f* **-1.** [de arcos] arcade; ~ **dentária** dental arch. **-2.** [arco] arch.

arcaico, ca [ax'kajku, ka] *adj* **-1.** [antigo] archaic. **-2.** [antiqüado] antiquated.

arcaizante [axkaj'zãntʃi] *adj* archaic.

arcanjo [ax'kãnʒu] *m* archangel.

arcar [12] [ax'ka(x)] *vi*: ~ **com algo** to take responsibility for sthg.

arcebispo [axse'biʃpu] *m* archbishop.

arco ['axku] *m* **-1.** [ger] arch; **em** ~ arched. **-2.** [arma, instrumento musical] bow; ~**-e-flecha** *ESP* archery. **-3.** *GEOM, ELETR & MAT* arc. **-4.** [de barril] hoop.

arco-da-velha [,axkuda'vɛʎa] *m*: **coisas do** ~ fantastic things; **história do** ~ tall story.

arco-e-flecha [axkuiflɛʃa] (*pl* **arcos-e-flechas**) *m* **-1.** *ESP* archery. **-2.** [arma] bow and arrow.

arco-íris [ax'kwiriʃ] (*pl* **arcos-íris**) *m inv* rainbow.

ar-condicionado [,a(x)kõndʒisjo'nadu] (*pl* **ares-condicionados**) *m* [aparelho] air conditioning.

ardência [ax'dẽnsja] *f* burning.

ardente [ax'dẽntʃi] *adj* burning.
arder [5] [ax'de(x)] *vi* **-1.** [ger] to burn; ~ **em chamas** to be in flames; ~ **em febre** [pessoa] to have a burning fever. **-2.** [ferimento] to sting.
ardido, da [ax'dʒidu, da] *adj* **-1.** [costas, olhos] stinging. **-2.** [pimenta, comida] hot.
ardil [ax'dʒiw] (*pl* **-is**) *m* cunning.
ardiloso, losa [axdʒi'lozu, lɔza] *adj* [pessoa] cunning.
ardor [ax'do(x)] (*pl* **-es**) *m* [paixão] ardour.
ardoroso, rosa [axdo'rozu, rɔza] *adj* amorous.
ardósia [ax'dɔzja] *f* slate.
árduo, dua ['axdwu, dwa] *adj* **-1.** [escarpado] arduous. **-2.** [difícil] hard. **-3.** [sofrimento] painful.
área ['arja] *f* **-1.** [ger] area; ~ **interditada** forbidden territory; ~ **de serviço** service point. **-2.** [de conhecimento etc] field.
areal [a'rejw] (*pl* **-ais**) *m* sandy area.
arear [15] [a'rja(x)] *vt* [polir] to polish.
areia [a'reja] *f* sand; ~ **movediça** quicksand; **ser muita ~ para o caminhão de alguém** to be too hot for sb to handle.
arejado, da [are'ʒadu, da] *adj* **-1.** [ventilado] airy. **-2.** [fig] [pessoa, cabeça] open-minded.
arena [a'rena] *f* **-1.** [ger] arena. **-2.** [de circo] ring. **-3.** [de teatro] amphitheatre.
arenito [are'nitu] *m* sandstone.
arenoso, osa [are'nozu, ɔza] *adj* sandy.
arenque [a'rẽŋki] *m* herring.
ares ['ariʃ] ⊳ **ar.**
aresta [a'rɛʃta] *f* [quina] edge.
arfar [4] [ax'fa(x)] *vi* **-1.** [ofegar] to pant. **-2.** *NÁUT* to pitch.
argamassa [axga'masa] *f* mortar.
Argel [ax'ʒɛw] *n* Algeria.
Argélia [ax'ʒɛlja] *n* Algeria.
argelino, na [axʒe'linu, na] ◇ *adj* Algerian. ◇ *m, f* Algerian.
Argentina [axʒẽn'tʃina] *n*: **(a)** ~ Argentina.
argentino, na [axʒẽn'tʃinu, na] ◇ *adj* Argentinian. ◇ *m, f* Argentinian.
argila [ax'ʒila] *f* clay.
argiloso, losa [axʒi'lozu, lɔza] *adj* [terreno] clay.
argola [ax'gɔla] *f* **-1.** [aro] ring. **-2.** [de porta] knocker.
argúcia [ax'gusja] *f* **-1.** [agudeza] shrewdness. **-2.** [sutileza] subtlety.
argüição [axgwi'sãw] (*pl* **-ões**) *f* oral exam.
argüir [75] [ax'gwi(x)] *vt* [alunos, candidatos] to examine.
argumentação [axgumẽnta'sãw] (*pl* **-ões**) *f* argument, reasoning.
argumentar [4] [axgumẽn'ta(x)] ◇ *vt* [alegar] to argue. ◇ *vi* [expor argumentos] to argue one's case.
argumento [axgu'mẽntu] *m* **-1.** [em teoria, debate] argument. **-2.** [de filme, TV, romance] theme, plot.
arguto, ta [ax'gutu, ta] *adj* **-1.** [agudo] shrewd. **-2.** [sutil] subtle.
ária ['arja] *f* *MÚS* aria.
ariano, na [a'rjãnu, na] ◇ *adj* Aryan. ◇ *m, f* **-1.** [pessoa] Aryan. **-2.** *ASTROL* Arian.
aridez [ari'deʒ] *f* **-1.** [de clima, estação] dryness. **-2.** [de terra, região] aridity. **-3.** *fig* [de teoria, pensamento] barrenness.
árido, da ['aridu, da] *adj* **-1.** [clima, estação] dry. **-2.** [terra, região] arid. **-3.** *fig* [teoria, pensamento] barren.
arisco, ca [a'riʃku, ka] *adj* **-1.** [insociável] antisocial. **-2.** [animal] untameable.
aristocracia [ariʃtokra'sia] *f* aristocracy.
aristocrata [ariʃto'krata] *mf* aristocrat.
aristocrático, ca [ariʃto'kratʃiku, ka] *adj* aristocratic.
aritmético, ca [aritʃ'mɛtʃiku, ka] *adj* arithmetic.
◆ **aritmética** *f* arithmetic.
arma ['axma] *f* **-1.** [ger] weapon; **depor as ~s** to lay down arms; ~ **biológica/química** biological/ chemical weapon; ~ **branca** knife *(or other weapon with a blade)*; ~ **de fogo** firearm; ~ **nuclear** nuclear weapon. **-2.** *MIL* [do Exército] force.
◆ **armas** *fpl* **-1.** [forças armadas] forces. **-2.** [brasão] arms.
armação [axma'sãw] (*pl* **-ões**) *f* **-1.** [de barraca, estrutura, peças] framework. **-2.** [estrutura] frame. **-3.** [de óculos] frames *(pl)*. **-4.** [de onda] *point near a shoreline where the waves start to break*. **-5.** [de tempestade] gathering. **-6.** *fam* [golpe] con. **-7.** *fam* [programa, aventura] move.
armada [ax'mada] ◆ **Armada** *f* navy.
armadilha [axma'diʎa] *f* trap; **cair numa ~** to fall into a trap.
armador, ra [axma'do(x), ra] *m, f* **-1.** [*NÁUT* - dono] shipowner; [- firma] ship chandler's. **-2.** [operário] ship chandler.
armadura [axma'dura] *f* **-1.** [de cavaleiro] armour. **-2.** [de ouriço, besouro] shell. **-3.** *ELETR* armature. **-4.** *CONSTR* framework.
armamentista [axmamẽn'tʃiʃta] *adj* ⊳ **corrida.**
armamento [axma'mẽntu] *m* **-1.** [armas] armament. **-2.** *NÁUT* fitting out.
armar [4] [ax'ma(x)] ◇ *vt* **-1.** [com arma] to arm. **-2.** [carregar] to load. **-3.** [gatilho] to cock. **-4.** [montar] to assemble. **-5.** [preparar] to set up. **-6.** [saia etc] to give body to. **-7.** *fam* [planejar - golpe] to plot; [- programa, aventura] to plan. **-8.** *fam* [provocar] to cause. **-9.** *NÁUT* to fit out. ◇ *vi fam* [urdir trama] to scheme; ~ **contra** to plot against.
◆ **armar-se** *vp* **-1.** [com armas] to arm o.s. **-2.** *fig* [munir-se]: **~-se de** to arm o.s with.
armarinho [axma'riɲu] *m* haberdasher's *UK*, notions store *US*.
armário [ax'marju] *m* **-1.** [de roupa] wardrobe; ~ **embutido** fitted wardrobe. **-2.** [de cozinha etc] cupboard.
armazém [axma'zẽj] (*pl* **-ns**) *m* **-1.** [depósito] warehouse. **-2.** [loja] store.
armazenagem [axmaze'naʒẽj] *f*, **armazenamento** *m* [axmazena'mẽntu] storage.
armazenar [4] [axmaze'na(x)] *vt* to store.
Armênia [ax'menja] *n* Armenia.
armênio, nia [ax'menju, nja] ◇ *adj* Armenian. ◇ *m, f* Armenian.

◆ **armênio** *m* [língua] Armenian.

arminho [ax'miɲu] *m* ermine.

armistício [axmiʃ'tʃisju] *m* armistice.

aro ['aru] *m* **-1.** [ger] rim. **-2.** [argola] ring. **-3.** [de porta] frame.

aroma [a'roma] *m* **-1.** [de perfume] scent. **-2.** [de café, comida] aroma.

aromático, ca [aro'matʃiku, ka] *adj* **-1.** [essência, erva] aromatic. **-2.** [tempero, comida] spicy.

arpão [ax'pãw] (*pl* **-ões**) *m* harpoon.

arpejo [ax'peʒu] *m* arpeggio.

arpoar [20] [ax'pwa(x)] *vt* to harpoon.

arpões [ax'põjʃ] *pl* ▷ **arpão**.

arqueado, da [ax'kjadu, da] *adj* **-1.** [pernas] bandy. **-2.** [sobrancelhas] arched.

arquear [16] [ax'kja(x)] *vt* to arch.

◆ **arquear-se** *vp* to bend.

arqueiro, ra [ax'kejru, ra] *m, f* **-1.** [atirador] archer. **-2.** [goleiro] goalkeeper.

arqueologia [axkjolo'ʒia] *f* archaeology.

arqueológico, ca [axkjo'lɔʒiku, ka] *adj* archaeological.

arqueólogo, ga [ax'kjɔlogu, ga] *m, f* archaeologist.

arquétipo [ax'kɛtʃipu] *m* archetype.

arquibancada [axkibãŋ'kada] *f* **-1.** [local] terrace; **ir de** ~ to sit on the terraces. **-2.** [público] terraces *(pl)*.

arquimilionário, ria [axkimiljo'narju, rja] ◇ *adj* multimillionaire. ◇ *m, f* [pessoa] multimillionaire.

arquipélago [axki'pɛlagu] *m* archipelago.

arquitetar [4] [axkite'ta(x)] *vt* to design.

arquiteto, ta [axki'tɛtu, ta] *m, f* architect.

arquitetônico, ca [axkite'toniku, ka] *adj* architectural.

arquitetura [axkite'tura] *f* architecture.

arquivamento [axkiva'mẽntu] *m* **-1.** [de documentos, fichas etc] filing. **-2.** [de projeto, processo] shelving.

arquivar [4] [axki'va(x)] *vt* **-1.** [ger] to file. **-2.** [projeto, processo] to shelve.

arquivista [axki'viʃta] *mf* archivist.

arquivo [ax'kivu] *m* **-1.** [ger] file; ~ **morto** dead file; **abrir/fechar um** ~ to open/close a file. **-2.** [local] archive. **-3.** [móvel] filing cabinet. **-4.** [de instituição] file.

arraia [a'xaja] *f* [peixe] ray.

arraial [axa'jaw] (*pl* **-ais**) *m* [povoado] village.

arraia-miúda [aˌxajami'uda] *f* hoi polloi *(pl)*.

arraigado, da [axaj'gadu, da] *adj* **-1.** [costume, idéia, mentalidade] deep-rooted. **-2.** *fig* [defensor, admirador] staunch.

arraigar [14] [axaj'ga(x)] *vi* [criar raízes] to put down roots.

◆ **arraigar-se** *vp* **-1.** [ger] to take root. **-2.** [pessoa] to settle down.

arrancada [axãŋ'kada] *f* **-1.** [puxão] tug. **-2.** [partida] start. **-3.** [em competição, disputa] spurt; **dar uma** ~ to jump ahead.

arrancar [12] [axãŋ'ka(x)] ◇ *vt* **-1.** [tirar]: ~ **algo de alguém** to pull sthg off sb; ~ **algo (de algo)** [pétala, botão] to pull sthg (off sthg); [folha] to tear sthg (out of sthg); [raiz] to pull sthg up (out of sthg). **-2.** [conseguir]: ~ **algo de alguém** to draw sthg from sb. **-3.** [fazer sair]: ~ **alguém de algum lugar** to turf sb out of somewhere. ◇ *vi* **-1.** [dar partida] to start off. **-2.** [em competição] to put on a spurt.

◆ **arrancar-se** *vt* *fam* [fugir]: ~**-se (de)** to scarper (from).

arranco [a'xãŋku] *m* [puxão] tug.

arranha-céu [aˌxãɲa'sɛw] (*pl* **arranha-céus**) *m* skyscraper.

arranhão [axã'ɲãw] (*pl* **-ões**) *m* scratch; **ele saiu sem muitos arranhões dessa situação** he came out of that situation relatively unscathed.

arranhar [4] [axa'ɲa(x)] ◇ *vt* **-1.** [ger] to scratch. **-2.** *fig* [tocar mal] to bash away at. **-3.** *fig* [idioma] to scratch by. ◇ *vi* [provocar arranhão] to scratch.

◆ **arranhar-se** *vp* to scratch o.s.

arranjador, ra [axãnʒa'dor, ra] *m, f* MÚS arranger.

arranjar [4] [axãn'ʒa(x)] *vt* **-1.** [ger] to arrange. **-2.** [resolver] to sort out. **-3.** [conseguir] to obtain. **-4.** [contrair] to catch. **-5.** [encontrar] to find.

◆ **arranjar-se** *vp* [virar-se] to get by.

arranjo [a'xãnʒu] *m* **-1.** [ger] arrangement. **-2.** [acordo] deal. **-3.** [mamata] scam.

arranque [a'xãŋki] *m* ▷ **motor**.

arrasado, da [axa'zadu, da] *adj* **-1.** [devastado] razed, devastated. **-2.** [arruinado] ruined. **-3.** [deprimido] devastated. **-4.** [muito cansado] worn out.

arrasador, ra [axaza'do(x), ra] *adj* **-1.** [devastador] crippling. **-2.** [notícia, crítica] devastating. **-3.** [vitória] overwhelming.

arrasar [4] [axa'za(x)] *vt* **-1.** [devastar] to raze. **-2.** [arruinar] to destroy. **-3.** [com críticas] to demolish.

◆ **arrasar-se** *vp* **-1.** [ser devastado] to be devastated. **-2.** [destruir-se] to be destroyed. **-3.** [arruinar-se] to collapse in ruins. **-4.** [em exame, competição] to flop.

arrastado, da [axaʃ'tadu, da] *adj* **-1.** [demorado] sluggish. **-2.** [lento] slow.

arrastão [axaʃ'tãw] (*pl* **-tões**) *m* **-1.** [PESCA - rede] dragnet; [- ato] haul. **-2.** [puxão] tug. **-3.** *fig* [assalto] mobbing.

arrasta-pé [aˌxaʃta'pɛ] (*pl* **arrasta-pés**) *m* *fam* shindig.

arrastar [4] [axaʃ'ta(x)] ◇ *vt* **-1.** [ger] to drag. **-2.** *fig* [impelir]: ~ **alguém a algo** to lead sb into sthg. ◇ *vi* [roçar] to drag.

◆ **arrastar-se** *vp* **-1.** [rastejar] to crawl. **-2.** [andar com dificuldade] to drag o.s. **-3.** [decorrer lentamente] to drag on.

arrasto [a'xaʃtu] *m* **-1.** [ato] dragging. **-2.** [rede] trawl. **-3.** FÍS [força] drag.

arrazoado, da [axa'zwadu, da] *adj* [discurso, argumento] reasoned.

◆ **arrazoado** *m* [defesa] defence.

arrazoar [20] [axa'zwa(x)] *vi* [argumentar] to argue.

arrear [15] [a'xja(x)] *vt* [montaria] to harness.

arrebanhar [4] [axeba'ɲa(x)] *vt* **-1.** [gado] to herd. **-2.** *fig* [reunir] to gather.
arrebatado, da [axeba'tadu, da] *adj* **-1.** [impetuoso] impetuous. **-2.** [exaltado] fiery.
arrebatador, ra [axebata'do(x), ra] *adj* fiery.
arrebatamento [axebata'mẽntu] *m* **-1.** [impetuosidade] impetuousness. **-2.** [exaltação] fervour.
arrebatar [4] [axeba'ta(x)] *vt* **-1.** [arrancar]: ~ **algo de algo/alguém** to grab sthg from sthg/sb. **-2.** [carregar] to drag off. **-3.** *fig* [aplausos] to draw. **-4.** *fig* [coração] to break.
◆ **arrebatar-se** *vp* **-1.** [exaltar-se] to get carried away. **-2.** [maravilhar-se] to be entranced.
arrebentação [axebẽnta'sãw] *f* [local] *point close to a shoreline at which the waves break.*
arrebentado, da [axebẽn'tadu, da] *adj* **-1.** [em mau estado] broken. **-2.** [ferido] battered. **-3.** [muito cansado] worn out.
arrebentar [4] [axebẽn'ta(x)] ◇ *vt* **-1.** [quebrar, romper] to break. **-2.** [estragar] to wreck. **-3.** [ferir] to smash; ~ **alguém** [surrar] to give sb a bashing; ~ **a cara de alguém** to smash sb's face in. ◇ *vi* **-1.** [quebrar-se, romper-se] to snap. **-2.** [bomba] to explode. **-3.** *fig* [guerra, revolução] to break out. **-4.** *fam fig* [fazer sucesso]: ~ **(em algo)** to have a smashing win (at sthg).
◆ **arrebentar-se** *vp* [ferir-se] to smash o.s.up.
arrebitado, da [axebi'tadu, da] *adj* **-1.** [para cima] turned up. **-2.** [bumbum, nariz] pert.
arrebitar [4] [axebi'ta(x)] *vt* to turn up.
arrecadação [axekada'sãw] (*pl* **-ões**) *f* **-1.** [coleta] collection. **-2.** [receita] revenue.
arrecadar [4] [axeka'da(x)] *vt* to collect.
arrecife [axe'sifi] *m* reef.
arredar [4] [axe'da(x)] *vt* [retirar] to remove; ~ **(o) pé (de)** [de lugar] to budge from; [de intenção, princípios] to budge (from).
◆ **arredar-se** *vp* [retirar-se] to withdraw.
arredio, dia [axe'dʒiu, dʒia] *adj* [pessoa] withdrawn.
arredondado, da [axedõn'dadu, da] *adj* round.
arredondar [4] [axedõn'da(x)] *vt* **-1.** [formato] to round off. **-2.** [conta] to round up.
arredores [axe'dɔriʃ] *mpl* **-1.** [cercanias] neighbourhood. **-2.** [periferia] outskirts.
arrefecer [25] [axefe'se(x)] ◇ *vt* **-1.** [tornar frio] to cool. **-2.** [febre] to lower. **-3.** *fig* [desanimar] to cool. ◇ *vi* **-1.** [tornar-se frio] to cool down. **-2.** [ger] to subside.
ar-refrigerado [ˌa(x)xefriʒe'radu] (*pl* **ares-refrigerados**) *m* **-1.** [aparelho] air-conditioner. **-2.** [sistema] air-conditioning.
arregaçar [13] [axega'sa(x)] *vt* to roll up.
arregalado, da [axega'ladu, da] *adj* staring.
arregalar [4] [axega'la(x)] *vt* to open wide.
arreganhado, da [axega'ɲadu, da] *adj* gaping.
arreganhar [4] [axega'ɲa(x)] *vt* **-1.** [gola de blusa] to open. **-2.** [boca] to open in a grin.
arregimentar [4] [axeʒimẽn'ta(x)] *vt* to drum up.
arreio [a'xeju] *m* [cavalo] harness.
arrematar [4] [axema'ta(x)] *vt* **-1.** [ger] to finish off. **-2.** [dizer concluindo] to conclude. **-3.** [em leilão - comprar] to bid successfully for; [- vender] to auction off.
arremate [axe'matʃi] *m* **-1.** [ger] finishing off. **-2.** [conclusão] finish.
arremessar [4] [axeme'sa(x)] *vt* to throw.
◆ **arremessar-se** *vp* to throw o.s.
arremesso [axe'mesu] *m* [lançamento] throw; ~ **de peso** *ESP* shot-put.
arremeter [5] [axeme'te(x)] *vi* to charge; ~ **contra** to attack.
arremetida [axeme'tʃida] *f* attack.
arrendamento [axẽnda'mẽntu] *m* leasing, hiring, rental.
arrendar [4] [axẽn'da(x)] *vt* **-1.** [dar] to let, to lease. **-2.** [tomar] to rent, to take a lease on.
arrepender-se [5] [axepẽn'dexsi] *vp* to repent; ~ **de algo/de fazer algo** to regret sthg/doing sthg.
arrependido, da [axepẽn'dʒidu, da] *adj* repentent, sorry.
arrependimento [axepẽndʒi'mẽntu] *m* **-1.** [remorso] regret. **-2.** [de crime] remorse. **-3.** *RELIG* repentance.
arrepiado, da [axe'pjadu, da] *adj* **-1.** [eriçado - cabelo] standing on end ***(depois de subst/verbo)***; [- pele] goose-pimpled. **-2.** *fig* [assustado] terrified.
arrepiar [16] [axe'pja(x)] *vt* **-1.** [eriçar - cabelo] to cause to stand on end; [- pele] to give goose pimples. **-2.** [fig] [assustar] to terrify; **(ser) de** ~ **os cabelos** to be enough to make your hair stand on end.
◆ **arrepiar-se** *vp* [ficar eriçado - cabelo] to stand on end; [- pessoa] to shiver.
arrepio [axe'piw] *m* shiver; **dar ~s (a alguém)** ***fig*** to send shivers up sb's spine.
arresto [a'xɛʃtu] *m JUR* confiscation.
arrevesado, da [axeve'zadu, da] *adj* **-1.** [obscuro] obscure. **-2.** [confuso] complicated.
arriado, da [a'xjadu, da] *adj* **-1.** [muito cansado] dead beat. **-2.** [devido a doença] drained.
arriar [16] [a'xja(x)] ◇ *vt* **-1.** [abaixar - cortina, calça] to lower; [- pneu] to let down. **-2.** [cansar muito] to exhaust. **-3.** [pôr de cama] to lay up. ◇ *vi* **-1.** [pneu, bateria] to go flat. **-2.** [vergar] to sag. **-3.** [desanimar] to lose heart.
arrimo [a'ximu] *m* support; ~ **de família** family support.
arriscado, da [axiʃ'kadu, da] *adj* **-1.** [perigoso] hazardous, risky. **-2.** [audacioso] daring.
arriscar [12] [axiʃ'ka(x)] ◇ *vt* **-1.** [pôr em perigo] to put at risk. **-2.** [palpite] to risk. ◇ *vi* [tentar] to take the risk; **quem não arrisca não petisca** *prov* nothing ventured nothing gained.
◆ **arriscar-se** *vp* [pôr-se em perigo] to take a risk; **~-se a fazer algo** to risk doing sthg.
arritmia [axitʃ'mia] *f* arrhythmia.
arrivista [axi'viʃta] ◇ *adj* opportunistic. ◇ *mf* opportunist.
arroba [a'xoba] *f COMPUT* at.
arrochado, da [axo'ʃadu, da] *adj* **-1.** [apertado] tight. **-2.** [difícil] tricky.

arrochar [4] [axo'ʃa(x)] *vt* **-1.** [apertar] to squeeze. **-2.** *fig* [diminuir] to shrink. **-3.** *fam fig* [pressionar] to grill.

arrocho [a'xoʃu] *m* **-1.** [diminuição] lessening; **~ salarial** wage squeeze. **-2.** [dificuldade financeira] hardship. **-3.** *fam fig* [pressão] grilling; **dar um ~ em alguém** to give sb a grilling.

arrogância [axo'gãnsja] *f* arrogance.

arrogante [axo'gãntʃi] *adj* arrogant.

arrogar-se [14] [axo'gaxsi] *vp* to claim.

arroio [a'xoju] *m* stream.

arrojado, da [axo'ʒadu, da] *adj* **-1.** [ger] bold. **-2.** [ousado] daring. **-3.** [temerário] rash.

arrojar [4] [axo'ʒa(x)] *vt* [atirar]: **~ algo (em/contra algo)** to hurl sthg (at/against sthg).

arrolamento [axola'mẽntu] *m* **-1.** [levantamento] register. **-2.** [lista] list.

arrolar [4] [axo'la(x)] *vt* [listar] to list.

arrolhar [4] [axo'ʎa(x)] *vt* [garrafa] to cork.

arromba [a'xõnba] ◆ **de arromba** *loc adj fam* fantastic.

arrombamento [axõnba'mẽntu] *m* [abertura forçada]: **foi necessário o ~ da porta** it was necessary to break down the door.

arrombar [4] [axõn'ba(x)] *vt* **-1.** [ger] to break into. **-2.** [porta] to break down.

arrotar [4] [axo'ta(x)] ◇ *vi* [dar arroto] to belch. ◇ *vt* **-1.** [cheiro] to burp. **-2.** *fam fig* [alardear] to boast about.

arroto [a'xotu] *m* burp; **dar** *ou* **soltar um ~** to let out a burp.

arroubo [a'xobu] *m* [enlevo] moment of ecstasy; **~ de algo** outpouring of sthg.

arroz [a'xoʒ] *m* rice; **~ à grega** Greek risotto, *rice with ham, smoked bacon, sweet peppers, onion and peas*; **~ doce** rice pudding.

arrozal [axo'zaw] (*pl* **-ais**) *m* paddy field.

arroz-doce [axoʒ'dosi] *m* CULIN *rice pudding sprinkled with cinnamon and cloves.*

arruaça [a'xwasa] *f* riot; **fazer ~** to run riot.

arruaceiro, ra [axwa'sejru, ra] ◇ *adj* rowdy. ◇ *m, f* rioter.

arruela [a'xwɛla] *f* washer.

arruinado, da [axwi'nadu, da] *adj* ruined.

arruinar [4] [axwi'na(x)] *vt* **-1.** [arrasar] to demolish. **-2.** [destruir] to destroy. **-3.** [causar falência] to ruin.
◆ **arruinar-se** *vp* [ruir] to be ruined.

arrulhar [4] [axu'ʎa(x)] *vi* **-1.** [pombo] to coo. **-2.** *fig* [namorados] to bill and coo.

arrulho [a'xuʎu] *m* **-1.** [de pombo] cooing. **-2.** [de namorados] wooing.

arrumação [axuma'sãw] *f* **-1.** [arranjo] arrangement. **-2.** [de quarto, armário] tidying; **fazer uma ~ em algo** to tidy sthg up. **-3.** [de malas, bagagem] packing.

arrumadeira [axuma'dejra] *f* [criada] maid.

arrumar [4] [axu'ma(x)] *vt* **-1.** [pôr em ordem] to arrange; **~ a vida** *fam fig* to set one's life in order. **-2.** [quarto, armário] to tidy. **-3.** [malas, bagagem] to pack. **-4.** [vestir, aprontar] to straighten up. **-5.** [conseguir] to get.
◆ **arrumar-se** *vp* **-1.** [vestir-se, aprontar-se] to get ready. **-2.** [na vida] to set o.s. up. **-3.** [virar-se] to fend for o.s. **-4.** *fam* [na vida amorosa]: **~-se (com alguém)** to hitch up (with sb).

arsenal [axse'naw] (*pl* **-ais**) *m* arsenal.

arsênico [ax'seniku] *m* arsenic.

arsênio [ax'senju] *m* arsenic.

arte ['axtʃi] *f* **-1.** [ger] art; **~ abstrata/figurativa** abstract/figurative art; **~ dramática** theatre; **~ moderna** modern art. **-2.** [arte-final] artwork. **-3.** [ofício] art. **-4.** [técnica] art; **~ culinária** cuisine; **~ marcial** martial art; **~s e ofícios** arts and crafts. **-5.** [primor]: **com ~** skilfully. **-6.** [astúcia] cunning. **-7.** *fam* [travessura] mischief; **fazer ~** to get up to mischief.
◆ **artes** *fpl* **-1.** [visuais] arts; **~s gráficas** graphic arts; **~s plásticas** plastic arts. **-2.** [curso]: **(belas) ~s** fine arts. **-3.** [artifício]: **por ~s de** through the artful wiles of.

artefato [axte'fatu] *m* **-1.** [instrumento] artefact. **-2.** [produto] goods (*pl*); **~s de madeira/couro** wooden/leather goods.

arteiro, ra [axẽtejru, ra] *adj* mischievous.

artéria [ax'tɛrja] *f* artery.

arterial [axte'rjaw] (*pl* **-ais**) *adj* arterial.

arteriosclerose [axterjoʃkle'rɔzi] *f* arteriosclerosis.

artesã [axte'zã] *f* ▷ **artesão**.

artesanal [axteza'naw] (*pl* **-ais**) *adj* craftwork.

artesanato [axteza'natu] *m* craftwork.

artesão, sã [axte'zãw, zã] (*mpl* **-ãos**, *fpl* **-s**) *m, f* craftsman (*f* craftswoman).

ártico, ca ['axtʃiku] *adj* Arctic.
◆ **Ártico** *n*: **o Ártico** the Arctic; **o Oceano Glacial Ártico** the Arctic Ocean.

articulação [axtʃikula'sãw] (*pl* **-ões**) *f* **-1.** [ligação] connection. **-2.** ANAT joint. **-3.** POL link.

articulado, da [axtʃiku'ladu, da] *adj* **-1.** [membro, boneco] articulated. **-2.** [pessoa - ao falar] articulate; [- bem relacionado] well connected.

articular [4] [axtʃiku'la(x)] *vt* **-1.** [ligar] to link. **-2.** [pronunciar] to articulate. **-3.** [organizar] to put together.
◆ **articular-se** *vp* **-1.** [ligar-se] to be joined. **-2.** [organizar-se] to organize o.s.; **~-se em** to be organised in.

articulista [axtʃiku'liʃta] *mf* JORN article writer.

artífice [ax'tʃifisi] *mf* **-1.** [artesão] craftsman (*f* craftswoman). **-2.** [criador, mentor] author.

artificial [axtʃifi'sjaw] (*pl* **-ais**) *adj* **-1.** [ger] artificial. **-2.** [dissimulado] false.

artificialidade [axtʃifisjali'dadʒi] *f* artificiality.

artifício [axtʃi'fisju] *m* **-1.** [processo] artifice. **-2.** [subterfúgio] trick. **-3.** [dissimulação] pretence.

artigo [ax'tʃigu] *m* article; **~ de luxo** luxury item; **~s esportivos** sports goods; **~s de toucador** toiletries; **~ de fundo** editorial.

artilharia [axtʃiʎa'ria] *f* artillery.

artilheiro, ra [axtʃi'ʎejru, ra] *m, f* **-1.** [atirador] gunner. **-2.** FUT striker.

artimanha [axtʃi'mãɲa] *m* **-1.** [estratagema]

stratagem. **-2.** [astúcia] cunning.
artista [ax'tʃiʃta] *mf* **-1.** [ger] artist. **-2.** [ator] actor (*f* actress). **-3.** [pessoa manhosa] crafty person.
artístico, ca [ax'tʃiʃtʃiku, ka] *adj* artistic.
artrite [ax'tritʃi] *f* arthritis.
artrose [ax'trɔzi] *f* arthrosis.
arvorar [4] [axvo'ra(x)] *vt* **-1.** [cruz, bandeira] to hoist. **-2.** [elevar]: ~ **alguém em algo** to hold sb up as sthg.
◆ **arvorar-se** *vp* [elevar-se]: ~**-se em algo** to claim to be sthg.
árvore ['axvori] *f* **-1.** [vegetal] tree; ~ **genealógica** family tree; ~ **de Natal** Christmas tree. **-2.** *TEC* shaft.
arvoredo [axvo'redu] *m* grove.
as [aʃ] ⊳ a.
ás, ases ['ajʃ, 'azeʃ] ◇ *mf* [pessoa exímia]: ~ **de algo** ace at sthg. ◇ *m* [carta] ace.
às [ajʃ] = **a** + **as**.
asa ['aza] *f* **-1.** [de pássaro, avião, inseto] wing; **dar** ~**s à imaginação** to give free rein to one's imagination. **-2.** [de xícara] handle.
asa-delta [ˌazaʒ'dɛwta] (*pl* **asas-delta**) *f* **-1.** [veículo] hang-glider. **-2.** [esporte] hang-gliding.
ascendência [asẽn'dẽnsja] *f* **-1.** [antepassados] descent. **-2.** [influência, domínio] influence; **ter** ~ **sobre** to hold sway over.
ascendente [asẽn'dẽntʃi] ◇ *adj* rising. ◇ *m, f* [antepassado] ancestor.
ascender [5] [asẽn'de(x)] *vi* to rise.
ascensão [asẽn'sãw] (*pl* **-ões**) *f* **-1.** [ger] rise. **-2.** [subida] climb.
ascensorista [asẽnso'riʃta] *mf* lift operator.
asceta [a'sɛta] *mf* ascetic.
ASCII (*abrev de* **American Standard Code for Information Interchange**) *m* ASCII.
asco ['aʃku] *m* disgust; **dar** ~ **a alguém** to make sb sick; **ser um** ~ to be a disgrace; **ter** ~ **de** to detest.
asfaltado, da [aʃfaw'tadu, da] *adj* asphalted.
asfaltar [4] [aʃfaw'ta(x)] *vt* to asphalt.
asfalto [aʃ'fawtu] *m* asphalt.
asfixia [aʃfik'sia] *f* asphyxia.
asfixiante [aʃfik'sjãntʃi] *adj* **-1.** [substância, ambiente] asphyxiating. **-2.** *fig* [calor] suffocating. **-3.** *fig* [regime, disciplina] oppressive.
asfixiar [16] [aʃfik'sja(x)] *vt* **-1.** [matar por asfixia] to asphyxiate. **-2.** [sufocar] to be suffocating. **-3.** *fig* [oprimir] to suppress.
◆ **asfixiar-se** *vp* **-1.** [morrer por asfixia] to be asphyxiated. **-2.** [sufocar-se] to gasp for breath.
Ásia ['azja] *n* Asia; ~ **Central** Central Asia.
asiático, ca [a'zjatʃiku, ka] ◇ *adj* Asian. ◇ *m, f* Asian.
asilo [a'zilu] *m* **-1.** [para orfãos, anciãos] home. **-2.** [refúgio] refuge. **-3.** *POL* asylum; ~ **político** political asylum.
asma ['aʒma] *f* asthma.
asmático, ca [aʒ'matʃiku, ka] ◇ *adj* asthmatic. ◇ *m, f* [pessoa] asthmatic.
asneira [aʒ'nejra] *f* **-1.** [ação] blunder; **dizer/fazer uma** ~ to say/do something stupid. **-2.** [condição] stupidity.
asno ['aʒnu] *m* **-1.** [animal] ass, donkey. **-2.** *fam fig & pej* [idiota] silly ass.
aspargo [aʃ'paxgu] *m* asparagus.
aspas ['aʃpaʃ] *fpl* quotation marks; **entre** ~ in inverted commas.
aspecto [aʃ'pɛktu] *m* **-1.** [aparência] look; **ter bom/mau** ~ [pessoa] to look right/dodgy; [coisa] to look good/bad. **-2.** [faceta] aspect; **em todos os** ~**s** in every way. **-3.** [ângulo] angle; **sob este** ~ from this angle. **-4.** [visão, detalhe] view.
aspereza [aʃpe'reza] *f* **-1.** [no tato] roughness. **-2.** *fig* [severidade, rispidez] harshness.
aspergir [64] [aʃpex'ʒi(x)] *vt* to sprinkle.
áspero, ra ['aʃperu, ra] *adj* **-1.** [ao tato] rough. **-2.** *fig* [severo, ríspido] harsh.
asperso, sa [aʃ'pexsu, sa] *pp* ⊳ **aspergir**.
aspiração [aʃpira'sãw] (*pl* **-ões**) *f* **-1.** [de ar - por pessoa] inhalation; [- por máquina] suction. **-2.** *LING* aspiration. **-3.** [desejo]: **ter** ~ **a algo** to aspire to sthg.
aspirador [aʃpira'do(x)] (*pl* **-es**) *m*: ~ **(de pó)** vacuum cleaner; **passar o** ~ **(em)** to vacuum, to hoover.
aspirante [aʃpi'rãntʃi] *mf* **-1.** [candidato]: **ser** ~ **(a algo)** to be a candidate (for sthg). **-2.** *MIL & NÁUT* cadet.
aspirar [4] [aʃpi'ra(x)] ◇ *vt* **-1.** [sugar] to aspirate, to suck in. **-2.** [ar - pessoa] to inhale; [- máquina] to suction. **-3.** *LING* to aspirate. ◇ *vi* **-1.** [desejar]: ~ **a algo** to aspire to sthg. **-2.** [respirar] to breathe. **-3.** [soprar brisa] to blow.
aspirina® [aʃpi'rina] *f* aspirin®.
asqueroso, osa [aʃke'rozu, ɔza] *adj* disgusting.
assadeira [asa'dejra] *f* roasting dish.
assado, da [a'sadu, da] *adj* roast.
◆ **assado** *m* roast.
assadura [asa'dura] *f* **-1.** [em bebê] nappy rash. **-2.** [em adulto] rash.
assalariado, da [asala'rjadu, da] ◇ *adj* wage-earning. ◇ *m, f* wage earner.
assaltante [asaw'tãntʃi] *mf* **-1.** [na rua] mugger. **-2.** [de banco] robber. **-3.** [de casa] burglar.
assaltar [4] [asaw'ta(x)] *vt* **-1.** [atacar] to attack. **-2.** [roubar - na rua] to mug; [- banco] to rob; [- casa] to break into. **-3.** *fig* [acometer] to assail.
assalto [a'sawtu] *m* **-1.** [ataque] attack. **-2.** [na rua] mugging. **-3.** [a banco] robbery. **-4.** [a casa] burglary.
assanhado, da [asa'ɲadu, da] *adj* **-1.** [excitado, irrequieto] excited. **-2.** [criança] excitable. **-3.** [desavergonhado] brazen. **-4.** [namorador] passionate.
assanhar [4] [asa'ɲa(x)] *vt* **-1.** [excitar, agitar] to excite. **-2.** [sensualmente] to arouse.
◆ **assanhar-se** *vp* **-1.** [excitar-se, agitar-se] to become excited. **-2.** [sensualmente] to become aroused.
assar [4] [a'sa(x)] ◇ *vt* **-1.** [no forno] to roast. **-2.** [na grelha] to grill. ◇ *vi* to roast.

assassinar [4] [asasi'na(x)] *vt* **-1.** [matar] to murder. **-2.** *POL* to assassinate.
assassinato [asasi'natu], **assassínio** [asa'sinju] *m* **-1.** [de pessoa comum] murder. **-2.** *POL* assassination.
assassino, na [asa'sinu, na] <> *adj* deadly. <> *m, f* **-1.** [de pessoa comum] killer, murderer. **-2.** *POL* assassin.
assaz [a'saʒ] *adv* quite.
asseado, da [a'sjadu, da] *adj* clean, neat.
assediar [16] [ase'dʒja(x)] *vt* **-1.** [sitiar] to besiege. **-2.** [perseguir] to hound. **-3.** [importunar]: ~ **alguém (com)** to pester sb (with). **-4.** [sexualmente] to harass.
assédio [a'sɛdʒju] *m* **-1.** [cerco] siege. **-2.** [insistência] hounding; **ele se acostumou com o ~ dos repórteres** he became used to being hounded by reporters; ~ **sexual** sexual harassment.
assegurar [4] [asegu'ra(x)] *vt* **-1.** [garantir] to ensure; ~ **alguém de algo** to assure sb of sthg; ~ **algo a alguém** to assure sb sthg; ~ **alguém de que** to assure sb that. **-2.** [afirmar] to give an assurance.
◆ **assegurar-se** *vp*: ~**-se de fazer algo** to make sure of doing sthg.
asseio [a'seju] *m* cleanliness, neatness.
assembléia [asẽn'blɛja] *f* **-1.** [reunião] meeting; ~ **geral** annual general meeting. **-2.** [órgão] assembly; **Assembléia Legislativa** Legislative Assembly.
assemelhar [4] [aseme'ʎa(x)] *vt* [tornar semelhante] to liken.
◆ **assemelhar-se** *vp* [ser parecido] to look alike; ~**-se a algo/alguém** to look like sthg/sb.
assenhorear-se [15] [aseɲo'rjaxsi] *vp*: ~ **de** to take possession of.
assentado, da [asẽn'tadu, da] *adj* **-1.** [firme] secure. **-2.** [combinado] arranged. **-3.** [ajuizado] sound. **-4.** [em terras] landed.
assentamento [asẽnta'mẽntu] *m* **-1.** [registro] registration. **-2.** [nota] entry. **-3.** [em terras] settling.
assentar [4] [asẽn'ta(x)] <> *vt* **-1.** [firmar] to set. **-2.** [colocar] to place. **-3.** [tijolos] to lay. **-4.** [em terras] to settle. **-5.** *fig* [basear] to base. **-6.** [anotar, registrar] to note down. **-7.** [estabelecer] to establish. **-8.** [determinar] to agree. **-9.** [decidir] to resolve. <> *vi* **-1.** [ger] to settle. **-2.** *fig* [cair]: ~ **a** *ou* **em alguém** to suit sb.
◆ **assentar-se** *vp* **-1.** [firmar-se] to be founded. **-2.** *fig* [basear-se] to be based. **-3.** *fig* [ajuizar-se] to settle down.
assente [a'sẽntʃi] <> *pp* ▷ **assentar**. <> *adj* [combinado, fixo] agreed.
assentir [56] [asẽn'tʃi(x)] *vi* **-1.** [concordar]: ~ **(em)** to agree (to). **-2.** [aceder]: ~ **(a)** to accede (to).
assento [a'sẽntu] *m* **-1.** [para sentar] seat. **-2.** *fig* [base]: **ter ~** to be based on.
assepsia [asep'sia] *f* *MED* asepsis.
asséptico, ca [a'sɛptʃiku, ka] *adj* aseptic.
assertiva [asex'tʃiva] *f* assertion.
assessor, ra [ase'so(x), ra] *m, f* **-1.** [consultor] consultant. **-2.** [assistente] adviser; ~ **de comunicação** public relations, PR; ~ **de imprensa** press adviser. **-3.** *POL* aide.
assessoramento [asesora'mẽntu] *m* assistance.
assessorar [4] [aseso'ra(x)] *vt* **-1.** [prestar consultoria]: ~ **alguém (em algo)** to advise sb (on sthg). **-2.** [assistir] to assist.
assessoria [aseso'ria] *f* **-1.** [consultoria] consultancy. **-2.** [assistência] assistance. **-3.** [setor, órgão, conselho] advisors *(pl)*; ~ **de comunicação** public relations, PR; ~ **de imprensa** press advisors *(pl)*.
asseveração [asevera'sãw] *(pl* **-ões)** *f* **-1.** [afirmação] assertion. **-2.** [garantia] affirmation.
asseverar [4] [aseve'ra(x)] *vt* **-1.** [afirmar] to assert. **-2.** [garantir] to affirm.
assexuado, da [asek'swadu, da] *adj* asexual.
assiduidade [asidwi'dadʒi] *f* **-1.** [a aulas, trabalho] regular attendance. **-2.** [diligência] diligence; **com ~** diligently.
assíduo, dua [a'sidwu, dwa] *adj* **-1.** [a aulas, trabalho] regularly attending. **-2.** [diligente] diligent.
assim [a'sĩ] <> *adv* **-1.** [deste modo] just like that; ~ **sendo** that being the case; **como ~?** how do you mean? **-2.** [igualmente] the same; **algo ~** [algo parecido] something similar; **e ~ por diante** and so on; ~ **como** [tal como] just like; [também] as well as. **-3.** [deste tamanho]: **ser grande ~** to be this big. <> *conj* [então] so; ~ **mesmo**, **mesmo ~** even so.
◆ **assim que** *loc conj* as soon as.
assimétrico, ca [asi'mɛtriku, ka] *adj* **-1.** [ger] asymmetrical. **-2.** *ESP* asymmetric.
assimilação [asimila'sãw] *(pl* **-ões)** *f* **-1.** [ger] assimilation. **-2.** [de alimento] absorbtion.
assimilar [4] [asimi'la(x)] *vt* **-1.** [ger] to assimilate. **-2.** [apropriar-se de] to absorb. **-3.** [comparar]: ~ **algo (a algo)** to compare sthg (to sthg).
assinalado, da [asina'ladu, da] *adj* **-1.** [marcado] marked. **-2.** [eminente] distinguished. **-3.** [notável] outstanding.
assinalar [4] [asina'la(x)] *vt* **-1.** [marcar] to mark. **-2.** [distinguir] to indicate. **-3.** [especificar] to specify. **-4.** [observar] to point out. **-5.** [celebrizar] to distinguish.
assinante [asi'nãntʃi] *mf* subscriber.
assinar [4] [asi'na(x)] <> *vt* **-1.** [firmar] to sign. **-2.** [ser assinante de] to subscribe to. <> *vi* [firmar] to sign.
assinatura [asina'tura] *f* **-1.** [firma] signature. **-2.** [subscrição] subscription.
assistência [asiʃ'tẽnsja] *f* **-1.** [ger] assistance, aid; ~ **jurídica** legal aid; ~ **médica** medical aid; ~ **técnica** technical assistance; ~ **social** social work. **-2.** [presença] attendance. **-3.** [espectadores] audience. **-4.** [ambulância] emergency assistance.
assistente [asiʃ'tẽntʃi] <> *adj* [auxiliar] assistant. <> *mf* **-1.** [auxiliar] assistant; ~ **social** social worker. **-2.** [espectador - em jogo] spectator; [- em teatro, cinema] member of the audience.

assistir [6] [asiʃ'tʃi(x)] <> *vt* **-1.** [socorrer] to assist. **-2.** [auxiliar] to assist. **-3.** [fazer companhia a] to attend. <> *vi* **-1.** [estar presente]: ~ **a** [ver] to watch; [testemunhar] to witness; [comparecer a] to attend. **-2.** [caber]: ~ **a alguém** to pertain to sb.
assoalho [a'swaʎu] *m* floor.
assoar [20] [a'swa(x)] *vt* to blow *(one's nose).*
assoberbado, da [asobex'badu, da] *adj* [de trabalho] snowed under.
assoberbar [4] [asobex'ba(x)] *vt*: ~ **alguém (de trabalho)** to overload sb (with work).
assobiar [aso'bja(x)] *m* = **assoviar**.
assobio [aso'biw] *m* = **assovio**.
associação [asosja'sãw] (*pl* **-ões**) *f* **-1.** [ger] association; ~ **de moradores** residents' association. **-2.** [parceria, aliança] partnership.
associado, da [aso'sjadu, da] <> *adj* **-1.** [relacionado] associated. **-2.** [sócio] associate. **-3.** [médico, advogado etc] associate. <> *m, f* [sócio] associate, partner.
associar [16] [aso'sja(x)] *vt* relacionar; ~ **algo a algo** to associate sthg with sthg.
◆ **associar-se** *vp* **-1.** *COM* [formar associação] to form a partnership. **-2.** [entrar de sócio]: **~-se a** to become a member of.
assolar [4] [aso'la(x)] *vt* to devastate.
assomar [4] [aso'ma(x)] *vi* **-1.** [aparecer]: ~ **(a)** to appear (at). **-2.** [subir]: ~ **a** to climb.
assombração [asõnbra'sãw] (*pl* **-ões**) *f* ghost.
assombrar [4] [asõn'bra(x)] *vt* **-1.** [assustar] to frighten. **-2.** [rondar] to haunt. **-3.** [impressionar] to amaze.
assombro [a'sõnbru] *m* **-1.** [admiração] astonishment. **-2.** [espanto, maravilha]: **ser um** ~ to be amazing.
assombroso, osa [asõn'brozu, rɔza] *adj* amazing.
assoprar [4] [aso'pra(x)] <> *vt* **-1.** [vela] to blow out. **-2.** [vidro] to blow. **-3.** *fam* [resposta, palpite] to whisper. <> *vi* [brisa, vento] to blow.
assoviar [16] [aso'vja(x)], **assobiar** [aso'bja(x)] *vi* & *vt* to whistle.
assovio [aso'viw], **assobio** [aso'bju] *m* whistling, whistle; **dar um** ~ to whistle.
assumido, da [asu'midu, da] *adj fam* **-1.** [declarado] acknowledged. **-2.** [homossexual]: **ser um gay** ~ to be openly gay.
assumir [6] [asu'mi(x)] <> *vt* **-1.** [chamar a si] to assume. **-2.** [reconhecer - filho] to recognize; [- erro] to admit. **-3.** [tomar posse de] to take up. **-4.** [adotar, adquirir] to take on. **-5.** [homossexualidade] to come out. <> *vi* [tomar posse] to take office.
Assunção [asũn'sãw] *n* [cidade] Asunción.
assuntar [4] [asũn'ta(x)] <> *vt* **-1.** [prestar atenção a] to notice. **-2.** [verificar] to find out about. <> *vi* [meditar]: ~ **(em)** to reflect (on).
assunto [a'sũntu] *m* [tema] subject; ~ **urgente** urgent business; **não ter** ~ *fig* to have nothing to talk about.
assustadiço, ça [asuʃta'dʒisu, sa] *adj* nervous.
assustador, ra [asuʃta'do(x), ra] (*mpl* **-es**, *fpl* **-s**) *adj* **-1.** [amedrontador] terrifying. **-2.** [alarmante] alarming.
assustar [4] [asuʃ'ta(x)] <> *vt* **-1.** [amedrontar] to frighten. **-2.** [alarmar] to alarm. <> *vi* **-1.** [amedrontar] to be terrifying. **-2.** [alarmar] to be alarming.
◆ **assustar-se** *vp*: **~-se (com)** [amedrontar-se] to be terrified (by); [alarmar-se] to be alarmed (by).
asteca [aʃ'tɛka] <> *adj* Aztec. <> *mf* Aztec.
asterisco [aʃte'riʃku] *m* asterisk.
astigmatismo [aʃtʃigma'tʃiʒmu] *m* astigmatism.
astral [aʃ'traw] (*pl* **-ais**) <> *adj ASTRO* astrological. <> *m* [humor, ambiente] mood.
astrologia [aʃtrolo'ʒia] *f* astrology.
astrólogo, ga [aʃ'trɔlogu, ga] *m, f* astrologist.
astronauta [aʃtro'nawta] *mf* astronaut.
astronáutica [aʃtro'nawtʃika] *f* astronautics *(sg).*
astronave [aʃtro'navi] *f* spaceship.
astronomia [aʃtrono'mia] *f* astronomy.
astronômico, ca [aʃtro'nomiku, ka] *adj* astronomical.
astúcia [aʃ'tusja] *f* **-1.** [esperteza] shrewdness. **-2.** [ardil] ruse.
astuto, ta [aʃ'tutu, ta] *adj* **-1.** [esperto] shrewd. **-2.** [ardiloso] cunning.
at. (*abrev de* **atenção a**) attn.
ata ['ata] *f* [de reunião] minutes *(pl).*
atacadista [ataka'dʒiʃta] <> *adj COM* [comércio, mercado, vendedor] wholesale. <> *mf* [vendedor] wholesaler.
atacado, da [ata'kadu, da] *adj fam* [pessoa]: **estar** *ou* **andar** ~ to be in a foul mood.
◆ **atacado** *m COM*: **no/por** ~ wholesale.
atacante [ata'kãntʃi] <> *adj* attacking. <> *mf* attacker.
atacar [12] [ata'ka(x)] <> *vt* **-1.** [lançar ataque contra] to attack. **-2.** [acometer] to strike at. **-3.** *fig* [combater] to tackle. **-4.** *fig* [criticar] to hit out at. <> *vi* **-1.** [lançar ataque] to attack. **-2.** [vírus] to strike. **-3.** *ESP* [time, jogador] to go on the attack. <> *interj*: **atacar!** charge!
atado, da [a'tadu, da] *adj* **-1.** [desajeitado] clumsy. **-2.** [confuso, perplexo] bewildered.
atadura [ata'dura] *f* bandage.
atalho [a'taʎu] *m COMPUT* shortcut.
atapetar [4] [atape'ta(x)] *vt* to carpet.
ataque [a'taki] *m* **-1.** [ger] attack; ~ **aéreo** air strike; ~ **cardíaco** heart attack; ~ **epilético** epileptic fit; ~ **histérico** fit of hysteria; ~ **de nervos** attack of nerves; ~ **de riso** fit of laughter; **ter um** ~ **(de raiva)** *fam* to have a fit (of rage). **-2.** [*FUT* - de time] attack; [- campo, ação]: **no** ~ on the attack.
atar [4] [a'ta(x)] *vt* to tie; **não** ~ **nem desatar** [pessoa] to shilly-shally; [negócio, namoro] to be getting nowhere.
atarantado, da [atarãn'tadu, da] *adj* **-1.** [dia] hectic. **-2.** [pessoa] flustered.
atarantar [4] [atarãn'ta(x)] *vt* to fluster.
atarefado, da [ˌatare'fadu, da] *adj* busy.
atarracado, da [ataxa'kadu, da] *adj* **-1.** [pessoa]

thickset. **-2.** [pescoço, perna] thick.

atarraxar [4] [ataxa'ʃa(x)] *vt* to screw.

ataúde [ata'udʒi] *m* coffin.

atávico, ca [a'taviku, ka] *adj* atavistic.

atazanar [4] [ataza'na(x)] *vt* to taunt.

até [a'tɛ] <> *prep* **-1.** [no espaço] as far as, up to; **de ... ~ ...** from ... to ... **-2.** [no tempo] until, till; **~ que enfim!** at long last!; **ir ~ o fim com algo** to see sthg through; **~ agora** so far, up until now. **-3.** [prazo - antes de] before; [- extensão] until. **-4.** [despedida]: **até!** see you!; **~ amanhã** until tomorrow; **~ já** see you soon; **~ logo** bye for now; **~ a vista** until next time. **-5.** [com quantidades] up to. <> *adv* [mesmo, inclusive] even.
◆ **até que** *loc conj* **-1.** [até quando] until. **-2.** [bem que]: **~ que** admittedly.

atear [15] [ate'a(x)] *vt* **-1.** [fogo]: **~ fogo a algo** to set fire to sthg. **-2.** *fig* [espalhar] to inflame.

atéia [a'tɛja] *f* ▻ **ateu.**

ateliê [ate'lje] *m* studio.

atemorizado, da [atemori'zadu, da] *adj* frightened.

atemorizador, ra [atemoriza'do(x), ra] *adj* alarming.

atemorizante [atemori'zãntʃi] *adj* frightening.

atemorizar [4] [atemori'za(x)] *vt* **-1.** [assustar] to frighten. **-2.** [intimidar] to alarm.

Atenas [a'tenaʃ] *n* Athens.

atenção [atẽn'sãw] (*pl* **-ões**) <> *f* **-1.** [interesse] attention; **chamar a ~ (de)** [atrair] to catch the eye (of); **chamar a ~ de alguém** [advertir] to warn sb; **prestar ~ (a)** to pay attention (to). **-2.** [cuidado] care. **-3.** [cortesia] consideration *(U)*. <> *interj*: **~!** [cuidado] beware!; [exigindo concentração] pay attention!; [em aeroporto, conferência] your attention please!

atencioso, osa [atẽn'sjozu, ɔsa] *adj* **-1.** [que presta atenção] attentive. **-2.** [polido, cortês] considerate.

atendente [atẽn'dẽntʃi] *mf* auxiliary.

atender [5] [atẽn'de(x)] <> *vt* **-1.** [satisfazer] to attend to. **-2.** [deferir] to grant. **-3.** [receber] to receive. **-4.** [responder] to answer. **-5.** [em loja] to serve. **-6.** [cuidar de - convidado, hóspede] to look after; [- paciente, ferido] to tend. <> *vi* **-1.** [satisfazer]: **~ a** to attend to. **-2.** [responder]: **~ (a)** to answer; **~ por** [por nome, apelido] to answer to. **-3.** [loja, vendedor] to serve; **~ bem/mal** to give good/bad service. **-4.** [dar atenção]: **~ a** to heed.

atendimento [atẽndʒi'mẽntu] *m* **-1.** [serviço] service; **~ médico** medical care; **horário de ~** opening times. **-2.** [recepção]: **tivemos pronto ~ no ministério** we were dealt with swiftly at the ministry.

ateniense [ate'njẽnsi] <> *adj* Athenian. <> *m, f* Athenian.

atentado [atẽn'tadu] *m* **-1.** [ataque] attack; **~ a bomba/tiros** bomb/gun attack; **~ terrorista** terrorist attack. **-2.** [contra pessoa] attempt on one's life. **-3.** [contra edifício, monumento]: **~ (a/contra)** attack (on/against). **-4.** [crime, ofensa]: **~ (a algo)** attack (on sthg); **~ ao pudor** indecent exposure.

atentar [4] [atẽn'ta(x)] *vi* **-1.** [prestar atenção]: **~ para** *ou* **a** to pay attention to. **-2.** [cometer atentado]: **~ contra (a vida de) alguém** to make an attempt on sb's life; **~ contra algo** [violar, ofender] to offend against sthg.

atento, ta [a'tẽntu, ta] *adj* **-1.** [interessado, concentrado] attentive. **-2.** [cuidadoso] painstaking.

atenuação [atenwa'sãw] (*pl* **-ões**) *f* **-1.** [de pressão, pena] reduction. **-2.** [de combate] subduing. **-3.** [de dor] easing.

atenuante [ate'nwãntʃi] <> *adj* extenuating. <> *m JUR* extenuating circumstance.

atenuar [4] [ate'nwa(x)] *vt* **-1.** [pressão, pena] to reduce. **-2.** [combate] to die down. **-3.** [dor] to ease.

aterrador, ra [atexa'do(x), ra] *adj* terrifying.

aterragem [ate'xaʒẽj] (*pl* **-ns**) *f* = **aterrissagem.**

aterrar [4] [ate'xar] *vt* [cobrir com terra] to level.

aterrissagem [atexi'saʒẽj] (*pl* **-ns**) *f* landing.

aterrissar [atexi'sa(x)], **aterrizar** [atexi'za(x)] [4] *vi* to land.

aterro [a'texu] *m* [área aterrada] levelling.

aterrorizado, da [atexori'zadu, da] *adj* terrified.

aterrorizante [atexori'zãntʃi] *adj* terrifying.

aterrorizar [4] [atexori'za(x)] *vt* to terrorize.

ater-se [1] [a'texsi] *vp* **-1.** [limitar-se]: **~ a** to keep to. **-2.** [fiar-se por] to rely on.

atestado, da [ateʃ'tadu, da] *adj* certified.
◆ **atestado** *m* **-1.** [certificado] certificate; **~ médico** medical certificate; **~ de óbito** death certificate; **passar um ~** to issue a certificate. **-2.** *fig* [prova] confirmation. **-3.** *JUR* testimony.

atestar [4] [ateʃ'ta(x)] *vt* **-1.** [certificar] to certify. **-2.** [provar] to confirm. **-3.** [testemunhar] to vouch for.

ateu, atéia [a'tew, a'tɛja] <> *adj* atheist. <> *m, f* atheist.

atinado, da [atʃi'nadu, da] *adj* [sensato] sensible.

atinar [4] [atʃi'na(x)] <> *vt* **-1.** [descobrir, acertar] to work out. **-2.** [perceber] to realize. <> *vi* **-1.** [encontrar]: **~ com** to come up with. **-2.** [ter consciência de]: **~ em** to be aware of.

atingir [52] [atʃĩn'ʒi(x)] *vt* **-1.** [ger] to reach. **-2.** [acertar] to hit. **-3.** [objetivo] to achieve. **-4.** *fig* [ferir] to wound. **-5.** [afetar] to affect. **-6.** [compreender] to grasp.

atingível [atʃĩn'ʒivew] (*pl* **-eis**) *adj* achievable, attainable.

atípico, ca [a'tʃipiku, ka] *adj* untypical, atypical.

atirado, da [atʃi'radu, da] *adj fam* [pessoa] forward.

atirador, ra [atʃira'do(x), ra] *m, f* shot, shooter.

atirar [4] [atʃi'ra(x)] <> *vt* **-1.** [lançar]: **~ algo (em)** to throw sthg (into); **~ algo (por)** to throw sthg (through). **-2.** [fig] [olhares, beijos] to cast. <> *vi* [dar disparo]: **~ (em)** to fire (at).
◆ **atirar-se** *vp* **-1.** [lançar-se]: **~-se (a/em)** to throw o.s. (at); *fig* [dedicar-se] to throw o.s. into; **~-se contra** to throw onself against. **-2.** *fam* [insinuar-se amorosamente] to come on to.

atitude [atʃi'tudʒi] *f* **-1.** [modo de agir] response; **tomar uma ~** [reagir, tomar uma providência] to take a stance. **-2.** [postura] attitude.
ativa [a'tʃiva] *f* ▷ **ativo**.
ativação [ativa'sãw] (*pl* **-ões**) *f* [aceleração, intensificação] acceleration.
ativar [4] [atʃi'va(x)] *vt* **-1.** [acionar] to turn on. **-2.** [bomba] to activate. **-3.** [estimular] to stimulate.
atividade [atʃivi'dadʒi] *f* **-1.** [ger] activity; **~ extracurricular** extracurricular activity; **entrar em ~** to be put into action; **em ~** [aparelho] functioning; [pessoa] on the go. **-2.** [ocupação] pursuit. **-3.** [movimento intenso] bustle.
ativo, va [a'tivu, va] *adj* **-1.** [ger] active. **-2.** [que trabalha] working. **-3.** [ágil, movimentado] lively.
◆ **ativo** *m COM* assets *(pl)*.
◆ **ativa** *f MIL*: **estar na ~** to be in active service; **da ~** staff *(antes de subst)*.
atlântico, ca [at'lãntʃiku, ka] *adj* Atlantic.
◆ **Atlântico** *n*: **o (oceano) Atlântico** the Atlantic Ocean.
atlas ['atlaʃ] *m inv* atlas.
Atlas ['atlaʃ] *n*: **o ~** the Atlas Mountains.
atleta [a'tlɛta] *mf* athlete.
atlético, ca [a'tlɛtʃiku, ka] *adj* athletic.
atletismo [atle'tʃiʒmu] *m* athletics *(sg)*.
atmosfera [atmoʃ'fɛra] *f* **-1.** *GEOGR* atmosphere. **-2.** *fig* [ambiente] mood.
atmosférico, ca [atmoʃ'fɛriku, ka] *adj* atmospheric.
ato ['atu] *m* **-1.** [ger] act; **~ sexual** sexual act; **~ falho** Freudian slip; **em ~ contínuo** straight away; **no ~** [imediatamente] on the spot. **-2.** [cerimônia] action; **~ público** public ceremony. **-3.** *POL* [decreto]: **~ (institucional)** act, law.
à-toa [a'toa] *adj* **-1.** [sem importância] insignificant. **-2.** [simples] simple.
atoalhado, da [atwa'ʎadu, da] *adj* towelling.
atolado, da [ato'ladu, da] *adj* **-1.** [carro, rua] muddy. **-2.** *fig* [pessoa]: **~ (de coisas para fazer)** snowed under (with things to do).
atolar [4] [ato'la(x)] *vt* to get bogged down.
◆ **atolar-se** *vp fig* [pessoa] to be snowed under.
atoleiro [ato'lejru] *m* **-1.** [de lama] quagmire. **-2.** *fig* [situação] morass.
atômico, ca [a'tomiku, ka] *adj* atomic.
atomizador [atomiza'do(x)] *m* atomizer, spray.
átomo ['atomu] *m* atom.
atonal, nais [a'tonaw, ajʃ] *adj MÚS* atonal.
atônito, ta [a'tonitu, ta] *adj* astonished.
ator, atriz [a'to(x), a'triʒ] (*mpl* **-res**, *fpl* **-zes**) *m, f* actor, actress.
atordoado, da [atox'dwadu, da] *adj* dazed.
atordoamento [atoxdwa'mẽntu] *m* bewilderment.
atordoante [atox'dwãntʃi] *adj* deafening.
atordoar [20] [atox'dwa(x)] *vt* to daze.
atormentado, da [atoxmẽn'tadu, da] *adj* tormented.
atormentar [4] [atoxmẽn'ta(x)] *vt* to torment.
atóxico, ca [a'tɔksiku, ka] *adj* non-toxic.
ATP (*abrev de* **Associação dos Tenistas Profissionais**) *f* ATP.
atração [atra'sãw] (*pl* **-ões**) *f* **-1.** *FÍS* attraction. **-2.** [de cinema, teatro] main attraction. **-3.** [propensão] pull. **-4.** [sexual] attraction.
atracar [12] [atra'ka(x)] *vt & vi NÁUT* to moor.
◆ **atracar-se** *vp* **-1.** *fig* [em briga] to come to blows. **-2.** *fam fig* [amorosamente] to clinch.
atraente [atra'ẽntʃi] *adj* **-1.** [objeto, efeito] eye-catching. **-2.** [proposta, vantagem] appealing. **-3.** [pessoa] attractive.
atraiçoar [20] [atraj'swa(x)] *vt* to betray.
atrair [68] [atra'i(x)] *vt* **-1.** [fascinar] to attract. **-2.** [chamar a si] to bring. **-3.** [aliciar] to entice.
atrapalhação [atrapaʎa'sãw] (*pl* **-ões**) *f* [confusão] muddle.
atrapalhar [4] [atrapa'ʎa(x)] ◇ *vt* **-1.** [confundir] to muddle. **-2.** [perturbar] to upset. **-3.** [dificultar] to confound. ◇ *vi* [perturbar] to be disturbing.
◆ **atrapalhar-se** *vp* [confundir-se] to get into a muddle.
atrás [a'trajʃ] *adv* **-1.** [posição] behind; **lá ~** back there. **-2.** [no tempo] ago. **-3.** [em classificação]: **estar/ficar ~ (de)** to be ranked behind; **não ficar ~** *fam fig* not to be far behind.
◆ **atrás de** *loc prep* **-1.** [posição] behind. **-2.** [em seguimento a] after; **logo ~ de** right behind. **-3.** [em busca de - pessoa] after; [- objeto, explicação] looking for.
atrasado, da [atra'zadu, da] *adj* **-1.** [ger] slow. **-2.** [tardio] late. **-3.** [país, povo, costume] backward. **-4.** [pagamento, conta] overdue. **-5.** [número, edição] back.
◆ **atrasados** *mpl* arrears.
atrasar [4] [atra'za(x)] ◇ *vt* **-1.** [fazer demorar] to delay. **-2.** [retardar] to hold back. **-3.** [relógio] to put back. **-4.** [pagamento] to be late with. ◇ *vi* **-1.** [demorar] to be delayed. **-2.** [publicação] to be late. **-3.** [relógio] to be slow. **-4.** [pagamento] to arrive late. **-5.** [em trabalho, encomenda] to fail to keep up.
◆ **atrasar-se** *vp* [pessoa]: **~-se (para)** to be late (for).
atraso [a'trazu] *m* **-1.** [demora] delay; **chegar com ~** to arrive late; **um ~ de vida** a drag. **-2.** [de pagamento] late payment. **-3.** [de país, povo, costumes] backwardness.
atrativo, va [atra'tʃivu, va] *adj* attractive.
◆ **atrativo** *m* attraction.
atravancar [12] [atravãŋ'ka(x)] *vt* **-1.** [bloquear] to block. **-2.** [lotar] to clutter.
através [atra'vɛʃ] *adv* [de lado a lado] through.
◆ **através de** *loc adv* **-1.** [por entre] amongst. **-2.** [pelo centro de] through. **-3.** [no decorrer de] through. **-4.** [por meio de] by means of. **-5.** [por via de] through.
atravessado, da [atrave'sadu, da] *adj* **-1.** [de través] askew; **~ sobre** (lying) across. **-2.** [cruzado] crossed. **-3.** [passado de lado a lado] (stuck) across. **-4.** *fig* [irritado] irritated; **estar com alguém ~ na garganta** to be fed up with sb.
atravessar [4] [atrave'sa(x)] *vt* **-1.** [ger] to cross.

-2. [pôr de través] to place across. **-3.** [transpassar] to pierce. **-4.** *fig* [passar por] to go through.

atrelar [4] [atre'la(x)] *vt* **-1.** [prender] to tie up, to tether. **-2.** [ligar] to attach; ~ **algo a algo** to attach sthg to sthg.

atrever-se [5] [atre'vexsi] *vp*: ~ **(a fazer algo)** to dare (to do sthg).

atrevido, da [atre'vidu, da] *adj* **-1.** [petulante] impertinent. **-2.** [ousado] bold.

atrevimento [atrevi'mẽntu] *m* **-1.** [petulância] insolence. **-2.** [ousadia - condição] boldness; [- ato] effrontery.

atribuição [atribwi'sãw] (*pl* **-ões**) *f* **-1.** [ato] attribution. **-2.** [prerrogativa] prerogative.
◆ **atribuições** *fpl* [poderes] powers.

atribuir [74] [atri'bwi(x)] *vt* **-1.** [imputar]: ~ **algo a alguém/algo** to attribute sthg to sb/sthg. **-2.** [conceder]: ~ **algo a alguém** to award sb sthg.

atribulação [atribula'sãw] (*pl* **-ões**) *f* adversity.

atribulado, da [atribu'ladu, da] *adj* wretched.

atribular [4] [atribu'la(x)] *vt* to afflict.
◆ **atribular-se** *vp* to be distressed.

atributo [atri'butu] *m* attribute.

átrio ['atriu] *m* **-1.** [vestíbulo] hallway. **-2.** [pátio] courtyard.

atritar [atri'ta(x)] *vt* to rub.

atrito [a'tritu] *m* **-1.** [fricção] friction. **-2.** *fig* [conflito] conflict; **entrar em** ~ to have a misunderstanding.

atriz [a'triʒ] *f* ▷ **ator**.

atrocidade [atrosi'dadʒi] *f* atrocity.

atrofia [atro'fia] *f* atrophy.

atrofiado, da [atro'fjadu, da] *adj* atrophied.

atrofiar [16] [atro'fja(x)] ◇ *vt* to cripple. ◇ *vi* to atrophy.
◆ **atrofiar-se** *vp* to become atrophied.

atropeladamente [atropelada'mẽntʃi] *adv* [atabalhoadamente] chaotically.

atropelamento [atropela'mẽntu] *m* [de pedestre] running over.

atropelar [4] [atrope'la(x)] *vt* **-1.** [pedestre] to run over. **-2.** [esbarrar em, empurrar] to crash into. **-3.** *fig* [precipitar]: ~ **as coisas** to rush things.

atropelo [atro'pelu] *m* **-1.** [confusão] turmoil. **-2.** [dificuldade, aflição] headache, problem.

atroz [a'trɔʒ] *adj* **-1.** [cruel] atrocious. **-2.** [terrível] terrible.

atuação [atwa'sãw] (*pl* **-ões**) [-õjʃ] *f* **-1.** [ger] performance. **-2.** [participação] role.

atual [a'twaw] (*pl* **-ais**) *adj* **-1.** [corrente] present. **-2.** [moderno] current.

atualidade [atwali'dadʒi] *f* **-1.** [período atual] present time. **-2.** [modernidade] modernity.
◆ **atualidades** *fpl* JORN news *(sg)*.

atualização [atwaliza'sãw] (*pl* **-ões**) *f* updating.

atualizado, da [atwali'zadu, da] *adj* up-to-date.

atualizar [4] [atwali'za(x)] *vt* to update.
◆ **atualizar-se** *vp* [pessoa] to bring o.s. up to date.

atualmente [atwaw'mẽntʃi] *adv* **-1.** [no momento] currently. **-2.** [hoje em dia] nowadays.

atuante [a'twãntʃi] *adj* active.

atuar [4] [a'twa(x)] *vi* **-1.** [ger] to act. **-2.** [participar de]: ~ **em** to act on/in. **-3.** [contribuir para]: ~ **para** *ou* **por** to work for *ou* towards. **-4.** [influenciar]: ~ **sobre** to influence.

atum [a'tũ] (*pl* **-ns**) *m* tuna.

aturar [4] [atu'ra(x)] *vt* to endure, to put up with.

aturdido, da [atur'dʒidu, da] *adj* stunned.

aturdir [6] [atux'dʒi(x)] ◇ *vt* to stun. ◇ *vi* to deafen.

audácia [aw'dasja] *f* **-1.** [intrepidez] boldness. **-2.** [insolência] audacity; **que** ~**!** what a cheek!

audacioso, sa [awda'sjozu, ɔza] *adj* **-1.** [pessoa] intrepid. **-2.** [ato] gallant. **-3.** [decisão] bold.

audaz [aw'daʒ] (*pl* **-es**) *adj* [intrépido] audacious.

audição [awdʒi'sãw] (*pl* **-ões**) *f* **-1.** [ger] hearing. **-2.** [concerto] audition.

audiência [aw'dʒjẽnsja] *f* **-1.** [ger] audience; **dar uma** ~ to grant an audience. **-2.** [mídia - RÁDIO] listeners *(pl)*; [- TV] viewers *(pl)*; **índices de** ~ ratings *(pl)*. **-3.** JUR hearing.

áudio ['awdʒu] *m* audio.

audiovisual [ˌawdʒuvi'zwaw] (*pl* **-ais**) ◇ *adj* audiovisual. ◇ *m* projector.

auditar [4] [awdʒi'ta(x)] *vt* FIN to audit.

auditivo, va [awdʒi'tʃivu, va] *adj* auditory.

auditor, ra [awdʒi'to(x), ra] *m, f* **-1.** FIN auditor. **-2.** [juiz] judge, magistrate. **-3.** [ouvinte] listener.

auditoria [awdʒito'ria] *f* **-1.** [servico] audit; **fazer a** ~ **de** to carry out an audit of. **-2.** [empresa] firm of accountants.

auditório [awdʒi'tɔrju] *m* **-1.** [recinto] courtroom. **-2.** [platéia] auditorium.

audível [aw'dʒivew] (*pl* **-eis**) *adj* audible.

auê [aw'e] *m fam* [confusão] uproar; **fazer um** ~ to create an uproar.

auferir [57] [awfe'ri(x)] *vt* to obtain.

auge ['awʒi] *m* height.

augurar [4] [awgu'ra(x)] *vt* **-1.** [prognosticar] to foretell. **-2.** [indicar] to augur. **-3.** [desejar] to wish.

augúrio [aw'gurju] *m* **-1.** [prognóstico] prophecy. **-2.** [sinal] indication.

aula ['awla] *f* [escola] **-1.** lesson; **dar** ~ to teach. **-2.** [universidade] lecture; ~ **inaugural** introductory lecture.

aumentar [4] [awmẽn'ta(x)] ◇ *vt* **-1.** [ger] to increase. **-2.** [adicionar]: ~ **algo (a)** to add sthg (to/onto). ◇ *vi* **-1.** [ger] to increase. **-2.** [crescer] to grow.

aumento [aw'mẽntu] *m* **-1.** [ger] price increase. **-2.** [de salário] rise *UK*, raise *US*. **-3.** [crescimento] increase. **-4.** [ampliação] magnification.

aura ['awra] *f* **-1.** [halo] halo. **-2.** *fig* [ar] aura.

áureo, rea ['awrju, rja] *adj* golden.

auréola [aw'rɛwla] *f* halo.

aurora [aw'rɔra] *f* dawn.

auscultar [4] [auʃkuw'ta(x)] *vt* **-1.** MED to sound, to auscultate. **-2.** *fig* [sondar] to sound (out).

ausência [aw'zẽnsja] *f* **-1.** [falta de presença] absence. **-2.** *fig* [inexistência] lack.

ausentar-se [7] [awzẽn'taxsi] *vp* to absent o.s.

ausente [aw'zẽntʃi] <> *adj* **-1.** [não-presente] absent. **-2.** [omisso] neglectful. <> *mf* [não-presente] absent.

auspiciar [16] [awʃpi'sja(x)] *vt* [prenunciar] to augur.

auspício [awʃ'pisju] *m* **-1.** [prenúncio] sign. **-2.** [patrocínio]: **sob os ~s de** under the auspices of.

auspicioso, osa [awʃpi'ʃjozu, ɔza] *adj* auspicious.

austeridade [awʃteri'dadʒi] *f* **-1.** [severidade, seriedade] severity. **-2.** [em gastos] austerity.

austero, ra [awʃ'tɛru, ra] *adj* **-1.** [severo] strict. **-2.** [em gastos] austere.

austral [awʃ'traw] (*pl* **-ais**) *adj* southern.

Austrália [awʃ'tralja] *n* Australia.

australiano, na [awʃtra'ljãnu, na] <> *adj* Australian. <> *m, f* Australian.

Áustria ['awʃtria] *n* Austria.

austríaco, ca [awʃ'triaku, ka] <> *adj* Austrian. <> *m, f* Austrian.

autarquia [awtax'kia] *f* autocracy.

autárquico, ca [aw'taxkiku, ka] *adj* autocratic.

autenticação [awtẽntʃi'kasãw] (*pl* **-ões**) *f* COMPUT verification.

autenticar [12] [awtẽntʃi'ka(x)] *vt* to authenticate.

autenticidade [awtẽntʃisi'dadʒi] *f* [genuinidade] authenticity.

autêntico, ca [aw'tẽntʃiku, ka] *adj* **-1.** [genuíno] authentic. **-2.** [original] original. **-3.** *(antes de subst) pej* [verdadeiro] real.

autismo [aw'tʃiʒmu] *m* autism.

autista [aw'tʃiʃta] <> *adj* autistic. <> *mf* autistic.

auto ['awtu] *m* **-1.** JUR (legal) brief. **-2.** TEATRO medieval allegorical play.

◆ **autos** *mpl* JUR legal papers.

auto-adesivo, va [ˌawtwade'zivu, va] (*mpl* **-s**, *fpl* **-s**) <> *adj* self-adhesive. <> *m* sticker.

auto-afirmação [ˌawtwafixma'sãw] *f* self-assertion.

autobiografia [awtobjogra'fia] *f* autobiography.

autobiográfico, ca [awtubjo'grafiku, ka] *adj* autobiographical.

autoconfiança [awtukõn'fjãnsa] *f* self-confidence.

autoconhecimento [awtukoɲesi'mẽntu] *m* self-knowledge.

autocontrole [awtukõn'troli] *m* self-control.

autocrata [awto'krata] <> *adj* autocratic. <> *mf* autocrat.

autocrítica [awto'kritika] *f* self-criticism; **fazer uma ~** to admit to one's faults.

autóctone [aw'tɔktoni] <> *adj* native. <> *mf* [nativo] native.

autodefesa [awtude'feza] *f* self-defence.

autodenominar-se [7] [awtudenomi'naxsi] *vp* to call o.s.

autodestruição [awtudeʃtruj'sãw] *f* self-destruction.

autodeterminação [awtudetexmina'sãw] *f* self-determination.

autodidata [awtodʒi'data] <> *adj* self-taught. <> *mf* self-taught person.

autodisciplina [awtudʒisi'plina] *f* self-discipline.

autodomínio [ˌawtodo'minju] *m* self-control.

autódromo [aw'tɔdromu] *m* racetrack.

auto-escola [ˌawtwiʃ'kɔla] (*pl* **auto-escolas**) *f* driving school.

auto-estima [ˌawtwiʃ'tʃima] *f* self-esteem.

auto-estrada [ˌawtwiʃ'trada] (*pl* **auto-estradas**) *f* motorway *UK*, freeway *US*.

autografar [4] [awtogra'fa(x)] *vt* to sign.

autógrafo [aw'tɔgrafu] *m* autograph.

automação [awtoma'sãw] *f* = **automatização**.

automático, ca [awto'matʃiku, ka] *adj* automatic.

automatização [awtomatʃiza'sãw] (*pl* **-ões**) *f* automation.

automatizar [4] [awtomatʃi'za(x)] *vt* to automate.

autômato [aw'tomatu] *m* **-1.** [aparelho] robot. **-2.** *fig* [pessoa] automaton.

automedicar-se [7] [awtumedʒi'kaxsi] *vp* to self-medicate.

automobilismo [awtomobi'liʒmu] *m* motor racing.

automobilista [awtomobi'liʃta] *mf* ESP racing driver.

automóvel [awto'mɔvɛw] (*pl* **-eis**) *m* car.

autonomia [awtono'mia] *f* **-1.** [independência] autonomy. **-2.** [de veículo] range; **~ de vôo** flight range.

autônomo, ma [aw'tonomu, ma] <> *adj* **-1.** [independente] autonomous. **-2.** [trabalhador] autonomist. <> *m, f* [trabalhador] autonomist.

autopeça [awto'pɛsa] *f* spare part *(for car)*.

autópsia [aw'tɔpsja] *f* autopsy.

autor, ra [aw'to(x), ra] (*mpl* **-es**, *fpl* **-s**) *m, f* author.

autoral [awto'raw] (*pl* **-ais**) *adj* authorial.

auto-retrato [ˌawtoxe'tratu] (*pl* **auto-retratos**) *m* self-portrait.

autoria [awto'ria] *f* **-1.** LITER authorship; **ser de ~ de alguém** to be written by sb. **-2.** [de crime] perpetration.

autoridade [awtori'dadʒi] *f* **-1.** [ger] authority; **ter/não ter ~** to have/not to have authority. **-2.** [perito]: **ser uma ~ em algo** to be an authority on sthg.

autoritário, ria [awtori'tarju, ja] *adj* authoritarian.

autoritarismo [awtorita'riʒmu] *m* authoritarianism.

autorização [awtoriza'sãw] (*pl* **-ões**) *f* permission; **dar ~ a alguém (para algo/para fazer algo)** to give sb permission (for sthg/to do sthg).

autorizar [4] [awtori'za(x)] *vt* **-1.** [permitir] to authorize. **-2.** [capacitar] to enable.

auto-serviço [ˌawtusex'visu] (*pl* **auto-serviços**) *m* self-service.

auto-suficiente [ˌawtusufi'sjẽntʃi] (*pl* **-s**) *adj*

self-sufficient; **ser ~ em algo** to be self-sufficient in sthg.
auto-sugestão [ˌawtusuʒeʃ'tãw] (*pl* -**ões**) *f* auto-suggestion.
autuar [4] [aw'twa(x)] *vt* to report; **~ alguém em flagrante** to catch sb red-handed.
auxiliar [16] [awsi'lja(x)] (*pl* -**es**) <> *adj* -**1.** [ger] assistant. -**2.** [enfermeiro] auxiliary. <> *mf* assistant; **~ administrativo** administrative assistant. <> *vt* to assist.
auxílio [aw'silju] *m* assistance; **prestar ~ a** to give assistance to.
auxílio-desemprego [awˌsiljudʒizĩn'pregu] (*pl* **auxílios-desemprego**) *m* unemployment benefit.
auxílio-doença [awˌsilju'dwẽnsa] (*pl* **auxílios-doença**) *m* sickness benefit.
auxílio-natalidade [awˌsiljunatali'dadʒi] (*pl* **auxílios-natalidade**) *m* maternity grant.
av. (*abrev de* **avenida**) *f* Av.
avacalhado, da [avaka'ʎadu, da] *adj* -**1.** [camisa, cabelo] dishevelled. -**2.** [trabalho] slipshod.
avacalhar [ava'kaʎa(x)] *vt* -**1.** [pôr em ridículo] ***fam*** to make a travesty of. -**2.** [executar com desleixo] ***fam*** to make a mess of.
aval [a'vaw] (*pl* -**ais**) *m* -**1.** [ger] backing. -**2.** [garantia] warranty.
avalanche [ava'lãnʃi], **avalancha** *f* avalanche.
avaliação [avalja'sãw] (*pl* -**ões**) *f* -**1.** [de preço, prejuízos] estimate. -**2.** [de qualidade, vantagens] appraisal. -**3.** [opinião] opinion. -**4.** EDUC assessment.
avaliar [16] [ava'lja(x)] *vt* -**1.** [preço, prejuízo] to estimate. -**2.** [imóvel] to value. -**3.** [qualidade, vantagens, idéia] to evaluate. -**4.** EDUC to assess.
avalista [ava'liʃta] *mf* backer.
avançado, da [avãn'sadu, da] *adj* -**1.** [adiantado] jutting out. -**2.** [hora] late. -**3.** [nível] advanced. -**4.** [idéia, pessoa] progressive.
avançar [13] [avã'sa(x)] <> *vi* -**1.** [adiantar-se] to move forward. -**2.** [estender-se] to spread. -**3.** [atacar, investir] to advance. -**4.** [atirar-se]: **~ em algo** to throw o.s. upon sthg. <> *vt* [adiantar] to advance.
avanço [a'vãsu] *m* -**1.** [de tropa] advance. -**2.** [adiantamento] headway. -**3.** [melhora] step in the right direction. -**4.** [progresso] progress.
avantajado, da [avãnta'ʒadu, da] *adj* imposing.
avante [a'vãntʃi] <> *adv* -**1.** [adiante] ahead. -**2.** [para diante] onward. <> *interj* forward!
avarento, ta [ava'rẽntu, ta] <> *adj* miserly. <> *m, f* miser.
avareza [ava'reza] *f* avarice.
avaria [ava'ria] *f* -**1.** [de veículo, máquina] breakdown. -**2.** [de carga, casco] damage.
avariado, da [ava'rjadu, da] *adj* -**1.** [veículo, máquina] broken down. -**2.** [carga, casco] damaged.
avariar [16] [ava'rja(x)] <> *vt* to break down. <> *vi* -**1.** to spoil. -**2.** [casco] to be damaged.
avaro, ra [a'varu, ra] <> *adj* avaricious. <> *m, f* miser.
ave ['avi] *f* bird; **~ de rapina** bird of prey.
aveia [a'veja] *f* oat.
avelã [ave'lã] *f* hazelnut.
aveludado, da [avelu'dadu, da] *adj* velvety.
avenida [ave'nida] *f* avenue.
avental [avẽn'taw] (*pl* -**ais**) *m* -**1.** [proteção] apron. -**2.** [vestido] pinafore dress.
aventar [4] [avẽn'ta(x)] *vt* to air.
aventura [avẽn'tura] *f* -**1.** [experiência] adventure. -**2.** [amorosa] love affair.
aventurar [4] [avẽntu'ra(x)] *vt* to risk.
◆ **aventurar-se** *vp* to venture (forth); **~-se a fazer algo** to dare to do sthg.
aventureiro, ra [avẽntu'rejru, ra] <> *adj* adventurous. <> *m, f* adventurer (*f* adventuress).
averiguação [averigwa'sãw] (*pl* -**ões**) *f* -**1.** [investigação] investigation. -**2.** [verificação] check.
averiguar [21] [averi'gwa(x)] *vt* -**1.** [investigar] to investigate. -**2.** [verificar] to check.
avermelhado, da [avexme'ʎadu, da] *adj* reddish.
aversão [avex'sãw] (*pl* -**ões**) *f* aversion; **ter ~ a algo** to have an aversion to sthg.
avesso, ssa [a'vesu] *adj* [lado] wrong.
◆ **avesso** *m* [lado] underside; **virar pelo ~** [blusa etc] to turn inside out; ***fig*** [revirar] to turn upside down.
◆ **às avessas** *loc adj* [oposto]: **ser um santo às avessas** to be anything but a saint.
avestruz [aveʃ'truʃ] (*pl* -**es**) *f* ostrich.
aviação [avja'sãw] *f* -**1.** [sistema] aviation. -**2.** [força aérea] air force.
aviador, ra [avja'do(x), ra] *m, f* pilot, aviator.
aviamento [avja'mẽntu] *m* -**1.** COST trimmings (*pl*). -**2.** [de receita médica] preparation.
avião [a'vjãw] (*pl* -**ões**) *m* -**1.** [veículo] aeroplane; **~ a jato** jet plane; **ir de ~** to fly. -**2.** ***fam*** [mulher] stunner. -**3.** ***gír*** [droga] drug pedlar.
aviar [16] [a'vja(x)] *vt* [receita médica] to make up.
avicultor, ra [avikuw'to(x), ra] *m, f* poultry breeder.
avicultura [avikuw'tura] *f* poultry breeding.
avidez [avi'deʒ] *f* -**1.** [desejo] eagerness; **com ~** eagerly. -**2.** [cobiça] greed.
ávido, da ['avidu, da] *adj* -**1.** [desejoso] eager. -**2.** [cobiçoso] greedy.
aviltamento [aviwta'mẽntu] *m* [degradação] degradation.
aviltar [4] [aviw'ta(x)] *vt* [degradar] to weaken.
◆ **aviltar-se** *vp* [degradar-se] to degenerate.
avinagrado, da [avina'gradu, da] *adj* sour.
avisar [4] [avi'za(x)] <> *vt* -**1.** [informar] to warn; **~ alguém de algo** to inform sb of sthg. -**2.** [advertir]: **~ alguém de algo** to warn sb about/of sthg. <> *vi* -**1.** [informar] to give warning. -**2.** [advertir] to give fair warning; **estou avisando ...** I'm warning you ...
aviso [a'vizu] *m* -**1.** [placa] notice. -**2.** [notificação] notification; **~ de crédito** credit note. -**3.** [informação] sign. -**4.** [advertência] warning sign; **~ prévio** [notificação, período] notice.
avistar [4] [aviʃ'ta(x)] *vt* to catch sight of.
◆ **avistar-se** *vp* [ter entrevista] to meet; **~-se**

com alguém to have a meeting with sb.
avivar [4] [avi'va(x)] *vt* **-1.** [ger] to revive. **-2.** [memória] to rekindle.
avizinhar-se [4] [avizi'ɲaxsi] *vp* [aproximar-se] to draw near.
avo ['avu] *m* [fração] fractional part.
avô [a'vo], **avó** [a'vɔ] *m, f* grandfather (*f* grandmother).
◆ **avós** *pl* grandparents.
avoado, da [avo'adu, da] *adj* scatty.
avolumar [4] [avolu'ma(x)] *vt* [aumentar - em volume] to swell; [- em quantidade] to increase.
◆ **avolumar-se** *vp* **-1.** [em volume] to rise. **-2.** [em quantidade] to increase.
avós [a'vɔʃ] *pl* ▻ **avô.**
avulso, sa [a'vuwsu, sa] *adj* loose.
◆ **avulso** *m* flyer.
avultado, da [avuw'tadu, da] *adj* large.
avultar [4] [avuw'ta(x)] ◇ *vt* [fazer crescer] to increase. ◇ *vi* **-1.** [sobressair] to tower above. **-2.** [crescer] to grow.
axila [ak'sila] *f* armpit.
axioma [ak'sjoma] *m* axiom.
axiomático, ca [aksio'matʃiku, ka] *adj* axiomatic.
azaléia [aza'lɛja] *f* azalea.
azar [a'za(x)] (*pl* **-es**) *m* bad luck; **~!** tough!; **que ~!** damn!; **~ o seu!** your loss!; **dar ~** to bring bad luck; **estar com ~** to be down on one's luck.
azaração [azara'sãw] (*pl* **-ões**) *f fam* flirtation.
azarado, da [aza'radu, da] *adj* jinxed.
azarar [4] [aza'ra(x)] *fam* ◇ *vt* to woo. ◇ *vi* to pull.
azedar [4] [aze'da(x)] ◇ *vt* **-1.** [comida, leite] to cause to go sour. **-2.** *fig* [pessoa] to irritate. ◇ *vi* [leite, vinho] to go sour.
azedo, da [a'zedu, da] *adj* **-1.** [sabor] sour. **-2.** *fig* [pessoa] bitter.
azedume [aze'dumi] *m* **-1.** [em sabor] bitterness. **-2.** *fig* [em pessoa] bitterness.
azeite [a'zejtʃi] *m*: **~ (de oliva)** (olive) oil.
azeitona [azej'tona] *f* olive.
Azerbaijão [azexbaj'ʒãw] *n* Azerbaijan.
azerbaijano, na [azexbaj'ʒãnu, na] ◇ *adj* Azerbaijani. ◇ *m, f* Azerbaijani.
azeviche [aze'viʃi] *m* [cor] jet black.
azia [a'zia] *f* heartburn.
aziago, ga [azi'agu, ga] *adj* ill-omened.
azucrinar [4] [azukri'na(x)] *vt* to annoy.
azul [a'zuw] (*pl* **azuis**) ◇ *adj* blue; **está tudo ~** *fig* everything is rosy. ◇ *m* blue.
azulado, da [azu'ladu, da] *adj* bluish.
azul-claro, ra [a'zuwklaru, ra] ◇ *adj* light blue. ◇ *m* light blue.
azulejado, da [azule'ʒadu, da] *adj* tiled.
azulejar [4] [azule'ʒa(x)] *vt* to tile.
azulejo [azu'leʒu] *m* (ornamental) tile.
azul-escuro, ra [a'zuwiʃkuru, ra] ◇ *adj* dark blue. ◇ *m* dark blue.
azul-marinho [a,zuwma'riɲu] ◇ *adj inv* ultramarine. ◇ *m* ultramarine.
azul-turquesa [a,zuwtux'keza] ◇ *adj inv* turquoise. ◇ *m* turquoise.

b, B [be] *m* [letra] b, B.
BA (*abrev de* **Estado da Bahia**) *n State of Bahia.*
B2B (*abrev de* **business-to-business**) *m* B2B.
baba ['baba] *f* dribble.
babá [ba'ba] *f* nursemaid.
babaca [ba'baka] *mfam adj* stupid.
baba-de-moça [,babadʒi'mosa] (*pl* **babas-de-moça**) *m, f* CULIN *egg and coconut pudding.*
babado, da [ba'badu, da] *adj* [molhado de baba] dribbly.
◆ **babado** *m* **-1.** [em roupa etc] frill. **-2.** *fam* [caso] gossip.
babador [baba'do(x)] *m* bib.
babaquice [baba'kisi] *f fam* [estupidez] stupidity.
babar [4] [ba'ba(x)] ◇ *vt* to dribble on. ◇ *vi* **-1.** [deitar baba] to dribble. **-2.** *fam* [ficar impressionado] to drool.
◆ **babar-se** *vp* **-1.** [deitar baba em si] to dribble. **-2.** *fig* [gostar muito de]: **~-se por** to drool over.
babosa [ba'bɔsa] *f* aloe.
baboseira [babo'zejra] *f* [tolice, bobagem] nonsense.
baby-sitter [,bejbi'site(x)] (*pl* **baby-sitters**) *mf* baby-sitter.
bacalhau [baka'ʎaw] *m* cod.
bacalhoada [bakaʎo'ada] *f a dish made with salt cod boiled with potatoes, cabbage, whole onions and other vegetables, mixed with hard-boiled eggs and olives and seasoned with vinegar and olive oil.*
bacana [ba'kãna] ◇ *adj* cool. ◇ *mf fam* [pessoa] toff.
bacanal [baka'naw] (*pl* **-ais**) *f* bacchanal.
BACEN (*abrev de* **Banco Central do Brasil**) *m central bank of Brazil.*
bacharel [baʃa'rɛw] (*pl* **-éis**) *mf*: **~ em Artes/Direito/Economia** Arts/Law/Economics graduate.
bacharelado [baʃare'ladu] *m* **-1.** [grau] degree. **-2.** [curso] undergraduate course.
bacharelar-se [4] [baʃare'laxsi] *vp*: **~ (em algo)** to obtain a degree (in sthg).
bacia [ba'sia] *f* **-1.** [ger] basin. **-2.** [sanitária] lavatory. **-3.** ANAT pelvis.
bacilo [ba'silu] *m* bacillus.

◆ **bacilos** *mpl* bacilli.

backbone [bak'boni] (*pl* **backbones**) *m* backbone.

background [bɛk'grawndʒi] (*pl* **-s**) *m* background.

backup [bɛ'kapi] (*pl* **-s**) *m* backup.

baço, ça ['basu, 'sa] ◇ *adj* **-1.** [pele] dull. **-2.** [metal] tarnished. ◇ *m* ANAT spleen.

bacon ['bejkõ] *m* bacon.

bactéria [bak'tɛrja] *f* bacterium.

◆ **bactérias** *fpl* bacteria.

badalação [badala'sãw] (*pl* **-ões**) *f fam* [movimento, diversão] movement.

badalado, da [bada'ladu, da] *fam adj* **-1.** [movimentado, divertido] swinging. **-2.** [famoso, falado] much talked about.

◆ **badalada** *f* [de sino] peal.

badalar [4] [bada'la(x)] ◇ *vt* [tocar] to ring. ◇ *vi* **-1.** [tocar] to peal. **-2.** *fam* [sair, divertir-se] to go out and enjoy o.s.

badalo [ba'dalu] *m* **-1.** [de sino] peal. **-2.** *fam* [diversão] fun.

badejo [ba'deʒu] *m* serran.

baderna [ba'dɛxna] *f* **-1.** [bagunça] mess. **-2.** [tumulto] revelry.

badulaque [badu'laki] *m* trinket.

◆ **badulaques** *mpl* odds and ends.

bafafá [bafa'fa] *m fam* [tumulto] hoo-ha.

bafo ['bafu] *m* breath; **~-de-onça** *fam* bad breath.

bafômetro [ba'fometru] *m* breathalyzer.

baforada [bafo'rada] *f* [fumaça] blast.

bagaço [ba'gasu] *m* [de fruta] remains of fruit *(once juice has been extracted)*; **estar/ficar um ~** *fig* to be drained, to be exhausted.

bagageiro [baga'ʒejru] *m* AUTO luggage rack.

bagagem [ba'gaʒẽ] (*pl* **-ns**) *f* **-1.** [equipagem] luggage. **-2.** *fig* [conhecimentos, experiência] experience.

bagatela [baga'tɛla] *f fig* [ninharia] next to nothing.

Bagdá [bag'da] *n* Baghdad.

bago ['bagu] *m* **-1.** [fruto] berry. **-2.** [uva] grape. **-3.** [de chumbo] shot. **-4.** *vulg* [testículo] ball.

baguete [ba'gɛtʃi] *f* baguette.

bagulho [ba'guʎu] *m* **-1.** [objeto] trinket. **-2.** *fig & pej* [pessoa]: **ser um ~** to be ugly.

bagunça [ba'gũnsa] *f* mess.

bagunçado, da [bagũn'sadu, da] *adj* cluttered.

bagunçar [bagũn'sa(x)], *vt* **-1.** [fazer confusão em] to clutter. **-2.** *fig* [atrapalhar, tumultuar] to upset.

bagunceiro, ra [bagũn'sejru, ra] *adj* [pessoa - desordeiro] disorderly; [- relaxado] untidy.

Bahamas [ba'amaʃ] *npl*: **as ~** the Bahamas.

Bahia [ba'ia] *n* Bahia.

BAHIA

Important state in north-east Brazil; Bahia was the main centre for the slave trade during colonial times. Founded in 1549, the city of Salvador was the capital of Brazil until the mid-eighteenth century. The decisive contribution of the Negroes endowed Bahia with an immense cultural wealth, as much in its many syncretic cults and African-inspired rhythms, as in the fundamental influence of Bahians in Brazilian art, from literature to popular music. Salvador is now one of the main tourist centres of the country, famous mainly for its churches and its carnival.

baia ['baja] *f* stall.

baía [ba'ia] *f* bay.

baiana [ba'jãna] *f*: **rodar a ~** to make a fuss.

baiano, na [baj'ãnu, na] ◇ *adj* Bahian. ◇ *m, f* Bahian.

baião [baj'ãw] (*pl* **-ões**) *m* [ritmo, dança] baião, *popular music from north-eastern Brazil.*

baila ['bajla] *f*: **trazer à ~** to raise (the issue); **vir à ~** to come to light.

bailado [baj'ladu] *m* dance.

bailar [4] [baj'la(x)] *vt & vi* to dance.

bailarino, na [bajla'rinu, na] *m, f* dancer.

baile ['bajli] *m* ball; **~ de carnaval** carnival ball; **~ à fantasia** fancy-dress party; **~ funk** funk party; **dar um ~ em** *fig* [superar] to crush.

bainha [ba'iɲa] *f* **-1.** [de arma] sheath. **-2.** COST hem.

baioneta [bajo'neta] *f* bayonet; **~ calada** bayoneted rifle.

bairrista [baj'xiʃta] ◇ *adj* **-1.** [que defende interesse do bairro] community-based. **-2.** [muito patriota] regionalistic. ◇ *mf* **-1.** [do local] local. **-2.** [patriota] regionalist.

bairro ['bajxu] *m* neighbourhood.

baita ['bajta] *adj (antes de subst)* **-1.** [soco, successo] tremendous. **-2.** [gripe, resfriado] terrible. **-3.** [abraço] huge.

baixa ['bajʃa] *adj* ▷ **baixo.**

baixada [baj'ʃada] *f* GEOGR valley.

baixa-mar [ˌbajʃa'ma(x)] (*pl* **baixa-mares**) *f* low tide.

baixar [4] [baj'ʃa(x)] *vt* COMPUT [fazer download]: **~ um arquivo** to download a file.

baixaria [bajʃa'ria] *f* **-1.** [ger] depravity. **-2.** [escândalo] disgrace.

baixela [baj'ʃɛla] *f* dinner service.

baixeza [baj'ʃeza] *f* low-mindedness.

baixio [baj'ʃiu] *m* sandbank.

baixista [baj'ʃiʃta] *mf* bass player.

baixo, xa ['bajʃu, ʃa] *adj* **-1.** [ger] low. **-2.** [pessoa] short. **-3.** [cabeça, olhar] lowered. **-4.** [bairro, cidade] lower. **-5.** [metal] base. **-6.** *(antes de subst)* [rio] downriver. **-7.** *(antes de subst)* [época] late. **-8.** *(antes de subst)* [vil, grosseiro] base; **~ nível** *fam* [baixaria] disgrace; **palavrão de ~ nível** swear word.

◆ **baixo** ◇ *m* **-1.** [MÚS - instrumento] bass; [- cantor] bass player. **-2.** *fam* [bairro] lower town. ◇ *adv* **-1.** [a pouca altura] low. **-2.** *fig* [em posição inferior]: **estar/ficar por ~** to be/become disheartened. **-3.** [falar] softly.

◆ **baixa** *f* **-1.** [ger] drop; **em baixa** falling. **-2.** [de serviço] sick-leave; **dar** *ou* **ter baixa (de)** to go on *ou* take sick-leave (from). **-3.** MIL loss.

◆ **para baixo** *loc adv* downwards.

◆ **por baixo (de)** *loc adv* underneath.

baixo-astral [ˌbajʃwaʃ'trawl] *m fam* glumness; **estar/ficar de ~** to be/become glum.
baixote, ta [baj'ʃɔtʃi, tal] <> *adj* shortish. <> *m, f* shortish person.
bajulação [baʒula'sãw] (*pl* **-ões**) *f* adulation.
bajulador, ra [baʒula'do(x), ral <> *adj* adulatory. <> *m, f* adulator.
bajular [4] [baʒu'la(x)] *vt* to adulate.
bala ['bala] *f* **-1.** [munição] bullet; **~ de festim** blank cartridge. **-2.** [doce] boiled sweet. **-3.** *loc*: **estar/ficar uma ~** *fam* to be/go ballistic.
balada [ba'lada] *f* ballad.
balaio [ba'laju] *m* basket.
balança [ba'lãnsa] *f* scales *(pl)*; **~ comercial** balance of trade.
◆ **Balança** *f* ASTRO Libra.
balançar [13] [balãn'sa(x)] <> *vt* **-1.** [fazer oscilar - bebê, navio] to rock; [- quadril] to wiggle; [- galho, carro, avião] to shake. **-2.** [compensar] to counterbalance. <> *vi* **-1.** [oscilar] to shake. **-2.** [em balanço, cadeira] to rock.
◆ **balançar-se** *vp* [sacudir-se] to sway.
balancear [15] [balãn'sja(x)] *vt* **-1.** AUTO to balance *(wheels)*. **-2.** [compensar] to counterbalance.
balancete [balãn'setʃi] *m* COM balance.
balanço [ba'lãnsu] *m* **-1.** [de criança] swing. **-2.** [ação] swinging. **-3.** ECON : **~ de pagamentos** balance of payments.
balangandã [balãngãn'dã] *m* amulet.
balão [ba'lãw] (*pl* **-ões**) *m* **-1.** [dirigível] airship. **-2.** [de brinquedo] balloon; **soltar um ~** to release a balloon. **-3.** [sonda] probe; **~ meteorológico** metereological balloon. **-4.** [tanque]: **~ de oxigênio** oxygen cylinder. **-5.** [em estrada etc] *place for doing U-turns*. **-6.** [em história em quadrinhos] bubble.
balão-de-ensaio [baˌlãwdʒĩn'saju] (*pl* **balões-de-ensaio**) *m* **-1.** [instrumento] pilot balloon. **-2.** *fig* [boato]: **soltar um ~** to spread a rumour.
balão-sonda [baˌlãw'sõnda] (*pl* **balões-sondas**) *m* pilot balloon.
balaustrada [balawʃ'trada] *f* balustrade.
balaústre [bala'uʃtri] *m* baluster.
balbuciar [16] [bawbu'sja(x)] <> *vt* to stammer. <> *vi* to babble.
balbúrdia [baw'buxdʒja] *f* hustle and bustle.
balcão [baw'kãw] (*pl* **-ões**) *m* **-1.** [sacada] balcony. **-2.** [de loja] counter. **-3.** DE TEATRO dress circle; **~ nobre** balcony; **~ simples** upper circle.
Balcãs ['bawkãʃ] *npl*: **os ~** the Balkans.
balcânico, ca [baw'kãniku, ka] <> *adj* Balkan. <> *m, f* Balkan.
balconista [bawko'niʃta] *mf* shop assistant.
balde ['bawdʒi] *m* bucket.
baldeação [bawdʒja'sãw] (*pl* **-ões**) *f* transfer; **fazer ~** to change.
baldio, dia [baw'dʒiu, dʒia] *adj* gone to wasteland.
balé [ba'lɛ] *m* ballet.
baleeira [bale'ejra] *f* whaler.
baleia [ba'leja] *f* **-1.** ZOOL whale. **-2.** *fam fig & pej* [pessoa]: **ser uma ~** to look like a beached whale.
baleiro, ra [ba'lejru, ra] <> *m, f* [vendedor] sweet seller. <> *m* [pote] sweet jar.
Bali ['bali] *n* Bali.
balido [ba'lidu] *m* bleating.
balística [ba'liʃtʃika] *f* ballistics *(sg)*.
baliza [ba'liza] *f* **-1.** [estaca] goalpost. **-2.** [bóia] buoy. **-3.** [luminosa] beacon. **-4.** ESP goal.
balizamento [baliza'mẽntu] *m* beaconing, signposting.
balneário [baw'njarju] *m* baths *(pl)*.
balões [ba'lõjʃ] *pl* ▷ **balão**.
balofo, fa [ba'lofu, fa] <> *adj* puffy. <> *m, f* puffed-up person.
balsa ['bawsa] *f* **-1.** [jangada] raft. **-2.** [barca] catamaran. **-3.** [salva-vidas] lifeboat.
bálsamo ['bawsamu] *m* balsam.
Báltico ['bawtʃiku] *n*: **o (mar) ~** the Baltic (Sea).
baluarte [ba'lwaxtʃi] *m* stronghold.
balzaquiana [bawza'kjana] *f* *woman in her late twenties or early thirties*.
bamba ['bãnba] *fam* <> *adj* [perito] expert. <> *mf* [perito] expert.
bambear [15] [bãn'bja(x)] <> *vt* [afrouxar] to loosen. <> *vi* **-1.** [tornar-se frouxo] to work itself loose. **-2.** *fig* [hesitar] to falter.
bambo, ba ['bãnbu, ba] *adj* **-1.** [corda, laço, parafuso] loose. **-2.** [perna] faltering.
bambolê [bãnbo'le] *m* hula hoop.
bamboleante [bãnbo'ljãntʃi] *adj* **-1.** [que balança] swaying. **-2.** [sem firmeza - parafuso, cordo] loose; [- estaca] wobbly.
bambolear [15] [bãnbo'lja(x)] <> *vt* [balançar] to sway. <> *vi* to sway.
bambu [bãn'bu] *m* **-1.** [planta] bamboo. **-2.** [vara] bamboo-stick.
bambuzal [bãnbu'zaw] (*pl* **-ais**)) *m* bamboo thicket.
banal [ba'naw] (*pl* **-ais**) *adj* mundane.
banalidade [banali'dadʒi] *f* simplicity.
banalizar [4] [banali'za(x)] *vt* to make commonplace.
banana [ba'nãna] <> *f* [fruta] banana; **dar uma ~ (para alguém)** *vulg fig* to say 'up yours!' (to sb). <> *mf fam fig & pej* [bobo, idiota] fool.
bananada [bana'nada] *f* banana sweetmeat.
bananal [bana'naw] (*pl* **-ais**)) *m* banana plantation.
bananeira [bana'nejra] *f* banana tree; **plantar ~** *fig* to do a handstand.
banca ['bãŋka] *f* **-1.** [de jogo] game of chance. **-2.** [estande]: **~ (de jornal)** newspaper stand. **-3.** [comissão]: **~ (examinadora)** (examination) board. **-4.** [escritório] desk. **-5.** [mesa de trabalho] worktop; **botar ~** to boss about.
bancada [bãŋ'kada] *f* **-1.** [banco] bench. **-2.** [POL - de partido] bench; [- de estado] representatives *(pl)*. **-3.** [mesa de trabalho] workbench.
bancar [12] [bãɲ'ka(x)] *vt* **-1.** [financiar] to back. **-2.** [comportar-se como] to play.

bancário, ria [bãŋ'karju, rja] ◇ *adj* bank. ◇ *m, f* [empregado] bank employee.

bancarrota [bãŋka'xota] *f* bankruptcy; **ir à ~** to go bankrupt.

banco ['bãŋku] *m* **-1.** [ger] bank; **~ 24 horas** 24-hour bank; **~ de sangue** blood bank. **-2.** [assento] bench; **~ dos réus** prisoners' dock. **-3.** *COMPUT*: **~ de dados** databank. **-4.** *GEOL*: **~ de areia** sandbank.

banda ['bãnda] *f*: *COMPUT* **~ larga** broadband.

bandagem [bãda'ʒẽ] (*pl* **-ns**) *f* bandage.

Band-aid® [bãn'dejdʒ] *m* Band-Aid®.

bandalheira [bãnda'ʎejra] *f* roguery.

bandear-se [15] [bãn'dʒjaxsi] *vp*: **~ para** *ou* **a** to side with.

bandeira [bãn'dejra, ra] *f* **-1.** [ger] flag; **~ branca** white flag; **~ a meio pau** flag at half-mast; **jurar a ~** to swear to the flag; **~ dois** taxi night-rate. **-2.** [estandarte] standard. **-3.** [de porta] fanlight. **-4.** *loc*: **dar ~ de que** to let it be known that.

bandeirante [bãndej'rãntʃi] ◇ *m* [explorador] expedition member. ◇ *f* [moça] Girl Guide.

bandeirinha [bãn'dejriɲa] *m ESP* linesman.

bandeirola [bãndej'rɔla] *f* banderole.

bandeja [bãn'deʒa] *f* tray; **dar de ~** to proffer.

bandejão [bãnde'ʒãw] (*pl* **-ões**) *m* [*UNIV* - refeição] meal on a tray; [- refeitório] canteen.

bandido, da [bãn'dʒidu, da] ◇ *m, f* **-1.** [marginal] bandit. **-2.** [mau-caráter] rogue. ◇ *adj fam fig* [malvado, ruim] cruel.

banditismo [bãndʒi'tʃiʒmu] *m* banditry.

bando ['bãndu] *m* **-1.** [de pessoas, animais] flock; **em ~** in flocks. **-2.** [quadrilha] gang. **-3.** [facção] group. **-4.** [monte] stack.

bandô [bãn'do] *m* pelmet.

bandoleiro, ra [bãndo'lejru, ra] *m, f* bandit.

bandolim [bãndo'lĩ] (*pl* **-ns**) *m* mandolin.

bandolinista [bãndoli'niʃta] *mf* mandolin player.

bangalô [bãŋga'lo] *m* bungalow.

Bangkok [bãŋg'kɔk] *n* Bangkok.

bangue-bangue [bãŋgi'bãŋgi] *m*: **(filme de) ~** Western (movie).

banguela [bãŋ'gɛla] *adj* toothless.

banha ['bãɲa] *f* **-1.** [no homem] fat. **-2.** [de porco] lard.

banhar [4] [bã'ɲa(x)] *vt* **-1.** [dar banho em] to bathe. **-2.** [mergulhar]: **~ algo (em)** to dip sthg (into). **-3.** [molhar]: **~ algo (com/em)** to bathe sthg (with/in). **-4.** [rio, mar] to wash.

◆ **banhar-se** *vp* **-1.** [tomar banho] to bathe. **-2.** [molhar-se]: **~-se em algo** to become bathed in sthg.

banheira [bã'ɲejra] *f* **-1.** [para banho] bathtub. **-2.** *fam fig* [carro] charabanc.

banheiro [bã'ɲejru] *m* toilet; **~ feminino/masculino** ladies'/men's toilet.

banhista [bã'ɲiʃta] *mf* bather.

banho ['bãɲu] *m* **-1.** [ger] immersion; **tomar um ~ de algo** to immerse o.s. in sthg. **-2.** [de entusiasmo] wave. **-3.** [para asseio]: **~ (de chuveiro)** shower; **tomar ~** to have a shower; **tomar ~ (de banheira)** to take a bath; **~ de assento** hip bath; **~ de espuma** foam bath. **-4.** [na praia, em clube etc]: **tomar um ~ de mar/piscina** to swim in the sea/pool; **tomar um ~ de sol** to sunbathe. **-5.** *fam fig* [surra]: **dar um ~ em alguém** to wipe sb out. **-6.** *loc*: **dar um ~ de algo em alguém** [derramar] to drench sb in sthg; **vai tomar ~!** *fam* get away!

banho-maria [ˌbãɲuma'ria] (*pl* **banhos-marias, banhos-maria**) *m CULIN* double boiler, bain-marie.

banimento [bani'mẽntu] *m* banishment.

banir [79] [ba'ni(x)] *vt* to banish.

banjo ['bãnʒu] *m* banjo.

banner ['banex] (*pl* **banners**) *m COMPUT* banner.

banqueiro, ra [bãɲ'kejru, ra] *m, f* banker.

banqueta [bãŋ'keta] *f* banquette.

banquete [bãŋ'ketʃi] *m* banquet.

banquetear [15] [bãŋke'tʃja(x)] *vt* [festejar] to give a banquet in honour of.

◆ **banquetear-se** *vp* [participar de banquete] to treat o.s. to a wonderful meal.

baque ['baki] *m* **-1.** [choque] shock; **levar um ~** to be given a shock; **ele levou um baque com a notícia** the news gave him a shock. **-2.** [ruído] thud. **-3.** [queda] fall.

baquear [15] [ba'kja(x)] *vi* **-1.** [cair] to fall. **-2.** *fig* [abalar-se] to be shaken.

bar ['ba(x)] (*pl* **-es**) *m* bar.

baralho [ba'raʎu] *m* pack.

barão [ba'rãw] (*pl* **-ões**) *m, f* baron.

barata [ba'rata] *f* cockroach; **estar entregue às ~s** [pessoa] to let o.s. go; [projeto, construção] to fall into a state of neglect.

baratear [15] [bara'tʃja(x)] *vt* to mark down.

barateiro, ra [bara'tejru, ra] *adj* cut-price.

baratinado, da [baratʃi'nadu, da] *adj* **-1.** [sobrecarregado, apressado] stressed. **-2.** [transtornado - pessoa] upset; [- idéia, atitude] disturbed.

baratinar [4] [baratʃi'na(x)] *vt* **-1.** [atrapalhar, assoberbar] to stress. **-2.** [transtornar] to upset.

barato, ta [ba'ratu, ta] ◇ *adj* **-1.** [produto, serviço, preço] cheap. **-2.** [barateiro] cut-price. **-3.** *fam* [ordinário] common or garden. ◇ *adv* [cobrar etc] cheaply. ◇ *m* **-1.** *gír droga* high. **-2.** *fam* [legal]: **que ~!** how cool!; **ser um ~** to be cool.

barba ['baxba] *f* **-1.** [de homem] beard; **fazer a ~** to shave; **fazer algo nas ~s de alguém** *fig* to do sthg under sb's nose; **pôr as ~s de molho** *fig* to lie low. **-2.** [de animal] whiskers.

barbada [bax'bada] *f* **-1.** *fam* [facilidade]: **ser uma ~** to be a piece of cake. **-2.** *gír turfe* [palpite] dead cert.

barbado, da [bax'badu, da] *adj* bearded.

Barbados [bax'baduʃ] *n* Barbados.

barbante [bax'bãntʃi] *m* string.

barbaramente [baxbara'mẽntʃi] *adv* **-1.** [cruelmente] brutally. **-2.** [demasiadamente] atrociously.

barbaridade [baxbari'dadʒi] *f* **-1.** [crueldade] barbarity. **-2.** [expressando espanto]: **que ~!** great! **-3.** [tolice] absurdity.

barbárie [bax'barje] *f* barbarity.

barbarismo [baxba'riʒmu] *m* barbarism.

bárbaro, ra ['baxbaru, ra] *adj* **-1.** [terrível] barbaric. **-2.** [ótimo] great.

barbatana [baxba'tãna] *f* fin.

barbeador [barbja'do(x)] (*pl* **-es**) *m* razor.

barbear [15] [bax'bja(x)] *vt* to shave.
◆ **barbear-se** *vp* to shave.

barbearia [baxbja'ria] *f* barbershop.

barbeiragem [baxbej'raʒẽ] *f* *fam* [no trânsito] bad driving; **fazer uma** ~ to drive badly.

barbeiro, ra [bax'bejru, ra] ◇ *adj* *fam* [motorista] careless. ◇ *m* **-1.** [quem corta cabelos, barba] barber. **-2.** [barbearia] barbershop. **-3.** [inseto] kissing bug.

barbicha [bax'biʃa] *fam* ◇ *f* [cavanhaque] goatee. ◇ *m* [pessoa de cavanhaque] man with a goatee.

barbitúrico [baxbi'turiku] *m* barbiturate.

barbudo, da [bax'budu, da] ◇ *adj* bearded. ◇ *m* bearded man.

barca ['baxka] *f* ship.

barcaça [bax'kasa] *f* barge.

barco ['baxku] *m* boat; ~ **a motor** motor boat; ~ **a remo** rowing boat; ~ **a vela** sailing boat; **deixar o** ~ **correr** *fig* to let matters run their course; **estar no mesmo** ~ *fig* to be in the same boat; **tocar o** ~ **para frente** *fig* to carry on with one's life.

barganha [bax'gãɲa] *f* bargain.

barganhar [4] [baxgã'ɲa(x)] *vt* & *vi* to bargain.

barítono, na [ba'ritonu, na] ◇ *adj* baritone. ◇ *m* baritone.

barlavento [baxla'vẽntu] *m* *NÁUT* windward; **a** ~ to windward.

barman ['baxmɛ] (*pl* **-s**) *m* barman.

barões [ba'rõjʃ] *pl* ▷ **barão.**

barômetro [ba'rometru] *m* barometer.

baronesa [baro'neza] *f* ▷ **barão.**

barqueiro, ra [bax'kejru, ra] *m, f* boatman.

barra ['baxa] *f* **-1.** [ger] bar; ~ **de chocolate** chocolate bar; ~**s paralelas** parallel bars. **-2.** [de metal] ingot; ~ **de direção** tiller. **-3.** [de madeira] pole. **-4.** [de balé] barre. **-5.** [traço] score. **-6.** [acabamento] trimming. **-7.** [faixa] strip. **-8.** *GEOGR* sandbar. **-9.** *loc*: **agüentar a** ~ *fam* to stick it out; **forçar a** ~ to make things difficult; **ser uma** ~ *fam* [ser difícil] to be a pain.

barraca [ba'xaka] *f* **-1.** [ger] tent. **-2.** [em feira] stall. **-3.** [de madeira] hut.

barracão [baxa'kãw] (*pl* **-ões**) *m* **-1.** [telheiro] shed. **-2.** [habitação] big house.

barraco [ba'xaku] *m* shack.

barragem [ba'xaʒẽ] (*pl* **-ns**) *f* **-1.** [represa] dam. **-2.** [barreira] barrage.

barranco [ba'xãŋku] *m* **-1.** [ribanceira] ravine. **-2.** [escarpa] escarpment. **-3.** [precipício] precipice.

barra-pesada [ˌbaxape'zada] (*pl* **barras-pesadas**) *fam* *adj* **-1.** [violento] threatening. **-2.** [difícil] tough.

barrar [4] [ba'xa(x)] *vt* **-1.** [obstruir] to block. **-2.** [excluir] to bar.

barreira [ba'xejra] *f* **-1.** [escarpa] embankment. **-2.** *fig* [dificuldade] barrier. **-3.** [fronteira] roadblock. **-4.** *ESP* hurdle.

barrento, ta [ba'xẽntu, ta] *adj* clayey.

barrete [ba'xetʃi] *m* [gorro] (woolly) hat.

barrica [ba'xika] *f* barrel.

barricada [baxi'kada] *f* barricade.

barriga [ba'xiga] *f* **-1.** *ANAT* belly. **-2.** [saliência] bulge. **-3.** *loc*: **chorar de** ~ **cheia** to complain for no reason; **tirar a** ~ **da miséria** to get one's fill.

barrigudo, da [baxi'gudu, da] *adj* pot-bellied.

barril [ba'xiw] (*pl* **-is**) *m* cask.

barro ['baxu] *m* clay.

barroco, ca [ba'xoku, ka] *adj* baroque.

barrote [ba'xɔtʃi] *m* beam.

barulheira [baru'ʎejra] *f* din.

barulhento, ta [baru'ʎẽntu, ta] *adj* noisy.

barulho [ba'ruʎu] *m* **-1.** [ruído] noise. **-2.** *fig* [confusão] fuss.

basco, ca ['baʃku, ka] ◇ *adj* Basque. ◇ *m, f* Basque.
◆ **basco** *m* [língua] Basque.

basculante [baʃku'lãntʃi] *m* swivel window.

base ['bazi] *f* **-1.** [ger] base; ~ **monetária** monetary base. **-2.** [camada] base coat. **-3.** *fig* [fundamento] basis; **com** ~ **em** based on; **na** ~ **de** with the support of.

baseado, da [ba'zjadu, da] *adj* [fundamentado] based.
◆ **baseado** *m* *fam* [droga] spliff.

basear [15] [ba'zja(x)] *vt*: ~ **algo em algo** to base sthg on sthg.
◆ **basear-se** *vp*: ~**-se em algo** to base o.s. on sthg.

básico, ca ['baziku, ka] *adj* basic.

basílica [ba'zilika] *f* basilica.

basquete [baʃ'kɛtʃi], **basquetebol** [baʃketʃi'bɔw] *m* basketball.

basta ['baʃta] ◇ *m*: **dar um** ~ **em** to stop. ◇ *interj* that's enough!

bastante [baʃ'tãntʃi] ◇ *adj* **-1.** [suficiente] enough. **-2.** [numeroso] many. ◇ *adv* enough.

bastão [baʃ'tãw] (*pl* **-ões**) *m* stick.

bastar [4] [baʃ'ta(x)] *vi* [ser suficiente] to be enough.
◆ **bastar-se** *vp* [ser auto-suficiente]: ~**-se a si próprio** to be self-sufficient.

bastardo, da [baʃ'taxdu, da] *adj* bastard.

bastião [baʃtʃi'ãw] (*pl* **-ões**) *m* **-1.** [fortificação] bastion. **-2.** *fig* [sustentáculo] bastion.

bastidor [baʃtʃi'do(x)] *m* [moldura] frame.
◆ **bastidores** *mpl* **-1.** *TEATRO* wings. **-2.** [lado secreto] shadowy side.

bastões [baʃ'tõjʃ] *pl* ▷ **bastão.**

bata ['bata] *f* **-1.** [blusa] blouse. **-2.** [jaleco] white coat, overall.

batalha [ba'taʎa] *f* **-1.** [ger] battle. **-2.** *fig* [esforço] struggle.

batalhador, ra [bataʎa'do(x), ra] *adj* hardworking.

batalhão [bata'ʎãw] (*pl* **-ões**) *m* **-1.** *MIL* battallion. **-2.** [multidão] crowd.
batalhar [4] [bata'ʎa(x)] *vi* **-1.** [combater] to battle. **-2.** *fig* [lutar] to fight.
batata [ba'tata] *f* potato; ~ **frita** chips *UK*, fries *US*; ~ **da perna** calf *(of the leg)*.
batata-doce [ba,tata'dosi] (*pl* **batatas-doces**) *f* sweet potato.
bate-boca [,batʃi'boka] (*pl* **bate-bocas**) *m* quarrel.
bate-bola [,batʃi'bɔla] (*pl* **bate-bolas**) *m* warm-up.
batedeira [bate'dejra] *f* **-1.** [para fazer bolos etc] whisk. **-2.** [para fazer manteiga] churn.
batedor [bate'do(x)] *m* **-1.** [polícia] escort. **-2.**: ~ **de carteiras** [ladrão] bag-snatcher.
batelada [bate'lada] *f* **-1.** [carregamento] boat-load. **-2.** *fig* [granda quantidade]: **uma** ~ **de** a large number of.
batente [ba'tẽntʃi] *m* **-1.** [ombreira] doorpost. **-2.** *fam* [trabalho] work; **pegar firme no** ~ to toil away.
bate-papo [,batʃi'papu] (*pl* **bate-papos**) *m fam* chat.
bater [5] [ba'te(x)] <> *vt* **-1.** [ger] to beat; ~ **o pé** to stamp one's foot. **-2.** [datilografar]: ~ **algo (à máquina)** to type sthg out. **-3.** [fechar com força] to slam. **-4.** [foto] to take. **-5.** [usar todo dia] to wear every day. **-6.** *fam* [furtar]: ~ **carteira** to pick-pocket. <> *vi* **-1.** [dar pancadas]: ~ **em alguém/algo** to hit sb/sthg. **-2.** [colidir]: ~ **em algo** to collide with sthg. **-3.** [horas, sino] to strike. **-4.** [coração] to beat. **-5.** *loc*: **não** ~ **bem** *fam* [ser meio doido] to be off one's rocker.
◆ **bater-se** *vp*: ~**-se por** to fight for.
bateria [bate'ria] *f* **-1.** [de cozinha] *set of kitchen utensils*. **-2.** [*MÚS* - instrumentos de percussão] percussion; [- conjunto de pratos, caixa e bombo] drum kit. **-3.** *ELETR* battery.
baterista [bate'riʃta] *mf* [*MÚS* - percussionista] percussionist; [- que toca bateria] drummer.
batido, da [ba'tʃidu, da] <> *adj* **-1.** [ger] beaten. **-2.** [comum demais] worn out. <> *adv* [às pressas] in a hurry.
◆ **batida** *f* **-1.** [ger] beat. **-2.** [de relógio, sino] strike. **-3.** [à porta] knock. **-4.** *AUTO* collision. **-5.** [bebida] crush.
batina [ba'tʃina] *f RELIG* cassock.
batismal [batʃiʒ'maw] (*pl* **-ais**) *adj* baptismal.
batismo [ba'tʃiʒmu] *m* baptism.
batistério [batʃiʃ'tɛrju] *m* baptistery.
batizado, da [batʃi'zadu, da] <> *adj* baptized. <> *m* baptism.
batizar [4] [batʃi'za(x)] *vt* **-1.** [ger] to baptize. **-2.** [apelidar] to nickname.
batom [ba'tõ] (*pl* **-ns**) *m* lipstick.
batucada [batu'kada] *f street gathering for samba music and expression.*
batucar [12] [batu'ka(x)] *vi* **-1.** *MÚS to dance and sing the batuque*. **-2.** [martelar] to hammer.
batuque [ba'tuki] *m Afro-Brazilian dance.*
batuta [ba'tuta] <> *f* [de maestro] baton. <> *adj fam* [exímio]: **ser** ~ **em algo** to be a maestro in sthg.
baú [ba'u] *m* trunk.
baunilha [baw'niʎa] *f* vanilla.
bazar [ba'za(x)] (*pl* **-es**) *m* **-1.** [ger] bazaar. **-2.** [loja] bazaar.
bazuca [ba'zuka] *f* bazooka.
BB (*abrev de* **Banco do Brasil**) *m Brazilian state-owned bank.*
BC (*abrev de* **Banco Central do Brasil**) *m central bank of Brazil.*
bê-á-bá [bea'ba] *m* **-1.** [abecedário] alphabet. **-2.** *fig* [noções básicas] ABC.
beatitude [beatʃi'tudʒi] *f* beatitude.
beato, ta [be'atu, ta] <> *adj* **-1.** [beatificado] blessed. **-2.** [fanático religioso] churchy. <> *m* **-1.** [quem foi beatificado] beatified person. **-2.** [devoto] worshipper.
bêbado, da ['bebadu, da] <> *adj* drunk. <> *m, f* **-1.** [que bebe regularmente] drunkard. **-2.** [que bebeu demais] drunk.
bebê [be'be] *m* baby.
bebedeira [bebe'dejra] *f* **-1.** [estado do bêbado] drunkenness; **tomar uma** ~ to get drunk. **-2.** [ato de se embebedar] drinking bout.
bêbedo ['bebedu] *adj* ▷ **bêbado**.
bebedouro [bebe'doru] *m* **-1.** [aparelho] drinking fountain. **-2.** [para animais] drinking trough.
beber [5] [be'be(x)] <> *vt* **-1.** [tomar líquido] to drink. **-2.** [absorver] to soak up. <> *vi* **-1.** [tomar bebida alcoólica] to have a drink. **-2.** [embriagar-se] to get drunk.
bebericar [12] [beberi'ka(x)] <> *vt* [beber degustando] to sip. <> *vi* [beber pouco] to sip.
beberrão, rrona [bebe'xãw, xona] <> *adj* [que bebe muito] heavy drinking. <> *m* [ébrio] heavy drinker.
bebida [be'bida] *f* **-1.** [líquido potável] drink. **-2.** [alcoólica] (alcoholic) drink.
bebível [be'bivew] (*pl* **-eis**) *adj* [tolerável] drinkable.
beca ['bɛka] *f* **-1.** [toga] robe. **-2.** *fig* [magistratura] magistrature.
beça ['bɛsa] *f*: **à** ~ [em grande quantidade] in large numbers; [ao extremo] **gostei à** ~ **da nova revista** I enjoyed the new magazine very much.
beco ['beku] *m* alley; **estar num** ~ **sem saída** to be in a catch-22 situation.
bedelho [be'deʎu] *m* latch; **meter o** ~ **em** [intrometer-se] to stick one's oar in.
beduíno, na [be'dwinu, na] <> *adj* Bedouin. <> *m, f* Bedouin.
bege ['bɛʒi] <> *adj inv* beige. <> *m* beige.
begônia [be'gonja] *f* begonia.
beiço ['bejsu] *m* lip.
beiçudo, da [bej'sudu, da] *adj* pouting.
beija-flor [,bejʒa'flo(x)] (*pl* **beija-flores**) *m* hummingbird.
beijar [4] [bej'ʒa(x)] *vt* to kiss.
◆ **beijar-se** *vp* to kiss.
beijo ['bejʒu] *m* kiss; **dar um** ~ **em alguém** to give sb a kiss.

beijoca [bej'ʒɔka] *f fam* smackeroo.
beira ['bejra] *f* edge; **à ~ de** [na borda] on the edge of; *fig* on the brink of.
beirada [bej'rada] *f* **-1.** [beira] side. **-2.** [bocado] slither.
beira-mar [ˌbejra'ma(x)] *f*: **à ~** by the sea.
beirar [4] [bej'ra(x)] *vt* **-1.** [caminhar à beira de] to walk alongside. **-2.** [estar à beira de] to be on the edge of. **-3.** [estar próximo de] to be close to.
Beirute [bej'rutʃi] *n* Beirut.
beisebol [bejze'bɔwl] *m* baseball.
belas-artes [ˌbɛla'zaxtʃiʃ] *fpl* fine arts..
beldade [bew'dadʒi] *f* **-1.** [beleza] beauty. **-2.** [mulher bonita] beautiful woman.
beleléu [bele'lɛw] *loc adv fam*: **ir para o ~** [morrer] to die; [desaparecer] to disappear; [fracassar] to fail.
Belém [be'lẽj] *n* **-1.** [no Brasil] Belém. **-2.** [na Palestina] Bethlehem.
beleza [be'leza] *f* **-1.** [de lugar etc] beauty. **-2.** [mulher bela] beautiful woman; **ser uma ~** [pessoa, lugar] to be beautiful.
belga ['bɛwga] ◇ *adj* Belgian. ◇ *m, f* Belgian.
Bélgica ['bɛwʒika] *n* Belgium.
Belgrado [bew'gradu] *n* Belgrade.
beliche [be'liʃi] *m* bunk bed.
bélico, ca ['bɛliku, ka] *adj* war *(antes de subst)*.
belicoso, cosa [beli'kozu, kɔza] *adj* **-1.** [aguerrido] quarrelsome. **-2.** [pronto para a guerra] bellicose. **-3.** [que incita à guerra] war-mongering.
beligerante [beliʒe'rãntʃi] *adj* belligerent.
beliscão [beliʃ'kãw] (*pl* **-ões**) *m* pinch; **dar um ~ alguém** to pinch sb.
beliscar [12] [beliʃ'ka(x)] ◇ *vt* **-1.** [pessoa] to pinch. **-2.** *fig* [comida] to pick at *(food)*. ◇ *vi fig* [comer] to pick at one's food.
beliscões [beliʃ'kõjʃ] *pl* ▷ **beliscão**.
Belize [be'lizi] *n* Belize.
belo, la ['bɛlu, la] ◇ *adj* **-1.** [perfeito] lovely. **-2.** [sublime] wonderful. **-3.** *(antes de subst)* [considerável] fine. **-4.** *(antes de subst)* [gratificante] excellent. **-5.** [indefinido]: **um ~ dia ...** one fine day ... ◇ *m* [estética] beauty.
Belo Horizonte [ˌbɛlori'zõntʃi] *n* Belo Horizonte.
bel-prazer [ˌbɛwpra'ze(x)] *m*: **ao seu ~** to one's heart's content.
beltrano [bew'trãnu] *m* so-and-so.
bem ['bẽj] ◇ *adv* **-1.** [ger] well. **-2.** [muito, bastante] very. **-3.** [exatamente] exactly; **~ ali** right there. **-4.** [de bom grado]: **~ que eu gostaria de ajudar, mas não posso** I'd very much like to help, but I can't. **-5.** [expressando opinião]: **estar ~** [de saúde] to be well; [de aspecto] to look good; [financeiramente] to be well-off; **cair ~** [comida] to go down well; **fazer ~ a alguém** [suj: exercício etc] to be good for sb; **ficar** *ou* **cair ~** [atitude] to be suitable; **ficar ~ em alguém** [roupa] to suit sb well. **-6.** [saudando]: **tudo ~?** *fam* how are you?; **tudo ~** [em resposta] fine. **-7.** [concordando]: **tá ~** all right. **-8.** [em conclusão, introdução] well now. **-9.** [em congratulação]: **muito ~!** well done! ◇ *m* **-1.** [ger] good. **-2.** [pessoa amada] loved one. **-3.** *fam* [forma de tratamento]: **meu ~** my darling. **-4.** [patrimônio] assets *(pl)*.
◆ **bens** *mpl* **-1.** [patrimônio] assets. **-2.** [produtos]: **~ de consumo** consumer goods.
◆ **bem como** *loc adv* as well as.
◆ **nem bem** *loc adv* scarcely.
◆ **se bem que** *loc conj* even though.
bem-acabado, da [bẽjaka'badu, da] (*mpl* **-s**, *fpl* **-s**) *adj* well-finished.
bem-agradecido, da [bẽjagrade'sidu, da] (*mpl* **-s**, *fpl* **-s**) *adj* grateful.
bem-apessoado, da [bẽjape'swadu, da] (*mpl* **-s**, *fpl* **-s**) *adj* presentable.
bem-arrumado, da [bẽjaxu'madu, da] (*mpl* **-s**, *fpl* **-s**) *adj* **-1.** [pessoa] well dressed. **-2.** [casa] well appointed.
bem-casado, da [bẽjka'zadu, da] (*mpl* **-s**, *fpl* **-s**) *adj* happily married.
bem-comportado, da [bẽjkõnpox'tadu, da] (*mpl* **-s** [-ʃ], *fpl* **-s** [-ʃ]) *adj* well behaved.
bem-conceituado, da [bẽjkõnsej'twadu, da] (*mpl* **-s** [-ʃ], *fpl* **-s** [-ʃ]) *adj* well respected.
bem-disposto, ta [bẽjdʒiʃ'poʃtu, ta] *adj* good-humoured.
bem-educado, da [bẽjedu'kadu, da] (*mpl* **-s**, *fpl* **-s**) *adj* well bred.
bem-estar [bẽjʃ'ta(x)] *m* well-being.
bem-feito, ta [bẽj'fejtu, ta] (*mpl* **-s**, *fpl* **-s**) *adj* **-1.** [bem-acabado] well made. **-2.** [de belas formas] elegant. **-3.** [quando algo ruim ocorre]: **~** serves you right!
bem-humorado, da [bẽjumo'radu, da] (*mpl* **-s**, *fpl* **-s**) *adj* good-humoured.
bem-intencionado, da [bẽjĩntẽnsjo'nadu, da] (*mpl* **-s**, *fpl* **-s**) *adj* well meaning.
bem-me-quer [bẽjmi'kɛ(x)] *m* daisy.
bem-nascido, da [bẽjna'sidu, da] (*mpl* **-s**, *fpl* **-s**) *adj* well born.
bem-passado, da [bẽjpa'sadu, da] (*mpl* **-s**, *fpl* **-s**) *adj* [carne] well cooked.
bem-sucedido, da [bẽjsuse'dʒidu, da] (*mpl* **-s**, *fpl* **-s**) *adj* successful.
bem-te-vi [bẽjtʃi'vi] (*pl* **bem-te-vis**) *m* great kiskadee.
bem-vindo, da [bẽj'vĩndu, da] *adj* welcome.
bem-visto, ta [bẽj'viʃtu, ta] (*mpl* **-s**, *fpl* **-s**) *adj* respected.
benchmarking [bɛnʃmarkiŋ] *m* ECON benchmarking.
bençāo [bẽnsãw] (*pl* **-ções**) *f* blessing.
bendito, ta [bẽn'dʒitu, ta] *adj* [abençoado] blessed.
bendizer [29] [bẽndʒi'ze(x)] *vt* **-1.** [falar bem de] to praise. **-2.** [abençoar] to bless.
beneficência [benefi'sẽnsja] *f* **-1.** [bondade] kindness. **-2.** [caridade] charity.
beneficente [benefi'sẽntʃi] *adj* **-1.** [bondoso] kind. **-2.** [caridoso] charitable.
beneficiado, da [benefi'sjadu, da] ◇ *adj* [que se beneficiou] benefitting. ◇ *m* [beneficiário] beneficiary.

beneficiar [16] [benefi'sja(x)] *vt* **-1.** [favorecer] to benefit. **-2.** [processar] to process. **-3.** [melhorar] to improve.
◆ **beneficiar-se** *vp* [favorecer-se] to profit.
beneficiário, ria [benefi'sjarju, rja] ◇ *adj* favoured. ◇ *m* [herdeiro beneficiado] beneficiary.
benefício [bene'fisju] *m* benefit.
benéfico, ca [be'nɛfiku, ka] *adj* **-1.** [ger] beneficial. **-2.** [favorável] favourable.
benemérito, ta [bene'mɛritu, ta] ◇ *adj* **-1.** [que merece o bem] deserving. **-2.** [digno de honras] praiseworthy. **-3.** [ilustre] renowned. ◇ *m* worthy person.
beneplácito [bene'plasitu] *m* [aprovação] approval.
benevolência [benevo'lẽnsja] *f* **-1.** [boa-vontade] benevolence. **-2.** [complacência] friendliness. **-3.** [afeto] kindness.
benevolente [benevo'lẽntʃi] *adj* **-1.** [bondoso] kindly. **-2.** [complacente] friendly.
benévolo, la [benɛ'volu, la] *adj* **-1.** [benevolente] benevolent. **-2.** [tolerante] tolerant.
benfazejo, ja [bẽnfa'zeʒu, ʒa] *adj* [benéfico] beneficial.
benfeitor, ra [bẽnfej'to(x), ra] ◇ *adj* [benévolo] benevolent. ◇ *m* [aquele que faz benfeitoria] benefactor.
benfeitoria [bẽnfejto'ria] *f* **-1.** [obra de melhoria] improvement. **-2.** [benefício] benefit.
bengala [bẽŋ'gala] *f* walking stick.
benigno, na [be'nignu, na] *adj* **-1.** [benévelo] gentle. **-2.** [complacente] friendly. **-3.** *MED* benign.
benjamim [bẽnʒa'mĩ] (*pl* **-ns**) *m ELETR* adaptor.
benquisto, ta [bẽn'kiʃtu, ta] *adj* **-1.** [querido] loved. **-2.** [bem-aceito] welcomed.
bens ['bẽjʃ] *pl* ▷ **bem**.
bento, ta ['bẽntu, ta] ◇ *pp* ▷ **benzer**. ◇ *adj* holy.
benzedeira [bẽnze'dejra] *f* healer.
benzer [5] [bẽn'ze(x)] *vt* [abençoar] to bless.
◆ **benzer-se** *vp* [fazer o sinal-da-cruz] to make the sign of the cross.
benzina [bẽn'zina] *f* benzine.
berbere [bex'bɛri], **berber** [bex'bɛ(x)] ◇ *adj* Berber. ◇ *mf* Berber.
◆ **berbere** *m* [língua] Berber.
berçário [bex'sarju] *m* nursery.
berço ['bexsu] *m* **-1.** cradle. **-2.** *loc*: **nascer em ~ de ouro** to be born with a silver spoon in one's mouth.
Berlim [bex'lĩ] *n* Berlin.
berimbau [berĩn'baw] *m MÚS* berimbau, *small Brazilian percussion instrument.*
berinjela [berĩn'ʒɛla] *f* aubergine *UK*, eggplant *US*.
berlinda [bex'lĩnda] *f*: **estar na ~** to be the butt of jokes.
berloque [bex'lɔki] *m* trinket.
bermuda [bex'muda] *f* Bermuda shorts *(pl)*.
berrante [bex'ãntʃi] *adj* gaudy.
barrar [4] [ba'xa(x)] *vt* to bar.
berreiro [be'xejru] *m* **-1.** [gritaria] shouting. **-2.** [choradeira] wailing.
berro ['bɛxu] *m* bellow; **estar aos ~s** to be bellowing; **falar aos ~s** to talk too loud.
besouro [be'zoru] *m* beetle.
besta ['beʃta] *fam* ◇ *adj* **-1.** [pedante] pedantic. **-2.** [idiota] idiotic; **fazer alguém de ~** to make a fool of sb. **-3.** [surpreso]: **ficar ~** to be dumbfounded. **-4.** [insignificante] insignificant. ◇ *f* **-1.** [animal] beast. **-2.** *fam* [pessoa pedante] pedant. **-3.** *fam* [pessoa idiota] fool.
bestalhão, lhona [beʃta'ʎãw, ʎona] (*mpl* **-lhões**, *fpl* **-s**) ◇ *adj* **-1.** [pateta] idiotic. **-2.** [ignorante] ignorant. ◇ *m* **-1.** [paspalhão] simpleton. **-2.** [ignorante] ignoramus.
bestial [beʃ'tjaw] (*pl* **-ais**) *adj* **-1.** [brutal] bestial. **-2.** [repugnante] depraved.
bestialidade [beʃtʃjali'dadʒi] *f* bestiality.
bestificar [12] [beʃtʃifi'ka(x)] *vt* **-1.** [bestializar] to bestialize. **-2.** [assombrar] to dumbfound. **-3.** [imbecilizar] to stupefy.
best-seller [ˌbɛʃt'sɛle(x)] (*pl* **-s**) *m* best-seller.
besuntar [4] [bezũn'ta(x)] *vt* **-1.** [untar]: **~ de** *ou* **com** to grease with. **-2.** [lambuzar]: **~ de** *ou* **com** to smear.
beterraba [bete'xaba] *f* beetroot.
betoneira [beto'nejra] *f* cement mixer.
betume [be'tumi] *m* bitumen.
bexiga [be'ʃiga] *f ANAT* bladder.
bezerro, rra [be'zexu, xa] *m, f* calf; **pensar na morte da bezerra** to daydream.
bibelô [bibe'lo] *m* [objeto decorativo] knick-knack.
bíblia ['biblja] *f* bible.
◆ **Bíblia** *f* Bible.
bíblico, ca ['bibliku, ka] *adj* biblical.
bibliografia [bibljogra'fia] *f* bibliography.
biblioteca [bibljo'tɛka] *f* library.
bibliotecário, ria [bibljote'karju, rja] *m, f* librarian.
biblioteconomia [bibljotekono'mia] *f* librarianship.
biboca [bi'bɔka] *f* **-1.** [casebre] hut. **-2.** [venda] small shop.
bica ['bika] *f* water outlet; **suar em ~s** to be streaming with perspiration.
bicada [bi'kada] *f* peck.
bicama [bi'kãma] *f* sofa bed.
bicampeão, peã [bikãnpjãw, pja] (*mpl* **-peões**, *fpl* **-s**) ◇ *adj* twice champion. ◇ *m* twice champion.
bicar [12] [bi'ka(x)] *vt* **-1.** [dar bicadas] to peck. **-2.** [bebericar] to sip.
bicarbonato [bikaxbo'natu] *m* bicarbonate.
bicentenário, ria [bisẽnte'narju, rja] ◇ *adj* bicentennial. ◇ *m* bicentenary.
bíceps ['biseps] *m (inv)* biceps.
bicha ['biʃa] *f* **-1.** [lombriga] earthworm. **-2.** *fam pej* [efeminado] fairy.
bichado, da [bi'ʃadu, da] *adj* worm-eaten.
bicheiro [bi'ʃejru] *m* [em jogo do bicho] bookie *(collecting money for illegal lottery bets).*

bicho ['biʃu] *m* **-1.** [animal] animal. **-2.** [inseto, piolho] insect. **-3.** *fam* [pessoa feia]: **ser um ~** to be enough to scare one's own mother. **-4.** *fam* [sujeito] mate. **-5.** [loc]: **ver que ~ dá** to see what will come of it; **virar ~** *fig* to turn nasty.

bicho-da-seda [ˌbiʃuda'seda] (*pl* **bichos-da-seda**) *m* silkworm.

bicho-de-sete-cabeças (*pl* **bichos-de-sete-cabeças**) *fam m* **-1.** [coisa difícil]: **ser um ~** to be hideous; **fazer um ~ de algo** to make a mountain out of a molehill. **-2.** [coisa que amedronta]: **ser um ~** to be a hideous thing.

bicho-do-mato [ˌbiʃudu'matu] (*pl* **bichos-do-mato**) *m fig* [pessoa] loner.

bicho-papão [ˌbiʃopa'pãw] (*pl* **bichos-papões**) *m* **-1.** [imagem] bogeyman. **-2.** *fig* [coisa ou pessoa que amedronta]: **o diretor é severo mas não é nenhum ~** the manager is strict but he won't eat you; **a idéia do fim do mundo é um ~** the idea of the end of the world is a terrifying prospect.

bicicleta [besi'klɛta] *f* bicycle; **~ ergométrica** ergonometric bicycle; **andar de ~** to ride a bike.

bicicletário [bisikle'tarju] *m* cycle rack.

bico ['biku] *m* **-1.** [de ave] beak. **-2.** [ponta] tip. **-3.** *fam* [boca] mouth; **abrir o ~** to pipe up; **calar o ~** to pipe down. **-4.** [chupeta] teat. **-5.** *fam* [biscate] odd job. **-6.** ANAT: **~ do peito** nipple. **-7.** [de gás] burner.

bico-de-papagaio [ˌbikudʒipapa'gaju] (*pl* **bicos-de-papagaio**) *m* **-1.** [doença] osteophyte on the spinal column. **-2.** [nariz adunco] hooked nose.

bicolor [biko'lo(x)] *adj* bicoloured.

bicudo, da [bi'kudu, da] ◇ *adj* **-1.** [que tem bico] beaked. **-2.** [pontiagudo] pointed. **-3.** *fam* [difícil] painful. ◇ *m* [peixe] boulengerella.

BID (*abrev de* **Banco Interamericano de Desenvolvimento**) *m* IDB.

bidê [bi'de] *m* bidet.

bidimensional [bidʒimẽnsjo'naw] (*pl* **-ais**) *adj* two-dimensional.

Bielo-Rússia [bjɛlo'xusja] *n* Belarus.

bielo-russo, sa, bielorusso, sa [bjɛlo'xusu, ˌsa] ◇ *adj* Belorussian. ◇ *m, f* Belorussian.

bienal [bje'naw] (*pl* **-ais**) ◇ *adj* biennial. ◇ *f* biennial.

biênio ['bjenju] *m* two years.

bife ['bifi] *m* **-1.** CULIN steak; **~ a cavalo** steak with a fried egg; **~ à milanesa** steak milanese. **-2.** [pele humana]: **tirar um ~** to nick one's skin.

bifocal [bifo'kaw] (*pl* **-ais**) *adj* bifocal.

bifurcado, da [bifux'kadu, da] *adj* forked.

bifurcar [12] [bifux'ka(x)] *vi* to fork.
◆ **bifurcar-se** *vp* to fork.

bigamia [biga'mia] *f* bigamy.

bígamo, ma ['bigamu, ma] ◇ *adj* bigamous. ◇ *m, f* bigamist.

bigode [bi'gɔdʒi] *m* moustache.

bigodudo, da [bigo'dudu, da] *adj* moustached.

bigorna [bi'gɔxna] *f* anvil.

bijuteria [biʒute'ria] *f* piece of jewellery.

bilateral [bilate'raw] (*pl* **-ais**) *adj* bilateral.

bilhão [bi'ʎãw] (*pl* **-ões**) *num* billion.

bilhar [bi'ʎa(x)] (*pl* **-es**) *m* **-1.** [jogo] billiards *(sg)*. **-2.** [estabelecimento] billiard hall.

bilhete [bi'ʎetʃi] *m* **-1.** [ger] ticket; **~ de ida** one-way ticket; **~ de ida e volta** return ticket. **-2.** [mensagem] note; **dar o ~ azul** to sack; **receber o ~ azul** to be given the sack.

bilheteiro, ra [biʎe'tejru, ra] *m, f* ticket clerk.

bilheteria [biʎete'ria] *f* ticket office.

bilhões [bi'ʎõjʃ] *pl* ▷ **bilhão.**

biliar [bili'a(x)] *adj* bilious; **vesícula ~** gall bladder.

bilíngüe [bi'lĩŋgwi] *adj* bilingual.

bilionário, ria [biljo'narju, rja] ◇ *adj* billionaire. ◇ *m, f* billionaire.

bílis ['biliʃ] *f (inv)* bile.

bimensal [bimẽn'saw] (*pl* **-ais**) *adj* fortnightly, twice-monthly.

bimestral [bimeʃ'traw] (*pl* **-ais**) *adj* two-monthly.

bimestre [bi'meʃtri] *m* two-month period.

bimotor [bimo'to(x)] ◇ *adj* twin-engined. ◇ *m* twin-engined plane.

binário, ria [bi'narju, rja] *adj* binary.

bingo ['bĩŋgu] *m* bingo.

binóculo [bi'nɔkulu] *m* binoculars *(pl)*.

binômio [bi'nomju] *m* MAT binomial.

biodegradável [bjwdegra'davew] (*pl* **-eis**) *adj* biodegradable.

biodiversidade [bjwdʒivexsi'dadʒi] *f* biodiversity.

BIODIVERSIDADE

Over 20% of the world's existing plants can be found in Brazil; the country's animal biodiversity is equally rich: Brazilian fauna includes not only 10% of all amphibians and mammals in the world, but also 17% of the planet's existing birds.

bioengenharia [biowẽnʒeɲa'ria] *f* bioengineering.

biofísica [bjo'fizika] *f* biophysics *(sg)*.

biografia [bjogra'fia] *f* biography.

biográfico, ca [bjo'grafiku, ka] *adj* biographical.

biógrafo, fa ['bjɔgrafu, fa] *m, f* biographer.

biologia [bjolo'ʒia] *f* biology.

biológico, ca [bjo'lɔʒiku, ka] *adj* biological.

biólogo, ga ['bjɔlogu, ga] *m, f* biologist.

biombo ['bjõnbu] *m* screen.

biônico, ca ['bjoniku, ka] *adj* **-1.** [relativo à biônica] bionic. **-2.** *irôn* & POL *undemocratically appointed politician*.

biópsia [bjɔp'sia] *f* biopsy.

bioquímica [bjo'kimika] *f* biochemistry.

biorritmo [bjo'xitʃmu] *m* biorhythm.

BIOS (*abrev de* **Basic Input/Output System**) *m* BIOS.

biosfera [bjos'fɛra] *f* biosphere.

bipartidário, ria [bipaxtʃi'darju, rja] *adj* bipartisan.

bipartidarismo [bipaxtʃida'riʒmu] *m* bipartisanship.
bípede ['bipedʒi] *adj* biped.
biqueira [bi'kejra] *f* **-1.** [ger] tip. **-2.** [calha] gutter.
biquíni [bi'kini] *m* bikini.
BIRD (*abrev de* **Banco Internacional de Reconstrução e Desenvolvimento**) *m* IBRD.
birita [bi'rita] *f fam* (alcoholic) drink.
Birmânia [bix'mãnja] *n* Burma.
birmanês, esa [bixma'neʃ, eza] ⬦ *adj* Burmese. ⬦ *m, f* Burmese.
◆ **birmanês** *m* [língua] Burmese.
birosca [bi'rɔʃka] *f* **-1.** [pequena mercearia] small shop. **-2.** [botequim] snack bar.
birra ['bixa] *f* **-1.** [teimosia] temper; **fazer ~** to throw a tantrum. **-2.** [irritação, zanga]: **ficar de ~ com alguém** to be at loggerheads with sb.
birrento, ta [bi'xẽntu, ta] *adj* wilful.
biruta [bi'ruta] ⬦ *adj* [pessoa] mad. ⬦ *m* [pessoa] madman. ⬦ *f* [dispositivo] windsock.
bis ['biʃ] ⬦ *m* encore; **pedir um ~** to demand an encore; **fazer** *ou* **dar um ~** to give an encore. ⬦ *interj* encore!
bisar [4] [bi'za(x)] *vt* **-1.** [pedir repetição de] to demand an encore. **-2.** [repetir] to give an encore.
bisavô, vó [biza'vo, vɔ] *m, f* great-grandfather (*f* great-grandmother).
◆ **bisavós** *mpl* great-grandparents.
bisbilhotar [4] [biʒbiʎo'ta(x)] ⬦ *vt* [examinar] to pry. ⬦ *vi fam* [fazer mexericos] to gossip.
bisbilhoteiro, ra [biʒbiʎo'tejru, ra] ⬦ *adj* **-1.** [curioso] nosy. **-2.** [mexeriqueiro] gossipy. ⬦ *m, f* **-1.** [pessoa curiosa] nosy parker. **-2.** [pessoa mexeriqueira] gossip.
bisbilhotice [biʒ'biʎo'tʃisi] *f* **-1.** [curiosidade] meddling. **-2.** [mexerico] gossip.
biscate [biʃ'katʃi] *m fam* odd job.
biscateiro, ra [biʃka'tejru, ra] *m, f* odd-job man.
biscoito [biʃ'kojtu] *m* biscuit; **~ amanteigado** buttery biscuit.
bisnaga [biʒ'naga] *f* **-1.** [pão] baguette. **-2.** [tubo] tube.
bisneto, ta [biʒ'nɛtu, ta] *m, f* great-grandchild.
bisonho, nha [bi'zɔɲu, ɲa] *adj* **-1.** [inexperiente] inexperienced. **-2.** [novato] novice.
bispado [biʃ'padu] *m* **-1.** [diocese] diocese. **-2.** [dignidade episcopal] episcopate.
bispo ['biʃpu] *m* bishop.
bissexto, ta [bi'sejʃtu, ta] *adj*: **ano ~** leap year.
◆ **bissexto** *m* 29 February.
bissexual [bisek'swaw] (*pl* **-ais**) ⬦ *adj* bisexual. ⬦ *m* bisexual.
bisturi [biʃtu'ri] *m* scalpel.
bit ['bitʃi] *m* COMPUT bit.
bitmap ['bitimapi] *m* COMPUT bitmap.
bitola [bi'tɔla] *f* gauge.
bizarro, a [bi'zaxu, xa] *adj* bizarre.
blablablá [blabla'bla] *m fam* chatter.
black-tie [blɛk'taj] *m* black tie, dinner jacket.
blasé [bla'ze] *adj* blasé.
blasfemar [4] [blaʃfe'ma(x)] ⬦ *vt* RELIG to take in vain. ⬦ *vi* **-1.** RELIG to swear. **-2.** [praguejar]: **~ contra** to defame.
blasfêmia [blaʃ'femja] *f* **-1.** RELIG blasphemy. **-2.** [ultraje] defamation.
blasfemo, ma [blaʃ'femu, ma] *adj* [palavras] blasphemous.
◆ **blasfemo** *m* [pessoa] blasphemer.
blazer ['blejzɛ(x)] (*pl* **-es**) *m* blazer.
blecaute [ble'kawtʃi] *m* blackout.
blefar [4] [ble'fa(x)] ⬦ *vi* **-1.** [em jogo] to bluff. **-2.** [tapear] to deceive. ⬦ *vt* [tapear] to trick.
blefe ['blɛfi] *m* **-1.** [truque] trick. **-2.** [no jogo] bluff.
blindado, da [blĩn'dadu, da] *adj* armoured.
blindagem [blĩn'daʒẽ] *f* armour.
blitz ['blitiʃ] (*pl* **blitze**) *f* blitz.
bloco ['blɔku] *m* **-1.** [ger] block. **-2.** [papel] pad. **-3.** [grupo]: **~ de Carnaval** group of carnival revellers.
◆ **em bloco** *loc adv* en bloc.
bloquear [15] [blo'kja(x)] *vt* **-1.** [cercar] to surround. **-2.** [impedir] to block off. **-3.** PSIC to block.
bloqueio [blo'keju] *m* **-1.** [cerco] blockade. **-2.** [obstrução] obstacle; MED, PSIC blockage. **-3.** ECON : **~ econômico** economic blockade.
blue chip [bluw'ʃipi] (*pl* **blue chips**) *f* ECON blue chip.
blues ['bluwʃ] *m (inv)* MÚS blues.
blusa ['bluza] *f* blouse.
BM (*abrev de* **Banco Mundial**) *m* World Bank.
BM & F (*abrev de* **Bolsa de Mercadorias e Futuros**) *f Brazilian commodities and futures market.*
BNDES (*abrev de* **Banco Nacional de Desenvolvimento Econômico e Social**) *m Brazilian bank for financing economic and social development.*
BNH (*abrev de* **Banco Nacional da Habitação**) *m national bank for financing low-paid workers to buy their own homes.*
BO (*abrev de* **Boletim de Ocorrência**) *m Brazilian crime report.*
boa ['boa] *f* ▻ **bom.**
boa-fé [ˌboa'fɛ] *f* **-1.** [ger] good faith; **agir de ~** to act in good faith. **-2.** [ingenuidade] naivety.
boa-gente [ˌboa'ʒẽntʃi] *adj (inv)* trustworthy.
boa-noite [ˌboa'nojtʃi] (*pl* **boas-noites**) *f* good night.
boa-pinta [ˌboa'pĩnta] (*pl* **boas-pintas**) *fam* ⬦ *adj* good-looking. ⬦ *m* looker.
boa-praça [ˌboa'prasa] (*pl* **boas-praças**) *UK fam adj* kind-hearted.
boas-festas [ˌboaʒ'fɛʃtaʃ] *fpl inv* [felicitações - no Natal] Happy Christmas; [- no Ano-Novo] Happy New Year.
boas-vindas [ˌboaʒ'vĩndaʃ] *fpl inv* welcome.
boa-tarde [ˌboa'taxdʒi] (*pl* **boas-tardes**) *f* good afternoon.
boataria [bwata'ria] *f* rumour.
boate ['bwatʃi] *f* nightclub.
boateiro, ra [bwa'tejru, ra] ⬦ *adj* gossipy. ⬦ *m, f* rumour-monger.

boato ['bwatu] *m* rumour.
boa-vida [ˌboa'vida] (*pl* **boas-vidas**) *m* bon vivant.
Boa Vista [ˌboa'viʃta] *n* Boa Vista.
bobagem [bo'baʒẽ] (*pl* **-ns**) <> *f* **-1.** [coisa supérflua] frippery. **-2.** [dito] rubbish. **-3.** [fato sem importância] trifle. <> *adj* [desaconselhável]: **ser ~ fazer algo** to be foolish to do sthg.
bobalhão, lhona [boba'ʎaw, ʎona] (*mpl* **-lhões**, *fpl* **-s**) *m, f* fool.
bobeada [bo'bjada] *f fam* foolishness; **dar uma ~** to be a fool.
bobear [15] [bo'bja(x)] *vi* **-1.** [fazer besteira] to make a mistake. **-2.** [deixar-se enganar] to be tricked. **-3.** [descuidar-se] to be careless. **-4.** [perder uma chance] to blow it.
bobeira [bo'bejra] *f* mistake; **marcar ~** *fam* [ser enganado] to be a fool; [perder uma chance] to blow it.
bobina [bo'bina] *f* bobbin.
bobo, ba ['bobu, ba] <> *adj* foolish. <> *m, f* fool.
◆ **bobo** *m*: **~ da corte** court jester.
bobó [bo'bɔ] *m* CULIN : **~ (de camarão)** *shrimp bobó.*
boboca [bo'bɔka] <> *mf* idiot. <> *adj* idiotic.
boca ['boka] *f* **-1.** [ger] mouth; **~ do estômago** MED cardia; **~ da noite** nightfall; **cala a ~!** *fam* shut up! **-2.** [de calça] top. **-3.** *fam* [emprego] opening. **-4.** *fam* [pessoa para alimentar] mouth to feed. **-5.** POL : **~ de urna** ballot-box slit. **-6.** *loc*: **bater ~** to argue; **botar a ~ no trombone** *fam* [denunciar] to complain loudly; **falar da ~ para fora** not to mean what one is saying.
◆ **de boca** *loc adv* unwritten.
boca-a-boca [ˌboka'boka] <> *m* MED mouth-to-mouth resuscitation. <> *adj*: **respiração ~** kiss of life.
boca-de-fumo [ˌbokadʒi'fumu] (*pl* **bocas-de-fumo**) *f fam* drug-dealing patch.
boca-de-sino [ˌbokadʒi'sinu] *adj inv* flared, bell-bottomed.
bocadinho [boka'dʒiɲu] *m* **-1.** [pequena quantidade]: **um ~ (de)** a little bit (of). **-2.** [tempo curto]: **um ~** a little bit.
bocado [bo'kadu] *m* **-1.** [grande quantidade]: **um ~ de** quite a lot of. **-2.** [pedaço, porção]: **um ~ (de)** a bit (of). **-3.** [mordida] mouthful.
◆ **um bocado** *loc adv* [bastante] quite.
bocal [bo'kaw] (*pl* **-ais**) *m* **-1.** [ger] mouth. **-2.** MÚS mouthpiece.
boçal [bo'saw] (*pl* **-ais**) *adj* **-1.** [ignorante] stupid. **-2.** [grosseiro] rude.
boçalidade [bosali'dadʒi] *f* **-1.** [ignorância] stupidity. **-2.** [grosseria] rudeness.
boca-livre [ˌboka'livri] (*pl* **bocas-livres**) *f* **-1.** [em evento] free meal. **-2.** [em serviços públicos] gravy train, *a place where a blind eye is turned to the misappropriation of public funds.*
bocejar [4] [bose'ʒa(x)] *vi* to yawn.
bocejo [bo'seʒu] *m* yawn.
boceta [bu'seta] *f vulg* [vulva] cunt.
bochecha [bu'ʃeʃa] *f* cheek.
bochechar [4] [boʃe'ʃa(x)] <> *vt* to rinse one's mouth with. <> *vi* to rinse one's mouth.
bochecho [bo'ʃeʃu] *m* mouthwash.
bochechudo, da [boʃe'ʃudu, da] *adj* chubby-cheeked.
bocó [bo'kɔ] *adj* **-1.** [infantil] childish. **-2.** [tolo] silly.
bodas ['bodaʃ] *fpl* wedding anniversary *(sg)*; **~ de ouro** golden wedding *(sg)*; **~ de prata** silver wedding *(sg)*.
bode ['bɔdʒi] *m* **-1.** ZOOL billy goat; **~ expiatório** *fig* scapegoat. **-2.** *fam* [problema]: **dar ~** to be hell to pay.
bodega [bo'dɛga] *f* **-1.** *fam* [coisa sem valor] rubbish. **-2.** [taberna] tavern.
boêmia [bo'emja] *f* bohemian lifestyle.
Boêmia [bo'emja] *n* Bohemia.
boêmio, mia [bo'emju, mja] <> *adj* **-1.** [vida etc] bohemian. **-2.** [da Boêmia] Bohemian. <> *m, f* **-1.** [pessoa boêmia] bohemian. **-2.** [da Boêmia] Bohemian.
bofe ['bɔfi] *m fam* **-1.** [pulmão] lungs *(pl)*. **-2.** *fam* [pessoa feia] monster.
bofetada [bofe'tada] *f* slap in the face.
bofetão [bofe'tãw] (*pl* **-ões**) *m* hard slap on the face.
Bogotá [bogo'ta] *n* Bogotá.
boi ['boj] *m* ox.
bói ['bɛj] *m* office boy.
bóia ['bɔja] *f* **-1.** NÁUT buoy; **~ salva-vidas** lifebuoy. **-2.** *fam* [comida] grub.
boiada [bo'jada] *f* drove of oxen.
bóia-fria [ˌbɔja'fria] (*pl* **bóias-frias**) *m* agricultural dayworker.
boiar [4] [bo'ja(x)] *vi* **-1.** [flutuar] to float. **-2.** *fam* [não entender]: **estar/ficar boiando** to be thrown by.
boicotar [4] [bojko'ta(x)] *vt* to boycott.
boicote [boj'kɔtʃi] *m* boycott.
boiler ['bɔjle(x)] (*pl* **-s**) *m* boiler.
boina ['bojna] *f* cap.
bojo ['boʒu] *m* **-1.** [saliência] bulge. **-2.** [de navio] belly.
bojudo, da [bo'ʒudu, da] *adj* rounded.
bola ['bɔla] *f* **-1.** [objeto] ball; **ser bom de ~** to play football very well; **~ de futebol** football; **~ de gude** marble; **~ de neve** snowball; *fig* [situação] snowball. **-2.** ESP [jogada] shot. **-3.** *fam fig* [cabeça]: **não ser bom da ~** to be not right in the head. **-4.** *fam fig* [pessoa engraçada]: **ser uma ~** to be a good laugh. **-5.** *loc*: **dar ~ para alguém** [flertar] to flirt with sb; **dar ~ para algo** [dar importância a] to care about sthg; **não dar ~ (para)** [ignorar] to ignore; **não dar ~ para algo** [não dar importância a] to ignore sthg; **pisar na ~** *fig* to make a mistake; **trocar as ~s** to get mixed up.
bolacha [bo'laʃa] *f* **-1.** [biscoito] biscuit; **~ d'água** water biscuit. **-2.** *fam* [bofetada]: **dar uma ~ em alguém** to slap sb; **levar uma ~ de alguém** to be slapped by sb. **-3.** [em bares, restaurantes] coaster.

bolada [bo'lada] *f* **-1.** [pancada] hit *(with a ball)*. **-2.** [vez]: **de uma ~ só** in one go. **-3.** [de dinheiro] jackpot.
bolar [4] [bo'la(x)] ◇ *vt* to devise. ◇ *vi* to be successful.
boléia [bo'lɛja] *f* lorry driver's seat.
boletim [bole'tʃĩ] (*pl* **-ns**) *m* **-1.** [publicação] bulletin. **-2.** *EDUC* school report. **-3.** [nota] memo; **~ médico** medical report.
boleto [bo'letu] *m* requisition.
bolha ['boʎa] ◇ *f* **-1.** [em líquido, material] bubble. **-2.** [na pele] blister. ◇ *mf fam* [pessoa] bore.
boliche [bo'liʃi] *m* **-1.** [jogo] pool. **-2.** [estabelecimento] pool room.
bolinagem [bolina'ʒẽ] (*pl* **-ns**) *f* *fam* touching up.
bolinar [4] [boli'na(x)] *vt fam* to touch up.
bolinho [bo'liɲu] *m* croquette; **~ de bacalhau** salt cod croquette.
Bolívia [bo'livja] *n* Bolivia.
boliviano, na [boli'vjãnu, na] ◇ *adj* Bolivian. ◇ *m, f* Bolivian.
bolo ['bolu] *m* **-1.** *CULIN* cake. **-2.** [quantidade]: **um ~ de** a load of. **-3.** *fam* [confusão] commotion; **dar o maior ~** to cause a commotion; **deu o maior ~ quando ...** there was a great to-do when ... **-4.** [em jogo etc] stake. **-5.** *loc*: **dar o ~ em alguém** to stand sb up.
bolor [bo'lo(x)] *m* mould.
bolorento, ta [bolo'rẽntu, ta] *adj* mouldy.
bolota [bo'lɔta] *f* **-1.** [fruto do carvalho] acorn. **-2.** [caroço] lump.
bolsa ['bowsa] *f* **-1.** [acessório] purse. **-2.** *EDUC*: **~ (de estudos)** bursary. **-3.** *FIN*: **~ (de valores)** stock market. **-4.** *MED*: **~ d'água** amniotic sac.
bolsista [bow'siʃta] *EDUC* ◇ *adj* scholarship *(antes de subst)*. ◇ *mf* scholarship holder.
bolso ['bowsu] *m* pocket; **de ~** pocket *(antes de subst)*.
bom, boa ['bõ, 'boa] (*mpl* **bons**, *fpl* **boas**) *adj* **-1.** [ger] good; **ser ~ em algo** to be good at sthg; **ficar ~** to be well made/done. **-2.** [curado] well. **-3.** [seguro] safe. **-4.** [amplo, confortável] spacious. **-5.** [em saudação]: **tudo ~?** how are you? **-6.** [pedindo opinião, permissão]: **está ~?** all right?
◆ **bom** ◇ *interj*: **que ~!** how great! ◇ *m*: **o ~ é que ...** the good thing is that ...
◆ **bons** *mpl* [pessoas honradas]: **os bons** the great.
◆ **boa** *fam* ◇ *adj f* [boazuda] sexy. ◇ *f irôn* [situação difícil]: **meter-se numa boa** to put o.s. in a tight spot; **livrar-se de uma boa** to get out of a tight spot.
◆ **às boas** *loc adv*: **viver às boas com alguém** to get on well with sb; **voltar às boas (com alguém)** to make up (with sb).
bomba ['bõnba] *f* **-1.** [explosivo] bomb; **~ atômica** atomic bomb; **~ de hidrogênio** hydrogen bomb. **-2.** [fogo de artifício] rocket. **-3.** [máquina, aparelho] pump; **~ d'água** water pump; **~ de ar** air pump; **~ de gasolina** petrol pump; **~ de incêndio** fire extinguisher. **-4.** *fig* [acontecimento] shock. **-5.** *fig* [coisa ruim]: **ser uma ~** to be a flop. **-6.** *EDUC*: **levar ~ (em algo)** to fail at sthg. **-7.** [trabalho mal-acabado]: **estar/ficar uma ~** to be/end up shoddy. **-8.** [doce] bombe.
bombachas [bõn'baʃaʃ] *fpl* gaucho pants.
bombardear [15] [bõnbax'dʒja(x)] *vt* to bombard.
bombardeio [bõnbax'deju] *m* bombardment.
bomba-relógio [ˌbõnbaxe'lɔʒju] (*pl* **bombas-relógios**, **bombas-relógio**) *f* time bomb.
bombástico, ca [bõn'baʃtʃiku, ka] *adj* **-1.** [estrondoso] deafening. **-2.** *fig* [empolado] bombastic.
bombear [15] [bõn'bja(x)] *vt & vi* to pump.
bombeiro [bõn'bejru] *m* **-1.** [de incêndios] firefighter. **-2.** [encanador] plumber.
bombom [bõn'bõ] (*pl* **-ns**) *m* sweetie.
bombordo [bõn'bɔxdu] *m NÁUT* port.
bom-tom [bõn'tõ] *m* good manners; **ser de ~** to be socially acceptable.
bonachão, ona [bona'ʃãw, ɔna] (*mpl* **-ões**, *fpl* **-s**) *adj* kind-hearted.
bonaerense [bonaj'rẽnsi] ◇ *adj* Buenos Aires *(antes de subst)*. ◇ *mf person from Buenos Aires*.
bonança [bo'nãnsa] *f* **-1.** *NÁUT* calm. **-2.** *fig* [tranqüilidade] calm.
bondade [bõn'dadʒi] *f* **-1.** [qualidade] kindness. **-2.** [benevolência] goodness; **ter a ~ de fazer algo** to be kind enough to do sthg.
bonde ['bõndʒi] *m* **-1.** [veículo] tram; **pegar o ~ andando** *fig* to come in (a conversation) half way. **-2.** *fam* [mulher feia] ugly woman.
bondoso, sa [bõn'dozu, ɔza] *adj* kind.
boné [bo'nɛ] *m* cap.
boneca [bo'nɛka] *f* **-1.** [ger] doll; **~ de pano** rag doll. **-2.** *fam* [homosexual] queen.
boneco [bo'nɛku] *m* **-1.** [ger] stencil. **-2.** [brinquedo] doll. **-3.** *fig* [fantoche] puppet.
bonificação [bonifika'sãw] (*pl* **-ões**) *f* **-1.** [gratificação] bonus. **-2.** [desconto] discount.
boníssimo, ma [bo'nisimu, ma] *superl* ▻ **bom**.
bonitão, tona [boni'tãw, tona] (*mpl* **-ões**, *fpl* **-s**) *adj* handsome.
bonito, ta [bo'nitu, ta] *adj* **-1.** [ger] beautiful. **-2.** *iron* [lamentável] lovely.
◆ **bonito** *adv* [bem] well.
bonitona [boni'tona] *f* ▻ **bonitão**.
bons ['bõjʃ] *pl* ▻ **bom**.
bônus ['bonuʃ] *m (inv)* **-1.** [prêmio] prize. **-2.** [debênture] share.
boot ['buti] (*pl* **boots**) *m COMPUT* [inicialização] boot-up; **dar ~** to reboot.
boquiaberto, ta [bokja'bɛxtu, ta] *adj* gaping.
boquinha [bo'kiɲa] *f* **-1.** [boca pequena] small mouth. **-2.** *fig* [refeição]: **fazer uma ~** snack.
borboleta [boxbo'leta] *f* **-1.** *ZOOL* butterfly. **-2.** [roleta] turnstile.
borboletear [15] [boxbole'tʃja(x)] *vi* **-1.** [vaguear] to flutter. **-2.** *fig* [devanear] to daydream.

borbotão [boxbo'tãw] (*pl* -**ões**) *m*: **aos borbotões** in spurts.

borbulhante [boxbu'ʎãntʃi] *adj* fizzy.

borbulhar [4] [boxbu'ʎa(x)] *vi* to bubble.

borda ['bɔxda] *f* **-1.** edge. **-2.** [lençol] hem. **-3.** [jardim] border. **-4.** [rio] bank. **-5.** [piscina] side.

bordadeira [boxda'dejra] *f* embroiderer.

bordado, da [box'dadu, da] *adj* embroidered.
◆ **bordado** *m* embroidery.

bordão [box'dãw] (*pl* -**ões**) *m* **-1.** [cajado] crook. **-2.** *fig* [arrimo] prop. **-3.** [MÚS - corda] bass string; [- nota] lowest note. **-4.** [frase] slogan.

bordar [4] [box'da(x)] *vt & vi* to embroider.

Bordeaux [box'do] *n* Bordeaux.

bordejar [4] [boxde'ʒa(x)] *vi* NÁUT to tack.

bordel [box'dɛw] (*pl* -**eis**) *m* brothel.

bordo ['bɔxdu] *m* **-1.** [de navio] board; **a ~** on board. **-2.** [ao bordejar] tack.

bordô [box'do] ◇ *adj* burgundy. ◇ *n* Bordeaux.

bordoada [box'dwada] *f* beating.

bordões [box'dõjʃ] *pl* ▻ **bordão**.

boreste [bo'rɛʃtʃi] *m* NÁUT starboard; **a ~** to starboard.

boricado, da [bori'kadu, da] *adj* boric.

borla ['bɔxla] *f* **-1.** [pendão] tassel. **-2.** [pompom] pompom.

borocoxô [boroko'ʃo] *adj* feeble.

borra ['boxa] *f* **-1.** [de café] grounds *(pl)*. **-2.** [de vinho] dregs *(pl)*.

borra-botas [ˌboxa'bɔtaʃ] *mf inv* good-for-nothing.

borracha [bo'xaʃa] *f* **-1.** [ger] rubber. **-2.** [para apagar] rubber, eraser. **-3.** [mangueira] hosepipe.

borrachudo [boxa'ʃudu] *m* black fly.

borracheiro [boxa'ʃejru] *m* **-1.** [pessoa] tyre fitter. **-2.** [oficina] tyre-fitting workshop.

borrado, da [bo'xadu, da] *adj* **-1.** [manchado] stained. **-2.** *fam* [de fezes] foul.

borrão [bo'xãw] (*pl* -**ões**) *m* stain.

borrar [4] [bo'xa(x)] *vt* **-1.** [manchar] to stain. **-2.** [riscar] to cross out. **-3.** [pintar] to smear. **-4.** *fam* [de fezes] to foul.
◆ **borrar-se** *vp vulg* [de fezes] to shit o.s.; **~-se (de medo)** *fig* to be shitting o.s.

borrasca [bo'xaʃka] *f* **-1.** [tempestade] thunderstorm. **-2.** [em alto mar] squall.

borrifar [4] [boxi'fa(x)] *vt* to spray.

borrifo [bo'xifu] *m* spray.

borrões [bo'xõjʃ] *pl* ▻ **borrão**.

Bósnia-Herzegovina [ˌbɔʒnjexzego'vina] *n* Bosnia-Herzegovina.

bósnio, nia ['bɔʒnju, nja], **bosniano, na** [boʒni'ãnu, na] ◇ *adj* Bosnian. ◇ *m, f* Bosnian.

bosque ['bɔʃki] *m* wood.

bossa ['bɔsa] *f* **-1.** [ger] bump. **-2.** *fam* [charme] appeal; **ter ~** to be appealing. **-3.** *fam* [aptidão]: **ter ~ (para algo)** to have an aptitude (for sthg). **-4.** MÚS: **~ nova** bossa nova.

BOSSA NOVA

Musical movement born in Rio de Janeiro in the late 50s; the bossa nova revolutionized the samba, condensing its rhythmic wealth into a syncopated beat with polished jazz chords for piano and guitar. The bossa nova's delicate melody and subtle song were to have a great influence on western popular music through two of the art form's greatest exponents, Tom Jobim and João Gilberto.

bosta ['bɔʃta] *f* **-1.** [de animal] dung. **-2.** [de ser humano] excrement.

bota ['bɔta] *f* boot; **~s de borracha** wellington boots, rubber boots; **bater as ~s** [morrer] to kick the bucket; **onde Judas perdeu as ~s** God-forsaken place.

bota-fora [ˌbɔta'fɔra] (*pl* **bota-foras**) *m* [despedida] send-off.

botânico, ca [bo'taniku, ka] ◇ *adj* botanic. ◇ *m, f* botanist.
◆ **botânica** *f* botany.

botão [bo'tãw] (*pl* -**ões**) *m* **-1.** [ger] button; **falar/pensar com os seus botões** to think to o.s. **-2.** [de jogo] counter. **-3.** [de flor] bud.

botar [4] [bo'ta(x)] ◇ *vt* **-1.** [ger] to put; **~ algo em dia** to bring sthg up to date; **~ fora** to throw away. **-2.** [roupa, sapatos] to put on. **-3.** [defeito] to point out. ◇ *vi loc*: **~ para quebrar** [empreender mudanças] to make sweeping changes; [fazer sucesso] to be a huge hit.

bote ['bɔtʃi] *m* **-1.** [barco] boat; **~ inflável** inflatable boat; **~ salva-vidas** lifeboat. **-2.** [golpe - com arma] thrust; [- salto] leap; [- de cobra] lunge; **dar o ~** to lunge.

boteco [bo'tɛku] (*pl* -**s**), **botequim** [bote'kĩ] (*pl* -**ns**) *m* tavern.

boticário, ria [botʃi'karju, rja] *m, f* dispensing chemist.

botijão [botʃi'ʒãw] (*pl* -**ões**) *m* cylinder.

botina [bo'tʃina] *f* ankle-boot.

botões [bo'tõjʃ] *pl* ▻ **botão**.

Bovespa (*abrev de* **Bolsa de Valores do Estado de São Paulo**) *f* *São Paulo stock exchange*.

bovino, na [bo'vinu, na] *adj* bovine.

boxe ['bɔksi] *m* **-1.** ESP boxing. **-2.** [em banheiro] shower cubicle.

boxeador [boksja'do(x)] *m* boxer.

boy ['bɔj] *m* = **bói**.

bps [bepe'esi] (*abrev de* **bit por segundo**) COMPUT bps.

BR *abrev de* **Brasil**.

braça ['brasa] *f* NÁUT fathom.

braçada [bra'sada] *f* **-1.** [de flores] armful. **-2.** [em natação] stroke.

braçadeira [brasa'dejra] *f* **-1.** [para o braço] armband. **-2.** [de cortina] tie-back. **-3.** [metálica] clasp. **-4.** ESP [correia] wristband.

braçal [bra'saw] (*pl* -**ais**) *adj* physical; **trabalho ~** physical work.

bracelete [brase'letʃi] *m* bracelet.

braço ['brasu] *m* **-1.** [ger] arm; **cruzar os ~s** to fold

one's arms; *fig* [ficar impassível] to do nothing; *fig* [fazer greve] to go on strike; **de ~s cruzados** with arms folded; *fig* [impassível] impassively; **dar o ~ a alguém** to give one's arm to sb; **de ~ dado** arm in arm; **no ~** [à força] by force; **~ direito** *fig* right arm. **-2.** [de toca-discos] arm. **-3.** [de balança] pointer. **-4.** [trabalhador] hand. **-5.** [ramo] limb. **-6.** *loc*: **meter o ~ em alguém** to beat sb up; **não dar o ~ a torcer** to stick to one's guns; **receber (alguém) de ~s abertos** to welcome (sb) with open arms.
bradar [4] [bra'da(x)] ◇ *vt* to proclaim. ◇ *vi* to shout.
Bradesco (*abrev de* **Banco Brasileiro de Descontos**) *m largest private Brazilian bank.*
brado ['bradu] *m* shout.
braguilha [bra'giʎa] *f* flies *UK (pl)*, fly *US*.
braile ['brajli] *m* Braille.
bramido [bra'midu] *m* **-1.** [ger] roar. **-2.** [grito] scream.
bramir [79] [bra'mi(x)] *vi* **-1.** [ger] to roar. **-2.** [gritar] to scream.
branco, ca ['brãŋku, ka] ◇ *adj* **-1.** [ger] white; **arma ~** weapon with a blade. **-2.** [versos] blank. ◇ *m, f* [pessoa] White.
◆ **branco** *m* **-1.** [cor] white; **~ do olho** white of the eye. **-2.** [espaço] blank space. **-3.** [esquecimento] blank; **me deu um ~** my mind went blank.
◆ **em branco** ◇ *loc adj* [espaço] blank. ◇ *loc adv* **-1.** [sem preencher]: **deixar algo em ~** to leave sthg blank. **-2.** [sem dormir]: **passar a noite em ~** to have a sleepless night. **-3.** [sem comemorar]: **passar uma data em ~** not to celebrate an important date.
brancura [brãŋ'kura] *f* whiteness.
brandir [79] [brãn'dʒi(x)] *vt* to brandish.
brando, da ['brãndu, da] *adj* **-1.** [ger] mild. **-2.** [fraco - ação] weak; [- febre] mild. **-3.** [fogo, forno] warm.
brandura [brãn'dura] *f* mildness.
branquear [15] [brãŋ'kja(x)] *vt & vi* to whiten.
brasa ['braza] *f* **-1.** [de carvão] embers *(pl)*; **na ~** in the embers. **-2.** [incandescência] heat; **em ~** red-hot. **-3.** *loc*: **mandar ~** *fam* to get cracking; **puxar a ~ para a sua sardinha** *fam* to look after number one.
brasão [bra'zãw] (*pl* **-ões**) *m* coat of arms.
braseiro [bra'zejru] *m* brazier.
Brasil [bra'ziw] *n*: **(o) ~** Brazil.
brasileiro, ra [brazi'lejru, ra] ◇ *adj* Brazilian. ◇ *m, f* Brazilian.
Brasília [bra'zilja] *n* Brasilia.

BRASÍLIA

Capital of Brazil since 1960; Brasilia is a landmark of Brazilian architecture. Designed in the shape of a plane, the city planned by Lúcio Costa became famous mainly through the daring architecture of Oscar Niemeyer.

brasões [bra'zõjʃ] *pl* ▻ **brasão**.
Bratislava [bratʃiʒ'lava] *n* Bratislava.
bravata [bra'vata] *f* bravado.
bravio, via [bra'viw, via] *adj* **-1.** [selvagem] wild. **-2.** [feroz] fierce.
bravo, va ['bravu, va] ◇ *adj* **-1.** [corajoso] brave. **-2.** [animal] wild. **-3.** [mar] rough. ◇ *m, f* [pessoa] intrepid person.
◆ **bravo** *interj* bravo!
bravura [bra'vura] *f* **-1.** [coragem] courage. **-2.** [de animal] wildness.
brecar [12] [bre'ka(x)] ◇ *vt* **-1.** [frear] to brake. **-2.** [conter] to curb. ◇ *vi* [frear] to brake.
brecha ['brɛʃa] *f* **-1.** [ger] gap. **-2.** [fenda, abertura] opening. **-3.** [prejuízo] hole. **-4.** *fam* [oportunidade] break.
brechó [bre'ʃɔ] *m* second-hand shop.
brega ['brɛga] *adj fam* [cafona] tacky.
brejo ['brɛʒu] *m* swamp; **ir para o ~** *fam* to go out the window.
brenha ['breɲa] *f* thicket.
breu ['brew] *m* **-1.** pitch; **escuro como ~** pitch black. **-2.** [escuridão] darkness.
breve ['brɛvi] ◇ *adj* **-1.** [ger] short. **-2.** [rápido] fleeting. **-3.** [conciso] brief; **ser ~** to be brief. **-4.** *MÚS* [nota] short. ◇ *adv* [dentro de pouco tempo] soon; **até ~** see you soon; **(dentro) em ~** soon. ◇ *m RELIG* [escapulário] scapular. ◇ *f MÚS* breve.
brevê [bre've] *m* diploma.
brevemente [ˌbrɛvi'mẽntʃi] *adv* **-1.** [dentro de pouco tempo] shortly. **-2.** [de modo conciso] concisely.
brevidade [brevi'dadʒi] *f* **-1.** [curteza] shortness. **-2.** [rapidez] brevity. **-3.** *CULIN* cassava-flour cake.
bricabraque [brika'braki] *m* **-1.** [conjunto] bric-a-brac. **-2.** [loja] junk shop.
bridge ['bridʒi] *m* bridge.
briga ['briga] *f* **-1.** [luta] brawl; **partir para a ~** to roll up one's sleeves; **~ de foice** long, drawn-out brawl; **~ de galo** cockfight. **-2.** [desavença] dispute. **-3.** [rixa] fight.
brigada [bri'gada] *f* brigade.
brigadeiro [briga'dejru] *m* **-1.** *MIL* brigadier. **-2.** *CULIN confectionery made with condensed milk and chocolate, very common at birthday parties.*
brigão, gona [bri'gãw, gɔna] (*mpl* **-ões**, *fpl* **-s**) ◇ *adj* brawling. ◇ *m, f* brawler.
brigar [4] [bri'ga(x)] *vi* **-1.** [ger] to fight; **~ por algo** to fight for sthg. **-2.** [desavir-se] to fall out.
brilhante [bri'ʎãntʃi] ◇ *adj* **-1.** [que reluz] sparkling. **-2.** *fig* [notável] brilliant. ◇ *m* [diamante] sparkler.
brilhar [4] [bri'ʎa(x)] *vi* **-1.** [reluzir] to shine. **-2.** *fig* [distinguir-se] to excel.
brilho ['briʎu] *m* **-1.** [luz] shine. **-2.** [de cor] brightness. **-3.** [de metal etc] gleam. **-4.** *fig* [distinção] excellence; **dar ~ a** to make sthg shine; **com ~** brilliantly. **-5.** *fig* [esplendor] splendour. **-6.** *gír droga* [cocaína] coke.
brim [brĩ] *m* coarse cloth.
brincadeira [brĩŋka'dejra] *f* **-1.** [divertimento] play. **-2.** [jogo] game. **-3.** [gracejo] joke; **de ~** as a joke;

~ **de mau gosto** joke in bad taste; **deixe de ~!** stop kidding!; **fora de ~** seriously. **-4.** *fam* [coisa fácil] child's play; **não ser ~** to be no joke.
brincalhão, ona [brĩŋka'ʎãw, ɔna] (*mpl* **-ões**, *fpl* **-s**) *adj* playful.
brincar [12] [brĩŋ'ka(x)] <> *vi* **-1.** [divertir-se] to play; **~ de algo/de fazer algo** to play with/at doing sthg; **~ de esconder** to play hide-and-seek. **-2.** [gracejar]: **~ com alguém** to joke with sb; **está brincando?** are you kidding?; **estar (só) brincando** to be (only) joking. **-3.** [no Carnaval] to party. <> *vt* [Carnaval] to celebrate.
brinco ['brĩŋku] *m* **-1.** [adorno] earring. **-2.** *fig* [primor]: **estar/ficar um ~** to be shiny.
brindar [4] [brĩn'da(x)] <> *vt* **-1.** [no ato de beber] to toast. **-2.** [presentear]: **~ alguém (com algo)** to make sb a present (of sthg). **-3.** [conceder]: **~ alguém com algo** to reward sb with sthg. <> *vi* [no ato de beber]: **~ a algo** to drink a toast to sthg.
brinde ['brĩndʒi] *m* **-1.** [no ato de beber] toast; **erguer um ~ (a)** to raise one's glass (to). **-2.** [presente] free gift.
brinquedo [brĩŋ'kedu] *m* toy.
brio ['briw] *m* **-1.** [honra, dignidade] honour; **mexer com os ~s de alguém** to attack sb's honour. **-2.** [galhardia] dignity.
brioche [bri'ɔʃi] *m* brioche.
brioso, osa ['brjozu, ɔza] *adj* noble.
brisa ['briza] *f* breeze.
brita ['brita] *f* CONSTR gravel.
britadeira [brita'dejra] *f* pneumatic drill.
britânico, ca [bri'tãniku, ka] <> *adj* British. <> *m, f* British person, Briton.
broa ['broa] *f* cornflour bread; **~ de milho** maize-flour bread.
broca ['brɔka] *f* drill.
brocado [bro'kadu] *m* brocade.
broche ['brɔʃi] *m* brooch.
brochura [bro'ʃura] *f* **-1.** [livro] binding; **em ~** in paperback. **-2.** [folheto] brochure.
brócolis ['brɔkoliʃ] *mpl* broccoli *(sg)*.
bronco, ca ['brõŋku, ka] *adj* **-1.** [rude] ill-mannered. **-2.** [burro] slow-witted.
◆ **bronca** *f fam* [repreensão] telling-off; **dar uma ~ em alguém** to give sb a telling-off; **levar uma ~ (de alguém)** to be given a telling-off (by sb).
bronquear [15] [brõŋ'kja(x)] *vi fam* to get furious; **~ com alguém** to tell sb off.
brônquio ['broŋkju] *m* bronchus.
bronquite [brõŋ'kitʃi] *f* bronchitis.
bronze ['brõnzi] *m* bronze.
bronzeado, da [brõn'zeadu, da] *adj* tanned.
◆ **bronzeado** *m* tan; **pegar um ~** to get a suntan.
bronzeador [brõnzea'do(x)] (*pl* **-es**) *adj* suntan *(antes de subst)*.
◆ **bronzeador** *m* suntan lotion.
bronzear [15] [brõn'zja(x)] *vt* to tan.
◆ **bronzear-se** *vp* to sunbathe.
brotar [4] [bro'ta(x)] *vi* **-1.** [germinar, desabrochar - planta] to sprout; [- muda] to begin; [- flor] to blossom. **-2.** [manar] to flow; **~ de** to spurt from. **-3.** *fig* [esperança, suspeita, paixão] to grow.
broto ['brotu] *m* **-1.** [de vegetal] sprout; **~ de bambu** bamboo shoot; **~ de feijão** bean sprout. **-2.** [de flor] shoot. **-3.** [jovem] sapling.
brotoeja [bro'tweʒa] *f* rash.
broxa [brɔ'ʃa] <> *f* [pincel] brush. <> *m vulg* [homem impotente] dickless guy. <> *adj vulg* [impotente] dickless.
bruços ['brusuʃ] *mpl*: **de ~** lying face down.
bruma ['bruma] *f* mist.
brumoso, osa [bru'mozu, ɔza] *adj* misty.
brusco, ca ['bruʃku, ka] *adj* **-1.** [repentino] sudden. **-2.** [tosco, grosseiro] coarse.
brutal [bru'taw] (*pl* **-ais**) *adj* **-1.** [violento, bárbaro] brutal. **-2.** [tremendo, grande] tremendous.
brutalidade [brutali'dadʒi] *f* brutality.
brutamontes [bruta'mõntʃiʃ] *m inv* [homem corpulento] hulk.
bruto, ta ['brutu, ta] *adj* **-1.** [rude, grosseiro] brutish. **-2.** [tosco] coarse. **-3.** *(antes de subst)* [tremendo, grande] tremendous. **-4.** [violento] brutal. **-5.** [produto] raw; **em ~** raw. **-6.** [sem decréscimo] gross.
bruxa ['bruʃa] *f* **-1.** [feiticeira] witch. **-2.** [mariposa] moth. **-3.** *fam pej* [mulher má] bad woman. **-4.** *fam pej* [mulher feia] hag.
bruxaria [bruʃa'ria] *f* witchcraft.
Bruxelas [bru'ʃɛlaʃ] *n* Brussels.
bruxo ['bruʃu] *m* sorcerer.
Bucareste [buka'rɛʃtʃi] *n* Bucharest.
bucha ['buʃa] *f* **-1.** [de parafuso] Rawlplug®. **-2.** [para buracos] lid. **-3.** [de arma] wad. **-4.** [de balão] wick.
◆ **na bucha** *loc adv fam* [sem demora] promptly.
bucho ['buʃu] *m* **-1.** [de boi] maw. **-2.** *fam* [pessoa feia]: **ser um ~** to look gross.
buço ['busu] *m* down.
bucólico, ca [bu'kɔliku, ka] *adj* bucolic.
Budapeste [buda'peʃtʃi] *n* Budapest.
budismo [bu'dʒiʒmu] *m* Buddhism.
budista [bu'dʒiʃta] <> *adj* Buddhist. <> *mf* Buddhist.
bueiro [bu'ejru] *m* gutter.
Buenos Aires [bwenu'zajriʃ] *n* Buenos Aires.
búfalo ['bufalu] *m* buffalo.
bufante [bu'fãntʃi] *adj* bouffant.
bufar [4] [bu'fa(x)] *vi* **-1.** [ofegar] to pant. **-2.** [de raiva] to fume.
bufê, buffet [bu'fe] *m* buffet.
bug ['bugi] (*pl* **bugs**) *m* COMPUT bug.
bugiganga [buʒĩŋ'gãŋga] *f* piece of junk.
bujão [bu'ʒãw] (*pl* **-ões**) *m* cylinder; **~ de gás** gas cylinder.
bula ['bula] *f* **-1.** MED information leaflet. **-2.** RELIG: **~ (papal)** papal bull.
bulbo ['buwbu] *m* bulb.
buldôzer [buw'doze(x)] (*pl* **-es**) *m* bulldozer.
bule ['buli] *m* pot.
Bulgária [buw'garja] *n* Bulgaria.
búlgaro, ra ['buwgaru, ra] <> *adj* Bulgarian. <> *m, f* Bulgarian.

◆ **búlgaro** *m* [língua] Bulgarian.
bulhufas [bu'ʎufaʃ] *pron fam* [coisa nenhuma]: **não entender/ouvir** ~ to understand/hear nothing.
buliçoso, osa [buli'sozu, ɔza] *adj* **-1.** [agitado] turbulent. **-2.** [vivo] lively.
bulimia [buli'mia] *f* bulimia.
bulir [61] [bu'li(x)] ◇ *vt* [mover] to ruffle. ◇ *vi* **-1.** [mover-se] to sway. **-2.** [tocar, mexer]: ~ **em** to fiddle with sthg. **-3.** [provocar]: ~ **com alguém** to taunt sb.
bumbum [bũn'bũ] (*pl* **-ns**) *m fam* bottom, bum.
bunda ['bũnda] (*pl* **-ns**) *f fam* bottom, bum.
bunda-mole [ˌbũnda'mɔli] (*pl* **bundas-moles**) *mf fam* wimp.
buquê [bu'ke] *m* bouquet; ~ **de flores** bouquet of flowers.
buraco [bu'raku] *m* **-1.** [ger] hole; ~ **da fechadura** keyhole. **-2.** [de agulha] eye. **-3.** [jogo] rummy.
burburinho [buxbu'riɲu] *m* **-1.** [agitação] clamour. **-2.** [rumor] murmur.
burguês, guesa [bux'geʃ, geza] ◇ *adj* bourgeois. ◇ *m, f* [pessoa] bourgeois.
burguesia [buxge'zia] *f* bourgeoisie; **alta** ~ upper middle class.
burilar [4] [buri'la(x)] *vt* **-1.** [lavrar] to engrave. **-2.** *fig* [aprimorar] to perfect.
burla ['buxla] *f* **-1.** [fraude] double-dealing. **-2.** [zombaria] jeering.
burlar [4] [bux'la(x)] *vt* **-1.** [fraudar, lesar] to cheat. **-2.** [enganar] to deceive. **-3.** [lei] to defraud.
burlesco, ca [bux'leʃku, ka] *adj* burlesque.
burocracia [burokra'sia] *f* bureaucracy.
burocrata [buro'krata] *m f* bureaucrat.
burocrático, ca [buro'kratʃiku, ka] *adj* bureaucratic.
burocratizar [4] [burokratʃi'za(x)] *vt* to bureaucratize.
burrice [bu'xisi] *f* **-1.** [estupidez] stupidity. **-2.** [ato, dito] something stupid; **foi** ~ **minha ter aceitado a proposta** it was silly of me to accept that offer.
burro, a ['buxu, xa] ◇ *adj* stupid. ◇ *m, f* [pessoa imbecil] ass.
◆ **burro** *m* ZOOL donkey; ~ **de carga** beast of burden; *fig* workhorse; **dar com os** ~**s n'água** to lose out.
◆ **pra burro** *fam loc adv*: **ele pinta mal pra** ~ he paints terribly; **a mulher do hotel era feia pra** ~ the woman in the hotel was terribly ugly.
bursite [bux'sitʃi] *f* bursitis.
busca ['buʃka] *f* search; **em** ~ **de** in search of; **dar** ~ **a** to search for.
buscador [buʃka'do(x)] *m* COMPUT search engine.
busca-pé [buʃka'pɛ] (*pl* **-s**) *m* firecracker.
buscar [12] [buʃ'ka(x)] *vt* **-1.** [procurar] to search for. **-2.** [tratar de obter] to seek. **-3.** [pegar, trazer] to fetch; **ir** ~ to go and fetch; **mandar** ~ to send for. **-4.** [esforçar-se por]: ~ **fazer algo** to try to do sthg. **-5.** COMPUT to search.
bússola ['busola] *f* compass.
bustiê [buʃ'tʃje] *m* bustier.
busto ['buʃtu] *m* **-1.** [ger] bust; **ela tem 85 cm de** ~ her bust size is 85 cm. **-2.** [torso] torso.
butique [bu'tʃiki] *f* boutique.
buzina [bu'zina] *f* horn, hooter.
buzinada [buzi'nada] *f* honk; **dar uma** ~ to honk.
buzinar [4] [buzi'na(x)] ◇ *vt* **-1.** AUTO to honk. **-2.** *fig* [dizer com insistência] to harp on; ~ **algo nos ouvidos de alguém** to harp on about sthg to sb. ◇ *vi* AUTO to honk.
búzio ['buzju] *m* [concha] conch; **jogar** ~**s** [espirit] to cast shells *(in fortune telling)*.
byte ['bajtʃi] *m* COMPUT byte.

c, C ['se] *m* [letra] c, C.
◆ **C** *abrev de* **celsius**.
cá ['ka] *adv* **-1.** [lugar] here; **vem** ~**!** come here!; **de** ~ **para lá** from here to there; **do lado de** ~ this side; **mais para** ~ closer. **-2.** [tempo]: **de uma semana para** ~ for the past week; **de uns tempos para** ~ recently; **de lá para** ~ since then. **-3.** [na intimidade]: ~ **comigo** to myself; ~ **entre nós** just between ourselves.
CA (*abrev de* **Centro Acadêmico**) *m centre in a Brazilian university where students meet to discuss problems concerning their course etc.*
caatinga [ka'tʃĩŋga] *f* caatinga.
cabal [ka'baw] (*pl* **-ais**) *adj* **-1.** [pleno, completo] utter. **-2.** [exato] complete. **-3.** [prova] ultimate.
cabala [ka'bala] *f* **-1.** [doutrina] cabbala. **-2.** *fig* [maquinação] cabal.
cabalístico, ca [kaba'liʃtʃiku, ka] *adj* cabalistic.
cabana [ka'bãna] *f* hut.
cabaré [kaba'rɛ] *m* cabaret.
cabeça [ka'besa] ◇ *f* **-1.** [ger] head; **de** ~ [calcular] in one's head; **de** ~ head first; **de** ~ **erguida** *fig* with one's head held high; **por** ~ per head; **só faz o que lhe dá na** ~ he only does what he has a mind to; **meter na** ~ to get into one's head; **não bater bem da** ~ to be off one's rocker; **não estar com** ~ **para fazer algo** not to be in the mood to do sthg; **passar pela** ~ to cross one's mind; **subir à** ~ [suj: sucesso, dinheiro] to go to one's head; **ter a** ~ **no lugar** [ser ajuizado] to be level-headed; ~ **fria** *fig* cool-headed; **com a** ~ **no ar** with one's head in the clouds; ~ **a** ~ neck and neck. **-2.** [inteligência] mind; **usar a** ~ to use one's head. **-3.** [pessoa inteligente] brains. **-4.** [topo, parte de cima]: **de** ~ **para baixo** upside down. **-5.**

[de lista] top. **-6.** *fam* [de glande] glans. **-7.** [loc]: **fazer a ~ de alguém** to influence sb's thinking; **levar na ~** *fam* to take a hard knock; **não esquentar a ~** *fam* not to get hot and bothered; **perder a ~** to lose one's head; **quebrar a ~** to rack one's brains. <> *mf* head.

cabeçada [kabe'sada] *f* **-1.** [pancada] headbutt; **dar uma ~ em alguém** to headbutt sb; **dar uma ~ em algo** to bang one's head on sthg; **dar uma ~** *fig* to take a knock. **-2.** *FUT* header.

cabeça-de-vento [ka,besadʒi'vẽntu] (*pl* **cabeças-de-vento**) *mf* scatterbrain.

cabeça-dura [ka,besa'dura] (*pl* **cabeças-duras**) <> *adj* [teimoso] headstrong. <> *mf* headstrong person.

cabeça-feita [ka,besa'fejta] (*pl* **cabeças-feitas**) *adj fam* [pessoa responsável] level-headed.

cabeçalho [kabe'saʎu] *m* **-1.** [de livro] title. **-2.** [de página, capítulo] heading.

cabecear [15] [kabe'sja(x)] *FUT vt* [bola] to head.

cabeceira [kabe'sejra] *f* head; **livro de ~** bedside book.

cabeçudo, da [kabe'sudu, da] *adj* **-1.** [de cabeça grande] big-headed. **-2.** *fam* [teimoso] pig-headed.

cabedal [kabe'daw] (*pl* **-ais**) *m* wealth.

cabeleira [kabe'lejra] *f* **-1.** [natural] head of hair. **-2.** [peruca] wig.

cabeleireiro, ra [kabelej'rejru, ra] *m, f* [profissional] hairdresser.
◆ **cabeleireiro** *m* [salão] hairdressing salon.

cabelo [ka'belu] *m* [ger] hair; **~ liso/crespo/pixaim** straight/curly/woolly hair; **de arrepiar os ~s** *fig* hair-raising.

cabeludo, da [kabe'ludu, da] *adj* **-1.** hairy. **-2.** *fam fig* [complicado, obsceno] hairy.
◆ **cabeludo** *m fam* [homem] hairy man.

caber [34] [ka'be(x)] *vi* **-1.** [ger] to fit; **não ~ em si de** *fam fig* to be overwhelmed with; **~ (em)** to fit (in); **~ por** to fit through; **~ fazer algo** to have to do sthg. **-2.** [ser oportuno] to be time to. **-3.** [ser compatível]: **~ em algo** to be compatible with sthg. **-4.** [competir]: **~ a alguém fazer algo** to be the responsibility of sb to so sthg. **-5.** [partilha]: **~ a alguém** to be allocated to sb.

cabide [ka'bidʒi] *m* [de armário] clothes hanger; [de pé] coat hanger; [de parede] coat hook; **~ de empregos** *fig* [pessoa] Jack-of-all-trades (but master of none); *fig* [empresa estatal] jobs-for-the-boys organisation.

cabideiro [kabi'dejru] *m* **-1.** [de pé] coat hanger. **-2.** [de parede] coat hook.

cabimento [kabi'mẽntu] *m* [adequação] sense; **ter/não ter ~** to make/not to make sense.

cabine [ka'bini] *f* **-1.** [ger] cabin. **-2.** [telefônica] phone box *UK*, phone booth *US*. **-3.** [guarita] sentry box. **-4.** *FERRO* [compartimento] carriage, compartment. **-5.** *AERON* [de comando] cockpit. **-6.** [vestuário] changing room.

cabisbaixo, xa [kabiʒ'bajʃu, ʃa] *adj* crestfallen.

cabível [ka'bivew] (*pl* **-eis**) *adj* fitting.

cabo ['kabu] *m* **-1.** [de panela, faca, vassoura] handle. **-2.** [fim] end. **-3.** *CORDA*: **~ de aço** iron cable. **-4.** *ELETR* cable. **-5.** *GEOGR* cape. **-6.** *MIL* corporal. **-7.** *POL*: **~ eleitoral** electoral canvasser. **-8.** [fim]: **dar ~ de** [pessoa] to kill; [problema] to put an end to; [tarefa] to finish; **levar algo a ~** [tarefa, projeto] to see sthg through; **ao ~ de** by the end of; **de ~ a rabo** [de uma extremidade a outra] from one end to the other; [do início ao fim] from the beginning to the end.

caboclo, cla [ka'boklu, kla] <> *adj* **-1.** [pele] copper-coloured. **-2.** [pessoa] bumpkinish. <> *m, f* **-1.** [mestiço de banco com índio] caboclo. **-2.** [pessoa da roça] bumpkin.

cabotino, na [kabo'tʃinu, na] <> *adj* theatrical. <> *m, f* show-off.

Cabo Verde [,kabu'vexdʒi] *n* Cape Verde.

cabra ['kabra] <> *f* [animal] goat. <> *m fam* **-1.** [homem] guy. **-2.** [capanga] gunman.

cabra-cega [,kabra'sɛga] (*pl* **cabras-cegas**) *f* blind man's buff.

cabra-macho [,kabra'maʃu] (*pl* **cabras-machos**) *m* tough guy.

cabreiro, ra [ka'brejru, ra] *adj fam* [desconfiado] suspicious.

cabresto [ka'breʃtu] *m* [para cavalos] halter.

cabrito [ka'britu] *m* kid.

caça ['kasa] <> *f* **-1.** [ato] hunt; **~ às bruxas** witch-hunt; **à ~ de** in pursuit of. **-2.** [animal - caçado por homem] game; [- caçado por outro animal] prey; game. **-3.** [passatempo] hunting. <> *m AERON* fighter.

caçada [ka'sada] *f* [jornada] hunting trip.

caçador, ra [kasa'do(x), ra] (*mpl* **-es**, *fpl* **-s**) *m, f* hunter.

caça-minas [,kasa'minaʃ] *m inv* minesweeper.

caça-níqueis [,kasa'nikejʃ] *m inv* **-1.** [máquina] slot-machine. **-2.** *fam* [empresa, loja] cowboy outfit.

cação [ka'sãw] (*pl* **-ões**) *m* dogfish.

caçapa [ka'sapa] *f* pocket *(on billiard table)*.

caçar [13] [ka'sa(x)] <> *vt* **-1.** [animais] to hunt. **-2.** [a tiro] to shoot. **-3.** [buscar - documentos, prova, tesouro] to search for; [- recompensa] to seek. **-4.** [perseguir] to hunt down. **-5.** *fam* [marido] to hunt for. <> *vi* [andar à caça] to hunt.

cacareco [kaka'rɛku] *m* piece of junk.
◆ **cacarecos** *mpl* junk *(sg)*.

cacarejar [4] [kakare'ʒa(x)] *vi* to cluck.

cacarejo [kaka'reʒu] *m* clucking.

caçarola [kasa'rɔla] *f* casserole.

cacau [ka'kaw] *m* **-1.** [fruto] cacao. **-2.** [semente] cocoa bean. **-3.** [pó] cocoa.

cacetada [kase'tada] *f* whack; **dar uma ~ (em algo/alguém)** to whack (sthg/sb).

cacete [ka'setʃi] <> *adj* [tedioso] tedious. <> *m* **-1.** [porrete] truncheon. **-2.** *vulg* [pênis] rod.
◆ **pra cacete** *mfam* <> *loc pron*: **gente pra ~** shitloads of people. <> *loc adv*: **chato/bom/forte pra cacete** bloody boring/good/strong.

cachaça [ka'ʃasa] *f* sugar-cane brandy.

CACHAÇA

Cachaça is the most popular alcoholic drink in Brazil; it is a fermented drink, obtained from the distillation of sugar-cane sap, and it is very high in alcohol. Its popularity can be measured by the many names that Brazilians give this drink, such as *pinga*, *caninha*, *branquinha*, *mel*, among many others.

cachaceiro, ra [kaʃa'sejru, ra] ◇ *adj* drunken. ◇ *m, f* drunkard.
cache [ka'ʃe] *m* COMPUT cache.
cachê [ka'ʃe] *m* fee *(for performance)*.
cacheado, da [ka'ʃjadu, da] *adj* curly.
cachecol [kaʃe'kɔw] (*pl* **-óis**) *m* scarf.
cachimbo [ka'ʃĩnbu] *m* pipe.
cacho ['kaʃu] *m* **-1.** [ger] bunch. **-2.** [de cabelos - anel] lock; [- mecha] strand.
cachoeira [ka'ʃwejra] *f* waterfall.
cachorra [ka'ʃoxa] *f* ▷ **cachorro**.
cachorrada [kaʃo'xada] *f* **-1.** [matilha] pack of dogs. **-2.** *fam fig* [canalhice] scam; **fazer uma ~ com alguém** to scam sb.
cachorrinho, nha [kaʃo'xiɲu, ɲa] *m, f* [filhote] puppy.
◆ **cachorrinho** *m* [nado] doggy-paddle.
cachorro, rra [ka'ʃoxu, xa] *m, f* **-1.** [cão] dog; **soltar os ~s (em cima de alguém)** *fig* to lash out (at sb); **estar matando ~ a grito** to be scraping the barrel. **-2.** *fam pej* [patife] bastard.
◆ **cachorra** *f*: **estar com a ~** *fig* to be in a bad mood.
cachorro-quente [ka,ʃoxu'kẽntʃi] (*pl* **cachorros-quentes**) *m* hot dog.
cacife [ka'sifi] *m* stake; **ter ~ para** *fig* [ter dinheiro para] to be able to afford; [ter condições de] to have what it takes.
cacique [ka'siki] *m* **-1.** [indígena] cacique, tribal chief. **-2.** *fig* [chefão] boss.
caco ['kaku] *m* **-1.** [de vidro etc] shard. **-2.** *fam* [pessoa]: **estar um ~** [estar velho] to be a wreck; [estar desgastado] to be a wreck; [estar exausto] to be wiped out.
caçoar [20] [ka'swa(x)] *vi* to mock; **~ de algo/alguém** to make fun of sthg/sb.
cações [ka'sõjʃ] *pl* ▷ **cação**.
cacoete [ka'kwetʃi] *m* tic.
cacto ['kaktu] *m* cactus.
caçula [ka'sula] ◇ *adj* youngest. ◇ *mf* youngest child.
CAD (*abrev de* **Computer Aided Design**) *m* CAD.
cada ['kada] *adj (inv)* **-1.** [valor de unidade] each; **uma coisa de ~ vez** one thing at a time; **~ (um)** [em preço] each; **~ qual, ~ um** each one. **-2.** [todo] every; **a ~** every; **aumentar a ~ dia** to increase from day to day; **em ~ dez pessoas, uma sofre de ...** one out of ten people suffers from ... **-3.** [valor progressivo]: **~ vez** more and more. **-4.** [valor intensivo] such; **me acontece ~ uma!** would you believe it!
cadafalso [kada'fawsu] *m* gallows *(pl)*.
cadarço [ka'daxsu] *m* shoelace.
cadastramento [kadaʃtra'mẽntu] *m* registration.
cadastrar [4] [kadaʃ'tra(x)] *vt* **-1.** [registrar] to register. **-2.** COMPUT [dados] to record.
◆ **cadastrar-se** *vp* [inscrever-se] to register o.s.
cadastro [ka'daʃtru] *m* **-1.** [registro] register. **-2.** [ato] registration. **-3.** [ficha de criminoso] criminal record. **-4.** [de banco, clientes] records *(pl)*. **-5.** [de imóveis] land registry. **-6.** COMPUT [de dados] data record.
cadáver [ka'davɛ(x)] (*pl* **-es**) *m* corpse.
cadavérico, ca [kada'vɛriku, ka] *adj* **-1.** [exame] post-mortem *(antes de subst)*. **-2.** [pessoa, palidez, rosto] cadaverous.
cadê [ka'de] *adv fam* where is/are.
cadeado [ka'dʒjadu] *m* padlock.
cadeia [ka'deja] *f* **-1.** [ger] chain. **-2.** [prisão] prison. **-3.** [série, seqüência] series *(inv)*; **~ de montanhas** mountain range. **-4.** [de emissoras de TV] network.
cadeira [ka'dejra] *f* **-1.** [ger] chair; **~ de balanço** rocking chair; **~ de rodas** wheelchair; **~ cativa** [em estádio] reserved place; **falar de ~** to speak with authority. **-2.** [disciplina] subject. **-3.** [em teatro] seat.
◆ **cadeiras** *fpl* ANAT hips.
cadela [ka'dɛla] *f* [cão] bitch ▷ **cão**.
cadência [ka'dẽnsja] *f* **-1.** [ritmo] rhythm. **-2.** [de estilo, fala] cadence.
cadenciado, da [kadẽn'sjadu, da] *adj* **-1.** [ritmado] rhythmic. **-2.** [pausado] measured.
cadente [ka'dẽntʃi] *adj* [estrela] falling.
caderneta [kadex'neta] *f* **-1.** [livrete] note pad. **-2.** [escolar] mark sheet. **-3.** FIN: **~ de poupança** savings account.
caderno [ka'dɛxnu] *m* **-1.** [de notas] notebook. **-2.** [de jornal] section.
cadete [ka'detʃi] *m* cadet.
cadinho [ka'dʒiɲu] *m* **-1.** [recipiente] crucible. **-2.** *fig* [local] melting pot.
caducar [12] [kadu'ka(x)] *vi* **-1.** [prazo, documento, lei] to expire. **-2.** [pessoa] to become senile.
caduco, ca [ka'duku, ka] *adj* **-1.** [prazo, documento, lei] expired. **-2.** [pessoa] senile. **-3.** BOT deciduous.
caduquice [kadu'kisi] *f* [senilidade] senility.
cães ['kãjʃ] *pl* ▷ **cão**.
cafajestada [kafaʒeʃ'tada] *f* *fam* con; **fazer uma ~ com alguém** to pull a fast one on sb.
cafajeste [kafa'ʒɛʃtʃi] *fam* ◇ *adj* **-1.** [canalha] crooked. **-2.** [vulgar] vulgar. ◇ *mf* [pessoa canalha] con man.
café [ka'fɛ] *m* **-1.** [ger] coffee; **~ (preto)** black coffee; **~ com leite** white coffee *UK*, coffee with cream *US*; **~ expresso** espresso; **~ pingado** *coffee with a tiny drop of milk*; **ser ~ pequeno** *fam* [tarefa] to be small beer; [pessoa] to be small fry. **-2.** [desjejum]: **~ (da manhã)** breakfast. **-3.** [estabelecimento] café.

CAFÉ

The *cafézinho*, so greatly enjoyed by the Brazilians, played a decisive role in the country's history. Coffee was the main export at the end of the nineteenth century; it propelled Brazilian industrialisation, bringing about the opening of roads and railways throughout the central south of the country. Coffee was a determining factor in the development of São Paulo as the industrial and financial centre of Brazil.

café-com-leite [ˌkafɛkõn'lejtʃi] *adj inv* [cor] coffee-coloured.

cafeeiro, ra [kafe'ejru, ra] ◇ *adj* [setor, indústria] coffee *(antes de subst)*. ◇ *m* coffee bush.

cafeicultor, ra [kafejkuw'to(x), ra] *m, f* coffee planter.

cafeína [kafe'ina] *f* caffeine.

cafetã [kafe'tã] *f* kaftan.

cafetão, tina [kafe'tãw, tʃina] (*mpl* **-ões**, *fpl* **-s**) *m, f* pimp.

cafeteira [kafe'tejra] *f* coffee pot.

cafetina [kafe'tʃina] *f* ▷ **cafetão**.

cafezal [kafe'zaw] (*pl* **-ais**) *m* coffee plantation.

cafezinho [kafɛ'ziɲu] *m* ***fam*** small black coffee.

cafona [ka'fona] ◇ *adj* [pessoa, roupa, música] tacky. ◇ *mf* [pessoa] tacky person.

cafonice [kafo'nisi] *f* tackiness.

cafundó-do-judas [kafũnˌdɔdu'ʒudaʃ] *m*: **no ~** out in the sticks.

cafuné [kafu'nɛ] *m*: **fazer ~ em alguém: fazer ~ em alguém** to scratch sb's head gently.

cagada [ka'gada] *f* ***vulg*** crap.

cágado ['kagadu] *m* terrapin.

caganeira [kaga'nejra] *f* ***vulg*** runs *(pl)*.

cagão, gona [ka'gãw, gona] (*mpl* **-ões**, *fpl* **-s**) *m, f* ***fam*** [medroso, tímido] wimp.

cagar [14] [ka'ga(x)] ***vulg*** ◇ *vi* **-1.** [defecar] to have a crap. **-2.** ***fig*** [menosprezar]: **~ para alguém/algo** not to give a shit about sb/sthg. ◇ *vt* ***fig*** [impôr]: **~ regras** to be full of shit.
◆ **cagar-se** *vp* [defecar nas calças] to shit o.s.; **~-se de medo** ***fig*** to be shit scared.

caiado, da [ka'jadu, da] *adj* ≃ whitewashed.

caiaque [ka'jaki] *m* kayak.

caiar [16] [ka'ja(x)] *vt* to whitewash.

caibro ['kajbru] *m* joist.

caído, da [ka'idu, da] *adj* **-1.** [derrubado] fallen. **-2.** [pendente] droopy. **-3.** ***fig*** [abatido] depressed. **-4.** ***fig*** [apaixonado]: **estar ~ por alguém** to be in love with sb. **-5.** ***fig*** [desanimado] subdued. **-6.** ***fig*** [feio] saggy.
◆ **caída** *f* [queda] fall.

caimento [kaj'mẽntu] *m* [de roupa] hang.

caipira [kaj'pira] ***fam*** ◇ *adj* provincial. ◇ *mf* [pessoa - do interior] country bumpkin; [- sem traquejo social] boor.

caipirinha [kajpi'riɲa] *f* caipirinha, *cocktail made with sugar-cane brandy and lime juice.*

CAIPIRINHA

One of the most typical alcoholic beverages of Brazil; *caipirinha* is prepared with slices or chunks of lemon, *cachaça*, ice and sugar. It is an essential accompaniment to Brazilian *feijoadas* and barbecues, and probably originates from the interior of the state of São Paulo, which would explain its name: *caipira* is the name given to those who were born there. Variations of *caipirinha* include *caipirosca* (made with vodka instead of *cachaça*) and *caipiríssima* (made with rum).

cair [68] [ka'i(x)] *vi* **-1.** [ger] to fall; **~ de joelhos** to fall to one's knees; **~ de quatro** to fall on all fours; ***fig*** [surpreender-se] to fall over backward; **estar caindo de sono** ***fig*** to be dropping with tiredness; **~ em** to fall into; **~ nas garras de alguém** ***fig*** to fall into sb's clutches. **-2.** [desabar] to collapse. **-3.** [desprender-se - dente, cabelo, folha] to fall out; [- botão] to fall off. **-4.** [deixar-se enganar] to fall for. **-5.** [entregar-se a]: **~ em** [na farra] to join in. **-6.** *EDUC* [em prova] to crop up. **-7.** ***loc*:** **~ bem/mal** [penteado, roupa, cor] to suit/not to suit; [frase, atitude] to go down well/badly; [comida, bebida] to agree/not to agree with; **estar caindo aos pedaços** to be falling to pieces; **~ em si** [reconhecer o erro] to accept one's mistake; [voltar à realidade] to come down to earth; **não ter onde ~ morto** to have nothing to one's name.

cais ['kajʃ] *m inv* quay.

Cairo ['kajru] *n* Cairo.

caixa ['kajʃa] ◇ *f* **-1.** [ger] box; **~ acústica** loudspeaker; **~ de fósforos** matchbox. **-2.** [para correspondência]: **~ de correio** postbox ***UK***, mailbox ***US***; **~ postal** *ou* **de coleta** postal box. **-3.** [mecanismo]: **~ de chave** console; **~ de luz** fuse-box; **~ de marchas** *ou* **de mudanças** gearbox. **-4.** [máquina]: **~ registradora** cash till. **-5.** [seção] till. **-6.** [banco] savings bank; **~ dois** undeclared assets; **~ econômica** national savings bank. **-7.** *ANAT*: **~ craniana** cranium; **~ torácica** thorax. **-8.** *TIP* : **~ alta/baixa** upper/lower case. ◇ *m* **-1.** [máquina]: **~ eletrônico** cashpoint. **-2.** [livro] ledger; **~ dois** fraudulent books *(pl)*. ◇ *mf* [funcionário] cashier.

caixa-d'água ['kajʃa'dagwa] (*pl* **caixas-d'água**) *f* water tank.

caixa-de-fósforos ['kajʃadʒi'fɔʃforuʃ] *f* ***fam*** [habitação, carro] matchbox.

caixa-forte ['kajʃa'fɔxtʃi] (*pl* **caixas-fortes**) *f* safe.

caixão [kaj'ʃãw] (*pl* **-ões**) *m* [ataúde] coffin.

caixa-preta ['kajʃa'preta] (*pl* **caixas-pretas**) *f* *AERON* black box.

caixeiro, ra [kaj'ʃejru, ra] *m, f* **-1.** [balconista] sales assistant. **-2.** [entregador] delivery person.

caixeiro-viajante, caixeira-viajante [kajˌʃejruvja'ʒãntʃi, kajˌʃejravja'ʒãntʃi] *m, f* commercial traveller.

caixilho [kaj'ʃiʎu] *m* [moldura] frame.

caixões [kaj'ʃõjʃ] *pl* ▷ **caixão**.

caixote [kaj'ʃɔtʃi] *m* crate.
caju [ka'ʒu] *m* cashew.
cajueiro [ka'ʒwejru] *m* cashew tree.
cal ['kaw] *f* **-1.** [substância] lime, quicklime. **-2.** [extinta] slaked lime. **-3.** [para caiar] whitewash.
calabouço [kala'bosu] *m* dungeon.
calada [ka'lada] *f*: **na ~ da noite** in the dead of night.
calado, da [ka'ladu, da] *adj* quiet.
calafetagem [kalafe'taʒẽ] (*pl* **-ns**) *f* caulking.
calafetar [4] [kalafe'ta(x)] *vt* to stop up.
calafrio [kala'friw] *m* shiver; **ter ~s** to have the shivers.
calamar [kala'ma(x)] *m* squid.
calamidade [kalami'dadʒi] *f* calamity.
calamitoso, tosa [kalami'tozu, tɔza] *adj* calamitous.
calão [ka'lãw] *m*: **(baixo) ~** foul language.
calar [4] [ka'la(x)] <> *vt* **-1.** [ocultar] to keep quiet about. **-2.** [silenciar] to silence; **cala a boca!** shut up! **-3.** [conter] to ignore. **-4.** *euf* [armas, canhões] to silence. <> *vi* **-1.** [manter-se em silêncio] to keep quiet. **-2.** [repercutir]: **~ em** to reverberate through.
◆ **calar-se** *vp* [parar de falar] to go quiet, to stop talking.
calça ['kawsa] *f* trousers ***UK*** *(pl)*, pants ***US*** *(pl)*.
calçada [kaw'sada] *f* pavement ***UK***, sidewalk ***US***.
calçadão [kawsa'dãw] (*pl* **-ões**) *m* pavement.
calçadeira [kawsa'dejra] *f* shoehorn.
calçado, da [kaw'sadu, da] *adj* **-1.** [caminho, rua] paved. **-2.** [pessoa, pé] with shoes on *(depois de subst)*.
◆ **calçado** *m* [sapato, tênis] footwear.
calçamento [kawsa'mẽntu] *m* paving.
calcanhar [kawka'ɲa(x)] (*pl* **-es**) *m* heel.
calcanhar-de-aquiles [kawka,ɲaxdʒia'kiliʃ] (*pl* **calcanhares-de-aquiles**) *m* Achilles' heel.
calção [kaw'sãw] (*pl* **-ões**) *m* shorts *(pl)*; **~ de banho** swim shorts *(pl)*.
calcar [12] [kaw'ka(x)] *vt* **-1.** [pisar] to tread on. **-2.** [comprimir]: **~ algo em** to press sthg into. **-3.** *fig* [basear]: **~ algo em** to base sthg on.
calçar [13] [kaw'sa(x)] *vt* **-1.** [sapatos, luvas] to put on; [tamanho] to take a size. **-2.** [pavimentar] to pave. **-3.** [pôr calço em] to wedge.
◆ **calçar-se** *vp* [pôr sapatos] to put one's shoes on.
calcário, ria [kaw'karju, rja] *adj* **-1.** [substância, pedra] chalky, calcareous. **-2.** [água] hard.
◆ **calcário** *m* [rocha] limestone.
calcificação [kawsifika'sãw] *f* calcification.
calcificar [12] [kawsifi'ka(x)] *vt* to calcify.
◆ **calcificar-se** *vp* to calcify.
calcinha [kaw'siɲa] *f* panties *(pl)*.
cálcio ['kawsju] *m* calcium.
calço ['kawsu] *m* [cunha] wedge.
calções [kal'sõiʃ] *pl* ▻ **calção**.
calculadora [kawkula'dora] *f* calculator.
calcular [4] [kawku'la(x)] <> *vt* **-1.** [fazer a conta de] to calculate. **-2.** [avaliar, estimar] to estimate. **-3.** [imaginar] to imagine. **-4.** [supor, prever]: **~ que** to guess that. <> *vi* [fazer contas] to calculate.
calculável [kawku'lavew] (*pl* **-eis**) *adj* calculable.
calculista [kawku'liʃta] <> *adj* calculating. <> *mf* opportunist.
cálculo ['kawkulu] *m* **-1.** [conta] calculation. **-2.** [estimativa] estimate. **-3.** *MAT* calculus. **-4.** *MED* stone; **~ renal** kidney stone.
calda ['kawda] *f* syrup.
caldeira [kaw'dejra] *f* *TEC* boiler.
caldeirão [kawdej'rãw] (*pl* **-ões**) *m* cauldron.
caldo ['kawdu] *m* **-1.** [sopa] broth; **~ verde** *green vegetable and potato soup*. **-2.** [sumo] juice; **~ de cana** sugar-cane juice. **-3.** [tempero]: **~ de carne/galinha** beef/chicken stock. **-4.** *fig* [mistura]: **~ de cultura** melting pot of cultures. **-5.** *fam* [mergulho]: **dar um ~ em alguém** to duck sb.
calefação [kalefa'sãw] *f* heating.
caleidoscópio [kalejdoʃ'kɔpju] *m* kaleidoscope.
calejado [kale'ʒadu] *adj* **-1.** [mão, pé] calloused. **-2.** *fig* [vivido] experienced. **-3.** *fig* [endurecido] hardened.
calejar [4] [kale'ʒa(x)] *vt* **-1.** [mãos, pés] to cause to become calloused. **-2.** *fig* [endurecer] to harden.
calendário [kalẽn'darju] *m* calendar.
calha [ka'ʎa] *f* **-1.** [sulco] channel. **-2.** [para a chuva] gutter.
calhamaço [kaʎa'masu] *m* tome.
calhambeque [kaʎãn'bɛki] *m* ***fam*** jalopy.
calhar [4] [ka'ʎa(x)] *vi* **-1.** [acontecer]: **~ que** to happen that. **-2.** [concidir] to happen that; **calhou de elas usarem vestidos iguais** they happened to be wearing the same dress. **-3.** [convir]: **vir a ~** to come at just the right time.
calhau [ka'ʎaw] *m* pebble.
calibrado, da [kali'bradu, da] *adj* **-1.** [pneu] balanced. **-2.** ***fam*** [meio embriagado] tipsy.
calibragem [kali'braʒẽj] (*pl* **-ns**) *f* calibration.
calibrar [4] [kali'bra(x)] *vt* **-1.** [pneu] to balance. **-2.** [instrumento] to calibrate.
calibre [ka'libri] *m* [de cano] calibre.
cálice ['kalisi] *m* **-1.** [taça] liqueur glass. **-2.** *RELIG* chalice.
cálido, da ['kalidu, da] *adj* warm.
caligrafia [kaligra'fia] *f* **-1.** [arte] calligraphy. **-2.** [letra] handwriting.
calista [ka'liʃta] *mf* chiropodist ***UK***, podiatrist ***US***.
calma ['kawma] *f* ▻ **calmo**.
calmante [kaw'mãntʃi] <> *adj* calming. <> *m* tranquillizer.
calmaria [kaw'maria] *f* lull.
calmo, ma ['kawmu, ma] *adj* [ger] calm.
◆ **calma** *f* **-1.** [quietude] tranquillity. **-2.** [serenidade] serenity; **calma!** just a moment!; **manter/perder a ~** to keep/lose one's composure.
calo ['kalu] *m* [endurecimento da pele] callus; [no pé] corn; **pisar nos ~s de alguém** *fig* to hit a raw nerve.
calombo [ka'lõnbu] *m* **-1.** [ger] lump. **-2.** [em estrada] bump.
calor [ka'lo(x)] *m* **-1.** [ger] heat; **estar com ~,**

sentir ~ to be/feel hot; **fazer** ~ to be hot. **-2.** [quentura] warmth.
calorão [kaloˈrãw] *m* [tempo] heatwave.
calorento, ta [kaloˈrẽntu, ta] *adj* **-1.** [pessoa] sensitive to heat. **-2.** [local] hot.
caloria [kaloˈria] *f* calorie.
caloroso, osa [kaloˈrozu, ɔza] *adj* **-1.** [ger] warm. **-2.** [manifestação, protesto] fervent.
calota [kaˈlɔta] *f* AUTO hubcap.
calote [kaˈlɔtʃi] *m* **fam** [de dívida] bad debt; **dar o** ~ **em alguém** to welsh on sb.
caloteiro, ra [kaloˈtejru, ra] ◇ *adj* unreliable. ◇ *m, f* bad payer.
calouro, ra [kaˈloru, ra] *m, f* **-1.** EDUC fresher *UK*, freshman *US*. **-2.** [novato] novice.
calúnia [kaˈlunja] *f* calumny.
caluniador, ra [kalunjaˈdo(x), ra] ◇ *adj* slanderous. ◇ *m, f* slanderer.
caluniar [16] [kaluˈnja(x)] *vt* to slander.
calunioso, niosa [kaluˈnjozu, njɔza] *adj* slanderous.
calvário [kawˈvarju] *m* **-1.** [via crucis] way of the cross. **-2.** *fig* [sofrimento] bitter trial.
calvície [kawˈvisi] *f* baldness.
calvo, va [ˈkawvu, va] *adj* bald.
cama [ˈkãma] *f* bed; ~ **de casal** double bed; ~ **de solteiro** single bed; **estar de** ~ [estar doente] to be bedridden.
camada [kaˈmada] *f* **-1.** [ger] layer. **-2.** [de tinta] coat.
camafeu [kamaˈfew] *m* cameo.
câmara [ˈkãmara] *f* **-1.** [ger] chamber; ~ **de gás** gas chamber; ~ **mortuária** burial chamber; ~ **alta/baixa** upper/lower house; ~ **de comércio** chamber of commerce; **Câmara dos Deputados** House of Representatives; ~ **municipal** town council. **-2.** CINE & FOTO camera; ~ **escura** darkroom. **-3.** TV television camera; **em** ~ **lenta** in slow motion. **-4.** [de pneu]: ~ **(de ar)** inner tube.
◆ **câmara** *mf* [cinegrafista] cameraman.
◆ **de câmara** *loc adj* MÚS chamber.
câmara-ardente [ˌkãmaraaxˈdẽntʃi] (*pl* **câmaras-ardentes**) *f*: **estar exposto em** ~ to lie in wake.
camarada [kamaˈrada] *adj* **-1.** [amigável] friendly. **-2.** [preço] good.
camaradagem [kamaraˈdaʒẽ] (*pl* **-ns**) *f* **-1.** [convivência] companionship. **-2.** [procedimento] good turn; **por** ~ out of friendship.
câmara-de-ar [ˌkãmaraˈdʒja(x)] (*pl* **câmaras-de-ar**) *f* inner tube.
camarão [kamaˈrãw] (*pl* **-ões**) *m* **-1.** [comum] shrimp. **-2.** [graúdo] prawn.
camareiro, ra [kamaˈrejru, ra] *m, f* **-1.** [in hotel] chambermaid, room cleaner. **-2.** [on boat] cabin cleaner.
camarilha [kamaˈriʎa] *f* clique.
camarim [kamaˈrĩ] (*pl* **-ns**) *m* dressing room.
Camarões [kamaˈrõjʃ] *n* Cameroon.
camaronês, esa [kamaroˈnejʃ, ɛza] ◇ *adj* Cameroonian. ◇ *m, f* Cameroonian.
camarote [kamaˈrɔtʃi] *m* **-1.** NÁUT cabin. **-2.** TEATRO box.
cambada [kãnˈbada] *f* **-1.** [porção] load. **-2.** [súcia] bunch.
cambalacho [kãnbaˈlaʃu] *m* scam.
cambaleante [kãnbaˈljãntʃi] *adj* unsteady.
cambalear [15] [kãnbaˈlja(x)] *vi* to stagger.
cambalhota [kãnbaˈʎɔta] *f* somersault; **dar uma** ~ to somersault.
cambial [kãnˈbjaw] (*pl* **-ais**) *adj* exchange.
cambiar [4] [kãnˈbja(x)] ◇ *vt* **-1.** [moeda] to exchange. **-2.** [transformar]: ~ **algo em** to change sthg into. ◇ *vi* [trocar]: ~ **de** to change.
câmbio [ˈkãnbju] *m* **-1.** [ger] exchange; ~ **livre** free trade; ~ **negro** black economy; ~ **oficial/paralelo** official/parallel exchange; [taxa] exchange rate. **-2.** AUTO [mudança] gear stick.
cambista [kãnˈbiʃta] *mf* **-1.** [de moeda] money changer. **-2.** [de ingressos] (ticket) tout.
Camboja [kãnˈbɔʒa] *n* Cambodia.
cambojano, na [kãnboˈʒãnu, na] ◇ *adj* Cambodian. ◇ *m, f* Cambodian.
camburão [kãnbuˈrãw] (*pl* **-ões**) *m* police van.
camélia [kaˈmɛlja] *f* camellia.
camelo [kaˈmelu] *m* **-1.** [animal] camel. **-2.** *fig* [pessoa burra] idiot.
camelô [kameˈlo] *m* pedlar.
câmera [ˈkãmera] ◇ *f* camera. ◇ *mf* [operador] camera operator.
cameraman [ˌkãmeraˈmẽj] (*pl* **cameramen**) *m* TV & CINE camera operator.
caminhada [kamiˈɲada] *f* **-1.** [passeio] walk. **-2.** [extensão] trek.
caminhão [kamiˈɲãw] (*pl* **-ões**) *m* lorry *UK*, truck *US*.
caminhar [kamiˈɲa(x)] *vi* **-1.** [andar] to walk. **-2.** [progredir] *fig* to progress; ~ **para** to lead to.
caminho [kaˈmiɲu] *m* **-1.** [via, estrada] road. **-2.** [extensão, direção] way; **havia um obstáculo no meio do** ~ there was an obstruction in the way; **cortar** ~ to take a short cut; **ser meio** ~ **andado** *fig* to be half way there. **-3.** *fig* [meio] way. **-4.** *fig* [rumo] route.
caminhoneiro, ra [kamiɲoˈnejru, ra] *m, f* lorry driver *UK*, truck driver *US*.
caminhonete [kamjoˈnɛtʃi], **camioneta** [kamioˈnɛta] *f* van.
camisa [kaˈmiza] *f* shirt; ~ **esporte** sports shirt; ~ **pólo** polo shirt; ~ **social** dress shirt; **mudar de** ~ ESP & *fig* to change sides.
camisa-de-força [kaˌmizadʒiˈfoxsa] (*pl* **camisas-de-força**) *f* straitjacket.
camisa-de-vênus [kaˌmizaʒdʒiˈvenuʃ] = **camisinha**.
camisão [kamiˈsãw] (*pl* **-ões**) *m* smock.
camiseta [kamiˈzeta] *f* T-shirt.
camisinha [kamiˈziɲa] *f* condom.
camisola [kamiˈzɔla] *f* nightdress.
camomila [kamoˈmila] *f* camomile; **de** ~ camomile.
campainha [kãmpaˈiɲa] *f* bell.

campal [kãn'paw] (*pl* **-ais**) *adj* **-1.** [relativo ao campo] rural. **-2.** [ao ar livre]: **missa** ~ open-air mass.
campanário [kãnpa'narju] *m* bell tower.
campanha [kãn'pãɲa] *f* **-1.** [ger] campaign; **fazer** ~ **(de/contra)** to campaign for/against. **-2.** [planície] plain.
campeão, ã [kãn'pjãw, ã] (*mpl* **-ões**, *fpl* **-s**) ◇ *adj* [time etc] champion. ◇ *m, f* champion.
campeonato [kãnpjo'natu] *m* championship.
campestre [kãn'pɛʃtri] *adj* rural.
campina [kãn'pina] *f* **-1.** [prado] meadow. **-2.** [planície] plain.
camping [kãn'pĩŋ] *m* **-1.** [atividade] camping. **-2.** [lugar] campsite.
campismo [kãn'piʒmu] *m* camping.
campista [kãn'piʃta] *mf* camper.
campo ['kãnpu] *m* **-1.** [ger] field. **-2.** [zona rural] countryside; **casa de** ~ country house. **-3.** [área] camp; ~ **de aviação** airfield; ~ **de concentração** concentration camp. **-4.** *ESP*: ~ **de futebol** football pitch; ~ **de golfe** golf course; ~ **de tênis** tennis court. **-5.** *fig* [âmbito] field; ~ **de ação** field of action. **-6.** *fig* [ocasião] scope. **-7.** *loc*: **embolar o meio de** ~ to mess it all up.
◆ **de campo** *loc adj* [pesquisa] field.
Campo Grande [ˌkãnpu'grãndʒi] *n* Campo Grande.
camponês, esa ['kãnpo'neʃ, eza] (*mpl* **-eses**, *fpl* **-s**) ◇ *adj* rural. ◇ *m, f* countryman (*f* countrywoman).
campus ['kãnpuʃ] *m inv* campus.
camuflado, da [kamu'fladu, da] *adj* camouflaged.
camuflagem [kamu'flaʒẽ] (*pl* **ns**) *f* camouflage.
camuflar [4] [kamu'fla(x)] *vt* **-1.** [dissimular] to camouflage. **-2.** *fig* [disfarçar] to disguise.
camundongo [kamũn'dõŋgu] *m* mouse.
camurça [ka'muxsa] *f* suede; **de** ~ suede.
cana ['kãna] *f* **-1.** [ger] cane. **-2.** *fam* [cachaça] gut-rot, cachaça, *sugar-cane brandy*. **-3.** *fam* [cadeia] jail; **ir em** ~ to be locked up.
Canadá [kana'da] *n*: **(o)** ~ Canada.
cana-de-açúcar [ˌkãnadʒja'suka(x)] (*pl* **canas-de-açúcar**) *f* sugar cane.
canadense [kana'dẽnsi] ◇ *adj* Canadian. ◇ *mf* Canadian.
canal [ka'naw] (*pl* **-ais**) *m* **-1.** [ger] canal; **canais competentes** proper channels. **-2.** *GEOGR, TV* channel. **-3.** [conduto] pipe. **-4.** *fig* [meio, via] channel.
canalha [ka'naʎa] ◇ *adj* despicable. ◇ *mf* rotter.
canalização [kanaliza'sãw] (*pl* **-ões**) *f* **-1.** [ato] piping. **-2.** [tubulação] plumbing.
canalizar [4] [kanali'za(x)] *vt* **-1.** [rios] to channel. **-2.** [pôr canos de esgotos] to lay with pipes. **-3.** [abrir canais] to canalize. **-4.** *fig* [dirigir] to channel.
canapé [kana'pɛ] *m* couch.
canapê [kana'pe] *m* canapé.
Canárias [ka'narjaʃ] *npl*: **as (Ilhas)** ~ the Canary Islands, the Canaries.
canário [ka'narju] *m* canary.
canastra [ka'naʃtra] *f* **-1.** [cesto] large basket. **-2.** [jogo] canasta.
canastrão, trona [kanaʃ'trãw, trona] (*mpl* **-ões**, *fpl* **-s**) *m, f* *TEATRO* ham actor.
canavial [kana'vjaw] (*pl* **-ais**) *m* cane field.
canavieiro, ra [kana'vjejru, ra] *adj* cane-growing.
Canberra [kãn'bɛxa] *n* Canberra.
canção [kãn'sãw] (*pl* **-ões**) *f* song.
cancela [kãn'sɛla] *f* gate.
cancelamento [kãnsela'mẽntu] *m* **-1.** [passagem] cancellation. **-2.** [processo] overruling.
cancelar [4] [kãnse'la(x)] *vt* **-1.** [anular] to cancel. **-2.** [riscar] to cross out. **-3.** [desistir de] to call off. **-4.** [suprimir - atividade, pagamento] to cancel; [- regalia] to revoke.
câncer ['kãse(x)] (*pl* **-es**) *m MED* cancer; ~ **de mama** breast cancer.
◆ **Câncer** *m ASTRO* Cancer; **ser** ~ to be a Cancer; **Trópico de** ~ Tropic of Cancer.
canceriano, na [kãnse'rjãnu, na] ◇ *adj ASTRO* Cancerian. ◇ *m, f* Cancerian.
cancerígeno, na [kãnse'riʒenu, na] *adj MED* carcinogenic.
cancerologista [kãnserolo'ʒiʃta] *mf* cancer specialist.
canceroso, rosa [kãnse'rozu, rɔza] ◇ *adj* cancerous. ◇ *m, f* cancer patient.
cancha ['kãnʃa] *f* **-1.** [raia] track. **-2.** *fig* [experiência] track record.
canções [kãn'sõjʃ] *pl* ▷ **canção**.
candeeiro [kãn'djejru] *m* lamp.
candelabro [kãnde'labru] *m* **-1.** [castiçal] candlestick. **-2.** [lustre] chandelier.
candente [kãn'dẽntʃi] *adj* **-1.** [ardente] red-hot. **-2.** *fig* [inflamado] inflamed.
candidatar-se [7] [kãndʒida'taxsi] *vp* **-1.** [à presidência da república] to stand for. **-2.** [à vaga] to apply for.
candidato, ta [kãndʒi'datu, ta] *m* **-1.** *POL* candidate. **-2.** [pretendente - a vaga] applicant; [- a exame] candidate.
candidatura [kãndʒida'tura] *f* **-1.** [ger] candidature. **-2.** [proposta] application.
cândido, da ['kãndʒidu, da] *adj* **-1.** [imaculado] candid. **-2.** *fig* [inocente] naive.
candomblé [kãndõn'blɛ] *m* **-1.** [religião] *Yoruba religious tradition in Bahia and its ceremony.* **-2.** [local] Candomblé shrine.

CANDOMBLÉ

Afro-Brazilian religion that worships West-African gods, known as *orixás*. The temples where *candomblé* ceremonies take place are called *terreiros* and the celebrations are held to the sound of percussion instruments, such as *atabaques*. One of the better known celebrations is the feast of Iemanjá, the queen of the oceans and seas, celebrated on 31st December in Rio de Janeiro and on 2nd February in Bahia, when devotees throw offerings into the sea.

candura [kãn'dura] *f* **-1.** [alvura] candour. **-2.** *fig* [inocência] naivety.
caneca [ka'nɛka] *f* mug.
caneco [ka'nɛku] *m* tankard.
canela [ka'nɛla] *f* **-1.** [especiaria] cinnamon. **-2.** ANAT shin.
canelada [kane'lada] *f* kick in the shins.
caneta [ka'neta] *f* pen; ~ **esferográfica** ballpoint pen; ~ **marca-texto** highlighter; ~ **pilot** felt-tip pen.
caneta-tinteiro [ka,netatʃĩn'tejru] (*pl* **canetas-tinteiros**) *f* fountain pen.
canga ['kãŋga] *f* [de praia] beach wrap.
cangaceiro [kãŋga'sejru] *m* bandit.
cangote [kãn'gɔtʃi] *m* (back of the) neck.
canguru [kãŋgu'ru] *m* kangaroo.
cânhamo ['kãɲamu] *m* hemp.
canhão [ka'ɲãw] (*pl* **-ões**) *m* **-1.** MIL cannon. **-2.** *fam fig* [mulher feia] hag.
canhestro, tra [ka'ɲeʃtru, tra] *adj* **-1.** [desajeitado] clumsy. **-2.** [acanhado] awkward.
canhões [ka'ɲõjʃ] *pl* ▷ **canhão**.
canhoto, ta [ka'ɲotu, ta] ◇ *adj* left-handed. ◇ *m, f* left-handed person.
◆ **canhoto** *m* [em talão] stub.
canibal [kani'baw] (*pl* **-ais**) ◇ *adj* cannibalistic. ◇ *m, f* cannibal.
canibalismo [kaniba'liʒmu] *m* cannibalism.
caniço [ka'nisu] *m* **-1.** PESCA rod. **-2.** *fam* [perna fina] pin.
canil [ka'niw] (*pl* **-is**) *m* kennel.
caninha [ka'niɲa] *f* sugar-cane alcohol.
canino, na [ka'ninu, na] *adj* **-1.** [ger] canine. **-2.** [fome] ravenous.
◆ **canino** *m* [dente] canine.
canivete [kani'vɛtʃi] *m* penknife.
canja ['kãnʒa] *f* **-1.** CULIN *thin broth of rice and chicken*. **-2.** *fig* [coisa fácil]: **ser** ~ to be a cinch. **-3.** MÚS: **dar uma** ~ to do a turn.
canjica [kãn'ʒika] *f a sweet dish of maize, coconut milk and cinnamon.*
cano ['kãnu] *m* **-1.** [tubo] pipe; ~ **de esgoto** sewer pipe. **-2.** [de arma] barrel. **-3.** [de bota] leg. **-4.** [trambique] swindle. **-5.** *loc*: **entrar pelo** ~ to come a cropper.
canoa [ka'noa] *f* canoe.
canoagem [ka'nwaʒẽ] *f* canoeing.
canoeiro, ra [ka'nwejru, ra] *m, f* canoeist.
canonização [kanoniza'sãw] (*pl* **-ões**) *f* canonization.
canonizar [4] [kanoni'za(x)] *vt* **-1.** [santificar] to canonize. **-2.** [consagrar] to endorse.
cansaço [kãn'sasu] *m* weariness.
cansado, da [kãn'sadu, da] *adj* **-1.** [fatigado] tired. **-2.** [enfastiado] weary.
cansar [4] [kãn'sa(x)] ◇ *vt* **-1.** [fatigar] to tire. **-2.** [entediar] to bore. **-3.** [aborrecer] to annoy. ◇ *vi* **-1.** [ficar cansado] to get tired; ~ **de algo/alguém** to get tired of sthg/sb; ~ **de fazer algo** to be tired of doing sthg. **-2.** [fazer ficar cansado] to be tiring. **-3.** [aborrecer] to be boring. **-4.** [desistir]: ~ **de fazer algo** to weary of doing sthg.
◆ **cansar-se** *vp* **-1.** [fatigar-se] to get tired. **-2.** [entediar-se]: ~**-se de algo** to get bored with sthg. **-3.** [aborrecer-se]: ~**-se de algo** to become weary of sthg.
cansativo, va [kãnsa'tʃivu, va] *adj* **-1.** [fatigante] tiring. **-2.** [enfadonho] boring.
canseira [kãn'sejra] *f* **-1.** [cansaço] weariness. **-2.** *fam* [esforço] hassle.
cantada [kãn'tada] *f* smooth talk.
cantado, da [kãn'tadu, da] *adj* sung.
cantar [4] [kãn'ta(x)] ◇ *vt* **-1.** [ger] to sing. **-2.** [dizer em voz alta] to sing out. **-3.** *fam* [tentar seduzir] to sweet talk. ◇ *vi* MÚS to sing.
cântaro ['kãntaru] *m* pitcher.
cantarolar [4] [kãntaro'la(x)] *vt & vi* to hum.
canteiro [kãn'tejru] *m* **-1.** [jardim]: ~ **de flores** flower bed. **-2.** [construção]: ~ **de obras** work site. **-3.** [operário] stone mason.
cantiga [kãn'tʃiga] *f* ballad.
cantil [kãn'tʃiw] (*pl* **-is**) *m* **-1.** [frasco] flask. **-2.** [ferramenta] plane.
cantina [kãn'tʃina] *f* canteen.
canto ['kãntu] *m* **-1.** [ger] corner. **-2.** [de triângulo] angle. **-3.** [lugar retirado] quiet corner. **-4.** [MÚS - som musical] song; ~ **gregoriano** Gregorian chant; [- arte] singing.
cantoneira [kãnto'nejra] *f* **-1.** [como reforço] angle iron. **-2.** [como enfeite] corner plate. **-3.** [para fotos] corner slot. **-4.** [prateleira] corner shelf.
cantor, ra [kãn'to(x), ra] (*mpl* **-es**, *fpl* **-s**) *m, f* singer.
cantoria [kãnto'ria] *f* singing.
canudo [ka'nudu] *m* **-1.** [tubo] tube. **-2.** [para beber] straw. **-3.** *fam* [diploma] certificate.
cão ['kãw] (*pl* **cães**) *mf* **-1.** ZOOL dog; ~ **de caça** hound; ~ **de guarda** guard dog. **-2.** *loc*: **quem não tem** ~ **caça com gato** there is more than one way to skin a cat.
◆ **de cão** *loc adj* [dia, férias etc] dreadful.
caolho, lha [ka'oʎu, ʎa] ◇ *adj* **-1.** [zarolho] one-eyed. **-2.** [estrábico] cross-eyed. ◇ *m, f* **-1.** [pessoa zarolha] one-eyed person; **ele é um** ~ he only has one eye. **-2.** [pessoa estrábica] cross-eyed person.
caos ['kawʃ] *m inv* chaos.
caótico, ca [ka'ɔtʃiku, ka] *adj* chaotic.
capa ['kapa] *f* **-1.** [ger] cover; ~ **dura** hard cover; **de** ~ **dura** hardback. **-2.** [roupa] cape; ~ **(de chuva)** rain cape. **-3.** *fig* [aparência] cloak.
capacete [kapa'setʃi] *m* helmet.
capacho [ka'paʃu] *m* **-1.** [tapete] door mat. **-2.** *fig* [pessoa servil] toady.
capacidade [kapasi'dadʒi] *f* **-1.** [ger] capacity. **-2.** [habilidade] ability. **-3.** *fig* [sumidade] genius.
capacitar [4] [kapasi'ta(x)] *vt* **-1.** [habilitar]: ~ **alguém a fazer algo** to prepare sb to do sthg. **-2.** [convencer]: ~ **alguém de algo** to convince sb of sthg.
◆ **capacitar-se** *vp* [convencer-se]: ~**-se de algo** to become convinced of sthg.
capado, da [ka'padu, da] ◇ *adj* [castrado]

castrated. ◇ *m* gelded pig.
capar [4] [ka'pa(x)] *vt* to castrate.
capataz [kapa'taʒ] *m* foreman.
capaz [ka'paʃ] (*pl* **-es**) *adj* **-1.** [competente] competent. **-2.** [apropriado] capable. **-3.** [provável]: **é ~ de nevar** it might snow. **-4.**: **ser ~ de fazer algo** [dispor-se a, ter coragem de] to be capable of doing sthg.
capcioso, osa [kap'sjozu, ɔza] *adj* [pergunta] trick.
capela [ka'pɛla] *f* chapel.
capelão [kape'lãw] (*pl* **-ães**) *m* chaplain.
capenga [ka'pẽŋga] ◇ *adj* lame. ◇ *mf* cripple.
capengar [14] [kapẽŋ'ga(x)] *vi* to limp.
CAPES (*abrev de* **Coordenação de Aperfeiçoamento de Pessoal de Nível Superior**) *f Brazilian educational body that finances postgraduate studies.*
capeta [ka'peta] *m* **-1.** [diabo] devil. **-2.** *fam* [traquinas] troublemaker.
capilar [kapi'la(x)] *adj* **-1.** [do cabelo] hair *(antes de subst)*. **-2.** [vaso] capillary.
capim [ka'pĩ] *m* grass.
capinar [4] [kapi'na(x)] *vt* [limpar] to weed.
capita ['kapita] ◆ **per capita** *loc adj* per capita.
capital [kapi'taw] (*pl* **-ais**) ◇ *adj* **-1.** [essencial] major. **-2.** [pena] capital. ◇ *m* ECON capital; **~ de giro** working capital; **~ de risco** venture capital. ◇ *f* [cidade] capital.
capitalismo [kapita'liʒmu] *m* capitalism.
capitalista [kapita'liʃta] ◇ *adj* capitalist. ◇ *mf* capitalist.
capitalização [kapitaliza'sãw] *f* ECON capitalization.
capitalizar [4] [kapitali'za(x)] *vt* **-1.** ECON to capitalize. **-2.** *fig* [tirar proveito de] to capitalize on.
capitanear [15] [kapita'nja(x)] *vt* **-1.** MIL to command. **-2.** [dirigir] to head.
capitania [kapitã'nia] ◆ **capitania do porto** *f* port authority.
capitão, ã [kapi'tãw, ã] (*mpl* **-ães**, *fpl* **-s**) *m, f* **-1.** [ger] captain. **-2.** [chefe] leader.
capitulação [kapitula'sãw] (*pl* **-ões**) *f* [rendição] surrender.
capitular [kapitu'la(x)] ◇ *vi* to capitulate. ◇ *adj* capitular. ◇ *f* [letra] capital.
capítulo [ka'pitulu] *m* chapter.
capô [ka'po] *m* AUTO bonnet ***UK***, hood ***US***.
capoeira [ka'pwejra] *f* [dança] capoeira, *acrobatic game in dance form that is very popular in north-eastern Brazil.*

CAPOEIRA

Of African origin, *capoeira* reached Brazil during colonial times, with the slaves shipped over from Angola. When *capoeira* was forbidden as a form of self-defence, it became a dance form, with very supple and graceful movements. From being very popular in Bahia, it has spread throughout the country and is performed to the accompaniment of various percussion instruments, especially the *berimbau*.

capoeirista [kapwej'riʃta] *mf person who does capoeira dancing.*
capota [ka'pɔta] *f* AUTO hood.
capotar [4] [kapo'ta(x)] *vi* to overturn.
caprichar [4] [kapri'ʃa(x)] *vi*: **~ (em)** to take delight in.
capricho [ka'priʃu] *m* **-1.** [esmero] care. **-2.** [vontade] whim. **-3.** [teimosia] obstinacy.
caprichoso, osa [kapri'ʃozu, ɔza] *adj* **-1.** [cuidadoso] meticulous. **-2.** [voluntarioso] capricious. **-3.** [teimoso] obstinate.
capricorniano, na [kaprikox'njãnu, na] ◇ *adj* Capricorn. ◇ *m, f* Capricorn.
Capricórnio [kapri'kɔxnju] *m* ASTRO Capricorn; **ser de ~** to be a Capricorn; **Trópico de ~** Tropic of Capricorn.
cápsula ['kapsula] *f* capsule.
captação [kapta'sãw] (*pl* **-ões**) *f* ECON: **~ de recursos** fund-raising.
captar [4] [kap'ta(x)] *vt* **-1.** [atrair] to win. **-2.** [sintonizar] to pick up. **-3.** [água] to collect. **-4.** [compreender] to catch.
captura [kap'tura] *f* capture.
capturar [kaptu'ra(x)] *vt* to capture.
capuz [ka'puʃ] (*pl* **-es**) *m* hood.
caquético, ca [ka'kɛtʃiku, ka] *adj* doddering.
caqui [ka'ki] *m inv* kaki fruit.
cáqui ['kaki] ◇ *adj inv* khaki. ◇ *m* drill.
cara ['kara] ◇ *f* **-1.** [rosto] face; **~ a ~** face to face; **ser a ~ de alguém** to be the image of sb. **-2.** [aspecto] look; **estar com uma ~ boa** [pessoa] to look well; [comida] to look good; **ficar com ~ de tacho** to be dumbfounded. **-3.** [de moeda] side. **-4.** *fam* [coragem] nerve. ◇ *m* **-1.** *fam* [sujeito] guy. **-2.** *loc*: **amarrar a ~** to sulk; **dar as ~s (em)** to show up for; **dar de ~ com alguém** to bump into sb; **encher a ~** *fam* to have a skinful; **estar com ~ de que** [parecer que] to look like; **estar na ~** to be staring one in the face; **meter a ~ em algo** *fig* to put one's back into sthg; **não ir com a ~ de alguém** not to be keen on sb.
carabina [kara'bina] *f* rifle.
Caracas [ka'rakaʃ] *n* Caracas.
caracol [kara'kɔw] (*pl* **-óis**) *m* **-1.** [molusco] snail. **-2.** [de cabelo] curl.
◆ **de caracol** *loc adj* [escada] spiral.
caractere [karak'tɛri] *m* character.
caracteres [karak'tɛriʃ] *pl* ▷ **caráter**.
◆ **caracteres** *mpl* **-1.** [características individuais] characteristics. **-2.** [legendas, créditos] credits.
característico, ca [karakte'riʃtʃiku, ka] *adj* characteristic.
◆ **característica** *f* characteristic.
caracterização [karakteriza'sãw] (*pl* **-ões**) *f* **-1.** [descrição] characterization. **-2.** [TEATRO - maquilagem] make-up; [- indumentária] wardrobe.
caracterizar [4] [karakteri'za(x)] *vt* **-1.** [descrever] characterize. **-2.** [TEATRO - maquilagem] to make up; [- indumentária] to dress.
◆ **caracterizar-se** *vp* [distinguir-se]: **~-se por** to be characterized by.

cara-de-pau [ˌkaradʒi'paw] fam ◇ *adj* shameless. ◇ *mf* shameless person.
caralho [kara'ʎu] *vulg* ◇ *interj* fuck!, fuck me! ◇ *m* [pênis] dick, cock.
caramanchão [karamãn'ʃãw] (*pl* **-ões**) *m* pergola.
caramba [ka'rãnba] *interj* my goodness! *UK*, gee! *US*; **está frio/quente pra** ~ it's incredibly cold/hot.
carambola [karãm'bɔla] *f* star fruit.
caramelado, da [karame'ladu, da] *adj* caramelized.
caramelo [kara'mɛlu] *m* **-1.** [calda] caramel. **-2.** [bala] toffee.
cara-metade [ˌkarame'tadʒi] (*pl* **caras-metades**) *f* better half.
caramujo [kara'muʒu] *m* shellfish.
caranguejo [karãŋ'gejʒu] *m* crab.
carão [ka'rãw] (*pl* **-ões**) *m* ticking off; **passar um ~ em alguém** to tick sb off.
carapaça [kara'pasa] *f* carapace.
carapuça [kara'pusa] *f* **-1.** [gorro] cap. **-2.** [indireta]: **enfiar a** ~ to take it personally.
caraquenho, nha [kara'kẽɲu, ɲã] ◇ *adj* Caracas *(antes de subst)*. ◇ *m, f person from Caracas.*
caratê [kara'te] *m* karate.
caráter [ka'rate(x)] (*pl* **-es**) *m* [índole, natureza, cunho] character; **uma pessoa de ~ /sem ~** a person of good moral fibre/with no moral fibre.
◆ **a caráter** *loc adv* [vestir-se] in character.
caravana [kara'vãna] *f* caravan.
carboidrato [kaxbwi'dratu] *m* carbohydrate.
carbônico, ca [kax'boniku, ka] *adj* carbonic.
carbonizar [4] [kaxboni'za(x)] *vt* to carbonize.
carbono [kax'bonu] *m* QUÍM carbon; **de** ~ carbon *(antes de subst)*.
carburador [kaxbura'do(x)] (*pl* **-es**) *m* carburettor *UK*, carburator *US*.
carcaça [kax'kasa] *f* **-1.** [esqueleto] carcass. **-2.** [armação] frame. **-3.** [de navio] hull.
cárcere ['kaxseri] *m* jail.
carcereiro, ra [kaxse'rejru, ra] *m* jailer.
carcomer [kaxko'me(x)] *vt* [roer] to eat into.
carcomido, da [kaxko'midu, da] *adj* **-1.** [roído] worm-eaten. **-2.** [gasto] frayed. **-3.** *fig* [rosto] pockmarked.
cardápio [kax'dapju] *m* menu.
cardeal [kax'dʒjaw] (*pl* **-ais**) ◇ *m* RELIG cardinal. ◇ *adj* [ponto] cardinal.
cardíaco, ca [kax'dʒiaku, ka] ◇ *adj* cardiac, heart; **ataque** ~ heart attack; **ser** ~ to have heart trouble. ◇ *m, f* heart patient, person with heart problems.
cardigã [kaxdʒi'gã] *m* cardigan.
cardinal [kaxdʒi'naw] (*pl* **-ais**) *adj* cardinal.
cardiologista [kaxdʒolo'ʒiʃta] *mf* cardiologist.
cardiovascular [ˌkaxdʒjovaʃku'la(x)] (*pl* **-es**) *adj* cardiovascular.
cardume [kax'dumi] *m* shoal.
careca [ka'rɛka] ◇ *adj* bald; **estar ~ de saber algo** to know sthg full well. ◇ *m* bald man. ◇ *f* bald patch.
carecer [25] [kare'se(x)] *vt* **-1.** [não ter]: ~ **de** to lack. **-2.** [precisar]: ~ **de** to need.
careiro, ra [ka'rejru, ra] *adj* pricey.
carência [ka'rẽnsja] *f* **-1.** [falta]: ~ **de** lack of. **-2.** [falta de afeto]: ~ **afetiva** lack of care. **-3.** [em seguro, financiamento]: **período de** ~ moratorium.
carente [ka'rẽntʃi] *adj* **-1.** [desprovido] lacking. **-2.** [pobre] needy.
carestia [kareʃ'tʃia] *f* **-1.** [custo alto] high cost. **-2.** [escassez] scarcity.
careta [ka'reta] ◇ *adj* **-1.** *fam* [conservador - pessoa] fuddy-duddy; [- roupa, festa] dated. **-2.** *fam* [que não usa drogas] clean. ◇ *f* [com o rosto] grimace; **fazer** ~ to pull faces.
caretice [kare'tʃisi] *f* *fam* [convencionalismo]: **meu pai é a ~ em pessoa** my father is as old-fashioned as they come.
carga ['kaxga] *f* **-1.** [ato] loading. **-2.** [carregamento] cargo; ~ **aérea** air freight. **-3.** [fardo] load. **-4.** [de arma de fogo] charge. **-5.** [de caneta] cartridge. **-6.** ELETR: ~ **elétrica** electric charge. **-7.** *fig* [peso] burden. **-8.** *fig* [responsabilidade] load; ~ **horária** working hours.
carga-d'água [ˌkaxga'dagwa] (*pl* **cargas-d'água**) *f* [chuva] downpour.
◆ **cargas-d'água** *fpl* [motivo]: **por que cargas-d'água ...?** why on earth ...?
cargo ['kaxgu] *m* **-1.** [função] post. **-2.** [responsabilidade] responsibility.
cargueiro, ra [kax'gejru, ra] *adj* cargo.
◆ **cargueiro** *m* cargo ship.
cariado, da [ka'riadu, da] *adj* [dente] decayed.
cariar [16] [ka'rja(x)] ◇ *vt* to rot. ◇ *vi* to decay.
Caribe [ka'ribi] *n*: **o (mar do)** ~ the Caribbean (Sea).
caribenho, nha [kari'bẽɲu, ɲa] ◇ *adj* Caribbean. ◇ *m, f* Caribbean.
caricatura [karika'tura] *f* **-1.** [desenho] caricature. **-2.** *fig* [reprodução mal-feita] distortion.
caricatural [karikatu'raw] (*pl* **-ais**) *adj* grotesque.
caricaturista [karikatu'riʃta] *mf* caricaturist.
carícia [ka'risja] *f* caress.
caridade [kari'dadʒi] *f* **-1.** [benevolência] charity. **-2.** [esmola] alms *(pl)*.
caridoso, osa [kari'dozu, ɔza] *adj* charitable.
cárie ['kari] *f* caries.
carimbar [4] [karĩn'ba(x)] *vt* to stamp.
carimbo [ka'rĩnbu] *m* stamp.
carinho [ka'riɲu] *m* **-1.** [afago] caress. **-2.** [cuidado] care.
carinhosamente [kariɲoza'mẽntʃi] *adv* **-1.** [afetuosamente] affectionately. **-2.** [cuidadosamente] carefully.
carinhoso, osa [kari'ɲozu, ɔza] *adj* affectionate.
carioca [ka'rjɔka] ◇ *adj* carioca. ◇ *mf* carioca.
carisma [ka'riʒma] *m* charisma.

carismático, ca [kariʒ'matʃiku, ka] *adj* charismatic.
caritativo, va [karita'tʃivu, va] *adj* charitable.
carnal [kax'naw] (*pl* **-ais**) *adj* **-1.** [da carne, do corpo] carnal. **-2.** [consanguíneo] blood- *(antes de subst)*.
carnaval [kaxna'vaw] (*pl* **-ais**) *m* **-1.** [festa popular] carnival. **-2.** *fig* [desordem] mess. **-3.** *fig* [estardalhaço] racket.

CARNAVAL

The greatest of all Brazilian festivals; *carnaval* officially lasts for four days, from Saturday until Shrove Tuesday. Although its most famous display is the parade of the Samba Schools of Rio de Janeiro, broadcast throughout the entire country, *carnaval* is celebrated in different ways in the various Brazilian states. In Salvador (BA), it is characterized by the parade of the *afoxés* and the *trios-elétricos*, drawing behind them vast numbers of revellers. Recife and Olinda (PE) celebrate *carnaval* with a parade of revellers partying to the sound of the *frevo*.

carnavalesco, ca [kaxnava'leʃku, ka] *adj* **-1.** [relativo ao carnaval] carnival. **-2.** [extravagante] over the top.
◆ **carnavalesco** *m* **-1.** [folião] reveller. **-2.** [organizador] carnival planner.
carne ['kaxni] *f* **-1.** [ger] flesh; **em ~ e osso** in the flesh; **em ~ viva** raw; **ser de ~ e osso** *fig* to be only human, after all. **-2.** CULIN meat; **~ assada** roast meat. **-3.** [parentesco] flesh and blood.
carnê [kax'ne] *m* [de pagamento] slate.
carne-de-sol [ˌkaxnidʒi'sɔw] (*pl* **carnes-de-sol**) *f* CULIN *lightly dried meat.*
carneiro [kax'nejru] *m* lamb.
carne-seca [ˌkaxni'seka] (*pl* **carnes-secas**) *f* CULIN dried meat.
carniça [kax'nisa] *f* carrion; **pular ~** to play leapfrog.
carnificina [kaxnifi'sina] *f* carnage.
carnívoro, ra [kax'nivoru, ra] *adj* carnivorous.
◆ **carnívoro** *m* carnivore.
carnoso, osa [kax'nozu, ɔza] *adj* **-1.** [semelhante à carne] meaty. **-2.** [fruto] fleshy. **-3.** [folha] pulpy.
carnudo, da [kax'nudu, da] *adj* **-1.** [lábios] full. **-2.** [fruta, perna] plump.
caro, ra ['karu, ra] *adj* **-1.** [ger] expensive. **-2.** [querido, custoso] dear.
◆ **caro** *adv* **-1.** [por alto preço] for a high price. **-2.** *fig* [com alto custo] dear.
carochinha [karɔ'ʃiɲa] *f* ▷ **história**.
caroço [ka'rosu] *m* stone.
carola [ka'rɔla] ◇ *adj* pious. ◇ *mf* pious person.
carona [ka'rona] *f* lift; **dar/pegar ~** to give/hitch a lift; **ir/viajar de ~** to hitchhike.
Cárpatos ['kaxpatuʃ] *npl*: **os ~** the Carpathians.
carpete [kax'pɛtʃi] *m* fitted carpet.
carpintaria [kaxpĩnta'ria] *f* **-1.** [ofício] carpentry. **-2.** [oficina] carpenter's shop.
carpinteiro, ra [kaxpĩn'tejru] *m, f* carpenter.
carranca [ka'xãŋka] *f* **-1.** *fam* [cara fechada] sour face. **-2.** [em embarcação] figurehead.
carrancudo, da [kaxãŋ'kudu, da] *adj* surly.
carrapato [kaxa'patu] *m* **-1.** [inseto] tick. **-2.** *fam* [pessoa dependente] hanger-on.
carrapicho [kaxa'piʃu] *m* **-1.** [arbusto] burr. **-2.** [carapinha] Afro hairstyle.
carrasco [ka'xaʃku] *m* **-1.** [algoz] executioner. **-2.** *fig* [tirano] tyrant.
carreata [ka'xjata] *f* motorcade.
carregado, da [kaxe'gadu, da] *adj* **-1.** [caminhão etc]: **~ (de)** laden with. **-2.** [fisionomia] sullen. **-3.** [ambiente] dismal. **-4.** [estilo] dark. **-5.** [céu] threatening.
carregador [kaxega'do(x)] (*pl* **-es**) *m, f* **-1.** [de bagagem] porter. **-2.** [transportador] carrier.
carregamento [kaxega'mẽntu] *m* **-1.** [ato] loading. **-2.** [carga] load.
carregar [14] [kaxe'ga(x)] ◇ *vt* **-1.** [ger] to load. **-2.** [levar] to transport. **-3.** *fig* [sentimento etc] to carry. **-4.** [bateria] to charge. **-5.** [impregnar] to fill. ◇ *vi* **-1.** [pôr em demasia]: **~ em** to overdo. **-2.** [exagerar]: **~ em** to overstate.
carreira [ka'xejra] *f* **-1.** [correria] run. **-2.** [profissão] career. **-3.** [fileira]: **~ de algo** row of sthg. **-4.** NÁUT slipway. **-5.** [turfe] racecourse. **-6.** [trilha] track.
carreirista [kaxej'riʃta] *mf* careerist.
carreta [ka'xeta] *f* **-1.** [caminhão] truck. **-2.** [carroça] cart.
carretel [kaxe'tɛw] (*pl* **-éis**) *m* **-1.** [cilindro] reel. **-2.** [molinete] fishing reel.
carretilha [kaxe'tʃiʎa] *f* **-1.** [roldana] pulley. **-2.** [cortadeira] pastry cutter.
carrilhão [kaxi'ʎãw] (*pl* **-ões**) *m* **-1.** [sinos] carillon. **-2.** [relógio] chime.
carrinho [ka'xiɲu] *m* **-1.** [para transportar criança] pushchair *UK*, stroller *US*. **-2.** [para transportar comida etc] trolley; **~ de chá** tea trolley *UK*, tea cart *US*; **~ de feira** shopping trolley; **~ de mão** handcart.
carro ['kaxu] *m* **-1.** [veículo] car; **~ alegórico** float; **~ de bombeiro** fire engine; **~ de passeio** car; **~ de praça** taxi. **-2.** [vagão] waggon. **-3.** [de bois] cart. **-4.** [de máquina de escrever] carriage. **-5.** *loc*: **pôr o ~ adiante dos bois** to put the cart before the horse.
carro-bomba [ˌkaxu'bõnba] (*pl* **carros-bombas, carros-bomba**) *m* car bomb.
carroça [ka'xɔsa] *f* **-1.** [de tração animal] cart. **-2.** [calhambeque] trap.
carroceria [kaxose'ria] *f* car body.
carro-chefe [ˌkaxũ'ʃɛfi] (*pl* **carros-chefes**) *m* leading float.
carrocinha [kaxɔ'siɲa] *f* dog wagon.
carro-forte [ˌkaxu'fɔxtʃi] (*pl* **carros-fortes**) *m* armoured car.
carrossel [kaxɔ'sɛw] (*pl* **-éis**) *m* roundabout *UK*, merry-go-round *US*.
carruagem [ka'xwaʒẽ] (*pl* **-ns**) *f* carriage.
carta ['kaxta] *f* **-1.** [missiva] letter; **~ registrada** registered letter. **-2.** [de baralho] playing card;

dar as ~s to deal the cards. -**3.** [mapa] map. -**4.** [constituição]: ~ **magna** charter.

◆ **carta branca** *f*: **dar/ter** ~ **branca** to give/have carte blanche.

carta-bomba [ˌkaxta'bõnba] (*pl* **cartas-bombas**, **cartas-bomba**) *f* letter bomb.

cartada [kax'tada] *f* -**1.** [em jogo] card play. -**2.** *fig* [ato arriscado] risk; **jogar a última** ~ to play one's last card.

cartão [kax'tãw] (*pl* -**ões**) *m* card; ~ **de crédito** credit card; ~ **de telefone** phone card; ~ **de embarque** boarding card; ~ **de visita** business card.

cartão-postal [kaxˌtãwpoʃtaw] (*pl* **cartões-postais**) *m* postcard.

cartaz [kax'taʃ] (*pl* -**es**) *m* -**1.** [anúncio] poster. -**2.** [popularidade]: **ter** ~ to be popular. -**3.** CINE & TEATRO: **estar em** ~ to be showing.

carteado [kax'tʃjadu] *m* card game.

carteira [kax'tejra] *f* -**1.** [para dinheiro]: ~ **(de notas)** wallet. -**2.** [mesa] desk. -**3.** [documento]: ~ **de identidade** identity card; ~ **de estudante** student card; ~ **de investimentos** ECON investment portfolio; ~ **de sócio** membership card; ~ **de motorista** driving licence *UK*, driver's license *US*; ~ **profissional** *ou* **de trabalho** employment contract. -**4.** [de cigarros] pack. -**5.** [de títulos, ações] portfolio.

carteiro, ra [kax'tejru, ra] *m, f* postman (*f* postwoman).

cartel [kax'tɛw] (*pl* -**éis**) *m* COM cartel.

cartela [kax'tɛla] *f* [mostruário] card.

cartilagem [kaxtʃi'laʒẽ] (*pl* -**ns**) *f* ANAT cartilage.

cartões [kax'tõjʃ] *mpl* ▷ **cartão**.

cartografia [kaxtogra'fia] *f* cartography.

cartola [kax'tɔla] ◇ *f* [chapéu] top hat. ◇ *m* -**1.** *fam* [pessoa importante] snob. -**2.** *pej* & FUT *club manager who abuses his position.*

cartolina [kaxto'lina] *f* card.

cartomante [kaxto'mãntʃi] *mf* card reader.

cartório [kax'tɔrju] *m* -**1.** [arquivo] archive. -**2.** [de registro civil] registry office. -**3.** [de registro de imóveis] Land Registry.

cartucho [kax'tuʃu] *m* -**1.** [de arma] cartridge. -**2.** [invólucro] tube; **queimar o último** ~ *fig* to play one's last card.

cartum [kax'tũ] (*pl* -**ns**) *m* cartoon.

cartunista [kaxtu'niʃta] *mf* cartoonist.

caruncho [ka'rũnʃu] *m* woodworm.

carvalho [kax'vaʎu] *m* oak.

carvão [kax'vãw] (*pl* -**ões**) *m* -**1.** [combustível] coal; ~ **vegetal** charcoal. -**2.** [tição] cinder.

casa ['kaza] *f* -**1.** [ger] house; ~ **de campo** country house; ~ **popular** council house; ~ **geminada** semi-detached house. -**2.** [lar] home; **em** ~ at home; **ir para** ~ to go home; **você é da** ~ [convidado, hóspede] make yourself at home. -**3.** [estabelecimento] building; ~ **de câmbio** bureau de change; **Casa da Moeda** Mint; ~ **noturna** nightclub; ~ **de saúde** hospital. -**4.** [de botões] buttonhole. -**5.** MAT place. -**6.** [instalação]: ~ **de máquinas** engine housing.

casaca [ka'zaka] *f* cloak; **virar a** ~ to be a turncoat.

casacão [kaza'kãw] (*pl* -**ões**) *m* overcoat.

casaco [ka'zaku] *m* coat; ~ **de pele** fur coat.

casa-grande [ˌkaza'grãndʒi] (*pl* **casas-grandes**) *f* main house.

casal [ka'zaw] (*pl* -**ais**) *m* -**1.** [homem e mulher] couple. -**2.** [de filhos] pair.

casamenteiro, ra [kazamẽn'tejru, ra] *adj* matchmaking; **Santo Antônio, o santo** ~ St Anthony the matchmaker.

casamento [kaza'mẽntu] *m* -**1.** [ger] marriage. -**2.** [cerimônia] wedding; ~ **civil/religioso** civil/religious wedding.

casar [4] [ka'za(x)] ◇ *vt* -**1.** [ger] to marry. -**2.** [emparelhar] to pair. ◇ *vi* [em matrimônio]: ~ **(com alguém)** to marry (sb); ~ **no civil/no religioso** to have a civil/religious wedding.

◆ **casar-se** *vp* -**1.** [em matrimônio] to marry. -**2.** [combinar-se] to go.

casarão [kaza'rãw] (*pl* -**ões**) *m* large house.

casca ['kaʃka] *f* -**1.** [de pão] crust. -**2.** [de ferida] scab. -**3.** [de ovo] shell. -**4.** [de fruta] peel. -**5.** *fig* [aparência] sullenness.

casca-grossa [ˌkaʃka'grɔsa] (*pl* **cascas-grossas**) *mf* uncouth person.

cascalho [kaʃ'kaʎu] *m* gravel.

cascão [kaʃ'kãw] (*pl* -**ões**) *m* -**1.** [crosta] hard crust. -**2.** [de sujeira] grime.

cascata [kaʃ'kata] *f* -**1.** [queda d'água] waterfall. -**2.** *fam* [mentira] fib. -**3.** *fam* [bazófia] bragging.

cascateiro, ra [kaʃka'tejru, ra] *fam* ◇ *adj* bullshit. ◇ *m, f* bullshitter.

cascavel [kaʃka'vɛw] (*pl* -**éis**) ◇ *m* ZOOL rattlesnake. ◇ *f* *fig* [mulher] cow.

casco ['kaʃku] *m* -**1.** [de navio] hull. -**2.** [de tartaruga] shell. -**3.** [garrafa] cask. -**4.** [crânio] scalp.

cascudo, da [kaʃ'kudu, da] *adj* [de casca dura] crusty.

◆ **cascudo** *m* -**1.** [inseto] horn-shelled insect. -**2.** [pancada] rap on the head; **dar um** ~ **em alguém** to rap sb on the head.

casebre [ka'zɛbri] *m* hovel.

caseiro, ra [ka'zejru, ra] ◇ *adj* -**1.** [produto] home-made. -**2.** [trabalho] home- *(antes de subst)*. -**3.** [roupa] homespun. -**4.** [pessoa] family man. ◇ *m, f* [empregado] caretaker.

caserna [ka'zɛxna] *f* MIL barracks *(pl)*.

casmurro, rra [kaʒ'muxu, xa] *adj* -**1.** [teimoso] stubborn. -**2.** [sorumbático] gloomy.

caso ['kazu] ◇ *m* -**1.** [fato] matter; **o** ~ **é que ...** the fact is that ... -**2.** [circunstância]: **em todo** ~ anyway; **neste** ~ in that case; **no** ~ **de** should there be; ~ **de emergência** emergency. -**3.** [história] story. -**4.** [amoroso] affair. -**5.** [problema]: **criar** ~ to cause a problem. -**6.** MED, GRAM case. -**7.** *loc*: **fazer pouco** ~ **de** to take little account of; **não vem ao** ~ it's not relevant; **ser um** ~ **perdido** to be a lost cause. ◇ *conj* if.

casório [ka'zɔrju] *m* *fam* splicing.

caspa [ˈkaʃpa] *f* dandruff.
Cáspio [ˈkaʃpju] *n*: **o (mar)** ~ the Caspian (Sea).
casquinha [kaʃˈkiɲa] *f* **-1.** [de sorvete] cone. **-2.** [de pele] scab.
cassado, da [kaˈsadu, da] *m, f person deprived of his/her civil rights.*
cassar [4] [kaˈsa(x)] *vt* **-1.** *POL* to annul. **-2.** [licença, direitos] to quash.
cassete [kaˈsɛtʃi] ◇ *adj inv* [fita, gravador] tape- *(antes de subst).* ◇ *m* [gravador] tape.
cassetete [kaseˈtɛtʃi] *m* truncheon.
cassino [kaˈsinu] *m* casino.
casta [ˈkaʃta] *f* **-1.** [camada social] caste. **-2.** *fig* [raça] race.
castanha [kaʃˈtãɲa] *f* ▷ **castanho.**
castanha-do-pará [kaʃˌtãɲadupaˈra] (*pl* **castanhas-do-pará**) *m* Brazil nut.
castanheiro [kaʃtãˈɲejru] *m* chestnut tree.
castanho, nha [kaʃˈtãɲu, ɲa] *adj* [olhos etc] brown.
◆ **castanha** *f* [fruto] chestnut; ~ **de caju** cashew.
castanholas [kaʃtãˈɲɔlaʃ] *fpl* castanets.
castelo [kaʃˈtɛlu] *m* castle.
castiçal [kaʃtʃiˈsaw] (*pl* **-ais**) *m* candlestick.
castiço, ça [kaʃˈtʃisu, sa] *adj* **-1.** [puro] top-breed. **-2.** [de boa casta] well-bred. **-3.** *fig* [vernáculo] vernacular.
castidade [kaʃtʃiˈdadʒi] *f* chastity.
castigar [14] [kaʃtʃiˈga(x)] *vt* **-1.** [punir] to punish. **-2.** *fam* [tocar] to bash out.
◆ **castigar-se** *vp* [penitenciar-se] to do penance.
castigo [kaʃˈtʃigu] *m* **-1.** [punição] punishment; **estar/ficar de** ~ to be being punished. **-2.** *fig* [mortificação] torture; **ser um** ~ to be torture.
casto, ta [ˈkaʃtu, ta] *adj* chaste.
castrado, da [kaʃˈtradu, da] *adj* castrated.
castrar [4] [kaʃˈtra(x)] *vt* **-1.** [capar] to castrate. **-2.** *fig* [impedir] to muzzle. **-3.** *fig* [personalidade] to castrate.
casual [kaˈzwaw] (*pl* **-ais**) *adj* chance *(antes de subst).*
casualidade [kazwaliˈdadʒi] *f* chance; **por** ~ by chance.
casulo [kaˈzulu] *m* **-1.** [de insetos] cocoon. **-2.** [de sementes] boll.
cata [ˈkata] *f*: **à** ~ **de algo/alguém** in search of sthg/sb.
cataclismo [kataˈkliʒmu] *m* **-1.** [dilúvio] flood. **-2.** *GEOL* cataclysm. **-3.** *fig* [desastre] cataclysm. **-4.** *fig* [convulsão social] revolt.
catacumbas [kataˈkũnbaʃ] *fpl* catacombs.
catalão, lã [kataˈlãw, lã] ◇ *adj* Catalan. ◇ *m, f* Catalan.
◆ **catalão** *m* [língua] Catalan.
catalisador, ra [katalizaˈdo(x), ra] *adj* catalytic.
◆ **catalisador** *m* catalyst.
catalogar [14] [kataloˈga(x)] *vt* to catalogue.
catálogo [kaˈtalogu] *m* catalogue; ~ **(de telefones)** telephone directory.
Catalunha [kataˈlũɲa] *n* Catalonia.
catapora [kataˈpɔra] *f* chickenpox.
catar [4] [kaˈta(x)] *vt* **-1.** [procurar] to search for. **-2.** [pegar, recolher] to pick up. **-3.** [tirar, limpar de] to pick out; ~ **piolhos** to delouse. **-4.** [escolher] to pick over; ~ **feijão/arroz** to pick over beans/ rice.
catarata [kataˈrata] *f* **-1.** [queda d'água] waterfall. **-2.** *MED* cataract.

CATARATAS DO IGUAÇU

Situated in the interior of the National Park of Iguaçu (PR), on the border between Brazil and Argentina, the Iguaçu falls pour out 13 million litres of water per second from an altitude that varies between 40 and 90 metres. Its 275 waterfalls are spread, on the Brazilian side, over a width of 800 metres. The almost 90m high *Garganta do Diabo* is its most famous fall.

catarro [kaˈtaxu] *m* catarrh.
catarse [kaˈtaxsi] *f* catharsis.
catástrofe [kaˈtaʃtrofi] *f* catastrophe.
catastrófico, ca [katаʃˈtrɔfiku, ka] *adj* catastrophic.
catatau [kataˈtaw] (*pl* **-ais**) *m fam*: **um** ~ **de** a pile of.
cata-vento [kataˈvẽntu] (*pl* **cata-ventos**) *m* weathervane.
catecismo [kateˈsiʒmu] *m* catechism.
cátedra [ˈkatedra] *f* **-1.** *UNIV* chair. **-2.** *RELIG* throne.
catedral [kateˈdraw] (*pl* **-ais**) *f* cathedral.
catedrático, ca [kateˈdratʃiku, ka] ◇ *m, f* chair. ◇ *adj* chair.
categoria [kategoˈria] *f* **-1.** [grupo] category. **-2.** [qualidade] quality; **de (alta)** ~ high quality. **-3.** [social] standing. **-4.** [cargo] position.
categórico, ca [kateˈgɔriku, ka] *adj* categoric.
categorização [kategorizaˈsãw] (*pl* **-ões**) *f* categorization.
categorizar [4] [kategoriˈza(x)] *vt* to classify.
catequese [kateˈkɛzi] *f* religious instruction.
catequizar [4] [katekiˈza(x)] *vt* **-1.** *RELIG* to teach doctrine to. **-2.** *fig* [doutrinar] to indoctrinate.
cateter [kateˈtɛ(x)] *m MED* catheter.
cateterismo [kateteˈriʒmu] *m MED* catheterization.
catinga [kaˈtʃĩŋga] *f* [mau-cheiro] stench.
cativante [katʃiˈvãntʃi] *adj* entrancing.
cativar [4] [katʃiˈva(x)] *vt* **-1.** [escravizar] to capture. **-2.** [seduzir] to captivate.
cativeiro [katʃiˈvejru] *m* **-1.** [escravidão] slavery. **-2.** [prisão] captivity.
cativo, va [kaˈtʃivu, va] ◇ *adj* **-1.** [preso] captive. **-2.** [sujeito]: ~ **a** attracted by. **-3.** [cadeira] exclusive. ◇ *m, f* **-1.** [escravo] slave. **-2.** [prisioneiro] prisoner.
catolicismo [katoliˈsiʒmu] *m* Catholicism.
católico, ca [kaˈtɔliku, ka] *adj* **-1.** *RELIG* Catholic. **-2.** *fig* [correto, tradicional]: **não ser muito** ~ to be unconventional. **-3.** *fig* [bem, de bom humor]: **ele não está muito** ~ he's not in a good mood.
catorze [kaˈtoxzi] *num* fourteen; *veja também* **seis.**

catucar [12] [katu'ka(x)] *vt* = **cutucar**.
caução [kaw'sãw] (*pl* **-ões**) *f* **-1.** [cautela] care. **-2.** [garantia] pledge. **-3.** *JUR* bail.
Cáucaso ['kawkazu] *n* Caucasus.
caucionar [4] [kawsjo'na(x)] *vt* **-1.** [garantir] to pledge. **-2.** *JUR* to stand bail for.
cauções [kaw'sõjʃ] *fpl* ▻ **caução**.
cauda ['kawda] *f* **-1.** [de animal] tail. **-2.** [de vestido] train.
caudaloso, osa [kawda'lozu, ɔza] *adj* torrential.
caudilho [kaw'dʒiʎu] *m* military commander.
caule ['kawli] *m* stem.
causa ['kawza] *f* **-1.** [ger] cause. **-2.** [motivo] reason; **por ~ de** because of.
causador, ra [kawza'do(x), ra] ◇ *adj* causal. ◇ *m, f* cause.
causar [4] [kaw'za(x)] *vt* to cause.
cáustico, ca ['kawʃtʃiku, ka] *adj* caustic.
cautela [kaw'tɛla] *f* **-1.** [precaução] precaution; **com ~** with care. **-2.** [título] share certificate. **-3.** [de penhor] pawn ticket.
cautelar [kawte'la(x)] *adj* precautionary.
cauteloso, osa [kawte'lozu, ɔza] *adj* cautious.
cauterizar [4] [kawteri'za(x)] *vt* to cauterize.
cava ['kava] *f* ▻ **cavo**.
cavaco [ka'vaku] *m*: **~s do ofício** part of the job.
cavala [ka'vala] *f* [peixe] mackerel.
cavalar [kava'la(x)] *adj* excessive.
cavalaria [kavala'ria] *f* **-1.** *MIL* cavalry. **-2.** [cavalos] herd of horses. **-3.** [ordem] chivalry.
cavalariça [kavala'risa] *f* [estrebaria] stable.
cavalariço [kavala'risu] *m* [estribeiro] groom *UK*, stableman *US*.
cavaleiro, ra [kava'lejru] *m, f* [quem monta] horseman (*f* horsewoman).
◆ **cavaleiro** *m* [medieval] knight.
cavalete [kava'letʃi] *m* **-1.** [de pintor] easel. **-2.** [de mesa] trestle. **-3.** [para instrumento] bridge.
cavalgar [14] [kavaw'ga(x)] *vt & vi* to ride.
cavalheiresco, ca [kavaʎej'reʃku, ka] *adj* noble.
cavalheiro [kava'ʎejru] ◇ *m* gentleman. ◇ *adj* [educado] well-bred.
cavalo [ka'valu] *m* **-1.** *ZOOL* horse; **a ~** on horseback. **-2.** [em xadrez] knight. **-3.** *fig* [pessoa agressiva] pig; **ele agiu como um ~** he behaved like a pig. **-4.** [cavalo-vapor] horsepower. **-5.** *loc*: **fazer um ~ de batalha** to make a fuss about nothing; **pode tirar o ~ da chuva que ela não vai aceitar sua proposta** you can forget that, as she's not going to accept your proposal.
cavalo-de-pau [kavaludʒi'paw] (*pl* **cavalos-de-pau**) *m* wheel spin.
cavalo-de-Tróia [ka'valudʒitrɔja] (*pl* **cavalos-de-Tróia**) *m COMPUT* Trojan horse.
cavalo-marinho [ka,valuma'riɲu] (*pl* **cavalos-marinhos**) *m* sea-horse.
cavanhaque [kava'ɲaki] *m* goatee.
cavaquinho [kava'kiɲu] *m* small guitar.
cavar [4] [ka'va(x)] ◇ *vt* **-1.** [ger] to dig. **-2.** [emprego] to search long and hard. ◇ *vi* [escavar] to dig.
cave ['kavi] *f* cellar.
caveira [ka'vejra] *f* **-1.** [crânio] skull. **-2.** *fig* [rosto macilento] cavernous face. **-3.** *loc*: **fazer a ~ de alguém** to run sb down.
caverna [ka'vɛxna] *f* cavern.
cavernoso, osa [kavex'nozu, ɔza] *adj* cavernous.
caviar [ka'vja(x)] *m* caviar.
cavidade [kavi'dadʒi] *f* cavity.
cavilha [ka'viʎa] *f* peg.
cavo, va ['kavu, va] *adj* [côncavo] hollow.
◆ **cava** *f* [de manga] armhole.
caxias [ka'ʃiaʃ] ◇ *adj (inv)* scrupulous. ◇ *mf (inv)* hard taskmaster.
caxumba [ka'ʃũnba] *f* mumps *(sg)*.
CBF (*abrev de* **Confederação Brasileira de Futebol**) *f Brazilian football federation.*
c/c (*abrev de* **conta corrente**) *f* c/a.
CD [se'de] (*abrev de* **Compact Disc**) *m* CD.
CDB (*abrev de* **Certificado de Depósito Bancário**) *m type of investment offered by Brazilian banks.*
CDC (*abrev de* **Código de Defesa do Consumidor**) *m Brazilian consumer protection legislation.*
CD-i (*abrev de* **Compact Disc-Interativo**) *m* CD-I.
CD-ROM (*abrev de* **Compact Disc-Read Only Memory**) *m* CD-ROM.
CE ◇ *f* (*abrev de* **Comunidade Européia**) EC. ◇ *m* (*abrev de* **Estado do Ceará**) *State of Ceará.*
cear [15] ['sja(x)] ◇ *vt* to have for supper. ◇ *vi* to have supper.
Ceará [sja'ra] *n* Ceará.
CEASA (*abrev de* **Companhia de Entrepostos e Armazéns S.A**) *m Brazilian company of fruit and vegetable wholesalers.*
cebola [se'bola] *f* onion.
cebolinha [sebo'liɲa] *f* chive.
CEBRAP (*abrev de* **Centro Brasileiro de Análise e Planejamento**) *m independent research centre for the study of Brazilian society.*
cê-cedilha [,sese'dʒiʎa] (*pl* **cês-cedilhas**) *m* c-cedilla.
cê-dê-efe [sede'ɛfi] (*pl* **cê-dê-efes**) *mf fam* **-1.** [com o trabalho] workaholic. **-2.** [com os estudos] swot.
cedente [se'dẽntʃi] *mf* transferor.
ceder [5] [se'de(x)] ◇ *vt* **-1.** [dar] to hand over. **-2.** [emprestar] to loan. ◇ *vi* **-1.** [aquiescer]: **~ a algo** to give in to sthg. **-2.** [diminuir] to fall. **-3.** [afrouxar-se] to loosen. **-4.** [curvar-se ao peso] to give way. **-5.** [sucumbir]: **~ a algo** to give way to sthg. **-6.** [transigir] to give in.
cedilha [se'diʎa] *f* cedilla.
cedo ['sedu] *adv* [de manhãzinha] early; **mais ~ ou mais tarde** sooner or later; **o mais ~ possível** as soon as possible; **quanto mais ~ melhor** the sooner the better.
cedro ['sɛdru] *m* cedar.
cédula ['sɛdula] *f* **-1.** [dinheiro] banknote. **-2.** [em votação]: **~ eleitoral** ballot paper.
CEF (*abrev de* **Caixa Econômica Federal**) *f Brazilian state-owned bank financing loans for house purchase.*
cefaléia [sefa'lɛja] *f* headache.

cegar [14] [se'ga(x)] *vt* **-1.** [ger] to blind. **-2.** [suj: paixão, raiva] to make blind. **-3.** [tesoura etc] to blunt.

cego, ga ['sɛgu, ga] ◇ *adj* **-1.** [ger] blind. **-2.** [tesoura] blunt. ◇ *m, f* blind person.

◆ **às cegas** *loc adv* **-1.** [sem ver] blindly. **-2.** [sem saber] in the dark.

cegonha [se'goɲa] *f* [ave] stork; **esperar a chegada da ~** *fam* to be pregnant.

cegueira [se'gejra] *f* blindness.

ceia ['seja] *f* supper; **a última ~** *RELIG* the Last Supper; **~ de Natal** Christmas Eve midnight supper.

ceifa ['sejfa] *f* **-1.** [ato] harvest. **-2.** [época] harvest-time. **-3.** *fig* [destruição, mortandade] death-toll.

ceifar [4] [sej'fa(x)] ◇ *vt* **-1.** [trigo, espigas] to harvest. **-2.** *fig* [vidas] to take. ◇ *vi* [colher] to harvest.

Ceilão [sej'lãw] *n* Ceylon.

cela ['sɛla] *f* cell.

celebração [selebra'sãw] (*pl* **-ões**) *f* **-1.** [realização] celebration. **-2.** [comemoração] commemoration.

celebrado, da [sele'bradu, da] *adj* [afamado] celebrated.

celebrar [4] [sele'bra(x)] *vt* **-1.** [ger] to celebrate. **-2.** [exaltar] to glorify.

célebre ['sɛlebri] *adj* famous.

celebridade [selebri'dadʒi] *mf* celebrity.

celebrizar [4] [selebri'za(x)] *vt* [conferir fama a] to make famous.

◆ **celebrizar-se** *vp* to become famous.

celeiro [se'lejru] *m* **-1.** [para cereais] granary. **-2.** [depósito] store.

célere ['sɛleri] *adj* quick.

celeste [se'lɛʃtʃi] *adj* heavenly.

celestial [seleʃ'tʃjaw] (*pl* **-ais**) *adj* celestial.

celeuma [se'lewma] *f* hubbub.

celibatário, ria [seliba'tarju, rja] ◇ *adj* celibate. ◇ *m, f* unmarried person.

celibato [seli'batu] *m* celibacy.

celofane [selo'fãni] ◇ *adj* [papel] cellophane. ◇ *m* cellophane.

celsius [sew'siuʃ] *adj* Celsius.

celta ['sɛwta] ◇ *adj* Celtic. ◇ *mf* [pessoa] Celt. ◇ *m* [língua] Celtic.

célula ['sɛlula] *f* cell; **~ fotoelétrica** photo-electric cell.

celular [selu'la(x)] ◇ *adj* cellular. ◇ *m* *TELEC* cellular phone.

celulite [selu'litʃi] *f* cellulite.

celulose [selu'lɔzi] *f* cellulose.

cem ['sẽ] *num* **-1.** [cardinal] one/a hundred; **~ por cento** one/a hundred per cent; *veja também* **seis**. **-2.** [muitos]: **~ vezes** hundreds of times.

◆ **cem por cento** ◇ *loc adj*: **ser ~ por cento** to be one hundred per cent. ◇ *loc adv* [totalmente] completely.

cemitério [semi'tɛrju] *m* cemetery.

cena ['sena] *f* **-1.** [de peça, filme, novela] scene; **~s externas** outdoor scenes. **-2.** [palco] stage; **levar à ~** to stage; **em ~** on stage. **-3.** [acontecimento] spectacle. **-4.** [escândalo]: **fazer uma ~** to make a scene.

cenário [se'narju] *m* **-1.** [ger] scene. **-2.** [em teatro, cinema, TV] scenery. **-3.** [panorama] sight.

cenho ['seɲu] *m* frown.

cênico, ca ['seniku, ka] *adj* *TEATRO* stage *(antes de subst)*; **artes cênicas** performing arts.

cenografia [senogra'fia] *f* scenography.

cenógrafo, fa [se'nɔgrafu, fa] *m, f* scenographer.

cenoura [se'nora] *f* carrot.

censo ['sẽnsu] *m* census.

censor, ra [sẽnso(x), ra] *m, f* censor.

censura [sẽn'sura] *f* **-1.** [crítica] criticism. **-2.** [repreensão] reprimand. **-3.** [condenação] condemnation. **-4.** [prática] censure. **-5.** [organismo] board of censors. **-6.** [proibição] censorship. **-7.** [corte] cut.

censurado, da [sẽnsu'radu, da] *adj* [proibido] censored.

censurar [4] [sẽnsu'ra(x)] *vt* **-1.** [criticar] to criticise. **-2.** [repreender] to reprove. **-3.** [condenar] to condemn. **-4.** [examinar] to censor. **-5.** [proibir] to ban. **-6.** [cortar] to cut.

censurável [sẽnsu'ravew] (*pl* **-eis**) *adj* [decisão, comportamento] open to criticism.

centavo [sẽn'tavu] *m* cent; **estar sem um ~** to be penniless.

centeio [sẽn'teju] *m* rye.

centelha [sẽn'teʎa] *f* spark.

centena [sẽn'tena] *f* hundred; **às ~s** in their hundreds; **uma ~ de vezes** a hundred times.

centenário, ria [sẽnte'narju, rja] ◇ *adj*: **um homem ~** a hundred-year-old man; **ele é ~** he is a hundred years old. ◇ *m, f* [pessoa] centenarian.

◆ **centenário** *m* [comemoração] centenary.

centésimo, ma [sẽn'tɛzimu, ma] ◇ *num* hundredth. ◇ *m, f* [pessoa] hundredth.

◆ **centésimo** *m* hundredth.

centígrado, da [sẽn'tʃigradu] *adj* centigrade *(depois de subst)*.

◆ **centígrado** *m* centigrade.

centilitro [sẽntʃi'litru] *m* centilitre.

centímetro [sẽn'tʃimetru] *m* centimetre.

cento ['sẽntu] *num*: **~ e dez** one/a hundred and ten; **por ~** per cent; *veja também* **seis**.

centopéia [sẽnto'pɛja] *f* centipede.

central [sẽn'traw] (*pl* **-ais**) ◇ *adj* **-1.** [ger] central. **-2.** *fig* [problema, ponto, argumento] central. ◇ *f* **-1.** [agência, delegacia]: **~ de polícia** police station; **~ de atendimento** call centre; **~ de correios** post office; **~ telefônica** telephone exchange. **-2.** [usina]: **~ elétrica** power station; **~ nuclear** nuclear power station.

centralização [sẽntraliza'sãw] *f* centralization.

centralizar [4] [sẽntrali'za(x)] *vt* to centralize.

centrar [4] [sẽn'tra(x)] ◇ *vt* **-1.** [ger] to centre. **-2.** *FUT* [bola, passe]: **~** to kick into the centre. ◇ *vi* *FUT* to shoot.

centrífuga [sẽntri'fuga], **centrifugadora** [sẽntri'fuga'dora] *f* centrifuge.

centro ['sẽntru] *m* **-1.** [ger] centre; **~ de gravidade** centre of gravity; **~ da Terra** centre of the

Earth; ~ **de mesa** centrepiece; **ser o ~ das atenções** to be the centre of attention; ~ **comercial** shopping centre *UK*, shopping mall *US*; ~ **cultural** cultural centre; ~ **espírita** spiritualist centre; ~ **financeiro** financial centre; ~ **industrial** industrial centre; ~ **produtor** manufacturing centre; ~ **de atendimento** service centre; ~ **de processamento de dados** data processing centre. **-2.** [de cidade] (city) centre; **ir ao** ~ to go downtown. **-3.** [metrópole] metropolis.

centroavante [ˌsẽntrw'vãntʃi] *m* centre forward.

CEP (*abrev de* **Código de Endereçamento Postal**) *m* ≃ post code *UK*, ≃ zip code *US*.

CEPAL (*abrev de* **Comissão Econômica para a América Latina**) *f* ECLAC.

cepo ['sepu] *m* **-1.** [toro] log. **-2.** [para decapitação] block.

cera ['sera] *f* **-1.** [ger] wax. **-2.** [para polir] wax polish. **-3.** *fam fig* [manha] sham; **fazer** ~ to sham.

cerâmica [se'rãmika] *f* **-1.** [ger] ceramics. **-2.** [fábrica] pottery. **-3.** [argila cozida] ceramic.

ceramista [sera'miʃta] *mf* potter, ceramicist.

cerca ['sexka] *f* [de arame, madeira, ferro] fence; ~ **viva** hedge.

◆ **cerca de** *loc prep* around.

cercado, da [sex'kadu, da] *adj* fenced.

◆ **cercado** *m* **-1.** [terreno] enclosure. **-2.** [para animais] pen. **-3.** [para crianças] playground.

cercanias [sexka'niaʃ] *fpl* **-1.** [arredores] outskirts. **-2.** [vizinhança] neighbourhood.

cercar [12] [sex'ka(x)] *vt* **-1.** [ger] to surround. **-2.** [pôr cerca em] to fence.

◆ **cercar-se** *vp* [rodear-se]: **~-se de** to surround o.s. with.

cercear [15] [sex'sja(x)] *vt* [liberdade, privilégios] to restrict.

cerco ['sexku] *m* [assédio] siege; **fechar o ~ a** to close in on, to clamp down on; **pôr ~ a** to lay siege to.

cerda ['sɛxda] *f* [de escova de dentes] bristle.

cereal [se'rjal] (*pl* **-ais**) *m* cereal.

cerebral [sere'braw] (*pl* **-ais**) *adj* **-1.** ANAT cerebral. **-2.** [intelectual] intellectual.

cérebro ['sɛrebru] *m* **-1.** ANAT brain. **-2.** *fig* [líder, mentor]: **o** ~ the brains *(sg)*.

cereja [se'reʒa] *f* cherry.

cerejeira [sere'ʒejra] *f* **-1.** [árvore] cherry tree. **-2.** [madeira] cherry wood.

cerimônia [seri'monja] *f* **-1.** [solenidade] ceremony; ~ **de posse** investiture. **-2.** [formalidade] formality; **fazer** ~ to stand on ceremony; **sirva-se sem ~!** just help yourself!

cerimonial [serimo'njaw] (*pl* **-ais**) *m* [protocolo] ceremonial.

cerimonioso, osa [serimo'njozu, ɔza] *adj* ceremonious.

cerne ['sɛxni] *m* **-1.** [de madeira] heartwood. **-2.** *fig* [de questão] heart.

ceroulas [se'rolaʃ] *fpl* long johns.

cerração [sexa'sãw] *f* [neblina] fog.

cerrado, da [se'xadu, da] *adj* **-1.** [fechado - porta, olhos] closed; [- punhos, dentes] clenched. **-2.** [intenso] [bombardeio] heavy. **-3.** [denso, espesso] thick.

◆ **cerrado** *m* [vegetação] *dense, low vegetation found in northern and central Brazil.*

cerrar [4] [se'xa(x)] *vt* [fechar - porta, olhos] to close; [-punhos, centes] to clench.

◆ **cerrar-se** *vp* **-1.** [fechar-se] to close; **~-se em** to shut oneself in. **-2.** [céu] to become dark.

certa ['sɛxta] *f* ⊳ **certo**.

certame [sex'tãmi] *m* [concurso, competição] contest.

certeiro, ra [sex'tejru, ra] *adj* accurate.

certeza [sex'teza] *f* certainty; **tem ~?** are you sure?; **ter ~ de algo** to be sure about sthg; **ter ~ de que** to be sure that; **com** ~ definitely.

certidão [sextʃi'dãw] (*pl* **-ões**) *f* certificate; ~ **de casamento** marriage certificate; ~ **de nascimento** birth certificate.

certificação [sextʃifika'sãw] (*pl* **-ões**) *f* certification.

certificado [sextʃifi'kadu] *m* certificate.

certificar [12] [sextʃifi'ka(x)] *vt* **-1.** [assegurar]: ~ **alguém de algo/de que** to assure sb of sthg/that. **-2.** [atestar] to affirm.

◆ **certificar-se** *vp*: **~-se de que/de algo** to make sure that/of sthg.

certo, ta ['sɛxtu, ta] ◇ *adj* **-1.** [ger] right. **-2.** [correto, certeiro] correct. **-3.** [sensato, acertado] sensible. **-4.** [infalível, seguro] certain; **ser ~ que** to be certain that. **-5.** [com razão]: **estar** ~ to be right. **-6.** [com certeza]: **estar ~ de que/de algo** to be sure that/of sthg. ◇ *pron* **-1.** *(antes de subst)* [um, algum] right; **certa vez** once. **-2.** *loc* : **dar** ~ to work; **está** ~ [está bem] all right.

◆ **certo** ◇ *m* **-1.** [correto] (what is) right; **ele não sabe distinguir entre o ~ e o errado** he doesn't know the difference between right and wrong. **-2.** [verdade] truth. ◇ *adv* **-1.** [certamente] certainly. **-2.** [corretamente] correctly.

◆ **certa** *f*: **na certa** definitely.

◆ **ao certo** *loc adv* for sure.

◆ **por certo** *loc adv* definitely.

cerveja [sex'veʒa] *f* [bebida] beer.

cervejaria [sexveʒa'ria] *f* **-1.** [fábrica] brewery. **-2.** [estabelecimento] *beer bar, usually serving food if wanted.*

cervical [sexvi'kaw] (*pl* **-ais**) *adj* cervical.

cerzir [58] [sex'zi(x)] ◇ *vt* to darn. ◇ *vi* to do invisible mending.

cesariana [seza'rjãna], **cesárea** [se'zarja] *f* Caesarean.

cessação [sesa'sãw] *f* ending.

cessão [se'sãw] (*pl* **-ões**) *f* **-1.** [cedência] assignment. **-2.** [transferência] transfer.

cessar [4] [se'sa(x)] ◇ *vi* to come to an end; ~ **com algo/de fazer algo** to stop sthg/doing sthg; **sem** ~ non-stop. ◇ *vt* **-1.** [fogo] to cease. **-2.** [trabalho] to stop.

cessar-fogo [seˌsax'fogu] *m (inv)* ceasefire.

cessões [se'sõjʃ] *pl* ⊳ **cessão**.

cesta ['seʃta] *f* **-1.** [ger] basket; ~ **básica** *basic* *monthly supplies that the average lower-middle-class family needs in order to survive.* **-2.** [conteúdo] basketful. **-3.** [*ESP* - aro] basket; [- ponto] stitch.

cesto ['seʃtu] *m* basket; **~ de roupa suja** laundry basket.

CETESB (*abrev de* **Companhia Estadual de Tecnologia de Saneamento Básico e Defesa do Meio Ambiente**) *f São Paulo environment agency.*

ceticismo [setʃi'siʒmu] *m* scepticism.

cético, ca ['sɛtʃiku, ka] ◇ *adj* sceptical. ◇ *m, f* sceptic.

cetim [se'tʃĩ] *m* satin.

cetro ['sɛtru] *m* sceptre.

céu ['sɛw] *m* **-1.** [firmamento] sky; **a ~ aberto** [ao ar livre] in the open; [mineração] open-cast; **cair do ~** *fig* to be heaven-sent; **mover ~s e terra** *fig* to move heaven and earth. **-2.** *RELIG* heaven. **-3.** *ANAT* : **~ da boca** roof of the mouth.

cevada [se'vada] *f* barley.

cevar [4] [se'va(x)] *vt* **-1.** [alimentar] to feed. **-2.** [fazer engordar] to fatten.

CFC (*abrev de* **clorofluorocarboneto**) *m* CFC.

chá ['ʃa] *m* **-1.** [ger] tea; **~ completo** afternoon tea; **~ de camomila/menta** camomile/mint tea; **~ preto** black tea. **-2.** [reunião] tea party; **~ beneficente** fund-raising tea; **~ dançante** tea dance. **-3.** *loc*: **depois de aparecer vários dias seguidos, ele tomou um ~ de sumiço** having turned up several days in a row he's gone missing; **tomar ~ de cadeira** to be a wallflower; **levei o maior ~ de cadeira no consultório ontem** I waited for ages at the doctor's yesterday.

chã ['ʃã] *f* plain.

chacal [ʃa'kaw] (*pl* **-ais**) *m* jackal.

chácara ['ʃakara] *f* **-1.** [no campo] smallholding. **-2.** [na cidade] large town house. **-3.** [casa de campo] country house.

chacina [ʃa'sina] *f* slaughter.

chacinar [4] [ʃasi'na(x)] *vt* to slaughter.

chacoalhar [4] [ʃakwa'ʎa(x)] ◇ *vt* [agitar] to shake. ◇ *vi* [sacudir] to shake.

chacota [ʃa'kɔta] *f* **-1.** [deboche] ridicule. **-2.** [objeto de deboche] butt of ridicule.

chacrinha [ʃa'kriɲa] *fam f* **-1.** [reunião] meeting. **-2.** *pej* [bagunça] mess.

chá-de-panela [ˌʃadʒipa'nɛla] (*pl* **chás-de-panela**) *m* (bridal) shower *US*, party at which presents are given to a bride-to-be.

chafariz [ʃafa'riʃ] (*pl* **-es**) *m* fountain.

chafurdar [4] [ʃafux'da(x)] *vi*: **~ em** [lama etc] to wallow in; *fig* [vícios etc] to become involved in.

chaga ['ʃaga] *f* **-1.** [ferida] wound. **-2.** *fig* [mal] scourge.

chalé [ʃa'lɛ] *m* cottage.

chaleira [ʃa'lejra] *f* kettle.

chama ['ʃãma] *f* flame; **em ~s** in flames.

chamada [ʃa'mada] *f* **-1.** [telefônica] call; **fazer uma ~ a cobrar** to make a reverse charge call *UK*, to call collect *US*. **-2.** [verificação de presença] roll call. **-3.** *JORN* headline. **-4.** [repreensão]: **dar uma ~ em alguém** to reprimand sb.

chamar [4] [ʃa'ma(x)] ◇ *vt* **-1.** [ger] to call; **ela decidiu chamá-la de Júlia** she decided to call her 'Júlia'. **-2.** [com gesto] to hail. **-3.** [convocar] to summon; [para função]: **~ alguém para algo** to call sb for sthg. **-4.** [convidar] to invite; **~ a atenção** [suj: pessoa, roupa] to attract attention; [para aspecto etc] to draw attention; **~ a atenção de alguém** [repreender] to reprimand sb. **-5.** [acordar] to wake. **-6.** [qualificar]: **~ algo/alguém de algo** to call sthg/sb sthg. ◇ *vi* **-1.** [dar sinal para vir] to call over; **chamei, mas ela não quis vir** I called her over but she didn't want to come. **-2.** [para acudir]: **~ por alguém** to call out for sb; **~ por socorro** to call for help. **-3.** [telefone] to ring.

◆ **chamar-se** *vp* [ter por nome] to be called; **como você se chama?** what's your name?

chamariz [ʃama'riʒ] *m* **-1.** [isca] bait. **-2.** [seta, anúncio] advert. **-3.** *fig* [engodo] illusion.

chamativo, va [ʃama'tʃivu, va] *adj* flashy.

chamego [ʃa'megu] *m* state of excitement; **estar/ficar de ~ com alguém** to caress sb.

chaminé [ʃami'nɛ] *f* chimney.

champanha [ʃãm'pãɲa], **champanhe** [ʃãm'-paɲi] *m ou f* champagne.

chamuscar [12] [ʃamuʃ'ka(x)] *vt* **-1.** [roupa] to scorch. **-2.** [cabelo] to singe. **-3.** [pessoa, braço] to burn.

◆ **chamuscar-se** *vp* to burn o.s.

chance ['ʃãnsi] *f* chance; **dar uma ~ a** *ou* **para alguém/algo** to give sb/sthg a chance; **ele tem boas ~s de ganhar** he has a good chance of winning.

chancela [ʃãn'sɛla] *f* seal.

chancelaria [ʃãnsela'ria] *f* **-1.** [repartição] chancery. **-2.** [ministério do exterior] foreign ministry.

chanceler [ʃãnse'lɛ(x)] *mf* **-1.** [ministro] minister. **-2.** [chefe de governo] head of government.

chanchada [ʃãn'ʃada] *f* **-1.** *CINE* blue movie. **-2.** *TEATRO* pornographic play.

chantagear [15] [ʃãnta'ʒja(x)] *vt* to blackmail.

chantagem [ʃãn'taʒẽ] (*pl* **-ns**) *f* blackmail.

chantagista [ʃãnta'ʒiʃta] *mf* blackmailer.

chão ['ʃãw] *m* **-1.** [piso] floor. **-2.** [solo] ground.

chapa ['ʃapa] ◇ *f* **-1.** [folha] sheet; **~ de metal/aço** metal/steel sheet. **-2.** [para grelhar] hotplate; **bife na ~** steak on the griddle. **-3.** *AUTO* [placa] number plate *UK*, license plate *US*; **~ fria** false number plate *UK*, false license plate *US*. **-4.** [de impressão] plate. **-5.** *FOT* shot. **-6.** [radiografia] X-ray. **-7.** *POL* [eleitoral] roll. ◇ *mf* [camarada] mate.

chapelaria [ʃapela'ria] *f* **-1.** [loja] hat shop. **-2.** [fábrica] millinery factory.

chapeleiro, ra [ʃape'lejru, ra] *m, f* milliner.

chapéu [ʃa'pɛw] *m* hat; **de tirar o ~** fantastic.

chapéu-coco [ʃaˌpɛw'koku] (*pl* **chapéus-cocos**) *m* bowler hat.

chapinha [ʃa'piɲa] *f* [de garrafa] stopper.

charada [ʃa'rada] *f* [enigma] puzzle; **matar uma ~** to solve a problem.

charco ['ʃaxku] *m* puddle.

charge [ˈʃaxʒi] *f* cartoon.
chargista [ʃaxˈʒiʃta] *mf* cartoonist.
charlatão, tã [ʃaxlaˈtãw, tã] (*mpl* **-ães**, *fpl* **-s**) ◇ *adj* charlatan. ◇ *m, f* impostor.
charme [ˈʃaxmi] *m* charm; **fazer ~** to play it cool.
charmoso, osa [ʃaxˈmozu, ɔza] *adj* charming.
charrete [ʃaˈxɛtʃi] *f* chariot.
charter [ˈʃarte(x)] ◇ *adj inv* charter. ◇ *m* charter plane.
charuto [ʃaˈrutu] *m* cigar.
chassi [ʃaˈsi] *m* **-1.** [ger] chassis. **-2.** *ARTE* [de tela] stretcher.
chateação [ʃatʃjaˈsãw] (*pl* **-ões**) *f* **-1.** [aborrecimento] boredom. **-2.** [maçada] bore.
chatear [15] [ʃaˈtʃja(x)] ◇ *vt* **-1.** [aborrecer] to annoy. **-2.** [incomodar] to bother. **-3.** [enfadar] to irritate. **-4.** [implicar com] to tease. ◇ *vi* **-1.** [aborrecer] to be boring. **-2.** [incomodar] to be annoying.
◆ **chatear-se** *vp* [aborrecer-se] to become bored.
chatice [ʃaˈtʃisi] *f* boredom.
chato, ta [ˈʃatu, ta] ◇ *adj* **-1.** [superfície, forma] flat; **ele tem pés ~s** he's got flat feet. **-2.** [filme, música] boring. **-3.** [desagradável] unwelcome. **-4.** [embaraçoso] tricky. ◇ *m, f* bore; **um ~ de galochas** a drag.
◆ **chato** *m* [coisa desagradável]: **o ~ é que vamos passar o final de semana trabalhando** the annoying thing is we're going to spend the weekend working.
◆ **chata** *f* [embarcação] boat.
chatura [ʃaˈtura] *f fam* drag.
chauvinismo [ʃawviˈniʒmu] *m* chauvinism.
chauvinista [ʃoviˈniʃta] *mf* chauvinist.
chavão [ʃaˈvãw] (*pl* **-ões**) *m* hackneyed phrase.
chave [ˈʃavi] *f* **-1.** [de fechadura] key; **~ mestra** master key. **-2.** [ferramenta] spanner; **~ de fenda** *ou* **para fusos** screwdriver; **~ de porcas** wrench; **~ inglesa** adjustable spanner *UK*, monkey wrench *US*. **-3.** *ELETR* switch. **-4.** [golpe] blow; **~ de braço** armlock. **-5.** [sinal gráfico] curly bracket. **-6.** *fig* [de problema] key.
-chave [ˈʃiiavi] *sufixo* key- *(prefixo)*.
chaveiro [ʃaˈvejru] *m* **-1.** [utensílio] key-rack. **-2.** [profissional] locksmith.
chavões [ʃaˈvõjʃ] *pl* ▷ **chavão**.
checar [12] [ʃeˈka(x);] *vt* to check.
check-up [ʃeˈkapi] (*pl* **check-ups**) *m* check-up.
chefe [ˈʃɛfi] *mf* **-1.** [superior] head; **~ de estado** head of state; **~ de família** head of the family; **~ de turma** shift supervisor. **-2.** *fam* [garçom] waiter. **-3.** *fam* [freguês] mate.
chefia [ʃeˈfia] *f* **-1.** [direção] management. **-2.** [repartição, sala] management office.
chefiar [16] [ʃeˈfja(x)] *vt* to lead.
chega [ˈʃega] *m fam* [repreensão]: **dar um ~ (para lá) em alguém** to tear a strip off sb.
chegada [ʃeˈgada] *f* **-1.** [vinda, regresso] arrival. **-2.** [aproximação] approach. **-3.** *ESP* finishing line.
chegado, da [ʃeˈgadu, da] *adj* **-1.** [ger] close. **-2.** [propenso]: **ser ~ a** to be very fond of.
chegar [14] [ʃeˈga(x)] ◇ *vi* **-1.** [a um lugar]: **~ em** to arrive at; **~ em casa** to arrive home; **~ de** to arrive from. **-2.** [aproximar-se] to approach; **chega aqui** *fam* come here; **chega para cá** move over here. **-3.** [afastar-se]: **chega para lá** [ir embora] go away; [deslocar-se] move over. **-4.** [verão, noite, hora] to arrive. **-5.** [bastar] to be enough; **chegar!** that's enough! **-6.** [alcançar] to reach; **não ~ aos pés de** [não ser comparável a] to come nowhere near. **-7.** [conseguir]: **~ a (ser) algo** to succeed in becoming sthg; **~ a fazer algo** to manage to do sthg. **-8.** [ir ao extremo]: **~ a fazer algo** to reach the point of doing sthg. **-9.** *fam* [partir]: **vou chegando** I'm pushing off. ◇ *vt* **-1.** [aproximar]: **~ algo para cá** to bring sthg over here. **-2.** [afastar]: **~ algo para lá/parao lado** to move sthg over there/to one side.
◆ **chegar-se** *vp* [aproximar-se] to come closer.
cheio, cheia [ˈʃeju, ˈʃeja] *adj* **-1.** [ger] full; **~ de** full of; **~ de manchas** covered in stains; **~ de dedos** *fam fig* [receoso] full of apprehension; [tímido] timid; **~ de frescura** *fam fig* finicky; **~ da nota** *fam* [rico] loaded; **~ de si** [orgulhoso] proud; [arrogante] full of o.s. **-2.** [gordo] plump. **-3.** *fam* [farto]: **estar ~ (de alguém/algo)** to be fed up with sb/sthg.
◆ **cheia** *f* **-1.** [de rio] flood. **-2.** [época] flood season.
◆ **em cheio** *loc adv*: **acertar em ~** to hit the mark.
cheirar [4] [ʃejˈra(x)] ◇ *vt* **-1.** [flor, perfume, comida] to smell. **-2.** [cocaína] to snort. ◇ *vi* **-1.** [flor, perfume, comida] to smell; **~ a** [ter cheiro de] to smell of; *fig* [parecer] to smack (of); **~ bem/mal** to smell nice/bad; **isto não me cheira bem** it makes me feel uncomfortable. **-2.** [cocaína]: **passou a noite cheirando** he spent the whole night snorting (coke).
cheiroso, osa [ʃejˈrosu, ɔza] *adj* scented; **estar ~** to be scented.
cheiro-verde [ˌʃejuˈvexdʒi] (*pl* **cheiros-verdes**) *m* parsley and spring onion.
cheque [ˈʃɛki] *m* cheque; **~ em branco** blank cheque; **~ compensado** cleared cheque; **~ cruzado** crossed cheque; **~ especial** guaranteed cheque; **~ nominal** nominative cheque; **~ ao portador** bearer cheque; **~ pré-datado** predated cheque; **~ voador** *ou* **sem fundos** bounced cheque.
chiado [ˈʃjadu] *m* **-1.** [de roda, porta] squeak. **-2.** [de passarinho] chirp.
chiar [16] [ˈʃja(x)] *vi* **-1.** [emitir chio - pessoa, respiração] to wheeze; [- vento] whistle. **-2.** *fam* [reclamar] to kick up a stink.
chibata [ʃiˈbata] *f* [vara] stick.
chiclete [ʃiˈklɛtʃi] *m* chewing gum; **~ de bola** bubble gum.
chicória [ʃiˈkɔrja] *f* chicory.
chicote [ʃiˈkɔtʃi] *m* whip.
chicotear [15] [ʃikoˈtʃja(x)] *vt* to whip.
chifrada [ʃiˈfrada] *f* horn thrust.

chifrar [4] [ʃi'fra(x)] *vt* **-1.** [toureiro, tronco] to gore. **-2.** *fam fig* [marido, namorada] to two-time.

chifre ['ʃifri] *m* [de animal] horn; **pôr ~s em** *fam fig* [em marido, namorada] to two-time.

chifrudo, da [ʃi'frudu, da] *adj* **-1.** [animal] large-horned. **-2.** *fam fig* [marido, namorada] two-timed.

Chile ['ʃili] *n* Chile.

chileno, na [ʃi'lenu, na] ◇ *adj* Chilean. ◇ *m, f* Chilean.

chilique [ʃi'liki] *m fam* faint; **ter um ~** to have a fit.

chilrear [15] [ʃiw'xja(x)] *vi* to chirp.

chilreio [ʃiw'xeju] *m* chirping.

chimarrão [ʃima'xãw] (*pl* **-ões**) *m herbal tea.*

chimpanzé [ʃĩnpãn'zɛ] *m* chimpanzee.

China ['ʃina] *n*: **(a) ~** China.

chinelo [ʃi'nɛlu] *m* slipper; **botar no ~** *fam* [superar] to outdo.

chinês, esa [ʃi'neʃ, eza] (*pl* **-eses**, *fpl* **-s**) ◇ *adj* Chinese. ◇ *m, f* [da China] Chinese.

chinfrim [ʃĩn'frĩ] (*pl* **-ns**) *adj* worthless.

chip ['ʃipi] *m COMPUT* microchip.

Chipre ['ʃipri] *n* Cyprus.

chique ['ʃiki] *adj* chic.

chiqueiro [ʃi'kejru] *m* **-1.** [de porcos] pigsty. **-2.** *fam fig* [bagunça] pigsty.

chispa ['ʃiʃpa] *f* [faísca] spark.

chispar [4] [ʃiʃ'pa(x)] *vi* [correr] to race.

chita ['ʃita] *f* printed cotton.

choça ['ʃɔsa] *f* hut.

chocalhar [4] [ʃoka'ʎa(x)] ◇ *vt* to rattle. ◇ *vi* [soar] to rattle.

chocalho [ʃo'kaʎu] *m* **-1.** *MÚS* maraca. **-2.** [brinquedo] rattle. **-3.** [de gado, cavalo] bell.

chocante [ʃo'kãntʃi] *adj* **-1.** [assustador, ofensivo] shocking. **-2.** *fam* [ótimo] wicked.

chocar [12] [ʃo'ka(x)] ◇ *vt* **-1.** [assustar, ofender] to shock. **-2.** *ZOOL* to hatch. ◇ *vi* **-1.** [causar espanto, ofensa] to shock. **-2.** *ZOOL* to brood.
◆ **chocar-se** *vp* **-1.** [colidir]: **~-se (contra)** to collide (with). **-2.** [assustar-se]: **~-se (com)** to be shocked (by). **-3.** [discordar]: **~-se em relação a** to clash over.

chocho, cha ['ʃoʃu, ʃa] *adj* **-1.** [sem graça] dull. **-2.** [fruta, ovo] rotten.

choco, ca ['ʃoku, ka] *adj* **-1.** [ave] sitting. **-2.** [ovo - fertilizado] fertilized; [- estragado] addled.

chocolate [ʃoko'latʃi] *m* chocolate.

chofer [ʃo'fɛ(x)] (*pl* **-es**) *mf* driver.

chofre ['ʃofri] ◆ **de chofre** *loc adv* [subitamente] suddenly.

chopada [ʃo'pada] *f fam* beer-drinking session.

chope ['ʃopi] *m* beer.

choque ['ʃɔki] *m* **-1.** [ger] shock; **estado de ~** state of shock; **dar um ~ (em alguém)** to give (sb) a shock; **levar** *ou* **tomar um ~** to get a shock. **-2.** [colisão] crash. **-3.** [conflito, confronto] clash.

choradeira [ʃora'dejra] *f* **-1.** [choro] crying. **-2.** [lamúria] grumbling. **-3.** [pedido] complaining.

choramingar [ʃoramĩŋ'ga(x)] *vi* to whine.

choramingas [14] [ʃora'mĩŋgaʃ] *mf* crybaby.

choramingo [ʃora'mĩŋgu] *m* whine.

chorão, ona [ʃo'rãw, ona] (*mpl* **-ões**, *fpl* **-onas**) ◇ *adj* moaning. ◇ *m, f* [pessoa] crybaby.
◆ **chorão** *m BOT* weeping willow.

chorar [4] [ʃo'ra(x)] ◇ *vi* **-1.** [verter lágrimas] to cry. **-2.** *fig* [barganhar] to haggle. ◇ *vt* **-1.** [lágrima] to cry; **~ a morte de alguém** to mourn the death of sb. **-2.** *fig* [barganhar] to haggle. **-3.** *loc*: **~ as mágoas** to pour out; **~ miséria** to moan about poverty.

chorinho [ʃo'riɲu] *m MÚS* = **choro.**

choro ['ʃoru] *m* **-1.** [pranto] crying. **-2.** *MÚS a type of traditional Brazilian music started at the end of the nineteenth century.*

CHORO

One of the more polished expressions of Brazilian music, the *choro*, or *chorinho*, is an instrumental musical genre characterized by virtuosity and improvisation. *Choro* originated in Rio de Janeiro towards the end of the nineteenth century and is derived from the polka and the maxixe, a precursor of the samba. It is generally performed to the accompaniment of percussion instruments, guitars, a *cavaquinho* (small four-stringed guitar), a mandolin and certain wind instruments such as the flute or the clarinet.

chorona [ʃo'rona] *f* ▷ **chorão.**

choroso, osa [ʃo'rozu, ɔza] *adj* tearful.

choupana [ʃo'pãna] *f* hut.

chouriço [ʃo'risu] *m* chorizo.

chove-não-molha [ˌʃɔvinãw'mɔʎa] *m inv fam* shilly-shallying.

chover [47] [ʃo've(x)] *v impess* **-1.** *METEOR* to rain; **~ a cântaros** to pour down with rain; **nem que chova canivete** *fig* come what may. **-2.** *fig* [cair do alto] to shower. **-3.** *fig* [sobrevir em demasia] to pour in.

chuchu [ʃu'ʃu] *m fruit-bearing climbing plant*; **está frio pra ~** *fam* it's bloody cold; **tinha comida pra ~** *fam* there was loads of food at the party.

chucrute [ʃu'krutʃi] *m* choucroute, sauerkraut.

chulé [ʃu'lɛ] *m* smell of feet.

chulear [15] [ʃu'lja(x)] *vt* to hem.

chulo, la ['ʃulu, la] *adj* vulgar.

chumaço [ʃu'masu] *m* **-1.** [enchimento] padding. **-2.** [de algodão, gaze] wadding.

chumbado, da [ʃũn'badu, da] *adj fam* worn out.

chumbar [4] [ʃũn'ba(x)] *vt* **-1.** [soldar] to solder. **-2.** [grade, portão] to secure. **-3.** [rede, anzol] to drop.

chumbo ['ʃũnbu] *m* lead.

chupado, da [ʃu'padu, da] *adj fam* [magro] skinny.
◆ **chupada** *f* [chupadela] suck.

chupão [ʃu'pãw] (*pl* **-ões**) *fam m* **-1.** [beijo] slurpy kiss. **-2.** [marca] love bite.

chupar [4] [ʃu'pa(x)] *vt* to suck.

chupeta [ʃu'peta] *f* **-1.** [de criança] dummy *UK*, comforter *US*. **-2.** *fam AUTO* **: fazer uma ~** to use jump-leads.

churrascaria [ʃuxaʃka'ria] *f restaurant specializing in grilled and spit-roasted meat*; ~

rodízio restaurant where diners may pick and choose from food offered.
churrasco [ʃu'xaʃku] *m* **-1.** [carne] barbecued meat. **-2.** [refeição] barbecue.
churrasqueira [ʃuxaʃ'kejra] *f* rotisserie.
churrasquinho [ʃuxaʃ'kiɲu] *m* kebab.
chutar [4] [ʃu'ta(x)] ◇ *vt* **-1.** [objeto, pessoa] to kick. **-2.** *fam* [resposta] to take a stab at. **-3.** *fam* [funcionário, namorado]: ~ **alguém** to give sb the push. ◇ *vi* **-1.** [dar chute] to kick. **-2.** *fam* [em prova] to take a pot shot. **-3.** *loc*: ~ **alto** to tell tall stories.
chute ['ʃutʃi] *m* **-1.** [pontapé] kick. **-2.** *fam* [mentira] bullshit. **-3.** *fam* [dispensa] push; **dar um ~ em alguém** to give sb the push.
chuteira [ʃu'tejra] *f* football boot; **pendurar as ~s** [aposentar-se] to hang up one's boots.
chuva ['ʃuva] *f* **-1.** *METEOR* rain; ~ **ácida** acid rain; ~ **fina** drizzle; ~ **de granizo** *ou* **pedra** hail; **tomar ~** to get wet in the rain; **estar na ~** *fig* to be drunk. **-2.** *fig* [de papel picado etc] shower.
chuvarada [ʃuva'rada] *f* downpour.
chuveirada [ʃuvej'rada] *f* shower.
chuveiro [ʃu'vejru] *m* shower.
chuviscar [12] [ʃuviʃ'ka(x)] *vi* to drizzle.
chuvisco [ʃu'viʃku] *m* **-1.** [chuva] drizzle. **-2.** *CULIN* *confection made of egg-yolk and sugar.*
chuvoso, osa [ʃu'vozu, ɔza] *adj* rainy.
Cia (*abrev de* **Companhia**) *f* Co.
cianeto [sja'netu] *m* cyanide.
cibercafé [sibex'kafe] *m* cybercafé.
ciberespaço [sibereʃ'pasu] *m* cyberspace.
cibernética [sibex'nɛtʃika] *f* cybernetics *(sg)*.
cibernético, ca [sibex'netʃiku, ka] *adj* cybernetic.
◆ **cibernética** *f* cybernetics.
ciberpunk [sibex'pũŋki] *mf* net hacker.
CIC (*abrev de* **Cartão de Identificação do Contribuinte**) *m* *Brazilian tax-payer's identity card for individual contributions.*
cicatriz [sika'triʃ] (*pl* **-es**) *f* scar.
cicatrização [sikatriza'sãw] *f* healing.
cicatrizar [4] [sikatri'za(x)] ◇ *vt* **-1.** [fechar] to heal. **-2.** [cobrir de cicatrizes] to scar. ◇ *vi* [fechar-se] to heal.
cicerone [sise'roni] *mf* guide.
ciceronear [sise'ronja(x)] *vt* to act as a guide for.
ciciar [16] [si'sja(x)] *vi* to whisper.
cíclico, ca ['sikliku, ka] *adj* cyclic.
ciclismo [si'kliʒmu] *m* cycling.
ciclista [si'kliʃta] *mf* cyclist.
ciclo ['siklu] *m* cycle; ~ **básico** *UNIV* foundation course.
ciclone [si'kloni] *m* cyclone.
ciclotimia [siclotʃi'mia] *f* *PSIC* cyclothymia.
ciclotímico, ca [siklo'tʃimiku, ka] ◇ *adj* cyclothymic. ◇ *m, f* cyclothymic.
ciclovia [siklo'via] *f* bicycle lane.
cidadã [sida'dã] *f* ▷ **cidadão**.
cidadania [sidada'nia] *f* citizenship.
cidadão, dã [sida'dãw, dã] (*pl* **-ãos**, *fpl* **-s**) *m, f* citizen.
cidade [si'dadʒi] *f* **-1.** [centro urbano] city; [pequena] small town; ~ **satélite** satellite town. **-2.** [bairro central] town. **-3.** *fig* [população] city.
Cidade do Cabo [si,dadʒidu'kabu] *n* Cape Town.
Cidade do México [si,dadʒidu'mɛʃiku] *n* Mexico City.
cidadela [sida'dɛla] *f* citadel.
cidra ['sidra] *f* citron.
ciência ['sjẽnsja] *f* **-1.** [saber] science; **~s econômicas** economics; **~s humanas** humanities; **~s ocultas** occultism *(sg)*; **~s sociais** social science *(sg)*. **-2.** [da vida, do amor] art. **-3.** [conhecimento] knowledge; **dar ~ de algo (a alguém)** to tell sb sthg; **tome ~** take this on board.
ciente ['sjẽntʃi] *adj* learned; **estar ~ (de algo)** to be aware of sthg.
cientificismo [sjẽntʃifi'siʒmu] *m scientific spirit.*
científico, ca [sjẽn'tʃifiku, ka] *adj* scientific.
cientista [sjẽn'tʃiʃta] *mf* scientist.
cifra ['sifra] *f* **-1.** [ger] cipher. **-2.** [soma, quantia] sum. **-3.** *MÚS* figure.
cifrão [si'frãw] (*pl* **-ões**) *m* dollar sign.
cifrar [si'fra(x)] *vt* to write in code.
cigano, na [si'gãnu, na] ◇ *adj* gipsy. ◇ *m, f* gipsy.
cigarra [si'gaxa] *f* **-1.** *ZOOL* cicada. **-2.** [campainha] buzzer.
cigarreira [siga'xejra] *f* [estojo] cigarette case.
cigarrilha [siga'xiʎa] *f* cheroot.
cigarro [si'gaxu] *m* cigarette.
cilada [si'lada] *f* **-1.** [ger] trap. **-2.** [emboscada] ambush.
cilindrada [silĩn'drada] *f* cubic capacity.
cilíndrico, ca [si'lĩndriku, ka] *adj* cylindrical.
cilindro [si'lĩndru] *m* *GEOM, AUTO* cylinder.
cílio ['silju] *m* eyelash.
cima ['sima] *f*: **lá em ~** [no topo, no alto] up there; [em andar superior] upstairs; **andar de ~** upstairs; **ainda por ~** on top of that; **de ~** from the top; **de ~ de** from the top of; **de ~ para baixo** from top to bottom; **em ~ de** on top of; **em ~ da mesa** on the table; **para ~** upwards; **por ~ de** over; **dar em ~ de alguém** to chat sb up; **estar por ~** to be quids in; **tudo em ~?** *fam* everything all right?
cimentado, da [simẽn'tadu, da] *adj* **-1.** *CONSTR* cemented. **-2.** [consolidado] sealed.
cimentar [4] [simẽn'ta(x)] *vt* to cement.
cimento [si'mẽntu] *m* cement; ~ **armado** reinforced concrete.
cimo ['simu] *m* top.
cinco ['sĩŋku] *num* five; *veja também* **seis**.
cindir [6] [sĩn'dʒi(x)] *vt* **-1.** [separar] to separate. **-2.** [cortar] to cut through.
cineasta [si'njaʃta] *mf* cinematographer.
cinéfilo, la [si'nɛfilu, la] *m, f* film enthusiast.
cinegrafista [sinegra'fiʃta] *mf* cameraman (*f* camerawoman).
cinema [si'nema] *m* cinema; ~ **mudo** silent film.

cinematografia [sinematogra'fia] *f* cinematography.
cinematográfico, ca [sinemato'grafiku, ka] *adj* cinematographic.
Cingapura [sĩŋga'pura] *n* Singapore.
cingir [52] [sĩn'ʒi(x)] *vt* **-1.** [ger] to encircle. **-2.** [pôr à cintura] to gird.
cínico, ca ['siniku, ka] ◇ *adj* shameless. ◇ *m, f* immoral person.
cinismo [si'niʒmu] *m* impudence.
cinqüenta [sĩŋ'kwẽnta] *num* fifty; *veja também* **seis**.
cinqüentão, tona [sĩŋkwẽn'tãw, tɔna] (*mpl* **-ões**, *fpl* **-s**) ◇ *adj* quinquagenarian. ◇ *m, f* quinquagenarian.
cinta ['sĩnta] *f* **-1.** [faixa] belt. **-2.** [feminina] girdle.
cinta-liga [ˌsĩnta'liga] (*pl* **cintas-ligas**) *f* suspender belt.
cintilante [sĩntʃi'lãntʃi] *adj* scintillating.
cintilar [4] [sĩntʃi'la(x)] *vi* to scintillate.
cinto ['sĩntu] *m* belt; ~ **de segurança** safety belt.
cintura [sĩn'tura] *f* waist.
cinturão [sĩntu'rãw] (*pl* **-ões**) *m* belt; ~ **verde** green belt.
cinza ['sĩnza] ◇ *adj inv* [cor] grey. ◇ *m* [cor] grey. ◇ *f* [de combustão] ash.
◆ **cinzas** *fpl* ashes.
cinzeiro [sĩn'zejru] *m* ashtray.
cinzel [sĩn'zɛw] (*pl* **-éis**) *m* chisel.
cinzelar [4] [sĩnze'la(x)] *vt* **-1.** [lavrar] to chisel. **-2.** [gravar] to engrave. **-3.** *fig* [frase, verso] to polish.
cinzento, ta [sĩn'zẽntu, ta] *adj* grey.
cio ['siw] *m* rut; **estar no** ~ to be in a rut.
cioso, ciosa ['sjozu, 'sjɔza] *adj* jealous.
CIPA (*abrev de* **Comissão Interna de Prevenção de Acidentes**) *f Brazilian commission for prevention of accidents at work*, ≃ HSE *UK*, ≃ OHSA *US*.
cipreste [si'prɛʃtʃi] *m* cypress.
cipriota [sipri'ɔta] ◇ *adj* Cypriot. ◇ *m, f* Cypriot.
circense [six'sẽnsi] *adj* circus *(antes de subst)*.
circo ['sixku] *m* circus.
circuito [six'kujtu] *m* circuit.
circulação [sixkula'sãw] *f* circulation.
circulante [sirku'lãntʃi] *adj* **-1.** [itinerante] itinerant. **-2.** *ECON*: **capital** ~ ready capital.
circular [4] [sixku'la(x)] (*pl* **-es**) ◇ *adj* [formato] circular. ◇ *m* [ônibus] shuttle. ◇ *f* [carta, ofício] circular. ◇ *vt* **-1.** [rodear] to circle. **-2.** [dar voltas por] to surround. ◇ *vi* **-1.** [ger] to circulate. **-2.** [percorrer] to wander.
círculo ['sixkulu] *m* **-1.** *GEOM* circle; ~ **vicioso** vicious circle. **-2.** *fig* [meio, grupo] circle.
circunavegação [sixkũnavega'sãw] *f* circumnavigation.
circunavegar [14] [sixkũnave'ga(x)] *vt* to circumnavigate.
circuncidado [sixkũnsi'dadu] *adj* circumcised.
circuncidar [4] [sixkũnsi'da(x)] *vt* to circumcise.
circuncisão [sixkũnsi'zãw] *f* circumcision.
circundante [sixkũn'dãntʃi] *adj* surrounding.
circundar [4] [sixkũn'da(x)] *vt* to surround.
circunferência [sixkũnfe'rẽnsja] *f* circumference.
circunflexo [sixkũn'flɛksu] *GRAM* ◇ *adj* circumflex. ◇ *m* circumflex.
circunscrever [6] [sixkũnʃkre've(x)] *vt* **-1.** [ger] to contain. **-2.** [inscrever] to circumscribe. **-3.** [restringir] to restrict.
◆ **circunscrever-se** *vp* [restringir-se] to be restricted.
circunscrição [sixkũnʃkri'sãw] (*pl* **-ões**) *f* [repartição] division; ~ **eleitoral** electoral constituency.
circunscrito, ta [sixkũnʃ'kritu, ta] ◇ *pp* ▷ **circunscrever**. ◇ *adj* circumscribed.
circunspe(c)ção [sixkũnʃpe(k)sãw] (*pl* **-ões**) *f* circumspection.
circunspecto, ta [sixkũnʃ'pɛktu, ta] *adj* circumspect.
circunstância [sixkũnʃ'tãnsja] *f* **-1.** [ger] circumstance. **-2.** *JUR* : ~**s atenuantes/agravantes** attenuating/aggravating circumstances. **-3.** [caso] event.
circunstanciado, da [sixkũnʃtãn'sjadu, da] *adj* detailed.
circunstantes [sixkũnʃ'tãntʃiʃ] *mpl* onlookers.
cirrose [si'xɔzi] *f* cirrhosis.
cirurgia [sirux'ʒia] *f* surgery; ~ **plástica** plastic surgery; ~ **estética** aesthetic surgery *UK*, esthetic surgery *US*; ~ **reconstrutora** *ou* **reparadora** reconstructive surgery.
cirurgião, ã [sirux'ʒjãwʒjã, a] (*pl* **-ões**, *fpl* **-s**) *m, f* surgeon.
cirurgião-dentista, cirurgiã-dentista [sirux,ʒjãwdẽn'tʃiʃta, sirux,ʒjãdẽntʃiʃta] (*mpl* **cirurgiões-dentistas**, *fpl* **cirurgiãs-dentistas**) *m, f* dental surgeon.
cirúrgico, ca [si'ruxʒiku, ka] *adj* surgical; **ataque** *ou* **bombardeio** ~ *fig* surgical strike.
cisão [si'zãw] (*pl* **-ões**) *f* **-1.** [divisão] split. **-2.** [discordância] division.
cisco ['siʃku] *m* dust.
cisma ['siʒma] ◇ *m* schism. ◇ *f* [mania] crazy idea.
cismado, da [siʒ'madu, da] *adj* wary.
cismar [4] [siʒ'ma(x)] ◇ *vt* [convencer-se de]: ~ **que** to be convinced that. ◇ *vi* **-1.** [decidir]: ~ **de** *ou* **em fazer algo** to determine upon doing sthg. **-2.** [implicar]: ~ **com** to clash with. **-3.** [insistir]: ~ **em** to insist on.
cisne ['siʒni] *m* swan.
cisões [si'zõjʃ] *pl* ▷ **cisão**.
cisterna [siʃ'tɛxna] *f* cistern.
cistite [siʃ'tʃitʃi] *f* cystitis.
citação [sita'sãw] (*pl* **-ões**) *f* **-1.** [de trecho, autor] quotation. **-2.** *JUR* citation.
citadino, na [sita'dʒinu, na] *adj* citizen.
citar [4] [si'ta(x)] *vt* **-1.** [trecho, autor] to quote. **-2.** *JUR* to summons.
cítrico, ca ['sitriku, ka] *adj* **-1.** [fruta] citrus. **-2.** [ácido] citric.

ciúme ['sjumi] *m* jealousy; **ficar com** ~ *ou* ~**s** to become jealous; **ter** ~ *ou* ~**s de alguém** to be jealous of sb.
ciumeira [sju'mejra] *f* jealousy.
ciumento, ta [sju'mẽntu, ta] *adj* jealous.
cívico, ca ['siviku, ka] *adj* civic.
civil [si'viw] (*pl* **-is**) <> *adj* **-1.** [direito, tribunal] civil. **-2.** [vida, traje] civilian. <> *mf* [pessoa] civilian. <> *m* [casamento civil]: **casar-se no** ~ to have a civil wedding.
civilidade [sivili'dadʒi] *f* courtesy.
civilização [siviliza'sãw] (*pl* **-ões**) *f* civilization.
civilizadamente [civilizada'mẽntʃi] *adv* **-1.** [com educação] politely. **-2.** [com ordem] in a civilized manner.
civilizador, ra [siviliza'do(x), ra] *adj* civilizing.
civilizar [4] [sivili'za(x)] *vt* to civilize.
◆ **civilizar-se** *vp* to become civilized.
civismo [si'viʒmu] *m* public spirit.
cl. (*abrev de* **centilitro**) *m* cl.
clã ['klã] (*pl* **clãs**) *m* clan.
clamar [4] [kla'ma(x)] <> *vt* to clamour. <> *vi*: ~ **por/contra algo** to clamour for/to protest against sthg.
clamor [kla'mo(x)] (*pl* **-es**) *m* clamour *UK*, clamor *US*.
clamoroso, osa [klamo'rozu, ɔza] *adj* clamorous.
clandestino, na [klãndeʃ'tʃinu, na] *adj* clandestine.
claque ['klaki] *f* **-1.** *TEATRO* paid participating audience. **-2.** [de fãs, seguidores] group of fans.
clara ['klara] *f* ▷ **claro.**
clarabóia [klara'bɔja] *f* skylight.
clarão [kla'rãw] (*pl* **-ões**) *m* **-1.** [de raio, flash] flash. **-2.** [claridade] brightness.
clarear [15] [kla'rja(x)] <> *vt* **-1.** [iluminar] to light up. **-2.** [dia, céu] to brighten. <> *vi* **-1.** [amanhecer] to get light. **-2.** [dia, céu] to brighten.
clareira [kla'rejra] *f* [em floresta] glade, clearing.
clareza [kla'reza] *f* clarity; **com** ~ clearly.
claridade [klari'dadʒi] *f* [luz] clarity.
clarim [kla'rĩ] (*pl* **-ns**) *m* bugle.
clarinete [klari'netʃi] *m* clarinet.
clarividência [klarivi'dẽnsja] *f* far-sightedness.
clarinetista [klarine'tʃiʃta] *mf* clarinettist *UK*, clarinetist *US*.
clarividente [klarivi'dẽntʃi] <> *adj* **-1.** [sagaz] wise. **-2.** [prudente] cautious. **-3.** [vidente] clairvoyant. <> *mf* [vidente] clairvoyant.
claro, ra ['klaru, ra] *adj* **-1.** [ger] bright; **dia** ~ daylight. **-2.** [límpido, nítido, explícito] clear; **deixar** ~ **que** to make explicit; **estar** ~ **(que/por que)** to be obvious (that/why); **ser** ~ **(que)** to be obvious (that); **ser** ~ **como água** to be crystal clear.
◆ **claro** <> *adv* [evidentemente]: **claro!** of course!; ~ **que sim!/que não!** of course!/of course not! <> *m* **-1.** [em escrita] space. **-2.** [em pintura] highlight.
◆ **clara** *f*: ~ **(de ovo)** egg white.
◆ **às claras** *loc adv* in broad daylight.
◆ **em claro** *loc adv*: **passar a noite em** ~ to have a sleepless night.
clarões [kla'rõjʃ] ▷ **clarão.**
classe ['klasi] *f* **-1.** [ger] class; ~ **média** middle class; ~ **trabalhadora** *ou* **operária** working class; ~ **executiva** business class; ~ **turística** tourist class; **primeira** ~ first class. **-2.** [categoria]: **de primeira** ~ first class; **ela tem** ~ she's got class; **com** ~ charmingly; **de** ~ classy.
clássico, ca ['klasiku, ka] *adj* **-1.** [ger] classic; **música** ~ classical music. **-2.** [da Antigüidade] classical.
◆ **clássico** *m* [obra-prima] classic.
classificação [klasifika'sãw] (*pl* **-ões**) *f* **-1.** [ger] classification. **-2.** [qualificação] label. **-3.** [para cinema e TV] rating.
classificado, da [klasifi'kadu, da] <> *adj* classified. <> *m, f* [em concurso, competição] classified entrant.
◆ **classificado** *m* [anúncio] classified advertisement, classified ad.
◆ **classificados** *mpl JORN* [seção] classifieds.
classificar [12] [klasifi'ka(x)] *vt* to classify.
◆ **classificar-se** *vp* **-1.** [ser aprovado] to pass. **-2.** [obter posição de]: ~**-se em primeiro lugar** to be first.
classificatório, ria [klasifika'tɔrju, rja] *adj* classifying.
classudo, da [kla'sudu, da] *adj fam* classy.
claudicante [klawdʒi'kãntʃi] *adj* [capengante] hobbling.
claudicar [12] [klawdʒi'ka(x)] *vi* **-1.** [mancar] to limp. **-2.** *fig* [ir mal] to limp along.
claustro ['klawʃtru] *m* cloister.
claustrofobia [klawʃtrofo'bia] *f* claustrophobia.
claustrofóbico, ca [klawʃtro'fɔbiku, ka] *adj* claustrophobic.
cláusula ['klawzula] *f* clause.
clausura [klaw'zura] *f* **-1.** [recinto] enclosure. **-2.** [vida] seclusion.
clave ['klavi] *f MÚS* clef.
clavícula [kla'vikula] *f* clavicle, collarbone.
clemência [kle'mẽnsja] *f* **-1.** [qualidade] leniency. **-2.** [perdão] clemency.
clemente [kle'mẽntʃi] *adj* clement.
cleptomaníaco, ca [klɛptoma'niaku, ka] *m, f* kleptomaniac.
clérigo ['klɛrigu] *m* clergyman.
clero ['klɛru] *m* clergy.
clicar [12] [kli'ka(x)] *vi* to click.
clichê [kli'ʃe] *m* **-1.** *FOT* proof. **-2.** [chavão] cliché. **-3.** [tipográfico] type. **-4.** *JORN* edition; **segundo** ~ second edition.
cliente [kli'ẽntʃi] *m COMPUT* client.
clientela [kliẽn'tɛla] *f* **-1.** clientele. **-2.** [de médico] patients *(pl)*.
clientelismo [kliẽnte'liʒmu] *m POL* political patronage.
clima ['klima] *m* **-1.** *METEOR* climate. **-2.** *fam fig* [atmosfera] atmosphere.

climático, ca [kli'matʃiku, ka] *adj* climatic.
clímax ['klimaks] *m inv* **-1.** [ger] climax. **-2.** [auge] peak.
clinicar [12] [klini'ka(x)] *vi* to be in clinical practice.
clínico, ca ['kliniku, ka] <> *adj* clinical. <> *m, f* [médico] doctor; ~ **geral** general practitioner, GP.
◆ **clínica** *f* **-1.** [local] clinic. **-2.** [prática] medicine; **clínica geral** general practice.
clipe ['klipi] *m* **-1.** [videoclipe] clip. **-2.** [para papéis] paper clip.
clitóris [kli'tɔriʃ] *m inv* clitoris.
clonagem [klo'naʒẽ] (*pl* **-ns**) *f* BIOL cloning.
clonar [klo'na(x)] *vt* BIOL to clone.
clone ['kloni] *m* clone.
cloro ['klɔru] *m* chlorine.
clorofila [kloro'fila] *f* chlorophyll.
clorofórmio [kloro'fɔxmju] *m* chloroform.
close ['klozi] *m* close-up; **dar um ~ (em)** to take a close-up (of).
CLT (*abrev de* **Consolidação das Leis do Trabalho**) *f* *Brazilian legislation regulating the rights and responsibilities of workers.*
clube ['klubi] *m* club.
cm (*abrev de* **centímetro**) *m* cm.
CNH (*abrev de* **Carteira Nacional de Habilitação**) *f* driving licence ***UK***, driver's license ***US***.
coabitar [4] [koabi'ta(x)] *vi*: ~ **(com alguém)** to live (with sb).
coação [koa'sãw] *f* force.
coadjuvante [kwadʒu'vãntʃi] <> *adj* back-up; **ator ~** supporting actor; **criminoso ~** accomplice. <> *mf* **-1.** CINE, TEATRO, TV supporting role. **-2.** [cúmplice] accomplice.
coadjuvar [4] [kwadʒu'va(x)] *vt* **-1.** [ajudar] to collaborate in. **-2.** CINE, TEATRO, TV to support.
coador [kwa'do(x)] (*pl* **-es**) *m* **-1.** [crivo] sieve. **-2.** [de café] filter. **-3.** [para legumes] colander.
coadunar [4] [koadu'na(x)] *vt* **-1.** [idéias, propostas] to combine. **-2.** [pessoas] to unite.
◆ **coadunar-se** *vp* [combinar-se] to be combined; **~-se com** to tie in with.
coagir [52] [kwa'ʒi(x)] *vt*: ~ **alguém (a fazer algo)** to coerce sb (into doing sthg).
coagulação [kwagula'sãw] (*pl* **-ões**) *f* [do sangue] clotting.
coagular [4] [kwagu'la(x)] <> *vt* [solidificar] to clot. <> *vi* **-1.** [sangue] to clot. **-2.** [leite] to curdle.
◆ **coagular-se** *vp* **-1.** [sangue] to clot. **-2.** [leite] to curdle.
coágulo ['kwagulu] *m* [de sangue] clot.
coalhado, da [kwa'ʎadu, da] *adj* [leite] curdled.
◆ **coalhada** *f* clabber.
coalhar [4] [kwa'ʎa(x)] *vt* & *vi* to curdle.
◆ **coalhar-se** *vp* to curdle.
coalho [ko'aʎu] *m* clot.
coalizão [kwali'zãw] (*pl* **-ões**) *f* coalition.
coar [20] ['kwa(x)] *vt* **-1.** [líquido] to filter. **-2.** [café] to percolate.
co-autor, ra [ˌkoaw'to(x), ra] (*mpl* **-res**, *fpl* **-ras**) *m, f* co-author.
co-autoria [ˌkoawto'ria] (*pl* **-s**) *f* co-authorship.
coaxar [4] [kwa'ʃa(x)] <> *m* [de sapo] croak. <> *vi* [sapo] to croak.
cobaia [ko'baja] *f* guinea pig.
cobalto [ko'bawtu] *m* cobalt.
coberto, ta [ko'bɛxtu, ta] <> *pp* ▷ **cobrir**. <> *adj* covered.
◆ **coberta** *f* **-1.** [colcha, cobertor] bed cover. **-2.** [cobertura] covering. **-3.** [telhado] roofing.
cobertor [kobex'to(x)] (*pl* **-es**) *m* [de lã] blanket; *fam* ~ **de orelha** lover.
cobertura [kobex'tura] *f* **-1.** [ger] cover; **dar ~ a** to cover up. **-2.** [apartamento] penthouse. **-3.** [calda] topping. **-4.** JORN coverage.
cobiça [ko'bisa] *f* greed.
cobiçar [13] [kobi'sa(x)] *vt* to covet.
cobiçoso, osa [kobi'sozu, ɔza] *adj* **-1.** [pessoa] greedy. **-2.** [olhar, interesse] avid.
cobra ['kɔbra] <> *adj fam* [perito] ace. <> *f* **-1.** ZOOL snake. **-2.** *pej* [mau-caráter] snake. <> *mf fam* [perito] ace.
cobrador, ra [kobra'do(x), ra] (*mpl* **-es**, *fpl* **-s**) *m, f* **-1.** [recebedor, caixa] debt collector; ~ **de impostos** tax collector. **-2.** [de ônibus] conductor.
cobrança [ko'brãnsa] *f* **-1.** [de taxa, passagem, ingresso] fee. **-2.** *fig* [exigência] demands (*pl*). **-3.** ESP penalty; ~ **de pênalti** FUT penalty kick.
cobrar [4] [ko'bra(x)] *vt* **-1.** [taxa, passagem, ingresso] to collect. **-2.** [preço] to charge. **-3.** *fig* [promessa, favor] to exact. **-4.** ESP to take a penalty; ~ **um pênalti** FUT to take a penalty.
cobre ['kɔbri] *m* **-1.** [metal] copper. **-2.** [dinheiro, moeda] coin.
cobrir [59] [ko'bri(x)] *vt* **-1.** [ger] to cover. **-2.** [ocultar] to conceal. **-3.** [envolver] to wrap up. **-4.** [exceder] to exceed. **-5.** [encher]: ~ **algo/alguém de algo** to cover sthg/sb with sthg. **-6.** ZOOL [fêmea] to breed.
◆ **cobrir-se** *vp* **-1.** [ocultar-se, resguardar-se] to hide o.s. **-2.** [com cobertor] to cover o.s. **-3.** [encher-se]: **~-se de** to cover o.s with.
coca ['kɔka] *f* coca.
cocada [ko'kada] *f* coconut ice ***UK***, coconut candy ***US***.
cocaína [koka'ina] *f* cocaine.
coçar [13] [ko'sa(x)] <> *vt* to scratch. <> *vi* to itch.
◆ **coçar-se** *vp* to scratch o.s; **não tenho tempo nem para me ~** I haven't got time to blink.
cocar [ko'ka(x)] *m* crest.
cóccix ['kɔksis] *m inv* coccyx.
cócegas ['kɔsigaʃ] *fpl*: **fazer ~ em alguém** to tickle sb; **sentir ~** to feel itchy.
coceguento, ta [kose'gẽntu, ta] *adj* ticklish.
coceira [ko'sejra] *f* [sensação] itch.
cocheira [ko'ʃejra] *f* stable; **informação de ~** *fam* inside information.
cocheiro [ko'ʃejru] *m* coachman.
cochichar [4] [koʃi'ʃa(x)] *vi* to whisper.
cochicho [ko'ʃiʃu] *m* whisper.
cochilar [4] [koʃi'la(x)] *vi* **-1.** [dormir um pouco] to

take a nap. **-2.** [dormitar] to doze off.

cochilo [koˈʃilu] *m* nap; **tirar um ~** to take a nap.

coco [ˈkoku] *m* **-1.** [fruta] coconut. **-2.** *fam fig* [cabeça] nut.

cocô [koˈko] *m fam* poo; **fazer ~** to have a poo.

cócoras [ˈkɔkoraʃ] ◆ **de cócoras** *loc adv* squatting.

cocoricar [12] [kokoriˈka(x)] *vi* to crow.

cocuruto [kokuˈrutu] *m* **-1.** [de morro] top. **-2.** [no chão] mound. **-3.** [da cabeça] crown.

codificação [kodʒiʃikaˈsãw] (*pl* **-ões**) *f* COMPUT coding.

codificador [kodʒifikaˈdo(x)] *m* COMPUT encoder.

codificar [12] [kodʒifiˈka(x)] *vt* **-1.** [ger] to encode. **-2.** [direito, leis] to codify.

código [ˈkɔdʒigu] *m* [ger] code; **~ de barras** bar code; **~ civil** civil code; **~ de ética profissional** code of professional ethics.

código-fonte [ˈkɔdiguˈfõntʃi] (*pl* **códigos-fonte**) *m* COMPUT source code.

codinome [kodʒiˈnɔmi] *m* code name.

codorna [koˈdɔxna] *f* quail.

co-editar [4] [koedʒiˈta(x)] *vt* to co-edit.

co-editor, ra [koedʒiˈto(x), ra] (*mpl* **-res**, *fpl* **-ras**) *m, f* co-editor.

coeficiente [koefiˈsjẽntʃi] *m* **-1.** MAT coefficient. **-2.** *fig* [fator] factor.

coelho [ˈkweʎu] *m* rabbit; **matar dois ~s de uma cajadada só** to kill two birds with one stone.

coentro [ˈkwẽntru] *m* coriander.

coerção [koexˈsãw] *f* coercion.

coercivo, va [koexˈsivu, va], **coercitivo, va** [koexsiˈtʃivu, va] *adj* coercive.

coerência [koeˈrẽnsja] *f* coherence.

coerente [koeˈrẽntʃi] *adj* coherent.

coesão [koeˈzãw] *f* cohesion.

coeso, sa [ˈkwɛzu, za] *adj* **-1.** [unido, ligado] united. **-2.** [coerente] coherent.

coexistência [koeziʃˈtẽnsja] *f* coexistence.

coexistir [6] [koeziʃˈtʃi(x)] *vi* to coexist.

COFINS (*abrev de* **Contribuição para o Financiamento da Seguridade Social**) *m Brazilian employer's social security contributions, based on profits.*

cofre [ˈkɔfri] *m* safe; **os ~s públicos** the public coffers.

cofre-forte [ˌkɔfriˈfoxtʃi] (*pl* **cofres-fortes**) *m* strongroom.

cogitar [4] [koʒiˈta(x)] <> *vt* **-1.** [considerar] to consider. **-2.** [planejar]: **~ fazer algo** to consider doing sthg. <> *vi* [refletir] to deliberate; **~ sobre algo** to think about sthg.

cognato [kogˈnatu] *m* cognate; **falso ~** false cognate.

cognome [kogˈnɔmi] *m* nickname.

cognominar [4] [kognomiˈna(x)] *vt*: **~ alguém** to give a cognomen to sb.

cogumelo [koguˈmɛlu] *m* **-1.** [comestível] mushroom. **-2.** [venenoso] toadstool.

COI (*abrev de* **Comitê Olímpico Internacional**) *m* IOC.

coibição [kojbiˈsãw] (*pl* **-ões**) *f* restraint.

coibir [77] [kojˈbi(x)] *vt* to restrain; **~ alguém de fazer algo** to restrain sb from doing sthg.

coice [ˈkojsi] *m* **-1.** [de animal] backward kick; **dar um ~ em** *fig* to give sb a kick in the teeth. **-2.** [de arma] butt.

coifa [ˈkojfa] *f* [para fogão] extractor hood.

coincidência [koĩnsiˈdẽnsja] *f* coincidence; **que ~!** what a coincidence!; **ser uma ~** to be a coincidence.

coincidente [koĩnsiˈdẽntʃi] *adj* coincidental.

coincidentemente [koĩnsidẽntʃiˈmẽntʃi] *adv* coincidentally.

coincidir [6] [koĩnsiˈdi(x)] *vi* **-1.** [eventos, datas] to coincide. **-2.** [concordar]: **~ (em)** to agree (upon).

coisa [ˈkojza] *f* **-1.** [ger] thing. **-2.** [assunto] topic. **-3.** *loc*: **~ do arco da velha** [feito] incredible thing; **deu uma ~ nele** *fam* sthg came over him; **ele não diz ~ com ~** he talks absolute rubbish; **que ~!** goodness me!; **a festa foi uma ~** [ser ótimo] the party was amazing; **ser uma ~** [ser terrível] to be dreadful.

◆ **coisa de** *loc adv* roughly.

◆ **coisas** *fpl fam* [genitais] private parts.

coisíssima [kojˈzisima] *f*: **ele não é corrupto ~ nenhuma** [de modo algum] no way is he corrupt; **ele não sabia ~ nenhuma** he knew absolutely nothing.

coitado, da [kojˈtadu, da] <> *adj* [pessoa] wretched; **coitado!** poor thing!; **coitado do povo que ...** poor people who ... <> *m, f* poor wretch.

coito [ˈkojtu] *m* sex; **~ anal** anal sex.

cola [ˈkɔla] *f* **-1.** [adesivo] glue. **-2.** *fam* EDUC [ato] cribbing. **-3.** *fam* EDUC [objeto] crib.

colaboração [kolaboraˈsãw] (*pl* **-ões**) *f* **-1.** [ajuda] cooperation. **-2.** [em jornal etc] freelance work.

colaborador, ra [kolaboraˈdo(x), ra] *m, f* **-1.** [ajudante] collaborator. **-2.** [de jornal etc] freelance.

colaborar [4] [kolaboˈra(x)] *vi* **-1.** [ajudar] to cooperate; **~ em algo/com alguém** to cooperate on sthg with sb. **-2.** [em jornal etc]: **~ em algo** to freelance on sthg.

colação [kolaˈsãw] (*pl* **-ões**) *f* [concessão] bestowal; **~ de grau** conferment of a degree.

colagem [koˈlaʒẽ] (*pl* **-ns**) *f* **-1.** [ato] glueing. **-2.** ARTE collage.

colante [koˈlãntʃi] *adj* [roupa] clinging.

colapso [koˈlapsu] *f* collapse; **entrar em ~** to collapse; **~ cardíaco** heart failure; **~ nervoso** nervous breakdown.

colar [4] [koˈla(x)] (*pl* **-es**) *vt* COMPUT to paste.

colarinho [kolaˈriɲu] *m* **-1.** [de camisa] collar. **-2.** *fam* [de cerveja] head; **com/sem ~** with/without a head.

colarinho-branco [kolaˌriɲuˈbrãŋku] (*pl* **colarinhos-brancos**) *m* white-collar worker; **crime do ~** white-collar crime.

colateral [kolateˈraw] (*pl* **-ais**) *adj* collateral.

colcha [ˈkowʃa] *f* bedspread; **~ de retalhos** *fig* mishmash.

colchão [kowˈʃãw] (*pl* **-ões**) *m* mattress.

colcheia [kow'ʃejal] *f MÚS* quaver *UK*, eighth note *US*.
colchete [kow'ʃetʃi] *m* **-1.** [de roupa] hook; ~ **de gancho** hook and eye; ~ **de pressão** press stud. **-2.** [sinal] bracket.
colchões [kow'ʃõjʃ] *pl* ▻ **colchão**.
colchonete [kowʃo'nɛtʃi] *m* bolster.
coleção [kole'sãw] (*pl* **-ões**) *f* collection.
colecionador, ra [kolesjona'do(x), ra] (*mpl* **-res**, *fpl* **-s**) *m, f* collector.
colecionar [4] [kolesjo'na(x)] *vt* to collect.
colega [ko'lɛga] *mf* **-1.** [amigo] friend. **-2.** [de escola] schoolfriend. **-3.** [de trabalho] colleague.
colegial [kole'ʒjaw] (*pl* **-ais**) ◇ *adj* school *(antes de subst)*. ◇ *mf* schoolboy (*f* schoolgirl).
colégio [ko'lɛʒju] *m* **-1.** [escola] school. **-2.** [de intelectuais] college. **-3.** [de clérigos] chapter. **-4.** [de eleitores]: ~ **eleitoral** electoral college.
coleguismo [kole'giʒmu] *m* esprit de corps.
coleira [ko'lejra] *f* dog collar.
cólera ['kɔlera] ◇ *f* [ira] anger. ◇ *m MED* cholera.
colérico, ca [ko'lɛriku, ka] ◇ *adj* [irado] angry. ◇ *m, f MED* cholera victim.
colesterol [koleʃte'rɔw] *m* cholesterol.
coleta [ko'lɛta] *f* collection; ~ **de dados** fact-gathering.
coletânea [kole'tãnja] *f* collectanea.
coletar [4] [kole'ta(x)] *vt* to collect.
colete [ko'letʃi] *m* waistcoat *UK*, vest *US*; ~ **salva-vidas** life jacket.
coletividade [koletʃivi'dadʒi] *f* community.
coletivo, va [kole'tʃivu, va] *adj* **-1.** [de muitos] collective. **-2.** [transporte, banheiro] public.
◆ **coletivo** *m* **-1.** [ônibus] public transport. **-2.** [futebol] trials. **-3.** [ling] collective noun.
coletor, ra [kole'to(x), ra] *m, f* [de impostos] collector.
colheita [ko'ʎejta] *f* **-1.** [ger] harvest. **-2.** [produto] crop.
colher [5] [ko'ʎɛ(x)] (*pl* **-es** [ko'ʎɛriʃ]) ◇ *f* **-1.** [talher] spoon; ~ **de chá** teaspoon; ~ **de sobremesa** dessertspoon; ~ **de sopa** tablespoon; **dar uma** ~ **de chá a alguém** *fig* to do sb a favour. **-2.** [ferramenta]: ~ **de pedreiro** trowel. ◇ *vt* **-1.** [fruta, verdura, safra] to pick. **-2.** [dados] to gather.
colherada [koʎe'rada] *f* spoonful.
colibri [koli'bri] *m* hummingbird.
cólica ['kɔlika] *f* colic; ~ **menstrual** period pains *(pl)*.
colidir [6] [koli'dʒi(x)] *vi* [chocar-se] to collide; ~ **com/contra** to collide with/against.
coligação [koliga'sãw] (*pl* **-ões**) *f* coalition; ~ **partidária** *ou* **eleitoral** political coalition.
coligar [14] [koli'ga(x)] *vt* to bind together.
◆ **coligar-se** *vp* to unite; ~**-se com** to align o.s with.
coligir [52] [koli'ʒi(x)] *vt* to compile.
colina [ko'lina] *f* hill.
colírio [ko'lirju] *m* eyewash; **ser um** ~ **para os olhos de alguém** *fam* to be a sight for sore eyes.
colisão [koli'zãw] (*pl* **-ões**) *f* collision.
colite [ko'litʃi] *f* colitis.
collant [ko'lã] *m* tights *(pl)*.
colméia [kow'mɛja] *f* beehive.
colo ['kɔlu] *m* **-1.** [ger] neck. **-2.** [regaço] lap; **no** ~ on one's lap.
colocação [koloka'sãw] (*pl* **-ões**) *f* **-1.** [ato] fitting. **-2.** [posição, emprego] position. **-3.** [em concurso, competição] place. **-4.** [observação] observation.
colocar [12] [kolo'ka(x)] *vt* **-1.** [ger] to place. **-2.** [dar emprego a] to employ. **-3.** [situar - no espaço] to site. **-4.** [instalar - ar-condicionado] to install; [- pneu] to fit; [- carpete] to lay; [- cortina] to hang. **-5.** [levantar] to raise.
◆ **colocar-se** *vp* **-1.** [pôr-se] to position o.s. **-2.** [em concurso, competição] to be placed. **-3.** [imaginar-se]: **coloque-se no meu lugar** put yourself in my place.
Colômbia [ko'lõnbja] *n* Colombia.
colombiano, na [kolõn'bjãnu, na] ◇ *adj* Colombian. ◇ *m, f* Colombian.
cólon ['kɔlõ] *m ANAT* colon.
colônia [ko'lonja] *f* **-1.** [ger] colony; **Brasil** ~ colonial Brazial. **-2.** [para crianças]: ~ **de férias** summer camp. **-3.** [perfume] cologne; **água de** ~ eau de cologne.
colonial [kolo'njaw] (*pl* **-ais**) *adj* colonial.
colonialismo [kolonja'liʒmu] *m* colonialism.
colonização [koloniza'sãw] *f* colonization.
colonizador, ra [koloniza'do(x), ra] ◇ *adj* [nação, esforço] colonizing. ◇ *m, f* [pessoa] settler.
colonizar [4] [koloni'za(x)] *vt* to colonize.
colono, na [ko'lɔnu, na] *m, f* **-1.** [povoador] colonist. **-2.** [cultivador] smallholder.
coloquial [kolo'kjaw] (*pl* **-ais**) *adj* colloquial.
coloquialismo [kolokja'liʒmu] *m* familiar tone.
colóquio [ko'lɔkju] *m* **-1.** [congresso] symposium. **-2.** *ant* [conversa] conversation.
coloração [kolora'sãw] (*pl* **-ões**) *f* colouration.
colorido, da [kolo'ridu, da] *adj* multi-coloured *UK*, multi-colored *US*.
◆ **colorido** *m* colour *UK*, color *US*.
colorir [79] [kolo'ri(x)] *vt* **-1.** [dar cor a] to colour *UK*, to color *US*. **-2.** *fig* [avivar] to brighten.
colossal [kolo'saw] (*pl* **-ais**) *adj* colossal.
colosso [ko'losu] *m* [ger] colossus.
coluna [ko'luna] *f* **-1.** [ger] column; ~ **social** society column. **-2.** [pilar] pillar. **-3.** *ANAT*: ~ **vertebral** spinal column.
colunável [kolu'navew] (*pl* **-eis**) ◇ *adj* [pessoa, festa] glamorous. ◇ *mf* [celebridade] celebrity.
colunista [kolu'niʃta] *mf* columnist; ~ **social** society columnist.
com [kõ] *prep* **-1.** with; **ela mora** ~ **um amigo** she lives with a friend; ~ **quem você vai?** who are you going with? **-2.** [relativo a modo] with; ~ **cuidado** with care; [relativo a instrumento] with; **ela escreve** ~ **a mão direita** she writes with her right hand; ~ **o tempo, a mulher conseguiu superar o trauma** with time, the woman managed to overcome the trauma **-3.** [indica causa] with,

because of; **só ~ muito esforço é que ele conseguiu** only with a lot of effort did he manage to do it; **estar ~ dor de cabeça** to have a headache; **estar ~ fome** to be hungry; **estar ~ pressa** to be in a hurry. **-4.** [apesar de] in spite of; **~ todo esse trabalho ele ainda encontra tempo para estudar** in spite of all that work, he still finds time to study; **você vai jogar bola ~ chuva?** are you going to play football in the rain?; **~ 86 anos, ele continua cheio de energia** at 86, he is still full of energy. **-5.** *(em loc prep)* with; **~ relação a** in relation to; **~ vistas a** with an aim to; **de acordo ~** in accordance with; **em parceria ~** in partnership with.

coma [ˈkoma] *m MED* coma; **estado de ~** comatose state; **em ~** in a coma.

comadre [koˈmadri] *f* **-1.** [madrinha] *a godmother in relation to her godchild's parents; a child's mother in relation to its godparents.* **-2.** [amiga] friend. **-3.** [urinol] bedpan.

comandante [komãnˈdãntʃi] *mf* **-1.** *MIL, NÁUT* commander. **-2.** [dirigente] leader.

comandar [4] [komãnˈda(x)] *vt* **-1.** *MIL, NÁUT* to command. **-2.** [dirigir] to head.

comando [koˈmãndu] *m* [ger] command.

comarca [koˈmaxka] *f* area of jurisdiction.

combalido, da [kõnbaˈlidu, da] *adj* enfeebled.

combate [kõnˈbatʃi] *m* **-1.** [luta, oposição] fight. **-2.** [bélico] skirmish; **fora de ~** *fig* flat on one's back.

combatente [kõnbaˈtẽntʃi] *mf* combatant.

combater [5] [kõnbaˈte(x)] ◇ *vt* [lutar contra, opor-se a] to struggle. ◇ *vi* [belicamente] to fight.

combinação [kõnbinaˈsãw] *(pl* **-ões***)* *f* **-1.** [ger] combination. **-2.** *QUÍM* compound. **-3.** [acordo, plano] agreement. **-4.** [peça de roupa] slip.

combinar [4] [kõnbiˈna(x)] ◇ *vt* **-1.** [associar, reunir] to combine. **-2.** [encontro, jantar] to fix; **combinado!** agreed! **-3.** [plano, fuga] to plan. ◇ *vi* **-1.** [planejar]: **combinamos de ir ao cinema** we fixed up to go to the cinema. **-2.** [cores, roupas] to match; **~ com algo** to go with sthg.

comboio [kõnˈboju] *m* **-1.** [ger] convoy. **-2.** *FERRO* train.

combustão [kõnbuʃˈtãw] *(pl* **-ões***)* *f* combustion.

combustível [kõnbuʃˈtʃivɛw] *(pl* **-eis***)* ◇ *adj* combustible. ◇ *m* fuel.

começar [13] [komeˈsa(x)] ◇ *vt* to start. ◇ *vi* to begin, to start; **~ a fazer algo** to start doing sthg, to start to do sthg; **~ por** to begin with; **para ~** [em primeiro lugar] first of all.

começo [koˈmesu] *m* beginning.

comédia [koˈmɛdʒja] *f* comedy.

comediante [komeˈdʒjãntʃi] *mf* comedian.

comedido, da [komeˈdʒidu, da] *adj* **-1.** [moderado] moderate. **-2.** [prudente] prudent.

comedimento [komedʒiˈmẽntu] *m* [moderação] moderation.

comedir-se [70] [komeˈdʒixsi] *vp* [conter-se] to restrain o.s.

comemoração [komemoraˈsãw] *(pl* **-ões***)* *f* celebration.

comemorar [4] [komemoˈra(x)] *vt* to celebrate.

comemorativo, va [komemoraˈtʃivu, va] *adj* commemorative.

comensal [komẽnˈsãw] *(pl* **-ais***)* *mf* dinner guest.

comentar [4] [komẽnˈta(x)] *vt* **-1.** [fato, festa, incidente] to comment on. **-2.** [observar]: **~ que** to remark that. **-3.** *ESP* [partida] to commentate.

comentário [komẽnˈtarju] *m* commentary; **fazer um ~** to do a commentary; **sem ~s** no comment; **~ esportivo** sports commentary; **~ político** political commentary.

comentarista [komẽntaˈriʃta] *mf* commentator; **~ esportivo** sports commentator; **~ político** political commentator.

comer [5] [koˈme(x)] *(pl* **-es***)* ◇ *vt* **-1.** [alimentar-se de] to eat. **-2.** *fig* [suprimir] to swallow. **-3.** *fig* [corroer] to corrode. **-4.** *fig* [consumir] to devour. **-5.** [em damas, xadrez] to take. **-6.** *vulg fig* [sexualmente] to fuck. ◇ *vi* [alimentar-se] to eat; **dar de ~ a alguém** to feed sb; **~ por quatro** [comer demais] to stuff o.s.

◆ **comer-se** *vp*: **~-se de raiva/vontade** to be consumed with anger/desire.

comercial [komexˈsjaw] *(pl* **-ais***)* ◇ *adj* commercial. ◇ *m* [anúncio] advertisement, commercial.

comercialização [komexsjalizaˈsãw] *(pl* **-ões***)* *f* commercialization.

comercializar [4] [komexsjaliˈza(x)] *vt* to market.

comercializável [komexsjaliˈzavɛw] *(pl* **-eis***)* *adj* marketable.

comerciante [komexˈsjãntʃi] *mf* businessman *(f* businesswoman).

comerciar [18] [komexˈsja(x)] *vi* to trade; **~ com** to trade with.

comerciário, ria [komexˈsjarju, rja] *m, f* trader.

comércio [koˈmɛxsju] *m* **-1.** [compra e venda] trade. **-2.** [tráfico] trafficking. **-3.** [estabelecimento] premises. **-4.** [mercado comercial] business. **-5.** *fig* [troca de idéias, influências] exchange.

comes [ˈkɔmiʃ] *mpl fam*: **~ e bebes** food and drink.

comestíveis [komeʃˈtʃivejʃ] *mpl* comestibles.

comestível [komeʃˈtʃivɛw] *(pl* **-eis***)* *adj* edible.

cometa [koˈmeta] *m* comet.

cometer [5] [komeˈte(x)] *vt* to commit.

cometimento [kometʃiˈmẽntu] *m* **-1.** [de crime, pecado, infração] committing. **-2.** [empreendimento] undertaking.

comichão [komiˈʃãw] *(pl* **-ões***)* *f* itch; **ter** *ou* **sentir ~** to have/feel an itch.

comicidade [komisiˈdadʒi] *f* comedy.

comício [koˈmisju] *m* rally; **~ relâmpago** short public rally.

cômico, ca [ˈkomiku, ka] ◇ *adj* comical. ◇ *m, f* [comediante] comedian.

comida [koˈmida] *f* **-1.** [alimento] food. **-2.** [refeição] meal; **~ caseira** home cooking.

comigo [koˈmigu] *pron*: **ela não fala ~** she won't speak to me; **o livro dele está ~** I've got his book; **matemática é ~ mesmo** maths is my thing; **ela acenou, mas pensei que não era ~** she nodded, but I thought that she didn't agree with me; **isto não é justo, pensei ~** that isn't fair, I thought to myself; **deixa ~!** leave it with me!

comilança [komi'lãnsa] *f* spread, blowout.

comilão, lona [komi'lãw, lona] (*mpl* **-ões**, *fpl* **-s**) <> *adj* gluttonous. <> *m, f* glutton.

cominho [ko'miɲu] *m* cumin.

comiserar-se [4] [komize'raxsi] *vp* to feel pity; **~ (de)** to feel pity for.

comissão [komi'sãw] (*pl* **-ões**) *f* **-1.** [comitê] committee; **Comissão Parlamentar de Inquérito** Parliamentary Investigative Committee. **-2.** [gratificação] commission.

comissário, ria [komi'sarju, rja] *m, f* agent; **~ de bordo** air steward (*f* air stewardess).

comissionar [4] [komisjo'na(x)] *vt* **-1.** [encarregar] to commission. **-2.** [confiar] to entrust.

comitê [komi'te] *m* committee; **~ executivo** executive committee.

comitiva [komi'tʃiva] *f* retinue.

commodity [comɔ'dʒitʃi] (*pl* **commodities**) *f* ECON commodity.

como ['komu] <> *adv* **-1.** [ger] as. **-2.** [de que modo] how; **~?** [o que você disse?] I'm sorry?; **~ assim?** how do you mean? **-3.** [comparativo]: **ser ~ algo/alguém** to be like sthg/sb. **-4.** [exclamativo]: **como!** what!; **e ~!** *fam* and how!; **~ não!** [pois não] of course! <> *conj* **-1.** [porque] because. **-2.** [conforme] as.

◆ **como que** *loc adv*: **~ que por um golpe de mágica, tudo desapareceu** as if by magic, everything disappeared.

◆ **como quer que** *loc conj* however.

◆ **como quiser** *loc adv* as; **fazer algo ~ quiser** to do as one wishes.

◆ **como se** *loc conj* as if.

comoção [komo'sãw] (*pl* **-ões**) *f* **-1.** [abalo] shock. **-2.** [revolta] unrest.

cômoda ['komoda] *f* chest of drawers.

comodidade [komodʒi'dadʒi] *f* **-1.** [conforto] comfort. **-2.** [conveniência] convenience.

comodismo [komo'dʒiʒmu] *m* indolence.

comodista [komo'dʒiʃta] <> *adj* passive. <> *mf* passive person.

cômodo, da ['komodu, da] *adj* **-1.** [confortável] comfortable. **-2.** [conveniente] appropriate.

◆ **cômodo** *m* [aposento] room.

comovente [komo'vẽntʃi], **comovedor, ra** [komove'do(x), ra] *adj* moving.

comover [5] [komo've(x)] <> *vt* to move. <> *vi* to be moving.

◆ **comover-se** *vp* to be moved.

comovido, da [komo'vidu, da] *adj* moved.

compactador [kõmpak'tado(x)] *m* COMPUT (file) compressor.

compactar [kõmpzk'ta(x)] *vt* COMPUT: **~ arquivos** to compress files.

compacto, ta [kõm'paktu, ta] *adj* **-1.** [pequeno] compact. **-2.** [denso, comprimido] dense.

◆ **compacto** *m* [disco] compact disc, CD.

compadecer-se [25] [kõnpade'sexsi] *vp*: **~ de** to take pity on.

compadecido, da [kõnpade'sidu, da] *adj* compassionate.

compadecimento [kõnpadesi'mẽntu] *m* [piedade] compassion.

compadre [kõn'padri] *m* **-1.** [padrinho do filho] *a godfather in relation to his godchild's parents* ou *a child's father in relation to its godparents.* **-2.** *fam* [companheiro] companion; **meu ~** my friend.

compaixão [kõnpaj'ʃãw] *f* **-1.** [piedade] compassion. **-2.** [misericórdia] mercy.

companheirismo [kõnpaɲej'riʒmu] *m* companionship.

companheiro, ra [kõnpa'ɲejru, ra] *m, f* **-1.** [que acompanha] companion; **~ de viagem** travelling companion. **-2.** [colega] colleague. **-3.** [marido, namorado] partner. **-4.** *fam* [amigo] mate.

companhia [kõnpa'ɲia] *f* [ger] company; **em ~ de** in the company of; **fazer ~ a alguém** to keep sb company.

comparação [kõnpara'sãw] (*pl* **-ões**) *f* comparison.

comparar [4] [kõnpa'ra(x)] *vt*: **~ algo/alguém (com)** to compare sthg/sb (with).

◆ **comparar-se** *vp*: **~-se com** to compare o.s. to; **isto não se compara com ...** this does not bear comparison with ...

comparável [kõnpa'ravew] (*pl* **-eis**) *adj* comparable.

comparecer [25] [kõnpare'se(x)] *vi*: **~ (a)** to appear (at).

comparecimento [kõnparesi'mẽntu] *m* presence; **~ às urnas** turnout at the ballot-boxes.

comparsa [kõn'paxsa] *mf* **-1.** [cúmplice] accomplice. **-2.** TEATRO extra.

compartilhar [4] [kõmpaxtʃi'ʎa(x)] <> *vt* [partilhar] to share. <> *vi* [participar]: **~ de** to share in.

compartimentar [4] [kõnpaxtʃimẽn'ta(x)] *vt* to split *(into separate rooms, parts etc).*

compartimento [kõnpaxtʃi'mẽntu] *m* **-1.** [divisão] compartment; **~ de carga** cargo bay. **-2.** [aposento] room.

compartir [6] [kõnpax'tʃi(x)] *vt* & *vi* = **compartilhar**.

compassado, da [kõnpa'sadu, da] *adj* **-1.** [pausado] measured. **-2.** [cadenciado] rhythmic. **-3.** [comedido] moderate.

compassivo, va [kõnpa'sivu, va] *adj* compassionate.

compasso [kõn'pasu] *m* **-1.** [instrumento] pair of compasses. **-2.** MÚS beat. **-3.** [ritmo] time; **dentro/fora do ~** in/out of time.

compatibilidade [kõnpatʃibili'dadʒi] *f* compatibility.

compatível [kõnpa'tʃivɛw] (*pl* **-eis**) *adj* compatible.

compatriota [kõnpatri'ɔta] *mf* compatriot.

compelir [57] [kõnpe'li(x)] *vt*: **~ alguém a**

fazer algo to force sb to do sthg.
compêndio [kõn'pẽndʒju] *m* **-1.** [livro] textbook. **-2.** [síntese] summary.
compenetração [kõnpenetra'sãw] *f* **-1.** [concentração] concentration. **-2.** [convicção] conviction.
compenetrado, da [kõnpene'tradu, da] *adj* **-1.** [concentrado] concentrated. **-2.** [convicto] convinced.
compenetrar [4] [kõnpene'tra(x)] *vt* [convencer] to convince.
◆ **compenetrar-se** *vp* **-1.** [convencer-se]: **~-se de** to become convinced of. **-2.** [concentrar-se] to concentrate.
compensação [kõnpẽnsa'sãw] (*pl* **-ões**) *f* **-1.** [reparação] compensation; **em ~** to make up for it. **-2.** [equilíbrio] balance. **-3.** [de cheque] clearance.
compensado [kõnpẽn'sadu] *m* [madeira] plywood.
compensador, ra [kõnpẽnsa'do(x), ra] *adj* compensatory.
compensar [4] [kõnpẽn'sa(x)] <> *vt* **-1.** [dar reparo a] to make up for. **-2.** [equilibrar] to compensate for. **-3.** [cheque] to clear. <> *vi* [valer a pena] to pay.
competência [kõnpe'tẽnsja] *f* **-1.** [habilidade] competence. **-2.** [responsabilidade] responsibility; **ser da ~ de alguém** to be the responsibility of sb.
competente [kõnpe'tẽntʃi] *adj* **-1.** [hábil] competent. **-2.** [responsável] responsible.
competição [kõnpetʃi'sãw] (*pl* **-ões**) *f* **-1.** [disputa, concorrência] competition. **-2.** *ESP* [prova] contest.
competidor, ra [kõnpetʃi'do(x), ra] *m, f* *ESP* competitor.
competir [57] [kõnpe'tʃi(x)] *vi* to compete; **~ com** to compete with.
competitividade [kõnpetʃitʃivi'dadʒi] *f* competitiveness.
competitivo, va [kõnpetʃi'tʃivu, va] *adj* competitive.
compilação [kõnpila'sãw] *f* compilation.
compilar [4] [kõnpi'la(x)] *vt* to compile.
complacência [kõnpla'sẽnsja] *f* complacency.
complacente [kõnpla'sẽntʃi] *adj* complacent.
compleição [kõnplej'sãw] (*pl* **-ões**) *f* build.
complementar [4] [kõnplemẽn'ta(x)] (*pl* **-es**) <> *adj* additional. <> *vt* to complement.
complemento [kõnple'mẽntu] *m* **-1.** [acréscimo] addition; **~ alimentar** food supplement; **~ salarial** additional wages. **-2.** *GRAM* object.
completamente [kõm,pleta'mẽntʃi] *adv* completely.
completar [4] [kõnple'ta(x)] *vt* **-1.** [terminar] to complete. **-2.** [idade] to reach. **-3.** [com gasolina etc] to fill up.
completo, ta [kõn'plɛtu, ta] *adj* **-1.** [trabalho] finished. **-2.** [idade]: **ele tem 16 anos ~s** he is 16 years old. **-3.** [tanque] full.
◆ **por completo** *loc adv* [inteiramente] completely.
complexado, da [kõnplek'sadu, da] *adj* hung-up; **estar/ficar ~** to have a complex.
complexidade [kõnpleksi'dadʒi] *f* complexity.
complexo, xa [kõm'plɛksu, sa] *adj* complex.
◆ **complexo** *m* complex; **~ de Édipo** Oedipus complex; **~ de inferioridade** inferiority complex.
complicação [kõnplika'sãw] (*pl* **-ões**) *f* **-1.** [ger] complexity. **-2.** *MED* complication.
complicado, da [kõnpli'kadu, da] *adj* complicated; **ser ~** to be complicated.
complicar [12] [kõnpli'ka(x)] *vt* [tornar complexo] to complicate.
◆ **complicar-se** *vp* to worsen.
complô [kõn'plo] *m* conspiracy.
componente [kõnpo'nẽntʃi] *m* component.
compor [45] [kõn'po(x)] <> *vt* **-1.** [formar, integrar] to comprise. **-2.** [música, versos] to compose. **-3.** [discurso, livro] to write. **-4.** [enfeitar] to arrange. **-5.** *POL* [aliança, acordo] to constitute. **-6.** *TIP* to typeset. <> *vi* **-1.** [música] to compose. **-2.** *TIP* to typeset.
◆ **compor-se** *vp* **-1.** [ser integrado por]: **~-se de** to consist of. **-2.** [controlar-se] to compose o.s.
comporta [kõn'pɔxta] *f* floodgate.
comportamento [kõnpoxta'mẽntu] *m* **-1.** [de pessoa] behaviour; **bom/mau ~** good/bad behaviour. **-2.** [reação] reaction.
comportar [4] [kõnpox'ta(x)] *vt* **-1.** [suportar] to hold. **-2.** [conter] to contain.
◆ **comportar-se** *vp* **-1.** [pessoa] to behave; **~ se bem/mal** to behave well/badly. **-2.** [reagir] to behave.
composição [kõnpozi'sãw] (*pl* **-ões**) *f* **-1.** [ger] composition. **-2.** [de trem, metrô] formation. **-3.** *TIP* typesetting.
compositor, ra [kõnpozi'to(x), ra] (*mpl* **-es**, *fpl* **-s**) *m, f* **-1.** *MÚS* composer. **-2.** *TIP* typesetter; **~ tipográfico** typesetter.
composto, ta [kõn'poʃtu, ta] <> *pp* ▻ **compor.** <> *adj* composed.
◆ **composto** *m* *QUÍM* compound.
compostura [kõnpoʃ'tura] *f* composure; **perder a ~** to lose one's composure.
compota [kõn'pɔta] *f* stewed fruit, fruit compote.
compra ['kõnpra] *f* **-1.** [ato] purchase; **fazer ~s** to shop; **ir às ~s** to go shopping. **-2.** [coisa comprada] shopping.
comprador, ra [kõnpra'do(x), ra] *m, f* purchaser, buyer.
comprar [4] [kõn'pra(x)] *vt* **-1.** [adquirir] to buy. **-2.** *fig* [subornar] to bribe. **-3.** *loc*: **~ briga** to pick a fight; **~ a briga de alguém** to take up sb's cause.
comprazer-se [32] [kõnpra'zexsi] *vp*: **~ com** *ou* **em fazer algo** to take pleasure in doing sthg.
compreender [5] [kõnprjẽn'de(x)] *vt* **-1.** [entender] to understand. **-2.** [abranger] to comprise.
compreensão [kõnprjẽ'sãw] *f* **-1.** [entendimento intelectual] comprehension. **-2.** [aceitação] understanding. **-3.** [percepção] realization.
compreensível [kõnprjẽ'sivew] (*pl* **-eis**) *adj* understandable.
compreensivo, va [kõnprjẽ'sivu, va] *adj* **-1.**

[pessoa, atitude] understanding. **-2.** [medida] comprehensive.
compressa [kõn'prɛsa] *f* compress.
compressão [kõnpre'sãw] (*pl* **-ões**) *f* compression.
compressor, ra [kõnpre'so(x), ra] *adj* ▻ **rolo**.
comprido, da [kõn'pridu, da] *adj* **-1.** [longo] long. **-2.** [alto] tall.
comprimento [kõnpri'mẽntu] *m* length; **três metros de ~** three metres in length, three metres long.
comprimido, da [kõnpri'midu, da] *adj* compressed.
◆ **comprimido** *m* tablet.
comprimir [6] [kõnpri'mi(x)] *vt* **-1.** [reduzir sob pressão - ar, volume] to compress; [- barriga] to pull in. **-2.** [apertar] to squeeze.
comprometedor, ra [kõnpromete'do(x), ra] *adj* compromising.
comprometer [5] [kõnprome'te(x)] *vt* **-1.** [ger] to compromise. **-2.** [empenhar] to commit.
◆ **comprometer-se** *vp* **-1.** [assumir compromisso]: **~-se (com)** to make a commitment (to). **-2.** [ser envolvido]: **~-se (em)** to become involved (in).
comprometido, da [kõnprome'tʃidu, da] *adj* **-1.** [ocupado] busy. **-2.** [amorosamente] engaged.
compromisso [kõnpro'misu] *m* **-1.** [encontro etc] appointment. **-2.** [promessa] promise; **assumir um ~** to undertake. **-3.** [obrigação] obligation; **sem ~** under no obligation. **-4.** [acordo] agreement; **solução de ~** compromise solution. **-5.** [namoro, noivado] engagement.
comprovação [kõnprova'sãw] (*pl* **-ões**) *f* **-1.** [prova] proof. **-2.** *ADMIN* [de gastos] evidence.
comprovante [kõnpro'vantʃi] <> *adj* confirming. <> *m* receipt.
comprovar [4] [kõnpro'va(x)] *vt* to confirm.
compulsão [kõnpuw'sãw] (*pl* **-ões**) *f* compulsion; **ter ~ por** to have a compulsion for.
compulsivo, va [kõnpuw'sivu, va] *adj* compulsive.
compulsório, ria [kõnpuw'sɔrju, rja] *adj* compulsory.
compunção [kõnpũn'sãw] *f* compunction.
compungir [52] [kõnpũn'ʒi(x)] <> *vt* to move. <> *vi* to be moving.
computação [kõnputa'sãw] *f* **-1.** [ato] computation. **-2.** [ciência, curso] computing.
computador [kõnputa'do(x)] (*pl* **-es**) *m* computer.
computadorizar [4] [kõnputadori'za(x)] *vt* to computerize.
computadorizado, da [kõmputa'dori'zadu, da] *adj* computerized.
computar [4] [kõnpu'ta(x)] *vt* **-1.** [contar] to count. **-2.** [calcular] to compute, to calculate. **-3.** [incluir] to include.
cômputo ['kõnputu] *m* **-1.** [contagem] counting. **-2.** [cálculo] estimate.
comum [ko'mũ] (*pl* **-ns**) <> *adj* **-1.** [ordinário] ordinary. **-2.** [mútuo] mutual; **ter algo em ~** to have sthg in common. **-3.** [usual] common. <> *m* [usual] usual thing; **o ~ é ficarmos em casa aos domingos** we usually stay at home on Sundays; **fora do ~** [extraordinário] out of the ordinary.
comuna [ko'muna] *mf fam* [comunista] Commie.
◆ **comuna** *f ADMIN* commune.
comungar [14] [komũn'ga(x)] *vi* **-1.** *RELIG* to receive Communion. **-2.** *fig* [partilhar]: **~ de algo** to share sthg.
comunhão [komu'ɲãw] (*pl* **-ões**) *f* **-1.** [união] unity; **~ de bens** [em matrimônio] joint ownership of property. **-2.** *RELIG* Communion.
comunicação [komunika'sãw] (*pl* **-ões**) *f* **-1.** [ato] communication. **-2.** [ciência] communications (*sg*); **~ de massa** mass media; **~ social** the media. **-3.** [mensagem] message. **-4.** [em congresso, simpósio] speech. **-5.** [ligação] link.
comunicador, ra [komunika'do(x), ra] *m, f* communicator.
comunicar [12] [komuni'ka(x)] <> *vt* **-1.** [informar sobre]: **~ algo a alguém** to inform sb of sthg. **-2.** [ligar] to link. <> *vi* [ligar-se]: **~ com** to be connected to.
◆ **comunicar-se** *vp* **-1.** [dialogar, entender-se] to communicate. **-2.** [entrar em contato]: **~-se com** to contact.
comunicativo, va [komunika'tʃivu, va] *adj* communicative.
comunidade [komuni'dadʒi] *f* community; **Comunidade Européia** European Community.
comunismo [komu'niʒmu] *m* communism.
comunista [komu'niʃta] <> *adj* communist. <> *mf* communist.
comunitário, ria [komuni'tarju, rja] *adj* community.
comutador [komuta'do(x)] *m* switch.
comutar [4] [komu'ta(x)] *vt* **-1.** *JUR* to commute. **-2.** [trocar] to exchange.
concatenação [kõnkatena'sãw] (*pl* **-ões**) *f* [encadeamento] (close) linkage.
concatenar [4] [kõnkate'na(x)] *vt* to link together.
côncavo, va ['kõnkavu, va] *adj* concave.
◆ **côncavo** *m* hollow.
conceber [5] [kõnse'be(x)] <> *vt* [gerar] to conceive. <> *vi* [engravidar] to conceive.
concebível [kõnse'bivew] (*pl* **-eis**) *adj* [imaginável] conceivable.
conceder [5] [kõnse'de(x)] *vt* **-1.** [dar, outorgar] to concede. **-2.** [permitir]: **~ que alguém faça algo** to allow sb to do sthg. **-3.** [admitir]: **~ que** to admit that.
conceito [kõn'sejtu] *m* **-1.** [idéia] concept. **-2.** [opinião] opinion. **-3.** [reputação] reputation. **-4.** *EDUC* [nota] grade.
conceituação [kõnsejtua'sãw] (*pl* **-ões**) *f* **-1.** [definição] conceptualization. **-2.** [avaliação] rating.
conceituado, da [kõsej'twadu, da] *adj* respected.
conceituar [4] [kõnsej'twa(x)] *vt* **-1.** [formular conceito de] to conceptualize. **-2.** [avaliar] to assess.

concentração [kõnsẽntra'sãw] (*pl* **-ões**) *f* **-1.** [ger] concentration. **-2.** ESP *athletic briefing and training usually the day before an important event.*

concentrado, da [kõsẽn'tradu, da] *adj* **-1.** [ger] concentrated. **-2.** [centralizado] centralized. **-3.** [aglomerado] gathered together.

◆ **concentrado** *m* [substância] concentrate.

concentrar [4] [kõnsẽn'tra(x)] *vt* **-1.** [ger] to concentrate. **-2.** [centralizar] to centralize. **-3.** [aglomerar] to bring together, to mass.

◆ **concentrar-se** *vp* **-1.** [aglomerar-se] to mass. **-2.** [pessoa, atenção, esforço]: **~-se (em algo)** to concentrate (on sthg).

concepção [kõnsep'sãw] (*pl* **-ões**) *f* **-1.** [geração] conception. **-2.** [conceito] concept. **-3.** [opinião] opinion.

concernente [kõnsex'nẽntʃi] *adj*: **~ a** concerning.

concernir [54] [kõnsex'ni(x)] *vi*: **~ a** to concern; **no que me concerne, ...** as far as I'm concerned, ...

concerto [kõn'sextu] *m* MÚS concert.

concessão [kõnse'sãw] (*pl* **-ões**) *f* **-1.** [ger] concession; **fazer uma ~ a** to make a concession to. **-2.** [entrega - de empréstimo, licença *etc*] granting; [- de prêmio] awarding. **-3.** [permissão] permission.

concessionário, ria [kõnsesjo'narju, rja] *m, f* concessionaire.

◆ **concessionária** *f* [empresa] agency.

concha ['kõnʃa] *f* **-1.** [de molusco] shell. **-2.** [para líquidos] ladle.

conchavo [kõn'ʃavu] *m* conspiracy; **fazer um ~** to form a conspiracy.

conciliação [kõnsilja'sãw] (*pl* **-ões**) *f* reconciliation.

conciliador, ra [kõnsilja'do(x), ra] ◇ *adj* conciliatory. ◇ *m, f* [pessoa] conciliator.

conciliar [16] [kõnsi'lja(x)] *vt* to reconcile.

conciliatório, ria [kõnsilja'tɔrju, rja] *adj* conciliatory.

conciliável [kõnsi'ljavew] (*pl* **-eis**) *adj* reconcilable.

concílio [kõn'silju] *m* RELIG council.

concisão [kõnsi'sãw] *f* concision.

conciso, sa [kõn'sizu, za] *adj* concise.

conclamar [4] [kõnkla'ma(x)] *vt* **-1.** [bradar] to shout. **-2.** [aclamar] to acclaim. **-3.** [convocar]: **~ alguém a fazer algo** to incite sb to do sthg; **~ alguém para algo** to call on sb for sthg.

conclave [kõn'klavi] *m* conclave.

concludente [kõnklu'dẽntʃi] *adj* conclusive.

concluir [74] [kõŋklu'i(x)] *vt* **-1.** [terminar] to conclude. **-2.** [deduzir] to deduce.

conclusão [kõŋklu'zãw] (*pl* **-ões**) *f* [ger] conclusion; **chegar a uma ~** [chegar a uma dedução] to reach a conclusion; [chegar a um acordo] to come to an agreement; **~:** *fam* [resultado] upshot.

conclusivo, va [kõnklu'zivu, va] *adj* conclusive.

concomitante [kõnkomi'tãntʃi] *adj* concomitant; **~ a** simultaneous with.

concordância [kõŋkox'dãnsja] *f* agreement.

concordante [kõŋkox'dãntʃi] *adj* corroborating.

concordar [4] [kõŋkox'da(x)] ◇ *vt*: **~ que** to agree that. ◇ *vi* to agree; **~ com algo/alguém** to agree with sthg/sb; **~ em fazer algo** to agree to do sthg; **não concordo!** I disagree!

concordata [kõŋkox'data] *f* **-1.** FIN composition; **entrar em ~** to make a composition; **pedir a ~** to seek a composition. **-2.** RELIG concordat.

concórdia [kõŋ'kɔxdʒja] *f* **-1.** [harmonia] concord. **-2.** [paz] peace.

concorrência [kõŋko'xẽnsja] *f* **-1.** [ger] competition. **-2.** *fig* [licitação] tender; **abrir uma ~** to call to tender.

concorrente [kõŋko'xẽntʃi] *adj* **-1.** [competidor] competitor. **-2.** [candidato] candidate.

concorrer [5] [kõŋko'xe(x)] *vi* **-1.** [ger] to compete; **~ com alguém** to compete with sb; **~ a algo** [ger] to apply for sthg; POL to be running for sthg. **-2.** [contribuir]: **~ para algo** to contribute to sthg.

concorrido, da [kõnko'xidu, da] *adj* **-1.** [disputado] disputed. **-2.** *fam* [festa, bar *etc*] popular.

concretamente [kõnkreta'mẽntʃi] *adv* [em termos reais] really, actually.

concretização [kõnkretʃiza'sãw] (*pl* **-ões**) *f* realization.

concretizar [4] [kõŋkreti'za(x)] *vt* to realize.

◆ **concretizar-se** *vp* [sonho, projeto, anseio] to be realized.

concreto, ta [kõŋ'krɛtu, ta] *adj* [sólido] concrete.

◆ **concreto** *m* concrete; **~ armado** reinforced concrete.

concretude [kõnkre'tudʒi] *f* concrete nature.

concunhado, da [kõnku'ɲadu, da] *m, f* the brother-in-law or sister-in-law of one's husband or wife.

concupiscência [kõnkupi'sẽnsja] *f* **-1.** [ambição] ambition. **-2.** [lascívia] lust.

concupiscente [kõŋkupis'sẽntʃi] *adj* materialistic.

concursado, da [kõŋkux'sadu, da] ◇ *adj referring to a person who has been successful in a competitive examination giving access to a position, particularly in public office.*

concurso [kõŋ'kuxsu] *m* **-1.** [exame] competitive examination; **~ público** public competitive examination. **-2.** [sorteio] lottery.

concussão [kõŋku'sãw] (*pl* **-ões**) *f* **-1.** MED concussion. **-2.** *fig* [desfalque] embezzlement.

condado [kõn'dadu] *m* county.

condão [kõn'dãw] *m* ▷ **varinha**.

conde, dessa ['kõndʒi, dʒesa] *m, f* count (*f* countess).

condecoração [kõndekora'sãw] (*pl* **-ões**) *f* **-1.** [cerimônia] investiture. **-2.** [insígnia] decoration.

condecorar [4] [kõndeko'ra(x)] *vt* to decorate.

condenação [kõndena'sãw] (*pl* **-ões**) *f* **-1.** JUR conviction. **-2.** [reprovação] condemnation.

condenar [4] [kõnde'na(x)] *vt* **-1.** [ger] to condemn; **~ alguém a algo** to sentence sb to sthg. **-2.** JUR [declarar culpado] to find guilty. **-3.** *fig* [interditar] to condemn. **-4.** *fig* [desenganar] to disillusion; ~ **um paciente** to give up hope of saving a patient.

condenável [kõnde'navew] (*pl* **-eis**) *adj* [reprovável] reprehensible.

condensação [kõndẽnsa'sãw] (*pl* **-ões**) *f* condensation.

condensar [4] [kõndẽn'sa(x)] *vt* to condense.
◆ **condensar-se** *vp* to condense.

condescendência [kõndesẽn'dẽnsja] *f* condescension.

condescendente [kõndesẽn'dẽntʃi] *adj* condescending.

condescender [5] [kõndesẽn'de(x)] *vi* to acquiesce; ~ **a** *ou* **em** to agree to.

condessa [kõn'desa] *f* ▻ **conde**.

condição [kõndʒi'sãw] (*pl* **-ões**) *f* **-1.** [ger] position; **de ~ humilde** of humble position; **de ~** [rico] wealthy; **na ~ de** in the capacity of. **-2.** [exigência] condition; **com a ~ de que** on condition that. **-3.** [natureza] nature; ~ **humana** human condition.
◆ **condições** *fpl* **-1.** [ger] conditions; **condições atmosféricas** atmospheric conditions; **condições próprias/impróprias de banho** [praia] suitable/unsuitable conditions for swimming; **condições de vida** living conditions; **condições de trabalho** working conditions. **-2.** [estado] condition *(sg)*; **em boas condições (de uso)** in good (working) order; **sem condições** [em mau estado] in poor condition. **-3.** [capacidade] requirement; **estar em condições de fazer algo** to be able do sthg; **ter condições de fazer algo** to be able to do sthg. **-4.** [meios] means.

condicionado, da [kõndʒisjo'nadu, da] *adj* conditioned; **estímulo/reflexo ~** conditioned stimulation/reflex; **venda ~** conditional sale.

condicionamento [kõndʒisjona'mẽntu] *m* conditioning; ~ **físico** physical condition.

condigno, na [kõn'dʒignu, na] *adj* **-1.** [adequado] adequate. **-2.** [merecido] worthy.

condimentar [4] [kõndʒimẽn'ta(x)] *vt* to season.

condimento [kõndʒi'mẽntu] *m* condiment.

condizente [kõndʒi'zẽntʃi] *adj*: ~ **com** appropriate for.

condizer [29] [kõndʒi'ze(x)] *vi*: ~ **com** to match.

condoer-se [28] [kõndo'exsi] *vp*: ~ **de** to be sorry for.

condolência [kõndo'lẽnsja] *f* sympathy.
◆ **condolências** *fpl* condolences.

condomínio [kõndo'minju] *m* **-1.** [conjunto de casas, apartamentos] condominium. **-2.** [pagamento] service charge.

condômino, na [kõn'dominu, na] *m, f* [co-proprietário] *person living in a condominium.*

condução [kõndu'sãw] (*pl* **-ões**) *f* **-1.** [ato] transportation. **-2.** [transporte] transport. **-3.** [ônibus] bus. **-4.** FÍSICA conduction.

conducente [kõndu'sẽntʃi] *adj*: ~ **a** conducive to.

conduta [kõn'duta] *f* conduct, behaviour; **má ~** bad behaviour.

conduto [kõn'dutu] *m* **-1.** [tubo] tube. **-2.** [cano] pipe. **-3.** [canal] channel.

condutor, ra [kõndu'to(x), ra] (*mpl* **-es**, *fpl* **-s**) ◇ *adj* [de eletricidade] conductor. ◇ *m, f* [de veículo] driver.
◆ **condutor** *m* ELETR conductor.

conduzir [72] [kõndu'zi(x)] ◇ *vt* **-1.** [levar]: ~ **algo/alguém (a)** to transport sthg/sb (to). **-2.** [empresa, equipe] to lead. **-3.** ELETR to conduct. ◇ *vi* [levar]: ~ **a** to lead to.
◆ **conduzir-se** *vp* [portar-se] to behave.

cone ['koni] *m* cone.

conectar [4] [konek'ta(x)] *vt* to connect.
◆ **conectar-se** *vp* to connect; ~ **à internet** to connect to the Internet.

conectividade [konektʃivi'dadʒi] *f* connectivity.

cônego ['konegu] *m* canon.

conexão [konek'sãw] (*pl* **-ões**) *f* **-1.** [ger & COMPUT] connection; ~ **discada** *ou* **dial-up** dial-up connection; ~ **a cabo** cable connection. **-2.** [nexo] link. **-3.** [relação] relationship.

conexo, xa [ko'nɛksu, sa] *adj* connected.

confabulação [kõnfabula'sãw] (*pl* **-ões**) *f* **-1.** [conspiração] conspiracy. **-2.** [conversa] chat.

confabular [4] [kõnfabu'la(x)] *vi* **-1.** [conspirar] to conspire. **-2.** [conversar] to chat; ~ **com** to chat with.

confecção [kõnfek'sãw] (*pl* **-ões**) *f* **-1.** [ger] making. **-2.** [fábrica de roupas] clothing factory.

confeccionar [4] [kõnfeksjo'na(x)] *vt* [fabricar, fazer] to make.

confederação [kõnfedera'sãw] (*pl* **-ões**) *f* confederation.

confeitar [4] [kõnfej'ta(x)] *vt* [bolo] to sugar-coat.

confeitaria [kõnfejta'ria] *f* cake shop.

confeiteiro, ra [kõnfej'tejru, ra] *m, f* confectioner.

conferência [kõnfe'rẽsja] *f* **-1.** [verificação] check. **-2.** [palestra] lecture; **fazer uma ~** to give a lecture.

conferencista [kõnferẽn'siʃta] *m f* [palestrante] speaker.

conferente [kõnfe'rẽntʃi] *mf* [em uma verificação] checker, controller.

conferir [57] [kõnfe'ri(x)] ◇ *vt* **-1.** [verificar] to check. **-2.** [cotejar, comparar] to compare. **-3.** [dar]: ~ **algo a alguém/algo** to invest sb/sthg with sthg. **-4.** [título, encargo] to confer. ◇ *vi* **-1.** [estar correto]: ~ **(com)** to agree (with). **-2.** [garantir] to make sure.

confessar [4] [kõnfe'sa(x)] ◇ *vt* **-1.** [fazer confissão de] to confess. **-2.** RELIG [ouvir confissão de] to hear confession. ◇ *vi* **-1.** [fazer confissão] to make a confession. **-2.** RELIG to confess.
◆ **confessar-se** *vp* **-1.** RELIG to confess. **-2.** [admitir ser] to confess to being; **~-se culpado** JUR to plead guilty.

confessionário [kõnfesjo'narju] *m* confessional.

confesso, sa [kõn'fesu, sa] *adj* confessed.

confessor [kõnfe'so(x)] *m* RELIG confessor.

confete [kõn'fɛtʃi] *m* confetti; **jogar ~** *fam* [bajular] to please sb.

confiabilidade [kõnfjabili'dadʒi] *f* [credibilidade] reliability.

confiado, da [kõn'fjadu, da] *adj* [atrevido] cheeky.

confiança [kõn'fjãnsa] *f* **-1.** [segurança] confidence. **-2.** [fé] trust; **digno de ~** worthy of trust; **ter ~ em alguém** to have confidence in sb; **de ~** trustworthy. **-3.** *fam* [intimidade] familiarity; **dar ~ a alguém** to allow sb to treat one in a familiar way.

confiante [kõn'fjãntʃi] *adj* **-1.** [seguro] confident. **-2.** [esperançoso]: **~ (em)** trusting (in).

confiar [16] [kõn'fja(x)] ◇ *vi*: **~ em** to trust in. ◇ *vt* **-1.** [entregar]: **~ algo a alguém** to entrust sthg to sb. **-2.** [contar]: **~ algo a alguém** to confide in sb about sthg.

confiável [kõn'fjavew] (*pl* **-eis**) *adj* reliable.

confidência [kõnfi'dẽnsja] *f* confidence; **em ~** in confidence.

confidencial [kõnfidẽn'sjaw] (*pl* **-ais**) *adj* confidential.

confidenciar [16] [kõnfidẽn'sja(x)] *vt*: **~ algo a alguém** to confide sthg to sb.

confidente [kõnfi'dẽntʃi] *m f* confidant (*f* confidante).

configuração [kõnfigura'sãw] (*pl* **-ões**) *f* **-1.** [disposição - de objetos, peças] arrangement; [- de astros] configuration. **-2.** [forma] shape. **-3.** *COMPUT* configuration.

configurar [4] [kõnfigu'ra(x)] *vt* to represent.

confinamento [kõnfina'mẽntu] *m* confinement.

confinar [4] [kõnfi'na(x)] ◇ *vt* [isolar, enclausurar]: **~ alguém/algo em** to confine sb/sthg to/in. ◇ *vi*

◆ **confinar-se** *vp* [isolar-se, enclausurar-se] to isolate o.s.

confins [kõn'fĩʃ] *mpl* [limite extremo] ends; **nos ~ de Judas** *fam* in the back of beyond.

confirmação [kõnfixma'sãw] (*pl* **-ões**) *f* confirmation.

confirmar [4] [kõnfix'ma(x)] *vt* [comprovar] to confirm.

◆ **confirmar-se** *vp* **-1.** [cumprir-se] to be confirmed. **-2.** [justificar-se] to be justified.

confiscar [12] [kõnfiʃ'ka(x)] *vt* to confiscate.

confisco [kõn'fiʃku] *m* confiscation.

confissão [kõnfi'sãw] (*pl* **-ões**) *f* [de falta, crime] confession.

conflagração [kõnflagra'sãw] (*pl* **-ões**) *f* **-1.** [guerra] war. **-2.** [revolução] revolution.

conflagrar [4] [kõnfla'gra(x)] *vt* [levar à guerra] to convulse.

conflitante [kõnfli'tãntʃi] *adj* conflicting.

conflito [kõn'flitu] *m* [ger] conflict; **~ de gerações** generation gap; **entrar em ~ (com)** to clash (with).

confluência [kõn'flwẽnsia] *f* **-1.** [de rios] confluence. **-2.** [de estradas, ruas] junction.

confluente [kõn'flwẽntʃi] *adj* **-1.** [rio] confluent. **-2.** [estrada, rua] merging.

confluir [kõn'flui(x)] *vi* to merge.

conformação [kõnfoxma'sãw] (*pl* **-ões**) *f* **-1.** [resignação] resignation. **-2.** [forma] shape.

conformado, da [kõnfox'madu, da] *adj* [resignado] resigned.

conformar [4] [kõnfox'ma(x)] *vt* [formar] to shape.

◆ **conformar-se** *vp* **-1.** [resignar-se]: **~-se com** to resign o.s. to. **-2.** [acomodar-se]: **~-se a** *ou* **com** to conform to *ou* with.

conforme [kõn'fɔxmi] ◇ *prep* [de acordo com, segundo] in accordance with. ◇ *conj* **-1.** [ger] as. **-2.** [de acordo com] according to. **-3.** [dependendo de] depending on.

◆ **conformes** *mpl*: **dentro dos ~s** *fam* in accordance with the requirements.

conformidade [kõnfoxmi'dadʒi] *f* [acordo] agreement; **em ~ com** in accordance with.

conformismo [kõnfox'miʒmu] *m* conformity.

conformista [kõnfox'miʃta] *mf* conformist.

confortante [kõnfox'tãntʃi] *adj* comforting.

confortar [4] [kõnfox'ta(x)] *vt* [consolar] to comfort.

confortável [kõnfox'tavɛw] (*pl* **-eis**) *adj* comfortable.

conforto [kõn'foxtu] *m* comfort.

confraria [kõnfra'ria] *f* fraternity.

confraternização [kõnfratexniza'sãw] (*pl* **-ões**) *f* fraternization.

confraternizar [4] [kõnfratexni'za(x)] ◇ *vt* **-1.** [reunir, ligar] to socialize. **-2.** [reconciliar] to reconcile. ◇ *vi* **-1.** [reunir-se, ligar-se] to unite. **-2.** [comemorar] to celebrate.

confrontação [kõnfrõnta'sãw] (*pl* **-ões**) *f* **-1.** [comparação] comparison. **-2.** [acareação] confrontation.

confrontar [4] [kõnfrõn'ta(x)] *vt* **-1.** [comparar] to compare. **-2.** [acarear] to confront.

◆ **confrontar-se** *vp* [defrontar-se] to face each other.

confronto [kõn'frõntu] *m* **-1.** [comparação] comparison. **-2.** [choque] confrontation.

confundir [6] [kõnfũn'di(x)] *vt* **-1.** [ger] to confuse; **~ algo com** to confuse sthg with. **-2.** [misturar] to muddle. **-3.** [trocar] to mix up.

◆ **confundir-se** *vp* to become confused; **~-se com** to become confused with.

confusão [kõnfu'zãw] (*pl* **-ões**) *f* **-1.** [mistura] muddle. **-2.** [troca] mixing up; **fazer ~** [confundir-se] to become confused. **-3.** [indistinção] confusion. **-4.** [caos] mess. **-5.** [problema] hassle; **dar ~** to cause a hassle. **-6.** [tumulto] melee.

confuso, sa [kõn'fuzu, za] *adj* **-1.** [obscuro] obscure. **-2.** [misturado] muddled. **-3.** [indistinto] hazy. **-4.** [atrapalhado] confused.

congelado, da [kõnʒe'ladu, da] *adj* frozen.

◆ **congelado** *m* frozen food *(inv)*.

congelador [kõnʒela'do(x)] (*pl* **-es**) *m* freezer.

congelamento [kõnʒela'mẽntu] *m* **-1.** [de água, alimento *etc*] freezing. **-2.** *ECON* [de preços, salários] freeze.

congelar [4] [kõnʒe'la(x)] ◇ *vt* [água, rio, alimento] to freeze. ◇ *vi* **-1.** [ficar congelado] to freeze. **-2.**

[sentir frio] to be freezing.
◆ **congelar-se** *vp* [ficar congelado] to freeze.
congênere [kõn'ʒeneri] *adj* similar.
congênito, ta [kõnʒenitu, ta] *adj* congenital.
congestão [kõnʒeʃ'tãw] *(pl* **-ões)** *f* congestion; ~ **nasal** nasal congestion.
congestionado, da [kõnʒeʃtjo'nadu, da] *adj* **-1.** [trânsito] congested. **-2.** [nariz, artéria] blocked.
congestionamento [kõnʒeʃtjona'mẽntu] *m* **-1.** [engarrafamento] congestion; ~ **de tráfego** traffic congestion. **-2.** [de nariz, artéria] blockage.
congestionar [4] [kõnʒeʃtʃjo'na(x)] *vt* **-1.** [trânsito]: ~ **o trânsito** to cause traffic congestion. **-2.** [nariz, artéria] to block.
◆ **congestionar-se** *vp* **-1.** [trânsito] to become congested. **-2.** [nariz, artéria] to become blocked.
conglomeração [kõŋglomera'sãw] *(pl* **-ões)** *f* conglomeration.
conglomerado [kõŋglome'radu] *m* conglomerate.
conglomerar [4] [kõŋglome'ra(x)] *vt* **-1.** [reunir] to conglomerate. **-2.** [empresas] to merge.
Congo ['kõŋgu] *n*: **o** ~ the Congo.
congolês, esa [kõŋgo'leʃ, eza] ◇ *adj* Congolese. ◇ *m, f* Congolese.
congratular [4] [kõŋgratu'la(x)] *vt*: ~ **alguém (por algo)** to congratulate sb (on sthg).
congregação [kõŋgrega'sãw] *(pl* **-ões)** *f* **-1.** *RELIG* congregation. **-2.** [reunião] coming together.
congregar [14] [kõŋgre'ga(x)] *vt* [reunir] to bring together.
◆ **congregar-se** *vp* [reunir-se] to congregate.
congressista [kõŋgre'siʃta] *m f* **-1.** [participante] delegate *(at a conference)*. **-2.** *POL* congressman (*f* congresswoman).
congresso [kõŋ'grɛsu] *m* **-1.** [conferência] conference. **-2.** *POL*: **o Congresso** Congress.
conhaque [ko'ɲaki] *m* cognac.
conhecedor, ra [koɲese'do(x), ra] *(mpl* **-es**, *fpl* **-s)** ◇ *adj* [ciente]: ~ **(de)** aware (of). ◇ *m, f* [especialista]: ~ **(de)** specialist (in).
conhecer [25] [koɲe'se(x)] *vt* **-1.** [ger] to know. **-2.** [entender de] to understand. **-3.** [pessoa pela primeira vez] to meet; ~ **alguém de nome/de vista** to know sb by name/sight. **-4.** [loja, casa *etc*] to see. **-5.** [país] to visit. **-6.** [reconhecer]: ~ **algo/alguém (por)** to recognize sthg/sb (by).
◆ **conhecer-se** *vp* **-1.** [a si próprio] to know o.s. **-2.** [pessoas] to know one another; [pela primeira vez] to meet.
conhecido, da [koɲe'sidu, da] ◇ *adj* **-1.** [famoso] well-known; ~ **por** known for. **-2.** [sabido] wise. **-3.** [notório] notorious. ◇ *m, f* [pessoa] acquaintance.
conhecimento [koɲesi'mẽntu] *m* **-1.** [saber] knowledge; ~ **de causa** due knowledge; **levar algo ao** ~ **de alguém** to bring sthg to the attention of sb; **não tomar** ~ **de** [não dar importância a] not to attach importance to; **ser de** ~ **geral que** to be general knowledge that; **ter** ~ **de** to be aware of; **tomar** ~ **de** to find out about. **-2.** [conhecido] acquaintance. **-3.** *COM*: ~ **aéreo** air waybill.
◆ **conhecimentos** *mpl* **-1.** [noções] knowledge *(sg)*. **-2.** [relações, conhecidos] friends.
cônico, ca ['koniku, ka] *adj* conical.
conivência [koni'vẽnsja] *f* connivance.
conivente [koni'vẽntʃi] *adj* conniving; **ser** ~ **com** to connive in.
conjetura [kõnʒe'tura] *f* conjecture; **fazer** ~**s (sobre)** to make conjectures (about).
conjeturar [4] [kõnʒetu'ra(x)] *vt* to conjecture.
conjugação [kõnʒuga'sãw] *(pl* **-ões)** *f* **-1.** [união] union. **-2.** *GRAM* conjugation.
conjugado, da [kõnʒu'gadu, da] *adj* **-1.** [apartamento, sala] adjoining. **-2.** *GRAM* conjugated.
◆ **conjugado** *m* [apartamento] adjoining apartment.
conjugal [kõnʒu'gaw] *(pl* **-ais)** *adj* marital; **vida** ~ married life.
conjugar [14] [kõnʒu'ga(x)] *vt* **-1.** [unir] to combine. **-2.** *GRAM* to conjugate.
◆ **conjugar-se** *vp* [unir-se] to be connected.
cônjuge ['kõnʒuʒi] *m* spouse.
conjunção [kõnʒũn'sãw] *(pl* **-ões)** *f* **-1.** [união] combination. **-2.** *GRAM* conjunction.
conjuntivite [kõnʒũntʃi'vitʃi] *f* conjunctivitis.
conjunto, ta [kõn'ʒũntu, ta] *adj* combined, joint.
◆ **conjunto** *m* **-1.** [grupo] combination. **-2.** [totalidade]: **o** ~ **de** the whole of; **em** ~ together. **-3.** *MÚS* group. **-4.** [residencial] complex; ~ **habitacional** housing complex. **-5.** [traje] suit. **-6.** *MAT* set.
conjuntura [kõnʒũn'tura] *f* conjuncture.
conluio [kõn'luju] *m* collusion.
conosco [ko'noʃku] *pron pess* with us.
conotação [konota'sãw] *(pl* **-ões)** *f* connotation.
conotar [4] [kono'ta(x)] *vt* to connote.
conquanto [kõŋ'kwãntu] *conj* although.
conquista [kõŋ'kiʃta] *f* conquest.
conquistador, ra [kõŋkiʃta'do(x), ra] ◇ *adj* **-1.** [exército, país] conquering. **-2.** [sedutor] seductive. ◇ *m, f* **-1.** [de terras, país] conqueror. **-2.** [sedutor - homem] lady-killer; [- mulher] femme fatale.
conquistar [4] [kõŋkiʃ'ta(x)] *vt* **-1.** [subjugar] to conquer. **-2.** [alcançar] to achieve. **-3.** [ganhar] to win. **-4.** [seduzir] to seduce.
consagração [kõnsagra'sãw] *(pl* **-ões)** *f* **-1.** [aclamação] acclaim. **-2.** [exaltação] acclamation; **fazer a** ~ **de** to be an acclamation of. **-3.** [dedicação] dedication. **-4.** [aceitação] acceptance. **-5.** *RELIG* consecration.
consagrar [4] [kõnsa'gra(x)] *vt* **-1.** [levar à aclamação] to lead to the acclamation of. **-2.** [exaltar] to glorify. **-3.** [dedicar] to dedicate. **-4.** [tornar aceito] to become accepted. **-5.** *RELIG* to consecrate.
◆ **consagrar-se** *vi* **-1.** [atingir a aclamação] to achieve acclaim. **-2.** [dedicar-se]: ~**-se a algo** to dedicate oneself to sthg.
consangüíneo, nea [kõnsãn'gwinju, nja] ◇ *adj* related by blood. ◇ *m, f* [parente] blood relation.

consciência [kõn'sjẽnsja] *f* **-1.** [conhecimento] awareness; ~ **de classe** class-consciousness; ~ **política** political awareness; **ter/tomar** ~ **de** to be/become aware of. **-2.** [sentidos]: **perder a** ~ to lose consciousness. **-3.** [moral] conscience; **estar com a** ~ **limpa/pesada** to have a clear/guilty conscience. **-4.** [cuidado, responsabilidade] care.

consciencioso, osa [kõnsjẽn'sjozu, ɔza] *adj* conscientious.

consciente [kõnʃ'sjẽntʃi] <> *adj* conscious. <> *m* PSIC consciousness.

conscientemente [kõnsjẽntʃi'mẽntʃi] *adv* consciously.

conscientizar [4] [kõnsjẽntʃi'za(x)] *vt* [dar conhecimento a]: ~ **alguém (de algo)** to raise sb's awareness (of something).

◆ **conscientizar-se** *vp* [tomar consciência de]: ~ **-se (de algo)** to become aware (of sthg).

côncio, cia ['kõnsju, sja] *adj* lucid.

consecução [kõnseku'sãw] *f* attainment.

consecutivo, va [kõnseku'tʃivu, va] *adj* consecutive.

conseguinte [kõnse'gĩntʃi] ◆ **por conseguinte** *loc conj* consequently.

conseguir [55] [kõnse'gi(x)] *vt* **-1.** [obter] to obtain. **-2.** [alcançar] to achieve; ~ **fazer algo** to manage to do sthg.

conselheiro, ra [kõnse'ʎejru, ra] *m, f* **-1.** [ger] adviser. **-2.** [membro de conselho] councillor.

conselho [kõ'seʎu] *m* **-1.** [advertência] advice; **dar um** ~ **a alguém** to give sb a piece of advice. **-2.** [órgão] council; ~ **administrativo** board of directors; ~ **de Estado** Council of State; ~ **de ministros** Cabinet; ~ **de guerra** council of war.

consenso [kõn'sẽnsu] *m* consensus.

consensual [kõnsẽn'swaw] (*pl* **-ais**) *adj* consensual.

consentimento [kõnsẽntʃi'mẽntu] *m* consent.

consentir [56] [kõnsẽn'tʃi(x)] <> *vt* **-1.** [permitir] to grant. **-2.** [aprovar] to approve. <> *vi* [concordar, anuir]: ~ **em algo** to consent to sthg; ~ **em fazer algo** to agree to do sthg.

conseqüência [kõnse'kwẽnsja] *f* [resultado] consequence; **em** ~ **de** because of, owing to; **por** ~ consequently.

conseqüente [kõnse'kwẽntʃi] *adj* **-1.** [resultante] consequent. **-2.** [coerente] coherent.

consertar [4] [kõnsex'ta(x)] *vt* **-1.** [reparar] to repair. **-2.** [remediar] to rectify.

conserto [kõn'sextu] *m* repair.

conserva [kõn'sɛrva] *f* preserve; **em** ~ preserved.

conservação [kõnsexva'sãw] *f* **-1.** [ger] conservation. **-2.** [preservação] preservation.

conservacionista [kõnsexvasjo'niʃta] <> *adj* conservationist. <> *mf* conservationist.

conservado, da [kõnsex'vadu, da] *adj* **-1.** [carro, casa] well kept. **-2.** [pessoa] well preserved.

conservador, ra [kõnsexva'do(x), ra] <> *adj* conservative. <> *m, f* conservative.

conservadorismo [kõnsexvado'riʒmu] *m* conservatism.

conservante [kõnser'vãntʃi] *m* preservative.

conservar [4] [kõnsex'va(x)] *vt* **-1.** [preservar] to preserve. **-2.** [sabor, qualidade *etc*] to conserve. **-3.** [manter] to maintain.

◆ **conservar-se** *vp* **-1.** [pessoa] to be well preserved. **-2.** [permanecer] to remain.

conservatório [kõnsexva'tɔrju] *m* conservatoire.

consideração [kõnsidera'sãw] (*pl* **-ões**) *f* **-1.** [ger] consideration; **levar em** ~ to take into consideration; **falta de** ~ **(com alguém)** lack of consideration (towards sb). **-2.** [pensamento] thought.

considerado, da [kõnside'radu, da] *adj* respected.

considerar [4] [kõnside'ra(x)] *vt* **-1.** [ger] to consider. **-2.** [respeitar, estimar]: ~ **muito alguém/algo** to have a high regard for sb/sthg.

◆ **considerar-se** *vp* [julgar-se] to consider o.s.

considerável [kõnside'ravɛw] (*pl* **-eis**) *adj* considerable.

consignação [kõnsigna'sãw] (*pl* **-ões**) *f* **-1.** [registro] report. **-2.** COM consignment; **venda por** ~ sale on consignment; **em** ~ on consignment. **-3.** [de verbas] allocation.

consignar [4] [kõnsig'na(x)] *vt* **-1.** [produtos] to consign. **-2.** [registrar] to record. **-3.** [verbas] to allocate.

consigo [kõn'sigu] *pron pess* with him/her/you/it.

consistência [kõnsiʃ'tẽnsja] *f* consistency; **ganhar** ~ to thicken.

consistente [kõnsiʃ'tẽntʃi] *adj* **-1.** [sólido] solid. **-2.** [espesso] thick. **-3.** [coerente, sólido] consistent.

consistir [6] [kõnsiʃ'tʃi(x)] *vi* [constituir-se]: ~ **em** to consist of; ~ **em fazer algo** to consist in doing sthg.

consoante [kõn'swãntʃi] <> *adj* LING consonant. <> *f* LING consonant. <> *prep* [de acordo com] according to.

consolação [kõnsola'sãw] (*pl* **-ões**) *f* comfort.

consolador, ra [kõnsola'do(x), ra] *adj* comforting.

consolar [4] [kõnso'la(x)] *vt* to comfort.

◆ **consolar-se** *vp*: ~**-se (com)** to console o.s. (with).

console [kõn'soli] *m* console.

consolidação [kõnsolida'sãw] (*pl* **-ões**) *f* [estabilização] consolidation.

consolidar [4] [kõnsoli'da(x)] <> *vt* **-1.** [estabilizar, ratificar] to consolidate. **-2.** [fratura] to calcify. <> *vi* [tornar-se sólido] to solidify.

consolo [kõn'solu] *m* **-1.** [consolação] comfort. **-2.** *vulg* [consolo-de-viúva] dildo.

consomê [kõnso'me] *m* consommé.

consonância [kõnso'nãnsja] *f* consonance; **em** ~ **com** in accordance with.

consórcio [kõn'sɔxsju] *m* **-1.** [união] partnership. **-2.** [de interesses, necessidades] uniting. **-3.** COM consortium.

consorte [kõn'sɔxtʃi] *m, f* consort.

conspícuo, cua [kõnʃ'pikwu, kwa] *adj* **-1.** [evidente] conspicuous. **-2.** [ilustre] remarkable.

conspiração [kõnʃpira'sãw] (*pl* **-ões**) *f* conspiracy.

conspirador, ra [kõnʃpira'do(x), ra] *m, f* conspirator.

conspirar [4] [kõnʃpi'ra(x)] ◇ *vi*: ~ **(contra)** to conspire (against). ◇ *vt* to plot.

conspiratório, ria [kõʃpira'tɔrju, rja] *adj* conspiratorial.

constância [kõnʃ'tãnsja] *f* **-1.** [de ruído, incômodo] persistence. **-2.** [no amor] constancy. **-3.** [perseverança] perseverance. **-4.** [de idéias, opiniões] constancy.

constante [kõnʃ'tãntʃi] *adj* **-1.** [ger] constant. **-2.** [pessoa, amor] faithful. **-3.** [que consta]: ~ **de** pertaining to.

constar [4] [kõnʃ'ta(x)] *vi* **-1.** [informação]: ~ **(em** *ou* **de)** to appear (in). **-2.** [ser assegurado]: ~ **que** to be said that. **-3.** [ser do conhecimento de]: **não lhe constava que o preço tivesse subido** he was not aware that the price had risen. **-4.** [constituir-se]: ~ **de** to consist of.

constatação [kõnʃtata'sãw] (*pl* **-ões**) *f* **-1.** [observação] observation. **-2.** [comprovação] confirmation.

constatar [4] [kõnʃta'ta(x)] *vt* **-1.** [observar] to notice. **-2.** [comprovar] to prove.

constelação [kõnʃtela'sãw] (*pl* **-ões**) *f* constellation.

consternação [kõnʃtexna'sãw] (*pl* **-ões**) *f* [desalento, desolação] dismay.

consternado, da [kõnʃter'nadu, da] *adj* dismayed.

consternar [4] [kõnʃtex'na(x)] *vt* to discourage.

constipação [kõnʃtʃipa'sãw] (*pl* **-ões**) *f* **-1.** [prisão de ventre] constipation. **-2.** [resfriado] cold.

constipado, da [kõnʃtʃi'padu, da] *adj* **-1.** [resfriado]: **estar** ~ to have a cold. **-2.** [com prisão de ventre] constipated.

constitucional [kõnʃtʃitusjo'naw] (*pl* **-ais**) *adj* constitutional.

constitucionalidade [kõnʃtʃitusionali'dadʒi] *f* constitutionality.

constituição [kõnʃtʃitwi'sãw] (*pl* **-ões**) *f* **-1.** [formação] make-up. **-2.** [consistência] composition. **-3.** *POL* [carta] constitution.

constituinte [kõnʃtʃi'twĩntʃi] ◇ *adj* **-1.** [componente] constituent. **-2.** *POL* representative. ◇ *mf* *POL* [deputado] deputy.

◆ **Constituinte** *f* *POL* [assembléia]: **a Constituinte** the Constituent Assembly.

constituir [74] [kõnʃtʃi'twi(x)] *vt* **-1.** [compor, ser] to constitute. **-2.** [criar, estabelecer] to establish.

◆ **constituir-se** *vp* **-1.** [estabelecer-se como]: ~**-se em algo** to establish o.s. as sthg. **-2.** [ser]: ~**-se em algo** to be sthg, to constitute sthg.

constitutivo, va [kõnʃtʃitu'tʃivu, va] *adj* **-1.** [formador] constituent. **-2.** [indispensável] essential. **-3.** [característico] characteristic.

constrangedor, ra [kõnʃtrãnʒe'do(x), ra] *adj* **-1.** [embaraçador] embarrassing. **-2.** [repressivo] repressive.

constranger [26] [kõnʃtrãn'ʒe(x)] *vt* **-1.** [embaraçar] to embarrass. **-2.** [reprimir, refrear] to curb. **-3.** [coagir]: ~ **alguém a fazer algo** to force sb to do sthg.

◆ **constranger-se** *vp* [ficar embaraçado] to be embarrassed.

constrangimento [kõnʃtrãnʒi'mẽntu] *m* **-1.** [embaraço] embarrassment. **-2.** [repressão] restriction.

construção [kõnʃtru'sãw] (*pl* **-ões**) *f* **-1.** [edifício] building; **em** ~ under construction *(depois de verbo)*. **-2.** [intelectual, imaginária] feat.

construir [73] [kõnʃtru'i(x)] *vt* to build.

construtivo, va [kõnʃtru'tʃivu, va] *adj* constructive.

construtor, ra [kõnʃtru'to(x), ra] (*mpl* **-es**, *fpl* **-s**) ◇ *adj* building *(antes de subst)*. ◇ *m, f* builder.

◆ **construtora** *f* [empresa] building company.

cônsul ['kõnsuw] (*pl* **-es**) *m* consul.

consulado [kõnsu'ladu] *m* consulate.

consulente [kõnsu'lẽntʃi] *mf* advice seeker.

cônsules ['kõnsuliʃ] *pl* ▷ **cônsul**.

consulesa [kõnsu'leza] *f* **-1.** [diplomata] consul. **-2.** [esposa] consul's wife.

consulta [kõn'suwta] *f* **-1.** [sobre problema, dúvida] query; **fazer uma** ~ **a alguém** to consult sb. **-2.** *MED* consultation; **horário de** ~ surgery hours; **ter uma** ~ **(com)** to have an appointment (with).

consultar [4] [kõnsuw'ta(x)] *vt* to consult; ~ **alguém sobre algo** to consult sb about sthg.

consultivo, va [kõnsuw'tʃivu, va] *adj* consultative.

consultor, ra [kõnsuw'to(x), ra] *m, f* consultant.

consultoria [kõnsuwto'ria] *f* [serviço] consultancy; **empresa de** ~ consultancy.

consultório [kõnsuw'tɔrju] *m* **-1.** *MED* consulting room. **-2.** *JORN*: ~ **sentimental** agony column.

consumação [kõnsuma'sãw] (*pl* **-ões**) *f* **-1.** [realização] realization, carrying out. **-2.** [completude] completion. **-3.** [de casamento] consummation. **-4.** [em restaurante, bar]: ~ **mínima** minimum order.

consumado, da [kõnsu'madu, da] *adj* **-1.** [realizado] realized, carried out. **-2.** [completado] completed. **-3.** [casamento] consummated.

consumar [4] [kõnsu'ma(x)] *vt* **-1.** [realizar] to realize, to carry out. **-2.** [completar] to complete. **-3.** [casamento] to consummate.

◆ **consumar-se** *vp* **-1.** [realizar-se] to be realized, to be carried out. **-2.** [completar-se] to be completed. **-3.** [casamento] to be consummated. **-4.** [profecia] to come true.

consumidor, ra [kõsumi'do(x), ra] (*mpl* **-es**, *fpl* **-s**) ◇ *adj* consumer. ◇ *m, f* consumer.

consumir [6] [kõnsu'mi(x)] ◇ *vt* **-1.** [ger] to consume. **-2.** [comprar] to purchase. **-3.** [corroer, devorar] to corrode. **-4.** *fig* [desgastar] to consume. ◇ *vi* [comprar] to consume.

◆ **consumir-se** *vp* **-1.** [combustível, fogo] to burn

itself out. **-2.** *fig* [pessoa] to wear o.s. out.

consumismo [kõnsu'miʒmu] *m* consumerism.

consumista [kõnsu'miʃta] *adj* consumerist.

consumo [kõn'sumu] *m* **-1.** [ger] consumption. **-2.** [compra] sale; **bens de ~** consumer goods; **sociedade de ~** consumer society. **-3.** [de drogas] use.

conta ['kõnta] *f* **-1.** [ger] account; **pôr na ~** to charge to one's account; **abrir uma ~** to open an account; **~ conjunta** joint account; **~ corrente** current account; **~ negativa** overdrawn account; **~ de poupança** savings account. **-2.** [cálculo] counting; **acertar** *ou* **ajustar contas com alguém** *fig* to settle a score with sb; **demais da ~** *fig* in excess; **fazer ~s** to make calculations; **pedir as ~s** *fig* [demitir-se] to resign; **perder a ~ de algo** to lose count of sthg; **ser a ~ certa** to be the correct amount; **afinal de ~s** after all. **-3.** [em restaurante] bill; **a ~, por favor!** the bill, please!; **pedir a ~** to ask for the bill. **-4.** [fatura] invoice; **~ de gás/luz/telefone** gas/electricity/telephone bill. **-5.** [consideração]: **levar algo em ~** to take sthg into account; **dar(-se) ~ de** to realize. **-6.** [justificação, razão]: **à ~ de** on account of; **por ~ de** because of. **-7.** [informação, satisfação] account; **dar ~ de** to give an account of; **prestar ~s de** to account for. **-8.** [responsabilidade, capacidade]: **dar ~ de** to manage; **deixar por ~ de alguém** to leave to sb; **não ser da ~ de alguém** to be nobody's business; **tomar ~ de alguém/algo** [cuidar, encarregar-se de] to look after sb/sthg; **tomar ~ de** [difundir-se por] to take over. **-9.** [de colar] bead. **-10.** *loc*: **dar ~ do recado** to do well; **fazer de ~ que** [imaginar] to pretend; [fingir] to pretend; **ficar por ~** to get angry; **ter alguém em alta ~** to hold sb in high esteem.

◆ **por conta própria** *loc adv* on one's own account; **trabalhar por ~ própria** to be self-employed.

contábil [kõn'tabiw] (*pl* **-eis**) *adj* accountancy *(antes de subst)*.

contabilidade [kõntabili'dadʒi] *f* **-1.** [ofício] accountancy; **~ de custos** cost accounting. **-2.** [setor] accounts department.

contabilista [kõntabi'liʃta] *m f* accountant.

contabilizar [4] [kõntabili'za(x)] *vt* **-1.** [registrar] to keep accounts. **-2.** [calcular] to count.

contado, da [kõn'tadu, da] *adj* accounted for; **estar com o dinheiro ~** to have every penny accounted for; **ele está com seus dias ~s** his days are numbered.

contador [kõnta'do(x)] (*pl* **-es**) *m, f* **-1.** COM accountant. **-2.** [narrador]: **~ de histórias** storyteller.

◆ **contador** *m* TEC meter.

contadoria [kõntado'ria] *f* accounts department.

contagem [kõn'taʒẽ] (*pl* **-ns**) *f* **-1.** [ato] counting; **~ regressiva** countdown. **-2.** [escore] score.

contagiante [kõnta'ʒjãntʃi] *adj* contagious.

contagiar [16] [kõnta'ʒja(x)] *vt* **-1.** [infectar] to infect. **-2.** *fig* [influenciar] to affect.

◆ **contagiar-se** *vp* **-1.** [infectar-se] to become infected. **-2.** *fig* [influenciar-se] to be affected.

contágio [kõn'taʒju] *m* contagion.

contagioso, osa [kõnta'ʒjozu, za] *adj* contagious.

conta-gotas [ˌkõnta'gotaʃ] *m inv* dropper.

contaminação [kõntamina'sãw] (*pl* **-ões**) *f* contamination.

contaminado, da [kõntami'nadu, da] *adj* **-1.** [infectado, poluído] contaminated. **-2.** [por doença] infected.

contaminar [4] [kõntami'na(x)] ◇ *vt* [contagiar] to contaminate. ◇ *vi fig* [corromper] to corrupt.

contanto [kõn'tãntu] ◆ **contanto que** *loc adv* provided that.

contar [4] [kõn'ta(x)] ◇ *vt* **-1.** [enumerar] to count. **-2.** [narrar] to tell. **-3.** [supor]: **~ que** to expect. ◇ *vi* **-1.** [fazer contas] to count. **-2.** [importar] to matter. **-3.**: **~ com** [ger] to count on; [dispor] to have. **-4.** [pretender]: **~ (em) fazer algo** to intend to do sthg. **-5.** [incluir]: **~ algo/alguém entre algo** to count sthg/sb as (being) sthg.

contatar [4] [kõnta'ta(x)] *vt* to contact.

contato [kõn'tatu] *m* contact.

contêiner [kõn'tejne(x)] *m* container.

contemplação [kõntẽnpla'sãw] *m* contemplation.

contemplar [4] [kõntẽn'pla(x)] *vt* **-1.** [olhar] to contemplate. **-2.** [premiar] to reward.

◆ **contemplar-se** *vp* [olhar-se] to look at o.s.

contemplativo, va [kõntẽnpla'tʃivu, va] *adj* contemplative.

contemporaneidade [kõntẽnporãnej'dadʒi] *f* contemporary nature.

contemporâneo, nea [kõntẽmpo'ranju, nja] ◇ *adj* contemporary. ◇ *m, f* contemporary.

contemporizar [4] [kõntẽnpori'za(x)] ◇ *vt* [acalmar] to calm. ◇ *vi* [transigir]: **~ (com)** to compromise (with).

contenção [kõntẽn'sãw] *f* **-1.** [diminuição - de despesas] cutback; [- de gestos, palavras] restraint. **-2.** [interrupção de fluxo] containment.

contencioso, osa [kõntẽn'sjozu, ɔza] *adj* contentious.

contenda [kõn'tẽnda] *f* dispute.

contentamento [kõntẽnta'mẽntu] *m* **-1.** [alegria] happiness. **-2.** [satisfação] contentment.

contentar [4] [kõntẽn'ta(x)] *vt* **-1.** [satisfazer] to content. **-2.** [agradar] to please.

◆ **contentar-se** *vp* [satisfazer-se]: **~-se com** to be satisfied with.

contente [kõn'tẽntʃi] *adj* happy.

contento [kõn'tẽntu] ◆ **a contento** *loc adv* satisfactorily.

conter [1] [kõn'te(x)] *vt* **-1.** [controlar] to control. **-2.** [ter] to contain.

◆ **conter-se** *vp* [controlar-se] to restrain o.s.

conterrâneo, nea [kõnte'xãnju, nja] ◇ *adj* fellow *(antes de subst)*; **é um amigo ~** he is a friend who comes from the same place as me. ◇ *m, f* compatriot.

contestação [kõnteʃta'sãw] (*pl* **-ões**) *f* **-1.** [negação] dispute. **-2.** [impugnação] challenge. **-3.** [oposição] opposition. **-4.** [réplica] reply.
contestar [4] [kõnteʃ'ta(x)] ◇ *vt* **-1.** [negar] to dispute. **-2.** [impugnar] to challenge. ◇ *vi* **-1.** [opor-se] to oppose. **-2.** [responder]: ~ **(a)** to reply (to).
contestatório, ria [kõnteʃta'tɔrju, rja] *adj* contentious; **movimento** ~ protest movement.
contestável [kõnteʃ'tavew] (*pl* **-eis**) *adj* questionable.
conteúdo [kõn'tjudu] *m* contents *(pl)*.
contexto [kõn'teʃtu] *m* context.
contextualização [kõnteʃtwaliza'sãw] (*pl* **-ões**) *f* contextualization.
contextualizar [kõnteʃtwali'za(x)] *vt* to put into context.
contido [kõn'tʃidu] *adj* **-1.** [encerrado] contained. **-2.** [reprimido] repressed.
contigo [kõn'tʃigu] *pron pess* with you.
contíguo, gua [kõn'tʃigwu, gwa] *adj* adjacent; ~ **a** next to.
continência [kõntʃi'nẽnsja] *f MIL* salute; **fazer** *ou* **bater** ~ **(a alguém)** to salute (sb).
continental [kõntʃinẽn'taw] (*pl* **-ais**) *adj* continental.
continente [kõntʃi'nẽntʃi] *m* continent.
contingência [kõntʃĩn'ʒẽnsja] *f* contingency.
contingente [kõntʃĩn'ʒẽntʃi] ◇ *adj* contingent. ◇ *m* contingent.
continuação [kõntʃinwa'sãw] (*pl* **-ões**) *f* continuation.
continuar [4] [kõntʃi'nwa(x)] ◇ *vt* [prosseguir] to continue. ◇ *vi* **-1.** [perdurar] to continue. **-2.** [prolongar-se] to go on. **-3.** [prosseguir]: ~ **em algo** to continue with sthg; ~ **fazendo algo** *ou* **a fazer algo** to continue doing sthg/to do sthg. ◇ *v de ligação (antes de adjetivo)* [expressa qualidade, estado]: **a cidade continua bonita** the city is still beautiful.
continuidade [kõntʃinwi'dadʒi] *f* continuity.
contínuo, nua [kõn'tʃinwu, nwa] ◇ *adj* **-1.** [sem interrupção] continuous. **-2.** [constante] constant. ◇ *m* [pessoa] office junior.
contista [kõn'tʃiʃta] *mf* story writer.
conto ['kõntu] *m* story; ~ **de fadas** *ou* **da carochinha** fairy tale.
conto-do-vigário ['kõntuduvi'garju] (*pl* **contos-do-vigário**) *m* confidence trick; **cair no** ~ to be tricked; **passar o** ~ **em alguém** to try to con sb.
contorção [kõntox'sãw] (*pl* **-ões**) *f* contortion.
contorcer [25] [kõntox'se(x)] *vt* to warp.
◆ **contorcer-se** *vp* to writhe.
contornar [4] [kõntox'na(x)] *vt* **-1.** [rodear] to go around. **-2.** *fig* [resolver] to get around.
contornável [kõntox'navew] (*pl* **-eis**) *adj* surmountable.
contorno [kõn'toxnu] *m* outline.
contra ['kõntra] ◇ *prep* [ger] against. ◇ *adv* against. ◇ *m* **-1.** [dificuldade] hard knock. **-2.** [contestação] objection; **dar o** ~ to object; **pesar os prós e os** ~**s** to weigh up the pros and the cons; **ser do** ~ to object on principle.
contra-almirante [ˌkõntraawmi'rãntʃi] (*pl* **contra-almirantes**) *m* rear admiral.
contra-argumento [ˌkõntraaxgu'mẽntu] (*pl* **contra-angumentos**) *m* counter-argument.
contra-atacar [12] [ˌkõntraata'ka(x)] *vt* to counter-attack.
contra-ataque [ˌkõntra'taki] (*pl* **contra-ataques**) *m* counter-attack.
contrabaixista [ˌkõntra'bajʃiʃta] *mf* double-bass player.
contrabaixo [ˌkõntra'bajʃu] *m* **-1.** [instrumento] double bass. **-2.** [músico] bassist.
contrabalançar [13] [ˌkõntrabalãn'sa(x)] *vt* to counterbalance; ~ **algo com algo** to compensate sthg with sthg.
contrabandear [15] [ˌkõntrabãn'dʒja(x)] *vt* to smuggle.
contrabandista [ˌkõntrabãn'dʒiʃta] *mf* smuggler.
contrabando [ˌkõntra'bãndu] *m* **-1.** [ato] smuggling. **-2.** [mercadoria] contraband; **fazer** ~ to smuggle.
contração [kõntra'sãw] (*pl* **-ões**) *f* contraction.
contracapa [ˌkõntra'kapa] *f* inside cover.
contracenar [4] [ˌkõntrase'na(x)] *vi*: ~ **(com)** to perform (with).
contracepção [ˌkõntrasep'sãw] (*pl* **-ões**) *f* contraception.
contraceptivo, va [ˌkõntrasep'tʃivu, va] *m* contraceptive.
contracheque [ˌkõntra'ʃɛki] *m* payslip.
contradição [ˌkõntradʒi'sãw] (*pl* **-ões**) *f* contradiction; **entrar** *ou* **cair em** ~ to contradict o.s.
contraditório, ria [ˌkõntradʒi'tɔrju, rja] *adj* contradictory.
contradizer [29] [ˌkõntradʒi'ze(x)] *vt* to contradict.
◆ **contradizer-se** *vp* to contradict o.s.
contrafeito, ta [ˌkõntra'fejtu, ta] *adj* constrained.
contrafilé [ˌkõntrafi'lɛ] *m* rump steak.
contragosto [kõntra'goʃtu] ◆ **a contragosto** *loc adv* unwillingly.
contraído, da [kõntra'idu, da] *adj* **-1.** [tenso] tense. **-2.** [assumido] agreed. **-3.** [adquirido] contracted.
contra-indicação [ˌkõntraĩndʒika'sãw] (*pl* **contra-indicações**) *f* [de remédio] contraindication.
contra-indicado [ˌkõntraĩndʒi'kadu] (*pl* **contra-indicados**) *adj* **-1.** [remédio] contraindicated. **-2.** [medida, solução] inadvisable.
contra-indicar [12] [ˌkõntraĩndʒi'ka(x)] *vt* to contraindicate.
contrair [68] [kõntra'i(x)] *vt* **-1.** [ger] to contract. **-2.** [assumir]: ~ **matrimônio** to get married; ~ **dívidas** to run up debts; ~ **compromisso** to take on responsibilities. **-3.** [adquirir - doenças] to catch; [- hábitos] to acquire.
◆ **contrair-se** *vp* [encolher-se] to contract.

contralto [kõn'trawtu] *m* **-1.** [voz] contralto. **-2.** [tom de instrumento] alto. **-3.** [cantora] contralto.

contramão [ˌkõntra'mãw] ◇ *adj* **-1.** [em sentido contrário] one-way. **-2.** [inconveniente] out of one's way. ◇ *f*: **na ~** on the wrong side of the road.

contramestre [ˌkõntra'mɛʃtri] *m* **-1.** [em fábrica etc] foreman. **-2.** [náut] first mate.

contra-ofensiva [ˌkõntraofẽn'siva] (*pl* **contra-ofensivas**) *f* counteroffensive.

contra-oferta [ˌkõntrao'fɛxta] (*pl* **contra-ofertas**) *f* counteroffer.

contraparente [ˌkõntrapa'rẽntʃi] *m* **-1.** [distante] distant relative. **-2.** [afim] in-law.

contrapartida [ˌkõntrapar'tʃida] *f* **-1.** [oposto] opposite. **-2.** [compensação]: **em ~** in compensation.

contrapeso [ˌkõntra'pezu] *m* counterbalance.

contrapor [45] [ˌkõntra'po(x)] *vt* [confrontar] to confront; **~ algo a algo** to set sthg against sthg.
◆ **contrapor-se** *vp* [opor-se]: **~-se a algo** to be opposed to sthg.

contraproducente [ˌkõntraprodu'sẽntʃi] *adj* counterproductive.

contra-regra [ˌkõntra'xɛgra] (*pl* **contra-regras**) *mf* stage manager.

contra-revolução [ˌkõntraxevolu'sãw] (*pl* **contra-revoluções**) *f* counter-revolution.

contrariado, da [kõntra'rjadu, da] *adj* annoyed.

contrariar [16] [kõntra'rja(x)] *vt* **-1.** [vontade, interesse] to thwart. **-2.** [declaração, informação] to contradict. **-3.** [desobedecer - ordem, instrução] to disobey; [- lei] to break. **-4.** [descontentar] to annoy.
◆ **contrariar-se** *vp* **-1.** [descontentar-se] to get annoyed. **-2.** [contradizer-se] to contradict o.s.

contrariedade [kõntrarje'dadʒi] *f* nuisance.

contrário, ria [kõn'trarju, rja] *adj* **-1.** [lado] opposite. **-2.** [ponto de vista, decisão] opposing; **ser ~ a algo** to be against sthg; **caso ~** otherwise.
◆ **contrário** *m* opposite; **do ~** otherwise; **pelo** *ou* **ao ~** on the contrary; **ao ~** [de outra maneira] the other way round; [roupa] back to front.

contra-senso [ˌkõntra'sẽnsu] (*pl* **contra-sensos**) *m* nonsense (*inv*).

contrastante [kõntraʃ'tãntʃi] *adj* contrasting.

contrastar [4] [kõntraʃ'ta(x)] ◇ *vt*: **~ algo com algo** to contrast sthg with sthg. ◇ *vi* to contrast; **~ em algo** to contrast in sthg.

contraste [kõn'traʃtʃi] *m* contrast.

contratação [kõntrata'sãw] (*pl* **-ões**) *f* recruitment.

contratante [kõntra'tãntʃi] ◇ *adj* contracting. ◇ *mf* contractor.

contratar [4] [kõntra'ta(x)] *vt* to recruit.

contratempo [ˌkõntra'tẽnpu] *m* **-1.** [imprevisto] setback. **-2.** [dificuldade] hurdle. **-3.** [aborrecimento] upset.

contrato [kõn'tratu] *m* **-1.** [documento] contract. **-2.** [acordo] agreement.

contratual [kõntra'twaw] (*pl* **-ais**) *adj* contractual.

contravenção [ˌkõntravẽn'sãw] (*pl* **-ões**) *f* contravention.

contraventor, ra [ˌkõntravẽn'to(x), ra] *m, f* offender.

contribuição [kõntribwi'sãw] (*pl* **-ões**) *f* **-1.** [ger] contribution. **-2.** [tributo - sindical] dues (*pl*); [- fiscal] tax.

contribuinte [kõntri'bwĩntʃi] *m f* **-1.** [colaborador] contributor. **-2.** [aquele que paga imposto] taxpayer.

contribuir [74] [kõntri'bwi(x)] *vi* **-1.** [ger] to contribute; **~ com algo (para algo)** [fornecer, colaborar] to contribute sthg (for/to sthg). **-2.** [ter parte em um resultado]: **~ para algo** to contribute to sthg.

contrição [kõntri'sãw] *f* contrition.

contrito, ta [kõn'tritu, ta] *adj* contrite.

controlar [4] [kõntro'la(x)] *vt* to control.
◆ **controlar-se** *vp* [dominar-se] to control o.s.

controlável [kõntro'lavew] (*pl* **-eis**) *adj* controllable.

controle [kõn'troli] *m* control; **~ remoto** remote control.

controvérsia [kõntro'vɛrsja] *f* controversy; **em ~** controversial.

controverso, sa [kõntro'vɛrsu, sa] *adj* controversial.

contudo [kõn'tudu] *conj* however.

contumácia [kõntu'masja] *f* **-1.** obstinacy. **-2.** JUR contempt of court.

contumaz [kõntu'majʒ] *adj* obstinate.

contundente [kõntũn'dẽntʃi] *adj* **-1.**: **por instrumento ~** with a blunt instrument. **-2.** *fig* [decisivo] decisive.

contundir [5] [kõntũn'dʒi(x)] *vt* to bruise.
◆ **contundir-se** *vp* to bruise o.s.

conturbação [kõntuxba'sãw] (*pl* **-ões**) *f* **-1.** [perturbação] commotion. **-2.** [motim] riot.

conturbar [4] [kõntux'ba(x)] *vt* **-1.** [perturbar] to disturb. **-2.** [amotinar] to stir up.
◆ **conturbar-se** *vp* **-1.** [perturbar-se] to become troubled. **-2.** [amotinar-se] to rebel.

contusão [kõntu'zãw] (*pl* **-ões**) *f* bruise.

conúbio [kõ'nubju] *m* [aliança] alliance.

convalescença [kõnvaleʃ'sẽnsa] *f* convalescence.

convalescente [kõnvale'sẽntʃi] ◇ *adj* convalescent. ◇ *mf* convalescent patient.

convalescer [25] [kõnvale'se(x)] *vi* to convalesce.

convenção [kõnvẽn'sãw] (*pl* **-ões**) *f* convention; **~ social** social convention.

convencer [25] [kõnvẽn'se(x)] ◇ *vt* [persuadir]: **~ alguém (de algo)** to convince sb (of sthg); **~ alguém a fazer algo** to persuade sb to do sthg. ◇ *vi fig* [agradar] to impress.
◆ **convencer-se** *vp* [persuadir-se]: **~-se de algo** to convince o.s. of sthg.

convencido, da [kõnvẽn'sidu, da] *adj* **-1.** [convicto] convinced. **-2.** *fig* [presunçoso] conceited.

convencimento [kõnvẽnsi'mẽntu] *m* **-1.** [convicção] conviction. **-2.** *fig* [presunção] conceit.

convencional [kõnvẽnsjo'naw] (*pl* **-ais**) *adj* **-1.** [ger] conventional. **-2.** *pej* [comum] commonplace.
convencionar [4] [kõnvẽnsjo'na(x)] *vt* to agree on.
conveniado, da [kõnve'njadu, da] <> *adj* associated. <> *m, f* associate.
conveniência [kõnve'njẽnsja] *f* convenience; **ser da ~ de alguém** to be suitable for sb.
◆ **conveniências** *fpl* [regras sociais] decorum; **loja de ~s** convenience store.
conveniente [kõnve'njẽntʃi] *adj* **-1.** [ger] convenient. **-2.** [oportuno] opportune.
convênio [kõn'venju] *m* **-1.** [acordo] agreement. **-2.** [entre instituições] accord.
convento [kõn'vẽntu] *m* convent.
convergência [kõnver'gẽnsja] *f* convergence.
convergente [kõnvex'ʒẽntʃi] *adj* convergent.
convergir [64] [kõnvex'ʒi(x)] *vi* **-1.** [mesma direção]: **~ para** to converge on. **-2.** [ter a mesma tendência]: **~ (para)** to aim (at). **-3.** [afluir]: **~ (de/para)** to converge (from/towards).
conversa [kõn'vɛxsa] *f* **-1.** [diálogo] chat; **~ fiada** *ou* **mole** chit-chat. **-2.** [mentira]: **~ (fiada)** nonsense (*inv*). **-3.** *loc*: **passar uma ~ em alguém** to soft-soap sb; **ir na ~ de alguém** to be taken in by sb.
conversação [kõnvexsa'sãw] (*pl* **-ões**) *f* conversation.
conversador, deira [kõnvexsa'do(x), dejra] *adj* chatty.
conversado [kõnvex'sadu] *adj* [problema, assunto] discussed; **estamos ~s** there is nothing more to be said.
conversa-fiada [kõn,vɛxsa'fjada] (*pl* **conversas-fiadas**) *mf* [pessoa] loudmouth.
conversão [kõnvex'sãw] (*pl* **-ões**) *f* conversion.
conversar [4] [kõnvex'sa(x)] *vi* to talk, to hold a conversation.
conversibilidade [kõnvexsibili'dadʒi] *f* convertibility.
conversível [kõnvex'sivew] (*pl* **-eis**) <> *adj* convertible. <> *m* AUTO convertible.
conversor [kõnvex'so(x)] *m* **-1.** [dispositivo] transformer. **-2.** COMPUT converter.
converter [5] [kõnvex'te(x)] *vt* **-1.** [transformar]: **~ algo/alguém em algo** to convert sthg/sb into sthg. **-2.** [trocar]: **~ algo em algo** to change sthg into sthg. **-3.** POL & RELIG: **~ alguém a** to convert sb to.
◆ **converter-se** *vp* POL & RELIG: **~-se (a)** to convert (to).
convertido, da [kõnvex'tʃidu, da] <> *adj* converted. <> *m, f* POL & RELIG convert.
convés [kõn'vɛʃ] (*pl* **-veses**) *m* deck.
convexo, xa [kõn'vɛksu, sa] *adj* convex.
convicção [kõnvik'sãw] (*pl* **-ões**) *f* conviction; **ter ~ de que** to be convinced that.
convicto, ta [kõn'viktu, ta] <> *adj* **-1.** [convencido] convinced. **-2.** [réu] convicted. <> *m, f* [presidiário] convict.
convidado, da [kõnvi'dadu, da] *m, f* guest.
convidar [4] [kõnvi'da(x)] <> *vt* **-1.** [ger] to invite. **-2.** *fig* [induzir]: **~ alguém a** to invite sb to. <> *vi fig* [induzir]: **~ a** to be conducive to.
◆ **convidar-se** *vp* **-1.** [invitar-se] to invite o.s. **-2.** [oferecer-se] to put o.s. forward.
convidativo, va [kõnvida'tʃivu, va] *adj* inviting.
convincente [kõnvĩn'sẽntʃi] *m* convincing.
convir [67] [kõn'vi(x)] *vi* **-1.** [concordar]: **~ (com alguém) em algo** to agree (with sb) about sthg; **você há de ~ que** you have to agree that. **-2.** [ser conveniente, proveitoso]: **~ a alguém** to be convenient for sb. **-3.** [condizer]: **~ a alguém** to be appropriate for sb.
convite [kõn'vitʃi] *m* invitation.
conviva [kõn'viva] *m f* guest.
convivência [kõnvi'vẽnsja] *f* **-1.** [convívio] closeness. **-2.** [familiaridade] familiarity.
conviver [5] [kõnvi've(x)] *vi* **-1.** [coexistir] to coexist. **-2.** [lidar]: **~ com** to cope with.
convívio [kõn'vivju] *m* [convivência] closeness.
convocação [kõnvoka'sãw] (*pl* **-ões**) *f* [chamamento] summons.
convocar [12] [kõnvo'ka(x)] *vt* **-1.** [chamar] to summon. **-2.** [reunir] to convene. **-3.** MIL to call up.
convosco [kõn'voʃku] *pron pess* with you.
convulsão [kõnvuw'sãw] (*pl* **-ões**) *f* **-1.** MED convulsion. **-2.** *fig* upheaval.
convulsionar [4] [kõnvuwsjo'na(x)] *vt* **-1.** [pôr em convulsão] to convulse. **-2.** *fig* [povo, país] to agitate.
convulsivo, va [kõnvuw'sivu, va] *adj* convulsive.
cookie ['kuki] (*pl* **cookies**) *m* COMPUT cookie.
cooper ['kupe(x)] *m* jogging; **fazer ~** to go jogging.
cooperação [kwopera'sãw] (*pl* **-ões**) *f* cooperation.
cooperante [kwope'rãntʃi] *adj* cooperative.
cooperar [4] [kwope'ra(x)] *vi*: **~ (com)** to cooperate (with).
cooperativo, va [kwopera'tʃivu, va] *adj* cooperative.
◆ **cooperativa** *f* cooperative.
coordenação [kooxdena'sãw] *f* [ato] coordination.
coordenada [kooxde'nada] *f* **-1.** *fam* [orientação] instructions. **-2.** GEOM coordinate.
coordenar [koorde'na(x)] *m* to coordinate.
copa ['kɔpa] *f* **-1.** [cômodo] pantry. **-2.** [parte superior] crown. **-3.** ESP cup.
◆ **copas** *fpl* [naipe] hearts.
copeiro, ra [ko'pejro, ra] *m, f* domestic servant (*who waits at table*).
Copenhague [kõpe'ɲagi] *n* Copenhagen.
cópia ['kɔpja] *f* **-1.** [ger] copy. **-2.** [fotocópia] photocopy.
copiadora [kopja'dora] *f* **-1.** [loja] print shop. **-2.** [máquina] photocopier.
copiar [16] [ko'pja(x)] *vt* to copy.
copidescar [kopi'deʃka(x)] *vt* [revisar] to copy edit.

copidesque [kopi'dɛʃki] ◇ *m* [redação final] copy-editing. ◇ *mf* [redator] copy editor.
co-piloto, ta [kopi'lotu, ta] (*mpl* **co-pilotos**, *fpl* **co-pilotas**) *m, f* copilot.
copioso, piosa [ko'pjozu, pjɔza] *adj* **-1.** [ger] copious. **-2.** [refeição] copious.
copista [ko'piʃta] *mf* [copiador] copyist.
copo ['kɔpu] *m* **-1.** [recipiente] glass. **-2.** [conteúdo] glassful. **-3.** *loc*: **ser um bom ~** to be a heavy drinker.
COPOM (*abrev de* **Comitê de Política Monetária**) [ko'põ] *m* [econ] Monetary Policy Committee.
cópula *f* [coito] copulation.
copular [ko'pula(x)] *vi* to copulate.
copyright [kopi'xajtʃi], **copirraite** [kopi'xajtʃi] *m* copyright.
coque ['kɔki] *m* bun.
coqueiro [ko'kejru] *m* coconut palm.
coqueluche [koke'luʃi] *f* **-1.** [doença] whooping cough. **-2.** *fig* [moda]: **o bambolê foi ~ nos anos setenta** the hula hoop was all the rage in the seventies.
coquete [ko'kɛtʃi] *adj* coquettish.
coquetel [koke'tɛw] (*pl* **-éis**) *m* **-1.** [drinque] cocktail. **-2.** [festa] cocktail party.
coqueteleira [kokete'lejra] *f* cocktail shaker.
cor ['ko(x)] (*pl* **-es**) *f* **-1.** [tom] colour; **~ de burro quando foge** *hum* undefinable color. **-2.** [de pele] complexion; **ficar sem ~** to go pale. **-3.** *fig* [feição] tone.
◆ **de cor** *loc adv* by heart.
coração [kora'sãw] (*pl* **-ões**) *m* [ger] heart; **abrir o ~** [confidenciar] to open one's heart; **ter um ~ de ouro** [ser bondoso] to have a good heart.
corado, da [ko'radu, da] *adj* **-1.** [na face] ruddy. **-2.** [avermelhado] reddish. **-3.** *fig* [envergonhado] shamefaced. **-4.** CULIN sautéed.
coragem [ko'raʒẽ] *f* courage.
corajoso, osa [kora'ʒozu, ɔza] *adj* courageous.
coral [ko'raw] (*pl* **-ais**) ◇ *m* **-1.** [ger] coral. **-2.** MÚS choir. ◇ *f* [cobra] coral snake. ◇ *adj* coral.
corante [ko'rãntʃi] ◇ *adj* colouring. ◇ *m* dye.
corar [4] [ko'ra(x)] ◇ *vt* CULIN to brown. ◇ *vi* [enrubescer] to blush.
corcova [kox'kɔva] *f* hump.
corcunda [kox'kũnda] ◇ *adj* hunchbacked. ◇ *mf* hunchback.
corda ['kɔrda] *f* **-1.** [ger] spring; **dar ~ em** to wind up. **-2.** [fio] rope; **pular ~** skipping. **-3.** [varal] clothesline. **-4.** *loc*: **dar ~ para alguém** *fig* [alimentar a conversa] to get sb going; [flertar] to flirt with sb; **estar com a ~ toda** *fig* to be really wound up.
◆ **cordas** *fpl* **-1.** ANAT: **~s vocais** vocal cords. **-2.** MÚS: **quarteto de ~s** string quartet.
cordão [kor'dãw] (*pl* **-ões**) *m* **-1.** [corda fina] twine. **-2.** [jóia] chain. **-3.** [cadarço] shoelace. **-4.** [bloco carnavalesco] carnival block. **-5.** ANAT: **~ umbilical** umbilical cord.
cordato, ta [kox'datu, ta] *adj* sensible.
cordeiro [kor'dejru] *m* lamb.
◆ **cordeiros** *mpl fig* [seguidores] disciples.
cordel [kor'dɛw] (*pl* **-éis**) *m* **-1.** [barbante] string. **-2.** LITER: **(literatura de) ~** popular Brazilian literature.

CORDEL

A popular form of literature, typical of the north-east of Brazil; the *cordel* ('string') consists of a small booklet, made up usually of a single sheet of paper folded over three times, to make eight pages. The *cordel* tells stories, in verse, of the people of the north-east. In order to sell these booklets in the street or at fairs, it is customary to hang them up with pieces of twine, hence the name *cordel*.

cor-de-rosa [ˌkordʒi'xɔza] ◇ *adj* **-1.** [cor] pink. **-2.** *fig* [feliz] rose-tinted. ◇ *m* [cor] pink.
cordial [kor'dʒjaw] (*pl* **-ais**) *adj* **-1.** [gentil] cordial. **-2.** [afetuoso] warm.
cordialidade [koxdʒjali'dadʒi] *f* **-1.** [gentileza] cordiality. **-2.** [afeição] warmth.
cordilheira [kordʒi'ʎejra] *f* mountain range.
cordões *pl* ▷ **cordão**.
coreano, na [ko'rjãnu, na] ◇ *adj* Korean. ◇ *m, f* Korean.
Coréia *n* Korea; **~ do Norte** North Korea; **~ do Sul** South Korea.
coreografia [korjogra'fia] *f* choreography.
coreógrafo, fa [ko'rjɔgrafu, fa] *m, f* choreographer.
coreto [ko'retu] *m* bandstand.
corisco [ko'riʃku] *m* **-1.** [ger] flash. **-2.** *fig* bright spark.
corista [ko'riʃta] *m, f* **-1.** [em coro] chorister. **-2.** [vedete] chorus girl.
coriza [ko'riza] *f* runny nose.
corja ['kɔxʒa] *f* gang.
córnea ['kɔxnja] *f* cornea.
cornear [15] [kox'nja(x)] *vt* **-1.** [com os chifres] to gore. **-2.** *fam* [trair] to two-time.
córner ['kɔxne(x)] *m* corner (kick).
corneta [kox'neta] *f* cornet.
corneteiro, ra [koxne'tejru, ra] *m, f* bugler.
cornija [kox'niʒa] *f* [em parede] cornice.
corno ['koxnu] *m* **-1.** [de animal] horn. **-2.** *vulg* [pessoa] cuckold.
cornudo, da [kox'nudu, da] ◇ *adj* [animal] horned.
◆ **cornudo** *m vulg* [pessoa] cuckold.
coro ['koru] *m* **-1.** [ger] chorus; **em ~** in chorus. **-2.** [cantores] choir. **-3.** [balcão] organ loft.
coroa [ko'roa] ◇ *f* **-1.** [ger] crown. **-2.** [de flores] garland. **-3.** [calvície] bald spot. ◇ *mf* [pessoa] *fam* old fogey.
coroação [korwa'sãw] (*pl* **-ões**) *f* coronation.
coroar [20] [koro'a(x)] *vt* **-1.** [ger] to crown. **-2.** [premiar] to reward.
coroinha *m* altar server.
corolário [koro'larju] *m* corollary.
coronário, ria [koro'narju, rja] *adj* coronary.
coronel [koro'nɛw] (*pl* **-éis**) *m* **-1.** MIL colonel. **-2.** POL political baron.

coronha [ko'roɲa] *f* butt.
coronhada [koro'ɲada] *f* blow with a rifle butt.
corpete [kox'petʃi] *m* bodice.
corpo ['koxpu] *m* **-1.** [ger] body; ~ **de baile** dance group; ~ **de bombeiros** fire department; ~ **diplomático** diplomatic corps; ~ **docente** faculty; [tronco] trunk; [carne] flesh; [formas] body. **-2.** [cadáver] corpse, body. **-3.** [consistência]: **tomar** ~ to thicken. **-4.** *JUR*: ~ **de delito** material fact. **-5.** *MED*: ~ **estranho** foreign body. **-6.** *loc*: **fazer** ~ **mole** to skulk; **tirar o** ~ **fora** to duck out.
corporação [koxpora'sãw] (*pl* **-ões**) *f* corporation.
corporal [koxpo'raw] (*pl* **-ais**) *adj* corporal.
corporativismo [koxporatʃi'viʒmu] *m* corporatism.
corporativista [koxporatʃi'viʃta] <> *adj* [relativo ao corporativismo] corporate. <> *mf* [partidário] corporatist.
corporativo, va [koxpo'ratʃivu, va] *adj* corporative.
corpulência [koxpu'lẽnsja] *f* corpulence.
corpulento, ta [koxpu'lẽntu, ta] *adj* corpulent.
correção [koxe'sãw] (*pl* **-ões**) *f* **-1.** [ato] marking; ~ **monetária** inflationary adjustment. **-2.** [qualidade] exactness.
corre-corre [kɔxi'kɔxi] *m* mad rush.
corredor, ra [koxe'do(x), ra] (*mpl* **-es**, *fpl* **-s**) *m, f* [atleta] runner.
◆ **corredor** *m* [passagem - em casa] corridor; [- em avião, etc] aisle.
córrego ['kɔxegu] *m* brook.
correia [ko'xeja] *f* **-1.** [tira] strap. **-2.** [em máquina] belt. **-3.** [em carro] fan belt.
correio [ko'xeju] *m* **-1.** [serviço] mail. **-2.** [correspondência] post; **agência dos** ~**s** post office. **-3.** *fig* [carteiro] postman *UK*, mailman *US*. **-4.** *COMPUT*: ~ **eletrônico** email.
correlação [koxela'sãw] (*pl* **-ões**) *f* correlation.
correlacionar [4] [koxelasjo'na(x)] *vt* to correlate.
◆ **correlacionar-se** *vp* to correlate.
correligionário, ria [koxeliʒjo'narju, rja] <> *adj* partisan. <> *m, f* **-1.** *POL* fellow party member. **-2.** *RELIG* coreligionist.
corrente [ko'xẽntʃi] <> *adj* **-1.** [atual] current. **-2.** [comum] common. **-3.** [fluente - língua] fluent; [- estilo] flowing. **-4.** [água] running. <> *f* **-1.** [ger] current; ~ **marítima** marine current; **remar contra a** ~ *fig* to swim against the tide. **-2.** [corrente] chain. **-3.** [vento]: ~ **de ar** draught.
correnteza [koxẽn'teza] *f* current.
correntista [koxẽn'tʃiʃta] *mf* account holder.
correr [5] [ko'xe(x)] <> *vi* **-1.** [ger] to run. **-2.** [passar] to fly past. **-3.** [circular] to circulate. **-4.** [espalhar-se] to spread. **-5.** [despesas]: ~ **por conta de alguém** to go on sb's tab. <> *vt* **-1.** [percorrer]: ~ **a fazenda** to go all over sthg. **-2.** [passar de leve] to run. **-3.** [olhar rapidamente]: **corri os olhos pela revista** I ran my eyes over the magazine. **-4.** [estar exposto a]: ~ **o risco de algo** to run the risk of sthg.
correria [koxe'ria] *f* rushing about.
correspondência [koxeʃpõn'dẽnsja] *f* correspondence.
correspondente [koxeʃpõn'dẽntʃi] <> *adj* corresponding. <> *mf* correspondent; ~ **de guerra** war correspondent.
corresponder [5] [koxeʃpõn'de(x)] *vi* **-1.** [ger]: ~ **a** to correspond to. **-2.** [retribuir]: ~ **a** to reciprocate.
◆ **corresponder-se** *vp* to correspond with.
corretagem [koxe'taʒẽ] *f* **-1.** [atividade] brokerage. **-2.** [remuneração] commission.
corretamente [koˌxɛta'mẽntʃi] *adv* correctly.
corretivo, va [koxe'tʃivu, va] *adj* [que corrige] corrective.
◆ **corretivo** *m* [castigo] punishment.
correto, ta [ko'xɛtu, ta] *adj* **-1.** [ger] correct. **-2.** [íntegro] honest.
corretor, ra [koxe'to(x), ra] (*mpl* **-es**, *fpl* **-s**) *m, f* [agente] broker; ~ **de imóveis** estate agent *UK*, realtor *US*; ~ **de Bolsa** stockbroker.
◆ **corretora** *f* [instituição] agency.
corrida [ko'xida] *f* **-1.** [ato] running. **-2.** *ESP* racing. **-3.** [de táxi] fare.
corrido, da [ko'xidu, da] *adj* [rápido] rushed.
corrigir [52] [koxi'ʒi(x)] *vt* **-1.** [retificar] to correct. **-2.** [eliminar] to repair. **-3.** [repreender] to tell off. **-4.** [atenuar] to attenuate.
◆ **corrigir-se** *vp* [emendar-se] to correct o.s.
corrimão [koxi'mãw] (*pl* **-ãos**, **-ões**) *m* handrail.
corrimento [koxi'mẽntu] *m* discharge.
corriqueiro, ra [koxi'kejru, ra] *adj* everyday.
corroborar [4] [koxobo'ra(x)] *vt* to corroborate.
corroer [28] [koxo'e(x)] *vt* **-1.** [carcomer] to eat away. **-2.** [danificar] to corrode. **-3.** *fig* [depravar] to undermine.
corromper [5] [koxõn'pe(x)] *vt* **-1.** [perverter] to pervert. **-2.** [subornar] to corrupt. **-3.** [adulterar] to tamper with.
◆ **corromper-se** *vp* [perverter-se] to become corrupt.
corrompido, da [koxõm'pidu, da] *adj* [pervertido] corrupted; **arquivo** ~ *COMPUT* corrupted file.
corrosão [koxo'sãw] (*pl* **-ões**) *f* **-1.** [de metais] corrosion. **-2.** *GEOL* erosion.
corrosivo, va [koxo'zivu, va] *adj* corrosive.
corrupção [koxup'sãw] (*pl* **-ões**) *f* **-1.** [perversão] pervertion. **-2.** [suborno] corruption.
corrupto, ta [ko'xuptu, ta] *adj* corrupt.
Córsega ['kɔxsega] *n* Corsica.
cortada [kox'tada] *f* *ESP* smash; **dar uma** ~ to smash the ball; **dar uma** ~ **em alguém** *fig* to cut sb short.
cortado, da [kox'tadu, da] *adj* **-1.** [ger] cut. **-2.** [relações] severed. **-3.** *fig* [coração] broken.
◆ **cortado** *m* *fig* [apuro] struggle.
cortador [koxta'do(x)] *m* cutter.
cortante [kox'tãntʃi] *adj* **-1.** [ger] cutting. **-2.** [que corta] sharp.
cortar [4] [kox'ta(x)] <> *vt* **-1.** [ger] to cut. **-2.** [árvore] to cut down. **-3.** [suprimir] to cut out. **-4.** *AUTO*

to stall. **-5.** [interromper] to interrupt. **-6.** [pôr fim a] to end. **-7.** [encurtar]: ~ **caminho** to take a short cut. ◇ *vi* **-1.** [ter bom gume] to cut. **-2.** *ESP* to smash the ball.

◆ **cortar-se** *vp* [ferir-se] to cut o.s.

corte[1] ['kɔxtʃi] *m* **-1.** [ger] cut. **-2.** [gume] cutting edge; **ter bom** ~ to be sharp; **estar sem** ~ to be blunt. **-3.** [porção de tecido]: ~ **de algo** length of sthg. **-4.** *ELETR*: ~ **de luz** power cut.

corte[2] ['koxtʃi] *f* **-1.** [ger] court. **-2.** *fig* [de admiradores *etc*] entourage. **-3.** [cortejar]: **fazer a** ~ **a alguém** to court sb.

cortejar [4] [koxte'ʒa(x)] *vt* to court.

cortejo [kox'teʒu] *m* **-1.** [séquito] cortege. **-2.** [procissão] procession.

cortês [kox'teʃ] *adj* polite.

cortesão, sã [koxte'zãw, zã] (*mpl* **-ãos, -ões**, *fpl* **-s**) ◇ *adj* courtly. ◇ *m, f* courtier. ◇ *f* courtesan.

cortesia [koxte'zia] *f* **-1.** [delicadeza] courtesy. **-2.** [presente] complimentary gift. **-3.** [mesura] bow.

cortiça [kox'tʃisa] *f* cork.

cortiço [kox'tʃisu] *m* **-1.** [para abelhas] beehive. **-2.** [habitação] slum dwelling.

cortina [kox'tʃina] *f* **-1.** [peça] curtain. **-2.** *fig* [nuvem] screen.

cortisona [koxtʃi'zona] *f* cortisone.

coruja [ko'ruʒa] ◇ *f ZOOL* owl. ◇ *adj* [pai, mãe] doting.

corvo ['koxvu] *m* crow.

cós ['kɔʃ] *m inv* **-1.** [tira de pano] waistband. **-2.** [cintura] waist.

coser [5] [ko'ze(x)] ◇ *vt* to stitch. ◇ *vi* to sew.

cosmético, ca [koʒ'mɛtʃiku, ka] *adj* cosmetic.

◆ **cosmético** *m* cosmetic.

cósmico, ca ['kɔʒmiku, ka] *adj* cosmic.

cosmo ['kɔʒmu] *m* cosmos.

cosmonauta [kɔʒmo'nawta] *mf* cosmonaut.

cosmopolita [koʒmopo'lita] ◇ *adj* cosmopolitan. ◇ *mf* [pessoa] cosmopolitan person.

costa ['kɔʃta] *f* [litoral] coast.

costado [koʃ'tadu] *m NÁUT* [forro] hull cladding.

Costa do Marfim [ˌkɔʃtadumax'fĩ] *n* Ivory Coast.

Costa Rica [ˌkɔʃta'xika] *n* Costa Rica.

costa-riquense [ˌkɔʃtaxi'kẽnsi], **costarriquenho, nha** [ˌkɔʃtaxi'kẽɲu, ɲa] ◇ *adj* Costa Rican. ◇ *m, f* Costa Rican.

costas ['kɔʃtaʃ] *fpl* **-1.** [ger] back. **-2.** [encosto] backrest. **-3.** *loc*: **carregar nas** ~ *fig* to shoulder the burden; **ter** ~ **quentes** *fig* to be under sb's wing.

costela [koʃ'tɛla] *f* rib.

costeleta [koʃte'leta] *f* **-1.** *CULIN* chop. **-2.** [suíças] sideburns.

costumar [4] [koʃtu'ma(x)] *vt* **-1.** [ter o hábito de]: ~ **fazer algo** to be in the habit of doing sthg; **costumo correr todas as manhãs** I usually go running every morning. **-2.** [habituar] to accustom.

costume [koʃ'tumi] *m* **-1.** [hábito] habit; **ter o** ~ **de fazer algo** to be in the habit of doing sthg; **como de** ~ as usual. **-2.** [roupa] costume.

◆ **costumes** *mpl* [de um povo] customs.

costumeiro, ra [koʃtu'mejru, ra] *adj* usual, customary.

costura [koʃ'tura] *f* **-1.** [ger] sewing; **alta** ~ haute couture. **-2.** [linha de junção] seam.

costurar [4] [koʃtu'ra(x)] ◇ *vt* **-1.** *COST* to stitch. **-2.** *fig* [texto] to tidy up. ◇ *vi* **-1.** *COST* to sew. **-2.** *fam AUTO* to weave in and out.

costureira [koʃtu'rejra] *f* seamstress.

costureiro [koʃtu'rejru] *m* [estilista] couturier.

cota ['kɔta] *f* **-1.** [quinhão] quota. **-2.** [prestacão, parcela] instalment.

cotação [kota'sãw] (*pl* **-ões**) *f* **-1.** [ato] quoting. **-2.** [preço] quote. **-3.** *fig* [possibilidade de êxito] chance. **-4.** *fig* [conceito] reputation.

cotado, da [ko'tadu, da] *adj* **-1.** [com bom preço] well priced. **-2.** *fig* [favorito] favourite. **-3.** *fig* [conceituado] respected. **-4.** [avaliado] valued.

cotar [4] [ko'ta(x)] *vt* **-1.** [ger] to quote. **-2.** [avaliar]: ~ **algo/alguém em** to value sthg/sb at.

cotejar [4] [kote'ʒa(x)] *vt* to compare.

cotejo [ko'teʒu] *m* comparison.

cotidiano, na [kotʃi'dʒjanu, na] *adj* everyday.

◆ **cotidiano** *m* routine.

cotizar [4] [kotʃi'za(x)] *vt* **-1.** [distribuir por cotas] to allocate. **-2.** [cotar] to value, to assess.

◆ **cotizar-se** *vp* to club together.

coto *m* **-1.** [mus] koto. **-2.** [zool] feather follicle.

cotonete [koto'nɛtʃi] *m* cotton bud.

cotovelada [kotove'lada] *f* **-1.** [batida] hefty nudge. **-2.** [cutucada] nudge.

cotovelo [koto'velu] *m* **-1.** *ANAT* elbow; **falar pelos** ~**s** *fig* to talk non-stop. **-2.** [de estrada *etc*] bend.

couraça [ko'rasa] *f* **-1.** [armadura] breastplate. **-2.** [de animal] plating. **-3.** *NÁUT* armour plate.

couraçado, da [kora'sadu, da] *adj* [que tem couraça] armoured.

◆ **couraçado** *m NÁUT* battleship.

couro ['koru] *m* **-1.** [de animal] hide; [curtido] leather; ~ **cru** rawhide; **de** ~ leather. **-2.** [humano]: ~ **cabeludo** scalp. **-3.** *loc*: **não dar no** ~ to underperform.

couve ['kovi] *f* spring greens.

couve-de-bruxelas [ˌkovidʒibru'ʃɛlaʃ] (*pl* **couves-de-bruxelas**) *f* Brussels sprout.

couve-flor [ˌkovi'flo(x)] (*pl* **couves-flores**) *f* cauliflower.

couvert [ko'vɛ(x)] *m* cover charge.

cova ['kɔva] *f* **-1.** [sepultura] grave. **-2.** [caverna] cavern. **-3.** [buraco] hole.

covarde [ko'vaxdʒi] ◇ *adj* cowardly. ◇ *mf* coward.

covardia [kovax'dʒia] *f* cowardice.

coveiro [ko'vejru] *m* gravedigger.

covil [ko'viw] (*pl* **-is**) *m* **-1.** [ger] den. **-2.** *fig* [casebre] hovel.

covinha [kɔ'viɲa] *f* dimple.

coxa ['koʃa] *f ANAT* thigh; ~ **de galinha** *CULIN*

chicken drumstick; **fazer (algo) nas ~s** *vulg* to do it any old how.
coxear [15] [ko'ʃja(x)] *vi* to limp.
coxia [ko'ʃia] *f* aisle.
coxo, xa ['koʃu, ʃa] *adj* **-1.** [ger] lame. **-2.** [móvel] wobbly *(on account of having one leg shorter than the others)*.
cozer [5] [ko'ze(x)] *vt* to cook.
cozido, da [ko'zidu, da] *adj* cooked.
◆ **cozido** *m* stew.
cozinha [ko'ziɲa] *f* **-1.** [cômodo] kitchen. **-2.** [arte] cookery; **~ brasileira** Brazilian cuisine; **aula/livro de ~** cookery class/book.
cozinhar [4] [kozi'ɲa(x)] ◇ *vt* **-1.** [cozer] to cook. **-2.** *fig* [adiar] to put off. ◇ *vi* to cook.
cozinheiro, ra [kozi'ɲejru, ra] *m, f* cook.
CPD (*abrev de* **Centro de Processamento de Dados**) *m data-processing department*.
CPF (*abrev de* **Cadastro de Pessoa Física**) *m Brazilian tax-payer's identity card for individual contributions*, ≃ NI number *UK*, ≃ social security number *US*.
CPMF (*abrev de* **Contribuição Provisória sobre Movimentação Financeira**) *f Brazilian tax on bank transactions*.
crachá [kra'ʃa] *m* badge.
crack[1] ['kraki] *m* crack (cocaine).
crack[2] ['kraki] (*pl* **cracks**) *m* COMPUT hack.
cracker (*pl* **crackers**) *m* COMPUT hacker.
crânio ['krãnju] *m* **-1.** ANAT skull. **-2.** *fam* [gênio]: **ser um ~** to be a brainbox.
crápula ['krapula] *mf* villain.
craque ['kraki] ◇ *mf* [pessoa exímia]: **ser um ~ em algo** to be an expert in sthg. ◇ *m* FUT football star *UK*, soccer star *US*.
crase ['krazi] *f* LING crasis.
crasso, ssa ['krasu, sa] *adj* **-1.** [grosseiro] crass. **-2.** [espesso] viscous.
cratera [kra'tɛra] *f* crater.
cravar [4] [kra'va(x)] *vt* **-1.** [fazer penetrar] to drive in. **-2.** [engastar] to set. **-3.** *fig* [fixar]: **~ os olhos em alguém** to stare at sb.
cravejar [4] [krave'ʒa(x)] *vt* **-1.** [com cravos] to nail. **-2.** [com pedras preciosas] to set.
cravo ['kravu] *m* **-1.** [flor] carnation. **-2.** [prego] nail. **-3.** MÚS harpsichord. **-4.** [especiaria] clove. **-5.** [na pele] blackhead.
crawl ['krɔw] *m* ESP crawl.
creche ['krɛʃi] *f* crèche.
credenciais [kredẽnsi'ajʃ] *fpl* [qualificações] credentials.
credenciamento [kredẽnsia'mẽntu] *m* accreditation.
credenciar [16] [kredẽn'sja(x)] *vt* **-1.** [dar credenciais a] to accredit. **-2.** [habilitar] to qualify.
◆ **credenciar-se** *vp* JORN to be accredited.
crediário [kre'dʒjarju] *m* hire purchase.
credibilidade [kredʒibili'dadʒi] *f* credibility.
creditar [4] [kredʒi'ta(x)] *vt* **-1.** [depositar] to deposit. **-2.** [inscrever como credor]: **~ alguém em** to credit sb with. **-3.** [atribuir]: **~ algo a algo/alguém** to put sthg down to sb/sthg.
crédito ['krɛdʒitu] *m* **-1.** [ger] credit; **digno de ~** creditworthy. **-2.** FIN credit; **venda a ~** sale on credit. **-3.** [boa reputação] credibility.
credo ['krɛdu] *m* **-1.** [crença] belief. **-2.** [reza]: **o Credo** the Creed.
credor, ra [kre'do(x), ra] (*mpl* **-es**, *fpl* **-s**) ◇ *adj* **-1.** FIN credit *(antes de subst)*. **-2.** [merecedor] deserving. ◇ *m, f* FIN creditor.
credulidade [kreduli'dadʒi] *f* credulity.
crédulo, ula ['krɛdulu, la] ◇ *adj* gullible. ◇ *m, f* gullible person.
cremação [krema'sãw] (*pl* **-ões**) *f* cremation.
cremar [4] [kre'ma(x)] *vt* to cremate.
crematório [krema'tɔrju] *m* crematorium.
creme ['kremi] ◇ *adj inv* [cor] cream. ◇ *m* **-1.** [ger] cream; **~ de leite** dairy cream; **~ chantilly** whipped cream. **-2.** [cosmético] face cream. **-3.** [pasta]: **~ dental** toothpaste. **-4.** [flavour]: **sorvete de ~** vanilla ice cream.
cremoso, osa [kre'mozu, ɔza] *adj* creamy.
crença ['krẽnsa] *f* **-1.** RELIG belief. **-2.** [convicção] conviction.
crendice [krẽn'diʃi] *f* superstition.
crente ['krẽntʃi] ◇ *adj* **-1.** [que tem fé] believing. **-2.** [protestante] Protestant. **-3.** [convencido]: **estar ~ que** to be sure that. ◇ *mf* **-1.** [quem tem fé] believer. **-2.** [protestante] Protestant.
crepitação [krepita'sãw] (*pl* **-ões**) *f* crackling.
crepitante [krepi'tãntʃi] *adj* crackling.
crepitar [4] [krepi'ta(x)] *vi* to crackle.
crepom [kre'põ] ◇ *adj* [papel] crêpe. ◇ *m* [tecido] crêpe.
crepuscular [krepuʃku'la(x)] *adj* twilight.
crepúsculo [kre'puʃkulu] *m* **-1.** [ao amanhecer] dawn. **-2.** [ao anoitecer] dusk. **-3.** *fig* [declínio] twilight.
crer [37] ['kre(x)] ◇ *vt* [ger] to believe. ◇ *vi* [acreditar]: **~ em** to believe in.
crescendo [kre'sẽndu] *m* crescendo.
crescente [kre'sẽntʃi] ◇ *adj* **-1.** [tamanho] growing. **-2.** [formato] crescent. ◇ *m* [fase da lua] crescent moon.
crescer [4] [kre'se(x)] *vi* **-1.** [aumentar] to grow. **-2.** CULIN to rise.
crescido, da [kre'sidu, da] *adj* grown-up.
crescimento [kresi'mẽntu] *m* growth.
crespo, pa ['kreʃpu, pa] *adj* **-1.** [anelado] curly. **-2.** [áspero] rough.
Creta ['krɛta] *n* Crete.
cretinice [kretʃi'nisi] *f* stupidity.
cretino, na [kre'tʃinu, na] ◇ *adj* cretinous. ◇ *m, f* cretin.
cria ['kria] *f* offspring *(inv)*.
criação [krja'sãw] (*pl* **-ões**) *f* **-1.** [ger] creation. **-2.** [de animais] raising. **-3.** [de filhos] upbringing.
◆ **de criação** *loc adj* adopted.
criado-mudo [ˌkrjadu'mudu] (*pl* **criados-mudos**) *m* bedside table.
criador, ra [kria'do(x), ra] (*mpl* **-es**, *fpl* **-s**) ◇ *adj* creative. ◇ *m, f* **-1.** [autor] creator. **-2.** [de animais] breeder.

◆ **Criador** *m* [Deus]: **o Criador** the Creator.
criança [kri'ãnsa] *f* **-1.** [infante] child. **-2.** [pessoa infantil] child.
criançada [krjãn'sada] *f*: **a** ~ the kids *(pl)*.
criancice [krjãn'sisi] *f* childishness.
criar [16] [kri'a(x)] *vt* **-1.** [produzir] to create. **-2.** [fundar] to found. **-3.** [educar] to bring up. **-4.** [animais] to raise. **-5.** [plantas] to cultivate.
◆ **criar-se** *vp* [educar-se] to grow up.
criatividade [kriatʃivi'dadʒi] *f* creativity.
criativo, va [kria'tʃivu, va] *adj* creative.
criatura [kria'tura] *f* creature.
crime ['krimi] *m* crime.
criminal [krimi'naw] (*pl* **-ais**) *adj* criminal.
criminalidade [kriminali'dadʒi] *f* criminality.
criminalista [krimina'liʃta] *m f* criminologist.
criminoso, osa [krimi'nozu, ɔza] ◇ *adj* criminal. ◇ *m, f* criminal.
crina ['krina] *f* mane.
crioulo, la ['krjolu, la] ◇ *adj* **-1.** [comida, dialeto] Creole. **-2.** [negro] black. ◇ *m, f* [pessoa negra] black person.
cripta ['kripta] *f* crypt.
criptografar [kriptogra'fa(x)] *vt* COMPUT to encrypt.
criptografia [kriptogra'fia] *f* COMPUT cryptography.
críquete ['kriketʃi] *m* cricket.
crisântemo [kri'zãntemu] *m* chrysanthemum.
crise ['krizi] *f* **-1.** MED attack. **-2.** [escassez] shortage. **-3.** [fase difícil] crisis. **-4.** *fig* [acesso] fit; **ter uma** ~ to have a fit.
crisma ['kriʒma] *f* confirmation.
crismar [kriʒ'ma(x)] *vt* RELto confirm.
crista ['kriʃta] *f* **-1.** [de galo] comb. **-2.** [cume] crest.
cristal [kriʃ'taw] (*pl* **-ais**) *m* crystal.
cristaleira [kriʃta'lejra] *f* display cabinet.
cristalino, na [kriʃta'linu, na] *adj* crystalline.
cristalização [kriʃtaliza'sãw] (*pl* **-ões**) *f* crystallization.
cristalizar [4] [kriʃtali'za(x)] ◇ *vt* [tornar cristalino] to crystallize. ◇ *vi* [tornar-se cristalino] to crystallize.
◆ **cristalizar-se** *vp* [consolidar-se] to crystallize.
cristandade [kriʃtãn'dadʒi] *f* Christianity.
cristão, ã [kriʃ'tãw, ã] ◇ *adj* Christian. ◇ *mf* Christian.
cristianismo [kriʃtʃjã'niʒmu] *m* Christianity.
cristo ['kriʃtu] *m* *fig* [vítima] victim.
Cristo ['kriʃtu] *m* Christ.
critério [kri'tɛrju] *m* criterion.
criterioso, osa [krite'rjozu, ɔza] *adj* selective.
criticar [12] [kritʃi'ka(x)] *vt* **-1.** [censurar] to criticize. **-2.** [analisar] to review.
crítico, ca ['kritʃiku, ka] ◇ *adj* critical. ◇ *m, f* [pessoa] critic.
◆ **crítica** *f* **-1.** [censura] criticism *(inv)*; **ser alvo de** ~**s** to be criticized. **-2.** [análise] review. **-3.** [os críticos]: **a** ~ critics *(pl)*.
crivar [4] [kri'va(x)] *vt* **-1.** [com balas, facadas] to riddle. **-2.** [fig] [com perguntas] to bombard.
crível ['krivew] (*pl* **-eis**) *adj* believable.
crivo ['krivu] *m* **-1.** [peneira] sieve. **-2.** *fig* [escrutínio] scrutiny.
Croácia [kro'asja] *n* Croatia.
croata [kro'ata] ◇ *adj* Croat. ◇ *mf* Croat.
crocante [kro'kãntʃi] *adj* crunchy.
crochê [kro'ʃe] *m* crochet.
crocodilo [kroko'dʒilu] *m* crocodile.
cromado, da [kro'madu, da] *adj* chromium-plated.
cromo ['kromu] *m* chrome.
cromossomo [kromo'somu] *m* [genética] chromosome.
cromoterapia [ˌkromotera'pia] *f* colour therapy.
crônica ['kronika] *f* **-1.** HIST & LITER chronicle. **-2.** JORN column.
crônico, ca ['kroniku, ka] *adj* **-1.** [ger] chronic. **-2.** [inveterado] inveterate.
cronista [kro'niʃta] *m f* **-1.** HIST & LITER chronicler. **-2.** JORN columnist.
cronograma [krono'grãma] *m* schedule.
cronologia [kronolo'ʒia] *f* chronology.
cronológico, ca [krono'lɔʒiku, ka] *adj* chronological.
cronometrar [4] [kronome'tra(x)] *vt* to time.
cronômetro [kro'nometru] *m* stopwatch.
croquete [kro'kɛtʃi] *m* croquette.
croqui [kro'ki] *m* sketch.
crosta ['kroʃta] *f* **-1.** [de pão, terra] crust. **-2.** [de ferida] scab.
cru, crua ['kru, 'krua] *adj* **-1.** [não cozido] raw. **-2.** [não refinado] crude. **-3.** *fig* [duro] harsh.
crucial [kru'sjaw] (*pl* **-ais**) *adj* **-1.** [ger] crucial. **-2.** [difícil] important.
crucificação [krusifika'sãw] (*pl* **-ões**) *f* RELIG: **a** ~ the Crucifixion.
crucificar [12] [krusifi'ka(x)] *vt* to crucify.
crucifixo [krusi'fiksu] *m* crucifix.
cruel [kru'ɛw] (*pl* **-éis**) *adj* **-1.** [perverso] cruel. **-2.** [doloroso] cruel. **-3.** [violento] violent.
crueldade [kruew'dadʒi] *f* cruelty.
cruento, ta [kru'ẽntu, ta] *adj* bloody.
crustáceos [kruʃ'tasjuʃ] *mpl* crustacea *(pl)*.
cruz ['kruʃ] (*pl* **-es** ['kruziʃ]) *f* cross.
◆ **Cruz Vermelha** *f* Red Cross.
cruzada [kru'zada] *f* crusade.
cruzado, da [kru'zadu, da] *adj* crossed.
◆ **cruzado** *m* [moeda] cruzado *(former Brazilian currency)*.
cruzador [kruza'do(x)] *m* NÁUT cruiser.
cruzamento [kruza'mẽntu] *m* **-1.** [de estradas] junction. **-2.** [de raças] crossbreeding.
cruzar [4] [kru'za(x)] ◇ *vt* **-1.** [ger] to cross. **-2.** [animais] to crossbreed. ◇ *vi* **-1.** [rua]: ~ **com** to intersect. **-2.** [navio] to cruise. **-3.** *fig* [encontrar]: ~ **com alguém** to bump into sb.
◆ **cruzar-se** *vp* [encontrar-se] to bump into each other.
cruzeiro [kru'zejru] *m* **-1.** NÁUT cruise. **-2.** [moeda]

cruzeiro *(former Brazilian currency).*

CTI (*abrev de* **Centro de Terapia Intensiva**) *m* ICU.

cu ['kul *m vulg* arse; **fazer ~-doce** to act cool; **~-do-mundo** arsehole.

cuba ['kubal *f* vat.

Cuba ['kubal *n* Cuba.

cubano, na ['kubãnu, nal <> *adj* Cuban. <> *m, f* Cuban.

cúbico, ca ['kubiku, kal *adj* cubic.

cubículo [ku'bikulul *m* cubicle.

cubismo [ku'biʒmul *m* cubism.

cubista [ku'biʃtal <> *adj* cubist. <> *mf* cubist.

cubo ['kubul *m* **-1.** [ger] cube. **-2.** *GEOM* hexahedron. **-3.** *MAT* cube. **-4.** *AUTO*: **~ de roda** wheel hub.

cuca ['kukal *fam f* **-1.** [cabeça] head. **-2.** [mente] intellect; **fundir a ~** [baratinar] to do one's head in; [confundir] to addle one's brain. **-3.** *CULIN* sponge cake.

cuca-fresca [ˌkuka'freʃkal (*pl* **cucas-frescas**) *mf fam* cool person.

cuco ['kukul *m* **-1.** [ave] cuckoo. **-2.** [relógio] cuckoo clock.

cucuia [ku'kujal *f fam*: **ir para a ~** to go out the window.

cu-de-ferro [ˌkudʒi'fɛxul (*pl* **cus-de-ferro**) *fam* <> *adj* anal-retentive. <> *mf* anal-retentive.

cueca ['kwɛkal *f* underpants *(pl).*

cueiro [ku'ejrul *m* nappy *UK*, diaper *US*.

Cuiabá [kuja'bal *n* Cuiabá.

cuíca ['kwikal *f* cuíca, *an instrument resembling a drum whose sound is produced by vibrating a cord on the inside.*

cuidado, da [kwi'dadu, dal *adj* [tratado]: **bem/mal ~** well/badly cared for.

◆ **cuidado** *m* **-1.** [ger] care; **~!** careful! **-2.** [encargo]: **sob os ~s de** in the care of.

cuidadoso, osa [kwida'dozu, ɔzal *adj* careful.

cuidar [4] [kwi'da(x)] *vi* [tratar]: **~ de alguém/algo** to take care of sb/sthg.

◆ **cuidar-se** *vp* **-1.** [tratar-se] to take care of o.s. **-2.** [prevenir-se] to be careful.

cujo, ja ['kuʒu, ʒal *pron rel* **-1.** [de quem] whose. **-2.** [de que] whose.

culatra [ku'latral *f* gun breech.

culinário, ria [kuli'narju, rjal *adj* culinary.

◆ **culinária** *f* cookery.

culminante [kuwmi'nãntʃil *adj* culminating.

culminar [4] [kuwmi'na(x)] *vi*: **~ com algo** to culminate with sthg.

culote [ku'lɔtʃil *m* **-1.** [calça] jodphurs *(pl).* **-2.** [nas coxas] big thighs *(pl).*

culpa ['kuwpal *f* **-1.** [falta] fault; **pôr a ~ em** to blame; **ter ~ de** to be to blame for. **-2.** *JUR* guilt.

culpabilidade [kuwpabili'dadʒil *f* guilt.

culpado, da [kuw'padu, dal <> *adj* guilty. <> *m, f* criminal.

culpar [4] [kuw'pa(x)] *vt*: **~ alguém (de)** [atribuir a culpa] to blame sb (for); [acusar] to accuse sb (of).

◆ **culpar-se** *vp* to take the blame o.s.

cultivar [4] [kuwtʃi'va(x)] *vt* to cultivate.

◆ **cultivar-se** *vp* [instruir-se] to cultivate one's mind.

cultivável [kuwtʃi'vavewl (*pl* **-eis**) *adj* arable.

cultivo [kuw'tʃivul *m* cultivation.

culto, ta ['kuwtu, tal *adj* **-1.** [instruído] well educated. **-2.** [civilizado] civilized.

◆ **culto** *m* **-1.** *RELIG* ritual. **-2.** [veneração] worship.

cultura [kuw'tural *f* **-1.** [conhecimento] culture. **-2.** [civilização] civilization. **-3.** [cultivo] culture. **-4.** [criação - de animais] breeding; [- de germes, bactérias] culture.

cultural [kuwtu'rawl (*pl* **-ais**) *adj* cultural.

cumbuca [kũn'bukal *f* gourd.

cume ['kumil *m* **-1.** [topo] summit. **-2.** *fig* [apogeu] apex.

cúmplice ['kũnplisil *mf* **-1.** [co-autor] accomplice. **-2.** *fig* [parceiro] partner.

cumplicidade [kũnplisi'dadʒil *f* complicity.

cumpridor, ra [kũnpri'do(x), ral *adj* [responsável]: **é ~ da sua palavra** he keeps his word.

cumprimentar [4] [kũnprimẽn'ta(x)] *vt* **-1.** [saudar] to greet. **-2.** [elogiar] to compliment.

◆ **cumprimentar-se** *vp* [saudar-se] to greet one another.

cumprimento [kũnpri'mẽntul *m* **-1.** [saudação] congratulation. **-2.** [elogio] compliment. **-3.** [realização] fulfilment.

cumprir [6] [kũn'pri(x)] <> *vt* **-1.** [dever, obrigação] to fulfill. **-2.** [lei] to obey. **-3.** [promessa] to keep. **-4.** [caber] to be sb's responsibility. <> *vi* [convir] to be necessary, to be convenient.

◆ **cumprir-se** *vp* [concretizar-se] to come true.

cumulativo, va [kumula'tʃivu, val *adj* cumulative.

cúmulo ['kumulul *m* height.

cunha ['kuɲal *f* wedge.

cunhado, da [ku'ɲadu, dal *m, f* brother-in-law, sister-in-law.

cunhar [4] [ku'ɲa(x)] *vt* **-1.** [moedas] to mint. **-2.** [palavras] to create.

cunho ['kuɲul *m* **-1.** [marca] mark. **-2.** *fig* [selo] stamp. **-3.** *fig* [caráter] nature.

cunilíngua [kuni'lĩŋgwal *f* cunnilingus.

cupê [ku'pel *m* coupé.

cupido [ku'pidul *m* cupid.

cupim [ku'pĩl (*pl* **-ns**) *m* termite.

cupincha [ku'pĩnʃal *m f* mate.

cupom [ku'põl (*pl* **-ns**) *m* coupon.

cúpula ['kupulal *f* **-1.** [abóbada] dome. **-2.** [chefia] leadership.

cura ['kural <> *f* **-1.** [ger] cure; **não ter ~** *fig* to be incurable. **-2.** [recuperação] recovery. <> *m* [pároco] curate.

curado, da [ku'radu, dal *adj* **-1.** [pessoa, doença] cured. **-2.** [ferimento] healed. **-3.** [carne, queijo] cured.

curador, ra [kura'do(x), ral *m, f* **-1.** *JUR* [de menores] guardian. **-2.** [de instituições] caretaker. **-3.** [de arte] curator.

curandeiro, ra [kurãn'dejru, ral *m* healer.

curar [4] [ku'ra(x)] ◇ *vt* **-1.** [pessoa, doença] to cure; ~ **alguém de algo** to cure sb of sthg. **-2.** [ferimento] to heal. ◇ *vi* [sarar] to heal.

◆ **curar-se** *vp* **-1.** [sarar] to heal. **-2.** [emendar-se] to mend one's ways.

curativo [kura'tʃivu] *m* dressing.

curável [ku'ravew] (*pl* **-eis**) *adj* curable.

Curdistão [kuxdʒiʃ'tãw] *n* Kurdistan.

curdo, da ['kurdu, da] ◇ *adj* Kurdish. ◇ *m, f* [pessoa] Kurd.

◆ **curdo** *m* [língua] Kurdish.

curetagem [kure'taʒẽ] (*pl* **-ns**) *f* curettage.

curinga [ku'rĩŋga] *m* **-1.** [ger] joker.- **2.** *COMPUT*: **(caractere)** ~ wild card.

curiosidade [kurjozi'dadʒi] *f* curiosity.

curioso, osa [ku'rjozu, ɔza] ◇ *adj* **-1.** [ger] curious. **-2.** [bisbilhoteiro] nosy. **-3.** [interesante] interesting. ◇ *m, f* **-1.** [pessoa interessada] bystander. **-2.** [amador] amateur.

◆ **curioso** *m* [coisa singular]: **o ~ é ...** the strange thing is ...

◆ **curiosos** *mpl* [espectadores] onlookers.

Curitiba [kuri'tʃiba] *n* Curitiba.

curral [ku'xaw] (*pl* **-ais**) *m* corral.

currar [4] [ku'xa(x)] *vt* ***fam*** to rape.

currículo [ku'xikulu] *m* **-1.** [histórico] curriculum vitae ***UK***, resume ***US***. **-2.** [matérias] curriculum.

curriculum vitae [ku,xiculũn'vitaj] *m (inv)* curriculum vitae ***UK***, resume ***US***.

cursar [4] [kux'sa(x)] *vt* **-1.** [curso] to study. **-2.** [escola] to attend.

cursinho [kur'siɲu] *m* [pré-vestibular] *preparatory course for university entry.*

cursivo, va [kux'sivu, va] *adj* [letra] cursive.

curso ['kursu] *m* **-1.** [ger] flow. **-2.** [rumo] course. **-3.** [andamento]: **em ~** current. **-4.** [*EDUC* - nível] key stage ***UK***, grade ***US***; [- estabelecimento] school; **~ de férias** summer school; **~ normal** teacher training course *(for primary school)*; **~ de primeiro grau** primary school ***UK***, grade school ***US***; **~ de segundo grau** secondary school ***UK***, high school ***US***; **~ superior** degree course; **~ supletivo** supplementary course.

cursor [kux'so(x)] (*pl* **-es**) *m COMPUT* cursor.

curta-metragem [,kuxtame'traʒẽ] (*pl* **curtas-metragens**) *m* short film.

curtição [kuxtʃi'sãw] *f* **-1.** [de couro] tanning. **-2.** ***fam*** [prazer] fun.

curtido, da [kux'tʃidu, da] *adj* **-1.** [couro] tanned. **-2.** ***fig*** [sofrido] fed up. **-3.** ***fig*** [endurecido] hard-boiled.

curtir [6] [kux'tʃi(x)] *vt* **-1.** [couro] to tan. **-2.** [sofrer] to suffer. **-3.** ***fam*** [desfrutar de] to enjoy.

◆ **curtir-se** *vp* ***fam***: **eles se curtem muito** they really hit it off.

curto, ta ['kuxtu, ta] ◇ *adj* **-1.** [com pouco comprimento] short. **-2.** [breve] brief. **-3.** [limitado] intellectually limited. ◇ *m ELETR* = **curto-circuito.**

curto-circuito [,kuxtusix'kujtu] (*pl* **curtos-circuitos**) *m ELETR* short circuit.

curva ['kuxva] *f* **-1.** [de rua *etc*] bend; **~ fechada** sharp bend, hairpin bend. **-2.** [arqueamento] curve. **-3.** *GEOM* arc. **-4.** [em gráfico] curve.

◆ **curvas** *fpl* [de mulher] curves.

curvado, da [kux'vadu, da] *adj* curved, bent.

curvar [4] [kux'va(x)] ◇ *vt* **-1.** [arquear] to arch. **-2.** ***fig*** [dominar] to subdue. ◇ *vi* [envergar] to stoop.

◆ **curvar-se** *vp* **-1.** [envergar-se] to bend down. **-2.** [prostrar-se] to bow. **-3.** ***fig*** [submeter-se]: **~-se a** to give in to.

curvatura [kuxva'tura] *f* curvature.

curvilíneo, nea [kuxvi'linju, nja] *adj* [forma, objeto, linha] curvilinear.

curvo, va ['kuxvu, va] *adj* **-1.** [arqueado] curved. **-2.** [sinuoso - estrada, caminho] bendy; [- rio] meandering.

cuscuz [kuʃ'kuʃ] *m* couscous.

cusparada [kuʃpa'rada] *f* gob of spittle.

cuspe ['kuʃpi] *m* spittle.

cuspida [kuʃ'pida] *f* ***fam***: **dar ~s em** to spit on *ou* at.

cuspido, da [kuʃ'pidu, da] *adj* **-1.** [telefone] crackling. **-2.** [pessoa] affronted.

cuspir [61] [kuʃ'pi(x)] ◇ *vt* to spit. ◇ *vi* to spit; **~ no prato em que comeu *fig*** to bite the hand that feeds you.

custa ['kuʃta] *f*: **à ~ de** at the expense of.

◆ **custas** *fpl JUR* costs.

custar [4] [kuʃ'ta(x)] ◇ *vt* **-1.** [preço] to cost; **custe o que ~** whatever the cost; ***fig* ~ os olhos da cara** to cost an arm and a leg. **-2.** ***fig*** [acarretar] to cause; **não ~ nada fazer algo** not to cost anything to do sthg. ◇ *vi* **-1.** [produto, serviço]: **~ barato/caro** to be cheap/expensive. **-2.** [ser difícil, penoso]: **não custava você ter ajudado ...** it wouldn't have hurt you to help me ...; **~ caro** to cost a great deal. **-3.** [ter dificuldade]: **~ a fazer algo** to find sthg hard to do. **-4.** [demorar] to be late; **~ a fazer algo** to take a lot of doing.

custear [15] [kuʃ'tja(x)] *vt* to defray.

custeio [kuʃ'teju] *m* defrayal.

custo ['kuʃtu] *m* **-1.** [preço] cost; **~ de vida** cost of living. **-2.** ***fig*** [dificuldade]: **ser um ~ fazer algo** to be difficult to do sthg; **a todo ~** at all costs.

custódia [kuʃ'tɔdʒja] *f* custody.

CUT (*abrev de* **Central Única dos Trabalhadores**) *f central trade union body,* ≃ TUC ***UK***.

cutelaria [kutela'ria] *f* cutlery.

cutelo [ku'tɛlu] *m* cutlass.

cutia [ku'tʃia] *f* agouti.

cutícula [ku'tʃikula] *f* cuticle.

cútis ['kutʃiʃ] *f inv* cutis.

cutucada [kutu'kada] *f* **-1.** [com o cotovelo] nudge. **-2.** [como o dedo] poke.

cutucar [12] [kutu'ka(x)], **catucar** [katu'ka(x)] *vt* **-1.** [com o cotovelo] to nudge. **-2.** [com o dedo] to poke.

C.V. (*abrev de* **curriculum vitae**) *m* CV.

CVM (*abrev de* **Comissão de Valores Mobiliários**) *f* *regulatory body overseeing the sale of shares,* ≃ FSA *UK*.

czar, ina ['kza(x), ina] *m, f* czar (*f* czarina).

d, D [de] *m* [letra] d, D.

da [da] = **de + a**.

DAC (**Departamento de Aviação Civil**) *m civil aviation department,* ≃ CAA.

dadaísmo [dada'iʒmu] *m* dadaism.

dadaísta [dada'iʃta] ◇ *adj* Dadaist. ◇ *mf* Dadaist.

dádiva ['dadiva] *f* **-1.** [donativo] donation. **-2.** [dom] gift.

dadivoso, osa [dadʒi'vozu, ɔza] *adj* generous.

dado, da ['dadu, da] *adj* **-1.** [ger] given. **-2.** [presenteado] presented. **-3.** [afável] friendly. **-4.** [afeito]: **ser ~ a algo** to be fond of sthg.
  ◆ **dado** *m* **-1.** [em jogo] dice. **-2.** [informação] data.
  ◆ **dados** *mpl* COMPUT data.
  ◆ **dado que** *loc conj* given that.

daí [da'i] = **de + aí**.

Dakar [da'ka(x)] *n* Dakar.

dali [da'li] = **de + ali**.

dália ['dalja] *f* dahlia.

dálmata ['dawmata] *m* Dalmatian.

daltônico, ca [daw'toniku, ka] ◇ *adj* colour-blind. ◇ *m, f* colour-blind person.

dama ['dãma] *f* **-1.** [mulher] lady; **~ de companhia** companion; **~ de honra** bridesmaid. **-2.** POL: **primeira-~** first lady. **-3.** [em uma área específica] grande dame. **-4.** [em xadrez, baralho] queen.
  ◆ **damas** *fpl* [jogo] checkers.

damasco [da'maʃku] *m* **-1.** [fruta] apricot. **-2.** [tecido] damask.

Damasco [da'maʃku] *n* Damascus.

danação [dana'sãw] *f* **-1.** [maldição] damnation. **-2.** *fam* [travessura] mischief.

danado, da [da'nadu, da] ◇ *adj* **-1.** [amaldiçoado] damned. **-2.** [zangado] annoyed. **-3.** [travesso] mischievous. **-4.** [incrível] unbelievable. **-5.** [hábil]: **ser ~ para algo** to be incredibly good at sthg. ◇ *m* **-1.** [pessoa amaldiçoada] cursed person. **-2.** *fam* [esperto] joker.

danar-se [4] [dã'naxsi] *vp* [zangar-se] to become furious; **dane-se!** *fam* to hell with it!

dança ['dãnsa] *f* dance; **~ folclórica** folkdance; **~ de salão** ballroom dance; **~ do ventre** belly dance.

dançante [dãn'sãntʃi] *adj* dancing; **chá ~** tea dance.

dançar [13] [dãn'sa(x)] ◇ *vi* **-1.** [bailar] to dance. **-2.** *fam* [sair-se mal] to flop. **-3.** *fam* [deixar de acontecer] to fall through. ◇ *vt* [bailar] to dance.

dançarino, na [dãnsa'rinu, na] *m, f* ballet dancer.

danceteria [dãnsete'ria] *f* dancehall.

danificar [12] [danifi'ka(x)] *vt* to damage.
  ◆ **danificar-se** *vp* to get damaged.

daninho, nha [da'niɲu, ɲa] *adj* harmful; **erva daninha** weed.

dano ['dãnu] *m* damage.

danoso, osa [da'nozu, ɔza] *adj* [nocivo]: **~ a** damaging to.

Danúbio [da'nubju] *n*: **o ~** the Danube.

daquela [da'kɛla] = **de + aquela** ▷ **aquele**.

daquele [da'keli] = **de + aquele** ▷ **aquele**.

daqui [da'ki] = **de + aqui** ▷ **aqui**.

daquilo [da'kilu] = **de + aquilo** ▷ **aquilo**.

dardo ['daxdu] *m* **-1.** [seta] dart. **-2.** ESP javelin.

dar [11] ['da(x)] ◇ *vt* **-1.** [entregar, presentear] to give; **~ algo a alguém** to give sb sthg, to give sthg to sb. **-2.** [produzir] to yield. **-3.** [causar, provocar] to give; **isto me dá sono/pena** this makes me sleepy/sad; **isto vai ~ muito que fazer** this is going to be a lot of work; **o amor só dá problemas** love is nothing but trouble. **-4.** [filme, programa]: **deu no noticiário hoje** it was on the news today. **-5.** [exprime ação] to give; **~ um berro** to cry out; **~ um pontapé em alguém** to kick sb; **~ um passeio** to go for a walk. **-6.** [festa, concerto] to have, to hold; **vão ~ uma festa** they're going to have *ou* throw a party. **-7.** [dizer] to say; **ele me deu boa-noite** he said good night to me. **-8.** [ensinar] to teach; **o que é que você está dando nas suas aulas?** what do you teach in your class?; **ela dá aula numa escola** she teaches at a school; **eu gostaria de ~ aulas de inglês** I would like to teach English. **-9.** [aprender, estudar] to do; **o que é que estão dando em Inglês?** what are you doing in English at the moment?; **estamos dando o verbo "to be"** we're doing the verb "to be". ◇ *vi* **-1.** [horas]: **já deram cinco horas** it's just gone five o'clock. **-2.** [condizer]: **~ com** to go with; **as cores não dão umas com as outras** the colours clash. **-3.** [proporcionar]: **~ de beber a alguém** to give sb sthg to drink; **~ de comer a alguém** to feed sb. **-4.** [em locuções]: **dá igual/no mesmo** it doesn't matter; **~ ares de** to look like; **~ à luz** to give birth; **~ de si** to give of o.s.
  ◆ **dar com** *v + prep* [encontrar, descobrir] to meet; **dei com ele no cinema** I met him at the movies.
  ◆ **dar em** *v + prep* [resultar]: **a discussão não vai ~ em nada** the discussion will come to nothing.
  ◆ **dar para** *v + prep* [servir para, ser útil para] to be good for; [suj: varanda, janela] to look onto; [suj: porta] to lead to; [ser suficiente para] to be enough for; [ser possível] to be possible; **dá para você fazer isso hoje?** could you do it today?; **dá para ir a pé?** is it

within walking distance?; **não vai ~ para eu chegar na hora** I won't be able to get there on time.

◆ **dar por** *v + prep* [aperceber-se de] to notice.

◆ **dar-se** *vp*: **~-se bem/mal com alguém** to get on well/badly with sb; **o professor deu-se mal com a brincadeira** the teacher did not appreciate the joke; **~-se por vencido** to give up.

das [daʃ] = **de + as**.

DAT (*abrev de* **digital audio tape**) *f* DAT.

data ['data] *f* **-1.** [em carta *etc*] date; **~ de nascimento** date of birth. **-2.** [época] time; **de longa ~** of long standing.

data-base [ˌdata'bazi] (*pl* **datas-bases**) *f* baseline date.

datação [data'sãw] (*pl* **-ões**) *f* dating.

data-limite [ˌdatali'mitʃi] (*pl* **datas-limites**) *f* deadline.

datar [4] [da'ta(x)] ◇ *vt* **-1.** [pôr data em] to date. **-2.** [considerar que existe]: **~ algo de** to date sthg at. ◇ *vi* [existir]: **~ de** to date from.

datilografar [4] [datʃilogra'fa(x)] *vt* to type.

datilografia [datʃilogra'fia] *f* typing.

datilógrafo, fa [datʃi'lɔgrafu, fa] *m, f* typist.

dativo [da'tʃivu] *m* GRAM dative.

DC (*abrev de* **Depois de Cristo**) AD.

DDT (*abrev de* **Dicloro-Difenil-Tricloretana**) *m* DDT.

de [dʒi] *prep* **-1.** [indica posse] of; **o lápis do Mário** Mário's pencil; **o carro daquele homem** that man's car; **a recepção do hotel** the hotel reception; **a casa é dela** it's her house, the house is hers; **as fases da lua** the phases of the moon. **-2.** [indica matéria] (made) of; **um bolo ~ chocolate** a chocolate cake; **um relógio ~ ouro** a gold watch. **-3.** [indica conteúdo] of; **um copo d'água** a glass of water. **-4.** [usado em descrições, determinações]: **uma camiseta ~ manga curta** a short-sleeved T-shirt; **uma nota ~ 50 reais** a 50-real note; **o senhor ~ preto** the man in black. **-5.** [indica assunto] about; **fale da viagem** tell me about the trip; **um livro ~ informática** a book about *ou* on computers; **um livro ~ geografia** a geography book. **-6.** [indica origem] from; **sou ~ Salvador** I'm from Salvador; **os habitantes do bairro** the locals; **um produto do Brasil** a Brazilian product. **-7.** [indica tempo]: **o jornal das nove** the nine o'clock news; **partimos às três da tarde** we left at three in the afternoon; **trabalho das nove às cinco** I work from nine to five. **-8.** [indica uso]: **a sala ~ espera** the waiting room; **uma máquina ~ calcular** a calculator; **a porta ~ entrada** the front door. **-9.** [usado em denominações, nomes] of. **-10.** [indica causa, modo]: **chorar ~ alegria** to cry with joy; **está tudo ~ pernas para o ar** everything is upside down; **morrer ~ frio** to freeze to death; **ele viajou ~ carro** he travelled by car. **-11.** [indica autor] by; **um filme ~ Glauber Rocha** a film by Glauber Rocha; **o último livro ~ Ferreira Gullar** Ferreira Gullar's latest book. **-12.** [introduz um complemento]: **cheio ~ gente** full of people, crowded; **desconfiar ~ alguém** to distrust sb; **difícil ~ esquecer** hard to forget; **gostar ~ algo/alguém** to like sthg/sb. **-13.** [em comparações]: **do que** than; **teu carro é mais rápido do que este** your car is faster than this one. **-14.** [em superlativos] of; **o melhor ~ todos** the best of all. **-15.** [dentre] of; **uma daquelas cadeiras** one of those chairs; **um dia destes** one of these days; **um desses hotéis serve** one of those hotels will do. **-16.** [indica série]: **~ dois em dois dias** every two days; **~ quinze em quinze minutos** every fifteen minutes; **~ três em três metros** every three metres.

deão [dʒi'ãw] (*pl* **deãos, deães**) *m* dean.

debaixo [de'bajʃu] *adv* underneath.

◆ **debaixo de** *loc prep* under.

debalde [de'bawdʒi] *adv* in vain.

debandada [debãn'dada] *f* **-1.** [fuga] stampede. **-2.** [confusão]: **em ~** in disarray.

debandar [4] [debãn'da(x)] ◇ *vt* [dispersar] to break up. ◇ *vi* [pôr-se em fuga] to scatter.

◆ **debandar-se** *vp* [dispersar-se] to break up.

debate [de'batʃi] *m* **-1.** [discussão] debate. **-2.** [disputa] discussion.

debatedor, ra [debate'do(x), ra] *m, f* debater.

debater [5] [deba'te(x)] ◇ *vt* **-1.** [discutir] to debate. **-2.** [questionar] to dispute. ◇ *vi* [discutir] to discuss.

◆ **debater-se** *vp* [agitar-se] to struggle.

débeis ['dɛbejʃ] *pl* ▷ **débil**.

debelar [4] [debe'la(x)] *vt* **-1.** [ger] to overcome. **-2.** [dominar] to defeat.

debênture [de'bẽnturi] *f* COM debenture.

débil ['dɛbiw] (*pl* **-eis**) ◇ *adj* **-1.** [fraco] weak. **-2.** PSIC retarded. ◇ *mf* PSIC: **~ mental** mentally retarded person; *fam* [idiota] fool.

debilidade [debili'dadʒi] *f* **-1.** [fraqueza] weakness. **-2.** PSIC: **~ mental** mental retardation.

debilitação [debilita'sãw] *f* [enfraquecimento] debilitation.

debilitante [debili'tãntʃi] *adj* debilitating.

debilitar [4] [debili'ta(x)] *vt* to debilitate.

◆ **debilitar-se** *vp* to weaken.

debilóide [debi'lɔjdʒi] *fam* ◇ *adj* stupid. ◇ *mf* dunderhead.

debitar [4] [debi'ta(x)] *vt* to debit.

débito ['dɛbitu] *m* debit.

debochado, da [debo'ʃadu, da] *adj* scornful.

debochar [4] [debo'ʃa(x)] *vi*: **~ de algo/alguém** to scorn sb/sthg.

deboche [de'bɔʃi] *m* scorn.

debruçar [13] [debru'sa(x)] *vt* to lean.

◆ **debruçar-se** *vp* to lean over.

debulhar [4] [debu'ʎa(x)] *vt* **-1.** [grãos] to thresh. **-2.** [casca] to shell.

◆ **debulhar-se** *vp* **~-se em lágrimas** *fig* to dissolve into tears.

debutante [debu'tãntʃi] *f* debutante.

debutar [4] [debu'ta(x)] *vi* to make one's debut.

década ['dɛkada] *f* decade.

decadência [deka'dẽnsja] *f* decadence.

decadente [deka'dẽntʃi] *adj* decadent.
decair [68] [deka'i(x)] *vi* **-1.** [deteriorar] to deteriorate. **-2.** [pender] to wither. **-3.** [diminuir] to diminish.
decalcar [12] [dekaw'ka(x)] *vt* to trace.
decalque [de'kawki] *m* tracing.
decano [de'kãnu] *m* **-1.** [membro mais antigo] oldest member. **-2.** [de universidade] dean.
decantar [4] [dekãn'ta(x)] *vt* **-1.** [líquido] to decant. **-2.** [exaltar] to sing the praises of.
decapitar [4] [dekapi'ta(x)] *vt* to decapitate.
decatleta [deka'tlɛta] *mf* ESP decathlete.
decatlo [de'katlu] *m* decathlon.
decência [de'sẽnsja] *f* decency.
decênio [de'senju] *m* decade.
decente [de'sẽntʃi] *adj* **-1.** [digno] decent. **-2.** [decoroso] demure. **-3.** [apropriado, asseado - roupa] decent; [- restaurante, casa] clean. **-4.** [bem-feito] well done.
decentemente [desẽntʃi'mẽntʃi] *adv* **-1.** [dignamente, com decoro] decently. **-2.** [adequadamente] satisfactorily.
decepar [4] [dese'pa(x)] *vt* to cut off.
decepção [desep'sãw] (*pl* **-ões**) *f* **-1.** [desapontamento] disappointment. **-2.** [desilusão] disillusion.
decepcionado, da [desepsjo'nadu, da] *adj* **-1.** [desapontado] disappointed. **-2.** [desiludido] disillusioned.
decepcionar [4] [desepsjo'na(x)] *vt* **-1.** [desapontar] to disappoint. **-2.** [desiludir] to disillusion.
◆ **decepcionar-se** *vp* [desapontar-se]: **~-se com algo/alguém** to be disappointed with sthg/sb.
decerto [dʒi'sɛxtu] *adv* surely.
decibel [desi'bɛw] (*pl* **-éis**) *m* decibel.
decididamente [desidʒida'mẽntʃi] *adv* **-1.** [com certeza] certainly. **-2.** [resolutamente] decidedly.
decidido, da [desi'dʒidu, da] *adj* **-1.** [resolvido] resolved. **-2.** [resoluto] resolute.
decidir [6] [desi'dʒi(x)] ◇ *vt* **-1.** [resolver] to resolve. **-2.** [deliberar] to decide; **~ que** to decide that; **~ fazer algo** to decide to do sthg. **-3.** [concluir] to decide. ◇ *vi* **-1.** [tomar decisão]: **~ (sobre algo)** to make a decision (about sthg). **-2.** [optar]: **~ entre** to decide between.
◆ **decidir-se** *vp* **-1.** [tomar decisão] to make a decision; **~-se a fazer algo** to decide to do sthg. **-2.** [optar]: **~-se por** to opt for.
decifrar [4] [desi'fra(x)] *vt* **-1.** [ler, interpretar] to decipher. **-2.** [entender] to unravel.
decifrável [desi'fravew] (*pl* **-eis**) *adj* decipherable.
décima ['dɛsima] ▷ **décimo**.
decimal [desi'maw] (*pl* **-ais** [dɛsi'majʃ]) ◇ *adj* decimal. ◇ *m* decimal.
décimo, ma ['dɛsimu, ma] *num* tenth.
◆ **décimo** *m* tenth part; *veja também* **sexto**.
decisão [desi'zãw] (*pl* **-ões**) *f* **-1.** [deliberação] decision; **tomar uma ~** to make a decision. **-2.** [qualidade] decisiveness.
decisivo, va [desi'zivu, va] *adj* **-1.** [deliberativo, crítico] decisive. **-2.** [terminante] deciding.
declamação [deklama'sãw] *f* recitation, declamation.
declamar [4] [dekla'ma(x)] ◇ *vt* [recitar] to recite. ◇ *vi* **-1.** [recitar] to declaim. **-2.** *pej* [falar com afetação] to posture.
declaração [deklara'sãw] (*pl* **-ões**) *f* **-1.** [documento] written declaration. **-2.** [depoimento] testimony; **~ de amor** declaration of love; **fazer uma ~** to make a declaration. **-3.** [inventário] statement; **~ de imposto de renda** income tax declaration.
declarado, da [dekla'radu, da] *adj* **-1.** [patenteado] declared. **-2.** [confessado] self-declared.
declarante [dekla'rãntʃi] *mf* JUR declarant.
declarar [4] [dekla'ra(x)] *vt* **-1.** [ger] to declare; **~ que** to declare that. **-2.** [confessar] to confess.
◆ **declarar-se** *vp* **-1.** [manifestar-se]: **~-se a favor de/contra** to declare o.s for/against. **-2.** [confessar-se] to confess o.s. to be. **-3.** [designar-se] to declare o.s.
declinação [deklina'sãw] (*pl* **-ões**) *f* **-1.** GRAM declension. **-2.** [diminuição] reduction. **-3.** [declive] slope.
declinar [4] [dekli'na(x)] ◇ *vt* **-1.** [ger] to decline. **-2.** [revelar] to disclose. ◇ *vi* **-1.** [astro] to set. **-2.** [mesa, terreno] to slope. **-3.** [dia, tarde] to draw to a close.
declínio [de'klinju] *m* decline.
declive [de'klivi] *m* [de terreno] slope.
decô [de'ko] *adj* decor.
decodificador [dekodʒifika'do(x)] *m* COMPUT & TV decoder.
decodificar [12] [dekodʒifi'ka(x)] *vt* COMPUT & TV to decode.
decolagem [deko'laʒẽ] (*pl* **-ns**) *f* take-off.
decolar [4] [deko'la(x)] *vi* to take off.
decompor [45] [dekõn'po(x)] *vt* **-1.** [separar elementos de] to break down. **-2.** [dividir em partes] to dissect. **-3.** [estragar] to rot. **-4.** [alterar] to change.
◆ **decompor-se** *vp* **-1.** [estragar-se] to rot. **-2.** [alterar-se] to change o.s.
decomposição [dekõnpozi'sãw] (*pl* **-ões**) *f* **-1.** [apodrecimento] rotting. **-2.** [divisão em partes] dissection. **-3.** [separação de elementos] breakdown. **-4.** [alteração] change. **-5.** [desorganização] breakup.
decomposto, ta [dekõn'poʃtu, ta] ◇ *pp* ▷ **decompor.** ◇ *adj* **-1.** [putrefato] rotten. **-2.** [dividido] dissected.
decoração [dekora'sãw] (*pl* **-ões**) *f* decoration.
decorador, ra [dekora'do(x), ra] *m, f* [profissional] decorator.
decorar [4] [deko'ra(x)] *vt* **-1.** [memorizar] to learn by heart. **-2.** [ornamentar] to decorate.
decorativo, va [dekora'tʃivu, va] *adj* decorative.
decoro [de'koru] *m* **-1.** [decência] decency; **com ~** properly. **-2.** [dignidade] dignity.
decoroso, osa [deko'rozu, ɔza] *adj* decent.
decorrência [deko'xẽnsja] *f* consequence; **em ~ de** as a consequence of.

decorrente [deko'xẽntʃi] *adj*: ~ **de** resulting from.
decorrer [5] [deko'xe(x)] <> *m* [decurso]: **no ~ de** in the course of, during. <> *vi* **-1.** [derivar]: **~ de** to stem from. **-2.** [passar] to pass.
decorrido, da [deko'xidu, da] *adj* [terminado]: **decorrida a votação, ...** once the voting was over, ...
decotado, da [deko'tadu, da] *adj* low-cut.
decotar [4] [deko'ta(x)] *vt* to cut a low neckline in.
decote [de'kɔtʃi] *m* décolletage.
decrépito, ta [de'krɛpitu, ta] *adj* decrepit.
decrepitude [dekrepi'tudʒi] *f* [caducidade] decrepitude.
decrescente [dekre'sẽntʃi] *adj* falling.
decrescer [25] [dekre'se(x)] *vi* to decrease.
decréscimo [de'krɛsimu] *m* decrease.
decretação [dekreta'sãw] (*pl* **-ões**) *f* decreeing.
decretar [4] [dekre'ta(x)] <> *vt* **-1.** [ordenar] to decree. **-2.** [determinar] to determine. <> *vi* [ordenar] to decree.
decreto [de'krɛtu] *m* **-1.** [ordem] decree; [judicial] fiat. **-2.** *loc*: **nem por ~** not for all the tea in China.
decreto-lei [de,krɛtu'lej] (*pl* **decretos-lei**) *m* law by decree.
decúbito [de'kubitu] *m*: **em ~ dorsal/lateral** lying on one's back/side.
decurso [de'kuxsu] *m* course; **no ~ de** in the course of.
dedal [de'daw] (*pl* **-ais**) *m* thimble.
dedão [de'dãw] (*pl* **-ões**) *m* **-1.** [polegar] thumb. **-2.** [do pé] big toe.
dedetização [dedetʃiza'sãw] (*pl* **-ões**) *f* fumigation.
dedetizar [4] [dedetʃi'za(x)] *vt* to fumigate.
dedicação [dedʒika'sãw] (*pl* **-ões**) *f* **-1.** [devotamento] dedication. **-2.** [amor] devotion.
dedicado, da [dedʒi'kadu, da] *adj* dedicated.
dedicar [12] [dedʒi'ka(x)] *vt* [devotar]: **~ algo a alguém** to devote sthg to sb; [oferecer] to dedicate.
◆ **dedicar-se** *vp* [devotar-se]: **~-se a algo/alguém** to devote o.s to sthg/sb; **~-se a fazer algo** to devote o.s to doing sthg.
dedicatória [dedʒika'tɔrja] *f* dedication.
dedilhar [4] [dedʒi'ʎa(x)] <> *vt* [cordas, música] to strum. <> *vi* [tamborilar] to drum one's fingers.
dedo ['dedu] *m* **-1.** [da mão] finger; **~ anular** ring finger; **~ indicador** forefinger; **~ mindinho** *ou* **mínimo** little finger; **~ polegar** thumb. **-2.** [do pé] toe. **-3.** [quantidade]: **um ~ de algo** a finger of sthg. **-4.** *loc*: **cheio de ~s** finicky; **não levantar um ~** not to lift a finger.
◆ **a dedo** *loc adv* [escolher] with care.
dedo-duro [,dedu'duru] (*pl* **dedos-duros**) *mf* **-1.** [*POL*, crime] squealer. **-2.** [criança] tell-tale.
dedões [de'dõjʃ] *pl* ▻ **dedão**.
dedução [dedu'sãw] (*pl* **-ões**) *f* deduction.
dedurar [4] [dedu'ra(x)] *fam vt* **-1.** [crime] to squeal. **-2.** [criança] to tell tales.
dedutível [dedu'tʃivew] (*pl* **-eis**) *adj* deductible.
dedutivo, va [dedu'tʃivu, va] *adj* deductive.
deduzir [72] [dedu'zi(x)] <> *vt* **-1.** [subtrair] to subtract. **-2.** [concluir] to deduce. <> *vi* [tirar dedução] to deduce.
defasado, da [defa'zadu, da] *adj* out of phase.
defasagem [defa'zaʒẽ] (*pl* **-ns**) *f* [discrepância] gap.
defecar [12] [defe'ka(x)] *vi* to defecate.
defecção [defek'sãw] (*pl* **-ões**) *f* defection.
defectivo, va [defek'tʃivu, va] *adj* defective.
defeito [de'fejtu] *m* **-1.** [físico] defect. **-2.** [moral] flaw. **-3.** [falha] fault; **com ~** out of order; **pôr ~ em algo** [criticar] to find fault with sthg.
defeituoso, osa [defej'twozu, ɔza] *adj* **-1.** [com falha] faulty. **-2.** [físico] defective.
defender [5] [defẽn'de(x)] *vt* **-1.** [proteger]: **~ algo/alguém (contra** *ou* **de)** to defend sthg/sb (against). **-2.** [sustentar] to stand up for.
◆ **defender-se** *vp* [proteger-se]: **~-se (contra** *ou* **de)** to defend o.s (against).
defensável [defẽn'savew] (*pl* **-eis**) *adj* defensible.
defensivo, va [defẽn'sivu, va] *adj* defensive.
◆ **defensiva** *f* **-1.** [meios de defesa] defences ***UK***, defenses ***US***. **-2.** [atitude]: **estar/ficar na ~** to be/stay on the defensive.
defensor, ra [defẽn'so(x), ra] (*mpl* **-es**, *fpl* **-s**) *m, f* **-1.** [de causa *etc*] defender. **-2.** *JUR* defendant.
deferência [defe'rẽnsja] *f* **-1.** [respeito] deference. **-2.** [condescendência] acquiescence.
deferente [defe'rẽntʃi] *adj* **-1.** [atencioso] deferential. **-2.** [condescendente] acquiescent.
deferir [57] [defe'ri(x)] <> *vt* **-1.** [atender] to grant. **-2.** [conceder]: **~ algo a alguém** to award sthg to sb. <> *vi* **-1.** [atender]: **~ a algo** to yield to sthg. **-2.** [acatar]: **~ a algo** to respect sthg.
defesa [de'feza] *f* **-1.** [proteção] defence. **-2.** *JUR* defence lawyer. **-3.** *FUT* defence. **-4.** *UNIV*: **~ de tese** viva.
defeso, sa [de'fezu, za] *adj* [proibido] forbidden.
deficiência [defi'sjẽnsja] *f* **-1.** [carência] deficiency. **-2.** *MED*: **~ física/mental** physical/mental disability.
deficiente [defi'sjẽntʃi] <> *adj* deficient. <> *mf* *MED*: **~ (físico/mental)** physically/mentally disabled.
déficit ['dɛfisitʃ] *m* *ECON*: **~ público** public deficit.
deficitário, ria [defisi'tarju, rja] *adj* [orçamento, saldo] negative; [empresa] loss-making.
definhamento [defiɲa'mẽntu] *m* [debilitação] debilitation, wasting away.
definhar [4] [defi'ɲa(x)] <> *vt* to drain. <> *vi* to waste away.
definição [defini'sãw] (*pl* **-ões**) *f* **-1.** [explicação] explanation. **-2.** [decisão] decision. **-3.** [de imagem] definition.
definido, da [defi'nidu, da] *adj* **-1.** [exato, claro] defined. **-2.** *GRAM* definite.
definir [6] [defi'ni(x)] *vt* **-1.** [fixar, explicar] to define. **-2.** [decidir] to determine.
◆ **definir-se** *vp* **-1.** [pronunciar-se]: **~-se sobre/contra/a favor de** to come out for/against/in favour of. **-2.** [decidir-se] to make up one's mind.

-3. [descrever-se]: **~-se como** to describe o.s. as.

definitivamente [definiˌtʃiva'mẽntʃi] *adv* **-1.** [para sempre] definitively. **-2.** [decididamente] definitely.

definitivo, va [defini'tʃivu, va] *adj* **-1.** [final] definitive. **-2.** [permanente] permanent; **em caráter ~** definitively.

deflagrar [4] [defla'gra(x)] ◇ *vt* **-1.** [causar a explosão] to ignite. **-2.** *fig* [provocar] to inflame. ◇ *vi* **-1.** [explodir] to explode. **-2.** *fig* [irromper] to erupt.

deflorar [4] [deflo'ra(x)] *vt* [mulher] to deflower.

deformação [defoxma'sãw] (*pl* **-ões**) *f* distortion.

deformar [4] [defox'ma(x)] *vt* **-1.** [tornar disforme] to deform. **-2.** [deturpar] to distort.

◆ **deformar-se** *vp* [tornar-se disforme] to become deformed.

deformidade [defoxmi'dadʒi] *f* deformity.

defraudar [4] [defraw'da(x)] *vt* to defraud.

defrontar [4] [defrõn'ta(x)] ◇ *vi* **-1.** [estar]: **~ com** to face onto. **-2.** [deparar]: **~ com** to come upon. ◇ *vt* **-1.** [encarar] to face. **-2.** [confrontar] to compare.

◆ **defrontar-se** *vp* [deparar-se]: **~-se com** to come face to face with.

defronte [de'frõntʃi] ◇ *adv* [em frente] opposite. ◇ *prep*: **~ a/de** in front of.

defumado, da [defu'madu, da] *adj* smoked.

defumador [defuma'do(x)] *m* **-1.** [recipiente] burner. **-2.** [substância] *substance used in burners for its smell.*

defumar [4] [defu'ma(x)] *vt* **-1.** [curar] to cure. **-2.** [perfumar] to perfume.

defunto, ta [de'fũntu, ta] ◇ *adj* [morto] dead. ◇ *m, f* [cadáver] corpse.

degelar [4] [deʒe'la(x)] ◇ *vt* [descongelar] to defrost. ◇ *vi* [derreter-se] to melt.

degelo [de'ʒelu] *m* thaw.

degeneração [deʒenera'sãw] *f* **-1.** [ger] degeneration. **-2.** [depravação] corruption.

degenerado, da [deʒene'radu, da] *adj* degenerate.

degenerar [4] [deʒene'ra(x)] *vi* **-1.** [ger] to degenerate. **-2.** [depravar-se] to become depraved.

◆ **degenerar-se** *vp* [depravar-se] to be led astray.

degenerativo, va [deʒenera'tʃivu, va] *adj* degenerative.

deglutição [deglutʃi'sãw] (*pl* **-ões**) *f* swallowing.

deglutir [6] [deglu'tʃi(x)] ◇ *vt* & *vi* to swallow.

degola [de'gɔla] *f* **-1.** [decapitação] decapitation. **-2.** [demissão] large-scale redundancy. **-3.** ESP sacking.

degolar [4] [dego'la(x)] *vt* to behead.

degradação [degrada'sãw] *f* degradation.

degradante [degra'dãntʃi] *adj* [aviltante] demeaning.

degradar [4] [degra'da(x)] *vt* **-1.** [privar] to strip. **-2.** [aviltar] to demean.

◆ **degradar-se** *vp* [aviltar-se] to demean o.s.

dégradé [degra'de] *adj* gradational.

degrau [de'graw] *m* **-1.** [de escada] step. **-2.** *fig* [meio] means.

degredar [degre'da(x)] *vt* to exile.

degredo [de'gredu] *m* **-1.** [pena] exile. **-2.** [lugar] place of exile.

degringolar [4] [degrĩŋgo'la(x)] *vi* **-1.** [cair] to fall down. **-2.** *fig* [deteriorar-se] to go off the rails. **-3.** *fig* [desordenar-se - esquema] to get in a mess; [- fila, jogo] to become disorderly. **-4.** [arruinar-se] to go bankrupt.

degustação [deguʃta'sãw] (*pl* **-ões**) *f* tasting.

degustar [4] [deguʃ'ta(x)] *vt* **-1.** [provar] to taste. **-2.** [saborear] to savour.

deificar [12] [dejfi'ka(x)] *vt* to deify.

deitada [dej'tada] *f fam*: **dar uma ~** to have a lie-down.

deitado, da [dej'tadu, da] *adj* **-1.** [pessoa] lying down *(depois de verbo)*. **-2.** [objeto] set down *(depois de verbo)*.

deitar [4] [dej'ta(x)] ◇ *vt* **-1.** [pessoa] to lay down. **-2.** [objeto] to set down. ◇ *vi* [pessoa] to lie down; **~ e rolar** *fig* to call the shots.

◆ **deitar-se** *vp* [pessoa] to go to bed.

deixa ['dejʃa] *f* **-1.** [dica] hint. **-2.** TEATRO cue. **-3.** [chance] opportunity.

deixar [4] [dej'ʃa(x)] ◇ *vt* **-1.** [ger] to leave. **-2.** [abandonar] to abandon. **-3.** [demitir-se de] to resign. **-4.** [consentir]: **~ alguém fazer/que alguém faça algo** to allow sb to do sthg; **~ passar algo** to overlook sthg. **-5.** [tornar possível]: **não ~ alguém fazer algo** not to allow sb to do sthg. **-6.** [esperar] to let. **-7.** [ignorar]: **~ algo/alguém pra lá** to let sthg/sb be. **-8.** [não considerar, esquecer] to forget; **me deixa (em paz)!** leave me alone! ◇ *vi* **-1.** [parar]: **~ de fazer algo** to stop doing sthg. **-2.** [não se preocupar]: **pode ~** it's fine; **deixa pra lá!** forget it! **-3.** [expressando pedido]: **não deixe de ir no concerto!** make sure you go to the concert! **-4.** *loc*: **~ (muito) a desejar** to leave much to be desired.

◆ **deixar-se** *vp* [permitir-se]: **~-se fazer algo** to allow o.s. to do sthg.

dejeto [de'ʒɛtu] *m* dejection.

dela ['dɛla] = **de** + **ella**.

delação [dela'sãw] (*pl* **-ões**) *f* **-1.** [denúncia] accusation. **-2.** [acusação] charge.

delas ['dɛlaʃ] = **de** + **ellas**.

delatar [4] [dela'ta(x)] *vt* **-1.** [denunciar] to denounce. **-2.** [acusar] to accuse. **-3.** [informar] to inform.

◆ **delatar-se** *vp* [denunciar-se] to betray o.s.

delator, ra [dela'to(x), ra] *m, f* informer.

délavé [dela've] *adj* faded.

dele ['deli] = **de** + **ele**.

delegação [delega'sãw] (*pl* **-ões**) *f* delegation; **~ de poderes** transfer of powers.

delegacia [delega'sia] *f* police station; **~ de polícia** police station.

delegado, da [dele'gadu, da] *m, f* delegate; **~ de polícia** chief of police.

delegar [14] [dele'ga(x)] *vt* **-1.** [dar]: ~ **algo a alguém** to delegate sthg to sb. **-2.** [enviar] to send sb as a delegate.

deleitar [4] [delej'ta(x)] *vt* to delight.

◆ **deleitar-se** *vp*: ~**-se com** to rejoice in.

deleite [de'lejtʃi] *m* delight.

deleitoso, osa [delej'tozu, ɔza] *adj* delightful.

deles ['deliʃ] = **de** + **eles**.

deletar [4] [dele'ta(x)] *vt* COMPUT to delete.

deletério, ria [dele'tɛrju, rja] *adj* harmful.

delgado, da [dew'gadu, da] *adj* **-1.** [fino] slim. **-2.** [esbelto] slender.

deliberação [delibera'sãw] (*pl* **-ões**) *f* **-1.** [discussão] discussion; **em** ~ under discussion. **-2.** [decisão] decision.

deliberadamente [deliberada'mẽntʃi] *adj* [propositalmente] deliberately.

deliberado, da [delibe'radu, da] *adj* **-1.** [decidido] wilful. **-2.** [propositado] deliberate.

deliberar [4] [delibe'ra(x)] ◇ *vt* [decidir] to decide. ◇ *vi* [refletir sobre]: ~ **sobre** to ponder upon.

deliberativo, va [delibera'tʃivu, va] *adj* deliberative.

delicadeza [delika'deza] *f* **-1.** [ger] delicacy. **-2.** [leveza] fineness. **-3.** [fragilidade] fragility. **-4.** [apuro]: ~ **de detalhes** attentiveness to detail. **-5.** [cortesia] politeness.

delicado, da [deli'kadu, da] *adj* **-1.** [ger] delicate. **-2.** [sensível] urbane. **-3.** [cortês] polite.

delícia [de'lisja] *f* **-1.** [deleite] delight. **-2.** [coisa saborosa]: **ser/estar uma** ~ to be delicious. **-3.** [pessoa encantadora]: **ser uma** ~ to be a delight.

deliciar [16] [deli'sja(x)] *vt* to delight.

◆ **deliciar-se** *vp*: ~**-se com algo** to be delighted with sthg.

delicioso, osa [deli'sjozu, ɔza] *adj* **-1.** [vinho, doce] delicious. **-2.** [passeio] delightful.

delimitação [delimita'sãw] (*pl* **-ões**) *f* demarcation.

delimitar [4] [delimi'ta(x)] *vt* **-1.** [demarcar] to mark the limits of. **-2.** [restringir] to outline.

delineador [delinja'do(x)] *m* eyeliner.

delinear [15] [deli'nja(x)] *vt* to outline.

delinqüência [delĩŋ'kwẽnsja] *f* delinquency.

delinqüente [delĩŋ'kwẽntʃi] ◇ *adj* delinquent. ◇ *mf* delinquent.

delirante [deli'rãntʃi] *adj* **-1.** PSIC delirious. **-2.** [extravagante, aloucado] wild. **-3.** [maravilhoso] wonderful.

delirar [4] [deli'ra(x)] *vi* **-1.** PSIC to be delirious. **-2.** [sentir intensamente]: ~ **de algo** to be overcome with sthg.

delírio [de'lirju] *m* **-1.** PSIC delirium. **-2.** [excitação] excitement. **-3.** [êxtase] ecstasy.

delirium tremens [de'lirjũ 'trɛmẽns] *m* delirium tremens.

delito [de'litu] *m* **-1.** [falta] sin. **-2.** [crime] crime.

delonga [de'lõŋga] *f* delay; **sem mais** ~ without further delay.

delongar [14] [de'lõŋ'ga(x)] *vt* [retardar] to postpone.

◆ **delongar-se** *vp* **-1.** [demorar-se] to delay. **-2.** [prolongar-se] to prolong.

delta ['dɛwta] *m* delta.

demagogia [demago'ʒia] *f* demagogy.

demagógico, ca [dema'gɔʒiku, ka] *adj* demagogic.

demagogo, ga [dema'gogu, ga] *m, f* demagogue.

demais [de'majʃ] ◇ *adv* **-1.** [em demasia, muitíssimo] too much. **-2.** *fam* [ótimo]: **estar/ser** ~ to be amazing. ◇ *pron* [outros]: **os/as** ~ the others.

demanda [de'mãnda] *f* **-1.** ECON demand. **-2.** JUR lawsuit. **-3.** [disputa] dispute. **-4.** [pedido] request.

demandar [4] [demãn'da(x)] *vt* **-1.** JUR to sue. **-2.** [exigir] to demand. **-3.** [pedir] to request.

demão [de'mãw] (*pl* **-s**) *f* coat.

demarcação [demaxka'sãw] (*pl* **-ões**) *f* **-1.** [delimitação] demarcation. **-2.** [separação] boundary.

demarcado, da [demax'kadu, da] *adj* **-1.** [delimitado] demarcated. **-2.** [separado] set apart.

demarcar [12] [demax'ka(x)] *vt* **-1.** [delimitar] to demarcate. **-2.** [fixar] to define. **-3.** [separar] to distinguish between.

demarcatório, ria [demaxka'tɔrju, rja] *adj* boundary *(antes de subst)*.

demasia [dema'zia] *f* excess; **em** ~ in excess.

demasiadamente [demazjada'mẽntʃi] *adv* **-1.** [demais] excessively. **-2.** [muito] too.

demasiado, da [dema'zjadu, da] ◇ *adj* excessive. ◇ *adv* too much; **por** ~ too.

demência [de'mẽnsja] *f* **-1.** MED dementia. **-2.** [loucura] insanity.

demente [de'mẽntʃi] *adj* **-1.** MED demented. **-2.** [louco] insane.

demérito, ta [de'mɛritu, ta] *adj* unworthy.

◆ **demérito** *m* [desmérito] unworthiness.

demissão [demi'sãw] (*pl* **-ões**) *f* **-1.** [solicitado pelo empregador] dismissal. **-2.** [solicitado pelo empregado] resignation; **pedir** ~ to tender one's resignation.

demissionário, ria [demisjo'narju, rja] *adj* resigning.

demitir [6] [demi'tʃi(x)] *vt* to dismiss.

◆ **demitir-se** *vp* to resign.

democracia [demokra'sia] *f* democracy.

democrata [demo'krata] *mf* democrat.

democrático, ca [demo'kratʃiku, ka] *adj* **-1.** [relativo a democracia] democratic. **-2.** [indiferente às classes sociais] egalitarian.

democratização [demokratʃiza'sãw] *f* democratization.

democratizar [4] [demokratʃi'za(x)] *f* **-1.** [tornar democrático] to democratize. **-2.** [popularizar] to make accessible.

◆ **democratizar-se** *vp* [tornar-se democrático] to become democratic.

démodé [demo'de] *adj* outmoded.

demografia [demogra'fia] *f* demography.

demográfico, ca [demo'grafiku, ka] *adj* demographic.
demolição [demoli'sãw] (*pl* **-ões**) *f* **-1.** demolition. **-2.** *fig* [ger] de reputação] destruction; [- de obstáculo] elimination.
demolidor, ra [demo'lido(x), ra] ◇ *adj* demolition *(antes de subst)*. ◇ *m,f* demolition expert.
demolir [79] [demo'li(x)] *vt* **-1.** [destruir] to demolish. **-2.** *fig* [- reputação] to destroy; [- obstáculo] to overcome.
demoníaco, ca [demo'niaku, ka] *adj* demonic.
demônio [de'monju] *m* demon.
demonstração [demõnʃtra'sãw] (*pl* **-ões**) *f* **-1.** [ger] demonstration. **-2.** [apresentação] display.
demonstrar [4] [demõnʃ'tra(x)] *vt* **-1.** [ger] to demonstrate. **-2.** [afeto, antipatia *etc*] to show. **-3.** [habilidades, talentos] to display.
◆ **demonstrar-se** *vp* [revelar-se] to show o.s.
demonstrativo, va [demõnʃtra'tʃivu, va] *adj* demonstrative.
demonstrável [demõnʃ'travew] (*pl* **-eis**) *adj* demonstrable.
demora [de'mɔra] *f* [atraso] delay; **sem** ~ without delay.
demorado, da [demo'radu, da] *adj* delayed.
demorar [4] [demo'ra(x)] ◇ *vt* [retardar] to delay. ◇ *vi* **-1.** [tardar] to be late; ~ **a fazer algo** to take a long time to do sthg. **-2.** [permanecer] to stay.
◆ **demorar-se** *vp* **-1.** [tardar] to be late; **~-se a fazer algo** to take a long time to do sthg. **-2.** [permanecer] to remain.
demover [5] [demo've(x)] *vt* **-1.** [dissuadir]: ~ **alguém de algo/fazer algo** to dissuade sb from sthg/doing sthg. **-2.** [remover] to move.
◆ **demover-se** *vp* [dissuadir-se]: **~-se de algo** to dissuade o.s. from sthg.
DENARC (*abrev de* **Departamento de Investigações sobre Narcóticos**) *m Brazilian police narcotics department.*
DENATRAN (*abrev de* **Departamento Nacional de Trânsito**) *m Brazilian national department responsible for transport law.*
dendê [dẽn'de] *m* **-1.** *BOT* palm. **-2.** [azeite] palm oil.
denegrir [58] [dene'gri(x)] *vt* [escurecer] to blacken.
dengo ['dẽngu] *m* **-1.** [faceirice] foppery. **-2.** [manha] affectation.
dengoso, osa [dẽn'gozu, ɔza] *adj* whining.
dengue ['dẽŋgi] *f MED* dengue.
denodado, da [deno'dadu, da] *adj* **-1.** [ousado] daring. **-2.** [impetuoso] impetuous.
denominação [denomina'sãw] (*pl* **-ões**) *f* **-1.** [nomeação] name. **-2.** [designação] designation. **-3.** *REL* denomination.
denominador, ra [denomina'do(x), ra] *adj* designatory.
◆ **denominador** *m MAT* denominator; ~ **comum** common denominator.
denominar [4] [denomi'na(x)] *vt* **-1.** [nomear] to name. **-2.** [designar] to designate.
◆ **denominar-se** *vp* to be called.
denotar [4] [deno'ta(x)] *vt* **-1.** [indicar] to indicate. **-2.** [significar] to denote.
densidade [dẽnsi'dadʒi] *f* density; **de alta/dupla** ~ high/double density.
denso, sa ['dẽnsu, sa] *adj* **-1.** [ger] dense. **-2.** [espesso] thick.
dentada [dẽn'tada] *f* bite.
dentado, da [dẽn'tadu, da] *adj* serrated.
dentadura [dẽnta'dura] *f* **-1.** [natural] set of teeth. **-2.** [postiça] denture.
dental [dẽn'taw] (*pl* **-ais**) *adj* dental; **pasta** ~ toothpaste.
dentário, ria [dẽn'tarju, rja] *adj* dental.
dente ['dẽntʃi] *m* **-1.** [ger] tooth; ~ **de leite** milk tooth; ~ **de siso** wisdom tooth; **falar entre os ~s** to mutter. **-2.** [de elefante] tusk. **-3.** [alho] clove.
dente-de-leão [dẽntʃidʒi'lãw] (*pl* **dentes-de-leão**) *m* dandelion.
dentição [dẽntʃi'sãw] *f* **-1.** [processo] dentition. **-2.** [as dentes] teething; **primeira/segunda** ~ milk/second teeth.
dentifrício, cia [dẽntʃi'frisju, sja] *adj* dental.
◆ **dentifrício** *m* toothpaste.
dentista [dẽn'tʃiʃta] *mf* dentist.
dentre ['dẽntri] *prep* among.
dentro ['dẽntru] ◇ *adv* in; **aí/lá** ~ in there. ◇ *prep* **-1.**: ~ **de** [no interior de] inside; [no tempo] within; **por** ~ [na parte interna] inside. **-2.** *loc*: **estar por** ~ **(de algo)** *fam* to be in touch (with sthg); **não dei uma** ~ *fam* I didn't get a single thing right.
dentuço, ça [dẽn'tusu, sa] ◇ *adj* buck-toothed. ◇ *m, f* [pessoa] buck-toothed person.
◆ **dentuça** *f* [arcada] buck-teeth.
denúncia [de'nũnsja] *f* **-1.** [acusação] accusation. **-2.** [à polícia] report. **-3.** [*JUR* - de pessoa, crime] condemnation; [- de contrato] termination; ~ **vazia** unfettered right to forfeiture.
denunciar [16] [denũn'sja(x)] *vt* **-1.** [acusar] to denounce. **-2.** [divulgar] to expose. **-3.** [*JUR* - pessoa, crime] to condemn; [- contrato] to terminate. **-4.** [evidenciar] to reveal.
◆ **denunciar-se** *vp* **-1.** [delatar-se] to confess. **-2.** [trair-se] to betray o.s.
deparar [4] [depa'ra(x)] *vi*: ~ **com** to come across.
departamental [depaxtamẽn'taw] (*pl* **-ais**) *adj* departmental.
departamento [departa'mẽntu] *m* department.
depauperado, da [depawpe'radu, da] *adj* **-1.** [empobrecido] impoverished. **-2.** [enfraquecido] exhausted.
depauperar [4] [depawpe'ra(x)] *vt* **-1.** [empobrecer] to impoverish. **-2.** [debilitar] to weaken.
◆ **depauperar-se** *vp* [debilitar-se] to become weak.
depenar [4] [depe'na(x)] *vt* **-1.** [ave] to pluck. **-2.** [pessoa] to lift. **-3.** [casa] to clean out.
dependência [depẽn'dẽnsja] *f* **-1.** [ger] dependency. **-2.** [cômodo] room.
dependente [depẽn'dẽntʃi] ◇ *adj* [subordinado]

dependent. <> *mf* dependant.
depender [5] [depẽn'de(x)] *vi* **-1.** [ger]: ~ **de** to depend upon. **-2.** [financeiramente]: ~ **de** to be dependent upon. **-3.** [de droga]: ~ **de** to be dependent on.
dependurar [4] [depẽndu'ra(x)] *vt* [pendurar]: ~ **algo (em algo)** to hang sthg (on sthg).
◆ **dependurar-se** *vp*: **~-se em algo** to hang from sthg.
depilação [depila'sãw] (*pl* **-ões**) *f* depilation.
depilador, ra [depila'do(x), ra] *m, f beautician who does hair-removal.*
depilar [4] [depi'la(x)] *vt* to remove hair from.
◆ **depilar-se** *vp* **-1.** [com cera - na estética] to have a wax; [- em casa] to wax. **-2.** [com lâmina] to shave.
depilatório, ria [depila'tɔrju, rja] *adj* hair-removing.
◆ **depilatório** *m* hair removal cream/wax.
deplorar [4] [deplo'ra(x)] *vt* to lament.
deplorável [deplo'ravew] (*pl* **-eis**) *adj* **-1.** [lamentável] lamentable. **-2.** [detestável] deplorable.
depoente [depo'ẽntʃi] *m JUR* witness.
depoimento [depoj'mẽntu] *m* **-1.** [ger] statement. **-2.** [ato] testimony.
depois [de'pojʃ] <> *adv* **-1.** [posteriormente] after; **logo** ~ straight after. **-2.** [além disso] besides. <> *prep*: ~ **de fazer algo** after doing sthg.
◆ **depois que** *loc conj* after.
depor [45] [de'po(x)] <> *vt* **-1.** [colocar] to put down. **-2.** [destituir] to depose. **-3.** *JUR*: ~ **que** to testify that. **-4.** [expressar] to express. <> *vi JUR*: ~ **(a favor/contra)** to testify (for/against).
◆ **depor-se** *vp* [depositar-se] to settle.
deportação [depoxta'sãw] (*pl* **-ões**) *f* deportation.
deportar [4] [depox'ta(x)] *vt* to deport.
deposição [depozi'sãw] (*pl* **-ões**) *f* [destituição] deposition.
depositante [depozi'tãntʃi] *mf* depositor.
depositar [4] [depozi'ta(x)] *vt* to deposit.
◆ **depositar-se** *vp* [assentar] to settle.
depositário, ria [depozi'tarju, rja] *m, f* **-1.** [quem recebe em depósito] depositary. **-2.** *fig* [confidente] confidant.
depósito [de'pɔzitu] *m* **-1.** [ger] deposit. **-2.** [reservatório] depository.
depravação [deprava'sãw] (*pl* **-ões**) *f* **-1.** [perversão] perversion. **-2.** [degeneração] degeneration.
depravado, da [depra'vadu, da] <> *adj* depraved. <> *m, f* depraved person.
depravar [4] [depra'va(x)] *vt* **-1.** [corromper] to corrupt. **-2.** [estragar] to ruin.
◆ **depravar-se** *vp* [corromper-se] to become corrupted.
depreciação [depresja'sãw] (*pl* **-ões**) *f* [desvalorização] depreciation.
depreciar [16] [depre'sja(x)] *vt* **-1.** [desvalorizar] to devalue. **-2.** [subestimar] to undervalue.
◆ **depreciar-se** *vp* **-1.** [desvalorizar-se] to fall in value. **-2.** [subestimar-se] to underestimate o.s.
depredação [depreda'sãw] (*pl* **-ões**) *f* **-1.** [destruição] destruction. **-2.** [pilhagem] robbery.
depredador, ra [depreda'do(x), ra] <> *adj* harmful, damaging. <> *m, f* damaging person.
depredar [4] [depre'da(x)] *vt* **-1.** [destruir] to destroy. **-2.** [saquear] to loot.
depreender [5] [deprjẽn'de(x)] *vt* **-1.** [compreender] to conclude. **-2.** [deduzir] to deduce.
depressa [de'prɛsa] *adv* quickly.
depressão [depre'sãw] (*pl* **-ões**) *f* **-1.** *PSIC* depression. **-2.** [en terreno, superfície] dip. **-3.** *fig* [abatimento] despondency.
depressivo, va [depre'sivu, va] *adj* depressive.
deprimente [depri'mẽntʃi] *adj* depressing.
deprimido, da [depri'midu, da] *adj* depressed.
deprimir [6] [depri'mi(x)] *vt* to depress.
◆ **deprimir-se** *vp* to become depressed.
depto (*abrev de* **departamento**) *m* dept.
depuração [depura'sãw] (*pl* **-ões**) *f* purification.
depurar [4] [depu'ra(x)] *vt* to purify.
◆ **depurar-se** *vp* to become purified.
deputado, da [depu'tadu, da] *m, f* **-1.** *POL* deputy. **-2.** [delegado] representative.
deque ['dɛki] *m* decking.
DER (*abrev de* **Departamento de Estradas de Rodagem**) *m Brazilian highways department.*
deriva [de'riva] *f* drift; **à ~** drifting; **ir à ~** to drift.
derivação [deriva'sãw] (*pl* **-ões**) *f* **-1.** *GRAM* derivation. **-2.** *fig* [origem] origin.
derivado, da [deri'vadu, da] *adj* [proveniente]: ~ **de** derived from.
◆ **derivado** *m* derivative.
◆ **derivada** *f MAT* derivative.
derivar [4] [deri'va(x)] *vi* **-1.** [resultar]: ~ **de** to derive from. **-2.** [ficar à deriva] to drift. **-3.** *GRAM*: ~ **de** to stem from.
derivativo, va [deriva'tʃivu, va] *adj* derivative.
◆ **derivativo** *m* [distração] distraction.
dermatologia [dexmatolo'ʒia] *f* dermatology.
dermatológico, ca [dexmato'lɔgiku, ka] *adj* dermatological.
dermatologista [dexmatolo'ʒiʃta] *mf* dermatologist.
derradeiro, ra [dexa'dejru, ra] *adj* final.
derramamento [dexama'mẽntu] *m* **-1.** [de água, leite] spillage. **-2.** [de lágrimas] flow; ~ **de sangre** bloodshed.
derramar [4] [dexa'ma(x)] *vt* **-1.** [ger] to spill **-2.** [espalhar] to strew
◆ **derramar-se** *vp* [verter] to spill.
derrame [de'xãmi] *m* **-1.** [de líquido] spillage. **-2.** [de lágrimas, sangue] flow. **-3.** *MED* haemorrhage; ~ **cerebral** brain haemorrhage.
derrapagem [dexa'paʒẽ] (*pl* **-ns**) *f* skid.
derrapar [4] [dexa'pa(x)] *vi* to skid.
derredor [dexe'do(x)] *adv fml*: **em ~ (de)** around.
derreter [5] [dexe'te(x)] <> *vt* to melt. <> *vi* [liquefazer-se] to melt.
◆ **derreter-se** *vp* **-1.** *fig* [comover-se]: ~ **(com algo)** to be moved (by sthg). **-2.** *fig* [apaixonar-se]: **~-se todo (por alguém)** to fall completely (for sb).
derretido, da [dexe'tʃidu, da] *adj* **-1.** [liquefeito]

melted. **-2.** *fig* [comovido] moved. **-3.** *fig* [apaixonado] besotted.
derrocada [dexo'kada] *f* **-1.** [desmoronamento] destruction. **-2.** [ruína] ruin.
derrota [de'xɔta] *f* **-1.** [fracasso] defeat. **-2.** NÁUT course.
derrotado, da [dexo'tadu, da] *adj* defeated.
derrotar [4] [dexo'ta(x)] *vt* to defeat.
derrotista [dexo'tʃiʃta] <> *adj* defeatist. <> *mf* defeatist.
derrubar [4] [dexu'ba(x)] *vt* **-1.** [fazer cair] to knock down. **-2.** [vencer] to overcome. **-3.** [destituir] to overthrow. **-4.** [destruir] to defame. **-5.** [prostrar] to lay low. **-6.** *fam* [prejudicar] to knock.
desabafar [4] [dʒizaba'fa(x)] <> *vt*: ~ **algo (com alguém)** to share sthg (with sb). <> *vi*: ~ **(com alguém)** to open up (to sb).
◆ **desabafar-se** *vp*: **~-se (com alguém)** to open up (to sb).
desabafo [dʒiza'bafu] *m* outpouring.
desabalado, da [dʒizaba'ladu, da] *adj* **-1.** [excessivo] enormous. **-2.** [espavorido]: **sair/correr** ~ to go/run headlong.
desabamento [dʒizaba'mẽntu] *m* collapse.
desabar [4] [dʒiza'ba(x)] *vi* **-1.** [ruir] to tumble down. **-2.** [cair com força] to fall heavily.
desabitado, da [dʒizabi'tadu, da] *adj* unoccupied.
desabituar [4] [dʒizabi'twa(x)] *vt*: ~ **alguém de algo/de fazer algo** to wean sb off sthg/doing sthg.
◆ **desabituar-se** *vp*: **~-se de algo/de fazer algo** to wean o.s. off sthg/doing sthg.
desabonar [4] [dʒizabo'na(x)] *vt* to discredit.
desabotoar [20] [dʒizabo'twa(x)] *vt* to unbutton.
◆ **desabotoar-se** *vp* to open up.
desabrigado, da [dʒizabri'gadu, da] <> *adj* **-1.** [sem casa] homeless. **-2.** [exposto] unsheltered. <> *m, f* [pessoa] homeless person; **os ~s** the homeless.
desabrigar [dʒiza'briga(x)] *vt* [tirar do abrigo] to leave without shelter.
desabrigo [dʒiza'brigu] *m* **-1.** [falta de abrigo] lack of shelter. **-2.** *fig* [abandono] lack of protection.
desabrochar [4] [dʒizabro'ʃa(x)] *vi* **-1.** [flor] to bloom. **-2.** *fig* [pessoa] to blossom.
desacatar [4] [dʒizaka'ta(x)] <> *vt* **-1.** [afrontar] to disrespect. **-2.** [desprezar] to disregard. <> *vi* *fam* [causar espanto] to stun.
desacato [dʒiza'katu] *m* **-1.** [afronta] disrespect. **-2.** [desprezo] disregard. **-3.** *fam* [pessoa]: **ser um** ~ to be a show-off.
desaceleração [dʒizaselera'sãw] *f* deceleration.
desacelerar [4] [dʒizasele'ra(x)] *vt* to slow down.
desacerto [dʒiza'sextu] *m* **-1.** [erro] mistake. **-2.** [tolice] blunder.
desacomodar [4] [dʒizakomo'da(x)] *vt* **-1.** [desorganizar] to disarrange. **-2.** [desalojar] to ask to leave.
desacompanhado, da [dʒizakõnpa'ɲadu, da] *adj* unaccompanied.
desaconselhar [4] [dʒizakõnse'ʎa(x)] *vt*: ~ **algo (a alguém)** to warn (sb) against sthg.
desaconselhável [dʒizakõnse'ʎavɛw] (*pl* **-eis**) *adj* not recommended *(depois de verbo)*.
desacordado, da [dʒizakox'dadu, da] *adj* senseless.
desacordo [dʒiza'koxdu] *m* **-1.** [falta de acordo] disagreement. **-2.** [desarmonia] disharmony.
desacostumado, da [dʒizakoʃtu'madu, da] *adj*: ~ **(a)** unaccustomed (to).
desacostumar [4] [dʒizakoʃtu'ma(x)] *vt*: ~ **alguém de algo** to wean sb off sthg.
◆ **desacostumar-se** *vp* [desabituar-se]: **~-se de algo/de fazer algo** to wean o.s. off sthg/doing sthg.
desacreditado, da [dʒizakredʒi'tadu, da] *adj* discredited.
desacreditar [4] [dʒizakredi'ta(x)] *vt* to discredit.
◆ **desacreditar-se** *vp* [perder o crédito] to become discredited.
desafeto [dʒiza'fɛtu] *m* opponent.
desafiador, ra [dʒizafja'do(x), ra] <> *adj* challenging. <> *m, f* challenger.
desafiar [16] [dʒiza'fja(x)] *vt* **-1.** [propor luta] to challenge. **-2.** [afrontar] to defy.
desafinação [dʒizafina'sãw] (*pl* **-ões**) *f* disharmony.
desafinado, da [dʒizafi'nadu, da] *adj* out of tune.
desafinar [4] [dʒizafi'na(x)] <> *vt*: ~ **un instrumento** to put an instrument out of tune. <> *vi* to be out of tune.
desafio [dʒiza'fiw] *m* **-1.** [provocação] challenge. **-2.** LITER & MÚS *literary/musical competition between two people.*
desafivelar [4] [dʒizafive'la(x)] *vt* to unclasp.
desafogado, da [dʒizafo'gadu, da] *adj* **-1.** [pessoa - de preocupações, de opressão] relieved; [- de trabalho] unencumbered. **-2.** [trânsito] clear.
desafogar [14] [dʒizafo'ga(x)] <> *vt* **-1.** [desoprimir - garganta] to clear; [- espírito] to free. **-2.** [desabafar] to relieve. **-3.** [aliviar]: ~ **alguém (de algo)** to relieve sb (of sthg). <> *vi* [desabafar-se]: ~ **(com alguém)** to open up (to sb).
◆ **desafogar-se** *vp* [desabafar-se] to unburden o.s.
desafogo [dʒiza'fogu] *m* **-1.** [alívio] relief; **dar ~ a algo** to relieve sthg. **-2.** [de trabalho] break.
desaforado, da [dʒizafo'radu, da] *adj* insulting.
desaforo [dʒiza'foru] *m* insult; **eu não levo ~ para casa** I'm not going to take it lying down.
desafortunado, da [dʒizafoxtu'nadu, da] *adj* unfortunate.
desagasalhado, da [dʒizagaza'ʎadu, da] *adj* unsheltered.
deságio [de'zaʒju] *m* ECON discount.
desagradar [4] [dʒizagra'da(x)] <> *vt* to displease. <> *vi*: ~ **a alguém** to displease sb.
◆ **desagradar-se** *vp* to be displeased.
desagradável [dʒizagra'davew] (*pl* **-eis**) *adj* unpleasant.

desagrado [dʒiza'gradu] *m* displeasure.
desagravo [dʒiza'gravu] *m* **-1.** [reparação de agravo] recompense; **de ~** to make amends. **-2.** *JUR* reparation.
desagregação [dʒizagrega'sãw] (*pl* **-ões**) *f* **-1.** [dissolução] break-up. **-2.** [separação] division.
desagregar [14] [dʒizagre'ga(x)] *vt* **-1.** [dissolver] to dissolve. **-2.** [separar] to split.
◆ **desagregar-se** *vp* [dissociar-se] to split.
desaguar [22] [dʒiza'gwa(x)] ◇ *vi* [vazar-se]: **~ em** to flow into. ◇ *vt* [drenar] to drain.
desajeitado, da [dʒizaʒej'tadu, da] *adj* clumsy.
desajuizado, da [dʒizaʒwi'zadu, -da] *adj* senseless.
desajustado, da [dʒizaʒuʃ'tadu, da] ◇ *adj* **-1.** *PSIC* maladjusted. **-2.** [desajuntado] in need of adjustment. ◇ *m, f PSIC* maladjusted person.
desajustamento [dʒizaʒuʃta'mẽntu] *m PSIC* maladjustment.
desajustar [4] [dʒizaʒuʃ'ta(x)] *vt* **-1.** *PSIC* to disturb. **-2.** [desajuntar] to undo.
desajuste [dʒiza'ʒuʃtʃi] *m* **-1.** *PSIC* maladjustment. **-2.** [de peças, máquina] loosening.
desalentado, da [dʒizalẽn'tadu, da] *adj* discouraged.
desalentar [4] [dʒizalẽn'ta(x)] ◇ *vt* to discourage. ◇ *vi* to lose heart.
◆ **desalentar-se** *vp* to become discouraged.
desalento [dʒiza'lẽntu] *m* discouragement.
desalinhado, da [dʒizali'ɲadu, da] *adj* dishevelled.
desalinhar [dʒiza'liɲa(x)] *vt* **-1.** [tirar do alinhamento] to break up. **-2.** [desarrumar] to mess up.
desalinho [dʒiza'liɲu] *m* dishevelment.
desalmado, da [dʒizaw'madu, da] *adj* soulless.
desalojar [4] [dʒizalo'ʒa(x)] ◇ *vt*: **~ alguém de** to remove sb from. ◇ *vi* to quit.
desamarrar [4] [dʒizama'xa(x)] ◇ *vt* [desfazer] to untie. ◇ *vi NÁUT* to lift anchor.
desamarrotar [4] [dʒizamaxo'ta(x)] *vt* to smooth.
desamassar [4] [dʒizama'sa(x)] *vt* to straighten out.
desambientado, da [dʒizãnbjẽn'tadu, da] *adj* disorientated.
desamor [dʒiza'mo(x)] *m* antipathy.
desamparado, da [dʒizãnpa'radu, da] *adj* **-1.** [pessoa - abandonado] abandoned; [- sem ajuda] unassisted. **-2.** [lugar] abandoned.
desamparar [4] [dʒizãnpa'ra(x)] *vt* [abandonar] to abandon.
desamparo [dʒizãn'paru] *m* **-1.** [abandono] abandonment. **-2.** [falta de ajuda] helplessness.
desandar [4] [dʒizãn'da(x)] *vi* **-1.** *fam* [clara, maionese] to separate. **-2.** [começar]: **~ a rir** to burst out laughing; **~ a chorar** to burst into tears; **~ a correr** to break into a run; **~ a falar** to start speaking.
desanimação [dʒizanima'sãw] *f* dejection.
desanimado, da [dʒizani'madu, da] *adj* despondent.
desanimador, ra [dʒizanima'do(x), ra] *adj* disheartening.
desanimar [4] [dʒizani'ma(x)] ◇ *vt* **-1.** [fazer perder o ânimo]: **~ alguém** to dishearten sb. **-2.** [desencorajar]: **~ alguém de fazer algo** to discourage sb from doing sthg. ◇ *vi* **-1.** [perder o ânimo] to become disheartened; **~ de fazer algo** to become disheartened about doing sthg. **-2.** [ser desencorajador] to be discouraging.
desânimo [dʒi'zãnimu] *m* despondency.
desanuviar [16] [dʒizanu'vja(x)] *vt* **-1.** [céu] to clear. **-2.** *fig* [pessoa, mente] to calm.
◆ **desanuviar-se** *vp* **-1.** [céu] to clear. **-2.** *fig* [pessoa, mente] to become calm.
desaparafusar [4] [dʒizaparafu'za(x)] *vt* to unscrew.
desaparecer [25] [dʒizapare'se(x)] *vi* to disappear.
desaparecido, da [dʒizapare'sidu, da] ◇ *adj* missing. ◇ *m, f* [pessoa] missing person.
desaparecimento [dʒizaparesi'mẽntu] *m* **-1.** [sumiço] disappearance. **-2.** [falecimento] loss.
desapegado, da [dʒizape'gadu, da] *adj* detached.
desapegar [14] [dʒizape'ga(x)] *vt*: **~ alguém de algo/alguém** to detach sb from sthg/sb.
◆ **desapegar-se** *vp*: **~-se de algo/alguém** to detach o.s. from sthg/sb.
desapego [dʒiza'pegu] *m* **-1.** [desamor] lack of love. **-2.** [indiferença] indifference.
desapertar [4] [dʒizapex'ta(x)] *vt* to loosen.
desapiedado, da [dʒizapje'dadu, da] *adj* ruthless.
desapontador, ra [dʒizapõnta'do(x), ra] *adj* disappointing.
desapontamento [dʒizapõnta'mẽntu] *m* disappointment.
desapontar [4] [dʒizapõn'ta(x)] *vt* to disappoint.
◆ **desapontar-se** *vp* to be disappointed.
desapossar [4] [dʒizapo'sa(x)] *vt*: **~ alguém de algo** to deprive sb of sthg.
◆ **desapossar-se** *vp*: **~-se de algo** to deprive o.s. of sthg.
desapreço [dʒiza'presu] *m* discontent.
desaprender [5] [dʒizaprẽn'de(x)] ◇ *vt* to forget. ◇ *vi*: **~ a fazer algo** to forget how to do sthg.
desapropriação [dʒizaproprja'sãw] (*pl* **-ões**) *f* dispossession.
desapropriar [16] [dʒizapro'prja(x)] *vt* **-1.** [desapossar]: **~ alguém de algo** to deprive sb of sthg. **-2.** [expropriar]: **~ algo (de alguém)** to expropriate sthg (from sb).
desaprovação [dʒizaprova'sãw] (*pl* **-ões**) *f* disapproval.
desaprovar [4] [dʒizapro'va(x)] *vt* **-1.** [reprovar] to disapprove. **-2.** [censurar] to censure.
desarmado, da [dʒizax'madu, da] *adj* **-1.** [ger] disarmed. **-2.** [sem arma] unarmed.
desarmamento [dʒizaxma'mẽntu] *m* disarmament.

desarmar [4] [dʒizax'ma(x)] *vt* **-1.** [ger] to disarm. **-2.** [barraca, brinqueda] to take down. **-3.** [arma] to disable.
◆ **desarmar-se** *vp* [criminoso] to hand over one's arms.
desarmonia [dʒizaxmo'nia] *f* **-1.** [falta de harmonia] disharmony. **-2.** *fig* [divergência] discord.
desarraigar [14] [dʒizaxaj'ga(x)] *vt* **-1.** [arrancar] to uproot. **-2.** [extinguir] to stamp out.
desarranjado, da [dʒizaxãn'ʒadu, da] *adj* **-1.** [desarrumado] untidy. **-2.** *MED*: **estar ~** to be queasy.
desarranjar [4] [dʒizaxãn'ʒa(x)] *vt* [desarrumar] to make untidy.
desarranjo [dʒiza'xãnʒu] *m* disorder.
desarregaçar [dʒizaxega'sa(x)] *vt* [mangas] to roll down.
desarrumado, da [dʒizaxu'madu, da] *adj* untidy.
desarrumar [4] [dʒizaxu'ma(x)] *vt* **-1.** [ger] to make untidy. **-2.** [mala] to unpack.
desarticulado, da [dʒizaxtʃiku'ladu, da] *adj* **-1.** [deslocado] dislocated. **-2.** [desfeito] broken up.
desarticular [4] [dʒizaxtʃiku'la(x)] *vt* to dislocate.
desarvorado, da [dʒizaxvo'radu, da] *adj* disorientated.
desassociar [16] [dʒizaso'sja(x)] *vt*: **~ algo/alguém (de)** to dissociate sthg/sb (from).
◆ **desassociar-se** *vp*: **~-se (de)** to dissociate o.s. (from).
desassossego [dʒizaso'segu] *m* uneasiness.
desastrado, da [dʒizaʃ'tradu, da] *adj* clumsy.
desastre [dʒi'zaʃtri] *m* **-1.** [acidente] accident. **-2.** *fig* [fracasso]: **ser um ~** to be a disaster.
desastroso, osa [dʒizaʃ'trozu, ɔza] *adj* disastrous.
desatar [4] [dʒiza'ta(x)] ◇ *vt* **-1.** [desfazer] to undo. **-2.** [desprender] to loosen. ◇ *vi* [começar]: **~ a fazer algo** to start to do sthg suddenly.
desatarraxar [4] [dʒizataxa'ʃa(x)] *vt* to undo.
desatenção [dʒizatẽn'sãw] *f* **-1.** [distração] lack of attention. **-2.** [descortesia] lack of courtesy.
desatento, ta [dʒiza'tẽntu, ta] *adj* inattentive.
desatinado, da [dʒizatʃi'nadu, da] ◇ *adj* mad. ◇ *m, f* mad person.
desatinar [4] [dʒizatʃi'na(x)] ◇ *vt* to drive mad. ◇ *vi* to go mad.
desatino [dʒiza'tʃinu] *m* idiocy.
desativar [4] [dʒizatʃi'va(x)] *vt* **-1.** [tornar inativo] to close down. **-2.** [desmontar] to deactivate.
desatolar [4] [dʒizato'la(x)] *vt* to pull out of the mud.
desatrelar [4] [dʒizatre'la(x)] *vt* **-1.** [cão] to unleash. **-2.** [cavalo] to unharness.
desatualizado, da [dʒizatwali'zadu, da] *adj* out-of-date.
desautorizar [4] [dʒizawtori'za(x)] *vt* **-1.** [não permitir] to disallow. **-2.** [fazer perder a autoridade] to discredit.
desavença [dʒiza'vẽnsa] *f* **-1.** [briga] enmity. **-2.** [dissensão] dissent.
desavergonhado, da [dʒizavexgo'ɲadu, da] *adj* unashamed.
desavisado, da [dʒizavi'zadu, da] *adj* not made aware.
desbancar [12] [dʒiʒbãŋ'ka(x)] *vt*: **~ alguém (em algo)** to outdo sb (at sthg).
desbaratar [4] [dʒiʒbara'ta(x)] *vt* **-1.** [dissipar]: **~ algo (em algo)** to squander sthg (on sthg). **-2.** [arruinar] to destroy. **-3.** [vencer] to defeat.
desbastar [4] [dʒiʒbaʃ'ta(x)] *vt* to thin (out).
desbocado, da [dʒiʒbo'kadu, da] *adj fig* lewd.
desbotado, da [dʒiʒbo'tadu, da] *adj* faded.
desbotar [4] [dʒiʒbo'ta(x)] *vt* to fade.
desbragadamente [dʒiʒbragada'mẽntʃi] *adv* shamelessly.
desbravador, ra [dʒiʒbrava'do(x), ra] *m, f* **-1.** [de terra, mata] explorer. **-2.** [de animais] tamer.
desbravar [4] [dʒiʒbra'va(x)] *vt* **-1.** [terras, matas] to explore. **-2.** [animais selvagens] to tame. **-3.** [cavalo] to break in.
desbundante [dʒiʒbũn'dãntʃi] *adj fam* amazing.
desbundar [4] [dʒiʒbũn'da(x)] *vi fam* [perder compostura] to freak out.
desbunde [dʒiʒ'bũndʒi] *m fam* sensation.
desburocratizar [4] [dʒiʒburokratʃi'za(x)] *vt* to get rid of bureacracy from.
descabelado, da [dʒiʃkabe'ladu, da] *adj* with untidy hair *(depois de subst)*.
descabelar [4] [dʒiʃkabe'la(x)] *vt fam* to ruffle the hair of.
◆ **descabelar-se** *vp fam* to ruffle one's hair.
descabido, da [dʒiʃka'bidu, da] *adj* **-1.** [absurdo] ridiculous. **-2.** [impróprio] inappropriate.
descadeirado, da [dʒiʃkadej'radu, da] *adj* **-1.** [com dor nas cadeiras]: **estar ~** to have painful hips. **-2.** [exausto] exhausted.
descalabro [dʒiʃka'labru] *m* disaster, ruin.
descalçar [13] [dʒiʃkaw'sa(x)] *vt* to take off.
◆ **descalçar-se** *vp* to take off one's shoes/gloves.
descalço, ça [dʒiʃ'kawsu, sa] *adj* barefoot.
descambar [4] [dʒiʃkãn'ba(x)] *vi* **-1.** [para o lado]: **~ para** to topple towards. **-2.** [degenerar]: **~ em** to degenerate into.
descampado, da [dʒiʃkãn'padu, da] *adj* uninhabited.
◆ **descampado** *m* open country.
descansado, da [dʒiʃkãn'sadu, da] *adj* **-1.** [tranqüilo] calm. **-2.** [lento] slow.
descansar [4] [dʒiʃkãn'sa(x)] ◇ *vt* **-1.** [ger] to rest. **-2.** *fig* [tranqüilizar] to calm. ◇ *vi* **-1.** [repousar] to rest. **-2.** *fig* [tranqüilizar-se] to calm down. **-3.** *ant & fig* [morrer] to be at rest.
descanso [dʒiʃ'kãnsu] *m* **-1.** [repouso] rest. **-2.** [folga] break. **-3.** [para travessa etc] trivet.
descaracterizar [4] [dʒiʃkara(k)teri'za(x)] *vt* to destroy the character of.
descarado, da [dʒiʃka'radu, da] ◇ *adj* shameless. ◇ *m, f* shameless person.

descaramento [dʒiʃkara'mẽntu] *m* shamelessness.

descarga [dʒiʃ'kaxga] *f* **-1.** [ato] unloading. **-2.** [vaso sanitário] flush; **dar a ~** to flush. **-3.** [de arma] fire. **-4.** *ELETR*: **~ elétrica** electrical discharge.

descarregar [14] [dʒiʃkaxe'ga(x)] ◇ *vt* **-1.** [carga] to unload. **-2.** [arma] to fire. **-3.** *ELETR* to discharge. **-4.** [desabafar] to give vent to. ◇ *vi* [bateria] to go flat.

descarrilamento [dʒiʃkaxila'mẽntu] *m* derailment.

descarrilar [4] [dʒiʃkaxi'la(x)] *vt & vi* to derail.

descartar [4] [dʒiʃkax'ta(x)] *vt* to discard.

◆ **descartar-se** *vp*: **~-se de** [de carta, pessoa] to get rid of; [de compromisso] to free o.s. of.

descartável [dʒiʃkax'tavɛw] (*pl* **-eis**) *adj* disposable.

descascador [dʒiʃkaʃka'do(x)] *m* peeler.

descascar [12] [dʒiʃkaʃ'ka(x)] ◇ *vt* to peel. ◇ *vi* **-1.** [perder a casca] to lose its shell. **-2.** [perder a pele] to peel; **com tanto sol, estou descascando todo** with all this sun, I'm peeling all over.

descaso [dʒiʃ'kasu] *m* negligence.

descendência [desẽn'dẽnsja] *f* descendancy.

descendente [desẽn'dẽntʃi] ◇ *adj* descendent; **ser ~ de** to be a descendant of. ◇ *mf* [pessoa] descendant.

descender [5] [desẽn'de(x)] *vi* **-1.** [pessoa]: **~ de** to be descended from. **-2.** [palavra]: **~ de** to stem from.

descentralização [dʒisẽntraliza'sãw] *f* decentralization.

descentralizar [4] [dʒiʃsẽntrali'za(x)] *vt* to decentralize.

descer [25] [de'se(x)] ◇ *vt* **-1.** [escada] to go down. **-2.** [carga] to take down. ◇ *vi* **-1.** [ger] to go down. **-2.** [de ônibus] to get off.

descida [de'sida] *f* [declive] descent.

desclassificação [dʒiʃklasifika'sãw] (*pl* **-ões**) *f* disqualification.

desclassificar [12] [dʒiʃklasifi'ka(x)] *vt* **-1.** [eliminar] to disqualify. **-2.** [desmoralizar] to disgrace.

descoberto, ta [dʒiʃko'bɛxtu, ta] ◇ *pp* ▷ **descobrir**. ◇ *adj* **-1.** [ger] discovered. **-2.** [exposto] uncovered. **-3.** *BANCO* [conta] overdrawn.

◆ **descoberta** *f* discovery.

◆ **a descoberto** *loc adv FIN* [saque] overdrawn, in the red.

descobridor, ra [dʒiʃkobri'do(x), ra] *m, f* discoverer.

descobrimento [dʒiʃkobri'mẽntu] *m* [de continentes] discovery.

descobrir [59] [dʒiʃko'bri(x)] *vt* **-1.** [ger] to discover. **-2.** [tirar a proteção de] to uncover. **-3.** [estátua] to unveil.

◆ **descobrir-se** *vp* [tirar a coberta] to appear.

descolado, da [dʒiʃko'ladu, da] *adj fam* trendy, cool.

descolar [4] [deʃko'lar] ◇ *vt* **-1.** [desgrudar]: **~ algo (de)** to detach sthg (from). **-2.** *fam* [conseguir] to fix up. ◇ *vi* [afastar-se]: **~ de alguém** to move away from sb.

descolorir [79] [dʒiʃkolo'ri(x)] ◇ *vt* [tirar a cor] to discolour. ◇ *vi* [perder a cor] to fade.

descomedido, da [dʒiʃkome'dʒidu, da] *adj* immoderate.

descompassado, da [dʒiʃkõnpa'sadu, da] *adj* **-1.** [ritmo] out of time. **-2.** [desmedido] excessive. **-3.** [desordenado] untidy.

descompor [45] [dʒiʃkõn'po(x)] *vt* [desordenar] to muddle.

descomposto, osta [dʒiʃkõn'poʃtu, ɔʃta] ◇ *pp* ▷ **descompor**. ◇ *adj* **-1.** [desalinhado] confused. **-2.** [desfeito] disordered. **-3.** [desfigurado] upset.

descompostura [dʒiʃkõnpoʃ'tura] *f* **-1.** [repreensão] reprimand; **passar uma ~ em alguém** to reprimand sb. **-2.** [insulto] affront.

descompressão [dʒiʃkõnpre'sãw] (*pl* **-ões**) *f* decompression.

descomprometido, da [dʒiʃkõnprome'tʃidu, da] *adj* no longer compromised *(depois de verbo)*.

descomunal [dʒiʃkomu'naw] (*pl* **-ais**) *adj* **-1.** [gigantesco] huge. **-2.** [fora do comum] unusual.

desconcentrar [4] [dʒiʃkõnsẽn'tra(x)] *vt* to distract.

◆ **desconcentrar-se** *vp* to lose concentration.

desconcentrado, da [dʒiʃkõnsex'tadu, da] *adj* lacking concentration.

desconcertado, da [dʒiʃkõnsex'tadu, da] *adj* **-1.** [confuso] confused. **-2.** [frustrado] upset.

desconcertante [dʒiʃkõnsex'tãntʃi] *adj* **-1.** [desorientador] confusing. **-2.** [frustrante] upsetting.

desconcertar [dʒiʃkõnsex'ta(x)] *vt* **-1.** [desorientar] to confuse. **-2.** [frustrar] to upset.

◆ **desconcertar-se** *vp* **-1.** [desarranjar-se] to break down. **-2.** [perturbar-se] to become bewildered. **-3.** [frustrar-se] to be upset.

desconectar [4] [dʒiʃkonek'ta(x)] *vt* to disconnect.

◆ **desconectar-se** *vp* [comput] to be disconnected.

desconexo, xa [dʒiʃko'nɛksu, ksa] *adj* **-1.** [incoerente] incoherent. **-2.** [desunido] disconnected.

desconfiado, da [dʒiʃkõn'fjadu, da] *adj* distrustful.

desconfiança [dʒiʃkõn'fjãnsa] *f* distrust.

desconfiar [16] [dʒiʃkõn'fja(x)] ◇ *vt* [conjeturar]: **~ que** to fear that. ◇ *vi* **-1.** [ficar suspeitoso] to suspect. **-2.** [não confiar em]: **~ de** to be distrustful of. **-3.** [suspeitar de]: **~ de** to be suspicious of.

desconfortável [dʒiʃkõnfor'tavɛw] (*pl* **-eis**) *adj* uncomfortable.

desconforto [dʒiʃkõn'foxtu] *m* discomfort.

descongelar [4] [dʒiʃkõnʒe'la(x)] *vt* to defrost.

descongestionante [dʒiʃkõnʒeʃtʃjo'nãntʃi] ◇ *adj* decongestant. ◇ *m* decongestant.

descongestionar [4] [dʒiʃkõnʒeʃtʃjo'na(x)] *vt* **-1.** to decongest. **-2.** *fig* [trânsito, rua] to clear.

desconhecer [25] [dʒiʃkoɲe'se(x)] *vt* **-1.** [ignorar]

not to know. **-2.** [estranhar] not to recognize. **-3.** [ser ingrato a] to be ungrateful for.
desconhecido, da [dʒiʃkoɲe'sidu, da] <> *adj* [incógnito] unknown. <> *m, f* [pessoa] unknown person.
desconhecimento [dʒiʃkoɲesi'mẽntu] *m* ignorance.
desconjuntado, da [dʒiʃkõnʒũn'tadu, da] *adj* dislocated.
desconjuntar [4] [dʒiʃkõnʒũn'ta(x)] *vt* to dislocate.
desconsideração [dʒiʃkõnsidera'sãw] (*pl* **-ões**) *f* **-1.** [desrespeito] disrespect. **-2.** [ofensa] insult.
desconsiderar [4] [dʒiʃkõnside'ra(x)] *vt* to overlook.
desconsolado, da [dʒiʃkõnso'ladu, da] *adj* disconsolate.
desconsolar [4] [dʒiʃkõnso'la(x)] <> *vt* to sadden. <> *vi* to become saddened.
◆ **desconsolar-se** *vp* to become dispirited.
descontar [4] [dʒiʃkõn'ta(x)] *vt* **-1.** [deduzir]: ~ **algo (de)** to deduct sthg (from). **-2.** [título de crédito - pagar] to pay off; [- receber] to receive. **-3.** *fam* [revidar]: ~ **algo (em alguém)** to pay sthg back (to sb). **-4.** *fig* [não fazer caso de] to take no notice of.
descontentamento [dʒiʃkõntẽnta'mẽntu] *m* **-1.** [desprazer] displeasure. **-2.** [insatisfação] dissatisfaction.
descontentar [4] [dʒiʃkõntẽn'ta(x)] *vt* to displease.
◆ **descontentar-se** *vp* to be displeased.
descontente [dʒiʃkõn'tẽntʃi] *adj* displeased.
descontínuo, nua [dʒiʃkõn'tʃinwu, nwa] *adj* discontinued.
desconto [dʒiʃ'kõntu] *m* discount; **com** ~ at a discount; **dar um** ~ *fig* to make allowances.
descontração [dʒiʃkõntra'sãw] *f* relaxation.
descontraído, da [dʒiʃkõntra'idu, da] *adj* relaxed.
descontrair [68] [dʒiʃkõntra'i(x)] *vt* to relax.
◆ **descontrair-se** *vp* to relax.
descontrolado, da [dʒiʃkõntro'ladu, da] *adj* uncontrolled.
descontrolar [4] [dʒiʃkõntro'la(x)] *vt* to lose control of.
◆ **descontrolar-se** *vp* **-1.** [pessoa] to lose control of o.s. **-2.** [situação] to get out of control.
descontrole [dʒiʃkõn'troli] *m* lack of control.
desconversar [4] [dʒiʃkõnvex'sa(x)] *vi* to change the subject.
descorar [4] [dʒiko'ra(x)] <> *vt* [desbotar] to discolour. <> *vi* [empalidecer] to turn pale.
descortês, tesa [dʒiʃkox'teʃ, teza] *adj* discourteous.
descortesia [dʒiʃkoxte'zia] *f* discourtesy.
descortinar [4] [dʒiʃkoxtʃi'na(x)] *vt* **-1.** [avistar] to reveal. **-2.** [correndo a cortina] to unveil. **-3.** [revelar]: ~ **algo a alguém** to reveal sthg to sb.
descoser [5] [dʒiʃko'ze(x)], **descosturar** [dʒiʃkoʃtu'ra(x)] <> *vt* to unstitch. <> *vi* to come unstiched.
descrédito [dʒiʃ'krɛdʒitu] *m* discredit.
descrença [dʒiʃ'krẽnsa] *f* disbelief.
descrente [dʒiʃ'krẽntʃi] *adj* disbelieving.
descrer [37] [dʒiʃ'kre(x)] *vi* to disbelieve: ~ **de algo/alguém** not to believe in sthg/sb.
descrever [5] [dʒiʃkre've(x)] *vt* **-1.** [expor] to describe. **-2.** [traçar] to trace.
descrição [dʒiʃkri'sãw] (*pl* **-ões**) *f* description.
descritivo, va [dʒiʃkri'tʃivu, va] *adj* descriptive.
descuidado, da [dʒiʃkuj'dadu, da] *adj* **-1.** [desleixado] uncared-for. **-2.** [irrefletido] careless.
descuidar [4] [dʒiʃkuj'da(x)] *vi*: ~ **de algo** to neglect sthg.
◆ **descuidar-se** *vp*: ~**-se de algo** to become careless about sthg.
descuido [dʒiʃ'kujdu] *m* **-1.** [ger] carelessness. **-2.** [erro] error.
desculpa [dʒiʃ'kuwpa] *f* **-1.** [ger] excuse. **-2.** [perdão] forgiveness; **pedir** ~**s a alguém por algo** to ask sb forgiveness for sthg.
desculpar [4] [dʒiʃkuw'pa(x)] *vt* **-1.** [perdoar]: ~ **alguém (por algo)** to forgive sb (for sthg). **-2.** [justificar] to give as an excuse.
◆ **desculpar-se** *vp* [justificar-se]: ~**-se (com alguém) por algo** to apologize (to sb) for sthg.
desculpável [dʒiʃkuw'pavew] (*pl* **-eis**) *adj* forgiveable.
descumprir [6] [dʒiʃkũn'pri(x)] *vt* to disobey.
desde ['deʒdʒi] *prep* **-1.** [tempo] since; ~ **então** from then on; ~ **já** straight away. **-2.** [espaço] from.
◆ **desde que** *loc conj* **-1.** [tempo] since. **-2.** [visto que] as. **-3.** [contanto que] as long as.
desdém [deʒ'dẽ] *m* disdain.
desdenhar [4] [deʒde'ɲa(x)] *vt* **-1.** [desprezar] to despise. **-2.** [escarnecer] to scorn.
desdenhoso, osa [deʒde'ɲozu, ɔza] *adj* disdainful.
desdentado, da [dʒiʒdẽn'tadu, da] *adj* toothless.
desdita [dʒiʒ'dʒita] *f* bad luck.
desdizer [29] [dziʒdʒi'ze(x)] *vt* **-1.** [negar] to deny. **-2.** [desmentir] to contradict.
◆ **desdizer-se** *vp* [negar o que havia dito] to retract.
desdobramento [dʒiʒdobra'mẽntu] *m* unfolding, development.
desdobrar [4] [dziʒdo'bra(x)] *vt* **-1.** [abrir] to unfold. **-2.** [dividir]: ~ **algo em algo** to divide sthg into sthg. **-3.** [aumentar] to develop.
◆ **desdobrar-se** *vp* **-1.** to unfold. **-2.** [empenhar-se]: ~**-se (em algo)** *fig* to make an effort (at sthg).
deseducar [12] [dʒizedu'ka(x)] *vt* **-1.** [educar mal] to educate poorly. **-2.** [estragar] to spoil.
desejar [4] [deze'ʒa(x)] <> *vt* **-1.** [querer] to wish; ~ **que** to hope that; ~ **fazer algo** to want to do sthg. **-2.** [ambicionar]: ~ **algo** to wish for sthg; ~ **fazer algo** to wish to do sthg. **-3.** [formulando votos]: ~ **algo a alguém** to wish sb sthg. **-4.** [sexualmente] to desire. <> *vi*: **deixar a** ~ to

leave sthg to be desired.

desejável [dese'ʒavew] (*pl* **-eis**) *adj* desirable.

desejo [de'zeʒu] *m* **-1.** [ger] desire. **-2.** [ambição] wish. **-3.** [de grávida] craving.

desejoso, osa [dese'ʒosu, ɔsa] *adj*: ~ **de algo/de fazer algo** keen for sthg/to do sthg.

deselegância [dʒizele'gãnsja] *f* inelegance.

deselegante [dʒizele'gãntʃi] *adj* inelegant.

desembaçar [13] [dʒizĩnba'sa(x)] *vt* to wipe the steam of.

desembainhar [4] [dʒizẽmbaj'ɲa(x)] *vt* to unsheathe; [sword] to draw.

desembalar [4] [dʒizĩnba'la(x)] *vt* to unwrap.

desembaraçado, da [dʒizẽmbara'sadu, da] *adj* **-1.** [desinibido] uninhibited. **-2.** [livre] free. **-3.** [expedito] prompt. **-4.** [cabelo, novelo] loose.

desembaraçar [13] [dʒizĩnbara'sa(x)] *vt* **-1.** [livrar] to free. **-2.** [desemaranhar] to loosen. **-3.** [liberar] to unencumber.

◆ **desembaraçar-se** *vp* **-1.** [desinibir-se] to open up. **-2.** [livrar-se]: **~-se de algo/alguém** to free o.s. of sthg/sb.

desembaraço [dʒizĩnba'rasu] *m* **-1.** [desinibição] ease. **-2.** [agilidade] agility.

desembarcar [12] [dʒizĩnbax'ka(x)] <> *vt* **-1.** [carga] to unload. **-2.** [passageiros] to disembark. <> *vi* [descer de transporte] to disembark.

desembargador, ra [dʒizẽmbaxga'do(x), ra] *m, f* high court judge.

desembarque [dʒizĩn'baxki] *m* disembarcation.

desembestar [dʒizĩnbeʃ'ta(x)] *vi* [disparar] to bolt.

desembocadura [dʒizĩnboka'dura] *f* discharge.

desembocar [12] [dʒizĩnbo'ka(x)] *vi* [rio, rua]: ~ **em** to discharge into.

desembolsar [4] [dʒizĩnbow'sa(x)] *vt* [gastar] to spend.

desembolso [dʒizĩn'bowsu] *m* [gasto] expenditure.

desembrulhar [4] [dʒizĩnbru'ʎa(x)] *vt* to unwrap.

desembuchar [4] [dʒizĩnbu'ʃa(x)] *fam* <> *vt* [confessar] to get off one's chest. <> *vi* to open up.

desempacotar [4] [dʒizĩnpako'ta(x)] *vt* to unpack.

desempatar [4] [dezĩnpa'ta(x)] <> *vt* ESP: ~ **a partida** to score a deciding point or goal in a match. <> *vi* to decide; **a eleição só desempatou no final** the election was only decided at the finish.

desempate [dʒizĩn'patʃi] *m* ESP decision.

desempenhar [4] [dʒizĩnpe'ɲa(x)] *vt* **-1.** [ger] to perform. **-2.** [cumprir] to carry out.

desempenho [dʒizĩn'peɲu] *m* performance.

desempregado, da [dʒizẽmpre'gadu, da] <> *adj* unemployed. <> *m, f* unemployed person.

desempregar [14] [dʒizĩnpre'ga(x)] *vt* to sack, to lay off.

◆ **desempregar-se** *vp* to lose one's job.

desemprego [dʒizĩn'pregu] *m* unemployment.

desencadear [15] [dʒizĩŋka'dʒja(x)] *vt* [provocar] to unleash.

◆ **desencadear-se** *vp* [irromper] to break out.

desencaixar [4] [dʒizĩŋkaj'ʃa(x)] *vt* to dislocate.

◆ **desencaixar-se** *vp* to become dislocated.

desencaixotar [4] [dʒizĩŋkajʃo'ta(x)] *vt* to take out of a box.

desencalhar [4] [dʒizĩŋka'ʎa(x)] <> *vt* NÁUT to set loose. <> *vi* **-1.** NÁUT to free itself. **-2.** *fam* [pessoa] to get hitched.

desencaminhar [4] [dʒizĩŋkami'ɲa(x)] *vt* to lead astray.

◆ **desencaminhar-se** *vp* to go astray.

desencantar [4] [dʒizĩŋkãn'ta(x)] *vt* **-1.** [desiludir] to disillusion. **-2.** [de feitiço *etc*] to free from a spell. **-3.** [encontrar] to unearth.

◆ **desencantar-se** *vp* [desiludir-se] to become disenchanted.

desencanto [dʒizĩŋ'kãntu] *m* [desilusão] disenchantment.

desencardir [6] [dʒizĩŋkax'di(x)] *vt* to clean.

desencargo [dʒizĩŋ'kaxgu] *m* [cumprimento] carrying out; **por ~ de consciência** to clear one's conscience.

desencarregar-se [14] [dʒizẽŋkaxe'gaxsi] *vp* [desobrigar-se]: ~ **de algo** to unburden o.s. of sthg.

desencavar [4] [dʒizĩŋka'va(x)] *vt* to dig up.

desencontrado, da [dʒizĩŋkõn'tradu, da] *adj* **-1.** [contrário] contrary. **-2.** [desalinhado] out of step.

desencontrar [4] [dʒizĩŋkõn'tra(x)] *vt* [fazer que não se encontrem] to send in different directions.

◆ **desencontrar-se** *vp* **-1.** [não se encontrar]: **~-se (de)** to diverge (from). **-2.** [perder-se um do outro] to fail to meet one another.

desencontro [dʒizĩŋ'kõntru] *m* **-1.** [falta de encontro] failure to meet. **-2.** [divergência] difference.

desencorajar [4] [dʒizĩŋkora'ʒa(x)] *vt* to discourage.

desencostar [4] [dʒizĩŋkoʃ'ta(x)] *vt*: ~ **algo/alguém (de)** to move sthg/sb away (from).

◆ **desencostar-se** *vp*: **~-se de algo** to stop leaning against sthg.

desenferrujar [4] [dʒizĩfexu'ʒa(x)] *vt* **-1.** [metal] to remove rust from. **-2.** *fig* [pernas] to stretch; [língua] to polish, brush up.

desenfreado, da [dʒizẽnfre'adu, da] *adj* wild.

desenganado, da [dʒizẽŋga'nadu, da] *adj* [sem cura] incurable; [desiludido] disenchanted.

desenganar [4] [dʒizĩŋga'na(x)] *vt* **-1.** [doente] to give up hope for. **-2.** [desiludir] to disillusion.

◆ **desenganar-se** *vp* [desiludir-se]: **~-se de algo/alguém** to have no illusions about sthg/sb.

desengano [dʒizĩn'gãnu] *m* [desilusão] disillusionment.

desengarrafar [4] [dʒizĩŋgaxa'fa(x)] *vt* **-1.** [líquido] to pour from a bottle. **-2.** *fig* [trânsito] to clear.

desengatar [4] [dʒizĩŋga'ta(x)] *vt* to uncouple.

desengonçado, da [dʒizẽŋgõ'sadu, da] *adj* **-1.** [desconjuntado] disjointed. **-2.** [desajeitado] clumsy.

desengrenado, da [dʒizĩŋgre'nadu, da] *adj* AUTO in neutral.
desengrenar [4] [dʒizĩŋgre'na(x)] *vt* AUTO to put into neutral.
desenhar [4] [deze'ɲa(x)] <> *vt* **-1.** [traçar] to outline. **-2.** TEC to design. **-3.** ARTE to draw. <> *vi* [traçar desenhos] to draw up.
◆ **desenhar-se** *vp* [figurar-se] to take shape.
desenhista [deze'ɲiʃta] *m, f* designer.
desenho [de'zeɲu] *m* **-1.** [expressão de formas] drawing. **-2.** ARTE & TEC design; ~ **industrial** technical drawing. **-3.** CINE: ~ **animado** (animated) cartoon.
desenlace [dʒizẽn'lasi] *m* unfolding, development.
desenredar [4] [dʒizẽnxe'da(x)] *vt* **-1.** [desembaraçar]: ~ **alguém de** to extricate sb from. **-2.** [resolver] to resolve. **-3.** [descobrir] to unravel.
◆ **desenredar-se** *vp* [desembaraçar-se]: ~**-se de** to extricate o.s. from.
desenrolar [4] [dʒizẽnxo'la(x)] <> *m* to progress. <> *vt* **-1.** [estender] to unroll. **-2.** [expor] to unfold.
◆ **desenrolar-se** *vp* **-1.** [desenroscar-se] to uncurl o.s. **-2.** [mostrar-se] to open out.
desentender-se [5] [dʒizẽntẽn'dexsi] *vp*: ~ **(com)** to disagree (with).
desentendido, da [dʒizẽntẽn'dʒidu, da] *adj*: **fazer-se de** ~ to pretend not to understand.
◆ **desentendido** *m* person who does not understand.
desentendimento [dʒizĩntẽndʒi'mẽntu] *m* misunderstanding.
desenterrar [4] [dʒizẽnte'xa(x)] *vt* **-1.** [ger] to dig up. **-2.** [exumar] to exhume. **-3.** [descobrir] to unearth.
desentortar [4] [dʒizẽntox'ta(x)] *vt* to straighten.
desentrosado, da [dʒizẽntro'zadu, da] *adj* out of line.
desentupir [61] [dʒizẽntu'pi(x)] *vt* to unblock.
desenvolto, ta [dʒizẽn'vowtu, ta] *adj* wanton.
desenvoltura [dʒizĩnvow'tura] *f* lack of inhibition.
desenvolver [5] [dʒizĩnvow've(x)] *vt* **-1.** [ger] to develop. **-2.** [melhorar] to improve. **-3.** [teorizar sobre] to expand on. **-4.** [correr] to run.
◆ **desenvolver-se** *vp* **-1.** [crescer] to develop. **-2.** [progredir] to progress.
desenvolvido, da [dʒizẽvow'vidu, da] <> *pp* ▷ **desenvolver**. <> *adj* **-1.** [concebido] conceived. **-2.** [adiantado] advanced. **-3.** [crescido] developed.
desenvolvimento [dʒizĩnvowvi'mẽntu] *m* **-1.** [crescimento] development. **-2.** [concepção] conception.
desequilibrado, da [dʒizekili'bradu, da] <> *adj* **-1.** [sem equilíbrio] unbalanced. **-2.** PSIC unstable. <> *m, f* PSIC unstable person.
desequilibrar [4] [dʒizekili'bra(x)] *vt* **-1.** [fazer perder o equilíbrio] to unbalance.
◆ **desequilibrar-se** *vp* **-1.** PSIC to become unstable. **-2.** *fig* [descontrolar] to get out of control.
desequilíbrio [dʒizeki'librju] *m* **-1.** [falta de equilíbrio] lack of balance. **-2.** PSIC instability.
deserção [dezex'sãw] (*pl* **-ões**) *f* desertion.
deserdar [4] [dezex'da(x)] *vt* to disinherit.
desertar [4] [dezex'ta(x)] <> *vt* [abandonar] to abandon. <> *vi* **-1.** MIL to desert. **-2.** [abandonar]: ~ **de algo** to abandon sthg. **-3.** [bandear]: ~ **para algo** to go over to sthg.
deserto, ta [de'zɛxtu, ta] *adj* deserted.
◆ **deserto** *m* desert.
desertor, ra [dezex'to(x), ra] *m, f* deserter.
desesperado, da [dʒiziʃpe'radu, da] *adj* **-1.** [sem esperança] desperate. **-2.** [irritado] irritated. **-3.** [intenso - briga, competição] fierce; [- amor] intense.
desesperador, ra [dʒiziʃpera'do(x), ra] *adj* **-1.** [sem esperança] hopeless. **-2.** [irritante] irritating.
desesperança [dʒiziʃpe'rãnsa] *f* despair.
desesperar [4] [dʒizeʃpe'ra(x)] <> *vt* **-1.** [arrasar] to dishearten. **-2.** [irritar] to drive mad. <> *vi* [perder a esperança] to give up hope.
◆ **desesperar-se** *vp* **-1.** [perder a esperança] to give up hope. **-2.** [afligir-se] to get upset.
desespero [dʒiziʃ'peru] *m* **-1.** [desesperança] despair. **-2.** [aflição] despondency; **levar alguém ao** ~ to lead sb to despair.
desestabilizar [4] [dʒiziʃtabili'za(x)] *vt* to destabilize.
◆ **desestabilizar-se** *vp* to become destabilized.
desestimulante [dʒiziʃtʃimulãntʃi] *adj* discouraging.
desestimular [4] [dʒiziʃtʃimu'la(x)] *vt* to discourage.
desfaçatez [dʒiʃfasa'teʃ] *f* effrontery.
desfalcar [12] [dʒiʃfaw'ka(x)] *vt* **-1.** [reduzir] to reduce. **-2.** [privar] to deprive. **-3.** [defraudar] to defraud.
desfalecer [25] [dʒiʃfale'se(x)] *vi* **-1.** [desmaiar] to faint. **-2.** [esmorecer] to lose heart.
desfalque [dʒiʃ'fawki] *m* **-1.** [redução] reduction. **-2.** [privação] loss. **-3.** [fraude] fraud.
desfavorável [dʒiʃfavo'ravɛw] (*pl* **-eis**) *adj* **-1.** [desvantajoso] unfavourable. **-2.** [oposto] adverse.
desfazer [31] [dʒiʃfa'ze(x)] <> *vt* **-1.** [desmanchar] to undo. **-2.** [dispersar] to disperse. **-3.** [acabar com] to put an end to. **-4.** [anular] to annul. <> *vi* ~ **de** *ou* **em** [desdenhar] to despise.
◆ **desfazer-se** *vp* **-1.** [desmanchar-se] to come undone. **-2.** [dispersar-se] to disperse. **-3.** [acabar-se] to end. **-4.** [desembaraçar-se]: ~**-se de algo** to get rid of sthg. **-5.** [despojar-se]: ~**-se de algo** to be stripped of sthg. **-6.** *fig* [desmanchar-se]: ~**-se em lágrimas** to burst into tears; ~**-se em sorrisos** to break into smiles; ~**-se em gentilezas** to be desperate to please.
desfechar [4] [dʒiʃfe'ʃa(x)] *vt* **-1.** [disparar] to fire. **-2.** [insultos] to loose off.
desfecho [dʒiʃ'feʃu] *m* ending.
desfeita [dʒiʃ'fejta] *f* insult.
desfeito, ta [dʒʃ'fejtu, ta] <> *pp* ▷ **desfazer**.

<> *adj* **-1.** [desmanchado] undone. **-2.** [acabado] ended. **-3.** [desarrumada] untidy. **-4.** [anulado] annulled.

desferir [57] [dʒiʃfe'ri(x)] *vt* [aplicar] to direct.

desfiado, da [dʒiʃ'fjadu, da] *adj* **-1.** [meia, tecido] frayed. **-2.** *fig* [assunto, tema] well-worn.

desfiar [16] [dʒiʃ'fja(x)] <> *vt* **-1.** [tecido *etc*] to unravel. **-2.** [terço] to unthread. **-3.** [galinha] to cut up. <> *vi* [tecido *etc*] to unravel.

desfigurar [4] [dʒiʃfigu'ra(x)] *vt* **-1.** [transformar] to disfigure. **-2.** *fig* [adulterar] to adulterate.

◆ **desfigurar-se** *vp* [transformar-se] to alter.

desfiladeiro [dʒiʃfila'dejru] *m* ravine.

desfilar [4] [dʒiʃfi'la(x)] <> *vt* [exibir] to parade. <> *vi* [passar em desfile - soldado] to march past; [- manequim, escola de samba] to parade.

desfile [dʒiʃ'fili] *m* [passar em desfile - soldado] march past; [- manequim, escola de samba] parade.

desforra [dʒiʃ'fɔxa] *f* revenge.

desfraldar [4] [dʒiʃfraw'da(x)] *vt* to unfurl.

desfrutar [4] [dʒiʃfru'ta(x)] <> *vt* to enjoy. <> *vi*: ~ **de algo** to enjoy sthg.

desfrute [dʒiʃ'frutʃi] *m* [prazer] enjoyment.

desgarrado, da [dʒiʒga'xadu, da] *adj* [perdido] lost.

desgarrar-se [4] [dʒiʒga'xaxsi] *vp* [perder-se]: ~ **de algo** to lose sight of sthg; ~ **(do caminho)** to lose one's way.

desgastante [dʒiʒgaʃ'tãntʃi] *adj* **-1.** [estressante] stressful. **-2.** [cansativo] tiring. **-3.** [desprestigiante] damaging.

desgastar [4] [dʒiʒgaʃ'ta(x)] *vt* **-1.** [ger] to wear out. **-2.** [gastar] to wear away. **-3.** [desprestigiar] to damage.

desgaste [dʒiʒ'gaʃtʃi] *m* **-1.** [deterioração] deterioration. **-2.** [dano] harm.

desgostar [4] [dʒiʒgoʃ'ta(x)] <> *vt* [contrariar] to displease. <> *vi* [não gostar]: ~ **de algo** to dislike sthg.

◆ **desgostar-se** *vp* [deixar de gostar]: **~-se de algo/de fazer algo** to no longer enjoy sthg/doing sthg.

desgosto [dʒiʒ'goʃtu] *m* **-1.** [desprazer] displeasure. **-2.** [pesar] regret.

desgostoso, osa [dʒiʒgoʃ'tozu, ɔza] *adj* **-1.** [triste] sad. **-2.** [contrariado] displeased.

desgovernado, da [dʒiʒgovex'nadu, da] *adj* **-1.** [país] misruled. **-2.** [veículo, animal] out of control.

desgraça [dʒiʒ'grasa] *f* **-1.** [infortúnio] misfortune. **-2.** [miséria] penury. **-3.** *fig* [pessoa inábil]: **ser uma** ~ to be a disgrace. **-4.** *loc*: **cair em** ~ [perder o prestígio] to fall from grace.

desgraçado, da [dʒiʒgra'sadu, da] <> *adj* **-1.** [desafortunado] unfortunate. **-2.** [miserável] wretched. **-3.** [vil] vile. **-4.** *m fam* [grande] hellish. <> *m, f* **-1.** [desafortunado] unfortunate. **-2.** [pessoa vil] beggar.

desgraçar [13] [dʒiʒgra'sa(x)] *vt* to disgrace.

desgravar [4] [dʒiʒgra'va(x)] *vt* to wipe.

desgrenhado, da [dʒiʒgre'ɲadu, da] *adj* **-1.** [despenteado] tousled. **-2.** [desarrumado] untidy.

desgrenhar [4] [dʒiʒgre'ɲa(x)] *vt* [despentear] to tousle.

desgrudar [4] [dʒiʒgru'da(x)] *vt* **-1.** [descolar]: ~ **algo de algo** to unstick sthg from sthg. **-2.** [afastar]: ~ **alguém de alguém/algo** *fig* to drag sb away from sb/sthg.

◆ **desgrudar-se** *vp* [afastar-se] to break away.

desguarnecer [25] [dʒiʒgwaxne'se(x)] *vt* **-1.** *MIL* to unman. **-2.** [despojar]: ~ **algo/alguém de algo** to take sthg/sb away from sthg.

desidratação [dezidrata'sãw] (*pl* **-ões**) *f* dehydration.

desidratante [dʒizidra'tãntʃi] *adj* dehydrating.

desidratar [4] [dʒizidra'ta(x)] *vt* to dehydrate.

◆ **desidratar-se** *vp* to become dehydrated.

design [dʒi'zajni] (*pl* **-s**) *m* design.

designação [dezigna'sãw] (*pl* **-ões**) *f* **-1.** [nome] designation. **-2.** [escolha] appointment.

designar [4] [dezig'na(x)] *vt* **-1.** [denominar] to designate. **-2.** [simbolizar] to symbolize. **-3.** [determinar] to award. **-4.** [escolher]: ~ **alguém para algo** to appoint sb as sthg.

designer [dʒi'zajnɛ(x)] (*pl* **-s**) *mf* designer.

desígnio [de'zignju] *m* design.

desigual [dezi'gwaw] (*pl* **-ais**) *adj* **-1.** [diferente] different. **-2.** [irregular] irregular. **-3.** [injusto] unfair.

desigualdade [dʒizigwaw'dadʒi] *f* **-1.** [diferença] difference. **-2.** [injustiça] inequality.

desiludir [6] [dʒizilu'dʒi(x)] *vt*: ~ **alguém (de algo /de fazer algo)** to dissuade sb (from sthg/from doing sthg); ~ **alguém (com algo)** to disappoint sb)with sthg).

◆ **desiludir-se** *vp*: **~-se (com algo)** to be disappointed (by sthg).

desilusão [dʒizilu'zãw] (*pl* **-ões**) *f* disappointment.

desimpedido, da [dʒizĩmpe'dʒidu, da] *adj* **-1.** [desatravancado] clear. **-2.** [livre de compromisso] unencumbered.

desimpedir [70] [dʒizĩnpe'dʒi(x)] *vt* to clear.

desinchar [4] [dʒizĩn'ʃa(x)] *vt* to reduce.

desincompatibilizar [4] [dʒizĩŋkõmpatʃibili'za(x)] *vt* to get rid of incompatibility between.

◆ **desincompatibilizar-se** *vp* to cease to be incompatible.

desincumbir-se [6] [dʒizĩŋkũn'bixsi] *vp*: ~ **de algo** to be released from sthg.

desinência *f GRAM* ending.

desinfetante [dʒizĩnfe'tãntʃi] <> *adj* disinfectant. <> *m* disinfectant.

desinfetar [4] [dʒizĩnfe'ta(x)] *vt MED* to disinfect.

desinflamar [4] [dʒizĩnfla'ma(x)] <> *vt* to reduce inflammation in/on. <> *vi* to become less inflamed.

desinibido, da [dʒizini'bidu, da] *adj* uninhibited.

desinibir [6] [dʒizini'bi(x)] *vt* to make less inhibited.

◆ **desinibir-se** *vp* to lose one's inhibitions, to come out of o.s.

desintegração [dʒizĩntegra'sãw] *f* disintegration.
desintegrar [4] [dʒizĩnte'gra(x)] *vt* to cause to disintegrate.
◆ **desintegrar-se** *vp* to disintegrate.
desinteressado, da [dʒizĩntere'sadu, da] *adj* **-1.** [sem interesse] disinterested. **-2.** [despreendido] detached.
desinteressar [4] [dʒizĩntere'sa(x)] *vt*: ~ **alguém de algo** to destroy sb's interest in sthg.
◆ **desinteressar-se** *vp*: ~**-se de algo** to lose interest in sthg.
desinteresse [dʒizĩnte'resi] *m* **-1.** [falta de interesse] lack of interest. **-2.** [despreendimento] detachment.
desintoxicação [dʒizĩntoksika'sãw] (*pl* **-ões**) *f* detoxification.
desintoxicar [12] [dʒizĩntoksi'ka(x)] *vt* to detoxify.
desistência [deziʃ'tẽnsja] *f* withdrawal.
desistir [6] [deziʃ'tʃi(x)] *vi* to give up; ~ **de algo /de fazer algo** to give up sthg/doing sthg.
desjejum [dʒiʒe'ʒũ] (*pl* **-ns**) *m* breakfast.
deslanchar [4] [dʒiʒlãn'ʃa(x)] *vi* **-1.** [dar partida] to set off. **-2.** [progredir rápido] to take off.
deslavado, da [dʒiʒla'vadu, da] *adj* brazen.
desleal [dʒiʒ'ljaw] (*pl* **-ais**) *adj* disloyal.
deslealdade [dʒiʒleaw'dadʒi] *f* disloyalty.
desleixado, da [dʒiʒlej'ʃadu, da] *adj* messy.
desleixo [dʒiʒ'lejʃu] *m* mess.
desligado, da [dʒiʒli'gadu, da] *adj* **-1.** ELETR switched off. **-2.** [desconectado] disconnected. **-3.** [afastado]: ~ **de** detached from. **-4.** *fig* [despreendido] indifferent. **-5.** *fig* [distraído] absent-minded.
desligar [14] [dʒiʒli'ga(x)] ◇ *vt* ELETR to switch off; ~ **o carro** to switch off the engine. ◇ *vi fam* [despreocupar-se] to switch off.
◆ **desligar-se** *vp* **-1.** [afastar-se]: ~**-se de** to switch off from. **-2.** *fig* [despreender-se]: ~**-se de** to abandon. **-3.** *fig* [distrair-se] to switch off.
deslizamento [dʒiʒliza'mẽntu] *m* slip; ~ **de terra** landslide.
deslizante [dʒiʒli'zãntʃi] *adj* slippery.
deslizar [4] [dʒiʒli'za(x)] *vi* **-1.** [movimentar-se - cisnes, dançarino] to glide; [- terra, encosta] to slide. **-2.** [escorregar] to slip. **-3.** *fig* [falhar] to make a slip.
deslize [dʒiʒ'lizi] *m* **-1.** [escorregão] slip. **-2.** *fig* [falha] blunder. **-3.** *fig* [engano] slip.
deslocado, da [dʒiʒlo'kadu, da] *adj* **-1.** MED dislocated. **-2.** [transferido] transferred. **-3.** *fig* [desambientado] out of place.
deslocamento [dʒiʒloka'mẽntu] *m* **-1.** MED dislocation. **-2.** [movimentação] movement.
deslocar [12] [dʒiʒlo'ka(x)] *vt* **-1.** MED to dislocate. **-2.** [transferir] to transfer. **-3.** [mover] to move.
◆ **deslocar-se** *vp* [mover-se] to move around.
deslumbrado, da [dʒiʒlũn'bradu, da] *adj* dazzled.
deslumbramento [dʒiʒlũnbra'mẽntu] *m* dazzle.
deslumbrante [dʒiʒlũn'brãntʃi] *adj* dazzling.
deslumbrar [4] [dʒiʒlũn'bra(x)] ◇ *vt* to dazzle. ◇ *vi* to be dazzling.
◆ **deslumbrar-se** *vp* to be dazzled.
desmaiado, da [dʒiʒmaj'adu, da] *adj* **-1.** MED unconscious. **-2.** [pálido] pale.
desmaiar [4] [dʒiʒmaj'a(x)] *vi* to faint.
desmaio [dʒiʒ'maju] *m* faint.
desmamar [4] [dʒiʒma'ma(x)] ◇ *vt* to wean. ◇ *vi* to be weaned.
desmancha-prazeres [dʒiʒˌmãnʃapra'zeriʃ] *mf inv* killjoy.
desmanchar [4] [dʒiʒmãn'ʃa(x)] *vt* **-1.** [desfazer] to undo. **-2.** [acabar com] to break off.
◆ **desmanchar-se** *vp* **-1.** [dissolver-se] to come undone. **-2.** *fig* [expandir-se]: ~**-se em algo** to be lavish with sthg.
desmantelar [4] [dʒiʒmãnte'la(x)] *vt* **-1.** [desmontar] to dismantle. **-2.** [desmoronar] to demolish.
◆ **desmantelar-se** *vp* **-1.** [desmontar-se] to fall apart. **-2.** [desmoronar-se] to collapse.
desmarcar [12] [dʒiʒmax'ka(x)] *vt* **-1.** [tirar as marcas de] to remove markings from. **-2.** [adiar] to postpone.
desmascaramento [dʒiʒmaʃkara'mẽntu] *m* unmasking.
desmascarar [4] [dʒiʒmaʃka'ra(x)] *vt* **-1.** [revelar] to reveal. **-2.** [desmoralizar] to demoralize.
desmatamento [dʒiʒmata'mẽntu] *m* deforestation.
desmatar [4] [dʒiʒma'ta(x)] *vt* to deforest.
desmazelado, da [dʒiʒmaze'ladu, da] *adj* slovenly.
desmazelar-se [7] [dʒiʒmaze'laxsi] *vp* to become slovenly.
desmazelo [dʒiʒma'zelu] *m* slovenliness.
desmedido, da [dʒiʒme'dʒidu, da] *adj* immense.
desmembramento [dʒiʒmẽnbra'mẽntu] *m* dismembering.
desmembrar [4] [dʒiʒmẽn'bra(x)] *vt* to divide up.
◆ **desmembrar-se** *vp* to divide.
desmemoriado, da [dʒiʒmemo'rjadu, da] *adj* forgetful.
desmentido [dʒiʒmẽn'tʃidu] *m* contradiction.
desmentir [56] [dʒiʒmẽn'tʃi(x)] *vt* **-1.** [negar] to deny. **-2.** [discrepar de] to disagree with. **-3.** [contradizer] to contradict.
◆ **desmentir-se** *vp* [contradizer-se] to contradict o.s.
desmerecer [25] [dʒiʒmere'se(x)] *vt* **-1.** [menosprezar] to despise. **-2.** [não merecer] not to deserve.
desmesurado, da [dʒiʒmezu'radu, da] *adj* excessive.
desmiolado, da [dʒiʒmjo'ladu, da] *adj* **-1.** [sem juízo] brainless. **-2.** [esquecido] forgetful.
desmistificação [dʒiʒmitʃifica'sãw] (*pl* **-ões**) *f* demystification.
desmistificar [12] [dʒiʒmiʃtʃifi'ka(x)] *vt* to demystify.
desmitificar [dʒiʒmitʃifi'ka(x)] *vt* to dispel the myth about.

desmontar [4] [dʒiʒmõn'ta(x)] ◇ *vt* **-1.** [separar as partes de] to dismantle. **-2.** *fig* [destruir] to destroy. ◇ *vi* [apear]: ~ **(de algo)** to dismount (from sthg).
desmontável [dʒiʒmõn'tavew] (*pl* **-eis**) *adj* that can be taken apart, knockdown *US*.
desmoralização [dʒiʒmoraliza'sãw] *f* demoralization.
desmoralizante [dʒiʒmorali'zãntʃi], **desmoralizador, ra** [dʒiʒmoraliza'do(x), ra] *adj* demoralizing.
desmoralizar [4] [dʒiʒmorali'za(x)] *vt* to demoralize.
◆ **desmoralizar-se** *vp* to be demoralized.
desmoronamento [dʒiʒmorona'mẽntu] *m* landslide.
desmoronar [4] [dʒiʒmoro'na(x)] ◇ *vt* to knock down. ◇ *vi* to collapse.
desmotivado, da [dʒiʒmotʃi'vadu, da] *adj* demotivated.
desmunhecar [12] [dʒiʒmuɲe'ka(x)] *vi fam* to be camp.
desnatado, da [dʒiʒna'tadu, da] *adj* skimmed.
desnecessário, ria [dʒiʒnese'sarju, rja] *adj* unnecessary.
desnível [dʒiʒ'nivɛw] (*pl* **-eis**) *m* unevenness.
desnivelar [4] [dʒiʒnive'la(x)] *vt* to make uneven.
desnorteado, da [dʒiʒnox'tʃjadu, da] *adj* [perturbado] bewildered.
desnorteante [dʒiʒnox'tʃjãntʃi] *adj* bewildering.
desnortear [15] [dʒiʒnox'tʃja(x)] *vt* **-1.** [desorientar] to disorientate. **-2.** *fig* [perturbar] to confuse.
◆ **desnortear-se** *vp* **-1.** [perder-se] to get lost. **-2.** *fig* [perturbar-se] to become confused.
desnudar [4] [dʒiʒnu'da(x)] *vt* **-1.** [despir] to undress. **-2.** *fig* [revelar] to reveal.
◆ **desnudar-se** *vp* [despir-se] to undress.
desnutrição [dʒiʒnutri'sãw] *f* malnutrition.
desnutrido, da [dʒiʒnu'tridu, da] *adj* malnourished.
desobedecer [25] [dʒizobede'se(x)] *vi*: ~ **(a)** to disobey.
desobediência [dʒizobe'dʒjẽnsja] *f* disobedience.
desobediente [dʒizobe'dʒjẽntʃi] *adj* disobedient.
desobrigar [14] [dʒizobri'ga(x)] *vt*: ~ **alguém de algo/de fazer algo** to release sb from sthg/doing sthg.
desobstruir [74] [dʒizobʃtru'i(x)] *vt* to clear.
desocupação [dʒizokupa'sãw] *f* emptiness.
desocupado, da [dʒizoku'padu, da] ◇ *adj* **-1.** [ocioso] idle. **-2.** [disponível] available. **-3.** [vazio] empty. ◇ *m, f* **-1.** [desempregado] unemployed person. **-2.** [vagabundo] layabout.
desocupar [4] [dʒizoku'pa(x)] *vt* **-1.** [deixar livre] to leave free. **-2.** [esvaziar] to empty.
desodorante [dʒizodo'rãntʃi] *m* deodorant.
desodorizar [4] [dʒizodori'za(x)] *vt* to deodorize.
desolação [dezola'sãw] *f* **-1.** [tristeza] sadness. **-2.** [devastação] devastation.
desolado, da [dezo'ladu, da] *adj* **-1.** [triste] sad. **-2.** [devastado] devasted.
desolador, ra [dezola'do(x), ra] *adj* [entristecedor] devastating.
desolar [4] [dezo'la(x)] *vt* to devastate.
desonestidade [dʒizoneʃtʃi'dadʒi] *f* dishonesty.
desonesto, ta [dʒizo'nɛʃtu, ta] ◇ *adj* **-1.** [indigno] contemptible. **-2.** [mentiroso] dishonest. ◇ *m, f* [pessoa indigna] despicable person.
desonra [dʒi'zõnxa] *f* dishonour.
desonrar [4] [dʒizõn'xa(x)] *vt* to dishonour.
◆ **desonrar-se** *vp* to disgrace o.s.
desonroso, osa [dʒizõn'xozu, ɔza] *adj* dishonourable.
desopilar [4] [dʒizopi'la(x)] *vt* **-1.** *MED* to clear an obstruction from. **-2.** [mente] to relieve.
desoprimir [6] [dʒizopri'mi(x)] *vt* to free from oppression.
desordeiro, ra [dʒizox'dejru, ra] ◇ *adj* rowdy. ◇ *m, f* rowdy person.
desordem [dʒi'zɔxdẽ] (*pl* **-ns**) *f* **-1.** [bagunça] mess. **-2.** [tumulto] commotion.
desordenar [4] [dʒizoxde'na(x)] *vt* to upset.
desorganização [dʒizoxganiza'sãw] *f* confusion.
desorganizar [4] [dʒizoxgani'za(x)] *vt* to throw into confusion.
◆ **desorganizar-se** *vp* to be disorganized.
desorientação [dʒizorjẽnta'sãw] *f* disorientation.
desorientar [4] [dʒizorjẽn'ta(x)] *vt* **-1.** [desnortear] to disorientate. **-2.** [perturbar] to bewilder. **-3.** *PSIC* to disturb.
◆ **desorientar-se** *vp* **-1.** [desnortear-se] to become disorientated. **-2.** [perturbar-se] to become disconcerted.
desossar [4] [dʒizo'sa(x)] *vt* to bone.
desovar [4] [dʒizo'va(x)] ◇ *vi* [pôr ovos] to lay eggs. ◇ *vt fig* [livrar-se de] to get rid of.
despachado, da [dʒiʃpa'ʃadu, da] *adj* **-1.** [enviado] dispatched. **-2.** [eficiente] efficient.
despachante [dʒiʃpa'ʃãntʃi] *mf* forwarding agent.
despachar [4] [dʒiʃpa'ʃa(x)] *vt* **-1.** [enviar] to send. **-2.** [resolver] to dispatch. **-3.** [atender] to attend to. **-4.** [mandar embora] to get rid of.
despacho [dʒiʃ'paʃu] *m* **-1.** [resolução] determination. **-2.** *ESPIRIT* religious offering.
despedaçar [13] [dʒiʃpeda'sa(x)] *vt* **-1.** [quebrar em pedaços] to smash. **-2.** *fig* [magoar]: ~ **o coração de alguém** to break sb's heart.
◆ **despedaçar-se** *vp* [quebrar-se em pedaços] to smash.
despedida [dʒiʃpe'dʒida] *f* [ato] farewell.
despedir [70] [dʒiʃpe'dʒi(x)] *vt* [demitir] to dismiss.
◆ **despedir-se** *vp* [dizer adeus]: **~-se (de alguém)** to say goodbye (to sb).
despeitado, da [dʒiʃpej'tadu, da] *adj* **-1.** [invejoso] envious. **-2.** *fam* [que tem o peito magro] flat.
despeito [dʒiʃ'pejtu] *m* [inveja] spite.

◆ **a despeito de** *loc conj* [apesar de] despite.
despejar [4] [dʒiʃpe'ʒa(x)] *vt* **-1.** [inquilino] to evict. **-2.** [entornar] to pour.
despejo [dʒiʃ'peʒu] *m* [de inquilino] eviction.
despencar [12] [dʒiʃpẽŋ'ka(x)] *vi* [cair]: ~ **de algo** to fall from sthg.
despender [5] [dʒiʃpẽn'de(x)] *vt* to spend.
despenhadeiro [dʒiʃpeɲa'dejru] *m* precipice.
despensa [dʒiʃ'pẽnsa] *f* pantry.
despentear [15] [dʒiʃpẽn'tʒja(x)] *vt* to tousle.
◆ **despentear-se** *vp* *fig* to let one's hair down.
despercebido, da [dʒiʃpexse'bidu, da] *adj* unnoticed.
desperdiçar [13] [dʒiʃpexdʒi'sa(x)] *vt* to waste.
desperdício [dʒiʃpex'dʒisju] *m* waste.
despersonalizar [4] [dʒiʃpexsonali'za(x)] *vt* to depersonalize.
despertador [dʒiʃpexta'do(x)] (*pl* **-es**) *m* alarm clock.
despertar [4] [dʒiʃpex'ta(x)] ◇ *m* awakening. ◇ *vt* **-1.** [acordar] to wake. **-2.** [provocar] to awaken. **-3.** *fig* [tirar]: ~ **alguém de algo** to rouse sb from sthg. ◇ *vi* **-1.** [ger] to wake up. **-2.** *fig* [sair]: ~ **de algo** to rouse o.s. from sthg.
desperto, ta [dʒiʃ'pɛxtu, ta] *adj* awake.
despesa [dʒiʃ'peza] *f* expense.
despido, da [dʒiʃ'pidu, da] *adj* **-1.** [nu] naked. **-2.** *fig* [desprovido]: ~ **de algo** lacking sthg.
despir [57] [dʒiʃ'pi(x)] *vt* [roupa, pessoa] to undress.
◆ **despir-se** *vp* **-1.** [tirar a roupa] to get undressed. **-2.** *fig* [despojar-se]: ~**-se de algo** to abandon sthg.
despistar [4] [dʒiʃpiʃ'ta(x)] *vt* to mislead.
desplante [dʒiʃ'plãntʃi] *m* *fig* cheek.
despojado, da [dʒiʃpo'ʒadu, da] *adj* **-1.** [privado]: ~ **de algo** stripped of sthg. **-2.** [desprendido] generous. **-3.** [sem enfeite] unadorned.
despojamento [dʒiʃpoʒa'mẽntu] *m* [privação, abandono] shedding.
despojar [4] [dʒiʃpo'ʒa(x)] *vt* **-1.** [roubar] to rob. **-2.** [espoliar] to clean out.
◆ **despojar-se** *vp* [privar-se]: ~**-se de algo** to renounce sthg.
despojos [dʒiʃ'pɔʒoʃ] *mpl* remains; ~ **mortais** mortal remains.
despoluir [74] [dʒiʃpo'lwi(x)] *vt* to clean up.
despontar [4] [dʒiʃpõn'ta(x)] *vi* to rise.
desportista [dʒiʃpox'tʃiʃta] ◇ *adj* sporty. ◇ *mf* sportsman (*f* sportswoman).
desporto [dʒiʃ'poxtu] *m* sport.
déspota ['dɛʃpota] ◇ *adj* despotic. ◇ *mf* despot.
despotismo [deʃpo'tʃiʒmu] *m* despotism.
despovoado, da [dʒiʃpo'vwadu, da] *adj* uninhabited.
desprazer [dʒiʃpra'ze(x)] *m* displeasure.
despregado, da [dʒiʃpre'gadu, da] *adj* loose.
despregar [14] [dʒiʃpre'ga(x)] ◇ *vt*: ~ **algo (de)** to unfasten sthg (from); **não despregou os olhos de mim** *fig* he didn't take his eyes off me. ◇ *vi* to come undone.
◆ **despregar-se** *vp* [soltar-se] to come loose.
desprender [5] [dʒiʃprẽn'de(x)] *vt* **-1.** [soltar]: ~ **alguém/algo (de algo)** to untie sthg (from sthg). **-2.** [escalar] to release.
◆ **desprender-se** *vp* **-1.** [soltar-se]: ~**-se (de algo)** to get free (from sthg). **-2.** [exalar]: ~**-se de algo** to extricate o.s. from sthg.
desprendido, da [dʒiʃprẽn'dʒidu, da] *adj* detached.
desprendimento [dʒiprẽndʒi'mẽntu] *m* [desapego] detachment.
despreocupado, da [dʒiʃpreoku'padu, da] *adj* carefree.
despreparado, da [dʒiʃprepa'radu, da] *adj* unprepared.
despreparo [dʒiʃpre'paru] *m* lack of preparation.
desprestigiar [16] [dʒiʃpreʃtʃi'ʒja(x)] *vt* to discredit.
despretensioso, osa [dʒiʃpretẽn'sjozu, ɔza] *adj* unpretentious.
desprevenido, da [dʒiʃpreve'nidu, da] *adj* [distraído] unaware; **ser pego** ~ to be taken by surprise.
desprezar [4] [dʒiʃpre'za(x)] *vt* **-1.** [menosprezar] to despise. **-2.** [não dar importância] to scorn. **-3.** [não considerar] to disregard.
desprezível [dʒiʃpre'zivew] (*pl* **-eis**) *adj* **-1.** [vil] despicable. **-2.** [ínfimo] least.
desprezo [dʒiʃ'prezu] *m* **-1.** [desdém] disdain. **-2.** [repulsa] revulsion.
desproporção [dʒiʃpropox'sãw] (*pl* **-ões**) *f* inequality.
desproporcional [dʒiʃpropoxsjo'naw] (*pl* **-ais**) *adj*: ~ **(a)** disproportionate (to).
despropositado, da [dʒiʃpropozi'tadu, da] *adj* unreasonable.
despropósito [dʒiʃpro'pɔzitu] *m* **-1.** [disparate] absurdity. **-2.** *fig* [excesso]: **un** ~ more than enough.
desproteger [26] [dʒiʃprote'ʒe(x)] *vt* to abandon.
desprotegido, da [dʒiʃprote'gidu, da] *adj* [desamparado] vulnerable.
desprover [41] [dʒiʃpro've(x)] *vt*: ~ **alguém (de algo)** to deprive sb (of sthg).
◆ **desprover-se** *vp*: ~**-se de algo** to strip o.s. of sthg.
desprovido, da [dʒiʃpro'vidu, da] *adj*: ~ **de algo** lacking sthg.
despudor [dʒiʃpu'do(x)] *m* shamelessness.
despudorado, da [dʒiʃpudo'radu, da] *adj* shameless.
desqualificar [12] [dʒiʃkwalifi'ka(x)] *vt* **-1.** [tornar indigno] to render unfit. **-2.** [inabilitar] to disqualify; ~ **alguém (para)** to disqualify sb (from).
◆ **desqualificar-se** *vp* [inabilitar-se]: ~**-se (para)** to be eliminated (from).
desquitar-se [4] [dʒiʃki'taxsi] *vp* to get divorced.
desquite [dʒiʃ'kitʃi] *m* divorce.
desratização [dʒiʒxatiza'sãw] *f* extermination of rats and mice.

desratizar [4] [dʒiʒxati'za(x)] *vt* to exterminate rats and mice.

desregrado, da [dʒiʒxe'gradu, da] <> *adj* **-1.** [desordenado] disorderly. **-2.** [devasso] dissolute. <> *m, f* [devasso] debauched person.

desregulado, da [dʒiʃregu'ladu, da] *adj* [motor, aparelho] poorly adjusted.

desregular [4] [dʒiʒxegu'la(x)] *vt* irregular.

desrespeitar [4] [dʒiʒxeʃpej'ta(x)] *vt* **-1.** [desacatar] to disregard. **-2.** [desobedecera] to disobey.

desrespeito [dʒiʒxeʃ'pejtu] *m*: ~ **(a)** disrespect (for).

desrespeitoso, osa [dʒiʒxeʃpej'tozu, ɔza] *adj* disrespectful.

dessa ['dɛsa] = **de + esse.**

desse ['desi] = **de + esse.**

destacado, da [dʒiʃta'kadu, da] *adj* **-1.** [separado] detached. **-2.** [proeminente] eminent.

destacamento [dʒiʃtaka'mẽntu] *m* detachment.

destacar [12] [dʒiʃta'ka(x)] *vt* **-1.** [ger] to detach. **-2.** [fazer sobressair] to highlight.

◆ **destacar-se** *vp* [fazer-se notar] to be outstanding.

destacável [dʒiʃta'kavɛw] (*pl* **-eis**) *adj* detachable.

destampado, da [dʒiʃtãn'padu, da] *adj* uncovered.

destampar [4] [dʒiʃtãn'pa(x)] *vt* to remove the lid from.

destapar [4] [dʒiʃta'pa(x)] *vt* to uncover.

destaque [dʒiʃ'taki] *m* **-1.** [realce] prominence. **-2.** [pessoa ou assunto relevante] highlight.

desta ['dɛʃta] = **de + esta.**

deste ['deʃtʃi] = **de + este.**

destemido, da [dʒiʃte'midu, da] *adj* fearless.

destempero [dʒiʃtẽn'peru] *m* **-1.** [disparate] blunder. **-2.** *fam* [diarréia] diarrhoea. **-3.** *fam* [grande quantidade] mountain.

desterrar [4] [dʒiʃte'xa(x)] *vt* to exile.

desterro [dʒiʃ'texu] *m* exile.

destilação [deʃtʃila'sãw] *f* distillation.

destilar [4] [deʃtʃi'la(x)] *vt* to distil.

destilaria [deʃtʃila'ria] *f* distillery.

destinação [deʃtʃina'sãw] (*pl* **-oes**) *f* destination.

destinar [4] [deʃtʃi'na(x)] *vt* **-1.** [reservar] to put aside. **-2.** [aplicar] to allocate.

◆ **destinar-se** *vp* **-1.** [ser designado]: **~-se a** to be intended for. **-2.** [dedicar-se] to dedicate oneslf.

destinatário, ria [deʃtʃina'tarju, rja] *m, f* addressee.

destino [deʃ'tʃinu] *m* **-1.** [direção] destination. **-2.** [aplicação] purpose. **-3.** [futuro] destiny.

destituição [deʃtʃitwi'sãw] *f* destitution.

destituir [74] [deʃtʃi'twi(x)] *vt* **-1.** [privar]: ~ **alguém de algo** to deprive sb of sthg. **-2.** [demitir]: ~ **alguém (de algo)** to deprive sb (of sthg).

destoante [dʒiʃto'ãntʃi] *adj* **-1.** [desafinado] discordant. **-2.** [divergente] divergent.

destoar [20] [dʒiʃto'a(x)] *vi* **-1.** [desafinar] to be out of tune. **-2.** [divergir]: ~ **de algo** to diverge from sthg. **-3.** [não condizer]: ~ **de algo** to clash with sthg.

destorcer [25] [dʒiʃtox'se(x)] *vt* [endireitar] to straighten.

destorcido, da [dʒiʃtox'sidu, da] *adj* untwisted.

destrambelhado, da [dʒiʃtrãnbe'ʎadu, da] *adj* **-1.** [aloprado] foolish. **-2.** [desajeitado] awkward. **-3.** [sem propósito] hair-brained.

destrancar [12] [dʒiʃtrãŋ'ka(x)] *vt* to unlock.

destratar [4] [dʒiʃtra'ta(x)] *vt* to offend.

destravar [4] [dʒiʃtra'va(x)] *vt* **-1.** [porta] to unlock. **-2.** [língua] to loosen.

destreza [deʃ'treza] *f* skill.

destrinchar [4] [dʒiʃtrĩn'ʃa(x)] *vt* **-1.** [resolver] to unravel. **-2.** [detalhar] to detail.

destro, tra ['dɛʃtru, tra] *adj* dexterous.

destroçar [13] [dʒiʃtro'sa(x)] *vt* **-1.** [ger] to destroy. **-2.** [despedaçar] to pull to pieces.

destroços [dʒiʃ'trɔsuʃ] *mpl* wreckage *(sg).*

destróier [dʒiʃ'trɔje(x)] *m* destroyer.

destronar [4] [dʒiʃtro'na(x)] *vt* to dethrone.

destroncar [12] [dʒiʃtrõŋ'ka(x)] *vt* **-1.** [deslocar] to dislocate. **-2.** [decepar] to cut off.

destruição [dʒiʃtruj'sãw] *f* destruction.

destruidor, ra [dʒiʃtruj'do(x), ra] <> *adj* destructive. <> *m, f* destroyer.

destruir [74] [dʒiʃtru'i(x)] <> *vt* **-1.** [ger] to destroy. **-2.** [aniquilar] to annihilate. <> *vi* [ter efeito negativo] to be destroying.

◆ **destruir-se** *vp* **-1.** [a si próprio] to destroy o.s. **-2.** [um ao outro] to destroy one another.

destrutivo, va [dʒiʃtru'tʃivu, va] *adj* destructive.

desumano, na [dʒizu'mãnu, na] *adj* inhuman.

desunião [dʒiʒun'jãw] *f* **-1.** [separação] separation. **-2.** [discórdia] discord.

desunir [6] [dʒizu'ni(x)] *vt* [separar] to separate.

desusado, da [dʒizu'zadu, da] *adj* out of date.

desvairado, da [dʒiʒvaj'radu, da] <> *adj* **-1.** [louco] crazy. **-2.** [descontrolado] uncontrolled. <> *m, f* **-1.** [pessoa louca] crazy person. **-2.** [pessoa descontrolada] person who is quite out of control.

desvalido, da [dʒiʒva'lidu, da] *adj* **-1.** [desamparado] destitute. **-2.** [miserável] wretched.

desvalorização [dʒiʒvaloriza'sãw] (*pl* **-ões**) *f* devaluation.

desvalorizar [4] [dʒiʃvalori'za(x)] *vt & vi* to devalue.

◆ **desvalorizar-se** *vp* to undervalue o.s.

desvanecer [25] [dʒiʒvane'se(x)] *vt* [dissipar] to dispel.

◆ **desvanecer-se** *vp* **-1.** [dissipar-se] to disappear. **-2.** [desbotar-se] to fade.

desvanecido, da [dʒiʒvane'sidu, da] *adj* **-1.** [dissipado] dispelled. **-2.** [desbotado] faded.

desvantagem [dʒiʒvãn'taʒẽ] (*pl* **-ns**) *f* disadvantage; **em** ~ at a disadvantage.

desvantajoso, osa [dʒiʒvãnta'ʒozu, ɔza] *adj* disadvantageous.

desvão [dʒiʒ'vãw] *m* loft.

desvario [dʒiʒva'riw] *m* madness.

desvelar [4] [dʒiʒve'la(x)] *vt* **-1.** [provocar vigília] to keep awake. **-2.** [descobrir] to uncover; **~ uma estátua** to unveil a statue. **-3.** [aclarar] to clear up.
◆ **desvelar-se** *vp* to stay awake.
desvelo [dʒiʒ'velu] *m* [zelo] zeal.
desvencilhar [4] [dʒiʒvẽnsi'ʎa(x)] *vt* [soltar]: **~ algo/alguém (de algo)** to save sthg/sb (from sthg).
◆ **desvencilhar-se** *vp* **-1.** [soltar-se]: **~-se (de algo)** to free o.s. (from sthg). **-2.** *fig* [livrar-se]: **~ de alguém/algo** to get rid of sb/sthg.
desvendar [4] [dʒiʒvẽn'da(x)] *vt* **-1.** [tirar a venda de] to remove the blindfold from. **-2.** [revelar] to reveal.
desventura [dʒiʒvẽn'tura] *f* misfortune.
desviar [16] [dʒiʒ'vja(x)] *vt* **-1.** [mudar a direção de] to deviate. **-2.** *fig* [roubar] to misappropriate.
◆ **desviar-se** *vp* [mudar a direção] to deviate.
desvincular [4] [dʒiʒvĩŋku'la(x)] *vt*: **~ algo de algo** to dissociate sthg from sthg.
◆ **desvincular-se** *vp*: **~-se de algo/alguém** to break ties with sthg/sb.
desvio [dʒiʒ'viw] *m* **-1.** [mudança de direção] diversion. **-2.** [da coluna vertebral] curvature. **-3.** *fig* deviation. **-4.** [roubo] misappropriation.
desvirar [4] [dʒiʒvi'ra(x)] *vt* to turn back to the normal position.
desvirginar [4] [dʒiʒvixʒi'na(x)] *vt* to deflower.
desvirtuar [4] [dʒiʒvix'twa(x)] *vt* to misconstrue.
detalhadamente [detaʎada'mẽntʃi] *adv* in detail.
detalhado, da [deta'ʎadu, da] *adj* detailed.
detalhar [4] [deta'ʎa(x)] *vt* to detail.
detalhe [de'taʎi] *m* detail; **entrar em ~s** to go into detail.
detalhista [deta'ʎiʃta] *adj* meticulous.
detecção [detek'sãw] *f* detection.
detectar [4] [detek'ta(x)] *vt* to detect.
detector [detek'to(x)] (*pl* **-es**) *m* detector.
detenção [detẽn'sãw] (*pl* **-ões**) *f* detention.
détente [de'tãntʃi] *f POL* détente.
detento, ta [de'tẽntu, ta] *m, f* prisoner.
detentor, ra [detẽn'to(x), ra] *m, f* holder.
deter [1] [de'te(x)] *vt* **-1.** [parar] to stop. **-2.** [prender] to detain. **-3.** [manter, reter] to keep. **-4.** [reprimir] to hold back. **-5.** [ter em seu poder] to retain.
◆ **deter-se** *vp* **-1.** [parar] to stop. **-2.** [ficar] to remain. **-3.** [reprimir-se] to hold back. **-4.** [ocupar-se]: **~-se em algo** to dwell on sthg.
detergente [detex'ʒẽntʃi] ◇ *adj* cleansing. ◇ *m* detergent.
deterioração [deterjora'sãw] *f* deterioration.
deteriorar [4] [deterjo'ra(x)] ◇ *vt* **-1.** [estragar] to spoil. **-2.** [piorar] to damage. ◇ *vi* [piorar] to worsen.
◆ **deteriorar-se** *vp* **-1.** [estragar] to become spoiled. **-2.** *fig* [piorar] to deteriorate.
determinação [detexmina'sãw] (*pl* **-ões**) *f* **-1.** [empenho] determination. **-2.** [ordem] order.
determinado, da [detexmi'nadu, da] *adj* **-1.** [resoluto] determined. **-2.** [estabelecido] fixed. **-3.** (*antes de subst*) [certo] certain; **em ~ momento ...** at a certain moment.
determinante [detexmi'nãntʃi] ◇ *adj* determining. ◇ *m MAT* determinant.
determinar [4] [detexmi'na(x)] *vt* **-1.** [ger] to determine. **-2.** [precisar] to state.
◆ **determinar-se** *vp* [decidir-se]: **~-se a fazer algo** to decide to do sthg.
detestar [4] [deteʃ'ta(x)] *vt* to detest.
◆ **detestar-se** *vp* to detest o.s.
detestável [deteʃ'tavew] (*pl* **-eis**) *adj* detestable.
detetive [dete'tʃivi] *mf* detective.
detidamente [detʃida'mẽntʃi] *adv* minutely.
detido, da [de'tʃidu, da] *adj* **-1.** [retido] retained. **-2.** [preso] detained.
detonação [detona'sãw] (*pl* **-ões**) *f* detonation.
detonar [4] [deto'na(x)] ◇ *vt* [arma, bomba] to detonate. ◇ *vi* **-1.** [arma, bomba] to detonate. **-2.** [trovão] to thunder.
DETRAN (*abrev de* **Departamento Estadual de Trânsito**) *m Brazilian state department responsible for licensing of drivers and vehicles,* ≃ DVLA.
detrás [de'trajʃ] *adv* behind.
◆ **detrás de** *loc prep* behind.
◆ **por detrás** *loc adv* from behind.
detrimento [detri'mẽntu] *m*: **em ~ de** to the detriment of.
detrito [de'tritu] *m* detritus.
deturpação [detuxpa'sãw] (*pl* **-ões**) *f* corruption.
deturpar [4] [detux'pa(x)] *vt* **-1.** [adulterar] to distort. **-2.** [corromper] to corrupt.
deus, sa ['dewʃ, sa] (*mpl* **-ses**, *fpl* **-sas**) *m, f* god.
◆ **Deus** *m* God; **Deus e o mundo** [todo o mundo] the world and his wife; **graças a Deus!** thank God!; **meu Deus do céu!** my goodness!
deus-dará [ˌdewʃda'ra] *m* **-1.**: **ficar ao ~** [à ventura] to be left unattended. **-2.**: **viver ao ~** [a esmo] to have no aims in one's life.
deus-nos-acuda [ˌdewʃnuʃa'kuda] *m* commotion.
devagar [dʒiva'ga(x)] ◇ *adv* slowly. ◇ *adj inv fam* **-1.** [lento] slow. **-2.** [sem graça] boring; **ser ~ quase parando** to go at a snail's pace.
devagarinho [dʒivaga'riɲu] *adv* nice and slowly.
devanear [15] [deva'nja(x)] *vi* to muse.
devaneio [deva'neju] *m* reverie.
devassa [de'vasa] *f* official inquiry.
devassado, da [deva'sadu, da] *adj* open.
devassidão [devasi'dãw] *f* licentiousness.
devasso, ssa [de'vasu, sa] ◇ *adj* debauched. ◇ *m, f* debauched person.
devastar [4] [devaʃ'ta(x)] *vt* **-1.** [assolar] to devastate. **-2.** [despovoar] to drive people out of.
deve ['dɛvi] *m COM* debit.
devedor, ra [deve'do(x), ra] ◇ *adj* [firma, pessoa] in debt. ◇ *m, f* debtor.
dever [5] [de've(x)] (*pl* **-es**) ◇ *m* **-1.** [obrigação] duty; **cumprir seu ~** to do one's duty. **-2.** *EDUC*: **~ (de casa)** homework; **fazer o ~ (de casa)** to do one's homework. ◇ *vt* **-1.** [dinheiro, favores]: **~**

algo (a alguém) to owe sthg (to sb). **-2.** [expressando probabilidade]: **deve fazer sol amanhã** it ought to be sunny tomorrow; **deve ser meia-noite** it must be midnight; **ela deve chegar à noite** she should arrive in the evening; **deve ter acontecido alguma coisa** something must have happened. **-3.** [expressando sugestão]: **você deve sair cedo** you ought to go out early. **-4.** [expressando necessidade]: **devo praticar mais esportes** I should do more sport. **-5.** [expressando obrigação]: **você deve ser pontual sempre** you must always be on time. <> *vi* [ter dívida]: **ele deve muito na praça** she owes a lot at the market; **ela deve a todos os amigos** she owes a lot to all her friends, she's in debt to all her friends.

◆ **dever-se a** *vp* [ser consequência de] to be due to.

deveras [de'vɛraʃ] *adv* really.

devidamente [de,vida'mẽntʃi] *adv* duly.

devido, da [de'vidu, da] *adj* due; **no ~ tempo** in due course.

◆ **devido a** *loc adv* due to.

devoção [devo'sãw] *f* **-1.** *RELIG* devotion. **-2.** [dedicação] dedication.

devolução [devolu'sãw] (*pl* **-ões**) *f* return.

devoluto, ta [devo'lutu, ta] *adj* **-1.** [vago, vazio] vacant. **-2.** [jur] repossessed.

devolver [5] [devow've(x)] *vt* **-1.** [restituir] to return. **-2.** [replicar] to respond to. **-3.** [vomitar] to throw up.

devorar [4] [devo'ra(x)] *vt* **-1.** [ger] to consume. **-2.** [comida] to devour. **-3.** *fig* [livro] to read voraciously.

devotar [4] [devo'ta(x)] *vt*: **~ algo a algo/alguém** to devote sthg to sthg/sb.

◆ **devotar-se** *vp*: **~-se a algo/alguém** to devote o.s. to sthg/sb.

devoto, ta [de'vɔtu, ta] <> *adj* devout. <> *m, f* devotee.

dez ['dɛʒ] *num* ten; *veja também* **seis**.

dez. (*abrev de* **dezembro**) Dec.

dezembro [de'zẽnbru] *m* December; *veja também* **setembro**.

dezena [de'zena] *f* **-1.** [ger] ten. **-2.** [em jogo]: **ganhei na ~** I got ten numbers right.

dezenove [deze'nɔvi] *num* nineteen; *veja também* **seis**.

dezesseis [deze'seiʃ] *num* sixteen; *veja também* **seis**.

dezessete [deze'sɛtʃi] *num* seventeen; *veja também* **seis**.

dezoito [de'zɔitu] *num* eighteen; *veja também* **seis**.

DF (*abrev de* **Distrito Federal**) *m* Federal District.

dia ['dʒia] *m* **-1.** [gen] day; **bom ~!** good morning!; **de um ~ para outro** from one day to the next; **no ~ anterior/seguinte** the previous/next day; **mais ~, menos dia** sooner or later; **o ~ todo** all day long; **todo ~, todos os ~s** all day, every day; **todo santo ~** every single day. **~ cheio** busy day; **um ~ daqueles** one of those days. **-2.** [data] date; **no ~ dez** on the tenth; **~ de Reis** Twelfth Night; **~ santo** feast day. **-3.** [luz do sol]: **de ~** in the daytime. **-4.** [atualidade]: **do ~** today's; **em ~** up-to-date; **hoje em ~** nowadays. **-5.** [horário de trabalho]: **~ de folga** day off; **~ útil** working day.

◆ **dias** *mpl* **-1.** [época]: **nos meus ~s** in my day. **-2.** [vida]: **ele está com seus ~s contados** his days are numbered.

dia-a-dia *m* daily routine.

diabetes [dʒja'bɛtʃiʃ] *m ou f* diabetes.

diabético, ca [dʒja'bɛtʃiku, ka] <> *adj* diabetic. <> *m, f* diabetic.

diabo ['dʒjabu] <> *m* devil; **aconteceu o ~** it all happened; **comer o pão que o ~ amassou** to go through hell; **dizer** *ou* **falar o ~ de alguém** to bad-mouth sb; **estar com o ~ no corpo** to be restless; **fazer o ~** to run riot. <> *adj fam*: **o ~ de carro parou** the damned car has stopped. <> *interj* damn!

◆ **como o diabo** *loc adv fam*: **é feia como o ~!** she's as ugly as sin!

diabólico, ca [dʒja'bɔliku, ka] *adj* diabolical.

diabrura [dʒja'brura] *f* devilish trick.

diacho ['dʒjaʃu] *interj fam* what the devil!

diácono ['dʒjakonu] *m* deacon.

diadema [dʒja'dema] *m* diadem.

diáfano, na ['dʒjafãnu, na] *adj* diaphanous.

diafragma [dʒja'fragma] *m* diaphragm.

diagnosticar [12] [dʒjagnoʃtʃi'ka(x)] *vt* diagnose.

diagnóstico [dʒjag'nɔʃtʃiku] *m* diagnosis.

diagonal [dʒjago'naw] (*pl* **-ais**) <> *adj* diagonal. <> *f* diagonal.

diagrama [dʒja'grãma] *m* diagram.

diagramador, ra [dʒjagrama'do(x), ra] *m, f* typesetter.

diagramar [4] [dʒjagra'ma(x)] *vt* to work as a typesetter.

dialética [dʒja'lɛtʃika] *f* dialectic.

dialeto [dʒja'lɛtu] *m* dialect.

diálise ['dʒjalizi] *f* dialysis.

dialogar [14] [dʒjalo'ga(x)] *vi* **-1.** [conversar]: **~ (com)** to talk (to). **-2.** [negociar]: **~ (com)** to negotiate (with).

diálogo ['dʒjalogu] *m* dialogue.

dial-up *m* *COMPUT* dial-up.

diamante [dʒja'mãntʃi] *m* diamond.

diâmetro ['dʒjãmetru] *m* diameter.

diante ◆ **por diante** *loc adv*: **e assim ~** and so on.

◆ **diante de** *loc adv* in the face of; **~ de algo /alguém** in front of sthg/sb.

◆ **daqui por diante** *loc adv* from now on.

dianteira [dʒjãn'tejra] *f* lead; **na ~** ahead.

dianteiro, ra [dʒjãn'tejru, ra] *adj* front.

diapasão [dʒjapa'zãw] *m* tuning fork.

diapositivo [dʒjapozi'tʃivu] *m* slide.

diário, ria ['dʒjarju, rja] *adj* daily.

◆ **diário** *m* **-1.** [caderno] diary; **~ de bordo** logbook. **-2.** [para viagem] journal. **-3.** [jornal] daily paper. **-4.** *COM* ledger.

◆ **diária** *f* [de hotel] daily rate.

◆ **Diário Oficial** *m* official gazette.

diarista [dʒja'riʃta] *m f* diarist.
diarréia [dʒja'xɛja] *f* diarrhoea.
dica ['dʒika] *f fam* hint.
dicção [dʒik'sãw] *f* diction.
dicionário [dʒisjo'narju] *m* dictionary.
dicionarista [dʒisjona'riʃta] *mf* lexicographer.
dicotomia [dʒikoto'mia] *f* dichotomy.
didata [dʒi'data] *mf* teacher.
didático, ca [dʒi'datʃiku, ka] *adj* **-1.** [pessoa] didactic. **-2.** [explicação] instructive.
◆ **didática** *f* didactics.
DIEESE (*abrev de* **Departamento Intersindical de Estatísticas e Estudos Sócio-Econômicos**) *m trade union body for the support of workers in São Paulo.*
diesel ['dʒizɛw] *m* diesel; **motor (a)** ~ diesel engine.
dieta ['dʒjɛta] *f* diet; **fazer** ~ to diet.
dietético, ca [dʒje'tɛtʃiku, ka] *adj* dietary; **chocolate** ~ diet chocolate; **bebida** ~ diet drink.
dietista [dʒje'tʃiʃta] *mf* dietician.
difamação [dʒifama'sãw] (*pl* **-ões**) *f* slander.
difamador, ra [dʒifama'do(x), ra] <> *adj* slanderous. <> *m, f* slanderer.
difamar [4] [dʒifa'ma(x)] *vt* to slander.
difamatório, ria [dʒifama'tɔrju, rja] *adj* defamatory.
diferença [dʒife'rẽnsa] *f* **-1.** [desigualdade] difference. **-2.** [distinção]: **fazer** ~ **entre** to distinguish between; **fazer** ~ to make a difference. **-3.** [prejuízo]: **fazer** ~ **para alguém** to matter to sb. **-4.** [discordância]: **ter** ~**(s) com alguém** to have one's differences with sb. **-5.** *MAT* remainder.
diferenciação [dʒiferẽnsja'sãw] *f*: **fazer** ~ **entre** to differentiate between.
diferencial [dʒiferẽn'sjaw] (*pl* **-ais**) <> *adj* differential. <> *m AUTO* differential. <> *f MAT* differential.
diferenciar [16] [dʒiferẽn'sja(x)] *vt*: ~ **algo/alguém (de)** to distinguish sthg/sb (from).
◆ **diferenciar-se** *vp* to differ.
diferente [dʒife'rẽntʃi] <> *adj* different; ~ **de** different from *UK*, different than *US*. <> *adv* differently.
diferir [57] [dʒife'ri(x)] *vi*: ~ **(em algo)** to differ (on sthg); ~ **de algo/alguém** to differ from sthg/sb.
difícil [dʒi'fisiw] (*pl* **-eis**) <> *adj* **-1.** [ger] difficult, hard. **-2.** [delicado] tricky. **-3.** [improvável]: **acho muito** ~ **ele vir hoje** I think it is very unlikely he will come today. <> *adv*: **falar /escrever** ~ to use fancy words. <> *m*: **o** ~ **é** the trouble is.
dificílimo, ma [dʒifi'silimu, ma] *superl* extremely difficult.
dificilmente [dʒifisiw'mẽntʃi] *adv*: ~ **voltarei a falar com ele** it will be hard for me ever to speak to him again.
dificuldade [dʒifikuw'dadʒi] *f* **-1.** [ger] problem; **pôr** ~ **em algo/em fazer algo** to object to sthg/to doing sthg; **ter** ~**s com algo** to have problems with sthg; **ter** ~ **em fazer algo** to have difficulty in doing sthg. **-2.** [qualidade de difícil] difficulty. **-3.** [impedimento] snag. **-4.** [relutância]: **ter** ~ **em fazer algo** to be loath to do sthg. **-5.** [situação crítica] trouble; **em** ~**(s)** in trouble; **meter-se em** ~**s** to get into trouble; **passar** ~**(s)** to have a hard time.
dificultar [4] [dʒifikuw'ta(x)] *vt* to complicate.
difteria [dʒifte'ria] *f* diphtheria.
difundir [6] [dʒifũn'di(x)] *vt* to spread.
difusão [dʒifu'zãw] *f* transmission.
difuso, sa [dʒi'fuzu, za] *adj* diffuse.
digerir [57] [dʒiʒe'ri(x)] *vt* to digest.
digestão [dʒiʒeʃ'tãw] *f* digestion.
digestivo, va [dʒiʒeʃ'tʃivu, va] *adj* digestive.
digitação [dʒiʒita'sãw] (*pl* **-ões**) *f COMPUT* keying-in.
digitador, ra [dʒiʒita'do(x), ra] *m, f* keyboarder.
digital [dʒiʒi'taw] (*pl* **-ais**) *adj* **-1.** [ger] digital. **-2.** [dos dedos] finger.
digitalizado, da [dʒiʒitali'zadu, da] *adj COMPUT* digitized.
digitalizar [4] [dʒiʒitali'za(x)] *vt COMPUT* to digitize.
digitar [4] [dʒiʒi'ta(x)] *vt COMPUT* to key in.
dígito ['dʒiʒitu] *m* digit.
digladiar-se [16] [dʒigla'dʒjaxsi] *vp* **-1.** [com espada] to fight with a sword. **-2.** *fig* [lutar] to battle it out.
dignamente [dʒigna'mẽntʃi] *adv* with dignity.
dignar-se [7] [dʒig'naxsi] *vp*: ~**-se a fazer algo** to deign to do sthg.
dignidade [dʒigni'dadʒi] *f* **-1.** [cargo] office. **-2.** [decência, honra] dignity; **com** ~ with dignity.
dignificar [12] [dʒignifi'ka(x)] *vt* to dignify.
dignitário, ria [dʒigni'tarju, rja] *m, f* dignitary.
digno, na ['dʒignu, na] *adj* worthy; **ser** ~ **de algo /de fazer algo** to be worthy of sthg/doing sthg.
digressão [dʒigre'sãw] (*pl* **-ões**) *f* digression.
dilaceração [dʒilasera'sãw] *f* laceration.
dilacerante [dʒilase'rãntʃi] *adj* agonizing.
dilacerar [4] [dʒilase'ra(x)] *vt* [despedaçar] to tear to pieces.
◆ **dilacerar-se** *vp* [afligir-se] to be torn apart.
dilapidação [dʒilapida'sãw] *f* **-1.** [destruição] dilapidation. **-2.** [esbanjamento] squandering.
dilapidar [4] [dʒilapi'da(x)] *vt* **-1.** [derrubar] to reduce to rubble. **-2.** [esbanjar] to squander.
dilatação [dʒilata'sãw] *f* dilation.
dilatador, ra [dʒitala'do(x), ra] <> *adj MED* dilator. <> *m MED* dilator.
dilatar [4] [dʒila'ta(x)] *vt* **-1.** [ampliar] to dilate. **-2.** [adiar] to delay.
dilema [dʒi'lema] *m* dilemma.
diletante [dʒile'tãntʃi] <> *adj* dilettantish. <> *mf* dilettante.
diletantismo [dʒiletãn'tʃiʒmu] *m* dilettantism.
diligência [dʒili'ʒẽnsja] *f* **-1.** [cuidado] diligence. **-2.** [presteza] promptness. **-3.** [pesquisa] enquiry. **-4.** [veículo] stagecoach. **-5.** *JUR* formality.
diligenciar [16] [dʒiliʒẽn'sja(x)] *vt* to strive for.
diligente [dʒili'ʒẽntʃi] *adj* diligent.

diluente [dʒil'wẽntʃi] ◇ *adj* diluent. ◇ *m* diluent.
diluição [dʒilwi'sãw] *f* dilution.
diluir [74] [dʒi'lwi(x)] *vt*: **~ algo (em algo)** to dilute sthg (in sthg).
dilúvio [dʒi'luviw] *m* flood.
dimensão [dʒimẽn'sãw] (*pl* **-ões**) *f* **-1.** [ger] dimension. **-2.** [tamanho] size.
dimensionar [4] [dʒimẽnsjo'na(x)] *vt* to dimension.
diminuição [dʒiminwi'sãw] *f* reduction.
diminuir [74] [dʒimi'nwi(x)] ◇ *vt* **-1.** [reduzir] to reduce. **-2.** [subtrair]: **~ algo de** *ou* **em algo** to deduct sthg from sthg. ◇ *vi* [reduzir-se] to lessen; **~ de peso/largura** to decrease in weight/width.
diminutivo [dʒiminu'tʃivu] *m* GRAM diminutive.
diminuto, ta [dʒimi'nutu, ta] *adj* minute.
dinâmico, ca [dʒi'nãmiku, ka] *adj* dynamic.
◆ **dinâmica** *f* **-1.** MEC dynamics *(pl)*. **-2.** *fig* [atividade] dynamic; **~ de grupo** teamwork.
dinamismo [dʒina'miʒmu] *m* dynamism.
dinamitar [4] [dʒinami'ta(x)] *vt* to dynamite.
dinamite [dʒina'mitʃi] *f* dynamite.
dinamizar [4] [dʒinami'za(x)] *vt* to motivate.
Dinamarca [dʒina'marka] *n* Denmark.
dinamarquês, esa [dʒinamax'keʃ, eza] ◇ *adj* Danish. ◇ *m, f* Dane.
◆ **dinamarquês** *m* [língua] Danish.
dínamo ['dʒinamu] *m* dynamo.
dinastia [dʒinaʃ'tʃia] *f* dynasty.
dinheirão [dʒiɲej'rãw] *m fam*: **um ~** a mint.
dinheiro [dʒi'ɲejru] *m* money; **~ vivo** hard cash.
dinossauro [dʒino'sawru] *m* dinosaur.
diocese [dʒjo'sɛzi] *f* diocese.
dióxido ['dʒjɔksidu] *m* QUÍM dioxide; **~ de carbono** carbon dioxide.
diploma [dʒi'ploma] *m* diploma.
diplomacia [dʒiploma'sia] *f* **-1.** [ciência] diplomacy. **-2.** [representantes] diplomatic corps. **-3.** *fig* [tato] tact; **com ~** tactfully.
diplomado, da [dʒiploma'du, da] ◇ *adj* [formado] graduated. ◇ *m,f* graduate.
diplomar [4] [dʒiplo'ma(x)] *vt* to graduate.
◆ **diplomar-se** *vp*: **~-se (em algo)** to get a diploma/degree (in sthg).
diplomata [dʒiplo'mata] *mf* **-1.** [representante] diplomat. **-2.** *fig* [negociador hábil] mediator.
diplomático, ca [dʒiplo'matʃiku, ka] *adj* diplomatic.
dique ['dʒiki] *m* dyke.
direção [dʒire'sãw] (*pl* **-ões**) *f* **-1.** [rumo, sentido] direction; **em ~ a** towards, headed for. **-2.** [de empresa] management. **-3.** [de partido] leadership. **-4.** [de filme, peça de teatro] direction. **-5.** [de jornal] editors. **-6.** [diretores] board of directors. **-7.** AUTO steering.
direcionamento [dʒiresiona'mẽntu] *m* COMPUT forwarding.
direcionar [4] *vt* to channel.
direita [dʒi'rejta] *f* ▷ **direito**.
direitinho [dʒirej'tʃiɲu] *adv* just right.
direitista [dʒirej'tʃiʃta] *mf* right-winger.
direito, ta [dʒi'rejtu, ta] *adj* **-1.** [lado] right-hand. **-2.** [destro] right. **-3.** [digno] honest. **-4.** [arrumado] straight.
◆ **direito** ◇ *m* **-1.** JUR law; **~ civil** civil law. **-2.** [prerrogativa] right. **-3.** [lado] right side. ◇ *adv* properly.
◆ **direita** *f* **-1.** [lado direito] right-hand side; **à ~** on *ou* to the right. **-2.** POL right; **ser de ~** to be right-wing.
◆ **direitos** *mpl*: **~ autorais** copyright *(sg)*; **~ humanos** human rights.
diretamente [dʒirɛta'mẽntʃi] *adv* straight.
diretas [dʒi'rɛtaʃ] *fpl* POL direct elections.
direto, ta [dʒi'rɛtu, ta] *adj* **-1.** [ger] direct. **-2.** TV [transmissão] live.
◆ **direto** *adv* straight.
diretor, ra [dʒire'to(x), ra] (*mpl* **-res**, *fpl* **-ras**) *m, f* **-1.** [de escola] head. **-2.** [de empresa, teatro, cinema] director. **-3.** [de jornal] editor.
diretoria [dʒireto'ria] *f* **-1.** [de escola] headship. **-2.** [de empresa] directorship.
diretório [dʒire'tɔriw] *m* **-1.** [conselho] board; **~ acadêmico** students' union. **-2.** COMPUT directory; **~ raiz** root directory.
diretriz [dʒire'triʒ] *f* directive.
DIRF (*abrev de* **Declaração de Imposto de Renda na Fonte**) *f* *Brazilian declaration of income tax at source.*
dirigente [dʒiri'ʒẽntʃi] *mf* leader.
dirigir [52] [dʒiri'ʒi(x)] ◇ *vt* **-1.** [administrar - empresa, hotel] to manage; [- filme, peça de teatro] to direct. **-2.** AUTO to drive. **-3.** [bicicleta] to ride. **-4.** [atenção, esforços]: **~ esforços para algo** to direct one's energy towards sthg. **-5.** [enviar] to address. ◇ *vi* AUTO to drive.
◆ **dirigir-se** *vp* **-1.** [encaminhar-se]: **~-se a** to go to. **-2.** [falar com]: **~-se a alguém** to speak to sb.
dirimir [6] [dʒiri'mi(x)] *vt* to settle.
discagem [dʒiʃ'kaʒẽ] *f* dialling; **~ direta** direct dialling.
discar [12] [dʒiʃ'ka(x)] *vt* to dial.
discente [dʒi'sẽntʃi] *adj* student.
discernimento [dʒisexni'mẽntu] *m* discernment.
discernir [54] [dʒisex'ni(x)] *vt* **-1.** [perceber] to recognize. **-2.** [distinguir]: **~ entre algo e algo** to distinguish between sthg and sthg.
discernível [dʒisex'nivew] (*pl* **-eis**) *adj* perceptible.
disciplina [dʒisi'plina] *f* discipline.
disciplinador, ra [dʒisiplina'do(x), ra] *adj* disciplinary.
disciplinar [4] [dʒisipli'na(x)] ◇ *adj* disciplinary. ◇ *vt* to discipline.
◆ **disciplinar-se** *vp* to discipline o.s.
discípulo, la [dʒi'sipulu, la] *m, f* disciple.
disc-jóquei [dʒisk'ʒɔkej] (*pl* **disc-jóqueis**) *mf* disc jockey.
disco ['dʒiʃku] *m* **-1.** [ger] disc; **~ voador** flying

saucer. **-2.** *MÚS* record; ~ **laser** compact disc; **mudar o** ~ *fig* to stop banging on; **não mudar o** ~ to keep banging on. **-3.** [de telefone] dial. **-4.** *COMPUT* disk; ~ **flexível/rígido** floppy/hard disk; ~ **de sistema** system disk.

discordância [dʒiʃkox'dãnsja] *f* **-1.** [ger] disagreement. **-2.** [resultados, opinião, gosto] difference.

discordante [dʒiʃkox'dãntʃi] *adj* at variance.

discordar [4] [dʒiʃkox'da(x)] *vi*: ~ **(de algo/alguém)** to disagree (with sthg/sb).

discórdia [dʒiʃ'kɔrdʒja] *f* discord.

discorrer [5] [dʒiʃko'xe(x)] *vi*: ~ **sobre algo** to talk about sthg (at length).

discoteca [dʒiʃko'tɛka] *f* **-1.** [boate] discotheque. **-2.** [coleção de discos] record collection.

discotecário, ria [dʒiʃkote'kariw, ria] *m, f* disc jockey.

discrepância [dʒiʃkre'pãnsja] *f* discrepancy.

discrepante [dʒiʃkre'pãntʃi] *adj* differing.

discrepar [4] [dʒiʃkre'pa(x)] *vi*: ~ **de algo/alguém** to differ from sthg/sb.

discretamente [dʒiʃkreta'mẽntʃi] *adv* discreetly.

discreto, ta [dʒiʃ'krɛtu, ta] *adj* **-1.** [roupa] modest. **-2.** [pessoa] discreet.

discrição [dʒiʃkri'sãw] *f* discretion.

discriminação [dʒiʃkrimina'sãw] *f* **-1.** [diferenciação] differentiation. **-2.** [segregação] discrimination.

discriminador, ra [dʒiʃkrimina'do(x), ra] *adj* biased.

discriminar [4] [dʒiʃkrimi'na(x)] *vt* **-1.** [listar] to itemize. **-2.** [segregar] to isolate.

discriminatório, ria [dʒiʃkrimina'tɔrju, rja] *adj* **-1.** [lista] itemized. **-2.** [medida] discriminatory.

discursar [4] [dʒiʃkux'sa(x)] *vi*: ~ **(sobre)** to make a speech (about).

discurso [dʒiʃ'kuxsu] *m* speech.

discussão [dʒiʃku'sãw] (*pl* **-ões**) *f* **-1.** [debate] discussion. **-2.** [briga] argument.

discutido, da [dʒiʃku'tʃidu, da] ◇ *pp* ▷ **discutir**. ◇ *adj* much-discussed.

discutir [6] [dʒiʃku'tʃi(x)] ◇ *vt* [debater]: ~ **algo (com alguém)** to discuss sthg (with sb). ◇ *vi* [brigar]: ~ **(com alguém)** to argue (with sb).

discutível [dʒiʃku'tʃivew] (*pl* **-eis**) *adj* arguable.

disenteria [dʒizẽnte'ria] *f* dysentery.

disfarçado, da [dʒiʃfax'sadu, da] *adj* disguised.
◆ **disfarçada** *f*: **dar uma** ~ **(em algo)** to mask (sthg).

disfarçar [13] [dʒiʃfax'sa(x)] *vt* [dissimular] to disguise.
◆ **disfarçar-se** *vp* [fantasiando-se]: ~**-se de algo** to disguise o.s. as sthg.

disfarce [dʒiʃ'faxsi] *m* disguise.

disfasia [dʒiʃfa'zia] *f MED* dysphasia.

disforme [dʒiʃ'fɔxmi] *adj* [horrendo] deformed.

disfunção [dʒiʃfũn'sãw] (*pl* **-ões**) *f* dysfunction.

dislexia [dʒiʒlek'sia] *f* dyslexia.

disléxico, ca [diʒ'lɛksiku, ka] *adj* dyslexic.

díspar ['dʒiʃpa(x)] *adj* disparate.

disparado, da [dʒiʃpa'radu, da] *adj* [lançado - tiro, flecha] fired; [- pedra] hurled.
◆ **disparado** *adv* **-1.** [a toda velocidade] at full speed. **-2.** [com grande superioridade] by far.
◆ **disparada** *f*: **em** ~ like a shot.

disparar [4] [dʒiʃpa'ra(x)] ◇ *vt* [desfechar, lançar - tiro, flecha] to fire; [- pedra] to hurl. ◇ *vi* **-1.** [descarregar-se] to fire. **-2.** [correr] to shoot off.

disparatado, da [dʒiʃpara'tadu, da] *adj* absurd.

disparate [dʒiʃpa'ratʃi] *m* nonsense.

disparidade [dʒiʃpari'dadʒi] *f* disparity.

disparo [dʒiʃ'paru] *m* shot.

dispêndio [dʒiʃ'pẽndʒu] *m* expense.

dispendioso, osa [dʒiʃpẽn'djozu, ɔza] *adj* costly.

dispensa [dʒiʃ'pẽnsa] *f* dispensation.

dispensar [4] [dʒiʃpẽn'sa(x)] *vt* **-1.** [prescindir] to do without. **-2.** [conceder]: ~ **algo a alguém** to grant sthg to sb. **-3.** [eximir]: ~ **alguém (de algo)** to excuse sb (from sthg).

dispensável [dʒiʃpẽn'savew] (*pl* **-eis**) *adj* expendable.

dispepsia [dʒiʃpep'sia] *f* dyspepsia.

dispersão [dʒiʃpex'sãw] *f* dispersal.

dispersar [4] [dʒiʃpex'sa(x)] *vt* to disperse.
◆ **dispersar-se** *vp* to disperse.

dispersivo, va [dʒiʃpex'sivu, va] *adj* **-1.** [pessoa] easily distracted. **-2.** [barulho] distracting.

display *m* display.

displicência [dʒiʃpli'sẽnsja] *f* carelessness.

displicente [dʒiʃpli'sẽntʃi] *adj* careless.

disponibilidade [dʒiʃponibili'dadʒi] *f* availability; **em** ~ openly available.

disponível [dʒiʃpo'nivɛw] (*pl* **-eis**) *adj* available.

dispor [45] [dʒiʃ'po(x)] ◇ *m*: **ao** ~ **de alguém** at sb's disposal. ◇ *vt* **-1.** [arrumar] to arrange. **-2.** [determinar] to decide. ◇ *vi* **-1.** [usar]: ~ **de** to have at one's disposal; **disponha!** go ahead! **-2.** [ter]: ~ **de** to have available.
◆ **dispor-se** *vp* **-1.** [decidir-se] to decide. **-2.** [propor-se] to be prepared.

disposição [dʒiʃpozi'sãw] *m* **-1.** [arrumação] arrangement. **-2.** [ânimo, vontade]: **minha** ~ **para trabalhar hoje é pouca** I don't feel much like working today. **-3.** [subordinação]: **à** ~ **de** available to.

dispositivo [dʒiʃpozi'tʃivu] *m* **-1.** [mecanismo] mechanism, device; ~ **intra-uterino** intrauterine device. **-2.** *JUR* provision. **-3.** *fig* [meio] measures *(pl)*.

disposto, ta [dʒiʃ'poʃtu, ta] *adj* **-1.** [arrumado] arranged. **-2.** [animado] in a good mood; ~ **a algo/a fazer algo** willing for sthg/to do sthg.

disputa [dʒiʃ'puta] *f* **-1.** [briga] dispute. **-2.** [competição] contest.

disputar [4] [dʒiʃpu'ta(x)] ◇ *vt* **-1.** [concorrer a] to enter. **-2.** [competir por] to compete for. ◇ *vi* [rivalizar]: ~ **com algo/alguém** to rival sthg/sb.

disquete [dʒiʃ'kɛtʃi] *m COMPUT* floppy disk.

dissabor [dʒisa'bo(x)] *m* annoyance.

dissecar [12] [dʒise'ka(x)] *vt* **-1.** [corpo] to dissect. **-2.** *fig* [analisar] to examine in detail.

disse-me-disse ['dʒisimi'dʒisi] *m inv* gossip.

disseminação [dʒisemina'sãw] *f* spread.

disseminar [4] [dʒisemi'na(x)] *vt* to spread.
◆ **disseminar-se** *vp* to spread.

dissensão [dʒisẽn'sãw] (*pl* **-ões**) *f* dissension.

dissentir [56] [dʒisẽn'tʃi(x)] *vi* **-1.** [discordar]: ~ **de algo/alguém** to disagree with sthg/sb. **-2.** [discrepar]: ~ **de algo** to be at odds with sthg.

dissertação [dʒisexta'sõw] (*pl* **-ões**) *f* **-1.** [tratado] dissertation. **-2.** [discurso] lecture.

dissertar [4] [dʒisex'ta(x)] *vi*: ~ **(sobre algo)** to lecture (on sthg).

dissidência [dʒisi'dẽnsja] *f* **-1.** [divergência] difference of opinion. **-2.** [cisão] breakaway. **-3.** [dissidentes] dissidents *(pl)*.

dissidente [dʒisi'dẽntʃi] ◇ *adj* dissident. ◇ *mf* dissident.

dissídio [dʒi'sidʒu] *m* dispute; ~ **coletivo** collective dispute.

dissimilar [4] [dʒisimi'la(x)] *vt* to dissimilate.

dissimulação [dʒisimula'sãw] *f* **-1.** [fingimento] pretence *UK*, pretense *US*. **-2.** [disfarce] disguise.

dissimular [4] [dʒisimu'la(x)] ◇ *vt* **-1.** [disfarçar] to disguise. **-2.** [fingir] to feign. ◇ *vi* [disfarçar] to dissimulate.

dissipação [dʒisipa'sãw] *f* dissipation.

dissipar [4] [dʒisi'pa(x)] *vt* **-1.** [dispersar] to disperse. **-2.** [esbanjar] to squander.
◆ **dissipar-se** *vp* to vanish.

disso ['dʒisu] = **de + isso**.

dissociação [dʒisosia'sãw] (*pl* **-ões**) *f* dissociation.

dissociar [16] [dʒiso'sja(x)] *vt*: ~ **algo de algo** to dissociate sthg from sthg.

dissolução [dʒisolu'sãw] *f* dissolution.

dissoluto, ta [dʒiso'lutu, ta] *adj* dissolute.

dissolver [5] [dʒisow've(x)] *vt* to dissolve.
◆ **dissolver-se** *vp* **-1.** [extinguir-se] to break up. **-2.** [desmanchar-se] to dissolve.

dissonância [dʒiso'nãnsja] *f* **-1.** *MÚS* discord. **-2.** [som desagradável] cacophony. **-3.** *fig* [desarmonia] incongruity.

dissonante [dʒiso'nãntʃi] *adj* **-1.** *MÚS* discordant. **-2.** [sons] jarring. **-3.** *fig* [desarmônico] incongruous.

dissuadir [6] [dʒiswa'di(x)] *vt*: ~ **alguém (de algo/de fazer algo)** to dissuade sb (from sthg/doing sthg).

dissuasão [dʒiswa'zãw] *f* dissuasion.

dissuasivo, va [dʒiswa'zivu, va] *adj* dissuasive.

distância [dʒiʃ'tãnsja] *f* **-1.** [espaço] distance; **manter-se à** ~ **de** to keep at a distance from. **-2.** *fig* [intervalo] gap. **-3.** [diferença] difference.

distanciamento [dʒiʃtãnsja'mẽntu] *m* separation.

distanciar [16] [dʒiʃtãn'sja(x)] *vt* to separate.
◆ **distanciar-se** *vp* to move away.

distante [dʒiʃ'tãntʃi] *adj* **-1.** [longe] distant. **-2.** *fig* [alheado] aloof.

distar [4] [dʒiʃ'ta(x)] *vi*: **a cidade não dista muito, estamos chegando lá** the city isn't very far, we're nearly there; *fig* **os poetas distam muito dos escritores de prosa** poets are very different from prose writers; **o Rio dista 420 km de São Paulo** Rio is 420 km from São Paulo.

distender [5] [dʒiʃtẽn'de(x)] *vt* [ger] to stretch; [músculo] to pull.

distensão [dʒiʃtẽn'sãw] (*pl* **-ões**) *f* **-1.** *MED* relaxation. **-2.** *POL* calm.

distinção [dʒiʃtĩn'sãw] (*pl* **-ões**) *f* [ger] distinction; [honraria] honour.

distinguir [53] [dʒiʃtĩŋ'gi(x)] *vt* **-1.** [caracterizar] to typify. **-2.** [discernir] to distinguish. **-3.** [separar] to differentiate. **-4.** [perceber] to make out. **-5.** [premiar] to decorate.
◆ **distinguir-se** *vp* [sobressair-se] to stand out.

distintivo, va [dʒiʃtʃĩn'tʃivu, va] *adj* distinctive.
◆ **distintivo** *m* badge.

distinto, ta [dʒiʃ'tʃintu, ta] *adj* **-1.** [diferente] different. **-2.** [perceptível] distinct. **-3.** [ilustre] distinguished. **-4.** [elegante - pessoa] refined; [- roupa] elegant; [- postura] distinguished.

disto ['dʒiʃtu] = **de + isto**.

distorção [dʒiʃtox'sãw] (*pl* **-ões**) *f* distortion.

distorcer [25] [dʒiʃtox'se(x)] *vt* to distort.

distração [dʒiʃtra'sãw] (*pl* **-ões**) *f* **-1.** [descuido] carelessness. **-2.** [diversão] distraction.

distraído, da [dʒiʃtra'idu, da] *adj* **-1.** [desatento] inattentive. **-2.** [alheio] absent-minded.

distrair [68] [dʒiʃtra'i(x)] *vt* **-1.** [divertir] to amuse. **-2.** [entreter] to entertain. **-3.** [desviar a atenção]: ~ **alguém (de)** to distract sb (from).
◆ **distrair-se** *vp* **-1.** [divertir-se] to amuse o.s. **-2.** [alhear-se] to lose concentration.

distribuição [dʒiʃtribwi'sãw] (*pl* **-ões**) *f* distribution.

distribuidor, ra [dʒiʃtribwi'do(x), ra] (*mpl* **-es**, *fpl* **-s**) *m, f* [pessoa] distributor.
◆ **distribuidor** *m AUTO* distributor.
◆ **distribuidora** *f FIN* broker.

distribuir [74] [dʒiʃtri'bwi(x)] *vt* **-1.** [repartir] to distribute. **-2.** [atribuir] to allocate. **-3.** [entregar] to deliver. **-4.** [dispor] to arrange. **-5.** [levar] to supply. **-6.** [dirigir] to bestow.

distrito [dʒiʃ'tritu] *m* **-1.** [divisão administrativa] district; ~ **eleitoral** electoral constituency. **-2.** [policial] *administrative area of a town or city in which there is at least one police station*, police district *US*.
◆ **Distrito Federal** *m* [no Brasil] Brasilia.

distúrbio [dʒiʃ'tuxbju] *m* **-1.** [agitação] disturbance. **-2.** [sublevação] riot. **-3.** *MED & PSIC* problem.

ditado [dʒi'tadu] *m* **-1.** [exercício escolar] dictation. **-2.** [provérbio] saying.

ditador, ra [dʒita'do(x), ra] (*mpl* **-es**, *fpl* **-s**) *m, f* **-1.** *POL* dictator. **-2.** *fig* [pessoa autoritária] despot.

ditadura [dʒita'dura] *f* dictatorship.

DITADURA MILITAR

In Brazil, in 1964, as happened in many South American countries throughout the 60s and 70s, a military coup deposed the country's president. The hardening of the military regime, especially from 1968 onwards, curtailed the civil liberties of the Brazilian people for two decades, stopping them from electing their rulers by direct vote until 1989. The growing protests of the civilian population, expressed through widespread popular demonstrations from the end of the 70s onwards, gradually restored the democratic freedoms of the country. The military government brought about some economic growth, but deepened foreign debt, increased the inequality of national income distribution and reinforced social inequality, evils which beset Brazil to this day.

ditame [dʒi'tãmi] *m* [preceito] rule.

ditar [4] [dʒi'ta(x)] *vt* **-1.** [texto] to dictate. **-2.** [impor] to impose.

ditatorial [dʒitato'rjaw] (*pl* **-ais**) *adj* [autoritário] dictatorial.

dito, ta ['dʒitu, ta] <> *pp* ▷ **dizer**. <> *adj* aforementioned.
◆ **dito** *m* [provérbio] saying.

dito-cujo, dita-cuja [ˌdʒitu'kuʒu, ˌdʒita'kuʒa] (*mpl* **ditos-cujos**, *fpl* **ditas-cujas**) *m, f fam*: **o** ~ the said person.

ditongo [dʒi'tõŋgu] *m* diphthong.

ditoso, osa [dʒi'tozu, ɔza] *adj* [venturoso] fortunate.

DIU (*abrev de* **Dispositivo Intra-Uterino**) *m* IUD.

diurético, ca [dʒju'rɛtʃiku, ka] *adj* diuretic.
◆ **diurético** *m* diuretic.

diurno, na ['dʒjuxnu, na] *adj* daytime.

divã [dʒi'vã] *m* couch.

divagação [dʒivaga'sãw] (*pl* **-ões**) *f* **-1.** [devaneio] daydream. **-2.** [digressão] digression.

divagar [14] [dʒiva'ga(x)] *vi* **-1.** [vaguear]: ~ **por** to wander about. **-2.** [devanear] to daydream. **-3.** [desviar-se do assunto] to digress.

divergência [dʒivex'ʒẽnsja] *f* **-1.** [discordância] divergence. **-2.** [desacordo] disagreement.

divergente [dʒivex'ʒẽntʃi] *adj* divergent.

divergir [64] [dʒivex'ʒi(x)] *vi* **-1.** [afastar-se] to branch off. **-2.** [discordar]: ~ **(de alguém)** to disagree (with sb).

diversão [dʒivex'sãw] (*pl* **-ões**) *f* **-1.** [entretenimento] entertainment, amusement. **-2.** [passatempo] pastime.

diversidade [dʒivexsi'dadʒi] *f* **-1.** [variedade] diversity. **-2.** [divergência] difference.

diversificação [dʒivexsifika'sãw] (*pl* **-ões**) *f* diversification.

diversificar [12] [dʒivexsifi'ka(x)] <> *vt* [tornar diverso] to diversify. <> *vi* [variar] to vary.

diverso, sa [dʒi'vɛxsu, sa] *adj* [diferente] different.
◆ **diversos** *adj pl* [vários] various.

divertido, da [dʒivex'tʃidu, da] *adj* entertaining, amusing.

divertimento [dʒivextʃi'mẽntu] *m* entertainment, amusement.

divertir [54] [dʒivex'tʃi(x)] *vt* to entertain, to amuse.
◆ **divertir-se** *vp* to have a good time.

dívida ['dʒivida] *f* debt; ~ **pública** national debt; ~ **externa** foreign debt.

dividendo [dʒivi'dẽndu] *m* dividend.

dividido, da [dʒivi'dʒidu, da] *adj* [em sentimento] divided.

dividir [6] [dʒivi'dʒi(x)] <> *vt* **-1.** [ger] to divide. **-2.** [repartir] to share. **-3.** [separar] to split. **-4.** [demarcar] to mark out. <> *vi MAT* to divide.
◆ **dividir-se** *vp* **-1.** [separar-se] to split up. **-2.** [divergir] to be divided.

divindade [dʒivĩn'dadʒi] *f* divinity.

divisa [dʒi'viza] *f* **-1.** [fronteira] border. **-2.** [insígnia] emblem. **-3.** [slogan] slogan.
◆ **divisas** *fpl FIN* foreign exchange *(sg)*.

divisão [dʒivi'zãw] (*pl* **-ões**) *f* **-1.** [partilha] sharing. **-2.** *MAT* division. **-3.** [discórdia] disagreement. **-4.** [compartimento] compartment.

divisar [4] [dʒivi'za(x)] *vt* **-1.** [avistar] to make out. **-2.** [marcar] to delimit.

divisível [dʒivi'zivew] (*pl* **-eis**) *adj* divisible.

divisor, ra [dʒivi'zo(x), ra] <> *adj* [separador] separating. <> *m MAT* divisor.

divisório, ria [dʒivi'zɔrju, rja] *adj* dividing.
◆ **divisória** *f* partition.

divorciado, da [dʒivox'sjadu, da] <> *adj* divorced. <> *m, f* divorcé (*f* divorcée).

divorciar [16] [dʒivox'sja(x)] *vt* **-1.** [cônjuge] to divorce. **-2.** [separar] to separate.
◆ **divorciar-se** *vp* **-1.** [cônjuges]: ~**-se (de)** to get divorced (from). **-2.** *fig* [afastar-se] to cut o.s. off.

divórcio [dʒi'vɔxsju] *m* divorce.

divulgação [dʒivuwga'sãw] *f* **-1.** [de notícias] publication. **-2.** [de doutrina, conhecimento, cultura] spread. **-3.** [de segredo] disclosure. **-4.** [de produto] marketing.

divulgador, ra [dʒivuwga'do(x), ra] *m, f* discloser.

divulgar [14] [dʒivuw'ga(x)] *vt* **-1.** [notícias] to publicize. **-2.** [doutrina, conhecimento, cultura] to spread. **-3.** [segredo] to disclose. **-4.** [produto] to market.

dizer [29] [dʒi'ze(x)] <> *vt* **-1.** [ger] to tell. **-2.** [falar] to say; ~ **que** to say that; ~ **que sim/não** to say yes/no; ~ **algo (a alguém)** to tell (sb) sthg; ~ **uma prece** to say a prayer. **-3.** [aconselhar, pensar, opinar] to say. **-4.** [significar] to mean; **esse título não me diz nada** the title means nothing to me; **querer** ~ to mean; **quer** ~**, ...** that is to say, ... **-5.** [atrair] to appeal. <> *vi* [falar]: **tive uma idéia! - diga!** I've had an idea! - tell me!; **dito e feito** no sooner said than done. <> *v impess* [afirmar]: **dizem que** it is said that; **a bem** ~ [na verdade] in fact; **que dirá** [quanto mais] let alone; [muito menos] even less.
◆ **dizer-se** *vp* [afirmar de si mesmo] to claim to be.
◆ **dizeres** *mpl* [dito] sayings.
◆ **até dizer chega** *loc adv* beyond belief.

◆ **por assim dizer** *loc adv* so to speak.
dizimar [4] [dʒizi'ma(x)] *vt* **-1.** [destruir em parte] to decimate. **-2.** *fig* [dissipar] to squander.
dízimo ['dizimu] *m* *RELIG* tithe.
DJ [di'ʒej] (*abrev de* **Disc jockey**) *m* DJ.
dl (*abrev de* **decilitro**) *m* dl.
DLL (*abrev de* **Dynamic Link Library**) *f* DLL.
dm (*abrev de* **decímetro**) *m* dm.
DNA (*abrev de* **ácido desoxirribonucleico**) *m* DNA.
do [du] = **de** + **o**.
dó ['dɔ] *m* **-1.** [piedade] pity; **ter ~ de alguém** to take pity on sb. **-2.** *MÚS* doh.
doação [dwa'sãw] (*pl* **-ões**) *f* donation.
doador, ra [dwa'do(x), ra] *m, f* donor.
doar [20] ['dwa(x)] *vt*: **~ algo (a alguém/algo)** to donate sthg (to sb/sthg).
dobra ['dɔbra] *f* **-1.** [parte voltada] fold. **-2.** [prega] pleat. **-3.** [vinco] crease.
dobradiça [dobra'disa] *f* hinge.
dobradinha [dobra'diɲa] *f* **-1.** *CULIN* tripe dish. **-2.** *fam* [dupla] pair.
dobrado, da [do'bradu, da] *adj* **-1.** [com dobras] folded. **-2.** [flexionado] bent. **-3.** [duplicado] doubled.
dobrar [4] [do'bra(x)] ◇ *vt* **-1.** [fazer dobras em] to fold. **-2.** [flexionar] to bend. **-3.** [duplicar] to double. **-4.** [circundar] to turn. **-5.** *fig* [fazer ceder] to win sb over. ◇ *vi* **-1.** [duplicar-se] to double. **-2.** [sino] to toll. **-3.** [envergar] to bend.
◆ **dobrar-se** *vp* **-1.** [curvar-se] to stoop. **-2.** *fig* [ceder] to give in.
dobro ['dobru] *m* double.
DOC (*abrev de* **Documento de Operação de Crédito**) *m Brazilian certificate of credit transfer between accounts.*
doca ['dɔka] *f* dock.
doce ['dosi] ◇ *adj* **-1.** [no sabor] sweet. **-2.** [terno] gentle. **-3.** [água] fresh. ◇ *m* **-1.** *CULIN* dessert, pudding. **-2.** [loc]: **fazer ~** *fam* to play hard to get; **ser um ~ (de pessoa)** to be a sweetie.
doce-de-coco [ˌdosidʒi'koku] (*pl* **doces-de-coco**) *m* [pessoa]: **ser um ~** to be a sweetie.
doceiro, ra [do'sejru, ra] *m, f* confectioner.
docemente [dosi'mẽntʃi] *adv* gently.
docência [do'sẽnsja] *f* teaching.
docente [do'sẽntʃi] ◇ *adj* teaching. ◇ *mf* teacher.
dócil ['dɔsiw] (*pl* **-eis**) *adj* docile.
docilidade [dosili'dadʒi] *f* docility.
documentação [dokumẽnta'sãw] *f* **-1.** [em arquivos] documentation. **-2.** [pessoal] papers.
documental [dokumẽn'taw] (*pl* **-ais**) *adj* documentary.
documentar [4] [dokumẽn'ta(x)] *vt* to document.
documentário [dokumẽn'tarju] *m* documentary.
documento [doku'mẽntu] *m* document.
doçura [do'sura] *f* **-1.** [gosto doce] sweetness. **-2.** [suavidade] gentleness.
doença ['dwẽnsa] *f* **-1.** *MED* illness. **-2.** *fig* [mania] obsession.
doente ['dwẽntʃi] ◇ *adj* **-1.** *MED* sick, ill. **-2.** *fam* [fanático] obsessed. ◇ *mf* [pessoa] patient.
doentio, tia [dwẽn'tʃiw, tʃia] *adj* **-1.** [débil] sickly. **-2.** [mórbido] unhealthy.
doer [48] ['dwe(x)] *vi* **-1.** [fisicamente] to hurt. **-2.** [causar pena, dó]: **~ (a alguém)** to distress (sb).
dogma ['dɔgma] *m* **-1.** *RELIG* doctrine. **-2.** [opinião] dogma.
dogmático, ca [dog'matʃiku, ka] *adj* dogmatic.
doidão, dona [doj'dãw, dɔna] (*mpl* **-ões**, *fpl* **-s**) *fam adj* **-1.** [maluco] crazy. **-2.** [sob efeito de droga]: **estar ~** to be high.
doideira [doj'dejra], **doidice** [doj'dʒizi] *f* **-1.** [ato de maluco] madness. **-2.** [imprudência] foolishness. **-3.** [exagero]: **ser uma ~** to be crazy.
doidivanas [dojdʒi'vãnaʃ] *mf inv fam* tearaway.
doido, da ['dojdu, da] ◇ *adj* **-1.** [maluco] mad. **-2.** [imprudente, insensato] foolish. **-3.** [excêntrico] crazy. **-4.** [exagerado] insane. **-5.** [apaixonado]: **ser ~ por** to be mad about. **-6.** [encantado] thrilled. ◇ *m, f* [pessoa] madman (*f* mad woman).
doído, da [do'idu, da] *adj* **-1.** [dolorido] sore. **-2.** [doloroso] painful. **-3.** [magoado] pained.
doidona [doj'dona] *adj f* ▷ **doidão**.
dois, duas ['dojʃ, 'duaʃ] *num* two; *veja também* **seis**.
dois-pontos [ˌdojʃ'põntuʃ] *m inv* colon *(punctuation mark).*
dólar ['dɔla(x)] (*pl* **-es**) *m* dollar.
dolarização [dolariza'sãw] *f* dollarization.
dolarizar [dolari'za(x)] *vt* to base on the dollar.
doleiro, ra [do'lejru, ra] *m, f* dollar dealer.
dolo ['dɔlu] *m* fraud.
dolorido, da [dolo'ridu, da] *adj* sore.
doloroso, osa [dolo'rozu, ɔza] *adj* painful.
◆ **dolorosa** *f fam* [conta] tab.
doloso, osa [do'lozu, ɔza] *adj* premeditated; **crime ~** premeditated crime.
dom ['dõ] (*pl* **-ns**) *m* **-1.** [dádiva] gift. **-2.** [aptidão] knack. **-3.** [virtude] talent.
dom. (*abrev de* **domingo**) *f* Sun.
domador, ra [doma'do(x), ra] (*mpl* **-es**, *fpl* **-s**) *m, f* tamer.
domar [4] [do'ma(x)] *vt* **-1.** [animal] to tame. **-2.** [subjugar] to subdue. **-3.** [reprimir] to repress.
doméstica [do'mɛʃtʃika] *f* ▷ **doméstico**.
domesticado, da [domeʃtʃi'kadu, da] *adj* domesticated.
domesticar [12] [domeʃtʃi'ka(x)] *vt* to domesticate.
doméstico, ca [do'mɛʃtʃiku, ka] *adj* domestic.
◆ **doméstica** *f* maid.
domiciliar [domisi'lja(x)] *adj* home; **prisão ~** house arrest.
domicílio [domi'silju] *m* residence; **entrega a ~** home delivery.
dominação [domina'sãw] *f* domination.
dominador, ra [domina'do(x), ra] ◇ *adj* domineering. ◇ *m, f* [pessoa] ruler.
dominante [domi'nãntʃi] *adj* dominant.

dominar [4] [domi'na(x)] ◇ *vt* **-1.** [controlar] to dominate. **-2.** [conhecer] to master. **-3.** [abranger] to overlook. ◇ *vi* **-1.** [ter influência]: **~ em** to hold sway over. **-2.** [predominar]: **~ em** to stand out in.
◆ **dominar-se** *vp* [controlar-se] to control o.s.
domingo [do'mĩŋgu] *m* Sunday; **~ de Páscoa** Easter Sunday; **~ de Ramos** Palm Sunday; *veja também* **sexta-feira.**
domingueiro, ra [domĩŋ'gejru, ra] *adj* Sunday.
dominical [domini'kaw] (*pl* **-ais**) *adj* **-1.** RELIG dominical. **-2.** [relativo a domingo] Sunday *(antes de subst).*
dominicano, na [domini'kãnu, na] ◇ *adj* Dominican. ◇ *m, f* Dominican.
domínio [do'minju] *m* **-1.** [dominação]: **~ (sobre)** control (over). **-2.** [posse] power. **-3.** [território] domain. **-4.** [controle] command. **-5.** [conhecimento] mastery. **-6.** COMPUT domain.
dom-juan (*pl* **dom-juans**) *m* Don Juan.
domo ['domu] *m* dome.
dona ['dona] *f* ▻ **dono.**
donatário, ria [dona'tarju, rja] *m, f* recipient.
donde ['dõnde] = **de + onde.**
dondoca [dõn'dɔka] *f fam* socialite.
dono, na ['donu, na] *m, f* [proprietário, senhor] owner; **~ da bola** *fam* big boss; **~ da verdade** know-all *UK*, know-it-all *US*; **ser ~ de seu nariz** to lead one's own life.
◆ **dona** *f* **-1.** [título - de casada] Mrs, Ms; [- de solteira] Miss, Ms. **-2.** *fam* [mulher] madam.
◆ **dona de casa** *f* housewife.
dons *pl* ▻ **dom.**
donzela [dõn'zɛla] *f* virgin.
dopado, da [do'padu, da] *adj* **-1.** [pessoa] drugged. **-2.** [cavalo] doped.
dopar [4] [do'pa(x)] *vt* **-1.** [pessoa] to drug. **-2.** [cavalo] to dope.
◆ **dopar-se** *vp* to take drugs.
doping *m* ESP doping.
dor ['do(x)] (*pl* **-es**) *f* **-1.** [física] pain. **-2.** [pesar] grief.
doravante [dora'vãntʃi] *adv* from now on.
dor-de-cotovelo [ˌdoxdʒikoto'velu] (*pl* **dores-de-cotovelo**) *f fam* jealousy.
dor-d'olhos ['do(x)dɔʎuʃ] (*pl* **dores-d'olhos**) *f fam* eye infection.
dormência [dox'mẽnsja] *f* numbness.
dormente [dor'mẽntʃi] *adj* numb.
◆ **dormente** *m* [ferro] sleeper.
dormida [dox'mida] *f* [sono] sleep; **dar uma ~** to have a sleep.
dormideira [doxmi'dejra] *f* **-1.** [sonolência] drowsiness. **-2.** BOT poppy.
dormido, da [dox'midu, da] *adj* **fam** [da véspera] yesterday's.
dorminhoco, ca [doxmi'ɲoku, ka] ◇ *adj* sleepy. ◇ *m, f* sleepyhead.
dormir [59] [dor'mi(x)] ◇ *vi* **-1.** [cair no sono] to sleep. **-2.** [ter relações sexuais]: **~ com alguém** to sleep with sb. ◇ *vt* **-1.** [sesta, noite]: **dormi uma deliciosa noite** I had a wonderful night's sleep; **dormimos uma sesta ótima esta tarde** we had a really good nap this afternoon. **-2.** *loc*: **~ como uma pedra** to sleep like a log; *fig* **~ no ponto** [bobear] to miss the boat.
dormitar [4] [doxmi'ta(x)] *vi* to doze.
dormitório [dormi'tɔrju] *m* **-1.** [coletivo] dormitory. **-2.** [quarto] bedroom.
dorsal [dox'saw] (*pl* **-ais**) *adj* dorsal; **coluna ~** spine, spinal column.
dorso ['doxsu] *m* back.
dos [duʃ] = **de + os.**
DOS (*abrev de* **Disc Operating System**) *m* DOS.
dosagem [do'zaʒẽ] (*pl* **-ns**) *f* dosage.
dosar [4] [do'za(x)] *vt* **-1.** [regular - medicamento, drinque] to measure out; [- palavras] to measure. **-2.** [misturar] to mix.
dose ['dɔzi] *f* **-1.** [remédio] dose. **-2.** [bebida] measure; **~ cavalar** massive dose; **ser ~ para leão** *fam* to be too much.
dossiê [do'sje] *m* dossier.
dotação [dota'sãw] (*pl* **-ões**) *f* allocation.
dotado, da [do'tadu, da] *adj* **-1.** [que tem dote] gifted. **-2.** [possuidor]: **~ de** endowed with.
dotar [4] [do'ta(x)] *vt* **-1.** [em casamento]: **~ alguém de algo** to give sthg to sb as a dowry. **-2.** [favorecer]: **~ alguém/algo de algo** to endow sb/sthg with sthg. **-3.** [prover]: **~ algo de algo** to provide sthg with sthg.
dote ['dɔtʃi] *m* **-1.** [bens] dowry. **-2.** *fig* [dom natural] gift.
DOU (*abrev de* **Diário Oficial da União**) *m official Brazilian government publication,* ≃ Weekly Information Bulletin *UK*, ≃ Federal Register *US.*
dourado, da [do'radu, da] *adj* golden; **peixinho ~** goldfish.
◆ **dourado** *m* **-1.** [cor] golden colour. **-2.** [peixe] gilthead.
dourar [4] [do'ra(x)] *vt* to gild; **~ a pílula** to sugar the pill.
douto, ta ['dotu, ta] *adj*: **~ (em)** learned (in).
doutor, ra [do'to(x), ra] (*mpl* **-es**, *fpl* **-s**) *m, f* **-1.** MED doctor. **-2.** UNIV: **~ (em)** doctor (of). **-3.** [conhecedor]: **~ em** expert on.
doutorado [doto'radu] *m* doctorate.
doutorando, da [doto'rãndu, da] *m* candidate for doctorate.
doutrina [do'trina] *f* doctrine.
doutrinar [dotri'na(x)] ◇ *vt* **-1.** [ensinar] to teach. **-2.** [convencer] to indoctrinate. ◇ *vi* to give instruction.
download [do'lodi] (*pl* **downloads**) *m* COMPUT download; **fazer (um) ~** to download.
doze ['dozi] *num* twelve; *veja também* **seis.**
DP (*abrev de* **Distrito Policial**) *m* police district.
Dr. (*abrev de* **Doutor**) *m* Dr.
Dra. (*abrev de* **Doutora**) *f* Dr.
draga ['draga] *f* dredger.
dragagem [dra'gaʒẽ] (*pl* **-ns**) *f* dredging.
dragão [dra'gãw] (*pl* **-ões**) *m* dragon.
drama ['drãma] *m* **-1.** TEATRO play. **-2.** *fig* [catástrofe]

tragedy. **-3.** *loc*: **fazer ~** to make a scene; **ser um ~** to be a nightmare.

dramalhão [drama'ʎãw] (*pl* **-ões**) *m pej* melodrama.

dramático, ca [dra'matʃiku, ka] *adj* dramatic.

dramatização [dramatʃiza'sãw] (*pl* **-ões**) *f* TEATRO dramatization.

dramatizar [4] [dramatʃi'za(x)] ◇ *vt* to dramatize. ◇ *vi fig* [ser dramático] to exaggerate.

dramaturgia [dramatux'ʒia] *f* play-writing.

dramaturgo, ga [drama'turgu, ga] *m, f* dramatist, playwright.

drapeado, da [dra'pjadu, da] *adj* draped.
◆ **drapeado** *m* [caimento] hang.

drástico, ca ['draʃtʃiku, ka] *adj* drastic.

drenagem [dre'naʒẽ] (*pl* **-ns**) *f* drainage.

drenar [4] [dre'na(x)] *vt* to drain.

dreno ['drenu] *m* **-1.** [tubo] drainpipe. **-2.** MED drain, drainage tube.

driblar [4] [dri'bla(x)] *vt* **-1.** FUT to dribble. **-2.** *fig* [enganar] to dodge.

drible ['dribli] *m* FUT dribble.

drinque ['drĩŋki] *m* drink.

drive ['drajvi] (*pl* **drives**) *m* COMPUT disk drive.

driver ['drive(x)] (*pl* **drivers**) *m* COMPUT driver; **~ de vídeo** video driver; **~ de impressora** printer driver.

droga ['drɔga] ◇ *f* **-1.** [medicamento, entorpecente] drug. **-2.** *fam fig* [coisa ruim]: **ser uma ~** to be a disaster. ◇ *interj fam* damn!

drogado, da [dro'gadu, da] ◇ *adj* drugged. ◇ *m, f* [pessoa] drug addict.

drogar [4] [dro'ga(x)] *vt* to drug.
◆ **drogar-se** *vp* to take drugs.

drogaria [droga'ria] *f* chemist's (shop) *UK*, drugstore *US*.

dromedário [drome'darju] *m* dromedary.

dropes ['drɔpiʃ] *m inv* drop *(sweet)*.

dualidade [ˌdwali'dadʒi] *f* duality.

duas ['duaʃ] *num* ▷ **dois**.

duas-peças [ˌduaʃ'pɛsaʃ] *mpl* two-piece.

dubiedade [dubje'dadʒi] *f* [ambigüidade] dubiousness.

dúbio, bia ['dubju, bja] *adj* dubious.

dublado, da [du'bladu, da] *adj* CINE dubbed.

dublador, ra [dubla'do(x), ra] *m, f* CINE dubber.

dublagem [du'blaʒẽ] (*pl* **-ns**) *f* CINE dubbing.

dublar [4] [du'blax] *vt* CINE to dub.

dublê [du'ble] *mf* double.

Dublin *n* Dublin.

dublinense [dubli'nẽnsi] ◇ *adj* Dublin *(antes de subst)*. ◇ *mf* Dubliner.

ducado [du'kadu] *m* duchy.

ducentésimo, ma [dusẽn'tɛzimu, ma] *num* two-hundredth.

ducha ['duʃa] *f* **-1.** [jorro de água] shower; **tomar uma ~** to take a shower. **-2.** [boxe] shower (cubicle).

duelar [dwe'la(x)] *vi* **-1.** [combater] to fight a duel. **-2.** *fig* [confrontar] to confront each other.

duelo ['dwɛlu] *m* duel.

duende ['dwẽndʒi] *m* goblin.

dueto ['dwetu] *m* duet.

dulcíssimo, ma [duw'sisimu, ma] *adj* very sweet.

dumping ['dãnpĩɲ] *m* COM dumping.

duo ['duw] *m* [dueto] duo.

duodeno [dwo'denu] *m* duodenum.

dupla ['dupla] *f* ▷ **duplo**.

duplex *m* duplex.

duplicação [duplika'sãw] (*pl* **-ões**) *f* [de receita etc] doubling.

duplicar [12] [dupli'ka(x)] ◇ *vt* **-1.** [dobrar] to double. **-2.** [aumentar] to redouble. ◇ *vi* [dobrar] to double.

duplicata [dupli'kata] *f* **-1.** [título] trade note. **-2.** [cópia] duplicate.

duplicidade [duplisi'dadʒi] *f fig* [falsidade] duplicity.

duplo, pla ['duplu, pla] *adj* double; **dupla cidadania** dual nationality.

duque, duquesa ['duki, du'keza] *m, f* duke (*f* duchess).

durabilidade [durabili'dadʒi] *f* durability.

duração [dura'sãw] *f* duration.

duradouro, ra [dura'doru, ra] *adj* lasting.

duramente [dura'mẽntʃi] *adv* **-1.** [severamente] strongly. **-2.** [cruelmente] harshly.

durante [du'rãntʃi] *prep* during.

durão, rona [du'rãw, rɔna] (*mpl* **-ões**, *fpl* **-s**) *adj* strict.

durar [4] [du'ra(x)] *vi* to last.

durável [du'ravew] (*pl* **-eis**) *adj* lasting, durable.

durex® [du'rɛkiʃ] *m* [fita adesiva] Sellotape® *UK*, Scotch tape® *US*.

dureza [du'reza] *f* **-1.** [rijeza] hardness. **-2.** [rigor] harshness. **-3.** [crueldade] callousness. **-4.** *fam* [dificuldade]: **ser uma ~** to be a hardship. **-5.** *fam* [falta de dinheiro]: **estar na maior ~** to be hard up.

duro, ra ['duru, ra] *adj* **-1.** [ger] harsh. **-2.** [carne, material, água] hard. **-3.** [vida, trabalho, tarefa] tough. **-4.** *fam* [sem dinheiro]: **estar ~** to be hard up. **-5.** *loc*: **dar ~ (para algo/ fazer algo)** to work flat out (for sthg/to do sthg).

durona [du'rona] *f* ▷ **durão**.

dúvida ['duvida] *f* doubt; **sem ~** without a doubt.

duvidar [4] [duvi'da(x)] ◇ *vt*: **~ que** to doubt that. ◇ *vi*: **~ de alguém/algo** to doubt sb/ sthg.

duvidoso, osa [duvi'dozu, ɔza] *adj* **-1.** [incerto] doubtful. **-2.** [suspeito] dubious.

duzentos, tas [du'zẽntuʃ, taʃ] *num* two hundred; *veja também* **seis**.

dúzia ['duzja] *f* dozen; **meia ~** half a dozen.

DVD (*abrev de* **Digital Video Disk**) *m* DVD.

E

e, E [ɛ] *m* [letra] e, E.
ébano ['ɛbanu] *m* ebony.
ébrio, ébria ['ɛbrju, 'ɛbrja] ◇ *adj* drunk. ◇ *m, f* drunkard.
EBTU (*abrev de* **Empresa Brasileira de Transportes Urbanos**) *f Brazilian company for urban transport planning.*
ebulição [ibuli'sãw] *f* **-1.** [de líquido] boiling. **-2.** *fig* [agitação] excitement.
e-business [ɛbusi'nɛesi] *m* ECON e-business.
eclampsia *f* eclampsia.
eclesiástico, ca [ekle'zjastʃiku, ka] *adj* ecclesiastical.
◆ **eclesiástico** *m* [membro do clero] clergyman.
eclético, ca [e'klɛtʃiku, ka] *adj* eclectic.
eclipsar [4] [eklip'sa(x)] *vt* to eclipse.
eclipse [e'klipsi] *m* eclipse.
eclodir [6] [eklo'dʒi(x)] *vi* **-1.** [surgir] to emerge. **-2.** [estourar] to break out.
eclosão [eklo'zãw] (*pl* **-ões**) *f* **-1.** [aparecimento] emergence. **-2.** [desenvolvimento] development. **-3.** [de flor] blooming.
eclusa [e'kluza] *f* lock *(on waterway)*.
eco ['ɛku] *m* echo.
ecoar [20] [e'kwa(x)] *vt & vi* to echo.
ecologia [ekolo'ʒia] *f* ecology.
ecológico, ca [eko'lɔʒiku, ka] *adj* ecological.
ecólogo, ga [e'kɔlogu, ga] *m, f* ecologist.
e-commerce [ɛko'mɛxsi] *m* ECON e-commerce.
economia [ekono'mia] *f* **-1.** [ger] economy; ~ **doméstica** domestic economy; ~ **dirigida** managed economy; ~ **de mercado** market economy; ~ **mista** mixed economy; **fazer** ~ to economize. **-2.** [estudo] economics; ~ **política** political economy.
◆ **economias** *fpl* [poupança] savings.
econômico, ca [eko'nomiku, ka] *adj* **-1.** [ger] economical. **-2.** [relativo à economia] economic.
economista [ekono'miʃta] *mf* economist.
economizar [4] [ekonomi'za(x)] ◇ *vt* **-1.** [gastar, usar com moderação] to economize on. **-2.** [acumular] to save. ◇ *vi* [fazer economia] to economize.
ecossistema [ˌɛkosiʃ'tema] *m* ecosystem.
ECT (*abrev de* **Empresa Brasileira de Correios e Telégrafos**) *f Brazilian postal service,* ≃ The Post Office *UK*, ≃ USPS *US*.
ecumênico, ca [eku'meniku, ka] *adj* ecumenical.
eczema [ek'zema] *m* eczema.
ed. (*abrev de* **edifício**) *m* building.
edema [e'dema] *m* oedema *UK*, edema *US*.
éden ['ɛdẽn] *m* Eden.
edição [edʒi'sãw] (*pl* **-ões**) *f* **-1.** [ger] edition; ~ **atualizada** revised edition; ~ **pirata** pirate copy. **-2.** [publicação] publication; **-3.** [seleção] editing.
edificação [edʒifika'sãw] (*pl* **-ões**) *f* **-1.** [ger] building. **-2.** *fig* [moral, religiosa] edification. **-3.** *fig* [instrução] instruction.
edificante [edʒifi'kãntʃi] *adj* **-1.** [moralizante] edifying. **-2.** [instrutivo] instructive.
edificar [12] [edʒifi'ka(x)] ◇ *vt* **-1.** [construir] to build. **-2.** *fig* [moralmente] to edify. ◇ *vi fig* [moralmente] to inspire.
edifício [edʒi'fisju] *m* building.
Édipo ['ɛdʒipu] *m* ▷ **complexo.**
edital [edʒi'taw] (*pl* **-ais**) *m* proclamation.
editar [4] [edʒi'ta(x)] *vt* **-1.** [ger] to produce. **-2.** [livro, revista] to publish. **-3.** [preparar texto] to edit.
edito [e'dʒitu] *m* edict.
editor, ra [edʒi'to(x), ra] ◇ *adj* [casa] publishing. ◇ *m, f* **-1.** [ger] editor. **-2.** [dono de editora] publisher. **-3.** RÁDIO & TV producer; ~ **de imagem** *ou* **de VT** video editor. **-4.** COMPUT: ~ **de texto** text editor.
◆ **editora** *f* [estabelecimento] publisher.
editoração [edʒitora'sãw] *f* editing; ~ **eletrônica** electronic publishing.
editorar [4] [edʒito'ra(x)] *vt* [editar] to edit.
editoria [edʒito'ria] *f* section.
editorial [edʒitor'jaw] (*pl* **-ais**) ◇ *adj* editorial. ◇ *m* editorial.
editorialista [edʒitorja'liʃta] *mf* editorial writer.
edredom [edre'dõ] (*pl* **-ns**) *m* eiderdown.
educação [eduka'sãw] *f* **-1.** [ensino] education; ~ **física/sexual** physical/sex education. **-2.** [criação] upbringing. **-3.** [polidez] manners; **falta de** ~ bad manners.
educacional [edukasjo'naw] (*pl* **-ais**) *adj* educational.
educado, da [edu'kadu, da] *adj* [polido] well-mannered.
educador, ra [eduka'do(x), ra] *m, f* instructor.
educandário [edukãn'darju] *m* educational establishment.
educar [12] [edu'ka(x)] *vt* **-1.** [instruir] to educate. **-2.** [criar] to bring up. **-3.** [adestrar] to instruct.
◆ **educar-se** *vp* [instruir-se] to teach o.s.
educativo, va [eduka'tʃivu, va] *adj* educational.
EEUU (*abrev de* **Estados Unidos da América do Norte**) *mpl* USA.
efeito [e'fejtu] *m* effect; **fazer** ~ to have an effect; **levar a** ~ to put into effect; **para todos os** ~**s** to all intents and purposes; **sob o** ~ **de** as a result of; ~ **colateral** side effect; ~**s especiais** CINE special effects; ~ **estufa** greenhouse effect.

efemérides [efe'mɛridʒizl] *fpl* **-1.** [notícia diária] daily news. **-2.** [registro] *section of a newspaper listing events that happened in the past on the day of issue.*
efêmero, ra [e'femeru, ra] *adj* [passageiro] ephemeral.
efervescência [efexve'sẽnsja] *f* **-1.** [de líquido] effervescence. **-2.** *fig* [agitação] excitement.
efervescente [eferve'sẽntʃi] *adj* **-1.** [líquido, comprimido] effervescent. **-2.** *fig* [agitado] excited.
efervescer [25] [efexve'se(x)] *vi* **-1.** [líquido] to effervesce. **-2.** *fig* [agitar-se] to become excited.
efetivamente [efɛˌtʃiva'mẽntʃi] *adv* **-1.** [permanentemente] permanently. **-2.** [realmente] actually.
efetivar [4] [efetʃi'va(x)] *vt* **-1.** [realizar] to carry out. **-2.** [admitir] to employ.
efetividade [efetʃivi'dadʒi] *f* effectiveness.
efetivo, va [efe'tʃivu, va] *adj* **-1.** [positivo] effective. **-2.** [permanente] permanent. **-3.** [seguro] certain.
◆ **efetivo** *m* **-1.** *MIL* military strength. **-2.** *COM* liquid assets.
efetuar [4] [efe'twa(x)] *vt* to carry out.
eficácia [efi'kasja] *f* **-1.** [de pessoa] efficiency. **-2.** [de medida, tratamento] effectiveness.
eficaz [efi'kaʃ] (*pl* **-es**) *adj* **-1.** [pessoa] efficient. **-2.** [medida, tratamento] effective.
eficiência [efi'sjẽnsja] *f* efficiency.
eficiente [efi'sjẽntʃi] *adj* efficient.
efígie [e'fiʒi] *f* effigy.
efusão [efu'zãw] (*pl* **-ões**) *f* **-1.** [de líquido, gás] spillage. **-2.** *fig* [demonstração] outburst.
efusivo, va [efu'zivu, va] *adj fig* [expansivo] effusive.
e.g. (*abrev de* **exempli gratia**) e.g.
Egeu [e'gew] *n*: **o (mar)** ~ the Aegean (Sea).
égide ['ɛʒidʒi] *f fig* [proteção]: **sob a** ~ **de** under the aegis of.
egípcio, cia [e'ʒipsju, ja] ◇ *adj* Egyptian. ◇ *m, f* Egyptian.
Egito [e'ʒitu] *n* Egypt.
ego ['ɛgu] *m* ego.
egocêntrico, ca [ego'sẽntriku, ka] ◇ *adj* egocentric. ◇ *m, f* egocentric person.
egocentrismo [egosẽn'triʒmu] *m* egocentricity.
egoísmo [e'gwiʒmu] *m* egoism.
egoísta [e'gwiʃta] ◇ *adj* egotistic. ◇ *mf* [pessoa] egotist.
egrégio, gia [e'greʒju, ʒja] *adj (antes de subst)* [ilustre] distinguished.
egresso, ssa [e'grɛsu, sa] *adj* graduate.
◆ **egresso** *m* **-1.** [ex-detento] ex-prisoner. **-2.** [ex-frade] former monk.
égua ['ɛgwa] *f* mare.
ei [ej] *interj* hey!
ei-lo ['ejlu] = **eis** + **o**.
eira ['ejra] *f*: **sem** ~ **nem beira** without a penny to one's name.
eis ['ejʃ] *adv* here is/are.
eixo ['ejʃu] *m* **-1.** [de rodas] axle. **-2.** [de máquina] shaft. **-3.** *MAT* axis. **-4.** [trecho] area *(between two points)*. **-5.** *loc*: **entrar nos** ~**s** to be on the right track; **sair dos** ~**s** to lose control.
ejaculação [eʒakula'sãw] (*pl* **-ões**) *f* ejaculation.
ejacular [4] [eʒaku'la(x)] *vt* & *vi* to ejaculate.
ejetar [4] [eʒe'ta(x)] *vt* to eject.
ela ['ɛla] ▷ **ele**.
elã [e'lã] *m* enthusiasm.
elaboração [elabora'sãw] (*pl* **-ões**) *f* preparation.
elaborador, ra [elabora'do(x), ra] *m, f* maker.
elaborar [4] [elabo'ra(x)] *vt* to prepare.
elasticidade [elaʃtʃisi'dadʒi] *f* elasticity.
elástico, ca [e'laʃtʃiku, ka] *adj* **-1.** [tecido etc] elastic. **-2.** *fig* [flexível] adaptable.
◆ **elástico** *m* **-1.** [para prender notas *etc*] rubber band. **-2.** [para roupa] elastic. **-3.** [para cabelo] elastic band.
ele, ela ['eli, 'ɛla] (*mpl* **eles**, *fpl* **elas**) *pron pess (de + ele = dele; de + ela = dela; em + ele = nele; em + ela = nela)* **-1.** [pessoa] he (*f* she); ~ **é médico** he is a doctor; **ela foi embora** she has gone away; **elas viajaram** they travelled; **eles têm uma filha** they have one daughter; **que só** ~ as only he can be/do; ~ **mesmo** *ou* **próprio** him himself. **-2.** [animal, coisa] it; **o cachorro?** ~ **uivou a noite inteira** the dog? it howled all night long; **ela dá flor em novembro** it flowers in November; **o relatório? aqui está** ~ the report? here it is; **eles já foram vendidos** they have already been sold; ~ **mesmo** itself. **-3.** *(depois de prep)* [pessoa] him, her, it; **este livro pertence a** ~ this book belongs to him; **jantei com** ~ I had dinner with them; **todos olharam para eles** ~ everybody looked at them; **sou mais velho que** ~ I am older than him; **decidimos ir sem ela** we decided to go without her; **deram um tiro nele** they shot him; **aquele é o carro dele** that's his car; **os jornais só falam dela** the newspapers talk about nothing but her. **-4.** *loc*: **agora é que são elas** there's the rub; **ser elas por elas** to be tit for tat.
elefante [ele'fãntʃi] *m* elephant; ~ **branco** *fig* white elephant.
elefantíase [elefãn'tʃiazi] *f* elephantiasis.
elefantino, na [elefãn'tʃinu, na] *adj* elephantine.
elegância [ele'gãnsja] *f* elegance; **com** ~ elegantly.
elegante [ele'gãntʃi] *adj* elegant.
eleger [26] [ele'ʒe(x)] *vt* **-1.** [por meio de votos] to elect. **-2.** [escolher] to select.
elegia [ele'ʒia] *f* elegy.
elegível [ele'ʒivew] (*pl* **-eis**) *adj* eligible.
eleição [elej'sãw] (*pl* **-ões**) *f* **-1.** [por meio de votos] election. **-2.** [escolha] selection.
eleito, ta [e'lejtu, ta] ◇ *pp* ▷ **eleger**. ◇ *adj* **-1.** [por votos] elected. **-2.** [escolhido] selected.
eleitor, ra [elej'to(x), ra] (*mpl* **-es**, *fpl* **-s**) *m, f* voter.
eleitorado [elejto'radu] *m* electorate; **conhecer o seu** ~ *fam fig* to know who one is dealing with.
eleitoral [elejto'raw] (*pl* **-ais**) *adj* electoral.
eleitoreiro, ra [elejto'rejru, ra] *adj pej* vote-catching.
elementar [elemẽn'ta(x)] (*pl* **-es**) *adj* **-1.** [rudimentar] elementary. **-2.** [fundamental] fundamental.

elemento [ele'mẽntu] *m* **-1.** [ger] element; **estar no seu ~** to be in one's element. **-2.** [indivíduo] individual; **bom/mau ~** good/bad lot.
◆ **elementos** *mpl* **-1.** [ger] elements. **-2.** [dados] facts.
elencar [elẽn'ka(x)] *vt* [listar] to list.
elenco [e'lẽnku] *m* **-1.** *TEATRO* cast list. **-2.** [rol] list.
elepê [eli'pe] *m* LP.
eletivo, va [ele'tʃivu, va] *adj* elective.
eletricidade [eletrisi'dadʒi] *f* electricity.
eletricista [eletri'siʃta] *mf* electrician.
elétrico, ca [e'lɛtriku, ka] *adj* **-1.** *ELETR* electric. **-2.** *fig* [agitado] excited.
eletrificar [4] [eletrifi'ka(x)] *vt* to electrify.
eletrizante [eletri'zãntʃi] *adj fig* electrifying.
eletrizar [4] [eletri'za(x)] *vt* **-1.** *ELETR* to electrify. **-2.** *fig* [arrebatar] to thrill.
Eletrobras (*abrev de* **Centrais Elétricas Brasileiras S/A**) *f Brazilian electricity company.*
eletrocardiograma [eˌlɛtrokaxdʒo'grãma] *m MED* electrocardiogram.
eletrochoque [elɛtro'ʃɔki] *m* electroconvulsive therapy.
eletrocutar [4] [eletroku'ta(x)] *vt* to electrocute.
eletrodinâmica [elɛtrodʒi'nãmika] *f FÍS* electrodynamics *(sg)*.
eletrodo [ele'trodu] *m* electrode.
eletrodomésticos [eletrodo'mɛʃtʃikuʃ] *mpl* domestic appliances.
eletroeletrônico, ra [elɛktro'eletroniko, ka] <> *adj* electronics. <> *m, f* electronic device.
eletroencefalograma [eˌlɛtrwẽnsɛfalo'grãma] *m* electroencephalogram.
eletromagnético, ca [elɛtromag'nɛtʃiku, ka] *adj* electromagnetic.
elétron *m* electron.
eletrônica [ele'tronika] *f* electronics *(sg)*.
eletrônico, ca [ele'troniku, ka] *adj* electronic.
elevação [eleva'sãw] (*pl* **-ões**) *f* **-1.** [ger] elevation. **-2.** [aumento] rise.
elevado, da [ele'vadu, da] *adj* **-1.** [alto] high. **-2.** [nobre] noble.
◆ **elevado** *m* [via] flyover.
elevador [eleva'do(x)] (*pl* **-es**) *m* lift *UK*, elevator *US*.
elevar [4] [ele'va(x)] *vt* **-1.** [erguer] to lift up. **-2.** [aumentar] to raise. **-3.** [exaltar] to acclaim.
◆ **elevar-se** *vp* to rise.
eliminação [elimina'sãw] (*pl* **-ões**) *f* elimination.
eliminar [4] [elimi'na(x)] *vt* **-1.** [ger] to eliminate. **-2.** [descartar] to exclude.
eliminatório, ria [elimina'tɔrju, rja] *adj* eliminatory.
◆ **eliminatória** *f* **-1.** *ESP* heat. **-2.** *EDUC* test.
elipse [e'lipsi] *f* ellipsis.
elite [e'litʃi] *f* elite.
elitismo [eli'tʃiʒmu] *m* elitism.
elitista [eli'tʃiʃta] *adj* elitist.
elitizar [4] [elitʃi'za(x)] *vt* to class among the elite.
elixir [eli'ʃi(x)] *m* elixir.
elo ['ɛlu] *m* link.
elocução [eloku'sãw] *f* elocution.
elogiar [16] [elo'ʒjar] *vt* to praise.
elogio [elo'ʒiu] *m* praise.
elogioso, osa [elo'ʒozu, ɔza] *adj* flattering.
El Salvador *n* El Salvador.
elucidação [elusida'sãw] (*pl* **-ões**) *f* clarification.
elucidar [4] [elusi'da(x)] *vt* to explain.
elucidativo, va [elusida'tʃivu, va] *adj* explanatory.
elucubração [elukubra'sãw] (*pl* **-ões**) *f* meditation.
elucubrar [4] [eluku'bra(x)] <> *vt* [intelectualmente] to dream up. <> *vi* [refletir, pensar] to muse.
em [ẽ] *prep (em + o = no; em + a = na)* **-1.** [lugar - dentro de] in; **no bolso/estojo/quarto** in the pocket/case/bedroom; **na bolsa/caixa/sala** in the purse/box/living room; [- num certo ponto de] at; **~ casa** at home; **no trabalho** at work; **nas ruas** on the streets; **moramos na capital** we live in the capital; **depositei o dinheiro no banco** I deposited the money in the bank; [- sobre] on; **o bife mal cabia no prato** the steak hardly fitted on the plate; **havia um vaso de flores na mesa** there was a vase of flowers on the table; [- cidade, país] in; **~ Londres/São Paulo** in London/São Paulo; **no Porto/Rio de Janeiro** in Oporto/Rio de Janeiro; **~ Portugal** in Portugal; **no Brasil** in Brazil; **na França** in France; **nos Estados Unidos** in the United States. **-2.** [tempo] in; **inaugurado ~ 1967** officially opened in 1967; **ele tirou férias ~ maio** he took his holidays in May; **~ 7 de setembro de 1622** on 7th September 1622; **comemoram a liberdade no 25 de abril** freedom is celebrated on 25th April; **no Natal** at Christmas; **na Semana Santa** during Holy Week; **ela fez tudo ~ uma semana** she did everything in one week; **o serviço ficará pronto ~ dois dias** the work will be ready in two days' time; **naquela época** at that time in those days; **~ breve** soon. **-3.** [introduzindo o objeto indireto] in; **enfiar/esquecer/guardar algo ~** to slip/forget/keep sthg in; **acreditar ~** to believe in; **pensar ~** to think of; **ele caiu num buraco** he fell in a hole; **ela caiu/no chão** she fell on the floor; **ela entrou na sala** she entered the room; **vou no jornaleiro e já volto** I am going to the newsagent's and I'll be right back. **-4.** [assunto] in; **doutorado ~ sociologia** graduated in sociology; **ele é perito ~ balistica** he is an expert in ballistics. **-5.** [modo] in; **ele falou ~ voz baixa** he spoke in a low voice; **ela falou ~ português** she spoke in Portuguese; **ele dirige ~ alta velocidade** he drives fast; **ela pagou ~ libras/reais** she paid in pounds sterling/reals; **o preço aumentou ~ 10%** the price has gone up by 10%; **ele gasta tudo o que ganha ~ livros** he spends all he earns on books; **bife na chapa** grilled steak. **-6.** [estado]: **a multidão ~ euforia** the rejoicing crowd; **ela ainda está ~ convalescença** she is still convalescing; **um carro usado ~ boas condições** a well-kept second-hand car; **países ~ guerra** countries at war. **-7.** [material]: **estátua ~ bronze**

bronze statue; **camisa ~ viscose** rayon shirt. **-8.** *(em loc adv, loc prep)* on; **com base ~** based on/in; **de tempos ~ tempos** from time to time; **~ busca de** in search of; **~ caso de** in case of; **~ geral** in general; **~ meio a** in the middle of; **na verdade** in truth; **no mínimo/máximo** at least/the most.

emagrecer [25] [emagre'se(x)] ◇ *vt* [causar perda de peso] to cause to lose weight. ◇ *vi* **-1.** [perder peso] to lose weight. **-2.** [definhar] to slim down.

emagrecimento [emagresi'mẽntu] *m* slimming.

e-mail *m* e-mail.

emanar [4] [ema'na(x)] *vi* **-1.** [exalar-se]: **~ de** to emanate from. **-2.** [originar-se]: **~ de** to stem from.

emancipação [emãnsipa'sãw] *(pl* **-ões**) *f* **-1.** [de mulheres, escravos] emancipation. **-2.** [de menor] coming of age. **-3.** [de país] liberation.

emancipado, da [emãnsi'padu, da] *adj* liberated.

emancipar [4] [emãnsi'pa(x)] *vt* **-1.** [ger] to emancipate. **-2.** [país] to liberate.

◆ **emancipar-se** *vp* **-1.** [mulheres] to become emancipated. **-2.** [menor] to come of age. **-3.** [país] to become free.

emaranhado, da [emarã'ɲadu, da] *adj* [embaraçado] tangled.

◆ **emaranhado** *m* [confusão] confusion.

emaranhar [4] [emarã'ɲa(x)] *vt* **-1.** [enredar] to tangle. **-2.** *fig* [complicar] to confuse.

◆ **emaranhar-se** *vp* [enredar-se] to become entangled.

embaçado, da [ẽnba'sadu, da] *adj* **-1.** [vidro] misted up. **-2.** [olhos] misty.

embaçar [13] [ẽnba'sa(x)] *vt* **-1.** [vidro] to mist up. **-2.** [olhos] to mist.

embaciado, da [ẽnba'sjadu, da] *adj* **-1.** [metal] tarnished. **-2.** [vidro] misted up. **-3.** [olhos] misty.

embaciar [16] [ẽnba'sja(x)] ◇ *vt* **-1.** [vidro] to mist up. **-2.** [olhos] to mist. ◇ *vi* **-1.** [metal] to tarnish. **-2.** [vidro, olhos] to cloud.

embainhar [4] [ẽnbaj'ɲa(x)] *vt* **-1.** [espada] to sheathe. **-2.** [roupa] to hem.

embaixada [ẽnbaj'ʃada] *f* **-1.** [local] embassy. **-2.** [cargo] ambassadorial duties. **-3.** [funcionários] embassy staff.

embaixador, ra [ẽnbajʃa'do(x), ra] *(mpl* **-es**, *fpl* **-s**) *m, f* ambassador.

embaixatriz [ẽnbajʃa'triʃ] *f* [esposa do embaixador] ambassadress.

embaixo [ẽn'bajʃu] *adv* **-1.**: **~ de** underneath. **-2.**: **aí ~** down there. **-3.**: **lá ~** downstairs.

◆ **embaixo de** *loc prep* under.

embalado, da [ẽnba'ladu, da] ◇ *adj* **-1.** [empacotado] wrapped, packed. **-2.** [acelerado] fast. **-3.** [drogado] high. ◇ *adv* [aceleradamente] more quickly.

embalagem [ẽnba'laʒẽ] *(pl* **-ns**) *f* **-1.** [ato] wrapping, packing. **-2.** [invólucro] package.

embalar [4] [ẽnba'la(x)] *vt* **-1.** [acondicionar] to wrap. **-2.** [berço] to rock. **-3.** [balanço] to swing.

◆ **embalar-se** *vp* [balançar-se] to rock o.s.

embalo [ẽn'balu] *m* **-1.** [balanço] rocking. **-2.** [impulso] push. **-3.** [euforia causada por droga] high. **-4.** *fam* [festa]: **festa de ~** swinging party.

embalsamado, da [ẽnbawsa'madu, da] *adj* **-1.** [cadáver] embalmed. **-2.** [perfumado] scented.

embalsamar [4] [ẽnbaws'ma(x)] *vt* **-1.** [cadáver] to embalm. **-2.** [perfumar] to perfume.

embananado, da [ẽnbana'nadu, da] *fam adj* **-1.** [situação] snarled up. **-2.** [pessoa] in a hole, in trouble.

embananar [4] [ẽnbana'na(x)] *vt* [situação] to complicate.

◆ **embananar-se** *vp fam* [pessoa] to be in a hole, to be in trouble.

embaraçar [13] [ẽnbara'sa(x)] *vt* **-1.** [obstruir] to block. **-2.** [acanhar] to embarrass. **-3.** [cabelos] to tangle. **-4.** [dificultar] to complicate.

◆ **embaraçar-se** *vp* [embaralhar-se] to become embroiled.

embaraço [ẽnba'rasu] *m* **-1.** [obstáculo] obstacle. **-2.** [acanhamento] embarrassment. **-3.** [dificuldade] difficult situation.

embaraçoso, osa [ẽnbara'sozu, ɔza] *adj* embarrassing.

embaralhar [4] [ẽnbara'ʎa(x)] *vt* **-1.** [cartas] to shuffle. **-2.** [confundir] to jumble.

◆ **embaralhar-se** *vp* [confundir-se] to become confused.

embarcação [ẽnbaxka'sãw] *(pl* **-ões**) *f* vessel.

embarcadouro [ẽnbaxka'doru] *m* quay.

embarcar [12] [ẽnbax'ka(x)] ◇ *vt* **-1.** [pessoa] to board. **-2.** [carga] to load. ◇ *vi* **-1.**: **~ (em)** [subir a bordo] to board; [viajar] to travel. **-2.** *fam* [cair na conversa]: **~ em algo** to fall for sthg.

embargado, da [ẽnbax'gadu, da] *adj* **-1.** [impedido] blocked. **-2.** [contido] carefully controlled.

embargar [14] [ẽnbax'ga(x)] *vt* **-1.** [*JUR* - apreender] to seize; [- impedir] to block. **-2.** [conter] to control.

embargo [ẽn'baxgu] *m* **-1.** *JUR* seizure. **-2.** [obstáculo] impediment.

embarque [ẽn'baxki] *m* **-1.** [de pessoa] boarding. **-2.** [de carga] loading.

embasamento [ẽnbaza'mẽntu] *m* **-1.** [base] foundation. **-2.** *fig* [fundamento] basis.

embasar [ẽnba'za(x)] *vt* **-1.** [alicerçar] to lay the foundations of. **-2.** [fundamentar] to base.

embasbacado, da [ẽnbaʒba'kadu, da] *adj* astounded.

embasbacar [12] [ẽnbaʒba'ka(x)] *vt* to astound.

◆ **embasbacar-se** *vp* to be astounded.

embate [ẽn'batʃi] *m* **-1.** [colisão] crash. **-2.** [choque] shock. **-3.** [resistência] resistance.

embebedar [4] [ẽnbebe'da(x)] *vt* & *vi* to intoxicate.

◆ **embebedar-se** *vp* to become intoxicated.

embeber [5] [ẽnbe'be(x)] *vt* **-1.** [ensopar]: **~ algo em algo** to soak sthg in sthg. **-2.** [absorver] to soak up.

◆ **embeber-se** *vp* [absorver-se]: **~-se em** to be absorbed in.

embelezador, ra [ẽnbeleza'do(x), ra] *adj* beautifying.
embelezar [4] [ẽnbele'za(x)] *vt* [tornar belo] to beautify.
◆ **embelezar-se** *vp* [enfeitar-se] to make o.s. beautiful.
embevecer [25] [ẽnbeve'se(x)] *vt* to delight.
◆ **embevecer-se** *vp* to be delighted.
embevecido, da [ẽnbeve'sidu, da] *adj* delighted.
embicar [12] [ẽnbi'ka(x)] ◇ *vt* [tornar bicudo] to sharpen. ◇ *vi* **-1.** [esbarrar] to meet. **-2.** [implicar]: ~ **com algo/alguém** to become entangled with sthg/sb. **-3.** [dirigir-se]: ~ **para** to head towards.
embirrar [4] [ẽnbi'xa(x)] *vi* **-1.** [teimar]: ~ **em** to insist upon. **-2.** [antipatizar]: ~ **com** to take a disliking to. **-3.** [ficar birrento] to be obstinate.
embocadura [ẽnboka'dura] *f* **-1.** [de rio] mouth. **-2.** [de instrumento] mouthpiece.
embolar [4] [ẽnbo'la(x)] ◇ *vt* [emaranhar] to entangle. ◇ *vi* **-1.** [engalfinhar-se]: ~ **com alguém** to grapple with sb. **-2.** [encaroçar] to make lumpy.
◆ **embolar-se** *vp* [engalfinhar-se]: **~-se (com alguém)** to become locked in battle (with sb).
embolia [ẽnbo'lia] *f* embolism.
êmbolo ['ẽnbolu] *m* **-1.** [bomba] piston. **-2.** [seringa] plunger. **-3.** *MED* embolism.
embolorado, da [ẽmbolo'radu, da] *adj* [mofado - pão, fruta] mouldy; [- roupa, casa] musty.
embolorar [4] [ẽnbolo'ra(x)] *vi* to become mouldy.
embolsar [4] [ẽnbow'sa(x)] *vt* **-1.** [receber] to pocket. **-2.** [pagar] to pay.
embonecar [12] [ẽnbone'ka(x)] *vt* to doll up.
◆ **embonecar-se** *vp* to doll o.s. up.
embora [ẽn'bɔra] ◇ *conj* although. ◇ *adv*: **ir** ~ to go; **vá-se ~!** go away!
emborcar [12] [ẽnbox'ka(x)] *vt* **-1.** [canoa] to overturn. **-2.** [vasilha] to turn upside down.
emboscada [ẽnboʃ'kada] *f* ambush.
embotado, da [ẽnbo'tadu, da] *adj* **-1.** [enfraquecido] weakened. **-2.** [insensível] numb.
embotar [4] [ẽnbo'ta(x)] *vt* to blunt.
Embraer (*abrev de* **Empresa Brasileira de Aeronáutica**) *f Brazilian aeronautical company.*
embranquecer [25] [ẽnbrãŋke'se(x)] ◇ *vt* to whiten. ◇ *vi* to turn white.
Embratel (*abrev de* **Empresa Brasileira de Telecomunicações S/A**) *f Brazilian telecommunications company.*
embravecer [25] [ẽnbrave'se(x)] ◇ *vt* to make wild. ◇ *vi* to become furious.
◆ **embravecer-se** ◇ *vp* to become furious.
embreagem [ẽnbre'aʒẽ] (*pl* **-ns**) *f* clutch.
embrear [15] [ẽm'brja(x)] ◇ *vt* to engage (the clutch). ◇ *vi* to engage the clutch.
embrenhar-se [15] [ẽnbre'ɲaxsi] *vp*: **~-se em/por** to conceal o.s. in.
embriagado, da [ẽnbrja'gadu, da] ◇ *adj* **-1.** [bêbado] drunk. **-2.** *fig* [enlevado] intoxicated. ◇ *m, f* [pessoa bêbada] drunk.
embriagante [ẽnbrja'gãntʃi] *adj* intoxicating.
embriagar [14] [ẽnbrja'ga(x)] ◇ *vt* to intoxicate. ◇ *vi* [embebedar] to intoxicate.
◆ **embriagar-se** *vp* [enlevar-se] to become intoxicated.
embriaguez [ẽnbrja'geʒ] *f* **-1.** [ebriedade] drunkenness. **-2.** *fig* [enlevo] intoxication.
embrião [ẽn'brjãw] (*pl* **-ões**) *m* embryo.
embrionário, ria [ẽnbrjo'narju, ja] *adj* [relativo a embrião] embryonic.
embromação [ẽnbroma'sãw] (*pl* **-ões**) *f* **-1.** [embuste] deception. **-2.** [protelação] delaying tactic.
embromador, ra [ẽmbroma'do(x), ra] *fam* ◇ *adj* **-1.** [enrolador] dishonest. **-2.** [trapaçeiro] fraudulent. ◇ *m, f* **-1.** [pessoa enroladora] cheat. **-2.** [pessoa trapaçeira] fraud.
embromar [4] [ẽnbro'ma(x)] ◇ *vt* **-1.** [enrolar] to fool. **-2.** [enganar] to bamboozle. ◇ *vi* **-1.** [protelar] to procrastinate. **-2.** [fazer rodeios] to beat about the bush.
embrulhada [ẽnbru'ʎada] *f fam* [confusão] muddle.
embrulhar [4] [ẽnbru'ʎa(x)] *vt* **-1.** [empacotar] to wrap. **-2.** *fig* [estômago] to upset. **-3.** [confundir] to screw up. **-4.** [enganar] to trick.
◆ **embrulhar-se** *vp* [enrolar-se] to get into a muddle.
embrulho [ẽn'bruʎu] *m* **-1.** [pacote] package. **-2.** [confusão] confusion.
embrutecer [25] [ẽnbrute'se(x)] ◇ *vt* to make brutal. ◇ *vi* to brutalize.
◆ **embrutecer-se** *vp* to become brutalized.
emburrado, da [ẽnbu'xadu, da] *adj* [aborrecido] sulky.
emburrar-se [4] [ẽnbu'xaxsi] *vp* [aborrecer-se] to sulk.
embuste [ẽn'buʃtʃi] *m* **-1.** [mentira] deception. **-2.** [armadilha] trick.
embusteiro, ra [ẽnbuʃ'tejru, ra] ◇ *adj* deceitful. ◇ *m, f* [pessoa] trickster.
embutido, da [ẽnbu'tʃidu, da] *adj* [armário, estante] built-in.
embutir [6] [ẽnbu'tʃi(x)] *vt* **-1.** [armário] to build in. **-2.** [pedra, marfim] to inlay.
emenda [e'mẽnda] *f* **-1.** [correção] correction. **-2.** *JUR* amendment. **-3.** *COST* repair. **-4.** [ligação] join.
emendar [4] [emẽn'da(x)] *vt* **-1.** [corrigir] to correct. **-2.** *JUR* to amend. **-3.** [reparar] to redress. **-4.** [ligar] to join.
◆ **emendar-se** *vp* [corrigir-se] to mend one's ways.
emergência [emex'ʒẽnsja] *f* **-1.** [ger] emergency. **-2.** [surgimento] emergence.
emergente [emex'ʒẽntʃi] *adj* emerging.
emergir [78] [emex'ʒi(x)] *vi* to emerge.
emérito, ta [e'mɛritu, ta] *adj* emeritus.
emigração [emigra'sãw] (*pl* **-ões**) *f* **-1.** [de pessoas] emigration. **-2.** [de aves] migration.
emigrado, da [emi'gradu, da] ◇ *adj* emigrant. ◇ *m, f* emigré.

emigrante [emi'grãntʃi] ◇ *adj* emigrant. ◇ *mf* emigré.

emigrar [4] [emi'gra(x)] *vi* **-1.** [pessoa] to emigrate. **-2.** [ave] to migrate.

eminência [emi'nẽnsja] *f* **-1.** [ger] eminence. **-2.** [título, tratamento] Eminence. **-3.** [pessoa importante] important person; ~ **parda** eminence grise.

eminente [emi'nẽntʃi] *adj* **-1.** [ilustre] eminent. **-2.** [elevado] high.

emir [e'mi(x)] *m* emir.

emirado [emi'radu] *m* emirate.

Emirados Árabes Unidos *n*: **os** ~ the United Arab Emirates.

emissão [emi'sãw] (*pl* **-ões**) *f* **-1.** [ger] emission. **-2.** [de moeda, títulos, passagens aéreas] issue. **-3.** *RÁDIO & TV* transmission.

emissário, ria [emi'sarju, rja] *m, f* [mensageiro] emissary.

◆ **emissário** *m* [esgoto] outlet.

emissor, ra [emi'so(x), ra] (*mpl* **-es**, *fpl* **-s**) *adj FIN* issuing.

◆ **emissor** *m* [transmissor] transmitter.

◆ **emissora** *f* transmitter.

emitente [emi'tẽntʃi] ◇ *adj FIN* issuing. ◇ *mf FIN* issuer.

emitir [6] [emi'tʃi(x)] ◇ *vt* **-1.** [ger] to issue. **-2.** [sons, raios] to emit. **-3.** [opinião, idéias] to transmit. ◇ *vi FIN* to issue money.

emoção [emo'sãw] (*pl* **-ões**) *f* emotion.

emocional [emosjo'naw] (*pl* **-ais**) *adj* emotional.

emocionante [emosjo'nãntʃi] *adj* **-1.** [comovente] moving. **-2.** [empolgante] gripping.

emocionar [4] [emosjo'na(x)] ◇ *vt* **-1.** [comover] to move. **-2.** [excitar] to thrill. ◇ *vi* [provocar emoção] to thrill.

◆ **emocionar-se** *vp* [comover-se]: **~-se com algo/alguém** to get emotional about sthg/sb.

emoldurar [4] [emowdu'ra(x)] *vt* to frame.

emoticom [ɛmo'tikõ] (*pl* **-ns**) *m COMPUT* emoticon.

emotividade [emotʃivi'dadʒi] *f* emotiveness.

emotivo, va [emo'tʃivu, va] *adj* emotional.

empacar [12] [ẽnpa'ka(x)] *vi* **-1.** [recusar-se a andar] to stand stock still. **-2.** [não progredir] to stand still. **-3.** [parar] to dry up; ~ **em algo** to get bogged down in sthg.

empacotar [4] [ẽnpako'ta(x)] ◇ *vt* [embalar] to wrap up. ◇ *vi fam* [morrer] to snuff it.

empada [ẽn'pada] *f CULIN* pie.

empadão [ẽnpa'dãw] (*pl* **-ões**) *m* pie.

empalhar [4] [ẽnpa'ʎa(x)] *vt* **-1.** [animal] to stuff. **-2.** [cadeira, garrafa] to cover in wickerwork.

empalidecer [25] [ẽnpalide'se(x)] ◇ *vt* [tornar pálido] to cause to turn pale. ◇ *vi* [perder a cor] to turn pale.

empanada [ẽnpa'nada] *f CULIN* large pie.

empanturrado, da [ẽnpãntu'xadu, da] *adj* stuffed full.

empanturrar [4] [ẽnpãntu'xa(x)] *vt*: ~ **alguém de algo** to stuff sb with sthg.

◆ **empanturrar-se** *vp*: **~-se de algo** to stuff o.s with sthg.

empapar [4] [ẽnpa'pa(x)] ◇ *vt* [ensopar] to drench. ◇ *vi* [fazer papo] to soak through.

◆ **empapar-se** *vp* [ensopar-se] to get drenched.

empapuçado, da [ẽnpapu'sadu, da] *adj* [olhos] puffy; [roupa] puffed.

empapuçar [ẽnpapu'sa(x)] *vt* [inchar] to stuff.

emparedar [4] [ẽnpare'da(x)] *vt* [enclausurar] to shut away.

◆ **emparedar-se** *vp* [isolar-se] to shut o.s. away.

emparelhado, da [ẽmpare'ʎadu, da] *adj* [lado a lado] paired.

emparelhar [4] [ẽnpare'ʎa(x)] ◇ *vt* [por em pares] to pair up. ◇ *vi* **-1.** [equivaler]: ~ **(em algo)** to be equal (in sthg). **-2.** [equiparar-se]: ~ **com** to be equal to. **-3.** [correr parelhas]: ~ **(com alguém)** to draw alongside.

◆ **emparelhar-se** *vp* [empatar] to become equal.

empastar [4] [ẽnpaʃ'ta(x)] *vt* **-1.** [ger] to plaster. **-2.** [tornar pastoso] to make a paste of.

empatar [4] [ẽnpa'ta(x)] ◇ *vi* [em jogo]: ~ **com** to draw with. ◇ *vt* **-1.** [impedir] to hinder. **-2.** [ocupar] to take up. **-3.** [aplicar] to tie up.

empate [ẽn'patʃi] *m* [jogo, votação] tie; **dar** ~ to end in a draw.

empatia [ẽnpa'tʃia] *f* empathy.

empecilho [ẽnpe'siʎu] *m* obstacle.

empedernido, da [ẽnpedex'nidu, da] *adj* harsh.

empedrar [4] [ẽnpe'dra(x)] *vt* [cobrir com pedras] to pave.

empenado, da [ẽmpe'nadu, da] *adj* **-1.** [deformado] warped. **-2.** [fora de prumo] leaning.

empenar [4] [ẽnpe'na(x)] ◇ *vt* [entortar] to warp. ◇ *vi* [entortar-se] to warp.

empenhado, da [ẽnpe'ɲadu, da] *adj* **-1.** [disposto] determined. **-2.** [penhorado] pawned.

empenhar [4] [ẽnpe'ɲa(x)] *vt* **-1.** [dar em penhor] to pawn. **-2.** [aplicar] to apply. **-3.** [comprometer] to pledge.

◆ **empenhar-se** *vp* [aplicar-se]: **~-se (para fazer algo)** to commit o.s. (to do sthg); **~-se em algo** to get into debt over sthg.

empenho [ẽn'peɲu] *m* **-1.** [diligência] commitment; **pôr todo o** ~ **em algo** to put all one's effort into sthg. **-2.** [compromisso] commitment. **-3.** [penhor] pledge.

emperiquitado, da [ẽnperiki'tadu, da] *adj* flashy.

emperiquitar-se [7] [ẽnperiki'taxsi] *vp* to get dolled up.

emperrado, da [ẽmpe'xadu, da] *adj* **-1.** [entravado] jammed. **-2.** [teimoso] stubborn.

emperrar [4] [ẽnpe'xa(x)] ◇ *vi* [tornar-se imóvel] to stick. ◇ *vt* **-1.** [entravar] to cause to stick. **-2.** [difcultar] to bog down.

empertigado, da [ẽnpextʃi'gadu, da] *adj* upright.

empertigar-se [14] [ẽnpextʃi'gaxsi] *vp* to stand up straight.

empestar [15] [ẽmpeʃ'ta(x)] *vt* **-1.** [contaminar] to infest. **-2.** [infectar com mau cheiro]: ~ **algo (com**

algo) to stink out sthg (with sthg).
empilhadeira [ẽnpiʎa'dejra] *f* fork-lift truck.
empilhar [4] [ẽnpi'ʎa(x)] *vt* [amontoar] to stack.
empinado, da [ẽnpi'nadu, da] *adj* straight.
empinar [4] [ẽnpi'na(x)] ◇ *vt* **-1.** [peito, corpo, nariz] to thrust out. **-2.** [pipa] to empty. ◇ *vi* [cavalo] to rear.
empipocado, da [ẽnpipo'kadu, da] *adj* spotty.
empipocar [12] [ẽnpipo'ka(x)] *vi* [corpo, superfície, massa] to come out in spots.
empírico, ca [ẽn'piriku, ka] *adj* empirical.
emplacar [12] [ẽnpla'ka(x)] *vt* **-1.** [veículo] to put a number plate on. **-2.** *fam fig* [idade] to make it to.
emplastrar [4] [ẽnplaʃ'tra(x)] *vt* to put in plaster.
emplastro [ẽn'plaʃtru] *m* [medicamento] plaster.
empobrecer [25] [ẽnpobre'se(x)] ◇ *vt* **-1.** [tornar pobre] to impoverish. **-2.** [o solo] to deplete. ◇ *vi* [tornar-se pobre] to become poor.
empobrecimento [ẽnpobresi'mẽntu] *m* **-1.** [ger] impoverishment. **-2.** [do solo] depletion.
empoeirado, da [ẽnpoej'radu, da] *adj* dusty.
empoeirar [4] [ẽnpoej'ra(x)] *vt* to cover in dust.
empolado, da [ẽnpo'ladu, da] *adj* **-1.** [pele] blistered. **-2.** *fig* [linguagem, estilo] pompous.
empolar [4] [ẽnpo'la(x)] ◇ *vt* [pele] to cause to swell. ◇ *vi* [pele] to blister.
◆ **empolar-se** *vp* **-1.** [pele] to become blistered. **-2.** [tornar-se soberbo] to become puffed up.
empolgação [ẽnpowga'sãw] *f* enthusiasm; **com** ~ with enthusiasm.
empolgante [ẽnpow'gãntʃi] *adj* thrilling.
empolgar [14] [ẽnpow'ga(x)] *vt* to fill with enthusiasm.
◆ **empolgar-se** *vp* [entusiasmar-se] to become enthusiastic.
emporcalhar [4] [ẽnpoxka'ʎa(x)] *vt* to dirty.
◆ **emporcalhar-se** *vp* [pessoa] to get dirty.
empório [ẽn'pɔrju] *m* **-1.** [mercado] market. **-2.** [armazém] department store.
empossado, da [ẽmpo'sadu, da] *adj* newly appointed.
empossar [4] [ẽnpo'sa(x)] *vt* [dar posse a] to install in office.
empreendedor, ra [ẽnprjẽnde'do(x), ra] ◇ *adj* [ativo] enterprising. ◇ *m, f* [pessoa] entrepreneur.
empreender [5] [ẽnprjẽn'de(x)] *vt* to undertake.
empreendimento [ẽnprjẽndʒi'mẽntu] *m* undertaking.
empregado, da [ẽnpre'gadu, da] *m, f* [funcionário] employee.
◆ **empregada** *f* [em casa de família]: **empregada (doméstica)** maid.
empregador, ra [ẽnprega'do(x), ra] *m, f* employer.
empregar [14] [ẽnpre'ga(x)] *vt* **-1.** [ger] to use. **-2.** [dar emprego a] to employ. **-3.** [ocupar] to put to use.
◆ **empregar-se** *vp* [obter trabalho] to get a job.
empregatício, cia [ẽnprega'tʃisju, sja] *adj* employment.
emprego [ẽn'pregu] *m* **-1.** [trabalho] job. **-2.** [local de trabalho] work. **-3.** [uso] use.
empreguismo [ẽnpre'giʒmu] *m* nepotism.
empreitada [ẽnprej'tada] *f* **-1.** [trabalho, empresa] contract. **-2.** [tarefa] venture. **-3.** [empresa] undertaking.
empreiteira [ẽnprej'tejra] *f* contracting company.
empreiteiro [ẽnprej'tejru] *m* contractor.
empresa [ẽn'preza] *f* **-1.** [firma] company; ~ **estatal/privada** state-owned/privately-owned company. **-2.** [empreendimento] enterprise.
empresariado [ẽnpreza'rjadu] *m* employers (*pl*).
empresarial [ẽnpreza'rjaw] (*pl* **-ais**) *adj* company.
empresário, ria [ẽnpre'zarju, rja] *m, f* **-1.** [dono de empresa] employer. **-2.** [de artista, jogador] agent.
emprestado, da [ẽnpreʃ'tadu, da] *adj* loaned; **pedir algo** ~ to borrow sthg.
emprestar [4] [ẽnpreʃ'ta(x)] *vt* to lend.
empréstimo [ẽn'prɛʃtʃimu] *m* [de dinheiro] loan.
emproado, da [ẽnpro'adu, da] *adj* arrogant.
empulhação [ẽnpuʎa'sãw] (*pl* **-ões**) *f* [logro] hoax.
empurra-empurra [ẽnpu,xẽn'puxa] (*pl* **empurras-empurras** *ou* **empurra-empurras**) *m* pushing and shoving.
empurrão [ẽnpu'xãw] (*pl* **-ões**) *m* shove; **dar um** ~ to give a shove; **levar um** ~ to be shoved.
empurrar [4] [ẽnpu'xa(x)] *vt* **-1.** [impelir com força] to shove; **'empurre'** [aviso] 'push' **-2.** [impingir] to palm off.
emudecer [25] [emude'se(x)] ◇ *vt* [fazer calar] to silence. ◇ *vi* [calar-se] to go quiet.
emulação [emula'sãw] *f* **-1.** [competição] rivalry. **-2.** [estímulo] ambition.
emular [4] [emu'la(x)] ◇ *vt* **-1.** [rivalizar com] to compete with. **-2.** [imitar] to emulate. ◇ *vi* [competir]: ~ **com** to compete with.
emulsão [emuw'zãw] (*pl* **-ões**) *f* QUÍM emulsion; ~ **fotográfica** photographic emulsion.
enaltecer [25] [enawte'se(x)] *vt* to honour.
enamorado, da [enamo'radu, da] *adj* in love.
enamorar-se [4] [enamo'raxsi] *vp*: ~**-se de** *ou* **por alguém** to fall in love with sb.
encabeçar [4] [ẽŋkabe'sa(x)] *vt* **-1.** [vir à frente de] to head. **-2.** [chefiar] to lead.
encabulação [ẽŋkabula'sãw] *f* **-1.** [acanhamento] embarrassment. **-2.** [constrangimento] constraint.
encabulado, da [ẽŋkabu'ladu, da] *adj* **-1.** [acanhado] embarrassed. **-2.** [envergonhado] ashamed.
encabular [4] [ẽŋkabu'la(x)] ◇ *vt* [envergonhar] to embarrass. ◇ *vi* [acanhar-se] to be embarrassed.
◆ **encabular-se** *vp* **-1.** [acanhar-se] to be embarrassed. **-2.** [envergonhar-se] to be ashamed.
encaçapar [ẽŋkasa'pa(x)] *vt* **-1.** [bola] to pocket. **-2.** *fam* [surrar] to spank.
encadeamento [ẽŋkadʒja'mẽntu] *m* chain.

encadear [15] [ẽŋka'dʒja(x)] *vt* [concatenar] to link.
◆ **encadear-se** *vp* [concatenar-se] to become linked.
encadernação [ẽŋkadexna'sãw] (*pl* **-ões**) *f* bookbinding.
encadernado, da [ẽŋkadex'nadu, da] *adj* bound.
encadernar [4] [ẽŋkadex'na(x)] *vt* to bind.
encaixar [4] [ẽŋkaj'ʃa(x)] ◇ *vt* **-1.** [inserir]: ~ **algo (em algo)** to fit sthg (into sthg). **-2.** [encaixotar] to box. ◇ *vi* [entrar no encaixe] to fit.
◆ **encaixar-se** *vp* to fit.
encaixe [ẽŋ'kajʃi] *m* **-1.** [ato] entrance. **-2.** [cavidade] groove. **-3.** [junção] joint.
encaixotar [4] [ẽŋkajʃo'ta(x)] *vt* to box.
encalacrado, da [ẽŋkala'kradu, da] *adj* in trouble.
encalacrar [4] [ẽŋkala'kra(x)] *vt* to lead into difficulties.
◆ **encalacrar-se** *vp* to get into difficulties.
encalço [ẽŋ'kawsu] *m*: **estar no ~ de algo/alguém** to be in pursuit of sthg/sb.
encalhado, da [ẽŋka'ʎadu, da] *adj* **-1.** [embarcação] aground. **-2.** [mercadoria] unsaleable. **-3.** *fam* [pessoa solteira] on the shelf.
encalhar [4] [ẽŋka'ʎa(x)] *vi* **-1.** [embarcação] to run aground. **-2.** [mercadoria] to remain unsold. **-3.** [processo] to grind to a halt. **-4.** *fam* [pessoa solteira] to be left on the shelf.
encaminhar [4] [ẽŋkami'ɲa(x)] *vt* **-1.** [dirigir] to direct. **-2.** [orientar] to guide. **-3.** [dar andamento] to get going.
◆ **encaminhar-se** *vp* [dirigir-se]: **~-se para/a** to set out for/to.
encampar [4] [ẽŋkãm'pa(x)] *vt* **-1.** JUR to rescind. **-2.** [empresa] to take into administration.
encanador, ra [ẽŋkana'dox, ra] (*mpl* **-es**, *fpl* **-s**) *m, f* plumber.
encanamento [ẽŋkana'mẽntu] *m* [sistema] plumbing.
encanar [4] [ẽŋka'na(x)] *vt* **-1.** [canalizar] to channel. **-2.** *fam* [prender] to lock up.
encantado, da [ẽŋkãn'tadu, da] (*mpl* **-es**, *fpl* **-s**) *adj* [ger] enchanted.
encantador, ra [ẽŋkãnta'do(x), ra] (*mpl* **-es**, *fpl* **-s**) *adj* **-1.** [fascinante] charming. **-2.** [deslumbrante] fantastic.
encantamento [ẽŋkãnta'mẽntu] *m* **-1.** [magia] enchantment. **-2.** [deslumbramento] fascination.
encantar [4] [ẽŋkãn'ta(x)] *vt* **-1.** [enfeitiçar] to bewitch. **-2.** [fascinar] to charm. **-3.** [deslumbrar] to fascinate.
◆ **encantar-se** *vp*: **~-se com algo** to be enchanted by sthg.
encanto [ẽŋ'kãntu] *m* **-1.** [ger] charm. **-2.** *fam* [pessoa]: **ser um ~** to be a charming person.
encapado, da [ẽŋka'padu, da] *adj* covered.
encapar [4] [ẽŋka'pa(x)] *vt* to cover.
encapetado, da [ẽŋkape'tadu, da] *adj* [criança] mischievous.
encapetar-se [ẽŋkape'ta(x)si] *vp* [endiabrar-se] to go into a tantrum.
encapotar [4] [ẽŋkapo'ta(x)] *vt* [cobrir] to wrap.
◆ **encapotar-se** *vp* [cobrir-se] to wrap o.s. up.
encaracolado, da [ẽŋkaraco'ladu, da] *adj* curly.
encaracolar [4] [ẽŋkarako'la(x)] ◇ *vt* [cabelo] to curl. ◇ *vi* [cabelo] to curl.
encarar [4] [ẽŋka'ra(x)] *vt* **-1.** [fitar] to stare at. **-2.** [enfrentar] to face up to. **-3.** [considerar] to consider.
encarcerar [4] [ẽŋkaxse'ra(x)] *vt* [prender] to incarcerate.
encardido, da [ẽŋkar'dʒidu, da] *adj* **-1.** [roupa] soiled. **-2.** [pele] grimy.
encardir [6] [ẽŋkax'dʒi(x)] ◇ *vt* **-1.** [roupa] to soil. **-2.** [pele] to make grimy. ◇ *vi* [ficar mal lavado] to be badly washed.
encarecer [25] [ẽŋkare'se(x)] ◇ *vt* **-1.** [tornar mais caro] to make more expensive. **-2.** [elogiar] to praise. ◇ *vi* [ficar mais caro] to go up in price.
encarecidamente [ẽŋkaresida'mẽntʃi] *adv* [insistentemente]: **pedir ~** to ask insistently.
encarecimento [ẽŋkaresi'mẽntu] *m* increase in price; **~ da vida** rise in the cost of living.
encargo [ẽŋ'kaxgu] *m* **-1.** [ger] duty. **-2.** [responsabilidade] responsibility.
encarnação [ẽŋkaxna'sãw] (*pl* **-ões**) *f* **-1.** [ger] incarnation. **-2.** [personificação]: **ser a ~ de algo** to be the embodiment of sthg. **-3.** *fam* [implicância] teasing.
encarnado, da [ẽŋkax'nadu, da] *adj* [vermelho] red.
encarnar [4] [ẽŋkax'na(x)] ◇ *vi* **-1.** [alma, espírito] to represent. **-2.** [implicar] *fam*: **~ em alguém** to tease sb. ◇ *vt* **-1.** [personificar] to personify. **-2.** TEATRO to play.
encaroçar [13] [ẽŋkaro'sa(x)] *vi* **-1.** [pele] to come up in bumps. **-2.** [molho, massa] to be lumpy.
encarregado, da [ẽŋkaxe'gadu, da] ◇ *adj*: **~ de algo/fazer algo** in charge of sthg/with doing sthg. ◇ *m, f* person in charge; **~ de negócios** chargé d'affaires.
encarregar [14] [ẽŋkaxe'ga(x)] *vt*: **~ alguém de algo** to put sb in charge of sthg.
◆ **encarregar-se** *vp*: **~-se de algo/fazer algo** to take charge of sthg/doing sthg.
encartar [4] [ẽŋkax'ta(x)] *vt* to insert.
encarte [ẽŋ'kaxtʃi] *m* **-1.** [em publicação] insertion. **-2.** [de disco, CD] insert.
encasquetar [4] [ẽŋkaʃke'ta(x)] *vt*: **~ que** to be convinced that; **~ uma idéia** to be obsessed with an idea.
encefalograma [ẽnsɛfalo'grãma] *m* encephalogram.
encenação [ẽnsena'sãw] *f* **-1.** TEATRO staging. **-2.** [produção] production. **-3.** *fig* [fingimento] play-acting.
encenar [4] [ẽnse'na(x)] *vt* **-1.** TEATRO to stage. **-2.** [produzir] to produce. **-3.** *fig* [fingir] to play-act.
enceradeira [ẽnsera'dejra] *f* floor-polisher.
encerado, da [ẽnse'radu, da] *adj* waxed.
◆ **encerado** *m* [oleado] tarpaulin.
encerar [4] [ẽnse'ra(x)] *vt* to polish.

encerramento [ẽnsexa'mẽntu] *m* closure.

encerrar [4] [ẽnse'xa(x)] *vt* **-1.** [acabar]: **~ algo (com algo)** to close sthg (with sthg). **-2.** [confinar] to shut. **-3.** [conter] to contain.

◆ **encerrar-se** *vp* [enclausurar-se]: **~-se (em)** to shut o.s. up (in).

encestar [4] [ẽnseʃ'ta(x)] *ESP* [basquete] *vt* & *vi* to score.

encetar [4] [ẽnse'ta(x)] *vt* [começar] to start.

encharcado, da [ẽnʃax'kadu, da] *adj* **-1.** [alagado] flooded. **-2.** [ensopado] soaking wet.

encharcar [12] [ẽnʃar'ka(x)] *vt* **-1.** [alagar] to flood. **-2.** [ensopar] to drench.

◆ **encharcar-se** *vp* [ensopar-se] to become soaked.

enchente [ẽn'ʃẽntʃi] *f* flood.

encher [5] [ẽn'ʃe(x)] ◇ *vt* **-1.** [ger] to fill; **~ o saco (de alguém)** *m fam* to piss sb off. **-2.** [fartar]: **~ algo (de)** to saturate sthg (with). **-3.** [balão, bola, pneu] to inflate. ◇ *vi* [tornar-se cheio] to become full.

◆ **encher-se** *vp* **-1.** [tornar-se cheio] to become full. **-2.** [fartar-se]: **~-se de** to have too much of. **-3.** [aborrecer-se] to become fed up.

enchimento [ẽnʃi'mẽntu] *m* **-1.** [ato] filling. **-2.** [coisa com que se enche] stuffing.

enchova [ẽn'ʃova] *f* anchovy.

encíclica [ẽn'siklika] *f* *RELIG* encyclical.

enciclopédia [ẽnsiklo'pɛdʒja] *f* **-1.** [obra] encyclopedia. **-2.** *fam* [pessoa sábia] walking encyclopedia.

enciclopédico, ca [ẽnsiklo'pɛdʒiku, ka] *adj* encyclopedic.

enciumar-se [4] [ẽnsju'maxsi] *vp* to be jealous.

enclausurar [4] [ẽŋklawzu'ra(x)] *vt* to shut away.

◆ **enclausurar-se** *vp* to shut o.s. away.

encoberto, ta [ẽŋko'bɛxtu, ta] ◇ *pp* ▷ **encobrir**. ◇ *adj* **-1.** [céu, tempo] overcast. **-2.** [escondido] hidden. **-3.** [disfarçado] concealed.

encobrir [59] [ẽŋko'bri(x)] *vt* **-1.** [ger] to conceal. **-2.** [esconder] to hide.

◆ **encobrir-se** *vp* **-1.** [esconder-se] to hide. **-2.** [disfarçar-se] to disguise o.s. **-3.** [céu, sol] to become overcast.

encolerizar [4] [ẽŋkoleri'za(x)] *vt* [pessoa] to enrage.

◆ **encolerizar-se** *vp* [pessoa] to get angry.

encolher [5] [ẽŋko'ʎe(x)] ◇ *vt* **-1.** [contrair] to tuck in; **~ os ombros** to shrug one's shoulders. **-2.** [diminuir o tamanho de] to shrink. ◇ *vi* [roupa] to shrink.

◆ **encolher-se** *vp* **-1.** [espremer-se] to squeeze up. **-2.** [de frio] to shrivel.

encomenda [ẽŋko'mẽnda] *f* **-1.** [mercadoria] order; **fazer uma ~** to order; **feito sob ~** made to order. **-2.** [pacote] parcel.

encomendar [4] [ẽŋkomẽn'da(x)] *vt* **-1.** [obra, compra]: **~ algo a alguém** to order sthg from sb. **-2.** *RELIG* to commend.

encompridar [4] [ẽŋkõnpri'da(x)] *vt* to lengthen.

encontrão [ẽŋkõn'trãw] (*pl* **-ões**) *m* **-1.** [esbarrão] bump; **dar um ~** to shove. **-2.** [empurrão] shove.

encontrar [4] [ẽŋkõn'tra(x)] ◇ *vt* **-1.** [pessoa - por acaso] to meet; [- em certa condição] to find. **-2.** [coisa perdida, procurada] to find. **-3.** [dificuldades] to come up against. **-4.** [solução, erro] to discover. ◇ *vi*: **~ com alguém** [por acerto] to meet up with sb; [por acaso] to meet sb.

◆ **encontrar-se** *vp* **-1.**: **~-se (com alguém)** [por acerto] to have a meeting (with sb); [por acaso] to meet (sb). **-2.** [estar] to be. **-3.** [colidir] to collide. **-4.** *PSIC* to find o.s.

encontro [ẽŋ'kõntru] *m* meeting; **ir ao ~ de** to go to meet; **de ~ a** [contra] against; **o carro foi de ~ ao muro** the car crashed into the wall; [em contradição a] in contrast with.

encorajamento [ẽŋkoraʒa'mẽntu] *m* encouragement.

encorajar [4] [ẽŋkora'ʒa(x)] *vt* to encourage.

encorpado, da [ẽŋkor'padu, da] *adj* **-1.** [forte] corpulent. **-2.** [espesso - tecido] thick; [- vinho] full-bodied.

encorpar [4] [ẽŋkox'pa(x)] *vt* **-1.** [fazer crescer] to make grow. **-2.** [engrossar] to thicken.

encosta [ẽŋ'kɔʃta] *f* hillside.

encostar [4] [ẽŋkoʃ'ta(x)] ◇ *vt* **-1.** [aproximar] to put against. **-2.** [quase fechar] to leave ajar. **-3.** [estacionar] to pull up. **-4.** [deitar] to rest. **-5.** *fig* [pôr de lado] to put aside. ◇ *vi* **-1.** [tocar]: **~ em algo/alguém** to lean against sthg/sb. **-2.** [bater]: **~ a mão em alguém** to hit sb with one's hand.

◆ **encostar-se** *vp* **-1.** [deitar-se] to recline. **-2.** [apoiar-se] to lean. **-3.** *fig* [aproveitar-se de]: **~-se em alguém** to lean on sb. **-4.** *fig* [fugir de trabalho] to lie back.

encosto [ẽŋ'koʃtu] *m* [espaldar] back.

encouraçado, da [ẽŋkora'sadu, da] *adj* ironclad.

◆ **encouraçado** *m* *NÁUT* battleship.

encravado, da [ẽŋkra'vadu, da] *adj* **-1.** [unha] ingrown. **-2.** [pêlo] ingrowing.

encravar [4] [ẽŋkra'va(x)] *vt*: **~ algo (em algo)** to imbed sthg (in sthg).

encrenca [ẽ'ŋkrẽnka] *f* **-1.** [problema] tight spot. **-2.** [briga] fight; **meter-se numa ~** to get caught up in a fight.

encrencar [12] [ẽŋkrẽn'ka(x)] ◇ *vt* [meter em complicação] to embarrass. ◇ *vi* **-1.** [quebrar - carro] to break down; [- computador] to go down. **-2.** [complicar-se] to become complicated. **-3.** *fam* [implicar]: **~ com alguém/algo** to take issue with sb/sthg.

encrenqueiro, ra [ẽŋkrẽn'kejru, ra] *adj* troublemaking.

encrespado, da [ẽŋkreʃ'padu, da] *adj* **-1.** [cabelo] tightly-curled. **-2.** [mar] choppy.

encrespar [4] [ẽŋkreʃ'pa(x)] *vt* **-1.** [cabelo] to curl. **-2.** [mar] to ripple.

◆ **encrespar-se** *vp* **-1.** [mar] to become choppy, to get choppy. **-2.** *fig* [irritar-se] to become angry, to get angry.

encruar [4] [ẽŋkru'a(x)] *vi* to harden.

encruzilhada [ẽŋkruzi'ʎada] *f* crossroads *(sg)*.
encucado, da [ẽŋku'kadu, da] *adj* perturbed.
encucar [12] [ẽŋku'ka(x)] *vi* to become confused.
encurralado, da [ẽŋkuxa'ladu, da] *adj* [cercado] cornered.
encurralar [4] [ẽŋkuxa'la(x)] *vt* to herd.
encurtar [4] [ẽŋkux'ta(x)] *vt* to shorten.
end. (*abrev de* **endereço**) *m* add.
endêmico, ca [ẽn'demiku, ka] *adj* endemic.
endemoninhado, da [ẽndemoni'ɲadu, da] *adj* **-1.** [pessoa - possuído] possessed; [- levado] mischievous. **-2.** [expressão, olhar] diabolical.
endereçamento [ẽnderesa'mẽntu] *m* **-1.** [ger] address. **-2.** *COMPUT* addressing.
endereçar [13] [ẽndere'sa(x)] *vt* **-1.** [sobrescrever] to address. **-2.** [enviar] to send.
endereço [ẽnde'resu] *m* address; ~ **eletrônico** e-mail address.
endeusar [4] [ẽndew'za(x)] *vt* to deify.
endiabrado, da [ẽndʒja'bradu, da] *adj* mischievous.
endinheirado, da [ẽndʒiɲej'radu, da] *adj* well-off.
endireitar [4] [ẽndʒirej'ta(x)] *vt* **-1.** [descurvar] to straighten. **-2.** [arrumar] to tidy.
◆ **endireitar-se** *vp* [corrigir-se] to go straight.
endividado, da [ẽndʒivi'dadu, da] *adj* in debt.
endividamento [ẽndʒivida'mẽntu] *m* state of being in debt.
endividar-se [4] [ẽndʒivi'daxsi] *vp* to fall into debt.
endócrino, na [ẽn'dɔkrinu, na] *adj* endocrine.
endocrinologia [ẽn,dokrinolo'ʒia] *f* endocrinology.
endocrinologista [ẽn,dokrinolo'ʒiʃta] *mf* endocrinologist.
endoidar [4] [ẽndoj'da(x)] *vi* to go mad; **meu relógio endoidou** my watch has gone haywire.
endoidecer [25] [ẽndojde'se(x)] <> *vt* to drive mad. <> *vi* to go mad.
endoscopia [ẽndoʃko'pia] *f* endoscopy.
endossar [4] [ẽndo'sa(x)] *vt* to endorse.
endosso [ẽn'dosu] *m* endorsement.
endurecer [25] [ẽndure'se(x)] <> *vt* to harden. <> *vi* **-1.** [ficar duro] to go hard. **-2.** [ficar difícil] to be hard. **-3.** *fig* [tornar-se frio]: ~ **(com alguém)** to harden (towards sb).
endurecimento [ẽnduresi'mẽntu] *m* hardening.
enegrecer [25] [enegre'se(x)] *vt* & *vi* to darken.
ENEM (*abrev de* **Exame Nacional do Ensino Médio**) *m exam taken at the end of middle education in Brazil.*
enema [e'nema] *m* enema.
energético, ca [enex'ʒɛtʃiku, ka] *adj* energizing.
◆ **energética** *f* energy.
energia [enex'ʒia] *f* energy; ~ **atômica/nuclear/solar** atomic/nuclear/solar energy.
enérgico, ca [e'nɛxʒiku, ka] *adj* energetic.
energizante [enexʒi'zãntʃi] *adj* energizing.
energizar [4] [enexʒi'za(x)] *vt* to energize.
enervante [enex'vãntʃi] *adj* annoying.
enervar [4] [enex'va(x)] *vt* to annoy.
◆ **enervar-se** *vp* to get annoyed.
enevoado, da [ene'vwadu, da] *adj* misty.
enfadar [4] [ẽnfa'da(x)] *vt* to bore.
◆ **enfadar-se** *vp* to get bored.
enfado [ẽn'fadu] *m* boredom.
enfadonho, nha [ẽnfa'doɲu, ɲa] *adj* boring.
enfaixar [4] [ẽnfaj'ʃa(x)] *vt* to bandage.
enfartar [4] [ẽnfax'ta(x)] *vi* to have a clot.
enfarte [ẽn'faxtʃi] *m MED* clot.
ênfase ['ẽnfazi] *f* emphasis; **dar** ~ **a** to emphasize.
enfastiado, da [ẽnfaʃ'tʃjadu, da] *adj* bored.
enfastiar [16] [ẽnfaʃ'tʃja(x)] *vt* to bore.
◆ **enfastiar-se** *vp* to get bored.
enfático, ca [ẽn'fatʃiku, ka] *adj* emphatic.
enfatizar [4] [ẽnfatʃi'za(x)] *vt* to emphasize.
enfear [15] [ẽnfe'a(x)] <> *vt* to make ugly. <> *vi* to become ugly.
enfeitar [4] [ẽnfej'ta(x)] *vt* to decorate.
◆ **enfeitar-se** *vp* to dress up.
enfeite [ẽn'fejtʃi] *m* decoration.
enfeitiçar [13] [ẽnfejtʃi'sa(x)] *vt* **-1.** [lançar feitiço] to bewitch. **-2.** *fig* [fascinar] to charm.
enfermagem [ẽnfex'maʒẽ] *f* nursing.
enfermaria [ẽnfexma'ria] *f* sickroom.
enfermeiro, ra [ẽnfex'mejru, ra] *m, f* nurse.
enfermidade [ẽnfexmi'dadʒi] *f* illness.
enfermo, ma [ẽn'fexmu, ma] <> *adj* sick. <> *m, f* sick person.
enferrujado, da [ẽnfexu'ʒadu, da] *adj* [oxidado] rusty.
enferrujar [4] [ẽnfexu'ʒa(x)] <> *vt* to rust. <> *vi* to go rusty.
enfezado, da [ẽnfe'zadu, da] *adj* annoyed.
enfezar [4] [ẽnfe'za(x)] *vt* to annoy.
◆ **enfezar-se** *vp* to get annoyed.
enfiar [16] [ẽn'fja(x)] *vt* **-1.** [introduzir]: ~ **algo (em algo)** to thread sthg (onto sthg). **-2.** [vestir] to slip on. **-3.** [pôr] to put.
◆ **enfiar-se** *vp* [meter-se]: **~-se em algo** to slip into sthg.
enfileirar [4] [ẽnfilej'ra(x)] *vt* to put in line.
◆ **enfileirar-se** *vp* to get in line.
enfim [ẽn'fĩ] *adv* finally; **até que** ~ finally; ~ **sós!** alone at last!
enfisema [ẽnfi'zema] *f* emphysema.
enfocar [12] [ẽnfo'ka(x)] *vt* to focus.
enfoque [ẽn'fɔki] *m* focus.
enforcamento [ẽnfoxka'mẽntu] *m* [de pessoa] hanging.
enforcar [ẽfox'ka(x)] *vt* **-1.** [pessoa] to hang. **-2.** *fam fig* [dia de trabalho, aula] to skip.
◆ **enforcar-se** *vp* [pessoa] to hang o.s.
enfraquecer [25] [ẽnfrake'se(x)] <> *vt* to weaken. <> *vi* to grow weak.
◆ **enfraquecer-se** *vp* to weaken o.s.
enfraquecido, da [ẽnfrake'sidu, da] *adj* weakened.
enfraquecimento [ẽnfrakesi'mẽntu] *m* weakening.

enfrentamento [ẽnfrẽnta'mẽntu] *m* clash, confrontation.
enfrentar [4] [ẽnfrẽn'ta(x)] *vt* to face.
enfronhado, da [ẽnfro'ɲadu, da] *adj*: **bem ~ em algo** well-versed in sthg.
enfronhar [4] [ẽnfro'ɲa(x)] *vt*: **~ alguém em algo** to instruct sb in sthg.
◆ **enfronhar-se** *vp*: **~-se em algo** to become knowledgeable about sthg.
enfumaçado, da [ẽnfuma'sadu, da] *adj* smoky.
enfumaçar [13] [ẽnfuma'sa(x)] *vt* to make smoky.
enfurecer [25] [ẽnfure'se(x)] *vt* to infuriate.
◆ **enfurecer-se** *vp* to get infuriated.
enfurecido, da [ẽnfure'sidu, da] *adj* infuriated.
enfurnar-se [4] [ẽnfux'naxsi] *vp*: **~-se em** to hide o.s. in.
engaiolar [4] [ẽŋgajo'la(x)] *vt* to put in a cage.
engajado, da [ẽŋga'ʒadu, da] *adj* engaged.
engajamento [ẽŋgaʒa'mẽntu] *m* **-1.** [ger] engagement. **-2.** [de trabalhadores] taking on.
engajar [4] [ẽŋga'ʒa(x)] *vt* [trabalhadores] to take on.
◆ **engajar-se** *vp* **-1.** *POL*: **~-se (em)** to engage o.s. (in). **-2.** *MIL*: **~-se (em)** to become engaged (in). **-3.** [em campanha, luta]: **~-se em** to get involved (in). **-4.** [trabalhador]: **~-se (em)** to be engaged (in).
engalfinhar-se [4] [ẽŋgawfi'ɲaxsi] *vp* to get entangled.
engambelar [4] [ẽŋgãnbe'la(x)] *vt* to deceive.
enganação [ẽŋgana'sãw] *f* deception.
enganador, ra [ẽŋgana'do(x), ra] *adj* deceptive.
enganar [4] [ẽŋga'na(x)] *vt* **-1.** [iludir] to deceive. **-2.** [trair] to cheat.
◆ **enganar-se** *vp* **-1.** [iludir-se] to fool o.s. **-2.** [cometer um erro] to make a mistake.
enganchar [4] [ẽŋgãn'ʃa(x)] ◇ *vt*: **~ algo (em algo)** to hook sthg up (to sthg). ◇ *vi*: **~ (em algo)** to catch (in sthg).
engano [ẽŋ'gãnu] *m* [equívoco] error; [em telefonema]: **ser ~** to be a wrong number.
engarrafado, da [ẽŋgaxa'fadu, da] *adj* **-1.** [bebida] bottled. **-2.** [rua, trânsito] blocked.
engarrafamento [ẽŋgaxafa'mẽntu] *m* **-1.** [de bebida] bottling. **-2.** [no trânsito] traffic jam.
engarrafar [4] [ẽŋgaxa'fa(x)] *vt* **-1.** [bebida] to bottle. **-2.** [rua, trânsito] to block.
engasgar [14] [ẽŋgaʒ'ga(x)] ◇ *vt* [na garganta] to choke. ◇ *vi* to choke.
◆ **engasgar-se** *vp* [na garganta] to choke o.s.
engasgo [ẽŋ'gaʒgu] *m* [na garganta] choking.
engastar [4] [ẽŋgaʃ'ta(x)] *vt* to set.
engaste [ẽŋ'gaʃtʃi] *m* [stone] setting.
engatar [4] [ẽŋga'ta(x)] *vt* **-1.** [atrelar]: **~ algo (em algo)** to couple sthg (with sthg). **-2.** [engrenar] to get into gear. **-3.** [iniciar] to start.
engate [ẽŋ'gatʃi] *m* connection.
engatilhar [4] [ẽŋgatʃi'ʎa(x)] *vt* **-1.** [arma] to cock. **-2.** *fig* [resposta *etc*] to prepare.
engatinhar [4] [ẽŋgatʃi'ɲa(x)] *vi* **-1.** [bebê] to crawl. **-2.** *fig* [ser principiante]: **~ em algo** to feel one's way in sthg.
engavetamento [ẽŋgaveta'mẽntu] *m* **-1.** [de carros] smash. **-2.** [de papéis] putting into a drawer. **-3.** [de projeto, processo] *fig* shelving.
engavetar [4] [ẽŋgave'ta(x)] ◇ *vt* **-1.** [papéis *etc*] to put into a drawer. **-2.** *fig* [processo, projeto] to shelve. ◇ *vi* [carros] to concertina.
◆ **engavetar-se** *vp* [carros] to concertina.
engendrar [4] [ẽnʒẽn'dra(x)] *vt* to create.
engenharia [ẽnʒeɲa'ria] *f* engineering; **~ genética** genetic engineering.
engenheiro, ra [ẽnʒe'ɲejru, ra] *m, f* engineer.
engenho [ẽn'ʒeɲu] *m* **-1.** [habilidade] inventiveness. **-2.** [máquina] engine. **-3.** [moenda] mill. **-4.** [fazenda de cana de açúcar] sugar plant.
engenhoca [ẽnʒe'ɲɔka] *f* ***pej*** [aparelho] Heath-Robinson device.
engenhoso, osa [ẽnʒe'ɲozu, ɔza] *adj* ingenious.
engessado, da [ẽne'sadu, da] *adj* plastered.
engessar [4] [ẽnʒe'sa(x)] *vt* to put in plaster.
englobar [4] [ẽŋglo'ba(x)] *vt* to encompass.
engodo [ẽŋ'godu] *m* **-1.** [isca] bait. **-2.** [farsa] flattery.
engolir [59] [ẽŋgo'li(x)] *vt* **-1.** [ger] to swallow. **-2.** *fig* [sobrepujar]: **~ alguém** to eclipse sb.
engomado, da [ẽŋgo'madu, da] *adj* starched.
engomar [4] [ẽŋgo'ma(x)] *vt* to starch.
engordar [4] [ẽŋgox'da(x)] ◇ *vt* to fatten. ◇ *vi* to put on weight; **açucar engorda** sugar is fattening.
engordurado, da [ẽŋgoxdu'radu, da] *adj* greasy.
engordurar [4] [ẽŋgoxdu'ra(x)] *vt* to grease.
engraçadinho, nha [ẽŋgrasa'dʒiɲu, ɲa] ◇ *adj* [pequeno, gracioso] cute. ◇ *m, f* ***pej*** clown.
engraçado, da [ẽŋgra'sadu, da] *adj* amusing.
engraçar-se [13] [ẽŋgra'saxsi] *vp*: **~ para o lado de alguém** to take advantage of sb.
engradado [ẽŋgra'dadu] *m* crate.
engrandecer [25] [ẽŋgrãnde'se(x)] *vt* to elevate.
◆ **engrandecer-se** *vp* to elevate o.s.
engravidar [4] [ẽŋgravi'da(x)] ◇ *vt* to make pregnant. ◇ *vi* to become pregnant.
engraxar [4] [ẽŋgra'ʃa(x)] *vt* to polish.
engraxate [ẽŋgra'ʃatʃi] *mf* shoe shiner.
engrenagem [ẽŋgre'naʒẽ] (*pl* **-ns**) *f* **-1.** *AUTO* gear. **-2.** *fig* [política, social] mechanism.
engrenar [4] [ẽŋgre'na(x)] *vt* **-1.** *AUTO* to put in gear. **-2.** [iniciar] to start.
engrossar [4] [ẽŋgro'sa(x)] ◇ *vt* **-1.** [aumentar] to enlarge. **-2.** [encorpar] to thicken. **-3.** [tornar grave] to deepen. ◇ *vi* ***fig*** [ser grosseiro]: **~ (com alguém)** to be rough (with sb).
enguia [ẽŋ'gia] *f* eel.
enguiçado, da [ẽŋgi'sadu, da] *adj* **-1.** [com defeito] broken down. **-2.** [emperrado] bogged down.
enguiçar [13] [ẽŋgi'sa(x)] *vi* **-1.** [carro] to break down. **-2.** [relógio] to stop.
enguiço [ẽŋ'gisu] *m* breakdown.
engulho [ẽŋ'guʎu] *m* nausea.
enigma [e'nigma] *m* enigma.

enigmático, ca [enigi'matʃiku, ka] *adj* enigmatic.
enjaular [19] [ẽnʒaw'la(x)] *vt* to put in a cage.
enjeitado, da [ẽnʒej'tadu, da] *adj* rejected.
enjeitar [4] [ẽnʒej'ta(x)] *vt* **-1.** [rejeitar] to reject. **-2.** [abandonar] to abandon.
enjoado, da [ẽn'ʒwadu, da] *adj* **-1.** [nauseado] nauseous. **-2.** *fig* [cansado]: ~ **de algo/de fazer algo** fed up with sthg/with doing sthg. **-3.** *fig* [chato] boring.
enjoar [20] [ẽn'ʒwa(x)] ◇ *vt* **-1.** [nausear] to make nauseous. **-2.** *fig* [cansar] to bore. ◇ *vi* **-1.** [nausear-se] to feel sick. **-2.** *fig* [cansar-se]: ~ **de algo /de fazer algo** to become bored with sthg/with doing sthg.
enjoativo, va [ẽnʒwa'tʃivu, va] *adj* nauseating.
enjôo [ẽn'ʒou] *m* **-1.** [náusea] sickness; ~ **de gravidez** morning sickness. **-2.** *fig* [aborrecimento]: **ser um** ~ to be a bore.
enlaçar [13] [ẽnla'sa(x)] *vt* **-1.** [prender com laço] to tie up. **-2.** [envolver] to bog down.
enlace [ẽn'lasi] *m* **-1.** [união] union. **-2.** [casamento] marriage.
enlameado, da [ẽnla'mjadu, da] *adj* **-1.** [com lama] muddy. **-2.** *fig* [vilipendiado] muddied.
enlamear [15] [ẽnla'mja(x)] *vt* to muddy.
enlatado, da [ẽnla'tadu, da] *adj* canned.
◆ **enlatado** *m* **-1.** [comida em lata] canned food. **-2.** *pej* [série de TV] trash TV.
enlatar [15] [ẽnla'ta(x)] *vt* to can.
enlevar [4] [ẽnle'va(x)] *vt* to entrance.
◆ **enlevar-se** *vp* **-1.** [extasiar-se] to become entranced. **-2.** [absorver-se]: **~-se em** to become absorbed in.
enlevo [ẽn'levu] *m* enchantment.
enlouquecer [25] [ẽnloke'se(x)] ◇ *vt* to drive mad. ◇ *vi* to go mad.
enlouquecido, da [ẽnloke'sidu, da] *adj* crazed.
enlouquecimento [ẽnlokesi'mẽntu] *m* (growing) insanity.
enluarado, da [ẽnlwa'radu, da] *adj* moonlit.
enobrecer [25] [enobre'se(x)] *vt* to ennoble.
◆ **enobrecer-se** *vp* to glorify o.s.
enojado, da [eno'ʒadu, da] *adj* disgusted.
enojar [4] [eno'ʒa(x)] *vt* to disgust.
◆ **enojar-se** *vp* [sentir nojo]: **enojava-se com o cheiro de frango** the smell of chicken made him/her sick.
enorme [e'nɔxmi] *adj* enormous.
enormidade [enoxmi'dadʒi] *f* enormity; **uma** ~ **de** a vast quantity of.
enquadramento [ẽŋkwadra'mẽntu] *m* CINE & FOTO frame.
enquadrar [4] [ẽŋkwa'dra(x)] ◇ *vt* **-1.** [ajustar]: ~ **algo em algo** to frame sthg in sthg. **-2.** [autuar] to charge. ◇ *vi* [combinar]: ~ **com** to fit in with.
◆ **enquadrar-se** *vp* [ajustar-se]: **~-se (em algo)** to fit in (with sthg).
enquanto [ẽŋ'kwãntu] *conj* **-1.** [ger] while. **-2.** [considerado como]: **isso é interessante** ~ **experiência** it's interesting as an experience; ~ **isso** meanwhile.
◆ **por enquanto** *loc adv* for the time being.
enquete [ẽn'kɛtʃi] *f* survey.
enraivecer [25] [ẽnxajve'se(x)] *vt* to anger.
◆ **enraivecer-se** *vp* to become angry.
enraizar [4] [ẽnxaj'za(x)] *vt* to root.
◆ **enraizar-se** *vp* to take root.
enrascada [ẽnxaʃ'kada] *f* tight spot; **meter-se numa** ~ to get into a tight spot.
enrascado, da [ẽnxaʃ'kadu, da] *adj* in a fix *(depois de verbo)*.
enrascar-se [12] [ẽnxaʃ'kaxsi] *vp* to get in a fix.
enredar [4] [ẽnre'da(x)] *vt* **-1.** [emaranhar] to twist. **-2.** *fig* [enganar] to deceive.
◆ **enredar-se** *vp* **-1.** [pessoa] to become entangled. **-2.** [peixe] to fall into a net.
enredo [ẽn'xedu] *m* plot.
enrijecer [25] [ẽnxiʒe'se(x)] *vt* to stiffen.
◆ **enrijecer-se** *vp* to become stiff.
enriquecer [25] [ẽnxike'se(x)] ◇ *vt* to enrich. ◇ *vi* to become rich.
◆ **enriquecer-se** *vp*: **~-se com algo** to become rich in sthg.
enriquecimento [ẽnxikesi'mẽntu] *m* **-1.** [financeiro] increase in wealth. **-2.** [cultural] enrichment.
enrolado, da [ẽnxo'ladu, da] *adj* **-1.** [embrulhado]: ~ **em algo** rolled up in sthg. **-2.** [cabelo] coiled. **-3.** *fam* [confuso] screwed up.
enrolar [4] [ẽnxo'la(x)] ◇ *vt* **-1.** [dar forma de rolo] to roll. **-2.** [embrulhar]: ~ **algo/alguém em algo** to wrap sthg/sb up in sthg. **-3.** *fam* [complicar] to screw up. **-4.** *fam* [enganar] to take in. ◇ *vi fam* [protelar] to put things off.
◆ **enrolar-se** *vp* **-1.** [agasalhar-se]: **~-se em algo** to wrap o.s. up in sthg. **-2.** *fam* [confundir-se] to screw things up.
enroscar [4] [ẽnxoʃ'ka(x)] *vt*: ~ **algo em** to entwine sthg in.
◆ **enroscar-se** *vp* **-1.** [encolher-se de frio] to curl up. **-2.** [embolar-se] to become entangled.
enrouquecer [25] [ẽnxoke'se(x)] ◇ *vt* to make hoarse. ◇ *vi* to become hoarse.
enrubescer [25] [ẽnxube'se(x)] ◇ *vt* to redden. ◇ *vi* to blush, go red.
enrugado, da [ẽnxu'gadu, da] *adj* wrinkled.
enrugar [14] [ẽnxu'ga(x)] *vt* & *vi* to wrinkle.
enrustido [ẽnxuʃ'tʃidu] *m* [homossexual] closet gay.
ensaboar [20] [ẽnsa'bwa(x)] *vt* to wash with soap.
◆ **ensaboar-se** *vp* to soap o.s.
ensaiar [4] [ẽnsa'ja(x)] *vt* to practise *UK*, to practice *US*.
ensaio [ẽn'saju] *m* **-1.** [experiência] trial. **-2.** TEATRO rehearsal. **-3.** LITER essay.
ensaísta [ẽnsa'iʃta] *mf* essayist.
ensangüentado, da [ẽnsãngwẽn'tadu, da] *adj* blood-stained.
ensangüentar [4] [ẽnsãngwẽn'ta(x)] *vt* to stain with blood.
enseada [ẽn'sjada] *f* inlet.
ensebado, da [ẽnse'badu, da] *adj* greasy.

ensebar [4] [ẽnse'ba(x)] *vt* to grease.
ensejar [4] [ẽnse'ʒa(x)] *vt*: ~ **algo a alguém** to offer the opportunity of sthg to sb.
ensejo [ẽn'seʒu] *m* opportunity.
ensimesmado, da [ẽnsimeʒ'madu, da] *adj* introverted.
ensinamento [ẽnsina'mẽntu] *m* instruction.
ensinar [4] [ẽnsi'na(x)] *vt*: ~ **alguém a fazer algo** to teach sb how to do sthg; ~ **algo a alguém** to teach sthg to sb.
ensino [ẽn'sinu] *m* **-1.** [transmissão de conhecimento] teaching. **-2.** [educação] education; ~ **fundamental/medio** primary/secondary education; ~ **superior** higher education; ~ **supletivo** *speeded-up education programme for adults who missed out on a full schooling.*
ensolarado, da [ẽnsola'radu, da] *adj* sunny.
ensombrecido, da [ẽnsõnbre'sidu, da] *adj* gloomy.
ensopado, da [ẽnso'padu, da] *adj* **-1.** *CULIN* stewed. **-2.** *fig* [encharcado] soaking.
◆ **ensopado** *m CULIN* stew.
ensopar [4] [ẽnso'pa(x)] *vt* to soak.
ensurdecedor, ra [ẽnsuxdese'dox, ra] (*mpl* **-es**, *fpl* **-s**) *adj* deafening.
ensurdecer [25] [ẽnsuxde'se(x)] *vt* to deafen.
entabular [4] [ẽntabu'la(x)] *vt* to open.
entalado, da [ẽnta'ladu, da] *adj* stuck.
entalar [4] [ẽnta'la(x)] <> *vt* [apertar] to squeeze. <> *vi* [encravar] to stick.
entalhador, ra [ẽntaʎa'do(x), ra] *m, f* woodcarver.
entalhar [4] [ẽnta'ʎa(x)] *vt* to carve.
entalhe [ẽn'taʎi] *m* groove.
entanto [ẽn'tãntu] ◆ **no entanto** *loc adv* however.
então [ẽn'tãw] *adv* then; **até** ~ up until then; **desde** ~ since then; **e** ~**?** well then?; **para** ~ so that; **pois** ~ then.
entardecer [25] [ẽntaxde'se(x)] <> *vi* to get late. <> *m* sunset.
ente ['ẽntʃi] *m* **-1.** [ser] being. **-2.** [corporação, órgão] entity.
enteado, da [ẽn'tʒjadu, da] *m, f* stepchild, stepson (*f* stepdaughter).
entediante [ẽnte'dʒjãntʃi] *adj* boring.
entediar [16] [ẽnte'dʒa(x)] *vt* to bore.
◆ **entediar-se** *vp* to get bored.
entendedor, ra [ẽntẽnde'do(x), ra] <> *adj* knowledgeable. <> *m, f* expert; **a bom** ~ **meia palavra basta** a word is sufficient to the wise.
entender [5] [ẽntẽn'de(x)] <> *vt* **-1.** [compreender] to understand; **dar a** ~ to give the impression. **-2.** [ouvir] to hear. **-3.** [interpretar] to perceive. **-4.** [deduzir]: ~ **que** to see (that). <> *vi* **-1.** [inferir]: **o que você** ~ **por isso?** what do you deduce from it? **-2.** [conhecer]: ~ **de** to know about. <> *m*: **no** ~ **de alguém** in the opinion of sb.
◆ **entender-se** *vp* **-1.** [comunicar-se] to get along. **-2.** [chegar a um acordo]: ~**-se (com alguém)** to see eye to eye (with sb). **-3.** [ter o uso da razão]: **desde que me entendo por gente, gosto de música** for as long as I can remember, I've liked music.
entendido, da [ẽntẽn'dʒidu, da] <> *adj* **-1.** [perito] expert; ~ **em algo** expert in sthg. **-2.** *fam* [homossexual] gay. <> *m, f* **-1.** [perito] expert. **-2.** *fam* [homossexual] gay.
◆ **bem entendido** *loc adv* understood.
entendimento [ẽntẽndʒi'mẽntu] *m* **-1.** [compreensão] understanding. **-2.** [juízo] perception. **-3.** [acordo] agreement.
enternecer [25] [ẽntexne'se(x)] *vt* to touch.
◆ **enternecer-se** *vp* to be touched.
enterrar [4] [ẽnte'xa(x)] *vt* **-1.** to bury. **-2.** *fig* [encerrar] to close. **-3.** *fig* [arruinar] to ruin. **-4.** [enfiar]: **enterrou a estaca no coração do vampiro** he rammed the stake into the vampire's heart; **enterrou o chapéu na cabeça** he rammed his hat on his head.
◆ **enterrar-se** *vp* **-1.** [isolar-se] to hide o.s. away. **-2.** [arruinar-se] to ruin o.s.
enterro [ẽn'texu] *m* **-1.** [sepultamento] burial. **-2.** [funeral] funeral.
entidade [ẽntʃi'dadʒi] *f* entity.
entoação [ẽntwa'sãw] *f* chanting.
entoar [20] [ẽn'twa(x)] *vt* to chant.
entonação [ẽntona'sãw] *f* intonation.
entornar [4] [ẽntox'na(x)] <> *vt* **-1.** [derramar] to spill. **-2.** [despejar] to pour. <> *vi fig* [embriagar-se] to drink heavily.
entorpecente [ẽntoxpe'sẽntʃi] *m* narcotic.
entorpecer [25] [ẽntoxpe'se(x)] *vt* **-1.** [causar torpor] to stupefy. **-2.** *fig* [insensibilizar] to numb.
entorpecido, da [ẽntoxpe'sidu, da] *adj* numb.
entorpecimento [ẽntoxpesi'mẽntu] *m* **-1.** [paralisia] stupor. **-2.** *fig* [estagnação] numbness.
entorse [ẽn'tɔxsi] *f* sprain.
entortar [4] [ẽntox'ta(x)] <> *vt* **-1.** [curvar] to bend. **-2.** [empenar] to jam. <> *vi* [empenar - porta] to warp; [- roda] to buckle.
entourage [ãntu'xaʒi] *m* entourage.
entrada [ẽn'trada] *f* **-1.** [ger] entry; **'proibida a** ~**'** 'no entry'. **-2.** [lugar] entrance; ~ **de serviço** service entrance. **-3.** [admissão] admission. **-4.** [porta] doorway. **-5.** [corredor] hallway. **-6.** *CULIN* starter. **-7.** [calvície] receding hairline. **-8.** [pagamento inicial] down payment. **-9.** [ingresso] ticket; ~ **gratuita** *ou* **franca** free admission; **meia** ~ half price. **-10.** [abertura] opening. **-11.** *TEC* inlet. **-12.** *COMPUT* input. **-13.** [início]: **dar** ~ **em algo** to institute sthg.
entra-e-sai [ˌẽntri'saj] *m inv* coming and going.
entranhado, da [ẽntra'ɲadu, da] *adj* deep-seated.
entranhar [4] [ẽntra'ɲa(x)] *vi*: ~ **(em algo)** to penetrate (sthg).
entranhas [ẽn'traɲaʃ] *fpl* **-1.** [vísceras] bowels. **-2.** *fig* [profundeza] depths.
entrar [4] [ẽn'tra(x)] *vi* **-1.** [adentrar]: ~ **(em)** to go/come (into). **-2.** [penetrar] to enter. **-3.** [começar a trabalhar] to begin. **-4.** [contribuir]: ~ **com algo** to

contribute sthg. **-5.** [começar]: ~ **de férias** to go on vacation. **-6.** [aprofundar-se]: ~ **em algo** to go into sthg. **-7.** [entabular]: ~ **em algo** to enter into sthg. **-8.** [envolver-se]: ~ **em algo** to become involved in sthg. **-9.** [caber]: ~ **em algo** to fit into sthg. **-10.** [ser componente]: ~ **em algo** to be part of sthg. **-11.** [ingressar]: ~ **para algo** [universidade] to go to sthg; [clube] to join sthg. **-12.** *COMPUT*: ~ **com algo** to enter sthg. **-13.** *loc*: ~ **bem** *fam* to get one's fingers burnt.

entrave [ẽn'travi] *m* obstacle.

entre ['ẽntri] *prep* between; **os dois dividiram o bolo ~ eles** the two shared the cake between them; **os alunos sempre conversavam ~ si** the schoolchildren always talked among themselves; **cá ~ nós** [confidencialmente] between you and me.

entreaberto, ta [ˌẽntrja'bɛxtu, ta] *adj* **-1.** [porta] ajar. **-2.** [olho] half-open.

entreabrir [6] [ẽntrja'bri(x)] *vt* to half-open.
◆ **entreabrir-se** *vp* to open up.

entrecortado, da [ẽntrekox'tadu, da] *adj* intermittent.

entrecortar [ẽntre'koxta(x)] *vt* **-1.** [cortar] to cut off. **-2.** [interromper] to interrupt.

entrega [ẽn'trɛga] *f* **-1.** [de carta, prêmio] delivery; ~ **em domicílio** home delivery; **pronta ~** speedy delivery. **-2.** [dedicação]: ~ **a algo/alguém** dedication to sthg/sb. **-3.** [rendição] surrender.

entregador, ra [ẽntrega'do(x), ra] *m, f* [funcionário] delivery person.

entregar [14] [ẽntre'ga(x)] *vt* **-1.** [passar às mãos de - mercadoria, carta] to deliver; [- presente] to give; [- prêmio] to award. **-2.** [delatar] to inform on. **-3.** [devolver] to return. **-4.** [confiar]: ~ **algo/alguém a alguém** to entrust sthg/sb to sb.
◆ **entregar-se** *vp* **-1.** [render-se - inimigo] to surrender; [- à dor *etc*]: **~-se a algo** to surrender to sthg. **-2.** [dedicar-se]: **~-se a algo** to dedicate o.s. to sthg. **-3.** [deixar-se seduzir]: **~-se a alguém** to give o.s. to sb. **-4.** *loc*: ~ **os pontos** to give up.

entregue [ẽn'trɛgi] *pp* ⊳ **entregar**.

entreguismo [ẽntre'giʒmu] *m* selling-out, *policy of allowing exploitation of the country's natural resources by foreign entities.*

entreguista [ẽntre'giʃta] *adj supportive or typical of selling-out.*

entrelaçamento [ẽntrelasa'mẽntu] *m* [união] interlinking.

entrelaçar [13] [ẽntrela'sa(x)] *vt* to entwine.

entrelinha [ẽntre'liɲa] *f* [espaço] line space.
◆ **entrelinhas** *fpl*: **nas ~s** *fig* [subentendido] between the lines.

entremear [15] [ẽntre'mja(x)] *vt*: ~ **algo com algo** to mix sthg with sthg.

entreolhar-se [7] [ẽntrjo'ʎaxsi] *vp* to exchange glances.

entrepor [45] [ẽntre'po(x)] *vt* to insert.
◆ **entrepor-se** *vp*: **~-se entre** to come between.

entreposto, ta [ẽntre'poʃtu, ta] *pp* ⊳ **entrepor**.
◆ **entreposto** *m* warehouse.

entressafra [ẽntri'safra] *f* period between harvests.

entretanto [ẽntri'tãntu] *conj* however.

entretenimento [ẽntriteni'mẽntu] *m* **-1.** [passatempo] pastime. **-2.** [diversão] entertainment.

entreter [1] [ẽntre'te(x)] *vt* **-1.** [ger] to entertain. **-2.** [ocupar] to occupy.
◆ **entreter-se** *vp* **-1.** [divertir-se] to amuse o.s. **-2.** [ocupar-se] to occupy o.s.

entretido, da [ẽntre'tʃidu, da] *adj* **-1.** [distraído] entertained. **-2.** [ocupado] occupied.

entrevar [4] [ẽntre'va(x)] *vt* to cripple.

entrever [40] [ẽntre've(x)] *vt* **-1.** [ver] to glimpse. **-2.** [prever] to foresee.

entrevero [ẽntre'vero] *m* mêlée *UK*, melee *US*.

entrevista [ẽntre'viʃta] *f* interview; ~ **coletiva** press conference.

entrevistado, da [ẽntre'viʃ'tadu, da] *m, f* interviewee.

entrevistador, ra [ẽntre'viʃtado(x), ra] (*mpl* **-es**, *fpl* **-s**) *m, f* interviewer.

entrevistar [4] [ẽntre'viʃ'ta(x)] *vt* to interview.

entristecedor, ra [ẽntriʃtese'do(x), ra] *adj* saddening.

entristecer [25] [ẽntriʃte'se(x)] ◇ *vt* to sadden. ◇ *vi* to become sad.
◆ **entristecer-se** *vp* to become sad.

entroncamento [ẽntrõŋka'mẽntu] *m* junction.

entrosado, da [ẽntro'zadu, da] *adj* [ambientado] integrated.

entrosamento [ẽntroza'mẽntu] *m* integration.

entrosar [4] [ẽntro'za(x)] *vt* **-1.** [endentar] to mesh. **-2.** [ambientar]: ~ **alguém com alguém** to integrate sb with sb.
◆ **entrosar-se** *vp* [entender-se]: **~-se (com alguém)** to get along (with sb).

entulhar [4] [ẽntu'ʎa(x)] *vt*: ~ **algo (de** *ou* **com)** to cram sthg with.

entulho [ẽn'tuʎu] *m* debris.

entupido, da [ẽntu'pidu, da] *adj* **-1.** [pia, nariz, ouvido] blocked. **-2.** [de comida] stuffed. **-3.** [de gente] packed.

entupimento [ẽntupi'mẽntu] *m* blockage.

entupir [60.61] [ẽntu'pi(x)] *vt* to block.
◆ **entupir-se** *vp*: **~-se de comida** to stuff o.s. with food; **~-se de bebida** to pump o.s. full of drink.

enturmar-se [7] [ẽntux'maxsi] *vp*: **~-se (com)** to make friends (with).

entusiasmado, da [ẽntuzjaʒ'madu, da] *adj* enthusiastic.

entusiasmar [4] [ẽntuzjaʒ'ma(x)] *vt* to fill with enthusiasm.
◆ **entusiasmar-se** *vp* to get enthusiastic.

entusiasmo [ẽntu'zjaʒmu] *m* enthusiasm.

entusiasta [ẽntu'zjaʃta] ◇ *adj* enthusiastic. ◇ *mf* enthusiast.

entusiástico, ca [ẽntu'zjaʃtʃiku, ka] *adj* enthusiastic.

enumeração [enumera'sãw] (*pl* **-ões**) *f* enumeration.

enumerar [4] [enume'ra(x)] *vt* to enumerate.
enunciado, da [enũ'sjadu, da] <> *adj* stated. <> *m* statement.
enunciar [16] [enũ'sja(x)] *vt* to state.
envaidecer [25] [ẽnvajde'se(x)] *vt* to flatter.
◆ **envaidecer-se** *vp* to feel flattered.
envelhecer [25] [ẽnveʎe'se(x)] <> *vt* **-1.** [tornar velho] to age. **-2.** [fazer parecer velho]: ~ **alguém** to make sb look older. <> *vi* **-1.** [ficar velho] to grow old. **-2.** [fazer parecer velho] to age.
envelhecido, da [ẽnveʎe'sidu, da] *adj* aged.
envelhecimento [ẽnveʎesi'mẽntu] *m* ageing.
envelopar [ẽnve'lopa(x)] *vt* to put in an envelope.
envelope [ẽnve'lɔpi] *m* envelope.
envenenado, da [ẽnvene'nadu, da] *adj* **-1.** [ger] poisoned. **-2.** *fam fig* [carro] souped up.
envenenamento [ẽnvenena'mẽntu] *m* poisoning.
envenenar [4] [ẽnvene'na(x)] *vt* **-1.** [intoxicar] to poison. **-2.** [corromper] to corrupt. **-3.** *AUTO* to soup up.
◆ **envenenar-se** *vp* [intoxicar-se] to poison o.s.
enveredar [4] [ẽnvere'da(x)] *vi* to make one's way; ~ **por/para** to head for.
envergadura [ẽnvexga'dura] *f* **-1.** [dimensão] wingspan. **-2.** *fig* [importância] scope. **-3.** *fig* [capacidade]: **é um poeta de pouca** ~ he's a poet of little talent.
envergar [14] [ẽnvex'ga(x)] <> *vt* **-1.** [entortar] to bend. **-2.** [vestir] to wear. <> *vi* [arquear] to warp.
envergonhado, da [ẽnvexgo'ɲadu, da] *adj* **-1.** [tímido] shy. **-2.** [por má ação] ashamed.
envergonhar [4] [ẽnvexgo'ɲa(x)] *vt* **-1.** [acanhar] to embarrass. **-2.** [com má ação] to disgrace.
◆ **envergonhar-se** *vp* **-1.** [acanhar-se] to be embarrassed. **-2.** [por má ação] to be ashamed.
envernizado, da [ẽnvexni'zadu, da] *adj* [com verniz] varnished.
envernizar [4] [ẽnvexni'za(x)] *vt* to varnish.
enviado, da [ẽn'vjadu, da] *m, f* envoy.
enviar [16] [ẽn'vja(x)] *vt*: ~ **algo a** *OU* **para alguém** to send sthg to sb.
envidar [4] [ẽnvi'da(x)] *vt* to endeavour *UK*, to endeavor *US*.
envidraçado, da [ẽnvidra'sadu, da] *adj* glazed.
envidraçar [13] [ẽnvidra'sa(x)] *vt* to glaze.
enviesado, da [ẽnvje'zadu, da] *adj* slanting.
enviesar [ẽnvje'za(x)] *vt* **-1.** [pôr obliquamente] to put at an angle. **-2.** [envesgar] to cross.
envio [ẽn'viu] *m* dispatch.
enviuvar [4] [ẽnvju'va(x)] *vi* to be widowed.
envolto, ta [ẽn'vowtu, ta] <> *pp* ▷ **envolver**. <> *adj* wrapped.
envoltório [ẽnvow'tɔrju] *m* wrapping.
envolvente [ẽnvow'vẽntʃi] *adj* compelling.
envolver [5] [ẽnvow've(x)] *vt* **-1.** [cobrir]: ~ **algo/alguém (em)** to wrap sthg/sb (in). **-2.** [comprometer]: ~ **alguém (em)** to involve sb (in). **-3.** [acarretar] to involve. **-4.** [abraçar] to embrace.
◆ **envolver-se** *vp* **-1.** [comprometer-se]: ~**-se em** *OU* **com** to get involved in *OU* with. **-2.** [intrometer-se]: ~**-se em** to get involved in.
envolvimento [ẽnvowvi'mẽntu] *m* involvement.
enxada [ẽn'ʃada] *f* hoe.
enxadrista [ẽnʃa'driʃta] *mf* chess player.
enxaguada [ẽnʃa'gwada] *f* rinse.
enxaguar [22] [ẽnʃa'gwa(x)] *vt* to rinse.
enxágüe *m* = **enxaguada**.
enxame [ẽn'ʃami] *m* swarm.
enxaqueca [ẽnʃa'keka] *f* migraine.
enxergar [14] [ẽnʃex'ga(x)] <> *vt* **-1.** [ver] to catch sight of. **-2.** *fig* [perceber] to make out. <> *vi* [ver] to see.
◆ **enxergar-se** *vp*: **ele não se enxerga** he doesn't know his limitations.
enxerido, da [ẽnʃe'ridu, da] *adj* nosy.
enxertar [4] [ẽnʃex'ta(x)] *vt* **-1.** [planta] to graft. **-2.** *fig* [inserir] to insert.
enxerto [ẽn'ʃextu] *m* **-1.** [de planta] grafting. **-2.** *MED* graft. **-3.** *fig* [inserção] insertion.
enxofre [ẽn'ʃofri] *m* sulphur *UK*, sulfur *US*.
enxotar [4] [ẽnʃo'ta(x)] *vt* to drive away.
enxoval [ẽnʃo'vaw] (*pl* **-ais**) *m* [de noiva] trousseau.
enxugador [ẽnʃuga'do(x)] *m* clothes dryer.
enxugar [14] [ẽnʃu'ga(x)] *vt* **-1.** [secar] to dry. **-2.** *fig* [diminuir] to rationalize.
enxurrada [ẽnʃu'xada] *f* **-1.** [torrente] torrent. **-2.** *fig* [amontoado] flood.
enxuto, ta [ẽn'ʃutu, ta] *adj* **-1.** [seco] dry. **-2.** *fig* [bonito] good-looking.
enzima [ẽn'zima] *f* enzyme.
epicentro [epi'sẽntru] *m* epicentre *UK*, epicenter *US*.
épico, ca ['ɛpiku, ka] *adj* epic.
◆ **épico** *m LITER* epic.
epidemia [epide'mia] *f* **-1.** *MED* epidemic. **-2.** *fig* [modismo] mania.
epidêmico, ca [epi'demiku, ka] *adj MED* epidemic.
epiderme [epi'dexmi] *f* epidermis.
epidural [epidu'raw] *adj* epidural.
epifania [epifa'nia] *f* Epiphany.
epígrafe [e'pigrafi] *f* epigraph; **em** ~ in epigraph.
epigrama [epi'grama] *f* epigram.
epilepsia [epilep'sia] *f* epilepsy.
epiléptico, ca [epi'lɛptʃiku, ka] <> *adj* epileptic. <> *m, f* epileptic.
epílogo [e'pilugu] *m* epilogue.
episcopado [epiʃko'padu] *m* bishopric.
episcopal [epiʃko'paw] (*pl* **-ais**) *adj* episcopal.
episódico, ca [epi'zɔdiku, ka] *adj* episodic.
episódio [epi'zɔdju] *m* episode.
epistemologia *f* epistemology.
epístola [e'piʃtola] *f* **-1.** [bíblia] Epistle. **-2.** [carta] letter.
epistolar [epiʃto'la(x)] *adj* epistolary.
epistolário [epiʃto'lariw] *m* collection of letters.
epitáfio [epi'tafju] *m* epitaph.
época ['ɛpoka] *f* **-1.** [período] age; **filme de** ~ period movie; **naquela** ~ at that time; **fazer** ~

to be epoch-making. **-2.** [estação] season.
epopéia [epo'pɛja] *f* epic.
equação [ekwa'sãw] (*pl* **-ões**) *f* equation.
equacionamento [ekwasiona'mẽntu] *m* rationalizing.
equacionar [4] [ekwasjo'na(x)] *vt* to set out.
equador [ekwa'do(x)] *m* equator.
Equador [ekwa'do(x)] *n* Ecuador.
equânime [e'kwãnimi] *adj* unbiased.
equatorial [ekwato'rjaw] (*pl* **-ais**) *adj* equatorial.
equatoriano, na ◇ *adj* Ecuadorean. ◇ *m, f* Ecuadorean.
eqüestre [e'kwɛʃtri] *adj* equestrian.
eqüidade [ekwi'dadʒi] *f* equity.
eqüidistante [ekwidʒiʃ'tãntʃi] *adj* equidistant.
eqüilátero, ra [ekwi'lateru, ra] *adj* equilateral.
equilibrado, da [ekili'bradu, da] *adj* balanced.
equilibrar [4] [ekili'bra(x)] *vt* to balance.
◆ **equilibrar-se** *vp* to balance.
equilíbrio [eki'libriw] *m* equilibrium.
equilibrista [ekili'briʃta] *mf* trapeze artist.
eqüino, na [e'kwinu, na] *adj* equine.
equinócio [eki'nɔsju] *m* equinox.
equipagem [ekipa'ʒẽ] *f* crew.
equipamento [ekipa'mẽntu] *m* equipment.
equipar [4] [eki'pa(x)] *vt*: ~ **algo/alguém (de)** to equip sthg/sb (with).
◆ **equipar-se** *vp*: **~-se (de)** to equip o.s. (with).
equiparação [ekipara'sãw] *m* parity.
equiparar [4] [ekipa'ra(x)] *vt*: ~ **algo (a** *ou* **com algo)** to compare sthg (against sthg).
◆ **equiparar-se** *vp* **-1.** [igualar-se]: **~-se (a** *ou* **com algo)** to compare o.s. (with sthg). **-2.** [comparar-se]: **~-se (a** *ou* **com alguém)** to compare o.s. (with sb).
equiparável [ekipa'ravew] (*pl* **-eis**) *adj* comparable.
equipe [e'kipi] *f* team; ~ **de socorros** rescue team.
equitação [ekita'sãw] *f* horse-riding.
eqüitativamente [ekwitatʃiva'mẽntʃi] *adv* equitably.
eqüitativo, va [ekwita'tʃivu, va] *adj* equitable.
equivalência [ekiva'lẽnsja] *f* equivalence.
equivalente [ekiva'lẽntʃi] *adj* equivalent.
equivaler [43] [ekiva'le(x)] *vi*: ~ **a** to be equivalent to.
◆ **equivaler-se** *vp* to be equal.
equivocado, da [ekivo'kadu, da] *adj* mistaken.
equivocar-se [12] [ekivo'kaxsi] *vp* to make a mistake.
equívoco [e'kivoku] *m* mistake.
era ['ɛra] *f* era.
erário [e'rarju] *m* exchequer.
ereção [ere'sãw] (*pl* **-ões**) *f* erection.
eremita [ere'mita] *mf* hermit.
ereto, ta [e'rɛtu, ta] *adj* erect.
erguer [27] [ex'ge(x)] *vt* **-1.** [levantar] to raise. **-2.** [construir] to erect.
◆ **erguer-se** *vp* [levantar-se] to get up.
eriçado, da [ẽri'sadu, da] *adj* standing on end.
eriçar [13] [eri'sa(x)] *vt* to make stand on end.
erigir [52] [eri'ʒi(x)] *vt* to erect.
ermo, ma ['exmu, ma] *adj* deserted.
erodir [6] [ero'dʒi(x)] *vt* to erode.
erógeno, na [e'rɔʒenu, na] *adj* erogenous.
erosão [ero'zãw] *f* erosion.
erótico, ca [e'rɔtʃiku, ka] *adj* erotic.
erotismo [ero'tʃiʒmu] *m* eroticism.
erradicação [exadʒika'sãw] *f* eradication.
erradicar [12] [exadʒi'ka(x)] *vt* to eradicate.
errado, da [e'xadu, da] *adj* **-1.** [incorreto] wrong. **-2.** [inadequado] inappropriate. **-3.** *loc*: **dar** ~ to go wrong.
errante [e'xãntʃi] *adj* wandering.
errar [4] [e'xa(x)] ◇ *vt* [não acertar - alvo] to miss; [- conta, resposta] to get wrong. ◇ *vi* **-1.** [enganar-se]: ~ **(em algo)** to be wrong (in sthg). **-2.** [proceder mal] to go wrong. **-3.** [vagar] to wander.
errata [e'xata] *f* erratum.
erro ['exu] *m* [ger] error; ~ **de impressão** printing error; ~ **de pronúncia** mispronunciation.
errôneo, nea [e'xonju, nja] *adj* erroneous.
erudição [erudʒi'sãw] *f* erudition.
erudito, ta [eru'dʒitu, ita] ◇ *adj* erudite. ◇ *m, f* scholar.
erupção [erup'sãw] (*pl* **-ões**) *f* eruption.
erva ['ɛxva] *f* **-1.** BOT herb; ~ **daninha** weed. **-2.** *fam* [maconha] grass.
erva-cidreira [ˌɛxva'sidrejra] (*pl* **ervas-cidreiras**) *f* lemon verbena.
erva-doce [ˌɛxva'dosi] (*pl* **ervas-doces**) *f* fennel.
erva-mate [ˌɛxva'matʃi] (*pl* **ervas-mates**) *f* matte.
ervilha [ex'viʎa] *f* pea.
ES (*abrev de* **Estado do Espírito Santo**) *m state of Espírito Santo.*
esbaforido, da [iʒbafo'ridu, da] *adj* breathless.
esbaldar-se [4] [iʒbaw'daxsi] *vp* to have great fun.
esbanjador, ra [iʒbãnʒa'do(x), ra] *adj* spendthrift.
esbanjamento [iʒbãnʒa'mẽntu] *m* [de dinheiro] squandering.
esbanjar [4] [iʒbãn'ʒa(x)] *vt* **-1.** [dinheiro] to squander. **-2.** [saúde] to be bursting with.
esbarrão [iʒba'xãw] *m* bump.
esbarrar [4] [iʒba'xa(x)] *vi*: ~ **em algo/alguém** to bump into sthg/sb.
esbelto, ta [iʒ'bɛwtu, ta] *adj* svelte.
esboçar [13] [iʒbo'sa(x)] *vt* **-1.** [ger] to sketch. **-2.** [sorriso] to trace.
esboço [iʒ'bosu] *m* **-1.** [desenho] sketch. **-2.** [primeira versão] draft. **-3.** [tentativa] hint. **-4.** [resumo] outline.
esbodegado, da [ˌiʒbode'gadu] *adj* **-1.** [estragado] worn out. **-2.** [exausto] exhausted.
esbodegar [iʒbode'ga(x)] ◆ **esbodegar-se** *vp fam* [descuidar-se] to let o.s. go.
esbofetear [15] [iʒbofe'tʃja(x)] *vt* to slap.
esbórnia [iʒ'bɔxnja] *f* wild party.

esborrachar-se [4] [iʒboxa'ʃaxsi] *vp* **-1.** [arrebentar-se] to burst. **-2.** [cair] to fall sprawling.
esbranquiçado, da [iʒbrãnki'sadu, da] *adj* whitish.
esbravejar [4] [iʒbrave'ʒa(x)] *vi*: ~ **(com alguém)** to shout (at sb).
esbugalhado, da [iʒbuga'ʎadu, da] *adj* bulging.
esbugalhar [4] [iʒbuga'ʎa(x)] *vt* to bulge.
esburacado, da [iʒbura'kadu, da] *adj* **-1.** [rua, jardim] potholed. **-2.** [rosto] pitted.
esburacar [12] [iʒbura'ka(x)] *vt* to make holes in.
escabeche [iʃka'bɛʃi] *m* marinade.
escabroso, sa [iʃka'brozu, za] *adj* **-1.** [difícil] tough. **-2.** [imoral] immoral.
escada [iʃ'kada] *f* **-1.** [interna] stairs (*pl*), staircase. **-2.** [externa] steps (*pl*); ~ **de armar** ladder; ~ **de caracol** spiral staircase; ~ **de incêndio** fire escape; ~ **rolante** escalator. **-3.** *fig* [meio] ladder.
escadaria [iʃkada'ria] *f* staircase.
escafandrista [iʃkafãn'driʃta] *mf* deep-sea diver.
escafandro [iʃka'fãndru] *m* diving suit.
escafeder-se [5] [iʃkafe'dexsi] *vp* to slip off.
escala [iʃ'kala] *f* **-1.** [ger] scale; **em grande** ~ on a grand scale. **-2.** [parada] stopover; **sem** ~ nonstop. **-3.** [turno] turn.
escalação [iʃkala'sãw] *f* [designação] selection.
escalada [iʃka'lada] *f* climbing.
escalão [iʃka'lãw] (*pl* **-ões**) *m* level; **o alto** ~ **do governo** the upper echelon of government.
escalar [4] [iʃka'la(x)] *vt* **-1.** [subir] to climb. **-2.** [designar] to select.
escaldado, da [iʃkaw'dadu, da] *adj* **-1.** [fervido] scalded. **-2.** *fig* [experiente] wary.
escaldar [4] [iʃkaw'da(x)] *vt* to scald.
escaler [iʃka'lɛ(x)] *m* launch.
escalonamento [iʃkalona'mẽntu] *m* scheduling.
escalonar [4] [iʃkalo'na(x)] *vt* to schedule.
escalope [iʃka'lɔpi] *m* escalope.
escalpelar [iʃkawpe'la(x)] *vt* [escalpar] to scalp.
escalpelo [iʃkaw'pelu] *m* scalpel.
escama [iʃ'kãma] *f* scale.
escamar [4] [iʃka'ma(x)] ◇ *vt* [peixe] to scale. ◇ *vi* [pele] to flake.
escamotear [15] [iʃkamo'tʃja(x)] *vt* to filch.
escancarado, da [iʃkãŋka'radu, da] *adj* **-1.** [aberto] wide open. **-2.** [evidente] brazen. **-3.** [franco] open.
escancarar [4] [iʃkãŋka'ra(x)] *vt* **-1.** [abrir] to open wide. **-2.** [exibir] to display openly.
escandalizar [4] [iʃkãndali'za(x)] *vt* to scandalize.
◆ **escandalizar-se** *vp* to be shocked.
escândalo [iʃ'kãndalu] *m* **-1.** [fato] scandal. **-2.** [indignação] outrage. **-3.** [alvoroço]: **fazer** *ou* **dar um** ~ to make a scene.
escandaloso, sa [iʃkãnda'lozu, ɔza] *adj* **-1.** [chocante] shocking. **-2.** [chamativo] outrageous.
Escandinávia [iʃkãndʒi'navja] *n* Scandinavia.
escandinavo, va [iʃkãndʒi'navu, va] ◇ *adj* Scandinavian. ◇ *m, f* Scandinavian.
escanear [15] [iʃkã'nea(x)] *vt* COMPUT to scan.
escangalhar [4] [iʃkãŋga'ʎa(x)] *vt* **-1.** [ger] to break. **-2.** [sapatos] to fall apart.
escaninho [iʃka'niɲu] *m* pigeon-hole.
escanteio [iʃkãn'teju] *m* corner.
escapada [iʃka'pada] *f* **-1.** [fuga] escape. **-2.** [ato leviano] escapade; **no meio da reunião, ele deu uma** ~ **para comprar flores para a mulher** in the middle of the meeting, he slipped out to buy flowers for his wife; **ele vive dando** ~**s com outras mulheres** he is always having affairs with other women; **a mulher sabe que ele dá umas** ~**s do casamento** his wife knows he has affairs outside marriage, his wife knows that he strays.
escapamento [iʃkapa'mẽntu] *m* **-1.** [de gás] leak. **-2.** [de veículo] exhaust.
escapar [4] [iʃka'pa(x)] *vi* **-1.** [sobreviver]: ~ **(de algo)** to escape (from sthg). **-2.**: ~ **a alguém** to escape (from) sb. **-3.** [fugir] to escape from. **-4.** [esquivar-se] to avoid; ~ **de fazer algo** to get out of doing sthg. **-5.** [soltar-se, cair]: ~ **de algo** to run away from sthg. **-6.** *loc*: ~ **de boa** to have a close shave; **deixar** ~ [não aproveitar] to miss; [revelar por descuido] to let drop.
escapatória [iʃkapa'tɔrja] *f* **-1.** [saída] way out. **-2.** [desculpa] excuse.
escape [iʃ'kapi] *m* [de veículo] exhaust pipe; **válvula de** ~ escape valve; **minha válvula de** ~ **é dançar todos os dias** *fig* my outlet is to dance every day.
escapismo [iʃka'piʒmu] *m* escapism.
escapulida [iʃkapu'lida] *f* [saída] outing; **dar uma** ~ to slip away.
escapulir [61] [iʃkapu'li(x)] *vi*: ~ **(de algo)** to escape (from sthg).
escarafunchar [4] [iʃkarafũn'ʃa(x)] *vt* to rummage in.
escaramuça [iʃkara'musa] *f* skirmish.
escaravelho [iʃkara'veʎu] *m* beetle.
escarcéu [iʃkax'sɛw] *m*: **fazer um** ~ to throw a fit.
escarlate [iʃkax'latʃi] *adj* scarlet.
escarlatina [iʃkaxla'tʃina] *f* scarlet fever.
escarnecer [25] [iʃkaxne'se(x)] *vi*: ~ **de algo/alguém** to mock sthg/sb, to make fun of sthg/sb.
escárnio [iʃ'karnju] *m* **-1.** [desdém] scorn. **-2.** [zombaria] mockery.
escarpa [iʃ'kaxpa] *f* escarpment.
escarpado, da [iʃkar'padu, da] *adj* steep.
escarrado, da [iʃka'xadu, da] *adj*: **o menino é o avô** ~ the boy is the spitting image of his grandfather.
escarrapachar-se [4] [iʃkaxapa'ʃaxsi] *vp* to sprawl.
escarrar [4] [iʃka'xa(x)] ◇ *vt* to spit. ◇ *vi* to hawk.
escarro [iʃ'kaxu] *m* phlegm.
escasseamento [iʃkasja'mẽntu] *m* shortage.
escassear [15] [iʃka'sja(x)] *vi* to become scarce.
escassez [iʃka'seʒ] *f* shortage.

escasso, a [iʃ'kasu, sa] *adj* scarce.
escavação [iʃkava'sãw] (*pl* **-ões**) *f* excavation.
escavadeira [iʃkava'dejra] *f* digger.
escavar [12] [iʃka'va(x)] *vt* to dig.
esclarecedor, ra [iʃklarese'do(x), ra] *adj* illuminating.
esclarecer [25] [iʃklare'se(x)] *vt* **-1.** [explicar] to clarify. **-2.** [elucidar] to explain. **-3.** [informar] to inform.
◆ **esclarecer-se** *vp* [informar-se] to find out.
esclarecido, da [iʃklare'sidu, da] *adj* **-1.** [resolvido] solved. **-2.** [informado] well informed.
esclarecimento [iʃklaresi'mẽntu] *m* **-1.** [explicação] explanation. **-2.** [informação] (piece of) information.
esclerosado, da [iʃklero'zadu, da] *adj* senile.
esclerose [iʃkle'rɔzi] *f* sclerosis; ~ **múltipla** multiple sclerosis.
esclerótica [iʃkle'rɔtʃika] *f* white of the eye, sclera.
escoadouro [iʃkoa'doru] *m* drain.
escoar [20] [iʃ'kwa(x)] *vi*: ~ **(por)** to drain (through).
escocês, esa [iʃko'seʒ, eza] ◇ *adj* Scottish. ◇ *m, f* Scot.
◆ **escocês** *m* [língua] Gaelic.
Escócia [iʃ'kɔsja] *n* Scotland.
escoicear [15] [iʃkoj'sja(x)] *vt & vi* to kick.
escola [iʃ'kɔla] *f* [ger] school; ~ **particular/pública** private/public school *US*, private/state school *UK*; ~ **naval** naval college; ~ **de samba** *group of musicians and samba dancers who perform in street parades during carnival celebrations in Brazil.*
escolado, da [iʃko'ladu, da] *adj* experienced.
escola-modelo [iʃˌkɔlamo'delu] (*pl* **escolas-modelo**) *f* model school.
escolar [iʃko'la(x)] (*pl* **-es**) *adj* school (*antes de subst*).
escolaridade [iʃkolari'dadʒi] *f* schooling.
escolarização [iʃkolariza'sãw] *f* school education.
escolarizar [4] [iʃkolari'za(x)] *vt* to educate.
escolha [iʃ'koʎa] *f* choice.
escolher [5] [iʃko'ʎe(x)] *vt* to choose.
escolhido, da [iʃko'ʎidu, da] *adj* selected, chosen.
escoliose [iʃkoli'ɔzi] *f MED* curvature of the spine.
escolta [iʃ'kɔwta] *f* escort.
escoltar [4] [iʃkow'ta(x)] *vt* to escort.
escombros [iʃ'kõnbruʃ] *mpl* ruins.
esconder [5] [iʃkõn'de(x)] *vt* to hide.
◆ **esconder-se** *vp* to hide.
esconderijo [iʃkõnde'riʒu] *m* hiding place.
escondidas [iʃkõn'dʒidaʃ] ◆ **às escondidas** *loc adv* secretly.
esconjurar [4] [iʃkõnʒu'ra(x)] *vt* **-1.** [juramento] to swear. **-2.** [maldição] to curse.
escopeta [iʃko'peta] *f* shotgun.
escopo [iʃ'kopu] *m* purpose.
escora [iʃ'kɔra] *f* prop.
escorar [4] [iʃko'ra(x)] *vt* [pôr escoras] to support, to prop up.
◆ **escorar-se** *vp* **-1.** [encostar-se]: **~-se (em)** to lean (on). **-2.** [fundamentar-se]: **~-se em** to go by. **-3.** [amparar-se]: **~-se em** to rely on.
escorbuto [iʃkox'butu] *m* scurvy.
escória [iʃ'kɔrja] *f* **-1.** [resíduo] slag. **-2.** *fig* [ralé] scum.
escoriação [iʃkorja'sãw] (*pl* **-ões**) *f* abrasion.
escorpiano, na [iʃkox'pjãnu, na] ◇ *adj* Scorpio. ◇ *m, f* Scorpio.
escorpião [iʃkox'pjãw] (*pl* **-ões**) *m ZOOL* scorpion.
◆ **Escorpião** *m ASTRO* Scorpio.
escorraçar [13] [iʃkoxa'sa(x)] *vt* to throw out.
escorredor [iʃkoxe'do(x)] *m* [para alimentos] colander; ~ **de pratos** dish drainer, draining board.
escorregadiço, dia [iʃkoxega'dʒisu, dʒia], **escorregadio, dia** [iʃkoxega'dʒiu, dʒia] *adj* slippery.
escorregador [iʃkoxega'do(x)] *m* slide.
escorregão [iʃkoxe'gãw] (*pl* **-ões**) *m* **-1.** [queda] slip. **-2.** *fig* [deslize] slip-up.
escorregar [14] [iʃkoxe'ga(x)] *vi* **-1.** [deslizar] to slip. **-2.** *fig* [errar]: ~ **em algo** to slip up on sthg.
escorrer [5] [iʃko'xe(x)] ◇ *vt* [tirar líquido de] to drain. ◇ *vi* [verter] to drip.
escorrido, da [iʃko'xidu, da] *adj* **-1.** [enxuto] dry. **-2.** [liso] straight, smooth.
escoteiro, ra [iʃko'tejru, ra] *m* scout.
escotilha [iʃko'tiʎa] *f* hatch, hatchway.
escova [iʃ'kova] *f* **-1.** [utensílio] brush; ~ **de dentes** toothbrush; ~ **de cabelo** hair brush. **-2.** [penteado]: **fazer uma** ~ [em si mesmo] to style one's hair.
escovar [4] [iʃko'va(x)] *vt* to brush.
escrachado, da [iʃkra'ʃadu, da] *adj fam* scruffy.
escrachar [iʃkra'ʃa(x)] *vt fam* **-1.** [desmascarar] to unmask. **-2.** [repreender] to tick off.
escracho [iʃ'kraʃu] *m fam* [bagunça] shambles.
escravatura [iʃkrava'tura] *f* slavery.
escravidão [iʃkravi'dãw] *f* slavery.
escravização [iʃkraviza'sãw] *f* enslavement.
escravizar [4] [iʃkravi'za(x)] *vt* **-1.** [tornar escravo] to enslave. **-2.** *fig* [subjugar] to dominate.
escravo, va [iʃ'kravu, va] ◇ *adj* **-1.** [ger] slave. **-2.** *fig* [dominado]: **ser** ~ **de alguém/algo** to be sb/sthg's slave. ◇ *m, f* slave.
escravocrata [iʃkravo'krata] ◇ *adj* slave-owning. ◇ *mf* slave-owner.
escrevente [iʃkre'vẽntʃi] *mf* clerk.
escrever [5] [iʃkre've(x)] *vt & vi* to write.
◆ **escrever-se** *vp* **-1.** [pessoas] to correspond. **-2.** [palavras] to spell; **esta palavra se escreve com x** this word is spelt with an 'x'.
escrevinhador, ra [iʃkreviɲa'do(x), ra] *m, f* hack (writer).
escrevinhar [4] [iʃkrevi'ɲa(x)] *vt* to scribble.
escrita [iʃ'krita] *f* **-1.** [letra] handwriting. **-2.** [tradição] tradition.
escrito, ta [iʃ'kritu, ta] ◇ *pp* ⊳ **escrever**. ◇ *adj* written; **por** ~ in writing; **ser algo/alguém**

~ to be the spitting image of sthg/sb.
◆ **escrito** *m* text.
◆ **escritos** *mpl* [obra literária] manuscripts.
escritor, ra [iʃkri'to(x), ra] (*mpl* **-es**, *fpl* **-s**) *m, f* writer.
escritório [iʃkri'tɔrju] *m* **-1.** COM office. **-2.** [em casa] study.
escritura [iʃkri'tura] *f* **-1.** JUR deed. **-2.** [na compra de imóvel] exchange of contracts.
escritura [iʃkri'tura] ◆ **Escrituras** *fpl*: **as ~** the Scriptures.
escriturar [4] [iʃkri'tura(x)] *vt* to draw up.
escriturário, ria [iʃkritu'rarju, rja] *m, f* clerk.
escrivã [iʃkri'vã] *f* ▷ **escrivão**.
escrivaninha [iʃkriva'niɲa] *f* desk.
escrivão, vã [iʃkri'vãw, vã] (*mpl* **-ões**, *fpl* **-s**) *m, f* registrar.
escroto, ta [iʃ'krotu, ta] *adj vulg* [ordinário] shitty.
◆ **escroto** *m* ANAT scrotum.
escrúpulo [iʃ'krupulu] *m* **-1.** [ger] scruple; **sem ~s** unscrupulous. **-2.** [cuidado] care.
escrupuloso, osa [iʃkrupu'lozu, ɔza] *adj* scrupulous.
escrutinar [4] [iʃkrutʃi'na(x)] *vt* to scrutinize.
escrutínio [iʃkru'tʃinju] *m* scrutiny.
escudar [4] [iʃku'da(x)] *vt* [proteger] to shield.
◆ **escudar-se** *vp* **-1.** [proteger-se] to shield o.s. **-2.** *fig* [amparar-se]: **~-se em algo/alguém** to shield o.s. with sthg/sb.
escudeiro [iʃku'dejru] *m* squire.
escudo [iʃkudu] *m* **-1.** [proteção] shield. **-2.** [moeda] escudo.
esculachado, da [iʃkula'ʃadu, da] *adj fam* messed up.
esculachar [4] [iʃkula'ʃa(x)] *fam vt* **-1.** [avacalhar] to mess up. **-2.** [repreender] to tell off.
esculacho [iʃku'laʃu] *m fam* [repreensão] telling-off.
esculhambado, da [iʃkuʎãn'badu, da] *adj* messed up.
esculhambar [4] [iʃkuʎãn'ba(x)] *fam vt* **-1.** [repreender] to tell off. **-2.** [avacalhar] to trash. **-3.** [desarrumar] to mess up. **-4.** [quebrar] to screw up.
esculpir [6] [iʃkuw'pi(x)] *vt* to sculpt.
escultor, ra [iʃkuw'to(x), ra] (*mpl* **-es**, *fpl* **-s**) *m, f* sculptor.
escultura [iʃkuw'tura] *f* sculpture.
escultural [iʃkuwtu'raw] (*pl* **-ais**) *adj* statuesque.
escumadeira [iʃkuma'dejra] *f* skimmer.
escuna [iʃ'kuna] *f* schooner.
escuras [iʃ'kuraʃ] *fpl* ▷ **escuro**.
escurecer [25] [iʃkure'se(x)] ◇ *vt* [tornar escuro] to darken. ◇ *vi* **-1.** [anoitecer] to go dark. **-2.** [ficar escuro] to get dark.
escuridão [iʃkuri'dãw] *f* darkness.
escuro, ra [iʃ'kuru, ra] *adj* **-1.** [ger] dark. **-2.** [pessoa] dark-skinned.
◆ **escuro** *m* [escuridão] darkness; **fazer algo no ~** *fig* to do sthg in the dark.
◆ **às escuras** *loc adv* **-1.** [sem luz] in the dark. **-2.** *fig* [às escondidas] on the quiet.
escusa [iʃ'kuza] *f* excuse.
escusado, da [iʃku'zadu, da] *adj* unnecessary.
escusar [4] [iʃku'za(x)] *vt* **-1.** [desculpar]: **~ alguém (de)** to excuse sb (for). **-2.** [dispensar]: **~ alguém de** to excuse sb from.
◆ **escusar-se** *vp* **-1.** [desculpar-se]: **~-se (de)** to excuse o.s. (for). **-2.** [dispensar-se]: **~-se de** to be excused from.
escusável [iʃku'zavew] (*pl* **-eis**) *adj* excusable.
escuso, sa [iʃ'kuzu, za] *adj* underhand.
escuta [iʃ'kuta] *f* listening; **~ telefônica** phone tap.
◆ **à escuta** *loc adv* listening.
escutar [4] [iʃku'ta(x)] ◇ *vt* **-1.** [ouvir] to hear; [prestar atenção] to listen to. **-2.** [dar ouvidos a] to hear out. **-3.** [atender a] to heed. ◇ *vi* [ouvir] to hear; [prestar atenção] to listen.
esdrúxulo, la [iʒ'druʃulu, la] *adj* weird.
esfacelar [4] [iʃfase'la(x)] *vt* to destroy.
◆ **esfacelar-se** *vp* to destroy o.s.
esfaimado, da [iʃfaj'madu, da] *adj* famished.
esfaltar-se [4] [iʃfaw'taxsi] *vp* to tire o.s. out.
esfaquear [15] [iʃfa'kja(x)] *vt* to stab.
esfarelar [4] [iʃfare'la(x)] *vt* to crumble.
◆ **esfarelar-se** *vp* to crumble.
esfarrapado, da [iʃfaxa'padu, da] *adj* **-1.** [roto] scruffy. **-2.** [não-convincente] unconvincing.
esfarrapar [4] [iʃfaxa'pa(x)] *vt* to tear up.
esfera [iʃ'fɛra] *f* **-1.** [ger] sphere. **-2.** [globo] globe.
esférico, ca [iʃ'fɛriku, ka] *adj* spherical.
esferográfica [iʃfero'grafika] *f* ballpoint pen.
esfiapar [4] [iʃfja'pa(x)] *vt & vi* to fray.
esfinge [iʃ'fĩnʒi] *f* sphinx.
esfolar [4] [iʃfo'la(x)] *vt* **-1.** [tirar a pele] to skin. **-2.** [arranhar] to graze. **-3.** [cobrar caro] to rip off.
◆ **esfolar-se** *vp* to graze o.s.
esfomeado, da [iʃfɔ'mjadu, da] *adj* starving.
esforçado, da [iʃfox'sadu, da] *adj* committed.
esforçar-se [13] [iʃfox'saxsi] *vp* to make an effort.
esforço [iʃ'foxsu] *m* effort.
esfregação [iʃfrega'sãw] *f* **-1.** [fricção] rubbing. **-2.** *fam* [bolinagem]: **estar na ~** to pet.
esfregão [iʃfre'gãw] (*pl* **-ões**) *m* mop.
esfregar [14] [iʃfre'ga(x)] *vt* **-1.** [friccionar] to scrub. **-2.** [lavar] to scrub.
◆ **esfregar-se** *vp* **-1.** [friccionar-se] to rub o.s. **-2.** [lavar-se] to scrub o.s. **-3.** *fam* [bolinar-se] to fondle each other.
esfriamento [iʃfrja'mẽntu] *m* cooling.
esfriar [16] [iʃfri'a(x)] ◇ *vt* to cool. ◇ *vi* **-1.** [perder o calor] to get cold. **-2.** *fig* [arrefecer] to cool.
esfumaçado, da [iʃfuma'sadu, da] *adj* smoky.
esfumaçar [13] [iʃfuma'sa(x)] *vt* to smoke out.
esfuziante [iʃfu'zjãntʃi] *adj* [alegre] effusive.
esganar [4] [iʒga'na(x)] *vt* to strangle.
esganiçado, da [iʒgani'sadu, da] *adj* shrill.
esgarçar [13] [iʒgax'sa(x)] ◇ *vt* to tear. ◇ *vi* to wear thin.
esgoelar [4] [iʒgwe'la(x)] *vt* [esganar] to strangle.
◆ **esgoelar-se** *vp* [gritar] to yell.

esgotado, da [iʒgo'tadu, da] *adj* **-1.** [exausto] exhausted. **-2.** [acabado - paciência, crédito] exhausted; [- reservas naturais] depleted; [- prazo] finished. **-3.** *fig* [esquadrinhado] scrutinized. **-4.** [totalmente vendido] sold out.

esgotamento [iʒgota'mẽntu] *m* [exaustão] exhaustion; ~ **nervoso** nervous breakdown.

esgotante [iʒgo'tãntʃi] *adj* exhausting.

esgotar [4] [iʒgo'ta(x)] *vt* **-1.** [ger] to exhaust. **-2.** [esquadrinhar] to scrutinize. **-3.** [esvaziar, secar] to drain.

◆ **esgotar-se** *vp* **-1.** [ger] to be exhausted. **-2.** [ser vendido totalmente] to be sold out.

esgoto [iʒ'gotu] *m* drain.

esgrima [iʒ'grima] *f* fencing.

esgrimir [6] [iʒgri'mi(x)] *vi* to fence.

esgueirar-se [4] [iʒgej'raxsi] *vp* to slip away.

esguelha [iʒ'geʎa] *f* slant.

◆ **de esguelha** *loc adv* obliquely; **olhar de esgelha** to cast a sidelong glance.

esguichar [4] [iʒgi'ʃa(x)] ◇ *vt* to squirt. ◇ *vi* to gush.

esguicho [iʒ'giʃu] *m* squirt.

esguio, guia [iʒ'giu, gia] *adj* willowy.

eslavo, va [iʒ'lavu, va] ◇ *adj* Slav. ◇ *m, f* Slav.

◆ **eslavo** *m* [língua] Slavic.

eslovaco, ca [iʒlo'vaku, ka] ◇ *adj* Slovakian. ◇ *m, f* Slovak.

◆ **eslovaco** *m* [língua] Slovak.

Eslováquia [iʒlo'vakja] *n* Slovakia.

Eslovênia [iʒlo'venja] *n* Slovenia.

esloveno, na [iʒlo'venu, na] ◇ *adj* Slovene. ◇ *m, f* Slovene.

◆ **esloveno** *m* [língua] Slovene.

esmagador, ra [iʒmaga'do(x), ra] (*mpl* **-es**, *fpl* **-s**) *adj fig* overwhelming.

esmagar [14] [iʒma'ga(x)] *vt* **-1.** [esmigalhar] to crush. **-2.** *fig* [vencer] to overpower.

esmaltado, da [iʒmaw'tadu, da] *adj* enamelled.

esmaltar [4] [iʒmaw'ta(x)] *vt* to enamel.

esmalte [iʒ'mawtʃi] *m* enamel; ~ **de unha** nail polish *UK*, nail enamel *US*.

esmerado, da [iʒme'radu, da] *adj* **-1.** [cuidadoso] meticulous. **-2.** [bem acabado - produção] accomplished; [- trabalho] well finished.

esmeralda [iʒme'rawda] *f* emerald.

esmerar-se [4] [iʒme'raxsi] *vp*: **~-se em algo/em fazer algo** to be meticulous about sthg/about doing sthg.

esmero ['iʒmeru] *m* meticulousness.

esmigalhar [4] [iʒmiga'ʎa(x)] *vt* **-1.** [fazer em migalhas] to crumble. **-2.** [despedaçar] to shatter. **-3.** [esmagar] to crush.

◆ **esmigalhar-se** *vp* **-1.** [fazer-se em migalhas] to crumble. **-2.** [despedaçar-se] to shatter.

esmiuçar [13] [iʒmju'sa(x)] *vt* **-1.** [explicar] to explain in great detail. **-2.** [investigar] to scrutinize.

esmo ['eʒmu] ◆ **a esmo** *loc adv* at random.

esmola [iʒ'mɔla] *f* alms *(pl)*.

esmolar [4] [iʒmo'la(x)] ◇ *vt* to beg for. ◇ *vi* to beg.

esmorecer [25] [iʒmore'se(x)] ◇ *vt* [pessoa] to discourage. ◇ *vi* **-1.** [pessoa] to lose heart. **-2.** [luz] to diminish.

esmorecimento [iʒmoresi'mẽntu] *m* discouragement.

esmurrar [4] [iʒmu'xa(x)] *vt* to punch.

esnobação [iʒnoba'sãw] *f* snobbery.

esnobar [4] [iʒno'ba(x)] ◇ *vt* to be snobbish towards. ◇ *vi* to be snobbish.

esnobe [iʒ'nɔbi] ◇ *adj* snobbish. ◇ *mf* snob.

esnobismo [iʒno'biʒmu] *m* snobbishness.

esôfago [e'zofagu] *m* oesophagus *UK*, esophagus *US*.

esotérico, ca [ezo'tɛriku, ka] *adj* esoteric.

esoterismo [ezote'riʃmu] *m* esotericism.

espaçado, da [iʃpa'sadu, da] *adj* **-1.** [com intervalos] spaced out. **-2.** [esparso] scattered.

espaçar [13] [iʃpa'sa(x)] *vt* to space out.

espacial [iʃpa'sjaw] (*pl* **-ais**) *adj* space *(antes do subst)*.

espaço [iʃ'pasu] *m* **-1.** [ger] space; ~ **aéreo** air space. **-2.** [o universo] outer space. **-3.** [de tempo] space.

espaçoso, osa [iʃpa'sozu, ɔza] *adj* spacious.

espada [iʃ'pada] *f* [arma] sword.

◆ **espadas** *fpl* [naipe] spades.

espadachim [iʃpada'ʃĩ] (*pl* **-ns**) *m* swordsman.

espádua [iʃ'padwa] *f* shoulder blade.

espaguete [iʃpa'gɛtʃi] *m* spaghetti.

espairecer [25] [iʃpajre'se(x)] *vt & vi* to relax.

espairecimento [iʃpajresi'mẽntu] *m* relaxation.

espaldar [iʃpaw'da(x)] *m* [de cadeira, sofá] back.

espalhafato [iʃpaʎa'fatu] *m* commotion.

espalhafatoso, osa [iʃpaʎafa'tozu, ɔza] *adj* **-1.** [roupa] gaudy. **-2.** [pessoa, jeito] loud.

espalhar [4] [iʃpa'ʎa(x)] *vt* **-1.** [ger] to spread. **-2.** [dispersar - semente] to scatter; [- fumaça, odor] to spread. **-3.** [difundir] to diffuse.

◆ **espalhar-se** *vp* **-1.** [dissipar-se] to dissipate. **-2.** [propagar-se] to be spread.

espalmado, da [iʃpaw'madu, da] *adj* splayed.

espalmar [4] [iʃpaw'ma(x)] *vt* **-1.** [abrir] to splay. **-2.** [desviar] to deflect.

espanador [iʃpana'do(x)] (*pl* **-es**) *m* duster.

espanar [4] [iʃpa'na(x)] *vt* to dust.

espancamento [iʃpãŋka'mẽntu] *m* beating.

espancar [12] [iʃpãŋ'ka(x)] *vt* to beat.

Espanha [iʃ'pãɲa] *n* Spain.

espanhol, la [iʃpã'ɲɔw, la] (*mpl* **-óis**, *fpl* **-s**) ◇ *adj* Spanish. ◇ *m, f* Spaniard.

◆ **espanhol** *m* [língua] Spanish.

espantado, da [iʃpãn'tadu, da] *adj* **-1.** [assustado] startled. **-2.** [surpreso] astonished.

espantalho [iʃpãn'taʎu] *m* [boneco] scarecrow.

espantar [4] [iʃpãn'ta(x)] ◇ *vt* **-1.** [assustar] to frighten. **-2.** [afugentar] to frighten (away). **-3.** [surpreender] to amaze. ◇ *vi* [surpreender] to be amazing.

◆ **espantar-se** *vp* **-1.** [assustar-se] to be frightened. **-2.** [surpreender-se] to be amazed.

espanto [iʃ'pãntu] *m* **-1.** [susto] fright. **-2.** [assombro] amazement.

espantoso, osa [iʃpãn'tozu, ɔza] *adj* **-1.** [surpreendente] startling. **-2.** [admirável] astounding.
esparadrapo [iʃpara'drapu] *m* sticking plaster *UK*, Band-Aid® *US*.
espargir [52] [iʃpax'ʒi(x)] *vt* to spray.
esparramado, da [iʃpaxa'madu, da] *adj* **-1.** [espalhado] scattered. **-2.** [derramado] splashed. **-3.** [refastelado] sprawled.
esparramar [4] [iʃpaxa'ma(x)] *vt* **-1.** [espalhar] to scatter. **-2.** [derramar] to splash.
◆ **esparramar-se** *vp* [refastelar-se] to sprawl.
esparramo [iʃpa'xamu] *m* scattering.
esparso, sa [iʃ'paxsu, sa] *adj* **-1.** [espalhado] sparse. **-2.** [raro] scarce.
espartano, na [iʃpax'tãnu, na] *adj* spartan.
espartilho [iʃpax'tiʎu] *m* corset.
espasmo [iʃ'paʒmu] *m* spasm.
espasmódico, ca [iʃpaʒ'mɔdʒiku, ka] *adj* spasmodic.
espatifar [4] [iʃpatʃi'fa(x)] *vt* & *vi* to smash.
◆ **espatifar-se** *vp* to shatter.
espátula [iʃ'patula] *f* spatula.
espavento [iʃpa'vẽntu] *m* fright.
espavorido, da [iʃpavo'ridu, da] *adj* terrified.
especial [iʃpe'sjaw] (*pl* **-ais**) *adj* special; **em ~** in particular.
especialidade [iʃpesjali'dadʒi] *f* speciality.
especialista [iʃpesja'liʃta] ◇ *adj* [perito]: **~ em** expert in. ◇ *mf* **-1.** [profissional] expert. **-2.** [perito]: **~ em** specialist in.
especialização [iʃpesjaliza'sãw] (*pl* **-ões**) *f* specialization.
especializado, da [iʃpesjali'zadu, da] *adj* **-1.** [treinado]: **~ (em)** specialized (in). **-2.** [específico] specialized.
especializar-se [4] [iʃpesjali'zaxsi] *vp*: **~ (em)** to specialize (in).
especiaria [iʃpesja'ria] *f* spice.
espécie [iʃ'pɛsji] *f* **-1.** *BIOL* species. **-2.** [tipo] kind.
◆ **em espécie** *loc adv FIN* (in) cash.
especificação [iʃpesifika'sãw] (*pl* **-ões**) *f* specification.
especificar [12] [iʃpesifi'ka(x)] *vt* to specify.
específico, ca [iʃpe'sifiku, ka] *adj* specific.
espécime [iʃ'pɛsimi] (*pl* **-es**), **espécimen** (*pl* **-ns**) *m* specimen.
espectador, ra [iʃpekta'do(x), ra] (*mpl* **-res**, *fpl* **-ras**) *m, f* **-1.** [testemunha] witness. **-2.** [de espetáculo *etc*] spectator.
◆ **espectadores** *mpl* viewers.
espectro [iʃ'pɛktru] *m* **-1.** [fantasma] ghost. **-2.** *FÍSICA* spectrum. **-3.** *fig* [pessoa esquálida] wretch.
especulação [iʃpekula'sãw] (*pl* **-ões**) *f* speculation.
especulador, ra [iʃpekula'do(x), ra] ◇ *adj* speculative. ◇ *m, f BOLSA & COM* speculator.
especular [4] [iʃpeku'la(x)] ◇ *vt* [averiguar] to speculate upon. ◇ *vi* **-1.** [informar-se]: **~ sobre algo** to speculate about sthg. **-2.** [teorizar]: **~ (sobre algo)** to speculate (about sthg). **-3.** *BOLSA & COM*: **~ (em)** to speculate (in).
especulativo, va [iʃpekula'tʃivu, va] *adj* speculative.
espelhar [4] [iʃpe'ʎa(x)] *vt* [mostrar] to reflect.
◆ **espelhar-se** *vp* **-1.** [refletir-se] to be reflected. **-2.** [mirar-se] to reflect.
espelho [iʃ'peʎu] *m* mirror; **~ retrovisor** rear-view mirror.
espelunca [iʃpe'lũŋka] *f* dump.
espera [iʃ'pɛra] *f* **-1.** [ato] wait; **à ~ de** waiting for. **-2.** [tempo] delay. **-3.** [tocaia] ambush.
esperado, da [iʃpe'radu, da] *adj* **-1.** [aguardado] awaited. **-2.** [previsto] expected.
esperança [iʃpe'rãnsa] *f* **-1.** [expectativa] expectation. **-2.** [confiança] hope.
esperançoso, osa [iʃperãn'sozu, ɔza] *adj* hopeful.
esperanto [iʃpe'rãntu] *m* Esperanto.
esperar [13] [iʃpe'ra(x)] ◇ *vt* **-1.** [aguardar] to wait for. **-2.** [bebê] to expect. **-3.** [desejar]: **~ que** to hope that; **~ fazer algo** to hope to do sthg. **-4.** [supor] to expect. **-5.** [estar destinado a] to await. **-6.** [contar obter] to expect. ◇ *vi* [aguardar]: to hope; **fazer alguém ~** to make sb wait; **espera (aí)!** wait (a moment)!
◆ **esperar-se** *vp*: **como era de se ~** as was to be expected.
esperável [iʃpe'ravew] (*pl* **-eis**) *adj* probable.
esperma [iʃ'pɛxma] *m* sperm.
espermatozóide *m* spermatozoon, spermatozoa (*pl*).
espermicida [iʃpexmi'sida] ◇ *adj* spermicidal. ◇ *m* spermicide.
espernear [15] [iʃpex'nja(x)] *vi* **-1.** [sacudir as pernas] to kick one's legs. **-2.** *fig* [protestar] to (put up a) protest.
espertalhão, ona [iʃpexta'ʎãw, ona] (*mpl* **-ões**, *fpl* **-s**) ◇ *adj* crafty. ◇ *m, f* smart operator.
esperteza [iʃpex'teza] *f* **-1.** [inteligência] intelligence. **-2.** [astúcia] shrewdness; **foi muita ~ dele fazer isso** it was very shrewd of him to do that.
esperto, ta [iʃ'pɛxtu, ta] *adj* **-1.** [inteligente] smart. **-2.** [ativo] lively. **-3.** [espertalhão] clever. **-4.** *fam* [bacana] groovy.
espesso, a [iʃ'pesu, sa] *adj* thick.
espessura [iʃpe'sura] *f* thickness.
espetacular [iʃpetaku'la(x)] (*pl* **-es**) *adj* amazing.
espetáculo [iʃpe'takulu] *m* **-1.** [show] show. **-2.** [maravilha]: **ser um ~** to be amazing. **-3.** [cena ridícula] spectacle; **ele deu o maior ~ aqui por causa da bebedeira** he made a spectacle of himself here being so drunk.
espetada [iʃpe'tada] *f* **-1.** [furada] prick. **-2.** [cul] kebab. **-3.** *fig* [implicância]: **dar ~ em alguém** to needle sb.
espetar [4] [iʃpe'ta(x)] *vt* to impale.
◆ **espetar-se** *vp* to prick o.s.
espeto [iʃ'petu] *m* **-1.** [utensílio de churrasco] (roasting) spit. **-2.** *fig* [pessoa magra] beanpole. **-3.** *fig* [situação difícil]: **ser um ~** to be difficult.
espevitado, da [iʃpevi'tadu, da] *adj* lively.

espevitar [iʃpevi'ta(x)] ◆ **espevitar-se** *vp* **-1.** [mostrar-se afetado] to show off. **-2.** [irritar-se] to fly off the handle.
espezinhar [4] [iʃpɛzi'ɲa(x)] *vt* **-1.** [implicar com] to put down. **-2.** [humilhar] to trample (on).
espiada [iʃ'pjada] *f* peep; **dar uma ~** to have a peep, to have a look-see.
espião, pia [iʃ'pjãw, pia] (*mpl* **-ões**, *fpl* **-s**) *m, f* spy.
espiar [16] [iʃ'pja(x)] ◇ *vt* **-1.** [olhar] to watch. **-2.** [espionar] to spy on. ◇ *vi* **-1.** [olhar]: **~ (por)** [pela fechadura] to look (through); [pelo canto do olho] to glance. **-2.** [espionar] to spy.
espicaçar [13] [iʃpika'sa(x)] *vt* ***fig*** [torturar] to torment.
espichado, da [iʃpi'ʃadu, da] *adj* **-1.** [pessoa] stretched out. **-2.** [corda] tight.
espichar [4] [iʃpi'ʃa(x)] ◇ *vt* [esticar] to stretch out. ◇ *vi* [crescer] to shoot up.
◆ **espichar-se** *vp* [espreguiçar-se] to stretch (out).
espiga [iʃ'piga] *f* ear.
espigão [iʃpi'gãw] (*pl* **-ões**) *m* **-1.** [pua] spike. **-2.** [pico] peak.
espinafrar [4] [iʃpina'fra(x)] *vt* **-1.** [repreender] to reprimand. **-2.** [criticar] to lambaste.
espinafre [iʃpi'nafri] *m* spinach.
espingarda [iʃpĩŋ'gaxda] *f* shotgun.
espinha [iʃ'piɲa] *f* **-1.** [na pele] pimple. **-2.** [de peixe] bone. **-3.** *ANAT* spine.
espinhento, ta [iʃpi'ɲẽntu, ta] *adj* **-1.** [planta] thorny. **-2.** [peixe] bony.
espinho [iʃ'piɲu] *m* **-1.** [de planta] thorn. **-2.** [de porco-espinho] quill. **-3.** [de ouriço] spine. **-4.** ***fig*** [dificuldade] snag.
espinhoso, osa [iʃpi'ɲozu, ɔza] *adj* thorny.
espionagem [iʃpio'naʒẽ] *f* espionage.
espionar [4] [iʃpio'na(x)] ◇ *vt* to spy on. ◇ *vi* to snoop.
espiral [iʃpi'raw] (*pl* **-ais**) ◇ *adj* spiral. ◇ *f* spiral; **em ~** in a spiral; **escada em ~** spiral staircase.
espírita [iʃ'pirita] ◇ *adj* spiritualistic. ◇ *mf* spiritualist.
espiritismo [iʃpiri'tʃiʒmu] *m* spiritualism.
espírito [iʃ'piritu] *m* **-1.** [ger] spirit. **-2.** [temperamento]: **~ esportivo** competitive spirit; **ter ~ forte/fraco** to be strong/weak willed; **ser ~ de porco** to be a busybody.
◆ **Espírito Santo** *m* Holy Spirit.
espiritual [iʃpiri'twaw] (*pl* **-ais**) *adj* spiritual.
espiritualidade [iʃpiritwali'dadʒi] *f* spirituality.
espirituoso, osa [iʃpiri'twozu, ɔza] *adj* witty.
espirrar [4] [iʃpi'xa(x)] ◇ *vi* **-1.** [dar espirro] to sneeze. **-2.** [jorrar] to squirt out. ◇ *vt* [jorrar] to squirt.
espirro [iʃ'pixu] *m* sneeze.
esplanada [iʃpla'nada] *f* esplanade.
esplêndido, da [iʃ'plẽndʒidu, da] *adj* splendid.
esplendor [iʃplẽn'do(x)] *m* splendour ***UK***, splendor ***US***.
espocar [12] [iʃpo'ka(x)] *vi* to explode.
espoleta [iʃpo'leta] *f* detonator.
espoliar [16] [iʃpo'lja(x)] *vt* to plunder.
espólio [iʃ'pɔlju] *m* **-1.** [herança] inheritance. **-2.** [restos] remains *(pl)*.
esponja [iʃ'põnʒa] *f* **-1.** [ger] sponge. **-2.** ***fig*** [beberrão] soak.
esponjoso, osa [iʃpõn'ʒozu, ɔza] *adj* spongy.
espontaneidade [iʃpõntanej'dadʒi] *f* spontaneity.
espontâneo, nea [iʃpõn'tãnju, nja] *adj* spontaneous.
espora [iʃ'pɔra] *f* spur.
esporádico, ca [iʃpo'radʒiku, ka] *adj* sporadic.
esporão [iʃpo'rãw] (*pl* **-ões**) *m* spur.
esporro [iʃ'poxu] *m* *vulg* **-1.** [barulho] racket. **-2.** [repreensão] tongue-lashing.
esporte [iʃ'pɔxtʃi] *m* sport.

ESPORTES

Although football is the absolute favourite sport of the Brazilian people, Brazil has excelled in other sports as well, including basketball, volleyball, sailing, swimming, judo, tennis and motor racing. Three Brazilian drivers have been Formula 1 world champions more than once: Emerson Fittipaldi ('72 and '74), Nelson Piquet ('81, '83 and '87) and Ayrton Senna ('88, '90 and '91).

esportista [iʃpox'tʃiʃta] ◇ *adj* sporty. ◇ *mf* sportsman (*f* sportswoman).
esportividade [iʃpoxtʃivi'dadʒi] *f* sportsmanship.
esportivo, va [iʃpox'tʃivu, va] *adj* sports *(antes de subst)*.
◆ **esportiva** *f* (sense of) fair play.
esposa [iʃpo'za] *f* wife.
esposar [4] [iʃ'poza(x)] *vt* to marry.
esposo [iʃ'pozu] *m* husband.
espraiar [4] [iʃpraj'a(x)] ◇ *vt* to spread. ◇ *vi* to sprawl, to wash ashore.
espreguiçadeira [iʃpregisa'dejra] *f* deckchair.
espreguiçar-se [13] [iʃpregi'saxsi] *vp* to stretch.
espreita [iʃ'prejta] *loc*: **à ~ (de)** on the lookout (for).
espreitar [4] [iʃprej'ta(x)] *vt* to peep at, to have a peep at.
espremedor [iʃpreme'do(x)] (*pl* **-es**) *m* masher; **~ de laranja** orange squeezer.
espremer [5] [iʃpre'me(x)] *vt* **-1.** [apertar] to squeeze. **-2.** [comprimir - fruta] to squeeze; [- toalha molhada] to wring out.
◆ **espremer-se** *vp* [apertar-se] to press together.
espuma [iʃ'puma] *f* foam.
espumante [iʃpu'mãntʃi] *adj* sparkling.
espumar [4] [iʃpu'ma(x)] *vi* to foam.
espumoso, osa [iʃpu'mozu, ɔza] *adj* foamy.
espúrio, ria [iʃ'purju, rja] *adj* spurious.
esquadra [iʃ'kwadra] *f* **-1.** *NAÚT* fleet. **-2.** *MIL* squadron.
esquadrão [iʃkwa'drãw] (*pl* **-ões**) *m* squadron.

esquadria [iʃkwa'dria] *f* frame.
esquadrilha [iʃkwa'driʎa] *f* flotilla.
esquadrinhar [4] [iʃkwadri'ɲa(x)] *vt* **-1.** [procurar] to search. **-2.** [analisar] to examine.
esquadro [iʃ'kwadru] *m* set square.
esqualidez [iʃkwali'deʃ] *f* squalour.
esquálido, da [iʃ'kwalidu, da] *adj* squalid.
esquartejar [4] [iʃkwaxte'ʒa(x)] *vt* to quarter.
esquecer [25] [iʃke'se(x)] ◇ *vt* to forget; ~ **que** to forget that. ◇ *vi*: ~ **(de algo/alguém)** to forget (sthg/sb); ~ **de fazer algo** to forget to do sthg.
◆ **esquecer-se** *vp*: **~-se (de algo)** to forget (about sthg); **~-se de fazer algo** to forget to do sthg.
esquecido, da [iʃke'sidu, da] *adj* **-1.** [não lembrado] forgotten. **-2.** [distraído] forgetful.
esquecimento [iʃkesi'mẽntu] *m* forgetfulness; **cair no** ~ to become a thing of the past.
esqueitista [iʃkej'tʃiʃta] *mf* skateboarder.
esquelético, ca [iʃke'lɛtʃiku, ka] *adj* skeletal.
esqueleto [iʃke'letu] *m* **-1.** [ossatura] skeleton. **-2.** [estrutura] skeleton. **-3.** [esboço] rough draft. **-4.** *fig* [pessoa magra] bag of bones, skeleton.
esquema [iʃ'kema] *m* **-1.** [gráfico] diagram. **-2.** [plano] plan; ~ **de segurança** security plan. **-3.** [resumo] schema.
esquemático, ca [iʃke'matʃiku, ka] *adj* schematic.
esquematização [iʃkematʃiza'sãw] (*pl* **-ões**) *f* schematization.
esquematizar [4] [iʃkematʃi'za(x)] *vt* **-1.** [representar em desenho] to sketch. **-2.** [planejar] to plan. **-3.** [sintetizar] to plan.
esquentado, da [iʃkẽn'tadu, da] *adj* **-1.** [aquecido] heated. **-2.** *fig* [exaltado] irritable.
esquentar [4] [iʃkẽn'ta(x)] ◇ *vt* [aquecer] to heat up. ◇ *vi* **-1.** [aquecer] to get hot. **-2.** *fig* [exaltar-se] to become irritable.
◆ **esquentar-se** *vp* **-1.** [aquecer-se] to warm o.s. up. **-2.** *fig* [exaltar-se] to get annoyed.
esquerdista [iʃkex'dʒiʃta] ◇ *adj* leftist. ◇ *mf* leftist.
esquerdo, da [iʃ'kexdu, da] *adj* left.
◆ **esquerda** *f* **-1.** [lado] left; **à** ~ on the left. **-2.** POL left wing.
esquete [iʃ'kɛtʃi] *m* sketch.
esqui [iʃ'ki] *m* **-1.** [patim] ski. **-2.** [esporte] skiing; ~ **aquático** water-skiing.
esquiador, ra [iʃkja'do(x), ra] *m, f* skier.
esquiar [16] [iʃ'kja(x)] *vi* to ski.
esquife [iʃ'kifi] *m* coffin.
esquilo [iʃ'kilu] *m* squirrel.
esquimó [iʃki'mɔ] ◇ *adj* Eskimo. ◇ *mf* Eskimo.
◆ **esquimó** *m* [língua] Eskimo.
esquina [iʃ'kina] *f* corner; **dobrar a** ~ to turn the corner; **minha rua faz** ~ **com a avenida principal** my street goes off the main street.
esquisitice [iʃkizi'tʃisi] *f* **-1.** [qualidade] eccentricity. **-2.** [ato, dito] incongruity.
esquisito, ta [iʃki'zitu, ta] *adj* **-1.** [incomum] strange. **-2.** [pessoa] strange.
esquivar-se [4] [iʃki'vaxsi] *vp*: **~-se de algo** to dodge sthg.
esquivo, va [iʃ'kivu, va] *adj* aloof.
◆ **esquiva** *f* dodge.
esquizofrenia [iʃkizofre'nia] *f* schizophrenia.
esquizofrênico, ca [iʃkizo'freniku, ka] ◇ *adj* schizophrenic. ◇ *m, f* schizophrenic.
esse, essa ['esi, 'ɛsa] ◇ *adj* that, those (*pl*). ◇ *pron* that (one), those (ones) (*pl*).
essência [e'sẽnsja] *f* essence.
essencial [esẽn'sjaw] (*pl* **-ais**) ◇ *adj* **-1.** [ger] essential. **-2.** [preocupação, benefício, trecho] main. ◇ *m*: **o** ~ [o mais importante] the main thing.
essencialmente [esẽnsjaw'mẽntʃi] *adv* **-1.** [substancialmente] essentially. **-2.** [basicamente] essentially.
esta ['ɛʃta] ▷ **este**.
estabanado, da [iʃtaba'nadu, da] *adj* careless.
estabelecer [25] [iʃtabele'se(x)] *vt* **-1.** [ger] to establish. **-2.** [instalar] to set up.
◆ **estabelecer-se** *vp* **-1.** [firmar-se] to establish o.s. **-2.** [instalar-se] to be established. **-3.** [em negócio] to become established. **-4.** [determinar-se]: **~-se (que)** to be established (that).
estabelecimento [iʃtabelesi'mẽntu] *m* establishment.
estabilidade [iʃtabili'dadʒi] *f* stability; ~ **financeira** financial stability.
estabilização [iʃtabiliza'sãw] *f* stabilization.
estabilizador [iʃtabiliza'do(x)] (*pl* **-es**) *m* COMPUT transformer.
estabilizar [4] [iʃtabili'za(x)] *vt* to stabilize.
◆ **estabilizar-se** *vp* to become stable.
estábulo [iʃ'tabulu] *m* stable.
estaca [iʃ'taka] *f* **-1.** [para cravar] stake. **-2.** [de construção] support. **-3.** [de barraca] post. **-4.** *loc*: **voltar à** ~ **zero** to go back to square one.
estacada [iʃta'kada] *f* **-1.** [de proteção] stockade. **-2.** [fileira] fence.
estação [iʃta'sãw] (*pl* **-ões**) *f* **-1.** [de trem, metrô, ônibus] station. **-2.** [período]: ~ **(do ano)** season (of the year); ~ **de chuvas** rainy season; [de colheita]: **frutas da** ~ fruits of the season. **-3.** [estância]: ~ **de águas** spa. **-4.** [para fins científicos] station. **-5.** RÁDIO & TV station.
estacar [12] [iʃta'ka(x)] *vi* to stop short.
estacionamento [iʃtasjona'mẽntu] *m* **-1.** [ato] parking. **-2.** [lugar] car park.
estacionar [4] [iʃtasjo'na(x)] ◇ *vt* AUTO to park. ◇ *vi* **-1.** AUTO to park. **-2.** [não evoluir] to remain stationary.
estacionário, ria [iʃtasjo'narju, rja] *adj* **-1.** [parado] stationary. **-2.** ECON [estagnado] stagnant.
estada [iʃ'tada], **estadia** [iʃ'tadʒa] *f* stay.
estádio [iʃ'tadʒju] *m* stadium.
estadista [iʃta'dʒiʃta] *mf* statesman.
estado [iʃ'tadu] *m* **-1.** [ger] state; **em bom/mau** ~ in good/bad condition; ~ **civil** marital status; ~ **de coisas** state of affairs; ~ **de espírito** state of

mind; ~ **de saúde** (state of) health; **em ~ interessante** in an interesting condition, pregnant; ~ **de sítio** state of siege; **em ~ de** in a state of; ~ **gasosa/líquido/sólido** gaseous/liquid/solid state. **-2.** *POL* state.

◆ **Estado** *m* [país] state.

estado-maior [iʃˌtaduma'jɔ(x)] (*pl* **estados-maiores**) *m MIL* general staff ***UK***, army/air staff ***US***.

Estados Unidos da América *n*: **os ~** the United States of America.

estadual [iʃta'dwaw] (*pl* **-ais**) *adj* [receita, constituição] state *(antes de subst)*.

estadunidense [iʃtaduni'dẽnsi] ◇ *adj* American. ◇ *mf* American.

estafa [iʃ'tafa] *f* **-1.** [esgotamento] exhaustion; **ter uma ~** to be exhausted. **-2.** [fadiga] exhaustion.

estafado, da [iʃta'fadu, da] *adj* exhausted.

estafante [iʃta'fãntʃi] *adj* exhausting.

estafar [4] [iʃta'fa(x)] *vt* to exhaust.

estafeta [iʃta'feta] *m* courier.

estagflação [iʃtag'flasãw] *f ECON* stagflation.

estagiar [16] [iʃta'ʒja(x)] *vi*: ~ **(em)** to train (in).

estagiário, ria [iʃta'ʒjarju, rja] *m, f* trainee.

estágio [iʃ'taʒu] *m* **-1.** [fase] stage. **-2.** [treinamento] training period.

estagnação [iʃtagna'sãw] *f* stagnation.

estagnado, da [iʃtag'nadu, da] *adj* stagnant.

estagnar [4] [iʃtag'na(x)] ◇ *vt* to make stagnant. ◇ *vi* to stagnate.

◆ **estagnar-se** *vp* to be stagnant.

estalagem [iʃta'laʒẽ] (*pl* **-ns**) *f* inn.

estalar [4] [iʃta'la(x)] ◇ *vt* **-1.** [dedos] to snap. **-2.** [nozes, ovos] to crack. ◇ *vi* **-1.** [rachar] to crack. **-2.** [crepitar] to crackle.

estaleiro [iʃta'lejru] *m* shipyard.

estalido [iʃta'lidu] *m* **-1.** [de dedos] snapping. **-2.** [de chicote, fogos] cracking.

estalo [iʃ'talu] *m* [de dedos] snap; [de chicote] crack; [de trovão] crash; [de foguete] bang; **dar um ~** to crack; **me deu um ~** *fig* I had a flash of inspiration; **de ~** [de repente] suddenly.

estampa [iʃ'tãnpa] *f* **-1.** [ger] print. **-2.** [aparência] appearance.

estampado, da [iʃtãn'padu, da] *adj* **-1.** [tecido] printed. **-2.** *fig* [evidente] etched.

◆ **estampado** *m* **-1.** [tecido] printed cloth. **-2.** [padrão impresso] print.

estampar [4] [iʃtãn'pa(x)] *vt* **-1.** [imprimir] to print. **-2.** [marcar] to imprint. **-3.** *fig* [mostrar]: **a mulher estampava no rosto seu desespero** the woman's despair was etched on her face.

estamparia [iʃtãnpa'ria] *f* **-1.** [oficina] print shop room. **-2.** [tecido] printed material.

estampido [iʃtãn'pidu] *m* bang.

estancar [12] [iʃtãŋ'ka(x)] *vt* & *vi* to stem ***UK***, to staunch ***US***.

estância [iʃ'tãnsja] *f* **-1.** [fazenda] estate. **-2.** [estação]: ~ **hidromineral** spa. **-3.** [estrofe] strophe, stanza.

estandarte [iʃtãn'daxtʃi] *m* standard.

estande [iʃ'tãndʒi] *m* stand.

estanho [iʃ'tãɲu] *m* tin.

estanque [iʃ'tãŋki] *adj* **-1.** [estancado] tight, watertight **-2.** [vedado]: **compartimento ~** airtight compartment.

estante [iʃ'tãntʃi] *f* **-1.** [móvel] bookcase. **-2.** [suporte] stand.

estapafúrdio, dia [iʃtapa'furdʒju, dʒja] *adj* outlandish.

estar [10] [iʃ'ta(x)] *vi* **-1.** [com lugar] to be; [em casa] to be at home, to be in; **ela estará lá à hora certa** she'll be there on time; **estarei no emprego às dez** I'll be at work at ten. **-2.** [exprime estado] to be; **está quebrado** it's out of order; ~ **bem/mal de saúde** to be well/unwell; **está muito calor/frio** it's very hot/cold. **-3.** [manter-se] to be; **estive em casa toda a tarde** I was at home all afternoon; **estive esperando** I was waiting; **estive fora três anos** I lived abroad for three years; **deixe ~ ...** let it be ... **-4.** [em locuções]: **está bem** *ou* **certo!** OK!, all right!

◆ **estar a** *v + prep* [relativo a preço] to cost, to be; **o camarão está a 25 reais o quilo** shrimp cost *ou* are 25 reals a kilo.

◆ **estar de** *v + prep*: ~ **de baixa/férias** to be on sick leave/vacation; ~ **de saia** to be wearing a skirt; ~ **de vigia** to keep watch.

◆ **estar para** *v + prep*: ~ **para fazer algo** to be about to do sthg; **estou para sair** I'm about to go out, I'm on my way out; **ele está para chegar** he'll be here any minute now; **não estou para brincadeiras** I'm not in the mood for silly games.

◆ **estar perante** *v + prep* [frente a] to be facing; **você está perante um gênio** you're in the presence of a genius.

◆ **estar por** *v + prep* [apoiar] to support; [por realizar]: **a cama está por fazer** the bed hasn't been made yet; **a limpeza está por fazer** the cleaning hasn't been done yet.

◆ **estar sem** *v + prep*: **estou sem tempo** I don't have time; **estou sem dinheiro** I don't have any cash; **ele está sem comer há dois dias** he hasn't eaten for two days.

estardalhaço [iʃtaxda'ʎasu] *m* **-1.** [bulha] racket. **-2.** [ostentação] flamboyance.

estarrecer [25] [iʃtaxe'se(x)] ◇ *vt* to appal ***UK***, to appall ***US***. ◇ *vi* to be appalled.

estarrecido, da [iʃtaxe'sidu, da] *adj* shaken.

estatal [iʃta'taw] (*pl* **-ais**) ◇ *adj* state *(antes de subst)*. ◇ *f* [empresa] state-owned company.

estatelado, da [iʃtate'ladu, da] *adj* [no chão] sprawled.

estatelar-se [4] [iʃtate'laxsi] *vp* [cair]: **~-se (em)** to fall flat (on).

estática [iʃ'tatʃika] *f FÍS* static.

estático, ca [iʃ'tatʃiku, ka] *adj* **-1.** [imóvel] still. **-2.** *FÍS* static.

estatístico, ca [iʃta'tʃiʃtʃiku, ka] ◇ *adj* statistical. ◇ *m, f* [profissional] statistician.

◆ **estatística** *f* statistics.

estatização [iʃtatʃiza'sãw] (*pl* **-ões**) *f* nationalization.

estatizar [4] [iʃtatʃi'za(x)] *vt* to nationalize.
estátua [iʃ'tatwa] *f* statue.
estatueta [iʃta'tweta] *f* statuette.
estatura [iʃta'tura] *f* **-1.** [física] stature; ~ **alta /baixa/mediana** tall/short/medium stature. **-2.** [intelectual, moral] standing.
estatutário, ria [iʃtatu'tarju, rja] *adj* **-1.** [norma] statutory. **-2.** [funcionário]: **funcionário** ~ civil servant.
estatuto [iʃta'tutu] *m* statute.
estável [iʃ'tavew] (*pl* **-eis**) *adj* **-1.** [ger] stable. **-2.** [cotação] fixed.
este[1] ['eʃtʃi] *m* east
este[2]**, esta** ['eʃtʃi] ◇ *adj* this, these (*pl*). ◇ *pron* this (one), these ones (*pl*).
esteio [iʃ'teju] *m* **-1.** [escora] prop. **-2.** *NÁUT* chock. **-3.** *fig* [amparo] breadwinner.
esteira [iʃ'tejra] *f* **-1.** [tecido] woven mat. **-2.** [usada na praia] reed mat. **-3.** [rolante] moving carpet. **-4.** *fig* [caminho] path; **na** ~ **de** in the course of.
estelionatário, ria [iʃteljona'tarju, rja] *m, f* swindler.
estelionato [iʃteljo'natu] *m* swindle.
estêncil [iʃ'tẽnsiw] (*pl* **-eis**) *m* stencil.
estender [5] [iʃtẽn'de(x)] *vt* **-1.** [ger] to spread. **-2.** [roupa] to hang out. **-3.** [corda, fio] to stretch out. **-4.** [massa] to roll out. **-5.** [pernas, braços, mãos] to stretch out. **-6.** [limites] to extend. **-7.** [oferecer]: ~ **algo para alguém** to give sthg to sb. **-8.** [prolongar] to prolong. **-9.** [fazer abranger]: ~ **algo a alguém/algo** to extend sthg to (include) sb/sthg.
◆ **estender-se** *vp* **-1.** [ocupar]: ~**-se por** to spread out over. **-2.** [durar]: ~**-se (por)** to last (for). **-3.** [alastrar-se]: ~**-se (por)** to spread (throughout). **-4.** [deitar-se]: ~**-se (em)** to lie down (on). **-5.** [falar, escrever muito]: ~**-se (sobre)** to enlarge (upon). **-6.** [abranger]: ~**-se a** to include.
estenodatilografia [iʃtenodatʃilɔgra'fia] *f* shorthand typing.
estenodatilógrafo, fa [iʃtenodatʃi'lɔgrafu, fa] *m, f* shorthand typist *UK*, stenographer *US*.
estenografar [4] [iʃtenogra'fa(x)] *vt* to write in shorthand.
estenografia [iʃtenogra'fia] *f* shorthand *UK*, stenography *US*.
estenógrafo, fa [iʃte'nɔgrafu, fa] *m, f* shorthand typist *UK*, stenographer *US*.
estepe [iʃ'tɛpi] ◇ *m* [pneu] spare wheel. ◇ *f* [vegetação] steppe.
esterco [iʃ'texku] *m* manure.
estéreo [iʃ'tɛrju] *adj* stereo.
estereofônico, ca [iʃterjo'foniku, ka] *adj* stereophonic.
estereotipado, da [iʃterjotʃi'padu, da] *adj* stereotypical.
estereotipar [4] [iʃterjotʃi'pa(x)] *vt* to stereotype.
estereótipo [iʃte'rjɔtʃipu] *m* stereotype.
estéril [iʃ'tɛriw] (*pl* **-eis**) *adj* **-1.** [ger] sterile. **-2.** [terreno] barren. **-3.** *fig* [inútil, infrutífero] pointless.
esterilidade [iʃterili'dadʒi] *f* **-1.** [infertilidade] sterility. **-2.** [da terra] barrenness. **-3.** [escassez] dearth.
esterilização [iʃteriliza'sãw] (*pl* **-ões**) *f* sterilization.
esterilizado, da [iʃterili'zadu, da] *adj* sterilized.
esterilizador [iʃteriliza'do(x)] *m* sterilizer.
esterilizar [4] [iʃterili'za(x)] *vt* to sterilize.
esterlino, na [iʃtex'linu, na] ◇ *adj*: **libra** ~ pound sterling. ◇ *m* sterling.
esteróide [iʃte'rɔjdʒi] *m* steroid.
esteta [iʃ'tɛta] *mf* aesthete *UK*, esthete *US*.
esteticista [iʃtetʃi'siʃta] *mf* beautician.
estético, ca [iʃ'tɛtʃiku, ka] *adj* **-1.** [artístico] aesthetic *UK*, esthetic *US*. **-2.** [harmonioso] tasteful.
◆ **estética** *f* **-1.** *FILOSOFIA* aestheticism *UK*, estheticism *US*. **-2.** [beleza] beauty; [do corpo] physical beauty.
estetoscópio [iʃtɛtoʃ'kɔpju] *m* stethoscope.
estiagem [iʃ'tʃjaʒẽ] (*pl* **-ns**) *f* **-1.** [período seco] dry spell. **-2.** [de rio, fonte] drying out.
estiar [16] [iʃ'tʃja(x)] *vi* **-1.** [parar de chover] to stop raining. **-2.** [faltar chuva] to be dry.
estibordo [iʃtʃi'bɔxdu] *m* starboard; **a** ~ to starboard.
esticada [iʃtʃi'kada] ◇ *f*: **dar uma** ~ [espichar-se] to have a stretch. ◇ *f*: **dar uma** ~ **em** *fam* to procede to.
esticar [12] [iʃtʃi'ka(x)] ◇ *vt* to stretch. ◇ *vi* **-1.** [distender-se] to stretch. **-2.** *fam* [prolongar saída]: ~ **(em)** to go on (to).
◆ **esticar-se** *vp* [pessoa] to stretch.
estigma [iʃ'tʃigma] *m* **-1.** [ger] stigma. **-2.** [ferrete] mark; **a Inquisição o condenou a usar o** ~ **de cristão-novo** the Inquisition branded him a neo-Christian.
estigmatizar [4] [iʃtʃigmatʃi'za(x)] *vt* **-1.** [com infâmia] to stigmatize; **eles o estigmatizaram de traidor** they branded him a traitor. **-2.** [com preconceito] to revile.
estilete *m* [punhal] stiletto.
estilhaçar [13] [iʃtʃiʎa'sa(x)] *vt* to shatter.
◆ **estilhaçar-se** *vp* to be shattered.
estilhaço [iʃtʃi'ʎasu] *m* **-1.** [de plástico, granada] splinter. **-2.** [de vidro] shard.
estilista [iʃtʃi'liʃta] *mf* **-1.** [escritor] stylist. **-2.** [de moda] fashion designer.
estilístico, ca [iʃtʃi'liʃtʃiku, ka] *adj* **-1.** [talento, característica] stylish. **-2.** [análise] stylistic.
estilização [iʃtʃiliza'sãw] (*pl* **-ões**) *f* stylization.
estilizar [4] [iʃtʃili'za(x)] *vt* to stylize.
estilo [iʃ'tʃilu] *m* style; ~ **de época** style of the period; **ter** ~ *fig* [ser autêntico] to have real style; **de** ~ [de época] fashionable; ~ **de vida** way of life; **em grande** ~ [com pompa] in grande style.
estima [iʃ'tʃima] *f* **-1.** [apreço] esteem. **-2.** [afeição] affection.
estimação [iʃtʃima'sãw] *f*: **de** ~ prized; **minha caneta de** ~ my favourite pen; **animal de** ~ (family) pet.
estimado, da [iʃtʃi'madu, da] *adj* **-1.** [avaliado] estimated. **-2.** [querido] esteemed.

estimar [4] [iʃtʃi'ma(x)] *vt* **-1.** [ger] to prize. **-2.** [avaliar]: ~ **algo (em)** to estimate sthg (at). **-3.** [desejar]: ~ **as melhoras de alguém** to hope sb gets better; ~ **que** to hope that.

estimativa [iʃtʃima'tʃiva] *f* estimation; ~ **de custo** to estimate; **fazer uma** ~ **de algo** to make an appraisal of sthg.

estimável [iʃtʃi'mavew] (*pl* **-eis**) *adj* **-1.** [avaliável]: ~ **em** reckoned at. **-2.** [digno de respeito] respectable.

estimulação [iʃtʃimula'sãw] *f* stimulation.

estimulante [iʃtʃimu'lãntʃi] <> *adj* stimulating. <> *m* stimulant.

estimular [4] [iʃtʃimu'la(x)] *vt* **-1.** [excitar, ativar] to stimulate. **-2.** [instigar] to incite. **-3.** [incentivar]: ~ **alguém (a fazer algo)** to encourage sb (to do sthg).

estímulo [iʃ'tʃimulu] *m* **-1.** [ger] stimulus. **-2.** [excitação] stimulant. **-3.** [incentivo] motivation.

estio [iʃ'tʃiu] *m* summer.

estipêndio [iʃtʃi'pẽndʒu] *m* stipend.

estipular [4] [iʃtipu'la(x)] *vt* to stipulate.

estiramento [iʃtʃira'mẽntu] *m* MED [distensão] strain.

estirar [4] [iʃtʃi'ra(x)] *vt* **-1.** [alongar] to stretch. **-2.** [estender ao comprido] to stretch out.

◆ **estirar-se** *vp* [deitar-se] to stretch o.s out.

estirpe [iʃ'tʃixpi] *f* lineage.

estiva [iʃ'tʃiva] *f* NÁUT stowage.

estivador, ra [iʃtʃiva'do(x), ra] (*mpl* **-es**, *fpl* **-s**) *m, f* stevedore.

estocada [iʃto'kada] *f* stab.

estocagem [iʃto'kaʒẽ] *f* [provisão] stock.

estocar [12] [iʃto'ka(x)] *vt* **-1.** [armazenar] to stock. **-2.** [dar estocada em] to stab.

Estocolmo [iʃto'kowmu] *n* Stockholm.

estofado, da [iʃto'fadu, da] <> *adj* **-1.** [forrado] upholstered. **-2.** [acolchoado] padded. <> *m* suite.

estofador, ra [iʃtofa'do(x), ra] *m, f* upholsterer.

estofar [4] [iʃto'fa(x)] *vt* **-1.** [revestir] to upholster. **-2.** [acolchoar] to stuff.

estofo [iʃ'tofu] *m* **-1.** [revestimento] reupholstery. **-2.** [acolchoamento] stuffing.

estoicismo [iʃtoj'siʒmu] *m* stoicism.

estóico, ca [iʃ'tɔjku, ka] <> *adj* **-1.** FILOSOFIA stoical, stoic. **-2.** *fig* [austero] stoical. <> *m, f fig* [pessoa austera] stoic.

◆ **estóica** *f* FILOSOFIA stoicism.

estojo [iʃ'toʒu] *m* case; ~ **de unhas** manicure set.

estola [iʃ'tɔla] *f* stole.

estomacal [iʃtoma'kaw] (*pl* **-ais**) *adj* stomach *(antes de subst)*.

estômago [iʃ'tomagu] *m* **-1.** ANAT stomach; **estar com o** ~ **embrulhado** to have an upset stomach; **forrar o** ~ to have a bite to eat. **-2.** *fig* [paciência]: **ter** ~ **para (fazer) algo** to have the stomach for (doing) sthg.

Estônia [iʃ'tonja] *n* Estonia.

estoniano, na [iʃto'njãnu, na] <> *adj* Estonian. <> *m, f* Estonian.

◆ **estoniano** *m* [língua] Estonian.

estonteante [iʃtõn'tʃãntʃi] *adj* stunning.

estopa [iʃ'topa] *f* tow.

estopim (*pl* **-ns**) *m* **-1.** [de bomba] fuse. **-2.** *fig* [de crise, revolta] trigger.

estoque [iʃ'tɔki] *m* **-1.** [provisão] stock; **em** ~ in stock. **-2.** [local] store.

estória [iʃ'tɔrja] *f* story.

estorricar [12] [iʃtoxi'ka(x)] *vt & vi* to scorch.

estorvar [4] [iʃtox'va(x)] *vt* **-1.** [obstruir] to obstruct. **-2.** [importunar] to disturb.

estorvo [iʃ'toxvu] *m* **-1.** [obstáculo] obstacle; [pessoa] hindrance. **-2.** [incômodo] disturbance.

estourado, da [iʃto'radu, da] *adj* **-1.** [temperamental] boisterous. **-2.** *fam* [fatigado] knackered.

estourar [4] [iʃto'ra(x)] <> *vi* **-1.** [bomba] to explode. **-2.** [pneu] to blow up. **-3.** [guerra, revolução] to break out. **-4.** [escândalo] to become public. **-5.** *fig* [rebentar] to burst; **estar estourando de raiva/alegria** to be bursting with rage/joy. **-6.** [ralhar]: ~ **(com alguém)** to explode (at sb). **-7.** [no mais tardar]: **estourando cinco e meia** no later than five-thirty. <> *vt* **-1.** [bomba] to explode. **-2.** [boca-de-fumo] to bust up.

estouro [iʃ'toru] *m* **-1.** [ger] explosion. **-2.** *fam*: **ser um** ~ [filme, pessoa] to be a hit; [notícia, carro] to be a sensation.

estouvado, da [iʃto'vadu, da] *adj* [desajuizado] foolhardy.

estrábico, ca [iʃ'trabiku, ka] *adj* cross-eyed.

estrabismo [iʃtra'biʒmu] *m* squint, strabismus.

estraçalhar [4] [iʃtrasa'ʎa(x)] *vt* **-1.** [livro, objeto] to tear to shreds. **-2.** [pessoa] to kill.

◆ **estraçalhar-se** *vp* **-1.** [objeto] to smash. **-2.** [pessoa] to smash one another.

estrada [iʃ'trada] *m* **-1.** road; ~ **principal** main road *UK*, highway *US*; ~ **secundária** secondary road, B road; ~ **de ferro** railway track *UK*, railroad *US*; ~ **de rodagem** public road; ~ **vicinal** link road. **-2.** *fig* [carreira] work; **estar na** ~ to be in the field.

estrado [iʃ'tradu] *m* **-1.** [de cama] frame. **-2.** [tablado] platform.

estragado, da [iʃtra'gadu, da] *adj* **-1.** [podre] rotten. **-2.** [danificado] damaged. **-3.** [mimado] spoilt.

estragão [iʃtra'gãw] *m* tarragon.

estraga-prazeres [iʃˌtragapra'zeriʃ] *mf inv* killjoy, spoilsport.

estragar [14] [iʃtra'ga(x)] <> *vt* **-1.** [ger] to spoil. **-2.** [danificar] to damage. <> *vi* [apodrecer] to go off.

◆ **estragar-se** *vp* **-1.** [deteriorar-se] to be ruined. **-2.** [avariar-se] to go wrong. **-3.** [apodrecer] to go rotten.

estrago [iʃ'tragu] *m* **-1.** [dano] damage; **fazer um** ~ **em algo** to cause damage to sthg. **-2.** [desperdício] disaster.

estrangeiro, ra [iʃtrãn'ʒejru, ra] <> *adj* foreign. <> *m, f* [pessoa] foreigner.

◆ **estrangeiro** *m*: **no** ~ abroad.

estrangulador, ra [iʃtrãngula'do(x), ra] *m, f* strangler.

estrangulamento [iʃtrãngula'mẽntu] *m* **-1.** [de pessoa] strangulation. **-2.** [obstrução] blocking.
estrangular [4] [iʃtrãŋgu'la(x)] *vt* to strangle.
estranhamento [iʃtrãɲa'mentu] *m* [espanto] surprise.
estranhar [4] [iʃtrã'ɲa(x)] ◇ *vt* **-1.** [achar fora do comum] to find strange. **-2.** [surpreender-se com] to be surprised by. **-3.** [não se habituar a] to be unaccustomed to. **-4.** [retrair-se diante de] to feel ill at ease with. **-5.** [hostilizar] to harass. ◇ *vi* [causar estranheza] to be strange.
◆ **estranhar-se** *vp* [hostilizar-se] to fall out with each other.
estranho, nha [iʃ'trãɲu, ɲa] *adj* **-1.** [diferente, estrangeiro] foreign. **-2.** [incomum, desconhecido] strange; **não ser ~ para alguém** to be familiar to sb.
estratagema [iʃtrata'ʒema] *m* stratagem.
estratégia [iʃtra'tɛʒja] *f* strategy.
estratégico, ca [iʃtra'tɛʒiku, ka] *adj* strategic.
estrategista [iʃtrate'ʒiʃta] *mf* strategist.
estratificar-se [12] [iʃtratʃifi'kaxsi] *vp* **-1.** [em camadas] to be stratified. **-2.** *fig* [cristalizar-se] to take shape.
estrato [iʃ'tratu] *m* stratum.
estratosfera [iʃtratoʃ'fɛra] *f* stratosphere.
estreante [iʃ'trjãntʃi] *adj* debut *(antes de subst)*.
estrear [15] [iʃtre'a(x)] ◇ *vt* **-1.** [roupa, carro] to try out for the first time. **-2.** [filme, show] to premiere. **-3.** [carreira] to start. ◇ *vi* **-1.** [filme, show] to premiere. **-2.** [artista, jogador] to debut.
estrebaria [iʃtreba'ria] *f* stable.
estrebuchar [4] [iʃtrebu'ʃa(x)] *vi* [em agonia] to writhe.
estréia [iʃ'trɛja] *f* **-1.** [de filme, show] premiere. **-2.** [de artista, jogador] debut. **-3.** [de roupa, carro] first time out.
estreitamento [iʃtrejta'mẽntu] *m* **-1.** [ger] narrowing. **-2.** [diminuição] shrinking. **-3.** [de relações] strengthening.
estreitar [4] [iʃtrej'ta(x)] ◇ *vt* **-1.** [diminuir] to shrink. **-2.** [apertar] to narrow. **-3.** [roupa] to constrict. **-4.** [relações, laços] to strengthen. **-5.** [tornar mais rigoroso] to tighten up. ◇ *vi* [estrada] to narrow.
◆ **estreitar-se** *vp* **-1.** [largura] to narrow. **-2.** [amizade, união] to strengthen.
estreiteza [iʃtrej'teza] *f* narrowness.
estreito, ta [iʃ'trejtu, ta] *adj* **-1.** [apertado] narrow. **-2.** [vestido, saia] straight. **-3.** [relação, amizade] strong.
◆ **estreito** *m* GEOGR strait.
estrela [iʃ'trela] *f* **-1.** [ger] star; **~ de cinema** film star *UK*, movie star *US*; **~ cadente** shooting star. **-2.** [sorte] lucky star; **ter boa/má ~** to have good/bad luck.
estrela-de-davi [iʃ'treladzidavi] (*pl* **estrelas-de-davi**) *f* Star of David.
estrelado, da [iʃtre'ladu, da] *adj* **-1.** [céu, noite] starry. **-2.** [ovo] fried.
estrela-do-mar [iʃtreladu'ma(x)] (*pl* **estrelas-do-mar**) *f* starfish.
estrelar [4] [iʃtre'la(x)] *vt* **-1.** [filme, peça] to star. **-2.** [ovos] to fry.
estrelato [iʃtre'latu] *m*: **o ~** stardom.
estrelinha [iʃtre'liɲa] *f* [fogo de artifício] sparkler.
estrelismo [iʃtre'liʒmu] *m prima donna-ish behaviour.*
estremecer [25] [iʃtreme'se(x)] ◇ *vt* to shake. ◇ *vi* **-1.** [tremer de espanto] to shiver. **-2.** [sacudir] to shudder. **-3.** [sofrer abalo] to be shaken.
estremecido, da [iʃtreme'sidu, da] *adj* [amizade, união] shaken.
estremecimento [iʃtremesi'mẽntu] *m* shaking.
estrepar-se [4] [iʃtre'paxsi] *vp* to come unstuck.
estrépito [iʃ'trɛpitu] *m* racket; **fazer ~** to make a racket; **com ~** noisily.
estrepitoso, osa [iʃtrepi'tozu, ɔza] *adj* **-1.** [ruidoso] noisy. **-2.** *fig* [sensacional] resounding.
estressado, da [iʃtre'sadu, da] *adj* stressed (out).
estressante [iʃtre'sãntʃi] *adj* stressful.
estressar [iʃtre'sa(x)] *vt* to cause stress to.
◆ **estressar-se** *vp* to become stressed.
estresse [iʃ'trɛʃi] *m* stress.
estria [iʃ'tria] *f* **-1.** [sulco] groove. **-2.** [na pele] stretch mark.
estribeira [iʃtri'bejra] *f*: **perder as ~s** *fam* to lose one's head.
estribilho [iʃtri'biʎu] *m* MÚS chorus.
estribo [iʃ'tribu] *m* **-1.** [de cavalo] stirrup. **-2.** [degrau] step.
estricnina [iʃtrik'nina] *f* strychnine.
estridente [iʃtri'dẽntʃi] *adj* strident.
estrilar [4] [iʃtri'la(x)] *vi fam* **-1.** [vociferar] to make a shrill noise. **-2.** [reclamar] to clamour.
estrilo [iʃ'trilu] *m fam*: **dar um ~** to fly off the handle.
estripulia [iʃtripu'lia] *f* mischief.
estritamente [iʃtrita'mẽntʃi] *adv* [à risca] to the letter.
estrito, ta [iʃ'tritu, ta] *adj* **-1.** [rigoroso] strict. **-2.** [exato] precise; **no sentido ~ da palavra** in the strict sense of the word.
estrofe [iʃ'trɔfi] *f* stanza.
estrogênio [iʃtro'ʒenju] *m* oestrogen.
estrogonofe [iʃtrogo'nɔfi] *m* CULIN stroganoff.
estrondo [iʃ'trõndu] *m* rumble.
estrondoso, osa [iʃtrõn'dozu, ɔza] *adj* **-1.** [ruidoso] roaring. **-2.** [espetacular] spectacular.
estropiado, da [iʃtro'pjadu, da] *adj* **-1.** [aleijado] crippled. **-2.** [exausto] worn out.
estropiar [16] [iʃtro'pja(x)] *vt* **-1.** [aleijar] to cripple. **-2.** [cansar] to tire out. **-3.** *fig* [mutilar] to mutilate. **-4.** *fig* [pronunciar mal] to mispronounce.
estrume [iʃ'trumi] *m* manure.
estrupício *m fam pej* [pessoa estúpida]: **ser um ~** to be an idiot.
estrutura [iʃtru'tura] *f* **-1.** CONSTR structure. **-2.** [armação] frame.
estruturação [iʃtrutura'sãw] (*pl* **-ões**) *f* structuring.
estrutural [iʃtrutu'raw] (*pl* **-ais**) *adj* structural.

estruturalismo [iʃtrutura'liʒmu] *m* structuralism.
estruturalista [iʃtrutura'liʃta] *adj* structuralist.
estruturar [4] [iʃtrutu'ra(x)] *vt* to structure.
estuário [iʃ'twarju] *m* estuary.
estudado, da [iʃtu'dadu, da] *adj* studied.
estudante [iʃtu'dãntʃi] *mf* student.
estudantil [iʃtudãn'tʃiw] (*pl* **-is**) *adj* student *(antes de subst).*
estudar [4] [iʃtu'da(x)] *vt & vi* to study.
estúdio [iʃ'tudʒju] *m* studio.
estudioso, osa [iʃtu'dʒjozu, ɔza] ◇ *adj* studious. ◇ *m, f* expert.
estudo [iʃ'tudu] *m* study; **ter muito** ~ to be very learned; ~ **de caso** case study; ~ **de viabilidade** feasibility study.
◆ **estudos** *mpl* [formação escolar] studies.
estufa [iʃ'tufa] *f* **-1.** [para plantas] greenhouse. **-2.** [aquecedor] stove.
estufar [4] [iʃtu'fa(x)] *vt* **-1.** [aquecer em estufa] to heat in the oven. **-2.** [encher] to stuff; **ele estufou o peito de orgulho** *fig* he puffed (his chest out) with pride; **o dinheiro estufava sua carteira** his wallet was stuffed with money. **-3.** *CULIN* [carne] to stew.
estupefação [iʃtupefa'sãw] *f* [espanto] amazement.
estupefato, ta [iʃtupe'fatu, ta] *adj* [espantado] amazed.
estupendo, da [iʃtu'pẽndu, da] *adj* **-1.** [maravilhoso] wonderful. **-2.** [espantoso] amazing.
estupidamente [iʃtupida'mẽntʃi] *adv* **-1.** [de maneira absurda] stupidly. **-2.** [extremamente] extremely; **uma cerveja estupidamente gelada, por favor** an extremely cold beer, please.
estupidez [iʃtupi'deʃ] *f* **-1.** [condição] stupidity. **-2.** [ato] stupid thing. **-3.** *fam* [grosseria]: **não é a primeira vez que ela me faz uma** ~ it is not the first time he's been rude to me.
estúpido, da [iʃ'tupidu, da] ◇ *adj* **-1.** [burro] stupid. **-2.** [grosseiro] rude; **um calor** ~ *fig* an unbearable heat. ◇ *m, f* **-1.** [pessoa burra] stupid person. **-2.** [pessoa grosseira] rude person.
estupor [iʃtu'po(x)] *m* **-1.** [estado] stupor. **-2.** [estarrecimento] amazement.
estuporado, da [iʃtupo'radu, da] *adj* **-1.** [paralisado] stupefied. **-2.** [estarrecido] stunned. **-3.** *fam* [estragado] messed up. **-4.** *fam* [cansado] wiped out. **-5.** *fam* [ferido] messed up.
estuporar [iʃtupo'ra(x)] *vt* **-1.** [cair em estupor] to paralise. **-2.** [assustar] to shock. **-3.** [arruinar] to smash.
estuprador [iʃtupra'do(x)] *m* rapist.
estuprar [4] [iʃtu'pra(x)] *vt* to rape.
estupro [iʃ'tupru] *m* rape.
estuque [iʃ'tuki] *m* stucco.
esturricado, da [iʃtuxi'kadu, da] *adj* dry.
esturricar [12] [iʃtuxi'ka(x)] ◇ *vt* to dry. ◇ *vi* to become dry.
esvair-se [68] [iʒva'ixsi] *vp* **-1.** [desaparecer] to disappear. **-2.** [desmaiar] to faint. **-3.** *loc:* ~ **em sangue** to bleed copiously; ~ **em lágrimas** to dissolve into tears.
esvaziamento [iʒvazja'mẽntu] *m* **-1.** [desocupação] emptying. **-2.** [evacuação] evacuation. **-3.** [perda de importância] nullification.
esvaziar [16] [iʒva'zja(x)] *vt* **-1.** [desocupar] to empty. **-2.** [beber de uma só vez] to drain. **-3.** [tirar a importância de] to nullify.
◆ **esvaziar-se** *vp* [tornar-se vazio] to empty.
esverdeado, da [iʒvex'dʒadu, da] *adj* greenish.
esvoaçante [iʒvwa'sãntʃi] *adj* fluttering.
esvoaçar [13] [iʒvwa'sa(x)] *vi* to flutter.
ET (*abrev de* **ExtraTerrestre**) *m* ET.
eta ['eta] *interj* blast; ~ **ferro!** gee whiz!
ETA (*abrev de* **Euskadi Ta Askatasuna**) *m* ETA.
etapa [e'tapa] *f* stage; **por** ~**s** in stages.
etário, ria [e'tarju, rja] *adj* aged.
etc. (*abrev de* **et cetera**) etc.
éter ['ɛte(x)] *m* ether.
etéreo, rea [e'tɛrju, rja] *adj* ethereal.
eternidade [etexni'dadʒi] *f* eternity.
eternizar [4] [etexni'za(x)] *vt* **-1.** [tornar eterno] to eternalize. **-2.** [imortalizar] to immortalize. **-3.** *fam* [prolongar] to drag out.
◆ **eternizar-se** *vp* **-1.** [tornar-se eterno] to become eternal. **-2.** [imortalizar-se] to become immortal. **-3.** *fam* [prolongar-se] to drag on.
eterno, na [e'tɛxnu, na] *adj* eternal.
Ethernet [etex'neti] *f COMPUT* Ethernet®.
ético, ca ['ɛtʃiku, ka] *adj* ethical.
◆ **ética** *f* ethics *(pl).*
etimologia [etʃimolo'ʒia] *f* etymology.
etíope [e'tʃiopi] ◇ *adj* Ethiopian. ◇ *mf* Ethiopian.
Etiópia [e'tʃi'ɔpja] *n* Ethiopia.
etiqueta [etʃi'keta] *f* **-1.** [ger] label; ~ **adesiva** sticky label. **-2.** [boas maneiras] etiquette. **-3.** [de preço] ticket; [de roupa] label.
etiquetar [4] [etʃike'ta(x)] *vt* to label.
etnia [etʃ'nia] *f* ethnic group.
étnico, ca ['ɛtʃniku, ka] *adj* ethnic.
etnocentrismo [etʃnosẽn'triʒmu] *m* ethnocentrism.
etnografia [etʃnogra'fia] *f* ethnography.
etnologia [etʃnolo'ʒia] *f* ethnology.
etos ['ɛtuʃ] *m inv* ethos.
eu ['ew] *pron* I; **e** ~ **?** what about me?; **sou** ~ it's me; ~ **mesmo** *ou* **próprio** (I) myself.
EUA (*abrev de* **Estados Unidos da América**) *n* USA.
eucalipto [ewka'liptu] *m* eucalyptus.
eucaristia [ewkariʃ'tʃia] *f* Eucharist.
eufemismo [ewfe'miʒmu] *m* euphemism.
eufonia [ewfo'nia] *f* euphony.
euforia [ewfo'ria] *f* euphoria.
eufórico, ca [ew'fɔriku, ka] *adj* euphoric.
eunuco [ew'nuku] *m* eunuch.
euro ['ewru] *m* [moeda] euro.
eurodólar [ewro'dɔla(x)] *m* Eurodollar.
Europa [ew'rɔpa] *n* Europe.
europeizar [4.19] [ewropeji'za(x)] *vt* to Europeanize.

◆ **europeizar-se** *vp* to become Europeanized.
europeu, péia [ewro'pew, pɛja] ◇ *adj* European. ◇ *m, f* European.
eutanásia [ewta'nazja] *f* euthanasia.
evacuação [evakwa'sãw] (*pl* **-ões**) *f* evacuation.
evacuar [4] [eva'kwa(x)] ◇ *vt* **-1.** [desocupar] to evacuate. **-2.** [expelir]: ~ **sangue** to bleed; ~ **fezes** to defecate. ◇ *vi* [defecar] to evacuate.
evadir [6] [eva'dʒi(x)] *vt* **-1.** [evitar] to avoid. **-2.** [eludir] to evade.
◆ **evadir-se** *vp* [escapar] to escape.
evanescente [evane'sẽntʃi] *adj* evanescent.
evangelho [evãn'ʒɛʎu] *m* Gospel; **o ~ segundo Mateus** the Gospel according to Matthew.
evangélico, ca [evãn'ʒɛliku, ka] ◇ *adj* evangelical. ◇ *m, f* [pessoa] evangelist.
evangelização [evãnʒeliza'sãw] (*pl* **-ões**) *f* conversion (to Christianity).
evangelizar [evãnʒeli'za(x)] *vt* to convert (to Christianity).
evaporação [evapora'sãw] (*pl* **-ões**) *f* evaporation.
evaporar [4] [evapo'ra(x)] ◇ *vt* [vaporizar] to evaporate. ◇ *vi* to evaporate.
◆ **evaporar-se** *vp* to evaporate.
evasão [eva'zãw] (*pl* **-ões**) *f* **-1.** [fuga] escape. **-2.** *fig* [evasiva] evasion.
evasivo, va [eva'zivu, va] *adj* evasive.
◆ **evasiva** *f* evasion.
evento [e'vẽntu] *m* event.
eventual [evẽn'twaw] (*pl* **-ais**) *adj* chance *(antes de subst)*.
eventualidade [evẽntwali'dadʒi] *f* eventuality.
eventualmente [evẽntwal'mẽntʃi] *adv* [às vezes] occasionally.
Everest [eve'rɛʃtʃi] *n*: **o ~** (Mount) Everest.
evidência [evi'dẽnsja] *f* evidence; **em ~** [destacado] obvious.
evidenciar [16] [evidẽn'sja(x)] *vt* **-1.** [comprovar] to prove. **-2.** [mostrar] to be evidence of. **-3.** [destacar] to show clearly.
◆ **evidenciar-se** *vp* **-1.** [comprovar-se] to be proven. **-2.** [destacar-se] to be shown clearly.
evidente [evi'dẽntʃi] *adj* obvious.
evidentemente [evidẽntʃi'mẽntʃi] *adv* clearly.
evitar [4] [evi'ta(x)] *vt* **-1.** [fugir a] to avoid; ~ **fazer algo** to avoid doing sthg. **-2.** [impedir] to prevent.
evitável [evi'tavew] (*pl* **-eis**) *adj* avoidable.
evocação [evoka'sãw] (*pl* **-ões**) *f* recollection.
evocar [12] [evo'ka(x)] *vt* [trazer à lembrança] to bring to mind.
evolução [evolu'sãw] (*pl* **-ões**) *f* **-1.** *BIOL* evolution. **-2.** [desenrolar] development. **-3.** [movimento] expansion. **-4.** *MIL* exercise.
evoluído, da [evo'lwidu, da] *adj* **-1.** [adiantado] advanced. **-2.** [aberto] open.
evoluir [74] [evo'lwi(x)] *vi* **-1.** [espécie] to evolve. **-2.** [adiantar-se] to progress.
ex. (*abrev de* **exemplo**) e.g.
exacerbação [ezaseba'sãw] *f* **-1.** [ger] exacerbation. **-2.** [irritação] provocation.
exacerbante [ezasex'bãntʃi] *adj* [intensificador] exacerbating.
exacerbar [4] [ezasex'ba(x)] *vt* **-1.** [intensificar] to exacerbate. **-2.** [irritar] to provoke.
◆ **exacerbar-se** *vp* **-1.** [intensificar-se] to be exacerbated. **-2.** [irritar-se] to be provoked.
exagerado, da [ezaʒe'radu, da] ◇ *adj* exaggerated. ◇ *m, f*: **o que ele diz é típico de um ~** what he says is typical of an exaggerator.
exagerar [4] [ezaʒe'ra(x)] *vt & vi* to exaggerate.
exagero [eza'ʒeru] *m* exaggeration.
exalação [ezala'sãw] (*pl* **-ões**) *f* exhalation.
exalar [4] [eza'la(x)] *vt* to exhale.
exaltação [ezawta'sãw] *f* **-1.** [engrandecimento] exaltation. **-2.** [irritação] irritation. **-3.** [excitação] excitement.
exaltado, da [ezaw'tadu, da] *adj* **-1.** [facilmente irritável] irritable. **-2.** [fanático] fanatical. **-3.** [exacerbado] irritated.
exaltar [4] [exaw'ta(x)] *vt* **-1.** [engrandecer] to exalt. **-2.** [irritar] to irritate. **-3.** [excitar] to excite.
◆ **exaltar-se** *vp* [irritar-se] to become irritated.
exame [e'zãmi] *m* **-1.** [ger] examination; **fazer um ~** to have an examination; ~ **de sangue** blood test. **-2.** *EDUC* [teste] examination, exam; **fazer um ~** to sit an examination; ~ **de direção** driving test. **-3.** [inspeção] inspection.
examinador, ra [ezamina'do(x), ra] ◇ *adj* examining. ◇ *m, f* examiner.
examinar [4] [ezami'na(x)] *vt* **-1.** [ger] to examine. **-2.** [inspecionar] to inspect.
exasperação [ezaʃpera'sãw] *f* exasperation.
exasperado, da [ezaʃpe'radu, da] *adj* exasperated.
exasperador, ra [ezaʃpera'do(x), ra] *adj* exasperating.
exasperante [ezaʃpe'rãntʃi] *adj* exasperating.
exasperar [4] [ezaʃpe'ra(x)] *vt* to exasperate.
◆ **exasperar-se** *vp* to become exasperated.
exatamente [ezata'mẽntʃi] *adv* exactly.
exatidão [ezatʃi'dãw] *f* **-1.** [precisão] accuracy. **-2.** [perfeição] perfection.
exato, ta [e'zatu, ta] *adj* **-1.** [preciso] exact. **-2.** [correto] correct, right.
exaurir [6] [ezaw'ri(x)] *vt* [esgotar] to exhaust.
◆ **exaurir-se** *vp* to be exhausted.
exaustão [ezawʃ'tãw] *f* exhaustion.
exaustivo, va [ezaws'tʃivu, va] *adj* **-1.** [esgotante] exhausting. **-2.** [completo] exhaustive.
exausto, ta [e'zawʃtu, ta] ◇ *pp* ▷ **exaurir**. ◇ *adj* exhausted.
exaustor [ezawʃ'to(x)] (*pl* **-es**) *m* extractor fan.
exceção [ese'sãw] (*pl* **-ões**) *f*: **com ~ de** except for, with the exception of.
excedente [ese'dẽntʃi] ◇ *adj* excess *(antes de subst)*. ◇ *m* **-1.** *COM* surplus. **-2.** [aluno] student on waiting list.
exceder [5] [ese'de(x)] *vt* exceed.
◆ **exceder-se** *vp* [cometer excessos] to go too far.

excelência [ese'lẽnsja] *f* **-1.** [primazia] excellence; **por ~** par excellence. **-2.** [tratamento]: **(Vossa) Excelência** Your Excellency.
excelente [ese'lẽntʃi] *adj* excellent.
excelentíssimo, ma [eselẽn'tʃisimu, ma] *adj superl* [tratamento] most excellent; **~ Senhor** Your Excellence; **o ~ senhor presidente da república** His Excellency, the president of the republic.
excelso, sa [e'sɛwsu, sa] *adj* **-1.** [sublime] sublime. **-2.** [excelente] excellent.
excentricidade [esẽntrisi'dadʒi] *f* eccentricity.
excêntrico, ca [e'sẽntriku, ka] ◇ *adj* eccentric. ◇ *m, f* eccentric.
excepcional [esepsjo'naw] (*pl* **-ais**) ◇ *adj* **-1.** [extraordinário, excelente] exceptional. **-2.** *MED* disabled. ◇ *mf MED* [pessoa] person with special needs.
excepcionalidade [esepsjonali'dadʒi] *f* **-1.** [condição de extraordinário] exceptional nature. **-2.** [excelência] exceptional quality.
excepcionalmente [esepsjonaw'mẽntʃi] *adv* exceptionally.
excerto [e'sextu] *m* excerpt.
excessivamente [esesiva'mẽntʃi] *adv* excessively.
excessivo, va [ese'sivu, va] *adj* excessive.
excesso [e'sɛsu] *m* **-1.** [ger] excess; **~ de peso** [obesidade] excess weight; [em bagagem] excess baggage; **~ de velocidade** excessive speed. **-2.** *COM* surplus. **-3.** [desmando]: **cometer ~s** to go too far.
exceto [e'sɛtu] *prep* except.
excetuar [4] [ese'twa(x)] *vt* to except.
excitação [esita'sãw] *f* **-1.** [agitação] excitement. **-2.** [sexual] arousal.
excitamento [esita'mẽntu] *m* [agitação] excitement.
excitado, da [esi'tadu, da] *adj* **-1.** [agitado] excited. **-2.** [sexualmente] aroused.
excitante [esi'tãntʃi] *adj* **-1.** [ger] stimulating; **uma droga ~** a stimulant. **-2.** [filme] exciting.
excitar [4] [esi'ta(x)] *vt* **-1.** [agitar] to excite. **-2.** [sexualmente] to arouse. **-3.** [incitar] to incite.
◆ **excitar-se** *vp* **-1.** [agitar-se] to become excited. **-2.** [sexualmente] to become aroused.
exclamação [iʃklama'sãw] (*pl* **-ões**) *f* exclamation.
exclamar [4] [iʃkla'ma(x)] *vi* to exclaim.
exclamativo, va [iʃklama'tʃivu, va] *adj* exclamatory; **ponto de ~** exclamation mark.
excluir [74] [iʃklu'i(x)] *vt* **-1.** [eliminar] to exclude. **-2.** [omitir]: **~ algo/alguém de** to exclude sthg/sb from. **-3.** [privar]: **~ algo/alguém de** to leave sthg/sb out of. **-4.** [por incompatibilidade] to preclude.
exclusão [iʃklu'zãw] (*pl* **-ões**) *f* exclusion.
exclusividade [iʃkluzivi'dadʒi] *f* **-1.** [uso, posse] exclusivity. **-2.** *COM* [direito] sole rights.
exclusivista [iʃkluzi'viʃta] ◇ *adj* [individualista] self-centred. ◇ *mf* self-centred person.
exclusivo, va [iʃklu'zivu, va] *adj* exclusive.
excomungado, da [iʃkomũŋ'gadu, da] ◇ *adj RELIG* excommunicated. ◇ *m, f* excommunicated person.
excomungar [14] [iʃkomũŋ'ga(x)] *vt* to excommunicate.
excreção [iʃkre'sãw] (*pl* **-ões**) *f* **-1.** *BIOL* excretion. **-2.** [substância excretada] excreta.
excremento [iʃkre'mẽntu] *m* excrement.
excretar [iʃkre'ta(x)] *vt* [expelir] to excrete.
excruciante [iʃkru'sjãntʃi] *adj* excruciating.
excursão [iʃkux'sãw] (*pl* **-ões**) *f* **-1.** [ger] excursion. **-2.** [em caminhada] walk, ramble.
excursionar [4] [iʃkuxsjo'na(x)] *vi*: **~ (por)** to tour.
excursionista [iʃkuxsjo'niʃta] *mf* [turista] tourist; [por um dia] day-tripper; [em caminhada] walker, rambler.
execrar [4] [eze'kra(x)] *vt* to execrate.
execrável [eze'kravew] (*pl* **-eis**) *adj* execrable.
execução [ezeku'sãw] (*pl* **-ões**) *f* **-1.** [ger] execution. **-2.** [de peça musical] performance.
executante [ezeku'tãntʃi] ◇ *adj* [de peça musical] performing. ◇ *mf* **-1.** [músico] performer. **-2.** [jur] executor.
executar [4] [ezeku'ta(x)] *vt* **-1.** [ger] to execute. **-2.** [peça musical] to perform. **-3.** [cumprir] to carry out.
executivo, va [ezeku'tʃivu, va] ◇ *adj* executive. ◇ *m, f* executive.
executor, ra [ezeku'to(x), ra] *m, f* executor.
exemplar [ezẽn'pla(x)] (*pl* **-es**) ◇ *adj* [modelar] exemplary. ◇ *m* **-1.** [de livro, jornal] copy. **-2.** [peça] example. **-3.** [modelo] model. **-4.** *BIOL* [espécie] specimen.
exemplificação [ezẽnplifika'sãw] (*pl* **-ões**) *f* exemplification.
exemplificar [ezẽnplifi'ka(x)] *vt* to exemplify.
exemplo [e'zẽnplu] *m* **-1.** [ger] example; **por ~** for example; **bom/mau ~** good/bad example; **dar o ~** to set an example; **seguir o ~ de** to follow the example of; **ser um ~ de algo** to be a model of sthg; **a ~ de** just like. **-2.** [lição]: **servir de ~ a alguém** to serve as a warning to sb.
exéquias [eˈzɛkjaʃ] *fpl* funeral rites.
exeqüível [eze'kwivew] (*pl* **-eis**) *adj* feasible.
exercer [25] [ezex'se(x)] *vt* **-1.** [desempenhar] to carry out; [profissão] to practise *UK*, to practice *US*. **-2.** [fazer sentir]: **~ algo (sobre)** to exert sthg (on).
exercício [ezex'sisju] *m* **-1.** [ger] exercise; **fazer ~** to exercise; **em ~** [presidente, diretor] in office; [professor] in service; [de profissão] practising; [de direitos] excercising; **em pleno ~ de suas faculdades mentais** in full command of one's mental faculties. **-2.** *EDUC* exercise. **-3.** *COM*: **~ anterior /corrente** previous/current financial year.
exercitar [4] [ezexsi'ta(x)] *vt* **-1.** [ger] to exercise. **-2.** [praticar, treinar] to practise *UK*, to practice *US*.
◆ **exercitar-se** *vp* [adestrar-se] to take exercise.
exército [e'zɛxsitu] *m* army.

exibição [ezibi'sãw] (*pl* **-ões**) *f* **-1.** [demonstração] exhibition; **ser pura ~** [ser falso] to be just for show. **-2.** [do corpo] exhibition. **-3.** [de filme, obra de arte] exhibition.
exibicionismo [ezibisjo'niʒmu] *m* **-1.** [ostentação] ostentation. **-2.** *PSIC* exhibitionism.
exibicionista [ezibisjo'niʃta] ◇ *adj* [ostentativo] ostentatious. ◇ *mf* **-1.** [pessoa] show-off. **-2.** *PSIC* exhibitionist.
exibido, da [ezi'bidu, da] *fam* ◇ *adj* [exibicionista] flamboyant. ◇ *m, f* [pessoa] exhibitionist.
exibidor, ra [ezibi'do(x), ra] ◇ *adj* [que exibe] exhibiting. ◇ *mf* [dono de cinema] cinema owner.
exibir [6] [ezi'bi(x)] *vt* **-1.** [ger] to show. **-2.** [ostentar] to exhibit. **-3.** [expor] [obra de arte] to exhibit.
◆ **exibir-se** *vp* **-1.** [mostrar-se] to show off. **-2.** [indecentemente] to expose o.s.
exigência [ezi'ʒẽnsja] *f* **-1.** [imposição] demand. **-2.** [requisito] requirement. **-3.** [rigor] urgent request.
exigente [ezi'ʒẽntʃi] *adj* [rigoroso] demanding.
exigir [52] [ezi'ʒi(x)] *vt* **-1.** [reclamar] to demand; **~ que alguém faça algo** to demand that sb do sthg. **-2.** [requerer] to require.
exíguo, gua [e'zigwu, gwa] *adj* **-1.** [diminuto] tiny. **-2.** [minguado] meagre.
exilado, da [ezi'ladu, da] ◇ *adj* [pessoa] exiled. ◇ *m, f* [pessoa] exile.
exilar [4] [ezi'la(x)] *vt* to exile.
◆ **exilar-se** *vp* to be exiled.
exílio [e'ziljul] *m* **-1.** [ger] exile. **-2.** [expatriação] deportation.
exímio, mia [e'zimju, mja] *adj* [excelente] excellent.
eximir [6] [ezi'mi(x)] *vt*: **~ alguém de algo** to exempt sb from sthg.
◆ **eximir-se** *vp*: **~-se de algo** to excuse o.s. from sthg.
existência [eziʃ'tẽnsja] *f* existence.
existencial [eziʃtẽn'sjãw] (*pl* **-ais**) *adj* existential.
existencialismo [eziʃtẽnsja'liʒmu] *m* existentialism.
existente [eziʃ'tẽntʃi] *adj* **-1.** [que existe] existing. **-2.** [vivente] living.
existir [6] [eziʃ'tʃi(x)] *vi* **-1.** [haver] to be. **-2.** [viver] to exist. **-3.** *loc* [ser fantástico]: **não ~** *fam* to be incredible; **este sorvete não existe!** this ice cream is incredible!
êxito ['ezitu] *m* **-1.** [sucesso] success; **ter/não ter ~ (em)** to be successful/unsuccessful (in). **-2.** [filme, música]: **ser um ~** to be a success, to be a hit.
êxodo ['ezodu] *m* exodus; **~ rural** rural exodus.
exoneração [ezonera'sãw] (*pl* **-ões**) *f* exoneration.
exonerar [4] [ezone'ra(x)] *vt* **-1.** [demitir]: **~ alguém de algo** to exonerate sb from sthg. **-2.** [desobrigar]: **~ alguém de algo** to exonerate sb from sthg.
◆ **exonerar-se** *vp* **-1.** [demitir-se]: **~-se de algo** to exonerate o.s. from sthg. **-2.** [desobrigar-se]: **~-se de algo** to release o.s. from sthg.
exorbitância [ezoxbi'tãnsja] *f* **-1.** [excesso] excess. **-2.** *fam* [preço excessivo] extortionate price.
exorcismo [ezox'siʒmu] *m* exorcism.
exorcista [ezox'siʃta] *mf* exorcist.
exorcizar [4] [ezoxsi'za(x)] *vt* to exorcize.
exortar [4] [ezox'ta(x)] *vt*: **~ alguém a fazer algo** to exhort sb to do sthg.
exótico, ca [e'zɔtʃiku, ka] *f* exotic.
exotismo [ezo'tʃiʒmu] *m* exoticism.
expandir [6] [iʃpãn'dʒi(x)] *vt* [ger] to spread.
◆ **expandir-se** *vp* **-1.** [dilatar-se] to spread, to be spread. **-2.** [ser expansivo] to be expansive.
expansão [iʃpãn'sãw] (*pl* **-ões**) *f* **-1.** [ato] expansion. **-2.** [efusão] outpouring.
expansionista [iʃpãsjo'niʃta] ◇ *adj* expansionist. ◇ *mf* expansionist.
expansividade [iʃpãnsivi'dadʒi] *f* expansiveness.
expansivo, va [iʃpã'sivu, va] *adj* expansive.
expatriação [iʃpatrja'sãw] (*pl* **-ões**) *f* expatriation.
expatriado, da [iʃpa'trjadu, da] ◇ *adj* [pessoa] expatriated. ◇ *m, f* [pessoa] expatriate.
expatriar [16] [iʃpa'trja(x)] *vt* to expatriate.
expectativa [iʃpekta'tʃiva] *f* expectation; **na ~ de** in the expectation of; **~ de vida** life expectancy.
expectorante [iʃpekto'rãntʃi] ◇ *adj* expectorant. ◇ *m* expectorant.
expectorar [4] [iʃpekto'ra(x)] *vt* & *vi* to expectorate.
expedição [iʃpedʒi'sãw] (*pl* **-ões**) *f* **-1.** [de mercadorias] dispatch. **-2.** [por navio] shipment. **-3.** [por correio] dispatch. **-4.** [viagem] expedition. **-5.** [de documento] issue.
expedidor, ra [iʃpedʒi'do(x), ra] *adj* forwarding.
expediência [iʃpe'dʒjẽnsja] *f* [desembaraço, diligência] efficiency.
expediente [iʃpe'dʒjẽntʃi] ◇ *adj* [desembaraçado, diligente] efficient; **ser ~** to be efficient. ◇ *m* **-1.** [horário] office hours; **durante o ~** during office hours; **fora do ~** out of office hours; **~ administrativo/bancário** banking/business hours; **meio ~** part-time. **-2.** [pessoal] resourceful. **-3.** [desembaraço, diligência]: **ter ~** to be resourceful. **-4.** [meios, recursos] expedient. **-5.** [correspondência] correspondence.
expedir [70] [iʃpe'dʒi(x)] *vt* **-1.** [carta, mercadoria] to send. **-2.** [documento etc] to issue.
expedito, ta [iʃpe'dʒitu, ta] *adj* **-1.** [pessoa] efficient. **-2.** [trabalho, solução] expeditious.
expelir [57] [iʃpe'li(x)] *vt* to expel.
experiência [iʃpe'rjẽnsja] *f* experience; **em ~** on trial.
experienciar [16] [iʃperjẽn'sja(x)] *vt* to experience.
experiente [iʃpe'rjẽntʃi] *adj* experienced.
experimentação [iʃperimẽnta'sãw] (*pl* **-ões**) *f* experimentation.
experimentado, da [iʃperimẽn'tadu, da] *adj* **-1.**

[experimento] experienced. **-2.** [testado] tested. **-3.** [provado] tried.

experimental [iʃperimẽn'tawl] (*pl* **-ais**) *adj* experimental.

experimentar [4] [iʃperimẽn'ta(x)] *vt* **-1.** [testar] to test. **-2.** [provar - comida, bebida] to try; [- roupa] to try on. **-3.** [sofrer] to go through. **-4.** [sentir] to experience.

experimento [iʃperi'mẽntu] *m* experiment.

expiação [iʃpja'sãw] (*pl* **-ões**) *f*: ~ **(de algo)** atonement (for sthg).

expiar [16] [iʃ'pja(x)] *vt* to atone for.

expiatório, ria [iʃpja'tɔrju, rja] *adj* ▷ **bode**.

expiração [iʃpira'sãw] (*pl* **-ões**) *f* **-1.** [de ar] exhalation. **-2.** [fim de prazo] expiry.

expirar [4] [iʃpi'ra(x)] ◇ *vt* [ar] to exhale. ◇ *vi* **-1.** [encerrar] to expire. **-2.** [morrer] to die.

explanação [iʃplana'sãw] (*pl* **-ões**) *f* explanation.

explanar [4] [iʃpla'na(x)] *vt* to explain.

explicação [iʃplika'sãw] (*pl* **-ões**) *f* explanation.

explicar [12] [iʃpli'ka(x)] *vt* & *vi* to explain.

◆ **explicar-se** *vp* [justificar-se] to explain o.s.

explicativo, va [iʃplika'tʃivu, va] *adj* explanatory.

explicável [iʃpli'kavew] (*pl* **-eis**) *adj* [justificável] explainable.

explicitar [4] [iʃplisi'ta(x)] *vt* to make explicit.

explícito, ta [iʃ'plisitu, ta] *adj* explicit.

explodir [6] [iʃplo'di(x)] ◇ *vi* **-1.** [bomba, avião, carro] to explode. **-2.** *fig* [não se conter] to burst; ~ **de** to be bursting with; ~ **em** to burst into. ◇ *vt* **-1.** [bomba] to detonate. **-2.** [edifício, avião] to blow up.

exploração [iʃplora'sãw] (*pl* **-ões**) *f* **-1.** [ger] exploration. **-2.** [emprego] use. **-3.** [de negócio] running. **-4.** [agrícola] cultivation, growing. **-5.** [abuso] exploitation. **-6.** [exorbitância]: **ser uma** ~ to be exorbitant.

explorador, ra [iʃplora'do(x), ra] ◇ *adj* **-1.** [pessoa, companhia] exploring, exploratory. **-2.** [aproveitador] exploitative. ◇ *m, f* **-1.** [desbravador] explorer. **-2.** [aproveitador] exploiter.

explorar [4] [iʃplo'ra(x)] *vt* **-1.** [ger] to exploit. **-2.** [empregar] to use. **-3.** [negócio] to run. **-4.** [desbravar] to explore.

exploratório, ria [iʃplora'tɔriu, ria] *adj* exploratory.

explosão [iʃplo'zãw] (*pl* **-ões**) *f* explosion.

explosivo, va [iʃplo'zivu, va] *adj* explosive.

◆ **explosivo** *m* [material] explosive.

EXPO (*abrev de* **Exposição**) *f* exhibition.

expoente [iʃ'pwẽntʃi] ◇ *mf* [figura ilustre] exponent. ◇ *m* *MAT* exponent.

expor [45] [iʃ'po(x)] *vt* **-1.** [mostrar] to display. **-2.** [explicar] to explain. **-3.** [exibir] to exhibit. **-4.** [revelar] to reveal. **-5.** [submeter]: ~ **algo (a algo)** to expose sthg (to sthg).

◆ **expor-se** *vp* **-1.** [submeter-se]: ~**-se a algo** to expose o.s. to sthg. **-2.** [exibir-se] to expose o.s.

exportação [iʃpoxta'sãw] (*pl* **-ões**) *f* **-1.** [ato] export. **-2.** [produtos] exports *(pl)*.

exportador, ra [iʃpoxta'do(x), ra] ◇ *adj* **-1.** [país, companhia] exporting. **-2.** [política] export *(antes de subst)*. ◇ *m, f* exporter.

exportar [4] [iʃpox'ta(x)] *vt* to export.

exposição [iʃpozi'sãw] (*pl* **-ões**) *f* **-1.** [mostra] display. **-2.** [explicação] explanation. **-3.** [narração] narrative. **-4.** *FOTO* exposure.

expositor, ra [iʃpozi'to(x), ra] *m, f* exhibitor.

exposto, osta [iʃ'poʃtu, ɔʃta] ◇ *pp* ▷ **expor**. ◇ *adj* [à vista - mercadoria] on show; [- corpo] exposed; [- fratura] compound.

expressão [iʃpre'sãw] (*pl* **-ões**) *f* **-1.** [ger] expression; ~ **escrita/oral** written/oral expression; ~ **artística** artistic expression; ~ **corporal** self-expression though movement. **-2.** [manifestação]: ~ **(de algo)** expression (of sthg). **-3.** [vivacidade] expressiveness.

expressar [4] [iʃpre'sa(x)] *vt* to express.

◆ **expressar-se** *vp* to express o.s.

expressionismo [iʃpresjo'niʒmu] *m* expressionism.

expressionista [iʃpresjo'niʃta] ◇ *adj* expressionist. ◇ *mf* expressionist.

expressividade [iʃpresivi'dadʒi] *f* expressiveness.

expressivo, va [iʃpre'sivu, va] *adj* expressive.

expresso, sa [iʃ'prɛsu, sa] ◇ *pp* ▷ **expressar**. ◇ *adj* express.

◆ **expresso** *m* express.

exprimir [6] [iʃpri'mi(x)] *vt* to express.

◆ **exprimir-se** *vp* to express o.s.

expropriação [iʃproprja'sãw] (*pl* **-ões**) *f* *JUR* expropriation.

expropriar [16] [iʃpropri'a(x)] *vt* *JUR* to expropriate.

expugnar [4] [iʃpugi'na(x)] *vt* to storm.

expulsão [iʃpuw'sãw] (*pl* **-ões**) *f* **-1.** [saída forçada] expulsion. **-2.** *ESP* sending-off.

expulsar [4] [iʃpuw'sa(x)] *vt* **-1.** [ger] to expel. **-2.** [inimigo] to drive out. **-3.** [deportar] to deport. **-4.** *ESP* to send off.

expulso, sa [iʃ'puwsu, sa] ◇ *pp* ▷ **expulsar**. ◇ *adj* expelled.

expurgar [14] [iʃpux'ga(x)] *vt* **-1.** [limpar] to clean. **-2.** [corrigir] to expurgate. **-3.** [livrar]: ~ **algo (de)** to purge sthg (of).

expurgo [iʃ'puxgu] *m* purge.

êxtase ['eʃtazi] *m* **-1.** [enlevo] ecstasy. **-2.** [transe]: **estar em** ~ to be in ecstasy.

extasiado, da [iʃta'zjadu, da] *adj* **-1.** [enlevado] ecstatic. **-2.** [pasmado] astounded.

extasiar [16] [iʃta'zja(x)] *vt* to enrapture.

◆ **extasiar-se** *vp* to be entranced.

extemporâneo, nea [iʃtẽnpo'rãnju, ja] *adj* extemporary, extemporaneous.

extensão [iʃtẽn'sãw] (*pl* **-ões**) *f* **-1.** [ger] extent; **em toda a** ~ **da palavra** in the full meaning of the word. **-2.** [dimensão, área] area. **-3.** [comprimento] length; **a vegetação cobria toda a** ~ **da praia** the vegetation covered the whole length and breadth of the beach. **-4.** [duração] duration. **-5.** [ampliação] scope. **-6.** [ramal telefônico, fio elétrico] extension.

extensivo, va [iʃtẽn'sivu, va] *adj* **-1.** [extensível] extending. **-2.** [amplo] extensive.

extenso, sa [iʃ'tẽnsu, sa] *adj* **-1.** [ger] long. **-2.** [amplo, abrangente] extensive. **-3.** *loc*: **por ~** in full.

extenuado, da [iʃte'nwadu, da] *adj* worn out.

extenuante [iʃte'nwãntʃi] *adj* **-1.** [cansativo] exhausting. **-2.** [debilitante] debilitating.

extenuar [4] [iʃtẽ'nwa(x)] *vt* **-1.** [cansar] to wear out. **-2.** [debilitar] to debilitate.

◆ **extenuar-se** *vp* **-1.** [cansar-se] to wear o.s. out. **-2.** [debilitar-se] to be debilitated.

exterior [iʃte'rjo(x)] (*pl* **-es**) ◇ *adj* **-1.** [externo] outer. **-2.** [com outros países] external. **-3.** [aparência] external. **-4.** [o estrangeiro]: **o ~** abroad; **estar no ~** to be abroad; **ser do ~** to be a foreigner. ◇ *m* [aparência] appearance.

exterioridade [iʃterjori'dadʒi] *f* external nature; [aparências] (outward) appearances

exteriorização [iʃterjoriza'sãw] (*pl* **-ões**) *f* manifestation.

exteriorizar [4] [iʃterjori'za(x)] *vt* to externalize.

exteriormente [iʃterjox'mẽntʃi] *adv* from the outside.

exterminação [iʃtexmina'sãw] (*pl* **-ões**) *f* extermination.

exterminar [4] [iʃtexmi'na(x)] *vt* **-1.** [aniquilar] to exterminate. **-2.** [erradicar] to eradicate.

extermínio [iʃtex'minju] *m* extermination.

externa [iʃ'tɛxna] *f* ▷ **externo**.

externato [iʃtɛx'natu] *m* day school.

externo, na [iʃtɛxnu, na] *adj* **-1.** [exterior - parede] exterior; [- lado] external. **-2.** [aparente] exterior. **-3.** [medicamento]: **uso ~** external use.

extinção [iʃtʃĩn'sãw] *f* extinction; **em ~** endangered.

extinguir [53] [iʃtʃĩŋ'gi(x)] *vt* **-1.** [fogo] to extinguish. **-2.** [exterminar] to exterminate. **-3.** [dissolver] to dissolve. **-4.** ECOL to endanger.

◆ **extinguir-se** *vp* **-1.** [fogo] to go out. **-2.** [desaparecer] to disappear. **-3.** ECOL to become extinct.

extinto, ta [iʃ'tʃĩntu, ta] *adj* **-1.** [ger] extinct. **-2.** [fogo] extinguished. **-3.** [associação] defunct.

extintor [iʃtʃĩn'to(x)] (*pl* **-res**) *m*: **~ (de incêndio)** (fire) extinguisher.

extirpar [4] [iʃtix'pa(x)] *vt* **-1.** [arrancar] to pull out. **-2.** [extrair - dente] to extract; [- tumor] to remove. **-3.** [erradicar] to eradicate.

extorquir [79] [iʃtox'ki(x)] *vt*: **~ algo (de alguém)** to extort sthg (from sb).

extorsão [iʃtox'sãw] (*pl* **-ões**) *f* extortion.

extorsivo, va [iʃtox'sivu, va] *adj* extortionate.

extra ['ɛʃtra] ◇ *adj* [extraordinário] extra. ◇ *mf* extra.

extração [iʃtra'sãw] (*pl* **-ões**) *f* **-1.** [ger] extraction. **-2.** [sorteio] draw.

extraconjugal [ɛʃtrakõnʒu'gaw] (*pl* **-ais**) *adj* extramarital.

extracurricular [ɛʃtrakuxiku'la(x)] *adj* extracurricular.

extradição [eʃtradʒi'sãw] (*pl* **-ões**) *f* extradition.

extraditar [4] [iʃtradʒi'ta(x)] *vt* to extradite.

extrair [68] [iʃtra'i(x)] *vt* [tirar]: **~ algo (de)** to extract sthg (from).

extrajudicial [ɛʃtraʒudʒi'sjaw] (*pl* **-ais**) *adj* extrajudicial.

extranet [ejʃtra'neti] *f* COMPUT extranet.

extra-oficial [ɛʃtraofi'sjaw] (*pl* **-ais**) *adj* unofficial.

extraordinário, ria [iʃtraordʒi'narju, rja] *adj* extraordinary.

extrapolação [eʃtrapola'sãw] (*pl* **-ões**) *f* extrapolation.

extrapolar [4] [iʃtrapo'la(x)] *vt* to go beyond.

extraterreno, na [iʃtra'texenu, na] *adj* extraterrestrial.

extraterrestre [eʃtrate'xɛʃtri] ◇ *adj* extraterrestrial. ◇ *mf* extraterrestrial.

extrato [iʃ'tratu] *m* **-1.** [ger] extract; **~ de tomate** tomato puree. **-2.** [resumo] excerpt; **~ bancário** bank statement.

extravagância [iʃtrava'gãnsja] *f* extravagance; **fazer uma ~** to be extravagant.

extravagante [iʃtrava'gãntʃi] ◇ *adj* [excêntrico] eccentric.

extravasar [4] [iʃtrava'sa(x)] ◇ *vt* [exteriorizar - sentimento, alegria] to show; [- raiva] to give vent to. ◇ *vi* **-1.** [expandir-se] to burst out. **-2.** [transbordar] to spill over.

extraviado, da [iʃtra'vjadu, da] *adj* missing.

extraviar [16] [iʃtra'vja(x)] *vt* **-1.** [perder] to lose. **-2.** [dinheiro] to embezzle. **-3.** *fig* [perverter] to lead astray.

◆ **extraviar-se** *vp* **-1.** [carta] to go astray; [processo] to get lost. **-2.** [pessoa - perder-se] to get lost; *fig* [perverter-se] to be led astray.

extravio [iʃtra'viw] *m* **-1.** [perda]: **~ (de algo)** loss (of sthg). **-2.** [roubo] embezzlement.

extremado, da [iʃtre'madu, da] *adj* extreme.

extremar-se [4] [iʃtre'maxsi] *vp*: **~ em esforços** to do one's utmost.

extrema-unção [iʃtremaũn'sãw] (*pl* **extrema-unções**) *f* extreme unction, sacrament of the sick.

extremidade [iʃtremi'dadʒi] *f* **-1.** [fim, limite] end. **-2.** [ponta] tip. **-3.** [beira] edge.

◆ **extremidades** *fpl* ANAT extremities.

extremista [iʃtre'miʃta] ◇ *adj* extremist. ◇ *mf* extremist.

extremo, ma [iʃ'tremu, ma] *adj* (*antes de subst*) **-1.** [ger] extreme; **o Extremo Oriente** the Far East. **-2.** [derradeiro, exagerado] extreme.

◆ **extremo** *m* **-1.** [limite, ponta] extreme; **de um ~ ao outro** from one extreme to another. **-2.** [máximo] utmost; **ao ~** to the utmost.

◆ **extremos** *mpl* [exagero] extremes.

extroversão [iʃtrovex'sãw] *f* extroversion.

extroverter-se [5] [iʃtrovex'texsi] *vp* to become (more) outgoing.

extrovertido, da [iʃtrɔvex'tʃidu, da] ◇ *adj* extrovert. ◇ *m, f* extrovert.
exu [e'ʃu] *m* devil *(in voodoo rituals).*
exuberância [ezube'rãnsja] *f* exuberance.
exuberante [ezube'rãntʃi] *adj* exuberant.
exultação [ezuwta'sãw] *f* exultation.
exultante [ezuw'tãntʃi] *adj* exultant.
exultar [4] [ezuw'ta(x)] *vi:* ~ **(de)** to exult (in).
exumação [ezu'masãw] (*pl* **-ões**) *f* exhumation.
exumar [4] [ezu'ma(x)] *vt* **-1.** [corpo] to exhume. **-2.** *fig* [lembranças] to dig up.
ex-voto [ɛks'vɔtu] (*pl* **ex-votos**) *m* icon.

f, F ['ɛfi] *m* [letra] f, F.
fá [fa] *m MÚS* F, fa(h).
fã [fã] (*pl* **fãs**) *mf* fan.
FAB (*abrev de* **Força Aérea Brasileira**) *m* Brazilian Air Force.
fábrica ['fabrika] *f* factory.
fabricação [fabrika'sãw] (*pl* **-ões**) *f* manufacture; **de ~ caseira** home-made.
fabricante [fabri'kãntʃi] *mf* manufacturer.
fabricar [12] [fabri'ka(x)] *vt* **-1.** [manufaturar] to manufacture. **-2.** [inventar] to fabricate.
fabril [fa'briw] (*pl* **-is**) *adj* manufacturing.
fábula ['fabula] *f* **-1.** [conto] fable. **-2.** *fam* [fortuna] fortune.
fabuloso, osa [fabu'lozu, ɔza] *adj* [ger] fabulous.
faca ['faka] *f* knife; **entrar na ~** *fam* to go under the knife; **estar com a ~ e o queijo na mão** *fam* to have things in hand; **ser uma ~ de dois gumes** *fam* to be a double-edged sword.
facada [fa'kada] *f* **-1.** [golpe] stab; **ser uma ~ pelas costas** *fig* to be a stab in the back. **-2.** *fam* cut; **dar uma ~ em alguém** [pedir dinheiro a alguém] to cadge money off sb.
façanha [fa'sãɲa] *f* exploit.
facão [fa'kãw] (*pl* **-ões**) *m* carving knife.
facção [fak'sãw] (*pl* **-ões**) *f* faction.
faccioso, sa [fak'sjozu, ɔza] *adj* factional.
face ['fasi] *f* **-1.** [ger] face; **fazer ~ a** *fig* [enfrentar] to face up to; [custear] to take on board; **~ a ~** face to face. **-2.** [lado] side. **-3.** [superfície]: **a ~ das águas** the surface of the water; **a ~ da terra** the face of the earth. **-4.** [aspecto] facet.
◆ **em face de** *loc prep* [diante de] faced with.
faceiro, ra [fa'sejru, ra] *adj* **-1.** [alegre - pessoa, sorriso] cheerful; [- dança] merry. **-2.** [elegante] smart.
fáceis ['fasejʃ] *pl* ▷ **fácil**.
faceta [fa'seta] *f* [aspecto] facet.
facetado, da [fase'tadu, da] *adj* [pedra] faceted.
fachada [fa'ʃada] *f* **-1.** [de prédio] façade. **-2.** *fig fam* [aparência] mug; **ser só ~** to be merely a façade.
facho ['faʃu] *m* beam.
facial [fa'sjaw] (*pl* **-ais**) *adj* facial.
fácil ['fasiw] (*pl* **-eis**) *adj* **-1.** [simples] easy. **-2.** [dócil] easy(-going). **-3.** *pej* [mulher] easy.
◆ **fácil** *adv* easily.
facilidade [fasili'dadʒi] *f* **-1.** [ausência de dificuldade] ease; **com ~** easily. **-2.** [aptidão]: **ter ~ (para algo)** to have an aptitude (for sthg).
◆ **facilidades** *fpl* [meios] facilities.
facílimo, ma [fa'silimu, ma] *adj superl* ▷ **fácil**.
facilitação [fasilita'sãw] *f* **-1.** [ato] facilitation. **-2.** [fornecimento] provision.
facilitar [4] [fasili'ta(x)] ◇ *vt* **-1.** [tornar fácil] to make easy. **-2.** [facultar] to facilitate. ◇ *vi* [descuidar-se] to be careless.
facínora [fa'sinora] *m* criminal.
fã-clube [fãn'klubi] (*pl* **fãs-clubes**) *m* fan club.
facões [fa'kõjʃ] *pl* ▷ **facão**.
fac-símile [fak'simili] (*pl* **fac-símiles**) *m* **-1.** [cópia] facsimile. **-2.** [máquina] fax machine.
factível [fak'tʃivew] (*pl* **-eis**) *adj* feasible.
factótum [fak'tɔtũ] *m* factotum.
faculdade [fakuw'dadʒi] *f* **-1.** [capacidade] faculty. **-2.** [propriedade] property. **-3.** [escola superior] faculty.
facultar [4] [fakuw'ta(x)] *vt* **-1.** [conceder] to grant. **-2.** [permitir] to permit.
facultativo, va [fakuwta'tʃivu, va] ◇ *adj* optional. ◇ *m, f* (medical) doctor.
fada ['fada] *f* fairy.
fadado, da [fa'dadu, da] *adj*: **estar ~ a algo** to be fated to sthg.
fada-madrinha [,fadama'driɲa] (*pl* **fadas-madrinhas**) *f* fairy godmother.
fadiga [fa'dʒiga] *f* fatigue.
fado ['fadu] *m* **-1.** [destino] fate. **-2.** *MÚS* fado, *type of Portuguese folk song.*
fagueiro, ra [fa'gejru, ra] *adj* **-1.** [meigo] sweet. **-2.** [agradável] pleasant. **-3.** [contente] happy.
fagulha [fa'guʎa] *f* spark.
fahrenheit [fare'najtʃi] *adj* Fahrenheit.
faia ['faja] *f* beech tree.
fair-play [fɛx'plej] *m* fair play.
faisão [faj'zãw] (*pl* **-ões**) *m* pheasant.
faísca [fa'iʃka] *f* spark.
faiscante [fajʃ'kãntʃi] *adj* **-1.** [fogo] flickering. **-2.** [olhos] sparkling.
faiscar [12] [fajʃ'ka(x)] *vi* **-1.** [fogo] to flicker. **-2.** [olhos] to flash.
faixa ['fajʃa] *f* **-1.** [tira] strip. **-2.** [para a cintura] belt. **-3.** [para o peito] sash; **~ de campeão/miss** champion's/beauty queen's sash; **~ presidencial** presidential sash. **-4.** [para pedestres]: **~ (de pedestres)** (pedestrian) crossing. **-5.** [pista] lane. **-6.** [atadura] bandage. **-7.** [de terra] strip.

-**8.** [para mensagem] banner. -**9.** [intervalo] interval; ~ **etária** age group; ~ **salarial** salary band. -**10.** [de disco] track.

faixa-título [ˌfajʃa'tʃitulu] (*pl* **faixas-título**) *f* [de disco] title track.

fajuto, ta [fa'ʒutu, ta] *adj fam* -**1.** [de má qualidade - tecido, equipamento] shoddy; [- político] second-rate. -**2.** [dinheiro] counterfeit.

fala ['fala] *f* -**1.** [ger] speech; **perder a** ~ to be struck dumb. -**2.** [parte de diálogo] words *(pl)*.

falação [fala'sãw] (*pl* **-ões**) *f fam* -**1.** [ato] talk. -**2.** [discurso] speech.

falácia [fa'lasja] *f* fallacy.

faladeira [fala'dejra] *adj & f* ▷ **falador**.

falado, da [fa'ladu, da] *adj* -**1.** [comentado] much talked about. -**2.** [famoso] well-known. -**3.** *fam* [de má fama] notorious.

falador, deira [fala'do(x), dejra] (*mpl* **-es**, *fpl* **-s**) ◇ *adj* [pessoa] talkative. ◇ *m,f* [pessoa] chatterbox.

falange [fa'lãnʒi] *f* phalanx.

falante [fa'lãntʃi] *adj* talking.

falar [4] [fa'la(x)] ◇ *vi* -**1.** [verbalmente] to speak; ~ **de** *ou* **em algo** to talk about sthg; ~ **com alguém** to speak to sb; ~ **alto/baixo** to speak loudly/softly; ~ **alto com alguém** *fig* to give sb a good talking-to; ~ **da boca para fora** *fam* not to mean a word one is saying; ~ **em inglês/espanhol** to speak in English/Spanish; ~ **mais alto** *fig* to win the day; ~ **para dentro** to mumble; ~ **pelos cotovelos** [falar muito] to talk one's head off; ~ **por alguém** to speak on behalf of sb; ~ **por** ~ to talk for the sake of talking; ~ **sozinho/dormindo** to talk to o.s./in one's sleep; **por** ~ **em ...** speaking *ou* talking of ...; **sem** ~ **de** *ou* **em ...** not to mention ...; **agora, falando sério, ...** but seriously, ...; **falou, está falado!** *fam* [OK] OK! -**2.** [discursar] to make a speech. -**3.** [tratar]: ~ **de** *ou* **sobre algo** to talk about sthg. -**4.** [confessar] to talk. ◇ *vt* -**1.** [idioma]: ~ **inglês/espanhol** to speak English/Spanish. -**2.** [dizer] to say; ~ **que** to say that; ~ **bem/mal de** to speak well/ill of; ~ **bobagem** to talk nonsense. -**3.** [contar]: ~ **algo (a alguém)** to tell (sb) sthg -**4.** *loc*: **dar o que** ~ [ser muito comentado] to cause a stir.

◆ **falar-se** *vp* -**1.** [dialogar] to talk. -**2.** [estar em boas relações] to be talking to one another; **não se** ~ to not be talking to one another.

falatório [fala'tɔrju] *m* -**1.** [ruído] voices *(pl)*. -**2.** [discurso] diatribe. -**3.** [maledicência] slander.

falcão [faw'kãw] (*pl* **-ões**) *m* falcon.

falcatrua [fawka'trua] *f* fraud.

falecer [25] [fale'se(x)] *vi* to pass away.

falecido, da [fale'sidu, da] ◇ *adj* [pessoa] deceased. ◇ *m, f* [pessoa] deceased.

falecimento [falesi'mẽntu] *m* decease.

falência [fa'lẽnsja] *f* bankruptcy; **abrir** ~ to declare o.s. bankrupt; **ir à** ~ to go bankrupt; **levar à** ~ to bankrupt.

falésia [fa'lɛzja] *f* cliff.

falha ['faʎa] *f* -**1.** [fenda] fault. -**2.** [defeito] defect. -**3.** [omissão] omission.

falhar [4] [fa'ʎa(x)] ◇ *vt* -**1.** [errar] to fail. -**2.** [faltar com - promessa] to break; [- obrigação] to fail. ◇ *vi* -**1.** [não funcionar, fracassar] to fail. -**2.** [não acertar] to miss.

falho, lha ['faʎu, ʎa] *adj* -**1.** [defeituoso] faulty. -**2.** [deficiente] flawed.

fálico, ca ['faliku, ka] *adj* phallic.

falido, da [fa'lidu, da] ◇ *adj* bankrupt. ◇ *m, f* bankrupt.

falir [79] [fa'li(x)] *vi* -**1.** [abrir falência] to go bankrupt. -**2.** [fracassar] to fail.

falível [fa'livew] (*pl* **-eis**) *adj* fallible.

falo ['falu] *m* phallus.

falsário, ria [faw'sarju, rja] *m* -**1.** [falsificador] forger. -**2.** [perjuro] perjurer.

falsear [15] [faw'sja(x)] ◇ *vt* [falsificar] to falsify. ◇ *vi* [pisar em falso] to miss one's step.

falsete [faw'setʃi] *m* MÚS falsetto.

falsidade [fawsi'dadʒi] *f* -**1.** [fingimento] hypocrisy. -**2.** [mentira] lie; ~ **ideológica** false declaration.

falsificação [fawsifika'sãw] (*pl* **-ões**) *f* forgery.

falsificador, ra [fawsifika'do(x), ra] *m, f* [pessoa] forger.

falsificar [12] [fawsifi'ka(x)] *vt* -**1.** [ger] to forge. -**2.** [adulterar - alimento, remédio] to adulterate; [- documento] to falsify. -**3.** [desvirtuar] to misrepresent.

falso, sa ['fawsu, sa] *adj* -**1.** [ger] false. -**2.** [falsificado] forged. -**3.** [fingido] deceitful. -**4.** [errôneo] erroneous. -**5.** *loc*: **pisar em** ~ to miss one's step.

falso-testemunho [ˌfawsoteʃte'muɲu] (*pl* **falsos-testemunhos**) *m* false witness.

falta ['fawta] *f* -**1.** [carência] lack; **ter** ~ **de** to be in need of; ~ **de água** water shortage; ~ **de ar** airlessness; ~ **de respeito** lack of respect; ~ **de responsabilidade** lack of responsibility. -**2.** [ausência] absence; **sentir** ~ **de algo/alguém** to miss sthg/sb; **na** ~ **de** for lack of; **sem** ~ without fail. -**3.** [erro, pecado] fault. -**4.** ESP foul; **cobrar/-cometer uma** ~ to commit a foul.

faltar [4] [faw'ta(x)] *vi* -**1.** [não haver]: **falta água/luz/comida** there's no water/electricity/food; **falta honestidade** there's a lack of honesty; ~ **sal/tempero** to need salt/seasoning. -**2.** [estar ausente] to be absent; **ontem faltaram cinco alunos** yesterday five students were absent; **falta o Hélio** Hélio's not here, Hélio's missing. -**3.** [ser escasso]: **falta-lhe dinheiro** he hasn't got enough money; **falta-lhe saúde** he's not too healthy; **faltou-lhe força de vontade** he lacked the willpower; **nada nos falta** we have everything we need, we want for nothing. -**4.** [restar - por fazer]: **só falta fazermos o bolo** all that's left for us to do is make the cake; **falta pintarmos a casa** we've still got to paint the house; [- por acontecer]: **só me faltava essa!** *fam* that's all I needed!; [- por decorrer]: **faltam dois meses para o**

festival there are two months to go before the festival; **falta uma semana para irmos embora** it's a week until we go. **-5.** [omitir-se]: **nunca faltou quando a família precisava** he was always there when the family needed him. **-6.** [morrer] to die.

falto, ta ['fawtu, ta] *adj*: ~ **de** lacking in.

faltoso, osa [faw'tozu, ɔza] *adj* **-1.** [culpado] guilty. **-2.** [que falta muito] frequently absent.

fama ['fãma] *f* **-1.** [celebridade] fame. **-2.** [reputação] reputation; **de** ~ by reputation; **de má** ~ of ill repute.

famigerado, da [famiʒe'radu, da] *adj* [célebre] famous.

família [fa'milja] ◇ *f* family; **de boa** ~ from a good family; **estar em** ~ to be one of the family; **ser de** ~ to run in the family. ◇ *adj fam* [decente]: **ser** ~ to be respectable.

familiar [fami'lja(x)] (*pl* **-es**) ◇ *adj* **-1.** [relativo à família] family *(antes de subst)*. **-2.** [conhecido] familiar. ◇ *mf* [pessoa da família]: **um** ~ a family member; **os** ~**es** the family *(sg)*.

familiaridade [familjari'dadʒi] *f* **-1.** [intimidade] familiarity. **-2.** [informalidade] informality.

familiarização [familjariza'sãw] *f* familiarization.

familiarizar [4] [familjari'za(x)] *vt* to familiarize.
◆ **familiarizar-se** *vp*: ~**-se com algo/alguém** to familiarize o.s. with sthg/sb.

faminto, ta [fa'mĩntu, ta] *adj* famished.

famoso, osa [fa'mozu, ɔza] *adj* famous.

fanático, ca [fa'natʃiku, ka] ◇ *adj* **-1.** POL & RELIG fanatical. **-2.** [apaixonado]: ~ **(por)** crazy (about). ◇ *m, f* [pessoa] fanatic.

fanatismo [fana'tʃiʒmu] *m* fanaticism.

fanfarrão, ona [fãfa'xãw, ɔna] (*mpl* **-ões**, *fpl* **-s**) ◇ *adj* boastful. ◇ *m, f* braggart.

fanfarronice [fãnwfaxo'nisi] *f* [gabarolice] boasting.

fanho, nha ['faɲu, ɲa], **fanhoso, sa** [fã'ɲozu, za] *adj* **-1.** [voz] nasal. **-2.** [pessoa] *with a nasal-sounding voice.*

faniquito [fani'kitu] *m fam* strop; **dar um** ~ to get into a strop.

fantasia [fãnta'zia] *f* **-1.** [coisa imaginada] fantasy; **jóia de** ~ [bijuteria] costume jewellery. **-2.** [imaginação] fancy. **-3.** [capricho] whim. **-4.** [traje] fancy dress; ~ **de Carnaval** fancy dress; ~ **de árabe/pirata** Arab/pirate costume. **-5.** MÚS fantasia.

fantasiar [16] [fãnta'zja(x)] *vt* **-1.** [imaginar] to imagine. **-2.** [pôr fantasia]: ~ **alguém de algo** to dress sb up as sthg. **-3.** [devanear] to daydream.
◆ **fantasiar-se** *vp*: ~**-se (de)** to dress up (as).

fantasioso, osa [fãta'zjozu, ɔza] *adj* fanciful.

fantasista [fãta'ziʃta] ◇ *adj* fanciful. ◇ *mf* whimsical person.

fantasma [fãn'taʒma] *m* **-1.** [espectro] ghost. **-2.** [alucinação] phantom. **-3.** *fig* [coisa terrível] spectre.

fantasmagórico, ca [fãtazma'gɔriku, ka] *adj* phantasmagorical.

fantástico, ca [fãn'taʃtʃiku, ka] *adj* **-1.** [ger] fantastic. **-2.** *fam* [ótimo] fantastic.
◆ **fantástico** *m* [fantasia]: **o** ~ the fantastic.

fantoche [fãn'tɔʃi] *m* puppet.

fanzoca [fãn'zɔka] *mf mfam* junkie.

FAQs (*abrev de* **Frequently Asked Questions**) *fpl* FAQs.

faqueiro [fa'kejru] *m* **-1.** [jogo de talheres] cutlery set. **-2.** [pessoa] cutler.

faquir [fa'ki(x)] *m* fakir.

faraó [fara'ɔ] *m* pharaoh.

faraônico, ca [fara'oniku, ka] *adj* **-1.** [relativo aos faraós] pharaonic. **-2.** *fig* [grandioso] grandiose.

FARC (*abrev de* **Forças Armadas Revolucionárias da Colômbia**) *f* FARC.

farda ['faxda] *f* [uniforme] uniform.

fardar [4] [fax'da(x)] *vt* to put in uniform.

fardo ['faxdu] *m* **-1.** [carga] load. **-2.** *fig* [peso] burden.

farejar [4] [fare'ʒa(x)] ◇ *vt* to sniff. ◇ *vi* [tomar o faro] to pick up the scent.

farelento, ta [fare'lẽntu, ta] *adj* crumbly.

farelo [fa'rɛlu] *m* **-1.** [de pão] crumb. **-2.** [de cereal] husk; ~ **de trigo** wheat bran.

farfalhante [faxfa'ʎãntʃi] *adj* rustling.

farfalhar [4] [faxfa'ʎa(x)] *vi* to rustle.

farináceo, cea [fari'nasju, sja] *adj* farinaceous.
◆ **farináceos** *mpl* [alimentos] starchy foods.

faringe [fa'rĩnʒi] *f* pharynx.

faringite [farĩn'ʒiti] *f* pharyngitis.

farinha [fa'riɲa] *f*: ~ **(de mesa** *ou* **de mandioca)** cassava flour; ~ **de rosca** toasted breadcrumbs; ~ **de trigo** wheat flour.

farinhento, ta [fari'ɲẽntu, ta] *adj* [que se esfarinha] floury.

farmacêutico, ca [farma'sewtiku, ka] ◇ *adj* pharmaceutical. ◇ *m, f* pharmacist.

farmácia [fax'masja] *f* **-1.** [ger] pharmacy. **-2.** [coleção de medicamentos] first-aid box *ou* cabinet.

farmacologia [faxmakolo'ʒia] *f* pharmacology.

farnel [fax'nɛw] (*pl* **-éis**) *m* **-1.** [provisões] packed meal. **-2.** [saco] lunch box.

faro ['faru] *m* **-1.** [olfato] sense of smell. **-2.** *fig* [intuição] nose.

faroeste [fa'rwɛʃtʃi] *m* **-1.** [filme] western. **-2.** [região] far west.

farofa [fa'rɔfa] *f* CULIN fried manioc flour

farofeiro, ra [faro'fejru, ra] *m, f fam* [de praia] beach bum.

farol [fa'rɔw] (*pl* **-óis**) *m* **-1.** [para navegantes] lighthouse. **-2.** AUTO headlight; ~ **alto/baixo** full/low beam.

faroleiro [faro'lejru] *m* lighthouse keeper.

farolete [farɔ'leti] *m* AUTO indicator; ~ **dianteiro** sidelight; ~ **traseiro** rear light.

farpa ['faxpa] *f* **-1.** [de madeira] splinter. **-2.** [metálica] shard. **-3.** *fam* [crítica] barb.

farpado, da [fax'padu, da] *adj* ▷ **arame**.

farra ['faxa] *f* binge; **cair na** ~ to paint the town red; **fazer algo de** *ou* **por** ~ to do sthg as a joke.

farrapo [fa'xapu] *m* [trapo] rag; **estar um** ~ *fig*

[coisa] to be ragged; [pessoa] to be in rags; ~ **humano** failure.
farrear [15] [fa'xja(x)] *vi* to rave.
farrista [fa'xiʃta] <> *adj* fun-loving. <> *mf* raver.
farsa ['faxsa] *f* **-1.** *TEATRO* farce. **-2.** *fig* [fraude] sham; **ser uma** ~ to be a sham.
farsante [fax'sãntʃi] *mf* **-1.** [pessoa sem palavra] fraud. **-2.** [pessoa brincalhona] buffoon.
farsesco, ca [fax'seʃku, ka] *adj* farsical.
fartar [4] [fax'ta(x)] *vt* **-1.** [saciar] to satiate; ~ **alguém com** to stuff sb with. **-2.** [cansar]: ~ **alguém (com)** to wear sb out (with).
◆ **fartar-se** *vp* **-1.** [saciar-se]: **~-se (de algo)** to gorge (on sthg). **-2.** [cansar-se]: **~-se (de algo/alguém)** to have had enough of sthg/sb.
farto, ta ['faxtu, ta] *adj* **-1.** [saciado] replete. **-2.** [abundante] lavish. **-3.** [cansado]: **estar** ~ **(de algo/alguém)** to be fed up (with sthg/sb).
fartura [fax'tura] *f* [abundância] abundance; ~ **de algo** abundance of sthg.
fascículo [fa'sikulu] *m* [de publicação] fascicle.
fascinação [fasina'sãw] *f* **-1.** [atração] fascination; **ter** ~ **por algo/alguém** to be fascinated by sthg/sb. **-2.** [deslumbramento] delight.
fascinante [fasi'nãntʃi] *adj* **-1.** [cativante] fascinating. **-2.** [deslumbrante] amazing.
fascinar [4] [fasi'na(x)] <> *vt* [cativar] to fascinate. <> *vi* [deslumbrar] to delight.
fascínio [fa'sinju] *m* [atração] fascination.
fascismo [fa'siʒmu] *m* fascism.
fascista [fa'siʃta] <> *adj* fascist. <> *mf* fascist.
fase ['fazi] *f* **-1.** [ger] phase; **ser só** ~ to be a passing phase. **-2.** *ASTRON*: **as ~s da Lua** the phases of the moon.
fastidioso, osa [faʃtʃi'dʒjozu, ɔza] *adj* fastidious.
fastígio [faʃ'tʃiʒu] *m* apex.
fastio [faʃ'tʃiu] *m* **-1.** [falta de apetite] lack of appetite. **-2.** [tédio] boredom.
FAT (*abrev de* **Fundo de Amparo ao Trabalhador**) *m* *Brazilan fund for the support of workers.*
fatal [fa'taw] (*pl* **-ais**) *adj* **-1.** [mortal] fatal. **-2.** [inevitável] inevitable.
fatalidade [fatali'dadʒi] *f* **-1.** [destino] fate. **-2.** [desgraça] misfortune.
fatalista [fata'liʃta] <> *adj* fatalistic. <> *mf* fatalist.
fatalmente [fataw'mẽntʃi] *adv* **-1.** [mortalmente] fatally. **-2.** [certamente] surely. **-3.** [inevitavelmente] inevitably.
fatia [fa'tʃia] *f* slice.
fatiado, da [fa'tʃiadu, da] *adj* sliced.
fatiar [4] [fa'tʃja(x)] *vt* to slice.
fatídico, ca [fa'tʃidʒiku, ka] *adj* fateful.
fatigante [fati'gãntʃi] *adj* **-1.** [cansativo] tiresome. **-2.** [enfadonho] tedious.
fatigar [14] [fati'ga(x)] *vt* **-1.** [cansar] to tire. **-2.** [enfadar] to bore.
◆ **fatigar-se** *vp* **-1.** [cansar-se] to tire. **-2.** [enfadar-se] to become bored.
fato ['fatu] *m* [ger] fact; ~ **consumado** fait accompli; **ser (um)** ~ to be a fact.
◆ **de fato** *loc adv* in fact.
fator [fa'to(x)] (*mpl* **-res**) *m* factor; ~ **Rh** rhesus factor.
fátuo, tua ['fatwu, twa] *adj* [vão] fatuous.
fatura [fa'tura] *f* invoice.
faturamento [fatura'mẽntu] *m* **-1.** *COM* turnover. **-2.** [fatura] invoicing.
faturar [4] [fatu'ra(x)] <> *vt* **-1.** [mercadorias]: ~ **algo a alguém** to invoice sb for sthg. **-2.** [dinheiro]: **faturou um bom dinheiro** he got a good price. **-3.** *fam* [obter] to land. <> *vi fam* [ganhar dinheiro] to rake it in; ~ **alto** to make loads of dosh.
fauna ['fawna] *f* fauna.
fausto, ta [fawʃtu, ta] *adj* fortunate.
◆ **fausto** *m* luxury.
faustoso, sa [fawʃ'tozu, ɔza] *adj* [luxuoso] sumptuous.
fava ['fava] *f*: **ser ~s contadas** to be a sure thing; **mandar alguém às ~s** to send sb on their way.
favela [fa'vɛla] *f* slum.

FAVELAS

Urban phenomenon common to all large cities of Brazil, *favelas* are nuclei of crude, improvised dwellings, found inside built-up areas or on the outskirts of the cities. Devoid of basic public amenities, such as water and sewerage, *favelas* are generally made up of conglomerations of dwellings known as *barracos*, built of various materials such as pieces of wood and pasteboard. In some cases, however, the houses can be made of masonry.

favelado, da [favɛ'ladu, da] *m, f* slum dweller.
favo ['favu] *m* honeycomb.
favor [fa'vo(x)] (*pl* **-es**) *m* **-1.** [ger] favour ***UK***, favor ***US***; **fazer um** ~ **para alguém** to do sb a favour ***UK***, to do sb a favor ***US***; **pedir um** ~ **a alguém** to ask a favour of sb ***UK***, to ask a favor of sb ***US***; **por** ~ please; **por ~, que horas são?** excuse me, what time is it?; *fam* [em reprimenda] do me a favour!; **quer fazer o** ~ **de se calar?** would you kindly shut up! **-2.** [benefício]: **a** ~ **de** in favour of ***UK***, in favor of ***US***; **em** ~ **de** for; **ter algo a seu** ~ to have sthg in one's favour ***UK*** *ou* favor ***US***.
favorável [favo'ravɛw] (*pl* **-eis**) *adj*: ~ **(a algo/a fazer algo)** favourable (to sthg/to doing sthg).
favorecer [25] [favore'se(x)] *vt* **-1.** [ger] to favour ***UK***, to favor ***US***. **-2.** [melhorar] to improve.
◆ **favorecer-se** *vp* [beneficiar-se] to take advantage of.
favorecido, da [favore'sidu, da] <> *adj* [protegido] favourite. <> *m, f* [beneficiário] beneficiary.
favoritismo [favori'tʃiʒmu] *m* favouritism ***UK***, favoritism ***US***.
favorito, ta [favo'ritu, ta] <> *adj* favourite ***UK***, favorite ***US***. <> *m, f* favourite ***UK***, favorite ***US***.
faxina [fa'ʃina] *f* bundle of twigs; **fazer uma** ~ to have a spring clean.
faxineiro, ra [faʃi'nejru, ra] *m, f* cleaner.

fax-modem (*pl* **-dens**) *m* fax-modem.

faz-de-conta [ˌfajʒdʒiˈkõnta] *m* make-believe.

fazenda [faˈzẽnda] *f* **-1.** [propriedade rural] fazenda. **-2.** [de gado] cattle ranch. **-3.** [de café, cacau] plantation. **-4.** [tecido] cloth. **-5.** *ECON* revenue.

fazenda-modelo [faˌzẽndamoˈdɛlu] (*pl* **fazendas-modelos, fazendas-modelo**) *f* model ranch.

fazendeiro, ra [fazẽnˈdejru, ra] *m, f* **-1.** [dono de fazenda] rancher. **-2.** [de café, cacau] planter. **-3.** [de gado] cattle rancher.

fazer [31] [faˈze(x)] <> *vt* **-1.** [produzir] to make; ~ **muito barulho** to make a lot of noise; ~ **planos/um vestido** to make plans/a dress; ~ **uma pergunta** to ask a question. **-2.** [comida] to cook.**-3.** [gerar] to produce. **-4.** [realizar]: **estou fazendo um curso de computadores** I'm taking a computer course; **vamos ~ uma festa** let's have a party. **-5.** [praticar] to do; **você devia ~ mais exercício** you should exercise more; **faço jogging todas as manhãs** I go jogging every morning. **-6.** [cama] to make; ~ **a cama** to make the bed. **-7.** [transformar] to make; ~ **alguém feliz** to make sb happy. **-8.** [anos]: **faço anos amanhã** it's my birthday tomorrow; **fazemos cinco anos de casados** we've been married (for) five years. **-9.** [obrigar] to make; ~ **alguém fazer algo** to make sb do sthg; ~ **alguém rir/chorar** to make sb laugh/cry. **-10.** [cálculo, conta] to do; **faz a conta para ver quanto é** work out the check to see what it comes to.<> *vi* **-1.** [causar]: ~ **bem/mal a algo** to be good/bad for sthg; ~ **bem/mal a alguém** [coisa] to be good/bad for sb; ~ **mal a alguém** [pessoa] to hurt sb. **-2.** [obrigar]: **faça (com) que ele venha** make him come; [imaginar]: ~ **de conta que ...** to pretend that ...<> *v impess* **-1.**: **faz frio/calor** it's cold/hot. **-2.** [tempo]: **faz um ano que não o vejo** it's been a year since I last saw him; **faz tempo que estou à espera** I've been waiting for a while; **o Sérgio partiu faz três meses** Sérgio left three months ago. **-3.** [importar]: **não faz mal se está quebrado** it doesn't matter if it's broken; **tanto faz** it doesn't matter.

◆ **fazer-se** *vp* [preparar-se] to be made; [ser correto]: **é assim que se faz** that's the way to do it; **~-se com** [ser preparado com] to be made with.

◆ **fazer-se de** *vp + prep* [pretender ser]: **ele gosta de ~-se de importante** he likes to act important; **~-se de tolo** to act stupid; **~-se de desentendido** to feign ignorance.

faz-tudo [fajʒˈtudu] *mf inv* handyman.

FBI (*abrev de* **Federal Bureau of Investigation**) *m* FBI.

fé [ˈfɛ] *f* [ger] faith; **de boa ~** in good faith; **de má ~** dishonestly; **fazer ~ em** to have faith in.

fealdade [feawˈdadʒi] *f* ugliness.

FEBEM (*abrev de* **Fundação Estadual do Bem-Estar do Menor**) *f organization set up by individual states in Brazil for the rehabilitation of young offenders.*

Febraban (*abrev de* **Federação Brasileira de Associações de Bancos**) *f Brazilian banking representative body.*

febrão [feˈbrãw] (*pl* **-ões**) *m* acute fever.

febre [ˈfɛbri] *f* **-1.** *MED* fever; ~ **amarela** yellow fever; ~ **do feno** hayfever. **-2.** *fig* [desejo]: ~ **de fortuna/poder** longing for fortune/power. **-3.** *fig* [mania] mania.

febril [feˈbriw] (*pl* **-is**) *adj* feverish.

fecal [feˈkaw] (*pl* **-ais**) *adj* faecal.

fechado, da [feˈʃadu, da] *adj* **-1.** [ger] closed. **-2.** [pessoa] reticent. **-3.** *AUTO* [sinal] red light. **-4.** [tempo, céu] overcast. **-5.** [mato] dense. **-6.** [expressão] blank.

◆ **fechada** *f AUTO*: **dar uma ~ em alguém** to cut in front of sb; **levei uma ~ de ele** he cut in front of me.

fechadura [feʃaˈdura] *f* lock.

fechamento [feʃaˈmẽntu] *m* closure.

fechar [4] [feˈʃa(x)] <> *vt* **-1.** [ger] to close. **-2.** *AUTO* to cut in front of. <> *vi* **-1.** [cicatrizar-se] to close. **-2.** [tempo] to turn close. **-3.** [sinal de trânsito] to turn red. **-4.** [parar de funcionar] to close down.

◆ **fechar-se** *vp* **-1.** [encerrar-se] to close o.s. off. **-2.** [retrair-se] to shut o.s. off.

fecho [ˈfeʃu] *m* **-1.** [de roupa] fastening; ~ **ecler** zip. **-2.** [de porta, bolsa] catch. **-3.** [término] end.

fécula [ˈfɛkula] *f* starch.

fecundação [fekũndaˈsãw] (*pl* **-ões**) *f* fertilization.

fecundar [4] [fekũnˈda(x)] *vt* to fertilize.

fecundidade [fekũndʒiˈdadʒi] *vt* fertility.

fecundo, da [feˈkũndu, da] *adj* **-1.** [ger] fertile. **-2.** *fig* [criador] creative.

fedelho, lha [feˈdeʎu, ʎa] *m, f fam* brat.

fedentina [fedẽnˈtʃina] *f* stench.

feder [5] [feˈde(x)] *vi* to stink; **não ~ nem cheirar** to be wishy-washy.

federação [federaˈsãw] (*pl* **-ões**) *f* federation.

federal [fedeˈraw] (*pl* **-ais**) *adj* **-1.** [da Federação] federal. **-2.** *fam* [enorme] huge.

federalismo [federaˈliʒmu] *m* federalism.

federalizar [4] [federaliˈza(x)] *vt* to federalize.

federativo, va [federaˈtʃivu, va] *adj* federalist.

fedido, da [feˈʒidu, da] *adj* stinking.

fedor [feˈdo(x)] *m* stench.

fedorento, ta [fedoˈrẽntu, ta] *adj* stinking.

feedback [ˌfidʒiˈbɛki] *m* feedback.

feição [fejˈsãw] (*pl* **-ões**) *f* **-1.** [forma] shape. **-2.** [natureza] character **à ~ de** [ao jeito de] in the manner of.

◆ **feições** *fpl* [face] features.

feijão [fejˈʒãw] (*pl* **-ões**) *m* bean.

feijão-fradinho [fejʒãwfraˈdʒiɲu] (*pl* **feijões-fradinhos**) *m* black-eyed bean.

feijão-mulatinho [fejʒãwmulaˈtʃiɲu] (*pl* **feijões-mulatinhos**) *m* kidney bean.

feijão-preto [fejʒãwˈpretu] (*pl* **feijões-pretos**) *m* black bean.

feijão-tropeiro [fejʒãwtroˈpejru] (*pl* **feijões-tropeiros**) *m* bean casserole.

feijoada [fej'ʒwada] *f typical Brazilian dish made with black beans, pork, sausage and vegetables.*

FEIJOADA

A typical Brazilian dish, *feijoada* consists of black beans stewed with pork (dried meat, rib, loin, tail, trotter, ear). It is generally served with chopped cabbage, *farofa* and orange. It is said that the *feijoada* was created by black slaves, who used up those parts of the pig disdained by their masters.

feijoeiro [fej'ʒwejru] *m* bean.
feio, feia ['fejo, 'feja] *adj* **-1.** [ger] ugly. **-2.** [tempo] nasty.
◆ **feio** *adv*: **fazer ~** [dar vexame] to behave badly; **ficar ~** [dar má impressão] to be rude; **perder ~** *ESP* to lose badly.
feioso, osa [fe'jozu, ɔza] *adj* plain.
feira ['fejra] *f* [ger] fair; **~ livre** vegetable market.
feirante [fej'rãntʃi] *mf* stallholder.
feita ['fejta] *f*: **certa ~** once; **de uma ~** once and for all.
feitiçaria [fejtʃisa'ria] *f* witchcraft.
feiticeiro, ra [fejtʃi'sejru, ra] <> *adj* [encantador] bewitching. <> *m, f* [pessoa] sorcerer (*f* witch).
feitiço [fej'tʃisu] *m* spell; **voltar-se o ~ contra o feiticeiro** to be hoist by one's own petard.
feitio [fej'tʃiw] *m* **-1.** [forma] shape. **-2.** [natureza] make-up. **-3.** [de roupa] cut.
feito, ta ['fejtu, ta] <> *pp* ▻ **fazer**. <> *adj* **-1.** [concluído, pronto] finished. **-2.** [adulto]: **homem ~/mulher feita** grown man/woman.
◆ **feito** <> *m* [façanha] deed. <> *conj* [tal qual] just like.
feitor, ra [fej'to(x), ra] *m, f* **-1.** [administrador] manager. **-2.** [capataz] steward.
feitura [fej'tura] *f* make-up.
feiúra [fej'ura] *f* ugliness.
feixe ['fejʃi] *m* **-1.** [molho] bunch. **-2.** [de luz] beam.
fel ['fɛw] *m* **-1.** [ger] bitterness. **-2.** [bílis] bile.
felação [fela'sãw] (*pl* **-ões**) *f* fellatio.
felicidade [felisi'dadʒi] *f* **-1.** [ventura] happiness. **-2.** [êxito] success. **-3.** [boa sorte] good luck.
◆ **felicidades** *fpl* congratulations.
felicíssimo, ma [feli'sisimu, ma] *superl* ▻ **feliz**.
felicitação [felisita'sãw] (*pl* **-ões**) *f* praise.
◆ **felicitações** *fpl* congratulations.
felicitar [4] [felisi'ta(x)] *vt*: **~ alguém (por algo)** to congratulate sb (on sthg).
felino, na [fe'linu, na] <> *adj* **-1.** [ger] feline. **-2.** *fig* [traiçoeiro] sly. <> *m* [animal] feline; **os ~s** the cat family (*sg*).
feliz [fe'liʒ] (*pl* **-es**) *adj* **-1.** [ger] happy; **ser ~ (em algo)** to be lucky (in sthg); **estar/ficar ~** to be happy; **~ aniversário** happy birthday; **Feliz Ano-Novo** happy new year; **Feliz Natal** happy Christmas *UK*, merry Christmas *US*; **ser ~** to be happy. **-2.** [oportuno] good. **-3.** [bem-sucedido] successful.
felizardo, da [feli'zaxdu, da] *m, f* very lucky person.
felizmente [feliʒ'mẽntʃi] *adv* **-1.** [por felicidade] luckily. **-2.** [de modo feliz] happily.
felonia [felo'nia] *f* felony.
felpa ['fewpa] *f* **-1.** [de tecido] nap. **-2.** [de animal] down.
felpudo, da [fɛw'pudu, da] *adj* downy.
feltro ['fewtru] *m* felt.
fêmea ['femja] *f* female.
feminilidade [feminili'dadʒi] *f* femininity.
feminino, na [femi'ninu, na] *adj* feminine.
◆ **feminino** *m GRAM* feminine.
feminismo [femi'niʒmu] *m* feminism.
feminista [femi'niʃta] <> *adj* feminist. <> *mf* feminist.
fêmur ['femu(x)] *m* femur.
fenda ['fẽnda] *f* **-1.** [rachadura] crack. **-2.** *GEOL* crevice.
fender [5] [fẽn'de(x)] *vt* to split.
◆ **fender-se** *vp* to split.
fenecer [25] [fene'se(x)] *vi* **-1.** [extingüir-se] to die out. **-2.** [morrer] to die. **-3.** [murchar] to wilt.
feno ['fenu] *m* hay.
fenomenal [fenome'naw] (*pl* **-ais**) *adj* **-1.** [maravilhoso] wonderful. **-2.** [surpreendente] phenomenal.
fenômeno [fe'nomenu] *m* phenomenon.
fenomenologia [fenomenolo'ʒia] *f* phenomenology.
fera ['fɛra] *f* **-1.** *fig* [ger] brute. **-2.** [animal] wild animal; **ficar uma ~ (com)** to be very angry (with). **-3.** *fam fig* [pessoa perita] ace; **ser (uma) ~ em algo** *fam fig* to be an ace at sthg.
féretro ['fɛretru] *m* coffin.
feriado [fe'rjadu] *m* (public) holiday; **~ bancário** bank holiday *UK*.
férias ['fɛrjaʃ] *fpl* holidays *UK*, vacation (*sg*) *US*; **de ~** on holiday *UK*, on vacation *US*; **entrar/sair de ~** to go on holiday *UK*, to go on vacation *US*; **passar as ~ em** to spend one's holiday in *UK*, to spend one's vacation in *US*; **tirar ~** to take one's holidays *UK*, to take one's vacation *US*.
ferida [fe'rida] *f* wound; **tocar na ~** *fig* to re-open the wound.
ferido, da [fe'ridu, da] <> *adj* **-1.** [machucado] wounded. **-2.** [magoado] wounded. <> *m, f* [pessoa] injured person; **os ~s** the injured.
ferimento [feri'mẽntu] *m* injury.
ferino, na [fe'rinu, na] *adj* **-1.** [cruel] cruel. **-2.** *fig* [mordaz] biting.
ferir [57] [fe'ri(x)] *vt* **-1.** [machucar] to wound. **-2.** *fig* [magoar] to wound.
◆ **ferir-se** *vp* **-1.** [machucar-se] to hurt o.s. **-2.** *fig* [magoar-se]: **~-se com** to be wounded by.
fermentação [fexmẽnta'sãw] (*pl* **-ões**) *f* fermentation.
fermentar [4] [fexmẽn'ta(x)] <> *vt* to ferment. <> *vi* to ferment.
fermento [fex'mẽntu] *m* yeast; **~ em pó** powdered yeast.

Fernando de Noronha *m National Marine Park situated off the coast of Rio Grande do Norte in Brazil.*

FERNANDO DE NORONHA

The archipelago Fernando de Noronha (PE) comprises 19 islands situated 345 km off the coast of Rio Grande do Norte, and totalling 26 km^2. The largest of these islands is the only inhabited one, and is also called Fernando de Noronha. Here is to be found the only urban centre of the islands, Vila dos Remédios. Because of its crystal-clear waters, dolphins, sharks and fifteen species of coral, Fernando de Noronha has been made into a National Marine Park.

ferocidade [ferosi'dadʒi] *f* ferocity.
ferocíssimo, ma [fero'sisimu, ma] *superl* ▷ **feroz.**
feroz [fe'rɔʃ] (*pl* **-es**) *adj* fierce.
ferrado, da [fe'xadu, da] *adj* **-1.** [cavalo] shod. **-2.** *fam fig* [em mau estado] falling apart.
ferradura [fexa'dura] *f* horseshoe.
ferragem [fe'xaʒẽj] (*pl* **-ns**) *f* **-1.** [peças] hardware. **-2.** [guarnição] ironwork.
ferramenta [fexa'mẽnta] *f* tool.
ferramental [fexa'mẽntaw] (*pl* **-ais**) *m* tool kit.
ferrão [fe'xãw] (*pl* **-ões**) *m* **-1.** [de inseto] sting. **-2.** [aguilhão] barb.
ferrar [4] [fe'xa(x)] *vt* **-1.** [ornar de ferro] to decorate with ironwork. **-2.** [cavalgadura] to shoe. **-3.** [marcar a ferro] to brand. **-4.** *fam fig* [prejudicar] to damage.
◆ **ferrar-se** *vp* [sair-se mal] to do badly.
ferreiro [fe'xejru] *m* blacksmith.
ferrenho, nha [fe'xeɲu, ɲa] *adj* **-1.** [inflexível] iron. **-2.** [obstinado] passionate.
férreo, rrea ['fexju, xja] *adj* iron.
ferrete [fe'xetʃi] *m* branding iron.
ferro ['fɛxu] *m* **-1.** [material] iron; **a ~ e fogo** *fig* by hook or by crook; **de ~** *fig* [vontade, punhos] of iron; [pessoa] made of iron; **~ batido** wrought iron; **~ fundido** cast iron; **~ ondulado** corrugated iron; **~ velho** [sucata] scrap metal. **-2.** [aparelho]: **~ (de passar)** iron; **passar a ~** to iron. **-3.** *loc*: **levar ~** to fail.
◆ **ferros** *mpl* [grilhões] chains.
ferroada [fe'xwada] *f* sting.
ferroar [20] [fe'xwa(x)] ◇ *vt* **-1.** [picar] to sting. **-2.** [criticar] to criticize. ◇ *vi* **-1.** [picar] to sting. **-2.** [latejar, doer] to really hurt.
ferrões [fe'xõjʃ] *pl* ▷ **ferrão.**
ferrolho [fe'xoʎu] *m* bolt.
ferroso, sa [fe'xozu, ɔza] *adj* [ferruginoso] rust coloured.
ferro-velho [ˌfɛxu'vɛʎu] (*pl* **ferros-velhos**) *m* **-1.** [estabelecimento] scrapyard. **-2.** [sucata] scrap metal.
ferrovia [fexo'via] *f* railway *UK*, railroad *US*.
ferroviário, ria [fexo'vjarju, ja] ◇ *adj* railway *UK*, railroad *US*. ◇ *m, f* railway employee *UK*, railroad employee *US*.
ferrugem [fe'xuʒẽj] *f* rust.
fértil ['fɛxtiw] (*pl* **-eis**) *adj* **-1.** [terreno, período] fertile. **-2.** [pessoa] productive.
fertilidade [fextʃili'dadʒi] *f* **-1.** [de terra, pessoa] fertility. **-2.** [abundância] abundance.
fertilização [fextʃiliza'sãw] (*pl* **-ões**) *f* fertilization.
fertilizante [fextʃili'zãntʃi] ◇ *adj* fertilizing; **método ~** method of fertilization. ◇ *m* fertilizer.
fertilizar [4] [fextʃili'za(x)] *vt* to fertilize.
fervente [fex'vẽntʃi] *adj* boiling.
ferver [5] [fex've(x)] ◇ *vt* to boil; **~ algo em fogo baixo** to simmer on a low heat. ◇ *vi* to become excited; **~ de raiva** *fig* to be steaming with anger.
fervilhar [4] [fexvi'ʎa(x)] *vi* **-1.** [ferver] to boil. **-2.** *fig* [pulular]: **~ (de)** to swarm (with). **-3.** *fig* [de excitação] to bubble.
fervor [fex'vo(x)] *m* fervour *UK*, fervor *US*.
fervoroso, osa [fexvo'rozu, ɔza] *adj* **-1.** [ardoroso] fervent. **-2.** [dedicado] devoted.
fervura [fex'vura] *f* **-1.** [ebulição] boiling. **-2.** *fig* [efervescência] fervour *UK*, fervor *US*.
festa ['fɛʃta] *f* **-1.** [reunião] party; **~ de arromba** thrash. **-2.** [comemoração]: **~ da Independência** Independence Day party; **~s juninas** *traditional celebrations held in Brazil in June.* **-3.** [alegria] thrill. **-4.** [carinho]: **fazer ~ (s) (em)** to cuddle up to. **-5.** *loc*: **fazer a ~** to have a field day.
◆ **festas** *fpl* [Natal e Ano-Novo] festive season (*sg*).

FESTAS JUNINAS

Popular religious festivals during the month of June; these festivals of ancient origin came over with the Portuguese, and mostly celebrate the feast days of St Anthony (13th), St John (24th) and St Peter (29th). They are celebrated with music, typical drinks and dishes, always including fires and bonfires. Nowadays these festivities are held mainly in the north and north-east of the country.

festança [feʃ'tãnsa] *fam* thrash.
festeiro, ra [feʃ'tejru, ra] *adj* party-going.
festejar [4] [feʃte'ʒa(x)] *vt* to celebrate.
festejo [feʃ'teʒu] *m* celebration.
festim [feʃ'tʃĩ] (*pl* **-ns**) *m* **-1.** [festa] feast. **-2.** [cartucho sem bala]: **tiro de ~** blank shot.
festival [feʃtʃi'vaw] (*pl* **-ais**) *m* **-1.** [festa] festival. **-2.** *fig* [grande quantidade] load.
festividade [feʃtʃivi'dadʒi] *f* festivity.
festivo, va [feʃ'tʃivu, va] *adj* festive.
fetal [fe'taw] (*pl* **-ais**) *adj* foetal *UK*, fetal *US*.
fetiche [fe'tʃiʃi] *m* fetish.
fetichismo [fetʃi'ʃiʒmu] *m* fetishism.
fetichista [fetʃi'ʃiʃta] ◇ *adj* fetishistic. ◇ *m, f* fetishist.
fétido, da ['fɛtʃidu, da] *adj* fetid.
feto ['fɛtu] *m* foetus *UK*, fetus *US*.
feudal [few'daw] (*pl* **-ais**) *adj* feudal.

feudalismo [fewda'liʒmu] *m* feudalism.
fev. (*abrev de* **fevereiro**) Feb.
fevereiro [feve'rejru] *m* February; *veja também* **setembro**.
fezes ['fɛziʃ] *fpl* faeces *UK*, feces *US*.
FGTS (*abrev de* **Fundo de Garantia por Tempo de Serviço**) *m monthly contribution towards the support of sacked and unemployed workers in Brazil.*
FGV (*abrev de* **Fundação Getúlio Vargas**) *f Brazilian private educational organization for improvement in public administration.*
FIA (*abrev de* **Federação Internacional de Automobilismo**) *f* FIA.
fiação [fja'sãw] (*pl* **-ões**) *f* **-1.** *ELETR* wiring; **fazer a ~ (de)** to wire (sthg). **-2.** [fábrica] spinning mill.
fiado, da ['fjadu, da] *adj* **-1.** [vendido a crédito] sold on credit *(depois do subst).* **-2.** [conversa]: **isso é conversa fiada** that's far-fetched.
◆ **fiado** *adv* [a crédito] on credit.
fiador, ra [fja'do(x), ra] *m, f* guarantor.
fiambre ['fjãnbri] *m* ham.
fiança ['fjãnsa] *f* **-1.** [garantia] guarantee. **-2.** *JUR* bail; **sob ~** on bail; **pagar ~** to post bail.
fiapo ['fjapu] *m* thread.
fiar [16] ['fja(x)] *vt* [reduzer a fio] to spin.
◆ **fiar-se** *vp* [confiar em]: **~-se em alguém/algo** to trust sb/sthg.
fiasco ['fjaʃku] *m* fiasco.
fibra ['fibra] *f* [ger] fibre *UK*, fiber *US*; **mulher de ~** gutsy woman; **~ óptica** fibre optics *(pl) UK*, fiber optics *(pl) US*; **~ de vidro** fibreglass *UK*, fiberglass *US*.
fibroma [fi'broma] *m* fibroma.
fibroso, sa [fi'brozu, ɔza] *adj* fibrous.
ficar [12] [fi'ka(x)] *vi* **-1.** [ger] to remain; **só ficaram duas garrafas de refrigerante** there are only two bottles of soda left. **-2.** [permanecer] to stay; **~ sentado/de pé** to remain seated/standing; **~ por isso mesmo** to remain the same; **~ sem** not to have. **-3.** [estar situado] to be. **-4.** [tornar-se] to become; **~ com frio** to be cold; **~ feliz com algo** to be happy about sthg; **~ de bem/de mal (com alguém)** to get on well/badly (with sb); **~ bom** [de doença] to recover; [pintura etc] to be good. **-5.** [ser adiado]: **~ para** to leave until. **-6.** [combinar]: **~ de fazer algo** to agree to do sthg. **-7.** [persistir]: **~ fazendo algo** to go on doing sthg. **-8.** [prometer]: **~ de fazer algo** to promise to do sthg. **-9.** [custar]: **~ em** to come to. **-10.** [comprar]: **fico com a verde** I'll take the green. **-11.** [manter sob posse, tutela]: **~ com** to be left with. **-12.** [assumir função]: **~ de** to work as. **-13.** [ser]: **não fica bem** it's not right. **-14.** [assentar a]: **~ bem em** *ou* **para alguém** to look good on sb; **~ bem de algo** to look good in sthg. **-15.** [vir a]: **~ sabendo de algo** to get to know sthg. **-16.** *loc*: **~ atrás** [ser inferior] to be behind; **~ sobrando** [ser relegado] to be left out; **~ sujo** [no conceito alheio] to get a bad name.
ficção [fik'sãw] (*pl* **-ões**) *f* fiction.
ficcional [fik'sionaw] (*pl* **-ais**) *adj LITER* fictional.
ficcionista [fiksjo'niʃta] *mf* fiction writer.
ficha ['fiʃa] *f* **-1.** [ger] file; **ter ~ na polícia** to have a police record. **-2.** [de telefone] plug. **-3.** [de jogo] token. **-4.** *fam* [informação]: **dar a ~ de** to give information on; **ter ~ limpa** to have a clean record.
fichado, da [fi'ʃadu, da] *adj*: **ser ~ (na polícia)** to have a police record.
fichar [4] [fi'ʃa(x)] *vt* to file.
fichário [fi'ʃarju] *m* **-1.** [ger] file. **-2.** [móvel] filing cabinet.
fichinha [fi'ʃiɲa] *f fam* cinch.
fictício, cia [fik'tʃisju, sja] *adj* fictitious.
fidalgo, ga [fi'dawgu, ga] *m, f* noble.
fidalguia [fidaw'gia] *f* nobility.
fidedigno, na [fide'dʒignu, na] *adj* trustworthy.
fidelidade [fideli'dadʒi] *f* **-1.** [lealdade] faithfulness. **-2.** [conjugal] fidelity. **-3.** [precisão] precision; **com ~** faithfully.
fiduciário, ria [fidu'sjarju, rja] *adj* fiduciary.
◆ **fiduciário** *m JUR* trustee.
fiel ['fjɛw] (*pl* **-éis**) *adj* **-1.** [ger] faithful. **-2.** [constante] loyal.
◆ **fiéis** *mpl RELIG*: **os fiéis** the faithful *(pl inv).*
fielmente [fjew'mẽntʃi] *adv* faithfully.
FIFA (*abrev de* **Féderation Internationale de Football Association**) *f* FIFA.
figa ['figaʃ] *f* charm.
◆ **de uma figa** *loc adj fam* effing.
fígado ['figadu] *m* liver; **desopilar o ~** *fig* to make one feel good.
figo ['figu] *m* fig.
figueira [fi'gejra] *f* fig tree.
figura [fi'gura] *f* **-1.** [ger] figure; **ser uma ~** *fam* to be a character; **mudar de ~** to change. **-2.** [em carta] picture card, court card. **-3.** *GRAM*: **~ de linguagem** figure of speech.
figura-chave [fi,gura'ʃavi] (*pl* **figuras-chave**) *f* key figure.
figurado, da [figu'radu, da] *adj* figurative.
figurante [figu'rãntʃi] *mf* extra.
figurão [figu'rãw] (*pl* **-ões**) *m* bigwig.
figurar [4] [figu'ra(x)] ◇ *vt* **-1.** [representar] to represent. **-2.** [ter a forma de] to look like. **-3.** [aparentar] to look. ◇ *vi* **-1.** [atuar]: **~ em** to act in. **-2.** [fazer parte]: **~ em/entre** to appear on/among.
figurinha [figu'riɲa] *f* **-1.** [cromo] sticker; **trocar ~s (com alguém)** *fig* to swap notes (with sb). **-2.** [pessoa]: **ele é uma ~ difícil** he's jumped up.
figurinista [figuri'niʃta] *mf* clothes designer.
figurino [figu'rinu] *m* **-1.** [molde] pattern. **-2.** [revista] fashion magazine. **-3.** *CINE, TEATRO & TV* [exemplo] model. **-4.** *fig*: **como manda o ~** as it should be.
Fiji ['fiʒi] *n* Fiji.
fila ['fila] *f* [fileira - de pessoas] queue *UK*, line *US*; [- de cadeiras] row; **em ~** in line; **fazer ~** to queue *UK*, to form a line *US*; **~ indiana** single file.

filamento [fila'mẽntu] *m* filament.
filantropia [filãntro'pia] *f* philanthropy.
filantrópico, ca [filãn'tropiku, ka] *adj* philanthropic.
filantropo, opa [filãn'tropu, ɔpa] *m, f* philanthropist.
filão [fi'lãw] (*pl* **-ões**) *m* *fig* [oportunidade] opportunity.
filar [16] [fi'la(x)] *vt* *fam* to cadge.
filarmônico, ca [filax'moniku, ka] *adj* philharmonic.
◆ **filarmônica** *f* philharmonic.
filatelia [filate'lia] *f* philately, stamp collecting.
filé [fi'lɛ] *m* fillet; ~ **mignon** filet mignon.
fileira [fi'lejra] *f* row.
◆ **fileiras** *fpl* MIL ranks.
filete [fi'lete] *m* fillet.
filha ['fiʎa] *f* ▷ **filho**.
filharada [fiʎa'rada] *f* many sons and daughters.
filhinho, nha [fi'ʎiɲu, ɲa] *m, f* young son; ~ **da mamãe** mummy's boy; ~ **de papai** spoilt brat.
filho, lha ['fiʎu, 'fiʎa] *m, f* **-1.** [descendente] son; ~ **adotivo** adopted son; ~ **de criação** adopted son; ~ **único** only son; ~ **da mãe** *vulg* bastard; ~ **da puta** *vulg* son of a bitch. **-2.** *loc*: **ter um** ~ *fig* to have a turn, to have a fainting fit; **ser** ~ **único de mãe solteira** *fig* to be unique.
filhote [fi'ʎɔtʃi] *m* **-1.** [de animal - de leão, urso] cub; [- de cachorro] puppy. **-2.** [filho] young son.
filiação [filja'sãw] (*pl* **-ões**) *f* **-1.** [pais] filiation. **-2.** [admissão] affiliation.
filial [fi'ljaw] (*pl* **-ais**) ◇ *adj* [amor] filial. ◇ *f* [sucursal] branch.
filiar [16] [fi'ʎa(x)] *vt*: ~ **alguém a algo** to sign sb up to sthg.
◆ **filiar-se** *vp*: ~**-se a algo** to sign o.s. up to sthg.
filigrana [fili'grãna] *f* filigree.
Filipinas [fili'pinaʃ] *npl*: **(as)** ~ the Philippines.
filipino, na [fili'pinu, na] ◇ *adj* Filipino. ◇ *m, f* Filipino.
◆ **filipino** *m* [língua] Filipino.
filmadora [fiwma'dora] *f* movie camera.
filmagem [fiw'maʒẽ] (*pl* **-ns**) *f* filming.
filmar [4] [fiw'ma(x)] ◇ *vt* to film. ◇ *vi* to film.
filme ['fiwmi] *m* **-1.** [obra cinematográfica] film *UK*, movie *US*; ~ **de bangue-bangue** Western; ~ **de época** period film *UK*, period movie *US*; ~ **mudo** silent film *UK*, silent movie *US*; ~ **de suspense** thriller. **-2.** *loc*: **queimar o** ~ to ruin one's image.
filmografia [fiwmogra'fia] *f* filmography.
filmoteca [fiwmo'tɛka] *f* film library.
filó [fi'lɔ] *m* voile.
filões [fi'lõjʃ] *mpl* ▷ **filão**.
filologia [filolo'ʒia] *f* philology.
filólogo, ga [fi'lɔlogu, ga] *m, f* philologist.
filosofar [4] [filozo'fa(x)] *vi* to philosophize.
filosofia [filozo'fia] *f* philosophy.
filosófico, ca [filo'zofiku, ka] *adj* philosophical.
filósofo, fa [fi'lɔzofu, fi'lɔzofa] *m, f* philosopher.
filtragem [fiwtra'ʒẽ] (*pl* **-ns**) *f* [filtração] filtration.
filtrar [4] [fiw'tra(x)] *vt* **-1.** [purificar] to filter. **-2.** [selecionar] to select.
filtro ['fiwtru] *m* filter; ~ **de ar** air filter.
fim ['fĩ] (*pl* **-ns**) *m* [ger] end; ~ **de semana** weekend; ~ **de mundo, do mundo** [cafundó] middle of nowhere; **no** ~ **das contas** after all; **ser o** ~ **(da picada)** to be the last straw; **por** ~ finally.
◆ **a fim de** *loc prep* in order to; **estar a** ~ **de fazer algo** to be planning on doing sthg; **estar a** ~ **de alguém** to be attracted to sb.
fimose [fi'mɔzi] *f* phimosis.
finado, da [fi'nadu, da] ◇ *adj* dead. ◇ *m, f* dead person.
◆ **finados** *mpl* RELIG: **os** ~**s** All Souls.
final [fi'naw] (*pl* **-ais**) ◇ *adj* final; **minuto** ~ last minute; **ponto** ~ full stop. ◇ *m* end; ~ **feliz** happy ending. ◇ *f* ESP final.
finalidade [finali'dadʒi] *f* end.
finalista [fina'liʃta] *mf* finalist.
finalização [finaliza'sãw] (*pl* **-ões**) *f* conclusion.
finalizar [4] [finali'za(x)] ◇ *vt* [concluir] to conclude. ◇ *vi* FUT [fazer gol] to score.
finanças [fi'nãnsaʃ] *fpl* **-1.** [ciência] finance *(sg)*. **-2.** [situação financeira] finances.
financeiro, ra [finãn'sejru, ra] *adj* financial.
◆ **financeira** *f* [firma] finance company.
financiamento [finãnsja'mẽntu] *m* financing.
financiar [16] [finãn'sja(x)] *vt* to finance.
financista [finãn'siʃta] *mf* financier.
fincar [12] [fĩŋ'ka(x)] *vt* [cravar] to stick.
findar [4] [fĩn'da(x)] *vt* & *vi* to end.
◆ **findar-se** *vp* to end.
findo, da ['fĩndu, da] *adj* finished.
fineza [fi'neza] *f* **-1.** [espessura] fineness. **-2.** [gentileza] politeness.
fingido, da [fĩn'ʒidu, da] ◇ *adj* fake. ◇ *m, f* dissembler.
fingimento [fĩnʒi'mẽntu] *m* pretence *UK*, pretense *US*.
fingir [52] [fĩ'ʒi(x)] ◇ *vt* to fake. ◇ *vi* to pretend.
◆ **fingir-se** *vp*: ~**-se de algo** to pretend to be sthg.
finito, ta [fi'nitu, ta] *adj* finite.
finitude [fini'tudʒi] *f* [limitação] finite nature.
finlandês, esa [fĩnlãn'dejʃ, eza] ◇ *adj* Finnish. ◇ *m, f* Finnish person, Finn.
◆ **finlandês** *m* [língua] Finnish.
Finlândia [fĩn'lãndʒja] *n* Finland.
fino, na ['finu, na] *adj* **-1.** [ger] fine. **-2.** [agudo] shrill. **-3.** [refinado] elegant. **-4.** *loc*: **ser o** ~ to be the best; **tirar um** ~ **de** to come within a hair's breadth of.
fins [fĩʃ] *mpl* ▷ **fim**.
finura [fi'nura] *f* **-1.** [espessura] fineness. **-2.** [refinamento] refinement.
fio ['fiw] *m* **-1.** [ger] thread. **-2.** ELETR wire. **-3.** [gume] blade. **-4.** [filete] trickle. **-5.** *loc*: **bater um** ~ *fam* to have a phone conversation.
◆ **a fio** *loc adj*: **dias/horas a** ~ days/hours on end.

◆ **por um fio** *loc adv*: **o emprego dele está por um ~** his job hangs by a thread; **escapou da morte por um ~** he escaped death by a hair's breadth.
fiorde ['fjoxdʒi] *m* fjord.
firma ['fixma] *f* **-1.** *COM* firm. **-2.** [assinatura] signature.
firmamento [fixma'mẽntu] *m* firmament.
firmar [4] [fix'ma(x)] <> *vt* **-1.** [fixar] to steady. **-2.** [assinar] to sign. **-3.** [estabelecer] to establish. **-4.** [basear]: **~ algo em algo** to base sthg on sthg. <> *vi* [estabilizar-se] to settle.
◆ **firmar-se** *vp* to settle.
firme ['fixmi] *adj* **-1.** [ger] firm. **-2.** [fixo] steady, stable. **-3.** [constante] settled. **-4.** [estável] stable.
firmeza [fix'meza] *f* **-1.** [ger] firmness. **-2.** [estabilidade] steadiness, stability. **-3.** [segurança] soundness.
fiscal [fiʃ'kaw] (*pl* **-ais**) <> *adj* [relativo ao fisco] fiscal. <> *mf* **-1.** [aduaneiro] customs officer. **-2.** [supervisor - de impostos] inspector; [- de prova] invigilator.
fiscalização [fiʃkaliza'sãw] (*pl* **-ões**) *f* overseeing.
fiscalizar [4] [fiʃkali'za(x)] *vt* **-1.** [estabelecimento, obras] to oversee. **-2.** [prova] to invigilate.
fisco ['fiʃku] *m*: **o ~** the public purse.
fisgada [fiʒ'gada] *f* stabbing pain.
fisgar [14] [fiʒ'ga(x)] *vt* **-1.** [peixe] to harpoon. **-2.** [pessoa] to understand.
físico, ca ['fiziku, ka] <> *adj* [ger] physical; **educação física** physical education. <> *m, f* *FÍSICA* physicist.
◆ **físico** *m* [corpo] physique.
◆ **física** *f* [ciência] physics *(sg)*.
fisiologia [fizjolo'ʒia] *f* physiology.
fisiológico, ca [fizjo'lɔʒiku, ka] *adj* **-1.** *MED* physiological. **-2.** *POL* self-serving.
fisiologismo [fizjolo'ʒiʒmu] *m* *POL* self-interest.
fisionomia [fizjono'mia] *f* features (*pl*), appearance; **ela está com boa ~** she's looking well.
fisionomista [fizjono'miʃta] *mf* *person who is good at remembering faces.*
fisioterapeuta [fizjotera'pewta] *mf* physiotherapist.
fisioterapia [fizjɔtera'pia] *f* physiotherapy.
fissura [fi'sura] *f* **-1.** *GEOL* fissure. **-2.** *fam* [gana] hankering.
fissurado, da [fisu'radu, da] *adj* **-1.** [rachado] cracked. **-2.** *fam* [maluco por]: **~ em** mad about.
fissurar [4] [fisu'ra(x)] *vt* to crack.
fístula ['fiʃtula] *f* fistula.
fita ['fita] *f* **-1.** [tira] ribbon; **~ crepe** crêpe bandage; **~ durex**® *OU* **colante** Sellotape® *UK*; Scotch tape® *US*; **~ de impressora** typewriter ribbon; **~ isolante** insulating tape; **~ magnética** magnetic tape; **~ métrica** tape measure, measuring tape. **-2.** [filme] tape. **-3.** [cassete]: **~ de vídeo** videotape; **~ virgem** blank tape. **-4.** [manha] play-acting.
fitar [4] [fi'ta(x)] *vt* to stare.
◆ **fitar-se** *vp* to stare at one another.
fiteiro, ra [fi'tejru, ra] *adj* play-acting.
fito ['fitu] *m* target.
fivela [fi'vɛla] *f* **-1.** [fecho] buckle. **-2.** [de cabelo] hair clip.
fixação [fiksa'sãw] (*pl* **-ões**) *f* fixation.
fixador [fiksa'do(x)] (*pl* **-es**) *m* **-1.** [de cabelo] hairspray. **-2.** [de essência] fixing agent.
fixar [4] [fik'sa(x)] *vt* **-1.** [prender] to fix. **-2.** [apreender] to make stick. **-3.** [estabelecer] to set.
◆ **fixar-se** *vp* **-1.** [estabilizar-se] to be fixed. **-2.** [estabelecer residência] to settle. **-3.** [fitar]: **~ em** to stare at.
fixo, xa ['fiksu, ksa] *adj* fixed.
flacidez [flasi'dejʒ] *f* flaccidity.
flácido, da ['flasidu, da] *adj* flaccid.
flagelado, da [flaʒe'ladu, da] *adj* flogged.
flagelante [flaʒe'lãntʃi] *adj* **-1.** [chicote] searing. **-2.** [isolamento] punishing.
flagelo [fla'ʒɛlu] *m* scourge.
flagrante [fla'grãntʃi] <> *adj* flagrant. <> *m*: **pegar em ~ (de algo)** to catch in the act (of sthg); **em ~** red-handed, in flagrante.
flagrar [4] [fla'gra(x)] *vt* to catch in the act.
flama ['flãma] *f* flame.
flambar [4] [flã'ba(x)] *vt* to flambé.
flamejante [flame'ʒãntʃi] *adj* flaming.
flamejar [4] [flame'ʒa(x)] *vi* to flame.
flamenco, ca [fla'mẽŋku, ka] <> *adj* flamenco.
◆ **flamenco** *m* flamenco.
flamengo, ga [fla'mẽŋgu, ga] *adj* Flemish.
◆ **flamengo** *m* [língua] Flemish.
flamingo [fla'mĩŋgu] *m* flamingo.
flâmula ['flãmula] *f* pennant.
flanco ['flãŋku] *m* flank.
flanela [fla'nɛla] *f* flannel.
flanelinha [flane'liɲa] *mf* *fam* *unofficial car-park attendant.*
flanquear [15] [flãŋ'kja(x)] *vt* **-1.** [atacar de flanco] to attack in the flank. **-2.** [ladear] to flank.
flash ['flɛʃi] (*pl* **-es**) *m* flash.
flash-back [flaʃ'baki] (*pl* **flash-backs**) *m* flashback.
flatulência [flatu'lẽnsja] *f* flatulence.
flauta ['flawta] *f* flute; **~ doce** tin whistle; **~ transversa** transverse flute; **levar algo na ~** to take sthg lightly.
flautim [flaw'tʃĩ] (*pl* **-ns**) *m* piccolo.
flautista [flaw'tʃiʃta] *mf* flautist.
flebite [fle'bitʃi] *f* phlebitis.
flecha ['flɛʃa] *f* arrow.
flechada [fle'ʃada] *f* **-1.** [arremesso] arrow shot. **-2.** [ferimento] arrow wound.
flertar [4] [flex'ta(x)] *vi*: **~ (com alguém)** to flirt (with sb).
flerte ['flextʃi] *m* flirt.
fleuma ['flewma] *f* phlegm.
fleumático, ca [flew'matʃiku, ka] *adj* phlegmatic.
flexão [flek'sãw] (*pl* **-ões**) *f* **-1.** [movimento] flexing. **-2.** *GRAM* inflexion.
flexibilidade [fleksibili'dadʒi] *f* flexibility.

flexibilização [fleksibiliza'sãw] (*pl* **-ões**) *f* relaxation.
flexibilizar [fleksibili'za(x)] *vt* to relax.
flexionado, da [fleksio'nadu, da] *adj* LING inflected.
flexionar [4] [fleksjo'na(x)] <> *vt* **-1.** [joelho etc] to flex. **-2.** GRAM to inflect. <> *vi* GRAM to inflect.
flexível [flek'sivɛw] (*pl* **-eis**) *adj* flexible.
flexões [flek'sõjʃ] *fpl* ▷ **flexão.**
fliperama [flipe'rãma] *m* **-1.** [máquina] pinball machine. **-2.** [estabelecimento] amusement arcade.
floco ['flɔku] *m* flake; ~ **de milho** cornflake; ~ **de neve** snowflake.
◆ **flocos** *mpl*: **sorvete de ~s** chocolate chip ice-cream.
flor ['flo(x)] (*pl* **-es**) *f* **-1.** BOT flower. **-2.** [pessoa boa]: **ser uma ~** to be a gem. **-3.** *loc*: **a fina ~ de** the flower of; **na ~ da idade** in the prime of life; **não ser ~ que se cheire** not to be trusted.
flora ['flɔra] *f* flora.
floral [flo'raw] (*pl* **-ais**) <> *adj* floral. <> *m* floral infusion; **florais de Bach** Bach flower remedies.
floreado, da [flo'rjadu, da] *adj* flowery.
florear [15] [flo'rja(x)] *vt* [rebuscar] to embellish.
floreio [flo'reju] *m* flourish.
Florença [flo'rẽnsa] *n* Florence.
florescente [flore'sẽntʃi] *adj* **-1.** [BOT - árvore] blossoming; [- planta] flowering. **-2.** *fig* [próspero] flowering.
florescer [25] [flore'se(x)] *vi* **-1.** [BOT - árvore] to blossom; [- planta] to flower. **-2.** *fig* [prosperar] to flower.
floresta [flo'rɛʃta] *f* forest.
florestal [floreʃ'taw] (*pl* **-ais**) *adj* forest *(antes de subst).*
Florianópolis [florja'nɔpoliʃ] *n* Florianópolis.
floricultor, ra [florikuw'to(x), ra] *m, f* floriculturist.
floricultura [florikuw'tura] *f* floriculture.
florido, da [flo'ridu, da] *adj* flower-filled.
florir [79] [flo'ri(x)] *vi* **-1.** [árvore] to blossom. **-2.** [planta] to flower.
florista [flo'riʃta] *mf* florist.
flotilha [flo'tiʎa] *f* flotilla.
fluência [flu'ẽnsja] *f* fluency.
fluente [flu'ẽntʃi] *adj* fluent.
fluidez [fluj'deʒ] *f* fluidity.
fluido, da [flu'idu, ida] *adj* **-1.** [substância] fluid. **-2.** *fig* [fácil] flowing; **tráfego ~** smooth-flowing traffic.
◆ **fluido** *m* fluid.
fluir [74] [flwi(x)] *vi* **-1.** [ger] to flow. **-2.** [derivar]: **~ de** to derive from.
flúor ['fluo(x)] *m* fluoride.
fluorescente [flworeʃ'sẽntʃi] *adj* fluorescent.
flutuação [flutwa'sãw] (*pl* **-ões**) *f* fluctuation.
flutuante [flu'twãntʃi] *adj* **-1.** [boiante] floating. **-2.** [oscilante] fluctuating.
flutuar [4] [flu'twa(x)] *vi* **-1.** [ger] to float. **-2.** [variar] to fluctuate.
fluvial [flu'vjaw] (*pl* **-ais**) *adj* river *(antes de subst).*
fluxo ['fluksu] *m* **-1.** [ger] flow. **-2.** COM: **~ de caixa** cash flow. **-3.** MED: **~ menstrual** menstrual flow. **-4.** FÍSICA: **~ de massa** flow rate.
fluxograma [flukso'grama] *m* flow chart.
FM (*abrev de* **freqüencia modulada**) *m* FM.
FMI (*abrev de* **Fundo Monetário Internacional**) *m* IMF.
fobia [fo'bia] *f* phobia.
foca ['fɔka] <> *f* ZOOL seal. <> *mf* [jornalista] cub reporter.
focal [fo'kaw] (*pl* **-ais**) *adj* focal.
focalização [fokaliza'sãw] *f* focusing.
focalizar [4] [fokali'za(x)], **focar** [4] [fo'ka(x)] *vt* to focus.
focinho [fo'siɲu] *m* **-1.** [de suíno] snout. **-2.** [de cão] muzzle.
foco ['fɔku] *m* focus.
foder [5] ['fode(x)] *vulg* ~ <> *vt* [copular com] to fuck. <> *vi* [copular] to fuck.
◆ **foder-se** *vp vulg* [dar-se mal] to fuck up.
fodido, da [fo'dʒidu, da] vulg *adj* **-1.** [ferrado] fucked; **~ e mal pago** up shit creek without a paddle. **-2.** [pobre] loser.
fofo, fa ['fofu, fa] *adj* **-1.** [macio] soft. **-2.** [gracioso] cute.
fofoca [fo'fɔka] *f* gossip; **fazer ~** to spread gossip.
fofocar [12] [fofo'ka(x)] *vi* to gossip.
fofoqueiro, ra [fofo'kejru, ra] <> *adj* gossipy. <> *m, f* gossip.
fofura [fo'fura] *f* cuteness; **ser uma ~** to be cute.
fogão [fo'gãw] (*pl* **-ões**) *m* stove, cooker.
fogareiro [foga'rejru] *m* (paraffin) cooker, coal pot.
fogaréu [foga'rɛw] *m* torch.
fogo ['fogu] (*pl* **fogos**) *m* **-1.** [ger] fire; **pegar ~** to catch fire; **brincar com ~** *fig* to play with fire; **ser ~ (na roupa)** to mean trouble. **-2.** [excitação] flame; **~ de palha** hot air. **-3.** [desejo sexual] sex drive. **-4.** [disparo]: **abrir ~** to open fire; **fogo!** fire!; **poder de ~** firepower. **-5.** [pirotecnia]: **~(s) de artifício** fireworks. **-6.** *loc*: **estar de ~** [estar embriagado] to be plastered.
fogões [fo'gõjʃ] *mpl* ▷ **fogão.**
fogo-fátuo [ˌfogu'fatwu] (*pl* **fogos-fátuos**) *m* will-o'-the-wisp.
fogoso, osa [fo'gozu, ɔza] *adj* **-1.** [arrebatado] fiery. **-2.** [sexualmente] aroused.
fogueira [fo'gejra] *f* bonfire.
foguete [fo'getʃi] *m* rocket; **soltar ~s antes da hora** *fig* to count one's chickens before they're hatched.
fogueteiro, ra [foge'tejru, ra] *m, f* pyrotechnist.
foguetório [foge'tɔrju] *m* noise of fireworks.
foice ['fojsi] *f* scythe.
folclore [fow'klɔri] *m* folklore.
folclórico, ca [fow'klɔriku, ka] *adj* folk.
fole ['fɔli] *m* bellows *(pl).*
fôlego ['folegu] *m* **-1.** [respiração] breath; **perder o ~** to lose one's breath; **tomar ~** to take a

breath. **-2.** *fig* [ânimo]: **recuperar o ~** to recover one's breath.

folga ['fɔwga] *f* **-1.** [descanso] break; **dia de ~** day off. **-2.** [abuso]: **que ~!** what a cheek! **-3.** [sobra de espaço] space. **-4.** [sobra de tempo] gap.

folgado, da [fow'gadu, da] *adj* **-1.** [largo] loose. **-2.** [abusado] cocky. **-3.** [despreocupado] easy.
◆ **folgado** *adv* easily.

folgazão, zona [fowga'zãw, zɔna] (*mpl* **-ões**, *fpl* **-s**) *adj* idler.

folha ['foʎa] *f* **-1.** *BOT* leaf. **-2.** [página] page; **~ de rosto** title page; **~ de pagamento** pay sheet. **-3.** [chapa] plate. **-4.** [jornal] newspaper. **-5.** [lâmina] blade. **-6.** [pedaço de papel] sheet.
◆ **em folha** *loc adv*: **novo em ~** brand new.

folhagem [fo'ʎaʒẽ] (*pl* **-ns**) *f* foliage.

folha-seca [ˌfoʎa'seka] (*pl* **folhas-secas**) *f* *FUT* lob.

folheado, da [fo'ʎadu, da] *adj* **-1.** [revestido]: **~ a ouro/prata** gold-/silver-plated. **-2.** *CULIN*: **massa folheada** puff pastry.

folhear [15] [fo'ʎja(x)] *vt* to leaf through.

folhetim [foʎe'tʃĩ] (*pl* **-ns**) *m* serialization.

folhetinesco, ca [foɲeti'neʃku, ka] *adj* [de folhetim] *published daily in a newspaper or magazine.*

folheto [fo'ʎetu] *m* pamphlet.

folhinha [fo'ʎiɲa] *f* [calendário] calendar.

folia [fo'lia] *f* revelry.

folião, ona [fo'ljãw, ɔna] (*mpl* **-ões**, *fpl* **-s**) *m, f* reveller.

folículo [fo'likulu] *m* follicle.

foliona [fo'ljɔna] *f* ▷ **folião**.

fome ['fɔmi] *f* [ger] hunger; **estar com ~** to be hungry; **passar ~** to go hungry.

fomentar [4] [fomẽn'ta(x)] *vt* to foment.

fomento [fo'mẽntu] *m* **-1.** *MED* poultice. **-2.** [estímulo] fomentation.

fominha [fɔ'miɲa] *adj* mean.

fonador, ra [fona'do(x), ra] *adj* phonic; **aparelho ~** speech apparatus.

fone ['foni] (*abrev de* **telefone**) *m* phone.

fonema [fo'nema] *m* phoneme.

fonético, ca [fo'nɛtʃiku, ka] *adj* phonetic.
◆ **fonética** *f* phonetics *(sg)*.

fônico, ca ['fɔniku, ka] *adj* phonic.

fonoaudiologia [fonawdʒiolo'gia] *f* speech therapy.

fonoaudiólogo, ga [ˌfonaw'dʒjɔlogu, ga] *m, f* speech therapist.

fonologia [fonolo'ʒia] *f* phonology.

fonte ['fõntʃi] ◇ *f* **-1.** [ger] source; **de ~ limpa** from a reliable source; **imposto retido na ~** taxed at source. **-2.** [chafariz] fountain. **-3.** *COMPUT* [tipo de caractere] font. ◇ *m* *COMPUT* source code.

fora [fɔra] ◇ *m* **-1.** [gafe] gaffe; **dar um ~** to commit a gaffe. **-2.** *fig* [dispensa]: **dar um ~ em alguém** to rebuff sb; **levar um ~ de alguém** to be rebuffed by sb; **fora!** get out! **-3.** *loc*: **dar o ~** [partir] to skedaddle. ◇ *adv* **-1.** [na parte exterior]: **do lado de ~** on the outside; **por ~** outside. **-2.** [ao ar livre]: **lá ~** outside. **-3.** [em outro lugar] away, out; **fui para ~ a semana** I went away last week; **jantei ~ ontem** I went out to dinner yesterday; **a família está ~ no momento** the family is out *ou* away at the moment; [no estrangeiro] abroad. **-4.** *fig* [distanciado]: **~ de** out of; **estar ~ de si** to be beside o.s. ◇ *prep* [exceto] except for, apart from.
◆ **de fora** *loc adv* **-1.** [nu] exposed; **ficar com as pernas de ~** to have one's legs exposed. **-2.** [sem participar]: **ficar de ~** to be left out.
◆ **para fora** *loc adv*: **ela costura para ~** she takes sewing in.
◆ **por fora** *loc adv* **-1.** [cobrar, pagar]: **cobrar por ~** to receive on the side; **pagar por ~** to pay on the side. **-2.** [ignorante]: **estar por ~ (de)** to be unaware (of).
◆ **fora de série** *loc adj* [excepcional] exceptional.

fora-da-lei [ˌfɔrada'lej] *mf inv* outlaw.

fora-de-estrada ['fɔradʒiʃ'trada] ◇ *adj* off-road. ◇ *m* all-terrain vehicle.

foragido, da [fora'ʒidu, da] ◇ *adj* fugitive. ◇ *m, f* fugitive.

foragir-se [52] [fora'ʒixsi] *vp* to flee.

forasteiro, ra [foraʃ'tejru, ra] *m, f* foreigner.

forca ['foxka] *f* gallows *(sg)*.

força ['foxsa] *f* **-1.** [ger] power. **-2.** [energia física, moral] strength; **ter ~ para fazer algo** to have (the) strength to do sthg; **~ de vontade** will power. **-3.** [violência] force; **à ~** by force; **com ~** violently. **-4.** [esforço]: **fazer ~** to try hard. **-5.** *MIL* force; **~s armadas** armed forces. **-6.** [causa]: **motivo de ~ maior** due to unavoidable circumstances; **por ~ de** by force of. **-7.** [ânimo, apoio]: **dar ~ a alguém** to give support to sb.
◆ **força de expressão** *f* understatement.

forcado [fox'kadu] *m* pitchfork.

forçado, da [fox'sadu, da] *adj* **-1.** [ger] forced. **-2.** [interpretação] far-fetched.

forçar [13] [fur'sar] *vt* **-1.** [obrigar]: **~ alguém (a algo/a fazer algo)** to force sb (to sthg/to do sthg). **-2.** [arrombar] to force. **-3.** [obter por força] to (obtain by) force. **-4.** [vista, voz] to strain. **-5.** [desvirtuar] to misinterpret. **-6.** *loc*: **~ a barra** [insistir, pressionar] to force sb's hand.
◆ **forçar-se** *vp*: **~-se a fazer algo** to force o.s. to do sthg, to make o.s. do sthg.

força-tarefa [ˌfoxsata'rɛfa] (*pl* **forças-tarefa**) *f* task force.

fórceps ['fɔxsepiʃ] *m inv* forceps *(pl)*.

forçosamente [foxsoza'mẽntʃi] *adv* necessarily.

forçoso, osa [fox'sozu, ɔza] *adj* necessary.

forense [fo'rẽnsi] *adj* judicial.

forja ['fɔxʒa] *f* forge.

forjado, da [fox'ʃadu, da] *adj* **-1.** [utensílio, metal] forged. **-2.** [notícia] fabricated.

forjar [4] [fox'sa(x)] *vt* to forge.

forma ['fɔxma] *f* **-1.** [ger] form; **desta ~** in this way, thus. **-2.** [estado físico, feitio] shape; **em ~ de** in the shape of; **estar em ~** to be in shape; **estar**

fora de ~ to be out of shape. **-3.** [fila]: **entrar em** ~ to fall into line.

◆ **formas** *fpl* [silhueta] figure *(sg)*.

◆ **de forma que** *loc conj* so that.

◆ **da mesma forma** *loc adv* similarly.

◆ **de forma alguma** *loc adv* in no way.

◆ **de qualquer forma** *loc adv* all the same.

◆ **de tal forma** *loc adv* in such a way.

fôrma ['foxma] *f* **-1.** *CULIN* mould. **-2.** [molde] mould, cast. **-3.** [de sapato] last.

formação [foxma'sãw] (*pl* **-ões**) *f* **-1.** [ger] formation. **-2.** [educação] upbringing.

formado, da [fox'madu, da] *adj* **-1.** [constituído]: ~ **por** made up of. **-2.** [graduado]: **ser** ~ **por** to be educated by.

formador, ra [foxma'do(x), ra] *adj*: ~ **de vício** habit-forming, addictive; ~ **de opinião** opinion-making.

formal [fox'maw] (*pl* **-ais**) *adj* formal.

formalidade [foxmali'dadʒi] *f* formality; **com** ~ formally.

formalismo [foxma'liʒmu] *m* **-1.** [convencionalismo] formality. **-2.** *ARTE* formalism.

formalizar [4] [foxmali'za(x)] *vt* **-1.** [ger] to formalize. **-2.** [estruturar] to formulate.

formando, da [fox'mãndu, da] *m, f* finalist.

formão [fox'mãw] (*pl* **-ões**) *m* chisel.

formar [4] [fox'ma(x)] ◇ *vt* **-1.** [ger] to form. **-2.** [educar] to educate. ◇ *vi MIL* [entrar em fila] to fall in.

◆ **formar-se** *vp* **-1.** [constituir-se] to form. **-2.** [graduar-se] to graduate.

formatar [4] [foxma'ta(x)] *vt COMPUT* to format.

formativo, va [foxma'tʃivu, va] *adj* formative.

formato [fox'matu] *m* **-1.** [forma] shape. **-2.** [modelo] format.

formatura [foxma'tura] *f EDUC* graduation.

fórmica ['fɔxmika] *f* formica®.

formidável [foxmi'davɛw] (*pl* **-eis**) *adj* **-1.** [fantástico] fantastic. **-2.** [imenso] formidable.

formiga [fox'miga] *f* ant.

formigamento [foxmiga'mẽntu] *m* pins and needles.

formigar [14] [foxmi'ga(x)] *vi* **-1.** [coçar] to have pins and needles. **-2.** *fig* [abundar]: ~ **de** to swarm with.

formigueiro [foxmi'gejru] *m* **-1.** [de formigas] anthill. **-2.** *fig* [multidão] swarm.

formol [fox'mɔw] (*pl* **-óis**) *m* formaldehyde.

formoso, osa [fox'mozu, ɔza] *adj* beautiful.

formosura [foxmo'zura] *f* beauty.

fórmula ['fɔxmula] *f* **-1.** [ger] formula. **-2.** [modo] (polite) phrase, (politeness) formula. **-3.** *AUTO*: ~ **um** Formula One.

formulação [foxmula'sãw] (*pl* **-ões**) *f* formulation.

formular [4] [foxmu'la(x)] *vt* to formulate.

formulário [foxmu'larju] *m* form; ~ **contínuo** *COMPUT* continuous stationery.

fornalha [fox'naʎa] *f* furnace.

fornecedor, ra [foxnese'do(x), ra] (*mpl* **-es**, *fpl* **-s**) ◇ *adj* supplying. ◇ *m, f* supplier.

fornecer [25] [foxne'se(x)] *vt* to supply.

fornecimento [foxnesi'mẽntu] *m* supply.

fornicar [12] [foxni'ka(x)] *vi* to fornicate.

forno ['foxnu] *m* **-1.** *CULIN* oven; ~ **de microondas** microwave (oven). **-2.** [fornalha] kiln. **-3.** *fig* [lugar quente]: **ser/estar um** ~ to be like an oven.

foro ['foru] *m* forum.

forquilha [fox'kiʎa] *f* pitchfork.

forra ['fɔxa] *f*: **ir à** ~ to take one's revenge.

forração [foxa'sãw] (*pl* **-ões**) *f* filling.

forragem [fo'xagẽ] (*pl* **-ns**) *f* forage.

forrar [4] [fo'xa(x)] *vt* **-1.** [ger] to line. **-2.** [sofá, chão] to cover. **-3.** [parede] to paper.

forro ['foxu] *m* **-1.** [interno] lining. **-2.** [externo] cover.

forró [fo'xɔ] *m typical Brazilian dance of the north-east.*

fortalecer [25] [foxtale'se(x)] *vt* to strengthen.

fortalecimento [foxtalesi'mẽntu] *m* strengthening.

fortaleza [foxta'leza] *f* **-1.** [forte] fortress. **-2.** *fig* [bastião] fortress.

Fortaleza [foxta'leza] *n* Fortaleza.

forte ['fɔxtʃi] ◇ *adj* **-1.** [ger] strong. **-2.** [piada, palavra, filme] crude. **-3.** [poderoso] powerful. **-4.** [versado]: **ser** ~ **em algo** to be strong at sthg. **-5.** [intenso - emoção, calor, dor] intense; [- chuva] heavy. **-6.** [violento] violent. ◇ *m* **-1.** [fortaleza] stronghold. **-2.** *fig* [ponto forte] strength. ◇ *adv* heavily.

fortificação [foxtʃifika'sãw] (*pl* **-ões**) *f* fortification.

fortificante [foxtʃifi'kãntʃi] ◇ *adj* fortifying. ◇ *m* fortifier.

fortificar [12] [foxtʃifi'ka(x)] *vt* to fortify.

◆ **fortificar-se** *vp* to fortify o.s.

fortuitamente [foxtwita'mẽntʃi] *adv* fortuitously.

fortuito, ta [fox'twitu, ta] *adj* fortuitous.

fortuna [fox'tuna] *f* fortune.

fosco, ca ['foʃku, ka] *adj* tarnished.

fosfato [foʃ'fatu] *m* phosphate.

fosforescente [foʃfore'sentʃi] *adj* phosphorescent.

fosforescer [25] [foʃfore'se(x)] *vi* to phosphoresce.

fósforo ['fɔʃfuru] *m* **-1.** *QUÍM* phosphor. **-2.** [palito] matchstick.

fossa ['fɔsa] *f* **-1.** [buraco] hole; ~ **nasal** nostril; ~ **das Marianas** Mariana Trench. **-2.** [esgoto] ditch. **-3.** *fig* [depressão] slump; **estar/entrar na** ~ to be down in the dumps.

fóssil ['fɔsiw] (*pl* **-eis**) *m* fossil.

fosso ['fosu] *m* ditch.

foto ['fɔtu] *f* photo.

fotocomposição [fotokõmpozi'sãw] (*pl* **-ões**) *f* photocomposition, filmsetting.

fotocópia [foto'kɔpja] *f* photocopy.

fotocopiar [16] [fotoko'pja(x)] *vt* to photocopy.

fotofobia [fotofo'bia] *f* photophobia.

fotofóbico, ca [foto'fɔbiku, ka] *adj* photophobic.
fotogênico, ca [foto'ʒeniku, ka] *adj* photogenic.
fotografar [4] [fotogra'fa(x)] *vt* to photograph.
fotografia [fotogra'fia] *f* **-1.** [técnica] photography. **-2.** [foto] photograph.
fotográfico, ca [foto'grafiku, ka] *adj* photographic.
fotógrafo, fa [fo'tɔgrafu, fa] *m, f* photographer.
fotolito [foto'litu] *m* plate.
fotômetro [fo'tometru] *m* light meter.
fotomontagem [foto'mõntaʒẽ] (*pl* **-ns**) *f* photomontage.
fóton ['fɔtõ] (*pl* **-tons, -nes**) *m* [fís] photon.
fotonovela [fotono'vɛla] *f* photo-strip story.
fotossíntese [foto'sĩntezi] *f* photosynthesis.
fototerapia [fototera'pia] *f* phototherapy.
foxtrote [fɔks'trɔtʃi] *m* foxtrot.
foyer [fwa'je] *m* foyer.
foz ['fɔʃ] *f* estuary.
fração [fra'sãw] (*pl* **-ões**) *f* **-1.** [pedaço] bit. **-2.** MAT fraction.
fracassar [4] [fraka'sa(x)] *vi* to fail.
fracasso [fra'kasu] *m* failure.
fracionar [4] [frasjo'na(x)] *vt* to fragment.
fracionário, ria [frasiona'riu, ria] *adj* MAT fractional.
fraco, ca ['fraku, ka] *adj* **-1.** [ger] weak. **-2.** [medíocre]: ~ **(em)** weak (at). **-3.** [não ativo - bebida] weak; [- cigarro] mild; [- perfume] delicate.
◆ **fraco** ◇ *adv* weakly. ◇ *m* **-1.** [ponto fraco] weak point. **-2.** [inclinação] weakness.
frade ['fradʒi] *m* friar.
fragata [fra'gata] *f* frigate.
frágil ['fraʒiw] (*pl* **-eis**) *adj* fragile.
fragilidade [fraʒili'dadʒi] *f* fragility.
fragilizar [4] [fraʒili'za(x)] *vt* to make vulnerable.
fragmentação [fragmẽnta'sãw] (*pl* **-ões**) *f* fragmentation.
fragmentar [4] [fragmẽn'ta(x)] *vt* to fragment.
◆ **fragmentar-se** *vp* to fragment.
fragmento [frag'mẽntu] *m* fragment.
fragrância [fra'grãnsja] *f* fragrance.
fragrante [fra'grãntʃi] *adj* fragrant.
fralda ['frawda] *f* **-1.** [cueiro] nappy *UK*, diaper *US*. **-2.** [de camisa] shirt tail.
framboesa [frãn'bweza] *f* raspberry.
frame ['frejmi] *m* COMPUT frame.
França ['frãnsa] *n* France.
francamente [ˌfrãŋka'mẽntʃi] *adv* frankly.
francês, esa [frã'seʃ, ezə] (*mpl* **-eses**, *fpl* **-s**) ◇ *adj* French. ◇ *m, f* Frenchman (*f* Frenchwoman).
◆ **francês** *m* [língua] French.
franco, ca ['frãŋku, ka] *adj* **-1.** [ger] free. **-2.** [sincero] frank. **-3.** [clara] candid.
◆ **franco** *m* [moeda] franc.
franco-atirador, ra ['frãnkuatriʃirado(x), ra] *m, f* sniper.
franco-brasileiro, ra [ˌfrãŋkobrazi'lejru, ra] (*mpl* **franco-brasileiros**, *fpl* **franco-brasileiras**) *adj* Franco-Brazilian.
francófono, na [frãn'kɔfonu, na] ◇ *adj* French-speaking. ◇ *m, f* French speaker.
franga ['frãŋga] *f* pullet.
frangalho [frãŋ'gaʎu] *m* [farrapo] tatter; **em ~s** *fig* in tatters.
frango ['frãŋgu] ◇ *m* ZOOL chicken. ◇ *m* FUT easy goal.
franja ['frãnʒa] *f* fringe.
franjado, da [frãn'ʒadu, da] *adj* **-1.** [cabelo, xale] fringed. **-2.** [rebuscado] recherché.
franqueado, da [frãn'keadu, da] *m* franchise.
franquear [15] [frãɲ'kja(x)] *vt* **-1.** [liberar]: **a entrada foi franqueada, vamos à festa!** they've opened the doors, let's party! **-2.** [isentar de imposto] to exempt (from). **-3.** [pagar o transporte] to pay transport costs (for). **-4.** [ceder franquia] to franchise.
franqueza [frãŋ'keza] *f* frankness.
franquia [frãŋ'kia] *f* **-1.** COM franchise. **-2.** [isenção] exemption; ~ **de bagagem** baggage allowance; ~ **postal** postage.
franzido, da [frãn'zidu, da] *adj* **-1.** [saia] gathered, pleated. **-2.** [pele] wrinkled.
franzino, na [frã'zinu, na] *adj* delicate.
franzir [6] [frãn'zi(x)] *vt* **-1.** [preguear] to pleat. **-2.** [enrugar] to wrinkle; ~ **a sobrancelha** to frown.
fraque ['fraki] *m* frock coat.
fraquejar [4] [frake'ʒa(x)] *vi* to weaken.
fraqueza [fra'keza] *f* weakness.
frasco ['fraʃku] *m* flask.
frase ['frazi] *f* **-1.** [oração] sentence; ~ **feita** aphorism. **-2.** MÚS phrase.
fraseado [fra'zjadu] *m* phrasing.
fraseologia [frazjolo'gia] *f* phraseology.
frasqueira [fraʃ'kejra] *f* bottle rack.
fraternal [fratex'naw] (*pl* **-ais**) *adj* fraternal, brotherly.
fraternidade [fratexni'dadʒi] *f* fraternity.
fraterno, na [fra'tɛxnu, na] *adj* fraternal, brotherly.
fratricida [fratri'sida] *mf* fratricide.
fratura [fra'tura] *f* fracture.
fraturar [4] [fratu'ra(x)] *vt* to fracture.
fraudar [4] [fraw'da(x)] *vt* to defraud.
fraude ['frawdʒi] *f* fraud.
fraudulento, ta [frawdu'lẽntu, ta] *adj* fraudulent.
freada [fre'ada] *f* braking; **dar uma ~** to brake.
frear [15] [fre'a(x)] ◇ *vt* **-1.** AUTO to brake. **-2.** *fig* [controlar] to curb. ◇ *vi* AUTO to brake.
freático, ca ['freatʃiku, ka] *adj*: **lençol ~** water table; **camada freática** aquifer.
freelance [fri'lãnsi] ◇ *adj* freelance. ◇ *mf* freelance, freelancer.
freeware [fri'wari] (*pl* **freewares**) *m* COMPUT freeware.
freezer ['frizɛx] (*pl* **-res**) *m* freezer.
frege ['frɛʒi] *m* quarrel.
freguês, esa [frɛ'geʃ, eza] (*mpl* **-eses**, *fpl* **-s**) *m, f* **-1.** [cliente] customer. **-2.** [paroquiano] parishioner.

freguesia [frege'zia] *f* **-1.** [clientela] clientele. **-2.** [paroquia] parish.
frei [frej] *m* friar.
freio ['freju] *m* **-1.** [cavalo] rein. **-2.** [carro] brake; ~ **de mão** handbrake; ~ **de pé** footbrake.
freira ['frejra] *f* nun.
freixo ['frejʃu] *m* ash.
fremir [6] [fre'mi(x)] *vi* **-1.** [rugir] to roar. **-2.** [tremer] to tremble.
frêmito ['fremitu] *m* shiver.
frenesi [frene'zi] *m* frenzy.
freneticamente [frenɛtʃika'mẽntʃi] *adv* frenetically.
frenético, ca [fre'nɛtʃiku, ka] *adj* frenetic.
frente ['frẽntʃi] *f* **-1.** [lado dianteiro]: **na** ~ **(de)** in front (of); **estar à** ~ **de** *fig* to be ahead of. **-2.** [avante]: **em** ~ ahead; **ir para a** ~ to move on; **levar algo à** ~ to make sthg succeed. **-3.** [resistência] front; ~ **de combate** frontline. **-4.** [presença] in front of; ~ **a** ~ face to face. **-5.** *METEOR*: ~ **fria/quente** cold/warm front.
frentista [frẽn'tʃiʃta] *mf* forecourt attendant.
freqüência [fre'kwẽnsja] *f* **-1.** [ger] frequency; **com** ~ frequently. **-2.** [pessoas] attendance.
freqüentador, ra [frekwẽnta'do(x), ra] *m, f* regular.
freqüentar [4] [frekwẽn'ta(x)] *vt* **-1.** [visitar] to frequent. **-2.** [cursar] to attend.
freqüente [fre'kwẽntʃi] *adj* recurrent.
freqüentemente [frekwẽntʃi'mẽntʃi] *adv* frequently.
fresa ['freza] *f MEC* milling cutter, drill.
fresca ['freʃka] *f* ⊳ **fresco**.
frescão [freʃ'kãw] (*pl* **-ões**) *m* de luxe coach.
fresco, ca ['freʃku, ka] *adj* **-1.** [ger] fresh. **-2.** [ameno] cool. **-3.** *fam* [luxento] posh. **-4.** *fam* [homossexual] camp.
◆ **fresca** *f* [aragem] breeze.
frescobol [freʃko'bɔw] (*pl* **-óis**) *m* beach tennis.
frescões [freʃ'kõjʃ] *mpl* ⊳ **frescão**.
frescor [freʃ'ko(x)] *m* [viço, vigor] freshness.
frescura [freʃ'kura] *f* **-1.** [frescor] freshness. **-2.** [afetação] affectation. **-3.** [formalidade] convention.
fresta ['frɛʃta] *f* slit.
fretado, da [fre'tadu, da] *adj* **-1.** [navio, caminhão] chartered. **-2.** [carro] hired.
fretar [4] [fre'ta(x)] *vt* to hire *UK*, to rent *US*.
frete ['frɛtʃi] *m* freight; **fazer** ~ to freight.
freudiano, na [frɔj'dʒanu, na] *adj* Freudian.
frevo ['frevu] *m Brazilian carnival street-dance, where dancers improvise their own dances.*
fria ['fria] *f fam* [apuros] fix; **entrar numa** ~ to be in a fix.
friagem ['frjaʒẽ] *f* cold.
fricção [frik'sãw] *f* friction.
friccionar [4] [friksjo'na(x)] *vt* to rub.
fricote [fri'kɔtʃi] *m*: **fazer** ~**s** to put on airs.
fricoteiro, ra [friko'tejru, ra] ◇ *adj* vain. ◇ *m, f* show-off.
frieira [fri'ejra] *f* chilblain.
frieza ['frjeza] *f* **-1.** [insensibilidade] coldheartedness. **-2.** [desinteresse] off-handedness.
frigideira [friʒi'dejra] *f* frying pan.
frigidez [friʒi'deʒ] *f* frigidity.
frígido, da ['friʒidu, da] *adj* frigid.
frigir [63] [fri'ʒi(x)] *vt* to fry.
frigorífico [frigo'rifiku] *m* **-1.** [loja] cold store. **-2.** [aparelho] fridge, refrigerator.
frila ['frila] *mf fam* freelance.
frio, fria ['friu, 'fria] *adj* **-1.** [sem calor] cold. **-2.** [insensível] cold. **-3.** [falso] fake. **-4.** [cor] cold. **-5.** [luz] cold.
◆ **frio** *m* [baixa temperatura] cold; **estar com** ~ to be cold; **fazer** ~ to be cold.
◆ **frios** *mpl* [carne] cold meats.
friorento, ta [frjo'rẽntu, ta] *adj* chilly.
frisa ['friza] *f TEATRO* box.
frisar [4] [fri'za(x)] *vt* **-1.** [salientar] to highlight. **-2.** [enrolar] to curl.
friso ['frizu] *m* **-1.** [borda] border. **-2.** *ARQUIT* frieze.
fritada [fri'tada] *f* fried food.
fritar [4] [fri'ta(x)] *vt* to fry.
frito, ta ['fritu, ta] *adj* **-1.** *CULIN* fried. **-2.** *fam* [em apuros]: **estar** ~ to be in hot water.
◆ **fritas** *fpl* chips *UK*, (French) fries *US*.
fritura [fri'tura] *f* fried food, fry-up *UK*.
frivolidade [frivoli'dadʒi] *f* frivolity.
frívolo, la ['frivolu, la] *adj* frivolous.
frondoso, osa [frõn'dozu, ɔza] *adj* leafy.
fronha ['froɲa] *f* pillowcase.
front [frõ] *m MIL* front.
frontal [frõn'taw] (*pl* **-ais**) *adj* frontal.
fronte ['frõntʃi] *f* forehead.
fronteira [frõn'tejra] *f* ⊳ **fronteiro**.
fronteiriço, ça [frõntej'risu, sa] *adj* border *(antes de subst)*.
fronteiro, ra [frõn'tejru, ra] *adj* facing.
◆ **fronteira** *f* **-1.** [extremidade] border. **-2.** *fig* [limite] border.
frontispício [frõntʃiʃ'pisju] *m* frontispiece.
frota ['frɔta] *f* fleet.
frouxo, xa ['froʃu, ʃa] *adj* **-1.** [folgado] loose. **-2.** [fraco, ineficiente] weak. **-3.** [condescendente]: **ser** ~ **com alguém** to be weak with sb. **-4.** [covarde] feeble.
frufru [fru'fru] *m* frill, frou-frou.
frugal [fru'gaw] (*pl* **-ais**) *adj* frugal.
frugalidade [frugali'dadʒi] *f* frugality.
fruição [frwi'sãw] *f* fruition.
fruir [74] ['frwi(x)] *vi*: ~ **de algo** to enjoy sthg.
frustração [fruʃtra'sãw] (*pl* **-ões**) *f* **-1.** [malogro] frustration. **-2.** [decepção] frustration.
frustrado, da [fruʃ'tradu, da] *adj* **-1.** [malogrado] frustrated. **-2.** [decepcionado] disappointed.
frustrante [fruʃ'trãntʃi] *adj* frustrating.
frustrar [4] [fruʃ'tra(x)] *vt* **-1.** [malograr] to frustrate. **-2.** [decepcionar] to cheat. **-3.** [privar]: ~ **alguém de algo** to deprive sb of sthg.
◆ **frustrar-se** *vp* **-1.** [malograr-se] to be frustrated. **-2.** [decepcionar-se] to be disappointed.

fruta ['fruta] *f* fruit.
fruta-de-conde [ˌfrutadʒi'kõndʒi] (*pl* **frutas-de-conde**) *f* custard apple.
fruta-pão [ˌfruta'pãw] (*pl* **frutas-pães**, **frutas-pão**) *f* breadfruit.
fruteiro, ra [fru'tejru, ra] *adj* fruit-loving.
◆ **fruteira** *f* fruit tree.
frutífero, ra [fru'tʃiferu, ra] *adj* **-1.** [árvore] fruit-bearing. **-2.** [proveitoso] fruitful.
fruto ['frutu] *m* **-1.** [fruta] fruit. **-2.** *fig* [resultado] fruit.
FTP (*abrev de* **File Transfer Protocol**) *m* FTP.
fubá [fu'ba] *m* **-1.** [de milho] maize flour. **-2.** [de arroz] rice flour.
fuça ['fusa] *f fam* [focinho] conk, nose; **nas ~s de** under the nose of.
fuçar [13] [fu'sa(x)] *fam* <> *vt* to meddle in. <> *vi* to meddle.
fuga ['fuga] *f* **-1.** [escapada] escape. **-2.** *fig* [alívio] escape. **-3.** *MÚS* fugue.
fugaz [fu'gaʒ] *adj* fleeting.
fugida [fu'ʒida] *f* escape; **dar uma ~** to make one's escape.
fugidio, dia [fu'ʒidio, dia] *adj* **-1.** [animal] skittish. **-2.** [pessoa, personalidade] retiring.
fugir [62] [fu'ʒi(x)] *vi* **-1.** [escapar]: **~ (de)** to escape (from). **-2.** [evitar]: **~ de algo/alguém** to avoid sthg/sb.
fugitivo, va [fuʒi'tʃivu, va] <> *adj* fugitive. <> *m, f* fugitive.
fulano, na [fu'lanu, na] *m, f* so-and-so; **~ de tal** some so-and-so; **~, beltrano e sicrano** Tom, Dick or Harry.
fuleiro, ra [fu'lejru, ra] *adj* shabby.
fúlgido, da ['fuwʒidu, da] *adj* dazzling.
fulgir [78] [fuw'ʒi(x)] *vi* to dazzle.
fulgor [fuw'go(x)] *m* brilliance.
fulgurante [fuwgu'rãntʃi] *adj* shining.
fuligem [fu'liʒẽ] *f* soot.
fulminante [fuwmi'nãntʃi] *adj* **-1.** [mortal] deadly. **-2.** *fig* [irado] vicious.
fulminar [4] [fuwmi'na(x)] *vt* **-1.** [matar] to kill. **-2.** [aniquilar] to annihilate.
fulo, la ['fulu, la] *adj*: **estar** *ou* **ficar ~ da vida** to be totally fed up.
fumaça [fu'masa] *f* smoke; **e lá vai ~** something or other.
fumaceira [fuma'sejra] *f* (cloud of) smoke.
fumante [fu'mãntʃi] *mf* smoker; **não ~** non-smoker.
fumar [4] [fu'ma(x)] <> *vt* to smoke. <> *vi* to smoke.
fumê [fu'me] *adj inv* smoky.
fumegante [fume'gãntʃi] *adj* steaming.
fumegar [4] [fume'ga(x)] *vi* **-1.** [fumaçar] to smoke. **-2.** *fig* [enfurecer-se] to blow up.
fumo ['fumu] *m* **-1.** [tabaco] tobacco. **-2.** [maconha] dope; **puxar ~** to draw (on a spliff). **-3.** [vício] smoking.
fumódromo [fu'mɔdromu] *m fam* smoking area.
FUNAI (*abrev de* **Fundação Nacional do Índio**) *f* *Brazilian government organization for the protection of the indigenous population.*
FUNARTE (*abrev de* **Fundação Nacional de Arte**) *f* *Brazilian government organization for the promotion of artistic activities.*
FUNASA (*abrev de* **Fundação Nacional de Saúde**) *f* *Brazilian government organization for health education and prevention of disease among indigenous peoples.*
função [fũn'sãw] (*pl* **-ões**) *f* **-1.** [cargo] function. **-2.** [responsabilidade] function. **-3.** [utilidade] role. **-4.** [espetáculo] performance. **-5.** [papel] function. **-6.** [atribuição] function. **-7.** *GRAM* function. **-8.** *MAT* function.
◆ **em função de** *loc prep* due to.
funcional [fũnsjo'naw] (*pl* **-ais**) *adj* **-1.** [ger] functional. **-2.** [público] civil-service. **-3.** [de carreira] service-related.
funcionalidade [fũnsjonali'dadʒi] *f* functionality.
funcionalismo [fũnsjona'liʒmu] *m* **-1.** [praticidade] practicality. **-2.** [servidores]: **~ público** civil service.
funcionamento [fũnsjona'mẽntu] *m* functioning; **horário de ~** opening hours, working hours.
funcionar [4] [fũsjo'na(x)] *vi* **-1.** [máquina *etc*] to work; **pôr algo para ~** to switch sthg on. **-2.** [loja *etc*] to be open. **-3.** [exercer função]: **~ como algo** to work as sthg. **-4.** [dar certo] to work.
funcionário, ria [fũsjo'narju, rja] *m, f* employee; **~ público** civil servant.
funções [fũn'sõjʃ] *fpl* ▷ **função**.
fundação [fũnda'sãw] (*pl* **-ões**) *f* **-1.** [alicerce] foundation. **-2.** [instituição] foundation. **-3.** [criação] founding.
fundador, ra [fũnda'do(x), ra] <> *adj* founding. <> *m, f* founder.
fundamentação [fũndamẽnta'sãw] (*pl* **-ões**) *f* foundation.
fundamental [fũndamẽn'taw] (*pl* **-ais**) *adj* fundamental.
fundamentalismo [fũndamẽnta'liʒmu] *m RELIG* fundamentalism.
fundamentalista [fũndamẽnta'liʃta] <> *adj* fundamentalist. <> *mf* fundamentalist.
fundamentar [4] [fũndamẽn'ta(x)] *vt* **-1.** [basear]: **~ algo em algo** to base sthg on sthg. **-2.** [justificar] to found.
◆ **fundamentar-se** *vp* [basear-se]: **~-se em algo** to be based on sthg.
fundamento [fũnda'mẽntu] *m* fundament; **sem ~** unfounded.
FUNDAP (*abrev de* **Fundação do Desenvolvimento Administrativo**) *f* *Brazilian organization for the coordination of training and educational programmes.*
fundar [4] [fũn'da(x)] *vt* **-1.** [instituir] to found. **-2.** [criar] to establish.
fundear [15] [fũn'dʒja(x)] *vi* to drop anchor.
fundição [fũdʒi'sãw] (*pl* **-ões**) *f* melting down.

fundilho [fũn'dʒiʎu] *m* seat, bottom.
fundir [6] [fũn'dʒi(x)] *vt* **-1.** [derreter] to melt. **-2.** [moldar] to cast. **-3.** [incorporar] to merge. **-4.** *fam* [perturbar]: ~ **a cuca de alguém** to do sb's head in.
◆ **fundir-se** *vp* **-1.** [derreter-se] to melt. **-2.** [incorporar-se] to merge.
fundo, da ['fũndu, da] *adj* **-1.** [profundo] deep. **-2.** [reentrante] sunken. **-3.** *fam* [despreparado]: ~ **(em algo)** weak (at sthg).
◆ **fundo** <> *m* **-1.** [base] bottom. **-2.** [de local] rear. **-3.** [segundo plano] background; **ao** ~ in the distance. **-4.** [de tecido, papel] background. **-5.** *MÚS*: ~ **musical** background music. **-6.** [íntimo]: **eu o perdoei do** ~ **da alma** I forgave him from the bottom of my heart. **-7.** *fig* [teor] element. **-8.** *FIN* fund; ~ **de garantia** security; ~ **de investimento** investment fund; **emprestei-lhe dinheiro a** ~ **perdidos** I lent him some money without expecting repayment. **-9.** *MED*: ~ **do olho** back of the eye. <> *adv* [profundamente] deeply; **a** ~ in depth.
◆ **fundos** *mpl* **-1.** [de casa] funds. **-2.** [capital] capital; **cheque sem** ~ unsecured cheque.
◆ **no fundo** *loc adv* [intrinsecamente] basically.
fundura [fũn'dura] *f* depth.
fúnebre ['funebri] *adj* funereal.
funeral [fune'raw] (*pl* **-ais**) *m* funeral.
funerário, ria [fune'rarju, rja] *adj* funeral *(antes de subst)*.
◆ **funerária** *f* funeral parlour.
funesto, ta [fu'nɛʃtu, ta] *adj* dire.
fungar [14] [fũŋ'ga(x)] *vi* to sniff.
fungicida [fũnʒi'sida] *m* fungicide.
fungo ['fũŋgu] *m* fungus.
funicular [funiku'la(x)] <> *adj* funicular. <> *m* **-1.** [sistema] funicular. **-2.** [veículo] cable car.
funil [fu'niw] (*pl* **-is**) *m* funnel.
funilaria [funi'laria] *f* panel beating.
funileiro [funi'lejru] *f* panel beater.
FUNRURAL (*de abrev* **Fundo de Assistência e Previdência ao Trabalhador Rural**) *m Brazilian fund for the assistance and support of rural workers.*
furacão [fura'kãw] (*pl* **-ões**) *m* **-1.** [ciclone] cyclone. **-2.** *fig* [turbilhão] maelstrom; **como um** ~ like a whirlwind.
furadeira [fura'dejra] *f* drill.
furado, da [fu'radu, da] *adj* **-1.** [pneu] punctured. **-2.** [orelha] pierced. **-3.** [sapato] holey. **-4.** *fam* [infrutífero] unsuccessful.
fura-greve ['furagrevi] *mf* blackleg.
furão, rona [fu'rãw, rɔna] (*mpl* **-ões**, *fpl* **-s**) *adj* [cavador] unreliable.
furar [4] [fu'ra(x)] <> *vt* **-1.** [pneu] to puncture. **-2.** [orelha] to pierce. **-3.** [sapato] to make a hole in. **-4.** [frustrar] to fail. **-5.** [não aderir a] to leave. <> *vi* **-1.** [perfurar] to puncture. **-2.** [sapato] to get a hole. **-3.** [malograr] to fail.
furgão [fux'gãw] (*pl* **-ões**) *m* van.
fúria ['furja] *f* fury; **estar/ficar uma** ~ to be in a fury.
furibundo, da [furi'bũndu, da] *adj* livid, incensed.
furioso, osa [fu'rjozu, ɔza] *adj* **-1.** [raivoso] furious. **-2.** [violento] furious.
furo ['furu] *m* **-1.** [buraco] puncture. **-2.** [orelha] hole. **-3.** [sapato] hole. **-4.** *fig* [falha] mistake; **dar um** ~ to put one's foot in it. **-5.** *JORN*: ~ **(de reportagem)** scoop.
furões [fu'rõjʃ] *mpl* ▻ **furão**.
furona [fu'rona] *f* ▻ **furão**.
furor [fu'ro(x)] *m* **-1.** [fúria] fury. **-2.** [arrebatamento]: **fazer algo com** ~ to do sthg furiously. **-3.** *loc*: **causar** ~ to cause fury.
furreca [fu'xɛka] *adj fam* mean.
furta-cor [ˌfuxta'ko(x)] (*pl* **furta-cores**) *adj* iridescent.
furtar [4] [fux'ta(x)] <> *vt* [roubar] to steal. <> *vi* [roubar] to steal.
◆ **furtar-se** *vp* [esquivar-se]: **~-se a algo** to dodge sthg.
furtivo, va [fux'tʃivu, va] *adj* **-1.** [às ocultas] furtive. **-2.** [dissimulado] furtive.
furto ['fuxtu] *m* theft.
furúnculo [fu'rũŋkulu] *m* boil.
fusão [fu'zãw] (*pl* **-ões**) *f* **-1.** [ger] fusion. **-2.** *COM* amalgamation. **-3.** [liga] amalgam.
fuseau [fu'zo] *m* leggings *(pl)*.
fuselagem [fuze'laʒẽ] (*pl* **-ns**) *f* fuselage.
fusível [fu'zivew] (*pl* **-eis**) *m* fuse.
fuso ['fuzu] *m* [peça] screw.
◆ **fuso horário** *m* time zone.
fusões [fu'zõjʃ] *fpl* ▻ **fusão**.
fustigar [14] [fuʃtʃi'ga(x)] *vt* to whip.
futebol [futʃi'bɔw] *m* football; ~ **de salão** five-a-side football.

FUTEBOL

Football is one of the great passions of the Brazilian people, who have made an art form of their most popular sport. Five times World Cup champions ('58, '62, '70, '94 and 2002), the Brazilians export their star players throughout the world, especially to Spain and Italy. The pride of the nation, Pelé, is considered the greatest football player of all time.

futebolismo [futʃibo'liʒmu] *m* [paixão] football mania.
futebolista [futʃibo'liʃta] *mf* **-1.** [jogador] footballer. **-2.** [fã] football fan. **-3.** [conhecedor] football expert.
futebolístico, ca [futʃibo'liʃtʃiku, ka] *adj* football *(antes de subst)*.
futevôlei [futʃi'volej] *m ESP sport practised on the beach and following the rules of volleyball but in which the hands are not allowed to touch the ball.*
fútil ['futʃiw] (*pl* **-eis**) *adj* **-1.** [leviano] frivolous. **-2.** [insignificante] trivial.
futilidade [futʃili'dadʒi] *f* **-1.** [leviandade] frivolity. **-2.** [insignificância] triviality. **-3.** [coisa fútil] triviality.

futrica [fu'trika] *f* rag; **correr ~s (com)** to rag.
futurista [futu'riʃta] *adj* futuristic.
futuro, ra [fu'turu, ra] *adj* future.
◆ **futuro** *m* **-1.** [tempo] future. **-2.** [destino] future. **-3.** GRAM future.
FUVEST (*abrev de* **Fundação do Vestibular do Estado de São Paulo**) *f organization regulating entrance examinations at some universities in São Paulo.*
fuxicar [12] [fuʃi'ka(x)] *vt* to gossip.
fuxico [fu'ʃiku] *m* gossip.
fuxiqueiro, ra [fuʃi'kejru, ra] ◇ *adj* gossipy. ◇ *m, f* gossip.
fuzil [fu'ziw] (*pl* **-is**) *m* rifle.
fuzilamento [fuzila'mẽntu] *m* shooting.
fuzilante [fuzi'lãntʃi] *adj* **-1.** [ameaçador] threatening. **-2.** [fatal] fatal.
fuzilar [4] [fuzi'la(x)] ◇ *vt* **-1.** [atirar] to shoot. **-2.** *fig* [ameaçar]: **~ alguém com os olhos** to look daggers at sb. ◇ *vi fig*: **~ (de ódio)** [pessoa] to radiate hatred; [olhos] to flash.
fuzileiro [fuzi'lejru] *m* rifleman; **~ naval** marine.
fuzuê [fu'zwe] *m* party.

g¹, G [ʒe] *m* [letra] g, G.
g² (*abrev de* **grama**) *m* g.
gabar-se [4] [gabax'si] *vp*: **~-se (de)** to boast (about).
gabardine [gabax'dʒini] *m* gaberdine.
gabaritado, da [gabari'tadu, da] *adj* high-calibre.
gabaritar [4] [gabari'ta(x)] *vt* to enable.
◆ **gabaritar-se** *vp* to be able.
gabarito [gaba'ritu] *m* **-1.** [qualidade] high calibre. **-2.** [respostas] results *(pl)*. **-3.** [limite] maximum size.
gabinete [gabi'netʃi] *m* **-1.** [escritório] study. **-2.** POL cabinet.
gado ['gadu] *m* cattle.
gaélico, ca [ga'ɛliku, ka] *adj* Gaelic.
◆ **gaélico** *m* [língua] Gaelic.
gafanhoto [gafã'ɲotu] *m* grasshopper.
gafe ['gafi] *f* gaffe.
gafieira [ga'fjejra] *f* **-1.** [baile] ball. **-2.** [dança] dance.
gagá [ga'ga] *adj* gaga.
gago, ga ['gagu, ga] ◇ *adj* stammering. ◇ *m, f* stammerer.
gagueira [ga'gejra] *f* stammer.
gaguejar [4] [gage'ʒa(x)] *vt & vi* to stammer.
gaiato, ta [ga'jatu, ta] *adj* mischievous.
gaiola [ga'jɔla] ◇ *f* **-1.** [clausura] cage. **-2.** *fam* [prisão] jail. ◇ *m* [vapor] steamboat.
gaita ['gajta] *f* **-1.** MÚS mouth organ; **~ de foles** bagpipe. **-2.** *fam fig* [dinheiro] dosh.
gaivota [gaj'vɔta] *f* seagull.
gala ['gala] *f*: **de ~** gala; **uniforme de ~** dress uniform.
galã [ga'lã] *m* **-1.** [ator] lead. **-2.** [sedutor] playboy.
galáctico, ca [ga'laktʃiku, ka] *adj* galactic.
galante [ga'lãntʃi] *adj* gallant.
galanteador [galãntʃja'do(x)] *adj* gallant.
galantear [15] [galãn'tʃja(x)] *vt* to play the gallant.
galanteio [galãn'teju] *m* gallantry.
galão [ga'lãw] (*pl* **-ões**) *m* **-1.** MIL stripe. **-2.** [enfeite] braid. **-3.** [medida] gallon.
Galápagos [ga'lapaguʃ] *npl*: **as (ilhas) ~** the Galapagos (Islands).
galardão [galax'dãw] (*pl* **-ões**) *m* reward.
galáxia [ga'laksja] *f* galaxy.
galé [ga'lɛ] *f* galley.
galera [ga'lɛra] *f* **-1.** NÁUT galley. **-2.** *fam* [grupo] crowd.
galeria [gale'ria] *f* **-1.** TEATRO circle. **-2.** [coleção] collection. **-3.** [canalização] drainage. **-4.** [loja de arte] gallery. **-5.** [centro comercial] shopping centre.
Gales ['galiʃ] *n*: **País de ~** Wales.
galês, esa [ga'leʃ, eza] ◇ *adj* Welsh. ◇ *m, f* Welshman (*f* Welshwoman).
◆ **galês** *m* [língua] Welsh.
galeto [ga'letu] *m* roast poussin.
galgar [14] [gaw'ga(x)] *vt* **-1.** [saltar] to jump across. **-2.** [subir] to climb. **-3.** *fig* [ascender] to move up.
galhardia [gaʎax'dʒia] *f* **-1.** [elegância] smartness. **-2.** [bravura] bravery.
galhardo, da [ga'ʎaxdu, da] *adj* **-1.** [elegante] smart. **-2.** [bravo] gallant.
galheta [ga'ʎeta] *f* cruet.
galheteiro [gaʎe'tejru] *m* cruet-stand.
galho ['gaʎu] *m* **-1.** BOT branch. **-2.** *fam* [problema] pickle; **dar ~** to cause a pickle; **quebrar um ~** to get out of a pickle.
Galícia [ga'lisja] *n* Galicia.
galicismo [gali'siʒmu] *m* Gallicism.
galináceos [gali'nasjuʃ] *mpl* Galliformes.
galinha [ga'liɲa] ◇ *f* **-1.** [ave] hen. **-2.** CULIN chicken. **-3.** *fam* [namorador] easy lay. **-4.** *loc*: **a ~ do vizinho é sempre mais gorda** the grass is always greener on the other side of the fence. ◇ *m, f fam* [covarde] chicken.
galinha-d'angola [ga,liɲadãŋ'gɔla] (*pl* **galinhas-d'angola**) *f* guinea-fowl.
galinhagem [gali'ɲaʒẽ] *f fam* [bolinação] touching up.
galinha-morta [ga,liɲa'mɔxta] (*pl* **galinhas-mortas**) *mf* [covarde] chicken.

galinheiro [gali'ɲejru] *m* poulterer.
galo ['galu] *m* **-1.** [ave] cockerel, rooster; ~ **de briga** *ou* **de rinha** fighting cock. **-2.** [inchaço] bump.
galocha [ga'lɔʃa] *f* galosh; **chato de** ~ drag.
galopante [galo'pãntʃi] *adj fig* galloping.
galopar [4] [galo'pa(x)] *vi* to gallop.
galope [ga'lɔpi] *m* gallop.
galpão [gaw'pãw] (*pl* **-ões**) *m* hangar.
galvanizado, da [gawvani'zadu, da] *adj* [ferro, chapa] galvanized.
galvanizar [4] [gawvani'za(x)] *vt* to galvanize.
gama ['gãma] *f* **-1.** *MÚS* scale. **-2.** *fig* [série] range.
gamado, da [ga'madu, da] *adj*: **ser/estar** ~ **por alguém** to be hooked on sb.
gamão [ga'mãw] *m* backgammon.
gamar [4] [ga'ma(x)] *vi* to be hooked; ~ **por algo/alguém** to fall for sthg/sb.
gambá [gãn'ba] *m ZOOL* opossum; **bêbado como um** ~ *fam* drunk as a skunk.
Gâmbia ['gãnbja] *n* Gambia.
gambito [gãn'bitu] *m* [xadrez] gambit.
gamela [ga'mɛla] *f* trough.
gana ['gãna] *f* **-1.** [desejo]: ~ **de algo/de fazer algo** desire for sthg/to do sthg. **-2.** [raiva]: **ter** ~ **de alguém** to be furious with sb.
Gana ['gãna] *n* Ghana.
ganância [ga'nãnsja] *f* greed.
ganancioso, osa [ganã'sjozu, ɔza] *adj* greedy.
gancho ['gãnʃu] *m* **-1.** [peça] hook. **-2.** *COST* hook. **-3.** *fig* [recurso] bait.
gandaia [gãn'daja] *f fig* dissipation; **ele passou a noite na** ~ he spent the night in dissipation; **ontem fomos para a** ~ yesterday we went on a binge, self-indulgence; **cair na** ~ to descend into a life of dissipation.
gandaiar [gãnda'ja(x)] *vi* **-1.** [farrear] to live it up, to party. **-2.** [vadiar] to idle about.
gânglio ['gãŋglju] *m* ganglion.
gangorra [gãŋ'goxa] *f* seesaw.
gangrena [gãŋ'grena] *f* gangrene.
gangrenar [4] [gãŋgre'na(x)] *vi* to become gangrenous.
gângster ['gãŋgiʃte(x)] *m* gangster.
gangue ['gãŋgi] *f* gang.
ganhador, ra [gaɲa'do(x), ra] ◇ *adj* winning. ◇ *m, f* winner.
ganha-pão [ˌgãɲa'pãw] (*pl* **ganha-pães**) *m* **-1.** [trabalho] living, livelihood. **-2.** [objeto de trabalho] livelihood.
ganhar [4] [ga'ɲa(x)] ◇ *vt* **-1.** [ger] to win. **-2.** [receber] to get. **-3.** [salário] to earn. **-4.** [lucrar] to gain; ~ **tempo** to gain time; **ganhou o dia quando recebeu a notícia** it made his day when he got the news. **-5.** [atingir] to reach. ◇ *vi* **-1.** [vencer]: ~ **de alguém** to beat sb; ~ **de alguém em algo** to outdo sb at sthg. **-2.** [como remuneração] to earn. **-3.** [lucrar]: ~ **(com)** to profit (from); **sair ganhando** to come out on top.
ganho ['gãɲu] ◇ *pp* ▷ **ganhar**. ◇ *m* **-1.** [salário] earnings *(pl)*. **-2.** [lucro] profit. **-3.** *COM*: ~ **de capital** capital gain. **-4.** *JUR*: ~ **de causa** successful lawsuit.
ganido [ga'nidu] *m* whine.
ganir [6] [ga'ni(x)] *vi* to whine.
ganso ['gãnsu] *m* goose.
GAPA (*abrev de* **Grupo de Apoio à Prevenção à Aids**) *m Brazilian non-governmental organization working in AIDS prevention.*
garagem [ga'raʒẽ] (*pl* **-ns**) *f* garage.
garagista [gara'ʒiʃta] *mf* **-1.** [manobrista] car jockey **-2.** [proprietário] garage owner.
garanhão [gara'ɲãw] (*pl* **-ões**) *m* **-1.** [cavalo] stallion. **-2.** *fig* [homem] stud.
garantia [garãn'tʃia] *f* **-1.** [ger] guarantee. **-2.** [de dívida] collateral.
garantir [6] [garãn'tʃi(x)] *vt* **-1.** [assegurar]: ~ **algo a alguém** to assure sb of sthg; ~ **que** to guarantee that. **-2.** [prometer]: ~ **algo a alguém** to promise sb sthg. **-3.** [asseverar] to guarantee.
◆ **garantir-se** *vp* [defender-se]: **~-se contra algo** to protect o.s. against sthg.
garatuja [garatu'ʒa] *f* scribble.
garbo ['gaxbu] *m* **-1.** [elegância] elegance. **-2.** [distinção] distinction.
garboso, osa [gax'bozu, ɔza] *adj* **-1.** [elegante] elegant. **-2.** [distinto] distinguished.
garça ['gaxsa] *f* heron.
garçom [gax'sõ] (*pl* **-ns**) *m* waiter.
garçonete [garso'nɛtʃi] *f* waitress.
garçonnière [gaxso'njɛ(x)] *f* love nest.
garfada [gax'fada] *f* forkful.
garfo ['gaxfu] *m* fork; **ser um bom** ~ *fig* to be a gourmet.
gargalhada [gaxga'ʎada] *f* burst of laughter; **cair na** ~ to fall about laughing; **dar** *ou* **soltar uma** ~ to burst out laughing.
gargalhar [gaxga'ʎa(x)] *vi* to roar with laughter.
gargalo [gax'galu] *m* **-1.** [de garrafa] neck. **-2.** [obstáculo] *fig* bottleneck.
garganta [gax'gãnta] *f* **-1.** *ANAT* throat; **molhar a** ~ *fam* [beber] to wet one's whistle; **não passar pela** ~ to stick in one's throat; **ter boa** ~ [ter boa voz] to have a good voice. **-2.** [desfiladeiro] mountain pass.
gargantilha [gaxgãn'tʃiʎa] *f* choker.
gargarejar [4] [gaxgare'ʒa(x)] *vi* to gargle.
gargarejo [gaxga'reʒu] *m* **-1.** [ato] gargling. **-2.** [líquido] gargle.
gari [ga'ri] *mf* roadsweeper.
garimpar [4] [garĩm'pa(x)] *vi* to prospect *(for precious metals or stones)*.
garimpeiro, ra [garĩn'pejru, ra] *m, f* prospector.
garimpo [ga'rĩnpu] *m* [mina] mining deposit.
garoa [ga'roa] *f* drizzle.
garoar [20] [gar'rwa(x)] *vi* to drizzle.
garota [ga'rota] *f* ▷ **garoto**.
garotada [garo'tada] *f*: **a** ~ the kids *(pl)*.
garoto, ta [ga'rotu, ta] *m, f* **-1.** [menino] boy, kid. **-2.** [prostituto]: ~ **de programa** prostitute.
◆ **garoto** *m* [chope] small glass of draught beer.
◆ **garota** *f* [namorada] girlfriend.

garoto-propaganda, garota-propaganda [gar,rotupropa'gãnda, gar,rotapropa'gãnda] (*mpl* **garotos-propaganda**, *fpl* **garotas-propaganda**) *m* cover-boy (*f* cover-girl).
garoupa [ga'ropa] *f* grouper.
garra ['gaxa] *f* **-1.** [de animal] claw. **-2.** *fig* [entusiasmo] enthusiasm; **ter ~** to be enthusiastic.
garrafa [ga'xafa] *f* bottle; **~ térmica** Thermos flask® *UK*, Thermos bottle® *US*.
garrafada [gaxa'fada] *f* [pancada]: **dar uma ~ em alguém** to hit sb with a bottle.
garrafal [gaxa'faw] (*pl* **-ais**) *adj fig* [imenso - letra] large; [- aviso] severe.
garrafão [gaxa'fãw] *m* flagon.
garrancho [ga'xãnʃu] *m* scrawl.
garrote [ga'xɔtʃi] *m* **-1.** [de tortura] garrotte *UK*, garrote *US*. **-2.** [torniquete] tourniquet.
garupa [ga'rupa] *f* **-1.** [de cavalo] hindquarters, rump. **-2.** [de bicicleta, moto] pillion; **andar na ~** to ride pillion.
gás ['gajʃ] (*pl* **gases**) *m* **-1.** [fluido] gas; **~ encanado** piped gas; **~ natural** natural gas; **~ carbônico** carbon dioxide; **~ lacrimogêneo** tear gas. **-2.** [do intestino] wind, flatulence. **-3.** *fam fig* [entusiasmo] go.
gaseificar [12] [gazejfi'ka(x)] *vt* to gasify.
◆ **gaseificar-se** *vp* to be gasified.
gasoduto [gazo'dutu] *m* gas pipeline.
gasóleo [ga'zɔlju] *m* diesel.
gasolina [gazo'lina] *f* petrol *UK*, gasoline *US*.
gasômetro [ga'zometru] *m* gasometer.
gasoso, osa [ga'zozu, ɔza] *adj* fizzy.
◆ **gasosa** *f* fizzy drink *UK*, soda *US*.
gastador, ra [gaʃta'do(x), ra] ◇ *adj* wasteful. ◇ *m, f* wasteful person.
gastar [4] [gaʃ'ta(x)] ◇ *vt* **-1.** [despender] to spend. **-2.** [consumir - energia, gasolina] to consume; [- tempo] to take up. **-3.** [usar - roupa, sapato] to wear; [- cosmético, produto] to use. **-4.** [desperdiçar] to waste. **-5.** [desgastar] to wear out. ◇ *vi* **-1.** [despender dinheiro] to spend money. **-2.** [desgastar-se] to wear out.
◆ **gastar-se** *vp* [desgastar-se] to wear out.
gasto, ta ['gaʃtu, ta] ◇ *pp* ▷ **gastar**. ◇ *adj* **-1.** [ger] worn out. **-2.** [consumido - tempo] spent; [- energia] used up; [- electricidade] consumed. **-3.** [despendido] spent. **-4.** [produto, cosmético] used up. **-5.** [desperdiçado] wasted. **-6.** [envelhecido] worn.
◆ **gasto** *m* [despesa] expense.
◆ **gastos** *mpl* [despesas] expenses; **~s públicos** public expenditure *(sg)*.
gástrico, ca ['gaʃtriku, ka] *adj* gastric.
gastrite [gaʃ'tritʃi] *f* gastritis *(inv)*.
gastroenterite [gaʃtrẽnte'ritʃi] *f* gastroenteritis *(inv)*.
gastronomia [gaʃtrono'mia] *f* gastronomy.
gastronômico, ca [gaʃtro'nomiku, ka] *adj* gastronomic.
gastrônomo, ma [gaʃ'tronomu, ma] *m, f* gastronome.
gata ['gata] *f* ▷ **gato**.
gateway [gejtʃi'wej] (*pl* **gateways**) *m* COMPUT gateway.
gatilho [ga'tʃiʎu] *m* trigger.
gatinhas [ga'tʃiɲaʃ] *fpl*: **andar de ~** to go on all fours, to crawl.
gato, ta ['gatu, ta] *m, f* **-1.** [animal] cat; **~ montês** wild cat; **~ escaldado tem medo de água fria** *prov* once bitten, twice shy; **vender ~ por lebre** to sell a pig in a poke. **-2.** *fam* [pessoa] sexy person.
◆ **gato** *m* ELETR *illegal electrical connection*; **fazer um ~** *to make an illegal electrical connection*.
gato-pingado [,gatupĩŋ'gadu] (*pl* **gatos-pingados**) *m*: **havia apenas uns gatos-pingados no cinema** there was hardly a soul in the cinema.
gato-sapato [,gatusa'patu] (*pl* **gatos-sapatos**) *m*: **fazer ~ de alguém** to treat sb like a doormat.
gatuno, na [ga'tunu, na] ◇ *adj* thieving. ◇ *m, f* thief.
gaúcho, cha [ga'uʃu, ʃa] ◇ *adj* Rio Grande do Sul *(antes de subst)*. ◇ *m, f person from Rio Grande do Sul*.
gaveta [ga'veta] *f* drawer.
gavetão [gave'tãw] (*pl* **-ões**) *m* large drawer.
gaveteiro [gave'tejru] *m* drawer-runner.
gavião [ga'vjãw] (*pl* **-ões**) *m* hawk.
gaze ['gazi] *f* **-1.** [tecido] gauze. **-2.** [para curativo] antiseptic gauze.
gazela [ga'zɛla] *f* gazelle.
gazeta [ga'zeta] *f* **-1.** [jornal] gazette. **-2.** [vadiação]: **fazer ~** to play truant.
gazua [ga'zua] *f* skeleton key.
GB (*abrev de* **Great Britain**) *n* GB.
geada ['ʒjada] *f* frost.
gear ['ʒia(x)] *vi* to freeze.
gel [ʒɛl] *f* gel.
geladeira [ʒela'dejra] *f* refrigerator, fridge.
gelado, da [ʒe'ladu, da] *adj* **-1.** [comida] frozen. **-2.** [bebida] chilled. **-3.** [mar, vento] icy.
gelar [4] [ʒe'la(x)] ◇ *vt* **-1.** [comida] to freeze. **-2.** [bebida] to chill. ◇ *vi* to be freezing.
gelatina [ʒela'tʃina] *f* **-1.** [gel] gelatine. **-2.** [sobremesa] jelly *UK*, Jell-O® *US*.
gelatinoso, osa [ʒelatʃi'nozu, ɔza] *adj* gelatinous.
geléia [ʒe'lɛja] *f* jam *UK*, jelly *US*.
geleira [ʒe'lejra] *f* glacier.
gélido, da ['ʒɛlidu, da] *adj* **-1.** [gelado] icy. **-2.** *fig* [imóvel] frozen.
gelo ['ʒelu] ◇ *adj inv* light grey *UK*, light gray *US*. ◇ *m* **-1.** [água solidificada] ice. **-2.** [cor] light grey *UK*, light gray *US*. **-3.** *fig* [indiferença]: **dar um ~ em alguém** to give sb the cold shoulder; **quebrar o ~** to break the ice. **-4.** *loc*: **estar um ~** to be freezing cold.
gelo-seco [,ʒelu'seku] (*pl* **gelos-secos**) *m* dry ice.
gema ['ʒema] *f* **-1.** [do ovo] yolk. **-2.** [pedra preciosa] gem.

◆ **da gema** *loc adv* [autêntico]: **ela é carioca da ~** she is a true carioca.
gemada [ʒe'mada] *f* eggnog.
gêmeo, mea ['ʒemju, mja] ◇ *adj* twin. ◇ *m, f* twin.
◆ **Gêmeos** *mpl* ASTRO Gemini; **ser Gêmeos** to be Gemini.
gemer [5] [ʒe'me(x)] *vi* **-1.** [de dor] to groan. **-2.** [lastimar-se] to moan. **-3.** [ranger] to wail. **-4.** *fig* [vento] to howl.
gemido [ʒe'midu] *m* **-1.** [de dor] groan. **-2.** [de animal] howl. **-3.** [lamento] wail.
geminiano, na [ʒemi'ɲanu, na] ◇ *adj* Gemini *(antes de subst).* ◇ *m, f* Gemini.
gene ['ʒeni] *m* gene.
genealogia [ʒenjalo'ʒia] *f* genealogy.
genealógico, ca [ʒenja'lɔʒiku, ka] *adj* genealogical; **árvore genelógica** family tree.
Genebra [ʒe'nɛbra] *n* Geneva.
general [gene'raw] (*pl* **-ais**) *m* general.
generalidade [ʒenerali'dadʒi] *f* **-1.** [totalidade] generality. **-2.** [maioria] majority.
◆ **generalidades** *fpl* [assuntos gerais] general matters.
generalização [ʒeneraliza'sãw] (*pl* **-ões**) *f* generalization.
generalizar [4] [generali'za(x)] ◇ *vi* [fazer generalizações] to generalize. ◇ *vt* [difundir] to spread.
◆ **generalizar-se** *vp* [difundir-se] to spread.
genérico, ca [ʒe'nɛriku, ka] *adj* generic.
gênero ['ʒenerul *m* **-1.** [ger] gender; **estudos de ~** gender studies. **-2.** [tipo] kind. **-3.** [estilo] style. **-4.** BIO genus. **-5.** *loc*: **fazer ~** to play up.
◆ **gêneros** *mpl* [mercadorias] goods; **~s alimentícios** foodstuffs; **~s de primeira necessidade** essentials.
generosidade [ʒenerozi'dadʒi] *f* generosity.
generoso, osa [ʒene'rozu, ɔza] *adj* generous.
gênese ['ʒenezi] *f* genesis *(inv).*
genética [ʒe'nɛtʃika] *f* genetics *(sg).*
genético, ca [ʒe'nɛtʃiku, ka] *adj* genetic.
gengibre [ʒẽn'ʒibri] *m* ginger.
gengiva [ʒẽn'ʒiva] *f* gum.
gengivite [ʒẽnʒi'vitʃi] *f* gingivitis.
genial [ʒe'njaw] (*pl* **-ais**) *adj* **-1.** [extraordinário] inspired. **-2.** *fam* [formidável] terrific.
genialidade [ʒenjali'dadʒi] *f* genius.
gênio ['ʒenju] *m* **-1.** [ger] genius; **ser um ~ (em algo)** to be a genius (at sthg). **-2.** [temperamento] nature; **~ bom/ruim** good-/bad-tempered. **-3.** MITOL genie.
genioso, osa [ʒe'njozu, ɔza] *adj* ill-natured.
genital [ʒeni'taw] (*pl* **-ais**) *adj* genital.
genitália [ʒeni'talja] *f* genitalia.
genitivo [ʒeni'tʃivu] *m* LING genitive.
genitor, ra [ʒeni'to(x), ra] *m, f* progenitor.
genocídio [ʒeno'sidʒju] *m* genocide.
genoma [geno'ma] *m* genome.

GENOMA

Brazil has played a significant part in 'Projeto Genoma', dedicated to the genetic sequencing of the DNA of living beings. The success of Brazilian researchers has contributed greatly towards the scientific recognition of the country in the field of biotechnology.

Gênova ['ʒenova] *n* Genoa.
genro ['ʒẽnxu] *m* son-in-law.
gentalha [ʒẽn'taʎa], **gentinha** [ʒẽn'tʃiɲa] *f* pleb.
gente ['ʒẽntʃi] ◇ *f* **-1.** [pessoas] people; **~ bem** upper classes; **~ grande** grown-ups; **minha ~** my family; **toda a ~** everybody; *fam* [amigos, colegas] folks; **oi/tchau, ~** hi/bye, folks. **-2.** [alguém] somebody, someone. **-3.** *fam* [nós]: **a ~ vai viajar** we're going travelling; **você quer ir com a ~?** do you want to come with us?; **o carro da ~ está enguiçado** our car has broken down. ◇ *interj* [exprimindo espanto] gosh!
gentil [ʒẽn'tʃiw] (*pl* **-is**) *adj* kind.
gentileza [ʒẽntʃi'leza] *f* kindness; **por ~ poderia me ajudar?** would you be so kind as to help me?
gentinha [ʒẽn'tʃiɲa] *f* = **gentalha**.
genuíno, na [ʒe'nwinu, na] *adj* genuine.
geofísica [ʒew'fizika] *f* geophysics *(sg).*
geografia [ʒjogra'fia] *f* geography.
geográfico, ca [ʒeo'grafiku, ka] *adj* geographical.
geógrafo, fa [ʒe'ɔgrafu, fa] *m, f* geographer.
geologia [ʒjolo'ʒia] *f* geology.
geológico, ca [geo'lɔgiku, ka] *adj* geological.
geólogo, ga [ʒe'ɔlogu, ga] *m, f* geologist.
geometria [ʒjome'tria] *f* geometry.
geométrico, ca [ʒeo'mɛtriku, ka] *adj* geometric.
geopolítica [geo'politika] *f* geopolitics.
geopolítico, ca [ʒeopo'litʃiku, ka] *adj* geopolitical.
geração [ʒɛra'sãw] (*pl* **-ões**) *f* generation; **~ espontânea** [biol] spontaneous generation; **de última ~** COMPUT & TEC latest generation.
gerador [ʒera'do(x)] (*pl* **-res**) *adj*: **empresa ~ a de empregos** job-creating company; **grupo ~ de problemas** problem-causing group.
◆ **gerador** *m* TEC generator.
geral [ʒe'raw] (*pl* **-ais**) ◇ *adj* [genérico] general; **de um modo ~** on the whole. ◇ *m* [o normal] normal thing. ◇ *f* **-1.** FUT & TEATRO gallery. **-2.** [revisão, arrumação] spring clean; **dar uma ~ em algo** to have a blitz on sthg.
◆ **em geral** *loc adv* in general.
geralmente [ʒeraw'mẽntʃi] *adv* generally.
gerânio [ʒe'rãnju] *m* geranium.
gerar [4] [ʒe'ra(x)] *vt* **-1.** [ger] to generate. **-2.** [ter filhos] to beget. **-3.** [causar] to breed.
gerativo, va [ʒera'tʃivu, va] *adj* generative.
gerência [ʒe'rẽnsja] *f* management.
gerenciador [ʒerẽnsja'do(x)] *m* COMPUT manager.
gerencial [ʒerẽn'sjaw] (*pl* **-ais**) *adj* management *(antes do subst).*

gerenciamento [ʒerẽnsja'mẽntu] *m* management.

gerenciar [16] [ʒerẽn'sja(x)] ◇ *vt* to manage. ◇ *vi* to manage.

gerente [ʒe'rẽntʃi] *mf* manager; ~ **de vendas** sales manager.

gergelim [ʒexʒe'lĩ] *m* sesame.

geriatra [ʒe'rjatra] *mf* geriatrician.

geriatria [ʒerja'tria] *f* geriatrics *(sg)*.

geriátrico, ca [ʒe'rjatriku, ka] *adj* geriatric.

geringonça [ʒerĩn'gõnsa] *f* contraption.

gerir [57] [ʒe'ri(x)] *vt* to manage.

germânico, ca [ʒex'maniku, ka] *adj* Germanic.

germanófono, na [gexma'nɔfonu, na] ◇ *adj* German-speaking. ◇ *m,f* German speaker.

germe ['ʒɛxmi] *m* germ; **ser o ~ de uma idéia** to be the germ of an idea.

germicida [ʒexmi'sida] *m* germicide.

germinação [ʒexmina'sãw] *(pl* **-ões***)* *f* germination.

germinar [4] [ʒexmi'na(x)] *vi* to germinate.

gerúndio [ʒe'rũndʒju] *m* gerund.

gesso ['ʒesu] *m* **-1.** [nas artes plásticas] plaster of Paris. **-2.** [em parede] cast.

gestação [ʒeʃta'sãw] *(pl* **-ões***)* *f* gestation.

gestante [ʒeʃ'tãntʃi] *f* pregnant woman.

gestão [ʒeʃ'tãw] *(pl* **-ões***)* *f* **-1.** [administração] administration. **-2.** [gerência] management.

gesticulação [ʒeʃtʃikula'sãw] *(pl* **-ões***)* *f* gesticulation.

gesticular [4] [ʒeʃtʃiku'la(x)] *vi* to gesticulate.

gesto ['ʒɛʃtu] *m* gesture; **fazer um ~** to make a gesture.

gestual [ʒeʃ'tuaw] *(pl* **-ais***)* *adj* gestural.

gibi [ʒi'bi] *m* comic; **não estar no ~** *fam* to be no joke.

Gibraltar [ʒibraw'ta(x)] *n* Gibraltar.

GIF *(abrev de* **Graphics Interchange Format***)* *m* GIF.

gigabyte [giga'baijtʃi] *(pl* **gigabytes***)* *m* COMPUT gigabyte.

gigante [ʒi'gãntʃi] ◇ *adj* gigantic. ◇ *m* giant.

gigantesco, ca [ʒigãn'teʃku, ka] *adj* gigantic.

gigolô [ʒigo'lo] *m* gigolo.

gilete® [ʒi'lɛtʃi] ◇ *f* [lâmina] razor blade. ◇ *m* *vulg* [bissexual] AC/DC.

gim ['ʒĩ] *(pl* **-ns***)* *m* gin.

ginasial [ʒina'ziaw] *(pl* **-ais***)* ◇ *adj* [relativo a ginásio] secondary school *UK*, high school *US*. ◇ *m* [curso] *dated* primary education.

ginásio [ʒi'nazju] *m* **-1.** EDUC secondary school. **-2.** [para esportes] gymnasium.

ginasta [ʒi'naʃta] *mf* gymnast.

ginástica [ʒi'naʃtʃika] *f* **-1.** [esporte] gymnastics *(sg)*. **-2.** [aeróbica, corretiva] exercises *(pl)*.

gincana [ʒĩŋ'kãna] *f* gymkhana.

ginecologia [ˌʒinɛkolo'ʒia] *f* gynaecology.

ginecológico, ca [ʒineko'lɔʒiku, ka] *adj* gynaecological.

ginecologista [ˌʒinekolo'ʒiʃta] *mf* gynaecologist.

ginete [ʒi'netʃi] *m* thoroughbred.

ginga ['ʒĩŋga] *f* **-1.** [remo] oar. **-2.** [movimento]: **ter ~** to be nimble.

gingar [14] [ʒĩn'ga(x)] *vi* to sway.

girafa [ʒi'rafa] *f* giraffe.

girar [4] [ʒi'ra(x)] ◇ *vi* **-1.** [rodar] to rotate. **-2.** *fig* [funcionar]: ~ **em torno de** to revolve around. ◇ *vt* [fazer rodar] to turn.

girassol [ˌʒira'sɔw] *(pl* **-óis***)* *m* sunflower.

giratório, ria [ʒira'tɔrju, rja] *adj* revolving; **cadeira giratória** swivel chair; **ponte giratória** swing bridge.

gíria ['ʒirja] *f* **-1.** [calão] slang. **-2.** [jargão] jargon.

giro, ra ['ʒiru, ra] *m* **-1.** [volta] rotation. **-2.** *fam* [passeio] stroll; **dar um ~** to take a stroll.

giz ['ʒiʒ] *m* chalk.

glacê [gla'se] *m* icing.

glaciação [glasia'sãw] *(pl* **-ões***)* *f* [período geológico] glaciation.

glacial [gla'sjaw] *(pl* **-ais***)* *adj* glacial.

gladiador [gladʒja'do(x)] *m* gladiator.

glamour [gla'mu(x)] *m* glamour *UK*, glamor *US*.

glamouroso, osa [glamu'rozu, ɔza] *adj* glamorous.

glande ['glãndʒi] *f* **-1.** [do carvalho] acorn. **-2.** ANAT glans.

glândula ['glãndula] *f* gland.

glandular [glãndu'la(x)] *adj* glandular.

glaucoma [glaw'koma] *m* glaucoma.

gleba ['glɛba] *f* field.

glicerina [glise'rina] *f* glycerine.

glicose [gli'kɔzi] *f* glucose.

global [glo'baw] *(pl* **-ais***)* *adj* **-1.** [total] total. **-2.** [relativo ao globo] global.

globalização [globaliza'sãw] *(pl* **-ões***)* *f* globalization.

globalizado, da [globali'zadu, da] *adj* globalized.

globalizante [globali'zãntʃi] *adj* globalizing.

globalizar [globa'liza(x)] *vt* to globalize.
◆ **globalizar-se** *vp* to become globalized.

globo ['globu] *m* globe; ~ **ocular** eyeball; ~ **terrestre** terrestrial globe.

globular [globu'la(x)] *adj* globular.

glóbulo ['glɔbulu] *m* globule; **~s brancos/vermelhos** white/red blood corpuscles.

glória ['glɔrja] *f* glory.

glorificação [glorifika'sãw] *(pl* **-ões***)* *f* glorification.

glorificar [12] [glorifi'ka(x)] *vt* **-1.** [honrar] to glorify. **-2.** [canonizar] to canonize.

glorioso, osa [glo'rjozu, ɔza] *adj* glorious.

glosa ['glɔza] *f* gloss.

glosar [4] [glo'za(x)] *vt* **-1.** [comentar] to gloss. **-2.** [conta] to scrap.

glossário [glo'sarju] *m* glossary.

glote ['glɔtʃi] *f* ANAT glottis.

GLP *(abrev de* **Gás Liquefeito de Petróleo***)* *m* LPG.

glucose [glu'kɔzi] *f* glucose.

glutão, ona [glu'tãw, ɔna] *(mpl* **-ões**, *fpl* **-s***)* ◇ *adj* [pessoa] greedy. ◇ *m, f* [pessoa] glutton.

glúten ['glutẽ] *(pl* **-s***)* *m* gluten.

glúteo, tea ['glutew, tʃia] ◇ *adj ANAT* gluteal. ◇ *m* gluteus.
glutões [glu'tõjʃ] *pl* ▷ **glutão**.
glutona [glu'tona] *f* ▷ **glutão**.
gnomo ['gnomu] *m* gnome.
GO (*abrev de* **Estado de Goiás**) *n State of Goiás*.
Gobi ['gɔbi] *m*: **o deserto de ~** the Gobi Desert.
godê [go'de] *adj* flared.
goela ['gwɛla] *f* throat.
gogó [go'gɔ] *m* ***fam*** [pomo-de-adão] Adam's apple.
goiaba [go'jaba] *f* guava.
goiabada [goja'bada] *f* guava jelly.
goiabeira [goja'bejra] *f* guava tree.
Goiânia [go'jãnja] *n* Goiânia.
Goiás [go'jaʃ] *n* Goiás.
gol ['gow] (*pl* **-es**) *m* goal; **marcar um ~** to score a goal.
gola ['gɔla] *f* collar; **~ rulê** polo neck.
golaço [go'lasu] *m* ***fam*** *FUT* great goal.
gole ['gɔli] *m* gulp; **de um ~ só** in one gulp; **tomar um ~** to take a sip.
goleada [go'ljada] *f FUT* hammering.
golear [15] [go'lja(x)] *vt FUT* to thrash.
goleiro [go'lejru] *m* goalkeeper.
golfada [gow'fada] *f* [jorro] spurt.
golfar [4] [gow'fa(x)] ◇ *vt* **-1.** [vomitar] to cough up. **-2.** [expelir] to spurt out. ◇ *vi* [sair em golfadas] to spurt out.
golfe ['gowfi] *m* golf.
golfinho [gow'fiɲu] *m* dolphin.
golfista [gow'fiʃta] *mf* golfer.
golfo ['gowfu] *m* gulf.
Golfo Pérsico [,gowfu'pɛxsiku] *n* Persian Gulf.
golinho [gɔ'liɲu] *m* sip; **aos ~s** in sips.
golpe ['gɔwpi] *m* **-1.** [ger] stroke; **~ de sorte** stroke of luck; **~ de vista** [olhar] glance; [no trânsito] knock; **~ de mestre** master stroke; **dar o ~ do baú** to marry for money. **-2.** [pancada, abalo moral] blow; [soco] punch; [de faca] slash; [de chicote] lash; **dar um ~ em alguém** to hit sb; **~ baixo** ***fam fig*** dirty trick; **~ mortal** mortal blow; **~ de vento** gust of wind. **-3.** *POL* coup; **~ de Estado** coup d'état.
golpear [15] [gow'pja(x)] *vt* **-1.** [dar pancada em] to hit; [com soco] to punch; [com chicote] to lash; [com faca] to slash. **-2.** [moralmente] to wound.
golpista [gow'piʃta] ◇ *adj* [pessoa] tricky. ◇ *mf* [pessoa] trickster.
goma ['goma] *f* gum, glue; **~ de mascar** chewing gum.
gomo ['gomu] *m* slice.
gôndola ['gõndula] *f* gondola.
gondoleiro [gõndo'lejru] *m* gondolier.
gongo ['gõŋgu] *m* **-1.** *MÚS* gong. **-2.** [sino] bell.
gonorréia [gono'xɛja] *f* gonorrhoea ***UK***, gonorrhea ***US***.
gorar [4] [go'ra(x)] ◇ *vt* [fracassar] to thwart. ◇ *vi* [fracassar] to fail.
gordo, da ['gordu, da] ◇ *adj* **-1.** [pessoa] fat; **nunca ter visto alguém mais ~** [não conhecer] not have seen sb before. **-2.** [carne] fatty. **-3.** ***fig*** [quantia] considerable. ◇ *m, f* fat person.
gorducho, cha [gox'duʃu, ʃa] ◇ *adj* plump. ◇ *m, f* plump person.
gordura [gox'dura] *f* **-1.** [banha] fat. **-2.** [líquida] grease. **-3.** [obesidade] fatness.
gordurento, ta [goxdu'rẽntu, ta] *adj* **-1.** [gordo] fatty. **-2.** [ensebado] greasy.
gorduroso, osa [goxdu'rozu, ɔza] *adj* **-1.** [ger] greasy. **-2.** [comida] fatty.
gorila [go'rila] *m* gorilla.
gorjear [15] [gox'ʒja(x)] *vi* to chirp.
gorjeio [gox'ʒeju] *m* chirp.
gorjeta [gox'ʒeta] *f* tip.
gororoba [goro'rɔba] *f* ***fam*** [comida] grub, nosh; [comida ruim] muck.
gorro ['goxu] *m* cap.
gosma ['gɔʒma] *f* spittle.
gosmento, ta [goʒ'mẽntu, ta] *adj* slimy.
gostar [4] [goʃ'ta(x)] *vi* **-1.** [ter prazer, gosto]**: ~ de** to enjoy; **~ de fazer algo** to enjoy doing sthg; **eu ~ ia de ir** I would like to go; **gostei de vê-lo feliz** it was good to see him happy; **~ mais de algo do que de** to prefer sthg to; **~ de alguém** [simpatizar com] to like sb; [sentir afeição por] to be fond of sb. **-2.** [aproveitar]**: ~ de** to enjoy. **-3.** [ter costume]**: ~ de fazer algo** to like doing sthg. **-4.** [aprovar]**: ~ de** to like.
◆ **gostar-se** *vp* [mutuamente] to be fond of each other *ou* one another.
gosto ['goʃtu] *m* **-1.** [ger] taste; **ter ~ de** to taste of; **de bom/mau ~** in good/bad taste; **a seu ~** to one's taste; **com ~** tastefully; **falta de ~** lack of taste; **para o meu ~** for my liking. **-2.** [prazer] pleasure; **ter ~ em fazer algo** to enjoy doing sthg; **tomar ~ por algo** to take a liking to sthg.
gostoso, osa [goʃ'tozu, ɔza] *adj* **-1.** [comida, bebida] tasty. **-2.** [cheiro] lovely. **-3.** [ambiente, música] pleasant. **-4.** [cama, cadeira] comfortable. **-5.** [risada] hearty. **-6.** ***fam*** [sensual, bonito] gorgeous.
gostosura [goʃto'zura] *f* ***fam*****: ser uma ~** to be lovely.
gota ['gota] *f* **-1.** [ger] drop; **ser a ~ d'água** to be the last straw; **ser uma ~ de água no oceano** to be a drop in the ocean. **-2.** [de suor] bead. **-3.** *MED* gout.
goteira [go'tejra] *f* [buraco no telhado] leak.
gotejante [gote'ʒãntʃi] *adj* dripping.
gotejar [4] [gote'ʒa(x)] *vt & vi* to drip.
gótico, ca ['gɛtʃiku, ka] *adj* Gothic.
◆ **gótico** *m*: **o ~** the Gothic style.
gotícula [go'tʃikula] *f* droplet.
gourmet [gux'me] (*pl* **-s**) *mf* gourmet.
governabilidade [govexnabili'dadʒi] *f* governability.
governador, ra [govexna'do(x), ra] *m, f* governor.
governamental [govexnamẽn'taw] (*pl* **-ais**) *adj* government (*antes de subst*), governmental.
governanta [govex'nãnta] *f* **-1.** [de criança] governess. **-2.** [de casa] housekeeper.
governante [govex'nãntʃi] ◇ *adj* [que governa] governing. ◇ *mf* [quem governa] governor.

governar [4] [govex'na(x)] ◇ *vt* **-1.** *POL* to govern. **-2.** [embarcação] to steer. **-3.** [dominar] to dominate. ◇ *vi POL* to govern.

governista [govex'niʃta] ◇ *adj* pro-government. ◇ *mf* government supporter.

governo [go'vexnu] *m* **-1.** *POL* government. **-2.** [controle]: **o carro estava sem ~** the car was out of control. **-3.** *NÁUT* steering. **-4.** *loc*: **para seu ~** for your information.

gozação [goza'sãw] (*pl* **-ões**) *f* teasing; **fazer uma ~ (com alguém)** to tease (sb).

gozado, da [go'zadu, da] *adj* **-1.** [engraçado] funny. **-2.** [estranho] strange.

◆ **gozada** *f fam*: **dar uma ~ em alguém** to pull sb's leg.

gozador, ra [goza'do(x), ra] ◇ *adj* comical. ◇ *m, f* joker.

gozar [4] [go'za(x)] ◇ *vt* **-1.** [desfrutar] to enjoy. **-2.** *fam* [troçar de] to make fun of. ◇ *vi* **-1.** [desfrutar]: **~ de** to enjoy. **-2.** *fam* [troçar] to mock; **~ da cara de alguém** to mock sb. **-3.** *fam* [ter orgasmo] to come.

gozo ['gozu] *m* **-1.** [prazer] pleasure. **-2.** [graça]: **ser um ~** to be a laugh. **-3.** [uso]: **~ de algo** use of sthg; **estar em pleno ~ das faculdades mentais** to be in full possession of one's mental faculties. **-4.** [orgasmo] orgasm.

GP (*abrev de* **Grande Prêmio**) *m* grand prix.

GPS (*abrev de* **Global Positioning System**) *m* GPS.

Grã-Bretanha [,grãnbre'tãɲa] *n*: **(a) ~** Great Britain.

graça ['grasa] *f* **-1.** [ger] grace. **-2.** [humor] wit; **achar ~ de** *ou* **em algo** to find sthg funny; **fazer ~** [gracejar] to joke; **ter ~** to be funny. **-3.** [encanto] charm; **cheio de ~** full of charm; **não ter ~ nenhuma** [ser chato] to be boring; [estar errado] to be wrong; **sem ~** dull; **ver ~ em alguém/algo** to see sthg funny in sb/sthg; **não sei que ~ ela vê nele** I don't know what she sees in him. **-4.** [favor, proteção] favour; **cair nas ~s de** to be in favour with. **-5.** [nome] name. **-6.** *loc*: **ficar sem ~** to be embarrassed.

◆ **graças a** *loc prep* **-1.** [devido a] due to, thanks to. **-2.** [agradecimento]: **dar ~s a** to give thanks to; **~s a Deus!** thank goodness!

◆ **de graça** *loc adj* **-1.** [grátis] free. **-2.** [muito barato] given away.

gracejar [4] [grase'ʒa(x)] *vi* to joke.

gracejo [gra'seʒu] *m* joke.

gracinha [gra'siɲa] *f*: **ser uma ~** [criança, rosto] to be sweet; [cidade, desenho] to be attractive; **que ~!** how sweet!

gracioso, osa [gra'sjozu, ɔza] *adj* gracious.

gradação [grada'sãw] (*pl* **-ões**) *f* gradient.

gradativo, va [grada'tʃivu, va] *adj* gradual.

grade ['gradʒi] *f* **-1.** [em janela] grille. **-2.** [no chão] grating. **-3.** *loc*: **atrás das ~s** *fam* [na cadeia] behind bars.

gradeado, da [gra'dʒiadu, da] *adj* [com grades - jardim] fenced; [- janela] with a grating *(antes de subst)*.

◆ **gradeado** *m* [gradeamento] fencing.

gradear [15] [gra'dʒa(x)] *vt* **-1.** [janela] to put bars on. **-2.** [área] to fence off.

grado ['gradu] *m* [vontade]: **de bom/mau ~** willingly/unwillingly.

graduação [gradwa'sãw] (*pl* **-ões**) *f* **-1.** [classificação] grading. **-2.** *MIL* rank. **-3.** [*EDUC* - colação] graduation; [- curso]: **curso de ~** degree course.

graduado, da [gra'dwadu, da] *adj* **-1.** [dividido em graus] graduated. **-2.** [diplomado] graduate. **-3.** [conceituado] graded. **-4.** *MIL* ranked.

gradual [gra'dwaw] (*pl* **-ais**) *adj* gradual.

graduar [4] [gra'dwa(x)] *vt* **-1.** [regular] to regulate. **-2.** [classificar]: **~ em** to classify according to. **-3.** [marcar os graus] to graduate. **-4.** *EDUC*: **~ alguém em algo** to confer a degree on sb in sthg. **-5.** *MIL*: **~ alguém em general/coronel** to promote sb to general/colonel.

◆ **graduar-se** *vp EDUC*: **~-se em algo** to graduate in sthg.

graduável [gra'dwavew] (*pl* **-eis**) *adj* adjustable.

grafar [4] [gra'fa(x)] *vt* [escrever] to write.

grafia [gra'fia] *f* **-1.** [escrita] writing. **-2.** [ortografia] spelling.

gráfico, ca ['grafiku, ka] ◇ *adj* **-1.** [visual] graphic. **-2.** [tipográfico] typographic. ◇ *m, f* [profissional] typesetter.

◆ **gráfico** *m* **-1.** [diagrama] diagram; **~ de barras** bar chart. **-2.** *MAT* graph.

◆ **gráfica** *f* [estabelecimento] graphics studio.

◆ **gráficos** *mpl COMPUT* graphics.

grã-finagem [grãnfi'naʒẽ] (*pl* **grã-finagens**) *f* [classe]: **a ~** the upper class.

grã-fino, na [grãn'finu, na] (*mpl* **grã-finos**, *fpl* **grã-finas**) ◇ *adj* posh. ◇ *m, f* toff.

grafite [gra'fitʃi] *f* **-1.** [material] graphite. **-2.** [de lápis] lead. **-3.** [pichação] graffiti.

grafologia [grafolo'ʒia] *f* graphology.

grama ['grãma] ◇ *f* [relva] grass. ◇ *m* [medida] gramme.

gramado [gra'madu] *m* **-1.** [de parque, jardim] lawn. **-2.** *FUT* pitch.

gramar [4] [gra'ma(x)] *vt* to sow with grass.

gramática [gra'matʃika] *f* ▷ **gramático**.

gramatical [gramatʃi'kãw] (*pl* **-ais**) *adj* grammatical.

gramático, ca [gra'matʃiku, ka] ◇ *adj* grammatical. ◇ *m, f* grammarian.

◆ **gramática** *f* **-1.** [disciplina] grammar. **-2.** [livro] grammar book.

gramofone [gramo'foni] *m* gramophone.

grampeador [grãnpja'do(x)] (*pl* **-es**) *m* stapler.

grampear [15] [grãm'pja(x)] *vt* **-1.** [prender com grampos] to staple. **-2.** [telefone] to tap.

grampo ['grãnpu] *m* **-1.** [para papel] staple. **-2.** [para cabelos] hairgrip. **-3.** [de chapéu] hatpin. **-4.** [de carpinteiro] clamp. **-5.** [de telefone] tap.

grana ['grãna] *f fam* dosh.

granada [gra'nada] *f* **-1.** [arma] projectile; **~ de mão** hand grenade. **-2.** [pedra] garnet.

Granada [gra'nada] *n* **-1.** [na Espanha] Granada. **-2.** [nas Antilhas] Grenada.

grandalhão, lhona [grãnda'ʎãw, ʎɔna] (*mpl* **-lhões**, *fpl* **-s**) *adj* large.

grandão, dona [grãn'dãw, dɔna] (*mpl* **-ões**, *fpl* **-s**) *adj* huge.

grande ['grãndʒi] *adj* **-1.** [em tamanho] large; **o Grande São Paulo** Greater São Paulo. **-2.** [em altura] tall. **-3.** [crescido] grown-up. **-4.** *(antes de subst)* [intenso] great. **-5.** *(antes de subst)* [excessivo] grand. **-6.** *(antes de subst)* [notável] great. **-7.** *(antes de subst)* [excepcional] great. **-8.** *(antes de subst)* [generoso] generous.
◆ **grandes** *mpl*: **os ~s** [os poderosos] the great.

grandeza [grãn'deza] *f* **-1.** [ger] greatness. **-2.** [ostentação] grandeur.

grandiloqüência [grãndʒilo'kwẽnsja] *f* grandiloquence.

grandiloqüente [grãndʒilo'kwẽntʃi] *adj* grandiloquent.

grandiosidade [grãndʒjozi'dadʒi] *f* magnificence.

grandioso, osa [grãn'dʒjozu, ɔza] *adj* grandiose.

granel [gra'nɛw] *m*: **a ~** in bulk; **comprar/vender a ~** to buy/sell in bulk.

granito [gra'nitu] *m* granite.

granizo [gra'nizu] *m* hailstone; **chover ~** to hail; **chuva de ~** hail.

granja ['grãnʒa] *f* farm.

granulado, da [granu'ladu, da] *adj* granulated.

grânulo ['grãnulu] *m* granule.

grão ['grãw] (*pl* **grãos**) *m* **-1.** [semente] seed; [de café] bean. **-2.** [de areia] grain.
◆ **grãos** *mpl* [cereais] cereal.

grão-de-bico [ˌgrãwdʒi'biku] (*pl* **grãos-de-bico**) *m* chick pea *UK*, garbanzo bean *US*.

grapefruit [ˌgreip'frutʃi] *m* grapefruit.

grasnar [4] [graʒ'na(x)] *vi* **-1.** [corvo] to caw. **-2.** [pato] to quack. **-3.** *fig* [gritar] to shout.

gratidão [gratʃi'dãw] *f* gratitude.

gratificação [gratʃifika'sãw] (*pl* **-ões**) *f* **-1.** [bônus] bonus. **-2.** [recompensa] reward. **-3.** [gorjeta] tip.

gratificante [gratʃifi'kãntʃi] *adj* gratifying.

gratificar [12] [gratʃifi'ka(x)] *vt* **-1.** [dar bônus] to give a bonus. **-2.** [dar gorjeta a] to tip. **-3.** [recompensar] to reward; **esse trabalho gratifica muito** this work is very rewarding.

gratinado, da [gratʃi'nadu, da] *adj* au gratin, gratiné.
◆ **gratinado** *m* **-1.** [prato] gratin. **-2.** [crosta] crust.

grátis ['gratʃiʃ] *adj* free.

grato, ta ['gratu, ta] *adj* **-1.** [agradecido]: **ficar ~ a alguém por algo/por fazer algo** to be grateful to sb for sthg/doing sthg. **-2.** *(antes de subst)* [agradável] pleasant.

gratuidade [gratwi'dadʒi] *f* gratuity.

gratuito, ta [gra'twitu, ta] *adj* **-1.** [grátis] free. **-2.** [sem fundamento] gratuitous.

grau ['graw] *m* **-1.** [ger] degree. **-2.** [nível, gradação] level.

graúdo, da [gra'udu, da] ◇ *adj* **-1.** [grande] large. **-2.** [influente] important. ◇ *m, f* [pessoa poderosa] bigwig.

gravação [grava'sãw] (*pl* **-ões**) *f* **-1.** [em fita, disco, telefone] recording. **-2.** [em madeira] carving.

gravador, ra [grava'do(x), ra] (*pl* **-es**) *m, f* [quem faz gravuras] engraver.
◆ **gravador** *m* [aparelho] tape recorder.
◆ **gravadora** *f* [empresa] record company.

gravar [4] [gra'va(x)] *vt* **-1.** [ger] to record. **-2.** [em pedra, metal, madeira] to carve. **-3.** [na memória] to memorize.

gravata [gra'vata] *f* **-1.** [adereço] tie. **-2.** [golpe] stranglehold; **dar uma ~ em alguém** to get sb in a stranglehold.

gravata-borboleta [graˌvataboxbo'leta] (*pl* **gravatas-borboletas, gravatas-borboleta**) *f* bow tie.

grave ['gravi] *adj* **-1.** [profundo] serious. **-2.** [sério] grave. **-3.** [rígido] grave. **-4.** MÚS deep. **-5.** LING [acento] grave.

gravemente [grave'mẽntʃi] *adv* seriously.

graveto [gra'vetu] *m* piece of kindling.

grávida ['gravida] *adj* pregnant.

gravidade [gravi'dadʒi] *f* gravity; **centro de ~** centre of gravity.

gravidez [gravi'deʒ] *f* pregnancy; **~ tubária** ectopic pregancy.

graviola [gra'vjɔla] *f* sweetsop.

gravitar [4] [gravi'ta(x)] *vi* **-1.** [orbitar] to gravitate. **-2.** *fig* [seguir]: **~ em torno de** to gravitate around.

gravura [gra'vura] *f* **-1.** [estampa] print. **-2.** [em madeira, metal] engraving.

graxa ['graʃa] *f* **-1.** [para couro] polish; **~ de sapatos** shoe polish. **-2.** [lubrificante] grease.

Grécia ['grɛsja] *f* Greece.

gregário, ria [gre'garju, rja] *adj* gregarious.

grego, ga ['gregu, 'ga] ◇ *adj* **-1.** [relativo à grécia] Greek. **-2.** *fig* [obscuro]: **isso para mim é ~** that's Greek to me. ◇ *m, f* [pessoa] Greek.
◆ **grego** *m* LING Greek; **falar ~** *fam* to speak a foreign language.

gregoriano, na [grego'rjanu, na] *adj* Gregorian.

grelha ['greʎa] *f* grill; **na ~** cooked on the grill.

grelhado, da [gre'ʎadu, da] *adj* grilled.
◆ **grelhado** *m* grilled food.

grelhar [4] [gre'ʎa(x)] *vt* to grill.

grêmio ['gremju] *m* **-1.** [associação] guild. **-2.** [clube] club.

grená [gre'na] ◇ *adj* dark red. ◇ *m* dark red.

greta ['greta] *f* crack.

greve ['grɛvi] *f* strike; **fazer ~** to strike; **~ de fome** hunger strike.

grevista [gre'viʃta] *mf* striker.

grifado, da [gri'fadu, da] *adj* italicized.

grifar [4] [gri'fa(x)] *vt* **-1.** [compor em grifo] to italicize. **-2.** [sublinhar] to underline. **-3.** *fig* [enfatizar] to emphasize.

grife ['grifi] *f* label.

grifo ['grifu] *m* italics.

grilado, da [gri'ladu, da] *adj fam*: **estar/ficar ~ (com)** to be/get worked up (about).
grilagem [grila'ʒẽ] (*pl* **-ns**) *f falsification of property deeds.*
grilar [4] [gri'la(x)] ◇ *vt fam* [preocupar] to worry. ◇ *vi fam* [chatear-se] to get annoyed.
◆ **grilar-se** *vp fam*: **~-se por** *ou* **com** to get worked up about.
grileiro, ra [gri'lejru, ra] *m, f forger of property deeds.*
grilhão [gri'ʎãw] (*pl* **-ões**) *m* chain.
grilo ['grilu] *m* **-1.** [inseto] cricket. **-2.** *fam* [problema] hiccup; **dar ~** to cause a hiccup.
grinalda [gri'nawda] *f* garland.
gringo, ga ['grĩŋgu, ga] *m, f fam pej* foreigner.
gripado, da [gri'padu, da] *adj*: **estar/ficar ~** to have/get flu.
gripar-se [4] [gri'paxsi] *vp* to catch flu.
gripe ['gripi] *f* flu; **pegar uma ~** to go down with flu.
grisalho, lha [gri'zaʎu, ʎa] *adj* greying *UK*, graying *US*.
gritante [gri'tãntʃi] *adj* **-1.** [evidente] glaring. **-2.** [de cor viva] dazzling.
gritar [4] [gri'ta(x)] *vt & vi* to shout; **~ com alguém** to shout at sb.
gritaria [grita'ria] *f* shouting.
grito ['gritu] *m* **-1.** [brado] shout; **falar aos ~s** to shout; **protestar aos ~s** to shout protests; **chegar aos ~s** to reach screaming point; **dar um ~** to give a shout. **-2.** [de animal] scream. **-3.** [de dor] scream. **-4.** [de pavor] scream.
◆ **no grito** *loc adv fam* by force.
Groenlândia [groẽn'lãndʒja] *n* Greenland.
grogue ['grɔgi] *adj* [pessoa] groggy.
grosa ['grɔza] *f* [doze dúzias] gross.
grosar [gro'za(x)] *vt* [limar, debastar] to file.
groselha [gro'zɛʎa] *f* redcurrant.
grosseiro, ra [gro'sejru, ra] *adj* **-1.** [rude] rude. **-2.** [chulo] vulgar. **-3.** [ordinário] coarse.
grosseria [grose'ria] *f* rudeness; **dizer/fazer uma ~** to say/do something rude.
grosso, ssa ['grosu, sa] *adj* **-1.** [ger] thick. **-2.** [áspero] rough. **-3.** [rude] rude. **-4.** *fam* [abundante]: **dinheiro ~** a considerable sum of money.
◆ **grosso** *adv*: **falar ~ com alguém** to get tough with sb.
◆ **grosso modo** *loc adv* roughly.
grossura [gro'sura] *f* **-1.** [espessura] thickness. **-2.** *fam* [grosseria] rudeness.
grotão [gro'tãw] (*pl* **-ões**) *m* gorge.
grotesco, ca [gro'teʃku, ka] *adj* grotesque.
◆ **grotesco** *m*: **o ~** the grotesque.
grua ['grua] *f* crane.
grudado, da [gru'dadu, da] *adj fig*: **ser ~ com alguém** to be very attached to sb.
grudar [4] [gru'da(x)] ◇ *vt*: **~ algo em algo** to stick sthg on sthg. ◇ *vi* to stick.
grude ['grudʒi] *m* **-1.** [cola] glue. **-2.** *fam* [comida ruim] muck.
grudento, ta [gru'dẽntu, ta] *adj* sticky.
grumete [gru'mɛtʃi] *m* cabin boy.
grunhido [gru'ɲidu] *m* grunt.
grunhir [6] [gru'ɲi(x)] *vi* **-1.** [porco] to grunt. **-2.** *fig* [resmungar] to grumble.
grupo ['grupu] *m* group; **~ étnico** ethnic group; **~ sanguíneo** blood group; **~ de discussão** *COMPUT* newsgroup.
gruta ['gruta] *f* cave, grotto.
guache ['gwaʃi] *m* gouache.
guaraná [gwara'na] *m* guarana; **~ em pó** powdered guarana; **~ natural** natural guarana.

GUARANÁ

A small fruit borne by a very common bush in Amazonas and Pará; it is used to make one of the most popular national drinks, *guaraná*. High in caffeine, it is considered by alternative medicine as an excellent source of energy. It is sold as a soft drink and can also be obtained in the form of a powder.

guarani [gwara'ni] (*pl* **guaranis**) ◇ *adj* Guarani (*antes de subst*). ◇ *m, f* Guarani. ◇ *m* **-1.** [língua] Guarani. **-2.** [moeda] guarani.
guarda ['gwaxda] ◇ *f* **-1.** [proteção] care; **ficar de ~** to stand guard. **-2.** *MIL* guard. ◇ *mf* [policial] police officer.
guarda-chuva [ˌgwaxda'ʃuva] (*pl* **guarda-chuvas**) *m* umbrella.
guarda-costas [ˌgwaxda'kɔʃtaʃ] *mf inv* **-1.** *NÁUT* coastguard. **-2.** *fig* [para defesa] bodyguard.
guardador, ra [gwaxda'do(x), ra] *m, f*: **~ (de automóveis)** (car) attendant.
guardados [gwax'daduʃ] *mpl* bits and pieces.
guarda-florestal [ˌgwaxdaflore'ʃtaw] (*pl* **guardas-florestais**) *mf* forest ranger.
guarda-louça [ˌgwaxda'losa] (*pl* **guarda-louças**) *m* dresser.
guarda-mor [ˌgwaxda'mɔ(x)] (*pl* **guardas-mores**) *m* head customs-officer.
guarda-móveis [ˌgwaxda'mɔvejʃ] *m (inv)* furniture warehouse.
guardanapo [ˌgwaxda'napu] *m* (table) napkin.
guarda-noturno [ˌgwaxdano'tuxnu] (*pl* **guardas-noturnos**) *mf* nightwatchman.
guardar [4] [gwax'da(x)] *vt* **-1.** [ger] to keep; **~ segredo sobre algo** to keep quiet about sthg; **~ silêncio** to keep silent. **-2.** [pôr no lugar]: **~ algo (em)** to put sthg away (in). **-3.** [reservar]: **~ algo (para)** to keep sthg (for); **~ lugar para alguém** [em teatro, ônibus] to keep a seat for sb. **-4.** [gravar na memória] to remember. **-5.** [vigiar] to guard. **-6.** [cuidar de] to look after. **-7.** [observar] to keep; **guardadas as (devidas) proporções** to a certain extent.
◆ **guardar-se** *vp* **-1.** [proteger-se]: **~-se de** to steer clear of. **-2.** [prevenir-se]: **~-se de** to watch out for.
guarda-roupa [ˌgwaxda'xopa] (*pl* **guarda-roupas**) *m* wardrobe.
guarda-sol [ˌgwaxda'sɔw] (*pl* **guarda-sóis**) *m* parasol.

guarda-volumes [ˌgwaxdavoˈlumiʃ] *m (inv)* left-luggage office.
guardião, diã [gwaxˈdʒjãw, dʒjã] (*mpl* **-ães, -ões**, *fpl* **-s**) *m, f* guardian.
guarida [gwaˈrida] *f* **-1.** [refúgio] den. **-2.** [proteção]: **dar ~ a alguém** to harbour sb.
guarita [gwaˈrita] *f* **-1.** [torre] watchtower. **-2.** [casinha] sentry box.
guarnecer [25] [gwaxneˈse(x)] *vt* **-1.** [abastecer] to supply; **~ alguém de algo** to supply sb with sthg. **-2.** *MIL* to occupy. **-3.** *NÁUT* to crew.
guarnição [gwaxniˈsãw] (*pl* **-ões**) *f* **-1.** [ger] garnish. **-2.** *MIL* garrison. **-3.** *NAUT* crew.
Guatemala [gwateˈmala] *n* Guatemala.
guatemalteco, ca [gwatemawˈtɛku, ka] ◇ *adj* Guatemalan. ◇ *m, f* Guatemalan.
gude [ˈgudʒi] *m* ▷ **bola**.
gueixa [ˈgejʃa] *f* geisha.
guelra [ˈgɛwxa] *f* gill.
guerra [ˈgɛxa] *f* **-1.** [ger] war; **declarar ~ a** to declare war on; **em ~** at war; **estar em pé de ~ (com)** to be ready for war (with); **~ civil** civil war; **~ fria** cold war; **~ mundial** world war; **~ nuclear** *OU* **atômica** nuclear war; **~ química** chemical warfare; **~ santa** holy war; **fazer ~ a** to do battle with; **~ de nervos** war of nerves. **-2.** *fig* [disputa] battle.
guerra-relâmpago [gɛxaˈxelãmpagu] (*pl* **-guerras-relâmpago**) *f* blitzkrieg.
guerrear [15] [geˈxja(x)] *vi*: **~ (com/contra)** to be at war (with/against).
guerreiro, ra [geˈxejru, ra] ◇ *adj* **-1.** [belicoso] warlike. **-2.** [espírito, índole] fighting. ◇ *m, f* [pessoa] warrior.
guerrilha [geˈxiʎa] *f* guerrilla warfare.
guerrilhar [4] [gexiˈʎa(x)] *vi* to engage in guerrilla warfare.
guerrilheiro, ra [gexiˈʎejru, ra] ◇ *adj* guerrilla *(antes de subst)*. ◇ *m, f* guerrilla.
gueto [ˈgetu] *m* ghetto.
guia [ˈgia] ◇ *f* guide. ◇ *m* [manual - turístico, cultural] guide; [- de instruções] manual. ◇ *mf* [pessoa] guide; **~ turístico** tourist guide.
Guiana [gwiˈjãna] *n* Guyana.
guianense [gwijaˈnẽnsi] ◇ *adj* Guyanese. ◇ *mf* Guyanese.
guiar [16] [ˈgja(x)] ◇ *vt* **-1.** [orientar] to guide. **-2.** [proteger] to watch over. **-3.** *AUTO* [dirigir] to drive. ◇ *vi AUTO* to drive.
◆ **guiar-se** *vp* [orientar-se] to orientate o.s.
guichê [giˈʃe] *m* **-1.** [no cinema, teatro] ticket office. **-2.** [em banco] counter.
guidom [giˈdõ] (*pl* **-ns**) *m* handlebars *(pl)*.
guilhotina [giʎoˈtʃina] *f* guillotine.
guilhotinar [4] [giʎotʃiˈna(x)] *vt* to guillotine.
guimba [ˈgĩnba] *f fam* [ponta de cigarro] stub.
guinada [giˈnada] *f* **-1.** *NÁUT* yaw. **-2.** *AUTO* veer; **dar uma ~** to veer. **-3.** *fig* [virada] change of direction; **dar uma ~** to change direction.
guinchar [4] [gĩnˈʃa(x)] ◇ *vt* [carro] to tow. ◇ *vi* [chiar] to squeal.
guincho [ˈgĩnʃu] *m* **-1.** [reboque] tow. **-2.** [chiado] squeal.
guindar [4] [gĩnˈda(x)] *vt* **-1.** [levantar] to raise. **-2.** *fig* [promover] to promote; **~ alguém a algo** to promote sb to sthg.
guindaste [gĩnˈdaʃtʃi] *m* crane.
guineano, na [gineˈãnu, na] ◇ *adj* Guinean. ◇ *m, f* Guinean.
Guiné-Bissau [giˌnɛbiˈsaw] *n* Guinea-Bissau.
Guiné Equatorial [giˌnɛkwatoˈrjaw] *n* Equatorial Guinea.
guirlanda [gixˈlãnda] *f* garland.
guisa [ˈgiza] *f*: **à ~ de** in the manner of.
guisado, da [giˈzadu, da] *m CULIN* stew.
guisar [4] [giˈza(x)] *vt* to stew.
guitarra [giˈtaxa] *f*: **~ (elétrica)** electric guitar.
guitarrista [gitaˈxiʃta] *mf* guitarist.
guizo [ˈgizu] *m* bell.
gula [ˈgula] *f* gluttony.
gulodice [guloˈdʒisi] *f* greediness.
guloseima [guloˈzejma] *f* titbit.
guloso, osa [guˈlozu, ɔza] *adj* greedy.
gume [ˈgumi] *m* blade.
guri, ria [guˈri, ria] *m* kid.
gurizada [guriˈzada] *f* [criançada] kids *(pl)*.
guru [guˈru] *m* guru.
gutural [gutuˈraw] (*pl* **-ais**) *adj* guttural.

h¹, H [aˈga] *m* [letra] h, H.
h² (*abrev de* **hora**) *f* hr., h.
ha (*abrev de* **hectare**) *m* ha.
hã [ã] *interj* **-1.** [reflexão]: **hã!** ah! **-2.** [pergunta]: **hã?** sorry?
habeas-corpus [ˌabjasˈkɔxpuʃ] *m inv* habeas corpus.
hábil [ˈabiw] (*pl* **-eis**) *adj* **-1.** [ger] skilful. **-2.** [sutil] subtle. **-3.** *loc*: **em tempo ~** in due course.
habilidade [abiliˈdadʒi] *f* **-1.** [aptidão] ability. **-2.** [competência] talent. **-3.** [astúcia] skill. **-4.** [sutileza] subtlety.
habilidoso, osa [abiliˈdozu, ɔza] *adj* skilful *UK*, skillful *US*.
habilitação [abilitaˈsãw] (*pl* **-ões**) *f* **-1.** [aptidão] aptitude. **-2.** [conhecimento formal] qualification. **-3.** *JUR* [documento] validation.
◆ **habilitações** *fpl* [qualificações] qualifications.
habilitado, da [abiliˈtadu, da] *adj* **-1.** [profissional liberal] qualified. **-2.** [operário] skilled.

habilitar [4] [abili'ta(x)] *vt* **-1.** [capacitar] to enable. **-2.** [preparar] to prepare. **-3.** [dar direito a] to entitle to.
◆ **habilitar-se** *vp* [capacitar-se] to prepare o.s.
habitação [abita'sãw] (*pl* **-ões**) *f* **-1.** [casa] house. **-2.** *POL* [moradia] housing.
habitacional [abitasjo'naw] (*pl* **-ais**) *adj* housing *(antes de subst)*.
habitante [abi'tãntʃi] *mf* inhabitant.
habitar [4] [abi'ta(x)] ◇ *vt* **-1.** [morar em] to live in. **-2.** [povoar] to inhabit. ◇ *vi* [viver] to live.
hábitat ['abitatʃ] *m* habitat; ~ **natural** natural habitat.
habitável [abi'tavew] (*pl* **-eis**) *adj* inhabitable.
hábito ['abitu] *m* habit; **ter o ~ de fazer algo** to be used to doing sthg; **por força do ~** through force of habit.
habituado, da [abi'twadu, da] *adj*: ~ **(a algo)** used (to sthg); ~ **a fazer algo** used to doing sthg.
habitual [abi'twaw] (*pl* **-ais**) *adj* habitual.
habituar [4] [abi'twa(x)] *vt* to accustom to; ~ **alguém a algo/a fazer algo** to get sb used to sthg/ to doing sthg.
◆ **habituar-se** *vp*: **~-se a (fazer) algo** to get used to (doing) sthg.
habitué [abi'twe] *m* habitué.
hacker [xake(x)ʃ] (*pl* **hackers**) *m COMPUT* hacker.
hadoque [a'dɔki] *m* haddock.
Haia ['aja] *n* The Hague.
Haiti [aj'tʃi] *n* Haiti.
hálito ['alitu] *m* breath; **mau ~** bad breath.
hall ['ɔw] *m* hall; ~ **de entrada** entrance hall.
halo ['alu] *m* halo.
haltere [aw'tɛri] *m* dumb-bell.
halterofilismo [awterofi'liʒmu] *m* weightlifting.
halterofilista [awterofi'liʃta] *mf* weight lifter.
hambúrguer [ãn'buxge(x)] (*pl* **-es**) *m* hamburger.
handicap [ãndʒi'kapi] *m* handicap.
hangar [ãŋ'ga(x)] (*pl* **-es**) *m* hangar.
Hanói [a'nɔj] *n* Hanoi.
Harare [a'rari] *n* Harare.
haras ['araʃ] *m inv* stud *(for racehorses)*.
hardware [ax'dwɛ(x)] *m COMPUT* hardware.
harém [a'rẽ] (*pl* **-ns**) *m* harem.
harmonia [axmo'nia] *f* harmony.
harmônico, ca [ax'moniku, ka] *adj* harmonic.
◆ **harmônica** *f* harmonica, mouth organ.
harmonioso, osa [axmo'njozu, ɔza] *adj* harmonious.
harmonizar [4] [axmoni'za(x)] *vt* **-1.** *MÚS* to harmonize. **-2.** [conciliar]: ~ **algo com algo** to reconcile sthg with sthg.
◆ **harmonizar-se** *vp*: **~-se (com algo)** to be in harmony (with sthg).
harpa ['axpa] *f* harp.
harpista [ax'piʃta] *mf* harpist.
haste ['aʃtʃi] *f* **-1.** [de bandeira] pole. **-2.** [caule] stalk.
hasteamento [aʃtʃja'mẽntu] *m* hoisting.
hastear [15] [aʃ'tʃja(x)] *vt* to raise.
Havaí [ava'i] *n* Hawaii.
havaiano, na [ava'jãnu, na] ◇ *adj* Hawaiian. ◇ *m, f* Hawaiian.
havana [a'vãna] ◇ *adj* [cor] beige. ◇ *m* [charuto] Havana cigar.
Havana [a'vãna] *n* Havana.
havanês, esa [ava'neʃ, eza] ◇ *adj* Havana *(antes de subst)*. ◇ *m, f person from Havana*.
haver [2] [a've(x)] *v impess* **-1.** [existir, estar, ter lugar]: **há** there is, there are *pl*; **havia** there was, there were *pl*; **há um café muito bom ao fim da rua** there's a very good café at the end of the street; **não há nada aqui** there's nothing here; **não há correio amanhã** there's no mail tomorrow. **-2.** [exprime tempo]: **estou esperando há dez minutos** I've been waiting for ten minutes; **há séculos que não vou lá** I haven't been there for ages; **há três dias que não o vejo** I haven't seen him for three days. **-3.** [exprime obrigação]: **há que esperar três dias** you'll have to wait three days. **-4.** [em locuções]: **haja o que houver** come what may; **não há de quê!** don't mention it! ◇ *v aux* [em tempos compostos] to have; **ele havia chegado há pouco** he had just arrived; **como não havia comido estava com fome** I was hungry because I hadn't eaten; **havíamos reservado com antecedência** we'd reserved in advance.
◆ **haver de** *v + prep* [dever] to have; [exprime intenção]: **hei de ir** I'll go.
◆ **haver-se com** *vp + prep*: **~-se com alguém** [prestar contas a] to answer to sb.
◆ **haveres** *mpl* [pertences] belongings; [bens] assets.
haxixe [a'ʃiʃi] *m* hashish.
HC (*abrev de* **Hospital das Clínicas**) *m famous teaching hospital in São Paulo*.
HD (*abrev de* **Hard Disk**) *m* HD.
hectare [ek'tari] *m* hectare.
hectograma [ekto'grãma] *m* hectogram, hectogramme.
hectolitro [ekto'litru] *m* hectolitre.
hedge [ɛdji] *m ECON* [proteção cambial] hedge.
hediondo, da [e'dʒõndu, da] *adj* hideous.
hedonista [edo'niʃta] ◇ *adj* hedonistic. ◇ *mf* hedonist.
hegemonia [eʒemo'nia] *f* hegemony.
hegemônico, ca [ege'moniku, ka] *adj* hegemonic.
hein [ẽj] *interj*: **~?** what?; **aí, ~?** *fam* [muito bem] not bad, eh?
hélice ['ɛlisi] *f* propeller.
helicóptero [eli'kɔpteru] *m* helicopter.
heliporto [eli'poxtu] *m* heliport.
Helsinki [ɛw'sĩŋki] *n* Helsinki.
hematologia [ematolo'ʒia] *f* haematology *UK*, hematology *US*.
hematoma [ema'toma] *f* bruise, haematoma *UK*, hematoma *US*.

hemisférico, ca [emiʃ'fɛriku, ka] *adj* hemispherical.
hemisfério [emiʃ'fɛrju] *m* hemisphere.
hemodiálise [emo'dʒjalizi] *f* dialysis.
hemofilia [emofi'lia] *f* haemophilia *UK*, hemophilia *US*.
hemofílico, ca [ɛmo'filiku, ka] ◇ *adj* haemophilic *UK*, hemophilic *US*. ◇ *m, f* haemophiliac *UK*, hemophiliac *US*.
hemoglobina [emoglo'bina] *f* haemoglobin *UK*, hemoglobin *US*.
hemograma [emo'grãma] *m* full blood count.
hemorragia [emoxa'ʒia] *f* haemorrhage *UK*, hemorrhage *US*.
hemorrágico, ca [emo'xagiku, ka] *adj* haemorrhagic.
hemorróidas [emo'xɔjdaʃ] *fpl* haemorrhoid *UK*, hemorrhoid *US*.
henê [e'ne], **hena** ['ɛna] *f* henna.
hepatite [epa'tʃitʃi] *f* hepatitis.
heptágono [ep'tagonu] *m* heptagon.
hera ['ɛra] *f* ivy.
heráldica [e'rawdʒika] *f* heraldry.
herança [e'rãnsa] *f* inheritance.
herbáceo, cea [ex'basju, sja] *adj* herbaceous.
herbanário [exba'narju] *m* herbarium.
herbicida [exbi'sida] *m* herbicide.
herbívoro, ra [ex'bivoru, ra] ◇ *adj* herbivorous. ◇ *m, f* herbivore.
hercúleo, lea [ex'kulju, lja] *adj* **fig** [muito forte] Herculean.
herdar [4] [ex'da(x)] *vt* **-1.** [ger]: **~ algo de alguém** to inherit sthg from sb. **-2.** [legar]: **~ algo a alguém** to pass sthg on to sb.
herdeiro, ra [ex'dejru, ra] *m, f* heir.
hereditariedade [eredʒitarje'dadʒi] *f* heredity.
hereditário, ria [eredʒi'tarju, rja] *adj* hereditary.
herege [e'rɛʒi] *mf* heretic.
heresia [ere'zia] *f* heresy.
herético, ca [e'rɛtʃiku, ka] ◇ *adj* heretical. ◇ *m, f* heretic.
hermafrodita [exmafro'dʒita] ◇ *adj* hermaphrodite, hermaphroditic. ◇ *mf* hermaphrodite.
hermético, ca [ex'mɛtʃiku, ka] *adj* **-1.** [bem fechado] hermetic, airtight. **-2.** **fig** [obscuro] hermetic.
hérnia ['ɛxnja] *f* hernia; **~ de disco** slipped disc.
herói [e'rɔj] *m* hero.
heróico, ca [e'rɔjku, ka] *adj* heroic.
heroína [e'rwina] *f* heroine.
heroísmo [e'rwiʒmu] *m* heroism.
herpes ['ɛxpiʃ] *m* herpes; **~ genital** genital herpes.
hertz ['ɛxts] *m* hertz.
hesitação [ezita'sãw] (*pl* **-ões**) *f* hesitation.
hesitante [ezi'tãntʃi] *adj* hesitant.
hesitar [4] [ezi'ta(x)] *vi*: **~ em fazer algo** to hesitate to do sthg.
heterodoxo, xa [etero'dɔksu, ksa] *adj* heterodox.
heterogêneo, nea [etero'ʒenju, nja] *adj* heterogeneous.
heterônimo [ete'ronimu] *m* pen-name, nom de plume.
heterossexual [eterosek'swaw] (*pl* **-ais**) ◇ *adj* heterosexual. ◇ *mf* heterosexual.
hexagonal [ezago'naw] (*pl* **-ais**) *adj* hexagonal.
hexágono [e'zagonu] *m* hexagon.
hiato ['jatu] *m* hiatus.
hibernação [ibexna'sãw] (*pl* **-ões**) *f* hibernation.
hibernar [4] [ibex'na(x)] *vi* to hibernate.
hibisco [i'biʃku] *m* hibiscus.
híbrido, da ['ibridu, da] *adj* [mesclado] hybrid.
◆ **híbrido** *m* [animal ou vegetal]: **ser um ~ (de)** to be a hybrid (of).
hidramático, ca [idra'matʃiku, ka] *adj* Hydra-Matic®.
hidratante [idra'tãntʃi] ◇ *adj* moisturizing. ◇ *m* moisturizer.
hidratar [4] [idra'ta(x)] *vt* **-1.** [pele] to moisturize. **-2.** MED to hydrate.
hidrato [i'dratu] *m*: **~ de carbono** carbohydrate.
hidráulico, ca [i'drawliku, ka] *adj* hydraulic.
◆ **hidráulica** *f* hydraulics *(sg)*.
hidrelétrica [idre'lɛtrika] *f* **-1.** [usina] hydroelectric power station. **-2.** [empresa] hydroelectric company.
hidrelétrico, ca [idre'lɛtriku, ka] *adj* hydroelectric.
hidroavião [ˌidrwa'vjãw] (*pl* **-ões**) *m* seaplane.
hidrocarboneto [idrokaxbo'netu] *m* hydrocarbon.
hidrodinâmica [idrodʒi'nãmika] *f* hydrodynamics *(sg)*.
hidrófilo, la [i'drɔfilu, la] *adj* absorbent.
hidrofobia [idrofo'bia] *f* hydrophobia, rabies.
hidrófobo, ba [i'drɔfobu, ba] ◇ *adj* hydrophobic. ◇ *m,f* hydrophobic person.
hidrogênio [idro'ʒenju] *m* hydrogen.
hidrografia [idrogra'fia] *f* hydrography.
hidromassagem [idruma'saʒẽ] (*pl* **-ns**) *f* hydromassage.
hidroplano [idro'plãnu] *m* hydroplane.
hidroterapia [idrotera'pia] *f* hydrotherapy.
hidrovia [idro'via] *f* waterway.
hiena ['jena] *f* hyena.
hierarquia [jerar'kia] *f* hierarchy.
hierárquico, ca [je'raxkiku, ka] *adj* hierarchical.
hierarquizar [4] [jeraxki'za(x)] *vt* to organize into a hierarchy.
hieróglifo [je'rɔgliful] *m* hieroglyph.
hífen ['ifẽ] (*pl* **-es**) *m* hyphen.
hifenizar [4] [ifeni'za(x)] *vt* hyphenate.
Hi-Fi (*abrev de* **High Fidelity**) *m* hi-fi.
higiene [i'ʒjeni] *f* hygiene.
higiênico, ca [i'ʒjeniku, ka] *adj* hygienic; **papel ~** toilet paper.
higienizar [4] [ʒjeni'za(x)] *vt* to sterilize.
hilariante [ila'rjãntʃi] *adj* hilarious.
hilário, ria [i'larju, rja] *adj* [hilariante] hilarious.

Himalaia [ima'lajal] *n*: **o** ~ the Himalayas *(pl)*.
hímen ['imẽ] (*pl* **-ns**) *m* ANAT hymen.
hindi ['ĩndʒi] *m* Hindi.
hindu [ĩn'du] (*pl* **hindus**) <> *adj* **-1.** [da Índia] Indian. **-2.** RELIG Hindu. <> *m, f* **-1.** [da Índia] Indian. **-2.** RELIG Hindu.
hinduísmo [ĩn'dwiʒmu] *m* Hinduism.
hino ['inu] *m* hymn; ~ **nacional** national anthem.
hiper ['ipe(x)] *prefixo* **-1.** [extremo, grande] hyper-. **-2.** *fam* [super] hyper-.
hipérbole [i'pɛxboli] *f* **-1.** MAT hyperbola. **-2.** [exagero] hyperbole.
hiperinflação [iperĩnfla'sãw] (*pl* **-ões**) *f* hyperinflation.
hiperlink [iper'linki] *m* COMPUT hyperlink.
hipermercado [ˌipexmex'kadu] *m* hypermarket.
hipermetropia [ipexmetro'pia] *f* hypermetropia, long-sightedness.
hipersensível [ipexsẽn'sivew] (*pl* **-eis**) *adj* hypersensitive.
hipertensão [ˌipextẽn'sãw] (*pl* **-ões**) *f* high blood pressure, hypertension.
hipertenso, sa [ipex'tẽsu, sa] *adj* with high blood-pressure; **ser** ~ to have high blood pressure.
hipertexto [ipex'tejʃtu] *m* COMPUT hypertext.
hipertrofia [ipextro'fia] *f* **-1.** MED hypertrophy. **-2.** [fig] excessive increase.
hipertrofiar [ipextro'fja(x)] *vt* to overstretch.
◆ **hipertrofiar-se** *vp* to become overdeveloped.
hípico, ca ['ipiku, ka] *adj* **-1.** [clube, competição] riding. **-2.** [sociedade] equestrian.
hipismo [i'piʒmu] *m* horse riding, equestrianism.
hipnose [ip'nɔzi] *f* hypnosis.
hipnótico, ca [ip'nɔtʃiku, ka] *adj* hypnotic.
◆ **hipnótico** *m* [substância] hypnotic.
hipnotizado, da [ipnotʃi'zadu, da] *adj* hypnotized.
hipnotizador, ra [ipnotʃiza'do(x), ra] <> *adj* hypnotizing. <> *m, f* hypnotist.
hipnotizar [4] [ipnotʃi'za(x)] *vt* to hypnotize.
hipocondria [ipokõn'dria] *f* hypochondria.
hipocondríaco, ca [ˌipɔkõn'driaku, ka] <> *adj* hypochondriac. <> *m, f* hypochondriac.
hipocrisia [ipokri'zia] *f* hypocrisy.
hipócrita [i'pɔkrita] <> *adj* hypocritical. <> *mf* hypocrite.
hipodérmico, ca [ipo'dɛxmiku, ka] *adj* hypodermic.
hipódromo [i'pɔdrumu] *m* racecourse.
hipófise [i'pɔfizi] *f* ANAT pituitary.
hipoglicemia [ipoglise'mia] *f* hypoglycaemia *UK*, hypoglycemia *US*.
hipopótamo [ipo'pɔtamu] *m* hippopotamus.
hipoteca [ipo'tɛka] *f* mortgage.
hipotecar [12] [ipote'ka(x)] *vt* to mortgage.
hipotecário, ria [ipote'karju, rja] *adj* mortgage *(antes de subst)*.
hipotenusa [ipote'nuza] *f* hypotenuse.
hipotermia [ipotex'mia] *f* hypothermia.
hipótese [i'pɔtezi] *f* **-1.** [conjectura] hypothesis. **-2.** [possibilidade] eventuality; **não abandonaria meus filhos em** ~ **alguma** I wouldn't abandon my children under any circumstances, under no circumstance would I abandon my children; **na melhor/pior das** ~**s** at best/worst.
hipotético, ca [ipo'tɛtʃiku, ka] *adj* hypothetical.
hirsuto, ta [ix'sutu, ta] *adj* hairy.
hispânico, ca [iʃ'paniku, ka] <> *adj* Hispanic. <> *m, f* Hispanic.
hispano, na [iʃ'pãnu, na] <> *adj* Hispanic. <> *m, f* Hispanic.
hispano-americano, na [iʃˌpãnwameri'kãnu, na] <> *adj* Spanish-American. <> *m, f* Spanish American.
histerectomia [iʃterekto'mia] *f* hysterectomy.
histeria [iʃte'ria] *f* hysteria.
histérico, ca [iʃ'tɛriku, ka] *adj* hysterical.
histerismo [iʃte'riʒmu] *m* MED hysteria.
histologia [iʃtolo'ʒia] *f* histology.
história [iʃ'tɔrja] *f* **-1.** [ger] history; ~ **antiga** ancient history; ~ **do Brasil** Brazilian history; ~ **natural** natural history. **-2.** [narração] story; ~ **do arco-da-velha** tall story; ~ **da carochinha** fairy tale; ~ **em quadrinhos** comic strip. **-3.** [lorota] nonsense; ~ **para boi dormir** empty talk. **-4.** [recato]: **deixa de** ~**!** come off it! **-5.** [explicação] excuse. **-6.** [idéia, proposta] suggestion. **-7.** [acontecimento] event; [caso amoroso] love affair. **-8.** [enredo] storyline. **-9.** [boato] rumour. **-10.** [tradição] tradition. **-11.** [problema] problem. **-12.** *fam* [abuso]: **que** ~ **é essa de ...?** what's the idea of ...?
historiador, ra [iʃtorja'do(x), ra] *m, f* historian.
historiar [16] [iʃto'rja(x)] *vt* to narrate.
historicidade [iʃtorisi'dadʒi] *f* historicity, historical authenticity.
histórico, ca [iʃ'tɔriku, ka] *adj* **-1.** [ger] historical. **-2.** [importante] historic.
◆ **histórico** *m* history.
historieta [iʃto'rjeta] *f* short story.
histrião [iʃtri'ãw] (*pl* **-ões**) *m* [comediante] comic.
histriônico, ca [iʃtri'oniku, ka] *adj* histrionic.
histrionismo [iʃrjo'niʒmu] *m* histrionics *(pl)*.
hit ['iti] *m* COMPUT hit.
HIV (*abrev de* **Human Immunodeficiency Virus**) *m* HIV.
hobby ['ɔbi] *m* hobby.
hoje ['oʒi] *adv* today; **ainda** ~ before the end of the day; **de** ~ **em diante** from today onwards, from this day forth; ~ **noite** tonight; ~ **em dia** nowadays; ~ **faz um mês** a month ago today.
Holanda [o'lãnda] *f* Holland, The Netherlands.
holandês, esa [olãn'deʃ, eza] (*mpl* **-eses** *fpl* **-s**) <> *adj* Dutch. <> *m, f* Dutchman (*f* Dutchwoman).
◆ **holandês** *m* [língua] Dutch.
holding ['xowdiŋ] *f* holdings *(pl)*.
holocausto [olo'kawʃtu] *m* holocaust.
holofote [olo'fɔtʃi] *m* searchlight.

holograma [olo'grãma] *m* hologram.
hombridade [õnbri'dadʒi] *f* decency.
home banking ['xomibãnkĩn] *m COMPUT* home banking.
homem ['ɔmẽ] (*pl* **-ns**) *m* **-1.** [ger] man; ~ **de negócios** businessman; ~ **do povo** man of the people. **-2.** [humanidade]: **o** ~ mankind. **-3.** [chefe]: **ser o** ~ **da casa** to be the man of the house.
homem-feito [ˌomẽn'fejtu] (*pl* **homens-feitos**) *m* grown man.
homem-rã [ˌomẽn'xã] (*pl* **homens-rãs**) *m* frogman.
homenageado, da [omena'ʒjadu, da] <> *adj* venerated. <> *m, f*: **o** ~ **da festa é ...** this party is being held in homage to ...
homenagear [15] [omena'ʒja(x)] *vt* to pay homage to.
homenagem [ome'naʒẽ] (*pl* **-ns**) *f* homage; **em** ~ **a algo/alguém** in homage to sthg/sb.
homenzarrão [omẽnza'xãw] (*pl* **-ões**) *m* strapping man.
homeopata [omjo'pata] <> *adj* homeopathic. <> *mf* homeopath.
homeopatia [omjopa'tʃia] *f* homeopathy.
homeopático, ca [omjo'patʃiku, ka] *adj* homeopathic.
homérico, ca [o'mɛriku, ka] *adj fig* [extraordinário] epic.
homicida [omi'sida] <> *adj* homicidal. <> *mf* murderer.
homicídio [omi'sidʒju] *m* homicide; ~ **culposo** manslaughter.
homogeneidade [omoʒenej'dadʒi] *f* homogeneity.
homogeneizado, da [omoʒenej'zadu, da] *adj* homogenized.
homogêneo, nea [omo'ʒenju, nja] *adj* homogeneous.
homologação [omologa'sãw] (*pl* **-ões**) *f* ratification.
homologar [14] [omolo'ga(x)] *vt* **-1.** [lei, casamento] to ratify. **-2.** [sociedade] to grant official recognition to.
homólogo, ga [o'mɔlogu, ga] <> *adj* **-1.** [ger] homologous. **-2.** [correspondente] equivalent. <> *m, f* [pessoa] counterpart, opposite number.
homônimo, ma [o'monimu, ma] *adj* homonymous.
◆ **homônimo** *m* **-1.** [pessoa] namesake. **-2.** *GRAM* homonym.
homossexual [omosek'swaw] (*pl* **-ais**) <> *adj* homosexual. <> *m, f* homosexual.
homossexualidade [omosekswali'dadʒi] *f* homosexuality.
homossexualismo [omosekswa'liʒmu] *m* homosexuality.
Honduras [õn'duraʃ] *n* Honduras.
hondurenho, nha [õndu'reɲu, ɲa] <> *adj* Honduran. <> *m, f* Honduran.
honestamente [oneʃta'mẽntʃi] *adv* honestly.
honestidade [oneʃtʃi'dadʒi] *f* honesty; **com** ~ honestly.
honesto, ta [o'nɛʃtu, ta] *adj* honest.
Honolulu [onolu'lu] *n* Honolulu.
honorário, ria [ono'rarju, rja] *adj* honorary.
honorários [ono'rarjuʃ] *mpl* fee *(sg)*.
honorífico, ca [ono'rifiku, ka] *adj* honorific.
honra ['õnxa] *f* **-1.** [ger] honour *UK*, honor *US*; **em** ~ **de alguém** in honour of sb *UK*, in honor of sb *US*. **-2.** [motivo de orgulho] credit.
◆ **honras** *fpl* honours *UK*, honors *US*; ~ **militares** military honours *UK*, military honors *US*; **fazer as** ~ **da casa** to do the honours *UK*, to do the honors *US*.
honradez [õnxa'deʒ] *f* honesty.
honrado, da [õ'xadu, da] *adj* **-1.** [digno] worthy. **-2.** [respeitado] respectable.
honrar [4] [õ'xa(x)] *vt* [respeitar] to honour *UK*, to honor *US*.
◆ **honrar-se** *vp* [lisonjear-se]: **~-se com algo/em fazer algo** to be honoured in sthg/to do sthg *UK*, to be honored in sthg/to do sthg *US*.
honraria [õnxa'ria] *f* honour *UK*, honor *US*.
honroso, osa [õ'xozu, ɔza] *adj* honourable *UK*, honorable *US*.
hóquei ['ɔkej] *m* hockey; ~ **sobre gelo** ice hockey.
hora ['ɔra] *f* **-1.** [do dia] hour; **de** ~ **em** ~ every hour. **-2.** [ger] time; **altas ~s** very late at night; **dar as ~s** to tell the time; ~ **legal** official time; **que ~s são?** what time is it?; ~ **extra** extra time; **~s vagas** spare time; **chegar a** ~ to arrive on time; **fazer algo fora de** ~ to do sthg at the wrong time; **em boa** ~ opportunely; **em má** ~ inopportunely; **estar na** ~ **de fazer algo** to be time to do sthg; **na** ~ **H** on the dot; **de última** ~ last minute *(antes de subst)*; **na última** ~ at the last minute; **não vejo a** ~ **de ir embora** I can't wait for the time to leave; **na** ~ on time; **em cima da** ~ dead on time; **perder a** ~ to be late. **-3.** [compromisso]: **marcar** ~ **com alguém** to make an appointment with sb. **-4.** [brincadeira]: **fazer** ~ **com alguém** to play with sb. **-5.** *loc*: **estar pela** ~ **da morte** to cost the earth; **fazer** ~ to waste time.
horário, ria [o'rarju, rja] *adj* hourly.
◆ **horário** *m* **-1.** [tabela] timetable. **-2.** [hora prefixada] time; ~ **nobre** prime time; ~ **de verão** summer time.
horda ['ɔxda] *f* horde.
horista [o'riʃta] <> *adj* paid by the hour *(depois de subst)*. <> *mf* employee paid by the hour.
horizontal [orizõn'taw] (*pl* **-ais**) <> *adj* horizontal. <> *f* [linha] horizontal.
horizonte [ori'zõntʃi] *m* horizon.
hormonal [oxmo'naw] (*pl* **-ais**) *adj* hormonal.
hormônio [ox'monju] *m* hormone.
horóscopo [o'rɔʃkopu] *m* horoscope.
horrendo, da [o'xẽndu, da] *adj* **-1.** [atemorizante] frightful. **-2.** [feio] horrendous.
horripilante [oxipi'lãntʃi] *adj* horrifying.

horripilar [4] [oxipi'la(x)] *vt* to horrify.
◆ **horripilar-se** *vp* to be horrified.
horrível [o'xivɛw] (*pl* **-eis**) *adj* **-1.** [ger] terrible. **-2.** [feio] horrible.
horror [o'xo(x)] (*pl* **-es**) *m* **-1.** [medo]: **ter ~ (de** *ou* **a algo)** to have a horror (of sthg). **-2.** [repulsa]: **ter ~ a algo/a fazer algo** to have a horror of sthg/doing sthg. **-3.** [coisa feia]: **fiquei um ~ com essa roupa** I looked a fright in those clothes. **-4.** [atrocidade]: **que ~!** how awful! **-5.** [ruim]: **ser um ~** to be terrible.
◆ **horrores** *mpl* **-1.** [palavras injuriosas]: **dizer ~ de algo/alguém** to say horrible things about sthg/sb. **-2.** [ações terríveis]: **fazer ~** to do horrible things. **-3.** [quantia vultuosa]: **ele está faturando ~es** he is raking it in. **-4.** [grande quantidade]: **~ de algo** vast amounts of sthg.
horrorizar [4] [oxori'za(x)] *vt* to terrify.
◆ **horrorizar-se** *vp* to be terrified.
horroroso, osa [oxo'rozu, ɔza] *adj* **-1.** [ger] terrible. **-2.** [feio] frightful.
horta ['ɔxta] *f* vegetable garden.
hortaliças [oxta'lisaʃ] *fpl* vegetables.
hortelã [oxte'lã] *f* mint.
hortelã-pimenta [oxte,lãpi'mẽnta] (*pl* **hortelãs-pimenta**) *f* peppermint.
hortênsia [ox'tẽnsja] *f* hydrangea.
horticultor, ra [oxtʃikuw'to(x), ra] (*mpl* **-es**, *fpl* **-s**) *m, f* horticulturist.
horticultura [oxtʃikuw'tura] *f* horticulture.
hortifrutigranjeiro, ra [oxtʃiʃrutʃigrãn'ʒejru, ra] *adj relating to fruit, vegetable and small farm production.*
◆ **hortifrutigranjeiro** *m* smallholder *(producing fruit and vegetables).*
hortigranjeiros [oxtʃigrãn'ʒeiruʃ] *mpl* farm produce.
horto ['oxtu] *m* allotment.
hospedagem [oʃpe'daʒẽ] (*pl* **-ns**) *f* **-1.** [acomodação] accommodation. **-2.** [diária] board and lodging. **-3.** [pensão] inn.
hospedar [4] [oʃpe'da(x)] *vt* to lodge.
◆ **hospedar-se** *vp* to lodge.
hospedaria [oʃpeda'ria] *f* guest house.
hóspede ['ɔʃpedʒi] *mf* guest.
hospedeiro, ra [oʃpe'dejru, ra] *m, f* host.
hospício [oʃ'pisju] *m* hospice.
hospital [oʃpi'taw] (*pl* **-ais**) *m* hospital.
hospitalar [oʃpita'la(x)] *adj* hospital *(antes de subst).*
hospitaleiro, ra [oʃpita'lejru, ra] *adj* hospitable.
hospital-escola [oʃpi,tawiʃ'kɔla] (*pl* **hospitais-escola, hospitais-escolas**) *m* teaching hospital.
hospitalidade [oʃpitali'dadʒi] *f* hospitality.
hospitalização [oʃpitaliza'sãw] *f* hospitalization.
hospitalizar [4] [oʃpitali'za(x)] *vt* to hospitalize.
host ['xoʃtʃi] *m* COMPUT host.
hostess ['ɔʃtes] *f* hostess.
hóstia ['ɔʃtʃia] *f* Host.
hostil [oʃ'tiw] (*pl* **-is**) *adj* **-1.** [contrário]: **~ a algo/alguém** hostile to sthg/sb. **-2.** [agressivo] hostile.
hostilidade [oʃtʃili'dadʒi] *f* [sentimento] hostility.
◆ **hostilidades** *fpl* MIL hostilities.
hostilizar [4] [oʃtili'za(x)] *vt* to be hostile towards.
hotel [o'tɛw] (*pl* **-éis**) *m* hotel; **~ de alta rotatividade** hotel of ill repute.
hotelaria [otela'ria] *f* **-1.** COM hotel management. **-2.** [conjunto de hotéis] hotels *(pl).*
hoteleiro, ra [ote'lejru, ra] ◇ *adj* hotel; **rede hoteleira** chain of hotels. ◇ *m, f* hotelier.
hp (*abrev de* **horsepower**) *m* hp.
HTML (*abrev de* **Hypertext Markup Language**) *m* HTML.
HTTP (*abrev de* **Hypertext Transfer Protocol**) *m* HTTP.
hum [ũ] *interj* hum!
humanamente [umãna'mẽntʃi] *adv* humanly; **~ impossível** humanly impossible.
humanidade [umani'dadʒi] *f* humanity.
humanismo [uma'niʒmu] *m* humanism.
humanista [uma'niʃta] ◇ *adj* humanistic. ◇ *mf* humanist.
humanitário, ria [umani'tarju, rja] *adj* humanitarian.
humanizar [4] [umani'za(x)] *vt* to humanize.
◆ **humanizar-se** *vp* to become humanized.
humano, na [u'manu, na] *adj* **-1.** [da humanidade] human; **ser ~** human being. **-2.** [bondoso] human, understanding.
humanóide [uma'nɔjdʒi] ◇ *adj* humanoid. ◇ *mf* humanoid.
humanos [u'mãnuʃ] *mpl* humans.
humildade [umiw'dadʒi] *f* **-1.** [pobreza] humbleness. **-2.** [modéstia] humility. **-3.** [submissão] humility; **com ~** humbly.
humilde [u'miwdʒi] *adj* humble; **os ~s** the poor *(pl).*
humildemente [umiwdʒi'mẽntʃi] *adv* humbly.
humilhação [umiʎa'sãw] (*pl* **-ões**) *f* humiliation.
humilhante [umi'ʎãntʃi] *adj* humiliating.
humilhar [4] [umi'ʎa(x)] *vt* to humiliate.
◆ **humilhar-se** *vp* to humble o.s.
humor [u'mo(x)] *m* **-1.** [ger] humour *UK*, humor *US*; **de ~** humorous; **~ negro** black humour. **-2.** [ânimo] mood; **estar de bom/mau ~** to be good-/bad-tempered; **estar com ~ de cão** to be in a foul mood. **-3.** [senso de humor] sense of humour *UK*, sense of humor *US*.
humorismo [umo'riʒmu] *m* humour *UK*, humor *US*.
humorista [umo'riʃta] *mf* comedian.
humorístico, ca [umo'riʃtʃiku, ka] *adj* comedy *(antes de subst).*
húmus ['umuʃ] *m inv* humus.
húngaro, ra ['ũŋgaru, ra] ◇ *adj* Hungarian. ◇ *m, f* Hungarian.
◆ **húngaro** *m* [língua] Hungarian.
Hungria [ũŋ'gria] *n* Hungary.
hurra ['uxa] *interj* hooray, hurrah.
Hz (*abrev de* **hertz**) *m* Hz.

i, I [i] *m* [letra] i, I.

ianque ['jãŋki] ◇ *adj* Yankee. ◇ *m, f* Yank.

iate ['jatʃi] *m* yacht.

iatismo [ja'tʃiʒmu] *m* yachting, sailing.

iatista [ja'tʃiʃta] *mf* yachtsman (*f* yachtswoman).

IBAMA (*abrev de* **Instituto Brasileiro do Meio Ambiente e dos Recursos Naturais Renováveis**) *m Brazilian organization responsible for preserving the country's natural environment.*

Ibase (*abrev de* **Instituto Brasileiro de Análises Sociais e Econômicas**) *m Brazilian institute for social and economic analysis.*

IBDF (*abrev de* **Instituto Brasileiro de Desenvolvimento Florestal**) *m Brazilian institute for forestry development.*

IBGE (*abrev de* **Instituto Brasileiro de Geografia e Estatística**) *m Brazilian institute of geography and statistics.*

ibidem [i'bidẽ] *adv* ibid., ibidem.

Ibope (*abrev de* **Instituto Brasileiro de Opinião Pública e Estatística**) *m Brazilian opinion poll institute.*

IBP (*abrev de* **Instituto Brasileiro de Petróleo**) *m Brazilian petroleum institute.*

içar [13] [i'sa(x)] *vt* to hoist.

iceberg [ajs'bɛxgi] *m* iceberg.

ICMS (*abrev de* **Imposto sobre a Circulação de Mercadorias e Serviços**) *m government tax on goods and services,* ≃ VAT *UK*.

ícone ['ikoni] *m* icon.

iconoclasta [ikono'klaʃta] ◇ *adj* iconoclastic. ◇ *mf* iconoclast.

iconografia [ikonogra'fia] *f* iconography.

icterícia [ikte'risja] *f* jaundice.

ida ['ida] *f* **-1.** [ato de ir] going; **~s e vindas** comings and goings. **-2.** [partida] departure. **-3.** [viagem] journey; **na ~** on the outward journet; **(bilhete de) ~ e volta** return ticket. **-4.** [bilhete]: **só comprei a ~** I only bought a single (ticket).

idade [i'dadʒi] *f* [ger] age; **de ~** [idoso] elderly; **ser menor/maior de ~** to be under/of age; **pessoa da terceira ~** senior citizen; **estar na ~ de fazer algo** to be of an age to do sthg; **~ adulta** adulthood; **~ escolar** school age; **Idade Média** Middle Ages (*pl*); **~ da pedra** Stone Age.

ideação [idea'sãw] *f* ideation.

ideal [i'deaw] (*pl* **-ais**) ◇ *adj* ideal. ◇ *m* **-1.** [valores] ideal. **-2.** [perfeição] ideal thing.

idealismo [idea'liʒmu] *m* idealism.

idealista [idea'liʃta] ◇ *adj* idealistic. ◇ *mf* idealist.

idealização [idealiza'sãw] (*pl* **-ões**) *f* **-1.** [endeusamento] idealization. **-2.** [planejamento] planning.

idealizador [idealiza'do(x)] *m, f* planner.

idealizar [4] [ideali'za(x)] *vt* **-1.** [endeusar] to idealize. **-2.** [planejar] to plan.

idear [4] ['idea(x)] *vt* [planejar] to plan.

ideário [ide'arju] *m* ideas (*pl*).

idéia [i'dɛja] *f* **-1.** [ger] idea; **~ de jerico** stupid idea; **estar com ~ de** to be thinking of; **~ fixa** idée fixe, fixed idea; **fazer uma ~ errada de alguém** to misjudge sb; **ter uma ~ errada de algo** to have the wrong idea about sthg; **fazer** *ou* **ter ~ de algo** to have an idea of sthg. **-2.** [mente, opinião] mind; **mudar de ~** to change one's mind.
◆ **idéias** *fpl* [concepções] ideas; **trocar ~** to exchange ideas.

idem ['idẽ] *pron* idem.

idêntico, ca [i'dʒẽntʃiku, ka] *adj* identical.

identidade [idẽntʃi'dadʒi] *f* identity; **(carteira de) ~** identity card.

identificação [idẽntʃifika'sãw] (*pl* **-ões**) *f* identification.

identificar [12] [idʒẽntʃifi'ka(x)] *vt* to identify.
◆ **identificar-se** *vp* **-1.** [revelar-se] to identify o.s. **-2.** [espelhar-se]: **~-se com algo/alguém** to identify o.s. with sthg/sb.

ideologia [ideolo'ʒia] *f* ideology.

ideológico, ca [ideo'lɔʒiku, ka] *adj* ideological.

ídiche ['idiʃi] *m* = **iídiche**.

idílico, ca [i'dʒiliku, ka] *adj* idyllic.

idílio [i'dʒilju] *m* idyll.

idioma [i'dʒjoma] *m* language.

idiomático, ca [idʒo'matʃiku, ka] *adj* idiomatic; **expressão idiomática** idiomatic expression.

idiossincrasia [idʒjosĩŋkra'zia] *f* idiosyncrasy.

idiota [i'dʒjɔta] ◇ *adj* idiotic. ◇ *mf* idiot.

idiotia [idʒjo'tʃia] *f* idiocy.

idiotice [idʒo'tʃisi] *f* idiocy.

ido, ida ['idu, 'ida] *adj* past.

idólatra [i'dɔlatra] ◇ *adj* idolatrous. ◇ *mf* [de ídolos] idol worshipper.

idolatrar [4] [idola'tra(x)] *vt* to idolize.

idolatria [idola'tria] *f* idolatry.

ídolo ['idulu] *m* idol.

idoneidade [idonej'dadʒi] *f* fitness.

idôneo, nea [i'donju, nja] *adj* **-1.** [pessoa, julgamento] fitting. **-2.** [empresa] suitable.

idos ['iduʃ] *mpl* bygone times.

idoso, osa [i'dozu, ɔza] *adj* aged.

Iemanjá [jemãn'ʒa] *f goddess of the sea and water, in Afro-Brazilian lore.*

iene ['jeni] *m* yen.

Ierevan [jere'vã] *n* Yerevan.

iglu [i'glu] *m* igloo.

ignaro, ra [igi'naru, ra] *adj* ignorant.
ignição [igni'sãw] *f* ignition.
ignóbil [ig'nɔbiw] (*pl* **-eis**) *adj* ignoble.
ignomínia [igno'minja] *f* ignominy.
ignominoso, osa [ignomi'nozu, ɔza] *adj* ignominious.
ignorado, da [igno'radu, da] *adj* unknown.
ignorância [igno'rãnsja] *f* **-1.** [desconhecimento] ignorance. **-2.** [grosseria] rudeness; **com ~** rudely. **-3.** [violência]: **apelar para a ~** to resort to violence.
ignorante [igno'rãntʃi] ◇ *adj* **-1.** [leigo]: **~ (em)** ignorant (of). **-2.** [grosseiro] rude. ◇ *mf* **-1.** [leigo] lay person. **-2.** [grosseiro] rude person.
ignorar [4] [igno'ra(x)] *vt* **-1.** [desconhecer] not to know. **-2.** [desprezar] to ignore.
ignoto, ta [ig'nɔtu, ta] *adj* unknown.
IGP (*abrev de* **Índice Geral de Preços**) *m general price index*.
IGP-M (*abrev de* **Índice Geral de Preços de Mercado**) *m general index of market prices*.
igreja [i'greʒa] *f* church.
Iguaçu [igwa'su] *n*: **as cataratas do ~** the Iguaçu Falls.
igual [i'gwaw] (*pl* **-ais**) ◇ *adj* **-1.** [idêntico] equal. **-2.** [uniforme] the same. ◇ *mf* equal; **de ~ para ~** as equals; **por ~** evenly. ◇ *adv* the same as.
igualar [4] [igwa'la(x)] *vt* **-1.** [tornar igual] to make equal. **-2.** [nivelar] to level.
◆ **igualar-se** *vp* **-1.** [tornar-se igual]: **~-se a algo/alguém** to equal sthg/sb. **-2.** [nivelar-se]: **~-se com algo** to equal sthg. **-3.** [comparar-se]: **~-se a algo/alguém** to bear comparison with sthg/sb.
igualdade [igwaw'dadʒi] *f* **-1.** [ger] equality. **-2.** [constância] regularity.
igualitário, ria [igwali'tarju, rja] *adj* egalitarian.
igualmente [igwaw'mẽntʃi] *adv* equally.
iguana [i'gwãna] *m* iguana.
iguaria [igwa'ria] *f* delicacy.
ih [i] *interj* eek!
iídiche ['jidiʃi], **ídiche** ['idiʃi] *m* Yiddish.
ilação [ila'sãw] (*pl* **-ões**) *f* inference.
ilegal [ile'gaw] (*pl* **-ais**) *adj* illegal.
ilegalidade [ilegali'dadʒi] *f* illegality.
ilegítimo, ma [ile'ʒitʃimu, ma] *adj* illegitimate.
ilegível [ile'ʒivɛw] (*pl* **-eis**) *adj* illegible.
ileso, sa [i'lezu, za] *adj* unharmed.
iletrado, da [ile'tradu, da] *adj* **-1.** [inculto] unlettered. **-2.** [analfabeto] illiterate.
ilha ['iʎa] *f* island.

ILHAS

Two of the world's largest islands are part of Brazil. The island of Marajó, in the mouth of the Amazon river in Pará, has an area of 50,000 km²; it is both a fluvial island and a marine island, as to the north it is washed by the Atlantic ocean. The breeding of buffalo is the island's main economic activity. In the state of Tocantins, two branches of the river Araguaia form the largest fluvial island in the world, with an area of 20,000 km²: the island of Bananal. Its fauna is extremely abundant and the island of Bananal is home to the National Park of Araguaia and two indigenous reserves: Carajás and Javaés.

ilhar [4] [i'ʎa(x)] *vt* to isolate.
ilharga [i'ʎaxga] *f* ANAT flank.
ilhéu, ilhoa [i'ʎɛw, i'ʎoa] *m, f* islander.
ilhós [i'ʎɔʃ] (*pl* **ilhoses**) *m* eyelet.
ilhota [i'ʎɔta] *f* islet.
ilícito, ta [i'lisitu, ta] *adj* illicit.
ilimitado, da [ilemi'tadu, da] *adj* unlimited.
ilógico, ca [i'lɔʒiku, ka] *adj* illogical.
iludir [6] [ilu'di(x)] *vt* to delude.
◆ **iludir-se** *vp* to delude o.s.
iluminação [ilumina'sãw] (*pl* **-ões**) *f* **-1.** [luzes] lighting. **-2.** *fig* [insight] inspiration.
iluminado, da [ilumi'nadu, da] *adj* **-1.** [que recebe luz - sala] lit; [- palco, estádio] floodlit. **-2.** *fig* [esclarecido] enlightened.
iluminante [ilumi'nãntʃi] *adj* illuminating.
iluminar [4] [ilumi'na(x)] *vt* **-1.** [alumiar] to light up. **-2.** *fig* [esclarecer] to enlighten.
◆ **iluminar-se** *vp* to light up.
Iluminismo [ilumi'niʒmu] *m* Enlightenment.
iluminista [ilumi'niʃta] ◇ *adj* Enlightenment (*antes de subst*). ◇ *mf member or follower of the Enlightenment*.
ilusão [ilu'zãw] (*pl* **-ões**) *f* illusion; **~ de ótica** optical illusion; **viver de ilusões** to delude o.s.
ilusionista [iluzjo'niʃta] *mf* illusionist.
ilusório, ria [ilu'zɔrju, rja] *adj* illusory.
ilustração [iluʃtra'sãw] (*pl* **-ões**) *f* illustration.
ilustrado, da [iluʃ'tradu, da] *adj* **-1.** [com figuras] illustrated. **-2.** [instruído] learned.
ilustrador, ra [iluʃtra'do(x), ra] ◇ *adj* illustrative. ◇ *m, f* illustrator.
ilustrar [4] [iluʃ'tra(x)] *vt* **-1.** [ger] to illustrate. **-2.** [instruir] to enlighten.
◆ **ilustrar-se** *vp* [instruir-se] to enlighten o.s.
ilustrativo, va [iluʃtra'tʃivu, va] *adj* illustrative.
ilustre [i'luʃtri] *adj* illustrious, distinguished; **um ~ desconhecido** a complete unknown.
ilustríssimo, ma [iluʃ'trisimu, ma] *superl* ▷ **ilustre**; **~ senhor** honourable gentleman ***UK***, honorable gentleman ***US***.
ímã ['imã] *m* magnet.
imaculado, da [imaku'ladu, da] *adj* immaculate.
imagem [i'maʒẽ] (*pl* **-ns**) *f* **-1.** [gen] image. **-2.** [TV] picture.
imagético, ca [ima'getiku, ka] *adj* fully illustrated.
imaginação [imaʒina'sãw] *f* imagination.
imaginar [4] [imaʒi'na(x)] ◇ *vt* **-1.** [fantasiar] to imagine. **-2.** [supor]: **~ que** to imagine that. ◇ *vi* to daydream; **imagina!** just imagine!
◆ **imaginar-se** *vp* [supor-se] to imagine o.s.
imaginário, ria [imaʒi'narju, rja] *adj* imaginary.
imaginativo, va [imaʒina'tʃivu, va] *adj* imaginative.

imaginável [imaʒi'navɛw] (*pl* **-eis**) *adj* imaginable.
imaginoso, osa [imaʒi'nozu, ɔza] *adj* fanciful.
imantar [4] [imãn'ta(x)] *vt* to magnetize.
imaturidade [imaturi'dadʒi] *f* immaturity.
imaturo, ra [ima'turu, ra] *adj* immature.
imbatível [ĩnba'tʃivɛw] (*pl* **-eis**) *adj* unbeatable.
imbecil [ĩnbe'siw] (*pl* **-is**) <> *adj* stupid, idiotic. <> *mf* imbecile.
imbecilidade [ĩnbesili'dadʒi] *f* stupidity.
imberbe [ĩn'bɛxbi] *adj* **-1.** [sem barba] beardless. **-2.** [juvenil] youthful.
imbricar [12] [ĩmbri'ka(x)] *vt* to overlap.
◆ **imbricar-se** *vp* to overlap.
imbuído, da [ĩmbu'idu, da] *adj* imbued.
imbuir [74] [ĩm'bwi(x)] *vt*: ~ **algo de algo** to impregnate sthg with sthg; ~ **alguém de algo** to instil sthg in sb.
imediações [imedʒja'sõiʃ] *fpl* vicinity *(sg)*; **nas ~ de** near, in the vicinity of.
imediatamente [ime,dʒjata'mẽntʃi] *adv* immediately.
imediatismo [imedʒja'tʃiʒmu] *m* immediacy.
imediatista [imedʒja'tʃiʃta] *adj* immediate.
imediato, ta [ime'dʒjatu, ta] *adj* immediate.
◆ **imediato** *m* second in command.
◆ **de imediato** *loc adv* at once.
imemorial [imemo'rjaw] (*pl* **-ais**) *adj* immemorial.
imensidão [imẽnsi'dãw], **imensidade** [imẽnsi'dadʒi] *f* immensity.
imenso, sa [i'mẽsu, sa] *adj* immense; **sinto uma saudade imensa dele** I miss him immensely.
imensurável [imẽnsu'ravew] (*pl* **-eis**) *adj* immeasurable.
imerecido, da [imere'sidu, da] *adj* undeserved.
imergir [78] [imex'ʒi(x)] <> *vt* to immerse. <> *vi* **-1.** [afundar] to sink. **-2.** *fig* [entrar]: ~ **em algo** to sink into sthg.
imersão [imex'sãw] (*pl* **-ões**) *f* immersion.
imerso, sa [i'mɛxsu, sa] *adj* immersed.
imigração [imigra'sãw] (*pl* **-ões**) *f* immigration.
imigrante [imi'grãntʃi] <> *adj* immigrant. <> *mf* immigrant.
imigrar [4] [imi'gra(x)] *vi* to immigrate.
iminência [imi'nẽnsja] *f* imminence; **em ~** imminent; **na ~ de fazer algo** on the point of doing sthg.
iminente [imi'nẽntʃi] *adj* imminent.
imiscuir-se [74] [imiʃ'kwixsi] *vp* to become involved.
imitação [imita'sãw] (*pl* **-ões**) *f* imitation.
imitador, ra [imita'do(x), ra] <> *adj* imitation *(antes de subst)*. <> *m, f* imitator.
imitar [4] [imi'ta(x)] *vt* **-1.** [arremedar] to imitate. **-2.** [falsificar] to forge.
imitativo, va [imita'tʃivu, va] *adj* imitative.
IML (*abrev de* **Instituto Médico Legal**) *m Brazilian institute of forensic medicine.*
imobiliário, ria [imobi'larju, rja] *adj* property *(antes de subst)*.
◆ **imobiliária** *f* estate agency.
imobilidade [imobili'dadʒi] *f* immobility.
imobilizar [4] [imobili'za(x)] *vt* to immobilize.
imoderação [imodera'sãw] *f* immoderation.
imoderado, da [imode'radu, da] *adj* immoderate.
imodéstia [imo'dɛʃtʃja] *f* immodesty.
imodesto, ta [imo'dɛʃtu, ta] *adj* immodest.
imolar [4] [imo'la(x)] *vt* **-1.** [sacrificar] to immolate. **-2.** [prejudicar] to damage.
imoral [imo'raw] (*pl* **-ais**) *adj* immoral.
imoralidade [imorali'dadʒi] *f* immorality.
imortal [imox'taw] (*pl* **-ais**) <> *adj* immortal. <> *mf member of the Academia Brasileira de Letras.*
imortalidade [imoxtali'dadʒi] *f* immortality.
imortalizar [4] [imoxtali'za(x)] *vt* to immortalize.
imóvel [i'mɔvɛw] (*pl* **-eis**) <> *adj* **-1.** [pessoa] immobile. **-2.** [olho, bem] fixed; **bens imóveis** real estate *(U)*. <> *m* property.
impaciência [ĩnpa'sjẽnsja] *f* impatience.
impacientar [4] [ĩmpasjẽn'ta(x)] *vt* to be impatient.
◆ **impacientar-se** *vp* to become impatient.
impaciente [ĩnpa'sjẽntʃi] *adj* **-1.** [sem paciência] impatient. **-2.** [ansioso] anxious.
impactante [ĩnpak'tãntʃi] *adj* [chocante] shattering.
impactar [4] [ĩnpak'ta(x)] <> *vt* **-1.** [impressionar, abalar] to shatter. **-2.** [colidir contra] to crash into. <> *vi* to have an impact.
impacto [ĩn'paktu] *m* impact.
impagável [ĩmpa'gavew] (*pl* **-eis**) *adj* priceless.
ímpar ['ĩnpa(x)] (*pl* **-es**) *adj* **-1.** [número] odd. **-2.** [único] peerless; **ele é um amigo ~** he's a friend in a million.
imparcial [ĩnpax'sjaw] (*pl* **-ais**) *adj* impartial.
imparcialidade [ĩnpaxsjali'dadʒi] *f* impartiality.
impasse [ĩn'pasi] *m* deadlock, impasse.
impassível [ĩnpa'sivew] (*pl* **-eis**) *adj* impassive.
impávido, da [ĩm'pavidu, da] *adj* undaunted.
impeachment [ĩnpitʃimẽnt] *m* impeachment.
impecável [ĩnpe'kavɛw] (*pl* **-eis**) *adj* impeccable.
impedido, da [ĩmpe'dʒidu, da] *adj* **-1.** [bloqueado] blocked. **-2.** FUT off-side. **-3.** [impossibilitado]: ~ **de fazer algo** prevented from doing sthg.
impedimento [ĩnpedʒi'mẽntu] *m* **-1.** FUT off-side. **-2.** *fig* [obstáculo] impediment. **-3.** POL impeachment.
impedir [70] [ĩmpe'dʒi(x)] *v* **-1.** [obstruir] to obstruct. **-2.** [coibir] to prevent; ~ **alguém de fazer algo** to prevent sb from doing sthg.
impelir [57] [ĩmpe'li(x)] *vt* **-1.** [empurrar] to thrust. **-2.** [instigar]: ~ **alguém a algo** to drive sb to sthg; ~ **alguém a fazer algo** to impel sb to do sthg.
impenetrável [ĩnpene'travɛw] (*pl* **-eis**) *adj* impenetrable.
impenitente [ĩnpeni'tẽntʃi] *adj* unrepentant.
impensado, da [ĩnpẽn'sadu, da] *adj* **-1.** [não-pensado] thoughtless. **-2.** [imprevisto] unthought of.

impensável [ĩnpẽn'savɛw] (*pl* **-eis**) *adj* unthinkable.
imperador [ĩnpera'do(x)] (*mpl* **-es**) *m* emperor (*f* empress).
imperar [4] [ĩmpe'ra(x)] *vi* **-1.** [reinar] to rule. **-2.** [prevalecer] to prevail.
imperativo, va [ĩmpera'tʃivu, va] *adj* **-1.** [urgente] imperative. **-2.** [autoritário] imperious.
◆ **imperativo** *m* imperative.
imperatriz [ĩnpera'triʃ] (*mpl* **-zes**) *f* ▷ **imperador**.
imperceptível [ĩnpexsep'tʃivew] (*pl* **-eis**) *adj* imperceptible.
imperdível [ĩnpex'dʒivew] (*pl* **-eis**) *adj* **-1.** [show, filme, aula] unmissable. **-2.** [jogo, eleição, questão] impossible to lose *(depois de verbo)*.
imperdoável [ĩnpex'dwavɛw] (*pl* **-eis**) *adj* unforgivable.
imperecível [ĩnpere'sivew] (*pl* **-eis**) *adj* imperishable.
imperfeição [ĩnpexfej'sãw] (*pl* **-ões**) *f* [defeito] imperfection.
imperfeito, ta [ĩnpex'fejtu, ta] *adj* imperfect.
◆ **imperfeito** *m* GRAM imperfect.
imperial [ĩnpe'rjaw] (*pl* **-ais**) *adj* imperial.
imperialismo [ĩnperja'liʒmu] *m* imperialism.
imperialista [ĩnperja'liʃta] ◇ *adj* imperialist. ◇ *mf* imperialist.
imperícia [ĩnpe'risja] *f* **-1.** [inabilidade] incompetence. **-2.** [inexperiência] inexperience.
império [ĩn'pɛrju] *m* empire.
imperioso, osa [ĩmpe'rjozu, ɔza] *adj* **-1.** [ger] imperious. **-2.** [urgente] imperative.
impermeabilizante [ĩnpexmjabili'zãntʃi] ◇ *adj* waterproofing. ◇ *m* waterproofer.
impermeabilizar [4] [ĩmpexmjabili'za(x)] *vt* to waterproof.
impermeável [ĩnpex'mjavɛw] (*pl* **-eis**) ◇ *adj* impermeable, waterproof. ◇ *m* [capa de chuva] raincoat.
impertinência [ĩnpextʃi'nẽnsja] *f* impertinence.
impertinente [ĩnpextʃi'nẽntʃi] *adj* impertinent.
imperturbável [ĩnpextux'bavɛw] (*pl* **-eis**) *adj* imperturbable.
impessoal [ĩnpe'swaw] (*pl* **-ais**) *adj* **-1.** [objetivo] objective. **-2.** GRAM impersonal.
impessoalidade [ĩnpeswali'dadʒi] *f* [impersonalidade] impersonal nature.
ímpeto ['ĩnpetu] *m* **-1.** [movimento brusco] sudden movement; **ele se levantou num ~** he stood up with a start. **-2.** [impulso] urge, impulse; **sentir um ~ de fazer algo** to feel an urge to do sthg.
impetrar [4] [ĩmpe'tra(x)] *vt* JUR: **~ algo** to petition for sthg.
impetuosidade [ĩnpetwozi'dadʒi] *f* impetuosity.
impetuoso, osa [ĩmpe'twozu, ɔza] *adj* **-1.** [pessoa] impetuous. **-2.** [chuva] driving. **-3.** [rio] fast-flowing.
impiedade [ĩnpje'dadʒi] *f* [crueldade] cruelty.
impiedoso, osa [ĩmpje'dozu, ɔza] *adj* merciless.
impingir [52] [ĩmpĩn'ʒi(x)] *vt*: **~ algo a alguém** to fob sthg off on sb.
ímpio, pia ['ĩmpiu, pia] ◇ *adj* pitiless. ◇ *m,f* pitiless person.
implacável [ĩnpla'kavɛw] (*pl* **-eis**) *adj* **-1.** [impiedoso] implacable. **-2.** [inexorável] unrelenting.
implantação [ĩnplãnta'sãw] *f* **-1.** [introdução] establishing. **-2.** [implementação] implementation. **-3.** MED implant.
implantar [4] [ĩmplãn'ta(x)] *vt* **-1.** [introduzir] to establish. **-2.** [implementar] to implement. **-3.** MED to implant.
implante [ĩn'plãntʃi] *m* MED implant.
implementação [ĩnplemẽnta'sãw] *f* implementation.
implementar [4] [ĩmplemẽn'ta(x)] *vt* to implement.
implemento [ĩnple'mẽntu] *m* implement.
implicação [ĩnplika'sãw] (*pl* **-ões**) *f* **-1.** [conseqüência] implication. **-2.** [envolvimento] involvement.
implicância [ĩnpli'kãnsja] *f* **-1.** [provocação] provoking; **meus filhos passam o dia inteiro de ~ um com o outro** my children spend the whole day provoking each other. **-2.** [antipatia]: **ter uma ~ com alguém** to dislike sb.
implicante [ĩnpli'kãntʃi] *adj* provocative.
implicar [12] [ĩmpli'ka(x)] ◇ *vt* [envolver]: **~ alguém em algo** to involve sb in sthg. ◇ *vi* **-1.** [pressupor]: **~ em algo** to involve sthg. **-2.** [acarretar]: **~ em algo** to result in sthg. **-3.** [provocar]: **~ com alguém** to torment sb.
implícito, ta [ĩn'plisitu, ta] *adj* implicit.
implodir [78] [ĩmplo'dʒi(x)] ◇ *vt* to implode. ◇ *vi* to implode.
implorar [4] [ĩmplo'ra(x)] *vt*: **~ algo (a alguém)** to beg (sb) for sthg.
implosão [ĩnplo'zãw] (*pl* **-ões**) *f* implosion.
impoluto, ta [ĩmpo'lutu, ta] *adj* unpolluted.
imponderado, da [ĩnpõnde'radu, da] *adj* rash.
imponderável [ĩnpõnde'ravew] (*pl* **-eis**) *adj* imponderable.
imponência [ĩnpo'nẽnsja] *f* impressiveness.
imponente [ĩnpo'nẽntʃi] *adj* impressive, imposing.
impontual [ĩnpõn'twaw] (*pl* **-ais**) *adj* unpunctual.
impopular [ĩnpopu'la(x)] (*pl* **-es**) *adj* unpopular.
impopularidade [ĩnpopulari'dadʒi] *f* unpopularity.
impor [45] [ĩm'po(x)] *vt* to impose; **~ algo a alguém** to impose sthg on sb.
◆ **impor-se** *vp* [afirmar-se] to establish o.s.
importação [ĩnpoxta'sãw] (*pl* **-ões**) *f* **-1.** [ato] importation. **-2.** [produtos] imports *(pl)*.
importador, ra [ĩnpoxta'do(x), ra] ◇ *adj* importing *(antes de subst)*. ◇ *m, f* importer.
◆ **importadora** *f* **-1.** [companhia] importer. **-2.** [loja] *shop selling imported goods*.
importância [ĩnpox'tãnsja] *f* **-1.** [mérito] importance; **não dar ~ a alguém/algo** to not care about sb/sthg; **ela não dá ~ ao que ele disse** she

doesn't care about what he said; **isso não tem ~** that doesn't matter. **-2.** [quantia] sum.
importante [ĩnpox'tãntʃi] *adj* important.
importar [4] [ĩmpox'ta(x)] <> *vt COM* to import. <> *vi* **-1.** [ser importante] to matter. **-2.** [resultar]: **~ em** to result in. **-3.** [atingir]: **~ em** to add up to.
◆ **importar-se** *vp* [fazer caso]: **não ~-se (com algo/de fazer algo)** not to mind sthg/about doing sthg.
importe [ĩn'pɔxtʃi] *m* **-1.** [soma] amount. **-2.** [preço] cost.
importunação [ĩnpoxtuna'sãw] *f* annoyance.
importunar [4] [ĩmpoxtu'na(x)] *vt* to annoy.
importuno, na [ĩnpox'tunu, na] *adj* annoying.
imposição [ĩnpozi'sãw] (*pl* **-ões**) *f* imposition.
impossibilidade [ĩnposibili'dadʒi] *f* impossibility.
impossibilitado, da [ĩnposibili'tadu, da] *adj*: **~ de fazer algo** unable to do sthg.
impossibilitar [4] [ĩmposi'bili'ta(x)] *vt*: **~ algo** to make sthg impossible; **~ alguém de fazer algo** to prevent sb from doing sthg.
impossível [ĩnpo'sivɛw] (*pl* **-eis**) *adj* impossible.
impostação [ĩnpoʃta'sãw] *f* diction.
imposto, osta [ĩm'poʃtu, ɔsta] *pp* ▷ **impor**.
◆ **imposto** *m* tax; **~ sobre Circulação de Mercadorias e Serviços** ≃ value added tax *UK*, ≃ sales tax *US*; **~ predial** ≃ council tax *UK*; **~ de renda** income tax.
impostor, ra [ĩnpoʃ'to(x), ra] (*mpl* **-es**, *fpl* **-s**) *m* impostor.
impostura [ĩnpoʃ'tura] *f* fraud.
impotência [ĩnpo'tẽnsja] *f* impotence.
impotente [ĩnpo'tẽntʃi] *adj* impotent.
impraticável [ĩnpratʃi'kavɛw] (*pl* **-eis**) *adj* **-1.** [impossível] impossible. **-2.** [inexeqüível] unworkable. **-3.** [intransitável] impassable.
imprecar [12] [ĩmpre'ka(x)] <> *vt* to curse. <> *vi* to curse.
imprecisão [ĩnpresi'zãw] (*pl* **-ões**) *f* imprecision.
impreciso, sa [ĩnpre'sizu, za] *adj* imprecise.
impregnar [4] [ĩmpreg'na(x)] <> *vt* to impregnate; **~ algo de algo** to impregnate sthg with sthg. <> *vi*: **~ en** to pervade.
imprensa [ĩn'prẽnsa] *f* **-1.** [ger] press; **~ marrom** gutter press. **-2.** [tipografia] printing press.
imprensar [ĩmprẽn'sa(x)] *vt* **-1.** [espremer] to crush. **-2.** [pressionar] to press.
imprescindível [ĩnpresĩn'dʒivɛw] (*pl* **-eis**) *adj* indispensable.
impressão [ĩnpre'sãw] (*pl* **-ões**) *f* **-1.** [marca] imprint; **~ digital** fingerprint. **-2.** [reprodução] printing. **-3.** [sensação] feeling; **ter boa/má impressão de alguém/algo** to have a good/bad impression of sb/sthg.
impressionante [ĩnpresjo'nãntʃi] *adj* impressive.
impressionar [ĩmpresju'na(x)] <> *vt* to impress. <> *vi* to impress.
◆ **impressionar-se** *vp*: **-se com alguém/algo** [comover-se] to be moved by sb/sthg.
impressionável [ĩnpresjo'navɛw] (*pl* **-eis**) *adj* impressionable.
impressionismo [ĩnpresjo'niʒmu] *m* Impressionism.
impressionista [ĩnpresjo'niʃta] <> *adj* Impressionist. <> *m, f* Impressionist.
impresso, a [ĩn'prɛsu, sa] <> *pp* ▷ **imprimir**. <> *adj* printed.
◆ **impresso** *m* printed matter *(sg)*.
impressora [ĩnpre'sora] *f* printer; **~ laser** laser printer; **~ a jato de tinta** ink-jet printer; **~ matricial** dot matrix printer.
imprestável [ĩnpreʃ'tavɛw] (*pl* **-eis**) *adj* **-1.** [inútil] unhelpful. **-2.** [estragado] useless.
impreterível [ĩnprete'rivew] (*pl* **-eis**) *adj* unavoidable.
imprevidente [ĩnprevi'dẽntʃi] *adj* **-1.** [imprudente] imprudent. **-2.** [que não soube prever] improvident.
imprevisão [ĩnprevi'zãw] *f* **-1.** [desleixo] carelessness. **-2.** [falta de previsão] improvidence.
imprevisível [ĩnprevi'zivɛw] (*pl* **-eis**) *adj* unforeseeable.
imprevisto, ta [ĩmpre'viʃtu, ta] *adj* unexpected.
◆ **imprevisto** *m*: **surgiu um ~ nos nossos planos** something unforeseen cropped up in our plans.
imprimir [ĩmpri'mi(x)] <> *vt* to print. <> *vi COMPUT* to print.
improbabilidade [ĩnprobabili'dadʒi] *f* improbability.
ímprobo, ba ['ĩmprobu, ba] *adj* dishonest.
improcedente [ĩnprose'dẽntʃi] *adj* unjustified.
improdutivo, va [ĩnprodu'tʃivu, va] *adj* unproductive.
improfícuo, cua [ĩnpro'fikwu, kwa] *adj* useless.
impropério [ĩnpro'pɛrju] *m* insult.
impróprio, pria [ĩn'prɔprju, prja] *adj* inappropriate.
improrrogável [ĩnproxo'gavew] (*pl* **-eis**) *adj* non-postponable.
improvável [ĩnpro'vavɛw] (*pl* **-eis**) *adj* improbable.
improvisação [ĩnproviza'sãw] *f* improvisation.
improvisado, da [ĩnprovi'zadu, da] *adj* improvised.
improvisar [4] [ĩmprovi'za(x)] <> *vt* to improvise. <> *vi* **-1.** to improvise. **-2.** *TEATRO* to ad-lib.
improviso [ĩnpro'vizu] *m* **-1.** [repente]: **de ~** [de repente] suddenly; [sem preparação] off the cuff; **falar de ~** to speak off the cuff. **-2.** *TEATRO* improvisation.
imprudência [ĩnpru'dẽnsja] *f* [descuido] carelessness.
imprudente [ĩnpru'dẽntʃi] *adj* careless.
impudico, ca [ĩnpu'dʒiku, ka] *adj* shameless.
impugnação [ĩnpugna'sãw] (*pl* **-ões**) *f* [contestação] challenge.
impugnar [4] [ĩmpug'na(x)] *vt* **-1.** [refutar] to refute. **-2.** [opor-se a] to oppose.

impulsionar [4] [ĩmpuwsju'na(x)] *vt* **-1.** [impelir] to propel. **-2.** [estimular] to speed up.
impulsividade [ĩnpuwsivi'dadʒi] *f* impulsiveness.
impulsivo, va [ĩnpuw'sivu, va] *adj* impulsive.
impulso [ĩn'puwsu] *m* **-1.** [ger] impulse, urge; **dar un novo ~ a** to give a new impetus to; **tomar ~** to gain strength; **por ~** on impulse. **-2.** [força] thrust; **tomar ~** to take a run.
impune [ĩn'puni] *adj* unpunished.
impunemente [ĩmpune'mẽntʃi] *adv* with impunity.
impunidade [ĩnpuni'dadʒi] *f* impunity.
impureza [ĩnpu'reza] *f* impurity.
impuro, ra [ĩm'puru, ĩm'pura] *adj* impure.
imputação [ĩmputa'sãw] (*pl* **-ões**) *f* [acusação] accusation.
imputar [4] [ĩmpu'ta(x)] *vt*: **~ algo a alguém** to attribute sthg to sb.
imundície [ĩmũn,dʒisji], **imundícia** [ĩmun'dʒisja] *f* [falta de asseio] filthiness.
imundo, da [i'mũndo, da] *adj* filthy.
imune [i'muni] *adj*: **~ (a)** immune to.
imunidade [imuni'dadʒi] *f* immunity.
imunização [imuniza'sãw] *f* immunization.
imunizar [4] [imuni'za(x)] *vt* to immunize.
imunologia [imunolo'ʒia] *f* immunology.
imutável [imu'tavew] (*pl* **-eis**) *adj* immutable.
inabalável [inaba'lavew] (*pl* **-eis**) *adj* unshakeable.
inábil [i'nabiw] (*pl* **-eis**) *adj* **-1.** [desajeitado] clumsy. **-2.** [incapaz] incapable.
inabilidade [inabili'dadʒi] *f* inability.
inabilidoso, osa [inabili'dozu, ɔza] *adj* inept.
inabilitar [4] [inabili'ta(x)] *vt* **-1.** [incapacitar] to disable. **-2.** [reprovar] to disqualify.
◆ **inabilitar-se** *vp* [reprovar-se] to fail.
inabitado, da [inabi'tadu, da] *adj* uninhabited.
inabitável [inabi'tavew] (*pl* **-eis**) *adj* uninhabitable.
inacabado, da [inaka'badu, da] *adj* unfinished.
inacabável [inaka'bavew] (*pl* **-eis**) *adj* unending.
inação [ina'sãw] *f* **-1.** [inércia] inaction. **-2.** [indecisão] indecision.
inaceitável [inasej'tavɛw] (*pl* **-eis**) *adj* unacceptable.
inacessível [inase'sivɛw] (*pl* **-eis**) *adj* inaccessible.
inacreditável [inakredʒi'tavɛw] (*pl* **-eis**) *adj* unbelievable.
inadaptado, da [inadap'tadu, da] *adj* maladjusted.
inadiável [ina'djavɛw] (*pl* **-eis**) *adj* pressing.
inadimplência [inadʒĩn'plẽnsja] *f* JUR noncompliance.
inadimplente [inadʒĩn'plẽntʃi] *adj* noncompliant.
inadmissível [inadʒimi'sivew] (*pl* **-eis**) *adj* unacceptable.
inadvertência [inadʒivex'tẽnsja] *f* inadvertence; **por ~** inadvertently.
inadvertidamente [inadʒivertʃida'mẽntʃi] *adv* inadvertently.
inadvertido, da [inadver'tʃidu, da] *adj* inadvertent.
inalação [inala'sãw] (*pl* **-ões**) *f* inhalation.
inalar [4] [ina'la(x)] *vt* to inhale.
inalcançável [inawkãn'savɛw] (*pl* **-eis**) *adj* inaccessible.
inalterado, da [inawte'radu, da] *adj* **-1.** [imudado] unaltered. **-2.** [calmo] composed.
inalterável [inawte'ravew] (*pl* **-eis**) *adj* **-1.** [imudável] immutable. **-2.** [impertubável] imperturbable.
inanição [inani'sãw] *f* starvation.
inanimado, da [inani'madu, da] *adj* inanimate.
inapetência [inape'tẽnsja] *f* loss of appetite.
inapetente [inape'tẽntʃi] *adj* lacking appetite *(depois de verbo)*.
inaplicável [inapli'kavew] (*pl* **-eis**) *adj* inapplicable.
inaproveitável [inaprovej'tavew] (*pl* **-eis**) *adj* useless.
inaptidão [inaptʃi'dãw] *f* inabilty.
inapto, ta [i'naptu, ta] *adj* unsuitable.
inatacável [inata'kavew] (*pl* **-eis**) *adj* unassailable.
inatenção [inatẽn'sãw] *f* inattention.
inatingível [inatʃĩn'ʒivɛw] (*pl* **-eis**) *adj* unattainable.
inatividade [inatʃivi'dadʒi] *f* **-1.** [ger] retirement. **-2.** [inércia] inactivity. **-3.** [desemprego] inactivity.
inativo, va [ina'tʃivu, va] *adj* **-1.** [ger] retired. **-2.** [parado] idle.
inato, ta ['inatu, ta] *adj* innate.
inaudito, ta [inaw'dʒitu, ta] *adj* unheard of.
inaudível [inaw'dʒivew] (*pl* **-eis**) *adj* inaudible.
inauguração [inawgura'sãw] (*pl* **-ões**) *f* inauguration.
inaugural [inawgu'rawl] (*pl* **-ais**) *adj* inaugural.
inaugurar [4] [inawgu'ra(x)] *vt* to open.
inca ['ĩŋka] ◇ *adj* Inca. ◇ *mf* Inca.
incalculável [ĩŋkawku'lavew] (*pl* **-eis**) *adj* incalculable.
incandescente [ĩŋkãnde'sẽntʃi] *adj* incandescent.
incansável [ĩŋkãn'savɛw] (*pl* **-eis**) *adj* tireless.
incapacidade [ĩŋkapasi'dadʒi] *f* **-1.** [deficiência] incapacity. **-2.** [incompetência] incompetence.
incapacitado, da [ĩŋkapasi'tadu, da] ◇ *adj* **-1.** [inválido] disabled. **-2.** [impedido] unable; **estar ~ de fazer algo** to be unable to do sthg. ◇ *m, f* disabled person.
incapacitar [4] [ĩŋkapasi'ta(x)] *vt* to incapacitate.
incapaz [ĩŋka'paʃ] (*pl* **-es**) *adj* **-1.** [incompetente]: **~ (para)** incompetent (for). **-2.** JUR incompetent. **-3.** [imprestativo]: **ser ~ de fazer algo** [não se dignar a] to be incapable of doing sthg.
incauto, ta [iŋ'kawtu, ta] *adj* **-1.** [imprudente] reckless. **-2.** [ingênuo] naive.
incendiar [17] [ĩsẽn'dʒja(x)] *vt* to set fire to.
◆ **incendiar-se** *vp* to catch fire.

incendiário, ria [ĩnsẽn'dʒjarju, rja] <> *adj* [bomba etc] incendiary. <> *m, f* arsonist.
incêndio [ĩn'sẽndʒju] *m* fire; ~ **provocado** *ou* **criminoso** arson.
incenso [ĩn'sẽnsu] *m* incense.
incentivador, ra [ĩnsẽntʃiva'do(x), ra] *adj* **-1.** [olhar, atitude] motivating. **-2.** [consumo, negócio] stimulating.
incentivar [4] [ĩsẽntʒi'va(x)] *vt* to stimulate.
incentivo [ĩnsẽn'tʃivu] *m* incentive.
incerteza [ĩnsex'teza] *f* uncertainty.
incerto, ta [ĩ'sɛxtu, ta] *adj* uncertain.
incessante [ĩnse'sãntʃi] *adj* incessant.
incesto [ĩn'sɛʃtu] *m* incest.
incestuoso, osa [ĩnseʃ'twozu, ɔza] *adj* incestuous.
inchação [ĩnʃa'sãw] *f* swelling.
inchaço [ĩn'ʃasu] *m fam* swelling.
inchado, da [ĩ'ʃadu, da] *adj* swollen.
inchar [4] [ĩ'sa(x)] <> *vt* to swell. <> *vi* to swell.
◆ **inchar-se** *vp* [envaidecer-se] to be puffed up (with pride).
incidência [ĩnsi'dẽnsja] *f* incidence.
incidente [ĩnsi'dẽntʃi] *m* incident.
incidir [6] [ĩnsi'dʒi(x)] *vi* **-1.** [refletir]: ~ **em** *ou* **sobre** to reflect in. **-2.** [recair]: ~ **em** *ou* **sobre** to be placed on. **-3.** [incorrer]: ~ **em** to fall into.
incinerador, ra [ĩnsine'rado(x), ra] <> *adj* incineration *(antes de subst).* <> *m* incinerator.
incinerar [4] [ĩnsine'ra(x)] *vt* to incinerate.
incipiente [ĩnsi'pjẽntʃi] *adj* incipient.
incisão [insi'zãw] (*pl* **-ões**) *f* **-1.** [corte] cut. **-2.** *MED* incision.
incisivo, va [ĩsi'zivu, va] *adj* **-1.** [cortante] cutting. **-2.** [direto] incisive.
incitação [ĩnsita'sãw] (*pl* **-ões**) *f* incitement.
incitamento [ĩnsita'mẽntu] *m* incitement.
incitar [4] [ĩsi'ta(x)] *vt* **-1.** [instigar]: ~ **alguém a algo** to incite sb to sthg; ~ **alguém a fazer algo** to incite sb to do sthg. **-2.** [suj: ambição *etc*]: ~ **alguém (a algo/a fazer algo)** to drive sb to sthg/to do sthg. **-3.** [animal] to urge on.
incivil [ĩnsi'viw] (*pl* **-is**) *adj* discourteous.
incivilidade [ĩnsivili'dadʒi] *f* discourtesy.
inclemência [ĩŋkle'mẽnsja] *f* **-1.** [impiedade] ruthlessness. **-2.** *fig* [rigor] mercilessness.
inclemente [ĩŋkle'mẽntʃi] *adj* **-1.** [impiedoso] ruthless. **-2.** *fig* [rigoroso] merciless.
inclinação [ĩŋklina'sãw] (*pl* **-ões**) *f* **-1.** [queda] inclination. **-2.** *fig* [propensão]: ~ **para** inclination towards. **-3.** [atração]: ~ **por** attraction towards.
inclinado, da [ĩŋkli'nadu, da] *adj* **-1.** [oblíquo] inclined. **-2.** *fig* [propenso]: **estar ~ a algo/a fazer algo** to be inclined towards sthg/to do sthg.
inclinar [4] [ĩŋkli'na(x)] *vt* **-1.** [fazer pender] to tilt. **-2.** [curvar] to bend.
◆ **inclinar-se** *vp* **-1.** [curvar-se] to bow. **-2.** [tender a]: **~-se a** to tend towards.
incluir [74] [ĩŋklu'i(x)] *vt* **-1.** [abranger] to include. **-2.** [inserir]: ~ **algo em algo** to insert sthg in sthg.
◆ **incluir-se** *vp* to include o.s.
inclusão [ĩŋklu'zãw] *f* inclusion.
inclusive [ĩŋklu'zivi] *adv* **-1.** [com inclusão de] including; **de segunda a sábado ~** from Monday to Saturday inclusive. **-2.** [até mesmo] even.
incluso, sa [ĩŋ'kluzo, za] *adj* included.
incoercível [ĩŋkwex'sivew] (*pl* **-eis**) *adj* uncontrollable.
incoerência [ĩŋkwe'rẽnsja] *f* **-1.** [ilogicidade] incoherence. **-2.** [discordância]: **ser uma ~ com algo** to conflict with sthg.
incoerente [ĩŋkwe'rẽntʃi] *adj* **-1.** [ilógico] illogical. **-2.** [discordante] conflicting. **-3.** [incompreensível] incoherent.
incógnito, ta [ĩŋ'kɔgnitu, ta] *adj* incognito *(depois de verbo).*
◆ **incógnita** *f* **-1.** *MAT* unknown quantity. **-2.** [mistério]: **ser uma ~** to be a mystery.
◆ **incógnito** *adv* incognito.
incolor [ĩŋko'lo(x)] (*pl* **-es**) *adj* colourless.
incólume [ĩŋ'kɔlumi] *adj* safe and sound.
incomensurável [ĩŋkomẽnsu'ravew] (*pl* **-eis**) *adj* unmeasurable.
incomodado, da [ĩŋkomo'dadu, da] *adj* [importunado] annoyed.
◆ **incomodada** *adj* & *f* [menstruada] having one's period.
incomodar [4] [ĩŋkomo'da(x)] <> *vt* to annoy. <> *vi* [irritar]: ~ **a** to annoy.
◆ **incomodar-se** *vp* **-1.** [irritar-se] to become annoyed. **-2.** [importar-se] to mind; **você se incomoda se eu fechar a porta?** would you mind if I closed the door?
incômodo, da [ĩŋ'komodu, da] *adj* **-1.** [ger] uncomfortable. **-2.** [enfadonho] boring.
◆ **incômodo** *m* **-1.** [embaraço] problem. **-2.** [menstruação] period, time of the month.
incomparável [ĩŋkõnpa'ravɛw] (*pl* **-eis**) *adj* incomparable.
incompatibilidade [ĩŋkonpatʃibili'dadʒi] *f* incompatibility.
incompatibilizar [4] [ĩnkõmpatʃibili'za(x)] *vt*: ~ **alguém com alguém** to put sb in sb's bad books.
◆ **incompatilibizar-se** *vp*: **~-se (com)** to clash (with).
incompatível [ĩŋkõnpa'tʃivɛw] (*pl* **-eis**) *adj* incompatible.
incompetência [ĩŋkõnpe'tẽnsja] *f* incompetence.
incompetente [ĩŋkõnpe'tẽntʃi] <> *adj* incompetent. <> *mf* incompetent.
incompleto, ta [ĩŋkõn'plɛtu, ta] *adj* incomplete, unfinished.
incompreendido, da [ĩŋkõnprjẽn'dʒidu, da] *adj* misunderstood.
incompreensão [ĩŋkõnprjẽn'sãw] *f* incomprehension.
incompreensível [ĩŋkõnprjẽn'sivew] (*pl* **-eis**) *adj* incomprehensible.
incompreensivo, va [ĩŋkõnprjẽn'sivu, va] *adj* uncomprehending.

incomum [ĩŋko'mũ] (*pl* **-ns**) *adj* uncommon.
incomunicável [ĩŋkomuni'kavɛw] (*pl* **-eis**) *adj* **-1.** [sem comunicação] cut off. **-2.** [que não deve se comunicar] incommunicado. **-3.** *fig* [insociável] uncommunicative.
inconcebível [ĩŋkõnse'bivɛw] (*pl* **-eis**) *adj* inconceivable.
inconciliável [ĩŋkõnsi'ljavew] (*pl* **-eis**) *adj* irreconcilable.
inconcludente [ĩŋkõŋklu'dẽntʃi] *adj* inconclusive.
inconcluso, sa [ĩŋkõŋ'kluzu, za] *adj* unfinished.
incondicional [ĩŋkõndʒisjo'naw] (*pl* **-ais**) *adj* **-1.** [total] unconditional. **-2.** [fiel] loyal.
inconfessável [ĩŋkõnfe'savew] (*pl* **-eis**) *adj* unconfessable.
inconfesso, ssa [ĩŋkõn'fɛsu, sa] *adj* unconfessed.
inconfidência [ĩŋkõnfi'dẽnsja] *f* disloyalty.
inconfidente [ĩŋkõnfi'dẽntʃi] ◇ *adj* disloyal. ◇ *mf* untrustworthy person.
inconformado, da [ĩŋkõnfox'madu, da] *adj*: **ela está ~** she has not come to terms with it.
inconfundível [ĩŋkõnfũn'dʒivɛw] (*pl* **-eis**) *adj* unmistakable.
incongruência [ĩŋkõŋ'grwẽnsja] *f* incongruity.
incongruente [ĩnkõŋ'grwẽntʃi], **incôngruo, grua** [ĩn'kõŋgrwu, grwa] *adj* incongruous.
inconsciência [ĩŋkõn'sjẽnsja] *f* **-1.** MED unconsciousness. **-2.** [leviandade] lack of awareness.
inconsciente [ĩŋkõn'sjẽntʃi] ◇ *adj* **-1.** [ger] unconscious. **-2.** [leviano] thoughtless. ◇ *m* PSIC: **o ~** the unconscious.
inconscientemente [ĩŋkõnsjẽntʃi'mẽntʃi] *adv* unconsciously.
inconseqüência [ĩŋkõnse'kwẽnsja] *f* **-1.** [incoerência] inconsistency. **-2.** [irresponsabilidade] irresponsibility.
inconseqüente [ĩŋkõnse'kwẽntʃi] ◇ *adj* **-1.** [incoerente] inconsistent. **-2.** [irresponsável] irresponsible. ◇ *mf* irresponsible person.
inconsistência [ĩŋkõnsiʃ'tẽnsja] *f* **-1.** [fraqueza] inconsistency. **-2.** [fluidez] weakness.
inconsistente [ĩŋkõnsiʃ'tẽntʃi] *adj* **-1.** [fraco] inconsistent. **-2.** [fluido] runny.
inconsolável [ĩŋkõnso'lavew] (*pl* **-eis**) *adj* inconsolable.
inconstância [ĩŋkõnʃ'tãnsja] *f* inconstancy.
inconstante [ĩŋkõnʃ'tãntʃi] *adj* **-1.** [instável] unstable. **-2.** [volúvel] inconstant.
inconstitucional [ĩŋkõnʃtʃitusjo'naw] (*pl* **-ais**) *adj* unconstitutional.
inconstitucionalidade [ĩŋkõnʃtʃitusjonali'dadʒi] *f* unconstitutionality.
incontável [ĩŋkõn'tavew] (*pl* **-eis**) *adj* countless.
incontestável [ĩŋkõnteʃ'tavɛw] (*pl* **-eis**) *adj* incontestable.
inconteste [ĩŋkõn'tɛʃtʃi] *adj* undisputed.
incontinência [ĩŋkõntʃi'nẽnsja] *f* MED incontinence.
incontinente [ĩŋkõntʃi'nẽntʃi] *adj* MED incontinent.
incontinênti [ĩnkõutʃi'nẽntʃi] *adv* at once.
incontrolável [ĩŋkõntro'lavew] (*pl* **-eis**) *adj* uncontrollable.
incontroverso, sa [ĩŋkõntro'vɛxsu, sa] *adj* incontrovertible.
inconveniência [ĩŋkõnve'njẽnsja] *f* **-1.** [falta de conveniência] inconvenience. **-2.** [grosseria] rudeness.
inconveniente [ĩŋkõnve'njẽntʃi] ◇ *adj* **-1.** [inoportuno] inconvenient. **-2.** [inadequado] unsuitable. **-3.** [incômodo] annoying. ◇ *m* **-1.** [desvantagem] disadvantage. **-2.** [obstáculo] obstacle.
INCOR (*abrev de* **Instituto do Coração do Hospital das Clínicas**) *m institute of coronary diseases at the Hospital das Clínicas in São Paulo.*
incorporação [ĩŋkoxpora'sãw] (*pl* **-ões**) *f* **-1.** COM incorporation. **-2.** [espirit] possession. **-3.** [inclusão] inclusion.
incorporado, da [ĩŋkoxpo'radu, da] *adj* **-1.** COM incorporated. **-2.** [espirit] possessed. **-3.** [embutido] incorporated.
incorporar [4] [ĩŋkoxpo'ra(x)] ◇ *vt* **-1.** COM to incorporate. **-2.** [espirit] to become possessed by. **-3.** [juntar]: **~ algo a algo** to include sthg in sthg. ◇ *vi* [espirit] to take possession of.
◆ **incorporar-se** *vp* [juntar-se] to join.
incorreção [ĩŋkoxe'sãw] (*pl* **-ões**) *f* inaccuracy.
incorrer [5] [ĩŋko'xe(x)] *vi*: **~ em algo** to fall into sthg.
incorreto, ta [ĩŋko'xɛtu, ta] *adj* incorrect.
incorrigível [ĩŋkoxi'ʒivɛw] (*pl* **-eis**) *adj* incorrigible.
incorruptível [ĩŋkoxup'tʃivew] (*pl* **-eis**) *adj* incorruptible.
INCRA (*abrev de* **Instituto Nacional de Colonização e Reforma Agrária**) *m Brazilian land reform institute.*
incredulidade [ĩŋkreduli'dadʒi] *f* incredulity.
incrédulo, la [ĩŋ'krɛdulu, la] *adj* incredulous.
incrementado, da [ĩŋkremẽn'tadu, da] *adj* **-1.** *fam* [melhorado - carro, computador] jazzed up; [- bebida, comida] fancy. **-2.** *fam* [moderno] trendy.
incrementar [4] [ĩŋkremẽn'ta(x)] *vt* **-1.** [aumentar] to increase. **-2.** [desenvolver] to develop. **-3.** *fam* [melhorar] to jazz up.
incremento [ĩŋkre'mẽntu] *m* **-1.** [aumento] increment. **-2.** [desenvolvimento] development.
incriminar [4] [ĩŋkrimi'na(x)] *vt* to incriminate.
incrível [ĩŋ'krivɛw] (*pl* **-eis**) *adj* **-1.** [inacreditável] incredible. **-2.** *fam* [maravilhoso] incredible.
incrustação [iŋkruʃta'sãw] (*pl* **-ões**) *f* inlay.
incrustar [4] [ĩŋkruʃ'ta(x)] *vt* to inlay.
incubação [ĩŋkuba'sãw] *f* incubation.
incubadora [ĩŋkuba'dora] *f* incubator.
incubar [4] [ĩŋku'ba(x)] *vt* & *vi* to incubate.
inculcar [12] [ĩŋkuw'ka(x)] *vt* to inculcate.
inculto, ta [ĩŋ'kuwtu, ta] *adj* **-1.** [terreno] uncultivated. **-2.** [pessoa] coarse.

incumbência [ĩŋkũn'bẽnsja] *f* incumbency.
incumbir [6] [ĩŋkũm'bi(x)] <> *vt*: ~ **alguém de algo** to put sb in charge of sthg. <> *vi*: ~ **a alguém fazer algo** to be sb's responsibility to do sthg.
◆ **incumbir-se** *vp*: ~**-se de algo** to take charge of sthg.
incurável [ĩŋku'ravɛw] (*pl* **-eis**) *adj* incurable.
incursão [ĩŋkux'sãw] (*pl* **-ões**) *f* incursion.
incutir [6] [ĩŋku'tʃi(x)] *vt*: ~ **algo (a** *ou* **em alguém)** to inspire sthg (in sb).
indagação [ĩndaga'sãw] *f* inquiry.
indagar [14] [ĩnda'ga(x)] <> *vt* to ask for. <> *vi* to make inquiries.
indébito, ta [ĩn'dɛbitu, ta] *adj* unreasonable.
indecência [ĩnde'sẽnsja] *f* **-1.** [indecoro] indecency. **-2.** [obscenidade] obscenity.
indecente [ĩnde'sẽntʃi] *adj* **-1.** [obsceno] indecent. **-2.** [imoral] unscrupulous.
indecifrável [ĩndesi'fravew] (*pl* **-eis**) *adj* indecipherable.
indecisão [ĩndesi'zãw] (*pl* **-ões**) *f* indecision.
indeciso, sa [ĩnde'sizu, za] *adj* indecisive.
indeclinável [ĩndekli'navew] (*pl* **-eis**) *adj* that cannot be refused *(depois de subst)*.
indecoroso, osa [ĩndeko'rozo, ɔza] *adj* indecent.
indefectível [ĩndefek'tʃivew] (*pl* **-eis**) *adj* that cannot fail *(depois de subst)*.
indefensável [ĩndefẽn'savew] (*pl* **-eis**) *adj* indefensible; **um pênalti** ~ an unstoppable penalty.
indeferido, da [ĩndefe'ridu, da] *adj* rejected.
indeferir [57] [ĩndefe'ri(x)] *vt* to reject.
indefeso, sa [ĩnde'fezu, za] *adj* defenceless.
indefinição [ĩndefini'sãw] (*pl* **-ões**) *f* indecision.
indefinido, da [ĩndefi'nidu, da] *adj* **-1.** [ger] indefinite. **-2.** [vago] vague.
indefinível [ĩndefi'nivew] (*pl* **-eis**) *adj* indefinable.
indelével [ĩnde'lɛvew] (*pl* **-eis**) *adj* indelible.
indelicadeza [ĩndelika'deza] *f* **-1.** [grosseria] rudeness. **-2.** [desfeita] bad manners *(pl)*.
indelicado, da [ĩndeli'kadu, da] *adj* indelicate.
indenização [ĩndeniza'sãw] (*pl* **-ões**) *f* indemnity, compensation.
indenizar [4] [ĩndeni'za(x)] *vt*: ~ **alguém (por algo)** to indemnify sb (for sthg), to compensate sb (for sthg).
independência [ĩndepẽn'dẽnsja] *f* independence.
independente [ĩndepẽn'dẽntʃi] *adj* **-1.** [ger] independent. **-2.** [separado, de livre acesso] separate. **-3.** [auto-suficiente] independent. **-4.** [financeiramente] of independent means, financially independent.
independer [5] [ĩndepẽn'de(x)] *vi*: ~ **de algo** to be independent of sthg.
indescritível [ĩndeʃkri'tʃivɛw] (*pl* **-eis**) *adj* indescribable.
indesculpável [ĩndʒiʃkuw'pavew] (*pl* **-eis**) *adj* unforgivable.
indesejável [ĩndeze'ʒavɛw] (*pl* **-eis**) *adj* undesirable.
indestrutível [ĩndeʃtru'tʃivɛw] (*pl* **-eis**) *adj* **-1.** [não destrutível] indestructible. **-2.** *fig* [inabalável] enduring.
indeterminado, da [ĩndetexmi'nadu, da] *adj* **-1.** [não fixado] indeterminate; **por tempo** ~ for an indefinite length of time. **-2.** [impreciso] imprecise.
indevassável [ĩndeva'savew] (*pl* **-eis**) *adj* impenetrable.
indevido, da [ĩnde'vidu, da] *adj* **-1.** [imerecido] undeserved. **-2.** [impróprio] inappropriate.
índex ['ĩndeks] *m* index.
indexação [ĩndeksa'sãw] (*pl* **-ões**) *f* **-1.** *ECON & COM* index-linking. **-2.** *COMPUT* index.
indexar [4] [ĩndek'sa(x)] *vt* **-1.** [ger] to index. **-2.** *ECON & COM* to index-link.
Índia ['ĩndʒja] *n* India.
indiano, na [ĩn'dʒjanu, na] <> *adj* [da Índia] Indian. <> *m, f* [habitante da Índia] Indian.
indicação [ĩndʒika'sãw] (*pl* **-ões**) *f* **-1.** [denotação] sign. **-2.** [de caminho *etc*] sign. **-3.** [recomendação] recommendation; ~ **de uso** instructions for use. **-4.** [menção] indication.
indicado, da [ĩndʒi'kadu, da] *adj* **-1.** [recomendado] recommended. **-2.** [apropriado] appropriate.
indicador, ra [ĩndʒika'do(x), ra] (*pl* **-es**, *fpl* **-s**) *adj* [que indica]: ~ **de** indicator of.
◆ **indicador** *m* **-1.** [ger] indicator. **-2.** [dedo] index finger.
indicar [4] [ĩndʒi'ka(x)] *vt* **-1.** [ger] to indicate. **-2.** [apontar]: ~ **algo com o dedo** to point to sthg. **-3.** [recomendar] to recommend. **-4.** [mencionar] to indicate. **-5.** [designar] to name.
indicativo, va [ĩndʒika'tʃivu, va] *adj* **-1.** [que indica] indicative. **-2.** *GRAM* indicative.
◆ **indicativo** *m GRAM* indicative.
índice ['ĩndʒisi] *m* **-1.** [lista] index; ~ **remissivo** subject index; ~ **onomástico** name index. **-2.** [medida] level; ~ **de audiência** ratings; ~ **do custo de vida** cost of living index. **-3.** [dedo] index finger.
indiciado, da [ĩndʒi'sjadu, da] *m, f* accused, defendant.
indiciar [16] [ĩndʒi'sja(x)] *vt* **-1.** [acusar] to accuse. **-2.** [submeter a inquérito] to investigate.
indício [ĩn'dʒisju] *m* **-1.** [vestígio] sign. **-2.** *JUR* [prova] evidence *(inv)*.
Índico *n*: **o (Oceano)** ~ the Indian Ocean.
indiferença [ĩndʒife'rẽnsa] *f* indifference.
indiferente [ĩndʒife'rẽntʃi] *adj*: ~ **(a algo)** indifferent (to sthg).
indígena [ĩn'dʒiʒena] <> *adj* indigenous. <> *mf* native.
indigência [ĩndʒi'ʒẽnsja] *f* **-1.** [miséria] poverty. **-2.** [indigentes]: **a** ~ **do país** the indigence of the country. **-3.** [falta] lack.
indigente [ĩndʒi'ʒẽntʃi] <> *adj* poverty-stricken. <> *mf* poor person.
indigestão [ĩndʒiʒeʃ'tãw] (*pl* **-ões**) *f* indigestion.

indigesto, ta [ĩndʒi'ʒɛʃtu, ta] *adj* indigestible.
indignação [ĩndʒigna'sãw] (*pl* **-ões**) *f* indignation.
indignado, da [ĩndʒig'nadu, da] *adj* indignant; **ficar ~ (com)** to be indignant (at).
indignar [4] [ĩndʒig'na(x)] *vt* to anger.
◆ **indignar-se** *vp*: **~-se (com)** to be indignant (about).
indignidade [ĩndʒigni'dadʒi] *f* **-1.** [falta de dignidade] indignity. **-2.** [ultraje] outrage.
indigno, gna [ĩn'dʒignu, gna] *adj* **-1.** [não merecedor]: **~ de algo** unworthy of sthg. **-2.** [vil] despicable.
índio, dia ['ĩndʒju, dʒja] ◇ *adj* Indian. ◇ *m,f* Indian; **programa de ~** *fig* boring programme.
indireto, ta [ĩndʒi'rɛtu, ta] *adj* indirect.
◆ **indireta** *f* hint; **dar uma ~** to make a hint.
indisciplina [ĩndʒisi'plina] *f* indiscipline.
indisciplinado, da [ĩndʒisipli'nadu, da] *adj* undisciplined.
indiscreto, ta [ĩndʒiʃ'krɛtu, ta] *adj* indiscreet.
indiscrição [ĩndʒiʃkri'sãw] (*pl* **-ões**) *f* indiscretion.
indiscriminado, da [ĩndʒiʃkrimi'nadu, da] *adj* indiscriminate.
indiscutível [ĩndʒiʃku'tʃivɛw] (*pl* **-eis**) *adj* incontestable.
indispensável [ĩndʒiʃpẽn'savɛw] (*pl* **-eis**) ◇ *adj* indispensable, essential. ◇ *m*: **o ~** the essentials.
indisponível [ĩndʒiʃpo'nivew] (*pl* **-eis**) *adj* unavailable.
indispor [45] [ĩndʒiʃ'po(x)] *vt* **-1.** [adoecer] to make ill, to upset. **-2.** [inimizar] to set at odds.
◆ **indispor-se** *vp* [inimizar-se]: **~-se com alguém** to fall out with sb.
indisposição [ĩndʒiʃpozi'sãw] (*pl* **-ões**) *f* [mal-estar] illness.
indisposto, osta [ĩndʒiʃ'poʃtu, ɔʃta] ◇ *pp* ▷ **indispor**. ◇ *adj* unwell.
indissolúvel [ĩndʒiso'luvew] (*pl* **-eis**) *adj* **-1.** [irrevogável] indissoluble. **-2.** [insolúvel] insoluble.
indistinguível [ĩndʒiʃtʃĩŋ'givew] (*pl* **-eis**) *adj* indistinguishable.
indistintamente [ĩndʒiʃtʃĩnta'mẽntʃi] *adv* **-1.** [vagamente] indistinctly. **-2.** [indiferentemente] without distinction.
indistinto, ta [ĩndʒiʃ'tʃĩntu, ta] *adj* indistinct.
individual [ĩndʒivi'dwaw] (*pl* **-ais**) *adj* individual.
individualidade [ĩndʒividwali'dadʒi] *f* individuality.
individualismo [ĩndʒividwa'liʒmu] *m* individualism.
individualista [ĩndʒividwa'liʃta] ◇ *adj* individualistic. ◇ *mf* individualist.
indivíduo [ĩndʒi'vidwu] *m* **-1.** [pessoa] individual. **-2.** *fam* [cara] person.
indivisível [ĩndʒivi'sivew] (*pl* **-eis**) *adj* indivisible.
indiviso, sa [ĩndʒi'vizu, za] *adj* undivided.
indizível [ĩndʒi'zivew] (*pl* **-eis**) *adj* **-1.** [inexprimível] inexpressible. **-2.** [extraordinário] extraordinary.
indócil [ĩn'dɔsiw] (*pl* **-eis**) *adj* **-1.** [rebelde] wayward. **-2.** [impaciente] restless.
indo-europeu, éia [ĩndwewro'pew, pɛja] *adj* Indo-European.
◆ **indo-europeu** *m* [língua] Indo-European.
índole ['ĩndoli] *f* **-1.** [temperamento] temperament. **-2.** [tipo] character.
indolência [ĩndo'lẽnsja] *f* indolence.
indolente [ĩndo'lẽntʃi] *adj* indolent.
indolor [ĩndo'lo(x)] (*pl* **-es**) *adj* painless.
indomável [ĩndo'mavew] (*pl* **-eis**) *adj* indomitable.
indômito, ta [ĩn'domitu, ta] *adj* indomitable, untamed.
Indonésia [ĩndo'nɛzja] *n* Indonesia.
indonésio, sia [ĩndo'nɛzju, zja] ◇ *adj* Indonesian. ◇ *m, f* Indonesian.
◆ **indonésio** *m* [língua] Indonesian.
indoor [ĩn'dɔ(x)] *adj inv* *ESP* indoor.
indubitável [ĩndubi'tavew] (*pl* **-eis**) *adj* indubitable; **é ~ que ...** it is beyond doubt that ...
indução [ĩndu'sãw] (*pl* **-ões**) *f* **-1.** [lógica] induction; **por ~** by induction. **-2.** [persuasão] persuasion.
indulgência [ĩnduw'ʒẽnsja] *f* **-1.** [tolerância] leniency. **-2.** [perdão] indulgence. **-3.** *JUR* clemency.
indulgente [ĩnduw'ʒẽntʃi] *adj* lenient.
indultar [4] [ĩnduw'ta(x)] *vt* *JUR* to reprieve.
indulto [ĩn'duwtu] *m* *JUR* reprieve.
indumentária [ĩndumẽn'tarja] *f* attire.
indústria [ĩn'duʃtria] *f* industry; **~ automobilística** car industry *UK*, automobile industry *US*; **~ fabril** manufacturing industry; **~ leve** *ou* **de consumo** light industry; **~ pesada** heavy industry; **~ brasileira** made in Brazil.
industrial [ĩnduʃ'trjaw] (*pl* **-ais**) ◇ *adj* industrial. ◇ *mf* industrialist.
industrialização [ĩnduʃtrjaliza'sãw] *f* industrialization.
industrializado, da [ĩnduʃtrjali'zadu, da] *adj* industrialized; **produto ~** manufactured product.
industrializar [4] [ĩnduʃtrjali'za(x)] *vt* **-1.** [ger] to industrialize. **-2.** [produto] to manufacture. **-3.** [usar na indústria] to put to industrial use.
◆ **industrializar-se** *vp* to become industrialized.
industrioso, osa [ĩnduʃ'trjozu, -ɔza] *adj* **-1.** [habilidoso] clever. **-2.** [diligente] industrious.
induzir [72] [ĩndu'zi(x)] *vt* **-1.** [levar]: **~ alguém a algo** to lead sb to sthg; **~ alguém a fazer algo** to persuade sb to do sthg. **-2.** [deduzir]: **~ algo de algo** to deduce sthg from sthg.
inebriante [ine'brjãntʃi] *adj* intoxicating.
inebriado, da [inebri'adu, da] *adj* [extasiado] intoxicated.
inebriar [16] [ine'brja(x)] *vt* to intoxicate.
◆ **inebriar-se** *vp* to be intoxicated.
ineditismo [inedʒi'tʃiʒmu] *m*: **o ~ dos contos** the fact that the stories are unpublished.

inédito, ta [i'nɛdʒitu, ta] *adj* **-1.** [não publicado] unpublished. **-2.** [novo] novel.
inefável [ine'favɛw] (*pl* **-eis**) *adj* ineffable.
ineficácia [inefi'kasja] *f* **-1.** [ger] ineffectiveness. **-2.** [de pessoa] inefficience.
ineficaz [inefi'kaʃ] (*pl* **-es**) *adj* **-1.** [ger] ineffective. **-2.** [pessoa] inefficient.
ineficiência [inefi'sjẽnsja] *f* inefficiency.
ineficiente [inefi'sjẽntʃi] *adj* inefficient.
inegável [ine'gavɛw] (*pl* **-eis**) *adj* undeniable.
inegociável [inego'sjavew] (*pl* **-eis**) *adj* non-negotiable.
inelegível [inele'givew] (*pl* **-eis**) *adj* unelectable.
inenarrável [inena'xavew] (*pl* **-eis**) *adj* inexpressible.
inépcia [i'nɛpsja] *f* ineptitude.
inepto, ta [i'nɛptu, ta] *adj* inept.
inequívoco, ca [ine'kivoku, ka] *adj* unmistakable.
inércia [i'nɛxsja] *f* inertia.
inerente [ine'rẽntʃi] *adj* inherent.
inerte [i'nɛxtʃi] *adj* inert.
inescrupuloso, osa [ineʃkrupu'lozu, ɔza] *adj* unscrupulous.
inescrutável [ineʃkru'tavew] (*pl* **-eis**) *adj* inscrutable.
inesgotável [inezgo'tavɛw] (*pl* **-eis**) *adj* **-1.** [inacabável] inexhaustible. **-2.** [copioso] profuse.
inesperado, da [ineʃpe'radu, da] *adj* unexpected.
◆ **inesperado** *m* surprise.
inesquecível [ineʃke'sivɛw] (*pl* **-eis**) *adj* unforgettable.
inestimável [ineʃtʃi'mavɛw] (*pl* **-eis**) *adj* **-1.** [ger] priceless. **-2.** [prejuízo] incalculable.
inevitabilidade [inevitabili'dadʒi] *f* inevitability.
inevitável [inevi'tavɛw] (*pl* **-eis**) <> *adj* inevitable. <> *m*: **o** ~ the inevitable.
inexatidão [ineza'tjidãw] (*pl* **-ões**) *f* inexactitude.
inexato, ta [ine'zatu, ta] *adj* inaccurate.
inexaurível [inezauw'rivew] (*pl* **-eis**) *adj* inexhaustible.
inexcedível [inese'dʒivew] (*pl* **-eis**) *adj* unsurpassable.
inexequível [ineze'kwivɛw] (*pl* **-eis**) *adj* unfeasible.
inexistência [ineziʃ'tẽnsja] *f* **-1.** [não existência] absence. **-2.** [carência] lack.
inexistente [ineziʃ'tẽntʃi] *adj* non-existent.
inexistir [6] [ineziʃ'ti(x)] *vi* not to exist.
inexorável [inezo'ravew] (*pl* **-eis**) *adj* inexorable.
inexperiência [ineʃpe'rjẽnsja] *f* inexperience.
inexperiente [ineʃpe'rjẽntʃi] *adj* inexperienced.
inexplicável [ineʃpli'kavew] (*pl* **-eis**) *adj* inexplicable.
inexplorado, da [ineʃplo'radu, da] *adj* unexplored.
inexpressivo, va [ineʃpre'sivu, va] *adj* **-1.** [rosto] expressionless. **-2.** [diferença] inexpressible.
inexpugnável [ineʃpug'navew] (*pl* **-eis**) *adj* **-1.** [invencível] insuperable. **-2.** *fig* [firme] unassailable.
infalível [ĩnfa'livɛw] (*pl* **-eis**) *adj* infallible.
infame [ĩn'fãmi] *adj* **-1.** [vil] shameful. **-2.** [péssimo] dreadful.
infâmia [ĩn'fãmja] *f* **-1.** [calúnia] slander. **-2.** [desonra] discredit. **-3.** [vilania] infamy.
infância [ĩn'fãnsja] *f* childhood; **primeira** ~ early childhood, infancy.
infantaria [ĩnfãnta'ria] *f* infantry.
infante, ta [ĩ'fãntʃi, tʃa] *m, f* **-1.** [príncipe] infante (*f* infanta), prince (*f* princess). **-2.** [criança] infant.
◆ **infante** *m* [soldado] infantryman.
infanticida [ĩnfãntʃi'sida] <> *adj* infanticide. <> *m, f* infanticide, child-killer.
infantil [ĩnfãn'tiw] (*pl* **-is**) *adj* **-1.** [próprio da infância] childhood *(antes de subst)*. **-2.** [para criança] children's *(antes de subst)*. **-3.** *fig* [imaturo] childish.
infantilidade [ĩnfãntʃili'dadʒi] *f* childishness.
infanto-juvenil [ĩn,fãntuʒuve'niw] (*pl* **infanto-juvenis**) *adj* children's *(antes de subst)*.
infarto [ĩn'faxtu] *m* = **enfarte**.
infatigável [ĩnfatʃi'gavew] (*pl* **-eis**) *adj* **-1.** [incansável] tireless. **-2.** [zeloso] untiring.
infecção [ĩnfek'sãw] (*pl* **-ões**) *f* infection.
infeccionar [4] [ĩfeksjo'na(x)] <> *vt* to infect. <> *vi* to become infected.
infeccioso, osa [ĩnfek'sjozu, ɔza] *adj* infectious.
infecto, ta [ĩ'fɛktu, ta] *adj* **-1.** [ger] contaminated. **-2.** *fig* [vil] sick.
infelicidade [ĩnfelisi'dadʒi] *f* **-1.** [tristeza] unhappiness. **-2.** [desgraça] misfortune. **-3.** [azar] bad luck; **por** ~ unfortunately.
infeliz [ĩnfe'liʒ] (*pl* **-es**) <> *adj* **-1.** [ger] unfortunate. **-2.** [triste] unhappy. **-3.** [desafortunado] wretched. <> *mf* **-1.** [triste] unfortunate person. **-2.** [desgraçado] wretch; **como um** ~ *fig* desperately.
infelizmente [ĩnfeliʒ'mẽntʃi] *adv* unfortunately.
infenso, sa [ĩ'fẽnsu, sa] *adj* adverse.
inferior [ĩnfe'rjo(x)] (*pl* **-es**) <> *adj* **-1.** [ger]: ~ **a** inferior to. **-2.** [que está mais baixo] lower. **-3.** [em valor]: ~ **(a)** lower (than). **-4.** [em quantidade]: ~ **(a)** fewer (than). **-5.** [em altura]: ~ **a** shorter (than). **-6.** [em qualidade]: ~ **(a)** inferior (to). <> *mf* [subalterno] inferior.
inferioridade [ĩnferjori'dadʒi] *f* **-1.** [condição, posição] inferiority. **-2.** PSIC: **complexo de** ~ inferiority complex.
inferiorizar-se [4] [ĩferjori'zaxsi] *vp* to degrade o.s.
inferir [57] [ĩfe'ri(x)] *vt*: ~ **algo (de)** to infer sthg (from).
infernal [ĩnfex'naw] (*pl* **-ais**) *adj fig* infernal.
inferninho [ĩnfɛx'niɲu] *m* dive.
infernizar [4] [ĩfexni'za(x)] *vt* to render hellish; ~ **a vida de alguém** to make sb's life hell.
inferno [ĩn'fɛxnu] *m* hell; **vá para o** ~**!** go to hell!
infértil [ĩ'fɛxtiw] *adj* infertile.

infertilidade [ĩnfextʃili'dadʒi] *f* infertility.
infestado, da [ĩnfeʃ'tadu, da] *adj* infested.
infestar [4] [ĩnfeʃ'ta(x)] *vt* to infest.
infidelidade [ĩnfideli'dadʒi] *f* infedility.
infiel [ĩn'fjɛw] (*pl* **-éis**) ◇ *adj* **-1.** [desleal] unfaithful. **-2.** [inexato] inaccurate. ◇ *mf* RELIG non-believer.
infiltração [ĩnfiwtra'sãw] (*pl* **-ões**) *f* infiltration.
infiltrar [4] [ĩfiw'tra(x)] *vt* [parede] to penetrate.
◆ **infiltrar-se** *vp* to infiltrate; **~-se em algo** to filter (into) sthg.
ínfimo, ma ['ĩfimu, ma] *adj* insignificant; **preço ~** rock-bottom price.
infindável [ĩnfĩn'davɛw] (*pl* **-eis**) *adj* **-1.** [inacabável] interminable. **-2.** [permanente] unending. **-3.** [energia] boundless.
infinidade [ĩnfini'dadʒi] *f*: **uma ~ de vezes/roupas** countless times/clothes.
infinitamente [ĩnfinita'mẽntʃi] *adv* infinitely.
infinitesimal [ĩnfinitezi'maw] (*pl* **-ais**) *adj* infinitesimal.
infinitivo, va [ĩnfini'tʃivu, va] GRAM *adj* infinitive.
◆ **infinitivo** *m* infinitive.
infinito, ta [ĩnfi'nitu, ta] *adj* **-1.** [ger] infinite. **-2.** [inumerável] countless.
◆ **infinito** *m* LING infinitive.
inflação [ĩnfla'sãw] *f* ECON inflation.
inflacionar [4] [ĩnflasjo'na(x)] *vt* ECON to inflate.
inflacionário, ria [ĩnflasjo'narju, rja] *adj* ECON inflationary.
inflamação [ĩnflama'sãw] (*pl* **-ões**) *f* MED inflammation.
inflamado, da [ĩnfla'madu, da] *adj* **-1.** MED inflamed. **-2.** *fig* [exaltado] heated.
inflamar [4] [ĩfla'ma(x)] ◇ *vt* to inflame. ◇ *vi* MED to become inflamed.
inflamatório, ria [ĩnflama'tɔrju, rja] *adj* inflammatory.
inflamável [ĩnfla'mavɛw] (*pl* **-eis**) *adj* inflammable.
inflar [4] [ĩ'fla(x)] *vt* **-1.** [balão, bóia] to inflate. **-2.** [vela] to fill. **-3.** [peito] to puff out.
inflexível [ĩnflek'sivɛw] (*pl* **-eis**) *adj* **-1.** [invergável] stiff. **-2.** *fig* [implacável] inflexible.
infligir [52] [ĩfli'ʒi(x)] *vt*: **~ algo (a alguém)** to inflict sthg (on sb).
influência [ĩnflu'ẽnsja] *f* influence.
influenciar [16] [ĩflwẽn'sja(x)] ◇ *vt* to influence. ◇ *vi*: **~ em algo** to influence sthg.
◆ **influenciar-se** *vp*: **~-se (com algo)** to be influenced by sthg; **~-se (por alguém/algo)** to be influenced (by sb/sthg).
influenciável [ĩnflwẽn'sjavɛw] (*pl* **-eis**) *adj* easily influenced.
influente [ĩnflu'ẽntʃi] *adj* influential.
influir [74] [ĩnflu'i(x)] *vi* **-1.** [importar] to matter, to be important. **-2.** [atuar]: **~ em algo** to interfere in sthg. **-3.** [influenciar]: **~ para algo** to play a role in sthg.
influxo [ĩn'fluksu] *m* **-1.** [convergência] influx. **-2.** [maré alta] high tide.
infográfico, ca [ĩnfo'grafiku, ka] *adj* computer graphic *(antes de subst)*.
◆ **infográfico** *m* computer graphics designer.
informação [ĩnfoxma'sãw] (*pl* **-ões**) *f* **-1.** [ger] information. **-2.** [notícia] news. **-3.** MIL intelligence. **-4.** COMPUT data *(inv)*.
informado, da [ĩnfox'madu, da] *adj* **-1.** [esclarecido] well-informed. **-2.** [notificado]: **~ de algo** informed of sthg.
informal [ĩnfox'maw] (*pl* **-ais**) *adj* informal.
informalidade [ĩnfoxmali'dadʒi] *f* informality.
informante [ĩnfox'mãntʃi] *mf* informant.
informar [4] [ĩfox'ma(x)] ◇ *vt* **-1.** [esclarecer] to inform. **-2.** [notificar]: **~ alguém de algo** to notify sb of sthg. ◇ *vi* [ser informativo] to inform.
◆ **informar-se** *vp* **-1.** [atualizar-se] to keep o.s. up to date. **-2.** [esclarecer-se]: **~-se sobre algo** to make inquiries about sthg, to inquire about sthg.
informático, ca [ĩnfox'matʃiku, ka] ◇ *adj* computer *(antes de subst)*. ◇ *m, f* [pessoa] IT specialist.
◆ **informática** *f* **-1.** [ciência] computer science. **-2.** [atividade] computing.
informativo, va [ĩnfoxma'tʃivu, va] *adj* informative.
informatização [ĩnfoxmatʃiza'sãw] *f* COMPUT computerization.
informatizar [ĩnfurmati'za(x)] *vt* to computerize.
informe [ĩn'fɔxmi] ◇ *adj* shapeless. ◇ *m* **-1.** [informações] information. **-2.** MIL (piece of) intelligence.
infortúnio [ĩnfox'tunju] *m* misfortune.
infração [ĩnfra'sãw] (*pl* **-ões**) *f* **-1.** [de lei etc] infringement; **~ de trânsito** driving offence *UK*, driving offense *US*. **-2.** ESP foul.
Infraero (*abrev de* **Empresa Brasileira de Infra-Estrutura Aeroportuária**) *f Brazilian company responsible for airport insfrastructure*, ≃ BAA *UK*.
infra-estrutura [ˌĩnfraʃtru'tura] (*pl* **infra-estruturas**) *f* infrastructure.
infrator, ra [ĩnfra'to(x), ra] (*mpl* **-es**, *fpl* **-s**) ◇ *adj* law-breaking. ◇ *m, f* infringer.
infravermelho, lha [ĩnfravex'meʎu, ʎa] *adj* infrared.
infreqüente [ĩnfre'kwẽntʃi] *adj* infrequent.
infringir [52] [ĩnfrĩ'ʒi(x)] *vt* to infringe.
infrutífero, ra [ĩnfru'tʃiferu, ra] *adj* fruitless.
infundado, da [ĩnfũn'dadu, da] *adj* unfounded, groundless.
infundir [6] [ĩnfũn'dʒi(x)] *vt* **-1.** [inspirar] to inspire. **-2.** [incutir] to instill.
infusão [ĩnfu'zãw] (*pl* **-ões**) *f* infusion.
ingenuidade [ĩnʒenwi'dadʒi] *f* ingenuousness, naivety.
ingênuo, nua [ĩn'ʒenwu, nwa] ◇ *adj* ingenuous, naive. ◇ *m, f* ingenuous person, naive person.
ingerência [ĩnʒe'rẽnsja] *f* intervention.

ingerir [57] [ĩnʒe'ri(x)] *vt* to ingest.
ingestão [ĩnʒeʃ'tãw] *f* ingestion.
Inglaterra [ĩŋgla'tɛxa] *n* England.
inglês, esa [ĩŋ'gleʃ, eza] (*mpl* **-eses**, *fpl* **-s**) ◇ *adj* English. ◇ *mf* Englishman (*f* Englishwoman).
◆ **inglês** *m* [língua] English.
inglório, ria [ĩŋ'glɔrju, rja] *adj* inglorious.
ingovernabilidade [ĩŋgovexnabili'dadʒi] *f* ungovernability.
ingovernável [ĩŋgovex'navew] (*pl* **-eis**) *adj* **-1.** [rebelde] unruly. **-2.** [fora de controle] ungovernable.
ingratidão [ĩŋgratʃi'dãw] *f* ingratitude.
ingrato, ta [ĩŋ'gratu, ta] *adj* **-1.** [sem gratidão] ungrateful. **-2.** [ruim] disagreeable.
ingrediente [ĩŋgre'djẽntʃi] *m* ingredient.
íngreme ['ĩŋgremi] *adj* steep.
ingressar [ĩŋgre'sa(x)] *vi*: ~ **em algo** to enter sthg.
ingresso [ĩŋ'grɛsu] *m* **-1.** [bilhete] (entrance) ticket. **-2.** [entrada] entry. **-3.** [admissão] entrance.
íngua ['ĩŋgwa] *f* bubo, *a swollen lymph node in the groin.*
inhame [i'ɲãmi] *m* yam.
inibição [inibi'sãw] (*pl* **-ões**) *f* inhibition.
inibido, da [ini'bidu, ini'bida] *adj* inhibited.
inibidor, ra [inibi'do(x), ra] *adj* inhibiting.
inibir [ini'bi(x)] *vt* **-1.** [embaraçar] to embarrass. **-2.** [dificultar] to inhibit. **-3.** [impedir]: ~ **alguém (de fazer algo)** to prevent sb (from doing sthg).
◆ **inibir-se** *vp* [ficar inibido] to become inhibited.
iniciação [inisja'sãw] (*pl* **-ões**) *f* initiation.
iniciado, da [ini'sjadu, da] ◇ *adj* [pessoa] initiated. ◇ *m, f* [pessoa] initiate.
inicial [ini'sjaw] (*pl* **-ais**) ◇ *adj* initial. ◇ *f* [letra] initial.
◆ **iniciais** *fpl* initials.
iniciante [ini'sjãntʃi] ◇ *adj* [pessoa] beginning. ◇ *mf* [pessoa] beginner.
iniciar [ini'sja(x)] *vt* **-1.** [começar] to initiate, to begin. **-2.** [introduzir]: ~ **alguém em algo** to introduce sb to sthg.
◆ **iniciar-se** *vp* [introduzir-se]: **~-se em algo** to get into sthg.
iniciativa [inisja'tʃiva] *f* initiative; **não ter** ~ to have no initiative; **por** ~ **própria** on one's own initiative; **tomar a** ~ to take the initiative; ~ **privada** private initiative.
início [i'nisju] *m* beginning; **desde o** ~ from the outset; **no** ~ in the beginning.
inigualável [inigwa'lavew] (*pl* **-eis**) *adj* unequalled.
inimaginável [inimaʒi'navew] (*pl* **-eis**) *adj* unimaginable.
inimigo, ga [ini'migu, ga] ◇ *adj* enemy *(antes de subst).* ◇ *m, f* enemy.
inimizade [inimi'zadʒi] *f* enmity.
ininteligível [inĩnteli'ʒivew] (*pl* **-eis**) *adj* unintelligible.
ininterrupto, ta [inĩnte'xuptu, ta] *adj* uninterrupted.
iniqüidade [inikwi'dadʒi] *f* iniquity.
iníquo, qua [i'nikwu, kwa] *adj* iniquitous.
injeção [ĩnʒe'sãw] (*pl* **-ões**) *f* injection.
injetado, da [ĩʒe'tadu, da] *adj* **-1.** [fluido] injected. **-2.** [corado de sangue]: **olhos ~s** bloodshot eyes.
injetar [4] [ĩʒe'ta(x)] *vt* to inject.
injunção [ĩnʒũn'sãw] (*pl* **-ões**) *f* **-1.** [ordem] injunction. **-2.** [pressão] pressure.
injúria [ĩn'ʒurja] *f* insult.
injuriado, da [ĩnʒu'rjadu, da] *adj* [pessoa] insulted.
injuriar [16] [ĩʒu'rja(x)] *vt* [insultar] to insult.
◆ **injuriar-se** *vp fam* [zangar-se] to get angry.
injurioso, osa [ĩnʒu'rjozu, ɔza] *adj* insulting.
injustiça [ĩnʒuʃ'tʃisa] *f* injustice.
injustiçado, da [ĩnʒuʃtʃi'sadu, da] ◇ *adj* unjustly treated. ◇ *m, f* victim of injustice.
injustificável [ĩnʒuʃtʃifi'kavew] (*pl* **-eis**) *adj* unjustifiable.
injusto, ta [ĩ'ʒuʃtu, ta] *adj* unfair.
INL (*abrev de* **Instituto Nacional do Livro**) *m* *Brazilian national book institute.*
INMETRO (*abrev de* **Instituto Nacional de Metrologia, Normalização e Qualidade Industrial**) *m* *Brazilian national institute of industrial standards,* ≃ TSI *UK*, ≃ NIST *US*.
inobservado, da [inobizex'vadu, da] *adj* unobserved.
inobservância [inobisex'vãnsja] *f* [violação] nonobservance.
inobservante [inobisex'vãntʃi] *adj* unobservant.
inocência [ino'sẽnsja] *f* innocence; **perder a** ~ to lose one's innocence.
inocentar [4] [inosẽn'ta(x)] *vt*: ~ **alguém de algo** to clear sb of sthg.
◆ **inocentar-se** *vp*: **inocentou-se por sua sinceridade** his sincerity showed that he was innocent.
inocente [ino'sẽntʃi] ◇ *adj* innocent. ◇ *mf* innocent person.
inoculação [inokula'sãw] (*pl* **-ões**) *f* innoculation.
inocular [4] [inoku'la(x)] *vt* to innoculate.
inócuo, cua [i'nɔkwu, kwa] *adj* innocuous.
inodoro, ra [ino'dɔru, ra] *adj* odourless.
inofensivo, va [inofẽ'sivu, va] *adj* inoffensive.
inolvidável [inowvi'davew] (*pl* **-eis**) *adj* unforgettable.
inominável [inomi'navew] (*pl* **-eis**) *adj fig* [vil] intolerable.
inoperante [inope'rãntʃi] *adj* inoperative.
inopinado, da [inopi'nadu, da] *adj* **-1.** [imprevisto] unexpected. **-2.** [extraordinário] extraordinary.
inoportuno, na [inopox'tunu, na] *adj* inopportune.
inorgânico, ca [inox'ganiku, ka] *adj* inorganic.
inóspito, ta [i'nɔʃpitu, ta] *adj* inhospitable.
inovação [inova'sãw] (*pl* **-ões**) *f* innovation.

inovador, ra [inova'do(x), ra] <> *adj* innovative. <> *m, f* innovator.
inovar [4] [ino'va(x)] *vt* to innovate.
inoxidável [inoksi'davɛw] (*pl* **-eis**) *adj* ▷ **aço**.
INPC (*abrev de* **Índice Nacional de Preços ao Consumidor**) *m* *national index of retail prices*, ≃ RPI *UK*.
inqualificável [ĩŋkwalifi'kavew] (*pl* **-eis**) *adj* indescribable.
inquebrantável [ĩŋkebrãn'tavew] (*pl* **-eis**) *adj* unbreakable.
inquérito [ĩŋ'kɛritu] *m* enquiry.
inquestionável [ĩŋkeʃtʃjo'navew] (*pl* **-eis**) *adj* unquestionable.
inquietação [ĩŋkjeta'sãw] (*pl* **-ões**) *f* anxiety.
inquietante [ĩŋkje'tãntʃi], **inquietador, ra** [ĩŋkjeta'do(x), ra] *adj* worrying.
inquietar [4] [ĩŋkje'ta(x)] *vt* to worry.
◆ **inquietar-se** *vp* to worry.
inquieto, ta [ĩŋ'kjɛtu, ta] *adj* **-1.** [apreensivo] worried. **-2.** [agitado] restless.
inquietude [ĩŋkje'tudʒi] *f* **-1.** [apreensão] worry. **-2.** [agitação] restlessness.
inquilino, na [ĩŋki'linu, na] *m, f* tenant.
inquirição [ĩŋkiri'sãw] (*pl* **-ões**) *f* inquiry.
inquirir [6] [ĩŋki'ri(x)] <> *vt* **-1.** [investigar] to enquire. **-2.** [interrogar] to question. **-3.** *JUR* to examine. <> *vi* [indagar] to investigate.
Inquisição [ĩŋkizi'sãw] *f*: **a ~** the Inquisition.
inquisitivo, va [ĩŋkizi'tʃivu, va] *adj* inquisitive.
insaciável [ĩnsa'sjavɛw] (*pl* **-eis**) *adj* insatiable.
insalubre [ĩnsa'lubri] *adj* **-1.** [local, clima] unhealthy. **-2.** [trabalho] damaging to the health. **-3.** [água] unfit for drinking.
insanidade [ĩnsani'dadʒi] *f* insanity.
insano, na [ĩ'sanu, na] <> *adj* **-1.** [demente] insane. **-2.** *fig* [incansável] relentless. <> *m, f* madman (madwoman).
insaciabilidade [ĩnsasjabili'dadʒi] *f* insatiable appetite.
insatisfação [ĩnsatʃiʃfa'sãw] (*pl* **-ões**) *f* dissatisfaction.
insatisfatório, ria [ĩnsatʃiʃfa'tɔrju, rja] *adj* unsatisfactory.
insatisfeito, ta [ĩnsatʃiʃ'fejtu, ta] *adj* dissatisfied.
inscrever [5] [ĩʃkre've(x)] *vt* **-1.** [gravar] to inscribe. **-2.** [pessoa]: **~ alguém (em algo)** to register sb (for sthg).
◆ **inscrever-se** *vp* [pessoa]: **~-se (em algo)** to register (for sthg).
inscrição [ĩnʃkri'sãw] (*pl* **-ões**) *f* **-1.** [mensagem] inscription. **-2.** [matrícula, assentamento] registration; **número de ~** registration number.
inscrito, ta [ĩ'ʃkritu, ta] <> *pp* ▷ **inscrever**. <> *adj* **-1.** [mensagem] inscribed. **-2.** [pessoa] registered.
insegurança [insegu'rãnsa] *f* **-1.** [falta de segurança] lack of safety. **-2.** [de pessoa] insecurity.
inseguro, ra [ĩnse'guru, ra] *adj* **-1.** [perigoso] unsafe. **-2.** [pessoa] insecure.
inseminação [ĩnsemina'sãw] (*pl* **-ões**) *f* insemination; **~ artificial** artificial insemination.
inseminar [4] [ĩsemi'na(x)] *vt* to inseminate.
insensatez [ĩnsẽnsa'teʒ] *f* foolishness.
insensato, ta [ĩnsẽn'satu, ta] *adj* foolish.
insensibilidade [ĩnsẽnsibili'dadʒi] *f* insensitivity.
insensibilizar [4] [ĩsẽsibili'ta(x)] *vt* [tornar insensível] to desensitize.
◆ **insensibilizar-se** *vp* [emocionalmente] to harden o.s.
insensível [ĩnsẽn'sivɛw] (*pl* **-eis**) *adj* **-1.** [sem sensibilidade] numb. **-2.** [impassível] insensitive.
inseparável [ĩnsepa'ravɛw] (*pl* **-eis**) *adj* inseparable.
inserção [ĩnsex'sãw] (*pl* **-ões**) *f* **-1.** [introdução]: **~ (de algo em algo)** insertion (of sthg into sthg). **-2.** *COMPUT* insertion.
inserir [57] [ĩse'ri(x)] *vt* **-1.**: **~ algo em algo** to insert sthg into sthg. **-2.** *COMPUT* to insert.
◆ **inserir-se** *vp*: **~ -em algo** to fit into sthg.
inseticida [ĩnsetʃi'sida] *m* insecticide.
inseto [ĩn'sɛtu] *m* insect.
insídia [ĩn'sidʒja] *f* ambush.
insidioso, osa [ĩnsi'dʒjozu, ɔza] *adj* insidious.
insight [ĩn'sajtʃi] *m* insight; **ter um ~** to have insight.
insigne [ĩn'signi] *adj* celebrated.
insígnia [ĩn'signja] *f* insignia.
insignificância [ĩnsignifi'kãnsja] *f* insignificance.
insignificante [ĩnsignifi'kãntʃi] *adj* insignificant.
insincero, ra [ĩnsĩ'sɛru, ra] *adj* insincere.
insinuação [ĩnsinwa'sãw] (*pl* **-ões**) *f* **-1.** [indireta, sugestão] insinuation. **-2.** [amorosa] advance.
insinuante [ĩnsi'nwãntʃi] *adj* [que se insinua] insinuating.
insinuar [4] [ĩnsi'nwa(x)] *vt* **-1.** [afirmar indiretamente] to hint at; **~ que** to insinuate that. **-2.** [sugerir]: **~ que** to suggest that.
◆ **insinuar-se** *vp* **-1.** [passar]: **~-se por** *ou* **entre** to insinuate o.s. in *ou* among. **-2.** [amorosamente]: **~-se (para alguém)** to make advances (to sb).
insípido, da [ĩn'sipidu, da] *adj* **-1.** [sem sabor] insipid. **-2.** *fig* [sem graça] insipid.
insistência [ĩnsiʃ'tẽnsja] *f* insistence.
insistente [ĩnsiʃ'tẽntʃi] *adj* insistent.
insistir [6] [ĩnsiʃ'ti(x)] *vi* [perseverar]: **~ em (fazer algo)** to insist on (doing sthg); **~ para alguém fazer algo** to insist that sb do sthg.
insociável [ĩnso'sjavɛw] (*pl* **-eis**) *adj* antisocial.
insolação [ĩnsola'sãw] (*pl* **-ões**) *f* sunstroke; **ter uma ~** to have sunstroke.
insolência [ĩnso'lẽnsja] *f* insolence.
insolente [ĩnso'lẽntʃi] <> *adj* insolent. <> *mf* insolent person.
insólito, ta [ĩn'sɔlitu, ta] *adj* unusual.
insolúvel [ĩnso'luvew] (*pl* **-eis**) *adj* insoluble.
insolvência [ĩnsow'vẽnsja] *f* insolvency.

insolvente [ĩnsow'vẽntʃi] *adj* insolvent.
insondável [ĩnsõn'davew] (*pl* **-eis**) *adj* unfathomable.
insone [ĩn'soni] *adj* **-1.** [pessoa] insomniac. **-2.** [noite] sleepless.
insônia [ĩn'sonja] *f* insomnia.
insosso, ssa [ĩn'sosu, sa] *adj* **-1.** [sem sal] unsalted. **-2.** [sem sabor] tasteless. **-3.** *fig* [sem graça] dull.
inspeção [ĩnʃpe'sãw] (*pl* **-ões**) *f* inspection.
inspecionar [4] [ĩʃpɛsjo'na(x)] *vt* to inspect.
inspetor, ra [ĩnʃpe'to(x), ra] (*mpl* **-es**, *fpl* **-s**) *m, f* inspector; ~ **da alfândega** customs officer.
inspetoria [ĩnʃpeto'ria] *f* inspectorate.
inspiração [ĩnʃpira'sãw] (*pl* **-ões**) *f* **-1.** [estímulo] inspiration. **-2.** [na respiração] breathing in.
inspirador, ra [ĩnʃpira'do(x), ra] (*mpl* **-es**, *fpl* **-s**) *adj* inspiring.
inspirar [4] [ĩʃpi'ra(x)] *vt* **-1.** [estimular] to inspire. **-2.** [ar] to breathe in.
◆ **inspirar-se** *vp* [obter estímulo] to be inspired.
instabilidade [ĩnʃtabili'dadʒi] *f* instability.
instalação [ĩnʃtala'sãw] (*pl* **-ões**) *f* **-1.** [ger] installation. **-2.** [sistema]: ~ **elétrica/hidráulica** electric/hydraulic plant.
◆ **instalações** *fpl* **-1.** [para esporte, lazer] facilities. **-2.** [de indústria] plant.
instalador, ra [ĩʃtala'do(x), ra] *m, f* fitter.
instalar [4] [ĩʃta'la(x)] *vt* **-1.** [ger] to install. **-2.** [estabelecer] to establish. **-3.** [num cargo]: ~ **alguém em** to install sb in.
◆ **instalar-se** *vp* **-1.** [alojar-se] to install o.s. **-2.** [em um cargo] to install o.s.
instância [ĩnʃ'tãnsja] *f* **-1.** [solicitação] demand; **em última** ~ as a last resort. **-2.** [jurisdição] jurisdiction. **-3.** JUR stages of a law suit; **tribunal de segunda** ~ court of second instance.
instantâneo, nea [ĩnʃtãn'tãnju, nja] *adj* instant.
◆ **instantâneo** *m* FOT snap, snapshot.
instante [ĩnʃ'tãntʃi] <> *m* moment; **a cada** ~ at any moment; **nesse** ~ at that moment; **num** ~ in a moment. <> *adj* **-1.** [iminente] imminent. **-2.** [urgente] urgent.
instar [4] [ĩ'ta(x)] <> *vt* [pedir]: ~ **que alguém faça algo** to request that sb do sthg. <> *vi* [insistir]: ~ **com alguém para que faça algo** to urge sb to do sthg; ~ **por algo** to insist on sthg.
instauração [ĩnʃtawra'sãw] (*pl* **-ões**) *f* establishment.
instaurar [4] [ĩʃtaw'ra(x)] *vt* **-1.** [estabelecer] to establish. **-2.** [criar] to set up.
instável [ĩnʃ'tavew] (*pl* **-eis**) *adj* **-1.** [ger] unstable. **-2.** [sem equilíbrio] wobbly.
instigação [ĩʃtʃiga'sãw] (*pl* **-ões**) *f* instigation.
instigar [14] [ĩʃtʃi'ga(x)] *vt* **-1.** [incitar]: ~ **alguém a fazer algo** to encourage sb to do sthg. **-2.** [provocar]: ~ **alguém contra alguém** to rouse sb against sb.
instilar [4] [ĩʃtʃi'la(x)] *vt* to instil.
◆ **instilar-se** *vp* [infiltrar-se]: **~-se em** to insinuate o.s. in.
instintivo, va [ĩnʃtʃĩn'tʃivu, va] *adj* instinctive.
instinto [ĩnʃ'tʃĩntu] *m* instinct; ~ **de sobrevivência** survival instinct.
institucional [ĩnʃtʃitusjo'naw] (*pl* **-ais**) *adj* institutional.
instituição [ĩnʃtʃitwi'sãw] (*pl* **-ões**) *f* institution; ~ **de caridade** charity, charitable institution.
instituir [74] [ĩʃtʃi'twi(x)] *vt* **-1.** [estabelecer] to institute. **-2.** [marcar] to set. **-3.** [nomear] to name.
instituto [ĩnʃtʃi'tutu] *m* institute; ~ **de beleza** beauty parlour.
instrução [ĩnʃtru'sãw] (*pl* **-ões**) *f* **-1.** [educação] education; **ter/não ter** ~ to be/not to be educated. **-2.** [ordem] instruction.
◆ **instruções** *fpl* instructions.
instruído, da [ĩʃ'trwidu, da] *adj* educated.
instruir [74] [ĩʃtru'i(x)] *vt* **-1.** [ger] to instruct. **-2.** [educar] to educate. **-3.** [informar]: ~ **alguém sobre algo** to instruct sb on sthg. **-4.** [adestrar] to train.
◆ **instruir-se** *vp* [educar-se] to become educated; **~-se em algo** to train in sthg.
instrumentação [ĩnʃtrumẽnta'sãw] (*pl* **-ões**) *f* MÚS instrumentation.
instrumentador, ra [ĩnʃtrumẽnta'do(x), ra] *m, f* **-1.** MÚS score writer. **-2.** [em uma cirurgia] theatre nurse.
instrumental [ĩnʃtrumẽn'taw] (*pl* **-ais**) <> *adj* MÚS instrumental. <> *m* [equipamento] instrument; ~ **cirúrgico** surgical instrument.
instrumentar [47] [ĩnʃtrumẽn'ta(x)] *vt* MÚS to write scores.
instrumentista [ĩnʃtrumẽn'tʃiʃta] *mf* instrumentalist.
instrumento [ĩnʃtru'mẽntu] *m* **-1.** [ger] instrument; ~ **de sopro** wind instrument. **-2.** [ferramenta] tool; ~ **de trabalho** work tool.
instrutivo, va [ĩnʃtru'tʃivu, va] *adj* educational.
instrutor, ra [ĩnʃtru'to(x), ra] (*mpl* **-es**, *fpl* **-s**) *m, f* instructor.
insubordinação [ĩnsuboxdʒina'sãw] (*pl* **-ões**) *f* insubordination.
insubordinado, da [ĩnsuboxdʒi'nadu, da] *adj* insubordinate.
insubordinar-se [4] [ĩnsuboxdʒi'naxsi] *vp* to rebel.
insubstituível [ĩnsubʃtʃi'twivɛw] (*pl* **-eis**) *adj* irreplaceable.
insucesso [ĩnsu'sɛsu] *m* failure.
insuficiência [ĩnsufi'sjẽnsja] *f* **-1.** [carência] lack. **-2.** MED insufficiency.
insuficiente [ĩnsufi'sjẽntʃi] <> *adj* **-1.** [não-suficiente] insufficient. **-2.** [incompetente] inadequate. <> *m* [nota escolar] fail; **tirar** ~ to fail.
insuflar [4] [ĩsu'fla(x)] *vt* **-1.** [soprar] to blow into. **-2.** *fig* [incutir]: ~ **algo em alguém** to provoke sthg in sb.
insular [4] [ĩsu'la(x)] <> *adj* insular. <> *vt* to isolate.
insulina [ĩnsu'lina] *f* insulin.

insultar [4] [isuw'ta(x)] *vt* to insult.
insulto [ĩn'suwtu] *m* insult.
insultuoso, osa [ĩn'suw'twozu, ɔza] *adj* insulting.
insumo [ĩn'sumu] *m* input.
insuperável [ĩnsupe'ravɛw] (*pl* **-eis**) *adj* **-1.** [invencível] insuperable. **-2.** [imbatível] unsurpassable.
insuportável [ĩnsupox'tavɛw] (*pl* **-eis**) *adj* unbearable.
insurgente [ĩnsux'ʒẽntʃi] ◇ *adj* insurgent. ◇ *mf* insurgent.
insurgir-se [52] [ĩsux'ʒixsi] *vp* to revolt.
insurreição [ĩnsuxej'sãw] (*pl* **-ões**) *f* insurrection.
insurreto, ta [ĩnsu'xɛtu, ta] ◇ *adj* insurgent. ◇ *m, f* insurgent.
insuspeito, ta [ĩnsuʃ'pejtu, ta] *adj* **-1.** [inocente] beyond suspicion. **-2.** [imparcial] impartial.
insustentável [ĩnsuʃtẽn'tavew] (*pl* **-eis**) *adj* untenable.
intacto, ta [ĩn'ta(k)tu, ta] *adj* = **intato.**
intangibilidade [ĩntãnʒibili'dadʒi] *f* intangibility.
intangível [ĩntãn'ʒivew] (*pl* **-eis**) *adj* **-1.** [impalpável] intangible. **-2.** *fig* [intocável] irreproachable.
intato, ta [ĩn'tatu, ta] *adj* **-1.** [ileso] intact. **-2.** *fig* [puro] inviolate.
íntegra ['ĩntegra] *f* entirety; **na ~** in entirety.
integração [ĩntegra'sãw] (*pl* **-ões**) *f* integration.
integral [ĩnte'graw] (*pl* **-ais**) *adj* [total] whole; **leite ~** full-cream milk; **cereal ~** wholegrain cereal; **arroz ~** brown rice; **pão ~** wholemeal bread; **trigo ~** wholewheat.
integralismo [ĩntegra'liʒmu] *m* Integralism, *Brazilian political movement of the 1930s.*
integralmente [ĩntegraw'mẽntʃi] *adv* fully.
integrante [ĩnte'grãntʃi] ◇ *adj* component. ◇ *mf* **-1.** [membro] constituent. **-2.** [parte] component. **-3.** GRAM conjunction.
integrar [4] [ĩnte'gra(x)] *vt* **-1.** [unir] to integrate. **-2.** [formar] to comprise. **-3.** [fazer parte] to be a member.
◆ **integrar-se** *vp* **-1.** [inteirar-se] to combine. **-2.** [juntar-se]: **~-se em** *ou* **a algo** to join sthg.
integridade [ĩntegri'dadʒi] *f* integrity.
íntegro, gra ['ĩntegru, gra] *adj* **-1.** [inteiro] entire. **-2.** [honesto] honest.
inteiramente [ĩn,tejra'mẽntʃi] *adv* entirely.
inteirar [4] [ĩntej'ra(x)] *vt* **-1.** [completar] to make up. **-2.** [informar]: **~ alguém de algo** to inform sb of sthg.
◆ **inteirar-se** *vp* [informar-se]: **~-se de algo** to find out about sthg.
inteireza [ĩntej'reza] *f* **-1.** [totalidade] entirety. **-2.** *fig* [retidão] integrity.
inteiriço, ça [ĩntej'risu, sa] *adj* all-in-one.
inteiro, ra [ĩn'tejru, ra] *adj* **-1.** [todo] whole. **-2.** [intacto] intact. **-3.** [completo] entire. **-4.** [ileso] in one piece *(depois de verbo).* **-5.** [inteiriço] all-in-one *(antes de subst)*; [total] complete. **-6.** *fam* [conservado] in good shape.
intelecto [ĩnte'lɛktu] *m* intellect.
intelectual [ĩntelɛ'twaw] (*pl* **-ais**) ◇ *adj* intellectual. ◇ *mf* intellectual.
intelectualidade [ĩntelektwali'dadʒi] *f* **-1.** [qualidade] intellect. **-2.** [o meio intelectual]: **a ~** the intelligentsia.
inteligência [ĩnteli'ʒẽnsja] *f* **-1.** [destreza mental] intelligence. **-2.** [entendimento] comprehension. **-3.** [pessoa] brain. **-4.** COMP: **~ artificial** artificial intelligence.
inteligente [ĩnteli'ʒẽntʃi] *adj* intelligent.
inteligível [ĩnteli'ʒivew] (*pl* **-eis**) *adj* intelligible.
intemperança [ĩntẽmpe'rãnsa] *f* intemperance.
intempérie [ĩntẽn'pɛri] *f* bad weather.
intempestivo, va [ĩntẽmpeʃ'tʃivu, va] *adj* untimely.
intenção [ĩntẽn'sãw] (*pl* **-ões**) *f* intention; **com boa ~** with good intentions, well meaning; **com má ~** with bad intentions; **segundas intenções** ulterior motives; **ter a ~ de fazer algo** to intend to do sthg, to have the intention of doing sthg.
intencional [ĩntẽnsjo'naw] (*pl* **-ais**) *adj* intentional.
intencionar [4] [ĩntẽsjo'na(x)] *vt* to intend.
intendente [ĩntẽn'dẽntʃi] *mf* **-1.** [administrador] administrator. **-2.** MIL quartermaster.
intensidade [ĩntẽnsi'dadʒi] *f* intensity.
intensificação [ĩntẽsifika'sãw] *f* intensification.
intensificar [12] [ĩntẽsifi'ka(x)] *vt* to intensify.
◆ **intensificar-se** *vp* to intensify.
intensivo, va [ĩntẽ'sivu, va] *adj* intensive.
intenso, sa [ĩn'tẽsu, sa] *adj* intense.
intentar [4] [ĩntẽn'ta(x)] *vt* **-1.** [tentar] to attempt. **-2.** [projetar] to plan. **-3.** [cometer] to commit. **-4.** JUR: **~ uma ação contra alguém** to take sb to court.
intento [ĩn'tẽntu] *m* intent.
interação [ĩntera'sãw] (*pl* **-ões**) *f* interaction.
interagir [52] [ĩntera'ʒi(x)] *vi*: **~ com algo/alguém** to interact with sthg/sb.
interatividade [ĩnteratʃivi'dadʒi] *f* COMPUT interactivity.
interativo, va [ĩntera'tʃivu, va] *adj* COMPUT interactive.
intercalar [4] [ĩntex'kala(x)] *vt* **-1.** [interpor]: **~ algo em** *ou* **entre** to place sthg in *ou* between. **-2.** [inserir]: **~ algo em** to insert sthg in(to).
◆ **intercalar-se** *vp* [interpor-se]: **~-se em** *ou* **entre** to intervene in/between.
intercambiar [4] [ĩnterkãn'bia(x)] *vt* to interchange.
intercambiável [ĩnterkãn'bjavɛw] (*pl* **-eis**) *adj* interchangeable.
intercâmbio [,ĩnter'kãnbju] *m* exchange.
interceder [5] [ĩntexse'de(x)] *vi*: **~ por alguém** to intercede on behalf of sb.
interceptar [4] [ĩntexsɛp'ta(x)] *vt* **-1.** [ger] to cut off. **-2.** [fazer parar] to stop. **-3.** [apoderar-se de] to intercept.
intercessão [ĩntexse'sãw] (*pl* **-ões**) *f* intercession.

interconexão [ĩntexkonek'sãw] (*pl* **-ões**) *f* interconnection.
intercontinental [ĩntexkõntʃinẽn'taw] (*pl* **-ais**) *adj* intercontinental.
interdependente [ĩntexdepẽn'dẽntʃi] *adj* interdependent.
interdição [ĩntexdʒi'sãw] (*pl* **-ões**) *f* **-1.** [proibição] ban. **-2.** [bloqueio] closure. **-3.** *JUR* injunction.
interdisciplinar [ĩntexdʒisipli'na(x)] *adj* interdisciplinary.
interdisciplinaridade [ĩntexdʒisiplinari'dadʒi] *f* interdisciplinary nature.
interditado, da [ĩntexdʒi'tadu, da] *adj* **-1.** [proibido] banned. **-2.** [bloqueado] closed.
interditar [4] [ĩntexdʒi'ta(x)] *vt* **-1.** [proibir] to ban. **-2.** [bloquear] to close. **-3.** *JUR* to interdict.
interessado, da [ĩntere'sadu, da] ◇ *adj* interested. ◇ *m, f* interested party.
interessante [ĩntere'sãntʃi] *adj* interesting.
interessar [4] [ĩntere'sa(x)] ◇ *vt* to interest. ◇ *vi* [despertar interesse] to be of interest; **a quem possa ~** *fml* to whom it may concern.
◆ **interessar-se** *vp* [ter interesse]: **~-se em** *ou* **por** to take an interest in.
interesse [ĩnte'resi] *m* **-1.** [ger] interest. **-2.** [vantagem] benefit; **no ~ de** in the interest of; **por ~ próprio** out of self-interest.
interesseiro, ra [ĩntere'sejru, ra] ◇ *adj* self-seeking. ◇ *m, f* egotist.
interestadual [ĩntereʃta'dwaw] (*pl* **-ais**) *adj* interstate.
interface [ˌĩntex'fasi] *f* *COMPUT* interface.
interferência [ĩntexfe'rẽnsja] *f* interference.
interferir [57] [ĩntexfe'ri(x)] *vi* **-1.** [intervir]: **~ em algo** to interfere in sthg. **-2.** [em rádio, televisão] to cause interference.
interfonar [4] [ĩntexfo'na(x)] *vi*: **~ a alguém** to call sb on the internal phone.
interfone [ˌĩntex'foni] *m* intercom.
ínterim ['ĩnterĩ] *m* interim; **nesse ~** meanwhile.
interior [ĩnte'rjo(x)] (*pl* **-es**) ◇ *adj* inner. ◇ *m* interior.
interiorano, na [ĩnterjo'rãnu, na] ◇ *adj* country *(antes de subst)*. ◇ *m,f* country dweller.
interiorizar [ĩnterjori'za(x)] *vt* to internalize.
interjeição [ĩntexʒej'sãw] (*pl* **-ões**) *f* exclamation.
interligação [ĩntexliga'sãw] (*pl* **-ões**) *f* interconnection.
interligar [14] [ĩntexli'ga(x)] *vt* to interconnect.
◆ **interligar-se** *vp* to be interconnected.
interlocutor, ra [ĩntexloku'to(x), ra] (*pl* **-es**, *fpl* **-s**) *m, f* interlocutor.
interlúdio [ĩntex'ludʒju] *m* interlude.
intermediar [17] [ĩntexme'dʒja(x)] *vt* **-1.** [servir como mediador] to mediate; **~ um debate entre** to chair a debate between. **-2.** [entremear, intercalar] to mix.
intermediário, ria [ĩntexme'dʒjarju, rja] ◇ *adj* intermediate. ◇ *m, f* **-1.** [mediador] mediator. **-2.** *COM* intermediary.
intermédio [ĩnter'mɛdʒu] *m*: **por ~ de** through.
interminável [ĩntexmi'navɛw] (*pl* **-eis**) *adj* endless.
intermitente [ĩntexmi'tẽntʃi] *adj* intermittent.
internação [ĩntexna'sãw] (*pl* **-ões**) *f* **-1.** [de doente] admission. **-2.** [de aluno] boarding.
internacional [ĩntexnasjo'naw] (*pl* **-ais**) *adj* international.
internacionalizar [4] [ĩntexnasjonali'za(x)] *vt* to internationalize.
◆ **internacionalizar-se** *vp* to become international.
internamento [ĩntexna'mẽntu] *m* admission.
internar [4] [ĩntex'na(x)] *vt* **-1.** *MED* to admit. **-2.** [aluno] to board. **-3.** *POL* to intern.
internato [ĩntex'natu] *m* *EDUC* boarding school.
internauta [ĩntex'nawta] *mf* *COMPUT* Internet user *ou* surfer.
Internet [ĩntex'nɛtʃi] *f*: **a ~** the Internet.
interno, na [ĩn'tɛxnu, na] ◇ *adj* **-1.** [interior] inside; **de uso ~** for internal use. **-2.** *POL* internal. **-3.** [aluno] boarding. ◇ *m, f* **-1.** *MED* houseman *UK*, intern *US*. **-2.** [aluno] boarder.
interpelação [ĩntexpela'sãw] (*pl* **-ões**) *f* **-1.** [indagação] questioning. **-2.** *JUR* summons *(sg)*.
interpelar [4] [ĩntexpe'la(x)] *vt* **-1.** [indagar]: **~ alguém sobre algo** to question sb about sthg. **-2.** [pedir explicações] to question. **-3.** *JUR* to summons.
interplanetário, ria [ĩntexplane'tarju, rja] *adj* interplanetary.
Interpol (*abrev de* **International Criminal Police Organization**) *f* Interpol.
interpolação [ĩntexpola'sãw] (*pl* **-ões**) *f* [inserção] insertion.
interpolar [4] [ĩntexpo'la(x)] *vt* **-1.** [texto, narrativa] to insert. **-2.** [intercalar] to interpolate.
interpor [45] [ĩntex'po(x)] *vt* **-1.** [entremeter] to put in. **-2.** [fazer intervir] to intervene with.
◆ **interpor-se** *vp* **-1.** [pôr-se entre, mediar]: **~-se entre** to intervene between. **-2.** [contrapor-se]: **~-se a algo/alguém** to oppose sthg/sb.
interposto, ta [ĩntex'poʃtu, ta] ◇ *pp* ▷ **interpor**. ◇ *adj* interposing.
interpretação [ĩntexpreta'sãw] (*pl* **-ões**) *f* **-1.** [ger] interpretation. **-2.** [tradução] interpreting.
interpretar [4] [ĩntexpre'ta(x)] *vt* **-1.** [ger] to interpret. **-2.** [traduzir] to interpret.
interpretativo, va [ĩntexpreta'tʃivu, va] *adj* interpretative.
intérprete [ĩn'tɛxpretʃi] *mf* **-1.** *LING* interpreter. **-2.** *CINE, TEATRO & TV* performer.
interregno [ĩnte'xegnu] *m* [intervalo] interlude.
inter-racial [ĩntexa'sjaw] (*pl* **-ais**) *adj* interracial.
inter-relacionado, da [ĩntexelasjo'nadu, da] *adj* interrelated.
inter-relacionar [4] [ĩntexelasjo'na(x)] *vt* to interrelate.
interrogação [ĩntexoga'sãw] (*pl* **-ões**) *f* interrogation; **ponto de ~** question mark.
interrogador, ra [ĩntexoga'do(x), ra] *m, f* interrogator.
interrogar [14] [ĩntexu'ga(x)] *vt* **-1.** [indagar]: **~**

alguém (sobre algo) to interrogate sb (about sthg). **-2.** *JUR* to put questions to.
interrogativo, va [ĩntexoga'tʃivu, va] *adj* **-1.** [indagativo] questioning. **-2.** *GRAM* interrogative.
interrogatório [ĩntexoga'tɔrju] *m* interrogation.
interromper [5] [ĩntexõm'pe(x)] *vt* to interrupt.
interrompido, da [ĩntexõn'pidu, da] *adj* interrupted.
interrupção [ĩntexup'sãw] (*pl* **-ões**) *f* interruption.
interruptor [ĩntexup'to(x)] (*pl* **-es**) *m* switch.
interseção [ĩntexse'sãw] (*pl* **-ões**) *f* intersection.
interstício [ĩntexʃ'tʃisju] *m* interstice.
interurbano, na [ˌĩnterux'bãnu, na] *adj* **-1.** intercity *UK*, inter-urban *US*. **-2.** [telefonema] long distance.
◆ **interurbano** *m* [telefonema] long distance call.
intervalo [ĩntex'valu] *m* **-1.** [ger] interval; **a ~s** at intervals; **~ comercial** commercial break. **-2.** [no espaço] distance.
intervenção [ĩntexvẽn'sãw] (*pl* **-ões**) *f* **-1.** [interferência] intervention; **~ cirúrgica** operation, surgical intervention. **-2.** *JUR* mediation.
intervencionismo [ĩntexvẽnsjo'niʒmu] *m* interventionism.
intervencionista [ĩntervẽnsjo'niʃta] <> *adj* interventionist. <> *mf* interventionist.
interventor, ra [ĩntexvẽn'to(x), ra] *m, f* interim governor.
intervir [67] [ĩntex'vi(x)] *vi* to intervene.
intestinal [ĩnteʃtʃi'naw] (*pl* **-ais**) *adj* intestinal.
intestino [ĩnteʃ'tʃinu] *m* intestine; **~ delgado** small intestine; **~ grosso** large intestine.
intimação [ĩntʃima'sãw] (*pl* **-ões**) *f* **-1.** [ordem] order. **-2.** *JUR* summons *(sg)*.
intimar [4] [ĩntʃi'ma(x)] *vt* **-1.** [ordenar]: **~ alguém (a fazer algo)** to order sb (to do sthg). **-2.** *JUR* to summons.
intimidação [ĩntʃimida'sãw] (*pl* **-ões**) *f* intimidation.
intimidade [ĩntʃimi'dadʒi] *f* **-1.** [vida íntima] privacy. **-2.** [familiaridade] intimacy; **ter ~ com alguém** to be close to sb.
intimidar [4] [ĩntʃimi'da(x)] *vt* to intimidate.
◆ **intimidar-se** *vp* to be intimidated.
íntimo, ma ['ĩntʃimu, ma] <> *adj* **-1.** [interior e profundo] intimate. **-2.** [privado] private. <> *m* **-1.** [âmago]: **no ~, ela sabia que estava errada** deep down, she knew that she was wrong. **-2.** [amigo] close friend.
intitular [4] [ĩntʃitu'la(x)] *vt* **-1.** [dar título a] to title; **~ algo de algo** to call sthg sthg. **-2.** [chamar]: **~ alguém de algo** to call sb sthg.
◆ **intitular-se** *vp* [denominar-se] to call o.s.
intocável [ĩnto'kavew] (*pl* **-eis**) *adj* untouchable.
intolerância [ĩntole'rãnsja] *f* intolerance.
intolerante [ĩntole'rãntʃi] *adj* intolerant.
intolerável [ĩntole'ravew] (*pl* **-eis**) *adj* intolerable.
intoxicação [ĩntoksika'sãw] (*pl* **-ões**) *f* poisoning; **~ alimentar** food poisoning.
intoxicar [12] [ĩntoksi'ka(x)] *vt* to poison.
◆ **intoxicar-se** *vp* to poison o.s.
intraduzível [ĩntradu'zivew] (*pl* **-eis**) *adj* **-1.** [que não tem tradução] untranslatable. **-2.** [inexprimível] inexpressible.
intragável [ĩntra'gavew] (*pl* **-eis**) *adj* unpalatable.
intranet ['ĩntranetʃi] *f* *COMPUT* intranet.
intranqüilidade [ĩntrãŋkwili'dadʒi] *f* disquiet.
intranqüilo [ĩntrãn'kwilu] *adj* restless.
intransferível [ĩntrãnʃfe'rivew] (*pl* **-eis**) *adj* **-1.** [bilhete, documento] non-transferable. **-2.** [inadiável] non-postponable.
intransigência [ĩntrãnsi'ʒẽnsja] *f* intransigence.
intransigente [ĩntrãnzi'ʒẽntʃi] *adj* **-1.** [intolerante] intransigent. **-2.** *fig* [austero] uncompromising.
intransitável [ĩntrãnzi'tavɛw] (*pl* **-eis**) *adj* impassable.
intransitivo, va [ĩntrãnzi'tʃivu, va] *adj* intransitive.
intransponível [ĩntrãnʃpo'nivɛw] (*pl* **-eis**) *adj* **-1.** [rio, barreira] impassable. **-2.** [problema, obstáculo] insurmountable.
intratável [ĩntra'tavɛw] (*pl* **-eis**) *adj* [insociável] intractable.
intra-uterino, intra-uterina [ˌĩntrawte'rinu, na] (*mpl* **intra-uterinos**, *fpl* **intra-uterinas**) *adj* intrauterine.
intravenoso, osa [ĩntrave'nozu, ɔza] *adj* intravenous.
intrépido, da [ĩn'trɛpidu, da] *adj* intrepid.
intricado, da [ĩntri'kadu, da] *adj* **-1.** [emaranhado] tangled. **-2.** [confuso] intricate.
intriga [ĩn'triga] *f* **-1.** [trama] intrigue. **-2.** [cilada] conspiracy. **-3.** [enredo] plot.
◆ **intrigas** *fpl* [fofoca] gossip *(sg)*.
intrigante [ĩntri'gãntʃi] *adj* intriguing.
intrigar [14] [ĩntri'ga(x)] <> *vt* [despertar curiosidade de] to intrigue. <> *vi* [excitar a curiosidade] to intrigue.
intrínseco, ca [ĩn'trĩnseku, ka] *adj* intrinsic.
introdução [ĩntrodu'sãw] (*pl* **-ões**) *f* introduction.
introdutório, ria [ĩntrodu'tɔrju, rja] *adj* introductory.
introduzir [72] [ĩntrodu'zi(x)] *vt* **-1.** [inserir]: **~ algo (em)** to introduce sthg (into). **-2.** [fazer adotar] to introduce.
◆ **introduzir-se** *vp*: **~ (em)** to find one's way (into).
intróito [ĩn'trɔjtu] *m* **-1.** [início] beginning. **-2.** *REL* introit.
intrometer-se [5] [ĩntrome'texsi] *vp*: **~-se em algo** to meddle in sthg.
intrometido, da [ĩntrome'tʃidu, da] <> *adj* meddlesome, interfering. <> *m, f* meddler.
intromissão [ĩntromi'sãw] (*pl* **-ões**) *f* meddling.
introspecção [ĩntroʃpek'sãw] *f* introspection.
introspectivo, va [ĩntroʃpek'tʃivu, va] *adj* introspective.

introversão [ĩntrovex'sãw] *f* introversion.
introvertido, da [ĩntrovex'tʃidu, da] ◇ *adj* introverted. ◇ *m, f* introvert.
intruso, sa [ĩn'truzu, za] *m, f* intruder.
intuição [ĩntwi'sãw] (*pl* **-ões**) *f* intuition.
intuir [74] [ĩn'twi(x)] ◇ *vt* to intuit. ◇ *vi* to be intuitive.
intuitivo, va [ĩntwi'tʃivu, va] *adj* intuitive.
intuito [ĩn'twitu] *m* **-1.** [objetivo] purpose. **-2.** [intento] intention.
intumescência [ĩntume'sẽnsja] *f* swelling.
intumescer-se [25] [ĩntume'sɛxsi] *vp* to swell (up).
intumescido, da [ĩntume'sidu, da] *adj* swollen.
inumano, na [inu'manu, na] *adj* inhuman.
inúmeros, ras [i'numeruʃ, raʃ] *adj pl* [antes de subst] innumerable.
inundação [inũnda'sãw] (*pl* **-ões**) *f* flood.
inundado, da [inũn'dadu, da] *adj* **-1.** [de água] flooded. **-2.** *fig* covered.
inundar [4] [inũn'da(x)] ◇ *vt* [alagar] to flood. ◇ *vt fig* [encher] to swamp. ◇ *vi* [transbordar] to flood.
◆ **inundar-se** *vp* [alagar-se] to become flooded.
inusitado, da [inuzi'tadu, da] *adj* unusual.
inútil [i'nutʃiw] (*pl* **-eis**) *adj* **-1.** [imprestável] useless. **-2.** [desnecessário] needless. **-3.** [vão] pointless; **ser ~ fazer algo** to be pointless to do sthg.
inutilidade [inutʃili'dadʒi] *f* uselessness.
inutilizar [4] [inutʃili'za(x)] *vt* **-1.** [tornar inútil] to render useless. **-2.** [danificar] to ruin. **-3.** [frustrar] to thwart.
inutilizável [inutʃili'zavew] (*pl* **-eis**) *adj* [não-utilizável] unusable.
inutilmente [iˌnutʃiwmẽntʃi] *adv* uselessly.
invadir [6] [ĩnva'di(x)] *vt* **-1.** [ger] to invade. **-2.** *fig* [dominar] to overwhelm.
invalidar [4] [ĩnvali'da(x)] *vt* **-1.** [anular] to invalidate. **-2.** [pessoa] to disable.
invalidez [ĩnvali'deʒ] *f* disability.
inválido, da [ĩnvalidu, da] ◇ *adj* **-1.** [nulo] invalid. **-2.** [pessoa] invalid, disabled. ◇ *m, f* [pessoa] invalid.
invariável [ĩnva'rjavɛw] (*pl* **-eis**) *adj* invariable.
invasão [ĩnva'zãw] (*pl* **-ões**) *f* invasion.
invasivo, va [ĩnva'zivu, va] *adj* **-1.** [agressivo] invasion *(antes de subst)*. **-2.** MED invasive.
invasor, ra [ĩva'zo(x), ra] ◇ *adj* invading. ◇ *m, f* invader.
inveja [ĩn'vɛʒa] *f* envy.
invejar [4] [ĩnvɛ'ʒa(x)] ◇ *vt* **-1.** [ter inveja de] to envy. **-2.** [cobiçar] to covet. ◇ *vi* [ter inveja] to be envious.
invejável [ĩnve'ʒavew] (*pl* **-eis**) *adj* enviable.
invejoso, osa [ĩnve'ʒozu, ɔza] ◇ *adj* [pessoa] envious. ◇ *m, f* [pessoa] envious person.
invenção [ĩnvẽn'sãw] (*pl* **-ões**) *f* **-1.** [ger] invention. **-2.** *fig* [mentira] fabrication.
invencibilidade [ĩnvẽnsibili'dadʒi] *f* invincibility.
invencionice [ĩnvẽnsjo'nisi] *f* [mentira, embuste] fabrication.
invencível [ĩnvẽn'sivew] (*pl* **-eis**) *adj* invincible.
inventar [4] [ĩnvẽn'ta(x)] ◇ *vt* to invent. ◇ *vi* [cismar]: **~ de fazer algo** to get it into one's head to do sthg.
inventariar [16] [ĩnvẽnta'rja(x)] *vt* to inventory.
inventário [ĩnvẽn'tarju] *m* inventory.
inventivo, va [ĩnvẽn'tʃivu, va] *adj* inventive.
inventor, ra [ĩnvẽn'to(x), ra] (*mpl* **-es**, *fpl* **-s**) *m, f* inventor.
inverdade [ĩnvex'dadʒi] *f* untruth.
invernada [ĩnvex'nada] *f* winter pasture.
invernal [ĩnvex'naw] (*pl* **-ais**) *adj* wintry.
inverno [ĩn'vɛxnu] *m* winter.
inverossímil [ĩnvero'simiw] (*pl* **-eis**) *adj* implausible.
inversão [ĩnvex'sãw] (*pl* **-ões**) *f* inversion.
inverso, sa [ĩn'vɛxsu, sa] *adj* **-1.** [invertido] inverse. **-2.** [oposto] opposite.
◆ **inverso** *m* [contrário] opposite.
invertebrado, da [ĩnvexte'bradu, da] ◇ *adj* [animal] invertebrate. ◇ *m* [animal] invertebrate.
inverter [5] [ĩnvex'te(x)] *vt* **-1.** [virar ao contrário] to reverse. **-2.** [trocar a ordem de] to invert. **-3.** [mudar] to alter.
invés [ĩn'vɛʃ] *m* inside out.
◆ **ao invés de** *loc prep* instead of.
investida [ĩnveʃ'tʃida] *f* **-1.** [ataque] attack. **-2.** *fig* [tentativa] attempt.
investidor, ra [ĩveʃtʃi'do(x), ra] *m, f* investor.
investidura [ĩnveʃtʃi'dura] *f* investiture.
investigação [ĩnveʃtʃiga'sãw] (*pl* **-ões**) *f* **-1.** [inquérito] investigation; **~ policial** police investigation. **-2.** [pesquisa] inquiry; **~ científica** scientific investigation.
investigador, ra [ĩnveʃtʃiga'do(x), ra] *m, f* [agente policial] detective.
investigar [14] [ĩnveʃtʃi'ga(x)] *vt* **-1.** [inquirir] to investigate. **-2.** [pesquisar] to research.
investimento [ĩnveʃtʃi'mẽntu] *m* investment.
investir [54] [ĩveʃ'tʃi(x)] ◇ *vt* **-1.** [dinheiro, verba] to invest. **-2.** [empossar]: **~ alguém diretor da empresa** to install sb as director of a company. ◇ *vi* **-1.** [aplicar dinheiro, verba]: **~ (em algo)** to invest (in sthg). **-2.** [atacar]: **~ contra algo** to storm sthg. **-3.** [atirar-se]: **~ para algo** to rush to sthg.
inveterado, da [ĩnvete'radu, da] *adj* [muito antigo] inveterate.
inviabilidade [ĩnvjabili'dadʒi] *f* impracticability.
inviabilizar [4] [ĩvjabili'za(x)] *vt* to make unviable.
◆ **inviabilizar-se** *vp* to become unviable.
inviável [ĩn'vjavɛw] (*pl* **-eis**) *adj* unviable.
invicto, ta [ĩn'viktu, ta] *adj* unbeaten.
inviolabilidade [ĩnviolabili'dadʒi] *f* inviolability.
inviolável [ĩnvjo'lavew] (*pl* **-eis**) *adj* inviolable.
invisível [ĩnvi'zivɛw] (*pl* **-eis**) *adj* invisible.
in vitro [ˌin'vitru] *loc adj* in vitro.

invocação [ĩvo'kasãw] (*pl* **-ões**) *f* invocation.

invocado, da [ĩvo'kadu, da] *adj fam* **-1.** [irritado] annoyed. **-2.** [cismado] preoccupied. **-3.** [incomum] bizarre. **-4.** [inconstante] inconsistent.

invocar [12] [ĩvo'ka(x)] ◇ *vt* **-1.** [chamar] to invoke. **-2.** *fam* [irritar] to wind up, to annoy. ◇ *vi fam* [antipatizar]: ~ **com alguém** to dislike sb.

invólucro [ĩn'vɔlukru] *m* **-1.** [envoltório] envelope. **-2.** [membrana] membrane. **-3.** [caixa] casing.

involuntário, ria [ĩnvolũn'tarju, rja] *adj* involuntary.

invulnerável [ĩvuwne'ravew] (*pl* **-eis**) *adj* invulnerable.

iodo ['jodu] *m* iodine.

IOF (*abrev de* **Imposto sobre Operações Financeiras**) *m Brazilian tax on financial transactions.*

ioga ['jɔga] *f* yoga.

iogue ['jogi] ◇ *adj* yoga *(antes de subst).* ◇ *mf* yogi.

iogurte [ju'guxtʃi] *m* yoghurt.

ioiô [jo'jo] *m* yo-yo.

íon ['iõ] (*pl* **íons**) *m* ion.

ionizar [joni'za(x)] *vt* to ionize.

IPC (*abrev de* **Índice de Preços ao Consumidor**) *m* consumer price index.

IPEM (*abrev de* **Instituto de Pesos e Medidas**) *m Brazilian institute of weights and measures.*

IPTU (*abrev de* **Imposto Predial e Territorial Urbano**) *m annual tax based on the value of a house.*

IPVA (*abrev de* **Imposto sobre Propriedade de Veículos Automotores**) *m tax paid annually on the value of a car,* ≃ road tax *UK*.

ir [66] ['i(x)] *vi* **-1.** [deslocar-se] to go; **fomos de ônibus** we went by bus; **iremos a pé** we'll go on foot, we'll walk; **vamos?** shall we go? **-2.** [assistir, freqüentar] to go; **ele nunca vai às reuniões** he never goes to the meetings; **você não vai à aula?** aren't you going to your class?; **vou ao cinema muitas vezes** I often go to the cinema. **-3.** [estender-se] to go; **o caminho vai até ao lago** the path leads to the lake. **-4.** [desenrolar-se] to go; **isto não vai nada bem** this isn't going at all well; **como vai você?** how are you?; **como vão as coisas?** how are things?; **os negócios vão mal** business is bad. **-5.** [exprime duração gradual]: ~ **fazendo algo** to continue doing sthg; **vá tentando!** keep trying! **-6.** [seguido de infinitivo]: **vou falar com ele** I'll speak to him; **você vai gostar** you'll like it; **não vou fazer nada** I'm not going to do anything. **-7.** [seguido de gerúndio]: **eu ia caindo** I almost fell. **-8.** [em locuções]: ~ **dar em** [desembocar] to lead to; ~ **ter com** [encontrar] to go and meet up with.

◆ **ir de** *v + prep* [ir disfarçado] to go as; [escolher]: **eu vou de filé com fritas, e você?** I'll have the steak and fries, what about you?

◆ **ir por** *v + prep* [auto-estrada, escadas] to take; ~ **pela esquerda/direita** to go (on the) left/right; ~ **pelo jardim** to go through the garden.

◆ **ir-se** *vp* [partir] to go; **ele já se foi** he's already left; ~**-se embora** to leave; **vai-te embora!** go away!

IR (*abrev de* **Imposto de Renda**) *m* income tax.

ira ['ira] *f* anger.

Irã [i'rã] *m*: **(o)** ~ Iran.

irado, da [i'radu, da] *adj* angry.

iraniano, na [ira'njãnu, na] ◇ *adj* Iranian. ◇ *m, f* Iranian.

Iraque [i'raki] *n*: **(o)** ~ Iraq.

iraquiano, na [ira'kjanu, na] ◇ *adj* Iraqi. ◇ *m, f* Iraqi.

irascível [ira'sivɛw] (*pl* **-eis**) *adj* irascible.

ir-e-vir [iri'vi(x)] (*pl* **ires-e-vires**) *m* coming and going.

iridescente [iride'sẽntʃi] *adj* iridescent.

íris ['iriʃ] *f inv* iris.

Irlanda [ix'lãnda] *n* Ireland; ~ **do Norte** Northern Ireland.

irlandês, esa [ixlãn'deʃ, eza] (*mpl* **-eses**, *fpl* **-s**) ◇ *adj* Irish. ◇ *m, f* Irishman (*f* Irishwoman).

◆ **irlandês** *m* [língua] Irish.

irmã [ix'mã] *f* ▷ **irmão**.

irmanar [4] [ixma'na(x)] *vt* to unite (as brothers).

◆ **irmanar-se** *vp*: ~**-se com algo/alguém** to join with sthg/sb.

irmandade [ixmãn'dadʒi] *f* **-1.** [*RELIG* - de irmãos] brotherhood; [- de irmãs] sisterhood. **-2.** [confraternidade] fraternity.

irmão, mã [ix'mãw, mã] *m, f* **-1.** [parente] brother (sister); ~ **de criação** stepbrother; ~ **gêmeo** twin brother; **irmãos siameses** siamese twins. **-2.** [afim] twin.

ironia [iro'nia] *f* irony.

irônico, ca [i'roniku, ka] *adj* ironic.

ironizar [4] [ironi'za(x)] *vt & vi* to mock.

IRPF (*abrev de* **Imposto de Renda de Pessoa Física**) *m income tax paid by individuals.*

IRPJ (*abrev de* **Imposto de Renda de Pessoa Jurídica**) *m corporation tax.*

irracional [ixasjo'naw] (*pl* **-ais**) *adj* irrational.

irracionalidade [ixasjonali'dadʒi] *f* irrationality.

irradiação [ixadʒja'sãw] (*pl* **-ões**) *f* **-1.** [transmissão] broadcast. **-2.** [propagação] diffusion. **-3.** *MED* irradiation.

irradiar [16] [ixa'dʒja(x)] *vt* **-1.** [transmitir] to broadcast. **-2.** [propagar] to spread. **-3.** *fig* [externar] to radiate.

◆ **irradiar-se** *vp* **-1.** [difundir-se] to be spread about. **-2.** [transmitir-se] to be broadcast.

irreal [i'xjaw] (*pl* **-ais**) *adj* unreal.

irrealizado, da [ixeali'zadu, da] *adj* unrealized.

irrealizável [ixeali'zavew] (*pl* **-eis**) *adj* unachievable.

irreconciliável [ixekõnsi'ljavɛw] (*pl* **-eis**) *adj* irreconcilable.

irreconhecível [ixekoɲe'sivɛw] (*pl* **-eis**) *adj* unrecognizable.

irrecorrível [ixeko'xivew] (*pl* **-eis**) *adj* [sentença] unappealable.

irrecuperável [ixekupe'ravɛw] (*pl* **-eis**) *adj* irrecoverable.
irrecusável [ixeku'zavew] (*pl* **-eis**) *adj which cannot be refused.*
irredutível [ixedu'tʃivew] (*pl* **-eis**) *adj* indomitable.
irrefletido, da [ixefle'tʃidu, da] *adj* rash.
irrefreável [ixefre'avew] (*pl* **-eis**) *adj* irrepressible.
irrefutável [ixefu'tavew] (*pl* **-eis**) *adj* irrefutable.
irregular [ixegu'la(x)] (*pl* **-es**) *adj* **-1.** [desigual] irregular. **-2.** [pouco convencional] unorthodox. **-3.** [irrecuperável] incurable.
irregularidade [ixegulari'dadʒi] *f* **-1.** [inconstância] unreliability. **-2.** [procedimento irregular] irregularity.
irrelevância [ixele'vãnsja] *f* irrelevance.
irrelevante [ixele'vãntʃi] *adj* irrelevant.
irremediável [ixeme'dʒjavɛw] (*pl* **-eis**) *adj* irreparable.
irremediavelmente [ixemedjavew'mẽntʃi] *adv* irremediably.
irremovível [ixemo'vivew] (*pl* **-eis**) *adj* immovable; **ser/estar ~ em algo** to be immovable in sthg.
irreparável [ixepa'ravew] (*pl* **-eis**) *adj* irreparable.
irrepreensível [ixeprjẽn'sivew] (*pl* **-eis**) *adj* irreproachable.
irreprimível [ixepri'mivɛw] (*pl* **-eis**) *adj* irrepressible.
irrequietação [ixikjeta'sãw] *f* restlessness.
irrequieto, ta [ixe'kjɛtu, ta] *adj* [desassossegado] restless.
irresistível [ixeziʃ'tʃivɛw] (*pl* **-eis**) *adj* irresistible.
irresoluto, ta [ixezo'lutu, ta] *adj* irresolute.
irresponsabilidade [ixeʃpõnsabili'dadʒi] *f* irresponsibility.
irresponsável [ixeʃpõn'savɛw] (*pl* **-eis**) <> *adj* irresponsible. <> *mf* irresponsible person.
irrestrito, ta [ixeʃ'tritu, ta] *adj* unlimited, limitless.
irreverência [ixeve'rẽnsja] *f* irreverence.
irreverente [ixeve'rẽntʃi] *adj* irreverent.
irreversível [ixevex'sivew] (*pl* **-eis**) *adj* irreversible.
irrevogável [ixevo'gavew] (*pl* **-eis**) *adj* irrevocable.
irrigação [ixiga'sãw] (*pl* **-ões**) *f* irrigation.
irrigar [14] [ixi'ga(x)] *vt* to irrigate.
irrisório, ria [ixi'zɔrju, rja] *adj* **-1.** [de zombaria] derisory. **-2.** *fig* [ínfimo] derisory.
irritabilidade [ixitabili'dadʒi] *f* irritability.
irritação [ixita'sãw] (*pl* **-ões**) *f* irritation.
irritadiço, ça [ixita'dʒisu, sa] *adj* irritable.
irritante [ixi'tãntʃi] *adj* irritating.
irritar [4] [ixi'ta(x)] *vt* to irritate.
◆ **irritar-se** *vp* [exasperar-se] to become irritated.
irritável [ixi'tavew] (*pl* **-eis**) *adj* irritable.
irromper [5] [ixõm'pe(x)] *vi* **-1.** [entrar]: **~ em** to burst into. **-2.** [surgir]: **~ de** to surge from; **~ em** to break out.
isca ['iʃka] *f* **-1.** [ger] bait. **-2.** CULIN morsel.
isenção [izẽn'sãw] (*pl* **-ões**) *f* **-1.** [dispensa] exemption. **-2.** [livramento] release. **-3.** [imparcialidade] impartiality.
isentar [4] [izẽn'ta(x)] *vt* **-1.** [dispensar]: **~ alguém de algo/de fazer algo** to exempt sb from sthg/from doing sthg. **-2.** [livrar]: **~ alguém de algo/fazer algo** to let sb off from sthg/from doing sthg.
◆ **isentar-se** *vp* to free o.s.
isento, ta [i'zẽntu, ta] *adj* **-1.** [dispensado] exempt. **-2.** [livre] free. **-3.** [imparcial] unbiased.
Islã [iʒ'lã] *m* Islam.
Islamabad [iʒlama'badʒi] *n* Islamabad.
islâmico, ca [iʒ'lamiku, ka] *adj* Islamic.
islamismo [iʒla'miʒmu] *m* Islam.
islamita [iʒla'mita] <> *adj* Islamic. <> *mf* Islamist.
islandês, esa [iʒlãn'deʃ, eza] <> *adj* Icelandic. <> *m, f* Icelander.
◆ **islandês** *m* [língua] Icelandic.
Islândia [iʒ'lãndʒja] *f* Iceland.
ISO (*abrev de* **International Standards Organization**) *f* ISO.
isolacionismo [izolasjo'niʒmu] *m* isolationism.
isolado, da [izo'ladu, da] *adj* **-1.** [separado] isolated. **-2.** [só] lone. **-3.** [afastado] remote. **-4.** ELETR insulated.
isolamento [izola'mẽntu] *m* **-1.** [ger] isolation. **-2.** ELETR insulation.
isolante [izo'lãntʃi] <> *adj* ELETR insulating. <> *m* insulator.
isolar [4] [izo'la(x)] <> *vt* **-1.** [ger] to isolate; **~ algo de algo** to isolate sthg from sthg. **-2.** ELETR to insulate. <> *vi* [afastar mau agouro]: **isola!** touch wood!
◆ **isolar-se** *vp* [afastar-se]: **~-se de alguém/algo** to isolate o.s from sb/sthg.
isonomia [izono'mia] *f* equality.
isopor [izo'pox] *m* polystyrene.
isqueiro [iʃ'kejru] *m* lighter.
Israel [iʒxa'ɛw] *n* Israel.
israelense [iʒxae'lẽnsi], **israelita** [iʒxae'lita] <> *adj* Israeli. <> *mf* Israeli.
isso ['isu] <> *pron* that; **é isso aí!** that's right!; **foi por isso que ele não veio** that's why he didn't come; **é por isso mesmo que en não vou!** that is exactly why I'm not going!; **isso não!** no way!; **não gosto disso** I don't like that; **não mexa nisso!** leave that alone!
◆ **por isso** *loc adv* therefore; **mem por ~** not really.
Istambul [iʃtãn'buw] *n* Istanbul.
istmo ['iʃtʃimu] *m* isthmus.
isto ['iʃtu] *pron* this; **disto eu não quero** I don't want any of this; **escreva nisto** write on this; **isto é** [quer dizer] that is (to say); **isto é que é vida!** this is the life!
Itália [i'talja] *n* Italy.

italiano, na [ita'ljanu, na] <> *adj* Italian. <> *m, f* Italian.
◆ **italiano** *m* [língua] Italian.
itálico, ca [i'taliku, ka] *adj TIPO* italic.
◆ **itálico** *m TIPO* italic.
Itamarati [itamara'tʃi] *m* Brazilian foreign ministry.
item ['itẽ] (*pl* **itens**) *m* **-1.** [ger] item. **-2.** *JUR* [artigo] point.
itinerante [itʃine'rãntʃi] <> *adj* itinerant. <> *mf* itinerant.
itinerário [itʃine'rarju] *m* **-1.** [roteiro] route. **-2.** [caminho] itinerary.
Iugoslávia [iwgo'ʒlavja] *f* Yugoslavia; **a ex-~** the ex-Yugoslavia.
iugoslavo, va [iwgoʒ'lavu, va] <> *adj* Yugoslav. <> *m, f* Yugoslav.

j, J ['ʒɔta] *m* [letra] j, J.
já ['ʒa] <> *adv* **-1.** [ger] already. **-2.** [agora] now. **-3.** [sem demora] just; **~ vou** just coming. **-4.** [até mesmo] even. **-5.** [daqui a pouco] soon; **até ~** see you soon. **-6.** [alguma vez] ever. <> *conj* however. <> *loc*: **~ era!** *fam* that's history!
◆ **desde já** *loc prep* from now on.
◆ **já que** *loc conj* since.
jabuti [ʒabu'tʃi] *m* jabuti, *indigenous Brazilian tortoise.*
jabuticaba [ʒabutʃi'kaba] *f* jaboticaba, *Brazilian evergreen tree or the fruit of this tree.*
jaca ['ʒaka] *f* jack fruit.
jacarandá [ʒakarãn'da] *f* jacaranda.
jacaré [ʒaka'rɛ] *m* **-1.** *ZOOL* Yacare caiman. **-2.** [surfe]: **pegar ~** to surf.
Jacarta [ʒa'kaxta] *n* Djakarta, Jakarta.
jacinto [ʒa'sĩntu] *m* hyacinth.
jactância [ʒak'tãnsja] *f* **-1.** [vaidade] boasting. **-2.** [arrogância] arrogance.
jactar-se [7] [ʒak'taxsi] *vp*: **~-se (de)** to boast (about).
jade ['ʒadʒi] *m* jade.
jaguar [ʒa'gwa(x)] (*pl* **-es**) *m* jaguar.
jaguatirica [ʒagwatʃi'rika] *f* leopard.
jagunço [ʒa'gũsu] *m* bodyguard.
jaleco [ʒa'lɛku] *m* coat.
Jamaica [ʒa'majka] *f* Jamaica.
jamais [ʒa'majʃ] *adv* never; *(com palavra negativa)* ever.
jamanta [ʒa'mãnta] *f* [caminhão] articulated truck.
jan. (*abrev de* **janeiro**) Jan.
janeiro [ʒa'nejru] *m* January; *veja também* **setembro**.
janela [ʒa'nɛla] *f* window.
janelão [ʒane'lãw] (*pl* **-ões**) *m* picture window.
jangada [ʒãŋ'gada] *f* raft.
jangadeiro, ra [ʒãŋga'dejru, ra] *m, f* raft owner.
janta ['ʒãnta] *f* dinner.
jantar [4] [ʒãn'ta(x)] (*pl* **-es**) <> *vt* to have for dinner. <> *vi* to have dinner. <> *m* dinner; **~ americano** buffet dinner.
Japão [ʒa'pãw] *n*: **(o) ~** Japan.
japona [ʒa'pona] *f* jacket.
japonês, esa [ʒapo'neʃ, eza] (*mpl* **-eses**, *fpl* **-s**) <> *adj* Japanese. <> *m, f* Japanese person.
◆ **japonês** *m* [língua] Japanese.
jaqueta [ʒa'keta] *f* jacket.
jaquetão [ʒake'tãw] (*pl* **-ões**) *m* double-breasted jacket.
jararaca [ʒara'raka] *f* **-1.** [cobra] viper. **-2.** *fig* [pessoa] harridan.
jarda ['ʒaxda] *f* yard.
jardim [ʒax'dʒĩ] (*pl* **-ns**) *m* garden; **~ botânico** botanical garden; **~ zoológico** zoo.
jardim-de-infância [ʒaxdʒĩndʒĩnfãnsja] (*pl* **jardins-de-infância**) *m* kindergarten.
jardim-de-inverno [ʒaxdʒĩndʒĩnvexnu] (*pl* **jardins-de-inverno**) *m* conservatory.
jardinagem [ʒaxdʒi'naʒẽ] *f* gardening.
jardineiro, ra [ʒaxdʒi'nejru, ra] *m, f* [pessoa] gardener.
◆ **jardineira** *f* **-1.** [móvel] jardinière. **-2.** [em parapeito] window box. **-3.** [roupa] overalls *(pl)*.
jargão [ʒax'gãw] (*pl* **-ões**) *m* jargon.
jarra ['ʒaxa] *f* [pote] carafe; [vaso] vase.
jarro ['ʒaxu] *m* jug.
jasmim [ʒaʒ'mĩ] (*pl* **-ns**) *m* jasmine.
jato ['ʒatu] *m* **-1.** [raio] beam. **-2.** [avião] jet. **-3.** [propulsão]: **a ~** jet propelled. **-4.** [jorro] stream.
jaula ['ʒawla] *f* cage.
Java ['ʒava] *n* Java.
javali [ʒava'li] *m* wild boar.
jazer [33] [ʒa'ze(x)] *vi* **-1.** [estar sepultado] to lie. **-2.** [estar deitado] to be lying.
jazida [ʒa'zida] *f* seam.
jazigo [ʒa'zigu] *m* grave.
jazz ['ʒajʃ] *m* jazz.
jazzista [ʒa'ziʃta] *mf* jazz artist.
JC (*abrev de* **Jesus Cristo**) *m* JC.
jeans ['ʒĩnʃ] *m inv* jeans *(pl)*.
jeca ['ʒɛka] *adj* rustic.
jeca-tatu ['ʒɛkatatu] (*pl* **-tus**) *m character from children's literature representing the village people of the Brazilian interior.*
jegue ['ʒɛgi] *m* ass.
jeitinho [ʒej'tʃiɲu] *m* touch; **dar um ~** to get something done one way or another.

JEITINHO BRASILEIRO

One of the more striking characteristics of the Brazilian people is their ability to rise to any occasion. Brazilians' adaptability to challenges and new situations is a cultural trait expressed in the famous *jeitinho brasileiro*, the belief that they will always have a special knack (*jeitinho*) for getting out of a tricky situation.

jeito ['ʒejtu] *m* **-1.** [modo] way; **ao ~ de** in the manner of; **de ~ algum!** no way!; **de qualquer ~** anyway; [sem cuidado] any old how. **-2.** [aspecto] air. **-3.** [índole] disposition. **-4.** [torção]: **dar um mau ~ em** to sprain. **-5.** [propensão]: **ter** *ou* **levar ~ para (fazer) algo** to be good at (doing) sthg. **-6.** [habilidade] aptitude; **falta de ~** clumsiness; **ter falta de ~ para (fazer) algo** to be bad at (doing) sthg. **-7.** [diplomacia] tact; **fazer algo com ~** to do sthg carefully. **-8.** [graça]: **ficar sem ~** to feel embarrassed. **-9.** [arrumação] clean up; **dar um ~ em algo** to tidy up. **-10.** [solução] solution; **dar um ~ em algo** to do something about sthg. **-11.** [corretivo]: **dar um ~ em alguém** to set sb straight. **-12.** [juízo]: **tomar ~** to grow up.

jeitoso, osa [ʒej'tozu, ɔza] *adj* **-1.** [habilidoso] dexterous. **-2.** [funcional] practical. **-3.** [diplomático] tactful.

jejuar [4] [ʒe'ʒwa(x)] *vi* to fast.

jejum [ʒe'ʒũ] (*pl* **-ns**) *m* fast; **em ~** fasting.

Jeová [ʒeo'va] *m*: **testemunha de ~** Jehovah's Witness.

jerico [ʒe'riku] *m* donkey; **idéia de ~** stupid idea.

jérsei ['ʒɛxsej] *m* jersey.

Jerusalém [ʒeruza'lẽ] *n* Jerusalem.

jesuíta [ʒe'zwita] <> *adj* Jesuit. <> *m* Jesuit.

jesuítico, ca [ʒezu'itʃiku, ka] *adj* [período, missão] Jesuitical.

jesus [ʒe'zuʃ] *interj* (good) heavens!

jetom [ʒe'tõ] (*pl* **-ns**) *m* **-1.** [remuneração] payment. **-2.** [ficha] jetton.

jet set [ʒet'sɛtʃi] *m* jet set.

jet ski [ʒɛtʃiʃ'ki] (*pl* **jet skis**) *m* jet ski.

jibóia [ʒi'bɔja] *f* [cobra] boa.

jiboiar [4] [ʒibo'ja(x)] *vi to rest and digest after a big meal.*

jiló [ʒi'lɔ] *m type of Brazilian vegetable.*

jingle ['ʒĩngow] *m* jingle.

jipe ['ʒipi] *m* jeep.

jiu-jitsu [ʒu'ʒitsu] *m* jiu-jitsu.

joalheiro, ra [ʒoa'ʎejru, ra] *m, f* jeweller ***UK***, jeweler ***US***.

joalheria [ʒwaʎe'ria] *f* jewellers ***UK***, jewelers ***US***.

joanete [ʒwa'netʃi] *m* bunion.

joaninha [ʒwa'niɲa] *f* **-1.** [inseto] ladybird. **-2.** [carro de polícia] patrol car.

joão-ninguém [ʒuãwnĩŋ'gẽ] (*pl* **joões-ninguém**) *m*: **um ~** a nobody, a nonentity.

joça ['ʒɔsa] *f fam* mess.

jocoso, sa [ʒoko'zu, za] *adj* [divertido, cômico] jocular.

joelheira [ʒwe'ʎeira] *f ESP* knee-pad.

joelho ['ʒweʎu] *m* knee; **de ~s** kneeling, on one's knees; **ficar de ~s** to kneel down.

jogada [ʒo'gada] *f* **-1.** [*ESP* - tática] strategy; [- lance] shot. **-2.** *fam* [esquema] scam. **-3.** *fam* [intenção] intention. **-4.** *loc*: **tirar alguém da ~** to eliminate sb from the equation.

jogado, da [ʒo'gadu, da] *adj* thrown.

jogador, ra [ʒoga'do(x), ra] *m, f* **-1.** [atleta] player; **~ de futebol** football player. **-2.** [apostador] gambler.

jogar [14] [ʒo'ga(x)] <> *vt* **-1.** [tomar parte em jogo de] to play. **-2.** [atirar] to throw. **-3.** [apostar]: **~ algo em algo** to gamble sthg on sthg. **-4.** [desfazer-se de]: **~ algo fora** to throw sthg out. **-5.** [desperdiçar]: **~ algo fora** to throw around. <> *vi* **-1.** [divertir-se num jogo] to play. **-2.** [apostar]: **~ em algo** to bet on sthg. **-3.** [na Bolsa]: **~ em** to speculate on. **-4.** [manipular]: **~ com algo** to play around with sthg. **-5.** [balançar] to toss.

◆ **jogar-se** *vp* **-1.** [lançar-se] to throw o.s. **-2.** [paquerar]: **~-se para cima de alguém** to be all over sb.

jogatina [ʒoga'tʃina] *f* gambling.

jogging ['ʒɔgĩŋ] *m* **-1.** [corrida] jogging; **fazer ~** to go jogging. **-2.** [roupa] tracksuit.

jogo ['ʒogu] (*pl* **jogos**) *m* **-1.** [ger] game; **~ limpo** clean game; **~ de azar** game of chance. **-2.** [partida] match. **-3.** [vício de jogar] gambling. **-4.** [conjunto] collection. **-5.** [aposta] bet. **-6.** *MEC* set. **-7.** *fig* [ardil] ruse. **-8.** [manipulação] play. **-9.** [movimentação] movement. **-10.** [balanço] tossing. **-11.** *AUTO* running. **-12.** *fam* [intenção] game. **-13.** *loc*: **abrir o ~** to lay one's cards on the table; **esconder o ~** to have a card up one's sleeve; **ter ~ de cintura para algo** to be quite capable of getting out of sthg.

jogo-da-velha [,ʒoguda'vɛʎa] (*pl* **jogos-da-velha**) *m* noughts and crosses ***UK***, tic-tac-toe ***US***.

joguete [ʒo'getʃi] *m* plaything; **fazer alguém de ~** to make a laughing stock of sb.

jóia ['ʒɔja] <> *adj fam* delightful. <> *f* **-1.** [enfeite] jewel. **-2.** [taxa] fee.

joio ['ʒoju] *m* darnel; **separar o ~ do trigo** to separate the wheat from the chaff.

jojoba [ʒo'ʒɔba] *f* jojoba.

jóquei ['ʒɔkej], **jóquei-clube** *m* Jockey Club.

jornada [ʒox'nada] *f* **-1.** [ger] journey. **-2.** [período] duration; **~ de trabalho** working day.

jornal [ʒox'naw] (*pl* **-ais**) *m* **-1.** [gazeta] newspaper. **-2.** [noticiário] news.

jornaleiro, ra [ʒoxna'lejru, ra] *m, f* [pessoa] newspaper vendor.

◆ **jornaleiro** *m* [banca] news-stand.

jornalista [ʒoxna'liʃta] *mf* journalist.

jornalístico, ca [ʒoxna'liʃtʃiku, ka] *adj* journalistic.

jorrar [4] [ʒo'xa(x)] <> *vt* to spurt. <> *vi* to gush.

jorro ['ʒoxu] *m* torrent.

jovem ['ʒɔvẽ] (*pl* **-ns**) <> *adj* **-1.** [juvenil] youthful. **-2.** [para jovens] young. <> *mf* young person.

jovial [ʒo'vjaw] (*pl* **-ais**) *adj* jovial.

jovialidade [ʒovjali'dadʒi] *f* joviality.
joystick [ʒɔj'ʃtʃik] (*pl* **joysticks**) *m* COMPUT joystick.
juazeiro [ʒwa'zejru] *m* jujube.
juba ['ʒuba] *f* mane.
jubilação [ʒubila'sãw] (*pl* **-ões**) UNIV *f* **-1.** [aposentadoria] retirement. **-2.** [desligamento] suspension.
jubilado, da [ʒubi'ladu, da] *adj* [aluno] barred *(from a course for not having fulfilled the formal requirements).*
jubilar [4] [ʒubi'la(x)] UNIV *vt* **-1.** [aposentar] to retire. **-2.** [desligar] to suspend.
jubileu [ʒubi'lew] *m* jubilee; ~ **de prata** silver jubilee.
júbilo ['ʒubilu] *m* elation.
jubiloso, osa [ʒubi'lozu, za] *adj* elated.
judaico, ca [ʒu'dajku, ka] *adj* Jewish.
judaísmo [ʒuda'iʒmu] *m* Judaism.
judas ['ʒudaʃ] *m* Judas, traitor.
judeu, dia [ʒu'dew, dʃia] ◇ *adj* Jewish. ◇ *m, f* Jewish person, Jew.
judiação [ʒudʒja'sãw] (*pl* **-ões**) *f* abuse, ill-treatment.
judiar [16] [ʒu'dʒja(x)] *vi*: ~ **de alguém** to abuse sb, to ill-treat sb.
judicial [ʒudʃi'sjaw] (*pl* **-ais**) *adj* judicial.
judiciário, ria [ʒudʒi'sjarju, rja] *adj* judicial.
◆ **Judiciário** *m*: **o** ~ the judiciary.
judicioso, osa [ʒudʒi'sjozu, ɔza] *adj* judicious.
judô [ʒu'do] *m* judo.
judoca [ʒu'dɔka] *mf* judoka.
jugo ['ʒugu] *m*: **sob o** ~ **de** under the yoke of.
juiz, íza ['ʒwiʃ, iza] (*mpl* **-es**, *fpl* **-s**) *m, f* **-1.** JUR judge; ~ **de direito** district judge; ~ **de menores** judge in a juvenile court; ~ **de paz** justice of the peace. **-2.** ESP referee.
juizado [ʒuj'zadu, da] *m* court; ~ **de menores** juvenile court; ~ **de pequenas causas** small claims court.
juízo ['ʒwizu] *m* **-1.** [julgamento] judgement. **-2.** [conceito] opinion. **-3.** [sensatez] prudence; **perder o** ~ to lose one's mind. **-4.** JUR [foro] tribunal.
Juízo Final [ˌʒwizufi'naw] *m*: **o** ~ Judgement Day.
jujuba [ʒu'ʒuba] *f* **-1.** BOT jujube. **-2.** [bala] *jujube-flavoured boiled sweet.*
jul. (*abrev de* **julho**) Jul.
julgador, ra [ʒuwga'do(x), ra] ◇ *adj* judging. ◇ *m, f* judge.
julgamento [ʒuwga'mẽntu] *m* **-1.** [juízo] judgement. **-2.** [audiência] hearing. **-3.** [sentença] sentence.
julgar [14] [ʒuw'ga(x)] *vt* **-1.** [sentenciar sobre] to judge. **-2.** [avaliar]: ~ **algo/alguém por algo** to judge sthg/sb by sthg. **-3.** [supor] to think; ~ **que** to think that.
◆ **julgar-se** *vp* [supor-se] to consider o.s.
julho ['ʒuʎu] *m* July; *veja também* **setembro**.
jumento [ʒu'mẽntu] *m* donkey.
jun. (*abrev de* **junho**) Jun.
junção [ʒũn'sãw] (*pl* **-ões**) *f* **-1.** [união] union. **-2.** [ponto] junction.
junco ['ʒũŋku] *m* reed.
junho ['ʒuɲu] *m* June; *veja também* **setembro**.
junino, na [ʒu'ninu, na] *adj* ▷ **festa**.
júnior ['ʒunjo(x)] (*pl* **juniores**) ◇ *adj* junior. ◇ *mf* ESP junior.
junta ['ʒũnta] *f* **-1.** [comissão] council. **-2.** POL junta. **-3.** [articulação] joint. **-4.** [órgão]: ~ **comercial** chamber of commerce. **-5.** [parelha]: ~ **de bois** yoke of oxen.
juntamente [ʒũnta'mẽntʃi] *adv*: ~ **com** together with.
juntar [4] [ʒũn'ta(x)] ◇ *vt* **-1.** [unir]: ~ **algo (a algo)** to mix sthg (with sthg). **-2.** [aproximar]: ~ **alguém (a alguém)** to unite sb (with sb). **-3.** [colocar junto] to mix (together). **-4.** [aglomerar] to assemble. **-5.** [recolher] to collect. ◇ *vi* [aglomerar-se] to cluster. ◇ *vi* [economizar]: ~ **(para)** to save (for).
◆ **juntar-se** *vp* [associar-se]: **~-se a** to mix with; **~-se com** to unite o.s with.
junto, ta ['ʒũntu, ta] ◇ *adj* together. ◇ *adv* at the same time; ~ **de** next to.
◆ **junto a, junto de** *loc prep* next to.
◆ **junto com** *loc prep* together.
jura ['ʒura] *f* vow.
jurado, da [ʒu'radu, da] ◇ *adj* sworn. ◇ *m, f* juror.
juramentado, da [ʒuramẽn'tadu, da] *adj* under oath.
juramento [ʒura'mẽntu] *m* oath; **fazer** ~ **a** to swear an oath to; **sob** ~ under oath.
jurar [4] [ʒu'ra(x)] ◇ *vt* **-1.** [prometer] to swear; ~ **fazer algo** to swear to do sthg; ~ **que** to swear that. **-2.** [sob juramento]: ~ **fazer algo** to take an oath to do sthg. ◇ *vi* [prestar juramento]: ~ **(por/sobre)** to swear (by/on).
júri ['ʒuri] *m* jury.
jurídico, ca [ʒu'ridʒiku, ka] *adj* legal.
jurisconsulto, ta [ʒurʃkõn'suwtu, ta] *m, f* legal expert **UK**, jurist **US**.
jurisdição [ʒuriʒdʒi'sãw] *f* jurisdiction.
jurisprudência [ʒuriʃpru'dẽnsja] *f* jurisprudence.
jurista [ʒu'riʃta] *mf* legal expert **UK**, jurist **US**.
juros ['ʒuruʃ] *mpl* interest *(sg)*; **empréstimo a** ~**/sem** ~**s** loan with/without interest; ~ **acumulados** accumulated interest; ~ **fixos/variáveis** fixed/variable interest.
jururu [ʒuru'ru] *adj* gloomy.
jus [ʒuʃ] *m*: **fazer** ~ **a algo** to do justice to sthg.
jusante [ʒu'zãntʃi] *f*: **a** ~ **de** downstream of.
justamente [ʒuʃta'mẽntʃi] *adv* **-1.** [com justiça] rightly. **-2.** [precisamente] precisely.
justapor [45] [ʒuʃta'po(x)] *vt*: ~ **algo (a algo)** to juxtapose sthg (with sthg).
◆ **justapor-se** *vp* to be juxtaposed.
justaposição [ʒuʃtapozi'sãw] (*pl* **-ões**) *f* juxtaposition.
justaposto, osta [ʒuʃta'poʃtu, ɔʃta] *pp* ▷ **justapor**.

justeza [ʒuʃ'teza] *f* precision.

justiça [ʒuʃ'tʃisa] *f* **-1.** [virtude] fairness; **com ~** justly; **fazer ~ a alguém/algo** to do justice to sb/sthg. **-2.** [eqüidade] equality; **~ social** social justice. **-3.** [tribunal] justice; **ir à ~** to go to court; **Justiça do Trabalho** Industrial Tribunal. **-4.** [poder judiciário]: **a Justiça** the judiciary.

justiceiro, ra [ʒuʃtʃi'sejru, ra] *adj* just.

justificação [ʒuʃtʃifika'sãw] (*pl* **-ões**) *f* justification.

justificar [12] [ʒuʃtʃifi'ka(x)] *vt* to justify.
◆ **justificar-se** *vp* [explicar-se]: **~-se por algo** to excuse o.s for sthg.

justificativa [ʒuʃtʃifika'tʃiva] *f* justification.

justificável [ʒuʃtʃifi'kavew] (*pl* **-eis**) *adj* justifiable.

justo, ta ['ʒuʃtu, ta] ◇ *adj* **-1.** [ger] fair. **-2.** [apertado] tight. **-3.** [exato] precise. **-4.** [merecido] just. ◇ *adv* just.

juta ['ʒuta] *f* jute.

juvenil [ʒuve'niw] (*pl* **-is**) ◇ *adj* **-1.** [de jovens] youth, teenage. **-2.** *ESP* junior. ◇ *m ESP* [campeonato] junior.

juventude [ʒuvẽn'tudʒi] *f* youth.

k, K [ka] *m* [letra] k, K.

kafkiano, na [kaf'kianu, na] *adj* Kafkaesque.

Kalahari [kala'xari] *n*: **o deserto de ~** the Kalahari Desert.

Kampala [kãn'pala] *n* Kampala.

karaokê [karaw'ke] *m* **-1.** [atividade] karaoke. **-2.** [casa noturna] karaoke bar.

kardecismo [kaxde'siʒmu] *m religious doctrine of the Frenchman Allan Kardec.*

kart ['kaxtʃi] *m* go-cart.

kartódromo [kax'tɔdromu] *m* go-kart track.

Katmandu [katʃimãn'du] *n* Kathmandu.

Kb (*abrev de* **kilobyte**) *m* Kb.

kg (*abrev de* **quilograma**) *m* kg.

ketchup [kɛ'tʃupi] *m* (tomato) ketchup.

Khartum [kax'tũ] *n* Khartoum.

Kíev ['kjɛvi] *n* Kiev.

Kingston ['kiŋgiʃtõ] *n* Kingston.

Kinshasa [kin'ʃaza] *n* Kinshasa.

kit ['kitʃi] *m* kit.

kitchenette [kitʃi'nɛtʃi] *f* kitchenette.

kitsch [kitʃi] *adj inv* kitsch.

kiwi ['kiwi] *m* [fruta] kiwi fruit.

kl (*abrev de* **quilolitro**) *m* kl.

km (*abrev de* **quilômetro**) *m* km.

km/h (*abrev de* **quilômetro por hora**) *m* km/h.

know-how [now'haw] *m* know-how.

Kuala Lumpur [kwalalãn'pu(x)] *n* Kuala Lumpur.

Kuwait [ku'ajtʃi] *n* Kuwait.

kW (*abrev de* **kilowatt**) *m* kW.

l, L ['ɛli] *m* [letra] l, L.

-la [la] *pron* **-1.** [pessoa] her; **-2.** [coisa] it; **-3.** [você] you.

lá ['la] *adv* there; **quero lá saber!** what do I care!; **sei lá!** how should I know; **para lá de** beyond.

lã ['lã] *f* wool; **calça de ~** woollen trousers; **de pura ~** pure wool; **~ de camelo** camel hair.

labareda [laba'reda] *f* flame.

lábia ['labja] *f* [conversa] smooth talk; **ter ~** to have the gift of the gab.

labial [la'bjaw] (*pl* **-ais**) *adj* labial.

lábio ['labju] *m* [*ANAT* - beiço] lip; [- genital] labium; **~ leporino** harelip, cleft lip.

labirinto [labi'rĩntu] *m* labyrinth.

laborar [4] [labo'ra(x)] *vi*: **~ em erro** to make a mistake.

laboratorial [laborato'riaw] (*pl* **-ais**) *adj* laboratory *(antes de subst)*.

laboratório [labora'tɔrju] *m* laboratory; **~ de línguas** language laboratory.

laborioso, osa [labo'rjozu, ɔza] *adj* **-1.** [trabalhador] hard-working. **-2.** [trabalhoso] laborious.

labuta [la'buta] *f* toil.

labutar [4] [labu'ta(x)] *vi* to toil.

laca ['laka] *f* lacquer; **de ~** lacquered.

laçar [13] [la'sa(x)] *vt* [animal] to lasso.

laçarote [lasa'rɔtʃi] *m* large bow.

laço ['lasu] *m* **-1.** [nó] bow; **dar um ~ em algo** to tie a bow in sthg. **-2.** [para laçar animais] lasso. **-3.** *fig* [vínculo] tie; **~s de família** family ties.

lacônico, ca [la'kɔniku, ka] *adj* laconic.

lacraia [la'kraja] *f* centipede.

lacrar [4] [la'kra(x)] *vt* to seal.

lacre ['lakri] *m* sealing wax.

lacrimal [lakri'maw] (*pl* **-ais**) *adj* lachrymal.

lacrimejante [lakrime'ʒãntʃi] *adj* tearful.

lacrimejar [4] [lakrime'ʒa(x)] *vi* **-1.** [olhos] to water. **-2.** [pessoa] to weep.

lacrimogêneo, nea [lakrimo'ʒenju, nja] *adj* ▻ gás.
lacrimoso, osa [lakri'mozu, ɔza] *adj* [olhos] tearful.
lactação [lakta'sãw] (*pl* **-ões**) *f* [amamentação] lactation.
lactante [lak'tãntʃi] ◇ *adj* lactating. ◇ *f* nursing woman.
lácteo, tea ['laktju, tja] *adj* **-1.** [produto] milky. **-2.** ▻ **via**.
lactose [lak'tɔzi] *f* lactose.
lacuna [la'kuna] *f* **-1.** [vão] gap. **-2.** [espaço em branco] blank. **-3.** [omissão] omission.
ladainha [lada'iɲa] *f* **-1.** [oração] litany. **-2.** *fig* [lengalenga] rigmarole.
ladear [15] [la'dʒja(x)] *vt* **-1.** [ger] to flank. **-2.** [correr paralelo a] to run alongside. **-3.** *fig* [contornar] to skirt.
ladeira [la'dejra] *f* **-1.** [rampa] slope. **-2.** [rua íngreme] steep road.
ladino, na [la'dʒinu, na] *adj* [esperto] sharp.
lado ['ladu] *m* **-1.** [ger] side; **do ~ avesso** inside out; **estar do ~ de alguém** to be on sb's side; **por um ~ ... por outro ~** on the one hand ... on the other hand. **-2.** [direção, local] direction; **de todos os ~s** everywhere; **de um ~ para outro** from one side to the other; **do ~ de fora** outside.
◆ **ao lado** *loc adv* **-1.** [na casa adjacente] next door. **-2.** [próximo] close by.
◆ **ao lado de** *loc prep* next to.
◆ **de lado** *loc adv* [sentar, andar] on the side; **deixar algo de ~** [pôr de reserva] to put sthg aside; [desconsiderar] to drop sthg; **deixar alguém de ~** [ignorar] to ignore sb; **olhar alguém de ~** [desdenhar] to look down on sb.
ladrão, ladra [la'drãw, 'ladra] (*mpl* **-ões**, *fpl* **-s**) ◇ *adj* thieving. ◇ *m, f* thief; **~ de loja** shoplifter.
◆ **ladrão** *m* [tubo] overflow pipe.
ladrar [4] [la'dra(x)] *vi* to bark.
ladrilhar [4] [ladri'ʎa(x)] *vt* to tile.
ladrilheiro, ra [ladri'ʎejru, ra] *m, f* tiler.
ladrilho [la'driʎu] *m* tile.
ladroagem [la'drwaʒẽ] (*pl* **-ns**), **ladroeira** [la'drwejra] *f* theft, robbery.
ladrões [la'drõjʃ] *pl* ▻ **ladrão**.
lagarta [la'gaxta] *f* *ZOOL* caterpillar.
lagartixa [lagax'tʃiʃa] *f* (small) lizard.
lagarto [la'gaxtu] *m* *ZOOL* lizard.
lago ['lagu] *m* **-1.** *GEOGR* lake. **-2.** [de jardim] pond. **-3.** *fig* [poça] puddle; **a cozinha está um ~** the kitchen is flooded.
lagoa [la'goa] *f* lake.
lagosta [la'goʃta] *f* lobster.
lagostim [lagoʃ'tʃĩ] (*pl* **-ns**) *m* crayfish.
lágrima ['lagrima] *f* tear; **derramar ~s** to cry.
laguna [la'guna] *f* lagoon.
laia ['laja] *f* kind, type.
laico, ca ['lajku, ka] *adj* **-1.** [pessoa] lay. **-2.** [ensino] secular.
laje ['laʒi] *f* **-1.** [pedra] flagstone. **-2.** *CONSTR* concrete flooring.
lajear [15] [la'ʒja(x)] *vt* to pave.
lajota [la'ʒɔta] *f* small flagstone.
lama ['lãma] *f* **-1.** [ger] mud. **-2.** *fig* [má situação]: **tirar alguém da ~** to help s.o. out of trouble.
lamaçal [lama'saw] (*pl* **-ais**), **lamaceiro** [lama'sejru] *m* muddy place.
lamacento, ta [lama'sẽntu, ta] *adj* muddy.
lambada [lãn'bada] *f* **-1.** [golpe] blow. **-2.** *fig* [descompostura] telling-off. **-3.** [dança] lambada.
lambança [lãn'bãnsa] *f* mess.
lamber [5] [lãm'be(x)] *vt* to lick.
lambida [lãn'bida] *f* lick; **dar uma ~ em algo** to have a lick of sthg, to lick sthg.
lambido, da [lãm'bidu, da] *adj* **-1.** [cara] clean. **-2.** [cabelo] straight.
lambiscar [12] [lãmbiʃ'ka(x)] ◇ *vt* to nibble. ◇ *vi* to pick.
lambreta® [lãn'breta] *f* motor scooter.
lambri [lãn'bri] (*pl* **-bris**) *m* panelling.
lambuja [lãn'buʒa] *f* [vantagem] advantage.
lambuzar [4] [lãmbu'za(x)] *vt*: **~ alguém/algo (de com algo)** to cover sb/sthg (in sthg).
lambuzeira [lãnbu'zejra] *f* mess.
lamentação [lamẽnta'sãw] (*pl* **-ões**) *f* complaint.
lamentar [4] [lamẽn'ta(x)] *vt* to regret; **lamento muito, mas ...** I am very sorry, but ...; **lamentamos comunicar-lhe ...** we regret to inform you ...
◆ **lamentar-se** *vp*: **~-se (de algo)** [lastimar-se] to feel sorry (about sthg).
lamentável [lamẽn'tavɛw] (*pl* **-eis**) *adj* **-1.** [lastimável] regrettable. **-2.** [deplorável] deplorable.
lamentavelmente [lamẽntavew'mẽntʃi] *adv* unfortunately.
lamento [la'mẽntu] *m* lament.
lâmina ['lãmina] *f* **-1.** [ger] blade; **~ de barbear** razor blade. **-2.** [de vidro] slide.
laminado, da [lami'nadu, da] *adj* laminated.
◆ **laminado** *m* laminate.
laminar [4] [lami'na(x)] *vt* [reduzir a lâminas] to shave.
lâmpada ['lãnpada] *f* **-1.** [bulbo] light; **~ (elétrica)** (light) bulb; **~ fluorescente** fluorescent light bulb; **~ neon** neon light. **-2.** [aparelho] lamp; **~ de mesa** table lamp.
lamparina [lãnpa'rina] *f* [aparelho] blowlamp.
lampejar [4] [lãmpe'ʒa(x)] *vi* to flash.
lampejo [lãn'peʒu] *m* flash.
lampião [lãn'pjãw] (*pl* **-ões**) *m* street light.
lamúria [la'murja] *f* lamentation.
lamuriante [lamu'rjãntʃi] *adj* whining.
lamuriar-se [16] [lamu'rjaxsi] *vp*: **~ (de algo)** to moan (about sthg).
LAN (*abrev de* **Local Area Network**) *f* LAN.
lança ['lãnsa] *f* spear.
lançador, ra [lãnsa'do(x), ra] *m, f* **-1.** *ESP* thrower. **-2.** [em leilão] bidder. **-3.** *COM* promoter.
lançamento [lãnsa'mẽntu] *m* **-1.** [arremesso] throw. **-2.** *ESP*: **~ de dardos** to play darts; **~ de disco** discus throwing. **-3.** [ger] launch; **novo ~** [livro] new title. **-4.** [escrituração] entry. **-5.** [de impostos] rate.

lança-perfume [ˌlãnsapex'fumi] (*pl* **lança-perfumes**) *m canister of perfumed ethyl chloride used during carnival.*

lançar [13] [lã'sa(x)] *vt* **-1.** [ger] to launch. **-2.** [atirar] to throw. **-3.** [pôr em voga] to start. **-4.** [escriturar] to enter. **-5.** [impostos] to set. **-6.** [dirigir] to cast.

◆ **lançar-se** *vp* **-1.** [atirar-se] to throw o.s. **-2.** [iniciar-se]: **~-se em algo** to take up sthg; **~-se como algo** to set o.s.up as sthg.

lance ['lãnsi] *m* **-1.** [episódio, passagem] moment. **-2.** [fato] incident. **-3.** [em leilão] bid. **-4.** [no jogo - aposta] bet; [- jogada] play. **-5.** [de escada] staircase. **-6.** [de casas] terrace. **-7.** [rasgo] surge.

lancha ['lãnʃa] *f* **-1.** *NÁUT* launch; **~ salva-vidas** lifeboat. **-2.** *fam* [pé] large foot. **-3.** *fam* [calçado] large shoe; **este sapato está uma ~** this shoe is like a boat.

lanchar [4] [lã'ʃa(x)] ◇ *vt* to snack on. ◇ *vi* to have tea.

lanche ['lãnʃi] *m* [refeição ligeira] snack *(in the afternoon).*

lancheira [lãn'ʃejra] *f* lunch box.

lanchonete [lãnʃo'nɛtʃi] *f* snack bar.

lancinante [lãnsi'nãntʃi] *adj* piercing.

languidez [lãŋgi'deʒ] *f* [debilitação] langour.

lânguido, da ['lãŋgidu, da] *adj* languid.

lanhar [4] [la'ɲa(x)] *vt* [ferir] to scratch.

◆ **lanhar-se** *vp* [ferir-se] to scratch o.s.

lanho ['lãɲu] *m* scratch.

lanígero, ra [la'niʒeru, ra] *adj* [animal] woolly.

lanolina [lãno'lina] *f* lanolin.

lantejoula [lãnte'ʒola] *f* sequin.

lanterna [lãn'tɛxna] *f* **-1.** [aparelho] lantern; **~ elétrica** torch *UK*, flashlight *US*. **-2.** *AUTO* light.

lanterninha [lãntex'niɲa] *mf* usher.

laparoscopia [laparoʃko'pia] *f* laparoscopy.

La Paz [la'paʃ] *n* La Paz.

lapela [la'pɛla] *f* lapel.

lapidar [4] [lapi'da(x)] *vt* to polish.

lápide ['lapidʒi] *f* **-1.** [comemorativa] plaque. **-2.** [tumular] tombstone.

lápis ['lapiʃ] *m inv* pencil; **~ de cera** wax crayon; **~ de cor** colouring pencil; **~ de olho** eye pencil.

lapiseira [lapi'zejra] *f* pencil case.

lápis-lazúli [ˌlapiʃla'zuli] (*pl* **lápis-lazúlis**) *m* lapis-lazuli.

Lapônia [la'ponja] *f* Lapland.

lapso ['lapsu] *m* **-1.** [falta] mistake. **-2.** [espaço de tempo] lapse.

laptop ['lapitopi] (*pl* **laptops**) *m COMPUT* laptop.

laquê [la'ke] *m* hairspray.

laqueadura [lakja'dura] *f MED* tubal ligation.

laquear [15] [la'kja(x)] *vt* **-1.** [com laca] to gloss. **-2.** *MED* to ligate.

lar ['la(x)] (*pl* **-es**) *m* home.

laranja [la'rãnʒa] ◇ *f* [fruta] orange. ◇ *m* **-1.** [cor] orange. **-2.** *fam* [testa-de-ferro] scapegoat. ◇ *adj (inv)* [cor] orange.

laranjada [larãn'ʒada] *f* orangeade.

laranjal [larãn'ʒaw] (*pl* **-ais**) *m* orange grove.

laranjeira [larãn'ʒejra] *f* orange tree.

larápio [la'rapju] *m* thief.

lareira [la'rejra] *f* fireplace.

larga ['laxga] *f* ⊳ **largo**.

largada [lax'gada] *f* [em corrida] start; **dar a ~** to start.

largado, da [lax'gadu, da] *adj* neglected.

largar [14] [lax'ga(x)] ◇ *vt* **-1.** [ger] to leave. **-2.** [soltar] to loosen. **-3.** [deixar cair] to drop. **-4.** [pôr em liberdade] to release. **-5.** [deixar em paz] to leave alone. **-6.** *fam* [dar] to give; **~ a mão em alguém** to slap sb. ◇ *vi* **-1.** [deixar]: **~ de algo/de ser algo** to stop doing sthg/being sthg. **-2.** *NÁUT* to set sail.

◆ **largar-se** *vp* **-1.** [desprender-se] to untie o.s. from. **-2.** [ir] to go.

largo, ga ['laxgu, ga] *adj* **-1.** [grande de lado a lado] wide. **-2.** [folgado] loose. **-3.** *(antes de subst)* [extenso] great, large. **-4.** *(antes de subst)* [prolongado] long. **-5.** *(antes de subst)* [abundante] abundant.

◆ **largo** *m* [praça] square.

◆ **larga** *f*: **viver à larga** to live lavishly.

◆ **largas** *fpl*: **dar largas a algo** to give free rein to sthg.

◆ **ao largo** *loc adv*: **passar ao ~ (de)** to give a wide berth (to); **avistar algo ao ~** to make something out in the distance; **ao ~ da costa brasileira** off the Brazilian coast; **fazer-se ao ~** to head for the open sea.

largueza [lax'geza] *f* largesse; **com ~** with largesse.

largura [lax'gura] *f* width; **tem 3 metros de ~** it is 3 metres wide; **~ de banda** *COMPUT* bandwidth.

larica [la'rika] *f fam* [fome] hunger.

laringe [la'rĩnʒi] *f* larynx.

laringite [larĩn'ʒitʃi] *f* laryngitis.

larva ['laxva] *f* larva.

lasanha [la'zãɲa] *f* lasagne.

lasca ['laʃka] *f* sliver.

lascado, da [laʃ'kadu, da] *adj* [rachado] cracked.

◆ **lascado** *adv fam* [a toda] full speed.

lascar [12] [laʃ'ka(x)] ◇ *vt* **-1.** [rachar] to break. **-2.** *fam* [dar]: **~ algo em alguém** suddenly to do sthg to sb. **-3.** *fam* [lançar]: **~ algo em algo/alguém** to throw sthg at sthg/sb. ◇ *vi* [rachar] to crack.

◆ **de lascar** *loc adj fam* [terrível]: **ser/estar de ~** to be nasty.

lascívia [la'sivja] *f* lasciviousness.

lascivo, va [la'sivu, va] *adj* lascivious.

laser ['lejze(x)] (*pl* **-es**) ◇ *adj (inv)* ⊳ **raio**. ◇ *m (inv)* laser.

lassidão [lasi'dãw], **lassitude** [lasi'tudʒi] *f* [fadiga] lassitude.

lasso, ssa ['lasu, sa] *adj* **-1.** [fatigado] weary. **-2.** [bambo] weak.

lástima ['laʃtʃima] *f* **-1.** [pessoa]: **ser/estar uma ~** to be pathetic; [coisa] to be a disgrace. **-2.** [pena]: **é uma ~ (que)** it is a pity (that); **que ~!** what a pity!

lastimar [4] [laʃtʃi'ma(x)] *vt* **-1.** [lamentar] to

regret. **-2.** [ter pena de] to pity.
◆ **lastimar-se** *vp* [lamentar-se]: **~-se (de algo)** to moan (about sthg).
lastimável [laʃtʃi'mavɛw] (*pl* **-eis**) *adj* **-1.** [lamentável] regrettable. **-2.** [deplorável] disgraceful.
lastimoso, osa [laʃtʃi'mozu, ɔza] *adj* pitiful.
lastro ['laʃtru] *m* **-1.** NÁUT ballast. **-2.** FIN guaranty. **-3.** *fig* [base] grounding.
lastro ['laʃtro] *m* ECON standard.
lata ['lata] *f* **-1.** [material] tin. **-2.** [recipiente] can; **~ de conserva** tin; **~ de lixo** rubbish bin **-3.** *fam* **na ~** straight.
latada [la'tada] *f* [treliça] lattice.
latão [la'tãw] (*pl* **-ões**) *m* [material] brass.
lataria [lata'ria] *f* **-1.** AUTO bodywork. **-2.** [latas] large quantity of tins.
latejante [late'ʒãntʃi] *adj* throbbing.
latejar [4] [late'ʒa(x)] *vi* to throb.
latejo [la'teʒu] *m* throb.
latente [la'tẽntʃi] *adj* latent.
lateral [late'raw] (*pl* **-ais**) ◇ *adj* lateral. ◇ *m* FUT outfielder. ◇ *f* ESP [linha] sideline.
látex ['latɛks] *m inv* latex.
laticínio [latʃi'sinju] *m* dairy produce.
latido [la'tʃidu] *m* bark.
latifundiário, ria [latʃifũn'dʒjarju, rja] ◇ *adj* landed. ◇ *m, f* landowner.
latifúndio [latʃi'fũndʒju] *m* large property.
latim [la'tʃĩ] *m* Latin; **gastar o seu ~** to waste one's breath.
latino, na [la'tʃinu, na] ◇ *adj* Latin. ◇ *m, f* Latin.
latino-americano, latino-americana [la,tʃinwameri'kanu, la,tʃinwameri'kana] ◇ *adj* Latin American. ◇ *m, f* Latin American.
latir [6] [la'tʃi(x)] *vi* to bark.
latitude [latʃi'tudʒi] *f* **-1.** [ger] latitude. **-2.** [amplitude] capacity.
◆ **latitudes** *fpl* [região] latitudes.
lato, ta ['latu, ta] *adj* broad.
latrina [la'trina] *f* latrine.
latrocínio [latro'sinju] *m* larceny.
lauda ['lawda] *f* page.
laudatório, ria [lawda'tɔrju, rja] *adj* laudatory.
laudo ['lawdu] *m* **-1.** [parecer] verdict. **-2.** [documento] written verdict.
laureado, da [law'rjadu, da] *adj* laureate.
laurel [law'rɛw] (*pl* **-éis**) *m* award, prize.
lauto, ta ['lawtu, ta] *adj* [farto] sumptuous.
lava ['lava] *f* lava.
lavabo [la'vabu] *m* **-1.** [pia] washbasin. **-2.** [local] bathroom.
lavadeira [lava'dejra] *f* **-1.** [trabalhadora] washerwoman. **-2.** [libélula] dragonfly.
lavadora [lava'dora] *f* washing machine.
lavagem [la'vaʒẽ] (*pl* **-ns**) *f* **-1.** [limpeza] washing; **~ a seco** dry-cleaning. **-2.** MED washout. **-3.** PSIC: **~ cerebral** brainwashing. **-4.** FIN: **~ de dinheiro** money laundering. **-5.** *fam* ESP: **dar uma ~ num time** to wipe out a team. **-6.** [comida de porcos] swill.
La Valetta [lava'leta] *n* Valletta.
lavanda [la'vãnda] *f* **-1.** BOT lavender. **-2.** [colônia] lavender water. **-3.** [recipiente com água] finger bowl.
lavanderia [lavãnde'ria] *f* laundry.
lavar [4] [la'va(x)] *vt* to wash; **~ a seco** to dry-clean.
◆ **lavar-se** *vp* to wash o.s.
lavatório [lava'tɔrju] *m* **-1.** [pia] washbasin. **-2.** [toalete] cloakroom.
lavoura [la'vora] *f* cultivation.
lavrador, ra [lavra'do(x), ra] (*mpl* **-es**, *fpl* **-s**) *m, f* ploughman.
lavrar [4] [la'vra(x)] ◇ *vt* **-1.** [terra] to plough. **-2.** [sentença, escritura, contrato] to draw up. **-3.** [madeira] to plane. ◇ *vi* [alastrar-se] to rage.
laxante [la'ʃãntʃi] *adj* laxative.
lazer [la'ze(x)] *m* **-1.** [descanso] pleasure. **-2.** [tempo de folga] leisure.
LBV (*abrev de* **Legião da Boa Vontade**) *f Brazilian charitable organization for support of the needy.*
leal [le'aw] (*pl* **-ais**) *adj* loyal.
lealdade [leaw'dadʒi] *f* loyalty.
leão [le'ãw] (*pl* **-ões**) *m, f* lion.
◆ **Leão** *m* **-1.** ASTRO Leo. **-2.** *fig* [fisco]: **o Leão** the taxman.
leão-de-chácara [leãwdʒi'ʃakara] (*pl* **leões-de-chácara**) *m fam* bouncer.
leão-marinho [le,ãwma'riɲu] (*pl* **leões-marinhos**) *m* sea lion.
leasing ['lisĩŋ] *m* ECON leasing.
lebre ['lɛbri] *f* hare.
lecionar [4] [lesjo'na(x)] ◇ *vt* to teach. ◇ *vi* to teach.
legado [le'gadu] *m* **-1.** [herança] legacy. **-2.** [enviado] envoy.
legal [le'gaw] (*pl* **-ais**) ◇ *adj* **-1.** JUR legal. **-2.** *fam* [bom, bonito] cool. **-3.** [hora] official time. ◇ *adv fam* [bem] well.
legalidade [legali'dadʒi] *f* legality.
legalização [legaliza'sãw] (*pl* **-ões**) *f* legalization.
legalizar [4] [legali'za(x)] *vt* to legalize.
legar [14] [le'ga(x)] *vt* **-1.** JUR to bequeath. **-2.** [transmitir] to pass on.
legenda [le'ʒẽnda] *f* **-1.** [em foto, desenho *etc*] caption. **-2.** CINE subtitle. **-3.** POL *number identifying political party on ballot sheet*; **votar na ~** to vote for the party.
legendado, da [leʒẽn'dadu, da] *adj* **-1.** [filme] subtitled. **-2.** [fotos] captioned.
legendar [le'ʒẽnda(x)] *vt* **-1.** [filme] to subtitle. **-2.** [fotos] to caption.
legendário, ria [leʒẽn'darju, rja] *adj* legendary.
legião [le'ʒjãw] (*pl* **-ões**) *f* [de fãs, leitores] legion.
legislação [leʒiʒla'sãw] (*pl* **-ões**) *f* legislation.
legislador, ra [leʒiʒla'do(x), ra] *m, f* legislator.
legislar [4] [leʒiʒ'la(x)] ◇ *vi* to legislate. ◇ *vt* to legislate.
legislativo, va [leʒiʒla'tʃivu, va] *adj* legislative.
◆ **Legislativo** *m*: **o Legislativo** the legislature.

legislatura [leʒiʒla'tura] *f* **-1.** [corpo] legislature. **-2.** [período] term.

legista [le'ʒiʃta] *mf* **-1.** [jurista] legal expert. **-2.** [médico] forensic scientist.

legitimar [4] [leʒitʃi'ma(x)] *vt* [legalizar] to legitimize.

legitimidade [leʒitʃimi'dadʒi] *f* legitimacy.

legítimo, ma [le'ʒitʃimu, ma] *adj* **-1.** [ger] legitimate; **em legítima defesa** in legitimate defense. **-2.** [autêntico] authentic.

legível [le'ʒivɛw] (*pl* **-eis**) *adj* **-1.** [nítido] legible. **-2.** [agradável de ler] readable.

légua ['lɛgwa] *f* [medida] league.
◆ **léguas** *fpl fig* [grande distância] miles.

legume [le'gume] *m* vegetable.

leguminosa [legumi'nɔza] *f* BOT leguminous plant.
◆ **leguminosas** *fpl* BOT leguminosae.

lei ['lej] *f* **-1.** [ger] law; **ditar a ~** to lay down the law; **promulgar a ~** to uphold the law; **violar a ~** to break the law; **~ marcial** martial law; **~ trabalhista** industrial law; **~ da oferta e da procura** the laws of supply and demand. **-2.** [de um metal]: **prata de ~** hallmarked silver.

leiaute [lej'awtʃi] *m* layout.

leigo, ga ['lejgu, ga] <> *adj* **-1.** RELIG secular. **-2.** *fig* [imperito]: **ser ~ em algo** to be a layperson in sthg. <> *m, f* [pessoa imperita] layperson.

leilão [lej'lãw] (*pl* **-ões**) *m* auction.

leiloar [20] [lej'lwa(x)] *vt* to auction.

leiloeiro, ra [lej'lwejru, ra] *m, f* auctioneer.

leitão, toa [lej'tãw, toa] (*pl* **-ões**) *m, f* suckling pig.

leite ['lejtʃi] *m* milk; **~ em pó** powdered milk; **~ de côco** coconut milk; **~ condensado** condensed milk; **~ desnatado** OU **magro** skimmed milk; **~ integral** full-cream milk; **~ de magnésia** Milk of Magnesia; **~ de soja** soya milk.

leiteiro, ra [lej'tejru, ra] <> *adj* [que produz leite] dairy. <> *m, f* [pessoa] milkman (*f* milkwoman).
◆ **leiteira** *f* **-1.** [para ferver leite] milk pan. **-2.** [para servir leite] milk jug.

leiteria [lejte'ria] *f* **-1.** [em fazenda] dairy. **-2.** [lanchonete] milk bar.

leito ['lejtu] *m* bed.

leitor, ra [lej'to(x), ra] (*mpl* **-es**, *fpl* **-s**) *m, f* **-1.** [quem lê] reader. **-2.** UNIV visiting lecturer.

leitoso, osa [lej'tozu, ɔza] *adj* milky.

leitura [lej'tura] *f* reading; **ter muita ~** to be well-read; **~ dinâmica** speed reading.

lelé [le'lɛ] *adj fam*: **~ (da cuca)** bonkers.

lema ['lema] *m* **-1.** [norma] maxim. **-2.** [político] motto.

lembrança [lẽn'brãsa] *f* **-1.** [recordação] souvenir. **-2.** [presente] gift.
◆ **lembranças** *fpl* [cumprimentos]: **(dê) ~s minhas à sua família** (give) my regards to your family.

lembrar [4] [lẽm'bra(x)] <> *vt* **-1.** [recordar] to remember. **-2.** [parecer] to look like. **-3.** [trazer à memória]: **~ algo a alguém** to remind sb of sthg. <> *vi* **-1.** [recordar]: **~ (de alguém/algo)** to remember (sb/sthg). **-2.** [advertir]: **~ a alguém de algo/de fazer algo** to remind sb of sthg/to do sthg; **~ a alguém (de) que** to remind sb that.
◆ **lembrar-se** *vp*: **~-se (de alguém/algo)** to remember (sb/sthg); **~-se (de) que** to remember that.

lembrete [lẽn'bretʃi] *m* memo.

leme ['lemi] *m* **-1.** [ger] helm. **-2.** [dispositivo] rudder.

lenço ['lẽnsu] *m* **-1.** [para limpar] handkerchief; **~ de papel** paper handkerchief, tissue. **-2.** [de cabeça] headscarf. **-3.** [de pescoço] neckerchief.

lençol [lẽn'sɔw] (*pl* **-óis**) *m* sheet; **~ d'água** water table; **estar em maus lençóis** *fig* to be in a fine mess.

lenda ['lẽnda] *f* **-1.** [história] legend. **-2.** *fig* [mentira] tall story.

lendário, ria [lẽn'darju, rja] *adj* legendary.

lêndea ['lẽndʒja] *f* nit.

lengalenga [lẽŋga'lẽŋga] *f* rigmarole.

lenha ['leɲa] *f* [para queimar] firewood; **botar ~ na fogueira** *fig* to add fuel to the fire; **fazer uma ~** [criar caso] to make a fuss.

lenhador [leɲa'do(x)] *m* woodcutter.

lenho ['leɲu] *m* **-1.** [tora] log. **-2.** [madeira] timber.

leninismo [leni'niʒmu] *m* Leninism.

leninista [leni'niʃta] <> *adj* Leninist. <> *mf* Leninist.

lenitivo, va [leni'tʃivu, va] *adj* [remédio, terapia] soothing.
◆ **lenitivo** *m* relief.

lenocínio [leno'sinju] *m* procuring.

lente ['lẽntʃi] *f* lens; **~ de aumento** magnifying glass; **~s de contato** contact lenses.

lentidão [lẽntʃi'dãw] *f* slowness.

lentilha [lẽn'tʃiʎa] *f* lentil.

lento, ta ['lẽntu, ta] *adj* slow.

leoa [le'oa] *f* ⊳ **leão**.

leões [le'õjʃ] *pl* ⊳ **leão**.

leonino, na [leo'ninu, na] <> *adj* **-1.** [caráter] leonine ; [contrato] fraudulent. **-2.** ASTRO Leo. <> *m, f* ASTRO Leo.

leopardo [ljo'paxdu] *m* leopard.

lépido, da ['lɛpidu, da] *adj* **-1.** [ágil] nimble. **-2.** [contente] happy.

leporino, na [lepo'rinu, na] *adj* ⊳ **lábio**.

lepra ['lɛpra] *f* leprosy.

leprosário [lepro'zarju] *m* leper colony.

leproso, osa [le'prozu, ɔza] <> *adj* leprous. <> *m, f* [pessoa] leper.

leque ['lɛki] *m* **-1.** [abano] fan. **-2.** *fig* [conjunto]: **um ~ de** a range of.

ler [42] ['le(x)] <> *vt* to read. <> *vi* to read.

lerdeza [lex'deza] *f* sluggishness.

lerdo, da ['lɛxdu, da] *adj* **-1.** [vagaroso] sluggish. **-2.** [idiota] slow.

lero-lero [lɛru'lɛru] *m* chit-chat.

lesado, da [le'zadu, da] *adj* [ferido] injured.

lesão [le'zãw] (*pl* **-ões**) *f* **-1.** MED lesion; **~ corporal** grievous bodily harm. **-2.** JUR [violação] violation.

lesar [4] [le'za(x)] *vt* **-1.** *fig* [prejudicar, enganar] to cheat. **-2.** *JUR* [violar] to violate.

lésbico, ca ['lɛʒbiku, ka] *adj* lesbian.
◆ **lésbica** *f* lesbian.

lesionar [4] [lezjo'na(x)] *vt* to injure.

lesivo, va [le'zivu, va] *adj* [prejudicial] harmful.

lesma ['leʒma] *f* **-1.** [animal] slug. **-2.** *fig* [pessoa] sluggard.

leso, sa [le'zu, za] *adj* [contundido] injured.

leste ['lɛʃtʃi] ◇ *m (inv)* [ger] east; **a ~ (de)** to the east (of); **para ~** eastward. ◇ *adj (inv)* easterly.

letal [le'taw] (*pl* **-ais**) *adj* lethal.

letão, tã [le'tãw, tã] ◇ *adj* Latvian. ◇ *m, f* Latvian.
◆ **letão** *m* [língua] Latvian.

letargia [letax'ʒia] *f* lethargy.

letárgico, ca [le'taxʒiku, ka] *adj* lethargic.

letivo, va [le'tʃivu, va] *adj* school *(antes de subst)*; **ano ~** academic year, school year.

Letônia [le'tonja] *n* Latvia.

letra ['letra] *f* **-1.** [caractere] letter; **~ de fôrma** block capital *(pl)*; **~ de imprensa** print; **~ maiúscula/minúscula** capital/small letter; **com todas as ~ s** [explicitamente] in detail. **-2.** [caligrafia] handwriting; **~ de mão** handwriting; **~ de médico** *fig* scrawl. **-3.** [de música] lyrics *(pl)*. **-4.** *COM*: **~ de câmbio** bill of exchange.
◆ **letras** *fpl* **-1.** [curso] arts. **-2.** [literatura] literature.
◆ **à letra, ao pé da letra** *loc adv* **-1.** [literalmente] literally. **-2.** [rigorosamente] to the letter.
◆ **de letra** *loc adv*: **tirar algo de ~** to do sthg with one's eyes closed.

letrado, da [le'tradu, da] *adj* **-1.** [culto] lettered. **-2.** [versado em literatura] well read.

letreiro [le'trejru] *m* notice; **~ luminoso** neon sign.

léu ['lɛw] ◆ **ao léu** *loc adv* **-1.** [à toa] aimlessly. **-2.** [à mostra] uncovered.

leucemia [lewse'mia] *f* leukaemia *UK*, leukemia *US*.

leva ['lɛva] *f* [conjunto] batch.

levadiço [leva'dʒisu] *adj* ▷ **ponte**.

levado, da [le'vadu, da] *adj*: **~ (da breca)** unruly.

leva-e-traz [ˌlɛvi'traʃ] ◇ *mf (inv)* [pessoa] gossip. ◇ *m (inv)* [fofoca] gossip.

levantador, ra [levãnta'do(x), ra] *m, f ESP*: **~ de pesos** weightlifter.

levantamento [levãnta'mẽntu] *m* **-1.** [pesquisa] survey. **-2.** [inventário] inventory. **-3.** *ESP*: **~ de pesos** weightlifting.

levantar [4] [levãn'ta(x)] ◇ *vt* **-1.** [ger] to raise; **~ os olhos** to look up. **-2.** [do chão] to lift; **~ vôo** to take off. **-3.** [tornar mais alto] to lift up. **-4.** [coletar] to collect. **-5.** [inventariar] to count. ◇ *vi* **-1.** [ficar de pé] to stand. **-2.** [sair da cama] to get up. **-3.** [avivar] to cheer.
◆ **levantar-se** *vp* **-1.** [ficar de pé] to stand up. **-2.** [sair da cama] to get up.

levante [le'vãntʃi] *m* **-1.** [revolta] uprising. **-2.** [leste] east.

levar [4] [le'va(x)] *vt* **-1.** [ger] to take; **isso leva algum tempo** that will take some time; **~ adiante** to carry on; **~ a cabo** to carry out. **-2.** [carregar] to carry. **-3.** [induzir] to lead; **~ alguém a algo/a fazer algo** to bring sb to sthg/to do sthg; **deixar-se ~ por algo** to let o.s. be led by sthg. **-4.** [retirar] to take away. **-5.** [lidar com] to deal with. **-6.** [vida]: **ele leva uma vida dura** he has a hard life; **~ a vida na flauta** to take life as it comes. **-7.** [susto, surra]: **~ um susto** to get a fright; **~ uma surra** to take a beating. **-8.** [ganhar] to win.

leve ['lɛvi] *adj* light; **de ~** lightly.

levedo [le'vedu] *m*, **levedura** *f* [leve'dura] yeast.

levemente [levi'mẽntʃi] *adv* lightly.

leveza [le'veza] *f* lightness.

leviandade [levjãn'dadʒi] *f* **-1.** [imprudência] rashness. **-2.** [falta de seriedade] frivolity.

leviano, na [le'vjanu, na] *adj* **-1.** [imprudente] rash. **-2.** [sem seriedade] frivolous.

levitar [4] [levi'ta(x)] *vi* to levitate.

lexical [leksi'kaw] (*pl* **-ais**) *adj* [função, unidade] lexical.

léxico, ca ['lɛksiku, ka] *adj* [análise, família] lexical.
◆ **léxico** *m* [vocabulário] lexicon.

lexicografia [leksikogra'fia] *f* lexicography.

lexicógrafo, fa [leksi'kografu, fa] *m* lexicographer.

lexicologia [leksikolo'ʒia] *f* lexicology.

lexicólogo, ga [leksi'kɔlogu, ga] *m* lexicologist.

lhama ['ʎãma] *mf* llama.

lhe [ʎe] (*pl* **lhes**) *pron pess* **-1.** [a ele, ela] (to) him/her/it; **dei-~ um presente** I gave him/her a present; **Maria ~ contou um segredo** Maria told him/her a secret; **acertaram-~ um tiro** they shot him/her; **isto lhes custou caro** this cost them a lot of money **-2.** [a você] (to) you; **telefonei-~ ontem** I phoned you yesterday; **o que ~ aconteceu?** what's happened to you?; **ouçam bem o que lhes digo!** listen carefully to what I say! **-3.** [indicando posse - dele, dela] his (*f* her); **roubaram-~ o carro** they stole his/her car; **ardia-lhes a vista** their eyes were stinging; [- de você] your; **beijei-~ as faces** I kissed your cheeks; **não lhes pesa a consciência?** doesn't your conscience trouble you? **-4.** [para enfatizar - a ele, ela] his (*f* her); **não sei como ele agüenta as confusões que sua namorada ~ a pronta** I don't know how he puts up with his girlfriend's nonsense; [- a você] you; **não sei como você agüenta as confusões que sua namorada ~ apronta** I don't know how you put up with your girlfriend's nonsense.

lhufas ['ʎufaʃ] *pron indef fam* zilch.

lia ['lia] *f* sediment.

liame ['ljãmi] *m* tie.

libanês, esa [liba'neʃ, eza] ◇ *adj* Lebanese. ◇ *m, f* Lebanese.

Líbano ['libanu] *n*: **o ~** Lebanon.

libelo [li'bɛlu] *m* **-1.** [ger] lampoon. **-2.** *JUR* indictment.

libélula [li'bɛlula] *f* dragonfly.

liberação [libera'sãw] *f* **-1.** [ger] release. **-2.** [libertação] liberation. **-3.** [de preços, câmbio] freedom from controls. **-4.** [de cheque] clearing. **-5.** [do aborto] legalization.
liberal [libe'raw] (*pl* **-ais**) <> *adj* liberal. <> *mf* POL liberal.
liberalidade [liberali'dadʒi] *f* [generosidade] liberality.
liberalismo [libera'liʒmu] *m* liberalism.
liberalização [liberaliza'sãw] *f* freedom from controls.
liberalizar [4] [liberali'za(x)] *vt* [preços, mercado] to liberalize.
liberar [4] [libe'ra(x)] *vt* **-1.** [ger] to release; ~ **alguém de algo** to release sb from sthg. **-2.** [libertar] to release. **-3.** [preço, câmbio] to free from controls. **-4.** [cheque] to clear. **-5.** [aborto] to legalize.
liberdade [libex'dadʒi] *f* freedom; **dar ~ a alguém (para fazer algo)** to give sb the freedom (to do sthg); **estar em ~** to be free; **pôr em ~** to set free; **ter ~ para fazer algo** to be at liberty to do sthg; **tomar a ~ de fazer algo** to take the liberty of doing sthg; **estar em ~ condicional** to be on parole; **~ de expressão** freedom of speech; **~ de imprensa** freedom of press; **~ de opinião** freedom of thought; **~ sob fiança** release on bail.
◆ **liberdades** *fpl* liberties; **tomar ~ com alguém** to take liberties with sb.
Libéria [li'bɛrja] *n* Liberia.
líbero ['liberu] *m* FUT sweeper.
libertação [libex'tasãw] (*pl* **-ões**) *f* liberation.
libertador, ra [libexta'do(x), ra] <> *adj* liberating. <> *m, f* liberator.
libertar [4] [libex'ta(x)] *vt* [tornar livre] to liberate.
libertinagem [libextʃi'naʒẽ] *f* loose living.
libertino, na [libex'tʃinu, na] <> *adj* libertine. <> *m, f* libertine.
liberto, ta [li'bextu, ta] <> *adj* **-1.** [escravo] liberated. **-2.** [salvo] free. <> *m,f* [escravo] freedman (*f* freedwoman).
Líbia ['libja] *n* Libya.
libidinoso, osa [libidʒi'nozu, ɔza] *adj* libidinous.
libido [li'bidu] *f* libido.
líbio, bia ['libju, bja] <> *adj* Libyan. <> *m, f* Libyan.
libra ['libra] *f* pound; **~ (esterlina)** pound (sterling).
◆ **Libra** *m* ASTRO Libra; **ser Libra** to be a Libran.
libreto [li'bretu] *m* libretto.
Libreville [ˌlibre'vili] *n* Libreville.
libriano, na [li'brjanu, na] <> *adj* Libran. <> *m, f* Libran.
lição [li'sãw] (*pl* **-ões**) *f* **-1.** EDUC lesson. **-2.** *fig* [ensinamento] lesson; **dar uma ~ a alguém** to teach sb a lesson; **servir de ~ a alguém** to be a lesson to sb. **-3.** *fig* [repreensão]**: dar uma ~ em alguém** to teach sb a lesson.
licença [li'sẽnsa] *f* **-1.** [permissão] permission; **dar ~ a alguém (para fazer algo)** to give sb permission (to do sthg); **com ~** excuse me; **~ poética** poetic licence. **-2.** [de trabalho] permit; **estar de ~** to be on leave; **tirar ~** to go on leave. **-3.** [documento] licence *UK*, license *US*.
licença-maternidade [li'sẽnsa'matexni'dadʒi] (*pl* **licenças-maternidade**) *f* maternity leave.
licença-prêmio [liˌsẽnsa'premju] (*pl* **licenças-prêmio**) *f six-months' leave from work, awarded every five years.*
licenciado, da [lisẽ'sjadu, da] <> *adj* **-1.** UNIV graduated. **-2.** [do trabalho] on leave. <> *m, f* UNIV graduate.
licenciar [16] [lisẽn'sja(x)] *vt* [do trabalho] to allow time off work.
◆ **licenciar-se** *vp* **-1.** UNIV: **~-se (em algo)** to obtain a degree (in sthg). **-2.** [do trabalho] to go on leave.
licenciatura [lisẽnsja'tura] *f* **-1.** [grau] degree. **-2.** [curso] degree course.
licencioso, osa [lisẽn'sjozu, ɔza] *adj* [obsceno] licentious.
licitação [lisita'sãw] (*pl* **-ões**) *f* **-1.** [em leilão] bid. **-2.** [concorrência] tender; **abrir uma ~** to put a project out to tender; **vencer uma ~** to win a tender.
licitante [lisi'tãntʃi] *mf* bidder.
lícito, ta ['lisitu, ta] *adj* **-1.** [legal] lawful. **-2.** [correto] licit.
lições [li'sõiʃ] *pl* ▷ **lição.**
licor [li'ko(x)] (*pl* **-es**) *m* liqueur.
licoroso, osa [liko'rozu, ɔza] *adj* sweet and strong.
lida ['lida] *f* **-1.** [trabalho] toil. **-2.** [leitura] read; **dar uma ~ em algo** to have a read of sthg.
lidar [4] [li'da(x)] *vi*: **~ com alguém/algo** [conviver com] to deal with sb/sthg; [tratar] to deal with sb/sthg; [trabalhar com] to deal with sb/sthg.
lide ['lidʒi] *f* **-1.** [combate] battle. **-2.** JUR case.
líder ['lide(x)] (*pl* **-es**) *mf* leader.
liderança [lide'rãnsa] *f* leadership.
liderar [4] [lide'ra(x)] *vt* to lead.
lido, da ['lidu, da] <> *pp* ▷ **ler.** <> *adj*: **muito ~** [culto] well read; [autor, obra] much read.
lifting ['liftĩŋ] *m* facelift.
liga ['liga] *f* **-1.** [associação] league. **-2.** [de meias] garter. **-3.** [de metais] alloy.
ligação [liga'sãw] (*pl* **-ões**) *f* **-1.** [ger] connection; **fazer a ~ entre algo e algo** to connect sthg with sthg. **-2.** TELEC (telephone) call; **a ~ caiu** we have been cut off; **completar a ~** to get through (on the phone); **fazer uma ~ (para alguém)** to make a call (to sb). **-3.** [relacionamento - amoroso] liaison; [- profissional] relationship.
ligado, da [li'gadu, da] *adj* **-1.** [ger] connected. **-2.** [absorto] immersed; **ser ~ em algo** to be knowledgeable in sthg. **-3.** [afeiçoado] attached.
◆ **ligada** *f* TELEC phonecall; **dar uma ~ para alguém** to call sb.
ligadura [liga'dura] *f* **-1.** [atadura] bandage. **-2.** MÚS ligature.

ligamento [liga'mẽntu] *m* **-1.** ANAT ligament. **-2.** MED: **~ de trompas** tubal ligation.

ligar [14] [li'ga(x)] ◇ *vt* **-1.** [ger] to connect. **-2.** [unir] to connect, to join. **-3.** [criar vínculos] to tie. **-4.** [dar importância a]: **não ~ a mínima (para alguém/algo)** to not pay the least bit of attention to sb/sthg. ◇ *vi* **-1.** [telefonar] to call; **~ para alguém/algum lugar** to call sb/somewhere (on the phone). **-2.** [dar importância] to care; **~ para alguém/algo** to care about sb/sthg. **-3.** [dar atenção] to notice; **~ para alguém/algo** to notice sb/sthg.

◆ **ligar-se** *vp* **-1.** [unir-se] to unite; **~-se a alguém/algo** to unite o.s. to sb/sthg. **-2.** [relacionar-se]: **~-se a algo** to be connected to sthg. **-3.** [afeiçoar-se] to become attached.

ligeireza [liʒej'reza] *f* **-1.** [rapidez] lightness. **-2.** [agilidade] agility.

ligeiro, ra [li'ʒejru, ra] *adj* **-1.** [rápido] light. **-2.** [ágil] agile. **-3.** *(antes de subst) fig* [sutil] slight.

◆ **ligeiro** *adv* **-1.** [rapidamente] swiftly. **-2.** [com agilidade] nimbly.

lilás [li'laʃ] (*pl* **lilases**) ◇ *adj* [cor] lilac. ◇ *m* lilac.

lima ['lima] *f* **-1.** [fruta] lime. **-2.** [ferramenta] file.

Lima ['lima] *n* Lima.

limão [li'mãw] (*pl* **-ões**) *m* lemon.

limbo ['lĩnbu] *m*: **estar no ~** *fig* to be in limbo.

limenho, nha [li'mẽɲu, ɲa] ◇ *adj* Lima *(antes de subst)*. ◇ *m, f* person from Lima.

limiar [li'mja(x)] *m* threshold.

liminar [4] [li'mi'na(x)] *f* JUR preliminary verdict.

limitação [limita'sãw] (*pl* **-ões**) *f* limitation.

limitado, da [limi'tadu, da] *adj* limited.

limitar [4] [limi'ta(x)] *vt* [restringir] to limit.

◆ **limitar-se** *vp* **-1.** [restringir-se]: **~-se a fazer algo** to limit o.s. to doing sthg. **-2.** [confinar-se]: **~-se com algo** to border on sthg.

limite [li'mitʃi] *m* [ger] limit; **~ de idade** age limit; **passar dos ~s** to go too far.

limítrofe [li'mitrofi] *adj* bordering.

limo ['limu] *m* BOT slime.

limoeiro [li'mwejru] *m* lemon tree.

limões [li'mõiʃ] *pl* ▷ **limão**.

limonada [limo'nada] *f* lemonade *UK*, lemon soda *US*.

limpador [lĩnpa'do(x)] (*pl* **-es**) *m* cleaner; **~ de chaminé** chimney sweep; **~ de pára-brisas** windscreen wiper *UK*, windshield wiper *US*.

limpa-pés [ˌlĩnpa'pɛʃ] *m inv* boot scraper.

limpar [4] [lĩm'pa(x)] *vt* **-1.** [ger] to clean. **-2.** *fig* [elevar]: **~ a imagem de alguém/algo** to clean up sb's/sthg's image. **-3.** [enxugar] to dry. **-4.** [esvaziar] to clean. **-5.** [roubar] to clean out. **-6.** *fig* [livrar] to rid.

◆ **limpar-se** *vp* **-1.** [assear-se] to wash o.s. **-2.** [moralmente] to make a clean start.

limpeza [lĩn'peza] *f* **-1.** [estado] cleanliness. **-2.** [ato] cleaning; **fazer uma ~ em algo** [livrar de excessos] to clear sthg out; [livrar de maus elemento] to clean sthg up; [roubar] to clean sthg out; **~ de pele** skin cleansing; **~ pública** refuse collection. **-3.** [esmero] neatness.

límpido, da ['lĩmpidu, da] *adj* **-1.** [translúcido] limpid. **-2.** [nítido] clear.

limpo, pa ['lĩnpu, pa] ◇ *pp* ▷ **limpar.** ◇ *adj* **-1.** [asseado] clean. **-2.** [esmerado] neat; **passar a ~** to make a clean copy. **-3.** *fig* [honrado] blameless. **-4.** [desanuviado] clear. **-5.** [sem dinheiro] broke. **-6.** [sem descontos]: **recebi 100 mil ~s** I received 100,000 clear. **-7.** *loc*: **tirar a ~** to get to the bottom of.

◆ **limpa** *f* **-1.** [limpeza]: **dar uma ~ em algo** to have a clean in sthg. **-2.** *fam fig* [roubo]: **fazer uma ~ (em algo)** to clean (sthg) out.

limusine [limu'zini] *f* limousine.

lince ['lĩnsi] *m* lynx; **ter olhos de ~** to have eyes like a hawk.

linchamento [lĩnʃa'mẽntu] *m* lynching.

linchar [4] [lĩn'ʃa(x)] *vt* to lynch.

lindeza [lĩn'deza] *f* beauty.

lindo, da ['lĩndu, da] *adj* beautiful; **ser ~ de morrer** *fam* to be a knockout.

linear [li'nja(x)] *adj* linear.

linearidade [linja'ridadʒi] *f* linearity.

linfático, ca [lĩn'fatʃiku, ka] *adj* lymphatic.

lingerie [lãnʒe'xi] *f* lingerie.

lingote [lĩŋ'gɔtʃi] *m* ingot.

língua ['lĩŋgwa] *f* **-1.** [órgão] tongue; **ter ~ presa** to be tongue-tied; **dar com a ~ nos dentes** to spill the beans; **ficar de ~ de fora** to be exhausted; **pagar pela ~** to pay dearly; **estar na ponta da ~** to be on the tip of one's tongue; **ter uma ~ comprida** to be a gossip; **dobrar a ~** to mind what one says. **-2.** [idioma] language; **~ materna** mother tongue; **~ morta** dead language.

LÍNGUA PORTUGUESA

The Portuguese language is spoken in Europe (Portugal), South America (Brazil), Africa (Cape Verde, São Tomé and Príncipe, Angola, Mozambique, Guinea-Bissau) and Asia (East Timor, Goa, and Macao). It is the sixth most spoken language in the world, mostly through the 200 million speakers of Portuguese in Brazil. Brazilian Portuguese has acquired specific characteristics through the incorporation of many words mainly of African and indigenous origin. It has, therefore, many differences in pronunciation, spelling, vocabulary and even grammar, in relation to the Portuguese spoken in other parts of the world, although it remains essentially the same language.

linguado [lĩŋ'gwadu] *m* [peixe] (Brazilian) flounder.

linguagem [lĩŋ'gwaʒẽj] (*pl* **-ns**) *f* language; **~ de máquina** machine language; **~ de programação** programming language.

linguajar [lĩŋgwa'ʒa(x)] *m* language.

linguarudo, da [lĩŋgwa'rudu, da] ◇ *adj* gossipy. ◇ *m, f* gossip.

lingüeta [lĩŋ'gweta] *f* **-1.** [de fechadura] catch. **-2.** [balança] pointer.

lingüiça [lĩŋˈgwisa] *f* chorizo; **encher** ~ *fam* to waffle.
lingüista [liŋˈgwiʃta] *mf* linguist.
lingüístico, ca [liŋˈgwiʃtʃiku, ka] *adj* linguistic.
◆ **lingüística** *f* linguistics *(pl)*.
linha [ˈlĩɲa] *f* **-1.** [ger] line; **as ~s gerais de algo** the general outlines of sthg; **em ~s gerais** in general terms; **~ de mira** line of sight; **~ de saque** service line; **~ de crédito** credit line; **~s inimigas** enemy lines; **~ de fogo** firing line; **~ de montagem** assembly line; **~ cruzada** crossed line; **não dar ~** to be dead; **~ de conduta** code of conduct; **andar na ~** *fig* to toe the line; **sair da ~** *fig* to be out of line. **-2.** [fio de costura] thread. **-3.** [via] route; **~ aérea** airline; **~ férrea** railway line *UK*, railroad *US*. **-4.** [elegância] flair; **é um homem de ~** he has a flair for things; **portar-se/vestir-se com muita ~** to behave/dress o.s. with a lot of flair; **perder a ~** to lose face. **-5.** *COMPUT*: **~ de comando** command line; **~ dedicada** dedicated line; **~ discada** dial-up line.
linhaça [liˈɲasa] *f* linseed.
linha-dura [ˌliɲaˈdura] (*pl* **linhas-duras**) ◇ *mf* hardliner. ◇ *adj (inv)* hard-line.
linhagem [liˈɲaʒẽ] *f* lineage.
linho [ˈlĩɲu] *m* **-1.** [tecido] linen. **-2.** [planta] flax.
link [ˈliŋnki] (*pl* **links**) *m* *COMPUT* link.
linóleo [liˈnɔlju] *m* linoleum.
lipoaspiração [lipuˈaʃpirasãw] (*pl* **-ões**) *f* liposuction.
liquefazer [31] [likefaˈze(x)] *vt* **-1.** [ger] to melt. **-2.** [tornar líquido] to liquefy.
◆ **liquefazer-se** *vp* to melt.
liquefeito, ta [likeˈfejtu, ta] ◇ *pp* ▷ **liquefazer**. ◇ *adj* molten.
líquen [ˈlikẽ] *m* *BOT* lichen.
liquidação [likidaˈsãw] (*pl* **-ões**) *f* **-1.** [dissolução] settlement. **-2.** *FIN* liquidation. **-3.** *COM* clearance sale; **(estar) em ~** (to be) in liquidation. **-4.** [destruição] elimination.
liquidar [4] [likiˈda(x)] ◇ *vt* **-1.** [ger] to liquidate. **-2.** [dissolver] to settle. **-3.** [destruir] to eliminate. ◇ *vi* **-1.** *COM* to hold a clearance sale. **-2.**: **~ com alguém/algo** [destruir] to destroy sb/sthg.
liquidez [likiˈdejʃ] *f* *ECON* liquidity.
liqüidificador [likwidʒifikaˈdo(x)] *m* liquidizer.
liqüidificar [likwidʒifiˈka(x)] *vt* to liquidize.
líquido, da [ˈlikidu, ˈlikida] *adj* **-1.** [estado] liquid. **-2.** [valor] net; **peso ~** *COM* net weight.
◆ **líquido** *m* [fluido] liquid.
lira [ˈlira] *f* **-1.** [instrumento] lyre. **-2.** *fig* [poesia] lyric poem. **-3.** [moeda] lira.
lírico, ca [ˈliriku, ka] *adj* **-1.** [gênero] lyrical. **-2.** *fig* [romântico] romantic.
◆ **lírica** *f* [coleção de poesia] lyrical poetry.
lírio [ˈlirju] *m* lily.
lírio-do-vale [ˌlirjuduˈvali] (*pl* **lírios-do-vale**) *m* lily of the valley.
lirismo [liˈriʒmu] *m* **-1.** [em poesia] lyricism. **-2.** *fig* [romantismo] romance.
Lisboa [liʒˈboa] *n* Lisbon.
lisboeta [liʒˈbweta] ◇ *adj* Lisbon *(antes de subst)*. ◇ *mf person from Lisbon*.
liso, sa [ˈlizu, ˈliza] *adj* **-1.** [superfície] smooth. **-2.** [cabelo] straight. **-3.** [tecido] plain. **-4.** *fam* [sem dinheiro] broke.
lisonja [liˈzõnʒa] *f* flattery.
lisonjeador, ra [lisõnʒjaˈdo(x), ra] ◇ *adj* flattering. ◇ *m, f* flatterer.
lisonjear [15] [lizõnˈʒja(x)] *vt* to flatter.
lisonjeiro, ra [lizõnˈʒejru, ra] *adj* flattering.
lista [ˈliʃta] *f* **-1.** [relação] list; **~ civil** civil list; **~ negra** black list; **~ de discussão** newsgroup; **~ telefônica** telephone directory. **-2.** [listra] stripe.
listagem [liʃˈtaʒẽ] (*pl* **-ns**) *f* listing.
listar [4] [liʃˈta(x)] *vt* *COMPUT* to list.
listra [ˈliʃtra] *f* stripe.
listrado, da [liʃˈtradu, da], **listado, da** [iʃˈtadu, da] *adj* striped.
lisura [liˈzura] *f* [de superfície] smoothness.
literal [liteˈraw] (*pl* **-ais**) *adj* literal.
literalmente [literawˈmẽntʃi] *adv* literally.
literário, ria [liteˈrarju, liteˈrarja] *adj* literary.
literato, ta [liteˈratu, ta] *m* writer.
literatura [literaˈtura] *f* literature; **~ comparada** comparative literature; **~ de cordel** *popular fairground novelettes*; **~ de ficção** fiction writing; **~ de vanguarda** avant-garde writing.

LITERATURA BRASILEIRA

Although not very widespread because of language difficulties, Brazilian literature has a wealth of good writers and poets. The great names of modern Brazilian poetry include Carlos Drummond de Andrade (1902-1987) from Minas Gerais and João Cabral de Melo Neto (1920-1999) from Pernambuco. Within prose writing, foremost are the novels of Machado de Assis (1839-1908) from Rio de Janeiro, the leading exponent of nineteenth century realism, those of Gumarães Rosa (1908-1967) from Minas Gerais, and those of Jorge Amado (1912-2001) from Bahia, the best known and most widely translated Brazilian author.

litigar [14] [litʃiˈga(x)] ◇ *vt* [pleitear] to litigate. ◇ *vi* [abrir processo] to litigate.
litígio [liˈtʃiʒju] *m* **-1.** *JUR* [questão] litigation. **-2.** *fig* [disputa] quarrel.
litigioso, osa [litʃiˈʒozu, ɔza] *adj* *JUR* contentious.
litografia [litograˈfia] *f* **-1.** [técnica] lithography. **-2.** [gravura] lithograph.
litogravura [ˌlitograˈvura] *f* [gravura] lithograph.
litoral [litoˈraw] (*pl* **-ais**) ◇ *adj* [costeiro] coastal. ◇ *m* [beira-mar] coast.
litorâneo, nea [litoˈranju, nja] *adj* coastal.
litro [ˈlitru] *m* [medida] litre *UK*, liter *US*.
Lituânia [liˈtwãnja] *f* Lithuania.
lituano, na [liˈtwãnu, na] ◇ *adj* Lithuanian. ◇ *mf* Lithuanian.
◆ **lituano** *m* [língua] Lithuanian.
liturgia [lituxˈʒia] *f* liturgy.
lívido, da [ˈlividu, da] *adj* pallid.

livrar [4] [li'vra(x)] *vt* **-1.** [libertar] to free. **-2.** [salvar]: **~ alguém/algo de algo** to save sb/sthg from sthg.
livrar-se *vp* **-1.** [libertar-se]: **~-se (de alguém/algo)** to free o.s. (from sb/sthg). **-2.** : **~-se de algo** [salvar-se] to escape from sthg; [evitar] to avoid sthg.
livraria [livra'ria] *f* bookshop *UK*, bookstore *US*.
livre ['livri] *adj* **-1.** [ger] free. **-2.** [independente] independent; **de ~ e espontânea vontade** of one's own free will. **-3.** [permitido] free. **-4.** [solto] free. **-5.** [isento]: **~ de algo** free of sthg; **~ de impostos** tax-free.
livre-arbítrio [ˌlivrjax'bitrju] (*pl* **livres-arbítrios**) *m* free will.
livre-docência [ˌlivrido'sẽnsja] (*pl* **livres-docências**) *f* [título universitário] *entitlement to teach and examine university lecturers.*
livre-docente ['livri'do'sẽntʃi] (*pl* **-s**) *mf* ≃ research professor. <> *m* [título] ≃ research professor.
livre-iniciativa ['livri'inisja'tʃiva] (*pl* **-s**) *m* ECON free enterprise.
livreiro, ra [liv'rejru, ra] *m,f* bookseller.
livre-pensador, ra [ˌlivripẽnsa'do(x), ra] (*pl* **livres-pensadores** *m* freethinker.
livresco, ca [li'vreʃku, ka] *adj* book *(antes de subst).*
livro ['livru] *m* **-1.** [ger] book; **~ de bolso** pocketbook; **~ brochado** paperback; **~ de capa dura** hardback; **~ de cozinha** cookery book; **~ didático** text book; **~ de cabeceira** favourite reading. **-2.** *loc*: **ser um ~ aberto** to be an open book.
livro-caixa [ˌlivro'kajʃa] (*pl* **livros-caixas**) *m* cash book.
lixa ['liʃa] *f* **-1.** [papel] sandpaper. **-2.** [de ferro] file; **~ de unhas** nail file.
lixadeira [liʃa'dejra] *f* sander.
lixar [4] [li'ʃa(x)] *vt* **-1.** [madeira] to sand. **-2.** [unhas] to file.
lixar-se *vp fam* [não se incomodar]: **ele está se lixando com a demissão** he couldn't care less about the resignation.
lixeira [li'ʃejra] *f* **-1.** [em prédio] rubbish chute *UK*, garbage chute *US*. **-2.** [local] rubbish dump *UK*, garbage dump *US*.
lixeiro [li'ʃejru] *m* refuse collector *UK*, dustman *UK*, garbage collector *US*.
lixo ['liʃu] *m* **-1.** [restos] rubbish *UK*, garbage *US*; **~ atômico** nuclear waste. **-2.** [coisa sem valor] rubbish *UK*, garbage *US*; **estar um ~** [estar ruim, feio] to be rubbish.
-lo [lu] *pron* [pessoa] him; [coisa] it; [você] you.
lobby ['lɔbi] (*pl* **lobbies**) *m* POL lobby.
lobinho [lo'biɲu] *m* [aprendiz de escoteiro] cub scout.
lobisomem [lobi'zɔmẽ] (*pl* **-ns**) *m* werewolf.
lobista [lo'biʃta] *mf* lobbyist.
lobo ['lobu] *m* wolf.
lobo-do-mar [ˌlobudu'ma(x)] (*pl* **lobos-do-mar**) *m* sea dog, old salt.
lobotomia [loboto'mia] *f* lobotomy.
lóbulo ['lɔbulu] *m* lobe; **~ de orelha** ear lobe.
locação [loka'sãw] (*pl* **-ões**) *f* **-1.** [de carro, vídeo] hire, rental. **-2.** [de telefone, imóvel] rental. **-3.** CINE location.
locador, ra [loka'do(x), ra] *m* **-1.** [de imóvel] landlord. **-2.** [de carro] lessor.
locadora *f* [agência] hire *ou* rental company; **~ de vídeo** video hire *ou* rental shop.
local [lo'kaw] (*pl* **-ais**) <> *adj* local. <> *m* place.
localidade [lokali'dadʒi] *f* **-1.** [lugar] locality. **-2.** [povoado] town.
localização [lokaliza'sãw] (*pl* **-ões**) *f* **-1.** [ato] tracking down, localization. **-2.** [lugar] positioning.
localizar [4] [lokali'za(x)] *vt* **-1.** [encontrar] to find. **-2.** [limitar a certo local] to site.
localizar-se *vp* [situar-se] to be sited.
loção [lo'sãw] (*pl* **-ões**) *f* lotion; **~ após-barba** aftershave.
locatário, ria [loka'tarju, rja] *m* **-1.** [carro] lessee. **-2.** [imóvel] tenant.
locomoção [lokomo'sãw] (*pl* **-ões**) *f* locomotion.
locomotiva [lokomo'tʃiva] *f* locomotive.
locomover-se [5] [lokomo'vexsi] *vp* to move.
locução [loku'sãw] (*pl* **-ões**) *f* **-1.** [expressão] expression. **-2.** [dicção] diction. **-3.** GRAM phrase.
locutor, ra [loku'to(x), ra] (*mpl* **-es**, *fpl* **-s**) *m,f* [profissional] presenter.
lodaçal [loda'saw] (*pl* **-ais**) *m* [lamaçal] mud.
lodacento, ta [loda'sẽntu, ta] *adj* muddy.
lodo ['lodu] *m* mud.
lodoso, osa [lo'dozu, ɔza] *adj* = **lodacento**.
logaritmo [loga'ritʃimu] *m* logarithm.
lógico, ca ['lɔʒiku, ka] *adj* logical; **(é) ~!** of course!
lógica *f* **-1.** [ger] logic. **-2.** [raciocínio] reasoning.
log-in (*pl* **logins**) *m* COMPUT login.
logística [lo'ʒiʃtʃika] *f* logistics *(pl).*
logo ['lɔgu] <> *adv* **-1.** [sem demora] at once; **~ de saída** *ou* **de cara** straight away; **vem ~!** come at once! **-2.** [em breve] soon; **até ~!** see you later!; **~ mais** in a while. **-3.** [exatamente]: **~ agora** right now; **~ ali** right there. **-4.** [pouco]: **~ antes/depois** just before/after. <> *conj* [portanto] therefore.
logo que *loc adv* as soon as.
tão logo *loc adv* as soon as.
logomarca [logo'maxka] *f* logo.
logotipo [logo'tʃipu] *m* logo.
logradouro [logra'doru] *m* public area.
lograr [4] [lo'gra(x)] *vt* **-1.** [conseguir] to achieve; **~ fazer algo** to manage to do sthg. **-2.** [empulhar] to trick.
logro ['logru] *m* fraud.
loiro, ra ['lojru, ra] *adj* = **louro**.
loja ['lɔʒa] *f* **-1.** COM shop *UK*, store *US*; **~ de antiguidades** antique shop; **~ de brinquedos** toy shop; **~ de departamentos** department store; ~

de ferragens ironmonger's *UK*, hardware store *US*; ~ **de produtos naturais** health food store. **-2.** [maçônica] lodge.

lojista [lo'ʒiʃta] *mf* shopkeeper.

lombada [lõn'bada] *f* **-1.** [de livro] spine. **-2.** [de boi] fillet. **-3.** [no solo] ridge.

lombalgia [lõnbaw'ʒia] *f* backache.

lombar [lõn'ba(x)] *adj* lumbar.

lombinho [lõn'biɲu] *m* [carne de porco] pork fillet.

lombo ['lõnbu] *m* **-1.** [dorso] lower back. **-2.** [carne] loin. **-3.** [elevação] ridge.

lombriga [lõn'briga] *f* roundworm.

lona ['lona] *f* **-1.** [tecido] canvas. **-2.** [cobertura] tarpaulin. **-3.** [de pneu] layer. **-4.** *loc*: **estar na** ~ *fam* to be wiped out.

Londres ['lõndriʃ] *n* London.

londrino, na ['lõn'drinu, na] ◇ *adj* London *(antes de subst)*. ◇ *m, f* Londoner.

longamente [lõŋga'mẽntʃi] *adv* **-1.** [em grande extensão] for a long way. **-2.** [por muito tempo] for a long time.

longa-metragem [ˌlõŋgame'traʒẽ] (*pl* **longas-metragens**) *m*: **(filme de)** ~ feature-length film.

longe ['lõnʒi] ◇ *adv* far (away); **é ~?** is it far?; **ir ~ demais** *fig* [exceder-se] to go too far; **ver ~** *fig* [ter visão] to look far ahead. ◇ *adj* remote.

◆ **ao longe** *loc adv* **-1.** [no espaço] in the distance. **-2.** [no tempo] a long way.

◆ **de longe** *loc adv* **-1.** [no espaço] from far away. **-2.** [no tempo]: **vir de ~** to be longstanding. **-3.** [sem comparação] by far.

◆ **longe de** ◇ *loc conj* far from; ~ **disso** far from it. ◇ *loc prep* far from.

longevidade [lõnʒevi'dadʒi] *f* longevity.

longevo, va [lõnʒe'vu, va] *adj* **-1.** [muito idoso] elderly. **-2.** [duradouro] long-lived.

longínquo, qua [lõ'ʒĩŋkwu, kwa] *adj* **-1.** [no espaço] distant, remote. **-2.** [no tempo] distant.

longitude [lõnʒi'tudʒi] *f* GEOGR longitude.

longitudinal [lõnʒitudʒi'naw] (*pl* **-ais**) *adj* longitudinal.

longo, ga ['lõŋgu, ga] *adj* **-1.** [ger] long. **-2.** *(antes de subst)* [duradouro] lasting.

◆ **longo** *m* [vestido] long dress.

◆ **ao longo de** *loc prep* **-1.** [no sentido longitudinal] along. **-2.** [à beira de] alongside. **-3.** [no tempo]: **ao ~ dos anos** over the years.

lontra ['lõntra] *f* otter.

loquacidade [lokwasi'dadʒi] *m* loquaciousness.

loquaz [lo'kwaʒ] *adj* **-1.** [falador] talkative. **-2.** [eloqüente] eloquent.

lorde ['lɔxdʒi] *m* **-1.** [título] Lord. **-2.** *fig* [homem refinado] refined gentleman.

lordose [lox'dɔzi] *f* MED lordosis, curvature of the spine.

lorota [lo'rɔta] *f fam* fib.

losango [lo'zãŋgu] *m* diamond, lozenge.

lotação [lota'sãw] (*pl* **-ões**) *f* **-1.** [capacidade] capacity; ~ **esgotada** [cinema, teatro] sold out, full house. **-2.** [quadro de pessoal] number of personnel. **-3.** [veículo] minibus.

lotado, da [lo'tadu, da] *adj* [cheio] full, crowded.

lotar [4] [lo'ta(x)] ◇ *vt* [encher] to fill. ◇ *vi* [encher]: ~ **(de)** to fill (with).

lote ['lɔtʃi] *m* **-1.** [parte] parcel. **-2.** [conjunto] set. **-3.** [terreno] plot.

loteamento [lotʃja'mẽntu] *m* division into plots.

lotear [15] [lo'tʃja(x)] *vt* to divide into plots.

loteca [lo'tɛka] *f fam* football pools *UK*, lottery *US*.

loteria [lote'ria] *f* lottery; **ganhar na** ~ to win the lottery; **jogar na** ~ to play the lottery; ~ **esportiva** (football) pools *UK*, lottery *US*.

loto ['lɔtu] *m* lottery.

louça ['losa] *f* china; **de** ~ china *(antes de subst)*; **lavar/secar a** ~ to wash/dry the dishes; ~ **de cerâmica** ceramics; ~ **de jantar** dinner service.

louco, ca ['loku, ka] ◇ *adj* **-1.** [ger] crazy. **-2.** [insano] mad. **-3.** [transtornado] crazed; **deixar alguém** ~ to drive sb mad; **ficar ~ com algo** to go mad with sthg; ~ **de fome** crazed with hunger. **-4.** [furioso]: ~ **(da vida com)** spitting mad (at). **-5.** [apaixonado]: **ser ~ por alguém/algo** to be crazy about sb/sthg. **-6.** [excêntrico] weird. **-7.** [intenso] extreme. **-8.** [extraordinário] unbelievable. ◇ *m, f* [insano] lunatic; ~ **varrido** *ou* **de pedra** *fam* stark raving mad.

◆ **louca** *f*: **dar a louca em alguém** to go mad.

loucura [lo'kura] *f* **-1.** [insanidade] insanity. **-2.** [imprudência] lunacy, madness; **ser (uma) ~ fazer algo** to be madness to do sthg. **-3.** [extravagância] antics *(pl)*; **fazer ~s** to get up to antics. **-4.** [paixão] passion; **ter ~ por alguém/algo** to be mad about sb/sthg.

louro, ra ['loru, ra] ◇ *adj* [cabelo, pessoa] fair. ◇ *m, f* [pessoa] fair-haired person.

◆ **louro** *m* **-1.** [cor] fair, blond. **-2.** [árvore] laurel. **-3.** CULIN bay leaf. **-4.** [papagaio] polly parrot.

◆ **louros** *mpl fig* [glórias] laurels.

lousa ['loza] *f* **-1.** [quadro-negro] blackboard. **-2.** [pedra] slate; ~ **tumular** tombstone.

louva-a-deus [ˌlova'dewʃ] *m inv* praying mantis.

louvação [lova'sãw] (*pl* **-ões**) *f* **-1.** [louvor] praise. **-2.** LITER *popular poetry written for a special occasion, sometimes set to music.*

louvar [4] [lo'va(x)] ◇ *vt* **-1.** [elogiar] to praise. **-2.** [glorificar] to exalt. ◇ *vi*: ~ **a Deus** to praise God.

louvável [lo'vavɛw] (*pl* **-eis**) *adj* praiseworthy.

louvor [lo'vo(x)] *m*: ~ **a alguém/algo** [elogio] praise for sb/sthg; [glorificação] glorification of sb/sthg.

Ltda (*abrev de* **Limitada**) *f* Ltd.

lua ['lua] *f* moon; ~ **cheia/nova** full/new moon; **estar no mundo da** ~ to be daydreaming; **ser de** ~ to have mood swings.

lua-de-mel [ˌluadʃi'mɛw] (*pl* **luas-de-mel**) *f* honeymoon.

Luanda ['lwãnda] *n* Luanda.

luar ['lwa(x)] *m* moonlight.

lubrificação [lubrifika'sãw] (*pl* -ões) *f* lubrication.
lubrificante [lubrifi'kãntʃi] <> *adj* lubricating. <> *m* lubricant.
lubrificar [12] [lubrifi'ka(x)] *vt* to lubricate.
lucidez [lusi'deʃ] *f* lucidity.
lúcido, da ['lusidu, da] *adj* lucid.
lucrar [4] [lu'kra(x)] <> *vt*: ~ **algo com** *ou* **em algo** [financeiramente] to make a profit of sthg from sthg; [tirar vantagem de] to enjoy sthg through sthg; ~ **algo em fazer algo** to gain sthg by doing sthg. <> *vi* [financeiramente] to make a profit; ~ **com algo** [tirar vantagem de] to benefit from sthg.
lucratividade [lukratʃivi'dadʒi] *f* profitability.
lucrativo, va [lukra'tʃivu, va] *adj* **-1.** [financeiramente] lucrative, profitable; **com/sem fins ~s** profit/non-profit-making. **-2.** [proveitoso] useful.
lucro ['lukru] *m* **-1.** [financeiro] profit; **ter ~** to make a profit; **~ bruto** gross profit; **~ líquido** net profit; **participação nos ~s** profit-sharing. **-2.** [proveito] gain.
ludibriar [16] [ludʒi'brja(x)] *vt* to swindle.
lúdico, da ['ludʒiku, ka] *adj* play *(antes de subst)*.
lufada [lu'fada] *f* gust.
lugar [lu'ga(x)] (*pl* -es) *m* **-1.** [ger] place; **em algum ~** somewhere; **em ~ nenhum** nowhere; **em outro ~** somewhere else; **~ de nascimento** place of birth; **em primeiro ~** [em competição] in first place; [em argumentação] in the first place; **tirar o primeiro/segundo ~** to come first/second. **-2.** [espaço] room. **-3.** [assento] seat. **-4.** [função, ocupação] position; **colocar-se no ~ de alguém** to put o.s. in sb else's shoes. **-5.** [situação]: **no seu ~ eu faria o mesmo** if I were you, I would do the same. **-6.** *log*: **dar ~ a** to give rise to; **ter ~** to take place.
◆ **em lugar de** *loc prep* instead of; **vá em meu ~** go instead of me.
lugar-comum [lu,gaxku'mũ] (*pl* **lugares-comuns**) *m* commonplace.
lugarejo [luga'reʒu] *m* small village.
lugar-tenente [lu,ga(x)te'nẽntʃi] *m* deputy.
lúgubre ['lugubri] *adj* gloomy.
lula ['lula] *f* squid.
lumbago [lũn'bagu] *m* lumbago.
lume ['lumi] *m* **-1.** *ant* [fogo] fire. **-2.** [luz] light.
luminária [lumi'narja] *f* lamp.
luminosidade [luminozi'dadʒi] *f* brightness.
luminoso, osa [lumi'nozu, ɔza] *adj* **-1.** [que emite luz] luminous. **-2.** *fig* [raciocínio, idéia, talento] brilliant.
lunar [lu'na(x)] (*pl* -es) *adj* lunar.
lunático, ca [lu'natʃiku, ka] *adj* lunatic.
luneta [lu'neta] *f* telescope.
lupa ['lupa] *f* magnifying glass.
lúpulo ['lupulu] *m* BOT hop.
Lusaka [lu'zaka] *n* Lusaka.
lusco-fusco [,luʃku'fuʃku] *m* twilight.
lusitano, na [luzi'tanu, na] <> *adj* Lusitanian. <> *m, f* Lusitanian.
luso, sa [za, 'luzu] <> *adj* Portuguese. <> *m, f* Portuguese person.
luso-brasileiro, ra ['luzubrazi'lejru, ra] (*mpl* -ros, *fpl* -ras) <> *adj* Luso-Brazilian. <> *m, f* Luso-Brazilian.
lusófono, na [na, lu'zɔfonu, na] <> *adj* Portuguese-speaking. <> *m, f* Portuguese speaker.
lustra-móveis [,luʃtra'mɔvejʃ] *m inv* furniture polish.
lustrar [4] [luʃ'tra(x)] *vt* [móvel] to polish.
lustre ['luʃtri] *m* **-1.** [polimento] polish; **dar um ~ em algo** to give sthg a polish. **-2.** [luminária] chandelier.
lustroso, osa [luʃ'trozu, ɔza] *adj* shiny.
luta ['luta] *f* **-1.** [ger] struggle; **~ de classes** class war; **ser uma ~ (fazer algo)** to be a struggle (to do sthg); **ir à ~** to fight for it. **-2.** [combate] fight; **~ armada** armed battle. **-3.** ESP: **~ de boxe** boxing; **~ livre** wrestling.
lutador, ra [luta'do(x), ra] <> *adj* [esforçado] tough. <> *m, f* **-1.** [ger] fighter. **-2.** BOXE boxer.
lutar [4] [lu'ta(x)] <> *vi* **-1.** [combater]: **~ (com/contra alguém)** to fight with/against sb; **~ por algo** to fight for sthg. **-2.** *fig* [combater]: **~ por/contra algo** to fight for/against sthg; **~ com algo** [enfrentar] to battle with sthg. **-3.** [empenhar-se] to use all one's forces; **~ (por algo/para fazer algo)** to fight (for sthg/to do sthg). **-4.** [resistir] to fight; **~ contra algo** to fight against sthg. <> *vt* [judô, caratê, capoeira, luta livre] to fight.
luterano, na [lute'ranu, na] <> *adj* [pessoa, igreja, doutrina] Lutheran. <> *m, f* [crente] Lutheran.
luto ['lutu] *m* mourning; **estar de ~ (por algo)** to be in mourning (over sthg); **estar de ~** to be in mourning; **tirar o ~** to come out of mourning; **pôr ~** to go into mourning.
luva ['luva] *f* glove; **cair como uma ~** to fit like a glove.
◆ **luvas** *fpl* [pagamento] payment.
luxação [luʃa'sãw] (*pl* -ões) *f* dislocation.
luxar [4] [lu'ʃa(x)] *vt* [deslocar] to dislocate.
Luxemburgo [luʃẽn'buxgu] *n* Luxemburg.
luxemburguês, esa [luʃẽnbux'geʃ, eza] <> *adj* Luxemburg *(antes de subst)*. <> *m, f person from Luxemburg*.
luxo ['luʃu] *m* **-1.** [pompa] ostentation; **de ~** luxury *(antes de subst)*. **-2.** [extravagância] luxury; **dar-se ao ~ de algo** to treat o.s. to sthg. **-3.** [afetação, cerimônia] ceremony; **cheio de ~** full of airs and graces; **fazer ~** to play hard to get.
luxuosidade [luʃwozi'dadʒi] *f* luxuriousness.
luxuoso, osa [lu'ʃwozu, ɔza] *adj* luxurious.
luxúria [lu'ʃurja] *f* [lascívia] lust.
luxuriante [luʃu'rjãntʃi] *adj* [vegetação] luxuriant.
luxurioso, osa [luʃu'rjozu, ɔza] *adj* = **luxuriante**.
luz ['luʃ] (*pl* -es) *f* **-1.** [claridade, fonte de luz] light; **acender a ~** to turn on the light; **apagar a ~** to turn off the light; **~ do dia** daylight; **~ (elétrica)** electric light; **~ de freio** brake light; **~ natural** natural light; **à ~ de vela** by candlelight. **-2.** [eletricidade] electricity; **corte de ~** power cut;

falta ~ **todos os dias aqui** the electricity gets cut off here every day. **-3.** *fig* [discernimento]: **ter uma** ~ to see the light. **-4.** *loc*: **dar à** ~ to give birth.
luzidio, dia [luzi'dʒiu, dʒia] *adj* gleaming.
luzir [72] [lu'zi(x)] *vi* to shine.
Lycra® ['lajkra] *f* Lycra®; **de** ~ Lycra®.

m, M ['emi] *m* [letra] m, M.
má [ma] ▷ **mau.**
MA (*abrev de* **Estado do Maranhão**) *m State of Maranhão.*
maca ['maka] *f* MED trolley.
maçã [ma'sã] *f* apple; ~ **ácida** cooking apple; ~ **do rosto** cheek; ~ **do amor** toffee apple.
macabro, bra [ma'kabru, ma'kabra] *adj* macabre.
macacão [maka'kãw] (*pl* **-ões**) *m* overalls *(pl) UK*, coveralls *(pl) US*.
macaco, ca [ma'kaku, ka] *m* [animal] monkey; ~ **velho** *fig* [pessoa experiente] old hand.
◆ **macaco** *m* AUTO jack.
◆ **macaca** *f*: **estar/acordar com a macaca** *fam* to be/wake up in a foul mood.
maçada [ma'sada] *f* [situação enfadonha] bore.
macadame [maka'dãmi] *m inv* tarmac.
macambúzio, zia [makãm'buzju, zja] *adj* sullen.
maçaneta [masa'neta] *f* handle.
maçante [ma'sãntʃi] *adj* boring.
Macapá [maka'pa] *n* Macapá.
macaquear [15] [maka'kja(x)] ◇ *vt* [imitar] to ape, to imitate. ◇ *vi* to monkey about.
macaquice [maka'kisi] *f*: **fazer** ~**s** to monkey around.
maçarico [masa'riku] *m* blow torch.
maçaroca [masa'rɔka] *f* **-1.** [emaranhado] tangle. **-2.** [mixórdia] mess.
macarrão [maka'xãw] *m* **-1.** [massa] pasta. **-2.** [em tiras] spaghetti.
macarrônico, ca [maka'xoniku, ka] *adj fam* [idioma] broken.
Maceió [masej'ɔ] *n* Maceió.
macerado, da [mase'radu, da] *adj* **-1.** [esmagado] crushed. **-2.** [impregnado] marinated. **-3.** *fig* [macilento] emaciated.
macerar [4] [mase'ra(x)] *vt* **-1.** [esmagar] to crush. **-2.** [impregnar]: ~ **algo em algo** to marinate sthg in sthg. **-3.** *fig* [mortificar] to torment.
macete [ma'setʃi] *m* **-1.** [instrumento] mallet. **-2.** *fam* [truque] trick; **cheio de** ~**s** [sofisticado] full of gadgets.
machadada [ma'ʃada] *f* axe blow.
machadinha [maʃa'dʒiɲa] *f* cleaver.
machado [ma'ʃadu] *m* axe.
machão, ona [ma'ʃãw, ɔna] (*mpl* **-ões**, *fpl* **-s**) *adj* **-1.** *pej* [ger] macho. **-2.** [corajoso] brave.
◆ **machão** *m* macho man.
◆ **machona** *f vulg* [lésbica] dyke.
machete [ma'ʃetʃi] *m* machete.
machismo [ma'ʃiʒmu] *m* machismo.
machista [ma'ʃiʃta] ◇ *adj* macho. ◇ *m* male chauvinist.
macho ['maʃu] ◇ *adj* **-1.** [ger] manly. **-2.** [gênero] male. ◇ *m* **-1.** [animal] male. **-2.** TEC tap. **-3.** [prega] box pleat.
machões [ma'ʃõjʃ] *pl* ▷ **machão.**
machona [ma'ʃona] *f* ▷ **machão.**
machucado, da [maʃu'kadu, da] *adj* **-1.** [ferido] hurt. **-2.** [contundido] injured. **-3.** [esmagado] bruised. **-4.** [lascado] scratched. **-5.** [magoado] hurt.
◆ **machucado** *m* [ferida] wound.
machucar [12] [maʃu'kax] ◇ *vt* **-1.** [ferir] to hurt. **-2.** [contundir] to injure. **-3.** [esmagar] to bruise. **-4.** [lascar] to scratch. **-5.** [magoar] to hurt. ◇ *vi* to hurt.
◆ **machucar-se** *vp* **-1.** [ferir-se] to injure o.s. **-2.** [contundir-se] to hurt o.s. **-3.** *fam* [sair-se mal]: ~**-se (com algo)** to get o.s. hurt (by sthg).
maciço, ça [ma'sisu, sa] *adj* **-1.** [sólido] massive. **-2.** [em quantidade] massive. **-3.** *fig* [sólido] solid.
◆ **maciço** *m* [cadeia montanhosa] massif.
macieira [ma'sjejra] *f* apple tree.
maciez [ma'sjeʒ] *f* softness.
macilento, ta [masi'lẽntu, ta] *adj* **-1.** [pálido] pale. **-2.** [sem brilho] dull.
macio, cia [ma'siu, sia] *adj* **-1.** [ger] smooth. **-2.** [fofo] soft.
maciota [ma'sjɔta] *f*: **na** ~ effortlessly.
maço ['masu] *m* **-1.** [de notas, folhas] bundle. **-2.** [de cartas] pack. **-3.** [de cigarros] packet.
maçom [ma'sõ] (*pl* **-ns**) *m* [membro da maçonaria] Freemason.
maçonaria [masona'ria] *f* freemasonary.
maconha [ma'koɲa] *f* **-1.** BOT hemp. **-2.** [droga] cannabis, to marijuana; **cigarro de** ~ spliff.
maconhado, da [mako'ɲadu, da] *adj* high *(on drugs)*.
maconheiro, ra [mako'ɲejru, ra] ◇ *adj* [viciado] addicted. ◇ *m, f* **-1.** [viciado] addict. **-2.** [vendedor] pusher.
maçônico, ca [ma'soniku, ka] *adj* Masonic.
má-criação [ˌmakrja'sãw] *f* = **malcriação.**
macro ['makru] *f* COMPUT macro.
macrobiótico, ca [makro'bjɔtʃiku, ka] *adj* macrobiotic.
◆ **macrobiótica** *f* **-1.** [doutrina] macrobiotics. **-2.** [dieta] macrobiotic diet.
macrocosmo [makro'kɔʒmu] *m* macrocosm.

macroeconomia [makrwekono'mia] *f* macroeconomics.
mácula ['makula] *f fig* [desonra, mancha] stain; **sem ~** untarnished.
maculado, da [maku'ladu, da] *adj* **-1.** [manchado] stained. **-2.** [desonrado] tarnished.
macumba [ma'kũnba] *f* [espirit- religião] macumba, *Afro-Brazilian religion*; [- despacho] sacrificial offering; **fazer uma ~ contra alguém** to put a macumba curse on sb.
macumbeiro, ra [makũm'bejru, ra] ◇ *adj* [relativo à macumba] macumba *(antes de subst)*. ◇ *m, f* [adepto] macumba initiate.
Madagascar [madagaʃ'ka(x)] *n* Madagascar.
madame [ma'dãmi], **madama** [ma'dama] *f* **-1.** [senhora] Madam. **-2.** *irôn* [mulher rica] lady. **-3.** *irôn* [esposa] ladyship. **-4.** [cafetina] madam.
madeira [ma'dejrã] *f* wood; **~ de lei** hardwood; **de ~** wooden; **bater na ~** to touch wood.
Madeira [ma'dejra] ◇ *n* Madeira ◇ *m* [vinho] Madeira (wine).
madeira-branca [ma,dejra'brãŋka] (*pl* **madeiras-brancas**) *f* softwood.
madeiramento [madejra'mẽntu] *m* [de casa, telhado] timber.
madeireiro, ra [madej'rejru, ra] ◇ *adj* timber *(antes de subst)*. ◇ *m, f* timber merchant.
◆ **madeireira** *f* [empresa] timber merchant's.
madeixa [ma'dejʃa] *f* [mecha] lock.
madona [ma'dona] *f* Madonna.
madrasta [ma'draʃta] *f* **-1.** [esposa do pai] stepmother. **-2.** *fig* [mãe má] unfit mother.
madre ['madri] *f* **-1.** [religiosa] nun. **-2.** [título] Mother; **~ superiora** Mother Superior, Reverend Mother.
madrepérola [,madre'pɛrula] *f* mother-of-pearl.
madressilva [,madre'siwva] *f BOT* honeysuckle.
Madri [ma'dri] *n* Madrid.
madrileno, na [madri'lenu, na] ◇ *adj* Madrid *(antes de subst)*. ◇ *m & f* *person from Madrid*.
madrinha [ma'driɲa] *f* **-1.** [*RELIG* - de batismo] godmother; [- de crisma] sponsor; [- de casamento] chief bridesmaid. **-2.** *fig* [protetora, patrocinadora] patroness.
madrugada [madru'gada] *f* early morning; **às três da ~** at three in the morning; **de ~** in the early hours.
madrugador, ra [madruga'do(x), ra] ◇ *adj* early rising. ◇ *m, f* early riser.
madrugar [14] [madru'ga(x)] *vi* **-1.** [acordar cedo] to wake up early. **-2.** [chegar cedo] to get in early.
maduro, ra [ma'duru, ra] *adj* **-1.** [fruto] ripe. **-2.** [pessoa, atitude, decisão] mature.
mãe ['mãj] *f* **-1.** [ger] mother; **~ adotiva** adoptive mother; **~ de criação** foster mother; **~ de família** wife and mother; **~ solteira** single mother. **-2.** [como forma de tratamento] mother. **-3.** [pessoa dedicada]: **ser uma ~ para alguém** to be a mother to sb.
mãe-benta [,mãj'bẽnta] (*pl* **mães-bentas**) *f CULIN* *small rice-flour cake*.
mãe-de-santo [,mãjʃdʒi'sãntu] (*pl* **mães-de-santo**) *f* [espirit] *high priestess in Afro-Brazilian religion*.
maestria [majʃ'tria] *f* mastery; **com ~** masterfully.
maestro, trina [ma'ɛʃtru, trina] *m, f* maestro.
má-fé [,ma'fɛ] *f inv* bad faith; **agir de ~** to act in bad faith.
máfia ['mafja] *f* **-1.** [bando do crime organizado] Mafia. **-2.** [grupo de corruptos] mafia.
mafioso, osa [ma'fjozu, ɔza] ◇ *adj* **-1.** [pessoa] Mafioso. **-2.** [ação] of the Mafia. ◇ *m, f* [membro da máfia] Mafioso.
má-formação [,mafoxma'sãw] *f* = **malformação**.
mafuá [ma'fwa] *m fam fig* [bagunça] shambles *(sg)*.
magazine [maga'zini] *m* **-1.** [loja] boutique. **-2.** [revista] magazine.
magérrimo, ma [ma'ʒɛximu, ma] *adj* [superl de magro] terribly thin, thinnest.
magia [ma'ʒia] *f* magic; **~ negra** black magic.
mágico, ca ['maʒiku, ka] ◇ *adj* magic. ◇ *m, f* [prestidigitador] magician.
◆ **mágica** *f* **-1.** [prestidigitação] magic. **-2.** [truque] trick; **fazer mágica** to perform magic; *fig* to work miracles.
magistério [maʒiʃ'tɛrju] *m* **-1.** [profissão] teaching. **-2.** [classe dos professores] teaching profession. **-3.** [ensino] teaching.
magistrado, da [maʒiʃ'tradu, da] *m* magistrate.
magistral [maʒiʃ'traw] (*pl* **-ais**) *adj* [exemplar] masterly.
magistralmente [maʒiʃtraw'mẽntʃi] *adv* [com maestria] masterfully.
magistratura [maʒiʃtra'tura] *f* [os magistrados] magistracy.
magnanimidade [magnãnimi'dadʒi] *f* magnanimity.
magnânimo, ma [mag'nanimu, ma] *adj* magnanimous.
magnata [mag'nata] *m* magnate.
magnésia [mag'nɛzja] *f* magnesia.
magnésio [mag'nɛzju] *m* magnesium.
magnético, ca [mag'nɛtʃiku, ka] *adj* magnetic.
magnetismo [magne'tʃiʒmu] *m* magnetism.
magnetizar [4] [magnetʃi'za(x)] *vt* **-1.** [imantar] to magnetize. **-2.** *fig* [atrair] to fascinate.
magnificência [magnifi'sẽnsja] *f* [suntuosidade] magnificence.
magnífico, ca [mag'nifiku, ka] *adj* magnificent.
magnitude [magni'tudʒi] *f* [dimensão] magnitude.
magnólia [mag'nɔlja] *f* magnolia.
mago, ga ['magu, ga] ◇ *m, f* wizard (*f* witch). ◇ *adj*: **os reis ~s** the Three Kings.
mágoa ['magwa] *f* **-1.** [ressentimento] grief. **-2.** [tristeza] sorrow.
magoado, da [ma'gwadu, da] *adj*: **estar/ficar ~ (com algo)** [ressentido] to be/feel offended (by sthg); [triste] to be hurt (by sthg).
magoar [20] [ma'gwa(x)] ◇ *vt* [ferir] to hurt. ◇ *vi* [ferir] to hurt.

magrela [ma'grɛla] *adj* skinny.

magreza [ma'greza] *f* thinness.

magricela [magri'sɛla] *adj* = **magrela**.

magro, gra ['magru, ra] *adj* **-1.** [franzino] slim. **-2.** [sem gordura - carne, presunto] lean; [- leite] skimmed. **-3.** *(antes de subst) fig* [parco] meagre *UK*, meager *US*.

mai. (*abrev de* **maio**) May.

mail [mejo] (*pl* **mails**) *m* COMPUT e-mail.

mainframe [mẽjn'frejmi] *m* COMPUT mainframe.

maio ['maju] *m* May; *veja também* **setembro**.

maiô [ma'jo] *m* swimming costume *UK*, swimsuit *US*.

maionese [majo'nɛzi] *f* mayonnaise.

maior [ma'jɔ(x)] (*pl* **-es**) ◇ *adj* **-1.** [comparativo]: ~ **(do) que** [de tamanho] bigger than; [de importância] more important than; [de número] larger than. **-2.** [superlativo]: **o/a** ~ **...** [de tamanho] the biggest ...; [de importância] the highest ...; [de número] the largest ...; **ser o** ~ **barato** [pessoa] to be really cool; [coisa] to be really great. **-3.** [adulto]: **ser** ~ **(de idade)** to be of age; **ser** ~ **de 21 anos** to be over 21. **-4.** MÚS: **em dó** ~ in C major. ◇ *mf* **-1.** [de tamanho]: **o/a** ~ the largest. **-2.** *fam* [superior]: **ser o/a** ~ to be the best. **-3.** [adulto] adult; **ser de** ~ to be an adult; **ser** ~ **e vacinado** *fam* to be grown up. ◇ *f* [notícia]: **você já soube da** ~**?** have you heard the latest?; **tenho a** ~ **para contar** have I got sthg to tell you!

maioral [majo'raw] (*pl* **-ais**) *mf*: **o** ~ the boss; **ele se acha o** ~ he thinks he's the greatest.

maioria [majo'ria] *f* majority; **a** ~ **de** the majority of; ~ **absoluta** absolute majority; **a** ~ **das pessoas acha ...** the majority think ...

maioridade [majori'dadʒi] *f* age of majority; **atingir a** ~ to come of age.

mais ['majʃ] ◇ *adv* **-1.** [em comparações] more; **a Ana é** ~ **alta/inteligente** Ana is taller/more intelligent; ~ **do que** more than; ~ **... do que ...** more ... than ...; **bebeu um copo a** ~**!** he's had one too many!; **deram-me dinheiro a** ~ they gave me too much money; **é** ~ **alta do que eu** she's taller than me. **-2.** [como superlativo]: **o/a** ~ **...** the most ...; **o** ~ **engraçado/inteligente** the funniest/most intelligent. **-3.** [indica adição] any more; **não necessito de** ~ **trabalho** I don't need any more work; **não necessito de** ~ **ninguém** I don't need anyone else. **-4.** [indica intensidade]: **que dia** ~ **feliz!** what a great day!; **que casa** ~ **feia!** what a horrible house! **-5.** [indica preferência]: **vale** ~ **a pena ficar em casa** it would be better to stay at home; **gosto** ~ **de comida chinesa** I prefer Chinese food. **-6.** [em locuções]: **de** ~ **a** ~ [ainda por cima] what's more; ~ **ou menos** more or less; **por** ~ **que se esforce** however hard he tries; **sem** ~ **nem menos** for no apparent reason; **uma vez** ~, ~ **uma vez** once *ou* yet again. ◇ *adj inv* **-1.** [em comparações] more; **eles têm** ~ **dinheiro** they have more money; **está** ~ **calor hoje** it's hotter today; ~ **... do que** more ... than. **-2.** [como superlativo] (the) most; **a pessoa que** ~ **discos vendeu** the person who sold (the) most records; **os que** ~ **dinheiro têm** those who have (the) most money. **-3.** [indica adição] more; ~ **água, por favor** I'd like some more water, please; ~ **alguma coisa?** anything else?; **tenho** ~ **três dias de férias** I have another three days of vacation left. ◇ *conj* and; **quero uma sopa** ~ **pão com manteiga** I'd like some soup and some bread and butter. ◇ *prep* [indica soma] plus; **dois** ~ **dois são quatro** two plus two is four.

maisena [maj'zena] *f*: **de** ~ cornflour *UK*, cornstarch *US*.

mais-valia [ˌmajʃva'lia] (*pl* **mais-valias**) *f* ECON surplus value.

maître ['mɛtri] *m* head waiter.

maiúsculo, la [ma'juʃkulu, la] *adj*: **letra maiúscula** capitals *(pl)*.

◆ **maiúscula** *f* capital letter.

majestade [maʒeʃ'tadʒi] *f* majesty.

◆ **Majestade** *f*: **Sua Majestade** Your Majesty, His Majesty, Her Majesty.

majestoso, osa [maʒeʃ'tozu, ɔza] *adj* [grandioso] majestic.

major [ma'ʒɔ(x)] (*pl* **-res**) *m* MIL major.

majoração [maʒora'sãw] *f* increase.

majorar [4] [maʒo'ra(x)] *vt* to increase.

majoritário, ria [maʒori'tarju, rja] *adj* majority *(antes de subst)*; **a opinião majoritária é que ...** the majority opinion is that ...

mal ['maw] (*pl* **-es**) *m* **-1.** [ger] evil; **cortar o** ~ **pela raiz** to stop things going from bad to worse; **a luta entre o bem e o** ~ the fight between good and evil. **-2.** [dano] damage; **fazer** ~ **(a)** [à saúde] to damage; **o cigarro faz** ~ **à saúde** smoking damages your health; **fazer** ~ **a alguém** [afetar] to upset sb; [deflorar] to deflower sb; **você fez** ~ **em se divorciar** you did the wrong thing in getting divorced; **não faz** ~ it doesn't matter; **querer** ~ **a alguém** to wish sb ill. **-3.** [doença] illness. **-4.** [sofrimento] stress. **-5.** [inconveniente]: **o** ~ **é que ...** the problem is that ... **-6.** [opinião desfavorável]: **falar** ~ **de alguém/algo** to speak ill of sb/sthg.

◆ **mal** ◇ *adv* **-1.** [ger] badly; **dar-se** ~ **(em algo)** to do badly (in sthg); **de** ~ **a pior** from bad to worse; ~ **e porcamente** lousily. **-2.** [quase não]: **ele** ~ **consegue dormir** he barely manages to sleep. **-3.** [injustamente] wrongly. **-4.** [rudemente] rudely. **-5.** [de maneira desfavorável] unfavourably; **levar alguém/algo a** ~ to take sb/sthg badly; **não me leve a** ~**, mas ...** don't get me wrong, but ... **-6.** PSIC [doente] down; **estar** ~ to feel down; **passar** ~ to feel sick. ◇ *conj* just; ~ **cheguei, ele saiu** just as I arrived, he left.

mala ['mala] *f* **-1.** [recipiente] suitcase; **fazer as** ~**s** to pack one's bags; ~ **de mão** hand luggage. **-2.** AUTO boot *UK*, trunk *US*. **-3.** COM: ~ **direta** mail order. **-4.** [serviço]: ~ **aérea** air mail; ~ **postal** mail. **-5.** *fam pej* [pessoa chata]: **ser uma** ~ to be a pain.

malabarismo [malaba'riʒmu] *m* **-1.** [arte] juggling. **-2.** *fig* [habilidade] deftness; **fazer ~s** to juggle.
malabarista [malaba'riʃta] *mf* juggler.
mal-acabado, da [ˌmawaka'badu] *adj* **-1.** [construção, móvel] poorly finished. **-2.** [corpo] in poor shape.
mala-direta [ˌmaladʒi'rɛta] (*pl* **malas diretas**) *f* [marketing] direct marketing.
mal-afamado, da [mawafa'madu, da] *adj* notorious.
mal-agradecido, da [mawagrade'sidu, da] (*pl* **-s**) <> *adj* ungrateful. <> *m, f*: **o ~ nem sequer me agradeceu** he's so ungrateful he didn't even thank me.
malagueta [mala'geta] *m* chilli pepper.
malaio, ia [ma'laju, ja] <> *adj* Malay. <> *m, f* Malay.
◆ **malaio** *m* [língua] Malay.
mal-ajambrado, da [mawaʒãm'bradu, da] (*pl* **-s**) *adj* scruffy.
malandragem [malãn'draʒẽ] (*pl* **-ns**), **malandrice** [malãn'drisi] *f* **-1.** [patifaria] double-dealing. **-2.** [astúcia] cunning. **-3.** [vadiagem] vagrancy. **-4.** [preguiça] laziness.
malandro, dra [ma'lãndru, dra] <> *adj* **-1.** [patife] crooked. **-2.** [astuto] sharp. **-3.** [vadio] vagrant. **-4.** [preguiçoso] idle. <> *m, f* **-1.** [patife] crook. **-2.** [astuto] swindler. **-3.** [vadio] vagrant. **-4.** [preguiçoso] layabout.
mal-apanhado, da [mawapa'ɲadu, da] (*pl* **-s**) *adj* = **mal-apessoado**.
mal-apessoado, da [mawape'swadu, da] (*pl* **-s**) *adj* unpleasant-looking.
malária [ma'larja] *f* malaria.
mal-arrumado, da [mawaxu'madu, da] (*pl* **-s**) *adj* untidy.
mala-sem-alça ['malasẽ'sãw] (*pl* **malas-sem-alça**) *mf fam* bore.
Malásia [ma'lazja] *n* Malaysia.
mal-assombrado, da [mawasõm'bradu, da] (*pl* **-s**) *adj* haunted.
malbaratar [4] [mawbara'ta(x)] *vt* to squander.
malcheiroso, osa [mawʃej'rozu, ɔza] *adj* foul-smelling.
malcomportado, da [mawkõmpox'tadu, da] *adj* badly behaved.
malconceituado, da [mawkõnsej'twadu, da] *adj* badly thought of.
malcriação [mawkrja'sãw] (*pl* **-ões**), **má-criação** [makrja'sãw] (*pl* **-ões**) *f* bad manners; **respondeu com ~** he replied rudely; **fazer ~** to behave badly.
malcriado, da [mawkri'adu, da] <> *adj* ill-mannered. <> *m, f* yob.
maldade [maw'dadʒi] *f* **-1.** [ger] cruelty; **bater em criança é uma ~** it's cruel to hit children; **ser uma ~** to be cruel. **-2.** [malícia] malice.
maldição [mawdi'sãw] (*pl* **-ões**) *f* curse.
maldito, ta [maw'dʒitu, ta] <> *pp* ▷ **maldizer**. <> *adj* **-1.** [amaldiçoado] damned. **-2.** [funesto] tragic. **-3.** [cruel] cruel. **-4.** *(antes de subst) fam* [para enfatizar]: **essa chuva maldita** this bloody rain.
maldizer [29] [mawdʒi'ze(x)] <> *vt* to curse. <> *vi*: **~ de algo** to curse sthg.
maldoso, osa [maw'dozu, ɔza] *adj* **-1.** [malvado] nasty. **-2.** *fig* [mordaz] vicious.
maleável [ma'ljavew] (*pl* **-eis**) *adj* malleable.
maledicência [malidʒi'sẽnsja] *f* **-1.** [ação] slander. **-2.** [difamação] defamation.
maledicente [malidʒi'sẽntʃi] <> *adj* slanderous. <> *m, f* slanderer.
mal-educado, da [ˌmaledu'kadu, da] <> *adj* rude. <> *m, f*: **o ~** the rude man; **a malcriada** the rude woman.
malefício [male'fisju] *m* **-1.** [ação] wrong. **-2.** [dano] harm.
maléfico, ca [ma'lɛfiku, ka] *adj* harmful.
mal-e-mal ['mawimaw] *adv* extremely poorly.
mal-encarado, da [ˌmalẽŋka'radu, da] (*pl* **-s**) *adj* shady.
mal-entendido [ˌmawẽntẽn'dʒidu] (*pl* **mal-entendidos**) <> *adj* [mal interpretado] misunderstood. <> *m* misunderstanding.
males ['maliʃ] *pl* ▷ **mal**.
mal-estar [maweʃ'ta(x)] (*pl* **mal-estares**) *m* **-1.** [indisposição] upset. **-2.** *fig* [embaraço] uneasiness.
maleta [ma'leta] *f* small suitcase.
malevolência [malevo'lẽnsja] *f* malevolence.
malevolente *adj* [malevo'lẽntʃi] malevolent.
malévolo, la [ma'lɛvolu, la] *adj* malevolent.
malfadado, da [mawfa'dadu, da] *adj* unlucky.
malfeito, ta [mal'fejtu, ta] *adj* **-1.** [mal-acabado] sloppy. **-2.** [deforme] misshapen. **-3.** *fig* [injusto] unjust.
malfeitor, ra [mawfej'to(x), ra] (*mpl* **-es**, *fpl* **-s**) *m* **-1.** [quem comete delito] wrongdoer. **-2.** [bandido] criminal.
malformação [mawfoxma'sãw] (*pl* **-ões**) *f* malformation.
malgrado [maw'gradu] *prep* despite.
malha ['maʎa] *f* **-1.** [tecido] jersey; **de ~** jersey; **roupas de ~** knitwear. **-2.** [de rede, tecido] mesh. **-3.** [de balé] leotard. **-4.** [suéter] sweatshirt.
mal-habituado, da [malabi'twadu, da] (*pl* **-s**) *adj* poorly trained.
malhação [maʎa'sãw] (*pl* **-ões**) *f fam* [crítica violenta] panning.
malhado, da [ma'ʎadu, ada] *adj* [animal] mottled.
malhar [4] [ma'ʎa(x)] <> *vt* **-1.** [ger] to beat. **-2.** [criticar] to knock. <> *vi* [fazer ginástica] *fam* to work out.
malharia [maʎa'ria] *f* **-1.** [loja] knitwear shop. **-2.** [fábrica] textile mill. **-3.** [artigos] knitted goods.
malho ['maʎu] *m* mallet.
mal-humorado, da [mawumo'radu, da] *adj* **-1.** [que tem mau humor] sullen. **-2.** [ranzinza] grumpy.
malícia [ma'lisja] *f* **-1.** [intenção maldosa] malice. **-2.** [intenção licenciosa] licentiousness; **pôr ~ em**

algo to misinterpret sthg. **-3.** [manha, marotice] cunning.
malicioso, osa [mali'sjozu, ɔza] *adj* **-1.** [maldoso] malicious. **-2.** [que vê licenciosidade] licentious. **-3.** [manhoso] sly.
malignidade [maligni'dadʒi] *f* **-1.** *MED* malignancy. **-2.** [ação] malice.
maligno, gna [ma'lignu, gna] *adj* **-1.** [mau] malicious. **-2.** [nocivo] harmful. **-3.** *MED* malignant.
má-língua [ˌma'lĩngwa] (*pl* **más-língua**) *f* scandalmonger; **dizem as más-línguas que ...** the scandalmongers are saying that ...
mal-intencionado, da [ˌmawĩntẽnsjo'nadu, da] (*pl* **-s**) *adj* malicious.
malmequer [mawmi'kɛ(x)] (*pl* **-es**) *m* marigold.
malnutrido, da [mawnu'tridu, da] *adj* malnourished.
maloca [ma'lɔka] *f* **-1.** [cabana] teepee. **-2.** [aldeia] encampment. **-3.** [esconderijo] hideout.
malogrado, da [malo'gradu, da] *adj* thwarted.
malograr [4] [malo'gra(x)] ◇ *vt* to thwart. ◇ *vi* to fall through.
malogro [ma'logru] *m* failure.
malote [ma'lɔtʃi] *m* **-1.** [bolsa] pouch. **-2.** [correspondência] mail. **-3.** [serviço] courier.
malpassado, da [mawpa'sadu, da] *adj* rare.
malproporcionado, da [mawpropoxsjo'nadu, da] *adj* out of proportion.
malquisto, ta [maw'kiʃtu, ta] *adj* disliked.
malsucedido, da [mawsuse'dʒidu, da] *adj* unsuccessful.
Malta ['mawta] *n* Malta.
malte ['mawtʃi] *m* malt.
maltês, esa [maw'teʃ, eza] ◇ *adj* Maltese. ◇ *m, f* Maltese.
maltrapilho, lha [mawtra'piʎu, ʎa] ◇ *adj* ragged. ◇ *m, f* **-1.** [mendigo] beggar. **-2.** [criança] urchin.
maltratar [4] [mawtra'ta(x)] *vt* **-1.** [fisicamente] to mistreat. **-2.** [verbalmente] to abuse. **-3.** [tratar com desleixo] to mishandle.
maluco, ca [ma'luku, ka] ◇ *adj* **-1.** *PSIC* crazy. **-2.** [adoidado] nuts. **-3.** [absurdo] mad. **-4.** [aficionado]: **ser ~ por algo** to be crazy about sthg. ◇ *m, f PSIC* insane.
maluquice [malu'kisi] *f* **-1.** *PSIC* madness. **-2.** [excentricidade]: **ser uma ~** to be madness.
malvadeza [mawva'deza], **malvadez** [mawva'deʒ] *f* wickedness.
malvado, da [maw'vadu, da] ◇ *adj* wicked. ◇ *m, f* thug.
malversação [mawvexsa'sãw] (*pl* **-ões**) *f* **-1.** [desvio]: **~ (de algo)** embezzlement (of sthg). **-2.** [mau gerenciamento] mismanagement.
Malvinas [maw'vinaʃ] *npl*: **as (ilhas) ~** the Falkland Islands, the Falklands.
malvisto, ta [maw'viʃtu, ta] *adj* **-1.** [malconceituado] badly thought of. **-2.** [antipatizado] disliked.
mama ['mãma] *f* breast.
mamadeira [mama'dejra] *f* baby's bottle.
mamãe [mã'mãj] *f* mummy, mum.
mamão [ma'mãw] (*pl* **-ões**) *m* papaya.
mamar [4] [ma'ma(x)] ◇ *vt* [sugar] to suck. ◇ *vi* **-1.** [alimentar-se] to feed; **dar de ~ a alguém** to breastfeed sb. **-2.** *fig* [tirar lucros ilícitos]: **ele está mamando nas tetas do governo** he's milking the government dry.
mamário, ria [ma'marju, rja] *adj* mammary.
mamata [ma'mata] *f* **-1.** *fam* [proveito ilícito] racket. **-2.** [facilidade] breeze; **ser uma ~** to be a piece of cake.
mambembe [mãn'bẽnbi] ◇ *adj* [circo, teatro] second-rate. ◇ *m* [grupo teatral ambulante] travelling theatre.
mameluco, ca [mame'luku, ka] *m mixed race person of native Indian and European extraction.*
mamífero, ra [ma'miferu, ra] *adj* mammalian.
◆ **mamífero** *m* mammal.
mamilo [ma'milu] *m* nipple.
maminha [ma'miɲa] *f* [carne] rump steak.
mamoeiro [ma'mwejru] *m* papaya tree.
mamões [ma'mõjʃ] *pl* ⊳ **mamão**.
mamografia [mãmogra'fia] *f* mammography.
manada [ma'nada] *f* herd.
Manágua [ma'nagwa] *n* Managua.
manancial [manãn'sjaw] (*pl* **-ais**) *m* **-1.** [fonte] spring. **-2.** *fig* [origem] source.
Manaus [ma'nawʃ] *n* Manaus.
mancada [mãŋ'kada] *f* **-1.** [erro] mistake. **-2.** [gafe] gaffe; **dar uma ~** to make a gaffe.
mancar [12] [mãŋ'ka(x)] *vi* [coxear] to limp.
◆ **mancar-se** *vp fam* [desconfiar] to take a hint.
mancha ['mãnʃa] *f* **-1.** [ger] stain. **-2.** [em pintura] blotch. **-3.** [marca] mark.
manchado, da [mã'ʃadu, da] *adj* **-1.** [com manchas] stained. **-2.** [pintura] blotched. **-3.** [malhado] mottled.
manchar [4] [mã'ʃa(x)] *vt* **-1.** [ger] to stain. **-2.** [deixar marca] to mark.
manchete [mãn'ʃɛtʃi] *f* headline; **o acidente virou ~ em todo o país** the accident hit the headlines nationwide.
manco, ca ['mãŋku, ka] ◇ *adj* lame. ◇ *m, f* disabled person.
mancomunado, da [mãŋkomu'nadu, da] *adj* hand in glove.
mancomunar [4] [mãŋkomu'na(x)] *vt*: **~ algo (com alguém)** to collude in sthg (with sb).
◆ **mancomunar-se** *vp*: **~-se (com alguém)** to collude (with sb).
mandachuva [mãnda'ʃuva] *mf* **-1.** [pessoa poderosa] boss. **-2.** [chefe, líder] chief.
mandado [mãn'dadu] *m* **-1.** [autorização] order. **-2.** *JUR* injunction; **~ de despejo** eviction order; **~ de prisão** arrest warrant; **~ de segurança** injunction.
mandamento [mãnda'mẽntu] *m* **-1.** [preceito] order. **-2.** *RELIG* commandment.
mandante [mãn'dãntʃi] *mf* **-1.** *JUR* person who grants a mandate. **-2.** [instigador] instigator.

mandão, ona [mãn'dãw, ɔna] (*mpl* **-ões**) *adj fam* [autoritário] bossy.
mandar [4] [mãn'da(x)] ◇ *vt* **-1.**: ~ **alguém fazer** *ou* **que alguém faça algo** [ordenar] to tell sb to do sthg; [recomendar] to order sb to do sthg; ~ **chamar alguém** to send for sb; ~ **dizer que** to send word that; ~ **embora** to send away. **-2.** [enviar] to send. ◇ *vi* **-1.** [chefiar, dominar]: ~ **(em alguém/algo)** to order (sb/sthg) around; **no escritório, é ele quem manda** he's the one who gives the orders in the office. **-2.** *fam* [noticiar]: **o que é que você manda?** what can I do for you?
◆ **mandar-se** *vp* **-1.** *fam* [ir-se embora] to get going. **-2.** [fugir] to take off.
mandarim [mãnda'rĩ] (*pl* **-ns**) *m* **-1.** [título] mandarin. **-2.** [dialeto] Mandarin.
mandatário, ria [mãnda'tarju, rja] *m* **-1.** [representante] deputy, representative. **-2.** [procurador] defence lawyer *UK*, defense lawyer *US*, counsel for the defence *UK*, defense attorney *US*.
mandato [mãn'datu] *m* **-1.** [procuração] mandate. **-2.** [missão] duty. **-3.** [ordem] order. **-4.** *POL* term of office.
mandíbula [mãn'dʒibula] *f* jaw.
mandinga [mãn'dʒĩŋga] *f* witchcraft.
mandioca [mãn'dʒjɔka] *f* cassava, manioc.
mando ['mãndu] *m* **-1.** [autoridade] authority. **-2.** [ordem] order; **a** ~ **de** at the orders of.
mandões [mãn'dõjʃ] *mpl* ▷ **mandão**.
mandona [mãn'dona] *f* ▷ **mandão**.
maneira [4] [ma'nejra] *f* manner; **à** ~ **(de)** like; **de** ~ **nenhuma** *ou* **alguma** no way; **não volto àquele clube de** ~ **alguma!** no way am I going back to that club!; **de** ~ **que** so that; **de qualquer** ~ [sem cuidado] anyhow; [a qualquer preço] at whatever cost; [de todo modo] whatever; **de qualquer** ~ **será útil** it'll be useful, whatever.
◆ **maneiras** *fpl* manners; **boas** ~**s** good manners; **ter boas** ~**s** to have good manners.
maneirar [4] [manej'ra(x)] ◇ *vt* **-1.** *fam* [contornar] to sort out. **-2.** [controlar] to control. ◇ *vi* **-1.** [acomodar as coisas] to get sorted. **-2.** [controlar-se] to control o.s.
maneiro, ra [ma'nejru, ra] *adj* **-1.** [de fácil uso] simple. **-2.** [fácil] easy. **-3.** *fam* [legal] great.
manejar [4] [mane'ʒa(x)] *vt* **-1.** [ger] to control. **-2.** [manusear] to handle. **-3.** [administrar] to manage.
manejável [mane'ʒavɛw] (*pl* **-eis**) *adj* **-1.** [fácil de usar] simple. **-2.** [controlável] controllable.
manejo [ma'neʒu] *m* **-1.** [manuseio] handling. **-2.** [uso] use. **-3.** [administração] management.
manequim [mane'kĩ] (*pl* **-ns**) ◇ *m* [boneco] dummy. ◇ *mf* [pessoa] model.
maneta [ma'neta] *adj* one-handed.
manga ['mãŋga] *f* **-1.** [de roupa] sleeve; **em** ~**s de camisa** in shirt-sleeves. **-2.** [fruto] mango. **-3.** [filtro] filter. **-4.** *loc*: **pôr as** ~**s de fora** to show one's true self; **arregaçar as** ~**s** to roll up one's sleeves.
manganês [mãŋga'neʃ] *m* manganese.
mangue ['mãŋgi] *m* **-1.** [terreno] mangrove swamp. **-2.** [planta] mangrove.
mangueira [mãŋ'gejra] *f* **-1.** *BOT* mango tree. **-2.** [cano] hose.
manha ['mãɲa] *f* **-1.** [habilidade] skill. **-2.** [esperteza] shrewdness. **-3.** *fam* [choro, birra] tantrum; **fazer** ~ to throw a tantrum.
manhã [mã'ŋã] (*pl* **-s**) *f* morning; **amanhã de** ~ tomorrow morning; **de** ~ **cedo** in the early morning; **de** *ou* **pela** ~ in the morning; **hoje de** ~ this morning; **seis horas da** ~ six o'clock in the morning.
manhãzinha [mãɲã'ziɲa] *f*: **de** ~ early in the morning.
manhoso, osa [ma'ɲozu, ɔza] *adj* **-1.** [esperto] sly. **-2.** [chorão, birrento] whingeing.
mania [ma'nia] *f* **-1.** *PSIC* mania; ~ **de perseguição** persecution complex. **-2.** [gosto exagerado] obsession; ~ **de algo** obsession with sthg. **-3.** [hábito] habit; **ter** ~ **de fazer algo** to have a habit of doing sthg. **-4.** [mau hábito] bad habit. **-5.** [peculiaridade, excentricidade] quirk.
maníaco, ca [ma'niaku, ka] ◇ *adj* **-1.** *PSIC* maniacal. **-2.** [fanático]: **ser** ~ **por algo** to be manic about sthg. ◇ *m, f PSIC* maniac; ~ **sexual** sex maniac.
maníaco-depressivo, maníaca-depressiva [ma,niakudepre'sivu, ma,niakadepre'siva] ◇ *adj* manic-depressive. ◇ *m, f* manic-depressive.
manicômio [mani'komju] *m* lunatic asylum.
manicuro, ra [mani'kuru, ra] *m, f* manicurist.
manicure [mani'kuri] *f* manicure.
manifestação [manifeʃta'sãw] (*pl* **-ões**) *f* **-1.** [ger] manifestation. **-2.** [expressão] display.
manifestadamente [manifeʃtada'mẽntʃi] *adv* quite clearly.
manifestante [manifeʃ'tãntʃi] *mf* demonstrator.
manifestar [4] [manifeʃ'ta(x)] *vt* **-1.** [exprimir] to express. **-2.** [revelar] to display.
◆ **manifestar-se** *vp* **-1.** [revelar-se] to reveal o.s. **-2.** [pronunciar-se]: ~**-se (sobre/a favor de/contra algo)** to express an opinion (on/in favour of/against sthg).
manifesto, ta [mani'fɛʃtu, ta] *adj* manifest.
◆ **manifesto** *m* manifesto.
Manila [ma'nila] *n* Manila.
manilha [ma'niʎa] *f* [tubo] pipe.
manipulação [manipula'sãw] *f* **-1.** [com as mãos] handling. **-2.** [ger] manipulation. **-3.** *FARM* preparation.
manipulador, ra [manipula'do(x), ra] *adj* manipulative.
manipular [manipu'la(x)] *vt* **-1.** [ger] to manipulate. **-2.** [com as mãos] to handle. **-3.** *FARM* to prepare.
maniqueísmo [manike'iʒmu] *m* Manicheism.
maniqueísta [manike'iʃta] ◇ *adj* seeing things in black and white. ◇ *mf* Manichaean.
manivela [mani'vɛla] *f* crank.
manjado, da [mã'ʒadu, da] *adj fam* well-known.

manjar [4] [mã'ʒa(x)] <> *m* [iguaria] delicacy. <> *vt fam* **-1.** [compreender] to grasp. **-2.** [observar] to watch. <> *vi* [conhecer]: **~ de algo** to know about sthg.
manjar-branco [mãn,ʒax'brãŋku] (*pl* **manjares-brancos**) *m* blancmange.
manjedoura [mãnʒe'dora] *f* manger.
manjericão [mãnʒeri'kãw] *m* basil.
manjerona [mãnʒe'rona] *f* marjoram.
mano, na ['manu, na] *m,f fam* **-1.** [irmão] brother (sister). **-2.** *fam* [camarada, amigo] buddy.
manobra [ma'nɔbra] *f* **-1.** [ger] manoeuvre *UK*, maneuver *US*. **-2.** *fig* [manipulação] manipulation.
◆ **manobras** *fpl MIL* manoeuvres *UK*, maneuvers *US*.
manobrar [mano'bra(x)] <> *vt* **-1.** [manejar] to manoeuvre *UK*, to maneuver *US*. **-2.** [dirigir] to direct. **-3.** *fig* [manipular] to manipulate. <> *vi MIL* to manoeuvre *UK*, to maneuver *US*.
manobrista [mano'briʃta] *mf* **-1.** [de carro] valet *UK*, car jockey *US*. **-2.** [de trem] shunter.
mansão [mãn'sãw] (*pl* **-ões**) *f* mansion.
mansidão [mãnsi'dãw] *f* **-1.** [brandura] gentleness; **ele falava com ~** he spoke gently. **-2.** [tranqüilidade] calmness.
mansinho, nha [mã'siɲu, ɲa] *adj* [diminutivo de manso] gentle.
◆ **de mansinho** *loc adv* **-1.** [de leve] gently. **-2.** [sorrateiramente]: **entrar/sair de ~** to creep in/out.
manso, sa ['mãsu, sa] *adj* **-1.** [brando] gentle. **-2.** [tranqüilo] calm. **-3.** [domesticado] tame.
mansões [man'sõjʃ] *pl* ▷ **mansão**.
manta ['mãnta] *f* **-1.** [cobertor] blanket. **-2.** [xale] shawl. **-3.** [de carne seca] cut.
manteiga [mãn'tejga] *f* butter; **passar ~ em algo** to spread butter on sthg; **~ de cacau** cocoa butter; **~ derretida** *fam fig* cry baby.
manteigueira [mãntej'gejra] *f* butter dish.
mantenedor, ra [mãntene'do(x), ra] *m, f* **-1.** [de filho, casa] supporter. **-2.** [de máquina] service engineer.
manter [4] [mãn'te(x)] *vt* **-1.** [ger] to keep. **-2.** [em bom estado - máquina] to service; [- casa, saúde] to keep. **-3.** [família] to support. **-4.** [opinião, posição] to hold. **-5.** [relações] to maintain; **~ boas relações com alguém** to maintain a good relationship with sb.
◆ **manter-se** *vp* **-1.** [sustentar-se] to support o.s. **-2.** [permanecer] to remain; **~-se a par de algo** to keep abreast of sthg.
mantilha [mãn'tʃiʎa] *f* **-1.** [véu] veil. **-2.** [manta] shawl.
mantimentos [mãntʃi'mẽntuʃ] *m* provisions *(pl)*.
manto ['mãntu] *m* **-1.** [vestimenta] cloak. **-2.** [de reis] robe. **-3.** *fig* [simulação] smokescreen.
mantô [mãn'to] *m* coat.
manual [ma'nwaw] (*pl* **-ais**) <> *adj* manual; **ter habilidade ~** to be good with one's hands. <> *m* manual.
manufatura [manufa'tura] *f* [fabricação] manufacture.
manufaturado, da [manufatu'radu, da] *adj* manufactured.
manufaturar [manufatu'ra(x)] *vt* to manufacture.
manuscrito, ta [manuʃ'kritu] *adj* handwritten.
◆ **manuscrito** *m* manuscript.
manusear [manu'zea(x)] *vt* **-1.** [manejar] to handle. **-2.** [folhear] to thumb.
manuseio [manu'zeju] *m* handling.
manutenção [manutẽn'sãw] *f* **-1.** [ger] maintenance. **-2.** [da casa] upkeep. **-3.** [da família] support.
mão ['mãw] (*pl* **mãos**) *f* **-1.** [ger] hand; **à ~** [perto] at hand; [com a mão] by hand; **feito à ~** handmade; **à ~ armada** armed; **dar a ~ a alguém** to hold sb's hand; **de ~s dadas** hand in hand; **de primeira ~** firsthand; **de segunda ~** second-hand; **entregar algo em ~s** to deliver sthg by hand; **~s ao alto!** hands up!; **~s à obra!** let's get to work!; **pôr a ~ em algo** to lay one's hands on sthg; **ter a ~ pesada** to be clumsy; **ter algo em ~** to have sthg to hand. **-2.** [no trânsito]: **esta rua dá ~ para a praia** this street takes you to the beach; **fora de ~** out of the way; **~ dupla** two-way; **~ única** one-way; **uma rua de ~ dupla/única** a two-way/one-way street. **-3.** [de tinta] coat. **-4.** [habilidade]: **com ~ de mestre** with a master touch; **ter uma ~ boa para algo** to be good at sthg. **-5.** [poder, controle]: **estar nas ~s de alguém** to be in sb's hands; **estar em boas ~s** t[o] be in good hands. **-6.** *loc*: **abrir ~ de algo** to giv[e] sthg up; **agüentar a ~** *fam* [suportar] to hold o[n]; [aguardar] to hang on; **dar a ~ à palmatóri[a]** admit one's mistake; **ficar na ~** to be du[...] **forçar a ~** to get nasty; **lançar ~ de algo** to [...] use of sthg; **largar a ~ em alguém** to hit [...] **gar alguém/algo de ~** to wash one's hand[s ...] sthg; **pedir a ~ de alguém (em casament[o])** for sb's hand (in marriage); **passar a** [...] [roubar] to nick sthg; **pôr a ~ no fo[go ...]** to stand up for sb; **ser um[a ...]** great help; **de ~ beijada** bucksh[ee ...] **a alguém** to give sb a hand; **pre[...]** need a hand.
mão-aberta [,mãwa'bɛxta] (*pl* [...] generous.
mão-boba [mãw'boba] (*pl* [...] [pro]pósito libidinoso]: **passar a** [...] sb up. <> *m* perv.
mão-cheia [,mãw'ʃeja] [...]
mão-de-obra [mãw'[...] *f* **-1.** [trabalho, custo] la[...] **~** *fig* to be hard [...] workforce; **~ esp**[...]
mão-de-vaca [...] skinflint.
mão-leve [,m[...]
maoísta [m[...] Maoist.
mapa ['m[...] disappe[...]

mapa-múndi [ˌmapaˈmũndʒi] (*pl* **mapas-múndi**) *m* world map.

Maputo [maˈputu] *n* Maputo.

maquete [maˈkɛtʃi] *f* model.

maquiado, da [maˈkjadu, da] *adj* [com maquiagem] made-up.

maquiador, ra [makjaˈdo(x), ra], **maquilador, ra** [makilaˈdo(x), ra] *m, f* make-up artist.

maquiagem [maˈkjaʒẽ] (*pl* **-ns**) *f* **-1.** [ger] make-up; **ele se encarregou da** ~ he was in charge of make-up. **-2.** [disfarce]: ~ **financeira** financial cover-up.

maquiar [16] [maˈkjax] *vt* **-1.** [pintar] to make up. **-2.** *fig* [mascarar] to cover up.

◆ **maquiar-se** *vp* [pintar-se] to put on one's make-up.

maquiavélico, ca [makjaˈvɛliku, ka] *adj* Machiavellian.

maquilador, ra [makilaˈdo(x), ra] *m, f* = **maquiador**.

maquilagem [makiˈlaʒẽ] *f* = **maquiagem**.

maquilar [4] [makiˈla(x)] *vt* [pintar] to make up.

◆ **maquilar-se** *vp* [pintar-se] to put on one's make-up.

máquina [ˈmakina] *f* **-1.** [ger] machine; **bater** *ou* **escrever à** ~ to type; **costurar à** ~ to machine-sew; **escrito à** ~ typewritten; **feito à** ~ machine-made; ~ **de calcular** calculator; ~ **de costura** sewing machine; ~ **de escrever** typewriter; ~ **fotográfica** camera; ~ **de lavar (roupa)** washing machine. **-2.** [locomotora] engine; ~ **a vapor** steam engine. **-3.** *fig* [de estado, partido *etc*] machinery.

◆ **máquinas** *fpl* machinery.

maquinação [makinaˈsãw] (*pl* **-ões**) *f* machination.

maquinar [4] [makiˈna(x)] ◇ *vt* to plot. ◇ *vi*: ~ **contra alguém/algo** to plot against sb/sthg.

maquinária [makiˈnarja], **maquinaria** [makiˈa'rial *f* [m quinas] machinery.

aquinár... ...iˈnarju] *m* = **maquinária**.

aquini... [makiˈniʃta] *mf* **-1.** *FERRO* engine river. -... *EATRO* stagehand.

r [ˈma(... *pl* **-es**) *m* sea; **em pleno** ~ on the gh sea ...**zer-se ao** ~ to set sail; ~ **aberto** en sea ~ by sea; ~ **Morto** Dead Sea; ~ gro B...ea; ~ **do Norte** North Sea; ~ **de** ...as [m... calm sea; *fig* bed of roses; **nem** ...to a... **tanto à terra** neither one way ... the

... (ab...**ço**) Mar.

...**aca**... *f* maracas (*pl*).

...**acu**... ...ʒa] *m* passion fruit.

...**ac**... ...arakuʒaˈzejru] *m* passion fruit ...t.

...**c**... ...ˈtaja] *f* dirty trick.

...**j**... **1.** [título] maharaja. **-2.** *fig* ...o has uses their position, ...stly, in order to become

... *n* Maranhão.

marasmo [maˈraʒmu] *m* **-1.** [desânimo] lethargy. **-2.** [estagnação] stagnation.

maratona [maraˈtona] *m* marathon.

maratonista [maratoˈniʃta] *mf* marathon runner.

maravilha [maraˈviʎa] *f* wonder; **às mil** ~**s** wonderfully; **ser uma** ~ to be wonderful.

maravilhado, da [maraviˈʎadu, da] *adj*: ~ **(com)** amazed (at).

maravilhar [4] [maraviˈʎa(x)] *vt* to astonish.

◆ **maravilhar-se** *vp*: ~**-se (de algo)** to be amazed (at sthg).

maravilhoso, osa [maraviˈʎozu, ɔza] *adj* wonderful.

marca [ˈmaxka] *f* **-1.** [ger] mark. **-2.** [*COM* - de carro] make; [- de café, queijo] brand; ~ **comercial** *ou* **de fábrica** trademark; ~ **registrada** registered trademark. **-3.** [de prata] hallmark.

◆ **de marca maior** *loc adj pej* of the first order.

marcação [maxkaˈsãw] (*pl* **-ões**) *f* **-1.** [ato de marcar - enxoval] marking; [- gado] branding. **-2.** *ESP* marking. **-3.** [perseguição, vigilância] scrutiny; **estar de** ~ **com alguém** to pick on sb.

marcado, da [maxˈkadu, da] *adj* **-1.** [assinalado - roupa, texto] marked; [- gado] branded. **-2.** [reservado] booked. **-3.** [com marca, mancha] marked. **-4.** [pessoa - traumatizada] marked; [- em evidência] watched.

marcador [maxkaˈdo(x)] *m* **-1.** [de livro] bookmark. **-2.** [*ESP* - quadro] scoreboard; [- jogador] scorer.

marcante [maxˈkãntʃi] *adj* marked.

marcapasso [maxkaˈpasu] *m MED* pacemaker.

marcar [12] [maxˈka(x)] *vt* **-1.** [ger] to mark; ~ **época** to make history. **-2.** [pôr marca em - livro, roupa] to mark; [- animal] to brand. **-3.** [data, hora, prazo] to fix; ~ **o tempo de algo** to time sthg. **-4.** [almoço, encontro] to arrange; ~ **uma consulta** to make an appointment. **-5.** [*ESP* - jogador] to mark; [- gol] to score. **-6.** [suj: relógio] to say. **-7.** [suj: termômetro] to show. **-8.** [demarcar] to demarcate.

marcenaria [maxsenaˈria] *f* **-1.** [arte] marquetry. **-2.** [trabalho] cabinet-making. **-3.** [oficina] cabinet-maker's workshop.

marceneiro, ra [maxseˈnejru, ra] *m, f* cabinet-maker.

marcha [ˈmaxʃa] *f* **-1.** [ato] marching; **pôr-se em** ~ to set off. **-2.** [passo] pace. **-3.** [ger] march. **-4.** *AUTO* gear; **dar** ~ **à ré** to reverse; ~ **à ré** reverse. **-5.** [*MÚS* - tradicional] march; ~ **fúnebre** funeral march; [- popular] festive march. **-6.** *fig* [progressão] course.

marchar [4] [maxˈʃa(x)] *vi* **-1.** *MIL* to march; ~ **sobre** [avançar] to march into. **-2.** [ir]: ~ **para** to go to.

marchetar [4] [maxʃeˈta(x)] *vt* [incrustar]: ~ **algo (de algo)** to inlay sthg (with sthg).

marchinha [maxˈʃiɲa] *f MÚS a satirical song in double time, in the main performed during carnival.*

marcial [max'sjaw] (*pl* **-ais**) *adj* martial; **corte ~** court martial.
marciano, na [max'sjanu, na] <> *adj* Martian. <> *m, f* Martian.
marco ['maxku] *m* **-1.** [ger] landmark. **-2.** [moeda] mark. **-3.** [da janela] frame.
março ['marsu] *m* March; *veja também* **setembro**.
maré [ma'rɛ] *f* **-1.** [do mar] tide; **~ alta/baixa** high/low tide; **remar contra a ~** *fig* to swim against the tide. **-2.** *fig* [ocasião] spell; **aproveitar a ~** to make the most of one's luck. **-3.** *fig* [tendência] tendency. **-4.** *fig* [humor]: **estar de ~ alta** to be in high spirits. **-5.** *fig* [multidão] sea.
mareado, da [ma'rjadu, da] *adj* **-1.** [enjoado] seasick. **-2.** [oxidado] tarnished.
marear [15] [ma'rja(x)] <> *vt* **-1.** [enjoar] to make seasick. **-2.** [oxidar] to tarnish. <> *vi* [enjoar] to be seasick.
marechal [mare'ʃaw] (*pl* **-ais**) *m* marshal.
maré-cheia [ma,rɛ'ʃeja] (*pl* **marés-cheias**) *f* high tide.
marejar [4] [mare'ʒa(x)] <> *vt* to shed. <> *vi* to flow.
◆ **marejar-se** *vp*: **~-se de lágrimas** to well up with tears.
maremoto [mare'mɔtu] *m* tidal wave.
maresia [mare'zia] *f* sea air.
marfim [max'fĩ] *m* ivory; **de ~** ivory *(antes de subst)*.
margarida [maxga'rida] *f* BOT daisy.
margarina [maxga'rina] *f* margarine.
margear [15] [max'ʒja(x)] *vt* **-1.** [seguir pela margem de] to follow. **-2.** [estar à margem de] to border.
margem ['maxʒẽ] (*pl* **-ns**) *f* **-1.** [ger] margin; **~ de lucro** profit margin. **-2.** [beira - de estrada, lago] edge; **à ~ de** alongside; [- de rio] bank; [- litoral] shore. **-3.** [latitude] room; **~ de erro** margin of error; **~ de segurança** safety margin. **-4.** [limites] edge; **à ~ da sociedade/lei** on the fringes of society/the law; **manter-se à ~ de algo** to remain distant from sthg. **-5.** [ocasião]: **dar ~ a alguém para fazer algo** to give sb the chance to do sthg.
marginal [maxʒi'naw] (*pl* **-ais**) <> *adj* **-1.** [pessoa] delinquent. **-2.** [nota] marginal. <> *mf* [pessoa] delinquent.
marginalidade [maxʒinali'dadʒi] *f* delinquency.
marginalizar [4] [maxʒinali'za(x)] *vt* [excluir] to marginalize.
◆ **marginalizar-se** *vp* [tornar-se fora-da-lei] to marginalize o.s.
maria-fumaça [ma,riafu'masa] (*pl* **marias-fumaças**) *m & f* steam train.
maria-mijona [ma,riami'ʒona] *adj inv* unfashionably long.
maria-mole [ma,ria'mɔli] (*pl* **-s**) *f* CULIN *marshmallow dessert covered with coconut.*
maria-sem-vergonha [ma,riasẽnvex'goɲa] (*pl* **marias-sem-vergonha**) *f* BOT busy lizzie.
maria-vai-com-as-outras [ma,riavajkwa'ʣ zowtraʃ] *mf inv* sheep.
maricas [ma'rikaʃ] *fam* <> *adj inv* [medroso] chicken. <> *m inv* [efeminado] pretty boy.
marido [ma'ridu] *m* husband.
marimbondo [marĩn'bõndu] *m* hornet.
marina [ma'rina] *f* marina.
marinar [4] [mari'nax] *vt* to marinate.
marinha [ma'riɲa] *f* ⊳ **marinho**.
marinheiro, ra [mari'ɲejru, ra] <> *adj* sailor's *(antes de subst)*. <> *m, f* sailor; **~ de primeira viagem** *fig* greenhorn.
marinho, nha [ma'riɲu, ɲa] *adj* [do mar] marine.
◆ **marinho** <> *adj inv* [cor] navy. <> *m* [cor] navy blue.
◆ **marinha** *f* **-1.** [força] navy; **marinha (de guerra)** navy; **marinha mercante** merchant navy. **-2.** [pintura] seascape.
marionete [marjo'nɛtʃi] *f* puppet.
mariposa [mari'poza] *f* moth.
marisco [ma'riʃku] *m* shellfish.
marital [mari'taw] (*pl* **-ais**) *adj* marital.
maritalmente [maritaw'mẽntʃi] *adv*: **viver ~ (com alguém)** to live together (with sb).
marítimo, ma [ma'ritʃimu, ma] *adj* maritime.
marketing ['maxketʃĩŋ] *m* marketing.
marmanjo [max'mãnʒu] *m* grown man.
marmelada [maxme'lada] *f* **-1.** [doce] quince jam. **-2.** *fam* [mamata] racket.
marmelo [max'mɛlu] *m* quince.
marmita [max'mita] *f* **-1.** [recipiente] casserole. **-2.** [refeição] packed lunch.
mármore ['maxmori] *m* marble; **de ~** marble *(antes de subst)*.
marmóreo, rea [max'mɔriu, ria] *adj* marble.
marola [ma'rɔla] *f* small wave.
maroto, ta [ma'rotu, ta] *adj* **-1.** [esperto] crafty. **-2.** [malicioso] malicious.
marquês, quesa [max'keʃ, eza] (*mpl* **-eses**, *fpl* **-esas**) *m, f* marquis (*f* marchioness).
marquise [max'kizi] *f* canopy.
marra ['maxa] *f*: **obedeceu na ~** he obeyed under pressure; **invadiram ~** they invaded in strength.
marreco [ma'xɛku] *m* wigeon.
Marrocos [ma'xɔkuʃ] *n* Morocco.
marrom [ma'xõ] (*pl* **-ns**) <> *adj* brown. <> *m* brown.
marrom-glacê [ma'xõ'gla'se] (*pl* **-s**) *m* marron glacé.
marroquino, na [maxo'kinu, na] <> *adj* Moroccan. <> *m, f* Morroccan.
Marte ['maxtʃi] *m* Mars.
martelada [maxte'lada] *f* **-1.** [pancada] blow. **-2.** [ruído] bang.
martelar [maxte'la(x)] <> *vt* **-1.** [com martelo] to hammer. **-2.** [afligir] to bother. **-3.** [repetir] to repeat. <> *vi* **-1.** [dar marteladas] to hammer. **-2.** [insistir]: **~ em algo** to keep on about sthg.
martelo [max'tɛlu] *m* hammer.
mártir ['maxti(x)] (*pl* **-es**) *mf* martyr.
martírio [max'tʃirju] *m* **-1.** [suplício] martyrdom.

-2. *fig* [tormento] torment; **ser um ~** to be a torment.
martirizante [maxtʃiri'zãntʃi] *adj* agonizing.
martirizar [4] [maxtʃiri'za(x)] *vt* **-1.** [torturar] to torture. **-2.** *fig* [atormentar] to torment.
◆ **martirizar-se** *vp* [atormentar-se] to agonize.
marujo [ma'ruʒu] *m* sailor.
marulhar [4] [maru'ʎa(x)] *vi* **-1.** [mar] to surge. **-2.** [ondas] to lap. **-3.** [barulho das ondas] to crash.
marulho [ma'ruʎu] *m* **-1.** [do mar] surge. **-2.** [das ondas] lapping.
marxismo [max'ksiʒmu] *m* Marxism.
marxista [max'ksiʃta] ◇ *adj* Marxist. ◇ *mf* Marxist.
marzipã [maxzi'pã] *m* marzipan.
mas [ma(j)ʃ] ◇ *conj* but; **~ que decepção!** how disappointing! ◇ *cont* = **me + as**.
◆ **mas também** *loc conj* but also; **não só ... ~ também** not only ... but also.
mascar [12] [maʃ'ka(x)] ◇ *vt* to chew. ◇ *vi* to chew.
máscara ['maʃkara] *f* **-1.** [ger] mask; **baile de ~s** masked ball; **~ de oxigênio** oxygen mask; **~ (de beleza)** face mask. **-2.** [fachada] disguise; **tirar a ~ de alguém** to unmask sb.
mascarado, da [maʃka'radu, da] *adj* **-1.** [fantasiado] masked. **-2.** *fig* [disfarçado]: **~ de mendigo** disguised as a beggar.
mascarar [4] [maʃka'ra(x)] *vt* to mask.
mascate [maʃ'katʃi] *m* hawker.
Mascate [maʃ'katʃi] *n* Muscat.
mascavo [maʃ'kavu] *adj* ▻ **açúcar**.
mascote [maʃ'kɔtʃi] *f* mascot.
masculinidade [maʃkulini'dadʒi] *f* masculinity.
masculinizado, da [maʃkulini'zadu, da] *adj* [mulher] masculine.
masculinizar [maʃkulini'za(x)] *vt* to masculinize.
masculino, na [maʃku'linu, na] *adj* **-1.** [sexo, população] male. **-2.** [modos, voz]: **esta foi uma reação tipicamente masculina** that was a typically male response. **-3.** *GRAM* masculine.
◆ **masculino** *m GRAM* masculine.
másculo, la ['maʃkulu, la] *adj* [viril] manly.
masmorra [maʒ'moxa] *f* **-1.** [calabouço] dungeon. **-2.** *fig* [aposento] hole.
masoquismo [mazo'kiʒmu] *m* masochism.
masoquista [mazo'kiʃta] ◇ *adj* masochistic. ◇ *mf* masochist.
massa ['masa] *f* **-1.** [ger] mass. **-2.** [culinária - de pão] dough; [- de bolo] mixture; [- de torta, empada] pastry; [- de tomate] paste. **-3.** [macarrão] pasta. **-4.** [grande quantidade]: **uma ~ de** a mass of. **-5.** *CONSTR*: **~ de vidraceiro** putty. **-6.** [maioria]: **a ~ de** the majority of.
◆ **massas** *fpl*: **as ~s** the masses.
◆ **em massa** *loc adv* en masse.
massa-corrida ['masako'xida] (*pl* **-s**) *f plaster skim applied before painting.*
massacrante [masa'krãntʃi] *adj* annoying.
massacrar [4] [masa'kra(x)] *vt* **-1.** [ger] to massacre. **-2.** [oprimir] to oppress. **-3.** *fig* [torturar] to torture.
massacre [ma'sakri] *m* massacre.
massagear [15] [masa'ʒea(x)] ◇ *vt* to massage. ◇ *vi* to do massage.
massagem [ma'saʒẽ] (*pl* **-ns**) *f* massage; **~ facial** facial.
massagista [masa'ʒiʃta] *mf* masseur (masseuse).
massificação [masifika'sãw] (*pl* **-ões**) *f* popularization.
massificado, da [masifika'du, da] *adj* popular *(antes de subst).*
massificar [12] [masifi'ka(x)] *vt* **-1.** [ensino universitário] to popularize. **-2.** [povo] to sell to the masses.
massinha [ma'siɲa] *f* **-1.** [para modelar] Plasticine®. **-2.** [comestível]: **sopa de ~** minestrone.
massudo, da [ma'sudu, da] *adj* **-1.** [pão, torta] heavy. **-2.** [documentação, livro] bulky.
mastectomia [maʃtekto'mia] *f* mastectomy.
mastigado, da [maʃtʃi'gadu, da] *adj* **-1.** [triturado] chewed. **-2.** [facilitado] well-explained.
mastigar [14] [maʃtʃi'ga(x)] ◇ *vt* [triturar] to chew. ◇ *vi* [triturar] to chew.
mastim [maʃ'tʃĩ] (*pl* **-ns**) *m* mastiff.
mastite [mas'tʃitʃi] *f* mastitis.
mastodonte [maʃto'dõntʃi] *m* **-1.** [mamífero] mammoth. **-2.** *fam* [pessoa] hulk.
mastro ['maʃtru] *m* **-1.** *NÁUT* mast. **-2.** [para bandeira] flagpole.
masturbação [maʃtuxba'sãw] *f* masturbation.
masturbar [4] [maʃtux'ba(x)] *vt* to masturbate.
◆ **masturbar-se** *vp* to masturbate.
mata ['mata] *f* forest; **~ virgem** virgin forest.
mata-baratas [mataba'rataʃ] *mpl* [inseticida] cockroach killer.
mata-borrão [ˌmatabo'xãw] (*pl* **mata-borrões**) *m* **-1.** [papel] blotting paper. **-2.** [artefato] blotter.
matacão [mata'kãw] (*pl* **-ões**) *f*: **uma ~ de algo** a big lump of sthg.
matado, da [ma'tadu, da] *adj* [serviço] lousy.
matador, ra [mata'do(x), ra] *m, f* killer.
◆ **matador** *m* [tourada] matador.
matadouro [mata'doru] *m* slaughterhouse.
matagal [mata'gaw] (*pl* **-ais**) *m* **-1.** [terreno] bush. **-2.** [mata espessa] thicket.
mata-moscas [ˌmata'moʃkaʃ] *m (inv)* fly-swat.
mata-mosquito [ˌmatamoʃ'kitu] (*pl* **mata-mosquitos**) *m* mosquito spray.
matança [ma'tãnsa] *f* **-1.** [de pessoas] massacre. **-2.** [de animais] slaughter.
matar [4] [ma'ta(x)] ◇ *vt* **-1.** [ger] to kill. **-2.** [saciar - fome] to satisfy; [- sede] to quench; [- curiosidade] to quell. **-3.** [gazetear] to skip. **-4.** [executar mal] to do badly. **-5.** [decifrar] to guess. **-6.** [fazer desaparecer] to crush. ◇ *vi* [causar morte] to kill.
◆ **matar-se** *vp* **-1.** [suicidar-se] to kill o.s. **-2.** [cansar-se]: **~-se de algo/fazer algo** to kill o.s. with sthg/doing sthg.

◆ **de matar** *loc adj fig* [terrível] terrible; **dor de** ~ excruciating pain; **ser de** ~ to be terrible.
mata-rato [ˌmata'xatu] (*pl* **mata-ratos**) *m* **-1.** [veneno] rat poison. **-2.** *fam* [cigarro] cancer stick.
mate ['matʃi] *m* [bebida] maté.
matelassê [matela'se] *adj* quilted.
matemático, ca [mate'matʃiku, ka] ◇ *adj* mathematical. ◇ *m, f* mathematician.
◆ **matemática** *f* [ciência] mathematics *(sg)*.
matéria [ma'tɛrja] *f* **-1.** [ger] matter; ~ **plástica** plastic. **-2.** [assunto] subject; **em** ~ **de política/esporte** in the area of politics/sports. **-3.** *EDUC* subject. **-4.** *JORN* article.
material [mate'rjaw] (*pl* **-ais**) ◇ *adj* material. ◇ *m* **-1.** [substância] material. **-2.** [utensílios] materials *(pl)*; ~ **de escritório** office stationery; ~ **de limpeza** cleaning products *(pl)*. **-3.** [bélico] armaments *(pl)*. **-4.** [informativo, didático] teaching material.
materialismo [materja'liʒmu] *m* materialism.
materialista [materja'liʃta] ◇ *adj* materialistic. ◇ *mf* materialist.
materializar [4] [materjali'za(x)] *vt* to materialize.
◆ **materializar-se** *vp* to materialize.
matéria-prima [maˌtɛrja'prima] (*pl* **matérias-primas**) *f* raw material.
maternal [matex'naw] (*pl* **-ais**) ◇ *adj* maternal. ◇ *m EDUC* nursery school.
maternidade [matexni'dadʒi] *f* **-1.** [qualidade] motherhood. **-2.** [hospital] maternity hospital.
materno, na [ma'tɛxnu, na] *adj* **-1.** [ger] maternal. **-2.** [língua]: **língua** ~ mother tongue.
matilha [ma'tʃiʎa] *f* [cães] pack.
matina [ma'tʃina] *f fam* morning.
matinal [matʃi'naw] (*pl* **-ais**) *adj* morning *(antes de subst)*.
matinê [matʃi'ne] *f* matinée.
matiz [ma'tʃiʒ] *m* **-1.** [tom] shade. **-2.** *fig* [traço] tinge.
matizar [4] [matʃi'za(x)] *vt* **-1.** [dar nuances a] to tinge. **-2.** [colorir] to colour *UK*, to color *US*.
mato ['matu] *m* **-1.** [área] scrubland. **-2.** [plantas] weeds *(pl)*. **-3.** [roça] countryside. **-4.** *loc*: **estar num** ~ **sem cachorro** *fam* to be up the creek without a paddle; **ser** ~ *fam* to be thick on the ground.
Mato Grosso do Sul [matuˌgrosudu'suw] *n* Mato Grosso do Sul.
matraca [ma'traka] *f* **-1.** [instrumento] rattle; **falar como uma** ~ to talk the hind legs off a donkey. **-2.** *fig* [pessoa] chatterbox.
matraquear [15] [matra'kja(x)] *vi* [tagarelar] to chatter.
matreiro, ra [ma'trejru, ra] *adj fam* [astuto, ardiloso] crafty.
matriarca [ma'trjaxka] *f* matriarch.
matriarcal [matrjax'kaw] (*pl* **-ais**) *adj* matriarchal.
matrícula [ma'trikula] *f* **-1.** [inscrição] enrolment *UK*, enrollment *US*; **fazer (a)** ~ to enrol *UK*, to enroll *US*; **qual é o seu número de** ~ what's your registration number? **-2.** [taxa] fee.
matricular [4] [matriku'la(x)] *vt*: ~ **alguém (em algo)** to enrol sb (in sthg) *UK*, to enroll sb (in sthg) *US*.
◆ **matricular-se** *vp*: ~**-se (em algo)** to enrol (in sthg) *UK*, to enroll (in sthg) *US*.
matrimonial [matrimo'njaw] (*pl* **-ais**) *adj* matrimonial.
matrimônio [matri'monju] *m* marriage; **contrair** ~ **(com alguém)** to be joined in marriage (to sb).
matriz [ma'triʃ] (*pl* **-es**) ◇ *adj* **-1.** [igreja, língua] mother *(antes de subst)*. **-2.** [idéia] original. ◇ *f* **-1.** [de empresa] head office. **-2.** [de igreja] mother church. **-3.** [molde] mould *UK*, mold *US*. **-4.** *MAT* matrix.
matrona [ma'trona] *f pej* matron; **estar uma** ~ to look like an old cow.
maturação [matura'sãw] (*pl* **-ões**) *f* **-1.** [de fruta] ripening. **-2.** *fig* [amadurecimento] maturation.
maturar [4] [matu'ra(x)] ◇ *vt* to mature. ◇ *vi* to mature.
maturidade [maturi'dadʒi] *f* maturity.
matusquela [matuʃ'kɛla] *mf fam* lunatic.
matutar [4] [matu'ta(x)] ◇ *vt* [planejar] to plan. ◇ *vi* [refletir] to think about; ~ **sobre algo** to turn sthg over in one's mind.
matutino, na [matu'tʃinu, na] *adj* morning.
◆ **matutino** *m* morning newspaper.
matuto, ta [ma'tutu, ta] ◇ *adj* **-1.** [da roça] country *(antes de subst)*. **-2.** *fam* [sabido] shrewd. ◇ *m, f* **-1.** [pessoa da roça] country bumpkin. **-2.** [pessoa rude] peasant.
mau, má ['maw, 'ma] ◇ *adj* **-1.** *(antes de subst)* [ger] bad. **-2.** *(antes de subst)* [incapaz] poor. ◇ *m, f* **-1.** [pessoa] bad person. **-2.** [em filme etc] baddy.
mau-caráter [ˌmawka'ratex] (*pl* **maus-caráteres**) ◇ *adj* disreputable. ◇ *mf* bad character.
mau-olhado [ˌmawo'ʎadu] (*pl* **maus-olhados**) *m* evil eye.
mauricinho [mawri'siɲu] *m fam* posh kid.
Maurício [maw'risju] *n* Mauritius.
máuser® ['mawze(x)] *m* mauser.
mausoléu [mawzo'lɛu] *m* mausoleum.
maus-tratos [mawʃ'tratuʃ] *mpl* abuse.
mavioso, osa [ma'vjozu, ɔza] *adj* affectionate.
maxidesvalorização [maksidʒiʒvaloriza'sãw] (*pl* **-ões**) *f* steep devaluation.
maxilar [maksi'la(x)] (*pl* **-es**) ◇ *m* jaw. ◇ *adj* maxillary.
máxima ['masima] *f* ⊳ **máximo**.
maximizar [4] [masimi'za(x)] *vt* **-1.** [aumentar ao máximo] to maximize. **-2.** *MAT* to round up.
máximo, ma ['masimu, ma] *adj* **-1.** [o maior possível] maximum. **-2.** [supremo] highest.
◆ **máximo** *m* [o mais alto grau] maximum; **ao** ~ to the maximum; **chegar ao** ~ to reach the peak; **no** ~ at most; **ser o** ~ [ser maravilhoso] to be the best.

◆ **máxima** *f* **-1.** [temperatura] maximum. **-2.** [sentença, princípio] maxim.
maxixe [ma'ʃiʃi] *m* **-1.** [legume] gourd. **-2.** [dança] *Brazilian dance, precursor of the samba.*
mazela [ma'zɛla] *f* **-1.** *fam* [doença]: **ela gosta de falar de suas ~s** she likes to talk about her aches and pains. **-2.** [infortúnio] misfortune.
MB (*abrev de* **Megabyte**) *m* MB.
MBA (*abrev de* **Master of Business Administration**) *m* MBA.
me [mi] *pron* [complemento direto] me; [complemento indireto] (to) me; [reflexo] myself; **eu nunca ~ engano** I'm never wrong; **eu ~ machuquei** I've hurt myself; **você já ~ contou essa história** you've already told me that story.
meado ['mjadu] *m*: **no ~ de** in the middle of; **em ~s de setembro** in mid-September.
meandro ['mjãndru] *m* meander.
◆ **meandros** *mpl* meanderings.
MEC (*abrev de* **Ministério da Educação e Cultura**) *m* Brazilian ministry of education and culture.
Meca ['mɛka] *n* Mecca.
mecânico, ca [me'kãniku, ka] <> *adj* mechanical. <> *m, f* [profissional] mechanic.
◆ **mecânica** *f* **-1.** [ger] mechanics *(pl)*. **-2.** *fig* [mecanismo] workings *(pl)*.
mecanismo [meka'niʒmu] *m* mechanism; **~ de defesa** defence mechanism; **~ de busca** *COMPUT* search engine.
mecanização [mekaniza'sãw] *f* mechanization.
mecanizar [4] [mekani'za(x)] *vt* to mechanize.
mecenas [me'senaʃ] *m inv* patron.
mecha ['mɛʃa] *f* **-1.** [de vela] wick. **-2.** [de explosivo] fuse. **-3.** [de cabelo] strand. **-4.** [cabelo tingido] streak; **fazer ~ (no cabelo)** to have one's hair streaked. **-5.** [em ferimento] wick.
medalha [me'daʎa] *f* medal.
medalhão [meda'ʎãw] (*pl* **-ões**) *m* **-1.** [jóia] medallion. **-2.** *fig* [figurão] high-flyer, big shot.
média ['mɛdʒja] *f* ▷ **médio**.
mediação [medʒja'sãw] *f* mediation; **por ~ de** through the mediation of.
mediador, ra [medʒja'do(x), ra] *m, f* mediator.
mediano, na [me'dʒjãnu, na] *adj* **-1.** [ger] average. **-2.** [linha] median.
◆ **mediana** *f GEOM* median.
mediante [me'dʒjãntʃi] *prep* **-1.** [por meio de] through; **~ ajuda de** with the help of; **~ a graça de Deus** by the grace of God. **-2.** [a troco de] in exchange for.
mediar [17] [me'dʒja(x)] <> *vt* [intervir em] to mediate; **~ um debate** to chair a debate. <> *vi* [intervir] to mediate; **~ entre/a favor de** to mediate between/in favour of.
medicação [medʒika'sãw] (*pl* **-ões**) *f* medication.
medicamento [medʒika'mẽntu] *m* medicine.
medição [medʒi'sãw] (*pl* **-ões**) *f* measurement.
medicar [12] [medʒi'ka(x)] <> *vt* to medicate. <> *vi* to practise medicine *UK*, to practice medicine *US*.
◆ **medicar-se** *vp* to take medicine.
medicina [medʒi'sina] *f* medicine; **~ alternativa** alternative medicine; **~ legal** forensic medicine.
medicinal [medʒisi'naw] (*pl* **-ais**) *adj* medicinal.
médico, ca ['mɛdʒiku, ka] <> *adj* medical. <> *m, f* doctor; **~ de família** family doctor, GP, general expert.
médico-hospitalar [ˌmɛdʒikwoʃpita'la(x)] (*pl* **médico-hospitalares**) *adj* hospital and medical *(antes de subst)*.
médico-legal [ˌmedʒikule'gaw] (*pl* **médico-legais**) *adj* forensic.
médico-legista, médica-legista [ˌmedʒikule'ʒiʃta] (*mpl* **médicos-legistas**, *fpl* **médicas-legistas**) *m, f* forensic expert.
medida [me'dʒida] *f* **-1.** [ger] measurement; **~ de capacidade** measure of capacity. **-2.** [tamanho] size; **feito sob ~** made to measure; **tomar as ~s de alguém/algo** to take the measurements of sb/sthg. **-3.** [grau] degree; **na ~ do possível** as far as possible. **-4.** [providência] measure; **tomar ~s** to take measures; **~ provisória** *JUR* emergency measure; **~ de segurança** safety measure. **-5.** [limite]: **passar das ~s** to go beyond the limits.
◆ **à medida que** *loc conj* as.
◆ **na medida em que** *loc conj* in so far as.
medidor [medʒi'do(x)] *m* meter; **~ de pressão** pressure gauge.
medieval [medʒje'vaw] (*pl* **-ais**) *adj* medieval.
médio, dia ['mɛdʒju, dja] *adj* **-1.** [entre dois pontos - ger] middle; [- tamanho] medium. **-2.** [resultado de cálculo] average. **-3.** [ensino] secondary.
◆ **média** *f* **-1.** *MAT* average; **em ~** on average. **-2.** *EDUC* secondary school. **-3.** [café com leite] white coffee. **-4.** *loc*: **fazer ~ com** to fawn over.
medíocre [me'dʒiwkri] <> *adj* mediocre. <> *mf* mediocrity.
mediocridade [medʒiwkri'dadʒi] *f* mediocrity.
medir [70] [me'dʒi(x)] *vt* **-1.** [ger] to measure; **~ alguém/algo por algo** to measure sb/sthg against sthg; **~ alguém/algo por alguém** to measure sb/sthg against sb. **-2.** [considerar, avaliar] to evaluate. **-3.** [moderar] to measure; **meça suas palavras!** watch what you say! **-4.** [olhar com desdém]: **~ alguém de alto a baixo** to look down on sb.
◆ **medir-se** *vp* **-1.** [tomar as medidas] to measure o.s. **-2.** [igualar-se]: **~-se com alguém em algo** to equal sb at sthg.
meditação [medʒita'sãw] (*pl* **-ões**) *f* meditation.
meditar [4] [me'dʒita(x)] *vi* to meditate; **~ sobre algo** to meditate on sthg.
meditativo, va [medʒita'tʃivu, va] *adj* meditative.
mediterrâneo, nea [medʒite'xãnju, nja] *adj* Mediterranean.
◆ **Mediterrâneo** *n*: **o (mar) ~** the Mediterranean (Sea).
médium ['mɛdʒjũ] (*pl* **-ns**) [espirit] *mf* medium.

mediúnico, ca [me'dʒjuniku, ka] *adj* of a medium *(depois de subst)*.

mediunidade [medʒjuni'dadʒi] *f* spiritualism.

medo ['medu] *m* **-1.** [pavor] fear; **dar ~** to frighten; **me dá ~ fazer algo** I am frightened of doing sthg; **estar com** *ou* **ter ~ (de)** to be afraid (of); **estar com** *ou* **ter ~ de fazer algo** to be afraid of doing sthg; **estar se cagando de ~** *vulg* to be shitting o.s. with fear; **feio de meter ~** as ugly as sin; **morrer de ~** to be frightened to death. **-2.** [receio]: **com ~ de/que** for fear of/that; **estar com** *ou* **ter ~ de** to be afraid of.

medonho, nha [me'doɲu, ɲa] *adj* **-1.** [assustador] terrifying. **-2.** [horrível] horrendous.

medrar [4] [me'dra(x)] *vi* **-1.** [planta] to grow. **-2.** *fam* [ficar com medo] to get scared.

medroso, osa [medrozu, ɔza] ◇ *adj* [temeroso] scared. ◇ *m, f* coward.

medula [me'dula] *f ANAT* marrow, medulla; **~ óssea** bone marrow.

megabyte [mɛga'bajtʃi] *m COMPUT* megabyte.

megaevento [mɛgae'vẽntu] *m* huge event.

megafone [mɛga'foni] *m* megaphone.

megahertz [mɛga'xɛxtʃiʃ] *m (inv)* megahertz.

megalomania [megaloma'nia] *f* megalomania.

megalomaníaco, ca [megaloma'njaku, ka] ◇ *adj* megalomaniac. ◇ *m, f* megalomaniac.

megalópole [mɛga'lɔpoli] *f* super-city.

megaton [mega'tõ] *m* megaton.

megera [me'ʒɛra] *f* shrew.

meia ['meja] *f* ▷ **meio**.

meia-calça [ˌmeja'kawsa] *(pl* **meias-calças**) *f* tights *(pl) UK*, pantyhose *(pl) US*.

meia-direita [ˌmejadʒi'rejta] *(pl* **meias-direitas**) *FUT* ◇ *f* inside right. ◇ *m* inside right.

meia-entrada [ˌmejaẽn'trada] *(pl* **meias-entradas**) *f* half-price ticket.

meia-esquerda [ˌmejaiʃ'kexda] *(pl* **meias-esquerdas**) *FUT* ◇ *f* inside left. ◇ *m* inside left.

meia-estação [ˌmejaiʃta'sãw] *(pl* **meias-estações**) *f* mid-season.

meia-idade [ˌmejej'dadʒi] *(pl* **meias-idades**) *f* middle age; **mulher de ~** middle-aged woman.

meia-lua [ˌmeja'lua] *f* **-1.** *ASTRO* half moon. **-2.** [semicírculo] semicircle.

meia-luz [ˌmeja'luʃ] *(pl* **meias-luzes**) *f* half light; **à ~** in the gloom.

meia-noite [ˌmeja'nojtʃi] *(pl* **meias-noites**) *f* midnight; **à ~** at midnight.

meia-volta [ˌmeja'vɔwta] *(pl* **meias-voltas**) *f* **-1.** [movimento] half turn. **-2.** *MIL* about-turn *UK*, about-face *US*; **fazer ~** to make an about-turn *UK*, to make an about-face *US*.

meigo, ga ['mejgu, ga] *adj* gentle.

meiguice [mej'gisi] *f* gentleness.

meio, meia ['meju, 'meja] *adj* half; **a ~ caminho** halfway; **meia dúzia** half a dozen; **meia hora** half an hour; **~ quilo** half a kilo; **são três e meia** it's half past three; **um quilo e ~** a kilo and a half.

◆ **meio** ◇ *adv* half-; **~ cansado** rather tired. ◇ *m* **-1.** [metade] half; **~ a ~** fifty-fifty; **veio ~ mundo à festa** *fig* half the world came to the party; **partir ao ~** to split *ou* break in half; **pelo ~** [inacabado] halfway through. **-2.** [centro] middle; **o filho do ~** the middle son; **no ~ (de)** in the middle (of). **-3.** [ambiente - social, profissional] circle; [- físico] milieu; **~ ambiente** environment. **-4.** [modo] way; **por ~ de** through, by means of; **por todos os ~s** in every way.

◆ **meios** *mpl* [recursos] means; **os ~s de comunicação** the media; **~s de transporte** means of transport.

◆ **meia** ◇ *num* six. ◇ *f* **-1.** [meia - de seda] stocking; [- soquete] sock. **-2.** [entrada] half-price ticket. **-3.** [ponto]: **ponto de meia** stocking stitch.

meio-campo [meju'kãmpu] *(pl* **meios-campo**) *m* **-1.** *FUT* [centro-médio] midfield player. **-2.** [zona] midfield.

meio-dia [ˌmeju'dʒia] *(pl* **meios-dias**) *m* midday; **ao ~** at midday.

meio-fio [ˌmejo'fiw] *(pl* **meios-fios**) *m* kerb *UK*, curb *US*.

meio-tempo [ˌmeju'tẽnpu] *(pl* **meios-tempos**) *m* **-1.** [ínterim]: **nesse ~** meanwhile. **-2.** *ESP* [período] half-time.

meio-termo [ˌmeju'texmu] *(pl* **meios-termos**) *m* **-1.** [posição]: **~ (entre)** mid point (between). **-2.** *fig* [consenso] compromise.

meio-tom [ˌmeju'tõ] *(pl* **meios-tons**) *m* **-1.** *MÚS* semitone. **-2.** [de cor] half-tone.

mel ['mɛw] *m* honey.

melado, da [me'ladu, da] *adj* [pegajoso] sticky.

◆ **melado** *m* [doce] molasses.

melancia [melãn'sia] *f* watermelon.

melancolia [melãŋko'lia] *f* melancholy.

melancólico, ca [melãŋ'kɔliku, ka] *adj* melancholic.

melão [me'lãw] *(pl* **-ões**) *m* melon.

melar [4] [me'la(x)] ◇ *vt* [sujar] to get sticky. ◇ *vi fig* [falhar] to flop.

◆ **melar-se** *vp* [sujar-se] to get sticky.

Melbourne [ˌmɛw'buxni] *n* Melbourne.

meleca [me'lɛka] *f* **-1.** *fam* [secreção] bogey; **ele está tirando ~ do nariz** he's picking his nose. **-2.** [coisa ruim]: **ser/ficar uma ~** to be rubbish. **-3.** *(enfático)*: **essa ~ dessa chuva** that dammed rain.

melhor [me'ʎɔ(x)] *(pl* **-es**) ◇ *adj* **-1.** *(comparativo de bom)*: **~ (do que)** better (than); **bem/muito ~** much better; **é ~ você ...** you had better ...; **quanto mais ~** the more the better. **-2.** *(superlativo de bom)*: **o/a ~** the best. ◇ *adv* **-1.** *(comparativo de bem)*: **~ (do que)** better (than); **estar ~** to be better; **estar ~ de vida** to be better off. **-2.** *(superlativo de bem)* best. ◇ *m, f*: **o/a ~** the best; **o ~ de todas** the best of all; **o ~ foi que ...** the best thing was that ...; **levar a ~** to come off best.

◆ **ou melhor** *loc adv* or rather.

◆ **tanto melhor** *loc adv* so much the better.

melhora [me'ʎɔra] *f* improvement; **estimo suas**

~**s** I hope you get better soon.
melhorada [meʎo'rada] *f fam*: **dar uma ~** to get better.
melhoramento [meʎora'mẽntu] *m* improvement.
melhorar [4] [meʎo'ra(x)] ◇ *vt* to improve. ◇ *vi* to improve; **~ de algo** to improve in sthg; **~ de vida** to get on in life.
melhoria [meʎo'ria] *f* improvement; **fazer ~s (em algo)** to make improvements (in sthg).
meliante [me'ljãntʃi] *mf* **-1.** [marginal] vagabond. **-2.** [ladrão] thief. **-3.** [patife] scoundrel.
melífluo, flua [me'liflwu, flwa] *adj fig* [suave] mellifluous.
Melilha [me'liʎa] *n* Melilla.
melindrar [4] [melĩn'dra(x)] *vt* to offend.
◆ **melindrar-se** *vp* to feel hurt.
melindre [me'lĩndri] *m* affection.
◆ **melindres** *mpl* [suscetibilidade] oversensitivity.
melindroso, osa [melĩn'drɔza, ozu] *adj* **-1.** [suscetível, frágil] sensitive. **-2.** [difícil, arriscado] tricky.
◆ **melindrosa** *f* [dos anos vinte] flapper dress.
melodia [melo'dʒia] *f* melody.
melódico, ca [me'lɔdʒiku, ka] *adj* melodic.
melodrama [melo'drama] *m* melodrama.
melodramático, ca [melodra'matʃiku, ka] *adj* melodramatic.
melões [me'lõjʃ] *pl* ▷ **melão**.
meloso, osa [me'lozu, ɔza] *adj* **-1.** *fig* [pessoa] sentimental. **-2.** [voz] honeyed.
melro ['mɛwxu] *m* blackbird.
membrana [mẽn'brãna] *f* membrane.
membro ['mẽnbru] *m* **-1.** [ANAT - braços, pernas] limb; [- pênis] (male) member, penis. **-2.** [parte] member.
memorando [memo'rãndu] *m* **-1.** [comunicação] memo. **-2.** [nota diplomática] memorandum.
memorável [memo'ravew] (*pl* **-eis**) *adj* memorable.
memória [me'mɔrja] *f* **-1.** [ger] memory; **de ~** by heart; **~ de elefante** *fig* memory like an elephant; **~ visual** visual memory; **ter ~ fraca** to have a poor memory; **vir à ~** to come to mind; **~ RAM/ROM** RAM/ROM memory. **-2.** [recordação] recollection; **em ~ de** in memory of.
◆ **memórias** *fpl* memoirs.
memorial [memo'rjaw] (*pl* **-ais**) *m* memorial.
memorização ['memori'zasãw] (*pl* **-ões**) *f* memorizing.
memorizar [4] [memori'za(x)] *vt* to memorize.
menção [mẽn'sãw] (*pl* **-ões**) *f* **-1.** [referência] mention; **fazer ~ a algo** to make mention of sthg; **digno de ~** worthy of mention. **-2.** [intento]: **fazer ~ de se levantar** to make as if to get up. **-3.** [distinção]: **~ honrosa** distinction.
mencionar [4] [mẽnsjo'na(x)] *vt* to mention; **(isso) sem mencionar ...** not to mention ...
mendicância [mẽndʒi'kãnsja] *f* begging.
mendicante [mẽndʒi'kãntʃi] ◇ *adj* begging. ◇ *mf* beggar.
mendigar [14] [mẽndʒi'ga(x)] ◇ *vt* **-1.** [esmola] to beg for. **-2.** [ajuda, favor] to beg. ◇ *vi* [pedir esmola] to beg.
mendigo, ga [mẽn'dʒigu, ga] *m, f* beggar.
menear [15] [me'nja(x)] *vt* to shake.
menina [me'nina] *f* ▷ **menino**.
meninada [meni'nada] *f* kids (*pl*).
meningite [menĩn'ʒitʃi] *f* meningitis.
meninice [meni'nisi] *f* **-1.** [período] childhood. **-2.** [criancice] childishness.
menino, na [me'ninu, na] ◇ *adj* young. ◇ *m, f* **-1.** [criança] child; **nasceu um ~** a boy was born; **os ~s** the children; **~ de rua** street child. **-2.** [jovem] youngster. **-3.** [como forma de tratamento] boy.
◆ **menina** *f*: **ser a menina dos olhos de alguém** to be the apple of sb's eye.
menopausa [meno'pawza] *f* menopause.
menor [me'nɔ(x)] (*pl* **-es**) ◇ *adj* **-1.** *(comparativo)*: **~ (do que)** [de tamanho] smaller (than); [de idade] younger (than); [de importância, número] less (than); **meu irmão ~** my younger brother. **-2.** *(superlativo)*: **o/a ~ ...** [ger] the least; [de tamanho] the smallest. **-3.** [jovem]: **ser ~ (de idade)** [para dirigir, votar] to be under age; JUR to be a minor, to be under age. **-4.** *(antes de subst)* [noção, paciência] slightest. **-5.** MÚS: **em dó ~** in C minor. ◇ *mf* **-1.** *(superlativo)*: **o/a ~** [de tamanho] the smallest; [de idade] the youngest; **proibido para ~es** prohibited to under 18s; **um ~ de 15 anos** a youth of 15. **-2.** [jovem] young person. **-3.** JUR minor.
menoridade [menori'dadʒi] *f* minority.
menos ['menuʃ] ◇ *adv* **-1.** [em comparações] less; **a Ana é ~ inteligente** Ana is less intelligent; **~ do que** less than; **~ ... do que ...** less ...than ...; **tenho ~ trabalho do que ele** I have less work than him; **tenho um livro a ~** I'm one book short; **deram-me 5 reais a ~** they gave me 5 reals too little, they short-changed me by 5 reals. **-2.** [como superlativo]: **o/a ~ ...** the least ...; **o ~ caro/interessante** the least expensive/interesting. **-3.** [em locuções]: **a ~ que** unless; **ao ~, pelo ~** at least; **isso é o de ~** that's the least of it; **pouco ~ de** just under. ◇ *adj inv* **-1.** [em comparações] less, fewer *pl*; **como ~ carne** I eat less meat; **eles têm ~ posses** they have fewer possessions; **está ~ frio do que ontem** it's less cold than it was yesterday; **~ ... do que** less ... than, fewer ... than *pl*. **-2.** [como superlativo] (the) least, (the) fewest *pl*; **as que ~ bolos comeram** those who ate (the) fewest cakes; **os que ~ dinheiro têm** those who have (the) least money. ◇ *prep* **-1.** [exceto] except (for); **todos gostaram ~ ele** they all liked it except (for) him; **tudo ~ isso** anything but that. **-2.** [indica subtração] minus; **três ~ dois é igual a um** three minus two equals one.
menosprezado, da [menoʃpre'zadu, da] *adj* underestimated.
menosprezar [4] [menoʃpre'za(x)] *vt* to disdain.

menosprezo [menoʃ'prezu] *m*: ~ **(por)** disdain (for).
mensageiro, ra [mẽsa'ʒejru, ra] *m, f* messenger.
mensagem [mẽnsa'ʒẽ] (*pl* **-ns**) *f* message.
mensal [mẽn'saw] (*pl* **-ais**) *adj* monthly; **ganho 1.000 reais mensais** I earn 1,000 reals a month.
mensalidade [mẽnsali'dadʒi] *f* monthly payment.
mensalmente [mẽnsaw'mẽntʃi] *adv* monthly.
menstruação [mẽnʃtrwa'sãw] (*pl* **-ões**) *f* menstruation.
menstruada [mẽnʃ'trwada] *adj f*: **estar/ficar** ~ to be menstruating.
menstrual [mẽnʃ'trwaw] (*pl* **-ais**) *adj* menstrual.
menstruar [4] [mẽnʃ'trwa(x)] *vi* to menstruate.
mensurável [mẽnsu'ravew] (*pl* **-eis**) *adj* measurable.
menta ['mẽnta] *f* mint; **de** ~ mint *(antes de subst)*.
mental [mẽn'taw] (*pl* **-ais**) *adj* mental.
mentalidade [mẽntali'dadʒi] *f* mentality.
mentalizar [4] [mẽntali'za(x)] *vt* **-1.** [pensar em] to think. **-2.** [conceber] to imagine.
mente ['mẽntʃi] *f* mind; **ter algo em** ~ to have sthg in mind; **ter em** ~ **fazer algo** to have it in mind to do sthg; **vir à** ~ to come to mind.
mentecapto, ta [mẽnte'kaptu, ta] *m, f* insane, foolish.
mentir [56] [mẽn'tʃi(x)] <> *vt*: ~ **que ...** to lie about ... <> *vi* to lie; ~ **a** *ou* **para alguém** to lie to sb.
mentira [mẽn'tʃira] *f* **-1.** [falsidade] lie; **de** ~ [como brincadeira] as a joke; [falso] fake; **embora pareça** ~ although it seems unlikely; ~ **deslavada** downright lie; ~**!** [mostrando surpresa] you don't say!; **parece** ~ **que ...** it seems unbelievable that ... **-2.** [ato, hábito] lying.
mentiroso, osa [mẽntʃi'rozu, ɔza] <> *adj* **-1.** [ger] untruthful. **-2.** [jornalista, artigo] lying. <> *m, f* [pessoa] liar.
mentol [mẽn'tɔw] *m* menthol.
mentolado, da [mẽnto'ladu, da] *adj* mentholated.
mentor, ra [mẽn'to(x), ra] *m, f* **-1.** [orientador] mentor. **-2.** [autor intelectual]: **o/a** ~ the brains.
menu [me'nu] *m* menu.
meramente [mɛra'mẽntʃi] *adv* merely.
mercadinho [mexka'dʒiɲu] *m* local shop *UK*, local store *US*.
mercado [mex'kadu] *m* market; ~ **de capitais** investment market; ~ **financeiro** financial market; ~ **negro** black market; ~ **de trabalho** job market; ~ **das pulgas** flea market.
◆ **Mercado Comum** *m* Common Market.
mercadologia [mexkadolo'ʒia] *f* marketing.
mercadológico, ca [mexkado'lɔʒiku, ka] *adj* marketing *(antes de subst)*.
mercador [mexka'do(x)] *m* merchant.
mercadoria [mexkado'ria] *f* commodity.
◆ **mercadorias** *fpl* merchandise, goods *(pl)*.
mercante [mex'kãntʃi] *adj* merchant *(antes de subst)*.
mercantil [mexkãn'tʃiw] (*pl* **-is**) *adj* mercantile.
mercantilismo [mexkãntʃi'liʒmu] *m* mercantilism.
mercantilista [mexkãntʃi'liʃta] *adj* mercantilist.
mercê [mex'se] *f*: **estar/ficar à** ~ **de alguém/algo** to be at the mercy of sb/sthg.
mercearia [mexsja'ria] *f* grocery shop.
mercenário, ria [mexse'narju, rja] <> *adj* mercenary. <> *m, f* mercenary.
Mercosul [mexko'suw] (*abrev de* **Mercado do Cone Sul**) *m South American common market.*

MERCOSUL

Created in 1991, the *Mercado Comum do Sul* brought Argentina, Brazil, Paraguay and Uruguay together with the aim of creating economic integration and customs union among the countries of the Southern Cone. Chile and Bolivia are associate members. Like the European Common Market and ALCA, Mercosul strives for the economic integration of its member countries and for the creation of an area of free trade.

mercúrio [mex'kurju] *m* mercury; ~ **cromo** merbromin, Mercurochrome®.
Mercúrio [mex'kurju] *m* Mercury.
merda ['mɛxda] *mfam* <> *f* **-1.** [ger] crap, shit; **essa** ~ **de ...** this crappy ...; **ser/estar uma** ~ to be crap; **mandar alguém à** ~ to tell sb to bugger off. **-2.** [excremento] shit. <> *mf* [pessoa] shit. <> *interj*: **(que)** ~**!** what crap!
◆ **de merda** *loc adj mfam*: **esta viagem de** ~ this shitty journey.
merecedor, ra [merese'do(x), ra] *adj*: ~ **de** deserving of.
merecer [25] [mere'se(x)] <> *vt* to deserve. <> *vi*: **ele ganhou o prêmio, mas não merecia** he won the prize but he didn't deserve to.
merecido, da [mere'sidu, da] *adj* deserved; **foi um castigo bem** ~ it was a well deserved punishment.
merecimento [meresi'mẽntu] *m* [mérito, valor] merit.
merenda [me'rẽnda] *f* snack; ~ **escolar** free school meal.
merendeira [merẽn'dejra] *f* [lancheira] snack box.
merengue [me'rẽŋgi] *m* meringue.
meretrício [mere'trisju] *m* prostitution.
meretriz [mere'triʒ] *f* prostitute.
mergulhador, ra [mexguʎa'do(x), ra] (*mpl* **-es**, *fpl* **-s**) <> *adj* diving. <> *m, f* diver.
mergulhar [4] [mexgu'ʎa(x)] <> *vt* [afundar]: ~ **algo (em algo)** to dip sthg (in sthg). <> *vi* **-1.**: ~ **(em algo)** [afundar] to dive (into sthg); [saltar] to spring (from sthg). **-2.**: ~ **em algo** [penetrar] to plunge into sthg; *fig* [concentrar-se] to plunge o.s. in sthg.
mergulho [mex'guʎu] *m* **-1.** [ger] dive; **dar um** ~ [na praia] to take a dip; [de trampolim] to spring. **-2.** *ESP* diving.
meridiano, na [meri'dʒjãnu, na] *adj* meridian.
◆ **meridiano** *m GEOGR* meridian.

meridional [merid͡ʒjo'naw] (*pl* **-ais**) *adj* southern.

meritíssimo, ma [meri'tʃisimu, ma] *adj* highly deserving.

mérito ['mɛritu] *m* merit; **julgar alguém por seus ~s** to judge sb by their merits.

meritório, ria [meri'tɔrju, rja] *adj* meritorious, deserving.

merluza [mex'luza] *f* hake.

mero, ra ['mɛru, ra] *adj* mere.

merreca [me'xɛka] *f*: **uma ~** a trifle; **custar/pagar uma ~** to cost/pay a trifle; **ser uma ~** [muito pequeno] to be a mere trifle.

mertiolate [mextʃjo'latʃi] *m* Merthiolate®, thiomersal.

mês ['meʃ] (*pl* **meses**) *m*: **de ~ em ~** monthly; **durante todo o ~ de setembro** throughout September; **no ~ que vem** next month; **recebo por ~** I am paid monthly; **uma vez por ~** once a month.

mesa ['meza] *f* **-1.** [móvel] table; **pôr/tirar a ~** to lay/clear the table; **~ de centro** centre table; **~ de jantar** dining table; **~ telefônica** switchboard. **-2.** [de uma assembléia etc] board; **~ eleitoral** polling station officials. **-3.** [apostas] **ganhar toda a ~** to sweep the table. **-4.** *loc*: **virar a ~** to turn the tables.

mesada [me'zada] *f* **-1.** [pagamento] monthly payment. **-2.** [de criança] pocket money *UK*, allowance *US*.

mesa-de-cabeceira [ˌmezad͡ʒikabi'sejra] (*pl* **mesas-de-cabeceira**) *f* bedside table.

mesa-redonda [ˌmezaxe'dõnda] (*pl* **mesas-redondas**) *f* round table.

mesário, ria [me'zarju, rja] *m, f* **-1.** [de mesa eleitoral] polling officer. **-2.** [de associação etc] committee member.

mescla ['mɛʃkla] ◇ *adj (inv)* [tecido, paletó] blend. ◇ *f* **-1.** [mistura] mixture. **-2.** [tecido] blend.

mesclar [4] [meʃ'kla(x)] *vt* **-1.** [misturar]: **~ algo (com algo)** to mix sthg (with sthg). **-2.** [incorporar]: **~ algo a algo** to combine sthg with sthg.

mesmice [meʒ'misi] *f* sameness.

mesmo, ma ['meʒmu, ma] ◇ *adj* **-1.** [ger] same; **o ~ batom** the same lipstick; **na mesma hora** [imediatamente] at once. **-2.** [próprio]: **eu ~ fiz isso** I made that myself; **ele ~** himself; **ela mesma** herself; **eles mesmos** themselves. **-3.** [para enfatizar] very. ◇ *pron*: **o ~ /a mesma** the same.

◆ **mesma** ◇ *f*: **continuar na mesma** [não mudar] to be exactly the same; **ficar na mesma** [não entender] to be none the wiser. ◇ *m* [a mesma coisa]: **o mesma** the same; **dá no mesma** it's all the same.

◆ **mesmo** *adv* **-1.** [precisamente]: **agora/aqui ~** right now/here; **é assim ~** that's just the way it is; **hoje/ontem ~** just today/yesterday; **por isso ~** for that very reason. **-2.** [realmente] really; **é ~?** really?; **só ~ você consegue fazer isso** only you can do it. **-3.** [até, ainda] even; **~ assim, assim ~** even so; **nem ~** not even.

◆ **mesmo que** *loc conj* even though.

Mesopotâmia [mezopo'tãmja] *n* Mesopotamia.

mesquinharia [meʃkiɲa'ria] *f* meanness.

mesquinhez [meʃki'ɲeʃ] *f* [] meanness.

mesquinho, nha [meʃ'kiɲu, ɲa] *adj* mean.

mesquita [meʃ'kita] *f* mosque.

messias [me'siaʃ] *m fig* messiah.

◆ **Messias** *m*: **o Messias** the Messiah.

mestiçagem [meʃtʃi'saʒẽ] (*pl* **-ns**) *f* **-1.** [cruzamento] cross-breeding. **-2.** [miscigenação] miscegenation.

mestiço, ça [meʃ'tʃisu, sa] ◇ *adj* mestizo. ◇ *m, f* mestizo.

mestra ['mɛʃtra] *f* ▷ **mestre**.

mestrado [meʃ'tradu] *m* **-1.** [grau] masters (degree). **-2.** [curso] masters; **fazer ~** to study for a masters.

mestrando, da [meʃ'trãndu, da] *m student about to complete a master's degree*.

mestre, tra ['mɛʃtri, tra] ◇ *adj* **-1.** [extraordinário] fantastic. **-2.** [principal] master. ◇ *m, f* **-1.** [ger] master; **ser ~ em fazer algo** *irôn* to be a past master at doing sthg. **-2.** [fonte de ensinamento] teacher. **-3.** [músico] maestro.

mestre-cuca [ˌmɛʃtri'kuka] (*pl* **mestres-cucas**) *m fam* chef.

mestre-de-cerimônias [ˌmɛʃtrid͡ʒiseri'monjaʃ] (*pl* **mestres-de-cerimônias**) *m* master of ceremonies.

mestre-de-obras [ˌmɛʃtri'd͡ʒjɔbraʃ] (*pl* **mestres de-obras**) *m* foreman.

mestre-sala [ˌmɛʃtri'sala] (*pl* **mestres-sala**) *m* [em escola de samba] *leader of samba group display during carnival*.

mestria [meʃ'tria] *f* = **maestria**.

mesura [me'zura] *f* reverence; **cheio de ~s** kowtowing.

meta ['mɛta] *f* **-1.** [objetivo] aim, goal. **-2.** [gol] goal. **-3.** [na corrida] finishing line.

metabolismo [metabo'liʒmu] *m* metabolism.

metade [me'tad͡ʒi] *f* half; **~ das pessoas** half the people; **cortar pela ~** to cut in half; **deixar pela ~** to leave halfway through; **na ~ do caminho** halfway; **na ~ do filme** halfway through the film; **pela ~ do preço** at half price.

metafísico, ca [meta'fiziku, ka] ◇ *adj* metaphysical. ◇ *m, f* [filósofo] metaphysicist.

◆ **metafísica** *f* [disciplina] metaphysics *(pl)*.

metáfora [me'tafora] *f* metaphor.

metafórico, ca [meta'fɔriku, ka] *adj* metaphorical.

metal [me'taw] (*pl* **-ais**) *m* metal.

◆ **metais** *mpl* MÚS brass instruments.

metálico, ca [me'taliku, ka] *adj* metallic.

metalinguagem [metalĩŋ'gwaʒẽ] (*pl* **-ns**) *f* metalanguage.

metalurgia [metalux'ʒia] *f* metallurgy.

metalúrgico, ca [meta'luxʒiku, ka] ◇ *adj* metallurgic. ◇ *m, f* [operário] metallurgist.

◆ **metalúrgica** *f* [oficina] foundry.

metamorfose [metamox'fɔzi] *f* metamorphosis.

metamorfosear [15] [metamoxfo'zja(x)] *vt*: ~ **alguém/algo (em)** to change sb/sthg (into).
◆ **metamorfosear-se** *vp* **-1.** *BIOL* to metamorphose. **-2.** *fig* [mudar]: **~-se (em)** to metamorphose (into).

metano [me'tãnu] *m* methane.

metástase [me'taʃtazi] *f MED* metastasis.

meteórico, ca [mete'ɔriku, ka] *adj* meteoric.

meteorito [metʃju'ritu] *m* meteorite.

meteoro [me'tjɔru] *m* meteor.

meteorologia [metʃjorolo'ʒia] *f* meteorology.

meteorológico, ca [metʃjoro'lɔʒiku, ka] *adj* meteorological.

meteorologista [metʃjorolo'ʒiʃta] *mf* **-1.** [especialista] meteorologist. **-2.** *RADIO* & *TV* weather forecaster.

meter [5] [me'te(x)] *vt* **-1.** [ger] to put. **-2.** [enfiar]: ~ **algo em** *ou* **dentro de algo** to put sthg in/inside sthg. **-3.** [inspirar]: **ele me mete pena** he makes me feel sorry for him; **ele é feio de ~ medo** he's so ugly it's frightening. **-4.** [envolver]: ~ **alguém em algo** to involve sb in sthg.
◆ **meter-se** *vp* **-1.** [ir, esconder-se] to hide. **-2.** [recolher-se]: **~-se em algum lugar** to shut o.s. in somewhere. **-3.** [intrometer-se]: **~-se (em algo)** to stick one's nose (in sthg); **não se meta!** don't interfere! **-4.** [desafiar]: **~-se com alguém** to provoke sb. **-5.** [associar-se]: **~-se com alguém** to get mixed up with sb. **-6.** [fazer-se de]: **~-se a algo** to play at being sthg; **~-se a valente** to pretend to be brave. **-7.** [aventurar-se]: **~-se a fazer algo** to start doing sthg. **-8.** [envolver-se]: **~-se em algo** to get involved in sthg.

meticulosidade [metʃikulozi'dadʒi] *f* meticulousness.

meticuloso, osa [metʃiku'lozu, ɔza] *adj* meticulous.

metido, da [me'tʃidu, da] *adj* **-1.** [abelhudo] meddlesome, nosy. **-2.** [presumido]: ~ **(a besta)** full of o.s. **-3.** [cheio de intimidades] inquisitive. **-4.** [envolvido]: ~ **com alguém** involved with sb; ~ **em algo** involved in sthg. **-5.** [em roupa] dressed.

metódico, ca [me'tɔdʒiku, ka] *adj* methodical.

metodismo [meto'dʒiʒmu] *m* **-1.** *RELIG* Methodism. **-2.** [procedimento] method.

metodista [meto'dʒiʃta] *RELIG* ◇ *adj* Methodist. ◇ *mf* Methodist.

método ['mɛtodu] *m* method.

metodologia [metodolo'ʒia] *f* methodology.

metodológico, ca [metodo'lɔʒiku, ka] *adj* methodological.

metonímia [meto'nimja] *f* metonymy.

metragem [me'traʒẽ] *f* **-1.** [medida] length in metres *UK* *ou* meters *US*. **-2.** *CINE*: **filme de curta/longa ~** short/feature-length film.

metralhadora [metraʎa'dora] *f* machine gun.

metralhar [4] [metra'ʎa(x)] *vt* **-1.** [atirar em] to machine-gun. **-2.** *fig* [bombardear]: ~ **alguém de perguntas** to fire questions at sb.

métrico, ca ['mɛtriku, ka] *adj* **-1.** [do metro] metric; **fita métrica** tape measure. **-2.** *LITER* metrical.
◆ **métrica** *f LITER* metre *UK*, meter *US*.

metro ['mɛtru] *m* metre *UK*, meter *US*; ~ **cúbico** cubic metre; ~ **quadrado** square metre.

metrô [me'tro] *m* underground *UK*, subway *US*.

metrópole [me'trɔpoli] *f* **-1.** [cidade principal] capital. **-2.** [cidade grande] metropolis. **-3.** [nação] mother country.

metropolitano, na [metropoli'tãnu, na] *adj* metropolitan.

metroviário, ria [metro'vjarju, rja] ◇ *adj* underground *UK (antes de subst)*, subway *US (antes de subst)*. ◇ *m, f* [funcionário] underground worker *UK*, subway worker *US*.

meu, minha ['mew, 'miɲa] ◇ *adj* **-1.** [ger] my; **este é o ~ carro** this is my car; ~ **Deus!** my God!; **minha nossa!** oh me, oh my!, gosh! **-2.** [caro a mim] my; **como vai, ~ caro Affonso?** how are you, my dear Affonso?; ~ **irmão** *fam* [tratamento] my friend. ◇ *pron*: **o ~ /a minha** mine; **um amigo ~** a friend of mine; **os ~s** [a minha família] my family; **este jeito de andar é bem ~** this manner of walking is quite me.

mexer [5] [me'ʃe(x)] ◇ *vt* **-1.** [ger] to move. **-2.** [misturar] to mix. ◇ *vi* **-1.** [mover] to move. **-2.**: ~ **em alguém/algo** [tocar] to touch sb/sthg; [mudar de posição, remexer] to fiddle with sb/sthg. **-3.**: ~ **com alguém** [caçoar] to tease sb; [provocar] to provoke sb; [afetar] to affect sb. **-4.** [trabalhar]: ~ **com algo** to work with sthg.
◆ **mexer-se** *vp* **-1.** [mover-se] to move. **-2.** [apressar-se] to hurry; **mexam-se!** get a move on! **-3.** [agir] to move.

mexerica [meʃe'rika] *f* tangerine.

mexericar [12] [meʃeri'ka(x)] *vi* to gossip.

mexerico [meʃe'riku] *m* **-1.** [ato] gossip. **-2.** [intriga] intrigue.

mexeriqueiro, ra [meʃeri'kejru, ra] ◇ *adj* gossipy. ◇ *m, f* busybody, gossip.

mexicano, na [meʃi'kãnu, na] ◇ *adj* Mexican. ◇ *m, f* Mexican.

México ['mɛʃiku] *n* Mexico.

mexido, da [me'ʃidu, da] *adj* **-1.** [papéis] muddled. **-2.** [ovos] scrambled.

mexilhão [meʃi'ʎãw] (*pl* **-ões**) *m* mussel.

mezanino [meza'ninu] *m* mezzanine.

mg (*abrev de* **miligrama**) *m* mg.

MG (*abrev de* **Estado de Minas Gerais**) *n State of Minas Gerais.*

mi [mi] *m MÚS* E, mi.

miado ['mjadu] *m* miaow.

miar [16] ['mja(x)] *vi* to mew.

miasma ['mjaʒma] *m* **-1.** [emanação] miasma. **-2.** *fig*: ~ **social** social miasma.

miau ['mjaw] *m* miaow.

miçanga [mi'sãŋga] *f* **-1.** [conta] glass bead. **-2.** [ornato] beads *(pl)*.

micção [mik'sãw] (*pl* **-ões**) *f* urination.

mico ['miku] *m ZOOL* capuchin monkey.

mico-leão [miku'ljãw] (*pl* **micos-leão**) *m* ZOOL golden lion tamarin.
micose [mi'kɔzi] *f* fungal infection, mycosis.
micro ['mikru] *m* COMPUT computer, PC.
micro- [mikru-] *prefixo* micro-.
micróbio [mi'krɔbju] *m* microbe.
microbiologia [mikrobjolo'ʒia] *f* microbiology.
microcirurgia [mikrosirux'ʒia] *f* microsurgery.
microcomputador [mikrokõnputa'do(x)] *m* microcomputer.
microcosmo [mikro'kɔʒmu] *m* microcosm.
microempresa [mikrowẽn'preza] *f* small business.
microempresário, ria [mikrwẽnpre'zarju, ria] *m* small-business owner.
microfilme [mikro'fiwmi] *m* microfilm.
microfone [mikro'foni] *m* microphone.
microfonia [mikro'fonia] *f* ELETRON *vibrations in a sound system.*
microinformática [mikrwĩnfox'matʃika] *f* microcomputing.
microonda [mikro'õnda] *f* microwave.
◆ **microondas** *mpl* [forno] microwave oven *(sg).*
microônibus [mikro'onibuʃ] *m inv* minibus.
microorganismo [mikrwoxga'niʒmu] *m* microorganism.
microprocessador [mikruprosesa'do(x)] *m* microprocessor.
microscópico, ca [mikroʃ'kɔpiku, ka] *adj* microscopic.
microscópio [mikroʃ'kɔpju] *m* microscope.
mictório [mik'tɔrju] *m* urinal.
mídia ['midʒja] *f* media.
migalha [mi'gaʎa] *f* [de pão, bolo] crumb.
◆ **migalhas** *fpl* [sobras] leftovers.
migração [migra'sãw] (*pl* **-ões**) *f* migration.
migrante [mi'grãntʃi] ◇ *adj* **-1.** [pássaro] migratory. **-2.** [população] migrant. ◇ *mf* migrant.
migrar [4] [mi'gra(x)] *vi* to migrate.
migratório, ria [migra'tɔrju, rja] *adj* migratory.
mijada [mi'ʒada] *f fam* pee; **dar uma ~** to have a pee.
mijar [4] [mi'ʒa(x)] *vi fam* to pee.
◆ **mijar-se** *vp mfam* to piss o.s.; **~-se de rir** to wet OU piss o.s. laughing.
mijo ['miʒu] *m fam* pee.
mil ['miw] *num* **-1.** [número] thousand; **três ~** three thousand. **-2.** [grande número] a thousand. **-3.** *loc*: **estar a ~** *fam* to be working flat out; **seis.**
milagre [mi'lagri] *m* miracle; **por ~** miraculously.
milagroso, osa [mila'grozu, ɔza] *adj* miraculous.
milanesa [mila'neza] *f*: **à ~** in breadcrumbs.
milenar [mile'na(x)] *adj* **-1.** [que tem um milênio] millenary. **-2.** *fig* [antigo] age-old.
milênio [mi'lenju] *m* millennium.
milésimo, ma [mi'lɛzimu, ma] *num* thousandth; **a milésima parte** the thousandth part.
mil-folhas [miw'foʎaʃ] *f inv* millefeuille.
milha ['miʎa] *f* mile; **~ marítima** nautical mile.
milhão [mi'ʎãw] (*pl* **-ões**) *num* million; **três milhões** three million.
milhar [mi'ʎa(x)] (*pl* **-es**) *m* thousand.
◆ **milhares** *mpl*: **~ es de pessoas** thousands of people.
milharal [miʎa'raw] (*pl* **-ais**) *m* maize field *UK*, corn field *US*.
milho ['miʎu] *m* **-1.** [planta] maize *UK*, corn *US*. **-2.** [grão] corn; **~ de pipoca** popcorn. **-3.** *loc*: **catar ~** to type very slowly.
milhões [mi'ʎõjʃ] *pl* ▷ **milhão.**
miliardário, ria [miljax'darju, rja] ◇ *adj* multimillionaire. ◇ *m, f* multimillionaire.
milícia [mi'lisja] *f* militia.
milico [mi'liku] *m fam pej* military type; **os ~s** the military.
miligrama [mili'grãma] *m* milligram.
mililitro [mili'litru] *m* millilitre *UK*, milliliter *US*.
milímetro [mi'limetru] *m* millimetre *UK*, millimeter *US*.
milionário, ria [miljo'narju, rja] ◇ *adj* millionaire. ◇ *m, f* millionaire.
milionésimo, ma [miljo'nɛʒimu, ma] *num* millionth; **a milionésima parte** the millionth part.
militância [mili'tãnsja] *f* militancy.
militante [mili'tãntʃi] ◇ *adj* militant. ◇ *mf* militant.
militar [4] [mili'ta(x)] ◇ *adj* military. ◇ *mf* career soldier; **os ~ es** the military *(inv)*. ◇ *vi* **-1.** [lutar]: **~ (por/contra)** to fight for/against. **-2.**: **~ em** MIL to serve in; POL to be active in.
militarismo [milita'riʒmu] *m* militarism.
militarista [milita'riʃta] ◇ *adj* militaristic. ◇ *mf* militarist.
militarizar [4] [militari'za(x)] *vt* to militarize.
mil-réis [miw'xɛjʃ] *m inv early Brazilian and Portuguese monetary unit.*
mim ['mĩ] *pron* **-1.** [com preposição: complemento indireto] me; **ela comprou um presente para ~** she bought a present for me, she bought me a present; **ele fez o serviço por ~** he did the work for me; **a ~ ele não faria isto** he wouldn't do that to me; **falaram mal de ~** they spoke ill of me; **o que você tem contra ~?** what have you got against me?; **eles foram embora sem ~** they left without me; **para ~, este é o melhor quadro** [para expressar opinião] for me, this is the best painting; **por ~, você pode ficar aqui** [de minha parte] as far as I'm concerned, you can stay here. **-2.** [com preposição: reflexo] myself; **a ~, você não engana** you don't fool me; **comprei-o para ~ (mesmo** OU **próprio)** I bought it for myself; **preciso cuidar mais de ~** I need to look after myself a bit better; **de ~ para ~** [comigo mesmo] to myself.
mimado, da [mi'madu, da] *adj* spoiled.
mimar [4] [mi'ma(x)] *vt* **-1.** [fazer todas as vontades de] to spoil. **-2.** [tratar com carinho] to pamper.
mimeografar [4] [mimjogra'fa(x)] *vt* to mimeograph.
mimeógrafo [mi'mjɔgrafu] *m* mimeograph.

mímico, ca ['mimiku, ka] <> *adj* imitative. <> *m, f* **-1.** [pessoa] mimic. **-2.** [ator] mime artist.
 ◆ **mímica** *f* mime; **fazer mímica** to mimic; **por mímica** in mime.
mimo ['mimu] *m* **-1.** [carinho] affection; **fazer ~s a alguém** to be affectionate towards sb. **-2.** [pessoa ou coisa graciosa]: **ser um ~** to be a delight.
mimoso, osa [mi'mozu, ɔza] *adj* **-1.** [carinhoso] affectionate. **-2.** [gracioso] delightful. **-3.** [delicado] delicate.
mina ['mina] *f* **-1.** [ger] mine; **~ de carvão/ouro** coal/gold mine. **-2.** ***fig*: ser uma ~** [de lucros] to be a goldmine; [preciosidade] to be precious; **ser uma ~ de informações** to be a mine of information. **-3.** ***fam*** [garota] girl.
minar [4] [mi'na(x)] <> *vt* **-1.** [pôr minas em] to mine. **-2.** [deteriorar, prejudicar] to undermine. <> *vi* [água]: **~ (de)** to stream (from).
minarete [mina'retʃi] *m* minaret.
Minas Gerais [ˌminaʒe'rajʃ] *n* Minas Gerais.
mindinho [mĩn'dʒiɲu] *m **fam*** pinky.
mineiro, ra [mi'nejru, ra] <> *adj* **-1.** [relativo a mina] mining. **-2.** [de Minas Gerais] from Minas Gerais. <> *m, f* **-1.** [operário] miner. **-2.** [de Minas Gerais] *person from Minas Gerais.*
mineração [minera'sãw] *f* **-1.** [exploração] mining. **-2.** [depuração] purifying.
minerador, ra [minera'do(x),ra] <> *adj* mining *(antes de subst)*. <> *m, f* miner.
 ◆ **mineradora** *f* mining company.
mineral [mine'raw] (*pl* **-ais**) <> *adj* mineral. <> *m* mineral.
mineralogia [mineralo'ʒia] *f* mineralogy.
minério [mi'nɛrju] *m* ore; **~ de ferro** iron ore.
mingau [mĩŋ'gaw] *m* **-1.** [papa] porridge. **-2.** ***fig*** [coisa mole] mush.
míngua ['mĩŋgwa] *f* lack; **estar à ~ de algo** to be short of sthg; **viver à ~ de algo** to live with a shortage of sthg.
minguado, da [mĩŋ'gwadu, da] *adj* **-1.** [escasso] scarce; **~ de algo** lacking sthg. **-2.** [pouco desenvolvido] flat.
minguante [mĩŋ'gwãntʃi] *m* ASTRON [moon] waning, last quarter.
minguar [4] [mĩŋ'gwa(x)] <> *vt* [reduzir] to reduce. <> *vi* [escassear] to dwindle.
minha ['miɲa] ▷ **meu.**
minhoca [mi'ɲɔka] *f* earthworm; **com ~s na cabeça** with strange ideas.
míni ['mini] <> *adj inv* mini. <> *m* [vestido] minidress. <> *f* [saia] miniskirt.
miniatura [minja'tura] *f* miniature; **em ~** in miniature.
mínima ['minima] *f* ▷ **mínimo.**
minimalista [minima'liʃta] *adj* minimalist.
minimizar [4] [minimi'za(x)] *vt* **-1.** [tornar mínimo] to minimize. **-2.** [subestimar] to underestimate. **-3.** [fazer pouco caso de] to play down.
mínimo, ma ['minimu, ma] *adj* **-1.** [ger] minimal. **-2.** [muito pequeno] tiny. **-3.** [o menor possível] smallest. **-4.** *(antes de subst)* [nenhum] slightest.
 ◆ **mínimo** *m* [limite] least; **o ~ que posso fazer** the least I can do; **no ~** at least.
 ◆ **mínima** *f* **-1.** METEOR minimum (temperature). **-2.** MÚS minim. **-3.** *loc*: **não dar a mínima (para alguém/algo)** not to have the least concern (for sb/sthg).
minissaia [ˌmini'saja] *f* miniskirt.
minissérie [ˌmini'sɛrji] *f* miniseries.
ministerial [miniʃte'rjaw] (*pl* **-ais**) *adj* ministerial.
ministeriável [miniʃterj'avɛw] (*pl* **-eis**) *mf* ministerial candidate.
ministério [miniʃ'tɛrju] *m* **-1.** [ger] ministry; **Ministério da Fazenda** ≃ HM Treasury *UK*, ≃ the Treasury *US*; **Ministério do Interior** Home Office *UK*, Department of the Interior *US*; **Ministério Público** public prosecution; **Ministério das Relações Exteriores** ≃ Foreign (and Commonwealth) Office *UK*, ≃ State Department *US*; **Ministério do Trabalho** ≃ Department of Employment *UK*, ≃ Department of Labor *US*; **Ministério da Educação e Cultura** ≃ Department of Education; **Ministério dos Transportes** ≃ Department of Transport. **-2.** [gabinete] cabinet.
ministra [mi'niʃtra] *f* ▷ **ministro.**
ministrar [4] [miniʃ'tra(x)] *vt* to administer.
ministro, tra [mi'niʃtru, tra] *m, f* minister; **~ sem pasta** minister without portfolio; **~ da Fazenda** ≃ Chancellor of the Exchequer *UK*, ≃ Secretary of the Treasury *US*; **~ do Interior** ≃ Home Secretary *UK*, ≃ Secretary of the Interior *US*; **~ das Relações Exteriores** ≃ Foreign Secretary *UK*, ≃ Secretary of State *US*; **~ da Educação e Cultura** ≃ Secretary for Education; **~ dos Transportes** ≃ Secretary for Transport.
minorar [4] [mino'ra(x)] *vt* to diminish.
minoria [mino'ria] *f* minority.
minoritário, ria [minori'tarju, rja] *adj* minority *(antes de subst)*.
minúcia [mi'nusja] *f* **-1.** [detalhe] detail. **-2.** [coisa sem importância] minutiae *(pl)*.
minuciosidade [minusjozi'dadʒi] *f* meticulousness.
minucioso, osa [minu'sjozu, ɔza] *adj* meticulous.
minúsculo, la [mi'nuʃkulu, la] *adj* **-1.** [tamanho] minuscule. **-2.** [letra] lower case *(antes de subst)*.
 ◆ **minúscula** *f* [letra] lower case.
minuta [mi'nuta] *f* **-1.** [rascunho] draft. **-2.** [prato] cooked to order.
minuteria [minute'ria] *f* timing device.
minuto [mi'nutu] *m* minute; **num ~ *fig*** [rapidamente] in a minute; **um ~!** one minute!
miolo ['mjolu] *m* **-1.** [pão] crumb. **-2.** [fruta] pulp.
 ◆ **miolos** *mpl* **-1.** CULIN brains. **-2.** ***fam*** [cérebro] brains.
mioma ['mjoma] *m* myoma.
míope ['mjupi] <> *adj* short-sighted, myopic. <> *mf* short-sighted person, myope.
miopia [mju'pia] *f* myopia.

miosótis [mjo'zɔtʃiʃ] *m inv BOT* forget-me-not.
mira ['mira] *f* **-1.** [ger] aim. **-2.** [de arma] sight.
mirabolante [mirabo'lãntʃi] *adj* **-1.** [surpreendente] incredible. **-2.** [espalhafatoso] gaudy.
miraculoso, osa [miraku'lozu, ɔza] *adj* [espantoso] miraculous.
mirada [mi'rada] *f* look.
miragem [mi'raʒẽ] (*pl* **-ns**) *f* **-1.** [efeito ótico] mirage. **-2.** *fig* [ilusão] illusion.
miramar [mira'ma(x)] *m* sea-view belvedere.
mirante [mi'rãntʃi] *m* belvedere.
mirar [4] [mi'ra(x)] ◇ *vt* **-1.** [fitar] to stare at. **-2.** [apontar para] to aim at. **-3.** [observar] to watch. ◇ *vi* [apontar]: ~ **(em algo)** to aim (at sthg).
◆ **mirar-se** *vp* **-1.** [olhar-se]: **~-se (em algo)** to look at o.s. (in sthg). **-2.** [seguir o exemplo de]: **~ se em alguém** to follow the example of sb.
miríade [mi'riadʒi] *f fig* myriad.
mirim [mi'rĩ] (*pl* **-ns**) *adj* little.
misantropo, pa [mizãn'tropu, pa] *m, f* misanthrope.
miscelânea [mise'lãnja] *f* **-1.** [coletânea] miscellany. **-2.** *fig* [mistura] assortment.
miscigenação [misiʒena'sãw] *f* interbreeding.
mise-en-plis [mizãn'pli] *m inv* shampoo and set.
miserável [mize'ravɛw] (*pl* **-eis**) ◇ *adj* **-1.** [ger] miserable. **-2.** [sovina] miserly. **-3.** [vil] despicable. **-4.** [terrível] dreadful. ◇ *mf* **-1.** [infeliz] miserable person. **-2.** [pessoa pobre] poor wretch. **-3.** [pessoa vil] despicable person.
miseravelmente [mizeravew'mẽntʃi] *adv* **-1.** [desgraçadamente] wretchedly. **-2.** [pobremente] in misery.
miséria [mi'zɛrja] *f* **-1.** [desgraça] misery. **-2.** [pobreza] poverty; **chorar** ~ to whinge. **-3.** [sovinice] meanness. **-4.** [ninharia]: **custar/ganhar uma** ~ to cost/to earn a pittance.
◆ **misérias** *fpl*: **fazer ~s** to do wonders; **fazer ~s com alguém** to cause sb misery.
misericórdia [mizeri'kɔrdʒja] *f*: ~ **(de/com)** mercy (on/for).
misericordioso, osa [mizerikox'dʒjozu, ɔza] *adj* compassionate.
mísero, ra ['mizeru, ra] *adj fig* [escasso] miserly.
misoginia [mizoʒi'nia] *f* misogyny.
misógino, na [mi'zɔʒinu, na] ◇ *adj* misogynous. ◇ *m, f* mysoginist.
missa ['misa] *f* **-1.** *RELIG* mass; ~ **do galo** midnight mass. **-2.** *loc*: **não saber da ~ a metade** *fam* to not know the half of it.
missal [mi'saw] (*pl* **-ais**) *m* missal.
missão [mi'sãw] (*pl* **-ões**) *f* mission.
misse ['misi] *f* beauty queen.
míssil ['misiw] (*pl* **-eis**) *m* missile; ~ **de curto/médio/longo alcance** short-/medium-/long-range missile.
missionário, ria [misjo'narju, rja] ◇ *adj* missionary. ◇ *m, f* missionary.
Mississippi [misi'sipi] *n*: **o** ~ the Mississippi.
missiva [mi'siva] *f* missive.
missões [mi'sõjʃ] *pl* ⊳ **missão**.
Missouri [mi'zuri] *n*: **o** ~ the Missouri.
mister [miʃ'te(x)] *m* **-1.** [ofício] office. **-2.** [necessidade] need; **ser ~ fazer algo** to be necessary to do sthg.
mistério [miʃ'tɛrju] *m* **-1.** [ger] mystery; **não ter ~** to be straightforward. **-2.** [segredo] secret; **fazer ~** to make a mystery.
misterioso, osa [miʃte'rjozu, ɔza] *adj* mysterious.
misticismo [miʃtʃi'siʒmu] *m* mysticism.
místico, ca ['miʃtʃiku, ka] ◇ *adj* mystic. ◇ *m, f* [pessoa] mystic.
mistificador, ra [miʃtʃifika'do(x), ra] ◇ *adj* mystifying *(antes de subst)*. ◇ *m, f* deceiver.
mistificar [12] [miʃtʃifi'ka(x)] *vt* to mystify.
misto, ta ['miʃtu, ta] *adj* mixed.
◆ **misto** *m* mixture.
misto-quente [ˌmiʃtu'kẽntʃi] (*pl* **mistos-quentes**) *m toasted cheese and ham sandwich.*
mistura [miʃ'tura] *f* mixture.

MISTURA DE RAÇAS

A large part of Brazil's cultural wealth is due to the many races that make up the Brazilian people. The Indians, Portuguese and Negroes of the colonial period were joined, from the mid-nineteenth century onwards, by millions of immigrants from, amongst many others, Italy, Germany, Spain, Syria, Lebanon and Japan.

misturar [4] [miʃtu'ra(x)] *vt* **-1.** [combinar, juntar] to mix. **-2.** [confundir] to mix up.
◆ **misturar-se** *vp* [socialmente]: **~-se com alguém** to mix with sb.
mistureba [miʃtu'rɛba] *f fam* hotchpotch.
mítico, ca ['mitʃiku, ka] *adj* mythical.
mitificar [12] [mitʃifi'ka(x)] *vt* to mythicize.
mitigar [14] [mitʃi'ga(x)] *vt* to mitigate.
mito ['mitu] *m* **-1.** [ger] myth. **-2.** [pessoa] legend.
mitologia [mitolo'ʒia] *f* mythology.
mitológico, ca [mito'lɔʒiku, ka] *adj* mythological.
miudeza [mju'deza] *f* **-1.** [pormenor] detail. **-2.** [insignificância] trifle.
miudezas [mju'dezaʃ] *fpl* **-1.** [objetos pequenos] odds and ends. **-2.** [quinquilharia] trinkets.
miúdo, da ['mjudu, da] *adj* [pequeno] small.
◆ **miúdos** *mpl* **-1.** [dinheiro] small change. **-2.** [de animal] giblets. **-3.** *loc*: **trocar em ~s** to put it simply.
mixagem [mik'saʒẽ] *f CINE & RÁDIO* mixing.
mixar[1] [4] [mi'ʃa(x)] *vi fam* [gorar] to go down the drain.
mixar[2] [4] [mi'ʃa(x)] *vt CINE & RÁDIO* to mix.
mixaria [miʃa'ria] *f* **-1.** *fam* [soma insignificante]: **uma ~** peanuts. **-2.** [coisa sem valor] rubbish.
mixórdia [mi'ʃɔxdʒja] *f* mess.
mixuruca [miʃu'ruka] *adj* **-1.** [presente] worthless. **-2.** [festa] lifeless.
ml (*abrev de* **mililitro**) *m* ml.

mm (*abrev de* **milímetro**) *m* mm.
mnemônico, ca [mne'moniku, ka] *adj* mnemonic.
mó ['mɔ] *f* **-1.** [de moinho] millstone. **-2.** [de afiar] whetstone.
moagem ['mwaʒẽ] *f* grinding.
móbile ['mɔbili] *m* mobile.
mobília [mo'bilja] *f* furniture; **sem ~** unfurnished.
mobiliar [16] [mobi'lja(x)] *vt* to furnish.
mobiliário [mobi'ljarju] *m* furniture.
mobilidade [mobili'dadʒi] *f* mobility; **~ social** social mobility.
mobilização [mobiliza'sãw] *f* mobilization.
mobilizar [14] [mobili'za(x)] *vt* to mobilize.
moça ['mosa] *f* ⊳ **moço**.
moçada [mo'sada] *f fam group of young people.*
Moçambique [mosãn'biki] *n* Mozambique.
moção [mo'sãw] *f* motion.
mocassim [moka'sĩ] (*pl* **-ns**) *m* moccasin.
mochila [mo'ʃila] *f* rucksack.
mocidade [mosi'dadʒi] *f* **-1.** [período] youth. **-2.** [os jovens]: **a ~** the young.
mocinho, nha [mo'siɲu, ɲa] *m, f* **-1.** [jovem] boy. **-2.** [herói] hero.
moço, ça ['mosu, sa] ◇ *adj* [pessoa] young. ◇ *m, f* **-1.** [jovem] young person. **-2.** [adulto] young boy (young girl). **-3.** [como forma de tratamento]: **ei, ~!** hey, man!
moções [mo'sõjʃ] *pl* ⊳ **moção**.
moda ['mɔda] *f* **-1.** [ger] fashion; **cair** *ou* **sair de ~** to fall out of fashion; **estar na ~** to be in fashion, to be fashionable; **fora de ~** out of fashion; **lançar uma ~** to start a fashion. **-2.** [coqueluche] craze. **-3.** [maneira] way; **faço tudo à minha ~** I do everything my way; **à ~ portuguesa** Portuguese-style. **-4.** *loc*: **inventar ~** to create a new fad.
modalidade [modali'dadʒi] *f* **-1.** [tipo] mode. **-2.** *ESP* event.
modelador [modela'do(x)] *m* [cinta] girdle.
modelagem [mode'laʒẽ] (*pl* **-ns**) *f* **-1.** [ato] modelling. **-2.** [produto] moulding *UK*, molding *US*. **-3.** [do corpo] shape.
modelar [4] [mode'la(x)] *vt* **-1.** [ger] to mould *UK*, to mold *US*. **-2.** *fig* [moldar]: **~ algo por algo** to model sthg on sthg.
modelista [mode'liʃta] *mf* designer.
modelo [mo'delu] ◇ *m* model; **~ econômico** economic model. ◇ *mf* model; **~ vivo** live model.
modem ['modẽ] (*pl* **-ns**) *m COMPUT* modem.
moderação [modera'sãw] *f* moderation.
moderado, da [mode'radu, da] *adj* moderate.
moderar [4] [mode'ra(x)] *vt* to moderate.
◆ **moderar-se** *vp* [comedir-se] to control o.s.
modernidade [modexni'dadʒi] *f* modernity.
modernismo [modex'niʒmu] *m* modernism.
modernização [modexniza'sãw] *f* modernization.
modernizar [4] [modexni'za(x)] *vt* to modernize.
◆ **modernizar-se** *vp* to keep o.s. up to date.
moderno, na [mo'dɛxnu, na] *adj* modern.
modernoso, osa [modex'nozu, ɔza] *adj* newfangled.
modess® ['mɔdeʃ] *m inv* sanitary towel *UK*, sanitary nakpin *US*.
modestamente [modeʃta'mẽntʃi] *adv* **-1.** [ger] modestly. **-2.** [sem pretensão] with modesty.
modéstia [mo'dɛʃtja] *f* modesty.
modesto, ta [mo'dɛʃtu, ta] *adj* modest.
módico, ca ['mɔdʒiku, ka] *adj* **-1.** [barato, parco] modest. **-2.** [moderado] moderate.
modificação [modʒifika'sãw] (*pl* **-ões**) *f* **-1.** [alteração] modification. **-2.** [transformação] transformation.
modificar [12] [modʒifi'ka(x)] *vt* **-1.** [ger] to modify. **-2.** [transformar] to change.
◆ **modificar-se** *vp* to alter.
modinha [mɔ'dʒiɲa] *f popular Brazilian song.*
modismo [mo'dʒiʒmu] *m* **-1.** [tendência] trend. **-2.** [moda] fashion.
modista [mo'dʒiʃta] *mf* dressmaker.
modo ['mɔdu] *m* **-1.** [ger] way; **de ~ algum** in no way; **desse ~** that way; **de um ~ geral** in general; **~ de usar** directions for use. **-2.** [jeito] manner; **~ de andar** gait. **-3.** *GRAM* mood.
◆ **modos** *mpl* manners.
◆ **de modo que** *loc conj* **-1.** [de maneira que] so (that). **-2.** [assim sendo] so that.
modorra [mo'doxa] *f* **-1.** [moleza] lethargy. **-2.** [sonolência] drowsiness.
modulação [modula'sãw] (*pl* **-ões**) *f* modulation; **~ de freqüência** frequency modulation.
modulado, da [modu'ladu, da] *adj* modular.
modular [4] [modu'la(x)] ◇ *adj* modular. ◇ *vt* to modulate.
módulo ['mɔdulu] *m* **-1.** [unidade] module. **-2.** [veículo]: **~ lunar** lunar module.
moeda ['mwɛda] *f* **-1.** [peça] coin; **uma ~ de 10 centavos** a 10 cent coin; **uma ~ falsa** a counterfeit coin. **-2.** [dinheiro] money; **~ forte** hard currency; **pagar na mesma ~** to pay sb back in their own coin; ⊳ **casa**.

MOEDA

The monetary unit in Brazil has undergone many changes throughout history, due to the various periods of high inflation that the country has gone through. In the post-war period, Brazil has adopted, successively, the cruzeiro, the cruzeiro novo, the cruzado, the cruzado novo and the cruzado real. Since 1994, with the relative economic stability of the country, the real has become the Brazilian monetary unit.

moedor [mwe'do(x)] *m* **-1.** [de café, pimenta] mill. **-2.** [de carne] mincer *UK*, grinder *US*.
moenda ['mwẽnda] *f* sugar mill.
moer [28] ['mwe(x)] ◇ *vt* **-1.** [café, pimenta] to grind. **-2.** [carne] to mince *UK*, to grind *US*. **-3.** [para extrair suco] to mill. ◇ *vi* [moinho] to grind.

mofado, da [mo'fadu, da] *adj* mouldy *UK*, moldy *US*.

mofar [4] [mo'fa(x)] ◇ *vt* [cobrir de mofo] to cover in mould *UK ou* mold *US*. ◇ *vi* **-1.** [criar mofo] to go mouldy *UK ou* moldy *US*. **-2.** *fig*: **~ (em)** [ficar esperando] to kick one's heels (in); [permanecer] to gather moss (in).

mofo ['mofu] *m* mould *UK*, mold *US*; **criar ~** to go mouldy *UK ou* moldy *US*; **o pão está cheio de ~** the bread is all mouldy *UK ou* moldy *US*; **esta camisa está com cheiro de ~** this shirt smells musty.

Mogadício [moga'disju] *n* Mogadishu.

mogno ['mɔgnu] *m* mahogany.

moído, da ['mwidu, da] *adj* **-1.** [café, pimenta] ground. **-2.** [carne] minced *UK*, ground *US*. **-3.** *fig* [doído]: **~ de algo** hurting from sthg; **~ de cansaço** shattered, tired out.

moinho ['mwiɲu] *m* mill; **~ de vento** windmill.

moisés [moj'zɛʃ] *m inv* carrycot.

moita ['mojta] *f* thicket.
◆ **na moita** *loc adv* [às escondidas] in secret; **ficar na ~** [fazer segredo] to keep quiet.

mola ['mɔla] *f* **-1.** [dispositivo] spring. **-2.** *fig* [impulsionador]: **~ (mestra)** driving force.

molambento, ta [molãn'bẽntu, ta] *adj* ragged.

molambo [mo'lãnbu] *m* [roupa em mau estado] rags *(inv)*.

molar [mo'la(x)] (*pl* **-es**) ◇ *adj* [dente] molar. ◇ *m* molar.

moldar [4] [mow'da(x)] *vt* **-1.** [fazer o molde de] to make a mould *UK ou* mold *US* of. **-2.** [modelar] to mould *UK*, to mold *US*. **-3.** *fig* [dar forma a] to shape.
◆ **moldar-se** *vp fig* [orientar-se]: **~-se por algo** to mould *UK ou* mold *US* o.s. on sthg.

Moldávia [mow'davja] *n* Moldova, Moldavia.

moldávio, via [mow'davju, vja] ◇ *adj* Moldovan, Moldavian. ◇ *m, f* Moldovan, Moldavian.

molde ['mɔwdʒi] *m* mould *UK*, mold *US*; **~ (de vestido)** (dress) pattern.

moldura [mow'dura] *f* **-1.** [de quadro, espelho] frame. **-2.** *ARQUIT* moulding *UK*, molding *US*.

mole ['mɔli] ◇ *adj* **-1.** [ger] soft. **-2.** [flácido] flabby. **-3.** [lento] languid. **-4.** [fraco] limp. **-5.** [indolente] lazy. **-6.** [condescendente]: **ser ~ com alguém** to be lenient with sb. **-7.** *fam* [fácil] a piece of cake. ◇ *adv* **-1.** [lentamente]: **falar ~** to speak languidly. **-2.** [facilmente] easily.

moleca [mo'lɛka] *f* ▷ **moleque**.

molecada [mole'kada] *f* bunch of kids.

molecagem [mole'kaʒẽ] (*pl* **-ns**) *f* **-1.** [travessura] prank. **-2.** [brincadeira] trick. **-3.** [patifaria]: **fazer uma ~ com alguém** to trick sb.

molécula [mo'lɛkula] *f* molecule.

molecular [moleku'la(x)] *adj* molecular.

moleira [mo'lejra] *f ANAT* fontanelle *UK*, fontanel *US*.

molejo [mo'leʒu] *m* **-1.** [de veículo] suspension. **-2.** *fam* [de pessoa, corpo] wiggle.

molenga [mo'lẽŋga] *adj* lazy.

moleque, leca [mo'lɛki, lɛka] ◇ *adj* **-1.** [travesso] wild. **-2.** [brincalhão] mischievous. ◇ *m, f* **-1.** [criança] youngster; **~ (de rua)** (street) urchin. **-2.** [criança travessa] rascal. **-3.** [patife] scoundrel.

molestador [moleʃta'do(x)] *m* molester.

molestar [4] [moleʃ'ta(x)] *vt* **-1.** [importunar] to annoy. **-2.** [ofender] to offend. **-3.** [sexualmente] to molest.

moléstia [mo'lɛʃtʃja] *f* ailment.

moletom [mole'tõ] *m* brushed cotton; **de ~** flannel *(antes de subst)*.

moleza [mo'leza] *f* **-1.** [maciez] softness. **-2.** [lentidão] slowness. **-3.** [fraqueza, falta de energia] limpness; **sentir ~** to feel limp. **-4.** *fam* [coisa fácil]: **ser uma ~** to be a piece of cake.

molhado, da [mo'ʎadu, da] *adj* wet.
◆ **molhado** *m* wet area.
◆ **molhada** *f*: **dar uma molhada em algo** to wet sthg.

molhar [4] [mo'ʎa(x)] *vt* **-1.** [banhar] to wet; **~ algo em algo** to dip *ou* dunk sthg in sthg. **-2.** [umedecer] to dampen. **-3.** [regar] to water. **-4.** *fam* [urinar] to wet.
◆ **molhar-se** *vp* **-1.** [cobrir-se de líquido] to wet o.s. **-2.** *fam* [urinar] to get wet.

molhe ['mɔʎi] *m* **-1.** [de defesa] breakwater. **-2.** [de atracação] jetty.

molheira [mo'ʎejra] *f* sauce boat.

molho[1] ['mɔʎu] *m* sauce; **~ de salada** salad dressing; **~ branco** white sauce; **~ inglês** Worcestershire sauce; **~ pardo** *gravy made with chicken blood and vinegar.*
◆ **de molho** ◇ *loc adv*: **pôr/deixar de ~** [roupa, feijão] to put/leave to soak. ◇ *loc adj*: **ficar de ~** *fig* [pessoa] to stay in bed.

molho[2] ['mɔʎu] *m* bunch.

molinete [moli'netʃi] *m PESCA* fishing reel.

molusco [mo'luʃku] *m* mollusc.

momentaneamente [momẽntãnja'mẽntʃi] *adv* momentarily.

momentâneo, nea [momẽn'tãnju, nja] *adj* momentary.

momento [mo'mẽntu] *m* **-1.** moment; **de um ~ para outro** from one moment to the next; **neste ~** [agora mesmo] just now; **a qualquer ~** any moment now; **(no) ~ oportuno** (at the) right moment. **-2.** [tempo presente]: **do ~** of the moment; **no ~** at the moment.

Mônaco ['monaku] *n*: **(o principado de) ~** (the principality of) Monaco.

monarca [mo'naxka] *mf* monarch.

monarquia [monax'kia] *f* monarchy.

monarquista [monax'kiʃta] ◇ *adj* monarchic. ◇ *mf* monarchist.

monastério [monaʃ'tɛrju] *m* monastery.

monástico, ca [mo'naʃtʃiku, ka] *adj* monastic.

monção [mõn'sãw] (*pl* **-ões**) *f* [vento] monsoon.

monetário, ria [mone'tarju, rja] *adj* monetary; ▷ **correção**.

monetarismo [moneta'riʒmu] *m* monetarism.
monetarista [moneta'riʃta] <> *adj* monetarist. <> *mf* [partidário] monetarist.
monge, ja ['mõnʒi, ʒa] *m, f* [monje] monk; [monja] nun.
mongol [mõŋ'gɔw] <> *adj* Mongol. <> *m* Mongol.
Mongólia [mõŋ'gɔlja] *n* Mongolia.
mongolismo [mõŋgo'liʒmu] *m* MED Down's syndrome.
mongolóide [mõŋgo'lɔjdʒi] MED <> *adj* Down's syndrome *(antes de subst)*. <> *mf* (person with) Down's syndrome.
monitor, ra [moni'to(x), ra] *(mpl* **-es**, *fpl* **-s**) *m, f* EDUC monitor.
◆ **monitor** *m* **-1.** [ger] monitor. **-2.** TV screen.
monitorar [4] [monito'ra(x)] *vt* to monitor.
monja ['mõnʒa] *f* ▷ **monge**.
monocromático, ca [monokro'matʃiku, ka] *adj* monochromatic.
monóculo [mo'nɔkulu] *m* monocle.
monocultura [monokuw'tura] *f* monoculture.
monogamia [monoga'mia] *f* monogamy.
monógamo, ma [mo'nɔgamu, ma] *adj* monogamous.
monografia [monogra'fia] *f* monograph.
monograma [mono'grãma] *m* monogram.
monolítico, ca [mono'litʃiku, ka] *adj* monolithic.
monologar [14] [monolo'ga(x)] *vi* **-1.** [falar consigo mesmo] to talk to o.s. **-2.** TEATRO to give a monologue.
monólogo [mo'nɔlogu] *m* monologue.
mononucleose [ˌmononukle'ɔzi] *f* mononucleosis.
monopólio [mono'pɔlju] *m* monopoly.
monopolista [monopo'liʃta] <> *adj* monopolistic. <> *mf* monopolist.
monopolizar [4] [monopoli'za(x)] *vt* to monopolize.
monossílabo, ba [mono'silabu, ba] *adj* monosyllabic.
◆ **monossílabos** *mpl* monosyllables.
monotonia [monoto'nia] *f* monotony.
monótono, na [mo'nɔtonu, na] *adj* monotonous.
monóxido [mo'nɔksidu] *m* monoxide; ~ **de carbono** carbon monoxide.
monsenhor [mõnse'ɲo(x)] *m* Monsignor.
monstrengo, ga [mõnʃ'treŋgu, ga] *m, f* [pessoa, coisa] monstrosity.
monstro ['mõnʃtru] <> *adj inv* [enorme] huge. <> *m* [criatura disforme] monster; **ser um** ~ [ser um prodígio] to be a wizard; [ser cruel, enorme, horrendo] to be monstrous.
monstruosidade [mõnʃtrwozi'dadʒi] *f* monstrosity.
monstruoso, osa [mõn'ʃtrwozu, ɔza] *adj* **-1.** [com conformação de monstro] deformed. **-2.** [enorme] enormous. **-3.** [horrendo] monstrous.
monta ['mõnta] *f*: **de pouca** ~ of little importance.
montador, ra [mõnta'do(x), ra] *m, f* CINE (film) editor.
montagem [mõn'taʒẽ] *(pl* **-ns**) *f* **-1.** [de equipamento, casa] assembly. **-2.** CINE (film) editing. **-3.** TEATRO (theatre) production.
montanha [mõn'tãɲa] *f* mountain.
montanha-russa [mõnˌtãɲa'rusa] *(pl* **montanhas-russas**) *f* roller coaster.
Montanhas Rochosas [mõnˌtãɲaʃxo'ʃɔzaʃ] *n*: **as** ~ the Rocky Mountains, the Rockies.
montanhês, esa [mõnta'ɲeʃ, eza] *(pl* **-eses**) <> *adj* mountain *(antes de subst)*. <> *m, f* highlander.
montanhismo [mõntã'ɲiʒmu] *m* mountaineering.
montanhista [mõntã'ɲiʃta] <> *adj* mountaineering. <> *mf* mountaineer.
montanhoso, osa [mõntã'ɲozu, ɔza] *adj* mountainous.
montante [mõn'tãntʃi] *m* **-1.** [soma] amount, sum. **-2.** [direção]: **a** ~ **de** upstream of.
montão [mõn'tãw] *(pl* **-ões**) *m* pile.
montar [4] [mõn'ta(x)] <> *vt* **-1.** [armar] to prime. **-2.** [instalar] to ready. **-3.** [pôr sobre]: ~ **alguém em algo** to mount sb on sthg. **-4.** CINE to edit. **-5.** TEATRO to produce. <> *vi* **-1.** [cavalgar]: ~ **(a cavalo)** to ride (horseback). **-2.** [pôr-se sobre]: ~ **em algo** to mount sthg. **-3.** [atingir]: ~ **a** *ou* **em algo** to amount to sthg.
montaria [mõnta'ria] *f* [cavalo] mount.
monte ['mõntʃi] *m* **-1.** [elevação] hill. **-2.** [pilha] pile. **-3.** *fig* [grande quantidade]: **um** ~ **de** a load of; **comida aos** ~**s** loads of food.
montepio [mõntʃi'piw] *m* trust fund.
montês [mõn'teʃ] *adj* mountain *(antes de subst)*; **cabra** ~ mountain goat.
Montevidéu [mõntevi'dɛw] *n* Montevideo.
montoeira [mõn'twjra] *f*: **uma** ~ **de** a heap of.
montões [mõn'tõjʃ] *pl* ▷ **montão**.
monumental [monumẽn'taw] *(pl* **-ais**) *adj* **-1.** [enorme] monumental. **-2.** [magnífico] magnificent.
monumento [monu'mẽntu] *m* monument.
moqueca [mo'kɛka] *f Brazilian fish or chicken stew made with coconut milk, onions and palm oil.*
moradia [mora'dʒia], **morada** [mo'rada] *f* dwelling.
morador, ra [mora'do(x), ra] *(mpl* **-es**, *fpl* **-s**) *m, f* resident.
moral [mo'raw] *(pl* **-ais**) <> *adj* moral. <> *m* [estado de espírito] morale; **levantar o** ~ **(de alguém)** to raise the morale (of sb). <> *f* **-1.** [ética] morals *(pl)*. **-2.** [de história, fato] moral. **-3.** [estado de espírito]: **estar de** ~ **baixa** to be demoralized.
moralidade [morali'dadʒi] *f* morality.
moralismo [mora'liʒmu] *m* moralism.
moralista [mora'liʃta] <> *adj* moralistic. <> *mf* moralist.
moralização [morali'zasãw] *(pl* **-ões**) *f* moralization.
moralizar [4] [morali'za(x)] <> *vt* [tornar mais

moral] to moralize. <> vi [pregar moral]: ~ **(sobre)** to moralize (on).
morango [mo'rãŋgu] *m* strawberry.
morar [4] [mo'ra(x)] *vi* **-1.** [habitar]: ~ **(em)** to live (in). **-2.** *fam* [entender] to catch on; **morou?** got it?
moratória [mora'tɔrja] *f* moratorium.
morbidez [moxbi'deʒ] *f* morbidity.
mórbido, da ['mɔxbidu, da] *adj* morbid.
morcego [mox'segu] *m* bat.
mordaça [mox'dasa] *f* **-1.** [de animal] muzzle. **-2.** *fig* [pano] gag.
mordaz [mox'daʒ] *adj* biting.
morder [5] [mox'de(x)] <> *vt* & *vi* to bite.
mordida [mox'dʒida] *f* bite; **dar uma** ~ **(em)** to bite (into).
mordomia [moxdo'mia] *f* **-1.** [num emprego] perks *(pl)*. **-2.** [conforto, luxo] comfort.
mordomo [mox'domu] *m* butler.
morena [mo'rena] *f* ▷ **moreno**.
morenaço, ça [more'nasu, sa] *m, f* dark-haired beauty.
moreno, na [mo'renu, na] <> *adj* **-1.** [tipo - de pele] dark-skinned; [- de cabelo] dark-haired. **-2.** [bronzeado] tanned; **ficar** ~ to tan; **estar** ~ to be tanned. <> *m, f* **-1.** [de pele] dark-skinned person. **-2.** [de cabelo] dark-haired person. **-3.** [cor] tan.
morfina [mox'fina] *f* morphine.
morfologia [moxfolo'ʒia] *f* GRAM morphology.
moribundo, da [mori'bũndu, da] *adj* dying.
moringa [mo'rĩŋga] *f* water-cooler.
mormacento, ta [moxma'sẽntu, ta] *adj* sultry.
mormaço [mox'masu] *m* sultry weather.
mormente [mɔx'mẽntʃi] *adv* especially.
mórmon ['mɔxmõ] *mf* Mormon.
morno, na ['moxnu, na] *adj* lukewarm.
morosidade [morozi'dadʒi] *f* slowness.
moroso, osa [mo'rozu, ɔza] *adj* slow.
morrer [5] [mo'xe(x)] *vi* **-1.** [ger] to die; ~ **afogado** to drown; **ele morreu atropelado** he was knocked down and killed. **-2.** [cair no esquecimento] to be dead. **-3.** AUTO to die. **-4.** *fig* [sentir intensamente]: **estou morrendo de calor/fome/frio** I'm dying of heat/hunger/cold; **morro de vontade de viajar** I'm dying to travel; **morri de medo** I was scared to death; **morri de rir** I died laughing. **-5.** *fam* [desembolsar]: ~ **em** to cough up.
morro ['moxu] *m* **-1.** [monte] hill. **-2.** [favela] slum.
mortadela [moxta'dɛla] *f* *salami-type sausage.*
mortal [mox'taw] (*pl* **-ais**) <> *adj* **-1.** [ger] mortal. **-2.** [terrível - dor] dreadful; [- pecado] deadly. <> *mf* mortal.
mortalha [mox'taʎa] *f* shroud.
mortalidade [moxtali'dadʒi] *f* mortality.
mortandade [moxtãn'dadʒi] *f* slaughter.
morte ['mɔxtʃi] *f* **-1.** [ger] death. **-2.** [fim] ending. **-3.** *fig*: **ser a** ~ **para alguém** [ser muito penoso] to be the end for sb. **-4.** *loc*: **pensar na** ~ **da bezerra** *fig* to daydream; **ser de** ~ *fam* to be impossible.
morteiro [mox'tejru] *m* mortar.
mortífero, ra [mox'tʃiferu, ra] *adj* lethal.
mortificar [12] [moxtʃifi'ka(x)] *vt* **-1.** [torturar] to torture. **-2.** [atormentar] to torment.
morto, ta ['moxtu, 'mɔxta] <> *pp* ▷ **matar.** <> *adj* **-1.** [ger] dead; **nem** ~ no way; **não ter onde cair** ~ to have nowhere to lay one's head. **-2.** [sem atividades] deadly. **-3.** [desbotado] faded. **-4.** [sentindo intensamente]: ~ **de fome** dying of hunger; ~ **de raiva** seething with rage. <> *m, f* [falecido] deceased.
◆ **morto** *m* [biriba] *pile of overturned playing cards.*
mosaico [mo'zajku] *m* mosaic.
mosca ['moʃka] *f* fly; **acertar na** ~ to hit the jackpot; **estar/viver às** ~**s** to be empty.
moscovita [moʃko'vita] <> *adj* Muscovite. <> *m, f* Muscovite.
Moscou [moʃ'kow] *n* Moscow.
mosquiteiro [moʃki'tejru] *m* mosquito net.
mosquito [moʃ'kitu] *m* mosquito.
mostarda [moʃ'taxda] *f* mustard.
mosteiro [moʃ'tejru] *m* [de monges] monastery; [de monjas] convent.
mostra ['mɔʃtra] *f* **-1.** [exposição] display. **-2.** [manifestação] sign; **dar** ~**s de algo** to show signs of sthg.
mostrador [moʃtra'do(x)] (*pl* **-es**) *m* dial.
mostrar [4] [moʃ'tra(x)] *vt* **-1.** [ger] to show. **-2.** [apontar] to point out.
◆ **mostrar-se** *vp* **-1.** [revelar-se] to show o.s. to be. **-2.** [exibir-se] to show off.
mostruário [moʃ'trwarju] *m* display case.
mote ['mɔtʃi] *m* LITER [tema] theme.
motel [mo'tɛw] (*pl* **-éis**) *m* motel.
motim [mo'tʃĩ] (*pl* **-ns**) *m* **-1.** [do povo] riot. **-2.** [de tropas] mutiny.
motivação [motʃiva'sãw] (*pl* **-ões**) *f* motivation.
motivado, da [motʃiva'du, da] *adj* [incentivado] motivated.
motivar [4] [motʃi'va(x)] *vt* **-1.** [estimular] to motivate. **-2.** [provocar] to provoke. **-3.** [induzir]: ~ **alguém a fazer algo** to motivate sb to do sthg.
motivo [mo'tʃivu] *m* **-1.** [causa]: ~ **(de/para)** cause (of/for); **dar** ~ **a** to give rise to; **por** ~**s de força maior** for reasons beyond our control; **sem** ~ without reason; **ser** ~ **de** to be a cause for; **(não) ter** ~ **para** to have (no) reason to. **-2.** [justificativa] reason. **-3.** ARTE, MÚS motif.
moto[1] ['mɔtu] *m* [lema] motto.
◆ **de moto próprio** *loc adv* of one's own accord.
moto[2] ['mɔtu] *f* [motocicleta] motorbike.
motoca [mo'tɔka] *f fam* (motor)bike.
motocicleta [,motosi'klɛta] *f* motorcycle, motorbike.
motociclismo [motosi'kliʒmu] *m* motorcycling.
motociclista [motosi'kliʃta] *mf* motorcyclist, biker.
motoneta [moto'neta] *f* motor scooter.
motoqueiro, ra [moto'kejru, ra] *m, f* **-1.** *fam*

[motociclista] biker. **-2.** [entregador] deliveryman *(on a bike).*

motor [mo'to(x)] (*pl* **-es**) <> *adj* **-1.** *TEC* driving. **-2.** *ANAT* motor. <> *m* engine; ~ **de arranque** starter (motor); ~ **diesel** diesel engine; ~ **de explosão** internal combustion engine; ~ **de popa** outboard motor.

motorista [moto'riʃta] *mf* driver.

motorizado, da [motori'zadu, da] *adj* motorized.

motorizar [4] [motori'za(x)] *vt* to motorize.

◆ **motorizar-se** *vp* [pessoa] to get one's own car.

motorneiro, ra [motox'nejru, ra] *m, f* tram driver *UK*, streetcar driver *US*.

motosserra [moto'sɛxa] *f* chainsaw.

motriz [mo'triʒ] *adj f* ▷ **motor**.

mouco, ca ['moku, ka] *adj ant* deaf.

mountain bike [ˌmawntẽn'bajki] *f* mountain bike.

mourisco, ca [mo'riʃku, ka] *adj* Moorish.

mouro, ra ['moru, ra] <> *adj* Moorish. <> *m, f* Moor.

mouse [ˌmawzi] *m COMPUT* mouse.

movediço, ça [move'dʒisu, sa] *adj TEC* moving; **areia movediça** quicksand.

móvel ['mɔvɛw] (*pl* **-eis**) <> *adj* movable. <> *m* piece of furniture.

◆ **móveis** *mpl* furniture *(sg).*

mover [5] [mo've(x)] *vt* **-1.** [ger] to move. **-2.** [começar] to set in motion.

◆ **mover-se** *vp* to move.

movido, da [mo'vidu, da] *adj* **-1.** [impelido]: ~ **a algo/a fazer algo** moved to sthg/ to do sthg; ~ **por algo** moved by sthg. **-2.** [promovido]: ~ **contra alguém/algo** started against sb/sthg. **-3.** [acionado]: ~ **a álcool/vapor** ethanol/steam-driven.

movimentação [movimẽnta'sãw] (*pl* **-ões**) *f* [ato] movement.

movimentado, da [movimẽn'tadu, da] *adj* **-1.** [bairro, loja, dia] busy. **-2.** [música, peça, show] lively.

movimentar [4] [movimẽn'ta(x)] *vt* **-1.** [ger] to move. **-2.** *fig* [animar] to liven up.

movimento [movi'mẽntu] *m* **-1.** [ger] movement. **-2.** [animação] bustle.

MP <> *m* (*abrev de* **Ministério Público**) *Brazilian state government.* <> *f* (*abrev de* **Medida Provisória**) *emergency law.*

MPB (*abrev de* **Música Popular Brasileira**) *f generic term for all popular Brazilian music.*

MS (*abrev de* **Estado do Mato Grosso do Sul**) *m State of Mato Grosso do Sul.*

MS-DOS (*abrev de* **Microsoft Disk Operating System**) *m* MS-DOS.

MST (*abrev de* **Movimento dos Trabalhadores Sem-Terra**) *m Brazilian movement for landless workers.*

MT (*abrev de* **Estado do Mato Grosso**) *m State of Mato Grosso.*

muamba ['mwãnba] *f* **-1.** *fam* [mercadoria contrabandeada] contraband. **-2.** [mercadoria roubada] loot.

muambeiro, ra [mwãn'bejru, ra] *m, f* **-1.** [contrabandista] smuggler. **-2.** [vendedor de objetos roubados] fence.

muco ['muku] *m* mucus.

mucosa [mu'kɔza] *f* mucous membrane.

muçulmano, na [musuw'mãnu, na] <> *adj* Muslim. <> *m, f* Muslim.

muda ['muda] *f* **-1.** *BOT* seedling. **-2.** *ZOOL* moult; **estar na** ~ to be moulting *UK*, to be molting *US*. **-3.** [vestuário]: ~ **(de roupa)** change (of clothes).

mudança [mu'dãnsa] *f* **-1.** [ger] move; **fazer a** ~ to move (house). **-2.** [modificação] change. **-3.** *AUTO* gear.

mudar [4] [mu'da(x)] <> *vt* to change. <> *vi* [modificar] to change; ~ **de algo** to change sthg; ~ **de casa** to move house; ~ **de roupa** to change clothes.

mudez [mu'deʒ] *f* muteness.

mudo, da ['mudu, da] <> *adj* **-1.** [ger] silent. **-2.** *MED* mute. **-3.** [telefone] dead. <> *m, f* mute.

mugido [mu'ʒidu] *m* moo.

mugir [52] [mu'ʒi(x)] *vi* [vaca] to moo.

muito, ta ['muĩntu, ta] <> *adj* **-1.** [grande quantidade - no sg] a lot of; ~ **problema** a lot of problems *(pl)*; **levou** ~ **tempo** it took a long time; **sinto muita fome** I'm very hungry; [- no pl] many; ~**s dias** many days; [- em frases interrogativas e negativas] much, many; **não tenho** ~ **tempo/**~**s alunos** I haven't much time/many pupils. **-2.** *(no sg)* [demais] too much; ~ **calor** too hot; **muita gente** too many people. <> *pron* *(no sg)* much; *(no pl)* a lot; **tenho** ~ **que fazer** I've got a lot to do; ~**s concordam comigo** many agree with me.

◆ **muito** *adv* **-1.** [intensamente] a lot; **gostei** ~ **de ir ao cinema** I enjoyed going to the cinema very much; **não gosto** ~ I don't like it very much; ~ **feliz** very happy; ~ **mais** much more; **sinto** ~**, mas não posso** I'm very sorry, but I can't. **-2.** [muito tempo] a long time; ~ **antes/depois** a long time before/afterwards; ~ **mais tarde** much later. **-3.** [freqüentemente] often; **ela faz** ~ **isso** she often does that; **você vem** ~ **aqui?** do you come here often? **-4.** *loc*: **quando** ~ at most.

◆ **por muito que** *loc conj* however much.

mula ['mula] *f* mule.

mulato, ta [mu'latu, ta] <> *adj* mulatto. <> *m, f* mulatto.

muleta [mu'leta] *f* **-1.** [para andar] crutch. **-2.** *fig* [apoio] support.

mulher [mu'ʎɛ(x)] (*pl* **-es**) *f* **-1.** [ser] woman; ~ **fatal** femme fatale; ~ **de negócios** businesswoman; ~ **da vida** prostitute. **-2.** [esposa] wife.

mulheraço [muʎe'rasu] (*pl* **-s**) **mulherão** [muʎe'rãw] (*pl* **-ões**) *f* fantastic woman.

mulherengo [muʎe'rẽŋgu] <> *adj* womanizing. <> *m* womanizer.

mulher-feita [mu,ʎɛx'fejta] (*pl* **mulheres-feitas**) *f* grown woman.

mulherio [muʎe'riw] *m* **-1.** [grupo de mulheres] group of women. **-2.** [as mulheres] women.

mulher-objeto [muɲe(x)'obʒetu] (*pl* **mulheres-objeto**) *f* female sex object.

multa ['muwta] *f* fine; **levar uma ~** to get fined; **dar uma ~** to fine.

multar [4] [muw'ta(x)] *vt*: **~ alguém (em R$ 100)** to fine sb (100 R$).

multicolor [muwtʃico'lo(x)] *adj* multicoloured *UK*, multicolored *US*.

multicultural [muwti'kuwturãw] (*pl* **-ais**) *adj* multicultural.

multidão [muwtʃi'dãw] (*pl* **-ões**) *f* **-1.** [de pessoas] crowd. **-2.** [grande quantidade] multitude; **uma ~ de** *fig* lots of.

multifacetado, da [muwtʃi'fasetadu, da] *adj* [personalidade, talento] multifaceted.

multiforme [muwtʃi'fɔxmi] *adj* multiform.

multilateral [muwtʃilate'raw] (*pl* **-ais**) *adj* multilateral.

multimilionário, ria [muwtʃimiljo'narju, rja] <> *adj* multimillionaire *(antes de subst)*. <> *m, f* multimillionaire.

multinacional [,muwtʃinasjo'naw] (*pl* **-ais**) <> *adj* multinational. <> *f* multinational.

multiplicação [muwtʃiplika'sãw] (*pl* **-ões**) *f* **-1.** [ger] multiplication. **-2.** [aumento] increase.

multiplicar [12] [muwtʃipli'ka(x)] <> *vt* **-1.** MAT to multiply; **x multiplicado por y é igual a z** x times y equals z. **-2.** [aumentar] to increase. <> *vi* MAT to multiply.

◆ **multiplicar-se** *vp* **-1.** [aumentar] to increase. **-2.** BIOL to multiply.

multiplicidade [muwtʃiplisi'dadʒi] *f* multiplicity.

múltiplo, pla ['muwtʃiplu, pla] *adj* multiple.

◆ **múltiplo** *m* multiple.

multiprocessamento [muwtʃiprosesa'mẽntu] *m* COMPUT multiprocessing.

multirracial [muwtʃixa'sjaw] (*pl* **-ais**) *adj* multiracial.

multiuso [muwtʃi'uzu] *adj inv* multipurpose.

multiusuário, ria [muwtʃiuz'arju, rja] *adj* COMPUT multiuser.

múmia ['mumja] *f* **-1.** [cadáver] mummy. **-2.** *fig* [pessoa] moron.

mundano, na [mũn'dãnu, na] *adj* mundane.

mundial [mũn'dʒjaw] (*pl* **-ais**) <> *adj* **-1.** [política, guerra] world *(antes de subst)*. **-2.** [organização, fama] worldwide. <> *m* [campeonato] world championship; [de futebol] World Cup.

mundo ['mũndu] *m* **-1.** [ger] world; **o outro ~** the next world; **vir ao ~** to come into the world. **-2.** [pessoas]: **todo o ~** everyone; **veio meio ~** loads of people came. **-3.** [quantidade]: **um ~ de** loads of. **-4.** *loc*: **abarcar o ~ com as pernas** to take on too much; **estar no ~ da lua** to be miles away; **prometer ~ s e fundos** to promise the world; **como este ~ é pequeno** what a small world; **desde que o ~ é ~** since time immemorial.

◆ **Mundo** *m*: **Novo Mundo** New World; **Terceiro Mundo** Third World.

munguzá [mũŋgu'za] *m* corn meal.

munheca [mu'ɲɛka] *f* **-1.** *fam* [mão] hand. **-2.** [pulso] wrist.

munição [muni'sãw] (*pl* **-ões**) *f* ammunition.

municipal [munisi'paw] (*pl* **-ais**) *adj* municipal.

municipalidade [munisipali'dadʒi] *f* local authority.

municipalizar [munisipali'za(x)] *vt* [instituições, serviços] to municipalize.

município [muni'sipju] *m* **-1.** [divisão administrativa] local authority. **-2.** [território] town.

Munique [mu'niki] *n* Munich.

munir [6] [mu'ni(x)] *vt*: **~ alguém de algo** to equip sb with sthg.

◆ **munir-se** *vp*: **~-se de algo** to equip o.s. with sthg; **~-se de coragem** to arm o.s. with courage; **~-se de paciência** to arm o.s. with patience.

muque ['muki] *m* brute force.

mural [mu'raw] (*pl* **-ais**) <> *adj* wall *(antes de subst)*. <> *m* [pintura] mural.

muralha [mu'raʎa] *f* wall.

murchar [4] [mux'ʃa(x)] <> *vt* **-1.** [planta] to wither. **-2.** [sentimento] to fade. **-3.** *fig* [retrair] to shrink. <> *vi* **-1.** [planta] to wilt. **-2.** *fig* [pessoa] to droop.

murcho, cha ['muxʃu, ʃa] *adj* **-1.** [planta] wilting. **-2.** [bola] soft. **-3.** [pessoa - sem energia] languid; [- triste] droopy.

murmurante [muxmu'rãntʃi] *adj* murmuring.

murmurar [4] [muxmu'ra(x)] <> *vt* [sussurar] to whisper. <> *vi* **-1.** [sussurar] to murmur. **-2.** [falar mal]: **~ a respeito de alguém** to complain about sb; **~ contra alguém** to speak ill of sb.

murmurinho [muxmu'riɲu] *m* **-1.** [de vozes] murmuring. **-2.** [de folhas] rustling. **-3.** [som confuso] murmur.

murmúrio [mux'murju] *m* **-1.** [de vozes] murmuring. **-2.** [de folhas] rustling. **-3.** [de água] trickling.

muro ['muru] *m* wall.

murro ['muxu] *m* punch; **dar um ~ em alguém/algo** to punch sb/sthg; **dar ~ em ponta de faca** *fig* to bang one's head against a brick wall.

musa ['muza] *f* muse.

musculação [muʃkula'sãw] *f* bodybuilding.

muscular [muʃku'la(x)] *adj* muscular.

musculatura [muʃkula'tura] *f* musculature.

músculo ['muʃkulu] *m* **-1.** ANAT muscle. **-2.** CULIN sinewy meat.

musculoso, osa [muʃku'lozu, ɔza] *adj* **-1.** [cheio de músculo - costas, pernas] muscular; [- carne de comer] tough. **-2.** *fig* [forte] tough.

museu [mu'zew] *m* museum; **~ de arte** art gallery.

musgo ['muʒgu] *m* moss.

musgoso, osa [muʒ'gozu, ɔza] *adj* mossy.

música ['muzika] *f* ▷ **músico**.

MÚSICA

The samba is, without doubt, the best known expression of Brazilian music. Yet it is far from being the only one. The size of a continent and with strong regional culture, Brazil has a huge variety of rhythms and dances, from the *baião* and *frevo* in the north-east to the gaucho *milonga*. Such a wealth of rhythms gives Brazil a prominent position in the international musical world, to which Brazil has contributed names that range from Heitor Villa-Lobos, in classical music, to Gilberto Gil and Milton Nascimento, in popular music, including famous musicians such as Egberto Gismonti, Toninho Horta and Naná Vasconcelos.

musicado, da [muzi'kadu, da] *adj* set to music.

musical [muzi'kaw] (*pl* **-ais**) ◇ *adj* musical. ◇ *m* musical.

musicalidade [muzikali'dadʒi] *f* musicality.

musicar [muzi'ka(x)] *vt* to set to music.

musicista [muzi'siʃta] *mf* **-1.** [músico] musician. **-2.** [especialista] musicologist.

músico, ca ['muziku, ka] ◇ *adj* [profissional] musical. ◇ *m, f* musician.

◆ **música** *f* **-1.** [ger] music; **~ de câmara** chamber music; **~ clássica** classical music; **~ folclórica** folk music. **-2.** [canção] song.

musicologia [muzikolo'ʒia] *f* musicology.

musicólogo, ga [muzi'kɔlogu, ga] *m* musicologist.

musse ['musi] *f* CULIN mousse.

musselina [muse'lina] *f* muslin.

mutabilidade [mutabili'dadʒi] *f* mutability.

mutação [muta'sãw] (*pl* **-ões**) *f* **-1.** BIOL mutation. **-2.** *fig* [transformação] change.

mutável [mu'tavew] (*pl* **-eis**) *adj* changeable.

mutilação [mutʃila'sãw] *f* **-1.** [orgânico] mutilation. **-2.** [de texto] cutting.

mutilado, da [mutʃi'ladu, da] ◇ *adj* mutilated. ◇ *m, f* cripple.

mutilar [4] [mutʃi'la(x)] *vt* **-1.** [pessoa] to mutilate. **-2.** [texto] to cut.

mutirão [mutʃi'rãw] (*pl* **-ões**) *m* joint effort.

mutreta [mu'treta] *f fam* cheating; **fazer (uma) ~** to cheat.

mutuamente [mutwa'mẽntʃi] *adv* mutually.

mútuo, tua ['mutwu, twa] *adj* mutual.

muxoxo [mu'ʃoʃu] *m* tutting; **fazer ~** to tut.

N

n, N ['eni] *m* **-1.** [letra] n, N. **-2.** [quantidade indeterminada] n; **contamos ~ vezes a mesma história** we told the story for the nth time.

na [na] = **em + a**.

-na [na] *pron* [pessoa] her; [coisa] it; [você] you.

nabo ['nabu] *m* turnip.

nação [na'sãw] (*pl* **-ões**) *f* nation.

nacional [nasjo'naw] (*pl* **-ais**) *adj* national.

nacionalidade [nasjonali'dadʒi] *f* nationality.

nacionalismo [nasjona'liʒmu] *m* nationalism.

nacionalista [nasjona'liʃta] ◇ *adj* nationalist. ◇ *mf* nationalist.

nacionalização [nasjonaliza'sãw] (*pl* **-ões**) *f* nationalization.

nacionalizar [4] [nasjonali'za(x)] *vt* **-1.** [estatizar] to nationalize. **-2.** [naturalizar] to naturalize.

naco ['naku] *m* [pedaço]: **um ~ (de)** a piece (of).

nações [na'sõjʃ] *fpl* ▷ **nação**.

◆ **Nações Unidas** *fpl* United Nations.

nada ['nada] ◇ *pron indef* [coisa alguma] nothing; **não li ~ desse autor** I haven't read anything by this author; **ele fez a barba? – fez ~!** has he had a shave? – no, he hasn't!; **antes de mais ~** first of all; **de ~!** [resposta a obrigado] not at all!, you're welcome!; **como se ~ tivesse acontecido** as if nothing had happened; **isso não é ~!** that's nothing!; **~ disso!** not at all!; **~ feito** nothing doing; **~ de novo** nothing new; **~ mais** nothing more; **não quero ~ mais com ele** I don't want anything more to do with him; **~ mau** not bad; **não dizer ~** to say nothing, not to say anything; **não foi ~** [resposta a desculpa!] don't mention it; **por ~ neste mundo** for love nor money; **quase ~** hardly anything, next to nothing; **que ~!** nonsense! ◇ *adv* [de modo algum] not at all; **não gostei ~ do filme** I didn't enjoy the film at all; **~ menos do que** nothing less than; **não é ~ difícil** it isn't at all difficult. ◇ *m* **-1.** [vazio]: **o ~** the void. **-2.** [ninharia]: **um ~** a trifle, nothing.

nada-consta [ˌnada'kõnʃta] *m inv deed of indemnity.*

nadadeira [nada'dejra] *f* **-1.** [de animal] fin. **-2.** [de mergulhador] flipper.

nadador, ra [nada'do(x), ra] (*mpl* **-es**, *fpl* **-s**) <> *adj* swimming. <> *m, f* swimmer.
nadar [4] [na'da(x)] *vi* **-1.** [em piscina, mar, rio] to swim. **-2.** [estar imerso] to be swimming; ~ **em dinheiro** *fig* to be rolling in money; **ficar nadando** *fig* to be out of one's depth.
nádegas ['nadegaʃ] *fpl* buttocks.
nado ['nadu] *m* swimming; **atravessar algo a** ~ to swim across sthg; ~ **borboleta** butterfly (stroke); ~ **cachorrinho** doggy paddle; ~ **de costas** backstroke; ~ **de peito** breaststroke; ~ **livre** freestyle.
NAFTA (*abrev de* **North American Free Trade Agreement**) *f* NAFTA.
naftalina [nafta'lina] *f* naphthaline.
náilon ['najlõ] *m* nylon.
naipe ['najpi] *m* **-1.** [cartas] suit. **-2.** *fig* [qualidade]: **de bom** ~ first class.
Nairóbi [naj'rɔbi] *n* Nairobi.
namoradeira [namora'dejra] *adj* flirtatious.
namorado, da [namo'radu, da] <> *adj* enamoured. <> *m, f* boyfriend (*f* girlfriend).
namorador, ra [namora'do(x), ra] *adj* flirtatious.
namorar [4] [namo'ra(x)] <> *vt* **-1.** [manter namoro] to be going out with. **-2.** [cobiçar] to covet. **-3.** [fitar] to stare longingly at. <> *vi* **-1.** [manter namoro] to be going out together. **-2.** [trocar carícias] to flirt.
namorico [na'moriku] *m* flirtation.
namoro [na'moru] *m* relationship.
nanico, ca [na'niku, ka] *adj* tiny.
nanquim [nãŋ'kĩ] *m* Indian ink.
não [nãw] <> *adv* **-1.** [resposta] no. **-2.** [negação] not; **ela** ~ **é fácil** she's not easy; **ela é médica,** ~ **é?** she's a doctor, isn't she?; **eu** ~ **tenho dinheiro** I haven't got any money; **agora** ~ not now; **como** ~? why not?; ~ **muito** not much; ~ **sei** I don't know; ~ **tem de quê** [resposta a obrigado] not at all, you're welcome; **pois** ~! [como interj] of course! <> *m* [recusa] refusal.
não-agressão [ˌnãwagre'sãw] *f*: **pacto de** ~ non-aggression pact.
não-alinhado, da [ˌnãwali'ɲadu, da] (*mpl* **-s**, *fpl* **-s**) *adj* non-aligned.
não-conformista [ˌnãwkõnfox'miʃta] (*pl* **-s**) <> *adj* non-conformist. <> *mf* non-conformist.
não-governamental [nãwgovernemẽn'taw] (*pl* **-ais**) *adj* non-governmental.
não-intervenção [ˌnãwĩntexvẽn'sãw] *f* JUR non-intervention.
napa ['napa] *f* nappa leather.
naquela [na'kɛla] = **em + aquela**.
naquele [na'keli] = **em + aquele**.
naquilo [na'kilu] = **em + aquilo**.
narcisismo [naxsi'ziʒmu] *m* narcissism.
narcisista [naxsi'ziʃta] *adj* narcissistic.
narciso [nax'sizu] *m* **-1.** BOT narcissus. **-2.** [pessoa] narcissist.
narcótico, ca [nax'kɔtʃiku, ka] *adj* narcotic.
◆ **narcótico** *m* narcotic.
narcotizar [4] [naxkotʃi'za(x)] *vt* to drug.
narcotráfico [naxko'trafiku] *m* drug traffic.
narigudo, da [nari'gudu, da] <> *adj* with a large nose; **ser** ~ to have a large nose. <> *m, f* large-nosed person.
narina [na'rina] *f* nostril.
nariz [na'riʃ] (*pl* **-es**) (*pl* **-es** [na'riziʃ]) *m* **-1.** [ger] nose. **-2.** *loc*: **dar com o** ~ **na porta** to find the doors closed; **meter o** ~ **em** to stick one's nose into; **torcer o** ~ **(para alguém/algo)** to turn up one's nose at sb/sthg; **sou dono do meu** ~ I know my own mind.
narração [naxa'sãw] (*pl* **-ões**) *f* **-1.** [conto] story. **-2.** [relato] narrative.
narrador, ra [naxa'do(x), ra] *m, f* narrator.
narrar [4] [na'xa(x)] *vt* **-1.** [contar] to describe. **-2.** [relatar] to recount.
narrativo, va [naxa'tʃivu, va] *adj* narrative.
◆ **narrativa** *f* = **narração**.
nas [naʃ] = **em + as**.
-nas [naʃ] *pron pl* [elas] them; [vocês] you.
NASA (*abrev de* **National Aeronautics and Space Administration**) *f* NASA.
nasal [na'zaw] (*pl* **-ais**) *adj* nasal.
nasalado, da [naza'ladu, da] *adj* nasal.
nascença [na'sẽnsa] *f* [nascimento] birth; **de** ~ from birth; **ela é surda de** ~ she has been deaf from birth; **marca de** ~ birthmark.
nascente [na'sẽntʃi] <> *adj* **-1.** [interesse, povo] emerging. **-2.** [planta] sprouting. <> *m* **-1.** [fonte] spring. **-2.** [nascer do sol] sunrise. **-3.** [leste] east.
nascer [25] [na'se(x)] *vi* **-1.** [vir ao mundo] to be born. **-2.** [brotar] to sprout. **-3.** [originar-se] to originate. **-4.** [surgir - sol, lua] to rise; [- dia] to dawn. **-5.** [formar-se] to be born. **-6.** [descender]: ~ **de** to be born into. **-7.** [ter aptidão]: **ele nasceu para o comércio** he is a born businessman. **-8.** [aparecer] to appear. **-9.** *loc*: ~ **em berço de ouro** to be born with a silver spoon in one's mouth; ~ **de novo** to take on a new lease of life; **eu não nasci ontem** I wasn't born yesterday.
nascido, da [na'sidu, da] *adj* [pessoa] born; **bem** ~ from a good family.
nascimento [nasi'mẽntu] *m* **-1.** [nascença] birth; **de** ~ since birth. **-2.** *fig* [origem] origin.
NASDAQ (*abrev de* **National Association of Securities Dealers Automated Quotation**) *f* NASDAQ.
Nassau [na'saw] *n* Nassau.
nata ['nata] *f* cream.
natação [nata'sãw] *f* swimming.
natal [na'taw] (*pl* **-ais**) *adj* native; **terra** ~ birthplace.
◆ **Natal** *m* Christmas; **Feliz Natal!** happy Christmas!, merry Christmas!
natalício, cia [nata'lisju, sja] *adj*: **aniversário** ~ birthday.
◆ **natalício** *m* birthday.
natalidade [natali'dadʒi] *f* birth rate; **índice de** ~ birth rate.
natalino, na [nata'linu, na] *adj* Christmas *(antes de subst)*; **festas natalinas** Christmas celebrations.

natimorto, ta [natʃi'moxtu, ta] *m, f* stillborn baby.
natividade [natʃivi'dadʒi] *f* nativity.
nativo, va [na'tʃivu, va] ◇ *adj* native. ◇ *m, f* native.
nato, ta ['natu, ta] *adj*: **ele é um escritor ~** he is a born writer.
natural [natu'raw] (*pl* **-ais**) ◇ *adj* **-1.** [ger] natural; **ao ~** CULIN uncooked; **de tamanho ~** life-size. **-2.** [nascido]: **ser ~ de** to be a native of. ◇ *mf* [nativo] native.
naturalidade [naturali'dadʒi] *f* **-1.** [espontaneidade] spontaneity; **agir com ~** to act naturally; **falar com ~** to speak naturally; **admiro sua ~** I admire your naturalness. **-2.** [local de nascimento]: **ele é de ~ brasileira** he is Brazilian by birth.
naturalismo [natura'liʒmu] *m* ARTE naturalism.
naturalista [natura'liʃta] *mf* naturalist.
naturalização [naturaliza'sãw] *f* naturalization.
naturalizado, da [naturali'zadu, da] ◇ *adj* naturalized. ◇ *m, f* naturalized citizen.
naturalizar-se [4] [naturali'zaxsi] *vp* to become naturalized.
naturalmente [naturaw'mẽntʃi] ◇ *adv* [evidentemente] naturally. ◇ *interj* of course!
natureba [natu'rɛba] *mf* health freak.
natureza [natu'reza] *f* **-1.** [ger] nature. **-2.** [espécie] kind.
natureza-morta [natu,reza'moxta] (*pl* **naturezas-mortas**) *f* still life.
nau ['naw] *f* LITER ship.
naufragar [4] [nawfra'ga(x)] *vi* **-1.** [embarcação] to be wrecked. **-2.** [pessoa] to be shipwrecked. **-3.** *fig* [fracassar] to fail.
naufrágio [naw'fraʒju] *m* **-1.** [de embarcação, pessoa] shipwreck. **-2.** *fig* [fracasso] failure.
náufrago, ga [ga, 'nawfragu] *m* (shipwreck) survivor, castaway.
náusea ['nawzja] *f* nausea; **dar ~s a alguém** to make sb sick; **sentir ~s** to feel sick.
nauseabundo, da [nawzja'bũndu, da], **nauseante** [naw'zjãntʃi] *adj* **-1.** [que produz náuseas] nauseating. **-2.** *fig* [nojento] sickening.
nauseado, da [naw'zjadu, da] *adj* [indisposto] nauseous.
nauseante [naw'zjãntʃi] *adj* = **nauseabundo**.
nausear [15] [naw'zja(x)] ◇ *vt* **-1.** [enjoar] to make sick. **-2.** [repugnar] to nauseate. ◇ *vi* [sentir náusea] to feel sick.
náutico, ca ['nawtʃiku, ka] *adj* nautical.
◆ **náutica** *f* ESP seamanship.
naval [na'vaw] (*pl* **-ais**) *adj* naval; **construção ~** shipbuilding.
navalha [na'vaʎa] *f* **-1.** [de barba] razor blade. **-2.** [faca] blade.
navalhada [nava'ʎada] *f* stab.
nave ['navi] *f* **-1.** [de igreja] nave. **-2.** LITER [embarcação] ship; **~ espacial** spaceship.
navegação [navega'sãw] (*pl* **-ões**) *f* voyage; **companhia de ~** shipping line; **~ costeira** coastal shipping; **~ fluvial** river navigation.
navegador, ra [navega'do(x), ra] *m, f* **-1.** [ger] navigator. **-2.** COMPUT surfer.
navegante [nave'gãntʃi] *mf* navigator.
navegar [14] [nave'ga(x)] ◇ *vt* to pilot. ◇ *vi* **-1.** [seguir viagem] to sail. **-2.** COMPUT to surf; **~ na Internet** to surf the net.
navegável [nave'gavew] (*pl* **-eis**) *adj* navigable.
navio [na'viw] *m* ship; **~ cargueiro** cargo vessel; **~ de guerra** warship; **~ mercante** merchant ship; **ficar a ver ~s** to be left high and dry.
navio-petroleiro [na,viwpetro'lejru] (*pl* **navios-petroleiros**) *m* oil tanker.
navio-tanque [na,viw'tãŋki] (*pl* **navios-tanques**) *m* tanker.
nazismo [na'ziʒmu] *m* Nazism.
nazista [na'ziʃta] ◇ *adj* Nazi. ◇ *mf* Nazi.
NBA (*abrev de* **National Basketball Association**) *f* NBA.
NE (*abrev de* **Nordeste**) *m* NE.
neblina [ne'blina] *f* mist.
nebulizador [nebuliza'do(x)] *m* nebulizer.
nebulosa [nebu'lɔza] *f* ▷ **nebuloso**.
nebulosidade [nebulozi'dadʒi] *f* cloudiness.
nebuloso, osa [nebu'lozu, ɔza] *adj* **-1.** [ger] cloudy. **-2.** *fig* [sombrio] dark. **-3.** *fig* [indefinido] nebulous. **-4.** *fig* [obscuro] nebulous.
◆ **nebulosa** *f* ASTRON nebula.
nécessaire [nese'sɛ(x)] *f* sponge bag.
necessariamente [nesesarja'mẽntʃi] *adv* necessarily.
necessário, ria [nese'sarju, rja] ◇ *adj* necessary; **ser ~ fazer algo** to be necessary to do sthg; **se for ~** if necessary. ◇ *m* necessities (*pl*); **o ~** the necessities.
necessidade [nesesi'dadʒi] *f* [o que se necessita] necessity; **gêneros de primeira ~** staple foods; **em caso de ~** in case of necessity, if need be; **não há ~ (de algo/fazer algo)** there is no need (for sthg/to do sthg).
◆ **necessidades** *fpl* **-1.** [privação] need (*sg*); **passar por muitas ~** to suffer many hardships. **-2.**: **fazer suas ~** *fam* [defecar, urinar] to spend a penny.
necessitado, da [nesesi'tadu, da] *adj*: **~ (de)** in need (of).
◆ **necessitados** *mpl*: **os ~** [miseráveis] the needy.
necessitar [4] [nesesi'ta(x)] ◇ *vt* to need. ◇ *vi* to be in need; **~ de** to need.
necrológio [nekro'lɔʒu] *m* obituary.
necrópole [ne'krɔpoli] *f* cemetery.
necrotério [nekro'tɛrju] *m* mortuary *UK*, morgue *US*.
néctar ['nɛkta(x)] (*pl* **-es**) *m* nectar.
nectarina [nekta'rina] *f* nectarine.
nefando, da [ne'fãndu, da] *adj* **-1.** [abominável] nefarious. **-2.** [sacrílego] iniquitous. **-3.** [malvado] wicked.
nefasto, ta [ne'faʃtu, ta] *adj* **-1.** [agourento] ominous. **-2.** [trágico] tragic. **-3.** [nocivo] harmful.

negação [nega'sãw] (*pl* **-ões**) *f* **-1.** [recusa] refusal. **-2.** [inaptidão]: **ser uma ~ em algo** to be hopeless at sthg. **-3.** [desmentido] denial.
negacear [15] [nega'sja(x)] *vt* **-1.** [menear] to shake. **-2.** [seduzir] to deceive. **-3.** [recusar] to refuse.
negar [14] [ne'ga(x)] *vt* **-1.** [ger] to deny. **-2.** [recusar, não permitir] to refuse.
◆ **negar-se** *vp* [recusar-se] to refuse.
negativo, va [nega'tʃivu, va] ◇ *adj* negative. ◇ *adv*: **negativo!** nope!
◆ **negativo** *m* FOT negative.
◆ **negativa** *f* [recusa] refusal.
negligé [negli'ge] *m* negligee.
negligência [negli'ʒẽnsja] *f* negligence.
negligenciar [16] [negli'ʒẽnsja(x)] *vt* to neglect.
negligente [negli'ʒẽntʃi] *adj* negligent.
nego, ga ['negu, ga] *m, f* **-1.** *fam* [negro] black. **-2.** [colega] mate.
negociação [negosja'sãw] (*pl* **-ões**) *f* **-1.** [transação] transaction. **-2.** [entendimento] negotiation.
negociador, ra [negosja'do(x), ra] ◇ *adj* negotiating. ◇ *m, f* negotiator.
negociante [nego'sjãntʃi] *mf* businessman (*f* businesswoman).
negociar [16] [nego'sja(x)] ◇ *vi* **-1.** COMM: **~ (com algo)** to trade (in sthg); **~ com alguém/algo** to negotiate with sb/sthg. **-2.** [discutir] to negotiate. ◇ *vt* **-1.** [combinar] to negotiate. **-2.** COM to trade.
negociata [nego'sjata] *f* crooked deal.
negociável [nego'sjavew] (*pl* **-eis**) *adj inv* negotiable.
negócio [ne'gɔsju] *m* **-1.** COM business; **homem de ~s** businessman; **o mundo dos ~s** the business world. **-2.** [transação] deal; **fazer um bom ~** to get a good deal; **fechar um ~** to make a deal; **~ da China** very profitable deal; **~ fechado!** it's a deal! **-3.** [caso] matter; **aconteceu um ~ estranho** something strange happened; **o ~ é o seguinte** the deal is as follows. **-4.** *fam* [coisa] thing; **o barco é um ~!** the boat is amazing!; **que ~ é esse?** what's the big idea?
negra ['negra] *f* ▻ **negro**.
negrito [ne'gritu] *m* bold type.
negritude [negri'tudʒi] *f* black awareness.
negro, gra ['negru, gra] ◇ *adj* black. ◇ *m, f* black.
◆ **negra** *f* ESP: **jogar a negra** to play a decider.
negrume [ne'grumi] *m* darkness.
negrura [ne'grura] *f* blackness.
nela ['nɛla] = **em + ela**.
nele ['neli] = **em + ele**.
nem [nẽ] *conj* nor; **nem ... nem ...** neither ... nor ...; **eles ~ (sequer) me convidaram** they didn't even invite me; **~ bem ela tinha saído, ele chegou** hardly had I left than someone else took my place; **~ eu!** nor was I!; **ele foi agressivo mas ~ por isso você deveria ter retrucado** he was aggressive but that was no reason for you to retaliate; **~ sempre** not always; **~ tanto** not so much; **~ todos** not all; **eles saíam sem ~ avisar** they would go out even without warning.
◆ **nem que** *loc conj* even if.
nenê [ne'ne] *m* [bebê] baby.
nenhum, ma [ne'ɲũ, ma] (*mpl* **-ns**, *fpl* **-s**) ◇ *adj* no; **ele não tomou nenhuma decisão** he has made no decision; **em ~ momento** at no time. ◇ *pron* none; **não comprei livro ~** I didn't buy a single book; **não comprei ~** I didn't buy any; **não quero nenhuma bebida** I don't want anything to drink; **não tive problema ~** I didn't have a single problem; **~ professor é perfeito** no teacher is perfect; **todos os professores são pessoas, ~ é perfeito** all teachers are human; none is/are perfect; **~ de** none of, not one of; **~ dos dois** neither of them, neither of the two; **~ dos cinco** none of the five, not one of the five.
neoclássico, ca [nɛw'klasiku, ka] *adj* neoclassical.
◆ **Neoclássico** *m* neoclassical period.
neofascismo [nɛwfa'siʒmu] *m* neo-fascism.
neofascista [nɛwfa'siʃta] ◇ *adj* neo-fascist. ◇ *mf* neo-fascist.
neófito, ta [ne'ɔfitu, ta] *adj* [principiante] beginner.
neolatino, na [nɛwla'tʃinu, na] *adj* Romance.
neoliberal [neo'liberaw] (*pl* **-ais**) ◇ *adj* neoliberal. ◇ *mf* neoliberal.
neoliberalismo [nɛw'liberaliʒmu] *m* neoliberalism.
neolítico, ca [neo'litʃiku, ka] *adj* neolithic.
neologismo [nɛwlo'giʒmu] *m* neologism.
néon ['nɛõ], **neônio** [ne'onju] *m* neon.
neonazismo [nɛw'naziʒmu] *m* neo-Nazism.
neonazista [nɛw'naziʒta] ◇ *adj* neo-Nazi. ◇ *mf* neo-Nazi.
neo-realismo [ˌnɛwxea'liʒmu] *m* neo-realism.
neozelandês, esa [ˌnɛwzelãn'deʃ, eza] ◇ *adj* New Zealand (*antes de subst*). ◇ *m, f* New Zealander.
Nepal [ne'paw] *n* Nepal.
nepalês, esa [nepa'leʃ, eza] ◇ *adj* Nepalese, Nepali. ◇ *m, f* Nepalese, Nepali.
◆ **nepalês** *m* [língua] Nepalese, Nepali.
nepotismo [nepo'tʃiʒmu] *m* nepotism.
nervo ['nexvu] *m* **-1.** ANAT nerve; **estar uma pilha de ~s** to be a bag of nerves; **ter ~s de aço** to have nerves of steel. **-2.** [na carne] sinew. **-3.** *fig* [força] driving force.
nervosismo [nexvo'ziʒmu] *m* **-1.** [ger] nervousness. **-2.** [irritabilidade] irritability.
nervoso, osa [nex'vozu, ɔza] *adj* **-1.** [ger] nervous. **-2.** [irritado] irritable; **isso me deixa ~!** that gets on my nerves!
nervura [nex'vura] *f* **-1.** [prega] rib. **-2.** BOT vein.
néscio, cia ['nɛʃju, ʃja] *adj* **-1.** [estúpido] stupid. **-2.** [insensato] foolish.
nesga ['neʒga] *f* [pedaço, tira]: **uma ~ (de)** a piece (of).
nessa ['nɛsa] = **em + essa**.
nessas ['nɛsaʃ] = **em + essas**.

nesse ['nesi] = **em + esse**.
nesses ['nɛsiʃ] = **em + esses**.
nesta ['nɛʃta] = **em + esta**.
nestas ['nɛstaʃ] = **em + estas**.
neste ['neʃtʃi] = **em + este**.
nestes ['nestʃiʃ] = **em + estes**.
net ['netʃi] *f COMPUT* net.
netiqueta [netʃi'keta] *f COMPUT* netiquette.
neto, ta ['nɛtu, ta] *m, f* grandson (*f* granddaughter).
◆ **netos** *mpl* grandchildren.
Netuno [ne'tunu] *n* Neptune.
neurastenia [newraʃte'nja] *f* **-1.** *PSIC* neurasthenia. **-2.** *fig* [mau humor] irritability.
neurastênico, ca [newraʃ'teniku, ka] ◇ *adj* **-1.** *PSIC* neurasthenic. **-2.** *fig* [irritado] irritated. ◇ *m, f* [pessoa irritadiça] irritable person.
neurocirurgião, giã [newrosirux'ʒjãw, ʒjã] (*mpl* **-iões**, *fpl* **-s**) *m, f* neurosurgeon.
neurolingüística [ˌnewroliŋ'gwiʃtʃika] *f* neurolinguistics.
neurologia [newrolo'ʒia] *f* neurology.
neurologista [newrolo'ʒiʃta] *mf* neurologist.
neurose [new'rɔzi] *f* neurosis.
neurótico, ca [new'rɔtʃiku, ka] ◇ *adj* neurotic. ◇ *m, f* neurotic.
neurovegetativo, va [newroveʒeta'tʃivu, va] *adj* neurovegetative.
neutralidade [newtrali'dadʒi] *f* neutrality.
neutralização [newtraliza'sãw] *f* neutralization.
neutralizar [4] ['newtrali'za(x)] *vt* to neutralize.
neutro, tra ['newtru, tra] *adj* neutral.
nêutron ['newtrõ] *m* neutron.
nevada [ne'vada] *f* snowfall.
nevado, da [ne'vadu, da] *adj* **-1.** [coberto de neve] snow-covered. **-2.** [branco] snow-white.
nevar [4] [ne'va(x)] *vi* to snow.
nevasca [ne'vaʃka] *f* snowstorm.
neve ['nɛvi] *f* snow; **branco feito ~** as white as snow.
névoa ['nɛvwa] *f* fog.
nevoeiro [ne'vwejru] *m* thick fog.
nevoento, ta [ne'vwẽntu, ta] *adj* foggy.
nevralgia [nevraw'ʒia] *f* neuralgia.
nevrálgico, ca [ne'vrawʒiku, ka] *adj* neuralgic.
newsgroup [neuʃ'grupi] (*pl* **-s**) *m COMPUT* newsgroup.
nexo ['nɛksu] *m* **-1.** [ligação] connection. **-2.** [coêrencia] coherence; **sem ~** incoherent.
nhenhenhém [ɲeɲe'ɲẽj] *m* **-1.** [resmungo] grumbling; **deixe de ~!** stop whinging! **-2.** [conversa] chattering.
nhoque ['ɲɔki] *m CULIN* gnocchi.
Niágara ['njagara] *n*: **as cataratas do ~** the Niagara Falls.
Niamey [nja'mej] *n* Niamey.
Nicarágua [nika'ragwa] *n* Nicaragua.
nicaragüense [nikara'gwẽnsi] ◇ *adj* Nicaraguan. ◇ *mf* Nicaraguan.
nicho ['niʃu] *m* niche.
nick (*abrev de* **nickname**) ['niki] *m COMPUT* nickname.
Nicósia [ni'kɔzja] *n* Nicosia.
nicotina [niko'tʃina] *f* nicotine.
Níger ['niʒe(x)] *n* Niger.
Nigéria [ni'ʒɛrja] *n* Nigeria.
niilista [nij'liʃta] ◇ *adj* nihilistic. ◇ *m,f* nihilist.
Nilo ['nilu] *n*: **o ~** the Nile.
nimbo ['nĩnbu] *m* **-1.** *METEOR* nimbus. **-2.** *fig* [auréola] halo.
ninar [4] [ni'na(x)] ◇ *vt* to sing to sleep. ◇ *vi* to fall asleep.
ninfeta [nĩn'feta] *f* nymphette.
ninfomaníaca [nĩnfoma'njaka] *f* nymphomaniac.
ninguém [nĩŋ'gẽj] ◇ *pron indef* **-1.** [nenhuma pessoa] nobody; **~ vai descobrir** nobody will find out; **não conte a ~!** don't tell anybody!, tell nobody!; **~ respeita mais ~** nobody respects anybody any more; **~ mais** nobody else. **-2.** *fig* [pessoa desimportante]: **ser ~** to be nobody. ◇ *m fig* [pessoa desimportante]: **esse (zé) ~** that nobody.
ninhada [ni'ɲada] *f* brood.
ninharia [niɲa'ria] *f* trifle.
ninho ['niɲu] *m* nest; **~ de rato** *fam* [bagunça] mess.
nipônico, ca [ni'poniku, ka] ◇ *adj* Nipponese. ◇ *m, f* Nipponese.
níquel ['nikew] (*pl* **-eis**) *m* nickel; **estar sem um ~** to be penniless.
niquelar [nike'la(x)] *vt* to nickel-plate.
nirvana [nix'vãna] *m inv* nirvana.
nissei [ni'sej] *mf child of Japanese parents born in Brazil*.
nisso ['nisu] = **en + isso**.
nisto ['niʃtu] = **em + isto**.
nitidez [nitʃi'deʃ] *f* **-1.** [precisão] sharpness. **-2.** [clareza] clarity. **-3.** [brilho] brightness.
nítido, da ['nitʃidu, da] *f* **-1.** [preciso] distinct. **-2.** [claro] clear. **-3.** [brilhante] bright.
nitrato [ni'tratu] *m* nitrate.
nítrico, ca ['nitriku, ka] *adj* nitric.
nitrogênio [nitro'ʒenju] *m* nitrogen.
nitroglicerina [nitroglise'rina] *f* nitroglycerine.
nível ['nivɛw] (*pl* **-eis**) *m* **-1.** [ger] level; **em ~ de** level with; **~ superior** *UNIV* higher education. **-2.** [condicões] standard; **alto/baixo ~** high/low standard; **~ de vida** standard of living. **-3.** [ferramenta] spirit level.
nivelamento [nivela'mẽntu] *m* **-1.** [aplanamento] levelling *UK*, leveling *US*. **-2.** [equiparação] comparison.
nivelar [4] [nive'la(x)] ◇ *vt* **-1.** [aplanar] to level. **-2.** [equiparar] to compare; **~ algo a** *ou* **por** *ou* **com algo** to put sthg on the same level as sthg. **-3.** [medir] to equal. ◇ *vi* [em altura]: **~ com algo** to be level with sthg.
◆ **nivelar-se** *vp* [equiparar-se]: **~-se a** *ou* **por** *ou* **com alguém** to measure up to sb; **~-se a** *ou*

por *ou* **com algo** to measure up to sthg.
no [nu] = **em + o**.
NO (*abrev de* **Noroeste**) *m* NW.
nó ['nɔ] *m* **-1.** [laço] knot; **dar um ~** to tie a knot; **~ cego** fast knot; **~ do dedo** knuckle; **ter um ~ na garganta** to have a lump in one's throat. **-2.** *fig* [dificuldade] knotty situation. **-3.** [ponto crucial] nub.
-no [nu] *pron* [pessoa] him; [coisa] it; [você] you.
nobilíssimo, ma [nobi'lisimu, ma] *adj* [superl de nobre] most noble.
nobilitar [4] [nobili'ta(x)] *vt* [dignificar] to ennoble.
nobre ['nɔbri] ◇ *adj* **-1.** [ger] noble; **bairro ~** smart area. **-2.** *(antes de subst)* [ilustre] honourable. **-3.** ▷ **horário**. ◇ *m, f* nobleman (*f* noblewoman).
nobreza [no'breza] *f* nobility.
noção [no'sãw] (*pl* **-ões**) *f* notion; **não ter a menor ~ de algo** not to have the slightest idea about sthg.
◆ **noções** *fpl* [rudimentos] basics.
nocaute [no'kawtʃi] *m* **-1.** *BOXE* knockout; **levar alguém a ~/pôr alguém em ~** *BOXE* to knock sb out; *fig* [prostrar] to lay sb out; **perder/vencer por ~** to lose/win by a knockout. **-2.** [soco] punch.
nocautear [15] [nokaw'tʃja(x)] *vt* to knock out.
nocivo, va [no'sivu, va] *adj* harmful.
noções [no'sõjʃ] *pl* ▷ **noção**.
noctívago [nok'tʃivagu] *adj & n* = **notívago**.
nódoa ['nɔdwa] *f* stain.
nódulo ['nɔdulu] *m ANAT* nodule.
nogueira [no'gejra] *f* walnut tree.
noitada [noj'tada] *f* **-1.** [período] night. **-2.** [de diversão] night out. **-3.**: **~ (de trabalho)** evening's work; **fazer uma ~** to work at night. **-4.** [de insônia] sleepless night.
noite ['nojtʃi] *f* **-1.** [período] night; **à** *ou* **de ~** at night; **a ~ passada** last night; **boa ~!** [cumprimento] good evening!; [despedida] good night!; **da ~ para o dia** from one day to the next, overnight; **esta ~** [a noite passada] last night; [a próxima noite] this evening, tonight; **ontem/hoje/amanhã a ~** yesterday/this/tomorrow evening; **passar a ~ em claro** to have a sleepless night; **tarde da ~** late at night; **~ de Natal** Christmas eve; **ao cair da ~** at nightfall. **-2.** [vida noturna] nightlife.
noitinha [noj'tʃiɲa] *f*: **à** *ou* **de ~** at dusk.
noivado [noj'vadu] *m* **-1.** [ger] engagement. **-2.** [festa] engagement party.
noivar [4] [noj'va(x)] *vi* **-1.** [comprometer-se] to become engaged; **~ com** to become engaged to. **-2.** [manter compromisso] to be engaged.
noivo, va ['nojvu, va] ◇ *adj* engaged. ◇ *m, f* **-1.** [comprometido]: **estar/ser ~ de alguém** to be sb's fiancé (*f* fiancée), to be engaged to sb. **-2.** [no altar] groom (*f* bride).
◆ **noivos** *mpl*: **os ~s** [no altar] the bride and groom; [na lua-de-mel] newly-weds.
nojeira [no'ʒejra] *f* filth; **estar/ficar uma ~** [coisa] to be/turn out foul; [serviço] to be/turn out appalling.
nojento, ta [no'ʒẽntu, ta] *adj* **-1.** [que enoja] disgusting. **-2.** [antipático] loathsome.
nojo ['noʒu] *m* **-1.** [náusea] nausea. **-2.** [repulsa] disgust; **estar um ~** [estar sujo, ruim] to be filthy; **ser um ~** [ser antipático] to be loathsome.
nômade ['nomadʒi] ◇ *adj* nomadic. ◇ *mf* nomad.
nome ['nɔmi] *m* **-1.** [designação] name; **~ de batismo** Christian name; **~ de família** surname; **~ feio** swearword; **~ de guerra** pseudonym; **de ~** [renome] of renown; [reputação] well known. **-2.** [autoridade]: **em ~ de algo** in the name of sthg; **em ~ de alguém** on behalf of sb. **-3.** *loc*: **dar ~ aos bois** to name the culprit.
nomeação [nomja'sãw] (*pl* **-ões**) *f* **-1.** [denominação] naming. **-2.** [para cargo] nomination.
nomeadamente [no,mjada'mẽntʃi] *adv* namely.
nomeado, da [nomea'du, da] *adj* nominated.
nomear [15] [no'mja(x)] *vt* **-1.** [proferir o nome, conferir o nome a] to name. **-2.** [conferir cargo a] to appoint.
nomenclatura [nomẽŋkla'tura] *f* nomenclature.
nominal [nomi'naw] (*pl* **-ais**) *adj* nominal.
nonagésimo, ma [nona'ʒɛzimu, ma] *num* ninetieth; *veja também* **sexto**.
nono, na ['nonu, na] *num* ninth; *veja também* **sexto**.
nora ['nɔra] *f* daughter-in-law.
nordeste [nox'dɛʃtʃi] ◇ *adj* north-east. ◇ *m* northeast.
◆ **Nordeste** *m* north-east region of Brazil.
nordestino, na [na, noxdɛʃ'tʃinu, na] ◇ *adj* **-1.** northeastern **-2.** *of north-eastern Brazil (depois de subst).* ◇ **-1.** Northeasterner *m, f* **-2.** *person from north-eastern Brazil.*
nórdico, ca ['nɔxdʒiku, ka] ◇ *adj* Nordic. ◇ *m, f* Nordic.
norma ['nɔxma] *f* **-1.** [padrão] norm. **-2.** [regra] rule; **ter como ~** to have as a norm.
normal [nox'maw] (*pl* **-ais**) *adj* **-1.** [ger] normal. **-2.** [no ensino]: **curso/escola ~** teacher-training course/college *UK*, normal school *US*.
normalidade [noxmali'dadʒi] *f* normality.
normalização [noxmaliza'sãw] *f* normalization.
normalizar [4] [noxmali'za(x)] *vt* to bring back to normal; **~ relações** to normalize relations.
◆ **normalizar-se** *vp* to return to normal.
normalmente [noxmaw'mẽntʃi] *adv* **-1.** [regularmente] as expected. **-2.** [geralmente] usually.
normativo, va [noxma'tʃivu, va] *adj* normative.
noroeste [no'rwɛʃtʃi] ◇ *adj* [relativo ao noroeste] north-west. ◇ *m* northwest.
norte ['nɔxtʃi] ◇ *adj* [relativo ao norte] north. ◇

m **-1.** [direção] north; **ao ~ de** to the north of. **-2.** [região] North. **-3.** [guia] guide.

norte-americano, na [ˌnɔxtʃjameri'kãnu, na] <> *adj* North American. <> *m & f* North American.

nortear [15] [nox'tʃja(x)] *vt* **-1.** [guiar] to guide. **-2.** *fig* [orientar] to guide.
◆ **nortear-se** *vp*: **~-se para** [dirigir-se] to head towards; **~-se por** *fig* [orientar-se] to be guided by.

nortista [nox'tʃiʃta] <> *adj* [do norte] northern. <> *mf* [pessoa] northerner.

Noruega [no'rwɛga] *n* Norway.

norueguês, esa [norwe'geʃ, eza] <> *adj* Norwegian. <> *m, f* Norwegian.
◆ **norueguês** *m* [língua] Norwegian.

nos[1] [noʃ] = **em + os**.

nos[2] [noʃ] *pron pess* **-1.** *(objeto direto)* us; **convidaram-~ para a festa** they invited us to the party. **-2.** *(objeto indireto)* us; **ele ~ deu um presente** he gave us a present; **isto ~ saiu caro** that cost us a lot of money; [para enfatizar] us; **não ~ faça mais isto!** don't do that to us again! **-3.** *(reflexivo)* ourselves; **ontem ~ matriculamos na Universidade** yesterday we registered at University. **-4.** [reciprocamente] each other; **olhamo-~ com ternura** we looked lovingly at each other. **-5.** [indicando posse] us; **ela ~ beijou as faces** she kissed us on the cheeks; **ardia-~ a vista** our eyes were stinging. **-6.** [ao autor] us; **parece-~ ...** it seems to us ...; **neste caso, o que ~ chama a atenção é ...** in this case, what draws our attention is ...

nós [nɔʃ] *pron pess (com + nós = conosco)* **-1.** [sujeito] we; **~ somos casados** we are married; **~, brasileiros/estudantes, somos ...** we Brazilians/students, are ...; **~, que gostamos de música, ...** we, who love music, ...; **não pude ver o jogo; ~ vencemos?** I couldn't watch the match; did we win?; **~ dois/quatro** the two/four of us, we two/four; **só ~ dois** just the two of us; **~ todos** all of us; **~ mesmos** *ou* **próprios** we ... ourselves; **~ mesmos pintaremos a casa** we shall paint the house ourselves. **-2.** *(depois de prep)* **us**; **chegou un convite para ~** an invitation arrived for us, we received an invitation; **o que ele tem contra ~?** what does he have against us?; **você fica para jantar conosco?** are you staying with us for dinner?; **alguns de ~ serão premiados** some of us will be rewarded; **entre ~** [duas pessoas] between the two of us, between you and me; [mais de duas pessoas] among us. **-3.** [o autor] we; **neste capítulo, o que ~ pretendemos é ...** in this chapter, what we are attempting to do is ... **-4.** *loc*: **cá entre ~** between ourselves.

-nos [noʃ] *pron pl* [eles] them; [vocês] you ▷ **nos**[2].

nosso, a ['nɔsu, a] <> *adj* our; **Nossa Senhora** Our Lady; **nossas coisas/brigas** our things/arguments; **um amigo ~** a friend of ours; **este iate é ~** this yacht is ours. <> *pron*: **o ~ /a nossa** ours; **um amigo ~** a friend of ours; **a nossa é maior** ours is bigger; **os ~s** [a nossa família] our family; [do nosso time] ours; **ser um dos ~s** *fam* [estar do nosso lado] to be one of ours; **à nossa!** here's to us!
◆ **nossa** *interj* [exprimindo espanto] God; **~ mãe!**, **~ senhora!** God!, Holy Mary!

nostalgia [noʃtaw'ʒia] *f* **-1.** [melancolia] nostalgia. **-2.** [da pátria] homesickness.

nostálgico, ca [noʃ'tawʒiku, ka] *adj* nostalgic.

nota ['nɔta] *f* **-1.** [ger] note; **digno de ~** noteworthy; **tomar ~** to take note; **~ de rodapé** footnote; **cheio da ~** loaded; **uma ~ (preta)** a fortune. **-2.** *COM* bill; **~ fiscal** invoice; **~ promissória** promissory note, IOU. **-3.** *EDUC* mark. **-4.** [comunicado] notice; **~ oficial** official statement.

notabilizar [4] [notabili'za(x)] *vt* to distinguish.
◆ **notabilizar-se** *vp*: **~-se (em/por)** to distinguish o.s. in/through.

notação [nota'sãw] *(pl* **-ões)** *f* [sistema] notation; **~ musical** (scale of) notation.

notadamente [notada'mẽntʃi] *adv* [em particular] in particular.

notar [4] [no'ta(x)] *vt* [reparar] to note; **fazer ~** to indicate.
◆ **notar-se** *vp*: **nota-se que ...** it is clear that ...; **é de se ~ que ...** it is noticeable that ...

notável [no'tavɛw] *(pl* **-eis)** *adj* notable.

notebook ['notʃibuki] *(pl* **-s)** *m COMPUT* notebook.

notícia [no'tʃisja] *f* news *(sg)*; **uma ~** a piece of news; **ter ~s** to have news; **ter ~s de alguém/algo** to have news of sb/sthg, to hear from sb/about sthg.

noticiar [16] [notʃi'sja(x)] *vt*: **~ algo a alguém** to inform sb of sthg; **~ algo** to report sthg; **~ a alguém que** to inform sb that.

noticiário [notʃi'sjarju] *m* **-1.** [de jornal] news section. **-2.** [rádio, tv] news bulletin. **-3.** [cinema] newsreel.

noticioso, osa [notʃi'sjozu, ɔza] *adj* news *(antes de subst)*.

notificação [notʃifika'sãw] *(pl* **-ões)** *f* **-1.** [comunicado] notification. **-2.** *JUR* instruction.

notificar [12] [notʃifi'ka(x)] *vt* **-1.** [comunicar]: **~ algo a alguém** to notify sb of sthg. **-2.** *JUR* to instruct.

notívago, ga [no'tʃivagu, ga] <> *adj* nocturnal. <> *m, f* [pessoa] sleepwalker.

notoriedade [notorje'dadʒi] *f* **-1.** [fama] fame. **-2.** [evidência] blatancy.

notório, ria [no'tɔrju, rja] *adj* **-1.** [famoso] famous, well-known. **-2.** [evidente] blatant; **é público e ~ que ...** it is public knowledge and blatantly clear that ...

noturno, na [no'tuxnu, na] *adj* **-1.** [trem, aula] night *(antes de subst)*; **vôo ~** night flight. **-2.** [animais, plantas] nocturnal.
◆ **noturno** *m* **-1.** *MÚS* nocturne. **-2.** [trem] night train.

noutro ['notru] = **em + outro**.

nov. *(abrev de* **novembro**) Nov.

nova ['nɔva] *f* ▷ **novo**.

Nova Déli [ˌnɔva'dɛli] *n* New Delhi.

nova-iorquino, na [ˌnovajox'kinu, na] <> *adj* New York *(antes de subst).* <> *m, f* New Yorker.

novamente [ˌnɔva'mẽntʃi] *adv* **-1.** [outra vez] once again. **-2.** [recentemente] recently.

novato, ta [no'vatu, ta] <> *adj* inexperienced. <> *m, f* novice.

Nova York [ˌnɔva'jɔxki] *n* New York.

Nova Zelândia [ˌnɔvaze'lãndʒja] *n* New Zealand.

nove ['nɔvi] *num* nine; *veja também* **seis**.

novecentos, tas [nɔve'sẽntuʃ, taʃ] *num* nine hundred; *veja também* **seiscentos**.

nove-horas [nɔ'vjɔraʃ] *fpl fam*: **cheio de ~** [complicado] fussy; [sofisticado] fancy.

novela [no'vɛla] *f* **-1.** *RÁDIO & TV* soap opera. **-2.** *LITER* story.

novelesco, ca [nove'lɛsku, ka] *adj pej* soppy.

novelista [nove'liʃta] *mf* **-1.** [roteirista] script writer. **-2.** [escritor] novelist.

novelo [no'velu] *m* ball of yarn.

novembro [no'vẽnbru] *m* November; *veja também* **setembro**.

novena [no'vena] *f RELIG* novena.

noventa [no'vẽnta] *num* ninety; *veja também* **sessenta**.

noviciado [novi'sjadu] *m RELIG* novitiate.

noviço, ça [no'visu, sa] *m, f RELIG* novice.

novidade [novi'dadʒi] *f* **-1.** [ger] novelty. **-2.** [notícia] news *(sg)*.

novilho, lha [no'viʎu, ʎa] *m, f* calf.

novinho, nha [no'viɲu, ɲa] *adj* **-1.** [pessoa] young. **-2.** [objeto] new.

novo, nova ['novu, 'nɔva] <> *adj* **-1.** [ger] new; **~ em folha** brand new; **o que há de ~?** what's new? **-2.** [jovem] young. **-3.** [outro] different. <> *m, f*: **a nova/o novo** the new one.

◆ **de novo** *loc adv* again.

◆ **novo** *m* unknown.

◆ **nova** *f*: **boa nova** good news; **nova economia** new economy.

novo-rico [novu'xiku] (*pl* **novos-ricos**) *m,f* nouveau riche.

noz ['nɔʃ] (*pl* **-es**) *f* nut.

noz-moscada [ˌnɔʒmoʃ'kada] (*pl* **nozes-moscadas**) *f* nutmeg.

nu, nua ['nu, 'nua] *adj* **-1.** [ger] bare. **-2.** [sem roupa] naked; **~ em pêlo** stark naked. **-3.** [sem rodeios]: **a verdade nua e crua** the naked truth; **a realidade nua e crua** the stark reality. **-4.** *loc*: **pôr algo a ~** *fig* to bring sthg out into the open.

◆ **nu** *m ARTE* nude.

nuança [nu'ãnsa], **nuance** [nu'ãsi] *f* nuance.

nublado, da [nu'bladu, da] *adj* cloudy.

nublar [4] [nu'bla(x)] *vt* to cloud.

◆ **nublar-se** *vp* to become cloudy.

nuca ['nuka] *f* nape.

nuclear [nukle'a(x)] (*pl* **-es**) *adj* **-1.** *TEC* nuclear. **-2.** *fig* [central] central.

núcleo ['nukljuı] *m* nucleus.

nudez [nu'deʃ] *f* **-1.** [de pessoa] nudity. **-2.** [de coisas] bareness.

nudismo [nu'dʒiʒmu] *m* nudism.

nudista [nu'dʒiʃta] <> *adj* nudist. <> *mf* nudist.

nulidade [nuli'dadʒi] *f* insignificance; **ser uma ~** [coisa] to amount to nothing; [pessoa] to be a nonentity.

nulo, la ['nulu, la] *adj* **-1.** [sem valor] invalid. **-2.** [nenhum] non-existent. **-3.** [inepto] useless; **ser ~ em algo** to be useless at sthg.

num [nũ] = **em + um**.

núm. (*abrev de* **número**) *m* no.

numa ['numa] *cont* = **em + uma**.

numeração [numera'sãw] (*pl* **-ões**) *f* **-1.** [ato] numbering. **-2.** [sistema] numbers; **~ arábica/decimal** Arabic/decimal figures; **~ romana** Roman numerals. **-3.** [de calçados, roupas] size.

numerado, da [nume'radu, da] *adj* numbered.

numeral [nume'raw] (*pl* **-ais**) *m GRAM* numeral.

numerar [4] [nume'ra(x)] *vt* **-1.** [pôr número em] to number. **-2.** [pôr em ordem numérica] to place in numerical order.

numerário [nume'rarju] *m* cash.

numérico, ca [nu'mɛriku, ka] *adj* numerical.

número ['numeru] *m* **-1.** [ger] number; **~ cardinal/ordinal** cardinal/ordinal number; **~ par/ímpar** even/odd number; **~ primo** prime number; **sem-~** countless; **um sem-~ de vezes** countless times; **~ de telefone/fax** telephone/fax number. **-2.** [tamanho]: **que ~ você calça?** what size shoe do you wear? **-3.** [edição] issue; **~ atrasado** back number. **-4.** [categoria]: **ser o ~ um** to be number one. **-5.** [quadro] act.

numeroso, osa [nume'rozu, ɔza] *adj* numerous.

nunca ['nũŋka] *adv* **-1.** [sentido negativo] never; **~ mais** never again; **ele quase ~ sorri** he hardly ever smiles. **-2.** [sentido afirmativo]: **como ~** as never before; **mais do que ~** more than ever.

núncio ['nũnsju] *m* nuncio.

nuns [nũʃ] = **em + uns**.

nupcial [nup'sjaw] (*pl* **-ais**) *adj* wedding *(antes de subst)*.

núpcias ['nupsjaʃ] *fpl* wedding.

nutrição [nutri'sãw] *f* nutrition.

nutricionista [nutrisjo'niʃta] *mf* nutritionist.

nutrido, da [nu'tridu, da] *adj* **-1.** [bem alimentado] well-fed. **-2.** [robusto] fit.

nutriente [nu'trjẽntʃi] <> *adj* nutritional. <> *m* nutrient.

nutrir [6] [nu'tri(x)] <> *vt* **-1.** [alimentar]: **~ (com/de)** to nourish (with). **-2.** *fig* [acalentar]: **~ algo por** to nurture sthg for. **-3.** *fig* [fornecer]: **~ algo de** to provide sthg with. <> *vi* to be nourishing; **~ de** to provide with.

◆ **nutrir-se** *vp* **-1.** [alimentar-se]: **~-se de** to obtain nourishment from; **~-se com** to feed on. **-2.** [prover-se] *fig*: **~-se de algo** to supply o.s. with.

nutritivo, va [nutri'tʃivu, va] *adj* nourishing; **valor ~** nutritional value.

nuvem ['nuvẽ] (*pl* **-ns**) *f* **-1.** [do céu] cloud. **-2.** *fig* [aglomeração - de pessoas] swarm; [- de insetos, gases, fumaça] cloud. **-3.** *loc*: **cair das nuvens** to come down to earth; **estar nas nuvens** to daydream; **passar em brancas nuvens** [data] to pass by unnoticed; **pôr nas nuvens** to praise to the skies.

O

o[1]**, O** [ɔ] *m* [letra] o, O.

o[2]**, a** [u, a] (*mpl* **os**, *fpl* **as**) <> *artigo definido* **-1.** [com substantivo genérico] the; **a casa** the house; **o hotel** the hotel; **os alunos** the students; **os noivos** the bride and groom. **-2.** [com substantivo abstrato]: **a vida** life; **o amor** love. **-3.** [com adjetivo substantivado]: **o melhor/pior** the best/worst; **vou fazer o possível** I'll do what I can. **-4.** [com nomes geográficos]: **a Inglaterra** England; **o Amazonas** the Amazon; **o Brasil** Brazil; **os Estados Unidos** the United States; **os Pirineus** the Pyrenees. **-5.** [indicando posse]: **quebrei o nariz** I broke my nose; **estou com os pés frios** my feet are cold. **-6.** [enfaticamente]: **ele pensa que é O gênio** he thinks he is THE genius; **ela é A supermãe** she is THE supermother; **Tentação, O perfume** Tentação, THE perfume. **-7.** [com nome de pessoa]: **o Alexandre** Alexandre; **a Helena** Helena; **o Sr. Mendes** Mr. Mendes. **-8.** [por cada] a, per; **3 reais a dúzia** 3 reals a dozen; **o linho é 5 reais o metro** linen is 5 reals per metre. **-9.** [em datas, períodos] the; **o dois de Abril** the second of April *UK*, April second *US*; **o pós-guerra** the post-war years. **-10.** [em títulos] the; **Alexandre o Grande** Alexander the Great; **D. Maria a louca** Queen Mary the madwoman. <> *pron pess* **-1.** [pessoa] him (*f* her), them *pl*; **eu a deixei ali** I left her there; **ela o amava muito** she loved him very much; **não os vi** I didn't see them. **-2.** [você, vocês] you; **eu o chamei, Dirceu, mas você não ouviu** I called you, Dirceu, but you didn't hear; **prazer em conhecê-los, meus senhores** pleased to meet you, gentlemen. **-3.** [coisa] it, them *pl*; **onde estão as chaves? não consigo achá-los** where are the keys? I can't find them; **este paletó é novo, comprei-o no mês passado** this jacket is new, I bought it last month. **-4.** [em locuções]: **o/a da esquerda** the one on the left; **os que desejarem vir terão de pagar** those who wish to come will have to pay; **o que (é que) ...?** what (is) ...?; **o que (é que) está acontecendo?** what's going on?; **era o que eu pensava** it's just as I thought; **o quê?** what? <> *pron dem* **-1.** [especificativo - com substantivo] the one; **feche a porta da frente e a dos fundos** close the front door and the one at the back; **compre o que for mais barato** buy the one that's cheapest; **2.** [- com adjetivo] the; **destas balas, adoro as vermelhas** out of these sweets, I prefer the red ones **3.** [indicando posse] one; **minha casa e a de Teresa** my house and Teresa's, mine and Teresa's house; **minha casa é grande e a de Teresa é pequena** my house is big and Teresa's one is small.

ó [ɔ] *interj* oh!

ô [o] *interj* oh!

OAB (*abrev de* **Ordem dos Advogados do Brasil**) *f Brazilian law society.*

oásis [ɔ'aziʃ] *m inv* oasis.

oba ['oba] *interj* **-1.** [de alegria] great! **-2.** [cumprimento] hi!

obcecado, da [obise'kadu, da] *adj* obsessive.

obcecar [12] [obise'ka(x)] *vt* to obsess.

◆ **obcecar-se** *vp*: ~ **(por/com)** to become obsessed by/with.

obedecer [25] [obede'se(x)] <> *vt* to obey. <> *vi*: ~ **a (alguém/algo)** to obey (sb/sthg).

obediência [obe'dʒjẽnsja] *f* obedience.

obediente [obe'dʒjẽntʃi] *adj* obedient.

obelisco [obe'liʃku] *m* obelisk.

obesidade [obezi'dadʒi] *f* obesity.

obeso, sa [o'bezu, za] <> *adj* obese. <> *m, f* obese person.

óbice ['ɔbisi] *m* obstacle.

óbito ['ɔbitu] *m* death.

obituário [obi'twarju] *m* obituary.

objeção [obʒe'sãw] (*pl* **-ões**) *f* **-1.** [contestação] objection. **-2.** [obstáculo] obstacle; **fazer** *ou* **pôr ~ a** to make an objection to.

objetar [4] [obʒe'ta(x)] <> *vt*: ~ **que** to contest (that). <> *vi*: ~ **(a)** to object (to).

objetiva [obʒe'tʃiva] *f FOT* lens.

objetivar [4] [obʒetʃi'va(x)] *vt* [visar a] to have as one's objective.

objetividade [obʒetʃivi'dadʒi] *f* objectivity.

objetivo, va [obʒe'tʃivu, va] *adj* objective.

◆ **objetivo** *m* objective, aim.

objeto [ob'ʒɛtu] *m* **-1.** [coisa] object. **-2.** [de estudo] subject.

oblíquo, qua [o'blikwu, kwa] *adj* **-1.** [diagonal - luz, chuva, traço] slanting; [- terreno, reta] sloping; [- ângulo] oblique. **-2.** *fig* [dissimulado] devious.

obliterar [4] [oblite'ra(x)] *vt* **-1.** [apagar] to obliterate. **-2.** *MED* to block.

oblongo, ga [ob'lõŋgu, ga] *adj* oblong.

oboé [o'bwɛ] *m* oboe.

oboísta [o'bwiʃta] *mf* oboist.

óbolo ['ɔbulu] *m* [esmola] alms *(pl)*.

obra ['ɔbra] *f* **-1.** [trabalho] work; ~ **de arte** work of art; ~ **de caridade** charitable work; **ser ~ de alguém** *fig* to be the work of sb. **-2.** *CONSTR* works *(pl)*; **em ~s** under repair.

obra-prima [ˌɔbra'prima] (*pl* **obras-primas**) *f* **-1.**

[melhor obra] masterpiece. **-2.** [perfeição]: **ser/estar uma ~** to be a work of art.
obrar [4] [o'bra(x)] <> *vt* [fazer] to perform. <> *vi* **-1.** [influir]: **~ sobre** to work on. **-2.** [trabalhar]: **~ (contra/a favor de)** to work (against/for).
obreiro, ra [o'brejru, ra] *m, f* worker.
obrigação [obriga'sãw] (*pl* **-ões**) *f* **-1.** [dever] obligation; **cumprir (com) suas ~s** to fulfil one's obligations *UK*, to fulfill one's obligations *US*. **-2.** *COM* bond.
obrigado, da [obri'gadu, da] *interj* [agradecimento]: **(muito) ~ (por)** thank you (very much) (for).
obrigar [14] [obri'ga(x)] *vt*: **~ alguém a fazer algo** [forçar] to force sb to do sthg; [impor] to require sb to do sthg; [induzir] to compel sb to do sthg.
◆ **obrigar-se** *vp* to take it upon o.s.
obrigatoriedade [obrigatorje'dadʒi] *f* obligatory nature.
obrigatório, ria [obriga'tɔrju, rja] *adj* obligatory.
obscenidade [obiseni'dadʒi] *f* obscenity; **ser uma ~** to be a disgrace.
obsceno, na [obi'senu, na] *adj* obscene.
obscurecer [25] [obiʃkure'se(x)] *vt* **-1.** [escurecer] to darken. **-2.** *fig* [entristecer] to trouble. **-3.** *fig* [prejudicar] to damage; *fig* [perturbar] to unsettle.
◆ **obscurecer-se** *vp* to become dark.
obscuridade [obiʃkuri'dadʒi] *f* **-1.** [escuridão] darkness. **-2.** [anonimato] obscurity. **-3.** *fig* [esquecimento] obscurity.
obscuro, ra [obi'ʃkuru, ra] *adj* **-1.** [escuro] dark. **-2.** *fig* [desconhecido, confuso] obscure.
obsequiar [16] [obize'kja(x)] *vt* **-1.** [fazer agrados a] to please. **-2.** [presentear]: **~ alguém (com algo)** to make a present (of sthg) to sb.
obséquio [obi'zɛkju] *m* favour *UK*, favor *US*; **por ~** please; **quer fazer o ~ de ...?** *irôn* would you kindly ...?
obsequioso, osa [obize'kjozu, ɔza] *adj* **-1.** [prestativo] obliging. **-2.** [respeitoso] respectful.
observação [obizexva'sãw] (*pl* **-ões**) *f* **-1.** [ato] observation. **-2.** [comentário] remark. **-3.** [cumprimento] observance.
observador, ra [obisexva'do(x), ra] (*pl* **-es**, *fpl* **-s**) <> *adj* [perspicaz] observant. <> *m, f* observer.
observância [obisex'vãnsja] *f* observance.
observar [4] [obisex'va(x)] *vt* **-1.** [ger] to observe. **-2.** [contemplar] to look at. **-3.**: **~ que** [notar] to notice that; [comentar] to remark that.
observatório [obisexva'tɔrju] *m* observatory.
observável [obisex'vavew] (*pl* **-eis**) *adj* observable.
obsessão [obse'sãw] (*pl* **-ões**) *f* obsession.
obsessivo, va [obse'sivu, va] *adj* obsessive.
obsoleto, ta [obso'letu, ta] *adj* obsolete.
obstáculo [obʃ'takulu] *m* obstacle; **corrida de ~s** *ESP* obstacle race.
obstante [obiʃ'tãntʃi] ◆ **não obstante** <> *loc conj* nevertheless. <> *loc prep* in spite of.
obstar [4] [obʃi'ta(x)] *vi*: **nada obsta a que ele viaje** there is nothing to prevent him from travelling.
obstetra [obʃ'tɛtra] *mf* obstetrician.
obstetrícia [obiʃte'trisja] *f* obstetrics *(sg)*.
obstinação [obiʃtʃina'sãw] (*pl* **-ões**) *f* obstinacy.
obstinado, da [obiʃtʃi'nadu, da] *adj* **-1.** [perseverante] obdurate. **-2.** [teimoso] obstinate.
obstinar-se [4] [obiʃtʃi'naxsi] *vp*: **~ em algo** to persist in sthg.
obstrução [obʃtru'sãw] (*pl* **-ões**) *f* **-1.** [entupimento] blockage. **-2.** [impedimento] obstruction.
obstruir [74] [obiʃ'trwi(x)] *vt* **-1.** [entupir] to block. **-2.** [impedir] to obstruct.
obtenção [obitẽn'sãw] (*pl* **-ões**) *f* **-1.** [aquisição] acquisition. **-2.** [consecução] achievement.
obtenível [obiteẽ'nivew] (*pl* **-eis**) *adj* achievable.
obter [1] [obi'te(x)] *vt* **-1.** [diploma, verbas, absolvição] to obtain. **-2.** [desempenho, sucesso] to achieve.
obturação [obtura'sãw] (*pl* **-ões**) *f* [de dente] filling.
obturador [obtura'do(x)] (*pl* **-es**) *m FOT* shutter.
obturar [4] [obtu'ra(x)] *vt* [dente] to fill.
obtuso, sa [obi'tuzu, za] *adj* **-1.** [arredondado] blunt. **-2.** [bronco] obtuse. **-3.** [obscuro] obscure.
obviedade [ob'vjedadʒi] *f*: **dizer ~s** to state the obvious.
óbvio, via ['ɔbvju, vja] *adj* obvious; **é ~ que ...** it's obvious that ...; **é ~!** of course!
◆ **óbvio** *m*: **o óbvio** the obvious; **ser o ~ ululante** to be blatantly obvious.
ocasião [oka'zjãw] (*pl* **-ões**) *f* **-1.** [ger] time; **em certas ocasiões** sometimes; **em duas ocasiões** twice; **certa ~ ...** once. **-2.** [oportunidade]: **aproveitar a ~** to seize the moment; **ter ~ de fazer algo** to have the opportunity to do sthg.
ocasional [okazjo'naw] (*pl* **-ais**) *adj* chance *(antes de subst)*.
ocasionar [4] [okazjo'na(x)] *vt* **-1.** [causar] to cause, to bring about. **-2.** [proporcionar]: **~ algo a alguém** to afford sb sthg.
ocaso [o'kazu] *m* **-1.** [do sol] sunset. **-2.** *fig* [fim] end. **-3.** *fig* [decadência] decline.
Oceania [osjã'nia] *n* Oceania.
oceânico, ca [o'sjãniku, ka] *adj* oceanic.
oceano [o'sjãnu] *m* [mar] ocean; **~ Antártico** Antarctic Ocean; **~ Atlântico** Atlantic Ocean; **~ Ártico** Arctic Ocean; **~ Índico** Indian Ocean; **~ Pacífico** Pacific Ocean.
oceanografia [osjanogra'fia] *f* oceanography.
ocidental [osidẽn'taw] (*pl* **-ais**) <> *adj* western. <> *m, f* westerner.
ocidentalizar [osidẽntali'za(x)] *vt* to westernize.
◆ **ocidentalizar-se** *vp* to become westernized.
ocidente [osi'dẽntʃi] *m* west.
◆ **Ocidente** *m*: **o Ocidente** the West.
ócio ['ɔsju] *m* **-1.** [tempo livre] free time. **-2.** [desocupação]: **estar no ~** to be unoccupied. **-3.** [indolência] idleness.
ociosidade [osjozi'dadʒi] *f* **-1.** [desocupação]:

estar na ~ to be unoccupied. **-2.** [indolência] idleness.
ocioso, sa [o'sjozu, za] *adj* **-1.** [desocupado] unoccupied. **-2.** [improdutivo] unproductive. **-3.** [indolente] idle. **-4.** [inútil] useless.
oco, oca ['oku, 'oka] *adj* **-1.** [vazio] hollow. **-2.** *fig* [fútil] empty.
ocorrência [oko'xẽnsja] *f* **-1.** [acontecimento] event; **~ policial** police matter. **-2.** [circunstância] circumstance.
ocorrer [5] [oko'xe(x)] *vi* **-1.** [acontecer] to occur. **-2.** [vir à memória]: **~ a alguém** to occur to sb.
ocre ['ɔkri] ◇ *adj* ochre *UK (antes de subst)*, ocher *US (antes de subst)*. ◇ *m* ochre.
octaedro [ˌokta'ɛdru] *m* octahedron.
octogenário, ria [oktoʒe'narju, rja] ◇ *adj* octogenarian. ◇ *m, f* octogenarian.
octogonal [oktogo'naw] (*pl* **-ais**) *adj* octagonal.
octógono [ok'tɔgonu] *m* octagon.
ocular [oku'la(x)] *adj* ocular.
oculista [oku'liʃta] *mf* oculist, ophthalmologist.
óculo ['ɔkulu] *m* **-1.** [de navio] porthole. **-2.** *ARQUIT* oculus.
◆ **óculos** *mpl* glasses *(pl)*; **~s escuros** sunglasses; **~s de natação** goggles.
ocultar [4] [okuw'ta(x)] *vt* to conceal.
◆ **ocultar-se** *vp* to hide.
ocultas [o'kuwtaʃ] ◆ **às ocultas** *loc adv* secretly.
ocultismo [okuw'tʃiʒmu] *m* occultism.
oculto, ta [o'kuwtu, ta] *adj* **-1.** [secreto, desconhecido] hidden. **-2.** [sobrenatural] occult.
ocupação [okupa'sãw] (*pl* **-ões**) *f* **-1.** [ger] occupation. **-2.** [de um espaço] occupancy.
ocupacional [okupasjo'naw] (*pl* **-ais**) *adj* occupational.
ocupado, da [oku'padu, da] *adj* **-1.** [ger] occupied. **-2.** [atarefado] busy. **-3.** *TELEC* engaged *UK*, busy *US*; **dar (sinal de) ~** to give the engaged tone *UK*, to give the busy signal *US*.
ocupante [oku'pãntʃi] *mf* occupant.
ocupar [4] [oku'pa(x)] *vt* **-1.** [ger] to occupy. **-2.** [atrair] to attract.
◆ **ocupar-se** *vp* **-1.** [preencher tempo] to keep o.s. occupied. **-2.** [cuidar de]: **~-se com alguém/algo** to look after sb/sthg.
odalisca [oda'liʃka] *f* odalisque.
ode ['ɔdʒi] *f* ode.
odiar [17] [o'dʒja(x)] ◇ *vt* to hate. ◇ *vi* to hate.
◆ **odiar-se** *vp* **-1.** [a si mesmo] to hate o.s. **-2.** [um ao outro] to hate one another.
odiento, ta [o'dʒjẽntu, ta] *adj* hateful.
ódio ['ɔdʒju] *m* hatred, hate; **ter ~ a/de alguém** to hate sb; **ter ~ a/de algo** to hate sthg.
odioso, osa [o'dʒjozu, ɔza] *adj* odious.
odisséia [odʒi'sɛja] *f* odyssey.
odontologia [odõntolo'ʒia] *f* odontology, dentistry.
odontologista [odõntolo'ʒiʃta] *mf* odontologist, dentist.
odor [o'do(x)] (*pl* **-es**) *m* odour.
OEA (*abrev de* **Organização dos Estados Americanos**) *f* OAS.
oeste ['wɛʃtʃi] ◇ *adj inv* west. ◇ *m*: **a ~ de** west of; **em direção ao ~** westwards.
ofegante [ofe'gãntʃi] *adj* **-1.** [arquejante] panting. **-2.** [cansado] breathless.
ofegar [12] [ofe'ga(x)] *vi* to pant.
ofender [5] [ofẽn'de(x)] *vt* to offend.
◆ **ofender-se** *vp* [sentir-se insultado] to be offended.
ofensa [o'fẽnsa] *f* **-1.** [insulto] insult. **-2.** [desrespeito] offence *UK*, offense *US*.
ofensivo, va [ofẽn'sivu, va] *adj* offensive; **~ à moral** morally offensive.
◆ **ofensiva** *f* offensive; **estar/ficar na ~** to be/get on the offensive; **tomar a ~** *MIL* to take the offensive.
oferecer [25] [ofere'se(x)] *vt* to offer.
◆ **oferecer-se** *vp* [propor seus serviços] to offer o.s.; **~-se para fazer algo** to offer to do sthg.
oferecido, da [ofere'sidu, da] *adj pej* easy.
oferecimento [oferesi'mẽntu] *m* offer.
oferenda [ofe'rẽnda] *f RELIG* offering.
oferta [o'fɛxta] *f* **-1.** [ger] offer; **em ~** on offer. **-2.** *ECON* supply; **a ~ e a demanda** supply and demand.
ofertar [4] [ofex'ta(x)] *vt* to offer.
off-line ['ɔflajni] *adv COMPUT* off-line.
off-set [ˌɔfi'sɛtʃi] *m* offset printing.
oficial [ofi'sjaw] (*pl* **-ais**) ◇ *adj* official. ◇ *mf* **-1.** *MIL* officer. **-2.** [funcionário] official; **~ de justiça** *JUR* bailiff.
oficializar [4] [ofisjali'za(x)] *vt* to officialize.
oficiar [16] [ofi'sja(x)] ◇ *vt* [endereçar ofício] to send officially; **~ algo a alguém** to address sthg officially to sb. ◇ *vi RELIG* to officiate.
oficina [ofi'sina] *f* workshop; **~ mecânica** garage.
ofício [o'fisju] *m* **-1.** [profissão] profession. **-2.** [incumbência] job. **-3.** *RELIG* office. **-4.** [correspondência] official letter. **-5.** [cartório]: **~ de notas** notary public.
oficioso, osa [ofi'sjozu, ɔza] *adj* [não-oficial] unofficial; **de caráter ~** unofficially.
oftalmologia [oftawmolo'ʒia] *f* ophthalmology.
oftalmológico, ca [oftawmo'lɔʒiku, ka] *adj* ophthalmological.
oftalmologista [oftawmolo'ʒiʃta] *mf* ophthalmologist.
ofuscante [ofuʃkãntʃi] *adj* dazzling.
ofuscar [12] [ofuʃ'ka(x)] ◇ *vt* **-1.** [encobrir] to conceal. **-2.** [suplantar em brilho] to outshine. **-3.** [olhos] to dazzle. **-4.** *fig* [apagar] to overshadow. ◇ *vi* [turvar a vista] to dazzle.
ogro ['ogru] *m* ogre.
ogum [o'gũ] *m god of war in Afro-Brazilian cults.*
oh [ɔ] *interj* oh!
oi ['oj] *interj* **-1.** [como saudação] hi! **-2.** [como resposta indagativa] mm?
oitava-de-final [ojˌtavadʒifi'naw] (*pl* **oitavas-de-final**) *f ESP round prior to quarter finals.*

oitavo, va [oj'tavu, va] <> *num* eighth; **a oitava parte** the eighth part. <> *m* eighth; *veja também* **sexto**.

oitenta [oj'tẽnta] *num* eighty; *veja também* **sessenta**.

oito ['ojtu] *num* eight; *veja também* **seis**; **ou ~ ou oitenta** all or nothing.

oitocentos, tas [ojtu'sẽntuʃ] *num* eight hundred; *veja também* **seiscentos**.

ojeriza [oʒe'riza] *f* loathing; **ter ~ a alguém/algo** to have a loathing for sb/sthg.

ola ['ɔla] *f* ESP Mexican wave.

olá [o'la] *interj* hello.

olaria [ola'ria] *f* [fábrica] pottery.

oleado [o'ljadu] *m* tarpaulin.

oleiro, ra [o'lejru, ra] *m, f* potter.

óleo ['ɔlju] *m* oil; **~ de bronzear** sun-tan oil; **~ de cozinha** cooking oil; **~ diesel** diesel oil; **~ de fígado de bacalhau** cod liver oil; **~ de rícino** castor oil.

oleoduto [oljo'dutu] *m* pipeline.

oleosidade [oljozi'dadʒi] *f* greasiness.

oleoso, osa [o'ljozu, ɔza] *adj* greasy.

olfato [ow'fatu] *m* smell.

olhada [o'ʎada] *f* look; **dar uma ~ (em)** to take a look (at).

olhadela [oʎa'dɛla] *f* glance.

olhar [4] [o'ʎa(x)] <> *vt* **-1.** [ger] to look at. **-2.** [cuidar de] to keep an eye on. **-3.** [ponderar] to look at. <> *vi* [ver] to look; **olha!** look!; **~ para alguém/algo** to look at sb/sthg; **~ por** [cuidar de] to keep an eye on. <> *m* look.

◆ **olhar-se** *vp* **-1.** [ver-se] to look at o.s. **-2.** [entreolhar-se] to look at each other.

olheiras [o'ʎejraʃ] *fpl* shadows under the eyes.

olho ['oʎu] (*pl* **olhos**) *m* **-1.** [ger] eye; **a ~ nu** to the naked eye; **de ~** [medir] by eye; **~ grande** *fig* envy; **pôr ~ grande em algo** to have one's eye on sthg; **~ de sogra** CULIN *Brazilian plum pudding with caramelized topping*; **ter ~ de peixe morto** to be glassy-eyed; **estar de ~ em alguém/algo** to have one's eye on sb/sthg. **-2.** [vista] glance; **dirigiu os ~s para todos durante o show** she cast her eyes over everyone during the show; **a ~s vistos** in front of one's very eyes; **passar os ~s por algo** to run one's eyes over sthg; **longe dos ~s, longe do coração** out of sight, out of mind. **-3.** [de queijo] hole. **-4.** [de agulha] eye; **~ mágico** magic eye. **-5.** *loc*: **abrir os ~s** to open one's eyes; **abrir os ~s de alguém** to open sb's eyes; **custar/pagar os ~s da cara** to cost/pay an arm and a leg; **não pregar o ~** not to sleep a wink; **não ver com bons ~s** to take a dim view of; **pôr alguém no ~ da rua** to fire sb; **ter o ~ maior do que a barriga** to have eyes bigger than one's stomach.

olho-de-gato [ˌoʎudʒi'gatu] (*pl* **olhos-de-gato**) *m* reflector.

oligarquia [oligax'kia] *f* oligarchy.

oligárquico, ca [oli'gaxkiku, ka] *adj* oligarchical.

oligopólio [oligo'pɔlju] *m* oligopoly.

olimpíada [olĩn'piada] *f* Olympiad; **as ~s** the Olympics.

olímpico, ca [o'lĩmpiku, ka] *adj* Olympic.

olmo ['owmu] *m* elm.

OLP (**Organização para Libertação da Palestina**) *f* PLO.

olvidar [4] [owvi'da(x)] *vt* to forget.

◆ **olvidar-se** *vp*: **~-se (de)** to forget.

Omã [o'mã] *n* Oman.

ombreira [õn'brejra] *f* **-1.** [de roupa] shoulder pad. **-2.** [de porta] doorpost.

ombro ['õnbru] *m* ANAT shoulder; **~ a ~** shoulder to shoulder; **encolher os ~s** to shrug.

OMC (*abrev de* **Organização Mundial de Comércio**) *f* WTO.

omelete [ome'lɛtʃi] *f* omelette *UK*, omelet *US*.

omissão [omi'sãw] (*pl* **-ões**) *f* omission.

omisso, ssa [o'misu, sa] *adj* **-1.** [negligente, ausente] negligent. **-2.** [faltando] omitted.

omitir [6] [omi'tʃi(x)] *vt* to omit.

◆ **omitir-se** *vp*: **~-se de algo** to refrain from sthg.

omoplata [omo'plata] *f* shoulder blade, scapula.

OMS (*abrev de* **Organização Mundial de Saúde**) *f* WHO.

onanismo [ona'niʒmu] *m* onanism.

onça ['õnsa] *f* **-1.** [animal] jaguar; **estar/ficar uma ~** to be wild. **-2.** [peso] ounce.

onça-parda [ˌõnsa'paxda] (*pl* **onças-pardas**) *f* ZOOL puma.

onça-pintada ['õnsapĩntada] (*pl* **-s**) *f* ZOOL jaguar.

oncologia [õŋkolo'ʒia] *f* oncology.

oncologista [õŋkolo'ʒiʃta] *mf* oncologist.

onda ['õnda] *f* **-1.** [ger] wave; **pegar ~** [surfar] to surf. **-2.** [moda] vogue; **estar na ~** to be in vogue. **-3.** *fam* [fingimento] lie. **-4.** FÍSICA: **~ curta/média/longa** short/medium/long wave; **~ sonora** sound wave. **-5.** *loc*: **deixar de ~** to stop messing about; **fazer ~** to make a fuss; **ir na ~ de alguém** to be taken in by sb.

onde ['õndʒi] (*a + onde = aonde*) <> *adv (interrogativo)* **-1.** where; **~ fica o museu?** where is the museum?; **não sei ~ deixei meus óculos** I don't know where I've left my glasses; **aonde vamos esta noite?** where are we going tonight?; **por ~ vieram?** which way did you come?; **~ quer que** wherever; **carregue sua carteira por ~ você for** keep your wallet with you wherever you go. **-2.** *loc*: **fazer por ~** to do what's necessary. <> *pron* **-1.** *(relativo)* where; **a casa ~ moro** the house where I live; **o vale por ~ passa o rio** the valley where the river flows. **-2.** *(indefinido)* where; **eles não têm ~ morar** they have nowhere to live, they don't have anywhere to live; **pretendo voltar ~ estivemos ontem** I intend to go back to where we were yesterday; **até ~ eu sei** as far as I know.

ondeado, da [õn'dʒjadu, da] *adj* **-1.** [saia, desenho] flowing. **-2.** [cabelo] wavy.

ondear [15] [õn'dʒja(x)] *vi* to ripple.

ondulação [õndula'sãw] (*pl* **-ões**) *f* undulation.

ondulado, da [õndu'ladu, da] *adj* **-1.** [cabelo] wavy. **-2.** [folha] curled.

ondulante [õndu'lãntʃi] *adj* wavy.

onerar [4] [one'ra(x)] *vt* **-1.** [impor ônus a] to burden. **-2.** [sobrecarregar] to put a burden upon.

oneroso, osa [one'rozu, ɔza] *adj* **-1.** [dispendioso] costly. **-2.** [pesado] burdensome.

ONG (*abrev de* **Organização Não-Governamental**) *f* NGO.

ônibus ['onibuʃ] *m inv* bus.

onipotência [onipo'tẽnsja] *f* omnipotence.

onipotente [ˌonipo'tẽntʃi] *adj* omnipotent.

onipresença [oni'prezẽnsa] *f* omnipresence.

onipresente [onipre'zẽntʃi] *adj* omnipresent.

onírico, ca [o'niriku, ka] *adj* dreamlike.

onisciência [oni'sjẽnsja] *f* omniscience.

onisciente [oni'sjẽntʃi] *adj* omniscient.

onívoro, ra [o'nivuru, ra] *adj* omnivorous.

ônix ['oniks] *m (inv)* onyx.

on-line ['õnlajni] *adv* COMPUT on-line.

onomástico, ca [ono'maʃtʃiku, ka] *adj* onomastic.

onomatopéia [onomato'pɛja] *f* onomatopoeia.

ontem ['õntẽ] *adv* yesterday; ~ **de manhã** yesterday morning; ~ **à noite/à tarde** yesterday evening/afternoon.

ONU ['ɔnu] (*abrev de* **Organização das Nações Unidas**) *f* UN.

ônus ['onuʃ] *m* **-1.** *(inv)* [peso] excess weight. **-2.** *fig* [encargo] obligation. **-3.** [imposto pesado] heavy tax.

onze ['õnzi] *num* eleven; *veja também* **seis**.

opa ['opa] *interj* [de admiração] wow!; [de saudação] hi!

opacidade [opasi'dadʒi] *f* opacity.

opaco, ca [o'paku, ka] *adj* opaque.

opala [o'pala] *f* **-1.** [mineral] opal. **-2.** [tecido] *fine cotton material*.

opção [op'sãw] (*pl* **-ões**) *f* **-1.** [escolha] choice. **-2.** [preferência] preference.

opcional [opsjo'naw] (*pl* **-ais**) *adj* optional.

open market ['opẽn'maxkitʃ] *m* open market.

OPEP (*abrev de* **Organização dos Países Exportadores de Petróleo**) *f* OPEC.

ópera ['ɔpera] *f* opera.

operação [opera'sãw] (*pl* **-ões**) *f* operation.

operacional [operasjo'naw] (*pl* **-ais**) *adj* operational.

operacionalidade [operasjionali'dadʒi] *f* operating efficiency.

operado, da [ope'radu, da] ◇ *adj* operated. ◇ *m, f person or animal having had an operation.*

operador, ra [opera'do(x), ra] (*mpl* **-es**, *fpl* **-s**) *m, f* operator.

operante [ope'rãntʃi] *adj* operative.

operar [4] [ope'ra(x)] ◇ *vt* **-1.** [fazer funcionar] to operate. **-2.** MED to operate on. **-3.** [realizar] to perform. ◇ *vi* **-1.** [ger] to operate. **-2.** MED to operate. **-3.** [trabalhar]: ~ **com algo** to work with sthg.

◆ **operar-se** *vp* [ocorrer] to take place.

operária [ope'rarja] *f* ▷ **operário**.

operariado [opera'rjadu] *m*: **o** ~ the working class.

operário, ria [ope'rarju, rja] ◇ *adj* **-1.** [greve] workers' *(antes de subst)*. **-2.** [classe] working. **-3.** [abelha] worker *(antes de subst)*. ◇ *m, f* [trabalhador] worker.

opereta [ope'reta] *m* operetta.

opinar [4] [opi'na(x)] ◇ *vi* [emitir opinião]: ~ **(sobre alguém/algo)** to give one's opinion (on sb/sthg); ~ **a favor de/contra algo** to make a statement in favour of/against sthg. ◇ *vt*: ~ **que** to declare that.

opinião [opi'njãw] (*pl* **-ões**) *f* opinion; **a ~ pública** public opinion; **dar uma ~** to give an opinion; **mudar de ~** to change one's mind; **ser de ~ que** to be of the opinion that.

ópio ['ɔpju] *m* opium.

oponente [opo'nẽntʃi] ◇ *adj* opposing. ◇ *mf* opponent.

opor [45] [o'po(x)] *vt* **-1.** [resistência, objeção] to oppose. **-2.** [argumento, razão] to set.

◆ **opor-se** *vp* **-1.** [ser contrário]: **~-se (a algo)** to be opposed (to sthg). **-2.** [contradizer]: **~-se a algo** to be in opposition to sthg.

oportunamente [opoxtuna'mẽntʃi] *adv* opportunely.

oportunidade [opoxtuni'dadʒi] *f* opportunity; **aproveitar a ~** to seize the opportunity; **na primeira ~** at the first opportunity.

oportunismo [opoxtu'niʒmu] *m* opportunism.

oportunista [opoxtu'niʃta] ◇ *adj* opportunistic. ◇ *mf* opportunist.

oportuno, na [opox'tunu, na] *adj* opportune; **momento ~** opportune moment.

oposição [opozi'sãw] (*pl* **-ões**) *f* **-1.** [objeção] opposition; **fazer ~ a** to oppose; **em ~ a** against. **-2.** POL: **a ~** the opposition.

oposicionista [opozisjo'niʃta] ◇ *adj* opposition *(antes de subst)*. ◇ *mf* member of the opposition.

oposto, ta [o'poʃtu, o'pɔʃta] *adj* **-1.** [contrário] opposite. **-2.** [em frente a] opposite.

◆ **oposto** *m* [inverso] opposite.

opressão [opre'sãw] (*pl* **-ões**) *f* **-1.** [ger] oppression. **-2.** [sufocação - no peito] tightness; [- no coração] oppression.

opressivo, va [opre'sivu, va] *adj* oppressive.

opressor, ra [opre'so(x), ra] *m, f* oppressor.

oprimido, da [opri'midu, da] *adj* oppressed.

oprimir [6] [opri'mi(x)] *vt* **-1.** [ger] to oppress. **-2.** [comprimir] to crush.

optar [4] [op'ta(x)] *vi*: ~ **(por/entre)** to opt (for/between); ~ **por fazer algo** to opt to do sthg, to choose to do sthg.

optativo, va [opta'tʃivu, va] *adj* optional.

óptico, ca ['ɔptʃiku, ka] ◇ *adj* optical. ◇ *mf* optician.

◆ **óptica** *f* **-1.** *FÍS* optics *(sg).* **-2.** [loja] optician's. **-3.** [ponto de vista] point of view.
opulência [opu'lẽnsja] *f* opulence.
opulento, ta [opu'lẽntu, ta] *adj* opulent.
opúsculo [o'puʃkulu] *m* **-1.** [livreto] booklet. **-2.** [folheto] pamphlet.
ora ['ɔra] <> *adv* [agora] now; **ela ~ quer uma coisa, ~ quer outra** first she wants one thing, then she wants another; **por ~** for now. <> *conj* now. <> *interj*: **~ bolas!** oh hell!; **~ viva!** hi there!
oração [ora'sãw] (*pl* **-ões**) *f* **-1.** [reza] prayer; **fazer uma ~** to say a prayer. **-2.** *GRAM* clause.
oráculo [o'rakulu] *m* oracle.
orador, ra [ora'do(x), ra] (*mpl* **-es**, *fpl* **-s**) *m, f* orator.
oral [o'raw] (*pl* **-ais**) <> *adj* oral. <> *f* oral (exam).
orangotango [orãŋgu'tãŋgu] *m* orang-utan.
orar [4] [o'ra(x)] *vi*: **~ (a/por)** to pray (to/for).
oratório, ria [ora'tɔrju, rja] <> *adj* oratorial. <> *m* **-1.** *RELIG* oratory. **-2.** *MÚS* oratorio.
◆ **oratória** *f* [arte de falar] oratory.
orbe ['ɔxbi] *m* orb.
órbita ['ɔxbita] *f* **-1.** *ASTRON* orbit; **a lua está em ~ da Terra** the moon orbits the Earth; **o satélite entrou em ~** the satellite entered into orbit; **entrar em ~** *fam fig* to be spaced out; **estar fora de ~** *fam fig* to be out of one's mind. **-2.** [de olho] socket. **-3.** *fig* [área] orbit.
orbitar [oxbi'ta(x)] *vi* **-1.** [descrever órbita] to orbit. **-2.** *fig* [em torno de alguém] to revolve around.
orçamentário, ria [oxsamẽn'tarju, rja] *adj* budget *(antes de subst).*
orçamento [oxsa'mẽntu] *m* **-1.** [de família, governo] budget. **-2.** [de obra] estimate; **~ sem compromisso** estimate without obligation, free estimate.
orçar [13] [ox'sa(x)] <> *vt* [calcular] to estimate. <> *vi* [avaliar] to make an estimate; **~ em** to estimate at.
ordeiro, ra [ox'dejru, ra] *adj* orderly.
ordem ['ɔxdẽ] (*pl* **-ns**) *f* **-1.** [ger] order; **dar uma ~ em algo** to tidy sthg up; **estar em ~** to be tidy; **~ do dia** agenda; **manter a ~** to maintain order; **tudo em ~?** everything OK?; **~ pública/social** public/social order; **às suas ordens** at your service; **até nova ~** until further notice; **dar ~ a alguém para fazer algo** to tell sb to do sthg; **~ de pagamento** money order; **~ de prisão** prison order. **-2.** [categoria]: **foi um prejuízo da ~ de bilhões** there was damage in the order of billions; **de primeira/segunda ~** first/second rate; **~ dos Advogados** Law Society; **~ de grandeza** *MAT* order of magnitude.
ordenação [oxdena'sãw] (*pl* **-ões**) *f* **-1.** *RELIG* ordination. **-2.** [ordem] ordering.
ordenado, da [oxde'nadu, da] *adj* **-1.** [organizado] organized. **-2.** *RELIG* ordained.
◆ **ordenado** *m* [salário] salary, wages *(pl).*
ordenança [oxde'nãnsa] <> *mf* [soldado] orderly. <> *f MIL* [regulamento] ordinance.
ordenar [4] [oxde'na(x)] *vt* to order.
◆ **ordenar-se** *vp* **-1.** *RELIG* to be ordained. **-2.** [organizar-se] to organize o.s.
ordenhar [4] [oxde'ɲa(x)] *vt* to milk.
ordinal [oxdʒi'naw] (*pl* **-ais**) *adj* ordinal.
ordinariamente [oxdʒinarja'mẽntʃi] *adv* usually.
ordinário, ria [oxdʒi'narju, rja] *adj* **-1.** [ger] ordinary. **-2.** [de má qualidade] poor. **-3.** [comum, freqüente] usual.
orégano [o'rɛganu] *m* oregano.
orelha [o'reʎa] *f* **-1.** *ANAT* ear; **estar de ~ em pé** *fam fig* to have one's wits about one; **~s de abano** protruding ears; **estar até as ~s com algo** to be up to one's ears in sthg. **-2.** [aba] flap.
orelhada [ore'ʎada] *f*: **de ~** by ear.
orelhão [ore'ʎãw] (*pl* **-ões**) *m* [cabine de telefone público] open telephone booth.
orelhudo, da [ore'ʎudu, da] *adj* **-1.** [de orelhas grandes] big-eared. **-2.** [estúpido] asinine. **-3.** [teimoso] stubborn.
orfanato [oxfa'natu] *m* orphanage.
orfandade [oxfãn'dadʒi] *f* orphanhood.
órfão, ã ['ɔxfãw, fã] <> *adj* orphaned; **~ de pai/mãe** fatherless/motherless. <> *m, f* orphan.
orfeão [ox'fjãw] (*pl* **-ões**) *m* choir.
organdi [oxgãn'dʒi] *m* organdie ***UK***, organdy ***US***.
orgânico, ca [ox'gãniku, ka] *adj* organic.
organismo [oxga'niʒmu] *m* **-1.** [ger] organism. **-2.** *fig* [instituição] organization.
organista [oxga'niʃta] *mf* organist.
organização [oxganiza'sãw] (*pl* **-ões**) *f* organization.
organizacional [oxganiza'sionaw] (*pl* **-ais**) *adj* organizational.
organizador, ra [oxganiza'do(x), ra] *m, f* organizer.
organizar [4] [oxgani'za(x)] *vt* to organize.
◆ **organizar-se** *vp* to get organized.
organograma [oxgano'grãma] *m* organization chart, organigram.
órgão ['ɔxgãw] (*pl* **-s**) *m* **-1.** [ger] organ. **-2.** [instituição] body; **~ de imprensa** news publication.
orgasmo [ox'gaʒmu] *m* orgasm.
orgia [ox'ʒia] *f* orgy.
orgulhar [4] [oxgu'ʎa(x)] *vt* to make proud.
◆ **orgulhar-se** *vp*: **~-se de** to pride o.s. on.
orgulho [ox'guʎu] *m* **-1.** [ger] pride. **-2.** [arrogância] arrogance.
orgulhoso, osa [oxgu'ʎozu, ɔza] *adj* **-1.** [brioso] self-satisfied. **-2.** [satisfeito] proud. **-3.** [arrogante] arrogant.
orientação [orjẽnta'sãw] (*pl* **-ões**) *f* **-1.** [ger] direction; **~ profissional** careers guidance. **-2.** [supervisão] supervision. **-3.** *fig* [linha, tendência] orientation.
orientador, ra [orjẽnta'do(x), ra] <> *adj* supervisory. <> *m, f* **-1.** [guia] adviser; **~ profissional** careers counsellor. **-2.** [supervisor] supervisor.

oriental [orjẽn'taw] (*pl* **-ais**) <> *adj* oriental. <> *mf* oriental.
orientar [4] [orjẽn'ta(x)] *vt* **-1.** [situar] to orient. **-2.** [nortear] to put in the right direction. **-3.** [supervisionar] to supervise. **-4.** *fig* [aconselhar] to advise.
◆ **orientar-se** *vp* **-1.** [nortear-se] to orient o.s.; **~-se por algo** to be guided by sthg. **-2.** [aconselhar-se, informar-se] to take advice.
oriente [o'rjẽntʃi] *m* east.
◆ **Oriente** *m*: **o Oriente** the East; **Extremo Oriente** Far East; **Oriente Médio** Middle East.
orifício [ori'fisju] *m* orifice.
origem [o'riʒẽ] (*pl* **-ns**) *f* **-1.** [início] origin; **ter ~ em** to originate from. **-2.** [ascendência] origin; **de ~ brasileira** of Brazilian descent; **país de ~** country of origin. **-3.** [causa] cause; **dar ~ a** to give rise to.
original [oriʒi'naw] (*pl* **-ais**) <> *adj* original. <> *m* [obra] original.
originalidade [oriʒinali'dadʒi] *f* **-1.** [origem] origin. **-2.** [excentricidade] originality.
originalmente [oriʒinaw'mẽntʃi] *adv* originally.
originário, ria [oriʒi'narju, rja] *adj* [proveniente]: **~ de** native of.
Orinoco [ori'noku] *n*: **o ~** the Orinoco.
oriundo, da [o'rjũndu, da] *adj*: **~ de** from.
orixá [ori'ʃa] *m Orisha, a Yoruba divinity that symbolizes the forces of nature and acts as an intermediary between worshippers and the highest divinity.*
orla ['ɔxla] *f* [faixa] edge; **~ marítima** coastline.
ornamentação [oxnamẽnta'sãw] (*pl* **-ões**) *f* decoration.
ornamental [oxnamẽn'taw] (*pl* **-ais**) *adj* ornamental.
ornamento [oxna'mẽntu] *m* ornament.
ornar [4] [ox'na(x)] *vt* to decorate.
ornato [ox'natu] *m* ornament.
ornitologia [oxnitolo'ʒia] *f* ornithology.
orquestra [ox'kɛʃtra] *f* orchestra; **~ de câmara** chamber orchestra; **~ sinfônica** symphony orchestra.
orquestração [oxkeʃtra'sãw] (*pl* **-ões**) *f* orchestration.
orquestrar [4] [oxkeʃ'tra(x)] *vt* to orchestrate.
orquídea [ox'kidʒja] *f* orchid.
ortodontista [oxtodõn'tʃiʃta] *mf* orthodontist.
ortodoxia [oxtodok'sia] *f* orthodoxy.
ortodoxo, xa [oxto'dɔksu, ksa] <> *adj* orthodox. <> *m, f* RELIG orthodox person.
ortografia [oxtogra'fia] *f* orthography, spelling.
ortográfico, ca [oxto'grafiku, ka] *adj* orthographic, spelling.
ortopedia [oxtope'dʒia] *f* orthopaedics *(pl)* **UK**, orthopedics *(pl)* **US**.
ortopédico, ca [oxto'pɛdʒiku, ka] *adj* orthopaedic **UK**, orthopedic **US**.
ortopedista [oxtope'dʒiʃta] *mf* orthopaedist **UK**, orthopedic **US**.
orvalhar [4] [oxva'ʎa(x)] *vi*: **orvalhou a noite inteira** the dew fell all night.
orvalho [ox'vaʎu] *m* dew.
os [uʃ] ⊳ **o**.
oscilação [osila'sãw] (*pl* **-ões**) *f* **-1.** [movimento] swinging. **-2.** [variação] swing. **-3.** *fig* [hesitação] hesitation.
oscilante [osi'lãntʃi] *adj* **-1.** *inv* [movimento] swinging. **-2.** [variável] variable. **-3.** *fig* [hesitante] hesitant.
oscilar [4] [osi'la(x)] *vi* **-1.** [ger] to swing. **-2.** *fig* [hesitar] to hesitate.
oscilatório, ria [osila'tɔrju, rja] *adj* swinging.
Oslo ['oʒlu] *n* Oslo.
osmose [oʒ'mɔzi] *f* osmosis.
ossatura [osa'tura] *f* **-1.** [esqueleto] skeletal structure. **-2.** [estrutura] framework.
ósseo, óssea ['ɔsju, 'ɔsja] *adj* bone *(antes de subst)*.
ossificação [osifika'sãw] *f* ossification.
osso ['osu] (*pl* **ossos**) *m* **-1.** ANAT bone. **-2.** *fig* [dificuldade]: **~s do ofício** occupational hazards; **ser um ~ duro de roer** to be a tough nut to crack.
ostensivo, va [oʃtẽn'sivu, va] *adj* **-1.** [pessoa, luxo] ostentatious. **-2.** [policiamento] overt.
ostentação [oʃtẽnta'sãw] (*pl* **-ões**) *f* ostentation.
ostentar [4] [oʃtẽn'ta(x)] *vt* **-1.** [exibir] to show off. **-2.** [alardear] to display.
ostentoso, osa [oʃtẽntozu, ɔza] *adj* ostentatious.
osteopata [oʃtʃjo'pata] *mf* osteopath.
osteoporose [oʃtʃjopo'rɔzi] *f* osteoporosis.
ostra ['oʃtra] *f* oyster.
ostracismo [oʃtra'siʒmu] *m* ostracism.
OTAN [o'tã] (*abrev de* **Organização do Tratado do Atlântico Norte**) *f* NATO.
otário, ria [o'tarju, rja] *m, f* sucker.
ótico, ca ['ɔtʃiku, ka] <> *adj* optic, optical. <> *m, f* [especialista] optician.
◆ **ótica** *f* **-1.** [loja] optician's. **-2.** *fig* [ponto de vista] viewpoint. **-3.** FÍSICA optics *(sg)*.
otimismo [otʃi'miʒmu] *m* optimism.
otimista [otʃi'miʃta] <> *adj* optimistic. <> *mf* optimist.
otimização [otʃimiza'sãw] (*pl* **-ões**) *f* optimization.
otimizar [otʃimi'za(x)] *vt* to optimize.
ótimo, ma ['ɔtʃimu, ma] <> *adj (superl de bom)* best. <> *interj* great!
otite [o'tʃitʃi] *f* otitis.
otorrinolaringologista [otoxinularĩngolo'ʒiʃta] *mf* ear, nose and throat specialist.
Ottawa [o'tawa] *n* Ottawa.
ou [ow] *conj* or; **~ ..., ~ ...** either ..., or ...; **~ seja** in other words.
ouriçado, da [ori'sadu, da] *adj fam* prickly.
ouriçar [13] [ori'sa(x)] *vt* [pessoa] to bristle.
◆ **ouriçar-se** *vp* to become excited.
ouriço [o'risu] *m* **-1.** [casca espinhosa] burr. **-2.** ZOOL hedgehog.
ouriço-do-mar [oˌrisudu'ma(x)] (*pl* **ouriços-do-mar**) *m* sea urchin.

ourives [o'rivi∫] *mf inv* goldsmith.
ourivesaria [oriveza'ria] *f* **-1.** [arte] goldworking. **-2.** [oficina, loja] goldsmith's.
ouro ['oru] *m* **-1.** [metal] gold; **de ~** *lit* gold; *fig* [coração] of gold; **~ branco** white gold; **valer ~** *fig* to be invaluable. **-2.** *fig* [dinheiro] money.
◆ **ouros** *mpl* [naipe] diamonds.

OURO PRETO

Ouro Preto is considered nowadays as a World Heritage Site; throughout the nineteenth century, it was the state capital of Minas Gerais. The city houses the masterpiece of Brazilian baroque: the church of St Francis of Assisi, created by Antônio Francisco Lisboa, the *Aleijadinho* (Cripple), who was also renowned for his soapstone sculptures.

ousadia [oza'dʒia] *f* daring; **ter a ~ de fazer algo** to have the audacity to do sthg.
ousado, da [o'zadu, da] *adj* **-1.** [audacioso] audacious. **-2.** [corajoso] daring.
ousar [4] [o'za(x)] ◇ *vt* to dare. ◇ *vi* to be daring.
out. (*abrev de* **outubro**) Oct.
outdoor [awt∫i'dɔr] *m* billboard, hoarding.
outeiro [o'tejru] *m* small hill.
outonal [oto'naw] (*pl* **-ais**) *adj* autumnal.
outono [o'tonu] *m* autumn.
outorgante [otox'gãnt∫i] ◇ *adj* granting. ◇ *mf* grantor.
outorgar [14] [otox'ga(x)] *vt*: **~ algo a alguém** to grant sthg to sb, to grant sb sthg.
outorgado, da [owtox'gadu, da] *adj* granted.
outra ['otra] *f* ▷ **outro**.
outrem [o'trẽ] *pron* **-1.** *inv (pl)* other people. **-2.** *(sg)* someone else.
outro, outra ['otru, 'otra] ◇ *adj* **-1.** [ger] other; **~ dia** the other day. **-2.** [diferente] another; **de ~ modo** in another way; **em ~ lugar** somewhere else; **entre outras coisas** among other things; **outra coisa** something else; **~s tipos** other sorts. **-3.** [novo, adicional] another; **no ~ dia** the next day; **outra vez** again. ◇ *pron* another; **o ~** the other; **de um momento para o ~** from one moment to the next; **tanto um quanto o ~** both of them; **(um) ~** another; **nem um, nem ~** neither one nor the other, neither of them; **os ~s** [pessoas] others; [objetos] the others; **dos ~s** [pessoas] other people's.
◆ **outra** *f*: **a outra** [amante] the other woman; **estar em outra** *fam* to be into something else; **... e não deu outra** *fam* ... and that's precisely what happened.
outrora [o'trɔra] *adv* in the past.
outrossim [otro'sĩ] *adv* likewise.
outubro [o'tubru] *m* October; *veja também* **setembro**.
ouvido [o'vidu] *m* **-1.** *ANAT* ear; **entrar por um ~ e sair pelo outro** to go in one ear and out the other. **-2.** [audição] hearing; **dar ~s a algo/alguém** to listen to sthg/sb; **de ~** by ear; **ser todo ~s** to be all ears; **ter bom ~ para algo** to have a good ear for sthg.
ouvinte [o'vĩnt∫i] *mf* **-1.** *RÁDIO* listener. **-2.** *UNIV* auditor.
ouvir [71] [o'vi(x)] ◇ *vt* **-1.** [pela audição] to hear. **-2.** [atentamente] to listen to. ◇ *vi* **-1.** [pela audição] to hear; **~ dizer que** to hear that; **~ falar de algo/alguém** to hear of sthg/sb. **-2.** [atentamente] to listen. **-3.** [ser repreendido] to get a telling off.
ova ['ɔva] *f* roe; **uma ~!** *fam* no way!
ovação [ova'sãw] (*pl* **-ões**) *f* ovation.
ovacionar [4] [ovasjo'na(x)] *vt* to applaud.
oval [o'vaw] (*pl* **-ais**) *adj* oval.
ovalado, da [ova'ladu, da] *adj* oval.
ovariano, na [ova'rjãnu, na] *adj* ovarian.
ovário [o'varju] *m* ovary.
ovelha [o'veʎa] *f* sheep; **~ negra** *fig* black sheep.
overdose [ˌovex'dɔzi] *f* overdose.
ovni ['ɔvni] *m* (*abrev de* **Objeto Voador Não-Identificado**) UFO.
ovo ['ovu] (*pl* **ovos**) *m ANAT* egg; **~ de codorna** quail egg; **~ cozido** hard-boiled egg; **~ estalado** *ou* **frito** fried egg; **~ de granja** free-range egg; **~ mexido** scrambled egg; **~ de Páscoa** Easter egg; **~ quente** boiled egg; **acordar/estar de ~ virado** *fam* to get out of bed on the wrong side; **pisar em ~s** to tread on egg shells; **ser um ~** [quarto, apartamento] to be tiny.
ovóide [o'vɔjdʒi] *adj* ovoid.
ovulação [ovula'sãw] *f* ovulation.
ovular [ovu'la(x)] ◇ *adj* oval. ◇ *vi* to ovulate.
óvulo ['ɔvulu] *m* ovum.
oxalá [o∫a'la] ◇ *interj* let's hope. ◇ *m RELIG highest Yoruba divinity in Afro-Brazilian cults.*
oxidação [oksida'sãw] (*pl* **-ões**) *f* **-1.** *QUÍM* oxidation. **-2.** [ferrugem] rust.
oxidar [4] [oksi'da(x)] *vt* **-1.** *QUÍM* to oxidize. **-2.** [enferrujar] to rust.
◆ **oxidar-se** *vp* [enferrujar] to rust.
óxido ['ɔksidu] *m* oxide; **~ de carbono** carbon monoxide.
oxigenado, da [oksiʒe'nadu, da] *adj* **-1.** [cabelo] bleached. **-2.** *QUÍM*: **água oxigenada** (hydrogen) peroxide.
oxigenar [4] [oksiʒe'na(x)] *vt* **-1.** [ger] to oxygenate. **-2.** [cabelo] to bleach.
oxum [o'∫ũ] *m Yoruba water goddess worshipped in Afro-Brazilian cults.*
ozônio [o'zonju] *m* ozone.
ozonizar [4] [ozoni'za(x)] *vt* to ozonize.

P

p, **P** [pe] *m* [letra] p, P.

pá ['pa] *f* **-1.** spade; ~ **de lixo** dustpan; ~ **mecânica** mechanical digger; ~ **para torta** cake slice. **-2.** [de hélice] blade. **-3.** *fam* [quantidade]: **uma** ~ **de** a mass of. **-4.** *loc*: **ser da** ~ **virada** to be of dubious character.

PA (*abrev de* **Estado do Pará**) *m State of Pará.*

PABX (*abrev de* **Private Automatic Branch Exchange**) *m* PABX.

paca ['paka] <> *mf* ZOOL paca. <> *adv fam* bloody; **isso está bom** ~ this is bloody good.

pacatez [paka'teʒ] *f* quietness.

pacato, ta [pa'katu, ta] *adj* quiet.

pachorra [pa'ʃoxa] *f* slowness.

pachorrento, ta [paʃo'xẽntu, ta] *adj* lumbering.

paciência [pa'sjẽnsja] *f* patience; **perder a** ~ to lose patience; **ter** ~ to be patient.

paciente [pa'sjẽntʃi] <> *adj* patient. <> *mf* MED patient.

pacificação [pasifika'sãw] *f* pacification.

pacificador, ra [pasifika'do(x), ra] <> *adj* pacifying. <> *m, f* peacemaker.

pacificar [12] [pasifi'ka(x)] *vt* to pacify.

pacífico, ca [pa'sifiku, ka] *adj* **-1.** [tranqüilo] tranquil. **-2.** [indiscutível] indisputable.

Pacífico [pa'sifiku] *n*: **o (oceano)** ~ the Pacific (Ocean).

pacifismo [pasi'fiʒmu] *m* pacifism.

pacifista [pasi'fiʃta] <> *adj* pacifist. <> *mf* pacifist.

paço ['pasu] *m* [palácio] palace.

paçoca [pa'sɔka] *f* **-1.** [doce] sweet made with peanuts and brown sugar. **-2.** *fig* [coisa amassada]: **estar uma** ~ to be all crumpled up.

pacote [pa'kɔtʃi] *m* **-1.** [embrulho] packet. **-2.** ECON package. **-3.** [turismo]: ~ **de viagem** package holiday.

pacto ['paktu] *m* [acordo] pact; ~ **social** social pact.

pactuante [pak'twãntʃi] *adj* cooperating.

pactuar [21] [pak'twa(x)] <> *vt* [combinar] to agree. <> *vi*: ~ **com alguém** to be in league with sb.

padaria [pada'ria] *f* bakery.

padecer [25] [pade'se(x)] <> *vt* to suffer. <> *vi*: ~ **de algo** to suffer from sthg.

padecimento [padesi'mẽntu] *m* suffering.

padeiro, ra [pa'dejru, ra] *m* baker.

padiola [pa'dʒjɔla] *f* stretcher.

padrão [pa'drãw] (*pl* **-ões**) <> *adj* [tamanho] standard. <> *m* **-1.** [ger] standard; ~ **de vida** standard of living. **-2.** [desenho] pattern.

padrasto [pa'draʃtu] *m* stepfather.

padre ['padri] *m* **-1.** [sacerdote] priest. **-2.** [como título] father.

◆ **Santo Padre** *m* Holy Father.

padrinho [pa'driɲu] *m* **-1.** [testemunha] godfather. **-2.** [paraninfo] guest of honour. **-3.** [protetor] protector.

◆ **padrinhos** *mpl* [padrinho e madrinha] godparents.

padroeiro, ra [pa'drwejru, ra] *m, f* patron saint.

padrões [pa'drõjʃ] *pl* ▷ **padrão.**

padronização [padroniza'sãw] (*pl* **-ões**) *f* standardization.

padronizado, da [padroni'zadu, da] *adj* [estandardizado] standardized.

padronizar [4] [padroni'za(x)] *vt* to standardize.

pães ['pãjʃ] *pl* ▷ **pão.**

paetê [pae'te] *m* sequin.

pág. (*abrev de* **página**) *f* p.

pagã [pa'gã] *f* ▷ **pagão.**

pagador, ra [paga'do(x), ra] <> *adj* paying. <> *m, f* payer; **ser bom/mau** ~ to be a good/bad payer.

pagamento [paga'mẽntu] *m* **-1.** [ger] payment. **-2.** [salário]: **dia de** ~ pay day. **-3.** COM [prestação, de dívida] repayment; ~ **contra entrega** cash on delivery; ~ **à vista** cash payment.

pagão, gã [pa'gãw, gã] (*mpl* **-s**, *fpl* **-s**) <> *adj* pagan. <> *m, f* pagan.

pagar [4] [pa'ga(x)] <> *vt* **-1.** [ger] to pay. **-2.** [compensar, reembolsar] to repay. <> *vi*: ~ **(a alguém)** to pay (sb); ~ **por algo** [desembolsar] to pay for sthg; *fig* [crime, pecado] to pay; **você me paga!** *fig* you'll pay for this!; ~ **caro** *fig* to pay dearly; ~ **para ver** *fig* to demand proof.

página ['paʒina] *f* page; ~ **de rosto** facing page.

paginação [paʒina'sãw] (*pl* **-ões**) *f* pagination.

paginar [4] [paʒi'na(x)] *vt* to paginate.

pago, ga ['pagu, ga] <> *pp* ▷ **pagar.** <> *adj* paid.

pagode [pa'gɔdʒi] *m* **-1.** [templo] pagoda. **-2.** MÚS *type of samba.* **-3.** [festa] *party where pagode is danced.*

pagodeiro, ra [pago'dejru, ra] [ra] *m pagode singer.*

págs. (*abrev de* **páginas**) *fpl* pp.

pai ['paj] *m* **-1.** [ger] father; ~ **adotivo** adoptive father; ~ **de criação** foster father; ~ **de família** paterfamilias. **-2.** [protetor] protector.

◆ **pais** *mpl* [pai e mãe] parents.

pai-de-santo [ˌpajdʒi'sãntu] (*pl* **pais-de-santo**) *m religious and spiritual candomblé leader.*

pai-dos-burros [ˌpajduʃ'buxuʃ] (*pl* **pais-dos-burros**) *m fam* wordbook.
painel [paj'nɛw] (*pl* **-éis**) *m* **-1.** [ger] panel. **-2.** [quadro, panorama] picture. **-3.** *ARQUIT* frame.
pai-nosso [ˌpaj'nɔsu] (*pl* **pais-nossos**) *m* Our Father, the Lord's Prayer.
paio ['paju] *m salami-like pork sausage.*
paiol [pa'jɔw] (*pl* **-óis**) *m* **-1.** [celeiro] store. **-2.** [depósito] arsenal; ~ **de pólvora** *fig* powder keg.
pairar [4] [paj'ra(x)] *vi* **-1.** [sustentar-se]: ~ **em/sobre** to hover in/over. **-2.** [ameaçar]: ~ **sobre** to hang over.
país [pa'iʃ] (*pl* **-es**) *m* country.
paisagem [paj'zaʒẽ] (*pl* **-ns**) *f* **-1.** [vista] view. **-2.** [pintura] landscape.
paisagista [pajza'ʒiʃta] <> *adj* landscape *(antes de subst)*. <> *mf* **-1.** *ARQUIT* landscape architect. **-2.** *ARTE* landscape painter.
paisano, na [paj'zãnu, na] *m, f* [civil] civilian.
◆ **à paisana** *loc adv* in mufti.
País Basco [paˌiʃ'baʃku] *n*: **o** ~ the Basque Country.
Países Baixos [paˌiziʃ'bajʃuʃ] *n*: **os** ~ the Netherlands.
paixão [paj'ʃãw] (*pl* **-ões**) *f* passion.
paixonite [pajʃo'nitʃi] *f fam*: **ter** ~ **aguda** to be madly in love.
pajé [pa'ʒɛ] *m Amerindian priest and medicine man.*
pajear [15] [pa'ʒja(x)] *vt* [tomar conta de] to look after.
pajem ['paʒẽ] (*pl* **-ns**) <> *m* page. <> *f* nanny.
PAL (*abrev de* **Phase Alternate Line**) *m* PAL.
pala ['pala] *f* **-1.** [de roupa] yoke. **-2.** [de boné] peak. **-3.** [de sapato] tongue. **-4.** *AUTO* sun visor. **-5.** *fam* [dica] tip.
palacete [pala'setʃi] *m* stately home.
palácio [pa'lasju] *m* **-1.** [residência] palace. **-2.** [sede] headquarters *(pl)*.
paladar [pala'da(x)] (*pl* **-es**) *m* **-1.** [ger] taste. **-2.** *ANAT* palate.
palafita [pala'fita] *f* **-1.** [habitação] house built on stilts. **-2.** [estacas] stilts *(pl)*.
palanque [pa'lãŋki] *m* **-1.** [de comício] seating. **-2.** [para espectadores] stand.
palato [pa'latu] *m ANAT* palate.
palavra [pa'lavra] *f* **-1.** [ger] word; ~**s cruzadas** crossword (puzzle) *(sg)*; **medir as** ~**s** *fig* to measure one's words; **não dar uma** ~ not to say a word; ~ **de ordem** watchword; **pessoa sem** ~ person who cannot be trusted; **ter** ~ to keep one's word; ~ **de honra** word of honour. **-2.** [fala] speaking. **-3.** [direito de falar] right to speak; **dar a** ~ **a alguém** to hand the floor to sb; **pedir a** ~ to ask permission to speak.
palavra-chave [paˌlavra'ʃavi] (*pl* **palavras-chaves, palavras-chave**) *f* keyword.
palavrão [pala'vrãw] (*pl* **-ões**) *m* swear word.
palavreado [pala'vrjadu] *m* chatter, gabble.
palco ['pawku] *m* **-1.** *TEATRO* stage. **-2.** *fig* [cenário] scene.
paleolítico, ca [paljo'litʃiku, ka] *adj* paleolithic.
paleontologia [paljõntolo'ʒia] *f* paleontology.
palerma [pa'lɛxma] <> *adj* foolish. <> *mf* fool.
Palestina [paleʃ'tʃina] *n* Palestine.
palestino, na [paleʃ'tʃinu, na] <> *adj* Palestinian. <> *m, f* Palestinian.
palestra [pa'lɛʃtra] *f* [conferência] lecture, talk.
palestrante [paleʃtrãntʃi] *mf* speaker *(at conference)*.
palestrar [4] [paleʃ'tra(x)] *vi* to give a talk.
paleta [pa'leta] *f* palette.
paletó [pale'tɔ] *m* overcoat.
palha ['paʎa] *f* straw; ~ **de aço** wire wool; **não mexer uma** ~ *fam fig* not to lift a finger.
palhaçada [paʎa'sada] *f* **-1.** [brincadeira] clowning; **fazer** ~**s** to clown around. **-2.** [cena ridícula] ridiculous sight.
palhaço, ça [pa'ʎasu, sa] *m, f* **-1.** [artista] clown. **-2.** *fam* [bobo] clown.
palheiro [pa'ʎejru] *m* [celeiro] hayloft.
palheta [pa'ʎeta] *f* **-1.** *ARTE* palette. **-2.** [lâmina - de veneziana] slat; [- de ventilador] blade. **-3.** [*MÚS* - para dedilhar] plectrum; [- embocadura] reed.
palhoça [pa'ʎɔsa] *f* straw hut.
paliativo, va [palja'tʃivu, va] <> *adj* palliative. <> *m* palliative.
paliçada [pali'sada] *f* **-1.** [tapume] palisade. **-2.** *MIL* stockade.
palidez [pali'deʒ] *f* **-1.** [de cor] paleness. **-2.** [de pessoa, rosto] pallor.
pálido, da ['palidu, da] *adj* pale.
palitar [4] [pali'ta(x)] *vt*: ~ **os dentes** to pick one's teeth.
paliteiro [pali'tejru] *m* toothpick holder.
palito [pa'litu] *m* **-1.** [para os dentes] toothpick. **-2.** [biscoito] straw. **-3.** [fósforo] matchstick. **-4.** [pessoa magra] matchstick.
PAL-M (*abrev de* **Phase Alternate Line-Modified**) *m* PAL-M.
palma ['pawma] *f* palm.
◆ **palmas** *fpl* [aplauso]: **bater** ~ to clap.
palmada [paw'mada] *f* smack; **dar/levar umas** ~**s** to smack/be smacked.
Palmas ['pawmaʃ] *n* Palmas.
palmatória [pawma'tɔrja] *f* ferule; ~ **do mundo** better than everyone else; **dar a mão à** ~ to climb down.
palmeira [paw'mejra] *f* palm tree.
palmilha [paw'miʎa] *f* inner sole.
palmito [paw'mitu] *m* Assai palm.
palmo ['pawmu] *m* handspan; **não enxergar um** ~ **adiante do nariz** not to be able to see past the end of one's nose; ~ **a** ~ inch by inch.
palmtop ['pawmitɔpi] (*pl* **palmtops**) *m COMPUT* palmtop.
palpável [paw'pavɛw] (*pl* **-eis**) *adj* [tangível] palpable.
pálpebra ['pawpebra] *f* eyelid.
palpitação [pawpita'sãw] (*pl* **-ões**) *f* throbbing.
◆ **palpitações** *fpl* palpitations.
palpitar [4] [pawpi'ta(x)] *vi* **-1.** [pulsar] to throb. **-2.**

[agitar-se] to quiver. **-3.** [opinar] to speculate.
palpite [paw'pitʃi] *m* **-1.** [opinião] speculation. **-2.** [intuição]: **ter um ~** to have a hunch. **-3.** [turfe] tip.
palpiteiro, ra [pawpi'tejru, ra] <> *adj* opinionated. <> *m, f* opinionated person.
paludismo [palu'dʒiʒmu] *m* malaria.
pamonha [pa'moɲa] <> *adj* sluggish, dull. <> *mf* sluggard, dullard.
pampa ['pãnpa] *m* **-1.** *GEOGR* pampas. **-2.**: **às ~s** [com substantivo] loads of; [com adjetivo] extremely; [com advérbio] really.
panaca [pa'naka] <> *adj* dim-witted. <> *mf* dimwit.
panacéia [pana'sɛja] *f* panacea.
Panamá [pana'ma] *n* Panama.
panamenho, nha [pana'meɲu, ɲa] <> *adj* Panamanian. <> *m, f* Panamanian.
pan-americano, na [ˌpãnameri'kãnu, na] *adj* pan-American.
pança ['pãnsa] *f fam* paunch.
pancada [pãŋ'kada] <> *adj fam* nuts. <> *f* **-1.** [golpe] blow; **dar uma ~ em alguém** to hit sb; **levar uma ~ de alguém** to be hit by sb. **-2.** [batida] hit. **-3.** [chuva]: **~ d'água** downpour.
pancadaria [pãŋkada'ria] *f* brawl.
pâncreas ['pãŋkrjaʃ] *m* pancreas.
pançudo, da [pãn'sudu, da] *adj* paunchy.
panda ['pãnda] *m ZOOL* panda.
pandarecos [pãnda'rɛkuʃ] *mpl fam*: **em ~** [exausto] shattered; [destruído] in pieces; [moralmente] thoroughly dejected.
pândego, ga ['pãndegu, ga] *adj* **-1.** [engraçado] funny. **-2.** [folião] reveller.
◆ **pândega** *f* [folia] revelry.
pandeiro [pãn'dejru] *m MÚS* tambourine.
pandemônio [pãnde'monju] *m* pandemonium.
pane ['pãni] *f* breakdown.
panegírico [pane'ʒiriku] *m* panegyric.
panela [pa'nɛla] *f* **-1.** [recipiente] saucepan; **~ de pressão** pressure cooker. **-2.** *fig* [conteúdo] saucepanful.
panelaço [pane'lasu] *m banging of pots and pans as a form of protest.*
panelinha [panɛ'liɲa] *f* clique.
panfletar [4] [pãnfle'ta(x)] *vi* to hand out pamphlets.
panfleto [pãn'fletu] *m* pamphlet.
pangaré [pãŋga'rɛ] *m* nag.
pânico ['pãniku] *m* panic; **estar/entrar em ~** to panic.
panificação [panifika'sãw] *f* **-1.** [padaria] bakery. **-2.** [fabrico] bread making.
pano ['pãnu] *m* **-1.** [tecido] cloth; **~ de chão** floor cloth; **~ de pó** duster; **~ de prato** tea towel; **por baixo/debaixo do ~** *fig* on the quiet; **dar ~ para mangas** *fig* to get people talking; **pôr ~s quentes em algo** *fig* to calm sthg down. **-2.** *TEATRO* curtain; **~ de fundo** backdrop.
panorama [pano'rãma] *m* panorama.
panorâmico, ca [pano'rãmiku, ka] *adj* panoramic.
◆ **panorâmica** *f* [exposição] panorama.
panqueca [pãŋ'kɛka] *f* pancake.
pantalonas [pãnta'lonaʃ] *fpl* **-1.** [calças] pantaloons. **-2.** [de bailarino] leggings.
pantanal [pãnta'naw] (*pl* **-ais**) *m* large swamp.

PANTANAL

The *pantanal* (swamp) of Mato Grosso extends over the south-west of Mato Grosso, the west of Mato Grosso do Sul and part of Paraguay. The swamp is periodically flooded by the many lakes and gullies that crisscross it; it is the largest flood plain in the world and one of Brazil's finest natural features. Within it can be found 650 species of birds, 60 species of mammals, 260 species of fish and 50 species of reptiles.

pântano ['pãntanu] *m* swamp.
pantanoso, osa [pãnta'nozu, ɔza] *adj* swampy.
panteão [pãn'tʃjãw] (*pl* **-ões**) *m* pantheon.
pantera [pãn'tɛra] *f ZOOL* panther.
pantomima [pãnto'mima] *f TEATRO* pantomime.
pantufa [pãn'tufa] *f* slipper.
pão ['pãw] (*pl* **pães**) *m* **-1.** [alimento] bread; **~ de carne** meat loaf; **~ de centeio** rye bread; **~ de fôrma** tin loaf; **~ de mel** honey bread; **~ dormido** stale bread; **~ francês** small baguette; **~ integral** wholemeal bread; **comer o ~ que o diabo amassou** to go through a bad patch; **com ele é ~, ~, queijo, queijo** you know where you stand with him. **-2.** [sustento] daily bread; **ganhar o ~** to earn a crust. **-3.** *RELIG* Eucharist.
pão-de-ló [ˌpãwdʒi'lɔ] (*pl* **pães-de-ló**) *m* sponge cake.
pão-durismo [ˌpãwdu'riʒmu] *m inv* stinginess.
pão-duro [ˌpãw'duru] (*pl* **pães-duros**) <> *adj* miserly. <> *m, f* miser.
pãozinho [pãw'ziɲu] *m* roll.
papa ['papa] *f* **-1.** [mingau] pap. **-2.** [pasta] mush; **não ter ~s na língua** to be outspoken.
◆ **Papa** *m RELIG* Pope.
papada [pa'pada] *f ANAT* double chin.
papagaiada [papaga'jada] *f fam* farce.
papagaio [papa'gaju] <> *m* **-1.** *ZOOL* parrot. **-2.** [pipa]: **soltar ~** to fly a kite. **-3.** *COM* promissory note. **-4.** *AUTO* provisional licence. <> *interj fam*: **~ (s)!** golly!
papaguear [papa'gja(x)] <> *vt* [repetir] to parrot. <> *vi* [tagarelar] to chatter away.
papai [pa'paj] *m* daddy; **o ~ aqui** *fam* [eu] yours truly.
◆ **Papai Noel** *m*: **o Papai Noel** Father Christmas.
papaia [pa'paja] *m* papaya, pawpaw.
papal [pa'paw] (*pl* **-ais**) *adj RELIG* papal.
papar [4] [pa'pa(x)] *fam* <> *vt* **-1.** [comer] to gobble. **-2.** [conseguir] to win. <> *vi* to eat.
paparicar [12] [papari'ka(x)] *vt* to mollycoddle.
paparicos [papa'rikuʃ] *mpl* smotherings.
papear [15] [pa'pja(x)] *vi*: **~ (com/sobre)** to chat (with/about).
papel [pa'pɛw] (*pl* **-éis**) *m* **-1.** [ger] role; **fazer o ~**

de to play the part of; **fazer ~ de bobo** *fig* to look like a fool. **-2.** [folha] paper; **~ crepon** crepe paper; **~ de carta** notepaper; **~ de embrulho** wrapping paper; **~ de seda** tissue paper; **~ higiênico** toilet paper; **~ laminado** *ou* **de alumínio** aluminium foil; **~ machê** papier mâché; **~ ofício** headed paper; **~ pardo** brown wrapping paper; **ficar no ~** to remain on the drawing board. **-3.** [documento] paper; **de ~ passado** officially. **-4.** *FIN* paper money. **-5.** *gír droga* twist.

papelada [pape'lada] *f* **-1.** [papéis] pile of paper. **-2.** [documentos] stack of papers.

papelão [pape'lãw] *m* **-1.** [papel] cardboard. **-2.** *fig* [fiasco] fiasco; **que ~!** what a fiasco!

papelaria [papela'ria] *f* stationer.

papel-bíblia [pa'pewbiblia] (*pl* **papéis-bíblia**) *m* India paper.

papel-carbono [pa,pɛwkax'bonu] (*pl* **papéis-carbono**) *m* carbon paper.

papel-manteiga [pa'pewmãntejga] (*pl* **papéis-manteiga**) *m* tracing paper.

papel-moeda [pa,pɛw'mwɛda] (*pl* **papéis-moeda**) *m* paper money.

papelote [pape'lɔtʃi] *m gír droga* twist.

◆ **papelotes** *mpl* [para o cabelo] curling paper.

papel-pergaminho [pa,pɛwpexga'miɲu] (*pl* **papéis-pergaminho**) *m* parchment.

papiro [pa'piru] *m* papyrus.

papo ['papu] *m* **-1.** [de ave] crop. **-2.** *fam* [de pessoa] double chin; **estar no ~** to be in the bag; **ficar de ~ para o ar** *fig* to sit on one's hands. **-3.** *fam* [conversa] chat; **ser bom ~** to be good company; **~ furado** [mentira] hot air; **ficar de ~ furado** [conversa] to stay and have a chat; **bater (um) ~** to (have a) natter.

papo-de-anjo [,papu'dʒjãnʒu] (*pl* **papos-de-anjo**) *m CULIN baked egg sweet.*

papo-furado [,papufu'radu] (*pl* **papos-furados**) ◇ *adj* full of hot air. ◇ *mf*: **ser um ~** to be full of hot air.

papoula [pa'pola] *f* poppy.

páprica ['paprika] *f* paprika.

Papua-Nova Guiné [pa,puanɔvagi'nɛ] *n* Papua New Guinea.

papudo, da [pa'pudu, da] *adj* double-chinned.

paquera [pa'kera] ◇ *f fam* [paqueração] casual affair. ◇ *mf* pick-up.

paquerar [4] [pake'ra(x)] *fam* ◇ *vt* to flirt with. ◇ *vi* to pull.

paquete [pa'ketʃi] *m ant* & *NÁUT* steamship.

Paquistão [pakiʃ'tãw] *n* Pakistan.

paquistanês, esa [pakiʃta'neʃ, eza] ◇ *adj* Pakistani. ◇ *m, f* Pakistani.

par ['pa(x)] (*pl* **-es**) ◇ *adj* **-1.** *MAT* even. **-2.** [parelho] paired. ◇ *m* **-1.** [dupla] pair; **de ~ em ~** wide (open); **~ a ~** side by side; **sem ~** peerless. **-2.** [casal] couple. **-3.** [em dança] partner. ◇ *f TELEC*: **~ trançado** twisted pair.

◆ **a par** *loc adj*: **estar a ~ de algo** to be well informed about sthg.

para ['para] *prep* **-1.** [exprime finalidade, destinação] for; **um telefonema ~ o senhor** a phone call for the gentleman; **esta água não é boa ~ beber** this water is not good for drinking; **eu queria algo ~ comer** I would like something to eat; **~ que serve isto?** what's this for? **-2.** [indica motivo, objetivo] (in order) to; **cheguei mais cedo ~ arranjar lugar** I arrived early (in order) to get a seat; **era só ~ lhe agradar** it was only to please you. **-3.** [indica direção] towards; **ela apontou ~ cima/baixo** she pointed upwards/downwards; **olhei ~ ela** I looked at her; **ele seguiu ~ o aeroporto** he headed for the airport; **vá ~ casa!** go home! **-4.** [relativo a tempo]: **de uma hora ~ a outra** from one hour to the next; **quero isso pronto ~ amanhã** I want it done by tomorrow; **estará pronto ~ a semana/o ano** it'll be ready next week/year; **são quinze ~ as três** it's a quarter of three *US*, it's a quarter to three *UK*. **-5.** [em comparações]: **é caro demais ~ as minhas posses** it's too expensive for my budget; **~ o que come, está magro** he's thin, considering how much he eats. **-6.** [relativo a opinião, sentimento]: **~ mim** as far as I'm concerned; **~ ele, você está errado** as far as he's concerned, you are wrong. **-7.** [exprime a iminência]: **estar ~ fazer algo** to be about to do sthg; **o ônibus está ~ sair** the bus is about to leave; **ele está ~ chegar** he'll be here any minute now. **-8.** [em locuções]: **~ com** towards; **~ mais de** well over; **~ que** so that; **é ~ já!** coming up!

Pará [pa'ra] *n* Pará.

parabenizar [4] [parabeni'za(x)] *vt*: **~ alguém por algo** to congratulate sb on sthg.

parabéns [para'bẽnʃ] *mpl* **-1.** [congratulações] congratulations; **dar ~ a alguém** to congratulate sb; **estar de ~ (por algo)** to be congratulated (on sthg); **meus ~!** congratulations! **-2.** [por aniversário] congratulations; **cantar ~** to sing 'Happy Birthday'.

parábola [pa'rabola] *f* **-1.** [narrativa] parable. **-2.** *MAT* parabola.

pára-brisa [,para'briza] (*pl* **pára-brisas**) *m* windscreen *UK*, windshield *US*.

pára-choque [,para'ʃɔki] (*pl* **pára-choques**) *m AUTO* bumper.

paradeiro [para'dejru] *m* whereabouts.

paradigma [para'dʒigma] *m* paradigm.

paradisíaco, ca [paradʒi'ziaku, ka] *adj fig* idyllic.

parado, da [pa'radu, da] *adj* **-1.** [imóvel] motionless. **-2.** [sem vida] dull. **-3.** [desativado] stopped. **-4.** [abandonado] axed. **-5.** [em greve] on strike. **-6.** [sem trabalhar] unemployed.

◆ **parada** *f* **-1.** [de ônibus, trem] stop. **-2.** [pausa] break; **dar uma ~ (em algo)** to have a break (from sthg); **~ cardíaca** cardiac arrest. **-3.** [desfile] parade. **-4.** *MÚS*: **~ de sucessos** hit parade. **-5.** *fam* [dificuldade] obstacle; **agüentar a ~** to take it. **-6.** *loc*: **ser uma ~** *fam* [ser difícil] to be difficult; [ser bonito] *fam* to be a knockout; **topar qualquer ~** to be ready for anything.

paradoxal [paradok'saw] (*pl* **-ais**) *adj* paradoxical.
paradoxo [para'dɔksu] *m* paradox.
paraestatal [parajʃta'taw] (*pl* **-ais**) ◇ *adj* public. ◇ *f* public organization.
parafernália [parafex'nalja] *f* **-1.** [tralha] paraphernalia. **-2.** [equipamento] equipment.
parafina [para'fina] *f* paraffin.
paráfrase [pa'rafrazi] *f* paraphrase.
parafrasear [15] [parafra'zja(x)] *vt* to paraphrase.
parafusar [4] [parafu'za(x)] *vt* to screw.
parafuso [para'fuzu] *m* screw; **entrar em ~** *fam* to be thrown off track; **ter um ~ de menos** *fam* to have a screw loose.
paragem [pa'raʒẽ] (*pl* **-ns**) *f* [local] stop; **em outras paragens** elsewhere.
parágrafo [pa'ragrafu] *m* paragraph.
Paraguai [para'gwaj] *n*: **(o) ~** Paraguay.
paraguaio, ia [para'gwaju, ja] ◇ *adj* Paraguayan. ◇ *m, f* Paraguayan.
Paraíba [para'iba] *n* Paraíba.
paraíso [para'izu] *m* paradise; **~ fiscal** *ECON fam* tax haven.
pára-lama [ˌpara'lãma] (*pl* **pára-lamas**) *m* mudguard.
paralela [para'lɛla] *f* ▷ **paralelo.**
paralelamente [paralela'mẽntʃi] *adv* **-1.** [em paralelo] in parallel. **-2.** [simultaneamente] as well as.
paralelepípedo [paralele'pipedu] *m* paving stone.
paralelo, la [para'lɛlu, la] *adj* parallel.
◆ **paralelo** *m* parallel; **traçar um ~** to draw a parallel.
◆ **paralela** *f MAT* parallel (line).
paralisação [paraliza'sãw] (*pl* **-ões**) *f* **-1.** [interrupção] stoppage. **-2.** [greve] strike.
paralisar [4] [parali'za(x)] *vt* [fazer parar] to paralyse.
◆ **paralisar-se** *vp* [obra] to be paralysed.
paralisia [parali'zia] *f* paralysis.
paralítico, ca [para'litʃiku, ka] ◇ *adj* paralytic. ◇ *m, f* paralytic.
Paramaribo [parama'ribu] *n* Paramaribo.
paramédico, ca [para'mɛdʒiku, ka] *adj* paramedic.
paramentado, da [paramẽn'tadu, da] *adj* dressed up.
paramentar [4] [paramẽn'ta(x)] *vt* [adornar] to decorate.
◆ **paramentar-se** *vp* [adornar-se] to dress o.s up.
paramento [para'mẽntu] *m* ornament.
◆ **paramentos** *mpl RELIG* vestments.
parâmetro [pa'rãmetru] *m* parameter.
paramilitar [paramili'ta(x)] *adj* paramilitary.
Paraná [para'na] *n* Paraná.
paraninfo [para'nĩnfu] *m* sponsor.
paranóia [para'nɔja] *f* **-1.** *PSIC* paranoia. **-2.** *fig* [coletiva] fear.
paranóico, ca [para'nɔiku, ka] *adj* paranoid.
paranormal [paranox'maw] (*pl* **-ais**) ◇ *adj* paranormal. ◇ *mf* psychic.
paranormalidade [paranoxmali'dadʒi] *f* paranormal nature.
parapeito [para'pejtu] *m* **-1.** [de janela] window sill. **-2.** [muro] parapet.
parapente [para'pẽntʃi] *m ESP* paragliding.
paraplégico, ca [para'plɛʒiku, ka] ◇ *adj* paraplegic. ◇ *m, f* paraplegic.
pára-quedas [ˌpara'kɛdaʃ] *m inv* parachute; **saltar de ~** to parachute.
pára-quedista [ˌparake'dʒiʃta] (*pl* **pára-quedistas**) *mf* **-1.** [quem salta] parachutist. **-2.** *MIL* paratrooper.
parar [4] [pa'ra(x)] ◇ *vi* **-1.** [deter-se] to stop; **~ de fazer algo** to stop doing sthg; **sem ~** non-stop. **-2.** [permanecer] to stay. **-3.** [acabar]: **ir ~** to end up. **-4.** [interromper-se] to stop. ◇ *vt* **-1.** [deter] to stop. **-2.** [paralisar] to bring to a standstill.
pára-raios [ˌpara'xajuʃ] *m inv* lightning conductor *UK*, lightning rod *US*.
parasita [para'zita] ◇ *adj* parasitic. ◇ *mf* parasite.
parceiro, ra [pax'sejru, ra] *m, f* partner.
parcela [pax'sɛla] *f* **-1.** [parte] portion. **-2.** [de pagamento] instalment. **-3.** [de terreno] plot. **-4.** [do eleitorado] section. **-5.** *MAT* factor.
parcelado, da [paxse'ladu, da] *adj* [pagamento] in instalments.
parcelamento [paxsela'mẽntu] *m* **-1.** [de pagamento] payment by instalments. **-2.** [de terra] distribution.
parcelar [4] [paxse'la(x)] *vt* to divide into instalments.
parceria [paxse'ria] *f* partnership; **fazer algo em ~** to do sthg in partnership.
parcial [pax'sjaw] (*pl* **-ais**) *adj* **-1.** [incompleto] partial. **-2.** [não-isento] biased.
parcialidade [paxsjali'dadʒi] *f* bias.
parcimônia [parsi'monja] *f* [moderação] parsimony; **com ~** frugally.
parcimonioso, osa [paxsimo'njozu, ɔza] *adj* parsimonious.
parco, ca ['paxku, ka] *adj* [escasso] scanty; **~ de algo** lacking in sthg.
pardacento, ta [paxda'sẽntu, ta] *adj* brownish.
pardal [pax'daw] (*pl* **-ais**) *m* sparrow.
pardieiro [pax'dʒjejru] *m* ruin.
pardo, da ['paxdu, da] *adj* **-1.** [escuro] dark. **-2.** [mulato] coloured.
parecer [25] [pare'se(x)] ◇ *m* judgement, opinion. ◇ *vi* **-1.** [ger] to seem; **~ a alguém** to seem to sb; **~ a alguém que** to think that; **~ (com) algo/alguém** to resemble sthg/sb. **-2.** [ser possível]: **~ que** to look like. **-3.** [aparentar]: **ao que parece** apparently.
◆ **parecer-se** *vp* [assemelhar-se] to resemble one another; **~-se com algo/alguém** to resemble sthg/sb.

parecido, da [pare'sidu, da] *adj*: **ser ~ (com alguém/algo)** to be similar (to sb/sthg).
paredão [pare'dãw] (*pl* **-ões**) *m* **-1.** [encosta] steep face. **-2.** [muro] high wall.
parede [pa'redʒi] *f* wall; **~ divisória** dividing wall; **subir pelas ~s** to go up the wall.
parelha [pa'reʎa] *f* **-1.** [de cavalos] team. **-2.** [par] pair.
parente, ta [pa'rẽntʃi, ta] <> *m, f* relative. <> *adj*: **ser ~ de alguém** to be related to sb.
parentela [parẽn'tɛla] *f* relatives *(pl)*.
parentesco [parẽn'teʃku] *m* kinship.
parêntese [pa'rẽntezi] *m* **-1.** [sinal] parenthesis; **abrir/fechar ~s** to open/close brackets. **-2.** [digressão] digression; **abrir um ~** to go off at a tangent.
páreo ['parju] *m* **-1.** [turfe] race. **-2.** [disputa] competition; **estar no ~** *fig* to be in the race; **um ~ duro** *fig* a hard nut to crack.
pária ['parja] *m* pariah.
paridade [pari'dadʒi] *f* parity; **abaixo/acima da ~** below/above par.
parir [6] [pa'ri(x)] <> *vt* to give birth to. <> *vi* to give birth.
Paris [pa'riʃ] *n* Paris.
parlamentar [4] [paxlamẽn'ta(x)] <> *adj* parliamentary. <> *mf* member of parliament. <> *vi* to discuss.
parlamentarismo [paxlamẽnta'riʒmu] *m* parliamentarianism.
parlamentarista [paxlamẽnta'riʃta] <> *adj* parliamentarian. <> *mf* parliamentarian.
parlamento [paxla'mẽntu] *m* POL parliament.
parmegiana [parme'ʒjãna] *f* CULIN: **à ~** *cooked in the oven with a filling of tomato sauce and mozzarella cheese.*
parmesão [paxme'zãw] *adj* parmesan.
pároco ['paroku] *m* RELIG parish priest.
paródia [pa'rɔdʒja] *f* parody.
parodiar [16] [paro'dʒja(x)] *vt* to parody.
paróquia [pa'rɔkja] *f* **-1.** RELIG parish. **-2.** *fig* [vizinhança] neighbourhood.
paroquial [paro'kjaw] (*pl* **-ais**) *adj* RELIG parochial, parish *(antes de subst)*.
paroquiano, na [paro'kjãnu, na] *m, f* parishioner.
paroxismo [parok'siʒmu] *m* **-1.** MED paroxysm. **-2.** *fig* [culminância] brink.
parque ['paxki] *m* park; **~ de diversões** amusement park; **~ industrial** industrial park; **~ nacional** national park.
parquímetro [pax'kimetru] *m* parking meter.
parreira [pa'xejra] *f* grapevine.
parricida [paxi'sida] <> *adj* parricidal. <> *mf* parricide.
parrudo, da [pa'xudu, da] *adj* squat.
parte ['paxtʃi] *f* **-1.** [fração] part; **a maior ~ de** the majority of, most; **em grande ~** largely; **em ~** in parts; **fazer ~ de algo** to belong to sthg; **por ~s** in sections; **tomar ~ em** to take part in. **-2.** [lado] side; **~ interna** inside; **à ~** [separadamente] separately; **à ~ de** [além de] apart from; **de ~ a ~** each other; **em alguma/qualquer ~** somewhere; **em ~ alguma** anywhere; **por toda (a) ~** everywhere. **-3.** [quinhão] share; **a ~ do leão** the lion's share. **-4.** JUR party. **-5.** [denúncia]: **dar ~ de algo/alguém** to report sthg/sb.
◆ **da parte de** *loc prep* from.
parteira [pax'tejra] *f* midwife.
partição [paxtʃi'sãw] *f* COMPUT partition.
participação [paxtʃisipa'sãw] (*pl* **-ões**) *f* **-1.** [atuação]: **~ em algo** participation in sthg. **-2.** [comunicação]: **fazer uma ~ (a alguém)sobre algo** to make a statement (to sb) about sthg. **-3.** COM share.
participante [paxtʃisi'pãntʃi] <> *adj* participating. <> *mf* participant.
participar [4] [paxtʃisi'pa(x)] <> *vi* **-1.** [tomar parte]: **~ de algo** to take part in sthg. **-2.** [compartilhar]: **~ de algo** to share in sthg. <> *vt* [anunciar]: **~ algo (a alguém)** to announce sthg (to sb).
participativo, va [paxtʃisipa'tʃivu, va] *adj* participatory; **orçamento ~** *a public-spending budget agreed upon after organized public discussion with the local electorate.*
particípio [paxtʃi'sipju] *m* participle; **~ passado/presente** past/present participle.
partícula [pax'tʃikula] *f* particle.
particular [paxtʃiku'la(x)] (*pl* **-es**) <> *adj* **-1.** [privado] private. **-2.** [especial] particular. <> *m* **-1.** [singularidade] detail. **-2.** *fam* [conversa] private talk.
◆ **em particular** *loc adv* in private.
◆ **particulares** *mpl fam* [detalhes íntimos] personal details.
particularidade [paxtʃikulari'dadʒi] *f* detail.
particularizar [4] [paxtʃikulari'za(x)] *vt* **-1.** [especificar] to specify. **-2.** [detalhar] to go into the details of.
particularmente [paxtʃikulax'mẽntʃi] *adv* [especialmente] particularly.
partida [pax'tʃida] *f* **-1.** [saída] departure. **-2.** [ESP - largada] start; **dar a ~** to give the off; [- jogo] game. **-3.** [COM - quantidade] shipment; [- remessa] consignment. **-4.** AUTO: **dar ~** to start.
partidário, ria [partʃi'darju, rja] *adj* **-1.** [de partido] party *(antes de subst)*. **-2.** [seguidor] follower.
partido, da [pax'tʃidu, da] *adj* [quebrado] broken.
◆ **partido** *m* **-1.** [político] party; **Partido dos Trabalhadores** Workers' Party. **-2.** [defesa]: **tomar o ~ de alguém** to take sb's side; **tomar ~ em algo** to take part in sthg. **-3.** [vantagem]: **tirar ~ de algo** to make the most of sthg. **-4.** [pretendente] catch.
partilha [pax'tʃiʎa] *f* sharing.
partilhar [4] [paxtʃi'ʎa(x)] <> *vt* **-1.** [dividir] to share. **-2.** [distribuir] to share out. <> *vi* [compartilhar]: **~ de algo** to share in sthg.
partir [6] [pax'tʃi(x)] <> *vt* to break. <> *vi* **-1.** [ir embora] to leave. **-2.**: **~ de** [originar-se em] to start from; [basear-se em] to take as one's starting

point. **-3.** *fam* [recorrer]: ~ **para** to resort to; ~ **para outra** to change tack.

◆ **a partir de** *loc prep* **-1.** [desde] from. **-2.** [dali em diante]: **a** ~ **daquele momento** from that moment on; **a** ~ **de agora** from now on.

◆ **partir-se** *vp* to break.

partitura [paxtʃi'tura] *f* score.

parto ['paxtu] *m* childbirth; **estar em trabalho de** ~ to be in labour *UK*, to be in labor *US*; **ser um** ~ *fig* [ser difícil] to be heavy going; ~ **prematuro** premature birth.

parturiente [paxtu'rjẽntʃi] *f* woman giving birth, parturient.

parvo, va ['paxvu, va] ◇ *adj* stupid. ◇ *m, f* fool.

Páscoa ['paʃkwa] *f* **-1.** *RELIG* Easter. **-2.** *GEOG*: **a ilha de** ~ Easter Island.

pasmaceira [paʒma'sejra] *f* apathy.

pasmado, da [paʒ'madu, da] *adj* amazed.

pasmar [4] [paʒ'ma(x)] ◇ *vt* to amaze. ◇ *vi* to be amazed.

◆ **pasmar-se** *vp* to be surprised.

pasmo, ma ['paʒmu, ma] *adj* amazed.

◆ **pasmo** *m* amazement.

paspalhão, lhona [paʃpa'ʎãw, ʎona] (*mpl* **-ões**, *fpl* **-s**) ◇ *adj* simple. ◇ *m, f* simpleton.

paspalho [paʃ'paʎu] *m* fool.

pasquim [paʃ'kĩ] (*pl* **-ns**) *m* [jornal] lampoon.

passa ['pasa] *f* raisin.

passada [pa'sada] *f* [passo] step; **dar uma** ~ **em** to drop by.

passadeira [pasa'dejra] *f* **-1.** [tapete] stair carpet. **-2.** [mulher] ironing woman.

passadiço [pasa'dʒisu] *m NÁUT* bridge.

passado, da [pa'sadu, da] *adj* **-1.** [que passou - tempo] past; [- semana, ano] last. **-2.** [ultrapassado]: **meio** ~ dated. **-3.** [fruta] overripe. **-4.** [carne]: **bem** ~ well done; **mal** ~ rare. **-5.** [vexado] infuriated.

◆ **passado** *m* past.

passageiro, ra [pasa'ʒejru, ra] ◇ *adj* passing. ◇ *m, f* passenger.

passagem [pa'saʒẽ] (*pl* **-ns**) *f* **-1.** [caminho] way; ~ **de nível** level crossing; ~ **de pedestres** pedestrian crossing; ~ **subterrânea** underpass. **-2.** [condução - preço] fare; [- bilhete] ticket; ~ **de ida** one-way ticket; ~ **de ida e volta** return ticket. **-3.** [trecho] passage. **-4.** [transição] transition.

◆ **de passagem** *loc adv* in passing; **diga-se de** ~ **...** I have to say ...; **estar de** ~ to be passing through.

passamento [pasa'mẽntu] *m* passing.

passaporte [pasa'pɔxtʃi] *m* passport.

passar [4] [pa'sa(x)] ◇ *vt* **-1.** [transpor] to cross. **-2.** [ultrapassar] to overtake; ~ **a frente de alguém** to get in front of sb; ~ **alguém para trás** *fig* [enganar] to dupe sb; [trair] to deceive sb. **-3.** [padecer] to endure. **-4.** [tarefa escolar] to set. **-5.** [reprimenda] to tell off. **-6.** [expedir] to send. **-7.** [entregar] to pass. **-8.** [deslizar]: ~ **algo em/por** to run sthg over/through. **-9.** [tempo] to spend. **-10.** [espalhar] to spread. **-11.** [coar] to sieve. **-12.** [grelhar] to grill. **-13.** [a ferro] to iron. ◇ *vi* **-1.** [ger] to pass; ~ **por algo** to pass o.s. off as sthg *ou* as being sthg; ~ **(de ano)** to go up (a year); ~ **raspando** to scrape through. **-2.** [ir] to go past; ~ **em/por** to go in/through; ~ **pela cabeça de alguém** *fig* to cross one's mind; ~ **por cima de alguém** *fig* to go over sb's head. **-3.** [cruzar]: ~ **por alguém/algo** to go by sb/sthg. **-4.** [sentir-se] to feel; **como está passando?** [cumprimentando] how do you do? **-5.** [viver]: ~ **sem algo** to do without. **-6.** [sofrer]: ~ **por algo** to go through sthg. **-7.** [trocar de lado] to cross over. **-8.** [ser mais tarde que] to be past. **-9.** [ter mais de] to be over; **ela já passou dos 40** she's over 40 now; **aos cinco anos, o menino não passara dos 18 quilos** at five years of age, the boy still didn't weigh more than 18kg. **-10.** [ser apenas]: **não** ~ **de** *pej* to be no more than. **-11.** [ser aceitável] to be passable.

◆ **passar-se** *vp* **-1.** [suceder-se] to happen. **-2.** [transcorrer] to go by.

passarela [pasa'rɛla] *f* **-1.** [para pedestre] footbridge. **-2.** [para manequim] catwalk.

passarinho [pasa'riɲu] *m* birdie.

pássaro ['pasaru] *m* bird.

passatempo [ˌpasa'tẽnpu] *m* hobby; **como** ~ as a hobby.

passável [pa'savew] (*pl* **-eis**) *adj* passable.

passe ['pasi] *m* **-1.** [licença] permit. **-2.** [*ESP* - de bola] pass; [- de jogador] transfer. **-3.** [lance]: ~ **de mágica** sleight of hand. **-4.** *REL* laying on of hands.

passear [15] [pa'sja(x)] *vi* **-1.** [ger] to go for a walk; **mandar alguém ir** ~ *fig* to send sb packing. **-2.** [cavalo, carro] to ride.

passeata [pa'sjata] *f* [protesto] demonstration.

passeio [pa'seju] *m* **-1.** [a pé] walk; **dar** *ou* **fazer um** ~ to go for a walk. **-2.** [a cavalo, de carro] ride; **fazer um** ~ to go for a ride. **-3.** [calçada] pavement *UK*, sidewalk *US*; ~ **público** public footpath.

passional [pasjo'naw] (*pl* **-ais**) *adj* **-1.** [discurso, atitude, artista] passionate. **-2.** [crime] of passion.

passista [pa'siʃta] *mf* samba dancer.

passível [pa'sivɛw] (*pl* **-eis**) *adj*: ~ **de algo** liable to sthg.

passividade [pasivi'dadʒi] *f* [condição] passivity.

passivo, va [pa'sivu, va] *adj* passive.

◆ **passivo** *m COM* liabilities *(pl)*.

passo ['pasu] *m* **-1.** [ger] step; **seguir os** ~**s de alguém** *fig* to follow in sb's footsteps; **dar um mau** ~ to go astray. **-2.** [medida]: **a uns seis** ~**s (de distância)** a short distance away; **a um** ~ **de** *fig* on the verge of. **-3.** [ruido de passos] footsteps. **-4.** [pegada] footprint. **-5.** [marcha] step; **apertar o** ~ to quicken one's step; **a** ~ **de tartaruga** at a snail's pace. **-6.** [modo de andar] walk.

◆ **ao passo que** *loc adv* **-1.** [enquanto] whilst. **-2.** [contudo] whereas.

pasta ['paʃta] *f* **-1.** [creme] paste; ~ **de atum** tuna paste; ~ **de dentes** toothpaste. **-2.** *CULIN*: ~ **de atum/ricota** tuna/ricotta cheese spread. **-3.** [de couro] briefcase. **-4.** [de cartolina] folder. **-5.** *POL* portfolio.

pastagem [paʃ'taʒẽ] (*pl* **-ns**) *f* pasture.

pastar [4] [paʃ'ta(x)] *vi* to graze; **vá** ~! *fig* & *pej* get lost!

pastel [paʃ'tɛw] (*pl* **-éis**) <> *adj* [cor] pastel. <> *m* **-1.** [ger] pastel. **-2.** [comida] pastie.

pastelão [paʃte'lãw] (*pl* **-ões**) *m* **-1.** *CULIN* [empadão] pie. **-2.** *CINE* slapstick.

pastelaria [paʃtela'ria] *f* cake shop.

pasteurizado, da [paʃtewri'zadu, da] *adj* pasteurized.

pasteurizar [4] [paʃtewri'za(x)] *vt* to pasteurize.

pastiche [paʃ'tʃiʃi] *m* pastiche.

pastilha [paʃ'tʃiʎa] *f* **-1.** [bala] pastille. **-2.** *MED* pill; ~ **de garganta** throat lozenge. **-3.** *COMPUT* chip. **-4.** *CONSTR* mosaic piece.

pasto ['paʃtu] *m* **-1.** [erva] grass. **-2.** [pastagem] pasture.

pastor, ra [paʃ'to(x), ra] (*mpl* **-es**, *fpl* **-s**) *m, f AGR* shepherd (*f* shepherdess).

◆ **pastor** *m RELIG* pastor.

pastoral [paʃto'raw] (*pl* **-ais**) *RELIG* <> *adj* pastoral. <> *f church body providing care and support in the community.*

pastorear [15] [paʃto'rja(x)] <> *vt* to tend. <> *vi* to take animals to pasture.

pastoril [paʃto'riw] (*pl* **-is**) *adj* pastoral.

pastoso, osa [paʃ'tozu, ɔza] *adj* pasty.

pata ['pata] *f* **-1.** [de animal - de cão, gato] paw; [- de cavalo] foot. **-2.** [ave] (female) duck.

patada [pa'tada] *f* kick; **dar/levar uma** ~ [de animal] to kick/to be kicked; *fig* [pessoa] to assault/be assaulted.

Patagônia [pata'gonja] *n*: **a** ~ Patagonia.

patamar [pata'ma(x)] (*pl* **-es**) *m* **-1.** [de escada] landing. **-2.** *fig* [nível] level.

patavina [pata'vina] *pron* nothing; **não entender/saber** ~ not to understand/know anything.

patê [pa'te] *m* pâté.

patente [pa'tẽntʃi] <> *adj* obvious. <> *f* **-1.** *COM* patent. **-2.** *MIL* rank; **altas/baixas** ~**s** high/low ranks.

patentear [15] [patẽn'tʃja(x)] *vt COM* to patent.

paternal [patex'naw] (*pl* **-ais**) *adj* paternal, fatherly.

paternalista [patexna'liʃta] *adj* paternalistic.

paternidade [patexni'dadʒi] *f* paternity.

paterno, na [pa'tɛxnu, na] *adj* paternal, father's *(antes de subst).*

pateta [pa'tɛta] <> *adj* foolish. <> *mf* fool.

patetice [pate'tʃisi] *f* foolishness.

patético, ca [pa'tɛtʃiku, ka] *adj* pathetic.

patíbulo [pa'tʃibulu] *m* gallows *(pl).*

patifaria [patʃifa'ria] *f* [ato] underhand trick.

patife [pa'tʃifi] <> *adj* roguish. <> *m* scoundrel.

patim [pa'tĩ] (*pl* **-ns**) *m* skate; **patins de rodas** roller skates.

patinação [patʃina'sãw] *f* skating; ~ **artística** figure skating; ~ **no gelo** ice skating.

patinador, ra [patʃina'do(x), ra] *m, f* skater.

patinar [4] [patʃi'na(x)] *vi* **-1.** [de patins] to skate. **-2.** [carro] to skid.

patinete [patʃi'nɛtʃi] *f* skateboard.

patinhar [4] [patʃi'ɲa(x)] *vi* [chafundar] to slosh about.

patinho [pa'tʃiɲu] *m* **-1.** *ZOOL* duckling. **-2.** [carne] leg of beef. **-3.** [urinol] bedpan.

pátio ['patʃju] *m* patio.

pato ['patu] *m* **-1.** *ZOOL* duck. **-2.** *fam* [otário] sucker; **cair como um** ~ to be a laughing stock. **-3.** *loc*: **pagar o** ~ to carry the can.

patologia [patolo'ʒia] *f* pathology.

patológico, ca [pato'lɔʒiku, ka] *adj* pathological.

patologista [patolo'ʒiʃta] *mf* pathologist.

patota [pa'tɔta] *f fam* gang.

patrão, roa [pa'trãw, roa] (*mpl* **-õe**, *fpl* **-oas**) *m, f* **-1.** [empregador] boss. **-2.** [de criados] master. **-3.** [como forma de tratamento] sir.

◆ **patroa** *f* **-1.** [mulher do patrão] master's/boss's wife. **-2.** *fam* [esposa] missus.

pátria ['patrja] *f* fatherland; **salvar a** ~ *fig* to save the day.

patriarca [pa'trjaxka] *m* patriarch.

patriarcal [patrjax'kaw] (*pl* **-ais**) *adj* patriarchal.

patricinha [patri'siɲa] *f pej* posh girl.

patrício, cia [pa'trisju, sja] *m, f* compatriot.

patrimonial [patrimo'njaw] (*pl* **-ais**) *adj* patrimonial.

patrimônio [patri'monju] *m* **-1.** [bens] patrimony. **-2.** [herança] inheritance; ~ **histórico** historical heritage.

PATRIMÔNIOS CULTURAIS

Apart from historical centres such as Salvador (BA), Olinda (PE), São Luís (MA), Goiás (GO), Ouro Preto and Diamantina (MG), Brazil has at least another ten localities recognized by UNESCO as World Heritage Sites. In Piauí, for example, the National Park of Serra da Capivara contains one of the most important archaeological sites in the world, with around 30,000 cave paintings.

patriota [pa'trjɔta] *mf* patriot.

patriótico, ca [pa'trjɔtʃiku, ka] *adj* patriotic.

patriotismo [patrjo'tʃiʒmu] *m* patriotism.

patroa [pa'troa] *f* ▻ **patrão**.

patrocinador, ra [patrosina'do(x), ra] (*mpl* **-es**, *fpl* **-s**) <> *adj* sponsoring. <> *m, f* sponsor.

patrocinar [4] [patrosi'na(x)] *vt* **-1.** [ger] to support. **-2.** [financiar] to sponsor.

patrocínio [patro'sinju] *m* **-1.** [financiamento] sponsorship. **-2.** [apoio] support.

patrões [pa'trõjʃ] *pl* ▻ **patrão**.

patrono [pa'tronu] *m* patron.

patrulha [pa'truʎa] *f* **-1.** [ronda] patrol. **-2.** [censura] censorship.

patrulhamento [patruʎa'mẽntu] *m* patrolling.
patrulhar [4] [patru'ʎa(x)] *vt* **-1.** [vigiar] to patrol. **-2.** [censurar] to censure.
patrulheiro [patru'ʎejru] *m* [navio] patrol boat.
pau ['paw] *m* **-1.** [bastão] stick. **-2.** [madeira]: **de ~** wooden. **-3.** [de bandeira] pole; **a meio ~** at half mast. **-4.** *fam* [briga] brawl; **o ~ comeu** all hell broke loose; **sair no ~** to start fighting. **-5.** *fam* [moeda] *slang for Brazilian currency.* **-6.** *mfam* [pênis] cock. **-7.** *loc fam*: **a dar com um ~** tons, loads; **meter o ~ em** [surrar] to beat up; [criticar] to run down; **ser ~ para toda obra** to be up for anything.
◆ **paus** *mpl* [naipe] clubs; **de ~s** of clubs.
◆ **pau a pau** *loc adj* on an equal footing.
pau-a-pique [ˌpawa'pikil] *m*: **de ~** of wattle and daub.
pau-brasil [ˌpawbra'ziw] *m* Brazil wood.

PAU-BRASIL

Pau-brasil was a very common tree on the Brazilian shoreline, from Rio de Janeiro to Rio Grande do Norte. Much sought after during colonial times, it was through constant reference to the name of this red-wooded tree that the Portuguese named the country Brazil.

pau-d'água [ˌpaw'dagwa] (*pl* **paus-d'água**) *m* [beberrão] soak.
pau-de-arara [ˌpawdʒja'rara] (*pl* **paus-de-arara**) *mf* [retirante do Nordeste] *migrant from northeastern Brazil.*
◆ **pau-de-arara** *m* [tortura] *form of torture where victim is suspended face down from a pole.*
pau-de-sebo [ˌpawdʒi'sebu] (*pl* **paus-de-sebo**) *m* [mastro de cocanha] greasy pole.
paulada [paw'lada] *f* blow (with a stick); **dar/levar uma ~** to hit/be hit with a stick.
paulatinamente [pawlatʃina'mẽntʃi] *adv* gradually.
paulatino, na [pawla'tʃinu, na] *adj* gradual.
Paulicéia [pawli'sɛja] *n* São Paulo.
paulista [paw'liʃta] ◇ *adj* São Paulo *(antes de subst).* ◇ *mf person from São Paulo.*
paupérrimo, ma [paw'pɛximu, ma] *adj* extremely poor.
pausa ['pawza] *f* **-1.** [interrupção, intervalo] break. **-2.** [descanso] rest.
pausadamente [pawzada'mẽntʃi] *adv* slowly and surely.
pausado, da [paw'zadu, da] *adj* **-1.** [lento] leisurely. **-2.** [cadenciado] rythmic.
◆ **pausado** *adv* unhurriedly.
pauta ['pawta] *f* **-1.** [linha] guideline; **sem ~** unruled. **-2.** [folha com linhas] ruled sheet. **-3.** [lista] list. **-4.** [ordem do dia] agenda; **em ~** on the agenda. **-5.** MÚS stave. **-6.** JORN issue, topic.
pautado, da [paw'tadu, da] *adj* ruled.
pautar [4] [paw'ta(x)] *vt* **-1.** [assuntos] to list. **-2.** *fig* [orientar]: **~ algo por algo** to guide sthg by sthg.
◆ **pautar-se** *vp fig* [orientar-se]: **~-se por algo** to guide o.s by sthg.
pauzinho [paw'ziɲu] *m fam*: **mexer os ~s** to pull strings.
pavão [pa'vãw] (*pl* **-ões**) *mf* peacock.
pavê [pa've] *m* CULIN *cream cake made of sponge soaked in liqueur.*
pavilhão [pavi'ʎãw] (*pl* **-ões**) *m* **-1.** [prédio] annex. **-2.** [de exposições] stand. **-3.** [tenda, abrigo] tent. **-4.** *fig* [bandeira] banner.
pavimentação [pavimẽnta'sãw] *f* paving.
pavimentar [4] [pavimẽn'ta(x)] *vt* to pave.
pavimento [pavi'mẽntu] *m* **-1.** [andar] storey *UK*, story *US*. **-2.** [chão] floor. **-3.** [de rua] pavement.
pavio [pa'viw] *m* wick; **ter o ~ curto** [ser de briga] to have a short fuse.
pavões [pa'võjʃ] *pl* ▷ **pavão**.
pavonear [15] [pavo'nja(x)] ◇ *vt pej* [ostentar] to show off. ◇ *vi pej* [desfilar] to strut.
◆ **pavonear-se** *vp* **-1.** [assoberbar-se] to parade. **-2.** [enfeitar-se] to dress up.
pavor [pa'vo(x)] *m* fear; **ter ~ de alguém/algo** to dread sb/sthg.
pavoroso, osa [pavo'rozu, ɔza] *adj* **-1.** [repulsivo] appalling. **-2.** [muito ruim, feio] dreadful.
paz ['paʃ] (*pl* **-es**) *f* peace; **acordo de ~** peace treaty; **assinar a ~** to sign a peace treaty; **deixar alguém em ~** to leave sb in peace; **fazer as pazes** to make up; **~ de espírito** peace of mind.
PB (*abrev de* **Estado da Paraíba**) *n State of Paraíba.*
PBX (*abrev de* **Private Branch Exchange**) PBX.
PC (*abrev de* **Personal Computer**) *m* PC.
Pça. (*abrev de* **Praça**) *f* Sq.
PC do B (*abrev de* **Partido Comunista do Brasil**) *m Brazilian communist party.*
PCI (*abrev de* **Placa de Circuito Interno**) *f internal circuit board.*
PDT (*abrev de* **Partido Democrático Trabalhista**) *m* Democratic Labour Party, *the second largest left-wing party in Brazil.*
PDV (*abrev de* **Programa de Demissão Voluntária**) *m Brazilian voluntary redundancy scheme.*
pé ['pɛ] *m* **-1.** [ger] foot; **não arredar o ~** not to budge; **~ chato** flat foot; **a ~** on foot; **com um ~ nas costas** with the greatest of ease; **em** *ou* **de ~** standing; **~ ante ~** on tiptoe; **açordar com o ~ direito/esquerdo** to wake up in a good/bad mood; **dar no ~** *fam* [fugir] to do a runner; **cuidado que aquela parte da piscina não dá ~** be careful because you will be out of your depth in that part of the pool; *fig* [ser possível] to be viable; **estar de ~** *fam* to still be on; **ficar com o ~ atrás** to be on one's guard; **meter os ~s pelas mãos** to go haywire; **não chegar aos ~s de** to be nowhere near as good as; **não largar do ~ de alguém** to stick like glue to sb; **não ter ~ nem cabeça** not to make any sense; **pegar no ~ de alguém** *fig* [implicar] to leave sb alone; [brincar] to pull sb's leg; **ser ~ no chão** to have one's feet firmly on the ground. **-2.** [base - de monumento, morro] foot; **ao ~ de** at the foot of; **ao ~ do ouvido** in secret; [- de mesa] leg; [- de copo] stem. **-3.** BOT plant. **-4.** [de calçado, meia] sole. **-5.**

[situação] state of affairs; **em que ~ estão as coisas?** what's the state of play?; **em ~ de guerra/igualdade** on a war/equal footing.
◆ **ao pé da letra** *loc adv* to the letter.
PE (*abrev de* **Estado de Pernambuco**) *n State of Pernambuco.*
peão ['pjãw] (*pl* **-ões**) *m* **-1.** [trabalhador] labourer *UK*, laborer *US*. **-2.** [xadrez] pawn.
peça ['pεsa] *f* **-1.** [ger] piece; **~ fundamental** *fig* vital part; *MÚS* **~ de resistência** pièce de résistance; [o forte de alguém] strong point. **-2.** *MEC* part; **~ de reposição** *ou* **~ sobressalente** replacement *ou* spare part. **-3.** [cômodo] room. **-4.** [brincadeira]: **pregar uma ~ em alguém** to play a practical joke on sb. **-5.** *TEATRO* play. **-6.** *JUR* document.
pecado [pe'kadu] *m* **-1.** *RELIG* sin; **~ capital** cardinal sin; **~ mortal** mortal sin; **~ original** original sin; **pagar os seus ~s** to pay for one's sins. **-2.** [pena]: **que ~!** what a sin!
pecador, ra [peka'do(x), ra] *m, f* sinner.
pecaminoso, osa [pekami'nozu, ɔza] *adj* sinful.
pecar [12] [pe'ka(x)] *vi* **-1.** *RELIG* to sin. **-2.** [errar]: **~ por algo** to err on the side of sthg.
pechincha [pe'ʃĩnʃa] *f* bargain; **ser uma ~** to be a bargain.
pechinchar [4] [pe'ʃĩnʃa(x)] *vi* to haggle.
peçonha [pe'soɲa] *f* poison.
pecuário, ria [pe'kwarju, rja] *adj* cattle.
◆ **pecuária** *f* [criação] cattle-raising.
pecuarista [pekwa'riʃta] *mf* cattle dealer.
peculiar [peku'lja(x)] (*pl* **-es**) *adj* **-1.** [característico] particular. **-2.** [curioso] peculiar.
peculiaridade [pekuljari'dadʒi] *f* peculiarity.
pecúlio [pe'kulju] *m* **-1.** [economias] nest egg. **-2.** [bens] belongings *(pl)*.
pedaço [pe'dasu] *m* **-1.** [parte] piece; **aos ~s** in pieces; **estar caindo aos ~s** to be falling to pieces. **-2.** [trecho] piece. **-3.** [lugar] area. **-4.** *fam* [beleza]: **ser um ~ (de mau caminho)** to be a bit of all right.
pedágio [pe'daʒju] *m* toll.
pedagogia [pedago'ʒia] *f* **-1.** [prática] teaching method. **-2.** [curso] education.
pedagógico, ca [peda'gɔʒiku, ka] *adj* teaching *(antes de subst)*.
pedagogo, ga [peda'gogu, ga] *m, f* educationalist.
pé-d'água [,pε'dagwa] (*pl* **pés-d'água**) *m* deluge.
pedal [pe'daw] (*pl* **-ais**) *m* pedal.
pedalada [peda'lada] *f* pedalling; **dar uma ~** to go for a bike ride.
pedalar [4] [peda'la(x)] ◇ *vt* to pedal. ◇ *vi* to pedal.
pedalinho [peda'liɲu] *m* pedalo.
pedante [pe'dãntʃi] ◇ *adj* pedantic. ◇ *m, f* pedant.
pedantismo [pedãn'tʃiʒmu] *m* pedantry.
pé-de-atleta [,pεdʒja'tlεta] *m* athlete's foot.
pé-de-cabra [pεdʒi'kabra] (*pl* **pés-de-cabra**) *m* **-1.** [alavanca] crowbar. **-2.** *fam* [diabo] devil.
pé-de-galinha [,pεdʒiga'liɲa] (*pl* **pés-de-galinha**) *m* crow's foot.
pé-de-meia [,pεdʒi'meja] (*pl* **pés-de-meia**) *m* nest egg; **fazer um ~** to get some savings together.
pé-de-moleque [,pεdʒimu'lεki] (*pl* **pés-de-moleque**) *m* **-1.** [doce] peanut brittle. **-2.** [calçamento] crazy paving.
pé-de-ouvido [,pεdʒio'vidu] (*pl* **pés-de-ouvido**) *m* [tapa] clip round the ear.
pé-de-pato [,pεdʒi'patu] (*pl* **pés-de-pato**) *m* **-1.** [nadadeira] flipper. **-2.** *fam* [diabo] Satan.
pedestal [pedeʃ'taw] (*pl* **-ais**) *m* pedestal.
pedestre [pe'dεʃtri] *mf* pedestrian.
pé-de-valsa [,pεdʒi'vawsa] (*pl* **pés-de-valsas**) *m* expert dancer.
pé-de-vento [,pεdʒi'vẽntu] (*pl* **pés-de-vento**) *m* squall.
pediatra [pe'dʒjatra] *mf* paediatrician *UK*, pediatrician *US*.
pediatria [pedʒja'tria] *f* paediatrics *UK*, pediatrics *US*.
pedicuro, re [pedʒi'kuru, ri] *m, f* pedicure.
pedido [pe'dʒidu] *m* **-1.** [ger] order. **-2.** [solicitação] request; **a ~** to an encore; **a ~ de alguém** at sb's request; **~ de casamento** marriage proposal; **~ de demissão** resignation; **~ de divórcio** divorce petition.
◆ **pedida** *f fam* suggestion; **ser uma boa pedida** to be a good idea.
pedigree [pedʒi'gri] *m* pedigree.
pedinte [pe'dʒĩntʃi] *mf* beggar.
pedir [70] [pe'dʒi(x)] ◇ *vt* **-1.** [solicitar] to ask for; **~ algo a alguém** to ask sb for sthg; **~ a alguém que faça algo** to ask sb to do sthg; **~ algo emprestado** to borrow sthg; **~ alguém em casamento** to ask for sb's hand in marriage; **~ desculpas** *ou* **perdão (por algo)** to apologize (for sthg). **-2.** [cobrar] to charge. **-3.** [necessitar] to call for. **-4.** [encomendar] to order. **-5.** [exigir, requerer] to demand; **~ satisfações (a alguém)** to demand an apology (from sb). ◇ *vi* [fazer pedidos] to make demands; **~ por alguém** to pray for sb.
pé-direito [,pεdʒi'rejtu] (*pl* **pés-direitos**) *m* height of a room.
pedra ['pεdra] *f* **-1.** [ger] stone. **-2.** [fragmento] pebble; **~ de amolar** grindstone; **~ de gelo** ice cube; **~ de toque** *fig* touchstone; **~ preciosa** precious stone; **dormir como uma ~** to sleep like a log; **pôr uma ~ em cima de** *fig* to bury; **ser de ~** to be made of stone; **vir com quatro ~s na mão** to jump down sb's throat. **-3.** [de açúcar] sugar lump.
pedrada [pe'drada] *f* **-1.** [com pedra] blow (with a stone). **-2.** *fig* [golpe] blow.
pedra-pomes [,pεdra'pɔmiʃ] (*pl* **pedras-pomes**) *f* pumice stone.
pedra-sabão [,pεdrasa'bãw] (*pl* **pedras-sabão**) *f* soapstone.
pedregoso, osa [pedre'gozu, ɔza] *adj* stony.

pedregulho [pedre'guʎu] *m* boulder.
pedreira [pe'drejra] *f* stone quarry.
pedreiro [pe'drejru] *m* CONSTR mason.
pé-frio [ˌpɛ'friw] (*pl* **pés-frios**) *m*: **ser um ~** to be jinxed.
pega ['pɛga] *m* **-1.** [briga] quarrel. **-2.** *fam* [corrida] illegal street race.
pegada [pe'gada] *f* footprint.
pegado, da [pe'gadu, da] *adj* **-1.** [contíguo] next door. **-2.** [unido] close.
pegajoso, osa [pega'ʒozu, ɔza] *adj* sticky.
pega-ladrão [ˌpɛgala'drãw] (*pl* **pega-ladrões**) *m* safety catch/switch.
pegar [14] [pe'ga(x)] <> *vt* **-1.** [ger] to pick up. **-2.** [surpreender] to catch. **-3.** [embarcar em] to catch. **-4.** [seguir por] to take. **-5.** [compreender] to take in. **-6.** [vivenciar] to experience. **-7.** [aceitar fazer] to take on. <> *vi* **-1.** [segurar] to catch; **~ em algo** to hold on to sthg. **-2.** [grudar]: **~ em algo** to stick to sthg. **-3.** [difundir-se - moda, mania] to catch on; [- doença] to be catching. **-4.** [fogo]: **a fogueira pega mais rápido com álcool** the fire lights quicker with alcohol; **ele pegou fogo na casa** he set fire to the house. **-5.** [planta] to take root. **-6.** RÁDIO & TV: **~ (bem/mal)** to have good/poor reception. **-7.** [motor] to start. **-8.** [iniciar]: **~ em algo** to start sthg. **-9.** [atitude]: **~ bem/mal** to go down well/badly; **não pega bem** it doesn't do. **-10.** [decidir-se]: **~ a fazer algo** to make up one's mind and do sthg.
◆ **pegar-se** *vp* [brigar]: **~-se (com)** to come to blows (with).
pega-rapaz [ˌpɛgaxa'paʒ] (*pl* **pega-rapazes**) *m* kiss-curl.
peia ['peja] *f* **ant** & *fig* [estorvo] hindrance.
peidar [4] [pej'da(x)] *vi* *mfam* to fart.
peido ['pejdu] *m* *mfam* fart.
peitar [4] [pej'ta(x)] *vt* **-1.** [enfrentar] to face. **-2.** [subornar] to bribe.
peitilho [pej'tʃiʎu] *m* shirt front.
peito ['pejtu] *m* **-1.** ANAT chest; **~ do pé** instep; **meter o ~ *fam*** to put one's heart into it. **-2.** [de mulher, ave] breast; **dar o ~** to breastfeed. **-3.** *fig* [coragem] courage; **no ~ (e na raça)** fearlessly.
peitoril [pejto'riw] (*pl* **-is**) *m* windowsill.
peitudo, da [pej'tudu, da] *adj* **-1.** [de peito grande] big-chested. **-2.** [valente] plucky.
peixada [pej'ʃada] *f* fish stew.
peixaria [pejʃa'ria] *f* fishmonger.
peixe ['pejʃi] *m* ZOOL fish; **não ter nada com o ~ *fam*** to have nothing to do with it; **vender o seu ~** [tratar de seus interesses] to look out for one's own interests; [opinar] to have one's say.
peixeira [pej'ʃejra] *f* [facão] *small, sharp knife.*
peixeiro, ra [pej'ʃejru, ra] *m, f* [vendedor] fishmonger.
Peixes ['pejʃiʃ] *mpl* [zodíaco] Pisces; **ser de ~** to be Pisces.
pejorativo, va [peʒora'tʃivu, va] *adj* pejorative.
pela ['pela] = **por + a**.
pelada [pe'lada] FUT *f* **-1.** [jogo informal] (friendly) match. **-2.** [jogo ruim] wasted game.
pelado, da [pe'ladu, da] *adj* **-1.** [nu] naked. **-2.** [sem pêlos] shorn.
pelanca [pe'lãŋka] *f* **-1.** [em pessoa] flabby skin. **-2.** [de carne] poor quality meat.
pelancudo, da [pelãŋ'kudu, da] *adj* **-1.** [pessoa, braço] flabby. **-2.** [carne] flaccid.
pelar [4] [pe'la(x)] <> *vt* **-1.** [animal] to skin. **-2.** [cabeça] to shave. <> *vi*: **estar pelando** [estar quentíssimo] to be scalding.
◆ **pelar-se** *vp fam*: **~-se de medo** to be scared stiff.
pelas ['pelaʃ] = **por + as**.
pele ['pɛli] *f* **-1.** [de pessoa] skin; **~ e osso** skin and bone; **cair na ~ de *fig fam*** to pester; **salvar a ~ de alguém *fig fam*** to save sb's skin; **sentir algo na ~ *fig*** to experience sthg first hand. **-2.** [animal] hide; **de ~** hide. **-3.** [couro] leather; **de ~** leather. **-4.** [agasalho] fur. **-5.** [de fruta, legume] skin, peel.
peleja [pe'leʒa] *f* battle.
pelejar [4] [pele'ʒa(x)] *vi* **-1.** [combater] to fight. **-2.** *fig* [lutar]: **~ (por/para algo)** to fight (for sthg).
pelerine [pele'rini] *f* cape.
pelica [pe'lika] *f* kid leather.
pelicano [peli'kãnu] *m* ZOOL pelican.
película [pe'likula] *f* **-1.** CINE film. **-2.** [de pele] membrane. **-3.** [camada fina] layer.
pelo ['pelu] = **por + o**.
pêlo ['pelu] *m* **-1.** [em pessoa] hair; **nu em ~** stark naked. **-2.** [de animal] fur.
pelos ['peluʃ] = **por + os**.
pelota [pe'lɔta] *f* **-1.** [bola] ball; **dar ~ a alguém/algo *fig*** to pay attention to sb/sthg. **-2.** [em molho, creme] lump. **-3.** [na pele] spot.
pelotão [pelo'tãw] (*pl* **-ões**) *m* platoon; **~ de fuzilamento** firing squad.
pelúcia [pe'lusja] *f* plush.
peludo, da [pe'ludu, da] *adj* hairy.
pélvico, ca ['pɛwviku, ka] *adj* pelvic.
pélvis ['pɛwviʃ] *f (inv)* ANAT pelvis.
pena ['pena] *f* **-1.** [de ave] feather. **-2.** [pesar] sorrow; **que ~!** what a pity!; **ser uma ~** to be a pity; **valer a ~ *fig*** [compensar] to be worthwhile; **a duras ~s** with great difficulty. **-3.** JUR punishment; **~ capital** *ou* **de morte** capital punishment *ou* death penalty; **cumprir ~** to serve a sentence; **sob ~ de *fig*** under penalty of. **-4.** [piedade] pity; **dar ~** to arouse pity; **ter ~ de** to be sorry for. **-5.** *ant* [caneta] pen.
penacho [pe'naʃu] *m* **-1.** [de plumas] plume. **-2.** [crista] crest.
penal [pe'naw] (*pl* **-ais**) *adj* JUR penal.
penalidade [penali'dadʒi] *f* **-1.** JUR penalty. **-2.** [castigo] punishment. **-3.** FUT: **~ máxima** penalty (kick).
penalizar [4] [penali'za(x)] *vt* **-1.** [dar pena a] to distress. **-2.** [castigar] to punish.
pênalti [pe'nawtʃi] *m* FUT penalty.

penar [4] [pe'na(x)] <> *m* [sofrimento] suffering. <> *vt* [sofrer] to hurt, to distress. <> *vi* [sofrer] to suffer.

penca ['pẽnka] *f* bunch; **uma ~ de algo** *fig* [quantidade] a bunch of sthg; **em ~** *fig* [quantidade] loads of.

pendão [pẽn'dãw] (*pl* **-ões**) *m* **-1.** [estandarte] pennant. **-2.** [bandeira] flag. **-3.** [de milho] tassel.

pendência [pẽn'dẽnsja] *f* **-1.** [contenda] dispute. **-2.** [algo por decidir] pending matter.

pendente [pẽn'dẽntʃi] <> *adj* **-1.** [ger] hanging. **-2.** [por decidir] pending. <> *m* [de jóia] pendant.

pender [5] [pẽn'de(x)] *vi* **-1.** [estar pendurado] to hang. **-2.** [inclinar-se]: **~ para/sobre** to hang towards/over. **-3.** [tender] to have a leaning; **o jovem pende para as letras** the young man has a leaning towards literature.

pendões [pẽn'dõjʃ] *pl* ▷ **pendão**.

pendor [pẽn'do(x)] *m* tendency.

pêndulo ['pẽndulu] *m* pendulum.

pendurado, da [pẽndu'radu, da] *adj* **-1.** [pendente]: **~ (em)** hanging (on). **-2.** *fig* [conta] on tick.

pendurar [4] [pẽndu'ra(x)] *vt* **-1.** [colocar] to hang. **-2.** *fig* [conta] to pay on tick.

◆ **pendurar-se** *vp* [pessoa] to hang.

penduricalho [pẽnduri'kaʎu], **penduricalho** [pẽnduru'kaʎu] *m* trinket.

penedo [pe'nedu] *m* boulder.

peneira [pe'nejra] *f* **-1.** [para peneirar] sieve. **-2.** *fig* [seleção]: **passar na** *ou* **pela ~** to pass the selection.

peneirar [4] [penej'ra(x)] <> *vt* [na peneira] to sieve. <> *vi fig* [chuviscar] to drizzle.

penetra [pe'nɛtra] *mf fam* gatecrasher; **entrar de ~** to gatecrash.

penetração [penetra'sãw] (*pl* **-ões**) *f* **-1.** [ger] penetration. **-2.** *fig* [difusão] circulation.

penetrante [pene'trãntʃi] *adj* penetrating.

penetrar [4] [pene'tra(x)] <> *vt* to penetrate. <> *vi* **-1.** [entrar, infiltrar-se]: **~ em/por/entre** to penetrate. **-2.** *fam* [em festa] to gatecrash.

penhasco [pe'ɲaʃku] *m* cliff.

penhoar [pe'ɲwa(x)] *m* dressing gown.

penhor [pe'ɲo(x)] *m* pawn; **fazer o ~ de algo** to pawn *ou* hock sthg, to leave sthg in pawn *ou* hock; **casa de ~es** pawnshop; **dar em ~** to pawn, to hock.

penhora [pe'ɲɔra] *f JUR* confiscation.

penhorado, da [peɲo'radu, da] *adj* pawned, hocked.

penhorar [4] [peɲo'ra(x)] *vt* to pawn, to hock.

penicilina [penisi'lina] *f* penicillin.

penico [pe'niku] *m* chamber pot, potty; **pedir ~** *fam fig* to eat humble pie.

península [pe'nĩnsula] *f* peninsula.

peninsular [penĩnsu'la(x)] *adj* peninsular.

pênis ['peniʃ] *m inv* penis.

penitência [peni'tẽnsja] *f RELIG* **-1.** [contrição] contrition. **-2.** [expiação] penance; **fazer ~** to do penance.

penitenciar [16] [penitẽn'sja(x)] *vt RELIG* **-1.** [impor penitência a] to give a penance to; **o arrependimento penitencia meu coração** my heart is mortified with remorse. **-2.** [expiar] to do penance.

◆ **penitenciar-se** *vp*: **~-se de/por** to punish o.s. for.

penitenciário, ria [penitẽn'sjarju, rja] <> *adj* penitentiary. <> *m, f* prisoner.

◆ **penitenciária** *f* penitentiary.

penitente [peni'tẽntʃi] <> *adj* penitent. <> *inf* penitent.

penoso, osa [pe'nozu, ɔza] *adj* **-1.** [assunto, trabalho] hard. **-2.** [tratamento, correção] harsh.

pensado, da [pẽn'sadu, da] *adj* considered; **de caso ~** on purpose.

pensador, ra [pẽnsa'do(x), ra] *m, f* thinker.

pensamento [pẽnsa'mẽntu] *m* **-1.** [ger] thought; **~ positivo** positive thinking; **fazer ~ positivo** to think positively. **-2.** [mente, opinião] mind. **-3.** [doutrina] thinking. **-4.** [idéia] idea.

pensante [pẽn'sãntʃi] *adj* thinking.

pensão [pẽn'sãw] (*pl* **-ões**) *f* **-1.** [pequeno hotel] boarding house. **-2.** [renda] pension; **~ alimentícia** maintenance allowance. **-3.** [restaurante] boarding house. **-4.** [refeição]: **dar ~** [hotel] to provide board; [cozinhar para fora] to provide meals; **~ completa** full board.

pensar [4] [pẽn'sa(x)] <> *vt* to think. <> *vi* **-1.** [ger] to think; **~ em/sobre algo** to think about sthg. **-2.** [tencionar] to intend.

pensativo, va [pẽnsa'tʃivu, va] *adj* thoughtful.

pênsil ['pẽnsiw] (*pl* **-seis**) *adj* [suspenso] hanging.

pensionato [pẽnsjo'natu] *m* hostel.

pensionista [pẽnsjo'niʃta] *mf* **-1.** [beneficiário] pensioner. **-2.** [morador] boarder.

penso, sa ['pẽnsu] *adj* hanging.

pentacampeão [ˌpẽntakãn'pjãw] (*pl* **-ões**) *m* five-times champion.

pentágono [pẽn'tagunu] *m GEOM* pentagon.

pentatlo [pẽn'tatlu] *m* pentathlon.

pente ['pẽntʃi] *m* **-1.** [de cabelo] comb. **-2.** [de pistola] cartridge.

penteadeira [pẽntʃja'dejra] *f* dressing table.

penteado, da [pẽn'tʃjadu] *adj* well groomed.

◆ **penteado** *m* hairstyle.

pentear [15] [pẽn'tʃja(x)] *vt* **-1.** [cabelo] to comb. **-2.** [fazer penteado] to style.

◆ **pentear-se** *vp* [pessoa] to do one's hair.

Pentecostes [pẽnte'kɔʃtiʃ] *m RELIG* Pentecost.

pente-fino [pẽntʃi'finu] (*pl* **pentes-finos**) *m* **-1.** [pente] fine-tooth comb. **-2.** *fam fig* [crivo] close scrutiny; **passar algo pelo ~** to go through sthg with a fine-tooth comb.

pentelhação [pẽnteʎa'sãw] (*pl* **-ões**) *f* [chateação] *fam* aggro, hassle.

pentelhar [4] [pẽnte'ʎa(x)] *vt fam* to aggravate.

pentelho, lha [pẽn'teʎu, ʎa] *fam* <> *adj* [chato] aggravating. <> *m, f* [pessoa chata] pain in the neck.

◆ **pentelho** *m fam* [pêlo] pubic hair.

penugem [pe'nuʒẽ] (*pl* **-ns**) *f* down.

penúltimo, ma [pe'nuwtʃimu, ma] *adj* penultimate, last but one.
penumbra [pe'nũnbra] *f* **-1.** [meia-luz] half-light. **-2.** *fig* [obscuridade] obscurity.
penúria [pe'nurja] *f* penury; **~ de algo** lack of sthg.
peões ['pjõjʃ] *pl* ▷ **peão**.
pepino [pe'pinu] *m* **-1.** [fruto] cucumber. **-2.** *fig* [problema] bit of a problem.
pepita [pe'pita] *f* [de ouro] nugget.
pequena [pe'kena] *f* ▷ **pequeno**.
pequenez [peke'neʒ] *f* **-1.** [de tamanho] smallness. **-2.** *fig* [mesquinhez] meanness.
pequenininho, nha [pekeni'niɲu, ɲa] *adj* tiny.
pequenino, na [peke'ninu, na] ◇ *adj* very small. ◇ *m, f* [criança] child.
◆ **pequeninos** *mpl*: **os ~s** [as crianças] the children; [os humildes] the little people.
pequeno, na [pe'kenu, na] ◇ *adj* **-1.** [tamanho] small. **-2.** [mesquinho] mean. ◇ *m, f* [criança] child.
◆ **pequena** *f* [namorada] girlfriend.
pequeno-burguês, pequeno-burguesa [pe,kenubux'geʃ, pe,kenabux'geza] (*pl* **pequenos-burgueses**) ◇ *adj* petit bourgeois. ◇ *m, f* petit bourgeois.
Pequim [pe'kĩ] *n* Beijing.
pequinês [peki'neʃ] *m* [cão] Pekinese.
pêra ['pera] (*pl* **pêras**) *f* pear.
peralta [pe'rawta] ◇ *adj* mischievous. ◇ *m, f* mischief-maker.
perambular [4] [perãnbu'la(x)] *vi*: **~ (por)** to wander (through).
perante [pe'rãntʃi] *prep* **-1.** [no espaço] before; **jurar ~ a Bíblia** to swear on the Bible. **-2.** [no sentido] faced with.
pé-rapado, da [,pɛxa'padu, da] (*mpl* **pés-rapados**, *fpl* **pés-rapadas**) *m, f* loser.
percalço [pex'kawsu] *m* pitfall.
per capita [pɛx'kapita] *loc adj* per capita.
perceber [5] [pexse'be(x)] *vt* **-1.** [através dos sentidos] to perceive. **-2.** [compreender] to realize. **-3.** [notar] to notice.
percentagem [pexsẽn'taʒẽ] (*pl* **-ns**) *f* percentage.
percentual [pexsẽn'twaw] (*pl* **-ais**) ◇ *adj* percentage. ◇ *m* [percentagem] percentage.
percepção [pexsep'sãw] *f* [dos sentidos] perception.
perceptível [pexsep'tʃivew] (*pl* **-eis**) *adj* perceptible.
perceptivo, va [pexsep'tʃivu, va] *adj* perceptive.
percevejo [pexse'veʒu] *m* **-1.** ZOOL bedbug. **-2.** [prego] drawing pin.
percorrer [5] [pexko'xe(x)] *vt* **-1.** [viajar] to travel through. **-2.** [passar por] to pass through. **-3.** [esquadrinhar] to search. **-4.** [consultar] to search through.
percurso [pex'kuxsu] *m* route.
percussão [pexku'sãw] (*pl* **-ões**) *f* percussion.
percussionista [pexkusjo'niʃta] *mf* drummer.
percutir [6] [pexku'tʃi(x)] *vt* to hit.
perda ['pexda] *f* **-1.** [ger] loss. **-2.** [desperdício]: **~ de tempo** waste of time. **-3.** [prejuízo] damage; **~s e danos** damages.
perdão [pex'dãw] (*pl* **-dões**) *m* [escusa] pardon; **pedir ~ a alguém** to apologize to sb; **perdão!** sorry!
perdedor, ra [pexde'do(x), ra] ◇ *adj* losing. ◇ *m, f* [de competição] loser.
perder [44] [pex'de(x)] ◇ *vt* **-1.** [ger] to lose. **-2.** [não chegar a tempo, não comparecer] to miss. **-3.** [desperdiçar] to waste; **pôr tudo a ~** to ruin everything. ◇ *vi* [ser vencido] to lose; **~ de** *ou* **para alguém** to lose to *ou* against sb; **saber ~** to be a good loser.
◆ **perder-se** *vp* **-1.** [extraviar-se] to get lost; **~-se de alguém** to wander away from sb. **-2.** [arruinar-se] to waste one's life. **-3.** *ant* [mulher] to lose one's virginity. **-4.** [atrapalhar-se] to get bogged down. **-5.** [absorver-se] to lose o.s.
perdição [pexdʒi'sãw] *f* **-1.** [ruína] decay. **-2.** [mau caminho] evil; **ser uma ~** *fig irôn* to be irresistible. **-3.** [desonra] fall from grace.
perdidamente [pexdʒida'mẽntʃi] *adv* desperately.
perdido, da [pex'dʒidu, da] ◇ *adj* **-1.** [ger] lost. **-2.** [amorosamente]: **~ (de amor) por alguém** desperately in love with sb. **-3.** [arruinado]: **nem tudo está ~** all is not lost; **meu pai descobriu que fui reprovado, estou ~!** my father's found out I've failed, I'm done for! ◇ *m, f* [pervertido] pervert.
perdigão [pexdʒi'gãw] (*pl* **-ões**) *m* [macho] male partridge.
perdigueiro [pexdʒi'gejru] *m* [cão] pointer.
perdiz [pex'dʒiʃ] (*pl* **-es**) *f* [fêmea] female partridge.
perdoar [20] [pex'dwa(x)] ◇ *vt* **-1.** [desculpar] to forgive; **~ algo (a alguém)** to forgive (sb for) sthg. **-2.** [eximir de] to pardon. **-3.** *fig* [desperdiçar]: **não ~** to make the most of. ◇ *vi* [desculpar] to forgive.
perdoável [pex'dwavew] (*pl* **-eis**) *adj* forgivable.
perdulário, ria [pexdu'larju, rja] *adj* wasteful.
perdurar [4] [pexdu'ra(x)] *vi* **-1.** [durar muito]: **~ (por/através de)** to last (for/throughout). **-2.** [permanecer] to carry on.
pereba [pe'rɛba] *f* sore.
perebento, ta [pere'bẽntu, ta] *adj* covered in sores.
perecer [25] [pere'se(x)] *vi* **-1.** [extingüir-se] to perish. **-2.** [morrer] to die. **-3.** *ant* [frustrar-se] to come to nothing.
perecível [pere'sivɛw] (*pl* **-eis**) *adj* perishable.
peregrinação [peregrina'sãw] (*pl* **-ões**) *f* **-1.** [viagem] journey. **-2.** RELIG pilgrimage.
peregrinar [4] [peregri'na(x)] *vi* **-1.** [viajar] to travel. **-2.** RELIG to go on a pilgrimage.
peregrino, na [pere'grinu, na] *m, f* **-1.** [viajante] traveller. **-2.** RELIG pilgrim.
pereira [pe'rejra] *f* pear tree.
peremptório, ria [perẽnp'tɔrju, rja] *adj* **-1.** [final]

decisive. **-2.** [taxativo] peremptory.
perene [pe'reni] *adj* **-1.** [eterno] eternal. **-2.** [incessante] unceasing. **-3.** *BOT* perennial.
perereca [pere'rɛka] *f* **-1.** *ZOOL* tree frog. **-2.** *mfam* [vulva] pussy.
perfazer [31] [pexfa'ze(x)] *vt* **-1.** [total] to reach. **-2.** [ação] to complete.
perfeccionismo [pexfeksjo'niʒmu] *m* perfectionism.
perfeccionista [pexfeksjo'niʃta] ◇ *adj* perfectionist. ◇ *mf* perfectionist.
perfeição [pexfej'sãw] *f* perfection; **ser uma ~** to be perfect; **à ~** to perfection.
perfeitamente [pex,fejta'mẽntʃi] ◇ *adv* perfectly. ◇ *interj* [de acordo] of course!
perfeito, ta [pex'fejtu, ta] *adj* **-1.** [ger] perfect. **-2.** *(antes de subst)* [completo] perfect.
◆ **perfeito** *m GRAM* perfect.
perfídia [pex'fidʒja] *f* [traição] treachery.
pérfido, da ['pɛxfidu, da] *adj* treacherous.
perfil [pex'fiw] (*pl* **-is**) *m* **-1.** [ger] profile; **de ~** in profile. **-2.** *fig* [retrato] outline. **-3.** [caráter] personality.
perfilar [4] [pexfi'la(x)] *vt* **-1.** [alinhar] to line up. **-2.** [aprumar] to straighten up.
◆ **perfilar-se** *vp* **-1.** [alinhar-se] to line up. **-2.** [aprumar-se] to stand to attention.
performance [pex'fɔxmãnsi] *f* performance.
perfumado, da [pexfu'madu, da] *adj* perfumed.
perfumar [4] [pexfu'ma(x)] *vt* to perfume.
◆ **perfumar-se** *vp* to put perfume on.
perfumaria [pexfuma'ria] *f* **-1.** [loja] perfume shop. **-2.** *fig* & *pej* [bobagem] nonsense.
perfume [pex'fumi] *m* perfume.
perfurado, da [pexfu'radu, da] *adj* perforated.
perfurar [4] [pexfu'ra(x)] *vt* to perforate.
perfuratriz [pexfura'triʒ] *f* drill.
pergaminho [pexga'miɲu] *m* [documento] parchment.
pérgula ['pɛxgula] *f* pergola.
pergunta [pex'gũnta] *f* question; **fazer uma ~ a alguém** to ask sb a question; **~ capciosa** trick question.
perguntador, ra [pexgũnta'do(x), ra] *adj pej* nosy.
perguntar [4] [pexgũn'ta(x)] ◇ *vt* **-1.** [indagar] to ask; **~ algo a alguém** to ask sb sthg. **-2.** [interrogar] to question. ◇ *vi* [indagar] to ask questions; **~ por alguém** to ask after sb.
◆ **perguntar-se** *vp* to wonder.
perícia [pe'risja] *f* **-1.** [ger] expertise. **-2.** [policial] investigation. **-3.** [examinadores] investigators.
pericial [peri'sjaw] (*pl* **-ais**) *adj* expert.
periclitante [perikli'tãntʃi] *adj* perilous.
periclitar [4] [perikli'ta(x)] *vi* to be in peril.
periculosidade [perikulozi'dadʒi] *f* peril; **de alta ~** highly perilous.
peridural [peridu'raw] (*pl* **-ais**) ◇ *adj* epidural. ◇ *f* epidural.
periferia [perife'ria] *f* **-1.** [contorno] periphery. **-2.** *GEOM* circumference. **-3.** [subúrbio] outskirts *(pl)*.
periférico, ca [peri'fɛriku, ka] *adj* **-1.** [que contorna] peripheral. **-2.** *fig* [marginal] superficial.
◆ **periférico** *m COMPUT* peripheral.
perigar [14] [peri'ga(x)] *vi* to be in danger; **~ com** to be endangered by; **periga ele ser morto** he may be dead; **~ chover** to look like it's going to rain.
perigo [pe'rigu] *m* danger; **correr ~** to be in danger; **estar a ~** *fam fig* [dinheiro] to be broke; *fig* [em dificuldade] to be in trouble; **estar em ~** to be in danger; **pôr em ~** to endanger; **fora de ~** out of danger; **ser um ~** [ser perigoso] to be dangerous; *fam fig* [ser uma tentação] to be tantalizing.
perigoso, osa [peri'gozu, ɔza] *adj* dangerous.
perímetro [pe'rimetru] *m* perimeter; **~ urbano** city limits *(pl)*.
periodicamente [perjɔdʒika'mẽntʃi] *adv* periodically.
periódico, ca [pe'rjɔdʒiku, ka] *adj* periodic.
◆ **periódico** *m* **-1.** [jornal] periodical (newspaper). **-2.** [revista] periodical (magazine).
período [pe'riwdu] *m* **-1.** [ger] period; **~ de carência** term. **-2.** *UNIV* semester; **~ letivo** school term.
peripécia [peri'pɛsja] *f* **-1.** [aventura] adventure. **-2.** [incidente] incident.
periquito [peri'kitu] *m* budgerigar.
periscópio [periʃ'kɔpju] *m* periscope.
perito, ta [pe'ritu, ta] ◇ *adj* [experiente, especialista] expert; **~ em algo** expert in sthg. ◇ *m, f* **-1.** [especialista] expert. **-2.** [quem faz perícia] investigator.
peritonite [perito'nitʃi] *f* peritonitis.
perjúrio [pex'ʒurju] *m* perjury.
permanecer [25] [pexmane'se(x)] *vi* to remain.
permanência [pexma'nẽnsja] *f* **-1.** [continuação, constância] endurance. **-2.** [estada] stay.
permanente [pexma'nẽntʃi] ◇ *adj* permanent. ◇ *m* [cartão] pass. ◇ *f* [penteado] perm; **fazer uma ~** to have a perm.
permeável [pex'mjavew] (*pl* **-eis**) *adj* permeable; **~ a algo** permeable to sthg.
permeio [pex'meju] *adv*: **de ~** in between.
permissão [pexmi'sãw] (*pl* **-ões**) *f* permission; **ter ~ (para fazer algo)** to have permission (to do sthg).
permissível [pexmi'sivew] (*pl* **-eis**) *adj* permissible.
permissivo, va [pexmi'sivu, va] *adj* permissive.
permitir [6] [pexmi'tʃi(x)] *vt* **-1.** [admitir] to allow; **~ a alguém fazer algo** to allow sb to do sthg. **-2.** [conceder]: **~ algo a alguém** to grant sb sthg.
◆ **permitir-se** *vp* [tomar a liberdade de] to allow o.s.
permuta [pex'muta] *f* exchange.
permutação [pexmuta'sãw] (*pl* **-ões**) *f* **-1.** *MAT* permutation. **-2.** [troca] exchange.
permutar [4] [pexmu'ta(x)] *vt*: **~ algo (por algo)** to exchange sthg (for sthg).
perna ['pɛxna] *f* leg; **~ de pau** wooden leg; **bater**

~ *fig* to wander; **passar a ~ em alguém** *fig* [enganar] to con sb; [trair] to cheat on sb; **trocar as ~s** *fam* [cambalear] to trip over one's feet.

perna-de-pau [ˌpɛxnadʒi'paw] (*pl* **pernas-de-pau**) *mf* **-1.** *fam pej* [perneta] one-legged man. **-2.** *FUT* & *pej*: **aquele jogador é um ~!** that player has two left feet!

Pernambuco [pexnãn'buku] *n* Pernambuco.

perneta [pex'neta] *fam pej* ◇ *adj* one-legged. ◇ *mf* one-legged person.

pernicioso, osa [pexni'sjozu, ɔza] *adj* **-1.** [nocivo] destructive. **-2.** *MED* pernicious.

pernil [pex'niw] (*pl* **-is**) *m CULIN* hock.

pernilongo [pexni'lõŋgu] *m* stilt.

pernoitar [4] [pexnoj'ta(x)] *vi* to spend the night.

pernoite [per'nojtʃi] *m*: **após um ~ na minha casa** after spending the night at my house.

pernóstico, ca [pex'nɔʃtʃiku, ka] ◇ *adj* pretentious. ◇ *mf* pretentious person.

pérola ['pɛrola] *f* **-1.** [de ostra] pearl. **-2.** *fig* [pessoa, peça rara] gem.

perpassar [4] [pexpa'sa(x)] *vt fig* [atravessar] to imbue.

perpendicular [pexpẽndʒiku'la(x)] (*pl* **-es**) ◇ *adj* perpendicular; **ser ~ a algo** to be at right angles to sthg. ◇ *f* perpendicular.

perpetrar [4] [pexpe'tra(x)] *vt* to perpetrate.

perpetuar [4] [pexpe'twa(x)] *vt* to prolong.

◆ **perpetuar-se** *vp* to survive.

perpétuo, tua [pex'pɛtwu, twa] *adj* **-1.** [eterno] eternal. **-2.** [vitalício] permanent. **-3.** *JUR*: **prisão perpétua** life imprisonment. **-4.** *(antes de subst)* [freqüente] on-going.

perplexidade [pexpleksi'dadʒi] *f* perplexity.

perplexo, xa [pex'plɛksu, sa] *adj* perplexed; **estar/ficar ~** to be perplexed.

perscrutar [4] [pexʃkru'ta(x)] *vt* [investigar] to scrutinize.

perseguição [pexsegi'sãw] (*pl* **-ões**) *f* **-1.** [ger] persecution. **-2.** *fig* [de um objetivo] pursuit.

perseguidor, ra [pexsegi'do(x), ra] *m, f* **-1.** [que acossa] pursuer. **-2.** *fig* [de um objetivo] seeker.

perseguir [55] [pexse'gi(x)] *vt* **-1.** [ger] to pursue. **-2.** *POL* & *RELIG* to persecute.

perseverança [pexseve'rãnsa] *f* perseverance.

perseverante [pexseve'rãntʃi] *adj* persevering.

perseverar [4] [pexseve'ra(x)] *vi* **-1.** [persistir]: **~ (em)** to persevere (with). **-2.** [permanecer] to last.

Pérsia ['pɛxsja] *n* Persia.

persiana [pex'sjãna] *f* blind.

persignar-se [7] [pexsig'naxsi] *vp* to cross o.s.

persistência [pexsiʃ'tẽnsja] *f* persistence.

persistente [pexsiʃ'tẽntʃi] *adj* persistent.

persistir [6] [pexsiʃ'tʃi(x)] *vi* [insistir]: **~ (em algo)** to persist (in sthg).

personagem [pexso'naʒẽ] (*pl* **-ns**) *m, f* **-1.** *CINE, LITER* & *TEATRO* character. **-2.** [celebridade] celebrity.

personalidade [pexsonali'dadʒi] *f* personality; **dupla ~** split personality.

personalizado, da [pexsonali'zadu, da] *adj* personalized.

personalizar [412] [pexsonali'za(x)] *vt* [tonar pessoal] to personalize.

personificação [pexsonifika'sãw] (*pl* **-ões**) *f* personification.

personificar [12] [pexsonifi'ka(x)] *vt* personify.

perspectiva [pexʃpek'tʃiva] *f* **-1.** [ger] perspective. **-2.** [probabilidade] prospect; **em ~** [em vista] in prospect; [a distância] in perspective.

perspicácia [pexʃpi'kasja] *f* insight.

perspicaz [pexʃpi'kaʃ] (*pl* **-es**) *adj* insightful.

perspirar [4] [pexʃpi'ra(x)] *vi* to perspire, to sweat.

persuadir [6] [pexswa'dʒi(x)] ◇ *vt* **-1.** [convencer]: **~ alguém (a fazer algo)** to persuade sb (to do sthg); **persuadiu a mulher de que tinha razão** he persuaded his wife that he was right. **-2.** [induzir]: **~ alguém a fazer algo** to persuade sb to do sthg. ◇ *vi* [induzir] to persuade.

◆ **persuadir-se** *vp* **-1.** [convencer-se]: **~-se (de algo)** to be persuaded (of sthg). **-2.** [resolver-se]: **~-se (a fazer algo)** to make up one's mind (to do sthg).

persuasão [pexswa'zãw] *f* persuasion.

persuasivo, va [pexswa'zivu, va] *adj* persuasive.

pertencente [pextẽn'sẽntʃi] *adj*: **~ a algo/alguém** belonging to sthg/sb.

pertencer [25] [pextẽn'se(x)] *vi*: **~ a** [ger] to belong to; [concernir] to refer to.

pertences [pex'tẽnsiʃ] *mpl* [objetos pessoais] belongings.

pertinácia [pextʃi'nasja] *f* persistence.

pertinaz [pextʃi'najʒ] *adj* persistent.

pertinência [pextʃi'nẽnsja] *f* pertinence.

pertinente [pextʃi'nẽntʃi] *adj* **-1.** [ger] pertinent. **-2.** [importante] relevant.

perto ['pɛxtu] ◇ *adj* nearby. ◇ *adv* near; **de ~** [a pouca distância] closely; *fig* [intimamente] first-hand; **~ de** [ger] close to; [em comparação] next to.

perturbação [pextuxba'sãw] (*pl* **-ões**) *f* **-1.** [ger] disturbance; **~ da ordem** breach of the peace. **-2.** [transtorno] perturbation. **-3.** *MED* trouble.

perturbado, da [pextux'badu, da] *adj* **-1.** [transtornado]: **~ (com algo)** perturbed (by sthg). **-2.** [desorientado] disorientated; **ser ~ (das idéias)** *irôn* to be addled.

perturbador, ra [pextuxba'do(x), ra] *adj* disturbing.

perturbar [4] [pextux'ba(x)] ◇ *vt* **-1.** [ger] to perturb. **-2.** [atrapalhar] to disturb. **-3.** [envergonhar] to embarass. ◇ *vi* [atordoar] to pester.

◆ **perturbar-se** *vp* **-1.** [atrapalhar-se] to be worried. **-2.** [incomodar-se] to worry. **-3.** [envergonhar-se] to be embarrassed.

peru, rua [pe'ru, rua] *m, f* [ave] turkey.

◆ **peru** *n mfam* [pênis] cock.

◆ **perua** *f* **-1.** [caminhonete] estate car *UK*, station wagon *US*. **-2.** *fam pej* [mulher] hussy.

Peru [pe'ru] *n*: **(o) ~** Peru.

peruada [pe'rwada] *f* **-1.** [palpite] tip. **-2.** [espiada] look-see.

peruano, na [pe'rwãnu, na] ◇ *adj* Peruvian. ◇ *m, f* Peruvian.

peruar [4] [pe'rwa(x)] *vi* **-1.** [palpitar] to speculate. **-2.** [espiar] to size up.

peruca [pe'ruka] *f* wig.

perueiro, ra [pe'ruejru, ra] *m* [motorista de perua] minibus driver.

perversão [pexvex'sãw] (*pl* **-ões**) *f* **-1.** [depravação] perversion. **-2.** [alteração] alteration.

perversidade [pexvexsi'dadʒi] *f* perversity.

perverso, sa [pex'vɛxsu, sa] *adj* perverse.

perverter [5] [pexvex'te(x)] *vt* **-1.** [corromper] to pervert. **-2.** [alterar] to alter. **-3.** [deturpar] to distort.
◆ **perverter-se** *vp* [corromper-se] to become depraved.

pervertido, da [pexvex'tʃidu, da] ◇ *adj* [corrompido] depraved. ◇ *m, f* pervert.

pesadelo [peza'delu] *m* nightmare.

pesado, da [pe'zadu, da] *adj* **-1.** [ger] heavy. **-2.** [tenso] tense. **-3.** [grosseiro] coarse.
◆ **pesado** *m*: **pegar no ~** to do hard work.

pesagem [pe'zaʒẽ] *f* weighing.

pêsames ['pezamiʃ] *mpl* condolences; **dar os ~ (a alguém)** to offer one's condolences (to sb).

pesar [4] [pe'za(x)] ◇ *m* sadness; **apesar dos ~es** in spite of everything. ◇ *vt* to weigh. ◇ *vi* **-1.** [ger] to weigh. **-2.** [recair]: **~ sobre alguém** to fall on sb. **-3.** [onerar] to be burdensome. **-4.** [influenciar]: **~ em algo** to influence sthg. **-5.** [causar tristeza]: **~ a alguém** to grieve sb. **-6.** [causar remorso] to weigh sb down.
◆ **pesar-se** *vp* [verificar o peso] to weigh o.s.

pesaroso, osa [peza'rozu, ɔza] *adj* **-1.** [triste] sorrowful. **-2.** [arrependido] sorry.

pesca ['pɛʃka] *f* **-1.** [ato] fishing; **ir à ~** to go fishing; **~ submarina** skin diving. **-2.** [o que se pescou] catch.

pescada [peʃ'kada] *f* whiting.

pescado [peʃ'kadu] *m* catch *(of fish)*.

pescador, ra [peʃka'do(x), ra] (*mpl* **-es**, *fpl* **-s**) *m, f* fisherman (*f* fisherwoman).

pescar [12] [peʃ'ka(x)] ◇ *vt* **-1.** [apanhar] to fish. **-2.** *fig* [conseguir] to get. **-3.** *fig* [conquistar] to catch. ◇ *vi fam* [entender]: **~ (de algo)** to catch on (to sthg).

pescoção [peʃko'sãw] (*pl* **-ões**) *m* **-1.** [pescoçada] blow on the neck; **levar um ~ de alguém** to be given a blow on the neck by sb. **-2.** [pescoço grande] large neck.

pescoço [peʃ'kosu] *m* neck; **até o ~** *fig* up to one's neck; **torcer o ~ de alguém** *fig* to wring sb's neck.

pescoçudo, da [peʃko'sudu, da] *adj* thick-necked.

peso ['pezu] *m* **-1.** [ger] weight; **~ bruto/líquido** gross/net weight; **~ pesado** heavyweight; **ter dois ~s e duas medidas** *fig* to have double standards; **ele é um intelectual de ~** he is a weighty intelectual. **-2.** [para papéis] paperweight. **-3.** [em atletismo] weights *(pl)*. **-4.** [moeda] peso. **-5.** *fig* [carga] burden.
◆ **em peso** *loc adj* en masse.

pespontar [4] [peʃpõn'ta(x)] *vt* COST to backstitch.

pesponto [peʃ'põntu] *m* backstitch.

pesqueiro, ra [peʃ'kejru, ra] *adj* fishing *(antes de subst)*.

pesquisa [peʃ'kiza] *f* **-1.** [investigação] search. **-2.**: **~ de mercado** market research; **~ de opinião** opinion poll. **-3.** [estudo] research; **~ de campo** field research; **~ e desenvolvimento** research and development.

pesquisador, ra [peʃkiza'do(x), ra] ◇ *adj* research *(antes de subst)*. ◇ *m, f* researcher.

pesquisar [4] [peʃki'za(x)] ◇ *vt* **-1.** [investigar] to investigate. **-2.** [estudar] to research. ◇ *vi* [estudar] to do research.

pêssego ['pesegu] *m* peach.

pessegueiro [pese'gejru] *m* peach tree.

pessimismo [pesi'miʒmu] *m* pessimism.

pessimista [pesi'miʃta] ◇ *adj* pessimistic. ◇ *mf* pessimist.

péssimo, ma ['pɛsimu, ma] *adj (superl de mau)* terrible; **ficou ~ com a notícia** the news made him feel terrible.

pessoa [pe'soa] *f* [ger] person; **em ~** personally; **~ física** JUR private individual; **~ jurídica** JUR legal entity.

pessoal [pe'swaw] (*pl* **-ais**) ◇ *adj* personal. ◇ *m* **-1.** [empregados] personnel *(pl)*, staff. **-2.** [grupo] people *(pl)*.

pessoalmente [peswaw'mẽntʃi] *adv* personally.

pestana [peʃ'tãna] *f* **-1.** [cílio] eyelash; **queimar as ~s** *fig* [estudar] to swot; **tirar uma ~** *fig* [dormir] to catch forty winks. **-2.** COST flap. **-3.** MÚS barré.

pestanejar [4] [peʃtane'ʒa(x)] *vi* to blink; **sem ~** *fig* without batting an eyelid.

peste ['pɛʃtʃi] *f* **-1.** [ger] plague. **-2.** *fig* [pessoa] pest. **-3.** *fig* [coisa perniciosa] scourge.

pesticida [peʃtʃi'sida] *f* pesticide.

pestilência [peʃtʃi'lẽnsja] *f* [fedor] stench.

pestilento, ta [peʃtʃi'lẽntu, ta] *adj* **-1.** [fedorento] stinking. **-2.** [infectado] pestilent.

pétala ['pɛtala] *f* petal.

petardo [pe'taxdu] *m* FUT powerful kick.

peteca [pe'tɛka] *f* [brinquedo] shuttlecock; **não deixar a ~ cair** *fam fig* to keep the ball rolling.

peteleco [pete'lɛku] *m* flick.

petição [petʃi'sãw] (*pl* **-ões**) *f* **-1.** [requerimento] petition. **-2.** [súplica] plea. **-3.** [estado]: **em ~ de miséria** in a pitiful state.

peticionário, ria [petʃisjo'narju, rja] *m, f* JUR petitioner.

petiscar [12] [petʃiʃ'ka(x)] ◇ *vt* to pick at. ◇ *vi* to snack; **quem não arrisca não petisca** he who dares wins.

petisco [pe'tʃiʃku] *m* titbit ***UK***, tidbit ***US***.

petit-pois [petʃi'pwa] *m inv* pea.

petrechos [pe'treʃuʃ] *mpl* **-1.** MIL munitions. **-2.** [utensílios] utensils.

petrificado, da [petrifi'kadu, da] *adj* petrified.

petrificar [12] [petrifi'ka(x)] *vt* **-1.** [tornar em pedra] to harden. **-2.** [insensibilizar] to numb. **-3.** [aterrorizar] to petrify.

Petrobras (*abrev de* **Petróleo Brasileiro S/A**) *f Brazilian state-owned petroleum company.*

petrodólar [petro'dɔla(x)] *m* petrodollar.

petroleiro, ra [petro'lejru] ◇ *adj*: **navio-** ~ (oil) tanker. ◇ *m, f* [pessoa] oilman.

petróleo [pe'trɔlju] *m* petroleum, oil; ~ **bruto** crude oil.

petrolífero, ra [petro'liferu, ra] *adj* oil.

petroquímico, ca [petro'kimiku, ka] ◇ *adj* petrochemical. ◇ *m, f* petroleum chemist.
◆ **petroquímica** *f* [indústria] petrochemicals *(pl)*.

petulância [petu'lãnsja] *f* petulance.

petulante [petu'lãntʃi] *adj* petulant.

petúnia [pe'tunja] *f* petunia.

PFL (*abrev de* **Partido da Frente Liberal**) *m* Party of the Liberal Front, *the largest, very right-wing party in Brazil.*

Phnom Penh [fnõn'pẽj] *n* Phnom Penh.

pia ['pia] *f* sink, washbasin; ~ **batismal** baptismal font.

piaçaba [pia'saba] *f* BOT *palm native to Brazil up to 15 meters in height producing a fibre used in the manufacture of brushes.*

piada ['pjada] *f* joke.

piadista [pja'dʒiʃta] *mf* joker.

piamente [pja'mẽntʃi] *adv* earnestly.

pianista [pja'niʃta] *mf* pianist.

piano ['pjãnu] *m* piano; ~ **de cauda** grand piano.

pianola [pja'nɔla] *f* pianola.

pião ['pjãw] (*pl* **-ões**) *m* spinning top.

piar [16] ['pja(x)] *vi* **-1.** [ave - pinto] to cheep; [- passarinho] to chirp; [- coruja] to hoot. **-2.** *fam* [falar]: **não** ~ not to make a peep.

PIB (*abrev de* **Produto Interno Bruto**) *m* GDP.

picada [pi'kada] *f* ▷ **picado**.

picadeiro [pika'dejru] *m* (circus) ring.

picadinho [pika'dʒiɲu] *m* CULIN **-1.** [de carne] minced meat. **-2.** [de legumes] vegetable stew.

picado, da [pi'kadu, da] *adj* **-1.** [ger] stung; **ser** ~ **por algo** to be bitten by sthg. **-2.** [em pedaços] chopped up. **-3.** [mar] choppy. **-4.** [vôo] nose-diving.
◆ **picada** *f* **-1.** [espetada] prick. **-2.** [mordida] bite. **-3.** [caminho] trail.

picanha [pi'kãɲa] *f* [carne bovina] rump.

picante [pi'kãntʃi] *adj* spicy.

pica-pau [,pika'paw] (*pl* **pica-paus**) *m* woodpecker.

picar [12] [pi'ka(x)] *vt* **-1.** [espetar] to prick. **-2.** [morder] to bite. **-3.** [cortar em pedaços] to chop. **-4.** [lascar] to splinter. **-5.** [bicar] to peck.
◆ **picar-se** *vp* **-1.** [espetar-se] to prick o.s. **-2.** [com droga] to inject o.s.

picardia [pikax'dʒia] *f* **-1.** [implicância] spitefulness. **-2.** [maldade] spite.

picaresco, ca [pika'reʃku, ka] *adj* [burlesco] burlesque.

picareta [pika'reta] ◇ *f* [instrumento] pickaxe *UK*, pickax *US*. ◇ *mf* [mau-caráter] con artist.

picaretagem [pikare'taʒẽ] (*pl* **-ns**) *f* con.

pichação [piʃa'sãw] (*pl* **-ões**) *f* **-1.** [grafite] graffiti. **-2.** *fam* [crítica] smear.

pichar [4] [pi'ʃa(x)] *vt* **-1.** [grafitar] to graffitti. **-2.** *fam* [criticar] to smear. **-3.** [aplicar piche em] to pitch.

piche ['piʃi] *m* pitch.

picles ['pikleʃ] *mpl* pickles.

pico ['piku] *m* **-1.** [cume] summit. **-2.** [de faca etc] point. **-3.** *fam* [de droga] shot.

picolé [piko'lɛ] *m* ice lolly.

picotar [4] [piko'ta(x)] *vt* to perforate.

picote [pi'kɔtʃi] *m* [perfuração] perforation.

pictórico, ca [pik'tɔriku, ka] *adj* pictorial.

picuinha [pi'kwiɲa] *f* [implicância] dispute; **estar de** ~ **com alguém** to be at odds with sb.

piedade [pje'dadʒi] *f* **-1.** [compaixão] pity; **ter** ~ **de alguém** to have pity on sb. **-2.** [religiosidade] piety.

piedoso, osa [pje'dozu, ɔza] *adj* pious.

piegas ['pjɛgaʃ] *adj inv* soppy.

pieguice [pje'gisi] *f* soppiness.

píer ['pie(x)] *m* pier.

pifado, da [pi'fadu, da] *fam adj* [enguiçado] broken down.

pifão [pi'fãw] (*pl* **-ões**) *m fam* drunk; **tomar um** ~ to have a skinful.

pifar [4] [pi'fa(x)] *vi fam* **-1.** [enguiçar] to break down. **-2.** [gorar] to fall through.

pigarrear [15] [piga'xja(x)] *vi* to hawk.

pigarro [pi'gaxu] *m* phlegm.

pigméia [pig'mɛja] *f* ▷ **pigmeu**.

pigmentação [pigmẽnta'sãw] *f* pigmentation.

pigmento [pig'mẽntu] *m* pigment.

pigmeu, méia [pig'mew, mɛja] ◇ *adj* [pequeno] pygmy. ◇ *m, f* pygmy.

pijama [pi'ʒãma] *m* pyjamas *(pl) UK*, pajamas *(pl) US*.

pilantra [pi'lãntra] *mf* rogue.

pilantragem [pilãn'traʒẽ] (*pl* **-ns**) *f* roguishness.

pilão [pi'lãw] (*pl* **-ões**) *m* pestle.

pilar [4] [pi'la(x)] (*pl* **-es**) ◇ *m* [coluna] pillar. ◇ *vt* to grind.

pilastra [pi'laʃtra] *f* pilaster.

pileque [pi'lɛki] *m* skinful; **estar de** ~ to be smashed; **tomar um** ~ to have a skinful.

pilha ['piʎa] *f* **-1.** [monte] pile. **-2.** ELETR battery. **-3.** [pessoa]: **estar/ser uma** ~ **(de nervos)** to be a bundle of nerves. **-4.** COMPUT stack.

pilhagem [pi'ʎaʒẽ] (*pl* **-ns**) *f* **-1.** [saque] pillage. **-2.** [objetos] booty.

pilhar [4] [pi'ʎa(x)] *vt* **-1.** [saquear] to pillage. **-2.** [roubar] to rob.

pilhéria [pi'ʎɛrja] *f* jest.

pilheriar [16] [piʎe'rja(x)] *vi* to jest.

pilões [pi'lõjʃ] *pl* ▷ **pilão**.

pilotagem [pilo'taʒẽ] *f* flying.

pilotar [4] [pilo'ta(x)] ◇ *vt* to steer. ◇ *vi* to steer.

pilotis [pilo'tʃiʃ] *mpl* ARQUIT stilts.

piloto [pi'lotu] ◇ *adj* [modelo] pilot. ◇ *m* **-1.** [ger] pilot; ~ **automático** automatic pilot. **-2.**

[de corrida] driver; ~ **de prova** racing driver. **-3.** [bico de gás] pilot light.

pílula ['pilula] *f* pill; ~ **anticoncepcional** contraceptive pill.

pimenta [pi'mẽnta] *f* **-1.** *CULIN* pepper. **-2.** *fig* [malícia] spite.

pimenta-do-reino [pi,mẽntadu'xejnu] (*pl* **pimentas-do-reino**) *f* black pepper.

pimenta-malagueta [pi,mẽntamala'geta] (*pl* **pimentas-malagueta**) *f* chilli pepper *UK*, chili pepper *US*.

pimentão [pimẽn'tãw] (*pl* **-ões**) *m*: ~ **verde/vermelho** green/red pepper; **estar/ficar um** ~ *fig* to be/go as red as a beetroot.

pimenteira [pimẽn'tejra] *f* **-1.** *BOT* pepper tree. **-2.** [recipiente] pepper pot.

pimpolho [pĩn'poʎu] *m* [criança] kid.

pinacoteca [pinako'tɛka] *f* **-1.** [coleção] art collection. **-2.** [museu] art gallery.

pináculo [pi'nakulu] *m* pinnacle.

pinça ['pĩnsa] *f* **-1.** *MED* forceps *(pl)*. **-2.** [de sobrancelha] tweezers *(pl)*.

pinçar [13] [pĩn'sa(x)] *vt* **-1.** [segurar] to grip (with pincers). **-2.** [sobrancelhas] to pluck. **-3.** *fig* [selecionar] to select.

píncaro ['pĩŋkaru] *m* **-1.** [cume] peak. **-2.** *fig* [apogeu] height.

pincel [pĩn'sɛw] (*pl* **-éis**) *m* brush; ~ **de barba** shaving brush.

pincelada [pĩnse'lada] *f* (brush) stroke.

pincelar [4] [pĩnse'la(x)] *vt* to paint.

pincenê [pĩnse'ne] *m* pince-nez.

pindaíba [pĩnda'iba] *f*: **estar na** ~ *fam* to be skint.

pinel [pi'nɛw] (*pl* **-éis**) *adj fam* crazy; **ficar** ~ to be driven crazy.

pinga ['pĩŋga] *f fam* [cachaça] booze.

pingado, da [pĩŋ'gadu, da] ◇ *adj* **-1.** [cheio de pingos]: ~ **de algo** splashed with sthg. **-2.** [leite] with a drop of coffee; [café] with a drop of milk. ◇ *m* [café] *coffee with a drop of milk*.

pingar [14] [pĩŋ'ga(x)] ◇ *vi* **-1.** [gotejar] to drip. **-2.** [chover] to spit. **-3.** [render] to trickle in. ◇ *vt* **-1.** [respingar] to spill. **-2.** [gotejar] to allow to drip through.

pingente [pĩn'ʒẽntʃi] *m* [objeto] pendant.

pingo ['pĩŋgu] *m* **-1.** [gota] drop. **-2.** [pequena quantidade]: **um** ~ **de** a little; ~ **de gente** [criança] little person. **-3.** [sinal ortográfico] dot; **pôr os** ~**s nos is** *fig* to dot the i's and cross the t's.

pingue-pongue [,pĩŋgi'põŋgi] (*pl* **pingue-pongues**) *m* ping-pong, table tennis.

pingüim [pĩŋ'gwĩ] (*pl* **-ns**) *m* penguin.

pinguinho [pĩŋ'giɲu] *m* **-1.** [pingo] droplet. **-2.** [pouquinho]: **um** ~ **(de)** a tiny bit (of).

pinha ['piɲa] *f* **-1.** [fruto do pinheiro] pine cone. **-2.** [fruta] pine nut.

pinhão [pi'ɲãw] (*pl* **-ões**) *m* pine nut.

pinheiral [piɲej'raw] (*pl* **-ais**) *m* pine forest.

pinheiro [pi'ɲejru] *m* pine tree.

pinho ['piɲu] *m* **-1.** *BOT* pine (tree). **-2.** [madeira] pine wood. **-3.** *fam* [violão] fiddle.

pinicada [pini'kada] *f* **-1.** [de ave] peck. **-2.** [de agulha, espinho] stab.

pinicar [12] [pini'ka(x)] *vt* **-1.** [comichar] to be itchy. **-2.** [bicar] to peck. **-3.** [cutucar] to jab.

pinimba [pi'nĩnba] *f fam* argument; **estar de** ~ **com alguém** to be at loggerheads with sb.

pino ['pinu] *m* **-1.** [peça] peg. **-2.** [*AUTO* - em motor] crankpin; [- tranca] lock; **bater** ~ to rattle; *fam fig* [estar mal] to fall apart. **-3.** [cume]: **a** ~ at the zenith; **sol a** ~ midday sun.

pinóia [pi'nɔja] *fam f* **-1.** [chatice]: **ser uma** ~ to be boring; **que** ~**!** what a bore! **-2.** [porcaria] junk. **-3.** [mentira]: **uma** ~**!** my foot!

pinote [pi'nɔtʃi] *m* buck; **dar** ~**s** to buck.

pinotear [15] [pino'tʃja(x)] *vi* to leap.

pinta ['pĩnta] *f* **-1.** [sinal] mole. **-2.** *fam* [aparência]: **o rapaz é boa** ~ the boy is looking good; **essa comida está com boa** ~ that food looks good; **ter** ~ **de algo** to look like sthg. **-3.** *fam* [indício]: **estar com** ~ **de (ser) difícil** to look (like being) difficult; **ela deu na** ~ **que ia nos assaltar** [demonstrar] she looked like she was going to attack us.

pinta-brava [pĩnta'brava] (*pl* **pintas-bravas**) *mf* [mau elemento] shady character.

pintado, da [pĩn'tadu, da] *adj* **-1.** [colorido - papel] coloured; [- parede, olhos, unhas] painted; [- face] painted, made-up; [- cabelo] dyed. **-2.** [sardento] freckled. **-3.** [idêntico]: **ser alguém** ~ to be the spitting image of sb.

pintar [4] [pĩn'ta(x)] ◇ *vt* **-1.** [ger] to paint. **-2.** [com tinta - ger] to paint; [- cabelo] to dye. **-3.** *fig* [conceber] to paint as. ◇ *vi* **-1.** *ARTE* to paint. **-2.** *fam* [aparecer] to turn up. **-3.** [exceder-se] to get overexcited; ~ **e bordar** *fig* to have a great time.

◆ **pintar-se** *vp* [maquilar-se] to make o.s. up.

pinto, ta ['pĩntu, ta] *m, f* **-1.** *ZOOL* chick; **ficar (molhado) como um** ~ to get soaked to the bone. **-2.** *mfam* [pênis] cock. **-3.** [coisa fácil]: **ser** ~ to be a pushover.

pintor, ra [pĩn'to(x), ra] (*mpl* **-es**, *fpl* **-s**) *m, f* painter.

pintura [pĩn'tura] *f* **-1.** *ARTE* painting; ~ **a óleo** oil painting. **-2.** [de casa etc] paintwork. **-3.** [maquiagem] make-up.

pio, pia ['piw, 'pia] *adj* **-1.** [devota] pious. **-2.** [caridoso] charitable.

◆ **pio** *m* [de ave] peep; **não dê um** ~**, senão atiro** not a peep, or else I'll shoot.

piões ['pjõjʃ] *pl* ▷ **pião**.

piolho ['pjoʎu] *m* louse.

pioneirismo [pjonej'riʒmu] *m* pioneering nature.

pioneiro, ra [pjo'nejru, ra] ◇ *adj* pioneering. ◇ *m, f* pioneer.

pior ['pjɔ(x)] (*pl* **-es**) ◇ *adj* **-1.** [comparativo]: ~ **(do que)** worse (than). **-2.** [superlativo]: **o/a** ~ **...** the worst ... ◇ *m*: **o** ~ **(de)** [inferior] the worst (of); **o** ~ **é que ...** the worst of it is that ... ◇ *f*: **o/a** ~ **(de)** the worst (of); **estar na** ~ to be in a jam;

levar a ~ to lose. <> *adv* [comparativo]: ~ **(do que)** worse (than); **ela está** ~ **de saúde** her health is worse.
piora ['pjɔra] *f* deterioration.
piorar [4] [pjo'ra(x)] *vi* to deteriorate.
pipa ['pipa] *f* **-1.** [vasilhame] barrel. **-2.** [de papel] kite; **soltar** ~ to fly a kite.
piparote [pipa'rɔtʃi] *m* flick.
pipi [pi'pi] *m fam* wee-wee *UK*, pee-pee *US*; **fazer** ~ to wee *UK*, to go pee-pee *US*.
pipilar [16] [pipi'la(x)] *vi* to chirp.
pipoca [pi'pɔka] *f* **-1.** [de milho] popcorn. **-2.** [em pele] blister.
pipocar [12] [pipo'ka(x)] *vi* **-1.** [estourar] to burst out. **-2.** [espocar] to crackle. **-3.** [surgir] to sprout up.
pipoqueiro, ra [pipo'keiru, ra] *m, f* [vendedor] popcorn seller.
◆ **pipoqueira** *f* [panela] popcorn-making pan.
pique ['piki] *m* **-1.** [brincadeira] catch. **-2.** [disposição] enthusiasm; **perder o** ~ to lose one's momentum; **ter** ~ to have what it takes. **-3.** [corte] notch. **-4.** *NÁUT*: **ir a** ~ to sink.
piquenique [,piki'niki] *m* picnic.
piquete [pi'ketʃi] *m* **-1.** [de greve] picket. **-2.** *MIL* squad.
pira ['pira] *f fam*: **dar o** ~ [ir-se embora] to scarper; [fugir] to abscond.
piração [pira'sãw] (*pl* **-ões**) *f fam* **-1.** [doidice] madness. **-2.** [ser excelente]: **aquele filme é uma** ~ that film is really great.
pirado, da [pi'radu, da] *adj* crazy.
pirâmide [pi'ramidʒi] *f* pyramid.
piranha [pi'rãɲa] *f* **-1.** [peixe] piranha. **-2.** *mfam pej* [mulher] hussy. **-3.** [prendedor de cabelo] hair clasp.
pirão [pi'rãw] (*pl* **-ões**) *m CULIN* cassava porridge.
pirar [4] [pi'ra(x)] *vi* **-1.** [endoidar] to go insane. **-2.** [fugir] to scarper.
pirata [pi'rata] <> *adj* pirate. <> *mf* pirate.
pirataria [pirata'ria] *f* [roubo] piracy.
piratear [pira'tea(x)] *vt*: ~ **um programa** to pirate a program.
Pireneus [pire'newʃ] *n*: **os** ~ the Pyrenees.
pires ['piriʃ] *m inv* saucer.
pirilampo [piri'lãnpu] *m* glow-worm.
pirotecnia [pirotek'nia] *f* **-1.** [arte] pyrotechnics (*sg*). **-2.** [fabricação] fireworks manufacturing.
pirotécnico, ca [piro'tɛkniku, ka] <> *adj* [com fogos de artifício] firework (*antes de subst*). <> *m, f* [fabricante] firework manufacturer.
pirraça [pi'xasa] *f*: **fazer algo por** ~ to do sthg out of spite; **fazer** ~ **a alguém** [fazer desfeita] to spite sb.
pirracento, ta [pixa'sẽntu, ta] *adj* spiteful.
pirralho, lha [pi'xaʎu, ʎa] *m, f* child.
pirueta [pi'rweta] *f* pirouette.
pirulito [piru'litu] *m* **-1.** [bala] lollipop. **-2.** *fam* [pênis] willy.
pisada [pi'zada] *f* **-1.** [passo] footstep; **dar uma** ~ **em algo/alguém** to tread on sthg/sb. **-2.** [pegada] footprint.
pisão [pi'sãw] (*pl* **-ões**) *m* [pisadela]: **dar um** ~ **no pé de alguém** to tread on sb's toes.
pisar [4] [pi'za(x)] <> *vt* **-1.** to tread on. **-2.** [esmagar] to crush. **-3.** [percorrer] to set foot on. <> *vi* **-1.** [andar]: ~ **(em)** to walk *ou* tread (on); **saber onde** ~ *fig* to know what one is getting into. **-2.**: ~ **em** [tocar com os pés] to step on; [ir, vir] to set foot in; [humilhar] to crush; ⊳ **bola**, **ovos**.
piscadela [piʃka'dɛla] *f* **-1.** [ato reflexo] blink. **-2.** [sinal] wink; **dar uma** ~ to give a wink.
pisca-pisca [,piʃka'piʃka] (*pl* **pisca-piscas**) *m AUTO* indicator.
piscar [12] [piʃ'ka(x)] <> *vt* [olho] to blink; ~ **o olho para alguém** [dar sinal] to wink at sb. <> *vi* **-1.** [pessoa, olho] to wink. **-2.** [trocar sinais]: ~ **para alguém** to wink at sb. **-3.** [tremeluzir] to twinkle. <> *m* twinkling; **num** ~ **de olhos** in a twinkling of an eye.
pisciano, na [pi'sjãnu, na] <> *adj*: **ser** ~ to be a Piscean. <> *m, f* Piscean.
piscicultura [pisikuw'tura] *f* fish farming, pisciculture.
piscina [pi'sina] *f* swimming pool.
piso ['pizu] *m* **-1.** [ger] floor. **-2.** [revestimento] flooring. **-3.** [salário]: ~ **(salarial)** minimum (professional) wage.
pisotear [15] [pizo'tʃja(x)] *vt* **-1.** [pisar] to trample (on). **-2.** [humilhar] to trample over.
píssico, ca ['pisiku, ka] <> *adj* crazy. <> *m, f* lunatic.
pista ['piʃta] *f* **-1.** [vestígio] trace. **-2.** [encalço]: **na** ~ **de** in pursuit of, on the trail of. **-3.** *fig* [informação] clue. **-4.** [de rua, estrada] track. **-5.** *AERON* runway. **-6.** [*ESP* - de automobilismo, atletismo] track; [- de esqui] piste; [- de equitação] ring; [- de tênis] court. **-7.** [de dança] floor.
pistache [piʃ'taʃi], **pistacho** [piʃ'taʃu] *m* pistachio.
pistola [piʃ'tɔla] *f* **-1.** [arma] pistol. **-2.** [para pintar] (spray) gun.
pistolão [piʃto'lãw] (*pl* **-ões**) *m* **-1.** [pessoa] connection. **-2.** [recomendação] recommendation.
pistoleiro, ra [piʃto'lejru, ra] *m, f* [criminoso] gunman.
◆ **pistoleira** *f mfam* [vagabunda] tart.
pistom [piʃ'tõ] (*pl* **-ns**) *m* **-1.** [instrumento] trumpet. **-2.** [de motor] piston.
pitada [pi'tada] *f* pinch.
pitanga [pi'tãŋga] *f* (red Brazil) cherry.
pitar [4] [pi'ta(x)] <> *vi* to smoke. <> *vt* to smoke.
piteira [pi'tejra] *f* cigarette-holder.
pito ['pitu] *m* **-1.** [cachimbo] pipe. **-2.** *fam* [repreensão] talking-to; **dar um** ~ **em alguém** to tell sb off; **levar um** ~ **de alguém** to be told off by sb. **-3.** *loc*: **sossegar o** ~ *fam* to calm down.
pitonisa [pito'niza] *f* fortune teller.
pitoresco, ca [pito'reʃku, ka] <> *adj* picturesque. <> *m* attraction.
pituitária [pituj'taria] *f ANAT* pituitary.

pivete [pi'vɛtʃi] *m* child thief.

pivô [pi'vo] *m* **-1.** [de dente] pivot. **-2.** *fig* [suporte] pivot. **-3.** *fig* [agente principal] central figure. **-4.** [jogador] centre.

pixaim [piʃa'ĩ] (*pl* **-ns**) ◇ *adj* frizzy. ◇ *m* frizzy hair.

pixote [pi'ʃɔtʃi] *m* small child.

pizza ['pitsa] *f* pizza.

pizzaria [pitsa'ria] *f* pizzeria.

plá [pla] *m*: **ter** *ou* **bater um ~ com alguém** to have a chat with sb.

placa ['plaka] *f* **-1.** [ger] plaque. **-2.** [lâmina] sheet. **-3.** [aviso] sign; **~ de sinalização** road sign. **-4.** *AUTO* number plate ***UK***, license plate ***US***; **~ fria** false number plate. **-5.** *COMPUT* & *ELECTRON* board; **~ de vídeo** video card. **-6.** [na pele] blotch.

placa-mãe ['plakamãj] (*pl* **placas-mãe** *ou* **placas-mães**) *f COMPUT* motherboard.

placar [pla'ka(x)] *m* **-1.** [escore] score. **-2.** [marcador] scoreboard.

placebo [pla'sebu] *m* placebo.

placenta [pla'sẽnta] *f ANAT* placenta.

placidez [plasi'deʒ] *f* quietness.

plácido, da ['plasidu, da] *adj* **-1.** [pessoa, olhar, semblante] placid. **-2.** [lugar, dia, vida] quiet.

plagiador, ra [plaʒja'do(x), ra] *m, f* plagiarist.

plagiar [16] [pla'ʒja(x)] *vt* to plagiarize.

plagiário, ria [ju, pla'ʒjarju, rja] *m, f* plagiarist.

plágio ['plaʒju] *m* plagiarism.

plaina ['plãjna] *f* [ferramenta] plane.

planador [plana'do(x)] (*pl* **-es**) *m* glider.

planalto [pla'nawtu] *m* plateau.

◆ **Planalto** *m* [palácio presidencial] president's office.

planar [4] [pla'na(x)] *vi* to glide.

planejador, ra [planeʒa'do(x), ra] *m, f* planner.

planejamento [planeʒa'mẽntu] *m* planning; **~ familiar** family planning.

planejar [4] [plane'ʒa(x)] *vt* **-1.** [ger] to plan. **-2.** *ARQUIT* to design.

planeta [pla'neta] *m* planet.

planetário, a [plane'tarju] *adj* planetary.

◆ **planetário** *m* planetarium.

plangente [plãn'ʒẽntʃi] *adj* plaintive.

planície [pla'nisji] *f* plain.

planificar [12] [planifi'ka(x)] *vt* **-1.** [ger] to plan out. **-2.** [tornar plano] to level.

planilha [pla'niʎa] *f* **-1.** [formulário] table. **-2.** *COMPUT* spreadsheet.

plano, na ['plãnu, na] ◇ *adj* **-1.** [superfície] flat. **-2.** [liso] smooth. ◇ *m* **-1.** [ger] plan; **~ piloto** outline plan. **-2.** [superfície plana] level surface. **-3.** [posição]: **em primeiro/segundo ~** in the foregound/background; **para ela isso fica em segundo ~** *fig* for her this takes second place. **-4.** [nível] level. **-5.** [seguro]: **~ de saúde** health plan. **-6.** *GEOM* plane.

planta ['plãnta] *f* **-1.** *BIOL* plant. **-2.** *ANAT*: **~ do pé** sole of the foot. **-3.** *ARQUIT* plan.

plantação [plãnta'sãw] *m* **-1.** [ato] planting. **-2.** [terreno] plantation. **-3.** [produtos] crops *(pl)*.

plantado, da [plãn'tadu, da] *adj* planted; **deixar alguém ~ em algum lugar** to leave sb standing somewhere.

plantão [plãn'tãw] (*pl* **-ões**) *m* **-1.** [serviço - diurno] duty; [- noturno] night duty; **estar de ~** to be on duty; **médico de ~** duty doctor. **-2.** [plantonista] person on duty.

plantar [4] [plãn'ta(x)] *vt* **-1.** [planta, árvore] to plant. **-2.** [semear] to sow. **-3.** [fincar] to drive in. **-4.** *fig* [estabelecer] to establish. **-5.** [incutir] to inspire. **-6.** [pôr] to set up.

◆ **plantar-se** *vp* [pôr-se] to remain.

plantões [plãn'tõjʃ] *pl* ▷ **plantão**.

plantonista [plãnto'niʃta] *mf* person on duty.

plaqueta [pla'keta] *f* **-1.** [placa pequena] small plaque, plaquette. **-2.** *AUTO* licensing badge. **-3.** *COMPUT* chip.

plasma ['plaʒma] *m* plasma.

plasmar [4] [plaʒ'ma(x)] *vt* to shape.

plástico, ca ['plaʃtʃiku, ka] *adj* plastic.

◆ **plástico** *m* [matéria] plastic; **de ~** plastic.

◆ **plástica** *f* **-1.** [cirurgia] plastic surgery; **fazer plástica** to have plastic surgery. **-2.** [corpo] build.

plastificado, da [plaʃtʃifi'kadu, da] *adj* laminated.

plastificar [12] [plaʃtʃifi'ka(x)] *vt* to laminate.

plataforma [plata'fɔxma] *f* **-1.** [ger] platform; **~ de exploração de petróleo** oil rig; **~ de lançamento** launch pad. **-2.** *GEOGR* shelf.

platéia [pla'tɛja] *f* **-1.** [espaço] stalls *(pl)* ***UK***, orchestra ***US***. **-2.** [público] audience.

platina [pla'tʃina] *f* [metal] platinum.

platinado, da [platʃi'nadu, da] *adj* platinum blond *(antes de subst)*.

◆ **platinado** *m AUTO* contact point.

platô [pla'to] *m* plateau.

platônico, ca [pla'toniku, ka] *adj* platonic.

plausível [plaw'zivɛw] (*pl* **-eis**) *adj* [aceitável] plausible.

playback [plej'bɛki] *m MÚS* playback.

playboy [plej'bɔj] *m* playboy.

playground [plej'grawndʒi] *m* playground.

plebe ['plɛbi] *f* common people.

plebeu, béia [ple'bew, bɛja] ◇ *adj* plebeian. ◇ *m, f* plebeian.

plebiscito [plebi'situ] *m* plebiscite.

plêiade ['plejadʒi] *f* [reunião] soirée.

pleitear [15] [plej'tʃja(x)] *vt* **-1.** [diligenciar] to strive for. **-2.** *JUR* to contest. **-3.** [concorrer a] to compete for.

pleito ['plejtu] *m* **-1.** *JUR* legal dispute, lawsuit. **-2.** [eleição]: **~ (eleitoral)** election.

plenamente [ˌplena'mẽntʃi] *adv* fully.

plenária [ple'naria] *f* plenary (session).

plenário [ple'narju] *m* **-1.** [assembléia] plenary session. **-2.** [local] chamber.

plenipotenciário, ria [plenipotẽn'sjarju, rja] ◇ *adj* plenipotentiary. ◇ *m, f* plenipotentiary.

plenitude [pleni'tudʒi] *f* fulfilment.

pleno, na ['plenu, na] *adj* **-1.** [cheio]: **~ de** full of.

-2. [total] complete; **em plena luz do dia** in broad daylight; **em plena rua** smack in the middle of the street; **em plena forma** on top form; **em ~ verão** in high summer; **~s poderes** full powers.

pleonasmo [pljo'naʒmu] *m* pleonasm.

pletora [ple'tɔra] *f fig* plethora.

pleurisia [plewri'zia] *f* pleurisy.

plissado, da [pli'sadu, da] *adj* pleated.

plugado, da [plu'gadu, da] *adj* **-1.** [aparelho] plugged. **-2.** [pessoa]: **passar o dia ~ no computador** to spend the day glued to the computer.

plugar [plu'ga(x)] *vt* to plug.

plug-in ['plugĩn] *m* COMPUT plug-in.

plugue ['plugi] *m* plug.

pluma ['pluma] *f* **-1.** [de ave] feather. **-2.** [para escrever] quill. **-3.** [adorno] plume.

plumagem [plu'maʒẽ] *f* plumage.

plural [plu'raw] (*pl* **-ais**) <> *adj* plural. <> *m* plural.

pluralidade [plurali'dadʒi] *f* **-1.** [diversidade] diversity. **-2.** [maioria] majority.

pluralismo [plura'liʒmu] *m* **-1.** [diversidade] diversity. **-2.** POL pluralism.

pluralista [plura'liʃta] *adj* **-1.** [diverso] diverse. **-2.** POL pluralist.

Plutão [plu'tãw] *n* Pluto.

plutocracia [plutokra'sia] *f* plutocracy.

plutocrata [pluto'krata] *mf* plutocrat.

plutônio [plu'tonju] *m* plutonium.

pluvial [plu'vjaw] (*pl* **-ais**) *adj* pluvial, rain *(antes de subst).*

pluviométrico, ca [pluvio'mɛtriku, ka] *adj* rainfall *(antes de subst).*

PM (*abrev de* **Polícia Militar**) *f* military police.

PMDB (*abrev de* **Partido do Movimento Democrático Brasileiro**) *m* Brazilian Party for Democratic Movement, *the largest party of the centre.*

PNB (*abrev de* **Produto Nacional Bruto**) *m* GNP.

pneu [pi'new] *m* **-1.** AUTO tyre *UK*, tire *US*; **~ sobressalente** spare tyre *UK*, spare tire *US*. **-2.** *fam* [gordura] spare tyre *UK*, spare tire *US*.

pneumático, ca [pinew'matʃiku, ka] *adj* pneumatic.

◆ **pneumático** *m* [pneu] tyre *UK*, tire *US*.

pneumonia [pinewmu'nia] *f* pneumonia.

pó ['pɔ] *m* **-1.** [poeira] dust; **tirar o ~ de algo** to dust sthg. **-2.** [substância pulverizada] powder; **em ~** powdered. **-3.** [pó-de-arroz] face powder. **-4.** *fam* [cocaína] snow.

pô [po] *interj* **-1.** *fam* [mostrando irritação] damn it! **-2.** [mostrando surpresa] blimey! *UK*, gee whiz! *US*.

pobre ['pɔbri] <> *adj* **-1.** [ger] poor. **-2.** [escasso]: **~ de/em algo** lacking in sthg. **-3.** *(antes do subst)* [digno de pena] poor. <> *m* [pessoa] poor person; **os ~s** the poor.

pobre-diabo [,pɔbri'dʒjabu] (*pl* **pobres-diabos**) *m* poor devil.

pobretão, tona [pobre'tãw, tona] (*mpl* **-ões**, *fpl* **-s**) *m, f* **-1.** [pessoa muito pobre] pauper. **-2.** *euf* poor thing.

pobreza [po'breza] *m* **-1.** [miséria] poverty. **-2.** [escassez]: **~ de** *ou* **em algo** lack of sthg; **~ de espírito** simplicity.

poça ['pɔsa] *f*: **~ (d'água)** puddle; **~ de sangue** pool of blood.

poção [po'sãw] (*pl* **-ões**) *f* potion.

pocilga [po'siwga] *f* **-1.** [chiqueiro] pigsty. **-2.** *fig* [lugar imundo] hovel.

poço ['posu] *f* **-1.** [cavidade] well; **~ de petróleo** oil well; **ir ao fundo do ~** *fig* to sink to the depths of despair. **-2.** [qualidade]: **ser um ~ de algo** *fig* to be a fount of sthg.

poda ['pɔda] *f* **-1.** [ato] pruning. **-2.** [época] pruning season.

podadeira [poda'dejra] *f* pruning knife.

podar [4] [po'da(x)] *vt* to prune.

pó-de-arroz [,pɔdʒja'xoʃ] (*pl* **pós-de-arroz**) *m* face powder.

poder [36] [po'de(x)] <> *m* **-1.** [político, influência] power; **estar no ~** to be in power; **~ de compra** purchasing power; **não tenho ~ nenhum** I'm powerless. **-2.** [possessão] power; **estar em ~ de alguém** to be in sb's power; **ter em seu ~ algo** to have sthg within one's power. <> *v aux* **-1.** [ser capaz de]: **~ fazer algo** to be able to do sthg; **posso fazê-lo** I can do it; **posso ajudar?** can I help?, may I help?; **você podia tê-lo feito antes** you could have done it earlier; **não posso mais!** [em relação a cansaço] I've had enough!; [em relação a comida] I'm full! **-2.** [estar autorizado para]: **~ fazer algo** to be allowed to do sthg; **posso fumar?** may I smoke?; **você não pode estacionar aqui** you can't park here; **não pude sair ontem** I wasn't allowed (to go) out yesterday. **-3.** [ser capaz moralmente] can; **não podemos magoar o gato** we can't hurt the cat. **-4.** [exprime possibilidade]: **você podia ter vindo de ônibus** you could have come by bus; **cuidado que você pode se machucar!** be careful, you might hurt yourself! **-5.** [exprime indignação, queixa]: **não pode ser!** this is outrageous!; **você podia ter nos avisado** you could have warned us!; **pudera!** I wish! <> *v impess* [ser possível]: **pode não ser verdade** it might not be true; **pode acontecer a qualquer um** it could happen to anybody; **pode ser que chova** it might rain.

◆ **poder com** *v + prep* **-1.** [suportar] to bear; **não posso com mentirosos** I cannot bear liars. **-2.** [rival, adversário] to bear. **-3.** [peso] to carry; **você não pode com tanto peso** you can't carry all that weight.

poderio [pode'riw] *m* power.

poderoso, sa [pode'rozu, za] *adj* **-1.** [influente] powerful. **-2.** [eficaz] powerful.

◆ **poderosos** *mpl*: **os ~** the powers that be.

pódio ['pɔdʒju] *m* podium.

podre ['podri] <> *adj* **-1.** [ger] rotten. **-2.** *fig* [corrupto] corrupt. **-3.** *fig* [cheio]: **estou ~ (de cansaço)** I am dog-tired; **~ de gripe** full of flu; **~ de rico** filthy rich. <> *m* **-1.** [parte]: **o ~ da maçã** the bad part of the apple. **-2.** *fig* [defeito] dark secret.

podridão [podri'dãw] (*pl* **-ões**) *f* **-1.** [estado de podre] decay. **-2.** *fig* [corrupção] corruption.

poeira ['pwejra] *f* dust; ~ **radioativa** fallout.

poeirento, ta [pwej'rẽntu, ta] *adj* dusty.

poema ['pwema] *m* poem.

poente ['pwẽntʃi] ◇ *adj* [sol] setting. ◇ *m* **-1.** [ocidente] west. **-2.** [do sol] sunset.

poesia [pwi'zia] *f* **-1.** [arte] poetry. **-2.** [poema] poem. **-3.** [encanto] charm.

poeta, tisa ['pwɛta, tʃiza] *m, f* poet.

poético, ca ['pwɛtʃiku, ka] *adj* poetic.

◆ **poética** *f* ARTE poetics *(sg)*.

poetizar [4] [pwetʃi'za(x)] ◇ *vi* [fazer versos] to write poetry. ◇ *vt* [tornar poético] to poeticize.

pogrom [po'grõ] *m* pogrom.

pois ['pojʃ] *conj* **-1.** [portanto] therefore. **-2.** [mas] well. **-3.** [porque] as.

◆ **pois bem** *loc adv* well then.

◆ **pois então** *loc adv* well then.

◆ **pois é** *loc adv* indeed.

◆ **pois não** ◇ *loc adv* [em loja, restaurante]: ~ **não?** can I help you? ◇ *interj* of course!

◆ **pois sim** *interj*: ~ **sim!** certainly not!, yeah right!

polaco, ca [po'laku, ka] ◇ *adj* Polish. ◇ *m, f* Pole.

◆ **polaco** *m* [língua] Polish.

polainas [po'lãjnaʃ] *fpl* gaiters.

polar [po'la(x)] *adj* polar.

polaridade [polari'dadʒi] *f* polarity.

polarizar [4] [polari'za(x)] *vt* to polarize.

polca ['pɔwka] *f* polka.

polegada [pole'gada] *f* inch.

polegar [pole'ga(x)] (*pl* **-es**) *m* thumb.

poleiro [po'lejru] *m* perch.

polêmico, ca [po'lemiku, ka] *adj* controversial.

◆ **polêmica** *f* controversy.

polemista [pole'miʃta] *adj* argumentative.

polemizar [4] [polemi'za(x)] *vi*: ~ **sobre algo** to debate on sthg.

pólen ['pɔlẽ] *m* pollen.

polenta [po'lẽnta] *f* polenta.

polia [po'lia] *f* pulley.

poliamida [polja'mida] *f* polyamide.

polichinelo [poliʃi'nɛlu] *m* Mr Punch.

polícia [po'lisja] ◇ *f* [corporação] police, police force; ~ **de choque** riot police; ~ **federal** federal police; ~ **militar** state police (force); ~ **rodoviária** traffic police. ◇ *mf* [policial] police officer.

policial [poli'sjaw] (*pl* **-ais**) ◇ *adj* police *(antes de subst)*. ◇ *mf* police officer.

policiamento [polisja'mẽntu] *m* policing.

policiar [16] [poli'sja(x)] *vt* **-1.** [vigiar] to police. **-2.** [controlar] to control.

◆ **policiar-se** *vp* [controlar-se] to control o.s.

policlínica [poli'klinika] *f* general hospital.

policultura [polikuw'tura] *f* mixed farming.

polidez [poli'deʒ] *f* [cortesia] politeness.

polido, da [po'lidu, da] *adj* **-1.** [cortês] polite. **-2.** [liso] polished. **-3.** [lustroso] shiny.

poliéster [po'ljɛʃte(x)] *m* polyester.

poliestireno [poljeʃtʃi'renu] *m* polystyrene.

polietileno [poljetʃi'lenu] *m* polythene.

poligamia [poli'gamia] *f* polygamy.

polígamo, ma [po'ligamu, ma] *adj* polygamous.

poliglota [poli'glɔta] ◇ *adj* polyglot. ◇ *m* polyglot.

polígono [po'ligonu] *m* GEOM polygon.

polimento [poli'mẽntu] *m* **-1.** [lustração] polishing. **-2.** *fig* [finura] refinement.

polinização [poliniza'sãw] (*pl* **-ões**) *f* pollination.

polinizar [4] [polini'za(x)] ◇ *vt* to pollinate. ◇ *vi* to pollinate.

polinômio [poli'nomju] *m* MAT polynomial.

poliomielite [poljo'mjelitʃi] *f* MED polio(myelitis).

pólipo ['pɔlipu] *m* MED polyp.

polir [60] [po'li(x)] *vt* **-1.** [ger] to polish. **-2.** *fig* [aprimorar - pessoa] to refine; [- linguagem] to polish up.

polissílabo [poli'silabu] (*f* **-ba**) [ba] *adj* polysyllabic.

◆ **polissílabo** *m* polysyllable.

politécnica [pɔli'tɛknika] *f* polytechnic.

política [po'litʃika] *f* ▷ **político**.

politicagem [politʃi'kaʒẽ] *f* politicking.

político, ca [po'litʃiku, ka] *adj* **-1.** POL political. **-2.** *fig* [hábil] astute.

◆ **político** *m* politician.

◆ **política** *f* **-1.** [ciência] politics *(pl)*. **-2.** [programa] policy; **politica econômica** economic policy; **politica de boa vizinhança** good neighbour policy *UK*, good neighbor policy *US*. **-3.** *fig* [habilidade] astuteness.

politiqueiro, ra [politʃi'kejru, ra] *pej* ◇ *adj* politicking. ◇ *m, f* political wheeler-dealer.

politização [politʃiza'sãw] (*pl* **-ões**) *f* politicization.

politizar [4] [politʃi'za(x)] *vt* to politicize.

◆ **politizar-se** *vp* to become politically aware.

polivalente [poliva'lẽntʃi] *adj* **-1.** [versátil] versatile. **-2.** MED polyvalent.

pólo ['pɔlu] *m* **-1.** [ger] pole. **-2.** *fig* [extremo] side. **-3.** ASTRON: ~ **magnético** magnetic pole. **-4.** [concentração] hub; ~ **petroquímico** petrochemicals complex. **-5.** ESP polo; ~ **aquático** water polo.

Polônia [po'lonja] *n* Poland.

polpa ['powpa] *f* pulp.

polpudo, da [pow'pudu, da] *adj* **-1.** [fruta] fleshy. **-2.** [vultuoso] sizeable.

poltrão, ona [pow'trãw, ɔna] (*mpl* **-ões**, *fpl* **-s**) *m, f* coward.

poltrona [pow'trona] *f* armchair.

poluente [po'lwẽntʃi] ◇ *adj* pollutant. ◇ *m* pollutant.

poluição [poluj'sãw] *f* pollution.

poluidor, ra [poluj'do(x), ra] *adj* polluting.

poluir [74] [po'lwi(x)] *vt* **-1.** [sujar] to pollute. **-2.** *fig* [corromper] to corrupt.

polvilhar [4] [powvi'ʎa(x)] *vt* **-1.** [cobrir de pó] to powder. **-2.** [salpicar] to sprinkle.

polvilho [pow'viʎu] *m* **-1.** [pó] powder. **-2.** [farinha] manioc flour.

polvo ['powvu] *m* octopus.
pólvora ['pɔwvora] *f* gunpowder; **descobrir a ~** *fig irôn* to do sthg highly original.
polvorosa [powvo'rɔza] *f*: **em ~** [agitado] in a flap; [desarrumado] in a mess.
pomada [po'mada] *f* ointment.
pomar [po'ma(x)] (*pl* **-es**) *m* orchard.
pombo, ba ['põnbu, ba] *m, f* dove, pigeon.
◆ **pomba** *interj* for heaven's sake!
pombo-correio [,põnbuko'xeju] (*pl* **pombos-correios**) *m* **-1.** [ave] carrier pigeon. **-2.** *fig* [pessoa] go-between.
pomo ['pomu] *m* pome; **~ de discórdia** bone of contention.
pomo-de-Adão [,pomudʒja'dãw] (*pl* **pomos-de-Adão**) *m* Adam's apple.
pompa ['põnpa] *f* splendour.
pomposo, osa [põn'pozu, ɔza] *adj* ostentatious.
ponche ['põnʃi] *m* punch.
poncheira [põn'ʃejra] *f* punchbowl.
poncho ['põnʃu] *m* poncho.
ponderação [põndera'sãw] *f* **-1.** [reflexão] reflection. **-2.** [prudência] care.
ponderado, da [põnde'radu, da] *adj* cautious.
ponderar [4] [põnde'ra(x)] ◇ *vi* **-1.** [refletir] to reflect. **-2.** [argumentar] to hold forth. ◇ *vt* **-1.** [avaliar] to weigh up. **-2.** [considerar] to consider.
pônei ['ponej] *m* pony.
ponta ['põnta] *f* **-1.** [extremidade] end; **na ~ do pé** on tiptoe; **na ~ do dedo** at one's fingertips. **-2.** [bico] point. **-3.** [canto] corner. **-4.** [vértice] apex. **-5.** *fig* [quantidade]: **estou com uma ~ de fome** I'm a touch hungry. **-6.** [de cigarro] cigarette end. **-7.** *CINE* & *TEATRO*: **fazer uma ~** to have a walk-on part. **-8.** *COM*: **~ de estoque** excess stock. **-9.** *GEOGR*: **~ de terra** point. **-10.** *loc*: **saber na ~ da língua** to have on the tip of one's tongue.
ponta-cabeça [,põntaka'besa] *f*: **de ~** head first.
pontada [põn'tada] *f* **-1.** [dor] twinge. **-2.** [ferroada] sting.
ponta-de-lança [,põntadʒi'lãnsa] (*pl* **pontas-de-lança**) *mf FUT* attacker.
ponta-direita [,põntadʒi'rejta] (*pl* **pontas-direitas**) *mf FUT* right-winger.
ponta-esquerda [,põntajʃ'kexda] (*pl* **pontas-esquerdas**) *mf FUT* left-winger.
pontal [põn'taw] (*pl* **-ais**) *m* [de terra] promontory.
pontão [põn'tãw] (*pl* **-ões**) *m* [plataforma] pontoon.
pontapé [põnta'pɛ] *m* **-1.** [chute] kick; **dar um ~ em alguém** to kick sb. **-2.** *fig* [rejeição]: **ele levou um ~ da namorada** his girlfriend kicked him out.
pontaria [põnta'ria] *f* aim.
ponte ['põntʃi] *f* **-1.** [ger] bridge; **~ levadiça** drawbridge; **~ suspensa** *ou* **pênsil** suspension bridge. **-2.** *AERON*: **~ aérea** air lift. **-3.** *MED*: **~ de safena** (heart) bypass operation.
pontear [15] [põn'tʃja(x)] *vt* **-1.** [pontilhar] to dot. **-2.** [dar pontos] to sew.
ponteira [põn'tejra] *f* tip.
ponteiro [põn'tejru] *m* **-1.** [de velocímetro] pointer. **-2.** [de bússola] needle. **-3.** [de relógio] hand.
pontiagudo, da [põntʃja'gudu, da] *adj* pointed.
pontificar [12] [põntʃifi'ka(x)] *vi* to pontificate.
pontífice [põn'tʃifisi] *m* pope.
pontilhado, da [põntʃi'ʎadu, da] ◇ *adj* dotted. ◇ *m* [conjunto de pontos] dotted line.
pontilhar [4] [põntʃi'ʎa(x)] *vt* to dot.
pontinha [põn'tʃiɲa] *f*: **estar/ficar com uma ~ de inveja de algo/alguém** to feel a little envious of sthg/sb.
ponto ['põntu] *m* **-1.** [ger] point; **~ final** terminus; **~ de ônibus** bus stop; **~ de táxi** taxi rank; **~ pacífico** established fact. **-2.** [costura, operação] stitch; **~ de meia** stocking stitch; **~ de tricô** garter stitch; **dar ~s** to put in stitches. **-3.** [sinal] spot. **-4.** [pontuação]: **~ (final)** full stop *UK*, period *US*; **dois ~s** colon; **~ de interrogação/exclamação** question/exclamation mark. **-5.** [mancha] mark. **-6.** [livro de presença] register; **assinar o ~** to sign in; **~ facultativo** optional day off. **-7.** [de calda] consistency. **-8.** [matéria escolar] topic. **-9.** *fig* [fim]: **pôr um ~ final em algo** to put and end to sthg. **-10.** *MÚS* (religious) chant. **-11.** *GEOGR*: **~ cardeal** cardinal point. **-12.** *AUTO*: **~ morto** neutral. **-13.** [espirit] spirit. **-14.** [boca-de-fumo] drugs den. **-15.** [traço]: **~ fraco** weak point. **-16.** *loc*: **dormir no ~** to miss the boat; **entregar os ~s** to give up; **não dar ~ sem nó** to look after number one.
◆ **a ponto de** *loc adv* on the point of.
pontocom [põntukõ] *adj ECON*: **empresa ~** dotcom company.
ponto-de-venda [,põntudʒi'venda] (*pl* **pontos-de-venda**) *m COM* outlet.
pontões [põn'tõjʃ] *pl* ▻ **pontão**.
ponto-e-vírgula [,pontwi'vixgula] (*pl* **ponto-e-vírgulas**) *m* semicolon.
pontuação [põntwa'sãw] (*pl* **-ões**) *f* punctuation.
pontual [põn'twaw] (*pl* **-ais**) *adj* punctual.
pontualidade [põntwali'dadʒi] *f* punctuality.
pontuar [4] [põn'twa(x)] ◇ *vi* to punctuate. ◇ *vt* to punctuate.
pontudo, da [põn'tudu, da] *adj* pointed.
poodle ['pudow] *m* poodle.
pool [puw] *m* pool.
POP (*abrev de* **Post Office Protocol**) *m* POP.
popa ['popa] *f* stern.
população [popula'sãw] (*pl* **-ões**) *f* population; **~ operária** working population; **~ escolar** school population.
populacional [populasjo'naw] (*pl* **-ais**) *adj* population *(antes de subst)*.
popular [popu'la(x)] (*pl* **-es**) ◇ *adj* popular. ◇ *m* [homem da rua] ordinary person.
popularidade [populari'dadʒi] *f* popularity.
popularizar [4] [populari'za(x)] *vt* to popularize.
◆ **popularizar-se** *vp* to become popular.
populismo [popu'liʒmu] *m POL* populism.
populista [popu'liʃta] *adj* populist.
populoso, osa [popu'lozu, ɔza] *adj* populous.

pôquer ['poke(x)] *m* poker.

por [po(x)] *prep* **-1.** [indica causa] because of, due to; **foi ~ sua causa** it was your fault; **~ falta de fundos** due to lack of funds; **~ hábito** through force of habit. **-2.** [indica objetivo] for; **lutar ~ algo** to fight for sthg. **-3.** [indica meio, modo, agente] by; **foi escrito pela Cristina** it was written by Cristina; **~ correio/fax** by post/fax; **~ escrito** in writing; **~ avião** [carta] (by) air mail. **-4.** [relativo a tempo] for; **ele partiu ~ duas semanas** he went away for two weeks. **-5.** [relativo a lugar] through; **entramos no Brasil pelo Paraguai** we crossed into Brazil via Paraguay; **está ~ aí** it's around there somewhere; **~ onde você vai?** which way are you going?; **vamos ~ aqui** we're going this way. **-6.** [relativo a troca, preço] for; **paguei apenas 20 reais ~ este casaco** I only paid 20 reals for this coat; **troquei o carro velho ~ um novo** I exchanged my old car for a new one. **-7.** [indica distribuição] per; **25 ~ cento** 25 per cent; **são 100 reais ~ dia/mês** it's 100 reals per day/month. **-8.** [em locuções]: **~ que** why; **~ que (é que) ...?** why (is it that) ...?; **~ mim tudo bem!** that's fine by me!

pôr [45] ['po(x)] *vt* **-1.** [ger] to put; **~ a mesa** to set the table; **~ a roupa** to put on clothes; **~ defeito em tudo** to find fault with everything; **~ a culpa em alguém** to put the blame on sb; **~ o dedo na ferida** *fig* to touch a raw nerve. **-2.** [incutir]: **não lhe ponha medo!** don't frighten him! **-3.** [guardar] to keep. **-4.** [desovar] to lay.

◆ **pôr-se** *vp* **-1.** [colocar-se] to stand; **~-se de pé** to stand up. **-2.** [sol] to set. **-3.** [começar]: **~-se a fazer algo** to start doing sthg; **~-se a caminho** to set off.

porão [po'rãw] (*pl* **-ões**) *f* **-1.** [de navio] hold. **-2.** [de casa] basement.

porca ['pɔxka] *f* **-1.** *ZOOL* sow. **-2.** [parafuso] nut.

porcalhão, lhona [poxka'ʎãw, ʎɔna] (*mpl* **-ões**, *fpl* **-s**) ◇ *adj* **-1.** [imundo] filthy. **-2.** [que faz sujeira] messy. **-3.** [que trabalha mal] bungling. ◇ *m, f* **-1.** [imundo] filthy person. **-2.** [quem faz sujeira] messy person. **-3.** [quem trabalha mal] bungler.

porção [pox'sãw] (*pl* **-ões**) *f* [parte] portion; **uma ~ de** a portion of; [grande quantidade] a lot of.

porcaria [poxka'ria] ◇ *adj* [sem valor] rubbishy. ◇ *f* **-1.** [imundície] filth. **-2.** *fig* [coisa malfeita] piece of junk. **-3.** *fig* [coisa sem valor] rubbish.

porcelana [poxse'lãna] *f* porcelain.

porcentagem [poxsẽn'taʒẽ] (*pl* **-ns**) *f* percentage.

porco, ca ['poxku, ka] ◇ *adj* **-1.** [suja] dirty. **-2.** [grosseiro] coarse. **-3.** [malfeito] shoddy. ◇ *m, f* **-1.** *ZOOL* pig. **-2.** *CULIN* pork. **-3.** [pessoa] *fam* pig.

porções [pox'sõjʃ] *pl* ⊳ **porção**.

pôr-do-sol [,poxdu'sɔw] (*pl* **pores-do-sol**) *m* sunset.

porco-espinho [,poxkwiʃ'piɲu] (*pl* **porcos-espinhos**) *m* porcupine.

porém [po'rẽj] ◇ *conj* [contudo] but, however. ◇ *m* [obstáculo] snag.

pormenor [poxme'nɔ(x)] (*pl* **-es**) *m* detail.

pormenorizar [4] [poxmenori'za(x)] *vt* to detail.

pornô [pox'no] ◇ *adj inv* ***fam*** porn. ◇ *m CINE* porn film.

pornochanchada [poxnoʃãn'ʃada] *m CINE* soft porn film ***UK***, soft porn movie ***US***.

pornografia [poxno'grafia] *f* pornography.

pornográfico, ca [poxno'grafiku, ka] *adj* pornographic.

poro ['pɔru] *m* pore.

porões [po'rõjʃ] *pl* ⊳ **porão**.

pororoca [poro'rɔka] *f* [onda] bore.

POROROCA

Word of Tupi origin, meaning 'thundering crash'; it describes the encounter of the waters of the Amazon with the Atlantic Ocean. Creating waves over 5m high and destroying everything in its passage, this phenomenon occurs mainly in March and is one of the main tourist attractions in Amazonia.

poroso, osa [po'rozu, ɔza] *adj* porous.

porquanto [pox'kwãntu] *conj* since.

porque [pux'ke] *conj* because; **ela trabalha ~ precisa** she works because she needs to; **~ sim** just because.

porquê [pux'ke] *m*: **o ~** the reason (for); **não entendo o ~ dessa atitude** I don't understand the reason for that attitude.

porquinho-da-Índia [pox,kiɲuda'ĩndʒja] (*pl* **porquinhos-da-Índia**) *m* guinea pig.

porra ['poxa] ◇ *f* ***vulg*** [esperma] spunk. ◇ *interj* ***vulg*** [exprime irritação] fucking hell!; **mas que ~!** fuck!

porrada [po'xada] ***mfam*** *f* **-1.** [pancada]: **ele deu uma ~ com o carro no muro** he smashed the car into the wall; **o garçom levou uma ~ do bêbado** the waiter took one hell of a beating from the drunkard. **-2.** [quantidade]: **uma ~ de** loads of. **-3.** ***fig*** [revés] fuck-up.

porra-louca [,poxa'loka] (*pl* **porras-loucas**) ***fam*** ◇ *adj* crazy. ◇ *mf* nutter.

porre ['pɔxi] ***fam*** *m* **-1.** [bebedeira] booze-up; **estar/ficar de ~** to be plastered; **tomar um ~** to get a skinful. **-2.**: **ser um ~** [pessoa, festa] to be a drag.

porretada [poxe'tada] *m* beating.

porrete [po'xetʃi] *m* club.

porta ['pɔxta] *m* **-1.** [peça] door; **~ corrediça** sliding door; **~ dos fundos** back door; **~ da frente/da rua** front/street door; **~ giratória** revolving door. **-2.** ***fig*** [possibilidade, saída] opportunity. **-3.** *COMPUT*: **~ paralela** parallel port; **~ serial** serial port.

porta-aviões [,pɔxta'vjõiʃ] *m inv* aircraft carrier.

porta-bandeira [,pɔxtabãn'dejra] (*pl* **porta-bandeiras**) *mf* standard-bearer.

portador, ra [poxta'do(x), ra] (*mpl* **-es**, *fpl* **-s**) ◇ *adj* **-1.** [de vírus, doença] carrying. **-2.** [de notícias] bearing. ◇ *m, f* **-1.** [de bagagem, AIDS] carrier.

-2. [de títulos, letras de câmbio, notícias] bearer; **ao ~** [cheque, ação] to the bearer.
porta-estandarte [ˌpɔxtiʃtãn'daxtʃi] (*pl* **porta-estandartes**) *mf* standard-bearer.
porta-guardanapos [ˌpɔxtagwaxda'napuʃ] *m inv* napkin holder.
porta-jóias [ˌpɔxta'ʒɔjaʃ] *m inv* jewellery box.
portal [pox'taw] (*pl* **-ais**) *m* **-1.** [pórtico] doorway. **-2.** COMPUT portal.
porta-luvas [ˌpɔxta'luvaʃ] *m inv* AUTO glove compartment.
porta-malas [ˌpɔxta'malaʃ] *m inv* AUTO boot *UK*, trunk *US*.
porta-moedas [ˌpɔxta'mwɛdaʃ] *m inv* [porta-níqueis] purse.
portanto [pox'tãntu] *conj* therefore.
portão [pox'tãw] (*pl* **-ões**) *m* gate.
portar [4] [pox'ta(x)] *vt* [carregar] to carry.
◆ **portar-se** *vp* [comportar-se] to behave.
porta-retratos [ˌpɔxtaxe'tratuʃ] *m (inv)* photo frame.
porta-revistas [ˌpɔxtaxe'viʃtaʃ] *m (inv)* magazine rack.
portaria [poxta'ria] *f* **-1.** [de edifício] entrance hall. **-2.** [documento oficial] order; **baixar uma ~** to issue a decree.
portátil [pox'tatʃiw] (*pl* **-eis**) *adj* portable.
porta-voz [ˌpɔxta'vɔjʃ] (*pl* **porta-vozes**) *mf* spokesperson.
porte ['pɔrtʃi] *m* **-1.** [transporte] carriage. **-2.** [preço] charge; **~ pago** post paid. **-3.** [postura] bearing. **-4.** [tamanho] scale; **de grande/médio/pequeno ~** large/medium/small-sized. **-5.** [importância] stature; **de grande ~** of great stature. **-6.** [licença]: **~ de arma** gun permit.
porteiro, ra [pox'tejru, ra] *m, f* [de edifício] caretaker *UK*, janitor *US*; **~ eletrônico** entryphone.
◆ **porteira** *f* [cancela] gate.
portento [pox'tẽntu] *m* marvel.
portentoso, osa [poxtẽn'tozu, ɔza] *adj* marvellous.
portfolio [port'fɔlju] *m* portfolio.
pórtico ['pɔxtʃiku] *m* portico.
portinhola [poxtʃi'ɲɔla] *f* **-1.** [pequena porta] small door, trapdoor. **-2.** [postigo] window.
Port Louis [ˌpɔxtʃ'lujʃ] *n* Port Louis.
Port Moresby [ˌpɔxtʃ'mɔreʒbi] *n* Port Moresby.
porto ['poxtu] *m* port; **~ de escala** port of call; **~ livre** freeport.
Porto Alegre [ˌpoxtwa'lɛgri] *n* Porto Alegre.
portões [pox'tõjʃ] *pl* ⊳ **portão**.
Porto Príncipe [ˌpoxtu'prĩnsipi] *n* Port-au-Prince.
Porto Rico [ˌpoxtu'xiku] *n* Puerto Rico.
Porto Velho [ˌpoxtu'vɛʎu] *n* Porto Velho.
portuário, ria [pox'twarju, rja] ◇ *adj* port *(antes de subst)*. ◇ *m, f* [funcionário] port official.
Portugal [poxtu'gaw] *n* Portugal.
português, esa [poxtu'geʃ, eza] (*mpl* **-eses**, *fpl* **-s**) ◇ *adj* Portuguese. ◇ *m, f* Portuguese person.
◆ **português** *m* [língua] Portuguese.
portunhol [poxtu'ɲɔw] *m mixture of Portuguese and Spanish.*
porventura [poxvẽn'tura] *adv* by chance; **se ~ você ...** if you happen to ...
porvir [pox'vi(x)] *m* future.
posar [4] [po'za(x)] *vi* **-1.** [fazer pose] to pose. **-2.** [bancar]: **~ de** to pose as.
pós-datado, da [ˌpɔjʃda'tadu, da] (*mpl* **-s**, *fpl* **-s**) *adj* post-dated.
pós-datar [ˌpɔjʃda'ta(x)] *vt* to postdate.
pose ['pozi] *f* **-1.** [de modelo etc] pose. **-2.** *pej* [afetação] affectedness; **ela está com muita ~ desde sua promoção** she's full of airs and graces since being promoted; **fazer ~ de** to pretend to be.
pós-escrito [ˌpɔjʃiʃ'kritu] (*pl* **pós-escritos**) *m* postscript, PS.
pós-graduação [ˌpɔjʃgradwa'sãw] (*pl* **pós-graduações**) *f qualifying for a degree as a postgraduate UK or graduate US student.*
pós-graduado, pós-graduada [ˌpɔjʃgra'dwadu, da] (*mpl* **pós-graduados**, *fpl* **pós-graduadas**) ◇ *adj* postgraduate *UK*, graduate student *US*. ◇ *m, f* postgraduate *UK*, graduate *US*.
pós-guerra [ˌpɔjʃ'gɛxa] (*pl* **pós-guerras**) *m* postwar *(antes de sust)*.
posição [pozi'sãw] (*pl* **-ões**) *f* **-1.** [ger] position; **tomar uma ~** to take a stand. **-2.** [arranjo] positioning.
posicionamento [pozisjona'mẽntu] *m* **-1.** [maneira de colocar] positioning. **-2.** [opinião] position.
posicionar [4] [pozisjo'na(x)] *vt* **-1.** [ger] to position. **-2.** [funcionário] to place.
◆ **posicionar-se** *vp* **-1.** [ger] to take up position. **-2.** [opinar] to take a stand. **-3.** [tomar atitude] to make a stand.
positivista [pozitʃi'viʃta] ◇ *adj* positivist. ◇ *mf* positivist.
positivo, va [pozi'tʃivu, va] *adj* positive.
◆ **positivo** ◇ *m* FOT positive. ◇ *interj fam* [sim] affirmative.
posologia [pozolo'ʒia] *f* dosage.
pós-operatório, a [ˌpɔjʃopera'tɔrju, rja] (*mpl* **-s**, *fpl* **-s**) ◇ *adj* post-operative. ◇ *m* post-operative period.
pós-parto [ˌpɔjʃ'paxtu] (*pl* **pós-partos**) *m* postnatal period.
pospor [45] [poʃ'po(x)] *vt* **-1.** [pôr depois] to put after. **-2.** [adiar] to postpone.
posposto, ta [poʃ'poʃtu, ta] *adj* **-1.** [posto depois] put after. **-2.** [adiado] postponed.
possante [po'sãntʃi] *adj* powerful.
posse ['pɔsi] *f* **-1.** [de bens] ownership; **pessoa de ~s** person of means. **-2.** [ocupação] possession; **tomar ~ de** to take possession of. **-3.** [investidura] swearing-in; **cerimônia de ~** swearing-in ceremony; **tomar ~** to take office.
◆ **posses** *fpl* [bens] possessions.
posseiro, ra [po'sejru, ra] *m, f* leaseholder.
possessão [pose'sãw] (*pl* **-ões**) *f* possession.

possessivo, va [pose'sivu, va] *adj* possessive.
◆ **possessivo** *m GRAM* possessive.
possesso, sa [po'sesu, sa] ◇ *adj* [furioso] enraged. ◇ *m, f* possessed person.
possibilidade [posibili'dadʒi] *f* **-1.** [gen] possibility. **-2.** [oportunidade] opportunity.
possibilitar [4] [posibili'ta(x)] *vt* to make possible.
possível [po'sivɛw] (*pl* **-eis**) ◇ *adj* possible. ◇ *m*: **o** ~ what is possible; **fazer o** ~ to do one's best.
possivelmente [posivew'mẽntʃi] *adv* possibly.
possuidor, ra [poswi'do(x), ra] *adj*: **ser** ~ **de** to be the owner of.
possuir [74] [po'swi(x)] *vt* [ter] to have.
posta ['pɔʃta] *f* [pedaço] piece; ~ **de peixe** piece of fish.
postal [poʃ'taw] (*pl* **-ais**) ◇ *adj* post, postage. ◇ *m* postcard.
postar [4] [poʃ'ta(x)] *vt* to post.
◆ **postar-se** *vp* to position o.s.
posta-restante [ˌpɔʃtaxeʃ'tãntʃi] (*pl* **postas-restantes**) *f* poste restante.
poste ['pɔʃtʃi] *m* **-1.** [haste] post. **-2.** *ELECTR*: ~ **de iluminação** lamp post; ~ **telegráfico** telegraph pole.
pôster ['poʃte(x)] (*pl* **-es**) *m* poster.
postergar [14] [poʃtex'ga(x)] *fml vt* **-1.** [adiar] to postpone. **-2.** [desprezar] to set aside.
posteridade [poʃteri'dadʒi] *f* posterity.
posterior [poʃte'rjo(x)] (*pl* **-es**) *adj* **-1.** [no tempo] later. **-2.** [traseiro] rear.
postiço, ça [poʃ'tʃisu, sa] *adj* false.
postigo [poʃ'tʃigu] *m* small door.
posto, ta ['poʃtu, 'pɔʃta] *pp* ▷ **pôr**.
◆ **posto** *m* **-1.** [ger] post; ~ **de gasolina** petrol station *UK*, gas station *US*; ~ **de salvamento** first-aid post; ~ **de saúde** health centre *UK*, health center *US*. **-2.** [de polícia] station. **-3.** [diplomático] posting.
◆ **a postos** *loc adv* at the ready.
◆ **posto que** *loc conj* since.
posto-chave [ˌpoʃtu'ʃavi] (*pl* **postos-chave**) *m* key position.
postulado [poʃtu'ladu] *m* assumption.
postulante [poʃtu'lãntʃi] ◇ *adj* candidate. ◇ *mf* applicant, candidate.
postular [4] [poʃtu'la(x)] *vt* **-1.** [pedir] to request. **-2.** [teorizar] to postulate. **-3.** *JUR* to apply for.
póstumo, ma ['pɔʃtumu, ma] *adj* posthumous.
postura [poʃ'tura] *m* **-1.** [ger] posture. **-2.** [municipal] position. **-3.** *fig* [atitude] point of view.
posudo, da [po'zudu, da] *adj* affected.
potássio [po'tasju] *m* potassium.
potável [po'tavɛw] (*pl* **-eis**) *adj*: **água** ~ drinking water.
pote ['pɔtʃi] *m* pot, jar.
potência [po'tẽnsja] *m* **-1.** [ger] power. **-2.** [sexual] potency.
potenciação [potẽnsia'sãw] (*pl* **-ões**) *f* [mat] exponentiation.
potencial [potẽn'sjaw] (*pl* **-ais**) ◇ *adj* potential. ◇ *m* potential; **o poder econômico em** ~ **do país é enorme** the country's potential economic power is great.
potencialidade [potẽnsjali'dadʒi] *f* [capacidade de realização] potencial.
potentado [potẽn'tadu] *m* potentate.
potente [po'tẽntʃi] *adj* powerful.
pot-pourri [pupu'xi] *m* pot-pourri.
potro ['potru] *m* colt.
pouca-vergonha [ˌpokavex'goɲa] (*pl* **poucas-vergonhas**) *f* **-1.** [ato] disgrace. **-2.** [falta de vergonha] shamelessness.
pouco, ca ['poku, ka] ◇ *adj* little; **de pouca importância** of little importance; **faz** ~ **tempo**, ~ **tempo (atrás)** a short time ago; *(pl)* few; **poucas pessoas** few people. ◇ *pron* little; *(pl)* few; **muito** ~**s** very few; ~**s** [pessoas] few; **dizer/ouvir poucas e boas** to tell/hear some home truths.
◆ **pouco** *m*: **um** ~ a little; **um** ~ **de** a little; **nem um** ~ **(de)** not at all; **aos** ~**s** gradually.
◆ **pouco** *adv* little; **dormi** ~ I hardly slept; **isso é** ~ **comum** that's uncommon, that's rare; **há** ~ a short time ago; **daqui a** ~, **dentro em** ~ shortly; **por** ~ **o carro não me atropelou** the car nearly ran me over; ~ **a** ~ little by little; **fazer** ~ **de** [zombar] to make fun of; [menosprezar] to belittle.
pouco-caso [ˌpoku'kazu] *m* contempt; **ele fez** ~ **da minha história** he treated my story with contempt.
poupador, ra [popa'do(x), ra] *adj* thrifty.
poupança [po'pãnsa] *f* **-1.** [economia] saving. **-2.** [fundo]: **(caderneta de)** ~ savings account (book).
poupar [4] [po'pa(x)] ◇ *vt* **-1.** [economizar] to save. **-2.** [resguardar]: ~ **alguém (de algo)** to spare sb (from sthg). **-3.** [respeitar] to spare. ◇ *vi* [economizar] to save.
◆ **poupar-se** *vp* [eximir-se] to spare o.s.
pouquinho [po'kiɲu] *m*: **um** ~ **(de algo)** a little (sthg).
pouquíssimo, ma [po'kisimu, ma] *superl* ▷ **pouco**.
pousada [po'zada] *f* **-1.** [hospedaria] inn. **-2.** [hospedagem] lodging.
pousar [4] [po'za(x)] ◇ *vi* **-1.** [aterrissar] to land. **-2.** [baixar] to settle. **-3.** [pernoitar] to spend the night. **-4.** [assentar] to rest. ◇ *vt* to put.
pouso ['pozu] *m* **-1.** [aterrissagem] landing; ~ **de emergência** emergency landing. **-2.** [lugar de descanso] bolt-hole.
povão [po'vãw] *m* hoi polloi *(pl)*.
povaréu [pova'rɛw] *m* [multidão] crowd.
povo ['povu] *m* **-1.** [habitantes] people. **-2.** [multidão] crowd. **-3.** [família, amigos] family.
povoação [povwa'sãw] (*pl* **-ões**) *f* **-1.** settlement. **-2.** [aldeia] village. **-3.** [habitantes] population.
povoado, da [po'vwadu, da] ◇ *adj* populated. ◇ *m* [aldeia] village.
povoamento [povwa'mẽntu] *m* settlement.

povoar [20] [po'vwa(x)] *vt* to populate.
poxa ['poʃa] *interj* gosh!
PPB (*abrev de* **Partido Progressista Brasileiro**) *m* Brazilian Progressive Party, *a right-wing party.*
PPS (*abrev de* **Partido Popular Socialista**) *m* Popular Socialist Party, *a centre-right party.*
PR (*abrev de* **Estado do Paraná**) *m State of Paraná.*
pra ['pra] *fam* = **para**, **para a**.
praça ['prasa] ◇ *f* **-1.** [largo] square. **-2.** [mercado financeiro] market. **-3.** *MIL*: ~ **de guerra** fortress. **-4.** [de touros] bull ring. ◇ *m MIL* [soldado] private (soldier).
pracinha [pra'siɲa] *m Brazilian soldier in World War II.*
prado ['pradu] *m* **-1.** [campo] meadow. **-2.** [hipódromo] racecourse.
pra-frente [ˌpra'frẽntʃi] *adj inv fam* trendy.
praga ['praga] *f* **-1.** [ger] curse; **rogar uma ~ a alguém** to curse sb. **-2.** [doença] scourge. **-3.** *ZOOL* plague. **-4.** [pessoa chata] pest.
Praga ['praga] *n* Prague.
pragmático, ca [prag'matʃiku, ka] *adj* pragmatic.
pragmatismo [pragma'tʃiʒmu] *m* pragmatism.
praguejar [4] [prage'ʒa(x)] *vi*: ~ **(contra)** to curse (at).
praia ['praja] *f* beach.
prancha ['prãnʃa] *f* **-1.** [tábua] plank. **-2.** [de surfe] board. **-3.** *NÁUT* gangplank. **-4.** *FERRO* open wagon.
prancheta [prãn'ʃeta] *f* **-1.** [mesa de desenho] drawing board. **-2.** [suporte para escrever] board.
pranto ['prãntu] *m* weeping.
prata ['prata] *f* **-1.** [metal] silver; **de ~** silver *(antes de subst)*; ~ **de lei** sterling silver. **-2.** *fam* [dinheiro] pennies *(pl)*.
prataria [prata'ria] *f* **-1.** [objetos de prata] silverware. **-2.** [pratos] crockery.
prateado, da [pra'tʃjadu, da] ◇ *adj* **-1.** [cor] silver *(antes de subst)*. **-2.** *fig* [brilhante] silvery. ◇ *m* silver.
pratear [15] [pra'tʃja(x)] *vt* [com prata] to silver.
prateleira [pratʃi'lejra] *f* shelf.
prática ['pratʃika] *f* ▻ **prático**.
praticamente [pratʃika'mẽntʃi] *adv* practically.
praticante [pratʃi'kãntʃi] ◇ *adj* practising *UK*, practicing *US*. ◇ *mf* practitioner.
praticar [12] [pratʃi'ka(x)] ◇ *vt* **-1.** [cometer] to commit. **-2.** [exercer] to practise *UK*, to practice *US*. ◇ *vi* [exercitar] to practise *US*, to practice *US*.
praticável [pratʃi'kavɛw] (*pl* **-eis**) *adj* **-1.** [realizável] feasible. **-2.** [transitável] passable.
prático, ca ['pratʃiku, ka] ◇ *adj* practical. ◇ *m, f NÁUT* pilot.
◆ **prática** *f* practice; **na ~** in practice; **pôr em ~** to put into practice.
prato ['pratu] *m* **-1.** [louça] plate; ~ **fundo** soup plate; ~ **raso** dinner plate; ~ **de sobremesa** dessert plate. **-2.** [comida] dish; ~ **do dia** dish of the day; ~ **principal/segundo** ~ main/second course; ~ **de resistência** *fig* pièce de résistance. **-3.** *MÚS* cymbal. **-4.** [de toca-disco] turntable. **-5.** [de balança] scale pan. **-6.** *loc*: **cuspir no ~ em que comeu** to bite the hand that feeds one; **vamos pôr isso em ~s limpos!** let's clear this up!; **ser um ~ cheio** to be manna from heaven.
praxe ['praʃi] *f* habit; **ter como ~** to be in the habit of; **ser de ~** to be customary.
prazenteiro, ra [prazẽn'tejru, ra] *adj* cheerful.
prazer [pra'ze(x)] (*pl* **-es**) *m* **-1.** pleasure. **-2.** [em apresentação]: **muito ~ (em conhecê-lo)** delighted (to meet you).
prazeroso, sa [prazeẽrozu, ɔza] *adj* pleasant.
prazo ['prazu] *m* **-1.** [tempo] period; **tenho um ~ de trinta dias para pagá-lo** I have thirty days in which to pay him, I have to pay him within thirty days; **a ~** on credit; **a curto/médio/longo ~** in the short/medium/long term. **-2.** [vencimento] deadline; ~ **final** final deadline.
preamar [prea'ma(x)] *f* high tide.
preâmbulo [pre'ãnbulu] *m* **-1.** [prefácio] foreword. **-2.** [introdução] preamble.
preaquecer [25] [prjake'se(x)] *vt* to preheat.
pré-aviso [prɛa'vizu] (*pl* **pré-avisos**) *m* (advance) notice.
precariedade [prekarje'dadʒi] *m* precariousness.
precário, ria [pre'karju, rja] *adj* **-1.** [ger] precarious. **-2.** [escasso] scarce.
precatória [preka'tɔrja] *f JUR* writ.
precaução [prekaw'sãw] (*pl* **-ões**) *f* caution.
precaver-se [50] [preka'vexsi] *vp* **-1.** [prevenir-se]: ~ **de** *ou* **contra algo** to be forearmed against sthg. **-2.** [preparar-se]: ~ **para algo** to prepare o.s. for sthg.
precavido, da [preka'vidu, da] *adj* cautious.
prece ['prɛsi] *f* **-1.** [oração] prayer. **-2.** [súplica] supplication.
precedência [presen'dẽsja] *f* precedence; **ter ~ sobre** to take precedence over.
precedente [prese'dẽntʃi] ◇ *adj* precedent. ◇ *m* precedent; **sem ~s** unprecedented.
preceder [5] [prese'de(x)] ◇ *vt* to precede; ~ **algo de** to precede sthg with. ◇ *vi*: ~ **a** to precede.
preceito [pre'sejtu] *m* precept.
preceptor [presep'to(x)] *m* tutor.
precificação [presifika'sãw] (*pl* **-ões**) *f* pricing policy.
precificar [presifi'ka(x)] *vt* to price.
preciosidade [presjozi'dadʒi] *f* gem.
preciosismo [presjo'ziʒmu] *m* preciosity.
precioso, osa [pre'sjozu, ɔza] *adj* **-1.** [ger] precious. **-2.** [importante] important. **-3.** [fino, rico] fine.
precipício [presi'pisju] *m* **-1.** [abismo] precipice. **-2.** *fig* [desgraça] hole.
precipitação [presipita'sãw] (*pl* **-ões**) *f* **-1.** [ger] haste. **-2.** *METEOR* precipitation.
precipitado, da [presipi'tadu, da] *adj* hasty.
precipitar [4] [presipi'ta(x)] ◇ *vt* [antecipar] to precipitate. ◇ *vi QUÍM* to precipitate.

◆ **precipitar-se** *vp* **-1.** [ger] to rush. **-2.** [apressar-se] to hurry. **-3.** [despenhar-se] to drop.

precisado, da [presi'zadu, da] *adj*: ~ **de** in need of.

precisamente [pre,siza'mẽntʃi] *adv* precisely.

precisão [presi'zãw] *f* **-1.** [exatidão] precision, accuracy. **-2.** [necessidade]: **ter ~ de** to be in need of.

precisar [4] [presi'za(x)] ◇ *vt* **-1.** [ger] to need; ~ **fazer algo** to need to do sthg; **preciso que me ajudem** I need you to help me. **-2.** [indicar] to specify. ◇ *vi* **-1.** [necessitar] to be in need; ~ **de alguém/algo** to be in need of sb/sthg. **-2.** [ser necessário]: **não precisa** there is no need; **fiz isso sem precisar** I did this when there was no need; '**precisam-se vendedores**' 'salespersons required'; **você precisa da chave para abrir a porta** you need a key to open the door.

preciso, sa [pre'sizu, za] *adj* **-1.** [ger] precise. **-2.** [necessário] necessary.

preço ['presu] *m* **-1.** [ger] price; ~ **de custo** cost price; ~ **à vista** [no comércio] cash price; [na bolsa] spot price; **vou comprar uma Ferrari por qualquer ~** I am going to buy a Ferrari whatever the cost; **a ~ de banana** for peanuts; **não ter ~** *fig* to be beyond price. **-2.** [importância] value.

precoce [pre'kɔsi] *adj* **-1.** [pessoa] precocious. **-2.** [fruto] early. **-3.** [calvície] premature.

precocidade [prekosi'dadʒi] *f* precociousness.

preconcebido, da [prɛkõnse'bidu, da] *adj* preconceived.

preconceito [prekõn'sejtu] *m* prejudice.

preconizar [4] [prekoni'za(x)] *vt* **-1.** [anunciar] to proclaim. **-2.** [propagar] to spread. **-3.** [elogiar] to praise.

precursor, ra [prekux'so(x), ra] (*mpl* **-es**, *fpl* **-s**) *m, f* precursor.

predador, ra [preda'do(x), ra] (*mpl* **-es**, *fpl* **-s**) ◇ *adj* predatory. ◇ *m, f* predator.

pré-datado, da [,prɛda'tadu, da] (*pl* **-s**) *adj* predated.

pré-datar [,prɛda'ta(x)] *vt* to predate.

predatório, ria [preda'tɔrju, rja] *adj* predatory.

predecessor, ra [predese'so(x), ra] (*mpl* **-es**, *fpl* **-s**) *m* predecessor.

predestinado, da [predeʃtʃi'nadu, da] *adj* predestined.

predestinar [4] [predeʃtʃi'na(x)] *vt* to predestine.

predeterminado, da [predetermi'nadu, da] *adj* predetermined.

predeterminar [predetermi'na(x)] *vt* to predetermine.

predial [pre'dʒjaw] (*pl* **-ais**) *adj* ▷ **imposto**.

predicado [predʒi'kadu] *m* **-1.** [qualidade] quality. **-2.** GRAM predicate.

predição [predʒi'sãw] (*pl* **-ões**) *f* prediction.

predileção [predʒile'sãw] (*pl* **-ões**) *f*: ~ **(por)** predilection (for).

predileto, ta [predʒi'lɛtu, ta] ◇ *adj* favourite *UK*, favorite *US*. ◇ *m, f* favourite *UK*, favorite *US*.

prédio ['prɛdʒju] *m* building; ~ **de apartamentos** block of flats *UK*, apartment house *US*; ~ **comercial** commercial building.

predispor [45] [predʒiʃ'po(x)] ◇ *vt* to predispose. ◇ *vi*: ~ **a** to predispose to.

◆ **predispor-se** *vp*: **~-se a fazer algo** to be predisposed to do sthg.

predisposição [predʒiʃpozi'sãw] *f* predisposition.

predisposto, osta [predʒiʃ'poʃtu, ɔʃta] *adj* **-1.** [ger] predisposed. **-2.** [à doença] prone.

predizer [29] [predʒi'ze(x)] ◇ *vt* to predict, to forecast. ◇ *vi* [profetizar] to make predictions.

predominância [predomi'nãnsja] *f* predominance.

predominante [predomi'nãntʃi] *adj* predominant.

predominar [4] [predomi'na(x)] *vi* to predominate.

predomínio [predo'minju] *m* **-1.** [supremacia] supremacy. **-2.** [influência] predominance.

pré-eleitoral [,prɛelejto'raw] (*pl* **-ais**) *adj* pre-election *(antes de subst)*.

preeminência [preemi'nẽnsja] *f* pre-eminence.

preeminente [preemi'nẽntʃi] *adj* pre-eminent.

preencher [5] [preẽn'ʃe(x)] *vt* **-1.** [completar - formulário, lacunas] to fill in; [- buracos] to fill. **-2.** [ocupar - tempo, férias] to spend; [- cargo, vaga] to fill. **-3.** [satisfazer] to fulfil *UK*, to fulfill *US*.

preenchimento [preẽnʃi'mẽntu] *m* **-1.** [de formulário, espaço em branco] filling in. **-2.** [de cargo, vaga, buraco] filling. **-3.** [de requisitos] fulfilment.

pré-escolar [,prɛiʃko'la(x)] (*pl* **pré-escolares**) *adj* pre-school *(antes de subst)*.

preestabelecer [25] [,preeʃtabele'se(x)] *vt* to pre-establish.

pré-estréia [,prɛiʃ'trɛja] (*pl* **-s**) *f* preview.

preexistente [preeziʃ'tẽntʃi] *m* pre-existing.

preexistir [6] [preeziʃ'tʃi(x)] *vi* to pre-exist; ~ **a algo** to pre-exist sthg.

pré-fabricado, da [,prɛfabri'kadu, da] *adj* prefabricated.

prefaciar [16] [prefa'sja(x)] *vt* to preface.

prefácio [pre'fasju] *m* preface.

prefeito, ta [pre'fejtu, ta] *m, f* mayor.

prefeitura [prefej'tura] *f* town hall.

preferência [prefe'rẽnsja] *f* **-1.** [precedência] priority; **dar ~ a** to give preference to. **-2.** AUTO: **ter ~** to have priority. **-3.** [predileção] preference; **de ~** preferably; **ter ~ por** to have a preference for.

preferencial [preferẽn'sjaw] (*pl* **-ais**) ◇ *adj* priority *(antes de subst)*. ◇ *f* main road.

preferido, da [prefe'ridu, da] *adj* favourite *UK*, favorite *US*.

preferir [57] [prefe'ri(x)] *vt*: ~ **algo (a algo)** to prefer sthg (to sthg); **prefiro que você fique** I would prefer you to stay.

preferível [prefe'rivew] (*pl* **-eis**) *adj*: ~ **(a)** preferable (to).

prefigurar [4] [prefigu'ra(x)] *vt* to prefigure.

prefixo [pre'fiksu] *m* prefix.

prega ['prɛga] *f* **-1.** [dobra - em papel, pano] fold; [- na saia] pleat. **-2.** [ruga] wrinkle.
pregado, da [pre'gadu, da] *adj* **-1.** [fixado] nailed. **-2.** [olhos] glued. **-3.** [cansado] exhausted.
pregador [prega'do(x)] *m* **-1.** [orador] preacher. **-2.** [utensílio]: ~ **de roupa** clothes peg.
pregão [pre'gãw] (*pl* **-ões**) *m* **-1.** [proclamação] cry. **-2.** BOLSA trading. **-3.** [em leilão] bidding.
pregar [14] [pre'ga(x)] ◇ *vt* **-1.** [ger] to fix; ~ **os olhos em alguém/algo** to stare at sb/sthg; **não preguei os olhos a noite toda** I didn't sleep a wink all night. **-2.** [com prego] to nail. **-3.** [infligir]: ~ **algo em alguém** to inflict sthg on sb; ~ **um susto em alguém** to give sb a fright; ~ **uma mentira em alguém** to tell sb a lie; ~ **uma peça em alguém** to play a trick on sb. **-4.** RELIG [louvar] to preach. ◇ *vi* **-1.** [pronunciar sermão] to preach. **-2.** [clamar]: ~ **por/contra algo** to preach for/against sthg. **-3.** [cansar-se] to collapse.
prego ['prɛgu] *m* **-1.** [peça] nail. **-2.** [casa de penhor] pawn shop; **pôr algo no** ~ to pawn sthg. **-3.** [cansaço] exhaustion; **dar o** ~ to collapse.
pregões [pre'gõjʃ] *pl* ⊳ **pregão**.
pré-gravado, da [,prɛgra'vadu, da] (*pl* **-s**) *adj* pre-recorded.
pregresso, sa [pre'grɛsu, sa] *adj* earlier.
preguear [15] [pre'gja(x)] *vt* **-1.** [saia] to pleat. **-2.** [calça] to put a crease in.
preguiça [pre'gisa] *f* **-1.** [indolência] laziness; **estar com** ~ **(de fazer algo)** to be too lazy (to do sthg). **-2.** [animal] sloth.
preguiçoso, osa [pregi'sozu, ɔza] ◇ *adj* lazy. ◇ *m, f* lazy person.
pré-história [,prɛiʃ'tɔrja] *f* prehistory.
pré-histórico, ca [prɛiʃ'tɔriku, ka] *adj* prehistoric.
preia ['prɛja] *f* prey.
preia-mar [,prɛja'ma(x)] (*pl* **preia-mares**) *f* high tide.
prejudicar [12] [preʒudʒi'ka(x)] *vt* **-1.** [afetar] to damage. **-2.** [transtornar] to disrupt. **-3.** [depreciar] to impair.
prejudicial [preʒudʒi'sjaw] (*pl* **-ais**) *adj* harmful.
prejuízo [pre'ʒwizu] *m* **-1.** [dano] damage. **-2.** [financeiro] loss.
prejulgar [14] [preʒuw'ga(x)] *vt* to prejudge.
prelado [pre'ladu] *m* prelate.
preleção [prele'sãw] (*pl* **-ões**) *f* lecture.
preliminar [prelimi'na(x)] ◇ *adj* preliminary. ◇ *f* [partida] preliminary.
prelo ['prɛlu] *m* (printing) press; **no** ~ in print.
prelúdio [pre'ludʒju] *m* prelude.
prematuro, ra [prema'turu, ra] *adj* **-1.** [bebê] premature. **-2.** [colheita, fruta] early.
pré-medicação [,prɛmedʒika'sãw] (*pl* **-ões**) *f* pre-medication.
premeditado, da [premedʒi'tadu, da] *adj* premeditated.
premeditar [4] [premedʒi'ta(x)] *vt* to premeditate.
premência [pre'mẽnsja] *f* urgency.
pré-menstrual [,prɛmẽnʃ'trwaw] (*pl* **-ais**) *adj* premenstrual.
premente [pre'mẽntʃi] *adj* urgent.
premiado, da [pre'mjadu, da] ◇ *adj* prize-winning. ◇ *m, f* prizewinner.
premiar [16] [pre'mja(x)] *vt* **-1.** [dar prêmio] to award a prize to. **-2.** [recompensar] to reward.
premiê [pre'mje], **premier** [pre'mje] *m* premier.
prêmio ['premju] *m* **-1.** [em concurso, jogo] prize; ~ **de consolação** consolation prize. **-2.** [recompensa] reward. **-3.** [seguro] premium. **-4.** ESP: **Grande Prêmio** [de turfe, automobilismo] Grand Prix.
premissa [pre'misa] *f* premise.
pré-moldado, da [,prɛmow'dadu, da] (*pl* **-s**) *adj* precast.
◆ **pré-moldado** *m* [bloco] breeze block *UK*, cinder block *US*.
premonição [premuni'sãw] (*pl* **-ões**) *f* premonition.
premonitório, ria [premuni'tɔrju, rja] *adj* premonitory.
pré-natal [,prɛna'taw] (*pl* **pré-natais**) *adj* antenatal *UK*, prenatal *US*.
prenda ['prẽnda] *f* **-1.** [presente] present. **-2.** [em jogo] forfeit.
◆ **prendas** *fpl*: ~**s domésticas** housework *(inv)*.
prendado, da [prẽn'dadu, da] *adj* gifted.
prendedor [prẽnde'do(x)] *m* peg; ~ **de papel** paper clip; ~ **de cabelo** hairgrip; ~ **de gravata** tie clip.
prender [5] [prẽn'de(x)] ◇ *vt* **-1.** [pregar] to fasten. **-2.** [amarrar] to tie. **-3.** [reter] to keep. **-4.** [capturar] to arrest. **-5.** [atrair] to capture. **-6.** [afetivamente] to unite. **-7.** [impedir] to restrict. ◇ *vi* [ficar preso]: ~ **em algo** to catch on sthg.
◆ **prender-se** *vp* **-1.**: ~**-se a alguém** [afeiçoar-se] to grow attached to sb; [em relacionamento] to tie o.s. down to sb. **-2.** [preocupar-se]: ~**-se a algo** to get caught up in sthg.
prenhe ['preɲi] *adj* pregnant.
prenome [pre'nɔmi] *m* forename.
prensa ['prẽnsa] *f* **-1.** [ger] press. **-2.** *fam*: **dar uma** ~ **em alguém** to tighten the screws on sb.
prensar [4] [prẽn'sa(x)] *vt* **-1.** [na prensa] to compress. **-2.** [fruta] to squeeze. **-3.** [pessoa]: ~ **alguém contra algo** to press sb against sthg.
prenunciar [16] [prenũn'sja(x)] *vt* to forewarn.
prenúncio [pre'nũnsjo] *m* harbinger; **essas nuvens são um** ~ **de chuva** clouds are a sign of rain.
preocupação [preokupa'sãw] (*pl* **-ões**) *f* concern.
preocupante [preoku'pãntʃi] *adj* worrying.
preocupar [4] [preoku'pa(x)] *vt* [inquietar] to worry.
◆ **preocupar-se** *vp*: ~**-se (com algo/alguém)** to worry (about sthg/sb).
preparação [prepara'sãw] (*pl* **-ões**) *f* [preparo] preparation.
preparado, da [prepa'radu, da] *adj* **-1.** [disposto] ready. **-2.** [instruído] well prepared.
◆ **preparado** *m* FARM preparation.

preparar [4] [prepa'ra(x)] *vt* to prepare.
◆ **preparar-se** *vp* **-1.** [aprontar-se] to get ready. **-2.** [instruir-se]: **~-se para algo** to train for sthg.

preparativos [prepara'tʃivuʃ] *mpl* preparations, arrangements.

preparo [pre'paru] *m* **-1.** [preparação] preparation. **-2.** [condição]: **~ físico** physical fitness.

preponderância [prepõnde'rãnsja] *f* preponderance.

preponderante [prepõnde'rãntʃi] *adj* preponderant, predominant.

preponderar [4] [prepõnde'ra(x)] *vi* to preponderate; **~ sobre algo** to prevail over sthg.

preposição [prepozi'sãw] (*pl* **-ões**) *f* preposition.

preposto, ta [pre'poʃtu, ta] *m, f* [representante] representative.

prepotência [prepo'tẽnsja] *f* **-1.** [grande poder] forcefulness. **-2.** [despotismo] tyranny.

prepotente [prepo'tẽntʃi] *adj* **-1.** [poderoso] forceful. **-2.** [despótico] overbearing.

prepúcio [pre'pusju] *m* prepuce.

prerrogativa [prexoga'tʃiva] *f* prerogative.

presa ['preza] *f* **-1.** [na guerra] spoils *(pl)*. **-2.** [preia] prey. **-3.** [dente] fang. **-4.** [garra] talon. **-5.** [vítima] slave. **-6.** [mulher encarcerada] (female) prisoner.

presbiteriano, na [preʒbite'rjãnu, na] ◇ *adj* Presbyterian. ◇ *m, f* Presbyterian.

presbítero [preʃ'biʃteru] *m* [padre] priest.

presciência [pre'sjẽnsja] *f* [previsão] prescience.

presciente [pre'sjẽntʃi] *adj* prescient.

prescindir [6] [presĩn'dʒi(x)] *vi*: **~ de algo** [dispensar] to do without sthg; [abstrair] to disregard sthg.

prescindível [presĩn'dʒivew] (*pl* **-eis**) *adj* dispensable.

prescrever [5] [preʃkre've(x)] ◇ *vt* **-1.** [ger] to prescribe. **-2.** [determinar] to decide. ◇ *vi* **-1.** [cair em desuso] to fall into disuse. **-2.** *JUR* to lapse.

prescrição [preʃkri'sãw] (*pl* **-ões**) *f* **-1.** [ordem] order. **-2.** *MED* prescription. **-3.** *JUR* lapse.

presença [pre'zẽnsa] *f* **-1.** [ger] presence; **~ de espírito** presence of mind; **marcar ~** to be present; **ter boa ~** to be well turned out. **-2.** [em curso etc] attendance.

presenciar [16] [prezẽn'sja(x)] *vt* to witness.

presente [pre'zẽntʃi] ◇ *adj* **-1.** [ger] present. **-2.** [evidente] obvious. **-3.** [interessado] concerned. ◇ *m* **-1.** [ger] present. **-2.** [pessoa]: **(entre) os ~s** (among) those present. **-3.** [regalo] present, gift; **de ~** as a present; **~ de grego** *fig* unwelcome gift.

presentear [15] [prezẽn'tʃja(x)] *vt*: **~ alguém (com algo)** to give sb (sthg as) a present.

presentemente [prezẽntʃi'mẽntʃi] *adv* at present.

presepada [preze'pada] *f* nonsense.

presépio [pre'zɛpju] *m* crib, Nativity scene.

preservação [prezexva'sãw] (*pl* **-ões**) *f* preservation.

preservar [4] [prezex'va(x)] *vt* to preserve.
◆ **preservar-se** *vp* to protect o.s.

preservativo [prezexva'tʃivu] *m* **-1.** [substância] preservative. **-2.** [camisinha] condom.

presidência [prezi'dẽnsja] *f* **-1.** [de país] presidency; **assumir a ~** to assume the presidency. **-2.** [de assembléia] chairmanship; **assumir a ~** to take the chair. **-3.** [tempo em excercício] time in office.

presidencial [prezidẽn'sjaw] (*pl* **-ais**) *adj* presidential.

presidencialismo [prezidẽnsja'liʒmu] *m* presidentialism.

presidenciável [prezidẽn'sjavew] (*pl* **-eis**) ◇ *adj* eligible to be president. ◇ *mf* presidential candidate.

presidente, ta [prezi'dẽntʃi, ta] *m, f* **-1.** [de país] president. **-2.** [de assembléia, empresa] chairman.
◆ **Presidente da República** *m* President of the Republic.

presidiário, ria [prezi'dʒjarju, rja] ◇ *adj* prison *(antes de subst)*. ◇ *m, f* convict.

presídio [pre'zidʒju] *m* prison.

presidir [6] [prezi'dʒi(x)] ◇ *vt* **-1.** [dirigir] to lead. **-2.** [reger] to rule. ◇ *vi*: **~ a algo** [dirigir] to preside over sthg; [reger] to rule sthg.

presilha [pre'ziʎa] *f* **-1.** [de suspensório, sapato] strap. **-2.** [de cabelo] hairslide.

preso, sa ['prezu, za] ◇ *adj* **-1.** [encarcerado] imprisoned. **-2.** [detido] detained, under arrest. **-3.** [atado] tied. **-4.** *fig* [em engarrafamento, casa] stuck. **-5.** *fig* [ligado]: **ficar ~ a detalhes** to get bogged down in detail. **-6.** *fig* [casado] spoken for. **-7.** *fig* [língua, voz] tongue-tied; **ele está com a voz presa** he has a catch in his voice. ◇ *m, f* [prisioneiro] prisoner.

pressa ['prɛsa] *f* **-1.** [velocidade] speed; **às ~s** quickly; **com ~** in a hurry; **sem ~** unhurriedly; **vir sem ~** to take one's time. **-2.** [urgência] rush; **não ter ~** not to be urgent; **ter ~ de algo/de fazer algo** to be in a hurry for sthg/to do sthg. **-3.** [precipitação] hastiness.

pressagiar [16] [presa'ʒja(x)] *vt* to foretell.

presságio [pre'saʒju] *m* **-1.** [indício] sign. **-2.** [pressentimento] premonition.

pressão [pre'sãw] (*pl* **-ões**) *f* **-1.** [ger] pressure; **fazer ~ sobre alguém** to put pressure on sb; **~ contra algo** pressure against sthg. **-2.** [colchete] press stud. **-3.** *MED*: **~ alta/baixa** high/low (blood) pressure; **~ arterial** blood pressure. **-4.** *FÍSICA*: **~ atmosférica** atmospheric pressure.

pressentimento [presẽntʃi'mẽntu] *m* premonition.

pressentir [56] [presẽn'tʃi(x)] *vt* **-1.** [pressagiar] to foresee. **-2.** [suspeitar] to suspect. **-3.** [perceber] to sense.

pressionar [4] [presjo'na(x)] *vt* **-1.** [apertar] to press. **-2.** *fig* [coagir]: **~ alguém (a fazer algo)** to pressurize sb (into doing sthg).

pressões [pre'sõjʃ] *pl* ⊳ **pressão**.

pressupor [45] [presu'po(x)] *vt* to assume.

pressuposto, osta [presu'poʃtu, ɔʃta] *pp* ⊳ **pressupor**.

◆ **pressuposto** *m*: **partir de um ~** to assume.

pressurização [presuriza'sãw] *f* pressurization.

pressurizado, da [presuri'zadu, da] *adj* pressurized.

prestação [preʃta'sãw] (*pl* **-ões**) *f* **-1.** [ger] instalment *UK*, installment *US*; **ele só compra à ~** he only buys on hire purchase. **-2.** [acerto]: **~ de conta** accounts rendered. **-3.** [trabalho]: **~ de serviço** services rendered.

prestamista [preʃta'miʃta] *mf* moneylender.

prestar [4] [preʃ'ta(x)] ◇ *vt* **-1.** [conceder]: **~ algo (a alguém)** [favores] to grant sthg (to sb); [informações] to provide (sb with) sthg. **-2.** [dispensar]: **~ algo (a alguém)** to provide (sb with) sthg. **-3.** [apresentar]: **~ algo (a alguém)** to present sthg (to sb). **-4.** [fazer]: **~ algo (a alguém/algo)** to provide sthg (to sb/sthg); **~ atenção** to pay attention. **-5.** [dedicar]: **~ algo a alguém** to pay sthg to sb. ◇ *vi* **-1.** [ser útil]: **essa caneta não presta** this pen isn't any good. **-2.** [ter bom caráter]: **ele não presta!** he's no good!

◆ **prestar-se** *vp* **-1.** [dispor-se]: **~-se a algo** to accept sthg. **-2.** [servir]: **~-se a algo** to be fit for sthg.

prestativo, va [preʃta'tʃivu, va] *adj* obliging.

prestes ['prɛʃtʃiʃ] *adj inv*: **estar ~ a fazer algo** to be about to do sthg.

presteza [preʃ'teza] *f* **-1.** [prontidão] promptness; **com ~** promptly. **-2.** [agilidade] agility.

prestidigitação [preʃtʃidʒiʒita'sãw] *f* conjuring.

prestidigitador, ra [preʃtʃidʒiʒita'do(x), ra] (*mpl* **-es**, *fpl* **-s**) *m, f* conjurer.

prestigiar [16] [preʃtʃi'ʒja(x)] *vt* to honour *UK*, to honor *US*.

prestígio [preʃ'tʃiʒju] *m* prestige; **é um escritor de ~** he is an eminent writer.

prestigioso, osa [preʃtʃi'ʒjozu, ɔza] *adj* prestigious.

préstimo ['prɛʃtʃimu] *m* [utilidade] use.

◆ **préstimos** *mpl* [favores]: **oferecer ~s a alguém** to offer one's services to sb.

presumido, da [prezu'midu, da] *adj* [presunçoso] presumptuous.

presumir [6] [prezu'mi(x)] *vt* [supor] to presume.

presunção [prezũn'sãw] (*pl* **-ões**) *f* presumption; **ter a ~ de ser algo** to believe o.s. to be sthg.

presunçoso, osa [prezũn'sozu, ɔza] *adj* presumptuous.

presunto [pre'zũntu] *m* **-1.** [de porco] ham. **-2.** *gír crime* [defunto] stiff.

prêt-à-porter [prɛtapox'te] *adj inv* ready-to-wear.

pretendente [pretẽn'dẽntʃi] ◇ *mf* [candidato]: **~ a algo** applicant for sthg. ◇ *m* [de uma mulher] suitor.

pretender [5] [pretẽn'de(x)] *vt* **-1.** [desejar]: **~ fazer algo** to want to do sthg. **-2.** [ter a intenção de]: **~ fazer algo** to intend to do sthg; **~ que** to intend (that).

pretensamente [pretẽnsa'mẽntʃi] *adv* supposedly.

pretensão [pretẽn'sãw] (*pl* **-ões**) *f* **-1.** [aspiração] pretension; **~ salarial** proposed salary. **-2.** [arrogância] pretentions *(pl)*. **-3.** [intenção] aim.

pretensioso, osa [pretẽn'sjozu, ɔza] *adj* pretentious.

pretenso, sa [pre'tẽsu, sa] *adj* [suposto] alleged.

preterir [prete'ri(x)] *vt* **-1.** [desprezar] to scorn. **-2.** [omitir] to omit. **-3.** [deixar de promover] to pass over. **-4.** [substituir] to replace.

pretérito, ta [pre'tɛritu] *adj* past.

◆ **pretérito** *m* GRAM preterite.

pretexto [pre'teʃtu] *m* [desculpa] pretext; **a ~ de** under the pretext of.

preto, ta ['pretu, ta] ◇ *adj* [cor] black; **estar/andar ~** *fig* to be/look gloomy; **ver as coisas pretas** to look on the dark side. ◇ *m, f* [pessoa] black (person).

◆ **preto** *m* [cor] black.

preto-e-branco [,pretwi'brãŋku] *adj inv* black and white.

pretume [pre'tumi] *m* blackness.

prevalecente [prevale'sẽntʃi] *adj* prevailing.

prevalecer [25] [prevale'se(x)] *vi* **-1.** [predominar] to prevail. **-2.** [ter primazia]: **~ (a/sobre)** to prevail (over).

◆ **prevalecer-se** *vp*: **~-se de algo** [aproveitar-se] to avail o.s. of sthg.

prevaricação [prevarika'sãw] (*pl* **-ões**) *f* JUR prevarication.

prevaricar [12] [prevari'ka(x)] *vi* **-1.** [faltar ao dever] to fail to do one's duty. **-2.** [proceder mal] to do wrong. **-3.** [cometer adultério] to stray.

prevenção [prevẽn'sãw] (*pl* **-ões**) *f* **-1.** [precaução]: **~ (a/contra/de)** prevention (against/of). **-2.** [implicância]: **estar de ~ contra** *ou* **com alguém** to pick on sb.

prevenido, da [previ'nidu, da] *adj* **-1.** [precavido] precautious. **-2.** [com dinheiro]: **estar ~** to be in pocket.

prevenir [58] [previ'ni(x)] *vt* **-1.** [avisar] to warn. **-2.** [evitar] to avoid. **-3.** [proibir] to prohibit.

◆ **prevenir-se** *vp* **-1.** [precaver-se]: **~-se contra alguém/algo** to protect o.s. against sb/sthg. **-2.** [equipar-se] **~-se de** to equip o.s. with.

preventivo, va [prevẽn'tʃivu, va] *adj* preventive.

◆ **preventivo** *m* [teste]: **(fazer um) ~** to have a check-up.

prever [40] [pre've(x)] *vt* **-1.** [conjeturar] to foresee; **~ que** to foresee (that). **-2.** [profetizar] to predict.

pré-vestibular [,prɛveʃtʃibu'la(x)] (*pl* **pré-vestibulares**) ◇ *adj preparing for university entrance exam.* ◇ *m* [curso] *university entrance-exam preparatory course.*

prévia ['prɛvja] *f* ▷ **prévio**.

previamente [,prɛvja'mẽntʃi] *adv* previously.

previdência [previ'dẽnsja] *f* precaution; **~ social** social security.

previdente [previ'dẽntʃi] *adj* **-1.** [que prevê] provident. **-2.** [cauteloso] cautious.

prévio, via ['prɛvju, vja] *adj* **-1.** [anterior] previous. **-2.** [preliminar] preliminary.

◆ **prévia** *f* **-1.** [pesquisa eleitoral] opinion poll. **-2.** [eleição interna de um partido] leadership elections.

previsão [previ'zãw] (*pl* **-ões**) *f* prediction; ~ **do tempo** weather forecast.

previsível [previ'zivɛw] (*pl* **-eis**) *adj* predictable.

previsto, ta [pre'viʃtu, ta] ◇ *pp* ▷ **prever**. ◇ *adj* **-1.** [prognosticado] foreseen. **-2.** [calculado] predicted. **-3.** [em lei] prescribed.

prezado, da [pre'zadu, da] *adj* **-1.** [estimado] prized. **-2.** [em carta]: **Prezado Senhor** Dear Sir.

prezar [4] [pre'za(x)] *vt* **-1.** [gostar muito] to cherish. **-2.** [respeitar] to respect.

◆ **prezar-se** *vp* [respeitar-se] to have self-respect.

primado [pri'madu] *m* [primazia] primacy.

prima-dona [ˌprima'dona] (*pl* **prima-donas**) *f* prima donna.

primar [4] [pri'ma(x)] *vi* **-1.** [destacar-se] to excel. **-2.** [esmerar-se]: ~ **em** to excel in.

primário, ria [pri'marju, rja] *adj* **-1.** [ger] primary. **-2.** [primitivo] primitive.

◆ **primário** *m* [curso] primary education *UK*, elementary education *US*.

primata [pri'mata] *m* primate.

primavera [prima'vɛra] *f* **-1.** [estação] spring. **-2.** *BOT* primrose.

primaveril [primave'riw] (*pl* **-is**) *adj* spring *(antes de subst)*.

primaz [pri'majʒ] *m* primate.

primazia [prima'zia] *f* **-1.** [prioridade] priority. **-2.** [superioridade] primacy.

primeira [pri'mejra] *f* ▷ **primeiro**.

primeira-dama [priˌmejra'dãma] (*pl* **primeiras-damas**) *f* first lady.

primeiranista [primejra'niʃta] *mf* first-year student.

primeiro, ra [pri'mejru, ra] ◇ *num* first. ◇ *adj* [inicial] first; ~ **grau** *EDUC* middle school; ~**s socorros** first aid; **à primeira vista** at first sight. ◇ *m, f* **-1.** [em ordem]: **ela foi o** ~ **a chegar** she was the first to arrive. **-2.** [o melhor]: **é o** ~ **na turma** he is the top of the class.

◆ **primeiro** ◇ *adv* [em primeiro lugar] first. ◇ *m* [andar] first.

◆ **primeira** *f AUTO* first; **passar a primeira** to get into first.

◆ **de primeira** ◇ *loc adj* **-1.** [hotel, restaurante] first-class. **-2.** [carne] prime. ◇ *loc adv* [viajar] first class.

primeiro-de-abril [priˌmejrudʒja'briw] (*pl* **primeiros-de-abril**) *m* April fool.

primeiro-ministro, primeira-ministra [priˌmejrumi'niʃtru, priˌmejrami'niʃtra] (*mpl* **primeiros-ministros**, *fpl* **primeiras-ministras**) *m, f* prime minister.

primeiro time [priˌmejro'tʃimi] *adj inv*: **de** ~ tip-top.

primitivo, va [primi'tʃivu, va] *adj* primitive.

primo, ma ['primu, ma] ◇ *adj* [número] prime. ◇ *m, f* [parente] cousin; ~ **em segundo grau** second cousin.

primogênito, ta [primo'ʒenitu, ta] ◇ *adj* first-born. ◇ *m, f* firstborn.

primo-irmão, prima-irmã [ˌprimwix'mãw, ˌprimajx'mã] (*mpl* **primos-irmãos**, *fpl* **primas-irmãs**) *m, f* first cousin.

primor [pri'mo(x)] *m* **-1.** [excelência] excellence. **-2.** [beleza] beauty. **-3.** [esmero]: **com** ~ thoroughly.

primordial [primox'dʒjaw] (*pl* **-ais**) *adj* **-1.** [primitivo] primordial. **-2.** [fundamental] fundamental.

primórdio [pri'mɔrdʒju] *m* [origem] origin.

primoroso, osa [primo'rozu, ɔza] *adj* perfect.

princesa [prĩn'seza] *f* princess.

principado [prĩnsi'padu] *m* principality.

principal [prĩnsi'paw] (*pl* **-ais**) ◇ *adj* **-1.** [mais importante - ator] principal; [- rua, praça, entrada] main. **-2.** [fundamental] main. ◇ *m* principal.

principalmente [prĩnsipaw'mẽntʃi] *adv* principally.

príncipe ['prĩnsipi] *m* prince.

principesco, ca [prĩnsi'peʃku, ka] *adj* princely.

principiante [prĩnsi'pjãntʃi] ◇ *adj* budding. ◇ *mf* beginner.

principiar [16] [prĩnsi'pja(x)] ◇ *vt* to begin. ◇ *vi* to begin.

princípio [prĩn'sipju] *m* **-1.** [ger] beginning; **a** ~ at first; **desde o** ~ from the start; **do** ~ **ao fim** from beginning to end. **-2.** [lei, norma, elemento] principle. **-3.** [premissa]: **partir do** ~ to assume.

◆ **princípios** *mpl* [morais] principles.

◆ **em princípio** *loc adv* in principle.

prior ['prio(x)] *m* prior.

prioridade [prjori'dadʒi] *f* [primazia] priority; **ter** ~ **sobre alguém/algo** to have priority over sb/sthg.

prioritário, ria [prjori'tarju, rja] *adj* priority *(antes de subst)*.

priorizar [prjori'za(x)] *vt* [dar prioridade a] to prioritize.

prisão [pri'zãw] (*pl* **-ões**) *f* **-1.** [captura] arrest. **-2.** [encarceramento] imprisonment; ~ **perpétua** life imprisonment; ~ **preventiva** protective custody. **-3.** [cadeia] prison. **-4.** *fig* [sufoco] (holy) deadlock. **-5.** *MED*: ~ **de ventre** constipation.

prisioneiro, ra [prizjo'nejru, ra] *m, f* prisoner.

prisma ['priʒma] *m* **-1.** [ger] prism. **-2.** *fig* [perspectiva]: **sob esse** ~ from that angle.

prisões [pri'zõjʃ] *pl* ▷ **prisão**.

privação [priva'sãw] (*pl* **-ões**) *f* privation.

◆ **privações** *fpl* [penúria] hardship.

privacidade [privasi'dadʒi] *f* privacy.

privada [pri'vada] *f* toilet.

privado, da [pri'vadu, da] *adj* **-1.** [particular] private. **-2.** [desprovido] deprived.

privar [4] [pri'va(x)] *vt*: ~ **alguém de algo** to deprive sb of sthg.

◆ **privar-se** *vp*: ~**-se de algo** to go without sthg.

privativo, va [priva'tʃivu, va] *adj* [exclusivo] private.

privatização [privatʃiza'sãw] (*pl* **-ões**) *f* privatization.

privatizar [4] [privatʃi'za(x)] *vt* to privatize.
privilegiado, da [privile'ʒjadu, da] *adj* **-1.** [favorecido] privileged. **-2.** [excepcional] exceptional.
privilegiar [16] [privile'ʒja(x)] *vt* to favour *UK*, to favor *US*.
privilégio [privi'lɛʒju] *m* privilege.
pro [pru] = **para + o**.
pró [prɔ] ◇ *prep* [a favor de] pro. ◇ *m* [vantagem] pro; **os ~s e os contras** the pros and cons.
pró- [prɔ] *prefixo* pro-.
proa ['proa] *f* bow.
probabilidade [probabili'dadʒi] *f* probability, likelihood.
problema [pro'blema] *m* problem.
problemático, ca [proble'matʃiku, ka] *adj* problematic.
◆ **problemática** *f* problematic.
problematizar [problematʃi'za(x)] *vt* **-1.** [colocar em dúvida] to cast doubt on. **-2.** [dar forma de problema a] to find problems in. **-3.** [tornar difícil] to complicate.
probo, ba ['probu, ba] *adj* honest.
procedência [prose'dẽnsja] *f* **-1.** [origem] origin. **-2.** [lugar de saída] point of departure. **-3.** [fundamento]: **não ter ~** to be unfounded.
procedente [prose'dẽntʃi] *adj* **-1.** [oriundo] originating. **-2.** [lógico] logical.
proceder [5] [prose'de(x)] *vi* **-1.** [ger] to proceed. **-2.** [prosseguir] to continue. **-3.** [comportar-se] to behave; **~ mal/bem** to behave badly/well. **-4.** [ter fundamento] to have foundation.
procedimento [prosedʒi'mẽntu] *m* **-1.** [comportamento] behaviour *UK*, behavior *US*. **-2.** [método] method. **-3.** *JUR* proceedings *(pl)*.
processador [prosesa'do(x)] *(pl* **-es***)* *m COMPUT* processor; **~ de texto** word processor.
processamento [prosesa'mẽntu] *m* processing; **~ de dados** data processing; **~ de texto** text processing.
processar [4] [prose'sa(x)] *vt* **-1.** *JUR* to sue, to prosecute. **-2.** *COMPUT* to process.
processo [pro'sɛsu] *m* **-1.** [*JUR* - ação] legal proceedings *(pl)*, lawsuit; **abrir** *ou* **mover um ~ contra** to instigate legal proceedings against, to file a lawsuit against; [- documentação] evidence. **-2.** [método] process. **-3.** [estágio] course.
procissão [prosi'sãw] *(pl* **-ões***)* *f* procession.
proclamação [proklama'sãw] *(pl* **-ões***)* *f* proclamation.
proclamar [4] [prokla'ma(x)] *vt* to proclaim.
Procon *(abrev de* **Fundação de Proteção e Defesa do Consumidor***)* *m Brazilian organization for the protection of consumers' rights.*
procrastinar [4] [prokraʃtʃi'na(x)] ◇ *vt* to put off. ◇ *vi* to procrastinate.
procriação [prokrja'sãw] *f* procreation.
procriar [16] [pro'krja(x)] ◇ *vt* [gerar] to engender. ◇ *vi* [multiplicar] to procreate.
proctologia [proktolo'ʒia] *f* proctology.
procura [pro'kura] *f* **-1.** [busca] search; **estar à ~ de** to be searching for. **-2.** *COM* demand; **a ~ e a oferta** supply and demand.
procuração [prokura'sãw] *(pl* **-ões***)* *f* power of attorney.
procurado, da [proku'radu, da] *adj* sought after; **ser ~ pela polícia** to be wanted by the police.
procurador, ra [prokura'do(x), ra] *(mpl* **-es**, *fpl* **-s***)* *m, f*: **Procurador Geral da República** ≃ state prosecutor.
procurar [4] [proku'ra(x)] ◇ *vt* **-1.** [buscar - objeto, pessoa] to look for; [- verdade] to seek. **-2.** [requerer] to look for. **-3.** [esforçar-se por]: **~ fazer algo** to try to do sthg. **-4.** [contatar] to call on. ◇ *vi* [buscar]: **~ (por)** to search (for).
prodigalidade [prodʒigali'dadʒi] *f* **-1.** [abundância] abundance. **-2.** [generosidade] generosity.
prodígio [pro'dʒiʒju] *m* **-1.** [pessoa] prodigy. **-2.** [maravilha] feat.
prodigioso, osa [prodʒi'ʒozu, ɔza] *adj* prodigious.
pródigo, ga ['prɔdʒigu, ga] *adj* prodigal.
produção [produ'sãw] *(pl* **-ões***)* *f* **-1.** [ger] production. **-2.** [volume, obra] output; **~ em massa** *ou* **em série** mass production.
produtividade [prudutʃivi'dadʒi] *f* productivity.
produtivo, va [produ'tʃivu, va] *adj* **-1.** [fértil] productive. **-2.** [rendoso] profitable.
produto [pro'dutu] *m* **-1.** [ger] product. **-2.** *AGR* produce. **-3.** *ECON*: **~ interno bruto** gross domestic product. **-4.** *fig* [conseqüência]: **ser ~ de** to be the product of.
produtor, ra [produ'to(x), ra] *(mpl* **-es**, *fpl* **-s***)* ◇ *adj* producing; **país ~ de petróleo** oil-producing country. ◇ *m, f* producer.
◆ **produtora** *f* [empresa] production company.
produzido, da [produ'zidu, da] *adj* [esmerado] trendy.
proeminência [projmi'nẽnsja] *f* prominence.
proeminente [projmi'nẽntʃi] *adj* prominent.
proeza [pro'eza] *f* feat.
profanação [profana'sãw] *(pl* **-ões***)* *f* profanity.
profanar [4] [profa'na(x)] *vt* to desecrate.
profano, na [pro'fãnu, na] *adj* profane.
profecia [profe'sia] *f* prophecy.
proferir [57] [profe'ri(x)] *vt* **-1.** [dizer] to utter. **-2.** [decretar] to pronounce.
professar [4] [profe'sa(x)] ◇ *vt* **-1.** [exercer profissão] to practise *UK*, to practice *US*. **-2.** [propagar] to profess. ◇ *vi RELIG* to take holy orders.
professo, ssa [pro'fɛsu, sa] *adj* **-1.** *RELIG* avowed. **-2.** *fig* [perito] seasoned.
professor, ra [profe'so(x), ra] *(mpl* **-es**, *fpl* **-s***)* *m, f* teacher; **~ titular** *ou* **catedrático** university professor.
professorado [profeso'radu] *m* **-1.** [magistério] professorship. **-2.** [conjunto de professores] teaching profession.
profeta, tisa [pro'fɛta, tʃiza] *m, f* prophet.
profético, ca [pro'fɛtʃiku, ka] *adj* prophetic.
profetisa [profe'tʃiza] *f* ⊳ **profeta**.
profetizar [4] [profetʃi'za(x)] ◇ *vt* to prophesy.

◇ *vi* to predict the future.
proficiência [profi'sjẽnsja] *f* proficiency.
proficiente [profi'sjẽntʃi] *adj* [capaz] proficient.
profícuo, a [pro'fikwu, kwa] *adj* useful.
profissão [profi'sãw] (*pl* **-ões**) *f* **-1.** [ofício] profession. **-2.** [carreira] professional life. **-3.** [declaração] statement; ~ **de fé** *RELIG* profession of faith.
profissional [profisjo'naw] (*pl* **-ais**) ◇ *adj* professional. ◇ *mf* professional; ~ **liberal** *person in a liberal profession.*
profissionalizante [profisjonali'zãntʃi] *adj* [ensino] vocational.
profissionalizar [4] [profisjonali'za(x)] *vt* to professionalize.
◆ **profissionalizar-se** *vp* **-1.** [pessoa] to turn professional. **-2.** [atividade] to become professional.
profundamente [profũnda'mẽntʃi] *adv* deeply.
profundezas [profũn'dezaʃ] *fpl* depths.
profundidade [profũndʒi'dadʒi] *f* depth; **o mar aqui tem 20 metros de** ~ here the sea is 20 metres deep.
profundo, da [pro'fũndu, da] *adj* **-1.** [ger] deep. **-2.** *fig* [intenso - sono, respeito, amor] deep; [- dor] intense; [- ódio] profound.
profusão [profu'zãw] *f* profusion.
profuso, sa [pro'fuzu, za] *adj* profuse.
progenitor, ra [proʒeni'to(x), ra] *m, f* progenitor.
◆ **progenitores** *mpl* parents.
prognosticar [12] [prognoʃtʃi'ka(x)] ◇ *vt* [predizer] to forecast. ◇ *vi MED* to make a prognosis.
prognóstico [prog'nɔʃtʃiku] *m* **-1.** [predição] prediction. **-2.** *MED* prognosis.
programa [pro'grãma] *m* **-1.** [plano] programme *UK*, program *US*; **fazer um** ~ to go out; ~ **de índio** *fam fig* boring activity. **-2.** *COMPUT* program.
programação [programa'sãw] (*pl* **-ões**) *f* **-1.** [ger] programming; ~ **orientada a objetos** object-orientated programming; ~ **visual** graphic design. **-2.** [organização] planning.
programador, ra [programa'do(x), ra] *m, f* **-1.** [de rádio, empresa] programme planner. **-2.** *COMPUT* programmer; ~ **visual** graphic designer.
programar [4] [progra'ma(x)] *vt* **-1.** [planejar] to plan. **-2.** *COMPUT* to program.
programável [progra'mavew] (*pl* **-eis**) *adj* programmable.
progredir [58] [progre'dʒi(x)] *vi* **-1.** [prosperar]: ~ **(em algo)** to progress (in sthg). **-2.** [agravar-se] to progress.
progressão [progre'sãw] (*pl* **-ões**) *f* progression.
progressista [progre'siʃta] ◇ *adj* progressive. ◇ *mf* progressive.
progressivo, va [progre'sivu, va] *adj* progressive.
progresso [pro'grɛsu] *m* progress; **fazer** ~**s em algo** to make progress in sthg.
proibição [projbi'sãw] (*pl* **-ões**) *f* prohibition.
proibir [77] [proj'bi(x)] *vt* **-1.** [impedir]: ~ **alguém (de fazer algo)** to prohibit sb (from doing sthg). **-2.** [interdizer] to ban. **-3.** [vedar] to prevent.
proibitivo, va [projbi'tʃivu, va] *adj* prohibitive.
projeção [proʒe'sãw] (*pl* **-ões**) *f* **-1.** [ger] projection; **tempo de** ~ running time. **-2.** *fig* [notoriedade] prominence.
projetar [4] [proʒe'ta(x)] *vt* **-1.** [ger] to project. **-2.** [planejar] to plan. **-3.** *ARQUIT* to design.
◆ **projetar-se** *vp* **-1.** [arremessar-se] to throw o.s. **-2.** [sombra] to be projected. **-3.** *fig* [ganhar notoriedade] to project o.s.
projétil [pro'ʒɛtʃiw] (*pl* **-teis**) *m* projectile.
projetista [proʒe'tʃiʃta] ◇ *adj* planning, design *(antes de subst)*. ◇ *mf* planner, designer.
projeto [pro'ʒɛtu] *m* **-1.** [ger] plan. **-2.** [empreendimento] project. **-3.** [esboço de texto] draft; ~ **de lei** bill.
projetor [proʒe'to(x)] (*pl* **-es**) *m* **-1.** [ger] projector. **-2.** [holofote] searchlight.
prol [prɔw] *m*: **em** ~ **de** in favour of.
pró-labore [ˌprɔla'bori] (*pl* **pró-labores**) *m* remuneration.
prolapso [pro'lapsu] *m MED* prolapse.
prole ['prɔli] *f* [filhos] offspring.
proletariado [proleta'rjadu] *m* proletariat.
proletário, ria [prole'tarju, rja] ◇ *adj* proletarian. ◇ *m, f* proletarian.
proliferação [prolifera'sãw] (*pl* **-ões**) *f* proliferation.
proliferar [4] [prolife'ra(x)] *vi* to proliferate.
prolífico, ca [pro'lifiku, ka] *adj* prolific.
prolixo, xa [pro'liksu, ksa] *adj* **-1.** [verboso] long-winded. **-2.** [muito longo] lengthy.
prólogo ['prɔlogu] *m* prologue.
prolongado, da [prolõŋgadu, da] *adj* prolonged.
prolongamento [prolõŋga'mẽntu] *m* extension.
prolongar [14] [prolõŋ'ga(x)] *vt* **-1.** [duração] to prolong. **-2.** [extensão] to extend. **-3.** [adiar] to put off.
◆ **prolongar-se** *vp* **-1.** [estender-se] to stretch. **-2.** [durar] to last.
promessa [pro'mɛsa] *f* promise.
prometer [5] [prome'te(x)] ◇ *vt* **-1.** [ger] to promise. **-2.** [comprometer-se]: ~ **algo a alguém** to promise sb sthg; ~ **fazer algo** to promise to do sthg. **-3.** [assegurar]: ~ **algo a alguém** to promise sb sthg. ◇ *vi* **-1.** [fazer promessa] to promise. **-2.** [ter potencial] to be promising.
prometido, da [prome'tʃidu, da] *adj* promised.
◆ **prometido** *m*: **aqui está o** ~ here's what was promised; **cumprir o** ~ to keep one's promise.
promiscuidade [promiʃkwi'dadʒi] *f* promiscuity.
promiscuir-se [74] [promiʃ'kwixsi] *vp* [misturar-se]: ~ **(com)** to mix (with).
promíscuo, cua [pro'miʃkwu, kwa] *adj* **-1.** [sem ordem] disorderly. **-2.** [sexualmente] promiscuous.
promissor, ra [promi'so(x), ra] (*mpl* **-es**, *fpl* **-s**) *adj* promising.
promissória [promi'sɔrja] *f* [nota] promissory note.

promoção [promo'sãw] (*pl* **-ões**) *f* promotion; **em ~** on special offer.
promocional [promo'sjonaw] (*pl* **-ais**) *adj* promotional.
promontório [promõn'tɔrju] *m* promontory.
promotor, ra [promo'to(x), ra] <> *adj* promoting. <> *m, f* promoter; **~ público** public prosecutor.
promotoria [promoto'ria] *f* [Ministério Público] state prosecutor's office.
promover [5] [promo've(x)] *vt* **-1.** [ger] to promote. **-2.** [funcionário]: **~ alguém (a)** to promote sb (to).
◆ **promover-se** *vp* [favorecer-se] to make o.s. look good.
promulgação [promuwga'sãw] *f* promulgation.
promulgar [14] [promuw'ga(x)] *vt* to promulgate.
pronome [pro'nɔmi] *m* pronoun; **~ oblíquo** objective pronoun; **~ pessoal** personal pronoun.
pronta-entrega [ˌprõntaẽn'trɛga] (*pl* **pronta-entregas**) *f* [departamento] immediate delivery department; **vocês têm ~** do you do immediate delivery?, do you have an immediate delivery department?
prontidão [prõntʃi'dãw] *f* **-1.** [alerta] readiness; **estar de ~** to be on the alert. **-2.** [rapidez] promptness.
prontificar-se [12] [prõntʃifi'kaxsi] *vp*: **~ para algo/a fazer algo** to volunteer for sthg/to do sthg.
pronto, ta ['prõntu, ta] *adj* **-1.** [concluído, preparado] ready. **-2.** *(antes de subst)* [imediato] prompt. **-3.** [rápido] prompt. **-4.** [disposto]: **~ a fazer algo** ready to do sthg. **-5.** *fam* [sem recursos] broke.
◆ **pronto** *adv* promptly; **de ~** promptly.
pronto-socorro [ˌprõntuso'koxu] (*pl* **prontos-socorros**) *m* [hospital] casualty unit *UK*, emergency unit *US*.
prontuário [prõn'twarju] *m* **-1.** [ficha] file. **-2.** [manual] handbook.
pronúncia [pro'nũnsja] *f* **-1.** *LING* pronunciation. **-2.** *JUR* pronouncement.
pronunciamento [pronũnsja'mẽntu] *m* **-1.** [declaração] pronouncement. **-2.** *JUR* judgment.
pronunciar [16] [pronũn'sja(x)] *vt* to pronounce.
◆ **pronunciar-se** *vp* [emitir juizo]: **~-se sobre/a favor de** to express an opinion about/in favour of.
propagação [propaga'sãw] (*pl* **-ões**) *f* **-1.** [ger] propagation. **-2.** [disseminação] spread.
propaganda [propa'gãnda] *f* **-1.** [*COM* - publicidade] advertising; [- anúncio] advert, advertisement; **fazer ~ de algo** to advertise sthg. **-2.** *POL* propaganda. **-3.** [divulgação] spreading.
propagar [14] [propa'ga(x)] *vt* **-1.** [disseminar] to spread. **-2.** *BIOL* to propagate.
◆ **propagar-se** *vp* **-1.** [ger] to propagate. **-2.** [disseminar-se] to spread.
propalado, da [propa'ladu, da] *adj (antes de subst)* known.
propalar [4] [propa'la(x)] *vt* to divulge.
propender [5] [propẽn'de(x)] *vi*: **~ para** *ou* **a** to lean towards.
propensão [propẽn'sãw] (*pl* **-ões**) *f* inclination.
propenso, sa [pro'pẽnsu, sa] *adj*: **~ a algo/a fazer algo** inclined to sthg/doing sthg.
propiciar [16] [propi'sja(x)] *vt* **-1.** [permitir, favorecer] to favour *UK*, to favor *US*. **-2.** [proporcionar]: **~ algo a alguém** to allow sb sthg.
propício, cia [pro'pisju, sja] *adj* **-1.** [favorável]: **~ a algo** propitious for sthg. **-2.** [oportuno] propitious.
propina [pro'pinaʃ] *f* **-1.** [gratificação] tip. **-2.** [ilegal] bribe.
propor [45] [pro'po(x)] *vt* **-1.** [ger] to propose; **~ (a alguém) que** to propose (to sb) that. **-2.** *JUR* [ação] to move.
◆ **propor-se** *vp*: **~-se a fazer algo** [visar] to aim to do sthg; [dispor-se] to offer to do sthg.
proporção [propox'sãw] (*pl* **-ões**) *f* proportion.
◆ **proporções** *fpl* **-1.** [tamanho] dimensions. **-2.** [importância] proportions.
◆ **à proporção que** *loc adv* as.
proporcionado, da [propoxsjo'nadu, da] *adj* proportionate.
proporcional [propoxsjo'naw] (*pl* **-ais**) *adj* proportional; **~ a algo** proportional to sthg.
proporcionar [4] [propoxsjo'na(x)] *vt* **-1.** [propiciar] to provide. **-2.** [harmonizar]: **~ algo com algo** to adjust sthg to sthg.
proporções [propox'sõjʃ] *pl* ▻ **proporção**.
proposição [propozi'sãw] (*pl* **-ões**) *f* **-1.** [proposta] proposal. **-2.** [enunciado] proposition.
propositadamente [propozitada'mẽntʃi] *adv* on purpose.
propositado, da [propozi'tadu, da] *adj* intentional.
propositai [propozi'taw] (*pl* **-ais**) *adj* intentional.
propósito [pro'pɔzitu] *m* intention; **de ~** on purpose.
◆ **a propósito** *loc adv* [aliás] by the way.
◆ **a propósito de** *loc prep* concerning.
◆ **fora de propósito** *loc adj* unreasonable.
proposto, osta [pro'poʃtu, ɔʃta] <> *pp* ▻ **propor**. <> *adj* proposed.
◆ **proposta** *f* **-1.** [proposição] proposition. **-2.** [oferta] proposal.
propriamente [prɔprja'mẽntʃi] *adv* **-1.** [exatamente] exactly; **~ dito** per se; **o Estado ~ dito** the actual State. **-2.** [adequadamente] suitably.
propriedade [proprje'dadʒi] *f* **-1.** [ger] property; **~ pública** public property; **~ privada** private property. **-2.** [direito de propriedade] ownership.
proprietário, ria [proprje'tarju, rja] *m, f* **-1.** [dono] owner. **-2.** [de imóvel de aluguel] landlord.
próprio, pria ['prɔprju, prja] *adj* **-1.** [ger] proper. **-2.** [particular] own; **meu ~ apartamento/carro** my own flat/car. **-3.** [apropriado]: **~ (para)** suitable (for). **-4.** [peculiar] characteristic. **-5.** [mesmo] -self; **o ~ cliente do banco** the customer of the bank himself; **falei com o ~ presidente** I spoke

to the president himself; **eu** ~ I myself; **é o** ~ [ser ele mesmo] speaking.
propulsão [propuw'sãw] *f* propulsion.
propulsor, ra [propuw'so(x), ra] *adj* propelling.
◆ **propulsor** *m* propellor.
prorrogação [proxoga'sãw] (*pl* **-ões**) *f* **-1.** [prolongação] deferment. **-2.** *FUT* extra time.
prorrogar [14] [proxo'ga(x)] *vt* to defer, to postpone.
prorrogável [proxo'gavew] (*pl* **-eis**) *adj* deferrable.
prorromper [5] [proxõn'pe(x)] *vi*: ~ **(de)** to burst (out of); ~ **em** to burst into.
prosa ['prɔza] ◇ *adj* [cheio de si] puffed up. ◇ *f* **-1.** *LITER* prose. **-2.** [conversa] chat. **-3.** [conversa fiada] chit-chat.
prosador, ra [proza'do(x), ra] *m, f* prose writer.
prosaico, ca [pro'zajku, ka] *adj* prosaic.
proscênio [pro'senju] *m* proscenium.
proscrever [5] [proʃkre've(x)] *vt* **-1.** [desterrar] to exile. **-2.** [expulsar] to ban. **-3.** [proibir] to prohibit. **-4.** [abolir] to do away with.
proscrito, ta [proʃ'kritu, ta] ◇ *pp* ▷ **proscrever**. ◇ *adj* **-1.** [desterrado] banished. **-2.** [expulso] outlawed. **-3.** [proibido] forbidden. ◇ *m, f* [exilado] exile.
prosear [15] [pro'zja(x)] *vi* to chat.
prosódia [pro'zɔdʒja] *f* *GRAM* prosody.
prosopopéia [prozopo'pɛja] *f* **-1.** [em retórica] prosopopoeia. **-2.** *fig* & *pej* [discurso] diatribe. **-3.** *fig* & *pej* [pose] airs and graces.
prospecção [proʃpek'sãw] (*pl* **-ões**) *f* *GEOL* prospecting; ~ **de petróleo** oil exploration.
prospecto [proʃ'pɛktu] *m* leaflet.
prospector, ra [proʃpek'to(x), ra] *m, f* *GEOL* prospector.
prosperar [4] [proʃpe'ra(x)] *vi* **-1.** [progredir]: ~ **(em algo)** [melhorar] to prosper (in sthg); [ter sucesso] to thrive (in sthg). **-2.** [enriquecer] to prosper.
prosperidade [proʃperi'dadʒi] *f* **-1.** [progresso] prosperity. **-2.** [sucesso] success.
próspero, ra ['prɔʃperu, ra] *adj* **-1.** [que progride] thriving. **-2.** [bem-sucedido] prosperous.
prosseguimento [prosegi'mẽntu] *m* continuation; **dar** ~ **a** to continue with.
prosseguir [55] [prose'gi(x)] ◇ *vt* to continue. ◇ *vi*: ~ **(em algo)** to continue (in sthg); ~ **fazendo algo** to continue doing sthg.
próstata ['prɔʃtata] *f* *ANAT* prostate.
prostíbulo [proʃ'tʃibulu] *m* brothel.
prostituição [proʃtʃitwi'sãw] *f* prostitution.
prostituir [74] [proʃtʃi'twi(x)] *vt* to prostitute.
◆ **prostituir-se** *vp* **-1.** [tornar-se prostituta] to turn to prostitution. **-2.** [ser prostituta] to be a prostitute. **-3.** *fig* [corromper-se] to prostitute o.s.
prostituta [prosʃtʃi'tuta] *f* prostitute.
prostração [proʃtra'sãw] *f* prostration.
prostrado, da [proʃ'tradu, da] *adj* prostrate.
prostrar [4] [proʃ'tra(x)] *vt* **-1.** [ger] to prostrate. **-2.** [derrubar] to floor.
◆ **prostrar-se** *vp* [com reverência] to prostrate o.s.
protagonista [protago'niʃta] *mf* protagonist.
protagonizar [4] [protagoni'za(x)] *vt* **-1.** *CINE* & *TEATRO* to feature in. **-2.** [acontecimento] to be at the centre of ***UK***, to be at the center of ***US***.
proteção [prote'sãw] (*pl* **-ões**) *f* **-1.** [resguardo] protection. **-2.** [favorecimento] favour ***UK***, favor ***US***. **-3.** [dispositivo] defence ***UK***, defense ***US***.
protecionismo [protesjo'niʒmu] *m* [econômico] protectionism.
proteger [26] [prote'ʒe(x)] *vt* to protect; ~ **alguém de/contra algo** to protect sb from/against sthg.
◆ **proteger-se** *vp* [resguardar-se] to protect o.s.
protegido, da [prote'ʒidu, da] ◇ *adj* [resguardado] protected. ◇ *m, f* [favorito] protégé (*f* protégée).
proteína [prote'ina] *f* protein.
protelar [4] [prote'la(x)] *vt* to postpone.
prótese ['prɔtezi] *f* *MED* prosthesis.
protestante [proteʃ'tãntʃi] ◇ *adj* Protestant. ◇ *mf* Protestant.
protestantismo [proteʃtãn'tʃiʒmu] *m* Protestantism.
protestar [4] [proteʃ'ta(x)] ◇ *vt* **-1.** [título, promissória] to contest. **-2.** [declarar] to profess. ◇ *vi* **-1.** [reclamar]: ~ **(contra/em favor de algo)** to protest (against/in favour of sthg); **protesto!** *JUR* I protest! **-2.** [clamar]: ~ **por algo** to call for sthg.
protesto [pro'tɛʃtu] *m* **-1.** [ger] protest. **-2.** *fml* [declaração] declaration.
protetor, ra [prote'to(x), ra] (*mpl* **-es**, *fpl* **-s**) ◇ *adj* protective. ◇ *m, f* protector.
protocolar [4] [protoko'la(x)] ◇ *adj* formal. ◇ *vt* to register.
protocolo [proto'kɔlu] *m* **-1.** [ger] protocol; **quebrar o** ~ to break with protocol. **-2.** [registro] registration. **-3.** [recibo] record. **-4.** [setor] registry.
protocolo [proto'kɔlu] *m* *COMPUT* protocol.
protótipo [pro'tɔtʃipu] *m* **-1.** [modelo] prototype. **-2.** *fig* [exemplo]: **ser o** ~ **de algo** to be the epitome of sthg.
protuberância [protube'rãnsja] *f* protuberance.
protuberante [protube'rãntʃi] *adj* protuberant.
prova ['prɔva] *f* **-1.** [ger] proof; **tirar a** ~ **dos noves** to cast out 9s. **-2.** *EDUC* exam. **-3.** [teste] test; **à** ~ **de água** waterproof; **à** ~ **de bala** bulletproof; **à** ~ **de fogo** fireproof; **pôr algo à** ~ to put sthg to the test. **-4.** *ESP* event. **-5.** *COST* fitting. **-6.** [de comida, bebida] taster.
provação [prova'sãw] (*pl* **-ões**) *f* ordeal.
provado, da [pro'vadu, da] *adj* **-1.** [ger] proven. **-2.** [experimentado] tried.
provador [prova'do(x)] *m* **-1.** [em loja] fitting room. **-2.** [de café, vinho] taster.
provar [4] [pro'va(x)] ◇ *vt* **-1.** [demonstrar] to prove; ~ **algo por A mais B** to demonstrate sthg step by step. **-2.** [testar] to test. **-3.** [roupa] to try on. **-4.** [comida, bebida] to taste. ◇ *vi*: ~ **(de algo)**

[comida, bebida] to have a taste (of sthg).

provável [pro'vavɛw] (*pl* **-eis**) *adj* [possível] probable; **é ~ que chova** it looks like rain; **é ~ que ela não chegue hoje** she's not likely to come today.

provavelmente [provavew'mẽntʃi] *adv* probably.

provedor, ra [prove'do(x), ra] *m, f* provider; **~ de acesso** Internet service provider.

proveito [pro'vejtu] *m* advantage; **em ~ de** in favour of; **tirar ~ de algo** to benefit from sthg.

proveitoso, osa [provej'tozu, ɔza] *adj* **-1.** [vantajoso] advantageous. **-2.** [lucrativo] profitable. **-3.** [útil] useful.

proveniência [prove'njẽnsja] *f* origin.

proveniente [prove'njẽntʃi] *adj*: **~ de** [originário] originating from; [resultante] arising from; **esta uva é ~ da Itália** these grapes come from Italy.

proventos [pro'vẽntuʃ] *mpl* proceeds.

prover [41] [pro've(x)] ◇ *vt* **-1.** [ger]: **~ algo/alguém de algo** to provide sthg/sb with sthg. **-2.** [providenciar] to provide. **-3.** [vaga, cargo] to fill. ◇ *vi* [atender]: **~ a algo** to take care of sthg.
◆ **prover-se** *vp* [abastecer-se]: **~-se de algo** to provide o.s. with sthg.

proverbial [provex'bjaw] *adj* proverbial.

provérbio [pro'vɛrbju] *m* proverb.

proveta [pro'veta] *f* test tube; **bebê de ~** test-tube baby.

providência [provi'dẽnsja] *f* [medida] measure; **tomar ~s** to take measures.
◆ **Providência** *f*: **Divina Providência** (divine) Providence.

providencial [providẽn'sjaw] (*pl* **-ais**) *adj* providential.

providenciar [16] [providẽn'sja(x)] ◇ *vt* **-1.** [prover] to provide. **-2.** [tomar providências para] to set into motion. ◇ *vi* **-1.** [cuidar]: **vamos ~ para que tudo dê certo** let's see to it that all works out. **-2.** [tomar providências]: **~ contra/para algo** to take measures against/for sthg.

provido, da [pro'vidu, da] *adj* [abastecido]: **~ de algo** supplied with sthg; **bem ~** well stocked; **uma conta bancária bem provida** a fat bank account.

provimento [provi'mẽntu] *m* **-1.** [provisão] stocking up. **-2.** *JUR* granting; **dar ~** to grant a petition.

província [pro'vĩnsja] *f* **-1.** [divisão administrativa] province. **-2.** [interior] provinces *(pl)*.

provincianismo [provĩnsja'niʒmu] *m* provincialism.

provinciano, na [provĩn'sjãnu, na] *adj pej* provincial.

provindo, da [pro'vĩndu, da] ◇ *pp* ▻ **provir**. ◇ *adj*: **~ de** (coming) from.

provir [67] [pro'vi(x)] *vi*: **~ de** to come from.

provisão [provi'zãw] (*pl* **-ões**) *f* supply.
◆ **provisões** *fpl* supplies.

provisoriamente [provizɔrja'mẽntʃi] *adv* provisionally.

provisório, ria [provi'zɔrju, rja] *adj* provisional.

provocação [provoka'sãw] (*pl* **-ões**) *f* **-1.** [implicância] provocation. **-2.** [sensual] attraction.

provocador, ra [provoka'do(x), ra] (*mpl* **-es**, *fpl* **-s**) ◇ *adj* provocative. ◇ *m, f* provoker.

provocante [provo'kãntʃi] *adj* [sensualmente] provocative.

provocar [12] [provo'ka(x)] *vt* **-1.** [ger] to provoke. **-2.** [incitar]: **~ alguém (a fazer algo)** to provoke sb (into doing sthg). **-3.** [chamar a atenção, atrair sensualmente] to arouse. **-4.** [promover] to cause.

provocativo, va [provoka'tʃivu, va] *adj* provocative.

proximidade [prosimi'dadʒi] *f* **-1.** [ger] proximity. **-2.** [afinidade] closeness.
◆ **proximidades** *fpl* [arredores] proximity *(sg)*.

próximo, ma ['prɔsimu, ma] ◇ *adj* **-1.** [no espaço]: **~ (a** *OU* **de)** close (to). **-2.** [no tempo] recent; **futuro ~** near future. **-3.** *(antes de subst)* [seguinte] next. **-4.** [chegado] close. ◇ *m, f* [em fila] next (one).
◆ **próximo** ◇ *m*: **o ~** [o semelhante] neighbour *UK*, neighbor *US*. ◇ *adv* close.
◆ **próxima** *f* [a próxima vez]: **até a próxima!** [em despedida] see you soon!; **fica para a próxima** until some other time.

proxy ['prɔʃi] (*pl* **proxies**) *m COMPUT* proxy.

prudência [pru'dẽnsja] *f* caution, prudence; **com ~** carefully.

prudente [pru'dẽntʃi] *adj* **-1.** [comedido] prudent. **-2.** [cauteloso] cautious.

prumo ['prumu] *m* **-1.** [instrumento] plumb line. **-2.** *NÁUT* lead.

prurido [pru'ridu] *m* **-1.** [comichão] itch. **-2.** *fig* [desejo] urge.

PS *m* **-1.** (*abrev de* **Post Scriptum**) PS. **-2.** (*abrev de* **Pronto Socorro**) *first aid*.

PSB (*abrev de* **Partido Socialista Brasileiro**) *m Brazilian socialist party.*

PSDB (*abrev de* **Partido da Social Democracia Brasileira**) *m Brazilian social democratic party, the second largest right-wing party in Brazil.*

pseudônimo [psew'donimu] *m* pseudonym.

psicanálise [psika'nalizi] *f* psychoanalysis.

psicanalista [psikana'liʃta] *mf* psychoanalyst.

psicanalítico, ca [psikana'litʃiku, ka] *adj* psychoanalitical.

psicodélico, ca [psiko'dɛliku, ka] *adj* psychedelic.

psicodrama [psiko'drãma] *m* psychodrama.

psicolingüístico, ca [ˌpsikolĩŋ'gwiʃtʃiku, ka] *adj* psycholinguistic.
◆ **psicolingüística** *f* psycholinguistics *(sg)*.

psicologia [psikolo'ʒia] *f* psychology.

psicológico, ca [psiko'lɔʒiku, ka] *adj* psychological.

psicólogo, ga [psi'kɔlogu, ga] *m, f* psychologist.

psicopata [psiko'pata] *mf* psychopath.

psicose [psi'kɔzi] *f* **-1.** *MED* psychosis. **-2.** *fig* [obsessão]: **~ de algo** obsession with sthg.

psicossomático, ca [psikoso'matʃiku, ka] *adj* psychosomatic.

psicotécnico, ca [psiko'tɛkniku, ka] *adj* response *(antes de subst)*.
◆ **psicotécnico** *m* [exame] response test.
psicoterapeuta [psikotera'pewta] *mf* psychotherapist.
psicoterapia [psikotera'pia] *f* psychotherapy.
psicótico, ca [psi'kɔtʃiku, ka] *adj* psychotic.
psique ['psiki] *f* psyche.
psiquiatra [psi'kjatra] *mf* psychiatrist.
psiquiatria [psikja'tria] *f* psychiatry.
psiquiátrico, ca [psi'kjatriku, ka] *adj* psychiatric.
psíquico, ca ['psikiku, ka] *adj* psychic.
psiu [psiw] *interj* **-1.** [para chamar] hey! **-2.** [para calar] hush!
psoríase [pso'rjazi] *f* psoriasis.
PT (*abrev de* **Partido dos Trabalhadores**) *m Brazilian workers' party, the largest left-wing party in Brazil.*
PTB (*abrev de* **Partido Trabalhista Brasileiro**) *m* Brazilian Workers' Party, *a large party of the centre.*
pua ['pua] *f* [de broca] bit; **sentar a ~ em alguém** *fig* to put the pressure on sb.
puberdade [puber'dadʒi] *f* puberty.
púbere ['puberi] *adj* pubescent.
púbico, ca ['pubiku, ka] *adj* pubic.
púbis ['pubiʃ] *m inv* pubis.
publicação [publika'sãw] (*pl* **-ões**) *f* publication.
publicar [12] [publi'ka(x)] *vt* **-1.** [ger] to publish. **-2.** [divulgar] to broadcast.
publicidade [publisi'dadʒi] *f* **-1.** [divulgação] publicity; **dar ~ a algo/alguém** to publicize sthg/sb. **-2.** *COM* advertising.
publicitário, ria [publisi'tarju, rja] ◇ *adj* advertising *(antes de subst)*. ◇ *m, f* advertiser.
público, ca ['publiku, ka] *adj* public.
◆ **público** *m* **-1.** [o povo] public. **-2.** [platéia] audience; **o grande ~** general public; **em ~** in public.
PUC (*abrev de* **Pontifícia Universidade Católica**) *f Pontifical Catholic university.*
pudico, ca [pu'dʒiku, ka] *adj* **-1.** [recatado] bashful. **-2.** *pej* prudish.
pudim [pu'dʒĩ] (*pl* **-ns**) *m* pudding; **~ de leite** milk pudding; **~ de pão** bread pudding.
pudor [pu'do(x)] *m* **-1.** [recato] modesty; **ter ~ de** [ter vergonha] to be ashamed of. **-2.** [decoro] decency; **atentado ao ~** indecent assault.
puericultura [pwerikuw'tura] *f* childcare.
pueril [pwe'riw] (*pl* **-is**) *adj* childish, puerile.
puerilidade [pwerili'dadʒi] *f* **-1.** [infantilidade] childishness, puerility. **-2.** *fig* [banalidade] foolish action.
pufe ['pufi] *m* pouffe.
pugilismo [puʒi'liʒmu] *m* boxing.
pugilista [puʒi'liʃta] *m* boxer.
pugnaz [pug'najʒ] *adj* pugnacious.
puído, da ['pwidu, da] *adj* frayed.
puir [74] [pwi(x)] *vt* to fray.
pujança [pu'ʒãnsa] *f* **-1.** [força, poderio] power. **-2.** [da vegetação] vitality.
pujante [pu'ʒãntʃi] *adj* powerful.
pula-pula [ˌpula'pula] (*pl* **pula-pulas**) *m* **-1.** [brinquedo] pogo (stick). **-2.** [cama elástica] bouncy castle. **-3.** [ave] golden-crowned warbler.
pular [4] [pu'la(x)] ◇ *vt* **-1.** [saltar] to jump (over); **~ corda** to skip; **~ a cerca** *fig* [trair] to be unfaithful. **-2.** [páginas, trechos] to skip. **-3.**: **~ Carnaval** to celebrate carnival. ◇ *vi* **-1.** [saltar] to jump; **~ de alegria** to jump for joy. **-2.** [palpitar] to skip a beat.
pulga ['puwga] *f* flea; **estar/ficar com a ~ atrás da orelha** to smell a rat.
pulgão [puw'gãw] (*pl* **-ões**) *m* aphid.
pulgueiro [puw'gejru] *m* [cinema] fleapit.
pulha ['puʎa] *m* creep.
pulmão [puw'mãw] (*pl* **-ões**) *m* lung.
pulmonar [puwmo'na(x)] *adj* pulmonary.
pulo ['pulu] *m* leap; **a um ~ de** *fig* [perto de] just a hop away from; **dar um ~ em** *fig* [ir] to stop off at.
pulôver [pu'love(x)] (*pl* **-es**) *m* pullover.
púlpito ['puwpitu] *m* pulpit.
pulsação [puwsa'sãw] (*pl* **-ões**) *f* **-1.** [batimento] pulsation. **-2.** *MED* [pulso] pulse; **medir as pulsações (cardíacas)** to take the pulse.
pulsar [4] [puw'sa(x)] *vi* [palpitar] to beat, to throb.
pulular [4] [pulu'la(x)] *vi* **-1.** [multiplicar-se] to proliferate. **-2.** [abundar]: **~ de** to swarm with, to teem with.
pulverizador [puwveriza'do(x)] *m* [para líquidos] spray.
pulverizar [4] [puwveri'za(x)] *vt* **-1.** [ger] to spray. **-2.** [reduzir a pó] [destruir] to pulverize.
pum [pũ] (*pl* **puns**) ◇ *m mfam* [peido] fart; **soltar um ~** to pass wind. ◇ *interj* bang!
pumba ['pũnba] *interj* [para ação rápida] whoosh!
punção [pũn'sãw] (*pl* **-ões**) ◇ *f MED* puncture. ◇ *m* [instrumento] stylus.
pungente [pũn'ʒẽntʃi] *adj* poignant.
pungir [78] [pũn'ʒi(x)] *vt ant* & *fig* [afligir] to afflict.
punguista [pũn'giʃta] *m* pickpocket.
punhado [pu'ɲadu] *m*: **um ~ de** a handful of.
punhal [pu'ɲaw] (*pl* **-ais**) *m* dagger.
punhalada [puɲa'lada] *f* stab.
punheta [pu'ɲeta] *f vulg* [masturbação] jacking off, wanking *UK*; **bater** *ou* **tocar ~** to jack off, to wank *UK*.
punho ['puɲu] *m* **-1.** *ANAT* fist; **de próprio ~** in one's own handwriting. **-2.** [de manga] cuff. **-3.** [de espada, punhal] hilt.
punição [puni'sãw] (*pl* **-ões**) *f* punishment.
punir [6] [pu'ni(x)] *vt* to punish.
punitivo, va [puni'tʃivu, va] *adj* punitive.
puns [pũnʃ] *mpl* ▷ **pum**.
pupila [pu'pila] *f ANAT* pupil.
pupilo, la [pu'pilu, la] *m, f* **-1.** [aluno] pupil. **-2.** [tutelado] ward.
purê [pu're] *m* purée, mash; **~ de batatas** mashed potato.
pureza [pu'reza] *f* purity.
purgação [puxga'sãw] (*pl* **-ões**) *f* **-1.** [expiação]

purge. **-2.** [de ferida] cleansing. **-3.** [purificação] purification.
purgante [pux'gãntʃi] *m* **-1.** [remédio] purgative. **-2.** *fam* [pessoa, trabalho] pain in the neck.
purgar [14] [pux'ga(x)] *vt* **-1.** [expiar] to purge. **-2.** [purificar]: ~ **algo (de algo)** to purge sthg (of sthg).
◆ **purgar-se** *vp*: **~-se (de algo)** to purge o.s. (of sthg).
purgativo, va [puxga'tʃivu, va] *adj* purgative.
◆ **purgativo** *m* [remédio] purgative.
purgatório [puxga'tɔrju] *m RELIG* purgatory.
purificação [purifika'sãw] (*pl* **-ões**) *f* **-1.** [depuração] purification. **-2.** *RELIG* [ritual] cleansing.
purificar [12] [purifi'ka(x)] *vt*: ~ **algo (de algo)** [depurar] to cleanse sthg (of sthg).
◆ **purificar-se** *vp* to cleanse o.s.
purista [pu'riʃta] *mf* purist.
puritanismo [puritã'niʒmu] *m* puritanism.
puritano, na [puri'tãnu, na] ◇ *adj* puritanical. ◇ *m, f* puritan.
puro, ra ['puru, ra] *adj* **-1.** [ger] pure. **-2.** *(antes de subst)* [mero] pure. **-3.** *(antes de subst)* [absoluto] plain.
puro-sangue [ˌpuru'sãŋgi] (*pl* **puros-sangues**) *mf* thoroughbred.
púrpura ['puxpura] *f* [cor] purple.
purpúreo, rea [pux'purju, rja] *adj* crimson.
purpurina [puxpu'rina] *f* purpurin.
purulento, ta [puru'lẽntu, ta] *adj* purulent.
pus ['puʃ] *m inv* pus.
pusilânime [puzi'lãnimi] *adj* pusillanimous.
pústula ['puʃtula] *f* **-1.** [vesícula] pustule. **-2.** *fig* & *pej* [pessoa] rat.
puta ['puta] *f* ▻ **puto**.
putaria [puta'ria] *f* *vulg* [prostíbulo] knocking shop.
putativo, va [puta'tʃivu, va] *adj* putative.
puto, ta ['putu, ta] *vulg adj* **-1.** [devasso] rotten; **o ~ de ...** *fam* the bloody ... **-2.** [zangado] mad; **estar/ficar ~ (da vida)** to be/get furious.
◆ **puto** ◇ *m vulg* [dinheiro] penny *UK*, dime *US* ◇ *adj* [extraordinário]: **um ~ (de um) ...** a brilliant/hell of a ....
◆ **puta** *vulg f* [prostituta] whore; **filho da puta** *fig* son of a bitch; **puta que pariu!** fucking hell!; **mandar alguém para a puta que pariu** to tell sb to fuck off.
putrefação [putrefa'sãw] *f* putrefaction.
putrefato, ta [putre'fatu, ta] *adj* rotten.
putrefazer [31] [putrefa'ze(x)] *vt* to putrefy.
◆ **putrefazer-se** *vp* to rot.
pútrido, da ['putridu, da] *adj* rotten.
puxa ['puʃa] *interj*: ~ **(vida)!** goodness (me)!, gosh.
puxado, da [pu'ʃadu, da] *adj* **-1.** [cansativo] exhausting. **-2.** [difícil] testing. **-3.** [caro] steep. **-4.** [amendoado] almond-shaped.
◆ **puxada** *f* **-1.** [puxão] tug. **-2.** [esforço]: **dar uma puxada** [em corrida] to put on a spurt; [nos estudos] to make an effort.
puxador [puʃa'do(x)] (*pl* **-es**) *mf* **-1.** [de samba] *the leading singer in an 'escola de samba', a group of musicians and samba dancers who perform in street parades during carnival celebrations in Brazil.* **-2.** [de fumo] (marijuana) smoker. **-3.** [ladrão] thief. ◇ *m* handle.
puxão [pu'ʃãw] (*pl* **-ões**) *m* tug; **dar um ~ em alguém** to pull s.b.
puxa-puxa [ˌpuʃa'puʃa] (*pl* **puxa-puxas**) ◇ *adj* toffee *(antes de subst)*. ◇ *m* toffee.
puxar [4] [pu'ʃa(x)] ◇ *vt* **-1.** [ger] to pull. **-2.** [arrancar, sacar] to pull out. **-3.** [iniciar - conversa] to start (up); [- briga] to break into; [- samba] to start (up), to break into; ~ **assunto** to bring up a subject. **-4.** [desencadear] to bring about; **uma coisa puxa a outra** one thing leads to another. **-5.** [adular]: ~ **o saco de alguém** *fam fig* to suck up to sb. **-6.** *gír droga* [fumo] to smoke. **-7.** *gír crime* [automóvel] to steal. ◇ *vi* **-1.** [impor esforço a]: ~ **por** to strain. **-2.** [ser parecido com]: ~ **a alguém** to take after sb. **-3.** [mancar]: ~ **de uma perna** to limp.
puxa-saco [ˌpuʃa'saku] (*pl* **puxa-sacos**) *fam* ◇ *adj* crawling. ◇ *mf* crawler.
puxões [pu'ʃõjʃ] *pl* ▻ **puxão**.
PV (*abrev de* **Partido Verde**) *m Brazilian green party.*
PVC (*abrev de* **Polyvinyl Chloride**) *m* PVC.

q, Q [ke] *m* [letra] q, Q.
Qatar [ka'ta(x)] *n* Qatar.
QG (*abrev de* **Quartel General**) *m* HQ.
QI (*abrev de* **Quociente de Inteligência**) *m* IQ.
QT (*abrev de* **Qualidade Total**) *f* TQM.
qua. (*abrev de* **quarta-feira**) *f* Wed.
quadra ['kwadra] *f* **-1.** [quarteirão] block; ~ **da praia** beachfront block. **-2.** [esportiva] court. **-3.** [em jogos] four. **-4.** [estrofe] quatrain. **-5.** *AGR* [medida] *area of 48,400m²*.
quadrado, da [kwa'dradu, da] *m*: **dois ao ~** two squared.
quadragésimo, ma [kwadra'ʒɛzimu, ma] *num* fortieth; *veja também* **sexto**.
quadrangular [kwadrãŋgu'la(x)] *adj GEOM* quadrangular.
quadrângulo [kwa'drãŋgulu] *m* quadrangle.
quadriculado, da [kwadriku'ladu, da] *adj* **-1.** [camisa, padrão] checked. **-2.** [papel] squared.

quadril [kwa'driw] (*pl* **-is**) *m* hip.

quadrilátero, ra [kwadri'lateru, ra] *adj* quadrilateral.

◆ **quadrilátero** *m* quadrilateral.

quadrilha [kwa'driʎa] *f* **-1.** [de ladrões etc] gang. **-2.** [dança] quadrille.

quadrimestral [kwadrimeʃ'traw] (*pl* **-ais**) *adj* quarterly.

quadrimotor [kwadrimo'to(x)] ◇ *adj* four-engined. ◇ *m* [avião] four-engined plane.

quadrinho [kwa'driɲu] *m* [das tiras] (cartoon) drawing.

◆ **quadrinhos** *mpl*: **(história em) ~s** cartoon strip.

quadro ['kwadru] *m* **-1.** [ger] frame. **-2.** [pintura] painting. **-3.** [quadro-negro] blackboard. **-4.** [mural] board; **~ de avisos** noticeboard. **-5.** [gráfico] chart. **-6.** *TEC* [painel] panel; **~ de luz** light panel. **-7.** *TEATRO* & *TV* scene. **-8.** [situação] picture; **~ clínico** clinical picture. **-9.** [de empresa, partido] staff. **-10.** *ESP* [equipe] team.

quadro-negro [ˌkwadru'negru] (*pl* **quadros-negros**) *m* blackboard.

quadrúpede [kwa'drupedʒi] ◇ *adj* [animal] quadrupedal, four-footed. ◇ *mf* **-1.** [animal] quadruped. **-2.** *mfam* [estúpido] clot *UK*, dumbhead *US*.

quadruplicar [12] [kwadrupli'ka(x)] ◇ *vt* to quadruple. ◇ *vi* to quadruple.

quádruplo, pla ['kwadruplu, pla] ◇ *adj* quadruple. ◇ *m, f* [quadrigêmeo] quad, quadruplet.

◆ **quádruplo** *m* quadruple.

quaisquer ▻ **qualquer**.

qual [kwaw] (*pl* **quais**) ◇ *adj* which; **~ perfume você prefere?** which perfume do you prefer?; **não sei ~ caminho devo seguir** I don't know which road I should follow. ◇ *conj fml* [como] like; **(tal) ~** exactly like. ◇ *interj* what!; **~!** [exprimindo espanto] what!; [exprimindo negação] no; **~ nada!**, **~ o quê!** yeah right! ◇ *pron* **-1.** [em interrogativa] what; **~ é o seu nome?** what's your name?; **~ a cor dos seus cabelos?** what is the colour of your hair?; **quais são suas intenções?** what are your intentions? **-2.** [especificando] which (one); **perguntei ~ seria a melhor opção** I asked which (one) would be the better option; **o/a ~** [suj: pessoa] who; [complemento: pessoa] whom; [suj, complemento: coisa] which; **ela teve três filhos, o mais velho dos quais tornou-se médico** she had three sons, the eldest of whom became a doctor; **este é o livro sobre o ~ lhe escrevi** this is the book (which/that) I wrote to you about; **cada ~** each and every one; **~ deles ...?** which one (of them) ...?

qualidade [kwali'dadʒi] *f* **-1.** [ger] quality; **~ de vida** quality of life; **de ~** good quality. **-2.** [tipo] grade. **-3.** *pej* [baixo nível] ilk. **-4.** [condição]: **na ~ de** in the capacity of.

qualificação [kwalifika'sãw] (*pl* **-ões**) *f* [avaliação] classification.

◆ **qualificações** *fpl* [formação, preparo] qualifications.

qualificado, da [kwalifi'kadu, da] *adj* **-1.** [preparado] qualified; **não ~** unqualified. **-2.** *JUR* [caracterizado] aggravated.

qualificar [12] [kwalifi'ka(x)] *vt* **-1.** [classificar] to qualify. **-2.** [avaliar] to describe.

◆ **qualificar-se** *vp* [classificar-se] to qualify.

qualificativo, va [kwalifika'tʃivu, va] *adj* qualifying.

◆ **qualificativo** *m* label.

qualitativo, va [kwalita'tʃivu, va] *adj* qualitative.

qualquer [kwaw'kɛ(x)] (*pl* **quaisquer**) ◇ *adj* **-1.** [algum]: **traga uma bebida ~** bring me any old drink; **comprei um jornal ~** I bought any old newspaper; **havia ~ coisa de errado** there was something wrong; **num ponto ~ da Sibéria** somewhere or other in Siberia; **~ dia venha me visitar** come and see me some day; **a ~ momento** any minute now; **um outro ~** [coisa] any other one; [pessoa] some; **ser ~ coisa** [ser ótimo, extraordinário] to be something else. **-2.** *(antes de subst)* [todo] any; **ele enfrenta quaisquer perigos** he braves all dangers; **~ pessoa sabe fazer arroz** anybody can cook rice; **~ que seja** whatever; **~ um** anybody; **todo e ~** each and every; **de ~ maneira** *ou* **jeito** [seja como for] somehow or other; [a todo custo] come what may. **-3.** *pej* [ordinário, sem importância]: **ele se contenta com ~ coisa** he's happy with any old thing; **de ~ maneira** *ou* **jeito** [sem cuidado] any (old) how. ◇ *pron* **-1.** [algum]: **~ (de)** any (of); **como não posso ter todas, terei de escolher ~** as I can't have them all, I'll have to chose any one; **prove quaisquer destas balas** try any one of these sweets; **um ~** *pej* [pessoa] a nobody. **-2.** [todo - coisa]: **~ (de)** any (of); **~ destas substâncias é perigosa** any of these substances is dangerous; [- pessoa] anyone; **~ de nós faria o mesmo** anyone of us would do the same.

quando ['kwãndu] ◇ *adv* when. ◇ *conj* when; [ao passo que] while; **de ~ em ~** from time to time; **de vez em ~** from time to time; **desde ~** how long; **~ mais não seja** at least, if only; **~ muito** at (the) most; **~ quer que** whenever.

quanta ▻ **quanto**.

quantia [kwãn'tʃia] *f* sum.

quantidade [kwãntʃi'dadʒi] *f* **-1.** [medida] amount. **-2.** [número] number. **-3.** [abundância]: **uma ~ de** a number of; **em ~** in large quantity.

quantificar [12] [kwãntʃifi'ka(x)] *vt* to quantify.

quantitativo, va [kwãntʃita'tʃivu, va] *adj* quantitative.

quanto, ta ['kwãntu, ta] ◇ *adj* **-1.** *(interrogativo)* how; **quantas maçãs você quer?** how many apples do you want?; **há ~ tempo você está esperando?** how long have you been waiting? **-2.** *(exclamativo)* how; **quantos livros!** how many books!, so many books!; **quanta gente!** how many people!, so many people! ◇ *pron* **-1.** *(interrogativo)* how; **quantos fugiram?** how many got away? **-2.** *(exclamativo)* how; **quantos não morrem antes de chegar à idade adulta!** how many died before reaching adulthood! **-3.** *(relativo)*: **tantos ... quantos ...** as many ... as ...; **faça tantas alterações quantas forem necessárias** make as many changes as necessary; **gosto de tudo ~é verdura** I like all green vegetables; **tudo ~é tipo de penteado** all kinds of hairstyles.

◆ **quanto** ◇ *pron (interrogativo)* [quantia, preço] how; **~ custa este casaco?** how much does this coat cost?; **a ~ está o dólar?** how much is the dollar?; [quantidade]: **~ de maionese devo acrescentar?** how much mayonnaise should I add?; **~ de combustível ainda temos?** how much fuel do we still have? ◇ *adv* [indicando intensidade, proporção] much; **esforcei-me o ~ pude** I tried as much/hard as I could; **sei o ~ você me ama** I know how much you love me; **um tanto ~** [meio] somewhat; **tanto ~** as much as; **tanto um quanto o outro são incompetentes** [ambos] both are equally incompetent; **tão ... ~ ...** as ... as ...; **~ mais tem, mais quer** the more he has, the more he wants; **~ mais rápido, melhor** the faster, the better; **~ mais** [especialmente] especially; [muito menos] especially not.

◆ **quanto a** *loc prep* [com relação] as for, as far as; **~ a mim** as for me, as far as I'm concerned.

◆ **quanto antes** *loc adv*: **o ~ antes** as soon as possible.

◆ **quantos** *pron pl fam*: **um certo Carlos não sei dos quantos** a certain Carlos something or other.

◆ **quantas** *pron pl fam*: **a quantas** [em que situação] at what stage; **não sei a quantas anda esse processo** I don't know what stage the trial is at.

quão [kwãw] *adv* how.

quarenta [kwa'rẽnta] *num* forty; *veja também* **sessenta**.

quarentão, tona [kwarẽn'tãw, tona] (*mpl* **-ões**, *fpl* **-s**) ◇ *adj* in one's forties. ◇ *m, f* person in their forties.

quarentena [kwarẽn'tena] *f* quarantine.

quarentona [kwarẽn'tona] *f* ⊳ **quarentão**.

quaresma [kwa'rɛʒma] *f* **-1.** *RELIG* Lent. **-2.** [flor] glory bush.

quarta ['kwaxta] *f* [quarta-feira] Wednesday; *veja também* **sábado**.

quarta-de-final [ˌkwaxtadʒifi'naw] (*pl* **quartas-de-final**) *f* quarter final.

quarta-feira [ˌkwaxta'fejra] (*pl* **quartas-feiras**) *f* Wednesday; **~ de cinzas** Ash Wednesday; *veja também* **sábado**.

quarteirão [kwaxtej'rãw] (*pl* **-ões**) *m* block.

quartel [kwax'tɛw] (*pl* **-éis**) *m MIL* barracks *(pl)*.

quartel-general [kwaxˌtɛwʒene'raw] (*pl* **quartéis-generais**) *m* general headquarters *(pl)*.

quarteto [kwax'tetu] *m* **-1.** *MÚS* quartet; **~ de cordas** string quartet. **-2.** *LITER* [em poesia] quatrain.

quarto, ta ['kwaxtu, ta] *num* fourth; **a quarta parte** a quarter; *veja também* **sexto**.

◆ **quarto** *m* **-1.** [a quarta parte] quarter; **passar um mau ~ de hora** *fig* to have a tough time (of it). **-2.** [aposento] bedroom; **~ de casal** double room; **~ de banho** bathroom; **~ de despejo** store cupboard; **~ de solteiro** single room. **-3.** *MIL* [plantão] watch; **estar/ficar de ~** to be/remain on duty. **-4.** [de boi] haunch. **-5.** *ASTRON* [da lua]: **~ crescente/minguante** first/last quarter.

◆ **quarta** *f* **-1.** [marcha] fourth; **passar a quarta** to shift into fourth. **-2.** *MÚS* perfect fourth. **-3.** [medida] quart.

quarto-e-sala [ˌkwaxtwi'sala] (*pl* **quarto-e-salas**) *m* studio apartment.

quarto-zagueiro [ˌkwaxtuza'gejru] (*pl* **-ros**) *m FUT* fullback.

quartzo ['kwaxtsu] *m* quartz.

quase ['kwazi] *adv* **-1.** [ger] nearly; **estou ~, ~ perdendo a paciência** I am on the verge of losing my temper; **tropecei e ~ caí** I tripped and almost fell. **-2.** [pouco mais, ou menos] almost, nearly; **ela tem ~ dez anos** she is almost *ou* nearly ten years old; **~ não trabalhei hoje** I hardly worked today; **~ nada/tudo** almost nothing/everything; **~ nunca** almost never, hardly ever; **~ sempre** nearly always.

quatro ['kwatru] *num* four; **de ~** on all fours; **estar/ficar de ~** [surpreso] to be astounded; **estar de ~ por alguém** [apaixonado] to be head over heels over sb; *veja também* **seis**.

quatrocentos, tas [ˌkwatru'sẽntuʃ, taʃ] *num* four hundred; *veja também* **seis**.

que [ki] ◇ *adj inv* **-1.** [em interrogativas] what, which; **~ livros você quer?** which books do you want?; **~ dia é hoje?** what day is it today?; **~ horas são?** what time is it? **-2.** [em exclamações]: **mas ~ belo dia!** what a beautiful day!; **~ fome!** I'm starving!; **~ maravilha!** how wonderful! ◇ *pron* **-1.** [em interrogativas] what; **~ é isso?** what's that?; **o ~ você quer?** what do you want?; **o ~ você vai comer?** what are you going to eat? **-2.** [uso relativo: sujeito-pessoa] who; **o homem ~ está correndo** the man who's running; [-coisa] which, that; **a guerra ~ começou em 1939** the war that started in 1939. **-3.** [uso relativo: complemento-pessoa] whom, that; **o homem ~ conheci** the man (whom) I met; [-coisa] which, that; **o bolo ~ comi era ótimo** the cake (that) I ate was great. ◇ *conj* **-1.** [com complemento direto] that; **ele disse-me ~ ia de férias** he told me (that) he was going on holiday. **-2.** [em comparações]: **(do) ~** than; **é mais caro (do) ~ o outro** it's more expensive than the other. **-3.** [exprime causa]: **leva o guarda-chuva ~ está chovendo** take an umbrella because it's raining; **vai depressa ~ você está atrasado** you'd better hurry because you're late. **-4.** [exprime conseqüência] that; **pediu-me tanto ~ acabei por lhe dar** he asked me for it so much that I ended up giving it to him. **-5.** [exprime tempo]: **há horas ~ estou à espera** I've been waiting for hours; **há muito ~ não vou lá** I haven't been there for ages. **-6.** [indica desejo] that; **espero ~ você se divirta** I hope (that) you have fun; **quero ~ você o faça** I want you to do it; **~ você seja feliz!** may you be happy! **-7.** [em locuções]: **~ nem** like; **ele chorou**

~ **nem um bebê** he cried like a baby; **ele é feio ~ nem o irmão** he's as ugly as his brother.

quê ['ke] ◇ *m* [algo]: **um ~** something; **um ~ de** [toque] a touch of; [sabor] slightly; **um não sei ~** a je ne sais quoi; **sem ~ nem por ~** [sem motivo] without rhyme or reason. ◇ *interj* [exprimindo espanto] what! ◇ *pron* ▷ **que**.

Quebec [ke'bɛki] *n*: **(o) ~** Quebec.

quebra ['kɛbra] *f* **-1.** [ger] break. **-2.** [despedaçamento] breakage. **-3.** [falência] bankruptcy. **-4.** *COMPUT*: **~ de página** page break.

◆ **de quebra** *loc adv* what's more.

quebra-cabeça [ˌkɛbraka'besa] (*pl* **quebra-cabeças**) *m* **-1.** [jogo] puzzle. **-2.** *fig* [problema] dilemma.

quebradiço, ça [kebra'dʒisu, sa] *adj* fragile.

quebrado, da [ke'bradu, da] *adj* **-1.** [vaso, vidro, braço] broken. **-2.** [enguiçado - carro, máquina] broken down; [- telefone] out of order. **-3.** [cansado] worn out. **-4.** [falido] bankrupt. **-5.** *fam* [sem dinheiro] broke.

◆ **quebrados** *mpl* [trocados] change *(sg)*.

quebra-galho [ˌkɛbra'gaʎu] (*pl* **quebra-galhos**) *m* **-1.** [pessoa] Mr Fixit. **-2.** [objeto] contrivance.

quebra-gelos [ˌkɛbra'ʒeluʃ] *m inv NÁUT* icebreaker.

quebra-mar [ˌkɛbra'ma(x)] (*pl* **quebra-mares**) *m* breakwater.

quebra-molas [ˌkɛbra'mɔlaʃ] *m inv* speed bump *ou* hump, sleeping policeman.

quebra-nozes [ˌkɛbra'nɔziʃ] *m inv* nutcracker.

quebranto [ke'brãntu] *m* **-1.** [mau- olhado] evil eye. **-2.** [abatimento] run-down state.

quebra-pau [ˌkɛbra'paw] (*pl* **quebra-paus**) *m fam* fisticuffs *(pl)*.

quebra-quebra [ˌkɛbra'kɛbra] (*pl* **quebra-quebras**) *m* riot.

quebrar [4] [ke'bra(x)] ◇ *vt* **-1.** [ger] to break; **~ algo ao meio** to split sthg in half. **-2.** [espancar] to beat up. **-3.** [enfraquecer] to weaken. **-4.** [interromper] to halt. **-5.** [desviar] to deflect. ◇ *vi* **-1.** [despedaçar-se] to break. **-2.** [enguiçar] to break down. **-3.** [falir] to go bankrupt. **-4.** *fam* [ficar sem dinheiro] to be broke.

◆ **quebrar-se** *vp* **-1.** [despedaçar-se] to break. **-2.** [desfazer-se] to be broken.

quebra-vento [ˌkɛbra'vẽntu] (*pl* **quebra-ventos**) *m AUTO* fanlight.

queda ['kɛda] *f* **-1.** [ger] fall; **~ livre** free fall; **~ de barreira** landslide; **em ~** falling. **-2.** [declínio] fall; **estar em ~** to be falling. **-3.** *fig* [inclinação]: **ter uma ~ para algo** to have a flair for sthg; **ter uma ~ por alguém** to have a soft spot for sb.

queda-d'água [ˌkɛda'dagwa] (*pl* **quedas-d'água**) *f* waterfall.

queda-de-braço [kɛdadʒibrasu] (*pl* **quedas-de-braço** [kɛdaʃibrasu]) *f* **-1.** [jogo] arm-wrestling. **-2.** *fig* [disputa] dispute.

queijada [kej'ʒada] *f* cheesecake.

queijadinha [kejʒa'dʒiɲa] *f* coconut ice.

queijeira [kej'ʒejra] *f* cheese cover.

queijo ['kejʒu] *m* cheese; **~ prato** (form of) processed cheese; **~ ralado** grated cheese.

queima ['kejma] *f* **-1.** [queimada] burning fire; **~ de fogos** fireworks display. **-2.** *COM* & *fig* [liquidação] clearance sale.

queimado, da [kej'madu, da] *adj* **-1.** [ger] burnt. **-2.** [de sol - bronzeado] tanned; [- ferido] sunburnt. **-3.** [plantas] scorched. **-4.** *fam fig* [malquisto] ruined.

◆ **queimado** *m* [coisa queimada]: **cheiro/gosto de ~** smell of burning/taste burnt.

◆ **queimada** *f* slash-and-burn.

queimadura [kejma'dura] *f* **-1.** [com fogo] burn; **~ de primeiro/segundo grau** first-/second-degree burn. **-2.** [de sol] sunburn.

queimar [4] [kej'ma(x)] ◇ *vt* **-1.** [ger] to burn. **-2.** [atear fogo a] to set on fire. **-3.** [abrasar, ferir - fogo, choque, sol] to burn; [- líquido] to scald. **-4.** [bronzear] to tan. **-5.** *COM* & *fig* [liquidar] to liquidate. **-6.** *fam fig* [tornar malquisto] to ruin. **-7.** *fig* [dinheiro] to blow. ◇ *vi* **-1.** [abrasar] to be burning hot. **-2.** [arder em febre] to burn (up). **-3.** [lâmpada, fusível] to blow. **-4.** *ESP* to hit the net. **-5.** [comida] to burn.

◆ **queimar-se** *vp* **-1.** [ferir-se - ger] to burn o.s.; [- com líquido fervente] to scald o.s. **-2.** [bronzear-se] to sunbathe. **-3.** *fam fig* [enfezar-se] to take offence. **-4.** *fam fig* [tornar-se malquisto] to blow it.

queima-roupa [ˌkejma'xopa] *f*: **à ~** [disparo] at point-blank range; *fig* [sem rodeios] point-blank.

queixa ['kejʃa] *f* **-1.** [reclamação] complaint; **dar ~ de algo/alguém** to complain about sthg/sb; **ter ~ de algo/alguém** to have a complaint against sthg/sb. **-2.** [lamento] grievance.

queixa-crime [ˌkejʃa'krimi] (*pl* **queixas-crime(s)**) *f JUR* citation.

queixada [kej'ʃada] *f* **-1.** [de animal] jaw. **-2.** [queixo grande] prominent jaw.

queixar-se [7] [kej'ʃaxsi] *vp* **-1.** [reclamar]: **~-se (de algo/alguém)** to complain (about sthg/sb). **-2.** [lamentar-se] to moan.

queixo ['kejʃu] *m* chin; **estava com tanto frio que chegava a bater o ~** [de frio] I was so cold my teeth started chattering; **ele ficou de ~ caído** [ficar admirado] his jaw dropped in amazement.

queixoso, osa [kej'ʃozu, ɔza] *adj* **-1.** [agravado] querulous. **-2.** [magoado] aggrieved.

queixudo, da [kej'ʃudu, da] *adj* big-jawed.

queixume [kej'ʃumi] *m* [lamentação] complaint.

quem ['kẽj] *pron* [interrogativo: sujeito] who; [interrogativo: complemento] who, whom; [indefinido] whoever; **~ diria!** who would have thought it!; **~ é?** [na porta] who's there?; **~ fala?** [no telefone] who's calling?, who's speaking?; **~ me dera ser rico!** if only I were rich!; **~ quer que** whoever; **seja ~ for** no matter who it is, whoever it is it is.

quentão [kẽn'tãw] *m* mulled wine.

quente ['kẽntʃi] ◇ *adj* **-1.** [ger] hot. **-2.** [roupa] warm. **-3.** [animado] vibrant. **-4.** *gír jornalismo* [notícia] reliable. ◇ *m* [moda]: **o ~ agora é usar cabelo comprido** the in thing now is to wear one's hair long.

quentinha [kẽn'tʃiɲa] *f* **-1.** [embalagem] *insulated carton for food.* **-2.** [refeição] snack.
quentura [kẽn'tura] *f* warmth.
quepe ['kɛpi] *m* kepi.
quer [kɛ(x)] <> *conj*: **~ ..., ~ ...** whether ... or ...; **~ você queira, ~ não** whether you want to or not. <> *v* ▻ **querer**.
◆ **onde quer que** *loc pron* wherever.
◆ **o que quer que** *loc pron* whatever.
◆ **quem quer que** *loc pron* whoever.
querela [ke'rɛla] *f* **-1.** [contenda] quarrel. **-2.** *JUR* charge.
querelar [4] [kere'la(x)] <> *vt JUR* to sue. <> *vi* [queixar-se]: **~ (contra/de)** to quarrel (with/about).
querer [38] [ke're(x)] <> *m* **-1.** [vontade] wanting. **-2.** [amor] love. <> *vt* **-1.** [ger] to want; **como queira/quiser** as you wish; **como quem não quer nada** casually; **estar querendo fazer algo** [estar na iminência de] to be about to do sthg; **não ~ nada com** to want nothing to do with; **~ dizer** to mean; **quer dizer** [em outras palavras] that is to say; **quer dizer que ...** [então] so that means ... **-2.** [ter a bondade de]: **queiram apertar seus cintos de segurança** please fasten your seatbelts; **quer me passar o vinho, por favor?** would you kindly pass me the wine, please? **-3.** [cobrar]: **quero dois mil pelo carro** I want two thousand for the car. **-4.** [ter afeição por] to love. **-5.** [conseguir]: **não ~ fazer algo** not to want to do sthg. <> *vi* **-1.** [desejar, ter vontade]: **não vou porque não quero** I am not going because I don't want to; **~ é poder** *prov* where there's a will, there's a way; **por ~** on purpose; **sem ~** unintentionally. **-2.** [amar] to love; **~ bem a alguém** to care about sb; **~ mal a alguém** to wish sb ill.
◆ **querer-se** *vp* [amar-se] to love one another.
querido, da [ke'ridu, da] <> *adj* **-1.** [caro] dear; **ele é muito ~ na cidade** he is much liked in town. **-2.** [em carta]: **Querido ...** Dear ... <> *m, f* **-1.** [preferido] favourite *UK*, favorite *US*. **-2.** [como forma de tratamento] darling.
quermesse [kex'mɛsi] *f* fête *UK*, kermis *US*.
querosene [kero'zeni] *m* kerosene.
querubim [keru'bĩ] (*pl* **-ns**) *m* cherub.
quesito [ke'zitu] *m* **-1.** [ponto, questão] question. **-2.** [requisito] requirement.
questão [keʃ'tãw] (*pl* **-ões**) *f* **-1.** [ger] question; **isso ocorreu há ~ de cinco meses** that happened some five months ago; **~ de honra** question of honour; **~ de tempo** question of time; **~ de vida ou morte** matter of life or death; **em ~** in question; **fazer ~ (de algo)** *fig* [insistir em] to insist (on sthg). **-2.** *JUR* case.
questionamento [keʃtʃjona'mẽntu] *m* [pôr em dúvida] questioning.
questionar [4] [keʃtʃjo'na(x)] *vt* **-1.** [debater] to dispute. **-2.** [fazer perguntas] to question.
questionário [keʃtʃjo'narju] *m* questionnaire.
questionável [keʃtʃjo'navew] (*pl* **-eis**) *adj* questionable.
questões [keʃ'tõjʃ] *pl* ▻ **questão**.
qui. (*abrev de* **quinta-feira**) *f* Thur.
quiabo ['kjabu] *m* okra.
quibe ['kibi] *m deep-fried meat dish with mint and other spices.*
quibebe [ki'bɛbi] *m* pumpkin purée.
quicar [12] [ki'ka(x)] <> *vt* [bola] to bounce. <> *vi* [bola] to bounce.
quiche ['kiʃi] *f* quiche.
quíchua ['kiʃwa] <> *adj* Quechuan. <> *m, f* Quechuan.
◆ **quíchua** *m* [língua] Quechuan.
quieto, ta ['kjɛtu, ta] *adj* **-1.** [em silêncio] quiet. **-2.** [tranqüilo] calm. **-3.** [imóvel] still.
quietude [kje'tudʒi] *f* tranquillity.
quilate [ki'latʃi] *m* **-1.** [de ouro] carat. **-2.** *fig* [excelência] calibre *UK*, caliber *US*.
quilha ['kiʎa] *f* keel.
quilo ['kilu] *m* kilo; **a ~** by the kilo.
quilobyte [kilo'bajtʃi] *m COMPUT* kilobyte.
quilohertz [kilo'hɛxtʃis] *m* kilohertz.
quilombo [ki'lõnbu] *m fortified village where runaway slaves lived.*
quilometragem [kilome'traʒẽ] (*pl* **-ns**) *f* **-1.** [distância percorrida] distance in kilometres *UK ou* kilometers *US*, ≃ mileage. **-2.** [distância entre dois pontos] distance in kilometres *UK ou* kilometers *US*.
quilometrar [4] [kilome'tra(x)] *vt* to measure in kilometres *UK ou* kilometers *US*.
quilométrico, ca [kilo'mɛtriku, ka] *adj fig* [longo] mile *(antes de subst)*.
quilômetro [ki'lometru] *m* kilometre *UK*, kilometer *US*.
quilowatt [kilo'vatʃi] *m* kilowatt.
quilowatt-hora [kilo,vatʃi'ɔra] (*pl* **-ras**) *m ELETR* kilowatt-hour.
quimbanda [kĩn'bãnda] *m* **-1.** [ritual] *macumba ritual.* **-2.** [feiticeiro] *priest of macumba.* **-3.** [terreiro] *place where macumba is practised.*
quimera [ki'mɛra] *f* [fantasia, ilusão] chimera.
químico, ca ['kimiku, ka] <> *adj* chemical. <> *m, f* [profissional] chemist.
◆ **química** *f* **-1.** [ger] chemistry. **-2.** [substância] chemical. **-3.** *fig* [segredo] secret.
quimioterapia [kimjotera'pia] *f* chemotherapy.
quimono [ki'monu] *m* kimono.
quina ['kina] *f* **-1.** [canto] corner; **de ~** side on. **-2.** [de jogo] jackpot.
quindim [kĩn'dʒĩ] (*pl* **-ns**) *m sweet made of egg, sugar and coconut.*
quinhão [ki'ɲãw] (*pl* **-ões**) *m* share.
quinhentista [kiɲẽn'tʃiʃta] *adj* sixteenth century *(antes de subst)*.
quinhentos, tas [ki'ɲẽntuʃ, taʃ] *num* five hundred; **ser outros ~** to be a different kettle of fish; *veja também* **seis**.
quinhões [ki'ɲõjʃ] *pl* ▻ **quinhão**.
quinina [ki'nina] *f* quinine.
qüinquagésimo, ma [kwiŋkwa'ʒɛzimu, ma] *num* fiftieth; *veja também* **sexto**.

qüinqüênio [kwiŋ'kwenju] *m* quinquennium.

quinquilharia [kĩŋkiʎa'ria] *f* **-1.** [bugiganga] junk. **-2.** [ninharia] trinket.
◆ **quinquilharias** *fpl* [miudezas] odds and ends.

quinta ['kĩnta] *f* **-1.** [quinta-feira] Thursday. **-2.** [sítio] estate; *veja também* **sábado**.

quinta-essência [ˌkintae'sẽnsja] *f* **-1.** [essência] quintessence. **-2.** [plenitude] epitome.

quinta-feira [ˌkĩnta'fejra] (*pl* **quintas-feiras**) *f* Thursday; *veja também* **sábado**.

quintal [kĩn'taw] (*pl* **-ais**) *m* [de casa] backyard.

quinteto [kĩn'tetu] *m* MÚS quintet.

quinto, ta ['kĩntu, ta] *num* fifth; *veja também* **sexto**.

quintuplicar [kĩntupli'ka(x)] *vt*: **quintuplicou o número de desempregados** the number of unemployed has multiplied by five.

quíntuplo, pla ['kĩntuplu, pla] *adj* quintuple.
◆ **quíntuplo** *m* quintuple.
◆ **quíntuplos** *mpl* [gêmeos] quins, quintuplets.

quinze ['kĩnzi] *num* fifteen; *veja também* **seis**.

quinzena [kĩn'zena] *f* **-1.** [tempo] fortnight. **-2.** [salário] fortnight's wages.

quinzenal [kĩnze'naw] (*pl* **-ais**) *adj* fortnightly.

quinzenalmente [kĩnzenaw'mẽntʃi] *adv* fortnightly.

quiosque ['kjɔʃki] *m* **-1.** [de jardim] gazebo. **-2.** [banca] kiosk.

qüiprocó [kwipro'kɔ] *m* [confusão] mix-up.

quiromancia [kiromãn'sia] *f* palmistry, chiromancy.

quiromante [kiro'mãntʃi] *mf* palm reader.

quisto ['kiʃtu] *m* cyst.

quitação [kita'sawl] (*pl* **-ões**) *f* **-1.** [remissão] discharge. **-2.** [pagamento] settlement. **-3.** [recibo] receipt.

quitanda [ki'tãnda] *f* grocer's shop *UK*, grocery store *US*.

quitandeiro, ra [kitãn'dejru, ra] *m, f* greengrocer.

quitar [4] [ki'ta(x)] *vt* **-1.** [pagar] to settle. **-2.** [perdoar] to cancel. **-3.** [devedor] to release.

quite ['kitʃi] *adj* **-1.** [com credor]: **estar/ficar ~ (com alguém)** to be quits (with sb). **-2.** [livre]: **~ de algo** free of sthg. **-3.** [igualado] even.

quitenho, nha [ki'teɲu, ɲa] ◇ *adj* Quito *(antes de subst)*. ◇ *m, f person from Quito*.

Quito ['kitu] *n* Quito.

quitute [ki'tutʃi] *m* titbit *UK*, tidbit *US*.

quizumba [ki'zũnba] *f fam* brawl.

quociente [kwo'sjẽntʃi] *m* MAT quotient; **~ de inteligência** intelligence quotient, IQ.

r, R ['ɛxi] *m* [letra] r, R.

rã ['xã] *f* frog.

rabada [xa'bada] *f* **-1.** [rabo] tail. **-2.** CULIN oxtail stew. **-3.** *fam* [de corrida]: **ele chegou na ~** he arrived at the tail end.

rabanada [xaba'nada] *f* **-1.** CULIN French toast. **-2.** [golpe com rabo] whack with the tail.

rabanete [xaba'netʃi] *m* radish.

Rabat [xa'batʃ] *n* Rabat.

rabeca [xa'bɛka] *f* MÚS fiddle.

rabecão [xabe'kãw] (*pl* **-ões**) *m* [carro fúnebre] hearse.

rabicho [xa'biʃu] *m* **-1.** [trança] pigtail. **-2.** *fam* [caso amoroso] passion.

rabino, na [xa'binu, na] *m* rabbi.

rabiscar [12] [xabiʃ'ka(x)] ◇ *vt* **-1.** [encher com rabiscos] to scribble over. **-2.** [riscos] to scribble. **-3.** [escrever às pressas] to scrawl. **-4.** [desenhar] to sketch. ◇ *vi* [fazer rabiscos] to doodle.

rabisco [xa'biʃku] *m* **-1.** [risco] scribble. **-2.** [esboço] sketch.
◆ **rabiscos** *mpl* [caligrafia ruim] scrawl *(sg)*.

rabo ['xabu] *m* **-1.** [cauda] tail; **~ de foguete** *fig* can of worms; **com o ~ do olho** out of the corner of one's eye; **meter o ~ entre as pernas** *fig* to be left with one's tail between one's legs. **-2.** *vulg* [nádegas] bum.

rabo-de-cavalo [ˌxabudʒika'valu] (*pl* **rabos-de-cavalo**) *m* ponytail.

rabo-de-saia [ˌxabudʒi'saja] (*pl* **rabos-de-saia**) *m fam* piece of skirt.

rabudo, da [xa'budu, da] *adj* [sortudo] lucky.
◆ **rabudo** *m fam* [diabo] devil.

rabugento, ta [xabu'ʒẽntu, ta] *adj* grumpy.

rabugice [xabu'ʒisi] *f* grumpiness.

raça ['xasa] *f* **-1.** [etnia] race. **-2.** [estirpe] lineage. **-3.** *pej* [laia] breed; **acabar com a ~ de alguém** [matar] to do away with sb. **-4.** *fig* [coragem, determinação] guts; **(no peito e) na ~** by sheer guts; **ter ~ (para algo)** to have the guts (for sthg). **-5.** [de animal] breed; **cão/cavalo de ~** pedigree dog/ thoroughbred horse.

ração [xa'sãw] (*pl* **-ões**) *f* **-1.** [de alimento] ration. **-2.** [para animal - para cão, gato] food; **~ para cachorro**

puppy food; [- para gado, cavalo] feed; ~ **para cavalo** horse feed.
racha ['xaʃa] *m* **-1.** *fam* [discórdia] split. **-2.** [em parede etc] crack.
rachadura [xaʃa'dura] *f* crack.
rachar [4] [xa'ʃa(x)] ◇ *vt* **-1.** [fender] to crack; **frio de** ~ bitterly cold; **ou vai ou racha** do or die; **sol de** ~ scorching sun. **-2.** [dividir]: ~ **algo (com alguém)** to split sthg (with sb). **-3.** *fig* [dividir] to split. **-4.** [cortar] to split. ◇ *vi* [fender-se] to crack.
racial [xa'sjaw] (*pl* **-ais**) *adj* racial.
raciocinar [4] [xasjosi'na(x)] *vi* to reason.
raciocínio [xasjo'sinju] *m* reasoning.
racional [xasjo'naw] (*pl* **-ais**) *adj* rational.
racionalidade [xasjonali'dadʒi] *f* racionality.
racionalização [xasjonaliza'sãw] *f* rationalization.
racionalizar [4] [xasjonali'za(x)] *vt* to rationalize.
racionalmente [xasjonaw'mẽntʃi] *adv* rationally, sensibly.
racionamento [xasjona'mẽntu] *m* rationing.
racionar [4] [xasjo'na(x)] *vt* to ration.
racismo [xa'siʒmu] *m* racism.
racista [xa'siʃta] ◇ *adj* racist. ◇ *mf* racist.
rack [xɛk] *m* rack.
rações [xa'sõjʃ] *pl* ⊳ **ração**.
radar [xa'da(x)] (*pl* **-es**) *m* radar.
radiação [xadʒja'sãw] (*pl* **-ões**) *f* radiation.
radiador [xadʒja'do(x)] (*pl* **-es**) *m* *AUTO* radiator.
radialista [xadʒja'liʃta] *mf* **-1.** [apresentador] (radio) announcer. **-2.** [da produção] (radio) producer.
radiante [xa'dʒjãntʃi] *adj* **-1.** [objeto] radiant. **-2.** [de alegria] ecstatic.
radical [xadʒi'kaw] (*pl* **-ais**) ◇ *adj* radical. ◇ *mf* **-1.** [ger] root. **-2.** *POL* & *QUÍM* radical; ~ **livre** free radical.
radicalismo [xadʒika'liʒmu] *m* radicalism.
radicalizar [4] [xadʒikali'za(x)] ◇ *vt* [aprofundar] to radicalize. ◇ *vi* [tornar-se radical] to become radical.
◆ **radicalizar-se** *vp* [tornar-se radical] to become radical.
radicar-se [12] [xadʒi'kaxsi] *vp* to settle.
rádio ['xadʒju] ◇ *m* **-1.** [aparelho] radio. **-2.** *QUÍM* radium. **-3.** *ANAT* [osso] radius. ◇ *f* [emissora] radio station.
radioamador, ra [xadʒjwama'do(x), da] *m, f* radio ham.
radioatividade [xadʒwatʃivi'dadʒi] *f* radioactivity.
radioativo, va [ˌxadʒwa'tʃivu, va] *adj* radioactive.
radiodifusão [xadʒodʒifu'zãw] *f* broadcasting.
radiodifusora [xadʒodʒifu'zora] *f* broadcasting station.
radioemissora [xadʒwemi'sora] *f* radio station.
radiografar [4] [xadʒogra'fa(x)] ◇ *vt* **-1.** *MED* to X-ray. **-2.** [notícia] to radio. ◇ *vi* [fazer contato] to radio.
radiografia [ˌxadʒjogra'fia] *f* **-1.** *MED* X-ray. **-2.** *fig* [análise] in-depth analysis.
radiograma [xadʒjo'grãma] *m* cablegram.
radiogravador [xadʒjugrava'do(x)] *m* radiocassette player.
radiojornal [xadʒjuʒox'naw] (*pl* **-ais**) *m* radio news *(sg)*.
radiologia [xadʒjolo'ʒia] *f* radiology.
radiologista [xadʒjolo'ʒiʃta] *mf* radiologist.
radionovela [xadʒjuno'vɛla] *f* radio soap.
radiooperador, ra [xadʒjoopera'do(x), ra] *m, f* radio operator.
radiopatrulha [xadʒjupa'truʎa] *f* **-1.** [serviço] radio patrol. **-2.** [viatura] patrol car.
radiorepórter [xadʒjuxe'pɔxte(x)] *mf* radio reporter.
radioso, osa [xa'dʒjozu, ɔza] *adj* radiant.
radiotáxi [ˌxadʒjo'taksi] *m* radio cab.
radioterapia [xadʒjotera'pia] *f* radiotherapy.
radiouvinte [xadʒjo'vĩntʃi] *mf* (radio) listener.
ráfia ['xafja] *f* raffia.
ragu [xa'gu] *m* ragout.
raia ['xaja] *f* **-1.** [linha] line. **-2.** [limite] boundary; **às** ~**s de algo** to the limits of sthg. **-3.** [pista - de piscina] (lane) marker; [- de tiro] firing range. **-4.** [peixe] ray. **-5.** *loc*: **fugir da** ~ to cut and run.
raiado, da [xa'jadu, da] *adj* **-1.** [pista] marked. **-2.** [cano] rifled. **-3.** [piscina] divided into lanes. **-4.** [bandeira] striped.
raiar [4] [xa'ja(x)] ◇ *vi* **-1.** [brilhar] to shine. **-2.** [despontar] to dawn. ◇ *vt* [com raias - pista] to mark; [- cano] to rifle; [- piscina] to lane off; [- pintar] to mark with stripes.
rainha [xa'iɲa] *f* queen.
rainha-mãe [xaˌiɲa'mãj] (*pl* **rainhas-mães**) *f* queen mother.
raio ['xaju] *m* **-1.** [ger] ray; ~ **laser** laser beam; ~ **X** X-ray. **-2.** [de luz] beam. **-3.** *METEOR* bolt of lightening. **-4.** *fam* [como ênfase]: **perdi o** ~ **da carteira** I lost my blasted wallet. **-5.** *GEOM* radius. **-6.**: ~ **de ação** [alcance] range; *fig* [área de atuação] range.
raiva ['xajva] *f* **-1.** [fúria] rage; **com** ~ **(de)** angry (at); **dar** ~ to drive mad; **morto de** ~ absolutely furious; **ter/tomar** ~ **de** to hate. **-2.** [doença] rabies *(sg)*.
raivoso, osa [xaj'vozu, ɔza] *adj* **-1.** [furioso] furious. **-2.** [doente] rabid.
raiz [xa'iʒ] (*pl* **-es**) *f* **-1.** [ger] root; **cortar o mal pela** ~ *fig* to root it out; **criar raízes** *fig* to put down roots; ~ **quadrada** square root. **-2.** [origem] roots *(pl)*.
rajada [xa'ʒada] *f* **-1.** [de vento] gust. **-2.** [de tiros] volley.
ralado, da [xa'ladu, da] *adj* **-1.** [moído] grated. **-2.** [esfolado] grazed.
ralador [xala'do(x)] (*pl* **-es**) *m* grater.
ralar [4] [xa'la(x)] *vt* **-1.** [com ralador] to grate. **-2.** [esfolar] to graze.
ralé [xa'lɛ] *f* [escória] riff-raff.

ralhar [4] [xa'ʎa(x)] *vi*: ~ **(com alguém)** to tell (sb) off.
rali [xa'li] *m* rally.
ralo, la ['xalu, la] *adj* **-1.** [cabelo, café, sopa] thin. **-2.** [vegetação] sparse.
◆ **ralo** *m* drainpipe.
Ram. (*abrev de* **ramal**) *m* ext.
RAM (*abrev de* **Random Access Memory**) *f* RAM.
rama ['xãma] *f* foliage; **em** ~ raw; **pela** ~ *fig* [superficialmente] superficially.
ramadã [xama'dã] *m* Ramadan, Ramadhan.
ramagem [xa'maʒẽ] *f* BOT branches *(pl)*.
ramal [xa'maw] (*pl* **-ais**) *m* **-1.** [de telefone] extension. **-2.** FERRO branch line. **-3.** [rodoviário] branch road.
ramalhete [xama'ʎetʃi] *m* [buquê] bunch.
rameira [xa'mejra] *f vulg* [prostituta] prostitute.
ramerrão [xame'xãw] *m* [rotina] grind.
ramificação [xamifika'sãw] (*pl* **-ões**) *f* [subdivisão] branch.
ramificar-se [12] [xamifi'kaxsi] *vp* **-1.** [subdividir-se] to be sub-divided. **-2.** [espalhar-se] to branch out.
ramo ['xãmu] *m* **-1.** [ger] branch. **-2.** [de flores] bouquet. **-3.** [área] field.
rampa ['xãnpa] *f* ramp.
rancheiro, ra [xãn'ʃejru, ra] *m, f* **-1.** [morador] farmer. **-2.** [zelador] tenant farmer. **-3.** [cozinheiro] cook.
rancho ['xãnʃu] *m* **-1.** [sítio] smallholding, farm. **-2.** [cabana] hut. **-3.** [refeição] mess. **-4.** MÚS [ritmo] carnival music.
ranço ['xãnsu] *m* **-1.** [sabor] rancid taste. **-2.** [cheiro] rank smell. **-3.** *fig* [atraso] age-old habit.
rancor [xãŋ'ko(x)] *m* **-1.** [ressentimento] resentment; **guardar** ~ **(de)** to be resentful (about). **-2.** [ódio] hatred.
rancoroso, osa [xãŋko'rozu, ɔza] *adj* resentful.
rançoso, osa [xãn'sozu, ɔza] *adj* rancid.
ranger [26] [xãn'ʒe(x)] ◇ *m* [ruído - de porta] creaking; [- de dentes] grinding. ◇ *vt* [os dentes] to grind. ◇ *vi* to creak.
rangido [xãn'ʒidu] *m* **-1.** [de porta] creak. **-2.** [de dente] grinding.
rango ['xãŋgu] *m fam* grub.
Rangun [xãŋ'gũ] *n* Rangoon.
ranheta [xã'ɲeta] *adj* surly.
ranhura [xã'ɲura] *f* **-1.** [entalhe] groove. **-2.** [canaleta] keyway. **-3.** [para moeda] slot.
ranzinza [xãn'zĩnza] *adj* bolshy.
rapa ['xapa] *m* **-1.** [de comida] scrap. **-2.** *fam* [fiscal] *policeman dealing with illegal street traders*. **-3.** *fam* [carro] *police patrol on the look-out for illegal street traders*.
rapadura [xapa'dura] *f* raw cane sugar.
rapagão, gona [xapa'gãw, gona] (*mpl* **-ões**, *fpl* **-onas**) *m, f* burly person.
rapapé [xapa'pɛ] *m* [bajulação] fawning; **fazer** ~**s a alguém** to kowtow to sb.
rapar [4] [xa'pa(x)] ◇ *vt* **-1.** [pelar] to shave. **-2.** *fam* [roubar] to nick. ◇ *vi fam* [ir embora] to scarper.
rapaz [xa'paʒ] (*pl* **-es**) *m* **-1.** [jovem] boy. **-2.** *fam* [cara] man.
rapaziada [xapa'zjada] *f* [rapazes] lads *(pl)*.
rapé [xa'pɛ] *m* snuff.
rapidamente [xapida'mẽntʃi] *adv* rapidly.
rapidez [xapi'deʃ] *f* speed; **com** ~ quickly, at speed.
rápido, da ['xapidu, da] *adj* **-1.** [veloz] fast, quick. **-2.** [breve] brief.
◆ **rápido** ◇ *m* [trem] express. ◇ *adv* [ligeiro] quickly.
rapina [xa'pina] *f* violent robbery; ▷ **ave**.
raposa [xa'poza] *f* **-1.** ZOOL vixen (*f* vixen). **-2.** *fig* [pessoa astuta] sly old fox.
rapsódia [xap'zɔdʒja] *f* rhapsody.
raptado, da [xap'tadu, da] ◇ *adj* kidnapped. ◇ *m, f* kidnap victim.
raptar [4] [xap'ta(x)] *vt* to kidnap.
rapto ['xaptu] *m* kidnapping.
raptor, ra [xap'to(x), ra] *m, f* kidnapper.
raquete [xa'kɛtʃi] *f* **-1.** [de tênis, squash] racket. **-2.** [de pingue-pongue] bat.
raquidiana [xaki͵dʒjãna] *f* [anestesia] epidural.
raquítico, ca [xa'kitʃiku, ka] *adj* **-1.** MED rachitic. **-2.** [magro] scrawny. **-3.** [escasso] sparse.
raquitismo [xaki'tʃiʒmu] *m* MED rickets *(sg or pl)*.
raramente [͵xara'mẽntʃi] *adv* rarely, seldom.
rarear [15] [xa'rja(x)] *vi* **-1.** [tornar-se raro] to become scarce. **-2.** [cabelos] to thin. **-3.** [vegetação, população] to thin out.
rarefazer [31] [xarefa'ze(x)] *vt* [tornar menos denso] to make thinner.
◆ **rarefazer-se** *vp* **-1.** [tornar-se menos denso] to get thinner. **-2.** [multidão] to disperse.
rarefeito, ta [xare'fejtu, ta] *adj* **-1.** [pouco denso] rarefied. **-2.** [disperso] dispersed.
raridade [xari'dadʒi] *f* **-1.** [qualidade] rareness. **-2.** [peça] rarity.
raro, ra ['xaru, ra] *adj* rare.
◆ **raro** *adv* [raramente] rarely; **não** ~ often.
rasante [xa'zãntʃi] ◇ *adj* low-flying. ◇ *adv*: **o avião passou** ~ the plane flew low.
rascunhar [4] [xaʃku'ɲa(x)] *vt* to draft.
rascunho [xaʃ'kuɲu] *m* draft.
rasgado, da [xaʒ'gadu, da] *adj* **-1.** [tecido, papel] torn. **-2.** *fig* [elogio, gesto] generous. **-3.** *fig* [ritmo, dança] flourishing.
rasgão [xaʒ'gãw] (*pl* **-ões**) *m* tear.
rasgar [14] [xaʒ'ga(x)] ◇ *vt* **-1.** [romper] to tear. **-2.** *fig* [elogios] to heap. ◇ *vi* [romper-se] to tear.
◆ **rasgar-se** *vp* **-1.** [romper-se] to be torn. **-2.** [pessoa] to be consumed.
rasgo ['xaʒgu] *m* **-1.** [rasgão] tear. **-2.** [traço] line. **-3.** *fig* [ação, ímpeto] burst.
rasgões [xaʒ'gõjʃ] *pl* ▷ **rasgão**.
raso, sa ['xazu, za] *adj* **-1.** [pouco fundo] shallow. **-2.** [colher etc] level. **-3.** [liso] even. **-4.** [rente] close-cropped. **-5.** [sapato] flat. **-6.** [soldado] private.
◆ **raso** *m* shallow end.

raspa ['xaʃpa] *f* **-1.** [lasca] shavings *(pl)*. **-2.** [de panela] scrapings *(pl)*.
raspadeira [xaʃpa'dejra] *f* scraper.
raspadinha [xaʃpa'dʒiɲa] *f* scratch card.
raspão [xaʃ'pãw] (*pl* **-ões**) *m* scratch; **o tiro pegou de ~ no braço** the shot grazed his arm.
raspar [4] [xaʃ'pa(x)] <> *vt* **-1.** [alisar] to smooth down. **-2.** [pêlos] to shave. **-3.** [limpar] to scrape; **~ o tacho** *fig* [as economias] to scrape the bottom of the barrel. **-4.** [arranhar] to scratch. **-5.** [de raspão] to graze. <> *vi* [de raspão]: **~ em** to strike a glancing blow at.
raspões [xaʃ'põjʃ] *pl* ▻ **raspão**.
rasteiro, ra [xaʃ'tejru, ra] *adj* **-1.** [vegetação] low-lying. **-2.** [vôo] low. **-3.** [que se arrasta] crawling. **-4.** *fig* [superficial] superficial.
◆ **rasteira** *f* trip; **dar uma ~ em alguém** [com pernada] to trip sb up; *fig* [trair] to double-cross sb.
rastejante [xaʃte'ʒãntʃi] *adj* **-1.** [que se arrasta - animal] crawling; [- planta] creeping. **-2.** *fig* [submisso] crawling.
rastejar [4] [xaʃte'ʒa(x)] <> *vi* **-1.** [arrastar-se - planta] to creep; [- animal] to crawl; [- cobra] to slide. **-2.** [andar de rastos] to crawl. **-3.** *fig* [rebaixar-se] to grovel. <> *vt* [rastrear] to track.
rastilho [xaʃ'tʃiʎu] *m* [de pólvora] fuse.
rasto ['xaʃtu] *m* **-1.** [pegada] track. **-2.** [de veículo] trail. **-3.** *fig* [vestígios] tracks *(pl)*.
◆ **rastos** *mpl*: **de rastos** on all fours.
rastrear [15] [xaʃ'trja(x)] <> *vt* **-1.** [seguir o rasto de] to track. **-2.** [investigar] to search for. <> *vi* [seguir o rasto] to track.
rastro ['xaʃtru] *m* = **rasto**.
rasura [xa'zura] *f* crossing out.
rasurar [4] [xazu'ra(x)] <> *vt* to cross out. <> *vi* to cross out.
rata ['xata] *f fam* [mancada] blunder; **dar uma ~** to make a stupid mistake; **rato**.
ratazana [xata'zãna] *f* Norway rat.
ratear [15] [xa'tʃja(x)] <> *vt* [dividir] to share out. <> *vi* [motor] to stall.
rateio [xa'teju] *m* **-1.** [divisão] sharing. **-2.** [turfe] [quantia] payout.
ratificação [xatʃifika'sãw] (*pl* **-ões**) *f* **-1.** [confirmação] ratification. **-2.** [comprovação] confirmation.
ratificar [12] [xatʃifi'ka(x)] *vt* **-1.** [confirmar] to ratify. **-2.** [comprovar] to confirm.
rato, ta ['xatu, ta] *m, f* rat; **~ de biblioteca** *fig* bookworm; **~ de praia** *fig* thief (on the beach).
ratoeira [xa'twejra] *f* **-1.** [para ratos] mousetrap. **-2.** *fig* [armadilha] trap.
ravina [xa'vina] *f* ravine.
ravióli [xa'vjɔli] *m* ravioli.
razão [xa'zãw] (*pl* **-ões**) <> *f* **-1.** [faculdade] reason; **~ de ser** raison d'être; **de viver** reason for living; **~ de Estado** reasons of state; **em ~ de** on account of. **-2.** [bom senso] (common) sense. **-3.** [justiça]: **dar ~ a alguém** to side with sb; **estar coberto de ~** to be absolutely right; **perder a ~** to lose one's mind; **ter/não ter ~ (de)** to be right/wrong (to); **com ~** with good reason; **sem ~** for no reason. **-4.** [*MAT* - proporção] ratio; [- quociente, fração] quotient; **à ~ de** at the rate of. **-5.** *FIN* account. <> *m COM* ledger.
◆ **razão social** *f COM* trade name.
razoável [xa'zwavew] (*pl* **-eis**) *adj* **-1.** [ger] reasonable. **-2.** [significativo] significant.
razoavelmente [xazwavew'mẽntʃi] *adv* reasonably.
ré ['xɛ] *f AUTO* reverse; **dar uma ~**, **dar marcha à ~** to reverse, to back up; ▻ **réu**.
reabastecer [25] [xejabaʃte'se(x)] *vt* **-1.** [tanque, carro, avião] to refuel. **-2.** [despensa, cozinha] to restock. **-3.** [energias] to rebuild.
◆ **reabastecer-se** *vp*: **~-se de algo** to replenish one's supply of sthg.
reabastecimento [xeabaʃtesi'mẽntu] *m* **-1.** [carro] refuelling. **-2.** [cidade] resupplying. **-3.** [despensa] restocking. **-4.** [energias] rebuilding.
reabertura [xeabex'tura] *f* reopening.
reabilitação [xeabilita'sãw] (*pl* **-ões**) *f* **-1.** [regeneração] rehabilitation. **-2.** [recuperação] rehabilitation; **~ motora** physiotherapy; [da forma física] recovery.
reabilitar [4] [xeabili'ta(x)] *vt* **-1.** [regenerar] to rehabilitate. **-2.** [recuperar] to recover.
◆ **reabilitar-se** *vp* **-1.** [regenerar-se] to be rehabilitated. **-2.** [recuperar-se] to recover.
reabrir [6] [xea'bri(x)] <> *vt* to reopen. <> *vi* to reopen.
reabsorver [5] [xeabsox've(x)] *vt* to reabsorb.
reaça *fam* [xe'asa] <> *adj* reactionary. <> *mf* [pessoa] reactionary.
reação [xea'sãw] (*pl* **-ões**) *f* **-1.** [ger] reaction; **~ em cadeia** chain reaction. **-2.** [recuperação] recovery.
reacender [5] [xeasẽn'de(x)] *vt* **-1.** [fogo, forno] to relight. **-2.** *fig* [ânimo, nacionalismo] to rekindle.
reacionário, ria [xeasjo'narju, rja] <> *adj* reactionary. <> *m, f* [pessoa] reactionary.
readaptação [xeadapta'sãw] (*pl* **-ões**) *f* readjustment.
readaptar [4] [xeadap'ta(x)] *vt* to readapt.
◆ **readaptar-se** *vp* to readapt.
readmissão [xeadʒimi'sãw] *f* readmission.
readmitir [6] [xeadʒimi'tʃi(x)] *vt* to readmit.
readquirir [6] [xeadʒiki'ri(x)] *vt* to regain.
reafirmar [4] [xeafix'ma(x)] *vt* to reaffirm.
reagir [52] [xea'ʒi(x)] *vi* **-1.** [responder]: **~ (a)** to react (to). **-2.** [protestar, resistir]: **~ (a** *OU* **contra)** to resist. **-3.** [recuperar-se] to rally. **-4.** *QUÍM*: **~ com** to react with.
reajustar [4] [xeaʒuʃ'ta(x)] *vt*: **~ algo (a algo)** to readjust sthg (to sthg).
◆ **reajustar-se** *vp*: **~-se a algo** to readjust to sthg.
reajuste [xea'ʒuʃtʃi] *m* adjustment; **~ salarial** wage adjustment.
real [xe'aw] (*pl* **-ais**) <> *adj* **-1.** [verdadeiro] true. **-2.** [régio] royal. <> *m* [realidade] reality.
realçar [13] [xeaw'sa(x)] *vt* to highlight.

realce [xe'awsi] *m* **-1.** [destaque] emphasis; **dar ~ a** to emphasize. **-2.** [brilho] highlight.
realejo [xea'leʒu] *m* barrel organ.
realeza [xea'leza] *f* **-1.** [dignidade de rei] royalty. **-2.** [grandeza] *fig* grandeur.
realidade [xeali'dadʒi] *f* reality; **na ~** actually.
realismo [xea'liʒmu] *m* realism.
realista [xea'liʃta] <> *adj* realistic. <> *mf* **-1.** [pessoa] realist. **-2.** [adepto] royalist.
realização [xealiza'sãw] (*pl* **-ões**) *f* **-1.** [ger] realization. **-2.** [execução - de projeto, negócios] realization; [- de congresso, espetáculo] holding; [- de reforma] enactment. **-3.** [pessoal] fulfilment *UK*, fulfillment *US*.
realizado, da [xeali'zadu, da] *adj* **-1.** [pessoa] fulfilled. **-2.** [obra] carried out. **-3.** [sonho] realized.
realizador, ra [xealiza'do(x), ra] (*mpl* **-es**, *fpl* **-s**) <> *adj* enterprising. <> *m, f* [pessoa] producer.
realizar [4] [xeali'za(x)] *vt* **-1.** [ger] to realize. **-2.** [executar] to carry out; **ser realizado** [conferência, festa] to take place.
◆ **realizar-se** *vp* **-1.** [concretizar-se] to be realized. **-2.** [ocorrer] to be carried out. **-3.** [alcançar seu ideal] to be fulfilled.
realizável [xeali'zavew] (*pl* **-eis**) *adj* achievable.
realmente [xeaw'mẽntʃi] <> *adv* **-1.** [de fato] in fact. **-2.** [muito] really. <> *interj* [expressando indignação] really!
reanimar [4] [xeani'ma(x)] *vt* **-1.** [fisicamente] to revive. **-2.** [moralmente] to cheer up. **-3.** MED to resuscitate.
◆ **reanimar-se** *vp* **-1.** [fisicamente] to come to. **-2.** [moralmente] to rally.
reaparecer [25] [xeapare'se(x)] *vi* to reappear.
reaparecimento [xeaparesi'mẽntu] *m* [ressurgimento] reappearance.
reaprender [5] [xeaprẽn'de(x)] <> *vt* to relearn. <> *vi*: **~ a fazer algo** to learn to do sthg again.
reapresentar [4] [xeaprezẽn'ta(x)] *vt* to represent.
◆ **reapresentar-se** *vp* to reappear.
reaproximação [xeaprosima'sãw] (*pl* **-ões**) *f* rapprochement.
reaproximar [4] [xeaprosi'ma(x)] *vt* to bring together again.
◆ **reaproximar-se** *vp* to grow closer again.
reaquecer [25] [xeake'se(x)] *vt* **-1.** [sopa, café] to reheat. **-2.** [relações] to re-establish.
reaquecimento [xcakesi'mẽntu] *m* **-1.** reheating. **-2.** ECON revival.
reassumir [6] [xeasu'mi(x)] <> *vt* to regain. <> *vi* to take over again.
reatar [4] [xea'ta(x)] *vt* **-1.** [nó] to retie. **-2.** [amizade, conversa, negócios] to resume.
reativar [4] [xeatʃi'va(x)] *vt* to revive.
reator [xea'to(x)] *m* reactor; **~ nuclear** nuclear reactor.
reavaliação [xeavalja'sãw] *f* **-1.** [ger] re-evaluation. **-2.** [de jóia] revaluation.
reavaliar [xeava'lja(x)] *vt* to reappraise.
reaver [51] [xea've(x)] *vt* to recover.
reavivar [4] [xeavi'va(x)] *vt* **-1.** [cor] to revive. **-2.** [passado] to reawaken.
rebaixado, da [xebaj'ʃadu, da] *adj* **-1.** [teto, terreno] lowered. **-2.** [preço] cut. **-3.** *fig* [pessoa] discredited. **-4.** FUT relegated.
rebaixar [4] [xebaj'ʃa(x)] *vt* **-1.** [teto, terreno] to lower. **-2.** [preço] to cut. **-3.** [pessoa] to discredit. **-4.** FUT to relegate.
◆ **rebaixar-se** *vp* [pessoa] to lower o.s.
rebanho [xe'bãɲu] *m* **-1.** [de bois, cabras] herd. **-2.** [de ovelhas] flock. **-3.** *fig* [de fiéis] flock.
rebater [5] [xeba'te(x)] <> *vt* **-1.** [bola] to kick back. **-2.** [golpe] to counter. **-3.** [argumentos, acusações] to rebut. **-4.** [à máquina] to retype. <> *vi* [chutar] to kick back.
rebelar-se [4] [xebe'laxsi] *vp*: **~-se (contra)** to rebel (against).
rebelde [xe'bɛwdʒi] <> *adj* rebellious. <> *mf* rebel.
rebeldia [xebew'dʒia] *f* **-1.** [qualidade] rebelliousness. **-2.** *fig* [oposição] defiance. **-3.** *fig* [obstinação] stubbornness.
rebelião [xebe'ljãw] (*pl* **-ões**) *f* [sublevação] rebellion.
rebentar [4] [xebẽn'ta(x)] <> *vi* **-1.** [ger] to break. **-2.** [não se conter]: **~ de** to burst with; **~ em** to burst into. **-3.** [surgir]: **~ (de/em)** to gush out (from/onto). **-4.** [guerra] to break out. <> *vt* **-1.** [romper] to tear. **-2.** [vidraça, louça] to smash.
rebento [xe'bẽntu] *m* [filho] offspring.
rebite [xe'bitʃi] *m* TEC rivet.
rebobinar [4] [xebobi'na(x)] *vt* [vídeo] to rewind.
rebocador [xeboka'do(x)] (*pl* **-es**) *m* NÁUT tug(-boat).
rebocar [12] [xebo'ka(x)] *vt* **-1.** [barco, carro] to tow. **-2.** [carro mal estacionado] to tow away. **-3.** CONSTR to plaster.
reboco [xe'boku] *m* CONSTR plaster.
rebolado [xebo'ladu] *m* swing of the hips.
rebolar [4] [xebo'la(x)] <> *vt* [corpo, quadris] to swing. <> *vi* **-1.** [pessoa, corpo] to sway. **-2.** *fam fig* [empenhar-se] to fight hard.
reboque [xe'bɔki] *m* **-1.** [ger] tow; **a ~** in tow. **-2.** [carro-guincho] towtruck.
rebordosa [xebox'dɔza] *f* **-1.** [situação difícil] tough situation. **-2.** [reincidência de doença] recurrence *(of an illness)*.
rebu [xe'bu] *m* *fam* rumpus.
rebuliço [xebu'lisu] *m* commotion.
rebuscado, da [xebuʃ'kadu, da] *adj* affected.
recado [xe'kadu] *m* message; **dar conta do ~** *fig* to deliver the goods.
recaída [xeka'ida] *f* relapse.
recair [68] [xeka'i(x)] *vi* **-1.** [tornar a fazer]: **~ em erro** to make the same mistake again. **-2.** [culpa, responsabilidade, suspeita]: **~ em** *ou* **sobre alguém** to fall (up)on sb. **-3.** [cair outra vez] to fall back.
recalcado, da [xekaw'kadu, da] PSIC <> *adj* repressed. <> *m, f* repressed person.
recalcar [12] [xekaw'ka(x)] *vt* **-1.** [comprimir] to

tread upon. **-2.** [reprimir] to repress. **-3.** *PSIC* to inhibit.
recalcitrante [xekawsi'trãntʃi] *adj* recalcitrant.
recalque [xe'kawki] *m PSIC* inhibition.
recanto [xe'kãntu] *m* nook.
recapitulação [xekapitula'sãw] *f* **-1.** [resumo] recapitulation. **-2.** [lembrança] recollection.
recapitular [4] [xekapitu'la(x)] *vt* **-1.** [resumir] to recap. **-2.** [relembrar] to recall.
recatado, da [xeka'tadu, da] *adj* **-1.** [pudico] modest. **-2.** [prudente] restrained.
recato [xe'katu] *m* **-1.** [pudor] modesty. **-2.** [prudência] restraint.
recauchutado, da [xekawʃu'tadu, da] *adj* [pneu] remoulded ***UK***, remolded ***US***.
recauchutagem [xekawʃu'taʒẽ] (*pl* **-ns**) *f* **-1.** [de pneu] remoulding ***UK***, remolding ***US***. **-2.** ***fig*** [em pessoa] plastic surgery; ~ **no rosto** facelift.
recauchutar [4] [xekawʃu'ta(x)] *vt* [pneu] to retread.
recear [15] [xe'sja(x)] ◇ *vt* **-1.** [temer] to fear; ~ **fazer algo** to be afraid to do sthg. **-2.** [preocupar-se com]: ~ **que** to be worried that. ◇ *vi* [preocupar-se]: ~ **por algo** to worry about sthg.
receber [5] [xese'be(x)] ◇ *vt* **-1.** [ger] to receive. **-2.** [recepcionar] to entertain. ◇ *vi* **-1.** [ser pago] to be paid; **a** ~ owing. **-2.** [recepcionar] to entertain.
recebimento [xesebi'mẽntu] *m* receipt; **acusar o** ~ **de** to acknowledge receipt of.
receio [xe'seju] *m* **-1.** [medo] fear. **-2.** [apreensão] concern; **ter** ~ **(de) que** to be afraid that.
receita [xe'sejta] *f* **-1.** [renda - pessoal] income; [- do Estado] tax revenue; ~ **pública** tax revenue. **-2.** *FIN* income. **-3.** *MED*: ~ **(médica)** prescription. **-4.** *CULIN* recipe. **-5.** ***fig*** [fórmula] way.
◆ **Receita** *f*: **a Receita (federal)** *Brazilian tax office*, ≃ Inland Revenue ***UK***, ≃ Internal Revenue Service ***US***.
receitar [4] [xesej'ta(x)] ◇ *vt* to prescribe. ◇ *vi* to issue prescriptions.
receituário [xesej'twarju] *m* prescription pad.
recém- [xesẽn] *prefixo* newly.
recém-casado, da [xe,sẽnka'zadu, da] ◇ *adj* newly-wed. ◇ *m, f* newly-wed; **os** ~**s** the newly-weds.
recém-chegado, da [xe,sẽʃe'gadu, da] ◇ *adj* recently arrived. ◇ *m, f* newcomer.
recém-formado, da [xe,sẽnfox'madu, da] (*pl* **-s**) ◇ *adj* newly qualified. ◇ *m,f* newly qualified person.
recém-nascido, da [xe,sẽna'sidu, da] ◇ *adj* newborn. ◇ *m, f* newborn child.
recém-publicado, da [xe,sẽnpubli'kadu, da] (*pl* **-s**) *adj* recently published.
recender [5] [xesẽn'de(x)] *vi*: ~ **a algo** to smell of sthg.
recenseamento [xesẽnsja'mẽntu] *m* census.
recensear [15] [xesẽn'sja(x)] *vt* to take a census of.
recente [xe'sẽntʃi] ◇ *adj* **-1.** [tempo] recent. **-2.** [novo] new; **este é o meu mais** ~ **hobby** this is my latest hobby. ◇ *adv* recently.
recentemente [xesẽntʃi'mẽntʃi] *adv* recently.
receoso, osa [xe'sjozu, ɔza] *adj* **-1.** [medroso] afraid. **-2.** [apreensivo] apprehensive; **estar** ~ **de algo/de fazer algo** to be worried about sthg/about doing sthg; **estar** ~ **de que** to be worried that.
recepção [xesep'sãw] (*pl* **-ões**) *f* reception.
recepcionar [4] [xesepsjo'na(x)] *vt* to entertain.
recepcionista [xesepsjo'niʃta] *mf* receptionist.
receptáculo [xesep'takulu] *m* receptacle.
receptador, ra [xesepta'do(x), ra] *m, f* fence.
receptar [4] [xesep'ta(x)] *vt* to fence.
receptividade [xeseptʃivi'dadʒi] *f* reception.
receptivo, va [xesep'tʃivu, va] *adj* receptive.
receptor [xesep'to(x)] (*pl* **-res**) *m* [aparelho] receiver.
recessão [xese'sãw] (*pl* **-ões**) *f* recession.
recesso [xe'sɛsu] *m* **-1.** [férias] recess. **-2.** [recanto] nook.
rechaçar [13] [xeʃa'sa(x)] *vt* **-1.** [opor-se a] to reject. **-2.** [repelir] to repel. **-3.** [negar] to decline.
recheado, da [xe'ʃjadu, da] *adj* **-1.** [comida]: ~ **(com** *ou* **de)** filled (with). **-2.** [repleto]: ~ **de algo** stuffed with sthg.
rechear [15] [xe'ʃja(x)] *vt* **-1.** [comida] to fill. **-2.** [encher muito]: ~ **algo de algo** to fill sthg with sthg.
recheio [xe'ʃeju] *m* **-1.** [de comida - de carne] stuffing; [- de bolo, pastel] filling. **-2.** ***fig*** [num texto] padding.
rechonchudo, da [xeʃõn'ʃudu, da] *adj* chubby.
recibo [xe'sibu] *m* receipt.
reciclagem [xesi'klaʒẽ] *f* **-1.** [de material] recycling. **-2.** [de pessoa] retraining.
reciclar [4] [xesi'kla(x)] *vt* **-1.** [material] to recycle. **-2.** [pessoa] to retrain.
recife [xe'sifi] *m* reef.
Recife [xe'sifi] *n* Recife.
recinto [xe'sĩntu] *m* area.
recipiente [xesi'pjẽntʃi] *m* recipient.
recíproca [xe'siproka] *f* ▷ **recíproco.**
reciprocar [12] [xesipro'ka(x)] *vt* to reciprocate.
reciprocidade [xesiprosi'dadʒi] *f* reciprocity.
recíproco, ca [xe'siproku, ka] *adj* reciprocal.
◆ **recíproca** *f*: **a reciproca** the reverse.
récita ['xɛsita] *f* performance.
recital [xesi'taw] (*pl* **-ais**) *m* recital.
recitar [4] [xesi'ta(x)] *vt* [declamar] to recite.
reclamação [xeklama'sãw] (*pl* **-ões**) *f* **-1.** [queixa] complaint. **-2.** *JUR* [petição] claim.
reclamante [xekla'mãntʃi] *mf JUR* claimant.
reclamar [4] [xekla'ma(x)] ◇ *vt* [exigir] to demand. ◇ *vi* **-1.** [protestar]: ~ **(de/contra)** to complain (about/against). **-2.** [exigir]: ~ **por** to demand.
reclame [xeklãmi] *m* advertisement.
reclinado, da [xekli'nadu, da] *adj* **-1.** [inclinado] bending over. **-2.** [recostado] lying back.
reclinar [4] [xekli'na(x)] *vt* [inclinar]: ~ **algo (em** *ou* **sobre)** to rest sthg (against *ou* on).
◆ **reclinar-se** *vp* [recostar-se] to lie back.
reclinável [xekli'navew] (*pl* **-eis**) *adj* reclining.

reclusão [xeklu'zãw] *f* **-1.** [isolamento] seclusion. **-2.** [em prisão] imprisonment. **-3.** [pena] solitary confinement.
recluso, sa [xe'kluzu, za] ◇ *adj* **-1.** [isolado] reclusive. **-2.** [preso] shut up. ◇ *m, f* **-1.** [pessoa que se isola] recluse. **-2.** [prisioneiro] prisoner.
recobrar [4] [xeko'bra(x)] *vt* to recover.
◆ **recobrar-se** *vp*: **~-se de algo** to recover from sthg.
recolher [5] [xeko'ʎe(x)] *vt* **-1.** [ger] to collect. **-2.** [do chão] to pick up. **-3.** [juntar] to gather (together). **-4.** [pôr ao abrigo] to bring in. **-5.** [levar] to gather. **-6.** [tirar de circulação] to withdraw. **-7.** [coligir] to gather. **-8.** [encolher] to pull back.
◆ **recolher-se** *vp* **-1.** [ger] to retire. **-2.** [ir para casa] to go home. **-3.** [absorver-se] to become absorbed.
recolhido, da [xeko'ʎidu, da] *adj* **-1.** [lugar] secluded. **-2.** [absorvido] absorbed. **-3.** [dentro de casa] housebound.
recolhimento [xekoʎi'mẽntu] *m* **-1.** [ato de levar] reception. **-2.** [arrecadação] collection. **-3.** [de circulação] withdrawal. **-4.** [coleta] gathering. **-5.** [devido a doença] confinement. **-6.** [refúgio] refuge. **-7.** [retraimento] seclusion.
recomeçar [13] [xekome'sa(x)] ◇ *vt* to restart. ◇ *vi* to start again; **~ a fazer algo** to start doing sthg again.
recomeço [xeko'mesu] *m* restart.
recomendação [xekomẽnda'sãw] (*pl* **-ões**) *f* [ger] recommendation; **por ~ de** on the recommendation of.
◆ **recomendações** *fpl* [saudações] regards.
recomendar [4] [xekomẽn'da(x)] *vt* **-1.** [ger] to recommend; **recomenda-se o uso de produtos naturais** the use of natural products is recommended. **-2.** [pedir] to ask. **-3.** [pedir proteção, favor]: **~ alguém a alguém** to recommend sb to sb. **-4.** [enviar cumprimentos] to send one's regards.
recomendável [xekomẽn'davɛw] (*pl* **-eis**) *adj* advisable; **é ~ que ...** it's advisable that ...
recompensa [xekõn'pẽnsa] *f* reward.
recompensador, ra [xekõnpẽnsa'do(x), ra] *adj* rewarding.
recompensar [4] [xekõnpẽn'sa(x)] *vt* **-1.** [premiar] to reward. **-2.** [remunerar]: **~ alguém de algo** to compensate sb for sthg.
recompor [45] [xekõn'po(x)] *vt* **-1.** [restabelecer] to reorganise. **-2.** [reordenar] to rearrange.
recôncavo [xe'kõŋkavu] *m* wide bay.
reconciliação [xekõnsilja'sãw] (*pl* **-ões**) *f* reconciliation.
reconciliar [16] [xekõnsi'lja(x)] *vt* to reconcile.
◆ **reconciliar-se** *vp*: **~-se com** [pessoa] to be reconciled with; [situação] to become reconciled to.
recondicionado, da [xekõdisio'nadu, da] *adj* reconditioned.
recondicionar [4] [xekõndʒisjo'na(x)] *vt* to recondition.
recôndito, ta [xe'kõndʒitu, ta] *adj* **-1.** [retirado] secluded. **-2.** [íntimo] innermost.
◆ **recôndito** *m fig* [âmago]: **no ~ da alma** in one's heart of hearts.
reconfortante [xekõnfox'tãntʃi] *adj* relaxing.
reconfortar [4] [xekõnfox'ta(x)] *vt* to comfort.
reconhecer [25] [xekoɲe'se(x)] *vt* **-1.** [ger] to recognize. **-2.** [mostrar-se agradecido por] [admitir] to acknowledge. **-3.** [constatar] to accept. **-4.** [autenticar] to authenticate; **~ firma num documento** to authenticate officially the signature on a document. **-5.** [explorar] to reconnoitre *UK*, to reconnoiter *US*.
reconhecido, da [xekoɲe'sidu, da] *adj* **-1.** [grato] thankful. **-2.** [firma] authenticated.
reconhecimento [xekoɲesi'mẽntu] *m* **-1.** [ger] recognition. **-2.** [admissão] acknowledgement. **-3.** [autenticação] authentication. **-4.** [gratidão] gratitude. **-5.** [exploração] reconnaissance.
reconhecível [xekoɲe'sivew] (*pl* **-eis**) *adj* recognizable.
reconquista [xekõŋ'kiʃta] *f* reconquest.
reconquistar [4] [xekõŋkiʃ'ta(x)] *vt* **-1.** [território] to reconquer. **-2.** [pessoa, confiança] to regain.
reconsiderar [4] [xekõnside'ra(x)] *vt* to reconsider.
reconstituição [xekõnʃtʃitwi'sãw] (*pl* **-ões**) *f* reconstruction.
reconstituir [74] [xekõnʃtʃi'twi(r)] *vt* **-1.** [regime, grupo] to reconstitute. **-2.** [enfermo] to revive. **-3.** [crime] to reconstruct.
reconstrução [xekõnʃtru'sãw] *f* rebuilding, reconstruction.
reconstruir [xekõnʃ'trwi(x)] *vt* to rebuild, to reconstruct.
recontar [4] [xekõn'ta(x)] *vt* to recount.
recordação [xekoxda'sãw] (*pl* **-ões**) *f* **-1.** [ato, lembrança] memory. **-2.** [objeto] souvenir.
recordar [4] [xekox'da(x)] *vt* **-1.** [lembrar] to remember. **-2.** [por semelhança]: **~ algo/alguém a alguém** to remind sb of sthg/sb. **-3.** [recapitular] to revise.
◆ **recordar-se** *vp* [lembrar]: **~-se de alguém/algo** to remember sb/sthg; **~-se (de) que** to remember that.
recorde [xe'kɔxdʒi] ◇ *adj inv* record *(antes de subst)*; **em tempo ~** in record time. ◇ *m* record; **bater/deter um ~** to break/hold a record.
recordista [xekox'dʒiʃta] ◇ *adj* record-breaking. ◇ *mf* **-1.** [quem detém um recorde] record-holder. **-2.** [quem bate um recorde] record-breaker.
recorrente [xeko'xẽntʃi] ◇ *adj* [que se repete] recurring. ◇ *mf* JUR appellant.
recorrer [5] [xeko'xe(x)] *vi* **-1.**: **~ a** to resort to. **-2.** JUR to appeal; **~ de algo** to appeal against sthg.
recortado, da [xekox'tadu, da] *adj* **-1.** [papel, desenho] cut out. **-2.** [borda, litoral] ragged.
recortar [4] [xekox'ta(x)] *vt* to cut out.
recorte [xe'kɔxtʃi] *m* [de jornal etc] cutting.
recostar [4] [xekoʃ'ta(x)] *vt* **-1.** [encostar] to rest. **-2.** [pôr meio deitado] to recline.

◆ **recostar-se** *vp* **-1.** [encostar-se] to lean against. **-2.** [pôr-se meio deitado] to lie back.

recreação [xekrja'sãw] *f* recreation.

recreativo, va [xekrja'tʃivu, va] *adj* recreational.

recreio [xe'kreju] *m* **-1.** [entretenimento] entertainment. **-2.** *EDUC* playtime *UK*, recess *US*; **hora do ~** breaktime.

recriação [xekrja'sãw] (*pl* **-ões**) *f* **-1.** [de história, mito] re-creation. **-2.** [de peça, ópera] new production. **-3.** [de filme] remake.

recriar [16] [xekri'a(x)] *vt* to recreate.

recriminação [xekrimina'sãw] (*pl* **-ões**) *f* recrimination.

recriminador, ra [xekrimina'do(x), ra] *adj* reproachful.

recriminar [4] [xekrimi'na(x)] *vt* to reproach.

recrudescer [25] [xekrude'se(x)] *vi* to intensify.

recrudescimento [xekrudesi'mẽntu] *m* intensification.

recruta [xe'kruta] *mf* recruit.

recrutamento [xekruta'mẽntu] *m* recruitment.

recrutar [4] [xekru'ta(x)] *vt* to recruit.

recuado, da [xe'kwadu, da] *adj* [edifício] set back.

recuar [4] [xe'kwa(x)] ◇ *vi* **-1.** [andar para trás] to step back. **-2.** [retirar-se] to retreat. **-3.** [voltar atrás - em intenção, decisão] to back out of; [- no tempo] to go back. **-4.** [canhão] to recoil. ◇ *vt* [mover para trás] to move back.

recuo [xe'kuw] *m* **-1.** [afastamento]: **com o ~, evitou ser atropelada** by stepping backwards, she avoided being run over; **o ~ do móvel, deu mais espaço na sala** moving this piece of furniture back has given the room more space. **-2.** [retirada] retreat. **-3.** [reconsideração - em intenção, decisão] reassessment; [- no tempo] going back. **-4.** [de canhão] recoil. **-5.** [em rua, terreno] setting back.

recuperação [xekupera'sãw] *f* **-1.** [reaquisição] recovery. **-2.** [restabelecimento] recuperation. **-3.** [reabilitação] rehabilitation. **-4.** [indenização] compensation.

recuperar [4] [xekupe'ra(x)] *vt* **-1.** [readquirir] to recover. **-2.** [restabelecer] to regain. **-3.** [reabilitar] to rehabilitate.

◆ **recuperar-se** *vp* [restabelecer-se] to recuperate.

recurso [xe'kuxsu] *m* **-1.** [ato]: **o ~ a algo** resorting to sthg. **-2.** [meio] recourse; **como** *ou* **em último ~** as a last resort. **-3.** [solução]: **~ contra algo** answer to sthg.

◆ **recursos** *mpl* [dinheiro] means.

recusa [xe'kuza] *f*: **~ (a/de algo)** refusal (to/of sthg); **~ a** *ou* **em fazer algo** refusal to do sthg.

recusar [4] [xeku'za(x)] *vt* **-1.** [não aceitar] to refuse. **-2.** [não conceder]: **~ algo (a alguém)** to deny (sb) sthg. **-3.** [negar-se a]: **~ fazer algo** to refuse to do sthg.

◆ **recusar-se** *vp* [negar-se a]: **~-se (a fazer algo)** to refuse (to do sthg).

redação [xeda'sãw] (*pl* **-ões**) *f* **-1.** [ato] writing. **-2.** [modo de redigir] composition. **-3.** *EDUC* essay. **-4.** [redatores] editorial staff. **-5.** [seção] editorial office.

redargüir [xedax'gwi(x)] ◇ *vt*: **~ que** to retort that. ◇ *vi* to retort; **~ a alguém/algo** to respond to sb/sthg.

redator, ra [xeda'to(x), ra] (*mpl* **-es**, *fpl* **-s**) *m, f* **-1.** *JORN* writer. **-2.** [de obra de referência] editor, compiler.

redator-chefe, redatora-chefe [xedatoxʃɛfi, xedatoraʃɛfi] (*mpl* **redatores-chefes**, *fpl* **redatoras-chefes**) *m, f* editor in chief.

rede ['xedʒi] *f* **-1.** [ger] network; **comunicar-se em ~** to network. **-2.** [para pesca, caça & *ESP*] net. **-3.** [para cabelo] hairnet. **-4.** [leito] hammock.

rédea ['xɛdʒja] *f* **-1.** [correia] rein. **-2.** *fig* [direção]: **tomar as ~s de algo** to take the reins of sthg. **-3.** *loc*: **dar ~ larga a algo** to give free rein to sthg.

redemoinho [xedʒi'mwiɲu] *m* **-1.** [de água] whirpool. **-2.** [de vento] whirlwind.

redenção [xedẽn'sãw] *f* redemption.

redentor, ra [xedẽn'to(x), ra] *m, f* [pessoa] redeemer.

◆ **Redentor** *m*: **o Redentor** *RELIG* the Redeemer.

redescobrir [59] [xedʒiʃko'bri(x)] *vt* to rediscover.

redigir [52] [xedʒi'ʒi(x)] ◇ *vt* to write. ◇ *vi* to write.

redimir [6] [xedʒi'mi(x)] *vt* **-1.** [*RELIG* - salvar] to redeem; [- expiar] to atone for. **-2.** [libertar] to set free.

◆ **redimir-se** *vp*: **~-se do castigo** to escape punishment; **redimiu-se dos seus erros da juventude** he made up for the errors of his youth.

redobrar [4] [xedo'bra(x)] ◇ *vt* **-1.** [dobrar de novo] to fold again. **-2.** [reduplicar, intensificar] to redouble. ◇ *vi* to intensify.

redoma [xe'doma] *f* bell jar.

redondamente [xe,dõnda'mẽntʃi] *adv* [totalmente]: **me enganei ~** I was utterly wrong.

redondeza [xedõn'deza] *f* [qualidade] roundness.

◆ **redondezas** *fpl* [arredores] surroundings.

redondo, da [xe'dõndu, da] *adj* **-1.** [circular] round. **-2.** [rechonchudo] plump.

redor [xe'dɔ(x)] *m*: **ao ~ de** around.

redução [xedu'sãw] (*pl* **-ões**) *f* **-1.** [ger] reduction. **-2.** [conversão] conversion.

redundância [xedũn'dãnsja] *f* redundancy.

redundante [xedũn'dãntʃi] *adj* redundant.

redundar [4] [xedũn'da(x)] *vi* [resultar]: **~ em algo** to result in sthg.

reduto [xe'dutu] *m* **-1.** [fortificação] fort. **-2.** *fig* [abrigo] shelter. **-3.** *fig* [lugar de reunião] meeting place.

reduzido, da [xedu'zidu, da] *adj* **-1.** [diminuído] reduced. **-2.** [pequeno] limited.

reduzir [72] [xedu'zi(x)] *vt* **-1.** [ger] to reduce. **-2.** [transformar]: **~ alguém/algo a algo** to reduce sb/sthg to sthg. **-3.** [converter]: **~ algo a algo** to convert sthg to sthg. **-4.** [levar]: **~ alguém a algo** to reduce sb to sthg.

◆ **reduzir-se** *vp*: ~**-se a algo** [resumir-se] to be reduced to sthg.
reedição [xeedʒi'sãw] (*pl* **-ões**) *f* **-1.** [de obra] reprint. **-2.** [de medida] reissue.
reeditar [4] [xeedʒi'ta(x)] *vt* to republish.
reeducar [12] [xeedu'ca(x)] *vt* to re-educate.
reeleger [26] [xeele'ʒe(x)] *vt* to re-elect.
◆ **reeleger-se** *vp* to be re-elected.
reeleição [xeelej'sãw] *f* re-election.
reembolsar [4] [xeẽnbow'sa(x)] *vt* **-1.** [reaver] to recover. **-2.** [restituir]: ~ **alguém (de algo)** to refund sb (sthg). **-3.** [indenizar]: ~ **algo a alguém**, ~ **alguém de algo** to reimburse sthg to sb, to reimburse sb for sthg.
reembolso [xeẽnbowsu] *m* **-1.** [recuperação] recovery. **-2.** [restituição] refund. **-3.** [indenização] reimbursement.
reencarnação [xeẽnkaxna'sãw] *f* reincarnation.
reencarnar [4] [xeẽnkax'na(x)] *vi*: ~ **(em)** to reincarnate (as).
◆ **reencarnar-se** *vp*: ~**-se (em)** to be reincarnated (as).
reencontrar [4] [xeẽnkõn'tra(x)] *vt* to meet again.
◆ **reencontrar-se** *vp*: ~**-se (com alguém)** to meet (sb) again.
reencontro [xeẽŋ'kõntru] *m* reunion.
reentrância [xeẽn'trãnsja] *f* recess.
reescalonamento [xeeʃkalona'mẽntu] *m* [of a debt] rescheduling.
reescalonar [4] [xeeʃkalo'na(x)] *vt* [dívida] to reschedule.
reescrever [5] [xeeʃkre've(x)] *vt* to rewrite.
reexaminar [4] [xeezami'na(x)] *vt* to re-examine.
refazer [31] [xefa'ze(x)] *vt* **-1.** [fazer de novo] to redo. **-2.** [reconstruir] to rebuild. **-3.** [recuperar] to recover.
◆ **refazer-se** *vp* **-1.** [recuperar-se]: ~**-se (de algo)** to recover (from sthg). **-2.** [indenizar-se]: ~**-se de algo** to be compensated for sthg.
refeição [xefej'sãw] (*pl* **-ões**) *f* meal; **fazer uma** ~ to have a meal.
refeito, ta [ta, xe'fejtu] ◇ *pp* ▷ **refazer**. ◇ *adj* **-1.** [feito de novo] redone. **-2.** [reconstruído] rebuilt. **-3.** [recuperado] recovered.
refeitório [xefej'tɔrju] *m* dining hall.
refém [xe'fẽ] (*pl* **-ns**) *mf* hostage.
referência [xefe'rẽnsja] *f* reference; **fazer** ~ **a** to refer to.
◆ **referências** *fpl* [informação] references.
referencial [xefe'rẽnsjaw] (*pl* **-ais**) *adj* reference *(antes de subst)*.
◆ **referencial** *m* [exemplo, modelo] yardstick.
referendar [457] [xeferẽn'da(x)] *vt* **-1.** [assinar] to countersign. **-2.** [validar] to endorse.
referendum [xefe'rẽndũ] *m* POL referendum.
referente [xefe'rẽntʃi] *adj*: ~ **a** concerning.
referido, da [xefe'ridu, da] *adj* **-1.** [mencionado] (afore)mentioned. **-2.** [referente]: ~ **a** in regard to.
referir [xefe'ri(x)] *vt* [narrar]: ~ **algo a alguém** to tell sb sthg.
◆ **referir-se** *vp*: ~**-se a** [aludir] to allude to; [dizer respeito] to refer to.
refestelado, da [xefeʃte'ladu, da] *adj* [estendido] sprawling.
refestelar-se [7] [xefeʃte'laxsi] *vp* [estender-se] to sprawl.
refil [xe'fiw] (*pl* **-is**) *m* refill.
refinado, da [xefi'nadu, da] *adj* refined.
refinamento [xefina'mẽntu] *m* **-1.** [ato] refining. **-2.** [requinte] refinement.
refinar [4] [xefi'na(x)] *vt* to refine.
refinaria [xefina'ria] *f* refinery.
refletido, da [xefle'tʃidu, da] *adj* **-1.** [espelhado] reflected. **-2.** [ponderado] considered.
refletir [65] [xefle'tʃi(x)] ◇ *vt* to reflect. ◇ *vi* **-1.** [luz]: ~ **de** to reflect off. **-2.** [pensar]: ~ **(em/sobre)** to reflect on/about. **-3.** [repercutir]: ~ **em** to reflect on.
◆ **refletir-se** *vp* **-1.** [espelhar-se] to be reflected. **-2.** [repercutir] to reflect on.
refletor [xefle'to(x)] (*pl* **-es**) *m* reflector.
reflexão [xeflek'sãw] (*pl* **-ões**) *f* reflection.
reflexivo, va [xeflek'sivu, va] *adj* reflective.
reflexo, xa [xe'flɛksu, sa] *adj* **-1.** [luz] reflected. **-2.** [movimento] reflex.
◆ **reflexo** *m* **-1.** [ger] reflection. **-2.** ANAT reflex.
◆ **reflexos** *mpl* [no cabelo] highlights.
reflorestamento [xefloreʃta'mẽntu] *m* reforestation.
reflorestar [4] [xefloreʃ'ta(x)] *vt* to reforest.
refluxo [xe'fluksu] *m* ebb.
refogado, da [xefo'gada, xefo'gadu] *adj* sautéed.
◆ **refogado** *m* **-1.** [molho] gravy. **-2.** [prato] stew.
refogar [14] [xefo'ga(x)] *vt* to sauté.
reforçado, da [xefox'sadu, da] *adj* **-1.** [ger] reinforced. **-2.** [refeição] hearty.
reforçar [13] [xefox'sa(x)] *vt* **-1.** [ger] to reinforce. **-2.** [ânimo] to invigorate.
reforço [xe'foxsu] *m* **-1.** [ger] reinforcement. **-2.** [a tropa, equipe] reinforcements *(pl)*. **-3.** [de vacina] booster.
reforma [xe'fɔxma] *f* **-1.** [modificação] reform; ~ **ministerial** ministerial reshuffle; ~ **agrária** land reform. **-2.** ARQUIT renovation; **estar em** ~ to be under repair. **-3.** MIL regrouping.
◆ **Reforma** *f*: **a Reforma** RELIG the Reformation.
reformado, da [xefox'madu, da] *adj* **-1.** [modificado - ensino, instituição] reformed; [- leis] amended; [- sofá] repaired. **-2.** ARQUIT renovated. **-3.** MIL regrouped.
reformar [4] [xefox'ma(x)] *vt* **-1.** [modificar - ensino, constituição] to reform; [- sofá] to repair; [- lei] to amend; [- empresa] to restructure. **-2.** ARQUIT to renovate. **-3.** MIL to regroup. **-4.** JUR to amend.
◆ **reformar-se** *vp* **-1.** MIL to retire. **-2.** [regenerar-se] to be reformed.
reformatar [4] [xefoxma'ta(x)] *vt* COMPUT to reformat.
reformatório [xefoxma'tɔrju] *m* young offender institution *UK*, reformatory *US*.

refrão [xe'frãw] (*pl* **-ões**) *m* **-1.** [estribilho] chorus. **-2.** [provérbio] saying.
refratário, ria [xefra'tarju, rja] *adj* **-1.** [material] heat-resistant. **-2.** [rebelde]: **ser ~ a algo** to be impervious to sthg; [imune] to be immune to sthg.
refrear [15] [xefri'a(x)] *vt* [reprimir] to suppress.
◆ **refrear-se** *vp* [conter-se] to contain o.s.
refrega [xe'frɛga] *f* [briga] fight.
refrescante [xefreʃ'kãntʃi] *adj* refreshing.
refrescar [12] [xefreʃ'ka(x)] ◇ *vt* **-1.** [tornar menos quente] to cool. **-2.** [avivar] to refresh. **-3.** [tranqüilizar] to refresh. ◇ *vi* [tempo] to cool down.
◆ **refrescar-se** *vp* [pessoa] to refresh o.s.
refresco [xe'freʃku] *m* fruit squash.
refrigeração [xefriʒera'sãw] *m* [de alimentos] refrigeration; [de ambiente] air conditioning.
refrigerado, da [xefriʒe'radu, da] *adj* [alimento] chilled; [ambiente] air conditioned.
refrigerador [xefriʒera'do(x)] *m* **-1.** [de alimentos] refrigerator. **-2.** [de máquina] cooler.
refrigerante [xefriʒe'rãntʃi] *m* soft drink.
refrigerar [4] [xefriʒe'ra(x)] *vt* **-1.** [bebidas, alimentos] to chill. **-2.** [ambiente] to cool. **-3.** [máquina] to refrigerate.
refugar [14] [xefu'ga(x)] ◇ *vt* **-1.** [recusar] to refuse. **-2.** [menosprezar] to reject. ◇ *vi* [recusar-se] to refuse.
refugiado, da [xefu'ʒjadu, da] ◇ *adj* refugee. ◇ *m, f* refugee.
refugiar-se [16] [xefu'ʒjaxsi] *vp* [abrigar-se] to take refuge; **~ em** [abrigar-se] to take cover in; [asilar-se] to take refuge in; *fig* [amparar-se] to seek solace in.
refúgio [xe'fuʒju] *m* **-1.** [local] hideaway. **-2.** *fig* [apoio] refuge.
refugo [xe'fugu] *m* **-1.** [resto] waste. **-2.** [mercadoria] rubbish *UK*, garbage *US*.
refulgir [52] [xefuw'ʒi(x)] *vi* **-1.** [resplandecer] to shine. **-2.** *fig* [destacar-se] to stand out.
refutação [xefuta'sãw] (*pl* **-ões**) *f* **-1.** [desmentido] refutation. **-2.** [contestação] denial.
refutar [4] [xefu'ta(x)] *vt* to refute.
regaço [xe'gasu] *m* [colo] lap.
regador [xega'do(x)] (*pl* **-es**) *m* watering can.
regalia [xega'lia] *f* privilege.
regalo [xe'galu] *m* **-1.** [presente] gift. **-2.** [prazer]: **ser um ~** to be a pleasure.
regar [14] [xe'ga(x)] *vt* **-1.** [aguar] to water. **-2.** [banhar] to wash. **-3.** [acompanhar] to wash down.
regata [xe'gata] *f* regatta.
regatear [15] [xega'tʃja(x)] ◇ *vt* to haggle over. ◇ *vi* to haggle.
regato [xe'gatu] *m* stream.
regência [xe'ʒẽnsja] *f* **-1.** *MÚS* conducting. **-2.** *GRAM* government. **-3.** [administração] rule.
regeneração [xeʒenera'sãw] *f* **-1.** [recomposição] regeneration. **-2.** [moral] reform.
regenerar [4] [xeʒene'ra(x)] *vt* **-1.** [recompor] to regenerate. **-2.** [moralmente] to reform.
◆ **regenerar-se** *vp* **-1.** [recompor-se] to be regenerated. **-2.** [moralmente] to be reformed.
regente [xe'ʒẽntʃi] *m* **-1.** *POL* regent. **-2.** *MÚS* conductor. **-3.** *UNIV* vice chancellor *UK*, president *US*.
reger [26] [xe'ʒe(x)] ◇ *vt* **-1.** [governar] to govern. **-2.** [regular] to rule. **-3.** *MÚS* to conduct. **-4.** *UNIV* to occupy. **-5.** *GRAM* to govern. ◇ *vi* **-1.** [governar] to rule. **-2.** *MÚS* to conduct.
região [xe'ʒjãw] (*pl* **-ões**) *f* **-1.** [território] region. **-2.** [de cidade, corpo] area.
regime [xe'ʒimi] *m* **-1.** [ger] system. **-2.** [dieta] diet; **estar de ~** to be on a diet; **fazer ~** to diet. **-3.** [regras] rules *(pl)*; **~ de vida** way of life.
regimento [xeʒi'mẽntu] *m* **-1.** [ger] regiment. **-2.** [normas] rules *(pl)*; **~ interno** [de escola] school rules; [de empresa] company rules.
regiões [xe'ʒjõjʃ] *mpl* ⊳ **região**.
regional [xeʒjo'naw] (*pl* **-ais**) *adj* regional.
regionalismo [xeʒjona'liʒmu] *m* regionalism.
regionalizar [xeʒjonali'za(x)] *vt* to regionalize.
registradora [xeʒiʃtra'dora] *f* [caixa] cash register.
registrar [4] [xeʒiʃ'tra(x)] *vt* **-1.** [ger] to register. **-2.** [anotar] to record. **-3.** [memorizar] to remember.
registro [xe'ʒiʃtru] *m* **-1.** [ger & *LING*] register. **-2.** [postal] registration. **-3.** [órgão]: **~ civil** registry office. **-4.** [torneira] tap *UK*, faucet *US*. **-5.** [relógio] meter. **-6.** *MÚS* range.
rego ['xegu] *m* **-1.** [valão] ditch. **-2.** [de arado] furrow. **-3.** *mfam ANAT* bum crack.
regozijar-se [4] [xegozi'ʒaxsi] *vp*: **~ com algo/por fazer algo** to be delighted with sthg/to do sthg.
regozijo [xego'ziʒu] *m* delight.
regra ['xɛgra] *f* **-1.** [norma] rule; **por via de ~** as a rule. **-2.** [rotina] routine; **sair da ~** to change one's routine. **-3.** [prudência]: **com ~** in moderation.
regrado, da [xe'gradu, da] *adj* sensible.
regrar [4] [xe'gra(x)] *vt* to regulate.
◆ **regrar-se** *vp*: **~-se por algo** to be guided by sthg.
regredir [57] [xegre'dʒi(x)] *vi*: **~ (a algo)** to regress (to sthg).
regressão [xegre'sãw] *f* **-1.** [retrocesso] regression. **-2.** *PSIC* relapse.
regressar [4] [xegre'sa(x)] *vi*: **~ (de/a)** to return from/to.
regressivo, va [xegre'sivu, va] *adj* regressive.
regresso [xe'grɛsu] *m* return.
régua ['xɛgwa] *f* ruler; **~ de cálculo** slide rule.
régua-tê [ˌxɛgwa'te] (*pl* **réguas-tê**) *f* *ARQUIT* T-square.
regulador, ra [xegula'do(x), ra] *adj* [força] regulating.
◆ **regulador** *m* [medicamento] regulator.
regulagem [xegu'laʒẽ] (*pl* **-ns**) *f* tuning.
regulamentação [xegulamẽnta'sãw] *f* **-1.** [ato] regulation. **-2.** [regras] regulations *(pl)*.
regulamentar [4] [xegula'mẽnta(x)] ◇ *adj* standardizing. ◇ *vt* to regulate.

regulamento [xegula'mẽntu] *m* rules *(pl)*.

regular [4] [xegu'la(x)] (*pl* **-es**) ◇ *adj* **-1.** [ger] regular. **-2.** [legal] legal. **-3.** [tamanho] medium. **-4.** [razoável] reasonable. ◇ *vt* **-1.** [ger] to regulate. **-2.** [ajustar] to adjust. **-3.** [conformar]: ~ **algo por algo** to check sthg against sthg. ◇ *vi* **-1.** [maquina]: ~ **bem/mal** to be well/badly adjusted. **-2.** [pessoa]: **não** ~ **(bem)** to not be quite right in the head. **-3.** [ter]: **ele** ~ **pelos 50** he's about 50. **-4.** [aproximar-se]: **meu filho regula em idade com o seu** my son is about the same age as yours.
◆ **regular-se por** *vp* [orientar-se] to be guided by.

regularidade [xegulari'dadʒi] *f* regularity.

regularizar [4] [xegulari'za(x)] *vt* **-1.** [legalizar] to legalize. **-2.** [normalizar] to regularize.
◆ **regularizar-se** *vp* [normalizar-se] to return to normal.

regurgitar [4] [xegux3i'ta(x)] *vt* & *vi* to regurgitate.

rei ['xej] *m* **-1.** [ger] king; **ser o** ~ **de algo** *fig* [da música, do crime] to be the king of sthg; [da bagunça] to be the world's worst for sthg. **-2.** *loc*: **ter o** ~ **na barriga** to be full of o.s.

Reikjavik [xejkʒa'viki] *n* Reykjavik.

reimpressão [xẽjnpre'sãw] (*pl* **-ões**) *f* reprint.

reimprimir [6] [xẽjnpri'mi(x)] *vt* to reprint.

reinado [xej'nadu] *m* reign.

reinante [xej'nãntʃi] *adj* prevailing.

reinar [4] [xej'na(x)] *vi* **-1.** [governar] to reign. **-2.** *fig* [dominar] to dominate.

reincidência [xẽjnsi'dẽnsja] *f* **-1.** [de doença] relapse. **-2.** [de crime] recidivism. **-3.** [de erro] repetition. **-4.** [na bebida] backsliding.

reincidente [xẽjnsi'dẽntʃi] ◇ *adj*: ~ **em algo** drawn back into sthg; **jamais perdoaremos os erros** ~**s** we shall never forgive repeated mistakes. ◇ *mf* reoffender.

reincidir [6] [xẽjnsi'dʒi(x)] *vi* to recur; ~ **em algo** to commit sthg again.

reingressar [4] [xẽjngre'sa(x)] *vt*: ~ **em** to re-enter.

reiniciar [16] [xejni'sja(x)] *vt* to restart.

reino ['xejnu] *m* **-1.** [ger] kingdom. **-2.** *fig* [âmbito] realm.

reintegrar [4] [xẽjnte'gra(x)] *vt* **-1.** [em cargo etc] to reinstate. **-2.** [reconduzir] to readmit.

reiterar [4] [xeite'ra(x)] *vt* to reiterate.

reitor, ra [xej'to(x), ra] *m, f* vice chancellor ***UK***, president ***US***.

reitoria [xejto'ria] *f* **-1.** [cargo] vice-chancellorship ***UK***, presidency ***US***. **-2.** [gabinete] vice chancellor's office ***UK***, president's office ***US***.

reivindicação [xejvĩndʒika'sãw] (*pl* **-ões**) *f* claim.

reivindicar [12] [xejvĩndʒi'ka(x)] *vt* to claim.

rejeição [xeʒej'sãw] (*pl* **-ões**) *f* rejection.

rejeitar [4] [xeʒej'ta(x)] *vt* **-1.** [recusar] to reject. **-2.** [vomitar] to vomit. **-3.** [desprezar] to ignore.

rejubilar-se [4] [xeʒubi'laxsi] *vp* to rejoice.

rejuvenescer [25] [xeʒuvene'se(x)] ◇ *vt* to rejuvenate. ◇ *vi* to be rejuvenating.
◆ **rejuvenescer-se** *vp* to be rejuvenated.

rejuvenescimento [xeʒuvenesi'mẽntu] *m* rejuvenation.

relação [xela'sãw] (*pl* **-ões**) *f* **-1.** [ligação] relationship; **em** ~ **a** in relation to; ~ **entre/com** relationship between/with. **-2.** [listagem] list.
◆ **relações** *fpl* [relacionamento] relationship *(sg)*; **ele não é pessoa de minhas relações** he's not sb I have anything to do with; **cortar relações com alguém** to break off with sb; **ter relações com alguém** [sexual] to sleep with sb; **relações públicas** public relations; **relações sexuais** sex, sexual intercourse.

relacionado, da [xelasjo'nadu, da] *adj* **-1.** [listado] listed. **-2.** [ligado] related. **-3.** [pessoa]: **bem** ~ well connected.

relacionamento [xelasjona'mẽntu] *m* **-1.** [ligação] relationship. **-2.** [trato]: **é uma garota de fácil** ~ she's a girl who's easy to get on with.

relacionar [4] [xelasjo'na(x)] *vt* **-1.** [listar] to list. **-2.** [confrontar]: ~ **algo com algo** to compare sthg with sthg. **-3.** [pessoa] to bring into contact with.
◆ **relacionar-se** *vp* **-1.** [ligar-se] to be related. **-2.** [pessoa]: ~**-se com alguém** to mix with sb.

relações-públicas [xela,sõjʃ'publikaʃ] *mf inv* [pessoa] PR officer.

relâmpago [xe'lãnpagu] ◇ *m* METEOR flash of lightning; **num** ~ [rapidamente] in a flash. ◇ *adj* [rápido] lightning *(antes de subst)*.

relampejar [4] [xelãnpe'ʒa(x)] *vi*: **relampejou esta noite** there was lightening last night.

relance [xe'lãnsi] *m*: **ver de** ~ to glance at.

relapso, sa [xe'lapsu, sa] ◇ *adj* negligent. ◇ *m, f* negligent person.

relatar [4] [xela'ta(x)] *vt* to relate.

relativamente [xelatʃiva'mẽntʃi] *adv* relatively.

relatividade [xelatʃivi'dadʒi] *f* relativity.

relativo, va [xela'tʃivu, va] *adj* relative; ~ **a algo** relative to sthg.

relato [xe'latu] *m* account.

relator, ra [xela'to(x), ra] *m, f* report writer.

relatório [xela'tɔrju] *m* report; ~ **anual** annual report.

relax [xi'lɛkiʃ] *m* relaxation.

relaxado, da [xela'ʃadu, da] *adj* **-1.** [desleixado] careless. **-2.** [descansado] relaxed.

relaxamento [xelaʃa'mẽntu] *m* **-1.** [desleixo] carelessness. **-2.** [repouso] relaxation.

relaxante [xela'ʃãntʃi] *adj* relaxing.

relaxar [4] [xela'ʃa(x)] ◇ *vt* to relax. ◇ *vi* **-1.** [desleixar-se]: ~ **em algo** to become careless with sthg. **-2.** [descansar] to relax. **-3.** [condescender]: ~ **com algo/alguém** to relent towards sthg/sb.
◆ **relaxar-se** *vp* **-1.** [desleixar-se]: ~**-se (com algo)** to be careless (with sthg). **-2.** [distender-se] to be relaxed.

relegar [14] [xele'ga(x)] *vt* to relegate.

relembrar [4] [xelẽn'bra(x)] *vt* to recall.

relento [xe'lẽntu] *m* dew; **ao** ~ outdoors.

reler [42] [xe'le(x)] *vt* to reread.

reles ['xɛliʃ] *adj inv* **-1.** [desprezível] despicable. **-2.** [mero] mere.
relevância [xele'vãnsja] *f* **-1.** [saliência] prominence. **-2.** [importância] relevance; **ser de ~** to be of importance, to be important.
relevante [xele'vãntʃi] *adj* **-1.** [saliente] prominent. **-2.** [importante] important.
relevar [4] [xele'va(x)] *vt* **-1.** [salientar] to emphasize. **-2.** [aliviar] to alleviate. **-3.** [perdoar] to forgive.
relevo [xe'levu] *m* **-1.** [em superfície] outstanding feature. **-2.** ARTE relief. **-3.** *fig* [destaque] importance; **pôr em ~** to emphasize.
relicário [xeli'karju] *m* reliquary.
religião [xeli'ʒjãw] (*pl* **-ões**) *f* religion.
religiosidade [xeliʒjozi'dadʒi] *f* piety; **pagar as contas com ~** to pay one's debts religiously.
religioso, osa [xeli'ʒozu, ɔza] ◇ *adj* religious. ◇ *m, f* [padre, freira] monk (*f* nun).
◆ **religioso** *m* [casamento] church wedding.
relinchar [4] [xelĩn'ʃa(x)] *vi* to neigh.
relincho [xe'lĩnʃu] *m* neigh.
relíquia [xe'likja] *f* relic; **~ de família** family heirloom.
relógio [xe'lɔʒju] *m* **-1.** [instrumento] clock; **~ de pé** grandfather clock; **~ de ponto** time clock; **~ de pulso** wrist watch; **~ de sol** sundial; **correr contra o ~** to race against the clock. **-2.** [registro] meter.
relojoaria [xeloʒwa'ria] *f* **-1.** ARTE watchmaking. **-2.** [loja] watchmaker's.
relojoeiro, ra [xelo'ʒwejru, ra] *m, f* watchmaker.
relutância [xelu'tãnsja] *f* reluctance.
relutante [xelu'tãntʃi] *adj* reluctant.
relutar [4] [xelu'ta(x)] *vi*: **~ (em fazer algo)** to be reluctant (to do sthg); **~ (contra algo)** to be reluctant (to accept sthg).
reluzente [xelu'zẽntʃi] *adj* shining.
reluzir [72] [xelu'zi(x)] *vi* [brilhar] to shine.
relva ['xɛwva] *f* grass.
remador, ra [xema'do(x), ra] *m, f* rower.
remanescente [xemane'sẽntʃi] ◇ *adj* remaining; **isto é ~ de práticas antigas** this is what remains of ancient customs. ◇ *m* remainder.
remanescer [25] [xemane'se(x)] *vi* to remain.
remanso [xe'mãnsu] *m* backwater.
remar [4] [xe'ma(x)] ◇ *vt* to row. ◇ *vi* to row; **~ contra a maré** *fig* to swim against the tide.
remarcação [xemaxka'sãw] (*pl* **-ões**) *f* adjustment.
remarcar [12] [xemax'ka(x)] *vt* to adjust.
rematado, da [xema'tadu, da] *adj* [concluído] completed.
rematar [4] [xema'ta(x)] *vt* **-1.** [concluir] to conclude. **-2.** [fazer o acabamento] to finish.
remate [xe'matʃi] *m* **-1.** [conclusão] end. **-2.** [acabamento] finishing touch. **-3.** [de piada] punchline.
remediado, da [xeme'dʒjadu, da] *adj* comfortably off.
remediar [17] [xeme'dʒja(x)] *vt* **-1.** [corrigir, solucionar] to put right. **-2.** [atenuar] to alleviate. **-3.** [evitar] to avoid.
remediável [xeme'dʒjavew] (*pl* **-eis**) *adj* rectifiable.
remédio [xe'mɛdʒju] *m* **-1.** [medicamento] remedy. **-2.** [solução] solution.
remela [xe'mɛla] *f* sleep.
remelento, ta [xeme'lẽntu, ta] *adj* bleary-eyed.
remelexo [xeme'leʃu] *m* swaying.
rememorar [4] [xememo'ra(x)] *vt* to remember.
remendar [4] [xemẽn'da(x)] *vt* **-1.** [roupa] to mend. **-2.** [erros] to rectify.
remendo [xe'mẽndu] *m* **-1.** [de pano] patch. **-2.** [de metal, couro] repair. **-3.** [emenda] correction.
remessa [xe'mɛsa] *f* **-1.** [ato] dispatch. **-2.** [de dinheiro] remittance; [de mercadorias] shipment.
remetente [xeme'tẽntʃi] *mf* [de carta] sender.
remeter [5] [xeme'te(x)] *vt* **-1.** [carta, encomenda] to send. **-2.** [dinheiro] to remit.
◆ **remeter-se** *vp* [referir-se] to refer to.
remexer [5] [xeme'ʃe(x)] ◇ *vt* **-1.** [mexer] to move. **-2.** [misturar] to mix. **-3.** [sacudir - braços] to shake; [- papéis, folhas] to shuffle. **-4.** [revolver] to stir up. **-5.** *fam* [rebolar] to roll. ◇ *vi* [mexer]: **~ em algo** to rummage through sthg.
◆ **remexer-se** *vp* **-1.** [mover-se] to stir. **-2.** [rebolar-se] to roll.
remição [xemi'sãw] *f* **-1.** [libertação] release. **-2.** [expiação] redemption.
reminiscência [xemini'sẽnsja] *f* reminiscence.
remir [80] [xe'mi(x)] *vt* **-1.** [ger] to redeem. **-2.** [livrar]: **~ alguém (de algo)** to free sb (from sthg). **-3.** [indenizar] to indemnify.
◆ **remir-se** *vp* [redimir-se] to redeem o.s.
remissão [xemi'sãw] (*pl* **-ões**) *f* **-1.** [ger] remission. **-2.** [em texto] cross-reference.
remo ['xemu] *m* **-1.** [instrumento] oar. **-2.** [esporte] rowing.
remoção [xemo'sãw] (*pl* **-ões**) *f* removal.
remoçar [13] [xemo'sa(x)] ◇ *vt* to rejuvenate. ◇ *vi* to be rejuvenated.
remoer [28] [xe'mwe(x)] *vt* **-1.** [moer novamente] to regrind. **-2.** [remastigar] to chew. **-3.** [refletir muito sobre] to chew over. **-4.** [afligir] to chew at.
◆ **remoer-se** *vp* [amofinar-se] to be consumed.
remontar [4] [xemõn'ta(x)] ◇ *vt* **-1.** [armar de novo] to reassemble. **-2.** TEATRO to restage. **-3.** [mobiliar] to refurnish. ◇ *vi* **-1.** [em cavalo] to remount. **-2.** [no tempo]: **~ a** to date back to; **~ ao passado** to return to the past.
remorso [xe'mɔxsu] *m* remorse.
remoto, ta [xe'mɔtu, ta] *adj* remote.
removedor [xemove'do(x)] *m* remover.
remover [5] [xemo've(x)] *vt* **-1.** [ger] to remove. **-2.** [transferir] to transfer. **-3.** [superar] to overcome.
remuneração [xemunera'sãw] (*pl* **-ões**) *f* remuneration.
remunerador, ra [xemunera'do(x), ra] *adj* [recompensador] remunerative.

remunerar [4] [xemune'ra(x)] *vt* to remunerate.
rena ['xena] *f* reindeer.
renal [xe'naw] (*pl* **-ais**) *adj* renal.
Renascença [xena'sẽnsa] *f*: **a** ~ the Renaissance.
renascentista [xenasẽn'tʃiʃta] *adj* Renaissance *(antes de subst)*.
renascer [25] [xena'se(x)] *vi* **-1.** [nascer de novo] to spring up again. **-2.** *fig* [recuperar-se, resurgir] to be reborn.
renascimento [xenasi'mẽntu] *m* rebirth.
◆ **Renascimento** *m*: **o Renascimento** the Renaissance.
renda ['xẽnda] *f* **-1.** [rendimento] income; **viver de** ~ to have a private income; ~ **bruta** gross income; ~ **fixa** fixed yield; ~ **líquida** net income. **-2.** [lucro] profit. **-3.** [tecido] lace.
rendado, da [xẽn'dadu, da] *adj* **-1.** [feito de renda] lace *(antes de subst)*. **-2.** [como renda] lacy.
◆ **rendado** *m* lacework.
rendeiro, ra [xẽn'dejru, ra] *m, f* **-1.** [fabricante de renda] lacemaker. **-2.** [de terra] tenant farmer.
render [5] [xẽn'de(x)] ◇ *vt* **-1.** [dominar] to overpower. **-2.** [substituir] to relieve. **-3.** [lucrar] to yield. **-4.** [causar] to bring about. **-5.** [prestar] to render. ◇ *vi* **-1.** [dar lucro] to be profitable. **-2.** [trabalho] to be productive. **-3.** [comida]: **a comida rendeu para toda a semana** there was enough food for the whole week; **vamos fazer sopa porque rende mais** let's make soup because it goes further. **-4.** [durar] to last.
◆ **render-se** *vp* [entregar-se]: **~-se (a algo/alguém)** to surrender (to sb/sthg).
rendição [xẽndʒi'sãw] *f* **-1.** [capitulação] surrender. **-2.** [substituição] changing.
rendido, da [xẽn'dʒidu, da] *adj fig*: ~ **a algo** overcome by sthg.
rendimento [xẽndʒi'mẽntu] *m* **-1.** [renda] rental. **-2.** [lucro] profit. **-3.** [desempenho] performance. **-4.** [juro] interest.
rendoso, osa [xẽn'dozu, ɔza] *adj* **-1.** [lucrativo] profitable. **-2.** [proveitoso] productive.
renegado, da [xene'gadu, da] ◇ *adj* renegade. ◇ *m, f* renegade.
renegar [14] [xene'ga(x)] *vt* **-1.** [ger] to renounce. **-2.** [negar] to deny. **-3.** [desprezar] to reject.
renhido, da [xe'ɲidu, da] *adj* hard-fought.
renitente [xeni'tẽntʃi] *adj* persistent.
renomado, da [xeno'madu, da] *adj* renowned.
renome [xe'nɔmi] *m*: **de** ~ renowned.
renovação [xenova'sãw] (*pl* **-ões**) *f* **-1.** [ger] renewal. **-2.** [de ensino, empresa] revamping. **-3.** ARQUIT renovation.
renovador, ra [xeno'vado(x), ra] ◇ *adj* reformist. ◇ *m, f* reformist.
renovar [4] [xeno'va(x)] *vt* **-1.** [ger] to renew. **-2.** [ensino, empresa] to revamp. **-3.** ARQUIT to renovate.
rentabilidade [xẽntabili'dadʒi] *f* **-1.** [lucro] profitability. **-2.** [proveito] productiveness.
rentável [xẽn'tavɛw] (*pl* **-eis**) *adj* profitable.
rente ['xẽntʃi] ◇ *adj* **-1.** [muito curto] close-cropped. **-2.** [junto]: ~ **a** right next to. ◇ *adv* **-1.** [muito curto] very short. **-2.** [junto]: **ele caiu** ~ **ao chão** he fell flat on the floor; **ele foi esmagado** ~ **ao muro** he was crushed right up against the wall.
renúncia [xe'nũnsja] *f* renouncement.
renunciar [16] [xenũn'sja(x)] *vi*: ~ **a algo** to renounce sthg.
reorganização [xeoxganiza'sãw] *f* reorganization.
reorganizar [4] [xeoxgani'za(x)] *vt* to reorganize.
reparação [xepara'sãw] (*pl* **-ões**) *f* **-1.** [conserto] repair. **-2.** [indenização] compensation. **-3.** [retratação] reparation.
reparar [4] [xepa'ra(x)] ◇ *vt* **-1.** [consertar] to repair. **-2.** [indenizar] to compensate. **-3.** [retratar-se de] to admit. **-4.** [notar] to notice. ◇ *vi* [notar]: ~ **em algo/alguém** to notice sthg/sb; **não repare na bagunça** pay no attention to the mess.
reparo [xe'paru] *m* **-1.** [conserto] repair. **-2.** [crítica] criticism.
repartição [xepaxtʃi'sãw] (*pl* **-ões**) *f* **-1.** [partilha] distribution. **-2.** [órgão governamental] department; ~ **pública** government department.
repartir [6] [xepax'tʃi(x)] *vt* **-1.** [dividir - em partes] to divide up; ~ **o cabelo** to part one's hair; [- entre vários] to distribute. **-2.** [compartilhar] to share.
repassar [4] [xepa'sa(x)] *vt* **-1.** [passar de novo] to cross again. **-2.** [revisar] to revise. **-3.** [verbas] to transfer.
repasse [xe'pasi] *m* [de verba] transfer.
repatriação [xepatrja'sãw] (*pl* **-ões**) *f* repatriation.
repatriar [16] [xepa'trja(x)] *vt* to repatriate.
◆ **repatriar-se** *vp* to return home.
repelente [xepe'lẽntʃi] ◇ *adj* [repugnante] repellent. ◇ *m* [inseticida] repellent.
repelir [57] [xepe'li(x)] *vt* **-1.** [fazer regressar] to drive away. **-2.** [expulsar] to repel. **-3.** [rechaçar, impedir de entrar] to refuse admission to. **-4.** [recusar] to refuse. **-5.** [repudiar] to reject. **-6.** [desmentir] to refute.
repensar [4] [xepẽn'sa(x)] ◇ *vt* to reconsider. ◇ *vi*: ~ **em algo** to reconsider sthg.
repente [xe'pẽntʃi] *m*: **num** ~ **tudo escureceu** all of a sudden everything went dark; **um** ~ **de carinho** a sudden show of affection.
◆ **de repente** *loc adv* **-1.** [repentinamente] suddenly. **-2.** *fam* [talvez] maybe.
repentinamente [xepẽntʃina'mẽntʃi] *adv* suddenly.
repentino, na [xepẽn'tʃinu, na] *adj* sudden.
repercussão [xepexku'sãw] (*pl* **-ões**) *f* **-1.** *fig* [de som] reverberation. **-2.** [efeito] repercussion; **o CD teve boa** ~ **no exterior** the CD was very successful abroad.
repercutir [6] [xepexku'tʃi(x)] ◇ *vt* [som] to re-echo. ◇ *vi* **-1.** [som] to reverberate. **-2.** *fig* [afetar]: ~ **em** to have repercussions on.

repertório [xepex'tɔrju] *m* **-1.** [conjunto] collection. **-2.** *MÚS* repertoire.
repetente [xepe'tẽntʃi] *EDUC* <> *adj* repeating. <> *mf student who repeats a year.*
repetição [xepetʃi'sãw] (*pl* **-ões**) *f* repetition.
repetido, da [xepe'tʃidu, da] *adj* repeated; **repetidas vezes** repeatedly.
repetir [57] [xepe'tʃi(x)] <> *vt* **-1.** [ger] to repeat. **-2.** [roupa] to wear again. **-3.** [refeição] to have a second helping of, to have seconds. **-4.** [tocar de novo]: ~ **uma música** to play an encore. <> *vi* to repeat.
◆ **repetir-se** *vp* **-1.** [fenômeno] to be repeated. **-2.** [pessoa] to repeat o.s.
repetitivo, va [xepetʃi'tʃivu, va] *adj* repetitive.
repicar [12] [xepi'ka(x)] *vt* & *vi* to ring.
repique [xe'piki] *m* **-1.** [de sino] peal. **-2.** *fig* [alarme] alarm bell; ~ **falso** false alarm.
replay [xi'plej] *m* replay.
repleto, ta [xe'plɛtu, ta] *adj* [cheio]: ~ **(de)** full (of).
réplica ['xɛplika] *f* **-1.** [cópia] replica. **-2.** [resposta] reply.
replicar [12] [xepli'ka(x)] <> *vt* **-1.** [responder] to reply. **-2.** [contestar] to answer. <> *vi* **-1.** [responder] to reply. **-2.** [contestar] to respond.
repolho [xe'poʎu] *m* cabbage.
repor [45] [xe'po(x)] *vt* **-1.** [recolocar] to replace. **-2.** [devolver] to repay.
◆ **repor-se** *vp* to recover.
reportagem [xepox'taʒẽ] (*pl* **-ns**) *f* **-1.** [ato] report. **-2.** [matéria]: ~ **(sobre)** report (on). **-3.** [repórteres] reporters *(pl)*, the press.
reportar [4] [xepox'ta(x)] *vt* **-1.** [atribuir] to attribute. **-2.** [retroceder] to take back. **-3.** [relatar] to report.
◆ **reportar-se** *vp* [referir-se] to refer.
repórter [xe'pɔxte(x)] (*pl* **-es**) *mf* reporter.
repórter-fotográfico, ca [xe'pɔxte(x)foto'grafiku, ka] (*pl* **-s**) *m* press photographer.
reposição [xepozi'sãw] (*pl* **-ões**) *f* [restituição] return; ~ **salarial** wage adjustment.
repositório [xepozi'tɔrju] *m* repository.
repousante [xepo'zãntʃi] *adj* restful.
repousar [4] [xepo'za(x)] <> *vt* to rest. <> *vi* **-1.** [descansar] to rest. **-2.** [basear-se]: ~ **em/sobre algo** to be based on sthg. **-3.** [não produzir] to rest, to lie fallow.
repouso [xe'pozu] *m* [descanso] rest; **em** ~ at rest.
repreender [5] [xeprjẽn'de(x)] *vt* to reprimand.
repreensão [xeprjẽn'sãw] (*pl* **-ões**) *f* reprimand.
repreensível [xeprjẽn'sivew] (*pl* **-eis**) *adj* reprehensible.
represa [xe'preza] *f* dam.
represália [xepre'zalja] *f* reprisal; **em** ~ in reprisal.
representação [xeprezẽnta'sãw] (*pl* **-ões**) *f* **-1.** [reprodução] representation. **-2.** [queixa]: ~ **contra algo/alguém** complaint against sthg/sb. **-3.** [delegação] representatives *(pl)*. **-4.** *TEATRO* performance. **-5.** *COM*: **ter a** ~ **de algo** to display sthg. **-6.** *fig* [fingimento] pretence *UK*, pretense *US*.
representante [xeprezẽn'tãntʃi] <> *adj* representative. <> *mf* representative.
representar [4] [xeprezẽn'ta(x)] <> *vt* **-1.** [ger] to represent. **-2.** [*TEATRO* - encenar] to perform; [- interpretar] to play. <> *vi TEATRO* [interpretar] to perform.
representatividade [xeprezẽntatʃivi'dadʒi] *f* representation.
representativo, va [xeprezẽnta'tʃivu, va] *adj* representative; ~ **de algo** representative of sthg.
repressão [xepre'sãw] (*pl* **-ões**) *f* repression.
repressivo, va [xepre'sivu, va] *adj* repressive.
repressor, ra [xepre'so(x), ra] *adj* repressive.
reprimido, da [xepri'midu, da] *adj* repressed.
reprimir [6] [xepri'mi(x)] *vt* **-1.** [conter - paixão] to contain; [- pensamento] to suppress. **-2.** [dissimular] to suppress. **-3.** *PSIC* to repress. **-4.** [proibir] to prohibit.
◆ **reprimir-se** *vp* [conter-se] to control o.s.
reprisar [4] [xepri'za(x)] *vt* to repeat.
reprise [xe'prizi] *f* repeat.
réprobo, ba ['xɛprobu, ba] <> *adj* reprobate. <> *m, f* reprobate.
reprodução [xeprodu'sãw] (*pl* **-ões**) *f* reproduction.
reprodutivo, va [xeprodu'tʃivu, va] *adj* reproductive.
reprodutor, ra [xeprodu'to(x), ra] *adj* reproductive.
◆ **reprodutor** *m* breeding animal.
reproduzir [72] [xeprodu'zi(x)] *vt* **-1.** [copiar, repetir] to copy. **-2.** [procriar] to breed. **-3.** [reeditar] to republish.
◆ **reproduzir-se** *vp* **-1.** [procriar-se] to breed. **-2.** [repetir-se] to be repeated.
reprovação [xeprova'sãw] (*pl* **-ões**) *f* **-1.** [censura] disapproval. **-2.** [em exame, seleção] failure.
reprovado, da [xepro'vadu, da] <> *adj* failed. <> *m, f* failure.
reprovar [4] [xepro'va(x)] <> *vt* **-1.** [censurar] to disapprove of. **-2.** [rejeitar] to reject. **-3.** [em exame, seleção] to fail. <> *vi* [em exame, seleção] to fail.
réptil ['xɛptʃiw] (*pl* **-eis**) *m* reptile.
república [xɛ'publika] *f* **-1.** *POL* republic. **-2.** *EDUC* students' residence.
República Centro-Africana [xe,publikasẽntrwafri'kãna] *n* Central African Republic.
República da África do Sul [xepublikada,afrikadu'suw] *n* Republic of South Africa.
República Dominicana [xe,publikadomini'kãna] *n* Dominican Republic.
republicano, na [xepubli'kãnu, na] <> *adj* republican. <> *m, f* republican.
República Tcheca [xe,publika'tʃɛka] *n* Czech Republic.
repudiar [16] [xepu'dʒjar] *vt* to repudiate.
repúdio [xe'pudʒju] *m* repudiation.

repugnância [xepug'nãsja] *f* **-1.** [ger] repugnance. **-2.** [oposição] opposition.
repugnante [xepug'nãntʃi] *adj* repugnant.
repugnar [4] [xepug'na(x)] ◇ *vt* to disgust. ◇ *vi*: ~ **(a)** to disgust, to be repugnant (to).
repulsa [xe'puwsa] *f* **-1.** [ato] repulsion. **-2.** [sentimento] repugnance. **-3.** [oposição] rejection.
repulsão [xepuw'sãw] (*pl* **-ões**) *f* **-1.** [repulsa] repulsion. **-2.** *FÍSICA* rejection.
repulsivo, va [xepuw'sivu, va] *adj* repulsive.
reputação [xeputa'sãw] (*pl* **-ões**) *f* reputation.
reputado, da [xepu'tadu, da] *adj* renowned.
reputar [4] [xepu'ta(x)] *vt* to consider, to regard as.
◆ **reputar-se** *vp* to consider o.s.
repuxado, da [xepu'ʃadu, da] *adj* **-1.** [esticado] tight; **cabelo** ~ pulled-back hair. **-2.** [amendoado] slanting.
repuxar [4] [xepu'ʃa(x)] ◇ *vt* [esticar - roupa, pele] to stretch; [- cabelo] to pull back tight. ◇ *vi* [retesar] to tense.
repuxo [xe'puʃu] *m* fountain.
requebrado [xeke'bradu] *m* swaying.
requebrar [4] [xeke'bra(x)] *vt* to wiggle.
◆ **requebrar-se** *vp* to wiggle one's hips.
requeijão [xekej'ʒãw] (*pl* **-ões**) *m* soft cheese.
requentado, da [xekẽn'tadu, da] *adj* reheated.
requentar [4] [xekẽn'ta(x)] *vt* to reheat.
requerente [xeke'rẽntʃi] *mf JUR* petitioner.
requerer [38] [xeke're(x)] ◇ *vt* **-1.** [pedir] to request. **-2.** [exigir] to demand. **-3.** [merecer] to deserve. **-4.** *JUR* to petition for. ◇ *vi JUR* to make a petition.
requerimento [xekeri'mẽntu] *m* **-1.** [ato de requerer] application. **-2.** [petição] petition.
réquiem ['xɛkjẽ] (*pl* **-ns**) *m* requiem.
requintado, da [xekĩn'tadu, da] *adj* refined.
requintar [4] [xekĩn'ta(x)] ◇ *vt* to refine. ◇ *vi*: ~ **em** to be refined in.
◆ **requintar-se** *vp* to be refined.
requinte [xe'kĩntʃi] *m* **-1.** [refinamento] refinement. **-2.** [excesso] excess.
requisição [xekizi'sãw] (*pl* **-ões**) *f* requisition.
requisitado, da [xekizi'tadu, da] *adj* **-1.** [pedido] requested. **-2.** [muito procurado] in demand.
requisitar [4] [xekizi'ta(x)] *vt* to demand.
requisito [xeki'zitu] *m* requirement.
rês [xeʃ] (*pl* **reses**) *m* head of cattle.
rescindir [6] [xesĩn'dʒi(x)] *vt* [contrato] to rescind.
rescrever [5] [xeʃkre've(x)] *vt* to rewrite.
resenha [xe'zaɲa] *f* **-1.** [de livro] review. **-2.** [relatório] report. **-3.** [resumo] summary.
resenhar [xeze'ɲa(x)] *vt* [sumariar] to write a summary of.
reserva [xe'zɛxva] ◇ *f* **-1.** [ger] reserve; ~ **internacionais** foreign reserves; ~ **natural** nature reserve; ~ **de mercado** protected market. **-2.** [em hotel, avião *etc*] reservation; **fazer** ~ **de algo** to reserve sthg. **-3.** [restrição]: **ter** ~ **a** *ou* **para com** to have reservations about. **-4.** [discrição] discretion. ◇ *mf ESP* reserve.
◆ **reservas** *fpl* [energia] reserves.
reservado, da [xezex'vadu, da] *adj* **-1.** [ger] reserved. **-2.** [íntimo] private.
◆ **reservado** *m* [privada] private room.
reservar [4] [xezex'va(x)] *vt* **-1.** [fazer reserva] to reserve. **-2.** [poupar] to save. **-3.** [destinar] to allow; **a vida lhe reserva muitas alegrias** life has much joy in store for him.
◆ **reservar-se** *vp* [preservar-se] to save o.s.
reservatório [xezexva'tɔrju] *m* **-1.** [depósito] tank. **-2.** [de água] reservoir.
reservista [xezex'viʃta] *mf* reservist.
resfriado, da [xeʃfri'adu, da] *adj* **-1.** [pessoa] cold; **estar** ~ to have a cold; **ficar** ~ to catch cold. **-2.** [carne] chilled.
◆ **resfriado** *m* cold; **pegar um** ~ to catch a cold.
resfriar [16] [xeʃ'frja(x)] *vt* [esfriar] to cool.
◆ **resfriar-se** *vp MED* to catch a cold.
resgatar [4] [xeʒga'ta(x)] *vt* **-1.** [ger] to rescue. **-2.** [restituir] to recover. **-3.** [pagar] to pay off. **-4.** [recuperar] to recoup. **-5.** [expiar] to redeem.
resgate [xeʒ'gatʃi] *m* **-1.** [dinheiro] ransom. **-2.** [libertação] release. **-3.** [salvamento] rescue. **-4.** *FIN* [retirada] withdrawal; ~ **automático** automatic withdrawal. **-5.** *COM* redemption.
resguardar [4] [xeʒgwax'da(x)] *vt* **-1.** [proteger]: ~ **(de)** to protect (from). **-2.** [vigiar] to protect.
◆ **resguardar-se** *vp* [proteger-se]: ~**-se de** to protect o.s. from.
resguardo [xeʒ'gwaxdu] *m* **-1.** [proteção] protection. **-2.** [cuidado] care. **-3.** [repouso] rest; **estar/ficar de** ~ to take it easy.
residência [xezi'dẽnsja] *f* residence; **fixar** ~ **em** to take up residence in.
residencial [xezidẽn'sjaw] (*pl* **-ais**) *adj* residential.
residente [xezi'dẽntʃi] ◇ *adj* resident. ◇ *mf* **-1.** [morador] resident. **-2.** [médico] senior registrar *UK*, resident *US*.
residir [6] [xezi'dʒi(x)] *vi* to reside.
resíduo [xe'zidwu] *m* **-1.** [resto] residue. **-2.** [bancário] surplus.
resignação [xezigna'sãw] *f*: ~ **(a/com)** resignation to.
resignadamente [xezignada'mẽntʃi] *adv* resignedly, with resignation.
resignado, da [xezig'nadu, da] *adj* resigned.
resignar-se [4] [xezig'naxsi] *vp* to resign o.s.; ~ **com algo** to resign o.s. to sthg; ~ **a fazer algo** to resign o.s. to doing sthg.
resiliente [xezi'ljẽntʃi] *adj* resilient.
resina [xe'zina] *f* resin.
resistência [xeziʃ'tẽnsja] *f* **-1.** [ger] resistance; **o carro não teve** ~ **para subir a ladeira** the car did not have the power to go up the slope. **-2.** [moral] stamina. **-3.** *fig* [oposição]: ~ **a** resistance to.
resistente [xeziʃ'tẽntʃi] *adj* **-1.** [forte] strong; ~ **ao calor** heat-resistant. **-2.** [durável] durable. **-3.** [que se opõe a]: ~ **a** resistant to.

resistir [6] [xeziʃ'tʃi(x)] *vi*: ~ **a algo** to resist sthg.
resma ['xeʒma] *f* ream.
resmungão, ona [xeʒmũɲ'gãw, ɔna] (*mpl* **-ões**, *fpl* **-nas**) <> *adj* [rabugento] cantankerous. <> *m,f* grouch.
resmungar [14] [xeʒmũŋ'ga(x)] *vt & vi* to grumble.
resmungo [xeʒ'mũŋgu] *m* grumble.
resolução [xezolu'sãw] (*pl* **-ões**) *f* **-1.** [decisão] decision; **tomar uma** ~ to take a decision. **-2.** [solução] solution. **-3.** [firmeza] resolve. **-4.** [de imagem] resolution; **de alta** ~ high-resolution, hi-res.
resoluto, ta [xezo'lutu, ta] *adj* resolute; ~ **a fazer algo** resolved to do sthg.
resolver [5] [xezow've(x)] <> *vt* **-1.** [solucionar] to solve. **-2.** [decidir]: ~ **fazer algo** to decide to do sthg. <> *vi* **-1.** [adiantar]: **a violência não resolve** violence doesn't solve anything. **-2.** [decidir] to decide.
◆ **resolver-se** *vp* [decidir] to make up one's mind; ~**-se a fazer algo** to decide to do sthg; ~**-se sobre** *ou* **quanto a algo** to make a decision about sthg.
resolvido, da [xezow'vidu, da] *adj* **-1.** [pessoa] determined; ~ **a fazer algo** determined to do sthg. **-2.** [assunto, questão] resolved.
respaldar [4] [xeʃpaw'da(x)] *vt* [apoiar] to back.
respaldo [xeʃ'pawdu] *m* **-1.** [de cadeira] back. **-2.** *fig* [apoio] backing.
respectivamente [xeʃpektʃiva'mẽntʃi] *adv* respectively.
respectivo, va [xeʃpek'tʃivu, va] *adj* respective; ~ **a** in respect of.
respeitador, ra [xeʃpejtado(x), ra] *adj* respectful.
respeitar [4] [xeʃpej'ta(x)] *vt* to respect.
respeitável [xeʃpej'tavɛw] (*pl* **-eis**) *adj* **-1.** [digno de respeito] respectable. **-2.** [considerável] considerable.
respeito [xeʃ'pejtu] *m* **-1.** [deferência]: ~ **a** *ou* **por** respect for; **falta de** ~ lack of respect; **dar-se ao** ~ to command respect; **em** ~ **a** out of respect for; **faltar ao** ~ **com alguém** to be rude to sb; **impor** ~ **a** to command the respect of. **-2.** [relação] respect; **dizer** ~ **a** to concern; **a** ~ **de** [sobre] about; **com** ~ **a** [no tocante a] as regards.
respeitoso, osa [xeʃpej'tozu, ɔza] *adj* respectful.
respingar [14] [xeʃpĩŋ'ga(x)] *vi* to splash.
respingo [xeʃ'pĩŋgu] *m* splash.
respiração [xeʃpira'sãw] *f* breathing; ~ **artificial** artificial respiration.
respirador [xeʃpira'do(x)] *m* respirator.
respirar [4] [xeʃpi'ra(x)] <> *vt* [ar] to breathe. <> *vi* **-1.** [absorver o ar] to breathe. **-2.** *fig* [descansar] to have time to breathe; **não deixar alguém** ~ to not give sb breathing space. **-3.** *fig* [sentir alívio] to breathe freely again.
respiratório, ria [xeʃpira'tɔrju, rja] *adj* respiratory.
respiro [xeʃ'piru] *m* **-1.** [respiração] breath. **-2.** *fig* [descanso] rest. **-3.** [abertura] vent.
resplandecente [xeʃplãnde'sẽntʃi] *adj* **-1.** [jóia] resplendent. **-2.** [dia] splendid.
resplandecer [25] [xeʃplãnde'se(x)] *vi* **-1.** [brilhar] to shine. **-2.** [sobressair] to outshine.
resplendor [xeʃplẽn'do(x)] *m* brilliance.
respondão, dona [xeʃpõn'dãw, dona] (*mpl* **-ões**, *fpl* **-s**) *m, f* cheeky person.
responder [5] [xeʃpõn'de(x)] <> *vt* [dar resposta] to reply. <> *vi* **-1.** [dar resposta]: ~ **(a algo/alguém)** to reply to sthg/sb. **-2.** [replicar] to answer. **-3.** [ser respondão] to answer back. **-4.** [reagir]: ~ **a algo** to respond to sthg. **-5.** [responsabilizar-se]: ~ **por algo/alguém** to answer for sthg/sb. **-6.** [submeter-se a]: ~ **a algo** to undergo sthg.
responsabilidade [xeʃpõnsabili'dadʒi] *f* **-1.** [obrigação] responsibility. **-2.** JUR liability.
responsabilizar [4] [xeʃpõnsabili'za(x)] *vt*: ~ **algo/alguém (por algo)** to hold sthg/sb responsible for sthg.
◆ **responsabilizar-se** *vp*: ~**-se (por algo/alguém)** to hold o.s. responsible (for sthg/sb).
responsável [xeʃpõn'savɛw] (*pl* **-eis**) <> *adj*: ~ **(por)** responsible (for). <> *mf* **-1.** [encarregado] person in charge. **-2.** [culpado] person responsible.
resposta [xeʃ'pɔʃta] *f* **-1.** [de pergunta] answer; **em** ~ **a algo** in response to sthg. **-2.** *fig* [reação] response.
resquício [xeʃ'kisju] *m* **-1.** [vestígio] fragment. **-2.** [fragmento] fragment.
ressabiado, da [xesa'bjadu, da] *adj* **-1.** [desconfiado] suspicious. **-2.** [ressentido] resentful.
ressabiar [xesa'bja(x)] ◆ **ressabiar-se** *vp* **-1.** [ficar assustado] to be startled. **-2.** [magoar-se] to be offended.
ressaca [xe'saka] *f* **-1.** [do mar] rough sea; **estar de** ~ to be rough. **-2.** *fig* [de bebida] hangover; **estar/ficar de** ~ to have/to get a hangover.
ressaibo [xe'sajbu] *m* **-1.** [mau gosto] unpleasant taste. **-2.** *fig* [indício] sign. **-3.** [ressentimento] resentment.
ressaltar [4] [xesaw'ta(x)] *vt* to emphasize.
ressalva [xe'sawva] *f* **-1.** [emenda] correction. **-2.** [restrição] proviso; **fazer uma** ~ **a algo** to make an exception to sthg.
ressarcimento [xesaxsi'mẽntu] *m* [compensação] reparation.
ressarcir [79] [xesax'si(x)] *vt* [compensar]: ~ **algo (de)** to compensate for sthg (with); ~ **alguém (de)** to compensate sb (with).
◆ **ressarcir-se** *vp* [compensar-se]: ~**-se de** to be compensated for.
ressecado, da [xese'kadu, da] *adj* dried up.
ressecar [12] [xese'ka(x)] *vt & vi* to dry up.
ressentido, da [xesẽn'tʃidu, da] *adj* resentful.
ressentimento [xesẽntʃi'mẽntu] *m* resentment.
ressentir-se [56] [xesẽn'tʃixsi] *vp* **-1.** [magoar-se]: ~ **(de algo)** to resent (sthg). **-2.** [sofrer consequência]: ~ **de algo** to feel the effects of sthg.
ressequido, da [xese'kidu, da] *adj* dried up.

ressoar [20] [xe'swa(x)] *vi* to resound.
ressonância [xeso'nãnsja] *f* **-1.** [ger] resonance. **-2.** *MED*: ~ **magnética** magnetic resonance. **-3.** *fig* [repercussão]: **ter ~ em algo** to be a success in sthg.
ressonante [xeso'nãntʃi] *adj* resonant.
ressurgimento [xesuxʒi'mẽntu] *m* resurgence.
ressurgir [52] [xesux'zi(x)] *vi* **-1.** [reaparecer] to reappear. **-2.** [revitalizar-se] to revive. **-3.** [ressuscitar] to be resurrected.
ressurreição [xesuxej'sãw] (*pl* **-ões**) *f* resurrection.
ressuscitar [4] [xesusi'ta(x)] ◇ *vt* **-1.** [pessoa, animal] to resuscitate. **-2.** [costume, moda] to revive. ◇ *vi* **-1.** [pessoa, animal] to be resuscitated. **-2.** [costume, moda] to be revived.
restabelecer [25] [xeʃtabele'se(x)] *vt* to restore.
◆ **restabelecer-se** *vp* to recover.
restabelecimento [xeʃtabelesi'mẽntu] *m* **-1.** [de ordem, tradição] restoration. **-2.** [de doente] recovery.
restante [xeʃ'tãntʃi] ◇ *adj* remaining. ◇ *m* [resto] remainder.
restar [4] [xeʃ'ta(x)] *vi* **-1.** [sobrar] to be left over. **-2.** [sobreviver] to survive. **-3.** [subsistir] to remain; **não me resta dúvida de que ...** I no longer have any doubt that ... **-4.** [faltar]: **faltam duas páginas para terminar** there are two pages left to finish.
restauração [xeʃtawra'sãw] (*pl* **-ões**) *f* restoration.
restaurador, ra [xeʃtawra'do(x), ra] *m, f* restorer.
restaurante [xeʃtaw'rãntʃi] *m* restaurant.
restaurar [4] [xeʃtaw'ra(x)] *vt* **-1.** [ger] to restore. **-2.** [recuperar] to recover.
réstia ['xɛʃtʃja] *m* [de luz] ray.
restinga [xeʃ'tʃĩŋga] *f* sandbank.
restituição [xeʃtʃitwi'sãw] (*pl* **-ões**) *f* **-1.** [devolução] return; ~ **do imposto de renda** refunding of income tax. **-2.** [pagamento] repayment.
restituir [74] [xeʃtʃi'twi(x)] *vt* **-1.** [devolver] to return. **-2.** [pagar] to repay. **-3.** [restabelecer] to restore.
resto ['xɛʃtu] *m* **-1.** [ger] remainder. **-2.** [restante] rest; **de ~** [além disso] besides.
◆ **restos** *mpl* [de comida] leftovers.
◆ **restos mortais** *mpl* (mortal) remains.
restrição [xeʃtri'sãw] (*pl* **-ões**) *f* restriction.
restringir [52] [xeʃtrĩn'ʒi(x)] *vt* to restrict.
◆ **restringir-se** *vp* to restrict o.s.
restrito, ta [xeʃ'tritu, ta] *adj* restricted.
resultado [xezuw'tadu] *m* **-1.** [ger] result. **-2.** [proveito]: **dar ~** to be effective; **o filme deu bom ~ publicitário** the film was good publicity.
resultante [xezuw'tãntʃi] ◇ *adj* resulting; ~ **de algo** resulting from sthg. ◇ *f* **-1.** [conseqüência] outcome. **-2.** *FÍSICA* result.
resultar [46] [xezuw'ta(x)] *vi* **-1.** [originar-se]: ~ **de algo** to result from sthg. **-2.** [redundar] to turn out to be; ~ **em algo** to lead to sthg.
resumido, da [xezu'midu, da] *adj* concise.
resumir [xezu'mi(x)] *vt* to summarize.
◆ **resumir-se** *vp*: **~-se em** *ou* **a algo** to consist of sthg.
resumo [xe'zumu] *m* summary; **em ~** in short.
resvalar [4] [xeʒva'la(x)] *vi* **-1.** [deslizar]: ~ **(de/por algo)** to slip (from/through sthg). **-2.** *fig* [incidir]: ~ **em algo** to slide into sthg.
reta ['xɛta] *f* ⊳ **reto**.
retaguarda [ˌxeta'gwaxda] *f* **-1.** [posição] rear. **-2.** *MIL* rearguard.
retalhar [4] [xeta'ʎa(x)] *vt* **-1.** [cortar em pedaços] to cut up. **-2.** [golpear] to slash. **-3.** [dividir] to divide.
retalho [xe'taʎu] *m* remnant; **colcha de ~s** patchwork quilt.
retaliação [xetalja'sãw] (*pl* **-ões**) *f* retaliation.
retaliar [16] [xeta'lja(x)] ◇ *vt* to repay. ◇ *vi* to retaliate.
retangular [xetãŋgu'la(x)] *adj* rectangular.
retângulo [xe'tãŋgulu] *m* rectangle.
retardado, da [xetax'dadu, da] ◇ *adj* **-1.** [atrasado]: **fui ~ pelo trânsito** I was delayed by traffic. **-2.** *PSIC* retarded. ◇ *m, f PSIC* retarded person; ~ **mental** mentally retarded person.
retardar [4] [xetax'da(x)] *vt* **-1.** [atrasar] to delay. **-2.** [adiar] to postpone.
◆ **retardar-se** *vp* [atrasar-se] to be delayed.
retardatário, ria [xetaxda'tarju, rja] ◇ *adj* tardy. ◇ *m, f* latecomer.
retardo [xe'taxdu] *m* **-1.** [atraso] delay. **-2.** *PSIC* retardedness.
retenção [xetẽn'sãw] *f* **-1.** [detenção] detention; **a ~ no trânsito é grande** there is a major traffic hold-up. **-2.** *MED* [de líquidos] retention.
reter [1] [xe'te(x)] *vt* **-1.** [ger] to retain. **-2.** [segurar, prender - rédeas, corda] to hold; [- ladrão, suspeito] to detain. **-3.** [guardar] to keep. **-4.** [reprimir, deter] to hold back.
◆ **reter-se** *vp* [reprimir-se] to restrain o.s.
retesado, da [xete'zadu, da] *adj* taut.
retesar [4] [xete'za(x)] *vt* to tense.
◆ **retesar-se** *vp* to tense.
reticência [xetʃi'sẽnsja] *f* reticence.
◆ **reticências** *fpl* [sinal] ellipsis *(sing)*, suspension points.
reticente [xetʃi'sẽntʃi] *adj* reticent.
retidão [xetʃi'dãw] *f* [lisura] rectitude.
retificar [12] [xetʃifi'ka(x)] *vt* **-1.** [corrigir] to rectify. **-2.** [purificar] to purify. **-3.** *AUTO* to repair.
retina [xe'tʃina] *f ANAT* retina.
retinir [6] [xetʃi'ni(x)] *vi* **-1.** [tinir] to clink. **-2.** [ressoar] to resound.
retinto, ta [xe'tʃĩntu, ta] *adj* [muito escuro] inky.
retirado, da [xetʃi'radu, da] *adj* [pessoa] retiring; [vida] retired; [lugar, casa] isolated.
◆ **retirada** *f* **-1.** [ger] withdrawal; **bater em retirada** [fugir] to beat a retreat. **-2.** [migração] migration.
retirante [xetʃi'rãntʃi] *mf* migrant.
retirar [4] [xetʃi'ra(x)] *vt* **-1.** [ger] to remove. **-2.** [retratar-se de] to take back. **-3.** [ganhar] to make. **-4.** [livrar, salvar] to get out.

◆ **retirar-se** *vp* **-1.** [ger] to leave. **-2.** [refugiar-se] to withdraw.

retiro [xe'tʃiru] *m* retreat.

reto, ta ['xɛtu, ta] *adj* **-1.** [ger] straight; **ângulo ~** right angle. **-2.** *fig* [justo] straightforward. **-3.** *fig* [honesto] honest.

◆ **reto** *m* ANAT rectum.

◆ **reta** *f* **-1.** MAT straight line. **-2.** [de estrada, pista] straight; **reta de chegada**, **reta final** home straight.

retocar [12] [xeto'ka(x)] *vt* **-1.** [pintura] to touch up. **-2.** [texto] to tidy up.

retomada [xeto'mada] *f* [recuperação] recovery.

retomar [4] [xeto'ma(x)] *vt* **-1.** [continuar] to resume. **-2.** [reaver] to take back.

retoque [xe'tɔki] *m* finishing touch; **dar um ~** to add a finishing touch.

retorcer [25] [xetox'se(x)] *vt* **-1.** [torcer de novo] to re-twist. **-2.** [contorcer-se] to twist.

◆ **retorcer-se** *vp* [contorcer-se] to writhe.

retorcido, da [xetox'sidu, da] *adj* **-1.** [muito torto] twisted. **-2.** [empolado] involved.

retórico, ca [xe'tɔriku, ka] *adj* **-1.** [sem conteúdo] rhetorical. **-2.** *fig* [afetado] affected.

◆ **retórico** *m* rhetorician.

◆ **retórica** *f* **-1.** [discurso] rhetoric. **-2.** *pej* [afetação] affectation.

retornar [4] [xetox'na(x)] *vi* [voltar] to return; **~ de algo** to return from sthg.

retorno [xe'toxnu] *m* **-1.** [ger] return. **-2.** [resposta] response; **dar um ~ (sobre algo)** to give one's response (to sthg). **-3.** [em estrada] turning place; **fazer o ~** to turn back.

retorquir [78] [xetox'ki(x)] ◇ *vt*: **~ que** to retort that. ◇ *vi* to answer back.

retrabalhar [xetraba'ʎa(x)] *vt* [aprimorar] to recondition.

retração [xetra'sãw] *f* **-1.** [de gengiva, de imagem] receding. **-2.** [em compras] contraction.

retraído, da [xetra'idu, da] *adj* *fig* [reservado, tímido] reserved.

retraimento [xetraj'mẽntu] *m* [reserva, timidez] reserve.

retrair [68] [xetra'i(x)] *vt* **-1.** [ger] to withdraw. **-2.** [tornar reservado] to make reserved.

◆ **retrair-se** *vp* **-1.** [afastar-se] to withdraw. **-2.** [tornar-se reservado] to become withdrawn.

retransmitir [6] [xetrãnʒmi'tʃi(x)] *vt* to show again.

retrasado, da [xetra'zadu, da] *adj* [ano, semana] before last.

retratar [4] [xetra'ta(x)] *vt* **-1.** [fazer retrato] to depict. **-2.** [descrever] to portray. **-3.** [desdizer] to retract. **-4.** [expressar] to express.

◆ **retratar-se** *vp* **-1.** [representar-se] to portray o.s. **-2.** [desdizer-se]: **~-se de algo** to retract sthg. **-3.** [confessar erro] to admit one's mistake.

retrátil [xe'tratʃiw] (*pl* **-eis**) *adj* retractable.

retratista [xetra'tʃiʃta] *mf* portrait painter.

retrato [xe'tratu] *m* **-1.** [ger] portrait; **~ falado** Identikit® picture; **ser o ~ de alguém** [parecer-se] to be the (spitting) image of sb. **-2.** *fig* [exemplo] picture.

retribuição [xetribwi'sãw] (*pl* **-ões**) *f* **-1.** [pagamento] remuneration. **-2.** [recompensa] reward. **-3.** [agradecimento] reciprocation.

retribuir [74] [xetri'bwi(x)] *vt* **-1.** [pagar] to pay. **-2.** [agradecer] to return. **-3.** [corresponder] to reciprocate.

retroagir [52] [xetrwa'ʒi(x)] *vi*: **~ (a algo)** to be retroactive (on sthg).

retroativo, va [xetrwa'tʃivu, va] *adj* retroactive.

retroceder [5] [xetrose'de(x)] *vi* **-1.** [recuar] to step back. **-2.** [desistir]: **~ (em algo)** to withdraw (from sthg). **-3.** [decair] to decline.

retrocesso [xetro'sɛsu] *m* **-1.** [retorno] return. **-2.** [declínio] step backwards. **-3.** [recaída] recurrence. **-4.** [tecla] backspace. **-5.** [na economia] slowdown.

retrógrado, da [xe'trɔgradu, da] *adj* **-1.** [idéia, movimento] retrograde, reactionary. **-2.** [pessoa] reactionary.

retroprojetor [ˌxɛtroproʒe'to(x)] *m* overhead projector.

retrós [xe'trɔʃ] *m* bobbin.

retrospectiva [xetroʃpek'tʃiva] *f* retrospective.

retrospectivamente [xetroʃpektʃiva'mẽntʃi] *adv* retrospectively.

retrospecto [xetroʃ'pɛktu] *m* [retrospetiva] retrospect; **em ~** in retrospect.

retrovisor [xetrovi'zo(x)] (*pl* **-es**) ◇ *adj* rear-view. ◇ *m* rear-view mirror.

réu [xɛw], **ré** [xɛ] *m, f* accused.

reumático, ca [xewma'tʃiku, ka] ◇ *adj* rheumatic. ◇ *m, f* rheumatism sufferer.

reumatismo [xewma'tʃiʒmu] *m* rheumatism.

reumatologia [xewmatolo'ʒia] *f* rheumatology.

reumatologista [xewmatolo'ʒiʃta] *mf* rheumatologist.

reunião [xew'njãw] (*pl* **-ões**) *f* **-1.** [encontro] meeting; **~ de cúpula** summit; **~ de diretoria** board meeting. **-2.** [festa] party. **-3.** [coletânea] collection.

reunir [6] [xew'ni(x)] *vt* **-1.** [juntar] to gather. **-2.** [congregar] to join together. **-3.** [aliar] to combine. **-4.** [unir] to unite.

◆ **reunir-se** *vp* **-1.** [juntar-se] to gather. **-2.** [aliar-se] to be combined. **-3.** [realizar reunião] to meet. **-4.** [incorporar-se] to join together.

reutilizar [4] [xewtʃili'za(x)] *vt* to reuse.

revalorizar [4] [xevalori'za(x)] *vt* to revalue.

revanche [xe'vãnʃi] *f* **-1.** [desforra] revenge. **-2.** ESP return match.

revanchismo [xevãn'ʃiʒmu] *m* retaliation.

reveillon [xeve'jõn] *m* New Year's Eve.

revelação [xevela'sãw] (*pl* **-ões**) *f* **-1.** [ger] revelation. **-2.** FOT developing.

revelador, ra [xevela'do(x), ra] *adj* revealing.

revelar [4] [xeve'la(x)] *vt* **-1.** [ger] to reveal. **-2.** [mostrar, demonstrar] to show. **-3.** FOT to develop.

◆ **revelar-se** *vp* [dar-se a conhecer] to turn out to be.

revelia [xeve'lia] *f* default.
◆ **à revelia** *loc adv* **-1.** *JUR* in absentia. **-2.** [despercebidamente] without anybody knowing.
◆ **à revelia de** *loc adv* without the knowledge/ consent of.
revenda [xe'vẽnda] *f* resale.
revendedor, ra [xevẽnde'do(x), ra] (*mpl* **-es**, *fpl* **-s**) <> *adj* resale *(antes de subst).* <> *m, f* [de automóveis] dealer.
revender [5] [xevẽn'de(x)] *vt* to resell.
rever [40] [xe've(x)] *vt* **-1.** [tornar a ver] to see again. **-2.** [examinar] to check. **-3.** [revisar] to revise.
reverberação [xevexbera'sãw] (*pl* **-ões**) *f* **-1.** [de som] reverberation. **-2.** [de luz, calor] reflection.
reverberar [4] [xevexbe'ra(x)] *vt* [refletir] to reflect.
reverência [xeve'rẽnsja] *f* **-1.** [respeito] reverence. **-2.** [saudação]: **fazer uma ~** to bow.
reverenciar [16] [xeverẽn'sja(x)] *vt* **-1.** [respeitar] to respect. **-2.** [saudar] to salute.
reverendo [xeve'rẽndu] *m* priest.
reverente [xeve'rẽntʃi] *adj* reverent.
reversão [xevex'sãw] (*pl* **-ões**) *f* reversion.
reversível [xevex'sivew] (*pl* **-eis**) *adj* reversible.
reverso, sa [xe'vɛxsu, sa] <> *adj* reverse. <> *m* [lado contrário] reverse.
reverter [5] [xevex'te(x)] *vi* **-1.** [retroceder]: **~ a** to return to. **-2.** [redundar]: **~ em favor de alguém** to revert in s.o.'s favour; **~ em benefício de** to benefit.
revertério [xevex'tɛrju] *m fam* turnabout.
revés [xe'vɛʃ] (*pl* **-eses**) *m* **-1.** [reverso] reverse; **ao ~** [às avessas] inside out. **-2.** *fig* [infortúnio] setback.
◆ **de revés** *loc adv* [olhar, sorrir] askance.
revestimento [xeveʃtʃi'mẽntu] *m* covering.
revestir [54] [xeveʃ'tʃi(x)] *vt* **-1.** [ger] to cover. **-2.** [munir]: **~ alguém de algo** to invest sb with sthg. **-3.** [vestir] to don, to put on.
◆ **revestir-se** *vp* [munir-se] to summon up.
revezamento [xeveza'mẽntu] *m* **-1.** [ato]: **para cuidar do bebê, o casal fez um ~** the couple took it in turns to look after the baby. **-2.** *ESP* relay.
revezar [4] [xeve'za(x)] <> *vt* to swap. <> *vi*: **~ (com)** to take turns (with).
◆ **revezar-se** *vp* to alternate.
revidar [4] [xevi'da(x)] <> *vt* **-1.** [responder] to return. **-2.** [contestar] to answer. <> *vi* [responder] to answer back.
revide [xe'vidʒi] *m* response.
revigorar [4] [xevigo'ra(x)] *vt* to reinvigorate.
◆ **revigorar-se** *vp* to regain one's strength.
revirado, da [xevi'radu, da] *adj* **-1.** [casa] untidy. **-2.** [revolto] choppy.
revirar [4] [xevi'ra(x)] *vt* **-1.** [tornar a virar] to turn over. **-2.** [mudar] to change. **-3.** [os olhos] to roll. **-4.** [remexer em] to turn out.
◆ **revirar-se** *vp* [virar-se] to toss and turn.
reviravolta [xe,vira'vɔwta] *f* **-1.** [mudança] turnabout. **-2.** [pirueta] pirouette.
revisão [xevi'zãw] (*pl* **-ões**) *f* **-1.** [de texto] revision; **~ de provas** proofreading. **-2.** [de máquina - ger] overhaul; [- carro, motor de carro] service. **-3.** [os revisores] review board. **-4.** *JUR* review.
revisar [4] [xevi'za(x)] *vt* **-1.** [texto] to revise. **-2.** [máquina - ger] to overhaul; [- motor de carro] to service. **-3.** [recapitular] to review.
revisor, ra [xevi'zo(x), ra] (*mpl* **-es**, *fpl* **-s**) <> *adj* examining. <> *m, f* [de provas] proofreader.
revista [xe'viʃta] *f* **-1.** [publicação] magazine; **~ feminina** women's magazine; **~ em quadrinhos** comic. **-2.** [acadêmica] journal. **-3.** *MIL* [inspeção] review. **-4.** [busca] search. **-5.** *TEATRO* revue.
revistar [4] [xeviʃ'ta(x)] *vt* to search.
revisto, ta [xe'viʃtu, ta] <> *pp* ▷ **rever**. <> *adj* checked.
revitalizar [4] [xevitali'za(x)] *vt* to revitalize.
reviver [5] [xevi've(x)] <> *vi* **-1.** [doente] to pick up. **-2.** [revigorar-se] to come back to life. <> *vt* [relembrar] to relive.
revocar [12] [xevo'ka(x)] *vt* **-1.** [lembrar] to recall. **-2.** [restituir]: **~ alguém a algo** to bring sb back to sthg. **-3.** [tirar]: **~ alguém de algo** to remove sb from sthg.
revogação [xevoga'sãw] (*pl* **-ões**) *f* repeal.
revogar [14] [xevo'ga(x)] *vt* to repeal.
revolta [xe'vɔwta] *f* **-1.** [ger] revolt. **-2.** [rebeldia]: **~ (contra)** rebellion (against). **-3.** [indignação]: **~ (diante de** *ou* **com)** indignation (at).
revolto, ta [xe'vowtu, ta] *adj* **-1.** [revirado] rough. **-2.** [conturbado] troubled. **-3.** [desarrumado] untidy.
revoltoso, osa [xevow'tozu, ɔza] *adj* rebellious.
◆ **revoltoso** *m* rebel.
revolução [xevolu'sãw] (*pl* **-ões**) *f* revolution.
revolucionar [4] [xevolusjo'na(x)] *vt* **-1.** [transformar] to revolutionize. **-2.** [sublevar] to stir up. **-3.** [agitar] to change completely.
revolucionário, ria [xevolusjo'narju, rja] <> *adj* revolutionary. <> *m, f* revolutionary.
revolver [5] [xevow've(x)] *vt* **-1.** [remexer] to rummage through. **-2.** [examinar, investigar] to search. **-3.** [revirar - olhos] to roll; [- corpo, terra] to turn over. **-4.** [agitar] to blow about. **-5.** [relembrar] to recall.
◆ **revolver-se** *vp* **-1.** [mexer-se] to roll over. **-2.** [agitar-se] to blow about.
revólver [xe'vɔwve(x)] (*pl* **-es**) *m* revolver.
reza ['xɛza] *f* prayer.
rezar [4] [xe'za(x)] <> *vt* **-1.** [orar] to pray. **-2.** [missa] to say mass. **-3.** [afirmar, preceituar] to state. <> *vi* [orar] to pray.
RG (*abrev de* **Registro Geral**) *m Brazilian identity card*, ≃ ID card.
RH (*abrev de* **Recursos Humanos**) *m* HR.
riacho ['xjaʃu] *m* stream.
Riad ['xjadʒi] *n* Riyadh.
ribalta [xi'bawta] *f* **-1.** [luzes] footlights *(pl).* **-2.** *fig* [palco] boards *(pl).*
ribanceira [xibãn'sejra] *f* **-1.** [margem elevada] steep river bank. **-2.** [despenhadeiro] ravine. **-3.** [rampa] steep slope.
ribeira [xi'bejra] *f* **-1.** [margem de rio] bank. **-2.** [riacho] stream.

ribeirão [xibej'rãw] (*pl* **-ões**) *m* stream.
ribeirinho, nha [xibej'riɲu, ɲa] ◇ *adj* riverside. ◇ *m, f* riverside dweller.
ribombar [4] [xibõn'ba(x)] *vi* **-1.** [trovão] to rumble. **-2.** [canhão, granada] to boom.
ricaço, ça [xi'kasu, sa] *m, f* very rich person.
ricamente [xika'mẽntʃi] *adv* richly.
rícino ['xisinu] *m* castor-oil plant; **óleo de ~** castor oil.
rico, ca ['xiku, ka] ◇ *adj* **-1.** [ger] rich. **-2.** [opulento] opulent. **-3.** [abundante]: **~ em algo** rich in sthg. **-4.** [esplêndido] splendid. **-5.** [valiosa] precious. ◇ *m, f* [pessoa] rich person.
ricochetear [15] [xikoʃe'tʃja(x)] *vi* to ricochet.
ricota [xi'kɔta] *f* ricotta.
ridicularizar [4] [xidʒikulari'za(x)] *vt* to ridicule.
ridículo, la [xi'dʒikulu, la] *adj* ridiculous.
◆ **ridículo** *m* ridicule.
rifa ['xifa] *f* raffle.
rifar [4] [xi'fa(x)] *vt* to raffle.
rifle ['xifli] *m* rifle.
Riga ['xiga] *n* Riga.
rigidez [xiʒi'deʒ] *f* **-1.** [dureza - de metais, parede] rigidity; [- de músculo, corpo] stiffness. **-2.** *fig* [severidade] harshness. **-3.** *fig* [inflexibilidade] strictness.
rígido, da ['xiʒidu, da] *adj* **-1.** [hirto] stiff. **-2.** [resistente] strong. **-3.** [severo - pessoa, rosto] severe; [- disciplina] strict.
rigor [xi'go(x)] (*pl* **-es**) *m* **-1.** [rigidez] rigour *UK*, rigor *US*. **-2.** [severidade] severity. **-3.** [exatidão] rigour *UK*, rigor *US*. **-4.** [meticulosidade] thoroughness; **com ~** strictly. **-5.** [preceito] good manners *(pl)*. **-6.** [auge] harshness.
◆ **a rigor** *loc adv* strictly speaking.
rigorosamente [xigorɔza'mẽntʃi] *adv* rigorously; **chega no trabalho ~ às 8 horas** he arrives at work at 8 o'clock sharp.
rigoroso, osa [xigo'rozu, ɔza] *adj* **-1.** [ger] strict. **-2.** [castigo] severe. **-3.** [exato] precise. **-4.** [meticuloso] meticulous. **-5.** *fig* [penoso] severe.
rijo, ja ['xiʒu, ʒa] *adj* **-1.** [rígido] firm. **-2.** [severo] severe.
rim ['xĩ] (*pl* **-ns**) *m* ANAT kidney.
◆ **rins** *mpl fam* [região lombar] lower back *(sg)*.
rima ['xima] *f* rhyme.
rimar [4] [xi'ma(x)] ◇ *vt* to set to rhyme. ◇ *vi* to rhyme.
rímel® ['ximɛw] (*pl* **-eis**) *m* mascara.
rinçagem [xĩn'saʒẽ] (*pl* **-ns**) *f* rinse.
rinçar [xĩn'sa(x)] *vt* to rinse.
ringue ['xĩŋgi] *m* ring.
rinha ['xiɲa] *f fam* [briga de galos] cockfight.
rinoceronte [xinose'rõntʃi] *m* rhinoceros.
rinque ['xĩŋki] *m* rink.
rins [xĩnʃ] *pl* ▷ **rim**.
rio ['xiw] *m* river; **gastar ~s de dinheiro** to spend lots of money.
Rio Branco [ˌxiw'brãŋku] *n* Rio Branco.
Rio de Janeiro [ˌxiwdʒiʒa'nejru] *n* Rio de Janeiro.

RIO DE JANEIRO

Capital of the republic until the foundation of Brasilia in 1960; Rio de Janeiro is one of the most beautiful and traditional icons of Brazil, thanks to its famous beaches, such as Copacabana and Ipanema, as well as the beauty of its natural landmarks, such as the Sugar Loaf Mountain and the Corcovado. In spite of its loss of political power following the move of the capital city, Rio de Janeiro still exerts a powerful influence on the culture of Brazil.

Rio da Prata [ˌxiwda'prata] *n* River Plate.
Rio Grande do Norte [ˌxiwgrãndʒidu'nɔxtʃi] *n* Rio Grande do Norte.
Rio Grande do Sul [ˌxiwgrãndʒidu'suw] *n* Rio Grande do Sul.
rio-platense [ˌxiwpla'tẽnsi] ◇ *adj* River Plate *(antes de subst)*. ◇ *mf person from the River Plate region*.
ripa ['xipa] *f* [de madeira] slat; **meter a ~ em alguém** *fig* [falar mal] to speak ill of sb.
riqueza [xi'keza] *f* **-1.** [ger] richness. **-2.** [fortuna, bens] wealth. **-3.** [beleza] beauty; **essa igreja é uma ~!** this church is beautiful!
rir [69] ['xi(x)] *vi* to laugh; **~ de algo/alguém** to laugh at sthg/sb; **~ para alguém** to smile at sb; **morrer de ~ (de algo/alguém)** to laugh one's head off (at sthg/sb), to laugh oneself silly (at sthg/sb).
risada [xi'zada] *f* **-1.** [riso] laughter. **-2.** [gargalhada] guffaw.
risca ['xiʃka] *f* **-1.** [listra] stripe. **-2.** [no cabelo] parting. **-3.** [traço] line.
◆ **à risca** *loc adv* to the letter.
riscar [12] [xiʃ'ka(x)] *vt* **-1.** [fazer riscas em - porta, pareded] to scratch; [- papel] to draw lines on. **-2.** [esboçar] to sketch. **-3.** [marcar] to draw. **-4.** [apagar] to cross out. **-5.** [acender] to scratch. **-6.** [eliminar]: **~ alguém/algo de algo** to eliminate sb/sthg from sthg. **-7.** [atritar] to scrape.
risco ['xiʃku] *m* **-1.** [traço] scratch. **-2.** [esboço] sketch. **-3.** [perigo] risk; **correr ~ de** to run the risk of; **pôr algo/alguém em ~** to put sthg/sb at risk.
risco-país [ˌxiʃkupa'jiʃ] *m* ECON country risk.
risível [xi'zivew] (*pl* **-eis**) *adj* laughable.
riso ['xizu] *m* laugh; **~ amarelo** forced laugh.
risonho, nha [xi'zoɲu, ɲa] *adj* **-1.** [que sorri] smiling. **-2.** [alegre] cheerful.
risoto [xi'zotu] *m* risotto.
rispidez [xiʃpi'deʒ] *f* harshness.
ríspido, da ['xiʃpidu, da] *adj* harsh.
rissole [xi'sɔli] *m* rissole.
riste ['xiʃtʃi] *m*: **dedo em ~** pointing finger; **orelhas em ~** pointed ears.
rítmico, ca ['xitʃmiku, ka] *adj* rhythmic.
ritmo ['xitʃimu] *m* rhythm.
rito ['xitu] *m* rite.
ritual [xi'twaw] (*pl* **-ais** [xi'twajʃ]) ◇ *adj* ritual. ◇ *m* **-1.** [ger] ritual. **-2.** [livro] service book.
rival [xi'vaw] (*pl* **-ais**) ◇ *adj* rival. ◇ *mf* rival.

rivalidade [xivali'dadʒi] *f* rivalry.
rivalizar [4] [xivali'za(x)] *vi*: ~ **com algo/alguém** to compete with sthg/sb; ~ **por algo/alguém** to compete for sthg/sb; ~ **em algo** to compete in sthg.
rixa ['xiʃa] *f* quarrel.
RJ (*abrev de* **Estado do Rio de Janeiro**) *n State of Rio de Janeiro.*
RN (*abrev de* **Estado do Rio Grande do Norte**) *n State of Rio Grande do Norte.*
RO (*abrev de* **Estado de Rondônia**) *n State of Rondônia.*
robalo [ro'balu] *m* sea bass.
robô [ro'bo] *m* robot.
robótica [xo'bɔtʃika] *f* robotics *(sg).*
robustecer [25] [xobuʃte'se(x)] ◇ *vt* to strengthen. ◇ *vi* to become stronger.
◆ **robustecer-se** *vp* to become stronger.
robustez [xobuʃ'teʒ] *f* robustness.
robusto, ta [xo'buʃtu, ta] *adj* robust.
roça ['xɔsa] *f* **-1.** [plantação] plantation. **-2.** [campo] country. **-3.** [mato] clearing.
roçado [xo'sadu] *m* **-1.** [terreno] cleared land. **-2.** [clareira] clearing. **-3.** [plantação] plantation.
rocambole [xokãn'bɔli] *m* roll.
roçar [13] [xo'sa(x)] ◇ *vt* **-1.** [cortar] to clear. **-2.** [tocar de leve] to brush. **-3.** [atritar] to scrape. ◇ *vi* [tocar de leve]: ~ **em** to brush against.
roceiro, ra [xo'sejru, ra] *m, f* **-1.** [lavrador] country worker. **-2.** [caipira] yokel.
rocha ['xɔʃa] *f* **-1.** [pedra] rock. **-2.** [rochedo] crag.
rochedo [xo'ʃedu] *m* crag.
rock ['xɔki] *m* MÚS rock.
roda ['xɔda] *f* **-1.** [ger] wheel. **-2.** [círculo] circle; **alta** ~ high society; ~ **de samba** *circle of samba dancers and musicians*; **brincar de** ~ to play in a circle. **-3.** [de saia] hoop.
roda d'água [xɔdadagwa] *f* waterwheel.
rodado, da [xo'dadu, da] *adj* **-1.** [que tem roda] full. **-2.** [percorrido] on the clock.
◆ **rodada** *f* **-1.** [giro] turn; **dar uma rodada** to turn round. **-2.** [de bebida] round. **-3.** ESP round.
rodagem [xo'daʒẽ] (*pl* **-ns**) *f* **-1.** [ato de rodar] driving. **-2.** [raio de roda] wheel ▷ **estrada**.
roda-gigante [xɔdaʒi'gãntʃi] (*pl* **rodas-gigantes**) *f* big wheel, Ferris wheel.
rodamoinho [xɔda'mwiɲu] *m* **-1.** [de água] whirlpool. **-2.** [de cabelo] swirl.
rodapé [xɔda'pɛ] *m* **-1.** [de parede] skirting board. **-2.** [de página] foot; **nota de** ~ footnote. **-3.** [artigo] article.
rodar [4] [xo'da(x)] ◇ *vt* **-1.** [fazer girar] to turn. **-2.** [percorrer] to travel. **-3.** [imprimir] to print. **-4.** [filmar] to film. **-5.** AUTO to do. **-6.** COMPUT to run. ◇ *vi* **-1.** [girar] to turn. **-2.** [percorrer]: ~ **por** [a pé] to wander around; [de carro] to drive around. **-3.** [ser impresso] to be printed. **-4.** *fam* [ser reprovado]: ~ **(em algo)** to fail (in sthg). **-5.** *fam* [sair]: ~ **(de algo)** to leave (sthg). **-6.** [decorrer] to move on.
roda-viva [ˌxɔda'viva] (*pl* **rodas-vivas**) *f* commotion.
rodear [15] [xo'dʒja(x)] *vt* **-1.** [contornar] to go round. **-2.** [cercar] to surround.
◆ **rodear-se** *vp* [cercar-se] to surround o.s.
rodeio [xo'deju] *m* **-1.** [circunlóquio] circumlocution. **-2.** [evasiva] evasiveness; **fazer** ~**s** to beat about the bush; **sem** ~**s** bluntly. **-3.** [de gado] rodeo.
rodela [xo'dɛla] *f* [pedaço] slice.
rodízio [xo'dʒizju] *m* **-1.** [revezamento] turn; **fazer** ~ to take turns. **-2.** [em restaurante] *type of service in a restaurant where you are served at your table as much meat or, sometimes, pizza as you can eat, and normally accompanied by a free buffet of salad, etc.*
rodo ['xodu] *m* **-1.** [para puxar água] brush. **-2.** [agrícola] rake.
◆ **a rodo** *loc adv* a lot.
rodoanel [rodo'anew] (*pl* **-éis**) *m* ring road *UK*, beltway *US*.
rododendro [xodo'dẽndru] *m* rhododendron.
rodopiar [16] [xodo'pja(x)] *vi* to spin around.
rodopio [xodo'piw] *m* spin.
rodovia [xodo'via] *f* motorway *UK*, highway *US*.
rodoviário, ria [xodo'vjarju, rja] *adj* road.
◆ **rodoviária** *f* [estação de ônibus] bus station.
roedor, ra [xwe'do(x), ra] *adj* gnawing.
◆ **roedor** *m* rodent.
roer [28] ['xwe(x)] *vt* **-1.** [com dentes] to gnaw; ~ **as unhas** to bite one's nails; **duro de** ~ *fam fig* a hard nut to crack. **-2.** [destruir] to eat away. **-3.** [corroer] to erode. **-4.** *fig* [atormentar] to eat away at, to gnaw at.
◆ **roer-se** *vp fig* [atormentar-se]: ~**-se de algo** to be eaten up with sthg.
rogado, da [xo'gadu, da] *adj*: **fazer-se de** ~ to play hard to get.
rogar [14] [xo'ga(x)] ◇ *vt* to ask; ~ **pragas (contra algo/alguém)** to curse (sthg/sb). ◇ *vi* to pray; ~ **a alguém que faça algo** to beg sb to do sthg.
rogo ['xogu] *m* **-1.** [súplica] request; **a** ~ **de** [a pedido] at the request of. **-2.** [oração] prayer.
rojão [xo'ʒãw] (*pl* **-ões**) *m* **-1.** [foguete] rocket. **-2.** *fig* [ritmo intenso] hectic pace; **aguentar o** ~ *fig* [resistir] to stand the pace.
rol [xɔw] (*pl* **róis**) *m* list.
rolagem [xo'laʒẽ] (*pl* **-ns**) *f* [de dívida] postponement.
rolamento [xola'mẽntu] *m* MEC ball bearing.
rolar [4] [xo'la(x)] ◇ *vt* **-1.** [fazer girar] to roll. **-2.** *fig* [dívida] to run up. ◇ *vi* **-1.** [cair, deslizar] to roll; ~ **de/por/em algo** to roll off/down/on sthg. **-2.** [na cama] to toss and turn. **-3.** *fam* [estender-se] to roll on. **-4.** *fam* [ser servido] to be served. **-5.** *fam* [acontecer] to go on.
roldana [xow'dãna] *f* pulley.
roleta [xo'leta] *f* **-1.** [jogo] roulette. **-2.** [borboleta] turnstile.
roleta-russa [xoˌleta'xusa] (*pl* **roletas-russas**) *f* Russian roulette.

rolha ['xoʎa] *f* **-1.** [peça] cork. **-2.** *fam fig* [censura] gag.
roliço, ça [xo'lisu, sa] *adj* **-1.** [redondo] round. **-2.** [gordo] chubby.
rolo ['xolu] *m* **-1.** [ger] roller; ~ **de pastel** rolling pin; ~ **compressor** steam roller. **-2.** [cilindro] roll. **-3.** [almofada] bolster. **-4.** *fam* [bafafá, confusão] brawl; **dar** ~ to cause trouble.
ROM (*abrev de* **Read Only Memory**) *f* ROM.
romã [xo'mã] *f* pomegranate.
Roma ['xoma] *n* Rome.
romance [xo'mãnsi] *m* **-1.** *LITER* novel; ~ **policial** detective story. **-2.** *fig* [amoroso] romance. **-3.** *fig* [saga] saga. **-4.** *fig* [exageração]: **fazer um** ~ **de algo** to make a song and dance about sthg.
romanceado, da [xomãn'sjadu, da] *adj* **-1.** *LITER* novelized. **-2.** [fantasiado] romanticized.
romancear [15] [xomãn'sja(x)] *vt* **-1.** *LITER* to novelize. **-2.** [fantasiar] to romanticize.
romancista [xomãn'siʃta] *mf* novelist.
românico, ca [xo'mãniku, ka] *adj* **-1.** *LING* Romance. **-2.** *ARQUIT & ARTE* Romanesque.
romano, na [xo'mãnu, na] <> *adj* Roman. <> *m, f* Roman.
romântico, ca [xo'mãntʃiku, ka] <> *adj* **-1.** *ARQUIT & LITER* Romantic. **-2.** [poético, sentimental] romantic. <> *m, f* **-1.** *ARQUIT & LITER* Romantic. **-2.** [pessoa] romantic.
romantismo [xomãn'tʃiʒmu] *m* **-1.** *ARQUIT & LITER* Romanticism. **-2.** [sentimentalismo] romance.
romantizar [4] [xomãntʃi'za(x)] *vt* [fantasiar] to romanticize.
romaria [xoma'ria] *f* **-1.** [peregrinação] pilgrimage. **-2.** [festa] popular festival. **-3.** *fig* [muita gente] flock.
rombo ['xõnbu] *m* **-1.** [furo] hole. **-2.** *fig* [desfalque] embezzlement. **-3.** *fig* [prejuízo] deficit.
rombudo, da [xõn'budu, da] *adj* [faca, agulha] blunt.
romeiro, ra [xo'mejru, ra] *m, f* pilgrim.
Romênia [xo'menja] *n* Rumania.
romeno, na [xo'menu, na] <> *adj* Rumanian. <> *m, f* Rumanian.
◆ **romeno** *m* [língua] Rumanian.
romeu-e-julieta [xo,mewiʒu'ljeta] *m CULIN guava preserve on cheese.*
rompante [xõn'pãntʃi] *m* outburst.
romper [5] [xõn'pe(x)] <> *vt* to break. <> *vi* **-1.** [quebrar] to burst. **-2.** [rasgar] to tear. **-3.** [despontar] to break. **-4.** [relações]: ~ **(com alguém)** to break up (with sb); ~ **com algo** [tradição] to break from sthg. **-5.** [começar]: ~ **em algo** to break into sthg.
◆ **romper-se** *vp* **-1.** [despedaçar-se] to break. **-2.** [interromper-se] to be broken off.
rompimento [xõnpi'mẽntu] *m* **-1.** [de cano, barragem] bursting. **-2.** [de contrato, relações] breaking.
roncar [12] [xõŋ'ka(x)] *vi* to snore.
ronco ['xõŋku] *m* **-1.** [no sono] snore. **-2.** *MED* rale. **-3.** [ruído] rumble. **-4.** [grunhido] grunt.
ronda ['xõnda] *f* beat; **fazer a** ~ to be on patrol.
rondar [4] [xõn'da(x)] <> *vt* **-1.** [andar vigiando] to patrol. **-2.** [espreitar] to prowl about. **-3.** [andar à volta de] to go round. **-4.** [cifra] to reach. <> *vi*: ~ **(por)** [andar vigiando] to be on patrol (throughout); [espreitar] to prowl (about).
Rondônia [xõn'donja] *n* Rondonia.
ronqueira [xõŋ'kejra] *f* wheeze.
ronrom [xõn'xõ] *m* purr.
ronronar [4] [xõnxo'na(x)] *vi* to purr.
roque ['xɔki] *m* **-1.** *MÚS* rock (and roll). **-2.** [dança] rock and roll.
roqueiro, ra [xo'kejru, ra] *m, f* **-1.** [músico] rock musician. **-2.** [cantor] rock singer.
Roraima [xo'rajma] *n* Roraima.
rosa ['xɔza] <> *adj inv* [cor] pink. <> *f BOT* rose. <> *m* [cor] pink.
rosado, da [xo'zadu, da] *adj* pink.
rosa-dos-ventos [,xɔzaduʃ'vẽntuʃ] *f inv* wind rose.
rosário [xo'zarju] *m* **-1.** [colar] string of beads. **-2.** [orações] rosary.
rosa-shocking [xɔza'ʃkĩŋ] *adj inv* shocking pink.
rosbife [xoʒ'bifi] *m* roast beef.
rosca ['xoʃka] *f* **-1.** [de parafuso, porca] thread. **-2.** [pão] twist. **-3.** [biscoito] biscuit.
roseira [xo'zejra] *f* rose bush.
róseo, sea ['xɔzju, zja] *adj* rosy.
roseta [xo'zeta] *f* **-1.** [ger] rosette. **-2.** [de espora] rowel.
rosnar [4] [xoʒ'na(x)] <> *vi* [cão] to growl. <> *m* [de cão] growl.
rosto ['xoʃtu] *m* face.
rota ['xɔta] *f* route.
ROTA (*abrev de* **Rondas Ostensivas Tobias de Aguiar**) *f shock police force of São Paulo.*
rotação [xota'sãw] (*pl* **-ões**) *f* rotation.
rotativa [xota'tʃiva] *f* ▷ **rotativo**.
rotatividade [xotatʃivi'dadʒi] *f* **-1.** [movimento] turning. **-2.** [rodízio] rotation ▷ **hotel**.
rotativo, va [xota'tʃivu, va] *adj* **-1.** [giratório] rotary. **-2.** [alternativo] rotating.
◆ **rotativa** *f TIP* rotary press.
roteador, ra [rotea'do(x),ra] *m COMPUT* router.
roteirista [xotej'riʃta] *mf* script writer.
roteiro [xo'tejru] *m* **-1.** [ger] script. **-2.** [de viagem] guide book. **-3.** [de trabalho] schedule.
rotina [xo'tʃina] *f* routine.
rotineiro, ra [xotʃi'nejru, ra] *adj* routine.
roto, ta ['xotu, ta] *adj* **-1.** [rasgado] torn. **-2.** [maltrapilho] ragged.
rótula ['xɔtula] *f ANAT* kneecap.
rotular [4] [xotu'la(x)] <> *adj ANAT* patellar. <> *vt* **-1.** [etiquetar] to label. **-2.** *fig* [qualificar]: ~ **alguém/algo (de algo)** to label sb/sthg (as sthg).
rótulo ['xɔtulu] *m* label.
rotundo, da [xo'tũndu, da] *adj* **-1.** [redondo] round. **-2.** [gordo] rotund.
◆ **rotunda** *f ARQUIT* rotunda.
roubada [xo'bada] *f FUT* [de bola] tackle.
roubalheira [xoba'ʎejra] *f* (outright) robbery.

roubar [4] [xo'ba(x)] <> *vt* **-1.** [ger] to steal. **-2.** [furtar] to rob. <> *vi* **-1.** [furtar] to steal. **-2.** [enganar] to cheat.
roubo ['xobu] *m* **-1.** [ato] theft. **-2.** [produto roubado] stolen goods *(pl)*. **-3.** *fig* [preço extorsivo]: **ser um ~** to be exorbitant.
rouco, ca ['xoku, ka] *adj* hoarse.
round ['xawndʒi] *m* *ESP* round.
roupa ['xopa] *f* clothes *(pl)*; **~ de baixo** underwear; **~ de cama/mesa** bed/table linen; **~ suja se lava em casa** *fig* don't wash your dirty linen in public.
roupagem [xo'paʒẽ] *f* clothing.
roupão [xo'pãw] *(pl* **-ões)** *m* dressing gown; **~ de banho** bathrobe.
rouparia [xopa'ria] *f* **-1.** [roupas] clothes *(pl)*. **-2.** [local] linen room.
rouquidão [xoki'dãw] *f* hoarseness.
rouxinol [xoʃi'nɔw] *(pl* **-óis)** *m* nightingale.
roxo, xa ['xoʃu, ʃa] *adj* **-1.** [cor] violet; **~ de inveja** *fig* green with envy; **estar ~ de saudades** *fig* to have the blues. **-2.** *MED* purple. **-3.** [apaixonado]: **ser ~ por** to be passionate about.
◆ **roxo** *m* [cor] violet.
royalty ['xɔjawtʃi] *(pl* **royalties)** *m* royalty.
RP *(abrev de* **Relações Públicas)** *f* PR.
RPM *(abrev de* **Rotações por Minuto)** *f* RPM.
RR *(abrev de* **Estado de Roraima)** *n State of Roraima.*
RS *(abrev de* **Estado do Rio Grande do Sul)** *n State of Rio Grande do Sul.*
RSVP *(abrev de* **répondez s'il vous plaît)** RSVP.
rua ['xua] *f* **-1.** [ger] street; **~ de mão única** one way street; **~ principal** main street; **~ sem saída** dead end. **-2.** *loc*: **ir para a ~** [sair] to go out; **pôr alguém na ~** [expulsar] to kick sb out; [demitir] to fire sb; **viver na ~** *fig* to go out a lot.
rubéola [xu'bɛwla] *f* German measles, rubella.
rubi [xu'bi] *m* ruby.
rubor [xu'bo(x)] *(pl* **-es)** *m* **-1.** [na face] flush. **-2.** [vergonha] blush.
ruborizar [4] [xubori'za(x)] *vt* [envergonhar] to embarrass.
◆ **ruborizar-se** *vp* to blush.
rubrica [xu'brika] *f* **-1.** [assinatura] initials *(pl)*. **-2.** [indicação de assunto *etc*] rubric.
rubricar [12] [xubri'ka(x)] *vt* to initial.
rubro, bra ['xubru, bra] *adj* **-1.** [ger] bright red. **-2.** [faces] ruddy.
ruço, ça ['xusu, sa] *adj* **-1.** [desbotado, surrado] faded. **-2.** *fam* [difícil] tricky.
rúcula ['xukula] *f* rocket (salad).
rude ['xudʒi] *adj* **-1.** [descortês] rude. **-2.** [primitivo] crude.
rudeza [xu'deza] *f* **-1.** [descortesia] rudeness. **-2.** [primitivismo] crudeness.
rudimentar [xudʒimẽn'ta(x)] *adj* rudimentary.
rudimentos [xudʒi'mẽntuʃ] *mpl* rudiments.
rueiro, ra ['xwejru, ra] *adj*: **ser ~** to be a gadabout.
ruela ['xwɛla] *f* alleyway.
rufar [4] [xu'fa(x)] <> *vt* [tambor] to beat. <> *vi* to drum.
rufião, fiona [xu'fjãw, fjona] *(mpl* **-ões**, *fpl* **-s)** *m, f* [gigolô] gigolo.
ruga ['xuga] *f* **-1.** [na pele] wrinkle; **cheio de ~s** covered in wrinkles. **-2.** [na roupa] crease.
rúgbi ['xugbi] *m* rugby.
ruge ['xuʒi] *m* rouge.
rugido [xu'ʒidu] *m* roar.
rugir [52] [xu'ʒi(x)] *vi* to roar.
ruído ['xwidu] *m* noise.
ruidoso, osa [xwi'dozu, ɔza] *adj* noisy.
ruim ['xuĩ] *(pl* **-ns)** *adj* **-1.** [nocivo] vile. **-2.** [malvado] wicked. **-3.** [imprestável, ineficiente] useless. **-4.** [podre] rotten. **-5.** [defeituoso] faulty. **-6.** [ordinário] poor. **-7.** [desagradável] bad; **achar ~** [zangar-se] to get upset.
ruína [ˌxwina] *f* **-1.** [ger] ruin; **levar alguém à ~** to ruin sb; **estar em ~s** to be in ruins. **-2.** [causa de destruição, queda] ruination. **-3.** [decadência] downfall.
◆ **ruínas** *fpl* [escombros] ruins.
ruindade [xwĩn'dadʒi] *f* **-1.** [qualidade] wickedness. **-2.** [ação] sin.
ruins [xu'ĩnʃ] *pl* ▷ **ruim**.
ruir [74] ['xwi(x)] *vi* to collapse.
ruivo, va ['xuivu, va] <> *adj* **-1.** [pessoa] redheaded. **-2.** [cabelo, barba] red. <> *m, f* redhead.
rulê [xu'le] *adj* ▷ **gola**.
rum ['xũ] *m* rum.
rumar [4] [xu'ma(x)] <> *vt*: **~ algo para** to steer sthg towards. <> *vi*: **~ para** to head for.
rumba ['xũnba] *f* rumba.
ruminante [xumi'nãntʃi] <> *adj* ruminant. <> *m* ruminant.
ruminar [4] [xumi'na(x)] <> *vt* to think over. <> *vi* to ruminate.
rumo ['xumu] *m* **-1.** [direção] course; **ir ~ a** to head for. **-2.** *fig* [destino] fate; **sem ~** *lit* adrift; *fig* aimless.
rumor [xu'mo(x)] *(pl* **-es)** *m* **-1.** [ruído] noise. **-2.** [boato] rumour.
rumorejante [xumore'ʒãntʃi] *adj* whispering.
ruptura [xup'tura] *f* **-1.** [ger] rupture. **-2.** [de fiação] break. **-3.** [de relações, negociações] break-up. **-4.** [de contrato] breach.
rural [xu'raw] *(pl* **-ais)** *adj* rural.
ruralista [xura'liʃta] <> *adj* rural. <> *mf landowner who protects the interests of rural life, and especially those of landowners themselves.*
rusga ['xuʒga] *f* brawl.
rush ['xãʃi] *m* heavy traffic; **a hora do ~** rush hour.
Rússia ['xusja] *n* Russia.
russo, sa ['xusu, sa] <> *adj* Russian. <> *m, f* Russian.
◆ **russo** *m* [língua] Russian.
rústico, ca ['xuʃtʃiku, ka] *adj* rustic.

S

s, S ['ɛsi] *m* [letra] s, S.
sã [sã] *f* ▻ **são**.
S.A. (*abrev de* **Sociedade Anônima**) *f limited company*, ≃ Ltd.
Saara [sa'ara] *n*: **o (deserto do)** ~ the Sahara (Desert).
saariano, na [saa'rjãnu, na] ◇ *adj* Saharan. ◇ *m, f* Saharan.
sáb. (*abrev de* **sábado**) *m* Sat.
sábado ['sabadu] *m* Saturday; **aos ~s** on Saturdays; **cair num** ~ to fall on a Saturday; **esse ~ agora** [próximo] next Saturday; **(no)** ~ (on) Saturday; **(no) ~ que vem/no próximo** ~ (on) the coming, next Saturday; ~ **de manhã** Saturday morning; ~ **de** *ou* **á tarde/noite** Saturday afternoon/evening; ~ **passado** *ou* **retrasado** last Saturday, Saturday just gone; ~ **sim,** ~ **não** every other Saturday; **todos os ~s** every Saturday; ~ **de aleluia** Easter Saturday.
sabão [sa'bãw] (*pl* **-ões**) *m* **-1.** [produto] soap; ~ **de coco** coconut soap; ~ **em pó** soap powder. **-2.** [repreensão]: **passar um ~ em alguém** to tell sb off.
sabatina [saba'tʃina] *f* revision test.
sabedoria [sabedo'ria] *f* wisdom; ~ **popular** popular wisdom.
saber [35] [sa'be(x)] ◇ *m* knowledge. ◇ *vt* to know. ◇ *vt* to know; ~ **de cor** to know (off) by heart; ~ **(como) fazer algo** to know how to do sthg; **que eu saiba** as far as I know; **sei lá!** *fam* who knows!; **você que sabe** *fam* it's up to you. ◇ *vi* **-1.** [ter erudição] to know. **-2.** [estar a par de]: ~ **(de algo)** to know (sthg). **-3.** [ter notícia]: ~ **de alguém** to hear from sb.
◆ **a saber** *loc adv* namely.
sabiá [sa'bja] *m* song thrush.
sabichão, chona [sabi'ʃãw, ʃona] (*mpl* **-chões**, *fpl* **-s**) *adj irôn* know-all.
sabido, da [sa'bidu, da] *adj* **-1.** [astuto] wise. **-2.** [conhecedor] knowledgeable. **-3.** [conhecido]: **como é** ~ as is generally known; **é ~ que ...** it is known that ...
sábio, bia ['sabju, bja] ◇ *adj* wise. ◇ *m, f* wise person.
sabões [sa'bõjʃ] *pl* ▻ **sabão**.
sabonete [sabo'netʃi] *m* toilet soap.
saboneteira [sabone'tejra] *f* soap dish.
sabor [sa'bo(x)] (*pl* **-es**) *m* taste; **ao ~ de** at the mercy of.
saborear [15] [sabo'rja(x)] *vt* to savour.
saboroso, osa [sabo'rozu, ɔza] *adj* tasty.
sabotador, ra [sabota'do(x), ra] *m, f* saboteur.
sabotagem [sabo'taʒẽ] (*pl* **-ns**) *f* sabotage.
sabotar [4] [sabo'ta(x)] *vt* to sabotage.
sabugo [sa'bugo] *m* ANAT nail root.
SAC (*abrev de* **Serviço de Atendimento ao Consumidor**) *m Brazilian consumer telephone service*.
saca ['saka] *f* [saco largo] sack.
sacação [saka'sãw] (*pl* **-ões**) *f fam* **-1.** [achado] find. **-2.** [invenção] clever idea.
sacada [sa'kada] *f* ARQUIT balcony.
sacado, da [sa'kadu, da] *m, f* COM drawee.
sacador, ra [saka'do(x), ra] *m, f* COM drawer.
sacal [sa'kaw] (*pl* **-ais**) *adj* boring; **ser** ~ to be boring.
sacana [sa'kana] *adj mfam* **-1.** [sujo]: **ser** ~ to be a bastard. **-2.** [esperto] sharp. **-3.** [libidinoso] randy. **-4.** [brincalhão] raffish.
sacanagem [saka'naʒẽ] (*pl* **-ns**) *f mfam* **-1.** [sujeira] dirty trick. **-2.** [libidinagem] screwing. **-3.** [brincadeira] joke.
sacanear [15] *mfam* [saka'nja(x)] *vt* **-1.** [amolar] to pester. **-2.** [fazer sujeira com] to screw.
sacar [12] [sa'ka(x)] ◇ *vt* **-1.** [arma, carteira] to pull out; ~ **algo de algo** to draw sthg from sthg. **-2.** [em banco] to draw. **-3.** *fam* [compreender] to twig. ◇ *vi* **-1.** [de arma]: ~ **de algo** to whip out sthg. **-2.** [em banco]: ~ **(contra/sobre)** to draw (against/from). **-3.** ESP to serve. **-4.** *fam* [compreender] to twig. **-5.** *fam* [mentir] to fib. **-6.** *fam* [falar sem saber] to talk through one's hat.
sacarina [saka'rina] *f* saccharin.
saca-rolha [ˌsaka'xoʎa] (*pl* **saca-rolhas**) *m* corkscrew.
sacerdócio [sasex'dɔsju] *m* priesthood.
sacerdote, tisa [sasex'dɔtʃi, tʃiza] *m, f* [pagão] priest (*f* priestess).
◆ **sacerdote** *m* RELIG priest.
sachê [sa'ʃe] *m* sachet.
saci-pererê [saˌsiper'ere] *m figure of Brazilian folklore who typically ambushes travellers*.
saciar [16] [sa'sja(x)] *vt* to satisfy.
saciedade [sasje'dadʒi] *f* [satisfação plena] satisfaction.
saco ['saku] *m* **-1.** [recipiente] bag. **-2.** [utensílio]: ~ **de água quente** hot-water bottle; ~ **de café** coffee filter; ~ **de dormir** sleeping bag. **-3.** [enseada] cove. **-4.** *vulg* [testículos] balls. **-5.** *fam* [amolação]: **encher o ~ (de alguém)** to get one's goat; **estar de ~ cheio (de alguém/algo)** to have a bellyful (of sb/sthg); **que ~!** what a bore!; **ser/estar um** ~ to be boring. **-6.** *fam* [paciência]: **haja ~!** keep your knickers on!, don't get your knickers in a twist!; **ter ~ (com alguém)** to be cool (with sb). **-7.** *fam* [disposição]: **estar com/sem**

~ **de fazer algo** to give/not to give a hoot about doing sthg.
sacola [sa'kɔla] *f* saddlebag.
sacolão [sako'lãw] *m* greengrocer's.
sacoleiro, ra [sako'lejru, ra] *m,f* pedlar *UK*, peddler *US*.
sacolejar [4] [sakole'ʒa(x)] *vt* **-1.** [sacudir] to shake. **-2.** [rebolar] to sway.
sacolejo [sako'leʒu] *m fam* jerk.
sacramentar [4] [sakramẽn'ta(x)] *vt* **-1.** *RELIG* to bless. **-2.** [ultimar] to close.
sacramento [sakra'mẽntu] *m RELIG* sacrament.
sacrificar [12] [sakrifi'ka(x)] *vt* **-1.** [ger] to sacrifice. **-2.** [prejudicar] to damage. **-3.** [matar] to put down.
◆ **sacrificar-se** *vp* **-1.** [ger] to sacrifice o.s. **-2.** [sujeitar-se] to give in to.
sacrifício [sakri'fisju] *m* sacrifice.
sacrilégio [sakri'lɛʒju] *m* sacrilege.
sacrílego, ga [sa'krilegu, ga] *adj* sacrilegious.
sacristão [sakriʃ'tãw] (*pl* **-ões**) *m* sacristan.
sacristia [sakriʃ'tʃia] *f* sacristy.
sacro, cra ['sakru, kra] *adj* **-1.** [sagrado] sacred. **-2.** *ANAT* sacral.
◆ **sacro** *m ANAT* sacrum.
sacrossanto, ta [sakro'sãntu, ta] *adj* sacrosanct.
sacudida [saku'dʒida] *f* shake.
sacudido, da [saku'dʒidu, da] *adj* [sacolejado] shaken.
sacudir [41] [saku'dʒi(x)] *vt* to shake.
◆ **sacudir-se** *vp* **-1.** [tremer] to shake. **-2.** [saracotear] to waggle.
sádico, ca ['sadʒiku, ka] ◇ *adj* sadistic. ◇ *m, f* sadist.
sadio, dia [sa'dʒiu, dʒia] *adj* healthy.
sadismo [sa'dʒiʒmu] *m* sadism.
sadomasoquismo [sadomazo'kiʒmu] *m* sadomasochism.
sadomasoquista [sadomazo'kiʃta] ◇ *adj* sadomasochistic. ◇ *mf* sadomasochist.
safadeza [safa'deza] *f* **-1.** [ger] mischief. **-2.** [devassidão] debauchery.
safado, da [sa'fadu, da] *adj* **-1.** [ger] mischievous. **-2.** [devasso] debauched. **-3.** [com raiva]: ~ **(da vida)** fed up to the back teeth.
safanão [safa'nãw] (*pl* **-ões**) *m fam* **-1.** [tranco, puxão] tug. **-2.** [cascudo] box *(on the ears)*.
safári [sa'fari] *m* safari.
safena [sa'fena] *f ANAT* saphena; **ponte de ~** coronary bypass.
safira [sa'fira] *f* sapphire.
safra ['safra] *f* **-1.** *AGR* harvest. **-2.** *fig* [de cantores *etc*] crop.
saga ['saga] *f* saga.
sagacidade [sagasi'dadʒi] *f* shrewdness.
sagaz [sa'gajʒ] *adj* shrewd.
sagitariano, na [saʒita'rjãnu, na] ◇ *adj* Sagittarian. ◇ *m, f* Sagittarian.
Sagitário [saʒi'tarju] ◇ *m* [zodíaco] Sagittarius; **ser ~** to be a Sagittarian. ◇ *mf* [pessoa] Sagittarian.
sagrado, da [sa'gradu, da] *adj* sacred.
saguão [sa'gwãw] (*pl* **-ões**) *m* **-1.** [entrada] lobby. **-2.** [pátio] courtyard.
saia ['saja] *f* **-1.** [roupa] skirt; ~ **escocesa** kilt. **-2.** [de mesa] (floor-length) tablecloth. **-3.** *fam fig* [mulher] skirt; ~ **justa** tight spot.
saia-calça [ˌsaja'kawsa] (*pl* **saias-calça**) *f* culottes *(pl)*.
saibro ['sajbru] *m* gravel.
saída [sa'ida] *f* **-1.** [ger] way out; **de ~** straight away; ~ **de emergência** emergency exit. **-2.** [ato] leaving; **dar uma ~** to pop out. **-3.** *COM*: **ter muita ~** to sell well. **-4.** [dito]: **ter boas ~s** to be witty. **-5.** [*COMPUT* - de programa] exit; [- de dados] output.
saída-de-praia [saˌidadʒi'praja] (*pl* **saídas-de-praia**) *f* beach wrap.
saideira [saj'dejra] *f* one for the road.
saiote [sa'jɔtʃi] *m* petticoat.
sair [68] [sa'i(x)] *vi* **-1.** [gen] to come out; ~ **do armário** *fig* to come out *(as being homosexual)*. **-2.** [ir para fora - de ônibus, trem, avião] to get off; [- de carro] to get out of. **-3.** [ir para a rua] to go out. **-4.** [ir embora, deixar] to leave; ~ **de fininho** to sneak off. **-5.** [fugir] to get out. **-6.** [escapar]: ~ **de** to get out of. **-7.** [aparecer] to appear. **-8.** [desaparecer]: ~ **de moda** to go out of fashion. **-9.** [parecer-se]: ~ **a alguém** to take after sb. **-10.** [resultar] to turn out; ~ **ganhando/perdendo** to end up winning/losing. **-11.** [custar]: ~ **(a** *ou* **por)** to come to; ~ **caro** to be expensive. **-12.** *COMPUT* to exit.
◆ **sair-se** *vp* **-1.** [obter resultado]: **~-se bem/mal** to come out well/badly. **-2.** [dizer]: **~-se com** to come out with.
sal ['saw] (*pl* **sais**) *m* salt; **sem ~** [manteiga *etc*] unsalted; [precisando de mais sal] bland; ~ **de banho** bath salts *(pl)*; ~ **de cozinha** kitchen salt; ~ **grosso** rock salt.
sala ['sala] *f* **-1.** [aposento] room; ~ **de embarque** departure lounge; ~ **de espera** waiting room; ~ **de estar** living room; ~ **de operações** operating theatre; ~ **de parto** delivery room. **-2.** [de espetáculos] concert hall. **-3.** *EDUC*: ~ **(de aula)** classroom; [alunos] class. **-4.** *fig*: **fazer ~ a alguém** [entreter] to entertain sb.
salada [sa'lada] *f* **-1.** *CULIN* salad; ~ **de frutas** fruit salad. **-2.** *fig* [confusão]: **fazer uma ~ de algo** to make a muddle of sthg.
saladeira [sala'dejra] *f* salad bowl.
sala-e-quarto [ˌsalaj'kwaxtu] (*pl* **sala-e-quartos**) *m* studio (flat).
salafrário, ria [sala'frarju, rja] *m, f fam* scoundrel.
salamaleque [salama'lɛki] *m* exaggerated greeting.
salame [sa'lãmi] *m* salami.
salaminho [salã'miɲu] *m* small salami.
salão [sa'lãw] (*pl* **-ões**) *m* **-1.** [aposento] lounge. **-2.** [estabelecimento]: ~ **de beleza** beauty salon; ~ **de chá** tea room. **-3.** [exposição] exhibition hall.
◆ **de salão** *loc adj* **-1.** [piada] tasteful. **-2.** [jogo]

indoor. **-3.** [dança] dance hall *(antes de subst)*.
salarial [sala'rjaw] (*pl* **-ais**) *adj* pay *(antes de subst)*.
salário [sa'larju] *m* wage; ~ **de fome** miserly wage; **décimo terceiro** ~ *Christmas bonus equal to one month's wages*; ~ **mínimo** minimum wage; ~ **líquido** net salary.
salário-base [sa,larju'bazi] (*pl* **salários-base**) *m* basic wage.
salário-família [sa,larjufa'milja] (*pl* **salários-família**) *m extra pro rata pay for employees with dependants*.
saldão [saw'dãw] (*pl* **-ões**) *m* [saldo] sale.
saldar [4] [saw'da(x)] *vt* to settle.
saldo ['sawdu] *m* **-1.** [ger] balance; ~ **credor/devedor** credit/debit balance; ~ **negativo/positivo** debit/credit balance; ~ **a receber/pagar** balance due/to pay. **-2.** *fig* [resultado] outcome.
saleiro [sa'lejru] *m* **-1.** [recipiente] salt cellar. **-2.** [moedor] salt mill.
saleta [sa'leta] *f* small living room.
salgadinho [sawga'dʒiɲu] *m* canapé.
salgado, da [saw'gadu, da] *adj* **-1.** [comida - com sal] salted; [- com excesso de sal] salty. **-2.** [anedota] salty. **-3.** [preço] steep.
salgar [14] [saw'ga(x)] *vt* to salt.
salgueiro [saw'gejru] *m* willow.
saliência [sa'ljẽnsja] *f* **-1.** [proeminência] projection. **-2.** *fig* [espevitamento] eagerness.
salientar [4] [saljẽn'ta(x)] *vt* **-1.** [ressaltar] to highlight. **-2.** [enfatizar] to stress.
◆ **salientar-se** *vp* [distinguir-se] to distinguish o.s.
saliente [sa'ljẽntʃi] *adj* **-1.** [ressaltado] salient. **-2.** *fig* [espevitado] eager.
salino, na [sa'linu, na] *adj* saline.
◆ **salina** *f* **-1.** [terreno] salt bed. **-2.** [empresa] salt works.
salitre [sa'litri] *m* saltpetre.
saliva [sa'liva] *f* saliva; **gastar** ~ to waste one's breath.
salivar [4] [sa'liva(x)] *vi* to salivate.
salmão [saw'mãw] (*pl* **-ões**) ◇ *m* [peixe] salmon. ◇ *m inv* [cor] salmon. ◇ *adj inv* [cor] salmon-pink.
salmo ['sawmu] *m* psalm.
salmões [saw'mõjʃ] *pl* ▷ **salmão**.
salmonela [sawmo'nɛla] *f* salmonella.
salmoura [saw'mora] *f* brine.
salobro, bra [sa'lobru, bra] *adj* brackish.
salões [sa'lõjʃ] *pl* ▷ **salão**.
salpicão [sawpi'kãw] (*pl* **-ões**) *m* **-1.** [paio] smoked sausage. **-2.** [prato]: ~ **(de galinha)** *cold shredded chicken and vegetable dish*.
salpicar [12] [sawpi'ka(x)] *vt* **-1.**: ~ **algo em algo**, ~ **algo de algo** [temperar] to season sthg with sthg; [sarapintar, sujar] to splash; ~ **alguém de algo** [sujar] to splash sb with sthg. **-2.** [entremear]: ~ **algo com** *ou* **de algo** to pepper sthg with sthg.
salsa ['sawsa] *f* **-1.** [erva] parsley. **-2.** *MÚS* salsa.
salsicha [saw'siʃa] *f* sausage.
salsichão [sawsi'ʃãw] (*pl* **-chões**) *m* large sausage.
saltado, da [saw'tadu, da] *adj* prominent.
saltar [4] [saw'ta(x)] ◇ *vt* **-1.** [ger] to jump. **-2.** *fam* [fazer vir] to send for. ◇ *vi* **-1.** [pular]: ~ **(de/sobre)** to jump (from/on). **-2.** [de ônibus, trem, cavalo]: ~ **(de)** to jump (from). **-3.** [brotar]: ~ **de** to pour from. **-4.** [rolha] to pop.
salteado, da [saw'tʃjadu, da] *adj* [alternado] alternate; **saber de cor e** ~ to know off by heart.
salteador, ra [sawtʃja'do(x), ra] *m, f* mugger.
saltimbanco [sawtʃĩn'bãŋku] *m* travelling acrobat.
saltitante [sawtʃi'tãntʃi] *adj* [ave, criança] hopping; ~ **de alegria** jumping for joy.
saltitar [4] [sawtʃi'ta(x)] *vi* **-1.** [pular] to hop. **-2.** *fig* [divagar]: ~ **de ... para ...** to jump from ... to ...
salto ['sawtu] *m* **-1.** [pulo] jump; **dar um** ~ to leap; **dar** ~**s de alegria** to leap for joy. **-2.** *ESP*: ~ **em altura** high jump; ~ **em distância** long jump; ~ **de vara** pole vault. **-3.** [de sapato] heel; ~ **alto/baixo** high/low heel.
salto-mortal [,sawtumox'taw] (*pl* **saltos-mortais**) *m* somersault.
salubre [sa'lubri] *adj* salubrious.
salutar [salu'ta(x)] (*pl* **-es**) *adj* **-1.** [saudável] healthy. **-2.** *fig* [moralizador] salutary.
salva ['sawva] *f* **-1.** *MIL*: ~ **(de tiros)** salvo (of gunshots). **-2.** *fig*: **uma** ~ **de palmas** a round of applause. **-3.** [bandeja] tray.
salvação [sawva'sãw] *f* salvation; **não ter** ~ to be without hope; **ser a** ~ **da pátria** *fam fig* to be one's salvation.
salvador, ra [sawva'do(x), ra] *m, f* [pessoa] saviour.
Salvador [sawva'do(x)] *n* Salvador.
salvadorenho, nha [sawvado'reɲu, ɲa] ◇ *adj* Salvadorean. ◇ *m, f* Salvadorean.
salvados [saw'vaduʃ] *mpl* salvage *(sg)*.
salvaguarda [sawva'gwaxda] *f* safeguard.
salvaguardar [4] [,sawvagwax'da(x)] *vt* to safeguard.
salvamento [sawva'mẽntu] *m* rescue; **equipe de** ~ rescue team.
salvar [4] [saw'va(x)] *vt* to save.
◆ **salvar-se** *vp* [escapar] to escape.
salva-vidas [,salva'vidaʃ] ◇ *adj inv* lifeguard; **lancha** ~ life boat. ◇ *m* **-1.** *inv* [bóia] lifebelt. **-2.** [pessoa] lifeguard. **-3.** [jaqueta] life jacket.
salve ['sawvi] *interj* cheers!
sálvia ['sawvja] *f BOT* sage.
salvo, va ['sawvu, va] ◇ *adj* safe; **estar a** ~ to be safe. ◇ *prep* except.
salvo-conduto [,sawvukõn'dutu] (*pl* **salvo-condutos, salvos-condutos**) *m* safe conduct.
samambaia [samãn'baja] *f* fern.
samaritano [samari'tãnu] *m*: **bom** ~ *RELIG* good Samaritan; *fig & pej* do-gooder.
samba ['sãnba] *m* samba.

SAMBA

Through its catchy rhythm and vitality, samba has become synonymous with Brazilian music. Afro-Brazilian in origin, it developed mainly in Bahia, Rio de Janeiro and São Paulo. It is characterized by a syncopated beat and is generally performed on percussion instruments, guitars and *cavaquinho* (small four-stringed guitar). There are many kinds of samba. One of the more traditional forms is the 'samba-de-roda' from Bahia; another very popular form is the 'sambas-enredo' of the carnival in Rio de Janeiro, which express the theme of each samba school's parade; finally, there is a fairly characteristic form of samba, known as the 'samba de breque', with a generally satirical content.

samba-canção [ˌsãnbakãn'sãw] (*pl* **sambas-canções**) ◇ *m* MÚS *type of samba*. ◇ *adj inv*: **cueca** ~ shorts *(pl)*.

samba-de-roda ['sãnbadʒi'xɔda] (*pl* **sambas-de-roda**) *m samba in which the dancers form a circle and each dances in turn*.

samba-enredo [ˌsãnbẽn'xedu] (*pl* **sambas-enredo**) *m samba describing the theme chosen by a samba school for the carnival*.

sambar [4] [sãn'ba(x)] *vi* to samba.

sambista [sãn'biʃta] *mf* **-1.** [dançarino] samba dancer. **-2.** [compositor] composer of sambas.

sambódromo [sãn'bɔdromu] *m track along which samba schools parade*.

samovar [samo'va(x)] *m* samovar.

Sana ['sana] *n* San'a.

sanar [4] [sa'na(x)] *vt* **-1.** [curar] to cure. **-2.** [remediar] to remedy.

sanatório [sana'tɔrju] *m* sanatorium.

sanável [sa'navew] (*pl* **-eis**) *adj* **-1.** [curável] curable. **-2.** [remediável] remediable.

sanção [sãn'sãw] (*pl* **-ões**) *f* **-1.** [ger] sanction. **-2.** [punição]: ~ **(contra)** sanction (against).

sancionar [4] [sãnsjo'na(x)] *vt* [aprovar] to sanction.

sanções [sãn'sõjʃ] *pl* ▷ **sanção**.

sandália [sãn'dalja] *f* sandal.

sândalo ['sãndalu] *m* sandalwood.

sanduíche [sãn'dwiʃi] *m* sandwich; ~ **americano** double-decker sandwich; ~ **misto** cheese and ham sandwich.

saneamento [sanja'mẽntu] *m* **-1.** [limpeza] sanitization. **-2.** *fig* [correção] purge.

sanear [15] [sa'nja(x)] *vt* **-1.** [tornar salubre] to sanitize. **-2.** *fig* [corrigir] to purge.

sanfona [sãn'fona] *f* **-1.** MÚS concertina. **-2.** [em suéter] ribbing.

sanfonado, da [sãnfo'nadu, da] *adj* **-1.** [porta] folding *(antes de subst)*. **-2.** [suéter] ribbed.

sangramento [sãŋgra'mẽntu] *m* **-1.** [de ferida] bleeding. **-2.** [de açude, represa] overflow.

sangrar [4] [sãŋ'gra(x)] ◇ *vi* [verter sangue] to bleed. ◇ *vt* **-1.** [ger] to bleed. **-2.** [açude, represa] to drain.

sangrento, ta [sãŋ'grẽntu, ta] *adj* **-1.** [ger] bloody. **-2.** CULIN [carne] rare.

sangria [sãŋ'gria] *f* **-1.** [bebida] sangria. **-2.** MED blood-letting. **-3.** *fig* [extorsão] extortion.

sangue ['sãŋgi] *m* **-1.** [ger] blood; **de** ~ [exame, transfusão] blood; **começou a sair muito** ~ **do corte** the cut started to bleed a lot; **tirar** ~ to take blood. **-2.** *fig* [raça]: **puro** ~ thoroughbred.

◆ **a sangue frio** *loc adv* in cold blood.

sangue-frio [ˌsãŋgi'friw] *m* sangfroid.

sanguessuga [ˌsãŋgi'suga] *f* leech.

sanguinário, ria [sãŋgi'narju, rja] *adj* bloodthirsty.

sanguíneo, nea [sãŋ'g(w)inju, nja] *adj* **-1.** [relativo ao sangue] blood *(antes de subst)*. **-2.** [pessoa] ruddy.

sanha ['sãɲa] *f*: ~ **(contra)** anger (against).

sanidade [sani'dadʒi] *f* [mental] sanity.

sanitário, ria [sani'tarju, rja] *adj* **-1.** [ger] sanitary. **-2.** [banheiro] bath *(antes de subst)*.

San José [ˌsãnxo'se] *n* San José.

San Marino [ˌsãnma'rinu] *n* San Marino.

San Salvador [ˌsãnsawva'do(x)] *n* San Salvador.

Santa Catarina [ˌsãntakata'rina] *n* Santa Catarina.

santidade [sãntʃi'dadʒi] *f* sanctity.

◆ **Santidade** *f* [Vossa Santidade] Holiness.

santificar [12] [sãntʃifi'ka(x)] *vt* to sanctify.

Santiago de Cuba [ˌsãnˌtʃjagudʒi'kuba] *n* Santiago de Cuba.

Santiago do Chile [sãnˌtʃagudu'ʃili] *n* Santiago de Chile.

santinho [sãn'tʃiɲu] *m* **-1.** [figura] religious figurine. **-2.** *fam* [pessoa] goody-goody.

santo, ta ['sãntu, ta] ◇ *adj* **-1.** [sagrado] holy; **todo o** ~ **dia** *fam fig* the whole blessed day long. **-2.** *(antes de subst)* [caridoso] kind. **-3.** [eficaz]: **um** ~ **remédio** an effective medicine. ◇ *m, f* **-1.** [ger] saint. **-2.** *loc*: ~ **de casa não faz milagre** a prophet is not without honour save in his own country; **ter** ~ **forte** *fam* to have the gods smiling on you.

SANTOS-DUMONT

Aviator and inventor from Minas Gerais; Alberto Santos-Dumont (1873-1832) invented the airship in 1901, with which he flew round the Eiffel Tower. In 1906, he built the 14-Bis, the first plane officially to fly over 25m above ground. Santos-Dumont also invented the wristwatch and is considered by Brazilians to be the inventor of the airplane.

Santo Domingo [ˌsãntudo'mĩŋgu] *n* Santo Domingo.

santuário [sãn'twarju] *m* sanctuary.

são, sã ['sãw, 'sã] *adj* **-1.** [ger] healthy. **-2.** PSIC sane. **-3.** [curado] well. **-4.** [ileso]: ~ **e salvo** safe and sound. **-5.** [sensato] sensible.

São [sãw] *m* Saint.

SÃO FRANCISCO

'Old Chico' is the nickname given to the largest river in Brazilian territory; its source is in Minas Gerais and it crosses the states of Bahia, Pernambuco, Alagoas and Sergipe, covering a total of 3,160 km. It is fundamental to the economy of the region, providing significant opportunities for hydroelectric output, fluvial access to certain areas, allowing agricultural activity on its banks and irrigation to distant areas.

São Luís [ˌsãwlu'iʒ] *n* São Luis.
São Paulo [ˌsãw'pawlu] *n* São Paulo.
São Tomé [ˌsãwto'mɛ] *n* São Tomé.
São Tomé e Príncipe [sãwtoˌmɛj'prĩnsipi] *n* São Tomé and Príncipe.
sapata [sa'pata] *f* **-1.** [suporte] prop. **-2.** [de freio] shoe.
sapatão [sapa'tãw] *m* ***mfam pej*** dyke.
sapataria [sapata'ria] *f* **-1.** [ofício] shoe trade. **-2.** [loja] shoe shop.
sapateado [sapa'tʃjadu] *m* tap dance.
sapateador, ra [sapatʃja'do(x), ra] *m, f* tap dancer.
sapatear [15] [sapa'tʃja(x)] *vi* **-1.** [dançar] to tap-dance. **-2.** [bater com os pés] to stamp.
sapateiro, ra [sapa'tejru, ra] *m, f* **-1.** [fabricante] shoemaker. **-2.** [quem conserta] cobbler.
◆ **sapateiro** *m* [loja] shoe shop.
◆ **sapateira** *f* [móvel] shoe cupboard.
sapatilha [sapa'tʃiʎa] *f* **-1.** [de balé] ballet shoe. **-2.** [sapato baixo] slipper.
sapato [sa'patu] *m* shoe.
sapê, sapé [sa'pe] *m* thatch; **telhado de ~** thatched roof.
sapeca [sa'pɛka] *adj* **-1.** [levado] mischievous. **-2.** [assanhado] irritable.
sapecar [15] [sape'ka(x)] *vt* [tapa, soco *etc*]: **~ algo em alguém** to hit sb with sthg.
sapiência [sa'pjẽnsja] *f* **-1.** [erudição] knowledge. **-2.** [bom julgamento] wisdom.
sapiente [sa'pjẽntʃi] *adj* [erudito] knowledgeable.
sapinho [sa'piɲu] *m* MED thrush.
sapo ['sapu] *m* toad; **engolir ~** *fig* to take the flak.
saque ['saki] *m* **-1.** FIN withdrawal; **~ a descoberto** overdraft. **-2.** ESP serve. **-3.** [de cidade, loja] ransacking. **-4.** *fam* [mentira] fib.
saquê [sa'ke] *m* sake.
saquear [15] [sa'kja(x)] *vt* to ransack.
saracotear [15] [sarako'tʃja(x)] *vt* to sway.
saraivada [saraj'vada] *f* hail storm; **uma ~ de** *fig* a shower of.
saraivar [4] [saraj'va(x)] *vi* to hail.
sarampo [sa'rãnpu] *m* measles.
sarapintado, da [sarapĩn'tadu, da] *adj* dotted.
sarar [4] [sa'ra(x)] ◇ *vt* [pessoa, doença, ferida] to heal. ◇ *vi* **-1.** [pessoa] to get better. **-2.** [ferida] to heal.
sarau [sa'raw] *m* soirée.
sarcasmo [sax'kaʒmu] *m* sarcasm.
sarcástico, ca [sax'kaʃtʃiku, ka] *adj* sarcastic.
sarcófago [sax'kɔfagu] *m* sarcophagus.
sarda ['saxda] *f* freckle.
Sardenha [sax'deɲa] *n* Sardinia.
sardento, ta [sax'dẽntu, ta] *adj* freckly.
sardinha [sax'dʒiɲa] *f* sardine.
sardônico, ca [sax'doniku, ka] *adj* sardonic.
sargento [sax'ʒẽntu] *mf* sergeant.
sári ['sari] *m* sari.
sarjeta [sax'ʒeta] *f* gutter.
sarna ['saxna] *f* scabies; **procurar ~ para se coçar** to look for trouble.
sarnento, ta [sax'nẽntu, ta] *adj* [com sarna] mangy.
sarrafo [sa'xafu] *m* batten; **baixar o ~ em alguém** *fam* to batter sb.
sarro ['saxu] *m* **-1.** [borra] residue. **-2.** [de nicotina] tartar. **-3.** [na língua] fur. **-4.** ***fam*** [pessoa, coisa]: **ser um ~** to be fun. **-5.** ***mfam*** [bolinagem]: **tirar um ~ (de alguém)** to grope (sb).
Satã [sa'tã], **Satanás** [sata'naʃ] *m* Satan.
satânico, ca [sa'tãniku, ka] *adj* **-1.** [culto] satanic. **-2.** *fig* [diabólico] devilish.
satélite [sa'tɛlitʃi] ◇ *m* satellite. ◇ *adj* [cidade, país] satellite *(antes de subst)*.
sátira ['satʃira] *f* satire.
satírico, ca [sa'tʃiriku, ka] *adj* satirical.
satirizar [4] [satʃiri'za(x)] *vt* to satirize.
satisfação [satʃiʃfa'sãw] (*pl* **-ões**) *f* **-1.** [alegria, prazer] pleasure; **dar ~ a alguém** to give sb pleasure; **ter ~ em fazer algo** to to be pleased to do sthg. **-2.** [de desejos, necessidades] satisfaction. **-3.** [explicação] explanation; **dar uma ~ a alguém** to give sb an explanation; **não dar satisfações a ninguém** to owe an explanation to nobody; **tomar satisfações de alguém** to get an explanation from sb.
satisfatório, ria [satʃiʃfa'tɔrju, rja] *adj* satisfactory.
satisfazer [31] [satʃiʃfa'ze(x)] ◇ *vt* to satisfy. ◇ *vi* **-1.** [ser satisfatório] to be satisfactory. **-2.** [contentar, convir]: **~ a** to satisfy.
◆ **satisfazer-se** *vp*: **~-se (com)** to be satisfied (with).
satisfeito, ta [satʃiʃ'fejtu, ta] ◇ *pp* ▷ **satisfazer**. ◇ *adj* **-1.** [ger] satisfied. **-2.** [alegre] pleased.
saturação [satura'sãw] *f* saturation.
saturado, da [satu'radu, da] *adj* **-1.**: **~ de algo** saturated with sthg. **-2.** *fig* [enfastiado]: **~ (de algo/alguém)** fed up (with sthg/sb).
saturar [4] [satu'ra(x)] *vt* **-1.**: **~ algo (de algo)** to saturate sthg (with sthg). **-2.** *fig* [enfastiar]: **~ alguém de algo** to wear sb out with sthg. **-3.** [saciar] to fill.
Saturno [sa'tuxnu] *m* Saturn.
saudação [sawda'sãw] (*pl* **-ões**) *f* **-1.** [cumprimento] greeting. **-2.** [homenagem] homage.
saudade [saw'dadʒi] *f* **-1.** [de pessoa, país, família] pining. **-2.** [do passado, de época] nostalgia; **estar morrendo de ~ (s) de alguém** to be pining for sb; **matar as ~s de alguém** to catch up with sb; **estava louco para as ~s da minha cama** I was dying to sleep in my own bed again; **sentir ~(s) de alguém/algo** to pine for sb/sthg.

saudar [19] [saw'da(x)] *vt* to greet.

saudável [saw'davɛw] (*pl* **-eis**) *adj* healthy.

saúde [sa'udʒi] <> *f* health; **estado de ~** state of health; **estar bem/mal de ~** to be in good/bad health; **não ter ~ para fazer algo** *fam fig* to not be fit to do sthg; **brindar à ~ de alguém** to drink to sb's health; **~ pública** public health; [órgão] health service. <> *interj* [para brindar] cheers!; [depois de um espirro] bless you!

saudita [saw'dʒita] (*pl* **sauditas**) <> *adj* Saudi. <> *mf* Saudi.

saudosismo [sawdo'ziʒmu] *m* nostalgia.

saudoso, osa [saw'dozu, ɔza] *adj* **-1.** [que causa saudades] dearly missed. **-2.** [que sente saudades]: **estar ~ de alguém/algo** to miss sb/sthg. **-3.** [que denota saudades] grieving.

sauna ['sawna] *f* **-1.** [ger] sauna; **fazer ~** to have a sauna. **-2.** *fig*: **estar uma ~** [estar muito quente] to be like a sauna.

saveiro [sa'vejru] *m* fishing boat.

saxão, xã [sak'sãw, sã] <> *adj* Saxon. <> *mf* Saxon.

saxofone [sakso'foni] *m* saxophone.

saxofonista [saksofo'niʃta] *mf* saxophonist.

sazonado, da [sazo'nadu, da] *adj* ripe.

sazonal [sazo'naw] (*pl* **-ais**) *adj* seasonal.

sazonalidade [sazonali'dadʒi] *f* seasonal variation.

SBT (*abrev de* **Sistema Brasileiro de Televisão**) *m the second most popular Brazilian television station.*

SC (*abrev de* **Estado de Santa Catarina**) *n State of Santa Catarina.*

scanner [iʃka'ne(x)] (*pl* **-s**) *m* COMPUT scanner.

script [iʃkriptʃi] (*pl* **-s**) *m* script.

se [si] <> *pron* **-1.** [reflexo: pessoa] himself (*f* herself); [você, vocês] yourself, yourselves *pl*; [impessoal] oneself; **lavar-~** to wash (oneself); **eles ~ perderam** they got lost; **vocês se perderam** you got lost. **-2.** [reflexo: coisa, animal] itself; **o vidro partiu-~** the glass broke. **-3.** [recíproco] each other; **escrevem-~ regularmente** they write to each other regularly. **-4.** [com sujeito indeterminado]: **'aluga-~ quarto'** 'room to let'; **'vende-~'** 'for sale'; **come-~ bem aqui** the food here is very good. <> *conj* **-1.** [indica condição] if; **~ tiver tempo, escrevo** I'll write if I have time; **~ fizer sol, iremos à praia** if it's sunny, we'll go to the beach. **-2.** [indica causa] if; **~ você está com fome, coma alguma coisa** if you're hungry, have something to eat; **~ ..., então ...** if ..., then ...; **~ diminui a oferta, então aumenta o preço** if demand diminishes, the cost goes up. **-3.** [indica comparação] if; **~ um é feio, o outro ainda é pior** if you think he's ugly, you should see the other one. **-4.** [em interrogativas]: **que tal ~ fôssemos ao cinema?** how about going to the movies?; **e ~ ela não vier?** and what if she doesn't come? **-5.** [exprime desejo] if; **~ pelo menos tivesse dinheiro!** if only I had the money! **-6.** [em interrogativa indireta] if, whether; **avisem-me ~ quiserem ir** let me know if you'd like to go; **perguntei-lhe ~ gostou** I asked him if he liked it. **-7.** [em locuções]: **~ bem que** even though, although.

sé ['sɛ] *f* cathedral.

◆ **Santa Sé** *f*: **a Santa Sé** the Holy See.

SE (*abrev de* **Estado de Sergipe**) *n State of Sergipe.*

seara ['sjara] *f* **-1.** [terra] sown field. **-2.** [de cereais] corn field.

sebáceo, cea [se'basju, sja] *adj* sebaceous.

sebento, ta [se'bẽntu, ta] *adj* [sujo] filthy.

sebo ['sebu] *m* **-1.** [substância] sebum. **-2.** [livraria] second-hand bookshop.

seborréia [sebo'xɛja] *f* seborrhoea *UK*, seborrhea *US*.

seboso, osa [se'bozu, ɔza] *adj* **-1.** [ger] greasy. **-2.** *fam fig* [pessoa] conceited.

SEBRAE (*abrev de* **Serviço de Apoio às Micro e Pequenas Empresas**) *m Brazilian support body for small and very small businesses.*

seca ['seka] *f* ▷ **seco**.

secador [seka'do(x)] (*pl* **-es**) *m* dryer; **~ (de cabelo)** hairdryer; **~ de pratos** drainer; **~ de roupa** [varal] clothes line.

secadora [seka'dora] *f* tumble-dryer.

secagem [se'kaʒẽ] *f* drying.

seção [se'sãw] (*pl* **-ões**) *f* section.

secar [12] [se'ka(x)] <> *vt & vi* to dry.

seccionar [4] [seksjo'na(x)] *vt* **-1.** [cortar] to cut into sections. **-2.** [dividir] to divide.

secessão [sese'sãw] *f* secession.

seco, ca ['seku, ka] *adj* **-1.** [ger] dry. **-2.** [magro] thin. **-3.** *fam* [ávido]: **estar ~ por algo/para fazer algo** to be dying for sthg/to do sthg.

◆ **seca** *f* drought.

SECA

Drought is one of the most long-standing and critical problems afflicting the Brazilian north-east. The semi-arid region known as the ***sertão nordestino*** covers parts of the states of Bahia, Pernambuco, Paraíba, Ceará, Piauí, Rio Grande do Norte, Sergipe and Alagoas. Its population suffers periodically from the lack of rain, and is forced to migrate to other states of the country in search of better conditions for survival.

seções [se'sõjʃ] *pl* ▷ **seção**.

secreção [sekre'sãw] (*pl* **-ões**) *f* secretion.

secretaria [sekreta'ria] *f* secretariat.

secretária [sekre'tarja] *f* ▷ **secretário**.

secretariado [sekreta'rjadu] *m* [cargo, curso] secretarial course.

secretariar [16] [sekreta'rja(x)] <> *vt* to take minutes of. <> *vi* to work as a secretary.

secretário, ria [sekre'tarju, rja] *m, f* [ger] secretary; **~ de Estado** Secretary of State.

◆ **secretária** *f* **-1.** [mesa] desk. **-2.** [aparelho]: **~ eletrônica** answering machine.

secretário-geral, secretária-geral [sekre,tarjuʒe'raw, sekre,tarjaʒe'raw] (*mpl* **secretários-gerais**, *fpl* **secretárias-gerais**) *m, f* secretary general.

secreto, ta [se'krɛtu, ta] *adj* secret.

sectário, ria [sɛk'tarju, rja] ◇ *adj* sectarian. ◇ *m, f* [seguidor] sectarian.

sectarismo [sekta'riʒmu] *m* sectarianism.

secular [seku'la(x)] (*pl* **-es**) *adj* **-1.** [ger] secular. **-2.** [antigo] age-old.

secularizar [4] [sekulari'za(x)] *vt* to secularize.

século ['sɛkulu] *m* century; **do** ~ [descoberta, romance] of the century.

◆ **séculos** *mpl fig* [longo tempo] ages; **há ~s** for ages; **há ~s que não viajava** it's ages since I travelled, I haven't travelled for ages; **~s atrás** ages ago.

secundar [4] [sekũn'da(x)] *vt* **-1.** [auxiliar] to help. **-2.** [reforçar] to reinforce.

secundário, ria [sekũn'darju, rja] *adj* secondary.

secura [se'kura] *f* **-1.** [ger] dryness. **-2.** *fam* [desejo]: ~ **por algo** longing for sthg.

seda ['seda] *f* **-1.** [material] silk; **de** ~ silk; ~ **crua/pura** raw/pure silk. **-2.** *fig* [pessoa]: **estar uma** ~ to be very friendly.

sedã [se'dã] *m* sedan.

sedar [4] [se'da(x)] *vt* to sedate.

sedativo, va [seda'tʃivu, va] *adj MED* sedative; *fig* [música, balanço, silêncio] soothing.

◆ **sedativo** *m MED* sedative.

sede[1] ['sedʒi] *f* **-1.** [secura] thirst; **estar com** ~ to be thirsty; **matar a** ~ to quench one's thirst. **-2.** *fig* [desejo]: ~ **de algo** thirst for sthg.

sede[2] ['sɛdʒi] *f* **-1.** [estabelecimento] headquarters. **-2.** [de governo] seat. **-3.** [centro, local] venue.

sedentário, ria [sedẽn'tarju, rja] *adj* sedentary.

sedento, ta [se'dẽntu, ta] *adj* **-1.** [de água] thirsty. **-2.** *fig* [ávido]: ~ **de algo** thirsty for sthg.

SEDEX (*abrev de* **Serviço de Encomenda Expressa**) *m Brazilian express mail delivery service.*

sediar [15] [se'dʒja(x)] *vt* to base.

sedição [sedʒi'sãw] (*pl* **-ões**) *f* sedition.

sedicioso, osa [sedʒi'sjozu, ɔza] *adj* seditious.

sedimentação [sedʒimẽnta'sãw] (*pl* **-ões**) *f* sedimentation.

sedimentar [4] [sedʒimẽn'ta(x)] *vi* to sediment.

sedimento [sedʒi'mẽntu] *m* sediment.

sedoso, osa [se'dozu, ɔza] *adj* silky.

sedução [sedu'sãw] (*pl* **-ões**) *f* **-1.** [ato] seduction. **-2.** [atração]: ~ **por algo/alguém** attraction towards sthg/sb.

sedutor, ra [sedu'to(x), ra] (*mpl* **-es**, *fpl* **-s**) ◇ *adj* seductive. ◇ *m, f* [sexualmente] seducer.

seduzir [72] [sedu'zi(x)] *vt* **-1.** [ger] to seduce. **-2.** [induzir] to encourage.

seg. (*abrev de* **segunda-feira**) *f* Mon.

segmentação [segmẽnta'sãw] (*pl* **-ões**) *f* segmentation.

segmentar [4] [segmẽn'ta(x)] *vt* to segment.

segmento [seg'mẽntu] *m* segment.

segredar [4] [segre'da(x)] *vt* & *vi* to whisper.

segredo [se'gredu] *m* **-1.** [ger] secret; **guardar** ~ to keep secret; ~ **de Estado** state secret. **-2.** [discrição] secrecy; **em** ~ in secret. **-3.** [dispositivo] secret lock.

segregação [segrega'sãw] *f* segregation.

segregar [14] [segre'ga(x)] *vt* **-1.** [ger] to segregate. **-2.** [expelir] to secrete.

seguidamente [se,gida'mẽntʃi] *adv* **-1.** [com freqüência] often. **-2.** [continuamente] continuously.

seguido, da [se'gidu, da] *adj* **-1.** [consecutivo] consecutive; **cinco dias ~s** five days running; **horas seguidas** hours on end. **-2.** [adotado] widely adopted. **-3.** [que se segue]: ~ **a** following. **-4.** [acompanhado]: ~ **de/por** followed by.

◆ **em seguida** *loc adv* **-1.** [consecutivamente] shortly after. **-2.** [imediatamente] straight away, at once.

seguidor, ra [segi'do(x), ra] *m, f* follower.

seguimento [segi'mẽntu] *m* continuation; **dar** ~ **a algo** to continue with sthg.

seguinte [se'gĩntʃi] ◇ *adj* **-1.** [subseqüente] following, next; ~ **a** following. **-2.** *(antes de subst)* [citando, explicando] following. ◇ *mf*: **o/a** ~ [numa fila, ordem] the next; [citando, explicando] as follows; **o negócio é o** ~ *fam* the matter is as follows; **pelo** ~ for the following reason.

seguir [55] [se'gi(x)] ◇ *vt* **-1.** [ger] to follow. **-2.** [perseguir] to chase. **-3.** [continuar] to continue. ◇ *vi* **-1.** [ger] to follow. **-2.** [continuar] to carry on, to keep going. **-3.** [direção] to continue; ~ **reto** to go straight ahead.

◆ **seguir-se** *vp* **-1.** [suceder]: **~-se (a algo)** to follow on (from sthg); **seguiram-se dias de euforia** there followed days of euphoria. **-2.** [em citações] to follow.

segunda [se'gũnda] *f* ▻ **segundo**.

segunda-feira [se,gũnda'fejra] (*pl* **segundas-feiras**) *f* Monday; *veja também* **sábado**.

segundanista [segũndã'niʃta] *mf second year (university) student.*

segundo, da [se'gũndu, da] ◇ *num adj* second; ~ **grau** *EDUC* secondary education; ~ **tempo** *FUT* second half. ◇ *num m, f* second. ◇ *adj* **-1.** [outro] second; **segundas intenções** ulterior motives; **de segunda mão** second-hand. **-2.** [inferior]: **de** ~ **time** second-rate.

◆ **segundo** ◇ *m* [medida de tempo] second; **(só) um ~!** *fig* just a second!, (just) one second! ◇ *prep* according to. ◇ *conj* [conforme] according to.

◆ **segunda** *f* **-1.** *AUTO* second (gear). **-2.** [segunda-feira] Monday.

◆ **de segunda** ◇ *loc adj* second class. ◇ *loc adv* [viajar] second class.

segurado, da [segu'radu, da] ◇ *adj* insured. ◇ *m, f* person insured.

segurador, ra [segura'do(x), ra] *m, f* [agente] insurance broker.

◆ **seguradora** *f* [companhia] insurance company.

seguramente [se,gura'mẽntʃi] *adv* **-1.** [com certeza] certainly. **-2.** [muito provavelmente] surely.

segurança [segu'rãnsa] ◇ *f* **-1.** [proteção, estabilidade] security; **de** ~ security; **cinto de** ~ safety belt; ~ **nacional** national security. **-2.** [ausência de perigo] safety. **-3.** [certeza, confiança] assurance. ◇ *mf* [pessoa] security guard.

segurar [4] [segu'ra(x)] ◇ *vt* **-1.** [pegar] to hold. **-2.** [firmar] to fix. **-3.** [sustentar] to hold up. **-4.** [pôr no seguro]: ~ **algo/alguém (contra)** to insure sthg/sb (against). ◇ *vi* [apoiar-se]: ~ **(em)** to hold on (to).

◆ **segurar-se** *vp* **-1.** [apoiar-se]: **~-se em** to hold on to. **-2.** [fazer seguro] to steady o.s. **-3.** [controlar-se] to control o.s.

seguro, ra [se'guru, ra] *adj* **-1.** [ger] safe. **-2.** [certo] sure; **estar ~ de algo** to be sure of sthg. **-3.** [confiante, firme] secure; ~ **de si** self-assured. **-4.** [infalível] foolproof.

◆ **seguro** ◇ *m* [contrato] insurance policy; **fazer ~** to take out an insurance policy; ~ **de automóvel** car insurance; ~ **contra incêndio** fire insurance; ~ **de vida** life insurance. ◇ *adv* steadily.

seguro-desemprego [se,gurudesẽn'pregu] (*pl* **seguros-desemprego**) *m* unemployment benefit *UK*, unemployment compensation *US*.

seguro-saúde [se,gurusa'udʒi] (*pl* **seguros-saúde**) *m* health insurance.

seio ['seju] *m* **-1.** *ANAT* breast. **-2.** *fig* [meio] heart.

seis ['sejʃ] *num* **-1.** [ger] six; **o (número) ~** the (number) six; **duzentos e ~** two hundred and six; **trinta e ~** thirty-six; **Rua das Acácias, (número) ~** number six, Rua das Acácias; **pacotes de ~** packets of six; ~ **de cada vez** six at a time; **somos ~** we are six, there are six of us; **vieram os ~** the six of them came; **tirar ~** [nos estudos] to get (a) six. **-2.** [hora]: **às ~ (horas)** at six o'clock; **são ~ horas** it is six o'clock; **são ~ e meia** it is half past six. **-3.** [data] sixth; **hoje é dia ~** today is the sixth; **(no) dia ~ de janeiro** (on the) sixth of January. **-4.** [idade]: **ele tem ~ anos (de idade)** he is six years old. **-5.** [temperatura]: ~ **graus abaixo de zero** six degrees below freezing. **-6.** *ESP* [jogador]: **o número ~** number six. **-7.** *ESP* [resultado]: **empatar de ~ a ~** to draw six all; ~ **a zero** six nil. **-8.** [em naipes]: ~ **de espadas** six of spades.

seiscentos, tas [sejʃ'sẽntuʃ, taʃ] *num* six hundred; *veja também* **seis**.

seita ['sejta] *f* sect.

seiva ['sejva] *f* sap.

seixo ['sejʃu] *m* pebble.

seja ['seʒa] *conj* whether it be; **ou ~** that is.

sela ['sɛla] *f* saddle.

selagem [se'laʒẽ] *f* [de carta] postage.

selar [4] [se'la(x)] *vt* **-1.** [ger] to seal. **-2.** [cavalo] to saddle. **-3.** [carta] to stamp.

seleção [sele'sãw] (*pl* **-ões**) *f* **-1.** [escolha] selection. **-2.** [equipe] team; **a ~ brasileira** the Brazilian team.

selecionado, da [selesjo'nadu, da] *adj* [escolhido] chosen.

◆ **selecionado** *m* [equipe] team.

selecionar [4] [selesjo'na(x)] *vt* to select.

seleta [se'lɛta] *f* ▷ **seleto**.

seletivo, va [sele'tʃivu, va] *adj* selective.

seleto, ta [se'lɛtu, ta] *adj* select.

◆ **seleta** *f* selection.

selim [se'lĩ] (*pl* **-ns**) *m* saddle.

selo ['selu] *m* **-1.** [carimbo, sinete] seal. **-2.** [postal] stamp. **-3.** *fig* [cunho] seal of approval.

selva ['sɛwva] *f* jungle.

selvagem [sew'vaʒẽ] (*pl* **-ns**) *adj* **-1.** [ger] wild. **-2.** [bárbaro] savage. **-3.** [ermo] desolate. **-4.** *fig* [grosseiro] rude.

selvageria [sewvaʒe'ria] *f* savagery.

sem [sẽ] *prep* without; ~ **algo/fazer algo** without sthg/doing sthg; ~ **ajuda** without help; ~ **dúvida** without doubt; **passar ~ algo** to go without sthg.

◆ **sem que** *loc conj* without.

semáforo [se'maforu] *m* **-1.** *AUTO* traffic lights (*pl*). **-2.** *FERRO* signal.

semana [se'mãna] *f* week; **há uma ~** a week ago; **uma ~ atrás** a week ago; **a ~ passada** last week; **a ~ retrasada** the week before last; **por ~** [número de vezes] per week; [ser pago] weekly.

◆ **Semana Santa** *f* Holy Week.

semanal [sema'naw] (*pl* **-ais**) *adj* weekly.

semanalmente [semanaw'mẽntʃi] *adv* weekly.

semanário [sema'narju] *m* weekly.

semântico, ca [se'mãntʃiku, ka] *adj* semantic.

◆ **semântica** *f* semantics (*pl*).

semblante [sẽn'blãntʃi] *m* [rosto] countenance.

sem-cerimônia [sẽnseri'monja] (*pl* **-s**) *f* **-1.** [informalidade] informality. **-2.** [grosseria] rudeness.

semeadura [semja'dura] *f* [semeação] sowing; **começaram a ~ do trigo** they began sowing the wheat.

semear [15] [se'mja(x)] *vt* **-1.** [ger] to sow. **-2.** *fig* [espalhar] to spread.

semelhança [seme'ʎãnsa] *f* resemblance; **ter ~ com** to resemble.

semelhante [seme'ʎãntʃi] ◇ *adj* **-1.** [parecido]: ~ **(a)** similar (to). **-2.** [tal] such. ◇ *m* (*ger pl*) [próximo] fellow man.

semelhar [4] [seme'ʎa(x)] *vt* to resemble.

sêmen ['semẽ] *m* semen.

semente [se'mẽntʃi] *f* seed.

semestral [semeʃ'trawl] (*pl* **-ais**) *adj* half-yearly.

semestralmente [semeʃtraw'mẽntʃi] *adv* every semester, every six months.

semestre [se'mɛʃtri] *m* semester; **todo ~** every six months; **todo o ~** the whole semester.

sem-fim [,sẽn'fĩ] *m*: **um ~ de** an endless amount of.

semi-aberto, ta [semja'bɛxtu, ta] (*mpl* **-s**, *fpl* **-s**) *adj* **-1.** [ger] half-opened. **-2.** [porta] ajar.

semi-analfabeto, ta [semjanawfa'bɛtu, ta] (*mpl* **-s**, *fpl* **-s**) *adj* semi-literate.

semibreve [semi'brɛvi] *f MÚS* semibreve.

semicerrar [semi'sexa(x)] *vt* to half-close.

semicírculo [semi'sixkulu] *m* semicircle.

semicolcheia [semikow'ʃeja] *f MÚS* semiquaver.

semiconsciente [semikõn'sjẽntʃi] *adj* semiconscious.

semifinal [semifi'naw] (*pl* **-ais**) *f* semi-final.
semifinalista [semifina'liʃta] ◇ *adj* semi-final (*antes de subst*). ◇ *mf* semi-finalist.
semi-internato [semiĩntex'natu] (*pl* **semi-internatos**) *m* day school.
seminal [semi'naw] (*pl* **-ais**) *adj* seminal.
seminário [semi'narju] *m* **-1.** RELIG seminary. **-2.** EDUC seminar.
seminarista [semina'riʃta] *mf* seminarist.
seminu, nua [semi'nu, nua] *adj* half-naked.
semiótica [se'mjɔtʃika] *f* semiotics.
semiprecioso, osa [semipre'sjozu, ɔza] *adj* semi-precious.
semita [se'mita] ◇ *adj* Semitic. ◇ *mf* Semite.
semítico, ca [se'mitʃiku, ka] *adj* Semitic.
semitom [semi'tõ] (*pl* **-ns**) *m* MÚS semitone.
sem-número [sẽn'numeru] *m*: **um ~ de** a countless number of.
semolina [semo'lina] *f* semolina.
sem-par [sẽn'pa(x)] *adj inv* peerless.
sempre ['sẽnpri] *adv* always; **como ~** as always; **de ~** usual; **para ~** for ever; **quase ~** nearly always.
◆ **sempre que** *loc conj* whenever.
sem-terra [sẽn'tɛxa] *mf inv* landless farm worker.
sem-teto [sẽn'tɛtu] *mf inv* homeless person.
sem-vergonha [sẽnvex'goɲa] ◇ *adj inv* shameless. ◇ *mf inv* shameless person.
SENAC (*abrev de* **Serviço Nacional de Aprendizagem Comercial**) *m Brazilian training body for people working in the general business sector.*
senado [se'nadu] *m* senate.
senador, ra [sena'do(x), ra] *m, f* senator.
SENAI (*abrev de* **Serviço Nacional de Aprendizagem Industrial**) *m Brazilian training body for people working in industry.*
senão [se'nãw] (*pl* **-ões**) ◇ *prep* [exceto] apart from. ◇ *conj* [caso contrário] or else. ◇ *m* hiccup.
senda ['sẽnda] *f* path.
Senegal [sene'gaw] *n*: **(o) ~** Senegal.
senhor, ra [se'ɲo(x), ɔra] (*mpl* **-es**, *fpl* **-s**) *adj* grand; **uma senhora indigestão** a bad case of indigestion.
◆ **senhor** *m* **-1.** [tratamento - antes de nome, cargo]: **~ X** Mr X; **o Senhor Ministro** (the) Minister; [- você]: **o ~** you; [mais formal] sir; [- em cartas]: **Prezado Senhor** Dear Sir. **-2.** [homem] man. **-3.** [cavalheiro] gentleman. **-4.** [homem idoso]: **~ (de idade)** elderly man. **-5.** [dono] master; **ser ~ de seu nariz** to be one's own master. **-6.** [patrão] boss. **-7.** RELIG: **o Senhor** the Lord.
◆ **senhora** *f* **-1.** [tratamento - antes de nome, cargo]: **senhora X** Mrs X; [- você]: **a senhora** you; [mais formal] madam; **senhoras e ~es!** ladies and gentlemen!; [- em cartas]: **Prezada Senhora** Dear Madam. **-2.** [mulher] woman. **-3.** [dama] lady. **-4.** [mulher idosa]: **senhora (de idade)** elderly woman. **-5.** [esposa] wife. **-6.** RELIG: **Nossa Senhora** Our Lady; **(Minha) Nossa (Senhora)!** *fam* Heavens (above)!, (My/Dear) Lord!
senhoria [seɲo'ria] *f* ▷ **senhorio**.
senhoril [seɲo'riw] (*pl* **-is**) *adj* distinguished.
senhorio, ria [seɲo'riu, ria] *m, f* [proprietário] landlord (*f* landlady).
◆ **Senhoria** *f* [em carta]: **Vossa Senhoria** Your Honour.
senhorita [seɲo'rita] *f* **-1.** [tratamento - antes de nome]: **~ X** Miss X; [- você]: **a ~** you. **-2.** [moça] young lady.
senil [se'niw] (*pl* **-is**) *adj* senile.
senilidade [senili'dadʒi] *f* senility.
sênior ['sẽnjo(x)] (*pl* **-s**) ◇ *adj* senior. ◇ *m* [desportista] senior.
senões [se'nõjʃ] *mpl* ▷ **senão**.
sensação [sẽnsa'sãw] (*pl* **-ões**) *f* **-1.** [ger] feeling; **ter a ~ de que** to have the feeling that. **-2.** [surpresa, agitação]: **causar ~** to cause a sensation.
sensacional [sẽnsasjo'naw] (*pl* **-ais**) *adj* sensational.
sensacionalismo [sẽnsasjona'liʒmu] *m* sensationalism.
sensacionalista [sẽnsasjona'liʃta] *adj* sensationalist.
sensatez [sẽnsa'teʒ] *f* common sense.
sensato, ta [sẽn'satu, ta] *adj* sensible.
sensibilidade [sẽnsibili'dadʒi] *f* sensitivity.
sensibilizar [4] [sẽnsibili'za(x)] *vt* **-1.** [comover] to move. **-2.** [impressionar] to sensitize.
◆ **sensibilizar-se** *vp* [comover-se] to be touched.
sensitivo, va [sẽnsi'tʃivu, va] *adj* sensitive.
sensível [sẽn'sivɛw] (*pl* **-eis**) *adj* **-1.** [ger] sensitive. **-2.** [evidente, considerável] marked.
sensivelmente [sẽnsivew'mẽntʃi] *adv* markedly.
senso ['sẽnsu] *m* [juízo] sense; **~ de humor** sense of humour; **bom ~**, good sense; **~ comum** common sense; **~ de responsabilidade** sense of responsibility.
sensor [sẽn'so(x)] *m* sensor.
sensorial [sẽnso'rjaw] (*pl* **-ais**) *adj* sensory.
sensual [sẽn'swaw] (*pl* **-ais**) *adj* sensual.
sensualidade [sẽnswali'dadʒi] *f* sensuality.
sentado, da [sẽn'tadu, da] *adj* **-1.** [pessoa] sitting. **-2.** [jantar] sit-down.
sentar [4] [sẽn'ta(x)] *vt & vi* to sit.
◆ **sentar-se** *vp* to sit down.
sentença [sẽn'tẽnsa] *f* JUR sentence; **~ de morte** death sentence.
sentenciar [sẽntẽn'sia(x)] ◇ *vt* [condenar] to sentence. ◇ *vi* [decidir] to decide.
sentencioso, sa [sẽntẽ'sjosu, sa] *adj* sententious.
sentido, da [sẽn'tʃidu, da] *adj* **-1.** [ressentido] offended. **-2.** [triste] hurt. **-3.** [lamentoso] sorrowful.
◆ **sentido** *m* **-1.** [ger] sense; **sexto ~** sixth sense. **-2.** [significado] meaning; **sem ~** meaningless; **duplo ~** double meaning; **~ figurado** figurative sense; **fazer ~** to make sense; **ter/não ter ~** to make/not make sense. **-3.** [direção] direction; **~ horário/anti-horário** clockwise/

anticlockwise. **-4.** [aspecto] way. **-5.** [atenção]: **estar com o ~ em algo/alguém** to have one's attention on sthg/sb. **-6.** [propósito] aim; **no ~ de** towards.

◆ **sentidos** *mpl* [consciência] senses; **perder/recobrar os ~s** to lose/regain consciousness.

sentimental [sẽntʃimẽn'taw] (*pl* **-ais**) ◇ *adj* **-1.** [ger] sentimental. **-2.** [amoroso] love *(antes de subst).* ◇ *mf* sentimental person.

sentimentalismo [sẽntʃimẽnta'liʒmu] *m* sentimentality.

sentimentalóide [sẽntʃimẽnta'lɔidʒi] *adj* oversentimental.

sentimento [sẽntʃi'mẽntu] *m* **-1.** [ger] feeling. **-2.** [emoção]: **com ~** with feeling. **-3.** [senso] sense.

◆ **sentimentos** *mpl* **-1.** [pêsames] condolences. **-2.** [índole]: **uma pessoa de bons ~s** a well-meaning person.

sentinela [sẽntʃi'nɛla] *f* guard.

sentir [56] [sẽn'tʃi(x)] ◇ *vt* **-1.** [ger] to feel. **-2.** [pelos sentidos] to sense. **-3.** [sofrer com] to be upset by. **-4.** [melindrar-se com] to resent. **-5.** [lamentar] to regret. ◇ *vi* **-1.** [sofrer] to suffer. **-2.** [lamentar] to regret; **sinto muito** I am very sorry. **-3.** [perceber]: **sem ~** without realizing.

◆ **sentir-se** *vp* to feel.

senzala [sẽn'zala] *f* slave quarters *(pl).*

separação [separa'sãw] (*pl* **-ões**) *f* separation; **~ de bens** *(contract of) separation of property (prior to marriage).*

separado, da [sepa'radu, da] *adj* **-1.** [apartado] separate. **-2.** [do cônjuge] separated.

separar [4] [sepa'ra(x)] *vt* **-1.** [ger] to separate. **-2.** [isolar] to isolate. **-3.** [reservar] to set aside.

◆ **separar-se** *vp* **-1.** [ger] to separate. **-2.** [cônjuges]: **~-se (de alguém)** to separate (from s.o.). **-3.** [estrada, rio]: **~-se em** to divide into.

separata [sepa'rata] *f* offprint.

separatismo [separa'tʃiʒmu] *m* separatism.

separatista [separa'tʃiʃta] ◇ *adj* separatist. ◇ *mf* separatist.

septicemia [septʃise'mia] *f* septicaemia ***UK***, septicemia ***US***.

séptico, ca ['sɛptʃiku, ka] *adj* septic.

septuagésimo, ma [septwa'ʒɛzimu, ma] *num* seventieth.

sepulcro [se'puwkru] *m* tomb.

sepultamento [sepuwta'mẽntu] *m* burial.

sepultar [4] [sepuw'ta(x)] *vt* to bury.

sepultura [sepuw'tura] *f* tomb, grave.

seqüela [se'kwɛla] *f* **-1.** [seqüência] sequel. **-2.** [conseqüência] consequence. **-3.** *MED* sequela.

seqüência [se'kwẽnsja] *f* sequence.

seqüenciador [sekwẽnsia'do(x)] *m* sequencer.

sequer [se'kɛ(x)] *adv* at least; **nem ~** not even; **não sabia ~ o nome de seus pais** he didn't even know his parents' name.

seqüestrador, ra [sekweʃtra'do(x), ra] (*mpl* **-res**, *fpl* **-s**) *m, f* **-1.** [de pessoa] kidnapper. **-2.** [de avião] hijacker.

seqüestrar [sekweʃ'tra(x)] *vt* **-1.** [pessoa] to kidnap. **-2.** [avião] to hijack. **-3.** *JUR* [bens] to sequestrate.

seqüestro [se'kwɛʃtru] *m* **-1.** [de pessoa] kidnapping. **-2.** [de avião] hijacking. **-3.** *JUR* [de bens] sequestration.

seqüestro-relâmpago [se,kweʃtruxe'lãnpagu] (*pl* **-gos**) *m kidnapping in which a person is held for a few hours while the kidnappers, having extracted passwords, use his bank cards to withdraw cash.*

sequioso, osa [se'kjozu, ɔza] *adj* thirsty.

séquito ['sɛkitu] *m* retinue.

ser [3] ['se(x)] (*pl* **-res**) ◇ *m* [criatura] being; **~ humano** human being. ◇ *vi* **-1.** [para descrever] to be; **é longo demais** it's too long; **são bonitos** they're pretty; **sou médico** I'm a doctor. **-2.** [para designar lugar, origem] to be; **ele é do Brasil** he's from Brazil; **é em São Paulo** it's in São Paulo; **sou brasileira** I'm Brazilian. **-3.** [custar] to be; **quanto é? - são 100 reais** how much is it? - (it's) 100 reals. **-4.** [com data, dia, hora] to be; **hoje é sexta** it's Friday today; **que horas são?** what time is it?; **são seis horas** it's six o'clock. **-5.** [exprime possessão] to be; **é do Ricardo** it's Ricardo's; **este carro é seu?** is this your car? **-6.** [em locuções]: **a não ~ que** unless; **que foi?** what's wrong?; **ou seja** in other words; **será que ele vem?** will he be coming? ◇ *v aux* [forma a voz passiva] to be; **ele foi visto na saída do cinema** he was seen on his way out of the cinema. ◇ *v impess* **-1.** [exprime tempo] to be; **é de dia/noite** it's daytime/night-time; **é tarde/cedo** it's late/early. **-2.** [com adjetivo] to be; **é difícil dizer** it's difficult to say; **é fácil de ver** it's easy to see; **eles são Fluminense** they're Fluminense fans.

◆ **ser de** *v + prep* [matéria] to be made of; [ser adepto de] to be a fan of.

◆ **ser para** *v + prep* to be for; **isto não é para comer** this isn't for eating.

serão [se'rãw] (*pl* **-ões**) *m* [trabalho noturno] night duty; **fazer ~** to work late.

sereia [se'reja] *f* mermaid.

serelepe [sere'lɛpi] *adj* lively.

serenar [4] [sere'na(x)] ◇ *vt* **-1.** [acalmar] to calm down. **-2.** [suavizar] to relieve. ◇ *vi* [acalmar] to calm down.

serenata [sere'nata] *f* serenade.

serenidade [sereni'dadʒi] *f* serenity.

sereno, na [se'renu, na] *adj* **-1.** [tranqüilo] serene. **-2.** [límpido] clear.

◆ **sereno** *m* night air; **apanhar ~** to get a chill; **no ~** in the open air.

seresta [se'rɛʃta] *f* serenade.

Sergipe [sex'ʒipi] *n* Sergipe.

seriado, da [se'rjadu, da] *adj* serialized.

◆ **seriado** *m TV* series.

serial [se'rjaw] (*pl* **-ais**) *adj COMPUT* serial.

série ['sɛrji] *f* **-1.** [ger] series; **uma ~ de** a series of; **número de ~** serial number. **-2.** *EDUC* year.

◆ **em série** *loc adv*: **fabricar em ~** to mass-produce.

◆ **fora de série** *loc adj* [excepcional] exceptional.

seriedade [serje'dadʒi] *f* **-1.** [ger] seriousness. **-2.** [circunspecção] sobriety. **-3.** [honestidade] integrity.

seringa [se'rĩŋga] *f* syringe.

seringal [serĩŋ'gaw] (*pl* **-ais**) *m* rubber-tree plantation.

seringueiro, ra [serĩŋ'gejru, ra] *m, f* rubber tapper.

◆ **seringueira** *f* rubber tree.

sério, ria ['sɛrju, rja] ◇ *adj* **-1.** [ger] serious. **-2.** [sóbrio] sober. **-3.** [sem rir] straight-faced. ◇ *adv* really; **falando ~** seriously.

◆ **a sério** *loc adv* seriously; **levar a ~** [dedicar-se] to take seriously; [magoar-se com] to take seriously.

sermão [sex'mãw] (*pl* **-ões**) *m* sermon; **levar um ~ de alguém** to be given a sermon by sb; **passar um ~ em alguém** to give sb a sermon.

serpente [sex'pẽntʃi] *f* **-1.** *ZOOL* serpent, snake. **-2.** *fig* [pessoa] snake (in the grass).

serpentear [15] [sexpẽn'tʃja(x)] *vi* **-1.** [rio, caminho] to meander. **-2.** [cobra] to snake.

serpentina [serpẽn'tʃina] *f* **-1.** [de papel] streamer. **-2.** [conduto] coil.

SERPRO (*abrev de* **Serviço Federal de Processamento de Dados**) *m Brazilian federal data-processing agency.*

serra ['sɛxa] *f* **-1.** [ferramenta] saw; **~ circular** circular saw. **-2.** [lâmina] serrated blade. **-3.** [montanhas] mountain range, sierra.

serrado, da [se'xadu, da] *adj* **-1.** [madeira] sawn. **-2.** [folha] serrated.

serragem [se'xaʒẽ] *f* [resíduo] sawdust.

Serra Leoa [ˌsexale'oa] *n* Sierra Leone.

serralheiro, ra [sexa'ʎejru, ra] *m, f* blacksmith.

serralheria [sexaʎe'ria] *f* **-1.** [ofício] smithery. **-2.** [oficina] smithy.

serrano, na [se'xãnu, na] ◇ *adj* mountain *(antes de subst)*. ◇ *m, f* mountain dweller.

serrar [4] [se'xa(x)] *vt* to saw.

serraria [sexa'ria] *f* sawmill.

serrote [se'xɔtʃi] *m* saw.

sertanejo, ja [sextanejʒu, ʒa] ◇ *adj of the sertão.* ◇ *m, f person who lives in the sertão.*

sertão [sex'tãw] *m* **-1.** [o interior do país] bush. **-2.** [região agreste] wilderness.

servente [sex'vẽntʃi] *mf* **-1.** [faxineiro] caretaker *UK*, janitor *US*. **-2.** [operário] labourer; **~ de pedreiro** bricklayer's labourer.

Sérvia ['sɛxvja] *n* Serbia.

serviçal [sexvi'saw] (*pl* **-ais**) ◇ *adj* [prestativo] obliging. ◇ *mf* [criado] servant.

serviço [sex'visu] *m* **-1.** [ger] service; **~ de bordo** ship's roster; **~ militar** military service; **~ de informações** information service; **Serviço Nacional de Saúde** National Health Service; **Serviço Público** Civil Service; **~s públicos** public services. **-2.** [trabalho, local de trabalho] work; **prestar ~s** [trabalhar] to render services; [fazer favores] to help out; **prestação de ~s** services rendered; **~ social** social services *(pl)*. **-3.** [iguarias] catering. **-4.** *loc*: **dar o ~** *fam* to spill the beans; **fazer um ~** *gír crime* to carry out a contract; **não brincar em ~** [ser eficiente] to be a stickler; [não desperdiçar oportunidade] to not miss an opportunity.

◆ **de serviço** *loc adj* [entrada, elevador] tradesmen's *(antes de subst)*.

servidão [sexvi'dãw] *f* **-1.** [escravidão] servitude. **-2.** *JUR* [de passagem] right of way.

servido, da [sex'vidu, da] *adj* **-1.** [que se serve] served. **-2.** [provido]: **bem ~ de** well-supplied with.

servidor, ra [sex'vido(x), ra] ◇ *m, f* [funcionário] official; **~ público** civil servant.

◆ **servidor** *m COMPUT* server.

servil [sex'viw] (*pl* **-is**) *adj* [subserviente]: **~ (a)** servile (to).

servir [54] [sex'vi(x)] ◇ *vt* **-1.** [jantar, bebida] to serve; **pedi para o garçom nos ~ duas cervejas** I asked the waiter to bring us a couple of beers; **~ algo a alguém**, **~ alguém de algo** to serve sthg to sb, to serve sb with sthg. **-2.** [ajudar] to help. ◇ *vi* **-1.** [ger] to serve. **-2.** [prestar serviço]: **~ a** to serve. **-3.** [prestar, ser útil] to be of use. **-4.** [ser adequado] to be good; **qualquer trem serve** any train will do; **não ~ para algo** to be no good for. **-5.** [caber] to fit. **-6.** [fazer as vezes de]: **~ de algo** to act as. **-7.** [ser apto] to be fit.

◆ **servir-se** *vp* **-1.** [de comida, bebida]: **~-se (de)** to help o.s. (to). **-2.** [usar]: **~-se de** to use.

servo, va ['sɛxvu, va] *m, f* **-1.** [escravo] slave. **-2.** [criado] servant.

SESC (*abrev de* **Serviço Social do Comércio**) *m Brazilian body providing social, sport and cultural facilities to people working in the general business sector.*

sessão [se'sãw] (*pl* **-ões**) *f* **-1.** [ger] session. **-2.** *CINE* performance; **primeira ~** first performance; **~ da tarde** matinée.

sessenta [se'sẽnta] *num* sixty; **os anos ~** the sixties; *veja também* **seis**.

sessões [se'sõjʃ] *pl* ▷ **sessão**.

sesta ['sɛʃta] *f* siesta, afternoon nap.

set. (*abrev de* **setembro**) Sept.

set ['sɛtʃi] *m ESP* set.

seta ['sɛta] *f* arrow.

sete ['sɛtʃi] *num* seven; **pintar o ~** *fig* to get up to mischief; *veja também* **seis**.

setecentos, tas [sɛtʃi'sẽntuʃ, taʃ] *num* seven hundred; *veja também* **seis**.

sete-e-meio [sɛtʃji'meju] (*pl* **sete-e-meios**) *m* [jogo] *kind of card game.*

setembro [se'tẽnbru] *m* September; **em ~**, **no mês de ~** in September/in the month of September; **em ~ do ano que vem/do ano passado** in September next year/last year; **em meados de ~** in mid-September; **dia primeiro/dois/**

seis de ~ first/second/sixth of September; **no dia três de ~** on the third of September; **no início/fim de ~** at the beginning/end of September; **todo ano em ~** every year in September.

setenta [se'tẽnta] *num* seventy; **os anos ~** the seventies; *veja também* **seis**.

setentrional [setẽntrjo'naw] (*pl* **-ais**) *adj* northern.

sétimo, ma ['sɛtʃimu, ma] *num* seventh; **a sétima parte** the seventh part.
◆ **sétima** *f MÚS* seventh.

setor [se'to(x)] (*pl* **-es**) *m* **-1.** [ger] sector. **-2.** [de repartição, estabelecimento] section.

setorial [seto'riaw] (*pl* **-ais**) [raijʃ] *adj* sector.

setorizar [setori'za(x)] *vt* to divide into sectors.

setuagésimo, ma [setwa'ʒɛsimu, ma] *num* seventieth.

seu, sua ['sew, 'sua] ◇ *adj* **-1.** [dele] his; [dela] her; [de você, vocês] your; [deles, delas] their; **ela trouxe o ~ carro** she brought her car; **onde estacionou a sua moto?** where did you park your motorcycle? **-2.** [de coisa, animal: singular] its; **o cachorro foi para o seu canil** the dog went into its kennel **-3.** [de coisa, animal: plural] their. ◇ *pron*: **o ~/a sua** [dele] his; [dela] hers; [deles, delas] theirs; [de coisa, animal: singular] its; [de coisa, animal: plural] theirs; **um amigo ~** a friend of his/hers; **os ~s** [a família de cada um] his/her etc. family. ◇ *m, f* **-1.** *pej*: **como vai, ~ Pedro?** how are you, mister Pedro?; **~ estúpido!** you fool!; **~s irresponsáveis!** you irresponsible lot! **-2.** [com malícia]: **~ malandro!** you cheeky one!, cheeky thing!; **sua danadinha!** you rotter!, rotten thing!

Seul [se'uw] *n* Seoul.

seus [sewʃ] ▻ **seu**.

severidade [severi'dadʒi] *f* **-1.** [ger] severity. **-2.** [com filho] strictness.

severo, ra [se'vɛru, ra] *adj* **-1.** [castigo] severe. **-2.** [pessoa] strict.

sex. (*abrev de* **sexta-feira**) *f* Fri.

sexagenário, ria [seksaʒe'narjo, rja] ◇ *adj*: **ser ~** to be a sexagenarian, to be in one's sixties. ◇ *m, f* sexagenarian.

sexagésimo, ma [seksa'ʒɛzimu, ma] *num* sixtieth.

sexo ['sɛksu] *m* sex.

sexólogo, ga [sek'sɔlogu, ga] *m, f* sexologist.

sexta ['seʃta] *f* ▻ **sexto**.

sexta-feira [ˌseʃta'fejra] (*pl* **sextas-feiras**) *f* Friday; *veja também* **sábado**.
◆ **Sexta-feira Santa** *f* Good Friday.

sexto, ta ['seʃtu, ta] *num* sixth; **a sexta parte** the sixth part.
◆ **sexta** *f* [sexta-feira] Friday.

sêxtuplos ['seʃtupluʃ] *mpl* sextuplets.

sexual [sek'swaw] (*pl* **-ais**) *adj* **-1.** [ger] sexual. **-2.** [educação, vida] sex *(antes de subst)*.

sexualidade [sekswali'dadʒi] *f* sexuality.

sexualmente [seksuaw'mẽntʃi] *adv* sexually.

sexy ['sɛksi] *adj* sexy.

Seychelles [sej'ʃɛliʃ] *npl*: **as (ilhas) ~** the Seychelles.

SFH (*abrev de* **Sistema Financeiro de Habitação**) *m* *Brazilian housing credit advisory service.*

shareware [ʃari'wari] (*pl* **-s**) *m COMPUT* shareware.

shopping ['ʃɔpĩŋ] *m* shopping centre *UK*, shopping mall *US*.

short ['ʃɔxtʃi] *m* shorts *(pl)*.

show ['ʃow] *m* **-1.** [espetáculo] show; **ser/estar um ~** *fig* to be spectacular. **-2.** *fig* [atuação brilhante]: **dar um ~ (de algo)** to give a brilliant performance (of sthg). **-3.** *fig* [escândalo]: **dar um ~** to create a scene.

showroom [ʃow'xũ] *m* showroom.

Sibéria [si'bɛrja] *n*: **(a) ~** Siberia.

siberiano, na [sibe'rjãnu, na] ◇ *adj* Siberian. ◇ *m, f* Siberian.

sibilante [sibi'lãntʃi] *adj* sibilant.

sibilar [sibi'la(x)] *vi* [silvar] to whistle; [zumbir] to buzz.

sicário [si'karju] *m* paid assassin.

Sicília [si'silja] *n* Sicily.

sicrano, na [si'krãnu, na] *m, f*: **fulano e ~** so-and-so.

sideral [side'raw] (*pl* **-ais**) *adj* sidereal.

siderurgia [si'derux'ʒia] *f* iron and steel industry.

siderúrgico, ca [side'ruxʒiku, ka] *adj* iron and steel *(antes de sust)*.
◆ **siderúrgica** *f* [usina] steelworks *(sg)*.

sidra ['sidra] *f* cider.

sifão [si'fãw] (*pl* **-ões**) *m* **-1.** [tubo] siphon. **-2.** [de aparelho sanitário] U-bend. **-3.** [garrafa] soda siphon.

sífilis ['sifiliʃ] *f inv* syphilis.

sifilítico, ca [sifi'litʃiku, ka] ◇ *adj* syphilitic. ◇ *m, f* syphilitic.

sifões [si'fõjʃ] *pl* ▻ **sifão**.

sigilo [si'ʒilu] *m* secrecy; **~ bancário** bank confidentiality.

sigiloso, osa [siʒi'lozu, ɔza] *adj* secret.

sigla ['sigla] *f* **-1.** [abreviatura] acronym. **-2.** [sinal] initial.

signatário, ria [signa'tarju, rja] *m, f* signatory.

significação [signifika'sãw] *f* **-1.** [significado] meaning. **-2.** [importância] significance.

significado [signifi'kadu, da] *m* **-1.** [sentido] meaning. **-2.** *LING* signified.

significante [signifi'kãntʃi] *adj* **-1.** [significativo] significant. **-2.** *LING* signifying.

significar [12] [signifi'ka(x)] ◇ *vt* **-1.** [ger] to mean. **-2.** [indicar] to signify. ◇ *vi* [ter importância] to mean.

significativo, va [signifika'tʃivu, va] *adj* significant.

signo ['signu] *m* sign; **~ do zodíaco** sign of the zodiac, star sign.

sílaba ['silaba] *f* syllable.

silenciador [silẽnsja'do(x)] *m* [de arma] silencer.

silenciar [16] [silẽn'sja(x)] ◇ *vt* **-1.** [calar] to silence. **-2.** [omitir] to conceal. ◇ *vi* **-1.** [calar-se]

to be quiet. **-2.** [omitir-se]: ~ **sobre** to keep quiet about.
silêncio [si'lẽnsju] *m* silence; **ficar em** ~ to remain silent.
silencioso, osa [silẽn'sjozu, ɔza] *adj* silent.
silhueta [si'ʎweta] *f* **-1.** [ger] silhouette. **-2.** [corpo] outline.
silício [si'lisju] *m* silicon.
silicone [sili'koni] *m* silicone.
silo ['silu] *m* silo.
silvar [4] [siw'va(x)] *vi* **-1.** [ger] to hiss. **-2.** [vento] to whistle.
silvestre [siw'vɛʃtri] *adj* wild.
silvícola [siw'vikola] *mf* forest dweller.
silvo ['siwvu] *m* **-1.** [ger] hiss. **-2.** [ventania] whistle.
sim ['sĩ] ◇ *adv* yes; **acho** *ou* **creio que** ~ I think *ou* believe so; **dizer que** ~ to say yes; **pelo** ~, **pelo não** just in case; **quero,** ~ yes, I'd like to; **vou,** ~ yes, I'm going. ◇ *m*: **dar o** ~ to consent.
simbiose [sĩn'bjɔzi] *f* symbiosis.
simbiótico, ca [sĩmbi'ɔtiku, ca] *adj* symbiotic.
simbólico, ca [sĩn'bɔliku, ka] *adj* symbolic.
simbolismo [sĩnbo'liʒmu] *m* **-1.** [representação] symbolism. **-2.** *ARTE & LITER* Symbolism.
simbolizar [4] [sĩnboli'za(x)] *vt* to symbolize.
símbolo ['sĩnbolu] *m* **-1.** [ger] symbol. **-2.** [insígnia] emblem.
simbologia [sĩnbolo'ʒia] *f* symbology.
simetria [sime'tria] *f* symmetry.
simétrico, ca [si'mɛtriku, ka] *adj* symmetrical.
similar [simi'la(x)] (*pl* **-es**) *adj*: ~ **(a)** similar (to).
similaridade [similari'dadʒi] *f* similarity.
símile ['simili] *m* **-1.** [de objeto] copy. **-2.** [de palavra] analogy, simile.
similitude [simili'tudʒi] *f* similitude.
simpatia [sĩnpa'tʃia] *f* **-1.** [qualidade] warmth. **-2.** [atração - por outrem, lugar] liking; **sentir** ~ **por alguém** to like sb. **-3.** [pessoa]: **ser uma** ~ to be friendly. **-4.** [solidariedade] sympathy. **-5.** [espirit] charm.
simpático, ca [sĩn'patʃiku, ka] *adj* **-1.** [pessoa - atraente] pleasant; [- amável] nice. **-2.** [agradável] pleasant. **-3.** [favorável]: ~ **a algo/alguém** favourable towards sthg/sb. **-4.** *ANAT* sympathetic.
simpatizante [sĩnpatʃi'zãntʃi] *adj*: ~ **com** sympathetic towards.
simpatizar [4] [sĩnpatʃi'za(x)] *vi*: ~ **com alguém/algo** to like sb/sthg; ~ **com uma causa** to sympathize with a cause.
simples ['sĩnpliʃ] ◇ *adj* **-1.** [ger] simple. **-2.** *(antes de subst)* [mero] mere; [único] single. ◇ *adv* simply.
simplesmente [sĩnpliʃ'mẽntʃi] *adv* simply.
simplicidade [sĩnplisi'dadʒi] *f* simplicity.
simplificação [sĩnplifika'sãw] *f* simplification.
simplificar [12] [sĩnplifi'ka(x)] *vt* to simplify.
simplista [sĩn'pliʃta] *adj* simplistic.
simplório, ria [sĩn'plɔrju, rja] *adj* simple.
simpósio [sĩn'pɔzju] *m* symposium.
simulação [simula'sãw] (*pl* **-ões**) *f* **-1.** [de combate, salvamento] simulation. **-2.** [de sentimento, desmaio] pretence. **-3.** [de animal, voz] imitation.
simulacro [simu'lakru] *m* **-1.** [ger] pretence. **-2.** [de exame] mock. **-3.** [de bosque] imitation.
simulador [simula'do(x)] *m* simulator.
simular [4] [simu'la(x)] *vt* **-1.** [combate, salvamento] to simulate. **-2.** [sentimento, desmaio] to feign. **-3.** [animal, vozes] to imitate.
simultaneamente [simuwtãnja'mẽntʃi] *adv* simultaneously.
simultâneo, nea [simuw'tãnju, nja] *adj*: ~ **(a** *ou* **com)** simultaneous (with).
sina ['sina] *f* fate.
sinagoga [sina'gɔga] *f* synagogue.
Sinai [si'naj] *n*: **o** ~ Sinai.
sinal [si'naw] (*pl* **-ais**) *m* **-1.** [ger] sign; **fazer um** ~ **(para alguém)** to signal (to sb); **dar** ~ **de vida** to give sign of life; **em** ~ **de** as a sign of. **-2.** [símbolo] signal; ~ **de pontuação** punctuation mark; ~ **de mais/menos** plus/minus sign. **-3.** [aviso]: **dar o** ~ *ESP* [para partida] to give the off; ~ **de alarme** alarm bell. **-4.** *TELEC* tone; ~ **de chamada** ringing tone; ~ **de discar** dialling tone; **dar** ~ **(de discar)** to give the (dialling) tone; **dar** ~ **de ocupado** to give the engaged tone. **-5.** *AUTO*: ~ **(luminoso de tráfego)** traffic lights *(pl)*; ~ **verde** green light; **avançar o** ~ to jump the lights. **-6.** [pinta] mole; [de nascença] birthmark. **-7.** *COM* deposit; **de** ~ as a deposit.
◆ **por sinal** *loc adv* **-1.** [a propósito] by the way. **-2.** [aliás] besides.
sinal-da-cruz [si,nawda'kruʒ] (*pl* **sinais-da-cruz**) *m* sign of the cross.
sinaleiro [sina'lejru] *m* *NÁUT* signalman.
sinalização [sinaliza'sãw] *f* **-1.** [sinais de tráfego - *AUTO*] traffic signs *(pl)*; [- *FERRO*] signals *(pl)*. **-2.** [indicação em estrada *etc*] road sign.
sinalizar [4] [sinali'za(x)] ◇ *vt* [avenida, estrada] to signpost. ◇ *vi* [pessoa] to signal.
sinceramente [sĩsera'mẽntʃi] *adv* sincerely.
sinceridade [sĩnseri'dadʒi] *f* sincerity; **com toda** ~ in all sincerity.
sincero, ra [sĩn'sɛru, ra] *adj* sincere.
sincopado, da [sĩŋko'padu, da] *adj* *MÚS* syncopated.
síncope ['sĩŋkopi] *f* *MED* syncope.
sincronia [sĩŋkro'nia] *f* synchrony.
sincronizar [4] [sĩŋkroni'za(x)] *vt* **-1.** [combinar] to synchronize. **-2.** *CINE* to sync.
sindical [sĩndʒi'kaw] (*pl* **-ais**) *adj* trade union *(antes de subst)*.
sindicalismo [sĩndʒika'liʒmu] *m* trade unionism.
sindicalista [sĩndʒika'liʃta] ◇ *adj* trade union *(antes de subst)*. ◇ *mf* trade unionist.
sindicalizado, da [sĩndʒikali'zadu, da] *adj* unionized.
sindicalizar-se [4] [sĩndʒikali'zaxsi] *vp* to join a trade union.

sindicância [sĩndʒi'kãnsja] f [inquérito]: ~ **(de/sobre)** enquiry (into).
sindicato [sĩndʒi'katu] m **-1.** [de profissionais] trade union. **-2.** [financeiro] syndicate.
síndico, ca ['sĩndʒiku, ka] m,f **-1.** [de prédio] residents' representative. **-2.** [de falência] receiver. **-3.** [de inquérito] leader.
síndrome ['sĩndromi] f syndrome; ~ **de abstinência** withdrawal symptoms *(pl)*.
sinecura [sine'kura] f sinecure.
sineta [si'neta] f small bell.
sinfonia [sĩnfo'nia] f symphony.
sinfônico, ca [sĩn'foniku, ka] adj symphonic.
◆ **sinfônica** f [orquestra] symphonic orchestra.
singeleza [sĩnʒe'leza] f simplicity.
singelo, la [sĩn'ʒɛlu, la] adj simple.
singular [sĩŋgu'la(x)] (pl **-es**) <> adj **-1.** [ger] singular. **-2.** [peculiar] strange. <> m GRAM singular.
singularidade [sĩŋgulari'dadʒi] f **-1.** [raridade] singularity. **-2.** [peculiaridade] oddness.
singularizar [4] [sĩŋgulari'za(x)] vt **-1.** [distinguir] to single out. **-2.** [detalhar] to list.
◆ **singularizar-se** vp [distinguir-se] to distinguish o.s.
sinistro, tra [si'niʃtru, tra] adj sinister.
◆ **sinistro** m **-1.** [acidente] disaster. **-2.** [dano] damage.
sino ['sinu] m bell.
sinônimo, ma [si'nonimu, ma] adj synonymous.
◆ **sinônimo** m synonym.
sinopse [si'nɔpsi] f synopsis.
sintagma [sĩn'tagma] m syntagma.
sintático, ca [sĩn'tatʃiku, ka] adj syntactic.
sintaxe [sĩn'tasi] f syntax.
síntese ['sĩntezi] f **-1.** [ger] synthesis. **-2.** [resumo] summary; **em** ~ in short.
sintético, ca [sĩn'tɛtʃiku, ka] adj **-1.** [artificial] synthetic. **-2.** [conciso] concise.
sintetizador [sĩntetʃiza'do(x)] m synthesizer.
sintetizar [4] [sĩntetʃi'za(x)] vt **-1.** [resumir] to summarize. **-2.** QUÍM to synthesize.
sintoma [sĩn'toma] m **-1.** MED symptom. **-2.** *fig* [indício] sign.
sintomático, ca [sĩnto'matʃiku, ka] adj symptomatic.
sintonia [sĩnto'nia] f **-1.** ELETRON tuning. **-2.** *fig* [entrosamento] harmony.
sintonizador [sĩntoniza'do(x)] m tuner.
sintonizar [4] [sĩntoni'za(x)] <> vt ELETRON to tune. <> vi **-1.** ELETRON: ~ **com** to tune into. **-2.** *fig* [entrosar-se]: ~ **(com)** to harmonise (with).
◆ **sintonizar-se** vp [harmonizar-se]: ~ **com** to be in tune with.
sinuca [si'nuka] f **-1.** ESP snooker. **-2.** [situação difícil]: **estar numa** ~ **(de bico)** to be snookered.
sinuosidade [sinwozi'dadʒi] f [tortuosidade]: **a** ~ **da estrada** the twistiness of the road.
sinuoso, osa [si'nwozu, ɔza] adj **-1.** [linha] wavy. **-2.** [estrada, rio] meandering. **-3.** [recorte] wavy.
sinusite [sinu'zitʃi] f sinusitis.
sionismo [sjo'niʒmu] m Zionism.
sionista [sjo'niʃta] <> adj Zionist. <> mf Zionist.
sirene [si'reni] f siren.
siri [si'ri] m crab; **casquinha de** ~ CULIN *stuffed crab shells*.
Síria ['sirja] n Syria.
sirigaita [siri'gajta] f *fam* shrew.
sírio, ria ['sirju, rja] <> adj Syrian. <> m, f Syrian.
sísmico, ca ['siʒmiku, ka] adj seismic.
sismógrafo [siʒ'mɔgrafu] m seismograph.
siso ['sizu] m **-1.** [juízo] wisdom. **-2.** [dente]: **(dente de)** ~ wisdom tooth.
sistema [siʃ'tema] m **-1.** [ger] system; ~ **nervoso** nervous system; ~ **solar** solar system; ~ **fiscal** tax system; ~ **operacional** COMPUT operating system. **-2.** [maneira] method.
sistemática [siʃte'matʃika] f **-1.** [sistematização] systematization. **-2.** [ciência] systematics *(sg)*.
sistemático, ca [siʃte'matʃiku, ka] adj systematic.
sistematização [siʃte'matʃiza'sãw] (pl **-ões**) f systematization.
sistematizar [4] [siʃtematʃi'za(x)] vt to systematize.
sisudo, da [si'zudu, da] adj wise.
site ['sajtji] (pl **-s**) m COMPUT site.
sitiante [si'tʃiãntʃi] mf settler.
sitiar [16] [si'tʃja(x)] vt **-1.** [cercar] to besiege. **-2.** [assediar] to harrass.
sítio ['sitʃju] m **-1.** [propriedade] farm. **-2.** MIL siege; **estado de** ~ state of siege; **em estado de** ~ under siege.
situação [sitwa'sãw] (pl **-ões**) f **-1.** [ger] situation. **-2.** [localização] position.
situacionista [sitwasjo'niʃta] <> adj ruling party. <> mf member of the ruling party.
situado, da [si'twadu, da] adj situated; **estar** ou **ficar** ~ to be situated.
situar [4] [si'twa(x)] vt to place.
◆ **situar-se** vp **-1.** [localizar-se - casa, filme] to be located; [- pessoa] to place o.s.; **tenho que me** ~ **para saber que rua seguir** I have to get my bearings in order to know which street to take. **-2.** [classificar-se] to be placed. **-3.** [em assunto, questão] to take a position.
skate [iʃ'kejtʃi] m **-1.** [esporte] skateboarding. **-2.** [prancha] skateboard.
slide [iʒ'lajdʒi] m slide, transparency.
slogan [iʒ'logãn] m slogan.
smart card [iʒimaxtʃi'kaxdʒi] (pl **smart cards**) m COMPUT smart card.
smoking [iʒ'mokĩŋ] m dinner jacket.
SNI (abrev de **Serviço Nacional de Informações**) m *Brazilian information service concerned particularly with state security*, ≃ MI5 UK, ≃ CIA US.
só ['sɔ] <> adj **-1.** [sozinho] alone; **a** ~**s** alone. **-2.** [solitário] lonely. **-3.** [único] single. <> adv [somente] only; **é** ~**?** is that all?; **é** ~**!** that's all!
SO (abrev de **Sudoeste**) m SW.

soalho ['swaʎu] *m* = **assoalho**.
soar [20] ['swa(x)] <> *vi* **-1.** [ger] to sound; ~ **a algo (a alguém)** to sound like sthg (to s.o.). **-2.** [ser pronunciado] to be voiced. **-3.** [hora] to strike. <> *vt* [suj: horas] to strike.
sob ['sobi] *prep* under; ~ **esse aspecto** from that perspective.
soberania [sobera'nia] *f* **-1.** [de nação] sovereignty. **-2.** *fig* [superioridade] supremacy.
soberano, na [sobe'rãnu, na] <> *adj* **-1.** [independente] sovereign. **-2.** [poderoso] powerful. **-3.** [supremo] supreme. **-4.** [altivo] haughty. <> *m, f* [monarca] sovereign.
soberba [so'bexba] *f* [altivez] arrogance.
soberbo, ba [so'bexbu, ba] *adj* **-1.** [arrogante] arrogant. **-2.** [magnífico] magnificent.
sobra ['sɔbra] *f* leftover; **dar de** ~ to be more than enough; **ter algo de** ~ to have sthg spare.
◆ **sobras** *fpl* leftovers.
sobraçar [13] [sobra'sa(x)] *vt* to carry under one's arm.
sobrado [so'bradu] *m* floor.
sobranceiro, ra [sobrãn'sejru, ra] *adj* **-1.** [que está acima]: ~ **a** above. **-2.** [arrogante] supercilious.
sobrancelha [sobrãn'seʎa] *f* eyebrow.
sobrar [4] [so'bra(x)] *vi* **-1.** [ger]: ~ to be left over; **me sobra tempo para ir ao cinema** I have some free time to go to the cinema; **o médico examinou duas crianças, sobrou uma** the doctor examined two children, there was one still left; **isso dá e sobra** that is more than enough. **-2.** [ficar de fora] to be left out.
sobre ['sobri] *prep* **-1.** [ger] on. **-2.** [por cima de] over. **-3.** [a respeito de] about.
sobreaviso [sobrja'vizu] *m*: **estar/ficar de** ~ to be on the alert.
sobrecapa [sobre'kapa] *f* dust jacket.
sobrecarga [sobre'kaxga] *f* overload.
sobrecarregar [4] [sobrekaxe'ga(x)] *vt* **-1.** [com carga] to overload. **-2.** [pessoa] to overburden.
sobre-humano, na [sobrju'mãnu, na] (*mpl* **-s**, *fpl* **-s**) *adj* superhuman.
sobreloja [sobre'lɔʒa] *f* mezzanine.
sobremaneira [sobrema'nejra] *adv* excessively.
sobremesa [sobre'meza] *f* dessert; **de** ~ for dessert.
sobrenatural [ˌsobrenatu'raw] (*pl* **-ais**) *adj* supernatural.
sobrenome [ˌsobri'nɔmi] *m* surname.
sobrepor [45] [sobre'po(x)] *vt* **-1.** [pôr em cima]: ~ **algo a algo** to put sthg on top of sthg. **-2.** *fig* [antepor]: ~ **algo a algo** to put sthg before sthg.
◆ **sobrepor-se** *vp* **-1.** [pôr-se em cima] to be put on top. **-2.** *fig* [antepor-se] to come before. **-3.** *fig* [a críticas] to overcome.
sobreposição [ˌsobrepozi'sãw] (*pl* **-ões**) *f* [de objetos] superimposition.
sobreposto, ta [sobre'poʃtu, ta] <> *pp* ▷ **sobrepor**. <> *adj* [posto em cima]: ~ **a** placed on top of.
sobrepujar [4] [sobrepu'ʒa(x)] *vt* **-1.** [ger] to overcome. **-2.** [ser superior a]: ~ **algo/alguém (em algo)** to outdo sthg/s.o. (in sthg).
sobrescrito [ˌsobreʃ'kritu] *m* address.
sobressair [68] [sobresa'i(x)] *vi* to stand out.
◆ **sobressair-se** *vp* to stand out.
sobressalente [sobresa'lẽntʃi] <> *adj* spare. <> *m* spare.
sobressaltado, da [sobresaw'tadu, da] *adj* **-1.** [assustado] startled; **acordar** ~ to wake up with a start. **-2.** [apreensivo] worried.
sobressaltar [4] [sobresaw'ta(x)] *vt* **-1.** [assustar] to startle. **-2.** [inquietar] to worry.
◆ **sobressaltar-se** *vp* **-1.** [assustar-se] to be startled. **-2.** [inquietar-se] to worry.
sobressalto [sobre'sawtu] *m* **-1.** [ger] start. **-2.** [inquietação] concern.
sobretaxa [ˌsobre'taʃa] *f* surcharge.
sobretudo [sobre'tudu] <> *m* overcoat. <> *adv* especially.
sobrevida [sobre'vida] *f*: **após o transplante, teve uma ~ de dez anos** after the transplant, he survived for another ten years.
sobrevir [67] [sobre'vi(x)] *vi*: ~ **(a algo)** to survive (sthg).
sobrevivência [sobrevi'vẽnsja] *f*: ~ **(a)** survival (from).
sobrevivente [sobrevi'vẽntʃi] <> *adj* surviving. <> *mf* survivor.
sobreviver [5] [sobrevi've(x)] *vi*: ~ **(a algo/alguém)** to survive (sthg/s.o.).
sobrevoar [20] [sobre'vwa(x)] *vt* to fly over.
sobrevôo [sobre'vow] *m* overflying.
sobriedade [sobrje'dadʒi] *f* **-1.** [moderação] moderation. **-2.** [ausência de embriaguez] sobriety.
sobrinho, nha [so'briɲu, ɲa] *m, f* nephew (*f* niece).
sóbrio, bria ['sɔbrju, brja] *adj* **-1.** [ger] sober. **-2.** [moderado]: ~ **(em)** moderate (in).
socado, da [so'kadu, da] *adj* **-1.** [esmagado] crushed. **-2.** [metido] stuck. **-3.** [pessoa] squat.
socador [soka'do(x)] *m* pestle; ~ **de alho** garlic crusher.
soçaite [so'sajtʃi] *m fam* high society.
socar [12] [so'ka(x)] *vt* **-1.** [dar socos em] to punch. **-2.** [esmagar] to crush. **-3.** [calcar] to grind. **-4.** [amassar] to knead. **-5.** [meter] to chuck.
sociabilidade [sosjabili'dadʒi] *f* sociability.
sociabilizar [4] [sosjabili'za(x)] *vt* to socialize.
social [so'sjaw] (*pl* **-ais**) *adj* **-1.** [ger] social. **-2.** [relativo a sócios] members' *(antes de subst)*. **-3.** [via de acesso] front *(antes de subst)*. **-4.** [banheiro] guest *(antes de subst)*. **-5.** [camisa] dress. **-6.** COM: **razão** ~ trade name.
◆ **sociais** *fpl* [em hipódromo *etc* - área] members' enclosure; [- cadeiras] members' seats.
socialdemocracia [soˌsjawdemokra'sia] *f* social democracy.
socialdemocrata [soˌsjawdemo'krata] <> *adj* social democratic. <> *mf* social democrat.
socialismo [sosja'liʒmu] *m* socialism.

socialista [sosja'liʃta] <> *adj* socialist. <> *mf* socialist.
socialite [sosja'lajtʃi] *mf* socialite.
socializar [4] [sosjali'za(x)] *vt* to socialize.
sociável [so'sjavew] (*pl* **-eis**) *adj* sociable.
sociedade [sosje'dadʒi] *f* **-1.** [ger] society; ~ **de consumo** consumer society; **a alta** ~ high society; **uma mulher da** ~ a woman of the world; **Sociedade Protetora dos Animais** *society for the protection of animals*, ≃ RSPCA *UK*. **-2.** [COM - empresa] company; [- entre sócios] partnership; ~ **anônima** limited company; ~ **(de responsabilidade) limitada** limited (liability) company. **-3.** [parceria] patnership; **em** ~ **com** in partnership with.
sócio, cia ['sɔsju, sja] *m, f* **-1.** [ger] partner. **-2.** [membro] member.
sociocultural ['sɔsjokuwtu'raw] (*pl* **-ais**) *adj* sociocultural.
sócio-econômico, ca [sosjoeko'nomiku, ka] (*mpl* **-s**, *fpl* **-s**) *adj* socio-economic.
sociolingüística [ˌsɔsjolĩŋ'gwiʃtʃika] *f* sociolinguistics *(sg)*.
sociologia [sosjolo'ʒia] *f* sociology.
sociológico, ca [sosjo'lɔʒiku, ka] *adj* sociological.
sociólogo, ga [so'sjɔlogu, ga] *m, f* sociologist.
sóciopolítico, ca [sosjopo'litʃiku, ka] (*mpl* **-s**, *fpl* **-s**) *adj* socio-political.
soco ['soku] *m* punch; **dar um** ~ **em algo/alguém** to punch sthg/sb.
soco-inglês [sokwĩn'gleʃ] (*pl* **socos-ingleses**) *m* knuckleduster.
socorrer [5] [soko'xe(x)] *vt* to rescue.
socorro [so'koxu] *m* rescue; **equipe de** ~ rescue team; **pedir** ~ to ask for help; **socorro!** help!; **primeiros** ~**s** first aid *(sg)*.
soda ['sɔda] *f* **-1.** [bebida] soda. **-2.** [substância]: ~ **cáustica** caustic soda.
sódio ['sɔdʒju] *m* sodium.
sodomia [sodo'mia] *f* sodomy.
sodomizar [sodomi'za(x)] *vt* to sodomize.
sofá [so'fa] *m* sofa.
sofá-cama [soˌfa'kãma] (*pl* **sofás-camas**) *m* sofa bed.
Sófia ['sɔfja] *n* Sofia.
sofisma [so'fiʒma] *m* **-1.** [em filosofia] sophism. **-2.** [falsidade] false statement.
sofista [so'fiʃta] <> *adj* sophist. <> *mf* sophist.
sofisticação [sofiʃtʃika'sãw] (*pl* **-ões**) *f* **-1.** [requinte] sophistication. **-2.** [aprimoramento] refinement.
sofisticado, da [sofiʃtʃi'kadu, da] *adj* **-1.** [requintado] sophisticated. **-2.** [aprimorado] fancy. **-3.** [afetado] refined.
sofisticar [12] [sofiʃtʃi'ka(x)] *vt* to refine.
sofredor, ra [sofre'do(x), ra] <> *adj* suffering. <> *m, f* [pessoa] sufferer.
sôfrego, ga ['sofregu, ga] *adj* **-1.** [ávido] eager. **-2.** [ao comer, beber] greedy. **-3.** [impaciente] impatient; **o pai aguardava** ~ **notícias sobre o filho** the father waited impatiently for news of his son.
sofreguidão [sofregi'dãw] *f* **-1.** [avidez] eagerness. **-2.** [ao comer, beber] greed. **-3.** [impaciência] impatience.
sofrer [5] [so'fre(x)] <> *vt* **-1.** [ger] to suffer. **-2.** [suportar] to bear. **-3.** [receber] to undergo. <> *vi* [padecer] to suffer; ~ **de** *MED* to suffer from.
sofrido, da [so'fridu, da] *adj* long-suffering.
sofrimento [sofri'mẽntu] *m* suffering.
sofrível [so'frivew] (*pl* **-eis**) *adj* bearable.
soft ['softʃi], **software** [sof'twe(x)] *m COMPUT* software.
sogro, gra [sogru, gra] *m, f* father-in-law (*f* mother-in-law).
sóis [sɔjʃ] *pl* ▻ **sol**.
soja ['sɔʒa] *f* soya.
sol ['sɔw] (*pl* **sóis**) *m* **-1.** [ger] sun; **fazer** ~ to be sunny; ~ **a pino** mid-day sun; **tomar (banho de)** ~ to sunbathe; **ao** ~ in the sun; **tapar o** ~ **com a peneira** to hide the truth. **-2.** *MÚS* [nota] soh, sol.
sola ['sɔla] *f* **-1.** [de sapato] sole. **-2.** *ANAT*: ~ **do pé** sole of the foot. **-3.** *loc*: **entrar de** ~ *FUT* to make an illegal tackle; [com garra] to enter aggressively.
solado, da [so'ladu, da] *adj* flat.
◆ **solado** *m* [de calçado] sole.
solão [so'lãw] *m* [sol quente] very hot sun.
solapar [4] [sola'pa(x)] *vt* **-1.** [minar] to undermine. **-2.** [abalar] to shake. **-3.** *fig* [arruinar] destroy.
solar [4] [so'la(x)] (*pl* **-es**) <> *adj* solar. <> *m* [moradia] manor house. <> *vt* [sapato] to sole. <> *vi* **-1.** [bolo] to fail to rise. **-2.** *MÚS* to perform a solo.
solavanco [sola'vãŋku] *m* jolt.
solda ['sɔwda] *f* **-1.** [substância] solder. **-2.** [soldadura] weld.
soldado [sow'dadu] *mf* **-1.** *MIL* soldier; ~ **de chumbo** tin soldier; ~ **raso** private (soldier). **-2.** [defensor] defender.
soldador, ra [sowda'do(x), ra] *m, f* welder.
soldadura [sowda'dura] *f* **-1.** [ato] welding. **-2.** [junta] weld.
soldagem [sow'daʒẽ] *f* welding.
soldar [4] [sow'da(x)] *vt* to weld.
soldo ['sowdu] *m MIL* pay.
soleira [so'lejra] *f* **-1.** [de porta] threshold. **-2.** [de ponte] foundation.
solene [so'leni] *adj* solemn.
solenemente [soleni'mẽntʃi] *adv* solemnly.
solenidade [soleni'dadʒi] *f* **-1.** [qualidade] solemnity. **-2.** [cerimônia] ceremony.
soletrar [4] [sole'tra(x)] *vt* **-1.** [letras] to spell. **-2.** [ler devagar] to read out slowly.
solicitação [solisita'sãw] (*pl* **-ões**) *f* [pedido] request.
◆ **solicitações** *fpl* [apelo] appeal *(sg)*.
solicitar [4] [solisi'ta(x)] *vt* **-1.** [pedir] to request; ~ **algo a alguém** to ask sb for sthg. **-2.** [requerer] to apply for. **-3.** [atenção, amizade] to seek.
solícito, ta [so'lisitu, ta] *adj* helpful.

solicitude [solisi'tudʒi] *f* **-1.** [zelo] care. **-2.** [boa-vontade] concern. **-3.** [empenho] commitment.
solidão [soli'dãw] *f* **-1.** [isolamento] solitude. **-2.** [ermo] desolation. **-3.** [sentimento] loneliness.
solidariedade [solidarje'dadʒi] *f* solidarity.
solidário, ria [soli'darju, rja] *adj* **-1.** [na dor] united; **mostrar-se ~** to show one's solidarity; **ser ~ com** to stand by. **-2.** [simpático]: **ser ~ a** to be sympathetic to.
solidarizar-se [4] [solidari'zaxsi] *vp*: **~-se com** to sympathise with.
solidez [soli'deʒ] *f* **-1.** [ger] strength. **-2.** [física] solidity. **-3.** [estabilidade] stability.
solidificar [12] [solidʒifi'ka(x)] *vt* **-1.** [fisicamente] to solidify. **-2.** *fig* [laços, amizade] to strengthen.
◆ **solidificar-se** *vp* **-1.** [fisicamente] to set. **-2.** *fig* [laços, amizade] to become strong.
sólido, da ['sɔlidu, da] *adj* **-1.** [ger] solid. **-2.** [moralmente] strong. **-3.** *fig* [firme - ger] strong; [- conhecimento] firm; [- argumento] sound.
◆ **sólido** *m MAT* solid.
solilóquio [soli'lɔkju] *m* soliloquy.
solista [so'liʃta] *m MÚS* soloist.
solitário, ria [soli'tarju, rja] ◇ *adj* solitary. ◇ *m, f* [eremita] solitary person.
◆ **solitário** *m* [diamante] solitaire.
◆ **solitária** *f* **-1.** [cela] solitary (confinement) cell. **-2.** [verme] tapeworm.
solo ['sɔlu] *m* **-1.** [chão] ground. **-2.** *MÚS* solo.
solstício [sowʃ'tʃisju] *m ASTRON* solstice; **~ de inverno/verão** winter/summer solstice.
soltar [4] [sow'ta(x)] *vt* **-1.** [libertar] to release; **~ os cachorros** *fig* to lash out. **-2.** [desatar] to untie. **-3.** [afrouxar] to loosen. **-4.** [largar] to let go. **-5.** [deixar cair (das mãos)] to drop. **-6.** [emitir] to let out. **-7.** [pronunciar] to utter; **~ um palavrão** to swear; **~ o verbo** *fig* to blow one's top. **-8.** [lançar] to let off; **~ pipa** to fly a kite.
◆ **soltar-se** *vp* [desprender-se]: **~-se (de algo)** to free o.s. (from sthg).
solteira [sow'tejra] *f* ▷ **solteiro**.
solteirão, rona [sowtej'rãw, rona] (*mpl* **-ões**, *fpl* **-s**) *m, f* bachelor (*f* spinster).
solteiro, ra [sow'tejru, ra] *adj* unmarried, single.
solteirona [sowtej'rona] *f* ▷ **solteirão**.
solto, ta ['sowtu, ta] ◇ *pp* ▷ **soltar**. ◇ *adj* [ger] loose; **ter a língua solta** *fam fig* to have a loose tongue.
◆ **à solta** *loc adv* on the loose.
soltura [sow'tura] *f* **-1.** [libertação] release. **-2.** [desregramento] looseness.
solução [solu'sãw] (*pl* **-ões**) *f* solution; **~ de continuidade** interruption; **sem ~ de continuidade** without interruption.
soluçar [13] [solu'sa(x)] *vi* **-1.** [chorar] to sob. **-2.** *MED* to hiccup.
solucionar [13] [solusjo'na(x)] *vt* to resolve.
soluço [su'lusu] *m* **-1.** [choro] sob; **aos ~s** sobbing. **-2.** *MED* hiccup.
solúvel [so'luvɛw] (*pl* **-eis**) *adj* soluble.
solvência [sow'vẽnsja] *f* **-1.** *FIN* [de dívida] solvency. **-2.** [dissolução] solubility.
solvente [sow'vẽntʃi] ◇ *adj* **-1.** [substância] soluble. **-2.** *FIN* [devedor] solvent. ◇ *m* [substância] solvent.
solver [5] [sow've(x)] *vt* **-1.** *FIN* [dívida] to pay. **-2.** [dissolver] to dissolve.
som ['sõ] (*pl* **-ns**) *m* **-1.** [ger] sound; **fazer um ~** *fam* to make music; **ao ~ de** to the sound of. **-2.** [aparelho] hi-fi.
soma ['soma] *f* **-1.** [ger] sum. **-2.** *fig* [conjunto] combination.
Somália [so'malja] *n* Somalia.
somar [4] [so'ma(x)] ◇ *vt* **-1.** [adicionar] to add; **~ algo a algo** to add sthg to sthg. **-2.** [totalizar] to add up to. ◇ *vi* to add (up).
◆ **somar-se** *vp* to gather together.
somatório [soma'tɔrju] *m* **-1.** [soma] sum total. **-2.** *fig* [total] total. **-3.** *fig* [conjunto] series.
sombra ['sõnbra] *f* **-1.** [projeção] shadow; **fazer ~ a alguém** *fig* to put sb in the shade; **ser a ~ de alguém** *fig* to shadow sb. **-2.** [área] shade; **à ~ de** in the shade of; *fig* [sob a proteção de] under the protection of; **querer ~ e água fresca** *fig* to want an easy life. **-3.** *fig* [sinal] shadow; **sem ~ de dúvida** without a shadow of a doubt. **-4.** *fig* [anonimato] in the shade.
sombreado, da [sõn'brjadu, da] *adj* shaded.
◆ **sombreado** *m ARTE* shading.
sombrear [15] [sõn'brja(x)] ◇ *vt* [com sombra] to shade; **a nuvem sombreou a praia** the cloud cast a shadow over the beach. ◇ *vi ARTE* to shade (in).
sombreiro [sõn'brejru] *m* hat.
sombrinha [sõn'briɲa] *f* umbrella.
sombrio, bria [sõn'briw, bria] *adj* **-1.** [escuro] dark. **-2.** [triste] gloomy. **-3.** [carrancudo] grim.
somente [sɔ'mẽntʃi] *adv* only.
sonambulismo [sonãnbu'liʒmu] *m* sleepwalking.
sonâmbulo, la [so'nãnbulu, la] ◇ *adj* sleepwalking. ◇ *m, f* sleepwalker.
sonata [so'nata] *f* sonata.
sonda ['sõnda] *f* **-1.** *MED* probe. **-2.** *MED* [de alimentação] drip. **-3.** *NÁUT* depth finder. **-4.** *TEC* [para mineiração] bore. **-5.** *TEC* [petrolífera] drill. **-6.** *METEOR* weather balloon.
◆ **sonda espacial** *f* space probe.
sondagem [sõn'daʒẽ] (*pl* **-ns**) *f* **-1.** [com sonda - biliar] exploration; [- marítima, meteorológica] sounding; [- petrolífera] drilling. **-2.** [de opinião] survey.
sondar [4] [sõn'da(x)] *vt* **-1.** [ger] to probe. **-2.** *NÁUT* to sound. **-3.** *TEC* [terreno] to bore. **-4.** *TEC* [petróleo] to drill. **-5.** *METEOR* [atmosfera] to take soundings of. **-6.** [opinião] to survey. **-7.** *fig* [investigar] to fathom.
soneca [so'nɛka] *f* nap; **tirar uma ~** to take a nap.
sonegação [sonega'sãw] *f* **-1.** [ocultação] withholding; **~ de impostos** *ou* **fiscal** tax evasion. **-2.** [roubo] theft.

sonegador, ra [sonega'do(x), ra] ◇ *adj* [de impostos] fraudulent. ◇ *m, f* [de impostos] tax dodger.

sonegar [14] [sone'ga(x)] *vt* **-1.** [dinheiro, bens] to conceal. **-2.** [impostos] to dodge. **-3.** [roubar] to steal. **-4.** [informações] to withhold.

soneto [so'netu] *m* sonnet.

sonhador, ra [soɲa'do(x), ra] (*mpl* **-es**, *fpl* **-s**) ◇ *adj* dreaming. ◇ *m, f* dreamer.

sonhar [4] [so'ɲa(x)] ◇ *vt* [ter sonho com] to dream. ◇ *vi* **-1.** [ter sonho] to dream; ~ **com algo/alguém** to dream about sthg/sb; **nem sonhando!** in your dreams!; ~ **acordado** to daydream. **-2.** [desejar]: ~ **com algo** to dream of sthg; ~ **em fazer algo** to dream of doing sthg.

sonho ['soɲu] *m* **-1.** [ger] dream. **-2.** *CULIN* doughnut.

sono ['sonu] *m* **-1.** [período] sleep; ~ **leve/pesado** light sleep/heavy sleep; **pegar no** ~ to fall asleep. **-2.** [vontade de dormir]: **estar caindo** *ou* **morrendo de** ~ to be dead on one's feet; **estar com** *ou* **sentir** ~ to be *ou* feel sleepy; **estar sem** ~ not to be sleepy.

sonolência [sono'lẽnsja] *f* drowsiness.

sonolento, ta [sono'lẽntu, ta] *adj* sleepy.

sonoridade [sonori'dadʒi] *f* **-1.** [timbre, altura] sound quality. **-2.** [ressonância] resonance.

sonorizar [sonori'za(x)] *vt* **-1.** [filme] to make the soundtrack for. **-2.** [sala] to set up the sound for.

sonoro, ra [so'nɔru, ra] *adj* **-1.** [de som] resonant. **-2.** *GRAM* voiced.

sonoterapia [sonotera'pia] *f* sleep therapy.

sons [sõʃ] *pl* ▷ **som**.

sonso, sa ['sõnsu, sa] *adj* sly.

sopa ['sopa] *f* **-1.** *CULIN* soup; ~ **de lentilhas** lentil soup. **-2.** *fam* [facilidade] easy life; **ser** ~ to be a piece of cake. **-3.** *loc*: **dar** ~ [descuidar-se] to be careless; [estar disponível] to be going spare; [abundar] to be in abundance.

sopapo [so'papu] *m* slap; **dar um** ~ **em alguém** to slap sb.

sopé [so'pɛ] *m* foot.

sopeira [so'pejra] *f* (soup) tureen.

soporífero, ra [sopo'riferu, ra], *adj* **-1.** [que faz dormir] soporific. **-2.** *fig* [chato] boring.
◆ **soporífero** *m* [substância] soporific.

soporífico [sopo'rifiku] = **soporífero**

soprano [so'prãnu] ◇ *adj* soprano *(antes de subst).* ◇ *mf* soprano.

soprar [4] [so'pra(x)] ◇ *vt* **-1.** [com sopro] to blow. **-2.** *fig* [segredar] to whisper. ◇ *vi* [vento] to blow.

sopro ['sopru] *m* **-1.** [ar] puff. **-2.** [som - de vento] sigh; [- de fole] puff; [- de saxofone] soft sound; **instrumento de** ~ wind instrument. **-3.** [aragem] breeze. **-4.** *fig* [ânimo] breath. **-5.** *MED* murmur; ~ **cardíaco** heart murmur.

soquete [so'kɛtʃi] *f* [meia] ankle sock.

sordidez [soxdʒi'deʒ] *f* **-1.** [imundície] squalor. **-2.** [torpeza] sordidness.

sórdido, da ['sɔrdʒidu, da] *adj* **-1.** [imundo] squalid. **-2.** [torpe] sordid.

soro ['soru] *m* **-1.** *MED* serum. **-2.** [de leite] whey.

soropositivo, va [soropozi'tʃivu, va] ◇ *adj* seropositive. ◇ *m, f* seropositive person.

sóror ['sɔro(x)] *f RELIG* sister.

sorrateiramente [soxatejra'mẽntʃi] *adv* stealthily.

sorrateiro, ra [soxa'tejru, ra] *adj* stealthy.

sorridente [soxi'dẽntʃi] *adj* smiling.

sorrir [69] [so'xi(x)] *vi* to smile; ~ **(para)** to smile (at); [destino, fortuna *etc*] to smile on.

sorriso [so'xizu] *m* smile; **dar um** ~ **(para alguém)** to smile (at sb); ~ **amarelo** wry smile.

sorte ['sɔxtʃi] *f* **-1.** [ventura] luck; **boa** ~**!** good luck!; **dar** ~ [ter sorte] to be lucky; **dar** ~ **(para alguém)** to bring (sb) luck; **estar com** *ou* **ter** ~ to be lucky; **má** ~ bad luck; **que** ~**!** what luck!; **de** ~ [sortudo] lucky; **tirar a** ~ to draw lots; **tirar a** ~ **grande** [na loteria] to hit the jackpot; [enriquecer] to become rich; [ser afortunado] to do the right thing. **-2.** [acaso] chance; **tentar a** ~ to try one's luck; **por** ~ by chance. **-3.** [sina] fate. **-4.** [situação] lot. **-5.** [maneira]: **desta** ~ in this way; **de** ~ **que** in such a way that. **-6.** [espécie] sort; **toda** ~ **de iguarias** all sorts of delicacies.

sorteado, da [sox'tʃjadu, da] *adj* winning.

sortear [15] [sox'tʃja(x)] *vt* **-1.** [pessoa, bilhete] to draw lots for. **-2.** [rifar] to raffle.

sorteio [sox'teju] *m* **-1.** [de pessoa, bilhete] draw. **-2.** [rifa] raffle.

sortido, da [sox'tʃidu, da] *adj* **-1.** [abastecido] stocked. **-2.** [variado] assorted.

sortilégio [soxtʃi'lɛʒu] *m* **-1.** [bruxaria] sorcery. **-2.** [encantamento] enchantment.

sortimento [soxtʃi'mẽntu] *m* [provisão] stock.

sortir [60] [sox'tʃi(x)] *vt* **-1.** [abastecer]: ~ **algo com** *ou* **de** to supply sthg with. **-2.** [variar] to vary.
◆ **sortir-se** *vp* [abastecer-se]: ~**-se com** *ou* **de** to supply o.s. with.

sortudo, da [sox'tudu, da] ◇ *adj* lucky. ◇ *m, f* lucky person.

sorumbático, ca [sorũn'batʃiku, ka] *adj* gloomy.

sorvedouro [soxve'doru] *m* **-1.** [redemoinho] whirlpool; ~ **de dinheiro** *fig* a drain on resources. **-2.** [abismo] chasm.

sorver [5] [sox've(x)] *vt* **-1.** [ger] to inhale. **-2.** [beber] to sip. **-3.** [absorver] to absorb.

sorvete [sox'vetʃi] *m* **-1.** [com leite] ice cream. **-2.** [sem leite] sorbet.

sorveteiro, ra [soxve'tejru, ra] *m, f* ice-cream man.

sorveteria [soxvete'ria] *f* ice-cream parlour.

sósia ['sɔzja] *mf* double.

soslaio [soʒ'laju] ◆ **de soslaio** *loc adv* sideways.

sossegado, da [sose'gadu, da] *adj* quiet.

sossegar [14] [sose'ga(x)] *vt* & *vi* to calm down.

sossego [so'segu] *m* peace (and quiet).

sotaina [so'tãjna] *f* cassock.

sótão ['sɔtãw] (*pl* **-ãos**) *m* attic.

sotaque [so'taki] *m* accent.

sotavento [sɔta'vẽntu] *m NÁUT* lee; **a** ~ leeward.

soterrar [4] [sote'xa(x)] *vt* to bury.

soturno, na [so'tuxnu, na] *adj* **-1.** [triste] sad. **-2.** [amedrontador] frightening.

soutien [su'tʃjã] *m* = **sutiã.**

sova ['sɔva] *f* **-1.** [amassamento - uva, cacau] crushing; [- de massa] keading. **-2.** [surra] beating; **dar uma ~ em alguém** to beat sb up; **levar uma ~ (de alguém)** to take a beating (from sb).

sovaco [so'vaku] *m* armpit.

sovado, da [so'vadu, da] *adj* **-1.** [trabalhado] kneaded. **-2.** [espancado] beaten. **-3.** [usado, fatigado] worn out.

sovar [4] [so'va(x)] *vt* **-1.** [amassar - uva, cacau] to crush; [- massa] to knead. **-2.** [surrar] to beat up. **-3.** *fig* [roupa, couro] to tan.

sovina [so'vina] ◇ *adj* miserly. ◇ *mf* miser.

sovinice [sovi'nisi] *f* meanness; **ser pura ~** to be utterly mean.

sozinho, nha [sɔ'ziɲu, ɲa] *adj* **-1.** [desacompanhado] alone. **-2.** [solitário] all alone. **-3.** [único] by itself. **-4.** [por si só] by myself/yourself/himself etc.

SP (*abrev de* **Estado de São Paulo**) *n State of São Paulo.*

spam ['ijpãm] (*pl* **-s**) *m* COMPUT spam.

SPC (*abrev de* **Serviço de Proteção ao Crédito**) *m Brazilian service providing information on credit credit rating.*

spot [iʃ'pɔtʃi] *m* spotlight.

spray [iʃ'prej] *m* spray.

SQL (*abrev de* **Structured Query Language**) *f* SQL.

Sr. (*abrev de* **senhor**) *m* ≃ Mr.

Sra. (*abrev de* **senhora**) *f* ≃ Mrs.

SRF (*abrev de* **Secretaria da Receita Federal**) *f department of the Brazilian ministry of finance responsible for taxes and customs and excise.*

Sri Lanka [ˌsri'lãŋka] *n* Sri Lanka.

Srs. (*abrev de* **senhores**) *mpl* Messrs, Mr and Mrs.

srta (*abrev de* **senhorita**) *f* ≃ Miss.

staff [iʃ'tafi] *m* staff.

standard [iʃ'tãndaxdʒi] *adj inv* standard.

status [iʃ'tatus] *m* status; **~ quo** status quo.

STF (*abrev de* **Supremo Tribunal Federal**) *m Brazilian supreme federal tribunal responsible for the enforcement of the constitution and also heading the judiciary.*

STJ (*abrev de* **Superior Tribunal de Justiça**) *m* Brazilian higher court of justice.

strip-tease [iʃˌtripi'tʃizi] *m* striptease; **fazer um ~** to do a striptease.

sua ['sua] ▻ **seu.**

suado, da ['swadu, da] *adj* **-1.** [da suor] sweaty. **-2.** *fam fig* [difícil de obter] hard-earned.

suador, ra [swa'do(x), ra] *m* **-1.** [sudorífero] sudorific. **-2.** [dificuldade, esforço] sweat, hard job.

suar [4] ['swa(x)] ◇ *vt* **-1.** [transpirar] to sweat. **-2.** [roupa] to make sweaty. ◇ *vi* **-1.** [transpirar] to sweat; **~ em bicas** to sweat buckets; **~ frio** to come out in a cold sweat. **-2.** [verter umidade] to sweat. **-3.** *fam fig* [esforçar-se]: **~ por algo/para fazer algo** to sweat blood for sthg/to do sthg; **ela suou por esse emprego** she had to work hard for that job.

suas ['suaʃ] ▻ **seu.**

suástica ['swaʃtʃika] *f* swastika.

suave ['swavi] *adj* **-1.** [ger] mild. **-2.** [vinho, pele, cabelos] smooth. **-3.** [brisa, ritmo] gentle. **-4.** [cor] delicate. **-5.** [música, tecido] soft. **-6.** [terno - pessoa] charming; [- carícia] gentle; [- voz] soft. **-7.** [leve - trabalho] light; [- vida] easy; **em ~s prestações** in easy instalments.

suavidade [swavi'dadʒi] *f* **-1.** [ger] mildness. **-2.** [de pele, cabelos] smoothness. **-3.** [de brisa, música, ritmo] gentleness. **-4.** [de tecido, cor, brisa, música] softness. **-5.** [ternura] charm.

suavizar [4] [swavi'za(x)] *vt* **-1.** [abrandar] to tone down. **-2.** [amenizar] to ease. **-3.** [amaciar - pele, cabelo] to smooth; [- tecido] to soften.

◆ **suavizar-se** *vp* [amenizar-se] to ease.

subalimentado, da [subalimẽn'tadu, da] *adj* undernourished.

subalterno, na [subaw'tɛxnu, na] ◇ *adj* subordinate. ◇ *m, f* subordinate.

subchefe [sub'ʃɛfi] *mf* assistant director.

subconsciente [subkõn'sjẽntʃi] ◇ *adj* subconscious. ◇ *m* subconscious.

subcutâneo, nea [subku'tãnju, nja] *adj* subcutaneous.

subdesenvolvido, da [subdʒizĩnvow'vidu, da] ◇ *adj* **-1.** [não-desenvolvido] underdeveloped. **-2.** *pej* [atrasado] moronic. ◇ *m, f pej* [pessoa] moron.

subdesenvolvimento [subdizĩnvowvi'mẽntu] *m* underdevelopment.

subdividir [6] [subdʒivi'dʒi(x)] *vt*: **~ algo (em)** to subdivide sthg (into).

◆ **subdividir-se** *vp*: **~-se (em)** to be subdivided (into).

subemprego [subẽn'pregu] *m* **-1.** [trabalho] underpaid job. **-2.** [condição] underpaid work.

subentender [5] [subẽntẽn'de(x)] *vt* to infer.

◆ **subentender-se** *vp* to be inferred; **subentende-se que ...** it can be inferred that ...

subentendido, da [subẽntẽn'dʒidu, da] *adj* inferred.

◆ **subentendido** *m* innuendo.

subestimar [4] [subeʃtʃi'ma(x)] *vt* to underestimate.

subida [su'bida] *f* **-1.** [ato] climb. **-2.** [ladeira] slope. **-3.** [de preços] rise.

subir [61] [su'bi(x)] ◇ *vt* **-1.** [galgar] to climb (up). **-2.** [ir para cima, percorrer] to go up. **-3.** [escalar] to climb, to scale. **-4.** [aumentar] to raise. **-5.** [ascender] to climb. **-6.** [voz] to raise. ◇ *vi* **-1.** [ger] to go up; **~ a** *ou* **até** to go up to; **~ em** [árvore] to climb (up); [telhado, cadeira] to climb onto; **~ por** to go up; **~ à cabeça** *fig* to go to one's head. **-2.** [ascender - balão, neblina, fumaça] to rise; [- elevador, teleférico] to go up; [- em ônibus] to get on. **-3.** [socialmente] to go up in the world; **~ a/de** to rise from; **~ na vida** to get on in life. **-4.** [aumentar] to rise.

súbito, ta ['subitu, ta] *adj* sudden.
◆ **súbito** *adv* suddenly; **de ~** suddenly.
subjacente [subʒa'sẽntʃi] *adj* underlying.
subjazer [subʒa'ze(x)] *vi*: **as tramas políticas que subjaziam** the underlying political plots.
subjetividade [subʒetʃivi'dadʒi] *f* subjectivity.
subjetivo, va [subʒɛ'tʃivu, va] *adj* subjective.
subjugar [14] [subʒu'ga(x)] *vt* **-1.** [derrotar] to overpower. **-2.** [dominar] to dominate. **-3.** [impor-se a] to supplant. **-4.** [moralmente] to subdue.
subjuntivo [subʒũn'tʃivu] *m* subjunctive.
sublevação [subleva'sãw] (*pl* **-ões**) *f* uprising.
sublevar [4] [suble'va(x)] *vt*: **~ alguém (contra algo)** to stir up sb (against sthg).
◆ **sublevar-se** *vp*: **~-se (contra algo)** to rebel (against sthg).
sublimação [sublima'sãw] (*pl* **-ões**) *f* **-1.** [engrandecimento] exaltation. **-2.** [de desejos] sublimation.
sublimar [4] [subli'ma(x)] *vt* **-1.** [engrandecer] to exalt. **-2.** [desejos] to sublimate.
sublime [su'blimi] *adj* sublime.
sublinhar [4] [subli'ɲa(x)] *vt* **-1.** [palavras] to underline. **-2.** [enfatizar] to emphasize.
sublocar [12] [sublo'ka(x)] *vt* to sublet.
sublocatário, ria [subloka'tarju, rja] *m, f* subtenant.
submarino, na [subma'rinu, na] *adj* underwater.
◆ **submarino** *m* submarine.
submergir [78] [submex'ʒi(x)] *vt & vi* to submerge.
submersão [submex'sãw] (*pl* **-ões**) *f* submersion.
submeter [5] [subme'te(x)] *vt* **-1.** [dominar] to subdue. **-2.** [para apreciação]: **~ algo a** to submit sthg to. **-3.** [sujeitar]: **~ alguém/algo a algo** to subject sb/sthg to sthg.
◆ **submeter-se** *vp* **-1.** [render-se] to surrender. **-2.** [sujeitar-se]: **~ a algo** to undergo sthg; **~ a alguém** to submit to sb.
submissão [submi'sãw] *f* **-1.** [sujeição, obediência] submission. **-2.** [apatia] lack of determination.
submisso, sa [sub'misu, sa] *adj* submissive.
submundo [sub'mũndu] *m* underworld.
subnutrição [subnutri'sãw] *f* malnutrition.
subnutrido, da [subnu'tridu, da] *adj* malnourished.
subordinado, da [suboxdʒi'nadu, da] <> *adj* subordinate. <> *m,f* [subalterno] subordinate.
subordinar [4] [suboxdʒi'na(x)] *vt* **-1.** [ger] to subordinate. **-2.** [sujeitar] to subject.
◆ **subordinar-se** *vp* [sujeitar-se]: **~-se a algo/alguém** to subject o.s. to sthg/sb.
subornar [4] [subox'na(x)] *vt* to bribe.
suborno [su'boxnu] *m* bribe.
subproduto [subpro'dutu] *m* by-product.
sub-reptício, cia [subxrep'tʃisju, sja] *adj* surreptitious.
subscrever [5] [subʃkre've(x)] <> *vt* **-1.** [assinar] to sign. **-2.** [aprovar] to subscribe to. **-3.** [arrecadar] to collect. <> *vi* **-1.** [aceder]: **~ a** to endorse *UK*, to indorse *US*. **-2.** [contribuir]: **~ (com algo) para algo** to contribute (sthg) to sthg.
◆ **subscrever-se** *vp* [assinar] to sign; **subscrevemo-nos** *fml* & *COM* we remain; **atenciosamente, subscrevemo-nos** *fml* & *COM* we remain, yours sincerely.
subscrição [subʃkri'sãw] (*pl* **-ões**) *f* **-1.** [ato de assinatura] signing. **-2.** [contribuição] contribution.
subscrito, ta [subʃ'kritu, ta] <> *pp* ▷ **subscrever**. <> *adj* undersigned. <> *m, f* undersigned.
subsecretário, ria [subsekre'tarju, rja] *m, f* undersecretary.
subseqüente [subse'kwẽntʃi] *adj* subsequent; **~ (a)** subsequent (to).
subserviência [subsexvjẽnsja] *f* subservience.
subserviente [subsex'vjẽntʃi] *adj* subservient, servile; **~ (a)** subservient (towards).
subsidiar [15] [subzi'dʒja(x)] *vt* to subsidize.
subsidiário, ria [subzi'dʒjarju, rja] *adj* subsidiary.
◆ **subsidiária** *f* [empresa] subsidiary.
subsídio [sub'zidʒju] *m* **-1.** [contribuição] contribution. **-2.** [estatal] subsidy.
◆ **subsídios** *mpl* [dados, contribuições] information *(sg)*.
subsistência [subziʃ'tẽnsja] *f* [sustento, subrevivência] subsistence; **de ~** subsistence *(antes de subst)*.
subsistir [6] [subziʃ'tʃi(x)] *vi* **-1.** [existir] to exist. **-2.** [persistir] to remain. **-3.** [sobreviver] to survive.
subsolo [sub'sɔlu] *m* **-1.** [da terra] subsoil. **-2.** [de prédio] basement.
substância [subʃ'tãnsja] *f* substance; **em ~** in essence.
substancial [subʃtãn'sjaw] (*pl* **-ais**) <> *adj* substantial. <> *m* [essência] essence.
substantivo, va [subʃtãn'tʃivu, va] *adj* **-1.** [essencial] essential. **-2.** *GRAM* substantive.
◆ **substantivo** *m GRAM* noun.
substituição [subʃtʃitwi'sãw] (*pl* **-ões**) *f* substitution, replacement.
substituir [74] [subʃtʃi'twi(x)] *vt* to substitute, to replace.
substituto, ta [subʃtʃi'tutu, ta] <> *adj* substitute *(antes de subst)*, replacement *(antes de subst)*. <> *m, f* substitute, replacement.
subterfúgio [subtex'fuʒju] *m* subterfuge.
subterrâneo, nea [subte'xãnju, nja] *adj* underground.
◆ **subterrâneos** *mpl* underground movements.
subtítulo [sub'tʃitulu] *m* subtitle.
subtotal [subto'taw] (*pl* **-ais**) *m* subtotal.
subtração [subtra'sãw] (*pl* **-ões**) *f* **-1.** [furto] theft. **-2.** [dedução] deduction. **-3.** *MAT* subtraction.
subtrair [68] [subtra'i(x)] <> *vt* **-1.** [furtar] to steal. **-2.** [deduzir] to deduct. **-3.** *MAT* to subtract. <> *vi MAT* to subtract.
◆ **subtrair-se** *vp* [esquivar-se]: **~-se a algo** to dodge sthg.
subumano, na [subju'mãnu, na] *adj* subhuman.
suburbano, na [subux'bãnu, na] <> *adj* **-1.** [do subúrbio] suburban. **-2.** *pej* [atrasado] backward.

◇ *m, f* **-1.** [morador] suburbanite. **-2.** *pej* [atrasado] moron.
subúrbio [su'buxbju] *m* suburb.
subvenção [subvẽn'sãw] (*pl* **-ões**) *f* subsidy.
subvencionar [4] [subvẽnsjo'na(x)] *vt* to subsidize.
subversão [subvex'sãw] *f* subversion.
subversivo, va [subvex'sivu, va] ◇ *adj* subversive. ◇ *m, f* [pessoa] subversive.
subverter [5] [subvex'te(x)] *vt* **-1.** [desordenar] to subvert. **-2.** [agitar] to incite. **-3.** [arruinar] to upset.
sucata [su'kata] *f* scrap metal.
sucção [suk'sãw] *f* suction.
sucedâneo, nea [suse'dãnju, nja] ◇ *adj* substitute. ◇ *m, f* substitute.
suceder [5] [suse'de(x)] *vi* **-1.** [acontecer] to happen. **-2.** [seguir-se a]: ~ **a algo/alguém** to follow (on from) sthg/sb.
◆ **suceder-se** *vp* **-1.** [seguir-se]: **sucedem-se os governantes, mas nada muda** rulers come and go but nothing changes. **-2.** [repetir-se]: **os dias se sucediam e ele não regressava** day followed day and still he didn't return.
sucedido, da [suse'dʒidu, da] *m*: **vou lhe contar o** ~ I'll tell you what happened.
sucessão [suse'sãw] (*pl* **-ões**) *f* succession.
sucessivo, va [suse'sivu, va] *adj* successive; **crimes** ~**s** a succession of crimes.
sucesso [su'sɛsu] *m* **-1.** [êxito] success; **fazer** *ou* **ter** ~ to be successful; **com/sem** ~ successfully/unsuccessfully; **de** ~ successful. **-2.** [música, filme] hit; **ser um** ~ to be a hit.
sucessor, ra [suse'so(x), ra] *m, f* successor.
sucinto, ta [su'sĩntu, ta] *adj* succinct.
suco ['suku] *m* juice.
suculento, ta [suku'lẽntu, ta] *adj* succulent.
sucumbir [6] [sukũn'bi(x)] *vi* **-1.** [vergar]: ~ **a algo** to yield to sthg. **-2.** [ceder]: ~ **a algo** to succumb to sthg. **-3.** [morrer]: ~ **(a algo)** to succumb (to sthg).
sucursal [sukux'saw] (*pl* **-ais**) *f* **-1.** [de empresa, loja] branch. **-2.** [de jornal, emissora] subsidiary.
SUDAM (**Superintendência do Desenvolvimento da Amazônia**) *f body overseeing the use of resources for the development of the Amazon region.*
sudanês, esa [suda'neʃ, eza] ◇ *adj* Sudanese. ◇ *m, f* Sudanese.
Sudão [su'dãw] *n* Sudan.
SUDENE (*abrev de* **Superintendência do Desenvolvimento do Nordeste**) *f body responsible for overseeing economic and financial incentives in northeastern Brazil.*
sudeste [su'dɛʃtʃi] ◇ *adj* south-east. ◇ *m* south-east.
súdito, ta ['sudʒitu, ta] *m, f* subject.
sudoeste [su'dwɛʃtʃi] ◇ *adj* south-west. ◇ *m* south-west.
Suécia ['swɛsja] *n* Sweden.
sueco, ca ['swɛku, ka] ◇ *adj* Swedish. ◇ *m, f* Swede.
◆ **sueco** *m* [língua] Swedish.
suéter ['swɛte(x)] (*pl* **-es**) *m ou f* sweater.
suficiência [sufi'sjẽnsja] *f* sufficiency.
suficiente [sufi'sjẽntʃi] ◇ *adj* sufficient. ◇ *m*: **tenho o** ~ **até amanhã** I have enough until tomorrow.
sufixo [su'fiksu] *m* suffix.
suflê [su'fle] *m* soufflé.
sufocação [sufoka'sãw] (*pl* **-ões**) *f* **-1.** [ger] suffocation. **-2.** *fig* [opressão] oppression.
sufocante [sufo'kãntʃi] *adj* **-1.** [ger] suffocating. **-2.** *fig* [opressivo] oppressive.
sufocar [12] [sufo'ka(x)] ◇ *vt* **-1.** [asfixiar] to suffocate. **-2.** *fig* [oprimir] to oppress. **-3.** *fig* [debelar] to crush. ◇ *vi* [asfixiar-se] to be stifled.
◆ **sufocar-se** *vp* [asfixiar-se] to be suffocated.
sufoco [su'foku] *m* **-1.** [aflição] dread; **que** ~**!** how dreadful!; **ser um** ~ to be dreadful. **-2.** [dificuldade] hassle; **deixar alguém no** ~ to leave sb in the lurch; **passar (por) um** ~ to have a hard time.
sufrágio [su'fraʒju] *m* **-1.** [voto] vote; ~ **universal** universal suffrage. **-2.** [apoio] support.
sugar [14] [su'ga(x)] *vt* **-1.** [por sucção] to suck. **-2.** *fig* [extorquir] to extort; ~ **o sangue de alguém** to get every last drop of blood out of sb.
sugerir [57] [suʒe'ri(x)] *vt* to suggest; ~ **algo a alguém** to suggest sthg to sb.
sugestão [suʒeʃ'tãw] (*pl* **-ões**) *f* **-1.** [ger] suggestion; **dar uma** ~ to make a suggestion. **-2.** [evocação, insinuação] hint.
sugestionar [4] [suʒeʃtʃjo'na(x)] *vt*: ~ **algo a alguém** to inspire sb with sthg.
◆ **sugestionar-se** *vp*: ~ **se con algo** to experience sthg.
sugestionável [suʒeʃtʃjo'navew] (*pl* **-eis**) *adj* impressionable.
sugestivo, va [suʒeʃ'tʃivu, va] *adj* **-1.** [evocativo] evocative. **-2.** [insinuante] suggestive.
Suíça ['swisa] *n* Switzerland.
suíças ['swisaʃ] *fpl* sideburns.
suicida [swi'sida] ◇ *adj* suicidal. ◇ *mf* [pessoa] suicidal person.
suicidar-se [7] [swisi'daxsi] *vp* to commit suicide.
suicídio [swi'sidʒju] *m* suicide; **ser** ~ *fig* [ser arriscado] to be suicide.
suíço, ça ['swisu, sa] ◇ *adj* Swiss. ◇ *m, f* Swiss.
sui generis [swi'ʒeneris] *adj inv* unique, sui generis.
suingar [swĩŋ'ga(x)] *vi* to dance the swing.
suingue ['swĩŋgi] *m* swing.
suíno, na ['swinu, na] *adj* pig *(antes de subst).*
◆ **suíno** *m* [porco] pig.
suíte ['switʃi] *f* suite.
sujar [4] [su'ʒa(x)] ◇ *vt* **-1.** [tornar sujo] to dirty. **-2.** *fig* [macular] to disgrace. ◇ *vi fam* [dar errado] to go wrong.
◆ **sujar-se** *vp* **-1.** [tornar-se sujo] to get dirty. **-2.** *fig* [macular-se] to disgrace o.s.
sujeição [suʒej'sãw] *f* **-1.** [subordinação] subordination. **-2.** [submissão] submission.

sujeira [su'ʒejra] *f* **-1.** [coisa suja] dirt. **-2.** [estado] dirtiness; **a sala estava uma ~ quando cheguei** the room was a dirty mess when I arrived. **-3.** *fam* [bandalheira] dirty trick; **fazer uma ~ com alguém** to play a dirty trick on sb.

sujeitar [4] [suʒej'ta(x)] *vt* **-1.** [submeter]: **~ algo/alguém a algo** to subject sthg/sb to sthg. **-2.** [apresentar]: **~ algo a algo** to submit sthg to sthg.
◆ **sujeitar-se** *vp* [submeter-se]: **~-se a algo** to subject o.s. to sthg.

sujeito, ta [su'ʒejtu, ta] <> *adj*: **~ a** subject to. <> *m, f* person.
◆ **sujeito** *m GRAM* subject.

sujo, ja ['suʒu, ʒa] <> *adj* **-1.** [imundo] dirty; **estar/ficar ~ com alguém** *fig* to be/fall out of favour with sb, to be in sb's bad books. **-2.** *fig* [mau-caráter] dishonest. <> *m, f fig* [pessoa] dishonest person.

sul ['suw] <> *adj* southern. <> *m* [região] south; **ao ~ de** to the south of.

sulcar [12] [suw'ka(x)] *vt* **-1.** [abrir sulcos em] to plough *UK*, to plow *US*. **-2.** [rosto] to line. **-3.** [singrar] to cut through.

sulco [suw'ku] *m* furrow.

sulfato [suw'fatu] *m* sulphate.

sulfúrico, ca [suw'furiku, ka] *adj* sulphuric.

sulista [su'liʃta] <> *adj* southern. <> *mf* southerner.

sultão, tana [suw'tãw, tãna] (*pl* **-ões**) *m, f* sultan (*f* sultana).

suma ['suma] ◆ **em suma** *loc adv* in short.

sumamente [suma'mẽntʃi] *adv* [extremamente] extremely.

sumário, ria [su'marju, rja] *adj* **-1.** [breve] brief. **-2.** [julgamento] summary. **-3.** [traje] skimpy.
◆ **sumário** *m* **-1.** [resumo] summary. **-2.** [no início de livro] table of contents. **-3.** *JUR*: **~ de culpa** indictment.

sumiço [su'misu] *m* disappearance; **dar (um) ~ em** to do away with.

sumidade [sumi'dadʒi] *f*: **~ (em algo)** authority (in sthg).

sumido, da [su'midu, da] *adj* **-1.** [desaparecido] vanished; **andar ~** to have disappeared. **-2.** [voz] low. **-3.** [apagado] faint.

sumir [61] [su'mi(x)] *vi* to disappear; **~ com algo** to disappear with sthg.

sumo, ma ['sumu, ma] *adj* extreme; **~ sacerdote** high priest.
◆ **sumo** *m* [suco] juice.

sundae ['sãndej] *m* sundae.

sunga ['sũŋga] *f* [de banho] (swimming) trunks.

suntuoso, osa [sũn'twozu, ɔza] *adj* sumptuous.

suor ['swɔ(x)] (*pl* **-es**) *m* **-1.** [transpiração] sweat. **-2.** *fig* [trabalho]: **fiz esta casa com o meu próprio ~** I built this house by the sweat of my brow.

super ['supe(x)] *fam* <> *adj* [ótimo] super. <> *interj* super!

superabundante [ˌsuperabũn'dãntʃi] *adj* excessive.

superação [supera'sãw] (*pl* **-ões**) *f* overcoming; **é fundamental para a ~ do estresse** it's essential for overcoming stress.

superado, da [supe'radu, da] *adj* **-1.** [ultrapassado] outmoded, old-fashioned. **-2.** [resolvido] overcome.

superalimentar [4] [4] [superalimẽn'ta(x)] *vt* **-1.** [animais, pacientes] to overfeed. **-2.** [indústria, sistema] to supercharge.

superaquecer [25] [ˌsuperake'se(x)] *vt* & *vi* to overheat.

superaquecimento [ˌsuperakesi'mẽntu] *m* overheating.

superar [4] [supe'ra(x)] *vt* **-1.** [sobrepujar]: **~ alguém (em algo)** to outdo sb (in sthg); **~ o inimigo** to defeat an enemy; **superou a todos em velocidade** he surpassed everyone in terms of speed. **-2.** [recorde] to beat. **-3.** [expectativa, objetivos *etc*] to exceed. **-4.** [ultrapassar] to surpass. **-5.** [resolver] to overcome.
◆ **superar-se** *vp* **-1.** [melhorar]: **~-se (em algo)** to excel o.s. (in sthg). **-2.** [exceder-se] to excel o.s.

superávit [supe'ravitʃi] *m COM* surplus.

supercílio [super'siljul] *m* eyebrow.

superdotado, da [ˌsupexdo'tadu, da] <> *adj* **-1.** [em inteligência] (exceptionally) gifted. **-2.** *fam* [sexualmente] well endowed. <> *m, f* [em inteligência] (exceptionally) gifted person.

superestimar [4] [ˌsupereʃtʃi'ma(x)] *vt* to overestimate.

superestrutura [ˌsupereʃtru'tura] *f* superstructure.

superficial [supexfi'sjaw] (*pl* **-ais**) *adj* superficial.

superficialidade [supexfisjali'dadʒi] *f* superficiality.

superfície [supex'fisji] *f* **-1.** [parte externa] surface. **-2.** [extensão] area.

supérfluo, lua [su'pɛxflu, lua] *adj* superfluous.
◆ **supérfluo** *m* [gasto]: **vamos cortar o ~** we're going to cut out what is superfluous.

super-homem [ˌsuper'ɔmẽ] (*pl* **-ns**) *m* superman.

superintendência [ˌsuperĩntẽn'dẽnsja] *f* [órgão] management.

superintendente [ˌsuperĩntẽn'dẽntʃi] *mf* manager.

superior [supe'rjo(x)] (*pl* **-es**) <> *adj RELIG* superior. <> *m, f* [em hierarquia] superior.
◆ **superior** *adj* **-1.** [de cima] upper. **-2.** [mais alto] higher. **-3.** [maior] greater. **-4.** [melhor] better; **~ a** better than. **-5.** [excelente] first class. **-6.** *EDUC* higher; **escola ~** senior school; **curso ~** degree course.

superioridade [superjori'dadʒi] *f* superiority.

superlativo, va [supexla'tʃivu] *adj* superlative.
◆ **superlativo** *m GRAM* superlative.

superlotado, da [ˌsupexlo'tadu, da] *adj*: **~ (de)** overcrowded (with).

superlotar [ˌsupexlo'ta(x)] *vt* to pack.

supermercado [ˌsupexmex'kadu] *m* supermarket.

superpotência [ˌsupexpo'tẽnsja] *f* superpower.

superpovoado, da [ˌsupexpo'vwadu, da] *adj* overpopulated.

superprodução [ˌsupexprodu'sãw] (*pl* **-ões**) *f* **-1.** ECON overproduction. **-2.** CINE mega-production.

superproteger [26] [ˌsupexprote'ʒe(x)] *vt* to overprotect.

supersensível [ˌsupexsẽn'sivew] (*pl* **-eis**) *adj* hypersensitive.

supersônico, ca [ˌsupex'soniku, ka] *adj* supersonic.

superstição [supexʃtʃi'sãw] (*pl* **-ões**) *f* superstition.

supersticioso, osa [superʃtʃi'sjozu, ɔza] ◇ *adj* superstitious. ◇ *m, f* superstitious person.

supervisão [ˌsupexvi'zãw] (*pl* **-ões**) *f* **-1.** [ato] supervision. **-2.** [instância] supervisory authority.

supervisionar [4] [ˌsupexvizjo'na(x)] *vt* to supervise.

supervisor, ra [ˌsupexvi'zo(x), ra] *m, f* supervisor.

supetão [supe'tãw] ◆ **de supetão** *loc adv* all of a sudden.

suplantar [4] [suplãn'ta(x)] *vt* [sobrepujar]: ~ **algo/alguém (em algo)** to supplant sthg/sb (in sthg).

suplementar [4] [suplemẽn'ta(x)] ◇ *adj* extra. ◇ *vt* **-1.** [fornecer] to provide. **-2.** [servir de suplemento a] to supplement.

suplemento [suple'mẽntu] *m* **-1.** [suprimento] supply. **-2.** [complemento] supplement; ~ **policial** police reinforcement. **-3.** JORN supplement.

suplente [su'plẽntʃi] *mf* substitute.

súplica ['suplika] *f* plea.

suplicar [12] [supli'ka(x)] ◇ *vt* to beg for; ~ **algo a/de alguém** to beg sb for sthg. ◇ *vi* to plead.

suplício [su'plisju] *m* torture.

supor [45] [su'po(x)] *vt* **-1.** [ger] to suppose; **suponho que sim** I suppose so; **suponhamos que** let's suppose (that), supposing. **-2.** [pressupor] to presuppose.
◆ **supor-se** *vp* to be assumed.

suportar [4] [supox'ta(x)] *vt* **-1.** [sustentar] to support. **-2.** [resistir a] to withstand. **-3.** [tolerar] to bear.

suportável [supox'tavew] (*pl* **-eis**) *adj* bearable.

suporte [su'pɔxtʃi] *m* support.

suposição [supozi'sãw] (*pl* **-ões**) *f* [conjetura] assumption.

supositório [supozi'tɔrju] *m* suppository.

supostamente [supɔʃta'mẽntʃi] *adv* supposedly.

suposto, osta [su'pɔʃtu, oʃta] ◇ *pp* ▷ **supor**. ◇ *adj* supposed.
◆ **suposto** *m* [pressuposto] assumption.

supracitado, da [suprasi'tadu, da] ◇ *adj* aforementioned. ◇ *m, f*: **o** ~ the abovementioned.

supra-sumo [ˌsupra'sumu] *m*: **o** ~ **de algo** [máximo] the culmination of sthg; [irôn] the height of sthg.

supremacia [suprema'sia] *f* supremacy.

supremo, ma [su'premu, ma] *adj* **-1.** [amor, perdão, tribunal] supreme. **-2.** [qualidade] superior.
◆ **Supremo** *m*: **o Supremo** the Supreme Court.

supressão [supre'sãw] (*pl* **-ões**) *f* **-1.** [corte] cutback. **-2.** [eliminação] deletion. **-3.** [abolição] abolition. **-4.** [omissão] suppression.

suprimento [supri'mẽntu] *m* supply.

suprimir [6] [supri'mi(x)] *vt* **-1.** [cortar] to cut back. **-2.** [eliminar] to delete. **-3.** [abolir] to abolish. **-4.** [omitir] to suppress.

suprir [6] [su'pri(x)] ◇ *vt* **-1.** [prover]: ~ **alguém de** *ou* **com algo** to supply sb with sthg. **-2.** [substituir]: ~ **algo por algo** to substitute sthg with sthg. **-3.** [fazer as vezes de] to replace. **-4.** [preencher] to meet; ~ **a falta de algo** to make up for the lack of sthg; ~ **a falta de alguém** to make up for sb's absence. **-5.** [perfazer] to make up. ◇ *vi* **-1.** [fazer as vezes de]: ~ **por** to stand in for. **-2.** [preencher]: ~ **a** to meet; ~ **a falta** to make up for the lack.

supurar [4] [supu'ra(x)] *vi* to suppurate, to fester.

surdez [sux'deʒ] *f* deafness.

surdina [sux'dʒina] *f* MÚS mute.
◆ **em surdina** *loc adv* on the quiet.

surdo, da ['suxdu, da] ◇ *adj* **-1.** MED deaf. **-2.** [som] muffled. **-3.** [consoante] voiceless. ◇ *m, f* [pessoa] deaf person.
◆ **surdo** *m* MÚS [de bateria] *kind of drum*.

surdo-mudo, surda-muda ['suxdu'mudu, 'suxda'muda] (*mpl* **surdos-mudos**, *fpl* **surdas-mudas**) ◇ *adj* [pessoa] deaf and dumb. ◇ *m, f* [pessoa] deaf mute.

surfar [4] [sux'fa(x)] *vi* to surf.

surfe ['suxfi] *m* surfing.

surfista [sux'fiʃta] *mf* surfer.

surgimento [suxʒi'mẽntu] *m* emergence.

surgir [52] [sux'ʒi(x)] *vi* **-1.** [aparecer] to appear. **-2.** [sobrevir] to arise; ~ **de** to come from.

Suriname [suri'nãmi] *n* Surinam.

surpreendente [surprjẽn'dẽntʃi] *adj* surprising.

surpreender [5] [surprjẽn'de(x)] ◇ *vt* **-1.** [ger] to surprise. **-2.** [apanhar em flagrante]: ~ **alguém (fazendo algo)** to catch sb (doing sthg). **-3.** [vislumbrar]: ~ **algo em algo** to glimpse sthg in sthg. ◇ *vi* [causar espanto] to be surprising.
◆ **surpreender-se** *vp* [espantar-se]: **~-se de/com algo** to be amazed by/at sthg.

surpreso, sa [sux'prezu, za] ◇ *pp* ▷ **surpreender**. ◇ *adj* surprised.
◆ **surpresa** *f* **-1.** [espanto] amazement. **-2.** [imprevisto] surprise; **fazer uma surpresa para alguém** to give sb a surprise; **que surpresa!** [em encontro casual] what a surprise!; **ser uma surpresa** to be a surprise; **de surpresa** by surprise. **-3.** [presente] surprise.

surra ['suxa] *f* thrashing; **dar uma** ~ **em alguém** to give sb a thrashing; **levar uma** ~ **(de alguém)** to get a thrashing (from sb).

surrado, da [su'xadu, da] *adj* **-1.** [espancado] beaten. **-2.** [muito usado] worn out.

surrar [4] [su'xa(x)] *vt* **-1.** [espancar] to beat up. **-2.** *ESP* to thrash. **-3.** [usar muito] to wear out.
surrealismo [suxea'liʒmu] *m* surrealism.
surrealista [suxea'liʃta] <> *adj* **-1.** *ARTE* surrealist. **-2.** *fig* [fora do normal] surreal. <> *mf* *ARTE* surrealist.
surrupiar [16] [suxu'pja(x)] *vt* to steal.
sursis [sux'si] *m (inv)* *JUR* suspended sentence.
surtar [sur'ta(x)] *vi* *fam* to go berserk.
surtir [6] [sux'tʃi(x)] <> *vt* [produzir] to bring about; ~ **efeito** to be effective. <> *vi* [funcionar] to work out.
surto ['suxtu] *m* **-1.** [irrupção] outburst. **-2.** [de doença] outbreak. **-3.** [de progresso, industrialização] surge.
suscetibilidade [susetʃibili'dadʒi] *f* **-1.** [melindre] touchiness. **-2.** [propensão] susceptibility.
suscetível [suse'tʃivɛw] (*pl* **-eis**) *adj* **-1.** [melindroso] sensitive. **-2.** [propenso]: ~ **a** susceptible to; ~ **de** liable to.
suscitar [4] [susi'ta(x)] *vt* **-1.** [provocar] to provoke. **-2.** [fazer surgir] to arouse. **-3.** [despertar] to awaken.
suspeição [suʃpej'sãw] (*pl* **-ões**) *f* suspicion.
suspeita [suʃ'pejta] *f* ▷ **suspeito.**
suspeitar [4] [suʃpej'ta(x)] <> *vt* [crer, supor]: ~ **que** to suspect (that). <> *vi* [desconfiar]: ~ **de alguém** to suspect sb; ~ **de que** to suspect that.
suspeito, ta [suʃ'pejtu, ta] <> *adj* **-1.** [que desperta suspeita] suspicious. **-2.** [de ser tendencioso]: **sou** ~ **para falar, mas ...** I'm biased in saying this but ... <> *m, f* [pessoa]: ~ **(de algo)** suspect (of sthg).
◆ **suspeita** *f* suspicion; **estar com suspeita de algo** to be suspected of having sthg.
suspender [6] [suʃpẽn'de(x)] *vt* **-1.** [ger] to suspend. **-2.** [levantar] to lift up. **-3.** [adiar] to postpone. **-4.** [encomenda] to cancel.
suspensão [suʃpẽn'sãw] (*pl* **-ões**) *f* **-1.** [ger] suspension. **-2.** [adiamento] postponement. **-3.** [de encomenda] cancellation. **-4.** [de sanções] lifting.
suspense [suʃ'pẽnsi] *m* suspense; **estamos assistindo um (filme de)** ~ we are watching a thriller; **fazer** ~ to create suspense.
suspenso, sa [suʃ'pẽnsu, sa] <> *pp* ▷ **suspender.** <> *adj* **-1.** [ger] suspended. **-2.** [levantado] held up. **-3.** [adiado] postponed. **-4.** [encomenda] cancelled. **-5.** [sanções] lifted.
suspensórios [suʃpẽn'sɔrjuʃ] *mpl* braces *UK*, suspenders *US*.
suspirar [4] [suʃpi'ra(x)] *vi* to sigh; ~ **de alívio** to sigh with relief; ~ **por algo** to long for sthg.
suspiro [suʃ'piru] *m* **-1.** [aspiração] sigh; **dar um** ~ to give a sigh. **-2.** *CULIN* meringue.
sussurrar [4] [susu'xa(x)] <> *vt & vi* to whisper.
sussurro [su'suxu] *m* whisper.
sustância [suʃ'tãnsja] *f* **-1.** [vigor] strength. **-2.** [de comida] sustenance.
sustar [4] [suʃ'ta(x)] *vt & vi* [deter-se] to stop.
sustentáculo [suʃtẽn'takulu] *m* **-1.** [base] support. **-2.** *fig* [base] mainstay.
sustentar [4] [suʃtẽn'ta(x)] *vt* **-1.** [ger] to support. **-2.** [afirmar]: ~ **que** to maintain (that). **-3.** [defender] to uphold.
◆ **sustentar-se** *vp* **-1.** [ger] to support o.s.; ~ **-se no ar** to hover. **-2.** [alimentar-se] to sustain o.s.
sustento [suʃ'tẽntu] *m* **-1.** [alimento] sustenance. **-2.** [manutenção] support.
suster [1] [suʃ'te(x)] *vt* **-1.** [sustentar] to hold up. **-2.** [conter] to keep in check.
◆ **suster-se** *vp* **-1.** [sustentar-se] to be supported. **-2.** [conter-se] to contain o.s. **-3.** [de pé] to hold o.s. up.
susto ['suʃtu] *m* fright; **dar um** ~ **em alguém** to give sb a fright; **levar** *ou* **tomar um** ~ to get a fright; **que** ~**!** what a fright!
sutiã [su'tʃjã] *m* bra.
sutil [su'tʃiw] (*pl* **-is**) *adj* subtle.
sutileza [sutʃi'leza] *f* subtlety.
sutilmente [sutʃiw'mẽntʃi] *adv* subtly.
Suva ['suva] *n* Suva.
suvenir [suve'ni(x)] *m* souvenir.

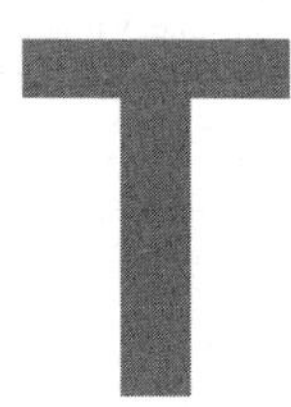

t, T *m* [letra] t, T.
tá ['ta] *fam* = **está.**
tabacaria [tabaka'ria] *f* tobacconist's.
tabaco [ta'baku] *m* tobacco.
tabagismo [taba'ʒiʒmu] *m* **-1.** [uso do tabaco] nicotine addiction. **-2.** [intoxicação] nicotine poisoning.
tabefe [ta'bɛfi] *m* *fam* slap; **dar um** ~ **em alguém** to slap sb; **levar um** ~ **de alguém** to be slapped by sb.
tabela [ta'bɛla] *f* **-1.** [quadro] table. **-2.** [lista] list; ~ **de preços** price list. **-3.: por** ~ [indiretamente] indirectly. **-4.** *loc*: **estar caindo pelas** ~**s** [estar fatigado, adoentado] to feel out of sorts; [estar em más condições] to be in a bad way.
tabelado, da [tabe'ladu, da] *adj* **-1.** [produtos] price-controlled. **-2.** [preços] controlled. **-3.** [dados] listed.
tabelamento [tabela'mẽntu] *m* [controle de preços]: ~ **de preços** price control.
tabelar [4] [tabe'la(x)] *vt* **-1.** [fixar o preço de] to set the price of. **-2.** [dados] to list.
tabelião, liã [tabe'ljãw, ljã] (*mpl* **-ães**, *fpl* **-s**) *m, f* notary public.

taberna [ta'bɛxna] *f* public house *UK*, tavern *US*.
tabique [ta'biki] *m* [parede divisória] dividing wall.
tablado [ta'bladu] *m* **-1.** [palco] stage. **-2.** [palanque] stand. **-3.** [estrado] dais.
tablete [ta'blɛtʃi] *m* **-1.** [de chocolate] bar. **-2.** [de manteiga] pat. **-3.** [medicamento] tablet.
tablóide [ta'blɔjdʒi] *m* tabloid.
tabu [ta'bu] <> *adj* taboo. <> *m* taboo.
tábua ['tabwa] *f* **-1.** [de madeira] board; ~ **corrida** *ARQUIT* wooden floor; ~ **de passar roupa** ironing board; ~ **de salvação** *fig* last resort. **-2.** [de mesa] leaf. **-3.** *MAT* table.
tabuada [ta'bwada] *f* **-1.** [tabela] multiplication table, times table. **-2.** [livro] book of tables.
tabulador [tabula'do(x)] *m* tab key.
tabular [4] [tabu'la(x)] *vt* to tabulate.
tabuleiro [tabu'lejru] *m* **-1.** [bandeja] tray. **-2.** *CULIN* baking tray. **-3.** [de jogo] board.
tabuleta [tabu'leta] *f* notice board.
taça ['tasa] *f* **-1.** [copo] glass. **-2.** [troféu] cup.
tacada [ta'kada] *f* **-1.** *ESP* strike. **-2.** *fig*: **de uma ~ só** [de uma só vez] in one go.
tacanho, nha [ta'kãɲu, ɲa] *adj* **-1.** [baixo] short. **-2.** [mesquinho] mean. **-3.** *fig* [sem visão] obtuse.
tacar [12] [ta'ka(x)] *vt* **-1.** *ESP* to strike. **-2.** [atirar] to hurl; ~ **um soco em alguém** to throw a punch at sb.
tacha ['taʃa] *f* **-1.** [prego] tack. **-2.** [em roupa, cadeira] stud.
tachar [4] [ta'ʃa(x)] *vt*: ~ **alguém/algo de algo** to brand sb/sth as sthg.
tacheado, da [ta'ʃjadu, da] *adj* studded.
tachinha [ta'ʃiɲa] *f* drawing pin *UK*, thumbtack *US*.
tacho ['taʃu] *m* [recipiente] pan, dish.
tácito, ta ['tasitu, ta] *adj* [implícito] tacit.
taciturno, na [tasi'tuxnu, na] *adj* [introverso, sério] taciturn.
taco ['taku] *m* **-1.** [*ESP* - bilhar] cue; [- golfe] club; [- hóquei] stick; [- pólo] mallet. **-2.** [de assoalho] block.
tadinho, nha [ta'dʒiɲu, ɲa] *interj fam* ▻ **coitado.**
tafetá [tafe'ta] *m* taffeta.
tagarela [taga'rɛla] <> *adj* prattling, chattering. <> *mf* chatterbox.
tagarelar [4] [tagare'la(x)] *vi* to prattle, to chatter.
tagarelice [tagare'lisi] *f* prattle, chatter.
tailandês, esa [tajlãn'deʃ, eza] <> *adj* Thai. <> *m, f* Thai.
◆ **tailandês** *m* [língua] Thai.
Tailândia [taj'lãndʒja] *n* Thailand.
tailleur [taj'ɛ(x)] *m* (woman's) suit.
tainha [ta'iɲa] *f* mullet.
taipa ['tajpa] *f*: **casa de ~** mud hut; **parede de ~** mud wall.
Taipei [taj'pej] *n* Taipei.
tais [tajʃ] *pl* ▻ **tal.**
Taiti [taj'tʃi] *n* Tahiti.
Taiwan [taj'wã] *n* Taiwan.
taiwanês, esa [tajwãneʃ, eza] <> *adj* Taiwanese. <> *m, f* Taiwanese.
tal ['taw] (*pl* **tais**) <> *adj* **-1.** [ger] such; **eu nunca diria ~ coisa** I would never say such a thing; **não me misturo com tais pessoas** I don't mix with such people; **isso nunca teve ~ repercussão** this never had such an effect; **a dor foi ~, que desmaiei** the pain was such that I fainted. **-2.** [este, aquele]: **não existe ~ hotel** there is no such hotel; **a ~ respeito** on that subject; **o ~ vizinho** that neighbour. **-3.** [valor indeterminado]: **na avenida ~** in such and such street. **-4.** [introduz um exemplo ou uma enumeração]: ~ **como** such as. **-5.** [introduz uma comparação]: ~ **qual** just like; ~ **pai,** ~ **filho** like father, like son. <> *pron indef* [isto, aquilo]: **por ~** for that reason; **fulano de ~** Joe Bloggs. <> *mf*: **ele se acha o ~** he thinks he's it.
◆ **que tal** *loc* [pedindo opinião]: **que ~?** what do you think?; **que ~ (tomarmos) um drinque?** what about (us having) a drink?
◆ **e tal** *loc*: **ele é simpático e ~, mas ineficiente** he's nice and all that, but inefficient; **ela tem trinta e ~ anos** she's thirty something.
◆ **um tal de** *loc*: **um ~ de João** John what's-his-name; **foi um ~ de gente reclamar** there were loads of people complaining.
◆ **a tal ponto que** *loc conj* such a point that.
◆ **de tal maneira que** *loc conj* in such a way that.
tala ['tala] *f MED* splint.
talão [ta'lãw] (*pl* **-ões**) *m* **-1.** [bloco] book; ~ **de cheques** cheque book *UK*, check book *US*. **-2.** [canhoto] stub.
talco ['tawku] *m* **-1.** [material] talc. **-2.** [produto de higiene] talcum powder.
talento [ta'lẽntu] *m* **-1.** [aptidão] ability; **uma pessoa de ~** a very able person. **-2.** [pessoa talentosa] talented person.
talentoso, osa [talẽn'tozu, ɔza] *adj* talented.
talhado, da [ta'ʎadu, da] *adj* **-1.** [leite] curdled. **-2.** [madeira] carved. **-3.** [apropriado] appropriate. **-4.** [cortado]: **um terno bem ~** a well-cut suit.
talhar [4] [ta'ʎa(x)] <> *vt* [madeira] to carve. <> *vi* [leite] to curdle.
talharim [taʎa'rĩ] (*pl* **-ns**) *m* tagliatelle.
talhe ['taʎi] *m* [de roupa] cut.
talher [ta'ʎɛ(x)] (*pl* **-es**) *m* place setting; ~ **es** cutlery *(sg)*.
talho ['taʎu] *m* [corte] cut.
talismã [taliʒ'mã] *m* talisman.
talo ['talu] *m BOT* stalk, stem.
talude [ta'ludʒi] *m* slope.
taludo, da [ta'ludu, da] *adj* **-1.** [corpulento - adulto] stout; [- criança] plump. **-2.** [de talo resistente] strong-stalked, thick-stemmed.
talvez [taw'veʒ] *adv* maybe, perhaps; ~ **ele esteja certo** maybe he is right.
tamanco [ta'mãŋku] *m* clog.
tamanduá [tamãn'dwa] *m* anteater.
tamanho, nha [ta'mãɲu, ɲa] *adj* **-1.** [tão grande]: **seu erro foi ~ que ele pediu desculpas** his

mistake was so great he apologized. **-2.** [tão notável]: **ele é um ~ escritor** he is such a great author.

◆ **tamanho** *m* size; **de que ~ é?** what size is it?; **em ~ natural** life-size, life-sized; **um prédio que não tem ~** *ou* **do ~ de um bonde** *fam* an enormous building.

tamanho-família [ta,mãɲufa'milja] *adj inv* **-1.** [garrafa, caixa] family-size. **-2.** *fig* [casa, carro] family *(antes de subst).*

tâmara ['tãmara] *f* date.

tamarindo [tama'rĩndu] *m* tamarind.

também [tãn'bẽ] <> *adv* **-1.** [igualmente] too; **ele ~ é inteligente** he's intelligent, too, he too is intelligent; **quero um café – eu ~** I want a coffee – so do I *ou* me too; **sou do Rio, e ele ~ é** I'm from Rio, and so is he; **ela não viajou, e eu ~ não** she didn't go, and neither did I; **ele não fala inglês, e eu ~ não** he doesn't speak English, and neither do I. **-2.** [além disso] too. <> *interj* [não é de surpreender] hardly surprising!

tambor [tãn'bo(x)] (*pl* **-es**) *m* drum.

tamborete [tãnbo'retʃi] *m* [banco] stool.

tamborilar [4] [tãnbori'la(x)] *vi* [tocar] to drum.

tamborim [tãnbo'rĩ] (*pl* **-ns**) *m* tambourine.

Tâmisa ['tãmiza] *n*: **o (rio) ~** the (river) Thames.

tampa ['tãnpa] *f* **-1.** [de caixa, privada, panela] lid. **-2.** [de garrafa] cap.

tampado, da [tãn'padu, da] *adj*: **a panela está tampada** the saucepan is covered.

tampão [tãn'pãw] (*pl* **-ões**) *m* **-1.** [de pia, banheira] plug. **-2.** MED compress. **-3.** [vaginal] tampon. **-4.** [de poço, esgoto] bung.

tampar [4] [tãn'pa(x)] *vt* **-1.** [com tampa - ger] to put a lid on; [- em garrafa] to put a top on. **-2.** [tapar] to cover.

tampinha [tãn'piɲa] <> *f* [tampa pequena] bottle top. <> *mf fam* [pessoa baixa] dumpy person.

tampo ['tãnpu] *m* **-1.** [de privada] seat, lid. **-2.** [de mesa] top.

tampouco [,tãn'poku] *adv*: **não foi à reunião e ~ justificou sua ausência** he didn't turn up at the meeting, nor did he justify his absence.

Tananarive [tanana'rivi] *n* Antananarivo.

tanga ['tãŋga] *f* **-1.** [roupa indígena] loincloth. **-2.** [biquíni] G-string.

Tanganica [tãŋga'nika] *n*: **o (lago) ~** Lake Tanganyika.

tangente [tãn'ʒẽntʃi] *f* tangent; **escapar pela ~** *fig* to narrowly escape.

tanger [26] [tãn'ʒe(x)] <> *vt* [instrumento] to play; [sinos] to ring. <> *vi* **-1.** [sinos] to ring. **-2.** [dizer respeito]: **no que tange a** with regard to, as regards.

tangerina [tãnʒe'rina] *f* tangerine.

tangível [tãn'ʒivew] (*pl* **-eis**) *adj fig* **-1.** [alcançável] attainable. **-2.** [real] tangible.

tango ['tãŋgu] *m* tango.

tanque ['tãŋki] *m* **-1.** MIL tank. **-2.** [de lavar roupa] washtub. **-3.** [reservatório] reservoir.

tantã [tãn'tã] *adj fam* [maluco] crazy.

tanto, ta ['tãntu, ta] <> *adj* **-1.** [tão grande] so much; **~ tempo** so much time. **-2.** [tão numeroso] so many; **ela tem trinta e ~s anos** he is thirty something; **~ ... quanto** as many ... as; **tanta gente** so many people. <> *pron* so much; **pode ficar com o lápis, já tenho ~s** you can keep the pencil, I already have so many.

◆ **tanto** <> *m*: **um ~ de** some. <> *adv* so much; **ela trabalha ~** she works so much; **~ quanto** as much as; **~ ... como** both ... and; **nem ~ assim** not that much; **~ melhor** all the better; **se ~** if that.

◆ **tantas** *fpl*: **às tantas** the early hours of the morning.

◆ **e tanto** *loc adj*: **é um professor e ~** he's an amazing teacher.

◆ **tanto que** *loc conj* so much so that.

◆ **tanto faz** *loc adv* it's all the same.

◆ **um tanto (ou quanto)** *loc adv*: **uma pessoa um ~ (ou quanto) difícil** a somewhat difficult person.

Tanzânia [tãn'zãnja] *n* Tanzania.

tão [tãw] *adv* so; **~ ... quanto** as... as; **~ logo** as soon as.

tão-só [tãw'sɔ] *adv* only.

tão-somente [tãosɔ'mẽntʃi] *adv* only.

tapa ['tapa] *m* [tabefe] slap; **dar um ~ em alguém** to slap sb; **levar um ~ de alguém** to be slapped by sb; **no ~** by force.

tapado, da [ta'padu, da] *adj* **-1.** [ger] covered. **-2.** *fam* [pessoa] thick.

tapar [4] [ta'pa(x)] *vt* **-1.** [ger] to cover. **-2.** [garrafa] to put the lid back on.

tapeação [tapja'sãw] (*pl* **-ões**) *f* **-1.** [engano] hoax. **-2.** [reparo, limpeza malfeitos] quick going-over.

tapear [15] [ta'pja(x)] *vt* [enganar] to fool.

tapeçaria [tapesa'ria] *f* **-1.** [tapete - de chão] rug; [- de parede] tapestry, wall hanging. **-2.** [loja] carpet shop. **-3.** [arte - de chão] rug-making; [- de parede] tapestry.

tapeceiro, ra [tape'sejru, ra] *m, f* **-1.** [vendedor] *seller of carpets and soft furnishings.* **-2.** [fabricante] *manufacturer of carpets and soft furnishings.*

tapete [ta'petʃi] *m* **-1.** [solto] rug; **~ de banheiro** bathmat. **-2.** [fixo] carpet.

tapioca [ta'pjɔka] *f* tapioca.

tapume [ta'pumi] *m* **-1.** [cerca de sebe] hedge. **-2.** [anteparo de madeira] fence. **-3.** [parede divisória] partition.

taquara [ta'kwara] *f* BOT bamboo; **voz de ~ rachada** gravelly voice.

taquicardia [takikax'dʒia] *f* palpitations *(pl)*, tachycardia.

taquigrafar [4] [takigra'fa(x)] <> *vt* to take shorthand. <> *vi* to write in shorthand.

taquigrafia [takigra'fia] *f* shorthand *UK*, stenography *US*.

taquígrafo, fa [ta'kigrafu, fa] *m, f* shorthand typist *UK*, stenographer *US*.

tara ['tara] *f* PSIC mania.

tarado, da [ta'radu, da] <> *adj* **-1.** [desequilibrado] unbalanced. **-2.** [sexualmente] depraved. **-3.** *fam fig* [fascinado]: **ser ~ por** to be mad about. <> *m, f* [desequilibrado] maniac; **~ (sexual)** (sexual) pervert.

tarar [4] [ta'ra(x)] *vi fam*: **~ por alguém/algo** to fall madly in love with sb/sthg.

tardar [4] [tax'da(x)] <> *vt* [retardar] to put off. <> *vi* [demorar-se, vir tarde] to delay; **~ a fazer algo** to take a long time to do sthg; **o mais ~** at the latest; **sem mais ~** without further delay.

tarde ['taxdʒi] <> *f* afternoon; **às cinco da ~** at five in the afternoon; **boa ~!** good afternoon!; **de** *ou* **à ~** in the afternoon; **hoje à ~** this afternoon; **ontem à ~** yesterday afternoon. <> *adv* late; **~ demais** too late; **mais ~** later; **antes ~ do que nunca** better late than never; **~ da noite** late at night.

tardinha [tax'dʒiɲa] *f* late afternoon; **à** *ou* **de ~** late in the afternoon.

tardio, dia [tax'dʒiu, dʒia] *adj* late.

tarefa [ta'rɛfa] *f* **-1.** [trabalho em geral] task. **-2.** [empreitada] job.

tarifa [ta'rifa] *f* **-1.** [preço - de gás, água] tariff; **~ alfandegária** customs duty; [- de transporte] fare. **-2.** [tabela de preços] price list.

tarifar [4] [tari'fa(x)] *vt* to price.

tarifaço [tari'fasu] *m general price rise in publicly-owned utilities.*

tarimba [ta'rĩnba] *f fig* [experiência] experience; **ter ~ (em/como algo)** to be an old hand at/as sthg.

tarimbado, da [tarĩn'badu, da] *adj*: **~ (em)** highly-experienced (in).

tarô [ta'ro] *m* tarot.

tarrafa [ta'xafa] *f* fishing net.

tarraxa [ta'xaʃa] *f* [rosca] screw.

tartaruga [taxta'ruga] *f* **-1.** [grande] turtle. **-2.** [pequena] tortoise; **pente de ~** tortoiseshell comb.

tascar [12] [taʃ'ka(x)] *vt fam*: **~ algo em alguém** to plant sthg on sb.

tasco ['taʃku] *m fam* bit.

Tasmânia [taʒ'mãnja] *n* Tasmania.

tataraneto, ta [tatara'nɛtu] *m* great-great-great-grandson (*f* -granddaughter).

tataravô, vó [tatara'vo, vɔ] *m, f* great-great grandfather (*f* -grandmother).

tatear [15] [ta'tʃja(x)] <> *vt* to feel. <> *vi* to feel one's way.

táteis ['tatejʃ] *pl* ⊳ **tátil**.

tatibitate [tatʃibi'tatʃi] *adj* [que troca consoantes - devido à idade] stumbling; [- por defeito] stammering.

tático, ca ['tatʃiku, ka] *adj* tactical.
◆ **tática** *f* **-1.** *MIL* tactic. **-2.** [ciência] tactics *(sg).* **-3.** *fam* [plano de ação] strategy.

tátil ['tatʃiw] (*pl* **-eis**) *adj* tactile.

tato ['tatu] *m* **-1.** [ger] touch. **-2.** *fig* [cautela]: **ter ~** to be tactful.

tatu [ta'tu] *m* armadillo.

tatuador, ra [tatwa'do(x), ra] *m, f* tattooist.

tatuagem [ta'twaʒẽ] (*pl* **-ns**) *f* **-1.** [desenho] tattoo. **-2.** [técnica] tattooing.

tatuar [4] [ta'twa(x)] *vt* to tattoo.

taurino, na [tawri'nu, na] <> *adj ASTRO* Taurus. <> *m, f ASTRO* Taurus.

tautologia [tawtolo'ʒia] *f* tautology.

taxa ['taʃa] *f* **-1.** [ger] rate; **~ de natalidade/crescimento** birth/growth rate; **~ de câmbio** exchange rate; **~ de conversão** *COM* conversion rate; **~ de juros** interest rate; **~ de retorno** *COM* rate of return; **~ bancária** bank rate; **~ fixa** *COM* flat rate; **~ de inscrição** registration fee; **~ de matrícula** enrolment fee. **-2.** [imposto] tax; **~ de embarque** airport tax; **~ de exportação** *COM* export duty; **~ rodoviária** road tax.

taxação [taʃa'sãw] *f* **-1.** [de impostos] taxation. **-2.** [de preços] fixing.

taxar [4] [ta'ʃa(x)] *vt* **-1.** [onerar com imposto] to tax. **-2.** [fixar o preço de] to fix.

taxativo, va [taʃa'tʃivu, va] *adj* [categórico] categorical; **ser ~ (em algo)** to be categorical (about sthg).

táxi ['taksi] *m* taxi *UK*, cab *US*; **~ aéreo** air taxi.

taxiar [tak'sja(x)] *vi* to taxi.

taxímetro [tak'simetru] *m* taxi meter.

taxinomia [taksino'mia] *f* taxonomy.

taxista [tak'siʃta] *mf* taxi driver *UK*, cab driver *US*.

tchã ['tʃã] *m fam* [charme] charm.

tchau ['tʃaw] *interj fam* bye, ciao.

tcheco, ca ['tʃɛku, ka] <> *adj* Czech. <> *m, f* Czech.
◆ **tcheco** *m* [língua] Czech.

tchecoslovaco, ca [tʃekoʒlo'vaku, ka] <> *adj* Czechoslovakian. <> *m, f* Czechoslovak.

Tchecoslováquia [tʃɛkoʒlo'vakja] *n* Czechoslovakia.

te ['tʃi] *pron pess* **-1.** [você] you. **-2.** [a, para, em você]: **~ mandei duas cartas** I sent you two letters.

tear [te'a(x)] (*pl* **-es**) *m* loom.

teatral [tʃja'traw] (*pl* **-ais**) *adj* **-1.** [ger] theatre *(antes de subst) UK*, theater *(antes de subst) US*. **-2.** *fig* [pessoa, comportamento] theatrical.

teatro ['tʃjatru] *m* **-1.** [ger] theatre *UK*, theater *US*; **~ de arena** theatre in the round; **~ de bolso** small theatre; **peça de ~** stage play; **~ de marionetes** puppet theatre; **~ rebolado** burlesque; **~ de variedades** variety show. **-2.** [*LITER* - gênero] playwriting; [- obras de um autor] plays *(pl).* **-3.** [curso] drama. **-4.** *MIL*: **~ de operações** theatre of war *UK*. **-5.** *fig* [palco] scene. **-6.** *fig*: **fazer ~** [exagerar] to dramatize.

teatrólogo, ga [tʃja'trɔlogu, ga] *m, f* dramatist.

teatro-revista [ˌtʃjatruxe'viʃta] (*pl* **teatros-revista**) *m* theatre review *UK*, theater review *US*.

tecelagem [tese'laʒẽ] (*pl* **-ns**) *f* weaving.

tecelão, lã [tese'lãw, lã] (*mpl* **-ões**, *fpl* **-s**) *m, f* weaver.

tecer [25] [te'se(x)] *vt* **-1.** [ger] to weave. **-2.** *fig* [fazer]: **~ elogios a alguém/algo** to praise sb/ sthg; **~ intrigas sobre/contra alguém** to create conspiracies about/against sb.
tecido [te'sidu] *m* **-1.** [têxtil] material. **-2.** *BIOL & ANAT* tissue.
tecla ['tɛkla] *f* **-1.** [ger] key; **~ de função** function key; **~ de saída** exit key; **~ de tabulação** tab key. **-2.** [de máquina de calcular, de gravador] button. **-3.** *loc:* **bater na mesma ~** *fig* to harp on about sthg.
tecladista [tekla'dʒiʃta] *mf MÚS* keyboard player.
teclado [te'kladu] *m* keyboard.
teclar [4] ['tekla(x)] ◇ *vt* to key (in) ◇ *vi COMPUT:* **~ (com alguém)** to chat (with sb); **você quer ~?** do you want to chat?
técnica ['tɛknika] *f* ⊳ **técnico**.
tecnicamente [tɛknika'mẽntʃi] *adv* technically.
técnico, ca ['tɛkniku, ka] ◇ *adj* technical. ◇ *m, f* **-1.** [profissional] technician. **-2.** [especialista] expert. **-3.** *ESP* coach.
◆ **técnica** *f* **-1.** [procedimentos, métodos] technique. **-2.** [conhecimento prático] skill.
tecnicolor [tekni'kɔlo(x)] *adj*: **em ~** (in) technicolour *UK*, (in) technicolor *US*.
tecnocrata [tekno'krata] *mf* technocrat.
tecnologia [tɛknolo'ʒia] *f* technology; **~ de ponta** latest technology.
tecnológico, ca [tɛkno'lɔʒiku, ka] *adj* technological.
teco ['tɛku] *m* [batida de uma bola em outra] hit; **dar um ~ em** [em bola] to hit; *fig* [em pessoa] to be angry with.
teco-teco [ˌtɛku'tɛku] (*pl* **teco-tecos**) *m* light aircraft.
tectônico, ca [katek'toniku, ka] *adj* tectonic.
◆ **tectônica** *f GEOL* tectonics *(sg)*.
tédio ['tɛdʒju] *m* tedium.
tedioso, osa [te'dʒjozu, ɔza] *adj* tedious.
Teerã [tee'rã] *n* Teheran.
Tegucigalpa [tegusi'kawpa] *n* Tegucigalpa.
teia ['teja] *f* **-1.** [ger] web; **~ de aranha** spider's web, cobweb. **-2.** *fig* [organização]: **~ de espionagem** espionage network.
teima ['tejma] *f* obstinacy.
teimar [4] [tej'ma(x)] ◇ *vt*: **~ que** to insist that. ◇ *vi* [insistir] to persist; **~ em fazer algo** to persist in doing sthg.
teimosia [tejmo'zia] *f* stubborness; **~ em fazer algo** obstinacy in doing sthg.
teimoso, osa [tej'mozu, ɔza] *adj* **-1.** [adulto] obstinate. **-2.** [criança] stubborn.
teipe ['tejpi] *m* magnetic tape.
Tejo ['tɛʒu] *n*: **o (rio) ~** the (river) Tagus.
tel. [tel] (*abrev de* **telefone**) *m* tel.
tela ['tɛla] *f* **-1.** [ger] canvas. **-2.** [de arame] wire netting. **-3.** *CINE, COMPUT & TV* screen.
telão [te'lãw] (*pl* **-ões**) *m* big screen.
tele ['tɛle] *pref* tele.
telecomandar [4] [tɛlekomãn'da(x)] *vt* to operate by remote control.
telecomando [tɛleko'mãndu] *m* remote control.
telecomunicação [tɛlekomunika'saw] (*pl* **-ões**) *f* telecommunication.
◆ **telecomunicações** *fpl* telecommunications.
teleconferência [telekõnferẽnsja] *f* teleconference.
telecurso [tɛle'kuxsu] *m* television course.
teleférico [tele'fɛriku] *m* **-1.** [de esqui] ski lift. **-2.** [bondinho] cable car.
telefonar [4] [telefo'na(x)] *vi* to (tele)phone, to call; **~ para alguém** to (tele)phone sb, to call sb.
telefone [tele'foni] *m* **-1.** [aparelho, linha] (tele)-phone; **estar/falar ao ~** to be on the phone; **~ celular** mobile phone *UK*, cellphone *US*; **~ sem fio** cordless phone; **~ público** public (tele)phone. **-2.** [número] (tele)phone number.
telefonema [telefo'nema] *m* (tele)phone call; **dar um ~ para alguém/algum lugar** to make a call to sb/somewhere.
telefonia [telefo'nia] *f* [sistema] telephone system.
telefônico, ca [tele'foniku, ka] *adj* telephone *(antes de subst)*; **chamada telefônica** (tele)phone call.
telefonista [telefo'niʃta] *mf* telephonist.
telefoto [tele'fɔtu] *f* telephoto.
telegrafar [4] [telegra'fa(x)] ◇ *vt* to telegraph. ◇ *vi* to telegraph; **~ a alguém** to telegraph sb.
telegrafia [telegra'fia] *f* telegraphy.
telegráfico, ca [tele'grafiku, ka] *adj* telegraphic.
telegrafista [telegra'fiʃta] *mf* telegraphist.
telégrafo [te'lɛgrafu] *m* **-1.** [aparelho] telegraph. **-2.** [local] telegraph office.
telegrama [tele'grãma] *m* telegram; **passar um ~** to send a telegram; **~ fonado** telemessage.
teleguiado, da [tɛle'gjadu, da] *adj* **-1.** [guiado a distância] remote-controlled; **míssil ~** guided missile. **-2.** *fig* [influenciado] (easily) led.
teleguiar [16] [tɛle'gja(x)] *vt* to operate by remote control.
telejornal [ˌtɛleʒox'naw] (*pl* **-ais**) *m TV* television news *(sg)*.
telejornalismo [tɛleʒoxna'liʒmu] *m* television journalism.
telenovela [ˌtɛleno'vɛla] *f TV* soap opera.

TELENOVELA

Telenovelas are very popular; episodes of these dramatized stories are broadcast daily on prime-time television. Although the main plot usually revolves around a love interest, the *telenovelas*, shown nationwide, often address important social issues. Having reached high technical standards, Brazilian *telenovelas* are currently exported to around 120 countries.

teleobjetiva [ˌtɛljobʒɛ'tʃiva] *f* telephoto lens.
telepatia [telepa'tʃia] *f* telepathy; **por ~** by telepathy.
telepático, ca [tele'patʃiku, ka] *adj* telepathic.
teleprocessamento [tɛleprosesa'mẽntu] *m* teleprocessing.

telescópico, ca [teleʃ'kɔpiku, ka] *adj* telescopic.
telescópio [teleʃ'kɔpju] *m* telescope.
telespectador, ra [tɛleʃpekta'do(x), ra] <> *adj* viewing. <> *m, f* viewer.
teletexto [tɛle'teʃtu] *m* teletext.
teletipo [tɛle'tʃipu] *m* teletype.
televisão [televi'zãw] (*pl* **-ões**) *f* **-1.** [ger] television; ~ **a cabo** cable television; ~ **a cores** colour television. **-2.** [empresa] television company.
televisionar [4] [televizjo'na(x)] *vt* to televise.
televisivo, va [televi'zivu, va] *adj* television *(antes de subst)*.
televisor [televi'zo(x)] (*pl* **-es**) *m* television.
telex [tɛ'lɛkiʃ] (*pl* **-es**) *m* telex; **passar um** ~ to send a telex.
telha ['teʎa] *f* **-1.** [de casa *etc*] tile. **-2.** *fam fig* [mente]: **dar na** ~ **de alguém fazer algo** to get it into sb's head to do sthg; **ter uma** ~ **de menos** to have a screw loose.
telhado [te'ʎadu] *m* roof.
telha-vã [ˌteʎa'vã] (*pl* **telhas-vãs**) *f* unlined roof.
telnet [tel'netji] (*pl* **-s**) *f* COMPUT telnet.
telões [tɛ'lõjʃ] *pl* = **telão**.
tema ['tema] *m* **-1.** [assunto - de redação, romance] theme; [- de palestra] subject. **-2.** MÚS theme. **-3.** [dever de casa] homework.
temático, ca [te'matʃiku, ka] *adj* thematic.
◆ **temática** *f* thematics *(sg)*.
temer [5] [te'me(x)] <> *vt* to fear; ~ **que** to fear that; ~ **fazer algo** to be afraid to do sthg, to be afraid of doing sthg. <> *vi* to be afraid; ~ **por alguém/algo** to fear for sb/sthg.
temerário, ria [teme'rarju, rja] *adj* **-1.** [audacioso, destemido] fearless. **-2.** [perigoso, arriscado] reckless.
temeridade [temeri'dadʒi] *f*: **ser uma** ~ [ser arriscado, perigoso] to be a foolhardy act; [ser atemorizador] to be terrifying.
temeroso, osa [teme'rozu, ɔza] *adj* **-1.** [medroso, receoso] afraid. **-2.** [amedrontador] dreadful.
temido, da [te'midu, da] *adj* [assustador] frightening.
temível [te'mivɛw] (*pl* **-eis**) *adj* fearsome.
temor [te'mo(x)] (*pl* **-es**) *m* fear.
tempão [tẽn'pãw] *m fam*: **um** ~ ages.
têmpera ['tẽnpera] *f* **-1.** [ger] tempera. **-2.** [de metais] tempering.
temperado, da [tẽnpe'radu, da] *adj* **-1.** [ferro, aço] hardened. **-2.** [clima] temperate. **-3.** [CULIN - condimentado] seasoned; [- marinado] marinated.
temperamental [tẽnperamẽn'taw] (*pl* **-ais**) <> *adj* temperamental. <> *mf* temperamental person.
temperamento [tẽnpera'mẽntu] *m* temperament.
temperança [tẽnpe'rãnsa] *f* temperance.
temperar [4] [tẽmpe'ra(x)] *vt* **-1.** [metal] to temper. **-2.** [CULIN - condimentar] to season; [- marinar] to marinate.
temperatura [tẽnpera'tura] *f* temperature; ~ **ambiente** room temperature.
tempero [tẽn'peru] *m* **-1.** [condimento] seasoning. **-2.** [vinha d'alho] marinade. **-3.** [sabor] flavour *UK*, flavor *US*.
tempestade [tẽnpeʃ'tadʒi] *f* storm; ~ **de areia** sandstorm; **fazer uma** ~ **em copo d'água** to make a mountain out of a molehill.
tempestuoso, osa [tẽnpeʃ'twozu, ɔza] *adj* [dia, tempo] stormy.
templo ['tẽnplu] *m* **-1.** [pagão] temple. **-2.** [cristão] church.
tempo ['tẽnpu] *m* **-1.** [ger] time; **o** ~ **todo** the whole time; **quanto** ~**?** how long?; **há quanto** ~ **você mora aqui?** how long have you been living here?; **não a vejo há muito** ~ it's a long time since I saw her; **há muito** ~ a long time ago; **não dá** ~ there isn't (enough) time; ~ **integral** full-time; **dar** ~ **ao** ~ to give things time; **ganhar/perder** ~ to gain/lose time; **em seu devido** ~ in due course; **em** ~ **hábil** in reasonable time; **a** ~ on time; **a** ~ **e a hora** at the appropriate time; **nos bons** ~**s** in the good times; **nesse meio** ~ in the meanwhile; **ao mesmo** ~ at the same time; **de** ~**s em** ~**s** from time to time; **esse vestido é do** ~ **do Onça** that dress went out with the ark. **-2.** METEOR weather; **previsão do** ~ weather forecast. **-3.** GRAM tense. **-4.** ESP: **primeiro/segundo** ~ first/second half. **-5.** [MÚS - divisão de compasso] time; [- velocidade de execução] timing.
tempo-quente [ˌtẽnpu'kẽntʃi] *m* [briga, discussão] heated words *(pl)*.
têmpora ['tẽnpora] *f* ANAT temple.
temporada [tẽnpo'rada] *f* **-1.** [ger] season; **baixa/alta** ~ high/low season. **-2.** [espaço de tempo] time.
temporal [tẽnpo'raw] (*pl* **-ais**) <> *adj* **-1.** [temporário] temporary. **-2.** [não-espiritual] temporal. <> *m* storm.
temporão, rã [tẽnpo'rãw, rã] *adj* [filho] premature.
temporário, ria [tẽnpo'rarju, rja] *adj* temporary.
tenacidade [tenasi'dadʒi] *f* tenacity.
tenaz [te'najʒ] <> *adj* [pessoa] tenacious. <> *f* [ferramenta] tongs *(pl)*.
tencionar [4] [tẽnsjo'na(x)] *vt*: ~ **algo/fazer algo** to be planning sthg/to do sthg.
tenda ['tẽnda] *f* tent; ~ **de oxigênio** oxygen tent.
tendão [tẽn'dãw] (*pl* **-ões**) *m* tendon.
tendência [tẽn'dẽnsja] *f* **-1.** [propensão] tendency; ~ **a** *ou* **para algo** tendency to *ou* towards sthg; ~ **a fazer algo** tendency to do sthg. **-2.** [vocação] inclination; ~ **a** *ou* **para algo** inclination towards sthg; ~ **a fazer algo** inclination to do sthg. **-3.** [da moda, música] trend.
tendencioso, osa [tẽndẽn'sjozu, ɔza] *adj* tendentious.
tendente [tẽn'dẽntʃi] *adj*: **ser** ~ **a fazer algo** to tend to do sthg.
tender [5] [tẽn'de(x)] *vt* **-1.** [ter tendência]: ~ **a** *ou* **para algo** to be inclined to *ou* towards sthg; ~

a fazer algo to tend to do sthg. **-2.** [ter vocação]: ~ **a** *ou* **para algo** to be inclined towards sthg; ~ **a fazer algo** to intend to do sthg. **-3.** [encaminhar-se]: ~ **a** *ou* **para algo** to move towards sthg; ~ **a fazer algo** to be closer to doing sthg.

têndertender ['tẽnde(x)] *m NÁUT* tender.

tendinite [tẽndʒi'nitʃi] *f MED* tendinitis.

tenebroso, sa [tene'brozu, za] *adj* **-1.** [ger] dark. **-2.** *fig* [terrível, horrível] horrendous.

tenente [te'nẽntʃi] *mf* lieutenant.

tenho ['teɲu] ⊳ **ter**.

tênis ['teniʃ] *m* **-1.** *inv ESP* tennis; ~ **de mesa** table tennis. **-2.** [calçado] trainer *UK*, sneaker *US*.

tenista [te'niʃta] *mf* tennis player.

tenor [te'no(x)] ◇ *m* tenor. ◇ *adj inv* [instrumento] tenor *(antes de subst)*.

tenro, ra ['tẽnxu, xa] *adj* **-1.** [ger] tender. **-2.** [recente, novo] new.

tensão [tẽn'sãw] (*pl* **-ões**) *f* **-1.** [ger] tension; ~ **pré-menstrual** pre-menstrual tension, PMT. **-2.** [pressão] pressure. **-3.** [voltagem] voltage.

tenso, sa ['tẽnsu, sa] *adj* **-1.** [ger] taut. **-2.** [pessoa, ambiente] tense.

tentação [tẽnta'sãw] (*pl* **-ões**) *f* temptation; ~ **de fazer algo** temptation to do sthg.

tentáculo [tẽn'takulu] *m* tentacle.

tentado, da [tẽn'tadu, da] *adj* **-1.** [atraído, seduzido] tempted; **estar** ~ **a fazer algo** to be tempted to do sthg. **-2.** [experimentado] attempted.

tentador, ra [tẽnta'do(x), ra] (*mpl* **-es**, *fpl* **-s**) *adj* tempting.

tentar [4] [tẽn'ta(x)] *vt* **-1.** [experimentar] to try. **-2.** [usar de meios para] to attempt; ~ **fazer algo** to try to do sthg. **-3.** [atrair] to tempt.

tentativa [tẽnta'tʃiva] *f* attempt; ~ **de fazer algo** attempt at doing sthg; ~ **de roubo** attempted robbery.

tênue ['tẽnwi] *adj* **-1.** [fraco - luz, voz, desejo] faint; [- sentimento] slight; [- argumento] tenuous. **-2.** [fino] flimsy. **-3.** [leve] slight.

teologia [tʃolo'ʒia] *f* theology.

teológico, ca [tʃjo'lɔʒiku, ka] *adj* theological.

teólogo, ga ['tʃjɔlogu, ga] *m, f* theologian.

teor ['tʃjo(x)] *m* **-1.** [conteúdo, significado] tenor. **-2.** [proporção de uma substância] content; **baixo** ~ **de nicotina** low nicotine content; ~ **alcoólico** alcohol content.

teorema [teo'rema] *m* theorem.

teoria [teo'ria] *f* theory.

teoricamente [ˌtjɔrika'mẽntʃi] *adv* theoretically.

teórico, ca [te'ɔriku, ka] ◇ *adj* theoretical. ◇ *m, f* theorist.

teorizar [4] [teori'za(x)] ◇ *vt* to theorize. ◇ *vi* **-1.** [expor teorias] to expound theories. **-2.** [discorrer teoricamente] to theorize; ~ **sobre algo** to theorize about sthg.

tépido, da ['tɛpidu, da] *adj* tepid, lukewarm.

ter [1] ['te(x)] ◇ *vt* **-1.** [ger] to have; ~ **razão** to be right. **-2.** [obter]: ~ **sucesso em algo** to be successful in sthg. **-3.** [sentir] to be; ~ **fome/pressa/calor** to be hungry/hurried/hot; **o que é que você tem?** what's wrong with you? **-4.** [contar]: **'quantos anos você tem?'** - **'tenho 30 anos'** [idade] 'how old are you?' - 'I'm 30'; **ele tem 2 metros de altura** [medida] he is 2 metres tall. **-5.** [proceder com]: ~ **cuidado** to be careful; **tenha calma!** calm down! **-6.** [considerar]: ~ **alguém por** *ou* **como algo** to consider sb as sthg. ◇ *v impess* [haver]: **tem algo/alguém** there is sthg/sb; **não tem problema** (it's) no problem; **não tem de quê** you're welcome; **tem três meses que não chove** it hasn't rained for three months; **tem três meses que cheguei** it's three months since I arrived. ◇ *v aux*: ~ **que** *ou* **de fazer algo** to have to do sthg; ~ **como fazer algo** to be able to do sthg; ~ **a ver com** to have sthg to do with; **não tenho nada a ver com isso** I have nothing to do with it; **não** ~ **onde cair morto** to have nowhere to turn.

ter. (*abrev de* **terça-feira**) *f* Tue.

terabyte [texa'baijtʃi] (*pl* **terabytes**) *m* terabyte.

terapeuta [tera'pewta] *mf* therapist.

terapêutico, ca [tera'pewtʃiku, ka] *adj* therapeutic.

◆ **terapêutica** *f* **-1.** [parte da medicina] therapeutics *(pl)*. **-2.** [tratamento] therapy.

terapia [tera'pia] *f* **-1.** [ger] therapy. **-2.**: ~ **de casal** marriage guidance.

terça ['texsa], **terça-feira** [texsa'fejra] (*pl* **terças-feiras** [texsaʃ'fejraʃ]) *f* Tuesday; ~ **gorda** Shrove Tuesday, Pancake Day; *veja também* **sexta-feira**.

terceirização [texsejriʒa'sãw] *f* outsourcing.

terceirizar [4] [texsejri'za(x)] *vt* to outsource.

terceiro, ra [tex'sejru, ra] ◇ *num* third; **o Terceiro Mundo** the Third World; *veja também* **sexto**. ◇ *m, f* **-1.** [ger] third party. **-2.** [aquele ou aquilo em terceiro lugar] third.

◆ **terceira** *f AUTO* third (gear).

◆ **terceiros** *mpl* [outras pessoas] others.

terciário, ria [tex'sjarju, rja] *adj* tertiary.

terço, ça ['texsu, sa] *num*: **a terça parte** the third part.

◆ **terço** *m* [rosário] rosary.

terçol [tex'sɔw] (*pl* **-óis**) *m* stye.

Tergal® [tex'gaw] *m* Terylene®.

tergiversar [4] [texʒivex'sa(x)] *vi* [usar de subterfúgios ou evasivas] to avoid the issue.

termas ['tɛxmaʃ] *fpl* spa *(sg)*.

termelétrica [texme'lɛtrika] *f* thermoelectric plant.

térmico, ca [tɛx'miku, ka] *adj* thermal.

terminação [texmina'sãw] (*pl* **-ões**) *f* **-1.** [ger] end. **-2.** [ato] termination. **-3.** *GRAM* ending.

terminal [texmi'naw] (*pl* **-ais**) ◇ *adj* terminal; **em estado** ~ terminally ill. ◇ *m* **-1.** [ger] terminal. **-2.** [fim da linha] terminus; ~ **marítimo** sea terminal.

terminante [texmi'nãntʃi] *adj* **-1.** [categórico] categorical. **-2.** [decisivo, inapelável] final. **-3.** [concludente] concluding.

terminantemente [texminãntʃimẽntʃi] *adv* categorically.

terminar [4] [texmi'na(x)] ◇ *vt* to finish. ◇ *aux*: ~ **de fazer algo** [finalmente] to finish doing sthg; [há pouco tempo] to have just done sthg. ◇ *vi* to finish; ~ **em algo** [em local, forma] to end in sthg.
término ['tεxminu] *m* end.
terminologia [texminolo'ʒia] *f* terminology.
terminológico, ca [texmino'lɔʒiku, ka] *adj* terminological.
termo ['texmu] *m* **-1.** [ger] term. **-2.** [fim] end; **pôr ~ a algo** to put an end to sthg; **a longo ~** in the long term; **meio ~** compromise.
◆ **termos** *mpl* terms; **em ~s de** in terms of; **em ~s gerais** in general terms; **em ~s** on terms; **estar em bons/maus ~s** to be on good/bad terms.
termodinâmica [texmodʒi'nãmika] *f* thermodynamics *(sg)*.
termômetro [ter'mɔmetru] *m* [instrumento] thermometer.
termonuclear [tεxmonukle'a(x)] ◇ *adj* thermonuclear. ◇ *f* [usina termonuclear] nuclear power station.
termostato [tεxmoʃ'tatu] *m* thermostat.
terninho [tεx'niɲu] *m* trouser suit ***UK***, pantsuit ***US***.
terno, na ['tεxnu, na] *adj* tender.
◆ **terno** *m* [traje] suit.
ternura [tex'nura] *f* tenderness.
terra ['tεxa] *f* **-1.** [ger] earth; ~ **vegetal** compost; **chão de ~ batida** earth floor. **-2.** [por oposição ao mar] [terreno] land; ~ **firme** terra firma. **-3.** [região, país]: **já me habituei a viver nesta ~** I've got used to living in this area; ~ **de ninguém** no-man's-land; **a ~ prometida** the promised land; **a Terra Santa** the Holy Land. **-4.** [pátria] homeland; ~ **natal** birthplace.
terraço [te'xasu] *m* **-1.** [varanda] terrace. **-2.** [cobertura plana de um edifício] roof terrace.
terracota [texa'kɔta] *f* [argila] terracotta.
Terra do Fogo [ˌtεxadu'fogu] *n* Tierra del Fuego.
Terra Nova [ˌtεxa'nɔva] *n* Newfoundland.
terraplenagem [texaple'naʒẽ] *f* site levelling ***UK***, site leveling ***US***.
terraplenar [texaple'na(x)] *vt* to level.
terreiro [te'xejru] *m* **-1.** [espaço de terra] yard. **-2.** [espirit] *place where Afro-Brazilian rites are performed*.
terremoto [texe'mɔtu] *m* earthquake.
terreno, na [te'xenu, na] *adj* [material, mundano] material.
◆ **terreno** *m* **-1.** [extensão de terra] land. **-2.** [para construção, plantação] site; ~ **baldio** wasteland. **-3.** GEOL terrain. **-4.** *loc*: **ganhar/perder ~** to lose/gain ground; **sondar o ~** to check the lie of the land.
térreo, ea ['tεxju, ja] *adj* [andar, casa] ground level *(antes de subst)*.
◆ **térreo** *m* [andar térreo] ground floor ***UK***, first floor ***US***.
terrestre [te'xεʃtri] *adj* **-1.** [relativo ou pertencente à Terra - globo, crosta] earth's, of the earth; [- seres, fenômenos] earthly. **-2.** [por oposição a aquático] land *(antes de subst)*.
terrificante [texifi'kãntʃi], **terrífico, ca** [te'xifiku, ka] *adj* terrifying.
terrina [te'xina] *f* tureen.
territorial [texito'rjaw] *adj* territorial.
território [texi'tɔrju] *m* **-1.** [ger] territory. **-2.** [parte de uma federação] district.
terrível [te'xivεw] (*pl* **-eis**) *adj* **-1.** [ger] terrible. **-2.** [muito forte, enorme] dreadful.
terror [te'xo(x)] (*pl* **-es**) *m* [medo] terror; **ser um ~** [ser amedrontador] to be terrifying; [ser horrível] to be awful.
terrorismo [texo'riʒmu] *m* terrorism.
terrorista [texo'riʃta] ◇ *adj* terrorist *(antes de subst)*. ◇ *mf* [pessoa] terrorist.
tesão [te'sãw] (*pl* **-ões**) *m* **-1.** ***mfam*** [desejo sexual] hots *(pl)*; **estar com ~** to have the hots, to be horny; **sentir ~ por alguém** to have the hots for sb; **ser um ~** [pessoa] to be sexy; [coisa] to be fantastic. **-2.** [ereção] stiffy, hard-on; **estar com ~** to have a hard-on.
tese ['tεzi] *f* thesis.
◆ **em tese** *loc adv* in theory.
teso, sa ['tezu, za] *adj* **-1.** [esticado] taut. **-2.** [ereto] stiff. **-3.** ***fam*** [sem dinheiro] skint.
tesões [te'zõjʃ] *pl* ▷ **tesão**.
tesoura [te'zora] *f* scissors *(pl)*.
tesourar [4] [tezo'ra(x)] *vt* **-1.** [cortar] to cut with scissors. **-2.** ***fam*** [falar mal de] to slag off.
tesouraria [tezora'ria] *f* **-1.** [departamento] finance department. **-2.** [cargo] finance director.
tesoureiro, ra [tezo'rejru, ra] *m, f* **-1.** [de banco] treasurer. **-2.** [de empresa] financial director.
tesouro [te'zoru] *m* **-1.** [ger] treasure. **-2.** [lugar onde são guardadas as riquezas] treasury.
◆ **Tesouro** *m*: **o Tesouro Nacional** the Treasury.
testa ['tεʃta] *f* forehead; **à ~ de** at the head of.
testa-de-ferro [ˌtεʃtadʒi'fεxu] (*pl* **testas-de-ferro**) *mf* figurehead.
testamentário, ria [tεʃtamẽntarju, rja] *adj* of a will.
testamento [teʃta'mẽntu] *m* will.
◆ **Novo Testamento** *m* New Testament.
◆ **Velho Testamento** *m* Old Testament.
testar [4] [teʃ'ta(x)] *vt* **-1.** [submeter a teste] to test. **-2.** [deixar em testamento] to bequeath.
teste ['tεʃtʃi] *m* test.
testemunha [teʃte'muɲa] *f* witness; ~ **ocular** eye witness; ~ **de acusação** witness for the prosecution.
testemunha-de-Jeová [teʃte'muɲadʒiʒeo'va] *mf* Jehovah's Witness.
testemunhar [4] [teʃte'muɲa(x)] ◇ *vt* **-1.** [ger] to witness. **-2.** JUR [depor sobre] to testify to. **-3.** [comprovar] to prove. **-4.** [manifestar] to display. ◇ *vi* JUR to testify; ~ **sobre/a favor de/contra algo** to give evidence about/for/against sthg; ~ **sobre/a favor de/contra alguém** to act as witness regarding/for/against sb.
testemunho [teʃte'muɲu] *m* testimony; **dar ~**

(sobre algo) to give evidence (about sthg).

testículo [teʃ'tʃikulu] *m* testicle.

testudo, da [teʃ'tudu, da] *adj* with a wide forehead.

teta ['teta] *f* [*ANAT* - de mulher] breast; [- de animal] teat; [- de vaca] udder.

tétano ['tɛtanu] *m* tetanus.

tête-à-tête [ˌtɛtʃja'tɛtʃi] *m* tête-à-tête.

tetéia [te'tɛja] *f fam* [pessoa] dish.

teto ['tɛtu] *m* **-1.** [ger] ceiling. **-2.** [de peça da casa] roof; ~ **solar** *AUTO* sunroof. **-3.** [habitação]: **sem** ~ homeless person.

tetracampeão, peã [tetrakãn'pjãw, pjã] *m, f* four times champion.

tetraplégico, ca [tetra'plɛʒiku, ka] ◇ *adj* quadriplegic. ◇ *m, f* quadriplegic.

tétrico, ca ['tɛtriku, ka] *adj* **-1.** [medonho, horrível] grim. **-2.** [triste, fúnebre] gloomy.

teu, tua ['tew, 'tua] ◇ *adj poss* your. ◇ *pron poss* yours.

tevê [te've] *f* = **televisão**.

têxtil ['teʃtʃiw] (*pl* **-teis**) *adj* textile.

texto ['teʃtu] *m* text.

textual [teʃ'twaw] *adj* **-1.** [relativo ao texto] textual. **-2.** *fig* [exato]: **foram estas minhas palavras textuais** those were my precise words.

textualmente [teʃtwaw'mẽntʃi] *adv* [exatamente, literalmente] verbatim.

textura [teʃ'tura] *f* texture.

texugo [te'ʃugu] *m ZOOL* badger.

tez ['teʃ] *f* [cútis] complexion.

ti ['tʃi] *pron pess* you; **trouxe este presente para** ~ I brought this present for you.

tia ['tʃia] *f* aunt.

tia-avó [ˌtʃia'vɔ] (*pl* **tias-avós**) *f* great-aunt.

tiara ['tʃjara] *f* tiara.

tibetano, na [tʃibe'tanu, na] ◇ *adj* Tibetan. ◇ *m, f* Tibetan.

◆ **tibetano** *m* [língua] Tibetan.

Tibete [tʃi'bɛtʃi] *n* Tibet.

tíbia ['tʃibja] *f ANAT* tibia.

tíbio, bia ['tʃibju, bja] *adj* lukewarm.

tição [tʃi'sãw] (*pl* **-ões**) *m* **-1.** [lenha] ember. **-2.** [negro] *fig & pej* nigger.

ticar [4] [tʃi'ka(x)] *vt* to tick.

tico ['tʃiku] *m*: **um** ~ **(de)** a bit (of).

tico-tico [ˌtʃiku'tʃiku] (*pl* **-s**) *m ZOOL* ruffous-collared sparrow.

tido, da ['tʃidu, da] *adj* [considerado]: ~ **como** considered.

◆ **tido** *pp* ▻ **ter**.

tietagem [tʃje'taʒẽ] (*pl* **-ns**) *f fam*: **fazer** ~ **para** to show admiration towards.

tiete ['tʃjɛtʃi] *mf fam* fan.

tifo ['tʃifu] *m* typhus.

tigela [tʃi'ʒɛla] *f* [vasilha] bowl.

tigre ['tʃigri] *m ZOOL* tiger.

tigresa [tʃi'greza] *f ZOOL* tigress.

tijolo [tʃi'ʒolu] *m* brick; **de** ~ **aparente** brick-faced; ~ **refratário** firebrick.

til ['tʃiw] *m* tilde.

tilintar [4] [tʃilĩn'ta(x)] ◇ *vt* [sino, chocalho] to jingle. ◇ *vi* [sino, moeda] to jingle. ◇ *m* jingle.

timaço [tʃi'masu] *m fam* [grande time] great team.

timão [tʃi'mãw] (*pl* **-ões**) *m NÁUT* helm, tiller.

timbrado, da [tʃĩn'bradu, da] *adj*: **papel** ~ headed paper.

timbre ['tʃĩnbri] *m* **-1.** [em papel de correspondência] heading. **-2.** [de voz] tone. **-3.** *MÚS* [tom] timbre. **-4.** [de vogal] sound.

time ['tʃimi] *m* **-1.** [ger] team. **-2.** *fig*: **de segundo** ~ second-rate. **-3.** *fam loc*: **tirar o** ~ **de campo** to pull out.

timer ['tajme(x)] *m* timer.

timidez [tʃimi'deʃ] *f* timidity.

tímido, da ['tʃimidu, da] *adj* **-1.** [avanço, governo] timid. **-2.** [pessoa, temperamento] timid, shy.

timões [tʃi'mõjʃ] *pl* ▻ **timão**.

timoneiro, ra [tʃimo'nejru, ra] *m, f NÁUT* helmsman.

tímpano ['tʃĩnpanu] *m* **-1.** *ANAT* eardrum. **-2.** [em campainha] bell.

tina ['tʃina] *f* **-1.** [para lavar roupa] trough. **-2.** [para banho] bathtub. **-3.** [para uso industrial] vat.

tíner ['tʃine(x)] *m* thinner.

tingido, da [tʃĩn'ʒidu, da] *adj* [tinto] dyed.

tingimento [tʃĩnʒi'mẽntu] *m* dyeing.

tingir [52] [tʃĩn'ʒi(x)] *vt* **-1.** [ger] to dye. **-2.** [parede, corpo] to paint.

tinha ['tʃiɲa] ▻ **ter**.

tinhoso, osa [tʃi'ɲozu, ɔza] *adj* **-1.** [teimoso] obstinate. **-2.** [persistente] stubborn.

tinido [tʃi'nidu] *m* ring.

tinir [6] [tʃi'ni(x)] *vi* **-1.** [ger] to ring. **-2.** *loc*: **estar tinindo** [estar em ótimo estado de limpeza] to be sparkling; [estar bem preparado] to be well-primed; [estar em ótimas condições] to be in excellent order; ~ **de fome/raiva** to be extremely hungry/furious.

tinjo ['tʃĩnʒu] *vb* ▻ **tingir**.

tino ['tʃinu] *m* **-1.** [juízo] common sense; **perder o** ~ to lose one's common sense. **-2.** [prudência] care. **-3.** : **ter** ~ **para algo** [ter queda para] to have a gift for sthg.

tinta ['tʃĩnta] *f* **-1.** [para imprimir, escrever] ink. **-2.** [para tingir] dye. **-3.** [para pintar] paint; ~ **a óleo** oil paint; ~ **plástica** emulsion.

tinteiro [tʃĩn'tejru] *m* inkwell.

tintim [tʃĩn'tʃĩ] *m*: **tintim!** cheers!

◆ **tintim por tintim** *loc adv* word for word.

tinto ['tʃĩntu] *adj* **-1.** [cabelos] dyed. **-2.**: **vinho** ~ red wine.

tintura [tʃĩn'tura] *f* **-1.** [tinta] dye. **-2.** [ato] dyeing.

tinturaria [tʃĩntura'ria] *f* **-1.** [ramo] dyeing. **-2.** [lavanderia] dry-cleaner's. **-3.** [onde se faz tingimento] dyer's.

tintureiro, ra [tʃĩntu'rejru, ra] *m, f* [profissional - que lava a seco] dry-cleaner; [- que tinge] dyer.

tio ['tʃiw] *m* uncle; **os meus** ~**s** [casal] my aunt and uncle.

tio-avô ['tʃiwa'vo] (*pl* **tios-avôs**) *m* great-uncle.

tipão [tʃi'pãw] *m* stunner.
tipicamente [tʃipika'mẽntʃi] *adv* typically.
típico, ca ['tʃipiku, ka] *adj* typical.
tipificar [12] [tʃipifi'ka(x)] *vt* to typify.
tipo, pa ['tʃipu, pa] *m* **-1.** [espécie] type; **~ sangüíneo** blood group. **-2.** [pessoa] sort. **-3.** *fam* [sujeito] guy (*f* girl). **-4.** [*TIP* - peça] type; [- letra] font.
tipografia [tʃipogra'fia] *f* **-1.** [arte] typography. **-2.** [estabelecimento] printer's.
tipográfico, ca [tʃipo'grafiku, ka] *adj* typographical; **erro ~** typo.
tipógrafo, fa [tʃi'pɔgrafu, fa] *m, f* [profissional - que imprime] printer; [- que compõe] typesetter.
tipóia [tʃi'pɔja] *f* [tira de pano] sling.
tique ['tʃiki] *m* tick; **~ nervoso** nervous tic.
tique-taque [ˌtʃiki'taki] (*pl* **tique-taques**) *m* tick-tock.
tíquete [tʃi'ketʃi] *m* ticket, voucher.
tíquete-restaurante ['tʃiketʃixeʃtaw'rãntʃi] (*pl* **tíquetes-restaurante**) *m* [vale-refeição] luncheon voucher.
tiquinho [tʃi'kiɲu] *m*: **um ~ (de)** a shred (of).
tira ['tʃira] <> *f* [ger] strip. <> *m gír* [agente de polícia] cop.
tiracolo [tʃira'kɔlu] *m*: **a ~** across the shoulder; **com os filhos a ~** with the children in tow.
tirada [tʃi'rada] *f* [dito] tirade.
tiragem [tʃi'raʒẽ] (*pl* **-ns**) *f* **-1.** [operação de imprimir] print run. **-2.** [número de exemplares] circulation.
tira-gosto ['tʃira'goʃtu] (*pl* **tira-gostos**) *m* savoury *UK*, savory *US*.
tira-manchas [ˌtʃira'mãnʃaʃ] *m inv* stain remover.
Tirana [tʃi'rãna] *n* Tirana.
tirania [tʃira'nia] *f* tyranny.
tirânico, ca [tʃi'rãniku, ka] *adj* tyrannical.
tiranizar [4] [tʃirani'za(x)] *vt* to tyrannize.
tirano, na [tʃi'rãnu, na] <> *adj* [cruel, injusto] tyrannical. <> *m, f* tyrant.
tirante [tʃi'rãntʃi] <> *adj*: **~ dois ou três problemas, o resto deu certo** except for a couple of problems, the rest worked out well; **uma cor ~ a verde** a greenish colour *UK*, a greenish color *US*. <> *m* **-1.** [correia] harness. **-2.** [viga] tie beam. **-3.** *MEC* connecting rod.
tirar [4] [tʃi'ra(x)] *vt* **-1.** [ger] to take. **-2.** [retirar] to take away. **-3.** [de cima] [despir, descalçar] to take off. **-4.** [de dentro] [sacar] to take out, to withdraw. **-5.** [trazer abaixo] to take down. **-6.** [extrair] to extract. **-7.** [eliminar] to remove. **-8.** [obter] to get; **~ proveito de** to make use of. **-9.** [mesa] to clear. **-10.** [para dançar] to ask. **-11.** *MÚS* to take down. **-12.** *TIP* [imprimir] to print. **-13.: ~ algo/alguém de algo** [afastar, fazer sair] to take sthg/sb away from sthg; **-14.** [loc]: **sem ~ nem pôr** exactly like; **ele é o pai sem ~ nem pôr** he's the spitting image of his father.
tiririca [tʃiri'rika] *adj fam*: **estar/ficar ~** to be hopping mad.
tiritar [4] [tʃiri'ta(x)] *vi* to shiver; **~ de frio** to shiver with cold.
tiro ['tʃiru] *m* **-1.** [ger] shot; **dar um ~ (em)** to fire a shot (at); **trocar ~s** to exchange fire; **~ ao alvo** target practice; **o ~ saiu pela culatra** *fig* it backfired. **-2.** [loc]: **ser ~ e queda** to be surefire.
tiro-de-guerra [tʃirudʒi'gɛxa] (*pl* **tiros-de-guerra**) *m army reserve training centre.*
tiroteio [tʃiro'teju] *m* **-1.** [tiros amiudados] shooting. **-2.** [troca de tiros] shootout.
tis [tʃiʃ] *pl* ▻ **til.**
tísico, ca ['tʃiziku, ka] <> *adj* consumptive. <> *m, f* consumptive.
titânio [tʃi'tãnju] *m* titanium.
títere ['tʃiteri] *m* [marionete] puppet.
titia [tʃi'tʃia] *f fam* aunty; **ficar para ~** to become an old maid.
Titicaca [tʃitʃi'kaka] *n*: **o (lago) ~** Lake Titicaca.
titio [tʃi'tʃiw] *m fam* uncle.
tititi [tʃitʃi'tʃi] *m* **-1.** *gír* [falatório] tittle-tattle. **-2.** [badalação] hubbub. **-3.** [discussão, briga] brawl.
titubeante [tʃitu'bjãntʃi] *adj* **-1.** [cambaleante] lurching. **-2.** [hesitante] hesitant.
titubear [15] [tʃitu'bja(x)] *vi* **-1.** [hesitar] to hesitate; **~ em algo/em fazer algo** to hesitate in sthg/at doing sthg. **-2.** [cambalear] to lurch.
titular [tʃitu'la(x)] <> *adj* [efetivo - juiz] incumbent; [- professor] tenured; [- oficial] official. <> *mf* **-1.** [ocupante efetivo de função ou cargo] incumbent. **-2.** *POL* [de ministério]: **o ~ do Ministério da Saúde** the Health Minister. **-3.** [possuidor] holder.
título ['tʃitulu] *m* **-1.** [ger] title. **-2.** [documento] (title) deed; **~ ao portador** *COM* bearer bond *ou* certificate; **~ de crédito** *COM* bond; **~ de propriedade** *JUR* title deed. **-3.** [motivo]: **a ~ de** by way of; **a ~ de curiosidade** out of curiosity; **a ~ de quê?** what for?
tive ['tʃivi] *v* ▻ **ter.**
tlintlim [tlĩn'tlĩn] *m* tinkle.
TM (*abrev de* **Trademark**) *f* TM.
TO (*abrev de* **Estado de Tocantins**) *n State of Tocantins.*
toa ['toa] *f NÁUT* towline.
◆ **à toa** *loc adv* **-1.** [ger] for no reason; **não é à ~ que** it's not by chance that. **-2.** [inutilmente] in vain. **-3.** [desocupado] at a loose end. **-4.** [sem rumo] aimlessly.
toada ['twada] *f MÚS* tune, melody.
toalete [twa'lɛtʃi] <> *m* [banheiro] toilet. <> *f* **-1.** [ato]: **fazer a ~** to get washed and dressed. **-2.** [traje] outfit.
toalha ['twaʎa] *f* towel; **~ de banho/rosto/praia** bath/hand/beach towel; **~ de mesa** tablecloth.
toalheiro [twa'ʎejru] *m* [utensílio] towel rail.
tobogã [tobo'gã] *m* **-1.** [trenó] toboggan. **-2.** [pista] slide.
toca ['tɔka] *f* **-1.** [covil] den. **-2.** *fig* [refúgio] bolthole.
toca-discos [ˌtɔka'dʒiʃkuʃ] *m inv* record player.
tocado, da [to'kadu, da] *adj* **-1.** *fam* [meio embriagado] tipsy. **-2.** [expulso] turfed out.
toca-fitas [ˌtɔka'fitaʃ] *m inv* cassette player.

tocaia [to'kaja] *f* ambush.

tocante [to'kãntʃi] *adj inv* [comovente] touching.
◆ **no tocante a** *loc prep* when it comes to.

Tocantins [tokãn'tʃĩn] *npl* Tocantins.

tocar [12] [to'ka(x)] ◇ *vt* -**1.** [ger] to touch. -**2.** *MÚS* to play. -**3.** [campainha, sino] to ring. -**4.** [buzina] to hoot. -**5.** [conduzir] to drive. -**6.** [fazer progredir]: ~ **algo (para frente)** to move (sthg) forward. -**7.** [expulsar]: ~ **alguém/algo de algum lugar** to throw sb/sthg out of somewhere. ◇ *vi* -**1.** [ger] to ring. -**2.** [apalpar, encostar]: ~ **(em) algo/alguém** to touch sthg/sb.
◆ **tocar a** *vi* [dizer respeito a]: **no** *ou* **pelo que me toca** as far as I am concerned.
◆ **tocar em** *vi* -**1.** [referir-se a] to touch (up)on. -**2.** [fazer escala em] to stop off in. -**3.** [caber a]: **toca a você fazer isso** it's up to you to do it.
◆ **tocar para** *vi* [telefonar] to ring.
◆ **tocar-se** *vp* -**1.** [pôr-se em contato] to touch. -**2.** [perceber] to notice. -**3.** [ofender-se] to be provoked.

tocha ['tɔʃa] *f* [facho] torch.

toco ['toku] *m* -**1.** [de árvore] stump. -**2.** [de cigarro, charuto] butt(-end), stub.

todavia [toda'via] *conj* however.

todo, da ['todu, da] ◇ *adj indef* [inteiro] all; **a Europa toda** the whole of Europe; **a equipe toda** the entire team; **o dia** ~, ~ **o dia** the whole day (long). ◇ *adv* [completamente] completely. ◇ *pron indef* [qualquer, cada] every; ~ **dia**, ~**s os dias** every day; **em** *ou* **por toda parte** everywhere; ~ **mundo** everyone; **em** ~ **caso** in any case; **de** ~ **jeito** all the same.
◆ **todo** *m* whole; **ao** ~ in all; **de** ~ entirely.
◆ **todos** *pron pl* [todas as pessoas] everyone *(sg)*.
◆ **a toda (velocidade)** *loc adv* at top speed.

todo-poderoso, osa [ˌtodupode'rozu, ɔza] *adj* all-powerful.
◆ **Todo-Poderoso** *m*: **o Todo Poderoso** the Almighty.

toga ['tɔga] *f* -**1.** *HIST* toga. -**2.** [jur] gown.

toicinho [toj'siɲu] *m* = **toucinho**.

toldo ['towdu] *m* awning.

tolerância [tole'rãnsja] *f* tolerance.

tolerante [tole'rãntʃi] *adj* tolerant.

tolerar [4] [tole'ra(x)] *vt* -**1.** [ger] to tolerate. -**2.** [suportar] to bear.

tolerável [tole'ravew] (*pl* -**eis**) *adj* -**1.** [aceitável] tolerable. -**2.** [suportável] bearable.

tolher [5] [to'ʎe(x)] *vt* -**1.** [dificultar] to impede. -**2.** [impedir]: ~ **alguém de algo/de fazer algo** to prevent sb from sthg/from doing sthg.

tolice [to'lisi] *f* -**1.** [ato] stupid thing. -**2.** [qualidade] idiocy. -**3.** [dito] rubbish.

tolo, la ['tolu, la] ◇ *adj* -**1.** [ger] stupid. -**2.** [pessoa - idiota] idiotic; [- ingênuo] foolish. ◇ *m, f* [pessoa] idiot.

tom ['tõ] (*pl* -**ns**) *m* -**1.** [ger] tone. -**2.** [altura de um som] pitch; ~ **agudo/grave** high/low pitch. -**3.** [matiz] shade. -**4.** [*MÚS* - intervalo entre duas notas] tone; [- escala] key; ~ **maior/menor** major/minor key. -**5.** *loc*: **ser de bom** ~ to be polite.

tomada [to'mada] *f* -**1.** [ato] taking; ~ **de decisão** decision making; ~ **de preços** tender; ~ **de posse** [de presidente] investiture; ~ **de posto oficial** taking office. -**2.** [*ELETR* - plugue] plug; [- na parede] socket. -**3.** [ocupação] taking. -**4.** *CINE* take.

tomar [4] [to'ma(x)] *vt* -**1.** [ger] to take; ~ **alguém em/por algo** to take sb in/by sthg; ~ **emprestado** to borrow; **toma!** there you are!; ~ **um susto** to get a fright. -**2.** [ocupar] to take. -**3.** [beber] to have. -**4.** [ocupar aspecto] to take up. -**5.** [satisfação]: ~ **satisfação de alguém** to get an explanation from sb. -**6.** [considerar]: ~ **algo como algo** to take sthg as sthg; ~ **alguém por algo** to take sb for sthg.
◆ **tomar-se** *vp*: ~**-se de algo (por)** [ser invadido por] to be full of sthg (for *ou* towards); ~**-se (de) horror a** to be filled with horror at.

tomara [to'mara] *interj* let's hope so!; ~ **que chova!** let's hope it rains!

tomara-que-caia [toˌmaraki'kaja] ◇ *adj inv* strapless. ◇ *m inv* strapless dress.

tomate [to'matʃi] *m* tomato.

tomateiro [toma'tejru] *m* tomato plant.

tombadilho [tõnba'dʒiʎu] *m* (poop) deck.

tombar [4] [tõn'ba(x)] ◇ *vt* -**1.** [derrubar] to knock down. -**2.** [para preservar] to list *(for the preservation of buildings)*. ◇ *vi*: ~ **(em/de/para)** [cair] to fall on/off/towards; [cair rolando] to tumble on/off/towards.

tombo ['tõnbu] *m* [queda] fall; **levar um** ~ to take a tumble.

tomilho [to'miʎu] *m* thyme.

tomo ['tomu] *m* -**1.** [parte] tome. -**2.** [volume] volume.

tomografia [tomogra'fia] *f MED* tomography; ~ **computadorizada** computerized axial tomography, CAT scanning.

tona ['tona] *f*: **à** ~ to the surface; **vir/trazer à** ~ *fig* [vir à baila] to come/bring up.

tonal [to'naw] (*pl* -**ais**) *adj MÚS* tonal.

tonalidade [tonali'dadʒi] *f* -**1.** [ger] shade. -**2.** [mus] tonality.

tonel [to'nɛw] (*pl* -**éis**) *m* [recipiente] cask.

tonelada [tone'lada] *f* -**1.** [medida] ton. -**2.** *fig* [grande quantidade de]: **uma** ~ **de** tons of.

tonelagem [tone'laʒẽ] *f* tonnage.

toner ['tone(x)] *m TEC* toner.

tônico, ca ['toniku, ka] *adj* tonic.
◆ **tônico** *m* [cosmético] tonic; ~ **para o cabelo** hair tonic.
◆ **tonica** *f* -**1.** [água tônica] tonic water. -**2.** *MÚS* tonic. -**3.** *fig* [idéia, assunto principal] keynote.

tonificante [tonifi'kãntʃi] *adj* invigorating.

tonificar [12] [tonifi'ka(x)] *vt* to tone.

tons [tõʃ] *pl* ▻ **tom**.

tontas ['tõntaʃ] *fpl*: **às** ~ [atarantadamente] in a fluster.

tontear [15] [tõn'tʃja(x)] ◇ *vt* -**1.** [suj: bebida, perfume] to make giddy. -**2.** [suj: pessoa, notícia, revelação] to stun. -**3.** [suj: barulho, confusão] to drive mad. <> *vi* **-1.** [bebida, perfume] to be intoxicating. **-2.** [notícia, revelação] to be shocking. **-3.** [barulho, confusão] to be maddening. **-4.** [pessoa - ficar tonto] to become dizzy; [- perturbar-se] to be stunned; [- ficar atordoado] to be maddened.

tonteira [tõn'tejra] *f* [vertigem] giddiness, dizziness; **ter ~** to suffer a dizzy spell.

tonto, ta ['tõntu, ta] *adj* **-1.** [zonzo] dizzy. **-2.** [perturbado, atordoado] giddy. **-3.** [tolo] giddy.

tontura [tõn'tura] *f* = **tonteira**.

tônus ['tonuʃ] *m inv*: **~ muscular** muscle tone.

top ['tɔpi] *m* **-1.** [bustiê] bodice. **-2.** [o melhor]: **~ de linha** top-of-the-range.

topada [to'pada] *f* trip; **dar uma ~ em algo** to trip over sthg.

topar [4] [to'pa(x)] <> *vt* [aceitar, concordar com]: **~ algo/fazer algo** to agree to sthg/to do sthg; **você topa ir à praia?** do you feel like going to the beach? <> *vi* [aceitar, concordar] to agree.

◆ **topar com** *vi* [encontrar] to come across.

◆ **topar em** *vi* [tropeçar em] to trip over.

◆ **topar-se** *vp* [deparar-se]: **~ com algo/alguém** to come across sthg/sb.

topázio [to'pazju] *m* topaz.

topete [to'pɛtʃi] *m* [cabelo levantado] quiff; **ter o ~ de fazer algo** to have the nerve to do sthg.

topetudo, da [topetu'du, da] *adj* **-1.** [que usa topete] with a quiff *(depois de subst)*. **-2.** [destemido] daring.

tópico, ca ['tɔpiku, ka] *adj* [questão, assunto] topical.

◆ **tópico** *m* [tema, assunto] topic.

topless [tɔpi'lɛʃ] <> *adj inv* topless. <> *m inv* topless bikini.

topo ['topu] *m* top.

topografia [topogra'fia] *f* topography.

topográfico, ca [topo'grafiku, ka] *adj* topographical.

topônimo [to'ponimu] *m* toponym, place name.

toque ['tɔki] <> *v* ▻ **tocar**. <> *m* **-1.** [ger] touch. **-2.** [de campainha] ring. **-3.** [de corneta] blast. **-4.** *MED* palpation. **-5.** [pequeno teor ou quantidade]: **um ~ de** a touch of. **-6.** [retoque] finishing touch. **-7.** *fam* : **dar um ~ em alguém** to have a word with sb. **-8.** *MIL*: **~ de recolher** curfew. **-9.** *loc*: **a ~ de caixa** hurriedly.

Tóquio ['tɔkju] *n* Tokyo.

tora ['tɔra] *f* **-1.** [de madeira] log. **-2.** [pedaço] piece; **tirar uma ~** [cochilar] to take a nap.

tórax ['tɔrakiʃ] *m inv* thorax.

torção [tox'sãw] *f* **-1.** [ato de torcer] twist(ing). **-2.** *MED* sprain.

torcedor, ra [toxse'do(x), ra] (*mpl* **-es**, *fpl* **-s**) *m, f* *ESP* supporter; **sou ~ do Flamengo** I am a Flamengo supporter.

torcedura [toxse'dura] *f MED* sprain.

torcer [25] [tox'se(x)] <> *vt* **-1.** [ger] to twist. **-2.** [espremer] to wring. **-3.** *MED* to sprain. <> *vi* **-1.** [ger] to twist **-2.** [num jogo] to do one's bit as a supporter.

◆ **torcer por** *vi ESP* [ser aficionado de] to be a supporter of.

◆ **torcer para, torcer por** *vi* [desejar o êxito de] to back.

torcicolo [toxsi'kɔlu] *m MED* stiff neck, wryneck; **estar com ~** to have a stiff neck.

torcida [tox'sida] *f* [*ESP* - ato] support; [- torcedores] supporters *(pl)*.

tormenta [tox'mẽnta] *f* **-1.** *METEOR* storm. **-2.** *fig* [transtorno] upheaval.

tormento [tox'mẽntu] *m* torment.

tormentoso, sa [toxmẽn'tozu, za] *adj* stormy.

tornado [tox'nadu] *m* tornado.

tornar [4] [tox'na(x)] <> *vt* [fazer ser] to make; **~ algo em algo** to turn sthg into sthg. <> *vi*: **~ a fazer algo** to do sthg again; **ela tornou a insistir** she again insisted.

◆ **tornar-se** *vp* [vir a ser] to become.

torneado, da [tox'njadu, da] *adj* [arredondado] turned; **bem ~** *fig* [corpo, pernas] well-turned, shapely.

tornear [15] [tox'nja(x)] *vt* to turn.

torneio [tox'neju] *m* [competição] tournament.

torneira [tox'nejra] *f* tap *UK*, faucet *US*.

torniquete [toxni'ketʃi] *m MED* tourniquet.

torno ['toxnu] *m TEC* lathe.

◆ **en torno de** *loc prep* around.

tornozeleira [toxnoze'lejra] *f* ankle strap.

tornozelo [toxnu'zelu] *m* ankle.

toró [to'rɔ] *m METEOR* downpour; **caiu um ~** there was a heavy downpour.

torpe ['toxpi] *adj* **-1.** [vil] foul. **-2.** [desonesto] shameful. **-3.** [obsceno] disgraceful.

torpedear [15] [toxpe'dʒja(x)] *vt* to torpedo.

torpedo [tox'pedu] *m* torpedo.

torpeza [tox'peza] *f* **-1.** [vileza] foulness. **-2.** [desonestidade] shamefulness. **-3.** [obscenidade] disgrace.

torpor [tox'po(x)] *m* **-1.** [entorpecimento] torpor. **-2.** [indiferença] inertia. **-3.** *MED* unresponsiveness.

torquês [tox'keʃ] *f* (pair of) pliers.

torrada [to'xada] *f* toast.

torradeira [toxa'dejra] *f* toaster.

torrão [to'xãw] (*pl* **-ões**) *m* **-1.** [de terra endurecida] clod. **-2.** [de açúcar] lump. **-3.** : **~ natal** birthplace.

torrar [4] [to'xa(x)] <> *vt* **-1.** [tostar] to toast. **-2.** [ressecar] to parch. **-3.** *fig* [mercadorias] to dump. **-4.** *fig* [dinheiro] to burn. **-5.** *fam fig* [irritar] to annoy; **~ a paciência de alguém** to try sb's patience. <> *vi* to be irritating.

torre ['toxi] *f* **-1.** [construção] tower; **~ de controle** *AERON* control tower; **~ de vigia** watchtower. **-2.** *ELETR* pylon. **-3.** *RÁDIO & TV* mast. **-4.** [xadrez] castle, rook.

torrefação [toxefa'sãw] (*pl* **-oes**) *f* **-1.** [de café, cacau] roast(ing). **-2.** [estabelecimento] roasting house.

torrencial [toxẽn'sjaw] *adj* torrential.

torrente [to'xẽntʃi] *f* torrent.

torresmo [to'xeʒmu] *m* CULIN crackling, pork scratchings *(pl)*.
tórrido, da ['tɔxidu, da] *adj* torrid.
torrone [to'xɔni] *m* nougat.
torso ['toxsu] *m* torso.
torta ['tɔxta] *f* [empadão, doce] pie; ~ **de limão/maçã** lemon/apple pie/tart.
torto, ta ['toxtu, ta] *adj* **-1.** [ger] crooked. **-2.** *loc:* **a ~ e a direito** left, right and centre; **cometer erros a ~ e a direito** to make mistakes left, right and centre.
tortuoso, osa [tox'twozu, ɔza] *adj* **-1.** [sinuoso] winding. **-2.** *(fig)* [que não segue uma linha reta] convoluted.
tortura [tox'tura] *f* [ger] torture; [lance difícil]: **ser uma ~** to be torture.
torturador, ra [toxtura'do(x), ra] *m, f* torturer.
torturante [toxtu'rãntʃi] *adj* **-1.** [dor] excruciating. **-2.** [espera] agonizing. **-3.** [viagem] harrowing.
torturar [4] [toxtu'ra(x)] *vt* [ger] to torment; [incomodar fisicamente] to kill.
torvelinho [toxve'liɲu] *m* [confusão] turmoil.
tosa ['tɔza] *f* **-1.** [de pêlo] trimming. **-2.** [de lã] shearing.
tosar [4] [to'za(x)] *vt* **-1.** [pêlo] to clip. **-2.** [cabelo] to crop.
tosco, ca ['toʃku, ka] *adj* crude.
tosquiar [16] [toʃ'kja(x)] *vt* [ovelha] to shear.
tosse ['tɔsi] *f* cough; ~ **de cachorro** *ou* **comprida** whooping cough; ~ **seca** dry cough.
tossir [59] [to'si(x)] *vi* **-1.** [ger] to cough. **-2.** [expelir] to cough up.
tostado, da [toʃ'tadu, da] *adj* **-1.** [levemente queimado] browned. **-2.** [moreno] tanned.
tostão [toʃ'tãw] *(pl* **-ões***)* *m* [dinheiro] cash; **estava sem um ~** I didn't have a penny; **fiquei sem um ~** I was left penniless.
tostar [4] [toʃ'ta(x)] *vt* **-1.** [ger] to brown. **-2.** [pele] to tan.
total [to'taw] *(pl* **-ais***)* ◇ *adj* total. ◇ *m* total; **no ~** in total.
totalidade [totali'dadʒi] *f* entirety; **a ~ da população** the entire population; **a ~ dos alunos** all the students; **em sua ~** in its/their entirety.
totalitário, ria [totali'tarju, rja] *adj* totalitarian.
totalitarismo [totalita'riʒmu] *m* totalitarianism.
totalizar [4] [totali'za(x)] *vt* **-1.** [calcular o total de] to total up. **-2.** [atingir o total de] to total.
totalmente [totaw'mẽntʃi] *adv* entirely, totally.
touca ['toka] *f* [de lã, malha] bonnet; ~ **de banho/natação** bathing/swimming cap.
toucador [toka'do(x)] *(mpl* **-es***)* *m* [cômoda] dressing table.
toucinho [to'siɲu] *m* uncured bacon; ~ **defumado** smoked bacon.
toupeira [to'pejra] *f* **-1.** ZOOL mole. **-2.** *fig* [ignorante] dimwit.
tourada [to'rada] *f* bullfight.
tourear [15] [to'rja(x)] ◇ *vt* to fight *(bulls)*. ◇ *vi* to be a bullfighter.
toureiro, ra [to'rejru, ra] *m, f* bullfighter.
touro ['toru] *m* **-1.** ZOOL bull. **-2.** *fig*: **ser um ~** [ser robusto] to be strong as an ox.
◆ **Touro** *m* ASTRO Taurus.
toxemia [tokse'mia] *f* toxaemia *UK*, toxemia *US*.
tóxico, ca ['tɔksiku, ka] *adj* toxic.
◆ **tóxico** *m* **-1.** [veneno] poison. **-2.** [droga] drug.
toxicômano, na [toksi'komanu, na] *m, f* drug addict.
toxina [tok'sina] *f* toxin.
TPM *(abrev de* **Tensão Pré-Menstrual***)* *f* PMT.
trabalhadeira [trabaʎa'dejra] *f* ▷ **trabalhador**.
trabalhado, da [traba'ʎadu, da] *adj* worked.
trabalhador, ra [trabaʎa'do(x), ra] *(mpl* **-es**, *fpl* **-s***)* ◇ *adj* [laborioso] hard-working; **classe trabalhadora** POL working class. ◇ *m, f* worker; **(~) autônomo** freelance (worker); ~ **braçal** manual worker.
trabalhão [traba'ʎãw] *m* = **trabalheira**.
trabalhar [4] [traba'ʎa(x)] ◇ *vt* **-1.** [ger] to work. **-2.** [aprimorar] to work on. **-3.** [elaborar] to develop. ◇ *vi* to work; ~ **em algo** [em projeto] to work at sthg; TEATRO to perform in sthg; ~ **com algo** [num ramo] to work in sthg; [comerciar com] to deal in; ~ **como algo** [exercer a profissão de] to work as sthg.
trabalheira [traba'ʎejra] *f* hard work; **ser** *ou* **dar uma ~** to be a lot of work.
trabalhista [traba'ʎiʃta] ◇ *adj* **-1.** [ger] labour *UK*, labor *US*; **Partido Trabalhista** Labour Party. **-2.** [que é especialista em direito do trabalho] employment *(antes de subst)*. ◇ *mf* [POL - partidário] Labour Party supporter; [- membro] Labour Party member.
trabalho [tra'baʎu] *m* **-1.** [ger] work; ~ **braçal** manual work; ~ **de campo** fieldwork; ~ **doméstico** domestic work; **~s forçados** forced labour *UK*, forced labor *US*; ~ **de parto** labour *UK*, labor *US*; ~ **artesanal** craftwork. **-2.** [tarefa] job. **-3.** ECON labour *UK*, labor *US*. **-4.** EDUC homework. **-5.** [espirit] spell; **fazer um ~** to cast a spell. **-6.:** **dar ~ (a alguém)** [exigir esforço] to be a lot of work (for sb); [causar transtorno] to be a bother (to sb).
trabalhoso, osa [traba'ʎozu, ɔza] *adj* arduous.
traça ['trasa] *f* **-1.** [de roupa] moth. **-2.** [de livro] bookworm.
traçado [tra'sadu] *m* **-1.** [conjunto de traços] sketch. **-2.** [planta] plan.
tração [tra'sãw] *f* traction; ~ **nas quatro rodas** four-wheel drive.
traçar [13] [tra'sa(x)] *vt* **-1.** [fazer com traços] to sketch. **-2.** [planejar] to draw up. **-3.** [demarcar] to mark out. **-4.** *fam* [devorar] to devour.
traço ['trasu] *m* **-1.** [linha] line. **-2.** [sinal de pontuação] (en) dash. **-3.** [modo de desenhar] style. **-4.** [característica] trait.
◆ **traços** *mpl* **-1.** [feições] features. **-2.** *fig* [vestígio] traces. **-3.** *fig* [laivos] traces. **-4.** [pequena quantidade de substância] traces.
tradição [tradʒi'sãw] *(pl* **-ões***)* *f* tradition.

tradicional [tradʒisjo'naw] (*pl* **-ais**) *adj* traditional.

tradicionalista [tradʒisjona'liʃta] <> *adj* traditionalist. <> *mf* traditionalist.

tradicionalmente [tradʒisjonaw'mẽntʃi] *adv* traditionally.

tradução [tradu'sãw] (*pl* **-ões**) *f* **-1.** [ger] translation. **-2.** *COMPUT:* ~ **eletrônica** machine translation, automatic translation.

tradutor, ra [tradu'to(x), ra] (*mpl* **-es**, *fpl* **-s**) <> *adj* translating. <> *m, f* translator; ~ **juramentado** accredited translator.

traduzir [72] [tradu'zi(x)] <> *vt* **-1.** [texto, código] to translate; ~ **algo do português para o inglês** to translate sthg from Portuguese into English. **-2.** [sentimento, pensamento] to express. <> *vi* **-1.** [saber traduzir] to translate. **-2.** [ser tradutor] to work as a translator.

◆ **traduzir-se** *vp* [manifestar-se]: **sua tristeza se traduz em agressão** her grief is expressed through aggression.

traduzível [tradu'zivew] (*pl* **-eis**) *adj* translatable.

trafegar [14] [trafe'ga(x)] *vi* [transitar] to be driven.

trafegável [trafe'gavew] (*pl* **-eis**) *adj* passable.

tráfego ['trafegu] *m* traffic; ~ **engarrafado** traffic jam; ~ **aéreo** air traffic.

traficante [trafi'kãntʃi] *mf* trafficker; ~ **de drogas** drug trafficker *ou* dealer.

traficar [12] [trafi'ka(x)] <> *vt* to traffic in. <> *vi* to traffic; ~ **com** to deal in.

tráfico ['trafiku] *m* traffic; ~ **de drogas** drug trafficking; ~ **de influência** backscratching.

tragada [tra'gada] *f* [em cigarro] drag.

tragar [14] [tra'ga(x)] <> *vt* **-1.** [engolir] to swallow. **-2.** [inalar] to inhale. **-3.** *fam* [tolerar] to tolerate. <> *vi* [inalar] to inhale.

tragédia [tra'ʒɛdʒja] *f* tragedy.

trágico, ca ['traʒiku, ka] <> *adj* **-1.** [ger] tragic. **-2.** *fig* [dado a fazer drama] over-dramatic. <> *m, f* [ator] tragic actor (*f* actress).

tragicomédia [traʒiko'mɛdʒa] *f* tragicomedy.

tragicômico, ca [traʒi'komiku, ka] *adj* tragicomic.

trago ['tragu] <> *v* ▻ **trazer**. <> *m* **-1.** [gole] mouthful; **de um só** ~ in one gulp. **-2.** [dose pequena] drop. **-3.** [em cigarro] puff; **dar um** ~ **(em)** to take a puff (of).

traguei [tra'gej] *v* ▻ **tragar**.

traição [traj'sãw] (*pl* **-ões**) *f* **-1.** [deslealdade] disloyalty. **-2.** [infidelidade] infidelity. **-3.** *POL* treason.

traiçoeiro, ra [traj'swejru, ra] *adj* **-1.** [pessoa] disloyal. **-2.** [ação] treacherous. **-3.** [mar, passagem] treacherous.

traidor, ra [traj'do(x), ra] (*mpl* **-es**, *fpl* **-s**) <> *adj* **-1.** [infiel] unfaithful. **-2.** [comprometedor] betraying. <> *m, f* [pessoa] traitor.

trailer ['trejle(x)] *m* **-1.** [ger] trailer. **-2.** [tipo casa] caravan *UK*, trailer *US*.

traineira [traj'nejra] *f NÁUT* trawler.

training ['trejnĩŋ] *m* tracksuit.

trair [68] [tra'i(x)] *vt* **-1.** [atraiçoar] to betray. **-2.** [ser infiel a] to be unfaithful to. **-3.** [não cumprir - promessa] to break; [- dever] to fail in. **-4.** [revelar] to betray.

◆ **trair-se** *vp*: ~**-se por algo/fazendo algo** [denunciar-se] to give o.s. away by sthg/doing sthg.

trajar [4] [tra'ʒa(x)] *vt* to wear.

◆ **trajar-se** *vp*: ~**-se de** to be dressed in.

traje ['traʒi] *m* dress; ~ **de banho** swimsuit; ~ **de passeio** smart dress; ~ **a rigor** evening dress; ~**s menores** underwear *(sg)*.

trajeto [tra'ʒɛtu] *m* distance, journey.

trajetória [traʒe'tɔrja] *f* **-1.** [trajeto] path. **-2.** *fig* [caminho] course.

tralha ['traʎa] *f* [traste] junk.

trama ['trãma] *f* **-1.** [ger] plot. **-2.** [de tecido] weft.

tramar [4] [tra'ma(x)] <> *vt* **-1.** [tecer] to weave. **-2.** [maquinar] to plot. <> *vi* [conspirar]: ~ **contra** to plot against.

trambique [trãn'biki] *m* *fam* [negócio fraudulento] con; **dar um** ~ **em** [burlar] to con.

trambiqueiro, ra [trãnbi'kejru, ra] <> *adj* slippery. <> *m, f* con artist.

trambolhão [tranbo'ʎãw] (*pl* **-ões**) *m* tumble; **levar um** ~ to be knocked down; **desceu as escadas aos trambolhões** he stumbled down the stairs; **abrir caminho aos trambolhões** to push one's way through.

trambolho [tran'boʎu] *m* [objeto grande e incômodo] encumbrance.

tramitar [4] [trami'ta(x)] *vi* to be dealt with.

trâmites ['trãmitʃiʃ] *mpl* *fig* [vias] procedures.

tramóia [tra'mɔja] *f* **-1.** [trama] scheme. **-2.** [trapaça] swindle.

trampolim [trãnpo'lĩ] (*pl* **-ns**) *m* **-1.** *ESP* diving board. **-2.** *fig* [meio] springboard.

tranca ['trãŋka] *f* **-1.** [de porta] bolt; **passar a** ~ **em** to bolt. **-2.** [de carro] lock; **passar a** ~ **em** to lock.

trança ['trãnsa] *f* **-1.** [ger] plaited bread. **-2.** [trançado] braid.

trançado, da [trãn'sadu, da] *adj* **-1.** [cabelo] plaited. **-2.** [cinto, galão, fita] braided. **-3.** [cesto] woven.

trancado, da [trãnka'du, da] *adj* [fechado] firmly shut.

trancafiar [16] [trãŋka'fja(x)] *vt* to lock up.

trancar [12] [trãŋ'ka(x)] *vt* **-1.** [chavear] to lock. **-2.** [prender] to lock up. **-3.** *EDUC & UNIV* [matrícula] to suspend. **-4.** *FUT* to shove (to one side).

◆ **trancar-se** *vp* **-1.** [fechar-se] to shut o.s. away. **-2.** [não se manifestar] to clam up.

trançar [13] [trãn'sa(x)] <> *vt* **-1.** [cabelo] to plait. **-2.** [palha, fita] to weave. <> *vi* *fam* [zanzar] to mope.

tranco ['trãŋku] *m* **-1.** [andadura de cavalo] trot. **-2.** [esbarrão] shove. **-3.** [solavanco] jolt. **-4.** *fam* [advertência] jolt.

◆ **aos trancos** *loc adv* [aos solavancos] jolting.

◆ **aos trancos e barrancos** *loc adv* [com dificuldade] with great difficulty.

tranqüilamente [trãŋkwila'mẽntʃi] *adv* **-1.** [com

calma] calmly. **-2.** [sossegadamente] peacefully. **-3.** [com facilidade, seguramente] easily.

tranqüilidade [trãŋkwili'dadʒi] *f* tranquillity; **preciso de ~ para fazer isso** I need peace and quiet to do this.

tranqüilizador, ra [trãŋkwiliza'do(x), ra] *adj* **-1.** [música] soothing. **-2.** [pessoa, notícia] reassuring.

tranqüilizante [trãŋkwili'zãntʃi] <> *adj* soothing. <> *m MED* tranquillizer.

tranqüilizar [trãŋkwili'za(x)] *vt* **-1.** [acalmar] to calm (down). **-2.** [despreocupar] to reassure.

◆ **tranqüilizar-se** *vp* to calm down.

tranqüilo, la [trãŋ'kwilu, la] *adj* **-1.** [mulher, criança] calm. **-2.** [lugar, sono] peaceful. **-3.** [consciência] clear. **-4.** [sem dificuldades] easy. **-5.** [certo] certain.

transa ['trãnza] *f fam* **-1.** [combinação] arrangement. **-2.** [relação] relationship. **-3.** [relação sexual] sex. **-4.** [assunto] matter. **-5.** [negócios] business.

transação [trãnza'sãw] (*pl* **-ões**) *f* **-1.** [combinação, acordo] agreement. **-2.** [negociação] deal. **-3.** *COM* business.

transamazônico, ca [trãnzama'zoniku, ka] *adj* trans-Amazonian.

transar [4] [trãn'za(x)] <> *vt* **-1.** *fam* [combinar] to arrange. **-2.** [arranjar] to obtain. **-3.** [drogas - tomar] to take; [- negociar] to deal in. <> *vi* **-1.** [ter relação sexual] to have sex; **~ com** to have sex with. **-2.** [relacionar-se]: **~ com** to hang out with. **-3.** [negociar, trabalhar]: **~ com** to deal in.

transatlântico, ca [trãnza'tlãntʃiku, ka] *adj* transatlantic.

◆ **transatlântico** *m* liner.

transbordamento [trãnʒboxda'mẽntu] *m* overflow.

transbordar [4] [trãnʒbox'da(x)] *vi*: **~ (de)** to overflow (from); **~ de felicidade** to be overjoyed.

transbordo [trãnʒ'bɔxdu] *m NÁUT* transfer.

transcendência [trãnsẽn'dẽnsja] *f* transcendence.

transcendental [trãnsẽndẽn'taw] (*pl* **-ais**) *adj* transcendental.

transcender [5] [trãnsẽn'de(x)] *vt*: **~ (a) algo** to transcend sthg.

transcodificar [5] [trãnʒkodʒifi'ka(x)] *vt* [videoteipe] to transcode.

transcorrer [trãnʃko'xe(x)] *vi* **-1.** [decorrer] to go by. **-2.** [decorrer em certo estado ou condição] to pass off.

transcrever [5] [trãnʃkre've(x)] *vt* **-1.** [ger] to transcribe. **-2.** [copiar] to copy.

transcrição [trãnʃkri'sãw] (*pl* **-ões**) *f* **-1.** [ato] transcription. **-2.** [texto transcrito] transcript; **~ fonética** phonetic transcription.

transcrito, ta [trãnʃ'kritu, ta] <> *pp* ▻ **transcrever**.

◆ **transcrito** *m* transcript.

transcurso [trãnʃ'kuxsu] *m* course.

transe ['trãnzi] *m* **-1.** [espirit] anguish. **-2.** [situação difícil] ordeal. **-3.** [hipnótico] trance.

transeunte [trãn'zeũntʃi] *mf* passer-by.

transferência [trãnʃfe'rẽnsja] *f* **-1.** [ger] transfer. **-2.** *PSIC* transference. **-3.** [adiamento] postponement.

transferir [57] [trãnʃfe'ri(x)] *vt* **-1.** [deslocar]: **~ algo/alguém para algum lugar** to transfer sthg/sb somewhere. **-2.** [transmitir]: **~ algo para alguém** to transfer sthg to sb; *PSIC* to transfer sthg onto sb. **-3.** [adiar] to postpone.

◆ **transferir-se** *vp* [mudar-se] to move.

transfigurar [4] [trãnʃfigu'ra(x)] *vt* [pessoa, rosto] to transfigure.

◆ **transfigurar-se** *vp* [pessoa, rosto] to be transfigured.

transformacão [trãnʃfoxma'sãw] (*pl* **-ões**) *f* transformation.

transformador, ra [trãnʃfoxma'do(x), ra] (*mpl* **-es**, *fpl* **-s**) *m ELETR* transformer.

transformar [4] [trãnʃfox'ma(x)] *vt* **-1.** [dar nova forma, modificar] to transform. **-2.** [converter]: **~ algo/alguémem** to turn sthg/sb into.

◆ **transformar-se** *vp* **-1.** [mudar, transfigurar-se] to be transformed. **-2.** [converter-se]: **~-se em** to turn into, to become. **-3.** [disfarçar-se]: **~-se em** to disguise o.s. as.

transformista [trãnʃfox'miʃta] *m* [travesti] transvestite.

transfusão [trãnʃfu'zãw] (*pl* **-ões**) *f* transfusion; **~ de sangue** blood transfusion.

transgredir [57] [trãnʒgre'dʒi(x)] *vt* [infringir] to transgress.

transgressão [trãnʒgre'sãw] (*pl* **-ões**) *f* transgression.

transgressor, ra [trãʒgre'so(x), ra] <> *adj* offending. <> *m, f* offender; **~ da lei** offender.

transição [trãnzi'sãw] (*pl* **-ões**) *f* [passagem de um estado a outro] transition; **fase de ~** transition stage.

transigente [trãnzi'ʒẽntʃi] *adj* compliant.

transigir [52] [trãnzi'ʒi(x)] *vi* **-1.** [ceder] to compromise; **~ com alguém** to meet sb halfway. **-2.** [condescender] to condescend; **~ com algo** to yield to sthg.

transitar [4] [trãnzi'ta(x)] *vi*: **~ (por)** [pessoa, carro] to travel (through); [documentos] to work one's way (through).

transitável [trãnzi'tavew] (*pl* **-eis**) *adj* passable.

transitivo, va [trãnzi'tʃivu, va] *adj GRAM* transitive.

trânsito ['trãnzitu] *m* **-1.** [ger] passage; **passageiro em ~** transit passenger. **-2.** [tráfego] traffic; **~ impedido** no entry. **-3.** [boa aceitação] acceptance; **ter bom ~ em** to be well-accepted in.

transitório, ria [trãnzi'tɔrju, rja] *adj* transitory.

transladar [4] [trãnʒla'da(x)] *vt* = **trasladar**.

translado [trãnʒ'ladu] *m* = **traslado**.

translúcido, da [trãnʒ'lusidu, da] *adj* **-1.** [que deixa passar a luz] translucent. **-2.** *fig* [claro] clear.

transmissão [trãnʒmi'sãw] (*pl* **-ões**) *f* **-1.** [ger]

transmission. **-2.** [de ordem, notícia, recado] sending; ~ **de pensamento** mind-reading. **-3.** [de bens, cargo] transfer. **-4.** [*RÁDIO* & *TV* - programa] broadcast; [- ato de transmitir] broadcasting; ~ **ao vivo** live broadcast.

transmissível [trãnʒmi'sivew] (*pl* **-eis**) *adj* [doença] transmittable.

transmissor, ra [trãnʒmi'so(x), ra] *adj* transmitting.

◆ **transmissor** *m* **-1.** [ger] transmitter. **-2.** [de doença] carrier.

transmitir [6] [trãnʒmi'tʃi(x)] *vt* **-1.** [ger] to transmit. **-2.** [comunicar] to send. **-3.** [transferir] to transfer. **-4.** *RÁDIO* & *TV* to broadcast.

transparecer [25] [trãnʃpare'se(x)] *vi* **-1.** [aparecer]: ~ **através/por trás de** to be visible through/behind. **-2.** *fig* [revelar-se]: ~ **(em)** to show through (in).

transparência [trãnʃpa'rênsja] *f* **-1.** [ger] transparency. **-2.** [usada em projetor] slide.

transparente [trãnʃpa'rêntʃi] *adj* **-1.** [ger] transparent. **-2.** [roupa] see-through. **-3.** *fig* [claro, evidente - sentimentos, intenções] clear; **o livro é de um moralismo** ~ the book is clearly moralistic; [- pessoa] transparent.

transpassar [4] [trãnʃpa'sa(x)] *vt* **-1.** [atravessar] to cross. **-2.** [penetrar, furar] to pierce. **-3.** [peça de vestuário] to overlap.

transpiração [trãnʃpira'sãw] *f* **-1.** [ato] perspiration. **-2.** [suor] perspiration.

transpirar [4] [trãnʃpi'ra(x)] ◇ *vt* **-1.** [suar] to perspire. **-2.** [exprimir] to exude. ◇ *vi* **-1.** [suar] to perspire. **-2.** [revelar-se] to transpire. **-3.** [divulgar-se] to become known.

transplantar [4] [trãnʃplãn'ta(x)] *vt*: ~ **algo (de/para)** to transplant sthg (from/to).

transplante [trãnʃ'plãntʃi] *m* transplant.

transpor [45] [trãnʃ'po(x)] *vt* **-1.** [ger] to transpose. **-2.** [atravessar] to cross. **-3.** *fig* [obstáculos] to overcome. **-4.** [mudar de lugar] to change the position of.

transportadora [trãnʃpoxta'dora] *f* haulage company.

transportar [trãnʃpox'ta(x)] *vt* **-1.** [levar] to transport. **-2.** *fig* [remontar mentalmente]: ~ **alguém a algum lugar/tempo** to take sb back to some place/time.

transporte [trãnʃ'pɔxtʃi] *m* **-1.** [ato] transport. **-2.** [condução] haulage; ~ **coletivo** public transport. **-3.** [soma] amount carried forward.

transposto, osta [trãnʃ'postu, ɔʃta] *pp* ▷ **transpor**.

transtornado, da [trãnʃtox'nadu, da] *adj* upset.

transtornar [4] [trãnʃtox'na(x)] *vt* **-1.** [abalar] to upset. **-2.** [alterar] to disrupt.

◆ **transtornar-se** *vp* to get upset.

transtorno [trãnʃ'toxnu] *m* **-1.** [perturbação] confusion. **-2.** [desordem, alteração] disruption. **-3.** [contrariedade, contratempo] upset.

transversal [trãnʒvex'saw] (*pl* **-ais**) ◇ *adj* **-1.** [corte, linha] transverse. **-2.** [rua]: **esta rua é** ~ **à avenida principal** this street crosses the main avenue. ◇ *f* [rua transversal] cross street.

transverso, sa [trãnʒ'vɛxsu, sa] *adj* transverse.

transviado, da [trãnʒ'vjadu, da] *adj* wayward.

transviar [16] [trãnʒ'vja(x)] *vt* to lead astray.

◆ **transviar-se** *vp* **-1.** [perder-se] to go astray. **-2.** [corromper-se] to become corrupted.

trapaça [tra'pasa] *f* cheating; **fazer ~s no jogo** to cheat during the game.

trapacear [15] [trapa'sja(x)] *vt* & *vi* to cheat.

trapaceiro, ra [trapa'sejru, ra] ◇ *adj* cheating. ◇ *m, f* cheat.

trapalhada [trapa'ʎada] *f* [confusão] confusion.

trapalhão, ona [trapa'ʎãw, ʎona] (*mpl* **-ões**, *fpl* **-s**) *adj* clumsy.

trapeiro, ra [tra'pejru, ra] *m, f* **-1.** [quem cata trapos] rag-and-bone-man. **-2.** [quem cata papéis] scavenger.

trapézio [tra'pɛzju] *m* **-1.** [aparelho] trapeze. **-2.** *GEOM* trapezium. **-3.** [*ANAT* - no pescoço] trapezius; [- do carpo] trapezium.

trapezista [trape'ziʃta] *mf* trapeze artist.

trapezoidal [trapezoj'daw] (*pl* **-ais**) *adj* trapezoidal.

trapo ['trapu] *m* **-1.** [pedaço de pano] rag. **-2.** *fig*: **estar um** ~ [estar mal física ou moralmente] to be down and out; [estar muito cansado] to be washed out.

◆ **trapos** *mpl* [roupa surrada] rags.

traquéia [tra'kɛja] *f* trachea, windpipe.

traquejo [tra'keʒu] *m* experience.

traqueotomia [trakjoto'mia] *f* tracheotomy.

traquinas [tra'kinaʃ] *adj inv* mischievous.

trarei [tra'rej] *v* ▷ **trazer**.

traria [tra'ria] *v* ▷ **trazer**.

trás ['trajʃ] *adv* & *prep* behind; **de** ~ **para frente** back to front; **andar para** ~ to walk backwards; **ficar para** ~ to fall behind; **de** ~ back; **por** ~ **de** behind; **dar para** ~ to back out.

traseira [tra'zejra] *f* **-1.** [parte posterior] rear. **-2.** *fam* [nádegas] bottom.

traseiro, ra [tra'zejru, ra] *adj* rear.

◆ **traseiro** *m fam* [nádegas] bottom.

trasladar [4] [traʒla'da(x)] *vt* **-1.** *JUR* to transfer. **-2.** [transferir]: ~ **algo (de ...) para** to transfer sthg (from ...) to.

traslado [traʒ'ladu] *m* **-1.** *JUR* transcript. **-2.** [transferência] transfer.

traspassar [trazpa'sa(x)] *vt* = **transpassar**.

traste ['traʃtʃi] *m* **-1.** [objeto de pouco valor] bauble. **-2.** [pessoa - inútil] no-hoper; [- de mau caráter] rogue; **estar um** ~ [estar mal fisicamente] to be a wreck.

tratado, da [tra'tadu, da] *m* **-1.** [acordo] treaty; ~ **de paz** peace treaty. **-2.** [obra] treatise.

tratador, ra [trata'do(x), ra] *m, f*: ~ **de cavalos** groom.

tratamento [trata'mẽntu] *m* **-1.** [ger] treatment; **forma de** ~ form of address; ~ **médico** medical treatment; ~ **de choque** shock treatment. **-2.** [de problema, tema] handling.

tratante [tra'tãntʃi] *mf* rogue.

tratar [4] [tra'ta(x)] *vt* **-1.** [ger] to treat. **-2.** [combinar] to deal with. **-3.** *MED*: **~ (de) alguém/algo** to treat sb/sthg. **-4.** [negociar] to organize. **-5.** [abordar] to deal with. **-6.** [forma de tratamento]: **~ alguém de** *ou* **por algo** to address sb as *ou* by sthg.
◆ **tratar com** *vi* [lidar com] to deal with.
◆ **tratar de** *vi* **-1.** [cuidar de - pessoa, planta] to care for; [- caso, negócio] to look after. **-2.** [organizar] to organize. **-3.** [discorrer, versar sobre] to deal with. **-4.** [empenhar-se]: **~ de fazer algo** to try to do sthg.
◆ **tratar-se** *vp* **-1.** [cuidar-se] to look after o.s. **-2.** *MED*: **~-se com alguém** to be under sb's care. **-3.** *loc*: **trata-se de ...** it's a matter of ...; **trata-se de uma moça de origem muito humilde** she happens to be a girl from a very humble background; **de que se trata?** what's it about?

tratável [tra'tavew] (*pl* **-eis**) *adj* **-1.** [pessoa] approachable. **-2.** [doença] treatable.

trato ['tratu] *m* **-1.** [tratamento] treatment. **-2.** [convivência, contato] dealings *(pl)*. **-3.** [acordo, combinação] agreement. **-4.** [modo]: **mulher de fino ~** a refined woman.

trator [tra'to(x)] (*pl* **-es**) *m* tractor.

trauma ['trawma] *m* **-1.** *MED* injury. **-2.** *PSIC* trauma.

traumático, ca [traw'matʃiku, ka] *adj* traumatic.

traumatismo [trawma'tʃiʒmu] *m MED* injury.

traumatizante [trawmatʃi'zãntʃi] *adj* traumatizing.

traumatizar [4] [trawmatʃi'za(x)] *vt* **-1.** *MED* to injure. **-2.** *PSIC* to traumatize. **-3.** *fig* [afetar] to affect.

trava ['trava] *f* [peça] stop.

travada [tra'vada] *f* [freada] braking; **dar uma ~ em algo** [frear] to put on the breaks; *fig* [interromper] to put the brakes on sthg.

travado, da [tra'vadu, da] *adj* **-1.** [preso] locked. **-2.** [freado] stopped.

travar [4] [tra'va(x)] ◇ *vt* **-1.** [fazer parar] to stop. **-2.** [frear] to brake. **-3.** [iniciar, desencadear - conversa, amizade] to strike up; [- luta] to start. **-4.** [movimento] to hinder. **-5.** [segurar] to take hold of. ◇ *vi* to stop.

trave ['travi] *f* **-1.** *CONSTR* beam. **-2.** *ESP* crossbar.

través [tra'vɛʃ] *m*: **olhar de ~ (para)** to look sideways (at).

travessa [tra'vɛsa] *f* **-1.** [rua] alleyway. **-2.** [prato] serving dish. **-3.** [prendedor de cabelo] slide.

travessão [trave'sãw] (*pl* **-ões**) *m GRAM* (em) dash.

travesseiro [trave'sejru] *m* pillow.

travessia [trave'sia] *f* **-1.** [ato] crossing. **-2.** [viagem] journey.

travesso, ssa [tra'vesu, sa] *adj* [criança] naughty.

travessura [trave'sura] *f* **-1.** [de criança] mischief; **fazer ~s** to get up to mischief. **-2.** [brincadeira] prank.

travesti [traveʃtʃi] *m* **-1.** [homossexual] transvestite. **-2.** [artista] drag artist.

trazer [30] [tra'ze(x)] *vt* **-1.** [ger] to bring; **~ de volta** to bring back. **-2.** [ter] to have. **-3.** [usar, trajar] to wear. **-4.** *loc*: **~ algo à baila** to air sthg.

TRE (*abrev de* **Tribunal Regional Eleitoral**) *m Regional Electoral Court.*

trecho ['treʃu] *m* **-1.** [parte do espaço de um lugar] stretch. **-2.** *LITER & MÚS* passage.

treco ['trɛku] *m fam* [coisa] thing; **ter um ~** [sentir-se mal] to have a nasty turn; [zangar-se] to have a fit.

trégua ['trɛgwa] *f* **-1.** *MIL* truce. **-2.** *fig* [descanso] rest.

treinado, da [trej'nadu, da] *adj* **-1.** [animal] trained. **-2.** [atleta] fit. **-3.** [acostumado] practised *UK*, practiced *US*.

treinador, ra [trejna'do(x), ra] (*mpl* **-es**, *fpl* **-s**) *m, f* trainer.

treinamento [trejna'mẽntu] *m* training.

treinar [4] [trej'na(x)] ◇ *vt* **-1.** [ger] to train. **-2.** [praticar] to practise *UK*, to practice *US*. ◇ *vi* [praticar] to train.

treino ['trejnu] *m* **-1.** [ger] training. **-2.** [destreza] skill.

trejeito [tre'ʒejtu] *m* **-1.** [gesto] gesture. **-2.** [gesto cômico] funny face.

trela ['trɛla] *f*: **dar ~ a** *ou* **para alguém** [conversar com] to keep chatting to sb; [dar confiança a] to encourage sb.

treliça [tre'lisa] *f* [para porta, planta] trellis.

trem ['trẽ] (*pl* **-ns**) *m* **-1.** *FERRO* train; **ir de ~** to go by train; **pegar um ~** to take a train; **~ de carga** goods train; **~ expresso** express train. **-2.** *AERON*: **~ de aterrissagem** landing gear, undercarriage. **-3.** *loc*: **~ da alegria** [nepotismo] jobs for the boys.

trema ['trema] *m* diaeresis *UK*, dieresis *US*.

trem-bala [ˌtrẽ'bala] (*pl* **trens-bala**) *m* high-speed train.

tremedeira [treme'dejra] *f* [tremor] trembling.

tremelicante [tremeli'kãntʃi] *adj* **-1.** [pessoa] shivering. **-2.** [bandeira] fluttering.

tremelicar [12] [tremeli'ka(x)] *vi* to tremble; **~ de frio** to shiver with cold.

tremelique [treme'liki] *m* trembling.

tremendo, da [tre'mẽndu, da] *adj* **-1.** [imenso] enormous. **-2.** [terrível] terrible. **-3.** [fantástico] amazing.

tremer [5] [tre'me(x)] *vi* to shake; **~ de frio/medo** to shake with cold/fear.

tremor [tre'mo(x)] (*pl* **-es**) *m* tremor; **~ de terra** earthquake.

tremular [4] [tremu'la(x)] *vi* **-1.** [bandeira] to flutter. **-2.** [luz] to flicker.

trêmulo, la ['tremulu, la] *adj* **-1.** [pessoa, mão] trembling. **-2.** [passo, voz] faltering.

trena ['trena] *f* [fita métrica] tape measure.

trenó [tre'nɔ] *m* sledge *UK*, sled *US*.

trepada [tre'pada] *f mfam* leg-over; **dar uma ~** to get laid.

trepadeira [trepa'dejra] *f* creeper.

trepar [4] [tre'pa(x)] *vi* **-1.** [subir]: **~ (em algo)** to climb (up sthg). **-2.** *mfam* [ter relações sexuais]: **~ (com alguém)** to get laid.

trepidação [trepida'sãw] *f* shaking.

trepidante [trepi'dãntʃi] *adj* **-1.** [que trepida] shaking. **-2.** *fig* [agitado] restless.

trepidar [4] [trepi'da(x)] *vi* to shake.

três ['trejʃ] ◇ *num* three. ◇ *m* three; *veja também* **seis**.

◆ **a três por dois** *loc adv* often.

tresloucado, da [treʒlo'kadu, da] *adj* crazy.

Três-Marias [ˌtrejʃma'riaʃ] *fpl* **-1.** *ASTRON* Orion's Belt. **-2.** *BOT* bougainvillea.

três-quartos [trejʃ'kwaxtuʃ] ◇ *adj inv* [manga, saia] three-quarter length. ◇ *m* [apartamento] three-room flat *UK* *ou* apartment *US*.

trevas ['trɛvaʃ] *fpl* [escuridão] darkness *(sg)*.

trevo ['trevu] *m* **-1.** *BOT* clover. **-2.** [de vias] intersection.

treze ['trezi] ◇ *num* thirteen. ◇ *m* [algarismo] thirteen; *veja também* **seis**.

trezentos, tas [tre'zẽntuʃ, taʃ] ◇ *num* three hundred. ◇ *m* [algarismo] three hundred; *veja também* **seis**.

triagem ['trjaʒẽ] *f* **-1.** [seleção] selection; **fazer uma ~** to make a selection. **-2.** [separação] sorting; **fazer uma ~** to sort out.

triangular [trjãŋgu'la(x)] *adj* triangular.

triângulo ['trjãŋgulu] *m* triangle.

triathlon ['trjatlu] *m* triathlon.

tribal [tri'baw] *adj* tribal.

tribo ['tribu] *m* tribe.

tribulação [tribula'sãw] *(pl* **-ões)** *f* tribulation.

tribuna [tri'buna] *f* **-1.** [de orador] rostrum. **-2.** [em espetáculos públicos] platform; **~ da imprensa** press gallery; **~ de honra** rostrum.

tribunal [tribu'naw] *(pl* **-ais)** *m* **-1.** [instituição] court; **Tribunal de Contas** Court of Accounts; **Tribunal do Júri** trial by jury; **Tribunal de Justiça** Court of Justice; **Tribunal do Trabalho** Industrial Tribunal. **-2.** [os magistrados] bench.

tributação [tributa'sãw] *f* taxation.

tributar [4] [tribu'ta(x)] *vt* **-1.** [ger] to tax. **-2.** [pagar como tributo] to pay tax on. **-3.** *fig* [render, prestar] to pay.

tributário, ria [tribu'tarju, rja] *adj* **-1.** [relativo a tributo] tax *(antes de subst)*. **-2.** [rio] tributary *(antes de subst)*.

◆ **tributário** *m* [afluente] tributary.

tributável [tribu'tavew] *(pl* **-eis)** *adj* taxable.

tributo [tri'butu] *m* **-1.** [imposto] tax. **-2.** *fig* [ônus] duty.

tricampeão, peã [trikãn'pjãw, pjã] *m, f* three-times champion.

triciclo [tri'siklu] *m* **-1.** [de criança] tricycle. **-2.** [usado para a entrega de mercadorias] (delivery) tricycle.

tricô [tri'ko] *m* knitting; **fazer ~** to knit; **de ~** knitted.

tricolor [triko'lo(x)] *adj* **-1.** [desenho, bandeira] three-coloured *UK*, three-colored *US*. **-2.** *FUT* tricolour *UK*, tricolor *US*.

tricotar [4] [triko'ta(x)] *vt* & *vi* to knit.

tridimensional [tridʒimẽnsjo'naw] *(pl* **-ais)** *adj* three-dimensional.

trienal [trje'naw] ◇ *adj* triennial. ◇ *f* [exposição] triennial.

triênio ['trjenju] *m* three-year period.

trigal [tri'gaw] *m* wheat field.

trigêmeo, mea [tri'ʒemju, mja] ◇ *adj* [criança] triplet *(antes de subst)*. ◇ *m, f* triplet.

trigésimo, ma [tri'ʒɛzimu, ma] ◇ *num* thirtieth. ◇ *m* thirtieth; *veja também* **sexto**.

trigo ['trigu] *m* wheat.

trigonometria [trigonome'tria] *f* trigonometry.

trilha ['triʎa] *f* **-1.** [caminho] path. **-2.** [rasto] trail. **-3.** *fig* [exemplo]: **seguir a ~ de alguém** to follow in sb's footsteps. **-4.** *COMPUT* track. **-5.** *CINE*: **~ sonora** soundtrack.

trilhado, da [tri'ʎadu, da] *adj* [percorrido] well-trodden.

trilhão [tri'ʎãw] *(pl* **-ões)** *num* trillion.

trilhar [4] [tri'ʎa(x)] *vt* [percorrer] to tread.

trilho ['triʎu] *m* **-1.** *FERRO* rail. **-2.** [caminho] track.

trilíngüe [tri'liŋgwe] *adj* trilingual.

trilogia [trilo'ʒia] *f* trilogy.

trimestral [trimeʃ'traw] *(pl* **-ais)** *adj* quarterly.

trimestralidade [trimeʃtrawi'dadʒi] *f* quarterly payment.

trimestralmente [trimeʃtraw'mẽntʃi] *adv* quarterly.

trimestre [tri'mɛʃtri] *m* quarter.

trinca ['trĩŋka] *f* **-1.** [de cartas] set of three. **-2.** *fam* [de pessoas] threesome.

trincar [12] [trĩŋ'ka(x)] ◇ *vt* **-1.** [cortar com os dentes] to crunch. **-2.** [cerrar] to grit. **-3.** [rachar] to crack. ◇ *vi* [rachar] to crack.

trinchar [4] [trĩn'ʃa(x)] *vt* [carne] to carve.

trincheira [trĩn'ʃejra] *f MIL* trench.

trinco ['trĩŋku] *m* **-1.** [ferrolho] latch. **-2.** [lingüeta] catch; **passar o ~ na porta** to put the door on the latch.

trindade [trĩn'dadʒi] *f*: **a Santíssima Trindade** the Holy Trinity.

◆ **trindades** *fpl* angelus *(sg)*.

Trinidad e Tobago [triniˌdadʒito'bagu] *n* Trinidad and Tobago.

trinta ['trĩnta] ◇ *num* thirty. ◇ *m* thirty; *veja também* **sessenta**.

trio ['triw] *m* trio; **~ elétrico** music float.

tripa [tri'pa] *f* **-1.** [intestino] intestine. **-2.** *CULIN* tripe *(inv)*. **-3.** *loc*: **fazer das ~s coração** to work one's guts out.

tripartir [6] [tripax'tʃi(x)] *vt* to divide into three parts.

tripé [tri'pɛ] *m* [suporte] tripod.

tríplex ['tripleks] ◇ *adj inv* three-storey *UK*, three-story *US*. ◇ *m inv* three-storey flat *UK*, three-storey apartment *US*.

triplicar [12] [tripli'ka(x)] ◇ *vt* **-1.** *MAT* to treble. **-2.** [aumentar muito] to triple. ◇ *vi* **-1.** [tornar-se triplo] to treble. **-2.** [aumentar muito] to triple.

tríplice ['triplisi] *adj* triple.

triplo, pla ['triplu, pla] *adj* triple.
◆ **triplo** *m*: **27 é o ~ de 9** 27 is three times 9; **este sofá é o ~ daquele** this sofa is three times the size of that one.
Trípoli ['tripoli] *n* Tripoli.
tripulação [tripula'sãw] (*pl* **-ões**) *f* crew.
tripulado, da [tripula'du, da] *adj* **-1.** [nave] manned. **-2.** [barco] crewed.
tripulante [tripu'lãntʃi] *mf* crew member.
tripular [4] [tripu'la(x)] *vt* **-1.** [prover de tripulação] to man. **-2.** [governar] to crew.
trisavô, vó [triza'vo, vɔ] *m, f* great-great-grandfather (*f* great-great-grandmother); **os ~s** great-great-grandparents.
triste ['triʃtʃi] *adj* **-1.** [ger] sad. **-2.** [entristecedor] depressing. **-3.** [sombrio, lúgubre] sombre. **-4.** *fam* [pessoa] sad.
tristeza [triʃ'teza] *f* **-1.** [de pessoa] sadness. **-2.** [de lugar] gloominess. **-3.**: **ser uma ~** [ser terrível] to be appalling.
tristonho, nha [triʃ'toɲu, ɲa] *adj* [pessoa, rosto, ar] melancholy.
triturar [4] [tritu'ra(x)] *vt* **-1.** [reduzir a fragmentos] to grind. **-2.** *fig* [afligir] to crush.
triunfal [trjũn'faw] (*pl* **-ais**) *adj* triumphal.
triunfante [trjũn'fãntʃi] *adj* triumphant.
triunfar [4] [trjũn'fa(x)] *vi* [vencer] to triumph.
triunfo ['trjũnfu] *m* triumph.
trivial [tri'vjaw] (*pl* **-ais**) ◇ *adj* **-1.** [comida] ordinary. **-2.** [assunto, preocupações] trivial. ◇ *m* [comida cotidiana] everyday food.
trivialidade [trivjali'dadʒi] *f* triviality.
triz ['triʃ] *m*: **por um ~** by a whisker; **escapar por um ~** to escape by the skin of one's teeth.
troca ['trɔka] *f* exchange; **em ~ de** in exchange for.
troça ['trɔsa] *f* [zombaria] ridicule; **fazer ~ de alguém** to make fun of sb.
trocadilho [troka'dʒiʎu] *m* pun.
trocado, da [tro'kadu, da] *adj* **-1.** [errado] wrong. **-2.** [dinheiro] in coins.
◆ **trocado** *m* small change.
trocador, ra [troka'do(x), ra] *m, f* [em ônibus] conductor.
trocar [12] [tro'ka(x)] ◇ *vt* **-1.** [ger] to change; **~ alguém/algo de lugar** to change the place of sb/sthg; **~ dinheiro** to change money. **-2.** [permutar] to swap. **-3.** [confundir] to mix up. **-4.** [cheque] to cash. **-5.** [reciprocar] to exchange. **-6.** [permutar]: **~ algo/alguém por algo**, **~ algo/alguém por alguém** to change sthg/sb for sthg, to change sthg/sb for sb; **~ o dia pela noite** to live at night. **-7.** [dar preferência]: **~ algo por algo** to exchange sthg for sthg. **-8.** *loc*: **~ as pernas** *fig* to trip over one's (own) feet. ◇ *vi*: **~ de algo** to change sthg; **~ de bem/mal** to make up/fall out.
◆ **trocar-se** *vp* [mudar de roupa] to get changed.
troçar [tro'sa(x)] *vt* to ridicule.
troca-troca [ˌtrɔka'trɔka] *m* swap.
troco ['troku] *m* **-1.** [dinheiro] change. **-2.** *fig* [revide] retort, rejoinder; **dar o ~ a alguém** to get one's own back; **a ~ de que ela fez isso?** [por quê, para quê] what on earth did she do that for?; **a ~ de algo/de fazer algo** [por causa de] by way of sthg/of doing sthg; [por meio de] by means of sthg/of doing sthg; **em ~ de** [em recompensa a] in exchange for.
troço ['trɔsu] *m* **-1.** *fam* [coisa] thing; **ter um ~** [sentir-se mal] to feel a pang; [ficar chocado, danado] to get a shock; **ser ~ em algum lugar/em algo** [ser influente] to have influence somewhere/in sthg; **ser um ~** [ser muito bonito, bom] to be amazing.
troféu [tro'fɛw] *m* trophy.
tromba ['trõnba] *f* **-1.** [de elefante] trunk. **-2.** *fam* [cara amarrada] long face; **estar de ~** to sulk.
trombada [trõn'bada] *f* crash; **dar uma ~** to crash.
tromba-d'água [ˌtrõnba'dagwa] (*pl* **trombas-d'água**) *f* [chuva] downpour; **caiu uma ~** there was a huge downpour.
trombadinha [trõnba'dʒiɲa] *mf gír* [pivete] very young thief.
trombeta [trõn'beta] *f* MÚS [instrumento] trumpet.
trombone [trõn'boni] *m* **-1.** MÚS trombone. **-2.**: **botar a boca no ~** *fam fig* to tell the whole world.
trombose [trõn'bɔzi] *f* thrombosis.
trombudo, da [trõn'budu, da] *adj fig* [emburrado] sulky.
trompa ['trõnpa] *f* **-1.** MÚS horn. **-2.** ANAT: **~ de Falópio** Fallopian tube; **ligar as ~s** to have one's tubes tied, to undergo tubal ligation.
troncho, cha ['trõnʃu, ʃa] *adj* **-1.** [torto] crooked. **-2.** [desajeitado] clumsy. **-3.** [mutilado]: **~ de uma perna** one-legged.
tronco ['trõŋku] *m* **-1.** [BOT - caule] trunk; [- ramo] branch. **-2.** ANAT trunk. **-3.** TELEC trunkline. **-4.** [de família, raça] lineage.
troncudo, da [trõŋ'kudu, da] *adj* stocky.
trono ['tronu] *m* **-1.** [cadeira] throne. **-2.** *fig* [poder] driving seat. **-3.** *fam* [latrina] throne.
tropa ['trɔpa] *f* **-1.** MIL army. **-2.** [conjunto de pessoas] troop. **-3.** [polícia]: **~ de choque** riot squad.
tropeção [trope'sãw] (*pl* **-ões**) *m* trip; **dar um ~ em algo** to trip over sthg.
tropeçar [13] [trope'sa(x)] *vi* to trip; **~ em algo** [dar topada em] to trip over sthg; *fig* [esbarrar em] to stumble on sthg.
tropeço [tro'pesu] *m fig* [obstáculo] setback.
tropeções [trope'sõjʃ] *pl* ▻ **tropeção**.
trôpego, ga ['tropegu, ga] *adj* unsteady; **estar ~ de sono** to be asleep on one's feet.
tropel [tro'pɛw] *m* **-1.** [multidão desordenada] mob. **-2.** [de animais] herd. **-3.** [ruído] clattering. **-4.** [grande confusão] hubbub.
tropical [tropi'kaw] (*pl* **-ais**) *adj* tropical.
tropicalismo [tropika'liʒmu] *m Brazilian musical movement.*

TROPICALISMO

Tropicalismo was a musical movement that renewed the so-called MPB (*Música Popular Brasileira*) in the midst of the cultural and political effervescence of the late 60s; it incorporated elements of the international cultural scene into the Brazilian music tradition. The movement also had an important influence on theatre and the arts. Two of its main exponents were Caetano Veloso and Gilberto Gil.

trópico ['trɔpiku] *m* tropic; **Trópico de Câncer/Capricórnio** Tropic of Cancer/Capricorn.
troquei [tro'kej] *v* ⊳ **trocar**.
trotar [4] [tro'ta(x)] *vi* to trot.
trote ['trɔtʃi] *m* **-1.** [de cavalo] trot. **-2.** [por telefone] hoax; **passar um ~ em alguém** to play a hoax on sb. **-3.** [em calouro] trick; **dar um ~ em alguém** to play a trick on sb.
trottoir [tro'twa(x)] *m*: **fazer ~** to walk the streets.
trouxa ['troʃa] ◇ *adj* ***fam*** [bobo] foolish. ◇ *mf* ***fam*** [bobo] fool. ◇ *f* bundle.
trouxe ['trosi] *v* ⊳ **trazer**.
trova ['trɔva] *f* **-1.** [cantiga] folksong. **-2.** [poesia] ballad.
trovador [trova'do(x)] *m* troubadour.
trovão [tro'vãw] (*pl* **-ões**) *m* thunder.
trovejar [4] [trove'ʒa(x)] *vi* METEOR to thunder.
trovoada [tro'vwada] *f* thunderstorm.
trucidar [trusi'da(x)] *vt* to slaughter, to massacre.
truculência [truku'lẽnsja] *f* horror.
truculento, ta [truku'lẽntu, ta] *adj* gruesome.
trufa ['trufa] *f* truffle.
truísmo [tru'iʒmu] *m* truism.
truncar [trũŋ'ka(x)] *vt* **-1.** [texto] to shorten. **-2.** [discurso] to cut off.
trunfo ['trũnfu] *m* trump card.
trupe ['trupi] *f* **-1.** [de artistas] troop. **-2.** ***pej*** [grupo] buch.
truque ['truki] *m* trick.
truste ['truʃtʃi] *m* **-1.** [organização financeira] trust. **-2.** [grupo de empresas] corporation.
truta ['truta] *f* trout.
TSE [te 'ɛsi ɛ] (*abrev de* **Tribunal Superior Eleitoral**) *m Brazilian higher electoral tribunal.*
TST [te 'ɛsi te] (*abrev de* **Tribunal Superior do Trabalho**) *m Brazilian higher employment tribunal.*
tu ['tu] *pron pess* you.
tua ['tua] *f* ⊳ **teu**.
tuba ['tuba] *f* MÚS tuba.
tubarão [tuba'rãw] (*pl* **-ões**) *m* shark.
tubário, ria [tu'barju, rja] *adj* [MED - gravidez] ectopic; [- infecção] tubal.
tuberculose [tubexku'lɔzi] *f* tubercolosis, TB.
tuberculoso, osa [tubexku'lozu, ɔza] ◇ *adj* tubercular. ◇ *m, f* person with TB.
tubinho [tu'biɲu] *m* **-1.** [tubo pequeno] small tube. **-2.** [vestido] tube dress.
tubo ['tubu] *m* **-1.** [ger] tube; **~ de ensaio** test tube. **-2.** [canal] pipe. **-3.** ANAT: **~ digestivo** digestive tract.
◆ **tubos** *mpl*: **gastar/custar os ~s** to spend/cost a bomb.
tubulação [tubula'sãw] *f* **-1.** [conjunto de tubos] pipework. **-2.** [colocação de tubos] plumbing.
tubular [tubu'la(x)] *adj* tubular.
TUCA (*abrev de* **Teatro da Universidade Católica**) *m theatre of the Catholic university in São Paulo.*
tucano [tu'kãnu] *m* **-1.** ZOOL toucan. **-2.** POL *member of Brazilian Social Democratic Party.*
tudo ['tudu] *pron indef* **-1.** [todas as coisas, a totalidade] everything; **~ (o) que** *ou* **quanto** everything that; **é ~** that's all; **~ isso** all that; **~ quanto é tipo de gente** all kinds of people. **-2.** [a coisa fundamental]: **ser ~** to be everything.
◆ **acima de tudo** *loc adv* above all.
◆ **antes de tudo** *loc adv* first of all.
◆ **apesar de tudo** *loc prep* despite everything.
◆ **depois de tudo** *loc adv* after all.
tufão [tu'fãw] (*pl* **-ões**) *m* typhoon.
tufo ['tufu] *m* **-1.** [de planta] shoot. **-2.** [de cabelo] lock. **-3.** [de terra, pedra] mound.
tulipa [tu'lipa] *f* **-1.** BOT tulip. **-2.** [chope servido em copo alto] *tall glass of draught beer.*
tumba ['tũnba] *f* [sepultura] tomb.
tumefação [tumefa'sãw] *f* swelling.
tumor [tu'mo(x)] (*pl* **-es**) *m* tumour ***UK***, tumor ***US***; **~ cerebral** brain tumour; **~ maligno/benigno** malignant/benign tumour.
túmulo ['tumulu] *m* **-1.** [monumento] tomb. **-2.** [cova] grave. **-3.** ***fig***: **ser um ~** [ser lúgubre] to be like a tomb; [ser discreto] to be very discreet.
tumulto [tu'muwtu] *m* **-1.** [grande movimento] commotion. **-2.** [confusão, balbúrdia] hubbub. **-3.** [motim] riot.
tumultuado, da [tumuw'twadu, da] *adj* **-1.** [vida] turbulent. **-2.** [rua] noisy.
tumultuar [4] [tumuw'twa(x)] ◇ *vt* [desordenar, agitar] to disrupt. ◇ *vi* **-1.** [fazer barulho] to make a noise. **-2.** [amotinar-se] to rise up.
túnel ['tunɛw] (*pl* **-eis**) *m* tunnel.
túnica ['tunika] *f* [vestimenta] tunic.
Túnis ['tuniʃ] *n* Tunis.
Tunísia [tu'nizja] *f* Tunisia.
tunisino, na [tuni'zinu, na] ◇ *adj* Tunisian. ◇ *m, f* Tunisian.
tupi [tu'pi] ◇ *adj* Tupi. ◇ *mf* Tupi Indian. ◇ *m* [língua] Tupi.

TUPI

The Tupi were an indigenous people in the north and central-west of the country and their language had a marked influence on Brazilian Portuguese. Many placenames derive from Tupi, such as the famous 'Ipanema', which, in Tupi, means 'thick-barked tree'. Other words have even reached the English language, such as 'cashew' (*caju* in Portuguese) and 'jaguar'.

tupi-guarani [tu,pigwara'ni] (*pl* **-is**) ◇ *adj* Tupi. ◇ *mf* [indígena] Tupi (Indian). ◇ *m* Tupi.
tupiniquim [tupini'kĩ] ◇ *adj* **-1.** [relativo aos tupiniquins] Brazilian Indian. **-2.** *pej* [brasileiro] Brazilian. ◇ *mf* Brazilian Indian.
turba ['tuxba] *f* **-1.** [multidão em desordem] mob. **-2.** [multidão] mass.
turbante [tux'bãntʃi] *m* turban.
turbar [4] [tux'ba(x)] *vt* [perturbar] to trouble.
◆ **turbar-se** *vp* [tornar-se sombrio] to darken.
turbilhão [tuxbi'ʎãw] (*pl* **-ões**) *m* **-1.** [de água] whirlpool. **-2.** [de ar] whirlwind. **-3.** *fig* [agitação] whirl.
turbina [tux'bina] *f* turbine.
turbinado, da [tuxbina'du, da] *adj fam* [motor, processador] turbocharged.
turbulência [tuxbu'lẽnsia] *f* **-1.** METEOR turbulence. **-2.** [desordem, inquietação] unrest.
turbulento, ta [tuxbu'lẽntu, ta] *adj* **-1.** METEOR stormy. **-2.** [tumultuoso] turbulent. **-3.** [que cria desordem] disorderly.
turco, ca ['tuxku, ka] ◇ *adj* Turkish. ◇ *m, f* Turk.
◆ **turco** *m* [língua] Turkish.
turfa ['tuxfa] *f* peat.
turfe ['tuxfi] *m* ESP horse-racing.
túrgido, da ['tuxʒidu, da] *adj* swollen, turgid.
turíbulo [tu'ribulu] *m* incense-burner.
turismo [tu'riʒmu] *m* tourism; **fazer** ~ to go sightseeing.
turista [tu'riʃta] *mf* **-1.** [quem faz turismo] tourist. **-2.** [aluno] persistent absentee.
turístico, ca [tu'riʃtʃiku, ka] *adj* tourist *(antes de subst).*
turma ['tuxma] *f* **-1.** [grupo] group. **-2.** [grupo de trabalhadores] shift. **-3.** EDUC class. **-4.** *fam* [grupo de amigos] gang.
turmalina [tuxma'lina] *f* tourmaline.
turnê [tux'ne] *f* tour.
turno ['tuxnu] *m* **-1.** [turma] group. **-2.** [horário - de trabalho] shift; [- de escola] class; ~ **da noite** night shift; ~ **da manhã** morning shift. **-3.** ESP round. **-4.** [de eleição] round. **-5.** [vez] turn; **por** ~**s** in turns; **por seu** ~ in turn.
turquesa [tux'keza] ◇ *adj inv* turquoise. ◇ *m* [cor] turquoise. ◇ *f* [pedra] turquoise.
Turquia [tux'kia] *n* Turkey.
turra ['tuxa] *f*: **viver às** ~**s** to argue all the time.
turrão, ona [tu'xãw, ɔna] *adj fam* [teimoso, pertinaz] stubborn.
turvar [4] [tux'va(x)] ◇ *vt* **-1.** [água, rio] to stir up. **-2.** [vista] to cloud. ◇ *vi* **-1.** [água, rio] to grow rough. **-2.** [vista] to become cloudy. **-3.** [vinho] to become cloudy.
turvo, va ['tuxvu, va] *adj* cloudy.
tusso ['tusu] *v* ▷ **tossir**.
tutano [tu'tãnu] *m* ANAT marrow.
tutela [tu'tɛla] *f* **-1.** JUR guardianship; **estar sob** ~ to be in care. **-2.** [proteção] protection. **-3.** [supervisão] supervision.
tutelar [4] [tute'la(x)] ◇ *adj* protective. ◇ *vt* **-1.** JUR to act as guardian to. **-2.** [proteger] to protect.
tutor, ra [tu'to(x), ra] (*mpl* **-es**, *fpl* **-s**) *m, f* guardian.
tutu [tu'tu] *m* **-1.** CULIN *Brazilian dish consisting of beans, bacon and cassava flour.* **-2.** *fam* [dinheiro] cash.
TV [te' ve] (*abrev de* **televisão**) *f* TV.
tweed ['twidʒi] *m* tweed.

u, U *m* [letra] u, U.
uai ['waj] *interj* **-1.** [espanto, surpresa, terror] oh! **-2.** [reforço, confirmação] yeah!
úbere ['uberi] ◇ *adj* [solo] fertile. ◇ *m* [mama] udder.
Ubes (*abrev de* **União Brasileira dos Estudantes Secundaristas**) *f Brazilian union of secondary students.*
ubiqüidade [ubikwi'dadʒi] *f* ubiquity.
ubíquo, qua [u'bikwu, kwa] *adj* ubiquitous.
Ucrânia [u'krãnja] *n* Ukraine.
ué ['wɛ] *interj* **-1.** [exprimindo surpresa] what? **-2.** [exprimindo ironia] hey!
UE (*abrev de* **União Européia**) *f* EU.
UEM (*abrev de* **União Econômica e Monetária**) *f* EMU.
UERJ (*abrev de* **Universidade Estadual do Rio de Janeiro**) *f state university of Rio de Janeiro.*
UF (*abrev de* **Unidade Federativa**) *f state.*
ufa ['ufa] *interj* phew!
ufanar-se [4] [ufa'naxsi] *vp*: ~ **de** to take inordinate pride in.
ufanismo [ufa'niʒmu] *m* **-1.** [por feitos pessoais] vainglory. **-2.** [pela pátria] national pride.
UFBA (*abrev de* **Universidade Federal da Bahia**) *f federal university of Bahia.*
UFMG (*abrev de* **Universidade Federal de Minas Gerais**) *f federal university of Minas Gerais.*
UFRGS (*abrev de* **Universidade Federal do Rio Grande do Sul**) *f federal university of Rio Grande do Sul.*
UFRJ (*abrev de* **Universidade Federal do Rio de Janeiro**) *f federal university of Rio de Janeiro.*
Uganda [u'gãnda] *n* Uganda.
UHF (*abrev de* **Ultra High Frequency**) *f* UHF.
ui ['uj] *interj* **-1.** [exprimindo dor] ouch! **-2.** [exprimindo surpresa] hey!
uísque ['wiʃki] *m* whisky.
uivada [uj'vada] *f* howl.

uivante [uj'vãntʃi] *adj* howling.

uivar [4] [uj'va(x)] *vi* [ger] to howl; ~ **(de)** to howl (with).

uivo ['ujvu] *m* howl.

UK (*abrev de* **United Kingdom**) *m* UK.

Ulan Bator [uˌlãnba'to(x)] *n* Ulan Bator.

úlcera ['uwsera] *f* ulcer; ~ **de estômago** gastric ulcer.

ulcerar [4] [uwse'ra(x)] ◇ *vt* to ulcerate. ◇ *vi* to develop an ulcer.

ulterior [uwte'rjo(x)] *adj* [que ocorre depois] subsequent.

ulteriormente [uwterjox'mẽntʃi] *adv* subsequently.

última ['uwtʃima] *f* ▷ **último**.

ultimamente [ˌuwtʃima'mẽntʃi] *adv* lately.

ultimar [4] [uwtʃi'ma(x)] *vt* to conclude.

últimas ['uwtʃimaʃ] *fpl* ▷ **último**.

ultimato [uwtʃi'matu], **ultimátum** [uwtʃi'matũ] *m* ultimatum.

último, ma ['uwtʃimu, ma] ◇ *adj* **-1.** [ger] last; **por** ~ [em último lugar] last; [finalmente] lastly. **-2.** [mais recente] latest. **-3.** [o pior] worst. **-4.** [gravíssimo] final. **-5.** [máximo] ultimate. ◇ *m, f* [em fila, competição] last.

◆ **última** *f* **-1.** [novidade] latest. **-2.** [asneira] latest blunder.

◆ **últimas** *fpl*: **dizer as últimas a alguém** to vilify sb; **estar nas últimas** [estar moribundo] to be on one's last legs; [estar na miséria] to be down and out.

ultrajante [uwtra'ʒãntʃi] *adj* outrageous.

ultrajar [4] [uwtra'ʒa(x)] *vt* to outrage.

ultraje [uw'traʒi] *m* outrage.

ultraleve [ˌuwtra'lɛvi] ◇ *adj* ultralight. ◇ *m* microlight.

ultramar [ˌuwtra'ma(x)] *m* overseas.

ultramarino, na [ˌuwtrama'rinu, na] *adj* overseas *(antes de subst)*.

ultramoderno, na [ˌuwtramo'dɛxnu, na] *adj* state-of-the-art.

ultrapassado, da [ˌuwtrapa'sadu, da] *adj* out-of-date.

ultrapassagem [ˌuwtrapa'saʒẽ] (*pl* **-ns**) *f* overtaking *UK*, passing *US*.

ultrapassar [4] [ˌuwtrapa'sa(x)] ◇ *vt* **-1.** [passar à frente de] to overtake *UK*, to pass *US*. **-2.** [transpor] to cross. **-3.** [em qualidade]: ~ **alguém (em algo)** to surpass sb (in sthg). **-4.** [exceder] to exceed. ◇ *vi* [passar à frente] to overtake *UK*, to pass *US*.

ultra-romântico, ca [ˌuwtraxo'mãntʃiku, ka] (*pl* **-s**) *adj* highly romantic.

ultra-secreto, ta [ˌuwtrase'krɛtu, ta] (*pl* **-s**) *adj* top secret.

ultra-sensível [ˌuwtrasẽn'sivew] (*pl* **-eis**) *adj* hypersensitive.

ultra-som [ˌuwtra'sõ] (*pl* **-s**) *m* ultrasound.

ultra-sônico, ca [ˌuwtra'soniku, ka] (*pl* **-s**) *adj* **-1.** [onda sonora] ultrasonic. **-2.** *MED* ultrasound *(antes de subst)*.

ultra-sonografia [ˌuwtrasonogra'fia] (*pl* **-s**) *f* ultrasound scanning.

ultravioleta [ˌuwtravjo'leta] *adj* ultraviolet.

ululante [ulu'lãntʃi] *adj* **-1.** [multidão] screaming. **-2.** *fig* [gritante] blatant; **o óbvio** ~ the glaring truth.

ulular [4] [ulu'la(x)] ◇ *vt* [protestos, insultos] to scream. ◇ *vi* **-1.** [vento] to howl. **-2.** [multidão] to scream.

um, uma [ũ, 'uma] (*mpl* **uns**, *fpl* **umas**) ◇ *artigo indefinido* a, an *(antes de vogal ou h mudo)*; ~ **homem** a man; **uma casa** a house; **uma mulher** a woman; **uma hora** an hour; **uma maçã** an apple. ◇ *adj* **-1.** [exprime quantidade, data indefinida] one, some *pl*; **comprei uns livros** I bought some books; ~ **dia voltarei** I'll be back one day; **estou saindo umas semanas de férias** I'm going on holidays for a few weeks. **-2.** [para indicar quantidades] one; **trinta e** ~ **dias** thirty-one days; ~ **litro/metro/quilo** one litre/metre/kilo. **-3.** [aproximadamente] about, around; **esperei uns dez minutos** I waited for about ten minutes; **estavam lá umas cinqüenta pessoas** there were about fifty people there. **-4.** [para enfatizar]: **está** ~ **frio/calor** it's so cold/hot; **estou com uma sede** I'm so thirsty; **foi** ~ **daqueles dias!** it's been one of those days! ◇ *pron* [indefinido] one, some *pl*; **me dê** ~ give me one; **pede mais uma** ask for another one; ~ **deles** one of them; ~ **a** ~, ~ **por** ~ one by one; **uns e outros** some/other people. ◇ *num* one ▷ *veja também* **seis**.

umbanda [ũn'bãnda] *f* [espirit] *Afro-Brazilian cult*.

umbigo [ũn'bigu] *m* navel.

umbilical [ũnbili'kaw] (*pl* **-ais**) *adj* ▷ **cordão**.

umbral [ũn'braw] (*pl* **-ais**) *m* **-1.** [de porta] doorway. **-2.** [limiar] threshold.

umedecer [25] [umide'se(x)] *vt* to dampen.

◆ **umedecer-se** *vp* to mist over.

umedecido, da [umide'sidu, da] *adj* damp.

umidade [umi'dadʒi] *f* **-1.** [de clima, ar] humidity. **-2.** [de parede, terra] damp.

úmido, da ['umidu, da] *adj* damp.

UN (*abrev de* **United Nations**) *f* UN.

UnB (*abrev de* **Universidade de Brasília**) *f university of Brasilia*.

unânime [u'nãnimi] *adj* unanimous.

unanimidade [unãnimi'dadʒi] *f* unanimity.

unção [ũn'sãw] *f* *RELIG* unction.

undécimo, ma [ũn'dɛsimu, ma] *num* eleventh.

UNE (*abrev de* **União Nacional dos Estudantes**) *f Brazilian national union of students*, ≃ NUS *UK*.

UNESCO (*abrev de* **United Nations Educational, Scientific and Cultural Organization**) *f* UNESCO.

ungir [78] [ũn'ʒi(x)] *vt* *RELIG* to anoint.

ungüento [ũn'gwẽntu] *m* ointment.

unha ['uɲa] *f* nail; **fazer as** ~**s** [com manicure] to do one's nails; ~ **encravada** ingrowing nail; **ser** ~ **e carne (com alguém)** to be hand in glove (with sb).

unhada [u'ɲada] *f* scratch.
unha-de-fome [ˌuɲadʒi'fɔmi] (*pl* **unhas-de-fome**) ◇ *adj* miserly. ◇ *mf* miser.
unhar [4] [u'ɲa(x)] *vt* to scratch.
união [u'njãw] (*pl* **-ões**) *f* **-1.** [ger] union. **-2.** [junção] joining.
◆ **União** *f* **-1.** [o governo federal]: **a União** the Union. **-2.** [confederação]: **a União Européia** the European Union.
unicamente [ˌunika'mẽntʃi] *adv* **-1.** [exclusivamente] exclusively. **-2.** [somente] only.
Unicamp (*abrev de* **Universidade Estadual de Campinas**) *f university of Campinas.*
UNICEF (*abrev de* **United Nations International Children's Emergency Fund**) *m* UNICEF.
único, ca ['uniku, ka] *adj* **-1.** [ger] unique. **-2.** [só] single; **ser filho ~** to be an only child; **ser o ~ que ...** to be the only one to ...
unicórnio [uni'kɔxnju] *m* unicorn.
unidade [uni'dadʒi] *f* **-1.** [ger] unit; **~ central de processamento** central processing unit; **~ de CD-ROM** CD-ROM drive; **~ de disco** disc drive. **-2.** [uniformidade, união, coesão] unity.
unidimensional [unidʒimẽnsjo'naw] (*pl* **-ais**) *adj* one-dimensional.
unido, da [u'nidu, da] *adj* **-1.** [ligado] joined. **-2.** *fig* [pessoas] united.
UNIFESP (*abrev de* **Universidade Federal de São Paulo**) *f federal university of São Paulo.*
unificação [unifika'sãw] *f* unification.
unificar [12] [unifi'ka(x)] *vt* **-1.** [unir] to unite. **-2.** [uniformizar] to unify.
uniforme [uni'fɔxmi] ◇ *adj* **-1.** [que só tem uma forma, semelhante] uniform. **-2.** [que não varia] regular. ◇ *m* [roupa] uniform; **de ~** in uniform.
uniformidade [unifoxmi'dadʒi] *f* uniformity.
uniformizado, da [unifoxmi'zadu, da] *adj* **-1.** [de uniforme] uniformed. **-2.** [uniforme] uniform.
uniformizar [4] [unifoxmi'za(x)] *vt* **-1.** [unificar] to standardize. **-2.** [pessoa] to put into uniform.
◆ **uniformizar-se** *vp* [vestir uniforme] to wear one's uniform.
unilateral [unilate'raw] (*pl* **-ais**) *adj* unilateral.
unir [6] [u'ni(x)] *vt* **-1.** [ger] to unite. **-2.** [juntar] [comunicar cidades] to join (together). **-3.** [combinar] to combine; **~ o útil ao agradável** to mix business with pleasure.
◆ **unir-se** *vp* **-1.** [juntar-se] to unite; **~-se a algo/alguém** to join sthg/sb. **-2.** [afetivamente] to be united. **-3.** [conciliar-se] to be reconciled. **-4.** [casar]: **~-se em matrimônio** to unite in marriage, to join in matrimony.
unissex [uni'sɛkiʃ] *adj inv* unisex.
uníssono, na [u'nisonu, na] *adj* unison; **em ~** in unison.
unitário, ria [uni'tarju, rja] *adj* **-1.** [preço] unit *(antes de subst)*. **-2.** POL unitary.
universal [univex'saw] (*pl* **-ais**) *adj* universal.
universalidade [univexsali'dadʒi] *f* universality.
universalizar [4] [univexsali'za(x)] *vt* to universalize.
universidade [univexsi'dadʒi] *f* **-1.** [ger] university. **-2.** [pessoal] faculty.
universitário, ria [univexsi'tarju, rja] ◇ *adj* university *(antes de subst)*. ◇ *m, f* **-1.** [professor] faculty member, university lecturer. **-2.** [aluno] university student.
universo [uni'vɛxsu] *m* **-1.** ASTRON universe. **-2.** *fig* [mundo] world.
uno, una ['unu, 'una] *adj* single.
uns [ũnʃ] ▷ **um**.
untar [4] [ũn'ta(x)] *vt*: **~ algo (com)** [fôrma] to grease sthg (with); [corpo] to oil sthg (with).
upa ['upa] *interj* [numa caída] oops!; [para pessoa se levantar] upsy-daisy!; [para incentivar animal] gee up!
update ['apdejtji] *m* COMPUT update.
upgrade ['apgrejdji] *m* COMPUT: **fazer um ~** to upgrade.
upload ['aplodji] *m* COMPUT: **fazer um ~** to upload.
Urais [u'rajʃ] *npl*: **os ~** the Urals.
urânio [u'rãnju] *m* uranium.
Urano [u'rãnu] *n* Uranus.
urbanismo [uxba'niʒmu] *m* town planning.
urbanista [uxba'niʃta] *mf* town planner.
urbanístico, ca [uxba'niʃtʃiku, ka] *adj* town planning *(antes de subst)*.
urbanização [uxbaniza'sãw] *f* urbanization.
urbanizado, da [uxbani'zadu, da] *adj* [área] built-up.
urbanizar [4] [uxbani'za(x)] *vt* **-1.** [área] to urbanize. **-2.** [pessoa] to refine.
urbano, na [ux'bãnu, na] *adj* **-1.** [da cidade] urban. **-2.** [pessoa - com hábitos citadinos] urban; [- cortês] urbane.
urbe ['uxbi] *f* city.
urdidura [uxdʒi'dura] *f* **-1.** [conjunto de fios] warp. **-2.** [enredo] plot.
urdir [6] [ux'dʒi(x)] *vt fig* [tramar] to plot.
urdu [ux'du] *m* [língua] Urdu.
uretra [u'rɛtra] *f* urethra.
urgência [ux'ʒẽnsja] *f* urgency; **com ~** urgently.
urgente [ux'ʒẽntʃi] *adj* urgent.
urgentemente [uxgẽntʃi'mẽntʃi] *adv* urgently.
urgir [52] [ux'ʒi(x)] ◇ *vt* **-1.** [pressionar]: **~ alguém (a/para) que** to urge sb to. **-2.** [exigir] to demand. ◇ *vi* **-1.** [tempo, circunstâncias] to press on. **-2.** [ser urgente] to be pressing; **~ fazer algo** to have to do sthg; **urge resolver a situação** the situation must be resolved; **uma situação que urge ser contornada** a situation that urgently needs to be turned around.
úrico, ca ['uriku, ka] *adj* [ácido] uric.
urina [u'rina] *f* urine.
urinar [4] [uri'na(x)] ◇ *vt* **-1.** [sangue] to pass. **-2.** [cama] to wet. ◇ *vi* [expelir urina] to urinate; **~ em** to wet.
◆ **urinar-se** *vp* [com urina] to wet o.s.
urinário, ria [uri'narju, rja] *adj* urinary.
urinol [uri'nɔw] (*pl* **-óis**) *m* chamber pot.
URL (*abrev de* **Universal Resources Locator**) *f* URL.
urna ['uxna] *f* [caixa] urn; **~ eleitoral** ballot box; **~ eletrônica** computerized vote.

◆ **urnas** *fpl fig* [pleito eleitoral] polls.
urologia [urolo'ʒia] *f* urology.
urologista [urolo'ʒiʃta] *mf* urologist.
urrar [4] [u'xa(x)] ◇ *vt* [gritar] to scream. ◇ *vi* **-1.** [animal] to roar. **-2.** [gritar]: ~ **de dor** to scream with pain.
urro ['uxu] *m* **-1.** [de animal] roar. **-2.** [grito] scream.
ursa ['uxsa] *f* ▷ **urso**.
ursada [ux'sada] *f fam*: **fazer uma ~ com alguém** to be disloyal to sb.
urso, sa ['uxsu, sa] *m, f* bear.
◆ **Ursa** *f*: **Ursa Maior/Menor** Ursa Major/ Minor.
urso-branco [ˌuxsu'brãŋku] *m* polar bear.
urso-polar [ˌuxsu'pola(x)] (*pl* **ursos-polares**) *m* polar bear.
urticária [uxtʃi'karja] *f* (nettle) rash, urticaria.
urtiga [ux'tʃiga] *f* nettle.
urubu [uru'bu] *m* black vulture.
urubuzar [urubu'za(x)] *vt fam* [com o olhar] to watch like a hawk.
urucubaca [uruku'baka] *f* bad luck; **estar com ~** to be unlucky.
Uruguai [uru'gwaj] *n*: **(o) ~** Uruguay.
uruguaio, ia [uru'gwaju, ja] ◇ *adj* Uruguayan. ◇ *m, f* Uruguayan.
urze ['uxzi] *f* heather.
usado, da [u'zadu, da] *adj* **-1.** [utilizado] used; **muito/pouco ~** much/little used. **-2.** [comum] usual. **-3.** [na moda] fashionable. **-4.** [gasto] worn out.
usar [4] [u'za(x)] ◇ *vt* **-1.** [ger] to use. **-2.** [gastar] to wear out. **-3.** [vestir, ter] to wear. **-4.** [costumar]: ~ **fazer algo** to be in the habit of doing sthg. ◇ *vi* [servir-se de]: ~ **de algo** to use sthg; **modo de ~** [em medicamento] directions for use.
Usenet (*abrev de* **Users Network**) [uze'ntʃi] *f* Usenet.
username [uzex'nejmi] (*pl* **usernames**) *m* COMPUT username.
usina [u'zina] *f* **-1.** [industrial] factory; ~ **de aço** steelworks *(pl)*. **-2.** [agrícola]: ~ **de açúcar** sugar mill. **-3.** [de energia elétrica]: ~ **hidrelétrica** hydroelectric power station; ~ **termonuclear** nuclear power station.
usineiro, ra [uzi'nejru, ra] ◇ *adj* plant *(antes de subst)*. ◇ *m, f* sugar mill owner.
uso ['uzu] *m* **-1.** [ger] use; **objetos de ~ pessoal** personal belongings; **de ~ fácil** easy to use; **fazer ~ de** to make use of; **para ~ externo/interno** FARM for external/internal use. **-2.** [vestir] wearing. **-3.** [costume] common practice. **-4.** [desgaste] wear. **-5.** LING usage.
USP (*abrev de* **Universidade de São Paulo**) *f university of São Paulo.*
usual [u'zwaw] (*pl* **-ais**) *adj* usual.
usualmente [uzwaw'mẽntʃi] *adv* usually.
usuário, ria [u'zwarju, rja] *m, f* user.
usucapião [uzuka'pjãw] *m* JUR prescription.
usufruir [74] [uzufru'i(x)] ◇ *vt* **-1.** [desfrutar] to enjoy. **-2.** JUR to hold in usufruct. ◇ *vi*: ~ **de** [desfrutar] to enjoy.
usufruto [uzu'frutu] *m* JUR usufruct.
usura [u'zura] *f* **-1.** [avareza] avarice. **-2.** [cobrança alta] usury. **-3.** [desgaste] wear.
usurário, ria [uzu'rarju, rja] ◇ *adj* [avaro] avaricious. ◇ *m, f* [agiota] usurer.
usurpação [uzuxpa'sãw] (*pl* **-ões**) *f* usurpation.
usurpar [4] [uzux'pa(x)] *vt* to usurp.
úteis ['utejʃ] *pl* ▷ **útil**.
utensílio [utẽn'silju] *m* **-1.** [instrumento] tool. **-2.** [de cozinha, doméstico] utensil.
uterino, na [ute'rinu, na] *adj* uterine.
útero ['uteru] *m* uterus, womb.
UTI (*abrev de* **Unidade de Terapia Intensiva**) *f* ICU.
útil ['utʃiw] (*pl* **-eis**) *adj* **-1.** [ger] useful. **-2.** [reservado ao trabalho]: **dia ~** working day.
utilidade [utʃili'dadʒi] *f* **-1.** [ger] usefulness; **de muita/pouca ~** of great/little use. **-2.** [utensílio]: **~s domésticas** domestic appliances.
utilitário, ria [utʃili'tarju, rja] *adj* **-1.** [objetivo, peça *etc*] practical. **-2.** AUTO & COMPUT utility.
◆ **utilitário** *m* COMPUT utility.
utilização [utʃiliza'sãw] (*pl* **-ões**) *f* use.
utilizar [4] [utʃili'za(x)] *vt* to use.
◆ **utilizar-se** *vp*: **~-se de** to make use of.
utilizável [utʃili'zavew] (*pl* **-eis**) *adj* **-1.** [máquina, instrumento] utilizable. **-2.** [sugestão] practical.
utopia [uto'pia] *f* Utopia.
utópico, ca [u'tɔpiku, ka] *adj* Utopian.
UV (*abrev de* **Ultravioleta**) *m* UV.
uva ['uva] *f* **-1.** [fruta] grape. **-2.** *fam* [pessoa, coisa]: **que ~ de ...!** what a delightful ...!; **uma ~** a delight; **uma ~ de criança** a delightful child.
úvula ['uvula] *f* uvula.

v, V *m* [letra] v, V.
vã [vã] *f* ▷ **vão**.
vaca ['vaka] *f* **-1.** ZOOL cow; **carne de ~** beef; **couro de ~** cowhide; ~ **leiteira** dairy cow; **a ~ foi para o brejo** it went out the window. **-2.** *fam pej* [pessoa] lump. **-3.** *loc*: **no tempo das ~s gordas** in times of plenty; **no tempo das ~s magras** during lean times.
vaca-fria [ˌvaka'fria] *f*: **voltar à ~** to get back to the point in question.
vacância [va'kãnsja] *f* vacancy.
vacante [va'kãntʃi] *adj* vacant.

vaca-preta [ˌvaka'preta] (*pl* **vacas-pretas**) *f* *Coca-Cola® float.*

vacilação [vasila'sãw] (*pl* **-ões**) *f* **-1.** [hesitação] hesitation. **-2.** [oscilação] swaying.

vacilada [vasi'lada] *f* slip-up; **dar uma ~** to slip up.

vacilante [vasi'lãntʃi] *adj* **-1.** [hesitante] hesitant. **-2.** [pouco firme] wobbly. **-3.** [luz] flickering.

vacilar [4] [vasi'la(x)] *vi* **-1.** [hesitar] to hesitate; **~ em algo/em fazer algo** to hesitate in sthg/in doing sthg. **-2.** [oscilar] to sway. **-3.** [cambalear] to totter. **-4.** [luz] to flicker.

vacilo [va'silu] *m* ***fam*** **-1.** [hesitação] havering, shilly-shallying. **-2.** [erro, falha] howler, blunder.

vacina [va'sina] *f* vaccine.

vacinação [vasina'sãw] (*pl* **-ões**) *f* vaccination.

vacinar [4] [vasi'na(x)] *vt* **-1.** *MED*: **~ alguém (contra)** to vaccinate sb (against). **-2.** ***fig*** [imunizar]: **~ alguém contra** to protect sb from.

◆ **vacinar-se** *vp* **-1.** *MED*: **~-se (contra)** to be vaccinated (against). **-2.** ***fig*** [imunizar-se]: **~-se contra** to be immune to.

vacum [va'kũ] *adj*: **gado ~** cattle.

vácuo ['vakwu] *m* **-1.** *FÍSICA* vacuum; **embalhado a ~** vacuum-packed. **-2.** *METEOR* low. **-3.** [espaço] space. **-4.** ***fig*** [vazio] void.

vadiagem [va'dʒjaʒẽ], **vadiação** [vadʒja'sãw] *f* vagrancy.

vadiar [16] [va'dʒja(x)] *vi* **-1.** [viver na ociosidade] to lounge about. **-2.** [suj: aluno, professional] to skive. **-3.** [perambular] to roam.

vadio, dia [va'dʒiu, ʒia] *adj* **-1.** [ocioso] idle. **-2.** [aluno, professional] skiving. **-3.** [vagabundo] vagrant.

vaga ['vaga] *f* ▷ **vago.**

vagabundagem [vagabũn'daʒẽ] *f* **-1.** [vagabundismo] roaming. **-2.** [vadiagem] loafing.

vagabundear [15] [vagabũn'dʒja(x)] *vi* **-1.** [vadiar] to drift. **-2.** [vaguear] to roam.

vagabundo, da [vaga'bũndu, da] ◇ *adj* **-1.** [errante] vagabond. **-2.** [vadio] idle. **-3.** [safado] shameless. **-4.** [mulher] easy. **-5.** [produto] shoddy. ◇ *m, f* **-1.** [pessoa errante] tramp. **-2.** [vadio] idler. **-3.** [safado] rogue.

vagalhão [vaga'ʎãw] (*pl* **-ões**) *m* breaker.

vaga-lume [ˌvaga'lumi] (*pl* **vaga-lumes**) *m* **-1.** *ZOOL* glow-worm. **-2.** [cine] usher.

vagão [va'gãw] (*pl* **-ões**) *m* **-1.** [de passageiros] carriage. **-2.** [de carga] wagon.

vagão-leito [vaˌgãw'lejtu] (*pl* **vagões-leito**) *m* sleeping car.

vagão-restaurante [vaˌgãwxeʃtaw'rãntʃi] (*pl* **vagões-restaurante**) *m* buffet car.

vagar [14] [va'ga(x)] ◇ *vi* **-1.** [ficar desocupado] to be vacant. **-2.** [vaguear] to drift. ◇ *m* [lentidão] slowness; **com mais ~** at greater leisure.

vagareza [vaga'reza] *f* slowness.

vagaroso, osa [vaga'rozu, ɔza] *adj* slow.

vagem ['vaʒẽ] (*pl* **-ns**) *f* green bean.

vagina [va'ʒina] *f* vagina.

vaginal [vaʒi'naw] (*pl* **-ais**) *adj* vaginal.

vago, ga ['vagu, ga] *adj* **-1.** [impreciso] vague. **-2.** [desocupado] vacant; **horas vagas** spare time. **-3.** [desabitado] empty.

◆ **vaga** *f* **-1.** [em hotel] vacancy. **-2.** [em empresa *etc*] vacancy; **abriu uma vaga para gerente** an opening has appeared for manager. **-3.** [para carro] space. **-4.** [onda] wave.

vagões [va'gõjʃ] *pl* ▷ **vagão.**

vaguear [15] [va'gja(x)] *vi* **-1.** [perambular] to drift. **-2.** [passear] to ramble.

vaia ['vaja] *f* boo.

vaiar [4] [va'ja(x)] *vt* & *vi* to boo.

vaidade [vaj'dadʒi] *f* **-1.** [orgulho] vanity. **-2.** [futilidade] futility.

vaidoso, osa [vaj'dozu, ɔza] *adj* vain; **ser ~ de alguém/algo** to be proud of sb/sthg.

vai-não-vai [vajnãw'vaj] *m inv* shilly-shallying.

vaivém [vaj'vẽ] (*pl* **-ns**) *m* **-1.** [de pessoas] to and fro. **-2.** [de pêndulo] swinging. **-3.** [de barco] rocking.

vala ['vala] *f* **-1.** [escavação] ditch. **-2.** [sepultura]: **~ comum** common grave.

vale ['vali] *m* **-1.** *GEOGR* valley. **-2.** [documento] receipt. **-3.** [postal] **~ postal** postal order.

valentão, ona [valẽn'tãw, ona] (*mpl* **-ões**, *fpl* **-s**) ◇ *adj* burly. ◇ *m, f* burly person.

valente [va'lẽntʃi] *adj* brave.

valentia [valẽn'tʃia] *f* **-1.** [coragem] courage. **-2.** [ação] feat.

valentona [valẽn'tona] *f* ▷ **valentão.**

valer [43] [va'le(x)] ◇ *vt* **-1.** [ger] to be worth; **~ a pena** to be worthwhile. **-2.** [acarretar]: **~ algo a alguém** to bring sb sthg. ◇ *vi* **-1.** [ger] to be worth; **mais vale ... (do que)** it is better to ... (than to); **valeu!** ***fam*** cheers! **-2.** [equivaler]: **~ por** to be worth the same as; **ou coisa que o valha** or something similar. **-3.** [ser válido] to be valid; [em jogos] to be fair; **assim não vale!** that's unfair!; **fazer ~ os direitos** to assert one's rights; **ser para ~** to be the real thing. **-4.** [vigorar] to be in force.

◆ **para valer** *loc adv* [muito]: **me diverti para ~** I had a really good time.

◆ **valer-se** *vp* [servir-se]: **~-se de** to make use of.

vale-refeição [ˌvalixefej'sãw] (*pl* **vales-refeição**) *m* [tíquete-refeição] meal ticket.

valeta [va'leta] *f* gutter.

valete [va'lɛtʃi] *m* [carta] jack.

vale-transporte [ˌvalitrãnʃ'pɔxtʃi] (*pl* **vales-transporte**) *m* travel voucher.

vale-tudo [ˌvali'tudu] *m inv* free-for-all.

valia [va'lia] *f* value; **de grande ~** [de grande valor] very valuable; [de grande utilidade] very useful.

validação [valida'sãw] *f* validation.

validade [vali'dadʒi] *f* validity; **prazo de ~** [em comida] expiry date.

validar [4] [vali'da(x)] *vt* to validate.

válido, da ['validu, da] *adj* valid.

valioso, osa [va'ljozu, ɔza] *adj* valuable.

valise [va'lizi] *f* case.

valor [va'lo(x)] (*pl* **-es**) *m* value; **de (grande)** ~ of (great) value; **objetos de** ~ valuables; **sem** ~ worthless; **ter** ~ to be valuable; ~ **de mercado** market value; ~ **nominal** *ECON* face value; **no** ~ **de** to the value of; **dar** ~ **a algo/alguém** to value sthg/sb.
◆ **valores** *mpl* **-1.** [princípios] values. **-2.** *BOLSA* securities.

valorização [valoriza'sãw] *f* appreciation.

valorizar [4] [valori'za(x)] *vt* **-1.** [imóvel, moeda] to push up the value of. **-2.** [pessoa, trabalho] to appreciate.
◆ **valorizar-se** *vp* to appreciate.

valoroso, osa [valo'rozu, ɔza] *adj* courageous.

valsa ['vawsa] *f* waltz.

valsar [4] [vaw'sa(x)] *vi* to waltz.

válvula ['vawvula] *f* valve; ~ **de escape** *fig* safety valve; ~ **de segurança** safety valve.

vampe ['vãnpi] *f* vamp.

vampiro [vãm'piru] *m* **-1.** [personagem] vampire. **-2.** *ZOOL* vampire bat.

vandalismo [vãnda'liʒmu] *m* vandalism.

vândalo, la ['vãndalu, la] *m, f* vandal.

vangloriar-se [16] [vãŋglo'rjaxsi] *vp*: ~**-se (de)** to boast (about).

vanguarda [vãŋ'gwaxda] *f* **-1.** *MIL* front line. **-2.** [cultural] avant-garde; **de** ~ avant-garde *(antes de subst)*.

vantagem [vãn'taʒẽ] (*pl* **-ns**) *f* **-1.** [ger] advantage; **levar** ~ **(em)** to get the upper hand (in); **tirar** ~ **de** to take advantage from. **-2.** [superioridade]: ~ **(sobre)** advantage (over); **contar** ~ to brag; **levar** ~ **(sobre)** to have an advantage (over).

vantajoso, osa [vãnta'ʒozu, ɔza] *adj* **-1.** [benéfico] advantageous. **-2.** [lucrativo] profitable.

vão, vã ['vãw, 'vã] *adj* **-1.** [frívolo] empty. **-2.** [inútil] vain; **em** ~ in vain. **-3.** [irreal] futile.
◆ **vão** *m* **-1.** [espaço] space. **-2.** [de porta *etc*] opening.

vapor [va'po(x)] (*pl* **-es**) *m* **-1.** [de água] steam; **a** ~ [máquina, ferro] steam *(antes de subst)*; **cozinhar no** ~ to steam. **-2.** *FÍSICA* vapour *UK*, vapor *US*.
◆ **a todo o vapor** *loc adv* at full speed.

vaporização [vaporiza'sãw] *f* **-1.** [nebulização] spray. **-2.** *FÍSICA* vaporization.

vaporizador [vaporiza'do(x)] (*pl* **-es**) *m* **-1.** [de perfume *etc*] spray. **-2.** *MED* vaporizer.

vaporizar [4] [vapori'za(x)] *vt* **-1.** [nebulizar] to spray. **-2.** *FÍSICA* to vaporize.

vaporoso, osa [vapo'rozu, ɔza] *adj* **-1.** [tecido, cortina] see-through, diaphanous. **-2.** [com vapor] steamy.

vapt-vupt [ˌvaptʃi'vuptʃi] <> *interj* zap! <> *m* [lençol] fitted sheet.

vaqueiro [va'kejru] *m* cowherd *UK*, cowboy *US*.

vaquinha [va'kiɲa] *f*: **fazer uma** ~ to have a whip-round.

vara ['vara] *f* **-1.** [pau] stick; ~ **de condão** magic wand. **-2.** [para salto] pole. **-3.** *TEC* rod. **-4.** [de trombone] slide. **-5.** *JUR* jurisdiction. **-6.** [de porcos] herd.

varal [va'raw] (*pl* **-ais**) *m* [de roupas] clothes line.

varanda [va'rãnda] *f* **-1.** [sacada] verandah. **-2.** [balcão] balcony.

varão [va'rãw] (*pl* **-ões**) <> *adj* male. <> *m* male.

varapau [vara'paw] *mf fam* [pessoa] beanpole.

varar [4] [va'ra(x)] <> *vt* **-1.** [furar] to pierce. **-2.** [passar por] to cross. <> *vi*: ~ **por** [passar por] to pass through; [atravessar] to go through.

varejeira [vare'ʒejra] *f* [mosca] bluebottle.

varejista [vare'ʒiʃta] <> *adj* retail *(antes de subst)*. <> *mf* [vendedor] retailer.

varejo [va'reʒu] *m COM* retail trade; **preço no** ~ retail price; **a loja vende a** ~ the shop sells retail.

variação [varja'sãw] (*pl* **-ões**) *f* [alteração] change, variation; ~ **cambial** *ECON* exchange-rate fluctuation.

variado, da [va'rjadu, da] *adj* **-1.** [diverso] varied. **-2.** [sortido] assorted.

variante [va'rjãntʃi] <> *adj* different. <> *f* **-1.** [variação] change. **-2.** [versão] variant.

variar [16] [va'rja(x)] <> *vt* [diversificar] to vary. <> *vi* **-1.** [ger] to vary; ~ **em algo** to vary in sthg. **-2.** [diversificar] to make changes; ~ **de** to change; **para** ~ [para diversificar] for a change; *irôn* and just for a change. **-3.** *fam* [delirar] to unhinge.

variável [va'rjavew] (*pl* **-eis**) <> *adj* changeable, variable. <> *f MAT* variable.

varicela [vari'sɛla] *f* chickenpox.

variedade [varje'dadʒi] *f* **-1.** [diversidade] variety. **-2.** [tipo] type.
◆ **variedades** *fpl* variety *(sg)*; **espetáculo/teatro de** ~**s** variety show *ou* theatre *UK ou* theater *US*.

varinha [va'riɲa] *f* stick; ~ **de condão** magic wand.

vário, ria ['varju, rja] *adj* [variado] diverse.
◆ **vários** <> *adj pl* several. <> *pron pl* several.

varíola [va'riwla] *f* smallpox.

varizes [va'riziʃ] *fpl* varicose veins.

varões [va'rõjʃ] *pl* ▻ **varão**.

varonil [varo'niw] (*pl* **-is**) *adj* virile.

varredor, ra [vaxe'do(x), ra] (*mpl* **-es**, *fpl* **-s**) *m, f* sweeper; ~ **de rua** road sweeper.

varredura [vaxe'dura] *f* **-1.** [ato] sweep. **-2.** *COMPUT* scan.

varrer [5] [va'xe(x)] *vt* **-1.** [com vassoura] to sweep. **-2.** [arrastar] to sweep away. **-3.** *fig* [devastar] to raze. **-4.** *fig* [livrar]: ~ **algo de** to sweep sthg from.

varrido, da [va'xidu, da] *adj*: **doido** ~ raving lunatic.

Varsóvia [vax'sɔvja] *n* Warsaw.

várzea ['vaxzja] *f* [vale] low, flat valley.

vascular [vaʃku'la(x)] (*pl* **-es**) *adj* vascular.

vasculhar [4] [vaʃku'ʎa(x)] *vt* **-1.** [pesquisar] to research. **-2.** [revirar] to rummage through.

vasectomia [vazekto'mia] *f* vasectomy.

vaselina® [vaze'lina] <> *f* [substância] vaseline. <> *mf fam pej* [pessoa]: **ser um** ~ to be smooth talker.

vasilha [va'ziʎa] *f* vessel.
vasilhame [vazi'ʎãmi] *m* **-1.** [para alimentos] storage jars *(pl)*. **-2.** [garrafa vazia] empties *(pl)*.
vaso ['vazu] *m* **-1.** [para plantas] pot; ~ **de flores** flower vase. **-2.** [privada] toilet; ~ **sanitário** toilet bowl. **-3.** ANAT vessel; ~ **sanguíneo** blood vessel.
vassalo, la [va'salu, la] *m, f* vassal.
vassoura [va'sora] *f* broom.
vastidão [vaʃtʃi'dãw] *f* vastness.
vasto, ta ['vaʃtu, ta] *adj* **-1.** [extenso] vast. **-2.** *fig* [considerável] wide.
vatapá [vata'pa] *m* CULIN *a very spicy Bahian dish made with fish, coconut milk, prawns, peanuts and cashew nuts*, vatapá.
vaticano, na [vatʃi'kãnu, na] *adj* Vatican *(antes de subst)*.
◆ **Vaticano** *m*: **o Vaticano** the Vatican.
vaticinar [4] [vatʃisi'na(x)] *vt* to foretell.
vaticínio [vatʃi'sinju] *m* prophecy.
vau [vaw] *m* **-1.** [de rio] ford. **-2.** NÁUT beam.
vazado, da [va'zadu, da] *adj* **-1.** [letra] outlined. **-2.** [círculo] hollow. **-3.** [moeda] embossed. **-4.** [olhos] sunken.
vazamento [vaza'mẽntu] *m* leakage.
vazante [va'zãntʃi] ◇ *adj* ebbing. ◇ *f* [maré] ebb tide.
vazão [va'zaw] (*pl* **-ões**) *f* **-1.** [vazamento] leak. **-2.** [escoamento] flow. **-3.** COM [venda] sale. **-4.** *loc*: **dar ~ a** [liberar] to give vent to; [atender a] to deal with; [solucionar] to sort out; COM to clear.
vazar [4] [va'za(x)] ◇ *vi* **-1.** [ger] to leak. **-2.** [maré] to go out. **-3.** *fig* [informação] to leak out. ◇ *vt* **-1.** [esvaziar] to empty. **-2.** [olhos] to gouge out. **-3.** [derramar]: ~ **algo (em)** to spill sthg (on). **-4.** *fig* [moldar] to model.
vazio, zia [va'ziu, zia] *adj* **-1.** [ger] empty. **-2.** [com pouca gente] deserted.
◆ **vazio** *m* **-1.** [vácuo] vacuum. **-2.** [lacuna] blank space. **-3.** *fig* [sentimento] void.
vazões [va'zõjʃ] *pl* ▷ **vazão.**
veado ['vjadu] *m* **-1.** [animal] deer; **carne de ~** venison. **-2.** *vulg pej* [homossexual] poof(ter) *UK*, fag(got) *US*.
vedado, da [ve'dadu, da] *adj* **-1.** [proibido, impedido] barred; ~ **a** prohibited to. **-2.** [hermeticamente fechado] sealed.
vedar [4] [ve'da(x)] *vt* **-1.** [proibir, impedir] to prohibit, to bar. **-2.** [sangue]: **vedou o sangramento com um lenço** he stopped the flow of blood with a handkerchief. **-3.** [hermeticamente] to seal.
vedete [ve'dɛtʃi] *f* **-1.** [de teatro] star. **-2.** *fam fig* [destaque] star.
veemência [veje'mẽnsja] *f* vehemence; **com ~** vehemently.
veemente [veje'mẽntʃi] *adj* vehement.
vegetação [veʒeta'sãw] (*pl* **-ões**) *f* vegetation.
vegetal [veʒe'taw] (*pl* **-ais**) ◇ *adj* plant *(antes de subst)*. ◇ *m* plant.
vegetar [4] [veʒe'ta(x)] *vi* **-1.** [planta] to grow. **-2.** *fig* [pessoa] to vegetate.
vegetarianismo [veʒetarjã'niʒmu] *m* vegetarianism.
vegetariano, na [veʒeta'rjãnu, na] ◇ *adj* vegetarian. ◇ *m, f* vegetarian.
vegetativo, va [veʒeta'tʃivu, va] *adj fig* vegetative.
veia ['veja] *f* **-1.** [ger] vein. **-2.** *fig* [tendência] streak.
veiculação [vejkula'sãw] (*pl* **-ões**) *f* **-1.** [de mercadorias, visitantes] transport *UK*, transportation *US*. **-2.** [de doença] transmission. **-3.** [de idéias, mensagens, doutrinas] spreading.
veicular [4] [vejku'la(x)] *vt* **-1.** [publicar, divulgar] to spread. **-2.** [anúncios] to distribute.
veículo [ve'ikulu] *m* **-1.** [de locomoção] vehicle. **-2.** [de informação] means *(sg)*.
veio ['veju] *m* **-1.** [de rocha] vein. **-2.** [de madeira] grain. **-3.** [em mina] seam.
vela ['vɛla] *f* **-1.** [de cera] candle; **segurar ~** *fam fig* to play gooseberry. **-2.** NÁUT sail; **à ~** sailing; **fazer-se à** OU **de vela** to set sail; ~ **mestra** mainsail. **-3.** [embarcação] yacht.
velame [velã'mi] *m* NÁUT sails *(pl)*.
velar [4] [ve'la(x)] ◇ *adj* LING velar. ◇ *f* LING velar. ◇ *vt* **-1.** [cobrir]: ~ **algo (com algo)** to cover sthg (with sthg). **-2.** [ocultar] to hide. **-3.** [dissimular] to disguise. **-4.** [doente, sono] to watch over. **-5.** [defunto] to keep vigil for, to hold a wake for. ◇ *vi* **-1.** [cuidar]: ~ **por algo/alguém** to watch over sthg/sb. **-2.** FOT [filme] to be damaged by exposure to light.
◆ **velar-se** *vp* **-1.** [cobrir-se] to keep o.s. covered. **-2.** [ocultar-se] to hide.
veleidade [velej'dadʒi] *f* **-1.** [capricho] whim. **-2.** [inconstância] fickleness.
veleiro [ve'lejru] *m* NÁUT sailing boat.
velejar [4] [vele'ʒa(x)] *vi* to sail.
velhaco, ca [ve'ʎaku, ka] ◇ *adj* dishonest. ◇ *m, f* crook.
velha-guarda [ˌveʎa'gwaxda] *f* old guard.
velharia [veʎa'ria] *f* **-1.** *pej* [grupo de idosos] old people *(pl)*. **-2.** [velhos objetos, trastes]: ~ **(s)** old stuff *(sg)*.
velhice [vɛ'ʎisi] *f* old age.
velho, lha ['vɛʎu, ʎa] ◇ *adj* old; **nos ~s tempos** in the old days. ◇ *m, f* **-1.** [pessoa] old person. **-2.** *fam* [pai] old man; **os ~s** [pai e mãe] one's folks. **-3.** *fam* [amigo]: **meu ~** old chap.
velhote, ta [ve'ʎɔtʃi, ta] ◇ *adj* old. ◇ *m, f* old person.
velocidade [velosi'dadʒi] *f* [ger] speed; **aumentar/diminuir a ~** to increase/reduce one's speed; ~ **de processamento** COMPUT processing speed; ~ **máxima** maximum speed; **a toda ~** at full speed; **em alta ~** at high speed.
velocímetro [velo'simetru] *m* speedometer.
velocípede [velo'sipedʒi] *m* velocipede.
velocíssimo, ma [velɔ'sisimu, ma] *adj superl* ▷ **veloz.**
velocista [velo'siʃta] *mf* sprinter.
velódromo [ve'lɔdrumu] *m* cycle track.

velório [ve'lɔrju] *m* wake.
veloz [ve'lɔʃ] (*pl* **-es**) *adj* **-1.** [ger] fast. **-2.** [movimento] quick.
velozmente [velɔʒ'mẽntʃi] *adv* quickly.
veludo [ve'ludu] *m* [tecido] velvet; ~ **cotelê** corduroy.
venal [ve'naw] (*pl* **-ais**) *adj* **-1.** [subornável] corrupt. **-2.**: valor ~ selling price.
vencedor, ra [vẽnse'do(x), ra] (*pl* **-es**, *fpl* **-s**) <> *adj* winning. <> *m, f* winner.
vencer [25] [vẽ'se(x)] <> *vt* **-1.** [ger] to win. **-2.** [superar, dominar, resistir a] to overcome. **-3.** [derrotar] to defeat. **-4.** [exceder]: ~ **algo/alguém (em algo)** to outdo sthg/sb (in sthg). **-5.** [conter] to contain. **-6.** [percorrer] to cross. <> *vi* **-1.** [ganhar] to win. **-2.** [expirar - prazo, garantia, contrato, validade] to expire; [- pagamento, conta, promissória] to become due.
vencido, da [vẽn'sidu, da] *adj* **-1.** [derrotado] beaten; **dar-se por** ~ to give up. **-2.** [expirado] expired.
vencimento [vẽnsi'mẽntu] *m* **-1.** [expiração] expiry. **-2.** [data] due date.
◆ **vencimentos** *mpl* [salário] earnings.
venda ['vẽnda] *f* **-1.** [vendagem] sale; **à** ~ on *ou* for sale; **pôr algo à** ~ to put sthg up for sale; **preço de** ~ selling price; ~ **a crédito** credit sale; ~ **a prazo** *ou* **prestação** sale in instalments. **-2.** [mercearia] general store. **-3.** [nos olhos] blindfold.
◆ **vendas** *fpl* [vendagem] sales.
vendagem [vẽn'daʒẽ] *f* [venda] sale.
vendar [4] [vẽn'da(x)] *vt*: ~ **(os olhos de) alguém** to blindfold sb.
vendaval [vẽnda'vaw] (*pl* **-ais**) *m* **-1.** [ventania] gale. **-2.** *fig* [turbilhão] whirlwind.
vendável [vẽn'davew] (*pl* **-eis**) *adj* saleable.
vendedor, ra [vẽnde'do(x), ra] (*mpl* **-es**, *fpl* **-s**) *m, f* **-1.** [dono] seller. **-2.** [em loja] sales assistant; ~ **ambulante** street vendor. **-3.** [de seguros] salesperson.
vender [5] [vẽn'de(x)] <> *vt* **-1.** [pôr à venda] to sell; ~ **no varejo** to sell retail; ~ **no/por atacado** to sell wholesale; **estar vendendo saúde** *fig* to be bursting with health. **-2.** [entregar em venda] to sell off; ~ **algo a/para alguém (por)** to sell sb sthg (for); ~ **algo a prazo** *ou* **prestação** to sell sthg on credit/in instalments; ~ **fiado** to give credit. <> *vi* to sell.
◆ **vender-se** *vp* **-1.** [estar à venda]: **vendem-se picolés** ice lollies for sale. **-2.** [deixar-se subornar]: **ele se vendeu por 30 mil dólares** he accepted a bribe of 30 thousand dollars.
vendeta [vẽn'deta] *f* vendetta.
vendido, da [vẽn'dʒidu, da] *pej* <> *adj* bribed. <> *m, f* grafter.
vendinha [vẽn'dʒiɲa] *f* corner shop.
veneno [ve'nenu] *m* **-1.** [peçonha] poison; **o cigarro é um** ~ **para a saúde** smoking is a health hazard. **-2.** [de cobra, inseto] venom. **-3.** *fig* [malícia] venom.
venenoso, osa [vene'nozu, ɔza] *adj* **-1.** [ger] poisonous. **-2.** *fig* [malicioso] venomous.
veneração [venera'sãw] *f*: ~ **(por)** veneration (for).
venerar [4] [vene'ra(x)] *vt* **-1.** [adorar] to revere. **-2.** *RELIG* to worship.
venéreo, rea [ve'nɛrju, rja] *adj* venereal.
veneta [ve'neta] *f*: **me deu na** ~ **que ...** [idéia] I took it into my head that ...; [impulso] I had a sudden impulse to ...; **fazer algo de** ~ to do sthg on impulse.
Veneza [ve'neza] *n* Venice.
veneziana [vene'zjana] *f* **-1.** [porta] louvred door *UK*, louvered door *US*. **-2.** [janela] louvred window *UK*, louvered window *US*.
veneziano, na [vene'zjãnu, na] <> *adj* Venetian. <> *m, f* Venetian.
Venezuela [vene'zwɛla] *n* Venezuela.
venezuelano, na [venezwɛ'lanu, na] <> *adj* Venezuelan. <> *m, f* Venezuelan.
vênia ['venja] *f* **-1.** [permissão] permission. **-2.** *JUR* [desculpa] pardon.
venial [ve'njaw] (*pl* **-ais**) *adj* **-1.** [desculpável] forgiveable. **-2.** *RELIG* [pecado] venial.
venta ['vẽnta] *f* [narina] nostril.
◆ **ventas** *fpl* [nariz] nose *(sg)*.
ventania [vẽnta'nia] *f* gale.
ventar [4] [vẽn'ta(x)] *vi*: **venta muito aqui** it is very windy here; **estar ventando** to be windy.
ventarola [vẽnta'rɔla] *f* fan.
ventilação [vẽntʃila'sãw] *f* **-1.** [de ambiente] ventilation. **-2.** *AUTO* [de motor] cooling.
ventilador [vẽntʃila'do(x)] (*pl* **-es**) *m* [elétrico] fan.
ventilar [4] [vẽntʃi'la(x)] *vt* [arejar] to air.
vento ['vẽntu] *m* **-1.** [ar] air. **-2.** [brisa] wind. **-3.** *loc*: **ir de** ~ **em popa** to go very well.
ventoinha [vẽn'twiɲa] *f* **-1.** [catavento] windmill. **-2.** [grimpa] weather vane. **-3.** *AUTO* fan.
ventoso, osa [vẽn'tozu, ɔza] *adj* windy.
◆ **ventosa** *f* **-1.** *MED* ventouse. **-2.** *ZOOL* sucker.
ventre ['vẽntri] *m* **-1.** *ANAT* belly. **-2.** *euf* [útero] womb.
ventríloquo, qua [vẽn'trilokwu, kwa] *m, f* ventriloquist.
ventura [vẽn'tura] *f* **-1.** [destino] fate; **por** ~ by chance. **-2.** [sorte] good fortune; **boa** ~ good luck.
venturoso, osa [vẽntu'rozu, ɔza] *adj* [feliz] happy.
Vênus ['venuʃ] *n* Venus.
ver [40] ['ve(x)] <> *vt* **-1.** [ger] to see; **já volto, viu?** I'll be back soon, OK? **-2.** [assistir] to watch. **-3.** [resolver] to see to. **-4.** [tomar cuidado em] to watch. **-5.** [em remissiva]: **veja ...** look ... <> *vi* **-1.** [enxergar] to see; **ela é bonita que só vendo** you wouldn't believe how pretty she is; ~ **em** *fig* [em situação, pessoa] to see in. **-2.** [pensar]: **deixa eu** ~ **...** let me see ... **-3.** [ger]: **ter a** *ou* **que** ~ **com** to have to do with; [ter envolvimento com] to be involved with; **são pessoas muito diferentes, não têm nada a** ~ **uma com a outra** they are two very different people, they are not at all alike; **este trabalho tem muito a** ~ **com você** that work is right up

your street. <> *m*: **a meu** ~ in my opinion.

◆ **ver-se** *vp* **-1.** [ger] to see o.s. **-2.** [avistar-se] to see one another. **-3.** [ter contato]: **há anos que não nos víamos** it's years since we saw each other, we hadn't seen each other for years. **-4.** [em dificuldade, lugar] to find o.s. **-5.** [entender-se]: **bem se vê que ...** it's obvious that ...; **~-se com alguém** to pay sb back.

◆ **pelo visto** *loc adv* by the look of it.

◆ **vai ver que** *loc adv* [talvez] perhaps.

veracidade [verasi'dadʒi] *f* truthfulness.

veranear [vera'nja(x)] *vi* to spend the summer.

veraneio [vera'neju] *m* summer holidays *(pl)* ***UK***, summer vacation ***US***; **cidade de** ~ holiday resort.

veranista [vera'niʃta] *mf* summer holidaymaker ***UK***, summer vacationer ***US***.

verão [ve'rãw] (*pl* **-ões**) *m* summer.

veraz [ve'rajʒ] *adj* truthful.

verba ['vɛxba] *f* funding.

verbal [vex'baw] (*pl* **-ais**) *adj* verbal.

verbalizar [4] [vexbali'za(x)] *vt* & *vi* to verbalize.

verbalmente [vexbaw'mẽntʃi] *adv* verbally.

verbete [vex'betʃi] *m* [em dicionário] entry.

verbo ['vɛxbu] *m* **-1.** *GRAM* verb; **deitar o** ~ *fam* to make a speech; **soltar o** ~ *fam* to shoot one's mouth off. **-2.** *RELIG*: **o Verbo** the Word.

verborragia [vexboxa'ʒia] *f* waffle.

verborrágico, ca [vexbo'xaʒiku, ka] *adj* verbose.

verdade [vex'dadʒi] *f* truth; **a** ~ **nua e crua** the naked truth; **não é** ~**?** *fam* isn't that right?; **na** ~ in fact; **para falar a** ~ to tell the truth; ~**?** *fam* really?

◆ **verdades** *fpl* home truths; **dizer umas** ~**s a alguém** *fam* to tell sb a few home truths.

◆ **de verdade** <> *loc adv* **-1.** [realmente]: **tudo o que relato aconteceu de** ~ everything I'm describing really happened. **-2.** [a sério] seriously. <> *loc adj* [autêntico]: **é um vencedor de** ~ he's a true winner.

verdadeiramente [vexdadejra'mẽntʃi] *adv* truly.

verdadeiro, ra [vexda'dejru, ra] *adj* **-1.** [ger] true. **-2.** [autêntico] real.

verde ['vexdʒi] <> *adj* **-1.** [cor] green; ~ **de fome** weak with hunger; ~ **de raiva** livid. **-2.** [fruta] unripe, green. <> *m* **-1.** [cor] green. **-2.** [natureza] country. **-3.** *loc*: **jogar (um)** ~ **(para colher maduro)** to get at the truth.

verde-abacate [ˌvexdʒjaba'katʃi] *adj (inv)* avocado-green.

verde-claro, ra ['vexdʒi'klaru, ra] (*pl* **-s**) <> *adj* light green. <> *m* light green.

verde-escuro, ra ['vexdʒiiʃ'kuru, ra] (*pl* **-s**) <> *adj* dark green. <> *m* dark green.

verdejante [vexde'ʒãntʃi] *adj* verdant.

verdejar [4] [vexde'ʒa(x)] *vi* to become green.

verde-oliva ['vexʒjo'liva] <> *adj inv* olive green. <> *m* olive green.

verdor [vex'do(x)] *m* **-1.** [cor verde] greenness. **-2.** [as plantas verdes] greenery. **-3.** *fig* [exuberância]: **o** ~ **da mocidade** the vigour of youth. **-4.** *fig* [inexperiência] inexperience.

verdugo [vex'dugu] *m* **-1.** [carrasco] executioner. **-2.** *fig* [pessoa cruel] beast.

verdura [vex'dura] *f* [hortaliça] greens *(pl)*.

verdureiro, ra [vexdu'rejru, ra] *m, f* greengrocer.

vereador, ra [verja'do(x), ra] *m, f* councillor ***UK***, councilor ***US***.

vereda [ve'reda] *f* path.

veredicto [vere'dʒiktu] *m* verdict.

verga ['vexga] *f* **-1.** [vara] stick. **-2.** [metálica] rod.

vergão [vex'gãw] (*pl* **-ões**) *m* [marca] weal.

vergar [14] [vex'ga(x)] <> *vt* [dobrar] to bend. <> *vi* **-1.** [dobrar] to bend. **-2.** [com peso] to sag.

vergões [vex'gõjʃ] *pl* ⊳ **vergão**.

vergonha [vex'goɲa] *f* **-1.** [acanhamento] shyness; **me dá** ~ **falar em público** I feel shy about speaking in public; **perder a** ~ to overcome one's shyness; **que** ~**!** how embarrassing!; **sentir** ~ to feel embarrassed; **ter** ~ **de fazer algo** to feel shy about doing sthg. **-2.** [brio, pudor] shame; **que falta de** ~**!** how disgraceful!; **ter** ~ **na cara** to be shameless; **tomar** ~ to swallow one's pride. **-3.** [desonra] shame. **-4.** [vexame] outrage; **passar por uma** ~ to be outraged.

vergonhoso, osa [vexgo'ɲozu, ɔza] *adj* **-1.** [indigno] disgraceful. **-2.** [indecoroso] indecent. **-3.** [que dá vergonha] shameful.

verídico, ca [ve'ridʒiku, ka] *adj* true.

verificação [verifika'sãw] (*pl* **-ões**) *f* **-1.** [averiguação] checking. **-2.** [comprovação] verification.

verificar [12] [verifi'ka(x)] *vt* **-1.** [averiguar] to check. **-2.** [comprovar] to confirm.

◆ **verificar-se** *vp*: **verifica-se um aumento na inflação** an increase in inflation has been confirmed.

verme ['vɛxmi] *m* worm.

vermelhidão [vexmeʎi'dãw] *f* redness.

vermelho, lha [vex'meʎu, ʎa] *adj* **-1.** [ger] red; **ficar** ~ **de raiva/vergonha** to flush with anger/embarrassment. **-2.** [ao chorar]: **olhos** ~**s** red eyes.

◆ **vermelho** *m* **-1.** [cor] red. **-2.** [déficit]: **estar no** ~ to be in the red.

vermicida [vexmi'sida], **vermífugo** [vex'mifugu] *m* vermicide.

vermute [vex'mutʃi] *m* vermouth.

vernáculo, la [vex'nakulu, la] *adj* vernacular.

◆ **vernáculo** *m* vernacular.

vernissage [vexni'saʒi] *f* opening.

verniz [vex'niʃ] (*pl* **-es**) *m* **-1.** [solução] varnish. **-2.** [couro] patent leather; **de** ~ [bolsa, sapatos] patent leather *(antes de subst)*. **-3.** *fig* [polidez] veneer.

verões [ve'rõjʃ] *pl* ⊳ **verão**.

verossímil [vero'simiw] (*pl* **-eis**) *adj* **-1.** [crível] credible. **-2.** [provável] likely.

verossimilhança [verosimi'ʎãnsa] *f* **-1.** [credibilidade] credibility. **-2.** [probabilidade] likelihood.

verruga [ve'xuga] *f* wart.

versado, da [vex'sadu, da] *adj*: ~ **em** versed in.
versão [vex'sãw] (*pl* **-ões**) *f* **-1.** [interpretação] version. **-2.** [tradução]: ~ **(para)** translation (into).
versar [4] [vex'sa(x)] *vi*: ~ **sobre** to be about.
versátil [vex'satʃiw] (*pl* **-eis**) *adj* versatile.
versatilidade [vexsatʃili'dadʒi] *f* versatility.
versejar [4] [vexse'ʒa(x)] ◇ *vt* to versify. ◇ *vi* to write in verse.
versículo [vex'sikulu] *m* **-1.** [de artigo] paragraph. **-2.** RELIG verse.
verso ['vɛxsu] *m* **-1.** [gênero] verse; **~s brancos** blank verse *(sg)*. **-2.** [linha de poema] line. **-3.** [poema] poem. **-4.** [de página] verso; **vide** ~ see over(leaf).
versões [vex'sõjʃ] *pl* ⊳ **versão**.
versus ['vɛxsuʃ] *prep* versus.
vértebra ['vɛxtebra] *f* vertebra.
vertebrado, da [vexte'bradu, da] *adj* vertebrate.
◆ **vertebrado** *m* vertebrate.
vertebral [vexte'braw] (*pl* **-ais**) *adj* vertebral.
vertente [vex'tẽntʃi] *f* **-1.** [declive] slope. **-2.** *fig* [aspecto] angle.
verter [5] [vex'te(x)] ◇ *vt* **-1.** [despejar - líquido] to pour; [- recipiente] to tip. **-2.** [derramar] to spill. **-3.** [lágrimas, sangue] to shed. **-4.** [traduzir]: ~ **(para)** to translate (into). ◇ *vi* [brotar]: ~ **de** [água] to spring from; [rio] to rise from.
vertical [vextʃi'kaw] (*pl* **-ais**) ◇ *adj* vertical. ◇ *f* vertical.
vértice ['vɛxtʃisi] *m* **-1.** GEOM vertex. **-2.** [de montanha *etc*] summit.
vertigem [vex'tʃiʒẽ] (*pl* **-ns**) *f* **-1.** MED vertigo. **-2.** [tonteira] giddiness, dizziness; **dar** ~ to make dizzy; **ter** ~ to feel giddy, to feel dizzy.
vertiginoso, osa [vextʃiʒi'nozu, ɔza] *adj* vertiginous.
verve ['vexvi] *f* verve.
vesgo, ga ['veʒgu, ga] *adj* cross-eyed.
vesícula [ve'zikula] *f*: ~ **(biliar)** gall bladder.
vespa ['veʃpa] *f* wasp.
véspera ['vɛʃpera] *f*: **na** ~ **de** the day before; ~ **de Natal** Christmas Eve.
◆ **vésperas** *fpl* [um tempo antes]: **nas ~s de** on the eve of; **estar nas ~s de** to be about to.
vesperal [veʃpe'raw] (*pl* **-ais**) ◇ *adj* evening *(antes de subst)*. ◇ *f* matinee.
vespertino, na [veʃpex'tʃinu, na] *adj* evening *(antes de subst)*.
◆ **vespertino** *m* evening paper.
veste ['veʃtʃi] *f* **-1.** [vestido] dress. **-2.** [eclesiástica] vestment.
vestiário [veʃ'tʃjarju] *m* **-1.** [onde se troca roupa] changing room. **-2.** [onde se deixa casacos *etc*] cloakroom.
vestibulando, da [veʃtʃibu'lãndu, da] *m, f* *university candidate*.
vestibular [veʃtʃibu'la(x)] *m* *university entrance exam*.

VESTIBULAR

Because of the limited number of places in Brazilian universities, a student who has finished middle school and wishes to enter one of the faculties has to sit an entrance exam: the *vestibular*. Highly competitive, the exam tests candidates' specific knowledge in various basic subjects: Portuguese, history, geography, mathematics, physics, biology and chemistry. The more sought-after places attract up to 60 candidates per vacancy.

vestíbulo [veʃ'tʃibulu] *m* **-1.** [de casa] hall. **-2.** [de teatro] foyer.
vestido, da [veʃ'tʃidu, da] *adj* **-1.** [com roupa]: ~ **(com/de)** dressed in. **-2.** [fantasiado]: ~ **de** dressed as.
◆ **vestido** *m* dress; ~ **de noiva** wedding dress.
vestígio [veʃ'tʃiʒju] *m* **-1.** [pegada] trail. **-2.** *fig* [indício] trace.
vestimenta [veʃtʃi'mẽnta] *f* **-1.** [roupa] garment. **-2.** RELIG vestment.
vestir [54] [veʃ'tʃi(x)] ◇ *vt* **-1.** [pôr sobre alguém] to put on. **-2.** [usar] to wear. **-3.** [costurar para] to make clothes for. **-4.** [dar vestuário para] to clothe. **-5.** [fantasiar]: ~ **alguém de** to dress sb as. **-6.** [fronha] to cover. ◇ *vi* [ter caimento]: ~ **bem/mal** to dress well/badly.
◆ **vestir-se** *vp* **-1.** [usar]: **ela só se veste de branco** she only wears white. **-2.** [aprontar-se] to get dressed. **-3.** [comprar roupa]: **~-se em** to buy clothes in. **-4.** [fantasiar-se]: **vestiu-se de pirata** he was dressed (up) as a pirate.
vestuário [veʃ'twarju] *m* **-1.** [roupas] clothing. **-2.** TEATRO costumes *(pl)*.
vetar [4] [ve'ta(x)] *vt* **-1.** [lei, proposta, candidato] to veto. **-2.** [acesso] to forbid.
veterano, na [vete'rãnu, na] ◇ *adj* veteran *(antes de subst)*. ◇ *m, f* veteran.
veterinário, ria [veteri'narju, rja] ◇ *adj* veterinary. ◇ *m, f* vet, veterinary surgeon.
veto ['vɛtu] *m* veto.
véu ['vɛu] *m* **-1.** [pano] veil. **-2.** ANAT: ~ **do paladar** soft palate.
vexame [ve'ʃãmi] *m* **-1.** [vergonha] shame; **dar um** ~ to make a fool of o.s.; **passar um** ~ to be disgraced. **-2.** [humilhação] humiliation. **-3.** [ultraje] outrage.
vexaminoso, sia [veʃami'nozu, za] *adj* **-1.** [vergonhoso] disgraceful. **-2.** [humilhante] humiliating. **-3.** [ultrajante] outrageous.
vexar [4] [ve'ʃa(x)] *vt* **-1.** [envergonhar] to embarrass. **-2.** [humilhar] to humiliate. **-3.** [ultrajar] to outrage.
◆ **vexar-se** *vp* [envergonhar-se] to be ashamed.
vexatório [veʃa'tɔrju] *adj* = **vexaminoso**.
vez ['veʃ] (*pl* **-es**) *f* **-1.** [freqüência, quantidade] time; **uma** ~ once; **duas** ~ **es** twice; **três** ~ **es** three times; **algumas** ~ **es** a few times; **às** ~ **es** sometimes; **cada** ~ **mais** more and more; **cada** ~ **mais alto** higher and higher; **cada** ~ **menos** less and less; **de** ~ **em quando** from time to

time; **mais ~ es** more often; **mais uma ~, outra ~** (once) again; **raras ~ es** seldom; **uma ~ ou outra** once in a while; **uma ~ na vida e outra na morte** once in a blue moon; **várias ~ es** several times. **-2.** [ocasião] time; **você já sentiu isso alguma ~?** have you ever felt that?; **cada ~ que, toda ~ que** every time; **desta ~** this time; **de uma ~ por todas** once and for all; **de uma ~ só** once only; **de ~** once and for all; **era uma ~ ...** once upon a time ...; **na maioria das ~ es** on most occasions, most times. **-3.** [turno] turn; **ter ~** to have a chance. **-4.** [multiplicação] times; **2 ~ es 4** 2 times 4.

◆ **vezes** *fpl* [função]: **fazer as ~ es de** to stand in for.

◆ **em vez de** *loc prep* instead of.

◆ **uma vez que** *loc conj* **-1.** [já que] since. **-2.** [se] if.

VHF (*abrev de* **Very High Frequency**) *f* VHF.

VHS (*abrev de* **Video Home System**) *m* VHS.

via ['via] ◇ *f* **-1.** [caminho, estrada] road; **~ de acesso** access road; **~ férrea** railway; **~ pública** thoroughfare. **-2.** [transporte]: **por ~ aérea** by air; [postal] by airmail; **por ~ terrestre** by land, overland. **-3.** [meio] route; **por ~ de** through (means of); **por ~ oficial** through official means. **-4.** [processo]: **em ~ (s) de** on the way to. **-5.** [de documento] copy; **primeira/segunda ~** original/duplicate (copy). **-6.** [de drenagem *etc*] channel. **-7.** ANAT tract; **por ~ oral** by mouth. **-8.** *loc*: **chegar às ~s de fato** to come to blows. ◇ *prep* via.

◆ **Via Láctea** *f* Milky Way.

◆ **por via das dúvidas** *loc adv* just in case.

◆ **via de regra** *loc adv*: **(por) ~ de regra** as a general rule.

viabilidade [vjabili'dadʒi] *f* feasibility, viability.

viabilizar [vjabili'za(x)] *vt* to make possible.

viação [vja'sãw] (*pl* **-ões**) *f* **-1.** [conjunto de estradas] highways, roads *(pl)*. **-2.** [companhia] bus company.

viaduto [vja'dutu] *m* viaduct.

viagem ['vjaʒẽ] (*pl* **-ns**) *f* **-1.** [ger] journey; **boa ~!** have a good journey!; **~ de ida e volta** return trip; **~ inaugural** NÁUT maiden voyage; **~ de negócios** business trip. **-2.** *fig* [sob efeito de droga] trip.

◆ **viagens** *fpl* travels.

viajado, da [vja'ʒadu, da] *adj* [pessoa] well-travelled *UK*, well-traveled *US*.

viajante [vja'ʒãntʃi] ◇ *adj* travelling *UK*, traveling *US*. ◇ *mf* traveller *UK*, traveler *US*.

viajar [4] [vja'ʒa(x)] *vi*: **~ (por)** to travel (across/through).

viário, ria ['vjarju, rja] *adj* road *(antes de subst)*.

viatura [vja'tura] *f* vehicle.

viável ['vjavɛw] (*pl* **-eis**) *adj* viable, feasible.

víbora ['vibora] *f* **-1.** ZOOL viper. **-2.** *fig* [pessoa] snake in the grass.

vibração [vibra'sãw] (*pl* **-ões**) *f* **-1.** [tremor] vibration. **-2.** *fig* [entusiasmo] thrill.

vibrador, ra [vibra'do(x),ra] *adj* [vibratório] vibrating.

◆ **vibrador** *m* [estimulador] vibrator.

vibrante [vi'brãntʃi] *adj fig* [entusiasmado] vibrant.

vibrar [4] [vi'bra(x)] ◇ *vt* **-1.** [fazer tremer] to shake. **-2.** [dedilhar] to vibrate. ◇ *vi* **-1.** [tremer] to shake. **-2.** *fig* [entusiasmar-se] to be thrilled.

vibrião [vi'brjãw] (*pl* **-ões**) *m* vibrio.

vice ['visi] *mf* deputy.

vice- [visi] *prefixo* vice-.

vice-campeão, peã [ˌvisikãn'pjãw, pjã] (*mpl* **-ões**, *fpl* **-s**) *m, f* runner-up.

vicejante [vise'ʒãntʃi] *adj* **-1.** [horta, pomar] lush. **-2.** [estilo, poesia] flowery.

vicejar [4] [vise'ʒa(x)] ◇ *vi* [vegetar] to flourish. ◇ *vt* [dar viço a] to cause to flourish.

vice-presidente, ta [ˌvisiprezi'dẽntʃi, ta] (*mpl* **-s**, *fpl* **-s**) *m, f* **-1.** POL vice-president. **-2.** [de comitê, empresa] deputy chairman.

vice-rei [ˌvisi'xej] (*pl* **vice-reis**) *m* viceroy.

vice-reitor, ra [ˌvisixej'to(x), ra] (*mpl* **-es**, *fpl* **-s**) *m, f* deputy head.

vice-versa [ˌvisi'vɛxsa] *adv* vice versa.

viciado, da [vi'sjadu, da] *adj* **-1.** [em droga *etc*]: **~ (em)** addicted (to); **ser ~ em drogas** to be hooked on drugs. **-2.** [adulterado] vitiated.

viciante [vi'sjãntʃi] *adj* addictive.

viciar [16] [vi'sja(x)] ◇ *vt* **-1.** [dar vício a] to addict. **-2.** [adulterar] to vitiate. ◇ *vi* [criar vício] to be addictive.

◆ **viciar-se** *vp* [tornar-se viciado]: **~-se (em)** to become addicted (to).

vicinal [visi'naw] (*pl* **-ais**) *adj*: **estrada ~** local route.

vício ['visju] *m* **-1.** [devassidão] vice. **-2.** [em droga, bebida] addiction. **-3.** [mau hábito] bad habit; **~ de linguagem** barbarism.

vicioso, osa [vi'sjozu, ɔza] *adj* **-1.** [sistema, hábito] corrupt. **-2.** [círculo] vicious.

vicissitude [visisi'tudʒi] *f* vicissitude; **as ~s da vida** the ups and downs of life.

viço ['visu] *m* **-1.** [de planta] vigour *UK*, vigor *US*. **-2.** [de pele] freshness.

viçoso, osa [vi'sozu, ɔza] *adj* **-1.** [planta] luxuriant. **-2.** [pele] glowing.

Victoria [vik'tɔrja] *n*: **o lago ~** Lake Victoria.

vida ['vida] *f* **-1.** [ger] life; **a outra ~** the life beyond; **dar a ~ por** *fig* to give anything for; **em ~** [doar *etc*] alive; **estar entre a ~ e a morte** to be at death's door; **estilo de ~** lifestyle; **feliz da ~** delighted; **para toda a ~** forever; **padrão de ~** standard of living; **que ~!** what a life!; **tratar da ~** to get on with one's life; **~ de cão** dog's life; **~ conjugal** married life; **~ doméstica** home life; **~ sentimental** love life; **~ útil** [de máquina *etc*] useful life. **-2.** [subsistência]: **custo de ~** cost of living; **estar bem de ~** to be well off; **ganhar a ~** to earn one's living; **meio de ~** means of living; **cheio de ~** full of life; **dar ~ a algo** to liven sthg up; **sem ~** lifeless. **-3.** [direção]: **seguir (reto) toda a ~** to continue straight on as far as you can go. **-4.**

[prostituição]: **cair na ~** to go on the game; **mulher da ~** prostitute.
vidão [vi'dãw] *m fam* life of Riley.
vide ['vidʒi] *vt* see; **~ verso** see over(leaf).
videira [vi'dejra] *f* grapevine.
vidente [vi'dãntʃi] *mf* seer.
vídeo ['vidʒju] *m* **-1.** [ger] video. **-2.** [tela] screen.
videocâmara [vidʒju'kãmara] *f* video camera.
videocassete [ˌvidʒjuka'sɛtʃi] *m* **-1.** [aparelho] video cassette recorder, VCR. **-2.** [fita] videotape.
videoclipe [ˌvidʒju'klipi] *m* music video.
videoclube [ˌvidʒju'klubi] *m* video club.
videoconferência ['vidʒjukõnʃe'rẽnsja] *f* TELEC video-conference.
vídeo game ['vidʒju'gejmi] *m* video game.
videolocadora [ˌvidʒjuloka'dora] *f* video rental.
videoteca [ˌvidʒju'tɛka] *f* video library.
videoteipe [ˌvidʒju'tejpi] *m* **-1.** [fita] videotape. **-2.** [processo] videotaping.
videotexto [ˌvidʒju'teʃtu] *m* teletext, videotex(t).
vidraça [vi'drasa] *f* window pane.
vidraçaria [vidrasa'ria] *f* **-1.** [loja] glazier's. **-2.** [fábrica] glass factory. **-3.** [vidraças] glazing.
vidraceiro [vidra'sejru] *m* glazier.
vidrado, da [vi'dradu, da] *adj* **-1.** [ger] glazed. **-2.** *fam* [encantado]: **~ em** crazy about.
vidrar [4] [vi'dra(x)] <> *vt* [cerâmica *etc*] to glaze. <> *vi fam* [encantar-se]: **~ (em)** to fall in love (with).
vidreiro, ra [vi'drejru, ra] *m, f* glass-maker.
vidro ['vidru] *m* **-1.** [material] glass; **~ aramado** reinforced glass; **~ fosco** frosted glass; **~ fumê** smoked glass. **-2.** [frasco] bottle.
viela ['vjɛla] *f* alley(way).
Viena ['vjena] *n* Vienna.
viés [vjɛʃ] *m* COST bias.
◆ **de viés** *loc adv* sideways.
Vietnã [vjɛt'nã] *n*: **(o) ~** Vietnam.
vietnamita [vjɛtna'mita] <> *adj* Vietnamese. <> *mf* Vietnamese.
◆ **vietnamita** *m* [língua] Vietnamese.
viga ['viga] *f* **-1.** [de madeira] beam. **-2.** [de concreto, ferro] girder.
vigamento [viga'mẽntu] *m* rafters *(pl)*.
vigarice [viga'risi] *f* swindle.
vigário [vi'garju] *m* vicar.
vigarista [viga'riʃta] *mf* swindler.
vigência [vi'ʒẽnsja] *f* validity; **estar em ~** to be in force.
vigente [vi'ʒẽntʃi] *adj* **-1.** [lei, contrato, norma] in force. **-2.** [situação política, costume] current.
viger [26] [vi'ʒe(x)] *vi* to be in force.
vigésimo, ma [vi'ʒɛzimu, ma] *num* twentieth; *veja também* **sexto**.
vigia [vi'ʒia] <> *f* **-1.** [vigilância] surveillance. **-2.** NÁUT porthole. <> *mf* [pessoa] nightwatchman.
vigiar [16] [vi'ʒja(x)] <> *vt* **-1.** [banco, presos] to guard. **-2.** [mala, criança] to keep an eye on. **-3.** [espreitar] to watch. <> *vi* to be on the lookout.
vigilância [viʒi'lãnsja] *f* surveillance.
vigilante [vi'ʒilãntʃi] <> *adj* alert. <> *mf* guard.
vigília [vi'ʒilja] *f* **-1.** [privação de sono]: **fez-se uma ~ para evitar ataques** a watch was kept in order to avoid attack. **-2.** [prática religiosa] vigil.
vigor [vi'go(x)] *m* **-1.** [energia - de corpo, espírito] vigour; [- para o trabalho] energy. **-2.** [veemência] vigour. **-3.** [vigência]: **em ~** in force; **entrar em ~** to come into force.
vigorar [4] [vigo'ra(x)] *vi* to be in force.
vigoroso, osa [vigo'rozu, ɔza] *adj* vigorous.
vil ['viw] *(pl* **vis**) *adj* vile.
vila ['vila] *f* **-1.** [povoação] town. **-2.** [conjunto residencial] residential block. **-3.** [casa] villa.
vilã [vi'lã] *f* ▻ **vilão**.
vilania [vila'nia] *f* villainy.
vilão, lã [vi'lãw, lã] *(mpl* **-ãos, -ães**, *fpl* **-s**) *m, f* villain.
vilarejo [vila'reʒu] *m* hamlet.
vileza [vi'leza] *f* **-1.** [ato] vileness. **-2.** [qualidade] meanness.
vilipendiar [vilipẽn'dʒja(x)] *vt* to belittle.
vime ['vimi] *m* osier, withy; **de ~** wicker.
vinagre [vi'nagri] *m* vinegar.
vinagreira [vina'grejra] *f* vinegar cruet.
vinagrete [vina'grɛtʃi] *m* vinaigrette.
vincar [12] [vĩn'ka(x)] *vt* **-1.** [roupa, papel] to crease. **-2.** [rosto] to wrinkle. **-3.** [terra] to furrow.
vinco ['vĩŋku] *m* **-1.** [em roupa, papel] crease. **-2.** [no rosto] wrinkle. **-3.** [sulco] furrow.
vinculação [vĩŋkula'sãw] *f* link, linking; **ele não quer a ~ do seu nome aos escândalos** he doesn't want his name to be linked to the scandals.
vincular [4] [vĩnku'la(x)] *vt* **-1.** [ligar] to tie. **-2.** [por obrigação] to bind.
vínculo ['viŋkulu] *m* **-1.** [pessoal, familiar] bond. **-2.** [profissional, entre países] tie; **~ empregatício** work contract.
vinda ['vĩnda] *f* ▻ **vindo**.
vindicar [12] [vĩndʒi'ka(x)] *vt* **-1.** [vingar] to avenge. **-2.** [defender] to vindicate. **-3.** [reivindicar] to claim.
vindima [vĩn'dʒima] *f* grape harvest.
vindo, da ['vĩndu, da] <> *pp* ▻ **vir**. <> *adj*: **~ (de)** originating (in).
◆ **vinda** *f* **-1.** [ger] arrival (in). **-2.** [regresso] return.
vindouro, ra [vĩn'doru, ra] *adj* **-1.** [ano, década] coming. **-2.** [geração] future.
vingador, ra [vĩŋga'do(x), ra] <> *adj* avenging. <> *m, f* avenger.
vingança [vĩŋ'gãnsa] *f* revenge.
vingar [4] [vĩŋ'ga(x)] <> *vt* [tirar desforra de] to avenge. <> *vi* **-1.** [medrar] to thrive. **-2.** [dar certo] to be successful.
◆ **vingar-se** *vp* [tirar desforra]: **~-se (de)** to take revenge (on/for).
vingativo, va [vĩŋga'tʃivu, va] *adj* vindictive.
vinha ['viɲa] *f* **-1.** [vinhedo] vineyard. **-2.** [planta] vine.
vinhedo [vi'ɲedu] *m* vineyard.

vinheta [vi'ɲeta] *f* vignette.
vinho ['viɲu] <> *adj inv* [cor] burgundy. <> *m* **-1.** [cor] burgundy. **-2.** [bebida] wine; ~ **branco** white wine; ~ **espumante** sparkling wine; ~ **de mesa** table wine; ~ **do Porto** port; ~ **rosado** rosé (wine); ~ **tinto** red wine.
vinícola [vi'nikula] *adj* wine-producing.
vinicultor, ra [ˌvinikuw'to(x), ra] (*mpl* **-es**, *fpl* **-s**) *m, f* wine producer.
vinicultura [vinikuw'tura] *f* winemaking.
vinil [vi'niw] *m* vinyl.
vinte ['vĩntʃi] *num* twenty; *veja também* **seis**.
vintém [vĩn'tẽ] (*pl* **-ns**) *m* **-1.** [moeda antiga] *old Brazilian coin*. **-2.** [dinheiro]: **estar sem um** ~ to be penniless.
vintena [vĩn'tena] *f*: **uma** ~ **de** a score of.
viola ['vjɔla] *f* viola.
violação [vjola'sãw] (*pl* **-ões**) *f* **-1.** [de lei, pacto, direitos] violation. **-2.** [invasão]: ~ **de domicílio** housebreaking. **-3.** [de pessoa] violation, rape. **-4.** [de correspondência] interference. **-5.** [de local sagrado] violation, desecration.
violão [vjo'lãw] (*pl* **-ões**) *m* guitar.
violar [4] [vjo'la(x)] *vt* **-1.** [lei, pacto, direitos] to violate. **-2.** [domicílio] to break in. **-3.** [pessoa] to violate, to rape. **-4.** [correspondência] to interfere with. **-5.** [local sagrado] to violate. **-6.** [segredo] to breach.
violeiro, ra [vjo'lejru, ra] *m, f* guitarist.
violência [vjo'lẽnsja] *f* **-1.** [ato] violence. **-2.** [agressividade] vehemence. **-3.** [força - de vendaval] force; [- de paixões] violence.
violentar [4] [vjolẽn'ta(x)] *vt* **-1.** [mulher] to violate, to rape. **-2.** [deturpar] to distort.
violento, ta [vjo'lẽntu, ta] *adj* violent.
violeta [vjo'leta] <> *f* [flor] violet. <> *adj inv* [cor] violet.
violinista [vjoli'niʃta] *mf* violinist.
violino [vjo'linu] *m* violin.
violoncelista [vjolõnse'liʃta] *mf* cellist.
violoncelo [vjolõn'sɛlu] *m* cello.
violonista [vjolo'niʃta] *mf* guitarist.
VIP (*abrev de* **Very Important Person**) [vipi] <> *adj* [pessoa, local] VIP. <> *mf* VIP.
vir [67] ['vi(x)] *vi* **-1.** [apresentar-se] to come; **veio me ver** he came to see me; **venho visitá-lo amanhã** I'll come and see you tomorrow. **-2.** [chegar] to arrive; **ele veio atrasado/adiantado** he arrived late/early; **ela veio no ônibus das onze** she came on the eleven o'clock bus. **-3.** [a seguir no tempo] to come; **a semana/o ano que vem** next week/year, the coming week/year. **-4.** [estar] to be; **vem escrito em português** it's written in Portuguese; **vinha embalado** it came in a package. **-5.** [regressar] to come back; **eles vêm de férias amanhã** they're coming back from holidays tomorrow; **hoje, venho mais tarde** today, I'll be coming later than usual. **-6.** [surgir] to come; **o carro veio não sei de onde** the car came out of nowhere; **veio-me uma idéia** I've got an idea. **-7.** [provir]: ~ **de** to come from; **venho agora mesmo de lá** I've just come from there. **-8.** [em locuções]: ~ **a ser** to become; **que vem a ser isto?** what's the meaning of this?; ~ **abaixo** [edifício, construção] to collapse; ~ **ao mundo** [nascer] to come into the world, to be born; ~ **a saber (de algo)** to find out (about sthg); ~ **sobre** [arremeter contra] to lunge at; ~ **a tempo de algo** to arrive in time for sthg; ~ **a tempo de fazer algo** to arrive in time to do sthg.
viração [vira'sãw] (*pl* **-ões**) *f* breeze.
vira-casaca [ˌviraka'zaka] (*pl* **vira-casacas**) *mf* turncoat.
virado, da [vi'radu, da] *adj* [voltado]: ~ **para** facing.
◆ **virado** *m* CULIN: ~ **de feijão** *sautéed beans with fried egg and sausage.*
◆ **virada** *f* **-1.** [viradela] turning. **-2.** [guinada] swerve. **-3.** ESP sudden turnaround. **-4.** [esforço]: **dar uma virada** to make a last effort.
vira-lata [ˌvira'lata] (*pl* **vira-latas**) *m* **-1.** [cachorro] mongrel. **-2.** [pessoa] down-and-out.
virar [4] [vi'ra(x)] <> *vt* **-1.** [volver]: ~ **algo (para)** to turn sthg (towards); ~ **as costas** to turn one's back. **-2.** [mostrar pelo verso] to turn over. **-3.** [entornar] to tip. **-4.** [emborcar] to capsize. **-5.** [contornar] to turn. **-6.** [apontar]: ~ **algo contra alguém** to turn sthg on sb. **-7.** [meter]: ~ **a mão em alguém** to attack sb. **-8.** [fazer mudar de opinião] to change. **-9.** [transformar-se] to turn into. <> *vi* **-1.** [volver] to turn; ~ **para** to turn towards; ~ **de bruços** to turn on to one's tummy; ~ **de costas** to turn on to one's back; ~ **do avesso** to turn inside out. **-2.** [emborcar] to capsize. **-3.** [contornar]: ~ **(em)** to turn (into); ~ **à direita/esquerda** to turn (to the) right/left. **-4.** [mudar] to change. **-5.** [mudar de direção] to change direction. **-6.** [rebelar-se, voltar-se]: ~ **contra** to turn against.
◆ **virar-se** *vp* **-1.** [volver-se] to turn around. **-2.** [rebelar-se] to rebel; **~-se contra** to turn against. **-3.** [defender-se] to stand up for o.s. **-4.** [empenhar-se] to struggle.
viravolta [ˌvira'vɔwta] *f* **-1.** [volta inteira] spin. **-2.** [sobre si mesmo] somersault. **-3.** *fig* [mudança] turnabout.
virgem ['vixʒẽ] (*pl* **-ns**) <> *adj* **-1.** [ger] virgin. **-2.** [fita, filme] blank. **-3.** [mel] pure. **-4.** [isento]: ~ **de algo** lacking sthg. <> *f* [pessoa] virgin.
◆ **Virgem** *f* **-1.** RELIG Virgin. **-2.** ARTE madonna. **-3.** [zodíaco] Virgo; **ser Virgem** to be a Virgo.
virginal [vixʒi'nawl] (*pl* **-ais**) *adj* virginal.
virgindade [vixʒĩn'dadʒi] *f* virginity.
virginiano, na [vixʒi'njãnu, na] <> *adj* Virgo (*antes de subst*). <> *m, f* Virgo.
vírgula ['vixgula] *f* **-1.** [entre palavras] comma. **-2.** [entre números] (decimal) point. **-3.** [mecha] curl. **-4.** [objetando-se]: **uma** ~! *fam* my foot!
viril [vi'riw] (*pl* **-is**) *adj* virile.
virilha [vi'riʎa] *f* groin.
virilidade [virili'dadʒi] *f* virility.
virose [vi'rɔzi] *f* viral infection.
virótico, ca [vi'rɔtʃiku, ka] *adj* viral.

virtual [vix'twaw] (*pl* **-ais**) *adj* **-1.** [possível] potential. **-2.** *COMPUT* virtual; **realidade ~** virtual reality.
virtualmente [vixtwaw'mẽntʃi] *adv* virtually.
virtude [vix'tudʒi] *f* **-1.** [qualidade] virtue. **-2.** [capacidade] knack. **-3.** [razão]: **em ~ de** due to.
virtuose [vix'twɔzi] *mf* virtuoso.
virtuosidade [vixtwozi'dadʒi] *f* virtuosity.
virtuosismo [vixtwo'ziʒmu] *m* virtuosity.
virtuoso, osa [vix'twozu, ɔza] <> *adj* [íntegro] virtuous. <> *m, f* [gênio] virtuoso.
virulência [viru'lẽnsja] *f* virulence.
virulento, ta [viru'lẽntu, ta] *adj* virulent.
vírus ['viruʃ] *m inv* virus.
vis [viʃ] *pl* ⊳ **vil**.
visado, da [vi'zadu, da] *adj* **-1.** [cheque] valid. **-2.** [pessoa] watched.
visão [vi'zãw] (*pl* **-ões**) *f* **-1.** [sentido] vision, sight. **-2.** [o que se vê] sight; **~ de conjunto** overall impression. **-3.** [alucinação] vision; **ter visões** to have visions. **-4.** [percepção, ponto de vista]: **~ (de/sobre)** view (on/about). **-5.** [revelação] vision.
visar [4] [vi'za(x)] <> *vt* **-1.** [cheque, passaporte] to stamp. **-2.** [objetivar] to look for; **~ (a) fazer algo** to aim to do sthg. <> *vi* [objetivar]: **~ a algo/a fazer algo** to aim for sthg/to aim to do sthg.
vis-à-vis [viza'viʃ] *adv* vis-à-vis.
víscera ['viseral] *f* viscus.
◆ **vísceras** *fpl* viscera, bowels.
visceral [vise'raw] (*pl* **-ais**) *adj* **-1.** [ger] visceral. **-2.** [arraigado] deep-rooted.
visconde, dessa [viʃ'kõndʒi, desa] *m, f* viscount.
viscoso, osa [viʃ'kozu, ɔza] *adj* viscous.
viseira [vi'zejra] *f* visor.
visibilidade [vizibili'dadʒi] *f* visibility.
visionário, ria [vizjo'narju, rja] <> *adj* visionary. <> *m, f* visionary.
visita [vi'zita] *f* **-1.** [ato] visit; **fazer uma ~ a alguém** to pay sb a visit; **~ de médico** *fig* flying visit. **-2.** [visitante] visitor; **ter ~s** to have visitors; **~ de cerimônia** official visit. **-3.** [vistoria] inspection.
visitação [vizita'sãw] (*pl* **-ões**) *f* [visita] visit; **aberto à ~ pública** open to the public.
◆ **Visitação** *f RELIG* Visitation.
visitante [vizi'tãntʃi] *mf* visitor.
visitar [4] [vizi'ta(x)] *vt* **-1.** [fazer visita a] to visit. **-2.** [vistoriar] to inspect.
◆ **visitar-se** *vp* [fazer visitas mútuas] to visit one another.
visível [vi'zivɛw] (*pl* **-eis**) *adj* visible.
visivelmente [vizivew'mẽntʃi] *adv* visibly.
vislumbrar [viʒlũm'bra(x)] *vt* to glimpse.
vislumbre [viʒ'lũnbri] *m* glimpse.
visões [vi'zõjʃ] *pl* ⊳ **visão**.
visom [vi'zõ] (*pl* **-s**) *m* mink; **casaco de ~** mink coat.
visor [vi'zo(x)] (*pl* **-es**) *m* viewfinder.
vista ['viʃta] *f* ⊳ **visto**.
vista-d'olhos [ˌviʃta'dɔʎuʃ] (*pl* **vistas-d'olhos**) *f* glance; **passar uma ~ (em)** to glance (at).
visto, ta ['viʃtu, ta] <> *pp* ⊳ **ver**. <> *adj* **-1.** [olhado]: **~ (de)** seen (from). **-2.** [considerado] thought of. **-3.** [estudado] looked at.
◆ **visto** *m* **-1.** [em documento] stamp. **-2.** [em passaporte] visa.
◆ **vista** *f* **-1.** [ger] view; **com vista para o mar** with sea view. **-2.** [sentido] sight. **-3.** [olhos, olhar] eyesight; **a perder de vista** as far as the eye can see; [pagamento] long-term; **à primeira vista** at first sight; **à vista** [visível] visible; [pagamento] in cash; **pôr à vista** to put on display; **até a vista!** see you later!; **conhecer de vista** to know by sight; **perder de vista** to lose sight of; **vista cansada** tired eyes. **-4.** [propósito]: **com vista a** with a view to; **ter em vista** to have in mind. **-5.** *loc*: **dar na vista** to be obvious; **fazer vista grossa (a)** to turn a blind eye (to); **saltar à vista** to be glaringly obvious, to stand out a mile.
◆ **em vista de** *loc prep* in view of.
◆ **pelo visto** *loc adv* by the look of it.
◆ **visto que** *loc conj* seeing.
vistoria [viʃto'ria] *f* inspection.
vistoriar [viʃto'rja(x)] *vt* to inspect.
vistoso, osa [viʃ'tozu, ɔza] *adj* eye-catching.
visual [vi'zwaw] (*pl* **-ais**) <> *adj* visual. <> *m fam* **-1.** [aspecto] appearance, look. **-2.** [vista] view.
visualizar [4] [vizwali'za(x)] *vt* to visualize.
visualmente [vizuaw'mẽntʃi] *adv* visually; **~ incapacitado** visually impaired.
vital [vi'taw] (*pl* **-ais**) *adj* vital.
vitalício, cia [vita'lisju, sja] *adj* lifelong *(antes de subst)*.
vitalidade [vitali'dadʒi] *f* vitality.
vitalizar [4] [vitali'za(x)] *vt* to vitalize.
vitamina [vita'mina] *f* vitamin.
vitaminado, da [vitami'nadu, da] *adj* with added vitamins.
vitamínico, ca [vita'miniku, ka] *adj* vitamin *(antes de subst)*.
vitela [vi'tɛla] *f* **-1.** *ZOOL* calf. **-2.** [carne] veal.
vítima ['vitʃima] *f* [pessoa] victim; **fazer-se de ~** to play the victim; **ser ~ de** to be the victim of.
vitimar [4] [vitʃi'ma(x)] *vt* **-1.** [matar] to claim the life of. **-2.** [sacrificar] to sacrifice. **-3.** [danificar] to destroy.
vitória [vi'tɔrja] *f* victory.
Vitória [vi'tɔrja] *n* Vitória.
vitória-régia [viˌtɔrja'xɛʒja] (*pl* **vitórias-régias**) *f* giant water lily.
vitorioso, osa [vito'rjozu, ɔza] *adj* victorious.
vitral [vi'traw] (*pl* **-ais**) *m* stained-glass window.
vítreo, trea ['vitrju, trja] *adj* **-1.** [de vidro] glass *(antes de subst)*. **-2.** [aspecto] glassy.
vitrificar [12] [vitrifi'ka(x)] <> *vt* **-1.** [converter em vidro] to vitrify. **-2.** [fazer tomar aparência de vidro] to make as smooth as glass. <> *vi* **-1.** [converter-se em vidro] to turn into glass. **-2.** [tomar aparência de vidro] to become as smooth as glass.
vitrine [vi'trini], **vitrina** [vi'trina] *f* **-1.** [de loja] shop window. **-2.** [armário] display case.
vitrinista [vitri'niʃta] *mf* window dresser.

vitrola [vi'trɔla] *mf fig fam* gossip.
◆ **vitrola** *f* gramophone.

viuvez [vju'veʒ] *f* widowhood.

viúvo, va ['vjuvu, va] <> *adj* widowed. <> *m, f* widower (*f* widow).

viva ['viva] <> *m* cheer. <> *interj* hooray!; ~ **a rainha!** long live the Queen!

vivacidade [vivasi'dadʒi] *f* vivacity.

vivalma [vi'vawma] *f*: **não tinha** ~ there wasn't a living soul about.

vivamente [viva'mẽntʃi] *adv* **-1.** [descrever, sentir] vividly. **-2.** [debater, discursar, protestar] vigorously.

vivaz [vi'vajʒ] *adj* lively.

viveiro [vi'vejru] *m* **-1.** [de plantas] nursery. **-2.** [de pássaros] aviary. **-3.** [de peixes] fish farm.

vivência [vi'vẽnsja] *f* **-1.** [existência] existence. **-2.** [experiência] experience; **ter** ~ **em algo** to have experience in sthg.

vivenciar [18] [vivẽn'sja(x)] *vt* to live through.

vivenda [vi'vẽnda] *f* (detached) house.

vivente [vi'vẽntʃi] <> *adj* living. <> *mf* living being.

viver [5] [vi've(x)] <> *vt* **-1.** [vida] to live. **-2.** [fase, situação] to experience. <> *vi* **-1.** [ger] to live; ~ **bem** [economicamente] to live comfortably; [em harmonia] to live happily. **-2.** [estar vivo] to be alive. **-3.** [perdurar] to last. **-4.** [sustentar-se]: ~ **de** to live off; ~ **à custa de** to live off. **-5.** [conviver]: ~ **com** to mingle with; [maritalmente] to live with. **-6.** [dedicar-se completamente]: ~ **para** to live for. **-7.** [residir]: ~ **(em)** to live (in). **-8.** [freqüentar muito]: ~ **(em)** to live (in). **-9.** [estar sempre] to always be; ~ **doente/gripado** to always be ill/ have a cold; ~ **trabalhando** to do nothing but work. <> *m* life.

víveres ['viveriʃ] *mpl* provisions.

vivido, da [vi'vidu, da] *adj* [pessoa] experienced.

vívido, da ['vividu, da] *adj* **-1.** [ger] vivid. **-2.** [expressivo] vivacious.

vivificar [12] [vivifi'ka(x)] *vt* to revive.

vivo, va ['vivu, va] *adj* **-1.** [ger] bright. **-2.** [existente] living; **estar** ~ to be alive. **-3.** [animado, buliçoso] lively. **-4.** [ardente] fervent.
◆ **vivos** *mpl*: **os** ~**s** the living.
◆ **ao vivo** *loc adv* live.

vizinhança [vizi'ɲãnsa] *f* neighbourhood *UK*, neighborhood *US*.

vizinho, nha [vi'ziɲu, ɲa] <> *adj* neighbouring *UK*, neighboring *US*. <> *m, f* neighbour *UK*, neighbor *US*.

voador, ra [vwa'do(x), ra] *adj* flying.

voar [20] ['vwa(x)] *vi* **-1.** [ger] to fly; ~ **em algo** to fly in sthg; **fazer algo voando** *fig* to do sthg quickly. **-2.** [explodir]: ~ **pelos ares** to explode; **fazer** ~ **pelos ares** to blow up. **-3.** *loc*: **estar/ficar voando** *fam* [ficar sem entender] to be thrown; ~ **alto** *fig* to aim high; ~ **para cima de alguém** [assediar] to mob sb; [atacar] to fly at sb.

vocabulário [vokabu'larju] *m* vocabulary.

vocábulo [vo'kabulu] *m* word.

vocação [voka'sãw] (*pl* **-ões**) *f* vocation.

vocacional [vokasjo'naw] (*pl* **-ais**) *adj* vocational.

vocal [vo'kaw] (*pl* **-ais**) *adj* vocal.

vocálico, ca [vo'kaliku, ka] *adj* vocal.

vocalista [voka'liʃta] *mf* vocalist.

você [vɔ'se] (*pl* **vocês**) *pron pess* **-1.** [tratamento] you; ~ **é médico?** are you a doctor?; ~ **está muito elegante** you're looking very elegant; **vocês precisam estudar** you need to study; ~ **mesmo** *ou* **próprio** you yourself. **-2.** *(depois de prep)*: **isto pertence a** ~**?** is this yours?; **quero ir com vocês** I want to go with you; **penso muito em** ~ I think about you a lot; **esta carta é para** ~ this letter is for you. **-3.** [em anúncios]: **'o novo Fiat Regatta** ~ **vai adorar'** 'the new Fiat Regatta - you'll love it'; **'o melhor para** ~**'** 'the best thing for you'. **-4.** [alguém qualquer um] one; **na Universidade,** ~ **tem que estudar muito** at university, one has to study a lot.

vocês [vo'seʃ] ▷ **você**.

vociferar [4] [vosife'ra(x)] <> *vt* [bradar] to shout. <> *vi* [reclamar]: ~ **(contra)** to complain (about).

vodca ['vɔdʒka] *f* vodka.

voga ['vɔga] <> *f* **-1.** [ger] fashion; **estar em** ~ to be in vogue. **-2.** *NÁUT* [cadência] rowing. <> *m* [remador] oarsman.

vogal [vo'gaw] (*pl* **-ais**) *f LING* vowel.

vogar [14] [vo'ga(x)] *vi* **-1.** [navegar] to sail. **-2.** [circular] to circulate. **-3.** [estar em moda] to be in vogue. **-4.** [vigorar] to be in force.

voile ['vwaw] (*pl* **voiles**) *m* voile; **cortina de** ~ net curtain.

volante [vo'lãntʃi] *m* **-1.** *AUTO* steering wheel; **estar no** ~ to be at the wheel. **-2.** [motorista, piloto] driver. **-3.** [para apostas] betting slip. **-4.** [de máquina] flywheel.

volátil [vo'latʃiw] (*pl* **-eis**) *adj* volatile.

volatilidade [volatʃili'dadʒi] *f ECON* volatility.

vôlei ['volej], **voleibol** [volei'bow] *m* volleyball.

voleio [vo'leju] *m* volley.

volt ['vɔwtʃi] *m* volt.

volta ['vɔwta] *f* **-1.** [giro] turn; **dar a** ~ **(a algo)** to go around (sthg); **dar uma** ~ [sobre si mesmo] to turn round. **-2.** [retorno] return; **de** ~ back; **estar de** ~ to be back; **na** ~ [voltando] on the way back; [ao chegar] on arrival. **-3.** [passeio]: **dar uma** ~ [a pé] to go for a walk; [de carro] to go for a drive. **-4.** *ESP* lap. **-5.** *MIL*: **dar meia** ~ to about-turn *UK*, to about-face *US*. **-6.** *AUTO*: **fazer a** ~ to make a U-turn, to turn back. **-7.** [mudança]: **dar** ~**s** [vida *etc*] to go round in circles. **-8.** [de espiral] twist. **-9.** [contorno] edge. **-10.** [curva] curve. **-11.** *fig* [troco] comeback. **-12.** *loc*: **dar a** ~ **por cima** *fig* to get over (it).
◆ **às voltas com** *loc prep*: **estar/andar às** ~**s com** to be struggling with.
◆ **em volta de** *loc prep* around.
◆ **por volta de** *loc prep* around.
◆ **volta e meia** *loc adv* every now and again.

voltado, da [vow'tadu, da] *adj* **-1.** [de frente para] facing. **-2.** [concentrado]: **estar** ~ **para** to be focussed on.

voltagem [vow'taʒẽ] *f* voltage.

voltar [4] [vow'ta(x)] ◇ *vt* **-1.** [dirigir]: **~ algo para** to turn sthg towards. **-2.** [mudar a posição de] to turn. **-3.** [mostrar pelo verso] to turn over. ◇ *vi* **-1.** [ger] to return; **~ a si** to come to; **~ atrás** *fig* to back out. **-2.** [mudar de direção]: **~ a** *ou* **para** to turn towards. **-3.** [repetir-se] to come back. **-4.** [tratar novamente]: **~ a algo** to return to sthg. **-5.** [recomeçar]: **~ a fazer algo** to do sthg again.
◆ **voltar-se** *vp* **-1.** [virar-se] to turn round. **-2.** [recorrer]: **~-se para** to turn to. **-3.** [rebelar-se]: **~-se contra** to turn against.

voltear [15] [vow'tʃja(x)] ◇ *vt* **-1.** [contornar] to go round. **-2.** [fazer girar] to turn. ◇ *vi* **-1.** [girar] to revolve. **-2.** [esvoaçar] to flutter.

volteio [vow'teju] *m* **-1.** [rodopio] spin. **-2.** [volta] bend. **-3.** [de equilibrista] movement.

voltímetro [vowtʃi'metru] *m* ELETR voltmeter.

volubilidade [volubili'dadʒi] *f* fickleness.

volume [vo'lumi] *m* **-1.** [ger] volume; **aumentar/diminuir o ~** to turn the volume up/down. **-2.** [pacote] package.

volumoso, osa [volu'mozu, ɔza] *adj* bulky.

voluntário, ria [volũn'tarju, rja] ◇ *adj* voluntary. ◇ *m, f* volunteer.

voluntarioso, osa [volũnta'rjozu, ɔza] *adj* headstrong.

volúpia [vo'lupja] *f* **-1.** [sexual] pleasure. **-2.** [ambição] desire.

voluptuoso, osa [volup'twozu, ɔza] *adj* voluptuous.

volúvel [vo'luvew] (*pl* **-eis**) *adj* changeable.

volver [5] [vow've(x)] ◇ *vt* to turn. ◇ *vi*: **~ a** to return to.

vomitar [4] [vomi'ta(x)] ◇ *vt* **-1.** [expelir] to vomit, to throw up. **-2.** [sujar com vômito] to vomit on, to be sick on. **-3.** *fig* [proferir] to spew out. ◇ *vi* [expelir vômito] to vomit, to be sick.

vômito ['vomitu] *m* **-1.** [ato] vomiting, throwing up. **-2.** [substância] vomit, sick.

vontade [võn'tadʒi] *f* **-1.** [determinação] will; **força de ~** will power; **por ~ própria** of one's own accord; **~ de ferro** iron will. **-2.** [desejo] wish; **dar ~ a alguém de fazer algo** to make sb feel like doing sthg; **me deu vontade de sair** I felt like going out; **o filme me deu vontade de viajar** the film made me feel like travelling; **fazer a ~ de alguém** to do what sb wants; **ter ~ de fazer algo** to feel like doing sthg; **contra a ~** unwillingly; **sem ~** reluctantly. **-3.** [necessidade] need. **-4.** [empenho, interesse]: **boa/má ~** good/ill will; **de boa/má ~** gladly/grudgingly.
◆ **vontades** *fpl* [caprichos]: **cheio de ~s** wilful; **fazer todas as ~s de alguém** to pander to sb.
◆ **à vontade** *loc adv* **-1.** [sem cerimônia]: **ficar à ~** to feel at ease; **fique à ~** make yourself at home. **-2.** [em quantidade] loads. **-3.** [quanto se quiser] as much as one wants.
◆ **com vontade** *loc adv* [comer *etc*] heartily.

vôo ['vow] *m* flight; **levantar ~** to take off; **~ cego** flying blind; **~ livre** ESP hang-gliding.

voragem [vo'raʒẽ] (*pl* **-s**) *f* **-1.** [abismo] chasm. **-2.** [de águas] maelstrom. **-3.** *fig* [de paixão, ambição] confusion.

voraz [vo'raʃ] (*pl* **-es**) *adj* **-1.** [pessoa, apetite] voracious. **-2.** *fig* [fogo *etc*] devastating.

vos [vuʃ] *pron pl* [complemento direto] you; [complemento indireto] (to) you; *fml* [reflexo] yourselves; *fml* [recíproco] each other, one another.

vós ['vɔʃ] *pron pess* [sujeito, complemento direto] you; [complemento indireto] (to) you; **~ mesmos** *ou* **próprios** you, yourselves.

vosso, vossa ['vɔsu, 'vɔsa] ◇ *adj* your. ◇ *pron*: **o ~/a vossa** yours; **um amigo ~** a friend of yours; **os ~s** [a vossa família] your family.

votação [vota'sãw] (*pl* **-ões**) *f* [ato] voting; [voto] vote; **decidir algo por ~** to decide sthg by ballot.

votado, da [vo'tadu, da] *adj*: **o mais ~** [chapa, senador etc] the one with the highest vote.

votante [vo'tãntʃi] *mf* voter.

votar [4] [vo'ta(x)] ◇ *vt* **-1.** [eleger] to vote. **-2.** [submeter a votação] to take a vote on. **-3.** [aprovar] to pass. ◇ *vi* **-1.** [dar voto] to vote; **~ em/contra/por** to vote on/against/for; **~ em branco** to abstain. **-2.** [ter direito a voto] to have a vote.

voto ['vɔtu] *m* **-1.** [votação] voting; **~ nulo/em branco** invalid/blank vote; **~ secreto** secret ballot. **-2.** [promessa] vow; **~ de castidade/pobreza** vow of chastity/poverty. **-3.** [desejo] wish; **fazer ~s por** to wish for; **fazer ~s que** to hope that; **~s de felicidade** best wishes.

vovó [vo'vɔ] *f* granny.

vovô [vo'vo] *m* grandpa.

voyeur [voj'ɛ(x)] (*pl* **-s**) *mf* voyeur.

voyeurismo [voje'riʒmu] *m* voyeurism.

voz ['vɔʃ] (*pl* **-es**) *f* **-1.** [ger] voice; **de viva ~** orally, viva (voce); **~ arrastada** drawling voice; **a meia ~** softly; **em ~ alta/baixa** in a loud/low voice; **levantar a ~ para alguém** to raise one's voice at sb; **~ de cana rachada** rasping voice. **-2.** [poder decisório, autoridade]: **ter ~ (ativa) em** to have a say in; **dar ~ de prisão** to announce an arrest. **-3.** *fig* [conselho]: **a ~ da experiência** the voice of experience. **-4.** MIL: **~ de comando** command. **-5.** GRAM: **~ ativa/passiva** active/passive voice.

vozeirão [vozej'rãw] (*pl* **-ões**) *m* thundering voice.

vozerio [voze'riw] *m* uproar.

vulcânico, ca [vuw'kãniku, ka] *adj* volcanic.

vulcão [vuw'kãw] (*pl* **-ões**) *m* volcano.

vulgar [vuw'ga(x)] (*pl* **-es**) *adj* **-1.** [comum] common. **-2.** [baixo, grosseiro] vulgar. **-3.** [medíocre] mediocre.

vulgaridade [vuwgari'dadʒi] *f* vulgarity.

vulgarizar [4] [vuwgari'za(x)] *vt* [popularizar] to popularize.
◆ **vulgarizar-se** *vp* **-1.** [popularizar-se] to become commonplace. **-2.** [tornar-se reles] to coarsen.

vulgarmente [vuwgax'mẽntʃi] *adv* commonly.

vulgo ['vuwgu] <> *m* common people. <> *adv* otherwise known as.
vulnerabilidade [vuwnerabili'dadʒi] *f* vulnerability.
vulnerável [vuwne'ravɛw] (*pl* **-eis**) *adj* vulnerable.
vulto ['vuwtu] *m* **-1.** [figura, sombra] figure. **-2.** [semblante] face. **-3.** *fig* [importância] stature; **de ~** important. **-4.**: **tomar ~** [desenvolver-se] to take shape.
vultoso, osa [vuw'tozu, ɔza] *adj* **-1.** [volumoso] bulky. **-2.** [obra, negócio] weighty. **-3.** [quantia] considerable.
vulva ['vuwva] *f* vulva.

w, W *m* [letra] w, W.
walkie-talkie [ˌwɔki'tɔki] (*pl* **walkie-talkies**) *m* walkie-talkie.
walkman® ['wɔkmɐ̃] *m* Walkman.
WAN (*abrev de* **Wide Area Network**) *f* WAN.
Washington ['wɔʃintõ] *n* Washington.
watt ['wɔtʃi] *m* watt.
WC (*abrev de* **water closet**) *m* WC.
Web [web] (**world wide web**) *f* COMPUT web.
webcam ['uɛbikɐ̃] (*pl* **webcams**) *f* COMPUT webcam.
webmail ['uɛbimejo] (*pl* **webmails**) *m* COMPUT webmail.
webmaster ['uɛbimaʃtɛ(x)] (*pl* **webmasters**) *mf* COMPUT webmaster.
webpage ['uɛbipejʒi] (*pl* **webpages**) *f* COMPUT webpage.
western ['wɛʃtexn] *m* western.
windsurfe [wĩndʒi'suxfi] *m* windsurfing.
windsurfista [wĩndʒisux'fiʃta] *mf* windsurfer.
workshop [woxki'ʃɔpi] *m* workshop.
WWW (*abrev de* **World Wide Web**) *f* WWW.

x, X *m* [letra] x, X.
xá [ʃa] *m* shah.
xadrez [ʃa'dreʃ] <> *m* **-1.** [jogo] chess. **-2.** [desenho] check. **-3.** [tecido] checked cloth; **de ~** checked. **-4.** *fam* [prisão] clink. <> *adj inv* checked.
xale ['ʃali] *m* shawl.
xampu [ʃɐ̃n'pu] *m* shampoo.
xará [ʃa'ra] *mf* namesake.
xaropada [ʃaro'pada] *f fam* drag.
xarope [ʃa'rɔpi] *m* syrup.
xaveco [ʃa'vɛku] *m* *fig* [objeto sem valor] piece of junk.
xaxim [ʃa'ʃĩ] *m* fibrous-stemmed plant.
xeique ['ʃejki] *m* sheikh.
xelim [ʃe'lĩ] (*pl* **-s**) *m* shilling.
xenofobia [ʃenofo'bia] *f* xenophobia.
xepa ['ʃepa] *f fam* [de feira] scraps *(pl)*.
xeque ['ʃɛki] *m* **-1.** [xadrez] check. **-2.** [xeique] sheikh. **-3.** *loc*: **pôr em ~** to threaten.
xeque-mate [ˌʃɛki'matʃi] (*pl* **xeque-mates**) *m* checkmate.
xereta [ʃe'reta] *adj fam* [bisbilhoteiro] busybody.
xeretar [4] [ʃere'ta(x)] <> *vt* to snoop into. <> *vi*: **~ (em/sobre)** to snoop (into/on).
xerez [ʃe'reʃ] *m* sherry.
xerife [ʃe'rifi] *m* sheriff.
xerocar [12] [ʃero'ka(x)], *vt* to photocopy.
xerocópia [ʃero'kɔpja] *f* photocopy.
xerocopiar [16] [ʃeroko'pja(x)] *vt* = **xerocar.**
xérox® [ʃe'rɔks] *m* **-1.** [cópia] photocopy. **-2.** [máquina] photocopier.
xexelento, ta [ʃeʃe'lẽntu, ta] *adj fam* gross.
xexéu [ʃe'ʃɛw] *m fam* pong.
xi [ʃi] *interj* **-1.** [exprimindo espanto] oh no! **-2.** [exprimindo inquietação] oh no!
xícara ['ʃikara] *f* cup; **~ de chá** cup of tea.
xiita [ʃi'ita] <> *adj* [muçulmano] Shiite. <> *mf* **-1.** [muçulmano] Shiite. **-2.** *fig* [radical] extremist.
xifópago, ga [ʃi'fɔpagu, ga] *adj* conjoined.
xilofone [ʃilo'foni] *m* xylophone.
xilografia [ʃilogra'fia] *f* **-1.** [técnica] wood engraving. **-2.** [gravura] woodcut.
xilogravura [ʃilogra'vura] *f* wood engraving.

xingação [ʃĩŋga'sãw] (*pl* **-ões**) *f* swearing.
xingamento [ʃĩŋga'mẽntu] *m* swearing.
xingar [14] [ʃĩŋ'ga(x)] ◇ *vt* to swear at; ~ **alguém de algo** to call sb sthg. ◇ *vi* to swear.
xinxim [ʃĩn'ʃĩ] (*pl* **-ns**) *m*: ~ **de galinha** chicken casserole.
xixi [ʃi'ʃi] *m fam* pee; **fazer** ~ to pee.
xodó [ʃo'dɔ] *m* **-1.** [pessoa querida] sweetheart. **-2.** [estima]: **ter** ~ **por alguém/algo** to be passionate about sb/sthg. **-3.** [flerte, namoro]: **estar de** ~ **com alguém** to be soft on sb.
xota ['ʃɔta] *f vulg* [vulva] pussy.
xoxota [ʃo'ʃɔta] *f vulg* [vulva] pussy.
xucro, cra ['ʃukru, kra] *adj* **-1.** [animal] untamed. **-2.** [grosseiro] coarse. **-3.** [ignorante] thick.

Z

z, Z *m* [letra] z, Z.
zabumba [za'bũnba] *m* [bombo] (big) bass drum.
zaga ['zaga] *f FUT* fullback.
zagueiro [za'gejru] *m FUT* fullback.
zaino ['zãjnu] *adj* [cavalo] dark brown.
Zaire ['zajri] *n* Zaire.
Zâmbia ['zãnbja] *m* Zambia.
zanga ['zãŋga] *f* **-1.** [irritação] annoyance. **-2.** [briga] anger.
zangado, da [zãŋ'gadu, da] *adj* **-1.** [aborrecido] angry; **estar** ~ **com alguém** [sem falar] to be angry with sb. **-2.** [irritado] annoyed. **-3.** [malhumorado] cross.
zangão ['zãŋgãw] (*pl* **-ões**) *m ZOOL* drone.
zangar [14] [zãŋ'ga(x)] ◇ *vt* [irritar] to annoy. ◇ *vi* **-1.** [irritar-se] to get angry. **-2.** [ralhar] to scold; ~ **com alguém** to tell sb off.
◆ **zangar-se** *vp* **-1.** [aborrecer-se] to get angry. **-2.** [irritar-se] to get annoyed.
zangões [zãŋ'gõjʃ] *pl* ▷ **zangão**.
zanzar [4] [zan'za(x)] *vi* to wander about.
zarcão [zar'kãw] *m* [tinta] red lead.
zarolho, lha [za'roʎu, ʎa] *adj* one-eyed.
zarpar [4] [zax'pa(x)] *vi* **-1.** [embarcação] to weigh anchor. **-2.** [partir] to set off. **-3.** [fugir] to run away.
zebra ['zebra] *f* **-1.** *ZOOL* zebra. **-2.** [faixa para pedestres] zebra crossing. **-3.** *fam pej* [pessoa] dunce. **-4.** *loc*: **dar** ~ to turn out badly.
zebu [ze'bu] *m ZOOL* zebu.
zelador, ra [zela'do(x), ra] (*pl* **-es**, *fpl* **-s**) *m, f* [de prédio] caretaker *UK*, janitor *US*.
zelar [4] [ze'la(x)] *vi*: ~ **por** to care for.
zelo ['zelu] *m* **-1.** [cuidado] care. **-2.** [empenho] zeal.
zeloso, osa [ze'lozu, za] *adj* **-1.** [cuidadoso]: ~ **(de/por)** caring (for), careful (of). **-2.** [diligente]: ~ **em** zealous in.
zé-mané [ˌzɛma'nɛ] (*pl* **-s**) *m fam* [otário, bobalhão] idiot, airhead.
zen [zẽ] *adj inv* zen.
zen-budismo [zẽn bu'dʒiʒmu] *m* Zen Buddhism.
zé-ninguém [ˌzɛnĩŋ'gẽ] (*pl* **zés-ninguém**) *m*: **um** ~ a nobody.
zênite ['zenitʃi] *m* zenith.
zepelim [ze'pelĩ] (*pl* **-ns**) *m* [balão] zeppelin.
zé-povinho [ˌzɛpo'viɲu] (*pl* **-s**) *m* **-1.** [homem comum] Joe Public, Joe Bloggs. **-2.** [povo] common people.
zerar [4] [ze'ra(x)] *vt* **-1.** [reduzir a zero] to reduce to zero. **-2.** [liquidar] to wipe out.
zerinho, nha [zɛ'riɲu, ɲa] *adj fam* spanking new.
zero ['zɛru] *num* **-1.** [ger] zero; ~ **erros** no mistakes; **abaixo/acima de** ~ below/above zero. **-2.** *ESP* nil; [em tênis] love. **-3.** *loc*: **começar do** ~ to start from scratch; **ser um** ~ **à esquerda** to be a nothing.
◆ **a zero** *loc adv*: **estar com a moral a** ~ to be at rock bottom; **ficar a** ~ to end up broke; *veja também* **seis**.
zero-quilômetro [ˌzɛruki'lɔmetru] ◇ *adj inv* brand new. ◇ *m inv* brand new car.
ziguezague [ˌzigi'zagi] *m* zigzag.
ziguezagueante [zigiza'gjãntʃi] *adj* zigzagging.
ziguezaguear [zigiza'gja(x)] *vi* to zigzag.
Zimbábue [zĩn'babwe] *n* Zimbabwe.
zinco ['zĩŋku] *m* zinc; **folha de** ~ corrugated iron.
zipar [4] [zi'pa(x)] *vt COMPUT* to zip.
zíper ['zipe(x)] (*pl* **-es**) *m* [fecho ecler] zip *UK*, zipper *US*.
ziquizira [ziki'zira] *f fam* bug.
zircônio [zix'konju] *m* zirconium.
zoada ['zwada] *f* = **zoeira**.
zoar ['zwa(x)] ◇ *vt* [caçoar] to make fun of. ◇ *vi* **-1.** [fazer grande ruído] to make a din. **-2.** [zumbir] to buzz. **-3.** [fazer troça] to make fun. **-4.** [promover confusão] to cause trouble.
zodiacal [zodʒja'kaw] *adj* of the zodiac *(depois de subst)*.
zodíaco [zo'dʒiaku] *m* zodiac.
zoeira ['zwejra] *f* din.
zombador, ra [zõnba'do(x), ra] *adj* mocking.
zombar [4] [zõm'ba(x)] *vi* **-1.** [debochar]: ~ **de alguém/algo** to make fun of sb/sthg. **-2.** [desdenhar]: ~ **de algo** to sneer at sthg.
zombaria [zonba'ria] *f* [deboche] ridicule.
zombeteiro, ra [zõnbe'tejru, ra] ◇ *adj* [zombador] joking. ◇ *m,f* joker.
zona ['zona] *f* **-1.** [ger] zone; ~ **eleitoral** electoral district; ~ **franca** free trade area. **-2.** *fam* [bagunça, confusão] mess; **fazer** ~ to make a mess.
zoneamento [zonja'mẽntu] *m* [divisão em zonas] zoning.

zonear [15] [zo'nja(x)] <> *vt* **-1.** *fam* [bagunçar] to mess up. **-2.** [dividir em zonas] to zone. <> *vi fam* [bagunçar] to mess up.

zonzeira [zõn'zejra] *f* dizziness, giddiness; **dar ~ em alguém** to make sb giddy; **sentir ~** to feel giddy.

zonzo, za ['zõnzu, za] *adj* **-1.** [tonto] dizzy. **-2.** [atordoado, confuso] giddy.

zôo ['zow] *m* zoo.

zoologia [zwolo'ʒia] *f* zoology.

zoológico, ca [zo'lɔʒiku, ka] *adj* zoological.
◆ **zoológico** *m* zoo.

zoólogo, ga ['zwɔlogu, ga] *m, f* zoologist.

zoom [zũ] *m* zoom.

zorra ['zoxa] *f fam* mess.

zum [zũ] *m* zoom.

zumbido [zũn'bidu] *m* **-1.** [de inseto] buzz. **-2.** [de motor, vozes *etc*] hum. **-3.** [no ouvido] ringing.

zumbir [6] [zũm'bi(x)] *vi* **-1.** [inseto] to buzz. **-2.** [motor, vozes] to hum. **-3.** [bala, vento] to whistle. **-4.** [ouvido] to ring.

zunido [zu'nidu] *m* **-1.** [de inseto] buzz. **-2.** [de motor] hum. **-3.** [de vento] whistle.

zunir [6] [zu'ni(x)] *vi* **-1.** [inseto] to buzz. **-2.** [motor] to hum. **-3.** [vento *etc*] to whistle.

zunzum [zũn'zũ] (*pl* **-ns**) *m* **-1.** [ruído] humming. **-2.** [boato] rumour.

zureta [zu'reta] *mf* halfwit.

zurrar [4] [zu'xa(x)] *vi* to bray.

zurro ['zuxu] *m* bray.

Vivendo no Reino Unido e nos Estados Unidos

ÍNDICE

Reino Unido

Estados Unidos

Reino Unido

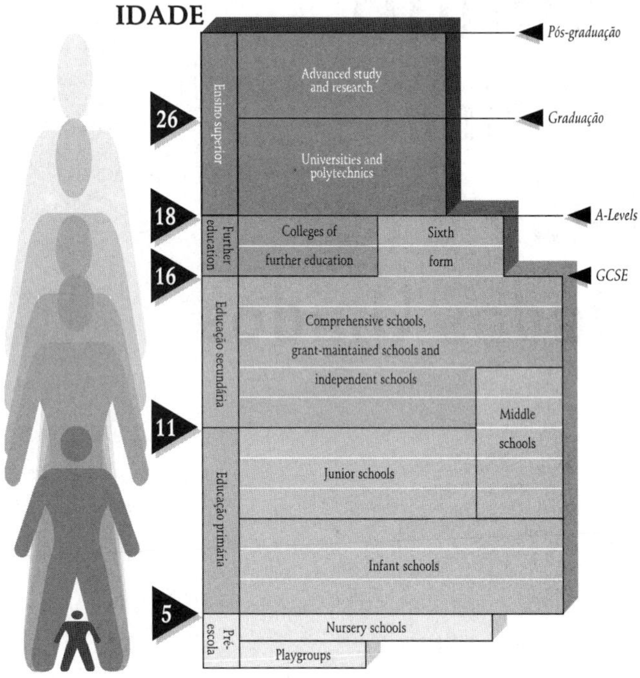

No Reino Unido, a educação é obrigatória dos 5 aos 16 anos de idade. O sistema educacional é, em grande parte, descentralizado, ou seja, de responsabilidade regional, e estrutura-se da seguinte maneira:

Educação pré-escolar (até 5 anos) Não é obrigatória, embora as crianças possam, a partir de dois anos de idade, matricular-se em escolas maternais (*nursery schools*). Muitas crianças em idade pré-escolar freqüentam grupos de atividades lúdico-educativas (*playgroups*), organizados pelos próprios pais.

Educação primária (dos 5 aos 11 anos) A educação primária subdivide-se em escolas para crianças dos 5 aos 7 anos (*infant schools*) e para aquelas dos 7 aos 11 anos (*junior schools*). Certas regiões optam por oferecer escolas para alunos dos 8 aos 14 anos (*middle schools*), que, depois, ingressam diretamente no nivel secundário (*upper secondary schools*). Alguns institutos particulares de educação primária são chamados *prep* (*preparatory*) *schools*.

Educação secundária (dos 11 aos 16/18 anos) É ministrada tanto em escolas públicas quanto nas escolas privadas.

- As ***comprehensive schools***, financiadas pelo Estado, oferecem educação genérica e gratuita para todos. Elas são freqüentadas pela maioria dos estudantes britânicos.
- As ***independent schools*** são instituições privadas, financiadas mediante semestralidade paga pelos pais. Elas também são chamadas *private schools* ou *public schools*, e

congregam apenas 16% das crianças em idade escolar. Dentre essas escolas, algumas são famosas, como *Eton* ou *Harrow*.

▸ As ***grant-maintained schools*** são escolas de administração autônoma, não sujeitas a autoridade regional, mas subvencionadas diretamente pelo Estado.

Currículo Durante os primeiros cinco anos da educação secundária, a maioria dos alunos segue um currículo comum, o chamado *national curriculum*, definido pelo governo central. Aos 16 anos, o aluno presta um exame chamado *General Certificate of Secondary Education* (*GCSE*). Cerca de 50% dos estudantes concluem nesse ponto seus estudos, independentemente de seu desempenho no exame.

▸ ***A-Levels*** Aqueles que desejarem ingressar na universidade devem prosseguir os estudos por mais dois anos, ao longo dos quais se preparam para prestar um exame chamado *GCE Advanced Level*. Em geral, desse exame constam três disciplinas. Os *A-Levels* são prestados na Inglaterra, no País de Gales e na Irlanda do Norte. Na Escócia, que possui sistema educacional próprio, os alunos concluem seus estudos prestando os chamados *Highers*, que são exames de várias disciplinas.

Educação secundária não-obrigatória (*Further Education*, dos 16 aos 18 anos)

Futher Education designa os estudos que se seguem ao ensino obrigatório. Os alunos que prosseguem seus estudos visando à obtenção de *A-Levels* costumam cursar na mesma escola os dois anos adicionais, também chamados *sixth form*. Mas podem ainda cursá-los nos *sixth-form colleges*. Cursos de orientação profissional são ministrados por instituições tais como os *colleges of further education*, que incluem escolas de arte, escolas agrícolas etc.

Ensino superior (dos 18 aos 26 anos) O ensino superior é ministrado pelas universidades. O acesso à universidade depende de uma quantidade mínima de *A-Levels* obtidos com boas notas, e a disputa por vagas é acirrada. Bolsas de estudo são oferecidas pelas autoridades regionais, mas, em geral, precisam ser complementadas, seja pelo auxílio financeiro dos pais ou por empréstimos bancários para estudantes, a juros menores. Normalmente, os cursos universitários estendem-se por três anos, conduzindo ao *undergraduate degree*. A partir daí, aqueles que desejarem prosseguir com seus estudos o fazem na qualidade de *post-graduates*, podendo concluí-los com o *higher degree* ou com um *doctorate*.

> **Oxbridge**
>
> *Oxbridge* é uma expressão utilizada para designar conjuntamente as famosas universidades de Oxford e Cambridge. Fundadas no século XIII, elas se distinguem tanto das universidades fundadas no Reino Unido na década de 60 - as *redbrick universities*, que visavam à expansão do número de vagas universitárias -, quanto das ex-escolas politécnicas, transformadas em universidades apenas na década de 1990. Ainda hoje, embora 50% dos alunos de Oxford e Cambridge provenham da escola pública, persiste a crença de que seus estudantes gozam de situação econômica privilegiada. Isso de deve à grande quantidade de graduados em *Oxbridge* que exercem cargos importantes em áreas como economia, política e direito.

Educacão de adultos A educação de adultos é proporcionada por centros de educação pós-escolar e por departamentos especiais de algumas universidades. Os adultos podem, ainda, realizar seus estudos na *Open University*, instituição de ensino a distância, fundada em 1969, que oferece cursos universitários de graduação e pós-graduação por correspondência. Para tanto, não existem pré-requisitos, e os estudos baseiam-se em livros e programas de rádio e televisão.

ADMINISTRAÇÃO 4

A sigla UK, *United Kingdom* (Reino Unido), é uma forma abreviada de Reino Unido da Grã-Bretanha e Irlanda do Norte. A Grã-Bretanha compõe-se de Inglaterra, País de Gales e Escócia. As chamadas Ilhas Britânicas, por sua vez, são formadas pela Grã-Bretanha, Irlanda e pelas ilhas adjacentes, como as do Canal da Mancha e a Ilha de Man. Os quatro países que integram o Reino Unido têm um governo comum, embora o parlamento escocês e a assembléia galesa cuidem dos assuntos internos da Escócia e do País de Gales, respectivamente. Cada uma dessas nações tem identidade cultural própria. No País de Gales, fala-se também o galês, língua de origem celta (há um canal de televisão que transmite em galês - ver **meios de comunicação** - e a maioria dos sinais de trânsito se vale dessa língua), mas o inglês é o idioma mais utilizado. A Escócia goza de maior autonomia do que o País de Gales, tendo também seu próprio sistema legal e educacional. O gaélico, língua celta da Escócia, tem uso menos generalizado do que o galês, mas é idioma corrente nas Terras Altas (*Highlands*) e nas ilhas escocesas. A Irlanda subdivide-se politicamente em Irlanda do Norte, de maioria protestante, e República da Irlanda (ou *Eire*, em gaélico irlandês), de maioria católica. A República da Irlanda é independente desde 1921.

País	Área (km2)	População
Inglaterra	130.400	46.161.000
País de Gales	20.800	2.798.000
Escócia	78.800	4.957.000
Irlanda do Norte	5.452	1.583.000

Geografia Cerca de mil quilômetros separam a costa sul da Inglaterra do extremo norte da Escócia; de leste a oeste do Reino Unido, a distância máxima atinge cerca de quinhentos quilômetros. Na Grã-Bretanha, nunca se está a mais de 120 km do mar. O interior da Inglaterra compõe-se de planícies, à exceção do norte e do sudoeste, ao passo que grande parte da Escócia e do País de Gales apresenta terreno montanhoso. A paisagem da Irlanda do Norte é formada de montanhas baixas e campos ondulados por colinas. Bem no centro, encontra-se Lough Neagh, o maior lago de água doce do Reino Unido, com cerca de 390 km^2. Nas áreas urbanas entre Londres e Manchester concentra-se 90% da população britânica.

Administração local O Reino Unido divide-se em condados (ou regiões, na Escócia), que, por sua vez, subdividem-se em distritos.

- ❑ A Inglaterra e o País de Gales têm seis condados metropolitanos (Grande Manchester, Merseyside, South Yorkshire, Tyne and Wear, West Midlands e West Yorkshire), os quais se subdividem em 36 distritos metropolitanos; há, ainda, 39 condados não-metropolitanos, que se subdividem em outros 296 distritos não-metropolitanos.
- ❑ A Grande Londres é uma área à parte, composta de 32 municípios (*boroughs*) e da *Corporation of the City of London*, o centro financeiro londrino.
- ❑ A Escócia possui 29 autoridades locais (*unitary authorities*) e três conselhos de ilhas (Órcadas, Shetland e Hébridas).
- ❑ A Irlanda do Norte subdivide-se em 26 conselhos distritais (*district councils*).

A maioria dos condados, regiões, distritos e municípios possui conselhos próprios. Em geral, seus representantes são eleitos a cada quatro anos. As autoridades metropolitanas, municipais e as dos condados respondem pelos serviços mais importantes: segurança, educação e transporte. As autoridades distritais ocupam-se de questões como habitação e coleta de lixo. Os serviços públicos são subvencionados por impostos municipais que taxam a propriedade de imóveis para habitação (*council tax*) e comércio (*non-domestic rates*).

Ir ao restaurante, ao cinema ou a um *pub* são as atividades preferidas da maioria dos britânicos, no que se refere ao lazer. O teatro e as danceterias são também populares, assim como assistir à televisão, praticar jardinagem ou dedicar-se a trabalhos manuais. Em anos mais recentes, a ginástica aeróbica e os exercícios físicos têm atraído uma maior quantidade de adeptos.

Feriados

1° de janeiro	Dia de Ano-Novo
2 de janeiro	Feriado de Ano-Novo (somente na Escócia)
17 de março	Dia de São Patrício (somente na Irlanda do Norte)
Março ou abril	Sexta-feira Santa e Páscoa Segunda-feira de Páscoa (exceto na Escócia)
Primeira segunda-feira de maio	Dia do trabalho
Última segunda-feira de maio	Feriado de primavera (*Spring Bank Holiday*, exceto na Escócia)
12 de julho	Batalha de Boyne (somente na Irlanda do Norte)
Primeira segunda-feira de agosto	Feriado de verão (*Summer Bank Holiday*, somente na Escócia)
Última segunda-feira de agosto	Feriado de verão (*Summer Bank Holiday*, exceto na Escócia)
25 de dezembro	Dia de Natal
26 de dezembro	*Boxing Day*

Festas populares A Grã-Bretanha tem poucas festas nacionais, que são também chamadas *bank holidays*, porque, nessas ocasiões, os bancos permanecem fechados, assim como as escolas e boa parte do comércio.

▸ **A Semana Santa e o Natal** são as únicas festas religiosas nacionais. No domingo de Páscoa, é comum presentear amigos e familiares com ovos de chocolate. Como ocorre em outros países europeus, a segunda-feira que sucede à Páscoa também é feriado no Reino Unido, à exceção da Escócia. O Natal é a festa popular mais importante. Costuma-se enviar cartões a parentes e amigos e decorar a árvore de Natal com bolas, fitas e luzes coloridas. A troca de presentes, depositados ao pé da árvore, acontece na manhã de 25 de dezembro, seguindo-se o almoço de Natal, que tradicionalmente consiste em peru recheado ao forno, batatas assadas e legumes. O dia 26, chamado *Boxing Day*, é feriado, e é costume passá-lo em casa, descansando, ou em visita a parentes ou amigos.

▸ **A véspera de Ano-Novo** (*Silvester* ou *Hogmanay*, na Escócia) caracteriza-se pelas festas que atravessam a noite. À meia-noite, é costume cantar uma canção chamada *Auld Lang Syne* ("Os velhos tempos").

Pubs Os *pubs* (forma abreviada de *public house*), os famosos bares da Grã-Bretanha, são parte importante da vida social do país. Em geral, dividem-se em uma área com mesas e cadeiras (*lounge bar*) e outra, em que se bebe em pé (*public bar*). Costuma-se pedir a bebida no balcão e pagar por ela de imediato. Nos *pubs*, não é hábito dar gorjetas. Em muitos deles, pode-se jogar dardos ou bilhar; karaokê e música ao vivo estão também entre as atrações oferecidas.

Off-licenses Bebidas alcoólicas em lata ou garrafa, como cerveja e vinho, podem ser compradas em lojas chamadas *off-licenses*. A maioria delas abre de segunda a sábado, das 10 horas da manhã às 10 horas da noite, ou mesmo aos domingos, em algumas regiões.

Restaurantes Na Grã-Bretanha, é grande a oferta de restaurantes e cafés dotados de excelente cozinha, tanto nacional quanto internacional. As lanchonetes de *fast food* são populares, mas o tradicional *fish and chips*, peixe frito com batatas fritas, continua sendo a opção preferida da maioria. A comida indiana também é muito popular, e são numerosos os restaurantes hindus existentes na Grã-Bretanha. De modo geral, os *pubs* também servem almoço barato e de boa qualidade. Nos restaurantes, o vinho pode custar o triplo do que se paga por ele nas lojas de bebidas, e a conta pode incluir um acréscimo de 10%, cobrado pelo serviço. Quando esse acréscimo não é cobrado, é costume deixar gorjeta correspondente a 10% ou 15% da conta.

7 MEIOS DE COMUNICAÇÃO

Nas horas vagas, ver televisão é a atividade preferida dos britânicos. Em geral, rádio e televisão desfrutam de sólida reputação de imparcialidade política na Grã-Bretanha.

Canais de televisão São cinco os canais nacionais de televisão:

- A **BBC** (*British Broadcasting Corporation*) transmite em dois canais para toda a Grã-Bretanha, BBC1 e BBC2, ambos financiados por um imposto anual, pago por todos os proprietários de aparelhos de televisão. A BBC1 oferece uma programação de alta qualidade, dirigida a um amplo público, que inclui filmes, notícias, esportes e programas humorísticos. A BBC2 atinge um público mais restrito, com programação voltada para a educação e a cultura, incluindo-se aí os programas relacionados à *Open University* (ver **educação**).

- A **ITV** (*Independent Television* ou canal 3) transmite programas de 15 emissoras regionais independentes, financiadas por publicidade. Em linhas gerais, sua programação se assemelha à da BBC1. Os dois canais travam feroz batalha por audiência.

- O ***Channel 4***, um canal comercial independente e de alcance nacional (à exceção do País de Gales), apresenta programas especializados para públicos específicos, buscando cobrir temas não explorados pela ITV. Em lugar do *Channel 4*, o País de Gales recebe o *S4C Welsh Fourth Channel*, que transmite seus programas em galês.

- O ***Channel 5*** é um canal comercial com um apelo jovem e descontraído, transmitindo programas culturais e informativos de caráter mais popular do que os de seus concorrentes.

TV por satélite e a cabo A *British Sky Broadcasting* (*BSkyB*) domina as transmissões por satélite, oferecendo programas esportivos, filmes, notícias, serviços de telecompras e concursos televisivos. Ela compete com diversos canais a cabo e companhias cuja programação apresenta atrações similares, além de filmes pelo sistema *pay-per-view*, televisão interativa e acesso à internet. Em 1998, foi introduzida na Grã-Bretanha a televisão digital, que oferece qualidade superior de imagem e de som.

Rádio A BBC tem cinco emissoras nacionais de rádio (ver quadro), além de estações na Escócia, País de Gales e Irlanda do Norte.

A Grã-Bretanha possui duas emissoras independentes: a *Classic FM* e a *Virgin Radio 1215 AM*. A Inglaterra conta ainda com 39 emissoras regionais da BBC, além de mais de uma centena de estações regionais independentes.

Radio nacional: BBC

- ***Rádio 1*** (1053/1089 kHz MW; 97.6-99.8 MHz FM) Música pop, rock, notícias e informação sobre o trânsito.
- ***Rádio 2*** (88-90.2 MHz FM) Música popular, entretenimento, comédias, programas culturais e notícias.
- ***Rádio 3*** (1215 kHz MW; 90.2-92.4 MHz FM) Música clássica, radioteatro e documentários.
- ***Rádio 4*** (198 kHz LW; 92.4-94.6 MHz FM) Notícias, documentários, atualidades, radioteatro, entretenimento e críquete.
- ***Rádio 5*** Live (693/909 kHz OM) Notícias e esportes 24 horas por dia.

Jornais Cerca de 56% dos adultos lêem jornal na Grã-Bretanha. Além dos jornais diários nacionais e das edições dominicais (ver quadro), algumas cidades publicam periódicos vespertinos, e há diversos jornais regionais, como o *Yorkshire Post* (de Leeds), o *Herald* (de Glasgow), *The Scotsman* (de Edimburgo), o *South Wales Echo* (de Cardiff) e *The Belfast Telegraph*. Existem também centenas de jornais semanais e numerosas publicações distribuídas gratuitamente. Os jornais podem ser entregues em domicílio ou podem ser adquiridos nos diversos postos de vendas, em pequenas lojas de bairro, nos supermercados e nos quiosques.

Os jornais britânicos podem ser classificados pelo formato grande ou pequeno. Em geral, os jornais de qualidade têm formato grande (*broadsheet*), embora alguns, como *The Guardian* e *The Times*, tragam suplementos com formato pequeno ou tablóide. Os jornais populares, sempre em formato tablóide, preferem trocar a seriedade das análises por notícias sobre a vida pessoal de personalidades públicas, crimes mórbidos, boatos sobre os famosos e cobertura obsessiva da vida da família real britânica.

▸ Em geral, não há espaço para questões políticas nos tablóides, cujas tiragens são bem maiores do que as da grande imprensa. Pode-se afirmar, contudo, que a maioria dos jornais britânicos situa-se à direita do espectro político.

▸ Os **jornais dominicais** são mais grossos do que os diários e, com freqüência, trazem dois ou mais suplementos, além de uma revista em cores.

Principais jornais britânicos

Jornais populares (diários)	Jornais populares (dominicais)
The Sun (1964) D 3 502.923 P	News of the World (1843) D 4.086.621 P
Daily Mail (1896) D 2 489.264 P	The Mail on Sunday (1982)D 2.342.860 P
Daily Mirror (1903) E 2 164.576 P	The Sunday Mirror (1963) D 1.845.860 P
Daily Express (1900)D 991.560 P	The People (1881) D 1.389.778 P
Daily Star (1978) D 706.554 P	The Sunday Express (1918) D 834,999 G
Daily Record (1895) C/E 584.290 P	Sunday Sport (1988) D 301.000 P
Grande imprensa (diários)	**Grande imprensa (dominicais)**
Daily Telegraph (1855) D 1.013.653 G	The Sunday Times (1822) D 1.405.430 G
The Times (1785) D 711,295 G	Sunday Telegraph (1961) D 784.069 G
Financial Times (1888) C 475.475 G	The Observer (1791) E 449.806 G
The Guardian (1821) E 411.386 G	The Independent on Sunday (1990)
The Independent (1985) C/E 224,655 G	C/E 231.869 G

Os números indicam circulação. Entre parênteses: ano de fundação. Orientação política: E = esquerda, D = direita, C = centro. Fomato: G = grande; P = pequeno (tablóide)

Revistas Os pontos de venda de jornais oferecem também uma ampla gama de revistas, que vão desde os semanários de análise político-econômica, como *The Economist*, até revistas de conteúdo satírico, como *Viz*. Milhares de publicações atendem a todo tipo de interesse. As revistas de maior vendagem são os guias da programação da televisão e publicações como *Reader's Digest*, *Computer Shopper*, *What Car* e *National Geographic*. Revistas femininas como *Woman's Own*, *Bella*, *Best* e *Prima* também vendem milhões de exemplares.

9 INTERNET

O uso da internet vem se ampliando cada vez mais no Reino Unido. Os domicílios conectados à rede já ultrapassam os 10 milhões, número superior à média européia, ainda que inferior àquele verificado na Escandinávia. Os britânicos passam, em média, mais tempo na rede do que a maioria dos europeus - mais de sete horas semanais. O Reino Unido encontra-se também entre os primeiros países da Europa no tocante às compras pela internet, embora muitos usuários ainda temam usar o cartão de crédito na rede.

Cerca de 74% dos internautas britânicos têm acesso à internet a partir de suas casas. O acesso desde o local de trabalho se dá também em proporções consideráveis, sendo menor o número daqueles que se valem de bibliotecas, centros educacionais ou cafés para o acesso à rede. Os principais provedores de acesso no Reino Unido são Freeserve, AOL, BT Internet, NTL, LineOne e VirginNet. A maioria das conexões se faz ainda por linha discada, mas os serviços de banda larga vêm se difundindo cada vez mais no mercado.

Embora o número de internautas do sexo masculino seja ainda superior ao de mulheres na rede, essa desproporção vem diminuindo progressivamente. No Reino Unido, o usuário típico da internet é do sexo masculino, jovem ou de meia-idade e de alto poder aquisitivo.

Uma grande porcentagem das empresas britânicas está conectada à rede (86%). Muitas fazem uso constante da internet em seus negócios, para envio e recebimento de mensagens de correio eletrônico, nas atividades relacionadas a marketing e publicidade, e nos setores de compras, vendas, administração e formação de pessoal.

TRABALHO 10

Na indústria manufatureira, a semana de trabalho oscila entre 38 e 40 horas, ao passo que, nos escritórios, a carga horária semanal é de 35 a 38 horas. Funcionários de hospitais, restaurantes e hotéis chegam a trabalhar cem horas por semana, embora a média esteja em torno de cinqüenta ou sessenta horas.

▸ Muitas empresas utilizam o sistema de **horário móvel**, sobretudo em escritórios. Seus empregados devem estar presentes em certos horários de maior demanda, o chamado *core time*: das 9 às 11.30 e das 13.30 às 16 horas, por exemplo. As pausas e os horários de entrada, saída e de almoço são flexíveis, podendo-se, assim, chegar mais tarde ao trabalho, desde que a diferença seja compensada ao final do expediente.

Férias A maioria dos britânicos dispõe de férias anuais remuneradas por um período de quatro a seis semanas. Em geral, as férias anuais são gozadas dentro do período correspondente, mas algumas empresas permitem que seus funcionários acumulem férias para o ano seguinte. Além das férias, há também os diversos feriados ao longo do ano (ver **lazer**).

Salários Os trabalhadores britânicos recebem o salário mensal depositado diretamente em suas contas bancárias. O pagamento é acompanhado de um contracheque (*wage slip*), detalhando o salário bruto e eventuais deduções, como o imposto retido, o desconto relativo à previdência social, aos fundos de pensão das empresas e à contribuição sindical. Trabalhadores manuais e temporários costumam receber por semana e em dinheiro. Em geral, o pagamento é realizado às sextas-feiras, também acompanhado de um demonstrativo, contendo os valores da remuneração e dos descontos.

Ausência por doença Em caso de ausência no trabalho por um período inferior a sete dias, basta ao trabalhador preencher um formulário (*self-certification form*) ao retornar, explicando o motivo da ausência. Períodos de tempo maiores, porém, demandam apresentação de atestado médico.

Imposto de renda O imposto é recolhido pelas autoridades fiscais (o *Inland Revenue*) e cobrado sobre o total dos ganhos anuais. O ano fiscal britânico começa em 6 de abril, estendendo-se até 5 de abril do ano seguinte. A maioria das pessoas não faz declaração de renda, uma vez que o imposto é recolhido na fonte pelas empresas, sistema que, no Reino Unido, chama-se *Pay-As-You-Earn* (*PAYE*). Os trabalhadores autônomos pagam seus impostos ao final do ano fiscal. O montante a pagar é definido com base nas informações contidas na declaração de renda, que devem ser devidamente documentadas.

Previdência social A assistência social pública é parcialmente financiada pelas contribuições à previdência social: a chamada *National Insurance* ou *NI*. Essas contribuições dão direito a aposentadoria, seguro-desemprego e outros benefícios. Elas são obrigatórias para a maioria dos residentes na Grã-Bretanha e, em geral, as empresas as deduzem diretamente dos salários.

Seguro-desemprego Para ter direito ao seguro-desemprego, o trabalhador precisa ter contribuído para a previdência social por determinado período de tempo. O benefício é pago a cada duas semanas, mediante cheque postal. Os requerentes devem renovar sua solicitação a cada duas semanas, comprovando sua situação. Aqueles que não são beneficiados pelo seguro-desemprego podem solicitar outros benefícios sociais destinados a pessoas de baixa renda, como o chamado *Income Support*. Centrais de trabalho (*job centres*) congregam ofertas de emprego, assessoram o desempregado em sua busca por uma nova colocação e orientam-no na solicitação dos benefícios.

TURISMO

O Reino Unido é visitado por mais de 25 milhões de pessoas por ano, que procuram seu patrimônio histórico-cultural, seus castelos, as cidades antigas e ruínas históricas, os museus e as galerias de arte, bem como sua beleza natural. A maior parte desses turistas - cerca de 12 milhões ao ano - dirige-se para Londres, atraída pelo caráter cosmopolita da cidade e por seus famosos monumentos. Londres oferece também muitas atrações culturais, como museus, teatros e espetáculos musicais. Muita gente aproveita a estada na capital inglesa para visitar as tradicionais cidades universitárias de Oxford e Cambridge. O interior da Inglaterra oferece muitos outros atrativos: cidades medievais, como York, as termas romanas e a elegância georgiana de Bath; Stratford-upon-Avon - a cidade-natal de William Shakespeare; Stonehenge e seu famoso monumento de pedras pré-históricas; ou a beleza natural de Lake District, a 160 km ao norte de Manchester, que serviu de cenário e inspiração a numerosos pintores e escritores.

Muitos turistas visitam também a Escócia, para desfrutar de sua beleza natural, da fauna e flora locais e, sobretudo, da sensação de amplidão e tranqüilidade propiciada pelas vastas paisagens. Numerosas atividades podem ser praticadas ao ar livre, como golfe, montanhismo, esqui, pesca e esportes aquáticos. Também o País de Gales atrai os que buscam atividade física e a prática de esportes, tais como o *tracking*, o montanhismo e o ciclismo pelas montanhas dos parques naturais de Snowdonia ou Breacon Beacons.

Uma importante categoria de visitantes compõem os estudantes de inglês. Todos os anos, milhares de jovens e adultos dirigem-se a diferentes pontos do Reino Unido com o intuito de fazer cursos de inglês e praticar o idioma. As cidades mais procuradas por esses estudantes de língua são Londres, Oxford, Cambridge, Bristol, Bath, Brighton e Edimburgo.

Boa parte dos visitantes chega ao Reino Unido de avião, embora o Eurostar tenha, nos últimos anos, popularizado o acesso por trem, a partir da França. Muitos ainda preferem cruzar o Canal da Mancha de balsa, sobretudo aqueles que viajam de carro, com suas famílias ou num grupo de pessoas.

Além dos hotéis, os turistas costumam hospedar-se também nos *bed & breakfast* - quartos em casas particulares, com café da manhã. Os *bed & breakfast* oferecem um ambiente mais íntimo e aconchegante do que os hotéis, além de maior economia. Essas acomodações estão sujeitas a inspeção por parte das autoridades responsáveis pelo turismo e por associações como a *AA* (*Automobile Association*, o automóvel-clube britânico). Elas são avaliadas pelo seu conforto, limpeza e qualidade dos serviços e recebem uma classificação, expressa em número de estrelas ou diamantes. Além disso, estão presentes em toda parte, até mesmo em áreas remotas do país.

Outra opção, bastante popular entre as famílias ou grupos que viajam para o campo, é o aluguel de *cottages*. Os *cottages* são, em geral, casas no campo - por vezes moinhos ou silos. Com freqüência, são construções antigas que foram reformadas para esse fim. Pode-se também optar pelo aluguel de uma casa flutuante, quando se deseja viajar pelos muitos rios e canais da Inglaterra.

Estados Unidos

Os Estados Unidos da América ocupam uma área de 9.809.155 km^2, sendo o quarto país do mundo em extensão territorial. Com 286.488.000 de habitantes, são também o terceiro país mais populoso do mundo, depois de China e Índia. Sua superfície cobre toda a faixa intermediária do continente norte-americano, estendendo-se por cerca de 4 mil quilômetros do Atlântico ao Pacífico, e por quase 2 mil quilômetros de norte a sul, desde a fronteira canadense até o Golfo do México. Fazem parte dos Estados Unidos o Alasca, situado a noroeste do Canadá, e o Havaí, no Pacífico central. Sob administração americana encontram-se, ainda, várias ilhas do Pacífico e do Caribe, incluindo-se aí Porto Rico, Guam, as Ilhas Virgens e a Samoa norte-americana.

As 10 maiores áreas metropolitanas dos EUA

Cidade	População	Estado
Nova York	20.124.000	Nova York
Los Angeles	15.781.000	Califórnia
Chicago	8.810.000	Illinois
Washington DC-Baltimore	6.726.000	DC/Maryland
São Francisco	6.278.000	Califórnia
Filadélfia	5.893.000	Pensilvânia
Boston	5.455.000	Massachusetts
Detroit	5.187.000	Michigan
Dallas	4.037.000	Texas
Houston	3.731.000	Texas

[Fonte: World Almanac]

Regiões Os EUA dividem-se em quatro regiões geográficas:

- ❑ Nordeste - Nova Inglaterra (formada pelos estados de Connecticut, New Hampshire, Maine, Massachusetts, Rhode Island e Vermont), Nova Jersey, Nova York, Pensilvânia, Maryland, Delaware e Washington DC.
- ❑ Centro-oeste (*Midwest*) - Illinois, Indiana, Iowa, Kansas, Michigan, Minnesota, Missouri, Nebraska, Dakota do Norte, Ohio, Dakota do Sul e Wisconsin.
- ❑ Sul - Alabama, Arkansas, Flórida, Georgia, Kentucky, Louisiana, Mississippi, Carolina do Norte, Oklahoma, Carolina do Sul, Tennessee, Texas, Virgínia e Virgínia Ocidental.
- ❑ Oeste - Alasca, Arizona, Califórnia, Colorado, Havaí, Idaho, Montana, Nevada, Novo México, Oregon, Utah, Washington e Wyoming.

Governos federal e estadual Os EUA são uma república federativa, formada por cinqüenta estados e o Distrito de Colúmbia, território situado no estado de Maryland, que abriga a capital do país, Washington DC. O poder se divide entre os governos federal, estadual e municipal.

- ❑ O governo federal constitui-se do presidente da República, do Congresso (formado pela Câmara de Representantes e pelo Senado) e da Corte Suprema. Sob seu controle estão áreas como defesa, relações exteriores, emissão de moeda e regulamentação do comércio.
- ❑ O poder estadual compõe-se do governador e de um congresso bicameral (*State Congress*). Estão sob sua responsabilidade a cobrança de impostos, a saúde pública, a educação e a legislação civil e penal.

❑ Os estados se dividem em condados, que, por sua vez, subdividem-se em municípios, cada um deles com administração própria. A maioria das cidades é governada por um prefeito e uma Câmara municipal (*city council*). As autoridades locais encarregam-se da administração de escolas, hospitais, serviços de emergência, da limpeza pública, do sistema viário e das leis que regulam a atividade comercial.

Estados Unidos

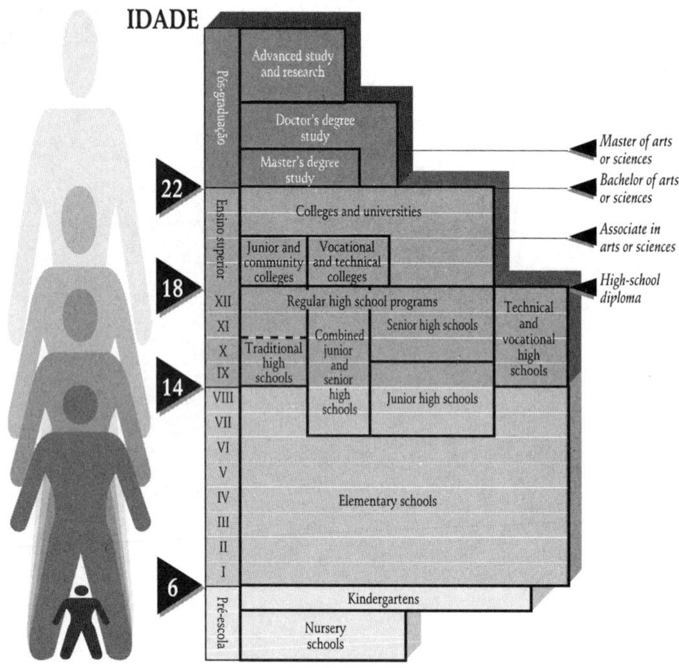

O governo central dos EUA exerce pouco controle direto sobre a educação. O sistema educacional varia de uma região para outra. A maioria das instituições de ensino compõe-se de escolas estaduais, mas cerca de 25% dessas escolas e 45% das faculdades estão nas mãos de grupos privados ou religiosos. O ensino é, em geral, obrigatório, e se estende dos 5 ou 6 anos até por volta dos 16 ou 18 anos de idade.

Educação pré-escolar (até 5 anos) Cerca de 35% das crianças de 3 e 4 anos freqüentam escolas maternais (*nursery schools*), e quase todas entre 4 e 5 vão ao jardim da infância.

Escola primária (dos 6 aos 13 anos) e escola secundária (até 18 anos) Nos dois casos, o número de anos de estudo varia de um estado para outro. Os modelos mais comuns são os seguintes:

- ❑ seis anos de escola primária, seguidos por três anos de *junior high school* (ensino fundamental) e três anos de *senior high school* (ensino médio).
- ❑ oito anos de escola primária (ensino fundamental), seguidos por quatro anos de escola secundária (ensino médio).
- ❑ quatro ou cinco anos de escola primária, seguidos por três ou quatro anos de *middle school* (ensino fundamental), e quatro anos de escola secundária ou *high school* (ensino médio).

OS ANOS ESCOLARES

	Escola Secundária		Faculdade
	Idade	Série	Idade
■ estudante de primeiro ano *(freshman)*	14-15	9ª	18
■ estudante de segundo ano *(sophomore)*	15-16	10ª	19
■ estudante de terceiro ano *(junior)*	16-17	11ª	20
■ estudante de último ano *(senior)*	17-18	12ª	21

Currículo Não há um currículo nacional nos EUA. A maioria dos estudantes das escolas secundárias (*high schools*) deve cursar algumas disciplinas obrigatórias, podendo, nas últimas séries, cursar matérias optativas.

Exames Os estudantes fazem provas ao final de cada curso semestral, mas, ao contrário do que ocorre em outros países, inexiste um exame nacional ao término do ensino secundário. As avaliações são contínuas, ao longo dos anos escolares, e o desempenho dos alunos é determinado pela média dessas avaliações, chamada *Grades Point Average* (*GPA*). Aqueles que desejarem ingressar na universidade fazem exames nacionais, tais como o *American College Test* (*ACT*) e o *Scholastic Aptitude Test* (*SAT*).

Escolas privadas Cerca de 12% dos estudantes estadunidenses freqüentam escolas privadas. Seus cursos organizam-se de forma idêntica ao das escolas públicas, mas o currículo tem por alvo prioritário assegurar o ingresso dos alunos nas melhores universidades e faculdades, como as que integram as chamadas *Ivy League* e *Seven Sisters* (ver quadro).

Ensino superior (dos 18 aos 26 anos) Mais de 50% dos graduados na escola secundária dão prosseguimento aos estudos em nível superior, onde podem obter os seguintes graus: *undergraduate*, *graduate* e *postgraduate*. Cursos superiores são oferecidos por *state colleges*, *community* ou *junior colleges* (que oferecem cursos de dois anos), *undergraduate colleges* (com cursos universitários de quatro anos de duração), escolas técnicas e as prestigiosas universidades e *graduate schools*. Os cursos são pagos pelos estudantes (ou por seus pais), mas cerca de 50% dos alunos conseguem ajuda econômica.

Instituições mais respeitadas de ensino superior

Universidades	Faculdades
Ivy League	***Seven Sisters***
Brown	Barnard
Columbia	Bryn Mawr
Cornell	Mount Holyoke
Dartmouth	Radcliffe
Harvard	Smith
Univ. of Pennsylvania	Vassar
Princeton	Wellesley
Yale	

Educação de adultos Nos EUA, milhões de adultos freqüentam universidades e outras instituições de ensino superior, seja em cursos de tempo integral ou de um único período. Cerca de 40% dos estudantes universitários têm mais de 25 anos.

MEIOS DE COMUNICAÇÃO 16

Os Estados Unidos têm a mais alta porcentagem *per capita* de televisores do mundo. Na prática, todos os lares americanos possuem pelo menos um aparelho de TV, e 70% deles possuem dois ou mais. Uma típica família americana vê sete horas de televisão por dia, e a média por pessoa é de trinta horas semanais.

Canais de televisão Existem quatro redes comerciais nacionais nos EUA:

- American Broadcasting Company (ABC)
- Columbia Broadcasting Service (CBS)
- National Broadcasting Company (NBC)
- Fox TV

Essas quatro redes respondem por 70% da audiência nos horários de maior demanda. Existem cerca de 1.300 canais comerciais, bem como por volta de quatrocentos canais estatais não-comerciais e canais educativos. A maioria dos canais comerciais é afiliada a uma rede nacional, porém existem mais de quatrocentos canais comerciais independentes, oferecendo uma programação especializada, composta, por exemplo, de filmes antigos.

Programação das redes A programação das tevês baseia-se quase exclusivamente no entretenimento, como competições televisivas, programas de entrevistas, comédias de costumes e filmes. De modo geral, apenas o noticiário local e os grandes eventos esportivos são transmitidos ao vivo.

Os índices de audiência e a publicidade O motor das grandes redes de televisão é sobretudo a publicidade, permitida à razão de 15 minutos por hora. Os índices de audiência são, portanto, o fator mais importante na televisão norte-americana. Índice baixo significa receita publicitária menor, o que pode fazer com que mesmo programas de relativa popularidade sejam tirados do ar, se assim exigirem as estatísticas.

TV a cabo e por satélite Cerca de 60% dos lares americanos possuem TV a cabo. Nas grandes cidades, há uma média de 35 canais disponíveis, além das redes nacionais e do *Public Broadcasting System* (PBS), a rede pública de televisão (ver abaixo). Ao contrário do que ocorre com as redes, a televisão a cabo não está sujeita às leis federais, razão pela qual pode, eventualmente, veicular material considerado impróprio. Em geral, cada canal especializa-se em determinado tema, como esportes, filmes, religião, notícias (como é o caso da CNN), compras, música (como a MTV), saúde, pornografia ou programas em língua estrangeira. Muitos hotéis, bares e clubes oferecem TV a cabo em seus estabelecimentos, um atrativo sobretudo quando da transmissão ao vivo de eventos esportivos.

Rede pública de televisão (*Public Broadcasting System*, PBS) O PBS compõe-se de uma rede de canais não-comerciais, financiada por fundos federais, pelo patrocínio de empresas e por doações de particulares. Suas transmissões oferecem programas de conteúdo educativo e cultural.

Rádio Há mais de 10 mil estações de rádio nos EUA, sendo que as principais cidades chegam a ter de cinqüenta a cem estações. Muitas delas são afiliadas a redes nacionais como a ABC, a NBC e a CBS, mas há também cerca de 100 redes regionais. Programas de conteúdo diferenciado podem ser encontrados na *National Public Radio* (NPR), especializada em notícias e em temas da atualidade, e na *American Public Radio* (APR), cuja especialidade são os programas de entretenimento. Assim como o PBS, a NPR e a APR sobrevivem com a ajuda de subsídios governamentais e do patrocínio privado.

Identificação das estações de rádio

As estações de rádio são identificadas por um prefixo de quatro letras, KLMN ou WBNS, por exemplo. As estações a leste do Mississippi e das Montanhas Rochosas têm por primeira letra o "W", e aquelas situadas a oeste, o "K". Em geral, a indicação AM ou FM sucede ao prefixo, como em WBNS FM.

Jornais Existem por volta de 1.700 jornais diários e 850 jornais dominicais nos EUA, perfazendo uma tiragem total superior a 68 milhões de exemplares. Jornais semanais e quinzenais somam cerca de 7.500 títulos. Os principais grupos étnicos têm também seus próprios jornais, e todas as regiões distribuem jornais gratuitos, contendo notícias das comunidades locais.

▸ **Imprensa nacional?** A maioria dos jornais americanos possui caráter regional. *Christian Science Monitor*, *USA Today* e *Wall Street Journal* são os únicos com circulação nacional, embora alguns jornais de prestígio, como o *New York Times*, o *Washington Post* e o *Los Angeles Times* publiquem edições nacionais. O *USA Today* destaca-se entre os jornais populares, com uma vendagem superior a 5 milhões de exemplares por dia. O *Wall Street Journal*, a mais importante publicação sobre negócios, é impresso em diversas cidades e tem quatro edições regionais, sendo o jornal de maior circulação nos EUA. Outras publicações regionais de qualidade, sobretudo em formato grande, são o *Boston Globe*, o *Chicago Tribune*, o *Denver Post*, o *Miami Herald* e o *San Francisco Herald*.

A compra do jornal

Um terço dos norte-americanos recebe seu jornal na porta de casa. Jornais são vendidos também em quiosques e máquinas. Nas máquinas, introduz-se o valor correspondente e retira-se o exemplar pelo qual se pagou.

▸ Os leitores podem optar entre jornais de formato grande ou pequeno. Assim como no Reino Unido, os jornais de conteúdo mais diferenciado são aqueles de formato grande, ao passo que os tablóides se concentram em temas como sexo, escândalos e esportes. A maioria das cidades publica seus próprios tablóides. Exemplos disso são o *Herald* (Boston), o *Sun Times* (Chicago) e o *Daily News* (Nova York). Os semanários mais escandalosos são o *National Enquirer*, o *Globe* e o *Star*.

▸ A maioria dos diários publica uma edição dominical, normalmente com diversas seções. Os jornais dominicais podem ser adquiridos no sábado à tarde (à exceção da seção de notícias), chegando a custar o triplo dos diários, embora, de modo geral, os jornais sejam baratos.

As revistas semanais de notícias, como *Newsweek*, *Time* e *US News and World Report*, são bastante populares e oferecem boa cobertura jornalística. Contudo, as revistas mais populares são as que tratam de moda, delinqüência, guerras e pessoas famosas.

Internet Nos EUA, muitas pessoas se conectam diariamente à internet, de suas casas, do trabalho ou da escola, enviando e recebendo milhões de mensagens de correio eletrônico - o serviço mais utilizado. Há centenas de provedores de acesso, dentre os quais destacam-se a *America Online* (AOL) e a MSN, que proporcionam aos usuários notícias de política, economia, finanças ou esportes, além de informações sobre os espetáculos em cartaz. Boa parte dos internautas conecta-se à rede por linha discada, mas é cada vez maior o número de usuários que se valem de modalidades mais rápidas de conexão, como ADSL e cabo. Bastante populares são os programas de troca de mensagens em tempo real, como o ICQ e o Instant Messenger, que permitem a comunicação rápida, por intermédio de texto ou de voz, além de possibilitar a transferência de arquivos em geral.

A semana de trabalho nos EUA tem de quarenta a 45 horas, embora os trabalhadores industriais cheguem a trabalhar 53 horas semanais. O horário típico de expediente vai das 8 às 17 horas, com uma hora para almoço.

▸ O sistema de horário móvel é menos utilizado nos EUA do que na Grã-Bretanha.

Férias Nos EUA, é comum ter apenas uma ou duas semanas de férias remuneradas ao ano, e muitos trabalhadores não têm direito a férias remuneradas durante o primeiro ano de trabalho. Cada ano de permanência num mesmo posto resulta num acréscimo do tempo de férias.

Imposto de renda Existem dois tipos de impostos: o federal e o estadual. Os impostos são recolhidos pelo *Internal Revenue Service* (IRS). O sistema baseia-se em cálculo individual (*self-assessment*), de responsabilidade exclusiva dos contribuintes. Às empresas, cabe deduzir o imposto do salário de seus empregados. Esse sistema de retenção do imposto na fonte chama-se *withholding*. Todos aqueles que recebem salário sujeito a retenção devem preencher uma declaração de renda relativa ao ano fiscal anterior (de janeiro a dezembro) e apresentá-la antes de 15 de abril. O imposto de renda recolhido pelos estados é, em geral, menor do que o imposto federal e varia de um estado a outro. Alguns estados não recolhem impostos.

Green Card

Todos os estrangeiros que desejem permanecer nos EUA necessitam de um visto. Em linhas gerais, existem dois tipos de visto: os concedidos para imigrantes (residência permanente) e os concedidos para não-imigrantes (residência temporária). Os imigrantes recebem um documento chamado *Alien Registration Receipt Card*, mais conhecido como *Green Card*, embora sua cor atual seja rosa. O trâmite para obtenção do *Green Card* é demorado e complicado. Para consegui-lo, o solicitante deve ser parente próximo de um cidadão americano ou funcionário de uma empresa sediada nos EUA. Do contrário, terá de comprovar que possui recursos suficientes para investir significativa importância em dinheiro na economia do país.

Previdência social A previdência norte-americana cobre a aposentadoria, compulsória ou por doença, pensões por invalidez e viuvez, e o programa de assistência chamado *Medicare*. Todos os cidadãos estadunidenses, bem como residentes estrangeiros, recebem uma carteira da chamada *social security*, contendo um número de identificação composto de nove dígitos. O pré-requisito para o direito à assistência consiste num número mínimo de anos de trabalho, que, em geral, é de cerca de dez anos.

As contribuições à previdência social são feitas por empregados e empresas, cada qual destinando ao sistema certa porcentagem do salário bruto. A contribuição dos trabalhadores é descontada diretamente pela empresa. Trabalhadores autônomos contribuem anualmente.

Desemprego Um fundo administrado conjuntamente pelo governo federal e pelos governos estaduais garante uma renda semanal por tempo limitado (em geral, 26 semanas) aos desempregados, que, para recebê-la, precisam se inscrever no órgão competente. O montante do auxílio depende da renda anterior do trabalhador, mas procura-se proporcionar-lhe uma renda equivalente à metade de seu salário semanal prévio.

O tempo livre de que desfrutam os norte-americanos é relativamente pequeno (ver **trabalho**).

Festas nacionais Além das festas nacionais, muitos estados têm suas próprias datas comemorativas.

- **Natal e Ano-Novo** No Natal, costuma-se enviar cartões a parentes e amigos e decorar a árvore de Natal com bolas, fitas e luzes coloridas. A troca de presentes, depositados ao pé da árvore, acontece na manhã de 25 de dezembro, seguindo-se o almoço de Natal, que tradicionalmente consiste em peru recheado ao forno, batatas assadas e legumes. A véspera de Ano-Novo (*Silvester*) caracteriza-se pelas festas que atravessam a noite.

- **Semana Santa** Nos EUA, as crianças associam a data ao coelho da Páscoa, que entrega cestas de doces e ovos de chocolate (*Easter baskets*) na manhã do domingo de Páscoa.

- O **dia de ação de graças** comemora, em sua origem, a colheita na colônia de Plymouth no ano de 1621, após um inverno de grandes privações. Hoje em dia, toda a família se reúne para compartilhar um almoço tradicional, que consiste, entre outros pratos, em peru recheado, purê de batatas e tortas de abóbora e maçã.

Feriados nacionais

1° de janeiro	Dia de Ano-Novo
Terceira segunda-feira de janeiro	Dia de Martin Luther King
Terceira segunda-feira de fevereiro	Dia dos presidentes (comemoram-se os aniversários de nascimento de Lincoln e Washington
Última segunda-feira de maio	*Memorial Day* (comemoração dos mortos na guerra)
4 de julho	Dia da independência
Primeira segunda-feira de setembro	Dia do trabalho
Segunda segunda-feira de outubro	Dia da hispanidade (Cristóvão Colombo)
11 de novembro	Dia do armistício
Quarta quinta-feira de novembro	Dia de ação de graças
25 de dezembro	Dia de Natal

Bares O melhor lugar para uma conversa tranqüila são os bares onde se servem coquetéis (*cocktail lounge*). A bebida é servida nas mesas e a conta pode ser paga a cada rodada ou ao final. Nos EUA, a prática mais comum é cada um pagar o que consumiu, e costuma-se deixar gorjeta, algo entre 15% a 20% do valor total da conta.

Restaurantes Os norte-americanos comem fora com bastante freqüência: cerca de 40% do orçamento de uma família típica americana são gastos em restaurantes. Os pratos são servidos em porções generosas e é bem ampla a oferta de comidas de diversos países. Em geral, a conta não inclui o serviço, sendo hábito deixar gorjeta equivalente a 15% ou 20% do valor total.

Esportes Os esportes individuais de maior popularidade são a natação, o ciclismo, o esqui, a pesca, a corrida para manter a forma, o *tracking* e a ginástica aeróbica. Os esportes coletivos que atraem maior público são o beisebol (o esporte nacional), o futebol americano e o basquetebol.

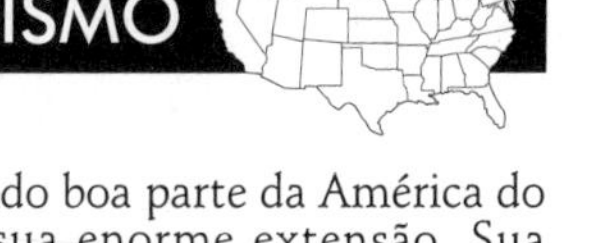

Desde o trópico de Câncer até o Ártico, abrangendo boa parte da América do Norte, os Estados Unidos se destacam por sua enorme extensão. Sua topografia caracteriza-se por grandes espaços abertos e pela diversidade da paisagem, que apresenta desde áridos desertos até os bosques mais densos, das imponentes montanhas às vastas pradarias.

Esse país gigantesco divide-se em cinqüenta estados, e viajar por eles significa apreciar as diferenças geográficas e culturais que os distinguem, cada um com seu sabor individual, mas todos contribuindo para o amálgama vital e dinâmico que deu forma ao país ao longo de sua história.

O turismo concentra-se sobretudo nos estados da Flórida, Califórnia e Havaí, nos centros de esqui em meio às montanhas e nas metrópoles. Mas são também bastante visitados os parques nacionais, como Yosemite e Yellowstone, os Grandes Lagos, e a impressionante paisagem dos cânions no Colorado e em Monument Valley. Entre as cidades norte-americanas destacam-se Nova York, com seus imponentes arranha-céus e suas muitas atrações culturais, além da energia e do dinamismo de sua gente; Nova Orleans, onde se pode desfrutar da típica cultura sulista e ouvir o jazz em sua terra-natal; e Las Vegas, um oásis no meio do deserto, com seus palácios de neon dedicados ao jogo e ao divertimento.

Viajar pelos Estados Unidos é fácil, ainda que as distâncias sejam grandes. A maneira mais simples de percorrer o país é por avião, sobretudo quando se deseja atravessar grandes extensões. Ônibus e trens são uma boa opção para aqueles que pretendem percorrer sem pressa uma área menor, como o noroeste do país, entre Boston e Washington. Mas o melhor meio de transporte para viajar pelo território americano é o carro, porque permite explorar as cidades pequenas e conhecer os locais de menor afluência turística. Além disso, o aluguel de veículos é simples, com preços bastante acessíveis, e o custo da gasolina é barato.

Não é difícil encontrar hospedagem, disponível em todos os níveis, desde pequenos motéis ao longo das estradas e nas cercanias das cidades até as grandes cadeias de hotéis. Outra opção de hospedagem são os *bed & breakfast*, ou *b&b*, normalmente situados em casas antigas transformadas em hospedarias. Muitos desses *b&b* são famosos pelos esplêndidos cafés-da-manhã que servem a seus hóspedes.

Living in Brazil

CONTENTS

BRAZIL AND THE BRAZILIANS 24

Brazil is a country the size of a continent, with an area of 8,514,205 km^2. Situated in South America, it is the largest country in the southern hemisphere. With the Atlantic Ocean on its east coast, Brazil shares borders with Argentina, Paraguay, Bolivia, Peru and Colombia in the west, Uruguay in the south and Venezuela, Guyana, Suriname and French Guyana in the north. The official language is Portuguese and its 170 million inhabitants make it the fifth most populous country in the world, after China, India, the USA and Indonesia.

Brazil is world famous for its natural beauty and talented football players; it is also becoming a valuable contributor to the world's scientific knowledge, supplying important research into agriculture, space, engineering, geosciences and physics. In addition, it has one of the most powerful economies in the world due to the size and strength of its industries, agriculture and cattle ranching.

The population of Brazil is characterized by its great ethnic and cultural diversity. It has developed from three basic ethnic groups: the indigenous, the White and the African (Black). The intensive intermarriage between these groups resulted in a large mixed-race population, and was added to in turn by various immigrant peoples, thus further broadening and diversifying the ethnic composition of the Brazilian population. Since independence from Portugal in 1822 there has been a huge influx of immigrants, coming mainly from Italy, Spain, Germany, Poland, Ukraine and Japan.

Indians In 1500, the indigenous population, speaking around one thousand different languages, exceeded 3 million. By the 1950s, this figure had been reduced to less than 100,000; this has since risen so that by 2001 there were 358,000 Indians, accounting for 0.21% of the Brazilian population. They live in 561 government-acknowledged reservations, which cover 1 million km^2, that is 12.26% of the entire country. These are spread throughout the country except for the states of Piauí and Rio Grande do Norte. Most of the indigenous people live in so-called Constitutional Amazonia (*Amazônia Legal*), comprising the states of Amazonas, Acre, Amapá, Pará, Rondônia, Roraima, Tocantins, Mato Grosso and part of Maranhão. Some tribes, such as the Ticuna, the Guarani and the Ianomâmi, are still quite large; others however, such as the Juma, the Xeta, the Caripuna and the Avá-canoeiro, are greatly reduced in number.

Black population In 1800, 47% of the Brazilian population was black, 30% mixed-race and 23% white. By 1880 this had changed: 20% were black, 38% white and 42% mixed-race. The ethnic composition of the Brazilian people was profoundly affected by a number of factors, including the end of the slave trade (slavery in Brazil was only abolished in 1888), the high mortality rate among the Black population, intense European immigration during the growth of the coffee industry, and the intense intermarrying between Whites and Blacks. The data from 2000 show that Blacks and mixed-race people make up 45.3% of the population in a proportion of 6.2% Black and 39.1 % mixed-race.

Immigration In 1808 the king of Portugal, Dom João VI, passed a decree permitting non-Portuguese to own land in Brazil. The first to take advantage of this were the Swiss, who founded the city of Nova Friburgo in the state of Rio de Janeiro in 1818. Throughout the 19th century, waves of immigrants entered the country. The Germans headed towards the states of Santa Catarina and Espírito Santo; the Italians went to São Paulo. The Japanese arrived in 1908, along with significant contingents of Swiss, Spaniards, Poles and Syrian-Lebanese. Over half these immigrants settled in the state of São Paulo, to work in the coffee plantations, replacing slave labour. In other areas of Brazil, immigration was characterized by the settling of the colonists in

Black Awareness Day

During the time Brazil was a colony, there were many conflicts between black slaves and whites. Rebellious slaves gathered in quilombos, fortified settlements. The most noteworthy quilombo was Palmares, situated in lands belonging to the states of Pernambuco and Alagoas. It contained up to eleven settlements, spread over an area of around 350 km^2. In the seventeenth century, Macaco, the most important centre of Palmares, comprised 1,500 dwellings and approximately 8,000 inhabitants. The chief of this quilombo, Zumbi, was killed in 1695 and became a symbol of the Black struggle against racial oppression; the date of his death – 20th November – is now Black Awareness Day.

small properties, as opposed to the vast fazendas of São Paulo. Nowadays, immigrants, for the most part Koreans and Bolivians, seek out the big cities, where they work illegally. There is also a significant number of highly qualified workers who are settling in Brazil in order to work for multinational firms.

Total population growth and proportion by sex

	1980	1990	1996	2000
Total Population	119,002,706	146,825,475	157,070,163	169,799,170
% Men	49.68	49.36	49.30	49.22
% Women	50.31	50.63	50.69	50.78

Source: IBGE (Instituto Brasileiro de Geografia e Estatística)

The majority of the Brazilian population is Roman Catholic. There are indicators, however, that show a decline in the number of practising Catholics, with a significant drift towards other Christian Protestant or free churches. Between 1970 and 1990, the number of Protestants increased by 10%; other free-church Christians, by 9%; and the number of Catholics by a mere 2%. One of the striking characteristics of Brazilian society is its religious syncretism. A large number of people not only profess the Christian faith, but also believe in spiritualism and the worship of Afro-Brazilian deities.

Religions in Brazil

Religion/Doctrine	Number of adherents (% of total population)
Roman Catholicism	73.60
Evangelical	15.41
Spiritualist (*espírita*)	1.38
Spiritualist (*espiritualista*)	0.02
Umbanda	0.25
Candomblé	0.08
Judaism	0.06
Buddhism	0.14
Other oriental religions	0.11
Islam	0.01
Hindu	--
Esoteric traditions	0.04
Indigenous traditions	0.01
Other religions	1.17
No religion	7.26
Indeterminate	0.23

Source: IBGE, Demographic Census 2000

The Regions of Brazil Brazil is divided into five regions, according to the physical, population and economic features of the states that make up the country:

- *Região Norte* (*Northern Region*): Rondônia, Acre, Amazonas, Roraima, Pará, Amapá and Tocantins
- *Região Nordeste* (*North-Eastern Region*): Maranhão, Piauí, Ceará, Rio Grande do Norte, Paraíba, Pernambuco, Alagoas, Sergipe and Bahia
- *Região Centro-Oeste* (*Central-Western Region*): Mato Grosso do Sul, Mato Grosso, Goiás, and Distrito Federal
- *Região Sudeste* (*South-Eastern Region*): Minas Gerais, Espírito Santo, Rio de Janeiro and São Paulo
- *Região Sul* (*Southern Region*): Paraná, Santa Catarina and Rio Grande do Sul

Norte The Northern Region has an area of 3,852,968 km^2 and a population of 12,893,561 (2000). The climate is equatorial, hot and humid, providing the ideal conditions for the survival of the Amazon forest, which covers nearly the whole region. The rubber boom, begun in the mid-nineteenth century, drew waves of people from the North-Eastern Region who settled along the region's rivers, which, until then, had remained practically undiscovered. In the 1970s, with the opening up of roadways and new projects in agriculture, livestock production and mineral exploitation, the population was enticed into the south of Pará, the north of Tocantins, the west of Amazonia, Rondônia and Acre. The economy of the region is based on plant produce such as latex, the Assai palm, various woods and cashew nuts, and on the extraction of minerals – most of the iron ore exported from Brazil comes from Carajás, in the state of Pará.

Nordeste The North-Eastern Region covers 1,553,918 km^2 and has a population of 47,693,253 (2000). This region is subdivided into four distinct areas, according to their geo-economic features: the *zona da mata*, *agreste*, the *sertão* and the *meio-norte*. The *zona da mata* corresponds to the coastal strip that stretches from the state of Rio Grande do Norte to the south of Bahia; most of the region's population is concentrated in this area, where the main urban centres of the *Nordeste* are to be found. The soil is fertile, due to the large rainfall, and it is here that the great sugarcane plantations are located, as well as the oil fields, the production of cocoa and the region's main industrial centres. The *agreste* is a narrow strip of land situated between the *zona da mata* and the *sertão*, stretching from Rio Grande do Norte to the north-east of Bahia. Although it is an area of lower rainfall, it is nevertheless very fertile. The *sertão*, on the other hand, is characterized by its semi-arid climate, with scarce and irregular rainfall; the harshness of this climate adversely affects the economic activities in the area, especially agriculture. The *sertão* covers a large part of the *Nordeste* region, forming a significant part of Piauí and almost the whole of Ceará. In spite of a greater vitality of the *Nordeste* economy over the past few years, the region still struggles with poverty and high infant mortality rates.

Centro-Oeste The Central-Western Region covers an area of 1,606,445 km^2 and has a population of 11,616,745 (2000). It includes most of the Central Plateau (*Planalto Central*), with extensive areas of wooded grassland and a tropical climate with a clearly-defined dry season. The vast plain of Pantanal is situated in Mato Grosso do Sul and provides natural pasture land, which is flooded by the river Paraguay and its tributaries during the rainy season. Part of the region is covered in equatorial forest, and shares features with the Amazon Rainforest. The main economy is agriculture, and the area produces vast quantities of soya, sorghum, cotton, sunflower, rice and corn. Beef farming is also an important endeavour here, with the country's largest herd, 57 million head of cattle, based mainly in the Mato Grosso do Sul. There are large mineral resources too, particularly manganese. The region is developing a growing tourist trade, encouraging interest in picturesque historic towns like Goiás and Pirenópolis, as well as the capital of Brazil, modern Brasilia.

Sudeste The South-Eastern Region is the most populous of the five Brazilian regions, with 72,297,351 inhabitants (2000). Its 924,574 km^2 are home to the largest cities of the country: São Paulo, Rio de Janeiro and Belo Horizonte. Interest in the area was first stimulated by the gold rush in Minas Gerais during the 18th century. The end of the mining boom saw the development of livestock production and agriculture, especially the cultivation of coffee, which spread from the *Baixada Fluminense* (the alluvial plain in the state of Rio de Janeiro), through the valley of Paraíba (which runs between the states of São Paulo and Rio de Janeiro), expanding then throughout the south of Minas Gerais, Espírito Santo and finally into the interior of São Paulo. Brazilian industrialization started at the turn of the 19th century in the Sudeste region, mainly in São Paulo, where the largest concentration of industries in the country is to be found. The *Sudeste* is considered the economic heart of Brazil, with its diverse industrial production, productive agriculture intensive, modern cattle farming and numerous mineral deposits. These deposits are concentrated in the Serra do Espinhaço (MG), where there is iron and manganese, and in the basin of Campos (RJ), where there is oil. The region has always attracted immigrants, especially from the *Nordeste*, although the influx has slowed recently.

Sul The Southern Region covers 576,300 km^2 and has a population of 25,089,783 (2000). The climate is colder than the rest of the country, with occasional frosts and snow in some parts of Rio Grande do Norte and Santa Catarina. The region was first settled by Portuguese missionaries, who remained only at certain isolated points along the coast and in the interior. European immigrants started to establish small farms in the region in the 19th century, and agriculture and livestock production formed the basis of its economy until the development of a car industry in Curitiba and Porto Alegre in the 1990s. However, agriculture and beef production remain important for the local economy, and Sul has some of the country's highest indices in health and education.

The Brazilian states and their capital cities

State	Abbr.	Capital City
ACRE	AC	Rio Branco
ALAGOAS	AL	Maceió
AMAPÁ	AP	Macapá
AMAZONAS	AM	Manaus
BAHIA	BA	Salvador
CEARÁ	CE	Fortaleza
DISTRITO FEDERAL	DF	Brasília
ESPÍRITO SANTO	ES	Vitória
GOIÁS	GO	Goiânia
MARANHÃO	MA	São Luís
MATO GROSSO	MT	Cuiabá
MATO GROSSO DO SUL	MS	Campo Grande
MINAS GERAIS	MG	Belo Horizonte
PARÁ	PA	Belém
PARAÍBA	PB	João Pessoa
PARANÁ	PR	Curitiba
PERNAMBUCO	PE	Recife
PIAUÍ	PI	Teresina
RIO DE JANEIRO	RJ	Rio de Janeiro
RIO GRANDE DO NORTE	RN	Natal
RIO GRANDE DO SUL	RS	Porto Alegre
RONDÔNIA	RO	Porto Velho
RORAIMA	RR	Boa Vista
SANTA CATARINA	SC	Florianópolis
SÃO PAULO	SP	São Paulo
SERGIPE	SE	Aracaju
TOCANTINS	TO	Palmas

Main cities of Brazil by population

São Paulo	10,405,867
Rio de Janeiro	5, 851,914
Salvador	2,440,828
Belo Horizonte	2,232,747
Fortaleza	2,138,234
Brasília	2,043,169
Curitiba	1,586,848
Recife	1,421,993
Manaus	1,403,796
Porto Alegre	1,360,033

Source: Almanaque Abril, data from 2000

Environment Between 15% and 20% of the earth's biological diversity is found in Brazil. It is estimated that, from a world total of 250,000 plant species, 55,000 can be found in Brazil, as can the world's greatest variety of primates, amphibians and vertebrates. This natural wealth could be exploited by the pharmaceutical or cosmetic industries, which represents a huge economic potential. However, these resources also attract plant and animal trafficking. Every year, 38 million animals are captured illegally in the country and 10% of international animal trafficking targets the fauna of Brazil.

In an effort to protect Brazilian fauna and flora the government has established so-called 'conservation units'. According to official figures, 5.05% of national territory is environmentally protected by these federal conservation units, which include national parks and biological reservations, as well as ecological stations and reserves.

Brazil's varied natural landscapes – the forests, bush, *caatinga*, the *Pantanal* (swamps) of Mato Grosso, fields, mangroves, sandbanks, coconut and pine plantations – are essential for the survival of its abundant flora. Some of the following areas form part of the greatest concentration of biodiversity in the world and deserve special mention:

Amazon Rainforest The largest tropical rainforest in the world, it has an area of 4.9 million km² and covers 54.4% of the country. Large projects such as the building of roads and hydroelectric plants have already resulted in the destruction of around 13.9% of its original area. Government organizations and the Brazilian scientific community have developed plans for the conservation and sustainable exploitation of species, in an attempt to broaden knowledge of the forest's biodiversity and how to protect it.

Atlantic woods Another important forested region, the Atlantic woods are now reduced to 7% of the area they occupied at the time the Portuguese arrived in Brazil. This is due to the fact that this area has been settled and populated the longest, and holds the greatest concentration of inhabitants in the country – from the coastline of the *Nordeste* to the interior of Rio Grande do Sul, stretching westwards through the states of São Paulo and Paraná. Once rich in rare woods such as Brazilian copal, peroba and tauari, the depletion of the region's riches began with the deforestation of Brazilwood, which is nowadays all but extinct. However, the Atlantic woods are still home to significant numbers of animal and plant species.

Pantanal The Pantanal, or swamp, is the largest floodplain in the world and has a wealth of relatively heterogeneous fauna and flora, with 650 species of birds, 80 species of mammals, 260 species of fish and 50 species of reptiles. Its rivers are thought to be the richest in fish in the world. In 2001, the Pantanal was declared a site of natural heritage for humanity by Unesco.

Cerrado This wooded grassland is a form of savannah, with abundant grasses and small, twisted, thick-barked trees. Around 20% of Brazilian territory is covered by this form of vegetation, which covers the whole of the country's central plateau (*Planalto Central*); it can also be found, less strikingly, in Amazônia, Minas Gerais, parts of São Paulo, Bahia, Maranhão and Piauí. An estimated 10,000 plant species, over 800 species of birds and 161 species of mammals are thought to live in the *cerrado*. Nowadays, extensive beef production, monocultures and road-building present the main threats to this environment.

Caatinga The *caatinga* has been reduced to half its original size and covers a mere 10% of the national territory. It is characteristic of the Brazilian *Nordeste*, and its vegetation is particularly adapted to a dry climate and poor, stony soil. The long peri-

ods of drought and the irregular rainfall in-between make life extremely hard for the *sertanejos*, as the inhabitants of the *sertão* (or *caatinga*) are known.

Apart from this wealth of vegetation, Brazil also has one of the world's largest river networks, due to its size, flatness and high rainfall in most regions. The more important water systems are the Amazon basin, with 3,904,393 km^2 in national territory (from a total of 7,050,000 km^2). The Amazon river is 6,868 km long and has around 7,000 tributaries; it is the largest river in the world in terms of water flow, and second only to the Nile in length. Other important water systems are formed by the basins of the rivers Paraná, Paraguai, Uruguai, São Francisco, Parnaíba and Tocantins-Araguaia. The São Francisco river is the longest river entirely within Brazilian territory.

Political administration The Federal Republic of Brazil comprises 26 states, 1 federal district and 5,561 municipalities; it has a presidential government. The political organization in Brazil is based on three independent bodies: the executive, the legislative and the judicial.

Executive body Within the federal framework, the executive body's leader is the President of the Republic, who has a four-year mandate, with a right to stand for re-election. Within the states, governors centralize executive power and, in the municipalities, this power is held by mayors (*prefeitos*). The President must be Brazilian-born and over 35 years of age to be eligible for election; he or she is elected through direct voting. If no candidate gets an absolute majority in the first round, a second round is held. The Vice-President is elected at the same time as the President.

Legislative body Responsible for making the laws that govern the country, the legislative body is formed at federal level by the National Congress, made up of the Chamber of Deputies and the Senate. At state level, it consists of Legislative Assemblies, led by state deputies. In the municipalities, it consists of Municipal Chambers, or town halls, led by councillors. The Chamber of Deputies is made up of 513 representatives elected by direct vote and proportional representation, for four-year mandates. Three Senators per state are elected to the Senate, with eight-year mandates. The Senate alternates the representation by one- and two-thirds every four years.

Judicial body At federal level, judicial power is exercised by the Supreme Federal Tribunal (the highest court in the country), the High Court of Justice, Regional Federal Tribunals, the Labour High Court, the Electoral High Court, the Military High Court and the Union Accounts Court. At regional level, there are Regional Labour Courts, Regional Electoral Courts and Military Courts.

Armed forces The Brazilian Armed Forces are made up of the Navy, the Army and the Air Force. Military service is compulsory for all male citizens. Young men are called up during the year of their eighteenth birthday. Nowadays, the three forces allow the voluntary enrolment of women in auxiliary roles.

The Brazilian economy In the past, the Brazilian economy was characterized by monoculture for exportation (Brazilwood, sugarcane, cotton, coffee, cocoa, rubber). Beef production and ore extraction have also been of great economic significance, being directly responsible for the development of Brazil's interior and for building up a transport network between its various regions. The cultivation of coffee was developed after independence and brought about the first stages of industrialization in the country during the nineteenth century. The crisis that followed the Wall Street Crash of 1929 saw the price of coffee plummet, yet it promoted industrialization by forcing the Brazilian government to take measures that were to accelerate the country's development. Since then, industry has continued to expand to such an extent that it overtook agriculture in terms of economic importance in the mid-1950s. Today, Brazil's GDP places the country amongst the top ten economies in the world, with the largest industrial park amongst so-called emergent countries.

GDP:	**US$ 529.3 billion (1999)**
GDP per sector:	Services 55.1%
	Industry 37.1%
	Agriculture 7.8%

Source: Banco Central do Brasil

Inflation Inflation has been a constant subject for debate in Brazilian economy, especially since the 1940s. Between 1915 and 1940, the rates of inflation varied greatly, though rarely reaching two figures, something that subsequently became a regular occurrence. In the 1960s, for the first time in history, the inflation index came very close to 100% per year. After the military coup in 1964 measures to fight inflation were implemented, especially wage control, which caused inflation indices to drop. In 1973, Brazilian inflation was 13.7% per year. However, international crises led to an increase in this rate, until it reached 76% per year in 1979. In the 1980s, rates of inflation increased dramatically, reaching three figures – in 1981, Brazilian inflation was 100% per year. In an attempt to contain the instability of the monetary system, there followed a number of governmental plans – the 'Cruzado' plan, the 'Collor 1' plan and the 'Collor 2' plan – but these were only partially successful. Finally, the 'Real' plan, implemented in July 1994, managed to contain inflation and provided the country with relative economic stability.

Income distribution In 2000, UN data relating to 174 nations placed Brazil amongst the countries of greatest income concentration in the world. The average income of the wealthiest 20% is 25.5 times greater than the average income of the poorest 20%. The first group receives 63.8% of national income, whereas the second receives a mere 2.5% of the total. This strong concentration of the country's wealth means that around 15% of Brazilians live in conditions of extreme poverty, a condition that affects mainly the Black and rural populations. Regional differences also have to be taken into consideration when looking at poverty in the country: the *Nordeste* region, with 30% of the national population, is home to 62% of the poorest people in Brazil. In spite of the social programmes that have been implemented, poverty in Brazil in 2002 has similar indices to those of the 1970s. One of the main factors in this unequal distribution of the country's wealth is the difficulty in gaining access to adequate education. In spite of the progress made in education in recent times, only a small proportion of the population can attend good schools and universities, thereby getting better jobs and higher income.

Work and employment Most labour relations in Brazil are ruled by the CLT ('Consolidation of Labour Laws'), created during the government of Getúlio Vargas (1930-1945). Since 1940, there has also been a minimum national wage, whose value is set by the federal government. The working day must not exceed 8 hours, or 44 hours a week. Data from 1999 shows an economically active population of 79.3 million people, and an unemployment figure of 9.6%. The Brazilian workplace has seen a dramatic fall in formal employment between 1989 and 1999: in 1999, there were around 38.9 million casual workers.

Women's social position There have been significant changes in the profile of the Brazilian woman and the family model. The census in 2000 and other studies have shown an increase in the number of women as principal earners in the family: in 1991, the proportion was 8.5%; by 2000, the number had increased to 13%. There has also been a dramatic fall in the birth rate and this coincides with the greater presence of women in the workplace. In spite of the continued difference in wages between men and women, women are increasingly active in the Brazilian workplace.

The Brazilian education system is divided into basic education and higher education. The former includes infant, primary and intermediate education. Higher education includes undergraduate and post-graduate studies, other university courses and further studies. These 'further studies', implemented in 1999, lead to earlier qualification than an undergraduate degree, but do not give access to post-graduate studies. Ongoing education for young people and adults, including professional and special training, are also supplied. Education is provided by both the public sector (municipal, state or federal) and by private schools and universities.

Infant education (*up to age 6*) This includes day-care nurseries for children from birth up to 3, and pre-school for children aged 4 to 6. Since 1996, infant education is no longer seen as a social service, being now considered part of basic education and, in the case of public schools, the responsibility of the municipalities. Nevertheless, infant education is not compulsory, and it remains a weak spot in the Brazilian education system: it provides for the needs of only a third of all children aged 6 or under. The Southern region has the highest proportion of pre-school attendance (99%), while the South-Eastern region has the most children in nurseries (78%). According to the schools' census of 2001, 6 million children aged 6 and under have access to infant education.

Basic education (*from age 7 to 14*) Basic education lasts eight academic years, or *series* – 1st to 4th *series* for children aged between 7 and 10, and 5th to 8th *series* for children between 11 and 14. According to the constitution of 1988, it is the duty of the state to provide free and compulsory basic education. There is a core curriculum common to the whole of Brazil, which is determined by the Federal Education Council of Brazil and takes regional differences into account, in order to make allowances for local characteristics. Many children fail to pass their final school exams, and many are forced to stay away from school. These problems have been addressed with some success by the educational policies of recent years. Data from 2000 shows that 94.9% of children aged between 7 and 14 attend school.

Intermediate education (*from age 15 to 17*) This takes place over three academic years, and most of those who attend go to public-sector schools. Figures from Unesco show that only 33.4% of the relevant age group attend school at this level in Brazil, though there has been some increase over the last decade.

Higher education (*from age 18 to 24*) There are 1,097 institutions for higher education in Brazil, provided by both private organisations and municipal, state and federal universities. In contrast to the other tiers of education, the public sector accounts for the majority of places – 65%. University candidates are selected primarily through an entrance exam, the *vestibular*, which is taken at the end of intermediate education.

Public Universities of Brazil

The Faculties of Law in São Paulo (1827) and Recife (1854), the Mining School of Ouro Preto (1854) and the Polytechnic of Rio de Janeiro (1870) developed from institutions that have existed in the country since 1808, and were the first universities in Brazil. Nowadays, with the exception of Tocantins, all Brazilian states have a public federal university. The more prominent of these are:

- Federal University of Bahia (UFBA)
- University of Brasília (UnB)
- Federal University of Minas Gerais (UFMG)
- Federal University of Rio de Janeiro (UFRJ)
- Federal University of Rio Grande do Sul (UFRGS)

The state of São Paulo also has three state public universities, which are among the most respected higher-education institutions in the country:

- São Paulo University (USP)
- Campinas State University (UNICAMP)
- São Paulo State University (UNESP)

Young people and adult education There are also courses and exams available for both young people and adults who did not finish their basic or intermediate education during their school years. The Brazilian education system thus enables these people to attend adult classes and resume their studies, so affording them greater professional possibilities.

Professional education Courses leading to professional qualifications are provided mainly by SENAC ('National Service for Commercial Training') and SENAI ('National Service for Industrial Training'), as well as by companies who are willing to take on trainees. These courses are geared towards employment. In 1999, there were 33,000 professional training courses in the whole country.

Special education Special education is intended for young people and adults with special needs; it is officially part of government policy, but its practical implementation is, as yet, in its early stages.

Illiteracy The 1999 data indicate 22.8 million illiterates in Brazil, that is, 13.8% of the population aged 15 or over. The country also has a rate of 30.5% functional illiterates, namely people aged 15 or over who have had less than four years of schooling, and who therefore read and write well below standard.

Schooling in Brazil				
Illiteracy rates	**1996**	**1997**	**1998**	**1999**
People aged 10 & over	13.7	13.9	12.9	12.3
People between 10 & 14	8.3	8.7	6.9	5.5
Years at school (people aged 10 or over) (% in 1999)	**Total**	**Men**	**Women**	
No education or less than 1 year	13.4	13.6	13.2	
1 to 3 years	18.3	19.4	17.2	
4 to 7 years	34.2	34.5	34.0	
8 to 10 years	14.8	14.7	14.9	
11 and over	19.0	17.5	20.4	

Source: IBGE

School curriculum The national curriculum includes: Portuguese, social studies (history and geography), mathematics, physics, biology and physical education. From the age of 11 (fifth *serie*), it is obligatory to learn at least one foreign language. In 1997, the Ministry of Education established educational guidelines ('National Curriculum Parameters', or PCNs), in an effort to redefine teaching in Brazil. They aim to encourage the critical and creative spirit of the pupil, stimulate ethical awareness and develop concern for health, the environment and multiculturalism, as well as to provide sex education.

Education versus work In Brazil, many young people are forced to leave school in order to work and help support the family. In the 1990s, however, there was a drop in the number of pupils forced to study part-time, or leave school altogether. Amongst 15 to 17 year-olds, the percentage of students who do not need to work as well rose from 38.9% in 1992 to 55.7% in 1999. Amongst young people aged between 20 and 24, the percentage of those who study full-time rose from 6.9% in 1992 to 10.9% in 1999.

Television In Brazil, the most popular means of communication, and the most far-reaching, is television; most advertising funds are channelled into this medium. The first televised broadcast took place in 1950, made by São Paulo's *TV Tupi*. In 1956, Brazilians watched their first football match on television and in 1972, colour television arrived. In 1996, subscription television was introduced, and now includes cable and satellite transmissions. Studies made in 2001 show that 97% of the population over the age of 10 watch television at least once a week. The biggest broadcasting station, *Rede Globo*, reaches most Brazilian municipalities (99.77%), and is famous for the quality of its soaps, which are exported to several countries worldwide. Other national commercial networks are *Rede Bandeirantes*, *Rede Record*, *SBT* (*Sistema Brasileiro de Televisão*) and *Rede TV!* Apart from these open-signal commercial stations, the country also has a public network of educational stations such as *TV Cultura* (in São Paulo) and *TVE* (in Rio de Janeiro).

Radio Much has changed since Brazil's first radio transmission, on September 7th 1922, when the speech of the then President of the Republic was broadcast over the airwaves while the country celebrated its first 100 years of Independence. Since then, radio has become the second most wide-reaching medium in the country after television, and it has evolved with the market, being also transmitted on the Brazilian internet. According to the Ministry of Communication, there are currently around 2,965 radio stations in the country.

Main Brazilian newspapers

The *Correio Braziliense* was the first Portuguese language newspaper to be distributed in Brazil; it was first published in London by Hipólito José da Costa between June 1808 and December 1822. The newspaper went against the interests of the Portuguese Crown. Free from censorship, it openly criticized Portuguese policies in Brazil and greatly influenced political journalism around Independence. Hipólito José da Costa was also the first famous Brazilian to defend the abolition of slavery.

Among the main present-day Brazilian newspapers are the following:

- *Folha de São Paulo* (SP)
- *O Estado de São Paulo* (SP)
- *O Globo* (RJ)
- *Jornal do Brasil* (RJ)
- *O Estado de Minas* (MG)
- *Correio Braziliense* (DF)
- *Zero Hora* (RS)

The press The history of the press in Brazil dates only from the nineteenth century, as Portugal would not allow it to exist in its colony. When the Portuguese Court moved to Brazil in 1808, it brought a printing plant with it; in the same year, the Royal Press was created. Editorial censorship was brought along too, and only came to an end in 1821. With the end of censorship, important newspapers emerged in opposition to the Portuguese Crown. During the reign of Dom Pedro II (1831-1889), there came a period of freedom and prosperity for the press; abolitionist and republican newspapers were printed, as were more humorous publications. Since the beginning of the 20th century the Brazilian press has gone from strength to strength; in 2000, there were around 500 daily newspapers being printed, with an average circulation in excess of 7 million, while weekly news and information magazines represent 32% of market: *Veja*, *Época* and *IstoÉ* being the three most widely-distributed. There are also specialized publications dedicated to a wide variety of subjects, which account for 22% of the market.

Telephone In 1877, just one year after Alexander Graham Bell's invention, some telephones were made in Rio de Janeiro by the Western and Brazilian Telegraph Company; one was installed in the residence of Emperor Dom Pedro II. Two years later the first grant to establish a telephone network was conceded, in Rio de Janeiro and Niterói (RJ). Phone networks in Brazil were managed by private foreign concession until 1970, and the service was unreliable; however, in 1972 the Ministry of Communication created *Telebrás* to manage the planning of public telecommunications services. By the 1990s, *Telebrás* had installed 10 million phone outlets in the country. Since 1995 the telecommunications network has been gradually privatized and in 1998 the *Telebrás* system, by then divided into 12 regional holdings for fixed and mobile telephony, was taken over by private enterprise. According to 2001 figures, Brazil now has 43.77 million land lines, around 26 million mobile phones and 1.3 million public telephones.

Internet Until 1994, the internet in Brazil was restricted to universities. However, once it became available to the general public, in 1996, and once the telephone lines had been improved, the internet grew rapidly. The country is already in the leading position in Latin America, both in terms of providers and of users, and is ninth in the world ranking of internet users. In 2001, 11.9 million people owned a home computer with access to the net, although these people belong mainly to the more affluent classes of the population – classes A (34%) and B (50%). The installation of broadband services, especially from 2000 onwards, has allowed faster navigation and file transfer. It is estimated that by the end of 2002, the number of users of this kind of service will have reached 634,000. At present, a huge effort is being made to take the internet into public-sector schools, in order to avoid so-called digital exclusion, namely the marginalizing of the poorer social layers in relation to access to information and technology. Brazil is also the third Latin American country to have access to Internet 2, a project that allows communication amongst the international scientific community via a high-tech network.

The Internet in South America

	Country	No. of hosts
1st	**Brazil (.br)**	**1,644,575**
2nd	Argentina (.ar)	465,359
3rd	Chile (.cl)	122,727
4th	Uruguay (.uy)	70,892
5th	Columbia (.co)	57,419
6th	Venezuela (.ve)	22,614
7th	Peru (.pe)	13,504
8th	Ecuador (.ec)	3,383
9th	Paraguay (.py)	2,704
10th	Bolivia (.bo)	1,522

Source: Network Wizards, January 2002

The calendar of Brazilian feast days is intimately linked to Christianity and, more especially, to Roman Catholicism. The celebrations of Easter, Christmas and the feast days in June (*festas juninas*) are popular. There are also secular celebrations such as Carnival, the greatest of all feasts in Brazil, and other civic feast days. The religious syncretism that characterizes the country becomes quite apparent during many religious feast days, when both Catholic saints and their Afro-Brazilian counterparts are honoured at the same time.

Groups and troupes: the birth of the samba schools

Groups (or *blocos*) were the most democratic way of celebrating Carnival. They were neither planned nor choreographed, and brought together friends, family and neighbours. Troupes (or *ranchos*) formed a much more organized parade, with a greater number of women and more instruments such as *cavaquinhos*, guitars, clarinets and flutes that played music especially composed for the occasion. The troupes also contained an element that was to become a feature of the samba schools: the standard-bearer. These groups and troupes were later to give rise to the samba schools. In 1899, the first *marcha-rancho* – a musical genre typical of carnival celebrations – to be recorded in the history of Brazilian carnivals was composed: *Ô abre alas*, by Chiquinha Gonzaga.

Carnival This is without doubt the most famous of all Brazilian celebrations. It was probably introduced into the country in the 17th century under the name of *entrudo*. This was a form of merrymaking where people pelted each other with water, dust, chalk and anything else that was to hand. However, the relative violence of this activity soon encountered strong opposition. Little by little, the missiles were replaced by more harmless ones, such as paper streamers and confetti. In 1840, in Rio de Janeiro, the first documented fancy-dress ball took place, inspired by similar events in European cities. In 1846, *Zé Pereira* emerged, a group of jesters that took to the streets, banging on *bumbos* and drums. Since then, Carnival has become a tradition in Rio de Janeiro. Its popularity helped it to spread throughout the various regions of the country. It officially takes place during the four days preceding Ash Wednesday (Saturday until Shrove Tuesday).

National Bank Holidays

- January 1st - *New Year's Day*
- Moveable Date - *Good Friday*
- April 21st - *Tiradentes**
- May 1st - *Labour Day*
- September 7th - *Independence Day*
- October 12th - *Nossa Senhora Aparecida***
- November 15th - *Proclamation of the Republic*
- December 25th - *Christmas Day*

* national hero, freedom fighter

** Patron saint of Brazil

Festas Juninas The *festas juninas* are also celebrated throughout the country, in commemoration of Saints Anthony, John and Peter. Originally these feast days were called *joaninas*, having reached Brazil through the Jesuits in the hope of luring the natives they intended to convert. The feast days occurred during the same period that the indigenous people celebrated their fertility rituals, namely the harvest season. The *festas juninas* became quite popular and the tradition spread. During these days, it is customary to have bonfires, fireworks, dancing and bunting, as well as traditional food and drink.

Feast of the Divine This feast is of Portuguese origin and was introduced into

Brazil during the 16th century; it celebrates the descent of the divine Holy Spirit to the apostles of Jesus Christ. It takes place on Whit Sunday, 50 days after Easter. The way it is celebrated varies very much from region to region, but all festivities have as a high point the crowning of the Emperor of the Divine. In the city of Pirenópolis (GO), where it is celebrated with great pomp, jousts are held as well, representing the battles between Christians and Moors. Some commemorations are accompanied by music and dances typical of the day, along with a glut of food for all.

Optional Bank Holidays

- Moveable Date - *Carnival*
- Moveable Date - *Ash Wednesday*
- Moveable Date - *Corpus Christi*
- November 2nd - *All Souls' Day*
- December 24th - *Christmas Eve*
- December 31st - *New Year's Eve*

Círio de Nazaré Our Lady of Nazareth is the patron saint of the city of Belém (Bethlehem), in Pará. Her feast day is one of the most important in the region and brings together thousands of locals and people from other regions as well. The procession of the Círio (candle) wends through the streets of Belém to the sound of prayers and chants, starting from the city's baroque cathedral and ending up at the basilica of Nazaré (Nazareth).

Bom Jesus dos Navegantes This celebration takes place on the São Francisco river in Alagoas and Salvador (BA). In Salvador, the statue of *Bom Jesus dos Navegantes* is taken by boat across the Baía de Todos os Santos accompanied by thousands of other highly-decorated sailing vessels, to the beach of Boa Viagem. A similar celebration takes place in Aracaju (SE). In Porto Alegre (RS), the celebration is held in honour of *Nossa Senhora dos Navegantes*.

Christian Celebrations

The Epiphany: January 6th
Ash Wednesday
Palm Sunday
Holy Saturday
Easter Sunday
Ascension Day
Pentecost
Corpus Christi
St John: June 24th
St Peter: June 29th
Nossa Senhora Aparecida: October 12th; patron saint of Brazil
All Souls' Day: November 2nd
Christmas Day: December 25th

Afro-Brazilian Celebrations

January 1st: *Day of Oxalá*
January 20th: *Day of Oxóssi (St Sebastian)*
February 2nd: *Day of Iemanjá*
April 23rd: *Ogum (St George)*
September 27th: *Ibeji (SS Cosmas and Damian)*

Manual de comunicação em inglês

Cartas

Início e término

A fórmula de despedida, utilizada ao término de uma carta, depende da saudação empregada em seu início.

Quando se sabe o nome do destinatário:
Dear Sir
Dear Madam

Quando não se sabe se o destinatário é homem ou mulher:
Dear Sir or Madam
ou
Dear Sir/Madam

Quando o destinatário é uma empresa ou organização:
Dear Sirs (UK)
Gentlemen (US)

Assim se conclui uma carta, quando não se sabe o nome do destinatário:
Yours faithfully (UK)

No inglês americano, a ordem das palavras é a inversa:
Faithfully yours (US)

Quando se sabe o nome do destinatário:
Dear Mr Robertson
Dear Mrs Dent
Dear Miss Carrington
Dear Ms Paton
Se o destinatário é uma mulher, a abreviatura *Ms* é cada vez mais utilizada, porque não especifica se ela é casada (*Mrs*) ou solteira (*Miss*).

Dear Dr Howells

Nos Estados Unidos, a abreviatura é normalmente seguida de um ponto: Mr., Mrs., Ms., Dr.

Yours sincerely (UK)
Sincerely yours (US)
Sincerely (US)

Mais amigável:
Yours very sincerely (UK)

Menos formal:
With best wishes
With kind regards
Kindest regards

Essas frases podem encerrar a carta ou preceder qualquer uma das fórmulas de despedida acima.

Quando o destinatário é um amigo ou parente:
Dear Bob
Dear Jane
Dear Martin and Kathryn
Dear All
Dear Mum and Dad
Dear Uncle John/Auntie Annie
My dear Chris
Dearest/My dearest Ruth

With love
Love
Love from
Love and best wishes

Mais afetuoso:
With all my/our love
Much love

Mais informal:
Lots of love

Mais formal:
Yours
All the best (UK)
Best wishes
Regards

Ao se escrever para o editor de um jornal:
Sir

Quando não se sabe o nome do destinatário:
Yours faithfully (UK)
Faithfully yours (US)

Para um membro do parlamento britânico:
Dear Mr/Mrs Brown

Quando se sabe o nome do destinatário:
Yours sincerely (UK)
Sincerely yours (US)
Sincerely (US)

Para um membro da Câmara ou do Senado americano:
Sir/Madam
Dear Congressman/ Congresswoman Fox
Dear Senator Mitcham

Menos comum:
Yours respectfully (UK)
Respectfully yours (US)
Respectfully (US)

Carta impressa formal

Os parágrafos não têm margem e são separados por um espaço.

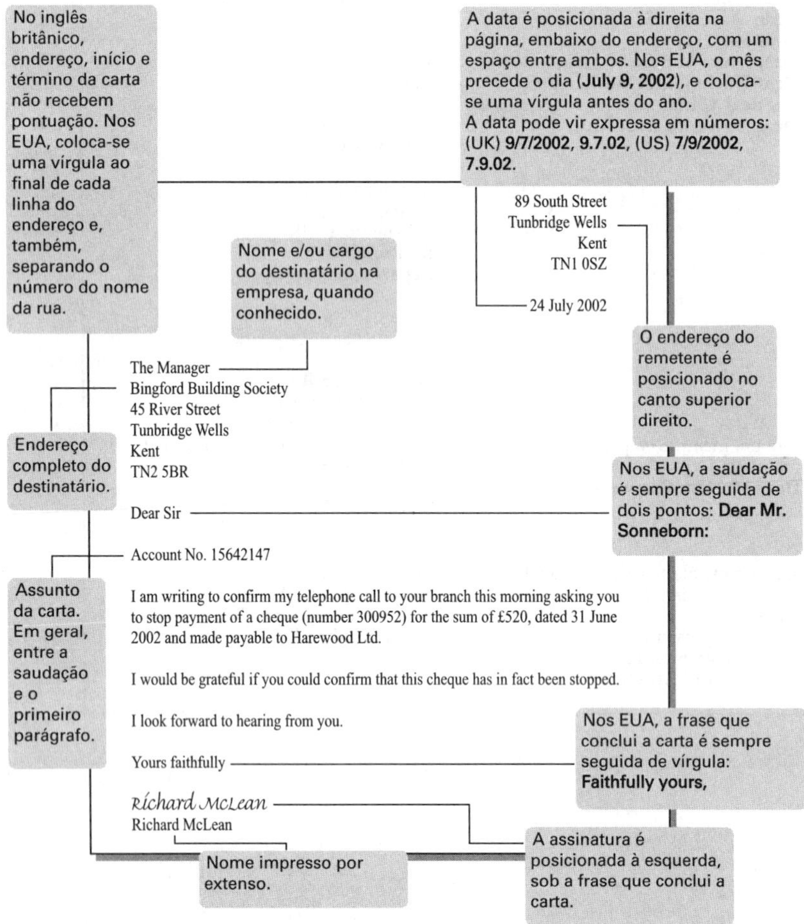

No inglês britânico, endereço, início e término da carta não recebem pontuação. Nos EUA, coloca-se uma vírgula ao final de cada linha do endereço e, também, separando o número do nome da rua.
A data é posicionada à direita na página, embaixo do endereço, com um espaço entre ambos. Nos EUA, o mês precede o dia (**July 9, 2002**), e coloca-se uma vírgula antes do ano.
A data pode vir expressa em números: (UK) **9/7/2002**, **9.7.02**, (US) **7/9/2002**, **7.9.02**.
Nome e/ou cargo do destinatário na empresa, quando conhecido.
O endereço do remetente é posicionado no canto superior direito.
Endereço completo do destinatário.
Nos EUA, a saudação é sempre seguida de dois pontos: **Dear Mr. Sonneborn:**
Assunto da carta. Em geral, entre a saudação e o primeiro parágrafo.
Nos EUA, a frase que conclui a carta é sempre seguida de vírgula: **Faithfully yours,**
A assinatura é posicionada à esquerda, sob a frase que conclui a carta.
Nome impresso por extenso.

89 South Street
Tunbridge Wells
Kent
TN1 0SZ

24 July 2002

The Manager
Bingford Building Society
45 River Street
Tunbridge Wells
Kent
TN2 5BR

Dear Sir

Account No. 15642147

I am writing to confirm my telephone call to your branch this morning asking you to stop payment of a cheque (number 300952) for the sum of £520, dated 31 June 2002 and made payable to Harewood Ltd.

I would be grateful if you could confirm that this cheque has in fact been stopped.

I look forward to hearing from you.

Yours faithfully

Richard McLean
Richard McLean

Carta para um amigo

Deixa-se uma margem no início de cada parágrafo.

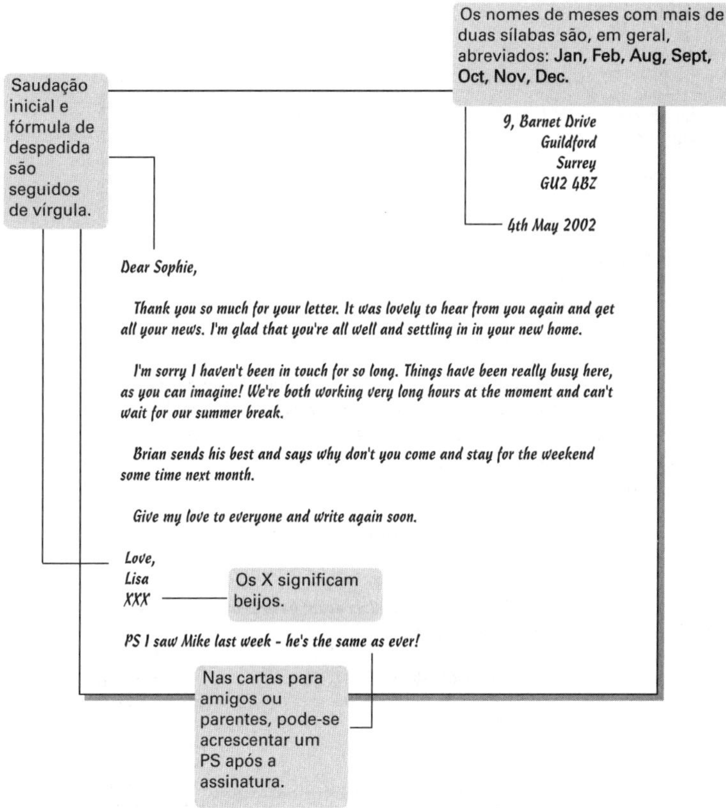

Os nomes de meses com mais de duas sílabas são, em geral, abreviados: **Jan, Feb, Aug, Sept, Oct, Nov, Dec.**
Saudação inicial e fórmula de despedida são seguidos de vírgula.
9, Barnet Drive
Guildford
Surrey
GU2 4BZ
4th May 2002
Dear Sophie,
Thank you so much for your letter. It was lovely to hear from you again and get all your news. I'm glad that you're all well and settling in in your new home.
I'm sorry I haven't been in touch for so long. Things have been really busy here, as you can imagine! We're both working very long hours at the moment and can't wait for our summer break.
Brian sends his best and says why don't you come and stay for the weekend some time next month.
Give my love to everyone and write again soon.
Love,
Lisa
XXX
Os X significam beijos.
PS I saw Mike last week - he's the same as ever!
Nas cartas para amigos ou parentes, pode-se acrescentar um PS após a assinatura.

Outro exemplo de carta para um amigo

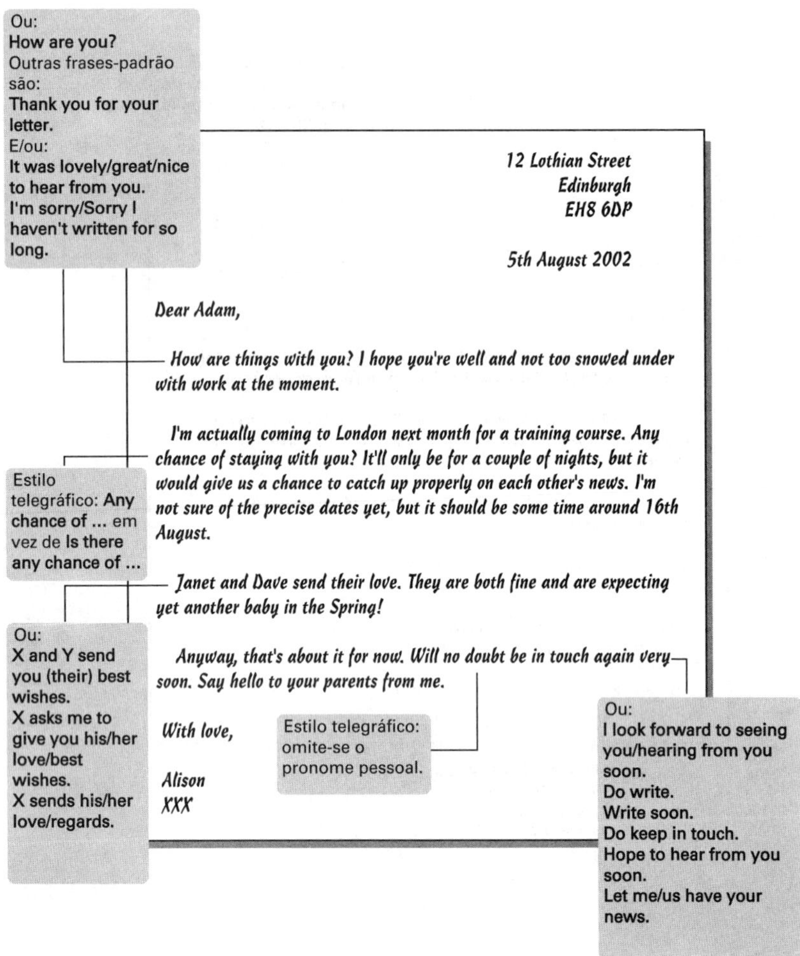
12 Lothian Street
Edinburgh
EH8 6DP

5th August 2002

Dear Adam,

How are things with you? I hope you're well and not too snowed under with work at the moment.

I'm actually coming to London next month for a training course. Any chance of staying with you? It'll only be for a couple of nights, but it would give us a chance to catch up properly on each other's news. I'm not sure of the precise dates yet, but it should be some time around 16th August.

Janet and Dave send their love. They are both fine and are expecting yet another baby in the Spring!

Anyway, that's about it for now. Will no doubt be in touch again very soon. Say hello to your parents from me.

With love,

Alison
XXX

Ou:
How are you?
Outras frases-padrão são:
Thank you for your letter.
E/ou:
It was lovely/great/nice to hear from you.
I'm sorry/Sorry I haven't written for so long.
Estilo telegráfico: Any chance of ... em vez de Is there any chance of ...
Ou:
X and Y send you (their) best wishes.
X asks me to give you his/her love/best wishes.
X sends his/her love/regards.
Estilo telegráfico: omite-se o pronome pessoal.
Ou:
I look forward to seeing you/hearing from you soon.
Do write.
Write soon.
Do keep in touch.
Hope to hear from you soon.
Let me/us have your news.

Convite de casamento

Modelo de convite

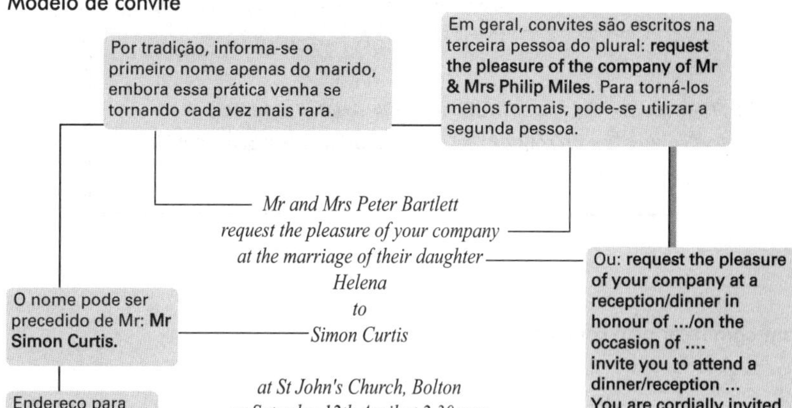

Por tradição, informa-se o primeiro nome apenas do marido, embora essa prática venha se tornando cada vez mais rara.

Em geral, convites são escritos na terceira pessoa do plural: **request the pleasure of the company of Mr & Mrs Philip Miles.** Para torná-los menos formais, pode-se utilizar a segunda pessoa.

Mr and Mrs Peter Bartlett
request the pleasure of your company
at the marriage of their daughter
Helena
to
Simon Curtis

at St John's Church, Bolton
on Saturday 12th April at 2.30 p.m.
and afterwards at the reception
at the Crown Hotel

RSVP
11 York Road
Bolton BL2 3XR

O nome pode ser precedido de Mr: **Mr Simon Curtis.**

Endereço para resposta.

Ou: **request the pleasure of your company at a reception/dinner in honour of .../on the occasion of .... invite you to attend a dinner/reception ... You are cordially invited to attend...**

Pode-se especificar uma data: **Please RSVP by 12th March.** Ou: **Your RSVP would be appreciated by 12th March.**

Para aceitar o convite

Não é necessário datar ou assinar a resposta. Se o convite estiver na terceira pessoa do plural, a resposta também deve empregar a terceira pessoa: **Mr & Mrs Mark Payne thank Mr & Mrs Peter Bartlett for their kind invitation to the marriage of their daughter Helena on 12th April, and to the reception afterwards. They have great pleasure in accepting.**

A resposta deve ser escrita à mão.

We thank you for your kind invitation to the marriage of your daughter Helena on 12th April, and to the reception afterwards. We have great pleasure in accepting.

Ou: **It is with great/much pleasure that we/they accept.**

Para declinar do convite

Ou, na terceira pessoa do plural: **Mr and Mrs Crosbie thank Mr and Mrs Bartlett for their kind invitation to their daughter's wedding, and to the reception afterwards, but regret that they will be unable to attend.**

We thank you for the kind invitation to your daughter's wedding and to the reception afterwards, but regret that we are unable to attend.

Para agradecer pelo comparecimento

45 Talbot Road
Leeds
LS11 9KY

1st February 2002

Dear Chris and Natalie,

Ou: **bought us ...**

Thank you so much for the beautiful coffee set you sent us as a wedding present. You must come and visit next week so that you can be the first to enjoy them.

Ou: **We were both delighted you could come...; It was really nice to see you at the wedding.**

I was so glad that you could come to the wedding. It was nice to have all our friends and family there, even Uncle George! Give my thanks to Tom for the catering: he did us proud.

Ou: **Say thank you to ...**

We had a wonderful honeymoon in the Maldives and are now trying to settle down to work again. Let us known when is good for you to come to dinner.

Many thanks once again!

With much love,

Sheila & Sam

XXX

Reservas

Cada vez mais, reservas de passagens ou hotel são feitas pela internet e por e-mail. Toda reserva feita por telefone precisa ser confirmada por escrito.

Para fazer uma reserva

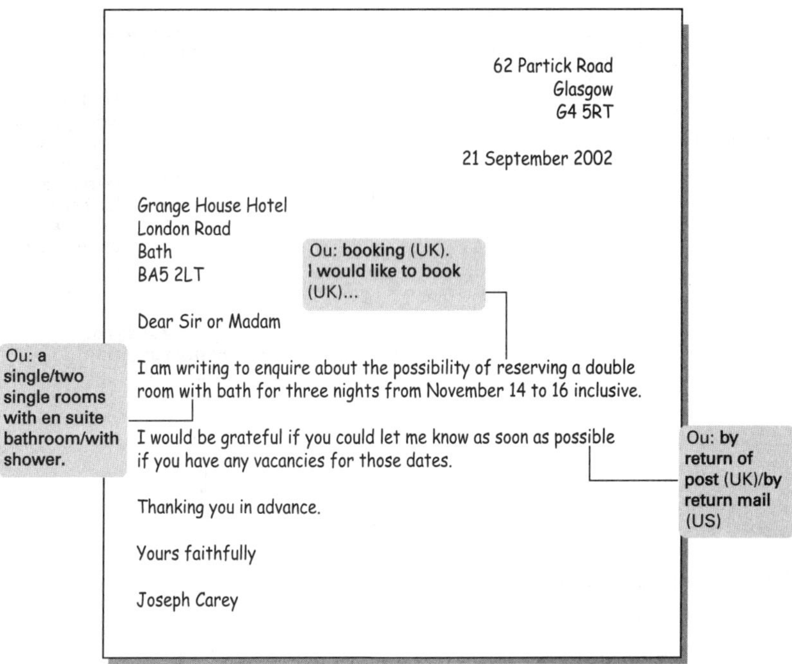

62 Partick Road
Glasgow
G4 5RT

21 September 2002

Grange House Hotel
London Road
Bath
BA5 2LT

Dear Sir or Madam

I am writing to enquire about the possibility of reserving a double room with bath for three nights from November 14 to 16 inclusive.

I would be grateful if you could let me know as soon as possible if you have any vacancies for those dates.

Thanking you in advance.

Yours faithfully

Joseph Carey

Ou: **booking** (UK). **I would like to book** (UK)...
Ou: **a single/two single rooms with en suite bathroom/with shower.**
Ou: **by return of post** (UK)/**by return mail** (US)

Para confirmar a reserva

622 Monroe Street
Philadelphia
PA 19145
USA

Tel: 215.617.1439

May 11, 2002

> Ou: **11 May 2002** (UK)

The Manager
The Pines Hotel
Denver
CO 80348
USA

Dear Sir:

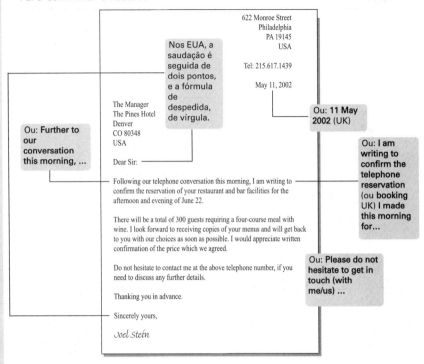

> Nos EUA, a saudação é seguida de dois pontos, e a fórmula de despedida, de vírgula.

Following our telephone conversation this morning, I am writing to confirm the reservation of your restaurant and bar facilities for the afternoon and evening of June 22.

> Ou: **Further to our conversation this morning, ...**

> Ou: **I am writing to confirm the telephone reservation** (ou **booking** UK) **I made this morning for...**

There will be a total of 300 guests requiring a four-course meal with wine. I look forward to receiving copies of your menus and will get back to you with our choices as soon as possible. I would appreciate written confirmation of the price which we agreed.

Do not hesitate to contact me at the above telephone number, if you need to discuss any further details.

> Ou: **Please do not hesitate to get in touch (with me/us) ...**

Thanking you in advance.

Sincerely yours,

Joel Stein

Para cancelar a reserva

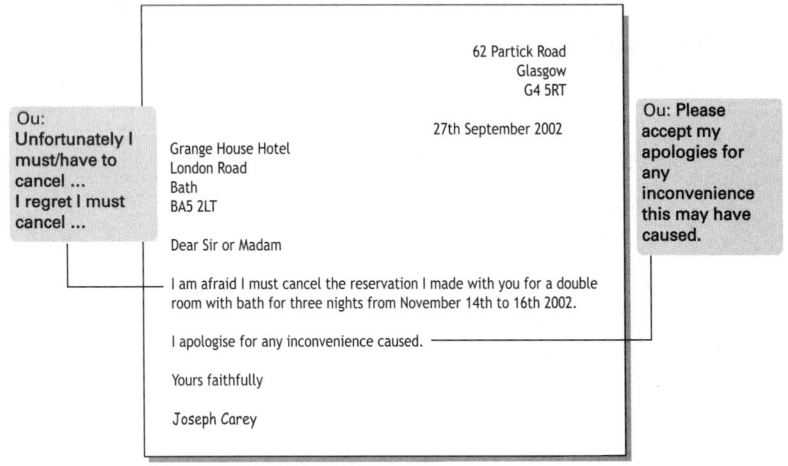

62 Partick Road
Glasgow
G4 5RT

27th September 2002

Grange House Hotel
London Road
Bath
BA5 2LT

Dear Sir or Madam

I am afraid I must cancel the reservation I made with you for a double room with bath for three nights from November 14th to 16th 2002.

> Ou: **Unfortunately I must/have to cancel ...**
> **I regret I must cancel ...**

I apologise for any inconvenience caused.

> Ou: **Please accept my apologies for any inconvenience this may have caused.**

Yours faithfully

Joseph Carey

Para solicitar informação

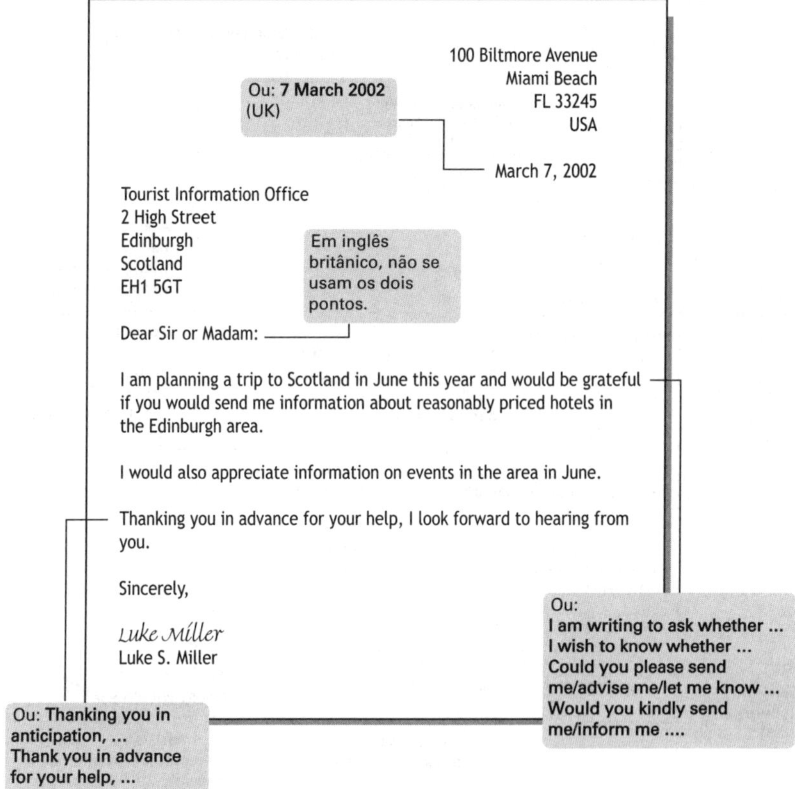

100 Biltmore Avenue
Miami Beach
FL 33245
USA

March 7, 2002

Tourist Information Office
2 High Street
Edinburgh
Scotland
EH1 5GT

Em inglês britânico, não se usam os dois pontos.

Dear Sir or Madam:

I am planning a trip to Scotland in June this year and would be grateful if you would send me information about reasonably priced hotels in the Edinburgh area.

I would also appreciate information on events in the area in June.

Thanking you in advance for your help, I look forward to hearing from you.

Sincerely,

Luke Miller
Luke S. Miller

Correspondência comercial

Para marcar reunião

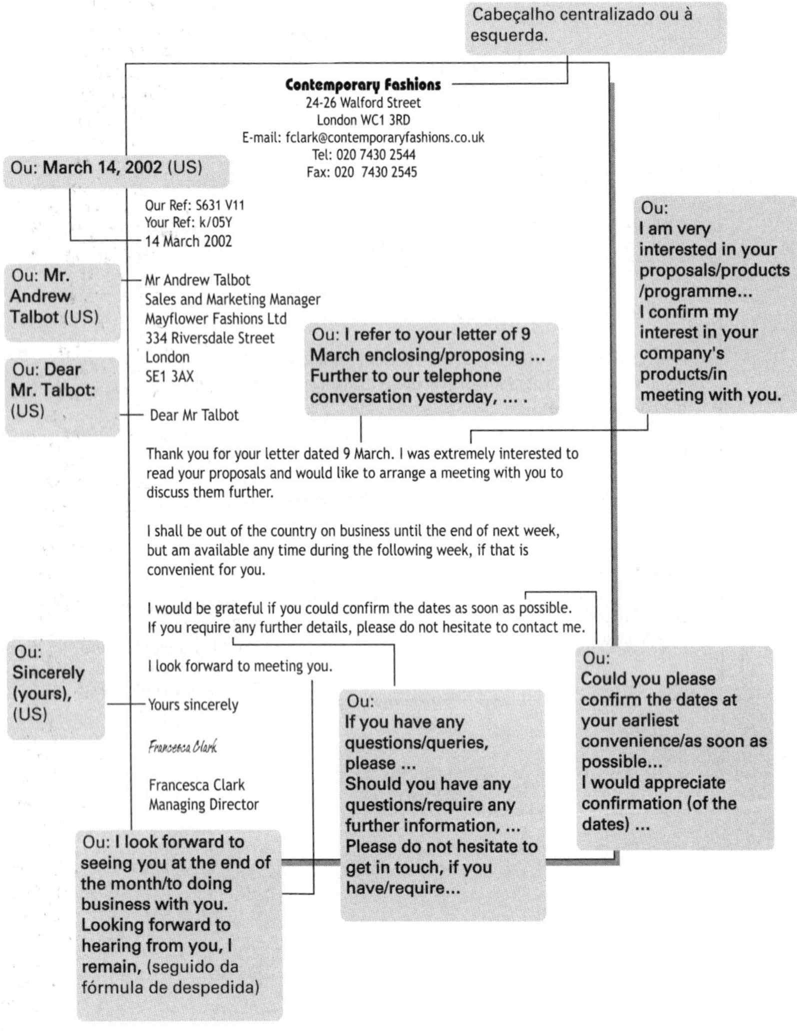

Cabeçalho centralizado ou à esquerda.

Contemporary Fashions
24-26 Walford Street
London WC1 3RD
E-mail: fclark@contemporaryfashions.co.uk
Tel: 020 7430 2544
Fax: 020 7430 2545

Ou: **March 14, 2002** (US)

Our Ref: S631 V11
Your Ref: k/05Y
14 March 2002

Ou: **Mr. Andrew Talbot** (US)

Mr Andrew Talbot
Sales and Marketing Manager
Mayflower Fashions Ltd
334 Riversdale Street
London
SE1 3AX

Ou: **Dear Mr. Talbot:** (US)

Dear Mr Talbot

Ou: **I refer to your letter of 9 March enclosing/proposing ... Further to our telephone conversation yesterday, ...**

Ou:
I am very interested in your proposals/products /programme...
I confirm my interest in your company's products/in meeting with you.

Thank you for your letter dated 9 March. I was extremely interested to read your proposals and would like to arrange a meeting with you to discuss them further.

I shall be out of the country on business until the end of next week, but am available any time during the following week, if that is convenient for you.

I would be grateful if you could confirm the dates as soon as possible. If you require any further details, please do not hesitate to contact me.

I look forward to meeting you.

Ou: **Sincerely (yours),** (US)

Yours sincerely

Francesca Clark

Francesca Clark
Managing Director

Ou:
If you have any questions/queries, please ...
Should you have any questions/require any further information, ...
Please do not hesitate to get in touch, if you have/require...

Ou:
Could you please confirm the dates at your earliest convenience/as soon as possible...
I would appreciate confirmation (of the dates) ...

Ou: **I look forward to seeing you at the end of the month/to doing business with you.**
Looking forward to hearing from you, I remain, (seguido da fórmula de despedida)

Para responder a um pedido de informação

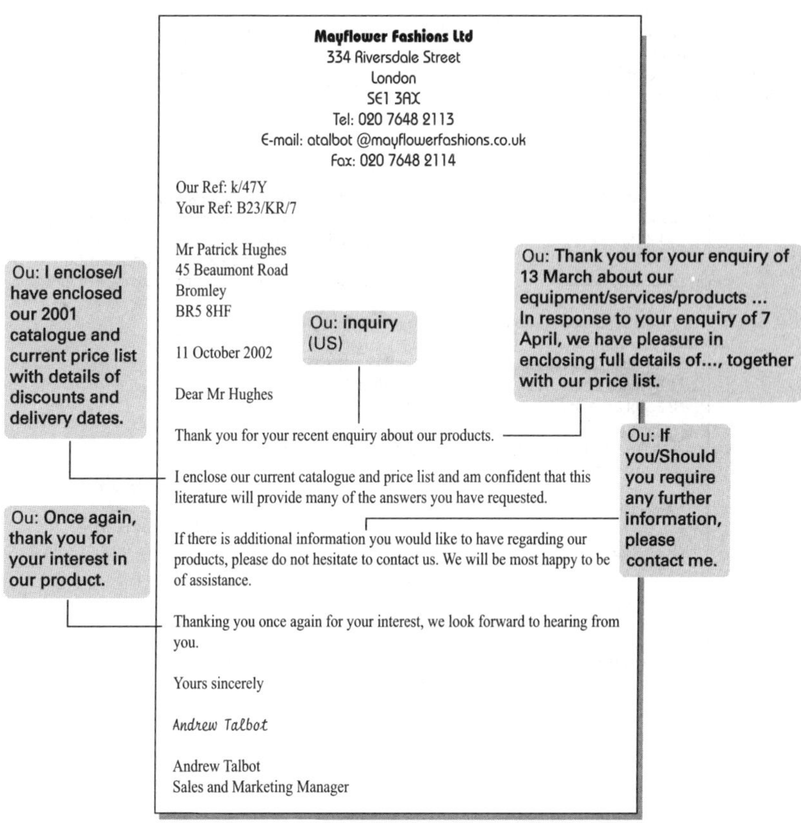

Mayflower Fashions Ltd
334 Riversdale Street
London
SE1 3AX
Tel: 020 7648 2113
E-mail: atalbot @mayflowerfashions.co.uk
Fax: 020 7648 2114

Our Ref: k/47Y
Your Ref: B23/KR/7

Mr Patrick Hughes
45 Beaumont Road
Bromley
BR5 8HF

11 October 2002

Dear Mr Hughes

Thank you for your recent enquiry about our products.

I enclose our current catalogue and price list and am confident that this literature will provide many of the answers you have requested.

If there is additional information you would like to have regarding our products, please do not hesitate to contact us. We will be most happy to be of assistance.

Thanking you once again for your interest, we look forward to hearing from you.

Yours sincerely

Andrew Talbot

Andrew Talbot
Sales and Marketing Manager

Ou: I enclose/I have enclosed our 2001 catalogue and current price list with details of discounts and delivery dates.
Ou: inquiry (US)
Ou: Thank you for your enquiry of 13 March about our equipment/services/products ... In response to your enquiry of 7 April, we have pleasure in enclosing full details of..., together with our price list.
Ou: If you/Should you require any further information, please contact me.
Ou: Once again, thank you for your interest in our product.

Para fazer um pedido de compra

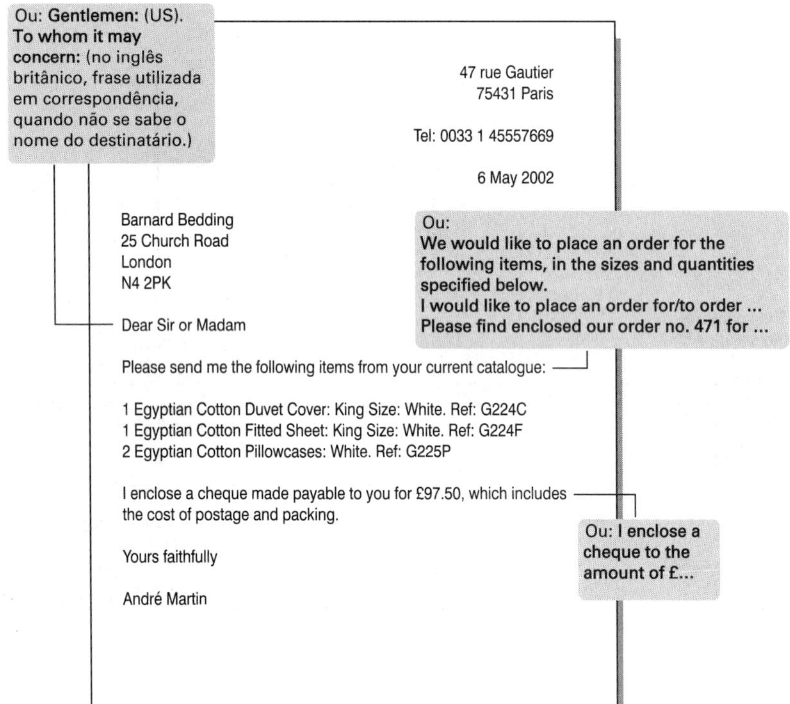

Ou: **Gentlemen:** (US). **To whom it may concern:** (no inglês britânico, frase utilizada em correspondência, quando não se sabe o nome do destinatário.)

47 rue Gautier
75431 Paris

Tel: 0033 1 45557669

6 May 2002

Barnard Bedding
25 Church Road
London
N4 2PK

Dear Sir or Madam

Please send me the following items from your current catalogue:

Ou:
We would like to place an order for the following items, in the sizes and quantities specified below.
I would like to place an order for/to order ...
Please find enclosed our order no. 471 for ...

1 Egyptian Cotton Duvet Cover: King Size: White. Ref: G224C
1 Egyptian Cotton Fitted Sheet: King Size: White. Ref: G224F
2 Egyptian Cotton Pillowcases: White. Ref: G225P

I enclose a cheque made payable to you for £97.50, which includes the cost of postage and packing.

Ou: **I enclose a cheque to the amount of £...**

Yours faithfully

André Martin

Emprego

Nos países de língua inglesa, cartas escritas com o intuito de candidatar-se a um emprego devem ser datilografadas ou impressas, a não ser quando em resposta a um anúnico solicitando que sejam escritas à mão.

Para candidatar-se a um estágio

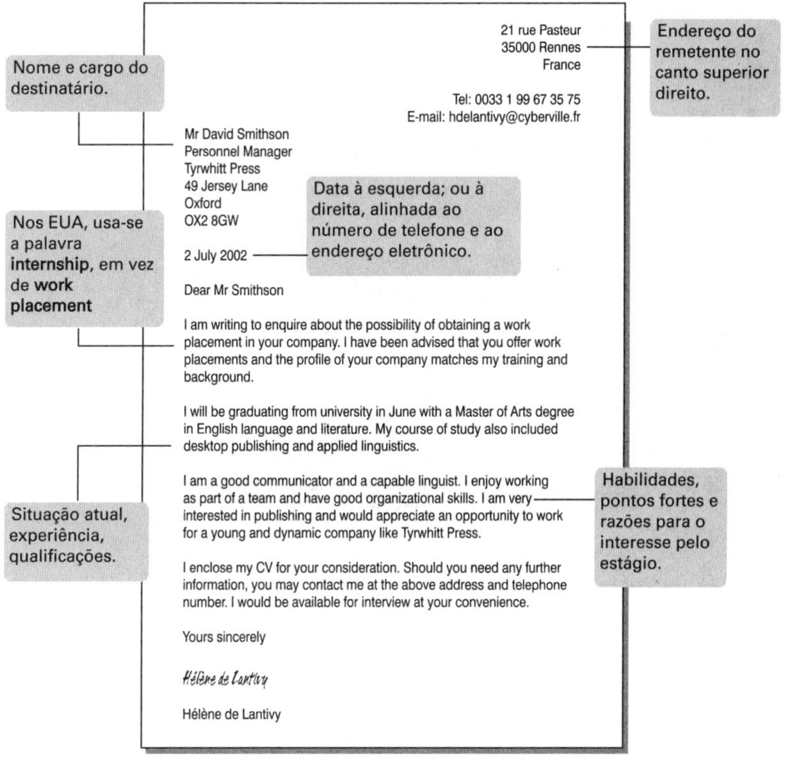

21 rue Pasteur
35000 Rennes
France

Tel: 0033 1 99 67 35 75
E-mail: hdelantivy@cyberville.fr

Mr David Smithson
Personnel Manager
Tyrwhitt Press
49 Jersey Lane
Oxford
OX2 8GW

2 July 2002

Dear Mr Smithson

I am writing to enquire about the possibility of obtaining a work placement in your company. I have been advised that you offer work placements and the profile of your company matches my training and background.

I will be graduating from university in June with a Master of Arts degree in English language and literature. My course of study also included desktop publishing and applied linguistics.

I am a good communicator and a capable linguist. I enjoy working as part of a team and have good organizational skills. I am very interested in publishing and would appreciate an opportunity to work for a young and dynamic company like Tyrwhitt Press.

I enclose my CV for your consideration. Should you need any further information, you may contact me at the above address and telephone number. I would be available for interview at your convenience.

Yours sincerely

Hélène de Lantivy

Hélène de Lantivy

Nome e cargo do destinatário.
Endereço do remetente no canto superior direito.
Data à esquerda; ou à direita, alinhada ao número de telefone e ao endereço eletrônico.
Nos EUA, usa-se a palavra **internship**, em vez de **work placement**
Situação atual, experiência, qualificações.
Habilidades, pontos fortes e razões para o interesse pelo estágio.

Para saber sobre vagas

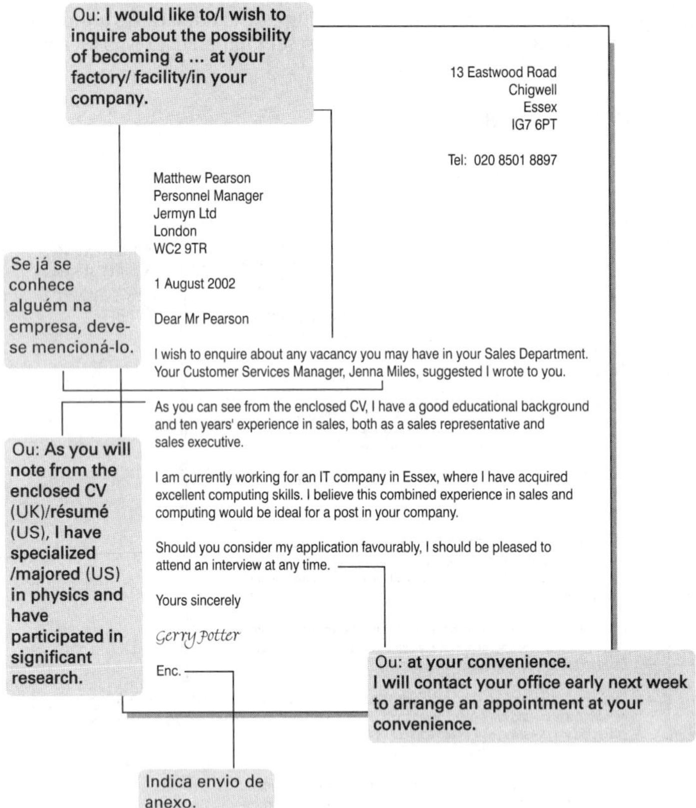

Ou: I would like to/I wish to inquire about the possibility of becoming a ... at your factory/ facility/in your company.
Se já se conhece alguém na empresa, deve-se mencioná-lo.
Ou: As you will note from the enclosed CV (UK)/résumé (US), I have specialized /majored (US) in physics and have participated in significant research.
Ou: at your convenience. I will contact your office early next week to arrange an appointment at your convenience.
Indica envio de anexo.

13 Eastwood Road
Chigwell
Essex
IG7 6PT

Tel: 020 8501 8897

Matthew Pearson
Personnel Manager
Jermyn Ltd
London
WC2 9TR

1 August 2002

Dear Mr Pearson

I wish to enquire about any vacancy you may have in your Sales Department. Your Customer Services Manager, Jenna Miles, suggested I wrote to you.

As you can see from the enclosed CV, I have a good educational background and ten years' experience in sales, both as a sales representative and sales executive.

I am currently working for an IT company in Essex, where I have acquired excellent computing skills. I believe this combined experience in sales and computing would be ideal for a post in your company.

Should you consider my application favourably, I should be pleased to attend an interview at any time.

Yours sincerely

Gerry Potter

Enc.

Para responder a um anúncio de jornal

12 Beaconsfield Street
London
W1 9JB

Tel: 020 7580 7095

Mr Nathan Richards
Chief Analyst
Pritchard Investments
Albert Street
London EC1 2KM

31 May 2002

Dear Mr Richards

Financial Analyst

I would like to apply for the above post as advertised in "The Financial Times" of 25 May, and I enclose my CV for your attention.

As you can see from my CV, I am an experienced financial analyst and consultant, having worked extensively in this sector in both London and Frankfurt. I am currently looking for a position that will allow me to develop my skills and experience in a dynamic environment such as Pritchard Investments.

I believe that my financial and academic background would be of benefit to your company. Should you consider me suitable for the post, I can provide the names of three referees.

I thank you for your consideration and remain at your disposal for any further information. I look forward to meeting you in the near future.

Your sincerely

Michael Griffin

Michael Griffin

Enc.

Ou: I would like to apply for the above post as recently advertised in the July issue of.../which was advertised in today's "Daily Post". I am writing to apply for the above post/for the post of ... (as) advertised in .... I am writing in response to your advertisement in ... for ... I would like to be considered for the above post which your company advertised in ...

Assunto da carta: função ou cargo.

Ou: **and (I) enclose my (current) CV** (UK)/**résumé** (US) **for your consideration.**

Ou:
Thank you for considering my application. If you would like to schedule an interview, please call me at .... I will be available at your convenience.
I would appreciate the chance to meet you (UK)/**meet with you** (US).
You may reach me at the above telephone number or e-mail address.

Ou: **I look forward to talking with you/to discussing matters with you (at a future interview).**

Frases úteis:

I know how to/I can operate a cash register/computer/power equipment.
I am computer literate/a good communicator/a good organizer.
I am a capable linguist/can speak fluent English and German.
I have good computer/IT/language/editing/communication/organisational skills.
I can learn new tasks and enjoy/can accept a challenge.
I enjoy working/can work with a variety of people.
I work well in team, and can also work under pressure.
I perform well under stress/am good with difficult customers.
I can handle multiple tasks simultaneously.

Curriculum Vitae

Recém-formado, com alguma experiência (UK)

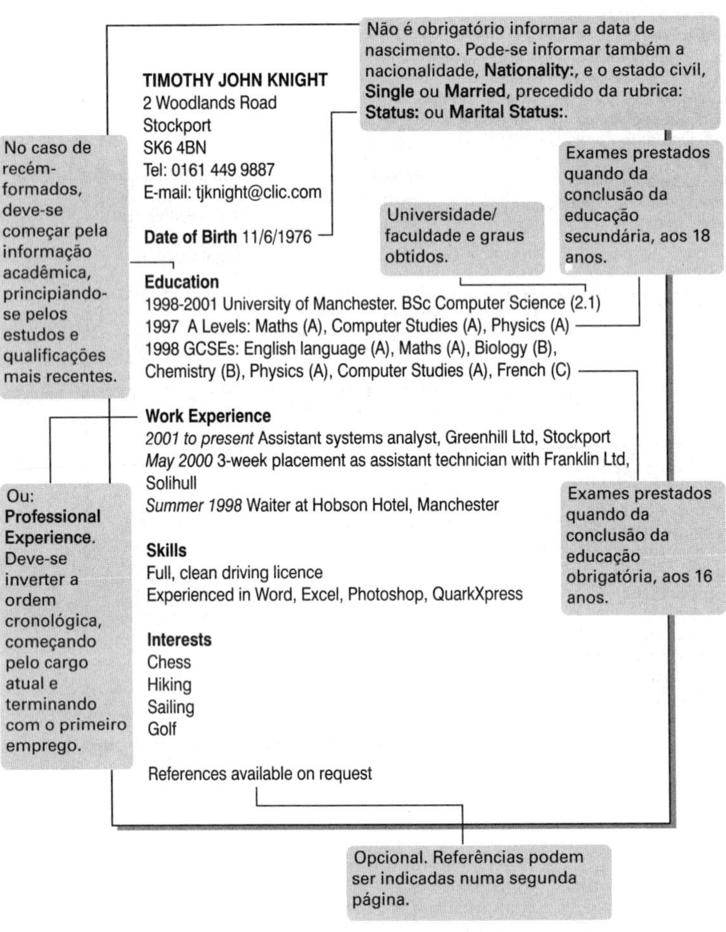

Não é obrigatório informar a data de nascimento. Pode-se informar também a nacionalidade, **Nationality:**, e o estado civil, **Single** ou **Married**, precedido da rubrica: **Status:** ou **Marital Status:**.
No caso de recém-formados, deve-se começar pela informação acadêmica, principiando-se pelos estudos e qualificações mais recentes.
Exames prestados quando da conclusão da educação secundária, aos 18 anos.
Universidade/ faculdade e graus obtidos.
Ou: **Professional Experience.** Deve-se inverter a ordem cronológica, começando pelo cargo atual e terminando com o primeiro emprego.
Exames prestados quando da conclusão da educação obrigatória, aos 16 anos.
Opcional. Referências podem ser indicadas numa segunda página.

TIMOTHY JOHN KNIGHT
2 Woodlands Road
Stockport
SK6 4BN
Tel: 0161 449 9887
E-mail: tjknight@clic.com

Date of Birth 11/6/1976

Education
1998-2001 University of Manchester. BSc Computer Science (2.1)
1997 A Levels: Maths (A), Computer Studies (A), Physics (A)
1998 GCSEs: English language (A), Maths (A), Biology (B), Chemistry (B), Physics (A), Computer Studies (A), French (C)

Work Experience
2001 to present Assistant systems analyst, Greenhill Ltd, Stockport
May 2000 3-week placement as assistant technician with Franklin Ltd, Solihull
Summer 1998 Waiter at Hobson Hotel, Manchester

Skills
Full, clean driving licence
Experienced in Word, Excel, Photoshop, QuarkXpress

Interests
Chess
Hiking
Sailing
Golf

References available on request

Cargo de gerência (UK)

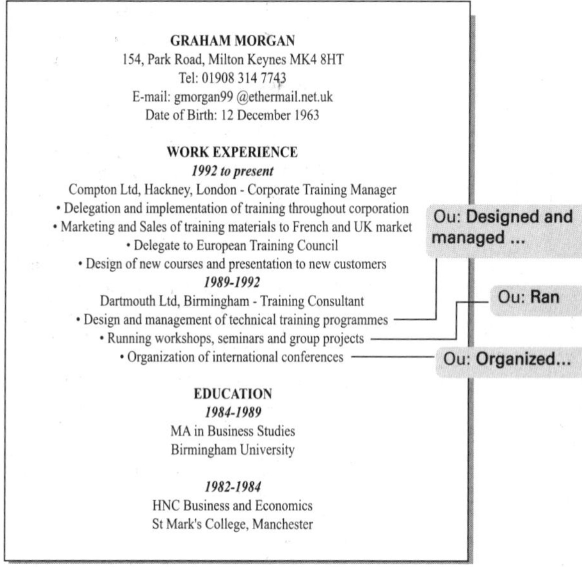

GRAHAM MORGAN
154, Park Road, Milton Keynes MK4 8HT
Tel: 01908 314 7743
E-mail: gmorgan99 @ethermail.net.uk
Date of Birth: 12 December 1963

WORK EXPERIENCE
1992 to present
Compton Ltd, Hackney, London - Corporate Training Manager
• Delegation and implementation of training throughout corporation
• Marketing and Sales of training materials to French and UK market
• Delegate to European Training Council
• Design of new courses and presentation to new customers
1989-1992
Dartmouth Ltd, Birmingham - Training Consultant
• Design and management of technical training programmes
• Running workshops, seminars and group projects
• Organization of international conferences

EDUCATION
1984-1989
MA in Business Studies
Birmingham University

1982-1984
HNC Business and Economics
St Mark's College, Manchester

Recém-formado, com alguma experiência (US)

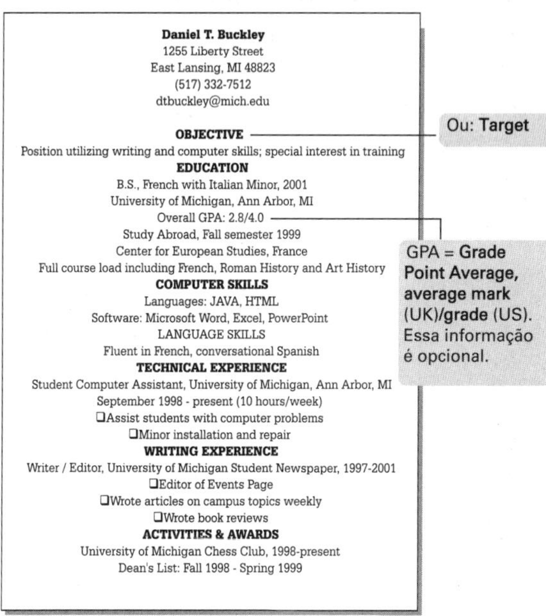

Daniel T. Buckley
1255 Liberty Street
East Lansing, MI 48823
(517) 332-7512
dtbuckley@mich.edu

OBJECTIVE
Position utilizing writing and computer skills; special interest in training
EDUCATION
B.S., French with Italian Minor, 2001
University of Michigan, Ann Arbor, MI
Overall GPA: 2.8/4.0
Study Abroad, Fall semester 1999
Center for European Studies, France
Full course load including French, Roman History and Art History
COMPUTER SKILLS
Languages: JAVA, HTML
Software: Microsoft Word, Excel, PowerPoint
LANGUAGE SKILLS
Fluent in French, conversational Spanish
TECHNICAL EXPERIENCE
Student Computer Assistant, University of Michigan, Ann Arbor, MI
September 1998 - present (10 hours/week)
❑Assist students with computer problems
❑Minor installation and repair
WRITING EXPERIENCE
Writer / Editor, University of Michigan Student Newspaper, 1997-2001
❑Editor of Events Page
❑Wrote articles on campus topics weekly
❑Wrote book reviews
ACTIVITIES & AWARDS
University of Michigan Chess Club, 1998-present
Dean's List: Fall 1998 - Spring 1999

Cargo de gerência (US)

TESSA PARKS
437 West 94th Street,
Chicago, IL 60637
(733) 702-1336
tessaparks@chicol.com

OBJECTIVE
Product Designer/Manager

EXPERIENCE

Computer Consultant and Systems Designer, Oakwood Inc., Chicago, IL, 1994-present
Troubleshoot hardware and software problems
Design and test new operating systems
Head up large team of consultants

Assistant Systems Consultant, Jones Davis Inc., Springfield, IL, 1990-1994
Created Web pages and customized computer systems for clients in the Springfield area

Intern, Roseberry Inc., Chicago, IL, June - August 1990
Worked as software design engineer intern.

EDUCATION
Bachelor of Science Degree in Computer Science, May 1990
University of Chicago, Chicago, IL

COMPUTER SKILLS
Languagues and Software : B, CC, Java, HTML, Excel, Word
Operating Systems : Unix, Windows, Mac OS

ACTIVITIES
Society of Manufacturing Engineers
Aircraft Owners and Pilots Association

Ou: Work Experience Employment History.

Quando a experiência profissional for mais relevante, não é necessário detalhar a formação acadêmica.

E-mail

Como o e-mail é uma forma bastante rápida de comunicação, o estilo das mensagens é, em geral, informal e telegráfico, contendo muitas abreviações e acrônimos.

As convenções que regem a comunicação pela internet - a chamada netiqueta - recomendam que não se escrevam mensagens em letras maiúsculas, pois isso é entendido como sinal de raiva.

Em geral, não se empregam as formas tradicionais de saudação (**Dear ...**). Quando se conhece bem o destinatário da mensagem, pode-se iniciá-la com uma saudação informal, **Hello** ou **Hi**, seguida do primeiro nome da pessoa em questão.

Na empresa

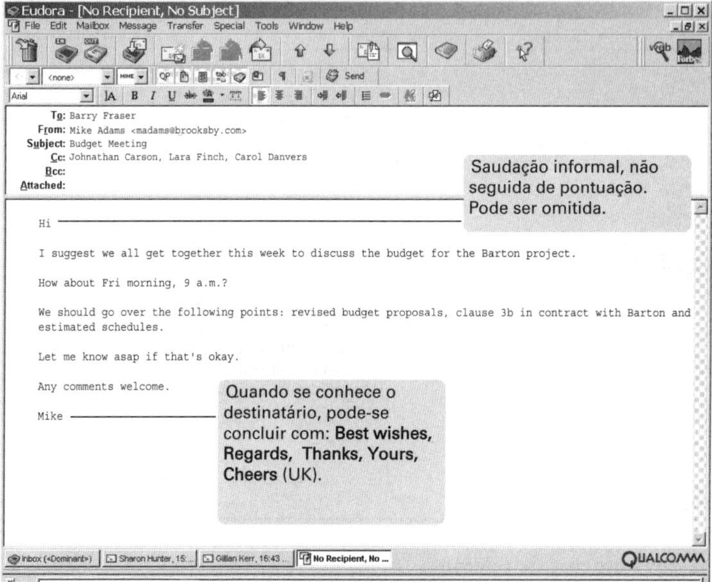

Entre empresas

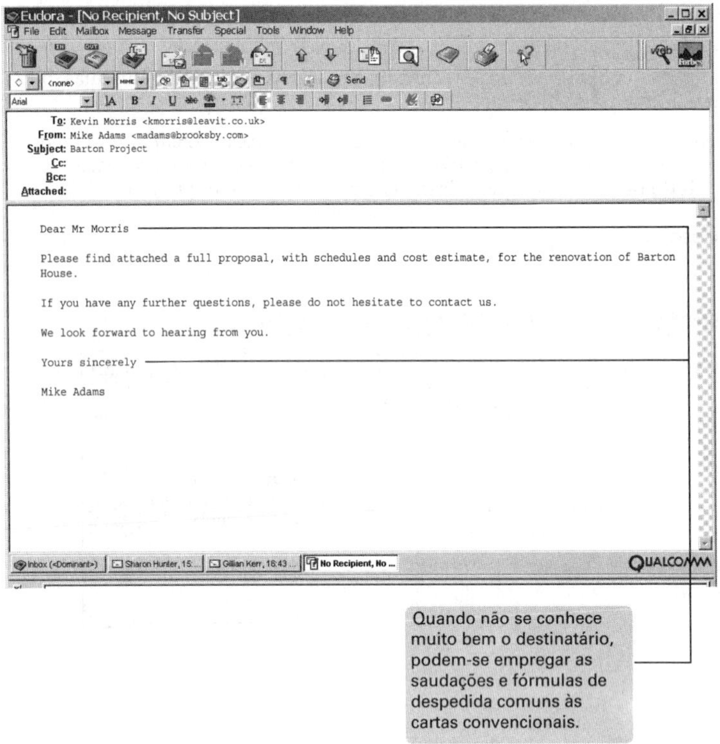

Eudora - [No Recipient, No Subject]

To: Kevin Morris <kmorris@leavit.co.uk>
From: Mike Adams <madams@brooksby.com>
Subject: Barton Project
Cc:
Bcc:
Attached:

Dear Mr Morris

Please find attached a full proposal, with schedules and cost estimate, for the renovation of Barton House.

If you have any further questions, please do not hesitate to contact us.

We look forward to hearing from you.

Yours sincerely

Mike Adams

Quando não se conhece muito bem o destinatário, podem-se empregar as saudações e fórmulas de despedida comuns às cartas convencionais.

Ao telefone

Pronúncia dos números de telefone:

20995 = Two oh double nine five (UK)
Two zero double nine five (US)

Frases típicas

Para pedir informação à telefonista:

- Can I have directory enquiries (UK)/directory assistance (US) please?
- I'm trying to get through to a London number.
- What is the (country) code for Canada?
- How do I get an outside line?

Para chamar alguém:
Hello,
- could I speak to ...?
- can I speak to ...?
- I'd like to speak to ...
- (could I have) extension 593 please?

Para atender a uma chamada:
- Robert McQueen speaking, can I help you?
- Hello, this is ...
- Yes, speaking *(confirmando que se é a pessoa chamada)*
- Hold on/hold please, I'll (just) get him/her.
- I'm sorry, he's/she's not here. Can I take a message?
- I'm afraid he's away on business/out of the office/off sick/on holiday/on vacation (US)

Para deixar um recado
Na secretária eletrônica:
- I'm returning your call...
- I'll be in London next week, perhaps we can...
- I'd like to talk to you about...
- Could you call me back, so we can discuss...?

Com outra pessoa:
- Could you ask him/her to call me on ...?
- Could you tell him/her I won't be able to...?
- I'll call back later.
- I need to speak to ... urgently
- Please ask him/her to confirm.... Thank you.

Para entender melhor:
- Could you spell that please?
- Could you speak a bit more slowly please?
- I'm sorry I didn't catch that. Could you repeat that please?
- Let me check, 11 a.m. Wednesday 10th ... Yes, that's fine.

Para concluir a chamada:
- Thank you, I look forward to seeing you on Wednesday. Goodbye.
- Thank you for your help.

Mensagem de secretária eletrônica:
- We are unable to take your call at the moment/I am not here at the moment. Please leave a message after the tone.

Portuguese Communication Guide

Letters

In Portuguese, informal letters to friends or relatives do not follow a very rigid pattern. But commercial letters and letters that require more formality are written according to given formats and rules, depending on their purpose. There are also specific ways for heading correspondence and addressing envelopes to given posts and authorities, as well as specific modes of address for a specific authority.

Beginnings and endings of formal letters

When you know the name of the person you are writing to:	*Endings:*
Prezado sr. Antonio Prezada sra. Carmem	Atenciosamente Muito atenciosamente Cordialmente Cordiais saudações Respeitosamente
When you do not know whether it is a man or woman that you are writing to:	
Prezado sr(a).	
When you are writing to a company or organization:	
Prezados senhores	

This is the abbreviation for **senhor(a)**. In Portuguese, pronouns agree with gender (masculine or feminine) and number (singular and plural).

Letters to authorities

In the case of authorities, letters should be headed and addressed according to the following conventions:

Presidents, governors, mayors, senators, deputies, councillors, ministers, ambassadors, judges, high-ranking military (general, admiral, marshal), university rectors:	*Pronouns of address:*
Exmo. Sr. Exmo. Sr. Governador Exmo. Sr. Deputado Exmo. Sr. Marechal Exmo. Sr. Ministro	V. Exa. (Vossa Excelência), *with verbs and pronouns inflected in the third person*
Other authorities: Ilmo. Sr. Ilma. Sra.	V.Sa. (Vossa Senhoria), senhor, senhora, *with verbs and pronouns inflected in the third person*

Informal letters

To friends and relatives, letters may start as follows:	*And end as follows:*
Querido Pedro	Um abraço
Meu querido Pedro	Um grande abraço
Querida Laura	Seu sobrinho/sua sobrinha
Minha querida Laura	
Queridos Pedro e Laura	*More affectionately:*
Meus queridos	Um beijo
Minha cara	Um grande beijo
Querido irmão/querida irmã	Muitos beijos
Querida mamãe/querido papai	Abraços e beijos
Queridos pais	Com muito carinho
Querido tio/querida tia	Com saudades
Queridos tios	Seu/sua
Caro/cara	
	More formally:
Or simply:	Com votos de
Pedro	Sinceramente
Laura	

Letters to friends

Below are two examples of letters to friends:

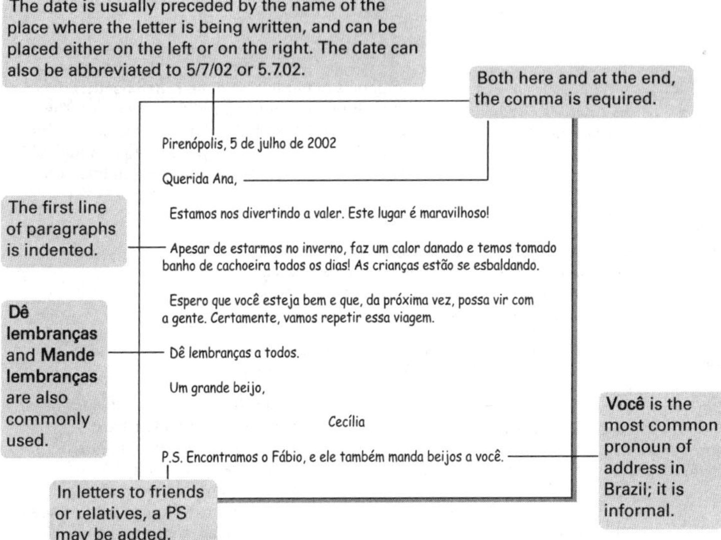

The date is usually preceded by the name of the place where the letter is being written, and can be placed either on the left or on the right. The date can also be abbreviated to 5/7/02 or 5.7.02.
Both here and at the end, the comma is required.
Pirenópolis, 5 de julho de 2002
Querida Ana,
The first line of paragraphs is indented.
Estamos nos divertindo a valer. Este lugar é maravilhoso!
Apesar de estarmos no inverno, faz um calor danado e temos tomado banho de cachoeira todos os dias! As crianças estão se esbaldando.
Espero que você esteja bem e que, da próxima vez, possa vir com a gente. Certamente, vamos repetir essa viagem.
Dê lembranças and **Mande lembranças** are also commonly used.
Dê lembranças a todos.
Um grande beijo,
Cecília
P.S. Encontramos o Fábio, e ele também manda beijos a você.
Você is the most common pronoun of address in Brazil; it is informal.
In letters to friends or relatives, a PS may be added.

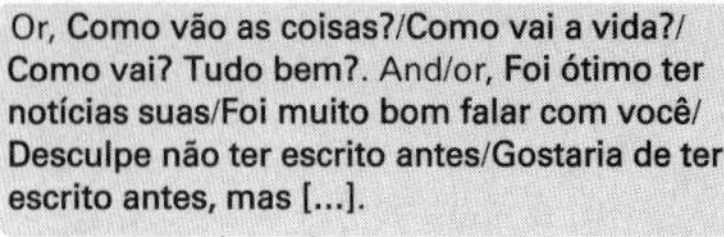
Or, **Como vão as coisas?/Como vai a vida?/ Como vai? Tudo bem?**. And/or, **Foi ótimo ter notícias suas/Foi muito bom falar com você/ Desculpe não ter escrito antes/Gostaria de ter escrito antes, mas [...]**.

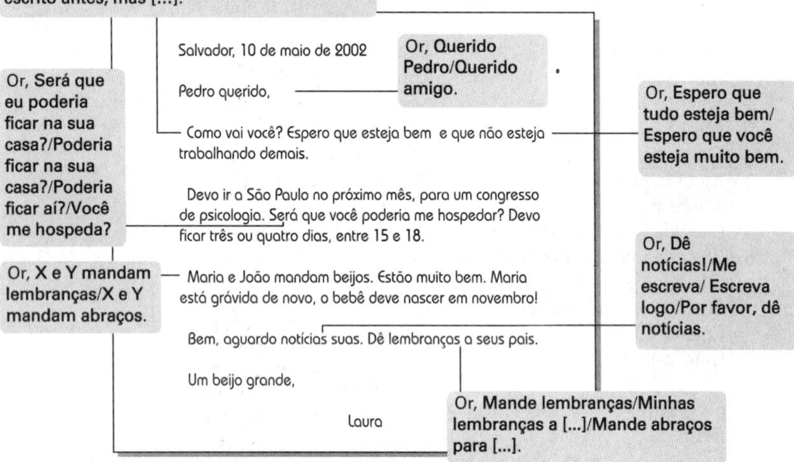
Salvador, 10 de maio de 2002

Pedro querido,

Como vai você? Espero que esteja bem e que não esteja trabalhando demais.

Devo ir a São Paulo no próximo mês, para um congresso de psicologia. Será que você poderia me hospedar? Devo ficar três ou quatro dias, entre 15 e 18.

Maria e João mandam beijos. Estão muito bem. Maria está grávida de novo, o bebê deve nascer em novembro!

Bem, aguardo notícias suas. Dê lembranças a seus pais.

Um beijo grande,

Laura

Or, **Querido Pedro/Querido amigo.**
Or, **Será que eu poderia ficar na sua casa?/Poderia ficar na sua casa?/Poderia ficar aí?/Você me hospeda?**
Or, **Espero que tudo esteja bem/ Espero que você esteja muito bem.**
Or, **X e Y mandam lembranças/X e Y mandam abraços.**
Or, **Dê notícias!/Me escreva/ Escreva logo/Por favor, dê notícias.**
Or, **Mande lembranças/Minhas lembranças a [...]/Mande abraços para [...].**

Commercial letters: format and language

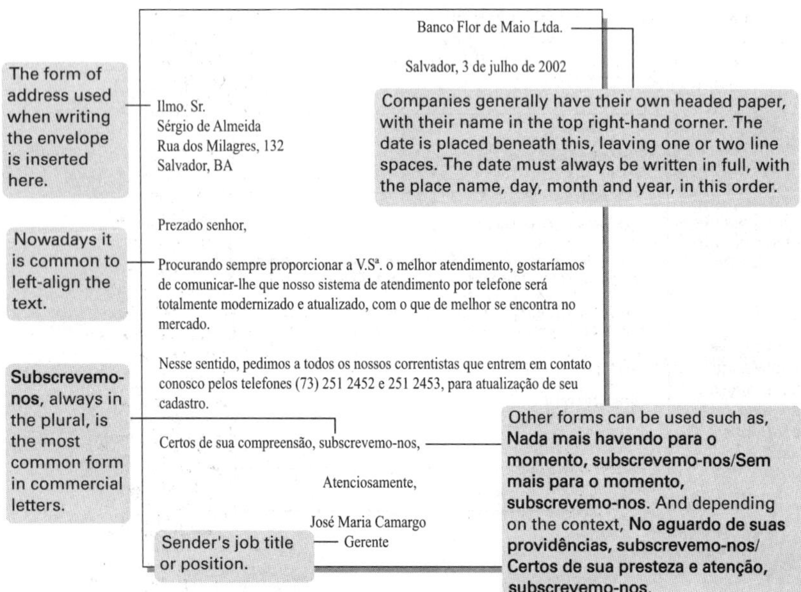
Banco Flor de Maio Ltda.

Salvador, 3 de julho de 2002

Ilmo. Sr.
Sérgio de Almeida
Rua dos Milagres, 132
Salvador, BA

Prezado senhor,

Procurando sempre proporcionar a V.S^{a}. o melhor atendimento, gostaríamos de comunicar-lhe que nosso sistema de atendimento por telefone será totalmente modernizado e atualizado, com o que de melhor se encontra no mercado.

Nesse sentido, pedimos a todos os nossos correntistas que entrem em contato conosco pelos telefones (73) 251 2452 e 251 2453, para atualização de seu cadastro.

Certos de sua compreensão, subscrevemo-nos,

Atenciosamente,

José Maria Camargo
Gerente

The form of address used when writing the envelope is inserted here.

Nowadays it is common to left-align the text.

Other forms can be used such as, **Nada mais havendo para o momento, subscrevemo-nos/Sem mais para o momento, subscrevemo-nos**. And depending on the context, **No aguardo de suas providências, subscrevemo-nos/ Certos de sua presteza e atenção, subscrevemo-nos**.
Sender's job title or position.

Requerimentos

A *requerimento* is a letter of petition to an authority. This also follows more rigid rules in terms of the structure and layout of the text.

This is the more commonly used form of address to people in this position; it is followed by the name of the institution. It could be, for instance, **Ilmo. Sr. Secretário da Saúde da Prefeitura do Município de São Paulo**, or **Ilmo. Sr. Diretor da Eletropaulo.**

Exmo. Sr. Reitor da Universidade Padre Manoel da Nóbrega

Mônica Batista, estudante do 3° ano da Faculdade de Economia desta Universidade, encontrando-se em sérias dificuldades financeiras, vem respeitosamente requerer a V. Exa. uma bolsa de estudo para que possa terminar seu curso.

Nestes termos,
pede deferimento.

Belo Horizonte, 5 de janeiro de 2002.

(Assinatura)

Wedding invitation

Sample invitation

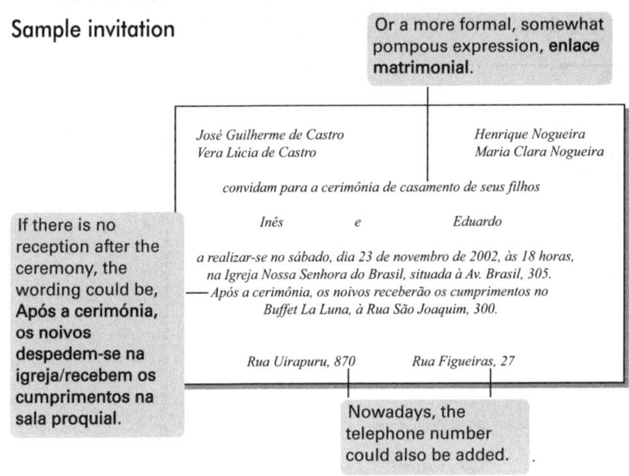

Or a more formal, somewhat pompous expression, enlace matrimonial.
José Guilherme de Castro
Vera Lúcia de Castro
Henrique Nogueira
Maria Clara Nogueira
convidam para a cerimônia de casamento de seus filhos
Inês e Eduardo
a realizar-se no sábado, dia 23 de novembro de 2002, às 18 horas, na Igreja Nossa Senhora do Brasil, situada à Av. Brasil, 305.
Após a cerimônia, os noivos receberão os cumprimentos no Buffet La Luna, à Rua São Joaquim, 300.
Rua Uirapuru, 870
Rua Figueiras, 27
If there is no reception after the ceremony, the wording could be, Após a cerimónia, os noivos despedem-se na igreja/recebem os cumprimentos na sala proquial.
Nowadays, the telephone number could also be added.

To thank someone for coming

Or, Muitíssimo agradecido/ Ficamos encantados com [...].

São Paulo, 2 de fevereiro de 2002

Queridos João e Maria,

Muito obrigado pelo lindo aparelho de café que vocês nos enviaram como presente de casamento. Venham nos visitar na próxima semana, para serem os primeiros a apreciá-lo.

Ficamos muito felizes com sua presença em nosso casamento. Adoramos ver todos os amigos e parentes, mesmo o tio Jorge!

Tivemos uma lua-de-mel deliciosa em Salvador e agora estamos tentando voltar à vida normal e ao trabalho. Avisem-nos sobre o melhor dia para vocês virem jantar conosco.

Muito obrigado mais uma vez,

Um grande beijo,

Inês e Eduardo

Or, Foi muito gostoso vê-los em nosso casamento.

Reservations

Travel and hotel reservations are increasingly being made by email or via the internet. However, reservations made by phone need to be confirmed in writing.

Making a reservation

Companies usually have their own headed notepaper, with their name or logo in the top right-hand corner. It is not common practice to write the sender's address in this spot; only the date.

São Paulo, 21 de setembro de 2002

Hotel Pitanga
Av. Ponta Negra, 450
Natal - Rio Grande do Norte

Prezados senhores,

Gostaria de reservar um apartamento para casal, com banheiro, para um período de três dias, de 14 a 16 de novembro.

Agradeceria se os senhores me respondessem o mais rápido possível sobre a disponibilidade de vagas nessas datas.

Desde já, agradeço sua atenção e subscrevo-me,

Atenciosamente,

Paula Moraes

Or, com cama de casal/um apartamento de solteiro/dois apartamentos de solteiro/uma suíte para casal/uma suíte para solteiro.

Confirming a reservation

São Paulo, 3 de julho de 2002

Ilmo. Sr.
Mário Loureiro
Gerente
Hotel Pinheiro

Prezado senhor,

De acordo com nossa conversa ao telefone esta manhã, escrevo para confirmar a reserva de seu restaurante para o dia 24 julho. Serão 300 pessoas, para três refeições. Assim que recebermos cópias de seu cardápio, entraremos em contato novamente para informá-lo de nossas escolhas. Gostaria que o senhor confirmasse por escrito o orçamento combinado.

Em caso de necessidade, queira entrar em contato comigo pelo telefone 7905643.

Desde já agradeço sua atenção,

Atenciosamente,

Miriam Muniz

Or, Não deixe de entrar em contato comigo pelo telefone [...] caso necessário.

Or, Certa(o) de sua atenção e pronto atendimento, subscrevo-me [...].

Cancelling a reservation

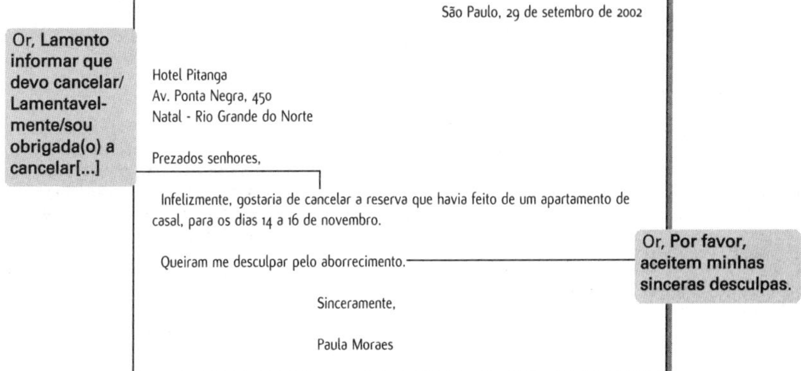

São Paulo, 29 de setembro de 2002

Hotel Pitanga
Av. Ponta Negra, 450
Natal - Rio Grande do Norte

Prezados senhores,

Infelizmente, gostaria de cancelar a reserva que havia feito de um apartamento de casal, para os dias 14 a 16 de novembro.

Queiram me desculpar pelo aborrecimento.

Sinceramente,

Paula Moraes

Or, Lamento informar que devo cancelar/ Lamentavelmente/sou obrigada(o) a cancelar[...]

Or, Por favor, aceitem minhas sinceras desculpas.

Requesting information

São Paulo, 11 de novembro de 2002

RioTour
Av. Copacabana, 50
Rio de Janeiro - RJ

Prezados senhores,

Tenho planos de fazer uma viagem ao Rio de Janeiro em dezembro, e gostaria de receber informações sobre hotéis com preços razoáveis.

Também gostaria de saber sobre eventos e festividades no Rio de Janeiro e cidades próximas nesse período.

Desde já, agradeço sua atenção e subscrevo-me,

Atenciosamente,

Marta Gomide

Or, **e gostaria de saber se/e agradeceria se vocês me enviassem informações sobre[...]**

Or, **sua ajuda.**

Business correspondence

Arranging a meeting

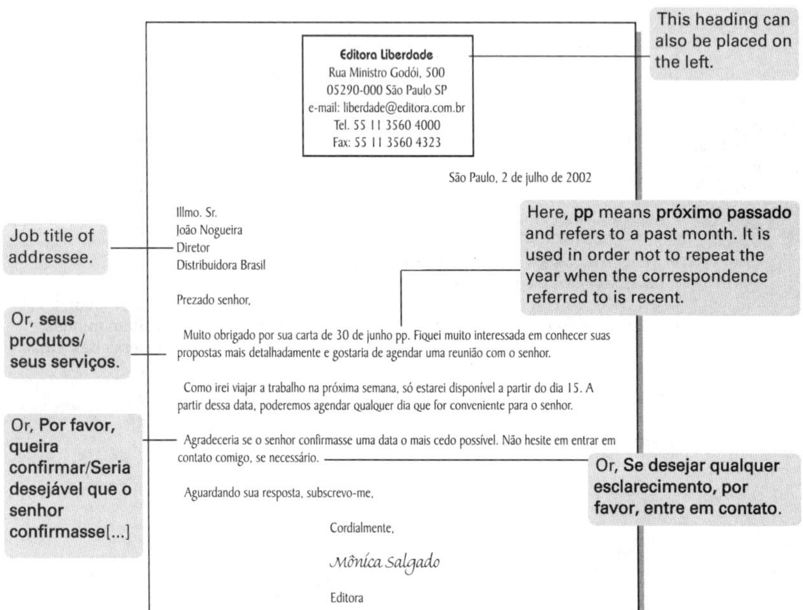

Editora Liberdade
Rua Ministro Godói, 500
05290-000 São Paulo SP
e-mail: liberdade@editora.com.br
Tel. 55 11 3560 4000
Fax: 55 11 3560 4323

São Paulo, 2 de julho de 2002

Illmo. Sr.
João Nogueira
Diretor
Distribuidora Brasil

Prezado senhor,

Muito obrigado por sua carta de 30 de junho pp. Fiquei muito interessada em conhecer suas propostas mais detalhadamente e gostaria de agendar uma reunião com o senhor.

Como irei viajar a trabalho na próxima semana, só estarei disponível a partir do dia 15. A partir dessa data, poderemos agendar qualquer dia que for conveniente para o senhor.

Agradeceria se o senhor confirmasse uma data o mais cedo possível. Não hesite em entrar em contato comigo, se necessário.

Aguardando sua resposta, subscrevo-me,

Cordialmente,

Mônica Salgado

Editora

This heading can also be placed on the left.
Job title of addressee.
Here, **pp** means **próximo passado** and refers to a past month. It is used in order not to repeat the year when the correspondence referred to is recent.
Or, **seus produtos/ seus serviços.**
Or, **Por favor, queira confirmar/Seria desejável que o senhor confirmasse[...]**
Or, **Se desejar qualquer esclarecimento, por favor, entre em contato.**

Placing an order

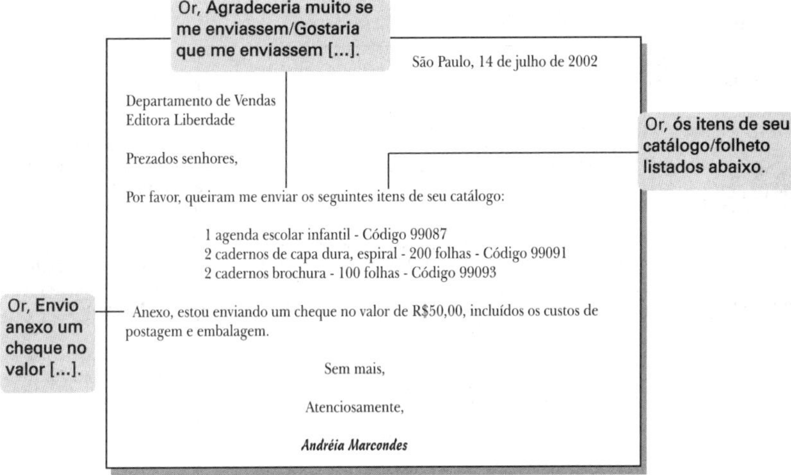

Or, Agradeceria muito se me enviassem/Gostaria que me enviassem [...].

São Paulo, 14 de julho de 2002

Departamento de Vendas
Editora Liberdade

Prezados senhores,

Or, ós itens de seu catálogo/folheto listados abaixo.

Por favor, queiram me enviar os seguintes itens de seu catálogo:

1 agenda escolar infantil - Código 99087
2 cadernos de capa dura, espiral - 200 folhas - Código 99091
2 cadernos brochura - 100 folhas - Código 99093

Or, Envio anexo um cheque no valor [...].

Anexo, estou enviando um cheque no valor de R$50,00, incluídos os custos de postagem e embalagem.

Sem mais,

Atenciosamente,

Andréia Marcondes

Replying to a request for information

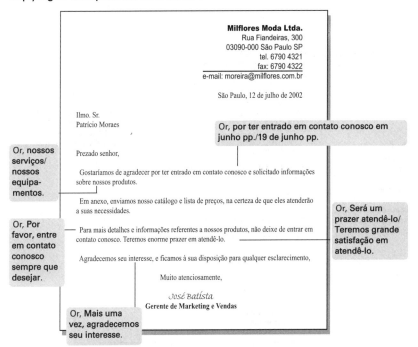

Milflores Moda Ltda.
Rua Fiandeiras, 300
03090-000 São Paulo SP
tel. 6790 4321
fax: 6790 4322
e-mail: moreira@milflores.com.br

São Paulo, 12 de julho de 2002

Ilmo. Sr.
Patrício Moraes

Or, por ter entrado em contato conosco em junho pp./19 de junho pp.

Prezado senhor,

Or, nossos serviços/ nossos equipamentos.

Gostaríamos de agradecer por ter entrado em contato conosco e solicitado informações sobre nossos produtos.

Em anexo, enviamos nosso catálogo e lista de preços, na certeza de que eles atenderão a suas necessidades.

Or, Por favor, entre em contato conosco sempre que desejar.

Para mais detalhes e informações referentes a nossos produtos, não deixe de entrar em contato conosco. Teremos enorme prazer em atendê-lo.

Or, Será um prazer atendê-lo/ Teremos grande satisfação em atendê-lo.

Agradecemos seu interesse, e ficamos à sua disposição para qualquer esclarecimento,

Muito atenciosamente,

José Batista
Gerente de Marketing e Vendas

Or, Mais uma vez, agradecemos seu interesse.

Employment

Making a speculative application

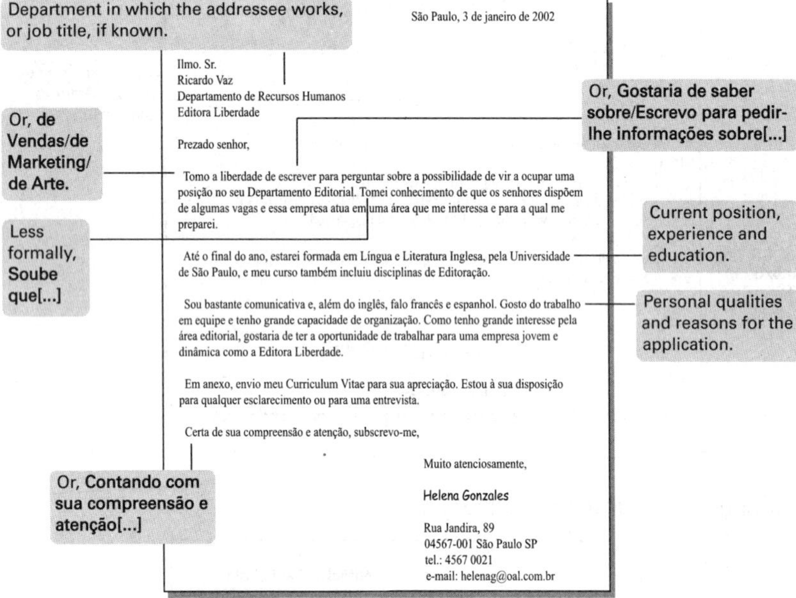

Department in which the addressee works, or job title, if known.
Or, de Vendas/de Marketing/ de Arte.
Less formally, Soube que[...]
Or, Gostaria de saber sobre/Escrevo para pedir-lhe informações sobre[...]
Current position, experience and education.
Personal qualities and reasons for the application.
Or, Contando com sua compreensão e atenção[...]

São Paulo, 3 de janeiro de 2002

Ilmo. Sr.
Ricardo Vaz
Departamento de Recursos Humanos
Editora Liberdade

Prezado senhor,

Tomo a liberdade de escrever para perguntar sobre a possibilidade de vir a ocupar uma posição no seu Departamento Editorial. Tomei conhecimento de que os senhores dispõem de algumas vagas e essa empresa atua em uma área que me interessa e para a qual me preparei.

Até o final do ano, estarei formada em Língua e Literatura Inglesa, pela Universidade de São Paulo, e meu curso também incluiu disciplinas de Editoração.

Sou bastante comunicativa e, além do inglês, falo francês e espanhol. Gosto do trabalho em equipe e tenho grande capacidade de organização. Como tenho grande interesse pela área editorial, gostaria de ter a oportunidade de trabalhar para uma empresa jovem e dinâmica como a Editora Liberdade.

Em anexo, envio meu Curriculum Vitae para sua apreciação. Estou à sua disposição para qualquer esclarecimento ou para uma entrevista.

Certa de sua compreensão e atenção, subscrevo-me,

Muito atenciosamente,

Helena Gonzales

Rua Jandira, 89
04567-001 São Paulo SP
tel.: 4567 0021
e-mail: helenag@oal.com.br

Enquiring about vacancies

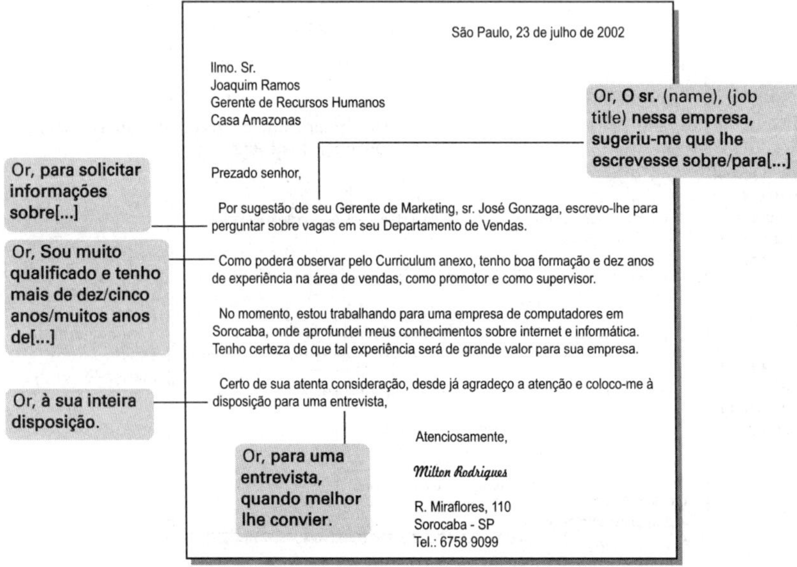

Or, O sr. (name), (job title) nessa empresa, sugeriu-me que lhe escrevesse sobre/para[...]
Or, para solicitar informações sobre[...]
Or, Sou muito qualificado e tenho mais de dez/cinco anos/muitos anos de[...]
Or, à sua inteira disposição.
Or, para uma entrevista, quando melhor lhe convier.

São Paulo, 23 de julho de 2002

Ilmo. Sr.
Joaquim Ramos
Gerente de Recursos Humanos
Casa Amazonas

Prezado senhor,

Por sugestão de seu Gerente de Marketing, sr. José Gonzaga, escrevo-lhe para perguntar sobre vagas em seu Departamento de Vendas.

Como poderá observar pelo Curriculum anexo, tenho boa formação e dez anos de experiência na área de vendas, como promotor e como supervisor.

No momento, estou trabalhando para uma empresa de computadores em Sorocaba, onde aprofundei meus conhecimentos sobre internet e informática. Tenho certeza de que tal experiência será de grande valor para sua empresa.

Certo de sua atenta consideração, desde já agradeço a atenção e coloco-me à disposição para uma entrevista,

Atenciosamente,

Milton Rodrigues

R. Miraflores, 110
Sorocaba - SP
Tel.: 6758 9099

Replying to a job advertisement

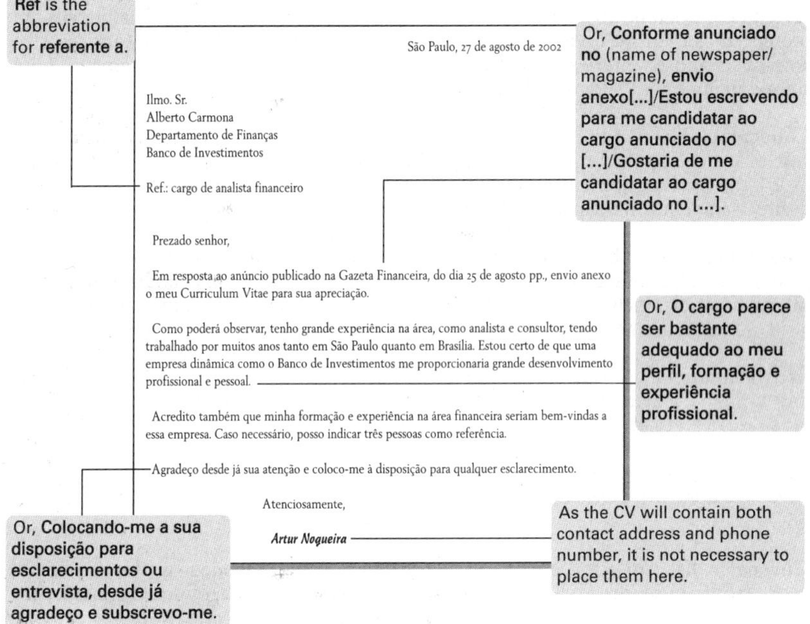
São Paulo, 27 de agosto de 2002

Ilmo. Sr.
Alberto Carmona
Departamento de Finanças
Banco de Investimentos

Ref.: cargo de analista financeiro

Prezado senhor,

Em resposta ao anúncio publicado na Gazeta Financeira, do dia 25 de agosto pp., envio anexo o meu Curriculum Vitae para sua apreciação.

Como poderá observar, tenho grande experiência na área, como analista e consultor, tendo trabalhado por muitos anos tanto em São Paulo quanto em Brasília. Estou certo de que uma empresa dinâmica como o Banco de Investimentos me proporcionaria grande desenvolvimento profissional e pessoal.

Acredito também que minha formação e experiência na área financeira seriam bem-vindas a essa empresa. Caso necessário, posso indicar três pessoas como referência.

Agradeço desde já sua atenção e coloco-me à disposição para qualquer esclarecimento.

Atenciosamente,

Artur Nogueira

Ref is the abbreviation for **referente a.**
Or, **Conforme anunciado no** (name of newspaper/magazine), **envio anexo[...]/Estou escrevendo para me candidatar ao cargo anunciado no [...]/Gostaria de me candidatar ao cargo anunciado no [...].**
Or, **O cargo parece ser bastante adequado ao meu perfil, formação e experiência profissional.**
Or, **Colocando-me a sua disposição para esclarecimentos ou entrevista, desde já agradeço e subscrevo-me.**
As the CV will contain both contact address and phone number, it is not necessary to place them here.

Useful phrases:

Tenho experiência em/no/na/com [...].
Sou bastante comunicativo(a)/muito organizado(a).
Sou fluente/Tenho fluência em inglês/espanhol/alemão/francês.
Tenho bons conhecimentos de informática/editoração/telecomunicações.
Estou apto a aprender novas tarefas/aceitar novos desafios.
Gosto de trabalhar em equipe/com pessoas diferentes.
Sou competente em [...].
Tenho competência para lidar com várias tarefas simultaneamente.
Meus pontos fortes são [...].
Tenho grande capacidade de organização/planejamento.

Currículum Vitae or Currículo

CVs nowadays tend to be quite concise and objective documents. Personal details are presented as clearly as possible in order to facilitate their assessment by prospective employers and/or interviewers. As a rule, apart from the candidate's experience, CVs should include the following details in the given order.

Cabeçalho: This is the first section on the CV. It displays the candidate's name, the title of the job applied for and the expected salary range. Note that it is advisable to insert up to three job titles related to the candidate's profile, and to indicate the desired salary, noting particularly the minimum acceptable wage.

Dados pessoais: This section displays the candidate's place and date of birth, full postal address, contact numbers (phone, mobile and/or fax), email address and marital status. It can include, for instance, the candidate's hobbies, whether or not he/she is a smoker, and whether he/she would accept to travel or even move for work.

Escolaridade: This shows the candidate's level of schooling and training, indicates any university attended, as well as listing qualifications, specializations and post-graduate degrees attained.

Idiomas: Languages spoken by the candidate, as well as the relevant level in each, need to be shown; levels can include fluent, spoken, spoken but not written, and so on.

Cursos: A list can also be given of any other courses attended by the candidate, apart from those already described under **Escolaridade**. These could include, for instance, professional and/or redeployment courses.

Experiência profissional: This section lists the posts held previously by the candidate, from the latest to the earliest, mentioning one or two past jobs or responsibilities of interest or relevance to the post applied for.

Habilidades/qualificações: This section describes the areas in which the candidate has the most aptitude and ability, and indicates the time spent acquiring each.

Capacitação profissional: A brief description is given here of the length of time the candidate has been working, the field he/she is currently working in, knowledge acquired, previously held posts, as well as training programmes and courses attended that are of relevance to his/her career.

Sample CV

It is important to date the CV or to indicate an update, such as **atualização: 15/07/02**, to show when the CV was either written or updated.

BERENICE BUENO

Analista de cobrança
Analista de orçamentos

15/07/2002

Mínimo aceitável: R$ 1.500,00/mês
Salário pretendido: R$ 2.000,00/mês

Dados pessoais

Data de nascimento: 21 de janeiro de 1970
Experiência profissional: 10 anos
Atualmente empregado
Hobbies: teatro, cinema e leitura
Não fumante

This is not obligatory, but nowadays this piece of information can be important for the prospective employer.

Endereço: R. José Vicente, 700
06543-000 São Paulo-SP
Tel. (11) 899-7766
e-mail: berebueno@oal.com.br

Aceita: transferência de cidade, de estado; viajar a trabalho
Informática: Word, Excel, Power Point, Access

Here you can indicate the level of knowledge of or proficiency in (**bom/ótimo/médio**) such programs.

Escolaridade

Pós-graduação incompleta – Contabilidade e Finanças – Unifesp - 2001/2003 – São Paulo
Superior completo – Ciências Contábeis – Universidade São Judas – 1991/1995 – São Paulo

Idiomas

Inglês: fluente
Espanhol: fluente

Cursos

Análise de risco – Universidade do Paraná – 1998 – 1 semana
Contabilidade Avançada – Senac – 1993 – 1 mês
Inglês - Cultura Inglesa – 1990 – 2 anos

You can list as many details as you want, provided they are relevant.

Experiência profissional

	Empresa	Cargo ocupado	Período
Emprego atual	Banco DBC	Consultor financeiro	De 1999 até hoje
Anterior	Cia. VVV	Analista financeiro	De 1995 a 1999
Outros:	Banco Finans	Analista financeiro	De 1990 a 1995

Habilidades/Qualificações

Área fiscal (ótimo) – última atualização: 1999 – Experiência: 9 anos
Área contábil (ótimo) – última atualização: 2001 – Experiência: 10 anos

Capacitação profissional

Profissional com 10 anos de experiência no mercado, sempre atuando na área financeira e contábil em empresas de médio e grande porte. Bons conhecimentos na área fiscal: ativo imobilizado, tesouraria, logística e expedição. Atuação na área contábil de contas patrimoniais, classificação e reclassificação contábil, participação em processos de diligências, fusões e aquisições.

Email

As emailing is a rapid and concise means of communication, the style of the messages themselves tends to be informal and telegraphic. According to internet conventions (netiquette), messages should never be written in capital letters, as this is interpreted as a sign of anger. Formal methods of address, such as, **Prezado(a) senhor(a)** are not normally used. If you are sending an email to someone you know well, the message can begin with a simple **Ola** or **Oi**, followed by the recipient's first name.

Within a company

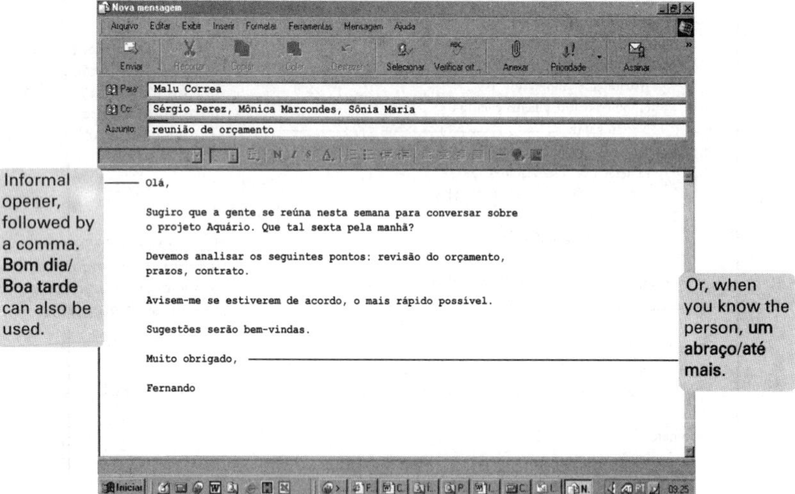

Para: Malu Correa
Cc: Sérgio Perez, Mônica Marcondes, Sônia Maria
Assunto: reunião de orçamento

Olá,

Sugiro que a gente se reúna nesta semana para conversar sobre o projeto Aquário. Que tal sexta pela manhã?

Devemos analisar os seguintes pontos: revisão do orçamento, prazos, contrato.

Avisem-me se estiverem de acordo, o mais rápido possível.

Sugestões serão bem-vindas.

Muito obrigado,

Fernando

Informal opener, followed by a comma. Bom dia/ Boa tarde can also be used.
Or, when you know the person, um abraço/até mais.

Business to business

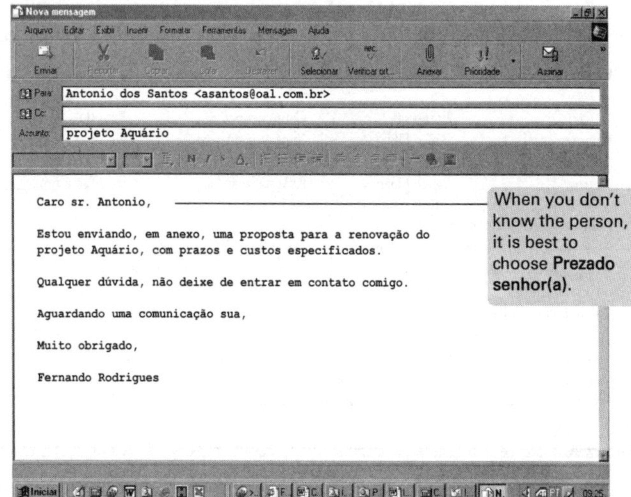

Para: Antonio dos Santos <asantos@oal.com.br>
Cc:
Assunto: projeto Aquário

Caro sr. Antonio,

Estou enviando, em anexo, uma proposta para a renovação do projeto Aquário, com prazos e custos especificados.

Qualquer dúvida, não deixe de entrar em contato comigo.

Aguardando uma comunicação sua,

Muito obrigado,

Fernando Rodrigues

When you don't know the person, it is best to choose Prezado senhor(a).

a¹ (*pl* **as** OR **a's**), **A** (*pl* **As** OR **A's**) [eɪ] *n* [letter] a, A *m*; **to get from A to B** ir de um lugar para outro; **from A to Z** de A a Z, de cabo a rabo.
◆ **A** *n* **-1.** MUS [note] lá *m* **-2.** SCH [mark] A *m*.

a² [*stressed* eɪ, *unstressed* ə] (*before vowel or silent 'h'* **an**) [*stressed* æn, *unstressed* ən] *indef art* **-1.** [non-specific] um *m*, uma *f*; **~ boy** um garoto; **~ table** uma mesa; **an orange** uma laranja **-2.** [referring to occupation]: **she's ~ teacher/actress** ela é professora/atriz **-3.** [one] um, uma; **~ hundred/thousand pounds** cem/mil libras **-4.** [to express prices, ratios etc] por; **£10 ~ day/person** £10 por dia/pessoa; **twice ~ week/month** duas vezes por semana/mês; **50 km an hour** 50 km por hora **-5.** [to express prices, ratios etc]: **20 cents ~ kilo** 20 centavos o quilo **-6.** [preceding person's name]: **~ Mr Smith phoned** um certo senhor Smith ligou; **do you know ~ Miss Costa?** você conhece alguma senhora Costa?

a. acre.

A-1 *adj inf* de primeira.

A4 *n UK* A4.

AA ◇ *adj* (*abbr of* **anti-aircraft**) antiaéreo(rea). ◇ *n* **-1.** (*abbr of* **Automobile Association**) *associação britânica que presta serviço de emergência a seus filiados em situações de problemas e acidentes automobilísticos*, ≃ Touring *m* Club do Brasil. **-2.** (*abbr of* **Associate in Arts**) *(titular de) diploma em ciências humanas nos Estados Unidos.* **-3.** (*abbr of* **Alcoholics Anonymous**) AA *mpl*.

AAA *n* **-1.** (*abbr of* **Amateur Athletic Association**) *federação britânica de atletas amadores.* **-2.** (*abbr of* **American Automobile Association**) *associação automobilística americana.*

AAU *n* (*abbr of* **Amateur Athletic Union**) *confederação norte-americana de atletas amadores.*

AAUP (*abbr of* **American Association of University Professors**) *n associação norte-americana de professores universitários*, ≃ ANDES *f*.

AB ◇ *n* (*abbr of* **Bachelor of Arts**) *(titular de) graduação em ciências humanas nos Estados Unidos.* ◇ *abbr of* **Alberta**.

aback [əˈbæk] *adv*: **to be taken ~ (by sthg)** ficar surpreso(sa) (com algo), ser surpreendido(da) (por algo).

abacus [ˈæbəkəs] (*pl* **-cuses** OR **-ci** [-saɪ]) *n* ábaco *m*.

abandon [əˈbændən] ◇ *vt* **-1.** [leave, desert] abandonar **-2.** [give up] desistir de. ◇ *n (U)*: **with ~** sem inibição, desenfreado(da).

abandoned [əˈbændənd] *adj* [deserted] abandonado(da).

abashed [əˈbæʃt] *adj* envergonhado(da).

abate [əˈbeɪt] *vi fml* [storm, noise, wind] abrandar; [pain, fear, anxiety] diminuir.

abattoir [ˈæbətwɑːʳ] *n* matadouro *m*.

abbess [ˈæbes] *n* abadessa *f*.

abbey [ˈæbɪ] *n* abadia *f*.

abbot [ˈæbət] *n* abade *m*.

abbreviate [əˈbriːvɪeɪt] *vt* abreviar.

abbreviation [əˌbriːvɪˈeɪʃn] *n* [short form] abreviatura *f*.

ABC *n* **-1.** [alphabet] abc *m*. **-2.** *fig* [basics]: **the ~ of** o abc de. **-3.** (*abbr of* **American Broadcasting Company**) *rede de televisão norte-americana*, ABC *f*.

abdicate [ˈæbdɪkeɪt] ◇ *vi* abdicar. ◇ *vt* [responsibility] abrir mão de.

abdication [ˌæbdɪˈkeɪʃn] *n* [of throne] abdicação *f*.

abdomen [ˈæbdəmen] *n* abdome *m*.

abdominal [æbˈdɒmɪnl] *adj* abdominal.

abduct [əbˈdʌkt] *vt* raptar.

abduction [əbˈdʌkʃn] *n* rapto *m*.

aberration [ˌæbəˈreɪʃn] *n* aberração *f*; **a mental ~** um desatino.

abet [əˈbet] (*pt* & *pp* **-ted**, *cont* **-ting**) *vt* ▷ **aid**.

abeyance [əˈbeɪəns] *n fml*: **in ~** em estado jacente.

abhor [əbˈhɔːʳ] (*pt* & *pp* **-red**, *cont* **-ring**) *vt* abominar.

abhorrent [əbˈhɒrənt] *adj* abominável.

abide [əˈbaɪd] *vt* suportar.
◆ **abide by** *vt fus* sujeitar-se a.

abiding [əˈbaɪdɪŋ] *adj* duradouro(ra).

ability [ə'bɪlətɪ] (*pl* **-ies**) *n* **-1.** *(U)* [capacity, level of capability] capacidade *f*; **to do sthg to the best of one's ~** fazer algo da melhor maneira possível **-2.** [skill, talent] habilidade *f*.

abject ['æbdʒekt] *adj* **-1.** [miserable, depressing] abjeto(ta) **-2.** [humble] servil.

ablaze [ə'bleɪz] *adj* **-1.** [on fire] em chamas **-2.** *fig* [bright]: **to be ~ with** estar iluminado(da) com.

able ['eɪbl] *adj* **-1.** [capable] capaz; **to be ~ to do sthg** ser capaz de fazer algo; [in a position to] poder fazer algo; [manage to] conseguir fazer algo **-2.** [accomplished, talented] competente.

able-bodied [-ˌbɒdɪd] *adj* **-1.** robusto(ta) **-2.** *MIL* (fisicamente) apto(ta).

ablutions [ə'blu:ʃnz] *npl fml* abluções *fpl*.

ably ['eɪblɪ] *adv* competentemente, habilmente.

abnormal [æb'nɔ:ml] *adj* anormal.

abnormality [ˌæbnɔ:'mælətɪ] (*pl* **-ies**) *n* anormalidade *f*.

abnormally [æb'nɔ:məlɪ] *adv* **-1.** [behave, develop, grow] irregularmente, de modo anormal **-2.** [cold, wide, loud]: **it's ~ cold for this time of the year** não é normal este frio nesta época do ano.

aboard [ə'bɔ:d] <> *adv* [on ship, plane] a bordo. <> *prep* [ship, plane] a bordo de; [bus, train] em.

abode [ə'bəʊd] *n fml*: **of no fixed ~** sem domicílio fixo.

abolish [ə'bɒlɪʃ] *vt* abolir.

abolition [ˌæbə'lɪʃn] *n* abolição *f*.

A-bomb (*abbr of* **atom bomb**) *n* bomba *f* atômica.

abominable [ə'bɒmɪnəbl] *adj* abominável.

abominable snowman *n*: **the ~** o abominável homem das neves.

abominably [ə'bɒmɪnəblɪ] *adv* abominavelmente.

aborigine [ˌæbə'rɪdʒənɪ] *n* aborígine *mf*.

abort [ə'bɔ:t] *vt & vi* abortar.

abortion [ə'bɔ:ʃn] *n* [of pregnancy] aborto *m*; **to have an ~** abortar.

abortive [ə'bɔ:tɪv] *adj* fracassado(da).

abound [ə'baʊnd] *vi* **-1.** [be plentiful] existir em abundância, abundar **-2.** [be full]: **to ~ with** *OR* **in sthg** ser rico(ca) em algo, ser cheio(cheia) de algo.

about [ə'baʊt] <> *adv* **-1.** [approximately] cerca de; **~ fifty/a hundred/a thousand** quase *OR* cerca de cinqüenta/cem/mil; **to be just ~ready** estar quase pronto(ta); **at ~ five o'clock** por volta das cinco horas **-2.** [referring to place] por perto; **to walk ~** andar por perto; **to jump ~** saltitar **-3.** [on the point of]: **to be ~ to do sthg** estar prestes a fazer algo. <> *prep* **-1.** [relating to, concerning] sobre; **a film ~ Paris** um filme sobre Paris; **what is it ~?** de que se trata?; **to talk ~ sthg** falar sobre algo **-2.** [referring to place] por; **to wander ~ the streets** vagar pelas ruas.

about-turn *esp UK*, **about-face** *esp US* *n* **-1.** *MIL* meia-volta *f* **-2.** *fig* [change of attitude] guinada *f* de 180 graus.

above [ə'bʌv] <> *adv* **-1.** [on top, higher up] de cima **-2.** [in text] acima; **the items mentioned ~** os itens acima mencionados **-3.** [more, over] acima de; **children aged five and ~** crianças de cinco anos ou mais. <> *prep* acima de.

◆ **above all** *adv* acima de tudo.

aboveboard [əˌbʌv'bɔ:d] *adj* **-1.** legítimo(ma) **-2.** limpo(pa).

abracadabra [ˌæbrəkə'dæbrə] *excl* abracadabra!

abrasion [ə'breɪʒn] *n fml* [graze] esfolamento *m*.

abrasive [ə'breɪsɪv] <> *adj* **-1.** [cleaner, cloth] abrasivo(va) **-2.** *fig* [person, manner] mordaz. <> *n* abrasivo *m*.

abreast [ə'brest] *adv* lado a lado.

◆ **abreast of** *prep*: **to keep ~ of sthg** estar a par de algo.

abridged [ə'brɪdʒd] *adj* resumido(da), compacto(-ta).

abroad [ə'brɔ:d] *adv* [overseas]: **to live ~** viver/morar no exterior; **to go ~** ir para o exterior.

abrupt [ə'brʌpt] *adj* **-1.** [sudden] repentino(na) **-2.** [brusque, rude] brusco(ca).

abruptly [ə'brʌptlɪ] *adv* **-1.** [suddenly] repentinamente **-2.** [brusquely, rudely] bruscamente.

ABS (*abbr of* **anti-lock breaking system**) *n* ABS *m*.

abscess ['æbsɪs] *n* abcesso *m*.

abscond [əb'skɒnd] *vi* esconder-se; **to ~ with sthg** sumir com algo.

abseil ['æbseɪl] *vi* praticar rappel; **to ~ down a rock** praticar rappel numa rocha.

absence ['æbsəns] *n* **-1.** [of person] ausência *f*; **in sb's ~** na ausência de alguém **-2.** [lack] falta *f*; **in the ~ of sthg** na falta de algo.

absent ['æbsənt] *adj* **-1.** [not present]: **~ (from)** ausente (de); **to be ~ without leave** *MIL* estar ausente sem autorização **-2.** [absent-minded] desatento(ta).

absentee [ˌæbsən'ti:] *n* ausente *mf*.

absenteeism [ˌæbsən'ti:ɪzm] *n* absenteísmo *m*.

absent-minded [-'maɪndɪd] *adj* distraído(da).

absent-mindedness *n* distração *f*.

absent-mindedly [-'maɪndɪdlɪ] *adv* distraidamente.

absinth(e) ['æbsɪnθ] *n* absinto *m*.

absolute ['æbsəlu:t] *adj* **-1.** [complete, utter] absoluto(ta) **-2.** [totalitarian] arbitrário(ria).

absolutely ['æbsəlu:tlɪ] <> *adv* [completely, utterly] absolutamente. <> *excl* [expressing agreement] sem dúvida.

absolute majority *n* maioria *f* absoluta.

absolution [ˌæbsə'lu:ʃn] *n RELIG* absolvição *f*.

absolve [əb'zɒlv] *vt* [free, clear]: **to ~ sb (of sthg)** absolver alguém (de algo).

absorb [əb'sɔ:b] *vt* **-1.** [soak up] absorver **-2.** *fig* [learn] assimilar **-3.** [interest] absorver; **to be ~ed in sthg** estar absorvido(da) em algo **-4.** [take over] incorporar.

absorbent [əb'sɔ:bənt] *adj* absorvente.

absorbing [əb'sɔ:bɪŋ] *adj* cativante.

absorption [əb'sɔ:pʃn] *n* **-1.** [soaking up] absorção *f* **-2.** [interest] concentração *f* **-3.** [taking over] incorporação *f*.

abstain [əb'steɪn] *vi* **-1.** [refrain]: **to ~ from sthg** abster-se de algo **-2.** [in vote] abster-se.

abstemious [æb'sti:mjəs] *adj fml* abstêmio(mia).

abstention [əb'stenʃn] *n* [in vote] abstenção *f*.

abstinence ['æbstɪnəns] *n*: **~ (from sthg)** abstinência *f* (de algo).

abstract [*adj* & *n* 'æbstrækt, *vb* æb'strækt] ◇ *adj* abstrato(ta). ◇ *n* [summary] resumo *m*. ◇ *vt* [summarize] resumir.

abstraction [æb'strækʃn] *n* **-1.** *(U)* [distractedness] distração *f* **-2.** [abstract idea] abstração *f*.

abstruse [æb'stru:s] *adj* confuso(sa).

absurd [əb'sɜ:d] *adj* absurdo(da).

absurdity [əb'sɜ:dətɪ] (*pl* **-ies**) *n* absurdo *m*.

absurdly [əb'sɜ:dlɪ] *adv* incrivelmente.

ABTA (*abbr of* **Association of British Travel Agents**) *n* *associação britânica de agentes de viagens*, ≃ ABAV *f*.

Abu Dhabi [ˌæbu:'dɑ:bɪ] *n* Abu Dabi.

abundance [ə'bʌndəns] *n* abundância *f*.

abundant [ə'bʌndənt] *adj* abundante.

abundantly [ə'bʌndəntlɪ] *adv* **-1.** [manifestly] suficientemente; **it is ~ clear that ...** está suficientemente claro que ...; **he made it ~ clear that ...** ele deixou mais do que claro que ... **-2.** [in large amounts] em abundância.

abuse [*n* ə'bju:s, *vb* ə'bju:z] ◇ *n* **-1.** [offensive remarks] insultos *mpl* **-2.** [maltreatment, misuse] abuso *m*. ◇ *vt* **-1.** [insult] insultar **-2.** [maltreat] maltratar **-3.** [misuse] abusar de.

abusive [ə'bju:sɪv] *adj* abusivo(va).

abut [ə'bʌt] (*pt* & *pp* **-ted**, *cont* **-ting**) *vi*: **to ~ on to** ser limítrofe a.

abysmal [ə'bɪzml] *adj* abismal.

abysmally [ə'bɪzməlɪ] *adv* terrivelmente.

abyss [ə'bɪs] *n* **-1.** abismo *m* **-2.** *fig* [gap] abismo *m*.

Abyssinia [ˌæbɪ'sɪnɪə] *n* Abissínia; **in/to ~** na/à Abissínia.

Abyssinian *adj* & *n* abissínio(nia).

a/c (*abbr of* **account (current)**) c.c. *f*.

AC (*abbr of* **alternating current**) *n* CA *f*.

acacia [ə'keɪʃə] *n* acácia *f*.

academic [ˌækə'demɪk] ◇ *adj* **-1.** [of college, university] acadêmico(ca) **-2.** [studious] intelectual **-3.** [hypothetical] conjetural. ◇ *n* [teacher, researcher] acadêmico *m*, -ca *f*.

academic year *n* ano *m* letivo.

academy [ə'kædəmɪ] (*pl* **-ies**) *n* **-1.** [school, college] academia *f*, escola *f* **-2.** [institution, society] academia *f*.

ACAS (*abbr of* **Advisory Conciliation and Arbitration Service**) *n organização britânica para conciliação entre sindicatos e empregadores*.

accede [æk'si:d] *vi* **-1.** *fml* [agree]: **to ~ to sthg** aceder a algo **-2.** [monarch]: **to ~ to the throne** subir ao trono.

accelerate [ək'seləreɪt] ◇ *vt* apressar. ◇ *vi* **-1.** [car, driver] acelerar **-2.** [inflation, growth] disparar.

acceleration [əkˌselə'reɪʃn] *n* **-1.** [of car] aceleração *f* **-2.** [of inflation, growth] disparada *f*.

accelerator [ək'seləreɪtə^r] *n* acelerador *m*.

accent ['æksent] *n* **-1.** [when speaking] sotaque *m* **-2.** [in writing] acento *m* **-3.** *fig* [emphasis] ênfase *f*.

accentuate [æk'sentjʊeɪt] *vt* [emphasize, stress] acentuar.

accept [ək'sept] *vt* **-1.** [agree to take, receive] aceitar **-2.** [agree to follow] assentir **-3.** [recognize as satisfactory] aprovar **-4.** [get used to] reconhecer **-5.** [admit, recognize as one's own] assumir **-6.** [person - as part of group] acolher; [- for job, as member of club] aceitar **-7.** [agree, believe]: **to ~ that** aceitar que **-8.** [process] aceitar.

acceptable [ək'septəbl] *adj* **-1.** [permissible] aceitável **-2.** [passable] admissível.

acceptably [ək'septəblɪ] *adv* apropriadamente.

acceptance [ək'septəns] *n* **-1.** [gen] aceitação *f* **-2.** [recognizing as satisfactory] aprovação *f*.

accepted [ək'septɪd] *adj* [recognized as correct, true] aceito(ta).

access ['ækses] ◇ *n* **-1.** [entry, way in] acesso *m*; **to gain ~ to** [place, building] obter acesso a **-2.** [opportunity to use, see]: **to have ~ to sthg** ter acesso a algo. ◇ *vt* COMPUT acessar.

accessibility [əkˌsesə'bɪlətɪ] *n* **-1.** [of place] acessibilidade *f* **-2.** [availability] acesso *m*.

accessible [ək'sesəbl] *adj* **-1.** [reachable, understandable] acessível **-2.** [available] disponível.

accession [æk'seʃn] *n* [of monarch] ascensão *f*.

accessory [ək'sesərɪ] (*pl* **-ies**) *n* **-1.** [extra part, device] acessório *m* **-2.** JUR cúmplice *mf*.

◆ **accessories** *npl* [to outfit] acessórios *mpl*.

access road *n* **-1.** [gen] rua *f* de acesso **-2.** *UK* [to motorway] via *f* de acesso.

access time *n* COMPUT tempo *m* de acesso.

accident ['æksɪdənt] *n* **-1.** acidente *m*; **to have an ~** sofrer um acidente **-2.** *(U)* [chance]: **by ~** por acaso; **it was an ~** foi sem querer.

accidental [ˌæksɪ'dentl] *adj* acidental.

accidentally [ˌæksɪ'dentəlɪ] *adv* **-1.** [drop, break] sem querer **-2.** [meet, find, discover] acidentalmente.

accident-prone *adj* propenso(sa) a acidentes.

acclaim [ə'kleɪm] ◇ *n (U)* aclamação *f*. ◇ *vt* aclamar.

acclamation [ˌæklə'meɪʃn] *n* aclamação *f*.

acclimatize, -ise [ə'klaɪmətaɪz], **acclimate** *US* ['æklɪmeɪt] *vi*: **to ~ (to sthg)** aclimatar-se (a algo).

accolade ['ækəleɪd] *n* honra *f*.

accommodate [ə'kɒmədeɪt] *vt* **-1.** [provide room for] acomodar **-2.** [oblige] comprazer a.

accommodating [ə'kɒmədeɪtɪŋ] *adj* complacente.

accommodation *UK* [əˌkɒmə'deɪʃn] *n*, **accommodations** *US* [əˌkɒmə'deɪʃnz] *npl* **-1.** [lodging] alojamento *m*, acomodação *f* **-2.** [work space] instalações *fpl*.

accompaniment [ə'kʌmpənɪmənt] *n* MUS acompanhamento *m*.

accompanist [ə'kʌmpənɪst] *n* MUS *pessoa que canta ou toca junto com alguém*.

accompany [ə'kʌmpənɪ] (*pt* & *pp* **-ied**) *vt* **-1.** acompanhar **-2.** MUS [with instrument]: **to ~ sb (on sthg)** acompanhar alguém (em algo).

accomplice [ə'kʌmplɪs] *n* cúmplice *m*.

accomplish [ə'kʌmplɪʃ] *vt* [achieve, manage] conseguir; [carry out, effect] realizar; [reach, attain] alcançar.

accomplished [ə'kʌmplɪʃt] *adj* [skilled] excelente, competente.

accomplishment [ə'kʌmplɪʃmənt] *n* **-1.** [achievement, finishing] realização *f*, conclusão *f* **-2.** [feat, deed] feito *m*.

◆ **accomplishments** *npl* [skills] habilidades *fpl*.

accord [ə'kɔ:d] *n* **-1.** [settlement] acordo *m* **-2.** [agreement, harmony]**: to be in ~ (with sb/sthg)** estar de acordo com alguém algo; **with one ~** unanimamente; **to do sthg of one's own ~** fazer algo por iniciativa própria.

accordance [ə'kɔ:dəns] *n*: **in ~ with sthg** de acordo com algo.

according to *prep* **-1.** [as stated or shown by] segundo; **to go ~ to plan** sair conforme o planejado **-2.** [with regard to, depending on] conforme.

accordingly [ə'kɔ:dɪŋlɪ] *adv* **-1.** [appropriately] de modo apropriado **-2.** [consequently] conseqüentemente.

accordion [ə'kɔ:djən] *n* acordeão *m*, sanfona *f*.

accordionist [ə'kɔ:djənɪst] *n* acordeonista *mf*, sanfoneiro *m*, -ra *f*.

accost [ə'kɒst] *vt* abordar.

account [ə'kaʊnt] *n* **-1.** [with bank, company] conta *f* **-2.** [with shop]**: I have an ~ at the butcher's** tenho conta no açougue **-3.** [report]**: to give an~ of sthg** fazer um relato de algo **-4.** *phr*: **to call sb to ~** fazer alguém se explicar; **to give a good ~ of o.s.** causar boa impressão; **to take ~ of sthg, to take sthg into ~** levar algo em consideração; **to be of no ~** não ter importância; **on no ~** de modo algum.

◆ **accounts** *npl* [of business] contabilidade *f*.

◆ **by all accounts** *adv* de acordo com a opinião geral.

◆ **on account of** *prep* devido a; **on my ~** por minha causa.

◆ **account for** *vt fus* **-1.** [explain] justificar; **a theory that ~s for all the facts** uma teoria que justifique os fatos **-2.** [represent] representar.

accountability [ə,kaʊntə'bɪlətɪ] *n* responsabilidade *f*.

accountable [ə'kaʊntəbl] *adj* [responsible]**: to be held ~ for sthg** ser responsabilizado(da) por algo; **~ to sb** [answerable] obrigado(da) a prestar contas a alguém.

accountancy [ə'kaʊntənsɪ] *n* [profession, business] contabilidade *f*.

accountant [ə'kaʊntənt] *n* contador *m*, -ra *f*.

accounting [ə'kaʊntɪŋ] *n* [skill, practice of accountancy] contabilidade *f*.

accounts department *n* setor *m* de contabilidade.

accoutrements *UK* [ə'ku:trəmənts], **accouterments** *US* [ə'ku:tərmənts] *npl hum* [baggage] parafernália *f*.

accredited [ə'kredɪtɪd] *adj* [authorized, recognized] acreditado(da).

accrue [ə'kru:] *vt* & *vi* FIN render.

accumulate [ə'kju:mjʊleɪt] ◇ *vt* acumular. ◇ *vi* acumular-se.

accumulation [ə,kju:mjʊ'leɪʃn] *n* **-1.** *(U)* [accumulating] acumulação *f* **-2.** [group of things] monte *m*.

accuracy ['ækjʊrəsɪ] *n* **-1.** [truth, correctness] exatidão *f* **-2.** [precision - of weapon, marksman] precisão *f*; [- of typing, figures, estimate] exatidão *f*.

accurate ['ækjʊrət] *adj* **-1.** [true, correct] exato(ta) **-2.** [precise - shot, marksman] preciso(sa); [- typist, figures, estimate] exato(ta).

accurately ['ækjʊrətlɪ] *adv* **-1.** [truthfully, correctly] com exatidão **-2.** [precisely - aim] com precisão; [- type, estimate] com exatidão.

accusation [,ækju:'zeɪʃn] *n* **-1.** [charge, criticism] acusação *f* **-2.** JUR [formal charge] incriminação *f*.

accuse [ə'kju:z] *vt* **-1.** [charge, criticize]**: to ~ sb of sthg/of doing sthg** acusar alguém de algo/de fazer algo **-2.** JUR **: to ~ sb of sthg/of doing sthg** incriminar alguém por algo/por fazer algo.

accused [ə'kju:zd] *n* JUR: **the ~** [defendant] o réu(a ré).

accusing [ə'kju:zɪŋ] *adj* acusador(ra).

accusingly [ə'kju:zɪŋlɪ] *adv* acusatoriamente.

accustomed [ə'kʌstəmd] *adj*: **to be ~ to sthg/to doing sthg** estar acostumado(da) a algo/a fazer algo.

ace [eɪs] ◇ *n* **-1.** [playing card] ás *m* **-2.** TENNIS ace *m* **-3.** *phr*: **to be within an ~ of victory** estar a um passo da vitória. ◇ *adj* [top-class]**: he's an ~ tennis player** ele é um tenista de primeira.

acerbic [ə'sɜ:bɪk] *adj* acerbo(ba).

acetate ['æsɪteɪt] *n* acetato *m*.

acetic acid [ə'si:tɪk-] *n (U)* ácido *m* acético.

acetone ['æsɪtəʊn] *n (U)* acetona *f*.

acetylene [ə'setɪli:n] *n (U)* acetileno *m*.

ache [eɪk] ◇ *n* [dull pain] dor *f*. ◇ *vi* **-1.** [be painful] doer **-2.** *fig* [want]**: to be aching for sthg/to do sthg** estar morrendo de vontade de algo/de fazer algo.

achieve [ə'tʃi:v] *vt* [success] conseguir ; [goal, ambition] realizar ; [victory, fame] conquistar.

achievement [ə'tʃi:vmənt] *n* **-1.** [feat, deed] conquista *f* **-2.** [process of achieving] realização *f*.

Achilles' heel [ə'kɪli:z-] *n* calcanhar *m* de Aquiles.

Achilles' tendon *n* tendão *m* de Aquiles.

acid ['æsɪd] ◇ *adj* **-1.** ácido(da) **-2.** *fig* [remark, tone] áspero(ra). ◇ *n* **-1.** ácido *m* **-2.** *inf* [LSD] ácido *m*.

acidic [ə'sɪdɪk] *adj* CHEM acidífero(ra).

acidity [ə'sɪdətɪ] *n* **-1.** CHEM acidez *f* **-2.** *fig* [of remark, tone] aspereza *f*.

acid rain *n* chuva *f* ácida.

acid test *n fig* [test of worth] prova *f* dos nove.

acknowledge [ək'nɒlɪdʒ] *vt* **-1.** [accept, recognize] reconhecer; **to ~ sb as sthg** reconhecer alguém como algo **-2.** [letter]: **to ~ (receipt of) sthg** acusar (o recebimento de algo) **-3.** [greet] cumprimentar.

acknowledg(e)ment [ək'nɒlɪdʒmənt] *n* **-1.** [acceptance, recognition] reconhecimento *m* **-2.** [of letter] aviso *m* de recebimento **-3.** [thanks, gratitude] retribuição *f*.

◆ **acknowledg(e)ments** *npl* [in book] agradecimentos *mpl*.

ACLU (*abbr of* **American Civil Liberties Union**) *n* *associação norte-americana para a defesa das liberdades civis.*

acme ['ækmɪ] *n* apogeu *m*.

acne ['æknɪ] *n* acne *f*.

acorn ['eɪkɔ:n] *n* bolota *f*, glande *m*.

acoustic [ə'ku:stɪk] *adj* acústico(ca).

◆ **acoustics** *npl* [of room, auditorium] acústica *f*.

acoustic guitar *n* violão *m* acústico.

acquaint [ə'kweɪnt] *vt*: **to ~ sb with sthg** [information] informar alguém sobre algo; **to be ~ed with sthg** [method, technique] estar por dentro de algo; **to be ~ed with sb** *fml* conhecer alguém.

acquaintance [ə'kweɪntəns] *n* **-1.** [personal associate] conhecido *m*, -da *f* **-2.** *(U) fml*: **to make sb's ~** conhecer alguém.

acquiesce [ˌækwɪ'es] *vi*: **to ~ (to** OR **in sthg)** aquiescer-se (a algo).

acquiescence [ˌækwɪ'esns] *n* aquiescência *f*.

acquire [ə'kwaɪəʳ] *vt* **-1.** [obtain] [property, company, object] adquirir **-2.** [information, document] obter **-3.** [skill, knowledge, habit] adquirir.

acquired taste [ə'kwaɪəd-] *n* gosto *m* adquirido.

acquisition [ˌækwɪ'zɪʃn] *n* **-1.** [of property, company, object] aquisição *f* **-2.** *(U)* [of information, document] obtenção *f* **-3.** *(U)* [of skill, knowlege, habit] aquisição *f*.

acquisitive [ə'kwɪzɪtɪv] *adj* ambicioso(sa), consumista.

acquit [ə'kwɪt] (*pt* & *pp* **-ted**, *cont* **-ting**) *vt* **-1.** JUR: **to ~ sb of sthg** absolver alguém de algo **-2.** [conduct]: **to ~ o.s. well/badly** desempenhar-se bem/mal.

acquittal [ə'kwɪtl] *n* JUR absolvição *f*.

acre ['eɪkəʳ] *n* [unit of measurement] acre *m (4046,9 m^2)*.

acreage *n* [size in acres] área *f* medida em acres.

acrid ['ækrɪd] *adj* **-1.** [smoke, smell, taste] acre **-2.** *fig* [remark] mordaz.

acrimonious [ˌækrɪ'məʊnjəs] *adj* acrimonioso(sa).

acrobat ['ækrəbæt] *n* [circus performer] acrobata *mf*.

acrobatic [ˌækrə'bætɪk] *adj* **-1.** [somersault, display] acrobático(ca) **-2.** [person] astuto(ta).

◆ **acrobatics** *npl* acrobacias *fpl*.

acronym ['ækrənɪm] *n* acrônimo *m*.

across [ə'krɒs] ◇ *adv* **-1.** [from one side to the other]: **they came ~ in a small boat** eles atravessaram num barco pequeno **-2.** [in the direction of]: **she looked ~ at me** ela olhou em minha direção; **he went ~ to speak to her** ele foi em sua direção para lhe falar **-3.** [in measurements] de um lado a outro **-4.** [in crosswords] cruzado(da) **-5.** *phr*: **to get sthg ~ (to sb)** fazer-se entender (por alguém). ◇ *prep* **-1.** [from one side to the other] de um lado a outro; **he drew a line ~ the page** ele traçou uma linha de um lado a outro da página; **there is a bridge ~ the river** há uma ponte sobre o rio; **she walked/ran ~ the road** ela atravessou a estrada caminhando/correndo; **he looked ~ the street** ele olhou pela rua **-2.** [on the other side of] no outro lado de.

◆ **across from** *prep* na frente de.

acrylic [ə'krɪlɪk] ◇ *adj* [fibre, jumper, paint] acrílico(-ca). ◇ *n (U)* [fibre] acrílico *m*.

act [ækt] ◇ *n* **-1.** [action, deed] ato *m*; **to catch sb in the ~** pegar alguém em flagrante **-2.** JUR lei *f* **-3.** [of play, opera] ato *m*; [in cabaret etc] número *m* **-4.** *fig* [pretence] fingimento *m*; **to put on an ~** agir com fingimento **-5.** *phr*: **to get in on the ~** aproveitar--se de algo iniciado por outrem; **to get one's ~ together** organizar-se. ◇ *vi* **-1.** [gen] agir; **to ~ as if/like** agir como se/como **-2.** [in play, film] representar, atuar **-3.** *fig* [pretend] fingir **-4.** [fulfil function]: **to ~ as sthg** atuar como algo; **to ~ for** OR **on behalf of sb** representar alguém. ◇ *vt* [role] desempenhar; **to ~ the fool/innocent** fazer-se de bobo/inocente.

◆ **act out** *vt sep* **-1.** [feeling] expressar **-2.** [event] representar.

◆ **act up** *vi inf* **-1.** [machine] emperrar **-2.** [person] comportar-se mal.

ACT (*abbr of* **American College Test**) *n exame realizado ao final do ensino médio em escolas norte-americanas.*

acting ['æktɪŋ] ◇ *adj* [interim] interino(na). ◇ *n (U)* [in play, film] atuação *f*; **to enjoy ~** gostar de atuar.

action ['ækʃn] *n* **-1.** *(U)* [fact of doing sthg] ação *f*; **to take ~** agir; **to put sthg into ~** pôr algo em ação; **in ~** [person, machine] em atividade; **out of ~** [person] fora de combate; [machine] desativado(da) **-2.** [deed] atividade *f* **-3.** *(U)* [in battle, war] ação *f*; **to be killed in ~** ser morto(ta) em ação **-4.** JUR ação *f* judicial; **to bring an ~ against sb** entrar com uma ação judicial contra alguém **-5.** [in play, book, film] história *f* **-6.** [effect] efeito *m*.

action group *n* [lobby] grupo *m* de ação.

action replay *n* replay *m*.

activate ['æktɪveɪt] *vt* [set off] ativar.

active ['æktɪv] *adj* **-1.** [lively, energetic] ativo(va) **-2.** [involved, hardworking] dinâmico(ca) **-3.** [positive] incessante **-4.** [volcano] ativo(va).

actively ['æktɪvlɪ] *adv* **-1.** [promote] ativamente **-2.** [seek, encourage] incessantemente.

active service *n (U)* MIL serviço *m* ativo; **to be killed on ~** ser morto(ta) em serviço.

activist ['æktɪvɪst] *n* [political campaigner] ativista *mf*.

activity [æk'tɪvətɪ] (*pl* **-ies**) *n (U)* atividade *f*.

◆ **activities** *npl* [actions, doings] ações *fpl*.

act of God *n* força *f* maior.

actor ['æktəʳ] *n* ator *m*.

actress ['æktrɪs] *n* atriz *f*.

actual ['æktʃʊəl] *adj* real; **in ~ fact** na verdade.

actuality [ˌæktʃʊ'ælətɪ] *n*: **in ~** de fato.

actually ['æktʃʊəlɪ] *adv* **-1.** [really, in truth] na verdade, realmente **-2.** [by the way] a propósito **-3.** [contradicting sb] pensando bem, de fato; **that's not true, ~** pensando bem, aquilo não é verdade.

actuary ['æktjʊərɪ] (*pl* **-ies**) *n* [statistician] estatístico *m*, -ca *f*.

actuate ['æktjʊeɪt] *vt* [activate] acionar.

acuity [ə'kju:ətɪ] *n fml* acuidade *f*.

acumen ['ækjʊmen] *n (U)*: **business ~** tino para os negócios.

acupuncture ['ækjʊpʌŋktʃəʳ] *n (U)* acupuntura *f*.

acute [ə'kju:t] *adj* **-1.** [severe, extreme] agudo(da) **-2.** [perceptive, intelligent] engenhoso(sa) **-3.** [keen, sensitive] aguçado(da) **-4.** LING: **e ~** e agudo **-5.** MATH agudo(da).

acute accent *n* acento *m* agudo.

acutely [ə'kju:tlɪ] *adv* [extremely] acentuadamente.

ad (*abbr of* **advertisement**) *n fam* **-1.** [in newspaper] anúncio *m*. **-2.** [on TV] propaganda *f*.

AD (*abbr of* **Anno Domini**) d.C.

adage ['ædɪdʒ] *n* adágio *m*.

adamant ['ædəmənt] *adj* [determined]: **to be ~**

(about sthg/that) estar inflexível (em relação a algo).

Adam's apple ['ædəmz-] *n* pomo-de-adão *m.*

adapt [ə'dæpt] ◇ *vt* adaptar. ◇ *vi*: **to ~ to sthg** adaptar-se a algo.

adaptability [əˌdæptə'bɪlətɪ] *n* adaptabilidade *f.*

adaptable [ə'dæptəbl] *adj* [person] maleável.

adaptation [ˌædæp'teɪʃn] *n* [of book, play] adaptação *f.*

adapter, adaptor [ə'dæptəʳ] *n* ELEC adaptador *m.*

ADAS (*abbr of* **Agricultural Development and Advisory Service**) *n organização britânica de pesquisa e consultoria para as indústrias do setor agrícola.*

ADC (*abbr of* **analogue to digital converter**) *n* ADC *m*, conversor *m* analógico-digital.

add [æd] *vt* **-1.** : **to ~ sthg to sthg** adicionar algo a algo **-2.** [total] somar; **6 ~ 3 equals 9** *US* 6 mais 3 é igual a 9 **-3.** [say as an afterthought] acrescentar.

◆ **add in** *vt sep* [include] incluir.

◆ **add on** *vt sep*: **to ~ sthg on (to sthg)** [to building] anexar algo (a algo); [to bill, total] incluir algo (em algo).

◆ **add to** *vt fus* [increase] aumentar.

◆ **add up** ◇ *vt sep* [total up] adicionar. ◇ *vi* **-1.** [make sense] fazer sentido **-2.** [accumulate] acumular.

◆ **add up to** *vt fus* [represent] representar.

addendum [ə'dendəm] (*pl* **-da**) *n* [additional section] adendo *m.*

adder ['ædəʳ] *n* [snake] víbora *f.*

addict ['ædɪkt] *n* **-1.** [to drug, harmful substance] viciado *m*, -da *f*, dependente *mf* **-2.** [exercise, TV etc.] fanático *m*, -ca *f.*

addicted [ə'dɪktɪd] *adj* **-1.** [to drug, harmful substance]: **~ (to sthg)** viciado(da) (em algo), dependente de algo **-2.** *fig* [to exercise, TV] fanático(ca) (por algo).

addiction [ə'dɪkʃn] *n (U)* **-1.** [to drug, harmful substance] vício *m*, dependência *f*; **~ to sthg** vício em algo, dependência de algo **-2.** *fig* [to exercise, food, TV] fanatismo *m*; **~ to sthg** fanatismo por algo.

addictive [ə'dɪktɪv] *adj* **-1.** [drug, harmful substance] que vicia **-2.** *fig* [exercise, food, TV] que vicia.

Addis Ababa ['ædɪs 'æbəbə] *n* Adis-Abeba; **in/to ~** em/para Adis-Abeba.

addition [ə'dɪʃn] *n* **-1.** *(U)* MATH adição *f* **-2.** [extra thing] acréscimo *m* **-3.** *(U)* [act of adding] adicionamento *m*; **in ~** além disso; **in ~ to** além de.

additional [ə'dɪʃənl] *adj* [extra] adicional.

additive ['ædɪtɪv] *n* aditivo *m.*

addled ['ædld] *adj* **-1.** [rotten] podre **-2.** *inf* [confused] confuso(sa).

add-on COMPUT ◇ *adj* adicional. ◇ *n* add-on *m*, *software ou hardware acrescentado a um computador para melhorar seu desempenho.*

address [ə'dres] ◇ *n* **-1.** [location] endereço *m* **-2.** [speech] discurso *m.* ◇ *vt* **-1.** [letter, parcel] endereçar **-2.** [give a speech to] discursar **-3.** [speak to, accost]: **to ~ sb as** dirigir-se a alguém como **-4.** [deal with] tratar; **to ~ o.s. to sthg** interessar-se por algo.

address book *n* agenda *f* de endereços.

addressee [ˌædre'siː] *n* [of letter, parcel] destinatário *m*, -ria *f.*

Aden ['eɪdn] *n* Áden; **in/to ~** em/à Áden.

adenoids ['ædɪnɔɪdz] *npl* adenóides *fpl.*

adept ['ædept] *adj*: **to be ~ at sthg/at doing sthg** ser perito(ta) em algo/em fazer algo.

adequacy ['ædɪkwəsɪ] *n (U)* **-1.** [sufficiency] suficiência *f* **-2.** [competence] adequação *f.*

adequate ['ædɪkwət] *adj* **-1.** [sufficient] suficiente **-2.** [competent] adequado(da).

adequately ['ædɪkwətlɪ] *adv* **-1.** [sufficiently] suficientemente **-2.** [competently] adequadamente.

adhere [əd'hɪəʳ] *vi* **-1.** [to surface, principle]: **to ~ (to sthg)** aderir (a algo) **-2.** [to regulation, decision]: **to ~ to sthg** respeitar algo.

adherence [əd'hɪərəns] *n* : **~ (to sthg)** [surface] aderência *f* (a algo); [principle] adesão *f* (a algo); [regulation, decision] respeito *m* (a algo).

adhesive [əd'hiːsɪv] ◇ *adj* [sticky] adesivo(va). ◇ *n* [glue] cola *f.*

adhesive tape *n* fita *f* adesiva.

ad hoc [ˌæd'hɒk] *adj* ad hoc.

ad infinitum [ˌædɪnfɪ'naɪtəm] *adv* ad infinitum.

adjacent [ə'dʒeɪsənt] *adj* adjacente; **~ to sthg** adjacente a algo.

adjective ['ædʒɪktɪv] *n* adjetivo *m.*

adjoin [ə'dʒɔɪn] *vt* unir.

adjoining [ə'dʒɔɪnɪŋ] ◇ *adj* [next-door] vizinho(-nha). ◇ *prep* ao lado de.

adjourn [ə'dʒɜːn] ◇ *vt* [postpone] adiar. ◇ *vi* **-1.** [come to a temporary close] ser/estar suspenso(sa) **-2.** *hum* [go]: **to ~ (to)** ir para.

adjournment [ə'dʒɜːnmənt] *n* adiamento *m*, suspensão *f.*

Adjt (*abbr of* **adjutant**) *assistente administrativo de oficial do exército.*

adjudge [ə'dʒʌdʒ] *vt* **-1.** [declare] decretar **-2.** JUR sentenciar.

adjudicate [ə'dʒuːdɪkeɪt] ◇ *vt* [contest, claim] adjudicar. ◇ *vi* [serve as judge, arbiter in contest] julgar; **to ~ on** *or* **upon sthg** deliberar sobre algo.

adjudication [əˌdʒuːdɪ'keɪʃn] *n* adjudicação *f.*

adjunct ['ædʒʌŋkt] *n* [something added] acessório *m.*

adjust [ə'dʒʌst] ◇ *vt* [alter, correct] ajustar. ◇ *vi*: **to ~ (to sthg)** adaptar-se (a algo).

adjustable [ə'dʒʌstəbl] *adj* [machine, chair] regulável.

adjustable spanner *n* chave *f* inglesa.

adjusted [ə'dʒʌstɪd] *adj* [emotionally stable]: **to be well ~** estar equilibrado(da).

adjustment [ə'dʒʌstmənt] *n* **-1.** [to heat, speed, machine] ajuste *m*; **to make an ~ to sthg** fazer um ajuste em algo **-2.** *(U)* [change of attitude] mudança *f*; **~ to sthg** adaptação a algo.

adjutant ['ædʒʊtənt] *n* ajudante *mf.*

ad lib [ˌæd'lɪb] (*pt & pp* **ad-libbed**, *cont* **ad-libbing**) ◇ *adj* [improvised] espontâneo(nea). ◇ *adv* [freely] de improviso. ◇ *n* [improvised joke, remark] improviso *m.*

◆ **ad-lib** *vi* [improvise] improvisar.

adman ['ædmæn] (*pl* **admen** ['ædmen]) *n* anunciante *m.*

admin ['ædmɪn] *n UK inf* administração *f.*

administer [əd'mɪnɪstəʳ] *vt* **-1.** [company, business]

administrar **-2.** [justice, punishment] aplicar **-3.** [drug, medication] ministrar.
administration [əd,mɪnɪ'streɪʃn] *n* **-1.** *(U)* [of company, business] administração *f* **-2.** *(U)* [of justice, punishment] aplicação *f.*
◆ **Administration** *n US* [government]: **the Administration** o Governo.
administrative [əd'mɪnɪstrətɪv] *adj* [job, work, staff] administrativo(va).
administrator [əd'mɪnɪstreɪtə^r] *n* administrador *m,* -ra *f.*
admirable ['ædmərəbl] *adj* admirável.
admirably ['ædmərəblɪ] *adv* admiravelmente.
admiral ['ædmərəl] *n* almirante *mf.*
Admiralty ['ædmərəltɪ] *n UK*: **the ~** o Ministério da Marinha.
admiration [,ædmə'reɪʃn] *n* admiração *f.*
admire [əd'maɪə^r] *vt* **-1.** [respect, like] admirar; **to ~ sb for sthg** admirar alguém por algo **-2.** [look at with pleasure] apreciar.
admirer [əd'maɪərə^r] *n* **-1.** [suitor] pretendente *mf* **-2.** [enthusiast, fan] fã *mf.*
admiring [əd'maɪərɪŋ] *adj* [look] de admiração.
admiringly [əd'maɪərɪŋlɪ] *adv* [gaze] com admiração.
admissible [əd'mɪsəbl] *adj JUR* [evidence] aceitável.
admission [əd'mɪʃn] *n* **-1.** [permission to enter] admissão *f* **-2.** [cost of entrance] entrada *f* **-3.** [confession] confissão *f*; **by his/her own ~** conforme ele/ela mesmo(ma) admitiu.
admit [əd'mɪt] (*pt* & *pp* **-ted**, *cont* **-ting**) ◇ *vt* **-1.** [acknowledge, confess] confessar, admitir; **to ~ that** admitir que; **to ~ doing sthg** admitir/confessar ter feito algo; **to ~ defeat** *fig* dar-se por vencido(-da) **-2.** [allow to enter] admitir; **to be admitted to hospital** *UK* OR **to the hospital** *US* dar entrada no hospital **-3.** [allow to join] admitir; **to ~ sb to sthg** admitir alguém em algo. ◇ *vi*: **to ~ to sthg/to doing sthg** admitir algo/fazer algo.
admittance [əd'mɪtəns] *n* [right to enter, entrance]: **to gain ~ to sthg** ser admitido(da) em algo; **'no ~'** 'entrada proibida'.
admittedly [əd'mɪtɪdlɪ] *adv* reconhecidamente.
admixture *n fml* mistura *f.*
admonish [əd'mɒnɪʃ] *vt fml* [tell off] repreender.
ad nauseam [,æd'nɔ:zɪæm] *adv* exaustivamente.
ado [ə'du:] *n*: **without further** OR **more ~** sem mais delongas OR preâmbulos.
adolescence [,ædə'lesns] *n* adolescência *f.*
adolescent [,ædə'lesnt] ◇ *adj* **-1.** [teenage] adolescente **-2.** *pej* [immature] imaturo(ra). ◇ *n* [teenager] adolescente *mf.*
adopt [ə'dɒpt] ◇ *vt* [recommendation, suggestion] aceitar. ◇ *vi* [give a home to a child] adotar.
adoption [ə'dɒpʃn] *n (U)* adoção *f.*
adoptive [ə'dɒptɪv] *adj* adotivo(va).
adorable [ə'dɔ:rəbl] *adj* adorável.
adoration [,ædə'reɪʃn] *n* adoração *f.*
adore [ə'dɔ:^r] *vt* adorar.
adoring [ə'dɔ:rɪŋ] *adj* **-1.** [look] de admiração **-2.** [smile, person] encantador(ra).
adorn [ə'dɔ:n] *vt* [decorate] adornar.
adornment [ə'dɔ:nmənt] *n* [decoration] adorno *m.*
ADP (*abbr of* **automatic data processing**) *n* PAD *m,* processamento *m* automático de dados.
adrenalin [ə'drenəlɪn] *n (U)* adrenalina *f.*
Adriatic [,eɪdrɪ'ætɪk] *n*: **the ~ (Sea)** o (Mar) Adriático.
adrift [ə'drɪft] ◇ *adj* [boat, ship] à deriva. ◇ *adv*: **to go ~** *fig* [go wrong] ir por água abaixo.
adroit [ə'drɔɪt] *adj* hábil.
ADT (*abbr of* **Atlantic Daylight Time**) *n horário de verão na costa leste dos Estados Unidos.*
adulation [,ædjʊ'leɪʃn] *n (U)* adulação *f.*
adult ['ædʌlt] ◇ *adj* **-1.** [mature, responsible] adulto(ta) **-2.** [for adults] para adultos, para maiores. ◇ *n* [person, animal] adulto *m,* -ta *f.*
adult education *n (U)* educação *f* para adultos.
adulterate [ə'dʌltəreɪt] *vt* adulterar.
adulteration [ə,dʌltə'reɪʃn] *n (U)* adulteração *f.*
adulterer [ə'dʌltərə^r] *n* adúltero *m,* -ra *f.*
adultery [ə'dʌltərɪ] *n (U)* adultério *m.*
adulthood ['ædʌlthʊd] *n* maioridade *f.*
advance [əd'vɑ:ns] ◇ *n* **-1.** [gen] avanço *m* **-2.** [money] adiantamento *m.* ◇ *comp* **-1.** [early] antecipado(da) **-2.** [prior]: **~ warning** aviso prévio. ◇ *vt* **-1.** [improve] progredir **-2.** [bring forward in time] adiantar **-3.** [money]: **to ~ sb sthg** adiantar algo a alguém. ◇ *vi* **-1.** [go forward] avançar; **to ~ on sb** avançar em alguém **-2.** [improve] progredir.
◆ **advances** *npl*: **to make ~s to sb** [sexual] assediar alguém; [business] propor um bom negócio para alguém.
◆ **in advance** *adv* com antecedência; **to book in ~** reservar antecipadamente; **to know in ~** saber de antemão; **half an hour in ~** meia hora antes.
◆ **in advance of** *prep* **-1.** [superior to] superior a **-2.** [prior to] antes de.
advanced [əd'vɑ:nst] *adj* avançado(da); **~ in years** *euph* [elderly] em idade avançada.
advancement [əd'vɑ:nsmənt] *n* **-1.** *(U)* [promotion in job] promoção *f* **-2.** [improvement] avanço *m.*
advantage [əd'vɑ:ntɪdʒ] *n* **-1.** vantagem *f*; **to be to one's ~** ser conveniente para alguém; **to have** OR **hold the ~ (over sb)** ter OR levar vantagem (sobre alguém) **-2.** *phr*: **to take ~ of sthg/sb** aproveitar-se de algo/alguém.
advantageous [,ædvən'teɪdʒəs] *adj* vantajoso(sa).
advent ['ædvənt] *n* [of invention, person, period] advento *m.*
◆ **Advent** *n RELIG* Advento *m.*
Advent calendar *n calendário com figuras decorativas em cada dia das quatro semanas antecedentes ao Natal, marcando o período do Advento.*
adventure [əd'ventʃə^r] *n* aventura *f*; **to have no sense of ~** não ter espírito de aventura.
adventure holiday *n* férias *fpl* de aventura.
adventure playground *n área de lazer para crianças que oferece materiais diversos para montar e brincar.*
adventurer [əd'ventʃərə^r] *n* **-1.** [adventurous person] aventureiro *m,* -ra *f* **-2.** [unscrupulous person] inescrupuloso *m,* -sa *f.*

adventurous [əd'ventʃərəs] *adj* **-1.** [person] intrépido(da) **-2.** [life, project] aventureiro(ra) **-3.** [menu, programme etc.] atraente, interessante.
adverb ['ædvɜ:b] *n* advérbio *m*.
adverbial ◇ *adj* adverbial. ◇ *n* adjunto *m* adverbial.
adversary ['ædvəsərɪ] (*pl* **-ies**) *n* adversário *m*, -ria *f*.
adverse ['ædvɜ:s] *adj* adverso(sa).
adversely ['ædvɜ:slɪ] *adv* negativamente.
adversity [əd'vɜ:sətɪ] *n (U)* adversidade *f*.
advert ['ædvɜ:t] *n UK* = **advertisement**.
advertise ['ædvətaɪz] ◇ *vt* [job, car, product] anunciar. ◇ *vi* [in newspaper, on TV, in shop window]: **they're advertising for sales representatives** estão anunciando vaga para representantes comerciais.
advertisement [əd'vɜ:tɪsmənt] *n* **-1.** [in newspaper, on TV, in shop window] anúncio *m* **-2.** *fig* [recommendation] propaganda *f*.
advertiser ['ædvətaɪzə^r] *n* anunciante *mf*.
advertising ['ædvətaɪzɪŋ] *n (U)* **-1.** [advertisements] propaganda *f* **-2.** [industry] publicidade *f*.
advertising agency *n* agência *f* de publicidade.
advertising campaign *n* campanha *f* publicitária.
advice [əd'vaɪs] *n (U)* conselho *m*; **to give sb ~** dar conselhos a alguém; **to take sb's ~** aceitar conselhos de alguém; **a piece of ~** um conselho.
advice note *n* aviso *m* de envio.
advisability [əd,vaɪzə'bɪlətɪ] *n (U)* conveniência *f*.
advisable [əd'vaɪzəbl] *adj* aconselhável.
advise [əd'vaɪz] ◇ *vt* **-1.** [give advice to]: **to ~ sb to do sthg/not to do sthg** aconselhar alguém a fazer algo/a não fazer algo **-2.** [professionally]: **to ~ sb on sthg** assessorar alguém em algo **-3.** *fml* [inform] avisar; **to ~ sb of sthg** avisar alguém sobre algo. ◇ *vi* **-1.** [give advice]: **to ~ against sthg/against doing sthg** desaconselhar algo/a fazer algo **-2.** [act as adviser]: **to ~ on sthg** assessorar em algo.
advisedly [əd'vaɪzɪdlɪ] *adv* deliberadamente.
adviser *UK*, **advisor** *US* [əd'vaɪzə^r] *n* assessor *m*, -ra *f*.
advisory [əd'vaɪzərɪ] *adj* [group, organization] de assessoria; **in an ~ capacity** *OR* **role** com função *OR* no papel de assessor(ra).
advocacy ['ædvəkəsɪ] *n (U)* [support] defesa *f*.
advocate [*n* 'ædvəkət, *vb* 'ædvəkeɪt] ◇ *n* **-1.** *Scot JUR* advogado *m*, -da *f* **-2.** [supporter] defensor *m*, -ra *f*. ◇ *vt fml* [recommend] defender.
AEC (*abbr of* **Atomic Energy Commission**) *n organismo norte-americano de energia nuclear*, ≃ CNEN *f*.
Aegean [i:'dʒi:ən] *n*: **the ~ (Sea)** o (Mar) Egeu; **in the ~** no Egeu.
aegis ['i:dʒɪs] *n*: **under the ~ of** sob a égide de.
aeon *UK*, **eon** *US* ['i:ən] *n* **-1.** *GEOL* éon *m* **-2.** *fig* [very long time] século *m*.
aerial ['eərɪəl] ◇ *adj* [of, from, in the air] aéreo(rea). ◇ *n UK* [antenna] antena *f*.
aerobatics [,eərəʊ'bætɪks] *n (U)* acrobacias *fpl* aéreas.
aerobics [eə'rəʊbɪks] *n (U)* aeróbica *f*, ginástica *f* aeróbica.
aerodrome ['eərədrəʊm] *n esp UK* aeródromo *m*.
aerodynamic [,eərəʊdaɪ'næmɪk] *adj* aerodinâmico(ca).
◆ **aerodynamics** ◇ *n (U) SCIENCE* aerodinâmica *f*. ◇ *npl* [aerodynamic qualities] aerodinâmicas *f*.
aerogramme ['eərəgræm] *n* aerograma *m*.
aeronautics [,eərə'nɔ:tɪks] *n (U)* aeronáutica *f*.
aeroplane *UK* ['eərəpleɪn], **airplane** ['eəpleɪn] *US n* avião *m*.
aerosol ['eərəsɒl] *n* aerossol *m*.
aerospace ['eərəʊspeɪs] *n*: **the ~ industry** a indústria aeroespacial.
aesthete, esthete *US* ['i:sθi:t] *n* esteta *mf*.
aesthetic, esthetic *US* [i:s'θetɪk] *adj* estético(ca).
aesthetically, esthetically *US* [i:s'θetɪklɪ] *adv* esteticamente.
aesthetics, esthetics *US* [i:s'θetɪks] *n (U)* estética *f*.
afar [ə'fɑ:^r] *adv*: **from ~** à distância.
AFC (*abbr of* **Association Football Club**) *n futebol clube britânico*, FC *f*.
AFDC (*abbr of* **Aid to Families with Dependent Children**) *n associação norte-americana para auxílio a famílias com crianças portadoras de necessidades especiais*, ≃ APAE *f*.
affable ['æfəbl] *adj* [pleasant] afável.
affair [ə'feə^r] *n* **-1.** [event] acontecimento *m* **-2.** [concern] assunto *m* **-3.** [extramarital relationship] caso *m*.
◆ **affairs** *npl* **-1.** [business, personal interests] negócios *mpl* **-2.** [matters] questões *fpl*.
affect [ə'fekt] *vt* **-1.** [influence, act upon] afetar **-2.** [imitate, put on] imitar **-3.** [feign] fingir.
affectation [,æfek'teɪʃn] *n* **-1.** [mannerism] afetação *f* **-2.** [pretence] fingimento *m*.
affected [ə'fektɪd] *adj* [mannered] afetado(da).
affection [ə'fekʃn] *n* afeição *f*.
affectionate [ə'fekʃnət] *adj* afetuoso(osa).
affectionately [ə'fekʃnətlɪ] *adv* afetuosamente.
affidavit [,æfɪ'deɪvɪt] *n* juramento *m*.
affiliate [*n* ə'fɪlɪət, *vb* ə'fɪlɪeɪt] ◇ *n* filiado *m*, -da *f*. ◇ *vt*: **to be ~d to** *OR* **with sthg** ser filiado(da) a algo.
affiliation [ə,fɪlɪ'eɪʃn] *n* afiliação *f*.
affinity [ə'fɪnətɪ] (*pl* **-ies**) *n* **-1.** *(U)* [attraction] atração *f*; **to have an ~ with sb/sthg** sentir atração por alguém/algo **-2.** [connection, similarity] afinidade *f*; **to have an ~ with sb/sthg** ter afinidade com alguém/algo.
affirm [ə'fɜ:m] *vt* afirmar.
affirmation [,æfə'meɪʃn] *n* afirmação *f*.
affirmative [ə'fɜ:mətɪv] ◇ *adj* afirmativo(va). ◇ *n* afirmativa *f*; **to reply in the ~** responder que sim/positivamente.
affix [ə'fɪks] *vt* [stamp] afixar.
afflict [ə'flɪkt] *vt* afligir; **to be ~ed with sthg** sofrer de algo.
affliction [ə'flɪkʃn] *n* **-1.** [distress] aflição *f* **-2.** [physical] doença *f*.
affluence ['æfluəns] *n (U)* riqueza *f*.

affluent ['æfluənt] *adj* rico(ca).
affluent society *n* sociedade *f* afluente.
afford [ə'fɔ:d] *vt* **-1.** [have enough money for]: **to be able to ~ sthg** poder pagar por algo **-2.** [time, energy]: **to be able to ~ the time (to do sthg)** ter tempo (para fazer algo) **-3.** [allow]: **we can't ~ to let this happen** não podemos nos dar ao luxo de deixar que isto aconteça **-4.** *fml* [provide, give] oferecer.
affordable [ə'fɔ:dəbl] *adj* acessível.
afforestation [æ,fɒrɪ'steɪʃn] *n (U)* florestamento *m*.
affray [ə'freɪ] *n UK fml* [disturbance] desordem *f*.
affront [ə'frʌnt] <> *n* afronta *f*. <> *vt* ofender.
Afghan ['æfgæn], **Afghani** [æf'gænɪ] <> *adj* afegão(gã) <> *n* afegão *m*, -gã *f*, afegane *mf*.
Afghan hound *n* Afghan hound *mf*.
Afghani *adj* & *n* = **Afghan**.
Afghanistan [æf'gænɪstæn] *n* Afeganistão; **in ~** no Afeganistão.
afield [ə'fɪəld] *adv*: **far ~** longe.
AFL-CIO (*abbr of* **American Federation of Labor and Congress of Industrial Organizations**) *n federação norte-americana de sindicatos da indústria.*
afloat [ə'fləʊt] *adj* **-1.** [above water] flutuante **-2.** *fig* [out of debt] em dia.
afoot [ə'fʊt] *adj* [present, happening] em ação.
aforementioned [ə,fɔ:'menʃənd], **aforesaid** [ə'fɔ:sed] *adj fml* acima mencionado(da).
afraid [ə'freɪd] *adj* **-1.** [frightened] assustado(da); **to be ~ (of sb/sth)** ter medo (de alguém/algo); **to be ~ of doing** *OR* **to do sthg** ter medo de fazer algo **-2.** [reluctant, apprehensive] apreensivo(va); **to be ~ (that)** ter medo (que); **to be ~ of sthg** ter medo de algo; **he was ~ of losing his job** tinha medo de perder seu emprego **-3.** [in apologies]: **to be ~ (that)** ter receio (que); **I'm ~ so/not** receio que sim/não.
afresh [ə'freʃ] *adv* novamente.
Africa ['æfrɪkəl *n* África; **in ~** na África.
African ['æfrɪkən] <> *adj* africano(na). <> *n* africano *m*, -na *f*.
African American <> *adj* afro-americano(na). <> *n* afro-americano *m*, -na *f*.
African violet *n* violeta *f* africana.
Afrikaans [,æfrɪ'kɑ:ns] *n* africâner *m*.
Afrikaner [,æfrɪ'kɑ:nə^r] *n* africâner *mf*.
aft [ɑ:ft] *adv* à popa *OR* ré.
after ['ɑ:ftə^r] <> *prep* **-1.** [following - in time] após; [- in order] após; **~ you!** atrás de você! **-2.** [as a result of] depois **-3.** [in spite of] apesar de **-4.** *inf* [in search of, looking for] atrás de **-5.** [with the name of] em homenagem a **-6.** [directed at sb moving away] atrás de **-7.** *ART* à moda de **-8.** *US* [telling the time]: **it's twenty ~ three** são três e vinte. <> *adv* em seguida, depois. <> *conj* depois que/de; **~ she left university ...** depois que deixou/de deixar a universidade, ela ...
◆ **afters** *npl UK* sobremesa *f*.
◆ **after all** *adv* **-1.** [in spite of everything] apesar de tudo **-2.** [it should be remembered] afinal.
afterbirth ['ɑ:ftəbɜ:θ] *n* placenta *f*.
aftercare ['ɑ:ftəkeə^r] *n (U) ajuda oficial para quem acabou de sair do hospital ou da prisão.*
after-effects *npl* efeitos *mpl* secundários, conseqüências *fpl*.
afterlife ['ɑ:ftəlaɪf] (*pl* **-lives** [-laɪvz]) *n* vida *f* após a morte.
aftermath ['ɑ:ftəmæθ] *n* conseqüências *fpl*.
afternoon [,ɑ:ftə'nu:n] *n* tarde *f*; **good ~** boa tarde.
◆ **afternoons** *adv esp US* à tarde.
after-sales service *n* serviço *m* pós-venda.
aftershave ['ɑ:ftəʃeɪv] *n* loção *f* após-barba.
aftershock ['ɑ:ftəʃɒk] *n* pequenos tremores *mpl (após terremoto).*
aftersun (lotion) *n* creme *m* hidratante após-sol.
aftertaste ['ɑ:ftəteɪst] *n* [of food, drink] ressaibo *m*, mau sabor *m*.
afterthought ['ɑ:ftəθɔ:t] *n* pensamento *m* a posteriori.
afterwards, afterward *US* ['ɑ:ftəwəd(z)] *adv* posteriormente, depois.
again [ə'gen] *adv* **-1.** [one more time] outra vez; **~ and ~** repetidas vezes; **all over ~** tudo de novo; **time and ~** mil vezes **-2.** [once more as before] de novo **-3.** [asking for information to be repeated]: **what was that ~?** o que foi mesmo que você disse? **-4.** *phr*: **half as much ~** cinqüenta por cento a mais; **(twice) as much ~** (duas) vezes mais; **come ~?** *inf* o que?; **then** *OR* **there ~** por outro lado.
against [ə'genst] <> *prep* **-1.** [gen] contra **-2.** [in contrast to]: **as ~** em comparação com, em vez de. <> *adv* contra.
age [eɪdʒ] (*cont* **ageing** *OR* **aging**) <> *n* **-1.** [of person, animal, thing] idade *f*; **what ~ are you?** quantos anos você tem?; **to be of ~** *US* ser maior de idade; **to come of ~** atingir à maioridade; **to be under ~** ser menor de idade; **act your ~!** pare de agir como criança! **-2.** *(U)* [state or process of ageing - of person] idade *f*; [- of object, cheese, wine] tempo *m*; **wine improves with ~** o vinho melhora com o tempo **-3.** [stage - of person's life] idade *f*, hora *f*; [- of history] era *f*. <> *vt* envelhecer. <> *vi* envelhecer.
◆ **ages** *npl* [a long time]: **~s ago** séculos atrás; **for ~s** há séculos.
aged [*adj sense 1* eɪdʒd, *adj sense 2 & npl* 'eɪdʒɪd] <> *adj* **-1.** [of the stated age] da idade de; **a person ~ 30** uma pessoa de 30 anos; **to be ~ 20** ter 20 anos (de idade) **-2.** [very old] envelhecido(da), antigo(ga). <> *npl*: **the ~** [the elderly] os idosos.
age group *n* grupo *m* etário.
ageing ['eɪdʒɪŋ] <> *adj* **-1.** [getting old - person] idoso(sa); **the ~ population** a população de idosos; [- thing] velho(lha), ultrapassado(da) **-2.** [thing] velho(lha), ultrapassado(da). <> *n (U)* [process of getting old] envelhecimento *m*.
ageless ['eɪdʒlɪs] *adj* [person, thing] imutável, eterno(na).
agency ['eɪdʒənsɪ] (*pl* **-ies**) *n* **-1.** [gen] agência *f* **-2.** [government organisation] órgão *m*.
agenda [ə'dʒendə] (*pl* **-s**) *n* pauta *f*, agenda *f*.
agent ['eɪdʒənt] *n* **-1.** [person] agente *mf* **-2.** [substance] reagente *m*.
age-old *adj* [very old] antigo(ga).

aggravate ['ægrəveɪt] *vt* **-1.** [make worse] agravar **-2.** [annoy] irritar.
aggravating ['ægrəveɪtɪŋ] *adj* [person, behaviour, problem] agravante, irritante.
aggravation [ˌægrə'veɪʃn] *n (U)* [irritation] agravo *m*, irritação *f*.
aggregate ['ægrɪgət] <> *adj* total. <> *n* **-1.** [total] total *m* **-2.** [material] agregado *m*.
aggression [ə'greʃn] *n (U)* agressão *f*.
aggressive [ə'gresɪv] *adj* **-1.** [belligerent] agressivo(-va) **-2.** [forceful - campaign] agressivo(va); [- person] audaz, empreendedor(ra).
aggressively [ə'gresɪvlɪ] *adv* [belligerently] agressivamente.
aggressor [ə'gresəʳ] *n* agressor *m*, -ra *f*.
aggrieved [ə'gri:vd] *adj* [upset, hurt] magoado(da).
aggro ['ægrəʊ] *n UK inf* arruaça *f*.
aghast [ə'gɑ:st] *adj* [horrified] espantado(da); ~ **at sthg** espantado(da) (com algo).
agile [*UK* 'ædʒaɪl, *US* 'ædʒəl] *adj* [body, person, mind] ágil.
agility [ə'dʒɪlətɪ] *n (U)* agilidade *f*.
aging *adj* & *n* = **ageing**.
agitate ['ædʒɪteɪt] <> *vt* **-1.** [disturb, worry] perturbar **-2.** [shake] agitar. <> *vi* [campaign actively]: **to ~ for/against sthg** fazer campanha pró/contra algo.
agitated ['ædʒɪteɪtɪd] *adj* [disturbed, anxious] agitado(-da).
agitation [ˌædʒɪ'teɪʃn] *n* [anxiety] agitação *f*.
agitator ['ædʒɪteɪtəʳ] *n* [political activist] agitador *m*, -ra *f*.
AGM (*abbr of* **annual general meeting**) *n UK* assembléia *f* geral anual *(de clube, empresa etc)*.
agnostic [æg'nɒstɪk] <> *adj* agnóstico(ca). <> *n* agnóstico *m*, -ca *f*.
ago [ə'gəʊ] *adv* atrás; **three days ~** três dias atrás; **years/long ~** anos/tempos atrás.
agog [ə'gɒg] *adj* ansioso(osa), impaciente; **to be all ~ (with)** estar ansioso(sa) (com).
agonize, -ise ['ægənaɪz] *vi* agonizar; **to ~ (over** *OR* **about sth)** atormentar-se (com algo).
agonized ['ægənaɪzd] *adj* [faces, screams] agoniado(-da).
agonizing ['ægənaɪzɪŋ] *adj* **-1.** [decision, wait] angustiante **-2.** [pain] agonizante.
agonizingly ['ægənaɪzɪŋlɪ] *adv* [difficult, painful] angustiosamente, dolorosamente.
agony ['ægənɪ] (*pl* **-ies**) *n* **-1.** [physical pain] dores *fpl*, agonia *f*; **to be in ~** estar morrendo de dor **-2.** [mental pain] angústia *f*; **to be in ~** estar angustiado(da).
agony aunt *n UK inf* conselheira *f* sentimental.
agony column *n UK inf* consultório *m* sentimental.
agoraphobia [ˌægərə'fəʊbjə] *n* agorafobia *f*.
agree [ə'gri:] <> *vi* **-1.** [concur] concordar; **to ~ with sb/sthg** concordar com alguém/algo; **to ~ on sthg** chegar a um acordo sobre algo; **to ~ about sthg** concordar sobre algo **-2.** [consent] concordar; **to ~ to sthg** concordar com algo **-3.** [statements] conferir **-4.** [food]: **to ~ with sb** combinar com alguém **-5.** *GRAMM* : **to ~ (with)** concordar (com). <> *vt* **-1.** [price, terms] concordar **-2.** [concur]: **to ~ that** concordar que **-3.** [arrange]: **to ~ to do sthg** combinar para fazer algo **-4.** [concede]: **to ~ (that)** concordar (que).
agreeable [ə'gri:əbl] *adj* **-1.** [weather, experience] agradável **-2.** [willing]: **to be ~ to sthg** ser favorável a algo.
agreeably [ə'grɪəblɪ] *adv* [pleasantly] agradavelmente.
agreed [ə'gri:d] <> *adj*: **to be ~ on sthg** estar de acordo sobre algo. <> *adv* **-1.** [decided] de acordo **-2.** [admittedly]: **~ (that)** sem dúvida (que).
agreement [ə'gri:mənt] *n* **-1.** [accord] acordo *m*; **to be in ~ with sb/sthg** estar de acordo com alguém/algo **-2.** [settlement, contract] acordo *m*; **to reach an ~** chegar a um acordo **-3.** [consent] aceitação *f* **-4.** *GRAMM* concordância *f*.
agricultural [ˌægrɪ'kʌltʃərəl] *adj* agrícola.
agriculture ['ægrɪkʌltʃəʳ] *n* [farming] agricultura *f*.
aground [ə'graʊnd] *adv*: **to run ~** encalhar.
ah [ɑ:] *excl* ah!
aha [ɑ:'hɑ:] *excl* ah! ah!
ahead [ə'hed] *adv* **-1.** [in front] à frente; **right** *OR* **straight ~** direto em frente **-2.** [forwards] em frente; **to go on ~** ir na frente; **to be sent on ~** ser mandado(da) antes *OR* primeiro **-3.** [in competition, game] à frente **-4.** [indicating success]: **to get ~** ir adiante, prosperar **-5.** [in time] à frente.
◆ **ahead of** *prep* **-1.** [gen] à frente de **-2.** [in time] antes de; **~ of schedule** adiantado(da).
ahoy [ə'hɔɪ] *excl NAUT* à vista!; **land/ship ~!** terra/barco à vista!
AI *n* **-1.** (*abbr of* **Amnesty International**) AI *f*. **-2.** (*abbr of* **artificial intelligence**) IA *f*. **-3.** (*abbr of* **artificial insemination**) IA *f*.
aid [eɪd] <> *n* **-1.** [help] socorro *m*, assistência *f*; **to go to the ~ of sb** socorrer alguém; **in ~ of sb/sthg** em benefício de alguém/algo; **with the ~ of sb/sthg** com a ajuda de alguém/algo **-2.** [device - for teaching, learning] ferramenta *f*; [- for walking, hearing etc] aparelho *m*. <> *vt* **-1.** [help] socorrer **-2.** *JUR* : **to ~ and abet** ser cúmplice de.
aide [eɪd] *n POL* assistente *mf*.
aide-de-camp [eɪddə'kɑɒ:] (*pl* **aides-de-camp**) *n* ajudante-de-ordens *mf*.
AIDS, Aids (*abbr of* **acquired immune deficiency syndrome**) <> *n* AIDS *f*. <> *comp*: **~ specialist** médico *mf* especialista em AIDS; **~ patient** aidético *m*, -ca *f*.
aid worker *n pessoa que presta assistência em áreas atingidas por catástrofes ou guerras.*
AIH (*abbr of* **artificial insemination by husband**) *n inseminação artificial com sêmen do marido.*
ail [eɪl] *vi* [be ill] estar doente.
ailing ['eɪlɪŋ] *adj* **-1.** [ill] doente **-2.** *fig* [economy] debilitado(da).
ailment ['eɪlmənt] *n* [illness] doença *f*.
AIM (*abbr of* **alternative investment market**) *n mercado financeiro britânico de investimentos alternativos.*
aim [eɪm] <> *n* **-1.** [objective] objetivo *m* **-2.** [in firing gun, arrow] mira *f*; **to take ~ at sthg** apontar para algo. <> *vt* **-1.** [gun, camera]: **to ~ sthg at sb/sthg** mirar algo em alguém/algo **-2.** [plan, programme]:

to be ~ed at doing sthg ser *OR* estar voltado(da) para algo **-3.** [remark, criticism]: **to be ~ed at sb** ser *OR* estar direcionado(da) para alguém. <> *vi* **-1.** [point weapon] mirar; **to ~ at sthg** mirar em algo **-2.** [intend]: **to ~ at** *OR* **for sthg** visar a algo; **to ~ to do sthg** pretender fazer algo.

aimless ['eɪmlɪs] *adj* [person, life, work] sem objetivo.

aimlessly ['eɪmlɪslɪ] *adv* [wander, look] a esmo, sem rumo.

ain't [eɪnt] *inf* = **am not, are not, is not, have not, has not.**

air [eəʳ] <> *n* **-1.** [for breathing] ar *m* **-2.** [sky]: **to be seen from the ~** ser visto(ta) do alto *OR* de cima; **to throw sthg into the ~** mandar algo pelos ares; **by ~** [travel] de avião; **to be (up) in the ~** *fig* ser avoado(da) **-3.** [distinctive quality] ar *m* **-4.** *literary* [tune] melodia *f* **-5.** *RADIO & TV*: **to be on the ~** estar no ar **-6.** *phr*: **to clear the ~** *fig* esclarecer as coisas. <> *comp* aéreo(rea). <> *vt* **-1.** [washing, room, bed] arejar **-2.** [feelings, opinions] manifestar **-3.** [broadcast] anunciar. <> *vi* [washing] arejar.
◆ **airs** *npl*: **~s and graces** ares *mpl*; **to give o.s. ~s, to put on ~s** fazer pose.

airbag ['eəbæg] *n AUT* airbag *m*.

airbase ['eəbeɪs] *n* base *f* aérea.

airbed ['eəbed] *n UK* [inflatable mattress] colchão *m* inflável.

airborne ['eəbɔ:n] *adj* **-1.** [troops, regiment] transportado(da) por via aérea **-2.** [plane] em vôo.

airbrake ['eəbreɪk] *n* freio *m* de ar comprimido.

airbrush ['eəbrʌʃ] <> *n ART* aerógrafo *m*. <> *vt* **-1.** *ART* pintar com aerógrafo **-2.** *PHOT* retocar com aerógrafo **-3.** *fig*: **an ~ed version** uma versão melhorada.

airbus ['eəbʌs] *n* airbus *m*.

air-conditioned [-kən'dɪʃnd] *adj* climatizado(-da).

air-conditioning [-kən'dɪʃnɪŋ] *n* ar *m* condicionado.

aircraft ['eəkrɑ:ft] (*pl inv*) *n* aeronave *f*, avião *m*.

aircraft carrier *n* porta-aviões *m inv*.

air cushion *n* **-1.** [inflatable cushion] almofada *f* inflável **-2.** [of hovercraft etc] colchão *m* de ar.

airfield ['eəfi:ld] *n* aeródromo *m*.

air force <> *n* força *f* aérea. <> *comp* da força aérea.

air freight *n* frete *m* aérea.

air freshener [-'freʃnəʳ] *n* purificador *m* de ar.

airgun ['eəgʌn] *n* pistola *f* de ar comprimido.

air hostess *n UK* aeromoça *f*.

airily ['eərəlɪ] *adv* [light-heartedly, casually] despreocupadamente, alegremente.

airing ['eərɪŋ] *n*: **to give sthg an ~** [clothes] dar uma arejada em algo; [room] ventilar algo; *fig* [opinion] refrescar algo.

airing cupboard *n UK* armário *m* para secar roupa.

air lane *n* rota *f* aérea.

airless ['eəlɪs] *adj* abafado(da).

air letter *n* aerograma *m*.

airlift ['eəlɪft] <> *n* transporte *m* aéreo. <> *vt* transportar por via áerea.

airline ['eəlaɪn] *n* companhia *f* aérea.

airliner ['eəlaɪnəʳ] *n* avião *m* de passageiros.

airlock ['eəlɒk] *n* **-1.** [in tube, pipe] retentor *m* de ar **-2.** [airtight chamber] câmara *f* de compressão.

airmail ['eəmeɪl] *n* correio *m* aéreo; **by ~** por via aérea.

airman ['eəmən] (*pl* **-men** [-mən]) *n* [aviator] aviador *m*.

air mattress *n* colchão *m* de ar.

air miles *npl* milhas *fpl* aéreas.

airplane ['eəpleɪn] *n US* = **aeroplane**.

airplay ['eəpleɪ] *n* [on radio] divulgação *m*.

air pocket *n* bolsa *f* de ar.

airport ['eəpɔ:t] <> *n* aeroporto *m*. <> *comp* de aeroporto.

air raid *n* ataque *m* aéreo.

air-raid shelter *n* abrigo *m* antiaéreo.

air rifle *n* espingarda *f* de ar comprimido.

airship ['eəʃɪp] *n* dirigível *m*.

airsick ['eəsɪk] *adj*: **to be ~** estar enjoado(da).

airspace ['eəspeɪs] *n* espaço *m* aéreo.

airspeed ['eəspi:d] *n* velocidade *f* no ar.

air steward *n* comissário *m* de bordo.

air stewardess *n* aeromoça *f*.

air strike *n MIL* ataque *m* aéreo.

airstrip ['eəstrɪp] *n* campo *m* de pouso.

air terminal *n* terminal *m* aéreo.

airtight ['eətaɪt] *adj* hermético(ca).

airtime ['eətaɪm] *n* [on radio] tempo *m* de transmissão.

air-to-air *adj* [missile] do ar para o ar.

air-traffic control *n* controle *m* de tráfego aéreo.

air-traffic controller *n* controlador *m* de tráfego aéreo.

air travel *n* viagem *f* aérea; **~ is cheaper now** viajar de avião é mais barato agora.

airwaves ['eəweɪvz] *npl* ondas *fpl* de rádio.

airy ['eərɪ] (*compar* **-ier**, *superl* **-iest**) *adj* **-1.** [room] arejado(da) **-2.** [notions, promises] leviano(na) **-3.** [nonchalant] indiferente.

aisle [aɪl] *n* **-1.** [in church] nave *f* lateral **-2.** [in plane, theatre, shop] corredor *m*.

ajar [ə'dʒɑ:ʳ] *adj* [door] entreaberto(ta).

AK *abbr of* **Alaska**.

aka (*abbr of* **also known as**) também conhecido(da) como.

akin [ə'kɪn] *adj* semelhante.

AL *abbr of* **Alabama**.

Alabama [ˌælə'bæməl] *n* Alabama.

alabaster [ˌælə'bɑ:stəʳ] *n* alabastro *m*.

à la carte *adj & adv* à la carte.

alacrity [ə'lækrətɪ] *n fml* [eagerness] prontidão *f*.

alarm [ə'lɑ:m] <> *n* **-1.** [fear] susto *m* **-2.** [device] alarme *m*; **to raise** *OR* **sound the ~** dar *OR* soar o alarme. <> *vt* [scare] alarmar.

alarm clock *n* despertador *m*.

alarming [ə'lɑ:mɪŋ] *adj* alarmante.

alarmingly [ə'lɑ:mɪŋlɪ] *adv* [worryingly] de forma alarmante.

alarmist [ə'lɑ:mɪst] *adj* [person, ideas] alarmista.

alas [ə'læs] *excl literary* ai!

Alaska [ə'læskəl] *n* Alasca.

Albania [æl'beɪnjəl] *n* Albânia; **in ~** na Albânia.
Albanian [æl'beɪnjən] ◇ *adj* albanês(nesa). ◇ *n* **-1.** [person] albanês *m*, -sa *f* **-2.** [language] albanês *m*.
albatross ['ælbətrɒs] (*pl inv* OR **-es**) *n* albatroz *m*.
albeit [ɔ:l'bi:ɪt] *conj fml* embora.
Alberta [æl'bɜ:tə] *n* Alberta.
Albert Hall *n*: **the ~** o Albert Hall.
alderman ['ɔ:ldəmən] (*pl* **-men** [-mən]) *n* vereador *m*.
ale [eɪl] *n* cerveja *f*.
alert [ə'lɜ:t] ◇ *adj* **-1.** [vigilant, aware] alerta; **to be ~ to sthg** estar alerta para algo **-2.** [perceptive] atento(ta). ◇ *n* [warning] alerta *f*; **on the ~** [watchful] em estado de alerta; **on ~** MIL em estado de alerta; **to give the ~** dar o sinal de alerta. ◇ *vt* **-1.** [warn] alertar, avisar **-2.** [make aware]: **to ~ sb to sthg** alertar alguém sobre algo.
Aleutian Islands [ə'lu:ʃjən-] *npl*: **the ~** as Ilhas Aleutas.
A level (*abbr of* **Advanced level**) *n* SCH *exame feito ao final do ensino médio na Grã-Bretanha*

A LEVEL

Na Grã-Bretanha (à exceção da Escócia), os *A-Levels* são exames prestados por aqueles que desejam dar prosseguimento a seus estudos, após a conclusão do ensino secundário. Em geral, o estudante faz os *A-Levels* aos 18 anos, após dois anos de curso preparatório, e pode escolher as disciplinas em que prestará seus exames. Normalmente, são necessários três *A-Levels* para ingressar na universidade, embora muita gente preste os exames apenas para melhorar seu currículo.

Alexander technique *n*: **the ~** a técnica de Alexander.
Alexandria [ˌælɪg'zɑ:ndrɪə] *n* Alexandria; **in ~** em Alexandria.
alfalfa [æl'fælfə] *n* alfalfa *f*.
alfresco [æl'freskəʊ] *adj, adv* [meal, eat] ao ar livre.
algae ['ældʒi:] *npl* algas *fpl*.
Algarve [æl'gɑ:v] *n*: **the ~** o Algarve; **in the ~** no Algarve.
algebra ['ældʒɪbrə] *n* álgebra *f*.
Algeria [æl'dʒɪərɪə] *n* Argélia; **in ~** na Argélia.
Algerian [æl'dʒɪərɪən] ◇ *adj* argelino(na). ◇ *n* argelino *m*, -na *f*.
Algiers [æl'dʒɪəz] *n* Argel; **in ~** em Argel.
algorithm ['ælgərɪðm] *n* algoritmo *m*.
alias ['eɪlɪəs] (*pl* **-es**) ◇ *adv* vulgo. ◇ *n* nome *m* falso.
alibi ['ælɪbaɪ] *n* álibi *m*.
alien ['eɪljən] ◇ *adj* **-1.** [foreign] estrangeiro(ra) **-2.** [from outer space] alienígena **-3.** [unfamiliar] estranho(nha). ◇ *n* **-1.** [from outer space] alienígena *mf* **-2.** JUR [foreigner] estrangeiro *m*, -ra *f*.
alienate ['eɪljəneɪt] *vt* [estrange] alienar.
alienation [ˌeɪljə'neɪʃn] *n* **-1.** [estrangement] afastamento *m* **-2.** [feeling of not belonging] alienação *f*.
alight [ə'laɪt] (*pt* & *pp* **-ed** OR **alit**) ◇ *adj* [on fire] em chamas. ◇ *vi fml* **-1.** [land] pousar **-2.** [from train, bus] descer; **to ~ from sthg** descer de algo.
align [ə'laɪn] *vt* **-1.** [line up] alinhar **-2.** [ally]: **to ~ o.s. with sb** aliar-se a alguém.
alignment [ə'laɪnmənt] *n* **-1.** [of car wheels, brakes, books] alinhamento *m* **-2.** [with an ally] aliança *f*.
alike [ə'laɪk] ◇ *adj* [two people, things] semelhante, parecido(da). ◇ *adv* [in a similar way] de forma semelhante; **they look ~** eles são parecidos.
alimentary canal [ˌælɪ'mentərɪ-] *n* tubo *m* digestivo.
alimony ['ælɪmənɪ] *n* pensão *f* (alimentícia).
A-line *adj* evasê.
alive [ə'laɪv] *adj* **-1.** [living] vivo(va); **to come ~** ganhar vida **-2.** [aware]: **to be ~ to sthg** estar consciente de algo **-3.** [full]: **to be ~ with sthg** estar cheio(cheia) de algo, fervilhar de algo.
alkali ['ælkəlaɪ] (*pl* **-s** OR **-es**) *n* álcali *m*.
alkaline ['ælkəlaɪn] *adj* alcalino(na).
all [ɔ:l] ◇ *adj* **-1.** [with singular noun] todo(da); **~ the money** o dinheiro todo; **~ the time** sempre; **we were out ~ day** estivemos fora o dia inteiro. **-2.** [with plural noun] todos(das); **~ the houses** todas as casas; **~ trains stop at Trenton** todos os trens param em Trenton. ◇ *adv* **-1.** [completely] completamente; **~ alone** completamente só. **-2.** [in scores]: **it's two ~** dois a dois *(empate)*. **-3.** [in phrases]: **~ but empty** quase vazio(zia); **~ over** [finished] terminado(da). ◇ *pron* **-1.** [everything] tudo; [people, things] todos *mpl*, -das *fpl*; **is that ~?** [in store] mais alguma coisa?; **the best of ~** o melhor de todos. **-2.** [everybody] todos, todo o mundo; **~ of us went** fomos todos. **-3.** [in phrases]: **can I help you at ~** posso ajudar em alguma coisa?; **in ~** [in total] ao todo; **in ~ it was a great success** resumindo, foi um grande êxito.
Allah ['ælə] *n* Alá *m*.
all-around *adj* US = **all-round**.
allay [ə'leɪ] *vt fml* **-1.** [calm] abrandar **-2.** [solve, settle] dirimir.
all clear *n* **-1.** [signal] *sinal de fim de estado de alerta* **-2.** *fig* [go-ahead] permissão *f* para prosseguir.
allegation [ˌælɪ'geɪʃn] *n* alegação *f*; **to make ~s (about sb/sthg)** fazer alegações (sobre alguém/algo).
allege [ə'ledʒ] *vt* [claim] alegar; **to ~ that** alegar que.
alleged [ə'ledʒd] *adj* suposto(ta).
allegedly [ə'ledʒɪdlɪ] *adv* supostamente.
allegiance [ə'li:dʒəns] *n*: **~ (to sb/sthg)** lealdade (a alguém/algo).
allegorical [ˌælɪ'gɒrɪkl] *adj* alegórico(ca).
allegory ['ælɪgərɪ] (*pl* **-ies**) *n* alegoria *f*.
alleluia [ˌælɪ'lu:jə] *excl* aleluia!
allergic [ə'lɜ:dʒɪk] *adj* alérgico(ca); **~ to sthg** *lit & fig* alérgico(ca) a algo.
allergy ['ælədʒɪ] (*pl* **-ies**) *n* alergia *f*; **to have an ~ to sthg** ter alergia a algo.
alleviate [ə'li:vɪeɪt] *vt* [ease] aliviar.
alley(way) ['ælɪ(weɪ)] *n* [narrow path] beco *m*.
alliance [ə'laɪəns] *n* **-1.** [agreement] acordo *m* **-2.** [union] aliança *f*.
allied ['ælaɪd] *adj* **-1.** [powers, troops] aliado(da) **-2.** [related] relacionado(da).
alligator ['ælɪgeɪtə[r]] (*pl inv* OR **-s**) *n* aligátor *m*.
all-important *adj* [crucial] crucial.

all-in *adj UK* [price] tudo incluído.
◆ **all in** ◇ *adj inf* [tired] exausto(ta). ◇ *adv UK* [inclusive] com extras incluído.

all-in-one *n* [garment - underwear or for cycling] macaquinho *m*; [- top and trousers] macacão *m*.

all-in wrestling *n* luta *f* livre.

alliteration [əˌlɪtəˈreɪʃn] *n* aliteração *f*.

all-night *adj* [party, vigil, session] que dura toda a noite; [chemist's, shop] 24 horas.

allocate [ˈæləkeɪt] *vt*: **to ~ sthg to sb/sthg** [money, resources, items] alocar algo para alguém/algo; [task] atribuir algo para alguém/algo.

allocation [ˌæləˈkeɪʃn] *n* **-1.** [sharing out - of money, resources, items] alocação *f*; [- of task, responsibility] atribuição *f* **-2.** [share - of money, resources] alocação *f*; [- of tickets, seats, places] atribuição *f*.

allot [əˈlɒt] (*pt* & *pp* **-ted**, *cont* **-ting**) *vt* [allocate - task] distribuir; [- money, resources] repartir; [- time] dedicar.

allotment [əˈlɒtmənt] *n* **-1.** *UK* [garden] lote *m* **-2.** [sharing out - of tasks, resources] distribuição *f*; [- of money] partilha *f*; [- of time] dedicação *f* **-3.** [share - of money, resources] cota *f*; [- of time] alocação *f*.

all-out *adj* [effort] supremo(ma) ; [war] total ; [attack] resoluto(ta).

allow [əˈlaʊ] *vt* **-1.** [permit] permitir; **to ~ sb to do sthg** permitir OR deixar alguém fazer algo; **~ me** permita-me, deixe-me **-2.** [allocate] destinar **-3.** [admit]: **to ~ (that)** admitir que.
◆ **allow for** *vt fus* levar em conta OR consideração.

allowable [əˈlaʊəbl] *adj* [acceptable] aceitável, permitido(da).

allowance [əˈlaʊəns] *n* **-1.** [grant] subsídio *m*, auxílio *m* **-2.** *Am* [pocket money] mesada *f* **-3.** FIN [tax exemption] isenção *f* **-4.** [excuse]: **to make ~s for sb/sthg** fazer concessões para alguém OR algo.

alloy [ˈælɔɪ] *n* [metal] liga *f*.

all-powerful *adj* onipotente, todo-poderoso(sa).

all right ◇ *adv* **-1.** [gen] bem **-2.** [indicating agreement] sim, o.k. **-3.** [do you understand?]: **all right?** certo? **-4.** [now then] certo, o.k. ◇ *adj* **-1.** [healthy, unharmed]: **to be ~** estar bem **-2.** *inf* [acceptable, satisfactory]: **how was the film? - ~, I suppose** como foi o filme? - legal, imagino; **sorry I'm late - that's ~** desculpe, estou atrasada - não tem importância **-3.** [permitted]: **is it ~ if...?** tudo bem se ...?, posso ...?

all-round *UK*, **all-around** *US adj* **-1.** [athlete, worker] versátil **-2.** [improvement] global.

all-rounder [-ˈraʊndə^r] *n* **-1.** [versatile person] pessoa *f* versátil **-2.** SPORT: **he is an ~ at football** no futebol, ele se destaca em várias posições.

all-terrain vehicle *n* (veículo) *m* fora-de-estrada *m*.

all-time *adj* [record, best]: **it was an ~ record** foi um recorde insuperável; **one of the ~ greatest songs** uma das melhores canções de todos os tempos.

allude [əˈluːd] *vi*: **to ~ to sthg** aludir a algo.

allure [əˈljʊə^r] *n* [attraction] fascinação *f*, encanto *m*.

alluring [əˈljʊərɪŋ] *adj* [attractive] fascinante, encantador(ra).

allusion [əˈluːʒn] *n* [reference] alusão *f*.

ally [*n* ˈælaɪ, *vb* əˈlaɪ] (*pl* **-ies**, *pt* & *pp* **-ied**) ◇ *n* **-1.** MIL & POL aliado *m*, -da *f* **-2.** [associate, helper] associado *m*, -da *f*. ◇ *vt*: **to ~ o.s. with sb** aliar-se a alguém.

almanac [ˈɔːlmənæk] *n* [book] almanaque *m*.

almighty [ɔːlˈmaɪtɪ] *adj inf* [enormous] enorme.
◆ **Almighty** ◇ *adj* onipotente. ◇ *n*: **the Almighty** o Todo-Poderoso.

almond [ˈɑːmənd] *n* **-1.** [nut] amêndoa *f* **-2.** [tree] amendoeira *f*.

almond paste *n* pasta *f* de amêndoas.

almost [ˈɔːlməʊst] *adv* quase, praticamente.

alms [ɑːmz] *npl dated* esmola *f*.

aloft [əˈlɒft] *adv* **-1.** [in the air] no ar, nas alturas **-2.** NAUT no topo do mastro.

alone [əˈləʊn] ◇ *adj* [without others] só, sozinho (nha); **to be ~ with sb** estar a sós com alguém. ◇ *adv* **-1.** [without others] só; **to go it ~** fazer algo por conta própria **-2.** [only] somente, só; **he ~ knows the answer** só OR somente ele sabe a resposta **-3.** [untouched, unchanged]: **to leave sthg ~** deixar algo em paz, parar de mexer em algo; **leave me ~!** deixe-me em paz!
◆ **let alone** *conj* sem falar em.

along [əˈlɒŋ] ◇ *adv*: **they went ~ to the demonstration** eles foram OR se dirigiram para a demonstração; **she insisted on coming ~** ela insistiu em vir junto OR também; **I took her ~ to the concert** levei-a comigo ao concerto. ◇ *prep* **-1.** [from one end to the other] ao longo de **-2.** [beside] ao lado de, junto de **-3.** [in] em.
◆ **all along** *adv* o tempo todo.
◆ **along with** *prep* junto com.

alongside [əˌlɒŋˈsaɪd] ◇ *prep* [next to] junto a; [beside] ao lado de. ◇ *adv* lado a lado.

aloof [əˈluːf] ◇ *adj* [reserved] reservado(da). ◇ *adv* [distant]: **to remain ~ (from sthg)** ficar indiferente (a algo).

aloud [əˈlaʊd] *adv* alto, em voz alta.

alpaca [ælˈpækə] *n* **-1.** [animal] alpaca *f* **-2.** [material] lã *f* de alpaca.

alphabet [ˈælfəbet] *n* alfabeto *m*.

alphabetical [ˌælfəˈbetɪkl] *adj* alfabético(ca); **in ~ order** em ordem alfabética.

alphabetically [ˌælfəˈbetɪklɪ] *adv* alfabeticamente, em ordem alfabética.

alphabetize, -ise [ˈælfəbətaɪz] *vt* alfabetizar.

alphanumeric key *n* COMPUT tecla *f* alfanumérica.

alpine [ˈælpaɪn] *adj* alpino(na).

Alps [ælps] *npl*: **the ~** os Alpes; **in the ~** nos Alpes.

already [ɔːlˈredɪ] *adv* já.

alright [ˌɔːlˈraɪt] *adv* & *adj* = **all right**.

Alsace [ælˈsæs] *n* Alsácia; **in ~** na Alsácia.

Alsatian [ælˈseɪʃn] ◇ *adj* alsaciano(na). ◇ *n* **-1.** [person] alsaciano *m*, -na *f* **-2.** [dog] pastor *m* alemão.

also [ˈɔːlsəʊ] *adv* [as well] também.

also-ran *n* **-1.** [gen] perdedor *m*, -ra *f* **-2.** [horse-racing] *cavalo que não chega entre os três primeiros*.

Alta *abbr of* **Alberta**.

altar [ˈɔːltə^r] *n* altar *m*.

alter ['ɔ:ltəʳ] <> *vt* [change, modify] alterar. <> *vi* alterar-se.

alteration [ˌɔ:ltə'reɪʃn] *n* **-1.** [act of changing] alteração *f*, modificação *f* **-2.** [change] alteração *f*, mudança *f*; **to make an ~** *OR* **~s to sthg** fazer uma alteração *OR* alterações em algo.

altercation [ˌɔ:ltə'keɪʃn] *n fml* altercação *f*.

alter ego (*pl* **-s**) *n* alter ego *m*.

alternate [*adj UK* ɔ:l'tɜ:nət, *US* 'ɒ:ltərnət, *vb* 'ɔ:ltərneɪt] <> *adj* alternado(da). <> *vt* alternar. <> *vi*: **to ~ (with)** alternar(com); **to ~ between sthg and sthg** alternar entre uma coisa e outra.

alternately [ɔ:l'tɜ:nətlɪ] *adv* [by turns] alternadamente.

alternating current ['ɔ:ltəneɪtɪŋ-] *n ELEC* corrente *f* alternada.

alternation [ˌɔ:ltə'neɪʃn] *n* alternação *f*, alternância *f*.

alternative [ɔ:l'tɜ:nətɪv] <> *adj* alternativo(va). <> *n* alternativa *f*; **an ~ to sb/sthg** uma alternativa a alguém/algo; **to have no ~ (but to do sthg)** não ter alternativa (a não ser fazer algo).

alternatively [ɔ:l'tɜ:nətɪvlɪ] *adv* por outro lado, de outro modo.

alternative medicine *n* medicina *f* alternativa.

alternator ['ɔ:ltəneɪtəʳ] *n ELEC* alternador *m*.

although [ɔ:l'ðəʊ] *conj* embora, apesar de.

altitude ['æltɪtju:d] *n* altitude *f*.

alto ['æltəʊ] (*pl* **-s**) <> *n* contralto *m*. <> *comp* [flute, saxophone] alto.

altogether [ˌɔ:ltə'geðəʳ] *adv* **-1.** [completely] completamente, totalmente **-2.** [in general] de modo geral, no geral **-3.** [in total] ao todo, no total.

altruism ['æltrʊɪzm] *n* altruismo *m*.

altruistic [ˌæltrʊ'ɪstɪk] *adj* altruista.

aluminium *UK* [ˌæljʊ'mɪnɪəm], **aluminum** *US* [ə'lu:mɪnəm] <> *n* alumínio *m*. <> *comp* de alumínio; **~ foil** papel-alumínio *m*.

alumnus [ə'lʌmnəs] (*pl* **-ni** [-naɪ]) *n* ex-aluno *m*, -na *f*.

always ['ɔ:lweɪz] *adv* sempre.

am [æm] *vb* ⊳ **be**.

a.m. (ante meridiem): **at three ~** às três da manhã.

AM (*abbr of* **amplitude modulation**) *n* **-1.** AM *f*. **-2.** (*abbr of* **Master of Arts**) *(titular de) diploma de mestre em ciências humanas nos Estados Unidos.*

AMA (*abbr of* **American Medical Association**) *n* *associação norte-americana de médicos*, ≃ AMB *f*.

amalgam [ə'mælgəm] *n* **-1.** *fml* [combination] amálgama *m OR f* **-2.** *TECH* [of metals] amálgama *m OR f*.

amalgamate [ə'mælgəmeɪt] <> *vt* [unite] amalgamar, misturar. <> *vi* [unite] unir-se.

amalgamation [əˌmælgə'meɪʃn] *n* [process] amalgamação *f*.

amass [ə'mæs] *vt* [fortune, power, information] acumular.

amateur ['æmətəʳ] <> *adj* amador(ra). <> *n* amador *m*, -ra *f*.

amateurish [ˌæmə'tɜ:rɪʃ] *adj pej* [unprofessional] malfeito(ta), mal-acabado(da).

amaze [ə'meɪz] *vt* [astonish] surpreender, assombrar.

amazed [ə'meɪzd] *adj* surpreso(sa), assombrado(-da).

amazement [ə'meɪzmənt] *n* surpresa *f*, assombro *m*.

amazing [ə'meɪzɪŋ] *adj* [incredible] incrível, surpreendente.

amazingly [ə'meɪzɪŋlɪ] *adv* [very] surpreendentemente.

Amazon ['æməzn] *n* **-1.** [river]: **the ~** o Amazonas **-2.** [region]: **in the ~** na Amazônia; **the ~ (Basin)** a bacia amazônica; **the ~ rainforest** a floresta amazônica **-3.** [woman] amazona *f*.

Amazonian [ˌæmə'zəʊnjən] *adj* amazônico(ca).

ambassador [æm'bæsədəʳ] *n* embaixador *m*, -ra *f*.

amber ['æmbəʳ] <> *adj* **-1.** [amber-coloured] ambárico(ca), ambariano(na) **-2.** *UK* [traffic light] amarelo(la). <> *n* **-1.** [substance] âmbar *m* **-2.** *UK* [colour of traffic light] amarelo *m*. <> *comp* [made of amber] de âmbar.

ambiance ['æmbɪəns] *n* = **ambience**.

ambidextrous [ˌæmbɪ'dekstrəs] *adj* ambidestro(-tra).

ambience ['æmbɪəns] *n* [atmosphere] ambiente *m*, atmosfera *f*.

ambiguity [ˌæmbɪ'gju:ətɪ] (*pl* **-ies**) *n* ambigüidade *f*.

ambiguous [æm'bɪgjʊəs] *adj* ambíguo(gua).

ambiguously [æm'bɪgjʊəslɪ] *adv* de modo ambíguo.

ambition [æm'bɪʃn] *n* ambição *f*.

ambitious [æm'bɪʃəs] *adj* ambicioso(sa).

ambivalence [æm'bɪvələns] *n* **-1.** [uncertainty] incerteza *f* **-2.** [ambiguity] ambivalência *f*.

ambivalent [æm'bɪvələnt] *adj* **-1.** [uncertain] incerto(ta) **-2.** [ambiguous] ambivalente.

amble ['æmbl] *vi* [walk] passear.

ambulance ['æmbjʊləns] <> *n* ambulância *f*. <> *comp* [service, driver] de ambulância.

ambush ['æmbʊʃ] <> *n* emboscada *f*. <> *vt* [attack] emboscar.

ameba *n US* = **amoeba**.

ameliorate [ə'mi:ljəreɪt] *vt & vi fml* melhorar.

amen [ˌɑ:'men] *excl* [at end of prayer] amém!

amenable [ə'mi:nəbl] *adj*: **~ (to sthg)** receptivo(-va) (a algo).

amend [ə'mend] *vt* [change] emendar, corrigir.

◆ **amends** *npl*: **to make ~s (for sthg)** compensar (por algo).

amendment [ə'mendmənt] *n* **-1.** [change] correção *f* **-2.** [act of changing] emenda *f*.

amenities [ə'mi:nətɪz] *npl* comodidades *fpl*, conforto *m*.

America [ə'merɪkə] *n* América, Estados Unidos (da América); **in ~** na América, nos Estados Unidos (da América).

◆ **Americas** *npl*: **the ~s** as Américas, a América.

American [ə'merɪkn] <> *adj* americano(na), estadunidense. <> *n* americano *m*, -na *f*, estadunidense *mf*.

American football *n UK* futebol *m* americano.
American Indian *n* ameríndio *m*.
Americanism [ə'merɪkənɪzm] *n* [word, phrase] americanismo *m*.
americanize, -ise [ə'merɪkənaɪz] *vt* americanizar.
amethyst ['æmɪθɪst] *n* ametista *f*.
Amex *n* (*abbr of* **American Stock Exchange**) *segunda maior bolsa de valores dos Estados Unidos.*
amiable ['eɪmjəbl] *adj* [pleasant, likable] amável.
amiably ['eɪmjəblɪ] *adv* amavelmente.
amicable ['æmɪkəbl] *adj* [friendly] amigável.
amicably ['æmɪkəblɪ] *adv* amigavelmente.
amid(st) [ə'mɪd(st)] *prep fml* [among] entre, no meio de.
amino acid [ə'mi:nəʊ-] *n* aminoácido *m*.
amiss [ə'mɪs] ◇ *adj* [wrong] errado(da). ◇ *adv* [wrongly]: **to take sthg** ~ levar algo a mal.
Amman *n* Amã; **in** ~ em Amã.
ammo ['æməʊ] *n inf* MIL munição *f*.
ammonia [ə'məʊnjə] *n* [liquid] amônia *f*; [gas] amoníaco *m*.
ammunition [ˌæmjʊ'nɪʃn] *n* **-1.** [bombs, bullets] munição *f* **-2.** *fig* [information, argument] argumento *m*.
ammunition dump *n* paiol *m*, depósito *m* de munição.
amnesia [æm'ni:zjə] *n* amnésia *f*.
amnesty ['æmnəstɪ] (*pl* **-ies**) *n* anistia *f*.
Amnesty International *n* Anistia *f* Internacional.
amniocentesis *n* amniocentese *f*.
amoeba *UK* (*pl* **-bas** OR **-bae** [-bi:]), **ameba** *US* (*pl* **-bas** OR **-bae** [-bi:]) [ə'mi:bə] *n* ameba *f*.
amok [ə'mɒk] *adv*: **to run** ~ *correr cega e furiosamente com o intuito de matar.*
among(st) [ə'mʌŋ(st)] *prep* **-1.** [surrounded by, in middle of] no meio de, entre **-2.** [within, between, included in] entre.
amoral [ˌeɪ'mɒrəl] *adj* [person, behaviour] amoral.
amorous ['æmərəs] *adj* amoroso(sa).
amorphous [ə'mɔ:fəs] *adj* amorfo(fa).
amortize [ə'mɔ:taɪz] *vt* FIN amortizar.
amount [ə'maʊnt] *n* **-1.** [quantity] quantidade *f*, volume *m* **-2.** [sum of money] quantia *f*.
◆ **amount to** *vt fus* **-1.** [total] totalizar, atingir a quantia de **-2.** [be equivalent to] equivaler.
amp *n* **-1.** (*abbr of* **ampere**) A. **-2.** *fam* (*abbr of* **amplifier**) amplificador *m*.
amperage ['æmpərɪdʒ] *n* ELEC amperagem *f*.
ampere ['æmpeəʳ] *n* ampère *m*.
ampersand ['æmpəsænd] *n* ampersand *m* (*nome do sinal gráfico '&'*)
amphetamine [æm'fetəmi:n] *n* anfetamina *f*.
amphibian [æm'fɪbɪən] *n* anfíbio *m*.
amphibious [æm'fɪbɪəs] *adj* [animal, vehicle] anfíbio(-bia).
amphitheatre *UK*, **amphitheater** *US* ['æmfɪˌθɪətəʳ] *n* anfiteatro *m*.
ample ['æmpl] *adj* **-1.** [enough] suficiente **-2.** [large] amplo(pla).
amplification [ˌæmplɪfɪ'keɪʃn] *n* **-1.** [of sound] amplificação *f* **-2.** [of idea, statement] ampliação *f*.
amplifier ['æmplɪfaɪəʳ] *n* [for radio, stereo] amplificador *m*.
amplify ['æmplɪfaɪ] (*pt* & *pp* **-ied**) ◇ *vt* **-1.** [sound] amplificar **-2.** [idea, statement] ampliar. ◇ *vi* [expand]: **to** ~ **(on sthg)** complementar (algo).
amply ['æmplɪ] *adv* **-1.** [sufficiently] amplamente **-2.** [considerably] consideravelmente.
ampoule *UK*, **ampule** *US* ['æmpu:l] *n* ampola *f*.
amputate ['æmpjʊteɪt] ◇ *vt* [limb] amputar. ◇ *vi* [perform amputation] amputar.
amputation [ˌæmpjʊ'teɪʃn] *n* amputação *f*.
Amsterdam [ˌæmstə'dæm] *n* Amsterdã; **in** ~ em Amsterdã.
Amtrak ['æmtræk] *n empresa pública de trens mais importante dos Estados Unidos no transporte de passageiros.*
amuck [ə'mʌk] *adv* = **amok**.
amulet ['æmjʊlɪt] *n* amuleto *m*.
amuse [ə'mju:z] *vt* **-1.** [cause to laugh, smile] divertir **-2.** [entertain] entreter; **to** ~ **o.s. (by doing sthg)** entreter-se (fazendo algo).
amused [ə'mju:zd] *adj* **-1.** [entertained, delighted] divertido(da), entretido(da); **to be** ~ **at** OR **by sthg** estar entretido(da) com algo **-2.** [entertained]: **to keep o.s.** ~ entreter-se.
amusement [ə'mju:zmənt] *n* **-1.** [enjoyment] divertimento *m* **-2.** [diversion, game] diversão *f*, entretenimento *m*.
amusement arcade *n* fliperama *m*.
amusement park *n* parque *m* de diversões.
amusing [ə'mju:zɪŋ] *adj* [funny] divertido(da).
an [*stressed* æn, *unstressed* ən] *indef art* ▷ **a²**.
anabolic steroid [ˌænə'bɒlɪk-] *n* esteróide *m* anabólico OR anabolizante.
anachronism [ə'nækrənɪzm] *n* anacronismo *m*.
anachronistic [əˌnækrə'nɪstɪk] *adj* anacrônico(ca).
anaemia *UK*, **anemia** *US* [ə'ni:mjə] *n* anemia *f*.
anaemic *UK*, **anemic** *US* [ə'ni:mɪk] *adj* [suffering from anaemia] anêmico(ca).
anaesthesia *UK*, **anesthesia** *US* [ˌænɪs'θi:zjə] *n* anestesia *f*.
anaesthetic *UK*, **anesthetic** *US* [ˌænɪs'θetɪk] *n* anestésico *m*; **under** ~ anestesiado(da).
anaesthetist *UK*, **anesthetist** *US* [æ'ni:sθətɪst] *n* anestesista *mf*.
anaesthetize *UK*, -ise *UK*, **anesthetize** *US* [æ'ni:sθətaɪz] *vt* anestesiar.
anagram ['ænəgræm] *n* anagrama *m*.
anal ['eɪnl] *adj* anal.
analgesic [ˌænæl'dʒi:sɪk] ◇ *adj* analgésico(ca). ◇ *n* analgésico *m*.
analog *adj* & *n US* = **analogue**.
analogous [ə'næləgəs] *adj fml* [comparable]: ~ **(to sthg)** análogo OR semelhante (a algo).
analogue, analog *US* ['ænəlɒg] ◇ *adj* [watch, clock] analógico(ca). ◇ *n fml* [similar object, device] análogo *m*.
analogy [ə'nælədʒɪ] (*pl* **-ies**) *n* [similarity] analogia *f*; **to draw an** ~ **with/between** fazer uma analogia com/entre; **by** ~ por analogia.
analyse *UK*, **analyze** *US* ['ænəlaɪz] *vt* [examine] analisar.

analysis [ə'næləsɪs] (*pl* **analyses** [ə'næləsi:z]) *n* **-1.** análise *f* **-2.** *phr:* **in the final** *OR* **last ~** afinal de contas.

analyst ['ænəlɪst] *n* **-1.** [political, computer, statistics] analista *mf* **-2.** [psychoanalyst] psicanalista *mf.*

analytic(al) [ˌænə'lɪtɪk(l)] *adj* [person, study, approach] analítico(ca).

analyze *vt US* = **analyse.**

anarchic [æ'nɑ:kɪk] *adj* [lacking control] anárquico(-ca).

anarchist ['ænəkɪst] *n POL* anarquista *mf.*

anarchy ['ænəkɪ] *n* [lawlessness, disorder] anarquia *f.*

anathema [ə'næθəmə] *n* [object of dislike, disapproval] anátema *m.*

anatomical [ˌænə'tɒmɪkl] *adj* anatômico(ca).

anatomy [ə'nætəmɪ] (*pl* **-ies**) *n* anatomia *f.*

ANC (*abbr of* **African National Congress**) *n* Congresso *m* Nacional Africano.

ancestor ['ænsestə^r] *n* **-1.** [person] ancestral *mf,* antepassado *m,* -da *f* **-2.** *fig* [of machine, vehicle] antecessor *m,* -ra *f.*

ancestral home [æn'sestrəl-] *n* casa *f* dos antepassados.

ancestry ['ænsestrɪ] (*pl* **-ies**) *n* linhagem *f.*

anchor ['æŋkə^r] ◇ *n* **-1.** *NAUT* âncora *f;* **to drop/weigh ~** lançar/içar âncora **-2.** *TV* [presenter] âncora *mf.* ◇ *vt* **-1.** [secure] assegurar **-2.** *TV* [present] apresentar. ◇ *vi NAUT* ancorar.

anchorage ['æŋkərɪdʒ] *n* **-1.** *NAUT* ancoradouro *m* **-2.** [means of securing] ancoragem *f.*

anchorman ['æŋkəmæn] (*pl* **-men** [-men]) *n TV* âncora *m.*

anchorwoman ['æŋkəˌwʊmən] (*pl* **women** [-ˌwɪmɪn]) *n TV* âncora *f.*

anchovy ['æntʃəvɪ] (*pl inv OR* **-ies**) *n* anchova *f.*

ancient ['eɪnʃənt] *adj* **-1.** [dating from distant past] antigo(ga) **-2.** *hum* [very old] pré-histórico(ca).

ancillary [æn'sɪlərɪ] *adj* [staff, workers, device] auxiliar.

and [*strong form* ænd, *weak form* ənd, ən] *conj* **-1.** [as well as, in addition to] e **-2.** [in numbers] e **-3.** *(with infinitive)* [in order to]: **come ~ see!** venha ver!; **try ~ come!** tente vir!; **to wait ~ see** esperar para ver.

◆ **and all that** *adv* e (todas) essas coisas.

◆ **and so on, and so forth** *adv* e assim por diante.

Andes ['ændi:z] *n*: **the ~** os Andes; **in ~** nos Andes.

Andorra [æn'dɔ:rə] *n* Andorra; **in ~** em Andorra.

androgynous [æn'drɒdʒɪnəs] *adj* andrógino(na).

android ['ændrɔɪd] *n* andróide *mf.*

anecdote ['ænɪkdəʊt] *n* anedota *f.*

anemia *n US* = **anaemia.**

anemic *adj US* = **anaemic.**

anemone [ə'nemənɪ] *n* anêmona *f.*

anesthetic *etc n US* = **anaesthetic etc.**

anew [ə'nju:] *adv* novamente.

angel ['eɪndʒəl] *n* **-1.** *RELIG* anjo *m* **-2.** *fig inf* [delightful person] anjo *m.*

Angeleno [ˌændʒə'li:nəʊ] *n habitante de ou nascido em Los Angeles.*

angelic [æn'dʒelɪk] *adj* angélico(ca).

anger ['æŋgə^r] ◇ *n* raiva *f.* ◇ *vt* irritar, zangar.

angina [æn'dʒaɪnə] *n* angina *f.*

angle ['æŋgl] ◇ *n* **-1.** *MATH* ângulo *m* **-2.** [corner] canto *m,* ângulo *m* **-3.** [point of view] ângulo *m* **-4.** [slope] ladeira *f;* **at an ~** [aslant] em ângulo. ◇ *vt* [slant] apresentar tendenciosamente. ◇ *vi* **-1.** [fish] pescar **-2.** [manoeuvre]: **to ~ for sthg** tramar para obter algo.

Anglepoise (lamp)® ['æŋglpɔɪz-] *n* luminária *f* de mesa *(flexível).*

angler ['æŋglə^r] *n* pescador *m,* -ra *f* (de linha e anzol).

Anglican ['æŋglɪkən] ◇ *adj* anglicano(na). ◇ *n* anglicano *m,* -na *f.*

anglicism ['æŋglɪsɪzm] *n* anglicismo *m.*

angling ['æŋglɪŋ] *n* [fishing] pesca *f* (com linha e anzol).

Anglo- *prefix* anglo-.

Anglo-Saxon [ˌæŋgləʊ'sæksn] ◇ *adj* anglo-saxão(ônica). ◇ *n* **-1.** [person] anglo-saxão *m,* -ônica *f* **-2.** [language] anglo-saxão *m.*

Angola [æŋ'gəʊlə] *n* Angola; **in ~** em Angola.

Angolan [æŋ'gəʊlən] ◇ *adj* angolano(na). ◇ *n* angolano *m,* -na *f.*

angora [æŋ'gɔ:rə] *n* **-1.** [goat] angorá *f;* [rabbit] angorá *mf* **-2.** [material] angorá *m.*

angrily ['æŋgrəlɪ] *adv* com irritação *OR* raiva.

angry ['æŋgrɪ] (*compar* **-ier**, *superl* **-iest**) *adj* zangado(da), furioso(sa); **to be ~ (with sb)** estar zangado(da) (com alguém); **to get ~ (with sb)** zangar-se (com alguém).

angst [æŋst] *n* ânsia *f.*

anguish ['æŋgwɪʃ] *n* angústia *f.*

anguished ['æŋgwɪʃt] *adj* angustiado(da).

angular ['æŋgjʊlə^r] *adj* [face, jaw, body] angular.

animal ['ænɪml] ◇ *adj* animal. ◇ *n* **-1.** [living creature] animal *m* **-2.** *inf pej* [brutal person] animal *m.*

animate ['ænɪmət] *adj* animado(da).

animated ['ænɪmeɪtɪd] *adj* animado(da).

animated cartoon *n* desenho *m* animado.

animation [ˌænɪ'meɪʃn] *n* animação *f.*

animosity [ˌænɪ'mɒsətɪ] (*pl* **-ies**) *n* animosidade *f.*

aniseed ['ænɪsi:d] *n* semente *f* de anis.

ankle ['æŋkl] ◇ *n* tornozelo *m.* ◇ *comp:* **~ deep** até o tornozelo.

annals ['ænlz] *npl fml* anais *mpl.*

annex ['æneks] *vt* anexar.

annexation [ˌænek'seɪʃn] *n* anexação *f.*

annexe ['æneks] *n* [building] anexo *m.*

annihilate [ə'naɪəleɪt] *vt* [destroy] aniquilar.

annihilation [əˌnaɪə'leɪʃn] *n* [destruction] aniquilação *f.*

anniversary [ˌænɪ'vɜ:sərɪ] (*pl* **-ies**) *n* aniversário *m (de casamento, de independência, etc.).*

annotate ['ænəteɪt] *vt fml* comentar.

annotated *adj*: **~ edition** edição *f* comentada.

announce [ə'naʊns] *vt* anunciar.

announcement [ə'naʊnsmənt] *n* [public statement] anúncio *m.*

announcer [ə'naʊnsə^r] *n*: **television/radio ~** locutor de televisão/rádio.

annoy [ə'nɔɪ] *vt* [irritate] irritar, amolar.

annoyance [ə'nɔɪəns] *n* irritação *f,* aborrecimento *m.*

annoyed [ə'nɔɪd] *adj* irritado(da); **to be ~ at sthg**

estar irritado(da) com algo; **to be ~ with sb** estar irritado(da) com alguém; **to get ~** irritar-se.
annoying [ə'nɔɪɪŋ] *adj* irritante.
annual ['ænjʊəl] <> *adj* anual. <> *n* **-1.** [plant] planta *f* sazonal **-2.** [book] anuário *m*, publicação *f* anual.
annual general meeting *n* reunião *f* geral anual.
annually ['ænjʊəlɪ] *adv* anualmente.
annuity [ə'nju:ɪtɪ] (*pl* **-ies**) *n* FIN anuidade *m*.
annul [ə'nʌl] (*pt* & *pp* **-led**, *cont* **-ling**) *vt* anular, invalidar.
annulment [ə'nʌlmənt] *n* anulação *f*.
annum ['ænəm] *n*: **per ~** por ano.
Annunciation [ə,nʌnsɪ'eɪʃn] *n*: **the ~** a Anunciação.
anode ['ænəʊd] *n* TECH ânodo *m*.
anoint [ə'nɔɪnt] *vt* RELIG ungir.
anomalous [ə'nɒmələs] *adj fml* anômalo(la).
anomaly [ə'nɒməlɪ] (*pl* **-ies**) *n* [different thing, person] anomalia *f*.
anon. (*abbr of* **anonymous**) anônimo(ma).
anonymity [,ænə'nɪmətɪ] *n* anonimato *m*, anonímia *f*.
anonymous [ə'nɒnɪməs] *adj* anônimo(ma).
anonymously [ə'nɒnɪməslɪ] *adv* anonimamente.
anorak ['ænəræk] *n esp UK* anoraque *m*.
anorexia (nervosa) [,ænə'reksɪə(nɜ:'vəʊsə)] *n* anorexia *f* nervosa.
anorexic [,ænə'reksɪk] <> *adj* anoréxico(ca). <> *n* anoréxico *m*, -ca *f*.
another [ə'nʌðə'] <> *adj* **-1.** [additional] outro(tra); **in ~ few minutes ...** dentro de alguns minutos ... **-2.** [different] outro(tra). <> *pron* **-1.** [an additional one] outro *m*, -tra *f*; **one after ~** um(a) depois do(da) outro(tra) **-2.** [a different one] outro *m*, -tra *f*; **to argue with one ~** discutir um com o outro/uma com a outra; **to love one ~** amar-se.
ANSI (*abbr of* **American National Standards Institute**) *n instituto norte-americano de padronização*, ≃ ABNT *f*.
answer ['ɑ:nsə'] <> *n* [reply] resposta *f*; **in ~ to sthg** em resposta a algo. <> *vt* **-1.** responder **-2.** [respond to]: **to ~ the door/phone** atender a porta/o telefone. <> *vi* [reply] responder.
◆ **answer back** <> *vt sep* retrucar. <> *vi* retrucar.
◆ **answer for** *vt fus* responder por.
answerable ['ɑ:nsərəbl] *adj* [accountable] responsável; **~ to sb** adequado(da) a alguém; **~ for sthg** responsável por algo.
answering machine, answerphone ['ɑ:nsərɪŋ-] *n* secretária *f* eletrônica.
ant [ænt] *n* formiga *f*.
antacid [,ænt'æsɪd] *n* antiácido *m*.
antagonism [æn'tægənɪzm] *n* antagonismo *m*.
antagonist [æn'tægənɪst] *n* antagonista *mf*.
antagonistic [æn,tægə'nɪstɪk] *adj* antagônico(ca).
antagonize, -ise [æn'tægənaɪz] *vt* hostilizar.
Antarctic [æn'tɑ:ktɪk] <> *n*: **the ~** o Antártico; **in the ~** no Antártico. <> *adj* antártico(ca).
Antarctica [æn'tɑ:ktɪkəl] *n* Antártica.
Antarctic Circle *n*: **the ~** o Círculo Polar Antártico.
Antarctic Ocean *n*: **the ~** o Oceano Antártico.
ante ['æntɪ] *n inf fig inf*: **to up** OR **raise the ~** jogar alto.
anteater ['ænt,i:tə'] *n* tamanduá *m*.
antecedent [,æntɪ'si:dənt] *n fml* [earlier event] antecedente *m*.
antediluvian [,æntɪdɪ'lu:vjən] *adj hum* [outdated] antidiluviano(na).
antelope ['æntɪləʊp] (*pl inv* OR **-s**) *n* antílope *m*.
antenatal [,æntɪ'neɪtl] *adj* pré-natal.
antenatal clinic *n* clínica *f* pré-natal.
antenna [æn'tenə] (*pl sense 1* **-nae** [-ni:], *pl sense 2* **-s**) *n* **-1.** [of insect, lobster] antena *f* **-2.** *US* [aerial] antena *f*.
anteroom ['æntɪrʊm] *n* **-1.** [antechamber] ante-sala *f* **-2.** [waiting room] sala *f* de espera.
anthem ['ænθəm] *n* [song, hymn] hino *m*.
anthill ['ænthɪl] *n* formigueiro *m*.
anthology [æn'θɒlədʒɪ] (*pl* **-ies**) *n* antologia *f*.
anthrax ['ænθræks] *n* antraz *m*.
anthropologist [,ænθrə'pɒlədʒɪst] *n* antropólogo *m*, -ga *f*.
anthropology [,ænθrə'pɒlədʒɪ] *n* antropologia *f*.
anti- ['æntɪ] *prefix* anti.
anti-aircraft [,æntɪ'eəkrɑ:ft] *adj* antiaéreo(a).
antiapartheid *adj* antiapartheid.
antiballistic missile [,æntɪbə'lɪstɪk-] *n* míssil *m* antibalístico.
antibiotic [,æntɪbaɪ'ɒtɪk] *n* [medicine] antibiótico *m*.
antibody ['æntɪ,bɒdɪ] (*pl* **-ies**) *n* BIOL anticorpo *m*.
anticipate [æn'tɪsɪpeɪt] *vt* **-1.** [expect, experience prematurely] prever **-2.** [preempt] antecipar-se a.
anticipation [æn,tɪsɪ'peɪʃn] *n* **-1.** [advance action] antecipação *f*; **thanking you in ~** antecipadamente grato(ta) **-2.** [expectation] expectativa *f*; **in ~ of** na expectativa de **-3.** [foresight] pressentimento *m*.
anticlimax [æntɪ'klaɪmæks] *n* [disappointment] anticlímax *m*.
anticlockwise *UK* [,æntɪ'klɒkwaɪz] <> *adj* [direction] em sentido anti-horário. <> *adv* em sentido anti-horário.
antics ['æntɪks] *npl* **-1.** [of children, animals] palhaçadas *fpl* **-2.** *pej* [of politician etc] trapaças *fpl*.
anticyclone [,æntɪ'saɪkləʊn] *n* METEOR anticiclone *m*.
antidepressant [,æntɪdɪ'presnt] <> *adj* antidepressivo(va). <> *n* [drug] antidepressivo *m*.
antidote ['æntɪdəʊt] *n* **-1.** [drug, medicine] antídoto *m*; **~ to sthg** antídoto contra algo **-2.** *fig* [relief] antídoto.
antifreeze ['æntɪfri:z] *n* anticongelante *m*.
Antigua [æn'ti:gəl] *n* Antígua; **in ~** em Antígua.
antihero ['æntɪ,hɪərəʊ] (*pl* **-es**) *n* [in literature] anti-herói *m*.
antihistamine [,æntɪ'hɪstəmɪn] <> *adj* anti-histamínico(ca). <> *n* anti-histamínico *m*.
antinuclear *adj* antinuclear.
antipathy [æn'tɪpəθɪ] *n* antipatia *f*; **~ to** OR **towards sb/sthg** antipatia por alguém/algo.
antipersonnel ['æntɪ,pɜ:sə'nel] *adj* MIL contra pessoas.

antiperspirant [ˌæntɪ'pɜ:spərənt] *n* desodorante *m*.

Antipodes [æn'tɪpədi:z] *npl*: **the ~** as Antípodas *(Austrália e Nova Zelândia)*.

antiquarian [ˌæntɪ'kweərɪən] ◇ *adj* [bookshop, bookseller] de antiguidades. ◇ *n* [antique collector] antiquário *m*.

antiquated ['æntɪkweɪtɪd] *adj* antiquado(da).

antique [æn'ti:k] ◇ *adj* [furniture, object] antigo(-ga). ◇ *n* [pece of furniture, object] antiguidade *f*.

antique dealer *n* antiquário *m*.

antique shop *n* loja *f* de antiguidades.

antiquity [æn'tɪkwətɪ] (*pl* **-ies**) *n* antiguidade *f*.

anti-Semitic [-sɪ'mɪtɪk] *adj* anti-semita.

anti-Semitism [ˌæntɪ'semɪtɪzm] *n* anti-semitismo *m*.

antiseptic [ˌæntɪ'septɪk] ◇ *adj* anti-séptico(ca). ◇ *n* anti-séptico *m*.

antisocial [ˌæntɪ'səʊʃl] *adj* anti-social.

antistatic [ˌæntɪ'stætɪk] *adj* antiestático(ca).

anti-tank *adj* MIL antitanque.

antithesis [æn'tɪθɪsɪs] (*pl* **-theses** [-θɪsi:z]) *n fml* [direct opposite] antítese *f*.

antlers ['æntləz] *npl* cornos *mpl*.

antonym ['æntənɪm] *n* antônimo *m*.

Antrim *n* [county] Antrim; **in ~** em Antrim.

Antwerp ['æntwɜ:p] *n* Antuérpia; **in ~** em Antuérpia.

anus ['eɪnəs] *n* ânus *m*.

anvil ['ænvɪl] *n* bigorna *f*.

anxiety [æŋ'zaɪətɪ] (*pl* **-ies**) *n* **-1.** [worry] ansiedade *f* **-2.** [cause of worry] angústia *f* **-3.** [keenness] anseio *m*.

anxious ['æŋkʃəs] *adj* **-1.** [worried] preocupado(da); **to be ~ about sb/sthg** estar preocupado(da) com alguém/algo **-2.** [keen]: **to be ~ to do sthg** estar ansioso(sa) por fazer algo; **to be ~ that** estar ansioso(sa) para que.

anxiously ['æŋkʃəslɪ] *adv* **-1.** [nervously] nervosamente **-2.** [eagerly] ansiosamente.

any ['enɪ] ◇ *adj* **-1.** *(with negative)* nenhum(ma); **I haven't got ~ money** não tenho dinheiro nenhum; **he never does ~ work** ele nunca faz trabalho algum **-2.** [some] *(with sg n)* algum(ma); *(with pl n)* alguns(mas); **can I be of ~ help?** posso ajudar (em algo)?; **have you got ~ money?** você tem algum dinheiro? **-3.** [no matter which] qualquer; **~ box will do** qualquer caixa serve. ◇ *pron* **-1.** *(with negative)* nenhum(ma); **I didn't buy ~ of them** não comprei nenhum deles **-2.** [some] algum(ma); **do you have ~?** você tem (algum)?; **if ~** se é que algum **-3.** [no matter which one or ones] qualquer um (uma); **take ~ you like** pegue qualquer um que você queira. ◇ *adv* **-1.** *(with negative)*: **I don't want it ~ more** não quero mais isto; **I can't stand it ~ longer** não agüento mais isto **-2.** [some, a little] um pouco; **is that ~ better/different?** está um pouco melhor/diferente?

anybody ['enɪˌbɒdɪ] *pron* = **anyone**.

anyhow ['enɪhaʊ] *adv* **-1.** [in spite of that] assim mesmo **-2.** [carelessly] de qualquer jeito **-3.** [returning to topic in conversation] seja como for.

anyone ['enɪwʌn] *pron* **-1.** *(in negative statements)* ninguém **-2.** *(in questions)* alguém **-3.** [someone] alguém **-4.** [any person] qualquer pessoa.

anyplace *adv US* = **anywhere**.

anything ['enɪθɪŋ] *pron* **-1.** *(in negative statements)* nada **-2.** *(in questions)* algo **-3.** [something] algo, qualquer coisa **-4.** [any object, event] qualquer coisa.

◆ **anything but** *adv*: **he wasn't friendly when I saw him, ~ but** ele não foi amigável quando o vi, muito pelo contrário; **she was ~ but complimentary about my painting** ela não foi nada elogiosa sobre meus quadros.

anyway ['enɪweɪ] *adv* [in any case] de qualquer forma.

anywhere ['enɪweə^r], **anyplace** *US* ['enɪpleɪs] *adv* **-1.** *(in negative statements)* nenhum lugar **-2.** *(in questions)* em/a algum lugar **-3.** [any place] (em) qualquer lugar **-4.** [unspecified amount, number] aproximadamente; **to last ~ from three weeks to two months** durar algo entre três semanas e dois meses.

Anzac (*abbr of* **Australia-New Zealand Army Corps**) *n corporação de soldados australianos ou neozeolandeses.*

AOB, a.o.b. (*abbr of* **any other business**) *questão que não foi incluída na pauta principal de uma reunião.*

Apache [ə'pætʃɪ] *n* [native American] apache *m*.

apart [ə'pɑ:t] *adv* **-1.** [separated in space] à parte, separadamente, distante; **we're living ~** estamos vivendo separados; **the houses were only a few yards ~ from each other** as casas ficavam a apenas algumas jardas de distância uma da outra; **I had to keep them ~** eu tinha que mantê-los à distância **-2.** [to pieces] em pedaços **-3.** [aside, excepted] à parte.

◆ **apart from** ◇ *prep* [except for] exceto, a não ser (por). ◇ *conj* [in addition to] além de.

apartheid [ə'pɑ:theɪt] *n* apartheid *m*.

apartment [ə'pɑ:tmənt] *n* apartamento *m*.

apartment building *n* prédio *m* de apartamentos.

apathetic [ˌæpə'θetɪk] *adj* apático(ca).

apathy ['æpəθɪ] *n* apatia *f*.

APB (*abbr of* **all points bulletin**) *n US mensagem de rádio da polícia sobre pessoa que está sendo procurada.*

ape [eɪp] ◇ *n* [animal] macaco *m*, -ca *f*. ◇ *vt pej* [imitate] imitar.

Apennines ['æpɪnaɪnz] *npl*: **the ~** os Apeninos.

aperitif [əperə'ti:f] *n* aperitivo *m*.

aperture ['æpəˌtjʊə^r] *n* abertura *f*.

apex ['eɪpeks] (*pl* **-es** OR **apices**) *n* [top] ápice *m*.

Apex (*abbr of* **advance purchase excursion**) *n UK passagem comprada com antecedência e que oferece descontos.*

aphid ['eɪfɪd] *n* pulgão *m*.

aphorism ['æfərɪzm] *n* aforismo *m*.

aphrodisiac [ˌæfrə'dɪzɪæk] ◇ *adj* afrodisíaco(ca). ◇ *n* afrodisíaco *m*.

apices ['eɪpɪsi:z] *pl* ▷ **apex**.

apiece [ə'pi:s] *adv* [each] cada.

aplomb [ə'plɒm] *n* [composure] compostura *f*.

apocalypse [ə'pɒkəlɪps] *n* apocalípse *m*.

apocalyptic [əˌpɒkəˈlɪptɪk] *adj* apocalíptico(ca).
apogee [ˈæpədʒiː] *n fig & fml* [peak] apogeu *m*.
apolitical [ˌeɪpəˈlɪtɪkəl] *adj* [non-political] apolítico (ca).
apologetic [əˌpɒləˈdʒetɪk] *adj* arrependido(da); **to be ~ about sthg** estar arrependido(da) em relação a algo, desculpar-se por algo.
apologetically [əˌpɒləˈdʒetɪklɪ] *adv* em tom de desculpas.
apologize, -ise [əˈpɒlədʒaɪz] *vi* [say sorry]: **to ~ to sb for sthg** pedir desculpas a alguém por algo.
apology [əˈpɒlədʒɪ] (*pl* **-ies**) *n* [spoken, written] desculpa *f*.
apoplectic [ˌæpəˈplektɪk] *adj* **-1.** *MED* apoplético(ca) **-2.** *inf* [very angry] furioso(sa).
apoplexy [ˈæpəpleksɪ] *n MED* apoplexia *f*.
apostle [əˈpɒsl] *n RELIG* apóstolo *m*.
apostrophe [əˈpɒstrəfɪ] *n GRAMM* apóstrofe *f*.
appal (*UK pt & pp* **-led**, *cont* **-ling**), **appall** *US* [əˈpɔːl] *vt* [shock deeply] horrorizar.
Appalachian [ˌæpəˈleɪtʃən] *n*: **the ~s** os Apalaches; **the ~ Mountains** os Montes Apalache.
appall *vt US* = **appal**.
appalled [əˈpɔːld] *adj* horrorizado(da).
appalling [əˈpɔːlɪŋ] *adj* **-1.** [shocking] espantoso(sa) **-2.** *inf* [very bad] terrível.
appallingly [əˈpɔːlɪŋlɪ] *adv* **-1.** [shockingly] espantosamente **-2.** *inf* [very badly] terrivelmente.
apparatus [ˌæpəˈreɪtəs] (*pl inv OR* **-es**) *n* **-1.** [equipment] aparelho *m* **-2.** [system, organization] organização *f*.
apparel [əˈpærəl] *n US* traje *m*.
apparent [əˈpærənt] *adj* aparente; **for no ~ reason** sem nenhuma razão aparente.
apparently [əˈpærəntlɪ] *adv* aparentemente.
apparition [ˌæpəˈrɪʃn] *n fml* [ghost] aparição *f*.
appeal [əˈpiːl] ◇ *vi* **-1.** [request] apelar; **to ~ to sb for sthg** apelar a alguém por algo **-2.** [to sb's honour, common sense]: **to ~ to sthg** apelar para algo **-3.** [contest a decision or verdict] recorrer; **to ~ against sthg** recorrer contra algo **-4.** [attract, interest]: **to ~ (to sb)** agradar a alguém. ◇ *n* **-1.** [request] apelo *m* **-2.** [contesting a decision or verdict] apelação *m* **-3.** [charm, interest] encanto *m*.
appealing [əˈpiːlɪŋ] *adj* [attractive] encantador(ra).
appear [əˈpɪəʳ] ◇ *vi* **-1.** [gen] aparecer **-2.** [act] atuar **-3.** *JUR* comparecer. ◇ *vt* [seem]: **to ~ to be/do sthg** aparentar ser/fazer algo; **it would ~ that ...** pareceria que.
appearance [əˈpɪərəns] *n* **-1.** [arrival] chegada *f* **-2.** [becoming visible - of person] aparecimento *m*; [- of object] chegada *f*; [- of rash etc. on skin] surgimento *m*; **to make an ~** aparecer; **to put in an ~** marcar presença **-3.** [outward aspect] aparência *f*; **to keep up ~s** manter as aparências; **by** *OR* **to all ~s** a julgar pelas aparências **-4.** [bodily features] aspecto *m* **-5.** [in play, film, on TV] participação *f*.
appease [əˈpiːz] *vt* **-1.** [placate] apaziguar **-2.** [satisfy] saciar.
appeasement [əˈpiːzmənt] *n* **-1.** [placating, pol] apaziguamento *m*, conciliação *f* **-2.** [satisfaction] satisfação *f*.
append [əˈpend] *vt fml* [add]: **to ~ sthg (to sthg)** anexar algo a algo.
appendage [əˈpendɪdʒ] *n* anexo *m*.
appendices [əˈpendɪsiːz] *pl* ▷ **appendix**.
appendicitis [əˌpendɪˈsaɪtɪs] *n* apendicite *f*.
appendix [əˈpendɪks] (*pl* **-dixes** *OR* **-dices**) *n* apêndice *m*; **to have one's ~ out** *OR* **removed** sofrer a remoção do apêndice.
appertain *vi fml*: **to ~ to sthg** ser pertinente a algo.
appetite [ˈæpɪtaɪt] *n* **-1.** [for food] apetite *m*; **~ for sthg** desejo por algo **-2.** *fig* [enthusiasm]: **~ for sthg** gosto por algo.
appetizer, -iser [ˈæpɪtaɪzəʳ] *n* [food] entrada *f*; [drink] aperitivo *m*.
appetizing, -ising [ˈæpɪtaɪzɪŋ] *adj* [food] apetitoso(sa).
applaud [əˈplɔːd] ◇ *vt* **-1.** [clap for] aplaudir **-2.** *fig* [approve] aplaudir. ◇ *vi* [clap] aplaudir.
applause [əˈplɔːz] *n* aplauso *m*.
apple [ˈæpl] *n* maçã *f*; **to be the ~ of sb's eye** ser a menina dos olhos de alguém.
apple pie *n* torta *f* de maçã.
apple tree *n* macieira *f*.
appliance [əˈplaɪəns] *n* [device] utensílio *m*.
applicable [əˈplɪkəbl] *adj* apropriado(da); **~ to sb/sthg** apropriado(da) a alguém/algo.
applicant [ˈæplɪkənt] *n* candidato *m*, -ta *f*; **~ for sthg** [job] candidato(ta) a algo; [state benefit] pretendente a algo *m*.
application [ˌæplɪˈkeɪʃn] *n* **-1.** [gen] aplicação *f* **-2.** [for job, college, club] inscrição *f*; **~ for sthg** inscrição para algo **-3.** *COMPUT* aplicativo *m*.
application form *n* ficha *f* de inscrição.
applicator [ˈæplɪkeɪtəʳ] *n* aplicador *m*.
applied [əˈplaɪd] *adj* [science] aplicado(da).
appliqué [əˈpliːkeɪ] *n SEWING* aplique *m*.
apply [əˈplaɪ] (*pt & pp* **-ied**) ◇ *vt* **-1.** [rule, skill] aplicar; **to ~ o.s. (to sthg)** dedicar-se a algo; **to ~ one's mind to sthg** concentrar-se em algo **-2.** [paint, ointment] aplicar **-3.** [brakes] usar. ◇ *vi* **-1.** [for work, grant] candidatar-se; **to ~ for sthg** candidatar-se a algo; **to ~ to sb for sthg** recorrer a alguém para algo **-2.** [be relevant] aplicar-se; **to ~ to sb/sthg** aplicar-se a alguém/algo.
appoint [əˈpɔɪnt] *vt* **-1.** [to job, position] nomear; **to ~ sb to/as sthg** nomear alguém para/como algo **-2.** *fml* [time, place] marcar.
appointment [əˈpɔɪntmənt] *n* **-1.** *(U)* [to job, position] nomeação *f*; **'by ~ to Her Majesty the Queen'** 'por indicação de Sua Majestade, a Rainha' **-2.** [job, position] posição *f* **-3.** [with doctor, hairdresser, in business] hora *f* marcada; **to have an ~** ter uma hora marcada; **to make an ~** marcar uma hora; **by ~** com hora marcada; **the doctor only sees patients by ~** o médico só atende (pacientes) com hora marcada.
apportion [əˈpɔːʃn] *vt* [money, blame] dividir.
apposite [ˈæpəzɪt] *adj fml* apropriado(da).
appraisal [əˈpreɪzl] *n* [report, opinion] apreciação *f*.
appraise [əˈpreɪz] *vt fml* [evaluate] apreciar.
appreciable [əˈpriːʃəbl] *adj* [noticeable] apreciável.

appreciably [ə'pri:ʃəblɪ] *adv* [noticeably] visivelmente.

appreciate [ə'pri:ʃɪeɪt] <> *vt* **-1.** [value] valorizar **-2.** [recognize, understand] reconhecer **-3.** [be grateful for] reconhecer. <> *vi FIN* [increase in value] valorizar.

appreciation [ə,pri:ʃɪ'eɪʃn] *n* **-1.** *(U)* [liking] apreciação *m* **-2.** *(U)* [recognition, understanding] reconhecimento *f* **-3.** *(U)* [gratitude] gratidão *m* **-4.** *FIN* [increase in value] valorização *f* **-5.** [assessment] avaliação *f*.

appreciative [ə'pri:ʃjətɪv] *adj* apreciativo(va).

apprehend [,æprɪ'hend] *vt fml* [arrest] deter.

apprehension [,æprɪ'henʃn] *n* [anxiety] apreensão *f*.

apprehensive [,æprɪ'hensɪv] *adj* [anxious]: **~ (about sthg)** apreensivo(va) com algo.

apprehensively [,æprɪ'hensɪvlɪ] *adv* apreensivamente.

apprentice [ə'prentɪs] <> *n* [trainee] aprendiz *mf*, estagiário(ria). <> *vt*: **to be ~d to sb** tornar-se aprendiz de alguém.

apprenticeship [ə'prentɪʃɪp] *n* estágio *m*.

appro. (*abbr of* **approval**) *n fam*: **on ~** sujeito(ta) à aprovação.

approach [ə'prəʊtʃ] <> *n* **-1.** [arrival] chegada *f* **-2.** [way in, access] acesso *m* **-3.** [method] abordagem *m* **-4.** [proposal]: **to make an ~ to sb** fazer uma proposta a alguém. <> *vt* **-1.** [come near to] aproximar-se de **-2.** [speak to]: **to ~ sb about sthg** abordar alguém sobre algo; *COMM* sondar alguém sobre algo **-3.** [deal with] abordar **-4.** [approximate, reach] alcançar. <> *vi* aproximar-se.

approachable [ə'prəʊtʃəbl] *adj* acessível.

approaching [ə'prəʊtʃɪŋ] *adj* [in time] próximo(ma) ; [in space] que se aproxima.

approbation [,æprə'beɪʃn] *n fml* [approval] sanção *f*.

appropriate [*adj* ə'prəʊprɪət, *vb* ə'prəʊprɪeɪt] <> *adj* [suitable] apropriado(da). <> *vt* **-1.** [steal] apropriar-se de **-2.** [allocate] destinar.

appropriately [ə'prəʊprɪətlɪ] *adv* adequadamente.

appropriation [ə,prəʊprɪ'eɪʃn] *n* **-1.** [stealing] apropriação *f* **-2.** [allocation] alocação *f*.

approval [ə'pru:vl] *n* **-1.** [liking, admiration] aprovação *f* **-2.** [official agreement] sanção *f* **-3.** *COMM* : **on ~** sob condição.

approve [ə'pru:v] <> *vi*: **to ~ (of sb/sthg)** ser a favor de alguém/algo. <> *vt* [ratify] aprovar.

approved [ə'pru:vd] *adj* aprovado(da).

approving [ə'pru:vɪŋ] *adj* [favourable] favorável.

approx. (*abbr of* **approximately**) aprox.

approximate [*adj* ə'prɒksɪmət, *vb* ə'prɒksɪmeɪt] <> *adj* aproximado(da). <> *vi*: **to ~ to sthg** aproximar-se de algo.

approximately [ə'prɒksɪmətlɪ] *adv* aproximadamente.

approximation [ə,prɒksɪ'meɪʃn] *n* **-1.** [estimate] aproximação *f* **-2.** [similar thing]: **~ (to sthg)** semelhança com algo.

Apr. (*abbr of* **April**) abr.

APR *n* **-1.** (*abbr of* **annualized percentage rate**) taxa *f* de juros anual. **-2.** (*abbr of* **annual purchase rate**) taxa *f* de aquisição anual.

après-ski [,æpreɪ'ski:] *n* après-ski *m*, *entretenimento noturno e atividades sociais que ocorrem nos lugares em que se costuma ir esquiar.*

apricot ['eɪprɪkɒt] <> *n* **-1.** [fruit] damasco *m* **-2.** [colour] laranja claro *m*. <> *comp* de damasco.

apricot tree *n* damasqueiro *m*.

April ['eɪprəl] *n* abril *m*; *see also* **September**.

April Fools' Day *n* primeiro *m* de abril.

APRIL FOOLS' DAY

Assim como no Brasil, também na Grã-Bretanha e nos Estados Unidos é costume pregar peças em amigos e conhecidos no 1° de abril. Nessa data, até mesmo os jornais mais sérios e as estações de rádio e TV brincam com seus leitores, ouvintes e espectadores, divulgando notícias falsas.

apron ['eɪprən] *n* **-1.** [clothing] avental *m*; **to be tied to sb's ~ strings** *inf* estar preso(sa) à saia de alguém **-2.** *AERON* pátio *m* de manobras.

apropos ['æprəpəʊ] *fml* <> *adj* [pertinent] concernente. <> *prep*: **~ (of)** a propósito de.

apt [æpt] *adj* **-1.** [pertinent] adequado(da) **-2.** [likely]: **to be ~ to do sthg** costumar fazer algo.

Apt. (*abbr of* **apartment**) apto.

aptitude ['æptɪtju:d] *n* [skill] aptidão *f*; **to have an ~ for sthg** ter aptidão para algo.

aptitude test *n* teste *m* de aptidão.

aptly ['æptlɪ] *adv* [suitably] apropriadamente.

aqualung ['ækwəlʌŋ] *n* aqualung *m*.

aquamarine [,ækwəmə'ri:n] *n* [colour] azul-turquesa *m*.

aquaplane ['ækwəpleɪn] *vi UK AUT* aquaplanar.

aquarium [ə'kweərɪəm] (*pl* **-riums** *OR* **-ria** [-rɪə]) *n* aquário *m*.

Aquarius [ə'kweərɪəs] *n* **-1.** [sign] Aquário *m* **-2.** [person] aquariano *m*, -na *f*.

aquatic [ə'kwætɪk] *adj* aquático(ca).

aqueduct ['ækwɪdʌkt] *n* aqueduto *m*.

AR *abbr of* **Arkansas**.

ARA (*abbr of* **Associate of the Royal Academy**) *n membro associado da Royal Academy, academia real britânica de artes.*

Arab ['ærəb] <> *adj* árabe. <> *n* [person, horse] árabe *mf*.

Arabia [ə'reɪbjə] *n* Arábia; **in ~** na Arábia.

Arabian [ə'reɪbjən] <> *adj* árabe. <> *n* [person] árabe *mf*.

Arabian desert *n*: **the ~** o deserto da Arábia.

Arabian Peninsula *n*: **the ~** a Península Arábica.

Arabian Sea *n*: **the ~** o Mar das Arábias.

Arabic ['ærəbɪk] <> *adj* arábico(ca). <> *n* [language] arábico *m*.

Arabic numeral *n* algarismo *m* arábico.

arable ['ærəbl] *adj* cultivável.

Arab League *n*: **the ~** a Liga Árabe.

arbiter ['ɑ:bɪtə[r]] *n fml* [judge] árbitro *m*.

arbitrary ['ɑ:bɪtrərɪ] *adj* [random] arbitrário(ria).

arbitrate ['ɑ:bɪtreɪt] *vi* arbitrar.

arbitration [ˌɑːbɪˈtreɪʃn] *n* arbitragem *f*; **to go to ~** ir à arbitragem.
arc [ɑːk] *n* [curve] arco *m*.
ARC (*abbr of* **AIDS-related complex**) *n* ARC *m*, complexo *m* relacionado à AIDS.
arcade [ɑːˈkeɪd] *n* arcada *f*.
arch [ɑːtʃ] ◇ *adj* [knowing] travesso(sa). ◇ *n* arco *m*. ◇ *vt* [back, eyebrow] arquear. ◇ *vi* arquear-se.
arch- [ɑːtʃ] *prefix* [chief] arqui.
archaeological [ˌɑːkɪəˈlɒdʒɪkl] *adj* arqueológico(-ca).
archaeologist [ˌɑːkɪˈɒlədʒɪst] *n* arqueólogo *m*, -ga *f*.
archaeology [ˌɑːkɪˈɒlədʒɪ] *n* arqueologia *f*.
archaic [ɑːˈkeɪɪk] *adj* **-1.** [ancient] arcaico(ca) **-2.** [old-fashioned] antiquado(da).
archangel [ˈɑːkˌeɪndʒəl] *n* arcanjo *m*.
archbishop [ˌɑːtʃˈbɪʃəp] *n* arcebispo *m*.
archduchess [ˌɑːtʃˈdʌtʃɪs] *n* arquiduquesa *f*.
archduke [ˌɑːtʃˈdjuːk] *n* arquiduque *m*.
arched [ɑːtʃt] *adj* **-1.** ARCHIT em arco **-2.** [curved] arqueado(da).
archenemy [ˌɑːtʃˈenɪmɪ] (*pl* **-ies**) *n* arqui-inimigo *m*, -ga *f*.
archeology etc [ˌɑːkɪˈɒlədʒɪ] *n* = **archaeology etc**.
archer [ˈɑːtʃəʳ] *n* arqueiro *m*.
archery [ˈɑːtʃərɪ] *n* arco-e-flecha *m*.
archetypal [ˌɑːkɪˈtaɪpl] *adj* [typical] arquetípico(ca).
archetype [ˈɑːkɪtaɪp] *n* arquétipo *m*.
archipelago [ˌɑːkɪˈpelɪgəʊ] (*pl* **-es** OR **-s**) *n* arquipélago *m*.
architect [ˈɑːkɪtekt] *n* **-1.** [of buildings] arquiteto *m*, -ta *f* **-2.** *fig* [of plan, event] idealizador *m*, -ra *f*.
architectural [ˌɑːkɪˈtektʃərəl] *adj* arquitetônico(-ca).
architecture [ˈɑːkɪtektʃəʳ] *n* arquitetura *f*.
archive file [ˈɑːkaɪv-] *n* COMPUT arquivo *m* armazenado.
archives [ˈɑːkaɪvz] *npl* [of documents] arquivo *m*.
archivist [ˈɑːkɪvɪst] *n* arquivista *mf*.
archway [ˈɑːtʃweɪ] *n* passagem *f* em arco.
Arctic [ˈɑːktɪk] ◇ *adj* **-1.** GEOGR ártico(ca) **-2.** *inf* [very cold] gélido(da). ◇ *n*: **the ~** o Ártico; **in the ~** no Ártico.
Arctic Circle *n*: **the ~** o Círculo Polar Ártico.
Arctic Ocean *n*: **the ~** o Oceano Ártico.
ardent [ˈɑːdənt] *adj* [passionate] ardente.
ardour *UK*, **ardor** *US* [ˈɑːdəʳ] *n* [zeal] ardor *m*.
arduous [ˈɑːdjʊəs] *adj* [difficult] árduo(a).
are [*stressed* ɑːʳ, *unstressed* əʳ] (cf **a, an**) *vb* ▷ **be**.
area [ˈeərɪəl] *n* **-1.** [gen] área *f*; **in the ~** na área **-2.** *fig* [approximate size, number]: **in the ~ of** ao redor de.
area code *n* *US* código *m* de área.
arena [əˈriːnəl] *n* **-1.** SPORT estádio *m* **-2.** *fig* [area of activity] área *f*.
aren't [ɑːnt] = **are not**.
Argentina [ˌɑːdʒənˈtiːnəl] *n* Argentina; **in ~** na Argentina.
Argentine [ˈɑːdʒəntaɪn], **Argentinian** ◇ *adj* argentino(na). ◇ *n* [person] argentino *m*, -na *f*.
arguable [ˈɑːgjʊəbl] *adj* [questionable] questionável.
arguably [ˈɑːgjʊəblɪ] *adv* indubitavelmente.
argue [ˈɑːgjuː] ◇ *vi* **-1.** [quarrel] discutir; **to ~ (with sb about sthg)** discutir (com alguém sobre algo) **-2.** [reason] argumentar; **to ~ for/against sthg** argumentar a favor/contra algo. ◇ *vt* [case, point] afirmar; **to ~ that** afirmar que.
argument [ˈɑːgjʊmənt] *n* **-1.** [quarrel] discussão *f*; **to have an ~ (with sb)** ter uma discussão (com alguém) **-2.** [reason] argumento *m* **-3.** [reasoning] argumentação *f*.
argumentative [ˌɑːgjʊˈmentətɪv] *adj* questionador(ra).
aria [ˈɑːrɪəl] *n* ária *f*.
arid [ˈærɪd] *adj* **-1.** [land] árido(da) **-2.** *fig* [subject, writing] árido(da).
Aries [ˈeəriːz] *n* **-1.** [sign] Áries *f* **-2.** [person] ariano(-na).
arise [əˈraɪz] (*pt* **arose**, *pp* **arisen** [əˈrɪzn]) *vi* [appear] surgir; **to ~ from sthg** surgir de algo; **if the need ~s** se houver necessidade.
aristocracy [ˌærɪˈstɒkrəsɪ] (*pl* **-ies**) *n* aristocracia *f*.
aristocrat [*UK* ˈærɪstəkræt, *US* əˈrɪstəkræt] *n* aristocrata *mf*.
aristocratic [*UK* ˌærɪstəˈkrætɪk, *US* əˌrɪstəˈkrætɪk] *adj* aristocrático(ca).
arithmetic [əˈrɪθmətɪk] ◇ *adj* aritmético(ca). ◇ *n* aritmética *f*.
Arizona [ˌærɪˈzəʊnəl] *n* Arizona; **in ~** no Arizona.
ark [ɑːk] *n* [ship] arca *f*.
Arkansas [ˈɑːkənsɔː] *n* Arkansas; **in ~** no Arkansas.
arm [ɑːm] ◇ *n* **-1.** [of person] braço *m*; **~ in ~** de braços dados; **to keep sb at ~'s length** *fig* manter alguém à distância; **to welcome sb/sthg with open ~s** *fig* receber alguém/algo de braços abertos; **to twist sb's ~** *fig* forçar alguém a fazer algo; **to cost an ~ and a leg** *fig* custar os olhos da cara **-2.** [of garment] manga *f* **-3.** [of chair] braço *m* **-4.** [of organization] ramo *m*. ◇ *vt* [with weapons] armar.
◆ **arms** *npl* [weapons] armas *fpl*; **to take up ~s** pegar em armas; **to be up in ~s (about sthg)** estar furioso(sa) em relação a algo.
armada [ɑːˈmɑːdəl] *n* [fleet of boats, ships] armada *f*.
armadillo [ˌɑːməˈdɪləʊ] (*pl* **-s**) *n* tatu *m*.
Armageddon [ˌɑːməˈgedn] *n* armagedom *m*.
armaments [ˈɑːməmənts] *npl* [weapons] armamento *m*.
armband [ˈɑːmbænd] *n* braçadeira *f*.
armchair [ˈɑːmtʃeəʳ] *n* poltrona *f*.
armed [ɑːmd] *adj* **-1.** [with weapon] armado(da) **-2.** *fig* [with information]: **~ with sthg** munido(da) de algo.
armed forces *npl* forças *fpl* armadas.
armed robbery *n* roubo *m* a mão armada.
Armenia [ɑːˈmiːnjəl] *n* Armênia; **in ~** na Armênia.
Armenian [ɑːˈmiːnjənl] ◇ *adj* armênio(a). ◇ *n* **-1.** [person] armênio *m*, -a *f* **-2.** [language] armênio *m*.
armhole [ˈɑːmhəʊl] *n* cava *f*.
armistice [ˈɑːmɪstɪs] *n* armistício *m*.
armour *UK*, **armor** *US* [ˈɑːməʳ] *n* **-1.** [for person] armadura *f* **-2.** [for military vehicle] blindagem *f*.

armoured *UK*, **armored** *US* ['ɑ:məd] *adj MIL* blindado(da).
armoured car [ɑ:məd-] *n MIL* carro *m* blindado.
armour-plated [-'pleɪtɪd] *adj MIL* blindado(da).
armoury *UK* (*pl* **-ies**), **armory** *US* (*pl* **-ies**) ['ɑ:mərɪ] *n* arsenal *m*.
armpit ['ɑ:mpɪt] *n* axila *f*.
armrest ['ɑ:mrest] *n* braço *m*.
arms control ['ɑ:mz-] *n* controle *m* armamentista.
army ['ɑ:mɪ] (*pl* **-ies**) *n* **-1.** *MIL* exército *m* **-2.** *fig* [large group] exército *m*.
A road *n UK* rodovia principal.
aroma [ə'rəʊmə] *n* [smell] aroma *m*.
aromatherapy [ərəʊmə'θerəpɪ] *n* aromaterapia *f*.
aromatic [ˌærə'mætɪk] *adj* aromático(ca).
arose [ə'rəʊz] *pt* ▷ **arise**.
around [ə'raʊnd] ◇ *adv* **-1.** [about, around] por aí **-2.** [on all sides] ao redor **-3.** [in circular movement] ao redor **-4.** *phr*: **to have been ~** *inf* ter experiência. ◇ *prep* **-1.** [encircling] ao redor de **-2.** [through, throughout] por todo(da) **-3.** [near] perto **-4.** [approximately] cerca de.
arousal [ə'raʊzl] *n* (*U*) [of feelings, emotions] despertar *m*.
arouse [ə'raʊz] *vt* **-1.** [excite - feeling] provocar; [- person] estimular **-2.** [wake] despertar.
arrange [ə'reɪndʒ] *vt* **-1.** [flowers, books, furniture] arrumar **-2.** [event, meeting, party] organizar; **to ~ to do sthg** combinar para fazer algo; **to ~ sthg for sb** arranjar algo para alguém; **to ~ for sb to do sthg** combinar com alguém para que faça algo **-3.** *MUS* fazer um arranjo.
arranged marriage [ə'reɪndʒd-] *n* casamento *m* arranjado.
arrangement [ə'reɪndʒmənt] *n* **-1.** [agreement] acordo *m*; **to come to an ~** chegar a um acordo **-2.** [of objects] arranjo *m*; **flower ~** arranjo de flores **-3.** *MUS* arranjo *m*.
◆ **arrangements** *npl* providências *fpl*; **to make ~s** tomar providências.
array [ə'reɪ] ◇ *n* **-1.** [of objects, people, ornaments] série *f* **-2.** *COMPUT* array *m*. ◇ *vt* [ornaments] enfeitar.
arrears [ə'rɪəz] *npl* [money owed] dívida *f*; **in ~** [retrospectively] retroativamente; [late] em atraso.
arrest [ə'rest] ◇ *n* [by police] prisão *f*; **under ~** preso(sa). ◇ *vt* **-1.** [subj: police] prender **-2.** *fml* [sb's attention] prender **-3.** *fml* [stop] deter.
arresting [ə'restɪŋ] *adj* [striking] impressionante.
arrival [ə'raɪvl] *n* [gen] chegada *f*; **late ~** [of train, bus, mail] chegada atrasada; **new ~** [person] recém-chegado(da); [baby] recém-nascido(da).
arrive [ə'raɪv] *vi* **-1.** [gen] chegar; **to ~ at a conclusion/decision** chegar a uma conclusão/decisão **-2.** [baby] nascer.
arrogance ['ærəgəns] *n* arrogância *f*.
arrogant ['ærəgənt] *adj* arrogante.
arrogantly ['ærəgəntlɪ] *adv* presunçosamente.
arrow ['ærəʊ] *n* **-1.** [weapon] flecha *f* **-2.** [symbol] seta *f*.
arrowroot *n* araruta *f*.
arse [*UK* ɑ:s], **ass** [*US* æs] *n vulg* [bottom] bunda *f*.
arsenal ['ɑ:sənl] *n* [of weapons] arsenal *m*.
arsenic ['ɑ:snɪk] *n* arsênico *m*.
arson ['ɑ:sn] *n* incêndio *m* premeditado.
arsonist ['ɑ:sənɪst] *n* incendiário *m*, -ria *f*.
art [ɑ:t] ◇ *n* (*U*) arte *f*. ◇ *comp* de artes.
◆ **arts** ◇ *npl* **-1.** *SCH & UNIV* [humanities] artes *fpl* **-2.** [fine arts]: **the ~s** as belas artes. ◇ *comp SCH & UNIV* de belas artes.
◆ **arts and crafts** *n* [school subject] artes *fpl*.
art deco [-'dekəʊ] *n* arte *f* deco.
artefact ['ɑ:tɪfækt] *n* = **artifact**.
arterial [ɑ:'tɪərɪəl] *adj* **-1.** [blood] arterial **-2.** [road] principal.
arteriosclerosis [ɑ:ˌtɪərɪəʊsklɪ'rəʊsɪs] *n* arterioesclerose *f*.
artery ['ɑ:tərɪ] (*pl* **-ies**) *n* artéria *f*.
artful ['ɑ:tfʊl] *adj* [cunning] astuto(ta).
art gallery *n* **-1.** [public] museu *m* de arte **-2.** [for selling paintings] galeria *f* de arte.
arthritic [ɑ:'θrɪtɪk] *adj* artrítico(ca).
arthritis [ɑ:'θraɪtɪs] *n* artrite *f*.
artic [ɑ:'tɪk] *n UK inf* = **articulated lorry**.
artichoke ['ɑ:tɪtʃəʊk] *n* alcachofra *f*.
article ['ɑ:tɪkl] *n* artigo *m*.
articled clerk ['ɑ:tɪkld-] *n UK* estagiário *m* de advocacia.
articles of association ['ɑ:tɪklz-] *npl* estatutos *mpl*.
articulate [*adj* ɑ:'tɪkjʊlət, *vb* ɑ:'tɪkjʊleɪt] ◇ *adj* [eloquent - person] articulado(da); [- speech] claro(ra). ◇ *vt* [give clear expression to] articular.
articulated lorry [ɑ:'tɪkjʊleɪtɪd-] *n UK* caminhão *m* articulado.
articulation [ɑ:ˌtɪkjʊ'leɪʃn] *n* **-1.** [enunciation] articulação *f* **-2.** [expression in words] expressão *f*.
artifact ['ɑ:tɪfækt] *n* artefato *m*.
artifice ['ɑ:tɪfɪs] *n* artifício *m*.
artificial [ˌɑ:tɪ'fɪʃl] *adj* artificial.
artificial insemination *n* inseminação *f* artificial.
artificial intelligence *n* inteligência *f* artificial.
artificially [ˌɑ:tɪ'fɪʃəlɪ] *adv* artificialmente.
artificial respiration *n* respiração *f* artificial.
artillery [ɑ:'tɪlərɪ] *n* [guns] artilharia *f*.
artisan [ˌɑ:tɪ'zæn] *n* artesão *m*, -sã *f*.
artist ['ɑ:tɪst] *n* artista *mf*.
artiste [ɑ:'ti:st] *n* artista *mf*.
artistic [ɑ:'tɪstɪk] *adj* artístico(ca).
artistically [ɑ:'tɪstɪklɪ] *adv* artisticamente.
artistry ['ɑ:tɪstrɪ] *n* [creative skill] talento *m* artístico.
artless ['ɑ:tlɪs] *adj* [naive, simple] ingênuo(nua), simples.
art nouveau [ˌɑ:nu:'vəʊ] *n* art nouveau *m*.
as [*stressed* æz, *unstressed* əz] ◇ *conj* **-1.** [referring to time] enquanto; **she rang (just) ~ I was leaving** ela ligou (bem) na hora em que eu estava saindo; **~ time goes by** com o passar do tempo **-2.** [referring to manner, way] como; **do ~ I say** faça como eu digo; **~ it is** como está; **~ it turns/turned out** no final; **~ things stand** pelo jeito **-3.** [introducing a statement] como; **~ you see, ...** como você pode ver; **~ you know, ...** como você sabe **-4.** [because]

como. <> *prep* **-1.** [referring to function, characteristic]: **he lived in Africa ~ a boy** ele viveu na África quando garoto; **he made his name ~ an actor** ele fez seu nome como ator; **she works ~ a nurse** ela trabalha como enfermeira **-2.** [referring to attitude, reaction] como; **she treats it ~ a game** ela trata isto como um jogo. <> *adv (in comparisons)*: **~ ... ~** tão ... quanto; **~ red ~ a tomato** tão vermelho quanto um tomate; **he's ~ tall ~ I am** ele é tão alto quanto eu; **~ much/many ~** tanto ... quanto; **~ much wine/chocolate ~ you want** tanto vinho/chocolate quanto você queira.
◆ **as it were** *adv* por assim dizer.
◆ **as for, as to** *prep* quanto a.
◆ **as from, as of** *prep* a partir de.
◆ **as if, as though** *conj* como se.
◆ **as to** *prep* sobre.

AS <> *n* (*abbr of* **Associate in Science**) *(titular de) graduação em ciências em universidade norte-americana.* <> *abbr of* **American Samoa**.

ASA (*abbr of* **American Standards Association**) *n* **-1.** *associação norte-americana de padronização,* ≃ ABNT *f.* **-2.** (*abbr of* **Advertising Standards Authority**) *órgão britânico que regula a propaganda,* ≃ CONAR *m.* **-3.** (*abbr of* **Amateur Swimming Association**) *associação britânica de nadadores amadores.*

asap (*abbr of* **as soon as possible**) o mais rápido possível.

asbestos [æs'bestəs] *n* asbesto *m.*

asbestosis [ˌæsbes'təʊsɪs] *n* asbestose *f.*

ascend [ə'send] <> *vt* ***fml*** [hill, staircase, ladder] subir; **to ~ the throne** ascender ao trono. <> *vi* [climb] subir, elevar-se.

ascendancy [ə'sendənsɪ] *n* [dominance] domínio *m.*

ascendant [ə'sendənt] *n*: **to be in the ~** [rising in power] estar em ascensão.

ascendency [ə'sendənsɪ] *n* = **ascendancy**.

ascending [ə'sendɪŋ] *adj* [increasing] ascendente; **in ~ order** em ordem ascendente.

ascension [ə'senʃn] *n* [to throne] ascensão *f.*
◆ **Ascension** *n* RELIG Ascensão *f.*

Ascension Island *n* Ilha *f* da Ascensão.

ascent [ə'sent] *n* **-1.** [climb] escalada *f* **-2.** [upward slope] subida *f* **-3.** *(U)* ***fig*** [progress] escalada *f.*

ascertain [ˌæsə'teɪn] *vt* averiguar.

ascetic [ə'setɪk] <> *adj* ascético(ca). <> *n* asceta *mf.*

ASCII (*abbr of* **American Standard Code for Information Interchange**) *n* ASCII *m.*

ascorbic acid [ə'skɔ:bɪk-] *n* ácido *m* ascórbico.

ascribe [ə'skraɪb] *vt* [attribute]: **to ~ sthg to sthg/sb** atribuir algo a algo/alguém.

aseptic [ˌeɪ'septɪk] *adj* [germ-free] asséptico(ca).

asexual [ˌeɪ'sekʃʊəl] *adj* BIOL assexuado(da).

ash [æʃ] *n* **-1.** [from cigarette, fire] cinza *f* **-2.** [tree] freixo *m.*
◆ **ashes** *npl* [from cremation] cinzas *fpl.*

ASH (*abbr of* **Action on Smoking and Health**) *n grupo britânico de combate ao tabagismo.*

ashamed [ə'ʃeɪmd] *adj* [embarrassed] envergonhado(da); **to be ~ of sb/sthg** estar envergonhado(da) por alguém/algo; **to be ~ to do sthg** estar com vergonha de fazer algo.

ashcan ['æʃkæn] *n* ***US*** lixeira *f.*

ashen-faced ['æʃnˌfeɪst] *adj* pálido(da).

ashore [ə'ʃɔ:ʳ] *adv* [go, swim] em direção à costa.

ashtray ['æʃtreɪ] *n* cinzeiro *m.*

Ash Wednesday *n* Quarta-feira *f* de Cinzas.

Asia ['eɪʒə] *n* Ásia; **in ~** na Ásia.

Asia Minor *n* Ásia Menor.

Asian ['eɪʒn] <> *adj* asiático(ca). <> *n* [person] asiático *m*, -ca *f.*

Asiatic [***UK*** ˌeɪʃɪ'ætɪk, ***US*** ˌeɪʒɪ'ætɪk] *adj* asiático(ca).

aside [ə'saɪd] <> *adv* **-1.** [to one side] para o lado; **to take sb ~** chamar alguém à parte; **to brush** OR **sweep sthg ~** ignorar algo **-2.** [apart] à parte; **~ from** com exceção de. <> *n* **-1.** [in play] aparte *m* **-2.** [remark] observação *f.*

ask [ɑ:sk] <> *vt* **-1.** [question] perguntar; **to ~ sb sthg** perguntar algo a alguém; **if you ~ me ...** se você quer saber ... **-2.** [enquire] perguntar; **to ~ a question** fazer uma pergunta **-3.** [request] pedir; **to ~ sb for sthg** pedir algo a alguém; **to ~ sb to do sthg** pedir a alguém para fazer algo **-4.** [invite] convidar **-5.** [set a price of]: **how much are they asking?** quanto estão pedindo? <> *vi* **-1.** [enquire] perguntar **-2.** [request] pedir.
◆ **ask after** *vt fus*: **to ~ sb** perguntar por alguém.
◆ **ask for** *vt fus* **-1.** [person] pedir por, chamar por **-2.** [thing] pedir por.

askance [ə'skæns] *adv* [disapprovingly]: **to look ~ at sb/sthg** olhar alguém/algo com desconfiança, olhar de soslaio para alguém/algo.

askew [ə'skju:] *adj* [not straight] torto(ta).

asking price ['ɑ:skɪŋ-] *n* [for house, car, item in sale] preço *m* estipulado.

asleep [ə'sli:p] *adj* [sleeping] adormecido(da); **to fall ~** pegar no sono; **to be fast** OR **sound ~** estar em sono profundo.

ASM (*abbr of* **air-to-surface missile**) *n* ASM *m*, míssil *m* ar-superfície.

asparagus [ə'spærəgəs] *n* aspargo *m.*

ASPCA (*abbr of* **American Society for the Prevention of Cruelty to Animals**) *n sociedade norte-americana protetora dos animais,* ≃ SUIPA *f.*

aspect ['æspekt] *n* **-1.** aspecto *m* **-2.** ARCHIT posição *f.*

aspen ['æspən] *n* álamo *m.*

aspersions [ə'spɜ:ʃnz] *npl* : **to cast ~ (on sb)** levantar calúnias (sobre alguém); **to cast ~ (on sthg)** levantar suspeitas (sobre algo).

asphalt ['æsfælt] *n* asfalto *m.*

asphyxiate [əs'fɪksɪeɪt] *vt* asfixiar.

aspic ['æspɪk] *n* geléia *f (de carne ou peixe).*

aspidistra *n* aspidistra *f.*

aspirate ['æspərət] <> *adj* LING aspirado(da). <> *vt* MED, LING aspirar.

aspiration [ˌæspə'reɪʃn] *n* aspiração *f.*

aspire [ə'spaɪəʳ] *vi*: **to ~ to sthg/to do sthg** aspirar algo, aspirar fazer algo.

aspirin ['æsprɪn] *n* aspirina *f.*

aspiring [ə'spaɪərɪŋ] *adj* aspirante.

ass [æs] *n* **-1.** [donkey] jumento *m* **-2.** ***UK inf*** [idiot] burro *m*, -ra *f* **-3.** ***US vulg*** = **arse**.

assail [ə'seɪl] *vt* **-1.** [attack physically] atacar **-2.** ***fig*** [beset] acometer.

assailant [ə'seɪlənt] *n* [attacker] agressor *m*, -ra *f*.
assassin [ə'sæsɪn] *n* assassino *m*, -na *f*.
assassinate [ə'sæsɪneɪt] *vt* assassinar; **to be ~ed** ser assassinado(da).
assassination [əˌsæsɪ'neɪʃn] *n* assassinato *m*.
assault [ə'sɔ:lt] ◇ *n* **-1.** *MIL* ataque *m*; **~ on sthg** ataque a algo **-2.** [physical attack] agressão *f*; **~ on sb** agressão a alguém; **~ and battery** *JUR* agressão *f* seguida de lesões. ◇ *vt* [attack - physically] agredir; [- sexually] violentar, estuprar.
assault course *n* pista *f* de combate.
assemble [ə'sembl] ◇ *vt* **-1.** [gather] reunir **-2.** [fit together] montar. ◇ *vi* [gather] reunir.
assembler language *n* = **assembly language**.
assembly [ə'semblɪ] (*pl* **-ies**) *n* **-1.** [meeting] reunião *f* **-2.** [law-making body] assembléia *f*, parlamento *m* **-3.** *(U)* [gathering together] assembléia *f* **-4.** *(U)* [fitting together] montagem *f*.
assembly language *n COMPUT* linguagem *f* assembly, linguagem *f* assembler.
assembly line *n* linha *f* de montagem.
assent [ə'sent] ◇ *n* [agreement] acordo *m*, aprovação *f*. ◇ *vi* concordar; **to ~ to sthg** aceitar algo.
assert [ə'sɜ:t] *vt* **-1.** [fact, belief] afirmar **-2.** [authority] impor; **to ~ o.s.** firmar-se.
assertion [ə'sɜ:ʃn] *n* [claim] afirmação *f*.
assertive [ə'sɜ:tɪv] *adj* positivo(va).
assess [ə'ses] *vt* **-1.** [judge] avaliar **-2.** [estimate] estimar.
assessment [ə'sesmənt] *n* **-1.** [judgment] avaliação *f* **-2.** [estimate] estimativa *f*.
assessor [ə'sesə^r] *n FIN* analista *mf*.
asset ['æset] *n* ativo *m*.
◆ **assets** *npl COMM* ativos *mpl*; **~s and liabilities** ativo *m* e passivo.
asset-stripping [-ˌstrɪpɪŋ] *n compra de uma empresa em baixa e venda lucrativa de seu capital, seguida de seu fechamento.*
assiduous [ə'sɪdjʊəs] *adj* [diligent] assíduo(dua).
assiduously [ə'sɪdjʊəslɪ] *adv* [diligently] com assiduidade.
assign [ə'saɪn] *vt* **-1.** [allot, allocate]: **to ~ sthg (to sb/sthg)** designar algo (a alguém/algo) **-2.** [appoint]: **to ~ sb (to sthg/to do sthg)** designar alguém (para algo/fazer algo).
assignation [ˌæsɪg'neɪʃn] *n fml* [secret meeting] encontro *m* amoroso.
assignment [ə'saɪnmənt] *n* **-1.** [task] tarefa *f* **-2.** *(U)* [act of appointing] designação *f* **-3.** [law] partilha *f*, transferência *f* de bens.
assimilate [ə'sɪmɪleɪt] *vt* **-1.** [ideas, facts] assimilar **-2.** [people]: **to ~ sb (into sthg)** absorver alguém (em algo) **-3.** [nutrients, food] absorver.
assimilation [əˌsɪmɪ'leɪʃn] *n* **-1.** [of ideas, facts] assimilação *f* **-2.** [of people, food] absorção *f*.
assist [ə'sɪst] *vt* [help] auxiliar; **to ~ sb with sthg/in doing sthg** auxiliar alguém em algo/a fazer algo.
assistance [ə'sɪstəns] *n* [help] auxílio *m*, ajuda *f*; **to be of ~ (to sb)** ser de alguma ajuda (para alguém).
assistant [ə'sɪstənt] ◇ *n* **-1.** [helper] assistente *mf* **-2.** [in shop] balconista *mf*, atendente *mf*. ◇ *comp* assistente *mf*; **~ manager** gerente adjunto.
assistant referee *n* árbitro *m* assistente, -tra assistente *f*.
associate [*adj* & *n* ə'səʊʃɪət, *vb* ə'səʊʃɪeɪt] ◇ *adj* [member] associado(da). ◇ *n* [business partner] sócio *m*, -cia *f*. ◇ *vt* [connect] associar-se; **to ~ o.s. with sb/sthg** associar-se a alguém/algo; **to ~ sthg with sb/sthg** associar algo a alguém/algo; **to be ~d with sb/sthg** ser associado a alguém/algo. ◇ *vi*: **to ~ with sb** relacionar-se com alguém.
association [əˌsəʊsɪ'eɪʃn] *n* **-1.** [organization] associação *f* **-2.** *(U)* [relationship, of ideas] associação *f*; **in ~ with sb/sthg** em associação com alguém/algo.
assonance ['æsənəns] *n* assonância *f*.
assorted [ə'sɔ:tɪd] *adj* [of various types] sortido(da), variado(da).
assortment [ə'sɔ:tmənt] *n* [mixture] diversidade *f*.
Asst (*abbr of* **assistant**) assistente *mf*.
assuage [ə'sweɪdʒ] *vt fml* [relieve] minorar.
assume [ə'sju:m] *vt* **-1.** [suppose] supor **-2.** [take on] assumir.
assumed name [ə'sju:md-] *n* nome *m* falso.
assuming [ə'sju:mɪŋ] *conj*: **~ that** supondo que.
assumption [ə'sʌmpʃn] *n* **-1.** [supposition] suposição *f* **-2.** [of power] tomada *f*.
◆ **Assumption** *n RELIG*: **the Assumption** a Ascensão *f*.
assurance [ə'ʃʊərəns] *n* **-1.** [promise] promessa *f* **-2.** *(U)* [confidence] segurança *f* **-3.** *(U) FIN* [insurance] seguro *m*.
assure [ə'ʃʊə^r] *vt* [reassure] assegurar; **to ~ sb of sthg** assegurar alguém de algo; **to be ~d of sthg** [be certain] estar seguro(ra de algo).
assured [ə'ʃʊəd] *adj* [confident] autoconfiante.
AST (*abbr of* **Atlantic Standard Time**) *n horário de inverno na costa leste dos Estados Unidos.*
asterisk ['æstərɪsk] *n* asterisco *m*.
astern [ə'stɜ:n] *adv NAUT* à popa.
asteroid ['æstərɔɪd] *n* asteróide *m*.
asthma ['æsmə] *n* asma *f*.
asthmatic [æs'mætɪk] ◇ *adj* asmático(ca). ◇ *n* asmático *m*, -ca *f*.
astigmatism [ə'stɪgmətɪzm] *n* astigmatismo *m*.
astonish [ə'stɒnɪʃ] *vt* [amaze] surpreender.
astonished *adj* surpreso(sa).
astonishing [ə'stɒnɪʃɪŋ] *adj* extraordinário(ria), surpreendente.
astonishment [ə'stɒnɪʃmənt] *n* espanto *m*, surpresa *f*.
astound [ə'staʊnd] *vt* [amaze] pasmar.
astounded *adj* pasmado(da).
astounding [ə'staʊndɪŋ] *adj* espantoso(sa).
astrakhan [ˌæstrə'kæn] *n* astracã *m*.
astray [ə'streɪ] *adv*: **to go ~** [become lost] extraviar-se; **to lead sb ~** *fig* [into bad ways] levar alguém para o mal caminho.
astride [ə'straɪd] *prep*: **sitting ~ a horse** montado(da) em um cavalo; **sitting ~ a chair** sentado(da) numa cadeira com uma perna de cada lado.
astringent [ə'strɪndʒənt] ◇ *adj* **-1.** [cosmetic lotion] adstringente **-2.** [criticism] severo(ra). ◇ *n* [cosmetic] adstringente *m*.
astrologer [ə'strɒlədʒə^r] *n* astrólogo *m*, -ga *f*.
astrological [ˌæstrə'lɒdʒɪkl] *adj* astrológico(ca).

astrologist [ə'strɒlədʒɪst] *n* = **astrologer**.
astrology [ə'strɒlədʒɪ] *n* astrologia *f*.
astronaut ['æstrənɔ:t] *n* astronauta *mf*.
astronomer [ə'strɒnəmə^r] *n* astrônomo *m*, -ma *f*.
astronomical [ˌæstrə'nɒmɪkl] *adj* **-1.** ASTRON astronômico(ca) **-2.** *inf fig* [very large] astronômico(ca).
astronomy [ə'strɒnəmɪ] *n* astronomia *f*.
astrophysics [ˌæstrəʊ'fɪzɪks] *n* astrofísica *f*.
astute [ə'stju:t] *adj* [shrewd] perspicaz.
asunder [ə'sʌndə^r] *adv literary* [apart]: **to tear ~** dilacerar.
ASV (*abbr of* **American Standard Version**) *n tradução da Bíblia adotada nos Estados Unidos.*
asylum [ə'saɪləm] *n* **-1.** *dated* [mental hospital] hospício *m* **-2.** *(U)* [protection] asilo *m*.
asymmetrical [ˌeɪsɪ'metrɪkl] *adj* assimétrico(ca).
at [*stressed* æt, *unstressed* ət] *prep* **-1.** [indicating place, position] em; **~ work** no trabalho; **~ my father's** na casa do meu pai; **~ home** em casa; **~ the top of the house** em cima de casa; **~ the bottom of the hill** ao pé da colina **-2.** [indicating direction] para, em direção a; **to smile ~ sb** sorrir para alguém; **to stare ~ sb/sthg** olhar para alguém/algo; **to shoot ~ sb/sthg** atirar em (direção a) alguém/algo **-3.** [indicating a particular time] em; **~ midnight/noon** à meia-noite, ao meio-dia; **~ eleven o'clock** às onze horas; **~ Christmas** no Natal; **~ night** à noite **-4.** [indicating age, speed, rate] a, em; **~ your age** na sua idade; **~ high speed** em alta velocidade; **~ 52 (years of age)** aos 52 anos (de idade); **~ 100 mph** a 100 milhas por hora **-5.** [indicating price] a; **~ £50** a OR por 50 libras **-6.** [indicating particular state, condition] a, em; **~ liberty** em liberdade; **~my invitation** a meu convite; **~ peace/war** em paz/guerra; **~ lunch/dinner** no almoço/jantar **-7.** [indicating tentativeness, noncompletion] em; **to snatch ~ sthg** tentar pegar algo; **to nibble ~ sthg** beliscar/mordiscar algo **-8.** *(after adjectives)* com; **amused/appalled/puzzled ~ sthg** entretido(da)/apavorado(da)/embaraçado(da) com algo; **to be bad/good ~ sthg** ser ruim/bom(boa) em algo.
◆ **at all** *adv* **-1.** *(with negative)*: **not ~ all** [when thanked] não há de que; [when answering a question] de forma alguma; **she's not ~ all happy** ela não está nem um pouco feliz **-2.** [in the slightest]: **anything ~ all will do** qualquer coisa está bem; **do you know her ~ all?** você a conhece de algum lugar?
ATC (*abbr of* **Air Training Corps**) *n unidade de formação e treinamento das forças aéreas britânicas.*
ate [*UK* et, *US* eɪt] *pt* ▷ **eat**.
atheism ['eɪθɪɪzm] *n* ateísmo *m*.
atheist ['eɪθɪɪst] *n* ateu *m*, -téia *f*.
Athenian [ə'θi:njən] ◇ *adj* ateniense *mf*. ◇ *n* ateniense *mf*.
Athens ['æθɪnz] *n* Atenas; **in ~** em Atenas.
athlete ['æθli:t] *n* atleta *mf*.
athlete's foot *n* MED pé-de-atleta *f*.
athletic [æθ'letɪk] *adj* atlético(ca).
◆ **athletics** *npl* atletismo *m*.
Atlantic [ət'læntɪk] ◇ *adj* atlântico(ca). ◇ *n*: **the ~ (Ocean)** o (Oceano) Atlântico.
Atlantis [ət'læntɪs] *n* Atlântida.
atlas ['ætləs] *n* atlas *m inv*.
Atlas ['ætləs] *n*: **the ~ Mountains** os Montes Atlas.
atm. (*abbr of* **atmosphere**) atm.
ATM (*abbr of* **automated teller machine**) *n* caixa *m* automático.
atmosphere ['ætməˌsfɪə^r] *n* atmosfera *f*.
atmospheric [ˌætməs'ferɪk] *adj* **-1.** [relating to the atmosphere] atmosférico(ca) **-2.** [attractive, mysterious] envolvente.
ATOL (*abbr of* **Air Travel Organisers' Licence**) *n organização britânica mantida pela CAA que defende os interesses das pessoas que utilizam a aviação comercial no Reino Unido.*
atoll ['ætɒl] *n* atol *m*.
atom ['ætəm] *n* **-1.** TECH átomo *m* **-2.** *fig* [tiny amount] ponta *f* pingo *m*.
atom bomb *n* bomba *f* atômica.
atomic [ə'tɒmɪk] *adj* atômico(ca).
atomic bomb *n* = **atom bomb**.
atomic energy *n* energia *f* atômica.
atomic number *n* PHYS número *m* atômico.
atomizer, -iser ['ætəmaɪzə^r] *n* vaporizador *m*.
atone [ə'təʊn] *vi*: **to ~ for sthg** redimir-se por algo.
atonement [ə'təʊnmənt] *n* remissão *f*; **~ for sthg** punição por algo.
A to Z *n* A a Z *m*.
ATP (*abbr of* **automatic train protection**) *n* **-1.** *sistema britânico para frear automaticamente um trem.* **-2.** (*abbr of* **Association of Tennis Professionals**) ATP *f*.
atrocious [ə'trəʊʃəs] *adj* **-1.** [cruel] desumano(na), atroz **-2.** [very bad] atroz.
atrocity [ə'trɒsətɪ] (*pl* **-ies**) *n* [terrible act] atrocidade *f*.
attach [ə'tætʃ] *vt* **-1.** [fasten] prender; **to ~ sthg to sthg** prender algo em algo **-2.** [to document] anexar; **to ~ sthg to sthg** anexar algo a algo **-3.** [importance, blame] atribuir; **to ~ sthg to sthg** atribuir algo a algo **-4.** COMPUT atachar, anexar.
attaché [ə'tæʃeɪ] *n* adido *m*.
attaché case [ə'tæʃeɪ-] *n* pasta *f*.
attached [ə'tætʃt] *adj* **-1.** [included] anexado(da) **-2.** [fastened]: **~ to sthg** preso(sa) a OR em algo **-3.** [assigned]: **~ to sthg** designado(da) para algo **-4.** [fond]: **~ to sb/sthg** apegado(da) a alguém/algo.
attachment [ə'tætʃmənt] *n* **-1.** [device] dispositivo *m* **-2.** [fondness]: **~ (to sb/sthg)** apego (a alguém/algo) **-3.** COMPUT anexo *m*.
attack [ə'tæk] ◇ *n* **-1.** [gen] ataque *f*; **~ on sb sthg** ataque contra OR a alguém/algo **-2.** [physical, verbal] agressão *f*; **~ on sb** agressão a alguém ◇ *vt* **-1.** [gen] atacar **-2.** [physically, verbally] agredir. ◇ *vi* atacar.
attacker [ə'tækə^r] *n* **-1.** [assailant] agressor *m*, -ra *f* **-2.** SPORT atacante *mf*.
attain [ə'teɪn] *vt* [reach] atingir.
attainment [ə'teɪnmənt] *n* **-1.** *(U)* [act of achieving] conquista *f* **-2.** [skill] capacitação *f*, qualificação *f*.
attempt [ə'tempt] ◇ *n* [try] tentativa *m*; **~ at sthg** tentativa de fazer algo; **~ on sb's life** atentado

contra a vida de alguém. ◇ *vt* [try] tentar; **to ~ to do sthg** tentar fazer algo.
attend [ə'tend] ◇ *vt* **-1.** [meeting, party] comparecer **-2.** [school, church] freqüentar. ◇ *vi* **-1.** [be present] comparecer **-2.** [pay attention]: **to ~ (to sthg)** prestar atenção (a algo).
◆ **attend to** *vt fus* **-1.** [deal with] cuidar de **-2.** [look after] atender a.
attendance [ə'tendəns] *n* **-1.** [number of people present] audiência *f* **-2.** *(U)* [presence] presença *f*.
attendant [ə'tendənt] ◇ *adj* [accompanying] relacionado(da). ◇ *n* [at museum, petrol station] atendente *mf*.
attention [ə'tenʃn] ◇ *n* **-1.** [gen] atenção *f*; **to attract sb's ~** atrair a atenção de alguém; **to bring sthg to sb's ~, to draw sb's ~ to sthg** chamar a tenção de alguém para algo; **to pay ~ to sb/sthg** prestar atenção a alguém/algo; **to pay no ~ to sb/sthg** não prestar atenção a alguém/algo **-2.** [care] atenção *f*, cuidados *mpl* **-3.** *COMM*: **for the ~ of** aos cuidados de **-4.** *MIL*: **to stand to ~** ficar em posição de sentido. ◇ *excl MIL* sentido!
attentive [ə'tentɪv] *adj* **-1.** [paying attention] atento(-ta) **-2.** [politely helpful] atencioso(sa).
attentively [ə'tentɪvlɪ] *adv* **-1.** [with attention] atentamente **-2.** [helpfully] cuidadosamente.
attenuate [ə'tenjʊeɪt] *fml* ◇ *vt* atenuar. ◇ *vi* atenuar.
attest [ə'test] ◇ *vt* [affirm] atestar. ◇ *vi*: **to ~ to sthg** [prove] dar testemunho de algo.
attic ['ætɪk] *n* sótão *m*.
attire [ə'taɪəʳ] *n fml* [clothing] traje *m*.
attitude ['ætɪtjuːd] *n* **-1.** [way of thinking/acting] atitude *f*; **~ to(wards) sb/sthg** atitude frente a alguém/algo **-2.** [posture] postura *f*.
attn (*abbr of* **for the attention of**) a/c.
attorney [ə'tɜːnɪ] *n US* [lawyer] advogado *m*, -da *f*.
attorney general (*pl* **attorneys general**) *n* procurador *m*, -ra *f* público, -ca *f*.
attract [ə'trækt] *vt* atrair; **to be ~ed to sb/sthg** ser atraído(da) por alguém/algo.
attraction [ə'trækʃn] *n* **-1.** *(U)* [liking] atração *f*; **~ to sb** atração por alguém **-2.** *(U)* [appeal, charm] graça *f* **-3.** [attractive feature, event] atração *f*.
attractive [ə'træktɪv] *adj* atraente.
attractively [ə'træktɪvlɪ] *adv* de modo atraente.
attributable [ə'trɪbjʊtəbl] *adj*: **~ to sb/sthg** atribuível a alguém/algo.
attribute [*vb* ə'trɪbjuːt, *n* 'ætrɪbjuːt] ◇ *vt*: **to ~ sthg to sb/sthg** atribuir algo a alguém/algo. ◇ *n* [quality] atributo *m*.
attribution *n* atribuição *f*; **~ to sb/sthg** atribuição a alguém/algo.
attrition [ə'trɪʃn] *n* desgaste *m*; **war of ~** guerra de desgaste.
attuned [ə'tjuːnd] *adj* **-1.** [accustomed] acostumado(da); **~ to sthg** familiarizado(da) a algo **-2.** [tuned in] sintonizado(da); **~ to sthg** ligado(da) em algo.
ATV *n* (*abbr of* **all-terrain vehicle**) off-road *m*.
atypical [ˌeɪ'tɪpɪkl] *adj* atípico(ca).
atypically [ˌeɪ'tɪpɪklɪ] *adv* atipicamente.
aubergine ['əʊbəʒiːn] *n UK* beringela *f*.
auburn ['ɔːbən] *adj* [hair] castanho avermelhado(-da).
auction ['ɔːkʃn] ◇ *n* [sale] leilão *m*; **at** *OR* **by ~** em leilão; **to put sthg up for ~** pôr algo em leilão. ◇ *vt* leiloar.
◆ **auction off** *vt sep* leiloar.
auctioneer [ˌɔːkʃə'nɪəʳ] *n* leiloeiro *m*, -ra *f*.
audacious [ɔː'deɪʃəs] *adj* [daring, impudent] audacioso(sa).
audacity [ɔː'dæsətɪ] *n* audácia *f*.
audible ['ɔːdəbl] *adj* audível.
audience ['ɔːdjəns] *n* **-1.** [of play, film, TV programme] platéia *f* **-2.** [formal meeting] audiência *f*.
audio ['ɔːdɪəʊ] *adj* áudio, auditivo(va).
audio frequency *n* freqüência *f* auditiva.
audiotyping *n* transcrição *f* de fitas de áudio.
audiotypist ['ɔːdɪəʊˌtaɪpɪst] *n* transcritor *m*, -ra *f* de fitas (de áudio).
audio-visual ['ɔːdɪəʊ-] *adj* audiovisual.
audit ['ɔːdɪt] ◇ *n* [of accounts] auditoria *f*. ◇ *vt* [accounts] auditorar.
audition [ɔː'dɪʃn] ◇ *n* audição *f*. ◇ *vi*: **she is ~ing for a part in a film** ela está fazendo um teste para um papel num filme.
auditor ['ɔːdɪtəʳ] *n* [of accounts] auditor *m*, -ra *f*.
auditorium [ˌɔːdɪ'tɔːrɪəm] (*pl* **-riums** *OR* **-ria** [-rɪə]) *n* auditório *m*.
au fait [ˌəʊ'feɪ] *adj*: **~ with sthg** estar a par de algo.
Aug. (*abbr of* **August**) ago.
augment [ɔːg'ment] *vt* [increase] aumentar.
augur ['ɔːgəʳ] *vi*: **to ~ well/badly** ser um bom/mau sinal.
august [ɔː'gʌst] *adj literary* [dignified] augusto(ta).
August ['ɔːgəst] *n* agosto *m*; *see also* **September**.
Auld Lang Syne [ˌɔːldlæŋ'saɪn] *n canção escocesa tradicionalmente cantada no ano-novo.*
aunt [ɑːnt] *n* tia *f*.
auntie, aunty ['ɑːntɪ] (*pl* **-ies**) *n inf* titia *f*.
au pair [ˌəʊ'peəʳ] *n* au pair *mf*.
aura ['ɔːrə] *n* aura *f*.
aural ['ɔːrəl] *adj* auditivo(va), auricular.
aurally ['ɔːrəlɪ] *adv* auditivamente.
auspices ['ɔːspɪsɪz] *npl*: **under the ~ of** sob o patrocínio de.
auspicious [ɔː'spɪʃəs] *adj* [promising] promissor(ra).
Aussie ['ɒzɪ] *inf* ◇ *adj* australiano(na). ◇ *n* australiano *m*, -na *f*.
austere [ɒ'stɪəʳ] *adj* **-1.** [person, life] duro(ra), austero(ra) **-2.** [room, building] austero(ra).
austerity [ɒ'sterətɪ] *n* austeridade *f*.
austerity measures *npl* medidas *fpl* austeras.
Australasia [ˌɒstrə'leɪʒə] *n* Australásia.
Australia [ɒ'streɪljə] *n* Austrália; **in ~** na Austrália.
Australian [ɒ'streɪljən] ◇ *adj* australiano(na). ◇ *n* australiano *m*, -na *f*.
Austria ['ɒstrɪə] *n* Áustria; **in ~** na Áustria.
Austrian ['ɒstrɪən] ◇ *adj* austríaco(ca). ◇ *n* austríaco *m*, -ca *f*.
authentic [ɔː'θentɪk] *adj* **-1.** [genuine] autêntico(ca) **-2.** [accurate] fidedigno(na).

authenticate [ɔː'θentɪkeɪt] *vt* autenticar.
authentication [ɔːˌθentɪ'keɪʃn] *n* autenticação *f*.
authenticity [ˌɔːθen'tɪsətɪ] *n* autenticidade *f*.
author ['ɔːθəʳ] *n* autor *m*, -ra *f*.
authoritarian [ɔːˌθɒrɪ'teərɪən] *adj* autoritário(ria).
authoritative [ɔː'θɒrɪtətɪv] *adj* **-1.** [person, voice] autoritário(ria) **-2.** [report] oficial.
authority [ɔː'θɒrətɪ] (*pl* **-ies**) *n* **-1.** [gen] autoridade *f*; ~ **on sthg** autoridade em algo **-2.** *(U)* [power] autoridade *f*; **in** ~ com autoridade **-3.** *(U)* [permission] autorização *f* **-4.** *phr*: **to have it on good** ~ receber de fonte segura.
◆ **authorities** *npl* [people in power]: **the authorities** as autoridades.
authorize, -ise ['ɔːθəraɪz] *vt* autorizar; **to** ~ **sb to do sthg** autorizar alguém a fazer algo.
Authorized Version ['ɔːθəraɪzd-] *n*: **the** ~ a Versão Autorizada *(da Bíblia)*.
authorship ['ɔːθəʃɪp] *n* autoria *f*.
autistic [ɔː'tɪstɪk] *adj* autista.
auto ['ɔːtəʊ] (*pl* **-s**) *n* ***US*** [car] auto *m*.
autobiographical ['ɔːtəˌbaɪə'græfɪkl] *adj* autobiográfico(ca).
autobiography [ˌɔːtəbaɪ'ɒgrəfɪ] (*pl* **-ies**) *n* autobiografia *f*.
autocrat ['ɔːtəkræt] *n* autocrata *mf*.
autocratic [ˌɔːtə'krætɪk] *adj* autocrático(ca).
autocross ['ɔːtəʊkrɒs] *n* ***UK*** autocross *m*.
Autocue® ['ɔːtəʊkjuː] *n* ***UK*** teleprompter *m*.
autofocus *n* autofoco *m*.
autograph ['ɔːtəgrɑːf] ◇ *n* autógrafo *m*. ◇ *vt* autografar.
Automat® *n* [restaurant] *tipo de restaurante americano comum nos anos 50 e 60, onde a comida era vendida em máquinas com a inserção de moedas*.
automata [ɔː'tɒmətə] *pl* ⊳ **automaton**.
automate ['ɔːtəmeɪt] *vt* automatizar.
automatic [ˌɔːtə'mætɪk] ◇ *adj* **-1.** [gen] automático(ca) **-2.** [fine, right of appeal] imediato(ta). ◇ *n* **-1.** [car] carro *n* automático **-2.** [gun] pistola *f* automática **-3.** [washing machine] máquina *f* de lavar automática.
automatically [ˌɔːtə'mætɪklɪ] *adv* automaticamente.
automatic pilot *n* AERON & NAUT piloto *m* automático; **on** ~ *fig* no automático.
automation [ˌɔːtə'meɪʃn] *n* [of process] automação *f*, automatização *f*.
automaton [ɔː'tɒmətən] (*pl* **-tons** OR **-ta**) *n* **-1.** [robot] autômata *mf*, robô *m* **-2.** *pej* [person] robô *m*.
automobile ['ɔːtəməbiːl] *n* ***US*** [car] automóvel *m*.
automotive [ˌɔːtə'məʊtɪv] *adj* [relating to automobiles] automotivo(va).
autonomous [ɔː'tɒnəməs] *adj* autônomo(ma).
autonomy [ɔː'tɒnəmɪ] *n* autonomia *f*.
autopilot ['ɔːtəʊpaɪlət] *n* = **automatic pilot**.
autopsy ['ɔːtɒpsɪ] (*pl* **-ies**) *n* autópsia *f*.
autumn ['ɔːtəm] ◇ *n* outono *m*; **in** ~ no outono. ◇ *comp* de outono, outonal.
autumnal [ɔː'tʌmnəl] *adj* outonal, de outono.
auxiliary [ɔːg'zɪljərɪ] (*pl* **-ies**) ◇ *adj* auxiliar. ◇ *n* [person] auxiliar *mf*.

AV ◇ *n* (*abbr of* **Authorized Version**) versão *f* autorizada. ◇ (*abbr of* **audio-visual**) audiovisual.
avail [ə'veɪl] ◇ *n*: **to no** ~ em vão. ◇ *vt*: **to** ~ **o.s. of sthg** aproveitar-se de algo.
availability [əˌveɪlə'bɪlətɪ] *n* disponibilidade *f*.
available [ə'veɪləbl] *adj* disponível.
avalanche ['ævəlɑːnʃ] *n* avalanche *f*.
avant-garde [ˌævɒŋ'gɑːd] ◇ *n* vanguarda *f*. ◇ *adj* de vanguarda.
avarice ['ævərɪs] *n* avareza *f*.
avaricious [ˌævə'rɪʃəs] *adj* avarento(ta).
avdp. (*abbr of* **avoirdupoids**) *sistema inglês de pesos baseado na libra*.
Ave. (*abbr of* **avenue**) Av.
avenge [ə'vendʒ] *vt* vingar.
avenue ['ævənjuː] *n* [wide road] avenida *f*.
average ['ævərɪdʒ] ◇ *adj* **-1.** [mean] média(dio) **-2.** [typical] comum **-3.** *pej* [mediocre] mediano(na). ◇ *n* [mean] média *f*; **on** ~ em média. ◇ *vt* [speed, distance, quantity]: **they** ~ **300 cars a day** eles atingem uma média de 300 carros por dia.
◆ **average out** ◇ *vt sep* calcular a média. ◇ *vi*: **to** ~ **out at** chegar à média de.
averse [ə'vɜːs] *adj*: **to be** ~ **to sthg/to doing sthg** ser contrário(ria) a algo/fazer algo.
aversion [ə'vɜːʃn] *n* **-1.** [dislike] aversão *f*; ~ **to sthg** aversão a algo **-2.** [object of dislike] aversão *f*.
avert [ə'vɜːt] *vt* [avoid] evitar.
aviary ['eɪvjərɪ] (*pl* **-ies**) *n* aviário *m*.
aviation [ˌeɪvɪ'eɪʃn] *n* aviação *f*.
aviator ['eɪvɪeɪtəʳ] *n* ***dated*** aviador *m*, -ra *f*.
avid ['ævɪd] *adj* [keen] ávido(da); ~ **for sthg** ávido(da) de/por algo.
avocado [ˌævə'kɑːdəʊ] (*pl* **-s** OR **-es**) *n*: ~ **(pear)** abacate *m*.
avoid [ə'vɔɪd] *vt* evitar; **to** ~ **doing sthg** evitar fazer algo.
avoidable [ə'vɔɪdəbl] *adj* evitável.
avoidance [ə'vɔɪdəns] *n* ⊳ **tax avoidance**.
avowed [ə'vaʊd] *adj* declarado(da).
AWACS (*abbr of* **airborne warning and control system**) *n sistema aéreo de monitoramento terrestre por radar*; ~ **planes** aviões *mpl* AWACS.
await [ə'weɪt] *vt* **-1.** [wait for] esperar **-2.** [be ready for] estar pronto(ta) para.
awake [ə'weɪk] (*pt* **awoke** OR **awaked**, *pp* **awoken**) ◇ *adj* [not sleeping] acordado(da); **to be wide** ~ estar totalmente desperto(ta). ◇ *vt* **-1.** [wake up] acordar **-2.** *fig* [provoke] despertar. ◇ *vi* [wake up] acordar.
awakening [ə'weɪknɪŋ] *n* **-1.** [from sleep] despertar *m* **-2.** *fig* [of feeling] despertar *m*.
award [ə'wɔːd] ◇ *n* **-1.** [prize] prêmio *m* **-2.** [compensation] recompensa *f*. ◇ *vt* [give] premiar; **to** ~ **sb sthg, to** ~ **sthg to sb** conceder algo a alguém.
aware [ə'weəʳ] *adj* **-1.** [conscious]: ~ **of sthg** consciente de algo; ~ **that** ciente de que **-2.** [informed, sensitive] consciente; ~ **of sthg** informado(da) sobre algo.
awareness [ə'weənɪs] *n* consciência *f*.
awash [ə'wɒʃ] *adj*: ~ **(with sthg)** cheio(a) (de algo).
away [ə'weɪ] ◇ *adv* **-1.** [indicating movement] embora; ~ **from** longe de; **to look/turn** ~

virar-se **-2.** [at a distance - in space]: **she lives 3 miles ~** ela mora a três milhas daqui; **we live 4 miles ~ from the city centre** moramos a 4 milhas do centro da cidade; [- in time]: **the exams were only two days ~** faltavam apenas dois dias para os exames **-3.** [separate from]: **to be kept ~ from sthg** ser mantido(da) afastado(da) de algo; **to give sthg ~** dar algo; **to take sthg ~** levar algo **-4.** [absent]: **to be ~** estar fora **-5.** [in a safe place]: **to put sthg ~** guardar algo **-6.** [indicating disappearance, cessation]: **the stain has faded ~** a mancha desapareceu; **the wood had rotted ~** a madeira tinha apodrecido **-7.** [continuously]: **to sing/work ~** cantar/trabalhar sem parar. ◇ *adj* SPORT: **~ team** time *m* visitante; **~ game** jogo fora de casa.

awe [ɔ:] *n* temor *m*; **to be in ~ of sb** estar intimidado(da) por alguém.

awesome ['ɔ:səm] *adj* [impressive] terrível.

awestruck ['ɔ:strʌk] *adj* aterrorizado(da).

awful ['ɔ:fʊl] *adj* **-1.** [terrible] horrível **-2.** *inf* [very great]: **to have an ~ lot of work to do** ter um bocado de coisas para fazer.

awfully ['ɔ:flɪ] *adv inf* [very] pra caramba; **to be ~ difficult** ser difícil pra caramba.

awhile [ə'waɪl] *adv literary* durante um tempo.

awkward ['ɔ:kwəd] *adj* **-1.** [clumsy] desajeitado(da) **-2.** [embarassing] embaraçoso(sa) **-3.** [embarrassed]: **to feel ~** sentir-se embaraçado(da) **-4.** [difficult to deal with] complicado(da) **-5.** [inconvenient] inadequado(-da).

awkwardly ['ɔ:kwədlɪ] *adv* **-1.** [clumsily] desajeitadamente **-2.** [in an embarrassed way] embaraçosamente **-3.** [inconveniently] inconvenientemente.

awkwardness ['ɔ:kwədnɪs] *n* **-1.** [clumsiness - of movement, position] falta *f* de jeito; [- of person] indelicadeza *f* **-2.** [unease] dificuldade *f* **-3.** [inconvenience] embaraço *m*.

awl [ɔ:l] *n* furador *m*.

awning ['ɔ:nɪŋ] *n* **-1.** [of tent] cobertura *f* **-2.** [of shop] toldo *m*.

awoke [ə'wəʊk] *pt* ⊳ **awake**.

awoken [ə'wəʊkn] *pp* ⊳ **awake**.

AWOL (*abbr of* **absent without leave**): **to go ~** MIL sair sem permissão; **the cat has gone ~** *hum* o gato sumiu.

awry [ə'raɪ] ◇ *adj* [twisted] desajeitado(da). ◇ *adv*: **to go ~** [wrong] dar errado.

axe *UK*, **ax** *US* [æks] ◇ *n* machado *m*; **to have an ~ to grind** ter um interesse pessoal. ◇ *vt* [project, jobs] cortar.

axes ['æksi:z] *pl* ⊳ **axis**.

axiom ['æksɪəm] *n* axioma *m*.

axis ['æksɪs] (*pl* **axes**) *n* eixo *m*.

axle ['æksl] *n* [shaft] eixo *m*.

ayatollah [ˌaɪə'tɒlə] *n* aiatolá *m*.

aye [aɪ] ◇ *adv* [yes] sim. ◇ *n* [affirmative vote] sim *m*.

AYH (*abbr of* **American Youth Hostels**) *n* Albergues *mpl* da Juventude *(nos Estados Unidos)*.

A-Z *n guia que contém mapas de ruas das cidades britânicas.*

AZ *abbr of* **Arizona**.

azalea [ə'zeɪljə] *n* azaléia *f*.

Azerbaijan [ˌæzəbaɪ'dʒɑ:n] *n* Azerbaijão; **in ~** no Azerbaijão.

Azerbaijani [ˌæzəbaɪ'dʒɑ:nɪ] ◇ *adj* azerbaijano(-na). ◇ *n* azerbaijano *m*, -na *f*.

Azeri [ə'zerɪ] ◇ *adj* azeri. ◇ *n* azeri *mf*.

Azores [ə'zɔ:z] *npl*: **the ~** os Açores; **in the ~** nos Açores.

AZT (*abbr of* **azidothymidine**) *n* AZT® *m*.

Aztec ['æztek] ◇ *adj* asteca. ◇ *n* asteca *mf*.

azure ['æʒə^r] *adj* [bright blue] azul-celeste.

B

b (*pl* **b's** OR **bs**), **B** (*pl* **B's** OR **Bs**) [bi:] *n* [letter] b, B *m*.
◆ **B** *n* **-1.** MUS si *m* **-2.** SCH [mark] B *m*.

b. (*abbr of* **born**) n.

BA *n* **-1.** (*abbr of* **Bachelor of Arts**) *titular de graduação em ciências humanas.* **-2.** (*abbr of* **British Academy**) *organismo público britânico para fomento de pesquisa em ciências humanas.*

BAA (*abbr of* **British Airports Authority**) *n organismo independente que controla os aeroportos britânicos*, ≃ INFRAERO *f*.

babble ['bæbl] ◇ *n* [noise] balbucio *m*. ◇ *vi* [person] balbuciar.

babe [beɪb] *n* **-1.** *literary* [baby] nenê *mf* **-2.** *inf* [term of affection] garota *f* **-3.** *inf* [beautiful woman] boneca *f*.

baboon [bə'bu:n] *n* [animal] babuíno *m*.

baby ['beɪbɪ] (*pl* **-ies**) *n* **-1.** [child] bebê *mf*, nenê *mf* **-2.** *pej* [feeble person]: **don't be such a ~!** não seja tão criança! **-3.** *esp US inf* [term of affection] pequeno(-na).

baby boomer [-ˌbu:mə^r] *n US pessoa nascida num período de explosão demográfica nos Estados Unidos, especialmente entre 1946 e 1954.*

baby buggy *UK*, **baby carriage** *UK n* [foldable pushchair] carrinho *m* de bebê

baby food *n* comida *f* de nenê.

babyish ['beɪbɪɪʃ] *adj pej* infantil.

baby-sit *vi* tomar conta de crianças, trabalhar como babá.

baby-sitter [-'sɪtə^r] *n* babá *f*, baby-sitter *f*.

bachelor ['bætʃələ^r] *n* [unmarried man] solteirão *m*; **confirmed ~** solteirão convicto.

Bachelor of Arts *n* [person]; [degree] *bacharelado em Artes, Ciências Humanas ou Sociais.*

Bachelor of Science *n* [person] Bacharel *m* em Ciências ; [degree] bacharelado *m* em ciências.

bachelor's degree *n* grau *m* de bacharel.

back [bæk] ◇ *adj (in compounds)* **-1.** [rear] traseiro (ra); ~ **legs** patas traseiras **- 2.** [at the back] de trás, dos fundos; ~ **seat** assento de trás; ~ **garden** jardim dos fundos **- 3.** [overdue] atrasado(da). ◇ *adv* **- 1.** [backwards] para trás **- 2.** [indicating return to former position or state] de volta; **is he ~ yet?** ele já está de volta?, ele já voltou?; **to go ~ to sleep** voltar a dormir; **to go ~ and forth** ficar indo e vindo **- 3.** [earlier]: ~ **in January** em janeiro passado **- 4.** [in reply, in return] de volta; **to phone ~** ligar de volta; **to pay ~** reembolsar; **to write ~** responder **- 5.** [in fashion again]: **to be ~ (in fashion)** estar de volta (à moda). ◇ *n* **- 1.** [of person, animal] costas *fpl*; **to break the ~ of sthg** *fig* conseguir terminar algo; **to do sthg behind sb's ~** fazer algo pelas costas de alguém; **to know somewhere like the ~ of one's hand** conhecer um lugar como a palma da mão; **to put sb's ~ up** encher o saco de alguém; **to stab sb in the ~** apunhalar pelas costas; **to turn one's ~ on sb/sthg** virar as costas para alguém/algo **- 2.** [reverse side - of page, envelope] verso *m*; [- of head] parte *f* de trás, parte *f* anterior **- 3.** [furthest point away from front - of room] fundos *mpl*; [- of cupboard, fridge]: **in the ~ of the fridge** na parte de trás geladeira; [- of car] traseira *f*; [- of chair] encosto *m*; **at the ~ of, in the ~ of** *US* atrás de; **in the ~ of beyond** *UK* no fim do mundo **- 4.** *SPORT* [player] zagueiro(ra). ◇ *vt* **- 1.** [reverse] recuar **- 2.** [support] apoiar **- 3.** [bet on] apostar **- 4.** [provide lining for] forrar. ◇ *vi* [reverse] retornar; **to ~ into sthg** [walking] voltar-se para algo; [in vehicle] entrar de ré em algo.

◆ **back to back** *adv* [with backs touching]: **to stand ~ to ~** ficar costas com costas.

◆ **back to front** *adv* [the wrong way round] de trás para frente, ao contrário.

◆ **back away** *vi* afastar-se.

◆ **back down** *vi* voltar atrás.

◆ **back off** *vi* afastar-se.

◆ **back onto** *vt fus UK* dar (com os fundos) para.

◆ **back out** *vi* [of promise, arrangement] dar para trás.

◆ **back up** ◇ *vt sep* **- 1.** [support] apoiar **- 2.** [reverse] dar marchar à ré **- 3.** *COMPUT* fazer cópia de segurança de. ◇ *vi* **- 1.** [reverse] dar marchar à ré **- 2.** *COMPUT* fazer cópia de segurança.

backache ['bækeɪk] *n* dor *f* nas costas.

backbencher [ˌbæk'bentʃəʳ] *n UK POL* *membro do Parlamento Britânico, sem cargo oficial no governo ou na oposição.*

backbenches [ˌbæk'bentʃɪz] *npl UK POL* : **the ~** *as cadeiras reservadas aos membros do Parlamento Britânico, sem cargo oficial no governo ou na oposição.*

backbiting ['bækbaɪtɪŋ] *n (U)* falar *m* pelas costas.

backbone ['bækbəʊn] *n* **- 1.** [spine] coluna *f* vertebral **- 2.** *(U) fig* [courage, force] tutano *m* **- 3.** *fig* [main support]: **the ~ of** a espinha dorsal de.

backbreaking ['bækˌbreɪkɪŋ] *adj* [exhausting] estafante.

back burner *n*: **to put sthg on the ~** *fig* deixar algo em segundo plano.

backchat *UK* ['bæktʃæt], **backtalk** *US* ['bæktɔːk] *n (U) inf* contestações *fpl*.

backcloth ['bækklɒθ] *n UK* = **backdrop**.

backcomb ['bækkəʊm] *vt UK* *pentear o cabelo em direção ao couro cabeludo para fazê-lo parecer mais volumoso.*

back copy *n* = **back number**.

backdate [ˌbæk'deɪt] *vt* antedatar.

back door *n* porta *f* dos fundos; **to get in through** *OR* **by the ~** *fig* conseguir algo por baixo do pano.

backdrop ['bækdrɒp] *n* **- 1.** *THEATRE* pano *m* de fundo **- 2.** *fig* [background] pano *m* de fundo.

backer ['bækəʳ] *n FIN* avalista *mf*.

backfire [ˌbæk'faɪəʳ] *vi* **- 1.** [motor vehicle] engasgar **- 2.** [go wrong] dar errado; **his plans ~d (on him)** seus planos não deram o resultado esperado.

backgammon ['bækˌgæmən] *n (U)* gamão *m*.

background ['bækgraʊnd] ◇ *n* **- 1.** [in picture, view] fundo *m*; **in the ~** *lit* ao fundo; *fig* [unnoticeable] em segundo plano **- 2.** [of event, situation] cenário *m* **- 3.** [upbringing] background *m*. ◇ *comp* **- 1.** [music, noise] de fundo **- 2.** [reading, information] preliminar.

backhand ['bækhænd] *n* backhand *m*.

backhanded ['bækhændɪd] *adj fig* [equivocal] falso(-sa).

backhander ['bækhændəʳ] *n UK inf* [bribe] suborno *m*.

backing ['bækɪŋ] *n* **- 1.** *(U)* [support] suporte *m* **- 2.** [lining] forro *m* **- 3.** *MUS* acompanhamento *m*.

backing group *n MUS* grupo *m* de acompanhamento.

back issue *n* = **back number**.

backlash ['bæklæʃ] *n* [adverse reaction] revolta *f*.

backless ['bæklɪs] *adj* frente-única.

backlog ['bæklɒg] *n* acúmulo *m*.

back number *n* número *m* atrasado.

backpack ['bækpæk] *n* mochila *f*.

backpacker ['bækpækəʳ] *n* mochileiro *m*, -ra *f*.

backpacking ['bækpækɪŋ] *n*: **to go ~** viajar com a mochila nas costas.

back passage *n euphemism* reto *m*.

back pay *n (U)* salário *m* atrasado.

backpedal [ˌbæk'pedl] (*UK pt* & *pp* **-led**, *cont* **-ling**, *US pt* & *pp* **-ed**, *cont* **-ing**) *vi fig* [change one's mind]: **to ~ (on sthg)** dar pra trás (em algo).

back seat *n* [in car] banco *m* de trás; **to take a ~** *fig* desempenhar um papel secundário.

back-seat driver *n* *carona que fica dizendo ao motorista como dirigir.*

backside [ˌbæk'saɪd] *n inf* traseiro *m*.

backslapping *n (U) inf* [congratulations] saudações *mpl*.

backslash ['bækslæʃ] *n COMPUT* barra *f* invertida.

backslide [ˌbæk'slaɪd] (*pt* & *pp* **-slid** [-'slɪd]) *vi* ter uma recaída.

backspace ['bækspeɪs] ◇ *n* [key] tecla *f* de retorno. ◇ *vi* [in typing] clicar o retorno, retornar.

backstage [ˌbæk'steɪdʒ] *adv* nos bastidores.

back street *n UK* ruela *f*.

back-street abortion *n UK* aborto *m* clandestino.

backstroke ['bækstrəʊk] *n* [in swimming] nado *m* (de) costas.

backtalk *n US* = **backchat**.

backtrack ['bæktræk] *vi* = **backpedal**.
backup ['bækʌp] <> *adj* **-1.** [reserve] de reserva **-2.** *COMPUT* de segurança. <> *n* **-1.** [support] suporte *m* **-2.** *COMPUT* backup *m*, cópia *f* de segurança.
backward ['bækwəd] <> *adj* **-1.** [directed towards the rear] para trás **-2.** *pej* [late in development - person] retardado(da); [- society, ideas] atrasado(da). <> *adv US* = **backwards**.
backward-looking [-,lʊkɪŋ] *adj pej* retrógrado(-da).
backwards ['bækwədz], **backward** *US* ['bækwəd] *adv* **-1.** [towards the rear] de trás para a frente; ~ **and forwards** de um lado para outro **-2.** [back to front] de trás para a frente, ao contrário.
backwash ['bækwɒʃ] *n* [of event, situation] repercussão *f*.
backwater ['bæk,wɔ:tə^r] *n* **fig** & **pej** [place behind the times] lugar *m* atrasado; **cultural** ~ atraso *m* cultural.
backwoods ['bækwʊdz] *npl* [remote place] confins *mpl*.
backyard [,bæk'jɑ:d] *n* **-1.** *UK* [yard] pátio *m*, quintal *m* **-2.** *US* [garden] jardim *m*.
bacon ['beɪkən] *n (U)* bacon *m*.
bacteria [bæk'tɪərɪə] *npl* bactérias *fpl*.
bacteriology [bæk,tɪərɪ'ɒlədʒɪ] *n (U)* bacteriologia *f*.
bad [bæd] (*compar* **worse**, *superl* **worst**) <> *adj* **-1.** [gen] ruim; **not** ~ nada mal; **too** ~ uma pena; **to be** ~ **at sthg** ser ruim em algo **-2.** [unfavourable] mau (má); **to go from** ~ **to worse** ir de mal a pior **-3.** [severe] grave, severo(ra) **-4.** [inadequate] ruim **-5.** [guilty]: **to feel** ~ **about sthg** sentir-se mal por algum motivo **-6.** [food, milk, meat] mal; **to go** ~ ir mal. <> *adv US* = **badly**.
bad blood *n (U)* [anger] ódio *m*.
bad cheque *UK*, **bad check** *US n* cheque *m* sem fundo.
bad debt *n* dívida *f* perdida.
baddy (*pl* **-ies**) *n inf* vilão *m*, vilã *f*.
bade [bæd] *pt* ▻ **bid**.
bad feeling *n (U)* [resentment] rancor *m*, ressentimento *m*.
badge [bædʒ] *n* **-1.** [metal, plastic] crachá *m* **-2.** [sewn on] distintivo *m* **-3.** [on car] selo *m*.
badger ['bædʒə^r] <> *n* [animal] texugo *m*. <> *vt* [pester]: **to** ~ **sb (to do sthg)** convencer alguém (a fazer algo).
badly ['bædlɪ] (*compar* **worse**, *superl* **worst**) *adv* **-1.** [poorly] mal; **to think** ~ **of sb** pensar mal de alguém **-2.** [severely] gravemente **-3.** [improperly] indevidamente **-4.** [cruelly] mal **-5.** [very much]: **to be** ~ **in need of sthg** precisar muito de algo.
badly-off *adj* **-1.** [poor] carente **-2.** [lacking]: **to be** ~ **for sthg** estar carente de algo.
bad-mannered [-'mænəd] *adj* mal-educado(da).
badminton ['bædmɪntən] *n (U)* badminton *m*.
bad-mouth *vt esp US inf* falar mal de.
badness ['bædnɪs] *n (U)* maldade *f*.
bad-tempered [-'tempəd] *adj* **-1.** [by nature] genioso(sa) **-2.** [in a bad mood] mal-humorado(da).
baffle ['bæfl] *vt* [puzzle] desnortear.
baffling ['bæflɪŋ] *adj* [puzzling] desnorteante.
BAFTA (*abbr of* **British Academy of Film and Television Arts**) *n organização britânica que promove e premia os melhores em filmes, televisão e outras mídias interativas*.
bag [bæg] (*pt* & *pp* **-ged**, *cont* **-ging**) <> *n* **-1.** [container] saco *m*; ~ **of bones** saco de ossos; **in the** ~ *inf* no papo; **to pack one's** ~**s** *fig* [leave] fazer as malas **-2.** [handbag] bolsa *f*; [when travelling] mala *f* **-3.** [bagful] sacola *f*. <> *vt* **-1.** [put into bags] ensacar **-2.** *UK inf* [get] pegar **-3.** *UK inf* [reserve] marcar.
◆ **bags** *npl* **-1.** [under eyes] bolsas *fpl* **-2.** [lots]: ~**s of sthg** *inf* um montão de algo.
bagel ['beɪgəl] *n* pão *m* enrolado.
baggage ['bægɪdʒ] *n (U)* bagagem *f*.
baggage car *n US* vagão *m* de bagagens.
baggage reclaim *n* esteira *f* de bagagem.
baggage room *n US* guarda-volumes *m inv*.
baggy ['bægɪ] (*compar* **-ier**, *superl* **-iest**) *adj* largo(ga).
Baghdad [bæg'dæd] *n* Bagdá; **in** ~ em Bagdá.
bag lady *n inf* mulher *f* de rua.
bagpipes ['bægpaɪps] *npl* gaita *f* de foles.
bagsnatcher ['bægsnætʃə^r] *n* batedor *m* de carteira.
baguette [bə'get] *n* [loaf] baguete *f*.
bah [bɑ:] *excl* bah!
Bahamas [bə'hɑ:məz] *npl*: **the** ~ as Bahamas; **in the** ~ nas Bahamas.
Bahrain, Bahrein [bɑ:'reɪn] *n* Barein; **in** ~ em Barein.
Bahraini, Bahreini [bɑ:'reɪnɪ] <> *adj* & *n* baraini. <> *n* baraini *mf*.
bail [beɪl] *n (U) JUR* fiança *f*; **on** ~ sob fiança.
◆ **bail out** <> *vt sep* **-1.** *JUR* [pay bail for] afiançar **-2.** [rescue] resgatar **-3.** [boat] tirar água. <> *vi* [from plane] saltar de pára-quedas.
bailiff ['beɪlɪf] *n* **-1.** [in court] oficial *mf* de justiça **-2.** [in charge of repossession] administrador *m*, -ra *f* de propriedades.
bait [beɪt] <> *n (U)* [food] isca *f*; **to rise to** *OR* **take the** ~ *fig* morder a isca. <> *vt* **-1.** [hook] pôr isca em **-2.** [mousetrap] armar **-3.** [tease, torment - person] atormentar; [- bear, badger] provocar.
baize [beɪz] *n (U)* feltro *m*.
bake [beɪk] <> *vt* **-1.** [cook] assar **-2.** [dry, harden] queimar. <> *vi* [food] assar.
baked beans [beɪkt-] *npl feijão cozido em molho de tomate*.
baked potato [beɪkt-] *n batata grande assada com casca e servida com recheio*.
Bakelite® ['beɪkəlaɪt] *n* baquelita *f*.
baker ['beɪkə^r] *n* padeiro *m*; ~**'s (shop)** padaria *f*.
bakery ['beɪkərɪ] (*pl* **-ies**) *n* padaria *f*.
baking ['beɪkɪŋ] <> *adj inf* [hot] escaldante. <> *n* [process] cozimento *m*.
baking powder *n (U)* fermento *m* em pó.
baking tin *n* fôrma *f*.
baking tray *n* assadeira *f*.
balaclava (helmet) [bælə'klɑ:və-] *n UK* balaclava *f*.
balance ['bæləns] <> *n* **-1.** [equilibrium] equilíbrio *m*; **to keep/lose one's** ~ manter/perder o equilíbrio; **off** ~ desequilibrado(da) **-2.** *fig* [counterweight] contra-peso *m* **-3.** *fig* [weight, force]: ~ **of evidence**

peso *m* da evidência **-4.** [scales] balança *f*; **to be** *OR* **hang in the ~** estar na balança **-5.** [remainder] restante *m* **-6.** [of bank account] saldo *m*. <> *vt* **-1.** [keep in balance] balancear **-2.** [compare]: **to ~ sthg against sthg** contrabalançar algo em relação a algo **-3.** [in accounting]: **to ~ the books/a budget** fazer o balanço dos livros/do orçamento. <> *vi* **-1.** [maintain equilibrium] equilibrar-se **-2.** [in accounting] fechar, bater.
◆ **on balance** *adv* de um modo geral.
balanced ['bælənst] *adj* equilibrado(da).
balanced diet ['bælənst-] *n* dieta *f* equilibrada.
balance of payments *n* balança *f* de pagamentos.
balance of power *n* equilíbrio *m* de forças.
balance of trade *n* balança *f* comercial.
balance sheet *n* balancete *m*.
balancing act ['bælənsɪŋ-] *n fig* [careful manoeuvre] malabarismo *m*.
balcony ['bælkənɪ] (*pl* **-ies**) *n* **-1.** [on building] sacada *f* **-2.** [in theatre] balcão *m*, galeria *f*.
bald [bɔ:ld] *adj* **-1.** [head, man, tyre] careca **-2.** *fig* [unadorned] curto(ta) e grosso(sa).
bald eagle *n* águia *f* americana *(símbolo dos Estados Unidos que aparece em todos os emblemas oficiais)*.
balding ['bɔ:ldɪŋ] *adj* careca, calvo(va).
baldness ['bɔ:ldnɪs] *n (U)* calvície *f*.
bale [beɪl] *n* fardo *m*.
◆ **bale out** *UK vt sep* = **bail out**.
Balearic Islands [ˌbælɪ'ærɪk-], **Balearics** [ˌbælɪ'ærɪks] *npl*: **the ~** as Ilhas Baleares; **in the ~** nas Ilhas Baleares.
baleful ['beɪlfʊl] *adj* fulminante.
Bali ['bɑ:lɪ] *n* Bali; **in ~** em Bali.
balk [bɔ:k] *vi* [recoil]: **to ~ (at sthg)** [person] recusar-se (a fazer algo).
Balkan ['bɔ:lkən] *adj* balcânico(ca).
Balkans ['bɔ:lkənz], **Balkan States** *npl*: **the ~** os Balcãs; **in the ~** nos Balcãs.
ball [bɔ:l] *n* **-1.** [in game] bola *f*; **to start/keep the ~ rolling** *fig* pôr/manter a bola em jogo; **to be on the ~** *fig* estar ligado(da) em tudo; **to play ~ with sb** *fig* colaborar (com alguém) **-2.** [sphere] novelo *m* **-3.** [dance] baile *m*; **to have a ~** *fig* divertir-se.
◆ **balls** *vulg* <> *n* [nonsense] merda *f*. <> *npl* [testicles] saco *m*; *fig* [courage]: **to have ~** ter colhões. <> *excl* caralho!
ballad ['bæləd] *n* balada *f*.
ball-and-socket joint *n* junta *f* articulada *(bola-e-soquete)*.
ballast ['bæləst] *n (U)* lastro *m*.
ball bearing *n* rolamento *m*.
ball boy *n* gandula *m*.
ballcock ['bɔ:lkɒk] *n* bóia *f*.
ballerina [ˌbælə'ri:nə] *n* bailarina *f*.
ballet ['bæleɪ] *n (U)* balé *m*.
ballet dancer *n* bailarino(na).
ball game *n* **-1.** *US* [baseball match] jogo *m* de beisebol **-2.** *fig* [situation]: **it's a whole new ~** *inf* é outra história.
ball girl *n* gandula *f*.
ballistic missile *n* míssil *m* balístico.
ballistics [bə'lɪstɪks] *n (U)* balística *f*.
balloon [bə'lu:n] <> *n* balão *m*. <> *vi* [swell] inflar.
ballooning [bə'lu:nɪŋ] *n (U)* balonismo *m*.
ballot ['bælət] <> *n* **-1.** [voting paper] voto *m* **-2.** [voting process] votação *f*. <> *vt* [canvass] caçar votos. <> *vi* [vote]: **to ~ for sthg** votar para algo.
ballot box *n* **-1.** [container] urna *f* **-2.** [voting process] urnas *fpl*.
ballot paper *n* cédula *f* de votação.
ball park *n US* estádio *m* de beisebal.
ball-park figure *n inf* [estimate] valor *m* estimado.
ballpoint (pen) ['bɔ:lpɔɪnt-] *n* caneta *f* esferográfica.
ballroom ['bɔ:lrʊm] *n* salão *m* de baile.
ballroom dancing *n (U)* dança *f* de salão.
balls-up *UK*, **ball-up** *US n v inf* cagada *f*.
balm [bɑ:m] *n* bálsamo *m*.
balmy ['bɑ:mɪ] (*compar* **-ier**, *superl* **-iest**) *adj* suave.
baloney [bə'ləʊnɪ] *n* **-1.** *inf* [rubbish] asneira *f* **-2.** *US* [sausage] mortadela *f*.
balsa ['bɒlsə] *n* = **balsawood**.
balsam ['bɔ:lsəm] *n (U)* [substance] bálsamo *m*.
balsawood ['bɒlsəwʊd] *n* balsa *f*.
Baltic ['bɔ:ltɪk] <> *adj* [port, coast] báltico(ca). <> *n*: **the ~ (Sea)** o (mar) Báltico.
Baltic Republic *n*: **the ~s** as Repúblicas Bálticas.
Baltic State *n*: **the ~s** os Estados Bálticos.
balustrade [ˌbælə'streɪd] *n* balaustrada *f*.
bamboo [bæm'bu:] *n* bambu *m*.
bamboozle [bæm'bu:zl] *vt inf* lograr.
ban [bæn] (*pt* & *pp* **-ned**, *cont* **-ning**) <> *n* proibição *f*; **~ on sthg** proibição de algo. <> *vt* banir; **to ~ sb from doing sthg** proibir alguém de fazer algo.
banal [bə'nɑ:l] *adj pej* banal.
banana [bə'nɑ:nə] *n* banana *f*.
banana republic *n* república *f* das bananas.
banana split *n* banana *f* split.
band [bænd] *n* **-1.** [musical group] banda *f* **-2.** [gang] bando *m* **-3.** [long strip] correia *f* **-4.** [broad stripe, range] faixa *f*.
◆ **band together** *vi* unir-se.
bandage ['bændɪdʒ] <> *n* faixa *f*. <> *vt* enfaixar.
Band-Aid® *n* band-aid *m*.
bandan(n)a [bæn'dænə] *n* bandana *f*.
b and b, B and B (*abbr of* **bed and breakfast**) *n tipo de acomodação típica da Grã-Bretanha em que residências privadas oferecem serviço de quarto e café da manhã*.
bandit ['bændɪt] *n* bandido *m*.
bandmaster ['bændˌmɑ:stəʳ] *n* maestro *m*, -trina *f*.
band saw *n* serra *f* de fita.
bandsman ['bændzmən] (*pl* **-men** [-mən]) *n* músico *m*.
bandstand ['bændstænd] *n* palanque *m*.
bandwagon ['bændwægən] *n*: **to jump on the ~** pegar carona na idéia.
bandy ['bændɪ] (*compar* **-ier**, *superl* **-iest**, *pt* & *pp* **-ied**) *adj* [bandy-legged] cambaio(a).
◆ **bandy about, bandy around** *vt sep* ficar repetindo.

bandy-legged [-ˌlegd] *adj* = **bandy**.
bane [beɪn] *n*: **the ~ of sb's life** a cruz da vida de alguém.
bang [bæŋ] ◇ *adv* **-1.** [right]: **~ in the middle** bem no meio; **~ on** certeiro(ra) **-2.** *phr*: **~ goes/go ...** *inf* lá se vai/vão ... ◇ *n* **-1.** [blow] golpe *m* **-2.** [loud noise] estrondo *m*; **to go with a ~** *inf fig* ser um estouro. ◇ *vt* **-1.** [hit] bater **-2.** [move noisily] bater. ◇ *vi* **-1.** [knock]: **to ~ on sthg** dar pancadas **-2.** [make a loud noise] bater **-3.** [crash]: **to ~ into sb/sthg** bater em alguém/algo. ◇ *excl* bum.
◆ **bangs** *npl US* franjas *fpl*.
◆ **bang down** *vt sep*: **to ~ sthg down on** bater algo com força em.
banger ['bæŋəʳ] *n UK* **-1.** *inf* [sausage] salsicha *f* **-2.** *inf* [old car] carroça *f* **-3.** [firework] rojão *m*.
Bangkok [bæŋ'kɒk] *n* Bangkok; **in ~** em Bangkok.
Bangladesh [ˌbæŋglə'deʃ] *n* Bangladesh; **in ~** em Bangladesh.
Bangladeshi [ˌbæŋglə'deʃɪ] ◇ *adj* bangladeshiano(na). ◇ *n* bangladeshiano *m*, -na *f*.
bangle ['bæŋgl] *n* pulseira *f*.
banish ['bænɪʃ] *vt* **-1.** [gen, fig] banir **-2.** *literary* [dismiss] afugentar.
banister ['bænɪstəʳ] *n*, **banisters** ['bænɪstəz] *npl* corrimão *m*.
banjo ['bændʒəʊ] (*pl* **-s** *OR* **-es**) *n* banjo *m*.
bank [bæŋk] ◇ *n* **-1.** [gen & *FIN*] banco *m*; **blood/data ~** banco *m* de sangue/dados **-2.** [alongside river, lake] margem *m* **-3.** [slope] monte *m* **-4.** [of clouds, fog] massa *f*. ◇ *vt FIN* depositar. ◇ *vi* **-1.** *FIN*: **to ~ with sb** ser correntista de **-2.** [plane] inclinar lateralmente.
◆ **bank on** *vt fus* contar com.
bank account *n* conta *f* corrente.
bank balance *n* saldo *m* bancário.
bankbook ['bæŋkbʊk] *n* extrato *m* bancário.
bank card *n* cartão *m* de garantia de cheque.
bank charges *npl* tarifas *fpl* bancárias.
bank draft *n* ordem *f* bancária.
banker ['bæŋkəʳ] *n FIN* banqueiro *m*, -ra *f*.
banker's order *n UK* débito *m* em conta.
bank holiday *n UK* feriado *m* bancário.
banking ['bæŋkɪŋ] *n (U)* serviços *mpl* bancários.
bank loan *n* empréstimo *m* bancário.
bank manager *n* gerente *mf* de banco.
bank note *n* cédula *f*.
bank rate *n* taxa *f* referencial de juros.
bankrupt ['bæŋkrʌpt] ◇ *adj* [financially] falido(da); **to go ~** ir à falência; **to be morally ~** *fig* estar desmoralizado(da). ◇ *n* falido *m*, -da *f*. ◇ *vt* falir.
bankruptcy ['bæŋkrəptsɪ] (*pl* **-ies**) *n* falência *f*; **moral ~** *fig* desmoralização *f*.
bank statement *n* extrato *m* bancário.
banner ['bænəʳ] *n* [made of cloth] faixa *f*.
bannister ['bænɪstəʳ] *n*, **bannisters** ['bænɪstəz] *npl* = **banister**.
banns [bænz] *npl*: **to publish the ~** proclamar os votos.
banquet ['bæŋkwɪt] *n* banquete *m*.
bantam ['bæntəm] *n* garnisé *m*.
bantamweight ['bæntəmweɪt] *n* peso-galo *m*.
banter ['bæntəʳ] ◇ *n (U)* brincadeiras *fpl*. ◇ *vi* brincar.
bap [bæp] *n UK* bisnaguinha *f*.
baptism ['bæptɪzm] *n* batismo *m*; **~ of fire** *fig* batismo de fogo.
Baptist ['bæptɪst] *n* batista *mf*.
baptize, -ise [*UK* bæp'taɪz, *US* 'bæptaɪz] *vt* batizar.
bar [bɑːʳ] (*pt* & *pp* **-red**, *cont* **-ring**) ◇ *n* **-1.** [of wood, metal, chocolate, soap etc] barra *f*; **to be behind ~s** estar atrás das grades **-2.** *fig* [obstacle] barreira *f* **-3.** [drinking place] bar *m* **-4.** [counter] balcão *m* **-5.** *MUS* compasso *m*. ◇ *vt* **-1.** [bolt] trancar **-2.** [block off] bloquear; **to ~ sb's way** bloquear a passagem de alguém **-3.** [ban] barrar; **to ~ sb (from somewhere/from doing sthg)** impedir alguém (de entrar em algum lugar/fazer algo). ◇ *prep* [except] exceto; **~ none** sem exceção.
◆ **Bar** *n* **-1.** *UK*: **the Bar** [barristers] o Magistrado; [profession] a Magistratura **-2.** *US*: **the Bar** [lawyers] advogados(das); [profession] a Advocacia.
Barbados [bɑː'beɪdɒs] *n* Barbados; **in ~** em Barbados.
barbarian [bɑː'beərɪən] *n* **-1.** *HIST* bárbaro *m* **-2.** *pej* & *fig* [uncultured person] bárbaro *m*, -ra *f*.
barbaric [bɑː'bærɪk] *adj pej* bárbaro(ra).
barbarous ['bɑːbərəs] *adj pej* bárbaro(ra).
barbecue ['bɑːbɪkjuː] ◇ *n* **-1.** [grill] churrasqueira *f* **-2.** [party] churrasco *m*. ◇ *vt* assar *(na churrasqueira)*.
barbed [bɑːbd] *adj* **-1.** [pointed, spiked] farpado(da) **-2.** [unkind] espinhento(ta).
barbed wire [bɑːbd-] *n UK (U)* arame *m* farpado.
barber ['bɑːbəʳ] *n* barbeiro *m*; **~'s (shop)** barbearia *f*.
barbiturate [bɑː'bɪtjʊrət] *n* barbitúrico *m*.
Barcelona [ˌbɑːsə'ləʊnə] *n* Barcelona; **in ~** em Barcelona.
bar chart, bar graph *US n* gráfico *m* de barras.
bar code *n* código *m* de barras.
bare [beəʳ] ◇ *adj* **-1.** [without covering] descoberto(-ta) **-2.** [basic] mínimo(ma); **the ~ essentials** o mínimo necessário **-3.** [empty] vazio(a) ◇ *vt* [reveal - chest, limbs] exibir, mostrar; **to ~ one's teeth** mostrar os dentes **to ~ one's head** tirar o chapéu.
bareback ['beəbæk] ◇ *adj* em pêlo. ◇ *adv* em pêlo.
barefaced ['beəfeɪst] *adj* deslavado(da).
barefoot(ed) [ˌbeə'fʊt(ɪd)] ◇ *adj* descalço(ça). ◇ *adv* descalço.
bareheaded [ˌbeə'hedɪd] ◇ *adj* sem chapéu. ◇ *adv* sem chapéu.
barelegged [ˌbeə'legd] ◇ *adj* de pernas de fora. ◇ *adv* de pernas de fora.
barely ['beəlɪ] *adv* [scarcely] mal.
bargain ['bɑːgɪn] ◇ *n* **-1.** [agreement] barganha *f*; **into the ~** ainda por cima **-2.** [good buy] pechincha *f*. ◇ *vi* barganhar; **to ~ with sb for sthg** pechinchar com alguém por algo.
◆ **bargain for, bargain on** *vt fus* esperar.
bargaining ['bɑːgɪnɪŋ] *n (U)* barganha *f*.
bargaining power *n (U)* poder *m* de barganha.
barge [bɑːdʒ] ◇ *n* barca *f*. ◇ *vi inf* **to ~ into sb/**

sthg esbarrar em alguém/algo; **to ~ past sb/sthg** passar empurrando alguém/algo.
◆ **barge in** *vi*: **to ~ in (on sb/sthg)** interromper (alguém/algo).
barge pole *n inf*: **I wouldn't touch it with a ~** não quero nem de graça.
bar graph *n US* = **bar chart**.
baritone ['bærɪtəʊn] *n* barítono *m*.
barium meal ['beərɪəm-] *n UK* (líquido de) contraste *m*.
bark [bɑːk] <> *n* **-1.** [of dog] latido *m*; **his ~ is worse than his bite** *inf* cão que late não morde **-2.** [on tree] casca *f*. <> *vt* [order] gritar. <> *vi* [dog] latir; **to ~ at sb/sthg** xingar alguém/algo.
barking ['bɑːkɪŋ] <> *n (U)* latidos *mpl*. <> *adj & adv*: **to be ~ (mad)** *UK inf* ser/estar completamente louco(ca); **to go ~ mad** *UK inf* pirar de vez.
barley ['bɑːlɪ] *n (U)* cevada *f*.
barley sugar *n UK* *bala feita com caramelo e cevada.*
barley water *n UK (U)* *bebida à base de cevada e suco de fruta.*
barmaid ['bɑːmeɪd] *n* garçonete *f*.
barman ['bɑːmən] (*pl* **-men** [-mən]) *n* barman *m*.
barmy ['bɑːmɪ] (*compar* **-ier**, *superl* **-iest**) *adj UK inf* doido(da).
barn [bɑːn] *n* celeiro *m*.
barnacle ['bɑːnəkl] *n* cirrípede *m*.
barn dance *n* **-1.** [occasion] ≃ baile *m* caipira **-2.** *UK* [type of dance] ≃ dança *f* caipira.
barn owl *n* coruja *f* branca.
barnstorm *US vi* **-1.** [politician] viajar em campanha (pelo país) **-2.** [performer] sair em turnê.
barnstorming *UK adj* vigoroso(sa).
barometer [bə'rɒmɪtə^r] *n* **-1.** [instrument] barômetro *m* **-2.** *fig* [way of measuring] ≃ termômetro *m*.
baron ['bærən] *n* barão *m*; **oil/press ~** *fig* magnata da imprensa/do petróleo.
baroness ['bærənɪs] *n* baronesa *f*.
baronet ['bærənɪt] *n* baronete *m*.
baroque [bə'rɒk] *adj* barroco(ca).
barrack ['bærək] *vt UK* interromper com gritos.
◆ **barracks** *npl* quartel *m*.
barracking ['bærəkɪŋ] *n (U) UK* gritaria *f*.
barracuda [ˌbærə'kuːdə] *n* barracuda *f*.
barrage ['bærɑːʒ] *n* **-1.** [of firing] bombardeio *m* **-2.** [of questions] bombardeio *m* **-3.** *UK* [dam] barragem *f*.
barred [bɑːd] *adj* [window, door] trancado(da).
barrel ['bærəl] *n* **-1.** [container] barril *m* **-2.** [of gun] cano *m*.
barrel organ *n* realejo *m*.
barren ['bærən] *adj* **-1.** [unable to have children] estéril **-2.** [unable to produce crops] improdutivo(va) **-3.** [dull] enfadonho(nha).
barrette [bə'ret] *n US* [for hair] fivela *f* passador *m*.
barricade [ˌbærɪ'keɪd] <> *n* barricada *f*. <> *vt* bloquear, obstruir com barricadas; **to ~ o.s. in** entrincheirar-se em.
barrier ['bærɪə^r] *n* **-1.** [fence, wall] barreira *f* **-2.** *fig* [obstacle] obstáculo *m*.
barrier cream *n UK* loção *f* protetora.
barring ['bɑːrɪŋ] *prep*: **~ accidents** a menos que haja imprevistos; **~ further complications** se não houver complicações.
barrister ['bærɪstə^r] *n UK* advogado *m*, -da *f*.
barroom ['bɑːrʊm] *n US* sala *f* de bar.
barrow ['bærəʊ] *n* [market stall] carrinho *m* de frutas/verduras.
bar stool *n* tamborete *m* de bar.
bartender ['bɑːtendə^r] *n US* garçom *m*, -nete *f*.
barter ['bɑːtə^r] <> *n* barganha *f*, troca *f*. <> *vt* trocar; **to ~ sthg for sthg** trocar algo por algo. <> *vi* barganhar.
base [beɪs] <> *n* base *f*. <> *vt* **-1.** [use as starting point]: **to ~ sthg (up)on sthg** basear algo em algo **-2.** [locate] estabelecer; **to be ~d in** viver/trabalhar em; **a New York-based company** uma empresa sediada em Nova York. <> *adj pej* [dishonourable] desprezível.
baseball ['beɪsbɔːl] *n (U)* beisebol *m*.
baseball cap *n* boné *m* de beisebol.
base camp *n* acampamento *m* de base.
baseless ['beɪslɪs] *adj* infundado(da).
baseline ['beɪslaɪn] *n SPORT* linha *f* de base.
basement ['beɪsmənt] *n* porão *m*.
base metal *n dated* metal *m* não-precioso.
base rate *n* taxa *f* de base.
bases ['beɪsiːz] *pl* ⊳ **basis**.
bash [bæʃ] *inf* <> *n* **-1.** [painful blow] pancada *f* **-2.** [attempt]: **to have a ~ (at sthg)** tentar fazer (algo) **-3.** [party] farra *f*. <> *vt* **-1.** [hit] bater **-2.** [criticize] xingar.
bashful ['bæʃfʊl] *adj* tímido(da).
basic ['beɪsɪk] *adj* [fundamental] básico(ca).
◆ **basics** *npl* **-1.** [rudiments] princípios *mpl* básicos **-2.** [essential foodstuffs] ≃ cesta *f* básica.
BASIC (*abbr of* **Beginners' All-purpose Symbolic Instruction Code**) *n* BASIC *m*.
basically ['beɪsɪklɪ] *adv* [essentially] basicamente, no fundo.
basic rate *n UK* taxa *f* básica.
basic wage *n* salário *m* base.
basil ['bæzl] *n (U)* manjericão *m*.
basin ['beɪsn] *n* **-1.** *UK* [bowl, container] tigela *f*; [for washing] pia *f* **-2.** *GEOGR* bacia *f*.
basis ['beɪsɪs] (*pl* **-ses**) *n* **-1.** [gen] base *f*; **on the ~ that** com base no fato de que, considerando que **-2.** [arrangement]: **on a weekly/monthly ~** numa base semanal/mensal; **on the ~ of** com base em.
bask [bɑːsk] *vi* **-1.** [sunbathe]: **to ~ in the sun** tomar banho de sol **-2.** *fig* [take pleasure]: **to ~ in sb's praise/approval** gozar do elogio/da aprovação de alguém.
basket ['bɑːskɪt] *n* [container - for rubbish] cesto *m*; [- for shopping] cesta *f*.
basketball ['bɑːskɪtbɔːl] <> *n (U)* basquete *m*. <> *comp* de basquete.
basket case *n inf* **-1.** [person] bagaço *m* **-2.** [failure] ruína *f*.
basketwork ['bɑːskɪtwɜːk] *n* **-1.** *(U)* [craft, activity] trabalho *m* em vime **-2.** *(U)* [articles] artigos *mpl* de vime.
basking shark ['bɑːskɪŋ-] *n* tubarão-frade *m*.
Basle [bɑːl] *n* Basiléia; **in ~** na Basiléia.

Basque [bɑ:sk] ◇ *adj* basco(ca). ◇ *n* **-1.** [person] basco *m*, -ca *f* **- 2.** [language] basco *m*.
bass¹ [beɪs] ◇ *adj* [part, singer] baixo(xa). ◇ *n* **-1.** [singer] baixo *m*, -xa *f* **- 2.** [double bass] duplo baixo *m* **- 3.** = **bass guitar**.
bass² [bæs] (*pl inv* OR **-es**) *n* [fish] perca *f*.
bass clef [beɪs-] *n* MUS clave *f* de fá.
bass drum [beɪs-] *n* MUS tambor *m* baixo.
basset (hound) ['bæsɪt-] *n* cão *m* bassê.
bass guitar [beɪs-] *n* MUS baixo *m*.
bassoon [bə'su:n] *n* MUS fagote *m*.
bassoonist *n* MUS fagotista *mf*.
bastard ['bɑ:stəd] *n* **-1.** [illegitimate child] bastardo *m*, -da *f* **- 2.** *v inf pej* [person] canalha *mf*, filho *m* da mãe.
baste [beɪst] *vt* CULIN regar.
bastion ['bæstɪən] *n fig* bastião *m*.
bat [bæt] (*pt* & *pp* **-ted**, *cont* **-ting**) ◇ *n* **-1.** [animal] morcego *m* **- 2.** [SPORT - for cricket] pá *f*; [- for baseball] bastão *m*; [- for table tennis] raquete *f* **- 3.** *phr*: **to do sthg off one's own** ~ fazer algo sem auxílio. ◇ *vt* & *vi* rebater.
batch [bætʃ] *n* **-1.** [of papers, letters] pilha *f* **- 2.** [of work] porção *f* **- 3.** [of products] lote *m* **- 4.** [of people] grupo *m* **- 5.** [of bread, cakes etc] fornada *f*.
batch file *n* COMPUT arquivo *m* em lote.
batch processing *n (U)* COMPUT processamento *m* em lote.
bated ['beɪtɪd] *adj*: **with** ~ **breath** [expectantly] segurando a respiração.
bath [bɑ:θ] ◇ *n* **-1.** [bathtub] banheira *f* **- 2.** [act of washing] banho *m*; **to have** OR **take a bath** tomar (um) banho. ◇ *vt* dar banho em.
◆ **baths** *npl* **UK** [public] banhos *mpl* públicos.
bath chair *n* cadeira *f* de banho.
bath cube *n* cubos *mpl* de sais de banho.
bathe [beɪð] ◇ *vt* **-1.** [wound] lavar **- 2.** [in light, sweat] banhar; **to be** ~**d in sthg** estar coberto(ta) de algo. ◇ *vi* **-1.** [swim] nadar **- 2. US** [take a bath] tomar (um) banho.
bather ['beɪðə^r] *n* [swimmer] banhista *m*.
bathing ['beɪðɪŋ] *n (U)* banho *m*; **safe for** ~ próprio(pria) para banho; **to go** ~ dar um mergulho.
bathing cap *n* touca *f* de banho.
bathing costume, bathing suit *n* maiô *m*.
bathing trunks *npl* calção *m* de banho.
bath mat *n* tapete *m* de banheiro.
bath oil *n* óleo *m* de banho.
bathrobe ['bɑ:θrəʊb] *n* **-1.** [made of towelling] roupão *m* de banho **- 2.** [dressing gown] **US** chambre *m*.
bathroom ['bɑ:θrʊm] *n* **UK** banheiro *m*.
bath salts *npl* sais *mpl* de banho.
bath towel *n* toalha *f* de banho.
bathtub ['bɑ:θtʌb] *n* banheira *f*.
batik [bə'ti:k] *n* batique *m*.
baton ['bætən] *n* **-1.** [of conductor] batuta *f* **- 2.** [in relay race] bastão *m* **- 3. UK** [of policeman] cassetete *m*.
baton charge *n* **UK** [by police] investida *f* policial.
batsman ['bætsmən] (*pl* **-men** [-mən]) *n* CRICKET batedor *m*.
battalion [bə'tæljən] *n* batalhão *m*.
batten ['bætn] *n* [piece of wood] tábua *f*.
◆ **batten down** *vt fus fig*: **to** ~ **down the hatches** preparar-se para momentos difíceis/ enfrentar uma crise.
batter ['bætə^r] ◇ *n* **-1.** CULIN massa *f* (mole) **- 2.** SPORT batedor *m*, -ra *f*. ◇ *vt* [child, woman] surrar. ◇ *vi* [beat] bater.
◆ **batter down** *vt sep* botar abaixo.
battered ['bætəd] *adj* **-1.** [child, woman] maltratado(-da) **- 2.** [old, worn-out - car] arruinado(da); [- hat] surrado(da) **- 3.** CULIN misturado(da).
battering ['bætərɪŋ] *n*: **to take a** ~ sofrer uma derrota.
battering ram *n* aríete *m*.
battery ['bætərɪ] (*pl* **-ies**) *n* **-1.** [gen] bateria *f* **- 2.** [ELEC - of car] bateria *f*; [- of radio, torch etc] pilha *f* **- 3.** [group - of people] grupo *m*; [- of things] série *f*, conjunto *m*.
battery charger *n* carregador *m* de bateria.
battery hen *n* frango *m* de granja.
battle ['bætl] ◇ *n* batalha *f*; ~ **for/against/with sthg** batalha por/contra/com algo; ~ **of wits** disputa de intelectos; **to be half the** ~ ser a metade do caminho; **to be fighting a losing** ~ estar lutando em vão. ◇ *vi* [fight] lutar; **to** ~ **for/against/with sthg** lutar por/contra/com algo.
battledress ['bætldres] *n* **UK** uniforme *m* de combate.
battlefield ['bætlfi:ld], **battleground** ['bætlgraʊnd] *n* MIL & *fig* campo *m* de batalha.
battlements ['bætlmənts] *npl* [of castle] ameias *fpl*.
battleship ['bætlʃɪp] *n* couraçado *m*.
bauble ['bɔ:bl] *n* bugiganga *f*.
baud [bɔ:d] *n* COMPUT baud *m*.
baud rate *n* COMPUT baud rate *m*, taxa *f* de bauds.
baulk [bɔ:k] *vi* = **balk**.
Bavaria [bə'veərɪə] *n* Baviera; **in** ~ na Baviera.
Bavarian [bə'veərɪən] ◇ *adj* bávaro(ra). ◇ *n* bávaro *m*, -ra *f*.
bawdy ['bɔ:dɪ] (*compar* **-ier**, *superl* **-iest**) *adj* obsceno(na).
bawl [bɔ:l] ◇ *vt* [shout] gritar. ◇ *vi* **-1.** [shout] gritar **- 2.** [weep] berrar.
bay [beɪ] ◇ *n* **-1.** GEOGR baía *f* **- 2.** [for loading] zona *m* de carga e descarga **- 3.** [for parking] vaga *f* **- 4.** [horse] baio *m* **- 5.** *phr*: **to keep sb/sthg at** ~ manter alguém/algo à distância. ◇ *vi* [dog, wolf] latir.
bay leaf *n* folha *f* de louro.
Bay of Biscay *n*: **the** ~ o Golfo de Biscaia.
bayonet ['beɪənɪt] *n* baioneta *f*.
bay tree *n* loureiro *m*.
bay window *n* bay window *f* janela *f* saliente.
bazaar [bə'zɑ:^r] *n* **-1.** [market] bazar *m* **- 2. UK** [charity sale] bazar *m* beneficente.
bazooka [bə'zu:kə] *n* bazuca *f*.
B & B *n abbr of* **bed and breakfast**
BBC (*abbr of* **British Broadcasting Corporation**) *n companhia estatal britânica de rádio e televisão*, BBC *f*.
BC - 1. (*abbr of* **before Christ**) a.C. **- 2.** *abbr of* **British Columbia**.
BCG (*abbr of* **Bacillus Calmette-Guérin**) *n* BCG *f*.
BD (*abbr of* **Bachelor of Divinity**) *n (titular de) graduação em teologia cristã protestante.*
BDS (*abbr of* **Bachelor of Dental Science**) *n (titular de) gradução em odontologia.*

be [bi:] (*pt* **was** *OR* **were**, *pp* **been**) <> *aux vb* **-1.** *(in combination with ppr: to form cont tense)* estar; **what is he doing?** o que ele está fazendo?; **it's snowing** está nevando **-2.** *(in combination with pp: to form passive)* ser; **to ~ loved** ser amado(da) **-3.** *(in question tags)* ser, estar; **the meal was delicious, wasn't it?** a comida estava deliciosa, não estava? **-4.** *(followed by to + infin)* dever; **I'm to ~ promoted** devo ser promovido(da); **you're not to tell anyone** você não deve contar a ninguém. <> *copulative vb* **-1.** *(with adj, n)* ser, estar; **to ~ a doctor/lawyer/plumber** ser médico/advogado/bombeiro; **she's intelligent/attractive** ela é inteligente/atraente; **~ quiet!** fique quieto!; **1 and 1 are 2** 1 e 1 são 2 **-2.** [referring to health] estar; **how are you?** como vai você? **-3.** [referring to age] ter; **how old are you?** quantos anos você tem? **-4.** [cost] custar; **how much was it?** quanto custou?; **that will ~ £10, please** são £10, por favor. <> *vi* **-1.** [exist] existir, haver, ser; **~ that as it may** seja como for **-2.** [referring to place] estar; **Toulouse is in France** Toulouse fica na França; **he will ~ here tomorrow** ele estará aqui amanhã **-3.** [referring to movement] estar; **I've been to the cinema/to France/to the butcher's** fui ao cinema/para a França/ao açougue. <> *v impers* **-1.** [referring to time, dates] ser; **it's two o'clock** são duas horas **-2.** [referring to distance] ser; **it's 3 km to the next town** são 3 quilômetros até a próxima cidade **-3.** [referring to the weather] estar; **it's hot/cold/windy** está quente *OR* frio *OR* ventando **-4.** [for emphasis] ser; **it's me** sou eu; **it's the milkman** é o leiteiro.

beach [bi:tʃ] <> *n* praia *f.* <> *vt* [boat, whale] encalhar.

beach ball *n* bola *f* de praia.

beach buggy *n* buggy *m.*

beachcomber ['bi:tʃˌkəʊməʳ] *n pessoa que ganha a vida catando e vendendo artigos deixados na praia.*

beachhead ['bi:tʃhed] *n MIL* cabeça-de-ponte *f.*

beachwear ['bi:tʃweəʳ] *n (U)* roupa *f* de praia.

beacon ['bi:kən] *n* **-1.** [warning fire] fogaréu *m* **-2.** [lighthouse] farol *m* **-3.** [radio beacon] radiofarol *m.*

bead [bi:d] *n* **-1.** [of wood, glass] conta *f* **-2.** [of sweat] gota *f.*

beaded *adj* [decorated with beads] enfeitado(da) com contas.

beading ['bi:dɪŋ] *n* [wood] moldura *f.*

beady ['bi:dɪ] (*compar* **-ier**, *superl* **-iest**) *adj* [eyes] pequeno(na) e brilhante; **to keep a ~ eye on sb/sthg** *fig* ficar de olho em alguém/algo.

beagle ['bi:gl] *n* bigle *m.*

beak [bi:k] *n* [of bird] bico *m.*

beaker ['bi:kəʳ] *n* copo *m (de plástico).*

be-all *n*: **the ~ and end-all** a razão de ser.

beam [bi:m] <> *n* **-1.** [of wood, concrete] viga *f* **-2.** [of light] raio *m*, feixe *m* **-3.** *US AUT*: **high/low ~s** luz alta/baixa. <> *vt* [signal, news] transmitir. <> *vi* **-1.** [smile] irradiar-se **-2.** [shine] irradiar.

beaming ['bi:mɪŋ] *adj* radiante.

bean [bi:n] *n CULIN* feijão *m*, grão *m*; **to be full of ~s** *inf* estar cheio (cheia) de vida; **to spill the ~s** *inf* dar com a língua nos dentes.

beanbag ['bi:nbæg] *n* [seat] *almofada grande e redonda, feita de flocos de espuma que se adapta ao corpo de quem senta.*

beanshoot ['bi:nʃu:t], **beansprout** ['bi:nspraʊt] *n* broto *m* de feijão.

bear [beəʳ] (*pt* **bore**, *pp* **borne**) <> *n* **-1.** [animal] urso *m*, -sa *f* **-2.** *ST EX* baixista *mf.* <> *vt* **-1.** [carry] carregar **-2.** [sustain] suportar **-3.** [accept] aceitar **-4.** [show] exibir **-5.** [produce, interest] produzir **-6.** [give birth to] parir **-7.** [feeling] guardar. <> *vi* **-1.** [turn] virar **-2.** [have effect]: **to bring pressure/influence to ~ on sb** exercer pressão/influência sobre alguém.

◆ **bear down** *vi*: **to ~ down on sb/sthg** abater-se sobre algo/alguém.

◆ **bear out** *vt sep* confirmar.

◆ **bear up** *vi* resistir.

◆ **bear with** *vt fus* tolerar.

bearable ['beərəbl] *adj* [tolerable] suportável.

beard [bɪəd] *n* [of man] barba *f.*

bearded *adj* [man, face] com barba.

bearer ['beərəʳ] *n* **-1.** [of stretcher, coffin] carregador *m*, -ra *f* **-2.** [of news, document] portador *m*, -ra *f* **-3.** [of name, title] detentor *m*, -ra *f.*

bear hug *n inf* abraço *m* forte.

bearing ['beərɪŋ] *n* **-1.** [connection] relação *f*; **~ on sthg** relação com algo **-2.** [deportment] conduta *f* **-3.** *TECH* mancal *m* **-4.** [on compass] direção *f*; **to get/lose one's ~s** *fig* achar/perder o rumo.

bear market *n ST EX* mercado *m* em baixa.

bearskin ['beəskɪn] *n* **-1.** [fur] pele *f* de urso **-2.** [hat] barretina *f* (de pele).

beast [bi:st] *n* **-1.** [animal] besta *m* **-2.** *inf pej* [person] besta *f.*

beastly ['bi:stlɪ] (*compar* **-ier**, *superl* **-iest**) *adj dated* abominável.

beat [bi:t] (*pt* **beat**, *pp* **beaten**) <> *n* **-1.** [gen] batida *f* **-2.** [of heart, pulse] batimento *m* **-3.** *MUS* [rhythm] ritmo *m* **-4.** [of policeman] ronda *f.* <> *adj inf* [exhausted] nocauteado(da). <> *vt* **-1.** [hit] bater em **-2.** [defeat] derrotar; **it ~s me** *inf* isto acaba comigo **-3.** [arrive ahead of] chegar antes; **she ~ me to it** ela me venceu **-4.** [be better than] superar **-5.** [eggs, wings] bater **-6.** *MUS* [time] marcar **-7.** *phr*: **~ it!** *inf* [go away] caia fora! <> *vi* **-1.** [rain] cair **-2.** [heart, pulse] bater.

◆ **beat down** <> *vi* **-1.** [sun] bater **-2.** [rain] cair uma pancada. <> *vt sep* [force to lower price] fazer baixar.

◆ **beat off** *vt sep* [resist] repelir.

◆ **beat up** *vt sep inf* [person] espancar.

beaten *adj* **-1.** [metal] forjado(da) **-2.** [path] batido(-da).

beater ['bi:təʳ] *n* **-1.** [for eggs, cream etc] batedeira *f* **-2.** [for carpet] batedor *m* **-3.** [of woman, child] agressor *m*, -ra *f.*

beat generation *n* geração *f* beat.

beating ['bi:tɪŋ] *n* [defeat, punishment] surra *f*; **to take a ~** levar uma surra; **to take some ~** *inf* ser difícil de superar.

beating up (*pl* **beatings up**) *n inf* [thrashing] espancamento *m.*

beatnik ['bi:tnɪk] *n* beatnik *m.*

beat-up *adj inf* [shabby] caindo aos pedaços.

beautician [bju:'tɪʃn] *n* esteticista *mf.*

beautiful ['bju:tɪfʊl] *adj* **-1.** [gen] bonito(ta) **-2.** [well executed] belo(la).
beautifully ['bju:təflɪ] *adv* **-1.** [attractively] belamente **-2.** *inf* [very well] esplendidamente.
beauty ['bju:tɪ] (*pl* **-ies**) ◇ *n* **-1.** *(U)* [attractiveness] beleza *f* **-2.** [beautiful woman] beldade *f* **-3.** *inf* [very good thing] maravilha *f.* ◇ *comp* [product] de beleza.
beauty contest *n* concurso *m* de beleza.
beauty parlour *n* salão *m* de beleza.
beauty queen *n* miss *f.*
beauty salon *n* = **beauty parlour.**
beauty spot *n* **-1.** [place] recanto *m* **-2.** [on skin] sinal *m.*
beaver ['bi:vəʳ] *n* castor *m.*
◆ **beaver away** *vi*: **to ~ away (at sthg)** dar duro (em algo).
becalmed [bɪ'kɑ:md] *adj* [ship] parado(da) por falta de vento.
became [bɪ'keɪm] *pt* ⊳ **become.**
because [bɪ'kɒz] *conj* porque.
◆ **because of** *prep* por causa de.
béchamel sauce [ˌbeɪʃə'mel-] *n* molho *m* bechamel *OR* branco.
beck [bek] *n*: **to be at sb's ~ and call** estar sempre à disposição de alguém.
beckon ['bekən] ◇ *vt* **-1.** [make a signal to] acenar **-2.** *fig* [call] chamar. ◇ *vi* [signal]: **to ~ to sb** acenar para alguém.
become [bɪ'kʌm] (*pt* **became**, *pp* **become**) *vt* **-1.** [grow] ficar; **what has ~ of ...?** o que foi feito de ...? **-2.** [acquire post of] tornar-se **-3.** [suit, be appropriate to] combinar com, ficar bem em; **sarcasm doesn't ~ you** o sarcasmo não combina com você.
becoming [bɪ'kʌmɪŋ] *adj* **-1.** [attractive] elegante **-2.** [appropriate] adequado(da).
bed [bed] (*pt* & *pp* **-ded**, *cont* **-ding**) *n* **-1.** [to sleep on] cama *f*; **to go to ~** ir para a cama; **to make the ~** arrumar a cama; **to make one's (own) ~** *fig* fazer a própria cama; **to go to ~ with sb** *euphemism* ir para a cama com alguém **-2.** [flowerbed] canteiro *m*; **a ~ of roses** *fig* [easy, pleasant] um mar de rosas **-3.** [bottom - of sea] fundo *m*; [- of river] leito *m.*
◆ **bed down** *vt* & *vi* acolher.
BEd (*abbr of* **Bachelor of Education**) *n (titular de) graduação que habilita para o magistério.*
bed and breakfast *n* **-1.** [service] hospedagem *f* com café da manhã **-2.** [hotel] bed and breakfast *m, acomodação típica da Grã-Bretanha (geralmente em casa de família) acompanhada de café da manhã.*
bed-bath *n* banho *m* na cama.
bedbug ['bedbʌg] *n* percevejo *m.*
bedclothes ['bedkləʊðz] *npl* roupa *f* de cama.
bedcover ['bedˌkʌvəʳ] *n* colcha *f.*
bedding ['bedɪŋ] *n* = **bedclothes.**
bedding plant *n* planta *f* de canteiro.
bedeck [bɪ'dek] *vt*: **to ~ sthg with sthg** decorar algo com algo.
bedevil [bɪ'devl] (*UK pt* & *pp* **-led**, *cont* **-ling**, *US pt* & *pp* **-ed**, *cont* **-ing**) *vt*: **to be bedevilled with sthg** estar atormentado(da) com algo.
bedfellow ['bedˌfeləʊ] *n fig* [colleague] aliado *m*, -da *f.*
bedlam ['bedləm] *n* [chaos] tumulto *m.*
bed linen *n* roupa *f* de cama.
Bedouin, Beduin ['bedʊɪn] ◇ *adj* beduíno(na). ◇ *n* beduíno *m*, -na *f.*
bedpan ['bedpæn] *n* comadre *f.*
bedraggled [bɪ'drægld] *adj* enlameado(da).
bedridden ['bedˌrɪdn] *adj* acamado(da).
bedrock ['bedrɒk] *n (U)* **-1.** GEOL leito *m* de rocha firme **-2.** *fig* [solid foundation] alicerce *m.*
bedroom ['bedrʊm] *n* quarto *m.*
bedside ['bedsaɪd] ◇ *n* beira *f* da cama. ◇ *comp* [lamp, table] de cabeceira.
bedside manner *n* [of doctor] jeito *m* para lidar com doentes.
bedside table *n* mesa *f* de cabeceira, criado-mudo *m.*
bed-sit(ter) *n UK* conjugado *m.*
bedsore ['bedsɔ:ʳ] *n* assadura *f.*
bedspread ['bedspred] *n* colcha *f.*
bedtime ['bedtaɪm] *n* hora *f* de dormir.
Beduin *adj* & *n* = **Bedouin.**
bed-wetting [-ˌwetɪŋ] *n* incontinência *f* urinária.
bee [bi:] *n* abelha *f*; **to have a ~ in one's bonnet about sthg** *fig* estar obcecado(da) por algo.
Beeb [bi:b] *n UK inf*: **the ~** a BBC.
beech [bi:tʃ] *n* faia *f.*
beef [bi:f] ◇ *n (U)* [meat] carne *f* de vaca. ◇ *vi inf* [complain]: **to ~ about sthg** reclamar de algo.
◆ **beef up** *vt sep inf* [strengthen] reforçar.
beefburger ['bi:fˌbɜ:gəʳ] *n* hambúrguer *m* bovino.
Beefeater ['bi:fˌi:təʳ] *n guarda da Torre de Londres.*
beefsteak ['bi:fˌsteɪk] *n* bife *m.*
beehive ['bi:haɪv] *n* **-1.** [for bees] colméia *f* **-2.** [hairstyle] ≃ pixaim *m.*
beekeeper ['bi:ˌki:pəʳ] *n* apicultor *m*, -ra *f.*
beeline ['bi:laɪn] *n*: **to make a ~ for sb/sthg** *inf* ir direto a alguém/algo.
been [bi:n] *pp* ⊳ **be.**
beep [bi:p] *inf* ◇ *n* bipe *m.* ◇ *vi* bipar.
beeper ['bi:pəʳ] *n* [device] bipe *m.*
beer [bɪəʳ] *n* cerveja *f.*
beer garden *n terraço de um bar em que geralmente se admite a presença de crianças.*
beer mat *n* bolacha *f.*
beeswax ['bi:zwæks] *n (U)* cera *f* de abelha.
beet [bi:t] *n* **-1.** [sugar beet] acelga *f* **-2.** *US* [beetroot] beterraba *f.*
beetle ['bi:tl] *n* besouro *m.*
beetroot ['bi:tru:t] *n* beterraba *f.*
befall [bɪ'fɔ:l] (*pt* **-fell** [-'fel], *pp* **-fallen** [-'fɔ:lən]) *literary* ◇ *vt* suceder. ◇ *vi* acontecer.
befit [bɪ'fɪt] (*pt* & *pp* **-ted**, *cont* **-ting**) *vt fml* convir a.
before [bɪ'fɔ:ʳ] ◇ *adv* [previously] antes. ◇ *prep* **-1.** [preceding in time] antes de **-2.** [in front of]: **the road stretched out ~ them** a estrada se abria diante *OR* à frente deles; **~ my very eyes** diante de meus próprios olhos; **standing ~ the door** parado(da) em frente à porta **-3.** [confronting] perante **-4.** [in the presence of] diante de, perante a. ◇

conj: ~ **leaving the country** antes de deixar o país; ~ **he entered the house** antes de entrar na casa.

beforehand [bɪˈfɔːhænd] *adv* [in advance] de antemão.

befriend [bɪˈfrend] *vt* **-1.** [make friends with] fazer amizade com **-2.** [support] favorecer.

befuddled [bɪˈfʌdld] *adj* [confused] atordoado(da).

beg [beg] (*pt* & *pp* **-ged**, *cont* **-ging**) ◇ *vt* **-1.** [money, food] mendigar, pedir **-2.** [favour, forgiveness, mercy] pedir; **I ~ your pardon** desculpe-me; **to ~ sb for sthg** pedir algo a alguém ; **to ~ sb to do sthg** pedir a alguém para fazer algo. ◇ *vi* **-1.** [for money, food] mendigar, pedir; **to ~ for sthg** mendigar *OR* pedir algo **-2.** [for favour, forgiveness, mercy] pedir; **to ~ for sthg** pedir algo.

began [bɪˈgæn] *pt* ▷ **begin**.

beggar [ˈbegəʳ] *n* mendigo *m*, -ga *f*.

begin [bɪˈgɪn] (*pt* **began**, *pp* **begun**, *cont* **-ning**) ◇ *vt* **-1.** [start] começar; **to ~ doing** *OR* **to do sthg** começar a fazer algo **-2.** [initiate] começar. ◇ *vi* [start] começar; **to ~ with, ...** para começar, ...

beginner [bɪˈgɪnəʳ] *n* [learner] principiante *mf*, aprendiz *mf*.

beginning [bɪˈgɪnɪŋ] *n* **-1.** [start] começo *m*; **in the ~** no começo **-2.** [origin] início *m*, origem *f*.

begonia [bɪˈgəʊnjə] *n* begônia *f*.

begrudge [bɪˈgrʌdʒ] *vt* **-1.** [envy]: **to ~ sb sthg** invejar algo de alguém **-2.** [give, do unwillingly]: **to ~ doing sthg** fazer algo de má vontade.

beguile [bɪˈgaɪl] *vt* [charm] encantar.

beguiling [bɪˈgaɪlɪŋ] *adj* [charming] encantador(ra).

begun [bɪˈgʌn] *pp* ▷ **begin**.

behalf [bɪˈhɑːf] *n*: **on ~ of sb** *UK*, **in ~ of sb** *US* em nome de alguém.

behave [bɪˈheɪv] ◇ *v refl*: **to ~ o.s.** comportar-se bem. ◇ *vi* **-1.** [in a particular way] comportar-se **-2.** [in an acceptable way] comportar-se bem.

behaviour *UK*, **behavior** *US* [bɪˈheɪvjəʳ] *n* comportamento *m*.

behaviourism *UK*, **behaviorism** *US* [bɪˈdˈheɪvjərɪzm] *n* behaviorismo *m*.

behead [bɪˈhed] *vt* degolar.

beheld [bɪˈheld] *pt* & *pp* ▷ **behold**.

behind [bɪˈhaɪnd] ◇ *prep* **-1.** [at the back of] atrás de **-2.** [causing, responsible for] por trás de **-3.** [supporting]: **to be ~ sb** apoiar alguém, estar com alguém **-4.** [indicating deficiency, delay] atrás de; **to run ~ schedule** estar atrasado(da). ◇ *adv* **-1.** [at, in the back] atrás **-2.** [late] para trás; **~ with sthg** com atraso em algo. ◇ *n inf* [buttocks] traseiro *m*.

behold [bɪˈhəʊld] (*pt* & *pp* **beheld**) *vt literary* contemplar.

beige [beɪʒ] ◇ *adj* bege. ◇ *n* bege *m*; **in ~** em bege.

Beijing [ˌbeɪˈdʒɪŋ] *n* Beijing; **in ~** em Beijing.

being [ˈbiːɪŋ] *n* **-1.** [creature] ser *m* **-2.** *(U)* [state of existing]: **in ~** em vigor; **to come into ~** nascer; **for the time ~** por enquanto.

Beirut [ˌbeɪˈruːt] *n* Beirute; **in ~** em Beirute.

belated [bɪˈleɪtɪd] *adj* tardio(dia).

belatedly [bɪˈleɪtɪdlɪ] *adv* tardiamente.

belch [beltʃ] ◇ *n* arroto *m*. ◇ *vt* [smoke, fire] expelir. ◇ *vi* [person] arrotar.

beleaguered [bɪˈliːgəd] *adj* **-1.** [*MIL* - city] sitiado(da); [- troops] cercado(da) **-2.** *fig* [harassed] assediado(da).

belfry [ˈbelfrɪ] (*pl* **-ies**) *n* campanário *m*.

Belgian [ˈbeldʒən] ◇ *adj* belga. ◇ *n* belga *mf*.

Belgium [ˈbeldʒəm] *n* Bélgica; **in ~** na Bélgica.

Belgrade [ˌbelˈgreɪd] *n* Belgrado; **in ~** em Belgrado.

belie [bɪˈlaɪ] (*cont* **belying**) *vt* **-1.** [disprove] desmentir **-2.** [give false idea of] esconder, disfarçar.

belief [bɪˈliːf] *n* **-1.** *(U)* crença *f*; **~ in sthg** crença em algo; **beyond ~** inacreditável **-2.** [opinion] opinião *f*; **in the ~ that** na certeza de que.

believable [bɪˈliːvəbl] *adj* **-1.** [creditable] crível **-2.** [possible] possível.

believe [bɪˈliːv] ◇ *vt* **-1.** [think] achar; **I ~ so** acho que sim **-2.** [person, statement] acreditar em; **~ it or not** acredite ou não. ◇ *vi* **-1.** [be religious] crer em **-2.** [know to exist]: **to ~ in sb/sthg** acreditar em alguém/algo.

believer [bɪˈliːvəʳ] *n* **-1.** *RELIG* crente *mf* **-2.** [supporter]: **~ in sthg** partidário(ria) de algo.

Belisha beacon [bɪˈliːʃə-] *n UK sinal laranja intermitente identificando local de travessia de pedestres*.

belittle [bɪˈlɪtl] *vt* [disparage] depreciar.

Belize [beˈliːz] *n* Belize; **in ~** em Belize.

bell [bel] *n* **-1.** [of church] sino *m* **-2.** [on door, bicycle] campainha *f*; **to ring a ~** *fig* trazer à lembrança.

bell-bottoms *npl* calça *f* boca-de-sino.

bellhop [ˈbelhɒp] *n US* mensageiro *m*, -ra *f* (de hotel).

belligerence [bɪˈlɪdʒərəns] *n* [aggression] agressividade *f*.

belligerent [bɪˈlɪdʒərənt] *adj* **-1.** [at war] beligerante **-2.** [aggressive] agressivo(va).

bellow [ˈbeləʊ] ◇ *vt* [order] gritar. ◇ *vi* **-1.** [person] gritar **-2.** [bull] mugir.

bellows [ˈbeləʊz] *npl* fole *m*.

bell push *n UK* campainha *f*.

bell-ringer *n* sineiro *m*, -ra *f*.

belly [ˈbelɪ] (*pl* **-ies**) *n* barriga *f*.

bellyache [ˈbelɪeɪk] ◇ *n* [stomachache] dor *f* de estômago. ◇ *vi inf* [complain] reclamar.

belly button *n inf* [navel] umbigo *m*.

belly dancer *n* dançarina *f* do ventre.

belly dancing *n* dança *f* do ventre.

belong [bɪˈlɒŋ] *vi* **-1.** [be property]: **to ~ to sb** pertencer a alguém **-2.** [be a member]: **to ~ to sthg** fazer parte *OR* ser membro de algo **-3.** [be situated in right place] encaixar-se.

belongings [bɪˈlɒŋɪŋz] *npl* pertences *mpl*.

Belorussia [ˌbeləʊˈrʌʃə] *n* Bielo-Rússia; **in ~** na Bielo-Rússia.

beloved [bɪˈlʌvd] ◇ *adj* amado(da), querido(da). ◇ *n* amado *m*, -da *f*.

below [bɪˈləʊ] ◇ *adv* **-1.** [in a lower position] de baixo **-2.** [in text or with numbers, quantities] abaixo **-3.** *NAUT*: **to go ~** descer. ◇ *prep* abaixo de.

belt [belt] ◇ *n* **-1.** [for clothing] cinto *m*; **to be below the ~** *fig* ser cruel, ser um golpe baixo; **to have sthg under one's ~** [as experience] ter algo

como experiência; [qualification] ter algo no currículo; **to tighten one's ~** apertar o cinto **-2.** *TECH* correia *f* **-3.** [of land, sea] faixa *f*, cinturão *m*. ◇ *vt* **-1.** *inf* [hit with a belt] dar uma surra de cinto em **-2.** *inf* [punch, beat] meter o couro em. ◇ *vi UK inf* [move at speed]: **to ~ along/down sthg** ir à toda por.
◆ **belt out** *vt sep inf* cantar a plenos pulmões.
◆ **belt up** *vi UK inf* [be quiet] botar zíper na boca, calar o bico.

beltway ['belt,weɪ] *n US* anel *m* viário, rodoanel *m*.

bemused [bɪ'mju:zd] *adj* bestificado(da).

bench [bentʃ] *n* **-1.** [seat] banco *m* **-2.** [in laboratory, workshop] bancada *f* **-3.** *UK JUR* magistratura *f*.

benchmark *n* **-1.** [standard] referência *f* **-2.** *COMPUT* padrão *m* de desempenho **-3.** *ECON* benchmark *m*, indicador *m*.

bend [bend] (*pt* & *pp* **bent**) ◇ *n* **-1.** curva *f* **-2.** *phr*: **round the ~** *inf* pirado(da), maluco(ca); **to drive sb round the ~** deixar alguém maluco(ca). ◇ *vt* dobrar. ◇ *vi* **-1.** [arm, leg] dobrar-se ; [tree, person] inclinar-se **-2.** [river, road] fazer uma curva.
◆ **bends** *npl MED* : **the ~s** o mal da descompressão.
◆ **bend down** *vi* curvar-se.
◆ **bend over** *vi* inclinar-se; **to ~ over backwards for sb** *fig* fazer todo o possível por alguém.

bendy ['bendɪ] (*compar* **-ier**, *superl* **-iest**) *adj UK* flexível.

beneath [bɪ'ni:θ] ◇ *adv* [below] debaixo. ◇ *prep* **-1.** [under] debaixo de, sob **-2.** [unworthy of]: **he felt the job was ~ him** ele sentia que o emprego estava aquém dele; **to be ~ sthg** não ser digno(na) de algo.

benediction [,benɪ'dɪkʃn] *n RELIG* bênção *f*.

benefactor ['benɪfæktə^r] *n* benfeitor *m*.

benefactress ['benɪfæktrɪs] *n* benfeitora *f*.

beneficial [,benɪ'fɪʃl] *adj* benéfico(ca); **~ to sb/sthg** benéfico(ca) para alguém/algo.

beneficiary [,benɪ'fɪʃərɪ] (*pl* **-ies**) *n JUR* beneficiário *m*, -ria *f*.

benefit ['benɪfɪt] ◇ *n* **-1.** [advantage] benefício *m*; **to be to sb's ~, to be of ~ to sb** ser benéfico(ca) para alguém; **for the ~ of** em benefício *OR* prol de **-2.** [good point] vantagem *f* **-3.** *ADMIN* [allowance of money] auxílio *m*. ◇ *comp* [concert, match, performance] beneficente. ◇ *vt* beneficiar. ◇ *vi*: **to ~ from sthg** beneficiar-se de algo.

Benelux ['benɪlʌks] *n* Benelux; **the ~ countries** os países Benelux.

benevolent [bɪ'nevələnt] *adj* [kind, generous] benevolente.

BEng [,bi:'eŋ] (*abbr of* **Bachelor of Engineering**) *n* (*titular de*) *graduação em engenharia*.

Bengal [,beŋ'gɔ:l] *n* Bengala; **in ~** em Bengala; **the Bay of ~** a Baía de Bengala.

benign [bɪ'naɪn] *adj* **-1.** [gen] benévolo(la) **-2.** [influence, conditions] agradável, propício(cia) **-3.** *MED* benigno(na).

Benin [be'nɪn] *n* Benim; **in ~** em Benim.

bent [bent] ◇ *pt* & *pp* ▷ **bend**. ◇ *adj* **-1.** [wire, bar] torto(ta) **-2.** [person, body] curvado(da) **-3.** *UK inf* [dishonest] corrupto(ta) **-4.** [determined]: **to be ~ on sthg/on doing sthg** ter inclinação para algo/fazer algo. ◇ *n* [natural aptitude] inclinação *f*; **to have a ~ for sthg** ter uma inclinação para algo.

bequeath [bɪ'kwi:ð] *vt* **-1.** [money, property] deixar; **to ~ sb sthg, to ~ sthg to sb** deixar algo para alguém **-2.** *fig* [idea, system] passar; **to ~ sb sthg, to ~ sthg to sb** passar algo para alguém.

bequest [bɪ'kwest] *n* [in will] herança *f*.

berate [bɪ'reɪt] *vt* [rebuke] repreender.

Berber ['bɜ:bə^r] ◇ *adj* berbere. ◇ *n* **-1.** [person] berbere *mf* **-2.** [language] berbere *m*.

bereaved [bɪ'ri:vd] (*pl inv*) ◇ *adj* enlutado(da). ◇ *npl*: **the ~** os enlutados.

bereavement [bɪ'ri:vmənt] *n* luto *m*.

bereft [bɪ'reft] *adj literary* desolado(da); **~ of sthg** privado(da) de algo.

beret ['bereɪ] *n* boina *f*.

Bering Sea ['berɪŋ-] *n*: **the ~** o Mar de Bering.

Bering Strait ['berɪŋ-] *n*: **the ~** o Estreito de Bering.

berk [bɜ:k] *n UK inf* palhaço *m*, -ça *f*.

Berlin [bɜ:'lɪn] *n* Berlim; **in ~** em Berlim; **in East/West ~** na Berlim Oriental/Ocidental; **the ~ Wall** o Muro de Berlim.

Berliner [bɜ:'lɪnə^r] *n* berlinense *mf*.

berm [bɜ:m] *n US* berma *f*.

Bermuda [bə'mju:də] *n* (Ilhas) Bermudas *fpl*.

Bermuda shorts *npl* bermuda *f*.

Bern [bɜ:n] *n* Berna; **in ~** em Berna.

berry ['berɪ] (*pl* **-ies**) *n* baga *f*.

berserk [bə'zɜ:k] *adj*: **to go ~** ficar furioso(sa).

berth [bɜ:θ] ◇ *n* **-1.** [in harbour] ancoradouro *m* **-2.** [in ship, train] beliche *m* **-3.** *phr*: **to give sb a wide ~** *fig* manter distância de alguém. ◇ *vt NAUT* ancorar, atracar. ◇ *vi* [ship] ancorar, atracar.

beseech [bɪ'si:tʃ] (*pt* & *pp* **besought** *OR* **beseeched**) *vt literary* [implore] suplicar; **to ~ sb to do sthg** suplicar a alguém para que faça algo.

beset [bɪ'set] (*pt* & *pp* **beset**, *cont* **-ting**) ◇ *adj*: **~ with** *OR* **by sthg** cercado (cercada) de algo. ◇ *vt* envolver.

beside [bɪ'saɪd] *prep* **-1.** [next to] ao lado de **-2.** [compared with] comparado(da) com **-3.** *phr*: **to be ~ o.s. with sthg** estar louco(ca) de algo.

besides [bɪ'saɪdz] ◇ *adv* além disso. ◇ *prep* [in addition to] além de.

besiege [bɪ'si:dʒ] *vt* **-1.** [town, fortress] sitiar **-2.** *fig*: **to be ~d by people** ser/estar assediado(da) de pessoas; **to be ~d with calls/complaints** ser bombardeado(da) com ligações/reclamações.

besotted [bɪ'sɒtɪd] *adj*: **~ (with sb)** obcecado(da) (por alguém).

besought [bɪ'sɔ:t] *pt* & *pp* ▷ **beseech**.

bespectacled [bɪ'spektəkld] *adj* com óculos.

bespoke [bɪ'spəʊk] *adj UK dated* **-1.** [clothes] feito (feita) sob medida **-2.** [tailor] que costura sob medida.

best [best] ◇ *adj* [in quality] melhor. ◇ *adv* **-1.** [better than all the others] melhor; **whoever does ~ in the exam** quem se sair melhor no exame **-2.** [more than all the others] mais; **which one did you like ~?** de qual deles você gostou mais? ◇ *n* **-1.** [highest standard possible] melhor *m*; **to do one's ~** fazer o melhor possível; **he is the ~ of friends**

ele é o melhor amigo do mundo **-2.** [utmost] máximo *m*; **she tried her best ~** ela fez o tudo o que podia **-3.** [most outstanding person, thing etc] melhor *mf* **-4.** *phr*: **to make the ~ of sthg** tirar o máximo de proveito de algo; **to be for the ~** ser melhor; **all the ~!** um abraço!; **the ~ of both worlds** o melhor de ambas as partes.
◆ **at best** *adv* na melhor das hipóteses.

bestial ['bestjəl] *adj* [disgusting] bestial.

best man *n* padrinho *m* de casamento.

bestow [bɪ'stəʊ] *vt fml*: **to ~ sthg on sb** outorgar *OR* conceder algo a alguém.

best-seller *n* **-1.** [article sold] mais vendido *m*, -da *f* **-2.** [book] best-seller *m*.

best-selling *adj* mais vendido(da).

bet [bet] (*pt* & *pp* **bet** *OR* **-ted**, *cont* **-ting**) <> *n* **-1.** [wager] aposta *f*; **a ~ on sthg** uma aposta em algo; **to hedge one's ~s** resguardar-se **-2.** *fig* [prediction] aposta *f*; **it's a safe ~ that ...** é certo que ...; **your best ~ is to ...** o melhor a se fazer é ... <> *vt* apostar. <> *vi* apostar; **to ~ on sthg** apostar em algo; **you ~!** *inf* pode apostar!, com certeza!

beta-blocker ['bi:təˌblɒkə^r] *n* bloqueador-beta *m*.

Bethlehem ['beθlɪhem] *n* Belém; **in ~** em Belém.

betray [bɪ'treɪ] *vt* **-1.** [person, principles] trair **-2.** [secret, emotion] revelar.

betrayal [bɪ'treɪəl] *n* **-1.** [of person, principles] traição *f* **-2.** [of secret, emotion] revelação *f*.

betrothed [bɪ'trəʊðd] *adj dated* [engaged to be married] prometido(da); **~ to sb** prometido(da) para alguém.

better ['betə^r] <> *adj* melhor; **to get ~** melhorar; **to get ~ and ~** ficar cada vez melhor. <> *adv* **-1.** [gen] melhor **-2.** [when giving advice, stating intention]: **you'd ~ phone her** é melhor você ligar para ela; **I'd ~ go now** é melhor eu ir embora. <> *n* [best one] melhor *mf*; **to get the ~ of sb** apoderar-se *OR* tomar conta de alguém; **her emotions got the ~ of her** suas emoções tomaram conta dela. <> *vt* [improve] melhorar; **to ~ o.s.** melhorar de vida, aprimorar-se.

better half *n inf* cara-metade *mf*.

better off *adj* **-1.** [financially] melhor de vida **-2.** [in a better situation] melhor; **you're ~ taking a taxi** será melhor você pegar um táxi.

betting ['betɪŋ] *n* **-1.** [bets] apostar *m* **-2.** [odds] chance *f*.

betting shop *n UK* casa *f* de apostas.

between [bɪ'twi:n] <> *prep* entre. <> *adv*: **(in) ~** entre.

bevelled *UK*, **beveled** *US* ['bevld] *adj* chanfrado(-da).

beverage ['bevərɪdʒ] *n fml* [drink] bebida *f*.

bevy ['bevɪ] (*pl* **-ies**) *n* [group] bando *m*.

beware [bɪ'weə^r] *vi* tomar cuidado, ter cautela; **to ~ of sthg** tomar cuidado com algo.

bewildered [bɪ'wɪldəd] *adj* [confused] confuso(sa), desnorteado(da).

bewildering [bɪ'wɪldərɪŋ] *adj* [confusing] desnorteante, desconcertante.

bewitched [bɪ'wɪtʃt] *adj* encantado(da).

bewitching [bɪ'wɪtʃɪŋ] *adj* encantador(ra).

beyond [bɪ'jɒnd] <> *prep* **-1.** além de; **it is ~ my responsibility** vai além de minha responsabilidade **-2.** [outside the range of] fora de; **it is ~ my control** está fora de meu controle; **the town has changed ~ all recognition** a cidade ficou irreconhecível. <> *adv* **-1.** [in space] mais além, mais adiante **-2.** [in time] mais além, mais um pouco.

b.f. (*abbr of* **brought forward**) cont.

BFPO (*abbr of* **British Forces Post Office**) *n código utilizado em cartas escritas para membros das forças britânicas.*

b.h.p. (*abbr of* **brake horsepower**) b.h.p.

bi- [baɪ] *prefix* bi.

biannual [baɪ'ænjʊəl] *adj* semestral.

bias ['baɪəs] *n* **-1.** [prejudice] preconceito *m* **-2.** [tendency] propensão *f*, tendência *f*.

biased ['baɪəst] *adj* **-1.** [prejudiced] preconceituoso(-sa); **to be ~ against sthg/sb** ser preconceituoso(sa) em relação a algo/alguém **-2.** [tendentious] tendencioso(sa); **to be ~ towards sthg** ser tendencioso(sa) em relação a algo; **to be ~ towards sb** pender para o lado de alguém.

bib [bɪb] *n* [for baby] babador *m*.

Bible ['baɪbl] *n*: **the ~** a Bíblia.
◆ **bible** *n* [copy of the Bible] bíblia *f*.

biblical ['bɪblɪkl] *adj* bíblico(ca).

bibliography [ˌbɪblɪ'ɒgrəfɪ] (*pl* **-ies**) *n* [list of books] bibliografia *f*.

bicarbonate of soda [baɪ'kɑ:bənət-] *n* bicarbonato *m* de sódio.

bicentenary *UK* [ˌbaɪsen'ti:nərɪ] (*pl* **-ies**), **bicentennial** *US* [ˌbaɪsen'tenjəl] *n* bicentenário *m*.

biceps ['baɪseps] (*pl inv*) *n* bíceps *m*.

bicker ['bɪkə^r] *vi* [quarrel] brigar.

bickering ['bɪkərɪŋ] *n (U)* [quarrelling] briga *f*.

bicycle ['baɪsɪkl] <> *n* bicicleta *f*. <> *vi* andar de bicicleta.

bicycle path *n* ciclovia *f*.

bicycle pump *n* bomba *f* de ar *(para bicicleta)*.

bid [bɪd] (*pt* & *pp vt sense 1* & *vi* **bid**, *cont* **bidding**, *pt vt senses 2* & *3* **bid** *OR* **bade**, *pp vt senses 2* & *3* **bid** *OR* **bidden** ['bɪdn], *cont* **bidding**) <> *n* **-1.** [attempt] tentativa *f*, intento *m*; **a ~ for power** uma busca pelo poder **-2.** [at auction] licitação *f* **-3.** *COMM* proposta *f*. <> *vt* **-1.** [at auction] licitar **-2.** *literary* [request]: **to ~ sb do sthg** convidar alguém a fazer algo **-3.** *fml* [say]: **to ~ sb good morning/farewell** dizer bom dia/adeus a alguém. <> *vi* **-1.** [at auction]: **to ~ (for sthg)** abrir licitação (para algo) **-2.** [attempt]: **to ~ for sthg** tentar algo.

bidder ['bɪdə^r] *n* [at auction] licitante *mf*.

bidding ['bɪdɪŋ] *n* [at auction] licitacão *f*.

bide [baɪd] *vt*: **to ~ one's time** esperar a vez.

bidet ['bi:deɪ] *n* bidê *m*.

biennial [baɪ'enɪəl] <> *adj* [every two years] bienal. <> *n* **-1.** [plant] planta *f* bienal **-2.** [festival] bienal *f*.

bier [bɪə^r] *n* caixão *m*.

bifocals [ˌbaɪ'fəʊklz] *npl* lentes *fpl* bifocais.

big [bɪg] (*compar* **-ger**, *superl* **-gest**) *adj* **-1.** [gen] grande **-2.** [older] mais velho(lha) **-3.** [successful] importante **-4.** *phr*: **in a ~ way** em grande estilo.

bigamist *n* bígamo *m*, -ma *f*.

bigamy ['bɪgəmɪ] *n (U)* bigamia *f*.
Big Apple *n*: **the ~** a Big Apple, Nova York.
Big Bang *n*: **the ~ theory** a teoria do big-bang.
Big Ben *n* Big Ben *m*.
big business *n (U)* [large companies] grandes negócios *mpl*.
big cat *n animal grande da família dos felinos.*
big deal *inf* <> *n* grande coisa *f*; **it's no ~** não é nada de mais; **what's the ~?** e daí? <> *excl* grande coisa!
Big Dipper [-'dɪpəʳ] *n* **-1.** *UK* [rollercoaster] montanha-russa *f* **-2.** *US ASTRON*: **the ~** a Ursa Maior.
big end *n AUT* cabeça *f* de biela.
big fish *n inf* [important person] peixe *m* grande.
big game *n (U)* animais *mpl* de grande porte.
big hand *n* **-1.** [on clock] ponteiro *m* dos minutos **-2.** *inf* [applause] salva *f* de palmas.
bighead ['bɪghed] *n inf* metido *m* a besta.
big-headed *adj inf* metido(da).
big-hearted [-'hɑːtɪd] *adj* gentil, generoso(sa).
big money *n (U) inf* bolada *f*; **to make ~** ganhar um dinheirão *ou* uma bolada.
big mouth *n inf* **-1.** [tendency to gossip] língua *f* solta **-2.** [person] linguarudo *m*, -da *f*.
big name *n inf* grande figura *f*.
bigot ['bɪgət] *n* fanático *m*, -ca *f*.
bigoted ['bɪgətɪd] *adj* fanático(ca).
bigotry ['bɪgətrɪ] *n (U)* fanatismo *m*.
big shot *n inf* figurão *m*, costa-larga *m*.
big time *n inf*: **the ~** o auge.
big toe *n* dedão *m* do pé.
big top *n* (lona do) circo *m*.
big wheel *n* **-1.** *UK* [at fairground] roda-gigante *f* **-2.** *inf* [big shot] peixe *m* grande.
bigwig ['bɪgwɪg] *n inf pej* figurão *m*, -rona *f*.
bike [baɪk] *n inf* **-1.** [cycle] bike *f*, bicicleta *f* **-2.** [motorcycle] moto *f*.
bikeway ['baɪkweɪ] *n US* ciclovia *f*.
bikini [bɪ'kiːnɪ] *n* biquíni *m*.
bilateral [ˌbaɪ'lætərəl] *adj* [talks] bilateral.
bilberry ['bɪlbərɪ] (*pl* **-ies**) *n* uva-do-monte *f*, mirtilo *m*.
bile [baɪl] *n* **-1.** [fluid] bílis *f* **-2.** [anger] irritação *f*.
bilingual [baɪ'lɪŋgwəl] *adj* bilíngüe.
bilious ['bɪljəs] *adj* **-1.** [sickening] bilioso(sa) **-2.** [nauseous] nauseado(da).
bill [bɪl] <> *n* **-1.** [statement of cost] conta *f*; **~ for sthg** conta de algo **-2.** [in parliament] projeto *m* de lei **-3.** [of show, concert] programa *m* **-4.** *US* [bank note] nota *f* **-5.** [poster]: **'post** *OR* **stick no ~s'** 'proibido colar cartazes' **-6.** [beak] bico *m* **-7.** *phr*: **to be given a clean ~ of health** *MED* obter um atestado de boa saúde. <> *vt* [send a bill to]: **to ~ sb (for sthg)** cobrar (algo) de alguém.
billboard ['bɪlbɔːd] *n* quadro *m* de anúncios.
billet ['bɪlɪt] <> *n* boleto *m*, alojamento *m*. <> *vt* aboletar, alojar.
billfold ['bɪlfəʊld] *n US* carteira *f*.
billiards ['bɪljədz] *n (U)* bilhar *m*.
billion ['bɪljən] *num* **-1.** [thousand million] bilhão *m* **-2.** *UK dated* [million million] trilhão *m*.
billionaire [ˌbɪljə'neəʳ] *n* bilionário *m*, -ria *f*.
bill of exchange *n* letra *f* de câmbio.
bill of lading [-'leɪdɪŋ] *n* conhecimento *m* de embarque marítimo.
Bill of Rights *n*: **the ~** *as dez primeiras emendas da Constituição norte-americana.*

BILL OF RIGHTS

É o nome que se dá às dez primeiras emendas da Constituição norte-americana, as quais garantem direitos fundamentais, tais como a liberdade de expressão, de credo e de reunião.

bill of sale *n* contrato *m* de venda.
billow ['bɪləʊ] <> *n* [of smoke] nuvem *f*. <> *vi* **-1.** [smoke, steam] formar nuvens **-2.** [skirt, sail] ondular.
billposter *n* **-1.** pessoa *f* que cola cartazes **-2.** [unauthorised] pichador *m*, -ra *f*.
billycan ['bɪlɪkæn] *n* caldeirão *m*.
billy goat ['bɪlɪ-] *n* bode *m*.
BIM (*abbr of* **British Institute of Management**) *n instituto britânico de administração.*
bimbo ['bɪmbəʊ] (*pl* **-s** *OR* **-es**) *n inf pej* ≃ burra *f* gostosa.
bimonthly [ˌbaɪ'mʌnθlɪ] <> *adj* **-1.** [every two months] bimestral **-2.** [twice a month] bimensal. <> *adv* **-1.** [every two months] bimestralmente **-2.** [twice a month] bimensalmente.
bin [bɪn] (*pt* & *pp* **-ned**, *cont* **-ning**) <> *n* **-1.** *UK* [for rubbish] lixeira *f* **-2.** [for storage] lata *f*. <> *vt inf* [discard] descartar.
binary ['baɪnərɪ] *adj* [system, code] binário(ria).
bind [baɪnd] (*pt* & *pp* **bound**) <> *vt* **-1.** [tie up] amarrar **-2.** [unite] ligar **-3.** [bandage] atar **-4.** [book] encadernar **-5.** [constrain] comprometer. <> *n inf* **-1.** *UK* [nuisance] saco *m* **-2.** [difficult situation] aperto *m*.
◆ **bind over** *vt sep JUR* obrigar legalmente.
binder ['baɪndəʳ] *n* **-1.** [machine] encadernadora *f* **-2.** [person] encadernador *m*, -ra *f* **-3.** [cover] encadernação *f*.
binding ['baɪndɪŋ] <> *adj* comprometedor(ra), obrigatório(ria). <> *n* **-1.** [of book - process] encadernação *f*; [- cover] capa *f* **-2.** [on dress, tablecloth] laço *m*.
binge [bɪndʒ] *inf* <> *n*: **to go on a ~** ir à farra. <> *vi*: **to ~ on sthg** empanturrar-se de algo.
bingo ['bɪŋgəʊ] *n* bingo *m*.
bin-liner *n UK* saco *m* de lixo.
binoculars [bɪ'nɒkjʊləz] *npl* binóculo *m*.
biochemistry [ˌbaɪəʊ'kemɪstrɪ] *n (U)* bioquímica *f*.
biodegradable [ˌbaɪəʊdɪ'greɪdəbl] *adj* biodegradável.
biodiversity [ˌbaɪəʊdaɪ'vɜːsətɪ] *n (U)* biodiversidade *f*.
bioethics [ˌbaɪəʊ'eθɪks] *n (U)* bioética *f*.
biographer [baɪ'ɒgrəfəʳ] *n* biógrafo *m*, -fa *f*.
biographic(al) [ˌbaɪə'græfɪk(l)] *adj* biográfico(ca).
biography [baɪ'ɒgrəfɪ] (*pl* **-ies**) *n* biografia *f*.
biofuel ['baɪəfjʊəl] *n* biocombustível *m*.
biological [ˌbaɪə'lɒdʒɪkl] *adj* biológico(ca); **~ washing powder** sabão em pó com enzimas.
biological clock *n* relógio *m* biológico.

biological warfare *n* guerra *f* biológica.

biological weapon *n* arma *f* biológica.

biologist [baɪ'ɒlədʒɪst] *n* biólogo *m*, -ga *f*.

biology [baɪ'ɒlədʒɪ] *n (U)* biologia *f*.

biopic ['baɪəʊpɪk] *n inf* filme *m* biográfico.

biopsy ['baɪɒpsɪ] (*pl* **-ies**) *n* biópsia *f*.

biosphere ['baɪəʊ,sfɪəʳ] *n* biosfera *f*.

biotech company ['baɪəʊtek-] *n* empresa *f* de biotecnologia.

biotechnology [,baɪəʊtek'nɒlədʒɪ] *n (U)* biotecnologia *f*.

bioterrorism [,baɪəʊ'terərɪzm] *n* bioterrorismo *m*.

bipartite [,baɪ'pɑ:taɪt] *adj* [treaty] bipartido(da).

biplane ['baɪpleɪn] *n* biplano *m*.

birch [bɜ:tʃ] *n* **-1.** [tree] bétula *f* **-2.** [for punishment]: **the ~** a vara.

bird [bɜ:d] *n* **-1.** [creature] pássaro *m*, ave *f*; **to kill two ~s with one stone** ≃ matar dois coelhos com uma cajadada só **-2.** *inf* [woman] perua *f*.

birdcage ['bɜ:dkeɪdʒ] *n* gaiola *f*.

birdie ['bɜ:dɪ] *n* **-1.** [bird] passarinho *m* **-2.** [in golf] birdie *m*.

bird of paradise *n* ave-do-paraíso *f*.

bird of prey *n* ave *f* de rapina.

birdseed ['bɜ:dsi:d] *n (U)* alpiste *m*.

bird's-eye view *n* vista *f* panorâmica.

birdwatcher *n* obeservador *m*, -ra *f* de pássaros.

biro® *n* caneta *f* esferográfica.

birth [bɜ:θ] *n* nascimento *m*; **to give ~ (to)** dar à luz (a); *fig* [of idea, system, country] dar origem(a).

birth certificate *n* certidão *f* de nascimento.

birth control *n (U)* controle *m* de natalidade.

birthday ['bɜ:θdeɪ] ◇ *n* aniversário *m*. ◇ *comp* de aniversário.

birthmark ['bɜ:θmɑ:k] *n* sinal *m* de nascença.

birthplace ['bɜ:θpleɪs] *n* local *m* de nascimento.

birthrate ['bɜ:θreɪt] *n* taxa *f* de natalidade.

birthright ['bɜ:θraɪt] *n* direito *m* inato.

Biscay ['bɪskɪ] *n*: **the Bay of ~** a Baía de Biscaia.

biscuit ['bɪskɪt] *n* **-1.** *UK* [crisp] biscoito *m*, bolacha *f* **-2.** *US* [bread-like cake] bolacha *f*.

bisect [baɪ'sekt] *vt* **-1.** GEOM cortar ao meio **-2.** [cut in two] dividir em duas partes.

bisexual [,baɪ'sekʃʊəl] ◇ *adj* bissexual. ◇ *n* bissexual *mf*.

bishop ['bɪʃəp] *n* bispo *m*.

bison ['baɪsn] (*pl inv* OR **-s**) *n* búfalo *f*.

bistro ['bɪstrəʊ] (*pl* **-s**) *n* bistrô *m*.

bit [bɪt] ◇ *pt* ▷ **bite**. ◇ *n* **-1.** [small piece] pedaço *m*; **~s and pieces** *UK inf* bugigangas; **to ~s** aos pedaços **-2.** [unspecified amount]: **a ~ of** um pouco de; **quite a ~ of** um bocado de **-3.** [short time]: **for a ~** por um instante/momento **-4.** [of drill] broca *f* **-5.** [of bridle] freio *m* **-6.** COMPUT bit *m* **-7.** *phr*: **to do one's ~** *UK* fazer a sua parte; **every ~ as ... as** exatamente tão ... quanto; **it's a ~ much** [overwhelming] é um pouco demais; **not a ~** nem um pouco.

◆ **a bit** *adv* um pouco.

◆ **bit by bit** *adv* pouco a pouco.

bitch [bɪtʃ] ◇ *n* **-1.** [female dog] cadela *f* **-2.** *v inf pej* [unpleasant woman] vaca *f*. ◇ *vi inf* **-1.** [complain] emputecer-se **-2.** [talk unpleasantly]: **to ~ about sb** falar mal de alguém.

bitchy ['bɪtʃɪ] (*compar* **-ier**, *superl* **-iest**) *adj inf* malicioso(sa).

bite [baɪt] (*pt* **bit**, *pp* **bitten**) ◇ *n* **-1.** [act of biting] mordida *f*, dentada *f* **-2.** *inf* [food]: **a ~ (to eat)** algo (para beliscar) **-3.** [wound] picada *f* **-4.** *UK* [sharp flavour] sabor *m* picante. ◇ *vt* **-1.** [subj: person, animal] morder; **to ~ one's nails** roer as unhas **-2.** [subj: insect, snake] picar. ◇ *vi* **-1.** [animal, person] morder; **to ~ into sthg** morder algo; **to ~ off sthg** abocanhar algo; **to ~ off more than one can chew** ≃ dar um passo maior que a perna; **to ~ the hand that feeds one** ≃ cuspir no prato em que comeu **-2.** [insect, snake] picar **-3.** [tyres, clutch] furar **-4.** *fig* [sanction, law] morder.

biting ['baɪtɪŋ] *adj* **-1.** [very cold] cortante **-2.** [caustic] mordaz.

bitmap *n* COMPUT bitmap *m*.

bit part *n* ponta *f*.

bitten ['bɪtn] *pp* ▷ **bite**.

bitter ['bɪtəʳ] ◇ *adj* **-1.** [gen] amargo(ga); **to the ~ end** até o fim **-2.** [acrimonious] pungente **-3.** [resentful] amargurado(da) **-4.** [icy] gelado(da). ◇ *n UK* [beer] cerveja *f* amarga.

bitter lemon *n* batida *f* de limão.

bitterly ['bɪtəlɪ] *adv* **-1.** [cold] amargamente **-2.** [intensely] duramente.

bitterness ['bɪtənɪs] *n (U)* **-1.** [gen] amargor *m* **-2.** [of wind, weather] rigor *m*.

bittersweet ['bɪtəswi:t] *adj* agridoce.

bitty ['bɪtɪ] (*compar* **-ier**, *superl* **-iest**) *adj UK inf* sem pé nem cabeça.

bitumen ['bɪtjʊmɪn] *n (U)* betume *m*.

bivouac ['bɪvʊæk] (*pt* & *pp* **-ked**, *cont* **-king**) ◇ *n* acampamento *m* sem barracas. ◇ *vi* dormir ao relento *(acampando)*.

biweekly [,baɪ'wi:klɪ] ◇ *adj* **-1.** [every two weeks] quinzenal **-2.** [twice a week]: **~ magazine** revista publicada duas vezes por semana. ◇ *adv* **-1.** [every two weeks] quinzenalmente **-2.** [twice a week] duas vezes por semana.

bizarre [bɪ'zɑ:ʳ] *adj* bizarro(ra), estranho(nha).

BL *n* **-1.** (*abbr of* **Bachelor of Law(s)**) *(titular de) graduação em direito*. **-2.** (*abbr of* **Bill of Lading**) *conhecimento de embarque marítimo*.

blab [blæb] (*pt* & *pp* **-bed**, *cont* **-bing**) *vi inf* fazer fofoca.

black [blæk] ◇ *adj* **-1.** [in colour] preto(ta); **to be beaten ~ and blue** ficar roxo(xa) de pancada; **~ and white** [films, photos] preto-e-branco **-2.** [person, skin] negro(gra) **-3.** [without milk] puro(ra), preto(ta) **-4.** [grim] sombrio(a); **~ humour** humor negro **-5.** [angry] furioso(sa). ◇ *n* **-1.** *(U)* [colour] preto *m*; **in ~ and white** [in writing] o preto no branco, por escrito; **in the ~** [solvent] sem dívidas **-2.** [person] negro *m*, -gra *f*. ◇ *vt UK* [boycott] boicotar.

◆ **black out** ◇ *vt sep* **-1.** [put out lights] ficar no escuro **-2.** [suppress] tirar do ar. ◇ *vi* [faint] desmaiar.

blackball ['blækbɔ:l] *vt* votar contra *(para excluir alguém de um clube)*.

black belt *n* faixa-preta *mf.*
blackberry ['blækbərɪ] (*pl* **-ies**) *n* amora *f.*
blackbird ['blækbɜ:d] *n* melro *m.*
blackboard ['blækbɔ:d] *n* quadro-negro *m*, lousa *f.*
black box *n* [flight recorder] caixa-preta *f.*
black comedy *n* tragicomédia *f*, comédia *f* de humor negro.
blackcurrant [ˌblæk'kʌrənt] *n* groselha-preta *f.*
black economy *n* economia *f* informal.
blacken ['blækn] ◇ *vt* **-1.** pretejar **-2.** *fig* [reputation, name] denegrir. ◇ *vi* [sky] escurecer.
black eye *n* olho *m* roxo.
Black Forest *n*: **the** ~ a Floresta Negra.
blackhead ['blækhed] *n* cravo *m.*
black hole *n* ASTRON buraco *m* negro.
black ice *n (U) camada fina e transparente de gelo sobre as ruas que dificulta a passagem de carros.*
blackjack ['blækdʒæk] *n* **-1.** *(U)* [card game] blackjack *m* **-2.** *Am* [weapon] cassetete *m.*
blackleg ['blækleg] *n pej* fura-greve *mf.*
blacklist ['blæklɪst] ◇ *n* lista *f* negra. ◇ *vt* incluir na lista negra.
black magic *n (U)* magia *f* negra.
blackmail ['blækmeɪl] ◇ *n lit* & *fig* chantagem *f.* ◇ *vt* chantagear.
blackmailer ['blækmeɪlə^r] *n* chantagista *mf.*
Black Maria [-mə'raɪə] *n inf* camburão *m.*
black mark *n* mancha *f* negra.
black market *n* mercado *m* negro.
blackout ['blækaʊt] *n* **-1.** [in wartime] blecaute *m* **-2.** [power cut] blecaute *m*, apagão *m* **-3.** [suppression of news] censura *f* **-4.** [fainting fit] desmaio *m.*
Black Power *n movimento que marcou a luta dos negros norte-americanos pelo direito à igualdade e liberdade.*
black pudding *n UK* morcela *f* preta.
Black Sea *n*: **the** ~ o Mar Negro.
black sheep *n fig* ovelha *f* negra.
blacksmith ['blæksmɪθ] *n* ferreiro *m.*
black spot *n* ponto *m* cego.
black-tie *adj* black-tie, de gala.
bladder ['blædə^r] *n* ANAT bexiga *f.*
blade [bleɪd] *n* **-1.** [of knife, saw] lâmina *f* **-2.** [of propeller] pá *f* **-3.** [of grass] folha *f.*
blame [bleɪm] ◇ *n (U)* [responsibility] culpa *f*; **to take the** ~ **for sthg** assumir a culpa por algo. ◇ *vt* culpar; **to** ~ **sthg on sb/sthg, to** ~ **sb/sthg for sthg** culpar alguém/algo de alguma coisa; **to be to** ~ **for sthg** ser culpado(da por algo).
blameless ['bleɪmlɪs] *adj* [innocent] inocente, irrepreensível.
blanch [blɑ:ntʃ] ◇ *vt* CULIN escaldar. ◇ *vi* [go white] empalidecer.
blancmange [blə'mɒndʒ] *n* manjar-branco *m.*
bland [blænd] *adj* **-1.** [person] agradável, meigo(ga) **-2.** [food] insosso(sa) **-3.** [music, style] suave.
blank [blæŋk] ◇ *adj* **-1.** em branco **-2.** *fig* [look] vazio(a). ◇ *n* **-1.** [empty space] espaço *m* em branco **-2.** MIL [cartridge] cartucho *m* **-3.** *phr*: **to draw a** ~ tirar leite de pedra.
blank cheque *n* **-1.** cheque *m* em branco **-2.** *fig* [free hand] carta *f* branca.
blanket ['blæŋkɪt] ◇ *adj* [comprehensive] na íntegra, completo(ta). ◇ *n* **-1.** [bed cover] cobertor *m*, colcha *f* **-2.** [layer] camada *f.* ◇ *vt* [cover] cobrir.
blanket bath *n UK* MED banho *m* na cama.
blankly ['blæŋklɪ] *adv* [stare] inexpressivamente.
blank verse *n (U)* verso *m* branco.
blare [bleə^r] *vi* soar.
◆ **blare out** *vi* soar.
blasé [*UK* 'blɑ:zeɪ, *US* ˌblɑ:'zeɪ] *adj* [unconcerned] indiferente.
blasphemous ['blæsfəməs] *adj* blasfemo(ma).
blasphemy ['blæsfəmɪ] (*pl* **-ies**) *n* blasfêmia *f.*
blast [blɑ:st] ◇ *n* **-1.** [of bomb] explosão *f* **-2.** [of air] corrente *f* **-3.** *US inf* [celebration] farra *f.* ◇ *vt* [hole, tunnel] dinamitar. ◇ *excl UK inf* diabos!
◆ **(at) full blast** *adv* **-1.** [maximum volume] a todo volume **-2.** [maximum effort, speed] a todo vapor.
◆ **blast off** *vi* SPACE decolar.
blasted ['blɑ:stɪd] *adj inf* [for emphasis] maldito(ta).
blast furnace *n* alto-forno *m.*
blast-off *n (U)* SPACE decolagem *f.*
blatant ['bleɪtənt] *adj* [shameless] descarado(da).
blatantly ['bleɪtəntlɪ] *adv* descaradamente.
blaze [bleɪz] ◇ *n* **-1.** [fire] incêndio *m* **-2.** *fig* [of colour, light] explosão *f*; **a** ~ **of publicity** uma grande onda de publicidade. ◇ *vi* **-1.** [fire] arder **-2.** *fig* [with colour, emotion] resplandecer.
blazer ['bleɪzə^r] *n* [jacket] blazer *m.*
blazing ['bleɪzɪŋ] *adj* **-1.** [sun, heat] abrasador(ra); **it was** ~ **hot** fazia um calor infernal **-2.** [row] acalorado(da).
bleach [bli:tʃ] ◇ *n* [chemical] alvejante *m.* ◇ *vt* **-1.** [hair] clarear **-2.** [clothes] alvejar. ◇ *vi* desbotar.
bleached [bli:tʃt] *adj* **-1.** [hair] descolorido(da), clareado(da) **-2.** [jeans] desbotado(da).
bleachers ['bli:tʃəz] *npl US* SPORT arquibancadas *fpl.*
bleak [bli:k] *adj* **-1.** [future] sombrio(a) **-2.** [place] escuro(ra) **-3.** [weather] gélido(da) **-4.** [face, person] triste.
bleary ['blɪərɪ] (*compar* **-ier**, *superl* **-iest**) *adj* [eyes] turvo(va).
bleary-eyed [ˌblɪərɪ'aɪd] *adj* com os olhos turvos.
bleat [bli:t] ◇ *n* [of sheep, goat] balido *m.* ◇ *vi* **-1.** [sheep, goat] balir **-2.** *fig* [person - speak] tagarelar; [- complain] balbuciar.
bleed [bli:d] (*pt* & *pp* **bled**) ◇ *vt* [drain] esvaziar. ◇ *vi* sangrar.
bleep [bli:p] ◇ *n* apito *m.* ◇ *vt* & *vi* apitar.
bleeper ['bli:pə^r] *n* bipe *m.*
blemish ['blemɪʃ] ◇ *n* **-1.** [flaw] mancha *f* **-2.** [pimple, scar] cicatriz *f* **-3.** *fig* [on name, reputation] mancha *f.* ◇ *vt* [reputation] manchar.
blend [blend] ◇ *n* mistura *f.* ◇ *vt* [mix] misturar; **to** ~ **sthg with sthg** misturar algo com algo. ◇ *vi* [colours, sounds] misturar-se; **to** ~ **with sthg** misturar com algo.
◆ **blend in** *vi* **-1.** [person] confundir-se **-2.** [colours, sounds] confundir-se.
◆ **blend into** *vt fus* confundir-se com.
blender ['blendə^r] *n* [food mixer] liquidificador *m.*
bless [bles] (*pt* & *pp* **-ed** OR **blest**) *vt* RELIG & *fig*

abençoar; **to be ~ed with sthg** ser abençoado(-da) com algo; **~ you!** [after sneezing] saúde!; [thank you] obrigado(da)!

blessed ['blesɪd] *adj* **-1.** *RELIG & fig* abençoado(da) **-2.** *inf* [for emphasis] bendito(ta).

blessing ['blesɪŋ] *n* benção *f*; **to count one's ~s** dar graças a Deus pelo que se tem; **a ~ in disguise** um mal que vem para bem; **to be a mixed ~** ter seus prós e contras.

blest [blest] *pt & pp* ▻ **bless.**

blew [blu:] *pt* ▻ **blow.**

blight [blaɪt] ◇ *n* **-1.** [plant disease] ferrugem *f* **-2.** *fig* [curse] desgraça *f* **-3.** *(U) fig* [decay] declínio *m*. ◇ *vt* arruinar.

blimey ['blaɪmɪ] *excl UK inf* minha nossa!, caramba!

blind [blaɪnd] ◇ *adj* **-1.** [gen] cego(ga) **-2.** *fig* [unaware]: **~ to sthg** cego(ga) para algo **-3.** *UK inf* [for emphasis]: **it doesn't make a ~ bit of difference to me** isso não faz a menor diferença para mim. ◇ *adv*: **~ drunk** completamente bêbado. ◇ *n* [for window] persiana *f*. ◇ *npl*: **the ~** os cegos. ◇ *vt* **-1.** cegar **-2.** *fig* [make unobservant] ofuscar; **to ~ sb to sthg** impedir alguém de ver algo.

blind alley *n* **-1.** [street] beco *m* **-2.** *fig* [dead end] beco *m* sem saída.

blind corner *n* curva *f* sem visibilidade.

blind date *n* encontro *m* às cegas.

blinders ['blaɪndəz] *npl US* antolhos *mpl*.

blindfold ['blaɪndfəʊld] ◇ *adv* de olhos vendados. ◇ *n* venda *f*. ◇ *vt* vendar.

blinding ['blaɪndɪŋ] *adj* **-1.** [light] ofuscante **-2.** [severe]: **~ headache** dor de cabeça de matar.

blindingly ['blaɪndɪŋlɪ] *adv* [clearly]: **~ obvious** totalmente óbvio(via).

blindly ['blaɪndlɪ] *adv* **-1.** [without seeing] às cegas **-2.** *fig* [without knowing] sem saber.

blindness ['blaɪndnɪs] *n (U)* cegueira *f*; **~ to sthg** falta *f* de visão para algo.

blind spot *n* [when driving] ponto *m* cego.

blink [blɪŋk] ◇ *n* **-1.** piscar *m*; **in the ~ of an eye** num piscar de olhos **-2.** *inf* [machine]: **on the ~** enguiçado(da). ◇ *vt* **-1.** [eyes] piscar **-2.** *Am AUT*: **to ~ one's lights** dar farol alto *OR* luz alta. ◇ *vi* **-1.** [person] piscar **-2.** [light] cintilar.

blinkered ['blɪŋkəd] *adj fig* [view, attitude] bitolado(-da).

blinkers ['blɪŋkəz] *npl UK* [for horse] antolhos *mpl*.

blinking ['blɪnkɪŋ] *adj UK inf* [for emphasis]: **that ~ phone!** que droga de telefone!

blip [blɪp] *n* **-1.** [sound] bipe *m* **-2.** [on radar] luz *f* intermitente **-3.** *fig* [temporary problem] problema *m* temporário.

bliss [blɪs] *n* êxtase *m*, bem-aventurança *f*.

blissful ['blɪsfʊl] *adj* abençoado(da); **~ ignorance** santa ignorância.

blissfully ['blɪsfʊlɪ] *adv* **-1.** [contentedly] maravilhosamente **-2.** [unknowingly]: **~ unaware** *OR* **ignorant** totalmente sem saber.

blister ['blɪstə^r] ◇ *n* [on skin] bolha *f*. ◇ *vi* formar bolhas.

blistering ['blɪstərɪŋ] *adj* **-1.** [very hot] abrasador(ra) **-2.** [scathing] mordaz.

blister pack *n* blíster *m*.

blithe [blaɪð] *adj* **-1.** [unworried] despreocupado(da) **-2.** *dated* [cheerful] alegre.

blithely ['blaɪðlɪ] *adv* **-1.** [without a care] despreocupadamente **-2.** [casually] tranqüilamente.

BLitt (*abbr of* **Bachelor of Letters (Baccalaureus Litterarum)**) *n (titular de) graduação em letras.*

blitz [blɪts] *n* **-1.** *MIL* bombardeio *m* aéreo **-2.** *UK fig* [attack]: **to have a ~ on sthg** dar uma geral em algo.

blizzard ['blɪzəd] *n* nevasca *f*.

BLM (*abbr of* **Bureau of Land Management**) *n instituto norte-americano de gestão territorial,* ≃ INCRA *m*.

bloated ['bləʊtɪd] *adj* **-1.** [swollen] inchado(da) **-2.** [having eaten too much] empanturrado(da).

blob [blɒb] *n* **-1.** [drop] pingo *m* **-2.** [shapeless thing] borrão *m*, mancha *f*.

bloc [blɒk] *n POL* bloco *m*.

block [blɒk] ◇ *n* **-1.** [gen] bloco *m* **-2.** [of buildings] quadra *f*, quarteirão *m* **-3.** [obstruction] bloqueio *m* **-4.** *TECH*: **~ and tackle** talha *f* patente. ◇ *vt* **-1.** bloquear **-2.** [hinder] barrar.

◆ **block off** *vt sep* bloquear.

◆ **block out** *vt sep* bloquear.

◆ **block up** ◇ *vt sep* [obstruct] entupir. ◇ *vi* entupir.

blockade [blɒ'keɪd] ◇ *n* bloqueio *m*. ◇ *vt* bloquear.

blockage ['blɒkɪdʒ] *n* [obstruction] obstrução *f*.

block booking *n* reserva *f* conjunta.

blockbuster ['blɒkbʌstə^r] *n inf* [book, film] estouro *m*.

block capitals *npl* maiúsculas *fpl*.

blockhead ['blɒkhed] *n inf* cabeça-dura *mf*.

block letters *npl* maiúsculas *fpl*.

block release *n UK na Inglaterra, liberação de estagiários de fábricas do trabalho para que possam estudar numa faculdade durante várias semanas.*

block vote *n UK* voto *m* em bloco.

bloke [bləʊk] *n UK inf* cara *m*.

blond [blɒnd] *adj* [hair, man] loiro(ra), claro(ra).

blonde [blɒnd] ◇ *adj* [hair, woman] loiro(ra), claro(ra). ◇ *n* [woman] loira *f*.

blood [blʌd] *n* sangue *m*; **new** *OR* **fresh ~** sangue novo; **in cold ~** a sangue frio; **it's in his ~** está em seu sangue; **to make one's ~ boil** deixar alguém danado(da) da vida; **to make sb's ~ run cold** gelar a alma de alguém.

blood bank *n* banco *m* de sangue.

bloodbath ['blʌdbɑ:θ] *n* banho *m* de sangue.

blood brother *n* irmão *m* de sangue.

blood cell *n* glóbulo *m* sangüíneo.

blood count *n* contagem *f* de glóbulos sangüíneos.

blood-curdling *adj* de gelar o sangue.

blood donor *n* doador *m*, -ra *f* de sangue.

blood group *n* grupo *m* sangüíneo.

bloodhound ['blʌdhaʊnd] *n* cão *m* de Santo Humberto.

bloodless ['blʌdlɪs] *adj* **-1.** [face, lips] pálido(da) **-2.** [coup, victory] sem derramamento de sangue.

bloodletting ['blʌd,letɪŋ] *n* [killing] matança *f*.

blood money *n* [money paid to killer] *dinheiro pago a um assassino.*
blood orange *n* laranja *f* sangüínea.
blood poisoning *n* septicemia *f.*
blood pressure *n* pressão *f* sangüínea *OR* arterial.
blood relation, blood relative *n* parente *mf* consangüíneo, -nea.
bloodshed ['blʌdʃed] *n* derramamento *m* de sangue.
bloodshot ['blʌdʃɒt] *adj* [eyes] injetado(da).
blood sports *npl esportes que envolvem a matança de animais.*
bloodstained ['blʌdsteɪnd] *adj* manchado(da) de sangue.
bloodstream ['blʌdstri:m] *n* corrente *f* sangüínea.
blood test *n* exame *m* de sangue.
bloodthirsty ['blʌd,θɜ:stɪ] *adj* sanguinário(ria).
blood transfusion *n* transfusão *f* de sangue.
blood type *n* tipo *m* sangüíneo.
blood vessel *n* vaso *m* sangüíneo.
bloody ['blʌdɪ] (*compar* **-ier**, *superl* **-iest**) ◇ *adj* **-1.** [war, conflict] sangrento(ta) **-2.** [face, hands] ensangüentado(da) **-3.** *UK v inf* [for emphasis]: **that ~ ...** essa droga de ...; **you ~ idiot!** seu imbecil! ◇ *adv UK v inf*: **~ good** bom pra caramba; **~ difficult** difícil para burro.
bloody-minded [-'maɪndɪd] *adj UK inf* do contra.
bloom [blu:m] ◇ *n* [flower] flor *f.* ◇ *vi* [plant, tree] florir.
blooming ['blu:mɪŋ] ◇ *adj* **-1.** *UK inf* [for emphasis]: **~ heck!** esse inferno miserável! **-2.** [healthy, attractive] radiante. ◇ *adv UK inf* pra caramba.
blossom ['blɒsəm] ◇ *n* [of tree] flor *f*; **in ~** em flor. ◇ *vi* **-1.** [tree] florescer **-2.** *fig* [person] desabrochar.
blot [blɒt] (*pt* & *pp* **-ted**, *cont* **-ting**) ◇ *n* **-1.** [of ink etc] borrão *m* **-2.** *fig* [- on character, reputation] mancha *f*; [- on landscape] estrago *m.* ◇ *vt* **-1.** [dry] secar **-2.** [stain with ink] borrar.
◆ **blot out** *vt sep* **-1.** [obscure] ocultar **-2.** [erase] apagar.
blotch *n* mancha *f.*
blotchy ['blɒtʃɪ] (*compar* **-ier**, *superl* **-iest**) *adj* manchado(da).
blotting paper ['blɒtɪŋ-] *n* papel *m* mata-borrão.
blouse [blaʊz] *n* blusa *f.*
blouson ['blu:zɒn] *n UK* blusão *m.*
blow [bləʊ] (*pt* **blew**, *pp* **blown**) ◇ *vi* **-1.** [wind] ventar **-2.** [through mouth] soprar **-3.** [fuse] estourar **-4.** [whistle] assoviar. ◇ *vt* **-1.** [subj: wind] soprar **-2.** [whistle, horn, trumpet] soar **-3.** *inf* [money] torrar **-4.** [clear]: **to ~ one's nose** assoar o nariz **-5.** *phr*: **to ~ bubbles** fazer bolas *OR* bolhas. ◇ *n* **-1.** [hit] golpe *m*; **to come to ~s** começar a brigar; **to strike a ~ for sthg** *fig* lutar por algo **-2.** [shock] choque *m*; **to soften the ~** amortecer o golpe.
◆ **blow away** *vi* [in wind] voar longe, sair voando.
◆ **blow out** ◇ *vt sep* apagar. ◇ *vi* **-1.** [candle] apagar **-2.** [tyre] estourar.
◆ **blow over** *vi* **-1.** [storm] cessar **-2.** [argument] esquecer-se.
◆ **blow up** ◇ *vt sep* **-1.** [inflate] encher **-2.** [with bomb] explodir **-3.** [enlarge] ampliar. ◇ *vi* [explode] explodir.
blow-by-blow *adj* detalhado(da).
blow-dry ◇ *n* secagem *f.* ◇ *vt* secar.
blowfly ['bləʊflaɪ] (*pl* **-flies**) *n* mosca-varejeira *f.*
blowgun *n US* = **blowpipe**.
blowlamp *UK* ['bləʊlæmp], **blowtorch** ['bləʊtɔ:tʃ] *n* maçarico *m.*
blown [bləʊn] *pp* ▷ **blow**.
blowout ['bləʊaʊt] *n* **-1.** [of tyre] furo *m* **-2.** *inf* [big meal] comilança *f.*
blowpipe *UK* ['bləʊpaɪp], **blowgun** *US* ['bləʊgʌn] *n* zarabatana *f.*
blowtorch *n* = **blowlamp**.
blowzy ['blaʊzɪ] (*compar* **-ier**, *superl* **-iest**) *adj Br*: **a ~ woman** uma mulher desalinhada.
BLS (*abbr of* **Bureau of Labor Statistics**) *n instituto norte-americano de economia e estatística do trabalho.*
BLT (*abbr of* **bacon, lettuce and tomato**) *n fam sanduíche de bacon, alface e tomate.*
blubber ['blʌbə^r] ◇ *n* [of whale] gordura *f.* ◇ *vi pej* [weep] choramingar.
bludgeon ['blʌdʒən] *vt* espancar; **to ~ sb into doing sthg** *fig* ameaçar alguém para que faça algo.
blue [blu:] ◇ *adj* **-1.** [in colour] azul **-2.** *inf* [sad] triste **-3.** [pornographic - film, movie] pornográfico(-ca); [- joke] obsceno(na). ◇ *n* azul *m*; **dressed in ~** vestido(da) de azul; **out of the ~** inesperadamente.
◆ **blues** *npl* **the ~s** *MUS* o blues; *inf* [sad feeling] a melancolia.
blue baby *n MED* bebê *m* cianótico.
bluebell ['blu:bel] *n* campainha *f* (azul).
blueberry ['blu:bərɪ] (*pl* **-ies**) *n* mirtilo *m.*
bluebird ['blu:bɜ:d] *n* azulão *m* norte-americano.
blue-black *adj* azul-ferrete.
blue-blooded [-'blʌdɪd] *adj* de sangue azul.
bluebottle ['blu:,bɒtl] *n* mosca-varejeira *f.*
blue channel *n*: **the ~** *acesso direto utilizado pelos membros da Comunidade Européia ao passar pelo controle de passaportes.*
blue cheese *n* queijo *m* azul.
blue chip *n ST EX* blue chip *f*, ação *f* de primeira ordem.
◆ **blue-chip** *comp ST EX* de primeira ordem.
blue-collar *adj* operário(ria).
blue-eyed boy [-aɪd-] *n inf* queridinho *m.*
blue jeans *npl US* jeans *m*, calça *f* jeans.
blue moon *n inf*: **once in a ~** uma vez a cada século.
blueprint ['blu:prɪnt] *n* **-1.** *CONSTR* planta *f* **-2.** *fig* [plan, programme] projeto *m.*
bluestocking ['blu:,stɒkɪŋ] *n pej* sabichona *f.*
blue tit *n UK* chapim-azul *m.*
blue whale *n* baleia *f* azul.
bluff [blʌf] ◇ *adj* [person, manner] expansivo(va). ◇ *n* **-1.** [deception] blefe *m*; **to call sb's ~** pagar para ver (o que alguém está ameaçando fazer)

-2. [cliff] penhasco *m.* <> *vt:* **to ~ one's way into/out of sthg** *trapacear para entrar em/sair de algo.* <> *vi* blefar.

blunder ['blʌndəʳ] <> *n* gafe *f.* <> *vi* **-1.** [make mistake] cometer um grande equívoco **-2.** [move clumsily] cambalear ; [stumble] tropeçar.

blundering ['blʌndərɪŋ] *adj* [stupid] desajeitado(-da).

blunt [blʌnt] <> *adj* **-1.** [gen] obtuso(sa) **-2.** [pencil] sem ponta **-3.** [knife] cego(ga) **-4.** [forthright] direto(ta). <> *vt* **-1.** [knife] cegar **-2.** *fig* [enthusiam, interest etc] murchar **-3.** [impact] amortecer.

bluntly ['blʌntlɪ] *adv* [say, reply] com franqueza, sem rodeios.

bluntness ['blʌntnɪs] *n* [forthrightness] franqueza *f.*

blur [blɜːʳ] (*pt* & *pp* **-red**, *cont* **-ring**) <> *n* borrão *m*, névoa *f.* <> *vt* **-1.** [outline, photograph] desfocar **-2.** [distinction, memory, vision] embaçar **-3.** [confuse] obscurecer.

blurb [blɜːb] *n inf* [on book] sinopse *f.*

blurred [blɜːd] *adj* **-1.** [outline, photograph] desfocado(da) **-2.** [distinction, memory, vision] obscuro(ra).

blurt [blɜːt] ◆ **blurt out** *vt sep* falar sem pensar.

blush [blʌʃ] <> *n* rubor *m.* <> *vi* corar.

blusher ['blʌʃəʳ] *n* ruge *m.*

bluster ['blʌstəʳ] <> *n* **-1.** [angry talk] discussão *f* **-2.** [boasting] bazófia *f.* <> *vi* **-1.** [speak angrily] vociferar **-2.** [boast] fanfarronar.

blustery ['blʌstərɪ] *adj* ventoso(sa).

BM *n* **-1.** (*abbr of* **Bachelor of Medicine**) *(titular de) graduação em medicina.* **-2.** (*abbr of* **British Museum**) Museu *m* Britânico.

BMA (*abbr of* **British Medical Association**) *n associação britânica de medicina,* ≃ AMB *f.*

BMJ (*abbr of* **British Medical Journal**) *n publicação da associação britânica de medicina.*

BMus (*abbr of* **Bachelor of Music**) *n (titular de) graduação em música.*

BNP (*abbr of* **British National Party**) *n partido britânico de extrema direita.*

BO (*abbr of* **body odour**) *n* cê-cê *m.*

boa constrictor ['bəʊəkən'strɪktəʳ] *n* jibóia *f.*

boar [bɔːʳ] *n* **-1.** [male pig] barrão *m* **-2.** [wild pig] javali *m.*

board [bɔːd] <> *n* **-1.** [plank] tábua *f* **-2.** [for notices] quadro *m* (de avisos) **-3.** [for games] tabuleiro *m* **-4.** [blackboard] quadro-negro *m* **-5.** ADMIN direção *f*; **~ of directors** conselho *m* de diretores; **examining ~** banca *f* examinadora; **~ of enquiry** comissão *f* de inquérito **-6.** *UK* [at hotel, guesthouse] pensão *f*; **~ and lodging** casa e comida; **full ~** pensão completa; **half ~** meia pensão **-7.** *phr*: **above ~** honesto(ta); **to go by the ~** ir por água abaixo; **to sweep the ~** ganhar todas. <> *vt* [get onto] embarcar em.

◆ **across the board** <> *adj* generalizado(da). <> *adv* de forma generalizada.

◆ **on board** <> *adj* a bordo. <> *adv* a bordo; **to take sthg on ~** aceitar algo.

◆ **board up** *vt sep* fechar com tábuas.

boarder ['bɔːdəʳ] *n* **-1.** [lodger] pensionista *mf* **-2.** [at school] interno *m*, -na *f.*

board game *n* jogo *m* de tabuleiro.

boarding card ['bɔːdɪŋ-] *n* cartão *m* de embarque.

boarding house *n* hospedaria *f.*

boarding school ['bɔːdɪŋ-] *n* colégio *m* interno.

board meeting *n* reunião *f* de conselho.

Board of Trade *n UK*: **the ~** ≃ Câmara *f* do Comércio, *na Inglaterra, comissão governamental responsável pela supervisão do comércio e pelo estímulo às exportações.*

boardroom ['bɔːdrʊm] *n* sala *f* da diretoria.

boardwalk ['bɔːdwɔːk] *n US* passeio *m* de tábuas.

boast [bəʊst] <> *n* alarde *m.* <> *vt* [special feature] ostentar. <> *vi* [show off] vangloriar-se; **to ~ about sthg** gabar-se de algo.

boastful ['bəʊstfʊl] *adj* presunçoso(sa).

boasting *n* presunção *f*, ostentação *f.*

boat [bəʊt] *n* [ship] barco *m*; [for rowing] bote *m*; [for sailing] veleiro *m*; **by ~** de barco; **in the same ~** *fig* no mesmo barco; **to rock the ~** *fig* complicar as coisas.

boater ['bəʊtəʳ] *n* [hat] chapéu *m* de palha.

boating ['bəʊtɪŋ] *n* passeio *m* de barco.

boat people *npl refugiados que escapam de seu país de barco.*

boatswain ['bəʊsn] *n* NAUT contramestre *m.*

boat train *n trem que leva as pessoas para embarcar num navio ou que recolhe as que desembarcaram.*

bob [bɒb] (*pt* & *pp* **-bed**, *cont* **-bing**) <> *n* **-1.** [hairstyle] corte *m* chanel **-2.** *UK inf dated* [shilling] xelim *m* **-3.** = **bobsleigh.** <> *vi* [boat, ship] balouçar-se.

bobbin ['bɒbɪn] *n* [spool] bobina *f.*

bobble ['bɒbl] *n* [fluffy ball] pompom *m.*

bobby ['bɒbɪ] (*pl* **-ies**) *n UK inf* [policeman] tira *m.*

bobby pin *n US* grampo *m* (de cabelo).

bobby socks, bobby sox *npl US* meias *fpl* soquete.

bobsleigh ['bɒbsleɪ] *n* trenó *m* de esporte.

bode [bəʊd] *vi literary*: **to ~ ill/well (for sb/sthg)** ser de mau/bom agouro (para alguém/algo).

bodice ['bɒdɪs] *n* [of dress] corpete *f.*

bodily ['bɒdɪlɪ] <> *adj* [needs] físico(ca). <> *adv* [carry, lift] em peso.

body ['bɒdɪ] (*pl* **-ies**) *n* **-1.** [gen] corpo *m*; **to keep ~ and soul together** ganhar o suficiente só para pagar as contas **-2.** [corpse] cadáver *m*; **over my dead ~!** só por cima do meu cadáver! **-3.** [organization] entidade *f* **-4.** [of car] carroceria *f* **-5.** [of plane] fuselagem *f* **-6.** *(U)* [of wine] corpo *m* **-7.** [garment] body *m.*

body bag *n* saco *m* mortuário.

body building *n* fisiculturismo *m.*

bodyguard ['bɒdɪgɑːd] *n* guarda-costas *mf inv.*

body odour *UK*, **body odor** *US* *n* odor *m* corporal.

body search *n* revista *f* corporal.

body shop *n* **-1.** [garage] oficina *f* mecânica **-2.** *Am inf* [gym] academia *f* (de ginástica).

body stocking *n* macaquinho *m* colante (*para ginástica, dança*).

bodywork ['bɒdɪwɜːk] *n* [of car] carroçeria *f.*

boffin ['bɒfɪn] *n UK inf* cientista *mf.*

bog [bɒg] *n* **-1.** [marsh] lodaçal *m* **-2.** *UK v inf* [toilet] privada *f*.
bogey ['bəʊgɪ] *n* **-1.** [spectre]: **the ~ of recession** o fantasma da recessão **-2.** *inf* [in nose] meleca *f*.
bogeyman *n* ≃ bicho-papão *m*.
bogged down [ˌbɒgd-] *adj* atolado(da).
boggle ['bɒgl] *vi*: **the mind ~s!** não dá para acreditar!
boggy ['bɒgɪ] (*compar* **-ier**, *superl* **-iest**) *adj* lamacento(ta), pantanoso(sa).
bogie *n* RAIL truque *m*.
Bogotá [ˌbɒgə'tɑ:] *n* Bogotá; **in ~** em Bogotá.
bog-standard *adj inf* comum.
bogus ['bəʊgəs] *adj* falso(sa).
Bohemia [bəʊ'hi:mjə] *n* Boêmia; **in ~** na Boêmia.
bohemian [bəʊ'hi:mɪən] ◇ *adj* boêmio(mia). ◇ *n* boêmio *m*, -mia *f*.
◆ **Bohemian** ◇ *adj* boêmio(mia). ◇ *n* boêmio *m*, -mia *f*.
boil [bɔɪl] ◇ *n* **-1.** MED [on skin] furúnculo *m* **-2.** [boiling point]: **to bring sthg to the ~** deixar algo ferver; **to come to the ~** começar a ferver. ◇ *vt* **-1.** [water, kettle] ferver **-2.** [food] cozinhar. ◇ *vi* [water, kettle] ferver.
◆ **boil away** *vi* [evaporate] evaporar.
◆ **boil down to** *vt fus fig* reduzir-se a.
◆ **boil over** *vi* **-1.** [liquid] derramar **-2.** *fig* [feelings] descontrolar-se.
boiled [bɔɪld] *adj* cozido(da); **~ sweet** *UK* caramelo *m*; **~ egg** ovo *m* cozido.
boiler ['bɔɪlə^r] *n* boiler *m*.
boiler suit *n UK* macacão *m*.
boiling ['bɔɪlɪŋ] *adj* **-1.** [liquid] fervente **-2.** *inf* [hot - person] morto(ta) de calor; [- weather] abrasador(ra) **-3.** [angry]: **~ with rage** fervendo de raiva.
boiling point *n* ponto *m* de ebulição.
boisterous ['bɔɪstərəs] *adj* [child, behaviour] irriquieto(ta).
bold [bəʊld] *adj* **-1.** [confident] audacioso(sa) **-2.** [brave] corajoso(sa) **-3.** ART [lines, design] arrojado(da) **-4.** [colour] nítido(da) **-5.** TYPO: **in ~ type** OR **print** em negrito.
boldly ['bəʊldlɪ] *adv* corajosamente.
Bolivia [bə'lɪvɪə] *n* Bolívia; **in ~** na Bolívia.
Bolivian [bə'lɪvɪən] ◇ *adj* boliviano(na). ◇ *n* boliviano *m*, -na *f*.
bollard ['bɒlɑ:d] *n* [on road] poste *m* de sinalização.
bollocks ['bɒləks] *UK vulg* ◇ *npl* saco *m*. ◇ *excl* saco!
Bolshevik ['bɒlʃɪvɪk] ◇ *adj* bolchevique. ◇ *n* bolchevique *mf*.
bolster ['bəʊlstə^r] ◇ *n* [pillow] travesseiro *m* longo. ◇ *vt* [encourage] alentar.
◆ **bolster up** *vt fus* [support] sustentar.
bolt [bəʊlt] ◇ *n* **-1.** [on door, window] ferrolho *m*, trinco *m* **-2.** [type of screw] parafuso *m*. ◇ *adv*: **to sit ~ upright** sentar direito. ◇ *vt* **-1.** [fasten together] aparafusar **-2.** [close] trancar **-3.** [food] devorar. ◇ *vi* [run] disparar.
bomb [bɒm] ◇ *n* [explosive device] bomba *f*. ◇ *vt* bombardear.
bombard [bɒm'bɑ:d] *vt* MIL & *fig* bombardear, **to ~ sb with sthg** bombardear alguém com algo.
bombardment [bɒm'bɑ:dmənt] *n* bombardeio *m*.
bombastic [bɒm'bæstɪk] *adj* bombástico(ca).
bomb disposal squad *n* esquadrão *m* antibombas.
bomber ['bɒmə^r] *n* **-1.** [plane] bombardeiro *m* **-2.** [person] *pessoa que pratica atentados a bomba.*
bomber jacket *n jaqueta curta ajustada ao peito e aos quadris.*
bombing ['bɒmɪŋ] *n* bombardeio *m*.
bombproof *adj* [shelter] à prova de bombas.
bombshell ['bɒmʃel] *n fig* [unpleasant surprise] bomba *f*; **to come as a ~** cair como uma bomba.
bombsite *n* área *f* bombardeada.
bona fide ['bəʊnə'faɪdɪ] *adj* [genuine] legítimo(ma).
bonanza [bə'nænzə] *n fonte, muitas vezes repentina ou inesperada, de sorte ou riqueza.*
bond [bɒnd] ◇ *n* **-1.** [emotional link] laço *m* **-2.** [binding promise] compromisso *m* **-3.** FIN título *m*. ◇ *vt* **-1.** [glue]: **to ~ sthg to sthg** colar algo a algo **-2.** *fig* [people] unir. ◇ *vi* **-1.** [stick together]: **to ~ (together)** colar **-2.** *fig* [people] unir-se.
bondage *n literary* [servitude] servidão *f*.
bonded warehouse ['bɒndɪd-] *n* depósito *m* da alfândega.
bone [bəʊn] ◇ *n* **-1.** [of body, material] osso *m*; **~ of contention** pomo *m* da discórdia; **to feel sthg in one's ~s** sentir algo na pele; **to know sthg in one's ~s** saber algo intuitivamente; **to make no ~s about sthg** não fazer cerimônia sobre algo **-2.** [of fish] espinha *f*. ◇ *vt* [fish, meat] desossar.
bone china *n porcelana fina e branca feita com cinzas de ossos.*
bone-dry *adj* completamente seco(ca).
bone-idle *adj inf* encostado(da).
boneless ['bəʊnlɪs] *adj* sem osso.
bone marrow *n* tutano *m*.
bonfire ['bɒnˌfaɪə^r] *n* fogueira *f* ao ar livre.
bonfire night *n UK noite de 5 de novembro, quando os ingleses lançam fogos de artifício e queimam a figura de Guy Fawkes numa fogueira ao ar livre.*
bongo ['bɒŋgəʊ] (*pl* **-s** OR **-es**) *n*: **~ (drum)** bongô *m*.
bonk [bɒŋk] *inf* ◇ *vt* [have sex with] transar com. ◇ *vi* [have sex] transar.
Bonn [bɒn] *n* Bonn; **in ~** em Bonn.
bonnet ['bɒnɪt] *n* **-1.** *UK* [of car] capô *m* **-2.** [hat] touca *f*.
bonus ['bəʊnəs] (*pl* **-es**) *n* **-1.** [extra money] bônus *m inv* **-2.** *fig* [added treat] vantagem *f* adicional.
bonus issue *n UK* FIN emissão *f* de títulos de bonificação.
bony ['bəʊnɪ] (*compar* **-ier**, *superl* **-iest**) *adj* **-1.** [person, hand, face] ossudo(da) **-2.** [meat] com osso; [fish] cheio (cheia) de espinhas.
boo [bu:] (*pl* **-s**) ◇ *excl* bu! ◇ *n* vaia *f*. ◇ *vt* & *vi* vaiar.
boob [bu:b] *n inf* [mistake] gafe *f*.
◆ **boobs** *npl UK inf* [breasts] tetas *fpl*.
boob tube *n* **-1.** *UK* [garment] tomara-que-caia *m inv* **-2.** *US inf* [TV] telinha *f*.
booby prize ['bu:bɪ-] *n* prêmio *m* de consolação.
booby trap ['bu:bɪ-] *n* **-1.** [bomb] bomba *f* camuflada **-2.** [prank] armadilha *f*.

◆ **booby-trap** *vt* [car, building] colocar explosivos em.

boogie ['bu:gɪ] *inf* <> *n* [dance]: **let's have a ~** vamos sacudir. <> *vi* [dance] sacudir.

book [bʊk] <> *n* **-1.** [for reading] livro *m*; **to do sthg by the ~** fazer algo como manda o figurino; **to throw the ~ at sb** fazer todas as acusações possíveis a alguém **-2.** [pack - of stamps] bloco *m*; [- of matches] caixa *f*; [- of cheques, tickets] talão *m*. <> *vt* **-1.** [reserve] reservar; **to be fully ~ed** estar totalmente cheio (cheia) *OR* esgotado(da) **-2.** *inf* [subj: police] autuar **-3.** *UK FTBL* dar cartão amarelo *OR* vermelho a. <> *vi* reservar, fazer uma reserva.

◆ **books** *npl COMM* registros *mpl*; **to do the ~s** escriturar, fazer a contabilidade; **to be in sb's good/bad ~s** ser bem/mal visto por alguém.

◆ **book in** <> *vt sep* registrar-se. <> *vi* [at hotel] registrar-se.

◆ **book up** *vt sep*: **to be ~ed up** [fully booked] estar completamente cheio (cheia); **the hotel is ~ed up** o hotel está lotado.

bookable ['bʊkəbl] *adj* **-1.** [seats, tickets] a ser reservado(da) **-2.** *FTBL*: **a ~ offence** uma falta digna de cartão.

book bag *n US* = **booksack**.

bookbinding ['bʊk,baɪndɪŋ] *n* encadernação *f*.

bookcase ['bʊkkeɪs] *n* estante *f* (para livros).

book club *n* clube *m* do livro.

bookends *npl* prateleiras *fpl*.

bookie ['bʊkɪ] *n inf* bookmaker *m*.

booking ['bʊkɪŋ] *n* **-1.** *esp UK* [reservation] reserva *f* **-2.** *esp UK FTBL* cartão *m* amarelo *OR* vermelho.

booking clerk *n esp UK* vendedor *m*, -ra *f* de ingressos.

booking office *n esp UK* bilheteria *f*.

bookish ['bʊkɪʃ] *adj* [person] aficionado(da) pelos livros.

bookkeeper ['bʊk,ki:pə^r] *n COMM* contador *m*, -ra *f*.

bookkeeping ['bʊk,ki:pɪŋ] *n COMM* contabilidade *f*.

booklet ['bʊklɪt] *n* [pamphlet] folheto *m*.

bookmaker ['bʊk,meɪkə^r] *n* bookmaker *m*.

bookmark ['bʊkmɑ:k] *n* marcador *m* de páginas.

booksack *n US* mochila *f*.

bookseller ['bʊk,selə^r] *n* vendedor *m*, -ra *f* de livros.

bookshelf ['bʊkʃelf] (*pl* **-shelves** [-ʃelvz]) *n* prateleira *f OR* estante *f* (para livros).

bookshop *UK* ['bʊkʃɒp], **bookstore** *US* ['bʊkstɔ:^r] *n* livraria *f*.

bookstall ['bʊkstɔ:l] *n UK* banca *f* de jornal.

bookstore *n US* = **bookshop**.

book token *n esp UK* vale-livro *m*.

bookworm ['bʊkwɜ:m] *n fig* [person] rato *m* de biblioteca.

boom [bu:m] <> *n* **-1.** [loud noise] estrondo *m* **-2.** [increase] boom *m*, crescimento *m* **-3.** *NAUT* retranca *f* **-4.** [for TV camera, microphone] bum *m*. <> *vi* **-1.** [make noise] ribombar **-2.** *ECON* [grow] crescer rapidamente.

boomerang ['bu:məræŋ] *n* bumerangue *m*.

boon [bu:n] *n* [help, advantage] ajuda *f*.

boor [bʊə^r] *n* pessoa *f* rude.

boorish ['bʊərɪʃ] *adj* rude.

boost [bu:st] <> *n* **-1.** [increase] incremento *m*; **to give a ~ to sthg** dar um empurrão em algo **-2.** [improvement] impulso *m*. <> *vt* **-1.** [increase] incrementar **-2.** [improve] levantar **-3.** *US inf* [steal] afanar.

booster ['bu:stə^r] *n MED* [vaccine] reforço *m*.

booster seat *n* cadeirinha *f* para automóvel, bebê-conforto *m*.

boot [bu:t] <> *n* **-1.** [footwear] bota *f* **-2.** *UK* [of car] porta-bagagem *m*. <> *vt* **-1.** *inf* [kick] dar um pé na bunda de **-2.** *COMPUT* inicializar, dar boot em.

◆ **to boot** *adv* também.

◆ **boot out** *vt sep inf* mandar às favas.

◆ **boot up** *vi COMPUT* inicializar, dar boot.

booth [bu:ð] *n* **-1.** [at fair] barraca *f* **-2.** [telephone booth] cabine *f* (telefônica) **-3.** [voting booth] cabine *f* eleitoral.

bootleg ['bu:tleg] *adj* [alcohol] de contrabando; [recording] pirata.

bootlegger ['bu:t,legə^r] *n inf* contrabandista *mf*.

booty ['bu:tɪ] *n literary* butim *m*.

booze [bu:z] *inf* <> *n* [alcohol] trago *m*. <> *vi* [drink alcohol] tomar umas e outras.

boozer ['bu:zə^r] *n inf* **-1.** [person] bebum *mf* **-2.** *UK* [pub] bar *m*.

bop [bɒp] (*pt* & *pp* **-ped**, *cont* **-ping**) *inf* <> *n* **-1.** [hit] batida *f* **-2.** [disco, dance] festa *f* dançante. <> *vt* [hit] bater. <> *vi* [dance] dançar.

border ['bɔ:də^r] <> *n* **-1.** [between countries] fronteira *f* **-2.** [edge] borda *f* **-3.** [hem] orla *f* **-4.** [outer boundary] limite *m* **-5.** [bank, shore] margem *f* **-6.** [for flowers] bordadura *f*. <> *vt* **-1.** [country] limitar-se com **-2.** [surround] cercar.

◆ **border on** *vt fus* [verge on] beirar em.

border collie *n* border collie *m*.

borderline ['bɔ:dəlaɪn] <> *adj*: **~ case** caso-limite *m*. <> *n fig* [division] limite *m*.

bore [bɔ:^r] <> *pt* ▷ **bear**. <> *n* **-1.** *pej* [tedious person] chato *m*, -ta *f*; [tedious situation, event] chatice *f* **-2.** [of gun] calibre *m*. <> *vt* **-1.** [not interest] entediar; **to ~ sb stiff** *OR* **to tears** *OR* **to death** *inf* matar alguém de tédio **-2.** [drill] furar.

bored [bɔ:d] *adj* entediado(da); **to be ~ with sthg** estar entediado(da) com algo.

boredom ['bɔ:dəm] *n* tédio *m*.

boring ['bɔ:rɪŋ] *adj* chato(ta).

born [bɔ:n] *adj* **-1.** [given life] nascido(da); **to be ~** nascer; **~ and bred (in)** nascido e criado (em), nascida e criada (em) **-2.** [for emphasis] nato(ta).

born-again *adj* **-1.** [Christian] convertido(da) **-2.** *fig* [earnestly enthusiastic] fanático(ca).

borne [bɔ:n] *pp* ▷ **bear**.

Borneo ['bɔ:nɪəʊ] *n* Bornéu; **in ~** em Bornéu.

borough ['bʌrə] *n* município *m*, distrito *m*.

borrow ['bɒrəʊ] *vt* [property, money] tomar emprestado(da); **to ~ sthg from sb** pegar algo emprestado de alguém.

borrower ['bɒrəʊə^r] *n* [of money] tomador *m*, -ra *f* de empréstimo.

borrowing ['bɒrəʊɪŋ] *n* [of money] empréstimo *m*.

borstal ['bɔ:stl] *n UK* instituto *m* correcional para jovens.

Bosnia ['bɒznɪə] *n* Bósnia; **in ~** na Bósnia.

Bosnia-Herzegovina [-ˌhɜ:tsəgə'vi:nə] *n* Bósnia-Herzegovina.

Bosnian ['bɒznɪən] <> *adj* bósnio(nia). <> *n* bósnio *m*, -nia *f*.

bosom ['bʊzəm] *n* **-1.** [of woman] peito *m* **-2.** *fig* [centre] seio *m*; **~ friend** amigo *m*, -ga *f* do peito.

Bosporus ['bɒspərəs], **Bosphorus** ['bɒsfərəs] *n*: **the ~** o Bósforo.

boss [bɒs] <> *n* **-1.** [of company, department, organization] chefe *mf*; **to be one's own ~** trabalhar por conta própria **-2.** *fig* [of gang] chefão *m*; **you're the ~!** você é quem manda! <> *vt pej* [give orders to] mandar.

◆ **boss about, boss around** *vt sep* mandar em.

bossy ['bɒsɪ] (*compar* **-ier**, *superl* **-iest**) *adj* mandão(ona).

bosun ['bəʊsn] *n* = **boatswain**.

botanic(al) [bə'tænɪk(l)] *adj* botânico(ca).

botanical garden *n* jardim *m* botânico.

botanist ['bɒtənɪst] *n* botânico *m*, -ca *f*.

botany ['bɒtənɪ] *n* botânica *f*.

botch [bɒtʃ] ◆ **botch up** *vt sep inf* fazer nas coxas.

both [bəʊθ] <> *adj* ambos(bas), os dois, as duas; **we ~ left** nós dois (duas) saímos, ambos saímos; **~ my brother and myself will be there** tanto meu irmão quanto eu estaremos lá, nós dois estaremos lá. <> *adv* não apenas ... como; **she is ~ witty and intelligent** ela não só é espirituosa, como também inteligente. <> *pron* ambos *mpl*, -bas *fpl*; **~ of us** nós dois (duas).

bother ['bɒðə^r] <> *vt* **-1.** [worry] preocupar; **I can't be ~ed to do that** não me disponho a fazer isso **-2.** [irritate, annoy] incomodar. <> *vi* [trouble o.s.] incomodar-se; **to ~ about sthg** incomodar-se com algo; **to ~ doing** OR **to do sthg** incomodar-se em fazer algo. <> *n* **-1.** *(U)* [inconvenience] aborrecimento *m* **-2.** [nuisance] incômodo *m* **-3.** [difficulty] dificuldade *f* **-4.** [obstacle] estorvo *m*. <> *excl* (que) droga!

bothered ['bɒðəd] *adj* **-1.** [worried] preocupado(da) **-2.** [annoyed] chateado(da).

Botswana [bɒ'tswɑ:nə] *n* Botsuana; **in ~** em Botsuana.

bottle ['bɒtl] <> *n* **-1.** [gen] garrafa *f* **-2.** [of medicine] frasco *m* **-3.** [of perfume] vidro *m* **-4.** [for baby] mamadeira *f* **-5.** *(U) UK inf* [courage]: **he didn't have the ~ to do it** ele não teve coragem de fazer isso. <> *vt* **-1.** [wine] engarrafar **-2.** [fruit] enfrascar.

◆ **bottle out** *vi UK inf* dar para trás.

◆ **bottle up** *vt sep* [feelings] reprimir.

bottle bank *n contêiner no qual se recolhem garrafas de vidro vazias para reciclagem.*

bottled ['bɒtld] *adj* engarrafado(da).

bottle-feed *vt* [baby] dar mamadeira para.

bottleneck ['bɒtlnek] *n* **-1.** [in traffic] engarrafamento *m* **-2.** [in production] gargalo *m*.

bottle-opener *n* abridor *m* (de garrafa).

bottle party *n festa informal em que cada convidado leva bebida.*

bottom ['bɒtəm] <> *adj* **-1.** [lowest] de baixo **-2.** [least successful] último(ma). <> *n* **-1.** [lowest part - of glass, bag, lake] fundo *m*; [- of page] fim *m*, final *m*; [- of mountain, hill] sopé *m*; **at the ~** embaixo; **at the ~ of** no fundo de **-2.** [far end] fim *m*, final *m* **-3.** [least successful level] nível *m* mais baixo **-4.** [buttocks] traseiro *m* **-5.** *fig* [root, cause]: **at the ~ of** por trás de; **to get to the ~ of sthg** ir até o fundo de algo.

◆ **bottom out** *vi* [prices, recession] estabilizar-se.

bottomless ['bɒtəmlɪs] *adj* **-1.** [very deep] sem fundo **-2.** [endless] infinito(ta).

bottom line *n fig*: **the ~ is that ...** a questão toda é que ...

botulism *n (U)* botulismo *m*.

bough [baʊ] *n* [of tree] galho *m*.

bought [bɔ:t] *pt & pp* ▻ **buy**.

boulder ['bəʊldə^r] *n* pedregulho *m*.

boulevard ['bu:ləvɑ:d] *n* alameda *f*.

bounce [baʊns] <> *vi* **-1.** [ball] quicar **-2.** [light, sound] refletir **-3.** [person - with energy, enthusiasm]: **she was bouncing with energy/enthusiasm** ela estava pulando de alegria/entusiasmo; **she bounced into the room, singing** ela entrou na sala radiante, cantando; [- jump up and down]: **to ~ on sthg** saltar sobre algo **-4.** *inf* [cheque] ser devolvido(da). <> *vt* [ball] bater. <> *n* **-1.** [of ball] pulo *m* **-2.** *fig* [vigour] vigor *m*, vivacidade *f*.

◆ **bounce back** *vi* [after illness, setback] recuperar-se.

bouncer ['baʊnsə^r] *n inf* [at club etc] leão-de-chácara *m*.

bouncy ['baʊnsɪ] (*compar* **-ier**, *superl* **-iest**) *adj* **-1.** [lively] vivaz **-2.** [bed, trampoline] com bom molejo **-3.** [ball] saltitante.

bound [baʊnd] <> *pt & pp* ▻ **bind**. <> *adj* **-1.** [certain]: **to be ~ to do sthg** fazer algo na certa **-2.** [forced, morally obliged]: **~ by sthg/to do sthg** obrigado(da) por algo/fazer algo; **I'm ~ to say/admit** devo dizer/admitir **-3.** [en route]: **to be ~ for** estar a caminho de. <> *n* [leap] salto *m*. <> *vt* [border]: **to be ~ed by** ser limitado(da) por. <> *vi* [leap] correr aos pulos.

◆ **bound up with** *prep* [connected] estreitamente ligado a.

◆ **bounds** *npl* [limits] limites *mpl*; **out of ~s** interditado(da).

boundary ['baʊndərɪ] (*pl* **-ies**) *n* **-1.** [of area of land] fronteira *f* **-2.** *fig* [of science, knowledge] fronteiras *fpl*.

boundless ['baʊndlɪs] *adj* ilimitado(da).

bountiful ['baʊntɪfʊl] *adj literary* [ample] abundante.

bounty ['baʊntɪ] *n (U) literary* [generosity] generosidade *f*.

bouquet [bəʊ'keɪ] *n* **-1.** [bunch] buquê *m* **-2.** [smell] buquê *m*.

bouquet garni ['bu:keɪgɑ:'ni:] *n* bouquet garni *m (ervas para tempero).*

bourbon ['bɜ:bən] *n* bourbon *m (uísque norte-americano).*

bourgeois ['bɔ:ʒwɑ:] *adj pej* burguês(esa).

bourgeoisie [ˌbɔ:ʒwɑ:'zi:] *n pej*: **the ~** a burguesia.

bout [baʊt] *n* **-1.** [attack] ataque *m* **-2.** [session] período *m* **-3.** [boxing match] assalto *m*.
boutique [bu:'ti:k] *n* butique *f*.
bow[1] [baʊ] <> *n* **-1.** [act of bowing] reverência *f* **-2.** [of ship] proa *f*. <> *vt* [lower] inclinar. <> *vi* **-1.** [make a bow] inclinar-se **-2.** [defer]: **to ~ to sthg** submeter-se a algo.
◆ **bow down** *vi* [give in]: **to ~ down (to sb)** render-se(a alguém).
◆ **bow out** *vi* afastar-se.
bow[2] [bəʊ] *n* **-1.** [gen & *MUS*] arco *m* **-2.** [knot] laço *m*.
bowels ['baʊəlz] *npl* **-1.** [intestines] intestinos *mpl* **-2.** *fig* [deepest part] entranhas *fpl*.
bowl [bəʊl] <> *n* **-1.** [container - gen] tigela *f*; [- for sugar] açucareiro *m*; [- for fruit] fruteira *f* **-2.** [bowl-shaped part - of toilet, sink] bacia *f*; [- of pipe] fornilho *m* **-3.** [bowlful] prato *m*. <> *vt & vi* [in cricket] atirar.
◆ **bowls** *n (U)* jogo *m* de bocha.
◆ **bowl over** *vt sep* **-1.** [knock over] derrubar **-2.** *fig* [surprise, impress] surpreender.
bow-legged [ˌbəʊ'legɪd] *adj* cambota.
bowler ['bəʊlə^r] *n* **-1.** [in cricket, bowls] lançador *m* **-2.** [headgear]: **~ (hat)** chapéu-coco *m*.
bowling ['bəʊlɪŋ] *n*: **(tenpin) ~** jogo *m* de boliche.
bowling alley *n* **-1.** [building] boliche *m* **-2.** [alley] pista *f* de boliche.
bowling green *n* cancha *m* de bocha.
bow tie [bəʊ-] *n* gravata-borboleta *f*.
bow window [bəʊ-] *n* janela *f* em arco.
box [bɒks] <> *n* **-1.** [gen] caixa *f* **-2.** [in theatre] camarote *m* **-3.** [in car races] box *m* **-4.** *UK inf* [television]: **the ~** a TV **-5.** [shrub, tree] buxo *m*. <> *vt* **-1.** [punch] esmurrar **-2.** [put in boxes] colocar em caixas. <> *vi* [fight] lutar.
◆ **box in** *vt sep* **-1.** [hem in]: **to get ~ed in** ficar espremido(da) **-2.** [build a box around] encaixotar, encaixar.
boxed [bɒkst] *adj* empacotado(da).
boxer ['bɒksə^r] *n* **-1.** [fighter] boxeador *m*, -ra *f* **-2.** [dog] boxer *mf*.
boxer shorts *npl* cuecas *fpl* samba-canção.
boxing ['bɒksɪŋ] *n (U)* boxe *m*.
Boxing Day *n dia seguinte ao Natal em que é feriado nacional no Reino Unido. Tradicionalmente, era o dia em que os empregados recebiam os presentes dos patrões, geralmente uma caixinha em dinheiro.*
boxing glove *n* luva *f* de boxe.
boxing ring *n* ringue *m* de boxe.
box junction *n UK cruzamento de ruas demarcado com faixas amarelas sobre o qual um veículo não pode avançar a menos que seu caminho esteja livre.*
box number *n* caixa *f* postal.
box office *n* bilheteria *f*.
boxroom ['bɒksrʊm] *n UK* quarto *m* de despejo.
boy [bɔɪ] <> *n* **-1.** [young male] menino *m* **-2.** [adult male] rapaz *m* **-3.** [son] filho *m* **-4.** [male friend]: **the ~s** os caras. <> *excl*: **(oh) ~!** *inf* nossa!
boycott ['bɔɪkɒt] <> *n* boicote *m*. <> *vt* boicotar.
boyfriend ['bɔɪfrend] *n* namorado *m*.
boyish ['bɔɪɪʃ] *adj* juvenil.
boy scout *n* escoteiro *m*.
Bp (*abbr of* **Bishop**) bispo *m*.
Br (*abbr of* **Brother**) *RELIG* Ir.
bra [brɑ:] *n* sutiã *f*.
brace [breɪs] (*pl sense 3 inv*) <> *n* **-1.** *MED* aparelho *m* **-2.** [pair] par *m*. <> *vt lit & fig* **to ~ o.s. (for sthg):** preparar-se (para algo).
◆ **braces** *npl UK* [for trousers] suspensórios *mpl*.
bracelet ['breɪslɪt] *n* bracelete *m*.
bracing ['breɪsɪŋ] *adj* revigorante.
bracken ['brækn] *n (U)* samambaia *f*.
bracket ['brækɪt] <> *n* **-1.** [support] suporte *m*, mão-francesa *f* **-2.** [parenthesis] parêntese *m*; **in ~s** entre parênteses **-3.** [group] faixa *f*. <> *vt* **-1.** [enclose in brackets] colocar entre parênteses **-2.** [group]: **to ~ sb/sth (together) with sb/sthg** equiparar alguém/algo a alguém/algo.
brackish ['brækɪʃ] *adj* salobre.
brag [bræg] (*pt & pp* **-ged**, *cont* **-ging**) *vi* [boast] gabar-se.
braid [breɪd] <> *n* **-1.** [on uniform] galão *m* **-2.** *US* [hairstyle] trança *f*. <> *vt US* trançar.
braille [breɪl] *n (U)* braile *m*.
brain [breɪn] *n* **-1.** [organ] cérebro *m* **-2.** [mind] cabeça *f*; **to have sthg on the ~** estar com algo na cabeça **-3.** *inf* [clever person] gênio *m*.
◆ **brains** *npl* [intelligence] sabedoria *f*; **to pick sb's ~s** recorrer à sabedoria de alguém; **to rack** *UK* *OR* **cudgel** *US* **one's ~s** *fig* queimar *OR* gastar os neurônios.
brainchild ['breɪntʃaɪld] *n* invenção *f*.
brain death *n (U)* morte *f* cerebral.
brain drain *n* evasão *f* de cérebros.
brainless ['breɪnlɪs] *adj* idiota, tolo(la).
brainstorm ['breɪnstɔ:m] *n* **-1.** *UK* [moment of aberration] bobeira *f* **-2.** *US* [brilliant idea] idéia *f* luminosa.
brainstorming ['breɪnˌstɔ:mɪŋ] *n (U)* brainstorming *m*.
brainteaser ['breɪnˌti:zə^r] *n* quebra-cabeça *m*.
brainwash ['breɪnwɒʃ] *vt* fazer lavagem cerebral em.
brainwave ['breɪnweɪv] *n* idéia *f* luminosa.
brainy ['breɪnɪ] (*compar* **-ier**, *superl* **-iest**) *adj inf* sabichão(chona).
braise [breɪz] *vt* refogar.
brake [breɪk] <> *n* **-1.** [on vehicle] freio *m* **-2.** *fig* [restraint] freio *m*. <> *vi* frear.
brake fluid *n (U)* líquido *m* de freio.
brake light *n* luz *f* de freio.
brake lining *n* lona *f* de freio.
brake pedal *n* pedal *m* do freio.
brake shoe *n* sapata *f* de freio.
bramble ['bræmbl] *n* [bush] amoreira *f* silvestre; [fruit] amora *f* silvestre.
bran [bræn] *n (U)* farelo *m*.
branch [brɑ:ntʃ] <> *n* **-1.** [of tree] galho *m* **-2.** [of river] braço *m* **-3.** [of railway] ramal *m* **-4.** [of company, bank, organization] sucursal *f* **-5.** [of subject] ramo *m*. <> *vi* [road] bifurcar-se.
◆ **branch off** *vi* [road, track] ramificar-se.
◆ **branch out** *vi* [person, company] expandir-se em nova direção.
branch line *n* [railway] ramal *m* secundário.
brand [brænd] <> *n* **-1.** *COMM* marca *f* **-2.** *fig* [type]

tipo *m* **-3.** [mark on cattle] marca *f* de ferro em brasa. ◇ *vt* **-1.** [cattle] marcar com ferro em brasa **-2.** *fig* [classify]: **to ~ sb (as) sthg** rotular alguém de algo.

brandish ['brændɪʃ] *vt* brandir.

brand leader *n* marca *f* dominante.

brand name *n* marca *f* registrada.

brand-new *adj* novo(va) em folha.

brandy ['brændɪ] (*pl* **-ies**) *n* conhaque *m*.

brash [bræʃ] *adj pej* atrevido(da).

Brasilia [brə'zɪljəl] *n* Brasília; **in ~** em Brasília.

brass [brɑ:s] *n* **-1.** *(U)* [type of metal] latão *m* **-2.** MUS: **the ~** os metais.

◆ **brasses** *npl* [ornaments] objetos *mpl* decorativos em latão.

brass band *n* fanfarra *f*.

brasserie ['bræsərɪ] *n restaurante simples e barato que serve comida em estilo francês.*

brassiere [*UK* 'bræsɪə[r], *US* brə'zɪr] *n* sutiã *m*.

brass knuckles *npl Am* soco-inglês *m*.

brass rubbing *n* [picture] gravura *f* em latão.

brass tacks *npl inf*: **to get down to ~** ir direto ao assunto.

brat [bræt] *n inf pej* capeta *m*.

bravado [brə'vɑ:dəʊ] *n (U)* bravata *f*.

brave [breɪv] ◇ *adj* corajoso(sa). ◇ *n* [warrior] guerreiro *m* índio, bravo *m*. ◇ *vt* enfrentar.

bravely ['breɪvlɪ] *adv* bravamente.

bravery ['breɪvərɪ] *n (U)* bravura *f*.

bravo [ˌbrɑ:'vəʊ] *excl* bravo!

brawl [brɔ:l] *n* briga *f*.

brawn [brɔ:n] *n (U)* [muscle] músculo *m*

brawny ['brɔ:nɪ] (*compar* **-ier**, *superl* **-iest**) *adj* musculoso(sa).

bray [breɪ] *vi* [donkey] zurrar.

brazen ['breɪzn] *adj* descarado(da).

◆ **brazen out** *vt sep*: **to ~ it out** encarar.

brazier ['breɪzjə[r]] *n* braseiro *m*.

Brazil [brə'zɪl] *n* Brasil; **in ~** no Brasil.

Brazilian [brə'zɪljən] ◇ *adj* brasileiro(ra). ◇ *n* brasileiro *m*, -ra *f*.

brazil nut *n* castanha-do-pará *f*.

breach [bri:tʃ] ◇ *n* **-1.** [act of disobedience] quebra *f*; **a ~ of an agreement** o rompimento de um acordo; **a ~ of the law** uma transgressão da lei; **to be in ~ of sthg** estar transgredindo algo; **~ of contract** quebra de contrato **-2.** [opening, gap] brecha *f*; **to step into the ~** *fig* ficar no lugar de alguém temporariamente **-3.** *fig* [in friendship, marriage] rompimento *m*. ◇ *vt* **-1.** [disobey] romper **-2.** [make hole in] abrir uma brecha em.

breach of the peace *n* atentado *m* à ordem pública.

bread [bred] *n* **-1.** [food] pão *m*; **~ and butter** [food] pão com manteiga; *fig* [main income] sustento *m* **-2.** *inf* [money] ganha-pão *m*.

bread bin *UK*, **bread box** *US* *n* caixa *f* para pão.

breadboard ['bredbɔ:d] *n* tábua *f* de pão.

breadcrumbs ['bredkrʌmz] *npl* farinha *f* de rosca.

breaded ['bredɪd] *adj* empanado(da).

breadline ['bredlaɪn] *n*: **to be on the ~** estar no limite da pobreza.

breadth [bretθ] *n* **-1.** [in measurements] largura *f* **-2.** *fig* [scope] alcance.

breadwinner ['bredˌwɪnə[r]] *n* arrimo *m* (de família).

break [breɪk] (*pt* **broke**, *pp* **broken**) ◇ *n* **-1.** [interruption] interrupção *f*; **a ~ in transmission** uma queda na transmissão **-2.** [gap] brecha *f* **-3.** [fracture] fratura *f* **-4.** [change] rompimento *m*; **~ with sthg** rompimento *m* com algo **-5.** [pause] pausa *f*; **tea/coffee/lunch ~** pausa para o chá/café/almoço; [rest] descanso *m*; **a weekend ~** um feriado curto; **give me a ~!** me dá um tempo/uma trégua!; **to have a ~ from sthg** dar uma parada em algo; **without a ~** sem parar **-6.** SCOL recreio *m* **-7.** *inf* [luck, chance] chance *f*; **lucky ~** golpe de sorte **-8.** *literary* [of day]: **at ~ of day** ao alvorecer, ao raiar do dia **-9.** COMPUT [key] tecla *f* break. ◇ *vt* **-1.** [gen] quebrar **-2.** [fracture] fraturar **-3.** [cause to malfunction] danificar **-4.** [burst through] romper; **to ~ sb's hold** esquivar-se de alguém **-5.** [interrupt] interromper **-6.** [destroy, cause to fail] arruinar **-7.** [undermine, cause to fail] furar **-8.** [announce]: **to ~ the news (of sthg to sb)** dar a notícia (de algo a alguém) **-9.** TENNIS : **to ~ sb's serve** quebrar o serviço de alguém. ◇ *vi* **-1.** [gen] quebrar **-2.** [split] partir-se **-3.** [burst through] romper **-4.** [pause] parar **-5.** [day] raiar **-6.** [weather] mudar **-7.** [escape]: **to ~ loose** OR **free** escapar **-8.** [voice - with emotion] perturbar-se; [- at puberty] mudar **-9.** [become known] ser divulgado(da) **-10.** *phr*: **to ~ even** ficar em ponto de equilíbrio.

◆ **break away** *vi* **-1.** [escape] escapar **-2.** [end relationship]: **to ~ away (from sb)** romper (com alguém).

◆ **break down** ◇ *vt sep* **-1.** [destroy, demolish] derrubar **-2.** [analyse] analisar **-3.** [bring to an end] acabar com. ◇ *vi* **-1.** [stop working] estragar **-2.** [end unsuccessfully] concluir sem sucesso **-3.** [collapse, disintegrate] terminar **-4.** [MED: collapse] sofrer um colapso; **to ~ down in tears** romper em lágrimas **-5.** [decompose] decompor-se.

◆ **break in** ◇ *vi* **-1.** [enter by force] arrombar **-2.** [interrupt] interromper; **to ~ in on sb/sthg** interromper alguém/algo. ◇ *vt sep* **-1.** [horse] domar **-2.** [person] acostumar **-3.** [shoes] amaciar.

◆ **break into** *vt fus* **-1.** [enter by force] arrombar **-2.** [begin suddenly] romper em **-3.** [become involved in] entrar em.

◆ **break off** ◇ *vt sep* **-1.** [detach] quebrar **-2.** [put an end to] acabar. ◇ *vi* **-1.** [become detached] quebrar-se **-2.** [stop talking] deter-se **-3.** [stop working] parar-se.

◆ **break out** *vi* **-1.** [begin suddenly] rebentar **-2.** [become covered]: **to ~ out in spots/a rash** aparecer com manchas/uma erupção; **to ~ out in a cold sweat** começar a suar frio **-3.** [escape]: **to ~ out (of)** fugir (de).

◆ **break through** ◇ *vt fus* [force a way through] abrir caminho por. ◇ *vi* [force a way through] romper.

◆ **break up** ◇ *vt sep* **-1.** [separate into smaller pieces - ice] partir; [- soil] repartir; [- car] desmontar **-2.** [bring to an end] acabar. ◇ *vi* **-1.** [separate into smaller pieces] partir-se **-2.** [come to an end] acabar-se; **to ~ up with sb** acabar com alguém **-3.**

[disperse] dispersar-se **-4.** [for school holiday] terminar.
◆ **break with** *vt fus* romper com.
breakable ['breɪkəbl] *adj* quebradiço(ça).
breakage ['breɪkɪdʒ] *n* quebra *f.*
breakaway ['breɪkəweɪ] *adj* dissidente.
break dancing *n (U)* break *m.*
breakdown ['breɪkdaʊn] *n* **-1.** [failure, ending] quebra *f* **-2.** [analysis] detalhamento *m* **-3.** *MED* **nervous ~** colapso *m* nervoso.
breaker ['breɪkəʳ] *n* [wave] rebentação *f.*
breakeven *n (U)* ponto *m* de equilíbrio.
breakfast ['brekfəst] ◇ *n* café *m* da manhã. ◇ *vi*: **to ~ (on sthg)** tomar (algo no) café da manhã.
breakfast cereal *n* cereal *m* matinal.
breakfast television *n UK* programa *m* de tv matutino.
break-in *n* arrombamento *m.*
breaking ['breɪkɪŋ] *n (U)*: **~ and entering** *JUR* invasão *m* de domicílio.
breaking point *n* limite *m.*
breakneck ['breɪknek] *adj*: **at ~ speed** em altíssima velocidade.
breakthrough ['breɪkθru:] *n* avanço *m.*
breakup ['breɪkʌp] *n* **-1.** [of system, group] dissociação *f* **-2.** [of relationship] rompimento *m.*
breakup value *n COMM* valor *m* de liquidação.
bream [bri:m] (*pl inv OR* **-s**) *n* brema *f*; **sea ~** pargo *m.*
breast [brest] *n* **-1.** [gen] peito *m* **-2.** [of woman] seio *m* **-3.** *fig*: **to make a clean ~ of it** desabafar.
breast-feed ◇ *vt & vi* amamentar.
breast pocket *n* bolso *m* superior.
breaststroke ['breststrəʊk] *n (U)* nado *m* de peito.
breath [breθ] *n* **-1.** *(U)* [air taken into lungs] respiração *f*; **out of ~** sem fôlego; **to get one's ~ back** retomar o fôlego; **to hold one's ~** [stop breathing] prender o fôlego; *fig* [wait anxiously] ficar apreensivo(va); **to save one's ~** poupar seu fôlego; **to say sthg under one's ~** dizer algo ao pé do ouvido; **to take one's ~ away** ser surpreendente; **to waste one's ~** gastar sua saliva; **to go out for a ~ of (fresh) air** sair para tomar ar (fresco) **-2.** [air breathed out] hálito *m*; **bad ~** mau hálito.
breathalyse *UK*, **-yze** *US* ['breθəlaɪz] *vt* aplicar o teste do bafômetro em.
Breathalyser® *UK*, **-yzer®** *US* ['breθəlaɪzəʳ] *n* bafômetro *m.*
breathe [bri:ð] ◇ *vi* respirar; **to ~ more easily** *fig* respirar aliviado(da). ◇ *vt* **-1.** [inhale] inalar **-2.** [whisper] murmurar.
◆ **breathe in** ◇ *vi* [inhale] respirar. ◇ *vt sep* [inhale] inalar.
◆ **breathe out** *vi* [exhale] exalar.
breather ['bri:ðəʳ] *n inf* respirada *f*, descanso *m.*
breathing ['bri:ðɪŋ] *n (U)* respiração *f.*
breathing space *n fig* pausa *f.*
breathless ['breθlɪs] *adj* **-1.** [physically] ofegante **-2.** [with excitement] radiante.
breathtaking ['breθˌteɪkɪŋ] *adj* **-1.** [beautiful] surpreendente **-2.** [extreme] incrível.
breath test *n* teste *m* de bafômetro.
breed [bri:d] (*pt & pp* **bred** [bred]) ◇ *n* **-1.** [of animal] raça *f* **-2.** *fig* [sort, style] tipo *m.* ◇ *vt* **-1.** [cultivate] criar **-2.** *fig* [provoke] gerar. ◇ *vi* [produce young] procriar.
breeder ['bri:dəʳ] *n* [of animals] criador *m.*
breeder reactor *n* reator *m* regenerador.
breeding ['bri:dɪŋ] *n (U)* **-1.** [raising animals, plants] criação *f* **-2.** [manners] boa educação *f*; **a person of good ~** uma pessoa de berço.
breeding-ground *n fig* [of ideas, activity] fonte *f.*
breeze [bri:z] ◇ *n* [light wind] brisa *f.* ◇ *vi*: **to ~ in/out** entrar/sair calmamente.
breezeblock ['bri:zblɒk] *n UK* tijolo *m* leve.
breezy ['bri:zɪ] (*compar* **-ier**, *superl* **-iest**) *adj* **-1.** [windy] ventoso(sa) **-2.** [cheerful] alegre.
Breton ['bretn] ◇ *adj* bretão(tã). ◇ *n* **-1.** [person] bretão *m*, -tã *f* **-2.** [language] bretão *m.*
brevity ['brevɪtɪ] *n* **-1.** [shortness] brevidade *f* **-2.** [conciseness] concisão *f.*
brew [bru:] ◇ *vt* [beer] fermentar; [tea] preparar. ◇ *vi* **-1.** [infuse] preparar-se **-2.** *fig* [develop - crisis, trouble] armar-se; [- storm] formar-se.
brewer ['bru:əʳ] *n* fabricante *mf* de cerveja.
brewery ['brʊərɪ] (*pl* **-ies**) *n* cervejaria *f.*
briar [braɪəʳ] *n BOT* urze *f* branca.
bribe [braɪb] ◇ *n* suborno *m.* ◇ *vt* subornar; **to ~ sb to do sthg** subornar alguém para fazer algo.
bribery ['braɪbərɪ] *n (U)* suborno *m.*
bric-a-brac ['brɪkəbræk] *n (U)* bugiganga *f.*
brick [brɪk] *n* [for building] tijolo *m.*
◆ **brick up** *vt sep* fechar com tijolos.
bricklayer ['brɪkˌleɪəʳ] *n* pedreiro *m.*
brickwork ['brɪkwɜ:k] *n (U)* alvenaria *f.*
bridal ['braɪdl] *adj* de noiva.
bride [braɪd] *n* noiva *f.*
bridegroom ['braɪdgrʊm] *n* noivo *m.*
bridesmaid ['braɪdzmeɪd] *n* dama *f* de honra.
bridge [brɪdʒ] ◇ *n* **-1.** [gen] ponte *f*; **I'll cross that ~ when I come to it** *fig* só vou me preocupar quando chegar a hora **-2.** [on ship] ponte *f* de comando **-3.** [of nose] cavalete *m* **-4.** [card game] bridge *m* **-5.** [for teeth] ponte *f.* ◇ *vt* [gap] transpor.
bridging loan ['brɪdʒɪŋ-] *n UK* empréstimo *m* bancário *(a curto prazo).*
bridle ['braɪdl] ◇ *n* [of horse] cabresto *m.* ◇ *vt* [put a bridle on] colocar cabresto em. ◇ *vi*: **to ~ (at sthg)** indignar-se (diante de algo).
bridle path *n* trilha *f.*
brief [bri:f] ◇ *adj* **-1.** [short, concise] breve; **in ~** em suma **-2.** [revealing, skimpy] reduzido(da). ◇ *n* **-1.** *JUR* [statement] declaração *f* **-2.** *UK* [instructions] instrução *f.* ◇ *vt* informar; **to ~ sb on sthg** [bring up to date] pôr alguém a par de algo; [instruct] treinar alguém sobre/em algo.
◆ **briefs** *npl* [underwear] cuecas *fpl.*
briefcase ['bri:fkeɪs] *n* pasta *f* executiva.
briefing ['bri:fɪŋ] *n* instruções *fpl.*
briefly ['bri:flɪ] *adv* **-1.** [for a short time] brevemente **-2.** [concisely] rapidamente.
Brig. (*abbr of* **brigadier**) brig..
brigade [brɪ'geɪd] *n* brigada *f.*
brigadier [ˌbrɪgə'dɪəʳ] *n* brigadeiro *m.*
bright [braɪt] *adj* **-1.** [full of light] claro(ra) **-2.** [colour] vivo(va) **-3.** [lively, cheerful] alegre **-4.** [intelligent]

inteligente **-5.** [hopeful, promising] radioso(sa).
◆ **brights** *npl US inf AUT* luz *f* alta.
◆ **bright and early** *adv* de manhã cedo.

brighten ['braɪtn] *vi* **-1.** [become lighter] iluminar-se **-2.** [become more cheerful] alegrar-se.
◆ **brighten up** ◇ *vt sep* alegrar. ◇ *vi* **-1.** [become more cheerful] alegrar-se **-2.** [weather] melhorar.

brightly ['braɪtlɪ] *adv* **-1.** [shine] fortemente **-2.** [cheerfully] alegremente **-3.** [coloured] em cores vivas.

brightness ['braɪtnɪs] *n (U)* brilho *m*.

brilliance ['brɪljəns] *n* **-1.** [cleverness] inteligência *f* **-2.** [of light, colour] brilho *m*.

brilliant ['brɪljənt] *adj* **-1.** [clever, successful] brilhante **-2.** [colour] vivo(va) **-3.** [light] brilhante **-4.** *inf* [wonderful, enjoyable] genial.

brilliantly ['brɪljəntlɪ] *adv* **-1.** [cleverly] inteligentemente, de forma brilhante **-2.** [coloured] em cores vivas **-3.** [shine] fortemente.

Brillo pad ['brɪləʊ-] *n* esfregão *m (de aço com sabão)*.

brim [brɪm] (*pt* & *pp* **-med**, *cont* **-ming**) ◇ *n* **-1.** [edge] borda *f* **-2.** [of hat] aba *f*. ◇ *vi*: **to ~ with enthusiasm** transbordar de entusiasmo.
◆ **brim over** *vi*: **to ~ over (with sthg)** transbordar (de algo).

brine [braɪn] *n (U)* salmoura *f*.

bring [brɪŋ] (*pt* & *pp* **brought**) *vt* **-1.** [gen] trazer; **to ~ sthg to an end** acabar com algo **-2.** *JUR*: **to ~ charges against sb** acusar alguém; **to be brought to trial** ser levado(da) a julgamento **-3.** *phr*: **I couldn't ~ myself to do it** não tive coragem de fazê-lo.
◆ **bring about** *vt sep* produzir.
◆ **bring along** *vt sep* trazer.
◆ **bring around** *vt sep* [make conscious]: **to bring sb around** fazer alguém recuperar os sentidos.
◆ **bring back** *vt sep* **-1.** [hand over] devolver **-2.** [carry, transport] trazer de volta **-3.** [recall] relembrar **-4.** [reinstate] trazer de volta.
◆ **bring down** *vt sep* **-1.** [cause to fall] derrubar **-2.** [reduce] baixar.
◆ **bring forward** *vt sep* **-1.** [in time] adiantar **-2.** [in bookkeeping] transportar.
◆ **bring in** *vt sep* **-1.** [introduce] apresentar **-2.** [earn] render **-3.** *JUR* [verdict] apresentar.
◆ **bring off** *vt sep* conseguir.
◆ **bring on** *vt sep* [cause] causar; **to ~ sthg on o.s.** causar algo a si próprio(pria).
◆ **bring out** *vt sep* **-1.** [produce and sell] lançar **-2.** [reveal] ressaltar.
◆ **bring round, bring to** *vt sep* = **bring around**.
◆ **bring up** *vt sep* **-1.** [educate] educar **-2.** [mention] mencionar **-3.** [vomit] vomitar.

brink [brɪŋk] *n*: **on the ~ of** à beira de.

brisk [brɪsk] *adj* **-1.** [walk, swim] rápido(da) **-2.** [business, trading] ativo(va) **-3.** [manner, tone] enérgico(ca) **-4.** [wind, weather] forte.

brisket ['brɪskɪt] *n* carne *f* de peito.

briskly ['brɪsklɪ] *adv* **-1.** [walk] rapidamente **-2.** [speak, act] desembaraçadamente.

bristle ['brɪsl] ◇ *n* **-1.** [hair] pêlo *m* **-2.** [on brush] cerda *f*. ◇ *vi* **-1.** [stand up] ficar em pé **-2.** [react angrily]: **to ~ (at sthg)** eriçar-se (diante de algo).
◆ **bristle with** *vt fus* estar apinhado(da) de.

bristly ['brɪslɪ] (*compar* **-ier**, *superl* **-iest**) *adj* [hairy] cabeludo(da).

Brit (*abbr of* **Briton**) *n fam* britânico *m*, -ca *f*.

Britain ['brɪtn] *n* Grã-Bretanha; **in ~** na Grã-Bretanha.

British ['brɪtɪʃ] ◇ *adj* britânico(ca). ◇ *npl*: **the ~** os britânicos.

British Columbia *n* Colúmbia Britânica.

British Council *n*: **the ~** o British Council, o Conselho Britânico.

British Isles *npl*: **the ~** as Ilhas Britânicas.

British Summer Time *n (U)* horário *m* britânico de verão.

British Telecom *n principal empresa britânica de telecomunicações.*

Briton ['brɪtn] *n* britânico *m*, -ca *f*.

Britpop ['brɪtpɒp] *n (U) tipo de música pop tocada por bandas britânicas, muito popular em meados dos anos 90.*

Brittany ['brɪtənɪ] *n* Bretanha; **in ~** na Bretanha.

brittle ['brɪtl] *adj* [easily broken] quebradiço(ça).

Bro = **Br.**

broach [brəʊtʃ] *vt* [subject] abordar.

broad [brɔːd] ◇ *adj* **-1.** [physically wide] largo(ga) **-2.** [wide-ranging, extensive] amplo(pla) **-3.** [general, unspecific] geral **-4.** [hint] explícito(ta) **-5.** [accent] forte. ◇ *n US inf* [woman] sujeita *f*.
◆ **in broad daylight** *adv* em plena luz do dia.

B road *n UK* estrada *f* secundária.

broad bean *n* fava *f*.

broadcast ['brɔːdkɑːst] (*pt* & *pp* **broadcast**) ◇ *n* transmissão *f*. ◇ *vt* transmitir.

broadcaster ['brɔːdkɑːstə^r] *n* locutor *m*, -ra *f*.

broadcasting ['brɔːdkɑːstɪŋ] *n (U)* transmissão *f*.

broaden ['brɔːdn] ◇ *vt* **-1.** [make physically wider] alargar **-2.** [make more general, wide-ranging] ampliar. ◇ *vi* [become physically wider] alargar-se.
◆ **broaden out** *vi* ampliar-se.

broadly ['brɔːdlɪ] *adv* **-1.** [generally] em geral; **~ speaking** em termos gerais **-2.** [smile] abertamente.

broadly-based [-'beɪst] *adj* de bases amplas.

broadminded [ˌbrɔːd'maɪndɪd] *adj* tolerante.

broadsheet ['brɔːdʃiːt] *n* jornal *m (de tamanho grande)*.

BROADSHEET/BROADSIDE

Broadsheet, na Grã-Bretanha, e *broadside*, nos Estados Unidos, são os termos empregados para designar os jornais de maior reputação e prestígio. Trata-se dos jornais impressos em formato grande, que apresentam as notícias com seriedade e oferecem seções importantes sobre cultura, esportes e finanças. De modo geral, esses jornais gozam de maior respeito do que os tablóides, que tendem a usar uma linguagem mais simples e direta, e são publicados em formato pequeno.

brocade [brə'keɪd] *n (U)* brocado *m*.

broccoli ['brɒkəlɪ] *n* brócolis *mpl*.

brochure ['brəʊʃəʳ] *n* folheto *m*.
brogue *n* **-1.** [accent] sotaque *m* **-2.** [shoe] chanca *f*.
broil [brɔɪl] *vt US* grelhar.
broiler ['brɔɪləʳ] *n* **-1.** [chicken for broiling] galeto *m* **-2.** *Am* [pan] grelha *f*.
broke [brəʊk] ◇ *pt* ▷ **break**. ◇ *adj inf* [penniless] falido(da); **to go** ~ ir à falência; **to go for** ~ arriscar tudo.
broken ['brəʊkn] ◇ *pp* ▷ **break**. ◇ *adj* **-1.** [damaged, in pieces] quebrado(da) **-2.** [fractured] fraturado(da) **-3.** [not working] estragado(da) **-4.** [interrupted] interrompido(da) **-5.** [unfulfilled] rompido(da) **-6.** [marriage, home] desfeito(ta) **-7.** [hesitant, inaccurate] incorreto(ta).
broken-down *adj* **-1.** [not working] avariado(da) **-2.** [dilapidated] arruinado(da).
broker ['brəʊkəʳ] *n* corretor *m*, -ra *f*.
brokerage ['brəʊkərɪdʒ] *n (U)* **-1.** [business] corretora *f* **-2.** [fee] corretagem *f*.
brolly ['brɒlɪ] (*pl* **-ies**) *n UK inf* guarda-chuva *m*.
bromine *n* bromo *m*.
bronchitis [brɒŋ'kaɪtɪs] *n (U)* bronquite *f*.
bronze [brɒnz] ◇ *n* **-1.** *(U)* [metal] bronze *m* **-2.** [sculpture] escultura *f* em bronze **-3.** = **bronze medal**. ◇ *comp* [made of bronze] em bronze. ◇ *adj* [bronze-coloured] bronzeado(da).
bronzed *adj* bronzeado(da).
bronze medal *n* medalha *f* de bronze.
brooch [brəʊtʃ] *n* broche *m*.
brood [bru:d] ◇ *n* **-1.** [of animals] ninhada *f* **-2.** *inf* [of children] penca *f*. ◇ *vi*: **to** ~ **(over** *OR* **about sthg)** matutar (sobre algo).
broody ['bru:dɪ] (*compar* **-ier**, *superl* **-iest**) *adj* **-1.** [sad] pensativo(va) **-2.** [bird] choco(ca).
brook [brʊk] ◇ *n* riacho *m*. ◇ *vt fml* tolerar.
broom [bru:m] *n* **-1.** [brush] vassoura *f* **-2.** [shrub] giesta *f*.
broomstick ['bru:mstɪk] *n* cabo *m* de vassoura.
Bros, bros (*abbr of* **brothers**) irmãos.
broth [brɒθ] *n (U)* caldo *m*.
brothel ['brɒθl] *n* bordel *m*.
brother ['brʌðəʳ] ◇ *n* **-1.** [gen & *RELIG*] irmão *m* **-2.** *fig* [associate, comrade] irmão *m*. ◇ *excl US inf* puxa vida!
brotherhood ['brʌðəhʊd] *n* **-1.** *(U)* [companionship] fraternidade *f* **-2.** [organization] irmandade *f*.
brother-in-law (*pl* **brothers-in-law**) *n* cunhado *m*.
brotherly ['brʌðəlɪ] *adj* fraternal.
brought [brɔ:t] *pt* & *pp* ▷ **bring**.
brow [braʊ] *n* **-1.** [forehead] testa *f* **-2.** [eyebrow] sobrancelha *f*; **to knit one's** ~**s** franzir a testa **-3.** [of hill] topo *m*.
browbeat ['braʊbi:t] (*pt* **browbeat**, *pp* **-en**) *vt* intimidar.
browbeaten ['braʊbi:tn] *adj* intimidado(da).
brown [braʊn] ◇ *adj* **-1.** [colour - hair, eyes] castanho(nha); [- object] marrom; ~ **bread** pão *m* integral **-2.** [tanned] bronzeado(da). ◇ *n* [colour] marrom *m*; **in** ~ em marrom. ◇ *vt* [food] tostar.
Brownie (Guide) *n escoteira junior de sete a dez anos.*
brownie point *n fig*: **to earn** ~**s** fazer média.
brown paper *n (U)* papel *m* pardo.
brown rice *n (U)* arroz *m* integral.
brown sugar *n (U)* açúcar *m* mascavo.
browse [braʊz] ◇ *vt COMPUT*: **to** ~ **the Web** navegar na Web. ◇ *vi* **-1.** [in shop] dar uma olhada **-2.** [read]: **to** ~ **through sthg** dar uma olhada em algo **-3.** [graze] pastar.
browser ['braʊzʳ] *n COMPUT* navegador *m*.
bruise [bru:z] ◇ *n* equimose *f*. ◇ *vt* **-1.** [leave a bruise on] machucar **-2.** *fig* [hurt, offend] ferir. ◇ *vi* machucar-se.
bruised [bru:zd] *adj* **-1.** [having bruise] machucado(da) **-2.** *fig* [hurt, offended] ferido(da).
Brummie, Brummy ['brʌmɪ] *UK inf* ◇ *adj* de Birmingham. ◇ *n* habitante *mf* de Birmimgham.
brunch [brʌntʃ] *n* brunch *m*, *combinação de café da manhã e almoço servido ao meio-dia.*
Brunei ['bru:naɪ] *n* Brunei; **in** ~ em Brunei.
brunette [bru:'net] *n* morena *f*.
brunt [brʌnt] *n*: **to bear** *OR* **take the** ~ **of sthg** suportar *OR* sofrer a força de algo.
brush [brʌʃ] ◇ *n* **-1.** [for hair] escova *f* **-2.** [of artist, for shaving, paint] pincel *m* **-3.** [encounter] atrito *m*. ◇ *vt* **-1.** [clean with brush] escovar **-2.** [move with hand] sacudir **-3.** [touch lightly] roçar.
◆ **brush aside** *vt sep* desprezar.
◆ **brush off** *vt sep* [dismiss] desprezar.
◆ **brush up** ◇ *vt sep* [revise] recapitular. ◇ *vi*: **to** ~ **up on sthg** treinar *OR* praticar algo.
brushed [brʌʃt] *adj* [fabric]: ~ **cotton** fio *m* de algodão penteado.
brush-off *n inf*: **to give sb the** ~ dar um chega pra lá em alguém, botar alguém de escanteio.
brush-up *n (U) inf*: **to have a wash and** ~ dar uma geral.
brushwood ['brʌʃwʊd] *n (U)* graveto *m*.
brushwork ['brʌʃwɜ:k] *n (U)* pincelada *f*.
brusque [bru:sk] *adj* brusco(ca).
Brussels ['brʌslz] *n* Bruxelas; **in** ~ em Bruxelas.
brussels sprout *n* couve-de-bruxelas *f*.
brutal ['bru:tl] *adj* brutal.
brutality [bru:'tælətɪ] (*pl* **-ies**) *n* **-1.** *(U)* [cruelty] brutalidade *f* **-2.** [cruel act] brutalidade *f*.
brutalize, -ise ['bru:təlaɪz] *vt* **-1.** [make brutal] brutalizar **-2.** [treat brutally] maltratar.
brute [bru:t] ◇ *adj* bruto(ta). ◇ *n* **-1.** [large animal] besta *f* **-2.** [bully] animal *mf*.
BS (*abbr of* **Bachelor of Science**) *n (titular de) graduação em ciências nos Estados Unidos.*
BSA (*abbr of* **Boy Scouts of America**) *n associação de escoteiros norte-americanos*, ≃ UEB *f*.
BSc (*abbr of* **Bachelor of Science**) *n (titular de) graduação em ciências.*
BSE (*abbr of* **bovine spongiform encephalopathy**) *n* EEB *f*.
BSI (*abbr of* **British Standards Institution**) *n instituto britânico de normatização*, ≃ ABNT *f*.
B-side *n* lado-B *m*.
BST (*abbr of* **British Summer Time**) *horário de verão britânico.*
BT (*abbr of* **British Telecom**) *n empresa de telefonia britânica.*

Btu (*abbr of* **British thermal unit**) *n unidade de calor britânica*, btu *m*.
bubble ['bʌbl] <> *n* bolha *f*. <> *vi* borbulhar.
bubble bath *n* **-1.** [liquid] espuma *f* de banho **-2.** [bath] banho *m* de espuma.
bubble gum *n (U)* chiclete *m* de bola.
bubblejet printer ['bʌbldʒet-] *n* impressora *f* a jato de tinta.
bubbly ['bʌblɪ] (*compar* **-ier**, *superl* **-iest**) <> *adj* [person] efervescente. <> *n inf* champanhe *m*.
Bucharest [ˌbu:kə'rest] *n* Bucareste; **in ~** em Bucareste.
buck [bʌk] (*pl sense 1 inv* OR **-s**) <> *n* **-1.** [male animal] macho *m* **-2.** *US inf* [dollar] pila *mf*; **to make a fast ~** fazer grana fácil OR rápido **-3.** *inf* [responsibility]: **the ~ stops here** a responsabilidade pára aqui; **to pass the ~** passar OR transferir a responsabilidade. <> *vt* **-1.** [subj: horse] derrubar **-2.** *inf* [oppose] ir contra. <> *vi* [horse] corcovear.
◆ **buck up** *inf* <> *vt sep* **-1.** [make more positive] avivar **-2.** [cheer up] animar. <> *vi* **-1.** [hurry up] apressar-se **-2.** [cheer up, become more positive] animar-se.
bucket ['bʌkɪt] *n* **-1.** [container] balde *m* **-2.** [bucketful] balde *m*.
◆ **buckets** *npl inf fig* [large quantity]: **~s of sthg** baldes de algo.
Buckingham Palace ['bʌkɪŋəm-] *n* Palácio *m* de Buckingham.
buckle ['bʌkl] <> *n* fivela *f*. <> *vt* **-1.** [fasten] afivelar **-2.** [bend] arquear. <> *vi* [bend] arquear-se, vergar-se.
◆ **buckle down** *vi* [work harder]: **to ~ down (to sthg)** empenhar-se (em algo).
buckshot ['bʌkʃɒt] *n (U)* chumbo *m* (de espingarda).
buckskin ['bʌkskɪn] *n (U)* pele *f* de cervo.
buckteeth [bʌk'ti:θ] *npl* dentes *mpl* salientes.
buckthorn *n* escambroeiro *m*, espinheiro *m*.
buckwheat ['bʌkwi:t] *n (U)* fagopiro *m*, trigo-mouro *m*.
bud [bʌd] (*pt* & *pp* **-ded**, *cont* **-ding**) <> *n* botão *m*; **to nip sthg in the ~** *fig* cortar algo pela raiz. <> *vi* florescer.
Budapest [ˌbju:də'pest] *n* Budapeste; **in ~** em Budapeste.
Buddha ['bʊdə] *n* Buda *m*.
Buddhism ['bʊdɪzm] *n (U)* budismo *m*.
Buddhist ['bʊdɪst] <> *adj* budista. <> *n* budista *mf*.
budding ['bʌdɪŋ] *adj* [aspiring] principiante.
buddy ['bʌdɪ] (*pl* **-ies**) *n US inf* [friend] camarada *mf*.
budge [bʌdʒ] <> *vt* **-1.** [move] mexer **-2.** [change mind of] dissuadir. <> *vi* **-1.** [move - object] mover-se; [- person] mudar-se **-2.** [change mind] mudar de opinião.
budgerigar ['bʌdʒərɪgɑ:ʳ] *n* periquito *m* (australiano).
budget ['bʌdʒɪt] <> *adj* [cheap] econômico(ca). <> *n* orçamento *m*; **the Budget** *UK* POL o Orçamento. <> *vt* estimar. <> *vi* calcular.
◆ **budget for** *vt fus* planejar os gastos com.
budget account *n* **-1.** [with shop] conta *f* (crediário) **-2.** [at bank] conta *f* orçamentária.
budgetary ['bʌdʒɪtrɪ] *adj* orçamentário(ria).
budgie ['bʌdʒɪ] *n inf* periquito *m* (australiano).
Buenos Aires [ˌbwenəs'aɪrɪz] *n* Buenos Aires; **in ~** em Buenos Aires.
buff [bʌf] <> *adj* [brown] pardo(da). <> *n inf* [expert] expert *mf*.
buffalo ['bʌfələʊ] (*pl inv* OR **-es** OR **-s**) *n* búfalo *m*.
buffer ['bʌfəʳ] *n* **-1.** [for trains] pára-choque *m* **-2.** [protection] proteção *f* **-3.** COMPUT buffer *m*.
buffer state *n* estado-tampão *m*.
buffet[1] [*UK* 'bʊfeɪ, *US* bə'feɪ] *n* **-1.** [meal] bufê *m* **-2.** [cafeteria] cantina *f*.
buffet[2] ['bʌfɪt] *vt* [physically] bater.
buffet car ['bʊfeɪ-] *n* vagão-restaurante *m*.
buffoon [bə'fu:n] *n* palhaço *m*.
bug [bʌg] (*pt* & *pp* **-ged**, *cont* **-ging**) <> *n* **-1.** *US* [small insect] inseto *m* **-2.** *inf* [germ] vírus *m* **-3.** *inf* [listening device] grampo *m* **-4.** COMPUT [fault in program] bug *m* **-5.** [enthusiasm]: **the travel ~** a febre de viajar. <> *vt inf* **-1.** [spy on] grampear **-2.** *Am* [annoy] chatear.
bugbear ['bʌgbeəʳ] *n* bicho-papão *m*.
bugger ['bʌgəʳ] *UK v inf* <> *n* **-1.** [unpleasant person, task] porre *mf* **-2.** [particular type of person] infeliz *mf*. <> *excl* merda! <> *vt*: **~ it!** dane-se!
◆ **bugger off** *vi*: **~ off!** vá à merda!
buggy ['bʌgɪ] (*pl* **-ies**) *n* [pushchair, stroller] carrinho *m* de bebê.
bugle ['bju:gl] *n* trombeta *f*.
build [bɪld] (*pt* & *pp* **built**) <> *vt* construir. <> *n* corpo *m*, constituição *f* física.
◆ **build into** *vt sep* embutir em.
◆ **build on** <> *vt fus* [further] ampliar. <> *vt sep* [base on] alicerçar.
◆ **build up** <> *vt sep* [strengthen] fortalecer. <> *vi* [increase] intensificar.
◆ **build upon** *vt fus* & *vt sep* = **build on**.
builder ['bɪldəʳ] *n* construtor.
building ['bɪldɪŋ] *n* **-1.** [structure] edifício *m*, prédio *m* **-2.** *(U)* [profession] construção *f*.
building and loan association *n US* associação *f* de financiamento imobiliário, ≃ sistema *m* financeiro de habitação.
building block *n* **-1.** [toy] bloco *m* para montar **-2.** *fig* [element] alicerce *f*.
building contractor *n* construtor *m*, -ra *f*.
building site *n* canteiro *m* de obras.
building society *n UK* sociedade *f* de financiamento imobiliário.

BUILDING SOCIETY

As *building societies* funcionam como bancos, embora não possuam um sistema de compensação. Elas se dedicam a conceder financiamentos imobiliários e, no passado, desempenharam papel muito importante na Grã-Bretanha. Hoje, muitas delas converteram-se em bancos.

build-up *n* [increase] intensificação *f*.
built [bɪlt] <> *pt* & *pp* ▷ **build**. <> *adj* [person]: **heavily ~** de forte constituição; **~ for sthg** de constituição apropriada para algo.

built-in *adj* **-1.** *CONSTR* embutido(da) **-2.** [inherent] embutido(da).

built-up *adj*: ~ **area** área *f* urbanizada.

bulb [bʌlb] *n* **-1.** [for lamp] lâmpada *f* **-2.** [of plant] bulbo *m*.

bulbous ['bʌlbəs] *adj* bulboso(sa).

Bulgaria [bʌl'geərɪə] *n* Bulgária; **in** ~ na Bulgária.

Bulgarian [bʌl'geərɪən] <> *adj* búlgaro(ra). <> *n* **-1.** [person] búlgaro *m*, -ra *f* **-2.** [language] búlgaro *m*.

bulge [bʌldʒ] <> *n* **-1.** [lump] protuberância *f* **-2.** [sudden increase] aumento *m*. <> *vi*: **to** ~ **(with sthg)** estar estourando(de algo).

bulging ['bʌldʒɪŋ] *adj* **-1.** abarrotado(da) **-2.** musculoso(sa).

bulimia (nervosa) [bjʊ'lɪmɪə-] *n (U)* bulimia *f* nervosa.

bulk [bʌlk] <> *n* **-1.** [mass] volume *m* **-2.** [of person] massa *f* **-3.** *COMM*: **in** ~ a granel **-4.** [majority, most of]: **the** ~ **of** a maior parte de. <> *adj* a granel.

bulk buying [-'baɪɪŋ] *n (U)* compra *f* a granel.

bulkhead ['bʌlkhed] *n* biombo *m*.

bulky ['bʌlkɪ] (*compar* **-ier**, *superl* **-iest**) *adj* volumoso(osa).

bull [bʊl] *n* **-1.** [male cow] touro *m* **-2.** [male animal] macho *m* **-3.** *ST EX* especulador *m*, -ra *f* **-4.** *(U) v inf US* [nonsense] tolice *f*.

bulldog ['bʊldɒg] *n* buldogue *m*.

bulldog clip *n* prendedor *m* de papel, clipe *m* buldogue.

bulldoze ['bʊldəʊz] *vt* **-1.** [with bulldozer] aplainar **-2.** *fig* [force]: **to** ~ **one's way** forçar sua passagem; **to** ~ **sb into sthg/into doing sthg** obrigar alguém a algo/a fazer algo.

bulldozer ['bʊldəʊzə^r] *n* escavadeira *f*.

bullet ['bʊlɪt] *n* **-1.** [for gun] bala *f* **-2.** [in text] marcador *m*.

bulletin ['bʊlətɪn] *n* **-1.** [brief report] boletim *m* **-2.** [regular publication] boletim *m*.

bulletin board *n* **-1.** *US* quadro *m* de avisos **-2.** *COMPUT* sistema *m* BBS.

bullet-proof *adj* à prova de bala.

bullfight ['bʊlfaɪt] *n* tourada *f*.

bullfighter ['bʊl,faɪtə[r]] *n* toureiro *m*.

bullfighting ['bʊl,faɪtɪŋ] *n* touradas *fpl*.

bullion ['bʊljən] *n (U)* barras *fpl* de ouro ou prata.

bullish ['bʊlɪʃ] *adj* **-1.** *ST EX*: ~ **market** mercado em alta **-2.** [optimistic] otimista.

bull market *n* mercado *m* em alta.

bullock ['bʊlək] *n* boi *m*.

bullring ['bʊlrɪŋ] *n* arena *f* de touros.

bullrush ['bʊlrʌʃ] *n* = **bulrush**.

bull's-eye *n* **-1.** [target] mosca *f* **-2.** [shot] mosca *f*.

bullshit ['bʊlʃɪt] (*pt* & *pp* **-ted**, *cont* **-ting**) *vulg* <> *n* papo *m* furado. <> *vi* falar abobrinhas.

bull terrier *n* bull terrier *mf*.

bully ['bʊlɪ] (*pl* **-ies**, *pt* & *pp* **-ied**) <> *n* brigão *m*, -gona *f*. <> *vt* amedontrar; **to** ~ **sb into doing sthg** amedrontar alguém para que faça algo.

bullying ['bʊlɪɪŋ] *n (U)* maus-tratos *mpl*.

bulrush ['bʊlrʌʃ] *n* papiro *m*.

bum [bʌm] (*pt* & *pp* **-med**, *cont* **-ming**) *n* **-1.** *esp UK v inf* [bottom] traseiro *m* **-2.** *US inf pej* [tramp] vagabundo *m* **-3.** *US inf pej* [idler] desocupado *m*, -da *f*.

◆ **bum around** *esp US vi inf* **-1.** [waste time] vadiar **-2.** [travel aimlessly] perambular.

bum bag *n inf* pochete *f*.

bumblebee ['bʌmblbi:] *n* abelhão *m*.

bumbling ['bʌmblɪŋ] *adj inf* inútil; ~ **incompetence** incompetência extraordinária.

bumf [bʌmf] *n UK inf* papelada *f*.

bump [bʌmp] <> *n* **-1.** [road] elevação *f* **-2.** [head] galo *m* **-3.** [leg] inchaço *m* **-4.** [knock, blow] batida *f* **-5.** [noise] pancada *f*. <> *vt* [knock, damage] bater. <> *vi* **-1.** [move unevenly] solavancar **-2.** [knock, hit]: **to** ~ **into sthg** topar em algo.

◆ **bump into** *vt fus* [meet by chance]: **to** ~ **into sb** topar com alguém.

◆ **bump off** *vt sep inf* apagar.

◆ **bump up** *vt sep inf* aumentar.

bumper ['bʌmpə[r]] <> *adj* super-. <> *n* **-1.** [on car] pára-choque *m* **-2.** *US RAIL* pára-choque *m*.

bumper-to-bumper *adj*: ~ **traffic** trânsito congestionado e lento.

bumph [bʌmf] *n* = **bumf**.

bumptious ['bʌmpʃəs] *adj pej* presunçoso(sa).

bumpy ['bʌmpɪ] (*compar* **-ier**, *superl* **-iest**) *adj* **-1.** [surface] esburacado(da) **-2.** [ride, journey] turbulento(-ta).

bun [bʌn] *n* **-1.** [cake] bolo *m* doce (*pequeno e com passas*) **-2.** [bread roll] pãozinho *m* **-3.** [hairstyle] coque *m*.

bunch [bʌntʃ] <> *n* [group - of people] grupo *m*; [- of flowers] ramalhete *m*; [- of fruit] cacho *m*; [- of keys] molho *m*. <> *vt* agrupar. <> *vi* unir.

◆ **bunches** *npl* [hairstyle] maria-chiquinha *f*.

bundle ['bʌndl] <> *n* **-1.** [clothes] trouxa **-2.** [paper] maço **-3.** [wood] feixe. <> *vt* socar.

◆ **bundle off** *vt sep* mandar, enviar.

◆ **bundle up** *vt sep* **-1.** [put into bundles] entrouxar **-2.** [dress warmly] agasalhar(-se).

bundled software ['bʌndld-] *n COMPUT* software *m* incluído.

bung [bʌŋ] <> *n* tampo *m*. <> *vt UK inf* **-1.** [give] passar **-2.** [put] deixar **-3.** [toss] jogar.

bungalow ['bʌŋgələʊ] *n* [single-storey house] casa *f* térrea.

bunged up [bʌŋd-] *adj* **-1.** [nose] congestionado -(da) **-2.** [sink, drains] entupido(da).

bungee jump *n* bungee jump *m*.

bungee-jumping ['bʌndʒɪ-] *n* bungee jumping *m*.

bungle ['bʌŋgl] *vt* fracassar.

bunion ['bʌnjən] *n* joanete *m*.

bunk [bʌŋk] *n* **-1.** [bed] beliche *m* **-2.** *inf* [nonsense] besteira *f* **-3.** *phr*: **to do a** ~ *inf* dar no pé.

bunk bed *n* beliche *m*.

bunker ['bʌŋkə[r]] *n* **-1.** *MIL* [shelter] abrigo *m* **-2.** [for coal] carvoeira *f* **-3.** [in golf] bunker *m*.

bunkhouse *n* alojamento *m*.

bunny ['bʌnɪ] (*pl* **-ies**) *n*: ~ **(rabbit)** coelhinho *m*.

bunny hill *n US SKIING morro baixo e sem obstáculos utilizado como pista para a prática de esqui na neve.*

Bunsen burner ['bʌnsn-] *n* bico *m* de Bunsen.

bunting ['bʌntɪŋ] *n* [flags] bandeirolas *fpl*.

buoy [*UK* bɔɪ, *US* 'bu:ɪ] *n* [float] bóia *f*.

◆ **buoy up** *vt sep* [encourage] animar.
buoyancy ['bɔɪənsɪ] *n (U)* **-1.** [ability to float] capacidade *f* de flutuar **-2.** [optimism] otimismo *m*.
buoyant ['bɔɪənt] *adj* **-1.** [able to float] capaz de flutuar, flutuante **-2.** [optimistic] otimista.
BUPA (*abbr of* **British United Provident Association**) *n plano de saúde privado existente na Grã-Bretanha.*
burden ['bɜ:dn] ◇ *n* **-1.** [physical load] carga *f* **-2.** *fig* [heavy responsibility] fardo *m*; **to be a ~ on sb** ser um peso para alguém; **to relieve the ~ on sb** aliviar a carga sobre alguém. ◇ *vt*: **to ~ sb with sthg** sobrecarregar alguém com algo.
bureau ['bjʊərəʊ] (*pl* **-x**) *n* **-1.** *US* [government department] departamento *m* **-2.** [office, branch] agência *f*, escritório *m* **-3.** *UK* [desk] escrivaninha *f* **-4.** *US* [chest of drawers] cômoda *f*.
bureaucracy [bjʊə'rɒkrəsɪ] (*pl* **-ies**) *n* **-1.** [system] burocracia *f* **-2.** *(U) pej* [rules] burocracia *f*.
bureaucrat ['bjʊərəkræt] *n pej* burocrata *mf*.
bureaucratic [ˌbjʊərə'krætɪk] *adj pej* burocrático(-ca).
bureau de change [ˌbjʊərəʊdə'ʃɒndʒ] (*pl* **bureaux de change** [ˌbjʊərəʊdə'ʃɒndʒ]) *n* casa *f* de câmbio.
bureaux ['bjʊərəʊz] *pl* ▷ **bureau**.
burger ['bɜ:gəʳ] *n* [hamburger] hambúrguer *m*.
burglar ['bɜ:gləʳ] *n* ladrão *m*, -dra *f*.
burglar alarm *n* alarme *m* anti-roubo.
burglarize *vt US* = **burgle**.
burglary ['bɜ:glərɪ] (*pl* **-ies**) *n* **-1.** [event] roubo *m (de casa)*, arrombamento *m (de casa)* **-2.** [activity] roubo *m (de casa)*, arrombamento *m (de casa)*.
burgle ['bɜ:gl], **burglarize** ['bɜ:gləraɪz] *US vt* roubar *(casa)*, arrombar *(casa)*.
Burgundy *n* Borgonha.
burial ['berɪəl] *n* enterro *m*.
burial ground *n* cemitério *m*.
burk [bɜ:k] *n UK inf* idiota *mf*.
Burkina Faso [bɜ:ˌki:nə'fæsəʊ] *n* Burquina Faso; **in ~** em Burquina Faso.
burly ['bɜ:lɪ] (*compar* **-ier**, *superl* **-iest**) *adj* robusto(ta).
Burma ['bɜ:mə] *n* Birmânia.
Burmese [ˌbɜ:'mi:z] ◇ *adj* birmanês(esa). ◇ *n* **-1.** [person] birmanês *m*, -esa *f* **-2.** [language] birmanês *m*.
burn [bɜ:n] (*pt* & *pp* **burnt** *OR* **-ed**) ◇ *vt* **-1.** [gen] queimar; **to ~ o.s.** queimar-se **-2.** [destroy by fire] incendiar ◇ *vi* **-1.** [gen] queimar **-2.** [be on fire] incendiar-se **-3.** *fig* [feel strong emotion]: **to ~ with sthg** arder de algo. ◇ *n* **-1.** [wound, injury] queimadura *f* **-2.** [mark] queimadura *f*.
◆ **burn down** ◇ *vt sep* [destroy by fire] incendiar. ◇ *vi* **-1.** [be destroyed by fire] incendiar-se **-2.** [burn less brightly] extinguir-se.
◆ **burn out** ◇ *vt sep* [exhaust]: **to ~ o.s. out** esgotar-se. ◇ *vi* [die down] extinguir-se.
◆ **burn up** ◇ *vt sep* [use up] queimar. ◇ *vi* [be destroyed by fire, heat] carbonizar.
burner ['bɜ:nəʳ] *n* [on cooker] queimador *m*.
burning ['bɜ:nɪŋ] *adj* **-1.** [on fire] em chamas **-2.** [very hot] escaldante; **to be ~ hot** estar ardendo *OR* derretendo de calor **-3.** [very red] em brasa **-4.** [intense] ardente.
burnish ['bɜ:nɪʃ] *vt* lustrar.
burnout *n* **-1.** *TECH* combustão *f* **-2.** *fig* [of person] exaustão *f*.
Burns Night *n festa celebrada na Escócia em 25 de janeiro para comemorar o aniversário do poeta Robert Burns.*
burnt [bɜ:nt] *pt* & *pp* ▷ **burn**.
burnt-out *adj* **-1.** [by fire] carbonizado(da) **-2.** *fig* [exhausted] esgotado(da).
burp [bɜ:p] *inf* ◇ *n* arroto *m*. ◇ *vi* arrotar.
burrow ['bʌrəʊ] ◇ *n* toca *f*. ◇ *vi* **-1.** [dig] entocar-se **-2.** *fig* [in order to search] remexer.
bursar ['bɜ:səʳ] *n* tesoureiro *m*, -ra *f*.
bursary ['bɜ:sərɪ] (*pl* **-ies**) *n UK* [scholarship, grant] bolsa *f (de estudos)*.
burst [bɜ:st] (*pt* & *pp* **burst**) ◇ *vi* **-1.** [break open] estourar **-2.** [explode] explodir **-3.** [door, lid]: **to ~ open** abrir-se de repente **-4.** [go suddenly] irromper. ◇ *vt* [break open] estourar. ◇ *n* [bout] estouro *m*.
◆ **burst into** *vt fus* **-1.** [gen] irromper em **-2.** [flower, leaf, blossom] desabrochar.
◆ **burst out** *vt fus* **-1.** [say suddenly] exclamar **-2.** [begin suddenly]: **to ~ out laughing/crying** começar a gargalhar/chorar.
bursting ['bɜ:stɪŋ] *adj* **-1.** [full] repleto(ta) **-2.** [with emotion]: **~ with sthg** repleto(ta) de algo **-3.** [eager]: **to be ~ to do sthg** estar morrendo de vontade de fazer algo.
Burundi [bʊ'rʊndɪ] *n* Burundi; **in ~** em Burundi.
bury ['berɪ] (*pt* & *pp* **-ied**) *vt* **-1.** [gen] enterrar **-2.** [hide - face, hands] esconder **-3.** *fig* [immerse]: **to ~ o.s. in sthg** enterrar-se em algo.
bus [bʌs] *n* ônibus *m*; **by ~** de ônibus.
bus conductor *n* cobrador *m*, -ra *f* de ônibus.
bus driver *n* motorista *mf* de ônibus.
bush [bʊʃ] *n* **-1.** [plant] arbusto *m* **-2.** [open country]: **the ~** a selva **-3.** *phr*: **to beat about the ~** fazer rodeios.
bushel ['bʊʃl] *n* alqueire *m*.
bushy ['bʊʃɪ] (*compar* **-ier**, *superl* **-iest**) *adj* espesso(-sa).
business ['bɪznɪs] ◇ *n* **-1.** *(U)* [commerce] negócios *mpl*; **on ~** a negócios; **to mean ~** *inf* falar sério; **to go out of ~** ir a falência **-2.** [company] negócio *m* **-3.** *(U)* [concern, duty] assunto *m*; **to have no ~ doing** *OR* **to do sthg** não ter o direito de fazer algo; **mind your own ~!** *inf* meta-se com sua vida! **-4.** [affair, matter] negócio *m*, assunto *m*. ◇ *comp* comercial *mf*.
business address *n* endereço *m* comercial.
business card *n* cartão *m* de visita.
business class *n (U)* classe *f* executiva.
businesslike ['bɪznɪslaɪk] *adj* profissional.
businessman ['bɪznɪsmæn] (*pl* **-men** [-men]) *n* [occupation] empresário *m*, homem *m* de negócios.
business school *n* escola *f* de comércio.
business trip *n* viagem *f* de negócios.
businesswoman ['bɪznɪsˌwʊmən] (*pl* **-women** [-ˌwɪmɪn]) *n* [occupation] empresária *f*, mulher *f* de negócios.
busker ['bʌskəʳ] *n UK* artista *mf* de rua.

bus lane *n* faixa *f* exclusiva para ônibus.
bus shelter *n* abrigo *m* de ônibus.
bus station *n* estação *f* rodoviária.
bus stop *n* parada *f* OR ponto *m* de ônibus.
bust [bʌst] (*pt* & *pp* **bust** OR **-ed**) <> *adj inf* **-1.** [broken] quebrado(da) **-2.** [bankrupt]: **to go ~** quebrar. <> *n* **-1.** [gen] busto *m* **-2.** *police sl* [raid] batida *f.* <> *vt inf* **-1.** [break] quebrar **-2.** [arrest] prender **-3.** *police sl* [raid] revistar. <> *vi inf* quebrar.
bustle ['bʌsl] <> *n* [activity] movimento *m.* <> *vi* apressar-se.
bustling ['bʌslɪŋ] *adj* movimentado(da).
bust-up *n inf* **-1.** [quarrel, fight] quebra-pau *m* **-2.** [breakup] rompimento *m.*
busy ['bɪzɪ] (*compar* **-ier**, *superl* **-iest**) <> *adj* **-1.** [gen & TELEC] ocupado(da); **to be ~ doing sthg** estar ocupado(da) fazendo algo **-2.** [hectic - time] agitado(da); [- place] movimentado(da) <> *vt*: **to ~ o.s. (doing sthg)** ocupar-se fazendo algo.
busybody ['bɪzɪˌbɒdɪ] (*pl* **-ies**) *n pej* intrometido *m*, -da *f.*
busy lizzie *n* maria-sem-vergonha *f.*
busy signal *n US TELEC* sinal *m* de ocupado.
but [bʌt] <> *conj* mas <> *prep* senão, a não ser; **you've been nothing ~ trouble** você só tem me dado trabalho; **the last ~ one** o penúltimo (a penúltima).
◆ **but for** *prep* se não fosse.
butane ['bju:teɪn] *n (U)* butano *m.*
butch [bʊtʃ] *adj UK inf* [woman] sapatão.
butcher ['bʊtʃəʳ] <> *n* **-1.** [shopkeeper] açougueiro *m*, -ra *f*; **~'s (shop)** açougue *m* **-2.** *fig* [indiscriminate killer] carniceiro *m*, -ra *f.* <> *vt* **-1.** [kill for meat] abater **-2.** *fig* [kill indiscriminately] exterminar, fazer uma carnificina com.
butchery ['bʊtʃərɪ] *n (U) fig* [indiscriminate killing] carnificina *f.*
butler ['bʌtləʳ] *n* mordomo *m.*
butt [bʌt] <> *n* **-1.** [of cigarette, cigar] bagana *f* **-2.** [of rifle] coronha *f* **-3.** [for water] tina *m* **-4.** [target] alvo *m* **-5.** *esp US inf* [bottom] traseiro *m.* <> *vt* [hit with head] dar cabeçada em.
◆ **butt in** *vi* [interrupt] atrapalhar, interromper; **to ~ in on sb/sthg** atrapalhar OR interromper alguém/algo.
butter ['bʌtəʳ] <> *n (U)* manteiga *f*; **~ wouldn't melt in her mouth** *inf* parece uma mosca morta. <> *vt* passar manteiga em.
◆ **butter up** *vt sep inf* bajular.
butter bean *n* feijão-manteiga *m*, feijão-de-lima *m.*
buttercup ['bʌtəkʌp] *n* botão-de-ouro *m.*
butter dish *n* manteigueira *f.*
buttered ['bʌtəd] *adj* com manteiga.
butterfingers ['bʌtəˌfɪŋgəz] (*pl inv*) *n inf* estabanado *m*, -da *f.*
butterfly ['bʌtəflaɪ] (*pl* **-ies**) *n* **-1.** [insect] borboleta *f*; **to have butterflies in one's stomach** *inf* estar com frio na barriga **-2.** *(U)* [swimming style] nado *m* borboleta.
buttermilk ['bʌtəmɪlk] *n (U)* soro *m (do leite).*
butterscotch ['bʌtəskɒtʃ] *n (U)* doce *m* de manteiga.
buttocks ['bʌtəks] *npl* nádegas *fpl.*
button ['bʌtn] <> *n* **-1.** [on clothes] botão *m* **-2.** [on machine] botão *m* **-3.** *US* [badge] button *m.* <> *vt* = **button up**.
◆ **button up** *vt sep* [fasten] abotoar.
button-down <> *adj* abotoado(da). <> *n.*
buttonhole ['bʌtnhəʊl] <> *n* **-1.** [hole] casa *f (de botão)* **-2.** *UK* [flower] flor *f (de lapela).* <> *vt inf* pegar para conversar.
button mushroom *n* cogumelo *m* de Paris.
buttress ['bʌtrɪs] <> *n* contraforte *m.* <> *vt* [wall] reforçar.
buxom ['bʌksəm] *adj* de corpo e seios grandes.
buy [baɪ] (*pt* & *pp* **bought**) <> *vt* **-1.** *lit* & *fig* comprar; **to ~ sthg from sb** comprar algo de alguém <> *n* compra *f*, aquisição *f.*
◆ **buy in** *vt sep UK* provisionar.
◆ **buy into** *vt fus* investir em.
◆ **buy off** *vt sep* subornar.
◆ **buy out** *vt sep* **-1.** [in business] comprar a parte de **-2.** [from army] pagar para sair; **he bought himself out** ele comprou sua saída do exército.
◆ **buy up** *vt sep* comprar a totalidade de.
buyer ['baɪəʳ] *n* **-1.** [purchaser] comprador *m*, -ra *f* **-2.** [profession] gerente *mf* de compras.
buyout ['baɪaʊt] *n* compra *f* majoritária de ações.
buzz [bʌz] <> *n* [noise - of insect, machinery] zumbido *m*; [- of conversation] murmúrio *m*; **to give sb a ~** *inf* [on phone] dar uma ligada para alguém. <> *vi* **-1.** zunir; *lit* & *fig* **to ~ (with sthg)** zunir (de algo) <> *vt* [on intercom] ligar, chamar.
◆ **buzz off** *vi UK inf*: **~ off!** dê o fora!
buzzard ['bʌzəd] *n* **-1.** *UK* [hawk] gavião *m* **-2.** *US* [vulture] abutre *m.*
buzzer ['bʌzəʳ] *n* campainha *f.*
buzzing ['bʌzɪŋ] *n* zumbido *m.*
buzzword ['bʌzwɜ:d] *n inf* palavra *f* da moda.
by [baɪ] <> *prep* **-1.** [expressing cause, agent] por; **he's worried ~ her absence** está preocupado com a sua ausência; **he was hit ~ a car** ele foi atropelado por um carro; **a book ~ Stephen King** um livro de Stephen King; **funded ~ the government** financiado pelo governo. **-2.** [expressing method, means]: **~ car/bus/plane** de carro/ônibus/avião; **~ phone/mail** pelo telefone/correio; **to pay ~ credit card/check** pagar com cartão de crédito/cheque; **to win ~ cheating** ganhar trapaceando. **-3.** [near to, beside] junto a; **~ the sea** à beira-mar, junto ao mar. **-4.** [past] por; **a car went ~ the house** um carro passou pela casa. **-5.** [via] por; **exit ~ the door on the left** saia pela porta do lado esquerdo. **-6.** [with time]: **be there ~ nine** esteja lá às nove horas; **~ day** de dia; **it should be ready ~ now** já deve estar pronto. **-7.** [expressing quantity] a; **sold ~ the dozen** vende-se à dúzia; **prices fell ~ 20%** os preços baixaram 20%; **we charge ~ the hour** cobramos por hora. **-8.** [expressing meaning] com; **what do you mean ~ that?** que quer dizer com isso? **-9.** [in division, multiplication] por; **about six feet ~ fifteen** aproximadamente dois metros por cinco. **-10.** [according to] segundo; **~ law** segundo a lei; **it's fine ~ me** por mim tudo bem. **-11.** [expressing gradual process] a; **one ~ one** um a

um; **day ~ day** dia a dia. **-12.** [in phrases]: **~ mistake** por engano; **~ oneself** sozinho; **~ profession** por profissão. ◇ *adv* [past]: **to go/drive ~** passar.

bye (-bye) [baɪ(baɪ)] *excl inf* tchau!

bye-election *n* = **by-election**.

byelaw ['baɪlɔ:] *n* = **bylaw**.

by-election *n eleição suplementar realizada para substituir um político que renunciou ao cargo parlamentar ou morreu.*

Byelorussia [bɪˌeləʊ'rʌʃə] *n* = **Belorussia**.

bygone ['baɪgɒn] *adj* decorrido(da).
◆ **bygones** *npl*: **to let ~s be ~s** deixar o que passou para trás.

bylaw ['baɪlɔ:] *n* estatuto *m*.

by-line *n linha no início de um artigo de jornal ou revista dando o nome do autor.*

BYOB (*abbr of* **bring your own bottle**) traga sua própria bebida.

bypass ['baɪpɑ:s] ◇ *n* **-1.** [road] rodoanel *m* **-2.** MED: **~ (operation)** (cirurgia de) ponte *f* de safena. ◇ *vt* **-1.** [place] passar ao redor de **-2.** [issue, person] passar por cima de.

by-product *n* **-1.** [product] subproduto *m* **-2.** *fig* [consequence] subproduto *m*.

bystander ['baɪˌstændəʳ] *n* espectador *m*, -ra *f*.

byte [baɪt] *n* COMPUT byte *m*.

byword ['baɪwɜ:d] *n* [symbol]: **to be a ~ for sthg** ser um exemplo de algo.

C

c[1] (*pl* **c's** OR **cs**), **C** (*pl* **C's** OR **Cs**) [si:] *n* [letter] c, C *m*.
◆ **C** *n* **-1.** MUS dó *m* **-2.** SCH [mark] C *m*, regular *m* **-3.** (*abbr of* **celsius, centigrade**) C.

c[2] **-1.** (*abbr of* **century**) séc. **-2.** (*abbr of* **cent(s)**) cent.

c., ca. (*abbr of* **circa**) c.

C/A -1. (*abbr of* **capital account**) *conta de empréstimos e investimentos.* **-2.** (*abbr of* **credit account**) conta *f* de crédito. **-3.** (*abbr of* **current account**) c/c *f*.

CA ◇ *n* (*abbr of* **chartered accountant**) *contador com certificado de qualificação profissional na Escócia e no Canadá.* ◇ **-1.** (*abbr of* **Central America**) América *f* Central. **-2.** *abbr of* **California**.

CAA *n* **-1.** (*abbr of* **Civil Aviation Authority**) *organismo regulador da aviação civil na Grã-Bretanha.* **-2.** (*abbr of* **Civil Aeronautics Authority**) *autoridade de aviação civil nos Estados Unidos.*

cab [kæb] *n* **-1.** [taxi] táxi *m* **-2.** [of lorry] cabine *f*.

CAB (*abbr of* **Citizens' Advice Bureau**) *n centro britânico de informação e assistência ao cidadão.*

cabaret ['kæbəreɪ] *n* cabaré *m*.

cabbage ['kæbɪdʒ] *n* [vegetable] repolho *m*.

cabbie, cabby ['kæbɪ] *n inf* taxista *mf*.

caber ['keɪbəʳ] *n*: **tossing the ~** *esporte praticado na Escócia no qual o vencedor é aquele que arremessar um tronco de pinheiro à maior distância.*

cabin ['kæbɪn] *n* **-1.** [on ship] camarote *m* **-2.** [in aircraft] cabine *f* **-3.** [house] cabana *f*.

cabin class *n* classe *f* cabina.

cabin crew *n* tripulação *f*.

cabin cruiser *n* iate *m*.

cabinet ['kæbɪnɪt] *n* **-1.** [cupboard] armário *m* **-2.** POL gabinete *m*.

cabinet-maker *n* marceneiro *m*, -ra *f*.

cabinet minister *n* ministro *m*, -tra *f* de gabinete.

cable ['keɪbl] ◇ *n* **-1.** [rope] cabo *m* **-2.** [telegram] telegrama *m* **-3.** ELEC cabo *m* **-4.** TV = **cable television**. ◇ *vt* [telegraph] telegrafar.

cable car *n* teleférico *m*.

cablegram *n* cabograma *m*.

cable railway *n* ferrovia *f* funicular.

cable television, cable TV *n (U)* televisão *f* a cabo.

caboodle [kə'bu:dl] *n inf*: **the whole (kit and) ~** a tralha toda.

cabriolet ['kæbrɪəʊleɪ] *n* [car] conversível *m*.

cache [kæʃ] ◇ *n* **-1.** [store] esconderijo *m* **-2.** COMPUT cache *f*. ◇ *vt* COMPUT armazenar em cache.

cachet ['kæʃeɪ] *n fml* prestígio *m*.

cackle ['kækl] ◇ *n* **-1.** [of hen] cacarejo *m* **-2.** [of person] gargalhada *f*. ◇ *vi* **-1.** [hen] cacarejar **-2.** [person] gargalhar.

cacophony [kæ'kɒfənɪ] *n* balbúrdia *f*.

cactus ['kæktəs] (*pl* **-tuses** OR **-ti** [-taɪ]) *n* cacto *m*.

CAD (*abbr of* **computer-aided design**) *n* CAD *m*.

caddie ['kædɪ] ◇ *n* carregador *m*, -ra *f* de tacos. ◇ *vi*: **to ~ for sb** carregar os tacos de golfe para alguém.

caddy ['kædɪ] (*pl* **-ies**) *n* porta-chá *m*.

cadence ['keɪdəns] *n* [of voice] cadência *f*.

cadet [kə'det] *n* [in police] cadete *m*.

cadge [kædʒ] *UK inf* ◇ *vt*: **to ~ sthg (off** OR **from sb)** filar algo (de alguém). ◇ *vi*: **to ~ off** OR **from sb** pedir esmolas a OR para alguém.

Cadiz [kə'dɪz] *n* Cádiz.

Caesar ['si:zəʳ] *n* César *m*.

caesarean (section) *UK*, **cesarean (section)** *US* [sɪ'zeərɪən-] *n* cesariana *f*; **she had a ~** ela fez uma cesariana.

CAF (*abbr of* **cost and freight**) custo *m* e frete.

cafe, café ['kæfeɪ] *n* café *m*.

cafeteria [ˌkæfɪ'tɪərɪə] *n* cantina *f*.

caffeine ['kæfi:n] *n (U)* cafeína *f*.

cage [keɪdʒ] *n* **-1.** [for animals] jaula *f* **-2.** [for birds] gaiola *f*.

caged [keɪdʒd] *adj* **-1.** [animals] enjaulado(da) **-2.** [birds] engaiolado(da).

cagey ['keɪdʒɪ] (*compar* **-ier**, *superl* **-iest**) *adj inf* cauteloso(sa), cuidadoso(sa).

cagoule [kə'gu:l] *n UK* capa *f* de chuva.

cahoots [kə'hu:ts] *n inf*: **to be in ~ with/against sb** estar de armação com/contra alguém.

CAI (*abbr of* **computer-aided instruction**) *n* CAI *f*, instrução *f* assistida por computador.

cairn [keən] *n* [heap of stones] marco *m* de pedras.

Cairo ['kaɪərəʊ] *n* Cairo.

cajole [kə'dʒəʊl] *vt*: **to ~ sb out of sthg** persuadir alguém a desistir de algo; **to ~ sb into doing sthg** persuadir alguém a fazer algo.

cake [keɪk] *n* **-1.** [type of sweet food] bolo *m*; **to sell like hot ~s** vender como água; **you can't have your ~ and eat it** não dá para assobiar e chupar cana ao mesmo tempo; **a piece of ~** *inf* uma moleza *OR* barbada **-2.** [of fish, potato] bolinho *m* *(achatado)* **-3.** [of soap] sabonete *m*.

caked [keɪkt] *adj*: **~ with sthg** empastado(da) de algo, coberto(ta) de algo.

cake pan *n US* fôrma *f (de bolo)*.

cake tin *n UK* [for baking] fôrma *f (de bolo)*; [for storing] pote *m*.

cal (*abbr of* **calorie**) *n* cal.

CAL (*abbr of* **computer-assisted learning**) *n* CAL *f*, aprendizagem *f* assistida por computador.

calamine lotion [kæləmaɪn-] *n (U)* loção *f* de calamina.

calamitous [kə'læmɪtəs] *adj fml* calamitoso(sa).

calamity [kə'læmɪtɪ] (*pl* **-ies**) *n fml* calamidade *f*.

calcium ['kælsɪəm] *n (U)* cálcio *m*.

calculate ['kælkjʊleɪt] *vt* **-1.** [work out - figures, result etc] calcular; [- consequences, risk etc] medir **-2.** [plan, intend]: **to be ~d to do sthg** ter o intuito de fazer algo.

◆ **calculate on** *vi*: **to ~ on sthg** contar com algo; **to ~ on sb doing sthg** contar com que alguém faça algo.

calculated ['kælkjʊleɪtɪd] *adj* [planned, intentional - risk] calculado(da); [- crime, deception] premeditado(da); [- insult] intencional.

calculating ['kælkjʊleɪtɪŋ] *adj pej* calculista.

calculation [ˌkælkjʊ'leɪʃn] *n MATH* cálculo *m*.

calculator ['kælkjʊleɪtəʳ] *n* calculadora *f*.

calculus [ˌkælkjʊləs] *n (U) MATH* cálculo *m*.

calendar ['kælɪndəʳ] *n* calendário *m*.

calendar month *n* mês *m* civil.

calendar year *n* ano *m* civil.

calf [kɑ:f] (*pl* **calves**) *n* **-1.** [young animal - cow] bezerro *m*, -ra *f*; [- elephant, whale] filhote *m* **-2.** *(U)* [leather] couro *m* de bezerro **-3.** [of leg] panturrilha *f*, barriga *f* da perna.

calf-length *adj* três-quartos.

calfskin *n* couro *m* de bezerro.

caliber *n US* = **calibre** *m*.

calibrate ['kælɪbreɪt] *vt* **-1.** [mark out] graduar **-2.** [adjust] calibrar.

calibre, caliber *US* ['kælɪbəʳ] *n* **-1.** [quality] nível *m* **-2.** [size] calibre *m*.

calico ['kælɪkəʊ] *n (U)* morim *m*.

California [ˌkælɪ'fɔ:njə] *n* Califórnia.

Californian [ˌkælɪ'fɔ:njən] ◇ *adj* californiano (na). ◇ *n* californiano *m*, -na *f*.

calipers *npl US* = **callipers**.

call [kɔ:l] ◇ *n* **-1.** [cry - of person] grito *m*; [- of animal, bird] canto *m* **-2.** [visit] visita *f*; **to pay a ~ on sb** fazer uma visita a alguém **-3.** [for flight] chamada *f*; **final ~** última chamada **-4.** [demand] pedido *m*; **~ for sthg** solicitação por algo; **there's no ~ for that** não há razão para isso **-5.** [summons] chamado *m* **-6.** [standby]: **on ~** de plantão **-7.** [telephone call] telefonema *m*, ligação *f*; **long-distance ~** chamada de longa distância; **to give sb a ~** telefonar para alguém, dar uma ligada para alguém **-8.** [lure, fascination] encanto *m*. ◇ *vt* **-1.** [gen] chamar; **disgraceful, I'd ~ it!** uma vergonha, eu diria!; **would you ~ what he does art?** você chamaria o que ele faz de arte?; **he ~ed me a liar** ele me chamou de mentiroso; **let's ~ it £10** a gente faz por £10 **-2.** [telephone] ligar para. ◇ *vi* **-1.** [shout] chamar **-2.** [animal, bird] cantar **-3.** [by telephone] ligar **-4.** [visit] visitar.

◆ **call back** ◇ *vt sep* **-1.** [on telephone] ligar de volta **-2.** [ask to return] chamar de volta. ◇ *vi* **-1.** [on phone] ligar de volta **-2.** [visit again] voltar outra vez.

◆ **call by** *vi inf* dar uma passada.

◆ **call for** *vt fus* **-1.** [collect] ir buscar **-2.** [demand] exigir.

◆ **call in** ◇ *vt sep* **-1.** [send for] chamar **-2.** *COMM* [goods] fazer um recall de; *FIN* [loan] resgatar. ◇ *vi*: **could you ~ in at the butcher's on your way home?** você pode passar no açougue ao voltar para casa?

◆ **call off** *vt sep* **-1.** [cancel] cancelar **-2.** [order not to attack] mandar voltar.

◆ **call on** *vt fus* **-1.** [visit] visitar **-2.** [ask]: **to ~ on sb to do sthg** convocar alguém para fazer algo.

◆ **call out** ◇ *vt sep* **-1.** [gen] convocar **-2.** [cry out] gritar. ◇ *vi* [cry out] gritar.

◆ **call round** *vi* dar uma passada.

◆ **call up** *vt sep* **-1.** *MIL* convocar **-2.** [on telephone] dar uma ligada **-3.** *COMPUT* chamar, buscar.

call box *n UK* cabine *f* telefônica, ≃ orelhão *m*.

caller ['kɔ:ləʳ] *n* **-1.** [visitor] visita *f* **-2.** [on telephone]: **I'm sorry ~, the number is engaged** sinto muito, senhor(ra), a linha está ocupada.

caller (ID) display *n* [on telephone] identificador *m* de chamadas.

call girl *n* garota *f* de programa.

calligraphy [kə'lɪgrəfɪ] *n (U)* caligrafia *f*.

call-in *n US RADIO & TV programa com participação por telefone de ouvintes ou telespectadores.*

calling ['kɔ:lɪŋ] *n* **-1.** [profession, trade] profissão *f* **-2.** [vocation] vocação *f*.

calling card *n US* cartão *m* de visita.

callipers *UK*, **calipers** *US* ['kælɪpəz] *npl* **-1.** *MATH* compasso *m* de calibre **-2.** *MED* aparelho *m* ortopédico.

callous ['kæləs] *adj* insensível.

callously ['kæləslɪ] *adv* insensivelmente.

callousness ['kæləsnɪs] *n (U)* insensibilidade *f*.

call-up *n UK* convocação *f*.

callus ['kæləs] (*pl* **-es**) *n* calo *m*.

calm [kɑ:m] ◇ *adj* [person, voice, weather] calmo(-ma), tranqüilo(la). ◇ *n (U)* [peaceful state] tranqüilidade *f*, calmaria *f*. ◇ *vt* acalmar, tranqüilizar.

◆ **calm down** ◇ *vt sep* acalmar, tranqüilizar. ◇ *vi* acalmar-se, tranqüilizar-se.
calmly ['kɑ:mlɪ] *adv* calmamente, tranqüilamente.
calmness ['kɑ:mnɪs] *n (U)* tranqüilidade *f*.
Calor gas® ['kæləʳ-] *n UK (U)* ≃ butano *m*.
calorie ['kælərɪ] *n* [in food] caloria *f*.
calorific [,kælə'rɪfɪk] *adj* [fattening] calórico(ca).
calumny *adj fml* calúnia *f*.
calve [kɑ:v] *vi* [cow] dar cria.
calves [kɑ:vz] *pl* ▷ **calf**.
cam [kæm] *n* came *f*.
CAM (*abbr of* **computer-aided manufacturing**) *n* CAM *f*, produção *f* assistida por computador.
camaraderie [,kæmə'rɑ:dərɪ] *n (U)* camaradagem *f*.
camber ['kæmbəʳ] *n* inclinação *f*.
Cambodia [kæm'bəʊdjəl] *n* Camboja; **in ~** no Camboja.
Cambodian [kæm'bəʊdjən] ◇ *adj* cambojano(-na). ◇ *n* cambojano *m*, -na *f*.
camcorder ['kæm,kɔ:dəʳ] *n* filmadora *f*.
came [keɪm] *pt* ▷ **come**.
camel ['kæml] ◇ *adj*: **~-coloured** da cor de camelo; **a ~ coat** um casaco de pele de camelo. ◇ *n* [animal] camelo *m*.
camellia [kə'mi:ljəl] *n* camélia *f*.
cameo ['kæmɪəʊ] (*pl* **-s**) *n* **-1.** [piece of jewellery] camafeu *m* **-2.** [in writing] descrição *f* breve e inteligente **-3.** [in acting] ponta *f*.
camera ['kæmərəl] *n* câmera *f*.
◆ **in camera** *adv fml* em câmara.
cameraman ['kæmərəmæn] (*pl* **-men** [-men]) *n* cameraman *m*, câmera *m*.
Cameroon [,kæmə'ru:n] *n* Camarões; **in ~** nos Camarões.
Cameroonian [,kæmə'ru:nɪən] ◇ *adj* camaronês(esa). ◇ *n* camaronês *m*, -esa *f*.
camisole ['kæmɪsəʊl] *n* camisola *f*.
camomile ['kæməmaɪl] ◇ *n* [plant, herb] camomila *f*. ◇ *comp*: **~ tea** chá de camomila.
camouflage ['kæməflɑ:ʒ] ◇ *n* comuflagem *f* ◇ *vt* camuflar.
camp [kæmp] ◇ *n* **-1.** [gen] acampamento *m*; **holiday ~** acampamento de férias; **training ~** campo *m* de treinamento; **concentration/refugee ~** campo de concentração/refugiados **-2.** *fig* [faction] facção *f*. ◇ *vi* acampar.
◆ **camp out** *vi* acampar.
campaign [kæm'peɪn] ◇ *n* campanha *f*. ◇ *vi*: **to ~ (for/against sthg)** fazer campanha (a favor de/contra algo).
campaigner [kæm'peɪnəʳ] *n* [activist] ativista *mf*; **old ~** veterano *m*, -na *f*.
camp bed *n* cama *f* de armar.
camper ['kæmpəʳ] *n* **-1.** [person] campista *mf* **-2.** [vehicle]: **~ (van)** trailer *m*.
campground ['kæmpgraʊnd] *n US* camping *m*.
camphor ['kæmfəʳ] *n (U)* cânfora *f*.
camping ['kæmpɪŋ] *n (U)* acampamento *m*; **to go ~** ir acampar.
camping site, campsite ['kæmpsaɪt] *n* camping *m*.
campus ['kæmpəs] (*pl* **-es**) *n* campus *m*.
camshaft ['kæmʃɑ:ft] *n* eixo *m* de came.
can¹ [kæn] ◇ *n* [container] lata *f*. ◇ *vt* enlatar.
can² [*weak form* kən, *strong form* kæn] (*pt* **was, were**, *pt & conditional* **could**) *aux vb* **-1.** [be able to] poder; **~ you help me?** pode me ajudar?; **I ~ see the mountains** posso ver as montanhas **-2.** [know how to] saber; **~ you drive?** você sabe dirigir?; **I ~ speak Portuguese** eu sei falar português **-3.** [be allowed to] poder; **you can't smoke here** você não pode fumar aqui **-4.** [in polite requests] poder; **~ you tell me the time?** pode me dizer as horas?; **~ I speak to the manager?** posso falar com o gerente? **-5.** [expressing occasional occurrence] poder; **it ~ get cold at night** às vezes a temperatura diminui bastante à noite **-6.** [expressing possibility] poder; **they could be lost** eles podem estar perdidos.
Canada ['kænədəl] *n* Canadá; **in ~** no Canadá.
Canadian [kə'neɪdjən] ◇ *adj* canadense. ◇ *n* canadense *mf*.
canal [kə'næl] *n* [waterway] canal *m*.
Canaries *npl*: **the ~** as Canárias.
canary [kə'neərɪ] (*pl* **-ies**) *n* canário *m*.
Canary Islands, Canaries [kə'neərɪz] *npl*: **the ~** as Ilhas Canárias; **in the ~** nas Ilhas Canárias.
Canberra *n* Canberra; **em ~** em Camberra.
cancel ['kænsl] (*UK pt & pp* **-led**, *cont* **-ling**, *US pt & pp* **-ed**, *cont* **-ing**) *vt* [call off, invalidate] cancelar.
◆ **cancel out** *vt sep* anular.
cancellation [,kænsə'leɪʃn] *n* cancelamento *m*.
cancer ['kænsəʳ] ◇ *n* [disease] câncer *m*. ◇ *comp*: **~ cell** célula cancerosa; **~ research** pesquisa sobre câncer; **~ specialist** especialista em câncer.
◆ **Cancer** *n* **-1.** [sign] Câncer *m* **-2.** [person] canceriano *m*, -na *f*; **I'm ~** sou de Câncer.
cancerous ['kænsərəs] *adj* canceroso(sa).
candelabra [,kændɪ'lɑ:brə] *n* candelabro *m*.
candid ['kændɪd] *adj* [frank] sincero(ra), franco(ca).
candidacy ['kændɪdəsɪ] *n (U)* candidatura *f*.
candidate ['kændɪdət] *n* **-1.** [for job]: **~ for sthg** candidato(ta) a algo **-2.** [taking exam] candidato *m*, -ta *f*.
candidature ['kændɪdətʃəʳ] *n* candidatura *f*.
candidly ['kændɪdlɪ] *adv* sinceramente, francamente.
candidness ['kændɪdnɪs] *n* = **candour**.
candied ['kændɪd] *adj* cristalizado(da).
candle ['kændl] *n* vela *f*; **to burn the ~ at both ends** *inf* dar duro dia e noite.
candlelight ['kændllaɪt] *n (U)* luz *f* de vela.
candlelit ['kændllɪt] *adj* à luz de velas.
candlestick ['kændlstɪk] *n* castiçal *m*.
candour *UK*, **candor** *US* ['kændəʳ] *n (U)* sinceridade *f*, franqueza *f*.
candy ['kændɪ] (*pl* **-ies**) *n esp US (U)* [confectionery] doce *m*, guloseima *f*.
candy bar *n US* barra *f* de doce.
candy box *n US* caixa *f* de doces.
candyfloss *UK* ['kændɪflɒs], **cotton candy** *US n (U)* algodão-doce *m*.
candy store *n US* confeitaria *f*.

cane [keɪn] ◇ *n* **-1.** *(U)* [for making furniture] palhinha *f* **-2.** [walking stick] bengala *f* **-3.** [for punishment]: **the ~** ≃ a palmatória **-4.** [for supporting plant] vara *f.* ◇ *comp* de palhinha. ◇ *vt* bater com vara em.
cane sugar *n (U)* cana-de-açúcar *f.*
canine ['keɪnaɪn] ◇ *adj* canino(na). ◇ *n*: **~ (tooth)** (dente *m*) canino *m.*
canister ['kænɪstəʳ] *n* lata *f* de metal; **a ~ of tear gas** uma bomba de gás lacrimogênio; **a smoke ~** uma bomba de fumaça.
cannabis ['kænəbɪs] *n (U)* maconha *f.*
canned [kænd] *adj* **-1.** [tinned - food] enlatado(da); [- drink] em lata, de latinha **-2.** *inf fig* [music] gravado(da).
cannelloni [ˌkænɪ'ləʊnɪ] *n (U)* canelone *m.*
cannery (*pl* **-ies**) *n* fábrica *f* de enlatados.
cannibal ['kænɪbl] *n* canibal *mf.*
cannibalize, -ise ['kænɪbəlaɪz] *vt* [vehicle, machine] desmanchar.
cannon ['kænən] (*pl inv* OR **-s**) *n* **-1.** [on ground] canhão *m* **-2.** [on aircraft] canhão *m.*
◆ **cannon into** *vt fus UK* esbarrar.
cannonball ['kænənbɔːl] *n* bala *f* de canhão.
cannot ['kænɒt] *vb fml* ▷ **can²**.
canny ['kænɪ] (*compar* **-ier**, *superl* **-iest**) *adj* [shrewd] astuto(ta).
canoe [kə'nuː] ◇ *n* canoa *f.* ◇ *vi* andar de canoa.
canoeing [kə'nuːɪŋ] *n (U)*: **to go ~** praticar canoagem.
canon ['kænən] *n* **-1.** [clergyman] cônego *m* **-2.** [general principle] cânone *m.*
◆ **Canon** *n* [of Mass]: **the Canon** o cânon.
canonize, -ise ['kænənaɪz] *vt* canonizar.
canoodle [kə'nuːdl] *vi UK inf* amassar-se.
can opener *n* abridor *m* de lata.
canopy ['kænəpɪ] (*pl* **-ies**) *n* **-1.** [over bed, seat] dossel *m* **-2.** [of trees, branches] cobertura *f.*
cant [kænt] *n pej* [insincere talk] papo-furado *m.*
can't [kɑːnt] = **cannot**.
Cantab (*abbr of* **Cantabrigiensis**) *da Universidade de Cambridge.*
Cantabrian Mountains [kæn'teɪbrɪən-] *npl*: **the ~** as Montanhas Cantábricas.
cantaloup *UK*, **cantaloupe** *US* ['kæntəluːp] *n* cantalupo *m.*
cantankerous [kæn'tæŋkərəs] *adj* rabugento(ta).
canteen [kæn'tiːn] *n* **-1.** [restaurant] cantina *f* **-2.** [box of cutlery] faqueiro *m.*
canter ['kæntəʳ] ◇ *n* meio *m* galope. ◇ *vi* andar a meio galope.
cantilever ['kæntɪliːvəʳ] *n* viga *f* em balanço, cantiléver.
Canton [kæn'tɒn] *n* Cantão.
Cantonese [ˌkæntə'niːz] ◇ *adj* cantonês(esa). ◇ *n* [language] cantonês *m.* ◇ *npl*: **the ~** os cantoneses.
canvas ['kænvəs] *n* **-1.** *(U)* [cloth] lona *f*; **under ~** [in a tent] em uma barraca **-2.** ART tela *f.*
canvass ['kænvəs] ◇ *vt* **-1.** POL pedir **-2.** [investigate] sondar. ◇ *vi* POL [campaign] pedir votos.
canvasser ['kænvəsəʳ] *n* **-1.** POL [campaigner] cabo *mf* eleitoral **-2.** [investigator] pesquisador *m*, -ra *f.*
canvassing ['kænvəsɪŋ] *n* **-1.** POL [campaigning] angariação *f* de votos **-2.** [investigation] pesquisa *f.*
canyon ['kænjən] *n* desfiladeiro *m.*
cap [kæp] (*pt* & *pp* **-ped**, *cont* **-ping**) ◇ *n* **-1.** [hat] boné *m* **-2.** [swimming, shower] touca *f*; **to go ~ in hand to sb** *fig* dirigir-se a alguém com o chapéu na mão **-3.** [lid, top] tampa *f* **-4.** *UK* [contraceptive device] diafragma *m.* ◇ *vt* **-1.** [cover top of] cobrir **-2.** [improve on]: **to ~ it all** para arrematar.
CAP (*abbr of* **Common Agricultural Policy**) *n política que permite que todos os países da União Européia organizem e controlem sua produção agrícola conjuntamente.*
capability [ˌkeɪpə'bɪlətɪ] (*pl* **-ies**) *n* **-1.** [ability] capacidade *f* **-2.** MIL poderio *m.*
capable ['keɪpəbl] *adj* **-1.** [able, having capacity]: **to be ~ of sthg/of doing sthg** ser capaz de algo/de fazer algo **-2.** [competent, skilful] competente, hábil.
capably ['keɪpəblɪ] *adv* habilmente.
capacious [kə'peɪʃəs] *adj fml* espaçoso(sa).
capacitor [kə'pæsɪtəʳ] *n* capacitor *m.*
capacity [kə'pæsɪtɪ] (*pl* **-ies**) ◇ *n* **-1.** *(U)* [limit, ability] capacidade *f*; **to be filled to ~** estar com a lotação esgotada; **~ for sthg** capacidade para algo; **~ for doing** OR **to do sthg** capacidade para OR de fazer algo **-2.** [position] qualidade *f*; **in my ~ as ...** na qualidade de ...; **in a ... ~** na condição de ... ◇ *comp* máximo(ma).
cape [keɪp] *n* **-1.** GEOGR cabo *m* **-2.** [cloak] capa *f.*
Cape Canaveral [-kə'nævərəl] *n* Cabo *m* Canaveral.
Cape of Good Hope *n*: **the ~** o Cabo da Boa Esperança.
caper ['keɪpəʳ] ◇ *n* **-1.** [for flavouring food] alcaparra *f* **-2.** *inf* [escapade] mutreta *f.* ◇ *vi* fazer travessuras, pular.
Cape Town *n* Cidade *f* do Cabo.
Cape Verde [-vɜːd] *n*: **the ~ Islands** as Ilhas de Cabo Verde; **in ~** em Cabo Verde.
capillary [kə'pɪlərɪ] (*pl* **-ies**) *n* capilar *m.*
capita ▷ **per capita**.
capital ['kæpɪtl] ◇ *adj* **-1.** [letter] maiúsculo(la) **-2.** [punishable by death] capital. ◇ *n* **-1.** [of country]: **~ (city)** capital *f* **-2.** *fig* [centre] capital *f* **-3.** TYPO : **~ (letter)** (letra) maiúscula; **in ~s** em letras maiúsculas **-4.** [money] capital *m*; **to make ~ (out) of sthg** *fig* aproveitar-se de algo.
capital allowance *n* margem *f* fiscal para investimentos.
capital assets *npl* ativos *mpl* fixos.
capital expenditure *n (U)* dispêndio *m* com ativos fixos.
capital gains tax *n* imposto *m* sobre lucros de capital.
capital goods *npl* bens *mpl* de capital.
capital-intensive *adj* de capital intensivo.
capitalism ['kæpɪtəlɪzm] *n (U)* capitalismo *m.*
capitalist ['kæpɪtəlɪst] ◇ *adj* capitalista. ◇ *n* capitalista *mf.*
capitalize, -ise ['kæpɪtəlaɪz] *vi*: **to ~ on sthg** [make most of] tirar proveito de algo, capitalizar algo.

capital punishment *n (U)* pena *f* de morte.
capital stock *n* estoque *m* de capital.
capital transfer tax *n* imposto *m* sobre transferência de capital.
Capitol ['kæpɪtl] *n*: **the ~** o Capitólio.
Capitol Hill ['kæpɪtl-] *n congresso norte-americano.*
capitulate [kə'pɪtjʊleɪt] *vi*: **to ~ (to sthg)** render-se (a algo), ceder (frente a algo).
capitulation [kə,pɪtjʊ'leɪʃn] *n (U)* capitulação *f.*
cappuccino [,kæpʊ'tʃi:nəʊ] *(pl* **-s**) *n* cappuccino *m.*
capricious [kə'prɪʃəs] *adj* inconstante.
Capricorn ['kæprɪkɔ:n] *n* **-1.** [sign] Capricórnio *m* **-2.** [person]: **I'm ~** sou de Capricórnio.
caps *(abbr of* **capital letters**) *npl* maiúsc.
capsicum ['kæpsɪkəm] *n* pimentão *m.*
capsize [kæp'saɪz] ◇ *vt* emborcar. ◇ *vi* emborcar-se.
capsule ['kæpsju:l] *n* cápsula *f.*
Capt. *(abbr of* **captain**) cap.
captain ['kæptɪn] ◇ *n* **-1.** [gen] capitão *m* **-2.** [of airliner] comandante *mf.* ◇ *vt* [ship] comandar.
caption ['kæpʃn] *n* legenda *f.*
captivate ['kæptɪveɪt] *vt* cativar.
captivating ['kæptɪveɪtɪŋ] *adj* cativante.
captive ['kæptɪv] ◇ *adj* **-1.** [imprisoned] de cativeiro **-2.** *fig* [unable to leave] cativo(va); **~ audience** audiência cativa. ◇ *n* prisioneiro *m*, -ra *f.*
captivity [kæp'tɪvətɪ] *n*: **in ~** em cativeiro.
captor ['kæptə[r]] *n* capturador *m*, -ra *f.*
capture ['kæptʃə[r]] ◇ *vt* **-1.** [gen] capturar **-2.** [gain, take control of] conquistar. ◇ *n (U)* captura *f.*
car [kɑ:[r]] ◇ *n* **-1.** [motor car] carro *m* **-2.** [on train] vagão *m.* ◇ *comp* de automóvel.
Caracas [kə'rækəs] *n* Caracas; **em ~** em Caracas.
carafe [kə'ræf] *n* garrafa *f* de mesa.
car alarm *n* alarme *m* de carro.
caramel ['kærəmel] *n* **-1.** *(U)* [burnt sugar] caramelo *m* **-2.** [sweet] caramelo *m.*
carat ['kærət] *n UK* quilate *m.*
caravan ['kærəvæn] ◇ *n* **-1.** *UK* [vehicle - towed by car] trailer *m*; [- towed by horse] carruagem *m* **-2.** [travelling group] caravana *f.* ◇ *comp* de trailer; **~ holiday** férias de trailer.
caravanning ['kærəvænɪŋ] *n UK* viagem *f* de trailer.
caravan site *n UK* área *f* para trailers.
caraway seed ['kærəweɪ-] *n* semente *f* de alcaravia.
carbohydrate [,kɑ:bəʊ'haɪdreɪt] *n (U)* [chemical substance] carboidrato *m.*
◆ **carbohydrates** *npl* [food] carboidratos *mpl.*
carbon ['kɑ:bən] *n* **-1.** *(U)* [element] carbono *m* **-2.** = **carbon copy -3.** = **carbon paper.**
carbonated ['kɑ:bəneɪtɪd] *adj* com gás.
carbon copy *n* **-1.** [document] cópia *f* em papel carbono **-2.** *fig* [exact copy] cópia *f* perfeita.
carbon dating [-'deɪtɪŋ] *n (U)* datação *f* por carbono 14.
carbon dioxide [-daɪ'ɒksaɪd] *n (U)* dióxido *m* de carbono.
carbon fibre *n (U)* fibra *f* de carbono.
carbon monoxide [-mɒ'nɒksaɪd] *n* monóxido *m* de carbono.
carbon paper *n* papel-carbono *m.*
car-boot sale *n UK feira em que objetos usados são vendidos no porta-malas de um carro.*
carburettor *UK*, **carburetor** *US* [,kɑ:bə'retə[r]] *n* carburador *m.*
carcass ['kɑ:kəs] *n* [of animal] carcaça *f.*
carcinogenic [,kɑ:'sɪnə'dʒenɪk] *adj* cancerígeno(-na).
card [kɑ:d] *n* **-1.** [playing card] carta *f*; **to play one's ~s right** *fig* agir de forma inteligente; **to put** *OR* **lay one's ~s on the table** *fig* pôr as cartas na mesa **-2.** [for information, greetings] cartão *m* **-4.** [postcard] postal *m*, cartão *m* postal **-5.** *(U)* [cardboard] papelão *m.*
◆ **cards** *npl* [game] cartas *fpl.*
◆ **on the cards** *UK*, **in the cards** *US adv inf*: **to be on the ~** estar na cara.
cardamom ['kɑ:dəməm] *n* cardamomo *m.*
cardboard ['kɑ:dbɔ:d] ◇ *n (U)* papelão *m.* ◇ *comp* [made of cardboard] de papelão *m.*
cardboard box *n* caixa *f* de papelão.
card-carrying [-'kærɪɪŋ] *adj* ativo(va).
card catalog *n US* fichário *m.*
cardiac ['kɑ:dɪæk] *adj* cardíaco(ca), do coração.
cardiac arrest *n* ataque *m* cardíaco.
cardigan ['kɑ:dɪgən] *n* cardigã *m.*
cardinal ['kɑ:dɪnl] ◇ *adj* primordial. ◇ *n RELIG* cardeal *m.*
cardinal number, cardinal numeral *n* número *m* cardinal.
card index *n UK* fichário *m.*
cardiograph ['kɑ:dɪəgrɑ:f] *n* cardiógrafo *m.*
cardiology [,kɑ:dɪ'ɒlədʒɪ] *n (U)* cardiologia *f.*
cardiovascular [,kɑ:dɪəʊ'væskjʊlə[r]] *adj* cardiovascular.
cardphone ['kɑ:dfəʊn] *n* telefone *m* (público) de cartão.
cardsharp ['kɑ:d,ʃɑ:p] *n* trapaceiro *m*, -ra *f.*
card table *n* mesa *f* de jogo.
card vote *n UK* voto *m* representativo da classe.
care [keə[r]] ◇ *n* **-1.** *(U)* [protection, looking after] cuidado *m*; **to be taken into ~** ser entregue aos cuidados de uma instituição social; **to take ~ of sb** [look after] cuidar de alguém; **to take ~ of sthg** [deal with] cuidar de algo; **take ~!** *inf* [when saying goodbye] cuide-se! **-2.** *(U)* [caution, carefulness] cuidado *m*; **to take ~ to do sthg** ter o cuidado de fazer algo; **take ~!** [be careful] tenha cuidado! **-3.** [cause of worry] preocupação *f.* ◇ *vi* **-1.** [be concerned] preocupar-se; **to ~ about sb/sthg** preocupar-se com alguém/algo **-2.** [mind] importar-se; **I couldn't ~ less** *inf* não dou a mínima.
◆ **care of** *prep* aos cuidados de.
◆ **care for** *vt fus* [like] gostar de.
CARE *(abbr of* **Cooperative for American Relief Everywhere**) *n organização humanitária norte-americana.*
career [kə'rɪə[r]] ◇ *n* carreira *f.* ◇ *comp* [professional] de carreira *f.* ◇ *vi* desgovernar-se; **to ~ into sthg** ir desgovernado(da) em direção a algo.
careerist [kə'rɪərɪst] *n pej* carreirista *mf.*

careers [kəˈrɪəz] *comp* de orientação vocacional.
careers adviser *n* orientador *m*, -ra *f* vocacional.
career woman *n* mulher *f* de carreira.
carefree [ˈkeəfriː] *adj* despreocupado(da).
careful [ˈkeəfʊl] *adj* **-1.** [cautious] cuidadoso(sa); **~ with sthg** cuidadoso(sa) com algo; **to be ~ to do sthg** ter o cuidado de fazer algo **-2.** [thorough] cuidadoso(sa).
carefully [ˈkeəflɪ] *adv* **-1.** [cautiously] cuidadosamente, com cuidado **-2.** [thoroughly] cuidadosamente.
careless [ˈkeəlɪs] *adj* **-1.** [inattentive] desatento(ta), descuidado(da) **-2.** [unconcerned] despreocupado(-da).
carelessly [ˈkeəlɪslɪ] *adv* **-1.** [inattentively] sem atenção, descuidadamente **-2.** [unconcernedly] despreocupadamente.
carelessness [ˈkeəlɪsnɪs] *n (U)* **-1.** [inattention] desatenção *f* **-2.** [lack of concern] descuido *m*.
carer [ˈkeərəl] *n pessoa que cuida de um familiar incapacitado ou doente*.
caress [kəˈres] ◇ *n* carícia *f*. ◇ *vt* acariciar.
caretaker [ˈkeəˌteɪkəʳ] *n UK* zelador *m*, -ra *f*.
caretaker government *n* governo *m* de transição.
car ferry *n* balsa *f*.
cargo [ˈkɑːgəʊ] (*pl* **-es** *OR* **-s**) ◇ *n* carregamento *m*. ◇ *comp* de carga.
car hire *n UK (U)* aluguel *m* de carros.
Carib [ˈkærɪb] *n* Caribe *m*.
Caribbean [*UK* kærɪˈbɪən, *US* kəˈrɪbɪən] ◇ *adj* caribenho(nha). ◇ *n* **-1.** [sea]: **the ~ (Sea)** o (Mar do) Caribe **-2.** [region]: **the ~** o Caribe; **in the ~** no Caribe.
caribou [ˈkærɪbuː] (*pl inv OR* **-s**) *n* caribu *m*.
caricature [ˈkærɪkəˌtjʊəʳ] ◇ *n* [cartoon, travesty] caricatura *f*. ◇ *vt* fazer caricatura de.
caries [ˈkeəriːz] *n (U)* cárie *f*.
caring [ˈkeərɪŋ] *adj* afetuoso(sa).
caring professions *npl*: **the ~** as profissões humanitárias.
carnage [ˈkɑːnɪdʒ] *n (U)* carnificina *f*.
carnal [ˈkɑːnl] *adj literary* carnal.
carnation [kɑːˈneɪʃn] *n* craveiro *m*.
carnival [ˈkɑːnɪvl] *n* **-1.** [festive occasion] carnaval *m* **-2.** [fair] parque *m* de diversões.
carnivore [ˈkɑːnɪvɔːʳ] *n* carnívoro *m*, -ra *f*.
carnivorous [kɑːˈnɪvərəs] *adj* carnívoro(ra).
carol [ˈkærəl] *n*: **(Christmas) ~** cântico *m* de Natal.
carouse [kəˈraʊz] *vi* farrear.
carousel [ˌkærəˈsel] *n* **-1.** *esp US* [at fair] carrossel *m* **-2.** [at airport] esteira *f*.
carp [kɑːp] (*pl inv OR* **-s**) ◇ *n* carpa *f*. ◇ *vi* queixar-se; **to ~ about sthg** queixar-se de algo.
car park *n UK* estacionamento *m*.
Carpathians [kɑːˈpeɪθɪənz] *npl*: **the ~** os Cárpatos.
carpenter [ˈkɑːpəntəʳ] *n* carpinteiro *m*, -ra *f*.
carpentry [ˈkɑːpəntrɪ] *n (U)* carpintaria *f*.
carpet [ˈkɑːpɪt] ◇ *n* **-1.** [floor covering] carpete *m*; **to sweep sthg under the ~** *fig* varrer algo para baixo do tapete **-2.** *fig* [of flowers, snow] tapete *m*. ◇ *vt* **-1.** [fit with floor covering] acarpetar **-2.** *fig* [with flowers, snow] cobrir.
carpet slipper *n* pantufas *fpl*.
carpet sweeper [-ˈswiːpəʳ] *n* limpador *m* de carpete, feiticeira *f*.
car phone *n* telefone *m* para automóvel.
car pool *n UK* [fleet of cars] frota *f*.
carport [ˈkɑːˌpɔːt] *n* garagem *f*.
car radio *n* rádio *m* de carro.
car rental *n Am* aluguel *m* de carro.
carriage [ˈkærɪdʒ] *n* **-1.** [horsedrawn vehicle] carruagem *f* **-2.** *UK* [railway coach] vagão **-3.** *(U)* [transport of goods] carregamento *m*; **~ paid** *OR* **free** *UK* frete pago; **~ forward** *UK* frete ao portador **-4.** [on typewriter] carro *m* **-5.** *(U) literary* [deportment] postura *f*.
carriage clock *n* relógio *m* com alça.
carriageway [ˈkærɪdʒweɪ] *n UK* pista *f* simples.
carrier [ˈkærɪəʳ] *n* **-1.** *COMM* transportador *m*, -ra *f* **-2.** [of disease] portador *m*, -ra *f* **-3.** *MIL*: **(aircraft) ~** porta-aviões *m inv* **-4.** [on bicycle] cestinha *f* **-5.** = **carrier bag**.
carrier bag *n* sacola *f*.
carrier pigeon *n* pombo-correio *m*.
carrion [ˈkærɪən] *n (U)* carniça *f*.
carrot [ˈkærət] *n* **-1.** [vegetable] cenoura *f* **-2.** *inf fig* [incentive] incentivo *m*.
carry [ˈkærɪ] (*pt* & *pp* **-ied**) ◇ *vt* **-1.** [transport - subj: person, animal] carregar; [- subj: water, wind, vehicle] levar **-2.** [be equipped with] dispor de; **all planes ~ lifejackets** todos os aviões dispõem de coletes salva-vidas **-3.** [weapon] portar **-4.** [disease] transmitir **-5.** [involve as a consequence] implicar; **the job carries considerable responsibility** o emprego implica em responsabilidades consideráveis **-6.** [motion, proposal] aprovar **-7.** [be pregnant with] carregar **-8.** *MATH* sobrar. ◇ *vi* [sound] projetar-se.
◆ **carry away** *vt sep*: **to get carried away** entrar no embalo.
◆ **carry forward** *vt sep* transportar.
◆ **carry off** *vt sep* **-1.** [make a success of] tornar um sucesso **-2.** [win] sair-se bem.
◆ **carry on** ◇ *vt fus* [continue] continuar; **to ~ on doing sthg** continuar a fazer algo. ◇ *vi* **-1.** [continue] continuar; **to ~ on with sthg** continuar algo **-2.** *inf* [make a fuss] criar caso **-3.** *inf* [have an affair]: **to ~ on with sb** estar de caso com alguém.
◆ **carry out** *vt fus* **-1.** [task, plan, experiment] levar a cabo **-2.** [promise, order, threat] cumprir.
◆ **carry through** *vt sep* [accomplish] completar.
carryall [ˈkærɪɔːl] *n US* bolsa *f* de viagem.
carrycot [ˈkærɪkɒt] *n esp UK* moisés *m inv*.
carry-on *n UK inf* bagunça *f*.
carryout *n US & Scot* **-1.** [food] comida *f* para viagem *OR* para levar **-2.** [drink] bebida *f* para viagem *OR* para levar.
carsick [ˈkɑːˌsɪk] *adj* enjoado(da) *(em carro)*.
cart [kɑːt] ◇ *n* **-1.** [vehicle] carroça *f* **-2.** (*abbr of* **cartridge**) *COMPUT* cartucho *m* **-3.** *US* [for shopping]: **(shopping** *OR* **grocery) ~** carrinho *m* (de compras). ◇ *vt inf* carregar.
carte blanche [ˈkartblãʃ] *n (U)* carta *f* branca.

cartel [kɑː'tel] *n* cartel *m*.
cartilage ['kɑːtɪlɪdʒ] *n (U)* cartilagem *f*.
carton ['kɑːtn] *n* **-1.** [brick-shaped] caixa *f* **-2.** [plastic] frasco *m*.
cartoon [kɑː'tuːn] *n* **-1.** [satirical drawing] cartum *m* **-2.** [comic strip] tira *f*, tirinha *f* **-3.** [film] desenho *m* animado.
cartoonist [kɑː'tuːnɪst] *n* cartunista *mf*.
cartridge ['kɑːtrɪdʒ] *n* **-1.** [for gun] cartucho *m* **-2.** [for pen] recarga *f* **-3.** [for camera] rolo *m* de filme **-4.** [for record player] cápsula *f*.
cartridge paper *n (U)* papel-manilha *m*.
cartwheel ['kɑːtwiːl] *n* [movement] pirueta *f*.
car valeting *n* lavagem *f* completa.
carve [kɑːv] ◇ *vt* **-1.** [shape, sculpt] esculpir **-2.** [slice] fatiar **-3.** [cut into surface] gravar. ◇ *vi* [slice joint] fatiar a carne.
◆ **carve out** *vt sep* [create, obtain] criar.
◆ **carve up** *vt sep* [divide] dividir.
carving ['kɑːvɪŋ] *n* [art, work, object] entalhe *m*.
carving knife *n* faca *f* de trinchar.
car wash *n* **-1.** [process] lavagem *f* de carro **-2.** [place] lava-rápido *m*.
cascade [kæ'skeɪd] ◇ *n* **-1.** [waterfall] cascata *f* **-2.** [of blossom, information] chuva *f*. ◇ *vi* [flow downwards] cair em cascatas.
case [keɪs] *n* **-1.** [gen] caso *m*; **a ~ in point** um exemplo típico; **to be the ~** ser o caso; **in that ~** nesse caso; **he may still come, in which ~ we can all leave together** pode ser que ele ainda venha, e neste caso todos podemos partir juntos; **as** *OR* **whatever the ~ may be** seja qual for o caso; **in ~ of** em caso de **-2.** [argument] razões *fpl*; **~ for/against sthg** razões a favor de/contra algo **-3.** *JUR* [trial, inquiry] causa *f* **-4.** [container, holder] estojo *m* **-5.** *UK* [suitcase] mala *f*.
◆ **in any case** *adv* seja como for.
◆ **in case** ◇ *conj* caso. ◇ *adv*: **(just) in ~** só por precaução.
case-hardened *adj* [person] calejado(da).
case history *n* prontuário *m*.
casement window *n* janela *f* de batente.
case study *n* estudo *m* de caso.
cash [kæʃ] ◇ *n (U)* **-1.** [notes and coins] dinheiro *m*; **to pay (in) ~** pagar em dinheiro **-2.** *inf* [money] dinheiro *m* **-3.** [payment]: **~ in advance** pagamento *m* adiantado/antecipado; **~ on delivery** pagamento contra entrega. ◇ *vt* descontar.
◆ **cash in** *vi*: **to ~ in on sthg** *inf* tirar proveito de algo.
cash and carry *n* sistema *f* pague e leve.
cashbook ['kæʃbʊk] *n* livro-caixa *m*.
cash box *n* cofre *m*.
cash card *n* cartão *m* de saque.
cash crop *n* plantação *f* para venda direta.
cash desk *n UK* caixa *m*.
cash discount *n* desconto *m* no pagamento à vista.
cash dispenser [-dɪ'spensəʳ] *n* = **cashpoint**
cashew (nut) ['kæʃuː-] *n* castanha *f* de caju.
cash flow *n* fluxo *m* de caixa.
cashier [kæ'ʃɪəʳ] *n* caixa *mf*.
cash machine *n* = **cash point**.
cashmere [kæʃ'mɪəʳ] ◇ *n (U)* caxemira *f*. ◇ *comp* de caxemira.
cashpoint ['kæʃpɔɪnt] *n* caixa *m* automático.
cash price *n* preço *m* à vista.
cash register *n* caixa *f* registradora.
cash sale *n* venda *f* à vista.
casing ['keɪsɪŋ] *n* [protective cover] invólucro *m*.
casino [kə'siːnəʊ] (*pl* **-s**) *n* cassino *m*.
cask [kɑːsk] *n* barril *m*.
casket ['kɑːskɪt] *n* **-1.** [for jewels] porta-jóias *m inv* **-2.** *US* [coffin] caixão *m*.
Caspian Sea ['kæspɪən-] *n*: **the ~** o mar Cáspio.
casserole ['kæsərəʊl] *n* **-1.** [stew] ensopado *m* (no forno) **-2.** [pot] prato *f* de ir ao forno.
cassette [kæ'set] *n* cassete *f*.
cassette deck *n* deck *m*.
cassette player *n* toca-fitas *m inv*.
cassette recorder *n* gravador *m*.
cassock ['kæsək] *n* batina *f*.
cast [kɑːst] (*pt* & *pp* **cast**) ◇ *n* **-1.** [of play, film] elenco *m* **-2.** *MED* gesso *m*. ◇ *vt* **-1.** [turn, direct] dar uma espiada em; **to ~ doubt on sthg** pôr algo em dúvida; **to ~ a spell (on sb)** lançar um feitiço (sobre alguém) **-2.** [light, shadow] lançar **-3.** [throw] arremessar **-4.** [choose for play, film] dar o papel a; **she ~ him in the role of Hamlet** ela deu-lhe o papel de Hamlet **-5.** *POL*: **to ~ one's vote** votar **-6.** [metal] moldar **-7.** [lose, shed] trocar. ◇ *vi* [in fishing] lançar.
◆ **cast about, cast around** *vi*: **to ~ about for sthg** procurar algo.
◆ **cast aside** *vt sep* rejeitar.
◆ **cast down** *vt sep fml* [make sad] deixar deprimido(da).
◆ **cast off** ◇ *vt* **-1.** *fml* [old practices, habits, burden] livrar-se de **-2.** [in knitting] arrematar. ◇ *vi* **-1.** *NAUT* soltar as amarras **-2.** [in knitting] arrematar os pontos.
◆ **cast on** ◇ *vt* [in knitting] montar. ◇ *vi* [in knitting] montar os pontos.
castanets [ˌkæstə'nets] *npl* castanholas *fpl*.
castaway ['kɑːstəweɪ] *n* náufrago *m*, -ga *f*.
caste [kɑːst] *n* [class] casta *f*.
caster ['kɑːstəʳ] *n* [wheel] rodízio *m*.
caster sugar *n (U) UK* açúcar *m* refinado.
castigate ['kæstɪgeɪt] *vt fml* [punish] castigar; [criticize severely] criticar severamente.
casting ['kɑːstɪŋ] *n* [object] peça *f* fundida.
casting vote ['kɑːstɪŋ-] *n* voto *m* de minerva.
cast iron *n (U)* ferro *m* fundido.
◆ **cast-iron** *adj* **-1.** [made of cast iron] de ferro fundido **-2.** *fig* [indisputable] incontestável.
castle ['kɑːsl] *n* **-1.** [building] castelo *m* **-2.** [in chess] torre *f*.
castoff *n*: **to wears sb's ~s** usar as roupas velhas de alguém.
castor ['kɑːstəʳ] *n* = **caster**.
castor oil *n (U)* óleo *m* de rícino.
castor sugar *n* = **caster sugar**.
castrate [kæ'streɪt] *vt* castrar.
castration [kæ'streɪʃn] *n (U)* castração *f*.
casual ['kæʒʊəl] *adj* **-1.** [relaxed, uninterested] despreocupado(da) **-2.** *pej* [offhand] deselegante, informal

-3. [chance] ocasional **-4.** [clothes] informal **-5.** [irregular] temporário(ria).

casually ['kæʒʊəlɪ] *adv* **-1.** [in a relaxed manner, without interest] casualmente **-2.** [dress] informalmente.

casualty ['kæʒjʊəltɪ] (*pl* **-ies**) *n* **-1.** [dead or injured person] vítima *mf*; *MIL* baixa *f* **-2.** *MED* = **casualty department** **-3.** *fig* [of change, policy, system] vítima *f*.

casualty department *n* pronto-socorro *m*.

cat [kæt] *n* **-1.** [domestic animal] gato *m*, -ta *f*; **to let the ~ out of the bag** abrir o bico; **to be like a ~ on hot bricks** *UK* OR **on a hot tin roof** *US* não estar à vontade; **to put the ~ among the pigeons** *UK* criar confusão; **to rain ~s and dogs** chover canivetes; **to think one is the ~'s whiskers** *UK* achar-se muito especial; **there's no room to swing a ~** não há espaço nem para respirar; **to play ~ and mouse** brincar de gato e rato **-2.** [wild animal] felino *m*, -na *f* **-3.** (*abbr of* **catalytic converter**) *AUT* catalisador *m*.

CAT (*abbr of* **computer-assisted testing**) *n* **-1.** CAT *f*, verificação *f* assistida por computador. **-2.** (*abbr of* **computer-assisted translation**) tradução *f* assistida por computador. **-3.** (*abbr of* **computerized axial tomography**) tomografia *f* axial computadorizada.

cataclysmic [ˌkætə'klɪzmɪk] *adj* cataclísmico(ca).

catacombs ['kætəku:mz] *npl* catacumbas *fpl*.

Catalan ['kætəˌlæn] ◇ *adj* catalão(lã). ◇ *n* **-1.** [person] catalão *m*, -lã *f* **-2.** [language] catalão *m*.

catalogue *UK*, **catolog** *US* ['kætəlɒg] ◇ *n* **-1.** [of items for sale] catálogo *m* **-2.** [in library, museum] catálogo *m* **-3.** *fig* [list] lista *f*. ◇ *vt* catalogar.

Catalonia [ˌkætə'ləʊnɪə] *n* Catalunha; **in ~** na Catalunha.

Catalonian [ˌkætə'ləʊnɪən] ◇ *adj* catalão(lã). ◇ *n* [person] catalão *m*, -lã *f*.

catalyst ['kætəlɪst] *n* **-1.** *CHEM* catalisador *m* **-2.** *fig* [cause] motivo *m*.

catalytic converter *n* conversor *m* catalítico.

catamaran [ˌkætəmə'ræn] *n* catamarã *f*.

catapult *UK* ['kætəpʊlt] ◇ *n* **-1.** [hand-held] atiradeira *f*, estilingue *m* **-2.** *HIST* [machine] catapulta *f*. ◇ *vt* **-1.** [hurl] catapultar **-2.** *fig* [promote] projetar.

cataract ['kætərækt] *n* catarata *f*.

catarrh [kə'tɑ:ʳ] *n* (*U*) catarro *m*.

catastrophe [kə'tæstrəfɪ] *n* catástrofe *f*.

catastrophic [ˌkætə'strɒfɪk] *adj* catastrófico(ca).

catatonic *adj* catatônico(ca).

cat burglar *n UK* *gatuno que entra e sai pela janela ou telhado*.

catcall ['kætkɔ:l] *n* vaia *f*.

catch [kætʃ] (*pt* & *pp* **caught**) ◇ *vt* **-1.** [gen] pegar **-2.** [ball etc] apanhar **-3.** [discover, surprise] flagrar; **to ~ sb doing sthg** flagrar alguém fazendo algo; **to ~ sb unawares** pegar alguém desprevenido(-da) **-4.** [hear clearly] compreender **-5.** [interest, imagination, attention] despertar **-6.** [sight]: **to ~ sight of sb/sthg, to ~ a glimpse of sb/sthg** conseguir avistar alguém/algo **-7.** [on hook, in door, in trap] prender **-8.** [strike] atingir. ◇ *vi* **-1.** [become hooked, get stuck] ficar preso(sa) em **-2.** [start to burn] pegar. ◇ *n* **-1.** [of ball etc] pegada *f* **-2.** [thing or amount caught] pesca *f* **-3.** [fastener] trinco *m* **-4.** [snag] armadilha *f*.

◆ **catch at** *vt fus* tentar agarrar.

◆ **catch on** *vi* **-1.** [become popular] pegar **-2.** *inf* [understand] entender; **to ~ on to sthg** dar-se conta de algo.

◆ **catch out** *vt sep* [trick] apanhar em erro.

◆ **catch up** ◇ *vt sep* **-1.** [come level with] alcançar **-2.** [involve]: **to get caught up in sthg** ser envolvido(da) em algo. ◇ *vi* alcançar; **to ~ up on sthg** por algo em dia.

◆ **catch up with** *vt fus* **-1.** [get to same point as] alcançar **-2.** [catch, find] pegar.

catch-22 *n* (*U*): **it's a ~ situation** é um beco sem saída.

catch-all *adj* que engloba tudo.

catching ['kætʃɪŋ] *adj* [infectious] contagioso(sa).

catchment area ['kætʃmənt-] *n* *região atendida por uma escola ou um hospital*.

catchphrase ['kætʃfreɪz] *n* [of entertainer] bordão *m*.

catchword ['kætʃwɜ:d] *n* [slogan] slogan *m*.

catchy ['kætʃɪ] (*compar* **-ier**, *superl* **-iest**) *adj* que pega com facilidade.

catechism ['kætəkɪzm] *n* catecismo *m*.

categorical [ˌkætɪ'gɒrɪkl] *adj* categórico(ca).

categorically [ˌkætɪ'gɒrɪklɪ] *adv* categoricamente.

categorize, -ise ['kætəgəraɪz] *vt* [classify]: **to ~ sb (as sthg)** classificar alguém (como algo).

category ['kætəgərɪ] (*pl* **-ies**) *n* categoria *f*.

cater ['keɪtəʳ] *vi* [provide food] fornecer comida.

◆ **cater for** *vt fus UK* **-1.** [provide for] satisfazer; **the magazine ~s for independent working women** a revista se destina a mulheres autônomas **-2.** [anticipate] contar com.

◆ **cater to** *vt fus* servir de instrumento a.

caterer ['keɪtərəʳ] *n* (serviço *m* de) bufê *m*.

catering ['keɪtərɪŋ] *n* bufê *m*; **a ~ college** uma escola de culinária.

caterpillar ['kætəpɪləʳ] *n* [insect] lagarta *f*.

catfish (*pl inv* OR **-es**) *n* peixe-gato *m*.

cat flap *n UK* portinhola *f* para gatos.

catgut *n* (*U*) categute *m*.

catharsis [kə'θɑ:sɪs] (*pl* **catharses** [kə'θɑ:si:z]) *n* *fml* [relief of tension] catarse *f*.

cathedral [kə'θi:drəl] *n* catedral *f*.

catheter ['kæθɪtəʳ] *n* catéter *m*.

cathode ray tube ['kæθəʊd-] *n* tubo *m* de raios catódicos.

Catholic ['kæθlɪk] ◇ *adj* católico(ca). ◇ *n* católico *m*, -ca *f*.

◆ **catholic** *adj* [broad] eclético(ca).

Catholicism [kə'θɒlɪsɪzm] *n* (*U*) catolicismo *m*.

catkin ['kætkɪn] *n* amento *m*.

cat litter *n* granulado *m* higiênico (para gatos).

Catseyes® ['kætsaɪz] *npl UK* olhos-de-gato *mpl*.

catsuit ['kætsu:t] *n UK* colante *m* feminino *(de corpo inteiro)*.

catsup ['kætsəp] *n US* ketchup *m*.

cattle ['kætl] *npl* gado *m*.

cattle grid *n UK* mata-burro *m*.

catty ['kætɪ] (*compar* **-ier**, *superl* **-iest**) *adj inf pej* [spiteful] rancoroso(sa).

catwalk ['kætwɔ:k] *n* passarela *f*.

Caucasian [kɔ:'keɪzjən] ◇ *adj* caucásio(sia). ◇ *n* **-1.** *GEOGR* caucásio *m*, -sia *f* **-2.** [white person] pessoa *f* de raça branca.

Caucasus ['kɔ:kəsəs] *n*: the ~ o Cáucaso.
caucus ['kɔ:kəs] *n* POL **-1.** *US* [meeting] cáucus *m* **-2.** [interest group] ala *f*.
caught [kɔ:t] *pt & pp* ⊳ **catch**.
cauldron *n* caldeirão *m*.
cauliflower ['kɒlɪˌflaʊə^r] *n* couve-flor *f*.
causal ['kɔ:zl] *adj* causal.
cause [kɔ:z] ◇ *n* **-1.** [gen] causa *f* **-2.** [grounds] razão *f*; **to have ~ for sthg** ter razão para algo; **to have ~ to do sthg** ter razão para fazer algo ◇ *vt* causar; **to ~ sb to do sthg** fazer com que alguém faça algo; **to ~ sthg to be done** fazer com que algo seja feito.
causeway ['kɔ:zweɪ] *n* caminho *m* elevado *(sobre a água)*.
caustic ['kɔ:stɪk] *adj* **-1.** CHEM cáustico(ca) **-2.** *fig* [comment] mordaz.
caustic soda *n* soda *f* cáustica.
cauterize, -ise ['kɔ:təraɪz] *vt* cauterizar.
caution ['kɔ:ʃn] ◇ *n* **-1.** *(U)* [care] cuidado *m*; **to do sthg with ~** fazer algo com cautela **-2.** [warning] aviso *m* **-3.** *UK* JUR injunção *f*. ◇ *vt* **-1.** [warn]: **to ~ sb against doing sthg** prevenir alguém para não fazer algo **-2.** *UK* JUR advertir; **to ~ sb for sthg** advertir alguém por algo.
cautionary ['kɔ:ʃənərɪ] *adj* preventivo(va).
cautious ['kɔ:ʃəs] *adj* cauteloso(sa).
cautiously ['kɔ:ʃəslɪ] *adv* com cautela.
cautiousness ['kɔ:ʃəsnɪs] *n (U)* cautela *f*.
cavalier [ˌkævə'lɪə^r] *adj* [offhand] arrogante.
cavalry ['kævlrɪ] *n (U)* **-1.** [on horseback] cavalaria *f* **-2.** [in armoured vehicles] cavalaria *f*.
cave [keɪv] *n* gruta *f*, caverna *f*.
◆ **cave in** *vi* **-1.** [physically collapse] desabar **-2.** [yield, stop arguing]: **to ~ in (to sthg)** ceder (a algo).
caveman ['keɪvmæn] (*pl* **-men** [-men]) *n* troglodita *mf*.
cavern ['kævən] *n* caverna *f*.
cavernous ['kævənəs] *adj* imenso(sa).
caviar(e) ['kævɪɑ:^r] *n (U)* caviar *m*.
caving ['keɪvɪŋ] *n (U) UK* espeleologia *f*; **to go ~** ir explorar cavernas.
cavity ['kævətɪ] (*pl* **-ies**) *n* **-1.** [in object, structure, body] cavidade *f*; **buccal ~** cavidade bucal; **nasal ~** fossas *fpl* nasais **-2.** [in tooth] cárie *f*.
cavort [kə'vɔ:t] *vi* saracotear.
cayenne (pepper) [keɪ'en-] *n (U)* pimenta-de--caiena *f*.
CB *n* **-1.** (*abbr of* **Citizens' Band**) CB, faixa *f* do cidadão. **-2.** (*abbr of* **Companion of (the Order of) the Bath**) *(titular de) distinção britânica de honra*.
CBC (*abbr of* **Canadian Broadcasting Corporation**) *n rede canadense de rádio e televisão*.
CBE (*abbr of* **Companion of (the Order of) the British Empire**) *n (beneficiário de) distinção britânica de honra*.
CBI (*abbr of* **Confederation of British Industry**) *n confederação britânica de empresários*, ≃ CNI *f*.
CBS (*abbr of* **Columbia Broadcasting System**) *n rede norte-americana de rádio e televisão*, CBS *f*.
cc ◇ *n* (*abbr of* **cubic centimetre**) *cm*. ◇ (*abbr of* **carbon copy**) cópia *f* carbono.
CC (*abbr of* **County Council**) *n* **-1.** *autoridade de estados administrativos britânicos*. **-2.** (*abbr of* **City Council**) *corpo administrativo de cidade britânica*.
CCTV (*abbr of* **closed-circuit television**) *n* CFT *m*.
CD ◇ *n* (*abbr of* **compact disc**) CD *m*. ◇ (*abbr of* **Corps Diplomatique**) corpo *m* diplomático.
CD-I (*abbr of* **compact disc (interactive)**) *n* CD-I *m*.
CD player *n* tocador *m* de CD.
Cdr. (*abbr of* **commander**) *n* com.
CD-R (*abbr of* **compact disc (rewritable)**) *n* CD-R *m*.
CD-R drive *n* unidade *f* de CD-R.
CD rewriter ['si:di:'i:ˌraɪtəl] = **CD-RW drive**.
CD-ROM (*abbr of* **compact disc read-only memory**) *n* CD-ROM *m*.
CD-RW (*abbr of* **compact disc rewritable**) *n* CD-RW *m*.
CD-RW drive *n* gravador *m* de CD.
CDT (*abbr of* **Central Daylight Time**) ◇ *n horário de verão na região central dos Estados Unidos*. ◇ (*abbr of* **craft, design and technology**) *disciplina de artes, desenho e tecnologia ensinada em escolas britânicas*.
CD tower *n* torre *f* para CDs.
CDV (*abbr of* **compact disc video**) *n* CDV *m*.
CE (*abbr of* **Church of England**) igreja anglicana.
cease [si:s] *fml* ◇ *vt* cessar; **to ~ doing** OR **to do sthg** parar de fazer algo; **~ fire!** cessar fogo! ◇ *vi* parar.
ceasefire *n* cessar-fogo *m*.
ceaseless ['si:slɪs] *adj fml* incessante.
ceaselessly ['si:slɪslɪ] *adv fml* incessantemente.
cedar *n* cedro *m*.
cede [si:d] *vt* [yield] ceder; **to ~ sthg to sb** ceder algo a alguém.
cedilla *n* cedilha *f*.
CEEB (*abbr of* **College Entry Examination Board**) *n organismo responsável pelo acesso ao ensino superior nos Estados Unidos*.
Ceefax® ['si:fæks] *n UK serviço de teletexto da BBC*.
ceilidh ['keɪlɪ] *n festa realizada na Escócia e na Irlanda na qual as pessoas cantam e dançam músicas regionais e contam histórias*.
ceiling ['si:lɪŋ] *n* **-1.** [of room] teto *m* **-2.** *fig* [limit] teto *m* máximo.
celebrate ['selɪbreɪt] ◇ *vt* celebrar. ◇ *vi* comemorar.
celebrated ['selɪbreɪtɪd] *adj* célebre, famoso(sa).
celebration [ˌselɪ'breɪʃn] *n* **-1.** *(U)* [activity, feeling] celebração *f* **-2.** [event] comemoração *f*.
celebrity [sɪ'lebrətɪ] (*pl* **-ies**) *n* [star] celebridade *f*.
celeriac [sɪ'lerɪæk] *n* aipo-rábano *m*.
celery ['selərɪ] *n (U)* aipo *m*.
celestial [sɪ'lestjəl] *adj* celestial.
celibacy ['selɪbəsɪ] *n (U)* celibato *m*.
celibate ['selɪbət] *adj* celibatário(ria).
cell [sel] *n* **-1.** BIOL & COMPUT célula *f* **-2.** [small room] cela *f* **-3.** [secret group] unidade *f*.
cellar ['selə^r] *n* **-1.** [basement] porão *m* **-2.** [stock of wine] adega *f*.
cellist ['tʃelɪst] *n* violoncelista *mf*.
cello ['tʃeləʊ] (*pl* **-s**) *n* [instrument] violoncelo *m*.

Cellophane® ['seləfeɪn] *n (U)* celofane *m*.
cellphone ['selfəʊn], **cellular phone** ['səljʊləʳ-] *n* (telefone *m*) celular *m*.
cellulite ['seljʊlaɪt] *n* celulite *f*.
celluloid *n (U)* [plastic] celulóide *m*.
cellulose ['seljʊləʊs] *n (U)* celulose *f*.
Celsius ['selsɪəs] *adj* Célsius.
Celt [kelt] *n* celta *mf*.
Celtic ['keltɪk] ◇ *adj* celta. ◇ *n* [language] celta *m*.
cement [sɪ'ment] ◇ *n (U)* **-1.** [for concrete] cimento *m*, argamassa *f* **-2.** [glue] cola *f*. ◇ *vt* **-1.** [cover with cement] cimentar **-2.** [glue] colar **-3.** *fig* [reinforce] fortalecer.
cement mixer *n* betoneira *f*.
cemetery ['semɪtrɪ] (*pl* **-ies**) *n* cemitério *m*.
cenotaph ['senətɑ:f] *n* cenotáfio *m*.
censor ['sensəʳ] ◇ *n* [of films, books, letters] censor *m*, -ra *f*. ◇ *vt* [film, book, letter] censurar.
censorship ['sensəʃɪp] *n (U)* censura *f*.
censure ['senʃəʳ] ◇ *n (U)* repreensão *f*. ◇ *vt* repreender.
census ['sensəs] (*pl* **censuses**) *n* [population survey] censo *m*.
cent [sent] *n* centavo *m*.
centenary *UK* [sen'ti:nərɪ] (*pl* **-ies**), **centennial** *US* [sen'tenjəl] *n* centenário *m*.
center *n*, *adj* & *vt US* = **centre**.
centigrade ['sentɪgreɪd] *adj* centígrado(da).
centigram(me) ['sentɪgræm] *n* centigrama *m*.
centilitre *UK*, **centiliter** *US* ['sentɪˌli:təʳ] *n* centilitro *m*.
centimetre *UK*, **centimeter** *US* ['sentɪˌmi:təʳ] *n* centímetro *m*.
centipede ['sentɪpi:d] *n* centopéia *f*.
central ['sentrəl] *adj* central; ~ **to sthg** [crucial] essencial para algo.
Central African ◇ *adj* centro-africano(na). ◇ *n* centro-africano *m*, -na *f*.
Central African Republic *n*: **the** ~ a República Centro-Africana; **in the** ~ na República Centro-Africana.
Central America *n* América Central.
Central American ◇ *adj* centro-americano(-na). ◇ *n* centro-americano *m*, -na *f*.
Central Asia *n* Ásia Central.
Central Europe *n* Europa Central.
central government *n (U)* governo *m* central.
central heating *n (U)* aquecimento *m* central.
centralization [ˌsentrəlaɪ'zeɪʃn] *n (U)* centralização *f*.
centralize, -ise ['sentrəlaɪz] *vt* centralizar.
centralized ['sentrəlaɪzd] *adj* centralizado(da).
central locking [-'lɒkɪŋ] *n* travamento *f* central (das portas).
centrally ['sentrəlɪ] *adv* no centro.
centrally heated *adj* com aquecimento central.
central nervous system *n* sistema *f* nervoso central.
central processing unit *n* COMPUT unidade *f* central de processamento.
central reservation *n UK* canteiro *m* central.
centre *UK*, **center** *US* ['sentəʳ] ◇ *n* **-1.** [gen] centro *m*; **health/leisure** ~ centro de saúde/lazer; ~ **of attention** centro das atenções; ~ **of gravity** centro de gravidade; **the** ~ POL o centro **-2.** SPORT [player] pivô. ◇ *adj* **-1.** [middle] central, do meio **-2.** POL de centro. ◇ *vt* [place centrally] centralizar.
◆ **centre around, centre on** *vt fus* centrar em.
centre back *n* SPORT centromédio *m*.
centrefold *n* página *f* central.
centre forward *n* SPORT centroavante *m*.
centre half *n* = **centre back**.
centrepiece *UK*, **centerpiece** *US* ['sentəpi:s] *n* **-1.** [decoration] centro *m* de mesa **-2.** [principal element] peça-chave *f*.
centre spread *n* = **centrefold**.
centrifugal force [sentrɪ'fju:gl-] *n* força *f* centrífuga.
century ['sentʃʊrɪ] (*pl* **-ies**) *n* **-1.** [one hundred years] século *m* **-2.** CRICKET: **to score a** ~ marcar cem pontos.
CEO (*abbr of* **chief executive officer**) *n* executivo *m*, -va *f* -chefe.
ceramic [sɪ'ræmɪk] *adj* de cerâmica, cerâmico(ca).
◆ **ceramics** *n* [craft, objects] cerâmica *f*.
cereal ['sɪərɪəl] *n* [crop, breakfast food] cereal *m*.
cerebral ['serɪbrəl] *adj* cerebral.
cerebral palsy *n (U)* MED paralisia *f* cerebral.
ceremonial [ˌserɪ'məʊnjəl] ◇ *adj* cerimonial, de cerimônia. ◇ *n* **-1.** [event] cerimônia *f* OR *m* **-2.** [pomp, formality] cerimonial *m*.
ceremonious [ˌserɪ'məʊnjəs] *adj* cerimonioso(sa).
ceremony ['serɪmənɪ] (*pl* **-ies**) *n* **-1.** [event] cerimônia *f*; **degree** ~ cerimônia *f* de colação de grau **-2.** *(U)* [pomp, formality] formalidade *f*; **without** ~ sem cerimônia; **to stand on** ~ fazer cerimônia.
cert [sɜ:t] *n UK inf* [certainty] barbada *f*.
cert. (*abbr of* **certificate**) certificado *m*.
certain ['sɜ:tn] *adj* **-1.** [gen] certo(ta); **she is** ~ **to be late** ela certamente vai se atrasar; **to be** ~ **of sthg/of doing sthg** ter a certeza de algo/fazer algo; **to make** ~ **of sthg/of doing sthg** assegurar-se de algo/fazer algo; **for** ~ com certeza; **to a** ~ **extent** até certo ponto **-2.** [named person]: **a** ~ **...** um certo ... (uma certa ...).
certainly ['sɜ:tnlɪ] *adv* com certeza; **do you agree? - I** ~ **do** com certeza (que sim); ~ **not!** de modo algum.
certainty ['sɜ:tntɪ] (*pl* **-ies**) *n (U)* certeza *f*.
CertEd (*abbr of* **Certificate in Education**) *n diploma universitário em educação*.
certifiable [ˌsɜ:tɪ'faɪəbl] *adj* [insane] demente.
certificate [sə'tɪfɪkət] *n* **-1.** [gen] certificado *m* **-2.** [of birth, marriage] certidão *f*; **death** ~ atestado *m* de óbito.
certification [ˌsɜ:tɪfɪ'keɪʃn] *n* certificação *f*.
certified ['sɜ:tɪfaɪd] *adj* **-1.** [professional person] habilitado(da) **-2.** [document] autenticado(da).
certified mail *n US* postagem *f* registrada.
certified public accountant *n US* perito-contador *m*, -ra *f*.
certify ['sɜ:tɪfaɪ] (*pt* & *pp* **-ied**) *vt* **-1.** [declare true]: **to** ~ **that** certificar OR atestar que **-2.** [give certificate

of qualification to]: **to be certified as** receber certificado de **-3.** [declare insane]: **to be certified** ser declarado(da) incapacitado(da).

cervical [sə'vaɪkl] *adj* cervical; ~ **cancer** câncer *m* de colo de útero.

cervical smear *n* exame *f* de lâmina.

cervix ['sɜ:vɪks] (*pl* **-ices** [-ɪsi:z]) *n* colo *m* do útero.

cesarean (section) *n US* = **caesarean (section)**.

cessation [se'seɪʃn] *n fml* [stopping] suspensão *f*.

cesspit ['sespɪt], **cesspool** ['sespu:l] *n* fossa *f*.

CET (*abbr of* **Central European Time**) *n* horário da Europa Central.

cf. (*abbr of* **confer**) cf., cfr.

CFC (*abbr of* **chlorofluorocarbon**) *n* CFC *m*.

cg (*abbr of* **centigram**) cg.

CGT (*abbr of* **capital gains tax**) *n imposto sobre ganhos de capital.*

ch (*abbr of* **central heating**) aquecimento *m* central.

ch. (*abbr of* **chapter**) cap.

CH (*abbr of* **Companion of Honour**) *n (beneficiário de) distinção de honra britânica.*

Chad [tʃæd] *n* Chade.

chafe [tʃeɪf] ◇ *vt* [rub] roçar. ◇ *vi* **-1.** [be sore] esfolar **-2.** *fig* [be annoyed]: **to** ~ **at sthg** irritar-se com algo.

chaff [tʃɑ:f] *n* [husks] palhiço *m*.

chaffinch ['tʃæfɪntʃ] *n* tentilhão *m*.

chain [tʃeɪn] ◇ *n* **-1.** [metal] corrente *f*; ~ **of office** *condecoração usada por oficiais em cerimônias* **-2.** [of islands] série *f*; ~ **of events** rede *f* de acontecimentos **-3.** [of mountains] cadeia *f* **-4.** [of shops, hotels] cadeia *f*, rede *f*. ◇ *vt* **-1.** [prisoner, bicycle] acorrentar **-2.** [hands] algemar **-3.** [dog] amarrar.

chain letter *n* carta *f* de corrente.

chain reaction *n* reação *f* em cadeia.

chainsaw *n* serra *f* articulada.

chain-smoke *vi* fumar um cigarro atrás do outro.

chain-smoker *n* fumante *mf* inveterado, -da.

chain store *n* filial *f*.

chair [tʃeəʳ] ◇ *n* **-1.** [for sitting in] cadeira *f* **-2.** [university post] cátedra *f* **-3.** [of meeting, organization - position] presidência *f*; **to take the** ~ presidir; [- person] presidente *mf*. ◇ *vt* [meeting, discussion] presidir.

chairlift *n* teleférico *m*.

chairman ['tʃeəmən] (*pl* **-men** [-mən]) *n* presidente *m*.

chairmanship ['tʃeəmənʃɪp] *n* presidência *f*.

chairperson ['tʃeə,pɜ:sn] (*pl* **-s**) *n* presidente *mf*.

chairwoman ['tʃeə,wʊmən] (*pl* **-women** [,wɪmɪn]) *n* presidenta *f*.

chaise longue [ʃeɪz'lɒŋ] (*pl* **chaises longues** [ʃeɪz'lɒŋ]) *n* espreguiçadeira *f*.

chalet ['ʃæleɪ] *n* chalé *f*.

chalice ['tʃælɪs] *n* cálice *m*.

chalk [tʃɔ:k] *n* **-1.** *(U)* [mineral] greda *f* **-2.** [for drawing] giz *m*.

◆ **by a long chalk** *adv* de longe.

◆ **not by a long chalk** *adv* nem de longe.

◆ **chalk up** *vt sep* [attain] obter.

chalkboard ['tʃɔ:kbɔ:d] *n UK* quadro-negro *m*.

challenge ['tʃælɪndʒ] ◇ *n* desafio *m*. ◇ *vt* **-1.** [to fight, competition]: **to** ~ **sb (to sthg)** desafiar alguém (para algo); **to** ~ **sb to do sthg** desafiar alguém a fazer algo **-2.** [question] questionar.

challenger ['tʃælɪndʒəʳ] *n* competidor *m*, -ra *f*.

challenging ['tʃælɪndʒɪŋ] *adj* **-1.** [difficult] desafiador(ra) **-2.** [aggressive] provocador(ra).

chamber ['tʃeɪmbəʳ] *n* **-1.** [room] gabinete *m*; **the council** ~ o gabinete do conselho **-2.** [body] câmara *f* **-3.** [of gun] tambor *m*.

◆ **chambers** *npl* [of barrister] sala *f* de audiências.

chambermaid ['tʃeɪmbəmeɪd] *n* camareira *f*.

chamber music *n (U)* música *f* de câmara.

chamber of commerce *n* câmara *f* de comércio.

chamber orchestra *n* orquestra *f* de câmara.

chameleon [kə'mi:ljən] *n* [animal] camaleão *m*, -oa *f*.

chamois¹ ['ʃæmɪ] (*pl inv*) *n* [animal] cabra *f* montês.

chamois² ['ʃæmɪ] *n*: ~ **(leather)** camurça *f*.

champ [tʃæmp] ◇ *n inf* [champion] campeão *m*, -ã *f*. ◇ *vi* [horse] mascar.

champagne [,ʃæm'peɪn] *n (U)* champanha *m*.

champion ['tʃæmpjən] *n* **-1.** [of competition] campeão *f*, -ã **-2.** [of cause] defensor *m*, -ra *f*.

championship ['tʃæmpjənʃɪp] *n* campeonato *m*.

chance [tʃɑ:ns] ◇ *n* **-1.** *(U)* [luck] acaso *m*, sorte *f*; **by** ~ por acaso; **by any** ~ por acaso **-2.** [likelihood, opportunity] chance *f*; **not to stand a** ~ **(of doing sthg)** não ter a menor chance (de fazer algo); **on the off-**~ **(that)** na esperança de que **-3.** [risk] risco *m*; **to take a** ~ **(on sthg/on doing sthg)** arriscar-se (em algo/a fazer algo). ◇ *adj* acidental. ◇ *vt* **-1.** [risk] arriscar **-2.** [happen]: **to** ~ **to do sthg** acontecer algo por acaso.

chancellor ['tʃɑ:nsələʳ] *n* **-1.** [chief minister] chanceler *m* **-2.** UNIV reitor *m*, -ra *f*.

Chancellor of the Exchequer *n UK* ≃ Ministro *m*, -tra *f* da Fazenda.

chancy ['tʃɑ:nsɪ] (*compar* **-ier**, *superl* **-iest**) *adj inf* [risky] arriscado(da).

chandelier [,ʃændə'lɪəʳ] *n* lustre *m*.

change [tʃeɪndʒ] ◇ *n* **-1.** [alteration, difference] mudança *f*, alteração *f*; ~ **in sb/sthg** mudança em alguém/algo **-2.** [contrast, for variety] diferença *f*; **to make a** ~ fazer diferença; **Peter arriving on time? That makes a** ~**!** Peter chegando na hora? Que mudança!; **for a** ~ para variar **-3.** [switch, replacement] mudança *f*; ~ **of clothes** muda *f* de roupa **-4.** *(U)* [money returned after payment, smaller units of money] troco *m* **-5.** *(U)* [coins] trocado *m*. ◇ *vt* **-1.** [gen] mudar; **to** ~ **sthg into sthg** transformar algo em algo; **to** ~ **one's mind** mudar de idéia; **to get** ~**d** mudar de roupa; **to** ~ **hands** COMM mudar de dono **-2.** [replace, exchange] trocar. ◇ *vi* **-1.** [gen] mudar; **to** ~ **into sthg** transformar-se em algo **-2.** [put on different clothes] trocar-se; **to** ~ **into sthg** trocar algo **-3.** [move to different train, bus] fazer conexão.

◆ **change over** *vi* [convert] trocar para; **to** ~ **over to sthg** trocar para algo.

◆ **change round** *vt sep* trocar.

changeable ['tʃeɪndʒəbl] *adj* **-1.** [mood] inconstante **-2.** [weather] instável.
changed [tʃeɪndʒd] *adj* [person] mudado(da); **to be a ~ person** ser uma outra pessoa.
change machine *n* máquina *f* de troco.
change of life *n*: **the ~** a menopausa.
changeover ['tʃeɪndʒ,əʊvəʳ] *n*: **~ (to sthg)** mudança *f* (para algo).
change purse *n US* porta-níqueis *m inv*, niqueleira *f*.
changing ['tʃeɪndʒɪŋ] *adj* variável, instável.
changing room *n* vestiário *m*.
channel ['tʃænl] (*UK pt* & *pp* **-led**, *cont* **-ling**, *US pt* & *pp* **-ed**, *cont* **-ing**) ◇ *n* canal *m*. ◇ *vt* canalizar.
◆ **Channel** *n*: **the (English) Channel** o Canal da Mancha.
◆ **channels** *npl*: **to go through the proper ~s** seguir os trâmites legais.
channel-hopping *n TV* troca *f* rápida de canal, zapping *m*.
Channel Islands *npl*: **the ~** as Ilhas Normandas.
Channel Tunnel *n*: **the ~** o Túnel do Canal da Mancha.
chant [tʃɑːnt] ◇ *n* **-1.** *RELIG* [song] canto *m* **-2.** [repeated words] coro *m*. ◇ *vt* **-1.** *RELIG* cantar, entoar **-2.** [words] entoar. ◇ *vi* **-1.** *RELIG* [sing] cantar **-2.** [repeat words] entoar.
chaos ['keɪɒs] *n* caos *m*.
chaotic [keɪ'ɒtɪk] *adj* caótico(ca).
chap [tʃæp] *n UK inf* [man] cara *m*, chapa *m*.
chapat(t)i [tʃə'pætɪ] *n pão indiano feito de farinha, água e sal, de formato arrendondado.*
chapel ['tʃæpl] *n* capela *f*.
chaperon(e) ['ʃæpərəʊn] ◇ *n* acompanhante *mf*. ◇ *vt* acompanhar.
chaplain ['tʃæplɪn] *n* capelão *m*.
chapped [tʃæpt] *adj* rachado(da).
chapter ['tʃæptəʳ] *n* **-1.** capítulo *m* **-2.** *phr*: **to give sb ~ and verse on sthg** falar tudo a alguém sobre algo.
char [tʃɑːʳ] (*pt* & *pp* **-red**, *cont* **-ring**) ◇ *vt* [burn] carbonizar, torrar. ◇ *vi* [work as cleaner] trabalhar como diarista.
character ['kærəktəʳ] *n* **-1.** [nature - of place] jeito *m*; [- of person] caráter *m*; **out of ~** atípico; **in ~** típico **-2.** *(U)* [unusual quality, style] estilo *m* **-3.** [in film, book, play] personagem *mf* **-4.** *inf* [unusual person] tipo *m* **-5.** [letter, symbol] caractere *m*.
character code *n COMPUT* código *m* de caracteres.
characteristic [,kærəktə'rɪstɪk] ◇ *adj* [typical] característico(ca). ◇ *n* [attribute] característica *f*.
characteristically [,kærəktə'rɪstɪklɪ] *adv* [typically] caracteristicamente.
characterization [,kærəktəraɪ'zeɪʃn] *n* caracterização *f*.
characterize, -ise ['kærəktəraɪz] *vt* **-1.** [typify] caracterizar **-2.** [portray]: **to ~ sthg as** caracterizar algo como.
charade [ʃə'rɑːd] *n* charada *f*.
◆ **charades** *n (U)* mímica *f*.
charcoal ['tʃɑːkəʊl] *n* carvão *m (vegetal)*.
charge [tʃɑːdʒ] ◇ *n* **-1.** [cost] preço *m*; **admission ~** entrada *f*; **telephone ~s** tarifas *fpl* telefônicas; **delivery ~** taxa *f* de entrega; **free of ~** grátis **-2.** [command, control] responsabilidade *f*; **to have ~ of sthg** estar no comando de algo; **to take ~ (of sthg)** tomar conta (de algo); **in ~** encarregado(-da); **in ~ of** no comando de **-3.** *JUR* acusação *f* **-4.** *ELEC* & *MIL* carga *f*. ◇ *vt* **-1.** [sum of money] cobrar; **to ~ sthg to sb/sthg** debitar algo de alguém/algo **-2.** [suspect, criminal] acusar; **to ~ sb with sthg** acusar alguém de algo **-3.** [attack] investir contra **-4.** *ELEC* carregar. ◇ *vi* **-1.** [ask for payment]: **to ~ (for sthg)** cobrar (por algo) **-2.** [rush] correr **-3.** [attack] investir.
chargeable ['tʃɑːdʒəbl] *adj* **-1.** [costs]: **~ (to sb/sthg)** debitável (de alguém/algo) **-2.** [offence] imputável.
charge account *n* conta *f* aberta.
charge card *n cartão de crédito de um estabelecimento comercial.*
charged [tʃɑːdʒd] *adj* [tense] carregado(da).
chargé d'affaires [,ʃɑːzeɪdæ'feəl] (*pl* **chargés d'affaires** [,ʃɑːzeɪdæ'feəl]) *n* encarregado *m*, -da *f* de negócios.
charge hand *n UK* capataz *m*.
charge nurse *n UK* enfermeiro *m*, -ra *f* -chefe.
charger ['tʃɑːdʒəʳ] *n* **-1.** [for batteries] carregador *m* **-2.** *literary* [soldier's horse] cavalo *m* de batalha.
charge sheet *n UK* boletim *m* de ocorrência.
chariot ['tʃærɪət] *n* biga *f*.
charisma [kə'rɪzmə] *n* carisma *m*.
charismatic [,kærɪz'mætɪk] *adj* [charming] carismático(ca).
charitable ['tʃærətəbl] *adj* **-1.** [person, remark] generoso(sa) **-2.** [organization] de caridade, beneficente.
charity ['tʃærətɪ] (*pl* **-ies**) *n* **-1.** *(U)* [gifts, money] caridade *f* **-2.** [organization] instituição *f* de caridade **-3.** [kindness] simpatia *f*.
charity shop *n* loja *f* beneficente.
charlatan ['ʃɑːlətən] *n* charlatão *m*, -tona *f*.
charm [tʃɑːm] ◇ *n* **-1.** *(U)* [appeal, attractiveness] charme *m*, encanto *m* **-2.** [spell] feitiço *m* **-3.** [on bracelet] amuleto *m*. ◇ *vt* encantar.
charm bracelet *n* pulseira *f* com berloques.
charmer ['tʃɑːməʳ] *n* [charming person] sedutor *m*, -ra *f*.
charming ['tʃɑːmɪŋ] *adj* encantador(ra).
charmingly ['tʃɑːmɪŋlɪ] *adv* encantadoramente.
charred [tʃɑːd] *adj* carbonizado(da).
chart [tʃɑːt] ◇ *n* **-1.** [diagram] gráfico *m* **-2.** [map] mapa *m*, carta *f*; **a star/sea ~** uma carta celeste/marítima. ◇ *vt* **-1.** [plot, map] cartografar **-2.** *fig* [record] registrar.
◆ **charts** *npl*: **the ~s** as paradas de sucesso.
charter ['tʃɑːtəʳ] ◇ *n* [document] carta *f*. ◇ *vt* [plane, boat] fretar.
chartered accountant ['tʃɑːtəd-] *n UK* contador *m* diplomado, contadora *f* diplomada.
charter flight *n* vôo *m* fretado.
charter plane *n* avião *m* fretado.
chary ['tʃeərɪ] (*compar* **-ier**, *superl* **-iest**) *adj*: **to be ~ of doing sthg** ser cuidadoso(sa) ao fazer algo.
chase [tʃeɪs] ◇ *n* **-1.** [pursuit] perseguição *f*; **to give ~** dar perseguição **-2.** [hunt] caça *f*. ◇ *vt*

-1. [pursue] perseguir **-2.** [drive away] enxotar **-3.** [money, jobs] correr atrás de. ◇ *vi*: **to ~ after sb/sthg** correr atrás de alguém/algo.
◆ **chase up** *vt sep UK* [person, information] correr *OR* sair atrás de.

chaser ['tʃeɪsəʳ] *n* [drink] *bebida suave tomada após uma bebida alcoólica mais forte ou mais fraca.*

chasm ['kæzml *n* abismo *m.*

chassis ['ʃæsɪ] (*pl inv*) *n* [of vehicle] chassi *m.*

chaste [tʃeɪst] *adj* casto(ta).

chasten ['tʃeɪsn] *vt* disciplinar.

chastise [tʃæ'staɪz] *vt fml* [scold] repreender.

chastity ['tʃæstətɪ] *n* castidade *f.*

chat [tʃæt] (*pt & pp* **-ted**, *cont* **-ting**) ◇ *n* bate-papo *m*, conversa *f*; **to have a ~** bater papo. ◇ *vi* bater papo, conversar.
◆ **chat up** *vt sep UK inf* bater papo.

chatiquette ['tʃætɪket] *n COMPUT* etiqueta *f* no bate-papo, chatiqueta *f.*

chat room *n COMPUT* sala *f* de bate-papo.

chat show *n UK* programa *m* de entrevistas.

chatter ['tʃætəʳ] ◇ *n* **-1.** [of person] tagarelice *f* **-2.** [of animal, bird] chilro *m.* ◇ *vi* **-1.** [person] tagarelar **-2.** [animal, bird] chilrar **-3.** [teeth] bater.

chatterbox ['tʃætəbɒks] *n inf* tagarela *mf.*

chattering classes *npl UK*: **the ~** os pseudo-formadores de opinião.

chatty ['tʃætɪ] (*compar* **-ier**, *superl* **-iest**) *adj* **-1.** [person] tagarela **-2.** [letter] informal.

chauffeur ['ʃəʊfəʳ] ◇ *n* chofer *m.* ◇ *vt* trabalhar como chofer.

chauvinist ['ʃəʊvɪnɪst] *n* chauvinista *mf.*

chauvinistic [ˌʃəʊvɪ'nɪstɪk] *adj* chauvinista.

cheap [tʃi:p] ◇ *adj* **-1.** [gen] barato(ta) **-2.** [despicable, vulgar] de mau gosto. ◇ *adv* barato. ◇ *n*: **on the ~** por uma ninharia.

cheapen ['tʃi:pn] *vt* [degrade] rebaixar; **to ~ o.s.** rebaixar-se.

cheaply ['tʃi:plɪ] *adv* [at a low price] barato.

cheapness ['tʃi:pnɪs] *n* **-1.** [low cost] baixo preço *m* **-2.** [vulgarity] mau gosto *m.*

cheapskate ['tʃi:pskeɪt] *n inf pej* pão-duro *m.*

cheat [tʃi:t] ◇ *n* trapaceiro *m*, -ra *f.* ◇ *vt* trapacear; **to ~ sb out of sthg** passar alguém para trás em algo; **to feel ~ed** sentir-se passado(da) para trás. ◇ *vi* [be dishonest] trapacear.
◆ **cheat on** *vt fus inf* [be unfaithful to] trair.

cheating ['tʃi:tɪŋ] *n* **-1.** [at cards] blefe *m* **-2.** [in exam] cola *f.*

check [tʃek] ◇ *n* **-1.** [gen]: **~ (on sthg)** checagem *f* (de algo) **-2.** [restraint]: **~ (on sthg)** controle *m* (sobre algo); **in ~** sob controle **-3.** *US* [bill] conta *f* **-4.** [pattern] xadrez *m* **-5.** [in chess] xeque *m.* ◇ *vt* **-1.** [test, verify] verificar, conferir **-2.** [restrain, stop] conter. ◇ *vi* verificar; **to ~ for sthg** verificar se há algo, procurar por algo; **to ~ on sthg** examinar algo.
◆ **check in** ◇ *vt sep* [luggage, coat] despachar. ◇ *vi* **-1.** [at hotel] registrar-se **-2.** [at airport] fazer check-in.
◆ **check off** *vt sep* [names on a list] marcar.
◆ **check out** ◇ *vt sep* **-1.** [luggage, coat] dar baixa em **-2.** [investigate] averiguar. ◇ *vi* [from hotel] fechar a conta e sair.
◆ **check up** *vi* informar-se; **to ~ up on sb/sthg** informar-se sobre alguém/algo.

checkbook *n US* = **chequebook**.

checked [tʃekt] *adj* [patterned] quadriculado(da).

checkered *adj US* = **chequered**.

checkers ['tʃekəz] *n US* (jogo *m* de) damas *fpl.*

check guarantee card *n US* cartão *m* de garantia de cheque.

check-in *n* check-in *m.*

checking account ['tʃekɪŋ-] *n US* conta *f* corrente.

checklist ['tʃeklɪst] *n* lista *f* de verificação.

checkmate ['tʃekmeɪt] *n* [in chess] xeque-mate *m.*

checkout ['tʃekaʊt] *n* **-1.** [in supermarket] caixa *m* **-2.** [in hotel] saída *f*, checkout *m.*

checkpoint ['tʃekpɔɪnt] *n* [place] posto *m* de controle.

check-up *n* check-up *m.*

Cheddar (cheese) ['tʃedəʳ-] *n* queijo *m* Cheddar.

cheek [tʃi:k] ◇ *n* **-1.** [of face] bochecha *f* **-2.** [buttock] nádega *f* **-3.** *inf* [impudence] audácia *f.* ◇ *vt inf* atrever-se a.

cheekbone ['tʃi:kbəʊn] *n* osso *m* malar, maçã *f* do rosto.

cheekily ['tʃi:kɪlɪ] *adv* descaradamente.

cheekiness ['tʃi:kɪnɪs] *n* descaramento *m.*

cheeky ['tʃi:kɪ] (*compar* **-ier**, *superl* **-iest**) *adj* descarado(da).

cheep *vi* piar.

cheer [tʃɪəʳ] ◇ *n* [shout] vivas *fpl.* ◇ *vt* **-1.** [shout approval, encouragement at] ovacionar **-2.** [gladden] animar. ◇ *vi* aclamar, aplaudir.
◆ **cheers** *excl* **-1.** [said before drinking] saúde! **-2.** *UK inf* [goodbye] tchau! **-3.** *UK inf* [thank you] valeu!
◆ **cheer on** *vt sep* torcer por.
◆ **cheer up** ◇ *vt sep* animar. ◇ *vi* animar-se.

cheerful ['tʃɪəfʊl] *adj* alegre.

cheerfully ['tʃɪəfʊlɪ] *adv* **-1.** [happily] alegremente **-2.** [willingly] de boa vontade.

cheerfulness ['tʃɪəfʊlnɪs] *n* [happiness] alegria *f.*

cheering ['tʃɪərɪŋ] ◇ *adj* [gladdening] animado(-da). ◇ *n* animação *f.*

cheerio [ˌtʃɪərɪ'əʊ] *excl UK inf* tchau!

cheerleader ['tʃɪəˌli:dəʳ] *n* animador *m*, -ra *f* de torcida.

cheerless ['tʃɪəlɪs] *adj* triste.

cheery ['tʃɪərɪ] (*compar* **-ier**, *superl* **-iest**) *adj* cordial.

cheese [tʃi:z] *n* queijo *m.*

cheeseboard ['tʃi:zbɔ:d] *n* **-1.** [board] tábua *f* de queijos **-2.** [on menu] variedade *f* de queijos.

cheeseburger ['tʃi:zˌbɜ:gəʳ] *n* xisburguer *m.*

cheesecake ['tʃi:zkeɪk] *n CULIN* torta *f* de queijo.

cheesed off *adj inf* chateado(da).

cheesy ['tʃi:zɪ] (*compar* **-ier**, *superl* **-iest**) *adj* **-1.** [tasting of cheese] de queijo **-2.** [grin] de chulé **-3.** *inf* [cheap, unpleasant] cafona.

cheetah ['tʃi:tə] *n* guepardo *m.*

chef [ʃef] *n* cozinheiro *m*, -ra *f*-chefe.

chemical ['kemɪkl] ◇ *adj* químico(ca). ◇ *n* substância *f* química.

chemically ['kemɪklɪ] *adv* quimicamente.

chemical weapons *npl* armas *fpl* químicas.

chemist ['kemɪst] *n* **-1.** *UK* [pharmacist] farmacêutico *m*, -ca *f*; ~ **'s (shop)** farmácia *f* **-2.** [scientist] químico *m*, -ca *f*.

chemistry ['kemɪstrɪ] *n* química *f*.

chemotherapy [ˌki:məʊ'θerəpɪ] *n* quimioterapia *f*.

cheque *UK*, **check** *US* [tʃek] *n* cheque *m*; **to pay by** ~ pagar com cheque.

cheque account *n* [at bank, building society] conta *f* corrente.

chequebook *UK*, **checkbook** *US* ['tʃekbʊk] *n* talão *m* de cheques.

cheque (guarantee) card *n UK* cartão *m* de garantia de cheque.

chequered *UK* ['tʃekəd], **checkered** *US* ['tʃekerd] *adj* **-1.** [patterned] xadrez **-2.** *fig* [varied] cheio (cheia) de altos e baixos.

cherish ['tʃerɪʃ] *vt* [treasure - hope, memory] acalentar; [- privilege, right] apreciar; [- person, thing] acariciar.

cherished ['tʃerɪʃt] *adj* [dear] precioso(sa).

cherry ['tʃerɪ] (*pl* **-ies**) *n* **-1.** [fruit] cereja *f* **-2.**: ~ **(tree)** cerejeira *f*.

cherry-pick *vt adquirir as empresas mais lucrativas durante a privatização de um setor da economia.*

cherub ['tʃerəb] (*pl* **-s** *OR* **-im** [-ɪm]) *n* **-1.** [angel] querubim *m* **-2.** [child] anjinho *m*, -nha *f*.

chervil ['tʃɜ:vɪl] *n (U)* [herb] cerefólio *m*.

chess [tʃes] *n* xadrez *m*.

chessboard ['tʃesbɔ:d] *n* tabuleiro *m* de xadrez.

chessman ['tʃesmæn] (*pl* **-men** [-men]), **chess piece** *n* peça *f* do jogo de xadrez.

chest [tʃest] *n* **-1.** *ANAT* peito *m*; **to get sthg off one's** ~ *inf* desabafar **-2.** [box, trunk] caixa *f* **-3.** [coffer] baú *m*.

chestnut ['tʃesnʌt] ◇ *adj* [colour] castanho(nha). ◇ *n* **-1.** [nut] castanha *f* **-2.**: ~ **(tree)** castanheiro *m*.

chest of drawers (*pl* **chests of drawers**) *n* [piece of furniture] cômoda *f*.

chesty ['tʃestɪ] (*compar* **-ier**, *superl* **-iest**) *adj* [cough] com catarro.

chevron ['ʃevrən] *n* **-1.** [on road] placa *f* de sinalização **-2.** [on uniform] divisa *f*.

chew [tʃu:] ◇ *n* [biting] mastigação *f*. ◇ *vt* **-1.** [food] mastigar **-2.** [nails, carpet] roer.

◆ **chew over** *vt sep fig* [think over] ponderar, refletir sobre.

◆ **chew up** *vt sep* [food, slippers] roer.

chewing gum ['tʃu:ɪŋ-] *n* chiclete *m*.

chewy [tʃu:ɪ] (*compar* **-ier**, *superl* **-iest**) *adj* [food] duro(ra).

chic [ʃi:k] ◇ *adj* chique. ◇ *n* elegância *f*.

chicanery [ʃɪ'keɪnərɪ] *n* [trickery] tramóia *f*; [deception] ilusão *f*.

chick [tʃɪk] *n* **-1.** [baby bird] filhote *m* (*de pássaro*) **-2.** *inf* [woman] garota *f*.

chicken ['tʃɪkɪn] ◇ *adj inf* [cowardly] galinha. ◇ *n* **-1.** [bird] galinha *f*; **it's a** ~ **and egg situation** é a história do ovo e da galinha **-2.** *(U)* [food] frango *m* **-3.** *inf* [coward] galinha *m*.

◆ **chicken out** *vi inf*: **to** ~ **out (of sthg/of doing sthg)** acovardar-se (de algo/de fazer algo).

chicken feed *n fig* [small sum of money] ninharia *f*.

chickenpox ['tʃɪkɪnpɒks] *n* catapora *f*.

chicken wire *n* tela *f* de arame *(para galinheiros)*.

chickpea ['tʃɪkpi:] *n* grão-de-bico *m*.

chicory ['tʃɪkərɪ] *n* [vegetable] chicória *f*.

chide [tʃaɪd] (*pt* **chided** *OR* **chid** [tʃɪd], *pp* **chid** *OR* **chidden** ['tʃɪdnl]) *vt literary* repreender.

chief [tʃi:f] ◇ *adj* **-1.** [most important] principal **-2.** [head] chefe; ~ **accountant** contador *m*, -ra *f* chefe. ◇ *n* **-1.** [of organization] chefe *mf* **-2.** [of tribe] chefe *m*, cacique *m*.

chief constable *n UK* chefe *mf* de polícia.

chief executive *n* [head of company] presidente *mf* executivo, -va.

◆ **Chief Executive** *n US* [US president]: **the Chief Executive** o (a) Chefe de Governo.

chief justice *n Am* ≃ presidente *mf* do Supremo Tribunal.

chiefly ['tʃi:flɪ] *adv* [mainly] principalmente.

chief of staff *n* chefe *mf* do estado-maior.

chieftain ['tʃi:ftən] *n* líder *m*, chefe *m*.

chiffon ['ʃɪfɒn] *n* chiffon *m*.

chihuahua [tʃɪ'wɑ:wə] *n* chihuahua *m*.

chilblain ['tʃɪlbleɪn] *n* frieira *f*.

child [tʃaɪld] (*pl* **children**) *n* **-1.** [boy, girl] criança *f* **-2.** [son, daughter] filho *m*, -lha *f*.

childbearing ['tʃaɪldˌbeərɪŋ] *n (U)* parto *m*.

child benefit *n UK benefício pago pelo governo britânico a todas as famílias de acordo com o número de filhos.*

childbirth ['tʃaɪldbɜ:θ] *n (U)* parto *m*.

childcare ['tʃaɪldkeə^r] *n* assistência *f* à infância; **they share the** ~ eles dividem as responsabilidades relativas às crianças.

childhood ['tʃaɪldhʊd] *n* infância *f*.

childish ['tʃaɪldɪʃ] *adj pej* infantil.

childishly ['tʃaɪldɪʃlɪ] *adv pej* de modo infantil.

childless ['tʃaɪldlɪs] *adj* sem filhos.

childlike ['tʃaɪldlaɪk] *adj* ingênuo(nua).

childminder ['tʃaɪldˌmaɪndə^r] *n UK* babá *mf*.

child prodigy *n* criança *f* prodígio.

childproof ['tʃaɪldpru:f] *adj* seguro(ra) para crianças, à prova de crianças.

children ['tʃɪldrən] *pl* ▻ **child**.

Chile ['tʃɪlɪ] *n* Chile; **in** ~ no Chile.

Chilean ['tʃɪlɪən] ◇ *adj* chileno(na). ◇ *n* chileno *m*, -na *f*.

chili ['tʃɪlɪ] *n* = **chilli**.

chill [tʃɪl] ◇ *adj* glacial. ◇ *n* **-1.** [illness] resfriado *m* **-2.** [in temperature]: **a** ~ **in the air** uma friagem **-3.** [feeling of fear] calafrio *m*. ◇ *vt* **-1.** [drink, food] gelar **-2.** [person] arrepiar-se de. ◇ *vi* [drink, food] esfriar.

chilli ['tʃɪlɪ] (*pl* **-ies**) *n* [vegetable] pimenta-malagueta *f*.

chilling ['tʃɪlɪŋ] *adj* **-1.** [very cold] gelado(da) **-2.** [frightening] arrepiante.

chilli powder *n* pimenta *f* em pó.

chilly ['tʃɪlɪ] (*compar* **-ier**, *superl* **-iest**) *adj* frio(fria).

chime [tʃaɪm] ◇ *n* [of bell, clock] batida *f*. ◇ *vt* [time] bater. ◇ *vi* [bell, clock] tocar.

◆ **chime in** *vi* concordar.
chimney ['tʃɪmnɪ] *n* chaminé *f*.
chimneypot ['tʃɪmnɪpɒt] *n* cano *m* de chaminé.
chimneysweep ['tʃɪmnɪswi:p] *n* limpador *m*, -ra *f* de chaminé.
chimp [tʃɪmp] *inf*, **chimpanzee** [ˌtʃɪmpən'zi:] *n* chimpanzé *mf*.
chin [tʃɪn] *n* queixo *m*.
china ['tʃaɪnə] <> *n (U)* **-1.** [substance] porcelana *f* **-2.** [crockery] louças *fpl* de porcelana. <> *comp* de porcelana.
China ['tʃaɪnə] *n* China; **in ~** na China; **the People's Republic of ~** a República Popular da China.
china clay *n (U)* caulim *m*.
China Sea *n*: **the ~** o Mar da China.
Chinatown ['tʃaɪnətaʊn] *n* bairro *m* chinês.
chinchilla [tʃɪn'tʃɪlə] *n* chinchila *f*.
Chinese [ˌtʃaɪ'ni:z] <> *adj* chinês(esa). <> *n* [language] chinês *m*. <> *npl*: **the ~** os chineses.
Chinese cabbage *n* repolho *m* chinês.
Chinese lantern *n* [light] lanterna *f* chinesa.
Chinese leaf *n UK* = **Chinese cabbage**.
chink [tʃɪŋk] <> *n* **-1.** [narrow opening] fresta *f* **-2.** [sound] tinido *m*. <> *vi* tilintar.
chinos ['tʃi:nəʊz] *npl calça de algodão grosso.*
chintz [tʃɪnts] <> *n (U)* tecido *m* de algodão estampado, chita *f*. <> *comp* de algodão estampado, de chita.
chinwag ['tʃɪnwæg] *n inf*: **to have a ~** bater um papo.
chip [tʃɪp] (*pt* & *pp* **-ped**, *cont* **-ping**) <> *n* **-1.** *UK* [hot, fried potato strip] batata *f* frita em palito **-2.** *US* [snack] batata *f* frita de pacote **-3.** [fragment] lasca *f* **-4.** [flaw] defeito *m* **-5.** *COMPUT* chip *m* **-6.** [token] ficha *f*; **when the ~s are down** quando chega a hora da verdade **-7.** *SPORT* tacada *f* **-8.** *phr*: **to have a ~ on one's shoulder** ficar ressentido(da). <> *vt* [damage] lascar.
◆ **chip in** *inf* <> *vt fus* [contribute] contribuir com. <> *vi* **-1.** [contribute] fazer uma vaquinha **-2.** [interrupt] interromper.
◆ **chip off** *vt sep* lascar.
chipboard ['tʃɪpbɔ:d] *n (U)* compensado *m*.
chipmunk ['tʃɪpmʌŋk] *n* tâmia *m*.
chipped ['tʃɪpt] *adj* [flawed] lascado(da).
chippings ['tʃɪpɪŋz] *npl* cavacos *mpl*; **'loose ~'** 'cascalho solto'.
chip shop *n UK loja onde se compram peixe com batatas fritas.*
chiropodist [kɪ'rɒpədɪst] *n* quiropodista *mf*.
chiropody [kɪ'rɒpədɪ] *n (U)* quiropodia *f*.
chiropractor *n* quiroprático *m*, -ca *f*.
chirp [tʃɜ:p] *vi* chilrar, piar.
chirpy ['tʃɜ:pɪ] (*compar* **-ier**, *superl* **-iest**) *adj esp UK inf* [cheerful] animado(da).
chisel ['tʃɪzl] (*UK pt* & *pp* **-led**, *cont* **-ling**, *US pt* & *pp* **-ed**, *cont* **-ing**) <> *n* **-1.** [for wood] formão *m* **-2.** [for stone] cinzel *m*. <> *vt* **-1.** [wood] esculpir com formão **-2.** [stone] cinzelar.
chit [tʃɪt] *n* [note] vale *m*.
chit-chat *n (U) inf* bate-papo *m*.
chivalrous ['ʃɪvlrəs] *adj* cavalheiresco(ca).
chivalry ['ʃɪvlrɪ] *n* **-1.** *literary* [of knights] cavalaria *f* **-2.** [courtesy] cavalheirismo *m*.
chives [tʃaɪvz] *npl* cebolinha *f*.
chivy (*pt* & *pp* **-ied**), **chivvy** (*pt* & *pp* **-ied**) ['tʃɪvɪ] *vt inf*: **to ~ sb along** dar uma apressada em alguém.
chloride ['klɔ:raɪd] *n* cloreto *m*.
chlorinated ['klɔ:rɪneɪtɪd] *adj* clorado(da).
chlorine ['klɔ:ri:n] *n (U)* cloro *m*.
chlorofluorocarbon ['klɔ:rəʊˌflʊərəʊ'kɑ:bən] *n* clorofluorcarbono *m*.
chloroform ['klɒrəfɔ:m] *n (U)* clorofórmio *m*.
chlorophyll *n* clorofila *f*.
choc-ice ['tʃɒkaɪs] *n UK bola de sorvete com cobertura de chocolate.*
chock [tʃɒk] *n* calço *m (para roda de veículo).*
chock-a-block, chock-full *adj inf*: **~ (with)** [people] apinhado(da) (de); [things] entupido(da) (de).
chocolate ['tʃɒkələt] <> *n (U)* chocolate *m*; **plain/milk ~** chocolate amargo/ao leite; **a box of ~s** uma caixa de bombons. <> *comp* [biscuit, cake, mousse] de chocolate.
choice [tʃɔɪs] <> *n* **-1.** [gen] escolha *f*, opção *f*; **to have no ~ but to do sthg** não ter outra escolha a não fazer algo; **it was my first ~** foi a minha primeira opção; **to do sthg by ~** fazer algo por vontade própria **-2.** [variety, selection] variedade *f*. <> *adj* selecionado(da).
choir ['kwaɪə^r] *n* [singers] coro *m*.
choirboy ['kwaɪəbɔɪ] *n* menino *m* de coro.
choke [tʃəʊk] <> *n AUT* afogador *m*. <> *vt* **-1.** [subj: person] estrangular **-2.** [subj: smoke, fumes] asfixiar, sufocar **-3.** [block] entupir, obstruir. <> *vi* [on food, water] engasgar.
◆ **choke back** *vt fus* segurar, controlar.
choker *n* gargantilha *f*.
cholera ['kɒlərə] *n (U)* cólera *f*.
cholesterol [kə'lestərɒl] *n (U)* colesterol *m*.
choose [tʃu:z] (*pt* **chose**, *pp* **chosen**) <> *vt* **-1.** [select] escolher; **there's little** *OR* **not much to ~ between them** não há muito o que escolher entre eles (elas) **-2.** [opt]: **to ~ to do sthg** optar por fazer algo. <> *vi* [select]: **to ~ (from sthg)** escolher (entre algo).
choos(e)y ['tʃu:zɪ] (*compar* **-ier**, *superl* **-iest**) *adj* exigente.
chop [tʃɒp] (*pt* & *pp* **-ped**, *cont* **-ping**) <> *n* **-1.** [meat] costeleta *f* **-2.** [blow] pancada *f*; **to be for the ~** [person] estar para ser demitido(da); [project] estar para ser cancelado(da). <> *vt* **-1.** [wood] retalhar **-2.** [vegetables, apple] picar **-3.** *inf* [funding, budget] cortar **-4.** *phr*: **to ~ and change** ser inconstante.
◆ **chop down** *vt sep* derrubar.
◆ **chop up** *vt sep* **-1.** [vegetables, fruit] picar **-2.** [wood, meat] cortar.
chopper ['tʃɒpə^r] *n* **-1.** [axe] machadinha *f* **-2.** *inf* [helicopter] helicóptero *m*.
chopping board ['tʃɒpɪŋ-] *n* tábua *f* de cozinha.
choppy ['tʃɒpɪ] (*compar* **-ier**, *superl* **-iest**) *adj* [sea] agitado(da).
chopsticks ['tʃɒpstɪks] *npl* hashi *mpl*.
choral ['kɔ:rəl] *adj* de coral.

chord [kɔ:d] *n MUS* acorde *m*; **to strike a ~ (with sb)** tocar fundo (em alguém).
chore [tʃɔ:ʳ] *n* afazeres *mpl*; **household ~s** afazeres domésticos.
choreographer [ˌkɒrɪ'ɒgrəfəʳ] *n* coreógrafo *m*, -fa *f*.
choreography [ˌkɒrɪ'ɒgrəfɪ] *n (U)* coreografia *f*.
chortle ['tʃɔ:tl] *vi* dar gargalhadas.
chorus ['kɔ:rəs] *n* **-1.** [gen] coro *m* **-2.** [part of song] refrão *m*.
chose [tʃəʊz] *pt* ▻ **choose**.
chosen ['tʃəʊzn] *pp* ▻ **choose**.
choux pastry [ʃu:-] *n (U) doce feito com ovos e em cujo interior se acrescenta creme.*
chow [tʃaʊ] *n* [dog] chow-chow *m inv*.
chowder ['tʃaʊdəʳ] *n (U)* sopa *f (de frutos do mar)*; **clam ~** sopa de mariscos.
Christ [kraɪst] ◇ *n* Cristo *m*. ◇ *excl* Jesus Cristo!, Minha Nossa!
christen ['krɪsn] *vt* batizar.
christening ['krɪsnɪŋ] ◇ *n* batizado *m*. ◇ *comp* de batismo.
Christian ['krɪstʃən] ◇ *adj* cristão(tã). ◇ *n* cristão *m*, -tã *f*.
Christian Democrat *n POL* democrata *mf* cristão, -tã.
Christianity [ˌkrɪstɪ'ænətɪ] *n (U)* cristianismo *m*.
Christian name *n* nome *m* de batismo.
Christmas ['krɪsməs] ◇ *n* Natal *m*; **Happy** *OR* **Merry ~!** Feliz Natal! ◇ *comp* de Natal.
Christmas cake *n UK bolo escuro e decorado que contém muitas frutas secas e que é coberto com marzipã e glacê e servido no Natal.*
Christmas card *n* cartão *m* de Natal.
Christmas carol *n* cântico *m* de Natal.
Christmas cracker *n UK cilindro de papel que produz um estalido ao ser aberto e que contém dentro um presente de Natal.*
Christmas Day *n* dia *m* de Natal.
Christmas Eve *n* noite *f* de Natal.
Christmas Island *n* Ilha de Natal.
Christmas pudding *n UK pudim rico e escuro feito com frutas secas, condimentos e gordura animal, servido no Natal.*
Christmas stocking *n* meias *fpl* de Natal *(penduradas na lareira).*
Christmas tree *n* árvore *f* de Natal.
chrome [krəʊm], **chromium** ['krəʊmɪəm] ◇ *n (U)* cromo *m*. ◇ *comp* de cromo, cromado(da).
chrome-plated *adj* cromado(da).
chromosome ['krəʊməsəʊm] *n* cromossomo *m*.
chronic ['krɒnɪk] *adj* **-1.** [long-lasting] crônico(ca) **-2.** [habitual] inveterado(da).
chronically ['krɒnɪklɪ] *adv* [ill] cronicamente.
chronicle ['krɒnɪkl] ◇ *n* crônica *f*. ◇ *vt* narrar.
chronological [ˌkrɒnə'lɒdʒɪkl] *adj* cronológico(-ca).
chronologically [ˌkrɒnə'lɒdʒɪklɪ] *adv* cronologicamente.
chronology [krə'nɒlədʒɪ] *n* [sequence] cronologia *f*.
chrysalis ['krɪsəlɪs] (*pl* **-lises** [-lɪsi:z]) *n* [insect] crisálida *f*.
chrysanthemum [krɪ'sænθəməm] (*pl* **-s**) *n* crisântemo *m*.
chub (*pl inv OR* **-s**) *n espécie de carpa.*
chubbiness *n (U)* fofice *f*.
chubby ['tʃʌbɪ] (*compar* **-ier**, *superl* **-iest**) *adj* rechonchudo(da).
chuck [tʃʌk] *vt inf* **-1.** [throw] jogar, atirar **-2.** *inf* **: to ~ sb** dar o fora em alguém; **to ~ sthg** largar algo.
◆ **chuck away, chuck out** *vt sep inf* jogar fora; **to ~ sthg out** botar algo fora; **to ~ sb out** botar alguém para fora.
chuckle ['tʃʌkl] ◇ *n* risadinha *f*. ◇ *vi* rir discretamente.
chuffed [tʃʌft] *adj UK inf*: **~ (with sthg/to do sthg)** muito contente (com algo/por fazer algo).
chug [tʃʌg] (*pt* & *pp* **-ged**, *cont* **-ging**) *vi* ratear.
chum [tʃʌm] *n inf* camarada *mf*, companheiro *m*, -ra *f*.
chummy ['tʃʌmɪ] (*compar* **-ier**, *superl* **-iest**) *adj inf*: **to be ~ (with sb)** ser legal (com alguém).
chump [tʃʌmp] *n inf* [fool] tonto *m*, -ta *f*.
chunk [tʃʌŋk] *n* **-1.** [piece] pedaço *m* **-2.** *inf* [large amount] grande parte *f*.
chunky ['tʃʌŋkɪ] (*compar* **-ier**, *superl* **-iest**) *adj* **-1.** [person] parrudo(da) **-2.** [jewellery, furniture] maciço(-ça) **-3.** [cardigan] grosso(sa).
church [tʃɜ:tʃ] *n* **-1.** [building] igreja *f*; **to go to ~** freqüentar a igreja **-2.** [organization]: **the Church** a Igreja.
churchgoer ['tʃɜ:tʃˌgəʊəʳ] *n* fiel *m*, devoto *m*, -ta *f*.
churchman ['tʃɜ:tʃmən] (*pl* **-men** [-mən]) *n* clérigo *m*, eclesiástico *m*.
Church of England *n*: **the ~** a Igreja Anglicana.

CHURCH OF ENGLAND

A Igreja Anglicana originou-se da disputa entre o rei Henrique VIII, que desejava divorciar-se, e a Igreja Católica, que lhe negou o divórcio, em meados do século XVI. Autoproclamando-se chefe da Igreja Anglicana, Henrique VIII separou-a da Igreja Católica. O chefe laico da Igreja Anglicana é o monarca, e seu chefe espiritual, o arcebispo de Canterbury.

Church of Scotland *n*: **the ~** a Igreja Presbiteriana da Escócia.
churchyard ['tʃɜ:tʃjɑ:d] *n cemitério ao redor de uma igreja.*
churlish ['tʃɜ:lɪʃ] *adj* indelicado(da).
churn [tʃɜ:n] ◇ *n* **-1.** [for making butter] batedeira *f* de manteiga **-2.** [for transporting milk] latão *m*. ◇ *vt* [stir up] agitar. ◇ *vi* revolver-se.
◆ **churn out** *vt sep inf* produzir em larga escala.
◆ **churn up** *vt sep* **-1.** [mud] agitar **-2.** [water] revolver.
chute [ʃu:t] *n* **-1.** [waterfall] queda *f* d'água, cachoeira *f* **-2.** [for escape] rampa *f* **-3.** [for rubbish] calha *f* **-4.** [in a pool] tobogã *m*.
chutney ['tʃʌtnɪ] *n (U) molho feito à base de frutas, sementes picantes e açúcar que se come com carne ou queijo.*

CI *abbr of* **Channel Islands.**
CIA (*abbr of* **Central Intelligence Agency**) *n* CIA *f.*
cicada [sɪ'kɑːdə] *n* cigarra *f.*
CID (*abbr of* **Criminal Investigation Department**) *n departamento de investigação criminal da polícia britânica.*
cider ['saɪdəʳ] *n* sidra *f.*
c.i.f. (*abbr of* **cost, insurance and freight**) c.i.f., custo, seguro e frete.
cigar [sɪ'gɑːʳ] *n* charuto *m.*
cigarette [ˌsɪgə'ret] *n* cigarro *m.*
cigarette butt, cigarette end *UK n* bagana *f.*
cigarette holder *n* piteira *f.*
cigarette lighter *n* isqueiro *m.*
cigarette paper *n* mortalha *f.*
C-in-C (*abbr of* **commander in chief**) *n* comandante-em-chefe *m.*
cinch [sɪntʃ] *n inf*: **it's a ~** é sopa *OR* canja.
cinder ['sɪndəʳ] *n* cinza *f.*
cinderblock ['sɪndəblɒk] *n US* bloco *m* de cimento e cinzas.
Cinderella [ˌsɪndə'relə] *n* Cinderela *f* gata-borralheira *f.*
cine camera *n* filmadora *f.*
cine film *n* filme *m*, película *f.*
cinema ['sɪnəmə] *n* [place, art] cinema *m.*
cinematic [ˌsɪnɪ'mætɪk] *adj* cinematográfico(ca).
cinnamon ['sɪnəmən] *n (U)* canela *f.*
cipher ['saɪfəʳ] *n* **-1.** [secret writing system] cifra *f* **-2.** *fig* [person] nulidade *f.*
circa ['sɜːkə] *prep* cerca de, aproximadamente.
circle ['sɜːkl] <> *n* **-1.** [gen] círculo *m*; **to come full ~** voltar ao ponto de partida; **to go round in ~s** andar em círculos **-2.** [seats in theatre, cinema] galeria *f.* <> *vt* **-1.** [draw a circle round] marcar com círculo **-2.** [move round] circundar. <> *vi* mover-se em círculos.
circuit ['sɜːkɪt] *n* **-1.** [gen] circuito *m* **-2.** [lap, movement round] volta *f.*
circuit board *n* placa *f* de circuito.
circuit breaker *n* disjuntor *m.*
circuitous [sə'kjuːɪtəs] *adj* tortuoso(sa).
circular ['sɜːkjʊləʳ] <> *adj* **-1.** [shape, object] redondo(da) **-2.** [argument] circular. <> *n* circular *f.*
circulate ['sɜːkjʊleɪt] <> *vi* circular. <> *vt* circular.
circulation [ˌsɜːkjʊ'leɪʃn] *n* circulação *f*; **in ~** em circulação.
circumcise ['sɜːkəmsaɪz] *vt* circuncidar.
circumcision [ˌsɜːkəm'sɪʒn] *n* circuncisão *f.*
circumference [sə'kʌmfərəns] *n* circunferência *f.*
circumflex ['sɜːkəmfleks] *n*: **~ (accent)** (acento) *m* circunflexo *m.*
circumnavigate [ˌsɜːkəm'nævɪgeɪt] *vt* circunavegar.
circumscribe ['sɜːkəmskraɪb] *vt fml* [restrict] circunscrever.
circumspect ['sɜːkəmspekt] *adj* circunspecto(ta).
circumstances *npl* circunstâncias *fpl*; **under** *OR* **in no ~** sob *OR* em nenhuma circunstância; **under** *OR* **in the ~** nas *OR* nestas circunstâncias.
circumstantial [ˌsɜːkəm'stænʃl] *adj fml*: **~ evidence** evidência *f* circunstancial.
circumvent [ˌsɜːkəm'vent] *vt fml* burlar.
circus ['sɜːkəs] *n* **-1.** [for entertainment] circo *m* **-2.** [in place names] *no Reino Unido, praça circular à qual convergem várias ruas.*
cirrhosis [sɪ'rəʊsɪs] *n (U)* cirrose *f.*
CIS (*abbr of* **Commonwealth of Independent States**) *n* CEI *f.*
cissy ['sɪsɪ] (*pl* **-ies**) *n UK inf* maricas *m inv.*
cistern ['sɪstən] *n* **-1.** *UK* [in roof] cisterna *f* **-2.** [on lavatory] caixa *f* de descarga.
citation [saɪ'teɪʃn] *n* **-1.** [quotation] citação *f* **-2.** [official praise]: **~ (for sthg)** menção *f* honrosa (por algo).
cite [saɪt] *vt* citar.
citizen ['sɪtɪzn] *n* [of country, of town] cidadão *m*, -dã *f.*
Citizens' Advice Bureau *n* Centro *m* de Apoio ao Cidadão.
Citizens' Band *n (U)* banda *f* do cidadão.
citizenship ['sɪtɪznʃɪp] *n (U)* cidadania *f.*
citric acid ['sɪtrɪk-] *n (U)* ácido *m* cítrico.
citrus fruit ['sɪtrəs-] *n* fruta *f* cítrica.
city ['sɪtɪ] (*pl* **-ies**) *n* cidade *f.*
◆ **City** *n UK*: **the City** *o bairro financeiro de Londres.*

THE CITY

A *City*, o bairro financeiro de Londres, compõe uma unidade administrativa autônoma da capital inglesa, dotada inclusive de sua própria polícia. É o bairro mais antigo da cidade, conhecido também como *Square Mile*, pelo fato de sua área total ter uma milha quadrada (ou 2,6 km^2). Por extensão, *the City* é hoje termo empregado para designar o mundo financeiro britânico.

city centre *n* centro *m* da cidade.
city hall *n US* prefeitura *f.*
city technology college *n UK centro de formação técnica profissional custeada por indústrias.*
civic ['sɪvɪk] *adj* cívico(ca).
civic centre *n UK* centro *m* cívico.
civil ['sɪvl] *adj* **-1.** [involving ordinary citizens] civil **-2.** [polite] educado(da).
civil defence *n (U)* defesa *f* civil.
civil disobedience *n (U)* desobediência *f* civil.
civil engineer *n* engenheiro *m*, -ra *f* civil.
civil engineering *n (U)* engenharia *f* civil.
civilian [sɪ'vɪljən] <> *n* civil *mf.* <> *comp* civil.
civility [sɪ'vɪlətɪ] *n (U)* civilidade *f.*
civilization [ˌsɪvɪlaɪ'zeɪʃn] *n (U)* civilização *f.*
civilize, -ise ['sɪvɪlaɪz] *vt* civilizar.
civilized ['sɪvɪlaɪzd] *adj* civilizado(da).
civil law *n (U)* [relating to private case] direito *m* civil.
civil liberties *npl* liberdades *fpl* civis.
Civil List *n UK verba anual designada pelo Parlamento inglês à Família Real.*
civil rights *npl* direitos *mpl* civis.
civil servant *n* funcionário *m* público, funcionária *f* pública.
civil service *n* serviço *m* público.
civil war *n* guerra *f* civil.

CJD (*abbr of* **Creutzfeldt-Jakob disease**) *n forma humana da doença da vaca louca*, doença *f* de Creutzfeldt-Jakob.

cl (*abbr of* **centilitre**) *n* cl.

clad [klæd] *adj literary* [dressed]: ~ **in sthg** vestido(da) de algo.

cladding ['klædɪŋ] *n (U) UK* revestimento *m*.

claim [kleɪm] <> *n* **-1.** [assertion] alegação *f* **-2.** [demand] reivindicação *f* **-3.** [rightful]: **to have a ~ on sb** ter direitos sobre alguém; **to have a ~ on sb's attention** reivindicar a atenção de alguém; **to lay ~ to sthg** reivindicar algo **-4.** [financial] reclamação *f*. <> *vt* **-1.** [assert, maintain] alegar; **to ~ (that)** alegar que **-2.** [apply for, assert one's rights to] reivindicar **-3.** [take] levar. <> *vi*: **to ~ on one's insurance** acionar o seguro; **to ~ for sthg** reclamar algo.

claimant ['kleɪmənt] *n* **-1.** [to the throne] pretendente *mf* **-2.** [of benefit, in law case] requerente *mf*.

claim form *n* formulário *m* de reclamação.

clairvoyant [kleə'vɔɪənt] <> *adj* clarividente. <> *n* vidente *mf*.

clam [klæm] (*pt* & *pp* **-med**, *cont* **-ming**) *n* marisco *m*.

◆ **clam up** *vi inf* fechar a boca.

clamber ['klæmbə^r] *vi* subir com dificuldade.

clammy ['klæmɪ] (*compar* **-ier**, *superl* **-iest**) *adj inf* melado(da).

clamor *n* & *vi US* = **clamour**.

clamorous ['klæmərəs] *adj* clamoroso(sa).

clamour *UK*, **clamor** *US* ['klæmə^r] <> *n (U)* **-1.** [noise] clamor *m* **-2.** [demand]: ~ **for sthg** queixa *f* por algo. <> *vi*: **to ~ for sthg** queixar-se por algo.

clamp [klæmp] <> *n* **-1.** [fastener] presilha *f*, braçadeira *f* **-2.** MED & TECH grampo *m*. <> *vt* **-1.** [with fastener] apertar **-2.** [parked car] pôr travas em.

◆ **clamp down** *vi*: **to ~ down (on sthg)** impor restrições (a algo).

clampdown ['klæmpdaʊn] *n*: ~ **(on sthg)** restrição *f* (sobre algo).

clan [klæn] *n* clã *m*.

clandestine [klæn'destɪn] *adj* clandestino(na).

clang [klæŋ] <> *n* som *m* metálico, tinido *m*. <> *vi* tinir.

clanger ['klæŋə^r] *n UK inf* mancada *f*; **to drop a ~** dar uma mancada.

clank [klæŋk] <> *n* ruído *m* metálico grave. <> *vi* retinir.

clap [klæp] (*pt* & *pp* **-ped**, *cont* **-ping**) <> *n* **-1.** [of hands] palmas *fpl* **-2.** [of thunder] estrondo *m*. <> *vt* **-1.**: **to ~ one's hands** bater palmas **-2.** *inf*: **to ~ eyes on sb/sthg** botar os olhos em alguém/algo. <> *vi* aplaudir.

clapboard ['klæpbɔːd] *n US tábua para revestimento externo da casa ou do edifício*.

clapped-out [klæpt-] *adj UK inf* [machine] caindo aos pedaços.

clapperboard ['klæpəbɔːd] *n* indicador *m* de cenas.

clapping ['klæpɪŋ] *n (U)* aplauso *m*.

claptrap ['klæptræp] *n (U) inf* conversa *f* mole.

claret ['klærət] *n* **-1.** [wine] clarete *m* **-2.** [colour] cor-de-vinho *f*.

clarification [ˌklærɪfɪ'keɪʃn] *n* [explanation] esclarecimento *m*.

clarify ['klærɪfaɪ] (*pt* & *pp* **-ied**) *vt* [explain, expand on] esclarecer.

clarinet [ˌklærə'net] *n* clarinete *m*.

clarity ['klærətɪ] *n (U)* clareza *f*.

clash [klæʃ] <> *n* **-1.** [of interests, personality] choque *m*; ~ **with sb** choque com alguém **-2.** [disagreement] divergência *f*; ~ **with sb** divergência com alguém **-3.** [noise] estrépito *m*. <> *vi* **-1.** [be incompatible - ideas, beliefs] chocar-se; [- colours] destoar; **to ~ with sthg** destoar de algo **-2.** [fight] chocar-se; **to ~ with sb** chocar-se com alguém **-3.** [disagree] divergir; **to ~ with sb** divergir de alguém **-4.** [coincide] coincidir; **to ~ with sthg** coincidir com algo **-5.** [make noise] soar.

clasp [klɑːsp] <> *n* [fastener] fecho *m*. <> *vt* [hold tight] apertar.

class [klɑːs] <> *n* **-1.** [gen] classe *f* **-2.** [lesson] aula *f* **-3.** [category] espécie *f*; **to be in a ~ of one's own** ser excelente. <> *comp* [relating to social groups] de classes. <> *vt* classificar; **to ~ sb as sthg** classificar alguém como algo.

class-conscious *adj pej* esnobe.

classic ['klæsɪk] <> *adj* clássico(ca). <> *n* clássico *m*.

◆ **classics** *npl*: **the ~** os clássicos.

classical ['klæsɪkl] *adj* clássico(ca).

classical music *n (U)* música *f* clássica.

classicism *n (U)* classicismo *m*.

classicist *n (U)* classicista *mf*.

classification [ˌklæsɪfɪ'keɪʃn] *n* classificação *f*.

classified ['klæsɪfaɪd] *adj* [secret] confidencial.

classified ad *n* (anúncio *m*) classificado *m*.

classify ['klæsɪfaɪ] (*pt* & *pp* **-ied**) *vt* classificar.

classless ['klɑːslɪs] *adj* sem classes.

classmate ['klɑːsmeɪt] *n* colega *mf* de classe.

classroom ['klɑːsrʊm] *n* sala *f* de aula.

classy ['klɑːsɪ] (*compar* **-ier**, *superl* **-iest**) *adj inf* bacana, chique.

clatter ['klætə^r] <> *n* **-1.** [of pans, dishes] tinido *m* **-2.** [of hooves] repique *m*. <> *vi* **-1.** [pans, dishes] retinir **-2.** [hooves] repicar **-3.** [person]: **to ~ in/out/down** entrar/sair/descer fazendo barulho.

clause [klɔːz] *n* **-1.** [in legal document] cláusula *f* **-2.** GRAMM oração *f*.

claustrophobia [ˌklɔːstrə'fəʊbjə] *n (U)* claustrofobia *f*.

claustrophobic [ˌklɔːstrə'fəʊbɪk] *adj* claustrofóbico(ca).

claw [klɔː] <> *n* **-1.** [of wild animal, bird] garra *f* **-2.** [of cat, dog] unha *f* **-3.** [of sea creature] pinça *f* **-4.** [of insect] ferrão *f*. <> *vt* arranhar; **to ~ one's way to** galgar seu caminho para. <> *vi*: **to ~ at sthg** agarrar-se a algo.

◆ **claw back** *vt sep UK* recuperar.

clay [kleɪ] *n* argila *f*, barro *m*.

clay pigeon shooting *n (U)* tiro *m* ao prato.

clean [kliːn] <> *adj* **-1.** [gen] limpo(pa); **to come ~ about sthg** *inf* confessar algo **-2.** [blank] em branco **-3.** [inoffensive] inofensivo(va) **-4.** [cut, break] preciso(sa). ◇ *adv* [completely] completamente. ◇ *vt* [make clean] limpar; **to ~ one's teeth** *UK* escovar os dentes. ◇ *vi* fazer faxina. ◇ *n* faxina *f*; **to give sthg a ~** dar uma limpada em algo.

◆ **clean out** *vt sep* **-1.** [clear out] fazer uma limpeza (em) **-2.** *inf fig* [leave penniless] deixar sem um centavo **-3.** *inf* [take everything from] depenar.

◆ **clean up** ◇ *vt sep* [clear up] arrumar. ◇ *vi inf* [win] limpar.

cleaner ['kli:nə^r] *n* **-1.** [person] faxineiro *m*, -ra *f* **-2.** [substance] produto *m* de limpeza **-3.** [shop]: **~'s** lavanderia *f*.

cleaning ['kli:nɪŋ] *n (U)* limpeza *f*, faxina *f*.

cleaning lady *n* faxineira *f*.

cleanliness ['klenlɪnɪs] *n (U)* limpeza *f*, asseio *m*.

clean-living *adj* de vida limpa.

cleanly ['kli:nlɪ] *adv* com precisão.

cleanness ['kli:nnɪs] *n (U)* limpeza *f*, asseio *m*.

cleanse [klenz] *vt* **-1.** [make clean] limpar **-2.** [make pure] purificar; **to ~ sb/sthg of sthg** livrar alguém/algo de algo.

cleanser ['klenzə^r] *n* **-1.** [for skin] creme *m* de limpeza **-2.** [detergent] detergente *m*.

clean-shaven [-'ʃeɪvn] *adj* de barba feita.

cleanup ['kli:nʌp] *n* limpeza *f*.

clear [klɪə^r] ◇ *adj* **-1.** [gen] claro(ra); **to make sthg ~ (to sb)** tornar algo claro (para alguém); **to make it ~ that** deixar claro que; **to make o.s. ~** fazer-se entender; **to be ~ about sthg** [understand] entender algo com clareza; [explain clearly] fazer-se entender sobre algo; **~ head** mente *f* lúcida **-2.** [obvious, unmistakable] óbvio(via) **-3.** [transparent] transparente **-4.** [water] límpido(da) **-5.** [unobstructed, free] livre **-6.** [conscience] tranqüilo(la) **-7.** [profit] líquido(da). ◇ *adv* [out of the way]: **to step ~** ficar fora do caminho; **stand ~!** afaste-se!; **to stay** *OR* **steer ~ of sb/sthg** afastar-se de alguém/algo. ◇ *n*: **in the ~** [out of danger] fora de perigo; [free from suspicion] acima de qualquer suspeita. ◇ *vt* **-1.** [remove obstacles from - way, path] desimpedir; [- pipe] limpar; [- table] tirar **-2.**: **to ~ one's throat** limpar a garganta **-3.** [take out of the way] retirar **-4.** [jump] transpor **-5.** [pay] saldar **-6.** [authorize] autorizar **-7.** [prove not guilty] livrar de culpa; **to be ~ed of sthg** ser declarado(da) inocente de algo **-8.** [accept for payment] liberar **-9.** [customs] desembaraçar. ◇ *vi* **-1.** [disperse, diminish - fog, smoke] dissipar-se; [- headache] passar **-2.** [brighten up] clarear.

◆ **clear away** *vt sep* arrumar.

◆ **clear off** *vi UK inf* dar o fora.

◆ **clear out** ◇ *vt sep* [tidy up] arrumar. ◇ *vi inf* [leave] dar o fora.

◆ **clear up** ◇ *vt sep* **-1.** [tidy] arrumar **-2.** [solve, settle] resolver. ◇ *vi* **-1.** [weather] clarear **-2.** [illness] desaparecer **-3.** [tidy up] arrumar.

clearance ['klɪərəns] *n (U)* **-1.** [removal] retirada *f*; **the ~ of mines** a remoção de minas terrestres; **land ~** a limpeza da terra **-2.** [of contents of house] desocupação *f* **-3.** [permission] autorização *f*; **customs ~** desembaraço *m* alfandegário **-5.** [free space] vão *m* livre; **the bridge has a 12m ~** a ponte tem um vão livre de 12m.

clearance sale *n* liquidação *f*.

clear-cut *adj* bem definido(da).

clear-headed [-'hedɪd] *adj* esperto(ta).

clearing ['klɪərɪŋ] *n* [in forest] clareira *f*.

clearing bank *n UK* banco *m* compensador.

clearing house *n* **-1.** [organization] central *f* de informações **-2.** [bank] carteira *f* de compensação.

clearing up *n (U)* limpeza *f*, arrumação *f*.

clearly ['klɪəlɪ] *adv* **-1.** [distinctly, lucidly] claramente **-2.** [obviously] evidentemente.

clearout ['klɪəraʊt] *n esp UK inf* faxina *f* geral.

clear-sighted [-'saɪtɪd] *adj* [person] perspicaz.

clearway ['klɪəweɪ] *n UK AUT* via *f* expressa.

cleavage ['kli:vɪdʒ] *n* **-1.** [between breasts] decote *m* **-2.** [division] rachadura *f*.

cleave *literary* ◇ *vt* [split] rachar. ◇ *vi* [be very attached to]: **to ~ to sb/sthg** ser fiel a alguém/algo.

cleaver ['kli:və^r] *n* cutelo *m* de açougueiro.

clef [klef] *n* clave *f*.

cleft [kleft] *n* fenda *f*, rachadura *f*.

cleft palate *n* fenda *f* palatina.

clematis ['klemətɪs] *n* clematite *f*.

clemency ['klemənsɪ] *n (U) fml* [mercy] clemência *f*.

clementine ['kleməntaɪn] *n* clementina *f*.

clench [klentʃ] *vt* cerrar; **to have sthg ~ed between one's teeth** ter algo preso entre os dentes.

clergy ['klɜ:dʒɪ] *npl*: **the ~** o clero.

clergyman ['klɜ:dʒɪmən] (*pl* **-men** [-mən]) *n* clérigo *m*.

cleric ['klerɪk] *n* clérigo *m*.

clerical ['klerɪkl] *adj* **-1.** [in office] de escritório **-2.** [in church] clerical.

clerk [*UK* klɑ:k, *US* klɜ:rk] *n* **-1.** [in office] auxiliar *mf* de escritório **-2.** [in court] escriturário *m*, -ria *f*, escrevente *mf* **-3.** *US* [shop assistant] balconista *mf*.

clever ['klevə^r] *adj* **-1.** [intelligent] inteligente **-2.** [ingenious] engenhoso(sa); **that's ~!** que engenhoso! **-3.** [skilful] hábil.

cleverly ['klevəlɪ] *adv* **-1.** [intelligently] inteligentemente **-2.** [ingeniously] engenhosamente **-3.** [skilfully] habilmente.

cleverness ['klevənɪs] *n* **-1.** [intelligence] esperteza *f*, inteligência *f* **-2.** [ingenuity] engenhosidade *f* **-3.** [skill] habilidade *f*.

cliché ['kli:ʃeɪ] *n* clichê *m*.

click [klɪk] ◇ *n* **-1.** [gen] clique *m* **-2.** [of tongue] estalo *m*. ◇ *vt* estalar. ◇ *vi* **-1.** [gen] estalar; **the door ~ed shut** a porta se fechou com um clique **-2.** *inf* [fall into place] cair a ficha **-3.** *COMPUT* clicar.

client ['klaɪənt] *n* cliente *mf*.

clientele [ˌkli:ən'tel] *n (U)* clientela *f*, freguesia *f*.

cliff [klɪf] *n* penhasco *m*.

cliffhanger ['klɪfˌhæŋə^r] *n inf* suspense *m*.

climactic [klaɪ'mæktɪk] *adj* culminante.

climate ['klaɪmɪt] *n* clima *m*.

climatic [klaɪ'mætɪk] *adj* climático(ca).

climate change *n* mudança *f* climática.

climax ['klaɪmæks] *n* clímax *m*.

climb [klaɪm] <> *n* [ascent] escalada *f.* <> *vt* [go up - tree, ladder] subir em; [- hill, mountain] escalar; [- fence] transpor. <> *vi* **-1.** [person]: **to ~ up/down/over sthg** subir em/descer de/transpor algo; **to ~ into/out of sthg** subir em/descer de algo **-2.** [plant] trepar **-3.** [road, plane, prices] subir.
◆ **climb down** *vi* [back down] admitir o erro.
climb-down *n* retratação *f.*
climber ['klaɪmə^r] *n* **-1.** [person] alpinista *mf* **-2.** [plant] trepadeira *f.*
climbing ['klaɪmɪŋ] <> *adj* [plant] trepadeira. <> *n (U)* alpinismo *m.*
climbing frame *n UK estrutura feita de metal, madeira ou corda na qual as crianças sobem para brincar.*
climes [klaɪmz] *npl literary* clima *m.*
clinch [klɪntʃ] *vt* [settle] fechar.
cling [klɪŋ] (*pt* & *pp* **clung**) *vi* **-1.** [person]: **to ~ to sb/sthg** [physically] agarrar-se a alguém/algo; *fig* [emotionally: to person] apegar-se a alguém/algo; [to beliefs, ideas, principles] aferrar-se a alguém/algo **-2.** [clothes]: **to ~ (to sb)** ajustar-se bem (a alguém) **-3.** [smell] impregnar.
clingfilm ['klɪŋfɪlm] *n (U) UK* filme *m* de PVC transparente.
clinging ['klɪŋɪŋ] *adj* **-1.** [person, child] apegado(da) **-2.** [clothes] colado(da).
clinic ['klɪnɪk] *n* [building] clínica *f.*
clinical ['klɪnɪkl] *adj* **-1.** MED clínico(ca) **-2.** *pej* [coldly rational] analítico(ca) **-3.** [functional] impessoal.
clinically ['klɪnɪklɪ] *adv* **-1.** MED clinicamente **-2.** *pej* [coldly] analiticamente.
clink [klɪŋk] <> *n* tilintar *m.* <> *vi* tilintar.
clip [klɪp] (*pt* & *pp* **-ped**, *cont* **-ping**) <> *n* **-1.** [fastener - for paper] clipe *m*; [- for hair] grampo *m*; [- for earring] fecho *m* **-2.** TV & CINEMA videoclipe *m* **-3.** *inf* [smack]: **to give sb a ~ around the ear** dar um tapa na orelha de alguém. <> *vt* **-1.** [fasten] prender **-2.** [cut - lawn, hedge, nails] cortar; [- newspaper cutting] recortar **-3.** *inf* [hit - person] dar um tapa em; [- car] bater em.
◆ **clip on** *vi* [fasten] segurar, prender.
clipboard ['klɪpbɔ:d] *n* prancheta *f* com prendedor.
clip-on *adj* de prender; **~ earrings** brincos *mpl* de pressão; **~ badge** button *m*; **~ bow tie** gravata-borboleta *f*.
clipped [klɪpt] *adj* [speech] entrecortado(da).
clippers ['klɪpəz] *npl* **-1.** [for hair] máquina *f* de cortar cabelo **-2.** [for nails] cortador *m* de unhas **-3.** [for plants, hedges] tesoura *f* de podar.
clipping ['klɪpɪŋ] *n* [newspaper cutting] recorte *m.*
◆ **clippings** *npl* [small pieces] fragmentos *mpl*; **grass/nail ~s** restos *mpl* de grama/unha cortada.
clique [kli:k] *n pej* panelinha *f.*
clitoris *n* clitóris *m inv.*
cloak [kləʊk] <> *n* **-1.** [garment] capa *f* **-2.** *fig* [cover for secret] disfarce *m.* <> *vt* [hide, disguise] ocultar; **to be ~ed in** estar envolto(ta) em.
cloak-and-dagger *adj* misterioso(sa).
cloakroom ['kləʊkrʊm] *n* **-1.** [for clothes] guarda-volumes *m inv* **-2.** *UK* [toilet - in public place] banheiro *m*; [- in house] lavabo *m.*
clobber ['klɒbə^r] *inf* <> *n* **-1.** *(U)* [things] tralhas *fpl* **-2.** *(U)* [clothes] trapos *mpl.* <> *vt inf* **-1.** [hit] bater **-2.** [defeat] massacrar **-3.** [affect very badly] afetar.
clock [klɒk] <> *n* **-1.** [timepiece] relógio *m*; **round the ~** dia e noite; **to put the ~ back** *lit* atrasar o relógio; *fig* fazer de conta que nada mudou; **to put the ~ forward** adiantar o relógio **-2.** [in vehicle - mileometer] hodômetro *m*; [- speedometer] velocímetro *m.* <> *vt* [reach time or speed] marcar.
◆ **clock in, clock on** *vi UK* [at work] bater o ponto OR cartão-de-ponto na entrada.
◆ **clock off, clock out** *vi UK* [at work] bater o ponto OR cartão-de-ponto na saída.
◆ **clock up** *vt fus* [amass] acumular.
clock radio *n* rádio-relógio *m.*
clockwise ['klɒkwaɪz] <> *adj* em sentido horário. <> *adv* em sentido horário.
clockwork ['klɒkwɜ:k] <> *n (U)*: **to go like ~** funcionar como um relógio. <> *comp* de corda.
clod [klɒd] *n* [of earth] torrão *m.*
clog [klɒg] (*pt* & *pp* **-ged**, *cont* **-ging**) *vt* entupir, bloquear.
◆ **clogs** *npl* tamancos *mpl.*
◆ **clog up** <> *vt sep* **-1.** [drains] entupir **-2.** [nose] congestionar. <> *vi* [drains] entupir; [roads] bloquear; [pores] fechar.
clogged [klɒgd] *adj* [drains] entupido(da); [roads] bloqueado(da); [pores] fechado(da).
cloister ['klɔɪstə^r] *n* ARCHIT claustro *m.*
cloistered *adj literary* [secluded] enclausurado(da), recluso(sa).
clone [kləʊn] <> *n* clone *m.* <> *vt* BIOL clonar.
close[1] [kləʊs] <> *adj* **-1.** [near] próximo(ma), perto; **~ to sb/sthg** perto de alguém/algo; **~ to tears** à beira das lágrimas; **it was a ~ shave** foi por um fio OR triz; **~ up**, **~ to** de perto; **~ by**, **~ at hand** bem perto **-2.** [in relationship] íntimo(ma); **~ to sb** apegado(da) a alguém **-3.** [in degree of connection - resemblance, family] próximo(ma); [- link, connection] estreito(ta) **-4.** [careful]: **a ~ watch** um olhar atento; **to pay ~ attention** prestar muita atenção; **~ questioning** uma pergunta detalhada; **a ~r look** um olhar mais de perto; **a ~r examination** um exame minucioso **-5.** [oppressive] carregado(-da) **-6.** [almost equal] com uma pequena margem de diferença. <> *adv* perto. <> *n* [street] rua *f* sem saída.
◆ **close on, close to** *prep* [almost] cerca de.
close[2] [kləʊz] <> *vt* **-1.** [shut, shut down] fechar **-2.** [bring to an end] encerrar, concluir. <> *vi* **-1.** [shut] fechar **-2.** [heal] cicatrizar **-3.** [end] terminar. <> *n* [end] fim *m*, final *m.*
◆ **close down** <> *vt sep* [shut] fechar. <> *vi* **-1.** [shut down] fechar **-2.** [end] terminar.
◆ **close in** *vi* **-1.** [night, fog] fechar **-2.** [person] cercar; **to ~ in on sb/sthg** cercar alguém/algo.
◆ **close off** *vt sep* interditar.
close-cropped [ˌkləʊs-] *adj* rente.
closed [kləʊzd] *adj* fechado(da).
closed circuit television *n* televisão *f* em circuito fechado.
closedown ['kləʊzdaʊn] *n* **-1.** *UK* [of TV, radio station] encerramento *m* da programação **-2.** [of factory, mine] fechamento *m.*

closed shop *n estabelecimento em que todos os trabalhadores devem pertencer a um determinado sindicato.*

close-fitting [ˌkləʊs-] *adj* justo(ta).

close-knit [ˌkləʊs-] *adj* muito unido(da).

closely [ˈkləʊslɪ] *adv* **-1.** [in degree of connection] intimamente; **to resemble sb/sthg ~** parecer muito com alguém/algo **-2.** [carefully] atentamente.

closeness [ˈkləʊsnɪs] *n (U)* **-1.** [of shops, facilities] proximidade *f* **-2.** [of relationship] intimidade *f.*

closeout [ˈkləʊzaʊt] *n US* liquidação *f.*

close quarters [ˌkləʊs-] *npl*: **at ~** [very close] muito próximo(ma); *MIL* em contato direto (com o inimigo).

close season [ˈkləʊs-] *n UK* temporada *f* de caça proibida.

closet [ˈklɒzɪt] ◇ *adj inf* inconfesso(sa). ◇ *n* **-1.** *Am* closet *m*, armário *m* **-2.** *fig*: **to come out of the ~** sair do armário. ◇ *vt*: **to be ~ed with sb** ficar trancado(da) com alguém.

close-up [ˈkləʊs-] *n* primeiro plano *m.*

closing [ˈkləʊzɪŋ] *adj* [final] final, de encerramento.

closing price *n* preço *m* OR cotação *f* de fechamento.

closing time *n* horário *m* de fechamento.

closure [ˈkləʊʒəʳ] *n* **-1.** [of business, company] fechamento *m* **-2.** [of road, railway line: temporarily] interdição *f.*

clot [klɒt] (*pt* & *pp* **-ted**, *cont* **-ting**) ◇ *n* **-1.** [of blood] coágulo *m* **-2.** *UK inf* [fool] idiota *mf.* ◇ *vi* [blood] coagular.

cloth [klɒθ] *n* **-1.** *(U)* [fabric] tecido *m* **-2.** [for cleaning] pano *m* **-3.** [tablecloth] toalha *f.*

clothe [kləʊð] *vt fml* [dress] vestir; **~d in** vestido(da) de.

clothes [kləʊðz] *npl* roupa *f*; **to put one's ~ on** vestir-se; **to take one's ~ off** tirar a roupa.

clothes basket *n* cesto *m* de roupa.

clothes brush *n* escova *f* de roupa.

clothes horse *n* **-1.** [for drying clothes] estendedor *m* de roupa **-2.** *pej* [person] *pessoa que só se preocupa em andar na moda, pouco inteligente e sem habilidades.*

clothesline [ˈkləʊðzlaɪn] *n* varal *m.*

clothes peg *UK*, **clothespin** *US* [ˈkləʊðzpɪn] *n* prendedor *m* de roupa.

clothing [ˈkləʊðɪŋ] *n (U)* roupa *f*; **~ allowance** auxílio-vestuário *m.*

clotted cream [ˌklɒtɪd-] *n (U) UK creme feito de nata muito espesso, típico da Cornualha.*

cloud [klaʊd] ◇ *n* [gen] nuvem *f*; **to be under a ~** ter má fama. ◇ *vt* **-1.** [mist up] embaçar **-2.** [make less pleasant] estragar **-3.** [make less clear]: **to ~ the issue** obscurecer a questão.

◆ **cloud over** *vi* **-1.** [sky] encobrir-se **-2.** [face] entristecer-se.

cloudburst [ˈklaʊdbɜːst] *n* temporal *m* repentino.

cloudless [ˈklaʊdlɪs] *adj* limpo(pa), sem nuvens.

cloudy [ˈklaʊdɪ] (*compar* **-ier**, *superl* **-iest**) *adj* **-1.** [sky] nublado(da) **-2.** [liquid] turvo(va).

clout [klaʊt] *inf* ◇ *n* **-1.** [blow] bofetão *m* **-2.** *(U)* [influence] influência *f.* ◇ *vt* [hit] dar um bofetão em.

clove [kləʊv] *n*: **a ~ of garlic** um dente de alho.

◆ **cloves** *npl* [spice] cravo-da-índia *m.*

clover [ˈkləʊvəʳ] *n (U)* trevo *m.*

clown [klaʊn] ◇ *n* **-1.** [performer] palhaço *m* **-2.** [fool] palhaço *m*, -ça *f.* ◇ *vi* fazer palhaçadas.

cloying [ˈklɔɪɪŋ] *adj* enjoativo(va).

club [klʌb] (*pt* & *pp* **-bed**, *cont* **-bing**) ◇ *n* **-1.** [association] clube *m* **-2.** [nightclub] boate *f*, casa *f* noturna **-3.** [weapon] bastão *m* **-4.** *SPORT* [equipment]: **(golf) ~** taco *m* (de golfe). ◇ *comp* do clube. ◇ *vt* [hit] espancar.

◆ **clubs** *npl* [playing cards] paus *mpl.*

◆ **club together** *vi UK* fazer vaquinha.

club car *n US RAIL* vagão-restaurante *m.*

clubhouse [ˈklʌbhaʊs] *n* clube *m.*

cluck [klʌk] *vi* [hen, person] cacarejar.

clue [kluː] *n* **-1.** [in crime] pista *f*, vestígio *m*; **I haven't (got) a ~** não tenho (a menor) idéia **-2.** [hint] dica *f* **-3.** [key to problem]: **the ~ (to sthg)** a chave (para algo) **-4.** [in crossword] pista *f.*

clued-up [kluːd-] *adj UK inf* antenado(da).

clueless [ˈkluːlɪs] *adj UK inf* tapado(da); **she's completely ~** ela é completamente tapada; **to be ~ about sth** não ter a menor idéia sobre algo.

clump [klʌmp] ◇ *n* [group - of trees] arvoredo *m*; [- of bushes] moita *m*; [- of flowers] ramalhete *m.* ◇ *vi* [move heavily] mover-se pesadamente.

clumsily [ˈklʌmzɪlɪ] *adv* **-1.** [move, express o.s.] desajeitadamente **-2.** [designed, executed] grosseiramente.

clumsy [ˈklʌmzɪ] (*compar* **-ier**, *superl* **-iest**) *adj* **-1.** [gen] desajeitado(da) **-2.** [unwieldy] tosco(ca).

clung [klʌŋ] *pt* & *pp* ▷ **cling.**

cluster [ˈklʌstəʳ] ◇ *n* [group - of people, houses, trees] grupo *m*; [- of grapes] cacho *m*; [- of flowers] ramalhete *m.* ◇ *vi* **-1.** [people] agrupar-se, reunir-se **-2.** [things] amontoar-se.

clutch [klʌtʃ] ◇ *n AUT* embreagem *f.* ◇ *vt* [with hands - object] agarrar; [- part of body] apertar. ◇ *vi*: **to ~ at sb/sthg** agarrar-se a alguém/algo.

◆ **clutches** *npl*: **in the ~es of** nas garras de.

clutch bag *n* bolsa *f* feminina.

clutter [ˈklʌtəʳ] ◇ *n* bagunça *f.* ◇ *vt* bagunçar.

cm (*abbr of* **centimetre**) *n* cm.

CNAA (*abbr of* **Council for National Academic Awards**) *n organismo britânico que outorga diplomas de cursos superiores de instituições que não possuem status de universidade.*

CND (*abbr of* **Campaign for Nuclear Disarmament**) *n organização britânica que realiza campanhas contra o armamento nuclear.*

c/o (*abbr of* **care of**) a/c.

co- [kəʊ] *prefix* co.

Co. **-1.** (*abbr of* **Company**) Cia. **-2.** (*abbr of* **County**) *área administrativa britânica, usada, em alguns casos, na representação de endereços.*

CO ◇ *n* **-1.** (*abbr of* **commanding officer**) com. **-2.** (*abbr of* **Commonwealth Office**) *ministério para as relações com o Commonwealth britânico.* **-3.** (*abbr of* **conscientious objector**) *aquele que não é voluntário para entrar nas forças armadas por* *razões morais.* ◇ *abbr of* **Colorado**.

coach [kəʊtʃ] ◇ *n* **-1.** *UK* [bus] ônibus *m inv* **-2.** *RAIL* vagão *m* **-3.** [horsedrawn] carruagem *f* **-4.** *SPORT* treinador *m*, -ra *f* **-5.** [tutor] professor *m*, -ra *f* particular. ◇ *vt* **-1.** *SPORT* treinar **-2.** [tutor] preparar; **to ~ sb in sthg** preparar alguém em algo.

coaching ['kəʊtʃɪŋ] *n (U)* **-1.** *SPORT* treinamento *m* **-2.** [tutoring] preparação *f*.

coach station *n UK* (estação *f*) rodoviária *f*.

coach trip *n UK* passeio *m* de ônibus.

coagulate [kəʊ'ægjʊleɪt] *vi* coagular.

coal [kəʊl] *n (U)* carvão *m*.

coalesce [,kəʊə'les] *vi fml* fundir-se.

coalface ['kəʊlfeɪs] *n* veio *m* de carvão.

coalfield ['kəʊlfi:ld] *n* jazida *f* de carvão.

coal gas *n (U)* gás *m* de carvão.

coalition [,kəʊə'lɪʃn] *n POL* coalizão *f*.

coal mine *n* mina *f* de carvão.

coal miner *n* minerador *m*, -ra *f* de carvão.

coal mining *n (U)* mineração *f* de carvão.

coarse [kɔ:s] *adj* **-1.** [rough] áspero(ra) **-2.** [vulgar] grosseiro(ra).

coarsen ['kɔ:sn] ◇ *vt* **-1.** [make vulgar] deixar grosso(sa) **-2.** [make rough] deixar áspero(ra). ◇ *vi* **-1.** [become vulgar] vulgarizar-se **-2.** [become rough] tornar-se áspero(ra).

coast [kəʊst] ◇ *n* costa *f*. ◇ *vi* **-1.** [car] ir em ponto morto **-2.** *fig* [through life, exam] passar; **to ~ through life** deixar a vida passar; **to be ~ing happily along** estar curtindo o momento.

coastal ['kəʊstl] *adj* costeiro(ra); **a ~ town** uma cidade litorânea.

coaster ['kəʊstə^r] *n* **-1.** [small mat] descanso *m* para copos **-2.** *UK* [ship] navio *m* costeiro.

coastguard ['kəʊstgɑ:d] *n* **-1.** [person] guarda *mf* costeiro, -ra **-2.** [organization]**: the ~** a guarda costeira.

coastline ['kəʊstlaɪn] *n* litoral *m*.

coat [kəʊt] ◇ *n* **-1.** [garment] casaco *m* **-2.** [of animal] pêlo *m* **-3.** [of paint, varnish] demão *f*. ◇ *vt*: **to ~ sthg (with sthg)** revestir algo (com algo).

coat hanger *n* cabide *m*.

coating ['kəʊtɪŋ] *n* [covering - of chocolate, icing] cobertura *f*; [- of dust] camada *f*.

coat of arms (*pl* **coats of arms**) *n* brasão *m*.

coat stand *n* cabide *m*.

coat-tails *npl* **-1.** abas *fpl* (de casaca); **on sb's ~** *fig* na esteira de alguém.

co-author ◇ *n* co-autor *m*, -ra *f*. ◇ *vt*: **to ~** ser co-autor(ra) de.

coax [kəʊks] *vt*: **to ~ sb (to do** *OR* **into doing sthg)** persuadir alguém (a fazer algo); **to ~ sthg out of sb** conseguir algo de alguém com jeitinho.

coaxial cable [kəʊ'æksɪəl-] *n COMPUT* cabo *m* coaxial.

cobalt ['kəʊbɔ:lt] *n* cobalto *m*.

cobble ◆ **cobble together** *vt sep* deixar alinhavado(da).

cobbled ['kɒbld] *adj* de pedras arredondadas.

cobbler ['kɒblə^r] *n* sapateiro *m*, -ra *f*.

cobbles ['kɒblz], **cobblestones** ['kɒblstəʊnz] *npl* *pedras arredondadas (para pavimentação).*

COBOL (*abbr of* **Common Business Oriented Language**) *n (U) COMPUT* COBOL.

cobra ['kəʊbrə] *n* naja *f*.

cobweb ['kɒbweb] *n* teia *f* de aranha.

Coca-Cola® [,kəʊkə'kəʊlə] *n* Coca-Cola® *f*.

cocaine [kəʊ'keɪn] *n (U)* cocaína *f*.

cock [kɒk] ◇ *n* **-1.** *UK* [male chicken] galo *m* **-2.** [male bird] pássaro *m* macho **-3.** *vulg* [penis] pinto *m*. ◇ *vt* **-1.** [gun] engatilhar **-2.** [head] virar.
◆ **cock up** *vt sep UK vulg*: **the project was going fine, but they ~ed it up** o projeto estava indo bem, mas eles acabaram fodendo tudo.

cock-a-hoop *adj inf* [delighted] exultante.

cock-and-bull story *n inf* história *f* para boi dormir.

cockatoo [,kɒkə'tu:] (*pl* **-s**) *n* cacatua *f*.

cockerel ['kɒkrəl] *n* frango *m*.

cocker spaniel [,kɒkə-] *n* cocker spaniel *mf*.

cockeyed ['kɒkaɪd] *adj inf* **-1.** [not straight] torto(ta) **-2.** [unlikely to succeed] absurdo(da).

cockfight ['kɒkfaɪt] *n* rinha *f*.

cockle ['kɒkl] *n* [shellfish] berbigão *m*.

Cockney ['kɒknɪ] (*pl* **Cockneys**) ◇ *n* **-1.** [person] *pessoa vinda da área leste de Londres, em geral da classe trabalhadora* **-2.** [accent] cockney *m*. ◇ *comp* de cockney.

cockpit ['kɒkpɪt] *n* **-1.** [in plane] cabine *f* de comando **-2.** [in F1 car] cockpit *m*.

cockroach ['kɒkrəʊtʃ] *n* barata *f*.

cocksure [,kɒk'ʃʊə^r] *adj* convencido(da).

cocktail ['kɒkteɪl] *n* [drink] coquetel *m*.

cocktail party *n* coquetel *m*.

cocktail shaker [-,ʃeɪkə^r] *n* coqueteleira *f*.

cocktail stick *n* garfo *m* para coquetéis.

cock-up *n v inf* cagada *f*.

cocky ['kɒkɪ] (*compar* **-ier**, *superl* **-iest**) *adj inf* petulante.

cocoa ['kəʊkəʊ] *n (U)* **-1.** [powder] cacau *m* **-2.** [drink] chocolate *m*.

coconut ['kəʊkənʌt] *n* coco *m*.

cocoon [kə'ku:n] ◇ *n* casulo *m*. ◇ *vt* [protect from reality] preservar.

cod [kɒd] (*pl inv OR* **-s**) *n* bacalhau *m*.

COD -1. (*abbr of* **cash on delivery**) entrega contra pagamento. **-2.** (*abbr of* **collect on delivery**) entrega contra pagamento.

code [kəʊd] ◇ *n* código *m*. ◇ *vt* **-1.** [encode] codificar **-2.** [give identifier to] identificar como.

coded ['kəʊdɪd] *adj* [written in code] em código.

codeine ['kəʊdi:n] *n (U)* codeína *f*.

code name *n* pseudônimo *m*.

code of practice *n* código *m* de conduta.

cod-liver oil *n (U)* óleo *m* de fígado de bacalhau.

codswallop ['kɒdz,wɒləp] *n (U) UK inf* asneira *f*.

coed ◇ *adj* (*abbr of* **co-educational**) *relativo à escola mista.* ◇ *n* **-1.** (*abbr of* **co-educational student**) *aluno de escola mista nos Estados Unidos.* **-2.** (*abbr of* **co-educational school**) *escola mista na Grã-Bretanha.*

coeducational [,kəʊedju:'keɪʃənl] *adj* [school] misto(ta).

coefficient [,kəʊɪ'fɪʃnt] *n* coeficiente *m*.

coerce [kəʊ'ɜ:s] *vt*: **to ~ sb (into doing sthg)**

coagir alguém(a fazer algo).
coercion [kəʊ'ɜːʃn] *n (U)* coerção *f.*
coexist [ˌkəʊɪg'zɪst] *vi* coexistir.
coexistence [ˌkəʊɪg'zɪstəns] *n (U)* coexistência *f.*
C. of E. (*abbr of* **Church of England**) *n* igreja anglicana.
coffee ['kɒfɪ] *n* [drink] café *m.*
coffee bar *n UK* lanchonete *f.*
coffee beans *npl* grãos *mpl* de café.
coffee break *n* intervalo *m* para o café, coffee break *m.*
coffee cup *n* xícara *f* de café.
coffee-maker *n* cafeteira *f.*
coffee mill *n* moedor *m* de café.
coffee morning *n UK evento social, realizado durante o café da manhã, cuja finalidade é arrecadar dinheiro para organizações beneficentes.*
coffee pot *n* bule *m* para café.
coffee shop *n* **-1.** *UK* [café] café *m* **-2.** *US* [restaurant] cafeteria *f* **-3.** [shop selling coffee] cafeteria *f.*
coffee table *n* mesinha *f* de centro.
coffee-table book *n* livro *m* de gravuras.
coffers ['kɒfəz] *npl* fundos *mpl*, quantia *f* disponível.
coffin ['kɒfɪn] *n* caixão *m.*
cog [kɒg] *n* [tooth on wheel] dente *m* de engrenagem; [wheel] roda *f* dentada; **a ~ in the machine** *fig* uma peça secundária.
cogent ['kəʊdʒənt] *adj* irrefutável.
cogitate ['kɒdʒɪteɪt] *vi fml* cogitar.
cognac ['kɒnjæk] *n* conhaque *m.*
cognitive ['kɒgnɪtɪv] *adj* cognitivo(va).
cogwheel ['kɒgwiːl] *n* roda *f* dentada.
cohabit [ˌkəʊ'hæbɪt] *vi*: **to ~ (with sb)** coabitar (com alguém).
coherent [kəʊ'hɪərənt] *adj* coerente.
coherently [kəʊ'hɪərəntlɪ] *adv* coerentemente.
cohesion [kəʊ'hiːʒn] *n (U)* [unity] coesão *f.*
cohesive [kəʊ'hiːsɪv] *adj* [united] coeso(sa).
cohort ['kəʊhɔːt] *n* **-1.** *pej* [companion] bando *m* **-2.** [in statistics] grupo *m.*
COI (*abbr of* **Central Office of Information**) *n serviço de informação do governo britânico.*
coil [kɔɪl] <> *n* **-1.** [of rope, wire] rolo *m* **-2.** [of smoke] espiral *f* **-3.** *ELEC* bobina *f* **-4.** *UK* [contraceptive device] DIU *m.* <> *vt* enrolar. <> *vi* enrolar-se, enroscar-se.
◆ **coil up** *vt sep* enrolar-se.
coiled [kɔɪld] *adj* enrolado(da).
coin [kɔɪn] <> *n* moeda *f.* <> *vt* [invent] criar; **to ~ a phrase** como se pode dizer.
coinage ['kɔɪnɪdʒ] *n* **-1.** *(U)* [currency] moeda *f* **-2.** *(U)* [system] sistema *m* monetário **-3.** [invented word, phrase] invenção *f.*
coincide [ˌkəʊɪn'saɪd] *vi* **-1.** [occur simultaneously]: **to ~ (with sthg)** coincidir (com algo) **-2.** [be in agreement] coincidir.
coincidence [kəʊ'ɪnsɪdəns] *n* [chance event] coincidência *f.*
coincidental [kəʊˌɪnsɪ'dentl] *adj* coincidente.
coincidentally [kəʊˌɪnsɪ'dentəlɪ] *adv* coincidentemente.
coin-operated [-'ɒpəˌreɪtɪd] *adj* que funciona com moedas.
coitus ['kəʊɪtəs] *n (U) fml* coito *m.*
coke [kəʊk] *n* **-1.** [fuel] coque *m* **-2.** *inf* [cocaine] coca *f.*
Coke® [kəʊk] *n* Coca® *f.*
Col. (*abbr of* **colonel**) cel.
cola ['kəʊlə] *n* refrigerante *m* de cola.
COLA (*abbr of* **cost-of-living adjustment**) *n na Grã-Bretanha, atualização salarial feita de acordo com o custo de vida.*
colander ['kʌləndə^r] *n* coador *m.*
cold [kəʊld] <> *adj* frio (fria); **to feel ~** [person] sentir frio; **to be ~** [person] estar com frio; **it's ~ today** está frio hoje; **to get ~** [person] ficar com frio; [food] esfriar. <> *n* **-1.** [illness] resfriado *m*; **to catch (a) ~** pegar um resfriado **-2.** *(U)* [low temperature]: **the ~** o frio.
cold-blooded [-'blʌdɪd] *adj* **-1.** *BIOL* de sangue frio **-2.** [unfeeling] frio (fria) **-3.** [ruthless - killer, murderer] de sangue frio; [- killing, murder] a sangue frio.
cold cream *n (U)* creme *m* para a pele.
cold cuts *npl US* frios *mpl.*
cold feet *npl*: **to have** *OR* **get ~** *inf* amarelar.
cold-hearted [-'hɑːtɪd] *adj* insensível.
coldly ['kəʊldlɪ] *adv* friamente.
coldness ['kəʊldnɪs] *n (U)* **-1.** [low temperature] friagem *f* **-2.** [attitude, response] frieza *f.*
cold shoulder *n*: **to give sb the ~** *inf* dar um gelo em alguém.
cold sore *n* herpes *m inv* bucal.
cold storage *n (U)* [of food] refrigeração *f.*
cold sweat *n* suor *m* frio; **to be in a ~ about sthg** suar frio por causa de algo.
cold war *n*: **the ~** a guerra fria.
coleslaw ['kəʊlslɔː] *n (U)* salada *f* de repolho.
colic ['kɒlɪk] *n (U)* cólica *f.*
collaborate [kə'læbəreɪt] *vi* **-1.** [work together] colaborar; **to ~ with sb** colaborar com alguém **-2.** *pej* [with enemy] conspirar; **to ~ with sb** conspirar com alguém.
collaboration [kəˌlæbə'reɪʃn] *n* **-1.** *(U)* [teamwork] colaboração *f*; **~ with sb** colaboração com alguém **-2.** *pej* [with enemy] conspiração *f*; **~ with sb** conspiração com alguém.
collaborative [kə'læbərətɪv] *adj* conjunto(ta).
collaborator [kə'læbəreɪtə^r] *n* **-1.** [colleague] colaborador *m*, -ra *f* **-2.** *pej* [traitor] traidor *m*, -ra *f.*
collage ['kɒlɑːʒ] *n* colagem *f.*
collagen ['kɒlədʒən] *n (U)* colágeno *m.*
collapse [kə'læps] <> *n (U)* **-1.** [gen] colapso *m* **-2.** [of building, roof] desmoronamento *m.* <> *vi* **-1.** [gen] desmoronar **-2.** [fail] fracassar **-3.** [person] ter um colapso; **his lung ~d** o pulmão dele entrou em falência; **to ~ with a heart attack** ter um ataque do coração; **I ~d into bed** desfaleci na cama **-4.** [folding table, chair] desmontar-se.
collapsible [kə'læpsəbl] *adj* desmontável.
collar ['kɒlə^r] <> *n* **-1.** [on garment - shirt] colarinho *m*; [- dress, jacket] gola *f* **-2.** [for dog] coleira *f* **-3.** *TECH* anel *m.* <> *vt inf* [detain] segurar.
collarbone ['kɒləbəʊn] *n* clavícula *f.*
collate [kə'leɪt] *vt* **-1.** [compare] confrontar **-2.** [put in order] ordenar.

collateral [kɒˈlætərəl] *n (U)* garantia *f* de empréstimo, caução *f.*
collation [kəˈleɪʃn] *n (U)* **-1.** [comparison] confrontação *f* **-2.** [ordering] ordenação *f.*
colleague [ˈkɒliːg] *n* colega *mf.*
collect [kəˈlekt] <> *vt* **-1.** [gather together - wood, bottles, belongings] juntar; [- material for book] colher, coletar: **to ~ o.s.** *OR* **one's thoughts** recompor-se **-2.** [as a hobby] colecionar **-3.** [fetch, pick up] buscar **-4.** [money, taxes] cobrar; **~ on delivery** *US* cobrar na entrega. <> *vi* **-1.** [crowd, people] reunir-se **-2.** [dust, dirt] juntar **-3.** [for charity, gift] arrecadar. <> *adv* ***US*** *TELEC*: **to call (sb) ~** ligar (para alguém) a cobrar.
◆ **collect up** *vt sep* juntar.
collectable [kəˈlektəbl] <> *adj* [desirable to collectors] de coleção. <> *n* [desirable object] colecionável *m.*
collected [kəˈlektɪd] *adj* **-1.** [person] controlado(da) **-2.** [works, poems] completo(ta).
collecting [kəˈlektɪŋ] *n (U)* [hobby] coleção *f*; **stamp ~** colecionar selos.
collection [kəˈlekʃn] *n* **-1.** [of objects] coleção *f* **-2.** [anthology] antologia *f* **-3.** *(U)* [act of collecting] coleta *f* **-4.** [of money] arrecadação *f*, vaquinha *f*; **they made a ~ to buy flowers for her** fizeram uma vaquinha para comprar flores para ela.
collective [kəˈlektɪv] <> *adj* coletivo(va). <> *n* cooperativa *f.*
collective bargaining *n (U)* negociações *fpl (entre empregadores e sindicatos).*
collectively [kəˈlektɪvlɪ] *adv* coletivamente.
collective ownership *n (U)* propriedade *f* conjunta.
collector [kəˈlektəʳ] *n* **-1.** [as a hobby] colecionador *m*, -ra *f* **-2.** [of taxes] coletor *m*, -ra *f* **-3.** [of debts, rent] cobrador *m*, -ra *f.*
collector's item *n* peça *f* de coleção.
college [ˈkɒlɪdʒ] *n* **-1.** [for further education] escola *f*; **a ~ of technology** um instituto de tecnologia; **art ~** escola de artes; **community ~** *US* escola politécnica **-2.** ***UK*** [of university] *instituição dentro de certas universidades britânicas que possui corpo docente, instalações e estudantes próprios* **-3.** [organized body] colégio *m*; **electoral ~** colégio eleitoral.
college of education *n* faculdade *f* de educação.
collide [kəˈlaɪd] *vi*: **to ~ (with sb/sthg)** colidir (com alguém/algo).
collie [ˈkɒlɪ] *n* collie *m.*
colliery [ˈkɒljərɪ] (*pl* **-ies**) *n* ***UK*** mina *f* de carvão *(incluindo suas instalações).*
collision [kəˈlɪʒn] *n* **-1.** [crash]: **~ (with sb/sthg)** colisão *f* (com alguém/algo); **~ between** colisão de **-2.** *fig* [conflict] conflito *m*; **head-on ~** colisão *f* frontal.
collision course *n*: **to be on a ~** estar em rota de colisão.
colloquial [kəˈləʊkwɪəl] *adj* coloquial.
colloquialism [kaˈləʊkwɪəlɪzm] *n* coloquialismo *m.*
collude [kəˈluːd] *vi*: **to ~ with sb** entrar em conluio com alguém.
collusion [kəˈluːʒn] *n*: **in ~ with** em conluio com.
cologne [kəˈləʊn] *n (U)* água-de-colônia *f.*
Colombia [kəˈlɒmbɪəl *n* Colômbia; **in ~** na Colômbia.
Colombian [kəˈlɒmbɪən] <> *adj* colombiano(na). <> *n* colombiano *m*, -na *f.*
colon [ˈkəʊlən] *n* **-1.** *ANAT* cólon *m* **-2.** [punctuation mark] dois-pontos *mpl.*
colonel [ˈkɜːnl] *n* coronel *m.*
colonial [kəˈləʊnjəl] *adj* [rule, power] colonial.
colonialism [kəˈləʊnjəlɪzm] *n (U)* colonialismo *m.*
colonist [ˈkɒlənɪst] *n* colonizador *m*, -ra *f.*
colonize, -ise [ˈkɒlənaɪz] *vt* colonizar.
colonnade [ˌkɒləˈneɪd] *n* colunata *f.*
colony [ˈkɒlənɪ] (*pl* **-ies**) *n* **-1.** [gen] colônia *f* **-2.** [of artists] retiro *m.*
color etc *US* = **colour etc.**
colorado beetle *n* dorífero *m.*
colossal [kəˈlɒsl] *adj* colossal.
colostomy [kəˈlɒstəmɪ] (*pl* **-ies**) *n* colostomia *f.*
colour *UK*, **color** *US* [ˈkʌləʳ] <> *n* cor *f*; **red/blue in ~** na cor vermelha/azul; **the photos are in ~** as fotos são coloridas. <> *adj* colorido(da); **~ television/diagram** televisão/diagrama em cores. <> *vt* **-1.** [food, liquid] tingir; [with pen, crayon] pintar, colorir **-2.** [dye] tingir **-3.** *fig* [affect] influenciar. <> *vi* [blush] corar.
◆ **colours** *npl* **-1.** [of school, team] cores *fpl* **-2.** [flag] bandeira *f.*
◆ **colour in** *vt sep* colorir.
colour bar *n* discriminação *f* racial.
colour blind *adj* **-1.** daltônico(ca) **-2.** *fig* [racially unprejudiced] que não faz discriminação racial.
colour-coded *adj* identificado(da) *OR* codificado(da) por cores.
coloured *UK*, **colored** *US* [ˈkʌləd] *adj* **-1.** [having colour] colorido(da) **-2.** [having stated colour]: **a cream-~ed jacket** uma jaqueta cor de creme; **a brightly ~ed shirt** uma camisa de cores vivas.
colourfast *UK*, **colorfast** *US* [ˈkʌləfɑːst] *adj* de cores firmes.
colourful *UK*, **colorful** *US* [ˈkʌləfʊl] *adj* **-1.** [brightly coloured] colorido(da) **-2.** [story] vivo(va) **-3.** [person] animado(da).
colouring *UK*, **coloring** *US* [ˈkʌlərɪŋ] *n* **-1.** [dye] corante *m* **-2.** *(U)* [complexion, hair] tonalidade *f* **-3.** [colours] cor *m.*
colourless *UK*, **colorless** *US* [ˈkʌləlɪs] *adj* **-1.** [not coloured] incolor **-2.** *fig* [uninteresting] sem graça.
colour scheme *n* distribuição *f* de cores.
colour supplement *n* ***UK*** suplemento *m* em cores.
colt [kəʊlt] *n* [young horse] potro *m.*
column [ˈkɒləm] *n* **-1.** [gen] coluna *f* **-2.** [of people, vehicles] fila *f.*
columnist [ˈkɒləmnɪst] *n* colunista *mf.*
coma [ˈkəʊmə] *n* coma *m.*
comatose [ˈkəʊmətəʊs] *adj* [in a coma] em coma.
comb [kəʊm] <> *n* [for hair] pente *m.* <> *vt* **-1.** [hair] pentear **-2.** *fig* [search] vasculhar.
combat [ˈkɒmbæt] <> *n* combate *m.* <> *vt* [fight] combater.
combative [ˈkɒmbətɪv] *adj* combativo(va).

combination [ˌkɒmbɪ'neɪʃn] *n* combinação *f*.

combination lock *n* fechadura *f* com segredo.

combine [*vb* kəm'baɪn, *n* 'kɒmbaɪn] <> *vt* [join together] agrupar; **to ~ sthg with sthg** [two substances] combinar algo com algo; [two qualities] reunir; [two activities] conjugar. <> *vi* [businesses, political parties]: **to ~ (with sb/sthg)** aliar-se (a alguém/algo). <> *n* **-1.** [group] associação *f* **-2.** = **combine harvester**.

combined *adj*: **~ (with sb/sthg)** conjunto(ta) (com alguém/algo).

combine harvester [-'hɑːvɪstəʳ] *n* colheitadeira *f*.

combustible [kəm'bʌstəbl] *adj* [substance] combustível.

combustion [kəm'bʌstʃn] *n (U)* combustão *f*.

come [kʌm] (*pt* **came**, *pp* **come**) *vi* **-1.** [move] vir; [arrive] chegar; **the news came as a shock** a notícia foi um choque; **coming!** estou indo; **the time has ~** chegou a hora; **he doesn't know whether he's coming or going** *fig* ele não sabe o que fazer **-2.** [reach]: **to ~ up/down to** chegar a **-3.** [happen] chegar a; **how did you ~ to fail your exam?** como que você foi rodar no exame?; **~ what may** haja o que houver **-4.** [become]: **to ~ true** tornar-se realidade; **to ~ undone/unstuck** se desfazer/soltar **-5.** [begin gradually]: **to ~ to do sthg** passar a fazer algo **-6.** [be placed in order] classificar-se; **P ~s before Q** o P vem antes do Q; **she came second in the exam** ela se classificou em segundo lugar no exame **-7.** *v inf* [sexually] gozar **-8.** *phr*: **~ to think of it** pensando bem.

◆ **to come** *adv* vindouro(ra); **in (the) days/years to ~** nos dias/anos vindouros.

◆ **come about** *vi* [happen] acontecer.

◆ **come across** <> *vt fus* [find] encontrar. <> *vi* [speaker, message] apresentar-se; **to ~ across as** parecer.

◆ **come along** *vi* **-1.** [arrive by chance] aparecer **-2.** [improve] desenvolver-se; **the project is coming along nicely** o projeto está se desenvolvendo bem **-3.** *phr*: **~ along!** [expressing encouragement] anda!; [hurry up] anda logo!

◆ **come apart** *vi* **-1.** [fall to pieces] desfazer-se **-2.** [come off] cair.

◆ **come at** *vt fus* [attack] avançar para.

◆ **come back** *vi* **-1.** [in talk, writing]: **to ~ back to sthg** voltar a algo **-2.** [memory]: **to ~ back (to sb)** lembrar(-se) de **-3.** [become fashionable again] voltar.

◆ **come by** *vt fus* **-1.** [get, obtain] conseguir **-2.** *US* [visit, drop in on] dar uma chegada.

◆ **come down** *vi* **-1.** [unemployment, prices] baixar **-2.** [aeroplane, parachutist] descer **-3.** [rain] cair.

◆ **come down to** *vt fus* resumir-se a.

◆ **come down with** *vt fus* [cold, flu] apanhar.

◆ **come forward** *vi* [witnesses, volunteers] apresentar-se.

◆ **come from** *vt fus* vir de.

◆ **come in** *vi* **-1.** [enter] entrar **-2.** [arrive, be received] chegar **-3.** [be involved] entrar.

◆ **come in for** *vt fus* [criticism] receber.

◆ **come into** *vt fus* **-1.** [inherit] receber **-2.** [begin to be]: **to ~ into being** surgir; **to ~ into sight** aparecer.

◆ **come of** *vt fus* [result from] dar em; **no good will ~ of it** isso não vai acabar bem.

◆ **come off** *vi* **-1.** [button, label, lid] abrir **-2.** [attempt, joke] dar certo **-3.** [finish]: **to ~ off well/badly** sair-se bem/mal **-4.** [stain] sair **-5.** *phr*: **~ off it!** *inf* deixa disso!

◆ **come on** *vi* **-1.** [start] começar **-2.** [light, heating] ligar-se **-3.** [progress, improve] ir; **how's the work coming on?** como está indo o trabalho? **-4.** *phr*: **~ on!** [expressing encouragement] vamos lá!; [hurry up] vamos; [expressing disbelief] que é isso.

◆ **come out** *vi* **-1.** [truth, fact] revelar-se **-2.** [product, book, film] ser lançado **-3.** [finish] acabar; **to ~ out well/badly** sair(-se) bem/mal **-4.** [go on strike] entrar em greve **-5.** [declare publicly]: **to ~ out for/against sthg** manifestar-se a favor/contra algo **-6.** [photograph] sair **-7.** [sun, moon, stars] aparecer.

◆ **come out in** *vt fus*: **to ~ out in spots** ficar com manchas.

◆ **come out with** *vt fus* [remark] sair com.

◆ **come over** *vt fus* [subj: sensation, emotion] tomar conta de.

◆ **come round** *vi* **-1.** [change opinion]: **to ~ round (to sthg)** concordar (com algo) **-2.** [regain consciousness] voltar a si **-3.** [Christmas, birthday, summer] chegar.

◆ **come through** <> *vt fus* [survive] sobreviver a. <> *vi* **-1.** [news, reports, results] chegar **-2.** [survive] sobreviver.

◆ **come to** <> *vt fus* **-1.** [reach]: **to ~ to an end** chegar ao fim; **to ~ to power** chegar ao poder; **to ~ to a decision** chegar a uma decisão **-2.** [amount to] chegar a. <> *vi* [regain consciousness] voltar a si.

◆ **come under** *vt fus* **-1.** [be governed by] ser de competência de **-2.** [heading] aparecer em **-3.** [suffer]: **to ~ under attack (from)** sofrer ataque (de).

◆ **come up** *vi* **-1.** [gen] surgir **-2.** [be imminent] estar próximo.

◆ **come up against** *vt fus* [opposition, difficulties] enfrentar.

◆ **come upon** *vt fus* [find] encontrar.

◆ **come up to** *vt fus* **-1.** [in space] chegar até ; [in time] estar chegando **-2.** [equal] comparar-se.

◆ **come up with** *vt fus* [answer, idea, solution] aparecer com.

comeback ['kʌmbæk] *n* [return] reaparecimento *m*; **to make a ~** reaparecer.

comedian [kə'miːdjən] *n* [comic] comediante *m*.

comedienne [kəˌmiːdɪ'en] *n* [comic] comediante *f*.

comedown ['kʌmdaʊn] *n inf* [anticlimax] retrocesso *m*.

comedy ['kɒmədɪ] (*pl* **-ies**) *n* comédia *f*.

comely ['kʌmlɪ] *adj literary* atraente.

come-on *n inf*: **to give sb the ~** estar a fim de alguém.

comet ['kɒmɪt] *n* cometa *m*.

come-uppance [ˌkʌm'ʌpəns] *n inf*: **to get one's ~** levar o troco.

comfort ['kʌmfət] <> *n* **-1.** *(U)* [ease] conforto *m*;

too close for ~ desconfortável devido à proximidade **-2.** [luxury] luxo *m* **-3.** [solace] consolo *m.* <> *vt* consolar.

comfortable ['kʌmftəbl] *adj* **-1.** [chair, room] confortável **-2.** [at ease] à vontade **-3.** [financially secure] bem de vida **-4.** [after operation, accident] bem **-5.** [ample] amplo(pla).

comfortably ['kʌmftəblɪ] *adv* **-1.** [sit, sleep] confortavelmente **-2.** [without financial difficulty] bem; **I can manage ~ on £50 a week** posso me virar bem com 50 libras por semana; **~ off** em boa situação **-3.** [win] com facilidade.

comforter ['kʌmfətəʳ] *n* **-1.** [person] consolador *m*, -ra *f* **-2.** *US* [quilt] edredon *m.*

comforting ['kʌmfətɪŋ] *adj* [thought, words] consolador(ra), confortante.

comfort station *n US euph* banheiro *m* público.

comfy ['kʌmfɪ] (*compar* **-ier**, *superl* **-iest**) *adj inf* **-1.** [chair, room] confortável **-2.** [person] à vontade.

comic ['kɒmɪk] <> *adj* [amusing] engraçado(da). <> *n* **-1.** [comedian] comediante *mf* **-2.** [magazine] história *f* em quadrinhos, gibi *m.*

◆ **comics** *npl US* [in newspaper] tira *f* em quadrinhos.

comical ['kɒmɪkl] *adj* [amusing] engraçado(da).

comic strip *n* tira *f* em quadrinhos.

coming ['kʌmɪŋ] <> *adj* [future] próximo(ma). <> *n*: **~s and goings** idas *fpl* e vindas.

comma ['kɒmə] *n* vírgula *f.*

command [kə'mɑːnd] <> *n* **-1.** [order] comando *m* **-2.** *(U)* [control] comando *m*; **in ~ of sthg** no comando de algo **-3.** [mastery] domínio *m*; **at one's ~** à disposição; **she has four languages at her ~** ela domina quatro idiomas **-4.** *COMPUT* comando *m.* <> *vt* **-1.** [order] mandar; **to ~ sb to do sthg** mandar alguém fazer algo **-2.** *MIL* [control] comandar **-3.** [deserve] merecer.

commandant [ˌkɒmən'dænt] *n* comandante *mf.*

commandeer [ˌkɒmən'dɪəʳ] *vt* confiscar.

commander [kə'mɑːndəʳ] *n* **-1.** [in army] comandante *mf* **-2.** [in navy] capitão *m*, -tã *f.*

commander in chief (*pl* **commanders in chief**) *n* comandante-chefe *m.*

commanding [kə'mɑːndɪŋ] *adj* **-1.** [lead, position] de comando **-2.** [voice, manner] autoritário(ria) **-3.** [view] dominante.

commanding officer *n* comandante *mf.*

commandment [kə'mɑːndmənt] *n RELIG* mandamento *m.*

command module *n* módulo *m* de comando.

commando [kə'mɑːndəʊ] (*pl* **-s** *OR* **-es**) *n* **-1.** [unit] unidade *f* de assalto **-2.** [soldier] soldado *m* da unidade de assalto.

command performance *n no Reino Unido, espetáculo feito por ordem superior.*

commemorate [kə'meməreɪt] *vt* homenagear.

commemoration [kəˌmemə'reɪʃn] *n*: **in ~ of** em homenagem a.

commemorative [kə'memərətɪv] *adj* comemorativo(va).

commence [kə'mens] *fml* <> *vt* principiar; **to ~ doing sthg** principiar algo. <> *vi* principiar.

commencement [kə'mensmənt] *n fml* [beginning] princípio *m.*

commend [kə'mend] *vt* **-1.** [praise]: **to ~ sb (on** *OR* **for sthg)** elogiar alguém (por algo) **-2.** [recommend]: **to ~ sthg (to sb)** recomendar algo (a alguém); **we ~ our souls to God** encomendamos nossas almas a Deus.

commendable [kə'mendəbl] *adj* louvável.

commendation [ˌkɒmen'deɪʃn] *n* [special award] condecoração *f.*

commensurate [kə'menʃərət] *adj fml*: **~ with sthg** proporcional a algo.

comment ['kɒment] <> *n* comentário *m*; **no ~** sem comentários. <> *vt*: **to ~ that** comentar que. <> *vi* comentar; **to ~ on sthg** comentar algo.

commentary ['kɒməntrɪ] (*pl* **-ies**) *n* **-1.** *RADIO & TV* comentário *m* **-2.** [written explanation, comment] crítica *f.*

commentate ['kɒmənteɪt] *vi RADIO & TV*: **to ~ (on sthg)** narrar (algo).

commentator ['kɒmənteɪtəʳ] *n* **-1.** [*RADIO & TV* - making comments] comentarista *mf*; [- describing] narrador *m*, -ra *f* **-2.** [expert] analista *mf*; **political ~** analista político.

commerce ['kɒmɜːs] *n (U)* comércio *m.*

commercial [kə'mɜːʃl] <> *adj* comercial. <> *n* [advertisement] comercial *m.*

commercial bank *n* banco *m* comercial.

commercial break *n* (intervalo *m*) comercial *m.*

commercialism [kə'mɜːʃəlɪzm] *n (U) pej* mercantilismo *m.*

commercialize, -ise [kə'mɜːʃəlaɪz] *vt* comercializar.

commercialized [kə'mɜːʃəlaɪzd] *adj pej* comercializado(da).

commercially [kə'mɜːʃəlɪ] *adv* comercialmente.

commercial vehicle *n UK* veículo *m* comercial.

commie ['kɒmɪ] *inf pej* <> *adj* comuna. <> *n* comuna *mf.*

commiserate [kə'mɪzəreɪt] *vi*: **to ~ (with sb)** compadecer-se (de alguém).

commiseration [kəˌmɪzə'reɪʃn] *n* compadecimento *m*, comiseração *f.*

commission [kə'mɪʃn] <> *n* **-1.** [gen] comissão *f* **-2.** [piece of work] encomenda *f.* <> *vt* [work] encomendar; **to ~ sb (to do sthg)** encarregar alguém (de fazer algo).

commissionaire [kəˌmɪʃə'neəʳ] *n UK* porteiro *m*, -ra *f.*

commissioner [kə'mɪʃnəʳ] *n* **-1.** [high-ranking public official] comissário *m*, -ria *f* **-2.** [member of commission] membro *m* de uma comissão, delegado *m*, -da *f.*

commit [kə'mɪt] (*pt* & *pp* **-ted**, *cont* **-ting**) *vt* **-1.** [carry out] cometer **-2.** [promise] comprometer; **to ~ o.s. (to sthg/to doing sthg)** comprometer-se (a algo/a fazer algo) **-3.** [person to institution] confinar **-4.**: **to ~ sthg to memory** confiar algo à memória.

commitment [kə'mɪtmənt] *n* **-1.** *(U)* [dedication] dedicação *f* **-2.** [responsibility] compromisso *m.*

committed [kə'mɪtɪd] *adj* [writer, artist, Christian] comprometido(da); **~ to sb/sthg** comprometido(da) com alguém/algo.

committee [kə'mɪtɪ] *n* comitê *m.*

commode [kə'məʊd] *n* comadre *f*.

commodity [kə'mɒdətɪ] (*pl* **-ies**) *n* **-1.** [gen] mercadoria *f* **-2.** *ECON* commodity *f*.

commodity exchange *n* bolsa *f* de mercadorias.

common ['kɒmən] ◇ *adj* **-1.** [gen] comum; ~ **to** comum a **-2.** *UK pej* [vulgar] vulgar. ◇ *n* [land] área *f* pública.
◆ **in common** *adv* em comum.

common denominator *n* **-1.** *MATH* denominador *m* comum **-2.** [characteristic in common] característica *f* em comum.

commoner ['kɒmənə^r] *n* plebeu *m*, -béia *f*.

common good *n*: **for the** ~ pelo bem comum.

common ground *n (U)* ponto *m* pacífico.

common knowledge *n (U)* conhecimento *m* geral.

common land *n (U)* área *f* pública.

common law *n* direito *m* consuetudinário, lei *f* comum.
◆ **common-law** *adj* concubinário(ria).

commonly ['kɒmənlɪ] *adv* [generally] geralmente.

commonplace ['kɒmənpleɪs] ◇ *adj* [everyday] trivial. ◇ *n* [frequent phenomenon] lugar-comum *m*.

common room *n* [in school, college] sala *f* de recreação.

Commons ['kɒmənz] *npl UK*: **the** ~ a Câmara dos Comuns.

common sense *n (U)* senso *m* comum.

Commonwealth ['kɒmənwelθ] *n* [former British colonies]: **the** ~ a Comunidade Britânica.

Commonwealth of Independent States *n*: **the** ~ a Comunidade dos Estados Independentes.

commotion [kə'məʊʃn] *n* comoção *f*.

communal ['kɒmjʊnl] *adj* comum.

commune [*n* 'kɒ'mju:n, *vb* kə'mju:n] ◇ *n* [group of people] comuna *f*. ◇ *vi*: **to** ~ **with** comungar com.

communicate [kə'mju:nɪkeɪt] ◇ *vt* comunicar. ◇ *vi* comunicar-se, relacionar-se; **to** ~ **with** comunicar-se com.

communicating [kə'mju:nɪkeɪtɪŋ] *adj* [doors, rooms] com comunicação.

communication [kə,mju:nɪ'keɪʃn] *n (U)* comunicação *f*.
◆ **communications** *npl* comunicações *fpl*.

communications satellite *n* satélite *m* de comunicações.

communications technology *n* tecnologia *f* de comunicação.

communicative [kə'mju:nɪkətɪv] *adj* [talkative] comunicativo(va).

communicator [kə'mju:nɪkeɪtə^r] *n*: **a good/bad** ~ um bom/mau comunicador, uma boa/má comunicadora.

communion [kə'mju:njən] *n (U)* [communication] comunhão *f*.
◆ **Communion** *n (U) RELIG* comunhão *f*.

communiqué [kə'mju:nɪkeɪ] *n* comunicado *m*.

communism *n (U)* comunismo *m*.

communist ◇ *adj* comunista. ◇ *n* comunista *mf*.

community [kə'mju:nətɪ] (*pl* **-ies**) *n* [group] comunidade *f*; **the** ~ a comunidade.

community centre *n* centro *m* comunitário.

community home *n UK* ≃ Febem *f*.

community policing *n (U)* policiamento *m* comunitário.

community service *n (U)* **-1.** [imposed on offender] prestação *m* de serviços à comunidade **-2.** *UK* [voluntary] trabalho *m* voluntário.

community spirit *n (U)* espírito *m* comunitário.

commutable [kə'mju:təbl] *adj JUR* [sentence] comutável.

commutation ticket [,kɒmju:'teɪʃn-] *n US* passagem *f* integrada.

commute [kə'mju:t] ◇ *vt JUR* comutar. ◇ *vi* [to work] *viajar regularmente entre a casa e o trabalho, especialmente de trem.*

commuter [kə'mju:tə^r] *n pessoa que viaja regularmente entre a casa e o trabalho, especialmente de trem.*

commy ['kɒmɪ] (*pl* **-ies**) *adj* & *n* = **commie**.

Comoro Islands *npl*: **the** ~ as Ilhas de Comoro.

compact [*adj* & *vb* kəm'pækt, *n* 'kɒmpækt] ◇ *adj* [small and neat] compacto(ta). ◇ *n* **-1.** [for face powder] estojo *m* **-2.** *US AUT*: ~ **(car)** carro *m* de médio porte. ◇ *vt* compactar.

compact disc *n* disco *m* compacto, CD *m*.

compact disc player *n* CD-player *m*, toca-CD *m*.

companion [kəm'pænjən] *n* **-1.** [gen] companheiro *m*, -ra *f* **-2.** [book] compêndio *m*.

companionable [kəm'pænjənəbl] *adj* amigável.

companionship [kəm'pænjənʃɪp] *n (U)* camaradagem *f*.

company ['kʌmpənɪ] (*pl* **-ies**) *n* **-1.** [gen] companhia *f*; **to keep sb** ~ fazer companhia a alguém; **to part** ~ **(with sb)** romper relações (com alguém) **-2.** [business] companhia *f*, empresa *f*.

company car *n* carro *m* da empresa.

company director *n* diretor *m*, -ra *f* de empresa *OR* companhia.

company secretary *n* secretário *m*, -ria *f* geral da empresa *OR* companhia.

comparable ['kɒmprəbl] *adj* comparável; ~ **to** *OR* **with** comparável a *OR* com.

comparative [kəm'pærətɪv] *adj* **-1.** [relative] relativo(va) **-2.** [study, literature] comparado(da) **-3.** *GRAM* comparativo(va).

comparatively [kəm'pærətɪvlɪ] *adv* [relatively] relativamente.

compare [kəm'peə^r] ◇ *vt* comparar; **to** ~ **sb/sthg with** *OR* **to** comparar alguém/algo com *OR* a; ~**d with** *OR* **to** comparado com *OR* a. ◇ *vi*: **to** ~ **(with sb/sthg)** comparar-se (com alguém/algo); **to** ~ **favourably/unfavourably with sthg** ser melhor/pior que algo.

comparison [kəm'pærɪsn] *n* comparação *f*; **in** ~ **(with** *OR* **to)** em comparação(com *OR* a).

compartment [kəm'pɑ:tmənt] *n* compartimento *m*.

compartmentalize, -ise [,kɒmpɑ:t'mentəlaɪz] *vt* compartimentar.

compass ['kʌmpəs] *n* **-1.** [for finding direction] bússola

f **-2.** *fml* [scope] alcance *f*; **within the ~ of sb/sthg** ao alcance de alguém/algo.
◆ **compasses** *npl* compasso *m*; **a pair of ~es** um compasso.
compassion [kəm'pæʃn] *n (U)* compaixão *f*.
compassionate [kəm'pæʃənət] *adj* compassível.
compassionate leave *n tempo que o empregador permite que o funcionário se ausente do trabalho por razões pessoais.*
compatibility [kəm,pætə'bɪlətɪ] *n (U)* ~ **(with)** compatibilidade *f* (com).
compatible [kəm'pætəbl] *adj* ~ **(with)** compatível (com).
compatriot [kəm'pætrɪət] *n* compatriota *mf*.
compel [kəm'pel] (*pt* & *pp* **-led**, *cont* **-ling**) *vt* **-1.** [force] compelir; **to ~ sb to do sthg** compelir alguém a fazer algo **-2.** [demand] impelir.
compelling [kəm'pelɪŋ] *adj* **-1.** [argument, reason] convincente **-2.** [book, film, performance] envolvente.
compendium [kəm'pendɪəm] (*pl* **-diums** OR **-dia** [-dɪə]) *n* [book] compêndio *m*.
compensate ['kɒmpenseɪt] ◇ *vt*: **to ~ sb for sthg** [financially] compensar alguém por algo. ◇ *vi*: **to ~ for sthg** compensar algo.
compensation [,kɒmpen'seɪʃn] *n*: ~ **(for sthg)** compensação *f* (por algo).
compere ['kɒmpeəʳ] *UK* ◇ *n* apresentador *m*, -ra *f*. ◇ *vt* apresentar.
compete [kəm'pi:t] *vi* **-1.** [vie]: **to ~ (for sthg)** competir (por algo); **to ~ with** OR **against sb (for sthg)** competir com OR contra alguém (por algo) **-2.** COMM: **to ~ (with sb/sthg)** concorrer (com alguém/algo); **to ~ for sthg** disputar algo **-3.** [take part]: **to ~ (in sthg)** participar (de algo).
competence ['kɒmpɪtəns] *n (U)* [proficiency] competência *f*.
competent ['kɒmpɪtənt] *adj* competente.
competently ['kɒmpɪtəntlɪ] *adv* competentemente.
competing [kəm'pi:tɪŋ] *adj* [conflicting] conflitante.
competition [,kɒmpɪ'tɪʃn] *n* **-1.** [gen] competição *f* **-2.** *(U)* COMM concorrência *f*.
competitive [kəm'petətɪv] *adj* competitivo(va).
competitively [kəm'petətɪvlɪ] *adv* competitivamente.
competitor [kəm'petɪtəʳ] *n* **-1.** [in business] concorrente *mf* **-2.** [in race, contest] competidor *m*, -ra *f*.
compilation [,kɒmpɪ'leɪʃn] *n* compilação *f*.
compile [kəm'paɪl] *vt* compilar.
complacency [kəm'pleɪsnsɪ] *n (U)* complacência *f*.
complacent [kəm'pleɪsnt] *adj* complacente.
complacently [kəm'pleɪsntlɪ] *adv* com complacência.
complain [kəm'pleɪn] *vi* [moan] queixar-se; **to ~ about sthg** queixar-se de algo.
complaining [kəm'pleɪnɪŋ] *adj* que reclama.
complaint [kəm'pleɪnt] *n* queixa *f*.
complement [*n* 'kɒmplɪmənt, *vb* 'kɒmplɪ,ment] ◇ *n* **-1.** [gen & GRAM] complemento *m* **-2.** [accompaniment] acompanhamento *m* **-3.** [number]: **a full ~ of** a totalidade de. ◇ *vt* **-1.** [gen] complementar **-2.** [accompany] acompanhar.
complementary [,kɒmplɪ'mentərɪ] *adj* complementar.
complete [kəm'pli:t] ◇ *adj* **-1.** [total, thorough] completo(ta); ~ **with** completo(ta) com **-2.** [finished, ended] concluído(da). ◇ *vt* **-1.** [collection, set, form] completar **-2.** [work, painting, book] concluir.
completely [kəm'pli:tlɪ] *adv* [totally] completamente.
completion [kəm'pli:ʃn] *n (U)* [of work] conclusão *f*.
complex ['kɒmpleks] ◇ *adj* complexo(xa). ◇ *n* complexo *m*.
complexion [kəm'plekʃn] *n* **-1.** [of face] aparência *f* **-2.** [aspect] caráter *m*.
complexity [kəm'pleksətɪ] (*pl* **-ies**) *n* complexidade *f*.
compliance [kəm'plaɪəns] *n (U)* [obedience] cumprimento *m*; ~ **with sthg** de acordo com algo.
compliant [kəm'plaɪənt] *adj* obediente.
complicate ['kɒmplɪkeɪt] *vt* complicar.
complicated ['kɒmplɪkeɪtɪd] *adj* complicado(da).
complication [,kɒmplɪ'keɪʃn] *n* complicação *f*.
complicity [kəm'plɪsətɪ] *n (U)*: ~ **(in sthg)** cumplicidade *f* (em algo).
compliment [*n* 'kɒmplɪmənt, *vb* 'kɒmplɪment] ◇ *n* cumprimento *m*, elogio *m*. ◇ *vt*: **to ~ sb (on sthg)** cumprimentar alguém (por algo).
◆ **compliments** *npl fml* cumprimentos *mpl*.
complimentary [,kɒmplɪ'mentərɪ] *adj* **-1.** [admiring] lisonjeiro(ra) **-2.** [free] gratuito(ta).
complimentary ticket *n* bilhete *m* gratuito.
compliments slip *n* bilhete *m* de saudação.
comply [kəm'plaɪ] (*pt* & *pp* **-ied**) *vi*: **to ~ with sthg** cumprir algo.
component [kəm'pəʊnənt] *n* componente *m*.
compose [kəm'pəʊz] *vt* **-1.** [constitute] compor; **to be ~d of sthg** ser composto(ta) por algo **-2.** [write, create] escrever **-3.** [make calm]: **to ~ o.s.** recompor-se.
composed [kəm'pəʊzd] *adj* [calm] tranqüilo(la).
composer [kəm'pəʊzəʳ] *n* compositor *m*, -ra *f*.
composite ['kɒmpəzɪt] ◇ *adj* composto(ta). ◇ *n* composto *m*.
composition [,kɒmpə'zɪʃn] *n* composição *f*.
compost [*UK* 'kɒmpɒst, *US* 'kɒmpəʊst] *n (U)* adubo *m*.
composure [kəm'pəʊʒəʳ] *n (U)* compostura *f*.
compound [*adj* & *n* 'kɒmpaʊnd, *vb* kəm'paʊnd] ◇ *adj* composto(ta). ◇ *n* **-1.** [gen] composto *m* **-2.** [enclosed area] complexo *m*. ◇ *vt* **-1.** [exacerbate] agravar **-2.** [mixture, substance]: **to be ~ed of sthg** ser composto(ta) por algo.
compound fracture *n* MED fratura *f* exposta.
compound interest *n (U)* juros *mpl* compostos.
comprehend [,kɒmprɪ'hend] *vt* [understand] compreender.
comprehension [,kɒmprɪ'henʃn] *n* **-1.** *(U)* [understanding] compreensão *f* **-2.** SCH [exercise] interpretação *f*.
comprehensive [,kɒmprɪ'hensɪv] ◇ *adj* **-1.** [wide-ranging] abrangente **-2.** [insurance] total. ◇ *n UK* [school] = **comprehensive school**.

comprehensively [ˌkɒmprɪ'hensɪvlɪ] *adv* completamente.
comprehensive school *n escola estadual de ensino médio que abrange todas as habilidades.*
compress [kəm'pres] ◇ *n* MED compressa *f.* ◇ *vt* **-1.** [squeeze, press] comprimir **-2.** [condense] sintetizar.
compression [kəm'preʃn] *n (U)* **-1.** [of air] compressão *f* **-2.** [of text] redução *f.*
comprise [kəm'praɪz] *vt* **-1.** [consist of]: **to be ~d of** ser constituído(da) de **-2.** [constitute] constituir.
compromise ['kɒmprəmaɪz] ◇ *n* [concession, agreement] meio-termo *m.* ◇ *vt* [undermine integrity of] comprometer; **to ~ o.s.** comprometer-se. ◇ *vi* [make concessions] fazer concessões.
compromising ['kɒmprəmaɪzɪŋ] *adj* [embarrassing] comprometedor(ra).
compulsion [kəm'pʌlʃn] *n* **-1.** [strong desire] compulsão *f* **-2.** *(U)* [force] coação *f.*
compulsive [kəm'pʌlsɪv] *adj* **-1.** [behaviour, gambler, liar] compulsivo(va) **-2.** [compelling] envolvente.
compulsory [kəm'pʌlsərɪ] *adj* compulsório(ria).
compulsory purchase *n UK* desapropriação *f.*
compunction [kəm'pʌŋkʃn] *n (U)* compunção *f.*
computation [ˌkɒmpju:'teɪʃn] *n* cômputo *m.*
compute [kəm'pju:t] *vt* computar.
computational linguistics *n (U)* lingüística *f* computacional.
computer [kəm'pju:tə^r] ◇ *n* computador *m.* ◇ *comp* de computador.
computer dating [-'deɪtɪŋ] *n* agência *f* de namoro por computador.
computer game *n* jogo *m* de computador.
computer graphics *npl* infografia *f.*
computerization [kəmˌpju:tərаɪ'zeɪʃn] *n (U)* informatização *f.*
computerize, -ise [kəm'pju:təraɪz] *vt* informatizar.
computerized [kəm'pju:təraɪzd] *adj* informatizado(da).
computer-literate *adj* com conhecimentos de informática.
computer science *n* ciência *f* da computação.
computing [kəm'pju:tɪŋ] *n (U)* computação *f,* informática *f.*
comrade ['kɒmreɪd] *n* companheiro *m,* -ra *f.*
comradeship ['kɒmreɪdʃɪp] *n (U)* companheirismo *m,* camaradagem *f.*
con (*pt* & *pp* **-ned**, *cont* **-ning**) *fam n* (*abbr of* **convict**) *fam* presidiário *m,* -a *f.*
concave [ˌkɒn'keɪv] *adj* côncavo(va).
conceal [kən'si:l] *vt* [hide - object, substance] esconder; [- information, feelings] ocultar; **to ~ sthg from sb** esconder algo de alguém.
concede [kən'si:d] ◇ *vt* [admit] conceder. ◇ *vi* aceitar.
conceit [kən'si:t] *n (U)* [arrogance] presunção *f.*
conceited [kən'si:tɪd] *adj* presunçoso(sa).
conceivable [kən'si:vəbl] *adj* concebível.
conceivably [kən'si:vəblɪ] *adv* possivelmente.
conceive [kən'si:v] ◇ *vt* conceber. ◇ *vi* **-1.** MED conceber **-2.** [imagine]: **to ~ of sthg** conceber algo.
concentrate ['kɒnsəntreɪt] ◇ *vt* concentrar. ◇ *vi* concentrar-se; **to ~ on sthg** concentrar-se em algo.
concentrated ['kɒnsəntreɪtɪd] *adj* concentrado(-da).
concentration [ˌkɒnsən'treɪʃn] *n* concentração *f.*
concentration camp *n* campo *m* de concentração.
concentric [kən'sentrɪk] *adj* concêntrico(ca).
concept ['kɒnsept] *n* conceito *m.*
conception [kən'sepʃn] *n* concepção *f.*
conceptual art *n* arte *f* conceitual.
conceptualize, -ise [kən'septʃʊəlaɪz] *vt* conceituar.
concern [kən'sɜ:n] ◇ *n* **-1.** [worry, anxiety] preocupação *f* **-2.** [matter of interest] assunto *m*; **it's no ~ of mine!** não é da minha conta! **-3.** COMM [company] negócio *m.* ◇ *vt* **-1.** [worry]: **to be ~ed (about sb/sthg)** estar preocupado(da) (com alguém/algo) **-2.** [involve] dizer respeito(a); **to be ~ed with sthg** [subj: person] estar envolvido(da) com algo; **to ~ o.s. with sthg** preocupar-se com algo; **as far as ... is ~ed** no que diz respeito a ... **-3.** [subj: book, report, film] tratar de.
concerning [kən'sɜ:nɪŋ] *prep* acerca de, sobre.
concert ['kɒnsət] *n* concerto *m.*
◆ **in concert** *adv* **-1.** MUS em concerto **-2.** *fml* [acting as one] conjuntamente.
concerted [kən'sɜ:tɪd] *adj* [effort] conjunto(ta).
concertgoer ['kɒnsətˌgəʊə^r] *n* freqüentador *m,* -ra *f* de concertos.
concert hall *n* casa *f* de concertos.
concertina [ˌkɒnsə'ti:nə] (*pt* & *pp* **-ed**, *cont* **-ing**) ◇ *n* concertina *f.* ◇ *vi* engavetar-se.
concerto [kən'tʃeətəʊ] (*pl* **-s**) *n* concerto *m.*
concession [kən'seʃn] *n* **-1.** [allowance, point won] concessão *f* **-2.** COMM [franchise] franquia *f* **-3.** [special price] desconto *m.*
concessionaire *n* concessionário *m,* -ria *f.*
concessionary [kən'seʃnərɪ] *adj* [fare, price] com desconto.
conciliation [kənˌsɪlɪ'eɪʃn] *n (U)* conciliação *f.*
conciliatory [kən'sɪlɪətrɪ] *adj* conciliatório(ria).
concise [kən'saɪs] *adj* conciso(sa).
concisely [kən'saɪslɪ] *adv* concisamente.
conclave ['kɒŋkleɪv] *n* conclave *m.*
conclude [kən'klu:d] ◇ *vt* **-1.** [bring to an end] concluir **-2.** [deduce]: **to ~ (that)** concluir (que) **-3.** [agree on] firmar. ◇ *vi* [finish] concluir.
conclusion [kən'klu:ʒn] *n* [ending, decision] conclusão *f*; **to jump to the wrong ~** chegar à conclusão errada; **a foregone ~** uma conclusão previsível.
conclusive [kən'klu:sɪv] *adj* conclusivo(va).
concoct [kən'kɒkt] *vt* **-1.** [story, excuse, alibi] forjar **-2.** [mixture, drink] preparar.
concoction [kən'kɒkʃn] *n* [mixture, drink] mistura *f.*
concord ['kɒŋkɔ:d] *n (U)* [peaceful agreement] acordo *m.*
concourse ['kɒŋkɔ:s] *n* [hall] hall *m.*
concrete ['kɒŋkri:t] ◇ *adj* concreto(ta). ◇ *n (U)* [building material] concreto *m.* ◇ *comp* [made of concrete] de concreto. ◇ *vt* [path, garden] concretar.

concrete mixer *n* betoneira *f.*
concur [kən'kɜːʳ] (*pt* & *pp* **-red**, *cont* **-ring**) *vi* [agree]: **to ~ (with sthg)** concordar (com algo).
concurrent *adj* simultâneo(nea).
concurrently [kən'kʌrəntlɪ] *adv* simultaneamente, concomitantemente.
concussed [kən'kʌst] *adj* que sofreu concussão.
concussion [kən'kʌʃn] *n (U)* concussão *f.*
condemn [kən'dem] *vt* **-1.** condenar; **to ~ sb for sthg** condenar alguém por algo **-2.** [force]: **to ~ sb to sthg/to do sthg** condenar alguém a algo/a fazer algo **-3.** *JUR* [sentence]: **to ~ sb to sthg** condenar alguém a algo.
condemnation [ˌkɒndem'neɪʃn] *n (U)* condenação *f.*
condemned [kən'demd] *adj* condenado(da).
condensation [ˌkɒnden'seɪʃn] *n (U)* condensação *f.*
condense [kən'dens] ◇ *vt* condensar. ◇ *vi* [gas, liquid] condensar-se.
condensed milk [kən'denst-] *n (U)* leite *m* condensado.
condescend [ˌkɒndɪ'send] *vi* **-1.** [behave patronizingly]: **to ~ to sb** condescender-se a alguém **-2.** [lower o.s.]: **to ~ to do sthg** condescender em fazer algo.
condescending [ˌkɒndɪ'sendɪŋ] *adj* condescendente.
condiments ['kɒndɪmənts] *npl fml* condimentos *mpl.*
condition [kən'dɪʃn] ◇ *n* **-1.** [of person] forma *f*; **out of ~** fora de forma **-2.** [of car] estado *m*; **in good/bad ~** em bom/mau estado **-3.** *MED* [disease, complaint] problema *m* **-4.** [provision] condição *f*; **on one ~** sob *OR* com uma condição; **on ~ that** desde que; **to agree to do sthg on one ~** concordar em fazer algo sob *OR* com uma condição. ◇ *vt* **-1.** condicionar **-2.** [hair] hidratar.
◆ **conditions** *npl* [circumstances] condições *fpl.*
conditional [kən'dɪʃənl] ◇ *adj* condicional; **~ (up)on sthg** condicionado(da) a algo. ◇ *n GRAM* condicional *m.*
conditionally [kən'dɪʃnəlɪ] *adv* condicionalmente.
conditioner [kən'dɪʃnəʳ] *n* **-1.** [for hair] condicionador *m* **-2.** [for clothes] amaciante *m.*
conditioning [kən'dɪʃnɪŋ] *n (U) PSYCH* condicionamento *m.*
condolences [kən'dəʊlənsɪz] *npl* condolências *fpl*, pêsames *mpl.*
condom ['kɒndəm] *n* camisinha *f*, preservativo *m.*
condominium [ˌkɒndə'mɪnɪəm] *n US* [apartment, building] condomínio *m.*
condone [kən'dəʊn] *vt* tolerar.
condor ['kɒndɔːʳ] *n* condor *m.*
conducive [kən'djuːsɪv] *adj*: **~ to sthg/to doing sthg** conducente a algo/a fazer algo.
conduct [*n* 'kɒndʌkt, *vb* kən'dʌkt] ◇ *n (U)* conduta *f.* ◇ *vt* **-1.** [research, survey & *PHYS*] conduzir **-2.** [behave]: **to ~ o.s. well/badly** comportar-se bem/mal **-3.** *MUS* reger. ◇ *vi MUS* reger.
conducted tour [kən'dʌktɪd-] *n* excursão *f* guiada.
conductor [kən'dʌktəʳ] *n* **-1.** [on bus] cobrador *m* **-2.** [on train] *US* condutor *m* **-3.** *PHYS* condutor *m* **-4.** *MUS* maestro *m*, -trina *f.*
conductress [kən'dʌktrɪs] *n* [on bus] cobradora *f.*
conduit ['kɒndɪt] *n* conduto *m.*
cone [kəʊn] *n* **-1.** [gen] cone *m* **-2.** [for ice cream] casquinha *f* **-3.** [from tree] pinha *f.*
◆ **cone off** *vt sep UK* bloquear com cones *(uma estrada).*
confectioner [kən'fekʃnəʳ] *n* confeiteiro *m*, -ra *f*; **~'s (shop)** confeitaria *f.*
confectionery [kən'fekʃnərɪ] *n (U)* confeito *m.*
confederacy *n* confederação *f.*
confederate *n* cúmplice *mf.*
confederation [kənˌfedə'reɪʃn] *n* [group] confederação *f.*
Confederation of British Industry *n*: **the ~** a Confederação das Indústrias Britânicas.
confer [kən'fɜːʳ] (*pt* & *pp* **-red**, *cont* **-ring**) ◇ *vt fml*: **to ~ sthg (on sb)** conferir algo (a alguém). ◇ *vi*: **to ~ (with sb on** *OR* **about sthg)** confabular (com alguém sobre *OR* a respeito de algo).
conference ['kɒnfərəns] *n* conferência *f*; **in ~** em reunião.
conference call *n* teleconferência *f.*
conference centre *n* centro *m* de conferências.
conference hall *n* salão *m* de conferências.
conferencing ['kɒnfərənsɪŋ] *n (U)* (sistema *m* de) teleconferência *f.*
confess [kən'fes] ◇ *vt* confessar; **to ~ (that)** confessar que. ◇ *vi* [gen] confessar; **to ~ to sthg** confessar *OR* admitir algo.
confession [kən'feʃn] *n* confissão *f.*
confessional [kən'feʃənl] *n* confessionário *m.*
confetti [kən'fetɪ] *n (U)* confete *m.*
confidant [ˌkɒnfɪ'dænt] *n* confidente *m.*
confidante [ˌkɒnfɪ'dænt] *n* confidente *f.*
confide [kən'faɪd] ◇ *vt* confiar ◇ *vi*: **to ~ in sb** confiar em alguém.
confidence ['kɒnfɪdəns] *n* **-1.** *(U)* [assurance] autoconfiança *f* **-2.** *(U)* [trust] confiança *f*; **to have ~ in sb** ter confiança em alguém **-3.** [secrecy]: **in ~** em segredo **-4.** [secret] confidência *f.*
confidence trick *n* conto-do-vigário *m.*
confident ['kɒnfɪdənt] *adj* **-1.** [assured] autoconfiante **-2.** [sure] confiante; **~ of sthg** confiante em algo.
confidential [ˌkɒnfɪ'denʃl] *adj* confidencial.
confidentiality ['kɒnfɪˌdenʃɪ'ælətɪ] *n (U)* sigilo *m*; **a breach of ~** uma quebra de sigilo.
confidentially [ˌkɒnfɪ'denʃəlɪ] *adv* **-1.** [in confidence] confidencialmente **-2.** [in private] em particular.
confidently ['kɒnfɪdəntlɪ] *adv* **-1.** [with assurance] com autoconfiança **-2.** [with certainty] com confiança.
configuration [kənˌfɪgə'reɪʃn] *n* configuração *f.*
confine [kən'faɪn] *vt* confinar; **to be ~d to** estar confinado(da) a; **to ~ o.s. to sthg/to doing sthg** confinar-se a algo/a fazer algo.
◆ **confines** *npl* confins *mpl.*
confined [kən'faɪnd] *adj* [space, area] confinado(da).

confinement [kən'faɪnmənt] *n* **-1.** *(U)* [imprisonment] confinamento *m* **-2.** *dated* & MED (trabalho *m* de) parto *m.*

confirm [kən'fɜ:m] *vt* **-1.** [gen] confirmar **-2.** RELIG crismar.

confirmation [ˌkɒnfə'meɪʃn] *n* **-1.** [gen] confirmação *f* **-2.** RELIG crisma *f.*

confirmed [kən'fɜ:md] *adj* [habitual] convicto(ta).

confiscate ['kɒnfɪskeɪt] *vt* confiscar.

confiscation [ˌkɒnfɪ'skeɪʃn] *n (U)* confisco *m.*

conflagration [ˌkɒnflə'greɪʃn] *n fml* conflagração *f.*

conflate *vt fml* fundir.

conflict [*n* 'kɒnflɪkt, *vb* kən'flɪkt] ◇ *n* [fighting, clash] conflito *m*; **~ of interest** conflito de interesses. ◇ *vi* [clash] entrar em conflito; **to ~ with sb/sthg** entrar em conflito com alguém/algo.

conflicting [kən'flɪktɪŋ] *adj* [contradictory] conflitante.

confluence *n* [of rivers] confluência *f.*

conform [kən'fɔ:m] *vi* **-1.** [behave as expected] conformar-se **-2.** [be in accordance]: **to ~ (to** OR **with sthg)** conformar-se (com algo).

conformist [kən'fɔ:mɪst] *pej* ◇ *adj* conformista. ◇ *n* conformista *mf.*

conformity [kən'fɔ:mətɪ] *n (U)* conformidade *f*; **~ to** OR **with sthg** conformidade com algo.

confound [kən'faʊnd] *vt* [confuse, defeat] confundir.

confounded [kən'faʊndɪd] *adj inf* [for emphasis] maldito(ta).

confront [kən'frʌnt] *vt* **-1.** [person] defrontar-se com **-2.** [task, problem] enfrentar **-3.** [present]: **to ~ sb (with sthg)** confrontar alguém (com algo).

confrontation [ˌkɒnfrʌn'teɪʃn] *n* confrontação *f.*

confrontational *adj* de confrontamento.

confuse [kən'fju:z] *vt* **-1.** [bewilder] confundir **-2.** [mix up]: **to ~ sb/sthg (with)** confundir alguém/algo (com) **-3.** [complicate, make less clear] complicar.

confused [kən'fju:zd] *adj* confuso(sa).

confusing [kən'fju:zɪŋ] *adj* confuso(sa).

confusion [kən'fju:ʒn] *n* confusão *f.*

conga ['kɒŋgə] *n*: **the ~** a conga.

congeal [kən'dʒi:l] *vi* **-1.** [blood] coagular **-2.** [food] congelar.

congenial [kən'dʒi:njəl] *adj* agradável.

congenital [kən'dʒenɪtl] *adj* MED congênito(ta).

conger eel ['kɒŋgər-] *n* enguia *f* marinha.

congested [kən'dʒestɪd] *adj* congestionado(da).

congestion [kən'dʒestʃn] *n (U)* **-1.** [overcrowding] congestionamento *m* **-2.** MED congestão *f.*

conglomerate [kən'glɒmərət] *n* COMM conglomerado *m.*

conglomeration [kənˌglɒmə'reɪʃn] *n fml* conglomeração *f.*

Congo ['kɒŋgəʊ] *n* **-1.** [country]: **the ~** o Congo; **in the ~** no Congo **-2.** [river]: **the ~** o Congo.

Congolese [ˌkɒŋgə'li:z] ◇ *adj* congolês(esa). ◇ *n* congolês *m*, -esa *f.*

congratulate [kən'grætʃʊleɪt] *vt*: **to ~ sb (on)** felicitar alguém (por); **to ~ o.s. (on)** congratular-se (por).

congratulations [kənˌgrætʃʊ'leɪʃənz] ◇ *npl* felicitações *fpl.* ◇ *excl* parabéns!

congratulatory [kən'grætʃʊlətrɪ] *adj* de felicitações.

congregate ['kɒŋgrɪgeɪt] *vi* congregar-se.

congregation [ˌkɒŋgrɪ'geɪʃn] *n* RELIG congregação *f.*

congress ['kɒŋgres] *n* [meeting] congresso *m.*
◆ **Congress** *n US* POL Congresso *m.*

CONGRESS

O órgão legislativo estadunidense compõe-se do Senado (*Senate*) e da Câmara de Representantes (*House of Representatives*). Os senadores são em número de 100; a Câmara conta hoje com 435 membros. Todo projeto de lei deve ser, obrigatoriamente, aprovado pelas duas casas, para que a lei possa entrar em vigor.

congressional [kəŋ'greʃənl] *adj US* POL parlamentar.

congressman ['kɒŋgresmən] (*pl* **-men** [-mən]) *n US* POL congressista *m.*

congresswoman ['kɒŋgresˌwʊmən] (*pl* **-women** [-ˌwɪmɪn]) *n US* POL congressista *f.*

conical ['kɒnɪkl] *adj* cônico(ca).

conifer ['kɒnɪfər] *n* conífera *f.*

coniferous [kə'nɪfərəs] *adj* conífero(ra).

conjecture [kən'dʒektʃər] ◇ *n* conjectura *f.* ◇ *vt*: **to ~ (that)** prever (que). ◇ *vi* conjecturar.

conjugal ['kɒndʒʊgl] *adj fml* conjugal.

conjugate ['kɒndʒʊgeɪt] *vt* conjugar.

conjugation [ˌkɒndʒʊ'geɪʃn] *n* conjugação *f.*

conjunction [kən'dʒʌŋkʃn] *n* **-1.** GRAM conjunção *f* **-2.** [combination] combinação *f*; **in ~ with** em conjunto com.

conjunctivitis [kənˌdʒʌŋktɪ'vaɪtɪs] *n (U)* conjuntivite *f.*

conjure ['kʌndʒər] ◇ *vt* [by magic] fazer aparecer. ◇ *vi* [by magic] fazer truques.
◆ **conjure up** *vt sep* [evoke] evocar.

conjurer ['kʌndʒərər] *n* [magician] mágico *m*, -ca *f.*

conjuring trick ['kʌndʒərɪŋ-] *n* [magic trick] truque *m* de mágica.

conjuror ['kʌndʒərər] *n* = **conjurer**.

conk [kɒŋk] *n inf* [nose] narigão *m.*
◆ **conk out** *vi inf* **-1.** [person] estar em frangalhos **-2.** [car, machine] escangalhar-se.

conker ['kɒŋkər] *n UK* castanha-da-índia *f.*

con man (*pl* **-men**) *n* vigarista *m.*

connect [kə'nekt] ◇ *vt* **-1.** [gen] ligar, conectar; **to ~ sthg (to sthg)** ligar algo (a algo); **I'm just ~ing you** [on telephone] estou completando sua ligação **-2.** [associate]: **to ~ sb/sthg to** OR **with** relacionar alguém/algo a OR com **-3.** ELEC [to power supply]: **to ~ sthg to** conectar algo a. ◇ *vi* [train, plane, bus]: **to ~ (with)** conectar com.

connected [kə'nektɪd] *adj* [related, associated] relacionado(da); **~ with** conectado(da) com.

Connecticut [kə'netɪkət] *n* Connecticut.

connecting [kə'nektɪŋ] *adj* [flight, train] de conexão.

connecting rod *n* AUT biela *f.*

connection [kə'nekʃn] *n* **-1.** [relationship] conexão *f*, relação *f*; **~ between/with sthg** relação entre /com algo; **in ~ with** em relação a **-2.** [plane, train,

bus & *ELEC*] conexão *f* **- 3.** [on telephone] ligação *f* **- 4.** [influential contact] contato *m*.
connective tissue [kə'nektɪv-] *n* tecido *m* conjuntivo.
connexion [kə'nekʃn] *n UK* = **connection.**
connive [kə'naɪv] *vi* **- 1.** [plot] conspirar; **to ~ with sb** tramar com alguém **- 2.** [allow to happen]: **to ~ at sthg** ser conivente em algo.
conniving [kə'naɪvɪŋ] *adj pej* traidor(ra).
connoisseur [ˌkɒnə'sɜːʳ] *n* conhecedor *m*, -ra *f*, especialista *mf*.
connotation [ˌkɒnə'teɪʃn] *n* conotação *f*.
conquer ['kɒŋkəʳ] *vt* **- 1.** [take by force] conquistar **- 2.** *fig* [overcome] dominar.
conqueror ['kɒŋkərəʳ] *n* conquistador *m*, -ra *f*.
conquest ['kɒŋkwest] *n* conquista *f*.
cons *npl* **- 1.** *Br fam* (*abbr of* **conveniences**): **all mod ~** com todas as comodidades. **- 2.** ▻ **pro.**
Cons. (*abbr of* **Conservative**) *partido político britânico de centro-direita.*
conscience ['kɒnʃəns] *n* consciência *f*; **to have a guilty ~** ter a consciência pesada; **in all ~** em sã consciência.
conscientious [ˌkɒnʃɪ'enʃəs] *adj* consciencioso(-sa).
conscientiously [ˌkɒnʃɪ'enʃəslɪ] *adv* conscienciosamente.
conscientiousness *n (U)* consciência *f*, escrúpulo *m*.
conscientious objector *n pessoa que, por razões morais ou religiosas, recusa-se a servir nas forças armadas.*
conscious ['kɒnʃəs] *adj* consciente; **~ of sthg** consciente de algo; **fashion-~** conhecedor(ra) da moda.
consciously ['kɒnʃəslɪ] *adv* [intentionally] deliberadamente.
consciousness ['kɒnʃəsnɪs] *n (U)* consciência *f*; **to lose/regain ~** perder/recobrar os sentidos.
conscript [*n* 'kɒnskrɪpt, *vb* kən'skrɪpt] *MIL* ◇ *n* recruta *mf*. ◇ *vt* recrutar.
conscription [kən'skrɪpʃn] *n (U)* serviço *m* militar obrigatório.
consecrate ['kɒnsɪkreɪt] *vt* **- 1.** *RELIG* [make holy] consagrar **- 2.** *fig* [dedicate] dedicar.
consecration [ˌkɒnsɪ'kreɪʃn] *n RELIG* consagração *f*.
consecutive [kən'sekjʊtɪv] *adj* consecutivo(va).
consecutively [kən'sekjʊtɪvlɪ] *adv* consecutivamente.
consensus [kən'sensəs] *n* consenso *m*.
consent [kən'sent] ◇ *n (U)* consentimento *m*. ◇ *vi*: **to ~ (to sthg)** consentir (em algo).
consenting [kən'sentɪŋ] *adj*: **~ adults** *adultos que aceitam ter relações sexuais.*
consequence ['kɒnsɪkwəns] *n* **- 1.** [result] conseqüência *f*; **to face the ~s** encarar as conseqüências; **in ~** em conseqüência **- 2.** [importance] importância *f*; **to be of little ~** não ter importância.
consequent ['kɒnsɪkwənt] *adj* conseqüente.
consequently ['kɒnsɪkwəntlɪ] *adv* conseqüentemente.
conservation [ˌkɒnsə'veɪʃn] *n* conservação *f*.
conservation area *n* área *f* de preservação permanente.
conservationist [ˌkɒnsə'veɪʃənɪst] *n* conservacionista *mf*.
conservatism [kən'sɜːvətɪzm] *n (U)* conservadorismo *m*.
◆ **Conservatism** *n (U) UK POL* Conservadorismo *m*.
conservative [kən'sɜːvətɪv] ◇ *adj* **- 1.** [traditional] conservador(ra) **- 2.** [cautious] cauteloso(sa). ◇ *n* conservador *m*, -ra *f*.
◆ **Conservative** *POL UK* ◇ *adj* conservador(ra). ◇ *n* conservador *m*, -ra *f*.
Conservative Party *n UK*: **the ~** o Partido Conservador.
conservatory [kən'sɜːvətrɪ] (*pl* **-ies**) *n* estufa *f*.
conserve [*n* 'kɒnsɜːv, *vb* kən'sɜːv] ◇ *n* conserva *f*. ◇ *vt* conservar.
consider [kən'sɪdəʳ] *vt* **- 1.** [gen] considerar; **all things ~ed** considerando tudo **- 2.** [believe] achar.
considerable [kən'sɪdrəbl] *adj* considerável.
considerably [kən'sɪdrəblɪ] *adv* consideravelmente.
considerate [kən'sɪdərət] *adj* [thoughtful] atencioso(sa); **that's very ~ of you** é muita consideração de sua parte.
consideration [kənˌsɪdə'reɪʃn] *n* **- 1.** *(U)* [gen] consideração *f*; **to take sthg into ~** levar algo em consideração; **to show no ~ for others** não mostrar consideração pelos outros **- 2.** [factor] fator *m* **- 3.** [discussion]: **under ~** em consideração; **your proposal is under ~** sua proposta está sendo considerada.
considered [kən'sɪdəd] *adj*: **~ opinion** opinião *f* sincera.
considering [kən'sɪdərɪŋ] ◇ *prep* considerando, em vista de. ◇ *conj* considerando que. ◇ *adv* apesar de tudo, pensando bem.
consign [kən'saɪn] *vt* [relegate]: **to ~ sb/sthg to sthg** consignar alguém/algo a algo.
consignee [ˌkɒnsaɪ'niː] *n* consignatário *m*, -ria *f*.
consignment [ˌkən'saɪnmənt] *n* [load] remessa *f*, despacho *m*.
consignment note *n* nota *f* de expedição.
consist [kən'sɪst] ◆ **consist in** *vt fus*: **to ~ in sthg/in doing sthg** consistir em algo/em fazer algo.
◆ **consist of** *vt fus* consistir em.
consistency [kən'sɪstənsɪ] (*pl* **-ies**) *n* **- 1.** *(U)* [coherence] consistência *f*, coerência *f* **- 2.** [texture] consistência *f*.
consistent [kən'sɪstənt] *adj* **- 1.** [gen] constante **- 2.** [growth, improvement] consistente **- 3.** [argument, facts, position]: **~ (with)** coerente (com).
consistently [kən'sɪstəntlɪ] *adv* **- 1.** [gen] constantemente **- 2.** [argue, reason] coerentemente.
consolation [ˌkɒnsə'leɪʃn] *n* consolação *f*.
consolation prize *n* [in competition] prêmio *m* de consolação.
console [*n* 'kɒnsəʊl, *vt* kən'səʊl] ◇ *n* [control panel] console *m*. ◇ *vt* consolar; **to ~ o.s. with sthg** contentar-se com algo.
consolidate [kən'sɒlɪdeɪt] ◇ *vt* **- 1.** [strengthen]

consolidar **-2.** *COMM* [merge] fundir-se. ◇ *vi COMM* fundir-se.

consolidation [kən,sɒlɪ'deɪʃn] *n (U)* **-1.** [strengthening] consolidação *f* **-2.** *COMM* [merging] fusão *f.*

consommé [*UK* kən'sɒmeɪ, *US* ,kɒnsə'meɪ] *n (U)* consomê *m.*

consonant ['kɒnsənənt] *n* consoante *f.*

consort [*vb* kən'sɔ:t, *n* 'kɒnsɔ:t] ◇ *n* **-1.** [spouse] consorte *mf* **-2.** *MUS* grupo *m.* ◇ *vi fml*: **to ~ with sb** ter ligações com alguém.

consortium [kən'sɔ:tjəm] (*pl* **-tiums** *OR* **-tia** [-tjə]) *n* consórcio *m.*

conspicuous [kən'spɪkjʊəs] *adj* conspícuo(cua).

conspicuously [kən'spɪkjʊəslɪ] *adv* conspicuamente.

conspiracy [kən'spɪrəsɪ] (*pl* **-ies**) *n* conspiração *f.*

conspirator [kən'spɪrətə^r] *n* conspirador *m,* -ra *f.*

conspiratorial [kən,spɪrə'tɔ:rɪəl] *adj* conspiratório(ria).

conspire [kən'spaɪə^r] ◇ *vt*: **to ~ to do sthg** conspirar para fazer algo. ◇ *vi* **-1.** [plan secretly]: **to ~ against/with sb** conspirar contra/com alguém **-2.** [combine] cooperar.

constable ['kʌnstəbl] *n UK* [policeman] guarda *m.*

constabulary [kən'stæbjʊlərɪ] (*pl* **-ies**) *n UK* força *f* policial.

constancy ['kɒnstənsɪ] *n (U)* **-1.** [continuity] constância *f* **-2.** *literary* [faithfulness] fidelidade *f.*

constant ['kɒnstənt] *adj* **-1.** [gen] constante **-2.** *literary* [faithful] fiel.

constantly ['kɒnstəntlɪ] *adv* constantemente.

constellation [,kɒnstə'leɪʃn] *n ASTRON* constelação *f.*

consternation [,kɒnstə'neɪʃn] *n (U)* consternação *f.*

constipated ['kɒnstɪpeɪtɪd] *adj* constipado(da).

constipation [,kɒnstɪ'peɪʃn] *n (U)* constipação *f,* prisão *f* de ventre.

constituency [kən'stɪtjʊənsɪ] (*pl* **-ies**) *n* **-1.** [area] distrito *m* eleitoral **-2.** [group] eleitorado *m.*

constituency party *n UK* partido *m* local.

constituent [kən'stɪtjʊənt] ◇ *adj* constituinte. ◇ *n* **-1.** [voter] eleitor *m,* -ra *f* **-2.** [element] constituinte *m.*

constitute ['kɒnstɪtju:t] *vt* constituir.

constitution [,kɒnstɪ'tju:ʃn] *n* **-1.** [health] constituição *f* (física) **-2.** [composition] constituição *f.*
◆ **Constitution** *n*: **the (United States) Constitution** a Constituição (dos Estados Unidos).

CONSTITUTION

Ao contrário da Constituição norte-americana, expressa num texto escrito e definitivo, a Constituição britânica não é um documento propriamente dito, mas resulta do conjunto das leis ao longo da história, tendo por base o princípio da jurisprudência.

constitutional [,kɒnstɪ'tju:ʃənl] *adj* constitucional.

constrain [kən'streɪn] *vt* **-1.** [person] coagir; **to ~ sb to do sthg** forçar alguém a fazer algo **-2.** [process, development] impedir, restringir.

constrained [kən'streɪnd] *adj* [inhibited] constrangido(da), contido(da).

constraint [kən'streɪnt] *n* **-1.** [restriction] restrição *f*; **~ on sthg** restrição a algo **-2.** *(U)* [control] força *f* **-3.** [coercion] coação *f.*

constrict [kən'strɪkt] *vt* **-1.** [part of body] apertar **-2.** [person] restringir.

constricting [kən'strɪktɪŋ] *adj* **-1.** [clothes] apertado(da) **-2.** [circumstances, lifestyle] limitado(da).

construct [*vb* kən'strʌkt, *n* 'kɒnstrʌkt] ◇ *vt* **-1.** [edifice, object] construir **-2.** [sentence, argument] formar. ◇ *n fml* [concept] constructo *m.*

construction [kən'strʌkʃn] ◇ *n* **-1.** [gen] construção *f* **-2.** *(U)* [building industry] construção *f* (civil). ◇ *comp* de construção.

construction industry *n* setor *m* da construção civil.

constructive [kən'strʌktɪv] *adj* construtivo(va).

constructively [kən'strʌktɪvlɪ] *adv* construtivamente.

construe [kən'stru:] *vt fml* [interpret]: **to ~ sthg as** interpretar algo como.

consul ['kɒnsəl] *n* [envoy] cônsul *m,* consulesa *f.*

consular ['kɒnsjʊlə^r] *adj* consular.

consulate ['kɒnsjʊlət] *n* [building] consulado *m.*

consult [kən'sʌlt] ◇ *vt* consultar. ◇ *vi*: **to ~ with sb** consultar-se com alguém.

consultancy [kən'sʌltənsɪ] (*pl* **-ies**) *n* [company] empresa *f* de consultoria.

consultancy fee *n* taxa *f* de consultoria.

consultant [kən'sʌltənt] *n* **-1.** [expert] consultor *m,* -ra *f* **-2.** *UK* [medical specialist] especialista *mf.*

consultation [,kɒnsəl'teɪʃn] *n* **-1.** [gen] consulta *f* **-2.** [of book, map] orientação *f.*

consulting room [kən'sʌltɪŋ-] *n* consultório *m.*

consume [kən'sju:m] *vt* consumir.

consumer [kən'sju:mə^r] ◇ *n* consumidor *m,* -ra *f.* ◇ *comp* do consumidor.

consumer credit *n (U)* crédito *m* ao consumidor.

consumer durables *npl* bens *mpl* duráveis.

consumer goods *npl* bens *mpl* de consumo.

consumerism [kən'sju:mərɪzm] *n (U) pej* [theory] consumismo *m.*

consumer society *n (U)* sociedade *f* de consumo.

consumer spending *n (U)* gastos *mpl* com bens de consumo.

consuming *adj* profundo(da); **a ~ passion** uma paixão ardente.

consummate [*adj* kən'sʌmət, *vb* 'kɒnsəmeɪt] ◇ *adj* **-1.** [perfect] consumado(da) **-2.** [highly skilled] perfeito(ta). ◇ *vt* consumar.

consummation [,kɒnsə'meɪʃn] *n (U)* consumação *f.*

consumption [kən'sʌmpʃn] *n (U)* **-1.** [use] consumo *m* **-2.** *dated* [tuberculosis] tuberculose *f.*

cont. (*abbr of* **continued**): **~ on page 10** continua na página 10.

contact ['kɒntækt] ◇ *n* **-1.** *(U)* [physical, eye, communication] contato *m*; **to lose ~ with sb** perder contato com alguém; **to make ~ with sb** fazer contato com alguém; **in ~** em contato; **in ~ with**

sb em contato com alguém **-2.** [person] contato *m.* ◇ *vt* contatar, entrar em contato com.

contact lens *n* lente *f* de contato.

contact number *n* telefone *m* para contato.

contagion *n* contágio *m.*

contagious [kən'teɪdʒəs] *adj* **-1.** *MED* contagioso(sa) **-2.** *fig* [laughter, good humour] contagiante.

contain [kən'teɪn] *vt* conter; **to ~ o.s.** conter-se.

contained [kən'teɪnd] *adj* [unemotional] contido(da).

container [kən'teɪnəʳ] *n* **-1.** [box, bottle etc] recipiente *m* **-2.** *COMM* [for transporting goods] contêiner *m.*

containerize, -ise [kən'teɪnəraɪz] *vt COMM* **-1.** [transport] transportar em contêiner **-2.** [pack] acondicionar em contêiner.

container ship *n* navio *m* de carga.

containment [kən'teɪnmənt] *n* contenção *f.*

contaminate [kən'tæmɪneɪt] *vt* contaminar.

contaminated [kən'tæmɪneɪtɪd] *adj* contaminado(da).

contamination [kən,tæmɪ'neɪʃn] *n (U)* contaminação *f.*

cont'd (*abbr of* **continued**) cont.

contemplate ['kɒntempleɪt] ◇ *vt* **-1.** [scheme, idea, proposal] considerar; **to ~ doing sthg** pensar em fazer algo **-2.** *literary* [sunset, flower] contemplar. ◇ *vi* [meditate] contemplar.

contemplation [,kɒntem'pleɪʃn] *n (U)* contemplação *f.*

contemplative [kən'templətɪv] *adj* contemplativo(va).

contemporary [kən'tempərərɪ] (*pl* **-ies**) ◇ *adj* contemporâneo(nea). ◇ *n* contemporâneo *m*, -nea *f.*

contempt [kən'tempt] *n (U)* **-1.** [gen] desprezo *m*; **~ for sb/sthg** desprezo por alguém/algo; **to hold sb in ~** menosprezar alguém **-2.** *JUR* : **~ (of court)** desacato *m* (à autoridade do tribunal).

contemptible [kən'temptəbl] *adj* vil.

contemptuous [kən'temptʃʊəs] *adj* desdenhoso(-sa); **to be ~ of sthg** fazer pouco caso de algo.

contend [kən'tend] ◇ *vt* **-1.** [deal]: **to ~ with sthg** lidar com algo; **to have enough to ~ with** ter muitos problemas para resolver **-2.** [compete]: **to ~ for sthg** disputar algo; **to ~ against sb** disputar com alguém. ◇ *vt fml* [claim]: **to ~ that** sustentar que.

contender [kən'tendəʳ] *n* **-1.** [in fight, race] oponente *mf* **-2.** [for political office] candidato *m*, -ta *f.*

content [*n* 'kɒntent, *adj & vb* kən'tent] ◇ *adj* contente; **~ with sthg** contente com algo; **to be ~ to do sthg** estar a fim de fazer algo. ◇ *n* **-1.** [amount contained] teor *m* **-2.** [subject matter] conteúdo *m.* ◇ *vt* : **to ~ o.s. with sthg/with doing sthg** contentar-se com algo/em fazer algo.

◆ **contents** *npl* **-1.** [of container, document] conteúdo *m* **-2.** [at front of book] sumário *m.*

contented [kən'tentɪd] *adj* satisfeito(ta).

contentedly [kən'tentɪdlɪ] *adv* com satisfação.

contention [kən'tenʃn] *n* **-1.** [argument, assertion] argumentação *f* **-2.** *(U)* [disagreement] discussão *f* **-3.** *(U)* [competition]: **to be in ~** estar em discussão; **the bone of ~** o pomo da discórdia.

contentious [kən'tenʃəs] *adj fml* contencioso(sa).

contentment [kən'tentmənt] *n (U)* contentamento *m.*

contest [*n* 'kɒntest, *vb* kən'test] ◇ *n* **-1.** [competition] concurso *m* **-2.** [for power, control] disputa *f.* ◇ *vt* **-1.** [compete for] concorrer **-2.** [dispute] questionar.

contestant [kən'testənt] *n* concorrente *mf.*

context ['kɒntekst] *n* contexto *m*; **out of ~** fora de contexto.

continent ['kɒntɪnənt] *n GEOGR* continente *m.*

◆ **Continent** *n UK*: **the Continent** o *Continente Europeu (excluindo-se a Grã-Bretanha).*

continental [,kɒntɪ'nentl] ◇ *adj* **-1.** *GEOGR* continental **-2.** *UK* [European] europeu(péia) (do continente). ◇ *n UK inf* europeu *m*, -péia *f* (do continente).

continental breakfast *n* café *m* da manhã continental.

contingency [kən'tɪndʒənsɪ] (*pl* **-ies**) *n* contingência *f.*

contingency plan *n* plano *m* de contingência.

contingent [kən'tɪndʒənt] ◇ *adj fml*: **~ (up)on sthg** dependente de algo. ◇ *n* contingente *m.*

continual [kən'tɪnjʊəl] *adj* contínuo(nua).

continually [kən'tɪnjʊəlɪ] *adv* continuamente.

continuation [kən,tɪnjʊ'eɪʃn] *n* **-1.** *(U)* [act of extending] prolongamento *m* **-2.** [sequel] continuação *f.*

continue [kən'tɪnju:] ◇ *vt* **-1.** [carry on] continuar, prosseguir; **to ~ doing** *OR* **to do sthg** continuar a fazer algo **-2.** [begin again] recomeçar **-3.** [resume speaking] prosseguir. ◇ *vi* **-1.** [carry on] continuar; **to ~ with sthg** continuar com algo **-2.** [begin again] recomeçar **-3.** [resume speaking, travelling] prosseguir.

continuity [,kɒntɪ'nju:ətɪ] *n (U)* [gen] continuidade *f*; **~ announcer** anunciante *m (que oferece um programa)*; **~ boy/girl** continuísta *mf.*

continuous [kən'tɪnjʊəs] *adj* [uninterrupted] contínuo(nua).

continuous assessment *n (U)* avaliação *f* contínua.

continuously [kən'tɪnjʊəslɪ] *adv* [without interruption] continuamente.

contort [kən'tɔ:t] *vt* contorcer.

contortion [kən'tɔ:ʃn] *n* contorção *f.*

contour ['kɒn,tʊəʳ] ◇ *n* **-1.** [outline] contorno *m* **-2.** [on map] relevo *m.* ◇ *comp* de relevo.

contraband ['kɒntrəbænd] ◇ *adj* contrabandeado(da). ◇ *n (U)* contrabando *m.*

contraception [,kɒntrə'sepʃn] *n (U)* contracepção *f.*

contraceptive [,kɒntrə'septɪv] ◇ *adj* anticoncepcional. ◇ *n* anticoncepcional *m.*

contraceptive pill *n* pílula *f* anticoncepcional.

contract [*n* 'kɒntrækt, *vb* kən'trækt] ◇ *n* contrato *m.* ◇ *vt* **-1.** [through legal agreement] contratar; **to ~ to do sthg** contratar para fazer algo **-2.** *COMM*: **to ~ sb (to do sthg)** contratar alguém (para fazer algo) **-3.** *fml* [illness, disease] contrair **-4.** [word] abreviar. ◇ *vi* [metal, plastic] contrair-se.

◆ **contract in** *vi esp UK* comprometer-se *(por contrato).*

◆ **contract out** ◇ *vt sep* terceirizar. ◇ *vi esp UK*: **to ~ out (of sthg)** desmanchar (algo).
contraction [kən'trækʃn] *n* contração *f*.
contractor [kən'træktəʳ] *n* contratante *mf*.
contractual [kən'træktʃʊəl] *adj* contratual.
contradict [ˌkɒntrə'dɪkt] *vt* **-1.** [challenge] contradizer **-2.** [conflict with]: **to ~ each other** contradizer-se.
contradiction [ˌkɒntrə'dɪkʃn] *n* contradição *f*; **~ in terms** contradição em termos.
contradictory [ˌkɒntrə'dɪktərɪ] *adj* contraditório(-ria).
contraflow ['kɒntrəfləʊ] *n* contrafluxo *m*.
contralto [kən'træltəʊ] (*pl* **-s**) *n* contralto *m*.
contraption [kən'træpʃn] *n* geringonça *f*.
contrary ['kɒntrərɪ, *adj sense 2* kən'treərɪ] ◇ *adj* [opposing] contrário(ria); **~ to sthg** contrário(ria) a algo. ◇ *n* contrário *m*; **on the ~** pelo contrário; **to the ~** em contrário.
◆ **contrary to** *prep* contrário a.
contrast [*n* 'kɒntrɑ:st, *vb* kən'trɑ:st] ◇ *n* **-1.** [difference]: **~ (between/with)** contraste *m* (entre/com); **by** *OR* **in ~** em comparação, por outro lado; **in ~ with** *OR* **to sthg** em comparação com algo **-2.** [something different]: **~ (to sb/sthg)** oposto *m*, -ta *f* (a alguém/algo). ◇ *vt*: **to ~ sthg with sthg** contrastar algo com algo. ◇ *vi*: **to ~ (with sthg)** contrastar *OR* dar contraste (com algo).
contrasting [kən'trɑ:stɪŋ] *adj* contrastante.
contravene [ˌkɒntrə'vi:n] *vt* violar.
contravention [kɒntrə'venʃn] *n* violação *f*.
contribute [kən'trɪbju:t] ◇ *vt* **-1.** [give] contribuir com **-2.** [to magazine, newspaper] colaborar com. ◇ *vi* **-1.** [give money]: **to ~ (to sthg)** contribuir (para algo) **-2.** [be part of cause]: **to ~ to sthg** contribuir para algo **-3.** [write material]: **to ~ to sthg** colaborar com algo.
contributing [kən'trɪbju:tɪŋ] *adj* [factor] contribuinte.
contribution [ˌkɒntrɪ'bju:ʃn] *n* **-1.** [gen]: **~ (to sthg)** contribuição *f* (para algo) **-2.** [written article] colaboração *f*.
contributor [kən'trɪbjʊtəʳ] *n* **-1.** [of money] contribuinte *mf* **-2.** [to magazine, newspaper] colaborador *m*, -ra *f*.
contributory [kən'trɪbjʊtərɪ] *adj* [factor] contribuinte.
contrite ['kɒntraɪt] *adj literary* contrito(ta).
contrivance [kən'traɪvns] *n* **-1.** [contraption] dispositivo *m* **-2.** [ploy] manobra *f*, artimanha *f*.
contrive [kən'traɪv] *fml vt* **-1.** [manoeuvre to put in place] manipular **-2.** [manage]: **to ~ to do sthg** dar um jeito de fazer algo **-3.** [invent, construct] improvisar.
contrived [kən'traɪvd] *adj pej* arranjado(da).
control [kən'trəʊl] (*pt* & *pp* **-led**, *cont* **-ling**) ◇ *n* **-1.** [gen] controle *m*; **to gain ~ (of sthg)** obter o controle (de algo); **to take ~ (of sthg)** tomar o controle (de algo); **beyond** *OR* **outside one's ~** fora do controle de alguém; **in ~ of** no controle de, no comando de; **out of ~** fora de controle; **under ~** sob controle; **to lose ~** [of emotions] perder o controle **-2.** *COMPUT* comando *m*. ◇ *vt* controlar. ◇ *comp* de controle.
◆ **controls** *npl* [of machine, vehicle] controles *mpl*.
control code *n COMPUT* código *m* de controle.
control group *n* [in experiment, survey] grupo *m* de controle.
control key *n COMPUT* tecla *f* control.
controlled [kən'trəʊld] *adj* controlado(da).
controller [kən'trəʊləʳ] *n* [person responsible] controller *mf*, diretor *m*, -ra *f*; **financial ~** contador *m*, -ra *f*.
controlling *adj* [factor] de controle.
controlling interest *n* controle *m* acionário.
control panel *n* painel *m* de controle.
control room *n* sala *f* de controle.
control tower *n* torre *f* de controle.
controversial [ˌkɒntrə'vɜ:ʃl] *adj* controverso(sa), polêmico(ca).
controversy ['kɒntrəvɜ:sɪ, *UK* kən'trɒvəsɪ] (*pl* **-ies**) *n* controvérsia *f*, polêmica *f*.
conundrum [kə'nʌndrəm] (*pl* **-s**) *n fml* [problem] enigma *m*.
conurbation [ˌkɒnɜ:'beɪʃn] *n* conurbação *f*.
convalesce [ˌkɒnvə'les] *vi* convalescer.
convalescence [ˌkɒnvə'lesns] *n (U)* convalescença *f*.
convalescent [ˌkɒnvə'lesnt] ◇ *adj* convalescente. ◇ *n* convalescente *mf*.
convection [kən'vekʃn] *n (U)* convecção *f*.
convector *n*: **~ heater** aquecedor *m* de convecção.
convene [kən'vi:n] ◇ *vt* [meeting, conference] convocar. ◇ *vi* [court, parliament] reunir-se.
convenience [kən'vi:njəns] *n* **-1.** *(U)* [gen] conveniência *f*; **at your earliest ~** assim que possível **-2.** [facility] comodidade *f*.
convenience food *n* alimentos *mpl* pré-prontos.
convenience store *n US* loja *f* de conveniências.
convenient [kən'vi:njənt] *adj* **-1.** [suitable] conveniente **-2.** [handy] cômodo(da); **~ for sthg** conveniente para algo.
conveniently [kən'vi:njəntlɪ] *adv* convenientemente.
convent ['kɒnvənt] *n* [building] convento *m*.
convention [kən'venʃn] *n* convenção *f*.
conventional [kən'venʃənl] *adj* convencional; **~ person** *pej* pessoa *f* sem graça; **~ weapons** armas *fpl* não-nucleares.
conventionally [kən'venʃnəlɪ] *adv* de maneira convencional.
convent school *n* colégio *m* de freiras.
converge [kən'vɜ:dʒ] *vi* convergir; **to ~ on sb/sthg** [to move towards] dirigir-se para alguém/algo.
convergence [kən'vɜ:dʒəns] *n* [in EU] convergência *f*; **~ criteria** critérios *mpl* de convergência.
conversant [kən'vɜ:sənt] *adj fml*: **~ with sthg** familiarizado(da) com algo.
conversation [ˌkɒnvə'seɪʃn] *n* conversação *f*, conversa *f*; **to make ~** puxar conversa.
conversational [ˌkɒnvə'seɪʃənl] *adj* [chatty] conversador(ra).

conversationalist [ˌkɒnvəˈseɪʃnəlɪst] *n* conversador *m*, -ra *f*.
converse [*n* & *adj* ˈkɒnvɜːs, *vb* kənˈvɜːs] ◇ *adj fml* [opposing] inverso(sa). ◇ *n* [opposite]: **the ~** o inverso. ◇ *vi fml* [talk] conversar; **to ~ with sb** conversar com alguém.
conversely [kənˈvɜːslɪ] *adv fml* inversamente.
conversion [kənˈvɜːʃn] *n* **-1.** [gen] conversão *f* **-2.** [converted building, room] reforma *f*.
conversion table *n* tabela *f* de conversão.
convert [*vb* kənˈvɜːt, *n* ˈkɒnvɜːt] ◇ *vt*: **to ~ sthg (in)to sthg** converter algo em algo; **to ~ sb (to sthg)** converter alguém (para algo); **I didn't like jazz much but she ~ed me to it** eu não gostava muito de jazz, mas ela me converteu. ◇ *vi* **-1.** [change]: **she's ~ed to Catholicism** ela se converteu ao catolicismo; **the seating ~s to a double bed** o sofá se transforma numa cama de casal **-2.** *SPORT* converter. ◇ *n* convertido *m*, -da *f*.
converted [kənˈvɜːtɪd] *adj* **-1.** [building, room, ship] transformado(da), adaptado(da) **-2.** *RELIG* [person] convertido(da).
convertible [kənˈvɜːtəbl] ◇ *adj* **-1.** [car, currency] conversível **-2.** [bed, sofa] dobrável. ◇ *n* [car] conversível *m*.
convex [kɒnˈveks] *adj* convexo(xa).
convey [kənˈveɪ] *vt* **-1.** *fml* [people, cargo] conduzir **-2.** [feelings, ideas, thoughts] expressar; **to ~ sthg to sb** transmitir algo a alguém.
conveyancing [kənˈveɪənsɪŋ] *n (U)* transferência *f* de posse.
conveyer belt [kənˈveɪə[r]-], **conveyor belt** *n* esteira *f* transportadora.
convict [*n* ˈkɒnvɪkt, *vb* kənˈvɪkt] ◇ *n* condenado *m*, -da *f*. ◇ *vt JUR*: **to ~ sb of sthg** condenar alguém por algo.
convicted [kənˈvɪktɪd] *adj JUR* condenado(da).
conviction [kənˈvɪkʃn] *n* **-1.** [gen] convicção *f* **-2.** *JUR* condenação *f*.
convince [kənˈvɪns] *vt* [persuade] convencer; **to ~ sb of sthg** convencer alguém de algo; **to ~ sb to do sthg** convencer alguém a fazer algo.
convinced [kənˈvɪnst] *adj*: **~ (of sthg)** convencido(da) (de algo).
convincing [kənˈvɪnsɪŋ] *adj* convincente.
convivial [kənˈvɪvɪəl] *adj* alegre, festivo(va).
convoluted [ˈkɒnvəluːtɪd] *adj* [tortuous] enrolado(da).
convoy [ˈkɒnvɔɪ] *n* [group] comboio *m*; **in ~** em comboio.
convulse [kənˈvʌls] *vt*: **to be ~d with** [laughter, pain] dobrar-se de.
convulsion [kənˈvʌlʃn] *n MED* convulsão *f*.
convulsive [kənˈvʌlsɪv] *adj* convulsivo(va).
coo [kuː] *vi* **-1.** [bird] arrulhar **-2.** [person] sussurrar.
cook [kʊk] ◇ *n* cozinheiro *m*, -ra *f*. ◇ *vt* **-1.** [food, meal] cozinhar; **I'll ~ dinner** vou preparar o jantar **-2.** *inf* [books, accounts] falsificar. ◇ *vi* cozinhar.
◆ **cook up** *vt sep* [plan, scheme, excuse] inventar.
cookbook [ˈkʊkˌbʊk] *n* = **cookery book**.
cooked [kʊkt] *adj* [food] cozido(da).
cooker [ˈkʊkə[r]] *n esp UK* [stove] fogão *m*.
cookery [ˈkʊkərɪ] *n (U)* culinária *f*.
cookery book *n* livro *m* de receitas.
cookie [ˈkʊkɪ] *n* **-1.** *esp US* [biscuit] biscoito *m* **-2.** *COMPUT* cookie *m*.
cooking [ˈkʊkɪŋ] ◇ *n (U)* **-1.** [activity] culinária *f*; **do you like ~?** você gosta de cozinhar? **-2.** [food] cozinha *f*; **her ~ is awful!** ela cozinha mal pra caramba! ◇ *comp* **-1.** [oil, utensils, salt] de cozinha **-2.** [sherry, chocolate] para cozinhar.
cooking apple *n* maçã *f* para cozinhar.
cookout [ˈkʊkaʊt] *n US* refeição *f* ao ar livre.
cool [kuːl] ◇ *adj* **-1.** [not warm] frio (fria) **-2.** [calm] tranqüilo(la) **-3.** [unfriendly] frio (fria) **-4.** *inf* [excellent] legal **-5.** *inf* [trendy] bacana. ◇ *vt* esfriar. ◇ *vi* **-1.** [food, liquid, room] esfriar **-2.** [enthusiasm, ardour] arrefecer. ◇ *n inf* [calm]: **to keep/lose one's ~** manter/perder a calma.
◆ **cool down** ◇ *vt sep* **-1.** [make less warm] esfriar **-2.** [make less angry] acalmar-se. ◇ *vi* **-1.** [become less warm] esfriar **-2.** [become less angry] acalmar-se.
◆ **cool off** *vi* **-1.** [become less warm] esfriar **-2.** [become less angry] acalmar-se.
coolant [ˈkuːlənt] *n* líquido *m* refrigerante.
cool bag *n* bolsa *f* térmica.
cool box *UK*, **cooler** *US n* caixa *f* de gelo.
cool-headed [-ˈhedɪd] *adj* calmo(ma), de sangue-frio.
cooling-off period [ˈkuːlɪŋ-] *n* período *m* de calmaria.
cooling tower [ˈkuːlɪŋ-] *n* torre *f* de resfriamento.
coolly [ˈkuːlɪ] *adv* **-1.** [calmly] calmamente **-2.** [coldly] friamente.
coolness [ˈkuːlnɪs] *n (U)* **-1.** [in temperature] friagem *f* **-2.** [unfriendliness] frieza *f*.
coop [kuːp] *n* gaiola *f*; **chicken ~** galinheiro *m*.
◆ **coop up** *vt sep inf* trancafiar.
co-op (*abbr of* **cooperative**) *n fam* coop.
cooperate [kəʊˈɒpəreɪt] *vi* cooperar; **to ~ with sb/sthg** cooperar com alguém/algo.
cooperation [kəʊˌɒpəˈreɪʃn] *n (U)* cooperação *f*.
cooperative [kəʊˈɒpərətɪv] ◇ *adj* cooperativo(va). ◇ *n* [enterprise] cooperativa *f*.
co-opt *vt*: **to ~ sb (into/onto sthg)** cooptar alguém (em algo).
coordinate [*n* kəʊˈɔːdɪnət, *vt* kəʊˈɔːdɪneɪt] ◇ *n* [on map, graph] coordenada *f*. ◇ *vt* coordenar.
◆ **coordinates** *npl* [clothes] conjuntos *mpl*.
coordination [kəʊˌɔːdɪˈneɪʃn] *n (U)* coordenação *f*.
coot *n* [bird] galeirão *m*.
co-ownership *n (U)* co-propriedade *f*.
cop [kɒp] (*pt* & *pp* **-ped**, *cont* **-ping**) *n inf* [policeman] tira *m*.
◆ **cop out** *vi inf*: **to ~ out (of sthg)** cair fora (de algo).
cope [kəʊp] *vi* suportar; **to ~ with sthg** lidar com algo.
Copenhagen [ˌkəʊpənˈheɪɡən] *n* Copenhague.
copier [ˈkɒpɪə[r]] *n* [photocopier] copiadora *f*.
copilot [ˈkəʊˌpaɪlət] *n* co-piloto *m*, -ta *f*.
copious [ˈkəʊpjəs] *adj* copioso(sa).
cop-out *n inf* desculpa *f* furada.

copper ['kɒpəʳ] *n* **-1.** *(U)* [metal] cobre *m* **-2.** *UK inf* [policeman] tira *m*.
coppice ['kɒpɪs], **copse** [kɒps] *n* capão *m*.
copulate ['kɒpjʊleɪt] *vi fml*: **to ~ (with)** copular (com).
copulation [ˌkɒpjʊ'leɪʃn] *n (U)* cópula *f*.
copy ['kɒpɪ] (*pt* & *pp* **-ied**) ◇ *n* cópia *f*. ◇ *vt* copiar. ◇ *vi* [cheat] colar.
◆ **copy down** *vt sep* anotar.
◆ **copy out** *vt sep* copiar.
copycat ['kɒpɪkæt] ◇ *n* **inf** maria-vai-com-as-outras *mf inv*. ◇ *comp* [crime, killing] idêntico(ca) a outro mais famoso.
copy protect *vt COMPUT* proteger contra cópias.
copyright ['kɒpɪraɪt] *n (U)* direitos *mpl* autorais, copyright *m*.
copy typist *n UK* digitador *m*, -ra *f*.
copywriter ['kɒpɪˌraɪtəʳ] *n* redator *m*, -ra *f* de material publicitário.
coral ['kɒrəl] ◇ *n (U)* coral *m*. ◇ *comp* de coral; **a ~ pink** uma rosa coral.
coral reef *n* recife *m* de corais.
Coral Sea *n*: **the ~** o Mar de Coral.
cord [kɔ:d] ◇ *n* **-1.** [string] cordão *m* **-2.** [wire] fio *m* **-3.** [fabric] veludo *m* cotelê. ◇ *comp* de veludo cotelê.
◆ **cords** *npl inf* calça *f* de veludo cotelê.
cordial ['kɔ:djəl] ◇ *adj* cordial. ◇ *n* cordial *m*.
cordially ['kɔ:dɪəlɪ] *adv* cordialmente.
cordless *adj* sem-fio.
cordon ['kɔ:dn] *n* [barrier] cordão *m* de isolamento.
◆ **cordon off** *vt sep* isolar *(com cordão)*.
cordon bleu [-'blɜ:] *adj*: **a ~ cook** cozinheiro *m*, -ra *f* de alto nível.
corduroy ['kɔ:dərɔɪ] ◇ *n* veludo *m* cotelê. ◇ *comp* de veludo cotelê.
core [kɔ:ʳ] ◇ *n* **-1.** [gen] centro *m* **-2.** [of apple, pear] caroço *m* **-3.** [of argument, policy] âmago *m* **-4.** *phr*: **to be English/royalist to the ~** ser inglês(esa)/monarquista até morrer; **to be shaken to the ~** ficar muito comovido(da). ◇ *vt* [fruit] descaroçar.
CORE (*abbr of* **Congress on Racial Equality**) *n organização norte-americana contra o racismo.*
corer ['kɔ:rəʳ] *n* [for fruit] descaroçador *m*.
co-respondent *n JUR* co-responsável *mf (em caso de divórcio por adultério)*.
Corfu [kɔ:'fu:] *n* Corfu; **in ~** em Corfu.
corgi ['kɔ:gɪ] (*pl* **-s**) *n pequeno cão do País de Gales de nariz alongado e pernas curtas.*
coriander [ˌkɒrɪ'ændəʳ] *n (U)* **-1.** [herb] coriandro *m* **-2.** [spice] coentro *m*.
cork [kɔ:k] *n* **-1.** *(U)* [material] cortiça *f* **-2.** [stopper] rolha *f*.
corkage ['kɔ:kɪdʒ] *n (U) taxa cobrada num restaurante pela abertura das garrafas trazidas pelos clientes.*
corked [kɔ:kt] *adj* com gosto de rolha.
corkscrew ['kɔ:kskru:] *n* saca-rolhas *m*.
cormorant ['kɔ:mərənt] *n* cormorão *m*.
corn [kɔ:n] *n* **-1.** *(U) UK* [wheat, barley, oats] cereais *mpl* **-2.** *(U) esp Am* [maize] milho *m* **-3.** [callus] calo *m*.
corn bread *n* broa *f* de milho.
cornea ['kɔ:nɪə] (*pl* **-s**) *n* córnea *f*.
corned beef [kɔ:nd-] *n (U)* carne *f* bovina enlatada.
corner ['kɔ:nəʳ] ◇ *n* **-1.** [gen] canto *m*; **to cut ~s** *fig* pular etapas **-2.** [in street, road] esquina *f* **-3.** *FTBL* escanteio *m*. ◇ *vt* **-1.** [trap] encurralar **-2.** [monopolize] monopolizar.
corner flag *n FTBL* bandeirinha *f* de escanteio.
corner kick *n FTBL* cobrança *f* de escanteio.
corner shop *n pequeno armazém de esquina que vende comida e artigos de limpeza.*
cornerstone ['kɔ:nəstəʊn] *n* **fig** [basis] fundamento *m*.
cornet ['kɔ:nɪt] *n* **-1.** [instrument] corneta *f* **-2.** *UK* [ice-cream cone] casquinha *f*.
cornfield ['kɔ:nfi:ld] *n* **-1.** *UK* [of wheat] campo *m* de trigo **-2.** *esp US* [of maize] milharal *m*.
cornflakes ['kɔ:nfleɪks] *npl* flocos *mpl* de cereais.
cornflour *UK* ['kɔ:nflaʊəʳ], **cornstarch** *US* ['kɔ:nstɑ:tʃ] *n (U)* amido *m* de milho.
cornice ['kɔ:nɪs] *n* cornija *f*.
Cornish ['kɔ:nɪʃ] ◇ *adj* da Cornualha.
corn oil *n* óleo *m* de milho.
corn on the cob *n* milho *m* cozido.
cornstarch *n US* = **cornflour**.
cornucopia [ˌkɔ:njʊ'kəʊpjə] *n* **literary** cornucópia *f*.
Cornwall ['kɔ:nwɔ:l] *n* Cornualha *f*; **in ~** na Cornualha.
corny ['kɔ:nɪ] (*compar* **-ier**, *superl* **-iest**) *adj* **inf** batido(da).
corollary [kə'rɒlərɪ] (*pl* **-ies**) *n* corolário *m*.
coronary ['kɒrənrɪ] (*pl* **-ies**), **coronary thrombosis** [-θrɒm'bəʊsɪs] (*pl* **coronary thromboses** [-θrɒm'bəʊsi:z]) *n* trombose *f* coronária.
coronation [ˌkɒrə'neɪʃn] *n* coroação *f*.
coroner ['kɒrənəʳ] *n oficial responsável por investigar as mortes das pessoas que morreram de forma violenta, brusca ou incomum.*
Corp. (*abbr of* **corporation**) Corp.
corpora ['kɔ:pərə] *pl* ▷ **corpus**.
corporal ['kɔ:pərəl] *n* cabo *m*.
corporal punishment *n (U)* castigo *m* corporal.
corporate ['kɔ:pərət] *adj* **-1.** [business] corporativo(-va) **-2.** [collective] coletivo(va).
corporate hospitality *n diversão proporcionada por uma empresa a seus clientes, como refeições especiais ou drinks em locais agradáveis.*
corporate identity, corporate image *n* imagem *f* da empresa.
corporation [ˌkɔ:pə'reɪʃn] *n* **-1.** [council] associação *f* **-2.** [large company] corporação *f*.
corporation tax *n UK* imposto *m* sobre renda de corporações.
corps [kɔ:ʳ] (*pl inv*) *n* **-1.** *MIL* unidade *f* **-2.** [group] corpo *m*.
corpse [kɔ:ps] *n* cadáver *m*.
corpulent ['kɔ:pjʊlənt] *adj fml* corpulento(ta).
corpus ['kɔ:pəs] (*pl* **-pora** *OR* **-puses**) *n* [collection of writings] corpus *m*.
corpuscle ['kɔ:pʌsl] *n* corpúsculo *m*.

corral [kɒ'rɑ:l] *n esp US* curral *m*.
correct [kə'rekt] <> *adj* **-1.** [right, accurate] certo(ta) **-2.** [appropriate, suitable] adequado(da). <> *vt* corrigir.
correction [kə'rekʃn] *n* **-1.** *(U)* [act of correcting] correção *f* **-2.** [change] emenda *f*.
correctly [kə'rektlɪ] *adv* **-1.** [accurately] corretamente **-2.** [appropriately, suitably] adequadamente.
correlate ['kɒrəleɪt] <> *vt* correlacionar. <> *vi*: **to ~ (with sthg)** corresponder (a algo).
correlation [ˌkɒrə'leɪʃn] *n*: **~ (between)** correlação (entre).
correspond [ˌkɒrɪ'spɒnd] *vi* **-1.** [be equivalent]: **to ~ (with** *OR* **to sthg)** corresponder (com *OR* a algo) **-2.** [tally]: **to ~ (with** *OR* **to sthg)** ajustar-se (a algo) **-3.** [write letters]: **to ~ (with sb)** corresponder-se (com alguém).
correspondence [ˌkɒrɪ'spɒndəns] *n* **-1.** [letters] correspondência *f* **-2.** [letter-writing]: **~ with/between sb** correspondência com/entre alguém **-3.** [relationship, similarity]: **~ with sthg** relação com algo.
correspondence course *n* curso *m* por correspondência.
correspondent [ˌkɒrɪ'spɒndənt] *n* [reporter] correspondente *mf*.
corresponding [ˌkɒrɪ'spɒndɪŋ] *adj* [relevant] correspondente.
corridor ['kɒrɪdɔ:ʳ] *n* [in building] corredor *m*.
corroborate [kə'rɒbəreɪt] *vt* corroborar.
corroboration [kəˌrɒbə'reɪʃn] *n (U)* corroboração *f*.
corrode [kə'rəʊd] <> *vt* corroer. <> *vi* corroer-se.
corrosion [kə'rəʊʒn] *n (U)* [of metal] corrosão *f*.
corrosive [kə'rəʊsɪv] *adj* [poison, substance] corrosivo(sa).
corrugated ['kɒrəgeɪtɪd] *adj* ondulado(da).
corrugated iron *n (U)* ferro *m* corrugado.
corrupt [kə'rʌpt] <> *adj* **-1.** [dishonest] corrupto(ta) **-2.** [depraved] depravado(da) **-3.** *COMPUT* [damaged] corrompido(da). <> *vt* corromper.
corruption [kə'rʌpʃn] *n (U)* **-1.** [gen] corrupção *f* **-2.** [depravity] depravação *f*.
corsage [kɔ:'sɑ:ʒ] *n* [flowers] *pequeno buquê utilizado pelas mulheres à altura dos ombros.*
corset ['kɔ:sɪt] *n* [undergarment] espartilho *m*.
Corsica ['kɔ:sɪkə] *n* Córsega; **in ~** na Córsega.
Corsican ['kɔ:sɪkən] <> *adj* córsico(ca). <> *n* **-1.** [person] córsico *m*, -ca *f*, **-2.** [language] córsico *m*.
cortege, cortège [kɔ:'teɪʒ] *n* séquito *m*.
cortisone ['kɔ:tɪzəʊn] *n (U)* cortisona *f*.
cos[1] [kɒz] *conj UK inf* = **because**.
cos[2] [kɒs] *n* = **cos lettuce**.
cosh [kɒʃ] <> *n* cacete *m*. <> *vt* dar cacetadas.
cosignatory [ˌkəʊ'sɪgnətrɪ] (*pl* **-ies**) *n* co-signatário(ria).
cosine ['kəʊsaɪn] *n* co-seno *m*.
cos lettuce [kɒs-] *n UK* alface *f* romana.
cosmetic [kɒz'metɪk] <> *adj fig* [superficial] superficial. <> *n* cosmético *m*.
cosmetic surgery *n (U)* cirurgia *f* estética.
cosmic ['kɒzmɪk] *adj* cósmico(ca).
cosmonaut ['kɒzmənɔ:t] *n* cosmonauta *mf*.
cosmopolitan [kɒzmə'pɒlɪtn] *adj* cosmopolita.
cosmos ['kɒzmɒs] *n*: **the ~** o cosmos.
Cossack ['kɒsæk] *n* cossaco *m*.
cosset ['kɒsɪt] *vt* acarinhar.
cost [kɒst] (*pt* & *pp senses 1 & 3* **cost**, *pt* & *pp sense 2* **-ed**) <> *n* **-1.** custo *m*; **at all ~s** a qualquer custo **-2.** <> *vt* **-1.** [in financial transactions - sum of money] custar; [- person] custar a **-2.** *COMM* [estimate price of] orçar; **to ~ a product** orçar um produto; **the work was ~ed at £65** o trabalho foi orçado em £65.
◆ **costs** *npl JUR* custas *fpl*.
cost accountant *n* contador *m*, -ra *f* de custos.
co-star ['kəʊ-] <> *n* coadjuvante *mf*. <> *vt* atuar como coadjuvante. <> *vi*: **to ~ (with)** contracenar (com).
Costa Rica [ˌkɒstə'ri:kə] *n* Costa Rica; **in ~** na Costa Rica.
Costa Rican [ˌkɒstə'ri:kən] <> *adj* costarriquenho(nha). <> *n* costarriquenho *m*, -nha *f*.
cost-benefit analysis *n (U)* análise *f* de custo-benefício.
cost-effective *adj* rentável, lucrativo(va).
cost-effectiveness *n (U)* rentabilidade *f*.
costing ['kɒstɪŋ] *n* estimativa *f* de custos.
costly ['kɒstlɪ] (*compar* **-ier**, *superl* **-iest**) *adj* **-1.** [expensive] oneroso(sa) **-2.** *fig* [involving loss, damage] dispendioso(sa).
cost of living *n*: **the ~** o custo de vida.
cost-of-living index *n* ≃ índice *m* de preços ao consumidor.
cost price *n* preço *m* de custo.
costume ['kɒstju:m] *n* **-1.** *THEATRE* roupa *f*; **lion ~** fantasia de leão; **in ~ and make-up** vestido(da) e maquiado(da) **-2.** *(U)* [dress] traje *m*; **swimming ~** maiô *m*.
costume jewellery *n (U)* bijuteria *f*.
cosy *UK*, **cozy** *US* ['kəʊzɪ] (*compar* **-ier**, *superl* **-iest**, *pl* **-ies**) <> *adj* **-1.** [clothes] confortável **-2.** [person] aconchegado(da); **to feel ~** sentir-se aconchegado(da) **-3.** [chat, atmosphere] aconchegante. <> *n* [for teapot] abafador *m*.
cot [kɒt] *n* **-1.** *UK* [for child] berço *m* **-2.** *US* [folding bed] cama *f* de campanha.
cot death *n* morte *f* no berço.
cottage ['kɒtɪdʒ] *n* cabana *f*, chalé *m*; **a country ~** uma casa de campo.
cottage cheese *n (U)* requeijão *m*.
cottage hospital *n UK* hospital *m* pequeno no campo.
cottage industry *n* indústria *f* caseira.
cottage pie *n UK* *bolo de carne picada coberto com purê de batata.*
cotton ['kɒtn] <> *n (U)* **-1.** [fabric, plants] algodão *m* **-2.** [thread] linha *f*. <> *comp* de algodão.
◆ **cotton on** *vi inf*: **to ~ on (to sthg)** sacar (algo).
cotton bud *UK*, **cotton swab** *US* *n* cotonete *m*.
cotton candy *n US* = **candyfloss**.
cotton swab *n US* = **cotton bud**.
cotton wool *n (U)* chumaço *m* de algodão.
couch [kaʊtʃ] <> *n* **-1.** [gen] sofá *m* **-2.** [psychiatrist's]

divã *m.* ◇ *vt fig*: **to ~ sthg in** [express] formular algo em.
couchette [kuː'ʃet] *n UK* cama *f (em trem ou navio).*
couch potato *n inf* folgado *m*, -da *f.*
cougar ['kuːgəʳ] (*pl inv* OR **-s**) *n* puma *m.*
cough [kɒf] ◇ *n* **-1.** [noise] tossida *f* **-2.** [illness] tosse *f.* ◇ *vi* tossir. ◇ *vt* expelir tossindo.
◆ **cough up** *vt sep* **-1.** [bring up] expelir tossindo **-2.** *v inf* [pay up] desembolsar.
coughing ['kɒfɪŋ] *n* tosse *f.*
cough mixture *n UK* xarope *m* para a tosse.
cough sweet *n UK* pastilha *f* para tosse.
cough syrup *n* = **cough mixture**.
could [kʊd] *pt* ⊳ **can²**.
couldn't ['kʊdnt] = **could not**.
could've ['kʊdəv] = **could have**.
council ['kaʊnsl] ◇ *n* **-1.** [local authority] câmara *f* municipal **-2.** [group, organization] conselho *m* **-3.** [meeting] assembléia *f.* ◇ *comp* [of local authority] de conselho.
council estate *n UK conjunto de casas de propriedade do município destinado à locação.*
council flat *n UK apartamento de propriedade do município para ser alugado a baixo custo.*
council house *n UK casa de propriedade do município para ser alugada a baixo custo.*
councillor ['kaʊnsələʳ] *n* vereador *m*, -ra *f.*
Council of Europe *n* Conselho *m* da Europa.
council of war *n* conselho *m* de guerra.
council tax *n UK* ≃ imposto *m* territorial urbano.
counsel ['kaʊnsəl] (*UK pt* & *pp* **-led**, *cont* **-ling**, *US pt* & *pp* **-ed**, *cont* **-ing**) ◇ *n* **-1.** *(U) fml* [advice] parecer *m* **-2.** [lawyer] conselheiro *m*, -ra *f*, advogado *m*, -da *f.* ◇ *vt* aconselhar; **to ~ sb to do sthg** *fml* aconselhar alguém a fazer algo.
counselling *UK*, **counseling** *US* ['kaʊnsəlɪŋ] *n (U)* aconselhamento *m*, orientação *f.*
counsellor *UK*, **counselor** *US* ['kaʊnsələʳ] *n* **-1.** [adviser, helper] conselheiro *m*, -ra *f*, orientador(ra) ra **-2.** *US* [lawyer] advogado *m*, -da *f.*
count [kaʊnt] ◇ *n* **-1.** [total] conta *f*; **to keep ~ of sthg** registrar algo; **to lose ~ of sthg** perder a conta de algo **-2.** [point] ponto *m* **-3.** JUR [charge] enquadramento *m* **-4.** [aristocrat] conde *m.* ◇ *vt* **-1.** [add up] contar **-2.** [consider, include]: **to ~ sb/sthg as sthg** considerar alguém/algo como algo. ◇ *vi* contar; **to ~ for** contar (para); **to ~ (up) to** contar até; **to ~ as sthg** contar como algo.
◆ **count against** *vt fus* pesar contra.
◆ **count in** *vt sep inf* incluir.
◆ **count on** *vt fus* [rely on, expect] contar com.
◆ **count out** *vt sep* **-1.** [money] contar um a um **-2.** *inf* [leave out] excluir.
◆ **count up** *vt fus* contar.
◆ **count upon** *vt fus* = **count on**.
countdown ['kaʊntdaʊn] *n* contagem *f* regressiva.
countenance ['kaʊntənəns] ◇ *n literary* [face] semblante *m.* ◇ *vt* [approve of] aprovar.
counter ['kaʊntəʳ] ◇ *n* **-1.** [in shop, kitchen] balcão *m* **-2.** [in board game] ficha *f* **-3.** [in post office, bank] guichê *m.* ◇ *vt*: **to ~ sthg with sthg** [respond to] responder algo com algo; **to ~ sthg by doing sthg** responder algo fazendo algo. ◇ *vi*: **to ~ with sthg / by doing sthg** responder com/fazendo algo.
◆ **counter to** *adv* ao contrário de; **to run ~ to sthg** ir contra algo/ser contrário a algo.
counteract [ˌkaʊntə'rækt] *vt* neutralizar.
counter-attack ◇ *n* contra-ataque *m.* ◇ *vt* & *vi* contra-atacar.
counterbalance [ˌkaʊntə'bæləns] *vt fig* [correct, balance] contrapeso *m.*
counterclaim ['kaʊntəkleɪm] *n* reivindicação *f.*
counterclockwise *US* [ˌkaʊntə'klɒkwaɪz] ◇ *adj* anti-horário(ria). ◇ *adv* em sentido anti-horário.
counter-espionage *n (U)* contra-espionagem *f.*
counterfeit ['kaʊntəfɪt] ◇ *adj* falsificado(da). ◇ *vt* falsificar.
counterfoil ['kaʊntəfɔɪl] *n* canhoto *m.*
counter-intelligence *n (U)* contra-espionagem *f.*
countermand [ˌkaʊntə'mɑːnd] *vt* revogar.
counter-measure *n* contramedida *f.*
counter-offensive *n* contra-ofensiva *f.*
counterpane ['kaʊntəpeɪn] *n* colcha *f.*
counterpart ['kaʊntəpɑːt] *n* contraparte *f.*
counterpoint ['kaʊntəpɔɪnt] *n (U)* MUS contraponto *m.*
counter-productive *adj* contraproducente.
counter-revolution *n* contra-revolução *f.*
countersank ['kaʊntəsæŋk] *pt* ⊳ **countersink**.
countersign ['kaʊntəsaɪn] *vt* [document] **-1.** referendar **-2.** [cheque] endossar.
countersink ['kaʊntəsɪŋk] (*pt* **-sank**, *pp* **-sunk** [-sʌŋk]) *vt* escarear.
countess ['kaʊntɪs] *n* condessa *f.*
countless ['kaʊntlɪs] *adj* inúmero(ra).
countrified ['kʌntrɪfaɪd] *adj pej* rústico(ca).
country ['kʌntrɪ] (*pl* **-ies**) ◇ *n* **-1.** [nation] país *m*; **to go to the ~** *UK* POL fazer uma eleição **-2.** [countryside]: **the ~** o campo **-3.** [area of land, region] região *f.* ◇ *comp* do campo.
country and western ◇ *n (U)* música *f* country. ◇ *comp* country *inv.*
country club *n* clube *m* de campo, country club *m.*
country dancing *n (U)* dança *f* tradicional.
country house *n* casa *f* de campo.
countryman ['kʌntrɪmən] (*pl* **-men** [-mən]) *n* [from same country] compatriota *m.*
country music *n* & *comp* = **country and western**.
country park *n UK* parque *m* regional.
countryside ['kʌntrɪsaɪd] *n (U)* campo *m.*
countrywoman ['kʌntrɪˌwʊmən] (*pl* **-women** [-ˌwɪmɪn]) *n* [from same country] compatriota *f.*
county ['kaʊntɪ] (*pl* **-ies**) *n* condado *m.*
county council *n UK* conselho *m* regional.
county court *n UK* tribunal *m* regional.
county town *UK*, **county seat** *US n capital de um condado.*
coup [kuː] *n* **-1.** [rebellion]: **~ (d'état)** golpe de

estado **-2.** [masterstroke] golpe *m* de mestre.
coupé ['ku:peɪ] *n AUT* cupê *m.*
couple ['kʌpl] <> *n* **-1.** [in relationship] casal *m* **-2.** [small number]: **a ~** alguns, algumas; **a ~ of** dois, duas. <> *vt* **-1.** [join]: **to ~ sthg (to sthg)** unir algo (a algo) **-2.** *fig* [associate]: **to ~ sthg with sthg** associar algo a algo; **~d with** aliado(da) a.
couplet ['kʌplɪt] *n* dístico *m.*
coupling ['kʌplɪŋ] *n RAIL* engate *m.*
coupon ['ku:pɒn] *n* **-1.** [voucher] vale *m* **-2.** [form] cupom *m.*
courage ['kʌrɪdʒ] *n (U)* coragem *f*; **to take ~ (from sthg)** tirar coragem (de algo); **to have the ~ of one's convictions** ter coragem de manter suas opiniões.
courageous [kə'reɪdʒəs] *adj* corajoso(sa).
courageously [kə'reɪdʒəslɪ] *adv* corajosamente.
courgette [kɔ:'ʒet] *n UK* abobrinha *f.*
courier ['kʊrɪə^r] *n* **-1.** [on holiday tour] *representante de uma agência de viagens que cuida das pessoas que estão a passeio* **-2.** [delivering letters, packages] mensageiro *m*, -ra *f*, courier *m.*
course [kɔ:s] <> *n* **-1.** [gen] curso *m* **-2.** *MED* [of treatment] tratamento *m* **-3.** [path, route] rota *f*; **to run** *OR* **take its ~** seguir *OR* tomar o curso natural; **to be on ~ for** [ship, plane] estar rumando para; *fig* [on target] em curso; **off ~** fora de curso **-4.** [plan]: **~ (of action)** curso (de ação) **-5.** [of time]: **in due ~** no tempo devido; **in the ~ of** no decorrer de **-6.** [in meal] prato *m* **-7.** *SPORT* campo *m.* <> *vi literary* [flow] correr.
◆ **of course** *adv* **-1.** [inevitably, not surprisingly] evidentemente **-2.** [certainly] claro que sim; **of ~ you can!** claro que pode!; **'do you want the job?' - 'of ~ I do!'** 'você quer o trabalho?' - 'claro que quero!'; **of ~ not** claro que não.
coursebook ['kɔ:sbʊk] *n* livro *m* de curso.
coursework ['kɔ:swɜ:k] *n (U)* trabalho *m* de curso.
court [kɔ:t] <> *n* **-1.** *JUR* tribunal *m*; **to appear in ~** comparecer perante um tribunal; **to settle out of ~** resolver fora dos tribunais; **to go to ~** processar; **to take sb to ~** levar alguém a julgamento; **the ~** o tribunal **-2.** *SPORT* quadra *f*; **on ~** na quadra **-3.** [courtyard] pátio *m* **-4.** [of king, queen etc] corte *f.* <> *vt* [seek] procurar. <> *vi dated* [go out together] cortejar.
court circular *n UK* ≃ diário *m* da corte.
courteous ['kɜ:tjəs] *adj* cortês.
courtesan [ˌkɔ:tɪ'zæn] *n* cortesã *f.*
courtesy ['kɜ:tɪsɪ] *n (U)* [polite behaviour] cortesia *f.*
◆ **(by) courtesy of** *prep* [thanks to] por cortesia de.
courtesy car *n* carro *m* de cortesia.
courtesy coach *n* ônibus *m* de cortesia.
courthouse ['kɔ:thaʊs] *n US* palácio *m* da justiça.
courtier ['kɔ:tjə^r] *n* cortesão *m.*
court-martial (*pl* **court-martials** *OR* **courts-martial**, *UK pt* & *pp* **-led**, *cont* **-ling**, *US pt* & *pp* **-ed**, *cont* **-ing**) <> *n* corte *m* marcial. <> *vt* submeter a uma corte marcial.
court of appeal *UK*, **court of appeals** *US n* tribunal *m* de apelação.
court of inquiry *n* **-1.** [investigation] tribunal *m* de investigação **-2.** [investigating group] comissão *f* de inquérito.
court of law *n* tribunal *m.*
courtroom ['kɔ:trʊm] *n* sala *f* de tribunal.
courtship ['kɔ:tʃɪp] *n (U)* **-1.** [of people] galanteio *m* **-2.** [of animals] requesta *f.*
court shoe *n* escarpim *m.*
courtyard ['kɔ:tjɑ:d] *n* pátio *m.*
cousin ['kʌzn] *n* primo *m*, -ma *f.*
couture [ku:'tʊə^r] *n*: **haute ~** alta-costura *f.*
cove [kəʊv] *n* [bay] enseada *f.*
coven ['kʌvən] *n* grupo *m* de bruxas.
covenant ['kʌvənənt] *n* **-1.** [promise of money] convênio *m* **-2.** [pact] pacto *m.*
Covent Garden [ˌkɒvənt-] *n área comercial e artística coberta no centro de Londres, que também inclui o Royal Opera House.*
Coventry ['kɒvəntrɪ] *n*: **to send sb to ~** pôr alguém no ostracismo.
cover ['kʌvə^r] <> *n* **-1.** [covering] capa *f* **-2.** [lid] tampa *f* **-3.** [blanket] coberta *f* **-4.** [protection, shelter] abrigo *m*; **to take ~** [from weather] abrigar-se; [from gunfire] proteger-se; **under ~** [from weather] abrigado(da); **under ~ of darkness** sob o manto da escuridão; **to break ~** sair do esconderijo **-5.** [disguise, front or insurance] cobertura *f.* <> *vt* cobrir; **to ~ sthg with sthg** cobrir algo com algo; **to ~ sb against sthg** [give insurance] cobrir alguém contra algo.
◆ **cover up** *vt sep* **-1.** [person, animal] cobrir **-2.** *fig* [story, scandal] encobrir.
coverage ['kʌvərɪdʒ] *n (U)* [of news] cobertura *f.*
coveralls ['kʌvərɔ:lz] *npl US* macacão *m.*
cover charge *n* couvert *m.*
cover girl *n* garota *f* da capa.
covering ['kʌvərɪŋ] *n* cobertura *f.*
covering letter *UK*, **cover letter** *US n carta ou nota contendo explicações ou informações adicionais que acompanha uma encomenda ou outra carta.*
cover note *n UK* nota *f* de cobertura.
cover price *n* [of book, magazine] preço *m* de capa.
covert ['kʌvət] *adj* secreto(ta), oculto(ta).
cover-up *n* encobrimento *m.*
cover version *n* regravação *f* de música.
covet ['kʌvɪt] *vt fml* ambicionar.
cow [kaʊ] <> *n* **-1.** [female type of cattle] vaca *f* **-2.** [female elephant, whale, seal] fêmea *f* **-3.** *UK inf pej* [woman] vaca *f.* <> *vt* intimidar.
coward ['kaʊəd] *n* covarde *mf.*
cowardice ['kaʊədɪs] *n (U)* covardia *f.*
cowardly ['kaʊədlɪ] *adj* covarde.
cowboy ['kaʊbɔɪ] <> *n* **-1.** [cattlehand] vaqueiro **-2.** *UK inf* [dishonest workman] patife *m.* <> *comp* [western] caubói *m.*
cower ['kaʊə^r] *vi* encolher-se de medo.
cowhide ['kaʊhaɪd] *n (U)* couro *m* de vaca.
cowl neck *n* capuz *m.*
co-worker *n* colega *mf* de trabalho.
cowpat ['kaʊpæt] *n* estrume *m* de vaca.
cowshed ['kaʊʃed] *n* estábulo *m.*
cox [kɒks], **coxswain** ['kɒksən] *n* timoneiro *m*, -ra *f.*

coy [kɔɪ] *adj* recatado(da).
coyly ['kɔɪlɪ] *adv* recatadamente.
coyote [kɔɪ'əʊtɪ] *n* coiote *m*.
cozy *adj & n US* = cosy.
CP (*abbr of* **Communist Party**) *n* partido *m* comunista.
CPA (*abbr of* **certified public accountant**) *n contador público certificado nos Estados Unidos.*
Cpl. (*abbr of* **corporal**) corporal.
cps (*abbr of* **characters per second**) cps.
CPS (*abbr of* **Crown Prosecution Service**) *n organismo britânico que decide quais casos policiais devem ser levados ao tribunal.*
CPU (*abbr of* **central processing unit**) *n* COMPUT CPU *f*.
Cr -1. *abbr of* **Councillor**. **-2.** *abbr of* **credit**.
crab [kræb] *n* **-1.** [sea creature] caranguejo *m* **-2.** [food] siri *m*.
crab apple *n* **-1.** [fruit] maçã *f* silvestre **-2.** [tree] macieira *f* silvestre.
crabby (*compar* **-ier**, *superl* **-iest**) *adj* mal-humorado(da).
crack [kræk] ◇ *n* **-1.** [fault - in cup, glass, mirror] trinca *f*; [- in wall, ceiling] rachadura *f*; [- in skin] arranhão *m* **-2.** [small opening, gap] fresta *f*; **at the ~ of dawn** no raiar do dia **-3.** [sharp noise] estalo *m* **-4.** [joke] piada *f* **-5.** *inf* [attempt]: **to have a ~ at sthg** tentar (fazer) algo **-6.** [cocaine] crack *m*. ◇ *adj* de primeira. ◇ *vt* **-1.** [damage - gen] arranhar; [- cup, glass] trincar; [- wall, ceiling] rachar **-2.** [open - egg] quebrar; [- bottle] abrir; [- safe] arrombar **-3.** [cause to make sharp noise] estalar **-4.** [bang, hit] bater **-5.** [solve - problem] resolver; [- code] decifrar **-6.** *inf* [make]: **to ~ a joke** soltar uma piada. ◇ *vi* **-1.** [split, be damaged - gen] arranhar; [- cup, glass] trincar; [- wall, ceiling,] rachar **-2.** [make sharp noise] estalar **-3.** [give way, collapse] ruir **-4.** *UK inf* [act quickly]: **to get ~ing** pôr mãos à obra.
◆ **crack down** *vi*: **to ~ down (on sb/sthg)** fazer linha dura (contra alguém/algo).
◆ **crack up** *vi* ter um colapso nervoso.
crackdown ['krækdaʊn] *n*: **~ (on sthg)** endurecimento *m* (em relação a algo).
cracked [krækt] *adj* **-1.** [damaged - cup, glass, skin] arranhado(da); [- wall, ceiling] rachado(da) **-2.** *inf* [mad] doido(da).
cracker ['krækə^r] *n* **-1.** [biscuit] biscoito *m* **-2.** *UK* [for Christmas] *tubo colorido que faz barulho ao abrir e contém um presente surpresa.*
crackers ['krækəz] *adj UK inf* [mad] doido(da).
cracking ['krækɪŋ] *adj inf*: **to walk at a ~ pace** andar a passos largos.
crackle ['krækl] ◇ *n* **-1.** [of fire, cooking] crepitação *f* **-2.** [of phone, radio] interferência *f*. ◇ *vi* **-1.** [fire, cooking] crepitar **-2.** [phone, radio] estar com interferência.
crackling ['kræklɪŋ] *n (U)* **-1.** [noise - on phone] tilintar *m*; [- on radio] interferência *f* **-2.** [pork skin] torresmo *m*.
crackpot ['krækpɒt] *inf* ◇ *adj* maluco(ca). ◇ *n* excêntrico *m*, -ca *f*.
cradle ['kreɪdl] ◇ *n* **-1.** [baby's bed, birthplace] berço *m* **-2.** [hoist] pedestal *m*. ◇ *vt* **-1.** [person] embalar **-2.** [object] segurar cuidadosamente.
craft [krɑːft] (*pl sense 2 inv*) *n* **-1.** [trade, skill] arte *f* **-2.** [boat] barco *m*.
craftsman ['krɑːftsmən] (*pl* **-men** [-mən]) *n* artesão *m*.
craftsmanship ['krɑːftsmənʃɪp] *n* destreza *f*, habilidade *f*.
craftsmen *pl* ▷ **craftsman**.
crafty ['krɑːftɪ] (*compar* **-ier**, *superl* **-iest**) *adj* astuto(-ta).
crag [kræg] *n* penhasco *m*.
craggy ['krægɪ] (*compar* **-ier**, *superl* **-iest**) *adj* **-1.** [rock] escarpado(da) **-2.** [face] de traços fortes.
Crakow ['krækaʊ] *n* Cracóvia; **in ~** em Cracóvia.
cram [kræm] (*pt & pp* **-med**, *cont* **-ming**) ◇ *vt* abarrotar; **to ~ sthg with sthg** abarrotar algo com algo; **to be crammed (with sthg)** estar abarrotado(da) (de algo). ◇ *vi* [study hard] rachar de estudar.
cramp [kræmp] ◇ *n* **-1.** [in leg, arm] cãibra *f* **-2.** [in stomach] cólica *f*. ◇ *vt* [restrict, hinder] limitar.
cramped [kræmpt] *adj* [confined] apertado(da).
crampon ['kræmpən] *n* ganho *m* de ferro.
cranberry ['krænbərɪ] (*pl* **-ies**) *n* uva-do-monte *f*.
crane [kreɪn] ◇ *n* **-1.** [machine] guindaste *m* **-2.** [bird] grou *m*. ◇ *vt* espichar. ◇ *vi* espichar-se.
crane fly *n* mosquito-berne *m*.
cranium ['kreɪnjəm] (*pl* **-niums** OR **-nia** [-njə]) *n* crânio *m*.
crank [kræŋk] ◇ *n* **-1.** TECH manivela *f* **-2.** *inf* [eccentric] extravagante *mf*. ◇ *vt* **-1.** [gen] dar manivela em **-2.** AUT dar partida em.
crankshaft ['kræŋkʃɑːft] *n* virabrequim *m*.
cranky ['kræŋkɪ] (*compar* **-ier**, *superl* **-iest**) *adj inf* **-1.** [odd] esquisito(ta) **-2.** [bad-tempered] irritadiço(ça).
cranny ['krænɪ] (*pl* **-ies**) *n* ▷ **nook**.
crap [kræp] *n (U) vulg* **-1.** [excrement] bosta *f* **-2.** *fig* [rubbish] asneira *f*.
crappy ['kræpɪ] (*compar* **-ier**, *superl* **-iest**) *adj vulg* de péssima qualidade.
crash [kræʃ] ◇ *n* **-1.** [accident] acidente *m* **-2.** [loud noise] estrépito *m* **-3.** FIN crash *m*. ◇ *vt* [cause to collide] bater com. ◇ *vi* **-1.** [collide] colidir; **to ~ into sthg** colidir em algo **-2.** [make loud noise - drums] soar; [- cymbals] retinir; [- waves] quebrar; [- china] espatifar **-3.** FIN [collapse] entrar em colapso **-4.** COMPUT dar pane.
crash barrier *n* cerca *f* de proteção.
crash course *n* curso *m* intensivo.
crash diet *n* dieta *f* rigorosa.
crash-dive *vi* submersão *f* súbita.
crash helmet *n* elmo *m*.
crash-land ◇ *vt* aterrisar forçosamente. ◇ *vi* aterrisar forçosamente.
crash-landing *n* aterrissagem *f* forçada.
crass [kræs] *adj* crasso(sa).
crate [kreɪt] *n* **-1.** [for carrying things] caixote *m* **-2.** [crateful] engradado *m*.
crater ['kreɪtə^r] *n* cratera *f*.
cravat [krə'væt] *n* cachecol *m*.
crave [kreɪv] ◇ *vt* ansiar. ◇ *vi*: **to ~ for sthg** ansiar por algo.
craving ['kreɪvɪŋ] *n*: **~ (for sthg/to do sthg)** desejo incontrolável (por algo/fazer algo).

crawl [krɔ:l] <> *vi* **-1.** [on hands and knees] engatinhar **-2.** [move slowly - insect] rastejar; [- vehicle, traffic] arrastar-se **-3.** *inf*: **to be ~ing with sthg** estar infestado(da) de algo **-4.** *inf* [grovel]: **to ~ (to sb)** rastejar (aos pés de alguém). <> *n* **-1.** [slow pace]: **at a ~** vagarosamente **-2.** *(U)* [swimming stroke]: **the ~** o crawl.

crawler lane ['krɔ:lə^r-] *n UK* faixa *f* para veículos lentos.

crayfish ['kreɪfɪʃ] (*pl inv* OR **-es**) *n* **-1.** [fish] lagostim *m* **-2.** [food] camarão-d'água-doce *m*.

crayon ['kreɪɒn] *n* lápis *m* de cera.

craze [kreɪz] *n* [fashion] moda *f*.

crazed [kreɪzd] *adj* enlouquecido(da); **~ with** louco(ca) de.

crazy ['kreɪzɪ] (*compar* **-ier**, *superl* **-iest**) *adj inf* [mad, enthusiastic] louco(ca); **to be ~ about sthg/sb** ser/estar louco(ca) por algo/alguém.

crazy paving *n UK* pavimento *m* irregular.

CRC (*abbr of* **camera-ready copy**) PRINT *n versão pronta para impressão.*

CRE (*abbr of* **Commission for Racial Equality**) *n* commissão para combater a desigualidade racial.

creak [kri:k] <> *n* rangido *m*. <> *vi* ranger.

creaky ['kri:kɪ] (*compar* **-ier**, *superl* **-iest**) *adj* que range.

cream [kri:m] <> *adj* [in colour] creme. <> *n* **-1.** creme *m* **-2.** [elite] **the ~** a nata. <> *vt* [puree] fazer purê com.

◆ **cream off** *vt sep* tirar o melhor de.

cream cake *n UK* bolo *m* de creme.

cream cheese *n (U)* queijo *m* cremoso.

cream cracker *n UK* bolacha *f* cream cracker.

cream of tartar *n (U)* cremor *m* de tártaro.

cream tea *n UK chá acompanhado de bolinhos com presunto, geléia e creme, comum na Inglaterra.*

creamy ['kri:mɪ] (*compar* **-ier**, *superl* **-iest**) *adj* **-1.** [texture, taste] cremoso(sa) **-2.** [colour] creme.

crease [kri:s] <> *n* [in fabric - deliberate] friso *m*; [- accidental] dobra *f*. <> *vt* [deliberately] amassar; [accidentally] amarrotar. <> *vi* **-1.** [fabric] amassar **-2.** [face, forehead] franzir-se.

creased [kri:st] *adj* **-1.** [fabric] amarrotado(da) **-2.** [face] franzido(da).

crease-resistant *adj*: **~ fabric** tecido *m* que não amassa.

create [kri:'eɪt] *vt* **-1.** [gen] criar **-2.** [noise, fuss, impression] causar.

creation [kri:'eɪʃn] *n* criação *f*.

creative [kri:'eɪtɪv] *adj* criativo(va); **~ writing** produção *f* literária.

creativity [ˌkri:eɪ'tɪvətɪ] *n (U)* criatividade *f*.

creator [kri:'eɪtə^r] *n* [person] criador *m*, -ra *f*.

creature ['kri:tʃə^r] *n* **-1.** [animal] criatura *f* **-2.** *literary* [person] ser *m*.

crèche [kreʃ] *n UK* creche *f*.

credence ['kri:dns] *n (U)* credibilidade *f*; **to give** OR **lend ~ to sthg** conferir credibilidade a algo.

credentials [krɪ'denʃlz] *npl* **-1.** [papers] credenciais *fpl* **-2.** *fig* [qualifications] credenciais *fpl* **-3.** [references] referências *fpl*.

credibility [ˌkredə'bɪlətɪ] *n (U)* credibilidade *f*.

credible ['kredəbl] *adj* crível.

credit ['kredɪt] <> *n* **-1.** *(U)* [financial aid] crédito *m*; **in ~** com saldo positivo; **on ~** a prazo **-2.** *(U)* [praise] honras *fpl*; **to his/her ~** [successfully completed] a seu favor; [in his/her favour] para o seu próprio bem; **to do sb ~** dizer muito em favor de alguém; **to give sb ~ for sthg** crer que alguém seja capaz de algo **-3.** SCH & UNIV crédito *m* **-4.** FIN [money credited] saldo *m* positivo. <> *vt* **-1.** FIN creditar **-2.** *inf* [believe] acreditar **-3.** [attribute]: **to ~ sb with sthg** atribuir a alguém o mérito por algo.

◆ **credits** *npl* CINEMA créditos *mpl*.

creditable ['kredɪtəbl] *adj fml* louvável.

credit account *n UK* conta *f* de crédito.

credit broker *n* intermediário *m* financeiro, intermediária *f* financeira.

credit card *n* cartão *m* de crédito.

credit control *n (U)* controle *m* de crédito.

credit facilities *npl* facilidades *fpl* de crédito.

credit limit *UK*, **credit line** *US n* limite *m* de crédito.

credit note *n* **-1.** COMM nota *f* promissória **-2.** FIN letra *f* de câmbio.

creditor ['kredɪtə^r] *n* credor *m*, -ra *f*.

credit rating *n* índice *f* de crédito.

credit squeeze *n* contenção *f* de crédito.

credit transfer *n* transferência *f* bancária.

creditworthy ['kredɪtˌwɜ:ðɪ] *adj* merecedor(ra) de crédito.

credulity [krɪ'dju:lətɪ] *n (U) fml* credulidade *f*.

credulous ['kredjʊləs] *adj* crédulo(la).

creed [kri:d] *n* **-1.** [political] doutrina *f* **-2.** RELIG credo *m*.

creek [kri:k] *n* **-1.** [inlet] enseada *f* **-2.** *US* [stream] riacho *m*.

creep [kri:p] (*pt* & *pp* **crept**) <> *vi* **-1.** [move slowly] arrastar-se **-2.** [move stealthily] andar furtivamente **-3.** [grovel]: **to ~ (to sb)** rastejar-se (diante de alguém). <> *n inf* [person] pegajoso *m*, -sa *f*.

◆ **creeps** *npl*: **to give sb the ~s** *inf* dar arrepios *mpl* em alguém.

◆ **creep in** *vi* [mistakes, doubts] surgir.

◆ **creep up on** *vt* **-1.** [subj: person, animal] aproximar-se furtivamente **-2.** [subj: feeling, state] aproximar-se.

creeper ['kri:pə^r] *n* [plant] trepadeira *f*.

creeping *adj* [gradual] gradual.

creepy ['kri:pɪ] (*compar* **-ier**, *superl* **-iest**) *adj inf* horripilante.

creepy-crawly [-'krɔ:lɪ] (*pl* **creepy-crawlies**) *n inf* bicho *m* rastejante.

cremate [krɪ'meɪt] *vt* cremar.

cremation [krɪ'meɪʃn] *n (U)* cremação *f*.

crematorium *UK* [ˌkremə'tɔ:rɪəm] (*pl* **-riums** OR **-ria** [-rɪə]), **crematory** *US* ['kremətrɪ] (*pl* **-ies**) *n* crematório *m*.

creosote ['krɪəsəʊt] <> *n (U)* creosoto *m*. <> *vt* aplicar creosoto em.

crepe [kreɪp] *n* crepe *m*.

crepe bandage *n UK* atadura *f*.

crepe paper *n (U)* papel *m* crepom.

crepe-soled shoes [-səʊld-] *npl UK* calçado *m* com sola emborrachada.
crept [krept] *pt & pp* ▷ **creep**.
Cres. *abbr of* **Crescent**.
crescendo [krɪ'ʃendəʊ] (*pl* **-s**) *n* crescendo *m*.
crescent ['kresnt] ◇ *adj* [shaped] crescente. ◇ *n* **-1.** [shape] crescente *mf* **-2.** [street] rua *f* em forma de arco.
cress [kres] *n (U)* agrião *m*.
crest [krest] *n* **-1.** [on bird's head, of wave] crista *f* **-2.** [of hill] cume *m* **-3.** [on coat of arms] brasão *m*.
crestfallen ['krest,fɔ:ln] *adj* desanimado(da).
Crete [kri:t] *n* Creta; **in ~** em Creta.
cretin ['kretɪn] *n inf offensive* [idiot] cretino *m*, -na *f*.
crevasse [krɪ'væs] *n* fissura *f*, fenda *f*.
crevice ['krevɪs] *n* fenda *f*, rachadura *f*.
crew [kru:] *n* **-1.** [of ship, plane, ambulance] tripulação *f* **-2.** CINEMA & TV equipe *f* **-3.** *inf* [gang] bando *m*.
crew cut *n* corte *m* de cabelo à escovinha.
crewman ['kru:mæn] (*pl* **-men** [-men]) *n* **-1.** [of aircraft] tripulante *mf* **-2.** [of film set] membro *m* da equipe.
crew neck *n* [on sweater] gola *f* redonda.
crew-neck(ed) [-nek(t)] *adj* de gola redonda.
crib [krɪb] (*pt & pp* **-bed**, *cont* **-bing**) ◇ *n* berço *m*. ◇ *vt inf* [copy]: **to ~ sthg off** OR **from sb** copiar algo de alguém.
cribbage ['krɪbɪdʒ] *n (U) jogo de cartas em que a pontuação é marcada com madeira num tabuleiro.*
crick [krɪk] ◇ *n* [in neck] torcicolo *m*. ◇ *vt* dar mau jeito em.
cricket ['krɪkɪt] ◇ *n* **-1.** *(U)* [game] críquete *m* **-2.** [insect] grilo *m*. ◇ *comp* de críquete.
cricketer ['krɪkɪtə[r]] *n* jogador *m*, -ra *f* de críquete.
crikey ['kraɪkɪ] *excl UK inf dated* caramba!
crime [kraɪm] ◇ *n* crime *m*. ◇ *comp*: **~ prevention** prevenção *f* contra o crime; **~ novel** novela *f* policial.
Crimea *n*: **the ~** a Criméia; **in the ~** na Criméia.
crime wave *n* onda *f* de criminalidade.
criminal ['krɪmɪnl] ◇ *adj* **-1.** [JUR - act] criminal; [- lawyer] criminalista; [offence] penal **-2.** *inf* [shameful] vergonhoso(sa). ◇ *n* criminoso *m*, -sa *f*.
criminalize, -ise ['krɪmɪnəlaɪz] *vt* criminalizar.
criminal law *n (U)* direito *m* penal.
criminology [,krɪmɪ'nɒlədʒɪ] *n (U)* criminologia *f*.
crimped *adj* ondulado(da).
crimson ['krɪmzn] ◇ *adj* **-1.** [in colour] carmesim **-2.** [with embarrassment] vermelho(lha). ◇ *n* carmesim *mf*.
cringe [krɪndʒ] *vi* **-1.** [out of fear] encolher-se **-2.** *inf* [with embarrassment]: **to ~ (at sthg)** encolher-se de vergonha (por algo).
crinkle ['krɪŋkl] ◇ *n* ruga *f*. ◇ *vt* enrugar. ◇ *vi* enrugar-se.
cripple ['krɪpl] ◇ *n offensive* aleijado *m*, -da *f*. ◇ *vt* **-1.** MED [disable] aleijar **-2.** [put out of action] inutilizar **-3.** *fig* [bring to a halt] paralisar.
crippling ['krɪplɪŋ] *adj* **-1.** MED [disease] devastador(-ra) **-2.** [taxes, prices, debts] excessivo(va).
crisis ['kraɪsɪs] (*pl* **crises** ['kraɪsi:z]) *n* crise *f*.
crisp [krɪsp] *adj* **-1.** [pastry, bacon] crocante; [fruit, vegetables] fresco(ca); [banknote] liso(sa); [snow] quebradiço(ça) **-2.** [weather] revigorante **-3.** [manner, toner] seco(ca).
◆ **crisps** *npl UK* batatas *fpl* fritas *(em pacote).*
crispbread ['krɪspbred] *n (U) biscoito de centeio ou trigo, que substitui o pão para quem está de dieta.*
crispy ['krɪspɪ] (*compar* **-ier**, *superl* **-iest**) *adj* [pastry, bacon] crocante; [fruit, vegetables] fresco(ca).
criss-cross ◇ *adj* [pattern] xadrez. ◇ *vt* [subj: roads] entrecruzar. ◇ *vi* [lines, pattern] entrecruzar-se.
criterion [kraɪ'tɪərɪən] (*pl* **-ria** [-rɪə], **-rions**) *n* critério *m*.
critic ['krɪtɪk] *n* crítico *m*, -ca *f*.
critical ['krɪtɪkl] *adj* **-1.** [serious] crítico(ca), grave **-2.** [crucial] fundamental **-3.** [analytical, disparaging] crítico(ca); **to be ~ of sb/sthg** criticar alguém/algo.
critically ['krɪtɪklɪ] *adv* **-1.** [seriously] criticamente, gravemente **-2.** [crucially] fundamentalmente **-3.** [analytically, disparagingly] criticamente.
criticism ['krɪtɪsɪzm] *n* crítica *f*.
criticize, -ise ['krɪtɪsaɪz] ◇ *vt* [judge unfavourably] criticar. ◇ *vi* [make unfavourable comments] criticar.
critique [krɪ'ti:k] *n* crítica *f*.
croak [krəʊk] ◇ *n* **-1.** [of frog] coaxo *m* **-2.** [of bird] grasnido *m* **-3.** [hoarse voice] rouquidão *f*. ◇ *vt* grunhir. ◇ *vi* **-1.** [animal] coaxar **-2.** [bird] granir **-3.** [person] ter rouquidão.
Croat ['krəʊæt], **Croatian** [krəʊ'eɪʃn] ◇ *adj* croata. ◇ *n* **-1.** [person] croata *mf* **-2.** [language] croata *m*.
Croatia [krəʊ'eɪʃə] *n* Croácia; **in ~** na Croácia.
crochet ['krəʊʃeɪ] ◇ *n (U)* crochê *m*. ◇ *vt* fazer de crochê.
crockery ['krɒkərɪ] *n (U)* louça *f (de barro).*
crocodile ['krɒkədaɪl] (*pl inv* OR **-s**) *n* [animal] crocodilo *m*.
crocus ['krəʊkəs] (*pl* **-cuses**) *n* açafrão *m*.
croft [krɒft] *n UK* sítio *m*.
croissant ['krwæsã] *n* croissant *m*.
crony ['krəʊnɪ] (*pl* **-ies**) *n inf* [friend] camarada *mf*.
crook [krʊk] ◇ *n* **-1.** [criminal] vigarista *mf* **-2.** *inf* [dishonest person] trapaceiro *m*, -ra *f* **-3.** [angle] curvatura *f* **-4.** [shepherd's staff] cajado *m*. ◇ *vt* entortar, dobrar.
crooked ['krʊkɪd] *adj* **-1.** [not straight - back] arqueado(da); [- teeth, smile] torto(ta); [- path] sinuoso(sa) **-2.** *inf* [dishonest] desonesto(ta).
croon [kru:n] ◇ *vt* [sing softly] cantarolar. ◇ *vi* [sing softly] cantarolar.
crop [krɒp] (*pt & pp* **-ped**, *cont* **-ping**) ◇ *n* **-1.** [kind of plant] cultura *f* **-2.** [harvested produce] colheita *f* **-3.** *inf fig* [group]: **a ~ of books** uma coleção de livros; **a ~ of graduates** um grupo de formandos **-4.** [whip] chicote *m* **-5.** [of bird] papo *m* **-6.** [haircut] cabelo *m* curto. ◇ *vt* **-1.** [cut short] tosar **-2.** [eat] mascar.
◆ **crop up** *vi* surgir.
cropper ['krɒpə[r]] *n inf*: **to come a ~** [fall] levar um tombo; [fail] entrar pelo cano.

crop spraying [-ˌspreɪɪŋ] *n (U)* pulverização *f.*

croquet [ˈkrəʊkeɪ] *n (U)* croqué *m.*

croquette [krɒˈket] *n* croquete *m.*

cross [krɒs] ◇ *adj* zangado(da). ◇ *n* **-1.** [gen] cruz *f* **-2.** [mixture] cruzamento *m*; **a Labrador ~** um cruzamento de labrador; **a ~ between two things** uma mistura de duas coisas. ◇ *vt* **-1.** [gen] cruzar **-2.** [move across - street, room] atravessar; [- subj: expression] trespassar; **a look of distaste ~ed her face** um olhar de desagrado trespassou-lhe o rosto **-3.** *RELIG*: **to ~ o.s.** fazer o sinal da cruz **-4.** *UK* [cheque] cruzar **-5.** [thwart] frustar, impedir. ◇ *vi* **-1.** [intersect] cruzar-se **-2.** [traverse] fazer uma travessia.

◆ **cross off, cross out** *vt sep* riscar.

crossbar [ˈkrɒsbɑːʳ] *n* **-1.** [of goal] trave *f* **-2.** [of bicycle] barra *f* transversal.

crossbow [ˈkrɒsbəʊ] *n* besta *f.*

crossbreed [ˈkrɒsbriːd] *n* cruza *f.*

cross-Channel *adj* [ferry, route] do Canal da Mancha; **~ travel** viagem pelo Canal da Mancha.

cross-check ◇ *n* verificação *f* cruzada. ◇ *vt* verificar de forma cruzada.

cross-country ◇ *adj* & *adv* através do campo. ◇ *n* [race, running] *esporte praticado através dos campos.*

cross-cultural *adj* intercultural.

cross-dress *vi* **-1.** [man] vestir-se de mulher **-2.** [woman] vestir-se de homem.

crossed line [krɒst-] *n* linha *f* cruzada.

cross-examination *n* **-1.** *JUR* interrogatório *m (para confirmar veracidade)* **-2.** *fig* [close questioning] interrogatório *m.*

cross-examine *vt* **-1.** *JUR* interrogar *(para confirmar veracidade)* **-2.** *fig* [question closely] interrogar.

cross-eyed [ˈkrɒsaɪd] *adj* vesgo(ga).

cross-fertilize *vt* [plant] fecundar por cruzamento.

crossfire [ˈkrɒsˌfaɪəʳ] *n (U)* fogo *m* cruzado.

crosshead [ˈkrɒsˌhed] *adj* [screw] com cabeça Philips®; **~ screwdriver** chave *f* de fenda Philips®.

crossing [ˈkrɒsɪŋ] *n* **-1.** [place to cross] faixa *f* de segurança **-2.** [sea journey] travessia *f.*

cross-legged [ˈkrɒslegd] *adv* de pernas cruzadas.

crossly [ˈkrɒslɪ] *adv* com irritação.

cross-ply *(pl* **-ies**) *adj* [tyre] de carcaça diagonal.

cross-purposes *npl* mal-entendido *m*; **to be at ~** não se entender.

cross-question *vt* interrogar novamente.

cross-refer ◇ *vt* remeter. ◇ *vi* fazer uma referência.

cross-reference *n* referência *f* cruzada.

crossroads [ˈkrɒsrəʊdz] *(pl inv) n* cruzamento *m*, encruzilhada *f*; **to be at a ~** *fig* estar numa encruzilhada.

cross-section *n* **-1.** [drawing] corte *m* transversal **-2.** [of population] amostra *f* representativa.

crosswalk [ˈkrɒswɔːk] *n US* faixa *f* de segurança.

crossways [ˈkrɒsweɪz] *adv* = **crosswise**.

crosswind [ˈkrɒswɪnd] *n* vento *m* contrário.

crosswise [ˈkrɒswaɪz] *adv* em diagonal, transversalmente.

crossword (puzzle) [ˈkrɒswɜːd-] *n* palavras *fpl* cruzadas.

crotch [krɒtʃ] *n* **-1.** [of person] entreperna *f* **-2.** [of garment] gancho *m.*

crotchet [ˈkrɒtʃɪt] *n* semínima *f.*

crotchety [ˈkrɒtʃɪtɪ] *adj UK inf* rabugento(ta).

crouch [kraʊtʃ] *vi* **-1.** [person] agachar-se **-2.** [animal] armar o bote.

croup [kruːp] *n* **-1.** [illness] crupe *m* **-2.** [of horse] garupa *f.*

croupier [ˈkruːpɪəʳ] *n* crupiê *mf.*

crouton [ˈkruːtɒn] *n pão torrado cortado em cubos que acompanha a sopa.*

crow [krəʊ] ◇ *n* corvo *m*; **as the ~ flies** em linha reta. ◇ *vi* **-1.** [cock] cantar **-2.** *inf* [gloat] gabar-se.

crowbar [ˈkrəʊbɑːʳ] *n* pé-de-cabra *m.*

crowd [kraʊd] ◇ *n* **-1.** [mass of people] multidão *f* **-2.** [social group] turma *f.* ◇ *vi* aglomerar-se. ◇ *vt* **-1.** [fill] lotar **-2.** [force into small space] empurrar; **to ~ everyone in** colocar todo mundo para dentro.

crowded [ˈkraʊdɪd] *adj* cheio (cheia), lotado(da); **~ with** cheio (cheia) de, repleto(ta) de.

crown [kraʊn] ◇ *n* **-1.** [gen] coroa *f* **-2.** [top - of hat] copa *f*; [- of head] topo *m*; [- of hill] cume *m.* ◇ *vt* **-1.** [monarch] coroar **-2.** [tooth] pôr uma coroa em **-3.** [cover top of] cobrir.

◆ **Crown** ◇ *n*: **the Crown** [monarchy] a Coroa. ◇ *comp* da Coroa.

crown court *n* tribunal *m (com júri).*

crowning [ˈkraʊnɪŋ] *adj* supremo(ma).

Crown Jewels *npl*: **the ~** as jóias da Coroa.

crown prince *n* príncipe *m* herdeiro.

crow's feet *npl* pés-de-galinha *mpl.*

crow's nest *n* cesto *m* de gávea.

crucial [ˈkruːʃl] *adj* [vital] crucial.

crucially [ˈkruːʃlɪ] *adv* [vitally] crucialmente; **~ important** de vital importância.

crucible [ˈkruːsɪbl] *n* [container] cadinho *m.*

crucifix [ˈkruːsɪfɪks] *n* crucifixo *m.*

Crucifixion [ˌkruːsɪˈfɪkʃn] *n*: **the ~** a Crucificação.

crucify [ˈkruːsɪfaɪ] (*pt* & *pp* **-ied**) *vt lit* & *fig* crucificar.

crude [kruːd] ◇ *adj* **-1.** [commodity] cru (crua) **-2.** [joke, person] grosseiro(ra) **-3.** [sketch] tosco(ca) **-4.** [method, shelter] primitivo(va). ◇ *n* = **crude oil**.

crudely [ˈkruːdlɪ] *adj* **-1.** [vulgarly] de maneira grosseira **-2.** [clumsily] toscamente.

crude oil *n (U)* petróleo *m* bruto.

cruel [krʊəl] (*compar* **-ler**, *superl* **-lest**) *adj* **-1.** [sadistic] cruel **-2.** [painful, harsh - disappointment] doloroso(sa); [- winter] rigoroso(sa).

cruelly [ˈkrʊəlɪ] *adv* **-1.** [sadistically] cruelmente **-2.** [painfully, harshly] dolorosamente.

cruelty [ˈkrʊəltɪ] *n (U)* crueldade *f.*

cruet [ˈkruːɪt] *n* galheta *f.*

cruise [kruːz] ◇ *n* cruzeiro *m.* ◇ *vi* **-1.** [sail] fazer um cruzeiro **-2.** [drive] ir à velocidade de cruzeiro **-3.** [fly] voar.

cruise missile *n* míssil *m* de cruzeiro.

cruiser [ˈkruːzəʳ] *n* **-1.** [warship] cruzador *m* **-2.** [cabin cruiser] iate *m.*

crumb [krʌm] *n* **-1.** [of food] migalha *f* **-2.** [of information] fragmento *m*.

crumble ['krʌmbl] ◇ *n doce de frutas coberto com uma mistura de farinha, manteiga e açúcar e cozido no forno.* ◇ *vt* esmigalhar. ◇ *vi* **-1.** [disintegrate - bread, cheese] esmigalhar-se; [- building, cliff] desmoronar **-2.** *fig* [collapse] desmoronar.

crumbly ['krʌmblɪ] (*compar* **-ier**, *superl* **-iest**) *adj* farelento(ta).

crummy ['krʌmɪ] (*compar* **-ier**, *superl* **-iest**) *adj* ***inf*** [bad] fajuto(ta).

crumpet ['krʌmpɪt] *n* **-1.** [food] *fatias de bolo tostadas que se come com manteiga* **-2.** *(U)* ***inf offensive*** [women] gostosona *f*.

crumple ['krʌmpl] ◇ *vt* amassar. ◇ *vi* **-1.** [crease, dent] amassar **-2.** [collapse] desmoronar.
◆ **crumple up** *vt sep* amassar.

crunch [krʌntʃ] ◇ *n* [sound] mastigação *f* barulhenta; **if/when it comes to the ~** *inf* se/quando chegar a hora da verdade. ◇ *vt* **-1.** [with teeth] mastigar ruidosamente **-2.** [underfoot] esmagar com o pé ao caminhar. ◇ *vi* [snow, gravel] estalar.

crunchy ['krʌntʃɪ] (*compar* **-ier**, *superl* **-iest**) *adj* **-1.** [food] crocante **-2.** [snow, gravel] que estala.

crusade [kru:'seɪd] ◇ *n* **-1.** [war] cruzada *f* **-2.** *fig* [campaign] campanha *f*. ◇ *vi*: **to ~ for/against sthg** fazer campanha em favor de/contra algo.

crusader [kru:'seɪdəʳ] *n* **-1.** HIST cavaleiro *m* das cruzadas **-2.** *fig* [campaigner] defensor *m*, -ra *f*.

crush [krʌʃ] ◇ *n* **-1.** [crowd] aglomeração *f* **-2.** *inf* [infatuation]: **to have a ~ on sb** estar obcecado(da) por alguém **-3.** *UK* [drink] batida *f*. ◇ *vt* **-1.** [squash, press, smash] esmagar **-2.** *fig* [destroy] acabar com.

crush barrier *n UK* barreira *f*.

crushing ['krʌʃɪŋ] *adj* esmagador(ra).

crust [krʌst] *n* **-1.** [on bread] casca *f* **-2.** [on pie] crosta *f* torrada **-3.** [hard covering] crosta *f*.

crustacean [krʌ'steɪʃn] *n* crustáceo *m*.

crusty ['krʌstɪ] (*compar* **-ier**, *superl* **-iest**) *adj* **-1.** [food] crocante **-2.** [person] ríspido(da).

crutch [krʌtʃ] *n* **-1.** [stick] muleta *f* **-2.** *fig* [support] apoio *m* **-3.** [crotch] gancho *m*.

crux [krʌks] *n* ponto *m* crucial.

cry [kraɪ] (*pl* **cries**, *pt* & *pp* **cried**) ◇ *n* **-1.** [weep] choro *m* **-2.** [shout] grito *m*; **to be a far ~ from** não se parecer em nada com **-3.** [of bird] canto *m*. ◇ *vt* **-1.** [weep] chorar **-2.** [shout] gritar. ◇ *vi* **-1.** [weep] chorar **-2.** [shout] gritar.
◆ **cry off** *vi* desistir de.
◆ **cry out** ◇ *vt* gritar. ◇ *vi* [call out] gritar.
◆ **cry out for** *vt fus* [be in need of]: **to be ~ing out for sthg** precisar de algo.

crybaby ['kraɪˌbeɪbɪ] (*pl* **-ies**) *n* ***inf pej*** chorão *m*, -rona *f*.

crying ['kraɪɪŋ] ◇ *adj* ***inf***: **it's a ~ shame** é uma vergonha enorme; **a ~ need for sthg** uma necessidade evidente de algo. ◇ *n (U)* choro *m*.

crypt [krɪpt] *n* cripta *f*.

cryptic ['krɪptɪk] *adj* [mysterious] enigmático(ca).

crypto- *prefix*: **a ~-communist** um comunista enrustido.

crystal ['krɪstl] ◇ *n* cristal *m*. ◇ *comp* [glass] de cristal.

crystal ball *n* bola *f* de cristal.

crystal clear *adj* **-1.** [water, voice] cristalino(na) **-2.** [motive, meaning] claro(ra).

crystallize, -ise ['krɪstəlaɪz] ◇ *vi* **-1.** [substance] cristalizar **-2.** [idea, plan] clarear. ◇ *vt* **-1.** [idea, plan] clarear **-2.** [fruit] cristalizar.

CSA (*abbr of* **Child Support Agency**) *n agência britânica responsável pela coleta de doações para auxílio a crianças carentes.*

CSC (*abbr of* **Civil Service Commission**) *n organização britânica responsável pela contratação de funcionários públicos.*

CSE (*abbr of* **Certificate of Secondary Education**) *n antigo certificado de conclusão de ensino médio na Grã-Bretanha.*

CS gas *n* gás *m* lacrimogêneo.

CST (*abbr of* **Central Standard Time**) *n horário oficial no centro dos Estados Unidos e do Canadá.*

ct (*abbr of* **carat**) ql.

CT *abbr of* **Connecticut**.

CTC (*abbr of* **city technology college**) *n escola de ensino médio que tem parceria com empresas e com o governo para ensino de tecnologia na Grã-Bretanha.*

cu. (*abbr of* **cubic**) cúbico(ca).

cub [kʌb] *n* **-1.** [young animal] filhote *m* **-2.** [boy scout] lobinho *m*.

Cuba ['kju:bə] *n* Cuba; **in ~** em Cuba.

Cuban ['kju:bən] ◇ *adj* cubano(na). ◇ *n* cubano *m*, -na *f*.

cubbyhole ['kʌbɪhəʊl] *n* cubículo *m*.

cube [kju:b] ◇ *n* cubo *m*. ◇ *vt* MATH elevar ao cubo.

cube root *n* raiz *f* cúbica.

cubic ['kju:bɪk] *adj* cúbico(ca).

cubicle ['kju:bɪkl] *n* **-1.** [shower] boxe *m* **-2.** [in shop] provador *m*.

cubism ['kju:bɪzm] *n (U)* cubismo *m*.

cubist ['kju:bɪst] *n* cubista *mf*.

cub reporter *n* jornalista *mf* novato, -ta.

Cub Scout *n* lobinho *m*.

cuckoo ['kʊku:] *n* cuco *m*.

cuckoo clock *n* (relógio *m* de) cuco *m*.

cucumber ['kju:kʌmbəʳ] *n* pepino *m*.

cud [kʌd] *n*: **to chew the ~** *lit* & *fig* ruminar.

cuddle ['kʌdl] ◇ *n* abraço *m*. ◇ *vt* abraçar. ◇ *vi* abraçar-se.
◆ **cuddle up** *vi*: **to ~ up (to sb)** aconchegar-se (em alguém).

cuddly ['kʌdlɪ] (*compar* **-ier**, *superl* **-iest**) *adj* [person] mimoso(sa).

cuddly toy ['kʌdlɪ-] *n* bicho *m* de pelúcia.

cudgel ['kʌdʒəl] (*UK pt* & *pp* **-led**, *cont* **-ling**, *US pt* & *pp* **-ed**, *cont* **-ing**) ◇ *n* cacete *m*; **to take up the ~s for sb/sthg** sair em defesa de alguém/algo. ◇ *vt* dar cacetadas.

cue [kju:] *n* **-1.** RADIO, THEATRE & TV deixa *f*; **on ~** no momento certo; **to take one's ~ from sb** seguir o exemplo de alguém **-2.** *fig* [stimulus, signal] sinal *f* **-3.** [in snooker, pool] taco *m*.

cuff [kʌf] ◇ *n* **-1.** [of sleeve] punho *m* **-2.** *US* [of

trouser] barra *f* **-3.** [blow] tapa *m.* ◇ *vt* [hit] bater.
cufflink *n* abotoadura *f.*
cu. in. *abbr of* **cubic inch(es).**
cuisine [kwɪ'zi:n] *n (U)* arte *f* culinária.
cul-de-sac ['kʌldəsæk] *n* beco *m* sem saída.
culinary ['kʌlɪnərɪ] *adj* culinária.
cull [kʌl] ◇ *n* [kill] extermínio *m.* ◇ *vt* **-1.** [kill] exterminar **-2.** *fml* [gather] reunir.
culminate ['kʌlmɪneɪt] *vi*: **to ~ in sthg** culminar em algo.
culmination [ˌkʌlmɪ'neɪʃn] *n* culminação *f.*
culottes [kju:'lɒts] *npl* saia-calça *f.*
culpable ['kʌlpəbl] *adj fml* culpável; **~ homicide** homicídio *m* culposo.
culprit ['kʌlprɪt] *n* culpado *m*, -da *f.*
cult [kʌlt] ◇ *n* **-1.** *RELIG* culto *m* **-2.** [book, film] objeto *m* de culto. ◇ *comp* [book, film] de culto.
cultivate ['kʌltɪveɪt] *vt* **-1.** [gen] cultivar **-2.** [get to know] fazer amizade com.
cultivated ['kʌltɪveɪtɪd] *adj* **-1.** [land] cultivado(da) **-2.** [person, accent] culto(ta).
cultivation [ˌkʌltɪ'veɪʃn] *n (U)* [farming] cultivo *m.*
cultural ['kʌltʃərəl] *adj* cultural.
culture ['kʌltʃə^r] *n* cultura *f.*
cultured ['kʌltʃəd] *adj* [educated] culto(ta).
cultured pearl *n* pérola *f* cultivada.
culture shock *n* choque *m* cultural.
culture vulture *n inf* amante *mf* da cultura.
culvert ['kʌlvət] *n* bueiro *m.*
cumbersome ['kʌmbəsəm] *adj* **-1.** [object] de difícil manejo **-2.** [system] ineficiente.
Cumbria *n* Cúmbria.
cumin ['kʌmɪn] *n (U)* cominho *m.*
cumulative ['kju:mjʊlətɪv] *adj* cumulativo(va).
cunning ['kʌnɪŋ] ◇ *adj* **-1.** [person] astuto(ta) **-2.** [method, idea] engenhoso(sa). ◇ *n (U)* astúcia *f.*
cup [kʌp] (*pt & pp* **-ped**, *cont* **-ping**) ◇ *n* **-1.** [gen] xícara *f*; **it's not my ~ of tea** *inf* não faz o meu gênero **-2.** [as prize, of bra] taça *f* **-3.** [competition] copa *f.* ◇ *vt* dispor (as mãos) em forma de concha.
cupboard ['kʌbəd] *n* armário *m.*
cupcake ['kʌpkeɪk] *n* bolinho *m* coberto com glacê.
Cup Final *n*: **the ~** o jogo final da copa.
cup holder *n SPORT* atual campeão *m*, -ã *f* da copa.
cupid ['kju:pɪd] *n* [figure] cupido *m.*
cupola ['kju:pələ] (*pl* **-s**) *n ARCHIT* cúpula *f.*
cup tie *n UK* jogo *m* eliminatório.
curable ['kjʊərəbl] *adj* curável.
curate ['kjʊərət] ◇ *n RELIG* coadjutor *m*, -ra *f.* ◇ *vt* [exhibition] organizar.
curator [ˌkjʊə'reɪtə^r] *n* [of museum] curador *m*, -ra *f.*
curb [kɜ:b] ◇ *n* **-1.** [control]: **~ (on sthg)** controle *m* (sobre algo) **-2.** *US* [of road] meio-fio *m.* ◇ *vt* controlar.
curd cheese [kɜ:d-] *n (U) UK* requeijão *m.*
curdle ['kɜ:dl] *vi* **-1.** [milk] coalhar **-2.** [blood] coagular.
cure [kjʊə^r] ◇ *n* **-1.** *MED*: **~ (for sthg)** cura *f* (de algo) **-2.** [solution]: **~ (for sthg)** solução *f* (para algo). ◇ *vt* **-1.** *MED* curar *f* **-2.** [solve] remediar **-3.** [rid]: **to ~ sb of sthg** *fig* livrar alguém de algo **-4.** [preserve] curtir.
cure-all *n* panacéia *f.*
curfew ['kɜ:fju:] *n* toque *m* de recolher.
curio ['kjʊərɪəʊ] (*pl* **-s**) *n* raridade *f*, curiosidade *f.*
curiosity [ˌkjʊərɪ'ɒsətɪ] *n* **-1.** *(U)* [inquisitiveness] curiosidade *f* **-2.** [rarity] raridade *f.*
curious ['kjʊərɪəs] *adj* curioso(sa); **~ about sb/sthg** curioso(sa) sobre alguém/algo.
curiously ['kjʊərɪəslɪ] *adv* curiosamente.
curl [kɜ:l] ◇ *n* **-1.** [of hair] cacho *m* **-2.** [of smoke] onda *f.* ◇ *vt* **-1.** [hair] encrespar, encaracolar **-2.** [tail, ribbon] enrolar. ◇ *vi* **-1.** [hair] encrespar, encaracolar **-2.** [paper, leaf, road, smoke, snake] enrolar; **to ~ into a ball** enrolar-se numa bola.
◆ **curl up** *vi* [person, animal] enrolar-se.
curler ['kɜ:lə^r] *n* rolo *m.*
curling ['kɜ:lɪŋ] *n SPORT* *jogo escocês que consiste em deslizar pedras sobre o gelo.*
curling tongs *npl* ferros *mpl* de frisar.
curly ['kɜ:lɪ] (*compar* **-ier**, *superl* **-iest**) *adj* [hair] encaracolado(da).
currant ['kʌrənt] *n* [dried grape] uva *f* passa.
currency ['kʌrənsɪ] (*pl* **-ies**) *n* **-1.** [money] moeda *f* corrente; **foreign ~** moeda *f* estrangeira **-2.** *fml* [acceptability]: **to gain ~** ganhar aceitação.
current ['kʌrənt] ◇ *adj* atual; **in ~ use** de uso corrente. ◇ *n* corrente *f.*
current account *n UK* conta *f* corrente.
current affairs *npl* atualidades *fpl.*
current assets *npl* ativo *m* corrente.
current liabilities *npl* passivo *m* circulante.
currently ['kʌrəntlɪ] *adv* atualmente.
curricular *adj* curricular.
curriculum [kə'rɪkjələm] (*pl* **-lums** *OR* **-la** [-lə]) *n* [course of study] currículo *m.*
curriculum vitae [-'vi:taɪ] (*pl* **curricula vitae**) *n* currículo *m*, curriculum *m* (vitae).
curried ['kʌrɪd] *adj* com molho de caril.
curry ['kʌrɪ] (*pl* **-ies**) *n* caril *m.*
curry powder *n (U)* caril *m* em pó.
curse [kɜ:s] ◇ *n* **-1.** [evil charm]: **~ (on sb/sthg)** maldição *f OR* praga *f* (sobre alguém/algo) **-2.** [swearword] palavrão *m* **-3.** [source of problems] desgraça *f.* ◇ *vt* **-1.** [wish misfortune on] maldizer **-2.** [complain about] xingar. ◇ *vi* [swear] praguejar.
cursor ['kɜ:sə^r] *n COMPUT* cursor *m.*
cursory ['kɜ:sərɪ] *adj* apressado(da); **a ~ glance** um olhada por cima.
curt [kɜ:t] *adj* brusco(ca).
curtail [kɜ:'teɪl] *vt* **-1.** [cut short] encurtar **-2.** [restrict, reduce] reduzir.
curtailment [kɜ:'teɪlmənt] *n (U) fml* [reduction] redução *f.*
curtain ['kɜ:tn] *n* cortina *f.*
◆ **curtain off** *vt sep* separar com uma cortina.
curtain call *n* *chamada à frente do palco para receber aplausos.*
curtain raiser *n fig* [warm-up] preâmbulo *m*, prelúdio *m.*
curts(e)y ['kɜ:tsɪ] (*pt & pp* **curtsied**) ◇ *n* reverência *f (feita por mulher).* ◇ *vi* fazer reverência.

curvaceous [kɜː'veɪʃəs] *adj inf* bom (boa) de curvas.
curvature ['kɜːvətjəʳ] *n (U)* curvatura *f.*
curve [kɜːv] ◇ *n* curva *f.* ◇ *vi* fazer uma curva.
curved [kɜːvd] *adj* curvo(va).
curvy ['kɜːvɪ] (*compar* **-ier**, *superl* **-iest**) *adj*: **a ~ blond** uma loira cheia de curvas.
cushion ['kʊʃn] ◇ *n* **-1.** [for sitting on] almofada *f* **-2.** [protective layer] colchão *m.* ◇ *vt* amortecer; **to be ~ed against sthg** estar protegido(da) de algo.
cushy ['kʊʃɪ] (*compar* **-ier**, *superl* **-iest**) *adj inf* mole.
custard ['kʌstəd] *n* [sauce] creme *m (para doces).*
custard pie *n* torta *f* de creme.
custard powder *n (U) pó desidratado que se mistura ao leite e ao açúcar para fazer creme.*
custodial *adj* [sentence] custódio(dia).
custodian [kʌ'stəʊdjən] *n* [of building, museum] guarda *m.*
custody ['kʌstədɪ] *n (U)* **-1.** [of child] custódia *f* **-2.** [of suspect]: **in ~** sob custódia.
custom ['kʌstəm] *n* **-1.** [tradition, habit] costume *m*, hábito *m* **-2.** *(U)* COMM [trade] preferência *f*; **thank you for your ~** agradecemos a preferência.
◆ **customs** *n (U)* [place, organization] alfândega *f*; **to go through ~** passar pela alfândega.
customary ['kʌstəmrɪ] *adj* costumeiro(ra), habitual.
custom-built *adj* personalizado(da).
customer ['kʌstəməʳ] *n* **-1.** [client] cliente *mf* **-2.** *inf* [person] tipo *m*; **an awkward ~** um tipo complicado.
customer services *npl* serviço *m* de atendimento ao consumidor.
customize, -ise ['kʌstəmaɪz] *vt* **-1.** [gen] personalizar **-2.** COMPUT customizar.
custom-made *adj* feito(ta) sob medida.
Customs and Excise *n (U) UK departamento do governo britânico responsável por coletar impostos sobre a compra e venda de bens e serviços ou sobre bens importados.*
customs duty *n (U)* imposto *m* alfandegário.
customs officer *n* fiscal *mf* de alfândega.
cut [kʌt] (*pt* & *pp* **cut**, *cont* **-ting**) ◇ *n* **-1.** [gen] corte *m*; **~ (in sthg)** corte (em algo) **-2.** *inf* [share] parte *f* **-3.** *phr*: **a ~ above (the rest)** melhor que os outros. ◇ *vt* **-1.** [gen] cortar **-2.** [tooth] romper **-3.** *inf* [miss] matar **-4.** *phr*: **to ~ sb dead** fazer que não se vê alguém; **~ and dried** definitivo(va). ◇ *vi* **-1.** cortar **-2.** *phr*: **to ~ both ways** ser uma faca de dois gumes.
◆ **cut across** *vt fus* **-1.** [as short cut] cortar caminho por **-2.** [transcend] transcender, estar acima de.
◆ **cut back** ◇ *vt sep* **-1.** [tree, bush] podar **-2.** [expenditure, budget] reduzir, diminuir. ◇ *vi*: **to ~ back (on sthg)** reduzir (algo).
◆ **cut down** ◇ *vt sep* **-1.** [chop down] cortar, derrubar **-2.** [reduce] reduzir, diminuir. ◇ *vi*: **to ~ down on sthg** reduzir algo.
◆ **cut in** *vi* **-1.** [interrupt]: **to ~ in (on sb)** interromper (alguém) **-2.** [in car] cortar (a frente de), fechar.
◆ **cut off** *vt sep* **-1.** [sever] cortar fora **-2.** [sever supply of] cortar; **I got ~ off** [on telephone] cortaram meu telefone **-3.** [isolate]: **to be ~ off (from sb/sthg)** ficar isolado(da) (de alguém/algo).
◆ **cut out** ◇ *vt sep* **-1.** [gen] cortar; **to ~ out the light** cortar a entrada de luz; **~ it out!** pare com isso! **-2.**: **to be ~ out for sthg** *fig* ser feito(ta) para algo. ◇ *vi* [stall] morrer.
◆ **cut up** *vt sep* [chop up] picar.
cut and paste COMPUT ◇ *vt* recortar e colar. ◇ *vi* recortar e colar.
cutback ['kʌtbæk] *n*: **~ (in sthg)** corte *m* (em algo).
cute [kjuːt] *adj esp US* [appealing] bonitinho(nha).
cut glass ◇ *n (U)* vidro *m* lapidado. ◇ *comp* de vidro lapidado.
cuticle ['kjuːtɪkl] *n* cutícula *f.*
cutlery ['kʌtlərɪ] *n (U)* talheres *mpl.*
cutlet ['kʌtlɪt] *n* costeleta *f.*
cut-off (point) *n* [limit] (ponto *m*) limite *m.*
cut-out *n* **-1.** [on machine] disjuntor *m* **-2.** [shape] figura *f* para recortar.
cut-price, cut-rate *US adj* com desconto.
cutter ['kʌtəʳ] *n* [tool] cortador *m.*
cut-throat *adj* [ruthless] acirrado(da).
cutting ['kʌtɪŋ] ◇ *adj* [sarcastic] mordaz. ◇ *n* **-1.** [of plant] chantão *m* **-2.** [from newspaper] recorte *m* **-3.** *UK* [for road, railway] corte *m.*
cutting edge *n* centro *m.*
cutting room *n* CINEMA sala *f* de edição.
cuttlefish ['kʌtlfɪʃ] (*pl inv*) *n* siba *m.*
cut up *adj UK inf* [upset] chateado(da).
CV (*abbr of* **curriculum vitae**) *n UK* CV *m.*
c.w.o. (*abbr of* **cash with order**) *pagamento no ato da ordem de compra.*
cwt. *abbr of* **hundredweight**.
cyanide ['saɪənaɪd] *n (U)* cianeto *m*, cianureto *m.*
cybercafé *n* COMPUT cibercafé *m.*
cybernetics [ˌsaɪbə'netɪks] *n (U)* cibernética *f.*
cyberspace ['saɪbəspeɪs] *n* COMPUT ciberespaço *m.*
cyclamen ['sɪkləmən] (*pl inv*) *n* ciclâmen *m.*
cycle ['saɪkl] ◇ *n* **-1.** [process] ciclo *m* **-2.** [bicycle] bicicleta *f.* ◇ *comp*: **~ path** ciclovia *f*; **~ track** pista *f* para ciclismo; **~ race** corrida *f* de bicicletas. ◇ *vi* andar de bicicleta.
cyclic(al) ['saɪklɪk(l)] *adj* cíclico(ca).
cycling ['saɪklɪŋ] *n (U)* ciclismo *m*; **to go ~** andar de bicicleta.
cycling helmet *n* capacete *m* de ciclismo.
cyclist ['saɪklɪst] *n* ciclista *mf.*
cyclone ['saɪkləʊn] *n* ciclone *m.*
cygnet ['sɪgnɪt] *n* filhote *m* de cisne.
cylinder ['sɪlɪndəʳ] *n* **-1.** [gen] cilindro *m* **-2.** [container] tambor *m.*
cylinder block *n* bloco *m* de cilindros.
cylinder head *n* cabeça *f* de cilindro, culatra *f.*
cylindrical [sɪ'lɪndrɪkl] *adj* cilíndrico(ca).
cymbals ['sɪmblz] *npl* címbalos *mpl.*
cynic ['sɪnɪk] *n* cético *m*, -ca *f.*
cynical ['sɪnɪkl] *adj* cético(ca).
cynically ['sɪnɪklɪ] *adv* ceticamente.
cynicism ['sɪnɪsɪzm] *n (U)* ceticismo *m.*
cypher ['saɪfəʳ] *n* = **cipher**.
cypress ['saɪprəs] *n* cipreste *m.*
Cypriot ['sɪprɪət] ◇ *adj* cipriota. ◇ *n* cipriota

mf; **Greek** ~ cipriota grego(ga); **Turkish** ~ cipriota turco(ca).
Cyprus ['saɪprəs] *n* Chipre; **in** ~ em Chipre.
cyst [sɪst] *n* cisto *m*.
cystic fibrosis [ˌsɪstɪkfaɪ'brəʊsɪs] *n (U)* fibrose *f* cística.
cystitis [sɪs'taɪtɪs] *n (U)* cistite *f*.
cytology [saɪ'tɒlədʒɪ] *n (U)* citologia *f*.
czar [zɑː'] *n* czar *m*.
Czech [tʃek] ◇ *adj* tcheco(ca). ◇ *n* **-1.** [person] tcheco *m*, -ca *f* **-2.** [language] tcheco *m*.
Czechoslovak *adj & n* = **Czechoslovakian**.
Czechoslovakia [ˌtʃekəslə'vækɪə] *n* Tchecoslováquia; **in** ~ na Tchecoslováquia.
Czechoslovakian [ˌtʃekəslə'vækɪən] ◇ *adj* tchecoslovaco(ca). ◇ *n* tchecoslovaco *m*, -ca *f*.
Czech Republic *n*: **the** ~ a República Tcheca.

d (*pl* **d's** *OR* **ds**), **D** (*pl* **D's** *OR* **Ds**) [diː] *n* [letter] d, D *m*.
◆ **D** ◇ *n* **-1.** *MUS* ré *m* **-2.** *SCH* [mark] D *m*. ◇ *US abbr of* **Democrat(ic)**.
d. (*abbr of* **died**) m.
DA (*abbr of* **district attorney**) *n promotor nos Estados Unidos.*
D/A (*abbr of* **digital to analogue**) *adj* D/A.
dab [dæb] (*pt & pp* **-bed**, *cont* **-bing**) ◇ *n* [small amount - of powder, ointment] pitada *f*; [- of paint] pincelada *f*. ◇ *vt* **-1.** [skin, wound] aplicar de leve **-2.** [eyes] tocar de leve **-3.** [cream, ointment]: **to** ~ **sthg on(to) sthg** aplicar algo em algo.
dabble ['dæbl] ◇ *vt* agitar *(com as mãos ou os pés)*. ◇ *vi*: **to** ~ **(in sthg)** atuar como amador (em algo).
dab hand *n UK inf*: **to be a** ~ **(at sthg)** ser um craque (em algo).
Dacca ['dækə] *n* Dacca.
dachshund ['dækshʊnd] *n* dachshund *m*.
dad [dæd] *n inf* pai *m*.
daddy ['dædɪ] (*pl* **-ies**) *n inf* papai *m*.
daddy longlegs [-'lɒŋlegz] (*pl inv*) *n* pernilongo *m*.
daffodil ['dæfədɪl] *n* narciso *m*.
daft [dɑːft] *adj UK inf* bobo(ba).
dagger ['dægə'] *n* adaga *f*.
dahlia ['deɪljə] *n* dália *f*.
daily ['deɪlɪ] (*pl* **-ies**) ◇ *adj* diário(ria). ◇ *adv* diariamente; **twice** ~ duas vezes por dia. ◇ *n* **-1.** [newspaper] diário *m* **-2.** *esp UK* [cleaning woman] diarista *f*.
daintily ['deɪntɪlɪ] *adv* delicadamente, suavemente; **to eat** ~ comer com delicadeza.
dainty ['deɪntɪ] (*compar* **-ier**, *superl* **-iest**) *adj* delicado(da).
dairy ['deərɪ] (*pl* **-ies**) *n* leiteria *f*.
dairy cattle *npl* gado *m* leiteiro.
dairy farm *n* fazenda *f* de gado leiteiro.
dairy products *npl* lacticínios *mpl*.
dais ['deɪɪs] *n* estrado *m*.
daisy ['deɪzɪ] (*pl* **-ies**) *n* margarida *f*.
daisy wheel *n* margarida *f* (de impressão).
daisy-wheel printer *n* impressora *f* de margarida.
Dakar ['dækɑː] *n* Dacar.
dale [deɪl] *n literary* vale *m*.
dalmatian [dæl'meɪʃn] *n* [dog] dálmata *m*.
dam [dæm] (*pt & pp* **-med**, *cont* **-ming**) ◇ *n* [across river] represa *f*, barragem *f*. ◇ *vt* [river] represar.
◆ **dam up** *vt sep* **-1.** [river] represar **-2.** [feelings] conter.
damage ['dæmɪdʒ] ◇ *n*: ~ **(to sthg)** [gen] dano *m* (a algo); [to health, skin] mal *m* (a algo). ◇ *vt* **-1.** [object] danificar **-2.** [person] machucar **-3.** *fig* [chances, reputation] prejudicar.
◆ **damages** *npl JUR* danos *mpl*.
damaging ['dæmɪdʒɪŋ] *adj fig* prejudicial, danoso(sa); ~ **to sthg** prejudicial a algo.
Damascus [də'mæskəs] *n* Damasco.
Dame [deɪm] *n UK título honorífico concedido a uma mulher pelos serviços prestados à sociedade.*
damn [dæm] ◇ *adj inf* maldito(ta). ◇ *adv inf* muito. ◇ *n inf*: **not to give** *OR* **care a** ~ **(about sthg)** não estar nem aí (para algo). ◇ *vt* **-1.** *RELIG* [condemn] condenar **-2.** *inf* [curse] amaldiçoar; ~ **you!** maldito seja! ◇ *excl inf* droga!
damnable ['dæmnəbl] *adj dated* [appalling] execrável.
damnation [dæm'neɪʃn] *n (U) RELIG* danação *f*.
damned [dæmd] *inf* ◇ *adj* maldito(ta); **I'm** ~ **if I'll do it** bem capaz que eu vou fazer isso; **well I'll be** *OR* **I'm** ~**!** ora veja só! ◇ *adv* muito.
damning ['dæmɪŋ] *adj* condenatório(ria), incriminatório(ria).
damp [dæmp] ◇ *adj* úmido(da). ◇ *n (U)* umidade *f*. ◇ *vt* [make wet] umedecer.
◆ **damp down** *vt sep* [restrain] controlar.
damp course *n UK* impermeabilização *f*.
dampen ['dæmpən] *vt* **-1.** [make wet] umedecer **-2.** *fig* [emotion] esfriar.
damper ['dæmpə'] *n* [for fire] abafador *m*; **to put a** ~ **on sthg** *inf* jogar um balde de água fria em algo.
dampness ['dæmpnɪs] *n* umidade *f*.
damp-proof course *n* = **damp course**.
damson ['dæmzn] *n* abrunheiro *m*.
dance [dɑːns] ◇ *n* **-1.** [gen] dança *f*; **shall we have a** ~**?** vamos dançar? **-2.** [social event] baile *m*. ◇ *vt* dançar. ◇ *vi* dançar.
dance floor *n* pista *f* de dança.
dance hall *n* salão *m* de baile.
dancer ['dɑːnsə'] *n* dançarino *m*, -na *f*.
dancing ['dɑːnsɪŋ] *n (U)* dança *f*; **to go** ~ ir dançar.

D & C (*abbr of* **dilation and curettage**) *n* D&C.
dandelion ['dændɪlaɪən] *n* dente-de-leão *m*.
dandruff ['dændrʌf] *n (U)* caspa *f*.
dandy ['dændɪ] (*pl* **-ies**) *n* almofadinha *m*.
Dane [deɪn] *n* dinamarquês *m*, -esa *f*.
danger ['deɪndʒə^r] *n* perigo *m*; **in ~** em perigo; **out of ~** fora de perigo; **~ to sb/sthg** perigo para alguém/algo; **to be in ~ of doing sthg** perigar fazer algo.
danger list *n UK*: **to be on the ~** estar em estado grave.
danger money *n (U) UK* adicional *m* por periculosidade.
dangerous ['deɪndʒərəs] *adj* perigoso(sa).
dangerous driving *n (U) JUR* direção *f* perigosa.
dangerously ['deɪndʒərəslɪ] *adv* **-1.** [riskily] perigosamente **-2.** *MED*: **~ ill** em estado grave.
danger zone *n* zona *f* de perigo.
dangle ['dæŋgl] *vt, vi* balançar.
Danish ['deɪnɪʃ] ◇ *adj* dinamarquês(quesa). ◇ *n* **-1.** [language] dinamarquês *m* **-2.** *US* = **Danish pastry.** ◇ *npl*: **the ~** os dinamarqueses.
Danish blue *n tipo de queijo azul.*
Danish pastry, Danish *US n torta recheada com maçãs, glacê e marzipã.*
dank [dæŋk] *adj* úmido e frio, úmida e fria.
Danube ['dænju:b] *n*: **the ~** o Danúbio.
dapper ['dæpə^r] *adj* garboso(sa).
dappled ['dæpld] *adj* **-1.** [animal] pintado(da), malhado(da) **-2.** [shade] pintado(da).
Dardanelles *npl*: **the ~** o estreito de Dardanelos.
dare [deə^r] ◇ *vt* **-1.** [be brave enough]: **to ~ to do sthg** ousar fazer algo **-2.** [challenge]: **to ~ sb to do sthg** desafiar alguém a fazer algo **-3.** *phr*: **I ~ say** ouso dizer (que). ◇ *vi* atrever-se; **how ~ you!** como se atreve! ◇ *n* desafio *m*.
daredevil ['deə,devl] *n* intrépido *m*, -da *f*.
daren't [deənt] = **dare not**.
Dar es-Salaam [,dɑ:ressə'lɑ:m] *n* Dar es-Salaam.
daring ['deərɪŋ] ◇ *adj* ousado(da). ◇ *n (U)* ousadia *f*.
dark [dɑ:k] ◇ *adj* **-1.** [gen] escuro(ra) **-2.** [gloomy] obscuro(ra) **-3.** [sinister] sombrio(bria). ◇ *n* **-1.** *(U)* [darkness]: **the ~** a escuridão, o escuro; **to be in the ~ about sthg** estar às escuras sobre algo **-2.** [night]: **before/after ~** antes/depois de escurecer.
Dark Ages *npl*: **the ~** a baixa Idade Média.
darken ['dɑ:kn] ◇ *vt* escurecer. ◇ *vi* **-1.** escurecer **-2.** *fig* [face] anuviar-se.
dark glasses *npl* óculos *m inv* escuros.
dark horse *n fig* [person] pessoa *f* enigmática.
darkness ['dɑ:knɪs] *n (U)* escuridão *f*, trevas *fpl*.
darkroom ['dɑ:krʊm] *n* câmara *f* escura.
darling ['dɑ:lɪŋ] ◇ *adj* **-1.** [dear] querido(da) **-2.** *inf* [cute] adorável. ◇ *n* **-1.** [loved person] querido *m*, -da *f*; **she's a little ~** é uma graça de criança **-2.** [favourite] preferido *m*, -da *f*.
darn [dɑ:n] ◇ *adj inf* maldito(ta). ◇ *adv inf* pra caramba. ◇ *n* remendo *m*. ◇ *vt* [repair] remendar, cerzir. ◇ *excl inf* [damn] que droga!
darning ['dɑ:nɪŋ] *n (U)* [work] remendagem *f*, cerzidura *f*; **I hate ~** odeio cerzir.
darning needle *n* agulha *f* de cerzir.
dart [dɑ:t] ◇ *n* **-1.** [arrow] dardo *m* **-2.** *SEWING* pence *f*. ◇ *vt* lançar. ◇ *vi* [move quickly] lançar-se.
◆ **darts** *n (U)* [game] dardos *mpl*.
dartboard ['dɑ:tbɔ:d] *n* alvo *m* para dardos.
dash [dæʃ] ◇ *n* **-1.** [of liquid] pingo *m* **-2.** [in punctuation] travessão *m* **-3.** *AUT* painel *m* (de instrumentos) **-4.** [rush]: **to make a ~ for sthg** sair em disparada por algo. ◇ *vt* **-1.** *literary* [hurl] arremessar **-2.** [hopes] frustar. ◇ *vi* correr; **I must ~!** preciso correr!
◆ **dash off** ◇ *vt sep* [write quickly] rabiscar. ◇ *vi* [rush off] chispar.
dashboard ['dæʃbɔ:d] *n* painel *m* de instrumentos.
dashing ['dæʃɪŋ] *adj* [handsome, energetic] atraente.
dastardly ['dæstədlɪ] *adj dated* cruel.
DAT [dæt] (*abbr of* **digital audio tape**) *n* DAT *m*.
data ['deɪtə] *n* dados *mpl*.
databank ['deɪtəbæŋk] *n* banco *m* de dados.
database ['deɪtəbeɪs] *n* base *f* de dados.
data capture *n (U)* captura *f* de dados.
data management *n COMPUT* gerenciamento *m* de dados.
data processing *n (U)* processamento *m* de dados.
data protection *n COMPUT* proteção *f* de dados.
data recovery *n COMPUT* recuperação *f* de dados.
data transmission *n (U)* transmissão *f* de dados.
date [deɪt] ◇ *n* **-1.** [in time] data *f*; **what's today's ~?** que dia é hoje?; **at a later ~** um outro dia; **to bring sb/sthg up to ~** atualizar alguém/algo; **to keep sb/sthg up to ~** manter alguém/algo atualizado(da); **to be out of ~** [dictionary, database] estar desatualizado(da); [passport] estar vencido(da); **to ~** até agora **-2.** [appointment] encontro *m* **-3.** [person] par *m* **-4.** [fruit] tâmara *f*, datil *m*. ◇ *vt* **-1.** [put a date on] datar **-2.** [go out with] sair com. ◇ *vi* [go out of fashion] cair de moda.
◆ **date back to, date from** *vt fus* datar de.
datebook *n US* agenda *f*.
dated ['deɪtɪd] *adj* antiquado(da).
date of birth *n* data *f* de nascimento.
date rape *n estupro realizado por um homem após ter se relacionado socialmente com uma mulher.*
date stamp *n* **-1.** [device] carimbo *m* datador **-2.** [mark] data *f* carimbada.
daub [dɔ:b] *vt*: **to ~ sthg with sthg** manchar algo.
daughter ['dɔ:tə^r] *n* filha *f*.
daughter-in-law (*pl* **daughters-in-law**) *n* nora *f*.
daunt [dɔ:nt] *vt* desalentar.
daunting ['dɔ:ntɪŋ] *adj* desalentador(ra).
dawdle ['dɔ:dl] *vi* fazer cera.
dawn [dɔ:n] ◇ *n* **-1.** [of day] amanhecer *m*, alvorada *f*; **at ~** ao amanhecer; **from ~ to dusk** do amanhecer ao pôr-do-sol **-2.** *fig* [of era, period] aurora *f*. ◇ *vi* **-1.** [day] amanhecer **-2.** *fig* [era, period] despertar.
◆ **dawn (up)on** *vt fus* dar-se conta de; **it finally**

~**ed on me that ...** finalmente me dei conta de que ...
dawn chorus *n* canto *m* dos pássaros ao amanhecer.
day [deɪ] *n* **-1.** [gen] dia *m*; **the ~ before** a véspera; **the ~ after** o dia seguinte; **the ~ before Christmas** a véspera de Natal; **the ~ before yesterday** anteontem; **the ~ after tomorrow** depois de amanhã; **any ~ now** qualquer dia destes; **let's call it a ~** por hoje chega; **to make sb's ~** ganhar o dia, guardar algo para dias mais difíceis; **it's early ~s yet: to save sthg for a rainy ~** é cedo para saber; **his ~s are numbered** seus dias estão contados; **~ and night** dia e noite **-2.** [age, era] tempo *m*; **in this ~ and age** hoje em dia; **one ~, some ~, one of these ~s** um dia (desses).
◆ **days** *adv* [work] durante o dia.
dayboy ['deɪbɔɪ] *n* **UK** *SCH* aluno *m* de semi-internato.
daybreak ['deɪbreɪk] *n* romper *m* do dia; **at ~** ao romper do dia.
day care *n assistência diurna proporcionada a idosos e/ou portadores de deficiência.*
day centre *n* **UK** *centro assistencial que proporciona cuidados e recreação durante o dia a idosos e/ou portadores de deficiência.*
daydream ['deɪdri:m] <> *n* devaneio *m*. <> *vi* devanear, sonhar acordado(da).
daygirl ['deɪgɜ:l] *n* **UK** *SCH* aluna *f* de semi-internato.
Day-Glo® ['deɪgləʊ] *adj* fluorescente.
daylight ['deɪlaɪt] *n* **-1.** *(U)* [light] luz *f* do dia **-2.** [dawn] amanhecer *m* **-3.** *phr inf*: **to scare the (living) ~s out of sb** quase matar alguém de susto.
daylight robbery *n (U) inf*: **50 pounds? that's ~!** 50 libras? isso é um roubo!
daylight saving time *n esp* **US** horário *m* de verão.
day nursery *n* creche *f*.
day off (*pl* **days off**) *n* dia *m* de folga.
day pupil *n* **UK** aluno *m*, -na *f* de semi-internato.
day release *n* **UK** *sistema na Inglaterra que permite que os trabalhadores se ausentem um dia por semana do serviço para estudar.*
day return *n* **UK** passagem *f* de ida e volta *(no mesmo dia)*.
day room *n* sala *f* de estar *(em hospital, asilo)*.
day school *n* escola *f* diurna *(particular)*.
day shift *n* turno *m* do dia.
daytime ['deɪtaɪm] <> *n* dia *m*; **in the ~** durante o dia. <> *comp* de dia; **~ flight** vôo *m* diurno.
day-to-day *adj* diário(ria).
daytrader ['deɪtreɪdəʳ] *n ST EX* day-trader *mf*.
day trip *n* viagem *f* de um dia.
day-tripper *n* **UK** *pessoa que sai em viagem de um dia.*
daze [deɪz] <> *n*: **in a ~** atordoado(da). <> *vt* atordoar.
dazed [deɪzd] *adj* [lit & fig] atordoado(da).
dazzle ['dæzl] *vt* **-1.** [blind] ofuscar **-2.** [impress] deslumbrar.
dazzling ['dæzlɪŋ] *adj* **-1.** [blinding] ofuscante **-2.** [impressive] deslumbrante.
DBE (*abbr of* **Dame Commander of the Order of the British Empire**) *n (beneficiária de) distinção de honra britânica.*
DBS *n* **-1.** (*abbr of* **direct broadcasting by satellite**) transmissão *f* direta via satélite. **-2.** (*abbr of* **direct-broadcast satellite**) satélite *f* de transmissão direta.
DC <> *n* (*abbr of* **direct current**) CC *f*. <> *abbr of* **District of Columbia**.
DD (*abbr of* **Doctor of Divinity**) *n (titular de) doutorado em teologia.*
D-day ['di:deɪ] *n* dia *m* D.
DDT (*abbr of* **dichlorodiphenyltrichloroethane**) *n* DDT *m*.
DE *abbr of* **Delaware**.
DEA (*abbr of* **Drug Enforcement Administration**) *n departamento da polícia norte-americana encarregado do controle de questões relacionadas a drogas*, ≃ DENARC *m*.
deacon ['di:kn] *n* **-1.** [minister] diácono *m* **-2.** [lay assistant] acólito *m*.
deaconess [ˌdi:kə'nes] *n* diaconisa *f*.
deactivate [ˌdi:'æktɪveɪt] *vt* desativar.
dead [ded] <> *adj* **-1.** [not alive] morto(ta); **to shoot sb ~** matar alguém com um tiro; **he wouldn't be seen ~ doing that** *inf* nunca seria visto fazendo aquilo **-2.** [numb] dormente, adormecido(da) **-3.** [*ELEC* - battery] descarregado(da); [- radio, TV] quebrado(da); [- telephone line] mudo(da) **-4.** [complete]: **~ silence** silêncio *m* mortal; **~ stop** parada *f* repentina **-5.** [not lively] morto(ta). <> *adv* **-1.** [directly, precisely] diretamente; **~ on time** bem na hora **-2.** *inf* [completely, very] totalmente; **to be ~ set on doing sthg** estar totalmente determinado(-da) a fazer algo; **to be ~ against sthg/doing sthg** ser totalmente contra algo/fazer algo **-3.** [suddenly]: **to stop ~** parar repentinamente. <> *n*: **at ~ of night** na calada da noite. <> *npl*: **the ~** os mortos.
deadbeat ['dedbi:t] *n* **US** *inf* malandro *m*, -dra *f*.
dead-beat *adj inf* morto(ta).
dead centre *n* ponto *m* morto.
dead duck *n inf* fracasso *m*.
deaden ['dedn] *vt* **-1.** [noise] amortecer **-2.** [feeling] abrandar.
dead end *n* **-1.** [street] rua *f* sem saída **-2.** *fig* [course of action] impasse *m*.
dead-end job *n* emprego *m* sem perspectivas.
deadhead ['dedhed] *vt* podar.
dead heat *n* empate *m*.
dead letter *n fig* [rule, law] letra *f* morta.
deadline ['dedlaɪn] *n* prazo *m* final.
deadlock ['dedlɒk] *n* impasse *m*.
deadlocked ['dedlɒkt] *adj* paralisado(da).
dead loss *n inf* **-1.** [person] traste *m* **-2.** [thing] porcaria *f*.
deadly ['dedlɪ] (*compar* **-ier**, *superl* **-iest**) <> *adj* **-1.** [lethal] letal **-2.** [mortal] mortal **-3.** [fatally precise] fatal. <> *adv* [extremely] terrivelmente.
deadly nightshade [-'naɪtʃeɪd] *n (U)* beladona *f*.
deadpan ['dedpæn] <> *adj* supostamente sério(-ria). <> *adv* afetadamente sério(ria).
Dead Sea *n*: **the ~** o Mar Morto.

dead wood *UK*, **deadwood** *US* ['dedwʊd] *n (U) fig* estorvo *m*.

deaf [def] ◇ *adj* **-1.** [unable to hear] surdo(da) **-2.** *fig* [unwilling to hear]: **to be ~ to sthg** ser surdo(da) a algo. ◇ *npl*: **the ~** os surdos.

deaf-aid *n UK* aparelho *m* de surdez.

deafen ['defn] *vt* ensurdecer.

deafening ['defnɪŋ] *adj* ensurdecedor(ra).

deaf mute ◇ *adj* surdo-mudo(da). ◇ *n* surdo-mudo *m*, -da *f*.

deafness ['defnɪs] *n (U)* surdez *f*.

deal [di:l] (*pt* & *pp* **dealt**) ◇ *n* **-1.** [business agreement] transação *f*, acordo *m*; **to do** *OR* **strike a ~ with sb** fazer um acordo com alguém **-2.** *inf* [treatment] tratamento *m*; **big ~!** *iron* grande coisa! **-3.** [quantity]: **a good** *OR* **great ~** muito; **a good** *OR* **great ~ of work** muito trabalho. ◇ *vt* **-1.** [strike]: **to ~ sb/sthg a blow** dar um golpe em alguém/algo; **to ~ a blow to sthg** *fig* ser um golpe em/para algo **-2.** [cards] repartir. ◇ *vi* **-1.** [in cards] repartir **-2.** [trade] negociar.

◆ **deal in** *vt fus* COMM negociar.

◆ **deal out** *vt sep* repartir.

◆ **deal with** *vt fus* **-1.** [handle, cope with, be faced with] lidar com **-2.** [be concerned with] tratar de.

dealer ['di:lə^r] *n* **-1.** [trader] negociante *m* **-2.** [in cards] carteador *m*, -ra *f*.

dealership ['di:ləʃɪp] *n* revendendor *m*, -ra *f*.

dealings *npl* [relations]: **~s with sb** relações *mpl* com alguém.

dealt [delt] *pt* & *pp* ▷ **deal**.

dean [di:n] *n* **-1.** [of church, cathedral] deão *m* **-2.** [of university] decano *m*, -na *f*.

dear [dɪə^r] ◇ *adj* **-1.** [loved] querido(da); **to be ~ to sb** ser precioso(sa) para alguém **-2.** [in letter]: **Dear Sir/Madam** Prezado Senhor/Prezada Senhora **-3.** *esp UK* [expensive] caro(ra). ◇ *n*: **my ~** meu querido, minha querida. ◇ *excl*: **oh ~!** oh céus!

dearly ['dɪəlɪ] *adv* **-1.**: **to love sb ~** amar muito alguém **-2.** [very much] muito; **I would ~ love to know ...** eu adoraria saber ... **-3.** [pay, cost] caro.

dearth [dɜ:θ] *n* carência *f*.

death [deθ] *n* morte *f*; **to frighten/worry sb to ~** quase matar alguém de susto/preocupação; **to be bored to ~ with sthg** *inf* morrer de tédio com algo; **to be sick to ~ of sthg/of doing sthg** *inf* estar de saco cheio de algo/de fazer algo; **to be put to ~** ser morto(ta); **to be at ~'s door** estar à beira da morte.

deathbed ['deθbed] *n* leito *m* de morte.

death certificate *n* certidão *f* de óbito.

death duty *UK*, **death tax** *US n* imposto *m* de transmissão causa mortis.

death knell *n fig*: **to sound the ~ for sb/sthg** soar o alarme para alguém/algo.

deathly ['deθlɪ] (*compar* **-ier**, *superl* **-iest**) ◇ *adj* [silence, hush] mortal. ◇ *adv* [pale, cold] mortalmente.

death penalty *n* pena *f* de morte.

death rate *n* taxa *f* de mortalidade.

death row *n US* corredor *m* da morte.

death sentence *n* sentença *f* de morte.

death squad *n* esquadrão *m* da morte.

death tax *n US* = **death duty**.

death toll *n* número *m* de mortos.

death trap *n inf*: **this car is a ~** este carro é um perigo.

Death Valley *n* Vale *m* da Morte.

deathwatch beetle ['deθwɒtʃ-] *n* caruncho *f*.

death wish *n* desejo *m* de morrer.

deb [deb] *n UK inf* debutante *mf*.

debacle *n* fracasso *m*.

debar [di:'bɑ:^r] (*pt* & *pp* **-red**, *cont* **-ring**) *vt*: **to ~ sb (from somewhere/from doing sthg)** privar alguém (do acesso a algum lugar/de fazer algo).

debase [dɪ'beɪs] *vt* [person, sport] degradar; **to ~ o.s.** degradar-se.

debasement [dɪ'beɪsmənt] *n* [of person, sport] degradação *f*.

debatable [dɪ'beɪtəbl] *adj* contestável, controverso(sa).

debate [dɪ'beɪt] ◇ *n (U)* debate *m*; **open to ~** aberto(ta) ao debate. ◇ *vt* [issue] debater; **to ~ whether to do sthg** discutir sobre o que fazer. ◇ *vi* debater.

debating society [dɪ'beɪtɪŋ-] *n* grupo *m* de discussão.

debauched [dɪ'bɔ:tʃt] *adj* devasso(sa), depravado(da).

debauchery [dɪ'bɔ:tʃərɪ] *n (U)* depravação *f*.

debenture [dɪ'bentʃə^r] *n* debênture *f*.

debilitate [dɪ'bɪlɪteɪt] *vt* enfraquecer.

debilitating [dɪ'bɪlɪteɪtɪŋ] *adj* enfraquecedor(ra).

debility [dɪ'bɪlətɪ] *n (U)* fraqueza *f*.

debit ['debɪt] ◇ *n* débito *m*. ◇ *vt* [account, sum of money] debitar.

debit card *n* cartão *m* de débito.

debonair [ˌdebə'neə^r] *adj* garboso(sa).

debrief [ˌdi:'bri:f] *vt* interrogar *(ao se terminar uma missão)*.

debriefing [ˌdi:'bri:fɪŋ] *n* interrogatório *m* (após o término de uma missão).

debris ['deɪbri:] *n* **-1.** escombros *mpl* **-2.** GEOL fragmento *m* de rocha.

debt [det] *n* **-1.** dívida *f*; **to be in ~** estar endividado(da) **-2.** [feeling of gratitude] dívida *f*; **to be in sb's ~** estar em débito com alguém.

debt collector *n* cobrador *m*, -ra *f* de dívidas.

debtor ['detə^r] *n* devedor *m*, -ra *f*.

debug [ˌdi:'bʌg] (*pt* & *pp* **-ged**, *cont* **-ging**) *vt* **-1.** [room] tirar microfones escondidos de **-2.** COMPUT [program] depurar.

debunk [ˌdi:'bʌŋk] *vt* derrubar.

debut ['deɪbju:] *n* debute *m*.

debutante ['debjʊtɑ:nt] *n* debutante *mf*.

dec. (*abbr of* **deceased**) m.

Dec. (*abbr of* **December**) dez.

decade ['dekeɪd] *n* década *f*.

decadence ['dekədəns] *n* decadência *f*.

decadent ['dekədənt] *adj* decadente.

decaf *n inf* café *m* descafeinado.

decaffeinated [dɪ'kæfɪneɪtɪd] *adj* descafeinado(-da).

decal ['di:kæl] *n US* adesivo *m*, decalque *m*.

decamp [dɪ'kæmp] *vi inf* safar-se.

decant [dɪ'kænt] *vt* decantar.
decanter [dɪ'kæntəʳ] *n* [container] licoreira *f*.
decapitate [dɪ'kæpɪteɪt] *vt* decapitar.
decathlete [dɪ'kæθli:t] *n* decatleta *mf*.
decathlon [dɪ'kæθlɒn] *n* decatlo *m*.
decay [dɪ'keɪ] <> *n* -**1.** [of tooth] cárie *f* -**2.** [of body, plant] decomposição *f* -**3.** *fig* [of building, society]: **to fall into** ~ [building] cair em ruínas; [system] entrar em decadência; [society] entrar em declínio; **urban** ~ decadência *f* urbana. <> *vi* -**1.** [tooth] criar cáries -**2.** [body, plant] decompor-se -**3.** *fig* [building, society] entrar em declínio.
deceased [dɪ'si:st] (*pl inv*) *fml* <> *adj* falecido(da). <> *n*: **the** ~ o falecido, a falecida. <> *npl*: **the** ~ os mortos.
deceit [dɪ'si:t] *n* engano *m*.
deceitful [dɪ'si:tfʊl] *adj* enganoso(sa).
deceive [dɪ'si:v] *vt* enganar; **to** ~ **o.s.** enganar-se.
decelerate [ˌdi:'seləreɪt] *vi* desacelerar.
December [dɪ'sembəʳ] *n* dezembro; *see also* **September**.
decency ['di:snsɪ] *n* -**1.** [respectability] decência *f* -**2.** [consideration]: **to have the** ~ **to do sthg** ter a decência de fazer algo.
decent ['di:snt] *adj* decente.
decently ['di:sntlɪ] *adv* decentemente.
decentralization [di:ˌsentrəlaɪ'zeɪʃn] *n* descentralização *f*.
decentralize, -ise [ˌdi:'sentrəlaɪz] *vt* descentralizar.
deception [dɪ'sepʃn] *n* -**1.** [lie, pretence] engano *m* -**2.** [act of lying, pretending] embuste *m*.
deceptive [dɪ'septɪv] *adj* enganoso(sa).
deceptively [dɪ'septɪvlɪ] *adv* enganosamente.
decibel ['desɪbel] *n* decibel *m*.
decide [dɪ'saɪd] <> *vt* -**1.** [resolve, determine] decidir; **to** ~ **to do sthg** decidir fazer algo; **to** ~ **that** decidir que -**2.** [settle] decidir, resolver. <> *vi* [make up one's mind] decidir-se.
◆ **decide (up)on** *vt fus* decidir-se por.
decided [dɪ'saɪdɪd] *adj* -**1.** [distinct] evidente -**2.** [resolute] decidido(da).
decidedly [dɪ'saɪdɪdlɪ] *adv* decididamente.
deciding [dɪ'saɪdɪŋ] *adj*: ~ **vote** voto *m* de Minerva.
deciduous [dɪ'sɪdjʊəs] *adj* decíduo(dua).
decimal ['desɪml] <> *adj* decimal. <> *n* (número *m*) decimal *m*.
decimal currency *n* moeda *f* de sistema decimal.
decimalize, -ise ['desɪməlaɪz] *vt* converter em decimal.
decimal place *n* casa *f* decimal.
decimal point *n* vírgula *f* decimal.
decimate ['desɪmeɪt] *vt* dizimar.
decipher [dɪ'saɪfəʳ] *vt* decifrar.
decision [dɪ'sɪʒn] *n* -**1.** [gen] decisão *f*; **to make a** ~ tomar uma decisão -**2.** [decisiveness] determinação *f*.
decision-maker *n* tomador *m*, -ra *f* de decisões.
decision-making *n* tomada *f* de decisão.
decisive [dɪ'saɪsɪv] *adj* -**1.** [person] decidido(da) -**2.** [factor, event] decisivo(va).
decisively [dɪ'saɪsɪvlɪ] *adv* -**1.** [confidently] decididamente -**2.** [conclusively] claramente.
decisiveness [dɪ'saɪsɪvnɪs] *n* [of person] determinação *f*.
deck [dek] <> *n* -**1.** [of ship] convés *m* -**2.** [of bus] piso *m* -**3.** [of cards] baralho *m* -**4.** *US* [of house] *área com piso e sem telhado junto a uma casa.* <> *vt* [decorate]: **to** ~ **sthg with** decorar algo com.
◆ **deck out** *vt sep* enfeitar.
deckchair ['dektʃeəʳ] *n* espreguiçadeira *f*.
deckhand ['dekhænd] *n* taifeiro *m*.
declaration [ˌdeklə'reɪʃn] *n* declaração *f*.
Declaration of Independence *n*: **the** ~ *a declaração da independência norte-americana em 1776.*
declare [dɪ'kleəʳ] *vt* declarar.
declared [dɪ'kleəd] *adj* [intention] declarado(da).
declassify [ˌdi:'klæsɪfaɪ] (*pt* & *pp* **-ied**) *vt* revelar, tornar público(ca).
decline [dɪ'klaɪn] <> *n* declínio *m*; **to be in** ~ estar em declínio; **on the** ~ em declínio. <> *vt* [refuse] recusar, declinar; **to** ~ **to do sthg** recusar-se a fazer algo. <> *vi* -**1.** [deteriorate] decair -**2.** [refuse] recusar-se.
declutch [dɪ'klʌtʃ] *vi AUT* soltar a embreagem.
decode [ˌdi:'kəʊd] *vt* decodificar.
decoder [ˌdi:'kəʊdəʳ] *n* decodificador *m*.
decommission [ˌdi:kə'mɪʃn] *vt* desmontar.
decompose [ˌdi:kəm'pəʊz] *vi* [decay] decompor.
decomposition [ˌdi:kɒmpə'zɪʃn] *n* [decay] decomposição *f*.
decompression chamber [ˌdi:kəm'preʃn-] *n* câmara *f* de descompressão.
decompression sickness [ˌdi:kəm'preʃn-] *n* mal *m* da descompressão.
decongestant [ˌdi:kən'dʒestənt] *n* descongestionante *m*.
decontaminate [ˌdi:kən'tæmɪneɪt] *vt* descontaminar.
décor ['deɪkɔ:ʳ] *n* decoração *f*.
decorate ['dekəreɪt] *vt* -**1.** [gen] decorar; **to** ~ **sthg with** decorar algo com -**2.** [with medal] condecorar.
decoration [ˌdekə'reɪʃn] *n* -**1.** [ornament] enfeite *m* -**2.** [activity, appearance] decoração *f* -**3.** [medal] condecoração *f*.
decorative ['dekərətɪv] *adj* decorativo(va).
decorator ['dekəreɪtəʳ] *n* decorador *m*, -ra *f*.
decorous ['dekərəs] *adj fml* decoroso(sa).
decorum [dɪ'kɔ:rəm] *n (U)* decoro *m*.
decoy [*n* 'di:kɔɪ, *vb* dɪ'kɔɪ] <> *n* chamariz *m*, isca *f*. <> *vt* atrair.
decrease [*n* 'di:kri:s, *vb* dɪ'kri:s] <> *n* diminuição *f*; ~ **in sthg** diminuição de algo. <> *vt* diminuir. <> *vi* diminuir.
decreasing [di:'kri:sɪŋ] *adj* decrescente.
decree [dɪ'kri:] <> *n* -**1.** [order, decision] decreto *m* -**2.** *US* [judgment] sentença *f*. <> *vt* decretar; **to** ~ **that** decretar que.
decree absolute (*pl* **decrees absolute**) *n UK JUR* sentença *f* definitiva de divórcio.
decree nisi [-'naɪsaɪ] (*pl* **decrees nisi**) *n UK JUR*

sentença *f* provisória de divórcio.

decrepit [dɪ'krepɪt] *adj* decrépito(ta).

decry [dɪ'kraɪ] (*pt* & *pp* **-ied**) *vt fml* depreciar, censurar.

dedicate ['dedɪkeɪt] *vt* **-1.** [book, song, poem]: **to ~ sthg to sb** dedicar algo a alguém **-2.** [life, career] dedicar; **to ~ o.s. to sthg** dedicar-se a algo.

dedicated ['dedɪkeɪtɪd] *adj* [gen & COMPUT] dedicado(da).

dedication [ˌdedɪ'keɪʃn] *n* dedicação *f*.

deduce [dɪ'dju:s] *vt* deduzir; **to ~ sthg from sthg** deduzir algo de algo.

deduct [dɪ'dʌkt] *vt* deduzir; **to ~ sthg from sthg** descontar OR deduzir algo de algo.

deduction [dɪ'dʌkʃn] *n* **-1.** [conclusion] dedução *f* **-2.** [sum deducted] desconto *m*.

deed [di:d] *n* **-1.** [action] ação *f*, feito *m* **-2.** JUR escritura *f*.

deed poll (*pl* **deed polls** OR **deeds poll**) *n UK*: **to change one's name by ~** trocar oficialmente de nome.

deem [di:m] *vt fml* julgar; **the building was ~ed to be unsafe** o edifício foi considerado inseguro; **to ~ it wise to do sthg** julgar sensato fazer algo.

deep [di:p] <> *adj* **-1.** [gen] profundo(da); **to be thrown in at the ~ end** *fig* ser posto(ta) numa situação nova sem preparação **-2.** [in measurements] de profundidade **-3.** [colour] intenso(sa) **-4.** [sound, voice] grave. <> *adv* fundo; **to go ~ into the forest** embrenhar-se floresta adentro; **to be ~ in thought** estar imerso(sa) em pensamentos; **to know ~ down** *fig* saber bem no fundo.

deepen ['di:pn] <> *vt* [hole, channel] aprofundar. <> *vi* **-1.** [river, sea] aprofundar-se **-2.** [crisis, recession, feeling] agravar-se **-3.** [darkness] tornar-se mais profundo(da).

deepening ['di:pnɪŋ] *adj* [crisis, recession] cada vez mais grave.

deep-fat fryer *n* fritadeira *f* por imersão.

deep freeze *n* freezer *m*.
◆ **deep-freeze** *vt* congelar.

deep-fry *vt* fritar *(com muito óleo)*.

deeply ['di:plɪ] *adv* **-1.** [dig, sigh] fundo **-2.** [profoundly, sincerely] profundamente.

deep-rooted *adj* arraigado(da).

deep-sea *adj* submarino(na).

deep-seated *adj* [belief, fear] profundamente arraigado(da).

deep-set *adj* [eyes] encovado(da).

deer [dɪəʳ] (*pl inv*) *n* veado *m*, cervo *m*.

deerstalker ['dɪəˌstɔ:kəʳ] *n* [hat] boné *m* com abas.

de-escalate [ˌdi:'eskəleɪt] <> *vt* suavizar. <> *vi* suavizar.

deface [dɪ'feɪs] *vt* danificar.

defamation [ˌdefə'meɪʃn] *n fml* difamação *f*.

defamatory [dɪ'fæmətrɪ] *adj fml* difamatório(ria).

default [dɪ'fɔ:lt] <> *n* **-1.** JUR falta *f*; **to declare s.o. in ~** declarar alguém inadimplente; **by ~** à revelia **-2.** COMPUT default *m*, padrão *m*. <> *adj* COMPUT default, OR padrão <> *vi* FIN, JUR: **to ~ on sthg** estar/ficar inadimplente com algo.

defaulter [dɪ'fɔ:ltəʳ] *n* [on payment] inadimplente *mf*.

default value *n* COMPUT valor-padrão *m*, valor *m* default.

defeat [dɪ'fi:t] <> *n* [gen] derrota *f*; **to admit ~** admitir a derrota. <> *vt* **-1.** [team, opponent] derrotar **-2.** [motion, proposal] rechaçar **-3.** [plans] frustrar.

defeatism [dɪ'fi:tɪzm] *n* derrotismo *m*.

defeatist [dɪ'fi:tɪst] <> *adj* derrotista. <> *n* derrotista *mf*.

defecate ['defəkeɪt] *vi fml* defecar.

defect [*n* 'di:fekt, *vb* dɪ'fekt] <> *n* [fault] defeito *m*. <> *vi* POL: **to ~ to the other side** ≃ passar para o outro lado, virar a casaca.

defection [dɪ'fekʃn] *n* deserção *f*.

defective [dɪ'fektɪv] *adj* defeituoso(sa).

defector [dɪ'fektəʳ] *n* desertor *m*, -ra *f*.

defence *UK*, **defense** *US* [dɪ'fens] *n* **-1.** [gen & SPORT] defesa *f*; **~ against sb/sthg** defesa contra alguém/algo **-2.** [protective device, system] proteção *f*; **~ against sb/sthg** proteção *f* contra alguém/algo **-3.** [JUR - lawyers]: **the ~** a defesa; [- denial of charge] defesa *f*; **in sb's ~** em defesa de alguém.
◆ **defences** *npl* [of country] defesas *fpl*.

defenceless *UK*, **defenseless** *US* [dɪ'fenslɪs] *adj* indefeso(sa).

defend [dɪ'fend] <> *vt* defender; **to ~ sb/sthg against sb/sthg** defender alguém/algo de alguém/algo; **to ~ o.s.** defender-se. <> *vi* SPORT defender-se.

defendant [dɪ'fendənt] *n* réu *m*, ré *f*.

defender [dɪ'fendəʳ] *n* **-1.** [gen] defensor *m*, -ra *f* **-2.** [SPORT - player] zagueiro *m*, -ra *f*; [- of title] defensor *m*, -ra *f*.

defense *n US* = **defence**.

defenseless *adj US* = **defenceless**.

defensive [dɪ'fensɪv] <> *adj* **-1.** [weapons, tactics] defensivo(va) **-2.** [person] receoso(sa). <> *n*: **on the ~** na defensiva.

defer [dɪ'fɜ:ʳ] (*pt* & *pp* **-red**, *cont* **-ring**) <> *vt* adiar, protelar. <> *vi*: **to ~ to sb** deferir a alguém.

deference ['defərəns] *n* deferência *f*.

deferential [ˌdefə'renʃl] *adj* deferente.

defiance [dɪ'faɪəns] *n* desafio *m*; **in ~ of sb/sthg** a despeito de alguém/algo.

defiant [dɪ'faɪənt] *adj* desafiador(ra).

defiantly [dɪ'faɪəntlɪ] *adv* desafiadoramente.

deficiency [dɪ'fɪʃnsɪ] (*pl* **-ies**) *n* **-1.** [lack] deficiência *f* **-2.** [inadequacy] deficiência *f*, imperfeição *f*.

deficient [dɪ'fɪʃnt] *adj* **-1.** [lacking]: **~ in sthg** deficiente em algo **-2.** [inadequate] deficiente.

deficit ['defɪsɪt] *n* déficit *m*.

defile [dɪ'faɪl] *vt* **-1.** [grave, church] profanar **-2.** [mind, purity] corromper.

define [dɪ'faɪn] *vt* definir.

definite ['defɪnɪt] *adj* **-1.** [date, plan] definido(da) **-2.** [improvement, difference] claro(ra) **-3.** [person] seguro(ra).

definitely ['defɪnɪtlɪ] *adv* sem dúvida.

definition [defɪ'nɪʃn] *n* **-1.** [of word, expression, concept] definição *f*; **by ~** por definição **-2.** [of problem, function] explicação *f* **-3.** [clarity] nitidez *f*.

definitive [dɪ'fɪnɪtɪv] *adj* definitivo(va).

deflate [dɪ'fleɪt] <> *vt* **-1.** [balloon, tyre] esvaziar **-2.**

fig [person] diminuir **-3.** *ECON* deflacionar. <> *vi* [balloon, tyre] esvaziar-se.
deflation [dɪ'fleɪʃn] *n ECON* deflação *f.*
deflationary [dɪ'fleɪʃnərɪ] *adj ECON* deflacionário(-ria).
deflect [dɪ'flekt] *vt* desviar.
deflection [dɪ'flekʃn] *n* desvio *m.*
defog [ˌdi:'fɒg] *vt US AUT* desembaçar.
defogger [ˌdi:'fɒgəʳ] *n US AUT* desembaçador *m.*
deforest [ˌdi:'fɒrɪst] *vt* desflorestar.
deforestation [di:ˌfɒrɪ'steɪʃn] *n* desflorestamento *m.*
deform [di:'fɔ:m] *vt* deformar.
deformed [dɪ'fɔ:md] *adj* deformado(da).
deformity [dɪ'fɔ:mətɪ] (*pl* **-ies**) *n* **-1.** [state of being deformed] deformidade *f* **-2.** [deformed part] má-formação *f* (congênita).
DEFRA (*abbr of* **Department for the Environment, Food and Rural Affairs**) *n divisão do governo britânico que trata de questões agrárias e do meio ambiente.*
defraud [dɪ'frɔ:d] *vt* fraudar.
defray [dɪ'freɪ] *vt* custear.
defrost [ˌdi:'frɒst] <> *vt* **-1.** [fridge] degelar **-2.** [frozen food] descongelar **-3.** *US* [*AUT* - de-ice] descongelar. <> *vi* **-1.** [fridge] degelar **-2.** [frozen food] descongelar.
deft [deft] *adj* **-1.** [movement, fingers] ágil **-2.** [handling of situation] hábil.
deftly ['deftlɪ] *adv* **-1.** [move] agilmente **-2.** [deal with situation] habilmente.
defunct [dɪ'fʌŋkt] *adj* extinto(ta).
defuse [ˌdi:'fju:z] *vt UK* **-1.** [bomb] desativar **-2.** *fig* [situation] acalmar.
defy [dɪ'faɪ] (*pt* & *pp* **-ied**) *vt* **-1.** [disobey] desafiar **-2.** [challenge]: **to ~ sb to do sthg** desafiar alguém a fazer algo **-3.** *fig* [elude - description] impossibilitar; [- efforts] tornar inútil.
degenerate [*adj* & *n* dɪ'dʒenərət, *vb* dɪ'dʒenəreɪt] <> *adj* degenerado(da). <> *n* degenerado *m*, -da *f.* <> *vi* degenerar; **to ~ into** degenerar para.
degradation [ˌdegrə'deɪʃn] *n* degradação *f.*
degrade [dɪ'greɪd] *vt* [debase] degradar.
degrading [dɪ'greɪdɪŋ] *adj* [debasing] degradante.
degree [dɪ'gri:] *n* **-1.** [unit of measurement, amount] grau *m*; **by ~s** gradualmente **-2.** [qualification] título *m* universitário; **to have/take a ~ (in sthg)** ter/obter graduação (em algo).
dehumanize, -ise [di:'hju:mənaɪz] *vt* desumanizar.
dehydrated [ˌdi:haɪ'dreɪtɪd] *adj* desidratado(da).
dehydration [ˌdi:haɪ'dreɪʃn] *n* desidratação *f.*
de-ice [di:'aɪs] *vt* descongelar.
de-icer [di:'aɪsəʳ] *n* substância *f* descongelante.
deign [deɪn] *vi*: **to ~ to do sthg** dignar-se a fazer algo.
deity ['di:ɪtɪ] (*pl* **-ies**) *n* divindade *f*, deidade *f.*
déjà vu [ˌdeʒɑ:'vju:] *n* déjà vu *m.*
dejected [dɪ'dʒektɪd] *adj* abatido(da), desanimado(da).
dejection [dɪ'dʒekʃn] *n* abatimento *m*, desânimo *m.*
Del. *abbr of* **Delaware.**
Delaware ['deləweəʳ] *n* Delaware; **in ~** em Delaware.
delay [dɪ'leɪ] <> *n* atraso *m*; **without ~** sem demora. <> *vt* **-1.** [cause to be late] atrasar **-2.** [postpone] adiar; **to ~ doing sthg** adiar (fazer) algo. <> *vi* demorar-se; **to ~ in doing sthg** demorar-se para fazer algo.
delayed [dɪ'leɪd] *adj* atrasado(da).
delayed-action [dɪ'leɪd-] *adj* de ação retardada; **~ shutter** *PHOT* obturador *m* automático.
delectable [dɪ'lektəbl] *adj* **-1.** [food] delicioso(sa) **-2.** [person] fabuloso(sa).
delegate [*n* 'delɪgət, *vb* 'delɪgeɪt] <> *n* delegado *m*, -da *f.* <> *vt* **-1.** [appoint to do job] delegar; **to ~ sb to do sthg** delegar alguém para fazer algo **-2.** [hand over responsibility for] delegar; **to ~ sthg to sb** delegar algo a alguém. <> *vi* delegar responsabilidades.
delegation [ˌdelɪ'geɪʃn] *n* delegação *f.*
delete [dɪ'li:t] *vt* **-1.** [remove] apagar **-2.** *COMPUT* deletar.
deletion [dɪ'li:ʃn] *n* exclusão *f.*
Delhi ['delɪ] *n* Delhi.
deli ['delɪ] (*abbr of* **delicatessen**) *n fam loja onde se vendem bebidas, frios, conservas e pães.*
deliberate [*adj* dɪ'lɪbərət, *vb* dɪ'lɪbəreɪt] <> *adj* **-1.** [intentional] deliberado(da) **-2.** [slow] pausado(da). <> *vi fml* deliberar.
deliberately [dɪ'lɪbərətlɪ] *adv* **-1.** [on purpose] deliberadamente **-2.** [slowly] pausadamente.
deliberation [dɪˌlɪbə'reɪʃn] *n* **-1.** [careful consideration] deliberação *f* **-2.** [slowness] morosidade *f.*
◆ **deliberations** *npl* deliberações *fpl.*
delicacy ['delɪkəsɪ] (*pl* **-ies**) *n* **-1.** *(U)* [gracefulness, tact] delicadeza *f* **-2.** [food] iguaria *f.*
delicate ['delɪkət] *adj* **-1.** [gen] delicado(da) **-2.** [flavour, colour] suave **-3.** [instrument] delicado(da), sensível.
delicately ['delɪkətlɪ] *adv* **-1.** [made, drawn] com delicadeza **-2.** [flavoured, coloured] suavemente **-3.** [hint, suggest] delicadamente.
delicatessen [ˌdelɪkə'tesn] *n* delicatessen *f.*
delicious [dɪ'lɪʃəs] *adj* **-1.** [tasty] delicioso(sa) **-2.** *fig* [delightful] encantador(ra).
delight [dɪ'laɪt] <> *n* **-1.** [great pleasure] prazer *m*, deleite *m*; **to take ~ in doing sthg** ter prazer em fazer algo **-2.** [wonderful thing, person] encanto *m.* <> *vt* encantar. <> *vi*: **to ~ in sthg/in doing sthg** encantar-se em algo/em fazer algo.
delighted [dɪ'laɪtɪd] *adj* muito contente; **~ by** *OR* **with sthg** encantado(da) com algo; **to be ~ to do sthg** estar muito feliz por fazer algo; **to be ~ that** ficar contente que.
delightful [dɪ'laɪtfʊl] *adj* encantador(ra).
delightfully [dɪ'laɪtfʊlɪ] *adv* encantadoramente.
delimit [di:'lɪmɪt] *vt fml* delimitar.
delineate [dɪ'lɪnɪeɪt] *vt fml* delinear.
delinquency [dɪ'lɪŋkwənsɪ] *n* delinqüência *f.*
delinquent [dɪ'lɪŋkwənt] <> *adj* delinqüente. <> *n* delinqüente *mf.*
delirious [dɪ'lɪrɪəs] *adj* delirante; **to be ~** estar delirando.
delirium [dɪ'lɪrɪəm] *n* delírio *m.*

deliver [dɪ'lɪvəʳ] ◇ *vt* **-1.** [distribute]: **to ~ sthg (to sb)** entregar algo (a alguém) **-2.** [give - speech, lecture] proferir; [- message] entregar; [- warning, ultimatum] dar **-3.** [blow] desferir **-4.** [baby] trazer ao mundo **-5.** *fml* [liberate]: **to ~ sb (from sthg)** libertar alguém (de algo) **-6.** *US POL* [votes] captar. ◇ *vi* **-1.** *COMM* repartir **-2.** [fulfil promise] cumprir *(o prometido)*.

deliverance [dɪ'lɪvərəns] *n fml* libertação *f*.

delivery [dɪ'lɪvərɪ] (*pl* **-ies**) *n* **-1.** [of goods, letters] entrega *f* **-2.** [goods delivered] remessa *f* **-3.** [way of speaking] elocução *f* **-4.** [birth] parto *m*.

delivery note *n* guia *f* de remessa.

delivery van *UK*, **delivery truck** *US n* camionete *f* de entrega.

delphinium [del'fɪnɪəm] (*pl* **-s**) *n* espora *f* de jardim.

delta ['deltə] (*pl* **-s**) *n GEOGR* delta *m*.

delude [dɪ'lu:d] *vt* enganar; **to ~ o.s.** enganar-se.

deluge ['delju:dʒ] ◇ *n* **-1.** [flood] dilúvio *m* **-2.** *fig* [huge number] mar *m*. ◇ *vt*: **to be ~d with sthg** ser inundado(da) por algo.

delusion [dɪ'lu:ʒn] *n* ilusão *f*; **~s of grandeur** delírios *mpl* de grandeza.

de luxe [də'lʌks] *adj* de luxo.

delve [delv] *vi* **-1.** [into mystery] pesquisar; **to ~ into sthg** investigar algo **-2.** [in bag, cupboard] remexer; **to ~ into** *OR* **inside sthg** revolver dentro de algo.

Dem. -1. (*abbr of* **Democrat**) Democrata *mf*. **-2.** (*abbr of* **Democratic**) Democrático(ca).

demagogue *UK*, **demagog** *US* ['deməgɒg] *n* demagogo *m*, -ga *f*.

demand [dɪ'mɑ:nd] ◇ *n* **-1.** [gen] exigência *f*; **wage ~** reivindicação *f* salarial; **on ~** [gen] a pedido; *COMM* sob demanda **-2.** [need & *COMM*]: **~ for sthg** demanda *f* por algo; **in ~** solicitado(da). ◇ *vt* **-1.** [gen] exigir; **to ~ to do sthg** exigir fazer algo **-2.** [enquire forcefully] inquirir.

demanding [dɪ'mɑ:ndɪŋ] *adj* **-1.** [exhausting] que exige muito esforço **-2.** [not easily satisfied] exigente.

demarcation [ˌdi:mɑ:'keɪʃn] *n* demarcação *f*.

demarcation dispute *n disputa entre sindicatos sobre as funções a serem realizadas por seus membros*.

dematerialize, -ise [di:mə'tɪərɪəlaɪz] *vi* desmaterializar-se.

demean [dɪ'mi:n] *vt* rebaixar; **to ~ o.s.** rebaixar-se, humilhar-se.

demeaning [dɪ'mi:nɪŋ] *adj* humilhante.

demeanour *UK*, **demeanor** *US* [dɪ'mi:nəʳ] *n fml* comportamento *m*.

demented [dɪ'mentɪd] *adj* demente.

dementia [dɪ'menʃə] *n* demência *f*.

demerara sugar [ˌdemə'reərə-] *n UK* açúcar *m* mascavo.

demigod ['demɪgɒd] *n* semideus *m*.

demijohn ['demɪdʒɒn] *n* garrafão *m*.

demilitarized zone, demilitarised zone [ˌdi:'mɪlɪtəraɪzd-] *n* zona *f* desmilitarizada.

demise [dɪ'maɪz] *n fml* **-1.** [death] falecimento *m* **-2.** *fig* [end] fim *m*.

demist [ˌdi:'mɪst] *vt UK AUT* desembaçar *m*.

demister [ˌdi:'mɪstəʳ] *n UK AUT* desembaçador *m*.

demo ['deməʊ] (*pl* **-s**) (*abbr of* **demonstration**) *n* **-1.** *fam* [protest] manifestação *f*. **-2.** [tape, video] demo *f*.

demobilize, -ise [ˌdi:'məʊbɪlaɪz] *vt fml* desmobilizar.

democracy [dɪ'mɒkrəsɪ] (*pl* **-ies**) *n* democracia *f*.

democrat ['deməkræt] *n* democrata *mf*.

◆ **Democrat** *n US* democrata *mf*.

democratic [demə'krætɪk] *adj* democrático(ca).

◆ **Democratic** *adj US* democrata.

democratically [ˌdemə'krætɪklɪ] *adv* democraticamente.

Democratic Party *n US*: **the ~** o Partido Democrata *(dos Estados Unidos)*.

democratize, -ise [dɪ'mɒkrətaɪz] *vt* democratizar.

demographic [ˌdemə'græfɪk] *adj* demográfico(-ca).

demolish [dɪ'mɒlɪʃ] *vt* **-1.** [knock down] demolir **-2.** [prove wrong] destruir, acabar com **-3.** *inf* [eat] acabar com.

demolition [ˌdemə'lɪʃn] *n* **-1.** [knocking down] demolição *f* **-2.** [proving wrong] destruição *f*.

demon ['di:mən] ◇ *n* [evil spirit] demônio *m*. ◇ *comp inf* [skilled] fantástico(ca).

demonstrable [dɪ'mɒnstrəbl] *adj* demonstrável.

demonstrably [dɪ'mɒnstrəblɪ] *adv* decididamente.

demonstrate ['demənstreɪt] ◇ *vt* **-1.** [gen] demonstrar **-2.** [appliance, machine] mostrar o funcionamento de. ◇ *vi* manifestar-se; **to ~ for/against sthg** manifestar-se a favor de/contra algo.

demonstration [demən'streɪʃn] *n* **-1.** [gen] demonstração *f* **-2.** [protest gathering, march] manifestação *f*.

demonstrative [dɪ'mɒnstrətɪv] *adj* efusivo(va).

demonstrator ['demənstreɪtəʳ] *n* **-1.** [of machine, product] demonstrador *m*, -ra *f* **-2.** [protester] manifestante *mf*.

demoralize, -ise [dɪ'mɒrəlaɪz] *vt* desmoralizar.

demoralized [dɪ'mɒrəlaɪzd] *adj* desmoralizado(-da).

demote [ˌdi:'məʊt] *vt* rebaixar *(na carreira profissional)*.

demotion [ˌdi:'məʊʃn] *n* rebaixamento *m (na carreira profissional)*.

demotivate [ˌdi:'məʊtɪveɪt] *vt* desmotivar.

demure [dɪ'mjʊəʳ] *adj* recatado(da).

demystify [ˌdi:'mɪstɪfaɪ] (*pt* & *pp* **-ied**) *vt* desmistificar.

den [den] *n* [lair] toca *f*.

denationalization ['di:ˌnæʃnəlaɪ'zeɪʃn] *n* desnacionalização *f*.

denationalize, -ise [ˌdi:'næʃnəlaɪz] *vt* desnacionalizar.

denial [dɪ'naɪəl] *n* **-1.** [refutation] contestação *f* **-2.** *(U)* [refusal] negação *f*.

denier ['denɪəʳ] *n* [of stockings, tights] denier *m*, *medida da espessura do fio de náilon ou de seda usado na fabricação de roupas*.

denigrate ['denɪgreɪt] *vt fml* difamar, denegrir.

denim ['denɪm] *n* brim *m*.

◆ **denims** *npl* jeans *m inv*.

denim jacket *n* jaqueta *f* jeans.
denizen ['denɪzn] *n literary or hum* habitante *mf.*
Denmark ['denmɑ:k] *n* Dinamarca; **in ~** na Dinamarca.
denomination [dɪ,nɒmɪ'neɪʃn] *n* **-1.** RELIG denominação *f*, seita *f* **-2.** FIN valor *m.*
denominator [dɪ'nɒmɪneɪtəʳ] *n* denominador *m.*
denote [dɪ'nəʊt] *vt fml* denotar.
denouement [deɪ'nu:mɒn] *n* desfecho *m.*
denounce [dɪ'naʊns] *vt* denunciar.
dense [dens] *adj* **-1.** [thick - trees, undergrowth] denso(sa); [- mist, fog] espesso(sa) **-2.** *inf* [stupid] estúpido(da).
densely ['densli] *adv* [thickly] densamente.
density ['densətɪ] (*pl* **-ies**) *n* densidade *f.*
dent [dent] ◇ *n* amassado *m.* ◇ *vt* [surface] amassar.
dental ['dentl] *adj* dentário(ria); **a ~ problem** um problema nos dentes.
dental floss *n (U)* fio *m* dental.
dental plate *n* dentadura *f* postiça, chapa *f.*
dental surgeon *n* cirurgião-dentista *m*, cirurgiã-dentista *f.*
dental surgery *n* cirurgia *f* dentária.
dental treatment *n (U)* tratamento *m* dentário.
dented ['dentɪd] *adj* amassado(da).
dentist ['dentɪst] *n* dentista *mf*; **to go to the ~'s** ir ao dentista.
dentistry ['dentɪstrɪ] *n (U)* odontologia *f.*
dentures ['dentʃəz] *npl* dentadura *f.*
denude *vt fml*: **to ~ sthg (of sthg)** despojar algo (de algo).
denunciation [dɪ,nʌnsɪ'eɪʃn] *n* denúncia *f.*
deny [dɪ'naɪ] (*pt* & *pp* **-ied**) *vt* negar; **to ~ sb sthg** negar algo a alguém.
deodorant [di:'əʊdərənt] *n* desodorante *m.*
depart [dɪ'pɑ:t] *vi fml* **-1.** [leave] partir; **to ~ from** partir de **-2.** [differ]: **to ~ from sthg** afastar-se de algo.
department [dɪ'pɑ:tmənt] *n* **-1.** [gen] departamento *m* **-2.** [of government] ministério *m.*
departmental [,di:pɑ:t'mentl] *adj* de departamento.
department store *n* loja *f* de departamentos.
departure [dɪ'pɑ:tʃəʳ] *n* **-1.** [leaving] partida *f* **-2.** [variation]: **~ (from sthg)** abandono *m* (de algo) **-3.** [orientation] início *m.*
departure lounge *n* sala *f* de embarque.
depend [dɪ'pend] *vi* **-1.** [rely - financially]: **to ~ on sb/sthg** depender de alguém/algo; [- emotionally]: **to ~ on sb** confiar em alguém **-2.** [be determined]: **it ~s** depende; **it ~s on** depende de; **~ing on** dependendo de.
dependable [dɪ'pendəbl] *adj* confiável.
dependant [dɪ'pendənt] *n* dependente *mf.*
dependence [dɪ'pendəns] *n* **-1.** [reliance]: **~ (on sb/sthg)** dependência *f* (de alguém/algo) **-2.** [addiction]: **~ (on sthg)** dependência (de algo).
dependent [dɪ'pendənt] *adj* **-1.** [reliant]: **to be ~ (on sb/sthg)** ser dependente (de alguém/algo) **-2.** [addicted] dependente **-3.** [determined by]: **to be ~ on sb/sthg** depender de alguém/algo.
depict [dɪ'pɪkt] *vt* **-1.** [show in picture] retratar **-2.** [describe]: **to ~ sb/sthg as sthg** retratar alguém/algo como algo.
depilatory [dɪ'pɪlətrɪ] *adj* depilatório(ria).
deplete [dɪ'pli:t] *vt* reduzir.
depletion [dɪ'pli:ʃn] *n (U)* redução *f.*
deplorable [dɪ'plɔ:rəbl] *adj* deplorável.
deplore [dɪ'plɔ:ʳ] *vt* deplorar.
deploy [dɪ'plɔɪ] *vt* dispor.
deployment [dɪ'plɔɪmənt] *n (U)* disposição *f.*
depopulated [,di:'pɒpjʊleɪtɪd] *adj* despovoado(-da).
depopulation [di:,pɒpjʊ'leɪʃn] *n (U)* despovoamento *m.*
deport [dɪ'pɔ:t] *vt* deportar.
deportation [,di:pɔ:'teɪʃn] *n* deportação *f.*
deportation order *n* ordem *f* de deportação.
depose [dɪ'pəʊz] *vt* [king, ruler] depor.
deposit [dɪ'pɒzɪt] ◇ *n* **-1.** GEOL [of gold, oil] jazida *f* **-2.** [of sediment, silt] depósito *m* **-3.** [fin] depósito *m*; **to make a ~** fazer um depósito **-4.** [down payment - on house, car] entrada *f*; [- on hotel room] depósito *m* **-5.** [returnable payment - on hired goods] caução *f*; [- on bottle, container] depósito *m.* ◇ *vt* **-1.** [gen] depositar **-2.** [bag, case, shopping] colocar.
deposit account *n UK* conta *f* remunerada.
depositor [də'pɒzɪtəʳ] *n* depositante *mf.*
depot ['depəʊ] *n* **-1.** [storage facility - for goods] armazém *m*; [- for vehicles] garagem *f* **-2.** *US* [bus or train terminus] terminal *m.*
depraved [dɪ'preɪvd] *adj* depravado(da).
depravity [dɪ'prævətɪ] *n (U)* depravação *f.*
deprecate ['deprɪkeɪt] *vt fml* censurar.
deprecating ['deprɪkeɪtɪŋ] *adj* desaprovador(ra).
depreciate [dɪ'pri:ʃɪeɪt] *vi* depreciar.
depreciation [dɪ,pri:ʃɪ'eɪʃn] *n (U)* depreciação *f.*
depress [dɪ'pres] *vt* **-1.** [sadden, discourage] deprimir **-2.** ECON depreciar **-3.** [slow down, reduce] reduzir.
depressant [dɪ'presənt] *n* MED sedativo *m.*
depressed [dɪ'prest] *adj* **-1.** [person] deprimido(da) **-2.** ECON em depressão **-3.** [area]: **~ point** ponto inferior.
depressing [dɪ'presɪŋ] *adj* deprimente.
depression [dɪ'preʃn] *n* depressão *f.*
◆ **Depression** *n*: **the (Great) Depression** a Grande Depressão.
depressive [dɪ'presɪv] *adj* depressivo(va).
deprivation [,deprɪ'veɪʃn] *n* [privation] privação *f.*
deprive [dɪ'praɪv] *vt*: **to ~ sb of sthg** privar alguém de algo.
deprived [dɪ'praɪvd] *adj* necessitado(da).
Dept. (*abbr of* **department**) Dep.
depth [depθ] *n* **-1.** profundidade *f*; **to be out of one's ~** [lit & fig] não dar pé para alguém; **in ~** em profundidade **-2.** [severity] gravidade *f*; **the ~ of sthg** a gravidade de algo.
◆ **depths** *npl*: **the ~s** [of sea, memory] as profundezas; [of winter] o auge; **to be in the ~s of despair** estar no auge do desespero.
depth charge *n* carga *f* de profundidade.
deputation [,depjʊ'teɪʃn] *n* delegação *f.*
deputize, -ise ['depjʊtaɪz] *vi*: **to ~ (for sb)** substituir oficialmente (alguém).
deputy ['depjʊtɪ] (*pl* **-ies**) ◇ *adj* adjunto(ta); ~

head subdiretor *m*, -ra *f*; ~ **chairman** vice-presidente *m*. <> *n* **-1.** [second-in-command] suplente *mf* **-2.** *US* [deputy sheriff] ajudante *mf* do delegado.

derail [dɪˈreɪl] *vt* [train] descarrilhar.

derailment [dɪˈreɪlmənt] *n* descarrilhamento *m*.

deranged [dɪˈreɪndʒd] *adj* perturbado(da), transtornado(da).

derby [*UK* ˈdɑːbɪ, *US* ˈdɜːbɪ] (*pl* **-ies**) *n* **-1.** [sports event] jogo *m* local **-2.** *US* [hat] chapéu-coco *m*.

deregulate [ˌdiːˈregjʊleɪt] *vt* desregulamentar.

deregulation [ˌdiːregjʊˈleɪʃn] *n (U)* desregulamentação *f*.

derelict [ˈderəlɪkt] *adj* abandonado(da).

deride [dɪˈraɪd] *vt* escarnecer de, zombar de.

derision [dɪˈrɪʒn] *n (U)* escárnio *m*, zombaria *f*.

derisive [dɪˈraɪsɪv] *adj* zombeteiro(ra).

derisory [dəˈraɪzərɪ] *adj* **-1.** [ridiculous] irrisório(ria) **-2.** [scornful] zombeteiro(ra).

derivation [ˌderɪˈveɪʃn] *n* [of word] origem *f*.

derivative [dɪˈrɪvətɪv] <> *adj pej* pouco original. <> *n* derivado *m*.

derive [dɪˈraɪv] <> *vt* **-1.** [pleasure]: **to ~ sthg from sthg** encontrar algo em algo **-2.** [word, expression]: **to be ~d from sthg** derivar de algo. <> *vi* [word, expression]: **to ~ from sthg** derivar-se de algo.

dermatitis [ˌdɜːməˈtaɪtɪs] *n (U)* dermatite *f*.

dermatologist [ˌdɜːməˈtɒlədʒɪst] *n* dermatologista *mf*.

dermatology [ˌdɜːməˈtɒlədʒɪ] *n (U)* dermatologia *f*.

derogatory [dɪˈrɒgətrɪ] *adj* depreciativo(va).

derrick [ˈderɪk] *n* **-1.** [crane] guindaste *m* **-2.** [over oil well] torre *f* de perfuração.

derv [dɜːv] *n UK* gasóleo *m*.

desalination [diːˌsælɪˈneɪʃn] *n (U)* dessalinização *f*.

descant [ˈdeskænt] *n* [tune] contraponto *m*.

descend [dɪˈsend] <> *vi* **-1.** *fml* [go down] descer **-2.** [fall]: **to ~ (on sb/sthg)** recair (sobre alguém/algo) **-3.** [invade]: **to ~ on** invadir **-4.** [stoop, lower o.s.]: **to ~ to sthg/to doing sthg** rebaixar-se a algo/a fazer algo. <> *vt fml* [go down] descer.

descendant [dɪˈsendənt] *n* [family member] descendente *mf*.

descended [dɪˈsendɪd] *adj*: **to be ~ from sb** ser descendente *OR* descender de alguém.

descending [dɪˈsendɪŋ] *adj*: **in ~ order** em ordem decrescente.

descent [dɪˈsent] *n* **-1.** [downwards movement] descida *f* **-2.** *(U)* [origin] ascendência *f*.

describe [dɪˈskraɪb] *vt* [recount] descrever.

description [dɪˈskrɪpʃn] *n* **-1.** [account] descrição *f* **-2.** [type] tipo *m*.

descriptive [dɪˈskrɪptɪv] *adj* descritivo(va).

desecrate [ˈdesɪkreɪt] *vt* profanar.

desecration [ˌdesɪˈkreɪʃn] *n (U)* profanação *f*.

desegregate [ˌdiːˈsegrɪgeɪt] *vt* dessegregar.

deselect [ˌdiːsɪˈlekt] *vt UK POL* [rejeitar (uma candidatura).

desert [*n* ˈdezət, *vb* & *npl* dɪˈzɜːt] <> *n* **-1.** *GEOGR* deserto *m* **-2.** *fig* [boring place] deserto *m*; **a cultural ~** um deserto cultural. <> *vt* abandonar. <> *vi MIL* desertar.

◆ **deserts** *npl*: **to get one's just ~s** receber aquilo que se merece.

deserted [dɪˈzɜːtɪd] *adj* [place] deserto(ta), abandonado(da).

deserter [dɪˈzɜːtə^r] *n* desertor *m*, -ra *f*.

desertion [dɪˈzɜːʃn] *n* **-1.** *(U) MIL* deserção *f* **-2.** [of person] abandono *m*.

desert island [ˈdezət-] *n* ilha *f* deserta.

deserve [dɪˈzɜːv] *vt* merecer; **to ~ sthg** merecer algo; **we ~ to win** merecemos vencer.

deserved [dɪˈzɜːvd] *adj* merecido(da).

deservedly [dɪˈzɜːvɪdlɪ] *adv* merecidamente.

deserving [dɪˈzɜːvɪŋ] *adj* merecedor(ra); **~ of sthg** *fml* merecedor(ra) de algo.

desiccated [ˈdesɪkeɪtɪd] *adj* desidratado(da).

design [dɪˈzaɪn] <> *n* **-1.** [plan, drawing] projeto *m* **-2.** *(U)* [art] design *m* **-3.** [pattern, motif] padrão *m* **-4.** [structure, shape] modelo *m* **-5.** *fml* [intention] intenção *f*; **by ~** por intenção; **to have ~s on sb/sthg** ter más intenções com relação a alguém/algo. <> *vt* **-1.** [building, car] projetar **-2.** [clothes, costumes] desenhar **-3.** [plan, system, test] projetar, criar; **to be ~ed for sthg/to do sthg** ser projetado(da) para algo/para fazer algo.

designate [*adj* ˈdezɪgnət, *vb* ˈdezɪgneɪt] <> *adj* designado(da). <> *vt* [appoint] designar; **to ~ sb as sthg/to do sthg** designar alguém como algo/para fazer algo.

designation [ˌdezɪgˈneɪʃn] *n fml* [name] designação *f*.

designer [dɪˈzaɪnə^r] <> *adj* [jeans, glasses, stubble] de marca. <> *n* **-1.** [of building, machine] projetista *mf* **-2.** [of theatre set] cenógrafo *m*, -fa *f* **-3.** [of clothes] estilista *mf*.

desirable [dɪˈzaɪərəbl] *adj* **-1.** *fml* [appropriate] apropriado(da) **-2.** [attractive] agradável **-3.** [sexually attractive] desejável.

desire [dɪˈzaɪə^r] <> *n* **-1.** [wish] desejo *m*, vontade *f*; **~ for sthg/to do sthg** desejo por algo/de fazer algo, vontade de algo/de fazer algo **-2.** *(U)* [sexual longing] desejo *m*. <> *vt* desejar; **it leaves a lot to be ~d** isso deixa muito a desejar.

desirous [dɪˈzaɪərəs] *adj fml*: **~ of sthg/of doing sthg** desejoso(sa) de algo/de fazer algo.

desist [dɪˈzɪst] *vi fml*: **to ~ (from doing sthg)** desistir (de fazer algo).

desk [desk] *n* **-1.** [piece of furniture - in office, study] escrivaninha *f*; [- in school] carteira *f* **-2.** [service point] balcão *m*.

desk clerk *n US* recepcionista *mf (de hotel)*.

desk diary *n* agenda *f (de mesa)*.

desk lamp *n* luminária *f (de mesa)*.

desktop [ˈdeskˌtɒp] *adj* [computer]: **a ~ computer** um computador de mesa *OR* desktop.

desktop publishing *n (U)* editoração *f* eletrônica.

desolate [ˈdesələt] *adj* desolado(da).

desolation [ˌdesəˈleɪʃn] *n* **-1.** [gen] desolação *f* **-2.** [despair] aflição *f*.

despair [dɪˈspeə^r] <> *n (U)* desespero *m*; **in ~** desesperado(da). <> *vi* desesperar-se; **to ~ of**

sb/sthg perder a esperança com alguém/algo; **to ~ of doing sthg** perder a esperança de fazer algo.

despairing [dɪ'speərɪŋ] *adj* desesperador(ra).

despairingly [dɪ'speərɪŋlɪ] *adv* desesperadamente.

despatch [dɪ'spætʃ] *n* & *vt* = **dispatch.**

desperate ['desprət] *adj* **-1.** [gen] desesperado(da); **to feel ~** sentir-se desperado(da) **-2.** [situation, problem] desesperador(ra) **-3.** [criminal] implacável **-4.** [in great need]: **to be ~ for sthg** estar louco(ca) por algo.

desperately ['desprətlɪ] *adv* **-1.** [gen] desesperadamente **-2.** [busy, sorry, in love] muito.

desperation [ˌdespə'reɪʃn] *n (U)* desespero *m*; **in ~** em desespero.

despicable [dɪ'spɪkəbl] *adj* desprezível.

despise [dɪ'spaɪz] *vt* desprezar.

despite [dɪ'spaɪt] *prep* apesar de.

despondent [dɪ'spɒndənt] *adj* desanimado(da).

despot ['despɒt] *n* déspota *mf.*

despotic [de'spɒtɪk] *adj* despótico(ca).

dessert [dɪ'zɜːt] *n* sobremesa *f.*

dessertspoon [dɪ'zɜːtspuːn] *n* **-1.** [spoon] colher *f* de sobremesa **-2.** [spoonful] colherada *f* de sobremesa.

dessert wine *n* vinho *m* doce *(servido com a sobremesa).*

destabilize, -ise [ˌdiː'steɪbɪlaɪz] *vt* desestabilizar.

destination [ˌdestɪ'neɪʃn] *n* destino *m.*

destined ['destɪnd] *adj* **-1.** [intended]: **~ for sthg/to do sthg** predestinado(da) a algo/a fazer algo **-2.** [bound]: **to be ~ for** estar indo para.

destiny ['destɪnɪ] (*pl* **-ies**) *n* destino *m.*

destitute ['destɪtjuːt] *adj* [extremely poor] necessitado(da), miserável.

destroy [dɪ'strɔɪ] *vt* **-1.** [gen] destruir **-2.** [animal] acabar com.

destroyer [dɪ'strɔɪəʳ] *n* **-1.** [ship] contratorpedeiro *m* **-2.** [person, thing] destruidor *m*, -ra *f.*

destruction [dɪ'strʌkʃn] *n (U)* destruição *f.*

destructive [dɪ'strʌktɪv] *adj* [harmful] destrutivo(-va).

destructively [dɪ'strʌktɪvlɪ] *adv* destrutivamente.

desultory ['desəltrɪ] *adj fml* sem propósito, desinteressado(da).

Det. (*abbr of* **Detective**) detetive *mf.*

detach [dɪ'tætʃ] *vt* **-1.** [remove] tirar; **to ~ sthg from sthg** tirar algo de algo ; [tear off] destacar **-2.** [dissociate]: **to ~ o.s. from sthg** afastar-se de algo.

detachable [dɪ'tætʃəbl] *adj* removível.

detached [dɪ'tætʃt] *adj* [unemotional] imparcial.

detached house *n* casa *f* separada.

detachment [dɪ'tætʃmənt] *n* **-1.** *(U)* [aloofness] desinteresse *m*, desapego *m* **-2.** MIL destacamento *m.*

detail ['diːteɪl] ◇ *n* **-1.** [small point] detalhe *m* **-2.** *(U)* [collection of facts, points] detalhe *m*, particularidade *f*; **to go into ~** entrar em detalhes; **in ~** detalhadamente **-3.** MIL destacamento *m.* ◇ *vt* [list] detalhar.

◆ **details** *npl* **-1.** [information] dados *mpl* **-2.** [personal information] dados *mpl* (pessoais).

detailed ['diːteɪld] *adj* detalhado(da).

detain [dɪ'teɪn] *vt* **-1.** [in hospital, police station] deter **-2.** [delay] retardar.

detainee [ˌdiːteɪ'niː] *n* detento *m*, -ta *f.*

detect [dɪ'tekt] *vt* **-1.** [subj: person] perceber **-2.** [subj: device] detectar.

detection [dɪ'tekʃn] *n* **-1.** *(U)* [discovery] detecção *f* **-2.** [investigation] investigação *f.*

detective [dɪ'tektɪv] *n* detetive *mf.*

detective novel *n* romance *m* policial.

detector [dɪ'tektəʳ] *n* detector *m.*

détente [deɪ'tɒnt] *n* POL détente *f.*

detention [dɪ'tenʃn] *n* **-1.** *(U)* [of suspect, criminal] detenção *f*; **in ~** em detenção **-2.** [at school] castigo *m (depois da aula)*; **to be in ~** ficar de castigo.

detention centre *n UK* centro *m* de detenção.

deter [dɪ'tɜːʳ] (*pt* & *pp* **-red**, *cont* **-ring**) *vt* dissuadir; **to ~ sb from doing sthg** dissuadir alguém de fazer algo.

detergent [dɪ'tɜːdʒənt] *n* detergente *m.*

deteriorate [dɪ'tɪərɪəreɪt] *vi* piorar.

deterioration [dɪˌtɪərɪə'reɪʃn] *n* **-1.** *(U)* [in health, economic situation] agravamento *f* **-2.** *(U)* [in weather] piora *f.*

determination [dɪˌtɜːmɪ'neɪʃn] *n* **-1.** *(U)* [resolve] determinação *f* **-2.** [establishing, fixing] definição *f.*

determine [dɪ'tɜːmɪn] *vt* **-1.** [gen] determinar **-2.** *fml* [resolve]: **to ~ to do sthg** determinar-se a fazer algo **-3.** [fix, settle] definir.

determined [dɪ'tɜːmɪnd] *adj* [person, effort] determinado(da); **~ to do sthg** determinado(da) a fazer algo.

deterrent [dɪ'terənt] ◇ *adj* dissuasivo(va). ◇ *n* dissuasão *f.*

detest [dɪ'test] *vt* detestar.

detestable [dɪ'testəbl] *adj* detestável.

dethrone [dɪ'θrəʊn] *vt* destronar.

detonate ['detəneɪt] ◇ *vt* detonar. ◇ *vi* detonar.

detonator ['detəneɪtəʳ] *n* detonador *m.*

detour ['diːˌtʊəʳ] *n* desvio *m.*

detox ['diːtɒks] *n inf* desintoxicação *f.*

detoxification *n* desintoxicação *f.*

detract [dɪ'trækt] *vi*: **to ~ from** [quality, achievement] depreciar; [enjoyment] perturbar.

detractor [dɪ'træktəʳ] *n* detrator *m*, -ra *f.*

detrain *vi* desembarcar *(de trem).*

detriment ['detrɪmənt] *n*: **to the ~ of sb/sthg** em detrimento de alguém/algo.

detrimental [ˌdetrɪ'mentl] *adj* prejudicial.

detritus [dɪ'traɪtəs] *n (U)* detrito *m.*

deuce [djuːs] *n* TENNIS empate *m.*

Deutschmark ['dɔɪtʃˌmɑːk] *n* marco *m* alemão.

devaluation [ˌdiːvæljʊ'eɪʃn] *n* FIN desvalorização *f.*

devalue [ˌdiː'væljuː] *vt* desvalorizar.

devastate ['devəsteɪt] *vt* **-1.** [place] devastar **-2.** *fig* [person] arrasar.

devastated ['devəsteɪtɪd] *adj* **-1.** [place] devastado(-da) **-2.** *fig* [person] arrasado(da).

devastating ['devəsteɪtɪŋ] *adj* **-1.** [disastrous] devastador(ra) **-2.** [very effective, attractive] avassalador(-ra).

devastation [ˌdevəˈsteɪʃn] *n (U)* [destruction] devastação *f.*
develop [dɪˈveləp] ◇ *vt* **-1.** [gen] desenvolver **-2.** [land, area, resources] explorar **-3.** [illness] contrair **-4.** *PHOT* revelar. ◇ *vi* **-1.** [gen] desenvolver **-2.** [problem, illness] aparecer.
developer [dɪˈveləpəʳ] *n* **-1.** [of land] empreendedor *m* imobiliário, empreendedora *f* imobiliária **-2.** [person]: **an early/a late ~** criança *f* com desenvolvimento precoce/tardio **-3.** *PHOT* [chemical] revelador *m.*
developing country [dɪˈveləpɪŋ-] *n* país *m* em desenvolvimento.
development [dɪˈveləpmənt] *n* **-1.** *(U)* [expansion, growth, conception - gen] desenvolvimento *m*; [- of business, company] crescimento *m* **-2.** *(U)* [of land, area] exploração *f* **-3.** [developed land] loteamento *m* **-4.** [further incident] acontecimento *m* **-5.** *(U)* [of illness, fault, habit] desenvolvimento *m* **-6.** *PHOT* revelação *f.*
development area *n UK* zona *f* de desenvolvimento urbano.
deviant [ˈdiːvjənt] ◇ *adj* anormal, pervertido(-da). ◇ *n* pervertido *m*, -da *f.*
deviate [ˈdiːvɪeɪt] *vi*: **to ~ (from sthg)** desviar-se (de algo).
deviation [ˌdiːvɪˈeɪʃn] *n* desvio *m*; **sexual ~** perversão *f* sexual.
device [dɪˈvaɪs] *n* **-1.** [apparatus] dispositivo *m*, aparelho *m* **-2.** [plan, method] artifício *m*; **to leave sb to their own ~s** deixar alguém à própria sorte **-3.** [bomb]: **(incendiary) ~** bomba *f* incendiária.
devil [ˈdevl] *n* **-1.** [evil spirit] demônio *m* **-2.** *inf* [person] diabo *m*, -ba *f*; **poor ~!** pobre diabo! **-3.** [for emphasis]: **who/where/why the ~ ...?** que/onde/por que diabos ...?
◆ **Devil** *n* [Satan]: **the Devil** o Diabo.
devilish [ˈdevlɪʃ] *adj* [fiendish] diabólico(ca).
devil-may-care *adj* inconseqüente, imprudente.
devil's advocate *n* advogado *m* do diabo.
devious [ˈdiːvjəs] *adj* **-1.** [gen] desonesto(ta) **-2.** [route] sinuoso(sa).
deviousness *n (U)* [dishonesty] desonestidade *f.*
devise [dɪˈvaɪz] *vt* conceber.
devoid [dɪˈvɔɪd] *adj fml*: **~ of sthg** desprovido(da) de algo.
devolution [ˌdiːvəˈluːʃn] *n (U) POL* descentralização *f.*
devolve [dɪˈvɒlv] *vi fml*: **to ~ (up)on sb** ser incumbência de alguém.
devote [dɪˈvəʊt] *vt*: **to ~ sthg to sthg** dedicar algo a algo; **to ~ o.s. to sthg** dedicar-se a algo.
devoted [dɪˈvəʊtɪd] *adj* [person] dedicado(da); **~ to sb/sthg** dedicado(da) a alguém/algo.
devotee [ˌdevəˈtiː] *n* **-1.** [disciple] devoto *m*, -ta *f* **-2.** [fan] fã *mf* **-3.** [enthusiast] entusiasta *mf.*
devotion [dɪˈvəʊʃn] *n* **-1.** *(U)* [commitment]: **~ to sb/sthg** dedicação *f* a alguém/algo **-2.** *RELIG* devoção *f.*
devour [dɪˈvaʊəʳ] *vt* **-1.** [eat, read avidly] devorar **-2.** *fig* [subj: fire] consumir.
devout [dɪˈvaʊt] *adj RELIG* devoto(ta).
dew [djuː] *n (U)* orvalho *m.*
dexterity [dekˈsterətɪ] *n (U)* agilidade *f*, destreza *f.*
dexterous [ˈdekstrəs] *adj* ágil.
dextrose [ˈdekstrəʊs] *n (U)* dextrose *f.*
dextrous [ˈdekstrəs] *adj* = **dexterous**.
diabetes [ˌdaɪəˈbiːtiːz] *n (U)* diabete *f.*
diabetic [ˌdaɪəˈbetɪk] ◇ *adj* **-1.** [person] diabético(ca) **-2.** [jam, chocolate] para diabéticos. ◇ *n* diabético *m*, -ca *f.*
diabolic(al) [ˌdaɪəˈbɒlɪk(l)] *adj* **-1.** [evil] diabólico(-ca) **-2.** *inf* [very bad] horroroso(sa).
diaeresis *UK*, **dieresis** *US* (*pl* **-eses**) [daɪˈerɪsɪs] *n* diérese *f.*
diagnose [ˈdaɪəgnəʊz] *vt* diagnosticar.
diagnosis [ˌdaɪəgˈnəʊsɪs] (*pl* **-oses** [-əʊsiːz]) *n* diagnóstico *m.*
diagnostic [ˌdaɪəgˈnɒstɪk] *adj MED* diagnóstico(ca).
diagonal [daɪˈægənl] ◇ *adj* [line] diagonal. ◇ *n* diagonal *f.*
diagonally [daɪˈægənəlɪ] *adv* diagonalmente.
diagram [ˈdaɪəgræm] *n* diagrama *m.*
diagrammatic [ˌdaɪəgrəˈmætɪk] *adj* diagramático(ca).
dial [ˈdaɪəl] (*UK pt* & *pp* **-led**, *cont* **-ling**, *US pt* & *pp* **-ed**, *cont* **-ing**) ◇ *n* **-1.** [of watch, clock, meter] mostrador *m* **-2.** [of radio] dial *m* **-3.** [of telephone] teclado *m.* ◇ *vt* [number] discar.
dialect [ˈdaɪəlekt] *n* dialeto *m.*
dialling code *UK*, **dialing code** *US* [ˈdaɪəlɪŋ-] *n* código *m* de discagem.
dialling tone *UK* [ˈdaɪəlɪŋ-], **dial tone** *US n* linha *f (no telefone).*
dialogue *UK*, **dialog** *US* [ˈdaɪəlɒg] *n* diálogo *m.*
dial tone *n US* = **dialling tone**.
dialysis [daɪˈælɪsɪs] *n (U)* diálise *f.*
diamanté *adj* de vidrilhos.
diameter [daɪˈæmɪtəʳ] *n* diâmetro *m.*
diametrically [ˌdaɪəˈmetrɪklɪ] *adv*: **~ opposed** diametralmente oposto(ta).
diamond [ˈdaɪəmənd] *n* **-1.** [gem] diamante *m* **-2.** [shape] losango *m.*
◆ **diamonds** *npl* [cards] ouros *mpl.*
diamond wedding *n* bodas *fpl* de diamante.
diaper [ˈdaɪpəʳ] *n US* fralda *f.*
diaphanous [daɪˈæfənəs] *adj* transparente.
diaphragm [ˈdaɪəfræm] *n* diafragma *m.*
diarrh(o)ea [ˌdaɪəˈrɪə] *n (U)* diarréia *f.*
diary [ˈdaɪərɪ] (*pl* **-ies**) *n* **-1.** [appointment book] agenda *f* **-2.** [personal record] diário *m.*
diatribe [ˈdaɪətraɪb] *n* crítica *f* violenta.
dice [daɪs] (*pl inv*) ◇ *n* [for games] dado *m*; **no ~** *US inf* de jeito nenhum. ◇ *vt* cortar em cubinhos.
dicey [ˈdaɪsɪ] (*compar* **-ier**, *superl* **-iest**) *adj UK inf* incerto(ta).
dichotomy [daɪˈkɒtəmɪ] (*pl* **-ies**) *n fml* dicotomia *f.*
Dictaphone® [ˈdɪktəfəʊn] *n* dictafone® *m.*
dictate [*vb* dɪkˈteɪt, *n* ˈdɪkteɪt] ◇ *vt* **-1.** [letter] ditar; **to ~ sthg to sb** ditar algo para alguém **-2.** [conditions, terms] ditar, impor. ◇ *vi*: **to ~ to sb** [read aloud] ditar para alguém; [give orders] impor a alguém. ◇ *n* ditado *m.*
dictation [dɪkˈteɪʃn] *n* ditado *m.*

dictator [dɪk'teɪtəʳ] *n POL* ditador *m*, -ra *f*.
dictatorship [dɪk'teɪtəʃɪp] *n* ditadura *f*.
diction ['dɪkʃn] *n (U)* [pronunciation] dicção *f*.
dictionary ['dɪkʃənrɪ] (*pl* **-ies**) *n* dicionário *m*.
did [dɪd] *pt* ▷ **do**.
didactic [dɪ'dæktɪk] *adj* didático(ca).
diddle ['dɪdl] *vt UK inf* passar a perna em.
didn't ['dɪdnt] = **did not**.
die [daɪ] (*pt* & *pp* **died**, *cont* **dying**, *pl sense 2 only* **dice**) ◇ *vi* **-1.** [person, animal, plant] morrer; **to be dying** estar morrendo; **to be dying for sthg/to do sthg** *inf* estar morrendo de vontade de algo/de fazer algo **-2.** *fig* [love, anger, memory] morrer. ◇ *n* **-1.** [for shaping metal] molde *m* **-2.** [dice] dado *m*.
◆ **die away** *vi* [sound, wind] desvanecer-se.
◆ **die down** *vi* **-1.** [fire] arrefecer **-2.** [sound, wind] abrandar.
◆ **die out** *vi* **-1.** [family, custom] desaparecer **-2.** [species] ser extinto(ta).
diehard ['daɪhɑːd] *n* teimoso(sa).
dieresis *n US* = **diaeresis**.
diesel ['diːzl] *n* **-1.** *(U)* [fuel, oil] diesel *m* **-2.** [vehicle] veículo *m* a diesel.
diesel engine *n* motor *m* a diesel.
diesel fuel, diesel oil *n* óleo *m* diesel.
diet ['daɪət] ◇ *n* **-1.** [gen] dieta *f* **-2.** [in order to lose weight] dieta *f*, regime *m*; **to be/go on a ~** estar de/entrar em dieta. ◇ *comp* [low-calorie] de baixa caloria; **a ~ Coke®** uma Coca® light. ◇ *vi* [in order to lose weight] fazer regime.
dietary ['daɪətrɪ] *adj* alimentar.
dietary fibre *n (U)* fibra *f* alimentar.
dieter ['daɪətəʳ] *n* pessoa *f* de regime.
dietician [ˌdaɪə'tɪʃn] *n* nutricionista *mf*.
differ ['dɪfəʳ] *vi* **-1.** [be different] diferir; **to ~ from sb/sthg** diferir/distinguir-se de alguém/algo **-2.** [disagree]: **to ~ with sb (about sthg)** discordar de alguém (sobre algo); **to agree to ~** parar de discutir.
difference ['dɪfrəns] *n* diferença *f*; **it doesn't make any ~** não faz a menor diferença; **to make all the ~** fazer toda a diferença.
different ['dɪfrənt] *adj* diferente; **~ from** diferente de.
differential [ˌdɪfə'renʃl] ◇ *adj* diferencial. ◇ *n* diferencial *m*.
differentiate [ˌdɪfə'renʃɪeɪt] ◇ *vt*: **to ~ sthg from sthg** diferenciar algo de algo. ◇ *vi*: **to ~ (between)** diferenciar (entre).
differently ['dɪfrəntlɪ] *adv* diferentemente.
difficult ['dɪfɪkəlt] *adj* difícil.
difficulty ['dɪfɪkəltɪ] (*pl* **-ies**) *n* dificuldade *f*; **to have ~ in doing sthg** ter dificuldade em fazer algo; **with ~** com dificuldade.
diffidence ['dɪfɪdəns] *n (U)* acanhamento *m*.
diffident ['dɪfɪdənt] *adj* acanhado(da).
diffuse [*adj* dɪ'fjuːs, *vb* dɪ'fjuːz] ◇ *adj* difuso(sa). ◇ *vt* **-1.** [light] difundir **-2.** [information] divulgar. ◇ *vi* difundir-se.
diffusion [dɪ'fjuːʒn] *n (U)* **-1.** [of light] difusão *f* **-2.** [of information] divulgação *f*.
dig [dɪg] (*pt* & *pp* **dug**, *cont* **digging**) ◇ *n* **-1.** *fig* [unkind remark] zombaria *f* **-2.** *ARCHAEOL* escavação *f*. ◇ *vt* **-1.** [in ground] cavar **-2.** [press, jab]: **to ~ sthg into sb/sthg** fincar algo em alguém/algo; **to ~ sb in the ribs** cutucar alguém. ◇ *vi* **-1.** [in ground] enterrar-se **-2.** [press, jab]: **to ~ into sthg** cravar-se em algo; **my strap's ~ging into me** a alça do vestido está me apertando.
◆ **dig out** *vt sep* **-1.** [car, accident victims] resgatar **-2.** *inf* [letter, document] desencavar.
◆ **dig up** *vt sep* **-1.** [from ground] desenterrar **-2.** *inf* [information] desencavar.
digest [*n* 'daɪdʒest, *vb* dɪ'dʒest] ◇ *n* [book] resenha *f*. ◇ *vt* [food, information] digerir.
digestible [dɪ'dʒestəbl] *adj* digerível.
digestion [dɪ'dʒestʃn] *n* digestão *f*.
digestive [dɪ'dʒestɪv] *adj* digestivo(va).
digestive biscuit [dɪ'dʒestɪv-] *n UK biscoito liso levemente adocicado muito comum na Grã-Bretanha*.
digestive system *n* sistema *m* digestivo.
digger *n* [machine] escavadeira *f*.
digit ['dɪdʒɪt] *n* **-1.** [figure] dígito *m* **-2.** [finger, toe] dedo *m*.
digital ['dɪdʒɪtl] *adj* [watch, readout] digital.
digital camera *n* câmera *f* digital.
digital recording *n* gravação *f* digital.
digital television, digital TV *n* televisão *f* digital.
digital watch *n* relógio *m* digital.
digitize, -ise ['dɪdʒɪtaɪz] *vt* digitalizar.
dignified ['dɪgnɪfaɪd] *adj* digno(na).
dignify ['dɪgnɪfaɪ] (*pt* & *pp* **-ied**) *vt* honrar.
dignitary ['dɪgnɪtrɪ] (*pl* **-ies**) *n* dignitário *m*, -ria *f*.
dignity ['dɪgnətɪ] *n* dignidade *f*.
digress [daɪ'gres] *vi* fugir do assunto, divagar; **to ~ (from sthg)** desviar-se (de algo).
digression [daɪ'greʃn] *n* digressão *f*.
digs [dɪgz] *npl UK inf* quarto *m* alugado.
dike [daɪk] *n* **-1.** [wall, bank] dique *m* **-2.** *inf pej* [lesbian] sapatão *m*.
diktat *n* [pol] imposição *f*.
dilapidated [dɪ'læpɪdeɪtɪd] *adj* em ruínas.
dilate [daɪ'leɪt] ◇ *vt* dilatar. ◇ *vi* dilatar-se.
dilated [daɪ'leɪtɪd] *adj* dilatado(da).
dilemma [dɪ'lemə] *n* dilema *m*.
dilettante [ˌdɪlɪ'tæntɪ] (*pl* **-tes** *OR* **-ti** [-tɪ]) *n pej* amador *m*, -ra *f*.
diligence ['dɪlɪdʒəns] *n (U)* [hard work] diligência *f*.
diligent ['dɪlɪdʒənt] *adj* diligente, aplicado(da).
dill [dɪl] *n (U)* aneto *m*.
dillydally ['dɪlɪdælɪ] (*pt* & *pp* **-ied**) *vi inf dated* embromar-se.
dilute [daɪ'luːt] ◇ *adj* diluído(da). ◇ *vt*: **to ~ sthg (with sthg)** diluir algo(com algo).
dilution [daɪ'luːʃn] *n*: **~ (with sthg)** diluição *f* (com algo).
dim [dɪm] (*compar* **-mer**, *superl* **-mest**, *pt* & *pp* **-med**, *cont* **-ming**) ◇ *adj* **-1.** [dark] sombrio(bria) **-2.** [indistinct - shape] indistinto(ta); [- sight, sound] fraco(ca); [- memory] vago(ga) **-3.** [weak] fraco(ca) **-4.** [gloomy]: **to take a ~ view of sthg** não levar fé em algo **-5.** *inf* [stupid] idiota. ◇ *vt* [light] diminuir. ◇ *vi* [beauty, hope, memory] extinguir-se.
dime [daɪm] *n US moeda de 10 centavos de dólar*;

cars are a ~ a dozen in the world today [common] hoje tem carros a dar com pau no mundo.
dimension [dɪ'menʃn] *n* dimensão *f.*
◆ **dimensions** *pl* [of room, object] dimensões *fpl.*
-dimensional [dɪ'menʃənl] *suffix* dimensional.
diminish [dɪ'mɪnɪʃ] ◇ *vt* [make less important] diminuir. ◇ *vi* diminuir.
diminished [dɪ'mɪnɪʃt] *adj* **-1.** [profits, budget] reduzido(da) **-2.** [reputation] em baixa **-3.** [person] menosprezado(da).
diminished responsibility *n (U) JUR* responsabilidade *f* diminuída.
diminishing returns [dɪ'mɪnɪʃɪŋ] *npl* rendimentos *mpl* decrescentes.
diminutive [dɪ'mɪnjʊtɪv] ◇ *adj fml* [tiny] diminuto(ta). ◇ *n GRAMM* diminutivo *m.*
dimly ['dɪmlɪ] *adv* **-1.** [shine] fracamente **-2.** [see, remember] vagamente.
dimmer ['dɪmə^r] *n* [switch] dimmer *m.*
◆ **dimmers** *npl US* **-1.** [dipped headlights] faróis *mpl* baixos **-2.** [parking lights] pisca-alerta *m.*
dimmer switch *n* = **dimmer**.
dimple ['dɪmpl] *n* covinha *f (no rosto).*
dimwit ['dɪmwɪt] *n inf* estúpido *m*, -da *f*, anta *mf.*
dim-witted [-'wɪtɪd] *adj inf* estúpido(da).
din [dɪn] *n inf* zoeira *f.*
dine [daɪn] *vi fml* jantar.
◆ **dine out** *vi* jantar fora.
diner ['daɪnə^r] *n* **-1.** [person] cliente *mf (de restaurante)* **-2.** *US* [restaurant] lanchonete *f (em beira de estrada).*
dingdong [ˌdɪŋ'dɒŋ] ◇ *adj inf* [battle, argument] tumultuado(da). ◇ *n* [of bell] badalada *f.*
dinghy ['dɪŋgɪ] (*pl* **-ies**) *n* [for sailing] barco *m* a vela *(pequeno)*; [for rowing] bote *m* a remo.
dingo ['dɪŋgəʊ] (*pl* **-es**) *n* dingo *m.*
dingy ['dɪndʒɪ] (*compar* **-ier**, *superl* **-iest**) *adj* [dirty, drab] sujo(ja).
dining car ['daɪnɪŋ-] *n* vagão-restaurante *m.*
dining room ['daɪnɪŋ-] *n* sala *f* de jantar.
dining table ['dəɪnɪŋ-] *n* mesa *f* de jantar.
dinner ['dɪnə^r] *n* **-1.** [meal - in evening] jantar *m*; [- at midday] almoço *m* **-2.** [formal event] jantar *m.*
dinner dance *n* jantar *m* dançante.
dinner jacket *n UK* smoking *m.*
dinner party *n* jantar *m (para poucas pessoas).*
dinner service *n* aparelho *m* de jantar.
dinner table *n*: the ~ a mesa de jantar.
dinnertime ['dɪnətaɪm] *n* hora *f* do jantar.
dinosaur ['daɪnəsɔː^r] *n* [reptile] dinossauro *m.*
dint [dɪnt] *n fml*: **by ~ of** por meio de.
diocese ['daɪəsɪs] *n* diocese *f.*
diode ['daɪəʊd] *n* diodo *m.*
dip [dɪp] (*pt* & *pp* **-ped**, *cont* **-ping**) ◇ *n* **-1.** [in road, ground] depressão *f* **-2.** [sauce] molho *m* cremoso **-3.** [swim]: **to go for a ~** dar um mergulho. ◇ *vt* **-1.** [into liquid]: **to ~ sthg in (to) sthg** mergulhar algo em algo **-2.** *UK* [headlights] baixar. ◇ *vi* **-1.** [sun, wing] baixar **-2.** [road, ground] descer **-3.** [temperature, price] cair.
Dip. *UK abbr of* **diploma**.
Dip. Ed. (*abbr of* **Diploma in Education**) *(titular de) diploma em educação na Grã-Bretanha.*
diphtheria [dɪf'θɪərɪəl *n (U)* difteria *f.*
diphthong ['dɪfθɒŋ] *n LING* ditongo *m.*
diploma [dɪ'pləʊmə] (*pl* **-s**) *n* diploma *m.*
diplomacy [dɪ'pləʊməsɪ] *n* diplomacia *f.*
diplomat ['dɪpləmæt] *n* diplomata *mf.*
diplomatic [ˌdɪplə'mætɪk] *adj* diplomático(ca).
diplomatic bag *n* mala *f* diplomática.
diplomatic corps *n* corpo *m* diplomático.
diplomatic immunity *n* imunidade *f* diplomática.
diplomatic relations *npl* relações *fpl* diplomáticas.
dipsomaniac [ˌdɪpsə'meɪnɪæk] *n* dipsomaníaco *m*, -ca *f.*
dipstick ['dɪpstɪk] *n AUT* vareta *f* do nível do óleo.
dipswitch ['dɪpswɪtʃ] *n UK AUT* chave *f* de luz alta e baixa.
dire ['daɪə^r] *adj* [serious] terrível.
direct [dɪ'rekt] ◇ *adj* **-1.** [gen] direto(ta) **-2.** [insurance] sem intermediários. ◇ *vt* **-1.** [aim]: **to ~ sthg at sb** dirigir algo a alguém **-2.** [person to place] guiar **-3.** [group, project, film, play] dirigir **-4.** [order]: **to ~ sb to do sthg** mandar alguém fazer algo. ◇ *adv* direto.
direct action *n* ação *f* direta.
direct current *n* corrente *f* contínua.
direct debit *n UK* débito *m* automático *(em conta corrente).*
direct dialling [-'daɪəlɪŋ] *n* discagem *f* direta.
direct hit *n*: **to score a ~ on the target** acertar em cheio no alvo.
direction [dɪ'rekʃn] *n* **-1.** [spatial] direção *f* **-2.** *fig* [orientation] rumo *m* **-3.** [of group, project, play, film] direção *f*; **under the ~ of** sob a direção de.
◆ **directions** *npl* **-1.** [instructions to place] indicações *fpl* **-2.** [instructions for use] instruções *fpl.*
directive [dɪ'rektɪv] *n* diretriz *f.*
directly [dɪ'rektlɪ] *adv* **-1.** [in straight line] diretamente, direto **-2.** [frankly, openly] diretamente **-3.** [exactly] logo, bem **-4.** [very soon] imediatamente.
direct mail *n* mala-direta *f.*
director [dɪ'rektə^r] *n* diretor *m*, -ra *f.*
directorate [dɪ'rektərət] *n* [board of directors] diretoria *f.*
director-general (*pl* **directors-general** *OR* **director-generals**) *n* diretor-geral *m*, diretora-geral *f.*
Director of Public Prosecutions *n UK* ≃ Procurador *m*, -ra *f* da República.
directorship [dɪ'rektəʃɪp] *n* **-1.** [position] cargo *m* de diretor, -ra *f* **-2.** [period] diretorado *m.*
directory [dɪ'rektərɪ] (*pl* **-ies**) *n* **-1.** [book, list] lista *f* **-2.** *COMPUT* diretório *m.*
directory enquiries *n UK* (serviço *m* de) auxílio *m* à lista.
direct rule *n* governo *m* central.
direct selling *n* vendas *f* diretas.
direct speech *n* discurso *m* direto.
direct taxation *n* imposto *m* direto.
dire straits *npl*: **in ~** em apuros.
dirge [dɜːdʒ] *n* música *m* fúnebre.
dirt [dɜːt] *n* **-1.** [mud, dust] sujeira *f* **-2.** [earth] terra *f.*

dirt cheap *inf* ◇ *adj* bem barato(ta). ◇ *adv* bem barato; **this was ~** isso foi uma ninharia.
dirt track *n* estrada *f* de terra.
dirty ['dɜ:tɪ] (*compar* **-ier**, *superl* **-iest**, *pt* & *pp* **-ied**) ◇ *adj* **-1.** [not clean] sujo(ja) **-2.** [unfair] baixo(xa); **~ trick** golpe *m* baixo **-3.** [smutty] obsceno(na); **~ joke** piada *f* suja. ◇ *vt* sujar.
disability [ˌdɪsə'bɪlətɪ] (*pl* **-ies**) *n* deficiência *f*.
disable [dɪs'eɪbl] *vt* [injure] incapacitar.
disabled [dɪs'eɪbld] ◇ *adj* [person] incapacitado(-da). ◇ *npl*: **the ~** os deficientes.
disablement [dɪs'eɪblmənt] *n* [of person] incapacidade *f*, deficiência *f*.
disabuse [ˌdɪsə'bju:z] *vt fml*: **to ~ sb (of sthg)** desiludir alguém (sobre algo).
disadvantage [ˌdɪsəd'vɑ:ntɪdʒ] *n* desvantagem *f*; **to be at a ~** estar em desvantagem; **to be to one's ~** pesar contra alguém.
disadvantaged [ˌdɪsəd'vɑ:ntɪdʒd] *adj* desfavorecido(da).
disadvantageous [ˌdɪsædvɑ:n'teɪdʒəs] *adj* desvantajoso(sa).
disaffected [ˌdɪsə'fektɪd] *adj* insatisfeito(ta).
disaffection [ˌdɪsə'fekʃn] *n (U)* insatisfação *f*.
disagree [ˌdɪsə'gri:] *vi* **-1.** [have different opinions] discordar, não estar de acordo; **to ~ with sb** discordar de alguém; **to ~ with sthg** discordar de algo **-2.** [differ] divergir **-3.** [subj: food, drink]: **to ~ with sb** fazer mal a alguém.
disagreeable [ˌdɪsə'gri:əbl] *adj* desagradável.
disagreement [ˌdɪsə'gri:mənt] *n* **-1.** [of opinions, records] divergência *f* **-2.** [argument] discussão *f*.
disallow [ˌdɪsə'laʊ] *vt* **-1.** *fml* [appeal, claim] rejeitar **-2.** [goal] anular.
disappear [ˌdɪsə'pɪə^r] *vi* desaparecer.
disappearance [ˌdɪsə'pɪərəns] *n* **-1.** [of person, object] desaparecimento *m* **-2.** [of species, civilization] extinção *f*.
disappoint [ˌdɪsə'pɔɪnt] *vt* [fail to satisfy] desapontar, decepcionar.
disappointed [ˌdɪsə'pɔɪntɪd] *adj* desapontado(da), decepcionado(da); **~ in** *OR* **with sthg** decepcionado(da) com algo.
disappointing [ˌdɪsə'pɔɪntɪŋ] *adj* desapontador(-ra), decepcionante.
disappointment [ˌdɪsə'pɔɪntmənt] *n* **-1.** *(U)* [feeling] desapontamento *m* **-2.** [letdown] decepção *f*.
disapproval [ˌdɪsə'pru:vl] *n (U)* desaprovação *f*.
disapprove [ˌdɪsə'pru:v] *vi*: **to ~ (of sb/sthg)** desaprovar (algo/alguém).
disapproving [ˌdɪsə'pru:vɪŋ] *adj* desaprovador(-ra).
disarm [dɪs'ɑ:m] *vt* & *vi* desarmar.
disarmament [dɪs'ɑ:məmənt] *n (U)* desarmamento *m*.
disarming [dɪs'ɑ:mɪŋ] *adj* [smile, person] que desarma, irresistível.
disarray [ˌdɪsə'reɪ] *n (U)*: **in ~** *fml* [clothes, hair] em desalinho; [room] em desordem; *POL* em desacordo.
disassociate [ˌdɪsə'səʊʃɪeɪt] *vt*: **to ~ o.s. from sb/sthg** desligar-se de alguém/algo.
disaster [dɪ'zɑ:stə^r] *n* **-1.** [gen] desastre *m*; **natural ~** desastre *m* natural **-2.** *(U)* [misfortune] azar *m*; **to court ~** procurar encrenca.
disaster area *n* [after natural disaster] área *f* de calamidade pública.
disastrous [dɪ'zɑ:strəs] *adj* [catastrophic] desastroso(sa).
disastrously [dɪ'zɑ:strəslɪ] *adv* [catastrophically] desastrosamente.
disband [dɪs'bænd] ◇ *vt* dispersar. ◇ *vi* dispersar-se.
disbelief [ˌdɪsbɪ'li:f] *n (U)*: **in** *OR* **with ~** com descrença.
disbelieve [ˌdɪsbɪ'li:v] *vt* [person, words] não acreditar em.
disc *UK*, **disk** *US* [dɪsk] *n* disco *m*.
discard [dɪ'skɑ:d] *vt* desfazer-se de, pôr fora.
discarded [dɪ'skɑ:dɪd] *adj* posto(ta) fora.
disc brake *n* freio *m* a disco.
discern [dɪ'sɜ:n] *vt* **-1.** [see] discernir **-2.** [detect] perceber.
discernible [dɪ'sɜ:nəbl] *adj* **-1.** [visible] discernível **-2.** [detectable] perceptível.
discerning [dɪ'sɜ:nɪŋ] *adj* perspicaz.
discharge [*n* 'dɪstʃɑ:dʒ, *vb* dɪs'tʃɑ:dʒ] ◇ *n* **-1.** [of patient] alta *f*; [of prisoner, defendant] libertação *f*; [from armed forces] dispensa *f* **-2.** *fml* [fulfilment] cumprimento *m* **-3.** [toxic emission] descarga *f* **-4.** *MED* [from nose, wound] secreção *f* **-5.** [payment] quitação *f*. ◇ *vt* **-1.** [allow to leave - patient] dar alta para; [- prisoner, defendant] libertar; [- from armed forces] dispensar **-2.** *fml* [fulfil] cumprir **-3.** [emit] emitir **-4.** [pay] quitar.
discharged bankrupt [dɪs'tʃɑ:dʒd-] *n pessoa falida que cumpriu as disposições legais e pode retornar aos negócios.*
disciple [dɪ'saɪpl] *n* **-1.** *RELIG* apóstolo *m* **-2.** *fig* [follower] discípulo *m*, -la *f*.
disciplinarian [ˌdɪsɪplɪ'neərɪən] *n* disciplinador *m*, -ra *f*.
disciplinary ['dɪsɪplɪnərɪ] *adj* disciplinar; **to take ~ action against sb** tomar ações disciplinares contra alguém.
discipline ['dɪsɪplɪn] ◇ *n* disciplina *f*. ◇ *vt* **-1.** [train] disciplinar **-2.** [punish] punir.
disciplined ['dɪsɪplɪnd] *adj* [controlled] disciplinado(da).
disc jockey *n* disc-jóquei *mf*.
disclaim [dɪs'kleɪm] *vt fml* negar.
disclaimer [dɪs'kleɪmə^r] *n* negação *f*.
disclose [dɪs'kləʊz] *vt* divulgar.
disclosure [dɪs'kləʊʒə^r] *n* **-1.** *(U)* [act of disclosing] divulgação *f* **-2.** [revealed fact] revelação *f*.
disco ['dɪskəʊ] (*pl* **-s**) (*abbr of* **discotheque**) *n* casa *f* noturna.
discoloration [dɪsˌkʌlə'reɪʃn] *n* [fading, staining] descoloração *f*.
discolour *UK*, **discolor** *US* [dɪs'kʌlə^r] *vt* & *vi* descolorir.
discoloured *UK*, **discolored** *US* [dɪs'kʌləd] *adj* descolorido(da).
discomfort [dɪs'kʌmfət] *n* **-1.** [gen] desconforto *m* **-2.** *(U)* [physical pain] mal-estar *m*.
disconcert [ˌdɪskən'sɜ:t] *vt* desconcertar.

disconcerting [ˌdɪskən'sɜːtɪŋ] *adj* desconcertante.
disconnect [ˌdɪskə'nekt] *vt* **-1.** [detach] desconectar **-2.** [from gas, electricity - appliance] desconectar, desligar; [- house, building] cortar **-3.** [on phone] cortar.
disconnected [ˌdɪskə'nektɪd] *adj* **-1.** [remarks, thoughts, events] desconexo(xa) **-2.** [telephone, wire] desconectado(da).
disconsolate [dɪs'kɒnsələt] *adj* inconsolável.
discontent [ˌdɪskən'tent] *n (U)*: **~ (with sthg)** descontentamento *m* (com algo).
discontented [ˌdɪskən'tentɪd] *adj*: **~ (with sthg)** descontente (com algo).
discontentment [ˌdɪskən'tentmənt] *n (U)*: **~ (with sthg)** descontentamento *m* (com algo).
discontinue [ˌdɪskən'tɪnjuː] *vt* suspender.
discontinued line [ˌdɪskən'tɪnjuːd-] *n* COMM (produto *m*) fora *f* de linha.
discord ['dɪskɔːd] *n* **-1.** *(U) fml* [conflict] discórdia *f* **-2.** MUS dissonância *f*.
discordant [dɪ'skɔːdənt] *adj* **-1.** [conflicting] discordante **-2.** MUS dissonante.
discotheque ['dɪskəʊtek] *n* discoteca *f*.
discount [*n* 'dɪskaʊnt, *vb* **UK** dɪs'kaʊnt, **US** 'dɪskaʊnt] <> *n* [price reduction] desconto *m*. <> *vt* **-1.** [disregard] desconsiderar **-2.** COMM [offer at lower price] dar desconto em; [price] abater.
discount house *n* **-1.** FIN casa *f* de câmbio **-2.** COMM [store] loja *f* que vende com descontos.
discount rate *n* taxa *f* de desconto.
discount store *n* COMM loja *f* que vende com descontos.
discourage [dɪ'skʌrɪdʒ] *vt* **-1.** [dishearten] desencorajar **-2.** [dissuade] dissuadir; **to ~ sb from doing sthg** desestimular alguém de fazer algo.
discouraging [dɪ'skʌrɪdʒɪŋ] *adj* desencorajador(-ra).
discourse ['dɪskɔːs] *n*: **~ (on sthg)** discurso *m* (sobre algo).
discourteous [dɪs'kɜːtjəs] *adj fml* descortês.
discourtesy [dɪs'kɜːtɪsɪ] *n (U)* descortesia *f*.
discover [dɪ'skʌvə^r] *vt* **-1.** [gen] descobrir **-2.** [realize] perceber, dar-se conta de.
discoverer [dɪ'skʌvərə^r] *n* descobridor *m*, -ra *f*.
discovery [dɪ'skʌvərɪ] (*pl* **-ies**) *n* **-1.** [gen] descoberta *f*; **the ~ of America** o descobrimento da América **-2.** [realization] compreensão *f*.
discredit [dɪs'kredɪt] <> *n (U)* [shame] descrédito *m*. <> *vt* **-1.** [person] desonrar **-2.** [idea, belief, theory] desacreditar.
discredited [dɪskredɪtɪd] *adj* desacreditado(da).
discreet [dɪ'skriːt] *adj* discreto(ta).
discreetly [dɪ'skriːtlɪ] *adv* discretamente.
discrepancy [dɪ'skrepənsɪ] (*pl* **-ies**) *n*: **~ (in/between)** discrepância *f* (em/entre).
discrete [dɪs'kriːt] *adj fml* distinto(ta).
discretion [dɪ'skreʃn] *n* **-1.** [tact] discrição *f* **-2.** [judgment] ponderação *f*; **at the ~ of** a critério de.
discretionary [dɪ'skreʃənərɪ] *adj* discricionário(-ria).
discriminate [dɪ'skrɪmɪneɪt] *vi* **-1.** [distinguish] discriminar; **to ~ between** fazer distinção entre **-2.** [treat unfairly]: **to ~ against sb** discriminar alguém.
discriminating [dɪ'skrɪmɪneɪtɪŋ] *adj* [discerning] criterioso(sa).
discrimination [dɪˌskrɪmɪ'neɪʃn] *n (U)* **-1.** [prejudice] discriminação *f* **-2.** [good judgment] discernimento *m*.
discus ['dɪskəs] (*pl* **-es**) *n* [sport] disco *m*.
discuss [dɪ'skʌs] *vt* discutir; **to ~ sthg with sb** discutir algo com alguém.
discussion [dɪ'skʌʃn] *n* **-1.** *(U)* [act of discussing] discussão *f*; **under ~** em discussão **-2.** [talk] debate *f*.
disdain [dɪs'deɪn] *fml* <> *n (U)* desdém *m*; **~ for sb/sthg** desprezo *m* por alguém/algo. <> *vt* desdenhar. <> *vi*: **to ~ to do sthg** não se dar ao trabalho de fazer algo.
disdainful [dɪs'deɪnfʊl] *adj* desdenhoso(sa).
disease [dɪ'ziːz] *n* doença *f*.
diseased [dɪ'ziːzd] *adj* doente.
disembark [ˌdɪsɪm'bɑːk] *vi* desembarcar.
disembarkation [ˌdɪsembɑː'keɪʃn] *n (U)* desembarque *m*.
disembodied [ˌdɪsɪm'bɒdɪd] *adj* **-1.** [spirit] desencarnado(da) **-2.** [voice] desincorporado(da).
disembowel [ˌdɪsɪm'baʊəl] (**UK** *pt* & *pp* **-led**, *cont* **-ling**, **US** *pt* & *pp* **-ed**, *cont* **-ing**) *vt* estripar.
disenchanted [ˌdɪsɪn'tʃɑːntɪd] *adj*: **~ (with sthg)** desencantado(da) (com algo).
disenchantment [ˌdɪsɪn'tʃɑːntmənt] *n (U)* desencantamento *m*.
disenfranchise [ˌdɪsɪn'fræntʃaɪz] *vt* = **disfranchise**.
disengage [ˌdɪsɪn'geɪdʒ] *vt* **-1.** [release]: **to ~ sthg (from sthg)** desprender algo (de algo); **to ~ o.s. (from sthg)** soltar-se (de algo) **-2.** TECH [gears, mechanism] desengatar.
disengagement *n* desligamento *m*.
disentangle [ˌdɪsɪn'tæŋgl] *vt*: **to ~ sthg from sthg** desemaranhar algo de algo; **to ~ o.s. from sthg** desenredar-se de algo.
disfavour **UK**, **disfavor** **US** [dɪs'feɪvə^r] *n*: **to look on sthg with ~** olhar para algo com desaprovação; **to fall into ~ with sb** cair em desgraça com alguém.
disfigure [dɪs'fɪgə^r] *vt* desfigurar.
disfranchise [ˌdɪs'fræntʃaɪz] *vt* caçar o direito de voto de.
disgorge [dɪs'gɔːdʒ] *vt* despejar.
disgrace [dɪs'greɪs] <> *n* **-1.** *(U)* [shame] desgraça *f*; **in ~** com vergonha **-2.** [cause for shame - thing] desgraça *f*; [- person] vergonha *f*. <> *vt* envergonhar; **to ~ o.s.** envergonhar-se.
disgraceful [dɪs'greɪsfʊl] *adj* vergonhoso(sa).
disgruntled [dɪs'grʌntld] *adj* decepcionado(da).
disguise [dɪs'gaɪz] <> *n* disfarce *m*; **in ~** disfarçado(da). <> *vt* disfarçar; **to ~ o.s. as sb/sthg** disfarçar-se de alguém/algo.
disgust [dɪs'gʌst] <> *n* nojo *m*; **~ at sthg** nojo de algo; **in ~** com nojo. <> *vt* enojar.
disgusting [dɪs'gʌstɪŋ] *adj* [very unpleasant] nojento(-ta).
dish [dɪʃ] *n* [container, food] prato *m*.
◆ **dishes** *npl* louça *f*; **to do** OR **wash the ~es** lavar a louça.

◆ **dish out** *vt sep inf* distribuir.
◆ **dish up** *vt sep inf* pôr na mesa.
dish aerial *UK*, **dish antenna** *US n* antena *f* parabólica.
disharmony [ˌdɪsˈhɑːmənɪ] *n (U)* desarmonia *f*.
dishcloth [ˈdɪʃklɒθ] *n* pano *m* de prato.
disheartened [dɪsˈhɑːtnd] *adj* desanimado(da).
disheartening [dɪsˈhɑːtnɪŋ] *adj* desanimador(ra).
dishevelled *UK*, **disheveled** *US* [dɪˈʃevəld] *adj* desalinhado(da).
dishonest [dɪsˈɒnɪst] *adj* desonesto(ta).
dishonesty [dɪsˈɒnɪstɪ] *n (U)* desonestidade *f*.
dishonor *n & vt US* = **dishonour**.
dishonorable *adj US* = **dishonourable**.
dishonour *UK*, **dishonor** *US* [dɪsˈɒnəʳ] *fml* <> *n* desonra *f*. <> *vt* desonrar.
dishonourable *UK*, **dishonorable** *US* [dɪsˈɒnərəbl] *adj* desonroso(sa).
dish soap *n US* detergente *m (para lavar louça)*.
dish towel *n US* pano *m* de prato.
dishwasher [ˈdɪʃˌwɒʃəʳ] *n* [machine] lava-louças *fpl inv*.
dishy [ˈdɪʃɪ] (*compar* **-ier**, *superl* **-iest**) *adj UK inf* [attractive] gato *m*, -ta *f*.
disillusioned [ˌdɪsɪˈluːʒnd] *adj* desiludido(da); ~ **with sb/sthg** desiludido(da) com alguém/algo.
disillusionment [ˌdɪsɪˈluːʒnmənt] *n (U)*: ~ **(with sb/sthg)** desilusão *f* (com alguém/algo).
disincentive [ˌdɪsɪnˈsentɪv] *n* desestímulo *m*.
disinclined [ˌdɪsɪnˈklaɪnd] *adj*: **to be ~ to do sthg** estar pouco disposto(ta) a fazer algo.
disinfect [ˌdɪsɪnˈfekt] *vt* desinfetar.
disinfectant [ˌdɪsɪnˈfektənt] *n* desinfetante *m*.
disinformation [ˌdɪsɪnfəˈmeɪʃn] *n (U)* desinformação *f*.
disingenuous [ˌdɪsɪnˈdʒenjʊəs] *adj* dissimulado(-da).
disinherit [ˌdɪsɪnˈherɪt] *vt* deserdar.
disintegrate [dɪsˈɪntɪgreɪt] *vi* **-1.** [object] desintegrar-se **-2.** *fig* [project, marriage] desmoronar.
disintegration [dɪsˌɪntɪˈgreɪʃn] *n (U)* **-1.** [of object] desintegração *f* **-2.** *fig* [of project, marriage] desmoronamento *m*.
disinterested [ˌdɪsˈɪntrəstɪd] *adj* **-1.** [objective] neutro(tra) **-2.** [uninterested]: ~ **(in sb/sthg)** desinteressado(da) (em alguém/algo).
disinvestment [ˌdɪsɪnˈvestmənt] *n (U)* desinvestimento *m*.
disjointed [dɪsˈdʒɔɪntɪd] *adj* desconjuntado(da).
disk [dɪsk] *n COMPUT*: **floppy ~** disquete *m*; **hard ~** disco *m* rígido.
disk drive *UK*, **diskette drive** *US n COMPUT* drive *m*, unidade *f* de disco.
diskette [dɪskˈet] *n COMPUT* disquete *m*.
diskette drive *n US* = **disk drive**.
disk operating system [-ɒpəreɪtɪŋ-] *n COMPUT* sistema *m* operacional de disco.
dislike [dɪsˈlaɪk] <> *n* **-1.** *(U)* [feeling] aversão *f*; ~ **of sb/sthg** aversão a alguém/algo; **to take a ~ to sb** não simpatizar com alguém; **to take a ~ to sthg** ter aversão a algo **-2.** [thing not liked] desgosto *m*. <> *vt* não gostar de.
dislocate [ˈdɪsləkeɪt] *vt* **-1.** *MED* deslocar **-2.** [disrupt] desorganizar.
dislodge [dɪsˈlɒdʒ] *vt* [remove - person]: **to ~ sb (from)** desalojar alguém (de); [- thing]: **to ~ sthg (from)** remover algo (de).
disloyal [ˌdɪsˈlɔɪəl] *adj*: ~ **(to sb)** desleal (a alguém).
dismal [ˈdɪzml] *adj* **-1.** [gloomy, depressing] sombrio(-bria), deprimente **-2.** [unsuccessful] frustrante.
dismantle [dɪsˈmæntl] *vt* [machine, structure] desmantelar.
dismay [dɪsˈmeɪ] <> *n (U)* consternação *f*; **to sb's ~** para desespero de alguém. <> *vt* consternar.
dismember [dɪsˈmembəʳ] *vt* desmembrar.
dismiss [dɪsˈmɪs] *vt* **-1.** [from job]: **to ~ sb (from sthg)** despedir alguém (de algo) **-2.** [refuse to take seriously] descartar **-3.** [allow to leave] dispensar **-4.** [*JUR* - case] encerrar; [- jury] dispensar.
dismissal [dɪsˈmɪsl] *n* **-1.** [from job] demissão *f* **-2.** [refusal to take seriously] descartamento *m* **-3.** [*JUR* - of case] encerramento *m*; [- of jury] dispensa *f*.
dismissive [dɪsˈmɪsɪv] *adj* [attitude, tone] de menosprezo; **to be ~ of sb/sthg** menosprezar algo/alguém.
dismount [ˌdɪsˈmaʊnt] *vi*: **to ~ (from sthg)** descer (de algo).
disobedience [ˌdɪsəˈbiːdjəns] *n* desobediência *f*.
disobedient [ˌdɪsəˈbiːdjənt] *adj* desobediente.
disobey [ˌdɪsəˈbeɪ] <> *vt* [person, rule] desobedecer a. <> *vi* desobedecer.
disorder [dɪsˈɔːdəʳ] *n* **-1.** [disarray]: **in ~** em desordem **-2.** [rioting] tumulto *m* **-3.** *MED* distúrbio *m*.
disordered [dɪsˈɔːdəd] *adj* **-1.** [in disarray] desordenado(da) **-2.** *MED*: **mentally ~** mentalmente perturbado(da).
disorderly [dɪsˈɔːdəlɪ] *adj* **-1.** [untidy] desordenado(da) **-2.** [unruly] indisciplinado(da).
disorderly conduct *n JUR* perturbação *f* da ordem.
disorganized, -ised [dɪsˈɔːgənaɪzd] *adj* desorganizado(da).
disorientated *UK* [dɪsˈɔːrɪənteɪtɪd], **disoriented** *US* [dɪsˈɔːrɪəntɪd] *adj* desorientado(da).
disown [dɪsˈəʊn] *vt* renegar.
disparage [dɪˈspærɪdʒ] *vt* depreciar.
disparaging [dɪˈspærɪdʒɪŋ] *adj* depreciativo(va).
disparate [ˈdɪspərət] *adj fml* diverso(sa).
disparity [dɪˈspærətɪ] (*pl* **-ies**) *n*: ~ **(between/in)** disparidade *f* (entre/em).
dispassionate [dɪˈspæʃnət] *adj* imparcial.
dispatch [dɪˈspætʃ] <> *n* [message] envio *m*. <> *vt* [send] enviar, despachar.
dispatch box *n UK POL* **-1.** [box] *caixa na qual se transporta documentos oficiais* **-2.** [in House of Commons]: **the ~** *local onde os parlamentares mais importantes fazem seus discursos*.
dispatch rider *n* emissário *m*, -ria *f*.
dispel [dɪˈspel] (*pt & pp* **-led**, *cont* **-ling**) *vt* [feeling] dissipar.
dispensable [dɪˈspensəbl] *adj* dispensável.
dispensary [dɪˈspensərɪ] (*pl* **-ies**) *n* dispensário *m*.
dispensation [ˌdɪspenˈseɪʃn] *n* [permission] dispensa *f*.

dispense [dɪ'spens] *vt* **-1.** [justice] administrar **-2.** [advice] oferecer **-3.** [drugs, medicine] preparar.
◆ **dispense with** *vt fus* dispensar.

dispenser [dɪ'spensəʳ] *n* [machine, container] máquina *f* automática; **cash ~** caixa *m* automático; **soap ~** sabão *m* líquido *(em banheiro público)*.

dispensing chemist *UK*, **dispensing pharmacist** *US* [dɪ'spensɪŋ-] *n* farmacêutico *m*, -ca *f*.

dispersal [dɪ'spɜːsl] *n* dispersão *f*.

disperse [dɪ'spɜːs] ◇ *vt* **-1.** [crowd] dispersar **-2.** [knowledge, news] disseminar **-3.** [substance, gas, oil slick] dispersar. ◇ *vi* [crowd] dispersar-se.

dispirited [dɪ'spɪrɪtɪd] *adj* desalentado(da).

dispiriting [dɪ'spɪrɪtɪŋ] *adj* desalentador(ra).

displace [dɪs'pleɪs] *vt* **-1.** [supplant] substituir **-2.** *CHEM & PHYS* deslocar.

displaced person [dɪs'pleɪst-] *n* exilado *m*, -da *f*.

displacement [dɪs'pleɪsmənt] *n* deslocamento *m*.

display [dɪ'spleɪ] ◇ *n* **-1.** [of goods, merchandise, ornaments] exposição *f*; **on ~** em exposição; **window ~** vitrine *f* **- 2.** [of feeling, courage, skill] demonstração *f* **- 3.** [performance] exibição *f* **- 4.** *COMPUT* exibição *f*. ◇ *vt* **-1.** [gen] expor **-2.** [feeling, courage, skill] demonstrar.

display advertising *n* propaganda *f* artística.

displease [dɪs'pliːz] *vt* descontentar.

displeasure [dɪs'pleʒəʳ] *n (U)* descontentamento *m*.

disposable [dɪ'spəʊzəbl] *adj* **-1.** [to be thrown away after use] descartável; **~ nappy** *UK*, **~ diaper** *US* fralda *f* descartável **-2.** [available] disponível.

disposal [dɪ'spəʊzl] *n (U)* **-1.** [getting rid] descarte *f* **-2.** [availability]: **at sb's ~** à disposição de alguém.

dispose ◆ **dispose of** *vt fus* [get rid of - rubbish, nuclear waste] descartar-se de; [- problem] livrar-se de.

disposed [dɪ'spəʊzd] *adj* **-1.** [willing]: **to be ~ to do sthg** estar disposto(ta) a fazer algo **-2.** [positive]: **to be well-~ to** *OR* **towards sb** estar bem-intencionado(da) com/em relação a alguém.

disposition [ˌdɪspə'zɪʃn] *n* **-1.** [temperament] temperamento *m* **- 2.** [willingness, tendency]: **~ to do sthg** disposição *f* para fazer algo.

dispossess [ˌdɪspə'zes] *vt fml*: **to ~ sb of sthg** despojar alguém de algo.

disproportion [ˌdɪsprə'pɔːʃn] *n* desproporção *f*.

disproportionate [ˌdɪsprə'pɔːʃnət] *adj* desproporcional; **~ to sthg** desproporcional a algo.

disprove [ˌdɪs'pruːv] *vt* [theory, idea]: **to ~ sthg** mostrar que algo está errado.

dispute [dɪ'spjuːt] ◇ *n* **-1.** [quarrel] disputa *f* **- 2.** *(U)* [disagreement] discussão *f*; **in ~** em discussão. ◇ *vt* **-1.** [question, challenge] discutir **-2.** [fight for] disputar.

disqualification [dɪsˌkwɒlɪfɪ'keɪʃn] *n*: **~ (from sthg)** desqualificação *f* (de algo); **~ from a sporting event** desqualificação de um evento esportivo; **~ from standing for election** ineligibilidade *f* para uma eleição; **~ from driving** *UK* proibição *f* para dirigir.

disqualify [ˌdɪs'kwɒlɪfaɪ] *(pt & pp* **-ied)** *vt* **-1.** [subj: authority, illness, criminal record]: **to ~ sb (from doing sthg)** desqualificar alguém (para fazer algo) **-2.** *SPORT* desqualificar **-3.** *UK* [from driving] ser proibido de.

disquiet [dɪs'kwaɪət] *n (U)* inquietação *f*.

disregard [ˌdɪsrɪ'gɑːd] ◇ *n*: **~ (for sthg)** desconsideração *f OR* indiferença *f* (por algo). ◇ *vt* desconsiderar.

disrepair [ˌdɪsrɪ'peəʳ] *n (U)* mau estado *m* de conservação; **to fall into ~** estar caindo aos pedaços.

disreputable [dɪs'repjʊtəbl] *adj* desacreditado(-da).

disrepute [ˌdɪsrɪ'pjuːt] *n*: **to bring sthg into ~** desacreditar algo; **to fall into ~** cair em descrédito.

disrespectful [ˌdɪsrɪ'spektfʊl] *adj* desrespeitoso(-sa).

disrupt [dɪs'rʌpt] *vt* transtornar.

disruption [dɪs'rʌpʃn] *n* transtorno *m*.

disruptive [dɪs'rʌptɪv] *adj* perturbador(ra).

dissatisfaction ['dɪsˌsætɪs'fækʃn] *n (U)* insatisfação *f*.

dissatisfied [ˌdɪs'sætɪsfaɪd] *adj* insatisfeito(ta); **~ with sthg** insatisfeito(ta) com algo.

dissect [dɪ'sekt] *vt* dissecar.

dissection [dɪ'sekʃn] *n* dissecação *f*.

disseminate [dɪ'semɪneɪt] *vt* [information] disseminar.

dissemination [dɪˌsemɪ'neɪʃn] *n (U)* [of information] disseminação *f*.

dissension [dɪ'senʃn] *n* divergência *f*.

dissent [dɪ'sent] ◇ *n (U)* [disagreement] divergência *f*. ◇ *vi*: **to ~ (from sthg)** divergir (de algo).

dissenter [dɪ'sentəʳ] *n* [protester] dissidente *mf*.

dissenting [dɪ'sentɪŋ] *adj* [not in agreement] dissidente.

dissertation [ˌdɪsə'teɪʃn] *n* dissertação *f*.

disservice [ˌdɪs'sɜːvɪs] *n*: **to do sb a ~** fazer um desserviço a alguém.

dissident ['dɪsɪdənt] *n* dissidente *mf*.

dissimilar [ˌdɪ'sɪmɪləʳ] *adj* diferente; **~ to** diferente de.

dissipate ['dɪsɪpeɪt] ◇ *vt* **-1.** [heat] dissipar **-2.** [efforts, money] dispersar. ◇ *vi* [heat, crowd] dissipar-se.

dissipated ['dɪsɪpeɪtɪd] *adj* [person, life] desregrado(-da).

dissociate [dɪ'səʊʃɪeɪt] *vt* dissociar; **to ~ o.s. from sthg** dissociar-se de algo.

dissolute ['dɪsəluːt] *adj* dissoluto(ta).

dissolution [ˌdɪsə'luːʃn] *n (U)* [of organization, relationship] dissolução *f*.

dissolve [dɪ'zɒlv] ◇ *vt* dissolver. ◇ *vi* **-1.** [substance] dissolver-se **-2.** *fig* [disappear] desaparecer.
◆ **dissolve in(to)** *vt fus* [tears, laughter] dissolver-se em.

dissuade [dɪ'sweɪd] *vt*: **to ~ sb (from doing sthg)** dissuadir alguém (de fazer algo).

distance ['dɪstəns] ◇ *n* **-1.** [between two places] distância *f* **-2.** [distant point]: **at a ~** à distância; **from a ~** de longe; **in the ~** ao longe. ◇ *vt*: **to ~ o.s. from sb/sthg** distanciar-se de alguém/algo.

distant ['dɪstənt] *adj* distante; **~ from** distante de.

distaste [dɪs'teɪst] *n (U)* repugnância *f*; ~ **for sthg** repugnância a algo.
distasteful [dɪs'teɪstfʊl] *adj* [unpleasant] desagradável, repugnante.
distemper [dɪ'stempə^{r}] *n (U)* **-1.** [paint] pintura *f* à têmpera **-2.** [disease] cinomose *f*.
distended [dɪ'stendɪd] *adj* dilatado(da).
distil *UK* (*pt* & *pp* **-led**, *cont* **-ling**), **distill** *US* [dɪ'stɪl] *vt* destilar.
distiller [dɪ'stɪlə^{r}] *n* destilador *m*.
distillery [dɪ'stɪlərɪ] (*pl* **-ies**) *n* destilaria *f*.
distinct [dɪ'stɪŋkt] *adj* **-1.** [different] distinto(ta); ~ **from** distinto(ta de); **as** ~ **from** em oposição a **-2.** [clear] nítido(da).
distinction [dɪ'stɪŋkʃn] *n* **-1.** [difference, excellence] distinção *f*; **to draw** *OR* **make a** ~ **between** fazer uma distinção entre **-2.** [in exam result] destaque *m*.
distinctive [dɪ'stɪŋktɪv] *adj* [flavour, voice] característico(ca).
distinctly [dɪ'stɪŋktlɪ] *adv* **-1.** [clearly] claramente **-2.** [considerably] excessivamente.
distinguish [dɪ'stɪŋgwɪʃ] <> *vt* **-1.** [tell apart]: **to** ~ **sthg from sthg** distinguir algo de algo **-2.** [discern, perceive, make different] distinguir; **to** ~ **o.s.** [perform well] distinguir-se. <> *vi*: **to** ~ **between** distinguir-se entre.
distinguished [dɪ'stɪŋgwɪʃt] *adj* ilustre.
distinguishing [dɪ'stɪŋgwɪʃɪŋ] *adj* [feature, mark] peculiar.
distort [dɪ'stɔ:t] *vt* distorcer.
distorted [dɪ'stɔ:tɪd] *adj* distorcido(da).
distortion [dɪ'stɔ:ʃn] *n* distorção *f*.
distract [dɪ'strækt] *vt* [person, attention]: **to** ~ **sb (from sthg)** distrair alguém(de algo).
distracted [dɪ'stræktɪd] *adj* [preoccupied] atordoado(da).
distraction [dɪ'strækʃn] *n* **-1.** [gen] distração *f* **-2.** *(U)*: **to drive sb to** ~ levar alguém à loucura.
distraught [dɪ'strɔ:t] *adj* transtornado(da).
distress [dɪ'stres] <> *n* **-1.** [suffering - mental] aflição *f*; [- physical] agonia *f*, dor *f*; **to be in** ~ estar em agonia **-2.** [danger]: **in** ~ em perigo. <> *vt* [upset] afligir.
distressed [dɪ'strest] *adj* [anxious, upset] angustiado(da).
distressing [dɪ'stresɪŋ] *adj* [news, account, image] angustiante.
distress signal *n* pedido *m* de socorro.
distribute [dɪ'strɪbju:t] *vt* distribuir.
distribution [ˌdɪstrɪ'bju:ʃn] *n* distribuição *f*.
distributor [dɪ'strɪbjʊtə^{r}] *n* **-1.** *COMM* distribuidor *m*, -ra *f* **-2.** *AUT* distribuidor *m*.
district ['dɪstrɪkt] *n* **-1.** [of country] distrito *m* **-2.** [of town] bairro *m*.
district attorney *n US JUR* promotor *m* público, promotora *f* pública.
district council *n UK ADMIN* conselho *m* de bairro.
district nurse *n UK* *enfermeira encarregada de atender a domicílio os pacientes de uma área.*
District of Columbia *n* Distrito *m* de Colúmbia.
distrust [dɪs'trʌst] <> *n* desconfiança *f*. <> *vt* desconfiar.
distrustful [dɪs'trʌstfʊl] *adj* desconfiado(da).
disturb [dɪ'stɜ:b] *vt* **-1.** [interrupt] incomodar **-2.** [upset, worry] preocupar **-3.** [cause to change] mexer em.
disturbance [dɪ'stɜ:bəns] *n* **-1.** [fight] distúrbio *m* **-2.** [interruption, disruption]: ~ **of the peace** *JUR* perturbação *f* da ordem **-3.** [distress, upset] perturbação *f*.
disturbed [dɪ'stɜ:bd] *adj* perturbado(da).
disturbing [dɪ'stɜ:bɪŋ] *adj* [news, image] perturbador(ra).
disunity *n (U)* desunião *f*.
disuse [ˌdɪs'ju:s] *n*: **to fall into** ~ cair em desuso.
disused [ˌdɪs'ju:zd] *adj* [factory, railway line] abandonado(da).
ditch [dɪtʃ] <> *n* fosso *m*. <> *vt inf* **-1.** [boyfriend, girlfriend] livrar-se de **-2.** [plan] descartar **-3.** [old car, clothes] desfazer-se de.
dither ['dɪðə^{r}] *vi* [be indecisive] hesitar.
ditto ['dɪtəʊ] *adv* idem.
diuretic [ˌdaɪjʊ'retɪk] *n* diurético *m*.
diva ['di:və] (*pl* **-s**) *n* diva *f*.
divan [dɪ'væn] *n* divã *m*.
divan bed *n* divã *m*.
dive [daɪv] (*UK pt* & *pp* **-d**, *US pt* & *pp* **-d** *OR* **dove**) <> *vi* **-1.** [gen] mergulhar; **to** ~ **(into sthg)** mergulhar (em algo) **-2.** [as sport] mergulhar, saltar **-3.** [into pocket, bag]: **to** ~ **into sthg** enfiar a mão em algo. <> *n* **-1.** [gen] mergulho *m* **-2.** [sudden movement] movimento *m* brusco **-3.** *inf pej* [bar, restaurant] espelunca *f*.
dive-bomb *vt* bombardear com caça de mergulho.
diver ['daɪvə^{r}] *n* mergulhador *m*, -ra *f*.
diverge [daɪ'vɜ:dʒ] *vi* **-1.** [opinions, interests] divergir; **to** ~ **from sthg** divergir de algo **-2.** [roads, paths] separar-se.
divergence [daɪ'vɜ:dʒəns] *n* [of opinions, interests] divergência *f*.
divergent [daɪ'vɜ:dʒənt] *adj* [opinions, interests] divergente.
diverse [daɪ'vɜ:s] *adj* diferente.
diversification [daɪˌvɜ:sɪfɪ'keɪʃn] *n (U)* [in industry] diversificação *f*.
diversify [daɪ'vɜ:sɪfaɪ] (*pt* & *pp* **-ied**) <> *vt* [products] diversificar. <> *vi* [in industry] diversificar-se.
diversion [daɪ'vɜ:ʃn] *n* **-1.** *(U)* [gen] desvio *m* **-2.** [distraction] diversão *f*.
diversionary [daɪ'vɜ:ʃnrɪ] *adj* [tactics] diversivo(va).
diversity [daɪ'vɜ:sətɪ] *n (U)* diversidade *f*.
divert [daɪ'vɜ:t] *vt* **-1.** [gen] desviar **-2.** [distract] distrair.
divest [daɪ'vest] *vt fml*: **to** ~ **sb of sthg** [take away] privar alguém de algo; **to** ~ **o.s. of sthg** [get rid of] livrar-se de algo.
divide [dɪ'vaɪd] <> *vt* **-1.** dividir; **to** ~ **sthg between** *OR* **among** dividir algo entre **-2.** [split up]: **to** ~ **sthg into** dividir algo em **-3.** *MATH*: **to** ~ **sthg by** dividir algo por. <> *vi* [split into two] dividir-se. <> *n* [difference] divisão *f*.
◆ **divide up** *vt sep* dividir.
divided [dɪ'vaɪdɪd] *adj* [disunited] dividido(da).

dividend [ˈdɪvɪdend] *n* [profit] dividendo *m*; **to pay ~s** trazer benefícios.
dividers [dɪˈvaɪdəz] *npl* compasso *m*.
dividing line [dɪˈvaɪdɪŋ-] *n* linha *f* divisória.
divine [dɪˈvaɪn] ◇ *adj* divino(na). ◇ *vt* **-1.** [gen] adivinhar **-2.** [water] descobrir.
diving [ˈdaɪvɪŋ] *n* [from board] salto *m (de trampolim)*; [underwater] mergulho *m*.
diving board *n* trampolim *m*.
diving suit *n* escafandro *m*.
divinity [dɪˈvɪnətɪ] (*pl* **-ies**) *n* **-1.** *(U)* [godliness] divindade *f* **-2.** *(U)* [study] teologia *f* **-3.** [god, goddess] deidade *f*.
divisible [dɪˈvɪzəbl] *adj MATH* divisível; **~ by** divisível por.
division [dɪˈvɪʒn] *n* **-1.** [gen] divisão *f* **-2.** *(U)* [sharing out, distribution] repartição *f* **-3.** [disagreement] discórdia *f*.
division sign *n* sinal *m* de divisão.
divisive [dɪˈvaɪsɪv] *adj* que causa divisão.
divorce [dɪˈvɔːs] ◇ *n JUR* divórcio *m*. ◇ *vt* **-1.** *JUR* [husband, wife] divorciar-se de **-2.** [separate]: **to ~ sthg from sthg** separar algo de algo.
divorced [dɪˈvɔːst] *adj* **-1.** *JUR* divorciado(da) **-2.** *fig* [separated]: **to be ~ from sthg** estar distante de algo.
divorcee [dɪvɔːˈsiː] *n* divorciado *m*, -da *f*.
divulge [daɪˈvʌldʒ] *vt* [information, secret] divulgar.
DIY (*abbr of* **do-it-yourself**) *n UK conceito utilizado para atividades do tipo faça-você-mesmo, como montar objetos ou fazer reparos em casa.*
dizziness [ˈdɪzɪnɪs] *n (U)* vertigem *f*, tontura *f*.
dizzy [ˈdɪzɪ] (*compar* **-ier**, *superl* **-iest**) *adj* **-1.** [giddy] tonto(ta) **-2.** *fig* [height, speed] vertiginoso(sa).
DJ *n* **-1.** (*abbr of* **disc jockey**) DJ *mf*. **-2.** (*abbr of* **dinner jacket**) smoking *m*.
Djakarta [dʒəˈkɑːtə] *n* Jacarta; **in ~** em Jacarta.
Djibouti [dʒɪˈbuːtɪ] *n* Djibouti; **in ~** no Djibouti.
dl (*abbr of* **decilitre**) dl.
DLit(t) [ˌdiːˈlɪt] (*abbr of* **Doctor of Letters**) *n (titular de) doutorado em letras.*
dm (*abbr of* **decimetre**) dm.
DM (*abbr of* **Deutschmark**) marco *m* alemão.
DMA (*abbr of* **direct memory access**) *n* DMA *m*.
DMus [ˌdiːˈmjuːz] (*abbr of* **Doctor of Music**) *n (titular de) doutorado em música.*
DMZ (*abbr of* **demilitarized zone**) *n US* zona *f* desmilitarizada.
DNA (*abbr of* **deoxyribonucleic acid**) *n* DNA *m*.
D-notice *n UK pedido oficial à imprensa para que uma determinada informação não se torne pública por razões de segurança nacional.*
DNS (*abbr of* **Domain Name System**) *n COMPUT* DNS *m*.
do[1] [duː] (*pt* **did**, *pp* **done**) *aux vb* **-1.** [in negatives]: **don't ~ that!** não faça isso!; **she didn't see it** ela não o viu. **-2.** [in questions]: **~ you like it?** você gosta?; **how ~ you do it?** como é que se faz? **-3.** [referring to previous verb]: **~ you smoke? - yes, I ~ / no, I don't** você fuma? sim/não; **I eat more than you ~** eu como mais do que você; **no, I didn't do it!** não fiz, não!; **so ~ I** eu também. **-4.** [in question tags]: **so, you like Scotland, ~ you?** então você gosta da Escócia, não gosta?; **the train leaves at five o'clock, doesn't it?** o trem sai às cinco, não é (verdade)? **-5.** [for emphasis]: **I ~ like this bedroom** eu realmente gosto deste quarto; **~ come in!** faça o favor de entrar!
◆ *vt* **-1.** [perform] fazer; **to ~ one's homework** fazer o dever de casa; **what is she doing?** o que ela está fazendo?; **what can I ~ for you?** em que posso ajudá-lo? **-2.** [clean, brush, etc]: **to ~ one's hair** pentear-se; **to ~ one's make-up** maquiar-se; **to ~ one's teeth** escovar os dentes. **-3.** [cause] fazer; **to ~ damage** fazer estragos; **to ~ sb good** fazer bem a alguém. **-4.** [have as job]: **what do you ~?** o que você faz? **-5.** [provide, offer] fazer; **we ~ pizzas for under $5** vendemos pizzas por menos de 5 dólares. **-6.** [subj: vehicle] ir a; **the car was ~ing 50mph** o carro ia a 80 km/h. **-7.** *inf* [visit] visitar; **we're doing Scotland next week** para a semana vamos visitar a Escócia.
◆ *vi* **-1.** [behave, act] fazer; **~ as I say** faça como eu lhe digo. **-2.** [progress]: **he did badly/well on his test** ele foi mal/bem no exame; **how did you ~?** como é que foi? **-3.** [be sufficient] chegar; **will $10 ~?** 10 dólares chega? **-4.** [in phrases]: **how ~ you ~?** [greeting] (muito) prazer (em conhecê-lo); **how are you ~ing?** como é que vão as coisas?; **what does that have to ~ with it?** o que é que isso tem a ver?
◆ *n* [party] festa *f*; **~s and don'ts** o que fazer e não fazer.
◆ **do up** *vt sep* [coat, shirt] abotoar; [shoes, laces] apertar, atar; [zip] fechar; [decorate] renovar.
◆ **do with** *vt fus* [need]: **I could ~ with a drink** eu bem que beberia alguma coisa.
◆ **do without** *vt fus* passar sem.
do[2] (*abbr of* **ditto**) ditto *m*.
DOA (*abbr of* **dead on arrival**) *adj diz-se do corpo que chega sem vida ao hospital.*
doable [ˈduːəbl] *adj inf* exeqüível.
d.o.b. (*abbr of* **date of birth**) data *f* de nascimento.
Doberman [ˈdəʊbəmən] (*pl* **-s**) *n*: **~ (pinscher)** dobermann *m* pinscher.
docile [*UK* ˈdəʊsaɪl, *US* ˈdɒsəl] *adj* dócil.
dock [dɒk] ◇ *n* **-1.** [in harbour] doca *f* **-2.** [in court] banco *m* dos réus. ◇ *vt* [wages] descontar. ◇ *vi* **-1.** [ship] atracar **-2.** [passengers] chegar.
docker [ˈdɒkəʳ] *n* estivador *m*, -ra *f*.
docket [ˈdɒkɪt] *n* **-1.** *UK documento que descreve o conteúdo de algo sendo entregue ou transportado* **-2.** *US JUR lista f das sentenças.*
docklands [ˈdɒkləndz] *npl UK* região *f* das docas.
dock worker *n* = **docker**.
dockyard [ˈdɒkjɑːd] *n* estaleiro *m*.
doctor [ˈdɒktəʳ] ◇ *n* **-1.** [of medicine] médico *m*, -ca *f*; **to go to the ~'s** ir ao médico **-2.** [holder of PhD] doutor *m*, -ra *f*. ◇ *vt* **-1.** [change, tamper with] adulterar **-2.** *UK* [neuter] castrar.
doctorate [ˈdɒktərət], **doctor's degree** *n* doutorado *m*.
Doctor of Medicine *n* doutor *m*, -ra *f* em medicina.
doctrinaire [ˌdɒktrɪˈneəʳ] *adj* doutrinário(ria).
doctrine [ˈdɒktrɪn] *n* doutrina *f*.
docudrama [ˌdɒkjʊˈdrɑːmə] (*pl* **-s**) *n TV* dramatização *f*.

document [*n* 'dɒkjʊmənt, *vb* dɒkjʊ'ment] <> *n* documento *m*. <> *vt* [record, detail] documentar.
documentary [ˌdɒkjʊ'mentərɪ] (*pl* **-ies**) <> *adj* [evidence] documental. <> *n* documentário *m*.
documentation [ˌdɒkjʊmen'teɪʃn] *n (U)* [evidence] documentação *f*.
DOD (*abbr of* **Department of Defense**) *n* departamento *m* de defesa *(norte-americano)*.
doddering ['dɒdərɪŋ], **doddery** ['dɒdərɪ] *adj* ***inf*** senil.
doddle ['dɒdl] *n* ***UK inf*** barbada *f*.
Dodecanese [ˌdəʊdɪkə'ni:z] *npl*: **the ~** o Dodecaneso.
dodge [dɒdʒ] <> *n* ***inf*** mutreta *f*; **a tax ~** uma mutreta para não pagar impostos. <> *vt* [avoid] fugir de. <> *vi* esquivar-se.
Dodgems® ['dɒdʒəmz] *npl* ***UK*** carros *m* de batida *(em parques de diversão)*.
dodgy ['dɒdʒɪ] *adj* ***UK inf*** **-1.** [dishonest] desonesto(ta) **-2.** [risky, unreliable] arriscado(da) **-3.** [weak, unhealthy] fraco(ca).
doe [dəʊ] *n* **-1.** [female deer] corça *f* **-2.** [female rabbit] coelha *f*.
doer ['du:ə^r] *n* ***inf***: **he's a ~!** ele põe a mão na massa!
does [*weak form* dəz, *strong form* dʌz] *vb* ▷ **do**.
doesn't ['dʌznt] = **does not**.
dog [dɒg] (*pt* & *pp* **-ged**, *cont* **-ging**) <> *n* **-1.** [animal] cão *m*, cachorro *m*; **it's a ~'s life** é uma vida de cão; **to go to the ~s** ***inf*** entrar pelo cano; **let sleeping ~s lie** não mexa em casa de marimbondo **-2.** ***UK*** [sport]: **the ~s** corrida *f* de cachorros **-3.** ***US*** [hot dog] cachorro-quente *m*. <> *vt* **-1.** [follow closely] seguir **-2.** [subj: problems, bad luck] atormentar.
dog biscuit *n* biscoito *m* canino.
dog collar *n* **-1.** [of dog] coleira *f* de cachorro **-2.** [of clergyman] gola *f* de padre.
dog-eared [-ɪəd] *adj* [book, page] com orelhas.
dog-eat-dog *adj* muito competitivo(va).
dog-end *n* ***inf*** [of cigarette] guimba *f*, bagana *f*.
dogfight ['dɒgfaɪt] *n* **-1.** [between dogs] briga *f* de cachorro **-2.** [between aircraft] combate *m* aéreo.
dogfish (*pl inv*) *n* cação *m*.
dog food *n* ração *f* para cachorro.
dogged ['dɒgɪd] *adj* [resistance, perseverance] persistente.
doggone ['dɒgɒn], **doggoned** ['dɒgɒnd] *adj* ***US inf*** maldito(ta).
doggy ['dɒgɪ] (*pl* **-ies**) *n* ***inf*** cachorrinho *m*.
doggy bag *n* ≃ quentinha *f*, *pequena sacola que os restaurantes oferecem para o cliente levar a comida que sobrou.*
dogma ['dɒgmə] *n* dogma *m*.
dogmatic [dɒg'mætɪk] *adj* dogmático(ca).
do-gooder [-'gʊdə^r] *n* ***pej*** *pessoa bem-intencionada, mas que acaba atrapalhando.*
dog paddle *n* nado *m* cachorrinho.
dogsbody ['dɒgzˌbɒdɪ] (*pl* **-ies**) *n* ***UK inf*** faz-tudo *mf*, burro *m* de carga.
dog tag *n* ***US*** *placa de identificação usada no pescoço de um soldado.*
doing ['du:ɪŋ] *n*: **is this your ~?** foi você que fez isso?
◆ **doings** *npl* [activities] atividades *fpl*.
do-it-yourself *n (U)* sistema *m* faça-você-mesmo.
doldrums ['dɒldrəmz] *npl*: **to be in the ~** ***fig*** estar estagnado(da).
dole [dəʊl] *n* ***UK*** [unemployment benefit] ≃ seguro-desemprego *m*; **to be on the ~** estar recebendo seguro-desemprego.
◆ **dole out** *vt sep* [food, money] repartir.
doleful ['dəʊlfʊl] *adj* lúgubre.
doll [dɒl] *n* [toy] boneca *f*.
dollar ['dɒlə^r] *n* dólar *m*.
dolled up [dɒld-] *adj* ***inf*** enfeitado(da), produzido(da).
dollhouse *n* ***US*** = **doll's house**.
dollop ['dɒləp] *n* ***inf*** monte *m*.
doll's house ***UK***, **dollhouse** ***US*** ['dɒlhaʊs] *n* casa *f* de bonecas.
dolly ['dɒlɪ] (*pl* **-ies**) *n* **-1.** [doll] bonequinha *f* **-2.** TECH [for TV or film camera] plataforma *f* móvel.
Dolomites ['dɒləmaɪts] *npl*: **the ~** os Dolomíticos.
dolphin ['dɒlfɪn] *n* golfinho *m*.
domain [də'meɪn] *n* [sphere of interest, land] domínio *m*.
domain name *n* COMPUT nome *m* de domínio.
dome [dəʊm] *n* ARCHIT domo *m*.
domestic [də'mestɪk] <> *adj* **-1.** [gen - flight] doméstico(ca); [- production] nacional **-2.** [person] caseiro(ra). <> *n* doméstico *m*, -ca *f*.
domestic appliance *n* eletrodoméstico *m*.
domesticated [də'mestɪkeɪtɪd] *adj* **-1.** [animal] domesticado(da) **-2.** ***hum*** [person] caseiro(ra).
domesticity [ˌdəʊme'stɪsətɪ] *n (U)* [home life] vida *f* caseira.
domicile ['dɒmɪsaɪl] *n* ***fml*** domicílio *m*.
dominance ['dɒmɪnəns] *n (U)* **-1.** [control, power] dominância *f* **-2.** [importance] predominância *f*.
dominant ['dɒmɪnənt] *adj* **-1.** [colour] predominante **-2.** [personality, group] influente.
dominate ['dɒmɪneɪt] *vt* dominar.
dominating ['dɒmɪneɪtɪŋ] *adj* [person] dominador(-ra).
domination [ˌdɒmɪ'neɪʃn] *n (U)* domínio *m*.
domineering [ˌdɒmɪ'nɪərɪŋ] *adj* [person, personality] dominador(ra).
Dominica [də'mɪnɪkə] *n* Domínica; **in ~** na Domínica.
Dominican Republic [də'mɪnɪkən-] *n*: **the ~** a República Dominicana; **in the ~** na República Dominicana.
dominion [də'mɪnjən] *n* **-1.** *(U)* [power] dominação *f* **-2.** [land] domínio *m*.
domino ['dɒmɪnəʊ] (*pl* **-es**) *n* peça *f* de dominó.
◆ **dominoes** *npl* [game] dominó *m*.
domino effect *n* efeito *m* dominó.
don [dɒn] (*pt* & *pp* **-ned**, *cont* **-ning**) <> *n* ***UK*** UNIV professor *m*, -ra *f* universitário, -ria *f*. <> *vt* ***fml*** [clothing] vestir.
donate [də'neɪt] *vt* [give] doar.
donation [də'neɪʃn] *n* doação *f*.
done [dʌn] <> *pp* ▷ **do**. <> *adj* **-1.** [finished] pronto(ta) **-2.** [cooked] assado(da) **-3.** [socially acceptable] socialmente aceito(ta); **it's not ~ to insult**

your host não é de bom tom insultar seu anfitrião; **it's the ~ thing to thank your host when leaving** é de bom tom agradecer seu anfitrião ao partir. <> *excl* [to conclude deal] combinado!

donkey ['dɒŋkɪ] (*pl* **donkeys**) *n* burro *m*, -ra *f*.

donkey jacket *n UK jaqueta feita de material resistente.*

donkey work *n UK inf* maçada *f*; **to do the ~** fazer a pior parte.

donor ['dəʊnəʳ] *n* doador *m*, -ra *f*.

donor card *n* carteira *f* de doador.

don't [dəʊnt] = **do not**.

doodle ['du:dl] <> *n* rabisco *m*. <> *vi* rabiscar.

doom [du:m] *n* destino *m*.

doomed [du:md] *adj* [plan, mission] condenado(da); **to be ~ to sthg/to do sthg** estar destinado(da) a algo/a fazer algo; **to be ~ to failure** estar fadado(da) ao fracasso.

door [dɔ:ʳ] *n* porta *f*; **the next ~ neighbour** o vizinho do lado; **the house next ~** a casa ao lado; **she showed him the ~** ela pediu para que ele saísse; **out of ~s** ao ar livre; **it's three miles ~ to ~** são três milhas de um ponto a outro; **as one ~ closes another one opens** quando se fecha uma porta, se abre uma janela; **to open the ~ to sthg** *fig* abrir as portas para algo.

doorbell ['dɔ:bel] *n* campainha *f*.

doorhandle ['dɔ:hændl] *n* maçaneta *f*.

doorknob ['dɔ:nɒb] *n* maçaneta *f*.

doorknocker ['dɔ:ˌnɒkəʳ] *n* aldrava *f*.

doorman ['dɔ:mən] (*pl* **-men** [-mən]) *n* porteiro *m*.

doormat ['dɔ:mæt] *n* **-1.** [mat] capacho *m* **-2.** *fig* [person] capacho *m*.

doorstep ['dɔ:step] *n* [step] degrau *m*; **there's a cinema right on the ~** há um cinema bem próximo de casa.

doorstop ['dɔ:stɒp] *n* encosto *m* para porta.

door-to-door *adj* [salesman, selling] de porta em porta.

doorway ['dɔ:weɪ] *n* vão *m* da porta.

dope [dəʊp] <> *n* **-1.** *drugs sl* [cannabis] maconha *f* **-2.** [for athlete, horse] estimulante *m* **-3.** *inf* [fool] babaca *mf*. <> *vt* [drug] dopar.

dope test *n* SPORT exame *m* antidoping.

dopey ['dəʊpɪ] (*compar* **-ier**, *superl* **-iest**) *adj inf* **-1.** [groggy] grogue **-2.** [stupid] tonto(ta).

dormant ['dɔ:mənt] *adj* inativo(va).

dormer (window) ['dɔ:məʳ-] *n* água-furtada *f*.

dormice ['dɔ:maɪs] *pl* ▷ **dormouse**.

dormitory ['dɔ:mətrɪ] (*pl* **-ies**) *n* **-1.** [room] dormitório *m* **-2.** *US* [in university] casa *f* de estudante.

Dormobile® ['dɔ:məˌbi:l] *n* motocasa *f*.

dormouse ['dɔ:maʊs] (*pl* **-mice**) *n* rato-silvestre *m*, rata-silvestre *f*.

DOS [dɒs] (*abbr of* **disk operating system**) *n* DOS *m*.

dosage ['dəʊsɪdʒ] *n* **-1.** [amount] dosagem *f* **-2.** [on label] posologia *f*.

dose [dəʊs] <> *n* **-1.** [of medicine, drug] dose *f* **-2.** [of illness] ataque *f*. <> *vt* [person]: **to ~ sb (with sthg)** medicar alguém (com algo).

doss [dɒs] ◆ **doss down** *vi UK inf* ajeitar-se para dormir *(num lugar qualquer)*.

dosser ['dɒsəʳ] *n UK inf pessoa que não tem onde morar e dorme na rua ou em pensões baratas.*

dosshouse ['dɒshaʊs, *pl* -haʊzɪz] *n UK inf* pensão *f* barata *(para os sem-teto)*.

dossier ['dɒsɪeɪ] *n* dossiê *m*.

dot [dɒt] (*pt* & *pp* **-ted**, *cont* **-ting**) <> *n* **-1.** [on material] mancha *f* **-2.** [in punctuation] ponto *m*; **since the year ~** desde que o mundo é mundo. <> *vt* [scatter - over surface] salpicar; [- over town, area, country] espalhar.

◆ **on the dot** *adv* em ponto.

DOT (*abbr of* **Department of Transportation**) *n departamento de transportes do governo norte-americano.*

dotage ['dəʊtɪdʒ] *n*: **to be in one's ~** estar fraco(ca) da cabeça.

dotcom ['dɒtkɒm] *adj* ponto-com.

dote ◆ **dote on** *vt fus* adorar; **to ~ on sb/sthg** babar por alguém/algo.

doting ['dəʊtɪŋ] *adj* babão(ona).

dot-matrix printer *n* impressora *f* matricial.

dotted line ['dɒtɪd-] *n* linha *f* pontilhada; **to sign on the ~** *fig* assinar na linha pontilhada.

dotty ['dɒtɪ] (*compar* **-ier**, *superl* **-iest**) *adj inf* [mad] doido(da).

double ['dʌbl] <> *adj* duplo(pla). <> *adv* **-1.** [twice] dobro **-2.** [two of the same] em dobro **-3.** [in two] em dois; **to bend ~** dobrar ao meio. <> *n* **-1.** [twice the amount] dobro *m* **-2.** [of alcohol] duplo *m*, -pla *f* **-3.** [look-alike] cópia *f* **-4.** CINEMA dublê *mf*. <> *vt* [increase twofold] dobrar. <> *vi* **-1.** [increase twofold] duplicar **-2.** [serve two purposes]: **to ~ as** fazer as vezes de.

◆ **doubles** *npl* TENNIS dupla *f*.

◆ **double up** <> *vt sep*: **to be ~d up with laughter** rachar de tanto rir; **to be ~d up in pain** dobrar-se de dor. <> *vi* [bend over] curvar-se, dobrar-se.

double act *n* dupla *f* cômica.

double agent *n* agente *mf* duplo.

double-barrelled *UK*, **double-barreled** *US* [-'bærəld] *adj* **-1.** [shotgun] de dois canos **-2.** [plan, question] de duplo sentido **-3.** [name]: **a ~ surname** um sobrenome composto.

double bass [-beɪs] *n* contrabaixo *m*.

double bed *n* cama *f* de casal.

double-breasted [-'brestɪd] *adj* [jacket] trespassado(da).

double-check <> *vt* verificar duas vezes. <> *vi* verificar duas vezes.

double chin *n* papada *f*.

double-click COMPUT <> *n* duplo clique *m*. <> *vt* dar um duplo clique em. <> *vi* dar um duplo clique.

double cream *n UK* creme *m* muito espesso.

double-cross *vt* passar para trás.

double-dealer *n* hipócrita *mf*.

double-decker [-'dekəʳ] *n* [bus] ônibus *m inv* de dois andares.

double-density *adj* COMPUT [disk] de dupla densidade.

double-dutch *n UK hum*: **to talk ~** falar grego.

double-edged *adj* **-1.** [blade] de dois gumes **-2.** *fig* [remark, compliment] ambíguo(gua).

double entendre [ˌdu:blɑɔ'tɑɔndr] *n* duplo sentido *m*.
double fault *n TENNIS* falta *f* dupla.
double figures *npl* números *mpl* de dois algarismos.
double-glazing [-'gleɪzɪŋ] *n* vidros *mpl* duplos.
double-jointed [-'dʒɔɪntɪd] *adj* [person, joint] de articulações flexíveis.
double-park *vi AUT* estacionar em fila dupla.
double-quick *inf* ◇ *adj* acelerado(da). ◇ *adv* de forma acelerada.
double room *n* quarto *m* de casal.
double-sided *adj COMPUT* [disk] de dupla face.
double standards *npl* critérios *mpl* tendenciosos; **to have ~** não medir as coisas segundo os mesmos critérios.
double take *n*: **to do a ~** dar uma segunda olhada.
double-talk *n* linguagem *f* confusa, algaravia *f*.
double time *n* pagamento *m* em dobro.
double vision *n* visão *f* dupla.
double whammy [-'wæmɪ] *n* golpe *m* duplo.
doubly ['dʌblɪ] *adv* duplamente.
doubt [daʊt] ◇ *n* dúvida *f*; **there is no ~ that** não há dúvida de que; **to cast ~ on sthg** lançar dúvida sobre algo; **no ~** sem dúvida; **without (a) ~** sem dúvida; **beyond (all) ~** sem dúvida alguma; **in ~** em dúvida. ◇ *vt* **-1.** [distrust] desconfiar de **-2.** [consider unlikely] duvidar; **to ~ whether** *OR* **if** duvidar se.
doubtful ['daʊtfʊl] *adj* **-1.** [unlikely] improvável **-2.** [uncertain] incerto(ta); **to be ~ about** *OR* **of sthg** estar em dúvida sobre algo **-3.** [dubious] duvidoso(sa).
doubtless ['daʊtlɪs] *adv* sem dúvida.
dough [dəʊ] *n (U)* **-1.** [for baking] massa *f* **-2.** *inf* [money] grana *f*.
doughnut ['dəʊnʌt] *n* **-1.** [without hole] sonho *m* **-2.** [with hole] rosca *f*.
dour [dʊəʳ] *adj* austero(ra).
douse [daʊs] *vt* **-1.** [put out] jogar água em **-2.** [drench] encharcar.
dove¹ [dʌv] *n* [bird] pomba *f*.
dove² [dəʊv] *pt US* ▻ **dive**.
dovecot(e) ['dʌvkɒt] *n* pombal *m*.
dovetail ['dʌvteɪl] ◇ *vt* combinar com. ◇ *vi* combinar.
dovetail joint *n* ensambladura *f* em cauda de andorinha.
dowager ['daʊədʒəʳ] *n literary* [old lady] senhora *f* digna.
dowdy ['daʊdɪ] (*compar* **-ier**, *superl* **-iest**) *adj* deselegante.
Dow-Jones average [ˌdaʊ'dʒəʊnz-] *n*: **the ~** o índice Dow Jones.
down [daʊn] ◇ *adv* **-1.** [downwards] para baixo; **to fall ~** cair; **~ here/there** aqui/ali em baixo **-2.** [along]: **I'm going ~ to the shops** estou indo fazer compras; **we walked ~ to the park** fomos até o parque **-3.** [southwards]: **we flew ~ from Recife to Rio** viajamos para o sul, do Recife até o Rio **-4.** [reduced, lower] baixo; **prices are coming ~** os preços estão baixando; **~ to the last detail** até o último detalhe **-5.** [as deposit]: **to pay £5 ~** pagar £5 de entrada **-6.** [in written form]: **get sthg ~ in writing** conseguir algo por escrito; **write it ~** tome nota. ◇ *prep* **-1.** [downwards] para baixo; **they ran ~ the hill** eles correram morro abaixo **-2.** [along]: **we walked ~ the street** caminhamos pela rua. ◇ *adj* **-1.** *inf* [depressed] desanimado(da) **-2.** [behind] por trás **-3.** [lower in amount] mais baixo(xa) **-4.** [not in operation] fora de operação. ◇ *n* **-1.** *(U)* [feathers, hair] penugem *f* **-2.** *US SPORT* tempo *m*. ◇ *vt* **-1.** [knock over] abater **-2.** [swallow] engolir.
◆ **Downs** *npl UK*: **the Downs** *chapada ao sul da Inglaterra*.
◆ **down with** *excl*: **~ with the king!** abaixo o rei!
down-and-out ◇ *adj* sem futuro. ◇ *n* mendigo *m*, -ga *f*.
down-at-heel *adj esp UK* desleixado(da).
downbeat ['daʊnbi:t] *adj inf* [gloomy] sombrio(-bria).
downcast ['daʊnkɑ:st] *adj fml* **-1.** [person] abatido(-da) **-2.** [eyes] cabisbaixo(xa).
downer ['daʊnəʳ] *n inf* **-1.** [drug] calmante *m* **-2.** [depressing event or situation] droga *f*; **to be on a ~** estar de baixo-astral.
downfall ['daʊnfɔ:l] *n* **-1.** *(U)* [ruin] queda *f* **-2.** [cause of ruin] ruína *f*.
downgrade ['daʊngreɪd] *vt* rebaixar.
downhearted [ˌdaʊn'hɑ:tɪd] *adj* desacorçoado(-da).
downhill [ˌdaʊn'hɪl] ◇ *adj* **-1.** [path] íngreme **-2.** *fig* [easy] canja; **it's ~ all the way now** daqui pra frente, é canja **-3.** [skier]: **he's a ~ skier** ele esquia morro abaixo. ◇ *adv* **-1.** [downwards] para baixo **-2.** *fig* [from bad to worse] de mau a pior. ◇ *n SKIING* descida *f*.
Downing Street ['daʊnɪŋ-] *n rua no centro de Londres onde fica a residência oficial do primeiro-ministro inglês*, governo *m* britânico.

DOWNING STREET

Situada no centro de Londres, e fechada ao público, a *Downing Street* abriga, no número 10, a residência oficial do primeiro-ministro britânico, e, no número 11, a do ministro das finanças. Por isso, a expressão é utilizada com freqüência para designar o governo britânico como um todo.

download [ˌdaʊn'ləʊd] *vt COMPUT* baixar, fazer download.
downmarket ◇ *adj* barato(ta), de baixa qualidade. ◇ *adv*: **to go ~** produzir mais barato com qualidade inferior.
down payment *n* entrada *f*.
downplay ['daʊnpleɪ] *vt* minimizar.
downpour ['daʊnpɔ:ʳ] *n* aguaceiro *m*.
downright ['daʊnraɪt] ◇ *adj* [lie, fool] inequívoco(ca). ◇ *adv* completamente.
downside ['daʊnsaɪd] *n* [disadvantage] desvantagem *f*.
downsize ◇ *vt* [workforce] reduzir o número

de. ◇ *vi* [subj: company] reduzir o número de empregados.

Down's syndrome *n (U)* síndrome *f* de Down.

downstairs [ˌdaʊnˈsteəz] ◇ *adj* do andar de baixo. ◇ *adv*: **to come ~** vir para *OR* andar de baixo; **to go ~** ir para *OR* andar de baixo; **to live ~** morar no andar de baixo.

downstream [ˌdaʊnˈstriːm] *adv* a jusante, rio abaixo.

downtime [ˈdaʊntaɪm] *n* tempo *m* ocioso.

down-to-earth *adj* realista.

downtown [ˌdaʊnˈtaʊn] *esp US* ◇ *adj* do centro; **~ New York** Nova York central. ◇ *adv*: **to go ~** ir ao centro; **to live ~** viver no centro.

downtrodden [ˈdaʊnˌtrɒdn] *adj* oprimido(da).

downturn [ˈdaʊntɜːn] *n* decréscimo *m*; **~ in sthg** queda em algo.

down under *adv* na *OR* para Austrália/Nova Zelândia.

downward [ˈdaʊnwəd] ◇ *adj* **-1.** [towards ground] para baixo **-2.** [decreasing] descendente. ◇ *adv US* = **downwards**.

downwards [ˈdaʊnwədz] *adv* **-1.** [look, move] para baixo; **the overall trend is ~** a tendência geral é de baixa **-2.** [in hierarchy] para baixo.

downwind [ˌdaʊnˈwɪnd] *adv* a favor do vento.

dowry [ˈdaʊərɪ] (*pl* **-ies**) *n* dote *m*.

doz. (*abbr of* **dozen**) dz.

doze [dəʊz] ◇ *n* soneca *f*; **to have a ~** tirar uma soneca. ◇ *vi* dormitar.

◆ **doze off** *vi* cochilar.

dozen [ˈdʌzn] ◇ *num adj* dúzia *f*. ◇ *n* [twelve] dúzia *f*; **50p a ~** 50p a dúzia.

◆ **dozens** *npl inf*: **~s of** um montão de.

dozy [ˈdəʊzɪ] (*compar* **-ier**, *superl* **-iest**) *adj* **-1.** [sleepy] sonolento(ta) **-2.** *UK inf* [stupid] retardado(da).

DP (*abbr of* **data processing**) *n* PD *m*.

DPhil [ˌdiːˈfɪl] (*abbr of* **Doctor of Philosophy**) *n* *(titular de) doutorado em ciências humanas.*

DPP (*abbr of* **Director of Public Prosecutions**) *n fiscal geral do estado na Grã-Bretanha.*

DPT (*abbr of* **diphtheria, pertussis, tetanus**) *n* (vacina *f*) tríplice *f*.

Dr (*abbr of* **Doctor**) Dr. (Dra.).

Dr. (*abbr of* **Drive**) *usado em nomes de rua na Grã-Bretanha.*

drab [dræb] (*compar* **-ber**, *superl* **-best**) *adj* **-1.** [buildings] sombrio(bria) **-2.** [colour, garment] apagado(da) **-3.** [life] monótono(na).

draconian [drəˈkəʊnjən] *adj fml* draconiano(na).

draft [drɑːft] ◇ *n* **-1.** [early version] rascunho *m* **-2.** [money order] ordem *f* de pagamento **-3.** *US MIL*: **the ~** o destacamento **-4.** *US* = **draught**. ◇ *vt* **-1.** [write] rascunhar, fazer um rascunho de **-2.** *US MIL* recrutar **-3.** [transfer] deslocar.

draft dodger [-dɒdʒəʳ] *n US o que tenta fugir do serviço militar.*

draftee [ˌdrɑːfˈtiː] *n US* recruta *m*.

draftsman *n US* = **draughtsman**.

draftsmanship *n US* = **draughtsmanship**.

drafty *adj US* = **draughty**.

drag [dræg] (*pt* & *pp* **-ged**, *cont* **-ging**) ◇ *vt* **-1.** [gen] arrastar **-2.** [search] dragar. ◇ *vi* **-1.** [trail] arrastar **-2.** [pass slowly] arrastar-se. ◇ *n* **-1.** *inf* [bore] chatice *f*; **what a ~!** que pé no saco! **-2.** *inf* [on cigarette] tragada *f* **-3.** [air resistance] resistência *f* aerodinâmica **- 4.** *(U)* [cross-dressing]: **in ~** vestido como mulher.

◆ **drag down** *vt sep fig* [debase]: **to ~ sb down** levar alguém para o buraco.

◆ **drag in(to)** *vt sep* [involve] meter em; **don't ~ me into this!** não me meta nisso!

◆ **drag on** *vi* arrastar-se.

◆ **drag out** *vt sep* **-1.** [protract] prolongar-se em demasia **-2.** [extract]: **to ~ sthg out of sb** arrancar algo de alguém.

dragnet [ˈdrægnet] *n* **-1.** [net] rede *f* de arrasto **-2.** *fig* [to catch criminal] batida *f*.

dragon [ˈdrægən] *n* **-1.** [beast] dragão *m* **-2.** *inf* [woman] bruxa *f*.

dragonfly [ˈdrægnflaɪ] (*pl* **-ies**) *n* libélula *f*.

dragoon [drəˈguːn] ◇ *n* dragão *m*. ◇ *vt*: **to ~ sb into doing sthg** forçar alguém a fazer algo.

drag racing *n (U)* corrida *f* de carros envenenados.

dragster [ˈdrægstəʳ] *n* carro *m* envenenado.

drain [dreɪn] ◇ *n* **-1.** [pipe] cano *m* de esgoto; **to go down the ~** ir para o brejo; [grating in street] bueiro *m* **-2.** [depletion]: **~ on sthg** sorvedouro de algo; **it's a ~ on my energy** esgota todas as minhas forças. ◇ *vt* **-1.** [remove water from] drenar **-2.** [deplete] esgotar, exaurir **-3.** [drink, glass] beber até o fim. ◇ *vi* **-1.** [dry] escoar **-2.** [disappear] desaparecer.

drainage [ˈdreɪnɪdʒ] *n* **-1.** [pipes, ditches] esgoto *m* **-2.** [draining] drenagem *f*.

draining board *UK* [ˈdreɪnɪŋ-], **drainboard** *US* [ˈdreɪnbɔːrd] *n* escorredor *m* de louça.

drainpipe [ˈdreɪnpaɪp] *n* cano *m* de esgoto.

drake [dreɪk] *n* pato *m* (macho).

dram [dræm] *n* [of whisky] trago *m*.

drama [ˈdrɑːmə] ◇ *n* **-1.** [play, excitement] drama *f* **-2.** *(U)* [art] teatro *m*. ◇ *comp* de teatro.

dramatic [drəˈmætɪk] *adj* **-1.** [concerned with theatre] teatral **-2.** [exciting] dramático(ca) **-3.** [sudden, noticeable] drástico(ca).

dramatically [drəˈmætɪklɪ] *adv* **-1.** [noticeably] drasticamente **-2.** [theatrically] teatralmente.

dramatist [ˈdræmətɪst] *n* dramaturgo *m*, -ga *f*.

dramatization [ˌdræmətaɪˈzeɪʃn] *n* [for theatre, film, television] dramatização *f*.

dramatize, -ise [ˈdræmətaɪz] *vt* **-1.** [rewrite as play] dramatizar **-2.** *pej* [make exciting] tornar dramático(ca).

drank [dræŋk] *pt* ▷ **drink**.

drape [dreɪp] *vt* colocar suavemente; **to be ~d with** *OR* **in sthg** estar/ser coberto(ta) com algo.

◆ **drapes** *npl US* cortinas *fpl*.

draper [ˈdreɪpəʳ] *n*: **~'s (shop)** loja *f* de cortinas e tecidos.

drastic [ˈdræstɪk] *adj* drástico(ca).

drastically [ˈdræstɪklɪ] *adv* drasticamente.

draught *UK*, **draft** *US* [drɑːft] *n* **-1.** [air current] corrente *f* **-2.** *literary* [gulp] golfada *f* **-3.** [from barrel]: **on ~** [beer] de barril.

◆ **draughts** *n UK* damas *fpl*.

draught beer *n UK* chope *m*.
draughtboard ['drɑ:ftbɔ:d] *n UK* tabuleiro *m* de damas.
draughtsman *UK*, **draftsman** *US* ['drɑ:ftsmən] (*pl* **-men** [-mən]) *n* [of technical drawings] desenhista *m* industrial.
draughtsmanship *UK*, **draftsmanship** *US* ['drɑ:ftsmənʃɪp] *n* **-1.** [of artist] habilidade *f* para o desenho **-2.** [of work] desenho *m* industrial.
draughtswoman *UK*, **draftswoman** *US* (*pl* **-women** [-wimin]) *n* [of technical drawings] desenhista *f* industrial.
draughty *UK* (*compar* **-ier**, *superl* **-iest**), **drafty** *US* (*compar* **-ier**, *superl* **-iest**) ['drɑ:ftɪ] *adj* pouco protegido(da) do frio.
draw [drɔ:] (*pt* **drew**, *pp* **drawn**) ◇ *vt* **-1.** [sketch] desenhar **-2.** [pull] puxar; **to ~ the curtains** [open] abrir as cortinas; [close] fechar as cortinas **-3.** [breath] inalar **-4.** [pull out] sacar **-5.** [arrive at, form] chegar a **-6.** [formulate] estabelecer **-7.** [attract] atrair; **to be** *OR* **feel drawn to** ser/sentir-se atraído(da) por; **to ~ sb's attention to sthg** chamar a atenção de alguém para algo. ◇ *vi* **-1.** [sketch] esboçar **-2.** [move]: **to ~ near** aproximar-se; **to ~ away** afastar-se; **to ~ to an end** *OR* **a close** tender para um final **-3.** *SPORT* empatar; **to ~ with sb** empatar com alguém. ◇ *n* **-1.** *SPORT* [result] empate *m* **-2.** [lottery] sorteio *m* **-3.** [attraction] atração *f*.
◆ **draw in** *vi* [days] declinar.
◆ **draw into** *vt sep*: **to ~ sb into sthg** envolver alguém em algo.
◆ **draw on** *vt fus* **-1.** = **draw upon -2.** [smoke] tragar.
◆ **draw out** *vt sep* **-1.** [encourage] desinibir **-2.** [prolong] prolongar **-3.** [withdraw] sacar.
◆ **draw up** ◇ *vt sep* [draft] redigir, preparar. ◇ *vi* [stop] parar.
◆ **draw upon** *vt fus* recorrer a.
drawback ['drɔ:bæk] *n* inconveniente *m*.
drawbridge ['drɔ:brɪdʒ] *n* ponte *f* levadiça.
drawer [drɔ:ʳ] *n* [in desk, chest] gaveta *f*.
drawing ['drɔ:ɪŋ] *n* **-1.** [picture] desenho *m*, croqui *m* **-2.** *(U)* [skill, act] ato *m* de desenhar.
drawing board *n* prancheta *f* de desenho; **back to the ~!** *inf* de volta ao ponto de partida!
drawing pin *n UK* percevejo *m*.
drawing room *n* [living room] sala-de-estar *f*.
drawl [drɔ:l] ◇ *n* fala *f* arrastada. ◇ *vt* arrastar. ◇ *vi* falar de forma arrastada.
drawn [drɔ:n] ◇ *pp* ⊳ **draw**. ◇ *adj* **-1.** [curtain, blind] fechado(da) **-2.** [face, person] abatido(da).
drawn-out *adj* esticado(da).
drawstring ['drɔ:strɪŋ] *n* cordão *m*.
dread [dred] ◇ *n (U)* medo *m*, pavor *m*. ◇ *vt* temer; **to ~ doing sthg** ter medo de fazer algo; **I ~ to think** tenho medo de pensar.
dreaded ['dredɪd] *adj* [feared] temido(da).
dreadful ['dredfʊl] *adj* **-1.** [terrible] terrível **-2.** [unpleasant] desagradável **-3.** [ill] horrível **-4.** [embarrassed] envergonhado(da) **-5.** [poor] fraco(ca) **-6.** [for emphasis] horroroso(sa).
dreadfully ['dredfʊlɪ] *adv* **-1.** [badly] terrivelmente **-2.** [extremely] extremamente.
dreadlocks ['dredlɒks] *npl* cabelo *m* rastafári.
dream [dri:m] (*pt* & *pp* **-ed** *OR* **dreamt**) ◇ *n* **-1.** [during sleep] sonho *m*; **bad ~** pesadelo *m* **-2.** [aspiration] sonho *m*; **to be beyond one's wildest ~s** ser muito melhor do que o esperado. ◇ *adj* almejado(da). ◇ *vt* [during sleep]: **to ~ (that)** sonhar que; **I never ~ed this would happen** jamais imaginei que isso pudesse acontecer. ◇ *vi* **-1.** [during sleep] sonhar; **to ~ of** *OR* **about sthg** sonhar com algo; **I wouldn't ~ of it** *fig* nem pensar, de maneira nenhuma **-2.** [aspire]: **to ~ of sthg/of doing sthg** sonhar com algo/em fazer algo.
◆ **dream up** *vt sep* bolar.
dreamer ['dri:məʳ] *n* [unrealistic person] sonhador *m*, -ra *f*.
dreamily ['dri:mɪlɪ] *adv* como em sonhos.
dreamlike ['dri:mlaɪk] *adj* de sonho.
dreamt [dremt] *pt* & *pp* ⊳ **dream**.
dream world *n* mundo *m* de sonhos.
dreamy ['dri:mɪ] (*compar* **-ier**, *superl* **-iest**) *adj* **-1.** [look, smile] distraído(da), sonhador(ra) **-2.** [music, feeling] sentimental.
dreary ['drɪərɪ] (*compar* **-ier**, *superl* **-iest**) *adj* **-1.** [gloomy, depressing] sombrio(a) **-2.** [dull, boring] chato(-ta).
dredge [dredʒ] *vt* [lake, harbour, river] dragar.
◆ **dredge up** *vt sep* **-1.** [with dredger] dragar **-2.** *fig* [from past] trazer à tona.
dredger ['dredʒəʳ] *n* [ship, machine] draga *f*.
dregs [dregz] *npl* **-1.** [of liquid] borra *f* **-2.** *fig* [of society] ralé *f*.
drench [drentʃ] *vt* encharcar; **to be ~ed in** *OR* **with sthg** estar encharcado(da) de algo.
Dresden ['drezdən] *n* Dresden; **in ~** em Dresden.
dress [dres] ◇ *n* **-1.** [frock] vestido *m* **-2.** [type of clothing] roupa *f*. ◇ *vt* **-1.** [clothe] vestir; **to be ~ed** estar vestido(da); **to be ~ed in** estar vestido(da) de; **to get ~ed** vestir-se **-2.** [bandage] fazer curativo em **-3.** *CULIN* temperar. ◇ *vi* vestir-se.
◆ **dress up** ◇ *vt sep* **-1.** [in costume] disfarçar-se **-2.** [in best clothes] vestir-se elegantemente **-3.** [in formal clothes] vestir-se a rigor **-4.** *fig* [embellish] enfeitar. ◇ *vi* **-1.** [in costume] fantasiar-se **-2.** [in best clothes] vestir-se elegantemente **-3.** [in formal clothes] vestir-se a rigor.
dressage ['dresɑ:ʒ] *n (U)* adestramento *m*.
dress circle *n THEATRE* balcão *m* nobre.
dresser ['dresəʳ] *n* **-1.** [for dishes] aparador *m* **-2.** *US* [chest of drawers] cômoda *f* **-3.** [person]: **to be a smart ~** vestir-se bem **-4.** *THEATRE* camareiro *m*, -ra *f*.
dressing ['dresɪŋ] *n* **-1.** [bandage] curativo *m* **-2.** [for salad] tempero *m*, molho *m* **-3.** *US* [for turkey etc] molho *m*.
dressing gown *n* **-1.** [man's] roupão *m* **-2.** [woman's] robe *f*.
dressing room *n* **-1.** *SPORT* vestiário *m* **-2.** *THEATRE* camarim *m*.
dressing table *n* penteadeira *f*.
dressmaker ['dres,meɪkəʳ] *n* costureiro *m*, -ra *f*.
dressmaking ['dres,meɪkɪŋ] *n (U)* costura *f*.
dress rehearsal *n THEATRE* ensaio *m* geral.
dress shirt *n* camisa *f* social.

dressy ['dresɪ] (*compar* **-ier**, *superl* **-iest**) *adj* [smart] chique.

drew [dru:] *pt* ⊳ **draw**.

dribble ['drɪbl] ◇ *n* **-1.** *(U)* [of saliva] filete *m* **-2.** [of other liquid] gota *f.* ◇ *vt* **-1.** *SPORT* [ball] driblar **-2.** [liquid] pingar. ◇ *vi* **-1.** [drool] babar **-2.** [trickle] derramar.

dribs [drɪbz] *npl*: **in ~ and drabs** aos poucos.

dried [draɪd] ◇ *pt & pp* ⊳ **dry**. ◇ *adj* **-1.** [powdered] em pó **-2.** [fruit, herbs, flowers] seco(ca).

dried fruit *n (U)* fruta *f* seca.

dried-up *adj* seco(ca).

drier ['draɪəʳ] *n* = **dryer**.

drift [drɪft] ◇ *n* **-1.** [movement, trend] tendência *f* **-2.** [of current] fluxo *m* **-3.** [geol] pressão *f* **-4.** [of people] curso *m* **-5.** [of snow, leaves, sand] monte *m* **-6.** [meaning] sentido *m*; **to get the general ~** pegar a idéia geral. ◇ *vi* **-1.** [boat] estar à deriva **-2.** [snow, sand, leaves] acumular-se **-3.** [person]: **they're ~ing towards bankruptcy** eles estão indo a caminho da falência; **to ~ into marriage** acabar se casando; **to ~ apart** acabar se afastando.

◆ **drift off** *vi* [fall asleep] cair de sono.

drifter ['drɪftəʳ] *n* [person] nômade *mf.*

driftwood ['drɪftwʊd] *n (U)* madeira *f* flutuante.

drill [drɪl] ◇ *n* **-1.** [tool] furadeira *f* **-2.** [industrial] perfuradora *f* **-3.** [dentist's] broca *f* **-4.** [exercise, training] treinamento *m.* ◇ *vt* **-1.** [metal, wood, hole] perfurar *f* **-2.** [instruct] instruir; **to ~ sthg into sb** ensinar algo a alguém *(repetindo a lição regularmente).* ◇ *vi* furar; **to ~ into sthg** penetrar em algo; **to ~ for sthg** procurar algo *(perfurando com broca).*

drilling platform ['drɪlɪŋ-] *n* plataforma *f* de perfuração.

drily ['draɪlɪ] *adv* = **dryly**.

drink [drɪŋk] (*pt* **drank**, *pp* **drunk**) ◇ *n* **-1.** [non-alcoholic beverage] bebida *f* **-2.** [alcoholic beverage] bebida *f* alcoólica; **to have a ~** tomar um drinque **-3.** *(U)* [alcohol] bebida *f.* ◇ *vt* beber. ◇ *vi* beber; **to ~ to sb/sb's success** brindar a alguém/ao sucesso de alguém.

drinkable ['drɪŋkəbl] *adj* **-1.** [safe to drink] potável **-2.** [tasty] saboroso(sa).

drink-driving *UK*, **drunk-driving** *US n (U)* ato *m* de dirigir bêbado, -da *f.*

drinker ['drɪŋkəʳ] *n* **-1.** [of alcohol] beberrão *m*, -rona *f* **-2.** [of tea, coffee]: **he's a great tea/coffee ~** ele gosta muito de tomar chá/café.

drinking ['drɪŋkɪŋ] ◇ *adj*: **I'm not a ~ man** não sou um homem que bebe; **~ laws** leis de consumo de bebida alcoólica. ◇ *n*: **to go ~** ir beber; **heavy ~** embriagamento.

drinking companion *n* companheiro *m*, -ra *f* de bebida.

drinking fountain *n* bebedouro *m.*

drinking-up time *n UK inf tempo concedido nos bares para acabar os drinks antes de fechar.*

drinking water ['drɪŋkɪŋ-] *n (U)* água *f* potável.

drip [drɪp] (*pt & pp* **-ped**, *cont* **-ping**) ◇ *n* **-1.** [drop] gota *f* **-2.** *MED* aparelho *m* de soro **-3.** *inf* [wimp] sonso *m*, -sa *f.* ◇ *vt* pingar. ◇ *vi* **-1.** [gen] pingar **-2.** [nose] escorrer **-3.** [person]: **to be ~ping with** [sweat, blood] estar encharcado(da) de; [diamonds, furs] *fig* estar coberto(ta) de.

drip-dry *adj* que não amarrota ao secar.

drip-feed ◇ *n* alimentação *f* por conta-gotas. ◇ *vt* alimentar por conta-gotas.

dripping ['drɪpɪŋ] ◇ *adj* **-1.** [person, clothes, hair]: **~ (wet)** encharcado(da) **-2.** [tap] que pinga. ◇ *n CULIN* [from meat] banha *f (de carne).*

drive [draɪv] (*pt* **drove**, *pp* **driven**) ◇ *n* **-1.** [journey] passeio *m*, volta *f* de carro **-2.** [urge] ímpulso *m* **-3.** [campaign] campanha *f* **-4.** *(U)* [energy] ímpeto *m* **-5.** [road to house] caminho *m (de entrada)* **-6.** *SPORT* [stroke] tacada *f* **-7.** *US AUT* [in automatic car] transmissão *f* automática. ◇ *vt* **-1.** [vehicle] dirigir; [passenger] levar *(de carro)* **-2.** *TECH* [operate] operar **-3.** [chase] seguir **-4.** [motivate] motivar **-5.** [force]: **to ~ sb to sthg/to do sthg** levar alguém a algo/a fazer algo; **to ~ sb mad** *OR* **crazy** [make insane] deixar alguém louco(ca) *OR* maluco(ca); [irritate] deixar alguém furioso(sa) **-6.** [hammer] bater **-7.** *SPORT* [hit] rebater. ◇ *vi AUT* **-1.** [driver] dirigir **-2.** [travel by car] viajar.

◆ **drive at** *vt fus* querer dizer, insinuar.

◆ **drive out** *vt sep* fazer sair.

drive-in *esp US* ◇ *adj* drive-in. ◇ *n* **-1.** [restaurant] drive-in *m* **-2.** [cinema] autocine *m.*

drivel ['drɪvl] *n inf* bobagem *f.*

driven ['drɪvn] *pp* ⊳ **drive**.

driver ['draɪvəʳ] *n* **-1.** [of vehicle] motorista *mf* **-2.** *COMPUT* driver *m.*

driver's license *n US* = **driving licence**.

drive shaft *n* eixo *m* de transmissão.

driveway ['draɪvweɪ] *n* acesso *m.*

driving ['draɪvɪŋ] ◇ *adj* [rain, wind] forte; **~ rain** chuva *f* torrencial. ◇ *n (U)* direção *f.*

driving force *n* força *f* motriz.

driving instructor *n* instrutor *m*, -ra *f* de direção.

driving lesson *n* aula *f* de direção.

driving licence *UK*, **driver's license** *US n* carteira *f* de motorista.

driving mirror *n* (espelho *m*) retrovisor *m.*

driving school *n* auto-escola *f.*

driving test *n* exame *m* de direção.

drizzle ['drɪzl] ◇ *n* garoa *f*, chuvisco *m.* ◇ *v impers* garoar, chuviscar.

drizzly ['drɪzlɪ] (*compar* **-ier**, *superl* **-iest**) *adj* chuvoso(sa); **~ rain** garoa *f* fina.

droll [drəʊl] *adj* engraçado(da).

dromedary ['drɒmədrɪ] (*pl* **-ies**) *n* dromedário *m.*

drone [drəʊn] ◇ *n* **-1.** [sound] zunido *m* **-2.** [bee] zangão *m.* ◇ *vi* zunir.

◆ **drone on** *vi* falar de forma monótona; **to ~ on about sthg** falar de forma monótona sobre algo.

drool [dru:l] *vi* **-1.** [dribble] babar **-2.** *fig* [admire]: **to ~ over sb/sthg** babar por alguém/algo.

droop [dru:p] *vi* **-1.** [hang down - shoulders] encurvar-se; [- head] inclinar-se; [- eyelids] fechar-se; [- flowers] murchar-se **-2.** *fig* [weaken, flag] desanimar-se.

drop [drɒp] (*pt & pp* **-ped**, *cont* **-ping**) ◇ *n* **-1.** [of liquid - water, blood, rain] gota *f*; [- tea, coffee, milk] gole m; [- alcohol] dose f **-2.** [sweet] bala f **-3.** [decrease] queda f; ~ **in sthg** queda de algo **-4.** [vertical distance] descida f. <> vt **-1.** [let fall - gen] deixar cair; [- bombs] lançar; [- stitch]: **she ~ped a stitch** escapou um ponto **-2.** [decrease, lower] reduzir **-3.** [voice] baixar **-4.** [leave, abandon] deixar **-5.** [leave out] excluir **-6.** [hint, remark] lançar **-7.** TENNIS [lose] perder **-8.** [write]: **to ~ sb a line** OR **note** escrever a alguém umas linhas OR um bilhete. <> vi **-1.** [fall] cair; **to ~ to one's knees** ajoelhar-se; **~ dead!** vai tomar banho! **-2.** [fall] baixar **-3.** [wind, attendance] diminuir.

◆ **drops** npl MED gotas fpl.

◆ **drop by** vi inf dar um pulo *(como visita)*.

◆ **drop in** vi inf passar na casa de; **to ~ in on sb** passar na casa de alguém.

◆ **drop off** <> vt sep deixar. <> vi **-1.** [fall asleep] cair no sono **-2.** [grow less] diminuir.

◆ **drop out** vi [withdraw] retirar-se; **to ~ out of** OR **from sthg** desligar-se de algo.

drop-in centre n *centro mantido pelos serviços sociais, pela igreja, etc., que as pessoas podem freqüentar se desejarem.*

droplet ['drɒplɪt] n gotícula f.

dropout ['drɒpaʊt] n **-1.** [from society] marginalizado m, -da f **-2.** [from university] pessoa f que largou os estudos.

dropper ['drɒpəʳ] n conta-gotas m inv.

droppings ['drɒpɪŋz] npl excremento m *(de animais)*.

drop shot n TENNIS deixada f.

dross [drɒs] n **-1.** TECH [waste material] refugo m **-2.** fig [rubbish] porcaria f.

drought [draʊt] n seca f.

drove [drəʊv] <> pt ▷ **drive**. <> n [of people] multidão f.

drown [draʊn] <> vt **-1.** [kill] afogar **-2.** [sound]: **to ~ sb/sthg (out)** abafar alguém/algo. <> vi afogar-se.

drowsy ['draʊzɪ] (compar **-ier**, superl **-iest**) adj [person] sonolento(ta).

drudge [drʌdʒ] n escravo m, -va f do trabalho.

drudgery ['drʌdʒərɪ] n (U) trabalho m pesado.

drug [drʌg] (pt & pp **-ged**, cont **-ging**) <> n **-1.** [medication] remédio m **-2.** [illegal substance] droga f. <> vt **-1.** [person, animal] drogar **-2.** [food, drink] adicionar droga a.

drug abuse n (U) abuso m de drogas.

drug addict n drogado m, -da f, viciado m, -da f em drogas.

drug addiction n (U) vício m em drogas, toxicomania f.

drug dealer n traficante mf de drogas.

druggist ['drʌgɪst] n US farmacêutico m, -ca f.

drugstore ['drʌgstɔːʳ] n US farmácia f, drogaria f.

druid ['druːɪd] n druida m.

drum [drʌm] (pt & pp **-med**, cont **-ming**) <> n **-1.** [instrument] tambor m **-2.** [container, cylinder] barril m. <> vt [fingers] tamborilar. <> vi **-1.** [on drums] tocar **-2.** [rain, fingers] tamborilar **-3.** [hooves] bater.

◆ **drums** npl [set of drums] bateria f.

◆ **drum into** vt sep: **to ~ sthg into sb** incutir algo em alguém.

◆ **drum up** vt sep angariar.

drumbeat ['drʌmbiːt] n rufo m *(de tambores)*.

drum brake n freio m de tambor.

drummer ['drʌməʳ] n baterista mf.

drumming ['drʌmɪŋ] n **-1.** [of drums] rufar m **-2.** [of rain, fingers] tamborilo m **-3.** [of hooves] batida f.

drum roll n rufar m de tambor.

drumstick ['drʌmstɪk] n **-1.** [for drum] baqueta f **-2.** [food] coxa f.

drunk [drʌŋk] <> pp ▷ **drink**. <> adj **-1.** [on alcohol] bêbado(da); **to get ~** embebedar-se; **to be charged with being ~ and disorderly** JUR ser acusado(da) de estar embriagado(do) **-2.** fig [excited, carried away]: **to be ~ with** OR **on sthg** estar encantado(da) com algo. <> n bêbado m, -da f.

drunkard ['drʌŋkəd] n beberrão m, -rona f.

drunk-driving n US = **drink-driving**.

drunken ['drʌŋkn] adj **-1.** [person] bêbado(da) **-2.** [state, event] = **de bêbado**.

drunken driving n = **drink-driving**.

drunkenness ['drʌŋkənnɪs] n (U) embriaguez f.

dry [draɪ] (compar **-ier**, superl **-iest**, pt & pp **dried**) <> adj **-1.** [gen] seco(ca) **-2.** [climate] árido(da) **-3.** [sense of humour] sarcástico(ca) **-4.** [tedious] monótono(na).
<> vt & vi secar.

◆ **dry out** <> vt sep secar completamente. <> vi [get dry - gen] secar; [- person] secar-se.

◆ **dry up** <> vt sep [dishes] secar. <> vi **-1.** [gen] secar **-2.** [supplies, inspiration] esgotar-se **-3.** [actor, speaker] calar-se.

dry-clean vt lavar a seco.

dry cleaner n: **~'s** tinturaria f.

dry cleaning n [work, service] lavagem f a seco.

dry dock n dique m seco.

dryer ['draɪəʳ] n [for clothes] secadora f.

dry ginger n (U) ginger ale m.

dry goods npl artigos mpl de armarinho.

dry ice n (U) gelo-seco m.

dry land n terra f firme.

dryly ['draɪlɪ] adv [wryly] secamente.

dryness ['draɪnɪs] n (U) **-1.** [lack of water] aridez f **-2.** [wryness] secura f **-3.** [tedium] monotonia f.

dry rot n (U) apodrecimento m da madeira *(de casa)*.

dry run n [practice] ensaio m.

dry ski slope n rampa f de esqui artificial.

dry-stone wall n parede f de pedra.

DSc (abbr of **Doctor of Science**) n *(titular de) doutorado em ciências.*

DST (abbr of **daylight saving time**) *horário de verão nos Estados Unidos.*

DTI (abbr of **Department of Trade and Industry**) n *ministério britânico da indústria e do comércio,* ≃ MDIC m.

DTLR (abbr of **Department for Transport, Local Government and the Regions**) n *departamento dos transportes do governo britânico e dos governos locais.*

DTP (abbr of **desktop publishing**) n DTP f.

DTs [ˌdiːˈtiːz] (abbr of **delirium tremens**) npl fam: **to have the ~** estar em crise de abstinência.

dual ['djuːəl] adj duplo(pla).

dual carriageway n UK pista f dupla.

dual control *n* controle *m* duplo.
dual nationality *n* dupla nacionalidade *f*.
dual-purpose *adj* que tem dupla finalidade.
Dubai [ˌdu:'baɪ] *n* Dubai.
dubbed [dʌbd] *adj* **-1.** *CINEMA* dublado(da) **-2.** [nicknamed] apelidado(da).
dubious ['dju:bjəs] *adj* **-1.** [suspect, questionable] duvidoso(sa) **-2.** [uncertain, undecided]: **to be ~ about doing sthg** estar indeciso(sa) sobre fazer algo.
Dublin ['dʌblɪn] *n* Dublin; **in ~** em Dublin.
Dublin Bay prawn *n* camarão *m* à Dublin Bay.
Dubliner ['dʌblɪnər] *n* dublinense *mf*.
duchess ['dʌtʃɪs] *n* duquesa *f*.
duchy ['dʌtʃɪ] (*pl* **-ies**) *n* ducado *m*.
duck [dʌk] ◇ *n* **-1.** [bird] pato *m*, -ta *f*; **to take to sthg like a ~ to water** tirar algo de letra; **like water off a ~'s back** sem nenhum efeito **-2.** *(U)* [food] pato *m*. ◇ *vt* **-1.** [lower] curvar **-2.** [try to avoid] esquivar-se de; **to ~ the issue** evitar a questão **-3.** [submerge] mergulhar. ◇ *vi* **-1.** [lower head] curvar-se **-2.** [move down quickly] abaixar-se.
◆ **duck out** *vi*: **to ~ out (of sthg/of doing sthg)** safar-se (de algo/de fazer algo).
duckling ['dʌklɪŋ] *n* **-1.** [animal] patinho *m*, -nha *f* **-2.** [food] pato *m* novo.
duct [dʌkt] *n* **-1.** [pipe - heating] tubo *m*; [- water] canal *m* **-2.** *ANAT* ducto *m*.
dud [dʌd] ◇ *adj* **-1.** [banknote, coin, cheque] falso(sa) **-2.** [machine, idea] imprestável **-3.** [bomb, shell, bullet] que falhou. ◇ *n* negação *f*; **to be a ~ at sthg** [person] ser uma negação em algo; **to be a ~** [banknote, cheque] não ter fundos; [bomb, shell, bullet] não prestar.
dude [dju:d] *n* **US** *inf* [man] cara *m*.
dude ranch *n* **US** rancho *m* para turistas.
due [dju:] ◇ *adj* **-1.** [expected] previsto(ta); **she's ~ back shortly** espera-se que ela volte logo; **when is the next train ~?** quando chega o próximo trem? **-2.** [proper] devido(da); **in ~ course** no tempo devido **-3.** [owed, owing]: **the rent is ~** o aluguel venceu; **she's ~ a pay rise** ela deve ganhar um aumento de salário; **how much are you ~?** quanto te devem? ◇ *n* [deserts] direito *m*; **to give him his ~, ...** para lhe fazer justiça, ... ◇ *adv* exatamente; **~ north** bem ao norte.
◆ **dues** *npl* direitos *mpl*.
◆ **due to** *prep* devido a.
due date *n* (data *f* de) vencimento *m*.
duel ['dju:əl] *n* duelo *m*.
duet [dju:'et] *n* dueto *m*.
duff [dʌf] *adj* **UK** *inf* inútil.
◆ **duff up** *vt sep* **UK** *inf* dar uma surra em.
duffel bag ['dʌfl-] *n* mochila *f*.
duffel coat ['dʌfl-] *n* casaco *m* grosso *(com capuz)*.
duffle bag ['dʌfl-] *n* = **duffel bag**.
duffle coat ['dʌfl-] *n* = **duffel coat**.
dug [dʌg] *pt* & *pp* ▷ **dig**.
dugout ['dʌgaʊt] *n* **-1.** [canoe] canoa *f* **-2.** *SPORT* fosso *m*.
duke [dju:k] *n* duque *m*.
dull [dʌl] ◇ *adj* **-1.** [boring] entediante **-2.** [colour, light] opaco(ca) **-3.** [day, weather] nublado(da) **-4.** [thud, boom] surdo(da) **-5.** [ache, pain] incômodo(da). ◇ *vt* **-1.** [deaden - pain] aliviar; [- senses, memory] enfraquecer; [- pleasure] diminuir **-2.** [make less bright] embaciar.
duly ['dju:lɪ] *adv* **-1.** [properly] devidamente **-2.** [as expected] como era de se esperar.
dumb [dʌm] *adj* **-1.** [unable to speak] mudo(da) **-2.** *esp* **US** *inf* [stupid] estúpido(da).
dumbbell ['dʌmbel] *n* [weight] haltere *m*.
dumbfound [dʌm'faʊnd] *vt* pasmar; **to be ~ed** ficar pasmado(da).
dumbstruck ['dʌmstrʌk] *adj* chocado(da), pasmado(da).
dumbwaiter [ˌdʌm'weɪtə^r] *n* [lift] elevador *m* de comida.
dumdum (bullet) ['dʌmdʌm-] *n* bala *f* dundum.
dummy ['dʌmɪ] (*pl* **-ies**) ◇ *adj* [fake] falso(sa). ◇ *n* **-1.** [model of human figure - tailor's] manequim *m*; [- ventriloquist's] boneco *m* **-2.** [copy, fake object] imitação *f* **-3.** **UK** [for baby] chupeta *f* **-4.** *SPORT* drible *m*. ◇ *vt SPORT* driblar.
dummy run *n* prova *f*, ensaio *m*.
dump [dʌmp] ◇ *n* **-1.** [for rubbish] lixeira *f* **-2.** [for ammunition] depósito *m* **-3.** *inf pej* [ugly place] espelunca *f*. ◇ *vt* **-1.** [put down] deixar cair **-2.** [dispose of] descarregar **-3.** *COMM* liquidar **-4.** *COMPUT* mover de um dispositivo para outro **-5.** *inf* [jilt] romper com.
◆ **dumps** *npl*: **to be (down) in the ~s** estar na fossa.
dumper (truck) ['dʌmpə^r-] **UK**, **dump truck** **US** *n* caminhão *m* basculante.
dumping ['dʌmpɪŋ] *n (U)* descarregamento *m*; **'no ~'** 'proibido jogar lixo'.
dumping ground *n* depósito *m*.
dumpling ['dʌmplɪŋ] *n CULIN* bolinho *m* de massa de pão.
dumpster *n* **US** caçamba *f* de lixo.
dump truck *n* **US** = **dumper (truck)**.
dumpy ['dʌmpɪ] (*compar* **-ier**, *superl* **-iest**) *adj inf* atarracado(da).
dunce [dʌns] *n* burro *m*, -ra *f*, ignorante *mf*.
dune [dju:n] *n* duna *f*.
dung [dʌŋ] *n (U)* esterco *m*.
dungarees [ˌdʌŋgə'ri:z] *npl* **UK** macacão *m*.
dungeon ['dʌndʒən] *n* masmorra *f*.
dunk [dʌŋk] *vt inf* molhar.
Dunkirk [dʌn'kɜ:k] *n* Dunquerque.
duo ['dju:əʊ] *n* **-1.** *MUS* dueto *m* **-2.** [couple] casal *m*.
duodenal ulcer ['dju:əʊ'di:nl-] *n* úlcera *f* duodenal.
dupe [dju:p] ◇ *n* [person] otário *m*, -ria *f*. ◇ *vt* [trick]: **to ~ sb (into doing sthg)** iludir alguém (a fazer algo).
duplex ['dju:pleks] *n* **US** dúplex *m inv*.
duplicate [*adj* & *n* 'dju:plɪkət, *vb* 'dju:plɪkeɪt] ◇ *adj* [document] duplicado(da); **~ key** cópia *f* de chave. ◇ *n* [of document] cópia *f*; **in ~** em duplicata. ◇ *vt* **-1.** [document] copiar **-2.** [double, repeat] repetir.
duplication [ˌdju:plɪ'keɪʃn] *n (U)* **-1.** [copying] duplicação *f* **-2.** [doubling, repetition] repetição *f*.

duplicity [dju:'plɪsətɪ] *n (U) fml* [deceit] duplicidade *f.*
durability [ˌdjʊərə'bɪlətɪ] *n (U)* durabilidade *f.*
durable ['djʊərəbl] *adj* durável, duradouro(ra).
duration [djʊ'reɪʃn] *n (U)* duração *f*; **for the ~ of** durante.
duress [djʊ'res] *n (U)*: **under ~** sob coerção.
Durex® ['djʊəreks] *n* [condom] preservativo *m*, camisinha *f.*
during ['djʊərɪŋ] *prep* durante.
dusk [dʌsk] *n (U)* crepúsculo *m*, anoitecer *m.*
dusky ['dʌskɪ] (*compar* **-ier**, *superl* **-iest**) *adj literary* [skin] moreno(na).
dust [dʌst] <> *n (U)* **-1.** [gen] pó *m*; **to gather ~** [get dusty] pegar pó; *fig* [be ignored] ser privado(da); **to let the ~ settle** deixar a poeira baixar; **to have bitten the ~** ser derrubado(da) por terra **-2.** [earth, sand] poeira *f*, pó *m.* <> *vt* **-1.** [clean] tirar o pó de **-2.** [cover]: **to ~ sthg with sthg** polvilhar algo com algo.
◆ **dust off** *vt sep* **-1.** [clean] sacudir a poeira de **-2.** *fig* [re-use] reaproveitar.
dustbin ['dʌstbɪn] *n UK* lata *f* de lixo.
dustbowl ['dʌstbəʊl] *n* zona *f* de desertificação.
dustcart ['dʌstkɑ:t] *n UK* caminhão *m* de lixo.
dust cover *n* **-1.** [for book] = **dust jacket -2.** [for furniture] = **dust sheet.**
duster ['dʌstə^r] *n* **-1.** [cloth] espanador *m* de pó **-2.** *US* [overall] guarda-pó *m.*
dust jacket, dust cover *n* [on book] sobrecapa *f.*
dustman ['dʌstmən] (*pl* **-men** [-mən]) *n UK* lixeiro *m.*
dust mite *n* ácaro *m (da poeira doméstica).*
dustpan ['dʌstpæn] *n* pá *f* de lixo.
dust sheet, dust cover *n UK* capa *f (para os móveis).*
dust storm *n* tempestade *f* de poeira.
dust-up *n inf* briga *f*, rinha *f.*
dusty ['dʌstɪ] (*compar* **-ier**, *superl* **-iest**) *adj* [covered in dust] empoeirado(da).
Dutch [dʌtʃ] <> *adj* holandês(esa). <> *n* [language] holandês *m.* <> *npl*: **the ~** os holandeses. <> *adv*: **let's go ~** cada um paga a sua parte.
Dutch auction *n UK leilão no qual vai se baixando o preço de venda até que haja um comprador.*
Dutch barn *n UK* celeiro *m* holandês.
Dutch cap *n UK* diafragma *m.*
Dutch courage *n* coragem *f (produzida pela embriaguez).*
Dutch elm disease *n (U) doença f do olmo holandês.*
Dutchman ['dʌtʃmən] (*pl* **-men** [-mən]) *n* holandês *m.*
Dutchwoman ['dʌtʃˌwʊmən] (*pl* **-women** [-ˌwɪmɪn]) *n* holandesa *f.*
dutiable ['dju:tjəbl] *adj* tributável.
dutiful ['dju:tɪfʊl] *adj* zeloso(sa).
duty ['dju:tɪ] (*pl* **-ies**) *n* **-1.** *(U)* [moral, legal responsibility] dever *m*; **to do one's ~** cumprir com o dever **-2.** *(U)* [work] obrigação *f*; **to be on/off ~** estar de plantão/folga **-3.** [tax] imposto *m.*
◆ **duties** *npl* [tasks, part of job] funções *fpl.*
duty bound *adj* [obliged] obrigado(da); **to be ~ to do sthg** ser obrigado(da) a fazer algo.
duty-free <> *n* **-1.** [goods] artigo *m* isento de impostos **-2.** [shop] loja *f* duty-free. <> *adj* [whisky, cigarettes] isento(ta) de impostos.
duty-free shop *n* loja *f* duty-free.
duty officer *n* oficial *mf* em serviço.
duvet ['du:veɪ] *n UK* edredom *m*, acolchoado *m.*
duvet cover *n UK* capa *f* do edredom.
DVD (*abbr of* **Digital Versatile Disk**) *n* DVD *m.*
DVD player *n* (reprodutor *m* de) DVD *m.*
DVD ROM (*abbr of* **Digital Versatile Disk read only memory**) *n* DVD-ROM *m.*
DVLA (*abbr of* **Driver and Vehicle Licensing Agency**) *n órgão britânico responsável pelo registro de automóveis e emissão de carteiras de motorista,* ≃ DENATRAN *m.*
DVM (*abbr of* **Doctor of Veterinary Medicine**) *n (titular de) doutorado em medicina veterinária.*
dwarf [dwɔ:f] (*pl* **-s** *OR* **dwarves** [dwɔ:vz]) <> *adj* [plant, animal] anão (anã). <> *n* anão *m*, anã *f.* <> *vt* [tower over] sobrepujar.
dwell [dwel] (*pt* & *pp* **dwelt** *OR* **-ed**) *vi literary* [live] morar.
◆ **dwell on** *vt fus* [past, problem] ficar dando voltas com.
-dweller ['dwelə^r] *suffix* [inhabitant] habitante *mf*; **city-~** habitante *mf* da cidade.
dwelling ['dwelɪŋ] *n literary* morada *f.*
dwelt [dwelt] *pt* & *pp* ⊳ **dwell.**
dwindle ['dwɪndl] *vi* [decrease, grow smaller] ir diminuindo.
dwindling ['dwɪndlɪŋ] *adj* [decreasing, growing smaller] decrescente.
DWP (*abbr of* **Department for Work and Pensions**) *n departamento britânico para administração de trabalhadores e pensionistas.*
dye [daɪ] <> *n* [colouring] tintura *f.* <> *vt* [change colour of] tingir.
dyed [daɪd] *adj* tingido(da).
dying ['daɪɪŋ] <> *cont* ⊳ **die.** <> *adj* **-1.** [about to die - person] agonizante; [- species] em vias de extinção **-2.** *fig* [declining] que está desaparecendo. <> *npl*: **the ~** os moribundos.
dyke [daɪk] *n* = **dike.**
dynamic [daɪ'næmɪk] *adj* [energetic] dinâmico(ca).
◆ **dynamics** *npl* [forces of change] dinâmica *f.*
dynamism ['daɪnəmɪzm] *n (U)* [energy] dinamismo *m.*
dynamite ['daɪnəmaɪt] <> *n (U)* **-1.** [explosive] dinamite *f* **-2.** *inf fig* [person, story, news]: **to be ~** ser uma bomba **-3.** *inf fig* [excellent] excelente. <> *vt* [blow up] dinamitar.
dynamo ['daɪnəməʊ] (*pl* **-s**) *n TECH* dínamo *m.*
dynasty [*UK* 'dɪnəstɪ, *US* 'daɪnəstɪ] (*pl* **-ies**) *n* [ruling family] dinastia *f.*
dysentery ['dɪsntrɪ] *n (U)* disenteria *f.*
dyslexia [dɪs'leksɪə] *n (U)* dislexia *f.*
dyslexic [dɪs'leksɪk] *adj* disléxico(ca).
dyspepsia [dɪs'pepsɪə] *n (U) MED* dispepsia *f.*
dystrophy ['dɪstrəfɪ] *n* ⊳ **muscular dystrophy.**

e (*pl* **e's** *OR* **es**), **E** (*pl* **E's** *OR* **Es**) [i:] *n* [letter] e, E *m*.
◆ **E** *n* **-1.** *MUS* mi *m* **-2.** (*abbr of* **east**) l **-3.** (*abbr of* **ecstasy**) ecstasy *m*.

E111 *n formulário que garante seguro saúde a cidadãos britânicos em estadas temporárias em outros países da União Européia.*

ea. (*abbr of* **each**) cada.

each [i:tʃ] <> *adj* [every] cada. <> *pron* [every one] cada um (uma); **two of ~** dois de cada; **~ other** um ao outro; **we know ~ other** nós nos conhecemos.

eager ['i:gəʳ] *adj* [keen, enthusiastic] animado(da); **to be ~ for sthg/to do sthg** estar ansioso(sa) por algo/para fazer algo.

eagerly ['i:gəlɪ] *adv* [talk, plan] animadamente.

eagle ['i:gl] *n* [bird] águia *f*.

eagle-eyed [-'aɪd] *adj* [person] com olhos de lince.

eaglet ['i:glɪt] *n* águia *f* nova.

E and OE (*abbr of* **errors and omissions excepted**) ≃ SEO, salvo erro ou omissão.

ear [ɪəʳ] *n* **-1.** [of person, animal] orelha *f*; **by ~** *MUS* de ouvido; **to go in one ~ and out the other** *inf* entrar por um ouvido e sair pelo outro; **to have** *OR* **keep one's ~ to the ground** *inf* estar/manter-se atento(ta) aos últimos acontecimentos; **to have sb's ~** ter a atenção de alguém; **to have an ~ for sthg** ter ouvido para algo; **to play it by ~** *fig* nadar de acordo com a maré **-2.** [of corn] espiga *f*.

earache ['ɪəreɪk] *n* dor *f* de ouvido.

eardrum ['ɪədrʌm] *n* tímpano *m*.

earl [3:l] *n* conde *m*.

earlier ['3:lɪəʳ] <> *adj* **-1.** [previous] anterior **-2.** [according to clock]: **let's take the ~ train** vamos pegar o trem que tem antes. <> *adv* antes; **~ on** antes; **~ that day** mais cedo naquele dia; **they arrived ~ than expected** eles chegaram antes do esperado.

earliest ['3:lɪəst] <> *adj* **-1.** [first] primeiro(ra); **at your ~ convenience** assim que puder **-2.** [according to clock] primeiro(ra). <> *adv*: **at the ~** no mínimo.

earlobe ['ɪələʊb] *n* lóbulo *m* da orelha.

early ['3:lɪ] (*compar* **-ier**, *superl* **-iest**) <> *adj* **-1.** [gen] adiantado(da); **the ~ train** o primeiro trem; **to make an ~ start** começar na primeira hora **-2.** [of the beginning of a period of time - old] antigo(ga); [- period]: **this chair is ~ Victorian** esta cadeira é do início da era Vitoriana; [- in career, life] os primeiros anos de; [- in time] no começo de; **~-morning** da madrugada; **the ~ chapters** os primeiros capítulos. <> *adv* **-1.** [before expected time] antes da hora **-2.** [in the morning, in a period of time] cedo; **to get up ~** madrugar; **as ~ as 1950** já em 1950; **~ on** cedo.

early closing *n* meio-feriado *m (para as lojas).*

early retirement *n* aposentadoria *f* antecipada.

early warning system *n MIL* sistema *m* de alerta imediato.

earmark ['ɪəmɑ:k] *vt*: **to be ~ed for sthg** ser destinado(da) para algo.

earn [3:n] *vt* **-1.** [as salary] ganhar **-2.** *COMM* gerar **-3.** *fig* [respect, praise] merecer.

earned income [3:nd-] *n* rendimento *m* do trabalho.

earner ['3:nəʳ] *n* **-1.** [person] assalariado *m*, -da *f* **-2.** [product] fonte *f* de recursos **-3.** *UK inf* [business]: **a nice little ~** um negócio da China.

earnest ['3:nɪst] *adj* [serious, sincere] sério(ria), sincero(ra).
◆ **in earnest** <> *adj* convicto(ta). <> *adv* para valer.

earnestly ['3:nɪstlɪ] *adv* **-1.** [talk] seriamente **-2.** [wish] de todo o coração.

earnings ['3:nɪŋz] *npl* [of person, business] rendimentos *mpl*.

earnings-related *adj* [pension, payment, benefit] proporcional aos rendimentos.

ear, nose and throat specialist *n* otorrinolaringologista *mf*.

earphones ['ɪəfəʊnz] *npl* [headset] fones *mpl* de ouvido.

earpiece *n* audiofone *m*.

earplugs ['ɪəplʌgz] *npl* protetores *mpl* de ouvido.

earring ['ɪərɪŋ] *n* brinco *m*.

earshot ['ɪəʃɒt] *n*: **within/out of ~** dentro/fora do alcance do ouvido.

ear-splitting *adj* ensurdecedor(ra).

earth [3:θ] <> *n* **-1.** [gen] terra *f*; **how/what on ~ ...?** como/o que é que ...?; **where/why on ~ ...?** onde/por que diabos ...?; **to cost the ~** *UK* custar uma fortuna **-2.** *(U)* [soil] solo *m* **-3.** *UK* [in electric plug, appliance] terra *m*. <> *vt UK*: **to be ~ed** estar aterrado(da).

earthenware ['3:θnweəʳ] <> *adj* de barro, de louça. <> *n (U)* cerâmica *f*.

earthling ['3:θlɪŋ] *n* habitante *mf* da terra.

earthly ['3:θlɪ] *adj* **-1.** [of material world] terreno(na) **-2.** *inf* [possible] concreto(ta).

earthquake ['3:θkweɪk] *n* terremoto *m*.

earth-shattering *adj UK inf* surpreendente.

earth tremor *n* tremor *m* de terra.

earthward(s) ['3:θwəd(z)] *adv* em direção à terra.

earthworm ['3:θw3:m] *n* minhoca *f*.

earthy ['3:θɪ] (*compar* **-ier**, *superl* **-iest**) *adj* **-1.** [humour, person] direto(ta) **-2.** [taste, smell] de terra.

earwax ['ɪəwæks] *n (U)* cera *f* de ouvido.

earwig ['ɪəwɪg] *n* lacraia *f*.

ease [i:z] ◇ *n (U)* **-1.** [lack of difficulty] facilidade *f*; **to do sthg with ~** fazer algo com facilidade **-2.** [comfort] comodidade *f*; **at ~** à vontade; **ill at ~** pouco(ca) à vontade. ◇ *vt* **-1.** [make less severe - pain, restrictions] aliviar; [- problems] atenuar **-2.** [move carefully] ajeitar; **to ~ sthg open** abrir algo com cuidado. ◇ *vi* [become less severe] aliviar; **to show signs of easing** mostrar sinais de alívio.
◆ **ease off** *vi* diminuir.
◆ **ease up** *vi* **-1.** [rain] acalmar **-2.** [relax] relaxar; **to ~ up on sb** *inf* ser menos duro(ra) com alguém.

easel ['i:zl] *n* cavalete *m*.

easily ['i:zɪlɪ] *adv* **-1.** [without difficulty] facilmente **-2.** [undoubtedly] sem sombra de dúvida **-3.** [in a relaxed manner] tranqüilamente.

easiness ['i:zɪnɪs] *n* [lack of difficulty] facilidade *f*.

east [i:st] ◇ *adj* **-1.** [in the east, facing the east] oriental **-2.** [from the east] leste. ◇ *adv* a leste; **~ of** ao leste de. ◇ *n* **-1.** [direction] leste *m* **-2.** [region]: **the ~** o leste.
◆ **East** *n*: **the East** [of country] o leste; [Asia, Eastern bloc] o Oriente.

eastbound ['i:stbaʊnd] *adj* em direção ao leste.

East End *n*: **the ~** *o leste de Londres.*

Easter ['i:stə^r] *n* Páscoa *f*.

Easter egg *n* ovo *m* de Páscoa.

Easter Island *n* Ilha da Páscoa.

easterly ['i:stəlɪ] *adj* **-1.** [towards the east, in the east] a leste **-2.** [from the east] do leste.

eastern ['i:stən] *adj* [part of country, continent] oriental, do leste.
◆ **Eastern** *adj* oriental.

Eastern bloc [-'blɒk] *n*: **the ~** o bloco Oriental.

Easter Sunday *n* Domingo *m* de Páscoa.

East German ◇ *adj* da Alemanha Oriental. ◇ *n* [person] alemão *m*, -mã *f* oriental.

East Germany *n*: **(the former) ~** (a antiga) Alemanha Oriental; **in ~** na Alemanha Oriental.

eastward ['i:stwəd] ◇ *adj* ao leste. ◇ *adv* = **eastwards**.

eastwards ['i:stwədz] *adv* em direção ao leste.

easy ['i:zɪ] (*compar* **-ier**, *superl* **-iest**) ◇ *adj* **-1.** [not difficult] fácil **-2.** [comfortable] cômodo(da) **-3.** [relaxed] sossegado(da). ◇ *adv*: **to go ~ on sb/sthg** *inf* [treat more kindly] ir com calma com alguém/algo; **to take it** OR **things ~** *inf* levar isso OR as coisas com calma.

easy-care *adj UK* [clothes] que não precisa ser passado(da).

easy chair *n* [armchair] poltrona *f*.

easygoing [ˌi:zɪ'gəʊɪŋ] *adj* [person, manner] descontraído(da).

eat [i:t] (*pt* **ate**, *pp* **eaten**) ◇ *vt* & *vi* comer.
◆ **eat away** *vt sep*, **eat into** *vt fus* **-1.** [corrode away] corroer **-2.** [deplete] destruir.
◆ **eat out** *vi* [at restaurant] comer fora.
◆ **eat up** *vt sep* **-1.** [food] comer tudo **-2.** *fig* [money, time] consumir um monte de.

eatable ['i:təbl] *adj* [palatable] comestível.

eaten ['i:tn] *pp* ▷ **eat**.

eater ['i:tə^r] *n* comedor *m*, -ra *f*.

eatery ['i:tərɪ] (*pl* **-ies**) *n* restaurante *m*.

eating apple ['i:tɪŋ-] *n* maçã *f (para a sobremesa).*

eau de cologne [ˌəʊdəkə'ləʊn] *n* água-de-colônia *f*, colônia *f*.

eaves ['i:vz] *npl* [of house] beirado *m*.

eavesdrop ['i:vzdrɒp] (*pt* & *pp* **-ped**, *cont* **-ping**) *vi* [listen, spy] bisbilhotar; **to ~ on sb** bisbilhotar alguém.

ebb [eb] ◇ *n (U)* [of tide, sea] vazante *f*; **the ~ and flow of sthg** *fig* os altos e baixos de algo; **to be at a low ~** *fig* estar cabisbaixo(xa). ◇ *vi* **-1.** [tide, sea] baixar **-2.** *literary* [strength, pain, feeling]: **to ~ (away)** desaparecer.

ebb tide *n* maré *f* baixa.

ebony ['ebənɪ] ◇ *adj literary* [colour] da cor do ébano. ◇ *n (U)* [wood] ébano *m*.

ebullient [ɪ'bʊljənt] *adj* [lively] entusiasmado(da).

e-business *n* **-1.** [company] empresa *f* de e-business **-2.** [electronic commerce] e-business *m*.

EC (*abbr of* **European Community**) *n* CE *f*.

e-cash *n* COMPUT dinheiro *m* eletrônico.

ECB (*abbr of* **European Central Bank**) *n* BCE *m*.

eccentric [ɪk'sentrɪk] ◇ *adj* [odd] excêntrico(ca). ◇ *n* [person] excêntrico *m*, -ca *f*.

eccentricity [ˌeksen'trɪsətɪ] (*pl* **-ies**) *n* excentricidade *f*.

ecclesiastic(al) [ɪˌkli:zɪ'æstɪ(l)] *adj* [of Christian church] eclesiástico(ca).

ECG *n* **-1.** (*abbr of* **electrocardiogram**) ECG *m*. **-2.** (*abbr of* **electrocardiograph**) eletrocardiógrafo *m*.

ECH (*abbr of* **electric central heating**) *n* aquecimento *m* central elétrico.

echelon ['eʃəlɒn] *n fml* [level in organization] escalão *m*.

echo ['ekəʊ] (*pl* **-es**, *pt* & *pp* **-ed**, *cont* **-ing**) ◇ *n* eco *m*. ◇ *vt* [repeat - words] repetir; [- opinion] repercurtir. ◇ *vi* ecoar.

éclair [eɪ'kleə^r] *n* [cake] bomba *f*.

eclectic [ɪ'klektɪk] *adj* eclético(ca).

eclipse [ɪ'klɪps] ◇ *n* **-1.** [of sun, moon] eclipse *m*; **total/partial ~** eclipse total/parcial **-2.** *fig* [decline] declínio *m*. ◇ *vt fig* [overshadow] eclipsar.

ECM (*abbr of* **European Common Market**) *n US* MCE *m*.

eco-friendly ['i:kəʊ'frendlɪ] *adj* ecológico(ca).

ecological [ˌi:kə'lɒdʒɪkl] *adj* ecológico(ca).

ecologically [ˌi:kə'lɒdʒɪklɪ] *adv* [from ecological point of view] ecologicamente.

ecologist [ɪ'kɒlədʒɪst] *n* ecologista *mf*.

ecology [ɪ'kɒlədʒɪ] *n (U)* ecologia *f*.

e-commerce *n* comércio *m* eletrônico.

economic [ˌi:kə'nɒmɪk] *adj* econômico(ca).

economical [ˌi:kə'nɒmɪkl] *adj* econômico(ca).

Economic and Monetary Union *n* União *f* Monetária e Econômica.

economics [ˌi:kə'nɒmɪks] ◇ *n (U)* [study] economia *f*. ◇ *npl* [of plan, business, trade] aspectos *mpl* econômicos.

economist [ɪ'kɒnəmɪst] *n* [expert] economista *mf*.

economize, -ise [ɪ'kɒnəmaɪz] *vi* [save money, resources] economizar; **to ~ on sthg** economizar em algo.

economy [ɪ'kɒnəmɪ] (*pl* **-ies**) *n* economia *f*; **economies of scale** economias de escala.
economy class *n* classe *f* econômica.
economy-size(d) *adj* [pack, jar] de tamanho econômico.
ecosystem ['i:kəʊˌsɪstəm] *n* ecossistema *m*.
ecotax ['i:kəʊtæks] *n* ecotaxa *f*.
ecotourism [ˌi:kəʊ'tʊərɪzm] *n* ecoturismo *m*.
ecstasy ['ekstəsɪ] (*pl* **-ies**) *n* **-1.** *(U)* [great happiness] êxtase *m* **-2.** [feeling of happiness]: **to go into ecstasies about sthg** entrar em êxtase por algo **-3.** [drug] ecstasy *m*.
ecstatic [ek'stætɪk] *adj* extasiado(da).
ecstatically [ek'stætɪklɪ] *adv* em êxtase.
ECT (*abbr of* **electroconvulsive therapy**) *n* terapia *f* de eletrochoque.
ectoplasm ['ektəplæzm] *n (U)* [of cell] ectoplasma *m*.
ECU, Ecu ['ekju:] (*abbr of* **European Currency Unit**) *n* Unidade *f* Monetária Européia.
Ecuador ['ekwədɔ:ʳ] *n* Equador; **in ~** no Equador.
Ecuadoran [ˌekwə'dɔ:rən], **Ecuadorian** [ˌekwə'dɔ:rɪən] <> *adj* equatoriano(na). <> *n* equatoriano *m*, -na *f*.
ecumenical [i:kjʊ'menɪkl] *adj* RELIG ecumênico(ca).
eczema ['eksɪməl] *n (U)* eczema *m*.
ed. **-1.** (*abbr of* **edited**) ed. **-2.** (*abbr of* **edition**) Ed. **-3.** (*abbr of* **editor**) ed.
eddy ['edɪ] (*pl* **-ies**, *pt* & *pp* **-ied**) <> *n* redemoinho *m*. <> *vi* redemoinhar.
Eden ['i:dn] *n*: **(the Garden of) ~** (o Jardim do) Éden.
edge [edʒ] <> *n* **-1.** [outer limit] borda *f*; **to be on the ~ of sthg** estar à beira de algo **-2.** [of blade] fio *m* **-3.** [advantage]: **to have an ~ over sb/sth, to have the ~ on sb/sthg** levar ligeira vantagem sobre alguém/algo **-4.** *(U)* ***fig*** [in voice] rispidez *f*. <> *vi* [move slowly] avançar lentamente.
◆ **on edge** *adj* **-1.** [person] nervoso(sa) **-2.** [nerves] à flor da pele.
edged [edʒd] *adj*: **~ with sthg** orlado(da) por algo.
edgeways ['edʒweɪz], **edgewise** ['edʒwaɪz] *adv* [sideways] de lado.
edging ['edʒɪŋ] *n* borda *f*.
edgy ['edʒɪ] (*compar* **-ier**, *superl* **-iest**) *adj* impaciente.
edible ['edɪbl] *adj* [safe to eat] comestível.
edict ['i:dɪkt] *n* [decree] edital *m*.
edifice ['edɪfɪs] *n* ***fml*** [building] edifício *m*.
edify ['edɪfaɪ] (*pt* & *pp* **-ied**) *vt* ***fml*** edificar.
edifying ['edɪfaɪɪŋ] *adj* ***fml*** edificante.
Edinburgh ['edɪnbrə] *n* Edimburgo.
Edinburgh Festival *n*: **the ~** o Festival de Edimburgo.
edit ['edɪt] *vt* **-1.** [gen] editar **-2.** [correct] revisar; **to need ~ing** precisar de revisão.
◆ **edit out** *vt sep* [word, sentence, passage] cortar.
edition [ɪ'dɪʃn] *n* edição *f*.
editor ['edɪtəʳ] *n* **-1.** [gen] editor *m*, -ra *f* **-2.** [copy editor] revisor *m*, -ra *f* **-3.** COMPUT editor *m* (de texto).
editorial [ˌedɪ'tɔ:rɪəl] <> *adj* editorial. <> *n* editorial *m*.
EDP (*abbr of* **electronic data processing**) *n* PED *m*.
EDT (*abbr of* **Eastern Daylight Time**) *n* *horário de verão na zona leste dos Estados Unidos.*
educate ['edʒʊkeɪt] *vt* **-1.** SCH & UNIV educar **-2.** [inform] informar.
educated ['edʒʊkeɪtɪd] *adj* [cultured] educado(da), culto(ta).
education [ˌedʒʊ'keɪʃn] *n (U)* **-1.** [activity, sector] educação *f*, ensino *m* **-2.** [process or result of teaching] educação *f*.
educational [ˌedʒʊ'keɪʃənl] *adj* **-1.** [establishment, policy] educacional **-2.** [toy, experience] educativo(-va).
educationalist [ˌedʒʊ'keɪʃnəlɪst] *n* especialista *mf* em educação.
educator ['edʒʊkeɪtəʳ] *n* ***US fml*** [teacher] educador *m*, -ra *f*.
Edwardian [ed'wɔ:dɪən] *adj* eduardiano(na), da época do rei Eduardo VII.
EEC (*abbr of* **European Economic Community**) *n* CEE *f*.
EEG *n* **-1.** (*abbr of* **electroencephalogram**) EEG *m*. **-2.** (*abbr of* **electroencephalograph**) eletrencefalógrafo *m*.
eel [i:l] *n* enguia *f*.
EEOC (*abbr of* **Equal Employment Opportunity Commission**) *n comissão norte-americana para a prevenção da discriminação no trabalho.*
eerie ['ɪərɪ] *adj* lúgubre, sinistro(tra).
EET (*abbr of* **Eastern European Time**) *n horário da Europa Oriental.*
efface [ɪ'feɪs] *vt* apagar.
effect [ɪ'fekt] <> *n* **-1.** [gen] efeito *m*; **to have an ~ on sb/sthg** ter um efeito sobre alguém/algo; **to take ~** [law, rule] entrar em vigor; [drug] fazer efeito; **to put sthg into ~** pôr algo em prática; **for ~** para impressionar **-2.** [meaning]: **to the ~ that** no sentido de que; **to that ~** neste sentido. <> *vt* **-1.** [recovery, change] causar **-2.** [reconcilition, comeback, repairs] fazer.
◆ **effects** *npl* **-1.** : **(special) ~s** efeitos (especiais) **-2.** [property] bens *mpl*.
◆ **in effect** *adv* na prática; **the law is in ~** a lei está em vigor.
effective [ɪ'fektɪv] *adj* **-1.** [successful] eficaz **-2.** [actual, real] efetivo(va) **-3.** [in operation] em vigor.
effectively [ɪ'fektɪvlɪ] *adv* **-1.** [well, successfully] eficazmente **-2.** [in fact] efetivamente.
effectiveness [ɪ'fektɪvnɪs] *n (U)* [success, efficiency] eficácia *f*.
effeminate [ɪ'femɪnət] *adj* ***pej*** efeminado(da).
effervesce [ˌefə'ves] *vi* efervescer.
effervescent [ˌefə'vesənt] *adj* [liquid] efervescente.
effete [ɪ'fi:t] *adj* ***pej*** [weak, effeminate] efeminado(da).
efficacious [efɪ'keɪʃəs] *adj* ***fml*** eficaz.
efficacy ['efɪkəsɪ] *n (U)* [effectiveness] eficácia *f*.
efficiency [ɪ'fɪʃənsɪ] *n (U)* eficiência *f*.
efficient [ɪ'fɪʃənt] *adj* eficiente.
efficiently [ɪ'fɪʃəntlɪ] *adv* [competently] eficientemente.
effigy ['efɪdʒɪ] (*pl* **-ies**) *n* efígie *f*.
effluent ['eflʊənt] *n* efluente *m*.
effort ['efət] *n* **-1.** *(U)* [physical or mental exertion] esforço *m*; **to be worth the ~** valer o esforço; **to make the ~ to do sthg** esforçar-se para fazer algo; **with ~** com esforço **-2.** [attempt] esforço *m*,

tentativa *f*; **to make an/no ~ to do sthg** empenhar-se/não se empenhar em fazer algo.
effortless ['efətlɪs] *adj* fácil, com desenvoltura.
effortlessly ['efətlɪslɪ] *adv* facilmente, sem esforço.
effrontery [ɪ'frʌntərɪ] *n (U)* atrevimento *m*.
effusive [ɪ'fju:sɪv] *adj* efusivo(va).
effusively [ɪ'fju:sɪvlɪ] *adv* efusivamente.
EFL (*abbr of* **English as a Foreign Language**) *n inglês para estrangeiros.*
EFTA ['eftə] (*abbr of* **European Free Trade Association**) *n associação para o livre comércio europeu.*
EFTS (*abbr of* **electronic funds transfer system**) *n sistema que processa transferência eletrônica de fundos de uma conta para a outra.*
e.g. (*abbr of* **exempli gratia**) *adv* e.g.
egalitarian [ɪ,gælɪ'teərɪən] *adj* igualitário(ria).
egg [eg] *n* **-1.** [gen] ovo *m* **-2.** [of woman] óvulo *m*.
◆ **egg on** *vt sep* instigar.
eggcup ['egkʌp] *n* oveiro *m*.
eggplant ['egplɑ:nt] *n US* berinjela *f*.
eggshell ['egʃel] *n* casca *f* de ovo.
egg timer *n* ampulheta *f (para marcar tempo de cozimento de um ovo).*
egg whisk *n* batedor *m* de ovos.
egg white *n* clara *f* de ovo.
egg yolk [-jəʊk] *n* gema *f* de ovo.
EGM (*abbr of* **extraordinary general meeting**) *n assembléia geral extraordinária*, AGE *f*.
ego ['i:gəʊ] (*pl* **-s**) *n* [opinion of self] ego *m*.
egocentric [,i:gəʊ'sentrɪk] *adj* ***fml*** & ***pej*** [selfish] egocêntrico(ca).
egoism ['i:gəʊɪzm] *n (U)* [self-interest] egoísmo *m*.
egoist ['i:gəʊɪst] *n* [self-centred person] egoísta *mf*.
egoistic [,i:gəʊ'ɪstɪk] *adj* [self-centred] egoísta.
egotism ['i:gətɪzm] *n (U)* egotismo *m*, egoísmo *m*.
egotist ['i:gətɪst] *n* egotista *mf*, egoísta *mf*.
egotistic(al) [,i:gə'tɪstɪk(l)] *adj* egotista, egoísta.
ego trip *n* ***inf*** massagem *f* no ego.
Egypt ['i:dʒɪpt] *n* Egito; **in ~** no Egito.
Egyptian [ɪ'dʒɪpʃn] ◇ *adj* egípcio(cia). ◇ *n* [person] egípcio *m*, -cia *f*.
eh [eɪ] *excl* ***UK inf*** **-1.** [inviting reply, agreement] ahã! **-2.** [what did you say?] hmm? **-3.** [expressing astonishment] ah!
eiderdown ['aɪdədaʊn] *n* ***UK*** [bed cover] edredom *m*.
eight [eɪt] *num* oito; *see also* **six**.
eighteen [,eɪ'ti:n] *num* dezoito; *see also* **six**.
eighteenth [,eɪ'ti:nθ] *num* décimo oitavo, décima oitava; *see also* **sixth**.
eighth [eɪtθ] *num* oitavo(va); *see also* **sixth**.
eightieth ['eɪtɪɪθ] *num* octagésimo(ma); *see also* **sixth**.
eighty ['eɪtɪ] (*pl* **-ies**) *num* oitenta; *see also* **sixty**.
Eire ['eərə] *n* (República da) Irlanda.
either ['aɪðə^r, 'i:ðə^r] ◇ *adj* **-1.** [one or the other] qualquer; **~ side could win** qualquer um dos lados poderia ganhar; **she couldn't find ~ jumper** ela não conseguiu achar nenhuma das blusas; **~ way** de qualquer jeito; **I don't mind ~ way** por mim tanto faz **-2.** [each] cada; **on ~ side** de cada lado. ◇ *pron*: **~ (of them) will do** qualquer um (deles) serve; **I don't like ~ (of them)** não gosto de nenhum (dos dois). ◇ *adv (after negative)* também não; **they don't smoke ~** eles também não fumam. ◇ *conj*: **~ ... or ...** [in positive sentence] ou ...ou ...; [in negative sentence] nem ...nem ...; **~ he leaves or I do** ou ele sai ou saio eu; **you are not being ~ clever or funny** você não está sendo nem inteligente nem engraçado.
ejaculate [ɪ'dʒækjʊleɪt] ◇ *vt* [exclaim] exclamar. ◇ *vi* [have orgasm] ejacular.
eject [ɪ'dʒekt] *vt* **-1.** [object] ejetar **-2.** [person]: **to ~ sb (from)** expulsar alguém (de).
ejector seat *UK* [ɪ'dʒektə^r-], **ejection seat** *US* [ɪ'dʒekʃn-] *n* assento *m* ejetor.
eke [i:k] ◆ **eke out** ◇ *vt sep* [save - money] esticar; [- food, supply] racionar. ◇ *vt fus*: **to ~ out a living** ganhar a vida com dificuldade.
EKG (*abbr of* **electrocardiogram**) *n US* ECG *m*.
el (*abbr of* **elevated railroad**) *n* ***US fam*** elevado *m* férreo.
elaborate [*adj* ɪ'læbrət, *vb* ɪ'læbəreɪt] ◇ *adj* [complicated, detailed] elaborado(da). ◇ *vi*: **to ~ (on sthg)** detalhar (algo).
elaborately [ɪ'læbərətlɪ] *adv* [in detail] detalhadamente.
elapse [ɪ'læps] *vi* [time] transcorrer.
elastic [ɪ'læstɪk] ◇ *adj* **-1.** [material, skin] elástico(ca) **-2.** ***fig*** [plan, timetable] elástico(ca). ◇ *n (U)* [material] elástico *m*.
elasticated [ɪ'læstɪkeɪtɪd] *adj* [waistband] elástico(ca).
elastic band *n UK* elástico *m*.
elasticity [,elæ'stɪsətɪ] *n (U)* [stretchiness] elasticidade *f*.
elated [ɪ'leɪtɪd] *adj* exultante.
elation [ɪ'leɪʃn] *n (U)* exultação *f*.
elbow ['elbəʊ] ◇ *n* cotovelo *m*. ◇ *vt*: **to ~ sb aside** empurrar alguém com os cotovelos.
elbow grease *n (U)* ***inf*** duro *m* danado.
elbowroom ['elbəʊrʊm] *n* ***inf*** [physical space] espaço *m (para trabalhar).*
elder ['eldə^r] ◇ *adj* [older] mais velho(lha), primogênito(ta). ◇ *n* **-1.** [older person] velho *m*, -lha *f* **-2.** [of tribe] ancião *m*, -ã *f* **-3.** [of church] presbítero *m* **-4.** BOT: **~ (tree)** sabugueiro *m*.
elderberry ['eldə,berɪ] (*pl* **-ies**) *n* **-1.** [fruit] fruto *m* do sabugueiro **-2.** [tree] sabugueiro *m*.
elderly ['eldəlɪ] ◇ *adj* [old - person] idoso(sa); [- thing] velho(lha), antigo(ga). ◇ *npl*: **the ~** os idosos.
elder statesman *n* estadista *mf* experiente.
eldest ['eldɪst] *adj* [oldest] mais velho(lha).
El Dorado *n* El Dorado.
elect [ɪ'lekt] ◇ *adj* eleito(ta). ◇ *vt* **-1.** [by voting] eleger; **to ~ sb (as) sthg** eleger alguém (como) algo **-2.** ***fml*** [choose]: **to ~ to do sthg** escolher fazer algo.
elected [ɪ'lektɪd] *adj* [president, chairperson] eleito(ta).
election [ɪ'lekʃn] *n* eleição *f*; **to have** OR **hold an ~** ter OR fazer uma eleição; **local ~s** eleições locais.

ELECTION

Nos EUA, as eleições presidenciais realizam-se a cada quatro anos. Por lei, o presidente não pode permanecer no cargo por mais de dois mandatos consecutivos. As eleições gerais britânicas realizam-se a cada cinco anos, mas o primeiro-ministro pode convocar eleições a qualquer momento. Tanto nos Estados Unidos como na Grã-Bretanha, o voto não é obrigatório.

election campaign *n* campanha *f* eleitoral.
electioneering [ɪˌlekʃəˈnɪərɪŋ] *n (U) pej* propaganda *f* eleitoral, eleitoralismo *m*.
elective [ɪˈlektɪv] *n SCH & UNIV* disciplina *f* opcional.
elector [ɪˈlektəʳ] *n* [voter] eleitor *m*, -ra *f*.
electoral [ɪˈlektərəl] *adj* eleitoral.
electoral college *n POL* colégio *m* eleitoral.
electoral register, electoral roll *n*: **the ~** o registro dos eleitores.
electorate [ɪˈlektərət] *n*: **the ~** o eleitorado.
electric [ɪˈlektrɪk] *adj* **-1.** [using or producing electricity] elétrico(ca) **-2.** *fig* [exciting] eletrizante.
◆ **electrics** *npl UK inf* [in car, machine] partes *fpl* elétricas.
electrical [ɪˈlektrɪkl] *adj* elétrico(ca).
electrical engineer *n* engenheiro *m*, -ra *f* eletricista.
electrical engineering *n (U)* engenharia *f* elétrica.
electrically [ɪˈlektrɪklɪ] *adv* [by electricity] eletricamente.
electrical shock *n US* = **electric shock**.
electric blanket *n* cobertor *m* elétrico.
electric chair *n*: **the ~** a cadeira elétrica.
electric cooker *n* fogão *m* elétrico.
electric current *n* corrente *f* elétrica.
electric drill *n* furadeira *f* elétrica.
electric fence *n* cerca *f* elétrica.
electric fire *n* estufa *f* elétrica.
electric guitar *n* guitarra *f* elétrica.
electrician [ˌɪlekˈtrɪʃn] *n* eletricista *mf*.
electricity [ˌɪlekˈtrɪsətɪ] *n* **-1.** *ELEC* eletricidade *f* **-2.** *fig* [excitement] excitação *f*.
electric light *n (U)* luz *f* elétrica.
electric shock *UK*, **electrical shock** *US* *n* choque *m* elétrico.
electric storm *n* tempestade *f* elétrica.
electrify [ɪˈlektrɪfaɪ] (*pt* & *pp* **-ied**) *vt* **-1.** [convert to electric power] eletrificar **-2.** *fig* [excite] deixar eletrizado(da).
electrifying [ɪˈlektrɪfaɪɪŋ] *adj fig* [exciting] eletrizante.
electro- [ɪˈlektrəʊ] *prefix* eletro-.
electrocardiogram *n MED* eletrocardiograma *m*.
electrocardiograph [ɪˌlektrəʊˈkɑːdɪəgrɑːf] *n MED* eletrocardiógrafo *m*.
electrocardiography *n MED* eletrocardiografia *f*.
electrocute [ɪˈlektrəkjuːt] *vt* eletrocutar; **to ~ o.s** eletrocutar-se.
electrode [ɪˈlektrəʊd] *n* eletrodo *m*.
electroencephalogram *n MED* eletrencefalograma *m*.
electroencephalograph [ɪˌlektrəʊenˈsefələgrɑːf] *n MED* eletrencefalógrafo *m*.
electroencephalography *n MED* eletrencefalografia *f*.
electrolysis [ˌɪlekˈtrɒləsɪs] *n (U)* eletrólise *f*.
electromagnet *n* eletroímã *m*.
electromagnetic [ɪˌlektrəʊmægˈnetɪk] *adj* eletromagnético(ca).
electron [ɪˈlektrɒn] *n* elétron *m*.
electronic [ˌɪlekˈtrɒnɪk] *adj* eletrônico(ca).
◆ **electronics** <> *n (U)* [technology] eletrônica *f*. <> *npl* [equipment] componentes *mpl* eletrônicos.
electronic banking *n* serviço *m* bancário via internet.
electronic data processing *n (U)* processamento *m* eletrônico de dados.
electronic mail *n (U)* correio *m* eletrônico.
electronic organizer *n* agenda *f* eletrônica.
electron microscope *n* microscópio *m* eletrônico.
electroplated [ɪˈlektrəʊˌpleɪtɪd] *adj* galvanizado(-da).
elegance [ˈelɪgəns] *n (U)* elegância *f*.
elegant [ˈelɪgənt] *adj* **-1.** [stylish, beautiful] elegante **-2.** [clever, neat] brilhante.
elegantly [ˈelɪgəntlɪ] *adv* **-1.** [stylishly, beautifully] elegantemente **-2.** [cleverly, neatly] brilhantemente.
elegy [ˈelɪdʒɪ] (*pl* **-ies**) *n* elegia *f*.
element [ˈelɪmənt] *n* **-1.** *SCIENCE* elemento *m* **-2.** [small amount, proportion] parcela *f* **-3.** [in heater, kettle] resistência *f* **-4.** *pej* [in society, group] elemento *m* **-5.** *phr*: **to be in one's ~** estar em seu meio.
◆ **elements** *npl* **-1.** [basics] conhecimentos *mpl* básicos **-2.** [weather]: **the ~s** os fenômenos atmosféricos.
elementary [ˌelɪˈmentərɪ] *adj* elementar.
elementary school *n US* escola *f* primária.
elephant [ˈelɪfənt] (*pl inv OR* **-s**) *n* elefante *m*
elevate [ˈelɪveɪt] *vt* **-1.** [give importance to, promote]: **to ~ sb/sthg to sthg, to ~ sb/sthg into sthg** elevar alguém/algo a algo **-2.** [raise physically] levantar.
elevated [ˈelɪveɪtɪd] *adj fml* **-1.** [person, situation] digno(na) **-2.** [idea, sentiment] elevado(da) **-3.** [platform, position] alto(ta).
elevated railway *n* ferrovia *f* elevada.
elevation [ˌelɪˈveɪʃn] *n fml* **-1.** *(U)* [promotion, raising - of person] promoção *f*; [- of standards] elevação *f* **-2.** [of hill, land] altitude *f*.
elevator [ˈelɪveɪtəʳ] *n US* elevador *m*.
eleven [ɪˈlevn] *num* onze; *see also* **six**.
elevenses [ɪˈlevnzɪz] *n (U) UK* lanche *m* rápido *(às 11 da manhã)*.
eleventh [ɪˈlevnθ] *num* décimo primeiro, décima primeira; *see also* **sixth**.
eleventh hour *n fig*: **the ~** a última hora.
elf [elf] (*pl* **elves**) *n* elfo *m*.
elicit [ɪˈlɪsɪt] *vt fml* **-1.** [response, reaction]: **to ~ sthg (from sb)** obter algo (de alguém) **-2.** [information]: **to ~ sthg (from sb)** extrair algo (de alguém).

eligibility [ˌelɪdʒəˈbɪlətɪ] *n (U)* **-1.** [suitability] eligibilidade *f* **-2.** ***dated*** [of bachelor] aptidão *f (para o casamento)*.
eligible [ˈelɪdʒəbl] *adj* **-1.** [suitable, qualified] elegível; **to be ~ for sthg/to do sthg** estar habilitado(da) a algo/a fazer algo **-2.** ***dated*** [marriageable]: **to be ~** ser um bom partido.
eliminate [ɪˈlɪmɪneɪt] *vt* **-1.** [remove]: **to ~ sb/sthg (from)** eliminar alguém/algo (de) **-2.** [in sport, competition]: **to be ~d from sthg** ser eliminado(da) de algo.
elimination [ɪˌlɪmɪˈneɪʃn] *n (U)* eliminação *f*.
elite [ɪˈli:t] ◇ *adj* de elite. ◇ *n* elite *f*.
elitism [ɪˈli:tɪzm] *n (U)* ***pej*** elitismo *m*.
elitist [ɪˈli:tɪst] ***pej*** ◇ *adj* elitista. ◇ *n* elitista *mf*.
elixir [ɪˈlɪksəʳ] *n* ***literary*** **-1.** [magic drink] elixir *m* **-2.** ***fig*** [magic cure] poção *f* mágica.
Elizabethan [ɪˌlɪzəˈbi:θn] ◇ *adj* elizabetano(na). ◇ *n* elizabetano *m*, -na *f*.
elk [elk] (*pl inv* OR **-s**) *n* alce *m*.
ellipse [ɪˈlɪps] *n* elípse *f*.
elliptical [ɪˈlɪptɪkl] *adj* **-1.** [in shape] elíptico(ca) **-2.** ***fml*** [phrase, remark] obscuro(ra).
elm [elm] *n*: **~ (tree)** olmo *m*.
elocution [ˌeləˈkju:ʃn] *n (U)* elocução *f*.
elongated [ˈi:lɒŋgeɪtɪd] *adj* alongado(da).
elope [ɪˈləʊp] *vi*: **to ~ (with sb)** fugir para casar (com alguém).
elopement [ɪˈləʊpmənt] *n* fuga *f (com o namorado)*.
eloquence [ˈeləkwəns] *n (U)* eloqüência *f*.
eloquent [ˈeləkwənt] *adj* eloqüente.
eloquently [ˈeləkwəntlɪ] *adv* eloqüentemente.
El Salvador [ˌelˈsælvədɔ:ʳ] *n* El Salvador; **in ~** em El Salvador.
else [els] *adv*: **anything ~** mais alguma coisa; **he doesn't need anything ~** ele não precisa de nada mais;. **everyone ~** todos os outros, todas as outras; **nothing ~** nada mais; **someone ~** alguma outra pessoa; **something ~** outra coisa; **somewhere ~** outro lugar; **who/what/where ~?** quem/que/onde mais?
◆ **or else** *conj* **-1.** [or if not] ou então, senão **-2.** [as threat] senão.
elsewhere [elsˈweəʳ] *adv* em outro lugar.
ELT (*abbr of* **English Language Teaching**) *n*. ensino *m* de língua inglese
elucidate [ɪˈlu:sɪdeɪt] ***fml*** ◇ *vt* elucidar. ◇ *vi* elucidar.
elude [ɪˈlu:d] *vt* escapar de; **his name ~s me completely** o nome dele me escapa totalmente.
elusive [ɪˈlu:sɪv] *adj* esquivo(va), evasivo(va).
elves [elvz] *pl* ▷ **elf**.
'em [əm] *cont inf* = **them**.
emaciated [ɪˈmeɪʃɪeɪtɪd] *adj* emagrecido (da).
e-mail *n* COMPUT e-mail *m*, correio *m* eletrônico.
e-mail address *n* endereço *m* (de correio) eletrônico, e-mail *m*.
e-mail phone *n* telefone *m* com correio eletrônico.
emanate [ˈeməneɪt] ***fml*** ◇ *vt* emanar. ◇ *vi*: **to ~ from** emanar de.
emancipate [ɪˈmænsɪpeɪt] *vt*: **to ~ sb (from sthg)** emancipar alguém (de algo).
emancipation [ɪˌmænsɪˈpeɪʃn] *n (U)*: **~ (from sthg)** emancipação *f* (de algo).
emasculate [ɪˈmæskjʊleɪt] *vt* ***fml*** [weaken] enfraquecer.
emasculation [ɪˌmæskjʊˈleɪʃn] *n (U)* ***fml*** [weakening] enfraquecimento *m*.
embalm [ɪmˈbɑ:m] *vt* [body] embalsamar.
embankment [ɪmˈbæŋkmənt] *n* **-1.** [along road, railway] barreira *f* **-2.** [along river] margem *f*.
embargo [emˈbɑ:gəʊ] (*pl* **-es**, *pt* & *pp* **-ed**, *cont* **-ing**) ◇ *n* **-1.** [gen]: **~ (on sthg)** embargo *m* (de algo) **-2.** ***fig*** [ban]: **~ (on sthg)** proibição *f* (de algo). ◇ *vt* **-1.** COMM & POL embargar **-2.** ***fig*** [ban] proibir.
embark [ɪmˈbɑ:k] *vi* **-1.** [board ship]: **to ~ (on)** embarcar(em) **-2.** [start]: **to ~ (up)on sthg** dar início (a algo).
embarkation [ˌembɑ:ˈkeɪʃn] *n* embarque *m*.
embarkation card *n* ***UK*** cartão *m* de embarque.
embarrass [ɪmˈbærəs] *vt* [shame] envergonhar.
embarrassed [ɪmˈbærəst] *adj* [self-conscious] envergonhado(da).
embarrassing [ɪmˈbærəsɪŋ] *adj* [shameful] embaraçoso(sa).
embarrassment [ɪmˈbærəsmənt] *n* vergonha *f*.
embassy [ˈembəsɪ] (*pl* **-ies**) *n* embaixada *f*.
embattled [ɪmˈbætld] *adj* [troubled] em dificuldade.
embedded [ɪmˈbedɪd] *adj* **-1.** [buried]: **~ in sthg** enterrado(da) em algo **-2.** COMPUT: **~ in sthg** embutido(da) em algo **-3.** ***fig*** [ingrained] enraizado(da).
embellish [ɪmˈbelɪʃ] *vt* **-1.** [room, garment]: **to ~ sthg with sthg** embelezar algo com algo **-2.** ***fig*** [story, account] enfeitar.
embers [ˈembəz] *npl* brasa *f*.
embezzle [ɪmˈbezl] *vt* [money] desviar.
embezzlement [ɪmˈbezlmənt] *n (U)* desvio *m (de dinheiro)*.
embezzler [ɪmˈbezləʳ] *n* defraudador *m*, -ra *f*.
embittered [ɪmˈbɪtəd] *adj* amargurado(da).
emblazoned [ɪmˈbleɪznd] *adj*: **~ (on sthg)** gravado(da) (em algo); **~ (with sthg)** ornado(da) (com algo).
emblem [ˈembləm] *n* [symbolic design] emblema *m*.
embodiment [ɪmˈbɒdɪmənt] *n* [epitome] personificação *f*.
embody [ɪmˈbɒdɪ] (*pt* & *pp* **-ied**) *vt* **-1.** [epitomize] personificar **-2.** [include]: **to be embodied in sthg** estar incorporado(da) em algo.
embolism [ˈembəlɪzm] *n* embolia *f*.
embossed [ɪmˈbɒst] *adj* **-1.** [material] em relevo **-2.** [design, lettering]: **~ (on sthg)** em relevo (sobre algo).
embrace [ɪmˈbreɪs] ◇ *n* abraço *m*. ◇ *vt* **-1.** [person] abraçar **-2.** ***fml*** [religion, way of life] converter-se a **-3.** ***fml*** [aspects, elements] conter. ◇ *vi* abraçar-se.
embrocation [ˌembrəˈkeɪʃn] *n (U)* ***fml*** [liquid] embrocação *f*.
embroider [ɪmˈbrɔɪdəʳ] ◇ *vt* **-1.** SEWING bordar **-2.** ***pej*** [embellish] enfeitar. ◇ *vi* SEWING bordar.
embroidered [ɪmˈbrɔɪdəd] *adj* SEWING bordado(da).

embroidery [ɪm'brɔɪdərɪ] *n (U)* bordado *m*.
embroil [ɪm'brɔɪl] *vt*: **to get/be ~ed (in sthg)** envolver-se/ser envolvido(da) (em algo).
embryo ['embrɪəʊ] *(pl* **-s**) *n* **-1.** BIOL embrião *m* **-2.** *fig* [beginnings]: **in ~** em estado embrionário.
embryonic [,embrɪ'ɒnɪk] *adj fig* [emergent] embrionário(ria).
emcee *(abbr of* **master of ceremonies**) *n US* mestre *mf* de cerimônias.
emend [ɪ'mend] *vt* corrigir.
emerald ['emərəld] ◇ *adj* [colour] esmeralda. ◇ *n* [stone] esmeralda *f*.
emerge [ɪ'mɜːdʒ] ◇ *vi* **-1.** [come out] aparecer; **to ~ from sthg** surgir de algo **-2.** [from experience, situation]: **to ~ from** surgir de **-3.** [become known - facts, truth] vir à tona; [- writer, movement] surgir. ◇ *vt*: **it ~s that** vem à tona que.
emergence [ɪ'mɜːdʒəns] *n (U)* surgimento *m*, aparecimento *m*.
emergency [ɪ'mɜːdʒənsɪ] *(pl* **-ies**) ◇ *adj* de emergência. ◇ *n* emergência *f*.
emergency brake *n US* [of car] freio *m* de mão.
emergency exit *n* saída *f* de emergência.
emergency landing *n* pouso *m* de emergência.
emergency number *n* número *m* de emergência.
emergency room *n US* [in hospital] sala *f* de emergência.
emergency services *npl* serviços *mpl* de emergência.
emergency stop *n* parada *f* de emergência.
emergent [ɪ'mɜːdʒənt] *adj* emergente.
emery board ['emərɪ-] *n* lixa *f (de unhas)*.
emetic [ɪ'metɪk] ◇ *adj* que provoca vômitos. ◇ *n* vomitório *m*.
emigrant ['emɪgrənt] *n* emigrante *mf*.
emigrate ['emɪgreɪt] *vi* emigrar; **to ~ to/from** emigrar para/de.
emigration [,emɪ'greɪʃn] *n (U)* emigração *f*.
émigré ['emɪgreɪ] *n fml* exilado *m* político, exilada *f* política.
eminence ['emɪnəns] *n (U)* [prominence] eminência *f*.
eminent ['emɪnənt] *adj* [distinguished] eminente.
eminently ['emɪnəntlɪ] *adv fml* [extremely] eminentemente.
emir [e'mɪə^r] *n* emir *m*.
emissary ['emɪsərɪ] *(pl* **-ies**) *n fml* emissário *m*, -ria *f*.
emission [ɪ'mɪʃn] *n fml* emissão *f*.
emit [ɪ'mɪt] *(pt & pp* **-ted**, *cont* **-ting**) *vt fml* emitir.
emollient [ɪ'mɒlɪənt] *n fml* emoliente *m*.
emolument [ɪ'mɒljʊmənt] *n fml* [payment fee] honorários *mpl*; [salary] remuneração *f*.
emoticon [ɪ'məʊtɪkɒn] *n* COMPUT emoticon *m*.
emotion [ɪ'məʊʃn] *n* emoção *f*.
emotional [ɪ'məʊʃənl] *adj* **-1.** [easily moved] emotivo(va) **-2.** [charged with emotion] emocionado(da) **-3.** [appealing to the emotions] comovente.
emotionally [ɪ'məʊʃnəlɪ] *adv* emocionalmente.
emotionless [ɪ'məʊʃnlɪs] *adj* sem emoção.
emotive [ɪ'məʊtɪv] *adj* emotivo(va), emocionante.
empathy ['empəθɪ] *n (U)*: **~ (with sb)** empatia *f* (com alguém).
emperor ['empərə^r] *n* imperador *m*.
emphasis ['emfəsɪs] *(pl* **-ases** [-əsiːz]) *n*: **~ (on sthg)** ênfase *f* (em algo); **to lay** OR **place ~ on sthg** dar ênfase a algo.
emphasize, -ise ['emfəsaɪz] *vt* enfatizar.
emphatic [ɪm'fætɪk] *adj* [forceful] enfático(ca).
emphatically [ɪm'fætɪklɪ] *adv* **-1.** [with emphasis] enfaticamente **-2.** [definitely] terminantemente.
emphysema [,emfɪ'siːməl] *n (U)* enfisema *m*.
empire ['empaɪə^r] *n* império *m*.
empire building *n* desenvolvimento *m* de impérios econômicos.
empirical [ɪm'pɪrɪkl] *adj* empírico(ca).
empiricism [ɪm'pɪrɪsɪzm] *n (U)* empirismo *m*.
employ [ɪm'plɔɪ] *vt* **-1.** [give work to] empregar; **to be ~ed as sthg** estar empregado(da) como algo **-2.** *fml* [use] empregar; **to ~ sthg as sthg/to do sthg** empregar algo como algo/para fazer algo.
employable [ɪm'plɔɪəbl] *adj* empregável.
employee [ɪm'plɔɪiː] *n* empregado *m*, -da *f*.
employer [ɪm'plɔɪə^r] *n* empregador *m*, -ra *f*.
employment [ɪm'plɔɪmənt] *n* **-1.** [being in work] emprego *m*; **to be in ~** estar empregado(da) **-2.** [work] trabalho *m*.
employment agency *n* agência *f* de empregos.
employment office *n* agência *m* de empregos.
emporium [em'pɔːrɪəm] *n* empório *m*.
empower [ɪm'paʊə^r] *vt fml*: **to be ~ed to do sthg** receber autoridade para fazer algo.
empress ['emprɪs] *n* imperatriz *f*.
emptiness ['emptɪnɪs] *n (U)* vazio *m*.
empty ['emptɪ] *(compar* **-ier**, *superl* **-iest**, *pt & pp* **-ied**, *pl* **-ies**) ◇ *adj* vazio(zia). ◇ *vt* esvaziar; **to ~ sthg into/out of sthg** despejar algo em/de dentro de algo. ◇ *vi* [become empty] esvaziar. ◇ *n inf* casco *m*.
empty-handed [-'hændɪd] *adv* de mãos vazias.
empty-headed [-'hedɪd] *adj pej* de cabeça vazia.
EMS *(abbr of* **European Monetary System**) *n* SMT *m*.
emu ['iːmjuː] *(pl inv* OR **-s**) *n* emu *f*.
EMU *(abbr of* **Economic and Monetary Union**) *n* UME *f*.
emulate ['emjʊleɪt] *vt* **-1.** [gen] imitar **-2.** COMPUT emular.
emulsion [ɪ'mʌlʃn] ◇ *n* **-1.**: **~ (paint)** tinta *f* plástica **-2.** PHOT emulsão *f*. ◇ *vt UK* [paint] pintar *(com tinta plástica)*.
enable [ɪ'neɪbl] *vt*: **to ~ sb to do sthg** permitir que alguém faça algo.
enact [ɪ'nækt] *vt* **-1.** JUR promulgar **-2.** [act] representar.
enactment [ɪ'næktmənt] *n* **-1.** JUR promulgação *f* **-2.** [of scene, play] representação *f*.
enamel [ɪ'næml] *n (U)* esmalte *m*.
enamelled *UK*, **enameled** *US* [ɪ'næmld] *adj* esmaltado(da).
enamel paint *n (U)* tinta *f* esmalte.
enamoured *UK*, **enamored** *US* [ɪ'næməd] *adj*: **~ of sb/sthg** encantado(da) por alguém/algo.
en bloc [ɑɒ'blɒk] *adv fml* em bloco.

enc. -**1.** (*abbr of* **enclosure**) anexo *m.* - **2.** (*abbr of* **enclosed**) anexo(xa).
encamp *vi* acampar, acampar-se.
encampment [ɪn'kæmpmənt] *n* [of soldiers, gipsies] acampamento *m.*
encapsulate [ɪn'kæpsjʊleɪt] *vt fig* [philosophy, idea]: **to ~ sthg (in)** resumir algo (em).
encase [ɪn'keɪs] *vt*: **~d in sthg** envolvido(da) em algo.
encash [ɪn'kæʃ] *vt UK* [cheque] descontar.
enchanted [ɪn'tʃɑ:ntɪd] *adj* -**1.** [delighted]: **~ (by** *OR* **with sthg)** encantado(da) (por *OR* com algo) -**2.** [under a spell] encantado(da).
enchanting [ɪn'tʃɑ:ntɪŋ] *adj* encantador(ra).
encircle [ɪn'sɜ:kl] *vt* cercar.
enclave ['enkleɪv] *n* [of country] enclave *m.*
enclose [ɪn'kləʊz] *vt* -**1.** [surround, contain] cercar; **~d by** *OR* **with sthg** cercado(da) por *OR* com algo -**2.** [put in envelope] anexar; **please find ~d ...** segue anexo(xa) ...
enclosure [ɪn'kləʊʒə^r] *n* -**1.** [place] cercado *m* -**2.** [in letter] anexo *m.*
encompass [ɪn'kʌmpəs] *vt fml* -**1.** [include] abranger -**2.** [surround] cercar.
encore ['ɒŋkɔ:^r] <> *n* [by singer, performer] bis *m.* <> *excl* bis!
encounter [ɪn'kaʊntə^r] <> *n* encontro *m.* <> *vt fml* -**1.** [person] encontrar, encontrar-se com -**2.** [problem, difficulty etc.] deparar-se com.
encourage [ɪn'kʌrɪdʒ] *vt* -**1.** [give confidence to]: **to ~ sb (to do sthg)** incentivar alguém (a fazer algo) -**2.** [foster] incentivar, estimular.
encouragement [ɪn'kʌrɪdʒmənt] *n (U)* incentivo *m*, estímulo *m.*
encouraging [ɪn'kʌrɪdʒɪŋ] *adj* incentivador(ra).
encroach [ɪn'krəʊtʃ] *vi*: **to ~ (up)on sthg** apossar-se de algo; [rights] abusar de algo; [privacy] invadir algo.
encrusted [ɪn'krʌstɪd] *adj*: **~ with sthg** incrustado(da) de algo.
encrypt [ɪn'krɪpt] *vt COMPUT* criptografar.
encumber [ɪn'kʌmbə^r] *vt fml*: **to be ~ed with sthg** estar carregado(da) de algo; [debts] estar sobrecarregado(da) de algo.
encyclop(a)edia [ɪnˌsaɪklə'pi:djə] *n* enciclopédia *f.*
encyclop(a)edic [ɪnˌsaɪkləʊ'pi:dɪk] *adj* enciclopédico(ca).
end [end] <> *n* -**1.** [last part, finish] fim *m*, final *m*; **to be at an ~** estar no fim; **to come to an ~** acabar, chegar ao fim; **to put an ~ to sthg** pôr fim a algo; **at the ~ of the day** *fig* no final das contas; **in the ~** [finally] finalmente -**2.** [tip, edge] extremidade *f* -**3.** [point, final section] ponta *f*; **from ~ to ~** de ponta a ponta -**4.** [side, one of two ends, of phone line] lado *m*; **which ~ does it open?** de que lado abre?; **to make ~s meet** conseguir que o dinheiro chegue -**5.** *fml* [purpose] fim *m*, objetivo *m*; **an ~ in itself** um fim em si mesmo -**6.** *literary* [death] fim *m.* <> *vt* acabar, terminar; **to ~ sthg with** acabar *OR* terminar algo com. <> *vi* [finish] acabar, terminar; **to ~ in** acabar em; **to ~ with** acabar *OR* terminar com.
◆ **on end** *adv* -**1.** [upright] em pé -**2.** [continuously] a fio.
◆ **no end** *adv inf*: **it cheered me up no ~** me alegrou o tempo inteirinho.
◆ **no end of** *prep inf* um mar de.
◆ **end up** *vi* acabar, terminar; **to ~ up doing sthg** acabar fazendo algo.
endanger [ɪn'deɪndʒə^r] *vt* pôr em perigo.
endangered species [ɪn'deɪndʒəd-] *n* espécie *f* em perigo de extinção.
endear [ɪn'dɪə^r] *vt*: **to ~ sb to sb** fazer com que alguém conquiste alguém; **to ~ o.s. to sb** conquistar a afeição de alguém.
endearing [ɪn'dɪərɪŋ] *adj* simpático(ca).
endearment [ɪn'dɪəmənt] *n fml* palavra *f* carinhosa.
endeavour *UK*, **endeavor** *US* [ɪn'devə^r] *fml* <> *n* tentativa *f*, esforço *m.* <> *vt*: **to ~ to do sthg** tentar fazer algo.
endemic [en'demɪk] *adj* endêmico(ca).
ending ['endɪŋ] *n* -**1.** [gen] final *m* -**2.** *GRAM* terminação *f.*
endive ['endaɪv] *n* -**1.** [salad vegetable] endívia *f* -**2.** [chicory] chicória *f.*
endless ['endlɪs] *adj* -**1.** [unending] interminável -**2.** [inexhaustible] inesgotável -**3.** [vast] sem fim.
endlessly ['endlɪslɪ] *adv* -**1.** [in time] interminavelmente -**2.** [in amount, degree] infinitamente.
endorse [ɪn'dɔ:s] *vt* -**1.** [approve] endossar -**2.** *UK* [driving licence]: **to have one's licence ~d** receber pontos na carteira.
endorsement [ɪn'dɔ:smənt] *n* -**1.** *(U)* [gen] endosso *m* -**2.** *UK* [on driving licence] pontos *mpl.*
endow [ɪn'daʊ] *vt* -**1.** [equip]: **to be ~ed with sthg** ser dotado(da) de algo -**2.** [donate money to] dotar.
endowment [ɪn'daʊmənt] *n* dote *m.*
endowment insurance *n* seguro *m* dotal.
endowment mortgage *n UK* hipoteca *f* dotal.
end product *n* produto *m* final.
end result *n* resultado *m* final.
endurable [ɪn'djʊərəbl] *adj* suportável.
endurance [ɪn'djʊərəns] *n (U)* resistência *f.*
endurance test *n* teste *m* de resistência.
endure [ɪn'djʊə^r] <> *vt* resistir, suportar. <> *vi fml* perdurar.
enduring [ɪn'djʊərɪŋ] *adj fml* perdurável.
end user *n* usuário *m*, -ria *f* final.
endways *UK* ['endweɪz], **endwise** *US* ['endwaɪz] *adv* -**1.** [lengthways] de frente -**2.** [end to end] ponta a ponta.
enema ['enɪmə] *n MED* enema *m.*
enemy ['enɪmɪ] (*pl* **-ies**) <> *n* -**1.** [person] inimigo *m*, -ga *f* -**2.** *MIL*: **the ~** o inimigo. <> *comp* inimigo(ga).
energetic [ˌenə'dʒetɪk] *adj* -**1.** [lively] ativo(va) -**2.** [physically taxing] vigoroso(sa) -**3.** [enthusiastic] ativo(-va).
energy ['enədʒɪ] (*pl* **-ies**) *n (U)* energia *f.*
energy-saving *adj* [device] que poupa energia.
enervating ['enəveɪtɪŋ] *adj fml* desgastante.
enfold [ɪn'fəʊld] *vt literary* -**1.** [engulf] envolver -**2.** [embrace]: **to ~ sb (in sthg)** envolver alguém (em algo).

enforce [ɪn'fɔːs] *vt* **-1.** [law] fazer cumprir, aplicar **-2.** [standards, discipline] impor.
enforceable [ɪn'fɔːsəbl] *adj* aplicável.
enforced [ɪn'fɔːst] *adj* **-1.** [obligatory] compulsório(-ria) **-2.** [unavoidable] inevitável.
enforcement [ɪn'fɔːsmənt] *n (U)* aplicação *f.*
enfranchise [ɪn'fræntʃaɪz] *vt* **-1.** [give vote to] conferir o direito de voto a **-2.** [set free] emancipar.
engage [ɪn'geɪdʒ] ◇ *vt* **-1.** [attract] atrair; **to ~ sb in conversation** travar conversa com alguém **-2.** *TECH* engrenar **-3.** *fml* [employ] contratar; **to be ~d in** *OR* **on sthg** dedicar-se a algo; [busy with] estar ocupado(da) em algo. ◇ *vi* [be involved]: **to ~ in** envolver-se em.
engaged [ɪn'geɪdʒd] *adj* **-1.** [couple] noivo(va); **~ to sb** noivo(va) de alguém; **to get ~** noivar **-2.** [busy, occupied] ocupado(da); **~ in sthg** envolvido(da) em algo **-3.** [phone, toilet] ocupado(da).
engaged tone *n UK* sinal *m* de ocupado.
engagement [ɪn'geɪdʒmənt] *n* **-1.** [of couple] noivado *m* **-2.** [appointment] compromisso *m.*
engagement ring *n* anel *m* de noivado.
engaging [ɪn'geɪdʒɪŋ] *adj* atraente.
engender [ɪn'dʒendəʳ] *vt fml* gerar.
engine ['endʒɪn] *n* **-1.** [of car, plane, ship] motor *m* **-2.** *RAIL* locomotiva *f.*
engine driver *n UK* maquinista *mf.*
engineer [ˌendʒɪ'nɪəʳ] ◇ *n* **-1.** [of roads, machines, bridges] engenheiro *m*, -ra *f* **-2.** [on ship] técnico *m*, -ca *f* **-3.** *US* [engine driver] maquinista *mf.* ◇ *vt* **-1.** [construct] construir **-2.** [contrive] tramar.
engineering [ˌendʒɪ'nɪərɪŋ] *n* engenharia *f.*
England ['ɪŋglənd] *n* Inglaterra; **in ~** na Inglaterra.
English ['ɪŋglɪʃ] ◇ *adj* inglês(esa). ◇ *n* [language] inglês *m.* ◇ *npl*: **the ~** os ingleses.
English breakfast *n* café *m* da manhã inglês.

ENGLISH BREAKFAST

Na Grã-Bretanha, o café da manhã tradicional consiste em um prato quente (ovos com bacon, por exemplo), cereais ou *porridge* (uma espécie de mingau de aveia) e torradas com geléia de laranja, além de café ou chá. Hoje em dia, os britânicos tendem a substituir seu desjejum tradicional por algo mais leve.

English Channel *n*: **the ~** o Canal da Mancha.
Englishman ['ɪŋglɪʃmən] (*pl* **-men** [-mən]) *n* inglês *m.*
English muffin *n US* *pãozinho redondo e chato que se costuma torrar antes de comer.*
Englishwoman ['ɪŋglɪʃˌwʊmən] (*pl* **-women** [-ˌwɪmɪn]) *n* inglesa *f.*
engrave [ɪn'greɪv] *vt* **-1.** [metal, glass] gravar **-2.** [design]: **to ~ sthg (on sthg)** gravar algo (em algo) **-3.** *fig* [on memory] gravar.
engraver [ɪn'greɪvəʳ] *n* gravador *m*, -ra *f.*
engraving [ɪn'greɪvɪŋ] *n* **-1.** [design] gravura *f* **-2.** *(U)* [skill] gravação *f.*
engrossed [ɪn'grəʊst] *adj*: **to be ~ (in sthg)** estar absorto(ta) (em algo).
engrossing [ɪn'grəʊsɪŋ] *adj* absorvente.
engulf [ɪn'gʌlf] *vt* **-1.** [cover, surround - subj: fire] devorar; [- subj: water] tragar **-2.** *fig* [overwhelm] tomar conta de.
enhance [ɪn'hɑːns] *vt* **-1.** [increase] aumentar **-2.** [improve] melhorar **-3.** [heighten: beauty, graphics] realçar.
enhancement [ɪn'hɑːnsmənt] *n* **-1.** *(U)* [increase] aumento *m* **-2.** [improvement] melhoria *f* **-3.** *COMPUT* realçamento *m.*
enigma [ɪ'nɪgmə] *n* enigma *m.*
enigmatic [ˌenɪg'mætɪk] *adj* enigmático(ca).
enjoy [ɪn'dʒɔɪ] ◇ *vt* **-1.** [like] gostar de; **to ~ doing sthg** gostar de fazer algo; **to ~ o.s.** divertir-se **-2.** *fml* [possess] desfrutar de. ◇ *vi US*: **~!** [enjoy yourself] divirta-se!; [before meal] bom apetite!
enjoyable [ɪn'dʒɔɪəbl] *adj* agradável.
enjoyment [ɪn'dʒɔɪmənt] *n* **-1.** *(U)* prazer *m* **-2.** *(U) fml* [possession] gozo *m*, desfrute *m.*
enlarge [ɪn'lɑːdʒ] *vt* ampliar.
◆ **enlarge (up)on** *vt fus* desenvolver.
enlargement [ɪn'lɑːdʒmənt] *n* **-1.** *(U)* [gen] ampliação *f* **-2.** *MED* dilatação *f.*
enlighten [ɪn'laɪtn] *vt fml* esclarecer.
enlightened [ɪn'laɪtnd] *adj* esclarecido(da).
enlightening [ɪn'laɪtnɪŋ] *adj* esclarecedor(ra).
enlightenment [ɪn'laɪtnmənt] *n (U)* esclarecimento *m.*
◆ **Enlightenment** *n*: **the Enlightenment** o Iluminismo.
enlist [ɪn'lɪst] ◇ *vt* **-1.** *MIL* [recruit] recrutar **-2.** [support, help] angariar. ◇ *vi MIL*: **to ~ (in)** alistar-se(em).
enlisted man [ɪn'lɪstɪd-] *n US* recruta *m.*
enliven [ɪn'laɪvn] *vt* animar.
en masse [ˌɒn'mæs] *adv* em massa.
enmeshed [ɪn'meʃt] *adj*: **to be ~ in sthg** estar enredado(da) em algo.
enmity ['enmətɪ] (*pl* **-ies**) *n (U)* inimizade *f.*
ennoble [ɪ'nəʊbl] *vt* **-1.** [elevate to nobility] nobilitar **-2.** [dignify] enobrecer.
enormity [ɪ'nɔːmətɪ] *n (U)* enormidade *f.*
enormous [ɪ'nɔːməs] *adj* enorme.
enormously [ɪ'nɔːməslɪ] *adv* enormemente.
enough [ɪ'nʌf] ◇ *adj* suficiente. ◇ *pron* suficiente; **to have had ~ (of sthg)** [expressing annoyance] estar farto(ta) (de algo); **more than ~** mais que suficiente; **~ is ~** já chega; **that's ~ (of that)!** chega! ◇ *adv* **-1.** [sufficiently] suficientemente, bastante; **to suffer ~** sofrer o bastante; **he hasn't tried hard ~** ele ainda não tentou o suficiente; **to be good ~ to do sthg** *fml* ter a bondade de fazer algo **-2.** [rather] bastante; **strangely ~** curiosamente.
enquire [ɪn'kwaɪəʳ] *vt & vi* = **inquire**.
enquiry [ɪn'kwaɪərɪ] (*pl* **-ies**) *n* = **inquiry**.
enraged [ɪn'reɪdʒd] *adj* enfurecido(da).
enrich [ɪn'rɪtʃ] *vt* enriquecer.
enrol *UK* (*pt* & *pp* **-led**, *cont* **-ling**), **enroll** *US* [ɪn'rəʊl] ◇ *vt* matricular. ◇ *vi*: **to ~ (on** *OR* **in sthg)** matricular-se (em algo).
enrolment *UK*, **enrollment** *US* [ɪn'rəʊlmənt] *n* **-1.** *(U)* [act of registering] inscrição *f* **-2.** [entry in register] matrícula *f.*

en route [ˌɒn'ru:t] *adv*: ~ **(from)** vindo de: ~ **(to)** a caminho de.
ensconced [ɪn'skɒnst] *adj fml* [in chair] acomodado(-da).
enshrine [ɪn'ʃraɪn] *vt*: **to be ~d in sthg** estar amparado(da) em algo, ser garantido(da) por algo.
ensign ['ensaɪn] *n* **-1.** [flag] bandeira *f* **-2.** *US* [sailor] guarda-marinha *mf.*
enslave [ɪn'sleɪv] *vt* escravizar.
ensue [ɪn'sju:] *vi fml* resultar.
ensuing [ɪn'sju:ɪŋ] *adj fml* subseqüente.
ensure [ɪn'ʃʊə^r] *vt* assegurar; **to ~ (that)** assegurar que.
ENT (*abbr of* **ear, nose and throat**) *n* otorrino *mf.*
entail [ɪn'teɪl] *vt* [involve] implicar.
entangled [ɪn'tæŋgld] *adj* **-1.** [ensnared]: **to be ~ in sthg** estar emaranhado(da) em algo **-2.** [involved]: **to be ~ in sthg** estar envolvido(da) em algo; **to be ~ with sb** estar envolvido(da) com alguém.
entanglement [ɪn'tæŋglmənt] *n* [involvement] envolvimento *m.*
enter ['entə^r] ◇ *vt* **-1.** [come or go into] entrar em **-2.** [join - competition, race, the church] entrar em; [- school, politics, parliament] ingressar em; [- armed forces] alistar-se em; [- university] matricular-se em **-3.** [register]: **to ~ sb/sthg for sthg** inscrever alguém/algo em algo **-4.** [write down] registrar **-5.** *COMPUT* inserir; **~ your name, please** insira seu nome. ◇ *vi* **-1.** [come or go in] entrar **-2.** [register]: **to ~ (for sthg)** inscrever-se (para algo).
◆ **enter into** *vt fus* **-1.** [begin] iniciar **-2.** [become involved in] comprometer-se em **-3.** [affect]: **money shouldn't ~ into it** o dinheiro não deveria contar aqui.
enteritis [ˌentə'raɪtɪs] *n (U)* enterite *f.*
enter key *n COMPUT* tecla *f* enter.
enterprise ['entəpraɪz] *n* **-1.** [company, business] empresa *f* **-2.** [venture] aventura *f* **-3.** *(U)* [initiative] empreendimento *m.*
enterprise culture *n* cultura *f* empresarial.
enterprise zone *n UK zona do Reino Unido na qual se fomenta a atividade cultural e empresarial.*
enterprising ['entəpraɪzɪŋ] *adj* empreendedor(-ra).
entertain [ˌentə'teɪn] ◇ *vt* **-1.** [amuse] entreter **-2.** [have as guest] receber **-3.** *fml* [consider] considerar **-4.** *fml* [harbour] nutrir. ◇ *vi* **-1.** [amuse] divertir **-2.** [have guests] receber.
entertainer [ˌentə'teɪnə^r] *n* animador *m*, -ra *f.*
entertaining [ˌentə'teɪnɪŋ] ◇ *adj* divertido(da). ◇ *n (U)* [receiving guests]: **she does a lot of ~** ela sempre recebe muitos convidados.
entertainment [ˌentə'teɪnmənt] ◇ *n* **-1.** *(U)* [amusement] divertimento *m*, entretenimento *m* **-2.** [show] espetáculo *m.* ◇ *comp* do espetáculo.
entertainment allowance *n* verba *f* de representação.
enthral (*pt* & *pp* **-led**, *cont* **-ling**), **enthrall** *US* [ɪn'θrɔ:l] *vt* fascinar.
enthralling [ɪn'θrɔ:lɪŋ] *adj* fascinante.
enthrone [ɪn'θrəʊn] *vt fml* entronizar.
enthuse [ɪn'θju:z] *vi*: **to ~ (about sthg)** entusiasmar-se (com algo).
enthusiasm [ɪn'θju:zɪæzm] *n* **-1.** *(U)* [passion, eagerness] entusiasmo *m*; **~ for sthg** entusiasmo por algo **-2.** [interest, hobby] paixão *f*, interesse *m.*
enthusiast [ɪn'θju:zɪæst] *n* [fan] entusiasta *mf.*
enthusiastic [ɪnˌθju:zɪ'æstɪk] *adj* entusiástico(ca).
enthusiastically [ɪnˌθju:zɪ'æstɪklɪ] *adv* entusiasticamente.
entice [ɪn'taɪs] *vt* atrair; **to ~ sb away from sthg** desviar alguém de algo; **to ~ sb into sthg** instigar alguém a algo.
enticing [ɪn'taɪsɪŋ] *adj* tentador(ra).
entire [ɪn'taɪə^r] *adj* inteiro(ra).
entirely [ɪn'taɪəlɪ] *adv* inteiramente; **that's ~ different** isso é completamente diferente.
entirety [ɪn'taɪrətɪ] *n (U) fml*: **in its ~** em sua totalidade.
entitle [ɪn'taɪtl] *vt* [allow]: **to ~ sb to sthg** dar a alguém o direito a algo; **to ~ sb to do sthg** autorizar alguém a fazer algo.
entitled [ɪn'taɪtld] *adj* **-1.** [having a right to]: **to be ~ to sthg/to do sthg** ter direito a algo/a fazer algo **-2.** [called] intitulado(da).
entitlement [ɪn'taɪtlmənt] *n* direito *m.*
entity ['entətɪ] (*pl* **-ies**) *n* entidade *f.*
entomology [ˌentə'mɒlədʒɪ] *n (U)* entomologia *f.*
entourage [ˌɒntʊ'rɑ:ʒ] *n* [of politician, popstar] séquito *m.*
entrails ['entreɪlz] *npl* entranhas *fpl.*
entrance [*n* 'entrəns, *vb* ɪn'trɑ:ns] ◇ *n* **-1.** [arrival] entrada *f* **-2.** [way in]: **~ (to sthg)** entrada (para *OR* de algo) **-3.** *(U)* [entry]: **to gain ~ to sthg** *fml* [to building] obter acesso a algo; [to society, university] ingressar em algo. ◇ *vt* [delight] encantar.
entrance examination *n* [for school, profession] exame *m* de admissão; [for university] ≃ vestibular *m.*
entrance fee *n* **-1.** [gen] (preço *m* do) ingresso *m* **-2.** [to club] taxa *f* de admissão.
entrancing [ɪn'trɑ:nsɪŋ] *adj* encantador(ra).
entrant ['entrənt] *n* **-1.** [gen] participante *mf* **-2.** [to profession] novato *m*, -ta *f* **-3.** [to university] calouro *m*, -ra *f.*
entreat [ɪn'tri:t] *vt*: **to ~ sb (to do sthg)** suplicar a alguém (para que faça algo).
entreaty [ɪn'tri:tɪ] (*pl* **-ies**) *n* súplica *f.*
entrenched *adj* [firm] arraigado(da).
entrepreneur [ˌɒntrəprə'nɜ:^r] *n* empresário *m*, -ria *f.*
entrepreneurial [ˌɒntrəprə'nɜ:rɪəl] *adj* empresarial.
entrust [ɪn'trʌst] *vt*: **to ~ sthg to sb**, **to ~ sb with sthg** confiar algo a alguém.
entry ['entrɪ] (*pl* **-ies**) *n* **-1.** [gen] entrada *f*; **~ (into)** entrada (em) **-2.** *(U)* [admission]: **~ (to)** acesso *m* (a); **to gain ~ to** conseguir acesso a; **'no ~'** [to room, building] 'proibida a entrada'; *AUT* 'não entre' **-3.** [in competition] inscrição *f* **-4.** [in diary] anotação *f* **-5.** [in ledger] lançamento *m* **-6.** *fig* [joining] ingresso *m.*
entry fee *n* ingresso *m.*
entry form *n* ficha *f* de inscrição.
entry phone *n* porteiro *m* eletrônico.

entryway ['entrɪˌweɪ] *n US* passagem *f* de entrada.
entwine [ɪn'twaɪn] ◇ *vt* entrelaçar. ◇ *vi* entrelaçar-se.
E number *n na Europa, número que representa a substância química adicionada a um alimento.*
enumerate [ɪ'nju:məreɪt] *vt* enumerar.
enunciate [ɪ'nʌnsɪeɪt] ◇ *vt* **-1.** [pronounce clearly] pronunciar **-2.** [express clearly] expor, enunciar. ◇ *vi* [speak clearly] enunciar.
envelop [ɪn'veləp] *vt*: **to ~ sb/sthg in sthg** envolver alguém/algo em algo.
envelope ['envələʊp] *n* [for letter] envelope *m*.
enviable ['envɪəbl] *adj* invejável.
envious ['envɪəs] *adj* invejoso(sa); **~ (of sb/ sthg)** invejoso(sa) (de alguém/algo).
enviously ['envɪəslɪ] *adv* com inveja.
environment [ɪn'vaɪərənmənt] *n* **-1.** [gen] ambiente *m* **-2.** [natural world]: **the ~** o meio ambiente; **Department of the Environment** *UK* ≃ Ministério *m* do Meio Ambiente.
environmental [ɪnˌvaɪərən'mentl] *adj* ambiental.
environmentalist [ɪnˌvaɪərən'mentəlɪst] *n* ambientalista *mf*.
environmentally [ɪnˌvaɪərən'mentəlɪ] *adv* ecologicamente; **~ friendly** que não prejudica o meio ambiente, ecológico(ca).
Environmental Protection Agency *n US*: **the ~** a Secretaria Especial do Meio Ambiente.
environs [ɪn'vaɪərənz] *npl* [of town, place] arredores *mpl*.
envisage [ɪn'vɪzɪdʒ], **envision** *US* [ɪn'vɪʒn] *vt* prever.
envoy ['envɔɪ] *n* enviado *m*, -da *f*.
envy ['envɪ] (*pt* & *pp* **-ied**) ◇ *n (U)* inveja *f*; **to be the ~ of** ser objeto de inveja de; **to be green with ~** estar morrendo de inveja. ◇ *vt* invejar; **to ~ sb sthg** invejar algo a alguém.
enzyme ['enzaɪm] *n* enzima *f*.
EOC (*abbr of* **Equal Opportunities Commission**) *n organismo do governo britânico que trata da discriminação sexual.*
eon *n US* = **aeon**.
EPA (*abbr of* **Environmental Protection Agency**) *n agência norte-americana de proteção ambiental,* ≃ APA *f*.
epaulet(te) ['epə'let] *n* dragona *f*.
ephemeral [ɪ'femərəl] *adj* efêmero(ra).
epic ['epɪk] ◇ *adj* épico(ca). ◇ *n* [book, film] épico *m*.
epicentre *UK*, **epicenter** *US* ['epɪsentəʳ] *n* epicentro *m*.
epidemic [ˌepɪ'demɪk] *n* [of disease] epidemia *f*.
epidural [ˌepɪ'djʊərəl] *n* [injection] epidural *f*.
epigram ['epɪgræm] *n* epigrama *f*.
epilepsy ['epɪlepsɪ] *n (U)* epilepsia *f*.
epileptic [ˌepɪ'leptɪk] ◇ *adj* [fit, person] epilético(-ca). ◇ *n* epilético *m*, -ca *f*.
epilogue *UK*, **epilog** *US* ['epɪlɒg] *n* [to play, book] epílogo *m*.
Epiphany [ɪ'pɪfənɪ] *n*: **(the) ~** (a) Epifania.
episcopal [ɪ'pɪskəpl] *adj* [of bishop] episcopal.
episode ['epɪsəʊd] *n* episódio *m*.
episodic [ˌepɪ'sɒdɪk] *adj* episódico(ca).
epistle [ɪ'pɪsl] *n literary* [letter] epístola *f*.
epitaph ['epɪtɑ:f] *n* epitáfio *m*.
epithet ['epɪθet] *n* epíteto *m*.
epitome [ɪ'pɪtəmɪ] *n*: **the ~ of sb/sthg** [person] o exemplo vivo de alguém/algo, a personificação de alguém/algo; **this hotel is the ~ of luxury** este hotel é o número um em termos de luxo.
epitomize, -ise [ɪ'pɪtəmaɪz] *vt* personificar, representar o paradigma de.
epoch ['i:pɒk] *n* época *f*.
epoch-making *adj* que marcou época.
eponymous [ɪ'pɒnɪməs] *adj* epônimo(ma).
EPOS (*abbr of* **electronic point of sale**) *n* ponto *m* eletrônico de venda, EPOS *m*.
equable ['ekwəbl] *adj* [calm, reasonable] calmo(ma).
equal ['i:kwəl] (*UK pt* & *pp* **-led**, *cont* **-ling**, *US pt* & *pp* **-ed**, *cont* **-ing**) ◇ *adj* **-1.** igual; **~ to sthg** [sum] igual a algo; **on ~ terms** em igualdade de condições **-2.** [capable]: **to be ~ to sthg** estar à altura de algo. ◇ *n* [person] igual *mf*; **he's her ~ in everything** ele é igual a ela em tudo. ◇ *vt* **-1.** *MATH* ser igual a **-2.** [in standard] igualar-se a.
equality [i:'kwɒlətɪ] *n (U)* igualdade *f*.
equalize, -ise ['i:kwəlaɪz] ◇ *vt* igualar. ◇ *vi* *SPORT* empatar.
equalizer ['i:kwəlaɪzəʳ] *n SPORT* gol *m* de empate.
equally ['i:kwəlɪ] *adv* **-1.** [to the same extent] igualmente **-2.** [in equal amounts] por igual **-3.** [by the same token] da mesma forma.
equal opportunities *npl* oportunidades *fpl* iguais.
Equal Opportunities Commission *n*: **the ~** *organismo do governo britânico que trata da discriminação sexual.*
equal(s) sign *n* sinal *m* de igual.
equanimity [ˌekwə'nɪmətɪ] *n (U)* equanimidade *f*.
equate [ɪ'kweɪt] *vt*: **to ~ sthg with sthg** equiparar algo com algo.
equation [ɪ'kweɪʒn] *n MATH* equação *f*.
equator [ɪ'kweɪtəʳ] *n*: **the ~** o equador.
equatorial [ˌekwə'tɔ:rɪəl] *adj* equatorial.
Equatorial Guinea *n* Guiné Equatorial.
equestrian [ɪ'kwestrɪən] *adj* eqüestre.
equidistant [ˌi:kwɪ'dɪstənt] *adj*: **~ (from)** eqüidistante (de).
equilateral triangle [ˌi:kwɪ'lætərəl-] *n* triângulo *m* equilátero.
equilibrium [ˌi:kwɪ'lɪbrɪəm] *n* equilíbrio *m*.
equine ['ekwaɪn] *adj* eqüino(na).
equinox ['i:kwɪnɒks] *n* equinócio *m*.
equip [ɪ'kwɪp] (*pt* & *pp* **-ped**, *cont* **-ping**) *vt* **-1.** [provide with equipment] equipar; **to ~ sb/sthg with sthg** equipar alguém/algo com algo **-2.** [prepare mentally]: **to ~ sb for sthg** preparar alguém psicologicamente para algo.
equipment [ɪ'kwɪpmənt] *n (U)* equipamento *m*.
equitable ['ekwɪtəbl] *adj* eqüitativo(va).
equity ['ekwətɪ] *n FIN* [market value] patrimônio *m* líquido.
◆ **equities** *npl ST EX* ações *fpl* ordinárias.
equivalent [ɪ'kwɪvələnt] ◇ *adj* equivalente; **to be**

~ **to sthg** ser equivalente a algo. <> *n* equivalente *m*.

equivocal [ɪ'kwɪvəkl] *adj* **-1.** [statement, remark] ambíguo(gua) **-2.** [behaviour, event] duvidoso(sa).

equivocate [ɪ'kwɪvəkeɪt] *vi* usar expressões ambíguas.

er [3:ʳ] *excl* **-1.** [in hesitation] ãhn! **-2.** [to attract attention] ei!

ER -1. (*abbr of* **Elizabeth Regina**) *emblema da rainha Elizabete* **- 2.** *n* **US** (*abbr of* **emergency room**) MED pronto-socorro *m*.

era ['ɪərə] (*pl* **-s**) *n* era *f*.

ERA (*abbr of* **Equal Rights Amendment**) *n lei norte-americana de igualdade de direitos para as mulheres*.

eradicate [ɪ'rædɪkeɪt] *vt* erradicar.

eradication [ɪˌrædɪ'keɪʃn] *n (U)* erradicação *f*.

erase [ɪ'reɪz] *vt* **-1.** [rub out] apagar **-2.** ***fig*** [drive away, eliminate] eliminar, extinguir.

eraser [ɪ'reɪzəʳ] *n* **US** borracha *f*.

erect [ɪ'rekt] <> *adj* ereto(ta). <> *vt* **-1.** [building, statue] erigir **-2.** [tent, roadblock] montar.

erection [ɪ'rekʃn] *n* **-1.** *(U)* [of building, statue] construção *f* **-2.** [erect penis] ereção *f*; **to get/have an ~** conseguir/ter uma ereção.

ergonomic [ˌ3:gə'nɒmɪk] *adj* ergonômico(ca).

ergonomics [ˌ3:gə'nɒmɪks] *n (U)* ergonomia *f*.

ERISA (*abbr of* **Employee Retirement Income Security Act**) *n lei norte-americana que trata de questões de aposentadoria*.

Eritrea [ˌerɪ'treɪə] *n* Eritréia; **in ~** na Eritréia.

Eritrean [ˌerɪ'treɪən] <> *adj* eritreu(tréia). <> *n* eritreu *m*, -tréia *f*.

ERM (*abbr of* **Exchange Rate Mechanism**) *n* MTC *m*.

ermine ['3:mɪn] *n (U)* [fur] arminho *m*.

erode [ɪ'rəʊd] <> *vt* **-1.** GEOL causar erosão em **-2.** ***fig*** [destroy] destruir. <> *vi* **-1.** GEOL sofrer erosão **-2.** ***fig*** [be destroyed] ser destruído(da).

erogenous zone [ɪ'rɒdʒɪnəs-] *n* zona *f* erógena.

erosion [ɪ'rəʊʒn] *n* **-1.** GEOL erosão *f* **-2.** ***fig*** [destruction] destruição *f*.

erotic [ɪ'rɒtɪk] *adj* erótico(ca).

eroticism [ɪ'rɒtɪsɪzml] *n (U)* erotismo *m*.

err [3:ʳ] *vi* errar; **to ~ on the side of caution** pecar por excesso de cautela; **to ~ is human** errar é humano.

errand ['erənd] *n* **-1.** [task] tarefa *f*; **to go on** OR **run an ~ (for sb)** encarregar-se de alguma tarefa (para alguém) **-2.** [message] recado *m*.

errand boy *n* menino *m* de recados.

erratic [ɪ'rætɪk] *adj* irregular.

erroneous [ɪ'rəʊnjəs] *adj* ***fml*** errôneo(nea).

error ['erəʳ] *n* **-1.** [mistake] erro *m*; **~ of judgment** erro de julgamento; **in ~** por engano **-2.** FIN: **~s and omissions excepted** salvo erro ou omissão.

error message *n* COMPUT mensagem *f* de erro.

erstwhile ['3:stwaɪl] *adj* ***literary*** anterior, antigo(-ga).

erudite ['eru:daɪt] *adj* erudito(ta).

erupt [ɪ'rʌpt] *vi* **-1.** [volcano] entrar em erupção **-2.** ***fig*** [violence, war] explodir.

eruption [ɪ'rʌpʃn] *n* **-1.** [of volcano] erupção *f* **-2.** [of violence, war] explosão *f*.

ESA (*abbr of* **European Space Agency**) *n agência espacial européia*.

escalate ['eskəleɪt] *vi* **-1.** [conflict, violence] intensificar-se **-2.** [costs, prices] aumentar.

escalation [ˌeskə'leɪʃn] *n* **-1.** [of conflict, violence] intensificação *f* **-2.** [of costs, prices] aumento *m*.

escalator ['eskəleɪtəʳ] *n* escada *f* rolante.

escalator clause *n* cláusula *f* de indexação.

escapade [ˌeskə'peɪd] *n* escapada *f*.

escape [ɪ'skeɪp] <> *n* **-1.** [gen] fuga *f*; **~ (from sb/sthg)** fuga (de alguém/algo); **to make an** OR **one's ~ (from)** fugir (de); **we had a narrow ~** escapamos por um triz **-2.** [leakage] escapamento *m* **-3.** COMPUT tecla *f* Esc. <> *vt* **-1.** [gen] fugir de **-2.** [death, injury] escapar a; **to ~ notice** passar desapercebido(da) **-3.** [subj: fact, name] escapar. <> *vi* **-1.** [from person, place, situation]: **to ~ (from sb/sthg)** fugir (de alguém/algo) **-2.** [from danger] escapar **-3.** [leak] vazar.

escape clause *n* cláusula *f* de exceção, *cláusula que permite revogação de um contrato*.

escape key *n* COMPUT tecla *f* Esc.

escape route *n* **-1.** [from prison] rota *f* de fuga **-2.** [from fire] saída *f* de emergência.

escapism [ɪ'skeɪpɪzm] *n (U)* escapismo *m*.

escapist [ɪ'skeɪpɪst] *adj* escapista.

escapologist [ˌeskə'pɒlədʒɪst] *n* ilusionista *mf*.

escarpment [ɪ'skɑ:pmənt] *n* escarpa *f*.

eschew [ɪs'tʃu:] *vt* ***fml*** evitar.

escort [*n* 'eskɔ:t, *vb* ɪ'skɔ:t] <> *n* **-1.** [guard] escolta *f*; **under ~** sob escolta **-2.** [companion] acompanhante *mf*. <> *vt* [accompany] acompanhar.

escort agency *n* agência *f* de acompanhantes.

Eskimo ['eskɪməʊ] (*pl* **-s**) <> *adj* esquimó. <> *n* **-1.** [person] esquimó *mf* **-2.** [language] esquimó *m*.

ESL (*abbr of* **English as a Second Language**) *n inglês para imigrantes que vivem permanentemente no Reino Unido e obtiveram cidadania britânica*.

esophagus *n* **US** = **oesophagus**.

esoteric [ˌesə'terɪk] *adj* esotérico(ca).

esp. (*abbr of* **especially**) espec.

ESP *n* **-1.** (*abbr of* **extrasensory perception**) percepção *f* extrasensorial. **-2.** (*abbr of* **English for Special Purposes** *inglês para fins específicos*.

espadrille [ˌespə'drɪl] *n* alpargata *f*.

especial *adj* especial.

especially [ɪ'speʃəlɪ] *adv* **-1.** [in particular, specifically] especialmente **-2.** [more than usually] excepcionalmente.

Esperanto [ˌespə'ræntəʊ] *n* esperanto *m*.

espionage ['espɪəˌnɑ:ʒ] *n (U)* espionagem *f*.

esplanade [ˌesplə'neɪd] *n* esplanada *f*.

espouse [ɪ'spaʊz] *vt* ***fml*** abraçar.

espresso [e'spresəʊ] (*pl* **-s**) *n* café *m* expresso.

Esq. (*abbr of* **esquire**) *n título formal utilizado após um nome masculino, especialmente se ele não tiver nenhum outro título*.

Esquire [ɪ'skwaɪəʳ] *n*: **James Smith, ~** Sr. James Smith.

essay ['eseɪ] *n* **-1.** SCH & UNIV trabalho *m* **-2.** LITERATURE ensaio *m*.

essayist ['eseɪɪst] *n* ensaísta *mf*.

essence ['esns] *n* essência *f*; **in ~** em essência.

essential [ɪ'senʃl] *adj* essencial; ~ **(to** *or* **for sthg)** essencial (para algo).

◆ **essentials** *npl* **-1.** [basic commodities] o essencial **-2.** [most important elements] fundamentos *mpl*, elementos *mpl* essenciais.

essentially [ɪ'senʃəlɪ] *adv* [basically] essencialmente, basicamente.

essential oil *n* óleo *m* essencial.

est. **-1.** (*abbr of* **established**) estabelecido(da). **-2.** (*abbr of* **estimated**) estimado(da).

EST (*abbr of* **Eastern Standard Time**) *n horário oficial na zona oriental dos Estados Unidos.*

establish [ɪ'stæblɪʃ] *vt* **-1.** [create, found] criar, estabelecer **-2.** [initiate]: **to ~ contact with sb** estabelecer contato com alguém **-3.** [ascertain] provar **-4.** [cause to be accepted] firmar; **to ~ o.s. (as)** estabelecer-se (como).

established [ɪ'stæblɪʃt] *adj* **-1.** [accepted] aceito(ta) **-2.** [founded] fundado(da).

establishment [ɪ'stæblɪʃmənt] *n* **-1.** *(U)* [creation, foundation] fundação *f*, criação *f* **-2.** [shop, business] estabelecimento *m*.

◆ **Establishment** *n* [status quo]: **the Establishment** a classe governante.

estate [ɪ'steɪt] *n* **-1.** [land, property] propriedade *f* **-2.** : **housing ~** loteamento *m* **-3.** : **industrial ~** zona *f* industrial **-4.** *JUR* [inheritance] herança *f*.

estate agency *n UK* agência *f* imobiliária.

estate agent *n UK* corretor *m*, -ra *f* de imóveis; **~'s** agência *f* imobiliária.

estate car *n UK* van *f*, perua *f*.

estd., est'd. (*abbr of* **established**) estabelecido(-da).

esteem [ɪ'sti:m] ◇ *n* estima *f*; **to hold sb/sthg in high ~** ter alguém/algo em alta estima. ◇ *vt* [respect] estimar.

esthetic etc *US* = **aesthetic etc.**

estimate [*n* 'estɪmət, *vb* 'estɪmeɪt] ◇ *n* **-1.** [calculation, reckoning] cálculo *m*, estimativa *f* **-2.** *COMM* orçamento *m*. ◇ *vt* calcular, estimar. ◇ *vi COMM*: **to ~ for sthg** fazer um orçamento de algo.

estimated ['estɪmeɪtɪd] *adj* estimado(da); **an ~ 5,000 people died** estima-se que 5.000 pessoas morreram.

estimation [ˌestɪ'meɪʃn] *n* **-1.** [opinion] opinião *f* **-2.** [calculation] cálculo *m*, estimativa *f*.

Estonia [e'stəʊnɪə] *n* Estônia; **in ~** na Estônia.

Estonian [e'stəʊnɪən] ◇ *adj* estoniano(na). ◇ *n* **-1.** [person] estoniano *m*, -na *f* **-2.** [language] estoniano *m*.

estranged [ɪ'streɪndʒd] *adj* separado(da); **his ~ son** o filho com o qual ele não fala.

estrogen *n US* = **oestrogen**.

estuary ['estjʊərɪ] (*pl* **-ies**) *n* estuário *m*.

ETA (*abbr of* **estimated time of arrival**) *n* hora *f* prevista de chegada.

e-tailer ['i:teɪlə^r] *n* varejista *mf* eletrônico(ca), e-tailer *mf*.

et al. [ˌet'æl] (*abbr of* **et alii**) et al.

etc. (*abbr of* **etcetera**) etc.

etcetera [ɪt'setərə] *adv* et cetera.

etch [etʃ] *vt* **-1.** [engrave] gravar com água-forte **-2.** *fig* [imprint]: **to be ~ed on sb's memory** estar gravado(da) na memória de alguém.

etching ['etʃɪŋ] *n* gravura *f* de água-forte.

ETD (*abbr of* **estimated time of departure**) *n* hora *f* prevista de partida.

eternal [ɪ'tɜ:nl] *adj* **-1.** [gen] eterno(na) **-2.** [truth, value] absoluto(ta).

eternally [ɪ'tɜ:nəlɪ] *adv* [forever] eternamente.

eternity [ɪ'tɜ:nətɪ] *n (U)* eternidade *f*.

eternity ring *n UK aliança que simboliza o amor eterno.*

ether ['i:θə^r] *n (U)* [solvent, anaesthetic] éter *m*.

ethereal [ɪ'θɪərɪəl] *adj literary* [unearthly] etéreo(rea).

ethic ['eθɪk] *n* ética *f*.

◆ **ethics** ◇ *n (U)* [study] ética *f*. ◇ *npl* [morals] moral *f*.

ethical ['eθɪkl] *adj* [morally right] ético(ca).

Ethiopia [ˌi:θɪ'əʊpɪə] *n* Etiópia; **in ~** na Etiópia.

Ethiopian [ˌi:θɪ'əʊpɪən] ◇ *adj* etíope. ◇ *n* etíope *mf*.

ethnic ['eθnɪk] *adj* **-1.** [traditions, groups, conflict] étnico(ca) **-2.** [clothes, food] folclórico(ca).

ethnic cleansing [-'klensɪŋ] *n* limpeza *f* étnica.

ethnic minority *n* minoria *f* étnica.

ethnology [eθ'nɒlədʒɪ] *n (U)* etnologia *f*.

ethos ['i:θɒs] *n* sistema *m* de valores.

etiquette ['etɪket] *n* etiqueta *f*.

ETV (*abbr of* **Educational Television**) *n rede norte-americana de televisão especializada em programas culturais e educacionais.*

etymology [ˌetɪ'mɒlədʒɪ] (*pl* **-ies**) *n* etimologia *f*.

EU (*abbr of* **European Union**) *n* UE *f*.

eucalyptus [ˌju:kə'lɪptəs] (*pl* **-tuses**) *n* eucalipto *m*.

eulogize, -ise ['ju:lədʒaɪz] *vt fml* elogiar, louvar.

eulogy ['ju:lədʒɪ] (*pl* **-ies**) *n fml* elogio *m*.

eunuch ['ju:nək] *n* eunuco *m*.

euphemism ['ju:fəmɪzm] *n* eufemismo *m*.

euphemistic [ˌju:fə'mɪstɪk] *adj* eufemístico(ca).

euphoria [ju:'fɔ:rɪə] *n* euforia *f*.

euphoric [ju:'fɒrɪk] *adj* eufórico(ca).

Eurasia [jʊə'reɪʒə] *n* Eurásia; **in ~** na Eurásia.

Eurasian [jʊə'reɪʒən] ◇ *adj* **-1.** [of Europe and Asia] eurásico(ca) **-2.** [of mixed European and Asian descent] eurasiático(ca). ◇ *n* eurasiático *m*, -ca *f*.

eureka [jʊə'ri:kə] *excl* heureca!

Euro- ['jʊərəʊ] *prefix* euro-.

Eurocheque ['jʊərəʊˌtʃek] *n* eurocheque *m*.

Eurocrat ['jʊərəˌkræt] *n* eurocrata *mf*.

Eurocurrency ['ju:rəʊˌkʌrənsɪ] (*pl* **-ies**) *n* moeda *f* européia.

Eurodollar ['jʊərəʊˌdɒlə^r] *n* eurodólar *m*.

Euro-elections *npl* eleições *fpl* do Parlamento Europeu.

Euro MP *n* membro *m* do Parlamento Europeu.

Europe ['jʊərəp] *n* Europa; **in ~** na Europa.

European [ˌjʊərə'pi:ən] ◇ *adj* europeu(péia). ◇ *n* europeu *m*, -péia *f*.

European Central Bank *n*: **the ~** o Banco Central Europeu.

European Community *n*: **the ~** a Comunidade Européia.

European Court of Human Rights *n*: **the ~** o Tribunal Europeu de Direitos Humanos.

European Court of Justice *n*: **the ~** o Tribunal Europeu de Justiça.
European Currency Unit *n* Unidade *f* Monetária Européia.
Europeanism [ˌjʊərəˈpiːənɪzm] *n* europeísmo *m*.
Europeanize, -ise [ˌjʊərəˈpiːənaɪz] *vt* europeizar.
European Monetary System *n*: **the ~** o Sistema Monetário Europeu.
European Parliament *n*: **the ~** o Parlamento Europeu.
European Union *n*: **the ~** a União Européia.
Eurosceptic [ˈʊərəʊˌskeptɪk] <> *adj* eurocético(-ca). <> *n* eurocético *m*, -ca *f*.
Eurostar [ˈʊərəʊstɑːʳ] *n* Eurostar *m*, *trem de alta velocidade que vai da Inglaterra à França passando sob o Canal da Mancha.*
euthanasia [ˌjuːθəˈneɪzjə] *n* eutanásia *f*.
evacuate [ɪˈvækjʊeɪt] *vt* evacuar.
evacuation [ɪˌvækjʊˈeɪʃn] *n* evacuação *f*.
evacuee [ɪˌvækjuːˈiː] *n* evacuado *m*, -da *f* (*devido a uma guerra*).
evade [ɪˈveɪd] *vt* **-1.** [pursuers, capture] fugir a **-2.** [issue, question] fugir de **-3.** [subj: love, success] escapar de.
evaluate [ɪˈvæljʊeɪt] *vt* avaliar.
evaluation [ɪˌvæljʊˈeɪʃn] *n* avaliação *f*.
evangelical [ˌiːvænˈdʒelɪkl] *adj* evangélico(ca).
evangelism [ɪˈvændʒəlɪzm] *n (U)* evangelismo *m*.
evangelist [ɪˈvændʒəlɪst] *n* evangelista *mf*.
evangelize, -ise [ɪˈvændʒəlaɪz] *vt* evangelizar.
evaporate [ɪˈvæpəreɪt] *vi* **-1.** [liquid] evaporar **-2.** *fig* [feeling] evaporar-se, dissipar-se.
evaporated milk [ɪˈvæpəreɪtɪd-] *n tipo de leite condensado por evaporação que não contém açucar.*
evaporation [ɪˌvæpəˈreɪʃn] *n* **-1.** [of liquid] evaporação *f* **-2.** *fig* [of feeling] dissipação *f*.
evasion [ɪˈveɪʒn] *n* **-1.** *(U)* [of responsibility, payment etc] evasão *f* **-2.** [lie] evasiva *f*.
evasive [ɪˈveɪsɪv] *adj* **-1.** [to avoid question, subject] evasivo(va) **-2.** [to avoid being hit]: **to take ~ action** tomar uma ação defensiva.
evasiveness [ɪˈveɪsɪvnɪs] *n (U)* atitude *f* evasiva.
eve [iːv] *n* [day before] véspera *f*.
even [ˈiːvn] <> *adj* **-1.** [regular] regular **-2.** [calm] equilibrado(da) **-3.** [flat, level] plano(na) **-4.** [equal] igual; **to get ~ with sb** ficar quite com alguém **-5.** : **~ number** número par. <> *adv* **-1.** [for emphasis] mesmo; **~ I** mesmo eu; **~ now** mesmo agora; **~ then** [at that time] mesmo então; [in spite of that] mesmo assim **-2.** [in comparisons] ainda **-3.** [indeed] até.
◆ **even as** *conj* [while] enquanto.
◆ **even if** *conj* mesmo se.
◆ **even so** *adv* [in spite of that] mesmo assim.
◆ **even though** *conj* ainda que.
◆ **even out** <> *vt sep* nivelar. <> *vi* nivelar-se.
even-handed [-ˈhændɪd] *adj* justo(ta).
evening [ˈiːvnɪŋ] *n* **-1.** [end of day - from 5 pm until 8 pm] tardinha *f*; **good ~** boa tarde; **in the ~** à tarde; [- from 8 pm onwards] noite *f*; **good ~** boa noite; **in the ~** à noite, ao anoitecer **-2.** [event, entertainment] noite *f*.
◆ **evenings** *adv US* à noite.
evening class *n* aula *f* noturna.
evening dress *n* **-1.** *(U)* [formal clothes] traje *m* a rigor **-2.** [woman's garment] vestido *m* de gala.
evening star *n*: **the ~** a estrela vespertina.
evenly [ˈiːvnlɪ] *adv* **-1.** [regularly] regularmente **-2.** [equally] igualmente **-3.** [calmly] tranqüilamente.
evenness [ˈiːvnnɪs] *n* **-1.** [regularity] regularidade *f* **-2.** [equality] igualdade *f*.
evensong [ˈiːvnsɒŋ] *n* culto *m* da tarde.
event [ɪˈvent] *n* **-1.** [happening] acontecimento *m*; **social ~** evento *m* social **-2.** *SPORT* evento *m* **-3.** [case] caso *m*; **in the ~ of** em caso de; **in the ~ that the train is cancelled** na eventualidade de o trem ser cancelado.
◆ **in any event** *adv* [all the same] em todo o caso.
◆ **in the event** *adv UK* na realidade.
even-tempered [-ˈtempəd] *adj* equilibrado(da).
eventful [ɪˈventfʊl] *adj* movimentado(da), agitado(da).
eventide home [ˈiːvntaɪd-] *n UK euphemism* lar *m* de idosos.
eventing [ɪˈventɪŋ] *n UK* [horseriding]: **(three-day) ~** concurso *m* hípico (de três dias).
eventual [ɪˈventʃʊəl] *adj* final.
eventuality [ɪˌventʃʊˈælətɪ] (*pl* **-ies**) *n* eventualidade *f*.
eventually [ɪˈventʃʊəlɪ] *adv* finalmente, no fim.
ever [ˈevəʳ] *adv* **-1.** [already, at some time] já, alguma vez; **have you ~ been to Scotland?** você já/alguma vez foi para a Escócia?; **the worst film I've ~ seen** o pior filme que eu já vi; **if ~** se por acaso **-2.** [with negative - gen] nunca; **no one ~ calls these days** ninguém nunca telefona por esses dias; **hardly ~** quase nunca; [- emphatic] jamais; **don't ~ speak to me like that!** jamais fale comigo desse jeito **-3.** [all the time] sempre; **as ~** como sempre; **for ~** para sempre **-4.** [for emphasis]: **why ~ did you do that?** por que cargas d'água você fez isso?; **how ~ did he get back?** como será que ele voltou?; **~ so kind** tão gentil; **~ such a mess** tamanha bagunça.
◆ **ever since** <> *adv* desde então. <> *conj* desde que. <> *prep* desde.
Everest [ˈevərɪst] *n*: **Mount ~** o Monte Everest.
Everglades [ˈevəˌgleɪdz] *npl*: **the ~** *região pantanosa da Flórida.*
evergreen [ˈevəgriːn] <> *adj* sempre-verde. <> *n* sempre-verde *m*.
everlasting [ˌevəˈlɑːstɪŋ] *adj* [lasting forever] eterno(-na).
every [ˈevrɪ] *adj* **-1.** [each] cada **-2.** [to express frequency]: **~ three hours** a cada três horas; **~ day** cada dia **-3.** [all] todo (da); **~ day** todos os dias.
◆ **every now and then, every so often** *adv* de vez em quando.
◆ **every other** *adj* [every alternate]: **~ other day** dia sim, dia não; **~ other week** cada duas semanas.
◆ **every which way** *adv US* para todos os lados.
everybody [ˈevrɪˌbɒdɪ] *pron* = **everyone**.
everyday [ˈevrɪdeɪ] *adj* diário(ria).

everyone ['evrɪwʌn] *pron* todo mundo, todos *mpl* -das *fpl*.
everyplace *adv US* = **everywhere**.
everything ['evrɪθɪŋ] *pron* tudo.
everywhere ['evrɪweəʳ], **everyplace** *US* ['evrɪ,pleɪs] *adv* por todo o lado; [with verbs of motion] para todo o lado; ~ **you go it's the same** onde quer que se vá é o mesmo.
evict [ɪ'vɪkt] *vt*: **to ~ sb (from)** despejar alguém (de).
eviction [ɪ'vɪkʃn] *n* despejo *m*.
eviction notice *n* aviso *m* de despejo.
evidence ['evɪdəns] *n* **-1.** [proof] evidência *f* **-2.** *JUR* prova *f*; **to give ~** prestar depoimento.
◆ **in evidence** *adj* [noticeable] em evidência.
evident ['evɪdənt] *adj* evidente.
evidently ['evɪdəntlɪ] *adv* evidentemente.
evil ['i:vl] ◇ *adj* [morally bad] mau(má). ◇ *n* **-1.** *(U)* [wicked behaviour] maldade *f* **-2.** [wicked thing] mal *m*.
evildoer *n* malfeitor *m*, -ra *f*.
evil-minded [-'maɪndɪd] *adj* malvado(da).
evince [ɪ'vɪns] *vt fml* evidenciar.
evocation [,evəʊ'keɪʃn] *n* evocação *f*.
evocative [ɪ'vɒkətɪv] *adj* evocativo(va).
evoke [ɪ'vəʊk] *vt* **-1.** [call up, summon] chamar **-2.** [elicit, provoke] evocar.
evolution [,i:və'lu:ʃn] *n* evolução *f*.
evolve [ɪ'vɒlv] ◇ *vt* [develop] desenvolver. ◇ *vi* **-1.** *BIOL*: **to ~ (into/from)** evoluir (para/de) **-2.** [develop] desenvolver-se.
ewe [ju:] *n* ovelha *f*.
ex- [eks] *prefix* ex-.
exacerbate [ɪg'zæsəbeɪt] *vt* exacerbar.
exact [ɪg'zækt] ◇ *adj* [precise] exato(ta); **to be ~** para ser exato(ta). ◇ *vt*: **to ~ sthg (from sb)** exigir algo (de alguém).
exacting [ɪg'zæktɪŋ] *adj* [demanding, rigorous] exigente.
exactitude [ɪg'zæktɪtju:d] *n (U) fml* exatidão *f*.
exactly [ɪg'zæktlɪ] ◇ *adv* [precisely] exatamente; **not ~** [not really] não exatamente. ◇ *excl* exatamente!
exaggerate [ɪg'zædʒəreɪt] ◇ *vt* exagerar. ◇ *vi* exagerar.
exaggerated [ɪg'zædʒəreɪtɪd] *adj* exagerado(da).
exaggeration [ɪg,zædʒə'reɪʃn] *n* exagero *m*.
exalted [ɪg'zɔ:ltɪd] *adj* [important] sublime.
exam [ɪg'zæm] (*abbr of* **examination**) *n* **-1.** *SCH* prova *f*; **to take** *OR* **sit an ~** fazer uma prova. **-2.** *MED US* exame *m*.
examination [ɪg,zæmɪ'neɪʃn] *n* **-1.** [gen] exame *m* **-2.** [inspection] investigação *f* **-3.** [consideration] análise *f* **-4.** *JUR* [of witness, suspect] interrogatório *m*.
examination board *n* banca *f* examinadora.
examination paper *n UK* [test] prova *f*, exame *m*.
examine [ɪg'zæmɪn] *vt* **-1.** [gen] examinar **-2.** [consider] estudar **-3.** *JUR* interrogar.
examiner [ɪg'zæmɪnəʳ] *n* examinador *m*, -ra *f*; **internal/external ~** examinador externo/interno, examinadora externa/interna.
example [ɪg'zɑ:mpl] *n* exemplo *m*; **for ~** por exemplo; **to follow sb's ~** seguir o exemplo de alguém; **to make an ~ of sb** fazer exemplo de alguém.
exasperate [ɪg'zæspəreɪt] *vt* exasperar.
exasperating [ɪg'zæspəreɪtɪŋ] *adj* exasperador(-ra), irritante.
exasperation [ɪg,zæspə'reɪʃn] *n (U)* exasperação *f*.
excavate ['ekskəveɪt] *vt* escavar.
excavation [,ekskə'veɪʃn] *n* escavação *f*.
excavator ['ekskə,veɪtəʳ] *n UK* [machine] escavadeira *f*.
exceed [ɪk'si:d] *vt* **-1.** [be bigger than] exceder **-2.** [go beyond, go over - limit] ultrapassar; [- expectations] superar.
exceedingly [ɪk'si:dɪŋlɪ] *adv* extremamente.
excel [ɪk'sel] (*pt* & *pp* **-led**, *cont* **-ling**) ◇ *vi*: **to ~ (in** *OR* **at sthg)** sobressair-se (em algo). ◇ *vt*: **to ~ o.s.** *UK* superar-se.
excellence ['eksələns] *n (U)* excelência *f*.
Excellency ['eksələnsɪ] (*pl* **-ies**) *n*: **Your/His ~** Sua Excelência.
excellent ['eksələnt] ◇ *adj* excelente. ◇ *excl* excelente!
except [ɪk'sept] ◇ *prep* exceto. ◇ *conj* exceto. ◇ *vt*: **to ~ sb (from sthg)** excluir alguém (de algo).
◆ **except for** ◇ *prep* com exceção de. ◇ *conj* exceto.
excepted [ɪk'septɪd] *prep*: **Jenny ~, everyone agreed** com a exceção de Jenny, todos concordaram.
excepting [ɪk'septɪŋ] *prep* & *conj* = **except**.
exception [ɪk'sepʃn] *n* **-1.** [exclusion] exceção *f*; **~ to sthg** exceção a algo; **with the ~ of** com a exceção de; **without ~** sem exceção **-2.** [offence]: **to take ~ to sthg** ofender-se com algo.
exceptional [ɪk'sepʃənl] *adj* [unusually clever, talented] excepcional.
exceptionally [ɪk'sepʃnəlɪ] *adv* [unusually] excepcionalmente.
excerpt ['eksɜ:pt] *n*: **~ (from sthg)** excerto *m* (de algo).
excess [ɪk'ses, *before nouns* 'ekses] ◇ *adj* excessivo(va). ◇ *n* excesso *m*; **to ~** em excesso; **debts in ~ of £200,000** débitos de mais de £200.000. ◇ *vt* *RAIL* sobretaxar.
excess baggage *n* excesso *m* de bagagem.
excess fare *n UK* sobretaxa *f*.
excessive [ɪk'sesɪv] *adj* excessivo(va).
excess luggage *n* = **excess baggage**.
exchange [ɪks'tʃeɪndʒ] ◇ *n* **-1.** *(U)* [act of swapping] troca *f*, intercâmbio *m*; **in ~** em troca; **in ~ for** em troca de **-2.** [swap] troca *f* **-3.** *FIN*: **stock ~** bolsa *f* (de valores) **-4.** *FIN*: **(foreign) ~** câmbio *m*, divisas *fpl* **-5.** *TELEC*: **(telephone) ~** central *f* telefônica **-6.** [educational visit] intercâmbio *m* **-7.** *fml* [conversation] diálogo *m*. ◇ *vt* [swap] trocar; **to ~ sthg for sthg** trocar algo por algo; **to ~ sthg with sb** trocar algo com alguém.
exchange rate *n FIN* taxa *f* de câmbio.
Exchequer [ɪks'tʃekəʳ] *n UK*: **the ~** o Ministério da Fazenda britânico.
excise ['eksaɪz] ◇ *n (U)* imposto *m*; **Customs and Excise** ≃ a Receita Federal. ◇ *vt fml* extrair.

excise duties *npl* impostos *mpl* indiretos OR de consumo.
excitable [ɪk'saɪtəbl] *adj* excitável.
excite [ɪk'saɪt] *vt* **-1.** [person] entusiasmar **-2.** [nerves, heart] agitar **-3.** [interest, suspicion] despertar.
excited [ɪk'saɪtɪd] *adj* **-1.** [enthused] entusiasmado(-da) **-2.** [agitated] agitado(da).
excitement [ɪk'saɪtmənt] *n* **-1.** *(U)* [state - enthusiasm] entusiasmo *m*; [- agitation] agitação *f* **-2.** [exciting thing] emoção *f*.
exciting [ɪk'saɪtɪŋ] *adj* emocionante.
excl. (*abbr of* **excluding**) exc.
exclaim [ɪk'skleɪm] ◇ *vt & vi* exclamar.
exclamation [ˌekskləˈmeɪʃn] *n* exclamação *f*.
exclamation mark *UK*, **exclamation point** *US n* ponto *m* de exclamação.
exclude [ɪk'sklu:d] *vt* excluir; **to ~ sb/sthg (from sthg)** excluir alguém/algo (de algo).
excluding [ɪk'sklu:dɪŋ] *prep* excluindo.
exclusion [ɪk'sklu:ʒn] *n (U)* exclusão *f*; **~ (from)** exclusão (de); **to the ~ of** a ponto de excluir.
exclusion clause *n* COMM cláusula *f* de exclusão.
exclusive [ɪk'sklu:sɪv] ◇ *adj* exclusivo(va). ◇ *n* PRESS artigo *m* exclusivo.
◆ **exclusive of** *prep*: **~ of sales tax** imposto sobre vendas não-incluído.
exclusively [ɪk'sklu:sɪvlɪ] *adv* exclusivamente.
excommunicate [ˌekskəˈmju:nɪkeɪt] *vt* excomungar.
excommunication [ˈekskəˌmju:nɪˈkeɪʃn] *n* excomungação *f*.
excrement [ˈekskrɪmənt] *n fml* excremento *m*.
excrete [ɪk'skri:t] *vt* excretar.
excruciating [ɪk'skru:ʃɪeɪtɪŋ] *adj* **-1.** [pain] insuportável **-2.** [emotion, performance] terrível.
excursion [ɪk'skɜ:ʃn] *n* [trip] excursão *f*.
excusable [ɪk'skju:zəbl] *adj* desculpável.
excuse [*n* ɪk'skju:s, *vb* ɪk'skju:z] ◇ *n* **-1.** [reason, explanation] desculpa *f* **-2.** [justification]: **~ (for sthg)** desculpa (para algo). ◇ *vt* **-1.** desculpar; **to ~ sb for sthg/for doing sthg** desculpar alguém por algo/por fazer algo **-2.** [let off, free] dispensar; **to ~ sb from sthg** dispensar alguém de algo **-3.** [allow to leave] dar licença **-4.** *phr*: **~ me** [to attract attention] com licença; [forgive me] desculpe; *US* [sorry] perdão.
ex-directory *adj UK* que não consta na lista telefônica.
exec [ɪg'zek] (*abbr of* **executive**) executivo(va).
execrable [ˈeksɪkrəbl] *adj fml* execrável.
execute [ˈeksɪkju:t] *vt* executar.
execution [ˌeksɪˈkju:ʃn] *n* execução *f*.
executioner [ˌeksɪˈkju:ʃnə[r]] *n* carrasco *m*, -ca *f*.
executive [ɪg'zekjʊtɪv] ◇ *adj* executivo(va). ◇ *n* **-1.** COMM executivo *m*, -va *f* **-2.** [of government] executivo *m* **-3.** [of political party] executiva *f*.
executive director *n* diretor *m* executivo, diretora *f* executiva.
executive toy *n brinquedo usado por executivos para ajudar na concentração.*
executor [ɪg'zekjʊtə[r]] *n* [of will] testamenteiro *m*, -ra *f*.
exemplary [ɪg'zemplərɪ] *adj* [perfect] exemplar.
exemplify [ɪg'zemplɪfaɪ] (*pt & pp* **-ied**) *vt* **-1.** [typify] ilustrar **-2.** [give example of] exemplificar.
exempt [ɪg'zempt] ◇ *adj*: **to be ~ (from sthg)** [tax] estar isento(ta) (de algo); [duty, rules] estar livre (de algo); [military service] estar dispensado(-da) (de algo). ◇ *vt*: **to ~ sb/sthg (from sthg)** [tax] isentar alguém/algo (de algo); [duty, rules, military service] dispensar alguém/algo (de algo).
exemption [ɪg'zempʃn] *n* **-1.** [from tax] isenção *f* **-2.** [from military service] dispensa *f*.
exercise [ˈeksəsaɪz] ◇ *n* exercício *m*; **to take ~** fazer exercício; **an ~ in sthg** um exercício de algo. ◇ *vt* **-1.** exercitar; **to ~ sb's mind** exercitar a mente de alguém **-2.** *fml* [use, practise] exercer. ◇ *vi* exercitar-se.
exercise bike *n* bicicleta *f* ergométrica.
exercise book *n* **-1.** [for notes] caderno *m (de anotações)* **-2.** [published book] livro *m* de exercícios.
exert [ɪg'zɜ:t] *vt* exercer; **to ~ o.s.** esforçar-se.
exertion [ɪg'zɜ:ʃn] *n* **-1.** [physical effort] esforço *m* **-2.** *fig* [committed effort] empenho *m* **-3.** *(U)* [of power, influence] exercício *m*.
ex gratia [eks'greɪʃə] *adj UK*: **~ payment** gratificação *f*.
exhale [eks'heɪl] ◇ *vt* exalar. ◇ *vi* exalar.
exhaust [ɪg'zɔ:st] ◇ *n* **-1.** [fumes] descarga *f*, escapamento *m* **-2.** [tube]: **~ (pipe)** (cano *m* de) descarga *f*. ◇ *vt* **-1.** [person, patience, subject] esgotar **-2.** [supply, money] usar.
exhausted [ɪg'zɔ:stɪd] *adj* exausto(ta).
exhausting [ɪg'zɔ:stɪŋ] *adj* exaustivo(va).
exhaustion [ɪg'zɔ:stʃn] *n (U)* exaustão *f*.
exhaustive [ɪg'zɔ:stɪv] *adj* exaustivo(va).
exhibit [ɪg'zɪbɪt] ◇ *n* **-1.** ART objeto *m* exposto **-2.** JUR [piece of evidence] prova *f*, evidência *f*. ◇ *vt* **-1.** *fml* [demonstrate] demonstrar **-2.** ART expor. ◇ *vi* ART expor.
exhibition [ˌeksɪˈbɪʃn] *n* **-1.** ART exposição *f* **-2.** [demonstration] demonstração *f* **-3.** *phr*: **to make an ~ of o.s.** *UK* fazer um escândalo.
exhibitionist [ˌeksɪˈbɪʃnɪst] *n* exibicionista *mf*.
exhibitor [ɪg'zɪbɪtə[r]] *n* expositor *m*, -ra *f*.
exhilarating [ɪg'zɪləreɪtɪŋ] *adj* estimulante.
exhort [ɪg'zɔ:t] *vt fml*: **to ~ sb to do sthg** exortar alguém a fazer algo.
exhume [eks'hju:m] *vt fml* exumar.
exile [ˈeksaɪl] ◇ *n* **-1.** [condition] exílio *m*; **in ~** no exílio **-2.** [person] exilado *m*, -da *f*. ◇ *vt*: **to ~ sb (from/to)** exilar alguém (de/para).
exiled [ˈeksaɪld] *adj* exilado(da).
exist [ɪg'zɪst] *vi* existir.
existence [ɪg'zɪstəns] *n (U)* existência *f*; **to come into ~** entrar em vigor; **to be in ~** existir.
existentialism [ˌegzɪˈstenʃəlɪzm] *n (U)* existencialismo *m*.
existentialist [ˌegzɪˈstenʃəlɪst] ◇ *adj* existencialista. ◇ *n* existencialista *mf*.
existing [ɪg'zɪstɪŋ] *adj* existente, atual.
exit [ˈeksɪt] ◇ *n* saída *f*. ◇ *vi* sair.
exit poll *n UK* POL pesquisa *f* de boca-de-urna.
exit visa *n* visto *m* de saída.

exodus ['eksədəs] *n* êxodo *m*.
ex officio [eksə'fɪʃɪəʊ] *fml* <> *adj* ex officio. <> *adv* em ex officio.
exonerate [ɪg'zɒnəreɪt] *vt*: **to ~ sb (from sthg)** exonerar alguém (de algo).
exorbitant [ɪg'zɔ:bɪtənt] *adj* exorbitante.
exorcism *n* exorcismo *m*.
exorcist ['eksɔ:sɪst] *n* exorcista *mf*.
exorcize, -ise ['eksɔ:saɪz] *vt* exorcizar.
exotic [ɪg'zɒtɪk] *adj* exótico(ca).
expand [ɪk'spænd] <> *vt* **-1.** [gen] expandir **-2.** [department, area] ampliar **-3.** [influence] aumentar. <> *vi* **-1.** [gen] expandir-se **-2.** [influence] aumentar **-3.** PHYS dilatar.
◆ **expand (up)on** *vt fus* entrar em detalhes.
expanse [ɪk'spæns] *n* vastidão *f*.
expansion [ɪk'spænʃn] *n* **-1.** *(U)* [gen] expansão *f* **-2.** [of department, area] ampliação *f* **-3.** [of influence] aumento *m* **-4.** PHYS dilatação *f*.
expansion card *n* COMPUT cartão *m* de expansão.
expansionism *n (U)* expansionismo *m*.
expansionist [ɪk'spænʃənɪst] *adj* expansionista.
expansion slot *n* COMPUT slot *m* de expansão.
expansive [ɪk'spænsɪv] *adj* [relaxed, talkative] expansivo(va).
expatriate [eks'pætrɪət] <> *adj* expatriado(da). <> *n* expatriado *m*, -da *f*.
expect [ɪk'spekt] <> *vt* **-1.** [gen] esperar; **to ~ to do sthg** esperar fazer algo; **to ~ sb to do sthg** esperar que alguém faça algo; **to ~ sthg from sb** esperar algo de alguém **-2.** [suppose]: **to ~ (that)** supor que; **I ~ so** suponho que sim; **what do you ~?** e o que você queria? <> *vi* [be pregnant]: **to be ~ing** estar esperando bebê.
expectancy *n* ▷ **life expectancy**.
expectant [ɪk'spektənt] *adj* [crowd, person] ansioso(-sa).
expectantly [ɪk'spektəntlɪ] *adv* ansiosamente.
expectant mother *n* gestante *f*.
expectation [ˌekspek'teɪʃn] *n* **-1.** [hope] expectativa *f* **-2.** [belief] convicção *f*; **against** OR **contrary to all ~(s)** ao contrário de todas as expectativas.
expectorant [ɪk'spektərənt] *n* expectorante *m*.
expedient [ɪk'spi:djənt] *fml* <> *adj* pertinente, conveniente. <> *n* expediente *m*.
expedite ['ekspɪdaɪt] *vt fml* expedir.
expedition [ˌekspɪ'dɪʃn] *n* **-1.** [organized journey] expedição *f* **-2.** [short trip, outing] passeio *m*.
expeditionary force [ˌekspɪ'dɪʃnərɪ-] *n* força *f* expedicionária.
expel [ɪk'spel] (*pt* & *pp* **-led**, *cont* **-ling**) *vt* **-1.** [from school, country]: **to ~ sb (from)** expulsar alguém (de) **-2.** [from container]: **to ~ sthg (from)** expelir algo (de).
expend [ɪk'spend] *vt*: **to ~ sthg (on sthg)** gastar algo (com/em algo).
expendable [ɪk'spendəbl] *adj* **-1.** [person] dispensável **-2.** [resources] consumível.
expenditure [ɪk'spendɪtʃə^r] *n* **-1.** [of money] gastos *mpl* **-2.** [of energy, resource] gasto *m*.
expense [ɪk'spens] *n* **-1.** [amount spent] despesa *f*, gasto *m* **-2.** *(U)* [cost] custo *m*; **to go to great ~ (to do sthg)** ter uma grande despesa (para fazer algo); **at the ~ of** em detrimento de, a custa de; **at his/her own ~** [financial] do seu próprio bolso; **at sb's ~** *fig* [in order to mock] às custas de alguém.
◆ **expenses** *npl* COMM despesas *fpl*; **on ~s** nas despesas.
expense account *n* relatório *m* de despesas.
expensive [ɪk'spensɪv] *adj* [financially] caro(ra).
experience [ɪk'spɪərɪəns] <> *n* experiência *f*. <> *vt* experimentar.
experienced [ɪk'spɪərɪənst] *adj* [well-practised] experiente; **~ at** OR **in sthg** experiente em algo.
experiment [ɪk'sperɪmənt] <> *n* **-1.** SCIENCE experimento *m*; **to carry out an ~** conduzir um experimento **-2.** [exploratory attempt] tentativa *f*. <> *vi* SCIENCE fazer experiências; **to ~ with sthg** fazer experiências com algo; **to ~ on sb/sthg** fazer experiências em alguém/algo.
experimental [ɪkˌsperɪ'mentl] *adj* SCIENCE experimental.
expert ['ekspɜ:t] <> *adj* especializado(da), perito(ta); **~ at sthg /at doing sthg** perito(ta) em algo/em fazer algo. <> *n* especialista *mf*, perito *m*, -ta *f*.
expertise [ˌekspɜ:'ti:z] *n (U)* excelência *f*, perícia *f*.
expert system *n* COMPUT sistema *m* especialista.
expiate *vt fml* expiar.
expire [ɪk'spaɪə^r] *vi* [run out] vencer.
expiry [ɪk'spaɪərɪ] *n (U)* vencimento *m*.
expiry date *n* data *f* de vencimento.
explain [ɪk'spleɪn] <> *vt* **-1.** [describe, clarify] explicar; **to ~ sthg to sb** explicar algo a alguém **-2.** [account for] justificar. <> *vi* explicar-se; **to ~ to sb (about sthg)** justificar-se (para alguém) sobre algo.
◆ **explain away** *vt sep* justificar.
explanation [ˌeksplə'neɪʃn] *n* **-1.** *(U)* [act of explaining] explicação *f* **-2.** [account]: **~ (for sthg)** justificativa *f* (por algo) **-3.** [description, clarification] explanação *f*.
explanatory [ɪk'splænətrɪ] *adj* explicativo(va).
expletive [ɪk'spli:tɪv] *n fml* imprecação *f*.
explicit [ɪk'splɪsɪt] *adj* [clearly expressed] explícito(ta).
explode [ɪk'spləʊd] <> *vt* **-1.** [set off] explodir **-2.** *fig* [disprove] derrubar. <> *vi* **-1.** [blow up] explodir **-2.** *fig* [with feeling] explodir.
exploit [*n* 'eksplɔɪt, *vb* ɪk'splɔɪt] <> *n* façanha *f*. <> *vt* explorar.
exploitation [ˌeksplɔɪ'teɪʃn] *n (U)* [of workers, resources] exploração *f*.
exploration [ˌeksplə'reɪʃn] *n* [of space, countries] exploração *f*.
exploratory [ɪk'splɒrətrɪ] *adj* exploratório(ria).
explore [ɪk'splɔ:^r] <> *vt* explorar. <> *vi* explorar.
explorer [ɪk'splɔ:rə^r] *n* explorador *m*, -ra *f*.
explosion [ɪk'spləʊʒn] *n* explosão *f*.
explosive [ɪk'spləʊsɪv] <> *adj* **-1.** [gen] explosivo(-va) **-2.** [controversial] controverso(sa). <> *n* explosivo *m*.
explosive device *n* dispositivo *m* explosivo.
exponent [ɪk'spəʊnənt] *n* **-1.** [gen] expoente *mf* **-2.** [supporter] defensor *m*, -ra *f*.
exponential [ˌekspə'nenʃl] *adj fml* [growth] exponencial.

export [n & comp 'ekspɔːt, vb ɪk'spɔːt] ◇ *n (U)* exportação *f.* ◇ *comp* de exportação. ◇ *vt* exportar.
◆ **exports** *npl* [goods] exportações *fpl.*
exportable [ɪk'spɔːtəbl] *adj* exportável.
exportation [ˌekspɔː'teɪʃn] *n (U)* exportação *f.*
exporter [ek'spɔːtə[r]] *n* exportador *m,* -ra *f.*
export licence *n UK COMM* licença *f* de exportação.
expose [ɪk'spəʊz] *vt* **-1.** [gen] expor; **to be ~d to sthg** estar exposto(ta) a algo; **to ~ o.s.** mostrar-se **-2.** [unmask] desmascarar.
exposé [eks'pəʊzeɪ] *n* exposição *f (de fatos reveladores).*
exposed [ɪk'spəʊzd] *adj* [unsheltered] desprotegido(-da).
exposition [ˌekspə'zɪʃn] *n fml* exposição *f.*
exposure [ɪk'spəʊʒə[r]] *n* **-1.** [gen] exposição *f* **-2.** *MED* [hypothermia]: **to die from ~** morrer de frio **-3.** [unmasking - of person] desmascaramento *m;* [- of corruption] descoberta *f* **-4.** [*PHOT* - time] exposição *f;* [- photograph] pose *f.*
exposure meter *n* fotômetro *m.*
expound [ɪk'spaʊnd] *fml* ◇ *vt* expor. ◇ *vi*: **to ~ on sthg** explanar sobre algo.
express [ɪk'spres] ◇ *adj* **-1.** *UK* [urgent letter, parcel] expresso(sa) **-2.** [transport] expresso(sa) **-3.** *fml* [specific] explícito(ta). ◇ *adv* por correio expresso. ◇ *n*: **~ (train)** (trem *m*) expresso *m.* ◇ *vt* **-1.** [show, state] expressar, exprimir; **to ~ o.s.** expressar-se **-2.** *MATH* representar.
expression [ɪk'spreʃn] *n* expressão *f.*
expressionism [ɪk'spreʃənɪzm] *n (U)* expressionismo *m.*
expressionist [ɪk'spreʃənɪst] ◇ *adj* expressionista. ◇ *n* expressionista *mf.*
expressionless [ɪk'spreʃənlɪs] *adj* sem expressão, inexpressivo(va).
expressive [ɪk'spresɪv] *adj* [full of feeling] expressivo(va).
expressively [ɪk'spresɪvlɪ] *adv* expressivamente.
expressly [ɪk'spreslɪ] *adv* [specifically] expressamente.
expressway [ɪk'spresweɪ] *n* via *f* expressa.
expropriate [eks'prəʊprɪeɪt] *vt fml* expropriar.
expropriation [eksˌprəʊprɪ'eɪʃn] *n fml* expropriação *f.*
expulsion [ɪk'spʌlʃn] *n* expulsão *f;* **~ (from)** expulsão (de).
exquisite [ɪk'skwɪzɪt] *adj* **-1.** [beautiful] fino(na) **-2.** [very pleasing] delicado(da).
exquisitely [ɪk'skwɪzɪtlɪ] *adv* [beautifully] finamente.
ex-serviceman *n UK* ex-combatente *m.*
ex-servicewoman *n UK* ex-combatente *f.*
ext., extn. (*abbr of* **extension**) extens.
extant [ek'stænt] *adj* existente.
extemporize, -ise [ɪk'stempəraɪz] *vi fml* improvisar.
extend [ɪk'stend] ◇ *vt* **-1.** [make bigger] ampliar **-2.** [make longer - in space] estender; [- in time] prolongar **-3.** [postpone] prorrogar **-4.** [make more wide-ranging] estender **-5.** *fml* [stretch out] esticar **-6.** [offer - welcome, help] estender; [- credit] conceder. ◇ *vi* **-1.** [stretch, reach] extender-se **-2.** [rule, law]: **to ~ to sb/sthg** extender-se a alguém/algo **-3.** [protrude] extender-se.
extendable [ɪk'stendəbl] *adj* **-1.** [in time] prorrogável **-2.** [in space] expansível.
extended-play [ɪk'stendɪd-] *adj* de grande duração.
extension [ɪk'stenʃn] *n* **-1.** [gen] aumento *m* **-2.** [longer time limit] prorrogação *f* **-3.** [development, growth] expansão *f* **-4.** *TELEC & ELEC* extensão *f* **-5.** *COMPUT*: **filename ~** extensão do arquivo.
extension cable, extension lead *n ELEC* extensão *f.*
extensive [ɪk'stensɪv] *adj* **-1.** [in amount] amplo(pla) **-2.** [in area, range] extenso(sa).
extensively [ɪk'stensɪvlɪ] *adv* **-1.** [in amount] amplamente **-2.** [in range] extensivamente.
extent [ɪk'stent] *n* **-1.** [gen] extensão *f* **-2.** [degree]: **to what ~ ...?** até que ponto ...?; **to the ~ that** [in that, in so far as] na medida em que; [to the point where] até o ponto em que; **to a certain ~** até um certo ponto; **to a large** *OR* **great ~** em grande parte; **to some ~** até certo ponto.
extenuating circumstances [ɪk'stenjʊeɪtɪŋ-] *npl* circunstâncias *fpl* atenuantes.
exterior [ɪk'stɪərɪə[r]] ◇ *adj* externo(na). ◇ *n* exterior *m.*
exterminate [ɪk'stɜːmɪneɪt] *vt* exterminar.
extermination [ɪkˌstɜːmɪ'neɪʃn] *n (U)* exterminação *f.*
external [ɪk'stɜːnl] *adj* **-1.** [outside] externo(na) **-2.** [foreign] exterior(ra).
◆ **externals** *npl* aparências *fpl.*
externally [ɪk'stɜːnəlɪ] *adv* externamente.
extinct [ɪk'stɪŋkt] *adj* extinto(ta).
extinction [ɪk'stɪŋkʃn] *n (U)* [of species] extinção *f.*
extinguish [ɪk'stɪŋgwɪʃ] *vt* **-1.** *fml* [put out] apagar **-2.** *fig* [eliminate] extinguir.
extinguisher [ɪk'stɪŋgwɪʃə[r]] *n*: **(fire) ~** extintor *m* (de incêndio).
extol (*pt & pp* **-led**, *cont* **-ling**), **extoll** *US* [ɪk'stəʊl] *vt* enaltecer.
extort [ɪk'stɔːt] *vt*: **to ~ sthg from sb** extorquir algo de alguém.
extortion [ɪk'stɔːʃn] *n* extorção *f.*
extortionate [ɪk'stɔːʃnət] *adj* extorsivo(va).
extra ['ekstrə] ◇ *adj* [additional] extra; **~ charge** sobrecarga *f.* ◇ *n* **-1.** [addition] acessório *m* **-2.** *CINEMA & THEATRE* extra *mf.* ◇ *adv* extra.
◆ **extras** *npl* [in price] extras *mpl.*
extra- ['ekstrə] *prefix* extra.
extract [*n* 'ekstrækt, *vb* ɪk'strækt] ◇ *n* **-1.** [excerpt] trecho *m* **-2.** *CHEM & CULIN* extrato *m.* ◇ *vt* **-1.** [take out]: **to ~ sthg (from sthg)** extrair algo (de algo) **-2.** [obtain, elicit]: **to ~ sthg (from sb)** arrancar algo (de alguém).
extraction [ɪk'strækʃn] *n* **-1.** [origin, descent] origem *f* **-2.** [removal] extração *f.*
extractor (fan) [ɪk'stræktə[r]-] *n UK* exaustor *m.*
extracurricular [ˌekstrəkə'rɪkjʊlə[r]] *adj* extracurricular.
extradite ['ekstrədaɪt] *vt*: **to ~ sb (from/to)** extraditar alguém (de/para).

extradition [ˌekstrəˈdɪʃn] <> *n* extradição *f*. <> *comp* de extradição.

extramarital [ˌekstrəˈmærɪtl] *adj* extraconjugal.

extramural [ˌekstrəˈmjʊərəl] *adj* UNIV de extensão universitária.

extraneous [ɪkˈstreɪnjəs] *adj* **-1.** [irrelevant] irrelevante **-2.** [outside] externo(na).

extraordinary [ɪkˈstrɔːdnrɪ] *adj* **-1.** [special] extraordinário(ria) **-2.** [strange] exquisito(ta).

extraordinary general meeting *n* assembléia *f* geral extraordinária.

extrapolate [ɪkˈstræpəleɪt] <> *vt* **-1.** MATH: **to ~ sthg from sthg** extrapolar algo a partir de algo **-2.** [deduce]: **to ~ sthg from sthg** inferir algo de algo. <> *vi* **-1.** MATH: **to ~ from sthg** extrapolar a partir de algo **-2.** [deduce]: **to ~ from sthg** inferir de algo.

extrasensory perception [ˌekstrəˈsensərɪ-] *n (U)* percepção *f* extrasensorial.

extraterrestrial [ˌekstrətəˈrestrɪəl] *adj* extraterrestre.

extra time *n UK* SPORT prorrogação *f*.

extravagance [ɪkˈstrævəgəns] *n* **-1.** [luxury] extravagância *f* **-2.** *(U)* [excessive spending] gasto *m* excessivo.

extravagant [ɪkˈstrævəgənt] *adj* **-1.** [excessive] extravagante **-2.** [elaborate] caprichado(da).

extravaganza [ɪkˌstrævəˈgænzə] *n espetáculo público de pompa.*

extreme [ɪkˈstriːm] <> *adj* extremo(ma). <> *n* [furthest limit] extremo *m*; **in the ~** ao extremo; **to ~s** aos extremos.

extremely [ɪkˈstriːmlɪ] *adv* [very] extremamente.

extreme sports *npl* esportes *mpl* radicais.

extremism [ɪkˈstriːmɪzm] *n (U)* extremismo *m*.

extremist [ɪkˈstriːmɪst] <> *adj* extremista. <> *n* extremista *mf*.

extremity [ɪkˈstremətɪ] (*pl* **-ies**) *n* **-1.** *(U)* *fml* [extreme adversity] suma gravidade *f* **-2.** *(U)* [extremeness] extremismo *m* **-3.** *fml* [end] extremidade *f*.
◆ **extremities** *npl* [of body] extremidades *fpl*.

extricate [ˈekstrɪkeɪt] *vt*: **to ~ sthg (from)** soltar algo (de); **to ~ o.s. (from)** livrar-se (de).

extrovert [ˈekstrəvɜːt] <> *adj* extrovertido(da). <> *n* extrovertido *m*, -da *f*.

extruded [ɪkˈstruːdɪd] *adj* TECH prensado(da).

exuberance [ɪgˈzjuːbərəns] *n (U)* exuberância *f*.

exuberant [ɪgˈzjuːbərənt] *adj* exuberante.

exude [ɪgˈzjuːd] <> *vt* **-1.** [ooze, give off] exsudar **-2.** *fig* [be full of] exalar. <> *vi* exsudar.

exult [ɪgˈzʌlt] *vi*: **to ~ (at** OR **in sthg)** alegrar-se (com algo).

exultant [ɪgˈzʌltənt] *adj* exultante.

eye [aɪ] (*cont* **eyeing** OR **eying**) <> *n* **-1.** , [gen & ANAT] olho *m*; **before my (very) ~s** bem debaixo dos meus olhos; **in my ~s** a meu ver; **to cast** OR **run one's ~ over sthg** passar os olhos em algo; **to catch sb's ~** chamar a atenção de alguém; **to clap** OR **lay** OR **set ~s on sb** pôr os olhos em alguém; **to cry one's ~s out** *inf* chorar muito; **to feast one's ~s on sthg** alimentar os olhos com algo; **to have an ~ for sthg** ter bons olhos para algo; **to have one's ~ on sb/sthg** ter os olhos sobre alguém/algo; **to keep one's ~s open (for)**, **to keep an ~ out (for)** ficar de olhos abertos (em); **to keep an ~ on sb/sthg** dar uma olhada em alguém/algo; **there is more to this than meets the ~** a coisa é mais complicada do que parece; **to open sb's ~s (to sthg)** abrir os olhos de alguém (em relação a algo); **not to see ~ to ~ with sb** não ver as coisas com os mesmos olhos de alguém; **to close** OR **shut one's ~s to sthg** fechar os olhos para algo; **to turn a blind ~ (to sthg)** fazer vista grossa (para algo); **to be up to one's ~s in sthg** *UK inf* estar até aqui de algo **-2.** [of needle] buraco *m*. <> *vt* olhar.
◆ **eye up** *vt sep UK* encarar, comer com os olhos.

eyeball [ˈaɪbɔːl] <> *n* globo *m* ocular. <> *vt US inf* encarar.

eyebath [ˈaɪbɑːθ] *n* copinho *m* para lavar os olhos.

eyebrow [ˈaɪbraʊ] *n* sobrancelha *f*; **to raise one's ~s (at sthg)** *fig* ficar surpreendido(da) (com algo).

eyebrow pencil *n* lápis *m inv* de sobrancelha.

eye-catching *adj* chamativo(va).

eye contact *n (U)*: **to make/avoid ~ (with sb)** fazer/evitar contato direto (com alguém).

eyedrops [ˈaɪdrɒps] *npl* colírio *m*.

eyeglasses [ˈaɪglɑsɪz] *npl US* óculos *m inv*.

eyelash [ˈaɪlæʃ] *n* cílio *m*.

eyelet [ˈaɪlɪt] *n* ilhó *m*.

eye-level *adj* à altura dos olhos.

eyelid [ˈaɪlɪd] *n* pálpebra *f*; **not to bat an ~** *inf* não dar a mínima.

eyeliner [ˈaɪˌlaɪnəʳ] *n* delineador *m (para os olhos)*.

eye-opener *n inf* revelação *f*.

eyepatch [ˈaɪpætʃ] *n* tapa-olho *m*.

eye shadow *n* sombra *f (para os olhos)*.

eyesight [ˈaɪsaɪt] *n* visão *f*.

eyesore [ˈaɪsɔːʳ] *n* horror *m*, monstruosidade *f*.

eyestrain [ˈaɪstreɪn] *n* vista *f* cansada.

eyetooth [ˈaɪtuːθ] (*pl* **-teeth**) *n*: **to give one's eyeteeth for sthg/to do sthg** dar tudo por algo/para fazer algo.

eyewash [ˈaɪwɒʃ] *n (U) inf* [nonsense] disparates *mpl*.

eyewitness [ˌaɪˈwɪtnɪs] *n* testemunha *mf* ocular.

eyrie [ˈɪərɪ] *n* ninho *m* de águia.

e-zine [ˈiːziːn] *n* revista *f* eletrônica.

F

f (*pl* **f's** OR **fs**), **F** (*pl* **F's** OR **Fs**) [ef] *n* [letter] f, F *m*.
◆ **F** *n* **-1.** MUS fá *m* **-2.** (*abbr of* **Fahrenheit**) F.

FA (*abbr of* **Football Association**) *n confederação de* *futebol da Inglaterra e do País de Gales,* ≃ CBF *f.*

FAA (*abbr of* **Federal Aviation Administration**) *n* *órgão federal norte-americano de aviação civil.*

fable ['feɪbl] *n* [traditional story] fábula *f.*

fabled ['feɪbld] *adj* lendário(ria).

fabric ['fæbrɪk] *n* **-1.** [cloth] tecido *m* **-2.** *fig* [of building, society] estrutura *f.*

fabricate ['fæbrɪkeɪt] *vt* **-1.** [invent] inventar **-2.** [manufacture] fabricar.

fabrication [ˌfæbrɪ'keɪʃn] *n* **-1.** [lie, lying] invenção *f* **-2.** *(U)* [manufacture] fabricação *f.*

fabulous ['fæbjʊləs] *adj* fabuloso(sa).

fabulously ['fæbjʊləslɪ] *adv* fabulosamente.

facade [fə'sɑːd] *n* fachada *f.*

face [feɪs] ◇ *n* **-1.** [of person] rosto *m*, cara *f*; **~ to ~** cara a cara; **to fall flat on one's ~** cair de cara no chão; **to look sb in the ~** olhar alguém na cara; **to say sthg to sb's ~** dizer algo na cara de alguém; **to show one's ~** mostrar a cara; **it was staring me in the ~** saltava aos meus olhos **-2.** [expression] expressão *f*; **to make** *OR* **pull a ~** fazer careta **-3.** [of building] fachada *f* **-4.** [of coin] lado *m* **-5.** [of clock, watch] mostrador *m* **-6.** [appearance, nature] cara *f* **-7.** [surface] face *f*; **on the ~ of it** à primeira vista **-8.** [respect]: **to lose ~** perder a reputação; **to save ~** livrar a cara **-9.** *phr*: **to fly in the ~ of sthg** ir de encontro a algo. ◇ *vt* **-1.** [gen] encarar **-2.** [look on to, point towards] dar para **-3.** [confront] enfrentar.

◆ **face down** *adv* [person] de bruços; [object] para baixo.

◆ **face up** *adv* [person] de costas; [object] para cima.

◆ **in the face of** *prep* [confronted with] diante de.

◆ **face up to** *vt fus* enfrentar.

facecloth ['feɪsklɒθ] *n UK* toalhinha *f* de rosto.

face cream *n (U)* creme *m* para o rosto.

faceless ['feɪslɪs] *adj* sem rosto, anônimo(ma).

facelift *n* **-1.** [on face] lifting *m* **-2.** *fig*: **to give sthg a ~** dar uma cara nova para algo.

face pack *n* máscara *f* facial.

face powder *n (U)* pó-de-arroz *m.*

face-saving [-'seɪvɪŋ] *adj* para salvar as aparências.

facet ['fæsɪt] *n* faceta *f.*

facetious [fə'siːʃəs] *adj* brincalhão(lhona).

facetiously *adv* de forma brincalhona.

face-to-face *adj* cara a cara.

face value *n* [of coin, stamp] valor *m* nominal; **to take sthg at ~** *fig* levar algo ao pé da letra.

facial ['feɪʃl] ◇ *adj* facial. ◇ *n* limpeza *f* de pele.

facile [*UK* 'fæsaɪl, *US* 'fæsl] *adj pej* [trivial] trivial.

facilitate [fə'sɪlɪteɪt] *vt fml* facilitar.

facility [fə'sɪlətɪ] (*pl* **-ies**) *n* **-1.** [ability]: **to have a ~ for sthg** ter facilidade para algo **-2.** [feature] recurso *m.*

◆ **facilities** *npl* **-1.** [amenities] instalações *fpl* **-2.** [services] serviços *mpl.*

facing ['feɪsɪŋ] *adj* [opposite] oposto(ta).

facsimile [fæk'sɪmɪlɪ] *n* fac-símile *m*; **a ~ edition** uma edição fac-similar.

facsimile machine *n fml* aparelho *m* de fax.

fact [fækt] *n* fato *m*; **the ~ is, ...** o fato é que ...; **the ~ remains that ...** a verdade que fica é que ...; **to know sthg for a ~** ter certeza de algo.

◆ **in fact** ◇ *conj* na verdade. ◇ *adv* na verdade.

fact-finding [-'faɪndɪŋ] *adj* de investigação.

faction ['fækʃn] *n* facção *f.*

factional ['fækʃənl] *adj* [dispute] faccional.

fact of life *n* fato *m* consumado.

◆ **facts of life** *npl euphemism*: **to tell sb (about) the ~s of life** contar a alguém como nascem as crianças.

factor ['fæktəʳ] *n* fator *m.*

factory ['fæktərɪ] (*pl* **-ies**) *n* fábrica *f.*

factory farming *n (U)* criação *f* intensiva.

factory ship *n* navio-fábrica *m.*

factotum [fæk'təʊtəm] (*pl* **-s**) *n* factótum *m.*

fact sheet *n UK* informativo *m.*

factual ['fæktʃʊəl] *adj* real, concreto(ta).

faculty ['fækltɪ] (*pl* **-ies**) *n* **-1.** [gen] faculdade *f* **-2.** *US* [in college]: **the ~** o corpo docente.

fad [fæd] *n* mania *f*, capricho *m.*

faddy ['fædɪ] (*compar* **-ier**, *superl* **-iest**) *adj inf pej* chato(ta).

fade [feɪd] ◇ *vt* [remove colour] desbotar. ◇ *vi* **-1.** [colour] desbotar **-2.** [sound] diminuir **-3.** [hope, memory, feeling] esvaecer **-4.** [smile, flower] murchar.

◆ **fade away, fade out** *vi* esvaecer.

faded ['feɪdɪd] *adj* desbotado(da).

faeces *UK*, **feces** *US* ['fiːsiːz] *npl* fezes *fpl.*

Faeroe, Faroe ['feərəʊ] *n*: **the ~ Islands**, **the ~s** as Ilhas Feroé; **in the ~ Islands** nas Ilhas Feroé.

faff [fæf] ◆ **faff about, faff around** *vi UK inf* enrolar.

fag [fæg] *n* **-1.** *UK inf* [cigarette] cigarro *m* **-2.** *UK inf* [chore] tarefa *f* chata **-3.** *US inf pej* [homosexual] bicha *f.*

fag end *n UK inf* bagana *f.*

fagged out [fægd-] *adj UK inf* acabado(da), moído(da).

faggot, fagot *US* ['fægət] *n* **-1.** *UK* *CULIN* almôndega *f* **-2.** *US inf pej* [homosexual] bicha *f.*

Fahrenheit ['færənhaɪt] *adj* Fahrenheit *inv.*

fail [feɪl] ◇ *vt* **-1.** [not succeed in]: **to ~ to do sthg** não conseguir fazer algo **-2.** [*SCH & UNIV* - exam, test] não passar em; [- candidate] rodar **-3.** [neglect]: **to ~ to do sthg** deixar de fazer algo **-4.** [let down] falhar. ◇ *vi* **-1.** [not succeed] não conseguir **-2.** *SCH & UNIV* rodar **-3.** [stop functioning] falhar **-4.** [weaken] enfraquecer.

failed [feɪld] *adj* [singer, writer etc] fracassado(da).

failing ['feɪlɪŋ] ◇ *n* [weakness] fraqueza *f.* ◇ *prep* na falta de; **or, ~ that, ...** ou, caso contrário, ...

fail-safe *adj* [device, system] protegido(da) contra falhas.

failure ['feɪljəʳ] *n* **-1.** fracasso *m* **-2.** [to attend, appear, act]: **I was surprised by her ~ to attend the meeting** fiquei surpreso pelo fato de ela não ter comparecido à reunião **-3.** [breakdown, malfunction] falha *f* **-4.** *MED*: **heart ~** falência *f* do coração.

faint [feɪnt] <> *adj* **-1.** [slight] vago(ga) **-2.** [half-hearted] desmaiado(da) **-3.** [dizzy] fraco(ca). <> *vi* desmaiar.
faint-hearted [-'hɑ:tɪd] *adj* covarde.
faintly ['feɪntlɪ] *adv* **-1.** [gen] tenuamente **-2.** [slightly] levemente.
faintness ['feɪntnɪs] *n (U)* **-1.** [dizziness] fraqueza *f* **-2.** [dimness - of image] imprecisão *f*; [- of sound, hope, memory] debilidade *f*.
fair [feəʳ] <> *adj* **-1.** [just] justo(ta); **it's not ~!** não é justo!; **to be ~, ...** para ser franco(ca), ... **-2.** [quite large] considerável **-3.** [quite good] bom (boa) **-4.** [hair, person] loiro(ra) **-5.** [skin, complexion] claro(ra) **-6.** [weather] claro(ra), bom (boa). <> *n* **-1.** *UK* [funfair] parque *m* de diversões **-2.** [trade fair] feira *f*. <> *adv* [fairly] limpo.
◆ **fair enough** *excl UK inf* tudo bem.
fair copy *n* cópia *f* passada a limpo.
fair game *n (U)* alvo *m* fácil; ~ **for sb/sthg** alvo fácil para alguém/algo.
fairground ['feəgraʊnd] *n* parque *m* de exposições.
fair-haired [-'heəd] *adj* [person] loiro(ra).
fairly ['feəlɪ] *adv* **-1.** [rather] bastante **-2.** [justly] justamente.
fair-minded [-'maɪndɪd] *adj* justo(ta).
fairness ['feənɪs] *n (U)* [justness] imparcialidade *f*, justiça *f*; **in ~ to sb** para ser justo(ta) com alguém.
fair play *n (U)* jogo *m* limpo.
fairway ['feəweɪ] *n* [on golf course] *parte lisa do campo de golfe entre os buracos*.
fairy ['feərɪ] (*pl* **-ies**) *n* [imaginary creature] fada *f*.
fairy lights *npl UK* lâmpadas *fpl* decorativas.
fairy tale *n* conto *m* de fadas.
fait accompli [ˌfeɪtə'kɒmplɪ] (*pl* **faits accomplis** [ˌfeɪtə'kɒmplɪ]) *n* fato *m* consumado.
faith [feɪθ] *n* **-1.** *(U)* [trust] fé *f*; ~ **in sb/sthg** fé em alguém/algo; **in good/bad ~** de boa/má fé **-2.** [religion] crença *f*, fé *f*.
faithful ['feɪθfʊl] <> *adj* fiel. <> *npl* RELIG: **the ~** os fiéis.
faithfully ['feɪθfʊlɪ] *adv* [loyally] fielmente; **Yours ~** *UK* [in letter] atenciosamente, cordialmente.
faithfulness ['feɪθfʊlnɪs] *n (U)* fidelidade *f*.
faith healer *n* curandeiro *m*, -ra *f*.
faithless ['feɪθlɪs] *adj* [disloyal] infiel.
fake [feɪk] <> *adj* falso(sa). <> *n* **-1.** [object, painting] falsificação *f* **-2.** [person] falsário *m*, -ria *f*. <> *vt* **-1.** [falsify] falsificar **-2.** [simulate] fingir. <> *vi* [pretend] fingir.
falcon ['fɔ:lkən] *n* falcão *m*.
Falkland Islands ['fɔ:klənd-], **Falklands** ['fɔ:kləndz] *npl*: **the ~** as (Ilhas) Malvinas; **in the ~** nas (Ilhas) Malvinas.
fall [fɔ:l] (*pt* **fell**, *pp* **fallen**) <> *vi* **-1.** [gen] cair; **to ~ flat** [joke] não surtir efeito **-2.** [become] ficar; **to ~ in love** apaixonar-se; **to ~ open** cair aberto(ta) **-3.** [be classified]: **to ~ into/under** pertencer a **-4.** [disintegrate]: **to ~ to bits** OR **pieces** cair aos pedaços **-5.** [city, country]: **to ~ (to sb)** cair (nas mãos de alguém) **-6.** [occur]: **to ~ on** cair em **-7.** *UK* POL [constituency]: **to ~ to sb** passar ao controle de alguém **-8.** [light, shadow] bater. <> *n* **-1.** [accident] tombo *m*, caída *f* **-2.** [of snow] nevasca *f* **-3.** [from power] queda *f* **-4.** [decrease] queda *f*; ~ **in sthg** queda de algo **-5.** *US* [autumn] outono *m*.
◆ **falls** *npl* [waterfall] cataratas *fpl*.
◆ **fall about** *vi UK inf*: **to ~ about (laughing)** cair na risada.
◆ **fall apart** *vi* **-1.** [book, chair] cair aos pedaços **-2.** *fig* [country, person] desmoronar.
◆ **fall away** *vi* **-1.** [plaster, paint] descolar **-2.** [land, slope] descer.
◆ **fall back** *vi* **-1.** [retreat, recede] retroceder **-2.** [lag behind] recuar.
◆ **fall back on** *vt fus* [resort to] recorrer a.
◆ **fall behind** *vi* **-1.** [in race] ficar para trás **-2.** [with rent, with work] atrasar-se.
◆ **fall down** *vi* **-1.** [person, picture, building] desabar **-2.** [fail] falhar.
◆ **fall for** *vt fus* **-1.** *inf* [fall in love with] ficar caído(da) por **-2.** [be deceived by] deixar-se enganar por.
◆ **fall in** *vi* **-1.** [roof, ceiling] desabar **-2.** MIL entrar em forma.
◆ **fall in with** *vt fus* [go along with] concordar com.
◆ **fall off** *vi* **-1.** [drop off] desprender-se **-2.** [diminish] diminuir.
◆ **fall on** *vt fus* **-1.** [subj: eyes, gaze] dirigir-se para **-2.** [attack] atacar, lançar-se sobre.
◆ **fall out** *vi* **-1.** [drop out] cair **-2.** [quarrel]: **to ~ out (with sb)** brigar (com alguém) **-3.** MIL sair de forma.
◆ **fall over** <> *vt fus* tropeçar em; **to be ~ing over o.s. to do sthg** *inf* desbobrar-se para fazer algo. <> *vi* [lose balance] cair.
◆ **fall through** *vi* [plan, deal] fracassar.
◆ **fall to** *vt fus* [devolve upon] recair; **it ~s to me to make a speech** toca para mim fazer o discurso.
fallacious [fə'leɪʃəs] *adj fml* falacioso(sa).
fallacy ['fæləsɪ] (*pl* **-ies**) *n* [misconception] falácia *f*.
fallen ['fɔ:ln] *pp* ▻ **fall**.
fall guy *n US inf* [scapegoat] bode *m* expiatório.
fallible ['fæləbl] *adj* falível.
falling ['fɔ:lɪŋ] *adj* [decreasing] em declínio.
fallopian tube [fə'ləʊpɪən-] *n* trompa *f* de Falópio.
fallout ['fɔ:laʊt] *n (U)* [radiation] chuva *f* radioativa.
fallout shelter *n* abrigo *m* antinuclear.
fallow ['fæləʊ] *adj* [land] alqueivado(da); **to lie ~** ficar sem cultivo.
false [fɔ:ls] *adj* **-1.** [gen] falso(sa) **-2.** [artificial] postiço(ça).
false alarm *n* alarme *m* falso.
falsehood ['fɔ:lshʊd] *n fml* **-1.** [lie] mentira *f* **-2.** *(U)* [lack of truth] falsidade *f*.
falsely ['fɔ:lslɪ] *adv* **-1.** [wrongly] erroneamente **-2.** [insincerely] falsamente.
false start *n* tentativa *f* frustrada.
false teeth *npl* dentadura *f* postiça.
falsetto [fɔ:l'setəʊ] (*pl* **-s**) <> *n* MUS falsete *m*. <> *adv* [sing] em falsete.
falsify ['fɔ:lsɪfaɪ] (*pt* & *pp* **-ied**) *vt* [facts, accounts] falsificar.

falter ['fɔ:ltəʳ] *vi* **-1.** [gen] vacilar **-2.** [hesitate, lose confidence] hesitar.
faltering ['fɔ:ltərɪŋ] *adj* [steps, voice] vacilante.
fame [feɪm] *n (U)* fama *f.*
familiar [fə'mɪljəʳ] *adj* **-1.** [known] familiar; ~ **to sb** familiar para alguém **-2.** [conversant]: ~ **with sthg** familiarizado(da) com algo; **to be on** ~ **terms with sb** ter relações amigáveis com alguém **-3.** *pej* [overly informal - person] que se dá muitas liberdades; [- tone, manner] amigável em excesso.
familiarity [fə,mɪlɪ'ærətɪ] *n* **-1.** [with book, rules, subject]: ~ **with sthg** conhecimento *m* de algo **-2.** [of place, face] familiaridade *f* **-3.** *pej* [excessive informality] liberdades *fpl.*
familiarize, -ise [fə'mɪljəraɪz] *vt*: **to** ~ **o.s. with sthg** familiarizar-se com algo; **to** ~ **sb with sthg** familiarizar alguém com algo.
family ['fæmlɪ] (*pl* **-ies**) <> *n* família *f.* <> *comp* **-1.** [belonging to family] familiar; ~ **car** carro da família **-2.** [suitable for all ages] para toda a família.
family business *n* negócio *m* familiar.
family credit *n (U) UK* auxílio-família *m.*
family doctor *n* médico *m*, -ca *f* de família.
family life *n (U)* vida *f* familiar.
family planning *n (U)* planejamento *m* familiar.
family tree *n* árvore *f* genealógica.
famine ['fæmɪn] *n* fome *f* extrema e coletiva.
famished ['fæmɪʃt] *adj inf* [very hungry] faminto(ta), morto(ta) de fome.
famous ['feɪməs] *adj* famoso(sa); ~ **for sthg** famoso(sa) por algo.
famously ['feɪməslɪ] *adv dated*: **to get on** *OR* **along** ~ **with sb** ficar íntimo(ma) de alguém.
fan [fæn] (*pt* & *pp* **-ned**, *cont* **-ning**) <> *n* **-1.** [of paper, silk] leque *m* **-2.** [electric or mechanical] ventilador *m* **-3.** [enthusiast] fã *mf*, admirador *m*, -ra *f.* <> *vt* **-1.** [cool] abanar; **to** ~ **o.s.** abanar-se **-2.** [stimulate] atiçar.
◆ **fan out** *vi* [army, search party] espalhar-se.
fanatic [fə'nætɪk] *n* fanático *m*, -ca *f.*
fanatical [fə'nætɪkl] *adj* fanático(ca).
fanaticism [fə'nætɪsɪzm] *n (U)* fanatismo *m.*
fan belt *n* correia *f* do ventilador.
fanciful ['fænsɪfʊl] *adj* **-1.** [odd] estapafúrdio(dia) **-2.** [elaborate] extravagante.
fan club *n* fã-clube *m.*
fancy ['fænsɪ] (*compar* **-ier**, *superl* **-iest**, *pl* **-ies**, *pt* & *pp* **-ied**) <> *adj* **-1.** [elaborate] caprichado(da) **-2.** [expensive] extravagante. <> *n* **-1.** [liking] gosto *m*; **to take a** ~ **to sb/sthg** ter simpatia por alguém/algo; **to take sb's** ~ cair nas graças de alguém **-2.** [whim] capricho *m* **-3.** [fantasy] fantasia *f.* <> *vt* **-1.** *inf* [want] querer; **I** ~ **going to the cinema** me agrada a idéia de ir ao cinema **-2.** [like] agradar-se de; **to** ~ **o.s.** estar cheio (cheia) de si **-3.** [imagine] imaginar; ~ **meeting you here!** imagina só, te encontrar por aqui!; **to** ~ **o.s. as sthg** imaginar-se como alguém; ~ **that!** imagina só!, quem diria!
fancy dress *n (U)* fantasia *f.*
fancy-dress party *n* festa *f* à fantasia.
fancy goods *npl* artigos *mpl* de luxo.
fanfare ['fænfeəʳ] *n MUS* fanfarra *f.*
fang [fæŋ] *n* **-1.** [of snake] presa *f* **-2.** [of carnivore] colmilho *m.*
fan heater *n* aquecedor *m* de ventoinha.
fanlight ['fænlaɪt] *n UK* clarabóia *f.*
fan mail *n (U)* cartas *fpl* de fãs.
fanny ['fænɪ] *n US inf* [backside] bunda *f.*
fanny pack *n US* pochete *f.*
fantasize, -ise ['fæntəsaɪz] *vi* fantasiar; **to** ~ **about sthg/about doing sthg** fantasiar sobre algo/sobre fazer algo.
fantastic [fæn'tæstɪk] *adj* **-1.** *inf* [gen] fantástico(ca) **-2.** [bizarre, strange] exótico(ca).
fantastically [fæn'tæstɪklɪ] *adv* **-1.** [extremely] extremamente **-2.** [bizarrely, strangely] exoticamente.
fantasy ['fæntəsɪ] (*pl* **-ies**) <> *n* fantasia *f.* <> *comp* de sonhos, imaginário(ria).
fanzine ['fænzi:n] *n* fanzine *m.*
fao (*abbr of* **for the attention of**) a/c.
FAO (*abbr of* **Food and Agriculture Organization**) *n* FAO *f.*
FAQ (*abbr of* **frequently asked questions**) *n* perguntas *fpl* mais freqüentes, FAQ *f.*
far [fɑ:ʳ] (*compar* **farther** *OR* **further**, *superl* **farthest** *OR* **furthest**) <> *adv* **-1.** [in distance] longe; **how** ~ **is it?** a que distância fica?; **how** ~ **have you come?** até onde você veio?; **is it** ~**?** é longe?; ~ **away** *OR* **off** muito longe; ~ **and wide** por todo o lugar; **as** ~ **as** até; **we walked as** ~ **as the river** caminhamos até o rio **-2.** [in time]: ~ **away** *OR* **off** muito longe; **as** ~ **back as 1900** já em 1900; **so** ~ até agora **-3.** [in degree or extent] muito; **how** ~ **have you got with your novel?** até onde você já foi no romance?; **he's not** ~ **wrong** *OR* **out** *OR* **off** ele não está tão errado; **as** ~ **as I know** até onde eu sei; **as** ~ **as I'm concerned** no que me diz respeito; **as** ~ **as possible** até onde é possível; ~ **and away**, **by** ~ de longe; ~ **from it** pelo contrário; **so** ~ até este ponto; **so** ~ **so good** até agora tudo bem; **to go so** ~ **as to do sthg** chegar ao ponto de fazer algo; **to go too** ~ ir longe demais. <> *adj* **-1.** [distant, extreme] extremo(ma) **-2.** [remote] distante, remoto(ta).
faraway ['fɑ:rəweɪ] *adj* **-1.** [distant] distante **-2.** [dreamy] ausente.
farce [fɑ:s] *n* farsa *f.*
farcical ['fɑ:sɪkl] *adj* ridículo(la).
fare [feəʳ] <> *n* **-1.** [payment, rate] tarifa *f* **-2.** [price of ticket] preço *m* **-3.** [person] passageiro *m*, -ra *f* **-4.** *fml* [food] comida *f.* <> *vi* [manage]: **to** ~ **well/badly** passar bem/mal.
Far East *n*: **the** ~ o Extremo Oriente.
fare stage *n UK parada na qual aumenta o preço da passagem.*
farewell [,feə'wel] <> *n* despedida *f*, adeus *m.* <> *excl literary* adeus!
farfetched [,fɑ:'fetʃt] *adj* forçado(da).
far-flung *adj* **-1.** [remote] longínquo(qua) **-2.** [extensive] vasto(ta).
farm [fɑ:m] <> *n* fazenda *f.* <> *vt* cultivar. <> *vi* cultivar a terra.
◆ **farm out** *vt sep* mandar fazer.
farmer ['fɑ:məʳ] *n* fazendeiro *m*, -ra *f.*
farmhand ['fɑ:mhænd] *n* peão *m*, -oa *f.*

farmhouse ['fɑ:mhaʊs, *pl* -haʊzɪz] *n* granja *f*, quinta *f*.
farming ['fɑ:mɪŋ] *n (U)* **-1.** [activity] agricultura *f* **-2.** [of animals] criação *f* **-3.** [of crops] cultivo *m*.
farmland ['fɑ:mlænd] *n (U)* terra *f* cultivada.
farmstead ['fɑ:msted] *n US* granja *f*.
farmyard ['fɑ:mjɑ:d] *n* terreiro *m (de fazenda)*.
Faroe *n* = **Faeroe**.
far-off *adj* distante.
far-reaching [-'ri:tʃɪŋ] *adj* **-1.** [implications] de longo alcance **-2.** [changes] abrangente.
farrier ['færɪə^r] *n* ferrador *m*, -ra *f*.
far-sighted *adj* **-1.** [person] prudente; [plan] perspicaz **-2.** *US* [longsighted] hipermetrope.
fart [fɑ:t] vulg ◇ *n* **-1.** [wind] peido *m* **-2.** [person] pé-no-saco *m*. ◇ *vi* peidar.
farther ['fɑ:ðə^r] *compar* ▷ **far**.
farthest ['fɑ:ðəst] *superl* ▷ **far**.
fascia ['feɪʃə] *n* **-1.** [on shop] fachada *m* **-2.** *AUT* painel *m* **-3.** [for mobile phone] frente *f*.
fascinate ['fæsɪneɪt] *vt* fascinar.
fascinating ['fæsɪneɪtɪŋ] *adj* fascinante.
fascination [ˌfæsɪ'neɪʃn] *n (U)* fascinação *f*.
fascism ['fæʃɪzm] *n (U)* fascismo *m*.
fascist ['fæʃɪst] ◇ *adj* fascista. ◇ *n* fascista *mf*.
fashion ['fæʃn] ◇ *n* **-1.** [current style] moda *f*; ~ **model** modelo *mf* (de passarela); **in/out of** ~ [vogue] na/fora de moda **-2.** [manner] maneira *f*; **after a** ~ até certo ponto. ◇ *vt fml* [shape] moldar.
fashionable ['fæʃnəbl] *adj* [in vogue] da moda.
fashion-conscious *adj* atento(ta) às tendências da moda.
fashion designer *n* estilista *mf*.
fashion show *n* desfile *m* de modas.
fast [fɑ:st] ◇ *adj* **-1.** [rapid] rápido(da); **she's in the ~ track** ela está indo pelo caminho mais rápido; **to pull a ~ one on sb** *inf* passar a perna em alguém **-2.** [clock, watch] adiantado(da) **-3.** [dye] permanente. ◇ *adv* **-1.** [rapidly] depressa; **how ~ does this car go?** a que velocidade este carro chega?; **I need help ~** preciso de ajuda rápido **-2.** [firmly] firmemente; **to hold ~ to sthg** [grip firmly] segurar firme algo; *fig* [stick to] manter-se firme em algo; **to be ~ asleep** dormir profundamente. ◇ *n* jejum *m*. ◇ *vi* jejuar.
fast breeder reactor *n* reator *m* super-regenerador.
fasten ['fɑ:sn] ◇ *vt* **-1.** [close - jacket, bag] fechar; [- seat belt] apertar **-2.** [attach]: **to ~ sthg to sthg** fixar algo em algo **-3.** [grasp] prender. ◇ *vi*: **to ~ on to sb/sthg** agarrar-se a alguém/algo.
fastener ['fɑ:snə^r] *n* **-1.** [dress, bag] fecho *m* **-2.** [necklace] presilha *f* **-3.** [door] fechadura *f*.
fastening ['fɑ:snɪŋ] *n* **-1.** [gen] fechadura *f* **-2.** [on window] trinco *m*.
fast food *n (U)* fast-food *m*.
fast-forward ◇ *n* avanço *m* rápido. ◇ *vt* avançar rapidamente. ◇ *vi* avançar rapidamente.
fastidious [fə'stɪdɪəs] *adj* [fussy] meticuloso(sa).
fast lane *n* **-1.** [on motorway] pista *f* de alta velocidade **-2.** *fig* [exciting lifestyle]: **life in the ~** vida *f* excitante.

fat [fæt] (*compar* **-ter**, *superl* **-test**) ◇ *adj* **-1.** [person, animal, face, legs, meat] gordo(da); **to get ~** engordar **-2.** [volume, file, wallet] pesado(da) **-3.** [*FIN* - profit, fee] avultado(da); [- cheque, bank account] gordo(da) **-4.** *iro* [small]: **that was a ~ lot of good** *OR* **use** não foi nada bom o que você fez!; **~ chance!** nem pensar! ◇ *n* **-1.** *(U) ANAT* gordura *f* **-2.** *(U)* [in food - raw] banha *f*; [- cooked] sebo *m*; [- in cooking, diet] gordura *f*.
fatal ['feɪtl] *adj* **-1.** [ruinous] fatal **-2.** [mortal] mortal.
fatalism ['feɪtəlɪzm] *n (U)* fatalismo *m*.
fatalistic [ˌfeɪtə'lɪstɪk] *adj* fatalista.
fatality [fə'tælətɪ] (*pl* **-ies**) *n* [accident victim] fatalidade *f*; [fatalism] fatalismo *m*.
fatally ['feɪtəlɪ] *adv* **-1.** [ruinously] fatalmente **-2.** [mortally] mortalmente.
fate [feɪt] *n* **-1.** *(U)* [destiny] destino *m*; **to tempt ~** brincar com a sorte **-2.** [of person, thing] sina *f*.
fated ['feɪtɪd] *adj* **-1.** [destined] predestinado(da); **to be ~ to do sthg** estar fadado(da) a fazer algo **-2.** [doomed] condenado(da).
fateful ['feɪtfʊl] *adj* [decisive] fatídico(ca).
fathead *n inf* estúpido *m*, -da *f*.
father ['fɑ:ðə^r] ◇ *n lit, fig* pai *m*. ◇ *vt* ser o pai de.
◆ **Father** *n* **-1.** [priest] padre *m* **-2.** [God]: **our Father** nosso Pai.
Father Christmas *n UK* Papai *m* Noel.
fatherhood ['fɑ:ðəhʊd] *n (U)* paternidade *f*.
father-in-law (*pl* **father-in-laws** *OR* **fathers-in-law**) *n* sogro *m*.
fatherly ['fɑ:ðəlɪ] *adj* paternal.
Father's Day *n* Dia *f* dos Pais.
fathom ['fæðəm] ◇ *n* braça *f*. ◇ *vt*: **to ~ sthg (out)** desvendar algo; **to ~ sb (out)** compreender alguém.
fatigue [fə'ti:g] ◇ *n (U)* fadiga *f*. ◇ *vt* [weary] fatigar.
◆ **fatigues** *npl* farda *f* de serviço.
fatless *adj* sem gordura.
fatness ['fætnɪs] *n (U)* [of person] gordura *f*.
fatten ['fætn] *vt* engordar.
◆ **fatten up** *vt sep* engordar.
fattening ['fætnɪŋ] *adj* que engorda; **to be very ~** engordar muito.
fatty ['fætɪ] (*compar* **-ier**, *superl* **-iest**, *pl* **-ies**) ◇ *adj* **-1.** [food] gorduroso(sa) **-2.** *BIOL* [tissue] adiposo(sa). ◇ *n inf pej* gorducho *m*, -cha *f*.
fatuous ['fætjʊəs] *adj* fátuo(tua).
fatuously *adv* tolamente.
fatwa ['fætwə] *n* mandado *m* religioso islâmico.
faucet ['fɔ:sɪt] *n US* torneira *f*.
fault [fɔ:lt] ◇ *n* **-1.** [responsibility] culpa *f* **-2.** [defect] defeito *m* **-3.** [mistake, imperfection] falha *f*; **to find ~ with sb/sthg** criticar algo/alguém; **to be at ~** equivocar-se; **through no ~ of my own I missed the train** perdi o trem, mas não foi culpa minha **-4.** *GEOL* falha *f* **-5.** [in tennis] falta *f*. ◇ *vt*: **to ~ sb (on sthg)** criticar alguém (em algo).
faultless ['fɔ:ltlɪs] *adj* impecável.
faulty ['fɔ:ltɪ] (*compar* **-ier**, *superl* **-iest**) *adj* **-1.** [machine, system] defeituoso(sa) **-2.** [reasoning, logic] falho(lha).

fauna ['fɔːnə] *n* fauna *f*.

faux pas [ˌfəʊ'pɑː] (*pl inv*) *n* gafe *f*.

favour *UK*, **favor** *US* ['feɪvə^{r}] ◇ *n* **-1.** *(U)* [approval] aprovação *f*; **in sb's ~** em favor de alguém; **to be in ~ (with sb)** contar com o apoio (de alguém); **to be out of ~ (with sb)** não contar com o apoio (de alguém); **to curry ~ with sb** puxar o saco de alguém **-2.** [kind act] favor *m*; **to do sb a ~** fazer um favor a alguém **-3.** *(U)* [favouritism] favoritismo *m* **-4.** [advantage]: **to rule in sb's ~** decidir a favor de alguém. ◇ *vt* **-1.** [gen] favorecer **-2.** *iro* [honour]: **to ~ sb with sthg** honrar alguém com algo.
◆ **in favour** *adv* [in agreement] a favor.
◆ **in favour of** *prep* **-1.** [in preference to] em favor de **-2.** [in agreement with]: **to be in ~ of sthg/of doing sthg** estar a favor de algo/de fazer algo.

favourable *UK*, **favorable** *US* ['feɪvrəbl] *adj* favorável.

favourably *UK*, **favorably** *US* ['feɪvrəblɪ] *adv* [well] favoralmente.

favoured *UK*, **favored** *US* ['feɪvəd] *adj* [with special advantages] favorecido(da).

favourite *UK*, **favorite** *US* ['feɪvrɪt] ◇ *adj* [preferred] favorito(ta). ◇ *n* favorito(ta).

favouritism *UK*, **favoritism** *US* ['feɪvrɪtɪzm] *n (U)* favoritismo *m*.

fawn [fɔːn] ◇ *adj* castanho(nha) claro(ra). ◇ *n* [animal] cervato *m*. ◇ *vi*: **to ~ on sb** bajular alguém.

fax [fæks] ◇ *n* fax *m*. ◇ *vt* **-1.** [send fax to] enviar um fax para **-2.** [send by fax] enviar por fax.

fax machine *n* (máquina *f* de) fax *m*.

fax number *n* número *m* de fax.

faze [feɪz] *vt inf* grilar.

FBI (*abbr of* **Federal Bureau of Investigation**) *n* FBI *m*.

FC (*abbr of* **Football Club**) *n* FC.

FCC (*abbr of* **Federal Communications Commission**) *n* *comissão federal norte-americana de comunicação audiovisual*.

FCO (*abbr of* **Foreign and Commonwealth Office**) *n* *ministério britânico de relações exteriores e com o Commonwealth*, ≃ MRE *m*.

FDA *n* (*abbr of* **Food and Drug Administration**) *órgão norte-americano que controla os medicamentos e produtos alimentícios*.

FE (*abbr of* **Further Education**) *n* *estudos de educação continuada após o término do ensino superior na Grã-Bretanha*.

fear [fɪə^{r}] ◇ *n* **-1.** [gen] medo *m* **-2.** [risk] risco *m*, perigo *m*; **for ~ of** por medo de. ◇ *vt* **-1.** [be afraid of] ter medo de, temer **-2.** [anticipate] temer, recear; **to ~ (that)** recear que. ◇ *vi* [be afraid]: **to ~ for sb/sthg** temer por alguém/algo.

fearful ['fɪəfʊl] *adj* **-1.** *fml* [frightened] temeroso(sa); **~ of sthg/of doing sthg** temeroso(sa) de algo/de fazer algo **-2.** [frightening] terrível, pavoroso(sa).

fearless ['fɪəlɪs] *adj* sem medo, destemido(da).

fearlessly ['fɪəlɪslɪ] *adv* destemidamente, sem medo.

fearsome ['fɪəsəm] *adj* terrível.

feasibility [ˌfiːzə'bɪlətɪ] *n (U)* [of plan] viabilidade *f*.

feasibility study *n* estudo *m* de viabilidade.

feasible ['fiːzəbl] *adj* [plan] viável.

feast [fiːst] ◇ *n* [meal] banquete *m*. ◇ *vi*: **to ~ on** *OR* **off sthg** banquetear-se com algo.

feat [fiːt] *n* façanha *f*.

feather ['feðə^{r}] *n* pena *f*; **a ~ in one's cap** motivo de muito orgulho.

feather bed *n* cama *f* de penas.

feather-brained *adj* disparatado(da); **a ~ person** um cabeça-de-vento.

featherweight ['feðəweɪt] *n* [boxer] peso-pena *m*.

feature ['fiːtʃə^{r}] ◇ *n* **-1.** [characteristic - of house] característica *f*; [- of machine] recurso *m*; [- of style, landscape] aspecto *m*; [- of face, personality] traço *m* **-2.** [article] reportagem *f* especial **-3.** *RADIO & TV* [programme] especial *m* **-4.** *CINEMA* longa-metragem *m*. ◇ *vt* [subj: film, exhibition] ter como atração principal; **a film featuring Juliette Binoche** um filme estrelando Juliette Binoche. ◇ *vi*: **to ~ (in sthg)** [appear, figure] figurar (em algo).

feature film *n* longa-metragem *m*.

featureless ['fiːtʃəlɪs] *adj* sem traços característicos.

Feb. [feb] (*abbr of* **February**) fev.

February ['februərɪ] *n* fevereiro *m*; *see also* **September**.

feces *npl US* = **faeces**.

feckless ['feklɪs] *adj* displicente.

fed [fed] *pt & pp* ▷ **feed**.

Fed [fed] ◇ *n* **-1.** *fam* (*abbr of* **Federal agent/official**) *oficial ou agente oficial norte-americano, especialmente do FBI*. **-2.** *fam* (*abbr of* **Federal Reserve Board**) *órgão de controle do banco central norte-americano*. ◇ **-1.** (*abbr of* **federal**) fed. **-2.** (*abbr of* **federation**) Fed.

federal ['fedrəl] *adj* federal.

Federal Bureau of Investigation *n* *polícia federal americana*, FBI *m*.

federalism ['fedrəlɪzm] *n (U)* federalismo *m*.

federation [ˌfedə'reɪʃn] *n* **-1.** [country] federação *f* **-2.** [association] liga *f*.

fed up *adj* farto(ta), cheio(a); **to be ~ with sb/sthg** estar cheio de alguém/algo.

fee [fiː] *n* [payment - school] (taxa *f* de) matrícula *f*; [- doctor] preço *m* da consulta; [- lawyer] honorários *mpl*; [- monthly membership] mensalidade *f*; [- annual membership] anuidade *f*; [- entrance] taxa *f* de admissão.

feeble ['fiːbəl] *adj* **-1.** [weak] fraco(ca) **-2.** [lacking conviction] débil.

feeble-minded *adj* [stupid] imbecil, de idéias curtas.

feebleness ['fiːblnɪs] *n (U)* **-1.** [weakness] fraqueza *f* **-2.** [lack of conviction] debilidade *f*.

feebly ['fiːblɪ] *adv* **-1.** [weakly] fracamente **-2.** [without conviction] sem convicção.

feed [fiːd] (*pt & pp* **fed**) ◇ *vt* **-1.** [give food to] alimentar **-2.** *fig* [fuel] alimentar **-3.** [put, insert]: **to ~ sthg into sthg** inserir algo em algo. ◇ *vi* **-1.** [take food] alimentar-se; **to ~ on** *OR* **off sthg** alimentar-se de algo **-2.** *fig* [be fuelled]: **to ~ on** *OR* **off sthg** crescer com algo. ◇ *n* **-1.** [meal] comida *f* **-2.** *(U)* [animal food] ração *f*.

feedback ['fiːdbæk] *n (U)* **-1.** [reaction] reação *f* **-2.** *ELEC* feedback *m*.

feedbag ['fi:dbæg] *n US* embornal *m*.
feeder road *n* via *f* de alimentação.
feeding bottle ['fi:dɪŋ-] *n UK* mamadeira *f*.
feel [fi:l] (*pt* & *pp* **felt**) ◇ *vt* **-1.** [touch] tocar **-2.** [believe, think] achar, acreditar; **to ~ (that)** achar que **-3.** [experience, be aware of] sentir; **to ~ o.s. doing sthg** sentir-se fazendo algo **-4.** *phr*: **I'm not ~ing myself today** não estou me sentindo bem hoje. ◇ *vi* **-1.** [have sensation, emotion] sentir-se; **to ~ like sthg/like doing sthg** [be in mood for] ter vontade de algo/de fazer algo **-2.** [seem] parecer **-3.** [by touch]: **to ~ for sthg** procurar algo com as mãos. ◇ *n* **-1.** [sensation, touch] sensação *f* **-2.** [atmosphere] clima *m* **-3.** *phr*: **to get/have a ~ for sthg** acostumar-se a algo.
feeler ['fi:lə^r] *n* **-1.** [of insect, snail] antena *f* **-2.** [of octopus] tentáculo *m*.
feeling ['fi:lɪŋ] *n* **-1.** [emotion] sensação *f*; **bad ~** mau pressentimento **-2.** [physical - of nausea, vertigo etc] sensação *f*; [- sensation] sensibilidade *f* **-3.** [awareness, impression] impressão *f* **-4.** [understanding] disposição *f*; **to have a ~ for sthg** levar jeito para algo.
◆ **feelings** *npl* sentimentos *mpl*; **to hurt sb's ~s** magoar alguém, magoar os sentimentos de alguém; **no hard ~s!** sem ressentimentos!
fee-paying [-'peɪɪŋ] *adj UK* pago(ga).
feet [fi:t] *pl* ▷ **foot**.
feign [feɪn] *vt fml* fingir.
feint [feɪnt] ◇ *n* finta *f*. ◇ *vi* fintar.
feisty ['faɪstɪ] (*compar* **-ier**, *superl* **-iest**) *adj esp US inf* determinado(da).
felicitous [fɪ'lɪsɪtəs] *adj fml* [fortunate] oportuno(na).
feline ['fi:laɪn] ◇ *adj* felino(na). ◇ *n fml* felino *m*, -na *f*.
fell [fel] ◇ *pt* ▷ **fall**. ◇ *vt* **-1.** [tree] cortar **-2.** [person] derrubar.
◆ **fells** *npl* GEOGR charneca *f*.
fellow ['feləʊ] ◇ *adj* companheiro *m*, -ra *f*. ◇ *n* **-1.** *dated* [man] cara *mf* **-2.** [comrade, peer] camarada *mf* **-3.** [of society or college] membro *m* honorário.
fellowship ['feləʊʃɪp] *n* **-1.** *(U)* [comradeship] companheirismo *m* **-2.** [organization] sociedade *f* **-3.** [in university - grant] bolsa *f* de pesquisa; [- post] pesquisador *m*, -ra *f*.
felony ['felənɪ] (*pl* **-ies**) *n* JUR delito *m* grave.
felt [felt] ◇ *pt* & *pp* ▷ **feel**. ◇ *n (U)* [textile] feltro *m*.
felt-tip pen *n* pincel *m* atômico.
female ['fi:meɪl] ◇ *adj* **-1.** [gen] feminino(na) **-2.** [plant] fêmeo(mea). ◇ *n* **-1.** [female animal] fêmea *f* **-2.** *inf pej* [woman] fêmea *f*.
feminine ['femɪnɪn] ◇ *adj* feminino(na). ◇ *n* GRAMM feminino *m*.
femininity [femɪ'nɪnətɪ] *n (U)* feminilidade *f*.
feminism ['femɪnɪzm] *n (U)* feminismo *m*.
feminist ['femɪnɪst] *n* feminista.
fence [fens] ◇ *n* [barrier] cerca *f*; **to sit on the ~** *fig* ficar em cima do muro. ◇ *vt* cercar.
◆ **fence in** *vt sep* **-1.** [garden] cercar **-2.** *fig* [person] prender; **she feels completely ~d in** ela se sente totalmente presa.
◆ **fence off** *vt sep* isolar.
fencing ['fensɪŋ] *n (U)* **-1.** SPORT esgrima *f* **-2.** [fences] cerca *f* **-3.** [material] material *m* para fazer cerca.
fend [fend] *vi*: **to ~ for o.s.** saber se virar.
◆ **fend off** *vt sep* rechaçar.
fender ['fendə^r] *n* **-1.** [round fireplace] guarda-fogo *m* **-2.** [on boat] proteção *f* **-3.** *US* [on car] pára-lama *f*.
fennel ['fenl] *n (U)* erva-doce *f*.
fens [fenz] *npl UK* pântano *m*.
feral ['fɪərəl] *adj* selvagem.
ferment [*n* 'fɜ:ment, *vb* fə'ment] ◇ *n (U)* [unrest] grande agitação *f*, polvorosa *f*; **in ~** em polvorosa. ◇ *vi* [change chemically] fermentar.
fermentation [ˌfɜ:mən'teɪʃn] *n (U)* fermentação *f*.
fermented [fə'mentɪd] *adj* fermentado(da).
fern [fɜ:n] *n* samambaia *f*.
ferocious [fə'rəʊʃəs] *adj* feroz.
ferociously [fə'rəʊʃəslɪ] *adv* ferozmente.
ferocity [fə'rɒsətɪ] *n (U)* ferocidade *f*.
ferret ['ferɪt] *n* [animal] furão *m*.
◆ **ferret about, ferret around** *vi inf* vasculhar.
◆ **ferret out** *vt sep inf* desenterrar.
ferris wheel ['ferɪs-] *n esp US* roda-gigante *f*.
ferry ['ferɪ] (*pl* **-ies**, *pt* & *pp* **-ied**) ◇ *n* balsa *f*. ◇ *vt* transportar.
ferryboat ['ferɪbəʊt] *n* = **ferry**.
ferryman ['ferɪmən] (*pl* **-men** [-mən]) *n* balseiro *m*.
fertile ['fɜ:taɪl] *adj* fértil.
fertility [fɜ:'tɪlətɪ] *n (U)* fertilidade *f*.
fertility drug *n* remédio *f* para infertilidade.
fertilization [ˌfɜ:tɪlaɪ'zeɪʃn] *n (U)* **-1.** [enrichment] fertilização *f* **-2.** [insemination] fecundação *f*.
fertilize, -ise ['fɜ:tɪlaɪz] *vt* **-1.** [enrich] fertilizar **-2.** [inseminate] fecundar.
fertilizer ['fɜ:tɪlaɪzə^r] *n* fertilizante *m*.
fervent ['fɜ:vənt] *adj* **-1.** [admirer, believer] fervoroso(-sa) **-2.** [belief, desire, hope] ardente.
fervour *UK*, **fervor** *US* ['fɜ:və^r] *n (U)* fervor *m*.
fester ['festə^r] *vi* **-1.** [wound] inflamar, inflamar-se **-2.** *fig* [situation, problem, feeling] inflamar.
festival ['festəvl] *n* **-1.** [series of organized events] festival *m* **-2.** [holiday] feriado *m*, dia *m* festivo.
festive ['festɪv] *adj* festivo(va).
festive season *n*: **the ~** a época do Natal.
festivities [fes'tɪvətɪz] *npl* festividades *fpl*.
festoon [fe'stu:n] *vt* enfeitar; **to be ~ed with sthg** estar enfeitado(da) com algo.
fetal ['fi:tl] *adj* = **foetal**.
fetch [fetʃ] *vt* **-1.** [go and get] ir buscar **-2.** [sell for] alcançar.
fetching ['fetʃɪŋ] *adj* atraente.
fete, fête [feɪt] ◇ *n* festa *f* beneficente. ◇ *vt* festejar (em honra de alguém).
fetid ['fetɪd] *adj* fétido(da).
fetish ['fetɪʃ] *n* **-1.** [sexual obsession] fetiche *m* **-2.** [mania] mania *f* **-3.** [object] amuleto *m*.
fetishism ['fetɪʃɪzm] *n (U)* fetichismo *m*.
fetlock ['fetlɒk] *n* machinho *m*.
fetter ['fetə^r] *vt* restringir.
◆ **fetters** *npl fig* [constraints] restrição *f*.
fettle ['fetl] *n (U)*: **in fine ~** [person] em forma.
fetus ['fi:təs] *n* = **foetus**.

feud [fju:d] ◇ *n* contenda *f.* ◇ *vi* brigar.

feudal ['fju:dl] *adj* feudal.

fever ['fi:vəʳ] *n* **-1.** *MED* febre *f* **-2.** *fig* [frenzy] frenesi *m*.

fevered ['fi:vəd] *adj* **-1.** [hot] febril **-2.** [wild, excited] exaltado(da).

feverish ['fi:vərɪʃ] *adj* **-1.** *MED* febril **-2.** [frenzied] frenético(ca).

fever pitch *n (U)* ponto *m* máximo.

few [fju:] ◇ *adj* [not many] pouco(ca); **a ~** alguns(mas); **a ~ more** mais alguns(mas); **quite a ~**, **a good ~** bastante; **~ and far between** pouquíssimos(mas). ◇ *pron* poucos *mpl*, -cas *fpl*; **a ~** poucos(cas); **quite a ~**, **a good ~** bastante.

fewer ['fju:əʳ] ◇ *adj* menos; **no ~ than** não menos do que. ◇ *pron* menos.

fewest ['fju:əst] *adj* o menos possível.

FHA (*abbr of* **Federal Housing Administration**) *n* *órgão norte-americano que controla a habitação social.*

fiancé [fɪ'ɒnseɪ] *n* noivo *m.*

fiancée [fɪ'ɒnseɪ] *n* noiva *f.*

fiasco [fɪ'æskəʊ] (*UK pl* **-s**, *US pl* **-s** *OR* **-es**) *n* fiasco *m.*

fib [fɪb] (*pt* & *pp* **-bed**, *cont* **-bing**) *inf* ◇ *n* lorota *f.* ◇ *vi* contar lorotas.

fibber ['fɪbəʳ] *n inf* mentiroso(sa).

fibre *UK*, **fiber** *US* ['faɪbəʳ] *n* **-1.** *(U)* [material, substance] fibra *f* **-2.** [thread] filamento *m* **-3.** *(U)* [strength] força *f.*

fibreboard *UK*, **fiberboard** *US* ['faɪbəbɔ:d] *n (U)* madeira *f* compensada.

fibreglass *UK*, **fiberglass** *US* ['faɪbəglɑ:s] ◇ *n (U)* fibra *f* de vidro. ◇ *comp* de fibra de vidro.

fibre optics *n (U)* fibra *f* óptica.

fibrositis [ˌfaɪbrə'saɪtɪs] *n (U)* fibrosite *f.*

FICA (*abbr of* **Federal Insurance Contributions Act**) *n* *lei norte-americana que regulamenta o pagamento obrigatório de contribuição social mensal por parte dos trabalhadores.*

fickle ['fɪkl] *adj* inconstante, volúvel.

fiction ['fɪkʃn] *n* **-1.** *(U)* [literature] ficção *f* **-2.** [fabrication, lie] invenção *f.*

fictional ['fɪkʃənl] *adj* **-1.** [literary] ficcional **-2.** [invented] imaginário(ria).

fictionalize, -ise ['fɪkʃənəlaɪz] *vt* romancear.

fictitious [fɪk'tɪʃəs] *adj* [false] fictício(cia).

fiddle ['fɪdl] ◇ *n* **-1.** [violin] rabeca *f*; **(as) fit as a ~** em excelente forma; **to play second ~ (to sb)** estar em segundo plano (para alguém) **-2.** *UK inf* [fraud] embuste *m.* ◇ *vt UK inf* falsificar. ◇ *vi* **-1.** [fidget]: **to ~ (about** *OR* **around)** enrolar; **to ~ (about** *OR* **around) with sthg** mexer em algo **-2.** [waste time]: **to ~ about** *OR* **around** perder tempo.

fiddler ['fɪdləʳ] *n* [violinist] violinista *mf.*

fiddly ['fɪdlɪ] (*compar* **-ier**, *superl* **-iest**) *adj UK inf* trabalhoso(sa).

fidelity [fɪ'delətɪ] *n (U)* **-1.** [loyalty] fidelidade *f* **-2.** [accuracy] veracidade *f.*

fidget ['fɪdʒɪt] *vi* estar irrequieto(ta), mover-se sem parar.

fidgety ['fɪdʒɪtɪ] *adj inf* inquieto(ta).

fiduciary [fɪ'du:ʃjərɪ] (*pl* **-ies**) ◇ *adj* fiduciário (ria). ◇ *n* fiduciário *m*, -ria *f.*

field [fi:ld] ◇ *n* **-1.** [gen] campo *m* **-2.** [of knowledge] área *f* **-3.** [real environment]: **in the ~** no campo de batalha **-4.** : **~ of vision** campo visual. ◇ *vt* [avoid answering] responder. ◇ *vi SPORT* interceptar.

field day *n* [for study, sport] dia *m* de atividades externas; **to have a ~** *fig* fazer a festa.

fielder ['fi:ldəʳ] *n* **-1.** [in baseball] jardineiro *m* **-2.** [in cricket] interceptador *m.*

field event *n* esporte *m* de campo.

field glasses *npl* binóculos *mpl.*

field marshal *n* marechal-de-campo *m.*

field mouse *n* ratazana *f.*

field trip *n* viagem *f* de estudos.

fieldwork ['fi:ldwɜ:k] *n (U)* pesquisa *f* de campo.

fieldworker ['fi:ldwɜ:kəʳ] *n* pesquisador *m*, -ra *f* de campo.

fiend [fi:nd] *n* **-1.** [cruel person] demônio *m* **-2.** *inf* [fanatic] fanático *m*, -ca *f.*

fiendish ['fi:ndɪʃ] *adj* **-1.** [evil] diabólico(ca) **-2.** *inf* [very difficult] cabeludo(da).

fierce [fɪəs] *adj* **-1.** [aggressive, ferocious] feroz **-2.** [wild, uncontrolled] violento(ta) **-3.** [intense - competition, battle] árduo(a); [- heat] intenso(sa); [- criticism] ferrenho(nha).

fiercely ['fɪəslɪ] *adv* **-1.** [aggressively, ferociously] ferozmente **-2.** [wildly] violentamente **-3.** [intensely] arduamente.

fiery ['faɪərɪ] (*compar* **-ier**, *superl* **-iest**) *adj* **-1.** [burning] ardente **-2.** [spicy] picante **-3.** [volatile] explosivo(-va) **-4.** [bright red] cor-de-fogo.

FIFA (*abbr of* **Fédération Internationale de Football Association**) *n* FIFA *f.*

fifteen [fɪf'ti:n] *num* quinze; *see also* **six**.

fifteenth [ˌfɪf'ti:nθ] *num* décimo quinto, décima quinta; *see also* **sixth**.

fifth [fɪfθ] *num* quinto, quinta; *see also* **sixth**.

Fifth Amendment *n*: **the ~** a Quinta Emenda, *emenda constitucional americana que estabelece direitos civis aos criminosos.*

fifth column *n* quinta-coluna *f.*

fiftieth ['fɪftɪəθ] *num* qüinquagésimo, qüinquagésima; *see also* **sixth**.

fifty ['fɪftɪ] (*pl* **-ies**) *num* cinqüenta; *see also* **sixty**.

fifty-fifty ◇ *adj*: **to have a ~ chance** ter cinqüenta por cento de chance. ◇ *adv*: **to split sthg ~** dividir algo meio a meio.

fig [fɪg] *n* figo *m.*

fight [faɪt] (*pt* & *pp* **fought**) ◇ *n* **-1.** [physical] briga *f*, luta *f*; **to have a ~ (with sb)** ter uma briga (com alguém); **to put up a ~** desencadear uma luta **-2.** *fig* [battle, struggle] luta *f*, batalha *f* **-3.** [argument] discussão *f*; **to have a ~ (with sb)** ter uma discussão (com alguém). ◇ *vt* **-1.** [gen] lutar (com), combater; [physically] brigar com **-2.** [combat, struggle against] lutar contra. ◇ *vi* **-1.** [physically, in war] lutar **-2.** *fig* [battle, struggle]: **to ~ for/against sthg** lutar por/contra algo **-3.** [argue] discutir sobre; **to ~ about** *OR* **over sthg** discutir sobre algo.

◆ **fight back** ◇ *vt fus* segurar. ◇ *vi* revidar.

◆ **fight off** *vt sep* **-1.** [deter physically] rechaçar **-2.** *fig* [overcome] superar.

◆ **fight out** *vt sep*: **to ~ it out** resolver a questão.
fighter ['faɪtəʳ] *n* **-1.** [plane] caça *m* **-2.** [soldier] guerreiro *m*, -ra *f* **-3.** [combative person] lutador *m*, -ra *f*.
fighting ['faɪtɪŋ] *n (U)* [in war, punch-up] luta *f*.
fighting chance *n*: **to have a ~** ter uma boa chance.
figment ['fɪgmənt] *n*: **a ~ of sb's imagination** um produto da imaginação de alguém.
figurative ['fɪgərətɪv] *adj* [language, art] figurado(da).
figuratively ['fɪgərətɪvlɪ] *adv* metaforicamente.
figure [*UK* 'fɪgəʳ, *US* 'fɪgjər] ◇ *n* **-1.** [statistic] índice *m*; **to put a ~ on sthg** declarar o valor total de algo **-2.** [symbol of number] número *m*; **in single/double ~s** em valores até dez/acima de dez **-3.** [human shape, outline] silhueta *f* **-4.** [diagram, representative personality] figura *f* **-5.** [famous person] personalidade *f* **-6.** [aesthetic shape of body] forma *f* **-7.** ◇ *vt esp US* [suppose] supor. ◇ *vi* **-1.** [feature] figurar **-2.** *US* [make sense]: **that ~s!** faz sentido!
◆ **figure out** *vt sep* compreender.
figure eight *n US* = **figure of eight**.
figurehead ['fɪgəhed] *n* **-1.** [on ship] carranca *f* de proa **-2.** [leader without real power] testa-de-ferro *m*.
figure of eight *UK*, **figure eight** *US n* forma *f* de oito.
figure of speech *n* figura *f* de linguagem.
figure-skating *n (U)* patinação *f* artística.
figurine [*UK* 'fɪgəri:n, *US* ˌfɪgjə'ri:n] *n* estatueta *f (de metal ou cerâmica)*.
Fiji ['fi:dʒi:] *n* Fiji; **in ~** em Fiji.
Fijian [ˌfi:'dʒi:ən] ◇ *adj* fijiano(na). ◇ *n* fijiano *m*, -na *f*.
filament ['fɪləmənt] *n* [in light bulb] filamento *m*.
filch [fɪltʃ] *vt inf* surrupiar.
file [faɪl] ◇ *n* **-1.** [folder] pasta *f* **-2.** [report] relatório *m*; **on ~, on the ~s** em arquivo, arquivado(da) **-3.** *COMPUT* arquivo *m* **-4.** [tool] lixa *f* **-5.** [line]: **in single ~** em fila indiana. ◇ *vt* **-1.** [put in folder] pôr na pasta **-2.** *JUR* dar entrada em **-3.** [shape, smooth] lixar. ◇ *vi* **-1.** [walk in single file] andar em fila única **-2.** *JUR*: **to ~ for divorce** dar entrada no divórcio.
file clerk *n US* = **filing clerk**.
filename ['faɪlˌneɪm] *n COMPUT* nome *m* de arquivo.
filet *n US* = **fillet**.
filibuster ['fɪlɪbʌstəʳ] *vi esp US POL* fazer discursos obstrucionistas.
filigree ['fɪlɪgri:] ◇ *adj* filigranado(da). ◇ *n (U)* filigrana *f*.
filing cabinet ['faɪlɪŋ-] *n* fichário *m*.
filing clerk *UK* ['faɪlɪŋ-], **file clerk** *US n* arquivista *mf*.
Filipino [ˌfɪlɪ'pi:nəʊ] (*pl* **-s**) ◇ *adj* filipino(na). ◇ *n* filipino *m*, -na *f*.
fill [fɪl] ◇ *vt* **-1.** [make full - container] encher; [- room, street] ocupar; **to ~ sthg (with sthg)** encher algo com algo **-2.** [fulfill] preencher **-3.** [tooth] obturar. ◇ *vi* encher-se. ◇ *n*: **to have had one's ~ of sthg** estar até o pescoço de algo; **to eat one's ~** fartar-se.
◆ **fill in** ◇ *vt sep* **-1.** [form] preencher **-2.** [hole] tapar **-3.** [inform]: **to ~ sb in (on sthg)** informar alguém (sobre algo). ◇ *vt fus*: **to be ~ing in time** fazer tempo. ◇ *vi* [substitute]: **to ~ in (for sb)** substituir alguém.
◆ **fill out** ◇ *vt sep* [complete] completar. ◇ *vi* [get fatter] engordar.
◆ **fill up** ◇ *vt sep* encher. ◇ *vi* lotar.
filled [fɪld] *adj* **-1.** [with sandwich filling] recheado(da) **-2.** [with emotion]: **~ (with sthg)** cheio(a) (de algo).
filler ['fɪləʳ] *n (U)* [for cracks] enchimento *m*.
filler cap *n UK* tampa *f* do tanque de combustível.
fillet *UK*, **filet** *US* ['fɪlɪt] *n* **-1.** [piece of meat] filé *m* **-2.** *(U)* [type of meat] lombo *m*.
fillet steak *n* filé *m*.
fill-in *n inf* [stopgap] tapa-buraco *m*.
filling ['fɪlɪŋ] ◇ *adj* [satisfying] que satisfaz. ◇ *n* **-1.** [in tooth] obturação *f* **-2.** [in cake, sandwich] recheio *m*.
filling station *n* posto *m* de gasolina.
fillip ['fɪlɪp] *n* estímulo *m*.
filly ['fɪlɪ] (*pl* **-ies**) *n* potranca *f*.
film [fɪlm] ◇ *n* **-1.** [cinema, TV, photographic] filme *m* **-2.** *(U)* [footage] cobertura *f* **-3.** [layer] película *f*. ◇ *vt* filmar. ◇ *vi* filmar.
filming ['fɪlmɪŋ] *n (U)* filmagem *f*.
film-maker *n* cineasta *mf*.
film star *n* astro *m* de cinema, estrela *f* de cinema.
filmstrip ['fɪlmˌstrɪp] *n* diafilme *m*.
film studio *n* estúdio *m* de cinema.
Filofax® ['faɪləʊfæks] *n* agenda *f (de folhas descartáveis)*.
filter ['fɪltəʳ] ◇ *n* filtro *m*. ◇ *vt* **-1.** [water, petrol] filtrar **-2.** [coffee] coar. ◇ *vi* [people] infiltrar-se.
◆ **filter out** *vt sep* [remove by filtering] filtrar.
◆ **filter through** *vi* infiltrar-se.
filter coffee *n* café *m* coado.
filter lane *n UK* faixa *f* de conversão *(à direita ou esquerda)*.
filter paper *n* filtro *m* de papel *(para café)*.
filter-tipped [-'tɪpt] *adj* com filtro.
filth [fɪlθ] *n (U)* **-1.** [dirt] sujeira *f* **-2.** [obscenity] obscenidade *f*.
filthy ['fɪlθɪ] (*compar* **-ier**, *superl* **-iest**) *adj* **-1.** [very dirty] imundo(da) **-2.** [obscene] obsceno(na).
filtration plant [fɪl'treɪʃn-] *n* unidade *f* de filtragem.
fin [fɪn] *n* **-1.** [on fish] barbatana *f* **-2.** *US* [for swimmer] nadadeira *f*.
final ['faɪnl] ◇ *adj* **-1.** [last in order] último(ma) **-2.** [at end, definitive] final. ◇ *n* final *f*.
◆ **finals** *npl UNIV* exames *mpl* finais; **to sit one's ~s** prestar os exames finais.
final demand *n* último aviso *m*.
finale [fɪ'nɑ:lɪ] *n* final *m*.
finalist ['faɪnəlɪst] *n* finalista *mf*.
finalize, -ise ['faɪnəlaɪz] *vt* finalizar.
finally ['faɪnəlɪ] *adv* **-1.** [at last] finalmente **-2.** [lastly] finalmente, por fim.
finance [*n* 'faɪnæns, *vb* faɪ'næns] ◇ *n (U)* **-1.** [money] financiamento *m* **-2.** [money management] finanças *fpl*. ◇ *vt* financiar.
◆ **finances** *npl* finanças *fpl*.

financial [fɪ'nænʃl] *adj* financeiro(ra).
financial adviser *n* assessor *m* financeiro, assessora *f* financeira.
financially [fɪ'nænʃəlɪ] *adv* financeiramente.
financial services *npl* serviços *mpl* financeiros.
financial year *UK*, **fiscal year** *US n* ano *m* fiscal.
financier [fɪ'nænsɪəʳ] *n UK* financista *mf*.
finch [fɪntʃ] *n* tentilhão *m*.
find [faɪnd] (*pt* & *pp* **found**) <> *vt* **-1.** [gen] encontrar, achar; **to ~ one's way** achar o caminho **-2.** [realize, discover]: **to ~ (that)** descobrir que **-3.** *JUR*: **to be found guilty/not guilty of sthg** ser declarado(da) culpado(da)/inocente de algo. <> *n* descoberta *f*.
◆ **find out** <> *vi* descobrir. <> *vt fus* **-1.** [information] informar-se **-2.** [truth] desmascarar. <> *vt sep* [person] descobrir.
findings ['faɪndɪŋz] *npl* constatações *fpl*.
fine [faɪn] <> *adj* **-1.** [good, high-quality] excelente **-2.** [perfectly satisfactory] ótimo(ma) **-3.** [healthy] bem **-4.** [not rainy] bom(boa) **-5.** [thin, smooth] fino(na) **-6.** [minute, exact] sutil. <> *adv* [quite well] bem. <> *n* multa *f*. <> *vt* multar.
fine arts *npl* belas-artes *fpl*.
finely ['faɪnlɪ] *adv* **-1.** [thinly, smoothly]: **to cut ~** cortar fino(na) **-2.** [tuned, balanced] com precisão.
fineness ['faɪnnɪs] *n (U)* **-1.** [high quality] excelência *f* **-2.** [thinness, smoothness] finura *f* **-3.** [precision] minúcia *f*.
finery ['faɪnərɪ] *n (U)* refinamento *m*.
finesse [fɪ'nes] *n (U)* finura *f*, delicadeza *f*.
fine-tooth comb ['faɪntu:θ-] *n*: **to go over sthg with a ~** passar o pente fino em algo.
fine-tune ['faɪntju:n] *vt* ajustar.
finger ['fɪŋgəʳ] <> *n* dedo *m*; **to keep one's ~s crossed** manter os dedos cruzados; **she didn't lay a ~ on him** ela não encostou um dedo nele; **he didn't lift a ~ to help** ele não levantou um dedo para ajudar; **to point a** *OR* **the ~ at sb** apontar um *OR* o dedo para alguém; **to put one's ~ on sthg** colocar o dedo na ferida de algo, identificar algo corretamente; **to slip through one's ~s** escorrer pelos dedos; **to twist sb round one's little ~** fazer alguém de gato e sapato. <> *vt* [feel] tocar com os dedos.
fingermark ['fɪŋgəmɑ:k] *n* marca *f* de dedo.
fingernail ['fɪŋgəneɪl] *n* unha *f (dos dedos da mão)*.
fingerprint ['fɪŋgəprɪnt] *n* impressão *f* digital; **to take sb's ~s** tirar as impressões digitais de alguém.
fingertip ['fɪŋgətɪp] *n* ponta *f* do dedo; **at one's ~s** ao alcance da mão.
finicky ['fɪnɪkɪ] *adj pej* [- person] meticuloso(sa); [- task] minucioso(sa).
finish ['fɪnɪʃ] <> *n* **-1.** [end] final *m* **-2.** [texture] acabamento *m*. <> *vt* **-1.** [conclude, complete] terminar; **to ~ doing sthg** terminar de fazer algo **-2.** [consume] acabar **-3.** [leave] terminar, acabar. <> *vi* **-1.** [gen] terminar **-2.** [complete task] terminar, acabar.
◆ **finish off** *vt sep* [conclude, complete, consume] terminar.
◆ **finish up** *vi* acabar, terminar.
◆ **finish with** *vt fus* [break off with] terminar com.
finished ['fɪnɪʃt] *adj* **-1.** [ready, completed] terminado(da), pronto(ta) **-2.** [no longer interested]: **to be ~ with sthg** não estar mais interessado(da) em algo **-3.** [over, no longer in existence] liquidado(da) **-4.** *inf* [done for] acabado(da).
finishing line ['fɪnɪʃɪŋ-] *n* linha *f* de chegada.
finishing school ['fɪnɪʃɪŋ-] *n* ≃ *colégio privado no qual se preparam as alunas da alta classe para entrar na sociedade.*
finite ['faɪnaɪt] *adj* **-1.** [limited] finito(ta) **-2.** *GRAMM* conjugado(da).
Finland ['fɪnlənd] *n* Finlândia; **in ~** na Finlândia.
Finn [fɪn] *n* [inhabitant of Finland] finlandês *m*, -esa *f*.
Finnish ['fɪnɪʃ] <> *adj* [of or relating to Finland] finlandês(esa). <> *n* [language] finlandês *m*.
fiord [fjɔ:d] *n* = **fjord**.
fir [fɜ:ʳ] *n* abeto *m*.
fire ['faɪəʳ] <> *n* **-1.** *(U)* [flames, burning] fogo *m*; **on ~** em chamas; **to catch ~** pegar fogo; **to set ~ to sthg** pôr fogo em algo **-2.** [for warmth, cooking] fogueira *f* **-3.** [blaze, conflagration] incêndio *m* **-4.** *UK* [heater, apparatus] aquecedor *m*, estufa *f* **-5.** *(U)* [shooting] fogo *m*; **to open ~ (on sb)** abrir fogo (contra alguém). <> *vt* **-1.** [shoot] disparar **-2.** [rap out] lançar **-3.** *esp US* [dismiss] demitir, despedir. <> *vi*: **to ~ (on** *OR* **at)** atirar em.
fire alarm *n* alarme *m* contra incêndio.
firearm ['faɪərɑ:m] *n* arma *f* de fogo.
fireball ['faɪəbɔ:l] *n* bola *f* de fogo.
firebomb ['faɪəbɒm] <> *n* bomba *f* incendiária. <> *vt* lançar bombas incendiárias em.
firebreak ['faɪəbreɪk] *n* aceiro *m*.
fire brigade *UK*, **fire department** *US n* corpo *m* de bombeiros.
fire chief *n US* = **fire master**.
firecracker ['faɪə,krækəʳ] *n* rojão *m*.
fire-damaged *adj* deteriorado(da) por incêndio.
fire department *n US* = **fire brigade**.
fire door *n* porta *f* corta-fogo.
fire drill *n* simulação *f* de incêndio.
fire-eater *n* [performer] engolidor *m*, -ra *f* de fogo.
fire engine *n* carro *m* de bombeiros.
fire escape *n* escada *f* de incêndio.
fire extinguisher *n* extintor *m* de incêndio.
fire fighter *n* bombeiro *m*, -ra *f*.
fireguard ['faɪəgɑ:d] *n* guarda-fogo *m*.
fire hazard *n* risco *m* de incêndio.
fire hydrant [-'haɪdrənt], **fireplug** *US* ['faɪəplʌg] *n* hidrante *m*.
firelight ['faɪəlaɪt] *n (U)* luz *f* de fogo.
firelighter ['faɪəlaɪtəʳ] *n* acendedor *m* de fogo.
fireman ['faɪəmən] (*pl* **-men** [-mən]) *n* bombeiro *m*.
fire master *UK*, **fire chief** *US n* chefe *mf* do corpo de bombeiros.
fireplace ['faɪəpleɪs] *n* lareira *f*.
fireplug *n US* = **fire hydrant**.
firepower ['faɪə,paʊəʳ] *n (U)* potência *f* de fogo.
fireproof ['faɪəpru:f] *adj* à prova de fogo.
fire-raiser [-,reɪzəʳ] *n UK* incendiário *m*, -ria *f*.

fire regulations *npl* medidas *fpl* contra incêndio.
fire service *n UK* corpo *m* de bombeiros.
fireside ['faɪəsaɪd] *n*: **by the ~** ao calor da lareira.
fire station *n* posto *m* de bombeiros.
firewood ['faɪəwʊd] *n (U)* lenha *f*.
firework ['faɪəwɜ:k] *n* fogo *m* de artifício.
◆ **fireworks** *npl fig* [outburst of anger] fogos *mpl* de artifício.
firework display *n* espetáculo *m* pirotécnico.
firing ['faɪərɪŋ] *n (U)* MIL tiroteio *m*.
firing squad *n* pelotão *m* de fuzilamento.
firm [fɜ:m] ◇ *adj* **-1.** [gen] firme; **to stand ~** manter-se firme **-2.** [definite] claro(ra) **-3.** [investment, rate] estável. ◇ *n* empresa *f*.
◆ **firm up** ◇ *vt sep* [make clearer, finalize] firmar. ◇ *vi* firmar.
firmly ['fɜ:mlɪ] *adv* firmemente.
firmness ['fɜ:mnɪs] *n (U)* firmeza *f*.
first [fɜ:st] ◇ *adj* primeiro(ra); **for the ~ time** pela primeira vez; **~ thing (in the morning)** à primeira hora (da manhã); **~ things ~** primeiro o mais importante; **I don't know the ~ thing about it** não tenho a mais remota idéia sobre isso. ◇ *adv* **-1.** [before anyone, anything else] primeiro; **~ of all** antes de mais nada, em primeiro lugar **-2.** [for the first time] pela primeira vez **-3.** [firstly, in list of points] primeiramente. ◇ *n* **-1.** [person] primeiro *m*, -ra *f* **-2.** [unprecedented event] acontecimento *m* sem precedentes **-3.** *UK* UNIV diploma *m* universitário **-4.** AUT: **~ (gear)** primeira *f* (marcha).
◆ **at first** *adv* no princípio.
◆ **at first hand** *adv* em primeira mão.
first aid *n (U)* primeiros socorros *mpl*.
first-aider [-'eɪdə^r] *n* socorrista *mf*.
first-aid kit *n* kit *m* de primeiros socorros.
first-class *adj* **-1.** [excellent] de primeira **-2.** *UK* UNIV com louvor **-3.** [letter, ticket] de primeira classe.
first-class mail *n (U) correio m de primeira classe.*
first course *n* entrada *f*.
first cousin *n* primo-irmão *m*, prima-irmã *f*.
first-day cover *n envelope com carimbo comemorativo de lançamento de um selo.*
first-degree *adj* **-1.** MED: **~ burn** queimadura *f* de primeiro grau **-2.** *US* JUR: **~ murder** homicídio *m* em primeiro grau.
first floor *n* **-1.** *UK* [above ground level] primeiro andar *m* **-2.** *US* [at ground level] andar *m* térreo.
firsthand [,fɜ:st'hænd] ◇ *adj* de primeira mão. ◇ *adv* em primeira mão.
first lady *n* POL primeira-dama *f*.
first language *n* língua *f* materna.
first lieutenant *n* primeiro-tenente *m*.
firstly ['fɜ:stlɪ] *adv* primeiramente.
first mate *n* primeiro piloto *m*, imediato *m*.
first name *n* nome *m* de batismo, nome *m*.
◆ **first-name** *adj*: **to be on first-name terms (with sb)** relacionar-se intimamente (com alguém).
first night *n* noite *f* de estréia.
first offender *n* delinqüente *mf* primário, -ria.
first officer *n* = **first mate**.
first-past-the-post system *n UK* sistema *m* de eleição por voto majoritário.
first-rate *adj* de primeira.
first refusal *n* primeira opção *f* de compra.
First World War *n*: **the ~** a Primeira Guerra Mundial.
firtree ['fɜ:tri:] *n* = **fir**.
fiscal ['fɪskl] *adj* fiscal.
fiscal year *n US* = **financial year**.
fish [fɪʃ] (*pl inv*) ◇ *n* peixe *m*. ◇ *vt* pescar em. ◇ *vi* **-1.** [try to catch fish] pescar; **to ~ for sthg** pescar algo **-2.** [try to obtain]: **to ~ for sthg** buscar algo.
◆ **fish out** *vt sep inf* [bring out] sacar.
fish and chips *npl UK* peixe *m* frito com batatas fritas.
fish and chip shop *n UK* barraca *f* de peixe frito com batatas fritas.
fishbowl ['fɪʃbəʊl] *n* aquário *m*.
fishcake ['fɪʃkeɪk] *n* bolinho *m* de peixe.
fisherman ['fɪʃəmən] (*pl* **-men** [-mən]) *n* pescador *m*.
fishery ['fɪʃərɪ] (*pl* **-ies**) *n* pescaria *f*.
fish-eye lens *n* lente *f* objetiva *(na câmera)*.
fish farm *n* viveiro *m* de peixes.
fish fingers *UK*, **fish sticks** *US npl* porções *fpl* de peixe empanado.
fishhook ['fɪʃ,hʊk] *n* anzol *m*.
fishing ['fɪʃɪŋ] *n (U)* pesca *f*; **to go ~** ir pescar.
fishing boat *n* barco *m* de pesca.
fishing line *n* linha *f* de pesca.
fishing rod *n* vara *f* de pescar.
fishmonger ['fɪʃ,mʌŋgə^r] *n esp UK* peixeiro *m*; **~'s (shop)** peixaria *f*.
fishnet ['fɪʃnet] *n* **-1.** [for fishing] rede *f* de pesca **-2.** *(U)* [material]: **~ stockings/tights** malhas *fpl*/meias *fpl* de malha.
fish pond *n* lagoa *f* de peixe.
fish shop *n* peixaria *f*.
fish slice *n UK* escumadeira *f*.
fish sticks *npl US* = **fish fingers**.
fish tank *n* aquário *m (usado como viveiro)*.
fishwife ['fɪʃwaɪf] (*pl* **-wives** [-waɪvz]) *n pej*: **to behave like a ~** comportar-se como uma lavadeira.
fishy ['fɪʃɪ] (*compar* **-ier**, *superl* **-iest**) *adj* **-1.** [like fish] de peixe **-2.** *fig* [suspicious] duvidoso(sa).
fission ['fɪʃn] *n (U)* fissão *f*.
fissure ['fɪʃə^r] *n* fissura *f*.
fist [fɪst] *n* punho *m*.
fit [fɪt] (*pt* & *pp* **-ted**, *cont* **-ting**) ◇ *adj* **-1.** [suitable] adequado(da); **to be ~ for sthg** estar apto(ta) para algo; **to be ~ to do sthg** estar apto(ta) a fazer algo; **to see** OR **think ~ (to do sthg)** julgar OR achar conveniente (fazer algo); **do as you think ~** faça como você achar melhor **-2.** [healthy] em forma; **to keep ~** manter-se em forma. ◇ *n* **-1.** [of clothes, shoes etc.] tamanho *m*; **it's a good ~** fica bem; **it's a tight ~** fica justo **-2.** [epileptic seizure] ataque *m*; **to have a ~** MED ter um ataque; *fig* [be angry] ter um ataque (de fúria) **-3.** [bout - of crying, depression] crise *f*; [- of rage, sneezing, giggles] acesso *m*; **in ~s and starts** aos trancos e barrancos. ◇

vt **-1.** [be correct size for] servir **-2.** [place]: **to ~ sthg into sthg** encaixar algo em algo **-3.** [provide]: **to ~ sthg with sthg** equipar algo com algo; **to have sthg ~ted** instalar algo **-4.** [be suitable for] adequar-se. ◇ *vi* **-1.** [be correct size] servir **-2.** [go] encaixar **-3.** [into container] caber.

◆ **fit in** ◇ *vt sep* [accommodate] arranjar tempo para. ◇ *vi* adaptar-se; **to ~ in with sb/sthg** adaptar-se com alguém/algo; **that ~s in with what she told me** isso vem ao encontro do que ela me contou.

◆ **fit out** *vt sep* equipar.

◆ **fit together** *vt sep* **-1.** [assemble] unir-se **-2.** [make sense] fazer sentido.

fitful ['fɪtfʊl] *adj* intermitente.

fitment ['fɪtmənt] *n* móvel *m (da casa)*.

fitness ['fɪtnɪs] *n (U)* **-1.** [health] bom estado *m* físico **-2.** [suitability] aptidão *f*; **~ for sthg** aptidão para algo.

fitted ['fɪtəd] *adj* **-1.** [suited]: **~ for** *OR* **to sthg** adequado(da) para algo; **to be ~ to do sthg** ser adequado(da) para fazer algo **-2.** [tailored] na medida **-3.** *UK* [built-in] embutido(da).

fitted carpet ['fɪtəd-] *n* carpete *m*.

fitted kitchen ['fɪtəd-] *n UK* cozinha *f* de módulos.

fitted sheet *n* lençol *m* com elástico.

fitter ['fɪtəʳ] *n* [mechanic] mecânico *m*, -ca *f*.

fitting ['fɪtɪŋ] ◇ *adj fml* apropriado(da). ◇ *n* **-1.** [part] acessório *m* **-2.** [for clothing] prova *f*.

◆ **fittings** *npl* acessórios *mpl*.

fitting room *n* provador *m*.

five [faɪv] *num* cinco; *see also* **six**.

five-day week *n* semana *f* de cinco dias.

fiver ['faɪvəʳ] *n inf* **-1.** *UK* [amount] *cinco libras*; [note] *cédula de cinco libras* **-2.** *US* [amount] *cinco dólares*; [note] *cédula de cinco dólares*.

five-star *adj* [of highest standard]: **~ hotel** hotel cinco estrelas; **~ treatment** tratamento de primeira.

fix [fɪks] ◇ *vt* **-1.** [attach, concentrate] fixar; **to ~ sthg to sthg** fixar algo em algo **-2.** [set, arrange] arranjar **-3.** [repair] consertar **-4.** *inf* [rig] manipular **-5.** *esp US* [food, drink] preparar. ◇ *n* **-1.** *inf* [difficult situation]: **to be in a ~** estar em apuro **-2.** *drugs sl* dose *f* de entorpecente.

◆ **fix up** *vt sep* **-1.** [provide]: **to ~ sb up with sthg** arranjar algo para alguém **-2.** [arrange] organizar, preparar.

fixation [fɪk'seɪʃn] *n* fixação *f*; **~ on** *OR* **about sb/sthg**, **~** fixação em *OR* por alguém/algo.

fixed [fɪkst] *adj* fixado(da).

fixed assets *npl* ativo *m* fixo.

fixture ['fɪkstʃəʳ] *n* **-1.** [in building] instalação *f* **-2.** *fig* [permanent feature] figura *f* constante **-3.** [sports event] encontro *m*.

fizz [fɪz] ◇ *vi* **-1.** [drink] espumar **-2.** [firework] crepitar. ◇ *n* **-1.** [sound] chiado *m* **-2.** *(U)* [of drinks] efervescência *f*.

fizzle ['fɪzl] ◆ **fizzle out** *vi* **-1.** [firework] falhar **-2.** *fig* [interest] sumir.

fizzy ['fɪzɪ] (*compar* **-ier**, *superl* **-iest**) *adj* gasoso(sa).

fjord [fjɔ:d] *n* fiorde *m*.

FL *abbr of* **Florida**.

flab [flæb] *n (U)* flacidez *f (do corpo)*.

flabbergasted ['flæbəgɑ:stɪd] *adj* estarrecido(da), pasmado(da).

flabby ['flæbɪ] (*compar* **-ier**, *superl* **-iest**) *adj* flácido(-da), gordo(da).

flaccid ['flæsɪd] *adj* flácido(da).

flag [flæg] (*pt* & *pp* **-ged**, *cont* **-ging**) ◇ *n* [banner] bandeira *f*. ◇ *vi* **-1.** [person] desanimar **-2.** [spirts] decair **-3.** [conversation] acabar.

◆ **flag down** *vt sep* fazer sinal para.

Flag Day *n 14 de junho, dia da bandeira nos Estados Unidos.*

flag of convenience *n* bandeira *f* de conveniência.

flagon ['flægən] *n* **-1.** [bottle] garrafão *m* **-2.** [jug] jarro *m*.

flagpole ['flægpəʊl] *n* mastro *m* de bandeira.

flagrant ['fleɪgrənt] *adj* flagrante.

flagship ['flægʃɪp] *n* **-1.** [ship] nau *f* capitânia **-2.** [main asset] carro-chefe *m*.

flagstone ['flægstəʊn] *n* laje *f*.

flail [fleɪl] ◇ *vt* agitar. ◇ *vi* agitar-se.

flair [fleəʳ] *n* **-1.** [talent] dom *m*; **to have a ~ for sthg** ter um dom para algo **-2.** *(U)* [stylishness] habilidade *f*.

flak [flæk] *n (U)* **-1.** [gunfire] fogo *m* antiaéreo **-2.** *inf* [criticism] críticas *fpl*.

flake [fleɪk] ◇ *n* [small piece - of snow] floco *m*; [- of paint, plaster] lasca *f*; [- of skin] pedaço *m*. ◇ *vi* descascar.

◆ **flake out** *vi inf* desfalecer.

flaky ['fleɪkɪ] (*compar* **-ier**, *superl* **-iest**) *adj* **-1.** [flaking - skin] com escamas; [- paintwork] lascado(da); [- texture] folhado(da) **-2.** *US inf* [person, idea] extravagante.

flaky pastry *n (U)* massa *f* folhada, mil-folhas *m inv*.

flambé ['flɑ:mbeɪ] (*pt* & *pp* **-ed**, *cont* **-ing**) ◇ *adj* flambado(da). ◇ *vt* flambar.

flamboyant [flæm'bɔɪənt] *adj* **-1.** [person, behaviour] extravagante **-2.** [clothes, design] chamativo(va).

flame [fleɪm] ◇ *n* chama *f*; **in ~s** em chamas; **to burst into ~s** irromper em chamas. ◇ *vi* **-1.** [be on fire] estar queimando **-2.** [redden] inflamar-se.

flameproof ['fleɪmpru:f] *adj* à prova de fogo.

flame-retardant [-rɪ'tɑ:dənt] *adj* resistente ao fogo.

flame-thrower [-'θrəʊəʳ] *n* lança-chamas *m inv*.

flaming ['fleɪmɪŋ] *adj* **-1.** [fire-coloured] em cor de fogo **-2.** *UK* [very angry] acalorado(da) **-3.** *UK inf* [for emphasis] maldito(ta).

flamingo [flə'mɪŋgəʊ] (*pl* **-s** *OR* **-es**) *n* flamingo *m*.

flammable ['flæməbl] *adj* inflamável.

flan [flæn] *n* torta *f*.

Flanders ['flɑ:ndəz] *n* Flanders; **in ~** em Flanders.

flange [flændʒ] *n* rebordo *m*.

flank [flæŋk] ◇ *n* **-1.** [of animal] lado *m* **-2.** [of army] flanco *m*. ◇ *vt*: **to be ~ed by sb/sthg** ser ladeado(da) por alguém/algo.

flannel ['flænl] *n* **-1.** *(U)* [fabric] flanela *f* **-2.** *UK* [face-cloth] luva *f* de banho.

◆ **flannels** *npl* calças *fpl* de flanela.
flannelette [flænə'let] *n (U)* baetilha *f.*
flap [flæp] (*pt* & *pp* **-ped**, *cont* **-ping**) ◇ *n* **-1.** [piece] dobra *f* **-2.** *inf* [state of panic]: **to get in a ~** ficar estérico(ca). ◇ *vt* **-1.** [wings] bater **-2.** [arms] agitar, mexer. ◇ *vi* **-1.** [wave - skirt, jacket] ondear, agitar-se; [- wings, bird] bater **-2.** *inf* [panic] estar estérico(ca).
flapjack ['flæpdʒæk] *n* **-1.** *UK* [biscuit] biscoito *m* de aveia **-2.** *US* [pancake] panqueca *f.*
flare [fleə^r] ◇ *n* [distress signal] sinal *m* luminoso. ◇ *vi* **-1.**: **to ~ (up)** [fire] chamejar; [person] enfurecer-se; [war, revolution, disease] deflagrar-se **-2.** [trousers, skirt] alargar-se **-3.** [nostrils] abrir-se.
◆ **flares** *npl UK* [trousers] calças *fpl* boca-de-sino.
flared [fleəd] *adj* [trousers, skirt] boca-de-sino.
flash [flæʃ] ◇ *adj* **-1.** *PHOT* com flash **-2.** *inf* [expensive-looking] ostentoso(sa). ◇ *n* **-1.** [of light, colour] brilho *m* **-2.** *PHOT* flash *m* **-3.** [sudden moment] instante *m*; **in a ~** num instante; **quick as a ~** rápido(da) como um raio. ◇ *vt* **-1.** [light, torch] brilhar *(numa direção específica)* **-2.** [look, smile]: **she flashed a smile at him** ela sorriu rapidamente para ele **-3.** [show on screen] projetar **-4.** [show briefly] mostrar rapidamente. ◇ *vi* **-1.** [gen] reluzir **-2.** [move fast] irromper; **it ~ed through his mind that ...** imediatamente lhe ocorreu que ...; **to ~ past** passar feito um raio.
flashback ['flæʃbæk] *n* flashback *m.*
flashbulb ['flæʃbʌlb] *n* (lâmpada *f* de) flash *m.*
flash card *n cartão no qual se aparecem uma palavra ou um desejo e que se utiliza como material didático.*
flashcube ['flæʃkju:b] *n* flash *m* de cubo.
flasher ['flæʃə^r] *n UK* **-1.** [light] pisca-pisca *m* **-2.** *inf* [man] exibicionista *m.*
flash flood *n* enchente *f.*
flashgun ['flæʃgʌn] *n* disparador *m* de flash.
flashlight ['flæʃlaɪt] *n* [torch] lanterna *f* (elétrica).
flashpoint *n* **-1.** [moment] ponto *m* de fulgor **-2.** [place] zona *f* de conflito.
flashy ['flæʃɪ] (*compar* **-ier**, *superl* **-iest**) *adj inf* ostentoso(sa).
flask [flɑ:sk] *n* **-1.** [to keep drinks hot] garrafa *f* térmica **-2.** [used in chemistry] frasco *m* **-3.** [hip flask] cantil *m.*
flat [flæt] (*compar* **-ter**, *superl* **-test**) ◇ *adj* **-1.** [level] plano(na); **~ feet** pés *mpl* chatos **-2.** [shoes] sem salto **-3.** [punctured] vazio(zia) **-4.** [categorical] categórico(ca) **-5.** [business, trade] estagnado(da) **-6.** [monotonous - voice] monótono(na); [- performance, writing] uniforme **-7.** [*MUS* - lower than correct note] abaixo do tom; [- lower than stated note] abemolado(da) **-8.** *COMM* [fare, fee] único(ca) **-9.** [no longer fizzy - beer] choco(ca); [- lemonade] que passou do ponto **-10.** [battery] descarregado(da). ◇ *adv* **-1.** [level] horizontalmente **-2.** [absolutely]: **~ broke** completamente quebrado(da) **-3.** [categorically] terminantemente **-4.** [exactly] precisamente **-5.** *MUS* abaixo do tom. ◇ *n* **-1.** *UK* [apartment] flat *m* **-2.** *MUS* bemol *m.*
◆ **flat out** *adv* a todo vapor.
flat cap *n UK* gorro *m.*
flat-chested [-'tʃestɪd] *adj* de seios pequenos.
flatfish ['flætfɪʃ] (*pl inv*) *n* linguado *m.*
flat-footed [-'fʊtɪd] *adj* [with flat feet] de pés chatos.
flatlet *n UK* flat *m.*
flatly ['flætlɪ] *adv* **-1.** [absolutely] categoricamente **-2.** [dully] de forma monótona.
flatmate ['flætmeɪt] *n UK* colega *mf* que divide o apartamento com outro.
flat-packed *adj* [furniture] para montar.
flat racing *n (U)* corrida *f* de cavalos sem obstáculos.
flat rate *n* preço *m* único.
flatscreen television, flatscreen TV ['flæt,skri:n] *n* tv *f* de tela plana.
flatten ['flætn] *vt* **-1.** [make flat - steel, bumps] aplanar; [- wrinkles] esticar; [- paper] alisar; **to ~ o.s. against sthg** prensar-se contra algo **-2.** [building] demolir **-3.** *inf* [opponent] esmagar.
◆ **flatten out** ◇ *vi* aplanar-se, nivelar-se. ◇ *vt sep* [wrinkles] esticar; [lumps, bumps] aplanar.
flatter ['flætə^r] *vt* **-1.** [compliment] adular, bajular; **I'm ~ed** sinto-me lisonjeado(da); **to ~ o.s. (that)** congratular-se de que **-2.** [suit] cair bem.
flatterer ['flætərə^r] *n* bajulador *m*, -ra *f.*
flattering ['flætərɪŋ] *adj* [remark, offer] lisonjeiro(ra); [dress, colour, neckline] que cai bem.
flattery ['flætərɪ] *n (U)* bajulação *f.*
flatulence ['flætjʊləns] *n (U)* flatulência *f.*
flatware ['flætweə^r] *n US* talheres *mpl.*
flaunt [flɔ:nt] *vt* ostentar.
flautist *UK* ['flaʊtɪst], **flutist** *US* ['flu:tɪst] *n* flautista *mf.*
flavour *UK*, **flavor** *US* ['fleɪvə^r] ◇ *n* **-1.** [taste] sabor *m* **-2.** *fig* [atmosphere] ar *m*, toque *m.* ◇ *vt* [food, drink] condimentar.
flavouring *UK*, **flavoring** *US* ['fleɪvərɪŋ] *n (U)* condimento *m.*
flaw [flɔ:] *n* [fault] imperfeição *f*; **~ in sthg** imperfeição em algo.
flawed [flɔ:d] *adj* imperfeito(ta), defeituoso(sa).
flawless ['flɔ:lɪs] *adj* impecável.
flax [flæks] *n* linho *m.*
flay [fleɪ] *vt* [skin] pelar.
flea [fli:] *n* pulga *f*; **to send sb away with a ~ in his/her ear** mandar alguém embora com forte reprovação.
flea market *n* mercado *m* das pulgas.
fleck [flek] ◇ *n* mancha *f.* ◇ *vt*: **~ed with sthg** manchado(da) com algo.
fled [fled] *pt* & *pp* ▷ **flee.**
fledg(e)ling ['fledʒlɪŋ] ◇ *adj* [new, young] novato(ta). ◇ *n* ave *f* recém-emplumada.
flee [fli:] (*pt* & *pp* **fled**) ◇ *vt* [country, enemy] fugir de. ◇ *vi* fugir.
fleece [fli:s] ◇ *n* **-1.** [material, of sheep] velo *m* **-2.** [garment] sobretudo *m* de lã. ◇ *vt inf* [cheat] trapacear.
fleet [fli:t] *n* frota *f.*
fleeting ['fli:tɪŋ] *adj* fugaz.
Fleet Street *n* Fleet Street *f.*

FLEET STREET

Essa rua, situada na *City* londrina (ver the *City*), era o antigo centro da imprensa inglesa. Embora muitos jornais tenham se mudado para outras regiões da cidade, *Fleet Street* continua sendo uma expressão utilizada para designar a imprensa em geral.

Fleming ['flemɪŋ] *n* flamengo *m*, -ga *f*.

Flemish ['flemɪʃ] ◇ *adj* flamengo(ga). ◇ *n* [language] flamengo *m*. ◇ *npl*: **the ~** os flamengos.

flesh [fleʃ] *n* **-1.** [of body] carne *f*; **to be only ~ and blood** ser de carne e osso; **to be sb's own ~ and blood** ser sangue do sangue de alguém; **in the ~** em carne e osso **-2.** [of fruit, vegetable] polpa *f*.
◆ **flesh out** *vt sep* detalhar.

flesh wound *n* ferimento *m* superficial.

fleshy ['fleʃɪ] (*compar* **-ier**, *superl* **-iest**) *adj* [fat] carnudo(da).

flew [flu:] *pt* ⊳ **fly**.

flex [fleks] ◇ *n* ELEC fio *m*, cabo *m*. ◇ *vt* [bend] flexionar.

flexibility [ˌfleksə'bɪlətɪ] *n (U)* flexibilidade *f*.

flexible ['fleksəbl] *adj* flexível.

flexitime ['fleksɪtaɪm] *n (U)* horário *m* flexível.

flick [flɪk] ◇ *n* **-1.** [of whip, towel] pancada leve **-2.** [with finger] peteleco *m*. ◇ *vt* **-1.** [whip, towel] dar uma pancada leve em **-2.** [with finger] dar um peteleco em **-3.** [switch - turn on] ligar; [- turn off] desligar.
◆ **flicks** *npl inf*: **the ~s** o cinema.
◆ **flick through** *vt fus* folhear.

flicker ['flɪkə^r] ◇ *n* **-1.** [of light, candle] oscilação *f* **-2.** *fig* [of hope, interest] centelha *f*. ◇ *vi* **-1.** [candle, light] tremeluzir **-2.** [shadow, eyelids] tremer.

flick knife *n UK* canivete *f* de mola.

flier ['flaɪə^r] *n* **-1.** [pilot] aviador *m* **-2.** [advertising leaflet] folheto *m* publicitário.

flight [flaɪt] *n* **-1.** [gen] vôo *m*; **~ of fancy** OR **of the imagination** *fig* vôo da imaginação **-2.** [of steps, stairs] lance *m* **-3.** [escape] fuga *f*.

flight attendant *n* comissário *m*, -ria *f* de bordo.

flight crew *n* tripulação *f* de vôo.

flight deck *n* **-1.** [of aircraft carrier] pista *f* de aterrissagem **-2.** [of aircraft] cabine *f* de comando.

flight path *n* trajetória *f* de vôo.

flight recorder *n* caixa-preta *f*.

flighty ['flaɪtɪ] (*compar* **-ier**, *superl* **-iest**) *adj* volúvel.

flimsy ['flɪmzɪ] (*compar* **-ier**, *superl* **-iest**) *adj* **-1.** [fabric, structure] frágil **-2.** [excuse, argument] furado(da).

flinch [flɪntʃ] *vi* encolher-se; **to ~ from sthg/from doing sthg** vacilar diante de algo/em fazer algo; **without ~ing** sem pestanejar.

fling [flɪŋ] (*pt* & *pp* **flung**) ◇ *n* [affair] caso *m*. ◇ *vt* [throw] atirar; **to ~ o.s. into an armchair/onto the ground** atirar-se numa poltrona/no chão.

flint [flɪnt] *n* **-1.** *(U)* [rock] sílex *m* **-2.** [in lighter] pedra *f*.

flip [flɪp] (*pt* & *pp* **-ped**, *cont* **-ping**) ◇ *vt* **-1.** [move with a flick] mover rapidamente, sacudir; **to ~ a coin** tirar cara ou coroa; **to ~ sthg open** abrir algo de supetão; **to ~ sthg over** virar algo bruscamente; **to ~ through sthg** folhear algo **-2.** [switch]: **to ~ on** ligar; **to ~ off** desligar **-3.** [throw] atirar, jogar. ◇ *vi inf* [become angry] perder o controle. ◇ *n* **-1.** [of coin] arremesso *m* rápido **-2.** [somersault] piparote *m* **-3.** *phr*: **at the ~ of a switch** ao toque de um interruptor.

flipchart *n* quadro *m* de folhas móveis.

flip-flop *n UK* [shoe] sandália *f* de dedo.

flippant ['flɪpənt] *adj* leviano(na).

flippantly ['flɪpəntlɪ] *adv* levianamente.

flipper ['flɪpə^r] *n* **-1.** [of animal] barbatana *f* **-2.** [for swimmer, diver] pé-de-pato *m*.

flipping ['flɪpɪŋ] *UK inf* ◇ *adj* maldito(ta). ◇ *adv* absolutamente.

flip side *n* [of record] lado *m* B.

flirt [flɜ:t] ◇ *n* [person] paquerador *m*, -ra *f*. ◇ *vi* **-1.** [with person] flertar; **to ~ with sb** flertar com alguém **-2.** [with idea] interessar-se por; **to ~ with sthg** interessar-se por algo.

flirtation [flɜ:'teɪʃn] *n* **-1.** *(U)* [flirting] flerte *m* **-2.** [love affair] caso *m* **-3.** [brief interest]: **~ with sthg** interesse *m* em algo.

flirtatious [flɜ:'teɪʃəs] *adj* galanteador(ra).

flit [flɪt] (*pt* & *pp* **-ted**, *cont* **-ting**) *vi* [move quickly - bird] esvoaçar; [- expression, idea] passar rapidamente.

float [fləʊt] ◇ *n* **-1.** [on fishing line, net] bóia *f* **-2.** [in procession] carro *m* alegórico **-3.** [money] caixa *m*. ◇ *vt* **-1.** [on water] fazer boiar **-2.** [idea, project] lançar. ◇ *vi* **-1.** [on water] boiar **-2.** [through air] flutuar.

floating ['fləʊtɪŋ] *adj* flutuante.

floating voter *n UK* eleitor *m* indeciso, eleitora *f* indecisa.

flock [flɒk] ◇ *n* **-1.** [of birds, people] bando *m* **-2.** [of sheep] rebanho *m*. ◇ *vi*: **to ~ to** ir em massa para.

floe [fləʊ] *n* banquisa *f*.

flog [flɒg] (*pt* & *pp* **-ged**, *cont* **-ging**) *vt* **-1.** [whip] chicotear **-2.** *UK inf* [sell] pôr no prego.

flood [flʌd] ◇ *n* **-1.** [of water] enchente *f* **-2.** *fig* [great amount] dilúvio *m*. ◇ *vt* **-1.** [with water] inundar **-2.** *fig* [overwhelm]: **to ~ sthg (with)** inundar algo (com); **to ~ the market** inundar o mercado **-3.** [with light] encher **-4.** AUT [engine] afogar. ◇ *vi* **-1.** [river] transbordar **-2.** [street, land] inundar-se **-3.** *fig* [arrive in great amounts] chegar aos montes; **to ~ back** retornar.
◆ **floods** *npl* **-1.** [from river, rain] enchentes *fpl* **-2.** *fig* [of tears] torrente *f*.

floodgates ['flʌdgeɪts] *npl*: **to open the ~** *fig* abrir caminho.

flooding ['flʌdɪŋ] *n (U)* [from river, rain] enchente *f*, inundação *f*.

floodlight ['flʌdlaɪt] *n* holofote *m*.

floodlit ['flʌdlɪt] *adj* iluminado(da) por holofotes.

flood tide *n* preamar *f*, maré *f* alta.

floor [flɔ:^r] ◇ *n* **-1.** [of room] piso *m*, chão *m* **-2.** [bottom] fundo *m* **-3.** [storey] andar *m*; **first** *US* OR **ground** *UK* **~** andar térreo **-4.** [at meeting, debate]: **from the ~** da platéia; **to have/give the ~** ter/dar a palavra **-5.** [for dancing] pista *f* **-6.** [of stock exchange] sala *f* de pregões; **to go through the ~** [share prices] atingir a cotação mais baixa. ◇ *vt* **-1.** [knock down] nocautear **-2.** [baffle] confundir.

floorboard ['flɔ:bɔ:d] *n* tábua *f* de assoalho.

floor cloth *n UK* pano *m* de chão.
flooring ['flɔ:rɪŋ] *n (U)* pavimentação *f*.
floor lamp *n US* abajur *m* de pé.
floor show *n* espetáculo *m* noturno *(em bar, restaurante, cabaré)*.
floorwalker ['flɔ:ˌwɔ:kəʳ] *n esp US* supervisor *m*, -ra *f* de seção *(em lojas)*.
floozy ['flu:zɪ] (*pl* **-ies**) *n dated & pej* mulher *f* promíscua.
flop [flɒp] (*pt & pp* **-ped**, *cont* **-ping**) *inf* <> *n* [failure] fracasso *m*. <> *vi* **-1.** [fail] fracassar **-2.** [fall] esparramar-se; **the book ~ed open at page 20** o livro caiu aberto na página 20.
floppy ['flɒpɪ] (*compar* **-ier**, *superl* **-iest**) *adj* desengonçado(da).
floppy (disk) *n* disquete *m*.
flora ['flɔ:rəl] *n* flora *f*; **~ and fauna** flora e fauna.
floral ['flɔ:rəl] *adj* **-1.** [made of flowers] floral **-2.** [patterned with flowers] florido(da), de flores.
Florence ['flɒrəns] *n* Florença; **in ~** em Florença.
floret ['flɒrɪt] *n* florzinha *f*.
florid ['flɒrɪd] *adj* **-1.** [face, complexion] corado(da) **-2.** [style] florido(da).
Florida ['flɒrɪdəl] *n* Flórida; **in ~** na Flórida.
florist ['flɒrɪst] *n* florista *mf*; **~'s (shop)** floricultura *f*.
floss [flɒs] <> *n (U)* **-1.** [dental floss] fio-dental *m* **-2.** [for embroidery] seda *f* crua. <> *vt* limpar com fio-dental. <> *vi* limpar os dentes com fio-dental.
flotation [fləʊ'teɪʃn] *n ST EX* levantamento *m* de capital.
flotilla [flə'tɪlə] *n* flotilha *f*.
flotsam ['flɒtsəm] *n (U)*: **~ and jetsam** [debris] entulho *m*; [people] gente *f* desocupada.
flounce [flaʊns] <> *n* [in cloth] babado *m*. <> *vi* [move] mover-se com ar de indignação; **he ~d out of the room** ele saiu indignado.
flounder ['flaʊndəʳ] (*pl inv* OR **-s**) <> *n* [fish] linguado *m*. <> *vi* **-1.** [in water, mud] debater-se **-2.** [in conversation, speech] atrapalhar-se.
flour ['flaʊəʳ] *n (U)* farinha *f*.
flourish ['flʌrɪʃ] <> *vi* **-1.** [grow healthily - plants, garden] florescer; [- child] crescer **-2.** [be successful] prosperar. <> *vt* movimentar. <> *n* **-1.** [movement]: **to do sthg with a ~** fazer algo de maneira a ser notado(da) **-2.** [of trumpets] fanfarra *f*.
flourishing ['flʌrɪʃɪŋ] *adj* **-1.** [growing healthily] viçoso(sa) **-2.** [successful] próspero(ra).
flout [flaʊt] *vt* desrespeitar.
flow [fləʊ] <> *n* fluxo *m*. <> *vi* **-1.** [liquid, electricity, air] correr *f* **-2.** [traffic, words, ideas] fluir **-3.** [tide] baixar **-4.** [hair, dress] ondear **-5.** [result]: **to ~ from sthg** brotar de algo.
flow chart, flow diagram *n* fluxograma *m*.
flower ['flaʊəʳ] <> *n BOT* flor *f*; **in ~** em flor. <> *comp* de flores. <> *vi* florescer.
flowerbed ['flaʊəbed] *n* canteiro *m* de flores.
flowered *adj* florido(da).
flowering ['flaʊərɪŋ] <> *adj BOT* florido(da). <> *n fig* [of artistic movement, talents] florescência *f*.
flowerpot ['flaʊəpɒt] *n* vaso *m* de flores.
flowery ['flaʊərɪ] (*compar* **-ier**, *superl* **-iest**) *adj* **-1.** [patterned] florido(da) **-2.** *pej* [elaborate] floreado(da) **-3.** [sweet-smelling] com odor de flores.
flowing ['fləʊɪŋ] *adj* **-1.** *fig* [writing, style] fluente **-2.** *fig* [hair, robes] esvoaçante.
flown [fləʊn] *pp* ⊳ **fly**.
fl. oz. *abbr of* **fluid ounce**.
flu [flu:] *n (U)* gripe *m*; **to have ~** estar com gripe.
fluctuate ['flʌktʃʊeɪt] *vi* oscilar, flutuar.
fluctuation [ˌflʌktʃʊ'eɪʃn] *n* [act of fluctuating] oscilação *f*, flutuação *f*.
flue [flu:] *n* fumeiro *m*.
fluency ['flu:ənsɪ] *n (U)* [in a foreign language] fluência *f*.
fluent ['flu:ənt] *adj* fluente; **he speaks ~ Spanish** ele fala espanhol fluentemente; **to be ~ in sthg** ser fluente em algo.
fluently ['flu:əntlɪ] *adv* fluentemente.
fluff [flʌf] <> *n (U)* **-1.** [down] felpa *f* **-2.** [dust] penugem *f*. <> *vt* **-1.** [puff up]: **to ~ sthg (up)** afofar **-2.** *inf* [do badly] fazer mal, não acertar.
fluffy ['flʌfɪ] (*compar* **-ier**, *superl* **-iest**) *adj* [downy] macio(cia).
fluid ['flu:ɪd] <> *n* fluido *m*. <> *adj* **-1.** [flowing] fluido(da) **-2.** [unfixed] mutável.
fluid ounce *n* onça *f* fluida *(0,028 litro)*.
fluke [flu:k] *n inf* [chance] obra *f* do acaso.
flummox ['flʌməks] *vt esp UK inf* bestificar.
flung [flʌŋ] *pt & pp* ⊳ **fling**.
flunk [flʌŋk] *esp US inf* <> *vt* [SCH & UNIV - exam, test] não passar em; [- student] reprovar. <> *vi* levar pau, ser reprovado(da).
fluorescent [flʊə'resnt] *adj* [colour] fluorescente.
fluorescent light *n* luz *f* fluorescente.
fluoridate *vt* adicionar flúor a.
fluoride ['flʊəraɪd] *n* fluoreto *m*.
fluorine ['flʊəri:n] *n (U)* flúor *m*.
flurry ['flʌrɪ] (*pl* **-ies**) *n* **-1.** [shower] lufada *f* **-2.** [sudden burst] erupção *f*.
flush [flʌʃ] <> *adj* **-1.** [level]: **~ with sthg** nivelado(da) com **-2.** *inf* [not short of money]: **to be ~ with money** estar sentado(da) no dinheiro. <> *n* **-1.** [in toilet] descarga *f* **-2.** [blush] rubor *m* **-3.** [sudden feeling] acesso *m*; **in the first ~ of sthg** *literary* no primeiro afluxo de algo. <> *vt* **-1.** [with water]: **to ~ the toilet** dar a descarga na privada; **to ~ sthg down the toilet** deixar algo cair na privada **-2.** *fig* [force out of hiding]: **to ~ sb out** fazer alguém sair. <> *vi* **-1.** [toilet] dar a descarga **-2.** [blush] ruborizar.
flushed [flʌʃt] *adj* **-1.** [red-faced] ruborizado(da) **-2.** [excited]: **~ with sthg** empolgado(da) com algo.
fluster ['flʌstəʳ] <> *n* atrapalhação *f*. <> *vt* atrapalhar.
flustered ['flʌstəd] *adj* atrapalhado(da).
flute [flu:t] *n MUS* flauta *f*.
fluted ['flu:tɪd] *adj ARCHIT* acanalado(da).
flutist *n US* = **flautist**.
flutter ['flʌtəʳ] <> *n* **-1.** [of wings] bater *m* **-2.** [of eyelashes] pestanejo *m* **-3.** [of heart] pulso *m* **-4.** *inf* [sudden feeling] agito *m* **-5.** *inf* [bet] aposta *f*. <> *vt* **-1.** [wings] bater, agitar **-2.** [eyelashes] pestanejar. <> *vi* **-1.** [bird, insect, wings] agitar **-2.** [flag] tremular **-3.** [dress] esvoaçar **-4.** [heart, pulse] pulsar.

flux [flʌks] *n* **-1.** *(U)* [change] fluxo *m*; **to be in a state of ~** mudar continuamente **-2.** *TECH* fundente *m*.
fly [flaɪ] (*pl* **flies**, *pt* **flew**, *pp* **flown**) <> *n* **-1.** [insect] mosca *f*; **a ~ in the ointment** *fig* ≃ um pequeno problema **-2.** [of trousers] braguilha *f*. <> *vt* **-1.** [cause to fly] fazer voar **-2.** [transport by air] transportar em avião **-3.** [flag] tremular. <> *vi* **-1.** [bird, insect, plane] voar **-2.** [pilot] pilotar **-3.** [travel by plane] ir de avião **-4.** [move fast] voar; **time flies** o tempo voa **-5.** [attack]: **to ~ at sb** voar para cima de alguém **-6.** [flag] tremular.
◆ **fly away** *vi* ir-se embora.
◆ **fly in** <> *vt sep* trazer em avião. <> *vi* chegar.
◆ **fly into** *vt fus*: **to ~ into a rage/temper** enfurecer-se.
◆ **fly out** <> *vt sep* levar de avião. <> *vi* sair de avião.
flyby *n US* = **flypast**.
fly-fishing *n (U)* pesca *f* com iscas artificiais.
fly half *n UK no rúgbi, jogador rápido cujo objetivo é passar a bola para uma linha de jogadores.*
flying ['flaɪɪŋ] <> *adj* **-1.** [able to fly] voador(ra) **-2.** [running] veloz. <> *n* [in plane]: **I hate ~** odeio viajar de avião.
flying colours *npl*: **to pass (sthg) with ~** passar (em algo) com louvor.
flying doctor *n médico que utiliza o avião para visitar seus pacientes em áreas mais isoladas.*
flying officer *n UK* tenente-aviador *m*.
flying saucer *n* disco *m* voador.
flying squad *n UK* radiopatrulha *f*.
flying start *n*: **to get off to a ~** começar muito bem.
flying visit *n* visita *f* rápida.
flyleaf ['flaɪli:f] (*pl* **-leaves**) *n* guarda *f*.
flyover ['flaɪˌəʊvə^r] *n UK* viaduto *m*.
flypast *UK* ['flaɪˌpɑ:st], **flyby** *US* ['flaɪˌbaɪ] *n* apresentação *f* aérea.
flysheet ['flaɪʃi:t] *n* [on tent] teto *m* duplo.
fly spray *n* inseticida *f*.
flyweight ['flaɪweɪt] *n* peso-mosca *m*.
flywheel ['flaɪwi:l] *n TECH* volante *m*.
FM -1. (*abbr of* **frequency modulation**) FM *f*. **-2.** (*abbr of* **field marshal**) mestre-de-campo *m*.
FMCS (*abbr of* **Federal Mediation and Conciliation Services**) *n serviço federal norte-americano que oferece serviços de conciliação entre empregadores e sindicatos em disputas industriais.*
FO (*abbr of* **Foreign Office**) *n* ≃ MRE *m*.
foal [fəʊl] *n* potro *m*.
foam [fəʊm] <> *n* **-1.** [bubbles] espuma *f* **-2.** [material]: **~ rubber** espuma de borracha. <> *vi* espumar.
foamy ['fəʊmɪ] (*compar* **-ier**, *superl* **-iest**) *adj* [with bubbles] espumoso(sa), espumante.
fob [fɒb] (*pt* & *pp* **-bed**, *cont* **-bing**) ◆ **fob off** *vt sep*: **to ~ sthg off on sb** empurrar algo para alguém; **to ~ sb off with sthg** enrolar alguém com algo.
FOB, f.o.b. (*abbr of* **free on board**) FOB *m*.
fob watch *n* relógio *m* de corrente.
focal ['fəʊkl] *adj* focal.
focal point ['fəʊkl-] *n* **-1.** [of view, room] ponto *m* central **-2.** *fig* [of report, study] foco *m*.
focus ['fəʊkəs] (*pl* **-cuses** *OR* **-ci** [-saɪ]) <> *n* [gen] foco *m*; **out of/in ~** fora de/em foco; **~ of attention** foco de atenção. <> *vt* **-1.** [lens, camera] focar; **to ~ sthg on sb/sthg** [lens, camera, eyes] focar algo em alguém/algo **-2.** [mentally]: **to ~ one's attention on sb/sthg** concentrar a atenção em alguém/algo. <> *vi* **-1.**: **to ~ on sb/sthg** enfocar alguém/algo **-2.** [mentally]: **to ~ on sthg** concentrar-se em algo.
focussed *adj* [mentally] concentrado(da).
fodder ['fɒdə^r] *n* [feed] forragem *f*.
foe [fəʊ] *n literary* inimigo *m*, -ga *f*, antagonista *mf*.
FOE *n* (*abbr of* **Friends of the Earth**) ≃ NAT *f*.
foetal ['fi:tl] *adj* fetal.
foetus ['fi:təs] *n* feto *m*.
fog [fɒg] *n* [mist] nevoeiro *m*, neblina *f*.
fogbound ['fɒgbaʊnd] *adj* fechado(da) por causa de nevoeiro.
fogey ['fəʊgɪ] *n* = **fogy**.
foggiest ['fɒgɪəst] *n inf*: **I haven't the ~** não tenho a menor idéia.
foggy ['fɒgɪ] (*compar* **-ier**, *superl* **-iest**) *adj* [misty] nevoento(ta).
foghorn ['fɒghɔ:n] *n* buzina *f* de nevoeiro.
fog lamp *n* farol *m* de neblina.
fogey ['fəʊgɪ] (*pl* **-ies**) *n inf*: **old ~** raposa *mf* velha.
foible ['fɔɪbl] *n* ponto *m* fraco.
foil [fɔɪl] <> *n* **-1.** *(U)* [metal sheet] papel *m* alumínio **-2.** [contrast]: **to act as a ~ to** *OR* **for sb/sthg** complementar alguém/algo, ser um complemento de alguém/algo. <> *vt* frustrar.
foist [fɔɪst] *vt*: **to ~ sthg on sb** impingir algo a alguém.
fold [fəʊld] <> *vt* **-1.** [gen] dobrar; **to ~ one's arms** cruzar os braços **-2.** [wrap] abraçar. <> *vi* **-1.** [bed, chair] dobrar **-2.** *inf* [newspaper, play] fracassar **-3.** *inf* [business] falir. <> *n* **-1.** [in material, paper] dobra *f* **-2.** [for animals] curral *m* **-3.** *fig* [group of people]: **the ~** o grupo.
◆ **fold up** <> *vt sep* dobrar. <> *vi* **-1.** dobrar **-2.** *inf* [newspaper, play] fracassar **-3.** *inf* [business] falir.
foldaway ['fəʊldəˌweɪ] *adj* dobrável.
folder ['fəʊldə^r] *n* **-1.** [gen & *COMPUT*] pasta *f* **-2.** [binder] fichário *f* **-3.** [brochure] folheto *f*.
folding ['fəʊldɪŋ] *adj* [chair, table] dobrável.
foliage ['fəʊlɪɪdʒ] *n (U)* folhagem *f*.
folk [fəʊk] <> *adj* popular. <> *n* [music] música *f* folk. <> *npl* [people] gente *f*.
◆ **folks** *npl inf* **-1.** [relatives] parentes *mpl* **-2.** [everyone] pessoal *m*.
folklore ['fəʊklɔ:^r] *n (U)* folclore *m*.
folk music *n (U)* música *m* folk.
folk singer *n* cantor *m*, -ra *f* folk.
folk song *n* canção *f* folk.
folksy ['fəʊksɪ] (*compar* **-ier**, *superl* **-iest**) *adj US inf* amigável.
follicle ['fɒlɪkl] *n* folículo *m*.
follow ['fɒləʊ] <> *vt* **-1.** [gen] seguir; **~ that taxi!** siga aquele táxi!; **(to be) ~ed by sthg** ser/vir

acompanhado(da) por algo, ser seguido(da) de algo **-2.** [pursue] perseguir **-3.** [go along with, understand] acompanhar. ◇ *vi* **-1.** [come after] seguir-se; **as ~s** conforme segue, da seguinte forma **-2.** [happen as logical result] vir em seguida **-3.** [be logical] proceder; **it ~s that** isso quer dizer que **-4.** [understand] acompanhar.

◆ **follow up** *vt sep* **-1.** [pursue] acompanhar **-2.** [supplement]: **to ~ sthg up with** responder a algo com.

follower ['fɒləʊə^r] *n* [disciple, believer] seguidor *m*, -ra *f*.

following ['fɒləʊɪŋ] ◇ *adj* seguinte. ◇ *n* [group of supporters, fans] séquito *m*. ◇ *prep* [after] depois de.

follow-up ◇ *adj* complementar. ◇ *n* [to visit, treatment, programme] continuação *f*.

folly ['fɒlɪ] *n (U)* [foolishness] loucura *f*.

foment [fəʊ'ment] *vt fml* fomentar.

fond [fɒnd] *adj* **-1.** [affectionate] carinhoso(sa); **to be ~ of sb** gostar muito de alguém; **to be ~ of sthg/of doing sthg** gostar muito de algo/de fazer algo **-2.** *fml* [hope, wish] ingênuo(nua).

fondle ['fɒndl] *vt* acariciar.

fondly ['fɒndlɪ] *adv* **-1.** [affectionately] carinhosamente **-2.** [naively] ingenuamente.

fondness ['fɒndnɪs] *n (U)* afeição *f*, carinho *m*; **~ for sb/sthg** gosto por alguém/algo.

fondue ['fɒndju:] *n* CULIN fondue *m*.

font [fɒnt] *n* **-1.** [in church] pia *f* batismal **-2.** COMPUT & TYPO fonte *f*.

food [fu:d] *n* comida *f*; **~ for thought** assunto para reflexão.

food chain *n* cadeia *f* alimentar.

food mill *n* processador *m* de alimentos.

food mixer *n* batedeira *f*.

food poisoning [-'pɔɪznɪŋ] *n (U)* intoxicação *f* alimentar.

food processor [-,prəʊsesə^r] *n* multiprocessador *m*.

food stamp *n US* vale-alimentação *m (fornecido pelo governo)*.

foodstuffs ['fu:dstʌfs] *npl* gêneros *mpl* alimentícios.

fool [fu:l] ◇ *n* **-1.** [idiot] idiota *mf*; **to make a ~ of sb** fazer alguém de bobo; **to make a ~ of o.s.** fazer papel de bobo; **to act** OR **play the ~** bancar o bobo **-2.** *UK* [dessert] musse *f*. ◇ *vt* enganar; **to ~ sb into doing sthg** enrolar alguém para que faça algo. ◇ *vi* brincar.

◆ **fool about, fool around** *vi* **-1.** [behave foolishly]: **to ~ about (with sthg)** fazer-se de bobo (em relação a algo) **-2.** [be unfaithful]: **to ~ about (with sb)** pular a cerca (com alguém) **-3.** *US* [tamper]: **to ~ around with sthg** brincar com algo.

foolhardy ['fu:l,hɑ:dɪ] *adj* temerário(ria).

foolish ['fu:lɪʃ] *adj* **-1.** [unwise, silly] bobo(ba), idiota **-2.** [laughable, undignified] tolo(la).

foolishly ['fu:lɪʃlɪ] *adv* **-1.** [unwisely, in a silly manner] de maneira idiota **-2.** [laughably, in an undignified manner] estupidamente.

foolishness ['fu:lɪʃnɪs] *n (U)* idiotice *f*.

foolproof ['fu:lpru:f] *adj* infalível.

foolscap ['fu:lzkæp] *n (U)* papel *m* ofício.

foot [fʊt] (*pl senses 1 and 2* **feet**, *pl sense 3 inv* OR **feet**) ◇ *n* **-1.** [of animal] pata *f* **-2.** [of person] pé *m*; **on ~** a pé; **to be on one's feet, to get to one's feet** ficar de pé; **to be back on one's feet** estar logo de pé; **to have/get cold feet** não ter coragem suficiente; **to have itchy feet** ter formiga nos pés; **to put one's ~ down** bater pé; **to put one's ~ in it** meter os pés pelas mãos; **to put one's feet up** descansar; **to be rushed off one's feet** ser massacrado(da); **to set ~ in** pôr os pés em; **to stand on one's own two feet** ser dono de seu próprio nariz **-3.** [bottom] pé *m* **-4.** [of hill] sopé *m* **-5.** [unit of measurement] pé *m (30,48 cm)*. ◇ *vt inf*: **to ~ the bill (for sthg)** pagar a conta (por algo).

footage ['fʊtɪdʒ] *n (U)* metragem *f*.

foot-and-mouth disease *n (U)* febre *f* aftosa.

football ['fʊtbɔ:l] *n* **-1.** *UK* [game] futebol *m* **-2.** *US* [American football] futebol *m* americano **-3.** [ball] bola *f* de futebol.

football club *n UK* time *m* de futebol.

footballer ['fʊtbɔ:lə^r] *n UK* jogador *m*, -ra *f* de futebol, futebolista *mf*.

football field *n US* campo *m* de futebol americano.

football game *n US* partida *f* de futebol americano.

football ground *n UK* campo *m* de futebol.

football match *n UK* partida *f* de futebol.

football player *n* jogador *m*, -ra *f* de futebol.

football pools *npl UK* ≃ loteria *f* esportiva.

football supporter *n* torcedor *m*, -ra *f*.

footbrake ['fʊtbreɪk] *n* freio *m* de pé.

footbridge ['fʊtbrɪdʒ] *n* passarela *f*.

footer ['fʊtə^r] *n* COMPUT rodapé *m*.

foot fault *n* TENNIS falta *f* de saque *(pé dentro da linha)*.

foothills ['fʊthɪlz] *npl* contraforte *m*.

foothold ['fʊthəʊld] *n* apoio *m* para os pés; **to get a ~** [on mountain, rockface] ter um ponto de apoio; [in organization, company] base *f* de operações.

footing ['fʊtɪŋ] *n* **-1.** [foothold] lugar *m* onde pôr o pé; **to lose one's ~** escorregar, perder a base **-2.** [basis] base *f*; **on an equal ~ (with sb/sthg)** em pé de igualdade (com alguém/algo).

footlights ['fʊtlaɪts] *npl* ribalta *f*.

footling *adj dated & pej* néscio(cia).

footman ['fʊtmən] (*pl* **-men** [-mən]) *n* lacaio *m*.

footmark ['fʊtmɑ:k] *n* pegada *f*.

footmen ['fʊtmən] *pl* ▷ **footman**.

footnote ['fʊtnəʊt] *n* nota *f* de rodapé.

footpath ['fʊtpɑ:θ, *pl* -pɑ:ðz] *n* trilha *f*.

footprint ['fʊtprɪnt] *n* pegada *f*.

footsie *n*: **to play ~** *tocar o pé de alguém com o próprio pé demonstrando interesse afetivo ou sexual.*

Footsie *n UK* FIN *inf* = **FTSE**

footsore ['fʊtsɔ:^r] *adj* com os pés doloridos.

footstep ['fʊtstep] *n* **-1.** [sound] passo *m* **-2.** [footprint] pegada *f*; **to follow in sb's ~s** seguir os passos de alguém.

footwear ['fʊtweə^r] *n (U)* calçado *m*.

footwork ['fʊtwɜ:k] *n* SPORT jogo *m* de pernas.

for [fɔ:r] *prep* **-1.** [expressing intention, purpose, reason] para; **this book is ~ you** este livro é para você; **what did you do that ~?** para que você fez isso?; **what's it ~?** para que é?; **to go ~ a walk** ir dar um passeio; **'~ sale'** 'vende-se'; **a town famous ~ its wine** uma cidade famosa pelo vinho; **~ this reason** por esta razão **-2.** [during] durante; **I'm going away ~ a while** vou estar fora durante OR por algum tempo; **I've lived here ~ ten years** vivo aqui há dez anos; **we talked ~ hours** falamos horas e horas **-3.** [by, before] para; **it'll be ready ~ tomorrow** estará pronto (para) amanhã; **be there ~ 8 p.m.** esteja lá antes das oito da noite **-4.** [on the occasion of] por; **I got socks ~ Christmas** ganhei meias de Natal; **~ the first time** pela primeira vez; **what's ~ dinner?** o que há para jantar?; **~ the moment** no momento **-5.** [on behalf of] por; **to do sthg ~ sb** fazer algo para alguém; **to work ~ sb** trabalhar para alguém **-6.** [with time and space] para; **there's no room ~ it** não há espaço para isso; **to have time ~ sthg** ter tempo para algo **-7.** [expressing distance]: **roadwork ~ 20 miles** obras na estrada ao longo de 32 quilômetros; **we drove ~ miles** dirigimos quilômetros e mais quilômetros **-8.** [expressing destination] para; **a ticket ~ Boston** um bilhete para Boston; **this train is ~ Newark only** este trem só vai até Newark **-9.** [expressing price] por; **I bought it ~ five dollars** comprei-o por cinco dólares **-10.** [expressing meaning]: **what's the Portuguese ~ boy?** como é que se diz boy em português? **-11.** [with regard to] para; **it's warm ~ November** para novembro está quente; **it's easy ~ you** para você é fácil; **respect ~ human rights** respeito pelos direitos humanos; **I feel sorry ~ them** sinto pena deles; **it's too far ~ us to walk** é longe demais para irmos a pé; **it's time ~ dinner** está na hora do jantar.

FOR (*abbr of* **free on rail**) FOR.

forage ['fɒrɪdʒ] *vi* [search] procurar; **to ~ for sthg** sair à procura de algo.

foray ['fɒreɪ] *n* **-1.** [raid] incursão *f* **-2.** *fig* [excursion] incursão *f*; **~ into sthg** incursão em algo.

forbad [fə'bæd], **forbade** [fə'beɪd] *pt* ▷ **forbid**.

forbearing [fɔ:'beərɪŋ] *adj* indulgente.

forbid [fə'bɪd] (*pt* **-bade** OR **-bad**, *pp* **forbid** OR **-bidden**, *cont* **-bidding**) *vt* [not allow] proibir; **to ~ sb to do sthg** proibir alguém de fazer algo; **God** OR **Heaven ~!** Deus me livre!

forbidden [fə'bɪdn] ◇ *pp* ▷ **forbid**. ◇ *adj* proibido(da).

forbidding [fə'bɪdɪŋ] *adj* **-1.** [severe] repulsivo(va) **-2.** [threatening] ameaçador(ra).

force [fɔ:s] ◇ *n* **-1.** [gen] força *f*; **~ of habit** força do hábito; **by ~** à força **-2.** [power, influence] poder *m*; **a ~ to be reckoned with** um poder a ser reconhecido **-3.** [group] equipe *f*; **sales ~** a equipe de vendas; **security ~s** as equipes de segurança; **task ~** orça-tarefa *f*; **in ~** em grande número **-4.** [effect]: **to be in/come into ~** estar/entrar em vigor. ◇ *vt* **-1.** [compel] forçar; **to ~ sb to do sthg** obrigar alguém a fazer algo; **to ~ sthg on sb** impor algo a alguém; **to ~ o.s.** forçar-se **-2.** [break open] forçar **-3.** [push] empurrar; **to ~ sthg open** forçar algo; **to ~ one's way through/into** abrir caminho (por entre) **-4.** [hurry] apressar **-5.** [smile, answer] arrancar.

◆ **forces** *npl*: **the ~s** as Forças Armadas; **to join ~s (with sb)** unir forças (com alguém).

◆ **by force of** *prep* mediante, por meio de.

◆ **force back** *vt sep* **-1.** [push back] fazer recuar **-2.** [suppress] reprimir.

◆ **force down** *vt sep* **-1.** [swallow] forçar-se a comer **-2.** [force to land] forçar a aterrissar.

forced [fɔ:st] *adj* forçado(da).

forced landing *n* aterrissagem *f* forçada.

force-feed *vt* alimentar à força.

forceful ['fɔ:sfʊl] *adj* **-1.** [strong, powerful] forte **-2.** [words, ideas] contundente **-3.** [support, recommendation] enérgico(ca).

forcefully ['fɔ:sfʊlɪ] *adv* vigorosamente, energicamente.

forcemeat ['fɔ:smi:t] *n esp UK* recheio *m* de carne.

forceps ['fɔ:seps] *npl* fórceps *m*.

forcible ['fɔ:səbl] *adj* **-1.** [using physical force] feito(ta) à força **-2.** [powerful] eficaz **-3.** [recommendation, argument] enérgico(ca).

forcibly ['fɔ:səblɪ] *adv* **-1.** [using physical force] à força **-2.** [powerfully] eficazmente **-3.** [eagerly] energicamente.

ford [fɔ:d] ◇ *n* vau *m*. ◇ *vt* vadear.

fore [fɔ:ʳ] ◇ *adj* NAUT dianteiro(ra). ◇ *n*: **to come to the ~** *fig* tornar-se influente.

forearm ['fɔ:rɑ:m] *n* antebraço *m*.

forebears ['fɔ:beəz] *npl fml* antepassados *mpl*.

foreboding [fɔ:'bəʊdɪŋ] *n* mau pressentimento *m*.

forecast ['fɔ:kɑ:st] (*pt* & *pp* **forecast** OR **-ed**) ◇ *n* [prediction] previsão *f*. ◇ *vt* [predict] prever.

forecaster ['fɔ:kɑ:stəʳ] *n* **-1.** ECON analista *mf* **-2.** METEOR meteorologista *mf*.

foreclose [fɔ:'kləʊz] ◇ *vt* executar. ◇ *vi*: **to ~ on sb** privar alguém do direito de resgatar uma hipoteca.

foreclosure [fɔ:'kləʊʒəʳ] *n* execução *f* de uma hipoteca.

forecourt ['fɔ:kɔ:t] *n* área *f* para estacionamento.

forefathers ['fɔ:ˌfɑ:ðəz] *npl* antepassados *mpl*.

forefinger ['fɔ:ˌfɪŋgəʳ] *n* indicador *m*.

forefront ['fɔ:frʌnt] *n*: **in** OR **at the ~ of sthg** em primeiro plano de algo.

forego [fɔ:'gəʊ] *vt* = **forgo**.

foregoing [fɔ:'gəʊɪŋ] ◇ *adj* anterior, precedente. ◇ *n fml*: **the ~** o supracitado.

foregone conclusion ['fɔ:gɒn-] *n*: **it's a ~** é um resultado inevitável.

foreground ['fɔ:graʊnd] *n* primeiro plano *m*; **in the ~** em primeiro plano.

forehand ['fɔ:hænd] *n* [tennis stroke] golpe *m* com a frente da mão.

forehead ['fɔ:hed] *n* testa *f*.

foreign ['fɒrən] *adj* **-1.** [from abroad] estrangeiro(ra) **-2.** [external] exterior **-3.** [alien] estranho(nha).

foreign affairs *npl* relações *fpl* exteriores.

foreign aid *n (U)* ajuda *f* internacional.

foreign body *n* corpo *m* estranho.

foreign competition *n (U)* competição *f* internacional.

foreign currency *n* moeda *m* estrangeira.
foreigner ['fɒrənəʳ] *n* [from abroad] estrangeiro *m*, -ra *f*.
foreign exchange *n (U)* câmbio *m*; ~ **markets** mercados de câmbio; ~ **rates** taxas de câmbio.
foreign investment *n (U)* investimento *m* estrangeiro.
Foreign Legion *n*: **the** ~ a Legião Estrangeira.
foreign minister *n* ministro *m* de relações exteriores.
Foreign Office *n UK*: **the** ~ ≃ o Ministério das Relações Exteriores.
Foreign Secretary *n UK* ≃ Ministro *m* das Relações Exteriores.
foreleg ['fɔːleg] *n* perna *f* dianteira.
foreman ['fɔːmən] (*pl* **-men** *n* **-1.** [of workers] capataz *m* **-2.** [of jury] primeiro jurado *m*.
foremost ['fɔːməʊst] ◇ *adj* principal. ◇ *adv*: **first and** ~ antes de mais nada.
forename ['fɔːneɪm] *n* prenome *m*.
forensic [fə'rensɪk] *adj* forense.
forensic medicine *n (U)* medicina *f* legal.
forensic science *n (U)* ciência *f* forense.
forerunner ['fɔːˌrʌnəʳ] *n* [precursor] precursor *m*, -ra *f*.
foresee [fɔː'siː] (*pt* **-saw** [-'sɔː], *pp* **-seen**) *vt* prever.
foreseeable [fɔː'siːəbl] *adj* previsível; **for/in the** ~ **future** num futuro próximo.
foreseen [fɔː'siːn] *pp* ▷ **foresee**.
foreshadow [fɔː'ʃædəʊ] *vt* prenunciar.
foreshortened [fɔː'ʃɔːtnd] *adj* condensado(da).
foresight ['fɔːsaɪt] *n (U)* previdência *f*.
foreskin ['fɔːskɪn] *n* prepúcio *m*.
forest ['fɒrɪst] *n* floresta *f*.
forestall [fɔː'stɔːl] *vt* prevenir.
forestry ['fɒrɪstrɪ] *n (U)* silvicultura *f*.
Forestry Commission *n UK*: **the** ~ *departamento do governo britânico responsável pela proteção e pelo desenvolvimento das florestas e matas do país.*
foretaste ['fɔːteɪst] *n* [sample] amostra *f*.
foretell [fɔː'tel] (*pt* & *pp* **-told**) *vt* predizer, prenunciar.
forethought ['fɔːθɔːt] *n (U)* premeditação *f*.
foretold [fɔː'təʊld] *pt* & *pp* ▷ **foretell**.
forever [fə'revəʳ] *adv* **-1.** [eternally] para sempre **-2.** *inf* [incessantly] sem parar, sempre **-3.** *inf* [a long time] para sempre.
forewarn [fɔː'wɔːn] *vt* prevenir.
foreword ['fɔːwɜːd] *n* apresentação *f*.
forfeit ['fɔːfɪt] ◇ *n* **-1.** [penalty] prenda *f* **-2.** [fine] multa *f*. ◇ *vt* [lose] perder.
forgave [fə'geɪv] *pt* ▷ **forgive**.
forge [fɔːdʒ] ◇ *n* [place] forja *f*. ◇ *vt* **-1.** [industry] forjar *f* **-2.** *fig* [create] forjar **-3.** [make illegal copy of] falsificar.
◆ **forge ahead** *vi* avançar continuamente.
forger ['fɔːdʒəʳ] *n* falsificador *m*, -ra *f*.
forgery ['fɔːdʒərɪ] (*pl* **-ies**) *n* falsificação *f*.
forget [fə'get] (*pt* **- got**, *pp* **-gotten**, *cont* **-getting**) ◇ *vt* **-1.** [gen] esquecer; **to** ~ **to do sthg** esquecer-se de fazer algo; **to** ~ **o.s.** esquecer-se de si mesmo **-2.** [leave behind] esquecer-se de. ◇ *vi* esquecer-se; **to** ~ **about sthg** esquecer-se de algo.
forgetful [fə'getfʊl] *adj* esquecido(da).
forgetfulness [fə'getfʊlnɪs] *n (U)* esquecimento *m*.
forget-me-not *n* não-te-esqueças-de-mim *f*, miosótis *f*.
forgive [fə'gɪv] (*pt* **-gave**, *pp* **-given**) *vt* perdoar; **to** ~ **sb for sthg/for doing sthg** perdoar alguém por algo/por fazer algo.
forgiveness [fə'gɪvnɪs] *n (U)* perdão *m*.
forgiving [fə'gɪvɪŋ] *adj* que perdoa, clemente.
forgo [fɔː'gəʊ] (*pt* **-went**, *pp* **-gone** [-'gɒn]) *vt* renunciar a, abrir mão de.
forgot [fə'gɒt] *pt* ▷ **forget**.
forgotten [fə'gɒtn] *pp* ▷ **forget**.
fork [fɔːk] ◇ *n* **-1.** [for food] garfo *m* **-2.** [for gardening] forquilha *f* **-3.** [in road, river] bifurcação *f*. ◇ *vi* bifurcar-se.
◆ **fork out** *inf* ◇ *vt fus* desembolsar; **to** ~ **out money on** *OR* **for sthg** desembolsar dinheiro em ou para algo. ◇ *vi*: **to** ~ **out (for sthg)** desembolsar uma grana (para algo).
forklift truck ['fɔːklɪft-] *n* empilhadeira *f*.
forlorn [fə'lɔːn] *adj* **-1.** [face, expression, cry] desesperado(da) **-2.** [desolate - person] desolado(da); [- place] abandonado(da) **-3.** [hope, attempt] desesperançado(da).
form [fɔːm] ◇ *n* **-1.** [shape] forma *f*; **in the** ~ **of** na forma de; **to take the** ~ **of** tomar a forma de **-2.** [type] tipo *m* **-3.** *(U)* [fitness] aparência *f*; **on** ~ *UK*, **in** ~ *US* em forma; **off** ~ fora de forma **-4.** [questionnaire] formulário *m* **-5.** [figure] imagem *f* **-6.** *UK SCH* [class] série *f* **-7.** *(U)* [usual behaviour]: **true to** ~ como era de se esperar. ◇ *vt* **-1.** [gen] formar **-2.** [constitute] constituir. ◇ *vi* formar-se.
formal ['fɔːml] *adj* **-1.** [gen] formal **-2.** [official] oficial.
formality [fɔː'mælətɪ] (*pl* **-ies**) *n* formalidade *f*.
formalize, -ise ['fɔːməlaɪz] *vt* formalizar.
formally ['fɔːməlɪ] *adv* **-1.** formalmente **-2.** [officially] oficialmente.
format ['fɔːmæt] (*pt* & *pp* **-ted**, *cont* **-ting**) ◇ *n* **-1.** [of book, magazine] formato *m* **-2.** [of meeting] estilo *m* **-3.** *COMPUT* formato. ◇ *vt COMPUT* formatar.
formation [fɔː'meɪʃn] *n* **-1.** [gen] formação *f* **-2.** *(U)* [establishment] estrutura *f*.
formative ['fɔːmətɪv] *adj* formativo(va).
former ['fɔːməʳ] ◇ *adj* **-1.** [earlier, previous] ex-; ~ **husband** ex-marido *m* **-2.** [time] passado(da) **-3.** [first] anterior. ◇ *n*: **the** ~ o primeiro.
formerly ['fɔːməlɪ] *adv* antigamente.
form feed *n* alimentação *f* de formulário.
Formica® [fɔː'maɪkəl *n (U)* fórmica® *f*.
formidable ['fɔːmɪdəbl] *adj* **-1.** [frightening] pavoroso(sa) **-2.** [impressive] impressionante.
formless ['fɔːmlɪs] *adj* [shapeless] disforme, sem forma.
Formosa [fɔː'məʊsəl *n* Formosa; **in** ~ em Formosa.
formula ['fɔːmjʊlə] (*pl* **-as** *OR* **-ae** [-iː]) *n* fórmula *f*.
formulate ['fɔːmjʊleɪt] *vt* formular.
formulation [ˌfɔːmjʊ'leɪʃn] *n* formulação *f*.

fornicate ['fɔ:nɪkeɪt] *vi fml* fornicar.
forsake [fə'seɪk] (*pt* **-sook**, *pp* **-saken**) *vt literary* abandonar.
forsaken [fə'seɪkn] *adj* abandonado(da).
forsook [fə'sʊk] *pt* ▻ **forsake**.
forsythia [fɔ:'saɪθjə] *n (U)* forsítia *f*.
fort [fɔ:t] *n* forte *m*; **to hold the ~ (for sb)** tomar conta de algo (para alguém).
forte ['fɔ:tɪ] *n* forte *m*.
forth [fɔ:θ] *adv literary* **-1.** [outwards, onwards] adiante **-2.** [into future]: **from that day ~** daquele dia em diante.
forthcoming [fɔ:θ'kʌmɪŋ] *adj* **-1.** [imminent] próximo(ma) **-2.** [available] disponível **-3.** [helpful] prestimoso(sa).
forthright ['fɔ:θraɪt] *adj* franco(ca).
forthwith [ˌfɔ:θ'wɪθ] *adv fml* incontinenti.
fortieth ['fɔ:tɪɪθ] *num* quadragésimo(ma); *see also* sixth.
fortification [ˌfɔ:tɪfɪ'keɪʃn] *n MIL* **-1.** [act of fortifying] fortificação *f* **-2.** [structure] forte *m*.
fortified wine ['fɔ:tɪfaɪd-] *n* vinho *m* licoroso.
fortify ['fɔ:tɪfaɪ] (*pt* & *pp* **-ied**) *vt* **-1.** [place] fortificar **-2.** *fig* [person, resolve] fortalecer.
fortitude ['fɔ:tɪtju:d] *n (U)* fortaleza *f*.
fortnight ['fɔ:tnaɪt] *n* quinzena *f*.
fortnightly ['fɔ:tˌnaɪtlɪ] ◇ *adj* quinzenal. ◇ *adv* quinzenalmente.
fortress ['fɔ:trɪs] *n* fortaleza *f*.
fortuitous [fɔ:'tju:ɪtəs] *adj fml* [accidental] fortuito(-ta).
fortunate ['fɔ:tʃnət] *adj* feliz; **it's ~ that ...** por sorte ...
fortunately ['fɔ:tʃnətlɪ] *adv* felizmente.
fortune ['fɔ:tʃu:n] *n* **-1.** [large amount of money] fortuna *f* **-2.** [luck] sorte *f* **-3.** [future]: **to tell sb's ~** ler a sorte de alguém.
◆ **fortunes** *npl* vicissitudes *fpl*.
fortune-teller [-ˌteləʳ] *n* **-1.** adivinho *m*, -nha *f* **-2.** [using cards] cartomante *mf*.
forty ['fɔ:tɪ] *num* quarenta; *see also* **sixty**.
forum ['fɔ:rəm] (*pl* **-s**) *n* **-1.** *HISTORY* praça *f* pública **-2.** [meeting place] fórum *m*.
forward ['fɔ:wəd] ◇ *adj* **-1.** [position] dianteiro(ra) **-2.** [movement] para frente **-3.** [advanced] avançado(da) **-4.** [impudent] impudente. ◇ *adv* **-1.** [in space] para a frente **-2.** [to earlier time]: **to bring sthg ~** trazer algo à baila **-3.** [to later time]: **to put a clock ~** adiantar um relógio. ◇ *n SPORT* atacante *mf*. ◇ *vt* **-1.** [send on - letter] remeter; [- parcels, goods] expedir; [- information] enviar; **please ~** favor enviar para novo endereço **-2.** [further] desenvolver.
forwarding address ['fɔ:wədɪŋ-] *n* endereço *m* para envio.
forward-looking [-'lʊkɪŋ] *adj* de visão.
forwardness ['fɔ:wədnɪs] *n (U)* [boldness] audácia *f*.
forwards ['fɔ:wədz] *adv* = **forward**.
forward slash *n TYPO* barra *f* inclinada *(para frente)*.
forwent [fɔ:'went] *pt* ▻ **forgo**.
fossil ['fɒsl] *n GEOL* fóssil *m*.
fossil fuel *n* combustível *m* fóssil.
fossilized, -ised ['fɒsɪlaɪzd] *adj GEOL* fossilizado(-da).
foster ['fɒstəʳ] ◇ *adj* de criação; **~ brother** irmão de criação. ◇ *vt* **-1.** [child] criar, cuidar de **-2.** [idea, hope] fomentar.
foster child *n* filho *m*, -lha *f* de criação.
foster parent *n* pais *mpl* de criação.
fought [fɔ:t] *pt* & *pp* ▻ **fight**.
foul [faʊl] ◇ *adj* **-1.** [dirty - linen] enlameado(da); [- water] imundo(da); [- air] poluído(da) **-2.** [food] estragado(da), podre; [taste] nojento(ta) ; [smell, breath] fétido(da) **-3.** [very unpleasant] péssimo(ma), horrível **-4.** [obscene] obsceno(na) **-5.** *phr*: **to fall ~ of sb** entrar em choque com alguém. ◇ *n SPORT* falta *f*. ◇ *vt* **-1.** [make dirty] sujar **-2.** *SPORT* cometer falta em **-3.** [entangle] enredar.
◆ **foul up** *vt sep inf* estragar.
foul-mouthed [-'maʊðd] *adj* desbocado(da).
foul play *n* **-1.** *SPORT* jogo *m* sujo **-2.** [criminal act] crime *m*.
found [faʊnd] ◇ *pt* & *pp* ▻ **find**. ◇ *vt* **-1.** [provide funds for] fundar **-2.** [start building] assentar os alicerces de **-3.** [base]: **to ~ sthg on** basear algo em.
foundation [faʊn'deɪʃn] *n* **-1.** *(U)* [gen] fundação *f* **-2.** [basis] base *f* **-3.** *(U)* [cosmetic]: **~ (cream)** base *f*.
◆ **foundations** *npl CONSTR* alicerces *mpl*.
founder ['faʊndəʳ] ◇ *n* [person] fundador *m*, -ra *f*. ◇ *vi* **-1.** [sink] afundar **-2.** *fig* [fail] fracassar.
founder member *n* sócio-fundador *m*, sócia-fundadora *f*.
founding father *n* [founder] fundador *m*.
foundry ['faʊndrɪ] (*pl* **-ies**) *n* fundição *f*.
fount [faʊnt] *n* [origin] fonte *f*.
fountain ['faʊntɪn] *n* **-1.** [man-made] chafariz *m* **-2.** *fig* [source] fonte *f*.
fountain pen *n* caneta-tinteiro *f*.
four [fɔ:ʳ] *num* quatro; *see also* **six**; **on all ~s** de quatro.
four-leaved clover [-li:vd-] *n* trevo *m* de quatro folhas.
four-letter word *n* palavrão *m*.
four-poster (bed) *n* cama *f* com dossel.
foursome ['fɔ:səm] *n* quarteto *m*.
four-star *adj* (de) quatro estrelas.
fourteen [ˌfɔ:'ti:n] *num* quatorze; *see also* **six**.
fourteenth [ˌfɔ:'ti:nθ] *num* décimo quarto, décima quarta; *see also* **sixth**.
fourth [fɔ:θ] *num* quarto(ta); *see also* **sixth**.
Fourth of July *n*: **the ~** o 4 de julho *(dia da Independência norte-americana)*.

FOURTH OF JULY

O 4 de julho, o dia da independência, é uma das mais importantes festas nacionais nos Estados Unidos. Como parte das comemorações, muitas cidades organizam paradas nas ruas e, à noite, queimas de fogos de artifício, em que predominam as cores azul, vermelho e branco. Os edifícios são decorados com enfeites nessas mesmas cores e com bandeiras americanas. Muita gente sai da cidade para fazer piquenique com a família e, conforme a tradição, comer cachorros-quentes e melancia.

four-way stop *n US* cruzamento *m (de quatro vias).*
four-wheel drive *n* **-1.** [vehicle] veículo *m* com tração nas quatro rodas **-2.** [system] tração *f* nas quatro rodas.
fowl [faʊl] (*pl inv* OR **-s**) *n* **-1.** CULIN ave *f* **-2.** [bird] ave *f* (doméstica).
fox [fɒks] <> *n* [animal] raposa *f.* <> *vt* **-1.** [outwit] lograr **-2.** [baffle] deixar atordoado(da).
foxcub *n* filhote *m* de raposa.
foxglove ['fɒksglʌv] *n* dedaleira *f.*
foxhole ['fɒkshəʊl] *n* **-1.** [for soldier] trincheira *f* **-2.** [for animal] toca *f* de raposa.
foxhound ['fɒkshaʊnd] *n* cão *m* de caça à raposa.
foxhunt ['fɒkshʌnt] *n* caça *f* à raposa.
foxhunting ['fɒks,hʌntɪŋ] *n (U)* caça *f* à raposa.
fox terrier *n* fox terrier *m.*
foxy ['fɒksɪ] *adj* [sexy] sexy.
foyer ['fɔɪeɪ] *n* **-1.** [of hotel, theatre] saguão *m* **-2.** *US* [of house] vestíbulo *m.*
FP *n* **-1.** (*abbr of* **former pupil**) ex-aluno *m*, -na *f.* **-2.** *US* (*abbr of* **fireplug**) hidrante *m.*
FPA (*abbr of* **Family Planning Association**) *n associação britânica que oferece serviço de planejamento familiar.*
fr. (*abbr of* **franc**) franco *m.*
Fr. (*abbr of* **father**) Pe.
fracas ['frækɑ:, *US* 'freɪkəs] (*UK pl inv, US pl* **fracases**) *n* rixa *f.*
fraction ['frækʃn] *n* **-1.** [gen] fração *f* **-2.** [a little bit]: **it's a ~ too big** é um pouquinho maior.
fractionally ['frækʃnəlɪ] *adv* levemente.
fractious ['frækʃəs] *adj* irritadiço(ça).
fracture ['fræktʃə^r] MED <> *n* fratura *f.* <> *vt* fraturar.
fragile ['frædʒaɪl] *adj* frágil.
fragility [frə'dʒɪlətɪ] *n* fragilidade *f.*
fragment [*n* 'frægmənt, *vb* 'frægment] <> *n* fragmento *m.* <> *vi* fragmentar-se.
fragmentary ['frægməntrɪ] *adj* fragmentário(ria).
fragmented [fræg'mentɪd] *adj* fragmentado(da).
fragrance ['freɪgrəns] *n* fragrância *f.*
fragrant ['freɪgrənt] *adj* perfumado(da).
frail [freɪl] *adj* frágil.
frailty ['freɪltɪ] (*pl* **-ies**) *n* **-1.** *(U)* [gen] fragilidade *f* **-2.** [imperfection] fraqueza *f.*
frame [freɪm] <> *n* **-1.** [of picture] moldura *f* **-2.** [of glasses] armação *f* **-3.** [structure - of door] marco *m*; [- of boat] estrutura *f*; [- of window, bicycle] quadro *m*; [- of bed, chair] armação *f* **-4.** [physique] constituição *f.* <> *vt* **-1.** [put in a frame] emoldurar **-2.** *fig* [surround] cercar **-3.** [formulate, express] expressar **-4.** *inf* [falsely incriminate] incriminar falsamente.
frame of mind *n* estado *m* de espírito.
framework ['freɪmwɜ:k] *n* **-1.** [physical structure] estrutura *f* **-2.** [basis] base *f.*
France [frɑ:ns] *n* França; **in ~** na França.
franchise ['fræntʃaɪz] *n* **-1.** POL [right to vote] direito *m* de voto **-2.** COMM [right to sell goods] franquia *f.*
franchisee [,fræntʃaɪ'zi:] *n* franqueado *m*, -da *f.*
franchisor *n* franqueador *m*, -ra *f.*
frank [fræŋk] <> *adj* franco(ca). <> *vt* franquear.
Frankfurt ['fræŋkfət] *n*: **~ (am Main)** Frankfurt (am Main); **in ~** em Frankfurt.
frankfurter ['fræŋkfɜ:tə^r] *n* salsicha *f* defumada.
frankincense ['fræŋkɪnsens] *n (U)* olíbano *m.*
franking machine ['fræŋkɪŋ-] *n* máquina *f* de selagem.
frankly ['fræŋklɪ] *adv* francamente.
frankness ['fræŋknɪs] *n (U)* franqueza *f.*
frantic ['fræntɪk] *adj* frenético(ca); **she was ~** ela estava fora de si.
frantically ['fræntɪklɪ] *adv* **-1.** [in an upset manner] furiosamente **-2.** [busily] ativamente.
fraternal [frə'tɜ:nl] *adj* **-1.** [brotherly] fraterno(na) **-2.** [friendly] fraternal.
fraternity [frə'tɜ:nətɪ] (*pl* **-ies**) *n* **-1.** [community] comunidade *f* **-2.** *US* [of students] fraternidade *f* **-3.** *(U)* [friendship] fraternidade *f.*

FRATERNITY

Os clubes de estudantes, masculinos (***fraternities***) e femininos (***sororities***), são elementos de destaque na vida universitária norte-americana. Muitos estudantes associam-se a eles desde o primeiro ano de faculdade, permanecendo membros desses clubes mesmo após o término dos estudos. Cada clube possui seu próprio nome, composto de letras do alfabeto grego, e tem sua sede no edifício em que reside a maioria de seus membros. Os clubes realizam trabalhos para instituições de assistência social, mas são famosos também por suas bebedeiras e cerimônias secretas. Algumas universidades proibiram essas cerimônias de iniciação, porque elas promoviam trotes cruéis e perigosos.

fraternize, -ise ['frætənaɪz] *vi* [be on friendly terms] confraternizar; **to ~ with sb** confraternizar-se com alguém.
fraud [frɔ:d] *n* **-1.** *(U)* [crime] fraude *f* **-2.** [deceitful act] trapaça *f* **-3.** *pej* [impostor] impostor *m*, -ra *f.*
fraudulent ['frɔ:djʊlənt] *adj* fraudulento(ta).
fraught [frɔ:t] *adj* **-1.** [full]: **~ with sthg** repleto(ta) de algo **-2.** *UK* [frantic] preocupado(da); **a ~ weekend** um fim de semana enlouquecido.
fray [freɪ] <> *vi* **-1.** [clothing, fabric, rope] esfiapar-se **-2.** *fig* [nerves, temper] desgastar-se. <> *n literary* rixa *f.*
frayed [freɪd] *adj* **-1.** [clothing, fabric, rope] esfiapado(-da) **-2.** *fig* [nerves, temper] desgastado(da).
frazzled ['fræzld] *adj inf* [harassed] estafado(da).
FRB (*abbr of* **Federal Reserve Board**) *n fundo de reserva federal norte-americano.*
FRCP (*abbr of* **Fellow of the Royal College of Physicians**) *membro do Royal College of Physicians, associação britânica de médicos.*
FRCS (*abbr of* **Fellow of the Royal College of Surgeons**) *membro do Royal College of Surgeons, associação britânica de cirurgiões.*
freak [fri:k] <> *adj* imprevisto(ta). <> *n* **-1.** [strange creature - in appearance] aberração *f*; [- in behaviour] excêntrico *m*, -ca *f* **-2.** [unusual event] anomalia *f* **-3.** *inf* [fanatic] fanático *m*, -ca *f.*
◆ **freak out** *inf* <> *vi* **-1.** [get angry] baratinar-se **-2.** [panic] apavorar-se. <> *vt sep* baratinar.
freakish ['fri:kɪʃ] *adj* [strange] esquisito(ta).
freckle ['frekl] *n* sarda *f.*

free [friː] (*compar* **freer**, *superl* **freest**, *pt* & *pp* **freed**) ◇ *adj* **-1.** [gen] livre; **to be ~ to do sthg** ser livre para fazer algo; **feel ~!** sinta-se à vontade!; **to set sb/sthg ~** libertar alguém/algo; **to give sb a ~ hand** dar a alguém carta branca **-2.** [not paid for] grátis; **~ of charge** sem despesas **-3.** [unattached] solto(ta) **-4.** [not affected by]: **~ of additives** sem aditivos; **~ from worry** sem preocupação **-5.** [generous]: **to be ~ with sthg** [money] ser generoso(sa) com algo; [advice, affection] ser generoso(sa) em algo. ◇ *adv* **-1.** [without payment] gratuitamente; **for ~** de graça **-2.** [without restraint] livremente. ◇ *vt* **-1.** [release] pôr em liberdade, libertar **-2.** [make available] liberar **-3.** [remove] livrar; **to ~ sb of** OR **from sthg** livrar alguém de algo.

-free [friː] *suffix*: **a salt-~ diet** uma dieta sem sal.

freebie [ˈfriːbɪ] *n inf* brinde *m*.

freedom [ˈfriːdəm] *n* liberdade *f*; **~ from sthg** ausência *f* de algo; **the right to ~ from hunger** o direito de não se passar fome.

freedom fighter *n* lutador *m*, -ra *f* pela liberdade.

free enterprise *n (U)* livre iniciativa *f*.

free-fall *n (U)* queda *f* livre.

Freefone® [ˈfriːfəʊn] *n UK (U)* discagem *f* gratuita.

free-for-all *n* **-1.** [brawl] tumulto *m* generalizado **-2.** [argument] discussão *f* generalizada.

free gift *n* oferta *f*.

freehand [ˈfriːhænd] ◇ *adj* à mão livre. ◇ *adv* à mão livre.

freehold [ˈfriːhəʊld] ◇ *adv*: **to buy ~** comprar como propriedade alodial. ◇ *n* propriedade *f* alodial.

freeholder [ˈfriːhəʊldəʳ] *n* possuidor *m*, -ra *f* de propriedade alodial.

free house *n bar não-controlado por uma única cervejaria.*

free kick *n* tiro *m* livre; **to take a ~** bater OR cobrar um tiro livre.

freelance [ˈfriːlɑːns] ◇ *adj* frila, autônomo(ma). ◇ *adv* como frila. ◇ *n* frila *mf*, autônomo *m*, -ma *f*. ◇ *vi* trabalhar como frila OR autônomo(-ma).

freeloader [ˈfriːləʊdəʳ] *n inf* bicão *m*.

freely [ˈfriːlɪ] *adv* **-1.** [without constraint] livremente; **~ available** fácil de obter **-2.** [generously] generosamente.

freeman [ˈfriːmən] (*pl* **-men** [-mən]) *n* [citizen] cidadão *m* honorário.

free-market economy *n* economia *f* de livre mercado.

Freemason [ˈfriːˌmeɪsn] *n* maçom *m*.

Freemasonry [ˈfriːˌmeɪsnrɪ] *n* maçonaria *f*.

freemen [ˈfriːmən] *pl* ▷ **freeman**.

freephone [ˈfriːfəʊn] *n* = **freefone**.

freepost *n (U)* porte *m* pago.

free-range *adj UK* caipira; **~ eggs** ovos caipira.

free sample *n* amostra *f* grátis.

freesia [ˈfriːzjə] *n* frésia *f*.

free speech *n (U)* liberdade *f* de expressão.

freestanding [ˌfriːˈstændɪŋ] *adj* independente.

freestyle [ˈfriːstaɪl] *n* [in swimming] estilo *m* livre.

freethinker [ˌfriːˈθɪŋkəʳ] *n* livre-pensador *m*, -ra *f*.

free time *n* tempo *m* livre.

free trade *n (U)* livre comércio *m*.

freeway [ˈfriːweɪ] *n US* auto-estrada *f*.

freewheel [ˌfriːˈwiːl] *vi* **-1.** [cyclist] andar sem pedalar **-2.** [motorist] ir em ponto morto.

freewheeling [ˌfriːˈwiːlɪŋ] *adj inf* [style, attitude] liberal.

free will *n (U)* vontade *f* própria; **to do sthg of one's own ~** fazer algo por vontade própria.

free world *n*: **the ~** o mundo livre.

freeze [friːz] (*pt* **froze**, *pp* **frozen**) ◇ *vt* **-1.** [gen] congelar **-2.** [engine, lock] emperrar **-3.** [pipes] entupir. ◇ *vi* **-1.** [turn to ice] congelar-se **-2.** METEOR esfriar muito **-3.** [stop moving] parar **-4.** *inf* [be cold] congelar. ◇ *n* **-1.** [cold weather] frio *m* intenso **-2.** [of wages, prices] congelamento *m*.

◆ **freeze over** *vi* congelar *(na superfície)*.

◆ **freeze up** *vi* **-1.** [river, lake] congelar **-2.** [lock, engine] emperrar.

freeze-dried [-ˈdraɪd] *adj* congelado(da) a vácuo.

freeze frame *n* **-1.** [photograph] pose *f* **-2.** [on video] imagem *f* congelada.

freezer [ˈfriːzəʳ] *n* **-1.** [machine] freezer *m*, frízer *m* **-2.** [part of fridge] congelador *m*.

freezing [ˈfriːzɪŋ] ◇ *adj* gelado(da); **it's ~ in here** está um gelo aqui; **I'm ~** estou congelando. ◇ *n* congelamento *m*; **5 degrees below ~** *inf* 5 graus abaixo de zero.

freezing point *n* ponto *m* de congelamento.

freight [freɪt] *n (U)* [goods] carga *f*.

freight train *n* trem *m* de carga.

French [frentʃ] ◇ *adj* francês(esa). ◇ *n* francês *m*, -esa *f*. ◇ *npl*: **the ~** os franceses.

French bean *n* vagem *f*.

French bread *n (U)* pão *m* francês, bisnaga *f*.

French Canadian ◇ *adj* franco-canadense. ◇ *n* [person] franco-canadense *mf*.

French chalk *n (U)* giz *m* de alfaiate.

French doors *npl* = **French windows**.

French dressing *n* **-1.** [in UK] molho *m* vinagrete **-2.** [in US] molho *m* rosé.

French fries *npl esp US* batatas *fpl* fritas.

Frenchman [ˈfrentʃmən] (*pl* **-men** [-mən]) *n* francês *m*.

French polish *n (U)* verniz *m (para móveis)*.

French Riviera *n*: **the ~** a Riviera Francesa.

French stick *n UK* baguete *f*.

French toast *n (U)* rabanada *f*.

French windows *npl* janela *f* de batente.

Frenchwoman [ˈfrentʃˌwʊmən] (*pl* **-women** [ˌwɪmɪn]) *n* francesa *f*.

frenetic [frəˈnetɪk] *adj* frenético(ca).

frenzied [ˈfrenzɪd] *adj* agitado(da), incontrolável.

frenzy [ˈfrenzɪ] (*pl* **-ies**) *n* frenesi *m*.

frequency [ˈfriːkwənsɪ] (*pl* **-ies**) *n* frequência *f*.

frequency modulation *n (U)* freqüência *f* modulada.

frequent [*adj* ˈfriːkwənt, *vb* frɪˈkwent] ◇ *adj* freqüente. ◇ *vt* freqüentar.

frequently [ˈfriːkwəntlɪ] *adv* freqüentemente.

fresco [ˈfreskəʊ] (*pl* **-es** OR **-s**) *n* afresco *m*.

fresh [freʃ] ◇ *adj* **-1.** [gen] fresco(ca); **~ from**

recém-saído(da) de **-2.** [water] doce **-3.** [another] novo(va); **to make a ~ start** começar tudo de novo **-4.** [not tired] bem-disposto(ta) **-5.** [complexion] revigorado(da) **-6.** [refreshing] refrescante **-7.** [original] original **-8.** *inf dated* [cheeky] atrevido(da); **to get ~ with sb** ser atrevido(da) com alguém **-9.** [bright] vivo(va). <> *adv* [recently] recém-; **~ cut flowers** flores recém-cortadas; **to be ~ out of sthg** *inf* acabar de ficar sem algo.
freshen ['freʃn] <> *vt* [refresh] renovar. <> *vi* [wind] tornar-se mais frio (fria).
◆ **freshen up** <> *vt sep* **-1.** [person] refrescar **-2.** [room, house] tornar mais atrativo(va). <> *vi* [person] refrescar-se *(com água)*.
fresher ['freʃəʳ] *n UK inf* calouro *m*, -ra *f*.
freshly ['freʃlɪ] *adv* [recently] recentemente, recém-.
freshman ['freʃmən] (*pl* **-men** [-mən]) *n* calouro *m*.
freshness ['freʃnɪs] *n* **-1.** [gen] frescor *m* **-2.** [originality] originalidade *f*.
freshwater ['freʃˌwɔːtəʳ] *adj* de água doce.
fret [fret] (*pt* & *pp* **-ted**, *cont* **-ting**) *vi* [worry] preocupar-se.
fretful ['fretfʊl] *adj* irritadiço(ça); **a ~ night** uma noite agitada.
fretsaw ['fretsɔː] *n* serra *f* tico-tico.
Freudian *adj* freudiano(na); **~ slip** ato *m* falho.
FRG (*abbr of* **Federal Republic of Germany**) *n* RFA *f*.
Fri. (*abbr of* **Friday**) sex.
friar ['fraɪəʳ] *n* frei *m*.
friction ['frɪkʃn] *n (U)* **-1.** [rubbing] fricção *f* **-2.** [conflict] atrito *m*.
Friday ['fraɪdɪ] *n* sexta-feira *f*; *see also* **Saturday**.
fridge [frɪdʒ] *n esp UK* refrigerador *m*.
fridge-freezer *n UK* refrigerador *m* com freezer.
fried [fraɪd] <> *pt* & *pp* ▷ **fry**. <> *adj* frito(ta); **~ egg** ovo frito.
friend [frend] *n* amigo *m*, -ga *f*; **to be ~s (with sb)** ser amigo(ga) (de alguém); **to make ~s (with sb)** fazer amizade (com alguém).
friendless ['frendlɪs] *adj* sem amigos.
friendly ['frendlɪ] (*compar* **-ier**, *superl* **-iest**, *pl* **-ies**) <> *adj* **-1.** [kind, pleasant] amável; **to be ~ with sb** ser amigável com alguém **-2.** [not enemy] amigo(-ga) **-3.** [not serious] amistoso(sa). <> *n esp UK* SPORT amistoso *m*.
friendly society *n UK organização com a qual as pessoas contribuem regularmente e que lhes dá dinheiro quando se aposentam ou ficam doentes.*
friendship ['frendʃɪp] *n* **-1.** [between people] amizade *f* **-2.** [between countries] boas relações *fpl*.
fries [fraɪz] *npl* = **French fries**.
Friesian (cow) ['friːzjən-] *n* vaca *f* holandesa.
frieze [friːz] *n* friso *m*.
frigate ['frɪgət] *n* fragata *f*.
fright [fraɪt] *n* **-1.** *(U)* [fear] medo *m*; **to take ~** ter medo **-2.** [shock] susto *m*; **to give sb a ~** dar um susto em alguém.
frighten ['fraɪtn] *vt* assustar; **to ~ sb into doing sthg** forçar alguém a fazer algo por medo.
◆ **frighten away** *vt sep* espantar.
◆ **frighten off** *vt sep* espantar.
frightened ['fraɪtnd] *adj* amedrontado(da); **to be ~ of sthg/of doing sthg** ter medo de algo/de fazer algo.
frightening ['fraɪtnɪŋ] *adj* assustador(ra).
frightful ['fraɪtfʊl] *adj dated* horrendo(da).
frigid ['frɪdʒɪd] *adj* [sexually cold] frígido(da).
frill [frɪl] *n* **-1.** [decoration] babado *m* **-2.** *inf* [extra] frescura *f*.
frilly ['frɪlɪ] (*compar* **-ier**, *superl* **-iest**) *adj* com babados.
fringe [frɪndʒ] <> *n* **-1.** [gen] franja *f* **-2.** *fig* [edge] orla *f*, margem *f* **-3.** *fig* [extreme] facção *f*. <> *vt* [border] cercar.
fringe benefit *n* benefício *m* adicional.
fringe group *n* facção *f*.
fringe theatre *n UK* teatro *m* de vanguarda.
Frisbee® ['frɪzbɪ] *n* jogo *m* de Frisbee®.
Frisian Islands ['frɪʒən-] *npl*: **the ~** as Ilhas Frísias.
frisk [frɪsk] <> *vt* [search] revistar. <> *vi* [play] brincar.
frisky ['frɪskɪ] (*compar* **-ier**, *superl* **-iest**) *adj inf* brincalhão(lhona).
fritter ['frɪtəʳ] *n* CULIN bolinho *m* frito.
◆ **fritter away** *vt sep* desperdiçar; **to ~ money/time away on sthg** desperdiçar dinheiro/tempo com algo.
frivolity [frɪ'vɒlətɪ] (*pl* **-ies**) *n* frivolidade *f*.
frivolous ['frɪvələs] *adj* frívolo(la).
frizzy ['frɪzɪ] (*compar* **-ier**, *superl* **-iest**) *adj* crespo(pa).
fro [frəʊ] *adv* ▷ **to**.
frock [frɒk] *n dated* vestido *m*.
frog [frɒg] *n* [animal] rã *f*; **to have a ~ in one's throat** estar com a garganta irritada.
frogman ['frɒgmən] (*pl* **-men** [-mən]) *n* homem-rã *m*.
frogmarch ['frɒgmɑːtʃ] *vt* levar à força.
frogspawn ['frɒgspɔːn] *n (U)* ova *f* de rã.
frolic ['frɒlɪk] (*pt* & *pp* **-ked**, *cont* **-king**) <> *n* brincadeira *f*. <> *vi* brincar.
from [frɒm] *prep* **-1.** [expressing origin, source] de; **I'm ~ California** sou da Califórnia; **the train ~ Chicago** o trem de Chicago; **I bought it ~ a supermarket** comprei-o num supermercado **-2.** [expressing removal, deduction] de; **away ~ home** longe de casa; **to take sthg (away) ~ sb** tirar algo de alguém; **10% will be deducted ~ the total** será deduzido 10% do total **-3.** [expressing distance] de; **five miles ~ here** a oito quilômetros daqui; **it's not far ~ here** não é longe daqui **-4.** [expressing position] de; **~ here you can see the valley** daqui se vê o vale **-5.** [expressing what sthg is made with] de; **it's made ~ stone** é feito de pedra **-6.** [expressing starting time] desde; **~ the moment you arrived** desde que chegou; **~ now on** de agora em diante; **~ next year** a partir do próximo ano; **open ~ nine to five** aberto das nove às cinco **-7.** [expressing change] de; **the price has gone up ~ $1 to $2** o preço subiu de um dólar para dois; **to translate ~ German into English** traduzir do alemão para o inglês **-8.** [expressing range] de; **it could take ~ two to six months** pode levar de dois a seis meses **-9.** [as a result of] de; **I'm tired ~ walking**

estou cansado de andar **-10.** [expressing protection] de; **sheltered ~ the wind** protegido do vento **-11.** [in comparisons]: **different ~** diferente de.

frond ['frɒnd] *n* fronde *m*.

front [frʌnt] ◇ *n* **-1.** [gen] frente *f*; **at the ~ of** à frente de **-2.** MIL front *m*, frente *f* **-3.** [promenade]: **(sea) ~** orla *f* marítima **-4.** [outward appearance] fachada *f* **-5.** [of book] capa *f*. ◇ *adj* [at front] da frente; **~ page** primeira página; **~ cover** capa. ◇ *vt* **-1.** [stand before] ser de frente para **-2.** [TV programme] estar à frente de. ◇ *vi*: **to ~ onto sthg** dar de frente para algo.

◆ **in front** *adv* **-1.** [further forward] na frente **-2.** [winning]: **to be in ~** estar na frente.

◆ **in front of** *prep* **-1.** [close to front of] em frente de **-2.** [in the presence of] na frente de.

frontage ['frʌntɪdʒ] *n* fachada *f* principal.

frontal ['frʌntl] *adj* frontal.

frontbench ['frʌnt'bentʃ] *n cadeiras dianteiras no parlamento britânico nas quais se sentam os líderes do governo e da oposição.*

front desk *n* recepção *f*.

front door *n* porta *f* da frente.

frontier ['frʌn,tɪə^r^, US frʌn'tɪər] *n* **-1.** [border] fronteira *f* **-2.** *fig* [furthest limit] fronteira *f*.

frontispiece ['frʌntɪspi:s] *n* frontispício *m*.

front line *n*: **the ~** a linha de frente.

front man *n* **-1.** [of group] representante *mf* **-2.** [of programme] apresentador *m*, -ra *f*.

front-page *adj* de primeira página.

front room *n* sala *f* de estar.

front-runner *n* favorito *m*, -ta *f*.

front-wheel drive *n* **-1.** [vehicle] veículo *m* com tração dianteira **-2.** [system] tração *f* dianteira.

frost [frɒst] ◇ *n* **-1.** *(U)* [layer of ice] geada *f* **-2.** [weather] frio *m* intenso. ◇ *vi*: **to ~ over** OR **up** cobrir-se de geada.

frostbite ['frɒstbaɪt] *n (U)* enregelamento *m*.

frostbitten ['frɒst,bɪtn] *adj* enregelado(da).

frosted ['frɒstɪd] *adj* **-1.** [opaque] fosco(ca) **-2.** **US** CULIN coberto(ta) com glacê.

frosting ['frɒstɪŋ] *n (U)* **US** CULIN cobertura *f (de glacê)*.

frosty ['frɒstɪ] (*compar* **-ier**, *superl* **-iest**) *adj* **-1.** [very cold] gelado(da) **-2.** [covered with frost] coberto(ta) de geada **-3.** *fig* [unfriendly] glacial.

froth [frɒθ] ◇ *n (U)* espuma *f*. ◇ *vi* espumar.

frothy ['frɒθɪ] (*compar* **-ier**, *superl* **-iest**) *adj* [covered in froth] espumante.

frown [fraʊn] ◇ *n* cenho *m*. ◇ *vi* franzir as sobrancelhas.

◆ **frown (up)on** *vt fus* não ver com bons olhos.

froze [frəʊz] *pt* ▷ **freeze**.

frozen [frəʊzn] ◇ *pp* ▷ **freeze**. ◇ *adj* **-1.** [gen] congelado(da) **-2.** [feeling very cold] gelado(da) **-3.** *fig* [rigid]: **~ with fear** gelado(da) de medo **-4.** [prices, salaries, assets] congelado(da).

FRS *n* **-1.** (*abbr of* **Fellow of the Royal Society**) *membro da Royal Society, organização britânica para pesquisa científica.* **-2.** (*abbr of* **Federal Reserve System**) ≃ BACEN *m*.

frugal ['fru:gl] *adj* **-1.** [small] frugal **-2.** [careful] regrado(da).

fruit [fru:t] (*pl inv* OR **fruits**) ◇ *n* **-1.** [food] fruta *f* **-2.** *fig* [result] fruto *m*; **to bear ~** dar resultados. ◇ *comp* de frutas; **a ~ tree** uma árvore frutífera. ◇ *vi* frutificar.

fruitcake ['fru:tkeɪk] *n* **-1.** bolo *m* com passas **-2.** *inf* [mad person] maluco *m*, -ca *f*.

fruiterer ['fru:tərə^r^] *n* **UK** fruteiro *m*, -ra *f*; **~'s (shop)** fruteira *f*.

fruitful ['fru:tfʊl] *adj* [successful] produtivo(va), proveitoso(sa).

fruition [fru:'ɪʃn] *n (U)*: **to come to ~** realizar-se.

fruit juice *n* suco *m* de fruta.

fruitless ['fru:tlɪs] *adj* [wasted] infrutífero(ra), vão (vã).

fruit machine *n* **UK** caça-níqueis *m inv*.

fruit salad *n* salada *f* de frutas.

frumpy ['frʌmpɪ] (*compar* **-ier**, *superl* **-iest**) *adj inf* antiquado(da).

frustrate [frʌ'streɪt] *vt* frustrar.

frustrated [frʌ'streɪtɪd] *adj* frustrado(da).

frustrating [frʌ'streɪtɪŋ] *adj* frustrante.

frustration [frʌ'streɪʃn] *n* frustração *f*.

fry [fraɪ] (*pt* & *pp* **fried**) ◇ *vt* [food] fritar. ◇ *vi* [food] fritar.

frying pan ['fraɪɪŋ-] *n* frigideira *f*; **to jump out of the ~ into the fire** saltar da frigideira e cair no fogo, ir de mal a pior.

ft. *abbr of* **foot, feet**.

FT (*abbr of* **Financial Times**) *n jornal diário britânico de economia.*

FTC (*abbr of* **Federal Trade Commission**) *n órgão norte-americano responsável por se fazer cumprir a legislação sobre monopólios.*

FTSE (*abbr of* **Financial Times Stock Exchange**) *n* FTSE *m*; **the ~ index** o índice FTSE; **the ~ 100** *as ações das 100 maiores empresas britânicas ponderadas com base em seu valor de mercado.*

fuchsia ['fju:ʃə] *n* fúcsia *f*.

fuck [fʌk] *vulg* ◇ *vt* [have sex with] trepar OR foder com. ◇ *vi* trepar, foder. ◇ *excl* merda!

◆ **fuck off** *vulg* ◇ *vi* foder-se. ◇ *excl* vá se foder!

fucking ['fʌkɪŋ] *adj vulg* [for emphasis] de merda; **a ~ idiot** um idiota de merda.

fuddled ['fʌdld] *adj* [confused] confuso(sa).

fuddy-duddy ['fʌdɪ,dʌdɪ] (*pl* **fuddy-duddies**) *n inf* careta *mf*.

fudge [fʌdʒ] ◇ *n (U)* [sweet] fondant *m*, *doce de açúcar, leite e manteiga.* ◇ *vt* **-1.** *inf* [falsify, tamper with] falsificar **-2.** [avoid, confuse] escapar-se de.

fuel [fjʊəl] (**UK** *pt* & *pp* **-led**, *cont* **-ling**, **US** *pt* & *pp* **-ed**, *cont* **-ing**) ◇ *n* combustível *m*; **to add ~ to the fire** *fig* botar lenha na fogueira. ◇ *vt* **-1.** [supply with fuel] abastecer **-2.** [increase] aumentar.

fuel cell *n* célula *f* a combustível.

fuel pump *n* bomba *f* de combustível.

fuel tank *n* tanque *m* de combustível.

fugitive ['fju:dʒətɪv] *n* fugitivo *m*, -va *f*.

fugue [fju:g] *n* MUS fuga *f*.

fulcrum ['fʊlkrəm] (*pl* **-crums** OR **-cra** [-krə]) *n* fulcro *m*.

fulfil (*pt* & *pp* **-led**, *cont* **-ling**), **fulfill** *US* [fʊl'fɪl] *vt* **-1.** [carry out] cumprir; **to ~ one's role** desempenhar seu papel **-2.** [satisfy] satisfazer; **to ~ o.s.** realizar-se.
fulfilling [fʊl'fɪlɪŋ] *adj* gratificante.
fulfilment, fulfillment *US* [fʊl'fɪlmənt] *n (U)* **-1.** [satisfaction] satisfação *f* **-2.** [carrying through - of ambition, dream] realização *f*; [- of role] desempenho *m*; [- of need, promise] cumprimento *m*.
full [fʊl] ◇ *adj* **-1.** [gen] cheio (cheia); **~ of** cheio (cheia) de **-2.** [with food] satisfeito(ta) **-3.** [complete - employment, use] integral; [- explanation, name, day, recovery] completo(ta), efetivo(va); [- member, professor] titular **-4.** [maximum] máximo(ma) **-5.** [sound] forte **-6.** [flavour] rico(ca) **-7.** [plump - mouth] cheio (cheia); [- figure] voluptuoso(sa) **-8.** [ample, wide] largo(ga). ◇ *adv* **-1.** [directly] em cheio **-2.** [very]: **to know ~ well that ...** saber muito bem que ... **-3.** [at maximum] no máximo. ◇ *n*: **in ~** [payment] na totalidade; [write] por extenso; **to the ~** ao máximo.
fullback ['fʊlbæk] *n* zagueiro *m*, -ra *f*.
full-blooded [-'blʌdɪd] *adj* **-1.** [pure-blooded] de raça pura **-2.** [wholehearted] vigoroso(sa).
full-blown [-'bləʊn] *adj* bem-caracterizado(da); **a ~ disease** uma doença bem-desenvolvida.
full board *n (U)* diária *f* completa.
full-bodied [-'bɒdɪd] *adj* [wine] encorpado(da).
full dress *n (U)* traje *m* a rigor.
full-face *adj* [portrait, photo] de frente.
full-fashioned *adj US* = **fully-fashioned**.
full-fledged *adj US* = **fully-fledged**.
full-frontal *adj* [photo, appearance] em nu frontal.
full-grown [-'grəʊn] *adj* adulto(ta).
full house *n* [at show, event] casa *f* cheia.
full-length ◇ *adj* **-1.** [portrait, mirror] de corpo inteiro **-2.** [dress, curtains] comprido(da) **-3.** [novel, film] extenso(sa); **a ~ film** um longa-metragem. ◇ *adv* ao comprido, completamente.
full moon *n* lua *f* cheia.
fullness ['fʊlnɪs] *n* **-1.** [of details, information] riqueza *f* **-2.** [of face, figure, lips] largura *f* **-3.** [of skirt, sleeves] comprimento *m* **-4.** *phr*: **in the ~ of time** no momento oportuno.
full-page *adj* de página inteira.
full-scale *adj* **-1.** [model, drawing, copy] em tamanho natural **-2.** [inquiry] completo(ta) **-3.** [war] total **-4.** [attack] maciço(ça).
full-size(d) *adj* **-1.** [life-size] de tamanho natural **-2.** [adult] adulto(ta) **-3.** *US AUT*: **~ car** carro *m* de passeio.
full stop ◇ *n* ponto *m* final. ◇ *adv UK* ponto final.
full time *n UK SPORT* final *m* de jogo.
◆ **full-time** ◇ *adj* de tempo integral. ◇ *adv* em tempo integral.
full up *adj* **-1.** [after meal] cheio(cheia) **-2.** [bus, train] lotado(da).
fully ['fʊlɪ] *adv* **-1.** [completely] completamente, totalmente; **to be ~ booked** estar com as reservas esgotadas **-2.** [in detail] em detalhes.
fully-fashioned *UK*, **full-fashioned** *US* [-'fæʃnd] *adj* justo(ta); **~ tights** meia-calça *f* justa.
fully-fledged *UK*, **full-fledged** *US* [-'fledʒd] *adj fig* [doctor, lawyer] experiente.
fulness ['fʊlnɪs] *n* = **fullness**.
fulsome ['fʊlsəm] *adj* exagerado(da).
fumble ['fʌmbl] *vi* tatear; **to ~ for sthg** procurar desajeitadamente por algo; **he ~d in his pockets for his keys** ele vasculhou os bolsos desajeitadamente à procura das chaves.
fume [fjuːm] *vi* [with anger] fumegar.
◆ **fumes** *npl* [gas - from car, fire] fumaça *f*; [- of paint] vapor *m*.
fumigate ['fjuːmɪgeɪt] *vt* desinfetar.
fun [fʌn] ◇ *n (U)* **-1.** [pleasure, amusement] diversão *f*; **we really had ~ at the party** nós realmente nos divertimos na festa; **what ~!** que divertido!; **for ~, for the ~ of it** por prazer, por brincadeira **-2.** [playfulness] alegria *f* **-3.** [ridicule]: **to make ~ of sb** caçoar de alguém; **to poke ~ at sb** zombar de alguém. ◇ *adj* divertido(da).
function ['fʌŋkʃn] ◇ *n* **-1.** [gen] função *f* **-2.** [formal social event] cerimônia *f*. ◇ *vi* funcionar; **to ~ as sthg** funcionar como algo.
functional ['fʌŋkʃnəl] *adj* **-1.** [furniture, design] funcional **-2.** [machine, system] operacional.
functionary ['fʌŋkʃnərɪ] (*pl* **-ies**) *n* funcionário *m* público, funcionária *f* pública.
function key *n COMPUT* tecla *f* de função.
fund [fʌnd] ◇ *n* **-1.** [amount of money] fundo *m* **-2.** *fig* [reserve] reserva *f*. ◇ *vt* financiar.
◆ **funds** *npl* recursos *mpl*.
fundamental [ˌfʌndə'mentl] *adj* **-1.** [basic] básico(-ca), fundamental **-2.** [vital] fundamental; **~ to sthg** fundamental para algo.
◆ **fundamentals** *npl* fundamentos *mpl*.
fundamentalism [ˌfʌndə'mentəlɪzm] *n (U)* fundamentalismo *m*.
fundamentally [ˌfʌndə'mentəlɪ] *adv* **-1.** [basically] basicamente, fundamentalmente **-2.** [radically] radicalmente.
funding ['fʌndɪŋ] *n (U)* recursos *mpl*.
fund-raising [-ˌreɪzɪŋ] ◇ *n (U)* angariação *f* de fundos. ◇ *comp* de angariação de fundos.
funeral ['fjuːnərəl] *n* funeral *m*.
funeral director *n* agente *mf* funerário, -ria.
funeral parlour *n* casa *f* funerária.
funeral service *n* cerimônia *f* de enterro.
funereal [fjuː'nɪərɪəl] *adj* fúnebre.
funfair ['fʌnfeəʳ] *n* parque *m* de diversões.
fungus ['fʌŋgəs] (*pl* **-gi** [-gaɪ], **-es**) *n BOT* fungo *m*.
funk [fʌŋk] *n (U)* **-1.** *MUS* funk *m* **-2.** *dated* [fear] pavor *m*.
funky ['fʌŋkɪ] (*compar* **-ier**, *superl* **-iest**) *adj MUS* ritmado(da), vibrante.
funnel ['fʌnl] (*UK pt* & *pp* **-led**, *cont* **-ling**, *US pt* & *pp* **-ed**, *cont* **-ing**) ◇ *n* **-1.** [tube] funil *m* **-2.** [on ship] chaminé *f*. ◇ *vt* **-1.** [liquid] passar por funil **-2.** [crowd, money] encaminhar. ◇ *vi* [crowd, people] encaminhar-se.
funnily ['fʌnɪlɪ] *adv* [strangely] estranhamente; **~ enough** curiosamente.
funny ['fʌnɪ] (*compar* **-ier**, *superl* **-iest**) *adj* **-1.** [amusing] engraçado(da) **-2.** [odd] esquisito(ta) **-3.** [ill]: **to feel ~** não se sentir bem.

◆ **funnies** *npl US* quadrinhos *mpl.*
funny bone *n* osso *m* do cotovelo.
funny farm *n esp US inf hum* pinel *f*, manicômio *m.*
fun run *n maratona que tem por objetivo angariar recursos para instituições de caridade.*
fur [fɜːʳ] *n* **-1.** [on animal] pêlo *m* **-2.** [garment] pele *f.*
fur coat *n* casaco *m* de pele.
furious ['fjʊərɪəs] *adj* **-1.** [very angry] furioso(sa) **-2.** [violent] violento(ta).
furiously ['fjʊərɪəslɪ] *adv* **-1.** [angrily] furiosamente **-2.** [fight, work, drive] violentamente.
furled [fɜːld] *adj* dobrado(da).
furlong ['fɜːlɒŋ] *n medida correspondente a um oitavo de milha.*
furnace ['fɜːnɪs] *n* [fire] fornalha *f.*
furnish ['fɜːnɪʃ] *vt* **-1.** [fit out] mobiliar **-2.** *fml* [provide] fornecer; **to ~ sb with sthg** fornecer algo a alguém.
furnished ['fɜːnɪʃt] *adj* [fitted out] mobiliado(da).
furnishings ['fɜːnɪʃɪŋz] *npl* mobiliário *m.*
furniture ['fɜːnɪtʃəʳ] *n (U)* móvel *m.*
furniture polish *n* lustrador *m* de móveis.
furore *UK* [fjʊ'rɔːrɪ], **furor** *US* ['fjʊrɔːr] *n* furor *m.*
furrier ['fʌrɪəʳ] *n* peleiro *m*, -ra *f.*
furrow ['fʌrəʊ] *n* **-1.** [in field] sulco *m* **-2.** [on forehead] ruga *f.*
furrowed ['fʌrəʊd] *adj* **-1.** [field, land] lavrado(da) **-2.** [brow] enrugado(da).
furry ['fɜːrɪ] (*compar* **-ier**, *superl* **-iest**) *adj* **-1.** [animal] peludo(da) **-2.** [material, toy] de pelúcia.
further ['fɜːðəʳ] ◇ *compar* ▷ **far.** ◇ *adv* **-1.** [gen] mais adiante; **how much ~ is it?** a que distância fica?; **~ on/back** mais adiante/atrás **-2.** [complicate, develop, enquire] mais; **to take sth ~** levar algo adiante; **to go ~** ir adiante; **this mustn't go any ~** isso tem que ficar entre nós **-3.** [in addition] além disso. ◇ *adj* adicional, novo(va); **until ~ notice** até novas ordens. ◇ *vt* [career, cause, aims] impulsionar.
◆ **further to** *prep fml* com referência a.
further education *n UK educação para adultos após deixar a escola excluindo-se a universidade.*
furthermore [ˌfɜːðə'mɔːʳ] *adv* além do mais, além disso.
furthermost ['fɜːðəməʊst] *adj* mais longe.
furthest ['fɜːðɪst] ◇ *superl* ▷ **far.** ◇ *adj* **-1.** [in distance] mais afastado(da) **-2.** [greatest] maior. ◇ *adv* **-1.** [in distance] mais longe **-2.** [to greatest degree, extent] maior.
furtive ['fɜːtɪv] *adj* furtivo(va).
furtively ['fɜːtɪvlɪ] *adv* furtivamente.
fury ['fjʊərɪ] *n* fúria *f*; **in a ~** num acesso de fúria.
fuse *esp UK*, **fuze** *US* [fjuːz] ◇ *n* **-1.** *ELEC* fusível *m* **-2.** [of bomb, firework] detonador *m.* ◇ *vt* **-1.** [gen] fundir **-2.** *ELEC* queimar. ◇ *vi* **-1.** [gen] fundir-se **-2.** *ELEC* queimar.
fusebox *n* caixa *f* de fusíveis.
fused [fjuːzd] *adj ELEC* [fitted with a fuse] com fusível.
fuselage ['fjuːzəlɑːʒ] *n* fuselagem *f.*
fuse wire *n* fio *m* de chumbo *(para fusível).*
fusillade [ˌfjuːzə'leɪd] *n* fuzilaria *f.*
fusion ['fjuːʒn] *n* fusão *f.*
fuss [fʌs] ◇ *n* [bother, agitation] alvoroço *m*; **to make a ~** fazer um estardalhaço; **to kick up** *OR* **to make a ~ about sthg** causar *OR* fazer confusão por algo; **to make a ~ of sb** *UK* tratar alguém com atenção. ◇ *vi* [become agitated] alvoroçar-se.
◆ **fuss over** *vt fus* alvoroçar-se com.
fusspot ['fʌspɒt] *n inf* exagerado *m*, -da *f.*
fussy ['fʌsɪ] (*compar* **-ier**, *superl* **-iest**) *adj* **-1.** [fastidious] exigente **-2.** [over-ornate] exagerado(da).
fusty ['fʌstɪ] (*compar* **-ier**, *superl* **-iest**) *adj* **-1.** [room, clothes] com cheiro de mofo **-2.** [person, idea, attitude] antiquado(da).
futile ['fjuːtaɪl] *adj* fútil.
futility [fjuː'tɪlətɪ] *n (U)* futilidade *f.*
futon ['fuːtɒn] *n colchão japonês.*
future ['fjuːtʃəʳ] ◇ *n* **-1.** [time ahead] futuro *m*; **in (the) ~** no futuro **-2.** *GRAMM*: **~ (tense)** futuro *m.* ◇ *adj* futuro(ra).
◆ **futures** *npl COMM* mercado *m* de futuros.
futuristic [ˌfjuːtʃə'rɪstɪk] *adj* [design] futurístico(ca).
fuze *n*, *vt* & *vi US* = **fuse.**
fuzz [fʌz] *n* **-1.** [hair] penugem *f* **-2.** *inf* [police]: **the ~** os tiras.
fuzzy ['fʌzɪ] (*compar* **-ier**, *superl* **-iest**) *adj* **-1.** [hair] encrespado(da) **-2.** [image, ideas] difuso(sa).
fwd. (*abbr of* **forward**) encaminhar.
fwy (*abbr of* **freeway**) *US* auto-estrada *f.*
FY (*abbr of* **fiscal year**) *n* **-1.** *US* ano *m* fiscal. **-2.** (*abbr of* **financial year**) *UK* ano *m* fiscal.
FYI (*abbr of* **for your information**) para sua informação.

G

g[1] (*pl* **g's** *OR* **gs**), **G** (*pl* **G's** *OR* **Gs**) [dʒiː] *n* [letter] g, G *m.*
◆ **G** ◇ *n MUS* sol *m.* ◇ **-1.** (*abbr of* **good**) B *m* **-2.** [film certificate] *US* (*abbr of* **general (audience)**) censura *f* livre.
g[2] **-1.** (*abbr of* **gram**) g **-2.** (*abbr of* **gravity**) G.
GA *abbr of* **Georgia.**
gab [gæb] *n* ▷ **gift.**
gabardine [ˌgæbə'diːn] *n* **-1.** *(U)* [material] gabardine *f* **-2.** [raincoat] gabardina *f.*
gabble ['gæbl] ◇ *vt* tagarelar. ◇ *vi* tagarelar. ◇ *n* tagarelice *f.*
gable ['geɪbl] *n* oitão *m.*
Gabon [gæ'bɒn] *n* Gabão; **in ~** no Gabão.
Gabonese [ˌgæbɒ'niːz] ◇ *adj* gabonense. ◇ *npl*: **the ~** os gabonenses.

gad ◆ **gad about** (*pt* & *pp* **-ded**, *cont* **-ding**) *vi inf* badalar.

gadget ['gædʒɪt] *n* aparelho *m*.

gadgetry ['gædʒɪtrɪ] *n (U)* aparelhagem *f*.

Gaelic ['geɪlɪk] ◇ *adj* gaélico(ca). ◇ *n* gaélico *m*, -ca *f*.

gaffe [gæf] *n* gafe *f*.

gaffer ['gæfə^r] *n UK inf* [boss] chefe *mf*.

gag [gæg] (*pt* & *pp* **-ged**, *cont* **-ging**) ◇ *n* **-1.** [for mouth] mordaça *f* **-2.** *inf* [joke] piada *f*. ◇ *vt* [put gag on] amordaçar. ◇ *vi* amordaçar.

gage *n* & *vt US* = **gauge**.

gaiety ['geɪətɪ] *n (U)* alegria *f*.

gaily ['geɪlɪ] *adv* **-1.** [cheerfully] alegremente **-2.** [without thinking] despreocupadamente.

gain [geɪn] ◇ *n* **-1.** [profit] ganho *m* **-2.** *(U)* [making a profit] lucro *m* **-3.** [increase] aumento *m*. ◇ *vt* **-1.** [gen] ganhar **-2.** [subj: watch, clock] adiantar-se; **my watch has ~ed ten minutes** meu relógio adiantou-se em dez minutos. ◇ *vi* **-1.** [increase]: **to ~ in sthg** crescer em algo **-2.** [profit] lucrar; **to ~ from/by sthg** lucrar com algo **-3.** [watch, clock] adiantar-se.

◆ **gain on** *vt fus* aproximar-se de.

gainful ['geɪnfʊl] *adj fml* [activity, employment] lucrativo(va), vantajoso(sa).

gainfully ['geɪnfʊlɪ] *adv fml* vantajosamente.

gainsay [ˌgeɪn'seɪ] (*pt* & *pp* **-said**) *vt fml* contradizer.

gait [geɪt] *n* maneira *f* de andar.

gaiters ['geɪtəz] *npl* polainas *fpl*.

gal. *abbr of* **gallon**.

gala ['gɑːlə] ◇ *n* **-1.** [celebration] festival *m* **-2.** *UK SPORT* festival *m*. ◇ *comp* [performance, occasion] de gala.

Galapagos Islands [gə'læpəgəs-] *npl*: **the ~** as Ilhas Galápagos; **in the ~** nas Ilhas Galápagos.

galaxy ['gæləksɪ] (*pl* **-ies**) *n* [group of planets and stars] galáxia *f*.

gale [geɪl] *n* [wind] ventania *f*.

Galicia [gə'lɪʃɪə] *n* **-1.** [in Central Europe] Galícia; **in ~** na Galícia **-2.** [in Spain] Galiza; **in ~** na Galiza.

gall [gɔːl] ◇ *n (U)* [nerve]: **to have the ~ to do sthg** ter a audácia de fazer algo. ◇ *vt* incomodar.

gall. *abbr of* **gallon**.

gallant [*sense 1* 'gælənt, *sense 2* gə'lænt] *adj* **-1.** [courageous] valente **-2.** [polite to women] galante.

gallantry ['gæləntrɪ] *n (U)* **-1.** [courage] valentia *f* **-2.** [politeness to women] galanteio *m*.

gall bladder *n* vesícula *f* biliar.

galleon ['gælɪən] *n* galeão *m*.

gallery ['gælərɪ] (*pl* **-ies**) *n* galeria *f*.

galley ['gælɪ] (*pl* **galleys**) *n* **-1.** [ship] galé *f* **-2.** [kitchen] cozinha *f (de navio ou avião)* **-3.** *TYPO*: **~ (proof)** prova *f* de granel.

Gallic ['gælɪk] *adj* gaulês(lesa).

galling ['gɔːlɪŋ] *adj* **-1.** [annoying] irritante **-2.** [humiliating] vergonhoso(sa).

gallivant [ˌgælɪ'vænt] *vi inf* perambular.

gallon ['gælən] *n* galão *m*.

gallop ['gæləp] ◇ *n* **-1.** [pace of horse] galope *m* **-2.** [horse ride] galopada *f*. ◇ *vi* galopar.

galloping ['gæləpɪŋ] *adj fig* [soaring] galopante.

gallows ['gæləʊz] (*pl inv*) *n* forca *f*.

gallstone ['gɔːlstəʊn] *n* cálculo *m* biliar.

Gallup poll® ['gæləp-] *n UK* ≃ pesquisa *f* do ibope.

galore [gə'lɔː^r] *adv* em abundância.

galoshes [gə'lɒʃɪz] *npl* galocha *f*.

galvanize, -ise ['gælvənaɪz] *vt* **-1.** *TECH* galvanizar **-2.** [impel]: **to ~ sb into action** estimular alguém a uma ação.

Gambia ['gæmbɪə] *n*: **(the) ~** a Gâmbia; **in (the) ~** na Gâmbia.

Gambian ['gæmbɪən] ◇ *adj* gambiano(na). ◇ *n* gambiano *m*, -na *f*.

gambit ['gæmbɪt] *n* **-1.** [remark, ploy] lábia *f* **-2.** [in chess] tática *f*, estratégia *f*.

gamble ['gæmbl] ◇ *n* [calculated risk] aposta *f*; **to take a ~** assumir o risco. ◇ *vi* **-1.** [bet] apostar; **to ~ on sthg** apostar em algo **-2.** [take risk]: **to ~ on sthg** arriscar em algo.

gambler ['gæmblə^r] *n* jogador *m*, -ra *f*.

gambling ['gæmblɪŋ] *n (U)* jogo *m (de azar)*.

gambol ['gæmbl] (*UK pt* & *pp* **-led**, *cont* **-ling**, *US pt* & *pp* **-ed**, *cont* **-ing**) *vi* cabriolar, saltar.

game [geɪm] ◇ *n* **-1.** [sport, amusement] jogo *m*; **a children's ~** uma brincadeira de criança **-2.** [contest, match] jogo *m*, partida *f* **-3.** [division of match - in tennis] game *m*; [- in bridge] jogada *f* **-4.** [playing equipment] brinquedo *m* **-5.** [scheme, trick] truque *m*; **stop playing ~s with me!** pare de brincar comigo! **-6.** *(U)* [hunted animals] caça *f* **-7.** *phr*: **to beat sb at their own ~** derrotar alguém usando suas próprias armas; **the ~'s up** acabou a brincadeira; **to give the ~ away** entregar o jogo. ◇ *adj* **-1.** [brave] corajoso(sa) **-2.** [willing] disposto(-ta); **~ for sthg/to do sthg** pronto(ta) para algo/ para fazer algo.

◆ **games** ◇ *n SCH* [physical education] jogos *mpl*. ◇ *npl* [sporting contest] jogos *mpl*.

gamekeeper ['geɪmˌkiːpə^r] *n* guarda-caça *mf*.

gamely ['geɪmlɪ] *adv* [bravely] corajosamente.

game reserve *n* reserva *f* de caça.

gamesmanship ['geɪmzmənʃɪp] *n (U)* artimanha *f (no jogo)*.

gamma rays ['gæmə-] *npl* raios *mpl* gama.

gammon ['gæmən] *n (U)* presunto *m*.

gammy ['gæmɪ] (*compar* **-ier**, *superl* **-iest**) *adj UK inf* manco(ca).

gamut ['gæmət] *n* gama *f*; **to run the ~ of sthg** recorrer a toda a gama de algo.

gander ['gændə^r] *n* [male goose] ganso *m*.

gang [gæŋ] *n* **-1.** [of criminals] quadrilha *f*, gangue *f* **-2.** [of young people] turma *f*.

◆ **gang up** *vi inf* mancomunar-se; **to ~ up on sb** mancomunar-se contra alguém.

Ganges ['gændʒiːz] *n*: **the (River) ~** o Rio Ganges.

gangland ['gæŋlænd] *n (U)* submundo *m (do crime)*.

gangling ['gæŋglɪŋ], **gangly** ['gæŋglɪ] (*compar* **-ier**, *superl* **-iest**) *adj* desajeitado(da).

gangplank ['gæŋplæŋk] *n* prancha *f (de desembarque)*, passadiço *m*.

gangrene ['gæŋgriːn] *n (U)* gangrena *f*.

gangrenous ['gæŋgrɪnəs] *adj* gangrenado(da).

gangster ['gæŋstə^r] *n* gângster *mf*.

gangway ['gæŋweɪ] *n* **-1.** *UK* [aisle] corredor *m* **-2.** [gangplank] passadiço *m*.
gannet ['gænɪt] (*pl inv OR* **-s**) *n* [bird] ganso-patola *m*.
gantry ['gæntrɪ] (*pl* **-ies**) *n* [for crane] cavalete *m*.
GAO (*abbr of* **General Accounting Office**) *n* departamento *m* de finanças públicas *(norte-americano)*.
gaol [dʒeɪl] *n & vt UK* = **jail**.
gap [gæp] *n* **-1.** [empty space] espaço *m*, brecha *f*; **her death left a ~ in our lives** sua morte deixou um vazio em nossas vidas; **fill in the ~s** preencher as lacunas **-2.** [in time] intervalo *m* **-3.** *fig* [in knowledge, report] falha *f* **-4.** *fig* [between theory and practice etc.] disparidade *f*.
gape [geɪp] *vi* **-1.** [person]: **to ~ (at sb/ sthg)** ficar boquiaberto(ta) (diante de alguém/algo) **-2.** [hole, shirt] abrir.
gaping ['geɪpɪŋ] *adj* **-1.** [person] boquiaberto(ta) **-2.** [hole, shirt, wound] todo aberto, toda aberta.
garage [*UK* 'gærɑ:ʒ, *US* gə'rɑ:ʒ] *n* **-1.** [for keeping car] garagem *f* **-2.** *UK* [for fuel] posto *m* de gasolina **-3.** [for car repair] oficina *f (mecânica)* **-4.** [for selling cars] revendedora *f*.
garage sale *n US* venda *f* de garagem.
garb [gɑ:b] *n (U) fml* traje *m*.
garbage ['gɑ:bɪdʒ] *n esp US (U)* **-1.** [refuse] lixo *m* **-2.** *inf* [nonsense] besteira *f*.
garbage can *n US* lata *f* de lixo.
garbage collector *n US* lixeiro *m*, -ra *f*.
garbage truck *n US* caminhão *m* de lixo.
garbled ['gɑ:bld] *adj* [message, account] adulterado(-da).
Garda (Síochána) *n Irish*: **the ~** *a polícia irlandesa*.
garden ['gɑ:dn] <> *n* jardim *m*. <> *comp* de jardim. <> *vi* jardinar.
◆ **gardens** *npl* jardim *m*.
garden centre *n* loja *f* de jardinagem.
garden city *n UK* cidade-jardim *f*.
gardener ['gɑ:dnəʳ] *n* jardineiro *m*, -ra *f*.
gardenia [gɑ:'di:njə] *n* gardênia *f*.
gardening ['gɑ:dnɪŋ] <> *n (U)* jardinagem *f*. <> *comp* de jardinagem; **~ expert** perito *m*, -ta *f* em jardinagem.
garden party *n* festa *f* ao ar livre.
gargantuan [gɑ:'gæntjʊən] *adj* gigantesco(ca).
gargle ['gɑ:gl] *vi* gargarejar.
gargoyle ['gɑ:gɔɪl] *n* gárgula *f*.
garish ['geərɪʃ] *adj* espalhafatoso(sa).
garland ['gɑ:lənd] *n* guirlanda *f (de flores)*.
garlic ['gɑ:lɪk] *n* alho *m*.
garlic bread *n* pão *m* de alho.
garlicky ['gɑ:lɪkɪ] *adj inf* **-1.** [in smell] com cheiro de alho **-2.** [in taste] com gosto de alho.
garment ['gɑ:mənt] *n* peça *f* de roupa.
garner ['gɑ:nəʳ] *vt fml* colher.
garnet ['gɑ:nɪt] *n* [red stone] granada *f*.
garnish ['gɑ:nɪʃ] *CULIN* <> *n* decoração *f*. <> *vt* decorar.
garret ['gærət] *n* sótão *m*.
garrison ['gærɪsn] <> *n* [soldiers] guarnição *f*. <> *vt* guarnecer.
garrulous ['gærələs] *adj* tagarela.
garter ['gɑ:təʳ] *n* **-1.** [band round leg] liga *f* **-2.** *US* [suspender] suspensório *m*.
gas [gæs] (*pl* **gases** *OR* **gasses**, *pt & pp* **-sed**, *cont* **-sing**) <> *n* **-1.** *CHEM* gás *m* **-2.** [domestic fuel] gás *m (de cozinha)* **-3.** *US* [fuel for vehicle] gasolina *f*; **to step on the ~** *inf* pisar no acelerador. <> *vt* [poison] envenenar (com gás).
gas chamber *n* câmara *f* de gás.
gas cooker *n UK* fogão *m* a gás.
gas cylinder *n* botijão *m* de gás.
gaseous *adj TECH* gasoso(sa).
gas fire *n UK* aquecedor *m* a gás.
gas fitter *n* encanador *m*, -ra *f* de gás.
gas gauge *n US* medidor *m* de gás.
gash [gæʃ] <> *n* corte *m (na pele)*, ferida *f*. <> *vt* cortar *(a pele)*, ferir.
gasket ['gæskɪt] *n* gaxeta *f*.
gasman ['gæsmæn] (*pl* **-men** [-men]) *n* vendedor *m*, -ra *f* de gás.
gas mask *n* máscara *f* antigás.
gasmen *pl* ▷ **gasman**.
gas meter *n* medidor *m* de gás.
gasoline ['gæsəli:n] *n US (U)* gasolina *f*.
gasometer [gæ'sɒmɪtəʳ] *n* gasômetro *m*.
gas oven *n* **-1.** [for cooking] forno *m* a gás **-2.** [gas chamber] câmara *f* de gás.
gasp [gɑ:sp] <> *n* arfada *f*. <> *vi* ofegar.
gas pedal *n US* acelerador *m*.
gasping ['gɑ:spɪŋ] *adj UK inf* [in great need]: **to be ~ for sthg** estar louco(ca) por algo.
gas pump attendant *n US* frentista *mf*.
gas station *n US* posto *m* de gasolina.
gas stove *n* = **gas cooker**.
gassy ['gæsɪ] (*compar* **-ier**, *superl* **-iest**) *adj pej* [water, beer] com muito gás.
gas tank *n US* tanque *m* de gasolina.
gas tap *n* torneira *f* de gás.
gastric ['gæstrɪk] *adj* gástrico(ca).
gastric ulcer *n* úlcera *f* gástrica.
gastritis [gæs'traɪtɪs] *n (U)* gastrite *f*.
gastroenteritis ['gæstrəʊˌentə'raɪtɪs] *n (U)* gastroenterite *f*.
gastronomic [ˌgæstrə'nɒmɪk] *adj* gastronômico(-ca).
gastronomy [gæs'trɒnəmɪ] *n (U)* gastronomia *f*.
gasworks ['gæswɜ:ks] (*pl inv*) *n* fábrica *f* de gás.
gate [geɪt] *n* portão *m*.

-GATE

Desde o escândalo de Watergate, em 1972, que resultou na primeira renúncia de um presidente dos Estados Unidos - Richard Nixon -, o sufixo *-gate* vem sendo acrescentado a outras palavras, para designar escândalos políticos nos Estados Unidos e na Grã-Bretanha. Assim, a palavra *Irangate* foi cunhada para referir-se á venda ilegal de armas dos Estados Unidos para o Irã, na década de 1980; e, ao final da década de 1990, a palavra *Monicagate* foi inventada para designar o escândalo sexual envolvendo o presidente Bill Clinton e a ex-estagiária da Casa Branca, Monica Lewinski.

gâteau ['gætəʊ] (*pl* **-x** [-z]) *n UK* bolo *m* recheado.

gatecrash ['geɪtkræʃ] *inf* <> *vt* entrar como penetra em. <> *vi* entrar como penetra.
gatecrasher ['geɪt,kræʃəʳ] *n inf* penetra *mf*.
gatehouse ['geɪthaʊs, *pl* -haʊzɪz] *n* portaria *f*.
gatekeeper ['geɪt,ki:pəʳ] *n* porteiro *m*, -ra *f*.
gatepost ['geɪtpəʊst] *n* mourão *m*.
gateway ['geɪtweɪ] *n* **-1.** [entrance] portão *m* **-2.** *fig* [means of access]: ~ **to** entrada *f* para; ~ **airport** aeroporto *m* de entrada.
gather ['gæðəʳ] <> *vt* **-1.** [collect - gen] colher; [- courage, strength] reunir: **to ~ together** reunir **-2.** [speed, momentum] ganhar **-3.** [understand]: **to ~ (that)** compreender que **-4.** [into folds] franzir. <> *vi* [come together] reunir.
◆ **gather up** *vt sep* [objects] juntar.
gathering ['gæðərɪŋ] *n* [meeting] assembléia *f*.
GATT [gæt] (*abbr of* **General Agreement on Tariffs and Trade**) *n acordo geral de tarifas e comércio*, GATT *m*.
gauche [gəʊʃ] *adj* desajeitado(da).
gaudy ['gɔ:dɪ] (*compar* **-ier**, *superl* **-iest**) *adj* chamativo(va).
gauge, gage *US* [geɪdʒ] <> *n* **-1.** [measuring instrument - for rain] pluviômetro *m*; [- for tyre pressure] calibrador *m*; [- for fuel] medidor *m* de combustível **-2.** [calibre] calibre *m* **-3.** [of rail] bitola *f*. <> *vt* **-1.** [estimate, measure] estimar, calcular **-2.** [predict] prever.
Gaul [gɔ:l] *n* **-1.** [country] Gália **-2.** [person] gaulês *m*, -lesa *f*.
gaunt [gɔ:nt] *adj* **-1.** [person, face] esquelético(ca) **-2.** [landscape, building] desolado(da).
gauntlet ['gɔ:ntlɪt] *n* [medieval glove] manopla *f*; [for motorcyclist] luva *f (de material resistente e punho largo)*; **to run the ~ of sthg** expor-se a algo; **to throw down the ~ (to sb)** lançar um desafio (a alguém).
gauze [gɔ:z] *n (U)* [fabric] gaze *f*.
gave [geɪv] *pt* ▷ **give**.
gawky ['gɔ:kɪ] (*compar* **-ier**, *superl* **-iest**) *adj* desengonçado(da).
gawp [gɔ:p] *vi* embasbacar-se; **to ~ at sb/sthg** embasbacar-se diante de alguém/algo.
gay [geɪ] <> *adj* **-1.** [homosexual] gay **-2.** [cheerful, brightly coloured] alegre. <> *n* [homosexual] gay *mf*.
Gaza Strip ['gɑ:zə-] *n*: **the ~** a Faixa de Gaza.
gaze [geɪz] <> *n* olhar *m* fixo. <> *vi*: **to ~ (at sb/sthg)** olhar fixamente (para alguém/algo).
gazebo [gə'zi:bəʊ] (*pl* **-s**) *n* mirante *m*.
gazelle [gə'zel] (*pl inv* OR **-s**) *n* gazela *f*.
gazette [gə'zet] *n* [newspaper] gazeta *f*.
gazetteer [,gæzɪ'tɪəʳ] *n* dicionário *m* geográfico.
gazump [gə'zʌmp] *vt UK inf concordar em vender uma casa a alguém e depois vendê-la a outro por um preço mais alto*; **to be ~ed** ser passado(da) pra trás na compra de um imóvel.
GB (*abbr of* **Great Britain**) *n* GB.
GBH (*abbr of* **grievous bodily harm**) *n UK* lesão *f* corporal grave.
GC (*abbr of* **George Cross**) *n (titular da) maior condecoração de bravura concedida a civis na Grã-Bretanha.*
GCE (*abbr of* **General Certificate of Education**) *n antigo exame final do ensino médio na Grã-Bretanha.*
GCH (*abbr of* **gas central heating**) *n UK* aquecimento *m* central a gás.
GCHQ (*abbr of* **Government Communications Headquarters**) *n centro de informações dos serviços secretos britânicos.*
GCSE (*abbr of* **General Certificate of Secondary Education**) *n exame final do ensino médio na Grã-Bretanha, em substituição ao nível O do GCE.*
Gdns (*abbr of* **Gardens**) Jd.
GDP (*abbr of* **gross domestic product**) *n* PIB *m*.
GDR (*abbr of* **German Democratic Republic**) *n* RDA *f*.
gear [gɪəʳ] <> *n* **-1.** *TECH* [mechanism] engrenagem *f* **-2.** [on car, bicycle] marcha *f*; **in ~** engatado(da), engrenado(da); **out of ~** desengatado(da), fora de funcionamento **-3.** *(U)* [equipment, clothes] apetrechos *mpl*. <> *vt*: **to ~ sthg to sb/sthg** encaminhar algo a alguém/algo.
◆ **gear up** *vi*: **to ~ up for sthg/to do sthg** preparar-se para algo/para fazer algo.
gearbox ['gɪəbɒks] *n* caixa *f* de câmbio.
gearing *n* [assembly of gears] engrenagem *f*.
gear lever, gear stick *UK*, **gear shift** *US n* alavanca *f* de mudança.
gear wheel *n* roda *f* de engrenagem.
gee [dʒi:] *excl* **-1.** [to horse]: **~ up!** eia! **-2.** *US inf* [expressing surprise, excitement]: **~ (whizz)!** puxa!, nossa!
geese [gi:s] *pl* ▷ **goose**.
Geiger counter ['gaɪgəʳ-] *n* contador *m* Geiger.
geisha (girl) ['geɪʃə-] *n* gueixa *f*.
gel [dʒel] (*pt* & *pp* **-led**, *cont* **-ling**) <> *n* [for hair] gel *m*. <> *vi* **-1.** *fig* [idea, plan] tomar forma **-2.** [liquid] engrossar.
gelatin ['dʒelətɪn], **gelatine** [,dʒelə'ti:n] *n* gelatina *f*.
gelding ['geldɪŋ] *n* cavalo *m* castrado.
gelignite ['dʒelɪgnaɪt] *n (U)* gelignite *f*.
gem [dʒem] *n* **-1.** [jewel] gema *f*, pedra *f* preciosa **-2.** *fig* [person, thing] jóia *f*.
Gemini ['dʒemɪnaɪ] *n* **-1.** [sign] Gêmeos **-2.** [person] geminiano *m*, -na *f*; **I'm ~** sou de Gêmeos.
gemstone ['dʒemstəʊn] *n* pedra *f* preciosa.
gen [dʒen] (*pt* & *pp* **-ned**, *cont* **-ning**) *n UK inf* informações *fpl*.
◆ **gen up** *vi UK inf*: **to ~ up (on sthg)** informar-se (sobre algo).
gen. -1. (*abbr of* **general**) ger. **-2.** (*abbr of* **generally**) em geral.
Gen. (*abbr of* **General**) Gen.
gender ['dʒendəʳ] *n* **-1.** [sex] sexo *m* **-2.** *GRAMM* gênero *m*.
gene [dʒi:n] *n* gene *m*.
genealogist [,dʒi:nɪ'ælədʒɪst] *n* genealogista *mf*.
genealogy [,dʒi:nɪ'ælədʒɪ] (*pl* **-ies**) *n* genealogia *f*.
genera ['dʒenərəl] *pl* ▷ **genus**.
general ['dʒenərəl] <> *adj* geral. <> *n MIL* general *mf*.
◆ **in general** *adv* **-1.** [as a whole] em geral **-2.** [usually] geralmente.
general anaesthetic *n* anestesia *f* geral.

general delivery *n (U) US* posta-restante *f*.
general election *n* eleições *fpl* gerais.
generality [ˌdʒenəˈrælətɪ] (*pl* **-ies**) *n* **-1.** [generalization] generalidade *f* **-2.** [majority] maioria *f*.
generalization [ˌdʒenərəlaɪˈzeɪʃn] *n* generalização *f*.
generalize, -ise [ˈdʒenərəlaɪz] *vi* generalizar; **to ~ about sthg** generalizar sobre algo.
general knowledge *n (U)* cultura *m* geral.
generally [ˈdʒenərəlɪ] *adv* **-1.** [usually] geralmente **-2.** [by most people] comumente **-3.** [in a general way] em geral.
general manager *n* gerente *mf* geral.
general practice *n* clínica *f* geral.
general practitioner *n* clínico *m*, -ca *f* geral.
general public *n*: **the ~** o público em geral.
general-purpose *adj* de uso geral.
general strike *n* greve *f* geral.
generate [ˈdʒenəreɪt] *vt* **-1.** [energy, power, heat] gerar **-2.** [interest, excitement] provocar ; [jobs, employment] gerar.
generation [ˌdʒenəˈreɪʃn] *n* geração *f*; **first/second ~** primeira/segunda geração.
generation gap *n* conflito *m* de gerações.
generator [ˈdʒenəreɪtəʳ] *n* gerador *m*.
generic [dʒɪˈnerɪk] *adj* [of whole group] genérico(ca).
generosity [ˌdʒenəˈrɒsətɪ] *n (U)* generosidade *f*.
generous [ˈdʒenərəs] *adj* generoso(sa).
generously [ˈdʒenərəslɪ] *adv* generosamente.
genesis [ˈdʒenəsɪs] (*pl* **-eses** [-əsiːz]) *n* [origin] gênese *f*.
genetic [dʒɪˈnetɪk] *adj* genético(ca).
◆ **genetics** *n (U)* genética *f*.
genetically modified [dʒɪˈnetɪkəlɪˈmɒdɪfaɪd] *adj* geneticamente modificado(da).
genetic engineering *n (U)* engenharia *f* genética.
genetic fingerprinting [-ˈfɪŋgəprɪntɪŋ] *n* impressão *f* genética.
Geneva [dʒɪˈniːvə] *n* Genebra; **in ~** em Genebra.
Geneva convention *n*: **the ~** a convenção de Genebra.
genial [ˈdʒiːnjəl] *adj* cordial, simpático(ca).
genie [ˈdʒiːnɪ] (*pl* **genies** *OR* **genii** [ˈdʒiːnɪaɪ]) *n* gênio *m*.
genitals [ˈdʒenɪtlz] *npl* genitais *mpl*.
genius [ˈdʒiːnjəs] (*pl* **-es**) *n* **-1.** [person] gênio *m* **-2.** [special ability]: **a stroke of ~** um golpe de mestre; **~ for sthg/for doing sthg** dom para algo/para fazer algo.
Genoa [dʒəˈnəʊə] *n* Gênova; **in ~** em Gênova.
genocide [ˈdʒenəsaɪd] *n (U)* genocídio *m*.
genre [ˈʒrə] *n* [in art, literature, film] gênero *m*.
gent [dʒent] *n UK dated inf* cavalheiro *m*.
◆ **gents** *n UK* [toilets] banheiro *m* masculino.
genteel [dʒenˈtiːl] *adj* **-1.** [refined] fino(na), refinado(da) **-2.** [affected] afetado(da).
gentile [ˈdʒentaɪl] ◇ *adj* gói, não-judeu(dia). ◇ *n* gói *mf*.
gentle [ˈdʒentl] *adj* **-1.** [gen] suave **-2.** [kind] gentil **-3.** [discreet] leve.
gentleman [ˈdʒentlmən] (*pl* **-men** [-mən]) *n* **-1.** [well-bred man] cavalheiro *m*, gentleman *m*; **~'s agreement** acordo *m* de cavalheiros **-2.** [man] senhor *m*.
gentlemanly [ˈdʒentlmənlɪ] *adj* cavalheiresco(ca).
gentleness [ˈdʒentlnɪs] *n* **-1.** [gen] suavidade *f* **-2.** [kindness] delicadeza *f*.
gently [ˈdʒentlɪ] *adv* **-1.** [gen] suavemente **-2.** [kindly] delicadamente, gentilmente **-3.** [slowly] lentamente.
gentry [ˈdʒentrɪ] *n* alta burguesia *f*.
genuflect [ˈdʒenjuːflekt] *vi fml* genuflectir.
genuine [ˈdʒenjʊɪn] *adj* **-1.** [antique, work of art] genuíno(na) **-2.** [person, feeling, mistake] autêntico(-ca).
genuinely [ˈdʒenjʊɪnlɪ] *adv* **-1.** [surprised, disappointed] genuinamente **-2.** [spoken, believed] sinceramente.
genus [ˈdʒiːnəs] (*pl* **genera** [ˈdʒenərə]) *n* gênero *m*.
geographer [dʒɪˈɒgrəfəʳ] *n* geógrafo *m*, -fa *f*.
geographical [ˌdʒɪəˈgræfɪkl] *adj* geográfico(ca).
geography [dʒɪˈɒgrəfɪ] *n* geografia *f*.
geological [ˌdʒɪəˈlɒdʒɪkl] *adj* geológico(ca).
geologist [dʒɪˈɒlədʒɪst] *n* geólogo *m*, -ga *f*.
geology [dʒɪˈɒlədʒɪ] *n* geologia *f*.
geometric(al) [ˌdʒɪəˈmetrɪk(l)] *adj* geométrico(-ca).
geometry [dʒɪˈɒmətrɪ] *n (U)* geometria *f*.
geophysics [ˌdʒiːəʊˈfɪzɪks] *n (U)* geofísica *f*.
Geordie [ˈdʒɔːdɪ] ◇ *adj de ou relativo a Tyneside.* ◇ *n* [person] *natural ou habitante de Tyneside.*
George Cross [ˈdʒɔːdʒ-] *n UK medalha de honra ao mérito.*
Georgia [ˈdʒɔːdʒə] *n* [in US, CIS] Geórgia *f*.
Georgian [ˈdʒɔːdʒjən] ◇ *adj* **-1.** *UK* [of Georgian period] georgiano(na) **-2.** *GEOGR:* [US, CIS] georgiano(-na). ◇ *n* [in US, CIS] georgiano *m*, -na *f*.
geranium [dʒɪˈreɪnjəm] (*pl* **-s**) *n* gerânio *m*.
gerbil [ˈdʒɜːbɪl] *n* gerbo *m*.
geriatric [ˌdʒerɪˈætrɪk] *adj* **-1.** [of old people] geriátrico(ca) **-2.** *pej* [very old, inefficient] ultrapassado(da).
germ [dʒɜːm] *n* **-1.** *BIO* germe *m* **-2.** *MED* bactéria *f* **-3.** *fig* [of idea, plan] embrião *m*.
German [ˈdʒɜːmən] ◇ *adj* alemão(mã). ◇ *n* **-1.** [person] alemão *m*, -mã *f* **-2.** [language] alemão *m*.
Germanic [dʒɜːˈmænɪk] *adj* germânico(ca).
German measles *n (U)* rubéola *f*.
German shepherd (dog) *n* pastor *m* alemão.
Germany [ˈdʒɜːmənɪ] (*pl* **-ies**) *n* Alemanha; **in ~** na Alemanha.
germicide [ˈdʒɜːmɪsaɪd] *n* germicida *f*, bactericida *f*.
germinate [ˈdʒɜːmɪneɪt] ◇ *vt* germinar. ◇ *vi* germinar.
germination [ˌdʒɜːmɪˈneɪʃn] *n (U)* germinação *f*.
germ warfare *n (U)* guerra *f* bacteriológica.
gerrymandering [ˈdʒerɪmændərɪŋ] *n (U) divisão de uma zona eleitoral de forma a beneficiar um partido em prejuízo de outro.*
gerund [ˈdʒerənd] *n GRAM* gerúndio *m*.
gestation [dʒeˈsteɪʃn] *n* gestação *f*.
gestation period *n* período *m* de gestação.
gesticulate [dʒesˈtɪkjʊleɪt] *vi* gesticular.

gesticulation [dʒe,stɪkjʊ'leɪʃn] *n* gesticulação *f.*

gesture ['dʒestʃəʳ] <> *n* gesto *m.* <> *vi*: **to ~ to** *OR* **towards sb** fazer gestos a alguém

get [get] (*pt* & *pp* **got**, *US pp* **gotten**) *vt* **-1.** [obtain] obter; [buy] comprar; **she got a job** ela arranjou emprego **-2.** [receive] receber; **I got a book for Christmas** ganhei um livro no Natal **-3.** [means of transportation] apanhar; **let's ~ a taxi** vamos apanhar um táxi **-4.** [find] ir buscar; **could you ~ me the manager?** [in store] podia chamar o gerente?; [on phone] pode me passar o gerente? **-5.** [illness] apanhar; **I got the flu over Christmas** peguei uma gripe no Natal **-6.** [cause to become]: **to ~ sthg done** mandar fazer algo; **to ~ sthg ready** preparar algo; **can I ~ my car repaired here?** posso mandar consertar o meu carro aqui? **-7.** [ask, tell]: **to ~ sb to do sthg** arranjar alguém para fazer algo **-8.** [move]: **to ~ sthg out of sthg** tirar algo de algo; **I can't ~ it through the door** não consigo passar com isso na porta **-9.** [understand] compreender; **to ~ a joke** contar uma piada **-10.** [time, chance] ter; **we didn't ~ the chance to see everything** não tivemos oportunidade de ver tudo **-11.** [idea, feeling] ter; **I ~ a lot of enjoyment from it** me divirto à beça com isso **-12.** [phone] atender **-13.** [in phrases]: **you ~ a lot of rain here in winter** chove muito aqui no inverno ⊳ **have.** <> *vi* **-1.** [become] ficar; **it's getting late** está ficando tarde; **to ~ ready** preparar-se; **to ~ lost** perder-se; **~ lost!** não enche o saco!, desapareça! **-2.** [into particular state, position] meter-se; **how do you ~ to El Paso from here?** como se vai daqui para El Paso?; **to ~ into the car** entrar no carro **-3.** [arrive] chegar; **when does the train ~ here?** quando é que o trem chega aqui? **-4.** [in phrases]: **to ~ to do sthg** ter a oportunidade de fazer algo. <> *aux vb* ser; **to ~ delayed** atrasar-se; **to ~ killed** ser morto.

◆ **get along (with sb)** *vi* dar-se bem (com alguém).

◆ **get back** *vi* [return] voltar.

◆ **get in** *vi* [arrive] chegar; (enter) entrar.

◆ **get off** *vi* [leave] sair.

◆ **get on** *vi* [enter train, bus] entrar.

◆ **get out** *vi* [of car, bus, train] sair.

◆ **get through** *vi* [on phone] completar a ligação.

◆ **get up** *vi* levantar-se.

getaway ['getəweɪ] *n* fuga *f*; **to make one's ~** escapar.

getaway car *n* carro *m* de fuga.

get-together *n inf* encontro *m* informal *(entre amigos)*.

getup ['getʌp] *n inf* traje *m.*

get-up-and-go *n (U) inf* iniciativa *f.*

get-well card *n* cartão *m* de melhoras.

geyser ['gi:zəʳ] *n* [hot spring] gêiser *m.*

Ghana ['gɑ:nə] *n* Gana; **in ~** em Gana.

Ghan(a)ian [gɑ:'neɪən] <> *adj* ganense. <> *n* ganense *mf.*

ghastly ['gɑ:stlɪ] (*compar* **-ier**, *superl* **-iest**) *adj* **-1.** *inf* [very bad, unpleasant] horrível **-2.** [horrifying, macabre] macabro(bra), horroroso(sa) **-3.** [ill] abatido(da).

gherkin ['gɜ:kɪn] *n* pepino *m* em conserva.

ghetto ['getəʊ] (*pl* **-s** *OR* **-es**) *n* gueto *m.*

ghetto blaster [-'blɑ:stəʳ] *n inf minisystem portátil de grande potência.*

ghost [gəʊst] <> *n* [spirit] fantasma *m*; **he doesn't have a ~ of a chance** ele não tem a menor chance. <> *vt* = **ghostwrite.**

ghostly ['gəʊstlɪ] (*compar* **-ier**, *superl* **-iest**) *adj* fantasmagórico(ca).

ghost town *n* cidade-fantasma *f.*

ghostwrite ['gəʊstraɪt] (*pt* **-wrote**, *pp* **-written**) *vt escrever anonimamente para outra pessoa.*

ghostwriter ['gəʊst,raɪtəʳ] *n* ghost-writer *mf.*

ghostwritten ['gəʊst,rɪtn] *pp* ⊳ **ghostwrite.**

ghostwrote ['gəʊstrəʊt] *pt* ⊳ **ghostwrite.**

ghoul [gu:l] *n* **-1.** [spirit] espírito *m* do mal **-2.** *pej* [ghoulish person] demônio *m.*

ghoulish ['gu:lɪʃ] *adj* [morbid] macabro(bra).

GHQ (*abbr of* **general headquarters**) *n* QG *m.*

GI (*abbr of* **government issue**) *n soldado raso norte-americano.*

giant ['dʒaɪənt] <> *adj* gigantesco(ca). <> *n* **-1.** [gen] gigante *m* **-2.** [business, organization] gigante *mf.*

giant-size(d) *adj* de tamanho família.

gibber ['dʒɪbəʳ] *vi* tagarelar.

gibberish ['dʒɪbərɪʃ] *n (U)* asneira *f.*

gibbon ['gɪbən] *n* gibão *m.*

gibe [dʒaɪb] <> *n* zombaria *f.* <> *vi*: **to ~ at sb/sthg** zombar de alguém/algo.

giblets ['dʒɪblɪts] *npl* miúdos *mpl (de ave).*

Gibraltar [dʒɪ'brɔ:ltəʳ] *n* Gibraltar; **in ~** em Gibraltar; **the Rock of ~** o Rochedo de Gibraltar.

giddy ['gɪdɪ] (*compar* **-ier**, *superl* **-iest**) *adj* [dizzy] tonto(ta).

gift [gɪft] *n* **-1.** [present] presente *m* **-2.** [talent] dom *m*; **to have a ~ for sthg/for doing sthg** ter o dom para algo/para fazer algo; **to have the ~ of the gab** ter o dom da fala; *pej* ter lábia.

GIFT (*abbr of* **gamete in fallopian transfer**) *n técnica de inseminação artificial.*

gift certificate *n US* = **gift token.**

gifted ['gɪftɪd] *adj* **-1.** [gen] talentoso(sa), de talento **-2.** [child] superdotado(da).

gift token, gift voucher *UK*, **gift certificate** *US n* vale-presente *m.*

gift wrap *n* papel *m* de presente.

gift-wrapped [-ræpt] *adj* enrolado(da) para presente.

gig [gɪg] *n inf* [concert] show *m.*

gigabyte ['gaɪgəbaɪt] *n COMPUT* gigabyte *m.*

gigantic [dʒaɪ'gæntɪk] *adj* gigantesco(ca).

giggle ['gɪgl] <> *n* **-1.** [laugh] risadinha *f*, risada *f* **-2.** *UK inf* [fun] diversão *f*; **to do sthg for a ~** divertir-se fazendo algo tolo; **to have the ~s** ter um ataque de riso. <> *vi* [laugh] dar risadinhas bobas.

giggly ['gɪglɪ] (*compar* **-ier**, *superl* **-iest**) *adj* com riso bobo.

GIGO ['gaɪgaʊ] (*abbr of* **garbage in, garbage out**) *COMPUT* GIGO *m*, entra lixo, sai lixo.

gigolo ['ʒɪgələʊ] (*pl* **-s**) *n pej* gigolô *m.*

gigot ['ʒi:gəʊ] *n* perna *f* de carneiro.

gilded ['gɪldɪd] *adj* = **gilt.**

gill [dʒɪl] *n* [unit of measurement] *0,142 litros.*
gills [gɪlz] *npl* [of fish] guelras *fpl.*
gilt [gɪlt] <> *adj* [covered in gold] dourado(da). <> *n (U)* [gold layer] dourado *m.*
◆ **gilts** *npl FIN* títulos *mpl* de máxima garantia.
gilt-edged *adj FIN* de máxima garantia.
gimme ['gɪmɪ] *inf* = **give me.**
gimmick ['gɪmɪk] *n pej* artimanha *f.*
gin [dʒɪn] *n* [drink] gim *m*; ~ **and tonic** gim-tônica *m.*
ginger ['dʒɪndʒəʳ] <> *adj UK* [colour - of hair] ruivo(va); [- of cat] avermelhado(da). <> *n (U)* **-1.** [root] gengibre *m* **-2.** [powder] gengibre *m* em pó.
ginger ale *n* [mixer] jinjibirra *f.*
ginger beer *n* [slightly alcoholic] cerveja *f* de gengibre.
gingerbread ['dʒɪndʒəbred] *n (U)* **-1.** [cake] pão *m* de gengibre **-2.** [biscuit] biscoito *m* de gengibre.
ginger group *n UK* grupo *m* de pressão.
ginger-haired [-'heəd] *adj* ruivo(va).
gingerly ['dʒɪndʒəlɪ] *adv* cuidadosamente.
gingham ['gɪŋəm] *n (U)* [cloth] guingão *m.*
gingivitis [ˌdʒɪndʒɪ'vaɪtɪs] *n (U) MED* gengivite *f.*
ginseng ['dʒɪnseŋ] *n (U)* ginseng *m.*
gipsy ['dʒɪpsɪ] (*pl* **-ies**) <> *adj* cigano(na). <> *n* [nomad] cigano *m*, -na *f.*
giraffe [dʒɪ'rɑːf] (*pl inv OR* **-s**) *n* girafa *f.*
gird [gɜːd] (*pt* & *pp* **-ed** *OR* **girt**) *vt* ▻ **loin.**
girder ['gɜːdəʳ] *n* viga *f.*
girdle ['gɜːdl] *n* [corset] espartilho *m.*
girl [gɜːl] *n* **-1.** [young female child] menina *f*, garota *f* **-2.** [young woman] moça *f* **-3.** [daughter] menina *f* **-4.** [female friend]: **the ~s** as amigas, as meninas.
girl Friday *n* auxiliar *f* de escritório.
girlfriend ['gɜːlfrend] *n* **-1.** [female lover] namorada *f* **-2.** [female friend] amiga *f.*
girl guide *UK*, **girl scout** *US n* [individual] escoteira *f*, bandeirante *f.*
girlie magazine ['gɜːlɪ-] *n inf* revista *f* erótica.
girlish ['gɜːlɪʃ] *adj* de menininha.
girl scout *n US* = **girl guide.**
giro ['dʒaɪrəʊ] (*pl* **-s**) *n UK* **-1.** *(U)* [system] transferência *f* de crédito **-2.**: *inf* ~ **(cheque)** seguro-desemprego *m.*
girt *pt* & *pp* ▻ **gird.**
girth [gɜːθ] *n* **-1.** [circumference] circunferência *f* **-2.** [of horse] cincha *f.*
gist [dʒɪst] *n* essência *f*; **to get the ~ (of sthg)** pegar a essência (de algo).
give [gɪv] (*pt* **gave**, *pp* **given**) <> *vt* **-1.** [gen] dar; **to ~ sb sthg** dar algo para *OR* a alguém **-2.** [hand over, pass] entregar; **to ~ sb sthg, to ~ sthg to sb** entregar algo para *OR* a alguém **-3.** [pay]: **to ~ sthg (for sthg)** dar *OR* pagar algo (por algo) **-4.** *phr*: **to be given to believe** *OR* **understand that** *fml* ser levado(da) a acreditar *OR* entender que; **I'd ~ anything** *OR* **my right arm to do that** eu daria tudo *OR* qualquer coisa para fazer isso. <> *vi* [collapse, break] ceder. <> *n (U)* [elasticity] elasticidade *f.*
◆ **give or take** *prep* mais ou menos.
◆ **give away** *vt sep* **-1.** [get rid of] desfazer-se de **-2.** [reveal] revelar.
◆ **give back** *vt sep* [return] devolver.
◆ **give in** *vi* **-1.** [admit defeat] render-se, dar-se por vencido(da) **-2.** [agree unwillingly]: **to ~ in to sthg** ceder frente a algo.
◆ **give off** *vt fus* [produce] exalar.
◆ **give out** <> *vt sep* [distribute] distribuir. <> *vi* **-1.** [be exhausted] esgotar-se **-2.** [fail] falhar, não funcionar.
◆ **give over** <> *vt sep* [dedicate]: **to be given over to sthg** ser destinado(da) a algo. <> *vi UK inf* [stop]: **~ over!** (já) chega!
◆ **give up** <> *vt sep* **-1.** [stop, abandon] abandonar; **to ~ up smoking** parar de fumar; **to ~ up chocolate** deixar de comer chocolate **-2.** [surrender]: **to ~ o.s. up (to sb)** render-se (a alguém). <> *vi* [admit defeat] render-se.
◆ **give up on** *vt fus* [abandon] abandonar *(por muito difícil).*
give-and-take *n (U)* [compromise] toma-lá-dá-cá *m.*
giveaway ['gɪvəˌweɪ] <> *adj* **-1.** [telltale] revelador(ra) **-2.** [very cheap] dado(da). <> *n* [telltale sign] sinal *m* óbvio.
given ['gɪvn] <> *pp* ▻ **give.** <> *adj* **-1.** [set, fixed] dado(da); **at any ~ time** num determinado momento **-2.** [prone]: **to be ~ to sthg/to doing sthg** ser dado(da) a algo/a fazer algo. <> *prep* [taking into account] dado(da); **~ the circumstances** dadas as circunstâncias; **~ that** dado que.
given name *n US* prenome *m.*
giver ['gɪvəʳ] *n* doador *m*, -ra *f.*
glacé cherry ['glæseɪ-] *n* cereja *f* glaçada.
glacial ['gleɪsjəl] *adj* glacial.
glacier ['glæsjəʳ] *n* geleira *f.*
glad [glæd] (*compar* **-der**, *superl* **-dest**) *adj* **-1.** [happy, pleased] feliz; **to be ~ about sthg** estar feliz por algo; **to be ~ that** estar feliz que **-2.** [willing]: **to be ~ to do sthg** ter vontade de fazer algo, desejar fazer algo **-3.** [grateful]: **to be ~ of sthg** ficar agradecido(da) por algo.
gladden ['glædn] *vt literary* contentar.
glade [gleɪd] *n literary* clareira *f.*
gladiator ['glædɪeɪtəʳ] *n* gladiador *m.*
gladioli [ˌglædɪ'əʊlaɪ] *npl* gladíolos *mpl.*
gladly ['glædlɪ] *adv* **-1.** [happily, eagerly] com prazer, alegremente **-2.** [willingly] com satisfação.
glamor *n US* = **glamour.**
glamorize, -ise ['glæməraɪz] *vt* fantasiar.
glamorous ['glæmərəs] *adj* [gen] glamouroso(sa); [job] atraente.
glamour *UK*, **glamor** *US* ['glæməʳ] *n (U)* [gen] glamour *m*; [of job] encanto *m.*
glance [glɑːns] <> *n* [quick look] olhadela *f*; **to cast** *OR* **take a ~ at sthg** dar uma olhada rápida em algo; **at a ~** de relance; **at first ~** à primeira vista. <> *vi* [look quickly]: **to ~ at sb/sthg** olhar alguém/algo de relance; **to ~ at** *OR* **through sthg** passar os olhos em algo.
◆ **glance off** *vt fus* **-1.** [light] desviar **-2.** [ball] rebater **-3.** [bullet] ricochetear.
glancing ['glɑːnsɪŋ] *adj* [oblique] oblíquo(qua).
gland [glænd] *n* glândula *f.*
glandular fever ['glændjʊləʳ-] *n (U)* mononucleose *f* infecciosa.
glare [gleəʳ] <> *n* **-1.** [scowl] olhar *m* penetrante,

encarada *f* **-2.** *(U)* [blaze, dazzle] brilho *m* **-3.** [of publicity] foco *m.* <> *vi* **-1.** [scowl]: **to ~ at sb/sthg** fulminar alguém/algo com o olhar, lançar um olhar fulminante sobre alguém/algo **-2.** [blaze, dazzle] ofuscar.

glaring ['gleərɪŋ] *adj* **-1.** [very obvious] evidente **-2.** [blazing, dazzling] ofuscante.

glasnost ['glæznɒst] *n (U)* glasnost *f.*

glass [glɑ:s] <> *n* **-1.** *(U)* [material] vidro *m* **-2.** [for drinking] copo *m* **-3.** *(U)* [glassware] objetos *mpl* de cristal. <> *comp* de vidro.

◆ **glasses** *npl* [spectacles] óculos *m inv*; [binoculars] binóculos *mpl.*

glassblowing ['glɑ:sˌbləʊɪŋ] *n (U)* modelagem *f* de vidro a quente.

glass fibre *n (U) UK* fibra *f* de vidro.

glasshouse ['glɑ:shaʊs, *pl* -haʊzɪz] *n UK* **-1.** [greenhouse] estufa *f* **-2.** *fig inf* [military prison] prisão *f* militar.

glassware ['glɑ:sweəʳ] *n (U)* objetos *mpl* de cristal.

glassy ['glɑ:sɪ] (*compar* **-ier**, *superl* **-iest**) *adj* **-1.** [smooth, shiny] cristalino(na) **-2.** [blank, lifeless] vidrado(da).

Glaswegian [glæz'wi:dʒjən] <> *adj de ou relativo a Glasgow.* <> *n* **-1.** [person] *natural ou habitante de Glasgow* **-2.** [dialect] *dialeto falado em Glasgow.*

glaucoma [glɔ:'kəʊmə] *n (U)* glaucoma *m.*

glaze [gleɪz] <> *n* **-1.** [on pottery] verniz *m*, esmalte *m* **-2.** CULIN glacê *m.* <> *vt* **-1.** [pottery] envernizar **-2.** CULIN cristalizar.

◆ **glaze over** *vi* apagar-se.

glazed [gleɪzd] *adj* **-1.** [dull, bored] vidrado(da) **-2.** [pottery] vitrificado(da) **-3.** CULIN cristalizado(da) **-4.** [with glass] envidraçado(da).

glazier ['gleɪzjəʳ] *n* vidraceiro *m*, -ra *f.*

gleam [gli:m] <> *n* **-1.** [glow] lampejo *m* **-2.** [fleeting expression] olhar *m.* <> *vi* **-1.** [surface, object] reluzir **-2.** [light] brilhar **-3.** [face, eyes] olhar.

gleaming ['gli:mɪŋ] *adj* **-1.** [surface, object] reluzente **-2.** [light] brilhante **-3.** [face, eyes] reluzente.

glean [gli:n] *vt* [gather] coletar.

glee [gli:] *n (U)* [joy, delight] alegria *f*; [gloating] regozijo *m.*

gleeful ['gli:fʊl] *adj* [joyful] alegre; [gloating] de regozijo.

glen [glen] *n Scot & Irish* vale *m.*

glib [glɪb] (*compar* **-ber**, *superl* **-best**) *adj pej* **-1.** [answer, excuse] de momento **-2.** [person] de muita lábia.

glibly ['glɪblɪ] *adv pej* [talk, reply] com muita lábia.

glide [glaɪd] *vi* **-1.** [move smoothly] deslizar **-2.** [fly] planar.

glider ['glaɪdəʳ] *n* [plane] planador *m.*

gliding ['glaɪdɪŋ] *n (U)* [sport] vôo *m* sem motor; **to go ~** voar de planador.

glimmer ['glɪməʳ] <> *n* **-1.** [faint light] luz *f* fraca **-2.** *fig* [trace, sign] sinal *m* mínimo; **a ~ of hope** um fio de esperança. <> *vi* tremeluzir.

glimpse [glɪmps] <> *n* **-1.** [sight, look] vislumbre *m*; **to catch a ~ of sb/sthg** ver alguém/algo de relance **-2.** [perception, idea, insight] noção *f.* <> *vt* **-1.** [catch sight of] ver de relance **-2.** [perceive] vislumbrar.

glint [glɪnt] <> *n* brilho *m.* <> *vi* **-1.** [metal, sunlight] brilhar **-2.** [eyes - greed, anger] faiscar; [- amusement] brilhar.

glisten ['glɪsn] *vi* brilhar.

glitch [glɪtʃ] *n inf* [in plan] falha *f* técnica, pane *f.*

glitter ['glɪtəʳ] <> *n* [gen] brilho *m.* <> *vi* **-1.** [object, light] brilhar **-2.** [eyes - with excitement] cintilar; [- with fury] faiscar.

glittering ['glɪtərɪŋ] *adj* **-1.** [object, light] reluzente, brilhante **-2.** [eyes] brilhante **-3.** [glamorous] deslumbrante.

glitzy ['glɪtsɪ] (*compar* **-ier**, *superl* **-iest**) *adj inf* [glamorous] deslumbrante.

gloat [gləʊt] *vi*: **to ~ (over sthg)** tripudiar (de algo).

global ['gləʊbl] *adj* [worldwide] mundial.

globalization [ˌgləʊbəlaɪ'zeɪʃn] *n* globalização *f.*

globally ['gləʊbəlɪ] *adv* **-1.** [worldwide] mundialmente **-2.** [generally] em geral.

global warming [-'wɔ:mɪŋ] *n (U)* aquecimento *m* global.

globe [gləʊb] *n* **-1.** [Earth]: **the ~** o globo **-2.** [spherical shape] globo *m.*

globetrotter ['gləʊbˌtrɒtəʳ] *n inf* globe-trotter *mf.*

globule ['glɒbju:l] *n* gota *f.*

gloom [glu:m] *n* **-1.** [darkness] escuro *m*, escuridão *f* **-2.** [unhappiness] desânimo *m.*

gloomy ['glu:mɪ] (*compar* **-ier**, *superl* **-iest**) *adj* **-1.** [place, landscape] sombrio(bria) **-2.** [weather] sombrio(bria), escuro(ra) **-3.** [atmosphere] deprimente; [mood] pessimista **-4.** [outlook, news] desanimador(ra).

glorification [ˌglɔ:rɪfɪ'keɪʃn] *n (U)* [act of glorifying] glorificação *f.*

glorified ['glɔ:rɪfaɪd] *adj pej* [jumped-up] incrementado(da).

glorify ['glɔ:rɪfaɪ] (*pt & pp* **-ied**) *vt* [overpraise, overesteem] glorificar.

glorious ['glɔ:rɪəs] *adj* **-1.** [illustrious] glorioso(sa) **-2.** [wonderful] magnífico(ca).

glory ['glɔ:rɪ] (*pl* **-ies**) *n* **-1.** [gen] glória *f* **-2.** *(U)* [splendour] esplendor *m.*

◆ **glories** *npl* glórias *fpl.*

◆ **glory in** *vt fus* [relish] desfrutar de.

gloss [glɒs] *n* **-1.** *(U)* [shine - of wood, furniture] lustre *m*; [- of hair] brilho *m* **-2.**: **~ (paint)** esmalte *m.*

◆ **gloss over** *vt fus* falar por alto sobre.

glossary ['glɒsərɪ] (*pl* **-ies**) *n* glossário *m.*

glossy ['glɒsɪ] (*compar* **-ier**, *superl* **-iest**) *adj* **-1.** [gen] lustroso(sa) **-2.** *fig* [spectacle, display] de luxo.

glossy magazine *n* revista *f* impressa em papel de luxo.

glove [glʌv] *n* luva *f.*

glove compartment *n* porta-luvas *m inv.*

glove puppet *n UK* fantoche *m.*

glow [gləʊ] <> *n* **-1.** [light] fulgor *m*, brilho *m* **-2.** [flush] rubor *m* **-3.** *fig* [feeling] arrebatamento *m.* <> *vi* **-1.** [fire] arder **-2.** [sky, light, brass] brilhar **-3.** [with colour] resplandecer **-4.** [person]: **to ~ (with sthg)** resplanceder (de algo).

glower ['glaʊəʳ] *vi*: **to ~ (at sb/sthg)** olhar

ameaçadoramente (para alguém/algo).

glowing ['gləʊɪŋ] *adj* [very favourable] inflamado(da).

glow-worm *n* vaga-lume *m*.

glucose ['glu:kəʊs] *n (U)* glicose *f*.

glue [glu:] (*cont* **glueing** *OR* **gluing**) ◇ *n (U)* cola *f*. ◇ *vt* [stick with glue] colar; **to ~ sthg to sthg** colar algo em algo; **to be ~d to sthg** *fig* [absorbed by] ficar grudado(da) em algo.

glue-sniffing [-ˌsnɪfɪŋ] *n (U)* inalação *f* de cola.

glum [glʌm] (*compar* **-mer**, *superl* **-mest**) *adj* [unhappy] melancólico(ca).

glut [glʌt] *n* excesso *m*.

gluten ['glu:tən] *n (U)* glúten *m*.

glutinous ['glu:tɪnəs] *adj* **-1.** [mud] pegajoso(sa) **-2.** [milk pudding, stew] glutinoso(sa) **-3.** [rice] empapado(da).

glutton ['glʌtn] *n* [greedy person] glutão *m*, -tona *f*; **to be a ~ for punishment** gostar de sofrer.

gluttony ['glʌtənɪ] *n (U)* gula *f*.

glycerin ['glɪsərɪn], **glycerine** ['glɪsəri:n] *n (U)* glicerina *f*.

gm (*abbr of* **gram**) g.

GMAT (*abbr of* **Graduate Management Admissions Test**) *n exame de admissão no segundo ciclo do ensino superior nos Estados Unidos.*

GM foods *npl* alimentos *mpl* geneticamente modificados.

GMO (*abbr of* **genetically modified organism**) ◇ *adj* OGM. ◇ *n* OGM *m*.

GMT (*abbr of* **Greenwich Mean Time**) *n horário oficial de Greenwich*, GMT *m*.

gnarled [nɑ:ld] *adj* **-1.** [tree] nodoso(sa) **-2.** [hands] áspero(ra).

gnash [næʃ] *vt*: **to ~ one's teeth** ranger os dentes.

gnat [næt] *n* mosquito *m*.

gnaw [nɔ:] ◇ *vt* [chew] roer. ◇ *vi* [worry] atormentar-se; **to ~ (away) at sb** atormentar alguém.

gnome [nəʊm] *n* gnomo *m*.

GNP (*abbr of* **gross national product**) *n* PNB *m*.

gnu [nu:] (*pl inv OR* **-s**) *n* gnu *m*.

GNVQ (*abbr of* **General National Vocational Qualification**) *n EDUC curso de formação profissional com duração de dois anos para maiores de 16 anos na Inglaterra e no País de Gales.*

go [gəʊ] (*pt* **went**, *pp* **gone**, *pl* **goes**) *vi* **-1.** [move, travel] ir; **to ~ home** ir para casa; **to ~ to Brazil** ir ao Brasil; **to ~ by bus** ir de ônibus; **to ~ for a walk** fazer um passeio; **to ~ and do sthg** ir fazer algo; **to ~ in** entrar; **to ~ out** sair **-2.** [leave] ir-se; **it's time for us to ~** é hora de irmos embora; **when does the bus ~?** quando é que ônibus sai?; **~ away!** vá embora! **-3.** [attend] ir; **to ~ to school** ir para a escola; **which school do you ~ to?** para que escola você vai? **-4.** [become] ficar; **she went pale** empalideceu; **the milk has gone sour** o leite azedou **-5.** [expressing future tense]: **to be going to do sthg** ir fazer algo **-6.** [function] funcionar; **the car won't ~** o carro não pega **-7.** [stop working] ir-se; **the fuse has gone** o fusível queimou **-8.** [time] passar **-9.** [progress] correr; **to ~ well** correr bem **-10.** [bell, alarm] tocar **-11.** [match] condizer; **to ~ with** condizer com; **red wine doesn't ~ with fish** vinho tinto não combina com peixe **-12.** [be sold] ser vendido; **'everything must ~'** 'liquidação total' **-13.** [fit] caber **-14.** [lead] ir; **where does this path ~?** aonde vai dar este caminho? **-15.** [belong] ir, ser **-16.** [in phrases]: **to let ~ of sthg** [drop] largar algo; **there are two days to ~** faltam dois dias; **to ~** *US* [to take away] para levar. ◇ *n* **-1.** [turn] vez *f*; **it's your ~** é a sua vez **-2.** [attempt] tentativa *f*; **to have a ~ at sthg** experimentar algo; **'50 cents a ~'** [for game] '50 centavos cada vez'.

◆ **go ahead** *vi* [take place] realizar-se; **~ ahead!** vá em frente!

◆ **go around** *vi* [revolve] rodar; **there isn't enough cake to ~ around** não tem bolo (suficiente) para todo mundo.

◆ **go back** *vi* voltar.

◆ **go down** *vi* [decrease] diminuir; [sun] pôr-se; [tire] esvaziar-se.

◆ **go in** *vi* entrar.

◆ **go off** *vi* [alarm, bell] tocar, soar; [go bad] azedar; [light, heating] apagar-se.

◆ **go on** *vi* [happen] passar-se; [light, heating] acender-se; **to ~ on doing sthg** continuar a fazer algo.

◆ **go out** *vi* [leave house] sair; [light, fire, cigarette] apagar-se; [have relationship]: **to ~ out with sb** sair com alguém; **to ~ out to eat** ir comer fora.

◆ **go over** *vt fus* [check] rever.

◆ **go through** *vt fus* [experience] passar por; [spend] gastar; [search] revistar.

◆ **go up** *vi* [increase] subir.

◆ **go without** *vt fus* passar sem.

goad [gəʊd] *vt* [provoke] provocar; **to ~ sb into doing sthg** incitar alguém a fazer algo.

go-ahead ◇ *adj* [dynamic] dinâmico(ca), empreendedor(ra). ◇ *n* [permission] permissão *f*; **to give sb the ~ (for sthg)** dar a luz verde a alguém (para algo).

goal [gəʊl] *n* **-1.** *SPORT* gol *m*; **to score a ~** fazer um gol, marcar um gol **-2.** [aim] meta *f*, objetivo *m*.

goalie ['gəʊlɪ] *n* **inf** goleiro *m*, -ra *f*.

goalkeeper ['gəʊlˌki:pəʳ] *n* goleiro *m*, -ra *f*.

goalless ['gəʊllɪs] *adj*: **~ draw** empate sem gols.

goalmouth ['gəʊlmaʊθ, pl -maʊðz] *n* boca *f* do gol.

goalpost ['gəʊlpəʊst] *n* trave *f*.

goat [gəʊt] *n* [animal] cabra *f*, bode *m*; **to act the ~** *UK* comportar-se de forma tola; **to get (on) sb's ~** encher o saco de agluém.

goatee (beard) *n* cavanhaque *m*.

goat's cheese *n* queijo *m* de cabra.

gob [gɒb] (*pt* & *pp* **-bed**, *cont* **-bing**) *v inf* ◇ *n* **-1.** *UK* [mouth] matraca *f*, bico *m* **-2.** *UK* [spit] escarro *m*. ◇ *vi* [spit] escarrar.

gobble ['gɒbl] *vt* devorar.

◆ **gobble down, gobble up** *vt sep* engolir rapidamente.

gobbledygook ['gɒbldɪgu:k] *n* **-1.** [incomprehensible language] linguagem *f* incompreensível, palavreado *m* sem sentido **-2.** *inf* [nonsense] asneiras *fpl*.

go-between *n* intermediário *m*, -ria *f*.

Gobi ['gəʊbɪ] *n*: **the ~ Desert** o Deserto de Gobi.

goblet ['gɒblɪt] *n* cálice *m*.

goblin ['gɒblɪn] *n* duende *m*.
gobsmacked ['gɒbsmækt] *adj UK v inf* embasbacado(da).
go-cart *n* = **go-kart**.
god [gɒd] *n* deus *m*.
◆ **God** ◇ *n* Deus *m*; **God knows** só Deus sabe; **for God's sake!** pelo amor de Deus!; **thank God** graças a Deus; **God willing** se Deus quiser. ◇ *excl*: **(my) God!** (meu) Deus!
◆ **gods** *npl UK inf*: **the ~s** THEATRE as galerias.
godchild ['gɒdtʃaɪld] (*pl* **-children** [-,tʃɪldrən]) *n* afilhado *m*, -da *f*.
goddam(n) ['gɒdæm] *esp US v inf* ◇ *adj* maldito(ta); **where's the ~ key?** cadê a porcaria da chave?; **what a ~ waste of time!** que perda de tempo imbecil! ◇ *excl* maldito!, maldita!
goddaughter ['gɒd,dɔːtə^r] *n* afilhada *f*.
goddess ['gɒdɪs] *n* deusa *f*.
godfather ['gɒd,fɑːðə^r] *n* padrinho *m*.
godforsaken ['gɒdfə,seɪkn] *adj* abandonado(da) por Deus, que Deus esqueceu.
godmother ['gɒd,mʌðə^r] *n* madrinha *f*.
godparents ['gɒd,peərənts] *npl* padrinhos *mpl*.
godsend ['gɒdsend] *n* dádiva *f* de Deus.
godson ['gɒdsʌn] *n* afilhado *m*.
goes [gəʊz] *vb* ⊳ **go**.
gofer ['gəʊfə^r] *n US inf* serviçal *m*.
go-getter [-'getə^r] *n* pessoa *f* dinâmica.
goggle ['gɒgl] *vi*: **to ~ (at sb/sthg)** arregalar os olhos (para alguém ou algo).
goggles ['gɒglz] *npl* óculos *m* de proteção.
go-go dancer *n dançarina sexy (de bar, boite)*.
going ['gəʊɪŋ] ◇ *adj* **-1.** [rate, salary] em vigor, atual **-2.** *UK* [available, in existence] disponível; **she's the biggest fool ~** ela é a maior trouxa do momento. ◇ *n* **-1.** [progress] avanço *m*, marcha *f*; **that's good ~** isso é que é andar rápido; **it was slow ~** estava indo devagar; **to be heavy ~** ser pesado(da); **to be easy ~** ser fácil (de lidar) **-2.** [in riding, horse-racing] condições *fpl* (do chão de corrida).
going concern *n* empresa *f* lucrativa e próspera.
goings-on *npl inf* coisas *fpl* estranhas.
go-kart [-kɑːt] *n UK* kart *m*.
Golan Heights ['gəʊ,læn-] *npl*: **the ~** os Altos de Golan.
gold [gəʊld] ◇ *adj* [gold-coloured] dourado(da). ◇ *n* **-1.** *(U)* [metal] ouro *m*; **to be as good as ~** ser bem comportado(da), ser de ouro **-2.** *(U)* [gold jewellery, ornaments, coins] riquezas *fpl* **-3.** [medal] dobrão *m*. ◇ *comp* [made of gold] de ouro.
golden ['gəʊldən] *adj* **-1.** [made of gold] de ouro **-2.** [gold-coloured] dourado(da).
golden age *n* idade *f* de ouro.
golden eagle *n* águia-real *f*.
golden handshake *n* bolada *f*.
golden opportunity *n* oportunidade *f* de ouro.
golden retriever *n* golden retriever *m*.
golden rule *n* regra *f* de ouro.
golden wedding *n* bodas *fpl* de ouro.
goldfish ['gəʊldfɪʃ] (*pl inv*) *n* peixe-dourado *m*.
goldfish bowl *n* aquário *m* para peixes-dourados.
gold leaf *n (U)* ouro *m* em folha.
gold medal *n* medalha *f* de ouro.
goldmine ['gəʊldmaɪn] *n lit, fig* mina *f* de ouro.
gold-plated [-'pleɪtɪd] *adj* banhado(da) a ouro.
gold standard *adj* padrão-ouro *m*.
goldsmith ['gəʊldsmɪθ] *n* ourives *mf*.
golf [gɒlf] *n (U)* golfe *m*.
golf ball *n* **-1.** [for golf] bola *f* de golfe **-2.** [for typewriter] esfera *f*.
golf club *n* **-1.** [association, place] clube *m* de golfe **-2.** [stick] taco *m* de golfe.
golf course *n* campo *m* de golfe.
golfer ['gɒlfə^r] *n* jogador *m*, -ra *f* de golfe.
golly ['gɒlɪ] *excl inf dated* Deus do céu!
gondola ['gɒndələ] *n* [boat] gôndola *f*.
gondolier [,gɒndə'lɪə^r] *n* gondoleiro *m*, -ra *f*.
gone [gɒn] ◇ *pp* ⊳ **go**. ◇ *adj* [no longer here] que já se foi. ◇ *prep* [past]: **it's just ~ mid-day** já passa do meio-dia; **she's ~ fifty** ela já passou dos cinqüenta.
gong [gɒŋ] *n* gongo *f*.
gonna ['gɒnə] *cont inf* = **going to**.
gonorrh(o)ea [,gɒnə'rɪə] *n (U)* gonorréia *f*.
goo [guː] *n (U) inf* meleca *f*.
good [gʊd] (*compar* **better**, *superl* **best**) ◇ *adj* **-1.** [gen] bom, boa; **it feels ~ to be in the fresh air** faz bem estar ao ar livre; **it's ~ that ...** é bom que ...; **to be ~ at sthg** ser bom em algo, ser boa em algo; **to be ~ with** [children, animals] ter jeito com; [one's hands] ter habilidade com **-2.** [kind] gentil; **to be ~ to sb** ser bom para alguém, ser boa para alguém; **to be ~ enough to do sthg** fazer o favor de fazer algo; **a ~ number of people** um bom número de pessoas **-3.** [morally correct] correto(ta) **-4.** [well-behaved] bem-comportado(da); **be ~!** comporte-se bem! **-5.** [beneficial]: **it's ~ for you** faz bem para você **-6.** [attractive] bonito(ta) **-7.** *phr*: **it's a ~ job** OR **thing (that) ...** ainda bem que ...; **~ for you!** que bom para você!; **to give as ~ as one gets** pagar na mesma moeda; **to make sthg ~** reparar algo. ◇ *n* **-1.** *(U)* [benefit, welfare] bem *m*; **for the ~ of** para o bem de; **for your own ~** para o seu próprio bem; **it will do him ~** fará bem a ele **-2.** [use]: **it's no ~** não adianta; **what's the ~ of ...?** qual é a vantagem de ...?; **will this be any ~?** isto serve? **-3.** [morality, virtue] bem *m*; **to be up to no ~** estar com más intenções. ◇ *excl* que bom!
◆ **goods** *npl* [merchandise] mercadorias *fpl*; **to come up with** OR **deliver the ~s** *UK inf* fazer o esperado.
◆ **as good as** *adv* quase; **it's as ~ as new** está praticamente novo.
◆ **for good** *adv* [forever] para sempre.
◆ **good afternoon** *excl* boa tarde!
◆ **good day** *excl dated* OR *Austr* tenha um bom dia!
◆ **good evening** *excl* boa noite!
◆ **good morning** *excl* bom dia!
◆ **good night** *excl* boa noite!
good behaviour *n* bom comportamento *m*.
goodbye [,gʊd'baɪ] ◇ *excl* até logo! ◇ *n* adeus *m*.

good deed *n* boa ação *f*.
good-for-nothing ◇ *adj* imprestável. ◇ *n* imprestável *mf*.
good fortune *n* boa sorte *f*.
Good Friday *n* Sexta-Feira *f* Santa.
good-humoured [-'hju:məd] *adj* bem-humorado(da).
good-looking [-'lʊkɪŋ] *adj* [person] bonito(ta).
good manners *npl* boas maneiras *fpl*.
good-natured [-'neɪtʃəd] *adj* **-1.** [person] de bom coração **-2.** [rivalry, argument] amigável.
goodness ['gʊdnɪs] ◇ *n* **-1.** [kindness] bondade *f* **-2.** [nutritive quality] valor *m* nutritivo. ◇ *excl*: **(my)** ~**!** minha nossa!; **for** ~ **sake!** pelo amor de Deus!; **thank** ~ graças a Deus!; ~ **gracious!** Santo Deus!
goods train [gʊdz-] *n UK* trem *m* de carga.
good-tempered [-'tempəd] *adj* calmo(ma).
good turn *n*: **to do sb a** ~ fazer um favor a alguém.
goodwill [,gʊd'wɪl] *n* **-1.** [kind feelings] boa vontade *f* **-2.** COMM fundo *m* de comércio.
goody ['gʊdɪ] (*pl* **-ies**) ◇ *n inf* [good person] mocinho *m*, -nha *f*. ◇ *excl* que ótimo!
◆ **goodies** *npl inf* **-1.** [delicious food] guloseimas *fpl* **-2.** [desirable objects] coisas *fpl* atraentes.
gooey ['gu:ɪ] (*compar* **gooier**, *superl* **gooiest**) *adj inf* [sticky] grudento(ta).
goof [gu:f] *US inf* ◇ *n* **-1.** [mistake] mancada *f* **-2.** [person] palerma *mf*. ◇ *vi* dar uma mancada.
◆ **goof off** *vi US inf* vadear.
goofy ['gu:fɪ] (*compar* **-ier**, *superl* **-iest**) *adj* **-1.** *inf* [person] pateta **-2.** *inf* [behaviour, clothes] simplório(ria).
goose [gu:s] (*pl* **geese** [gi:s]) *n* [bird] ganso *m*, -sa *f*.
gooseberry ['gʊzbərɪ] (*pl* **-ies**) *n* **-1.** [fruit] groselha *f* **-2.** *UK inf* [unwanted person]: **to play** ~ segurar a vela.
gooseflesh ['gu:sfleʃ], **goose pimples** *UK n*, **goosebumps** *US* ['gu:sbʌmps] *npl* arrepio *m*.
goosestep ['gu:s,step] (*pt* & *pp* **-ped**, *cont* **-ping**) ◇ *n* passo *m* de ganso. ◇ *vi* andar a passo de ganso.
GOP (*abbr of* **Grand Old Party**) *n US partido republicano norte-americano.*
gopher ['gəʊfə^r] *n pequeno roedor semelhante a uma ratazana encontrado nos Estados Unidos.*
gore [gɔ:^r] ◇ *n (U) literary* [blood] sangue *m (derramado)*. ◇ *vt* [subj: bull] ferir com os chifres.
gorge [gɔ:dʒ] ◇ *n* garganta *f*, desfiladeiro *m*. ◇ *vt*: **to** ~ **o.s. on** OR **with sthg** empanturrar-se com algo.
gorgeous ['gɔ:dʒəs] *adj* **-1.** [place, present, weather] magnífico(ca), maravilhoso(sa) **-2.** *inf* [person] deslumbrante.
gorilla [gə'rɪlə] *n* gorila *m*.
gormless ['gɔ:mlɪs] *adj UK inf* burro(ra).
gorse [gɔ:s] *n (U)* tojo *m*.
gory ['gɔ:rɪ] (*compar* **-ier**, *superl* **-iest**) *adj* sangrento(-ta).
gosh [gɒʃ] *excl inf* por Deus!
go-slow *n UK* operação *f* tartaruga.
gospel ['gɒspl] ◇ *n* **-1.** [doctrine] evangelho *m* **-2.**: ~ **(truth)** verdade absoluta. ◇ *comp* gospel *inv*; ~ **music/singer** música/cantor(ra) gospel.
◆ **Gospel** *n* [in Bible] Evangelho *m*.
gossamer ['gɒsəmə^r] *n* **-1.** [spider's thread] teia *f* de aranha **-2.** [material] *tecido muito fino*.
gossip ['gɒsɪp] ◇ *n* **-1.** [conversation] conversa *f*, bate-papo *m*; **to have a** ~ bater papo **-2.** [person] fofoca *f*. ◇ *vi* fofocar.
gossip column *n* coluna *f* social.
got [gɒt] *pt* & *pp* ▻ **get**.
Gothic ['gɒθɪk] *adj* gótico(ca).
gotta ['gɒtə] *cont inf* = **got to**.
gotten ['gɒtn] *pp US* ▻ **get**.
gouge [gaʊdʒ] ◆ **gouge out** *vt sep* **-1.** [hole] abrir **-2.** [eyes] arrancar.
goulash ['gu:læʃ] *n (U)* gulash *m (prato típico húngaro)*.
gourd [gʊəd] *n* cabaço *m*.
gourmet ['gʊəmeɪ] ◇ *n* gourmet *m*. ◇ *comp* gastrônomo *m*, -ma *f*.
gout [gaʊt] *n (U)* gota *f*.
govern ['gʌvən] ◇ *vt* **-1.** POL governar **-2.** [determine] controlar. ◇ *vi* POL governar.
governable *adj* POL governável.
governess ['gʌvənɪs] *n* governanta *f*.
governing ['gʌvənɪŋ] *adj* POL governante.
governing body *n* conselho *m* administrativo.
government ['gʌvnmənt] ◇ *n* **-1.** [group of people] governo *m* **-2.** *(U)* [process] governo *m*; **the art of** ~ a arte de governar. ◇ *comp* do governo.
governmental [,gʌvn'mentl] *adj* governamental.
government stock *n* títulos *mpl* do governo.
governor ['gʌvənə^r] *n* **-1.** POL governador *m*, -ra *f* **-2.** [of school] diretor *m*, -ra *f* **-3.** [of prison] diretor *m*, -ra *f*.
governor-general (*pl* **governor-generals** OR **governors-general**) *n* governador geral *m*.
govt (*abbr of* **government**) gov.
gown [gaʊn] *n* **-1.** [dress] vestido *m* **-2.** UNIV & JUR beca *f* **-3.** MED avental *m*.
GP (*abbr of* **general practitioner**) *n* clínico *m* geral.
GPO *n* **-1.** (*abbr of* **General Post Office**) *antigo serviço britânico de correios*. **-2.** (*abbr of* **Government Printing Office**) *departamento de imprensa do governo (norte-americano)*.
gr. -1. *abbr of* **gross**. **-2.** (*abbr of* **gram**) g.
grab [græb] (*pt* & *pp* **-bed**, *cont* **-bing**) ◇ *vt* **-1.** [with hands - person, arm] agarrar; [- money] pegar **-2.** *fig* [opportunity, sandwich] pegar; **to** ~ **the chance to do sthg** aproveitar a oportunidade de fazer algo **-3.** *inf* [appeal to] arrebatar; **how does this** ~ **you?** o que você me diz disso? ◇ *vi*: **to** ~ **at sthg** [with hands] tentar agarrar. ◇ *n*: **to make a** ~ **at** OR **for sthg** tentar apoderar-se de algo.
grace [greɪs] ◇ *n* **-1.** *(U)* [elegance] graça *f*, elegância *f* **-2.** [graciousness]: **to have the** ~ **to do sthg** ter finura para fazer algo; **to do sthg with good** ~ fazer algo de bom grado **-3.** *(U)* [extra time] prazo *m* **-4.** [prayer] graças *fpl*. ◇ *vt* **-1.** *fml* [honour] agraciar **-2.** [adorn] enfeitar.

◆ **Grace** *n* [title] Eminência *f.*
graceful ['greɪsfʊl] *adj* **-1.** [beautiful] elegante **-2.** [gracious] amável.
graceless ['greɪslɪs] *adj* **-1.** [lacking charm] sem graça **-2.** [ill-mannered] deselegante.
gracious ['greɪʃəs] <> *adj* **-1.** [polite] afável **-2.** [elegant] elegante. <> *excl*: **(good) ~!** Santo Deus!, Nossa (Senhora)!
graciously ['greɪʃəslɪ] *adv* [politely] afavelmente.
gradation [grə'deɪʃn] *n* [of colour, light] gradação *f.*
grade [greɪd] <> *n* **-1.** [level] nível *m* **-2.** [quality] qualidade *f*; **high-~** de alta qualidade; **low-~** de baixa qualidade; **to make the ~** obter sucesso **-3.** *US* [in school] série *f* **-4.** [mark] classificação *f* **-5.** *US* [gradient] declive *m.* <> *vt* **-1.** [classify] classificar **-2.** [mark, assess] avaliar.
grade crossing *n US* passagem *f* de nível.
grade school *n US* escola *f* primária.
grade school teacher *n US* professor *m*, -ra *f* de nível primário.
gradient ['greɪdjənt] *n* **-1.** [of road] declive *m* **-2.** *MATH* gradiente *m.*
gradual ['grædʒʊəl] *adj* gradual.
gradually ['grædʒʊəlɪ] *adv* gradualmente.
graduate [*n* 'grædʒʊət, *vb* 'grædʒʊeɪt] <> *n* **-1.** [person with a degree] graduado *m*, -da *f*, licenciado *m*, -da *f* **-2.** *US*: **to be a high-school ~** ter completado o segundo grau. <> *comp US* [postgraduate] pós-graduado(da). <> *vi* **-1.** [with a degree]: **to ~** graduar-se **-2.** *US* [from high school]: **to ~** formar-se **-3.** [progress]: **to ~ from sthg (to sthg)** passar *OR* evoluir de algo (para algo).
graduated ['grædjʊeɪtɪd] *adj* [gen] graduado(da); [pension, tax] retroativo(va).
graduate school *n US* escola *f* de pós-graduação.
graduation [ˌgrædʒʊ'eɪʃn] *n* **-1.** [completion of course] formatura *f* **-2.** [ceremony - at university] colação *f* de grau; *US* [at high school] formatura *f.*
graffiti [grə'fi:tɪ] *n (U)* pichação *f.*
graft [grɑ:ft] <> *n* **-1.** [gen] enxerto *m* **-2.** *UK inf* [hard work] labuta *f* **-3.** *US inf* [corruption] suborno *m.* <> *vt* **-1.** enxertar; **to ~ sthg onto sthg** enxertar algo em algo **-2.** [idea, system] combinar; **to ~ sthg onto sthg** combinar algo com algo.
grain [greɪn] *n* **-1.** [of corn, rice, salt] grão *m* **-2.** *(U)* [crops] cereais *mpl* **-3.** *fig* [small amount] parcela *f* mínima; **there wasn't a ~ of truth in what he said** não havia uma palavra de verdade no que ele disse **-4.** *(U)* [of wood] veio *m*; **it goes against the ~ for me** *fig* vai contra a minha natureza.
gram [græm] *n* grama *f.*
grammar ['græmə^r] *n* gramática *f.*
grammar school *n* **-1.** [in UK] ginásio *m* **-2.** [in US] escola *f* primária.
grammatical [grə'mætɪkl] *adj* gramatical.
gramme [græm] *n UK* = **gram**.
gramophone ['græməfəʊn] *dated* <> *n* gramofone *m.* <> *comp* de gramofone.
gran [græn] *n UK inf* vovó *f.*
Granada [grə'nɑ:də] *n* Granada; **in ~** em Granada.
granary ['grænərɪ] (*pl* **-ies**) *n* celeiro *m.*
granary bread *n* pão *m* de trigo.
grand [grænd] (*pl inv*) <> *adj* **-1.** [impressive, imposing] magnífico(ca) **-2.** [ambitious, large-scale] ambicioso(-sa) **-3.** [socially important] ilustre **-4.** *inf dated* [excellent] excelente. <> *n inf* [thousand pounds] mil libras *fpl*; [thousand dollars] mil dólares *mpl.*
grandad *n inf* vovô *m.*
Grand Canyon *n*: **the ~** o Grand Canyon.
grandchild ['græntʃaɪld] (*pl* **-children** [-ˌtʃɪldrən]) *n* neto *m*, -ta *f.*
granddad ['grændæd] *n inf* = **grandad**.
granddaughter ['grænˌdɔ:tə^r] *n* neta *f.*
grand duchess *n* [noblewoman] grã-duquesa *f.*
grand duke *n* [nobleman] grão-duque *m.*
grandeur ['grændʒə^r] *n* grandeza *f.*
grandfather ['grændˌfɑ:ðə^r] *n* avô *m.*
grandfather clock *n* relógio *m* de pêndulo.
grandiose ['grændɪəʊz] *adj pej* espalhafatoso(sa).
grand jury *n US* júri *m* principal.
grandma ['grænmɑ:] *n inf* vovó *f*, vó *f.*
grand master *n* grão-mestre *m.*
grandmother ['grænˌmʌðə^r] *n* avó *f.*
Grand National *n*: **the ~** a Grand National, *corrida de cavalos realizada anualmente em Liverpool, na Inglaterra.*
grandpa ['grænpɑ:] *n inf* vovô *m*, vô *m.*
grandparents ['grænˌpeərənts] *npl* avós *mpl.*
grand piano *n* piano *m* de cauda.
grand prix [ˌgrɒn'pri:] (*pl* **grands prix**) *n* grande prêmio *m.*
grand slam *n SPORT* grand slam *m.*
grandson ['grænsʌn] *n* neto *m.*
grandstand ['grændstænd] *n* tribuna *f* de honra.
grand total *n* total *m* geral.
granite ['grænɪt] *n (U)* granito *m.*
granny ['grænɪ] (*pl* **-ies**) *n inf* vovó *f*, vó *f.*
granny flat *n UK local dentro ou próximo à casa de uma pessoa, feito para que um parente de idade possa viver nele.*
granola [grə'nəʊlə] *n US* granola *f.*
grant [grɑ:nt] <> *n* [money - for renovations] subsídio *m*; [- for study] bolsa *f.* <> *vt fml* **-1.** [agree to] conceder **-2.** [accept as true] admitir; **I ~ (that) ...** eu admito que ... **-3.** *phr*: **to take sb/sthg for ~ed** não dar o devido valor a alguém/algo; **to take it for ~ed that ...** tomar como certo que ...
granulated sugar ['grænjʊleɪtɪd-] *n (U)* açucar *m* -cristal.
granule ['grænju:l] *n* grânulo *m.*
grape [greɪp] *n* uva *f.*
grapefruit ['greɪpfru:t] (*pl inv OR* **-s**) *n* pomelo *m.*
grape picking [-'pɪkɪŋ] *n (U)* colheita *f* de uvas.
grapevine ['greɪpvaɪn] *n* **-1.** [plant] parreira *f* **-2.** *fig* [information channel]: **I heard on the ~ that ...** um passarinho me contou que ...
graph [grɑ:f] *n* gráfico *m.*
graphic ['græfɪk] *adj* **-1.** [vivid] vívido(da) **-2.** *ART* pitoresco(ca).
◆ **graphics** *npl* [pictures] artes *fpl* gráficas; **computer ~s** gráfico *m* de computador.
graphic artist *n* artista *mf* gráfico, -ca.
graphic design *n (U)* projeto *m* gráfico.

graphic designer *n* projetista *mf* gráfico, -ca.
graphic equalizer *n* equalizador *m* gráfico.
graphics card *n* COMPUT placa *f* gráfica.
graphite ['græfaɪt] *n (U)* grafita *f.*
graphology [græ'fɒlədʒɪ] *n (U)* grafologia *f.*
graph paper *n (U)* papel *m* quadriculado.
grapple ['græpl] ◆ **grapple with** *vt fus* **-1.** [physically] atracar-se com **-2.** *fig* [mentally] estar às voltas com.
grappling iron ['græplɪŋ-] *n* arpéu *m.*
grasp [grɑ:sp] ◇ *n* **-1.** [grip] agarramento *m* **-2.** [power to achieve]: **in** OR **within one's ~** ao alcance de alguém **-3.** [understanding] compreensão *f*; **to have a good ~ of sthg** ter um bom domínio de algo. ◇ *vt* **-1.** [with hands] segurar **-2.** [understand] compreender **-3.** *fig* [seize] agarrar.
grasping ['grɑ:spɪŋ] *adj pej* [greedy - person] ganancioso(sa); [- attitude] avaro(ra).
grass [grɑ:s] ◇ *n* **-1.** [common green plant] grama *f* **-2.** *(U) drugs sl* [marijuana] maconha *f.* ◇ *vi UK crime sl*: **to ~ (on sb)** dedurar alguém.
grasshopper ['grɑ:s,hɒpə^r] *n* gafanhoto *m.*
grassland ['grɑ:slænd] *n* pastagem *f.*
grass roots ◇ *npl* [ordinary people] plebe *f.* ◇ *comp* popular.
grass snake *n* cobra *f* d'água.
grassy ['grɑ:sɪ] (*compar* **-ier**, *superl* **-iest**) *adj* coberto(ta) de grama.
grate [greɪt] ◇ *n* [fireplace] grade *f.* ◇ *vt* CULIN ralar. ◇ *vi* [irritate] irritar; **to ~ on sb's nerves** deixar alguém com os nervos à flor da pele.
grateful ['greɪtfʊl] *adj* agradecido(da); **to be ~ to sb (for sthg)** ser grato(ta) a alguém (por algo).
gratefully ['greɪtfʊlɪ] *adv* agradecidamente.
grater ['greɪtə^r] *n* ralador *m.*
gratification [,grætɪfɪ'keɪʃn] *n* **-1.** [pleasure] gratificação *f* **-2.** [satisfaction] satisfação *f.*
gratify ['grætɪfaɪ] (*pt* & *pp* **-ied**) *vt* **-1.** [please]: **to be gratified** sentir-se gratificado(da) **-2.** [satisfy] satisfazer.
gratifying ['grætɪfaɪɪŋ] *adj* [pleasing] gratificante.
grating ['greɪtɪŋ] ◇ *adj* áspero(ra). ◇ *n* [grille] grade *f.*
gratitude ['grætɪtju:d] *n (U)* gratidão *f*; **~ to sb (for sthg)** gratidão por alguém (por algo).
gratuitous [grə'tju:ɪtəs] *adj fml* [unjustified] gratuito(ta).
gratuity [grə'tju:ɪtɪ] (*pl* **-ies**) *n fml* [tip] gratificação *f.*
grave [greɪv] ◇ *adj* grave. ◇ *n* túmulo *m*; **to turn in one's ~** revirar-se no túmulo; **to dig one's own ~** cavar a própria sepultura.
grave accent [grɑ:v-] *n* acento *m* grave.
gravedigger ['greɪv,dɪgə^r] *n* coveiro *m*, -ra *f.*
gravel ['grævl] ◇ *n (U)* cascalho *m.* ◇ *comp* de cascalho.
gravelled *UK*, **graveled** *US* ['grævld] *adj* de cascalho.
gravestone ['greɪvstəʊn] *n* lápide *f.*
graveyard ['greɪvjɑ:d] *n* cemitério *m.*
gravitate ['grævɪteɪt] *vi*: **to ~ towards sb/sthg** *fig* [be attracted to] ser atraído(da) por alguém/algo.
gravity ['grævətɪ] *n* **-1.** [force] gravidade *f* **-2.** *fml* [seriousness, worrying nature] seriedade *f*, gravidade *f* **-3.** [solemnity] gravidade *f.*
gravy ['greɪvɪ] *n* **-1.** [meat juice] molho *m* de carne; [sauce] caldo *m* de carne **-2.** *US v inf* [easy money] grana *f* fácil.
gravy boat *n* molheira *f.*
gravy train *n inf*: **the ~** a mina de ouro.
gray *adj* & *n US* = **grey**.
grayscale *n US* = **greyscale**.
graze [greɪz] ◇ *n* [wound] machucado *m*, ferimento *m.* ◇ *vt* **-1.** [feed on] pastar **-2.** [cause to feed] pastorear **-3.** [break surface of] esfolar **-4.** [touch lightly] tocar de leve. ◇ *vi* [animals] pastar.
grease [gri:s] ◇ *n* **-1.** [animal fat] gordura *f* **-2.** [lubricant] graxa *f* **-3.** [dirt] sebo *m.* ◇ *vt* **-1.** [gen] engraxar **-2.** [baking tray] untar.
grease gun *n* bomba *f* engraxadeira.
greasepaint ['gri:speɪnt] *n (U)* maquilagem *f* para o teatro.
greaseproof paper [,gri:spru:f-] *n (U) UK* papel *m* parafinado.
greasy ['gri:zɪ] (*compar* **-ier**, *superl* **-iest**) *adj* **-1.** [food] gorduroso(sa); [tools] engordurado(da); [hair, hands, skin] seboso(sa) **-2.** [clothes] sujo(ja) **-3.** [road] escorregadio(dia).
greasy spoon *n hum* [cafe] boteco *m.*
great [greɪt] ◇ *adj* **-1.** [gen] grande **-2.** *inf* [really good, really nice] ótimo(ma). ◇ *n* grande *mf.* ◇ *excl* ótimo!
Great Barrier Reef *n*: **the ~** a Grande Barreira.
Great Bear *n*: **the ~** (a) Ursa Maior.
Great Britain *n* Grã-Bretanha; **in ~** na Grã-Bretanha.
greatcoat ['greɪtkəʊt] *n* sobretudo *m* pesado.
Great Dane *n* pastor *m* dinamarquês.
Great Depression *n*: **the ~** a Grande Depressão.
great-grandchild *n* bisneto *m*, -ta *f.*
great-grandfather *n* bisavô *m.*
great-grandmother *n* bisavó *f.*
Great Lakes *npl*: **the ~** os Grandes Lagos.
greatly ['greɪtlɪ] *adv* imensamente; **~ exaggerated** muito exagerado(da); **~ different** extremamente diferente.
greatness ['greɪtnɪs] *n* grandeza *f.*
Great Wall of China *n*: **the ~** a Grande Muralha da China.
Great War *n*: **the ~** a Grande Guerra.
Greece [gri:s] *n* Grécia; **in ~** na Grécia.
greed [gri:d] *n* **-1.** [for food] gula *f* **-2.** *fig* [for money, power]: **~ (for sthg)** ganância (por algo).
greedily ['gri:dɪlɪ] *adv* gulosamente.
greedy ['gri:dɪ] (*compar* **-ier**, *superl* **-iest**) *adj* **-1.** [for food] guloso(sa) **-2.** *fig* [for money, power]: **~ for sthg** ganancioso(sa) por algo.
Greek [gri:k] ◇ *adj* grego(ga); **the ~ Islands** as Ilhas Gregas. ◇ *n* **-1.** [person] grego *m*, -ga *f* **-2.** [language] grego *m.*
green [gri:n] ◇ *adj* **-1.** [gen] verde **-2.** *inf* [with nausea, fear] pálido(da) **-3.** *inf* [inexperienced] novato(ta) **-4.** *inf* [jealous]: **~ (with envy)** morto(ta) de ciúme. ◇ *n* **-1.** [colour] verde; **in ~** de verde **-2.** [in village] praça *f* **-3.** GOLF green *m.*

◆ **Green** *n POL* Verde; **the Greens** os Verdes.
◆ **greens** *npl* [vegetables] verduras *fpl*.
greenback ['gri:nbæk] *n US inf* [banknote] nota *f* de dólar.
green bean *n* vagem *f*.
green belt *n UK* área *f* verde.
Green Beret *n US inf*: **the ~s** os Green Berets, *membros das Forças Especiais norte-americanas.*
green card *n* **-1.** *UK* [for insuring vehicle] *seguro que protege veículos e motoristas no exterior* **-2.** *US* [resident's permit] green card *m*, visto *m* permanente *(nos Estados Unidos)*.

GREEN CARD

Assim se denomina o documento que permite a um estrangeiro viver e trabalhar nos Estados Unidos. A despeito do nome, hoje o *green card* já não é verde. O processo para sua obtenção é longo e complexo. O interessado deve possuir um parente próximo que seja cidadão estadunidense ou estar empregado numa companhia do país. Do contrário, precisará comprovar que tem condições de fazer investimentos financeiros nos Estados Unidos.

greenery ['gri:nərɪ] *n (U)* folhagem *f*.
green fingers *npl UK*: **to have ~** ter dom/mão boa para jardinagem.
greenfly ['gri:nflaɪ] (*pl inv* OR **-ies**) *n* pulgão *m*.
greengage ['gri:ngeɪdʒ] *n* rainha-cláudia *f*.
greengrocer ['gri:n,grəʊsə'] *n* verdureiro(ra); **~'s (shop)** quitanda *f*.
greenhorn ['gri:nhɔ:n] *n US* **-1.** [immigrant, new arrival] recém-chegado *m*, -da *f* **-2.** [novice] novato *m*, -ta *f*.
greenhouse ['gri:nhaʊs, *pl* -haʊzɪz] *n* estufa *f*.
greenhouse effect *n*: **the ~** o efeito estufa.
greenhouse gas *n* gás *m* de efeito estufa.
greenish ['gri:nɪʃ] *adj* esverdeado(da).
Greenland ['gri:nlənd] *n* Groenlândia; **in ~** na Groenlândia.
Greenlander ['gri:nləndə'] *n* groenlandês *m*, -esa *f*.
green light *n*: **the ~** o sinal verde.
green paper *n POL projeto de lei.*
Green Party *n*: **the ~** o Partido Verde.
green salad *n* salada *f* verde.
green thumb *n US*: **to have a ~** ter dom/mão boa para jardinagem.
greet [gri:t] *vt* **-1.** [say hello to] cumprimentar **-2.** [speech, announcement, remark] saudar **-3.** [subj: sight, smell] receber.
greeting ['gri:tɪŋ] *n* [salutation] cumprimento *m*, saudação *f*.
◆ **greetings** *npl* [on card] votos *mpl*.
greetings card *UK* ['gri:tɪŋz-], **greeting card** *US n* cartão *m* de comemoração.
gregarious [grɪ'geərɪəs] *adj* gregário(ria).
gremlin ['gremlɪn] *n inf duende que supostamente provoca o mau funcionamento de motores ou outros equipamentos*, gremlin *m*.
Grenada [grə'neɪdə] *n* Granada; **in ~** em Granada.
grenade [grə'neɪd] *n*: **(hand) ~** granada *f* (de mão).
Grenadian [grə'neɪdjən] ◇ *adj* granadino(na). ◇ *n* granadino *m*, -na *f*.
grenadier [,grenə'dɪə'] *n* granadeiro *m*.
grew [gru:] *pt* ▷ **grow**.
grey *UK*, **gray** *US* [greɪ] ◇ *adj* **-1.** [colour, weather] cinzento(ta) **-2.** [hair, beard] grisalho(lha); **to go ~** ficar grisalho(lha) **-3.** [complexion - with fatigue, nausea] desolado(da); [- skin] envelhecido(da) **-4.** *fig* [life, situation] preto(ta). ◇ *n* cinza *m*; **in ~** de cinza.
grey area *n* área *f* cinzenta.
grey-haired [-'heəd] *adj* grisalho(lha).
greyhound ['greɪhaʊnd] *n* galgo *m*.
greying *UK*, **graying** *US* ['greɪɪŋ] *adj* acinzentado(da).
grey matter *n* **-1.** *MED* massa *f* cinzenta **-2.** *inf* [brain power] inteligência *f*.
greyscale *UK*, **grayscale** *US* ['greɪskeɪl] *n COMPUT* escala *f* de tons.
grey squirrel *n* esquilo *m* cinzento.
grid [grɪd] *n* **-1.** [grating] gradeamento *m* **-2.** [system of squares] grade *f* **-3.** *ELEC* rede *f*.
griddle ['grɪdl] *n* chapa *f* de ferro *(para assar)*.
gridiron ['grɪd,aɪən] *n* **-1.** [in cooking] grelha *f* **-2.** *US* [game] futebol *m* americano; [field] campo *m* de futebol americano.
gridlock ['grɪdlɒk] *n* empasse *m*.
grid reference *n* coordenadas *fpl*.
grief [gri:f] *n* **-1.** [sorrow] pesar *m*, tristeza *f* **-2.** *inf* [trouble] chateação *f* **-3.** *phr*: **to come to ~** fracassar; **good ~!** credo!
grief-stricken *adj* agoniado(da).
grievance ['gri:vns] *n* [complaint] queixa *m*, agravo *m*.
grieve [gri:v] ◇ *vt fml*: **it ~s me to say that** me dói dizer que. ◇ *vi*: **to ~ (for sb/sthg)** estar de luto por alguém/algo.
grieving ['gri:vɪŋ] *n (U)* luto *m*.
grievous ['gri:vəs] *adj fml* [serious, harmful] doloroso(sa).
grievous bodily harm *n (U)* lesão *f* corporal.
grievously ['gri:vəslɪ] *adv fml* gravemente.
grill [grɪl] ◇ *n* **-1.** [for cooking] grelha *f* **-2.** [food] grelhado *m*. ◇ *vt* **-1.** [cook on grill] grelhar **-2.** *inf* [interrogate] interrogar.
grille [grɪl] *n* grade *f*.
grim [grɪm] (*compar* **-mer**, *superl* **-mest**) *adj* **-1.** [stern] severo(ra), rígido(da) **-2.** [gloomy] deprimente.
grimace [grɪ'meɪs] ◇ *n* careta *f*. ◇ *vi* fazer caretas.
grime [graɪm] *n (U)* sujeira *f*.
grimly ['grɪmlɪ] *adv* **-1.** [unhappily] severamente **-2.** [with determination] rigidamente.
grimy ['graɪmɪ] (*compar* **-ier**, *superl* **-iest**) *adj* imundo(da).
grin [grɪn] (*pt* & *pp* **-ned**, *cont* **-ning**) ◇ *n* sorriso *m* aberto. ◇ *vi*: **to ~ (at sb/sthg)** abrir um sorriso (para alguém/algo); **to ~ and bear it** aceitar (algo) e aguentar firme.
grind [graɪnd] (*pt* & *pp* **ground**) ◇ *vt* **-1.** [coffee, pepper, grain] moer; **freshly ground coffee** café

moído na hora **-2.** [ash, dirt]: **to ~ sthg into sthg** esmagar algo em algo **-3.** [rub together] ranger. <> *vi* [scrape] arranhar. <> *n* **-1.** [hard, boring work] rotina *f* **-2.** *US inf*: **to go ~** ficar grisalho(lha).
◆ **grind down** *vt sep* [oppress] oprimir.
◆ **grind up** *vt sep* **-1.** [bottles] triturar **-2.** [knife] afiar **-3.** *US* [meat] picar **-4.** [gemstone] lapidar.
grinder ['graɪndə^r] *n* [machine] moedor *m*.
grinding ['graɪndɪŋ] *adj* [oppressive] opressivo(va).
grinning *adj* sorridente.
grip [grɪp] (*pt* & *pp* **-ped**, *cont* **-ping**) <> *n* **-1.** [physical hold]: **to have a ~ on sb/sthg** ter o controle sobre alguém/algo; **to keep a ~ on the handrail** segurar-se no corrimão; **to get a good ~** dar um bom aperto; **to release one's ~ on sb/sthg** deixar de controlar alguém/algo **-2.** [control, domination] domínio *m*; **~ on sb/sthg** controle sobre alguém/algo; **in the ~ of sthg** nas garras de algo; **to get to ~s with sthg** encarar algo; **to get a ~ on o.s.** controlar-se; **to lose one's ~** *fig* perder a eficiência **-3.** *(U)* [adhesion] aderência *f* **-4.** [handle] punho *m* **-5.** *dated* [bag] valise *f*. <> *vt* **-1.** [grasp] agarrar **-2.** [subj: tyres] ter aderência a **-3.** [imagination, attention] controlar.
gripe [graɪp] *inf* <> *n* [complaint] queixa *f*; **the ~s** cólicas *fpl*. <> *vi*: **to ~ (about sthg)** resmungar (por causa de algo).
gripping ['grɪpɪŋ] *adj* [story, film] emocionante.
grisly ['grɪzlɪ] (*compar* **-ier**, *superl* **-iest**) *adj* [horrible, macabre] horrendo(da), medonho(nha).
grist [grɪst] *n (U)*: **it's all ~ to sb's** *OR* **the mill** tudo vale *OR* serve.
gristle ['grɪsl] *n (U)* cartilagem *f*.
gristly ['grɪslɪ] (*compar* **-ier**, *superl* **-iest**) *adj* cartilaginoso(sa).
grit [grɪt] (*pt* & *pp* **-ted**, *cont* **-ting**) <> *n* **-1.** [stones] areia *f* **-2.** *inf* [courage] coragem *f*. <> *vt* [road, steps] pôr areia em.
◆ **grits** *npl US* canjica *f*.
gritter ['grɪtə^r] *n veículo que espalha areia nas estradas congeladas.*
gritty ['grɪtɪ] (*compar* **-ier**, *superl* **-iest**) *adj* **-1.** [stony] arenoso(sa) **-2.** *inf* [brave] corajoso(sa).
grizzled ['grɪzld] *adj* acinzentado(da).
grizzly ['grɪzlɪ] (*pl* **-ies**) *n*: **~ (bear)** urso-cinzento *m*.
groan [grəʊn] <> *n* gemido *m*. <> *vi* **-1.** [moan] gemer **-2.** [creak] ranger **-3.** [complain] resmungar.
grocer ['grəʊsə^r] *n* dono *m*, -na *f* de mercearia; **~'s (shop)** mercearia *f*.
groceries ['grəʊsərɪz] *npl* [foods] comestíveis *mpl*.
grocery ['grəʊsərɪ] (*pl* **-ies**) *n* [shop] mercearia *f*.
groggy ['grɒgɪ] (*compar* **-ier**, *superl* **-iest**) *adj* grogue.
groin [grɔɪn] *n ANAT* virilha *f*.
groom [gru:m] <> *n* **-1.** [of horses] cavalariço *m* **-2.** [bridegroom] noivo *m*. <> *vt* **-1.** [horse, dog] tratar **-2.** [candidate]: **to ~ sb (for sthg)** preparar alguém (para algo).
groomed *adj*: **well/badly ~** bem/mal tratado(-da).
groove [gru:v] *n* **-1.** [in metal, wood] entalhe *m* **-2.** [in record] ranhura *f*.
grope [grəʊp] <> *vt* **-1.** [sexually] acariciar **-2.** [try to find]: **to ~ one's way** tatear o caminho. <> *vi*: **to ~ (about) for sthg** [object] tatear por algo; *fig* [solution, remedy] tentar algo às cegas.
gross [grəʊs] (*pl inv OR* **-es**) <> *adj* **-1.** [total] bruto(ta) **-2.** *fml* [serious, inexcusable] grave **-3.** *inf* [coarse, vulgar] indecente **-4.** *inf* [obese] balofo(fa) **-5.** *inf* [disgusting] nojento(ta). <> *n* grosa *f*. <> *vt* [subj: person] receber em bruto; [subj: store, film] arrecadar em bruto.
gross domestic product *n* produto *m* interno bruto.
grossly ['grəʊslɪ] *adv* [for emphasis] extremamente.
gross national product *n* produto *m* nacional bruto.
gross profit *n* lucro *m* bruto.
grotesque [grəʊ'tesk] *adj* [strange, unnatural] grotesco(ca).
grotto ['grɒtəʊ] (*pl* **-es** *OR* **-s**) *n* gruta *f*.
grotty ['grɒtɪ] (*compar* **-ier**, *superl* **-iest**) *adj UK inf* asqueroso(sa).
grouchy ['graʊtʃɪ] (*compar* **-ier**, *superl* **-iest**) *adj inf* mal-humorado(da).
ground [graʊnd] <> *pt* & *pp* ▷ **grind**. <> *n* **-1.** [surface of earth] terra *f*, chão *m*; **above/below ~** em cima/embaixo da terra; **on the ~** no chão; **to be thin on the ~** ser pouco numeroso(sa); **to get sthg off the ~** *fig* iniciar algo com sucesso **-2.** *(U)* [area of land] terreno *m* **-3.** [area used for a particular purpose] campo *m* **-4.** [subject area] área *f*; **to break fresh** *OR* **new ~** dar o primeiro passo **-5.** [advantage]: **to gain/lose ~** ganhar/perder terreno **-6.** *phr*: **to cut the ~ from under sb's feet** puxar o tapete de alguém; **to go to ~** esconder-se; **to run sb/sthg to ~** encontrar alguém/algo; **to run o.s. into the ~** trabalhar até a exaustão; **to stand one's ~** defender seu ponto de vista. <> *vt* **-1.** [base]: **to be ~ed on** *OR* **in sthg** ter algo como base; **to be well-~ed in sthg** estar bem baseado em algo **-2.** [aircraft, pilot] ficar retido(da) **-3.** *esp US inf* [child] ficar de castigo **-4.** *US ELEC*: **to be ~ed** ter um fio-terra.
◆ **grounds** *npl* **-1.** [reason] razão *f*, motivo *m*; **~s for sthg/for doing sthg** motivo para algo/para fazer algo; **on the ~s of** com o pretexto de; **on the ~s that** com o motivo de que **-2.** [land round building] jardins *mpl* **-3.** [area for specific purpose] área *f* **-4.** [of coffee] borra *f*.
ground control *n* controle *m* de terra.
ground cover *n (U)* vegetação *f* rasteira.
ground crew *n* equipe *f* de terra.
ground floor *n* (andar *m*) térreo *m*.
ground-in *adj* impregnado(da).
grounding ['graʊndɪŋ] *n*: **~ (in sthg)** conhecimentos *mpl* básicos (sobre algo).
groundless ['graʊndlɪs] *adj* infundado(da).
ground level *n*: **at ~** ao nível do solo.
groundnut ['graʊndnʌt] *n* amendoim *m*.
ground plan *n* [of building] planta *f* baixa.
ground rent *n* aluguel *m* residencial.
ground rules *npl* regras *fpl* básicas.
groundsheet ['graʊndʃi:t] *n* lona *f*.
groundsman ['graʊndzmən] (*pl* **-men** [-mən]) *n UK* zelador *m* de campo esportivo.

ground staff *n* **-1.** [at sports ground] equipe *f* de campo **-2.** *UK* [at airport] pessoal *m* de terra.
groundswell ['graʊndswel] *n* [of feeling] acirramento *m*.
groundwork ['graʊndwɜːk] *n (U)* base *f*, fundamento *m*.
group [gruːp] ◇ *n* **-1.** [gen] grupo *m* **-2.** *MUS* banda *f*. ◇ *vt* agrupar; [classify] classificar. ◇ *vi*: **to ~ (together)** agrupar-se.
group captain *n UK* ≃ coronel *m (de aviação)*.
groupie ['gruːpɪ] *n inf* tiete *mf*.
group practice *n prática médica empreendida por um grupo de médicos associados que trabalham juntos como colegas ou como especialistas de áreas diferentes.*
group therapy *n (U)* terapia *f* de grupo.
grouse [graʊs] (*pl sense 1 inv* OR **-s**, *pl sense 2* **-s**) ◇ *n* **-1.** [bird] galo-silvestre *m* **-2.** *inf* [complaint] queixa *f*. ◇ *vi inf* queixar-se.
grove [grəʊv] *n* **-1.** [of trees] arvoredo *m* **-2.** [of fruit trees] pomar *m*.
grovel ['grɒvl] (*UK pt* & *pp* **-led**, *cont* **-ling**, *US pt* & *pp* **-ed**, *cont* **-ing**) *vi* **-1.** *pej* [humble o.s.] humilhar-se; **to ~ to sb** humilhar-se diante de alguém **-2.** [crawl on floor] rastejar.
grow [grəʊ] (*pt* **grew**, *pp* **grown**) ◇ *vt* **-1.** [plants] cultivar **-2.** [hair, beard] deixar crescer. ◇ *vi* **-1.** [plant, hair, person] crescer; [company, city, economy, plan] desenvolver-se **-2.** [seeds] germinar **-3.** [increase] aumentar **-4.** [become] tornar-se; **to ~ tired of sthg** cansar-se de algo **-5.** [do eventually]: **to ~ to do sthg** passar a fazer algo.
◆ **grow apart** *vi* [become less friendly] distanciar-se.
◆ **grow into** *vt fus* [clothes, shoes] crescer o suficiente para poder vestir.
◆ **grow on** *vt fus inf* [please more and more]: **this book is growing on me** gosto cada vez mais deste livro.
◆ **grow out** *vi* [perm, dye] desbotar.
◆ **grow out of** *vt fus* **-1.** [clothes, shoes]: **he's grown out of all his clothes** as roupas dele ficaram pequenas **-2.** [habit] perder.
◆ **grow up** *vi* crescer.
grower ['grəʊə[r]] *n* [person] produtor *m*, -ra *f*, agricultor *m*, -ra *f*.
growl [graʊl] ◇ *n* **-1.** [of dog] rosnar *m* **-2.** [of lion] rugido *m* **-3.** [of engine] rangido *m* **-4.** [of person] resmungo *m*. ◇ *vi* **-1.** [dog] rosnar **-2.** [lion] rugir **-3.** [engine] ranger **-4.** [person] resmungar.
grown [grəʊn] ◇ *pp* ▷ **grow**. ◇ *adj* crescido(-da).
grown-up ◇ *adj* **-1.** [fully grown, full-sized] crescido(da) **-2.** [mature, sensible] maduro(ra). ◇ *n* adulto *m*, -ta *f*.
growth [grəʊθ] *n* **-1.** *(U)* [development, increase] crescimento *m* **-2.** *MED* [lump] tumor *m*, abscesso *m*.
growth rate *n* taxa *f* de crescimento.
grub [grʌb] *n* **-1.** [insect] larva *f* **-2.** *(U) inf* [food] rango *m*.
grubby ['grʌbɪ] (*compar* **-ier**, *superl* **-iest**) *adj* encardido(da).
grudge [grʌdʒ] ◇ *n* ressentimento *m*; **to bear sb a ~, to bear a ~ against sb** guardar rancor contra alguém. ◇ *vt* ressentir, lamentar; **to ~ sb sthg** invejar alguém por algo; **to ~ doing sthg** fazer algo com má vontade.
grudging ['grʌdʒɪŋ] *adj* relutante.
grudgingly ['grʌdʒɪŋlɪ] *adv* com relutância.
gruelling *UK*, **grueling** *US* ['grʊəlɪŋ] *adj* árduo(-dua).
gruesome ['gruːsəm] *adj* horrível.
gruff [grʌf] *adj* **-1.** [hoarse] rouco(ca) **-2.** [rough, unfriendly] brusco(ca).
grumble ['grʌmbl] ◇ *n* **-1.** [complaint] resmungo *m* **-2.** [rumble - thunder, stomach] ronco *m*; [- train] rebôo *m*. ◇ *vi* **-1.** [complain] resmungar; **to ~ about sthg** resmungar por algo **-2.** [rumble - thunder, stomach] roncar; [- train] reboar.
grumbling ['grʌmblɪŋ] *n* **-1.** [complaining] resmungo *m* **-2.** [rumbling] ronco *m*.
grumpy ['grʌmpɪ] (*compar* **-ier**, *superl* **-iest**) *adj* **-1.** *inf* [person] resmungão(ona) **-2.** *inf* [face] rabugento(ta).
grunt [grʌnt] ◇ *n* **-1.** [of pig] grunhido *m* **-2.** [of person] resmungo *m*. ◇ *vi* **-1.** [pig] grunhir **-2.** [person] resmungar.
G-string *n* **-1.** *MUS* corda *f* G **-2.** [clothing] tanga *f* tapa-sexo.
Guadeloupe [ˌgwɑːdəˈluːp] *n* Guadalupe; **in ~** em Guadalupe.
Guam *n* Guam; **in ~** em Guam.
guarantee [ˌgærənˈtiː] ◇ *n* garantia *f*; **under ~** sob garantia. ◇ *vt* **-1.** *COMM* dar garantia para **-2.** [promise] garantir.
guarantor [ˌgærənˈtɔː[r]] *n* fiador *m*, -ra *f*.
guard [gɑːd] ◇ *n* **-1.** [person] guarda *mf* **-2.** [group of guards] guarda *f* **-3.** [supervision] proteção *f*; **to be on ~** estar em guarda; **to stand ~** estar de guarda; **to be on (one's) ~ (against sthg)** estar alerta (em relação a algo); **to catch sb off ~** pegar alguém desprevenido(da) **-4.** *UK RAIL* chefe *mf* de trem **-5.** [protective device] dispositivo *m* de segurança **-6.** [in boxing] proteção *f*. ◇ *vt* **-1.** [protect] proteger **-2.** [prevent from escaping] vigiar.
◆ **guard against** *vt fus* prevenir-se contra.
guard dog *n* cão *m* de guarda.
guarded ['gɑːdɪd] *adj* [careful] cauteloso(sa).
guardian ['gɑːdjən] *n* **-1.** *JUR* [of child] guardião *m*, -diã *f* **-2.** [protector] curador *m*, -ra *f*.
guardian angel *n* anjo *m* da guarda.
guardianship ['gɑːdjənʃɪp] *n (U)* tutela *f*.
guard rail *n US* [on road] proteção *f* lateral.
guardsman ['gɑːdzmən] (*pl* **-men** [-mən]) *n* sentinela *mf*.
guard's van *n UK* vagão *m* de freio.
Guatemala [ˌgwɑːtəˈmɑːlə] *n* Guatemala; **in ~** na Guatemala.
Guatemalan [ˌgwɑːtəˈmɑːlən] ◇ *adj* guatemalteco(ca). ◇ *n* guatemalteco *m*, -ca *f*.
guava ['gwɑːvə] *n* **-1.** [fruit] goiaba *f* **-2.** [tree] goiabeira *f*.
guerilla [gəˈrɪlə] *n* = **guerrilla**.
Guernsey ['gɜːnzɪ] *n* **-1.** [place] Guernsey; **in ~** em Guernsey **-2.** [sweater] pulôver *m* de lã *(originalmente usado por pescadores)* **-3.** [cow] Guernsey.

guerrilla [gəˈrɪlə] *n* guerrilheiro *m*, -ra *f*; **urban ~** guerrilheiro urbano, guerrilheira urbana.

guerrilla warfare *n (U)* guerrilha *f*.

guess [ges] <> *n* **-1.** [at facts, figures] suposição *f*; **to take a ~** adivinhar **-2.** [hypothesis] hipótese *f*; **it's anybody's ~** não há como saber. <> *vt* [assess correctly] adivinhar; **~ what!** adivinha! <> *vi* **-1.** [attempt to answer] chutar; **to ~ at sthg** tentar adivinhar algo; **to keep sb ~ing** não contar a alguém **-2.** [think, suppose]: **I ~ (so)** eu acho (que sim).

guesstimate [ˈgestɪmət] *n inf* estimativa *f* aproximada.

guesswork [ˈgeswɜːk] *n (U)* adivinhação *f*.

guest [gest] *n* **-1.** [visitor - at home] visita *mf*; [- at club, restaurant, concert] convidado *m*, -da *f* **-2.** [at hotel] hóspede *mf* **-3.** [in show] convidado *m*, -da *f* especial **-4.** *phr*: **be my ~!** seja meu convidado!

guesthouse [ˈgesthaʊs, pl -haʊzɪz] *n* pensão *f*.

guest of honour *n* convidado *m*, -da *f* de honra.

guestroom [ˈgestrʊm] *n* quarto *m* de hóspedes.

guest star *n* ator *m* convidado, atriz *f* convidada.

guffaw [gʌˈfɔː] <> *n* gargalhada *f*. <> *vi* gargalhar, dar gargalhadas.

Guiana [gaɪˈænə] *n* Guiana; **in ~** na Guiana.

guidance [ˈgaɪdəns] *n* **-1.** [help] orientação *f* **-2.** [leadership] liderança *f*; **under the ~ of** sob a orientação de.

guide [gaɪd] <> *n* **-1.** [person, book for tourist] guia *mf* **-2.** [manual] manual *m* **-3.** [indication] estimativa *f* (aproximada) **-4.** = **girl guide**. <> *vt* **-1.** [show by leading] guiar; **the waiter ~d them to a table** o garçom os conduziu até a mesa **-2.** [plane, missile] orientar **-3.** [influence]: **to be ~d by sb/sthg** ser orientado(da) por alguém/algo.

Guide Association *n*: **the ~** as Escoteiras.

guide book *n* guia *m*.

guided missile [ˈgaɪdɪd-] *n* míssil *m* guiado.

guide dog *n* cão-guia *m*.

guided tour *n* **-1.** [of city] excursão *f* guiada **-2.** [of cathedral, museum etc] visita *f* guiada.

guidelines [ˈgaɪdlaɪnz] *npl* princípios *mpl*, diretrizes *fpl*.

guiding [ˈgaɪdɪŋ] *adj* norteador(ra).

guild [gɪld] *n* **-1.** HIST guilda *f* **-2.** [association] associação *f*.

guildhall [ˈgɪldhɔːl] *n* guilda *f*.

guile [gaɪl] *n (U) literary* astúcia *f*.

guileless [ˈgaɪllɪs] *adj literary* cândido(da).

guillotine [ˈgɪləˌtiːn] <> *n* **-1.** [gen] guilhotina *f* **-2.** *UK* POL *estipulação de um tempo determinado para discutir um projeto de lei*. <> *vt* guilhotinar.

guilt [gɪlt] *n* culpa *f*.

guiltily [ˈgɪltɪlɪ] *adv* com a consciência pesada.

guilty [ˈgɪltɪ] (*compar* -ier, *superl* -iest) *adj* **-1.** [remorseful] culpado(da); **to have a ~ conscience** ter a consciência pesada **-2.** [causing remorse] condenável, que causa remorso **-3.** JUR culpado(da); **to be found ~/not ~** ser declarado culpado(da)/inocente **-4.** *fig* [culpable] culpável; **to be ~ of sthg** ser culpado(da) de algo.

guinea [ˈgɪnɪ] *n* guinéu *m*.

Guinea [ˈgɪnɪ] *n* Guiné; **in ~** em Guiné.

Guinea-Bissau [-bɪˈsəʊ] *n* Guiné-Bissau; **in ~** em Guiné-Bissau.

guinea fowl *n* galinha *f* d'angola.

guinea pig [ˈgɪnɪ-] *n* **-1.** [animal] porquinho-da-Índia *m* **-2.** [subject of experiment] cobaia *mf*.

guise [gaɪz] *n fml* aparência *f*, aspecto *m*.

guitar [gɪˈtɑːʳ] *n* violão *m*, guitarra *f*.

guitarist [gɪˈtɑːrɪst] *n* violonista *mf*, guitarrista *mf*.

gulch [gʌltʃ] *n US* ravina *f*.

gulf [gʌlf] *n* **-1.** [sea] golfo *m* **-2.** [deep hole]: **~ (between)** abismo (entre) **-3.** *fig* [separation] abismo *m*.

◆ **Gulf** *n*: **the Gulf** o Golfo Pérsico; **the Gulf of Aden** o Golfo de Áden; **the Gulf of Mexico** o Golfo do México.

Gulf States *npl*: **the ~** [around Persian Gulf] os países do Golfo Pérsico; [in US] *os estados norte-americanos que têm costa para o Golfo do México (Flórida, Alabama, Mississippi, Louisiana e Texas)*.

Gulf Stream *n*: **the ~** a corrente do Golfo.

gull [gʌl] *n* [bird] gaivota *f*.

gullet [ˈgʌlɪt] *n* esôfago *m*.

gullible [ˈgʌləbl] *adj* ingênuo(nua).

gully [ˈgʌlɪ] (*pl* **-ies**) *n* **-1.** [valley] barranco *m* **-2.** [ditch] vala *f*.

gulp [gʌlp] <> *n* gole *m*. <> *vt* engolir. <> *vi* engolir em seco.

◆ **gulp down** *vt sep* engolir.

gum [gʌm] (*pt* & *pp* **-med**, *cont* **-ming**) <> *n* **-1.** *(U)* [chewing gum] chiclete *m* **-2.** [adhesive] goma *f* **-3.** ANAT gengiva *f*. <> *vt* **-1.** [cover with adhesive] passar goma em **-2.** [stick] colar.

gumboil [ˈgʌmbɔɪl] *n* abscesso *m* nas gengivas.

gumboots [ˈgʌmbuːts] *npl UK* galocha *f*.

gummed *adj* adesivo(va).

gumption [ˈgʌmpʃn] *n (U) inf* [resourcefulness] senso *m* prático.

gumshoe [ˈgʌmʃuː] *n US crime sl* detetive *mf*.

gun [gʌn] (*pt* & *pp* **-ned**, *cont* **-ning**) *n* **-1.** [gen] arma *f* **-2.** [specific type - revolver] revólver *m*; [- pistol] pistola *f*; [- shotgun] espingarda *m*; [- rifle] rifle *m*; [- cannon] canhão *m*; **to stick to one's ~s** não dar o braço a torcer **-3.** SPORT [starting pistol] revólver *m*; **to jump the ~** *fig* precipitar-se **-4.** [tool] pistola *f*.

◆ **gun down** *vt sep* balear.

gunboat [ˈgʌnbəʊt] *n* canhoeira *f*.

gundog [ˈgʌndɒg] *n* cão *m* de caça.

gunfire [ˈgʌnfaɪəʳ] *n (U)* tiroteio *m*.

gunge [gʌndʒ] *n (U) UK inf* substância *f* nojenta e pegajosa.

gung-ho [ˌgʌŋˈhəʊ] *adj UK inf* impulsivo(va).

gunk [gʌŋk] *n inf* meleca *f*.

gunman [ˈgʌnmən] (*pl* **-men** [-mən]) *n* pistoleiro *m*.

gunner [ˈgʌnəʳ] *n* MIL artilheiro *m*, -ra *f*.

gunpoint [ˈgʌnpɔɪnt] *n*: **at ~** na mira.

gunpowder [ˈgʌnˌpaʊdəʳ] *n (U)* pólvora *f*.

gunrunning [ˈgʌnˌrʌnɪŋ] *n (U)* contrabando *m* de armas.

gunshot [ˈgʌnʃɒt] *n* [firing of gun] tiro *m*.

gunsmith [ˈgʌnsmɪθ] *n* armeiro *m*, -ra *f*.

gurgle [ˈgɜːgl] <> *n* **-1.** [of water] gorgolejo *m* **-2.** [of baby] gugu *m.* ◇ *vi* **-1.** [water] gorgolejar **- 2.** [baby] fazer gugu.

guru ['gʊru:] *n* **-1.** [spiritual leader] guru *m* **- 2.** [adviser] conselheiro *m*, -ra *f.*

gush [gʌʃ] ◇ *n* jorro *m.* ◇ *vt* jorrar. ◇ *vi* **-1.** [flow out] verter **- 2.** *pej* [enthuse] entusiasmar-se.

gushing ['gʌʃɪŋ] *adj pej* [over-enthusiastic] efusivo(va).

gusset ['gʌsɪt] *n* **-1.** SEWING nesga *f* **- 2.** [in tights] entreperna *m.*

gust [gʌst] ◇ *n* rajada *f.* ◇ *vi* dar uma rajada.

gusto ['gʌstəʊ] *n (U)*: **with ~** com garra.

gusty ['gʌstɪ] (*compar* **-ier**, *superl* **-iest**) *adj* tempestuoso(sa).

gut [gʌt] (*pt* & *pp* **-ted**, *cont* **-ting**) ◇ *n* **-1.** MED intestino *m* **- 2.** *inf* [stomach] bucho *m.* ◇ *vt* **-1.** [remove organs from] destripar **- 2.** [destroy] destruir.
◆ **guts** *npl inf* **-1.** [intestines] tripas *fpl*; **to hate sb's ~s** ter alguém atravessado(da) na garganta **- 2.** [courage] coragem *f*; **to have ~s** ter estômago.

gut feeling *n* pressentimento *m.*

gut reaction *n* reação *f* instintiva.

gutter ['gʌtə^r] *n* **-1.** [ditch] sarjeta *f* **- 2.** [on roof] calha *f.*

guttering ['gʌtərɪŋ] *n (U)* calhas *fpl.*

gutter press *n pej* imprensa-marrom *f.*

guttural ['gʌtərəl] *adj* gutural.

guv [gʌv] *n UK inf* chefe *m.*

guy [gaɪ] *n* **-1.** *inf* [man] cara *mf* **- 2.** *esp US* [person] galera *f inv* **- 3.** *UK* [dummy] *boneco que se queima na Grã-Bretanha na Noite da Conspiração da Pólvora.*

Guyana [gaɪ'ænə] *n* Guiana; **in ~** na Guiana.

Guy Fawkes Night *n* Noite *f* da Conspiração da Pólvora.

GUY FAWKES NIGHT

Festividade britânica celebrada na noite de 5 de novembro, em comemoração ao complô católico encabeçado por Guy Fawkes, em 1605, que tinha por objetivo explodir as casas do Parlamento. Nessa noite, os britânicos acendem fogueiras, nas quais queimam uma efígie de Guy Fawkes, e soltam fogos de artifício, razão pela qual a noite é também conhecida como *Fireworks Night* ou *Bonfire Night*.

guy rope *n* amarra *f.*

guzzle ['gʌzl] ◇ *vt pej* - [food] devorar com gula; [- drink] beber com gula. ◇ *vi* engolir com gula.

gym [dʒɪm] *n inf* **-1.** [gymnasium - in school] ginásio *m*; [- in hotel, health club] sala *f* de ginástica **- 2.** *(U)* [exercises] ginástica *f*, ginásio *m.*

gymkhana [dʒɪm'kɑ:nə] *n* gincana *f.*

gymnasium [dʒɪm'neɪzjəm] (*pl* **-siums** OR **-sia** [-zjə]) *n* ginásio *m.*

gymnast ['dʒɪmnæst] *n* ginasta *mf.*

gymnastics [dʒɪm'næstɪks] *n (U)* ginástica *f.*

gym shoes *npl* sapatilha *f* de ginástica.

gymslip ['dʒɪm,slɪp] *n UK* bata *f* escolar.

gynaecological *UK*, **gynecological** *US* [,gaɪnəkə'lɒdʒɪkl] *adj* ginecológico(ca).

gynaecologist *UK*, **gynecologist** *US* [,gaɪnə'kɒlədʒɪst] *n* ginecologista *mf.*

gynaecology *UK*, **gynecology** *US* [,gaɪnə'kɒlədʒɪ] *n (U)* ginecologia *f.*

gypsy ['dʒɪpsɪ] (*pl* **-ies**) *adj* & *n* = **gipsy**.

gyrate [dʒaɪ'reɪt] *vi* girar.

gyration [dʒaɪ'reɪʃn] *n* giro *m*, rotação *f.*

gyroscope ['dʒaɪrəskəʊp] *n* giroscópio *m.*

h (*pl* **h's** OR **hs**), **H** (*pl* **H's** OR **Hs**) [eɪtʃ] *n* [letter] h, H *m.*

ha [hɑ:] *excl* ah!

habeas corpus [,heɪbjəs'kɔ:pəs] *n (U)* habeas corpus *m.*

haberdashery ['hæbədæʃərɪ] (*pl* **-ies**) *n* **-1.** *(U)* [goods] materiais *mpl* de costura, artigos *mpl* de armarinho **- 2.** [shop] armarinho *m.*

habit ['hæbɪt] *n* **-1.** [customary practice] hábito *m*, costume *m*; **to be in the ~ of doing sthg** ter o hábito de fazer algo, ter o costume de fazer algo; **to make a ~ of sthg** tornar algo um hábito; **to make a ~ of doing sthg** ter por hábito fazer algo **- 2.** [drug addiction] vício *m* **- 3.** [garment] hábito *m.*

habitable ['hæbɪtəbl] *adj* habitável.

habitat ['hæbɪtæt] *n* hábitat *m.*

habitation [hæbɪ'teɪʃn] *n* **-1.** *(U)* [occupation] habitação *f* **- 2.** *fml* [house] moradia *f.*

habit-forming [-,fɔ:mɪŋ] *adj* que vicia; **marijuana is ~** a maconha vicia.

habitual [hə'bɪtʃʊəl] *adj* **-1.** [customary] habitual, costumeiro(ra) **- 2.** [offender, smoker, drinker] inveterado(da).

habitually [hə'bɪtʃʊəlɪ] *adv* habitualmente.

hack [hæk] ◇ *n* **-1.** *pej* [writer] escritorzinho *m*, -razinha *f* **- 2.** *US inf* [taxi] táxi *m.* ◇ *vt* **-1.** [cut] cortar **- 2.** *inf* [cope with] enfrentar. ◇ *vi* [cut] talhar.
◆ **hack into** *vt fus* COMPUT invadir ilegalmente.
◆ **hack through** *vt fus* [cut] abrir caminho; **to ~ (one's way) through sthg** abrir caminho através de algo.

hacker ['hækə^r] *n* COMPUT: **(computer) ~** hacker *mf* (de computador).

hackie *n US inf* taxista *mf.*

hacking ['hækɪŋ] *n* COMPUT invasão *m* ilegal de sistemas de computação.

hacking cough *n* tosse *f* seca.

hackles ['hæklz] *npl* [on animal] pêlos *mpl* eriçados do dorso; **to make sb's ~ rise** enfurecer alguém.

hackney cab, hackney carriage ['hæknɪ-] *n fml* [taxi] carro *m* de praça.

hackneyed ['hæknɪd] *adj pej* batido(da), banal.

hacksaw ['hæksɔ:] *n* serra *f* para metais.

had [*weak form* həd, *strong form* hæd] *pt & pp* ▷ have.
haddock ['hædək] (*pl inv*) *n* hadoque *m*.
hadn't ['hædnt] = **had not**.
haematology [ˌhi:mə'tɒlədʒɪ] *n* = **hematology**.
haemoglobin [ˌhi:mə'gləʊbɪn] *n* = **hemoglobin**.
haemophilia [ˌhi:mə'fɪlɪə] *n* = **hemophilia**.
haemophiliac [ˌhi:mə'fɪlɪæk] *n* = **hemophiliac**.
haemorrhage ['hemərɪdʒ] *n & vi* = **hemorrhage**.
haemorrhoids ['hemərɔɪdz] *npl* = **hemorrhoids**.
hag [hæg] *n pej* bruxa *f*, megera *f*.
haggard ['hægəd] *adj* abatido(da).
haggis ['hægɪs] *n lingüiça escocesa, normalmente com o formato de uma bola, feita de carne de carneiro picada e embutida na pele do estômago do carneiro.*
haggle ['hægl] *vi* pechinchar, regatear; **to ~ over** OR **about sthg** pechinchar acerca de algo; **to ~ with sb** pechinchar com alguém.
haggling ['hæglɪŋ] *n (U)* regateio *m*.
Hague [heɪg] *n*: **The ~** Haia.
hail [heɪl] ◇ *n* **-1.** *(U)* [frozen rain] granizo *m* **-2.** *fig* [torrent - of bullets] rajada *f*; [- of criticism] chuva *f*; [- of abuse] onda *f*. ◇ *vt* **-1.** [call] chamar **-2.** [acclaim]: **to ~ sb/sthg as sthg** aclamar alguém/algo como algo. ◇ *v impers* METEOR chover granizo.
hailstone ['heɪlstəʊn] *n* granizo *m*.
hailstorm *n* chuva *f* de granizo.
hair [heə[r]] ◇ *n* **-1.** *(U)* [on human head] cabelo *m*; **to do one's ~** pentear-se; **to let one's ~ down** relaxar e curtir; **to make sb's ~ stand on end** deixar alguém de cabelos em pé; **to split ~s** debater minúcias **-2.** [on animal, insect, plant] pêlo *m* **-3.** [on human skin] pêlo *m*. ◇ *comp* **-1.** [oil, lotion] capilar **-2.** [conditioner] de cabelos.
hairbrush ['heəbrʌʃ] *n* escova *f* de cabelo.
haircut ['heəkʌt] *n* corte *m* de cabelo.
hairdo ['heədu:] (*pl* **-s**) *n inf* penteado *m*.
hairdresser ['heəˌdresə[r]] *n* cabeleireiro *m*, -ra *f*; **~'s (salon)** (salão *m* de) cabeleireiro *m*.
hairdressing ['heəˌdresɪŋ] ◇ *n (U)* profissão *f* do cabeleireiro. ◇ *comp* de cabeleireiro.
hairdryer ['heəˌdraɪə[r]] *n* secador *m* de cabelos.
hair gel *n (U)* gel *m* fixador.
hairgrip ['heəgrɪp] *n UK* grampo *m* de cabelo.
hairline ['heəlaɪn] *n* [of the hair] contorno *m* do cabelo.
hairline fracture *n* fratura *f* muito fina.
hairnet ['heənet] *n* rede *f* de cabelo.
hairpiece ['heəpi:s] *n* cabelo *m* postiço.
hairpin ['heəpɪn] *n* grampo *m* de cabelo.
hairpin bend *n* curva *f* fechada.
hair-raising [-ˌreɪzɪŋ] *adj* assustador(ra); **a ~ story** uma história de deixar os cabelos em pé.
hair remover [-rɪˌmu:və[r]] *n* (creme *m*) depilatório *m*.
hair-restorer *n* loção *f* capilar.
hair's breadth *n*: **by a ~** por um triz.
hair slide *n UK* passador *m*, presilha *f*.
hair-splitting *n (U) pej* sutilezas *fpl*.
hairspray ['heəspreɪ] *n* laquê *m*.
hairstyle ['heəstaɪl] *n* penteado *m*.
hairstylist ['heəˌstaɪlɪst] *n* cabeleireiro *m*, -ra *f*.
hairy ['heərɪ] (*compar* **-ier**, *superl* **-iest**) *adj* **-1.** [covered in hair - person] cabeludo(da); [- animal, legs] peludo(-da) **-2.** *inf* [dangerous] arriscado(da).
Haiti ['heɪtɪ] *n* Haiti; **in ~** no Haiti.
Haitian ['heɪʃn] ◇ *adj* haitiano(na). ◇ *n* haitiano *m*, -na *f*.
hake [heɪk] (*pl inv* OR **-s**) *n* merluza *f*.
halal [hə'lɑ:l] ◇ *adj que foi abatido conforme a lei islâmica.* ◇ *n (U) carne de animal abatido conforme a lei islâmica.*
halcyon *adj literary*: **~ days** dias *mpl* venturosos.
hale [heɪl] *adj*: **~ and hearty** firme e forte.
half [*UK* hɑ:f, *US* hæf] (*pl senses 1, 2 and 3* **halves**, *pl senses 4, 5 and 6* **halves** OR **halfs**) ◇ *adj* meio (meia); **~ my salary** metade *f* do meu salário. ◇ *adv* **-1.** [partly, almost] meio, quase; **I ~ expected him to say yes** eu meio que esperava que ele dissesse sim; **not ~!** *UK inf* e como! **-2.** [by half]: **to increase sthg by ~** acrescentar a metade ao valor de algo **-3.** [in equal measure] meio; **~-and-~** meio a meio **-4.** [in telling the time]: **~ past ten** *UK*, **~ after ten** *US* dez e meia; **it's ~ past ten/one** são dez e meia/é uma e meia. ◇ *n* **-1.** [one of two equal parts] metade *f*; **by ~** pela metade; **in ~** ao meio; **to be too clever by ~** *pej* ser muito astuto(ta); **he doesn't do things by halves** ele não faz as coisas pela metade; **to go halves (with sb)** rachar as despesas (com alguém) **-2.** [fraction] meio *m* **-3.** SPORT [of sports match] tempo *m* **-4.** SPORT [halfback] meio-campo *mf* **-5.** [of beer] meia cerveja *f* **-6.** [child's ticket] meia entrada *f*. ◇ *pron* [one of two equal parts] metade de; **~ of** metade de.
halfback ['hɑ:fbæk] *n* meio-campo *mf*.
half-baked [-'beɪkt] *adj inf* mal-elaborado(da).
half board *n (U) UK* meia pensão *f*.
half-breed ◇ *adj* mestiço(ça). ◇ *n* mestiço *m*, -ça *f*.
half-brother *n* meio-irmão *m*.
half-caste [-kɑ:st] ◇ *adj* mestiço(ça). ◇ *n* mestiço *m*, -ça *f*.
half cock *n*: **to go off (at) ~** ir com muita sede ao pote.
half-day *n* meio turno *m*.
half-fare *n* meia passagem *f*.
half-hearted [-'hɑ:tɪd] *adj* desanimado(da).
half-heartedly [-'hɑ:tɪdlɪ] *adv* sem entusiasmo.
half hour *n* meia hora *f*.
◆ **half-hour** *adj* = **half-hourly**.
half-hourly *adj* a cada meia hora.
half-length *adj* de meio corpo.
half-light *n (U)* meia-luz *f*.
half-mast *n UK*: **at ~** [flag] a meio pau.
half measures *npl* meios-termos *mpl*.
half moon *n* meia-lua *f*.
half note *n US* MUS mínima *f*.
halfpenny ['heɪpnɪ] (*pl* **-pennies** OR **-pence**) *n* meio pêni *m*.
half-price *adj* a metade do preço.
◆ **half price** *adv* pela metade do preço.
half-sister *n* meia-irmã *f*.
half step *n US* MUS semitom *m*.
half term *n UK* recesso *m* escolar.

half time *n (U)* meio-tempo *m.*
half tone *n US MUS* meio-tom *m*, semitom *m.*
half-truth *n* meia verdade *f.*
halfway [hɑ:f'weɪ] <> *adj* no meio do caminho. <> *adv* **-1.** [in space] a meio caminho **-2.** [in time] no meio **-3.** *phr*: **to meet sb ~** *fig* [compromise] chegar a um acordo com alguém.
half-wit *n* idiota *mf.*
half-yearly *adj* semestral.
◆ **half yearly** *adv* semestralmente.
halibut ['hælɪbət] (*pl inv* OR **-s**) *n* halibute *m.*
halitosis [ˌhælɪ'təʊsɪs] *n (U)* halitose *f.*
hall [hɔ:l] *n* **-1.** [in house] entrada *f*, hall *m* **-2.** [meeting room] salão *m* **-3.** [public building] sala *f*; **town ~** prédio *m* da prefeitura **-4.** *UK* [UNIV & hall of residence] alojamento *m*, casa *f* do estudante; **to live in ~** morar em casa do estudante **-5.** [country house] mansão *m.*
halleluja [ˌhælɪ'lu:jə] *excl* aleluia!
hallmark ['hɔ:lmɑ:k] *n* **-1.** [typical feature] marca *f* distintiva **-2.** [on metal] selo *m* de autenticidade.
hallo [hə'ləʊ] *excl* = **hello.**
hall of residence (*pl* **halls of residence**) *n UK UNIV* casa *f* do estudante.
hallowed ['hæləʊd] *adj* [respected] sagrado(da), santo(ta).
Hallowe'en, Halloween, [ˌhæləʊ'i:n] n Dia *m* das Bruxas.

HALLOWE'EN

O *Halloween* é celebrado nos Estados Unidos e na Grã-Bretanha na noite de 31 de outubro. As crianças, vestidas de bruxas, fantasmas etc., vão de porta em porta, pedindo doces às pessoas. Marca registrada dessa festa são as abóboras ocas, com o interior iluminado por uma vela.

hallucinate [hə'lu:sɪneɪt] *vi* alucinar.
hallucination [ˌhəlu:sɪ'neɪʃn] *n* alucinação *f.*
hallucinogenic [həˌlu:sɪnə'dʒenɪk] *adj* alucinógeno(na).
hallway ['hɔ:lweɪ] *n* **-1.** [at entrance of house] saguão *m*, hall *m* **-2.** [corridor] corredor *m.*
halo ['heɪləʊ] (*pl* **-es** OR **-s**) *n* **-1.** [of saint, angel] auréola *f* **-2.** *fig* [circle of light] halo *m.*
halogen ['hælədʒen] <> *n (U)* halogênio *m.* <> *comp* halógeno *m*, -na *f.*
halt [hɔ:lt] <> *n* [stop]: **to come to a ~** [vehicle, horse] fazer uma parada; [development, activity] interromper-se; **to call a ~ to sthg** pôr fim a algo; **to grind to a ~** [stop moving] parar lentamente; [stop working] estagnar-se. <> *vt* [stop - person] deter; [- development, activity] interromper. <> *vi* [stop - person, train] parar; [- development, activity] interromper-se.
halter ['hɔ:ltə^r] *n* [for horse] cabresto *m.*
halterneck ['hɔ:ltənek] *adj*: **~ dress** vestido *m* de frente-única.
halting ['hɔ:ltɪŋ] *adj* vacilante.
halve [*UK* hɑ:v, *US* hæv] *vt* **-1.** [reduce by half] reduzir à metade **-2.** [divide] partir ao meio.
halves [*UK* hɑ:vz, *US* hævz] *pl* ▷ **half.**
ham [hæm] (*pt* & *pp* **-med**, *cont* **-ming**) <> *n* **-1.** [meat] presunto *m* **-2.** *pej* [actor] canastrão *m* **-3.** [radio fanatic]: **(radio) ~** radioamador *m*, -ra *f.* <> *comp* de presunto. <> *vt*: **to ~ it up** *THEATRE* exagerar na atuação.
Hamburg ['hæmbɜ:g] *n* Hamburgo.
hamburger ['hæmbɜ:gə^r] *n* **-1.** [burger] hambúrguer *m* **-2.** *US* [mince] carne *f* moída.
ham-fisted [-'fɪstɪd] *adj* desajeitado(da).
hamlet ['hæmlɪt] *n* aldeia *f.*
hammer ['hæmə^r] <> *n* [tool] martelo *m.* <> *vt* **-1.** [with tool] martelar **-2.** [with fist] bater em **-3.** *inf fig* [fact, order]: **to ~ sthg into sb** meter algo na cabeça de alguém **-4.** *inf fig* [defeat] dar uma surra em. <> *vi* **-1.** [with tool] martelar **-2.** [with fist]: **to ~ (on sthg)** bater com insistência (em algo) **-3.** *phr*: **to ~ away at sthg** *fig* [task] trabalhar com afinco em algo.
◆ **hammer into** *vt sep*: **to ~ sthg into sb** *fig* meter algo na cabeça de alguém.
◆ **hammer out** <> *vt fus* [draw up] alcançar com muito esforço. <> *vt sep* [with tool] malhar.
hammock ['hæmək] *n* rede *f* de dormir.
hamper ['hæmpə^r] <> *n* **-1.** [for picnic] cesta *f* **-2.** *US* [for laundry] cesto *m* de roupa. <> *vt* [impede] dificultar.
hamster ['hæmstə^r] *n* hamster *m.*
hamstring ['hæmstrɪŋ] (*pt* & *pp* **-strung** [-strʌŋ]) <> *n ANAT* tendão *m* do jarrete. <> *vt fig* [thwart] impedir, dificultar.
hand [hænd] <> *n* **-1.** [part of body] mão *f*; **to hold ~s** dar as mãos; **by ~** à mão; **~ in ~** [people] de mãos dadas; **with his bare ~s** com suas próprias mãos; **at the ~s of** nas mãos de; **~s up!** mãos ao alto!; **to change ~s** trocar de mãos; **to force sb's ~** forçar alguém a agir; **to get** OR **lay one's ~s on sb** colocar OR pôr as mãos em alguém; **to get** OR **lay one's ~s on sthg** colocar OR pôr as mãos em algo; **to give sb a free ~** dar carta branca a alguém; **to go ~ in ~** [things] andar de mãos dadas; **to have one's ~s full** estar muito atarefado(da); **to try one's ~ at sthg** tentar fazer algo; **to wait on sb ~ and foot** dar tudo de bandeja para alguém; **to wash one's ~s of sthg** lavar as mãos sobre algo **-2.** [help] mão *f*; **to give** OR **lend sb a ~ (with sthg)** dar uma mão para alguém (em algo) **-3.** [control, management] mão *f*; **in the ~s of** nas mãos de; **to take sb in ~** controlar alguém **-4.** [influence] dedo *m*; **to have a ~ in sthg/in doing sthg** interferir em algo/ao se fazer algo **-5.** [worker - on farm] peão *m*, -ona *f*; [- on ship] tripulante *mf* **-6.** [of clock, watch] ponteiro *m* **-7.** [handwriting] caligrafia *f* **-8.** [of cards] mão *f*; **I overplayed my ~** *fig* superestimei minha situação **-9.** *inf* [applause] palmas *fpl.* <> *vt*: **to ~ sthg to sb, to ~ sb sthg** entregar algo a alguém.
◆ **(close) at hand** *adv* próximo.
◆ **in hand** *adv* **-1.** [time, money]: **to have sthg in ~** ter algo sobrando **-2.** [problem, situation]: **to have sb/sthg in ~** ter alguém/algo sob controle.
◆ **on hand** *adv* em prontidão.
◆ **on the one hand** *adv* por um lado.
◆ **on the other hand** *adv* por outro lado.
◆ **out of hand** <> *adj* [situation]: **to get out of ~** sair de controle. <> *adv* [completely] completamente.
◆ **to hand** *adv* à mão.

◆ **hand down** *vt sep* [to next generation] legar.
◆ **hand in** *vt sep* entregar.
◆ **hand on** *vt sep* passar adiante.
◆ **hand out** *vt sep* distribuir.
◆ **hand over** ◇ *vt sep* **-1.** [baton, money] entregar **-2.** [responsibility, power] transferir, ceder **-3.** *TELEC* passar a ligação. ◇ *vi* [government minister, chairman] transferir; **to ~ over to sb** transferir para alguém.
handbag ['hændbæg] *n* bolsa *f.*
handball ['hændbɔ:l] *n (U)* [game] handebol *m.*
handbill ['hændbɪl] *n* panfleto *m.*
handbook ['hændbʊk] *n* manual *m.*
handbrake ['hændbreɪk] *n* freio *m* de mão.
handclap ['hændklæp] *n*: **slow ~** *aplauso lento e ritmado em forma de protesto.*
handcrafted ['hænd,krɑ:ftɪd] *adj* artesanal.
handcuff ['hændkʌf] *vt* algemar.
handcuffs ['hændkʌfs] *npl* algemas *fpl.*
handful ['hændfʊl] *n* **-1.** *lit & fig* punhado *m* **-2.** *inf* [difficult person, animal]: **to be a ~** ser um demônio.
handgun ['hændgʌn] *n* arma *f* de mão.
handheld PC ['hændheld-] *n* computador *m* de bolso, handheld *m.*
handicap ['hændɪkæp] (*pt & pp* **-ped**, *cont* **-ping**) ◇ *n* **-1.** [physical or mental disability] deficiência *f* **-2.** *fig* [disadvantage] obstáculo *m* **-3.** *SPORT* handicap *m.* ◇ *vt* [hinder] estorvar, atrapalhar.
handicapped ['hændɪkæpt] ◇ *adj* [physically or mentally disabled] deficiente. ◇ *npl*: **the ~** os deficientes.
handicraft ['hændɪkrɑ:ft] *n* [skill] artesanato *m.*
handiwork ['hændɪwɜ:k] *n (U)* [work produced by o.s.] trabalho *m* manual.
handkerchief ['hæŋkətʃɪf] (*pl* **-chiefs** *OR* **-chieves** [-tʃi:vz]) *n* lenço *m.*
handle ['hændl] ◇ *n* **-1.** [for opening and closing - of window] trinco *m*; [- of door] maçaneta *f* **-2.** [for holding] cabo *m* **-3.** [for carrying] alça *f*; **to fly off the ~** perder a cabeça. ◇ *vt* **-1.** [with hands] manusear **-2.** [control, operate - car] guiar; [- ship] comandar; [- gun] manejar; [- words] articular **-3.** [manage, process] manejar **-4.** [cope with] tratar de. ◇ *vi* **-1.** governar **-2.** [ship] comandar **-3.** [car] guiar.
handlebars ['hændlbɑ:z] *npl* guidom *m.*
handler ['hændlə^r] *n* **-1.** [of animal] treinador *m*, -ra *f* **-2.** [of luggage]: **(baggage) ~** carregador *m*, -ra *f* (de bagagem) **-3.** [of stolen goods] receptor *m*, -ra *f.*
handling charges ['hændlɪŋ-] *npl* [at bank] taxas *fpl* de manutenção.
hand lotion *n* creme *m* para as mãos.
hand luggage *n UK* bagagem *f* de mão.
handmade [,hænd'meɪd] *adj* feito(ta) à mão.
hand-me-downs *npl inf* roupas *fpl* usadas.
handout ['hændaʊt] *n* **-1.** [gift] donativo *m* **-2.** [leaflet] folheto *m* informativo **-3.** [for lecture, discussion] polígrafo *m.*
handover ['hændəʊvə^r] *n* transferência *f.*
handpicked [,hænd'pɪkt] *adj* [people] escolhido(da) a dedo.
handrail ['hændreɪl] *n* corrimão *m.*
handset ['hændset] *n TELEC* fone *m (do telefone).*
handshake ['hændʃeɪk] *n* aperto *m* de mão.
hands-off *adj* sem inteferência.
handsome ['hænsəm] *adj* **-1.** [man] bonito(ta) **-2.** *literary* [woman] bela, bonita **-3.** [reward, profit] considerável.
handsomely ['hænsəmlɪ] *adv* [generously] generosamente.
hands-on *adj* [training, experience] prático(ca).
handstand ['hændstænd] *n*: **to do a ~** plantar bananeira.
hand-to-mouth *adj* precário(ria).
◆ **hand to mouth** *adv* precariamente.
hand towel *n* toalha *f* de mão.
handwriting ['hænd,raɪtɪŋ] *n* letra *f*, caligrafia *f.*
handwritten ['hænd,rɪtn] *adj* escrito(ta) à mão.
handy ['hændɪ] (*compar* **-ier**, *superl* **-iest**) *adj inf* **-1.** [useful] prático(ca); **to come in ~** vir a calhar **-2.** [skilful] hábil **-3.** [near] à mão; **to keep sthg ~** manter algo à mão.
handyman ['hændɪmæn] (*pl* **-men** [-men]) *n* faz-tudo *mf.*
hang [hæŋ] (*pt & pp sense 1* **hung**, *pt & pp sense 2* **hung** *OR* **hanged**) ◇ *vt* **-1.** [suspend] pendurar **-2.** [execute] enforcar. ◇ *vi* **-1.** [be suspended] estar suspenso(sa) **-2.** [be executed] ser enforcado(da). ◇ *n*: **to get the ~ of sthg** *inf* pegar o jeito de algo.
◆ **hang about, hang around** *vi* **-1.** [loiter] demorar-se **-2.** [wait] rondar.
◆ **hang down** *vi* pender.
◆ **hang on** ◇ *vt fus* [depend on] depender de. ◇ *vi* **-1.** [keep hold]: **to ~ on (to sb/sthg)** segurar-se (em alguém/algo) **-2.** *inf* [continue waiting] aguardar **-3.** [persevere] resistir, agüentar.
◆ **hang onto** *vt fus* **-1.** [keep hold of] segurar-se a **-2.** [keep] manter.
◆ **hang out** ◇ *vt sep* [washing] estender. ◇ *vi inf* [spend time] passar um tempo, frequentar.
◆ **hang round** *vi* = **hang about.**
◆ **hang together** *vi* [alibi, argument] ser consistente.
◆ **hang up** ◇ *vt sep* [suspend] pendurar. ◇ *vi* [on telephone] desligar.
◆ **hang up on** *vt fus TELEC* desligar; **he hung up on me** ele desligou o telefone na minha cara.
hangar ['hæŋə^r] *n* hangar *m.*
hangdog ['hæŋdɒg] *adj* envergonhado(da).
hanger ['hæŋə^r] *n* [coat hanger] cabide *m.*
hanger-on (*pl* **hangers-on**) *n* bajulador *m*, -ra *f*, aproveitador *m*, -ra *f.*
hang glider *n* [apparatus] asa-delta *f.*
hang gliding *n (U)* vôo *m* livre *(com asa delta).*
hanging ['hæŋɪŋ] *n* **-1.** *(U)* [form of punishment] forca *f* **-2.** [execution] enforcamento *m* **-3.** [drapery] tapeçaria *f (para parede).*
hangman ['hæŋmən] (*pl* **-men** [-mən]) *n* carrasco *m*, -ca *f.*
hangover ['hæŋ,əʊvə^r] *n* **-1.** [from drinking] ressaca *f*; **to have a ~** estar de ressaca **-2.** [from past]: **~ (from sthg)** vestígio *m* (de algo).
hang-up *n inf PSYCH* complexo *m.*
hank *n* **-1.** [of wool] novelo *m* **-2.** [of rope, wire] meada *m.*
hanker ['hæŋkə^r] ◆ **hanker after, hanker for** *vt fus* ansiar por, desejar ardentemente.

hankering ['hæŋkərɪŋ] *n*: ~ **after** *OR* **for** anseio *m* por.

hankie, hanky ['hæŋkɪ] (*pl* **-ies**) (*abbr of* **handkerchief**) *n inf* lencinho *m*.

hanky-panky *n inf* [sexual behaviour] sem-vergonhice *f*.

Hanoi [hæ'nɔɪ] *n* Hanói.

Hansard ['hænsɑːd] *n atas oficiais dos debates realizados no parlamento britânico,* ≃ Diário Oficial.

haphazard [ˌhæp'hæzəd] *adj* caótico(ca), desordenado(da).

haphazardly [ˌhæp'hæzədlɪ] *adv* desordenadamente, de qualquer maneira.

hapless ['hæplɪs] *adj literary* desafortunado(da).

happen ['hæpən] *vi* **-1.** [occur] acontecer; **to ~ to sb** acontecer com alguém **-2.** [chance]: **I ~ed to see him yesterday** por acaso eu o vi ontem; **do you ~ to have a pen on you?** você não teria por acaso uma caneta?; **as it ~s** por acaso.

happening ['hæpənɪŋ] *n* [occurrence] acontecimento *m*.

happily ['hæpɪlɪ] *adv* **-1.** [contentedly]: **to be ~ doing sthg** fazer algo alegremente **-2.** [fortunately] felizmente **-3.** [willingly] com satisfação.

happiness ['hæpɪnɪs] *n (U)* felicidade *f*.

happy ['hæpɪ] (*compar* **-ier**, *superl* **-iest**) *adj* **-1.** [contented] feliz, contente **-2.** [causing contentment] feliz; **Happy Christmas/New Year/Birthday!** Feliz Natal/Ano Novo/Aniversário!; **to be ~ with** *OR* **about sthg** estar feliz com algo; **to be ~ to do sthg** estar muito disposto(ta) a fazer algo; **I'd be ~ to do it** eu faria isso com muito gosto.

happy event *n* nascimento *m*; **when's the ~ event** quando nasce a criança?

happy-go-lucky *adj* despreocupado(da).

happy hour *n inf* happy hour *f*.

happy medium *n* meio-termo *m*.

harangue [hə'ræŋ] ◇ *n* arenga *f*, ladainha *f*. ◇ *vt* arengar.

Harare [hə'rɑːrɪ] *n* Harare.

harass ['hærəs] *vt* [pester - with questions, problems] atormentar; [- sexually] molestar.

harassed ['hærəst] *adj* [stressed] tenso(sa).

harassment ['hærəsmənt] *n* **-1.** [persecution] perseguição *f* **-2.** [sexual] assédio *m*.

harbinger ['hɑːbɪndʒə^r] *n literary* precursor *m*, -ra *f*.

harbour *UK*, **harbor** *US* ['hɑːbə^r] ◇ *n* porto *m*. ◇ *vt* **-1.** [feeling] abrigar **-2.** [person] dar refúgio a.

harbour master *n* capitão *m*, -tã *f* do porto.

hard [hɑːd] ◇ *adj* **-1.** [very firm, not soft] duro(ra) **-2.** [difficult] difícil **-3.** [strenuous, stressful] duro(ra), pesado(da) **-4.** [forceful] forte **-5.** [harsh, unkind] ríspido(da); **to be ~ on sb/sthg** ser duro com alguém/algo **-6.** [winter, frost] rigoroso(sa) **-7.** [water] duro(ra) **-8.** [fact, news] concreto(ta) **-9.** *UK POL* [extreme]: **~ left/right** extrema esquerda/direita. ◇ *adv* **-1.** [strenuously] muito, duro **-2.** [forcefully] com força **-3.** [rain, snow] intensamente **-4.** *phr*: **to be ~ pushed** *OR* **put** *OR* **pressed to do sthg** ver-se em apuros para fazer algo; **to feel ~ done by** sentir-se injustiçado(da) por.

hard-and-fast *adj* rígido(da).

hardback ['hɑːdbæk] ◇ *adj* de capa dura. ◇ *n* [book] edição *f* de capa dura.

hard-bitten *adj* duro(ra), inflexível.

hardboard ['hɑːdbɔːd] *n (U)* madeira *f* compensada.

hard-boiled *adj* **-1.** [egg] cozido(da) **-2.** [person] impassível.

hard cash *n (U)* dinheiro *m* vivo.

hard cider *n US* sidra *f*.

hard copy *n COMPUT* cópia *f* impressa.

hard-core *adj* [pornography] explícito(ta).
◆ **hard core** *n* [of group] núcleo *m*.

hard court *n* quadra *f* rápida.

hard currency *n* moeda *f* forte.

hard disk *n* disco *m* rígido.

hard drugs *npl* drogas *fpl* pesadas.

harden ['hɑːdn] ◇ *vt* **-1.** [steel, arteries] endurecer **-2.** *fig* [person] endurecer **-3.** [attitude, ideas, opinion] fortalecer. ◇ *vi* **-1.** [glue, concrete, arteries] endurecer, endurecer-se **-2.** *fig* [person] endurecer-se **-3.** [attitude, ideas, opinion] fortalecer-se.

hardened ['hɑːdnd] *adj* **-1.** [steel, arteries] endurecido(da) **-2.** [criminal] habitual **-3.** [accustomed]: **~ to sthg** acostumado(da) a algo.

hardening ['hɑːdnɪŋ] *n* **-1.** [of steel, arteries] endurecimento *m* **-2.** [of attitude, ideas, opinion] fortalecimento *m*.

hard hat *n* [for protection] capacete *m*.

hard-headed [-'hedɪd] *adj* realista.

hard-hearted [-'hɑːtɪd] *adj* insensível; **a ~ person** uma pessoa sem coração.

hard-hitting [-'hɪtɪŋ] *adj* chocante.

hard labour *n (U)* trabalhos *mpl* forçados.

hard line *n*: **to take a ~ on sthg** manter a linha dura em relação a algo.
◆ **hard-line** *adj* linha-dura.
◆ **hard lines** *npl UK*: **hard lines!** que azar!

hard-liner *n* linha-dura *mf*.

hardly ['hɑːdlɪ] *adv* **-1.** [scarcely, not really] dificilmente; **~ ever/anything** quase nunca/nada; **I can ~ move/wait** mal posso me mover/esperar **-2.** [only just] apenas.

hardness ['hɑːdnɪs] *n* **-1.** [firmness, also of water] dureza *f* **-2.** [difficulty] dificuldade *f* **-3.** [of heart, person] insensibilidade *f*.

hard-nosed [-'nəʊzd] *adj* obstinado(da), contundente.

hard return *n COMPUT* retorno *m* de hardware.

hard sell *n* venda *f* agressiva.

hardship ['hɑːdʃɪp] *n* **-1.** *(U)* [difficult conditions] privações *fpl* **-2.** [difficult circumstance] dificuldade *f*.

hard shoulder *n UK AUT* acostamento *m*.

hard up *adj inf* desprovido(da); **~ for sthg** desprovido(da) de algo.

hardware ['hɑːdweə^r] *n* **-1.** [tools, equipment] ferragens *fpl* **-2.** *COMPUT* hardware *m*.

hardware shop *n* ferragem *f*.

hardwearing [ˌhɑːd'weərɪŋ] *adj UK* resistente.

hardwood ['hɑːdwʊd] *n (U)* madeira *f* de lei.

hardworking [ˌhɑːd'wɜːkɪŋ] *adj* trabalhador(ra).

hardy ['hɑːdɪ] (*compar* **-ier**, *superl* **-iest**) *adj* **-1.** [person, animal] forte, robusto(ta) **-2.** [plant] resistente.

hare [heəʳ] <> *n* lebre *f.* <> *vi UK inf*: **to ~ off** correr a toda.
harebell *n* campainha *f.*
harebrained [ˈheəˌbreɪnd] *adj inf* tolo(la).
harelip [ˌheəˈlɪp] *n* lábio *m* leporino.
harem [*UK* hɑːˈriːm, *US* ˈhærəm] *n* harém *m.*
haricot (bean) [ˈhærɪkəʊ-] *n* feijão *m.*
hark [hɑːk] ◆ **hark back** *vi*: **to ~ back to sthg** voltar a algo.
harlequin [ˈhɑːləkwɪn] <> *n* arlequim *m.* <> *comp* arlequinal, de arlequim.
Harley Street [ˈhɑːlɪ-] *n rua no centro de Londres famosa pelos seus médicos especialistas.*
harm [hɑːm] <> *n* [physical] mal *m*; [psychological] dano *m*; **to do ~ to sb/sthg, to do sb/sthg ~** fazer mal a alguém/algo; **to mean no ~** não ter má intenção; **there's no ~ in it** não há mal nenhum nisso; **to be out of ~'s way** estar a salvo; **to come to no ~** [person] chegar são e salvo, chegar sã e salva; [thing] ficar a salvo. <> *vt* [physically] ferir; [psychologically] danificar, prejudicar.
harmful [ˈhɑːmfʊl] *adj* [physically] nocivo(va) ; [psychologically] prejudicial.
harmless [ˈhɑːmlɪs] *adj* inofensivo(va).
harmlessly [ˈhɑːmlɪslɪ] *adv* [without causing damage] sem causar dano.
harmonic [hɑːˈmɒnɪk] *adj* harmônico(ca).
harmonica [hɑːˈmɒnɪkəl] *n* gaita-de-boca *f.*
harmonious [hɑːˈməʊnjəs] *adj* harmonioso(sa).
harmonium [hɑːˈməʊnjəm] (*pl* **-s**) *n* harmônio *m.*
harmonize, -ise [ˈhɑːmənaɪz] <> *vt* harmonizar. <> *vi* harmonizar; **to ~ with sthg** harmonizar-se com algo.
harmony [ˈhɑːmənɪ] (*pl* **-ies**) *n* harmonia *f*; **in ~ with sthg** em harmonia com algo.
harness [ˈhɑːnɪs] <> *n* **-1.** [for horse] arreio *m* **-2.** [for person, child] andador *m.* <> *vt* **-1.** [horse] arrear, pôr arreios em **-2.** [energy, solar power] aproveitar.
harp [hɑːp] *n MUS* harpa *f.*
◆ **harp on** *vi*: **to ~ on (about sthg)** bater sempre na mesma tecla (sobre algo).
harpist [ˈhɑːpɪst] *n* harpista *mf.*
harpoon [hɑːˈpuːn] <> *n* arpão *m.* <> *vt* arpoar.
harpsichord [ˈhɑːpsɪkɔːd] *n* clavicórdio *m.*
harrowing [ˈhærəʊɪŋ] *adj* angustiante.
harry [ˈhærɪ] (*pt* & *pp* **-ied**) *vt* **-1.** [badger] importunar; **to ~ sb for sthg** importunar alguém para obter algo **-2.** *MIL* [attack] saltear.
harsh [hɑːʃ] *adj* **-1.** [cruel, severe] severo(ra), duro(ra) **-2.** [conditions, weather] duro(ra) **-3.** [cry, voice] áspero(ra) **-4.** [colour, contrast, light] forte **-5.** [landscape] desolado(da) **-6.** [taste] azedo(da).
harshly [ˈhɑːʃlɪ] *adv* **-1.** [treat, punish, judge] severamente, duramente **-2.** [cry, shout] asperamente **-3.** [shine] ofuscantemente.
harshness [ˈhɑːʃnɪs] *n (U)* **-1.** [of person, treatment] severidade *f*, dureza *f* **-2.** [of climate] rigor *m* **-3.** [of cry, voice] aspereza *f* **-4.** [of colour, contrast, light] forte constraste *m* **-5.** [of landscape] desolação *f.*
harvest [ˈhɑːvɪst] <> *n* colheita *f.* <> *vt* [crops] colher.
harvest festival *n festividade religiosa que celebra o início da colheita.*
has [*weak form* həz, *strong form* hæz] *vb* ▷ **have**.
has-been *n inf pej*: **that man is a ~** aquele homem já era.
hash [hæʃ] *n* **-1.** *(U)* [meat] picadinho *m* **-2.** *inf* [mess]: **to make a ~ of sthg** fazer uma confusão em algo **-3.** *drugs sl* [hashish] haxixe *m.*
◆ **hash up** *vt sep UK inf* [make a mess of] fazer uma confusão em.
hash browns *npl US prato feito com batatas esmagadas e fritas.*
hashish [ˈhæʃiːʃ] *n (U)* haxixe *m.*
hasn't [ˈhæznt] = **has not**.
hassle [ˈhæsl] *inf* <> *n* [annoyance] amolação *f.* <> *vt* amolar, aborrecer.
haste [heɪst] *n (U)* **-1.** [rush] pressa *f*; **to do sthg in ~** fazer algo às pressas **-2.** [speed] rapidez *f*; **to make ~** *dated* apressar-se.
hasten [ˈheɪsn] <> *vt* acelerar. <> *vi* apressar-se; **I ~ to add that ...** apresso-me a acrescentar que ...
hastily [ˈheɪstɪlɪ] *adv* **-1.** [rashly] apressadamente **-2.** [quickly] rapidamente, às pressas.
hasty [ˈheɪstɪ] (*compar* **-ier**, *superl* **-iest**) *adj* **-1.** [rash] precipitado(da) **-2.** [quick] breve.
hat [hæt] *n* chapéu *m*; **keep it under your ~** mantenha isso entre nós; **to be talking through one's ~** só dizer besteira; **that's old ~** isso é mais velho que andar para frente.
hatbox [ˈhætˌbɒks] *n* chapeleira *f.*
hatch [hætʃ] <> *vt* **-1.** [chick] incubar **-2.** [egg] chocar **-3.** *fig* [scheme, plot] conceber, idealizar. <> *vi* **-1.** [chick] sair do ovo **-2.** [egg] chocar. <> *n* [for serving food] portinhola *f*, janela *f* de comunicação.
hatchback [ˈhætʃˌbæk] *n* carro *m* com porta traseira.
hatchet [ˈhætʃɪt] *n* machadinha *f*; **to bury the ~** fazer as pazes.
hatchet job *n inf* crítica *f* destrutiva.
hatchway [ˈhætʃˌweɪ] *n* escotilha *f.*
hate [heɪt] <> *n* **-1.** [emotion] ódio *m* **-2.** [person, thing hated] aversão *f.* <> *vt* [dislike] detestar, odiar; **to ~ doing sthg** odiar fazer algo.
hateful [ˈheɪtfʊl] *adj* detestável.
hatred [ˈheɪtrɪd] *n (U)* ódio *m.*
hat trick *n SPORT série de três pontos marcados pelo mesmo jogador na mesma partida.*
haughty [ˈhɔːtɪ] (*compar* **-ier**, *superl* **-iest**) *adj* arrogante.
haul [hɔːl] <> *n* **-1.** [of drugs, stolen goods] carregamento *m* **-2.** [distance]: **long ~** longo trajeto *m.* <> *vt* **-1.** [pull] arrastar, puxar **-2.** [by lorry] transportar.
haulage [ˈhɔːlɪdʒ] *n* **-1.** [gen] transporte *m* **-2.** [cost] gasto *m* com transporte.
haulage contractor *n* transportadora *f.*
haulier *UK* [ˈhɔːlɪəʳ], **hauler** *US* [ˈhɔːlər] *n* **-1.** [business] transportadora *f* **-2.** [person] transportador *m*, -ra *f.*
haunch [hɔːntʃ] *n* **-1.** [of person] quadril *m* **-2.** [of animal] lombo *m.*
haunt [hɔːnt] <> *n* [place] lugar *m* preferido. <> *vt* **-1.** [subj: ghost] assombrar **-2.** [subj: memory, fear, problem] perseguir.

haunted ['hɔ:ntɪd] *adj* **-1.** [house, castle] assombrado(da) **-2.** [look] espantado(da).
haunting ['hɔ:ntɪŋ] *adj* inesquecível, obcecante.
Havana [hə'vænə] *n* Havana; **in ~** em Havana.
have [hæv] (*pt* & *pp* **had**) *aux vb* **-1.** [to form perfect tenses]: **I ~ finished** acabei; **~ you been there? - no, I ~n't** você já esteve lá? - não; **they hadn't seen it** não o tinham visto; **we had already left** nós já tínhamos saído **-2.** [must]: **to ~ (got) to do sthg** ter de fazer algo; **do you ~ to pay?** é preciso pagar? <> *vt* **-1.** [possess]: **to ~ (got)** ter; **do you ~** *OR* **~ you got a double room?** você tem um quarto de casal?; **she's got brown hair** ela tem o cabelo castanho **-2.** [experience] ter; **to ~ a cold** estar resfriado; **to ~ a great time** divertir-se a valer **-3.** [replacing other verbs] ter; **to ~ breakfast** tomar o café da manhã; **to ~ dinner** jantar; **to ~ lunch** almoçar; **to ~ a bath** tomar banho; **to ~ a drink** tomar qualquer coisa, tomar um drinque; **to ~ a shower** tomar um banho; **to ~ a swim** nadar **-4.** [feel] ter; **I ~ no doubt about it** não tenho dúvida alguma *OR* nenhuma sobre isso **-5.** [cause to be]: **to ~ sthg done** mandar fazer algo; **to ~ one's hair cut** cortar o cabelo **-6.** [be treated in a certain way]: **I've had my wallet stolen** roubaram a minha carteira.
haven ['heɪvn] *n* [refuge] abrigo *m*.
haven't ['hævnt] = **have not**.
haversack ['hævəsæk] *n dated* mochila *f*.
havoc ['hævək] *n (U)* destruição *f*, estragos *mpl*; **to play ~ with sthg** causar estragos em algo.
Hawaii [hə'waii:] *n* Havaí; **in ~** no Havaí.
Hawaiian [hə'waɪjən] <> *adj* havaiano(na). <> *n* havaiano *m*, -na *f*.
hawk [hɔ:k] <> *n* **-1.** [bird] falcão *m*; **to watch sb like a ~** observar alguém com olhos de lince **-2.** *POL* não-pacifista *mf*. <> *vt* [in the street] vender de forma ambulante ; [door to door] vender *(de porta em porta)*.
hawker ['hɔ:kə^r] *n* **-1.** [street vendor] camelô *mf* **-2.** [door-to-door] vendedor *m*, -ra *f* ambulante.
hawthorn ['hɔ:θɔ:n] *n* pilriteiro *m*.
hay [heɪ] *n (U)* feno *m*; **to make ~ while the sun shines** aproveitar uma oportunidade.
hay fever *n (U)* febre *f* do feno.
haymaking *n (U)* preparo *m* do feno.
haystack ['heɪˌstæk] *n* feixe *m* de feno.
haywire ['heɪˌwaɪə^r] *adj inf*: **to go ~** ficar louco (ca).
hazard ['hæzəd] <> *n* [danger] perigo *m*. <> *vt* **-1.** [life, reputation] arriscar, pôr em perigo **-2.** [guess, suggestion] atrever-se a fazer.
hazardous ['hæzədəs] *adj* perigoso(sa), arriscado(-da).
hazard warning lights *npl UK* pisca-alerta *m*.
haze [heɪz] *n* **-1.** [mist] neblina *f* **-2.** [state of confusion] confusão *f* mental.
hazel ['heɪzl] <> *adj* castanho-claro. <> *n* [tree] aveleira *f*.
hazelnut ['heɪzlˌnʌt] *n* avelã *f*.
hazy ['heɪzɪ] (*compar* **-ier**, *superl* **-iest**) *adj* **-1.** [misty] nebuloso(sa) **-2.** [vague, confused - ideas, memory] vago(ga); [- person, facts] confuso(sa).
H-bomb *n* bomba *f* H.
h & c (*abbr of* **hot and cold (water)**) (água) q e f.
HCA (*abbr of* **health care assistant**) *n* auxiliar *mf* de enfermagem.
he [hi:] <> *pers pron* ele; **he's tall** ele é alto.
HE -1. (*abbr of* **high explosive**) altamente explosivo(va). **-2.** (*abbr of* **His (or Her) Excellency**) S.Exª.
head [hed] <> *n* **-1.** [gen] cabeça *f*; **a** *OR* **per ~** por pessoa, por cabeça; **off the top of one's ~** de improviso; **to bite** *OR* **snap sb's ~ off** xingar/insultar alguém sem motivos; **to laugh/sing/shout one's ~ off** rir/cantar/gritar a plenos pulmões; **to be banging one's ~ against a brick wall** dar murro em ponta de faca; **I can't make ~ nor tail of it** isto não tem pé nem cabeça; **on your own ~ be it** que seja por sua própria conta e risco, você que arque com as conseqüências; **to have a ~ for heights** não ter medo de altura; **to be off one's ~** *UK*, **to be out of one's ~** *US* estar fora de seu juízo; **we put our ~s together** tratamos de resolver juntos; **to go to one's ~** subir à cabeça; **to keep one's ~** manter a cabeça no lugar; **to lose one's ~** perder a cabeça; **to be soft in the ~** ter o miolo mole **-2.** [of table, bed, river] cabeceira *f* **-3.** [of page] cabeçalho *m* **-4.** [of stairs] topo *m* **-5.** [of queue, procession] frente *f* **-6.** [of flower] corola *f* **-7.** [head teacher] diretor *m*, -ra *f* **-8.** *ELEC* cabeçote *m* **-9.** *phr*: **to come to a ~** chegar a um ponto crítico. <> *vt* **-1.** [be at front of, top of] encabeçar **-2.** [be in charge of] comandar **-3.** *FTBL* cabecear. <> *vi* dirigir-se, ir; **we gave up and ~ed home** nós desistimos e fomos para casa; **the ship was ~ing due north** o navio rumava para o norte.
◆ **heads** *npl* [on coin] cara *f*; **~s or tails?** cara ou coroa?
◆ **head for** *vt fus* **-1.** [place] dirigir-se para **-2.** *fig* [trouble, disaster] encaminhar-se para.
◆ **head off** <> *vt sep* **-1.** [intercept] deter **-2.** [forestall] antecipar-se a. <> *vi* [leave] esquivar-se.
headache ['hedeɪk] *n* dor *f* de cabeça; **to have a ~** ter uma dor de cabeça.
headband ['hedbænd] *n* faixa *f (para a cabeça)*.
headboard ['hedˌbɔ:d] *n* cabeceira *f*.
head boy *n UK* [at school] representante *m* discente.
head cold *n* resfriado *m*.
head count *n* contagem *f (das pessoas presentes)*.
headdress ['hedˌdres] *n* touca *f*.
header ['hedə^r] *n* **-1.** *FTBL* cabeçada *f* **-2.** [at top of page] cabeçalho *m*.
headfirst [ˌhed'fɜ:st] *adv* de cabeça.
headgear ['hedˌgɪə^r] *n* proteção *f* para a cabeça.
head girl *n UK* [in school] representante *f* discente.
headhunt ['hedhʌnt] *vt* [recruit] contratar *(novos talentos)*.
headhunter ['hedˌhʌntə^r] *n* [recruiter] caça-talentos *mf inv*.
heading ['hedɪŋ] *n* título *m*, cabeçalho *m*.
headlamp ['hedlæmp] *n UK* farol *m (de carro)*.
headland ['hedlənd] *n* promontório *m*.
headlight ['hedlaɪt] *n* farol *m (de carro)*.
headline ['hedlaɪn] *n* **-1.** [in newspaper] manchete *f* **-2.** [of news broadcast] notícia *f* principal.

headlong ['hedlɒŋ] <> *adv* -1. [at great speed] apressadamente -2. [impetuously] precipitadamente -3. [dive, fall] abruptamente. <> *adj* [impetuous] precipitado(da).

headmaster [ˌhed'mɑːstəʳ] *n* diretor *m (de colégio)*.

headmistress [ˌhed'mɪstrɪs] *n* diretora *f (de colégio)*.

head office *n* sede *f*.

head-on <> *adj* frontal, de frente. <> *adv* de frente.

headphones ['hedfəʊnz] *npl* fones *mpl* de ouvido.

headquarters [ˌhed'kwɔːtəz] *npl* -1. FIN sede *f*, matriz *f* -2. MIL quartel-general *m*.

headrest ['hedrest] *n* apoio *m* para a cabeça.

headroom ['hedrʊm] *n (U)* -1. [in car] espaço *m (entre a cabeça e o teto)* -2. [below bridge] altura *f* livre.

headscarf ['hedskɑːf] (*pl* **-scarves** [-skɑːvz] OR **-scarfs**) *n* lenço *m (para a cabeça)*.

headset ['hedset] *n* fones *mpl* de ouvido com microfone.

headship ['hedʃɪp] *n* direção *f (de colégio)*.

head start *n* vantagem *f* inicial; ~ **on** OR **over sb** vantagem sobre alguém.

headstone ['hedstəʊn] *n* lápide *f*.

headstrong ['hedstrɒŋ] *adj* cabeça-dura, obstinado(da).

head teacher *n* diretor *m*, -ra *f* de colégio.

head waiter *n* maître *m*.

headway ['hedweɪ] *n*: **to make** ~ fazer progressos.

headwind ['hedwɪnd] *n* vento *m* contrário.

headword *n* [in dictionary, reference book] entrada *f*, verbete *m*.

heady ['hedɪ] (*compar* **-ier**, *superl* **-iest**) *adj* -1. [exciting] emocionante -2. [causing giddiness] inebriante, estonteante.

heal [hiːl] <> *vt* -1. [mend, cure - person] curar; [- wound] cicatrizar -2. *fig* [breach, division] cicatrizar. <> *vi* [be mended, cured] cicatrizar.

◆ **heal up** *vi* [be mended, cured] cicatrizar.

healing ['hiːlɪŋ] <> *adj* curativo(va). <> *n (U)* cura *f*.

health [helθ] *n (U)* -1. [condition of body] saúde *f*; **to be in good/poor** ~ estar bem/mal de saúde; **to drink (to) sb's** ~ brindar à saúde de alguém -2. *fig* [of country, organization] bom estado *m*.

health centre *n* centro *m* de saúde.

health-conscious *adj* preocupado(da) com a saúde.

health farm *n* spa *m*.

health food *n* alimentos *mpl* naturais.

health food shop *n* loja *f* de alimentos naturais.

health hazard *n* risco *m* à saúde.

health service *n* serviço *m* de saúde.

health visitor *n UK* enfermeiro *m* comunitário, enfermeira *f* comunitária.

healthy ['helθɪ] (*compar* **-ier**, *superl* **-iest**) *adj* -1. [gen] saudável -2. *fig* [thriving] saneado(da) -3. [substantial] substancial.

heap [hiːp] <> *n* monte *m*, pilha *f*; **in a** ~ amontoado(da). <> *vt* -1. [pile up] amontoar; **to** ~ **sthg on (to) sthg** amontoar algo sobre algo -2. *fig* [lavish]: **to** ~ **sthg on sb** cobrir alguém de algo.

◆ **heaps** *npl inf*: ~**s of** montes OR pilhas de.

hear [hɪəʳ] (*pt* & *pp* **heard** [hɜːd]) <> *vt* -1. [perceive] ouvir -2. [learn of] escutar; **to** ~ **(that)** ouvir dizer que -3. JUR [listen to] ver. <> *vi* -1. [perceive sound] ouvir -2. [know]: **to** ~ **about sthg** ouvir falar sobre algo -3. [receive news] ter notícias de; **to** ~ **from sb** ter notícias de alguém -4. *phr*: **I've never heard of him/it!** nunca ouvi falar dele/disto!; **I won't** ~ **of it!** não quero saber nada sobre isto!

◆ **hear out** *vt sep* escutar *(sem interromper)*.

hearing ['hɪərɪŋ] *n* -1. [sense] audição *f*; **hard of** ~ com problemas de audição; **in/within sb's** ~ ao alcance dos ouvidos de alguém -2. JUR [trial] audiência *f*, julgamento *m*; **to give sb a fair** ~ *fig* dar a alguém a oportunidade de falar.

hearing aid *n* aparelho *m* auditivo.

hearsay ['hɪəseɪ] *n (U)* rumor *m*, boato *m*.

hearse [hɜːs] *n* carro *m* funerário.

heart [hɑːt] *n* -1. [gen] coração *m*; **to have a** ~ **of gold** ter um coração de ouro; **his** ~ **isn't in it** ele não colocou o coração nisto; **it's a subject close to my** ~ é um assunto que me encanta; **from the** ~ de coração; **from the bottom of my** ~ do fundo do meu coração; **in one's** ~ **of** ~**s** no fundo do coração; **to do sthg to one's** ~**'s content** fazer algo até que se tenha vontade; **my** ~ **leapt/sank** meu coração pulou/entristeceu-se; **to break sb's** ~ partir o coração de alguém; **to set one's** ~ **on sthg/on doing sthg** colocar o coração em algo/ao fazer algo; **to take sthg to** ~ levar algo a sério -2. *(U)* [courage]: **to have the** ~ **to do sthg** ter coragem de fazer algo; **to lose** ~ perder o ímpeto -3. [of problem] centro *m* -4. [of cabbage, celery, lettuce] miolo *m*.

◆ **hearts** *npl* [playing cards] copas *fpl*; **the six of** ~**s** o seis de copas.

◆ **at heart** *adv* de coração.

◆ **by heart** *adv* de cor.

heartache ['hɑːteɪk] *n* sofrimento *m*, angústia *f*.

heart attack *n* ataque *m* cardíaco.

heartbeat ['hɑːtbiːt] *n* pulsação *f*.

heartbreaking ['hɑːtˌbreɪkɪŋ] *adj* de partir o coração.

heartbroken ['hɑːtˌbrəʊkn] *adj* de coração partido.

heartburn ['hɑːtbɜːn] *n (U)* azia *f*.

heart disease *n (U)* doença *f* cardíaca.

heartening ['hɑːtnɪŋ] *adj* animador(ra).

heart failure *n (U)* parada *f* cardíaca.

heartfelt ['hɑːtfelt] *adj* sincero(ra), de todo coração.

hearth [hɑːθ] *n* -1. [of fireplace] base *f* -2. [fireplace] lareira *f*.

heartland ['hɑːtlænd] *n* área *f* central.

heartless ['hɑːtlɪs] *adj* desumano(na); ~ **person** pessoa sem coração.

heartrending ['hɑːtˌrendɪŋ] *adj* consternador(ra).

heart-searching *n (U)* exame *m* de consciência.

heartthrob ['hɑːtθrɒb] *n* galã *m*.

heart-to-heart <> *adj* franco(ca). <> *n* conversa *f* franca.

heart transplant *n* transplante *m* de coração.

heartwarming ['hɑ:t,wɔ:mɪŋ] *adj* enternecedor(-ra), gratificante.

hearty ['hɑ:tɪ] (*compar* **-ier**, *superl* **-iest**) *adj* **-1.** [loud, energetic] caloroso(sa) **-2.** [substantial - meal] farto(ta); [- appetite] bom (boa) **-3.** [strongly felt] profundo(da).

heat [hi:t] ◇ *n* **-1.** *(U)* [gen] calor *m* **-2.** *(U)* [specific temperature] temperatura *f* **-3.** *(U)* [fire, source of heat] fogo *m* **-4.** *(U) fig*: **in the ~ of the moment** no calor do momento **-5.** [eliminating round] rodada *f* **-6.** *ZOOL*: **on ~** *UK*, **in ~** no cio. ◇ *vt* esquentar.
 ◆ **heat up** ◇ *vt sep* [make warm] esquentar. ◇ *vi* [become warm] ficar quente, esquentar.

heated ['hi:tɪd] *adj* **-1.** [room, swimming pool] aquecido(da) **-2.** [argument, discussion, person] esquentado(-da).

heater ['hi:təʳ] *n* aquecedor *m*.

heath [hi:θ] *n* [open place] charneca *f*.

heathen ['hi:ðn] ◇ *adj* pagão(gã). ◇ *n* pagão *m*, -gã *f*.

heather ['heðəʳ] *n (U)* urze *f*.

heating ['hi:tɪŋ] *n (U)* calefação *f*.

heat rash *n* brotoeja *f (pelo calor)*.

heat-resistant *adj* refratário(ria), resistente ao calor.

heat-seeking [-,si:kɪŋ] *adj* detector(ra) de calor.

heatstroke ['hi:tstrəʊk] *n (U)* insolação *f*.

heat wave *n* onda *f* de calor.

heave [hi:v] ◇ *vt* **-1.** [pull] puxar, arrastar ; [push] empurrar **-2.** *inf* [throw] atirar, arremessar **-3.** [give out]: **to ~ a sigh** dar um suspiro. ◇ *vi* **-1.** [pull] puxar **-2.** [rise and fall - boat, shoulders] sacudir--se; [- waves] ondular; [- chest] arfar **-3.** [retch] embrulhar. ◇ *n* **-1.** [pull] puxão *m* **-2.** [push] empurrão *m*.

heaven ['hevn] *n* **-1.** [Paradise] paraíso *m*; **~ (alone) knows!** sabe Deus! **-2.** *(U)* [something delightful] paraíso *m*.
 ◆ **heavens** ◇ *npl*: **the ~s** *literary* os céus. ◇ *excl*: **(good) ~s!** céus!

heavenly ['hevnlɪ] *adj* **-1.** *inf dated* [delightful] divino(na) **-2.** *literary* [of the skies] celestial.

heavily ['hevɪlɪ] *adv* **-1.** [for emphasis - to rain, smoke, drink, tax] excessivamente; [- laden, booked, dependent] totalmente; [- in debt] seriamente; [- populated] densamente **-2.** [solidly] solidamente **-3.** [noisily, ponderously] pesadamente **-4.** [deeply] profundamente.

heaviness ['hevɪnɪs] *n* **-1.** [of object] peso *m* **-2.** [of sleep] profundidade *f* **-3.** [of movement] dureza *f*, intensidade *f* **-4.** [of mixture] densidade *f* **-5.** [of feeling] abatimento *m*.

heavy ['hevɪ] (*compar* **-ier**, *superl* **-iest**) *adj* **-1.** [gen] pesado(da); **how ~ is it?** quanto pesa? **-2.** [intense, deep] intenso(sa); **to be a ~ sleeper** ter o sono muito profundo **-3.** [in quantity] em grande número **-4.** [person - fat] gordo(da); [- solidly built] sólido(da) **-5.** [laden]: **~ with fruit** *literary* carregado(da) de fruta **-6.** [ponderous - movement] brusco(-ca); [- fall] feio (feia) **-7.** [oppressive] carregado(da) **-8.** [sad]: **with a ~ heart** com o coração partido **-9.** [excessive]: **to be a ~ smoker/drinker** fumar/ beber em excesso; **this car's ~ on petrol** este carro consome muita gasolina **-10.** [grave, serious] grande **-11.** [busy] cheio (cheia).

heavy cream *n US* nata *f* para enfeitar.

heavy-duty *adj* para grandes cargas/esforços; [material] resistente.

heavy goods vehicle *n UK* veículo *m* de carga pesada.

heavy-handed [-'hændɪd] *adj* [clumsy - tactics, policy, person] desastrado(da); [- compliment, treatment] grosseiro(ra).

heavy industry *n* indústria *f* pesada.

heavy metal *n (U) MUS* heavy-metal *m*.

heavyweight ['hevɪweɪt] ◇ *adj SPORT* peso pesado. ◇ *n* peso *m* pesado.

Hebrew ['hi:bru:] ◇ *adj* hebraico(ca). ◇ *n* **-1.** [person] hebraico *m*, -ca *f* **-2.** [language] hebraico *m*.

Hebrides ['hebrɪdi:z] *npl*: **the ~** as Hébridas; **in the ~** nas Hébridas.

heck [hek] *excl*: **what/where/why the ~ ...?** o que/
onde/por que diabos ...?; **a ~ of a lot of** uma montanha de; **a ~ of a nice guy** um cara e tanto.

heckle ['hekl] ◇ *vt* ficar interrompendo. ◇ *vi* ficar interrompendo.

heckler ['hekləʳ] *n pessoa que fica interrompendo (um orador, um comediante, um político etc)*.

hectare ['hekteəʳ] *n* hectare *m*.

hectic ['hektɪk] *adj* muito agitado(da).

hector ['hektəʳ] ◇ *vt* intimidar com bravatas. ◇ *vi* bravatear.

he'd [hi:d] = **he had**, **he would**.

hedge [hedʒ] ◇ *n* [shrub] cerca *f* viva. ◇ *vi* [prevaricate] dar evasivas.

hedgehog ['hedʒhɒg] *n* porco-espinho *m*.

hedgerow ['hedʒrəʊ] *n* linha *f* de cerca viva.

hedonism ['hi:dənɪzm] *n (U)* hedonismo *m*.

hedonist ['hi:dənɪst] *n* hedonista *mf*.

heed [hi:d] ◇ *n*: **to pay ~ to sb** prestar atenção em alguém; **to take ~ of sthg** levar algo em consideração. ◇ *vt fml* ter em conta.

heedless ['hi:dlɪs] *adj*: **to be ~ of sthg** não fazer caso de algo.

heel [hi:l] *n* **-1.** [of foot] calcanhar *m*; **to dig one's ~s in** fincar o pé; **to follow hard on the ~s (of sb/sthg)** ficar na cola (de alguém/algo); **to take to one's ~s** dar no pé; **to turn on one's ~** dar meia volta **-2.** [of shoe] salto *m*.

hefty ['heftɪ] (*compar* **-ier**, *superl* **-iest**) *adj inf* **-1.** [person] robusto(ta) **-2.** [salary, fee, fine] vultoso(sa), alto(ta).

heifer ['hefəʳ] *n* vitela *f*, novilha *f*.

height [haɪt] *n* **-1.** [gen] altura *f*; **in ~** de altura; **what ~ is it/are you?** que altura tem isto/você tem?; **to gain/lose ~** ganhar/perder altura **-2.** [zenith] apogeu *m*; **the ~ of** [fight, fame, tourist season] o auge de; [stupidity, ignorance, bad manners] o cúmulo de.
 ◆ **heights** *npl* **-1.** [limits] limites *mpl* **-2.** [high places] alto *m*; **are you afraid of ~?** você tem medo de altura?; **the Golan Heights** o Planalto do Golã.

heighten ['haɪtn] ◇ *vt* intensificar. ◇ *vi* intensificar-se.

heinous ['heɪnəs] *adj fml* hediondo(da).

heir [eəʳ] *n* herdeiro *m*.
heir apparent (*pl* **heirs apparent**) *n* sucessor *m* direto.
heiress ['eərɪs] *n* herdeira *f*.
heirloom ['eəlu:m] *n* herança *f* de família.
heist [haɪst] *n inf* roubo *m*.
held [held] *pt & pp* ▷ **hold**.
helices ['helɪsi:z] *pl* ▷ **helix**.
helicopter ['helɪkɒptəʳ] *n* hepicóptero *m*.
heliport ['helɪpɔ:t] *n* heliporto *m*.
helium ['hi:lɪəm] *n (U)* hélio *m*.
helix ['hi:lɪks] (*pl* **-es** OR **helices**) *n* [spiral] hélice *f*.
hell [hel] ◇ *n* **-1.** inferno *m* **-2.** *inf* [for emphasis]: **what/where/why the ~ ...?** o que/onde/por que diabos ...?; **it was one ~ of a mess** estava uma bagunça total; **he's a ~ of a nice guy** ele é um cara simpático e tanto; **like ~** como o diabo; **like ~ you will!** com os diabos que você vai!; **let's get the ~ out (of here!)** vamos cair fora daqui! **-3.** *phr*: **to ~ with...!** *v inf* pro inferno com ...!; **all ~ broke loose** *inf* o mundo veio abaixo; **to do sthg for the ~ of it** *inf* fazer algo por gosto; **to give sb ~** *inf* [verbally] fazer alguém passar poucas e boas; **go to ~! v inf** vá para o inferno!; **to play ~ with sthg** *inf* infernizar algo. ◇ *excl inf* diabos!, droga!
he'll [hi:l] = **he will**.
hell-bent *adj*: **to be ~ on doing sthg** estar totalmente decidido(da) a fazer algo.
hellish ['helɪʃ] *adj inf* infernal.
hello [hə'ləʊ] *excl* [greeting] olá!, oi!; [answering telephone, attracting attention] alô!
helm [helm] *n* **-1.** [of ship] leme *m*, timão *m* **-2.** *fig* [of company, organization] direção *f*; **at the ~** na direção.
helmet ['helmɪt] *n* capacete *m*.
helmsman ['helmzmən] (*pl* **-men** [-mən]) *n* NAUT timoneiro *m*, -ra *f*.
help [help] ◇ *n* **-1.** *(U)* [assistance] ajuda *f*; **to be of ~** ajudar; **with the ~ of sb/sthg** com a ajuda de alguém/algo **-2.** *(U)* [in an emergency] socorro *m* **-3.** [useful person or object]: **to be a ~** ser útil. ◇ *vt* **-1.** [gen] ajudar; **to ~ sb (to) do sthg** ajudar alguém a fazer algo; **to ~ sb with sthg** ajudar alguém em algo; **can I ~ you?** [in shop, at reception] pois não? **-2.** [avoid] evitar; **I can't ~ feeling sad** não posso evitar ficar triste; **I couldn't ~ laughing** eu não conseguia parar de rir **-3.** *phr*: **to ~ o.s. (to sthg)** servir-se (de algo). ◇ *vi* [gen] ajudar; **to ~ with sthg** ajudar em algo. ◇ *excl* socorro!
◆ **help out** ◇ *vt sep* dar uma mão para. ◇ *vi* dar uma mão.
helper ['helpəʳ] *n* ajudante *mf*.
helpful ['helpfʊl] *adj* **-1.** [willing to help] prestativo(va) **-2.** [useful] proveitoso(sa).
helping ['helpɪŋ] *n* porção *f (de comida)*; **would you like a second ~?** quer repetir?
helping hand *n*: **if you need a ~, just call** se precisar de uma mãozinha, é só chamar.
helpless ['helplɪs] *adj* indefeso(sa).
helplessly ['helplɪslɪ] *adv* **-1.** [uncontrollably] sem parar **-2.** [in a helpless manner] sem se poder fazer nada.
helpline ['helplaɪn] *n* (linha *f* de) suporte *m*.
Helsinki ['helsɪŋkɪ] *n* Helsinque; **in ~** em Helsinque.
helter-skelter [ˌheltə'skeltəʳ] *UK* ◇ *n* tobogã *m* gigante. ◇ *adv* desordenadamente.
hem [hem] (*pt & pp* **-med**, *cont* **-ming**) ◇ *n* bainha *f*. ◇ *vt* abainhar, fazer a bainha de.
◆ **hem in** *vt sep* cercar.
he-man *n inf hum* macho *m*.
hematology [ˌhi:mə'tɒlədʒɪ] *n (U)* hematologia *f*.
hemisphere ['hemɪˌsfɪəʳ] *n* [of Earth] hemisfério *m*.
hemline ['hemlaɪn] *n* (altura *f* da) bainha *f*.
hemoglobin [ˌhi:mə'gləʊbɪn] *n (U)* hemoglobina *f*.
hemophilia [ˌhi:mə'fɪlɪə] *n (U)* hemofilia *f*.
hemophiliac [ˌhi:mə'fɪlɪæk] *n* hemofílico *m*, -ca *f*.
hemorrhage ['hemərɪdʒ] ◇ *n* hemorragia *f*. ◇ *vi* ter uma hemorragia.
hemorrhoids ['hemərɔɪdz] *npl* hemorróidas *fpl*.
hemp [hemp] *n (U)* [plant or fibre] cânhamo *m*.
hen [hen] *n* **-1.** [female chicken] galinha *f* **-2.** [female bird] fêmea *f*.
hence [hens] *adv fml* **-1.** [therefore] por isso, assim **-2.** [from now]: **ten years ~** daqui a dez anos.
henceforth [ˌhens'fɔ:θ] *adv fml* doravante.
henchman ['hentʃmən] (*pl* **-men** [-mən]) *n pej* capanga *m*, jagunço *m*.
henna ['henə] ◇ *n (U)* hena *f*. ◇ *vt* passar OR aplicar hena em.
hen party *n UK inf* despedida *f* de solteira.
henpecked ['henpekt] *adj pej* submisso(sa), dominado(da).
hepatitis [ˌhepə'taɪtɪs] *n (U)* hepatite *f*.
her [hɜ:ʳ] ◇ *pers pron* **-1.** *(direct)* a; **I know ~** eu a conheço **-2.** *(indirect)* lhe; **send it to ~** mande isso para ela; **tell ~** diga-lhe **-3.** *(after prep)* ela; **Lucy brought it with ~** a Lucy trouxe-o consigo OR com ela. ◇ *poss adj* o seu (a sua), dela; **~ books** o livros dela, os seus livros.
herald ['herəld] ◇ *n* [messenger] mensageiro *m*, -ra *f*. ◇ *vt fml* **-1.** [signify, usher in] anunciar **-2.** [proclaim] conclamar.
heraldry ['herəldrɪ] *n (U)* heráldica *f*.
herb [*UK* hɜ:b, *US* ɜ:b] *n* erva *f*.
herbaceous [hɜ:'beɪʃəs] *adj* herbáceo(cea).
herbal [*UK* 'hɜ:bl, *US* ɜ:bl] *adj* à base de ervas.
herbalist ['hɜ:blɪst] *n* herbanário *m*, -ria *f*.
herbicide *n* herbicida *f*.
herbivore ['hɜ:bɪvɔ:ʳ] *n* herbívoro *m*, -ra *f*.
herb tea *n (U)* infusão *f* de ervas.
herd [hɜ:d] ◇ *n* **-1.** [gen] rebanho *m*; [of elephants] manada *f* **-2.** [of people] multidão *f*. ◇ *vt* **-1.** [drive] pastorear **-2.** *fig* [push] conduzir *(em grupo)*.
herdsman ['hɜ:dzmən] (*pl* **-men** [-mən]) *n* **-1.** [of sheep, goats] pastor *m* **-2.** [of cattle] boiadeiro *m*, vaqueiro *m*.
here [hɪəʳ] *adv* **-1.** [in, at this place] aqui; **~ he is/they are** aqui está ele/estão eles; **~ it is** aqui está; **~ you are!** toma!; **Christmas is nearly ~** o Natal está próximo; **~ and there** aqui e acolá **-2.** [from this place]: **from ~** daqui; **he left ~ a while ago** ele saiu daqui há pouco **-3.** [to this place]: **come ~!** vem aqui!; **~ they come** lá vêm eles **-4.** [in toasts]: **~'s to** um brinde a.

hereabouts *UK* ['hɪərəˌbaʊts], **hereabout** *US* [ˌhɪərə'baʊt] *adv* por aqui.

hereafter [ˌhɪər'ɑ:ftə[r]] <> *adv fml* de agora em diante, a partir de agora. <> *n*: **the ~** o além.

hereby [ˌhɪə'baɪ] *adv* **-1.** *fml* [in documents] por meio deste (desta) **-2.** *fml* [when speaking]: **I ~ declare this theatre open** neste momento, declaro este teatro aberto.

hereditary [hɪ'redɪtrɪ] *adj* hereditário(ria).

heredity [hɪ'redətɪ] *n (U)* hereditariedade *f*.

heresy ['herəsɪ] (*pl* **-ies**) *n* heresia *f*.

heretic ['herətɪk] *n* **-1.** RELIG herege *mf* **-2.** *fig* [unorthodox thinker] rebelde *mf*.

herewith [ˌhɪə'wɪð] *adv fml* [with letter]: **please find ~ ...** segue anexo ...

heritage ['herɪtɪdʒ] *n (U)* herança *f*.

heritage centre *n* museu *m (em local histórico)*.

hermaphrodite [hɜ:'mæfrədaɪt] ZOOL <> *adj* hermafrodita. <> *n* hermafrodita *mf*.

hermetic [hɜ:'metɪk] *adj* [airtight] hermético(ca).

hermetically [hɜ:'metɪklɪ] *adv*: **~ sealed** hermeticamente fechado(da).

hermit ['hɜ:mɪt] *n* eremita *mf*.

hernia ['hɜ:njə] *n* hérnia *f*.

hero ['hɪərəʊ] (*pl* **-es**) *n* **-1.** [gen] herói *m* **-2.** [idol] ídolo *m*.

heroic [hɪ'rəʊɪk] *adj* heróico(ca).
 ◆ **heroics** *npl pej* patetices *fpl*.

heroin ['herəʊɪn] *n* [drug] *(U)* heroína *f*.

heroine ['herəʊɪn] *n* heroína *f*.

heroism ['herəʊɪzml] *n (U)* heroísmo *m*.

hero worship *n (U)* idolatria *f*, veneração *f*.

heron ['herən] (*pl inv* OR **-s**) *n* garça *f* real.

herpes ['hɜ:pi:z] *n (U)* herpes *m inv*.

herring ['herɪŋ] (*pl inv* OR **-s**) *n* arenque *m*.

herringbone ['herɪŋbəʊn] *adj* [pattern] em espinha de peixe.

hers [hɜ:z] *poss pron* o seu (a sua), (o/a) dela; **a friend of ~** um amigo dela OR seu; **those shoes are ~** estes sapatos são dela OR seus; **these are mine - where are ~?** estes são os meus - onde estão os dela?

herself [hɜ:'self] *pron* **-1.** *(reflexive)* se; **she hurt ~** ela se machucou **-2.** *(after prep)* si própria OR mesma; **she did it ~** foi ela mesma que o fez.

he's [hi:z] = **he is, he has**.

hesitant ['hezɪtənt] *adj* hesitante.

hesitate ['hezɪteɪt] *vi* [pause] hesitar; **to ~ to do sthg** hesitar em fazer algo.

hesitation [ˌhezɪ'teɪʃn] *n* hesitação *f*; **without ~** sem hesitação; **to have no ~ in doing sthg** não ter dúvidas ao fazer algo.

hessian ['hesɪən] *n UK* aniagem *f*, juta *f*.

heterogeneous [ˌhetərə'dʒi:njəs] *adj fml* heterogêneo(nea).

heterosexual [ˌhetərəʊ'sekʃʊəl] <> *adj* heterossexual. <> *n* heterossexual *mf*.

het up [het-] *adj inf* nervoso(sa), como uma pilha de nervos.

hew [hju:] (*pt* **-ed**, *pp* **-ed** OR **hewn**) *vt literary* [stone, wood] talhar.

HEW (*abbr of* **(Department of) Health, Education and Welfare**) *n ministério norte-americano de educação, saúde e bem-estar social.*

hex [heks] *n* **-1.** [curse] praga *f*, urucubaca *f* **-2.** COMPUT: **~ (code)** (código *m*) hexadecimal *m*.

hexagon ['heksəgən] *n* hexágono *m*.

hexagonal [hek'sægənl] *adj* hexagonal.

hey [heɪ] *excl* ei!

heyday ['heɪdeɪ] *n* auge *m*, apogeu *m*.

hey presto [-'prestəʊ] *excl* tadá!

HF (*abbr of* **high frequency**) HF.

HGV (*abbr of* **heavy goods vehicle**) *n veículos pesados, como ônibus e caminhão*; **an ~ licence** ≃ uma carteira categoria C.

hi [haɪ] *excl inf* [hello] oi!, olá!

HI *abbr of* **Hawaii**.

hiatus [haɪ'eɪtəs] (*pl* **-es**) *n fml* [pause] pausa *f*.

hibernate ['haɪbəneɪt] *vi* hibernar.

hibernation [ˌhaɪbə'neɪʃn] *n (U)* hibernação *f*; **to be in ~** estar hibernando.

hiccough, hiccup ['hɪkʌp] (*pt & pp* **-ped**, *cont* **-ping**) <> *n* **-1.** [sound] soluço *m*; **to have ~s** estar com soluços **-2.** *fig* [difficulty] contratempo *m*. <> *vi* soluçar.

hick [hɪk] *n esp US inf pej* caipira *mf*.

hid [hɪd] *pt* ▻ **hide**.

hidden ['hɪdn] <> *pp* ▻ **hide**. <> *adj* **-1.** [from view] escondido(da) **-2.** [not apparent - disadvantages, dangers] escondido(da); [- problems] não aparente; [- cost] embutido(do) **-3.** [deliberately concealed - weapons] secreto; [- feelings] oculto.

hidden agenda *n pej* segunda intenção *f*.

hide [haɪd] (*pt* **hid**, *pp* **hidden**) <> *n* **-1.** [animal skin] pele *f* **-2.** [for watching birds, animals] esconderijo *m*. <> *vt* **-1.** [conceal] esconder; **to ~ sthg (from sb)** esconder algo (de alguém) **-2.** [cover] cobrir. <> *vi* [conceal o.s.] esconder-se.

hide-and-seek *n (U)* esconde-esconde *m*; **to play ~** brincar de esconde-esconde.

hideaway ['haɪdəweɪ] *n inf* refúgio *m*.

hidebound ['haɪdbaʊnd] *adj pej* **-1.** [institution] antiquado(da) **-2.** [person] careta.

hideous ['hɪdɪəs] *adj* horrível.

hideout ['haɪdaʊt] *n* esconderijo *m*.

hiding ['haɪdɪŋ] *n* **-1.** *(U)* [concealment]: **to be in ~** estar escondido(da) **-2.** *inf* [beating]: **to give sb a (good) ~** dar uma (boa) surra em alguém; **to get a (good) ~ from sb** levar uma (boa) surra de alguém.

hiding place *n* esconderijo *m*.

hierarchical [ˌhaɪə'rɑ:kɪkl] *adj* hierárquico(ca).

hierarchy ['haɪərɑ:kɪ] (*pl* **-ies**) *n* hierarquia *f*.

hieroglyphics [ˌhaɪərə'glɪfɪks] *npl* hieróglifos *mpl*.

hi-fi ['haɪfaɪ] *n* sistema *f* hi-fi.

higgledy-piggledy [ˌhɪgldɪ'pɪgldɪ] *inf* <> *adj* desordenado(da). <> *adv* desordenadamente, de qualquer maneira.

high [haɪ] <> *adj* **-1.** [gen] alto(ta); **to have a ~ opinion of sb/sthg** ter alguém/algo em alta conta; **how ~ is it?** qual é a altura? **-2.** [greater than normal - speed] alto(ta); [- wind] forte; [- prices, unemployment] elevado(da); **temperatures in the ~ twenties** temperaturas bem acima dos 20 graus **-3.** [important, influential] importante **-4.** [honourable] nobre **-5.** [high-pitched] agudo(da) **-6.** ***drugs sl*** [on drugs] baratinado(da) **-7.** ***inf*** [drunk] alto(ta). <> *adv* **-1.** [above ground level] a grande altura **-2.** [in degrees] em alto grau; **to search ~ and low** procurar em tudo quanto é lugar. <> *n* [highest point] pico *m*; **to reach a new ~** atingir um novo pico; **to be on a ~** estar animadíssimo(ma).

highball ['haɪbɔ:l] *n* ***US*** uísque *m* com soda e gelo.

highbrow ['haɪbraʊ] *adj* erudito(ta).

high chair *n* cadeira *f* de bebê.

high-class *adj* [superior - person] de alta classe; [- hotel, restaurant] de alta categoria; [- performance] de alto nível.

high command *n* alto comando *m*.

high commission *n* alta comissão *f*.

high commissioner *n* alto comissário *m*, alta comissária *f*.

High Court *n* ***UK*** *JUR* Corte *f* Suprema.

high-density *adj* *COMPUT* de alta densidade.

higher ['haɪəʳ] *adj* [exam, qualification] superior(ra).
◆ **Higher** *n*: **Higher (Grade)** *SCH na Escócia, exame realizado ao final da escola secundária.*

higher education *n (U)* ensino *m* superior.

high explosive *n* explosivo *m* de alta potência.

high-fidelity *adj* de alta-fidelidade.

high finance *n* altas finanças *fpl*.

high-flier *n* pessoa *f* ambiciosa.

high-flying *adj* [ambitious] ambicioso(sa).

high ground *n*: **to have** *OR* **hold the ~** ter *OR* levar vantagem; **to take the moral ~** acreditar possuir valores morais superiores.

high-handed [-'hændɪd] *adj* despótico(ca).

high-heeled [-'hi:ld] *adj* de salto alto.

high horse *n* ***inf***: **to get on one's ~** estar por cima.

high jump *n* *SPORT* salto *m* em altura; **to be for the ~** ***UK inf*** merecer uma punição.

Highland Games ['haɪlənd-] *npl* Jogos *mpl* das Terras Altas.

Highlands ['haɪləndz] *npl*: **the ~** [of Scotland] as Terras Altas.

high-level *adj* **-1.** [talks, discussions] de alto nível **-2.** [diplomats, officials] do alto escalão.

high life *n (U)*: **the ~** a vida da alta sociedade.

highlight ['haɪlaɪt] <> *n* [of event, occasion] ponto *m* alto, destaque *m*. <> *vt* **-1.** [with pen] realçar **-2.** [emphasize] enfatizar.
◆ **highlights** *npl* [in hair] realces *mpl*.

highlighter (pen) ['haɪlaɪtəʳ-] *n* caneta *f* marca-texto.

highly ['haɪlɪ] *adv* **-1.** [very, extremely] altamente **-2.** [very well, at high level] muito bem **-3.** [favourably] favoravelmente; **I ~ recommend it** realmente recomendo isso.

highly-strung *adj* irritadiço(ça).

high mass *n* missa *f* solene.

high-minded [-'maɪndɪd] *adj* nobre.

Highness ['haɪnɪs] *n*: **His/Her/Your (Royal) ~** Sua Alteza (Real); **Their (Royal) ~es** Suas Altezas (Reais).

high-octane *adj* de alto índice de octana.

high-pitched [-'pɪtʃt] *adj* [shrill] agudo(da).

high point *n* [of occasion] ponto *m* alto.

high-powered [-'paʊəd] *adj* **-1.** [powerful] de alta potência **-2.** [dynamic] dinâmico(ca).

high-pressure *adj* **-1.** [air, gas] de alta pressão **-2.** [persuasive] persuasivo(va).

high priest *n* *RELIG* sumo sacerdote *m*.

high-ranking [-'ræŋkɪŋ] *adj* de destaque.

high-resolution *adj* *COMPUT* de alta resolução.

high-rise *adj* de muitos andares; **a ~ building** um espigão.

high-risk *adj* de alto risco.

high school *n* **-1.** ***UK*** [for 11- to 18-year-olds] ≃ escola *f* secundária **-2.** ***US*** [for 15- to 18-year-olds] ≃ segundo grau *m*.

high seas *npl*: **the ~** o alto-mar.

high season *n (U)* alta estação *f*.

high-speed *adj* **-1.** [train] de alta velocidade **-2.** *PHOT* [film] para alta velocidade.

high-spirited *adj* [person] alegre, vivaz.

high spot *n* ponto *m* de relevo.

high street *n* ***UK*** avenida *f* principal.

hightail ['haɪteɪl] *vt esp* ***US***: **they ~ed it back home** eles se mandaram rapidinho para casa.

high tea *n (U)* ***UK*** chá *f* ao fim da tarde *(servido no lugar do jantar)*.

high-tech <> *adj* [method, industry] de alta tecnologia. <> *n* (*abbr of* **high technology**) alta tecnologia *f*.

high technology *n (U)* alta tecnologia *f*.

high-tension *adj* de alta tensão.

high tide *n (U)* [of sea] maré *f* alta.

high treason *n (U)* alta traição *f*.

high water *n (U)* preamar *f*.

highway ['haɪweɪ] *n* **-1.** ***US*** [main road between cities] auto-estrada *f* **-2.** ***UK*** [any main road] rodovia *f*.

Highway Code *n* ***UK***: **the ~** ≃ o Código Nacional de Trânsito.

high wire *n* cabo *m* de aço.

hijack ['haɪdʒæk] <> *n* [of aircraft, car] seqüestro *m*. <> *vt* [aircraft, car] seqüestrar.

hijacker ['haɪdʒækəʳ] *n* seqüestrador *m*, -ra *f*.

hike [haɪk] <> *n* [long walk] caminhada *f*. <> *vi* [go for a long walk] caminhar.

hiker ['haɪkəʳ] *n* caminhante *mf*, andarilho *m*.

hiking ['haɪkɪŋ] *n (U)* excursões *fpl* a pé; **to go ~** fazer excursões.

hilarious [hɪ'leərɪəs] *adj* hilariante, engraçado(da).

hilarity [hɪ'lærətɪ] *n (U)* ***fml*** hilaridade *f*; **to cause much ~** causar muitos risos.

hill [hɪl] *n* **-1.** [mound] colina *f* **-2.** [slope] ladeira *f*.

hillbilly ['hɪl,bɪlɪ] (*pl* **-ies**) *n* ***US inf pej*** jeca *m*.

hillock ['hɪlək] *n* pequena colina *f*, outeiro *m*.

hillside ['hɪlsaɪd] *n* encosta *f*.

hill start *n* partida *f* do carro em uma lomba.

hilltop ['hɪltɒp] <> *adj* no topo do morro. <> *n* topo *m* do morro.

hilly ['hɪlɪ] (*compar* **-ier**, *superl* **-iest**) *adj* montanhoso(sa).

hilt [hɪlt] *n* punho *m*; **to the ~** ao extremo; **to support/defend sb to the ~** apoiar/defender alguém com unhas e dentes.

him [hɪm] *pers pron* **-1.** *(direct)* o; **I know ~** eu o conheço **-2.** *(indirect)* lhe; **tell ~** diga-lhe **-3.** *(after prep)* ele; **send it to ~** mande isso para ele; **Tony brought it with ~** Tony trouxe-o consigo *OR* com ele.

Himalayan [ˌhɪmə'leɪən] *adj* do Himalaia, himalaico(ca).

Himalayas [ˌhɪmə'leɪəz] *npl*: **the ~** as montanhas do Himalaia; **in the ~** nas montanhas do Himalaia.

himself [hɪm'self] *pron* **-1.** *(reflexive)* se; **he hurt ~** machucou-se **-2.** *(after prep)* si próprio *OR* mesmo; **he did it ~** foi ele mesmo que o fez.

hind [haɪnd] *(pl inv OR* **-s**) <> *adj* traseiro(ra). <> *n* [deer] corça *f*.

hinder ['hɪndəʳ] *vt* retardar, atrapalhar.

Hindi ['hɪndɪ] *n (U)* [language] hindi *m*.

hindmost ['haɪndməʊst] *adj* último(ma).

hindquarters ['haɪndkwɔ:təz] *npl* traseiro *m*.

hindrance ['hɪndrəns] *n* **-1.** [obstacle] obstáculo *m* **-2.** *(U)* [delay] atrasos *mpl*.

hindsight ['haɪndsaɪt] *n (U)*: **with the benefit of ~** olhando em retrospecto.

Hindu ['hɪndu:] *(pl* **-s**) <> *adj* hindu. <> *n* hindu *m*.

Hinduism ['hɪndu:ɪzm] *n (U)* hinduísmo *m*.

hinge [hɪndʒ] *(cont* **hingeing**) *n* [on door, window, lid] dobradiça *f*.

◆ **hinge (up)on** *vt fus* [depend on] depender de.

hint [hɪnt] <> *n* **-1.** [indirect suggestion] alusão *f*; **to drop a ~** dar uma indireta; **to take the ~** pegar uma indireta **-2.** [useful suggestion, tip] dica *f* **-3.** [small amount, trace] sinal *m*. <> *vi*: **to ~ at sthg** fazer alusão a algo. <> *vt*: **to ~ that** insinuar que.

hinterland ['hɪntəlænd] *n* [area around coast, river] hinterlândia *f*, interior *m*.

hip [hɪp] <> *adj* ***inf*** [fashionable] moderno(na). <> *n* [part of body] quadril *m*.

hip bath *n* banheira *f* de assento.

hip bone *n* osso *m* ilíaco.

hip flask *n* garrafa *f* de bolso.

hip-hop *n (U)* [music] hip-hop *m*.

hippie ['hɪpɪ] *n* hippie *m*.

hippo ['hɪpəʊ] *(pl* **-s**) *n* hipopótamo *m*.

hippopotamus [ˌhɪpə'pɒtəməs] *(pl* **-muses** *OR* **-mi** [-maɪ]) *n* hipopótamo *m*.

hippy ['hɪpɪ] *(pl* **-ies**) *n* = **hippie**.

hire ['haɪəʳ] <> *n (U)* [of car, equipment] aluguel *m*; **for ~** aluga-se; **bicycles for ~** alugam-se bicicletas; **taxi for ~** táxi livre. <> *vt* **-1.** [rent] alugar **-2.** [employ] contratar.

◆ **hire out** *vt sep* alugar.

hire car *n UK*: **to have a ~** alugar um carro.

hired help *n* [domestic staff] assessoria *f* doméstica.

hire purchase *n (U) UK* compra *f* a prazo; **to buy sthg on ~** comprar algo a prazo.

his [hɪz] <> *poss pron* o seu (a sua), (o/a) dele; **~ books** os livros dele, os seus livros <> *poss adj* o seu (a sua), dele; **a friend of ~** um amigo dele *OR* seu; **these shoes are ~** estes sapatos são dele *OR* seus; **these are mine - where are ~?** estes são os meus - onde estão os dele?

Hispanic [hɪ'spænɪk] <> *adj* hispânico(ca). <> *n esp US* hispânico *m*, -ca *f*.

hiss [hɪs] <> *n* **-1.** [of animal, person] silvo *m* **-2.** [of audience] vaia *f* **-3.** [of steam, gas] assobio *m*. <> *vt* [actor, speaker] vaiar. <> *vi* **-1.** [animal, person] silvar; **she ~ed angrily at him** ela o vaiou irritada **-2.** [steam, gas] assobiar.

histogram ['hɪstəgræm] *n* histograma *m*.

historian [hɪ'stɔ:rɪən] *n* historiador *m*, -ra *f*.

historic [hɪ'stɒrɪk] *adj* [significant] histórico(ca).

historical [hɪ'stɒrɪkəl] *adj* histórico(ca).

history ['hɪstərɪ] *(pl* **-ies**) *n* **-1.** [gen] história *f*; **to go down in ~** entrar para a história; **to make ~** fazer história **-2.** [past record] histórico *m*.

histrionics [hɪstrɪ'ɒnɪks] *npl pej* melodrama *m*.

hit [hɪt] *(pt & pp* **hit**, *cont* **-ting**) <> *n* **-1.** [blow] golpe *m*, pancada *f* **-2.** [successful strike] tiro *m* certeiro **-3.** [success] sucesso *m* **-4.** COMPUT [of website] visita *f*. <> *comp* de sucesso. <> *vt* **-1.** [strike a blow at] bater em **-2.** [crash into] bater contra **-3.** [score] ferir **-4.** [reach] alcançar; **the thought suddenly ~ me that ...** de repente me dei conta de que ... **-5.** [affect badly] atingir **-6.** *phr*: **to ~ it off (with sb)** dar-se bem (com alguém).

◆ **hit back** *vi*: **to ~ back (at sb/sthg)** ***fig*** revidar aos ataques (de alguém/algo).

◆ **hit on** *vt fus* **-1.** = **hit upon -2.** ***US inf*** [chat up] dar uma cantada em.

◆ **hit out** *vi*: **to ~ out at sb/sthg** [physically] tentar bater em alguém/algo; [in speech, writing] rebater veementemente.

◆ **hit upon** *vt fus* [think of] achar, descobrir.

hit-and-miss *adj* = **hit-or-miss**.

hit-and-run <> *adj* **-1.** [driver] que não presta socorro **-2.** [accident] em que não se presta socorro. <> *n* [accident] acidente no qual não se presta socorro.

hitch [hɪtʃ] <> *n* [problem, snag] dificuldade *f*. <> *vt* **-1.** [solicit]: **to ~ a lift** pegar carona **-2.** [fasten]: **to ~ sthg on(to) sthg** amarrar algo em algo. <> *vi* [hitchhike] viajar de carona.

◆ **hitch up** *vt sep* [pull up] levantar.

hitchhike ['hɪtʃhaɪk] *vi* viajar de carona.

hitchhiker ['hɪtʃhaɪkəʳ] *n* caroneiro *m*, -ra *f*.

hi-tech [ˌhaɪ'tek] *adj* = **high-tech**.

hither ['hɪðəʳ] *adv literary* aqui; **~ and thither** em muitas direções, aqui e acolá.

hitherto [ˌhɪðə'tu:] *adv* ***fml*** até agora.

hit list *n* lista *f* negra.

hit man *n* matador *m* de aluguel.

hit-or-miss *adj* aleatório(ria).

hit parade *n* ***dated*** parada *f* de sucessos.

HIV (*abbr of* **human immunodeficiency virus**) *n (U)* HIV *m*; **to be ~-positive** ser soropositivo(va).

hive [haɪv] *n* [for bees] colméia *f*; **a ~ of activity** ***fig*** um centro de atividades.

◆ **hive off** *vt sep* [separate] transferir.

HK (*abbr of* **Hong Kong**) HK.

hl (*abbr of* **hectolitre**) hl.

HM (*abbr of* **His (or Her) Majesty**) S.M.

HMG (*abbr of* **His (or Her) Majesty's Government**) *expressão utilizada nos documentos oficiais da Grã-Bretanha*, governo *m* de sua majestade.

HMI (*abbr of* **His (or Her) Majesty's Inspector**) *n inspetor de escolas na Grã-Bretanha.*

HMO (*abbr of* **health maintenance organization**) *n* órgão norte-americano de saúde pública.

HMS (*abbr of* **His (or Her) Majesty's Ship**) *prefixo utilizado nos navios da marinha real britânica*, navio *m* de sua majestade.

HMSO (*abbr of* **His (or Her) Majesty's Stationery Office**) *n serviço oficial de imprensa da Grã-Bretanha.*

HNC (*abbr of* **Higher National Certificate**) *n certificado de qualificação em disciplinas técnicas na Grã-Bretanha.*

HND (*abbr of* **Higher National Diploma**) *n diploma de qualificação em disciplinas técnicas na Grã-Bretanha.*

hoard [hɔːd] <> *n* [store] provisão *f*. <> *vt* [collect, save] estocar.

hoarding ['hɔːdɪŋ] *n UK* [for advertisements, posters] outdoor *m*.

hoarfrost ['hɔːfrɒst] *n (U)* geada *f*.

hoarse [hɔːs] *adj* rouco(ca).

hoax [həʊks] *n* trote *m*.

hoaxer ['həʊksə^r] *n* trotador *m*, -ra *f*; **bomb ~** *pessoa que passa um trote de bomba.*

hob [hɒb] *n UK* [on cooker] mesa *f*.

hobble ['hɒbl] *vi* [limp] coxear.

hobby ['hɒbɪ] (*pl* **-ies**) *n* [leisure activity] hobby *m*.

hobby horse *n* **-1.** [toy] cavalinho-de-pau *m* **-2.** [favourite topic] assunto *m* favorito.

hobnob ['hɒbnɒb] (*pt* & *pp* **-bed**, *cont* **-bing**) *vi* [socialize]: **to ~ with sb** enturmar-se com alguém.

hobo ['həʊbəʊ] (*pl* **-es** OR **-s**) *n US* [tramp] vagabundo *m*, -da *f*.

Ho Chi Minh City ['həʊˌtʃiː'mɪn-] *n* Ho Chi Minh.

hock [hɒk] *n (U)* [wine] vinho *m* branco do Reno.

hockey ['hɒkɪ] *n* **-1.** [on grass] hóquei *m* **-2.** *US* [ice hockey] hóquei *m* no gelo.

hockey stick *n* bastão *m* de hóquei.

hocus-pocus [ˌhəʊkəs'pəʊkəs] *n (U)* [trickery] tapeação *f*.

hod [hɒd] *n* [for bricks] cocho *m (de pedreiro).*

hodgepodge *n US* = **hotchpotch**.

hoe [həʊ] <> *n* enxada *f*. <> *vt* capinar.

hog [hɒg] (*pt* & *pp* **-ged**, *cont* **-ging**) <> *n* **-1.** *US lit & fig* porco *m*, -ca *f* **-2.** *phr*: **to go the whole ~** ir até o fim. <> *vt inf* [monopolize] monopolizar.

Hogmanay ['hɒgməneɪ] *n denominação escocesa para a Noite de Ano Novo.*

hoi-polloi *npl pej*: **the ~** a gentalha, a ralé.

hoist [hɔɪst] <> *n* guindaste *f*. <> *vt* **-1.** [load, person] levantar **-2.** [sail, flag] içar.

hokum ['həʊkəm] *n US inf* palhaçada *f*.

hold [həʊld] (*pt* & *pp* **held**) <> *n* **-1.** [grasp, grip]: **to have a firm ~ on sthg** segurar algo firme; **to keep ~ of sthg** segurar algo; **to take** OR **lay ~ of sthg** começar a ter efeito de algo; **to get ~ of sthg** [obtain] arranjar algo; **to get ~ of sb** [find] encontrar **-2.** [of ship, aircraft] porão *m* **-3.** [control, influence] influência *f*; **to take ~** [fire] tomar conta. <> *vt* **-1.** [in hand, arms] segurar **-2.** [maintain in position] manter; **to ~ sb prisoner** manter alguém como prisioneiro(ra); **to ~ sb hostage** tomar alguém como refém **-3.** [have, possess] ter, possuir **-4.** [conduct, stage] conduzir **-5.** *fml* [consider] julgar; **to ~ (that)** sustentar que; **to ~ sb responsible for sthg** responsabilizar alguém por algo; **to ~ sthg dear** ter afeição por algo **-6.** [on telephone]: **please ~ the line** aguarde na linha, por favor **-7.** [keep, sustain] manter **-8.** MIL ocupar **-9.** [support, have space for] suportar **-10.** [contain] guardar **-11.** *phr*: **~ it!**, **~ everything!** espera aí!; **to ~ one's own** virar-se. <> *vi* **-1.** [remain unchanged] manter-se; **to ~ still** OR **steady** segurar firme **-2.** [on phone] esperar.

◆ **hold against** *vt sep*: **to ~ sthg against sb** *fig* ter algo que pese contra alguém.

◆ **hold back** <> *vi* [hesitate] hesitar; **to ~ back from doing sthg** hesitar em fazer algo. <> *vt sep* **-1.** [gen] reter **-2.** [prevent progress of]: **to ~ sb back (from doing sthg)** impedir alguém (de fazer algo).

◆ **hold down** *vt sep* [job] manter.

◆ **hold off** <> *vt sep* [fend off] manter à distância. <> *vi* [rain] parar.

◆ **hold on** *vi* **-1.** [gen] esperar **-2.** [grip]: **to ~ on (to sthg)** segurar-se firme (em algo).

◆ **hold onto** *vt fus* [retain] reter.

◆ **hold out** <> *vt sep* [hand, arms] estender. <> *vi* **-1.** [last] durar **-2.** [resist]: **to ~ out (against sb/sthg)** resistir (a alguém/algo).

◆ **hold out for** *vt fus* insistir em.

◆ **hold up** *vt sep* **-1.** [raise] levantar **-2.** [delay] atrasar **-3.** *inf* [rob] assaltar.

◆ **hold with** *vt fus* [approve of] aprovar.

holdall ['həʊldɔːl] *n UK* mochila *f*.

holder ['həʊldə^r] *n* **-1.** [gen] suporte *m*, recipiente *m*; **cigarette ~** boquilha *f*; **candle ~** castiçal *m* **-2.** [owner - gen] titular *mf*; [- of ticket] portador *m*, -ra *f*; [- position, title] detentor *m*, -ra *f*.

holding ['həʊldɪŋ] <> *adj* [action, operation] controlador(ra). <> *n* **-1.** [investment] participação *f* acionária **-2.** [farm] propriedade *f*.

holding company *n* empresa *f* controladora, holding *f*.

hold-up *n* **-1.** [robbery] assalto *m* à mão armada **-2.** [delay] empecilho *m*, atraso *m*.

hole [həʊl] *n* **-1.** [gen] buraco *m*; **~ in one** um buraco numa só tacada; **to pick ~s in sthg** [criticize] achar defeito em algo; [in sock, shoe] furo *m* **-2.** *inf* [horrible place] buraco *m* **-3.** *inf* [predicament] apuro *m*.

◆ **hole up** *vi* [hide, take shelter] hibernar.

holiday ['hɒlɪdeɪ] *n* **-1.** [vacation] férias *fpl*; **to be/go on ~** estar de/sair de férias **-2.** [public holiday] feriado *m*.

holiday camp *n UK* colônia *f* de férias.

holidaymaker ['hɒlɪdeɪˌmeɪkə^r] *n UK* excursionista *mf*.

holiday pay *n UK* férias *fpl* remuneradas.

holiday resort *n UK* cidade *f* turística.

holiday season *n UK* temporada *f* de férias.

holiness ['həʊlɪnɪs] *n (U)* [holy quality] santidade *f*.

◆ **Holiness** *n* [in titles]: **His/Your Holiness** Sua Santidade.

holistic [həʊ'lɪstɪk] *adj* holístico(ca).

Holland ['hɒlənd] *n* Holanda *f*; **in ~** na Holanda.

hollandaise sauce [ˌhɒlən'deɪz-] *n (U)* molho *m* holandês.
holler ['hɒlə^r] *inf* <> *vt* gritar. <> *vi esp US* gritar.
hollow ['hɒləʊ] <> *adj* **-1.** [gen] oco (oca), vazio(-zia) **-2.** [gaunt - eyes] fundo(da); [- cheeks] magro(gra) **-3.** [empty of meaning or value - laugh, optimism] falso(sa); [- promise, victory] vão (vã). <> *n* **-1.** [gen] buraco *m* **-2.** [in ground, pillow] buraco *m*, cavidade *f*.
◆ **hollow out** *vt sep* **-1.** [make hollow] tornar oco (oca) **-2.** [make by hollowing] escavar.
holly ['hɒlɪ] *n (U)* azevinho *m*.
hollyhock *n* malva-rosa *f*.
Hollywood ['hɒlɪwʊd] <> *n* [film industry] Hollywood. <> *comp* de Hollywood.
holocaust ['hɒləkɔ:st] *n* [destruction] holocausto *m*.
◆ **Holocaust** *n*: **the Holocaust** o Holocausto.
hologram ['hɒləgræm] *n* holograma *m*.
hols [hɒlz] *npl UK inf* folgas *fpl*.
holster ['həʊlstə^r] *n* coldre *m*.
holy ['həʊlɪ] (*compar* **-ier**, *superl* **-iest**) *adj* **-1.** [sacred] sagrado(da), santo(ta); ~ **water** água *f* benta **-2.** [pure and good] puro(ra).
Holy Communion *n (U)* Sagrada Comunhão *f*.
Holy Father *n*: **the** ~ o Papa.
Holy Ghost *n*: **the** ~ o Espírito Santo.
Holy Grail [-'greɪl] *n*: **the** ~ o Santo Graal.
Holy Land *n*: **the** ~ a Terra Santa.
holy orders *npl* votos *mpl* sagrados; **to take** ~ ordenar-se sacerdote.
Holy Spirit *n*: **the** ~ o Espírito Santo.
homage ['hɒmɪdʒ] *n fml* **-1.** [respect] homenagem *f*; **to pay** ~ **to sb/sthg** prestar homenagem a alguém/algo **-2.** [tribute] tributo *m*.
home [həʊm] <> *adj* **-1.** [not foreign] nacional **-2.** *SPORT* interno(na). <> *adv* **-1.** [to or at one's house] para casa **-2.** [from abroad] para casa (do exterior) **-3.** *phr*: **to bring sthg** ~ **(to sb)** fazer alguém enxergar algo; **to drive** *OR* **hammer sthg** ~ **(to sb)** deixar algo bem claro (para alguém). <> *n* **-1.** [one's house, place of residence] casa *f*; **to make one's** ~ fazer a casa; **it's a** ~ **from** ~ *UK*, **it's a** ~ **away from** ~ *US* é um lugar onde a gente se sente em casa **-2.** [place of origin] terra *f* natal **-3.** [family unit, Institution] lar *m*; **to leave** ~ sair de casa.
◆ **at home** *adv* **-1.** [gen] em casa; **at** ~ **with sthg** à vontade com algo; **to make o.s. at** ~ sentir-se à vontade *OR* em casa **-2.** [in one's own country] no meu país **-3.** *SPORT*: **to play at** ~ jogar em casa.
◆ **home in** *vi*: **to** ~ **in on sthg** dirigir-se diretamente a algo.
home address *n* endereço *m* residencial.
home banking *n (U)* home banking *m*.
home brew *n (U)* [beer] cerveja *f* caseira.
homecoming ['həʊmˌkʌmɪŋ] *n* **-1.** [return] volta *f* ao lar **-2.** *US SCH & UNIV* regresso *m* dos ex-alunos às suas faculdades.
home computer *n* computador *m* pessoal.
home cooking *n* comida *f* caseira.
Home Counties *npl UK*: **the** ~ *os condados ao redor de Londres*.
home delivery *n* entrega *m* a domicílio.
home economics *n (U)* economia *f* doméstica.
home fries *npl US* batatas *fpl* fritas.
home ground *n* **-1.** [gen]: **to be on** ~ estar em seu território **-2.** *SPORT* campo *m* do time da casa.
home-grown *adj* plantado(da) em casa.
home help *n UK empregada que auxilia pessoas idosas ou doentes*.
home improvements *npl* reformas *fpl* na casa.
homeland ['həʊmlænd] *n* **-1.** [country of birth] terra *f* natal **-2.** [in South Africa] gueto *m*.
homeless ['həʊmlɪs] <> *adj* sem-teto. <> *npl*: **the** ~ os sem-teto, os desabrigados.
homelessness ['həʊmlɪsnəs] *n (U)*: **the problem of** ~ o problema dos sem-teto.
home loan *n* financiamento *m* para habitação.
homely ['həʊmlɪ] *adj* **-1.** [simple, unpretentious] simples **-2.** [ugly] feio (feia).
home-made *adj* caseiro(ra); ~ **bread** pão *m* feito em casa.
home movie *n* filmagem *f* caseira.
Home Office *n UK*: **the** ~ ≃ o Ministério do Interior.
homeopathic [ˌhəʊmɪəʊ'pæθɪk] *adj* homeopático(ca).
homeopathy [ˌhəʊmɪ'ɒpəθɪ] *n (U)* homeopatia *f*.
homeowner ['həʊmˌəʊnə^r] *n* proprietário *m*, -ria *f* da casa.
home page *n COMPUT* homepage *f*, página *f* inicial.
home rule *n (U)* autonomia *f* interna.
home run *n US inf tacada que permite ao jogador de beisebol completar o circuito das bases*.
Home Secretary *n UK* ≃ Ministro *m*, -tra *f* do Interior.
homesick ['həʊmsɪk] *adj* com saudade de casa; **to feel** ~ estar com saudades de casa.
homesickness ['həʊmˌsɪknɪs] *n (U)* saudade *f* de casa.
homespun ['həʊmspʌn] *adj fig* [unsophisticated] tosco(ca).
homestead ['həʊmsted] *n US* fazenda *f*.
home straight *n*: **the** ~ [of race] a reta de chegada; [of task] última etapa *f*.
hometown ['həʊmtaʊn] *n* cidade *f* natal.
home truth *n* verdades *fpl* desagradáveis; **to tell sb a few** ~**s** dizer algumas verdades para alguém.
homeward ['həʊmwəd] <> *adj* de regresso. <> *adv* = **homewards**.
homewards ['həʊmwədz] *adv* para casa.
homework ['həʊmwɜ:k] *n* **-1.** *SCH* dever *m* de casa, tema *m* **-2.** *inf fig* [preparation] dever *m* de casa.
homey, homy ['həʊmɪ] *US adj US* familiar.
homicidal [ˌhɒmɪ'saɪdl] *adj* homicida.
homicide ['hɒmɪsaɪd] *n fml (U)* homicídio *m*.
homily ['hɒmɪlɪ] (*pl* **-ies**) *n* [lecture] homilia *f*.
homing ['həʊmɪŋ] *adj* **-1.** [instinct] que se refere ao instinto do lar; ~ **instinct** instinto *m* doméstico **-2.** [device] autodirecional.
homing pigeon *n* pombo-correio *m*.
homoeopathy *etc n* = **homeopathy** *etc*.

homogeneous [ˌhɒmə'dʒiːnjəs] *adj* homogêneo(-nea).

homogenize, -ise [hə'mɒdʒənaɪz] *vt UK* homogeneizar.

homophobic ['həʊməʊ'fəʊbɪk] *adj* homofóbico(-ca).

homosexual [ˌhɒmə'sekʃʊəl] <> *adj* homossexual. <> *n* homossexual *mf*.

homosexuality [ˌhɒməˌsekʃʊ'ælətɪ] *n (U)* homossexualidade *f*.

homy *adj US* = **homey**.

Hon. **-1.** (*abbr of* **Honourable**) honorável **-2.** (*abbr of* **Honorary**) hon.

Honduran [hɒn'djʊərən] <> *adj* hondurenho(-nha). <> *n* hondurenho *m*, -nha *f*.

Honduras [hɒn'djʊərəs] *n* Honduras; **in ~** em Honduras.

hone [həʊn] *vt* **-1.** [knife, sword] afiar **-2.** [intellect, wit] aprimorar.

honest ['ɒnɪst] <> *adj* **-1.** [trustworthy] honesto(ta) **-2.** [frank, truthful] sincero(ra); **to be ~, ...** para ser franco(ca), ... **-3.** [legal] legal. <> *adv inf*: **I didn't steal your pencil, ~!** eu não roubei o seu lápis, juro!

honestly ['ɒnɪstlɪ] <> *adv* **-1.** [in a trustworthy manner] honestamente **-2.** [frankly, truthfully] sinceramente. <> *excl* [expressing impatience, disapproval] ora, francamente!

honesty ['ɒnɪstɪ] *n* **-1.** *(U)* [trustworthiness] honestidade *f* **-2.** [frankness, truthfulness] sinceridade *f*.

honey ['hʌnɪ] *n* **-1.** *(U)* [food] mel *m* **-2.** *esp US* [dear] querido *m*, -da *f*.

honeybee ['hʌnɪbiː] *n* abelha *f* operária.

honeycomb ['hʌnɪkəʊm] *n* **-1.** [in wax] favo *m* *(de mel)* **-2.**: **~ pattern** formato *m* de favo de mel.

honeymoon ['hʌnɪmuːn] <> *n lit & fig* lua-de-mel *f*. <> *vi* sair em lua-de-mel.

honeysuckle ['hʌnɪˌsʌkl] *n* madressilva *f*.

Hong Kong [ˌhɒŋ'kɒŋ] *n* Hong Kong; **in ~** em Hong Kong.

honk [hɒŋk] <> *n* **-1.** [of horn] buzinada *f* **-2.** [of goose] grasnada *f*. <> *vi* **-1.** [motorist] buzinar **-2.** [goose] grasnar. <> *vt*: **to ~ a horn** tocar a buzina.

honky ['hɒŋkɪ] (*pl* **-ies**) *n US v inf offensive* branquelo *m*, -la *f*.

Honolulu [ˌhɒnə'luːluː] *n* Honolulu; **in ~** em Honolulu.

honor etc *n & vt US* = **honour etc**.

honorary [*UK* 'ɒnərərɪ, *US* ɒnə'reərɪ] *adj* honorário(-ria).

honor roll *n US* [sch] [univ] relação *f* dos melhores alunos.

honour *UK*, **honor** *US* ['ɒnə^r] <> *n* honra *f*; **in ~ of sb/sthg** em honra de alguém/algo. <> *vt* honrar.

◆ **Honour** *n* [in titles]: **Your ~** Vossa Senhoria, Vossa Excelência.

◆ **honours** *npl* **-1.** [gen] honras *fpl* **-2.** UNIV *tipo de grau universitário concedido por universidades britânicas* **-3.** *phr*: **to do the ~s** fazer as honras da casa.

honourable *UK*, **honorable** *US* ['ɒnrəbl] *adj* honrado(da).

◆ **Honourable** *adj* [in titles]: **the Honourable ...** o Honorável ...

honourably *UK*, **honorably** *US* ['ɒnərəblɪ] *adv* honrosamente.

honour bound *adj*: **to be ~ to do sthg** ver-se moralmente obrigado(da) a fazer algo.

honours degree *n UK* [univ] = **honours 2**.

honours list *n UK na Inglaterra, relação de pessoas importantes que recebem condecorações como sinal de respeito.*

Hons. (*abbr of* **honours degree**) *n tipo de grau universitário concedido por universidades britânicas.*

Hon. Sec. (*abbr of* **honorary secretary**) *n* secretário *m* honorário, secretária *f* honorária.

hooch [huːtʃ] *n inf* bebida *f* alcoólica ilegal.

hood [hʊd] *n* **-1.** [on cloak, jacket] capuz *f* **-2.** *US* [of car] capota *f* **-3.** [of pram] toldo *m* **-4.** [of cooker] aba *f* **-5.** *US* [car bonnet] capô *m*.

hooded ['hʊdɪd] *adj* **-1.** [wearing a hood] encapuzado(da) **-2.** [eyes] mascarado(da).

hoodlum ['huːdləm] *n* [youth] *US inf* arruaceiro *m*, -ra *f*; [gangster] gângster *mf*.

hoodwink ['hʊdwɪŋk] *vt* lograr.

hooey ['huːɪ] *n US inf* bobagem *f*.

hoof [huːf, hʊf] (*pl* **-s** OR **hooves**) *n* pata *f*, casco *m*.

hook [hʊk] <> *n* **-1.** [for coat, picture, curtain] gancho *m* **-2.** [for catching fish] anzol *m* **-3.** [fastener] fecho *m*; **~ and eye** colchete *m*. <> *vt* **-1.** [fasten with hook] enganchar **-2.** [fish] fisgar **-3.** [arm, leg] dar um gancho em.

◆ **off the hook** *adv* **-1.** [phone] fora do gancho **-2.** [out of trouble] sem problemas; **to get sb off the ~** livrar alguém de um problema.

◆ **hook up** *vt sep*: **to ~ sthg up to sthg** COMPUT & TELEC conectar algo em algo.

hooked [hʊkt] *adj* **-1.** [shaped like a hook] curvado(da) **-2.** *inf* [addicted]: **to be ~ (on sthg)** ser viciado(da) (em algo).

hooker ['hʊkə^r] *n US inf* prostituta *f*.

hook(e)y ['hʊkɪ] *n (U) US inf*: **to play ~** matar aula.

hooligan ['huːlɪgən] *n* arruaceiro *m*, -ra *f*, hooligan *m*.

hooliganism ['huːlɪgənɪzm] *n (U)* arruaça *f*.

hoop [huːp] *n* argola *f*.

hoop-la ['huːplɑː] *n (U)* [game] jogo *m* de argolas.

hooray [hʊ'reɪ] *excl* = **hurray**.

hoot [huːt] <> *n* **-1.** [of owl] pio *m* **-2.** [of horn] buzinada *f* **-3.** [of laughter] grito *m* **-4.** *UK inf* [amusing thing, person]: **she's a real ~** ela é o máximo. <> *vi* **-1.** [owl] piar **-2.** [horn] buzinar **-3.** *inf* [person] gritar. <> *vt* [horn] buzinar.

hooter ['huːtə^r] *n* **-1.** [horn - of car] buzina *f*; [- of factory] sirene *f* **-2.** *UK inf* [nose] narigão *m*.

Hoover® ['huːvə^r] *n UK* aspirador *m*.

◆ **hoover** <> *vt* passar o aspirador em. <> *vi* passar o aspirador.

hooves [huːvz] *pl* ▷ **hoof**.

hop [hɒp] (*pt & pp* **-ped**, *cont* **-ping**) <> *n* **-1.** [of person] pulo *m* num pé só **-2.** [of small animal, bird] pulinho *m* **-3.** *inf* [trip] viagem *f* rápida. <> *vt inf*

-1. ***US*** [bus, train] pegar **-2.** ***phr*****: ~ it!** dê o fora. <> *vi* **-1.** [jump on one leg] pular com um pé só **-2.** [small animal, bird] dar pulinhos **-3.** ***inf*** [move nimbly] pular; **she ~ped on a plane to New York** ela foi dar um pulo em Nova York.
◆ **hops** *npl* [for making beer] lúpulos *mpl*.

hope [həʊp] <> *n* esperança *f*; **in the ~ of** na esperança de; **I don't hold out much ~** não tenho muita esperança; **to pin one's ~s on sb/sthg** depositar a esperança em alguém/algo; **to raise sb's ~s** dar esperança a alguém. <> *vt*: **to ~ (that)** esperar que; **to ~ to do sthg** esperar fazer algo. <> *vi* esperar; **to ~ for sthg** esperar (por) algo; **I ~ so/not** espero que sim/não; **to ~ for the best** esperar que tudo dê certo.

hope chest *n* ***US*** baú *m* do enxoval.

hopeful ['həʊpfʊl] <> *adj* **-1.** [full of hope] esperançoso(sa), otimista; **to be ~ of sthg/of doing sthg** ter esperanças de algo/de fazer algo **-2.** [encouraging] promissor(ra). <> *n* aspirante *mf (a um cargo)*.

hopefully ['həʊpfəlɪ] *adv* **-1.** [in a hopeful way] esperançosamente **-2.** [with luck] com sorte.

hopeless ['həʊplɪs] *adj* **-1.** [despairing] desesperado(da) **-2.** [impossible] impossível **-3.** ***inf*** [useless] inútil.

hopelessly ['həʊplɪslɪ] *adv* **-1.** [despairingly] desesperançosamente **-2.** [completely] totalmente.

hopper ['hɒpəʳ] *n* [bin] tremonha *f*.

hopping ['hɒpɪŋ] *adv*: **to be ~ mad** estar soltando fogo pelas ventas.

hopscotch ['hɒpskɒtʃ] *n (U)* amarelinha *f*.

horde [hɔ:d] *n* horda *f*.
◆ **hordes** *npl*: **~s of** uma multidão de.

horizon [hə'raɪzn] *n* [of sky] horizonte *m*; **on the ~** no horizonte.
◆ **horizons** *npl*: **to broaden one's ~s** ampliar os horizontes.

horizontal [ˌhɒrɪ'zɒntl] <> *adj* horizontal. <> *n*: **the ~** a horizontal.

hormone ['hɔ:məʊn] *n* hormônio *m*.

hormone replacement therapy *n* terapia *f* de reposição hormonal.

horn [hɔ:n] *n* **-1.** [of animal] chifre *m* **-2.** ***MUS*** [instrument] trompa *f* **-3.** [of car] buzina *f* **-4.** [of ship] apito *m*.

hornet ['hɔ:nɪt] *n* vespão *m*.

horn-rimmed [-'rɪmd] *adj* feito(ta) com aros de chifre.

horny ['hɔ:nɪ] (*compar* **-ier**, *superl* **-iest**) *adj* **-1.** [scale, body, armour] feito(ta) de chifre **-2.** [hand] calejado(-da) **-3.** ***vinf*** [sexually excited] com tesão.

horoscope ['hɒrəskəʊp] *n* horóscopo *m*.

horrendous [hɒ'rendəs] *adj* horrendo(da).

horrible ['hɒrəbl] *adj* horrível.

horribly ['hɒrəblɪ] *adv* **-1.** [horrifically] horrivelmente **-2.** ***inf*** [very] terrivelmente, muito.

horrid ['hɒrɪd] *adj* **-1.** *esp* ***UK*** [person] antipático(ca) **-2.** [idea, place] horroroso(sa).

horrific [hɒ'rɪfɪk] *adj* horroroso(sa), horrível.

horrify ['hɒrɪfaɪ] (*pt* & *pp* **-ied**) *vt* horrorizar.

horrifying ['hɒrɪfaɪɪŋ] *adj* horripilante.

horror ['hɒrəʳ] *n* **-1.** [gen] horror *m*; **to my/his ~** para o meu/seu espanto **-2.** [strong dislike]: **to have a ~ of sthg** ter horror a algo.

horror film *n* filme *m* de terror.

horror-struck *adj* horrorizado(da).

hors d'oeuvre [ɔ:'dɜ:vr] (*pl* **-s**) *n* hors d'oeuvre *m*, entrada *f*.

horse [hɔ:s] *n* [animal] cavalo *m*.

horseback ['hɔ:sbæk] <> *adj*: **~ riding** ***US*** equitação *f*. <> *n*: **on ~** a cavalo.

horsebox ***UK*** ['hɔ:sbɒks], **horsecar** ***US*** ['hɔ:skɑ:ʳ] *n* reboque *m* para transportar cavalos.

horse chestnut *n* **-1.** [tree]: **~ (tree)** castanheiro-da-índia *m* **-2.** [nut] castanha-da-índia *f*.

horse-drawn *adj* puxado(da) a cavalo.

horsefly ['hɔ:sflaɪ] (*pl* **-flies**) *n* mutuca *f*.

horsehair ['hɔ:sheəʳ] *n (U)* pêlo *m* de cavalo.

horseman ['hɔ:smən] (*pl* **-men** [-mən]) *n* **-1.** [non-professional] cavaleiro *m* **-2.** [professional] ginete *m*.

horse opera *n* ***US hum*** filme *m* de faroeste.

horseplay ['hɔ:spleɪ] *n (U)* grosseria *f*.

horsepower ['hɔ:sˌpaʊəʳ] *n (U)* cavalo-vapor *m*.

horse racing *n (U)* corrida *f* de cavalos.

horseradish ['hɔ:sˌrædɪʃ] *n (U)* [plant] raiz-forte *f*.

horse riding *n (U)* equitação *f*; **to go ~** andar a cavalo, montar.

horseshoe ['hɔ:sʃu:] *n* ferradura *f*.

horse show *n* concurso *m* hípico, rodeio *m*.

horse-trading *n (U)* ***fig*** & ***pej*** negociação *f*.

horse trials *npl* concurso *m* hípico, rodeio *m*.

horsewhip ['hɔ:swɪp] (*pt* & *pp* **-ped**, *cont* **-ping**) *vt* chicotear.

horsewoman ['hɔ:sˌwʊmən] (*pl* **-women** [-ˌwɪmɪn]) *n* amazona *f*.

horticultural [ˌhɔ:tɪ'kʌltʃərəl] *adj* hortícola.

horticulture ['hɔ:tɪkʌltʃəʳ] *n (U)* horticultura *f*.

hose [həʊz] <> *n* [hosepipe] mangueira *f*. <> *vt* regar com mangueira.
◆ **hose down** *vt sep* lavar com mangueira.

hosepipe ['həʊzpaɪp] *n* mangueira *f*.

hosiery ['həʊzɪərɪ] *n (U)* artigos *mpl* de malha, lingeries *fpl*.

hospice ['hɒspɪs] *n* [for the terminally ill] hospício *m*.

hospitable [hɒ'spɪtəbl] *adj* hospitaleiro(ra).

hospital ['hɒspɪtl] *n* hospital *m*.

hospitality [ˌhɒspɪ'tælətɪ] *n (U)* hospitalidade *f*.

hospitality suite *n* copa *f* livre *(em conferência, hotel)*.

hospitalize, -ise ['hɒspɪtəlaɪz] *vt* hospitalizar.

host [həʊst] <> *n* **-1.** [at private party] anfitrião *m*, -ã *f* **-2.** [place, organization] sede *f*; **~ city/country** cidade-/país-sede **-3.** [compere] apresentador *m*, -ra *f* **-4.** ***literary*** [large number]: **a ~ of sthg** um monte de algo. <> *vt* apresentar.
◆ **Host** *n* ***RELIG***: **the ~** a hóstia.

hostage ['hɒstɪdʒ] *n* refém *mf*; **to be taken/held ~** ser levado(a)/mantido(a) como refém.

hostel ['hɒstl] *n* albergue *m*, alojamento *m*; **(youth) ~** albergue (da juventude).

hostelry ['hɒstəlrɪ] (*pl* **-ries**) *n* ***hum*** [pub] estalagem *f*.

hostess ['həʊstes] *n* **-1.** [at party] anfitriã *f* **-2.** [escort] acompanhante *f*.

hostile [*UK* 'hɒstaɪl, *US* 'hɒstl] *adj* **-1.** [gen] hostil; **~ to sb/sthg** hostil com alguém/algo **-2.** [unfavourable] adverso(sa), desfavorável.

hostility [hɒ'stɪlətɪ] *n (U)* [antagonism, unfriendliness] hostilidade *f.*

◆ **hostilities** *npl* hostilidades *fpl.*

hot [hɒt] (*compar* **-ter**, *superl* **-test**, *pt* & *pp* **-ted**, *cont* **-ting**) *adj* **-1.** [gen] quente; **I'm ~** estou com calor **-2.** [spicy] picante **-3.** *inf* [expert] bom (boa); **to be ~ on** *OR* **at sthg** ser bom (boa) em algo **-4.** [recent] recente, quente **-5.** [temper] veemente.

◆ **hot up** *vi inf* **-1.** [situation, campaign] esquentar **-2.** [party] animar-se **-3.** [pace]: **the pace is ~ting up** as coisas estão indo rápido demais.

hot-air balloon *n* balão *m* de ar quente.

hotbed ['hɒtbed] *n fig* [centre] foco *m.*

hotchpotch *UK* ['hɒtʃpɒtʃ], **hodgepodge** *US* ['hɒdʒpɒdʒ] *n inf* mixórdia *f.*

hot-cross bun *n pão doce feito com passas e enfeitado com uma cruz que se come na Semana Santa.*

hot dog *n* cachorro-quente *m.*

hotel [həʊ'tel] ◇ *n* hotel *m.* ◇ *comp* de hotel; **~ industry** setor *m* hoteleiro.

hotelier [həʊ'telɪəʳ] *n* hoteleiro *m*, -ra *f.*

hot flush *UK*, **hot flash** *US n* calorão *m (da menopausa).*

hotfoot *adv literary* apressadamente.

hotheaded [ˌhɒt'hedɪd] *adj* temerário(ria).

hothouse ['hɒthaʊs, *pl* -haʊzɪz] ◇ *n* [greenhouse] estufa *f.* ◇ *comp* de estufa.

hot line *n* **-1.** [between government heads] linha *f* direta **-2.** [24-hour phone line] linha *f* de emergência.

hotly ['hɒtlɪ] *adv* **-1.** [argue, debate] calorosamente **-2.** [deny] veementemente **-3.** [pursue]: **to be ~ pursued** ser seguido(da) de perto.

hotplate ['hɒtpleɪt] *n* chapa *f* elétrica.

hotpot ['hɒtpɒt] *n UK ensopado de cordeiro típico de Lancashire.*

hot potato *n inf fig* [controversial topic] batata *f* quente.

hot rod *n AUT* carro *m* envenenado.

hot seat *n inf*: **to always be in the ~** ser sempre quem tem de descascar o abacaxi.

hot spot *n* **-1.** [exciting place] lugar *m* da moda **-2.** [politically unsettled area] área *f* de tensão.

hot-tempered *adj* esquentado(da).

hot water *n (U) inf fig*: **to be in/get into ~** estar/ficar em maus lençóis.

hot-water bottle *n* bolsa *f* de água quente.

hot-wire *vt inf*: **to ~ a car** dar partida num carro fazendo ligação direta.

hound [haʊnd] ◇ *n* [dog] cão *m* de caça. ◇ *vt* **-1.** [persecute] perseguir **-2.** [drive out]: **to ~ sb out (of somewhere)** conseguir tirar alguém (de algum lugar).

hour ['aʊəʳ] *n* **-1.** [gen] hora *f*; **half an ~** meia hora; **per** *OR* **an ~** por hora; **on the ~** nas horas cheias, nas horas fechadas; **in the small ~s** em altas horas da madrugada **-2.** *literary* [specific moment] momento *m.*

◆ **hours** *npl* **-1.** [of business] expediente *m*; **bank ~** expediente bancário **-2.** [routine] horário *m*; **to work long ~** trabalhar por horas a fio.

hourly ['aʊəlɪ] ◇ *adj* **-1.** [happening every hour] de hora em hora, a cada hora **-2.** [per hour] por hora. ◇ *adv* **-1.** [every hour] a cada hora **-2.** [per hour] por hora **-3.** *fig* [constantly] continuamente.

house [*n* & *adj* haʊs, *pl* 'haʊzɪz, *vb* haʊz] ◇ *adj* **-1.** *COMM* caseiro(ra) **-2.** [wine] da casa. ◇ *n* **-1.** [gen] casa *f*; **it's on the ~** é oferta da casa; **to put** *OR* **set one's ~ in order** pôr *OR* colocar as coisas em ordem; **to bring the ~ down** *inf* fazer a casa vir abaixo, ser muito aplaudido(da) **-2.** [people in house] família *f* **-3.** *POL* câmara *f* **-4.** [in debates]: **this ~ believes that ...** os participantes do debate acreditam que ... **-5.** [in school] dormitório *m.* ◇ *vt* [accommodate - people, family] alojar; [- department, library, office] abrigar.

house arrest *n (U)*: **under ~** sob prisão domiciliar.

houseboat ['haʊsbəʊt] *n* casa *f* flutuante.

housebound ['haʊsbaʊnd] *adj* confinado(da) em casa.

housebreaking ['haʊsˌbreɪkɪŋ] *n (U)* arrombamento *m* da casa.

housebroken ['haʊsˌbrəʊkn] *adj US* [pet] domesticado(da).

housecoat ['haʊskəʊt] *n* chambre *m.*

household ['haʊshəʊld] ◇ *adj* **-1.** [domestic] doméstico(ca) **-2.** [familiar] familiar. ◇ *n* família *f*, lar *m.*

householder ['haʊsˌhəʊldəʳ] *n* **-1.** [owner] dono *m*, -na *f* da casa **-2.** [head of family] chefe *mf* da casa.

househunting ['haʊsˌhʌntɪŋ] *n (U)* procura *f* de casa; **to go ~** procurar casa para morar/alugar.

househusband *n* dono *m* de casa.

housekeeper ['haʊsˌkiːpəʳ] *n* governanta *f.*

housekeeping ['haʊsˌkiːpɪŋ] *n* **-1.** [work] tarefas *fpl* domésticas **-2.** [budget]: **~ (money)** dinheiro *m* para os gastos da casa.

houseman ['haʊsmən] (*pl* **-men** [-mən]) *n UK* interno *m*, -na *f.*

house martin *n* andorinha-de-casa *f.*

housemen *pl* ▻ **houseman.**

house music *n* house music *f.*

House of Commons *n UK*: **the ~** a Câmara dos Comuns.

HOUSE OF COMMONS

House of Commons e *House of Lords* são as duas casas que compõem o Parlamento britânico. A *House of Commons*, com seus 650 membros, é a que desfruta de maior poder. Seus *Members of Parliament* (MPs) são eleitos pelo povo para um mandato de cinco anos. O governo é formado pelos MPs pertencentes ao partido que obteve maioria nas eleições

House of Lords *n UK*: **the ~** a Câmara dos Lordes.

HOUSE OF LORDS

A *House of Lords* conta com mais de mil membros. Seus componentes não são eleitos: em sua maioria, eles ou herdaram seus títulos de nobreza ou desfrutam do título em caráter vitalício, mas não hereditário. A *House of Lords* tem menos poder do que a *House of Commons*, mas possui a prerrogativa de modificar leis aprovadas por essa última. É a mais alta corte de apelações do Reino Unido, excetuando-se a Escócia, que desfruta de sistema jurídico próprio.

House of Representatives *n US*: **the ~** a Câmara dos Representantes.

HOUSE OF REPRESENTATIVES

Juntamente com o Senado, a *House of Representatives* constitui o corpo legislativo dos Estados Unidos. Seus deputados são eleitos em sistema de votação proporcional, de acordo com a população de cada estado.

house-owner *n* proprietário *m*, -ria *f (da casa)*.
houseplant ['hauspla:nt] *n* planta *f* de interior.
house-proud *adj* fanático(ca) pela aparência da casa.
Houses of Parliament *npl UK*: **the ~** o Parlamento britânico.
house-to-house *adj* de casa em casa.
house-train *vt UK ensinar o local onde fazer as necessidades a (gato, cachorro)*.
housewarming (party) ['haus,wɔ:mɪŋ-] *n* festa *f* de inauguração de uma casa.
housewife ['hauswaɪf] (*pl* **-wives** [-waɪvz]) *n* dona *f* de casa.
housework ['hausw3:k] *n (U)* afazeres *mpl* domésticos.
housing ['hauzɪŋ] <> *n* **-1.** *(U)* [accommodation] alojamento *m* **-2.** *(U)* [topic, study] habitação *f* **-3.** *TECH* cárter *m*. <> *comp* habitacional.
housing association *n UK organização que possui casas e ajuda seus membros a alugá-las ou comprá-las por um preço mais barato.*
housing benefit *n UK* auxílio-moradia *m*.
housing development *n* conjunto *m* habitacional.
housing estate *UK*, **housing project** *US n* conjunto *m* habitacional.
hovel ['hɒvl] *n* [house] choupana *f*.
hover ['hɒvəʳ] *vi* **-1.** [fly] pairar, flutuar no ar **-2.** [linger] permanecer.
hovercraft ['hɒvəkra:ft] (*pl inv* OR **-s**) *n* aerodeslizador *m*.
hoverport ['hɒvəpɔ:t] *n* porto *m* para aerodeslizador.
how [hau] *adv* **-1.** [referring to way or manner] como; **~ do you get there?** como se chega lá?; **~ does it work?** como funciona?; **tell me ~ to do it** me diga como fazer isso. **-2.** [referring to health, quality] como; **~ are you?** como vai?; **~ are you doing?** como vai você?; **~ are things?** como vão as coisas?; **~ is your room?** como é o seu quarto? **-3.** [referring to degree, amount] quanto; **~ far?** a que distância?; **~ long?** quanto tempo?; **~ many?** quantos?; **~ much?** quanto?; **~ much is it?** quanto custa?; **~ old are you?** quantos anos você tem? **-4.** [in phrases]: **~ about a drink?** que tal uma bebida?; **~ lovely!** que lindo!
howdy ['haudɪ] *excl US inf* olá!
however [hau'evəʳ] <> *conj* [in whatever way] como quer que; **~ you want** como quiser. <> *adv* **-1.** [nevertheless] contudo, no entanto **-2.** [no matter how]: **~ difficult it is** por mais difícil que seja; **~ many/much** não importa quantos/quanto **-3.** [how] de que modo, como.
howl [haul] <> *n* **-1.** [of pain, anger] grito *m* **-2.** [of laughter] gargalhada *f*. <> *vi* **-1.** [animal, wind] uivar **-2.** [person - in pain] gritar; [- with laughter] gargalhar.
howler ['hauləʳ] *n inf* asneira *f*.
howling ['haulɪŋ] *adj inf* [success] imenso(sa).
hp (*abbr of* **horsepower**) *n* hp *m*.
HP *n* **-1.** *UK* (*abbr of* **hire purchase**) a prazo; **to buy sthg on ~** comprar algo a prazo **-2.** = **hp**.
HQ (*abbr of* **headquarters**) *n* QG.
hr (*abbr of* **hour**) h.
HRH (*abbr of* **His/Her Royal Highness**) Sua A. Real.
hrs (*abbr of* **hours**) h.
HRT (*abbr of* **hormone replacement therapy**) *n* TRH *f*.
HS (*abbr of* **high school**) *US escola de ensino médio.*
HST (*abbr of* **Hawaiian Standard Time**) *horário oficial do Havaí.*
ht (*abbr of* **height**) altura *f*.
HT (*abbr of* **high tension**) *ELEC* alta-tensão *f*.
hub [hʌb] *n* **-1.** [of wheel] cubo *m* **-2.** [of activity] centro *m*.
hub airport *n US* aeroporto *m* principal.
hubbub ['hʌbʌb] *n* algazarra *f*.
hubcap ['hʌbkæp] *n* calota *f*.
huddle ['hʌdl] <> *vi* **-1.** [crouch, curl up] amontoar-se **-2.** [crowd together] apertar-se uns contra os outros. <> *n* [of people] amontoado *m*.
hue [hju:] *n* [colour] matiz *f*.
huff [hʌf] <> *n*: **in a ~** com raiva. <> *vi*: **to ~ and puff** estar ofegante, bufar.
huffy ['hʌfɪ] (*compar* **-ier**, *superl* **-iest**) *adj inf* **-1.** [offended] ressentido(da) **-2.** [touchy] sensível.
hug [hʌg] (*pt & pp* **-ged**, *cont* **-ging**) <> *n* abraço *m*; **to give sb a ~** dar um abraço em alguém. <> *vt* **-1.** [embrace] abraçar **-2.** [stay close to] manter-se perto de.
huge [hju:dʒ] *adj* enorme.
huh [hʌ] *excl* **-1.** [after questions] hein! **-2.** [expressing surprise] como!, hein! **-3.** [expressing scorn] hum!
hulk [hʌlk] *n* **-1.** [of ship] carcaça *f* **-2.** [person] brutamontes *mpl*.
hulking ['hʌlkɪŋ] *adj* gigantesco(ca).
hull [hʌl] *n* [of ship] casco *m*.
hullabaloo [,hʌləbə'lu:] *n inf* bagunça *f*.
hullo [hə'ləu] *excl* = **hello**.
hum [hʌm] (*pt & pp* **-med**, *cont* **-ming**) <> *vi* **-1.** [buzz] zumbir **-2.** [sing] cantarolar **-3.** [be busy] estar em atividade **-4.** *phr*: **to ~ and haw** gaguejar, titubear. <> *vt* [tune] zunir. <> *n (U)* **-1.** [of bee, machine] zumbido *m* **-2.** [of car] barulho *m* **-3.** [of conversation] murmúrio *m*.
human ['hju:mən] <> *adj* humano(na). <> *n*: **~ (being)** (ser *m*) humano *m*.

humane [hju:'meɪn] *adj* [compassionate] humano(na), humanitário(ria).
humanely [hju:'meɪnlɪ] *adv* humanamente.
human error *n (U)* erro *m* humano.
humanist ['hju:mənɪst] *n* PHILOSOPHY humanista *mf.*
humanitarian [hju:ˌmænɪ'teərɪən] ◇ *adj* humanitário(ria). ◇ *n* pessoa *f* que luta pela justiça social.
humanity [hju:'mænətɪ] *n* humanidade *f.*
◆ **humanities** *npl*: **the humanities** as humanidades.
humanly ['hju:mənlɪ] *adv*: ~ **possible** humanamente possível.
human nature *n (U)* natureza *f* humana.
human race *n*: **the** ~ a raça humana.
human resources *npl* recursos *mpl* humanos.
human rights *npl* direitos *mpl* humanos.
humble ['hʌmbl] ◇ *adj* humilde. ◇ *vt* humilhar; **to** ~ **o.s.** humilhar-se.
humbly ['hʌmblɪ] *adv* humildemente.
humbug ['hʌmbʌg] *n* **-1.** *(U)* ***dated*** [hypocrisy] hipocrisia *f* **-2.** ***UK*** [sweet] caramelo *m* de menta.
humdrum ['hʌmdrʌm] *adj* monótono(na).
humid ['hju:mɪd] *adj* úmido(da).
humidity [hju:'mɪdətɪ] *n (U)* umidade *f.*
humiliate [hju:'mɪlɪeɪt] *vt* humilhar.
humiliating [hju:'mɪlɪeɪtɪŋ] *adj* humilhante.
humiliation [hju:ˌmɪlɪ'eɪʃn] *n (U)* humilhação *f.*
humility [hju:'mɪlətɪ] *n (U)* humildade *f.*
hummingbird ['hʌmɪŋbɜ:d] *n* beija-flor *m.*
humor *n & vt* ***US*** = **humour**.
humorist ['hju:mərɪst] *n* humorista *mf.*
humorous ['hju:mərəs] *adj* humorístico(ca).
humour ***UK***, **humor** ***US*** ['hju:mə^r] ◇ *n (U)* [gen] humor *m*; **in bad/good** ~ ***dated*** de mau/bom humor. ◇ *vt* fazer a vontade de.
hump [hʌmp] ◇ *n* **-1.** [hill] elevação *f* **-2.** [on back of animal, person] corcova *f.* ◇ *vt* ***inf*** [carry] carregar.
humpbacked bridge ['hʌmpbækt-] *n* ponte *f* encurvada.
humus ['hju:məs] *n (U)* humo *m.*
hunch [hʌntʃ] ◇ *n* ***inf*** pressentimento *m.* ◇ *vt* curvar. ◇ *vi* curvar-se.
hunchback ['hʌntʃbæk] *n* corcunda *mf.*
hunched [hʌntʃt] *adj* encurvado(da).
hundred ['hʌndrəd] *num* cem; **a** OR **one hundred** cem; *see also* **six**.
◆ **hundreds** *npl* centenas *fpl.*
hundredth ['hʌndrətθ] *num* centésimo(ma); *see also* **sixth**.
hundredweight ['hʌndrədweɪt] *n* **-1.** [in UK] quintal *m* métrico *(50,8 kg)* **-2.** [in US] quintal *m* métrico *(45,3 kg)*.
hung [hʌŋ] ◇ *pt & pp* ▷ **hang**. ◇ *adj* POL sem maioria.
Hungarian [hʌŋ'geərɪən] ◇ *adj* húngaro(ra). ◇ *n* **-1.** [person] húngaro *m*, -ra *f* **-2.** [language] húngaro *m.*
Hungary ['hʌŋgərɪ] *n* Hungria; **in** ~ na Hungria.
hunger ['hʌŋgə^r] *n* **-1.** [desire for food, starvation] fome *f* **-2.** ***literary*** [strong desire] sede *f.*
◆ **hunger after, hunger for** *vt fus* ***literary*** ter fome de.
hunger strike *n* greve *f* de fome.
hung over *adj inf*: **to be** ~ estar com ressaca.
hungry ['hʌŋgrɪ] (*compar* **-ier**, *superl* **-iest**) *adj* **-1.** [for food] faminto(ta); **to go** ~ ficar com fome **-2.** ***literary*** [eager]: **to be** ~ **for sthg** ter sede de algo.
hung up *adj inf*: **to be** ~ **(on sb/sthg)**, **to be** ~ **(about sb/sthg)** ficar complexado(da) (por causa de alguém/algo).
hunk [hʌŋk] *n* **-1.** [large piece] naco *m* **-2.** ***inf*** [attractive man] pedaço *m* de mau caminho.
hunky-dory [ˌhʌŋkɪ'dɔ:rɪ] *adj inf* satisfatório(ria) para todos.
hunt [hʌnt] ◇ *n* **-1.** [SPORT- activity] caça *f*; [- hunters] grupo *m* de caçadores **-2.** [search] busca *f.* ◇ *vi* **-1.** [for food, sport] caçar **-2.** [search]: **to** ~ **(for sthg)** procurar (algo). ◇ *vt* **-1.** [animals, birds] caçar **-2.** [person] procurar.
◆ **hunt down** *vt sep* encurralar.
hunter ['hʌntə^r] *n* caçador *m*, -ra *f.*
hunting ['hʌntɪŋ] ◇ *n* **-1.** SPORT caça *f* **-2.** ***UK*** [foxhunting] caça *f* à raposa **-3.** [pursuit] busca *f.* ◇ *comp* de caça.
huntsman ['hʌntsmən] (*pl* **-men** [-mən]) *n* caçador *m.*
hurdle ['hɜ:dl] ◇ *n* **-1.** [in race] barreira *f* **-2.** [obstacle] obstáculo *m.* ◇ *vt* [jump over] saltar.
◆ **hurdles** *npl* SPORT corrida *f* de obstáculos.
hurl [hɜ:l] *vt* **-1.** [throw] arremessar **-2.** [shout] proferir.
hurrah [hʊ'rɑ:] *excl* ***dated*** viva!, hurra!
hurray [hʊ'reɪ] *excl* viva!
hurricane ['hʌrɪkən] *n* furacão *m.*
hurried ['hʌrɪd] *adj* [hasty] apressado(da), precipitado(da).
hurriedly ['hʌrɪdlɪ] *adv* apressadamente, precipitadamente.
hurry ['hʌrɪ] (*pt & pp* **-ied**) ◇ *vt* apressar. ◇ *vi* apressar-se; **to** ~ **to do sthg** apressar-se para fazer algo. ◇ *n* [rush] pressa *f*; **to be in a** ~ estar com pressa; **to do sthg in a** ~ fazer algo com pressa; **to be in no** ~ **to do sthg** [unwilling] não estar com pressa nenhuma de fazer algo.
◆ **hurry off** *vi* sair correndo.
◆ **hurry up** ◇ *vi* apressar-se; **hurry!** vamos de uma vez! ◇ *vt sep* apressar, acelerar.
hurt [hɜ:t] (*pt & pp* **hurt**) ◇ *vt* **-1.** [cause physical pain to] machucar **-2.** [injure] ferir **-3.** [upset] magoar **-4.** [be detrimental to] prejudicar. ◇ *vi* **-1.** [gen] doer; **my feet** ~ os meus pés doem; **ouch, you're** ~**ing!** ai, você está me machucando **-2.** [be detrimental] prejudicar. ◇ *adj* **-1.** [injured] machucado(da) **-2.** [upset] magoado(da). ◇ *n (U)* [emotional pain] dor *f.*
hurtful ['hɜ:tfʊl] *adj* ofensivo(va).
hurtle ['hɜ:tl] *vi* precipitar-se; **to** ~ **over** precipitar-se por; **to** ~ **past** passar como um raio.
husband ['hʌzbənd] *n* marido *m.*
husbandry ['hʌzbəndrɪ] *n (U)* ***fml*** criação *f.*
hush [hʌʃ] ◇ *n* [quietness] silêncio *m.* ◇ *vt* [silence] silenciar. ◇ *excl* silêncio!
◆ **hush up** *vt sep* **-1.** [affair] silenciar a respeito de **-2.** [noisy person] ficar quieto(ta).
hush money *n (U)* ***inf*** suborno *m* *(para comprar o silêncio de alguém)*.

husk [hʌsk] *n* [of seed, grain] casca *f*.
husky ['hʌskɪ] (*compar* **-ier**, *superl* **-iest**) ◇ *adj* [hoarse] rouco(ca). ◇ *n* [dog] husky *m*.
hustings ['hʌstɪŋz] *npl UK* campanha *f* eleitoral.
hustle ['hʌsl] ◇ *vt* **-1.** [hurry] empurrar **-2.** *US* [persuade, trick]: **to ~ sb into doing sthg** pressionar alguém a fazer algo *OR* para que faça algo. ◇ *n (U)* [business]: **~ and bustle** grande atividade *f*.
hut [hʌt] *n* **-1.** [rough house] cabana *f* **-2.** [shed] barraca *f*.
hutch [hʌtʃ] *n* arapuca *f*.
hyacinth ['haɪəsɪnθ] *n* jacinto *m*.
hybrid ['haɪbrɪd] ◇ *adj* híbrido(da). ◇ *n* híbrido *m*.
hydrangea [haɪ'dreɪndʒəl *n* hortênsia *f*.
hydrant ['haɪdrənt] *n* hidrante *m*.
hydraulic [haɪ'drɔ:lɪk] *adj* hidráulico(ca).
◆ **hydraulics** *n (U)* hidráulica *f*.
hydro *n UK* [spa] estância *f* hidromineral.
hydrocarbon [ˌhaɪdrə'kɑ:bən] *n* hidrocarboneto *m*.
hydrochloric acid [ˌhaɪdrə'klɔ:rɪk-] *n (U)* ácido *m* clorídrico.
hydroelectric [ˌhaɪdrəʊɪ'lektrɪk] *adj* hidrelétrico(-ca).
hydroelectricity [ˌhaɪdrəʊɪlek'trɪsətɪ] *n (U)* hidreletricidade *f*.
hydrofoil ['haɪdrəfɔɪl] *n* embarcação *f* com hidrofólio.
hydrogen ['haɪdrədʒən] *n (U)* hidrogênio *m*.
hydrogen bomb *n* bomba *f* de hidrogênio.
hydrophobia [ˌhaɪdrə'fəʊbjə] *n (U) fml* [rabies] hidrofobia *f*.
hydroplane ['haɪdrəpleɪn] *n* [speedboat] hidroplano *m*.
hyena [haɪ'i:nə] *n* hiena *f*.
hygiene ['haɪdʒi:n] *n (U)* higiene *f*.
hygienic [haɪ'dʒi:nɪk] *adj* higiênico(ca).
hygienist [haɪ'dʒi:nɪst] *n* [at dentist's] higienista *mf* bucal.
hymn [hɪm] *n* hino *m*.
hymn book *n* hinário *m*.
hype [haɪp] *inf* ◇ *n (U)* propaganda *f* exagerada. ◇ *vt* fazer propaganda exagerada de.
hyped up [haɪpd-] *adj inf* como uma pilha de nervos.
hyper ['haɪpə^r] *adj inf* enérgico(ca), ativo(va).
hyperactive [ˌhaɪpər'æktɪv] *adj* hiperativo(va).
hyperbole [haɪ'pɜ:bəlɪ] *n (U)* hipérbole *f*.
hyperinflation *n (U)* hiperinflação *f*.
hyperlink ['haɪpəˌlɪŋk] *n COMPUT* hyperlink *m*.
hypermarket ['haɪpəˌmɑ:kɪt] *n* hipermercado *m*.
hypersensitive [ˌhaɪpə'sensɪtɪv] *adj* **-1.** [easily offended]: **~ (to/about sthg)** hipersensível (a algo) **-2.** *MED* hipersensível.
hypertension [ˌhaɪpə'tenʃn] *n MED (U)* hipertensão *f*.
hypertext ['haɪpətekst] *n COMPUT* hipertexto *m*.
hyperventilate [ˌhaɪpə'ventɪleɪt] *vi* hiperventilar.
hyphen ['haɪfn] *n* hífen *m*.
hyphenate ['haɪfəneɪt] *vt* hifenizar.
hypnosis [hɪp'nəʊsɪs] *n (U)* hipnose *f*; **under ~** hipnotizado(da).
hypnotic [hɪp'nɒtɪk] *adj* hipnótico(ca).
hypnotism ['hɪpnətɪzm] *n (U)* hipnotismo *m*.
hypnotist ['hɪpnətɪst] *n* hipnotizador *m*, -ra *f*.
hypnotize, -ise ['hɪpnətaɪz] *vt* hipnotizar.
hypoallergenic ['haɪpəʊˌælə'dʒenɪk] *adj* hipoalergênico(ca).
hypochondriac [ˌhaɪpə'kɒndrɪæk] *n* hipocondríaco *m*, -ca *f*.
hypocrisy [hɪ'pɒkrəsɪ] *n (U)* hipocrisia *f*.
hypocrite ['hɪpəkrɪt] *n* hipócrita *mf*.
hypocritical [ˌhɪpə'krɪtɪkl] *adj* hipócrita.
hypodermic needle [ˌhaɪpə'dɜ:mɪk-] *n* agulha *f* hipodérmica.
hypodermic syringe [ˌhaɪpə'dɜ:mɪk-] *n* seringa *f* hipodérmica.
hypothermia [ˌhaɪpəʊ'θɜ:mɪə] *n (U)* hipotermia *f*.
hypothesis [haɪ'pɒθɪsɪs] (*pl* **-theses** [-θɪsi:z]) *n* hipótese *f*.
hypothesize, -ise [haɪ'pɒθɪsaɪz] ◇ *vt* fazer hipóteses sobre. ◇ *vi* fazer hipóteses.
hypothetical [ˌhaɪpə'θetɪkl] *adj* hipotético(ca).
hysterectomy [ˌhɪstə'rektəmɪ] (*pl* **-ies**) *n* histerectomia *f*.
hysteria [hɪs'tɪərɪə] *n* histeria *f*.
hysterical [hɪs'terɪkl] *adj* **-1.** [gen] histérico(ca) **-2.** *inf* [very funny] hilariante.
hysterics [hɪs'terɪks] *npl* **-1.** [panic, excitement] crise *f* histérica, histeria *f* **-2.** *inf* [fits of laughter] ataque *m* de riso; **to be in ~** arrebentar-se de tanto rir.
Hz (*abbr of* **hertz**) Hz.

i (*pl* **i's** *OR* **is**), **I** (*pl* **I's** *OR* **Is**) [aɪ] *n* [letter] i, I *m*.
I[1] [aɪ] (*abbr of* **Island, Isle**) ilha *f*.
I[2] [aɪ] *pers pron* eu; **she and ~ were at college together** eu e ela fomos ao colégio juntos(tas); **it is ~** *fml* sou eu; **~ can't do it** eu não posso fazer isso.
IA *abbr of* **Iowa**.
IAEA (*abbr of* **International Atomic Energy Agency**) *n* AIEA *f*.
IATA (*abbr of* **International Air Transport Association**) *n associação internacional de transporte aéreo*, IATA *f*.
IBA (*abbr of* **Independent Broadcasting Authority**) *n órgão britânico de regulamentação das redes privadas de rádio e televisão*.
Iberian [ai'bi:riən] ◇ *adj* ibérico(ca). ◇ *n* ibérico *m*, -ca *f*.

Iberian peninsula *n*: **the ~** a Península Ibérica.
ibid (*abbr of* **ibidem**) ib.
i/c (*abbr of* **in charge**) resp.; **to be ~ sthg** ser responsável por.
ICA (*abbr of* **Institute of Contemporary Arts**) *n* *instituto de arte contemporânea de Londres.*
ICBM (*abbr of* **intercontinental ballistic missile**) *n* míssil *m* balístico intercontinental.
ICC *n* **-1.** (*abbr of* **International Chamber of Commerce**) ICC *f*, Câmara *f* de Comércio Internacional **-2.** (*abbr of* **Interstate Commerce Commission**) *órgão federal norte-americano que regula o comércio entre os estados.*
ice [aɪs] ◇ *n* **-1.** *(U)* [gen] gelo *m*; **to break the ~** *fig* quebrar o gelo; **to put sthg on ~** *fig* colocar algo de lado **-2.** *UK* [ice cream] sorvete *m*. ◇ *vt UK* [cover with icing] cobrir com glacê.
◆ **ice over, ice up** *vi* congelar.
ice age *n* era *f* glacial.
iceberg ['aɪsbɜːg] *n* iceberg *m*.
iceberg lettuce *n* alface *f* americana.
icebox ['aɪsbɒks] *n* **-1.** *UK* [in refrigerator] congelador *m* **-2.** *US* [refrigerator] geladeira *f*, refrigerador *m*.
icebreaker ['aɪsˌbreɪkəʳ] *n* [ship] navio *m* quebra-gelo.
ice bucket *n* balde *m* de gelo.
ice cap *n* calota *f* glacial.
ice-cold *adj* gelado(da).
ice cream *n* sorvete *m*.
ice cream bar *n US* picolé *m* com casquinha de chocolate.
ice cube *n* cubo *m* de gelo.
iced [aɪst] *adj* **-1.** [cooled with ice] com gelo **-2.** [covered in icing] coberto(ta) com glacê.
ice floe *n* banquisa *f*.
ice hockey *n (U)* hóquei *m* sobre o gelo.
Iceland ['aɪslənd] *n* Islândia; **in ~** na Islândia.
Icelander ['aɪsləndəʳ] *n* islandês *m*, -esa *f*.
Icelandic [aɪs'lændɪk] ◇ *adj* islandês(esa). ◇ *n* [language] islandês *m*.
ice lolly *n UK* picolé *m*.
ice pick *n* picador *m* de gelo.
ice rink *n* rinque *m* (de patinação).
ice skate *n* patim *m* para o gelo.
◆ **ice-skate** *vi* patinar sobre o gelo.
ice-skater *n* patinador *m*, -ra *f* sobre o gelo.
ice-skating *n (U)* patinação *f* sobre o gelo; **to go ~** praticar patinação.
icicle ['aɪsɪkl] *n* pingente *m* de gelo.
icily ['aɪsɪlɪ] *adv* [in unfriendly way] friamente.
icing ['aɪsɪŋ] *n (U)* glacê *m*; **the third goal was the ~ on the cake** *fig* o terceiro gol foi para coroar a vitória.
icing sugar *n UK* açúcar *m* de confeiteiro.
ICJ (*abbr of* **International Court of Justice**) *n* TIJ *m*.
icon ['aɪkɒn] *n* ícone *m*.
iconoclast [aɪ'kɒnəklæst] *n* iconoclasta *mf*.
ICR (*abbr of* **Institute for Cancer Research**) *n instituto norte-americano para pesquisa do câncer*, ≃ INCA *m*.
ICU (*abbr of* **intensive-care unit**) *n* UTI *f*.
icy ['aɪsɪ] (*compar* **-ier**, *superl* **-iest**) *adj* **-1.** [very cold] gelado(da) **-2.** [covered in ice] coberto(ta) de gelo **-3.** *fig* [unfriendly] frio (fria).
id [ɪd] *n* id *m*.
I'd [aɪd] = **I would, I had**.
ID ◇ *n* (*abbr of* **identification**) identificação *f*; **~ card** (carteira *f* de) *f* identidade, ≃ RG *m*. ◇ *abbr of* **Idaho**.
Idaho ['aɪdəˌhəʊ] *n* Idaho.
ID card *n* = **identity card**.
IDD (*abbr of* **international direct dialling**) *n* DDI *m*.
idea [aɪ'dɪə] *n* **-1.** [gen] idéia *f*; **to get the ~** *inf* pegar a idéia; **wherever did you get the ~ that I don't like him?** de onde você tirou a idéia de que eu não gosto dele?; **to have an ~ of sthg** ter idéia de algo; **to have an ~ that** ter a sensação de que; **to have no ~** não ter idéia; **the ~ is to ...** a idéia é ... **-2.** [suspicion] impressão *f*.
ideal [aɪ'dɪəl] ◇ *adj* [perfect] ideal; **to be ~ for sthg** ser ideal para algo. ◇ *n* [principle] ideal *m*.
idealism [aɪ'dɪəlɪzm] *n* [high principles] idealismo *m*.
idealist [aɪ'dɪəlɪst] *n* idealista *mf*.
idealize, -ise [aɪ'dɪəlaɪz] *vt* idealizar.
ideally [aɪ'dɪəlɪ] *adv* **-1.** [perfectly] perfeitamente **-2.** [preferably] idealmente.
identical [aɪ'dentɪkl] *adj* idêntico(ca).
identical twins *npl* gêmeos *mpl* idênticos.
identifiable [aɪ'dentɪfaɪəbl] *adj* identificável.
identification [aɪˌdentɪfɪ'keɪʃn] *n* identificação *f*; **~ with sb/sthg** identificação com alguém/algo.
identify [aɪ'dentɪfaɪ] (*pt* & *pp* **-ied**) ◇ *vt* **-1.** [gen] identificar **-2.** [connect]: **to ~ sb with sthg** relacionar alguém a algo. ◇ *vi* [empathize]: **to ~ with sb/sthg** identificar-se com alguém/algo.
Identikit picture® [aɪ'dentɪkɪt-] *n* retrato *m* falado.
identity [aɪ'dentətɪ] (*pl* **-ies**) *n* identidade *f*.
identity card *n* (carteira *f* de) identidade *f*.
identity parade *n* identificação *f (de um criminoso).*
ideological [ˌaɪdɪə'lɒdʒɪkl] *adj* ideológico(ca).
ideology [ˌaɪdɪ'ɒlədʒɪ] (*pl* **-ies**) *n* ideologia *f*.
idiom ['ɪdɪəm] *n* **-1.** [phrase] expressão *f* idiomática **-2.** *fml* [style, language] linguagem *f*.
idiomatic [ˌɪdɪə'mætɪk] *adj* [natural-sounding] idiomático(ca).
idiosyncrasy [ˌɪdɪə'sɪŋkrəsɪ] (*pl* **-ies**) *n* idiossincrasia *f*.
idiot ['ɪdɪət] *n* [fool] idiota *mf*.
idiotic [ˌɪdɪ'ɒtɪk] *adj* idiota.
idle ['aɪdl] ◇ *adj* **-1.** [person - inactive] ocioso(sa); [- lazy] preguiçoso(sa) **-2.** [not in use] parado(da) **-3.** [empty] vão (vã) **-4.** [casual] casual **-5.** [futile] inútil. ◇ *vi* [engine] estar em ponto morto.
◆ **idle away** *vt sep* desperdiçar.
idleness ['aɪdlnɪs] *n (U)* [laziness] preguiça *f*.
idler ['aɪdləʳ] *n* preguiçoso(sa), desocupado(da).
idly ['aɪdlɪ] *adv* **-1.** [lazily] preguiçosamente **-2.** [casually] casualmente.
idol ['aɪdl] *n* ídolo *m*.
idolize, -ise ['aɪdəlaɪz] *vt* idolatrar.
idyl(l) ['ɪdɪl] *n* idílio *m*.
idyllic [ɪ'dɪlɪk] *adj* idílico(ca).
i.e. (*abbr of* **id est**) i.e.

IEE (*abbr of* **Institution of Electrical Engineers**) *n* *instituto britânico de engenheiros eletricistas.*
if [ɪf] <> *conj* **-1.** [gen] se; ~ **I were you** se eu fosse você **-2.** [though] ainda que; **a good,** ~ **rather expensive, restaurant** um bom restaurante, ainda que caro **-3.** [that] que. <> *n*: ~**s and buts** poréns *mpl.*
◆ **if not** *conj* se não.
◆ **if only** <> *conj* **-1.** [providing a reason] ao menos, nem que seja; **let's stop at the next services,** ~ **to stretch our legs** vamos parar no próximo posto, ao menos OR nem que seja para esticar as pernas **-2.** [expressing regret] se ao menos. <> *excl* quem dera!
iffy ['ɪfɪ] (*compar* **-ier**, *superl* **-iest**) *adj inf* inseguro(ra).
igloo ['ɪglu:] (*pl* **-s**) *n* iglu *m.*
ignite [ɪg'naɪt] <> *vt* acender. <> *vi* acender, acender-se.
ignition [ɪg'nɪʃn] *n* ignição *f.*
ignition key *n* chave *f* de ignição.
ignoble [ɪg'nəʊbl] *adj fml* ignóbil.
ignominious [ˌɪgnə'mɪnɪəs] *adj fml* ignominioso(-sa).
ignominy ['ɪgnəmɪnɪ] *n (U) fml* ignomínia *f.*
ignoramus [ˌɪgnə'reɪməs] (*pl* **-es**) *n* ignorante *mf.*
ignorance ['ɪgnərəns] *n (U)* ignorância *f.*
ignorant ['ɪgnərənt] *adj* **-1.** [uneducated] ignorante; [lacking information] desinformado(da) **-2.** *fml* [unaware]: **to be** ~ **of sthg** ignorar algo **-3.** *inf* [rude] ignorante.
ignore [ɪg'nɔ:ʳ] *vt* [take no notice of] ignorar.
iguana [ɪ'gwɑ:nə] (*pl inv* OR **-s**) *n* iguana *f.*
ikon ['aɪkɒn] *n* = **icon**.
IL *abbr of* **Illinois**.
ILEA (*abbr of* **Inner London Education Authority**) *n* *antigo órgão responsável pela educacão em Londres.*
ileum ['ɪlɪəm] (*pl* **ilea** ['ɪlɪə]) *n* íleo *m.*
ilk [ɪlk] *n fml*: **of that** ~ [of that sort] do mesmo tipo.
ill [ɪl] <> *adj* **-1.** [sick, unwell] doente; **to feel** ~ sentir-se doente; **to be taken** ~, **to fall** ~ ficar doente **-2.** [bad, unfavourable] mau (má). <> *adv* mal; **to speak/think** ~ **of sb** falar/pensar mal de alguém; **we can** ~ **afford such luxuries** mal conseguimos pagar esses luxos.
◆ **ills** *npl* males *mpl.*
ill. (*abbr of* **illustration**) il.
I'll [aɪl] = **I will**, **I shall**.
ill-advised [-əd'vaɪzd] *adj* **-1.** [not sensible] imprudente, insensato(ta); **to be** ~ **to do sthg** ser imprudente fazer algo **-2.** [unwise] pouco aconselhável.
ill at ease *adj*: **he always felt shy and** ~ **at parties** ele sempre se sentia intimidado e pouco àvontade nas festas.
ill-bred *adj* malcriado(da).
ill-considered *adj* imponderado(da).
ill-disposed *adj*: **to be** ~ **towards sb** estar de má vontade com alguém.
illegal [ɪ'li:gl] *adj* ilegal; ~ **immigrant/alien** imigrante/estrangeiro ilegal.
illegally [ɪ'li:gəlɪ] *adv* ilegalmente.
illegible [ɪ'ledʒəbl] *adj* ilegível.
illegitimate [ˌɪlɪ'dʒɪtɪmət] *adj* ilegítimo(ma).
ill-equipped [-ɪ'kwɪpt] *adj* despreparado(da).
ill-fated [-'feɪtɪd] *adj* malfadado(da).
ill feeling *n (U)* ressentimento *f*, rancor *m.*
ill-founded [-'faʊndɪd] *adj* infundado(da).
ill-gotten gains [-'gɒtən-] *npl fml* ganhos *mpl* ilícitos.
ill health *n (U)* má saúde *f.*
illicit [ɪ'lɪsɪt] *adj* ilícito(ta).
illicitly [ɪ'lɪsɪtlɪ] *adv* ilicitamente.
ill-informed *adj* mal informado(da).
Illinois *n* Illinois; **in** ~ em Illinois.
illiteracy [ɪ'lɪtərəsɪ] *n (U)* analfabetismo *m.*
illiterate [ɪ'lɪtərət] <> *adj* analfabeto(ta). <> *n* analfabeto *m*, -ta *f.*
ill-mannered *adj* mal-educado(da).
illness ['ɪlnɪs] *n* doença *f.*
illogical [ɪ'lɒdʒɪkl] *adj* ilógico(ca).
ill-suited *adj* inadequado(da); **an** ~ **couple** um casal desajustado; **to be** ~ **to sthg** ser inadequado(da) para algo.
ill-tempered *adj* mal-humorado(da), genioso(-sa).
ill-timed [-'taɪmd] *adj* inoportuno(na).
ill-treat *vt* maltratar.
ill-treatment *n (U)* maus tratos *mpl.*
illuminate [ɪ'lu:mɪneɪt] *vt* **-1.** [light up] iluminar **-2.** [explain] ilustrar, esclarecer.
illuminated [ɪ'lu:mɪneɪtɪd] *adj* [sign, notice] iluminado(da).
illuminating [ɪ'lu:mɪneɪtɪŋ] *adj* [enlightening] esclarecedor(ra).
illumination [ɪˌlu:mɪ'neɪʃn] *n (U)* [lighting] iluminação *f.*
◆ **illuminations** *npl UK* luzes *fpl* decorativas.
illusion [ɪ'lu:ʒn] *n* **-1.** [gen] ilusão *f*; **to have no** ~**s about sb/sthg** não ter ilusões com alguém/algo; **to be under the** ~ **that** estar com a ilusão de que **-2.** [magic trick] truque *m* de ilusionismo.
illusionist [ɪ'lu:ʒənɪst] *n fml* ilusionista *mf.*
illusory [ɪ'lu:sərɪ] *adj fml* ilusório(ria).
illustrate ['ɪləstreɪt] *vt* ilustrar.
illustration [ˌɪlə'streɪʃn] *n* ilustração *f.*
illustrator ['ɪləstreɪtəʳ] *n* ilustrador *m*, -ra *f.*
illustrious [ɪ'lʌstrɪəs] *adj fml* ilustre.
ill will *n (U)* animosidade *f.*
ill wind [-wɪnd] *n*: **it's an** ~ **(that blows nobody any good)** *proverb* há males que vêm para o bem.
ILO (*abbr of* **International Labour Organization**) *n* OIT *f.*
I'm [aɪm] = **I am**.
image ['ɪmɪdʒ] *n* [gen] imagem *f*; **to be the** ~ **of sb** ser a cara de alguém.
imagery ['ɪmɪdʒrɪ] *n* imagens *fpl.*
imaginable [ɪ'mædʒɪnəbl] *adj* imaginável.
imaginary [ɪ'mædʒɪnrɪ] *adj* imaginário(ria).
imagination [ɪˌmædʒɪ'neɪʃn] *n* imaginação *f.*
imaginative [ɪ'mædʒɪnətɪv] *adj* imaginativo(va).
imagine [ɪ'mædʒɪn] *vt* imaginar; **to** ~ **doing sthg** imaginar fazer algo; ~ **(that)!** imagine!
imaginings [ɪ'mædʒɪnɪŋz] *npl literary* fantasias *fpl.*
imbalance [ˌɪm'bæləns] *n* desequilíbrio *m.*

imbecile [ˈɪmbɪsiːl] *n* imbecil *mf.*
imbue [ɪmˈbjuː] *vt fml*: **to be ~d with sthg** estar imbuído(da) de algo.
IMF (*abbr of* **International Monetary Fund**) *n* FMI *m.*
imitate [ˈɪmɪteɪt] *vt* imitar.
imitation [ˌɪmɪˈteɪʃn] <> *n* imitação *f.* <> *adj* de imitação.
imitator [ˈɪmɪteɪtəʳ] *n* imitador *m*, -ra *f.*
immaculate [ɪˈmækjʊlət] *adj* **-1.** [clean and tidy] imaculado(da) **-2.** [impeccable] impecável.
immaculately [ɪˈmækjʊlətlɪ] *adv* **-1.** [cleanly, tidily] de maneira imaculada **-2.** [impeccably] impecavelmente.
immaterial [ˌɪməˈtɪərɪəl] *adj* [irrelevant, unimportant] irrelevante.
immature [ˌɪməˈtjʊəʳ] *adj* **-1.** [childish] imaturo(ra) **-2.** *BOT & ZOOL* jovem.
immaturity [ˌɪməˈtjʊərətɪ] *n* **-1.** [childishness] imaturidade *f* **-2.** *BOT & ZOOL* juventude *f.*
immeasurable [ɪˈmeʒrəbl] *adj* incomensurável.
immediacy [ɪˈmiːdjəsɪ] *n (U)* imediatidade *f*, urgência *f.*
immediate [ɪˈmiːdjət] *adj* **-1.** [gen] imediato(ta) **-2.** [closest in relationship] próximo(ma).
immediately [ɪˈmiːdjətlɪ] <> *adv* **-1.** [gen] imediatamente **-2.** [directly, closely] diretamente. <> *conj* [as soon as] assim que.
immemorial [ˌɪmɪˈmɔːrɪəl] *adj*: **from time ~** desde tempos imemoráveis.
immense [ɪˈmens] *adj* imenso(sa).
immensely [ɪˈmenslɪ] *adv* imensamente.
immensity [ɪˈmensətɪ] *n (U)* imensidão *f.*
immerse [ɪˈmɜːs] *vt* **-1.** [plunge into liquid]: **to ~ sthg in sthg** mergulhar algo em algo **-2.** *fig* [involve]: **to ~ o.s. in sthg** envolver-se em algo.
immersion heater [ɪˈmɜːʃn-] *n* ebulidor *m.*
immigrant [ˈɪmɪgrənt] <> *n* imigrante *mf.* <> *comp* de imigrantes.
immigration [ˌɪmɪˈgreɪʃn] <> *n (U)* imigração *f.* <> *comp* de imigração; **~ restrictions** restrições *fpl* para imigração.
imminence [ˈɪmɪnəns] *n (U)* iminência *f.*
imminent [ˈɪmɪnənt] *adj* iminente.
immobile [ɪˈməʊbaɪl] *adj* imóvel.
immobilization [ɪˌməʊbɪlaɪˈzeɪʃn] *n (U)* imobilização *f.*
immobilize, -ise [ɪˈməʊbɪlaɪz] *vt* imobilizar.
immobilizer *n AUT* corta-corrente *m.*
immodest [ɪˈmɒdɪst] *adj* **-1.** [vain] vaidoso(sa) **-2.** [indecent] indecente.
immoral [ɪˈmɒrəl] *adj* imoral.
immorality [ˌɪməˈrælətɪ] *n (U)* imoralidade *f.*
immortal [ɪˈmɔːtl] <> *adj* imortal. <> *n* **-1.** [god] deus *m* **-2.** [hero] imortal *mf.*
immortality [ˌɪmɔːˈtælətɪ] *n* imortalidade *f.*
immortalize, -ise [ɪˈmɔːtəlaɪz] *vt* imortalizar.
immovable [ɪˈmuːvəbl] *adj* **-1.** [fixed] fixo(xa) **-2.** [obstinate] inflexível.
immune [ɪˈmjuːn] *adj* **-1.** *MED* imune; **to be ~ to sthg** ser imune a algo **-2.** *fig* [impervious]: **to be ~ to sthg** não ser suscetível a algo **-3.** [exempt] isento(ta), livre; **to be ~ from sthg** estar protegido(da) de algo.
immune system *n* sistema *m* imunológico.
immunity [ɪˈmjuːnətɪ] *n* **-1.** *(U) MED*: **~ (to sthg)** imunidade *f* (a algo) **-2.** *(U) fig* [imperviousness]: **~ to sthg** falta *f* de suscetibilidade a algo **-3.** [exemption] isenção *f*; **~ from sthg** proteção *f* contra algo.
immunization [ˌɪmjuːnaɪˈzeɪʃn] *n MED* imunização *f.*
immunize, -ise [ˈɪmjuːnaɪz] *vt*: **to ~ sb (against sthg)** *MED* imunizar alguém (contra algo).
immunodeficiency [ˌɪmjuːnəʊdɪˈfɪʃənsɪ] *n (U)* imunodeficiência *f.*
immunology [ˌɪmjuːˈnɒlədʒɪ] *n (U)* imunologia *f.*
immutable [ɪˈmjuːtəbl] *adj fml* imutável.
imp [ɪmp] *n* **-1.** [creature] diabinho *m* **-2.** [naughty child] diabinho *m*, -nha *f.*
impact [*n* ˈɪmpækt, *vb* ɪmˈpækt] <> *n* impacto *m*; **on ~** ao impacto; **to make an ~ on sb/sthg** causar impacto em alguém/algo. <> *vt* **-1.** [collide with] colidir com **-2.** [influence] influenciar.
impair [ɪmˈpeəʳ] *vt* prejudicar, debilitar.
impaired [ɪmˈpeəd] *adj* prejudicado(da), debilitado(da).
impale [ɪmˈpeɪl] *vt* perfurar; **to ~ sb/sthg on sthg** empalar alguém/algo em algo.
impart [ɪmˈpɑːt] *vt fml* **-1.** [information]: **to ~ sthg (to sb)** transmitir algo (a alguém) **-2.** [feeling, quality] conferir; **to ~ flavour to the dish** conferir sabor ao prato.
impartial [ɪmˈpɑːʃl] *adj* imparcial.
impartiality [ɪmˌpɑːʃɪˈælətɪ] *n (U)* imparcialidade *f.*
impassable [ɪmˈpɑːsəbl] *adj* intransitável.
impasse [æmˈpɑːs] *n* impasse *m*; **to reach an ~** chegar a um impasse.
impassioned [ɪmˈpæʃnd] *adj* veemente.
impassive [ɪmˈpæsɪv] *adj* impassível.
impatience [ɪmˈpeɪʃns] *n* impaciência *f.*
impatient [ɪmˈpeɪʃnt] *adj* impaciente; **to be ~ to do sthg** estar impaciente para fazer algo; **to be ~ for sthg** esperar algo com impaciência.
impatiently [ɪmˈpeɪʃntlɪ] *adv* impacientemente.
impeach [ɪmˈpiːtʃ] *vt JUR* impugnar.
impeachment [ɪmˈpiːtʃmənt] *n (U) JUR* impeachment *m.*
impeccable [ɪmˈpekəbl] *adj* impecável.
impeccably [ɪmˈpekəblɪ] *adv* impecavelmente.
impecunious [ˌɪmpɪˈkjuːnjəs] *adj fml* indigente.
impede [ɪmˈpiːd] *vt* impedir.
impediment [ɪmˈpedɪmənt] *n* impedimento *m*; **a speech ~** um defeito de fala.
impel [ɪmˈpel] (*pt* & *pp* **-led**, *cont* **-ling**) *vt*: **to ~ sb to do sthg** impelir alguém a fazer algo.
impending [ɪmˈpendɪŋ] *adj* iminente.
impenetrable [ɪmˈpenɪtrəbl] *adj* **-1.** [impossible to penetrate] impenetrável **-2.** [impossible to understand] incompreensível.
imperative [ɪmˈperətɪv] <> *adj* [essential] indispensável. <> *n* imperativo *m.*
imperceptible [ˌɪmpəˈseptəbl] *adj* imperceptível.
imperfect [ɪmˈpɜːfɪkt] <> *adj* [not perfect] imperfeito(ta). <> *n GRAM*: **~ (tense)** (pretérito *m*) imperfeito *m.*

imperfection [ˌɪmpəˈfekʃn] *n* imperfeição *f*.
imperial [ɪmˈpɪərɪəl] *adj* **-1.** [of an empire or emperor] imperial **-2.** [system of measurement]: **~ system** *sistema britânico de medidas.*
imperialism [ɪmˈpɪərɪəlɪzm] *n (U)* imperialismo *m*.
imperialist [ɪmˈpɪərɪəlɪst] ◇ *adj* imperialista. ◇ *n* imperialista *mf*.
imperil [ɪmˈperɪl] (*UK pt* & *pp* **-led**, *cont* **-ling**, *US pt* & *pp* **-ed**, *cont* **-ing**) *vt fml* pôr em perigo.
imperious [ɪmˈpɪərɪəs] *adj* imperioso(sa).
impersonal [ɪmˈpɜːsnl] *adj* impessoal.
impersonate [ɪmˈpɜːsəneɪt] *vt* **-1.** [mimic, imitate] imitar **-2.** [pretend to be] fazer-se passar por.
impersonation [ɪmˌpɜːsəˈneɪʃn] *n* [by mimic] imitação *f*; **to do ~s (of sb)** fazer imitações (de alguém).
impersonator [ɪmˈpɜːsəneɪtə^r] *n* **-1.** [mimic] imitador *m*, -ra *f* **-2.** [impostor] impostor *m*, -ra *f*.
impertinence [ɪmˈpɜːtɪnəns] *n (U)* impertinência *f*.
impertinent [ɪmˈpɜːtɪnənt] *adj* [rude] impertinente.
imperturbable [ˌɪmpəˈtɜːbəbl] *adj* imperturbável.
impervious [ɪmˈpɜːvjəs] *adj* [not influenced]: **~ to sthg** imune a algo.
impetuous [ɪmˈpetʃʊəs] *adj* impetuoso(sa).
impetus [ˈɪmpɪtəs] *n* **-1.** [momentum] ímpeto *m* **-2.** [stimulus] estímulo *m*.
impinge [ɪmˈpɪndʒ] *vi*: **to ~ on sb/sthg** afetar alguém/algo.
impish [ˈɪmpɪʃ] *adj* travesso(sa).
implacable [ɪmˈplækəbl] *adj* implacável.
implant [*n* ˈɪmplɑːnt, *vb* ɪmˈplɑːnt] ◇ *n* implante *m*. ◇ *vt*: **to ~ sthg in(to) sb** implantar algo em alguém.
implausible [ɪmˈplɔːzəbl] *adj* implausível.
implement [*n* ˈɪmplɪmənt, *vt* ˈɪmplɪment] ◇ *n* [tool] ferramenta *f*. ◇ *vt* implementar.
implementation [ˌɪmplɪmenˈteɪʃn] *n (U)* implementação *f*.
implicate [ˈɪmplɪkeɪt] *vt*: **to ~ sb in sthg** implicar alguém em algo.
implication [ˌɪmplɪˈkeɪʃn] *n* **-1.** *(U)* [involvement] implicação *f*, envolvimento *m* **-2.** [inference] implicação *f*; **by ~** por conseqüência.
implicit [ɪmˈplɪsɪt] *adj* **-1.** [inferred] implícito(ta) **-2.** [inherent]: **~ in sthg** inerente a algo **-3.** [complete] absoluto(ta).
implicitly [ɪmˈplɪsɪtlɪ] *adv* **-1.** [by inference] implicitamente **-2.** [completely] absolutamente.
implied [ɪmˈplaɪd] *adj* subentendido(da).
implode [ɪmˈpləʊd] *vi* implodir.
implore [ɪmˈplɔː^r] *vt*: **to ~ sb (to do sthg)** implorar a alguém (para que faça algo).
imply [ɪmˈplaɪ] (*pt* & *pp* **-ied**) *vt* **-1.** [suggest] pressupor **-2.** [involve] implicar.
impolite [ˌɪmpəˈlaɪt] *adj* descortês, indelicado(da).
imponderable [ɪmˈpɒndrəbl] *adj* imponderável.
◆ **imponderables** *npl* imponderáveis *mpl*.
import [*n* ˈɪmpɔːt, *vt* ɪmˈpɔːt] ◇ *n* **-1.** COMM importação *f* **-2.** *fml* [meaning] significado *m*, sentido *m* **-3.** *(U) fml* [importance] importância *f*. ◇ *comp* de importação. ◇ *vt* importar.
importance [ɪmˈpɔːtns] *n (U)* importância *f*.
important [ɪmˈpɔːtnt] *adj* importante; **to be ~ to sb** ser importante para alguém.
importantly [ɪmˈpɔːtntlɪ] *adv*: **more ~** o que é mais importante.
importation [ˌɪmpɔːˈteɪʃn] *n (U)* importação *f*.
imported [ɪmˈpɔːtɪd] *adj* importado(da).
importer [ɪmˈpɔːtə^r] *n* importador *m*, -ra *f*.
impose [ɪmˈpəʊz] ◇ *vt* [force]: **to ~ sthg (on sb/sthg)** impor algo (a alguém/algo). ◇ *vi* [cause trouble]: **to ~ (on sb)** causar problemas (para alguém).
imposing [ɪmˈpəʊzɪŋ] *adj* imponente.
imposition [ˌɪmpəˈzɪʃn] *n* imposição *f*.
impossibility [ɪmˌpɒsəˈbɪlətɪ] (*pl* **-ies**) *n* impossibilidade *f*.
impossible [ɪmˈpɒsəbl] ◇ *adj* impossível. ◇ *n*: **to do the ~** fazer o impossível.
impostor, imposter *US* [ɪmˈpɒstə^r] *n* impostor *m*, -ra *f*.
impotence [ˈɪmpətəns] *n* impotência *f*.
impotent [ˈɪmpətənt] *adj* impotente.
impound [ɪmˈpaʊnd] *vt* JUR apreender.
impoverished [ɪmˈpɒvərɪʃt] *adj lit & fig* empobrecido(da).
impracticable [ɪmˈpræktɪkəbl] *adj* impraticável.
impractical [ɪmˈpræktɪkl] *adj* pouco prático(ca).
imprecation [ˌɪmprɪˈkeɪʃn] *n fml* imprecação *f*.
imprecise [ˌɪmprɪˈsaɪs] *adj* impreciso(sa).
impregnable [ɪmˈpregnəbl] *adj* **-1.** [impenetrable] invulnerável **-2.** *fig* [in very strong position] imbatível.
impregnate [ˈɪmpregneɪt] *vt* **-1.** [introduce substance into]: **to ~ sthg with sthg** impregnar algo de algo **-2.** *fml* [fertilize] fecundar.
impresario [ˌɪmprɪˈsɑːrɪəʊ] (*pl* **-s**) *n* empresário *m*, -ria *f* teatral.
impress [ɪmˈpres] ◇ *vt* **-1.** [influence, affect] impressionar **-2.** [make clear]: **to ~ sthg on sb** convencer alguém da importância de algo. ◇ *vi* impressionar.
impression [ɪmˈpreʃn] *n* **-1.** [gen] impressão *f*; **to make an ~** impressionar; **to be under the ~ (that)** ter a impressão de que **-2.** [impersonation] imitação *f*.
impressionable [ɪmˈpreʃnəbl] *adj* impressionável.
Impressionism *n (U)* ART Impressionismo *m*.
impressionist [ɪmˈpreʃənɪst] *n* [entertainer] imitador *m*, -ra *f*.
◆ **Impressionist** ART ◇ *adj* impressionista. ◇ *n* impressionista *mf*.
impressive [ɪmˈpresɪv] *adj* impressionante.
imprint [ˈɪmprɪnt] ◇ *n* **-1.** [mark] marca *f*, impressão *f* **-2.** [publisher's name] ≃ selo *m* da editora. ◇ *vt* [mark] imprimir, marcar.
imprinted [ɪmˈprɪntɪd] *adj* **-1.** [marked] marcado(da) **-2.** *fig* [on mind, memory]: **~ on sthg** impresso(sa) em algo, marcado(da) em algo.
imprison [ɪmˈprɪzn] *vt* [put in prison] aprisionar.
imprisonment [ɪmˈprɪznmənt] *n (U)* aprisionamento *m*.

improbable [ɪm'prɒbəbl] *adj* **-1.** [unlikely] improvável **-2.** [strange] estranho(nha).
impromptu [ɪm'prɒmptju:] *adj* de improviso, improvisado(da).
improper [ɪm'prɒpə^r] *adj* **-1.** [unsuitable] inadequado(da) **-2.** [dishonest] desonesto(ta) **-3.** [rude, shocking] impróprio(pria).
impropriety [ɪmprə'praɪətɪ] *n* indecoro *m*.
improve [ɪm'pru:v] <> *vi* [get better] melhorar; **to ~ (up)on sthg** melhorar algo. <> *vt* **-1.** [gen] melhorar **-2.** [cultivate] desenvolver.
improved [ɪm'pru:vd] *adj* [better] melhorado(da).
improvement [ɪm'pru:vmənt] *n* melhoria *f*; **~ in/on sthg** melhoria em algo.
improvisation [ˌɪmprəvaɪ'zeɪʃn] *n* improvisação *f*.
improvise ['ɪmprəvaɪz] *vt* & *vi* improvisar.
imprudent [ɪm'pru:dənt] *adj* imprudente.
impudence *n* impudência *f*.
impudent ['ɪmpjʊdənt] *adj* impudente.
impugn [ɪm'pju:n] *vt fml* impugnar.
impulse ['ɪmpʌls] *n* impulso *m*; **on ~** sem pensar.
impulse buying [-'baɪɪŋ] *n (U)* compra *f* impulsiva.
impulsive [ɪm'pʌlsɪv] *adj* impulsivo(va).
impunity [ɪm'pju:nətɪ] *n* impunidade *f*; **with ~** impunemente.
impure [ɪm'pjʊə^r] *adj* impuro(ra).
impurity [ɪm'pjʊərətɪ] (*pl* **-ies**) *n* impureza *f*.
IMRO ['ɪmrəʊ] (*abbr of* **Investment Management Regulatory Organization**) *n órgão britânico regulador de empresas que lidam com fundos de investimento e pensões.*
in [ɪn] *prep* **-1.** [indicating place, position] em; **it comes ~ a box** vem numa caixa; **~ the hospital** no hospital; **~ Scotland** na Escócia; **~ Boston** em Boston; **~ the middle** no meio; **~ the sun/rain** no sol/na chuva; **~ here/there** aqui/ali (dentro); **~ front** à frente. **-2.** [appearing in] em; **who's ~ the play?** quem está na peça? **-3.** [indicating arrangement] em; **they come ~ packs of three** vêm em embalagens de três; **~ a row** em fila; **cut it ~ half** corte-o ao meio. **-4.** [during]: **~ April** em abril; **~ the afternoon** à OR de tarde; **~ the morning** de manhã; **ten o'clock ~ the morning** dez (horas) da manhã; **~ 1994** em 1994; **~ summer/winter** no verão/inverno. **-5.** [within] em; [after] dentro de, daqui a; **it'll be ready ~ an hour** estará pronto daqui a OR dentro de uma hora; **she did everything ~ ten minutes** ela fez tudo em dez minutos; **they're arriving ~ two weeks** chegam dentro de OR daqui a duas semanas. **-6.** [indicating means]: **~ writing** por escrito; **they were talking ~ English** estavam falando (em) inglês; **write ~ ink** escreva a tinta. **-7.** [wearing] de; **dressed ~ red** vestido de vermelho; **the man ~ the blue suit** o homem com o terno azul. **-8.** [indicating state] em; **to be ~ a hurry** estar com pressa; **to be ~ pain** ter dores; **to cry out ~ pain** gritar de dor OR com dores; **~ ruins** em ruínas; **~ good health** com boa saúde. **-9.** [with regard to] de; **a rise ~ prices** uma subida dos preços; **to be 50 meters ~ length** ter 50 metros de comprimento. **-10.** [with numbers]: **one ~ ten** um em cada dez. **-11.** [indicating age]: **she's ~ her twenties** ela está na casa dos vinte. **-12.** [with colours]: **it comes ~ green or blue** vem em verde ou azul. **-13.** [with superlatives] de; **the best ~ the world** o melhor do mundo. <> *adv* **-1.** [inside] dentro; **you can go ~ now** pode entrar agora. **-2.** [at home, work]: **she's not ~** (ela) não está; **to stay ~** ficar em casa. **-3.** [train, bus, plane]: **the train's not ~ yet** o trem ainda não chegou. **-4.** [tide]: **the tide is ~** a maré está cheia. <> *adj inf* [fashionable] na moda, in *(inv)*.
in. *abbr of* **inch**.
IN *abbr of* **Indiana**.
inability [ˌɪnə'bɪlətɪ] *n* incapacidade *f*; **~ to do sthg** incapacidade para fazer algo.
inaccessible [ˌɪnək'sesəbl] *adj* inacessível.
inaccuracy [ɪn'ækjʊrəsɪ] (*pl* **-ies**) *n* imprecisão *f*.
inaccurate [ɪn'ækjʊrət] *adj* impreciso(sa).
inaction [ɪn'ækʃn] *n* inação *f*.
inactive [ɪn'æktɪv] *adj* inativo(va).
inactivity [ˌɪnæk'tɪvətɪ] *n (U)* inatividade *f*.
inadequacy [ɪn'ædɪkwəsɪ] (*pl* **-ies**) *n* **-1.** *(U)* [state of being inadequate] insuficiência *f* **-2.** [weakness - of system] imperfeição *f*; [- of person] incapacidade *f*.
inadequate [ɪn'ædɪkwət] *adj* **-1.** [insufficient] insuficiente **-2.** [person] incapaz.
inadmissible [ˌɪnəd'mɪsəbl] *adj* inadmissível.
inadvertent [ˌɪnəd'vɜ:tnt] *adj* acidental.
inadvertently [ˌɪnəd'vɜ:təntlɪ] *adv* acidentalmente.
inadvisable [ˌɪnəd'vaɪzəbl] *adj* desaconselhável.
inalienable [ɪn'eɪljənəbl] *adj fml* inalienável.
inane [ɪ'neɪn] *adj* vazio(zia), fútil.
inanely [ɪ'neɪnlɪ] *adv* futilmente.
inanimate [ɪn'ænɪmət] *adj* inanimado(da).
inanity [ɪ'nænətɪ] *n (U)* futilidade *f*.
inapplicable [ˌɪnə'plɪkəbl] *adj* inaplicável.
inappropriate [ˌɪnə'prəʊprɪət] *adj* inapropriado(da).
inarticulate [ˌɪnɑ:'tɪkjʊlət] *adj* **-1.** [person] incapaz de se expressar (bem) **-2.** [words, sounds] inarticulado(da).
inasmuch [ˌɪnəz'mʌtʃ] ◆ **inasmuch as** *conj fml* [because] visto que; [to the extent that] na medida em que.
inattention [ˌɪnə'tenʃn] *n (U)* desatenção *f*; **~ to sthg** desatenção a algo.
inattentive [ˌɪnə'tentɪv] *adj* desatento(ta); **~ to sthg** desatento(ta) a algo.
inaudible [ɪ'nɔ:dɪbl] *adj* inaudível.
inaugural [ɪ'nɔ:gjʊrəl] *adj* [opening] inaugural.
inaugurate [ɪ'nɔ:gjʊreɪt] *vt* **-1.** [leader, president] empossar **-2.** [building, system] inaugurar.
inauguration [ɪˌnɔ:gjʊ'reɪʃn] *n* **-1.** [of leader, president] posse *f* **-2.** [of building, system] inauguração *f*.
inauspicious [ˌɪnɔ:'spɪʃəs] *adj* de mau agouro, pouco propício(cia).
in-between *adj* intermediário(ria).
inboard *adj* interno(na).
inborn [ˌɪn'bɔ:n] *adj* inato(ta).
inbound ['ɪnbaʊnd] *adj* **US**: **an ~ ship** um navio que se aproxima; **the ~ flight from Miami** o vôo que chega de Miami.

inbred [ˌɪnˈbred] *adj* **-1.** [family, group] endogâmico(-ca), consangüíneo(nea) **-2.** [characteristic, quality] inato(ta).
inbreeding [ˈɪnˌbriːdɪŋ] *n (U)* endogamia *f*.
inbuilt [ˌɪnˈbɪlt] *adj* **-1.** [device] embutido(da), incorporado(da) **-2.** [quality, defect] inerente.
inc. (*abbr of* **inclusive**) inclusive.
Inc. [ɪŋk] (*abbr of* **incorporated**) ≃ S.A.
Inca [ˈɪŋkə] ◇ *adj* inca. ◇ *n* inca *mf*.
incalculable [ɪnˈkælkjʊləbl] *adj* [very great] incalculável.
incandescent [ˌɪnkænˈdesnt] *adj lit* incandescente ; *fig* [with rage] vermelho(lha).
incantation [ˌɪnkænˈteɪʃn] *n* **-1.** [magic words] palavras *fpl* mágicas **-2.** [spell] feitiço *m*.
incapable [ɪnˈkeɪpəbl] *adj* **-1.** [unable]: **to be ~ of sthg/of doing sthg** ser incapaz de algo/de fazer algo **-2.** [incompetent] incompetente.
incapacitate [ˌɪnkəˈpæsɪteɪt] *vt* incapacitar.
incapacitated [ˌɪnkəˈpæsɪteɪtɪd] *adj* incapacitado(-da).
incapacity [ˌɪnkəˈpæsətɪ] *n (U)* incapacidade *f*; **~ for sthg** incapacidade para algo.
incarcerate [ɪnˈkɑːsəreɪt] *vt fml* encarcerar.
incarceration [ɪnˌkɑːsəˈreɪʃn] *n (U) fml* encarceramento *m*.
incarnate [ɪnˈkɑːneɪt] *adj* encarnado(da); **he is generosity ~** ele é a generosidade em pessoa.
incarnation [ˌɪnkɑːˈneɪʃn] *n* encarnação *f*.
incendiary device [ɪnˈsendjərɪ-] *n* artefato *m* incendiário.
incense [*n* ˈɪnsens, *vt* ɪnˈsens] ◇ *n (U)* [perfume] incenso *m*. ◇ *vt* [anger] enfurecer, enraivecer.
incentive [ɪnˈsentɪv] *n* incentivo *m*.
incentive scheme *n* plano *m* de incentivos.
inception [ɪnˈsepʃn] *n fml* começo *m*, origem *f*.
incessant [ɪnˈsesnt] *adj* incessante.
incessantly [ɪnˈsesntlɪ] *adv* incessantemente.
incest [ˈɪnsest] *n* incesto *m*.
incestuous [ɪnˈsestjʊəs] *adj* **-1.** [sexual] incestuoso(-sa) **-2.** *fig* [too close] fechado em si mesmo, fechada em si mesma.
inch [ɪntʃ] ◇ *n* polegada *f*. ◇ *vi* avançar gradualmente.
incidence [ˈɪnsɪdəns] *n* incidência *f*.
incident [ˈɪnsɪdənt] *n* [occurrence, event] incidente *m*.
incidental [ˌɪnsɪˈdentl] *adj* [minor] acessório(ria), secundário(ria).
incidentally [ˌɪnsɪˈdentəlɪ] *adv* **-1.** [by chance] por acaso **-2.** [by the way] a propósito.
incidental music *n* música *f* de fundo.
incinerate [ɪnˈsɪnəreɪt] *vt* incinerar.
incinerator [ɪnˈsɪnəreɪtə^r] *n* incinerador *m*.
incipient [ɪnˈsɪpɪənt] *adj fml* incipiente.
incision [ɪnˈsɪʒn] *n fml* incisão *f*.
incisive [ɪnˈsaɪsɪv] *adj* incisivo(va).
incisor [ɪnˈsaɪzə^r] *n* incisivo *m*.
incite [ɪnˈsaɪt] *vt* incitar; **to ~ sb to do sthg** incitar alguém a fazer algo.
incitement [ɪnˈsaɪtmənt] *n (U)* incitamento *m*; **~ to sthg/to do sthg** incitamento a algo/a fazer algo.
incl. **-1.** (*abbr of* **including**) incluindo **-2.** (*abbr of* **inclusive**) inclusive.
inclement [ɪnˈklemənt] *adj fml* [weather] inclemente.
inclination [ˌɪnklɪˈneɪʃn] *n* **-1.** *(U)* [liking, preference] vontade *f* **-2.** [tendency]: **~ to do sthg** tendência *f* OR inclinação *f* para fazer algo.
incline [*n* ˈɪnklaɪn, *vb* ɪnˈklaɪn] ◇ *n* [slope] ladeira *f*. ◇ *vt* [lean, bend] inclinar. ◇ *vi* [tend]: **to ~ to sthg** tender para algo.
inclined [ɪnˈklaɪnd] *adj* **-1.** [tending] inclinado(da), propenso(sa); **to be ~ to sthg** estar propenso(sa) a algo; **to be ~ to do sthg** estar inclinado(da) a fazer algo **-2.** [wanting, willing]: **to be ~ to do sthg** estar disposto(ta) a fazer algo **-3.** [sloping] inclinado(da).
include [ɪnˈkluːd] *vt* **-1.** [contain] abranger **-2.** [add, count] incluir.
included [ɪnˈkluːdɪd] *adj* incluído(da).
including [ɪnˈkluːdɪŋ] *prep* inclusive; **six died, ~ a child** seis morreram, incluindo uma criança.
inclusion [ɪnˈkluːʒn] *n* inclusão *f*.
inclusive [ɪnˈkluːsɪv] *adj* inclusive; **1 to 9, ~** de um a nove, inclusive; **£150 ~** £150, tudo incluído; **~ of** incluindo.
incognito [ˌɪnkɒgˈniːtəʊ] *adv* incógnito(ta).
incoherent [ˌɪnkəʊˈhɪərənt] *adj* incoerente.
income [ˈɪŋkʌm] *n* **-1.** [earnings] renda *f* **-2.** [profit] lucro *m*.
incomes policy *n UK* política *f* de rendimentos.
income support *n UK auxílio dado pelo governo a pessoas desempregadas ou de renda muito baixa.*
income tax *n* imposto *m* de renda.
incoming [ˈɪnˌkʌmɪŋ] *adj* **-1.** [tide] ascendente **-2.** [plane, passengers] de chegada **-3.** [mail, report, phone call] recebido(da) **-4.** [government, official] novo(va).
incommunicado [ˌɪnkəmjuːnɪˈkɑːdəʊ] *adv* incomunicável.
incomparable [ɪnˈkɒmpərəbl] *adj* incomparável.
incompatible [ˌɪnkəmˈpætɪbl] *adj* incompatível; **~ with sb/sthg** incompatível com alguém/algo.
incompetence [ɪnˈkɒmpɪtəns] *n (U)* incompetência *f*.
incompetent [ɪnˈkɒmpɪtənt] *adj* incompetente.
incomplete [ˌɪnkəmˈpliːt] *adj* incompleto(ta).
incomprehensible [ɪnˌkɒmprɪˈhensəbl] *adj* incompreensível.
inconceivable [ˌɪnkənˈsiːvəbl] *adj* inconcebível.
inconclusive [ˌɪnkənˈkluːsɪv] *adj* **-1.** [meeting, outcome, debate] sem conclusões claras **-2.** [evidence, argument] pouco convincente.
incongruous [ɪnˈkɒŋgrʊəs] *adj* incongruente.
inconsequential [ˌɪnkɒnsɪˈkwenʃl] *adj* [insignificant] insignificante.
inconsiderable [ˌɪnkənˈsɪdərəbl] *adj*: **not ~** nada desprezível.
inconsiderate [ˌɪnkənˈsɪdərət] *adj* **-1.** [attitude, treatment] impensado(da), irrefletido(da) **-2.** [person] sem consideração.
inconsistency [ˌɪnkənˈsɪstənsɪ] (*pl* **-ies**) *n* **-1.** *(U)*

[state of being inconsistent] inconsistência *f* **-2.** [contradictory point] contradição *f.*

inconsistent [ˌɪnkənˈsɪstənt] *adj* **-1.** [not agreeing, contradictory] inconsistente; **~ with sthg** contraditório(ria) com algo **-2.** [erratic] irregular.

inconsolable [ˌɪnkənˈsəʊləbl] *adj* inconsolável.

inconspicuous [ˌɪnkənˈspɪkjʊəs] *adj* discreto(ta).

incontinence [ɪnˈkɒntɪnəns] *n (U)* incontinência *f.*

incontinent [ɪnˈkɒntɪnənt] *adj* incontinente.

incontrovertible [ˌɪnkɒntrəˈvɜːtəbl] *adj* incontestável.

inconvenience [ˌɪnkənˈviːnjəns] <> *n* **-1.** *(U)* [difficulty, discomfort] incômodo *m* **-2.** [inconvenient thing] inconveniência *f.* <> *vt* incomodar.

inconvenient [ˌɪnkənˈviːnjənt] *adj* incoveniente.

incorporate [ɪnˈkɔːpəreɪt] *vt* **-1.** [include] incorporar; **to ~ sb/sthg in (to) sthg** incluir alguém/algo em algo **-2.** [blend] combinar.

incorporated company *n* COMM sociedade *f* anônima.

incorporation [ɪnˌkɔːpəˈreɪʃn] *n* **-1.** [integration] integração *f* **-2.** COMM [of company] incorporação *f.*

incorrect [ˌɪnkəˈrekt] *adj* incorreto(ta).

incorrigible [ɪnˈkɒrɪdʒəbl] *adj* incorrigível.

incorruptible [ˌɪnkəˈrʌptəbl] *adj* [person] incorruptível.

increase [*n* ˈɪnkriːs, *vb* ɪnˈkriːs] <> *n*: **~ (in sthg)** aumento *m* (de algo); **to be on the ~** estar aumentando, estar em crescimento. <> *vt* & *vi* aumentar.

increased [ɪnˈkriːst] *adj* intensificado(da), em crescimento.

increasing [ɪnˈkriːsɪŋ] *adj* crescente.

increasingly [ɪnˈkriːsɪŋlɪ] *adv* cada vez mais.

incredible [ɪnˈkredəbl] *adj inf* incrível.

incredulous [ɪnˈkredjʊləs] *adj* incrédulo(la).

increment [ˈɪnkrɪmənt] *n* incremento *m.*

incriminate [ɪnˈkrɪmɪneɪt] *vt* incriminar; **to ~ o.s.** incriminar-se.

incriminating [ɪnˈkrɪmɪneɪtɪŋ] *adj* incriminatório(ria).

incrusted *adj* = **encrusted**.

incubate [ˈɪnkjʊbeɪt] *vt* & *vi* **-1.** [gen] incubar **-2.** [egg] chocar.

incubation [ˌɪnkjʊˈbeɪʃn] *n* incubação *f.*

incubator [ˈɪnkjʊbeɪtə^r] *n* [for baby] incubadora *f.*

inculcate [ˈɪnkʌlkeɪt] *vt fml*: **to ~ sthg in (to) sb** inculcar algo em alguém.

incumbent [ɪnˈkʌmbənt] *fml* <> *adj*: **to be ~ (up)on sb to do sthg** incumbir alguém de fazer algo. <> *n* [postholder] titular *mf.*

incur [ɪnˈkɜː^r] (*pt* & *pp* **-red**, *cont* **-ring**) *vt* **-1.** [wrath, criticism] incorrer em **-2.** [expenses] contrair.

incurable [ɪnˈkjʊərəbl] *adj lit & fig* incurável.

incursion [*UK* ɪnˈkɜːʃn, *US* ɪnˈkɜːʒn] *n* MIL incursão *f*; *fig* [unwelcome] invasão *f.*

indebted [ɪnˈdetɪd] *adj* **-1.** [grateful]: **to be ~ to sb** estar em dívida com alguém **-2.** [owing money]: **to be ~ to sb** estar devendo a alguém.

indecency [ɪnˈdiːsnsɪ] *n (U)* indecência *f.*

indecent [ɪnˈdiːsnt] *adj* **-1.** [obscene] indecente **-2.** [unreasonable] inadequado(da).

indecent assault *n* atentado *m* contra o pudor.

indecent exposure *n (U)* ato *m* obsceno.

indecipherable [ˌɪndɪˈsaɪfərəbl] *adj* indecifrável.

indecision [ˌɪndɪˈsɪʒn] *n (U)* indecisão *f.*

indecisive [ˌɪndɪˈsaɪsɪv] *adj* indeciso(sa).

indeed [ɪnˈdiːd] *adv* **-1.** [certainly] realmente, certamente **-2.** [in fact] na verdade **-3.** [for emphasis] realmente; **very big ~** estupidamente grande; **very few ~** pouquíssimos(mas) **-4.** [to express surprise, disbelief] mesmo; **~?** é mesmo?

indefatigable [ˌɪndɪˈfætɪgəbl] *adj* incansável.

indefensible [ˌɪndɪˈfensəbl] *adj* [behaviour, argument] indefensável.

indefinable [ˌɪndɪˈfaɪnəbl] *adj* indefinível.

indefinite [ɪnˈdefɪnɪt] *adj* **-1.** [indeterminate] indefinido(da) **-2.** [imprecise] impreciso(sa).

indefinitely [ɪnˈdefɪnətlɪ] *adv* [for indeterminate period] indefinidamente.

indelible [ɪnˈdeləbl] *adj* **-1.** [gen] indelével **-2.** [memory] que não se pode apagar.

indelicate [ɪnˈdelɪkət] *adj* indelicado(da).

indemnify [ɪnˈdemnɪfaɪ] (*pt* & *pp* **-ied**) *vt* **-1.** [insure]: **to ~ sb for** OR **against sthg** segurar alguém contra algo **-2.** [compensate]: **to ~ sb for sthg** indenizar alguém por algo.

indemnity [ɪnˈdemnətɪ] *n* **-1.** *(U)* [insurance] garantia *f* **-2.** [compensation] indenização *f.*

indent [ɪnˈdent] *vt* **-1.** [text] recuar **-2.** [edge, surface] recortar.

indentation [ˌɪndenˈteɪʃn] *n* **-1.** [in text] recuo *m* de parágrafo novo **-2.** [in edge, coastline, surface] reentrância *f.*

indenture [ɪnˈdentʃə^r] *n* contrato *m* de aprendizagem.

independence [ˌɪndɪˈpendəns] *n* independência *f.*

Independence Day *n festa nos Estados Unidos em comemoração à sua independência, no dia 4 de julho em 1776.*

independent [ˌɪndɪˈpendənt] *adj* independente; **~ of sb/sthg** independente de alguém/algo.

independently [ˌɪndɪˈpendəntlɪ] *adv* **-1.** [govern, rule] independentemente; **~ of sb/sthg** independentemente de alguém/algo **-2.** [live, think, act] de forma independente.

independent school *n UK* escola *f* privada.

in-depth *adj* em profundidade, exaustivo(va).

indescribable [ˌɪndɪˈskraɪbəbl] *adj* indescritível.

indestructible [ˌɪndɪˈstrʌktəbl] *adj* indestrutível.

indeterminate [ˌɪndɪˈtɜːmɪnət] *adj* [indefinite] indeterminado(da).

index [ˈɪndeks] (*pl senses 1 and 2* **-es**, *pl sense 3* **-es** OR **indices**) <> *n* **-1.** [of book] índice *m* remissivo **-2.** [in library] catálogo *m* **-3.** ECON [value system] índice *m.* <> *vt* **-1.** [book] acrescentar índice remissivo a **-2.** [econ] indexar.

index card *n* ficha *f* de indexação.

index finger *n* (dedo *m*) indicador *m.*

index-linked [-lɪŋkt] *adj* indexado(da).

India [ˈɪndjə] *n* Índia; **in ~** na Índia.

India ink *n US* = **Indian ink**.

Indian [ˈɪndjən] <> *adj* **-1.** [from India] indiano(na) **-2.** [from the Americas] índio(dia). <> *n* **-1.** [from India] indiano *m*, -na *f* **-2.** [from the Americas] índio *m*, -dia *f*.

Indiana [ˌɪndɪ'ænəl] *n* Indiana; **in ~** em Indiana.

Indian ink *UK*, **India ink** *US* *n* (tinta *f*) nanquim *m*.

Indian Ocean *n*: **the ~** o Oceano Índico.

Indian summer *n* [warm weather] veranico *m*.

india rubber *n* borracha *f*.

indicate ['ɪndɪkeɪt] <> *vt* **-1.** [gen] indicar **-2.** [suggest] sugerir. <> *vi* [when driving]: **to ~ left/right** sinalizar à esquerda/direita.

indication [ˌɪndɪ'keɪʃn] *n* **-1.** [suggestion] indicação *f* **-2.** [sign] indício *m*.

indicative [ɪn'dɪkətɪv] <> *adj*: **~ of sthg** indicativo(va) de algo. <> *n* *GRAM* indicativo *m*.

indicator ['ɪndɪkeɪtə^r] *n* **-1.** [sign] indicador *m* **-2.** [on car] pisca-pisca *m*.

indices ['ɪndɪsi:z] *pl* ▷ **index**.

indict [ɪn'daɪt] *vt* indiciar; **to ~ sb for sthg** indiciar alguém por algo.

indictable [ɪn'daɪtəbl] *adj* passível de ser indiciado(da).

indictment [ɪn'daɪtmənt] *n* **-1.** *JUR* indiciamento *m* **-2.** [criticism] crítica *f* dura.

indie ['ɪndɪ] *adj inf* independente.

indifference [ɪn'dɪfrəns] *n (U)* indiferença *f*.

indifferent [ɪn'dɪfrənt] *adj* **-1.** [uninterested] indiferente; **~ to sthg** indiferente a algo **-2.** [mediocre] medíocre.

indigenous [ɪn'dɪdʒɪnəs] *adj* nativo(va), indígena.

indigestible [ˌɪndɪ'dʒestəbl] *adj* **-1.** [food] indigesto(ta) **-2.** [facts] incompreensível.

indigestion [ˌɪndɪ'dʒestʃn] *n (U)* indigestão *f*.

indignant [ɪn'dɪgnənt] *adj* indignado(da); **to be ~ at sthg** estar indignado(da) com algo.

indignantly [ɪn'dɪgnəntlɪ] *adv* com indignação.

indignation [ˌɪndɪg'neɪʃn] *n (U)* indignação *f*.

indignity [ɪn'dɪgnətɪ] (*pl* **-ies**) *n* **-1.** *(U)* [feeling of humiliation] afronta *f* **-2.** [humiliating situation] indignidade *f*.

indigo ['ɪndɪgəʊ] <> *adj* [in colour] da cor de anil. <> *n* [colour] anil *m*.

indirect [ˌɪndɪ'rekt] *adj* indireto(ta).

indirect costs *npl* gastos *mpl* indiretos.

indirect lighting *n* luz *f* *OR* iluminação *f* indireta.

indirectly [ˌɪndɪ'rektlɪ] *adv* indiretamente.

indirect speech *n* *GRAM* discurso *m* indireto.

indirect taxation *n* impostos *mpl* indiretos.

indiscreet [ˌɪndɪ'skri:t] *adj* indiscreto(ta); [tactless] indelicado(da).

indiscretion [ˌɪndɪ'skreʃn] *n* indiscrição *f*.

indiscriminate [ˌɪndɪ'skrɪmɪnət] *adj* indiscriminado(da).

indiscriminately [ˌɪndɪ'skrɪmɪnətlɪ] *adv* indiscriminadamente.

indispensable [ˌɪndɪ'spensəbl] *adj* indispensável.

indisposed [ˌɪndɪ'spəʊzd] *adj fml* [unwell] indisposto(ta).

indisputable [ˌɪndɪ'spju:təbl] *adj* inquestionável.

indistinct [ˌɪndɪ'stɪŋkt] *adj* **-1.** [words] indistinto(ta) **-2.** [memory] confuso(sa) **-3.** [picture, marking] borrado(da).

indistinguishable [ˌɪndɪ'stɪŋgwɪʃəbl] *adj* indistinguível; **~ from sb/sthg** indistinguível de alguém/algo.

individual [ˌɪndɪ'vɪdʒʊəl] <> *adj* **-1.** [gen] individual **-2.** [private] particular **-3.** [distinctive] pessoal. <> *n* indivíduo *m*.

individualist [ˌɪndɪ'vɪdʒʊəlɪst] *n* individualista *mf*.

individualistic ['ɪndɪˌvɪdʒʊə'lɪstɪk] *adj* individualista.

individuality ['ɪndɪˌvɪdʒʊ'ælətɪ] *n (U)* individualidade *f*.

individually [ˌɪndɪ'vɪdʒʊəlɪ] *adv* [separately] individualmente.

indivisible [ˌɪndɪ'vɪzəbl] *adj* indivisível.

Indochina [ˌɪndəʊ'tʃaɪnə] *n* Indochina; **in ~** na Indochina.

indoctrinate [ɪn'dɒktrɪneɪt] *vt* doutrinar.

indoctrination [ɪnˌdɒktrɪ'neɪʃn] *n (U)* doutrinação *f*.

indolent ['ɪndələnt] *adj fml* indolente.

indomitable [ɪn'dɒmɪtəbl] *adj* indomável.

Indonesia [ˌɪndə'ni:zjə] *n* Indonésia; **in ~** na Indonésia.

Indonesian [ˌɪndə'ni:zjən] <> *adj* indonésio(sia). <> *n* **-1.** [person] indonésio *m*, -sia *f* **-2.** [language] indonésio *m*.

indoor ['ɪndɔ:^r] *adj* **-1.** [plant] de interior **-2.** [shoes] para dentro de casa **-3.** [sports] em local coberto; **~ swimming pool** piscina *f* coberta.

indoors [ˌɪn'dɔ:z] *adv* dentro de casa; **to go ~** entrar, ir para dentro.

indubitably [ɪn'dju:bɪtəblɪ] *adv* indubitavelmente, sem dúvida.

induce [ɪn'dju:s] *vt*: **to ~ sb to do sthg** induzir alguém a fazer algo.

inducement [ɪn'dju:smənt] *n* [incentive] estímulo *m*, incentivo *m*.

induction [ɪn'dʌkʃn] *n* **-1.** [into official position]: **~ into sthg** posse *m* em algo **-2.** *(U)* *MED, ELEC* indução *f* **-3.** [introduction to job] apresentação *f*.

induction course *n* curso *m* de integração *OR* de iniciação.

indulge [ɪn'dʌldʒ] <> *vt* **-1.** [whim, passion] satisfazer **-2.** [child, person] fazer a vontade de; **to ~ o.s.** permitir-se um luxo. <> *vi*: **to ~ in sthg** permitir-se algo.

indulgence [ɪn'dʌldʒəns] *n* **-1.** *(U)* [tolerance, kindness] indulgência *f* **-2.** [special treat] vício *m*, prazer *m*.

indulgent [ɪn'dʌldʒənt] *adj* [liberal, kind] indulgente.

Indus *n*: **the (River) ~** o (Rio) Indus.

industrial [ɪn'dʌstrɪəl] *adj* **-1.** [of industry] industrial **-2.** [industrialized] industrializado(da).

industrial action *n*: **to take ~** declarar-se em greve.

industrial estate *UK*, **industrial park** *US* *n* parque *m* industrial.

industrial injury *n* acidente *m* de trabalho.

industrialist [ɪn'dʌstrɪəlɪst] *n* industrialista *mf*.

industrialization [ɪnˌdʌstrɪəlaɪ'zeɪʃn] *n* industrialização *f*.

industrialize, -ise [ɪn'dʌstrɪəlaɪz] <> *vt* industrializar. <> *vi* industrializar-se.

industrial park *n US* = **industrial estate.**
industrial relations *npl* relações *fpl* de trabalho.
industrial revolution *n* revolução *f* industrial.
industrial tribunal *n* justiça *f* do trabalho.
industrious [ɪnˈdʌstrɪəs] *adj* trabalhador(ra), diligente.
industry [ˈɪndəstrɪ] (*pl* **-ies**) *n* **-1.** [gen] indústria *f*; **the coal ~** o setor carvoeiro **-2.** *(U)* [hard work] laboriosidade *f*.
inebriated [ɪˈniːbrɪeɪtɪd] *adj fml* inebriado(da).
inedible [ɪnˈedɪbl] *adj* **-1.** [unpleasant to eat] não-comestível **-2.** [poisonous] venenoso(sa).
ineffective [ˌɪnɪˈfektɪv] *adj* ineficaz, inútil.
ineffectual [ˌɪnɪˈfektʃʊəl] *adj* ineficaz, inútil.
inefficiency [ˌɪnɪˈfɪʃnsɪ] *n (U)* ineficiência *f*.
inefficient [ˌɪnɪˈfɪʃnt] *adj* ineficiente.
inelegant [ɪnˈelɪgənt] *adj* deselegante.
ineligible [ɪnˈelɪdʒəbl] *adj* inelegível; **to be ~ for sthg** não estar qualificado(da) para algo.
inept [ɪˈnept] *adj* **-1.** [incompetent] inepto(ta); **~ at sthg** incapaz de algo **-2.** [clumsy] malfeito(ta).
ineptitude [ɪˈneptɪtjuːd] *n (U)* [incompetence] inépcia *f*, incompetência *f*.
inequality [ˌɪnɪˈkwɒlətɪ] (*pl* **-ies**) *n* desigualdade *f*.
inequitable [ɪnˈekwɪtəbl] *adj fml* injusto(ta).
ineradicable *adj fml* inextirpável.
inert [ɪˈnɜːt] *adj* inerte.
inertia [ɪˈnɜːʃə] *n* inércia *f*.
inertia-reel seat belt *n* cinto *m* de segurança retrátil.
inescapable [ˌɪnɪˈskeɪpəbl] *adj* inevitável.
inessential [ˌɪnɪˈsenʃl] *adj*: **~ (to sthg)** dispensável (para algo).
inestimable [ɪnˈestɪməbl] *adj fml* inestimável.
inevitable [ɪnˈevɪtəbl] <> *adj* inevitável. <> *n*: **the ~** o inevitável.
inevitably [ɪnˈevɪtəblɪ] *adv* inevitavelmente.
inexact [ˌɪnɪgˈzækt] *adj* inexato(ta).
inexcusable [ˌɪnɪkˈskjuːzəbl] *adj* imperdoável.
inexhaustible [ˌɪnɪgˈzɔːstəbl] *adj* inesgotável.
inexorable [ɪnˈeksərəbl] *adj fml* [unpreventable] inexorável.
inexorably [ɪnˈeksərəblɪ] *adv* inexoravelmente.
inexpensive [ˌɪnɪkˈspensɪv] *adj* barato(ta), econômico(ca).
inexperience [ˌɪnɪkˈspɪərɪəns] *n (U)* inexperiência *f*.
inexperienced [ˌɪnɪkˈspɪərɪənst] *adj* inexperiente.
inexpert [ɪnˈekspɜːt] *adj* inábil.
inexplicable [ˌɪnɪkˈsplɪkəbl] *adj* inexplicável.
inexplicably [ˌɪnɪkˈsplɪkəblɪ] *adv* inexplicavelmente.
inextricably [ˌɪnɪkˈstrɪkəblɪ] *adv* inextricavelmente.
infallible [ɪnˈfæləbl] *adj* infalível.
infamous [ˈɪnfəməs] *adj* infame.
infamy *n (U) fml* infâmia *f*.
infancy [ˈɪnfənsɪ] *n (U)* primeira infância *f*; **to be in its ~** *fig* estar engatinhando.
infant [ˈɪnfənt] *n* **-1.** [baby] bebê *m* **-2.** [young child] criança *f* pequena.
infantile [ˈɪnfəntaɪl] *adj* infantil.
infant mortality *n* mortalidade *f* infantil.
infantry [ˈɪnfəntrɪ] *n (U)* infantaria *f*.
infantryman [ˈɪnfəntrɪmən] (*pl* **-men** [-mən]) *n* soldado *m* de infantaria.
infant school *n UK na Grã-Bretanha, escola para crianças entre 5 e 7 anos.*
infatuated [ɪnˈfætjʊeɪtɪd] *adj*: **~ (with sb/sthg)** obcecado(da) (por alguém/algo).
infatuation [ɪnˌfætjʊˈeɪʃn] *n*: **~ (with sb/sthg)** obsessão *f* (por alguém/algo).
infect [ɪnˈfekt] *vt* **-1.** *MED* infectar; **to become ~ed** [wound] infeccionar; **to ~ sb with sthg** infectar alguém com algo **-2.** *fig* [spread to] contagiar.
infected [ɪnˈfektɪd] *adj* **-1.** [food, patient] infectado(-da); **~ with sthg** infectado(da) por algo **-2.** [wound] infeccionado(da).
infection [ɪnˈfekʃn] *n* **-1.** [disease] infecção *f* **-2.** *(U)* [spreading of germs] contágio *m*.
infectious [ɪnˈfekʃəs] *adj* **-1.** [disease] infeccioso(sa) **-2.** *fig* [feeling, laugh] contagioso(sa).
infer [ɪnˈfɜːʳ] (*pt* & *pp* **-red**, *cont* **-ring**) *vt* **-1.** [deduce]: **to ~ (that)** inferir que; **to ~ sthg (from sthg)** deduzir *OR* inferir algo (de algo) **-2.** *inf* [insinuate] insinuar.
inference [ˈɪnfrəns] *n* **-1.** [conclusion] conclusão *f* **-2.** *(U)* [deduction]: **by ~** por dedução.
inferior [ɪnˈfɪərɪəʳ] <> *adj* [gen] inferior; **~ to sb/sthg** inferior a alguém/algo. <> *n* [in status] inferior *mf*.
inferiority [ɪnˌfɪərɪˈɒrətɪ] *n (U)* inferioridade *f*.
inferiority complex *n* complexo *m* de inferioridade.
infernal *adj inf dated* infernal.
inferno [ɪnˈfɜːnəʊ] (*pl* **-s**) *n* inferno *m*, incêndio *m* incontrolável.
infertile [ɪnˈfɜːtaɪl] *adj* **-1.** [woman, animal] estéril **-2.** [soil] infértil.
infertility [ˌɪnfəˈtɪlətɪ] *n (U)* **-1.** [of woman, animal] esterilidade *f* **-2.** [of soil] infertilidade *f*.
infestation [ˌɪnfeˈsteɪʃn] *n* infestação *f*, praga *f*.
infested [ɪnˈfestɪd] *adj*: **~ with sthg** infestado(da) por algo.
infidelity [ˌɪnfɪˈdelətɪ] *n* [of partner] infidelidade *f*.
infighting [ˈɪnˌfaɪtɪŋ] *n (U)* disputa *f* interna.
infiltrate [ˈɪnfɪltreɪt] <> *vt* infiltrar. <> *vi*: **to ~ into sthg** infiltrar-se em algo.
infinite [ˈɪnfɪnət] *adj* infinito(ta).
infinitely [ˈɪnfɪnətlɪ] *adv* infinitamente.
infinitesimal [ˌɪnfɪnɪˈtesɪml] *adj* infinitesimal.
infinitive [ɪnˈfɪnɪtɪv] *n GRAM* infinitivo *m*.
infinity [ɪnˈfɪnətɪ] *n* **-1.** *(U)* [gen] infinito *m* **-2.** *MATH* [incalculable number] infinidade *f*.
infirm [ɪnˈfɜːm] <> *adj* [unhealthy] enfermo(ma). <> *npl*: **the ~** os enfermos.
infirmary [ɪnˈfɜːmərɪ] (*pl* **-ies**) *n* **-1.** [hospital] hospital *m* **-2.** [room] enfermaria *f*.
infirmity [ɪnˈfɜːmətɪ] (*pl* **-ies**) *n* enfermidade *f*.
inflamed [ɪnˈfleɪmd] *adj MED* inflamado(da).
inflammable [ɪnˈflæməbl] *adj* [burning easily] inflamável.
inflammation [ˌɪnfləˈmeɪʃn] *n MED* inflamação *f*.

inflammatory [ɪn'flæmətrɪ] *adj* [provocative] incendiante.
inflatable [ɪn'fleɪtəbl] *adj* inflável.
inflate [ɪn'fleɪt] *vt* **-1.** [fill with air] inflar **-2.** *ECON* [increase] inflacionar.
inflated [ɪn'fleɪtɪd] *adj* **-1.** [filled with air] inflado(da) **-2.** *pej* [exaggerated] exagerado(da) **-3.** *ECON* [unreasonably high] inflacionado(da).
inflation [ɪn'fleɪʃn] *n (U) ECON* inflação *f*.
inflationary [ɪn'fleɪʃnrɪ] *adj ECON* inflacionário(ria).
inflationary spiral *n* espiral *f* inflacionária.
inflation-proof *adj* que não é afetado(da) pela inflação.
inflation rate *n ECON* taxa *f* de inflação.
inflection *n GRAM* flexão *f*.
inflexible [ɪn'fleksəbl] *adj* **-1.** [gen] inflexível **-2.** [fixed] imutável.
inflict [ɪn'flɪkt] *vt*: **to ~ sthg on sb** infligir algo a alguém.
in-flight *adj* de bordo.
inflow ['ɪnfləʊ] *n* afluência *f*.
influence ['ɪnflʊəns] <> *n* **-1.** *(U)* [power]: **~ (on sb/sthg)**, **~ (over sb/sthg)** influência *f* (sobre alguém/algo); **under the ~ of** [person, group] sob a influência de; [alcohol, drugs] sob o efeito de **-2.** [influential person, thing]: **~ (on sb/sthg)** influência para alguém/algo. <> *vt* influenciar.
influential [,ɪnflʊ'enʃl] *adj* influente.
influenza [,ɪnflʊ'enzə] *n (U) fml* influenza *f*.
influx ['ɪnflʌks] *n* afluxo *m*.
info ['ɪnfəʊ] (*abbr of* **information**) *n (U) inf* info *f*.
inform [ɪn'fɔ:m] *vt* informar; **to ~ sb of/about sthg** informar alguém de/sobre algo.
◆ **inform on** *vt fus* denunciar, delatar.
informal [ɪn'fɔ:ml] *adj* informal.
informally [ɪn'fɔ:məlɪ] *adv* informalmente.
informant [ɪn'fɔ:mənt] *n* informante *mf*.
information [,ɪnfə'meɪʃn] *n (U)* informações *fpl*; **to give sb ~** dar informações a alguém; **to get ~** obter informações; **that's a useful piece of ~** esta é uma informação útil; **to have some ~ on** *OR* **about sthg** ter alguma informação sobre algo; **'Information'** 'Informações'; **for your ~** para seu conhecimento.
information desk *n* (balcão *m* de) informações *fpl*.
information office *n* (balcão *m* de) informações *fpl*.
information retrieval *n* recuperação *f* de informações.
information technology *n* tecnologia *f* da informação.
informative [ɪn'fɔ:mətɪv] *adj* instrutivo(va).
informed [ɪn'fɔ:md] *adj* **-1.** [having information] informado(da) **-2.** [based on good information] bem-informado(da); **~ guess** conjectura *f* bem-fundamentada.
informer [ɪn'fɔ:mə^r] *n* [denouncer] informante *mf*, delator *m*, -ra *f*.
infrared [,ɪnfrə'red] *adj* infravermelho(lha).
infrastructure ['ɪnfrə,strʌktʃə^r] *n* infra-estrutura *f*.
infrequent [ɪn'fri:kwənt] *adj* infreqüente.
infringe [ɪn'frɪndʒ] (*cont* **infringeing**) <> *vt* **-1.** [right] transgredir, violar **-2.** [law, agreement] infringir. <> *vi* **-1.** [on right]: **to ~ on sthg** transgredir *OR* violar algo **-2.** [on law, agreement]: **to ~ on sthg** infringir algo.
infringement [ɪn'frɪndʒmənt] *n* **-1.** [of right] transgressão *f*, violação *f* **-2.** [of law, agreement] infração *f*.
infuriate [ɪn'fjʊərɪeɪt] *vt* enfurecer.
infuriating [ɪn'fjʊərɪeɪtɪŋ] *adj* enfurecedor(ra).
infuse [ɪn'fju:z] <> *vt*: **to ~ sb with sthg** infundir algo em alguém. <> *vi* estar em infusão.
infusion [ɪn'fju:ʒn] *n* infusão *f*.
ingenious [ɪn'dʒi:njəs] *adj* engenhoso(sa).
ingenuity [,ɪndʒɪ'nju:ətɪ] *n (U)* engenhosidade *f*.
ingenuous [ɪn'dʒenjʊəs] *adj fml* ingênuo(nua).
ingest [ɪn'dʒest] *vt fml* ingerir.
ingot ['ɪŋgət] *n* lingote *m*.
ingrained [,ɪn'greɪnd] *adj* **-1.** [ground in] entranhado(da) **-2.** [deeply rooted] arraigado(da).
ingratiate [ɪn'greɪʃɪeɪt] *vt*: **to ~ o.s. with sb** congraçar-se com alguém.
ingratiating [ɪn'greɪʃɪeɪtɪŋ] *adj* insinuante, lisonjeiro(ra).
ingratitude [ɪn'grætɪtju:d] *n (U)* ingratidão *f*.
ingredient [ɪn'gri:djənt] *n* ingrediente *m*.
ingrowing ['ɪn,grəʊɪŋ], **ingrown** ['ɪn,grəʊn] *adj* encravado(da).
inhabit [ɪn'hæbɪt] *vt* habitar.
inhabitant [ɪn'hæbɪtənt] *n* habitante *mf*.
inhalation [,ɪnhə'leɪʃn] *n (U)* inalação *f*.
inhale [ɪn'heɪl] <> *vt* inalar. <> *vi* [breathe in - smoker] tragar; [- patient] inspirar.
inhaler [ɪn'heɪlə^r] *n MED* inalador *m*.
inherent [ɪn'hɪərənt, ɪn'herənt] *adj* inerente; **~ in sthg** inerente a algo.
inherently [ɪn'hɪərentlɪ, ɪn'herəntlɪ] *adv* intrinsecamente.
inherit [ɪn'herɪt] <> *vt*: **to ~ sthg (from sb)** herdar algo (de alguém). <> *vi* herdar.
inheritance [ɪn'herɪtəns] *n* herança *f*.
inheritor [ɪn'herɪtə^r] *n* [of debt, problem, tradition] herdeiro *m*, -ra *f*.
inhibit [ɪn'hɪbɪt] *vt* **-1.** [restrict] impedir **-2.** *PSYCH* [repress] inibir.
inhibited [ɪn'hɪbɪtɪd] *adj* inibido(da).
inhibition [,ɪnhɪ'bɪʃn] *n* inibição *f*.
inhospitable [,ɪnhɒ'spɪtəbl] *adj* **-1.** [unwelcoming] inospitaleiro(ra) **-2.** [climate, area] inóspito(ta).
in-house <> *adj* **-1.** [journal, report, magazine] de circulação interna **-2.** [staff, group] interno(na), da casa; **~ staff** quadro *m* interno. <> *adv* internamente.
inhuman [ɪn'hju:mən] *adj* **-1.** [cruel] desumano(na) **-2.** [not human] inumano(na).
inhumane [,ɪnhju:'meɪn] *adj* desumano(na).
inimitable [ɪ'nɪmɪtəbl] *adj* inimitável.
iniquitous [ɪ'nɪkwɪtəs] *adj fml* iníquo(qua).
iniquity [ɪ'nɪkwətɪ] (*pl* **-ies**) *n* **-1.** *(U) fml* [wickedness, injustice] iniqüidade *f* **-2.** [wicked or unjust act] injustiça *f*.
initial [ɪ'nɪʃl] (*UK pt* & *pp* **-led**, *cont* **-ling**, *US pt* & *pp* **-ed**, *cont* **-ing**) <> *adj* inicial. <> *vt* rubricar.
◆ **initials** *npl* iniciais *fpl*.

initialize, -ise [ɪ'nɪʃəlaɪz] *vt* COMPUT inicializar.
initially [ɪ'nɪʃəlɪ] *adv* inicialmente.
initiate [ɪ'nɪʃɪeɪt] ◇ *vt* **-1.** [start] iniciar **-2.** [teach]: **to ~ sb (into sthg)** iniciar alguém (em algo). ◇ *n* iniciado *m*, -da *f*.
initiation [ɪ,nɪʃɪ'eɪʃn] *n (U)* **-1.** [start] início *m* **-2.** [introduction, teaching] iniciação *f*.
initiative [ɪ'nɪʃətɪv] *n* **-1.** [gen] iniciativa *f*; **to use one's ~** fazer uso de sua própria iniciativa; **on one's own ~** por iniciativa própria **-2.** [first move]: **to take the ~** tomar a iniciativa **-3.** [advantage]: **to have the ~** ter a vantagem.
inject [ɪn'dʒekt] *vt* **-1.** MED: **to ~ sb with sthg, to ~ sthg into sb** injetar algo em alguém **-2.** *fig* [add]: **to ~ sthg into sthg** injetar algo em algo.
injection [ɪn'dʒekʃn] *n* injeção *f*.
injudicious [,ɪndʒuː'dɪʃəs] *adj fml* injudicioso(sa).
injunction [ɪn'dʒʌŋkʃn] *n* JUR mandado *m* judicial, interdito *m*.
injure ['ɪndʒəʳ] *vt* **-1.** [hurt physically] machucar; **to ~ o.s.** machucar-se, ferir-se **-2.** [reputation, chances] prejudicar **-3.** [offend] ferir.
injured ['ɪndʒəd] ◇ *adj* **-1.** [physically hurt] machucado(da), ferido(da) **-2.** [reputation, chances] prejudicado(da) **-3.** [offended] ferido(da). ◇ *npl*: **the ~** os feridos.
injurious [ɪn'dʒʊərɪəs] *adj fml*: **~ (to sb/sthg)** pernicioso(sa) (a alguém/algo).
injury ['ɪndʒərɪ] (*pl* **-ies**) *n* **-1.** *(U)* [physical harm] lesão *f* **-2.** [wound] ferimento *m*; **to do o.s. an ~** machucar-se **-3.** *(U)* [to one's reputation] dano *m* **-4.** [to one's pride, feelings] golpe *m*.
injury time *n (U)* tempo *m* de descontos *(num jogo)*.
injustice [ɪn'dʒʌstɪs] *n* injustiça *f*; **to do sb an ~** fazer uma injustiça a alguém.
ink [ɪŋk] ◇ *n (U)* tinta *f*. ◇ *comp* de tinta; **~ pen** caneta-tinteiro *f*.
◆ **ink in** *vt sep* repassar a caneta.
ink-jet printer *n* impressora *f* jato de tinta.
inkling ['ɪŋklɪŋ] *n*: **to have an ~ of sthg** ter uma vaga idéia de algo; **to have an ~ that** ter a vaga idéia de que.
inkpad ['ɪŋkpæd] *n* almofada *f* para carimbos.
inkwell ['ɪŋkwel] *n* tinteiro *m*.
INLA (*abbr of* **Irish National Liberation Army**) *n* *grupo terrorista que luta pela reunificação da Irlanda*, Exército *m* de Libertação Nacional Irlandês.
inlaid [,ɪn'leɪd] *adj* incrustado(da); **~ with sthg** incrustado(da) de algo.
inland [*adj* 'ɪnlənd, *adv* ɪn'lænd] ◇ *adj* interior. ◇ *adv* **-1.** [drive, head, walk] para o interior **-2.** [be positioned] no interior.
Inland Revenue *n UK*: **the ~** o fisco, ≃ a Receita Federal.
in-laws *npl inf* sogros *mpl*.
inlet ['ɪnlet] *n* **-1.** [stretch of water] enseada *f* **-2.** [way in] entrada *f*.
inmate ['ɪnmeɪt] *n* **-1.** [mental hospital] interno *m*, -na *f* **-2.** [prison] preso *m*, -sa *f*.
inmost ['ɪnməʊst] *adj literary* [deepest] mais íntimo(-ma).
inn [ɪn] *n* pousada *f*.
innards ['ɪnədz] *npl* entranhas *fpl*.
innate [,ɪ'neɪt] *adj* inato(ta).
inner ['ɪnəʳ] *adj* **-1.** [most central] interno(na); **Inner London** o centro de Londres **-2.** [unexpressed, secret - feelings, doubts] íntimo(ma); [- peace, meaning] interior.
inner city ◇ *n*: **the ~** o centro urbano decadente. ◇ *comp* do centro urbano decadente.
innermost ['ɪnəməʊst] *adj* = **inmost**.
inner tube *n* câmara *f* de ar.
innings ['ɪnɪŋz] (*pl inv*) *n UK* [in cricket] turno *m*; **to have had a good ~** *fig* ter aproveitado bem a vida.
innocence ['ɪnəsəns] *n (U)* **-1.** JUR [gen] inocência *f* **-2.** [naivety] ingenuidade *f*.
innocent ['ɪnəsənt] ◇ *adj* **-1.** [gen] inocente; **~ of sthg** inocente de algo **-2.** [harmless] ingênuo(nua). ◇ *n* [naive person] inocente *mf*.
innocuous [ɪ'nɒkjʊəs] *adj* [harmless] inócuo(cua).
innovation [,ɪnə'veɪʃn] *n* inovação *f*.
innovative ['ɪnəvətɪv] *adj* inovador(ra).
innovator ['ɪnəveɪtəʳ] *n* inovador *m*, -ra *f*.
innuendo [,ɪnjuː'endəʊ] (*pl* **-es** OR **-s**) *n* **-1.** [individual remark] insinuação *f*, indireta *f* **-2.** *(U)* [style of speaking] insinuações *fpl*.
innumerable [ɪ'njuːmərəbl] *adj* inumerável.
inoculate [ɪ'nɒkjʊleɪt] *vt* inocular; **to ~ sb with sthg** inocular algo em alguém; **to ~ sb against sthg** vacinar alguém contra algo.
inoculation [ɪ,nɒkjʊ'leɪʃn] *n* **-1.** [injection] inoculação *f* **-2.** *(U)* [disease prevention] vacinação *f*.
inoffensive [,ɪnə'fensɪv] *adj* inofensivo(va).
inoperable [ɪn'ɒprəbl] *adj* **-1.** MED que não se pode operar **-2.** *fml* [unworkable] impraticável.
inoperative [ɪn'ɒprətɪv] *adj* **-1.** [unworkable] impraticável **-2.** [not working] que não funciona.
inopportune [ɪn'ɒpətjuːn] *adj fml* inoportuno(na).
inordinate [ɪ'nɔːdɪnət] *adj fml* **-1.** [gen] excessivo(-va) **-2.** [pleasure] desmesurado(da).
inordinately [ɪ'nɔːdɪnətlɪ] *adv fml* [extremely] de forma desmesurada.
inorganic [,ɪnɔː'gænɪk] *adj* [substance] inorgânico(-ca).
in-patient *n* paciente *mf* interno, -na.
input ['ɪnpʊt] (*pt* & *pp* **input** OR **-ted**, *cont* **-ting**) ◇ *n (U)* **-1.** [contribution] contribuição *f* **-2.** COMPUT, ELEC entrada *f*. ◇ *vt* COMPUT entrar.
input/output *n* COMPUT entrada/saída *f*.
inquest ['ɪnkwest] *n* JUR inquérito *m*.
inquire [ɪn'kwaɪəʳ] ◇ *vt*: **to ~ when/whether/if/how ...** inquirir quando/se/como ... ◇ *vi* [ask for information] informar-se; **to ~ about sthg** pedir informações sobre algo.
◆ **inquire after** *vt fus* perguntar por.
◆ **inquire into** *vt fus* investigar.
inquiring [ɪn'kwaɪərɪŋ] *adj* inquisitivo(va); **an ~ mind** uma mente curiosa.
inquiry [ɪn'kwaɪərɪ] (*pl* **-ies**) *n* **-1.** [question] pergunta *f*; **'Inquiries'** 'Informações' **-2.** [investigation] investigação *f*, inquérito *m* **-3.** *(U)* [questioning]: **this spirit of ~** este espírito de questionar.

inquiry desk *n* (balcão *m* de) informações *fpl*.
inquisition [ˌɪnkwɪ'zɪʃn] *n pej* inquisição *f*.
◆ **Inquisition** *n*: **the Inquisition** a Inquisição.
inquisitive [ɪn'kwɪzətɪv] *adj* curioso(sa).
inroads ['ɪnrəʊdz] *npl*: **to make ~ into sthg** abrir caminho em algo.
insane [ɪn'seɪn] ◇ *adj* **-1.** MED [mad] insano(na) **-2.** *fig* [very stupid] louco(ca). ◇ *npl*: **the ~** os deficientes mentais.
insanitary [ɪn'sænɪtrɪ] *adj* insalubre, anti-higiênico(ca).
insanity [ɪn'sænətɪ] *n (U)* **-1.** MED [madness] insanidade *f* **-2.** *fig* [great stupidity] loucura *f*.
insatiable [ɪn'seɪʃəbl] *adj* insaciável.
inscribe [ɪn'skraɪb] *vt* **-1.** [on wall, headstone, plaque] escrever; **to ~ sthg with sthg** escrever algo com algo; **to ~ sthg on sthg** gravar algo em algo **-2.** [in book]: **to ~ sthg in sthg** escrever algo em algo.
inscription [ɪn'skrɪpʃn] *n* **-1.** [gen] inscrição *f* **-2.** [in book] dedicatória *f*.
inscrutable [ɪn'skru:təbl] *adj* inescrutável, impenetrável.
insect ['ɪnsekt] *n* inseto *m*.
insect bite *n* picada *f* de inseto.
insecticide [ɪn'sektɪsaɪd] *n* inseticida *m*.
insect repellent *n* repelente *m* para insetos.
insecure [ˌɪnsɪ'kjʊə^r] *adj* **-1.** [not confident] inseguro(ra) **-2.** [not safe] pouco seguro(ra).
insecurity [ˌɪnsɪ'kjʊərətɪ] *n (U)* **-1.** [lack of confidence] insegurança *f* **-2.** [uncertainty] instabilidade *f*.
insensible [ɪn'sensəbl] *adj* **-1.** [unconscious] inconsciente **-2.** [unaware]: **to be ~ of sthg** não ter consciência de algo **-3.** [unable to feel]: **to be ~ to sthg** ser insensível a algo.
insensitive [ɪn'sensətɪv] *adj* **-1.** [unkind, thoughtless] insensível **-2.** [unresponsive]: **~ to sthg** indiferente a algo **-3.** [unable to feel]: **~ to sthg** insensível a algo.
insensitivity [ɪnˌsensə'tɪvətɪ] *n (U)* **-1.** [unkindness, thoughtlessness] insensibilidade *f* **-2.** [lack of sensation]: **~ to sthg** insensibilidade a algo.
inseparable [ɪn'seprəbl] *adj* **-1.** [subjects, facts]: **~ (from sthg)** inseparável (de algo) **-2.** [people] inseparável.
insert [*vb* ɪn'sɜ:t, *n* 'ɪnsɜ:t] ◇ *n* encarte *m*. ◇ *vt* [put in]: **to ~ sthg (in** OR **into sthg)** inserir algo (em algo).
insertion [ɪn'sɜ:ʃn] *n (U)* inserção *f*.
in-service training *n UK* treinamento *m* no serviço.
inset ['ɪnset] *n* [detail] detalhe *m*.
inshore [*adj* 'ɪnʃɔ:^r, *adv* ɪn'ʃɔ:^r] ◇ *adj* costeiro(ra). ◇ *adv* **-1.** [towards shore] em direção à costa **-2.** [close to shore] perto da costa.
inside [ɪn'saɪd] ◇ *adj* [interior, near centre] interno(-na). ◇ *adv* **-1.** [in, within - place, object, building] para dentro; **there was sthg ~** havia alguma coisa dentro; [- body, mind] por dentro **-2.** [prison] *sl* preso(sa). ◇ *prep* dentro de; **get some food ~ you!** coma alguma coisa!; **~ three weeks** em menos de três semanas. ◇ *n* **-1.** [interior, inner part]: **the ~** o lado de dentro; **~ out** [clothes] do avesso; **to know sthg ~ out** *fig* conhecer algo de cabo a rabo; **to turn sthg ~ out** virar algo do avesso **-2.** AUT: **the ~** [in UK] a faixa da esquerda; [in mainland Europe, US, Brazil etc] a faixa da direita.
◆ **insides** *npl inf* [intestines] tripas *fpl*.
◆ **inside of** *prep US* [building, object] dentro de.
inside information *n (U)* informação *f* confidencial.
inside job *n inf roubo cometido com a ajuda de um empregado da empresa ou do local roubado.*
inside lane *n* AUT **-1.** [in UK] faixa *f* da esquerda **-2.** [in mainland Europe, US, Brazil etc] faixa *f* da direita.
insider [ˌɪn'saɪdə^r] *n* pessoa *f* bem-informada *(numa organização)*.
insider dealing, insider trading *n (U) uso indevido de informações privilegiadas na bolsa de valores.*
inside story *n* história *f* íntima.
insidious [ɪn'sɪdɪəs] *adj* insidioso(sa).
insight ['ɪnsaɪt] *n* **-1.** *(U)* [wisdom]: **~ (into sthg)** discernimento *m* (sobre algo) **-2.** [glimpse]: **~ (into sthg)** insight *m* (sobre algo); **the book gave me an ~ into the problem** o livro me fez ter algumas idéias sobre o problema.
insignia [ɪn'sɪgnɪə] *(pl inv) n* insígnia *f*.
insignificance [ˌɪnsɪg'nɪfɪkəns] *n* insignificância *f*.
insignificant [ˌɪnsɪg'nɪfɪkənt] *adj* insignificante.
insincere [ˌɪnsɪn'sɪə^r] *adj* insincero(ra).
insincerity [ˌɪnsɪn'serətɪ] *n (U)* insinceridade *f*.
insinuate [ɪn'sɪnjʊeɪt] *pej vt* **-1.** [imply]: **to ~ (that)** insinuar que **-2.** [install]: **to ~ o.s. into sthg** infiltrar-se em algo.
insinuation [ɪnˌsɪnjʊ'eɪʃn] *n pej* **-1.** [suggestion] insinuação *f* **-2.** *(U)* [act of insinuating] insinuação *f*.
insipid [ɪn'sɪpɪd] *adj pej* **-1.** [dull, boring] insosso(sa) **-2.** [flavourless - drink] insípido(da); [- food] insosso(-sa).
insist [ɪn'sɪst] ◇ *vt*: **to ~ (that)** insistir que. ◇ *vi*: **to ~ on sthg** insistir em algo; **to ~ on doing sthg** insistir em fazer algo.
insistence [ɪn'sɪstəns] *n (U)* [act of demanding] insistência *f*; **~ on sthg/on doing sthg** insistência em algo/em fazer algo.
insistent [ɪn'sɪstənt] *adj* insistente; **~ on sthg** insistente em algo.
in situ [ˌɪn'sɪtju:] *adv* no local.
insofar [ˌɪnsəʊ'fɑ:^r] ◆ **insofar as** *conj* na medida em que.
insole ['ɪnsəʊl] *n* [in shoe] palmilha *f*.
insolence ['ɪnsələns] *n (U)* insolência *f*.
insolent ['ɪnsələnt] *adj* insolente.
insoluble *UK* [ɪn'sɒljʊbl], **insolvable** *US* [ɪn'sɒlvəbl] *adj* insolúvel.
insolvable *adj US* insolúvel.
insolvency [ɪn'sɒlvənsɪ] *n (U)* insolvência *f*.
insolvent [ɪn'sɒlvənt] *adj* insolvente.
insomnia [ɪn'sɒmnɪə] *n (U)* insônia *f*.
insomniac [ɪn'sɒmnɪæk] *n* insone *mf*.
insomuch [ˌɪnsəʊ'mʌtʃ] ◆ **insomuch as** *conj fml* na medida em que.
inspect [ɪn'spekt] *vt* **-1.** [letter, person] examinar **-2.** [factory] inspecionar, vistoriar **-3.** [troops] passar revista em.

inspection [ɪn'spekʃn] *n* **-1.** [examination] exame *m* **-2.** [official check] inspeção *f*, vistoria *f*.
inspector [ɪn'spektəʳ] *n* **-1.** [official] fiscal *mf* **-2.** [of police] inspetor *m*, -ra *f*.
inspector of taxes *n* fiscal *mf* da Receita.
inspiration [ˌɪnspə'reɪʃn] *n* **-1.** *(U)* [source of ideas] inspiração *f*; ~ **(for sthg)** inspiração (para algo) **-2.** [brilliant idea] idéia *f*.
inspire [ɪn'spaɪəʳ] *vt* [stimulate, encourage]: **to ~ sb (to do sthg)** inspirar alguém (a fazer algo); **to ~ sb with sthg, to ~ sthg in sb** inspirar algo a alguém.
inspired [ɪn'spaɪəd] *adj* inspirado(da).
inspiring [ɪn'spaɪərɪŋ] *adj* [stimulating, exciting] inspirador(ra).
inst. [ɪnst] (*abbr of* **instant**) *do corrente mês*.
instability [ˌɪnstə'bɪlətɪ] *n (U)* instabilidade *f*.
install *UK*, **instal** *US* [ɪn'stɔːl] *vt* **-1.** [machinery, equipment] instalar **-2.** [appoint]: **to ~ sb (as sthg)** nomear alguém (como algo) **-3.** [settle] instalar-se; **to ~ o.s. in front of the fire** acomodar-se em frente ao fogo.
installation [ˌɪnstə'leɪʃn] *n* instalação *f*.
installment *n US* = **instalment**.
installment plan *n US* compra *f* a prazo.
instalment *UK*, **installment** *US* [ɪn'stɔːlmənt] *n* **-1.** [payment] prestação *f*; **in ~s** em prestações **-2.** [episode] episódio *m*.
instance ['ɪnstəns] *n* [example, case] caso *m*, exemplo *m*; **for ~** por exemplo; **in the first ~** *fml* em primeira instância.
instant ['ɪnstənt] ◇ *adj* instantâneo(nea). ◇ *n* [moment] instante *m*; **the ~ (that) ...** no mesmo instante em que ...; **at that** *OR* **the same ~** naquele *OR* no mesmo instante; **this ~** agora mesmo.
instantaneous [ˌɪnstən'teɪnjəs] *adj* instantâneo(-nea).
instantly ['ɪnstəntlɪ] *adv* instantaneamente.
instead [ɪn'sted] *adv* em vez disso.
◆ **instead of** *prep* em vez de, em lugar de.
instep ['ɪnstep] *n* [of foot] peito *m* do pé.
instigate ['ɪnstɪgeɪt] *vt* [initiate] instigar.
instigation [ˌɪnstɪ'geɪʃn] *n*: **at the ~ of** por solicitação de.
instigator ['ɪnstɪgeɪtəʳ] *n* instigador *m*, -ra *f*.
instil *UK* (*pt* & *pp* **-led**, *cont* **-ling**), **instill** *US* (*pt* & *pp* **-ed**, *cont* **-ing**) [ɪn'stɪl] *vt*: **to ~ sthg in(to) sb** instilar algo em alguém.
instinct ['ɪnstɪŋkt] *n* instinto *m*; **first ~** primeiro impulso *m*.
instinctive [ɪn'stɪŋktɪv] *adj* instintivo(va).
instinctively [ɪn'stɪŋktɪvlɪ] *adv* instintivamente.
institute ['ɪnstɪtjuːt] ◇ *n* [establishment] instituto *m*. ◇ *vt* instituir.
institution [ˌɪnstɪ'tjuːʃn] *n* instituição *f*.
institutional [ˌɪnstɪ'tjuːʃənl] *adj* **-1.** [of organization] institucional **-2.** [of psychiatric hospital, children's home] para uma instituição beneficiente.
institutionalize *vt* institucionalizar.
institutionalized, -ised [ˌɪnstɪ'tjuːʃnəˌlaɪzd] *adj* institucionalizado(da).
instruct [ɪn'strʌkt] *vt* **-1.** [tell, order]: **to ~ sb to do sthg** instruir alguém a fazer algo **-2.** [teach] instruir; **to ~ sb in sthg** instruir alguém em algo.
instruction [ɪn'strʌkʃn] *n* instrução *f*.
◆ **instructions** *npl* [for use] instruções *fpl*.
instruction manual *n* manual *m* de instruções.
instructive [ɪn'strʌktɪv] *adj* instrutivo(va).
instructor [ɪn'strʌktəʳ] *n* **-1.** [in driving, skiing] instrutor *m* **-2.** [in swimming] professor *m*.
instructress [ɪn'strʌktrɪs] *n* **-1.** [in driving, skiing] instrutora *f* **-2.** [in swimming] professora *f*.
instrument ['ɪnstrʊmənt] *n* **-1.** instrumento *m* **-2.** *literary* [means] instrumento *m*.
instrumental [ˌɪnstrʊ'mentl] ◇ *adj* **-1.** [important, helpful]: **to be ~ in sthg** desempenhar um papel fundamental em algo **-2.** [music] instrumental.
◇ *n MUS* instrumental *m*.
instrumentalist [ˌɪnstrʊ'mentəlɪst] *n MUS* instrumentalista *mf*.
instrument panel *n* painel *m* de instrumentos.
insubordinate [ˌɪnsə'bɔːdɪnət] *adj fml* insubordinado(da).
insubordination ['ɪnsəˌbɔːdɪ'neɪʃn] *n (U) fml* insubordinação *f*.
insubstantial [ˌɪnsəb'stænʃl] *adj* **-1.** [fragile] frágil **-2.** [unsatisfying] pouco substancioso(sa).
insufferable [ɪn'sʌfərəbl] *adj* insuportável.
insufficient [ˌɪnsə'fɪʃnt] *adj fml* insuficiente; **~ for sthg/to do sthg** insuficiente para algo/para fazer algo.
insular ['ɪnsjʊləʳ] *adj* **-1.** [narrow-minded] limitado(da) **-2.** [isolated] isolado(da).
insulate ['ɪnsjʊleɪt] *vt* isolar; **to ~ sb against** *OR* **from sthg** isolar alguém de algo.
insulating tape ['ɪnsjʊleɪtɪŋ-] *n (U) UK* fita *f* isolante.
insulation [ˌɪnsjʊ'leɪʃn] *n (U)* [material, substance] isolamento *m*.
insulin ['ɪnsjʊlɪn] *n (U)* insulina *f*.
insult [*vt* ɪn'sʌlt, *n* 'ɪnsʌlt] ◇ *n* insulto *m*; **to add ~ to injury** para piorar ainda mais as coisas. ◇ *vt* insultar, ofender.
insulting [ɪn'sʌltɪŋ] *adj* ofensivo(va).
insuperable [ɪn'suːprəbl] *adj fml* insuperável.
insurance [ɪn'ʃʊərəns] ◇ *n* **-1.** [against fire, accident, theft] seguro *m*; **~ against sthg** seguro contra algo **-2.** *fig* [safeguard, protection] proteção *f*; **~ against sthg** proteção contra algo. ◇ *comp* de seguro.
insurance broker *n* corretor *m*, -ra *f* de seguros.
insurance policy *n* apólice *f* de seguros.
insurance premium *n* prêmio *m* do seguro.
insure [ɪn'ʃʊəʳ] ◇ *vt* **-1.** [against fire, accident, theft]: **to ~ sb/sthg against sthg** segurar alguém/algo contra algo **-2.** *US* [make certain] assegurar. ◇ *vi* [protect]: **to ~ against sthg** prevenir-se contra algo.
insured [ɪn'ʃɔːd] ◇ *adj* **-1.** [against fire, accident, theft]: **~ (against** *OR* **for sthg)** segurado(da) (contra algo) **-2.** *US* [certain] assegurado(da). ◇ *n*: **the ~** o segurado, a segurada.
insurer [ɪn'ʃʊərəʳ] *n* segurador *m*, -ra *f*.

insurgent [ɪn'sɜːdʒənt] *n* insurgente *mf*.
insurmountable [ˌɪnsə'maʊntəbl] *adj* intransponível.
insurrection [ˌɪnsə'rekʃn] *n* insurreição *f*.
intact [ɪn'tækt] *adj* intacto(ta).
intake ['ɪnteɪk] *n* **-1.** [amount consumed] ingestão *f* **-2.** [people recruited - *SCH, UNIV*] ingresso *m*; [- *MIL*] recrutamento *m* **-3.** [inlet] entrada *f*.
intangible [ɪn'tændʒəbl] *adj* intangível.
integral ['ɪntɪgrəl] *adj* [essential] essencial; **to be ~ to sthg** ser parte integrante de algo.
integrate ['ɪntɪgreɪt] <> *vi* integrar; **to ~ with** *OR* **into sthg** integrar-se em algo. <> *vt* integrar; **to ~ sb with** *OR* **into sthg** integrar alguém em algo; **to ~ sthg with** *OR* **into sthg** integrar algo em algo.
integrated ['ɪntɪgreɪtɪd] *adj* [multiracial] integrado(-da).
integrated circuit *n* circuito *m* integrado.
integration [ˌɪntɪ'greɪʃn] *n (U)*: **~ (with** *OR* **into sthg)** integração *f* (em algo).
integrity [ɪn'tegrətɪ] *n (U)* **-1.** [honour] integridade *f* **-2.** *fml* [wholeness] integridade *f*.
intellect ['ɪntəlekt] *n* **-1.** [gen] inteligência *f*, intelecto *m* **-2.** [mind] inteligência *f*.
intellectual [ˌɪntə'lektjʊəl] <> *adj* intelectual. <> *n* [person] intelectual *mf*.
intellectualize, -ise [ˌɪntə'lektjʊəlaɪz] *vt* intelectualizar.
intelligence [ɪn'telɪdʒəns] *n (U)* **-1.** [ability to think and reason] inteligência *f* **-2.** [information service] serviço *m* de inteligência **-3.** [information] informações *fpl* secretas.
intelligence quotient *n* quociente *m* de inteligência.
intelligence test *n* teste *m* de inteligência.
intelligent [ɪn'telɪdʒənt] *adj* [clever] inteligente.
intelligent card *n* cartão *m* inteligente.
intelligently [ɪn'telɪdʒəntlɪ] *adv* inteligentemente.
intelligentsia [ɪnˌtelɪ'dʒentsɪə] *n*: **the ~** a intelligentsia.
intelligible [ɪn'telɪdʒəbl] *adj* inteligível.
intemperate [ɪn'tempərət] *adj fml* **-1.** [excessive] excessivo(va) **-2.** [uncontrolled] descomedido(da) **-3.** [climate] intemperado(da).
intend [ɪn'tend] *vt* [mean] pretender, propor-se a; **to be ~ed for/as sthg** ser destinado(da) para algo; **to be ~ed for sb** ser destinado(da) a alguém; **it wasn't ~ed to be a criticism** não pretendia ser uma crítica; **it was ~ed to be a surprise** era para ser uma surpresa; **to ~ doing sthg/to do sthg** pretender fazer algo.
intended [ɪn'tendɪd] *adj* [planned] planejado(da); **the ~ victim** a vítima almejada.
intense [ɪn'tens] *adj* **-1.** [gen] intenso(sa) **-2.** [person - serious] muito sério(ria); [- emotional] forte.
intensely [ɪn'tenslɪ] *adv* **-1.** [very] enormemente **-2.** [very much] intensamente.
intensify [ɪn'tensɪfaɪ] (*pt* & *pp* **-ied**) <> *vt* intensificar. <> *vi* intensificar-se.
intensity [ɪn'tensətɪ] *n* **-1.** [gen] intensidade *f* **-2.** [of person - seriousness] seriedade *f*; [- of emotional nature] força *f*.
intensive [ɪn'tensɪv] *adj* [concentrated] intensivo(va).
intensive care *n (U)* tratamento *m* intensivo.
intensive care unit *n* unidade *f* de tratamento intensivo.
intent [ɪn'tent] <> *adj* **-1.** [absorbed] atento(ta) **-2.** [determined]: **to be ~ (up)on doing sthg** estar determinado(da) a fazer algo. <> *n fml* [intention] intenção *f*; **to all ~s and purposes** para todos os efeitos.
intention [ɪn'tenʃn] *n* intenção *f*.
intentional [ɪn'tenʃənl] *adj* intencional.
intentionally [ɪn'tenʃənəlɪ] *adv* intencionalmente.
intently [ɪn'tentlɪ] *adv* atentamente.
inter [ɪn'tɜː[r]] (*pt* & *pp* **-red**, *cont* **-ring**) *vt fml* sepultar.
interact [ˌɪntər'ækt] *vi* **-1.** [people]: **to ~ (with sb)** interagir (com alguém) **-2.** [forces, ideas]: **to ~ (with sthg)** interagir (com algo).
interaction [ˌɪntər'ækʃn] *n* interação *f*.
interactive [ˌɪntər'æktɪv] *adj COMPUT* interativo(va).
intercede [ˌɪntə'siːd] *vi fml*: **to ~ (with/for sb)** interceder (junto a/em favor de alguém).
intercept [ˌɪntə'sept] *vt* [message, missile] interceptar.
interception [ˌɪntə'sepʃn] *n (U)* interceptação *f*.
interchange [*n* 'ɪntətʃeɪndʒ, *vb* ˌɪntə'tʃeɪndʒ] <> *n* **-1.** [exchange] intercâmbio *m* **-2.** [road junction] trevo *m* rodoviário. <> *vt* trocar, intercambiar; **to ~ sthg with sb/sthg** trocar algo com alguém/algo.
interchangeable [ˌɪntə'tʃeɪndʒəbl] *adj*: **~ (with sb/sthg)** intercambiável (com alguém/algo).
intercity [ˌɪntə'sɪtɪ] *adj UK* intermunicipal.
intercom ['ɪntəkɒm] *n* interfone *m*.
interconnect [ˌɪntəkə'nekt] *vi* interligar-se; **to ~ with sthg** interligar-se com algo.
interconnecting *adj* [rooms] interligado(da).
intercontinental ['ɪntəˌkɒntɪ'nentl] *adj* intercontinental.
intercontinental ballistic missile *n* míssil *m* balístico intercontinental.
intercourse ['ɪntəkɔːs] *n (U)* [sexual] relação *f* sexual.
interdenominational ['ɪntədɪˌnɒmɪ'neɪʃənl] *adj* de diferentes grupos religiosos.
interdepartmental ['ɪntəˌdiːpɑːt'mentl] *adj* interdepartamental.
interdependent [ˌɪntədɪ'pendənt] *adj* interdependente.
interdict ['ɪntədɪkt] *n* **-1.** *JUR* interdição *m* **-2.** *RELIG* interdito *m*.
interest ['ɪntrəst] <> *n* **-1.** [gen] interesse *m*; **~ in sb/sthg** interesse em alguém/algo **-2.** [hobby] hobby *m*; **in the ~s of** [in order to benefit] em benefício de; [in order to achieve] com a finalidade de; **in the ~s of peace** em nome da paz **-3.** *(U)* [financial charge] juro *m* **-4.** [share in company] participação *f*. <> *vt* [appeal to] interessar; **to ~ sb in sthg/in doing sthg** chamar alguém para algo/para fazer algo; **can I ~ you in a drink?** posso te convidar para um drinque?
interested ['ɪntrəstɪd] *adj* interessado(da); **to be ~ in sb/sthg** estar interessado(da) em alguém/algo; **to be ~ in doing sthg** estar interessado(da) em fazer algo.
interest-free *adj* sem juros.

interesting ['ɪntrəstɪŋ] *adj* interessante.
interest rate *n* taxa *f* de juros.
interface [*n* 'ɪntəfeɪs, *vb* ɪntə'feɪs] <> *n* **-1.** *COMPUT* interface *f* **-2.** [junction, boundary] zona *f* de interação. <> *vt COMPUT* conectar por interface.
interfere [ˌɪntə'fɪə^r] *vi* **-1.** [meddle] interferir, intrometer-se; **to ~ in sthg** interferir em algo, intrometer-se em algo **-2.** [cause disruption] interferir; **to ~ with sthg** interferir em algo.
interference [ˌɪntə'fɪərəns] *n (U)* **-1.** [meddling]: **~ (with** *OR* **in sthg)** intrometimento *m* (em algo) **-2.** *RADIO & TV* interferência *f.*
interfering [ˌɪntə'fɪərɪŋ] *adj pej* intrometido(da).
intergalactic *adj* intergaláctico(ca).
interim ['ɪntərɪm] <> *adj* provisório(ria). <> *n*: **in the ~** neste ínterim.
interior [ɪn'tɪərɪə^r] <> *adj* **-1.** [inner] interno(na), interior **-2.** *POL* do interior. <> *n* **-1.** [inside] interior *m* **-2.** [of country]: **the ~** [inland part] o interior.
interior decorator *n* decorador *m*, -ra *f* de interiores.
interior designer *n* decorador *m*, -ra *f* de interiores.
interject [ˌɪntə'dʒekt] *fml* <> *vt* **-1.** [add] interpor **-2.** [interrupt] interromper. <> *vi* intervir.
interjection [ˌɪntə'dʒekʃn] *n* **-1.** [remark] interrupção *f* **-2.** *GRAM* interjeição *f.*
interleave [ˌɪntə'li:v] *vt*: **to ~ sthg with sthg** intercalar algo com algo.
interlock [ˌɪntə'lɒk] <> *vi* **-1.** *TECH* encaixar; **to ~ with sthg** encaixar com algo **-2.** [entwine] entrelaçar. <> *vt* **-1.** *TECH* engatar; **to ~ sthg with sthg** engatar algo em algo **-2.** [entwine] entrelaçar.
interloper ['ɪntələʊpə^r] *n* intruso *m*, -sa *f.*
interlude ['ɪntəlu:d] *n* **-1.** [gen] intervalo *m* **-2.** *MUS* interlúdio *m.*
intermarry [ˌɪntə'mærɪ] (*pt* & *pp* **-ied**) *vi*: **to ~ (with sb)** unir-se (com alguém) pelo casamento *(parentes ou pessoas de raças, religiões, etc. distintas).*
intermediary [ˌɪntə'mi:djərɪ] (*pl* **-ies**) *n* intermediário *m*, -ria *f*, mediador *m*, -ra *f.*
intermediate [ˌɪntə'mi:djət] *adj* intermediário *m*, -ria *f.*
interminable [ɪn'tɜ:mɪnəbl] *adj* interminável.
intermingle [ˌɪntə'mɪŋgl] *vi*: **to ~ (with people)** misturar-se (com as pessoas).
intermission [ˌɪntə'mɪʃn] *n* intervalo *m.*
intermittent [ˌɪntə'mɪtənt] *adj* intermitente.
intern [*vb* ɪn'tɜ:n, *n* 'ɪntɜ:n] <> *n US* [trainee - teacher] estagiário *m*, -ria *f*; [- doctor] interno *m*, -na *f.* <> *vt* internar.
internal [ɪn'tɜ:nl] *adj* interno(na); **~ affairs** relações *fpl* interiores.
internal-combustion engine *n* motor *m* de combustão interna.
internally [ɪn'tɜ:nəlɪ] *adv* internamente.
Internal Revenue *n US*: **the ~** a receita pública.
international [ˌɪntə'næʃənl] <> *adj* internacional. <> *n UK SPORT* **-1.** [match] partida *f* internacional **-2.** [player] atleta *mf* da seleção.
international date line *n*: **the ~** a linha internacional de data.
internationally [ˌɪntə'næʃnəlɪ] *adv* internacionalmente.
International Monetary Fund *n*: **the ~** o Fundo Monetário Internacional.
international relations *npl* relações *fpl* internacionais.
internecine [*UK* ˌɪntə'ni:saɪn, *US* ˌɪntər'ni:snl] *adj fml* interno(na); **the ~ quarrels in the party** as disputas internas no partido.
internee [ˌɪntɜ:'ni:] *n* recluso *m*, -sa *f (por motivos políticos).*
Internet ['ɪntənet] *n*: **the ~** a Internet.
Internet access *n* acesso *m* à Internet.
Internet café *n* cibercafé *m.*
Internet connection *n* conexão *f* com a Internet.
Internet Service Provider *n* provedor *m* de serviços de Internet.
Internet start-up company *n* empresa *f* eletrônica que surgiu com a Internet.
Internet television, Internet TV *n* televisão *f* via Internet.
internment [ɪn'tɜ:nmənt] *n (U)* reclusão *f (por motivos políticos).*
interpersonal [ˌɪntə'pɜ:sənl] *adj* interpessoal.
interplay ['ɪntəpleɪ] *n (U)*: **~ (of/between)** interação *f* (de/entre).
Interpol ['ɪntəpɒl] *n* Interpol *f.*
interpolate [ɪn'tɜ:pəleɪt] *vt fml* **-1.** [add]: **to ~ sthg (into sthg)** interpolar algo (em algo) **-2.** [interrupt] interpolar.
interpose [ˌɪntə'pəʊz] *vt fml* **-1.** [add] interpor **-2.** [interrupt] intervir.
interpret [ɪn'tɜ:prɪt] <> *vt* **-1.** [understand] interpretar; **to ~ sthg as** interpretar algo como **-2.** [translate] servir de intérprete em **-3.** *fml* [perform] interpretar. <> *vi* [translate] interpretar.
interpretation [ɪnˌtɜ:prɪ'teɪʃn] *n* interpretação *f.*
interpreted language *n COMPUT* linguagem *f* de programação interpretada.
interpreter [ɪn'tɜ:prɪtə^r] *n* [person] intérprete *mf.*
interpreting [ɪn'tɜ:prɪtɪŋ] *n* [occupation] interpretação *f.*
interracial [ˌɪntə'reɪʃl] *adj* inter-racial.
interrelate [ˌɪntərɪ'leɪt] <> *vt* correlacionar. <> *vi*: **to ~ (with sthg)** correlacionar-se (com algo).
interrogate [ɪn'terəgeɪt] *vt* **-1.** [question] interrogar **-2.** *COMPUT* consultar.
interrogation [ɪnˌterə'geɪʃn] *n* **-1.** *(U)* [questioning] interrogação *f* **-2.** [interview] interrogatório *m.*
interrogation mark *n US* ponto *m* de interrogação.
interrogative [ˌɪntə'rɒgətɪv] *GRAM* <> *adj* interrogativo(va). <> *n* **-1.** [form]: **the ~** a forma interrogativa **-2.** [word] pronome *m* interrogativo.
interrogator [ɪn'terəgeɪtə^r] *n* interrogador *m*, -ra *f.*
interrupt [ˌɪntə'rʌpt] <> *vt* interromper. <> *vi* interromper, incomodar.
interruption [ˌɪntə'rʌpʃn] *n* interrupção *f.*
interrupter *n ELEC* interruptor *m.*

intersect [ˌɪntəˈsekt] ◇ *vi* cruzar-se. ◇ *vt* cruzar.
intersection [ˌɪntəˈsekʃn] *n* [junction] interseção *f.*
intersperse [ˌɪntəˈspɜːs] *vt*: **to be ~ed with sthg** ser entremeado(da) por algo.
interstate (highway) *n US* rodovia *f* interestadual.
interval [ˈɪntəvl] *n* **-1.** [period of time]: **~ (between)** intervalo *m* (entre); **at ~s** em intervalos; **at monthly/yearly ~s** em intervalos de um mês/um ano **-2.** *UK* [at play, concert] intervalo *m* **-3.** *MUS* pausa *f.*
intervene [ˌɪntəˈviːn] ◇ *vt* intervir. ◇ *vi* **-1.** [gen] intervir; **to ~ in sthg** intervir em algo **-2.** [time] transcorrer **-3.** [interrupt] interferir.
intervening [ˌɪntəˈviːnɪŋ] *adj* [period of time] transcorrido(da).
intervention [ˌɪntəˈvenʃn] *n* intervenção *f.*
interventionist [ˌɪntəˈvenʃənɪst] ◇ *adj* intervencionista. ◇ *n* intervencionista *mf.*
interview [ˈɪntəvjuː] ◇ *n* entrevista *f.* ◇ *vt* entrevistar.
interviewee [ˌɪntəvjuːˈiː] *n* entrevistado *m*, -da *f.*
interviewer [ˈɪntəvjuːəʳ] *n* entrevistador *m*, -ra *f.*
interweave [ˌɪntəˈwiːv] (*pt* **-wove**, *pp* **-woven**) *fig* ◇ *vt* entrelaçar. ◇ *vi* entrelaçar-se.
intestate [ɪnˈtesteɪt] *adj*: **to die ~** morrer intestado(da).
intestine [ɪnˈtestɪn] *n* intestino *m.*
◆ **intestines** *npl* intestinos *mpl.*
intimacy [ˈɪntɪməsɪ] (*pl* **-ies**) *n (U)* [closeness]: **~ (between/with)** intimidade *f* (entre/com).
◆ **intimacies** *npl* [personal thoughts] intimidades *fpl.*
intimate [*adj* & *n* ˈɪntɪmət, *vb* ˈɪntɪmeɪt] ◇ *adj* **-1.** íntimo(ma) **-2.** *fml* [sexually]: **to be ~ with sb** ter intimidades com alguém **-3.** [personal] pessoal **-4.** [thorough] profundo(da) **-5.** [direct] direto(ta). ◇ *n fml* [close friend] amigo *m* íntimo, amiga *f* íntima. ◇ *vt fml* [hint, imply] insinuar; **to ~ that** insinuar que, dar a entender que.
intimately [ˈɪntɪmətlɪ] *adv* intimamente.
intimation [ˌɪntɪˈmeɪʃn] *n fml* [suggestion] insinuação *f.*
intimidate [ɪnˈtɪmɪdeɪt] *vt* intimidar.
intimidation [ɪnˌtɪmɪˈdeɪʃn] *n (U)* intimidação *f.*
into [ˈɪntʊ] *prep* **-1.** [inside - referring to object] em; [- referring to place, vehicle] em direção a; **to get ~ a car** entrar num carro **-2.** [against] contra; **to bump ~ sb/sthg** tropeçar em alguém/algo; **to crash ~ sb/sthg** chocar-se com alguém/algo **-3.** [indicating transformation, change] em; **to translate ~ Spanish** traduzir para o espanhol **-4.** [concerning, about] sobre **-5.** *MATH* [indicating division] por; **6 ~ 2 is 3** 6 dividido por 2 é 3 **-6.** [indicating elapsed time]: **~ the night** noite adentro; **I was a week ~ my holiday when ...** eu estava há uma semana de férias quando ... **-7.** *inf* [interested in]: **to be ~ sthg** gostar de algo.
intolerable [ɪnˈtɒlrəbl] *adj fml* intolerável.
intolerance [ɪnˈtɒlərəns] *n (U)* [lack of respect] intolerância *f.*
intolerant [ɪnˈtɒlərənt] *adj* intolerante; **to be ~ of sb/sthg** ser intolerante com alguém/algo.
intonation [ˌɪntəˈneɪʃn] *n* entonação *f.*
intone *vt literary* entoar.
intoxicated [ɪnˈtɒksɪkeɪtɪd] *adj* **-1.** [drunk]: **to be ~** estar embriagado(da) **-2.** *fig* [excited]: **to be ~ by** *OR* **with sthg** estar inebriado(da) com algo.
intoxicating [ɪnˈtɒksɪkeɪtɪŋ] *adj* **-1.** [alcoholic] embriagante **-2.** *fig* [exciting] inebriante.
intoxication [ɪnˌtɒksɪˈkeɪʃn] *n (U) fml* **-1.** [drunkenness] embriaguez *f* **-2.** [excitement] excitação *f.*
intractable [ɪnˈtræktəbl] *adj fml* **-1.** [stubborn] intratável **-2.** [insoluble] insolúvel.
intramural *adj* intramuros.
Intranet *n COMPUT* Intranet *f.*
intransigent [ɪnˈtrænzɪdʒənt] *adj fml* intransigente.
intransitive [ɪnˈtrænzətɪv] *adj* intransitivo(va).
intrauterine device [ˌɪntrəˈjuːtəraɪn-] *n* dispositivo *m* intra-uterino.
intravenous [ˌɪntrəˈviːnəs] *adj* intravenoso(sa).
in-tray *n* bandeja *f* de entrada *(para documentos em escritório).*
intrepid [ɪnˈtrepɪd] *adj literary* intrépido(da).
intricacy [ˈɪntrɪkəsɪ] (*pl* **-ies**) *n* **-1.** *(U)* [complexity] complexidade *f* **-2.** [detail] pormenor *m.*
intricate [ˈɪntrɪkət] *adj* intricado(da).
intrigue [ɪnˈtriːg] ◇ *n* intriga *f.* ◇ *vt* intrigar. ◇ *vi*: **to ~ against sb** fazer intriga contra alguém.
intriguing [ɪnˈtriːgɪŋ] *adj* intrigante.
intrinsic [ɪnˈtrɪnsɪk] *adj* intrínseco(ca).
intro [ˈɪntrəʊ] (*pl* **-s**) (*abbr of* **introduction**) *n inf* introdução *f.*
introduce [ˌɪntrəˈdjuːs] *vt* **-1.** [present, make aware of] apresentar; **to ~ sb to sb/sthg** apresentar alguém a alguém/algo **-2.** [bring in]: **to ~ sthg (to** *OR* **into)** introduzir algo (em).
introduction [ˌɪntrəˈdʌkʃn] *n* **-1.** [start, initiation] introdução *f*; **~ to sthg** introdução a algo **-2.** [presentation]: **~ (to sb)** apresentação *f* (a alguém).
introductory [ˌɪntrəˈdʌktrɪ] *adj* introdutório(ria).
introspective [ˌɪntrəˈspektɪv] *adj* introspectivo(va).
introvert [ˈɪntrəvɜːt] *n* introvertido *m*, -da *f.*
introverted [ˈɪntrəvɜːtɪd] *adj* introvertido(da).
intrude [ɪnˈtruːd] *vi* intrometer-se; **to ~ (up)on sb/sthg** intrometer-se em alguém/algo.
intruder [ɪnˈtruːdəʳ] *n* intruso *m*, -sa *f.*
intrusion [ɪnˈtruːʒn] *n* intrometimento *m.*
intrusive [ɪnˈtruːsɪv] *adj* **-1.** [person] intrometido(da) **-2.** [presence, interest] inoportuno(na).
intuition [ˌɪntjuːˈɪʃn] *n* intuição *f.*
intuitive [ɪnˈtjuːɪtɪv] *adj* intuitivo(va).
Inuit [ˈɪnʊɪt] ◇ *adj* inuit. ◇ *n* inuit *mf.*
inundate [ˈɪnʌndeɪt] *vt* inundar; **to be ~d with sthg** estar cheio (cheia) de algo.
inured [ɪˈnjʊəd] *adj fml*: **to be/become ~ to sthg** estar habituado(da)/habituar-se a algo.
invade [ɪnˈveɪd] *vt* invadir.
invader [ɪnˈveɪdəʳ] *n MIL* invasor *m*, -ra *f.*
invading *adj* invasor(ra).
invalid [*adj* ɪnˈvælɪd *n* & *vb* ˈɪnvəlɪd] ◇ *adj* [not

acceptable] inválido(da). <> *n* [ill person] inválido *m*, -da *f*.

◆ **invalid out** *vt sep*: **to be ~ed out (of)** aposentar-se por invalidez (por).

invalidate [ɪn'vælɪdeɪt] *vt* **-1.** [claim, theory] invalidar, refutar **-2.** [contract, agreement] anular.

invalid chair *n* cadeira *f* de rodas.

invaluable [ɪn'væljʊəbl] *adj*: **~ (to sb/sthg)** inestimável (para alguém/algo).

invariable [ɪn'veərɪəbl] *adj* invariável.

invariably [ɪn'veərɪəblɪ] *adv* [always] invariavelmente.

invasion [ɪn'veɪʒn] *n* invasão *f*.

invective [ɪn'vektɪv] *n (U) fml* invectiva *f*.

inveigle [ɪn'veɪgl] *vt*: **to ~ sb into sthg** aliciar alguém para algo; **to ~ sb into doing sthg** enganar alguém para que faça algo.

invent [ɪn'vent] *vt* inventar.

invention [ɪn'venʃn] *n* invenção *f*.

inventive [ɪn'ventɪv] *adj* inventivo(va).

inventor [ɪn'ventə^r] *n* inventor *m*, -ra *f*.

inventory ['ɪnventrɪ] (*pl* **-ies**) *n* **-1.** [list] inventário *m* **-2.** *US* [goods] estoque *m*.

inventory control *n* controle *m* de estoque.

inverse [ɪn'vɜ:s] <> *adj* [proportion, relation] inverso(sa). <> *n fml* inverso *m*.

invert [ɪn'vɜ:t] *vt fml* inverter.

invertebrate [ɪn'vɜ:tɪbreɪt] *n* invertebrado *m*.

inverted commas [ɪn'vɜ:tɪd-] *npl UK* aspas *fpl*; **in ~** entre aspas.

inverted snob [ɪn'vɜ:tɪd-] *n pessoa que finge não gostar de coisas caras ou de boa qualidade*.

invest [ɪn'vest] <> *vt* **-1.** [gen]: **to ~ sthg in sthg/in doing sthg** investir algo em algo/para fazer algo **-2.** *fml* [endow]: **to ~ sb with sthg** outorgar algo a alguém, investir alguém de algo. <> *vi* **-1.** [financially] investir; **to ~ in sthg** investir em algo **-2.** *fig* [in sthg useful]: **to ~ in sthg** investir em algo.

investigate [ɪn'vestɪgeɪt] *vt & vi* investigar.

investigation [ɪn,vestɪ'geɪʃn] *n*: **~ (into sthg)** investigação *f* (sobre algo).

investigative [ɪn'vestɪgətɪv] *adj* investigador(ra), de investigação.

investigator [ɪn'vestɪgeɪtə^r] *n* investigador *m*, -ra *f*.

investiture [ɪn'vestɪtʃə^r] *n* investidura *f*.

investment [ɪn'vestmənt] *n* investimento *m*.

investment analyst *n* analista *mf* financeiro, -ra.

investment trust *n* fundo *m* de investimento.

investor [ɪn'vestə^r] *n* investidor *m*, -ra *f*.

inveterate [ɪn'vetərət] *adj* inveterado(da).

invidious [ɪn'vɪdɪəs] *adj* **-1.** [unfair] injusto(ta) **-2.** [unpleasant] desagradável.

invigilate [ɪn'vɪdʒɪleɪt] *UK* <> *vt* fiscalizar *(um exame)*. <> *vi* fiscalizar um exame.

invigilator [ɪn'vɪdʒɪleɪtə^r] *n UK* fiscal *mf*.

invigorating [ɪn'vɪgəreɪtɪŋ] *adj* **-1.** [gen] revigorante **-2.** [experience] estimulante.

invincible [ɪn'vɪnsɪbl] *adj* [unbeatable] invencível.

inviolate *adj* inviolado(da).

invisible [ɪn'vɪzɪbl] *adj* invisível.

invisible assets *npl* ativos *mpl* intangíveis.

invisible earnings *npl* ganhos *mpl* invisíveis.

invisible ink *n (U)* tinta *f* invisível.

invitation [,ɪnvɪ'teɪʃn] *n* convite *m*; **an ~ to sthg/to do sthg** um convite para algo/para fazer algo.

invite [ɪn'vaɪt] *vt* **-1.** [request to attend] convidar; **to ~ sb to sthg** convidar alguém para algo **-2.** [ask politely]: **to ~ sb to do sthg** convidar alguém para fazer algo **-3.** [solicit] solicitar **-4.** [encourage] estimular.

inviting [ɪn'vaɪtɪŋ] *adj* convidativo(va), tentador(-ra).

in vitro fertilization [,ɪn'vi:trəʊ-] *n (U)* fertilização *f* in vitro.

invoice ['ɪnvɔɪs] <> *n* fatura *f*. <> *vt* **-1.** [send an invoice to] enviar uma fatura para **-2.** [prepare an invoice for] faturar.

invoke [ɪn'vəʊk] *vt* **-1.** *fml* [quote as justification] invocar **-2.** [cause] evocar, suscitar.

involuntary [ɪn'vɒləntrɪ] *adj* [unintentional] involuntário(ria).

involve [ɪn'vɒlv] *vt* **-1.** [entail, require] envolver; **to ~ doing sthg** envolver fazer algo **-2.** [concern, affect] atingir, afetar; **to be ~ed in sthg** estar envolvido(-da) em algo **-3.** [make part of sthg]: **to ~ sb in sthg** envolver alguém em algo; **to ~ o.s. in sthg** meter-se em algo.

involved [ɪn'vɒlvd] *adj* **-1.** [complex] complicado(da) **-2.** [participating]: **to be ~ in sthg** estar metido(da) em algo **-3.** [in a relationship]: **to be/get ~ with sb** envolver-se com alguém **-4.** [entailed]: **~ (in sthg)** envolvido(da) (em algo).

involvement [ɪn'vɒlvmənt] *n (U)* [gen] envolvimento *m*; **~ in sthg** envolvimento em algo.

invulnerable [ɪn'vʌlnərəbl] *adj*: **to be ~ (to sthg)** ser invulnerável (a algo).

inward ['ɪnwəd] <> *adj* **-1.** [feelings, satisfaction] interno(na), interior **-2.** [flow, movement] para dentro. <> *adv US* = **inwards**.

inward investment *n* investimento *m* externo.

inwardly ['ɪnwədlɪ] *adv* [pleased, upset] por dentro.

inwards ['ɪnwədz], **inward** *US adv* para dentro.

I/O (*abbr of* **input-output**) *n* E/S *f*.

IOC (*abbr of* **International Olympic Committee**) *n* COI *m*.

iodine [*UK* 'aɪədi:n, *US* 'aɪədaɪn] *n (U)* iodo *m*.

ion ['aɪən] *n* íon *m*.

Ionian Sea [aɪ'əʊnjən-] *n*: **the ~** o Mar Jônio.

iota [aɪ'əʊtə] *n* pouquinho *m*; **not an ~** nem um pouquinho.

IOU (*abbr of* **I owe you**) *n documento assinado no qual se reconhece uma dívida*.

Iowa ['aɪəʊə] *n* Iowa; **in ~** em Iowa.

IPA (*abbr of* **International Phonetic Alphabet**) *n* AFI *m*.

IQ (*abbr of* **intelligence quotient**) *n* QI *m*.

IRA *n* **-1.** (*abbr of* **Irish Republican Army**) IRA *m* **-2.** (*abbr of* **individual retirement account**) *plano de previdência privada nos Estados Unidos*.

Iran [ɪ'rɑ:n] *n* Irã; **in ~** no Irã.

Iranian [ɪ'reɪnjən] <> *adj* iraniano(na). <> *n* [person] iraniano *m*, -na *f*.

Iraq [ɪ'rɑ:k] *n* Iraque; **in ~** no Iraque.

Iraqi [ɪ'rɑ:kɪ] <> *adj* iraquiano(na). <> *n* [person] iraquiano, -na *f.*
irascible [ɪ'ræsəbl] *adj* irascível.
irate [aɪ'reɪt] *adj* irado(da).
Ireland ['aɪələnd] *n* Irlanda; **in** ~ na Irlanda; **the Republic of** ~ a República da Irlanda.
iridescent [ˌɪrɪ'desənt] *adj literary* iridescente.
iris ['aɪərɪs] (*pl* **-es**) *n MED, BOT* íris *f inv.*
Irish ['aɪrɪʃ] <> *adj* irlandês(esa). <> *n* [language] gaélico-irlandês *m.* <> *npl*: **the** ~ os irlandeses.
Irish coffee *n* café *m* irlandês.
Irishman ['aɪrɪʃmən] (*pl* **-men** [-mən]) *n* irlandês *m.*
Irish Sea *n*: **the** ~ o Mar da Irlanda.
Irish setter *n* séter *m* irlandês.
Irish stew *n ensopado de carne e verduras típico da Irlanda.*
Irish wolfhound *n* wolfhound *m* irlandês.
Irishwoman ['aɪrɪʃˌwʊmən] (*pl* **-women** [-ˌwɪmɪn]) *n* irlandesa *f.*
irk [ɜ:k] *vt dated* aborrecer.
irksome ['ɜ:ksəm] *adj fml* aborrecido(da).
IRO *n* **-1.** (*abbr of* **International Refugee Organization**) *organização humanitária para refugiados* **-2.** (*abbr of* **Inland Revenue Office**) *departamento britânico de arrecadação de impostos,* ≃ Secretaria *f* da Fazenda.
iron ['aɪən] <> *adj* **-1.** [made of iron] de ferro **-2.** *fig* [very strict] duro(ra). <> *n* **-1.** *(U)* [metal] ferro *m* **-2.** [for clothes] ferro *m* (de passar roupa) **-3.** [golf club] ferro *m.* <> *vt* passar (a ferro).
◆ **iron out** *vt sep fig* [overcome] resolver.
Iron Age <> *n*: **the** ~ a Idade do Ferro. <> *comp* da Idade do Ferro.
Iron Curtain *n*: **the** ~ a Cortina de Ferro.
ironic(al) [aɪ'rɒnɪk(l)] *adj* irônico(ca); **how** ~**!** que ironia!
ironically [aɪ'rɒnɪklɪ] *adv* ironicamente.
ironing ['aɪənɪŋ] *n (U)* **-1.** [activity]: **to do the** ~ passar roupa **-2.** [clothes to be ironed] roupa *f* para passar.
ironing board *n* tábua *f* de passar roupa.
iron lung *n* pulmão *m* de aço.
ironmonger ['aɪənˌmʌŋgə^r] *n UK* ferrageiro *m,* -ra *f*; ~**'s (shop)** ferragem *f.*
ironworks ['aɪənwɜ:ks] (*pl inv*) *n* siderúrgica *f.*
irony ['aɪrənɪ] (*pl* **-ies**) *n* ironia *f*; **the** ~ **of it all is that ...** o curioso disso tudo é que ...
irradiate [ɪ'reɪdɪeɪt] *vt* irradiar.
irrational [ɪ'ræʃənl] *adj* irracional.
irreconcilable [ɪˌrekən'saɪləbl] *adj* [completely different] irreconciliável.
irredeemable [ˌɪrɪ'di:məbl] *adj fml* **-1.** [irreplaceable] irrecuperável **-2.** [hopeless] irreparável.
irrefutable [ˌɪrɪ'fju:təbl] *adj fml* irrefutável.
irregular [ɪ'regjʊlə^r] *adj* irregular.
irregularity [ɪˌregjʊ'lærətɪ] (*pl* **-ies**) *n* irregularidade *f.*
irregularly [ɪ'regjʊləlɪ] *adv* [spasmodically] de forma irregular.
irrelevance [ɪ'reləvəns], **irrelevancy** [ɪ'reləvənsɪ] (*pl* **-ies**) *n* irrelevância *f.*
irrelevant [ɪ'reləvənt] *adj* irrelevante.
irreligious [ˌɪrɪ'lɪdʒəs] *adj* descrente.
irremediable [ˌɪrɪ'mi:djəbl] *adj fml* irremediável.
irreparable [ɪ'repərəbl] *adj* irreparável.
irreplaceable [ˌɪrɪ'pleɪsəbl] *adj* insubstituível.
irrepressible [ˌɪrɪ'presəbl] *adj* irreprimível.
irreproachable [ˌɪrɪ'prəʊtʃəbl] *adj* irrepreensível.
irresistible [ˌɪrɪ'zɪstəbl] *adj* irresistível.
irresolute [ɪ'rezəlu:t] *adj fml* irresoluto(ta).
irrespective ◆ **irrespective of** *prep* independente de.
irresponsible [ˌɪrɪ'spɒnsəbl] *adj* irresponsável.
irretrievable [ˌɪrɪ'tri:vəbl] *adj* **-1.** [data] irrecuperável **-2.** [loss, situation] irreparável.
irreverent [ɪ'revərənt] *adj* irreverente.
irreversible [ˌɪrɪ'vɜ:səbl] *adj* irreversível.
irrevocable [ɪ'revəkəbl] *adj* irrevogável.
irrigate ['ɪrɪgeɪt] *vt* [land] irrigar.
irrigation [ˌɪrɪ'geɪʃn] <> *n (U)* [of land] irrigação *f.* <> *comp* de irrigação.
irritable ['ɪrɪtəbl] *adj* [bad-tempered] irritável.
irritant ['ɪrɪtənt] <> *adj* irritante. <> *n* **-1.** [irritating situation, person] motivo *m* de irritação **-2.** [substance] agente *m* irritante.
irritate ['ɪrɪteɪt] *vt* irritar.
irritated *adj* irritado(da).
irritating ['ɪrɪteɪtɪŋ] *adj* irritante.
irritation [ɪrɪ'teɪʃn] *n* **-1.** [gen] irritação *f* **-2.** [cause of anger] motivo *m* de irritação.
IRS (*abbr of* **Internal Revenue Service**) *n departamento norte-americano de arrecadação de impostos,* ≃ Secretaria *f* da Fazenda.
is [ɪz] *vb* ▷ **be.**
ISA (*abbr of* **individual savings account**) *n sistema britânico de aplicações financeiras isentas de impostos.*
ISBN (*abbr of* **International Standard Book Number**) *n* ISBN *m.*
ISDN (*abbr of* **Integrated Services Delivery Network**) *n COMPUT* RDSI *f,* ISDN *f.*
Islam ['ɪzlɑ:m] *n (U)* [religion] Islã *m.*
Islamabad [ɪz'lɑ:məbæd] *n* Islamabad; **in** ~ em Islamabad.
Islamic [ɪz'læmɪk] *adj* islâmico(ca).
island ['aɪlənd] *n* **-1.** [in water] ilha *f* **-2.** [in traffic] passagem *m* para pedestres.
islander ['aɪləndə^r] *n* ilhéu *m,* ilhoa *f.*
isle [aɪl] *n* ilha *f,* ilhota *f.*
Isle of Man *n*: **the** ~ a Ilha de Man.
Isle of Wight [-waɪt] *n*: **the** ~ a Ilha de Wight.
Isles of Scilly *npl* = **Scilly Isles.**
isn't ['ɪznt] = **is not.**
ISO (*abbr of* **International Organization for Standardization**) *n* ISO *f.*
isobar ['aɪsəbɑ:^r] *n METEOR* isóbara *f.*
isolate ['aɪsəleɪt] *vt*: **to** ~ **sthg/sb (from sthg)** isolar algo/alguém (de algo).
isolated ['aɪsəleɪtɪd] *adj* isolado(da).
isolation [aɪsə'leɪʃn] *n (U)* [solitariness] isolamento *m*; **in** ~ [live] em isolamento; [happen, consider] isoladamente.
isolationism [ˌaɪsə'leɪʃənɪzm] *n* isolacionismo *m.*
isosceles triangle [aɪ'sɒsɪli:z-] *n* triângulo *m* isósceles.

isotope ['aɪsətəʊp] *n* isótopo *m*.
ISP (*abbr of* **Internet Service Provider**) *n* ISP *m*.
Israel ['ɪzreɪəl] *n* Israel; **in ~** em Israel.
Israeli [ɪz'reɪlɪ] <> *adj* israelense. <> *n* israelense *mf*.
Israelite ['ɪzrəlaɪt] <> *adj* israelita. <> *n* israelita *mf*.
issue ['ɪʃu:] <> *n* **-1.** [important subject] assunto *m*, questão *f*; **at ~** em questão; **to make an ~ of sthg** dar importância demasiada a algo **-2.** [edition] número *m*, edição *f* **-3.** [bringing out] emissão *f*. <> *vt* **-1.** [statement, decree, warning] expedir **-2.** [stamps, bank notes, shares] emitir, pôr em circulação **-3.** [passport, documents, uniforms] expedir; **to ~ sthg to sb, to ~ sb with sthg** expedir algo a alguém. <> *vi fml* [come out, go out]: **to ~ from** vir de.
Istanbul [ˌɪstæn'bʊl] *n* Istambul; **in ~** em Istambul.
isthmus ['ɪsməs] *n* istmo *m*.
it [ɪt] *pron* **-1.** [referring to specific thing, subject after prep] ele *m*, ela *f* **-2.** [direct object] o *m*, a *f* **-3.** [indirect object] lhe; **a free book came with ~** veio acompanhado de um livro grátis; **give ~ to me** me dê isso; **he gave ~ a kick** ele deu um chute nele; **~'s big** é grande; **~'s here** está aqui; **she hit ~** ela deu uma pancada nele; **she lost ~** ela o perdeu. **-4.** [referring to situation, fact]: **~'s a difficult question** é uma questão difícil; **I can't remember ~** não me lembro; **tell me about ~** conte-me. **-5.** [used impersonally]: **~'s hot** está calor; **~'s six o'clock** são seis horas; **~'s Sunday** é domingo. **-6.** [referring to person]: **~'s me** sou eu; **who is ~?** quem é?
IT (*abbr of* **information technology**) *n* TI *f*.
Italian [ɪ'tæljən] <> *adj* italiano(na). <> *n* **-1.** [person] italiano *m*, -na *f* **-2.** [language] italiano *m*.
italic [ɪ'tælɪk] *adj* itálico *m*.
◆ **italics** *npl*: **in ~** em itálico.
Italy ['ɪtəlɪ] *n* Itália; **in ~** na Itália.
ITC (*abbr of* **Independent Television Commission**) *n órgão britânico que monitora todos os canais de televisão independentes, a cabo e via satélite.*
itch [ɪtʃ] <> *n* coceira *f*. <> *vi* **-1.** [be itchy] coçar **-2.** *fig* [be impatient]: **to be ~ing to do sthg** estar se coçando para fazer algo.
itchy ['ɪtʃɪ] (*compar* **-ier**, *superl* **-iest**) *adj* que coça.
it'd ['ɪtəd] = **it would, it had**.
item ['aɪtəm] *n* **-1.** [single thing] item *m* **-2.** [article in newspaper] artigo *m*.
itemize, -ise ['aɪtəmaɪz] *vt* detalhar, especificar.
itemized bill ['aɪtəmaɪzd-] *n* conta *f* discriminada.
itinerant [ɪ'tɪnərənt] *adj* itinerante.
itinerary [aɪ'tɪnərərɪ] (*pl* **-ies**) *n* itinerário *m*.
it'll [ɪtl] = **it will**.
ITN (*abbr of* **Independent Television News**) *n agência britânica de notícias para os canais independentes de televisão.*
its [ɪts] *poss adj* o seu (a sua), dele (dela).
it's [ɪts] = **it is, it has**.
itself [ɪt'self] *pron* **-1.** (*reflexive*) se **-2.** (*after prep*) si mesmo *m*, -ma *f* **-3.** (*stressed*): **the house ~ is fine** o casa em sí e boa.
ITV (*abbr of* **Independent Television**) *n canal privado de televisão na Grã-Bretanha.*
IUCD (*abbr of* **intrauterine contraceptive device**) *n* DIU *m*.
IUD (*abbr of* **intrauterine device**) *n* DIU *m*.
I've [aɪv] = **I have**.
IVF (*abbr of* **in vitro fertilization**) *n* FIV *f*.
ivory ['aɪvərɪ] <> *adj* [ivory-coloured] marfim *inv*. <> *n* (*U*) marfim *m*. <> *comp* [made of ivory] de marfim.
Ivory Coast *n*: **the ~** a Costa do Marfim; **in the ~** na Costa do Marfim.
ivory tower *n fig* ≃ torre *f* de marfim.
ivy ['aɪvɪ] *n* (*U*) hera *f*.
Ivy League *n US grupo formado pelas oito universidades mais prestigiadas do leste norte-americano.*

j (*pl* **j's** *OR* **js**) **J** (*pl* **J's** *OR* **Js**) [dʒeɪ] *n* [letter] j, J *m*.
J/A (*abbr of* **joint account**) conta *f* conjunta.
jab [dʒæb] (*pt* & *pp* **-bed**, *cont* **-bing**) <> *n* **-1.** [push] golpe *m* **-2.** *UK inf* [injection] injeção *f*. <> *vt*: **to ~ sthg at sb/sthg** espetar algo em alguém/algo; **to ~ sthg into sb/sthg** cravar algo em alguém/algo. <> *vi*: **to ~ at sb/sthg** apunhalar alguém/algo.
jabber ['dʒæbə^r] <> *vt* algaraviar. <> *vi* tagarelar.
jack [dʒæk] *n* **-1.** [device] macaco *m* **-2.** [playing card] valete *m*.
◆ **jack in** *vt sep UK inf* largar.
◆ **jack up** *vt sep* **-1.** [lift with a jack] macaquear **-2.** [force up] aumentar.
jackal ['dʒækəl] *n* chacal *m*.
jackdaw ['dʒækdɔ:] *n* gralha *f*.
jacket ['dʒækɪt] *n* **-1.** [garment] casaco *m*, jaqueta *f* **-2.** [potato skin] casca *f* **-3.** [book cover] sobrecapa *f* **-4.** *US* [of record] capa *f* **-5.** [of boiler] camisa *f*.
jacket potato *n* batata *f* assada com pele.
jackhammer ['dʒækˌhæmə^r] *n US* britadeira *f*.
jack-in-the-box *n* caixa *f* de surpresa.
jack knife *n* [tool] canivete *m* grande.
◆ **jack-knife** *vi* [truck, lorry] derrapar a parte dianteira.
jack-of-all-trades (*pl* **jacks-of-all-trades**) *n* pau-para-toda-obra *m*.
jack plug *n* pino *m*.
jackpot ['dʒækpɒt] *n* bolada *f*.
Jack Russell (terrier) *n* Jack Russell terrier *m*.
Jacobean [ˌdʒækə'bɪən] *adj* jacobino(na).
Jacobite ['dʒækəbaɪt] <> *adj* jacobita. <> *n* jacobita *mf*.
Jacuzzi® [dʒə'ku:zɪ] *n* banheira *f* de hidromassagem.

jade [dʒeɪd] ◇ *adj* [jade-coloured] jade *inv.* ◇ *n* **-1.** [stone] jade *f* **-2.** [colour] cor *f* jade. ◇ *comp* [made of jade] de jade.

jaded ['dʒeɪdɪd] *adj* estafado(da).

jagged ['dʒægɪd] *adj* dentado(da).

jaguar ['dʒægjʊəʳ] *n* jaguar *m.*

jail [dʒeɪl] ◇ *n* prisão *f*, cadeia *f.* ◇ *vt* prender.

jailbird ['dʒeɪlbɜːd] *n inf* preso *m*, -sa *f* reincidente.

jailbreak ['dʒeɪlbreɪk] *n* fuga *f* da prisão.

jailer ['dʒeɪləʳ] *n* carcereiro *m*, -ra *f.*

Jakarta [dʒə'kɑːtə] *n* Jacarta; **in ~** em Jacarta.

jam [dʒæm] (*pt* & *pp* **-med**, *cont* **-ming**) ◇ *n* **-1.** *(U)* [preserve] geléia *f* **-2.** [of traffic] engarrafamento *m* **-3.** *inf* [difficult situation]: **to get into/be in a ~** meter-se/estar em apuros. ◇ *vt* **-1.** [place roughly]: **to ~ sthg onto sthg** enfiar algo em algo **-2.** [fix, cause to stick - window]: **to ~ the window shut** trancar a janela; [- mechanism] emperrar **-3.** [fill, pack tightly] apinhar, abarrotar; **to ~ sthg into sthg** socar algo em algo **-4.** *TELEC* bloquear **-5.** *RADIO* interferir. ◇ *vi* [stick] emperrar.

◆ **jam on** *vt* [brakes] pisar.

Jamaica [dʒə'meɪkə] *n* Jamaica; **in ~** na Jamaica.

Jamaican [dʒə'meɪkn] ◇ *adj* jamaicano(na). ◇ *n* jamaicano *m*, -na *f.*

jamb [dʒæm] *n* batente *m.*

jamboree [ˌdʒæmbə'riː] *n* [celebration] farra *f.*

jamming ['dʒæmɪŋ] *n RADIO* interferência *f.*

jam-packed [-'pækt] *adj inf* apinhado(da).

jam session *n sessão improvisada de jazz ou de rock.*

Jan. [dʒæn] (*abbr of* **January**) jan.

jangle ['dʒæŋgl] ◇ *n* [of keys, bells] som *m* estridente, estrépido *m.* ◇ *vt* fazer soar de forma estridente. ◇ *vi* retinir.

janitor ['dʒænɪtəʳ] *n* ***US*** & ***Scot*** [caretaker] zelador *m*, -ra *f.*

January ['dʒænjʊərɪ] *n* janeiro; *see also* **September**.

Japan [dʒə'pæn] *n* Japão; **in ~** no Japão.

Japanese [ˌdʒæpə'niːz] (*pl inv*) ◇ *adj* japonês(esa). ◇ *n* **-1.** [person] japonês *m*, -esa *f* **-2.** [language] japonês *m.* ◇ *npl* [people]: **the ~** os japoneses.

jape [dʒeɪp] *n* ***dated*** pilhéria *f.*

jar [dʒɑːʳ] (*pt* & *pp* **-red**, *cont* **-ring**) ◇ *n* pote *m.* ◇ *vt* [shake] sacudir. ◇ *vi* **-1.** [noise, voice]: **to ~ (on sb)** dar nos nervos (de alguém) **-2.** [colours] destoar.

jargon ['dʒɑːgən] *n (U)* jargão *m.*

jarring ['dʒɑːrɪŋ] *adj* **-1.** [noise, voice] enervante **-2.** [colours] destoante.

jasmine ['dʒæzmɪn] *n* jasmim *m.*

jaundice ['dʒɔːndɪs] *n (U)* icterícia *f.*

jaundiced ['dʒɔːndɪst] *adj* ***fig*** [attitude, view] pessimista.

jaunt [dʒɔːnt] *n* excursão *f.*

jaunty ['dʒɔːntɪ] (*compar* **-ier**, *superl* **-iest**) *adj* **-1.** [hat, wave] vistoso(sa) **-2.** [person] animado(da).

Java ['dʒɑːvə] *n* Java; **in ~** em Java.

javelin ['dʒævlɪn] *n* dardo *m.*

jaw [dʒɔː] ◇ *n* **-1.** [of person] maxilar *m* **-2.** [of animal] mandíbula *f.* ◇ *vi* ***inf*** tagarelar.

jawbone ['dʒɔːbəʊn] *n* osso *m* maxilar.

jay [dʒeɪ] *n* gaio *m.*

jaywalk ['dʒeɪwɔːk] *vi* atravessar a rua imprudentemente.

jaywalker ['dʒeɪwɔːkəʳ] *n* pedestre *mf* imprudente.

jazz [dʒæz] *n* **-1.** *MUS* jazz *m* **-2.** ***US inf*** [insincere talk] balela *f.*

◆ **jazz up** *vt sep inf* alegrar, animar.

jazz band *n* banda *f* de jazz.

jazz singer *n* cantor *m*, -ra *f* de jazz.

jazzy ['dʒæzɪ] (*compar* **-ier**, *superl* **-iest**) *adj* **-1.** [bright] chamativo(va) **-2.** [music] jazzístico(ca).

JCS (*abbr of* **Joint Chiefs of Staff**) *n conselho militar do presidente dos Estados Unidos.*

jealous ['dʒeləs] *adj* **-1.** [envious]: **to be ~ (of sb/sthg)** ter inveja (de alguém/algo) **-2.** [possessive]: **to be ~ (of sb/sthg)** estar com ciúmes (de alguém/algo).

jealously ['dʒeləslɪ] *adv* **-1.** [enviously] invejosamente **-2.** [possessively] zelosamente.

jealousy ['dʒeləsɪ] *n (U)* **-1.** [envy] inveja *f* **-2.** [resentment] ciúmes *mpl.*

jeans [dʒiːnz] *npl* jeans *m inv.*

Jeep® *n* jipe *m.*

jeer [dʒɪəʳ] ◇ *vt* **-1.** [mock] zombar de **-2.** [boo] vaiar. ◇ *vi* **-1.** [boo] vaiar; **to ~ at sb** vaiar alguém **-2.** [mock] zombar; **to ~ at sb** zombar de alguém.

◆ **jeers** *npl* vaias *fpl.*

jeering ['dʒɪərɪŋ] ◇ *adj* zombeteiro(ra). ◇ *n* zombarias *fpl.*

Jehovah's Witness [dʒɪ'həʊvəz-] *n* Testemunha *f* de Jeová.

Jello® *n (U)* ***US*** ≃ gelatina *f.*

jelly ['dʒelɪ] (*pl* **-ies**) *n* **-1.** [dessert] gelatina *f* **-2.** [jam] geléia *f.*

jelly baby *n* ***UK*** *caramelo em forma de boneco.*

jelly bean *n* bala *f* de jujuba.

jellyfish ['dʒelɪfɪʃ] (*pl inv* OR **-es**) *n* água-viva *f.*

jelly roll *n* ***US*** rocambole *m.*

jemmy ***UK*** ['dʒemɪ], **jimmy** ***US*** ['dʒɪmɪ] (*pl* **-ies**) *n* pé-de-cabra *m.*

jeopardize, -ise ['dʒepədaɪz] *vt* pôr em perigo, arriscar.

jeopardy ['dʒepədɪ] *n*: **in ~** em perigo.

jerk [dʒɜːk] ◇ *n* **-1.** [movement] guinada *f*, movimento *m* brusco **-2.** ***inf pej*** [fool] estúpido *m*, -da *f.* ◇ *vt* mover abruptamente; **he ~ed the door open** ele abriu a porta bruscamente. ◇ *vi* dar solavancos.

jerkily ['dʒɜːkɪlɪ] *adv* abruptamente.

jerkin ['dʒɜːkɪn] *n* colete *m.*

jerky ['dʒɜːkɪ] (*compar* **-ier**, *superl* **-iest**) *adj* abrupto(-ta).

jerry-built ['dʒerɪ-] *adj* mal construído(da).

jerry can *n* lata *f.*

jersey ['dʒɜːzɪ] (*pl* **jerseys**) *n* **-1.** [sweater] suéter *m* **-2.** *(U)* [cloth] jérsei *m.*

Jersey ['dʒɜːzɪ] *n* Jersey; **in ~** em Jersey.

Jerusalem [dʒə'ruːsələm] *n* Jerusalém; **in ~** em Jerusalém.

Jerusalem artichoke *n* tupinambor *m.*

jest [dʒest] *n* brincadeira *f*; **in ~** de brincadeira.

jester ['dʒesteʳ] *n* bufão *m.*

Jesuit ['dʒezjʊɪt] ◇ *adj* jesuíta. ◇ *n* jesuíta *m*.
Jesus (Christ) ['dʒi:zəs-] ◇ *n* Jesus Cristo. ◇ *interj inf* Jesus Cristo!
jet [dʒet] (*pt* & *pp* **-ted**, *cont* **-ting**) ◇ *n* **-1.** [gen] jato *m* **- 2.** [nozzle, outlet] cano *m* de descarga. ◇ *vi* [travel by jet] voar num avião a jato.
jet-black *adj* da cor de azeviche.
jet engine *n* motor *m* a jato.
jetfoil ['dʒetfɔɪl] *n* hidroavião *m*.
jet lag *n (U)* jet lag *m*.
jet-propelled [-prə'peld] *adj* de propulsão a jato.
jetsam ['dʒetsəm] *n* ⊳ **flotsam**.
jet set *n*: **the ~** o jet set.
jettison ['dʒetɪsən] *vt* **-1.** [cargo, bombs] alijar **- 2.** *fig* [discard] descartar.
jetty ['dʒetɪ] (*pl* **-ies**) *n* quebra-mar *m*.
Jew [dʒu:] *n* judeu *m*.
jewel ['dʒu:əl] ◇ *n* **-1.** [gemstone] pedra *f* preciosa **- 2.** [piece of jewellery] jóia *f* **- 3.** [in watch] rubi *m*. ◇ *comp* de jóias.
jeweller *UK*, **jeweler** *US* ['dʒu:ələʳ] *n* joalheiro *m*, -ra *f*; **~'s (shop)** joalheria *f*.
jewellery *UK*, **jewelry** *US* ['dʒu:əlrɪ] *n (U)* jóias *fpl*.
Jewish ['dʒu:ɪʃ] *adj* judeu(dia).
JFK (*abbr of* **John Fitzgerald Kennedy International Airport**) *n* (aeroporto *m*) JFK *m*.
jib [dʒɪb] (*pt* & *pp* **-bed**, *cont* **-bing**) ◇ *n* **-1.** [NAUT - beam] vau *m*; [- sail] bujarrona *f* **- 2.** [of crane] braço *m* de guindaste. ◇ *vi*: **to ~ at sthg** hesitar em fazer algo.
jibe [dʒaɪb] *n* zombaria *f*.
jiffy ['dʒɪfɪ] *n inf*: **in a ~** num instante.
Jiffy bag® *n* envelope *m* acolchoado.
jig [dʒɪg] (*pt* & *pp* **-ged**, *cont* **-ging**) ◇ *n* [dance] jiga *f*. ◇ *vi* **-1.** [dance] dançar jiga **- 2.** [jump] saracotear, gingar.
jiggle ['dʒɪgl] *vt* sacudir.
jigsaw (puzzle) ['dʒɪgsɔ:-] *n* quebra-cabeça *m*.
jihad [dʒɪ'hɑ:d] *n* jihad *f*.
jilt [dʒɪlt] *vt* deixar plantado(da).
jimmy *n US* = **jemmy**.
jingle ['dʒɪŋgl] ◇ *n* **-1.** [sound] tilintar *m* **- 2.** [song] jingle *m*. ◇ *vi* tilintar.
jingoism ['dʒɪŋgəʊɪzm] *n (U)* jingoísmo *m*.
jinx [dʒɪŋks] *n* pé-frio *m*.
jinxed ['dʒɪŋkst] *adj* de má sorte.
jitters ['dʒɪtəz] *npl inf*: **to have the ~** ficar com os nervos à flor da pele.
jittery ['dʒɪtərɪ] *adj inf* nervoso(sa).
jive [dʒaɪv] ◇ *n* **-1.** [dance] swing *m* **- 2.** *US inf* [glib talk] burburinho *m*. ◇ *vi* dançar swing.
job [dʒɒb] *n* **-1.** [paid employment] emprego *m* **- 2.** [task, piece of work] trabalho *m*; **to do a good ~** fazer um bom trabalho; **to make a good ~ of sthg** fazer algo muito bem **- 3.** [difficult time]: **to have a ~ doing sthg** ter trabalho para fazer algo **- 4.** [function, role] tarefa *f*, função *f* **- 5.** *inf* [plastic surgery]: **to have a nose ~** fazer uma plástica no nariz **- 6.** *inf* [crime] trabalho *m* **- 7.** *phr*: **that's just the ~** *UK inf* isso vem bem a calhar.
jobbing ['dʒɒbɪŋ] *adj UK* que trabalha por empreitada.
job centre *n UK* agência *f* de empregos.
job creation scheme *n* projeto *m* de geração de empregos.
job description *n* descrição *f* do cargo.
jobless ['dʒɒblɪs] ◇ *adj* desempregado(da). ◇ *npl*: **the ~** os desempregados.
job lot *n* lote *m (de mercadorias variadas)*.
job satisfaction *n (U)* satisfação *f* profissional.
job security *n (U)* segurança *f* no trabalho.
Job Seekers Allowance *n UK seguro-desemprego concedido a pessoas que comprovadamente estão buscando um novo trabalho.*
jobsharing ['dʒɒbʃeərɪŋ] *n (U) prática de dividir um trabalho de tempo integral entre duas pessoas de forma que cada uma cumpra apenas meio turno, especialmente para permitir que mulheres com filhos possam trabalhar.*
Joburg, Jo'burg ['dʒəʊbɜ:g] *n inf* Joanesburgo; **in ~** em Joanesburgo.
jockey ['dʒɒkɪ] (*pl* **-s**) ◇ *n* jóquei *m*. ◇ *vi*: **to ~ for position** competir por uma melhor posição.
jockstrap ['dʒɒkstræp] *n* sunga *m*.
jocular ['dʒɒkjʊləʳ] *adj* **-1.** [person] divertido(da) **- 2.** [remark] engraçado(da).
jodhpurs ['dʒɒdpəz] *npl* culote *m*.
Joe Public [dʒəʊ-] *n UK inf* população *f* em geral.
jog [dʒɒg] (*pt* & *pp* **-ged**, *cont* **-ging**) ◇ *n* [run] corrida *f*, jogging *m*. ◇ *vt* [nudge] cutucar; **to ~ the table** sacudir a mesa; **to ~ sb's memory** refrescar a memória de alguém. ◇ *vi* [run] fazer cooper.
jogger ['dʒɒgəʳ] *n* [runner] corredor *m*, -ra *f*, praticante *mf* de cooper.
jogging ['dʒɒgɪŋ] *n* [running] cooper *m*.
joggle ['dʒɒgl] *vt* embalar.
Johannesburg [dʒəʊ'hænɪsbɜ:g] *n* Joanesburgo; **in ~** em Joanesburgo.
john [dʒɒn] *n US inf* [toilet] banheiro *m*.
John Hancock [-'hænkɒk] *n US inf* assinatura *f*, jamegão *m*.
join [dʒɔɪn] ◇ *n* junção *f*. ◇ *vt* **-1.** [connect] juntar **- 2.** [get together with] juntar-se a; **do ~ us for lunch** venha almoçar com a gente **- 3.** [become a member of - political party] filiar-se a; [- club] associar-se a; [- army] alistar-se em **- 4.** [take part in] unir-se a; **to ~ a queue** *UK*, **to ~ a line** *US* entrar numa fila; **to ~ forces** juntar forças; **~ the club!** juntem-se ao clube! ◇ *vi* **-1.** [connect - rivers] unir-se; [- pieces] encaixar-se **- 2.** [become a member - of library] inscrever-se; [- of club] associar-se.
◆ **join in** *vt fus* & *vi* participar.
◆ **join up** *vi* MIL alistar-se.
joiner ['dʒɔɪnəʳ] *n* marceneiro *m*, -ra *f*.
joinery ['dʒɔɪnərɪ] *n (U)* marcenaria *f*.
joint [dʒɔɪnt] ◇ *adj* conjunto(ta). ◇ *n* **-1.** ANAT articulação *f* **- 2.** [where things are joined] encaixe *m* **- 3.** *UK* [of meat] corte *m* **- 4.** *inf pej* [place] espelunca *f* **- 5.** *drugs sl* [cannabis cigarette] baseado *m*.
joint account *n* conta *f* conjunta.
Joint Chiefs of Staff *npl*: **the ~** o Alto Comando das Forças Armadas *(nos Estados Unidos)*.
jointed ['dʒɔɪntɪd] *adj* articulado(da).

jointly ['dʒɔɪntlɪ] *adv* conjuntamente.
joint ownership *n (U)* co-propriedade *f.*
joint-stock company *n* ≃ sociedade *f* anônima.
joint venture *n* joint-venture *f.*
joist [dʒɔɪst] *n* viga *f* de madeira.
jojoba [hə'həʊbə] *n (U)* jojoba *f.*
joke [dʒəʊk] <> *n* **-1.** [funny story or action] piada *f*, anedota *f*; **to go beyond a ~** perder a graça; **to play a ~ on sb** pregar uma peça em alguém; **it's no ~** [not easy] não é fácil **-2.** [referring to situation, person]: **to be a ~** ser uma piada. <> *vi* brincar; **to ~ about sthg** brincar em relação a algo; **to ~ with sb** brincar com alguém.
joker ['dʒəʊkə^r] *n* **-1.** [person] brincalhão *m*, -lhona *f* **-2.** [playing card] curinga *m.*
jollity ['dʒɒlətɪ] *n (U)* alegria *f.*
jolly ['dʒɒlɪ] (*compar* **-ier**, *superl* **-iest**) <> *adj* alegre, divertido(da). <> *adv UK inf* muito; **~ easy!** barbada!; **~ good!** excelente!
jolt [dʒəʊlt] <> *n* **-1.** [jerk] empurrão *m*, solavanco *m* **-2.** [shock] sacudida *f.* <> *vt* **-1.** [jerk] sacudir **-2.** [shock] chocar; **to ~ sb into doing sthg** forçar alguém a fazer algo. <> *vi* sacolejar.
Joneses ['dʒəʊnzɪz] *npl*: **to keep up with the ~** não ser menos que os outros.
Jordan ['dʒɔ:dn] *n* Jordânia; **in ~** na Jordânia; **the (River) ~** o (Rio) Jordão.
Jordanian [dʒɔ:'deɪnjən] <> *adj* jordaniano(na). <> *n* jordaniano *m*, -na *f.*
joss stick [dʒɒs-] *n* incenso *m* aromático.
jostle ['dʒɒsl] <> *vt* acotovelar. <> *vi* acotovelar-se.
jot [dʒɒt] (*pt* & *pp* **-ted**, *cont* **-ting**) *n* tiquinho *m*; **there isn't a ~ of truth in ...** não há um pingo de verdade em ...; **I don't care a ~ what the rest of you think** não ligo a mínima para o que vocês pensam.
◆ **jot down** *vt sep* anotar.
jotter ['dʒɒtə^r] *n* bloco *m* de anotações.
jottings ['dʒɒtɪŋz] *npl* recadinhos *mpl.*
journal ['dʒɜ:nl] *n* **-1.** [magazine] revista *f* especializada **-2.** [diary] diário *m.*
journalese [,dʒɜ:nə'li:z] *n (U) pej* jargão *m* jornalístico, jornalês *m.*
journalism ['dʒɜ:nəlɪzm] *n (U)* jornalismo *m.*
journalist ['dʒɜ:nəlɪst] *n* jornalista *mf.*
journey ['dʒɜ:nɪ] (*pl* **-s**) *n* jornada *f.*
joust [dʒaʊst] <> *n* justa *f.* <> *vi* justar.
jovial ['dʒəʊvjəl] *adj* jovial.
jowls [dʒaʊlz] *npl* bochechas *fpl.*
joy [dʒɔɪ] *n* **-1.** *(U)* [happiness] alegria *f* **-2.** [cause of happiness] prazer *m*, deleite *m.*
joyful ['dʒɔɪfʊl] *adj* alegre.
joyfully ['dʒɔɪfʊlɪ] *adv* alegremente.
joyous ['dʒɔɪəs] *adj literary* deleitante, jubiloso(sa).
joyously ['dʒɔɪəslɪ] *adv literary* com deleite.
joypad *n COMPUT* joystick *m.*
joyride ['dʒɔɪraɪd] <> *n* volta *f* num carro roubado. <> *vi* andar num carro roubado.
joyrider ['dʒɔɪraɪdə^r] *n* ladrão *m*, -dra *f* de carro.
joystick ['dʒɔɪstɪk] *n* **-1.** [in aircraft] manche *m* **-2.** [for computers, video games] joystick *m.*

JP *n abbr of* **Justice of the Peace.**
Jr. (*abbr of* **Junior**) Jr.
jubilant ['dʒu:bɪlənt] *adj* jubilante.
jubilation [,dʒu:bɪ'leɪʃn] *n (U)* júbilo *m.*
jubilee ['dʒu:bɪli:] *n* jubileu *m.*
Judaism [dʒu:'deɪɪzm] *n (U)* judaísmo *m.*
judder ['dʒʌdə^r] *vi UK* sacudir intensamente.
judge [dʒʌdʒ] <> *n* juíz *m*, -za *f.* <> *vt* **-1.** *JUR* julgar **-2.** [decide result of] sentenciar **-3.** [estimate] estimar. <> *vi* [decide] julgar; **to ~ from** *OR* **by** a julgar por, julgando-se por.
judg(e)ment ['dʒʌdʒmənt] *n* **-1.** *JUR* julgamento *m*; **to pass ~ (on sb)** condenar (alguém) **-2.** [opinion] parecer *m*; **to pass ~ (on sb/sthg)** julgar (alguém/algo); **to reserve ~** adiar um julgamento **-3.** *(U)* [ability to form opinion] opinião *f*; **against my better ~** contra a minha vontade **-4.** [punishment] sentença *f.*
judg(e)mental [dʒʌdʒ'mentl] *adj pej* crítico(ca).
judicial [dʒu:'dɪʃl] *adj* judicial.
judiciary [dʒu:'dɪʃərɪ] *n*: **the ~** o judiciário.
judicious [dʒu:'dɪʃəs] *adj* judicioso(sa).
judo ['dʒu:dəʊ] *n (U)* judô *m.*
jug [dʒʌg] *n* [container] jarro *m.*
juggernaut ['dʒʌgənɔ:t] *n* [truck] jamanta *f.*
juggle ['dʒʌgl] <> *vt* **-1.** [throw] fazer malabarismos com **-2.** [rearrange] reorganizar **-3.** [commitments] equilibrar **-4.** [figures, ideas] maquiar. <> *vi* [as entertainment] fazer malabarismos.
juggler ['dʒʌglə^r] *n* malabarista *mf.*
jugular (vein) ['dʒʌgjʊlə^r-] *n* (veia *f*) jugular *f.*
juice [dʒu:s] *n* **-1.** [from fruit, vegetables] suco *m* **-2.** [from meat] molho *m.*
◆ **juices** *npl* [in stomach] suco *m* gástrico.
juicy ['dʒu:sɪ] (*compar* **-ier**, *superl* **-iest**) *adj* **-1.** [full of juice] suculento(ta) **-2.** *inf* [scandalous] escandaloso(-sa) **-3.** *inf* [enjoyable, desirable] desejável.
jujitsu [dʒu:'dʒɪtsu:] *n (U)* jiu-jitsu *m.*
jukebox ['dʒu:kbɒks] *n* juke-box *f.*
Jul. (*abbr of* **July**) jul.
July [dʒu:'laɪ] *n* julho; *see also* **September.**
jumble ['dʒʌmbl] <> *n* [mixture] mistura *f.* <> *vt*: **to ~ (up)** confundir.
jumble sale *n UK* venda *f* de objetos usados.
jumbo jet ['dʒʌmbəʊ-] *n* jumbo *m.*
jumbo-sized ['dʒʌmbəʊsaɪzd] *adj* gigantesco(ca).
jump [dʒʌmp] <> *n* **-1.** [leap] salto *m* **-2.** [fence in horse-jumping] obstáculo *m* **-3.** [rapid increase] alta *m* **-4.** *phr*: **to keep one ~ ahead of sb** manter um passo à frente de alguém. <> *vt* **-1.** [cross by leaping] pular; **the train ~ed the rails** o trem descarrilhou **-2.** *inf* [attack] atacar **-3.** *US* [train, bus] viajar sem passagem em. <> *vi* **-1.** [leap] saltar **-2.** [make a sudden movement] sobressaltar; **the noise made me ~** o barulho me fez dar um sobressalto **-3.** [increase rapidly] ter uma alta.
◆ **jump at** *vt fus fig* agarrar.
◆ **jump in** *vi* [get in quickly]: **~ in!** entra rápido!
◆ **jump out** *vi* [get out quickly]: **~ out!** salta fora!
◆ **jump up** *vi* [rise hurriedly] levantar-se rapidamente.
jumped-up ['dʒʌmpt-] *adj UK inf pej* pretencioso(-sa).

jumper ['dʒʌmpəʳ] *n* **-1.** *UK* [pullover] suéter *m* **-2.** *US* [dress] avental *m*.

jump jet *n* aeronave *f* de decolagem vertical.

jump leads *npl* cabos *mpl* para ligação da bateria.

jump-start *vt* fazer ligação direta.

jumpsuit ['dʒʌmpsu:t] *n* macacão *m*.

jumpy ['dʒʌmpɪ] (*compar* **-ier**, *superl* **-iest**) *adj* nervoso(sa).

Jun. -1. (*abbr of* **June**) jun. **-2.** = **Junr**.

junction ['dʒʌŋkʃn] *n* [meeting point] junção *f*, entroncamento *m*.

junction box *n* caixa *f* de ligação.

juncture ['dʒʌŋktʃəʳ] *n* ***fml*: at this ~** nesta conjuntura.

June [dʒu:n] *n* junho; *see also* **September**.

jungle ['dʒʌŋgl] *n* selva *f*; **the Amazon ~** a floresta amazônica.

jungle gym *n* ***US*** trepa-trepa *f*.

junior ['dʒu:njəʳ] ◇ *adj* **-1.** [younger] jovem **-2.** [lower in rank] júnior **-3.** ***US*** [after name] júnior. ◇ *n* **-1.** [person of lower rank] júnior *mf* **-2.** [younger person] jovem *mf*; **he's five years her ~** ele é cinco anos mais jovem que ela **-3.** ***US SCH & UNIV*** aluno *m*, -na *f* do penúltimo ano.

junior college *n* ***US*** *escola universitária para os dois primeiros anos de curso.*

junior doctor *n* médico *m*, -ca *f* residente.

junior high school *n* ***US*** escola *f* de ensino intermediário *(para alunos de 13 a 15 anos)*.

junior minister *n* ***UK*** subsecretário *m*, -ria *f*.

junior school *n* ***UK*** escola *f* primária.

juniper ['dʒu:nɪpəʳ] *n* junípero *m*.

junk [dʒʌŋk] ◇ *n* **-1.** ***inf*** [unwanted things] traste *m* **-2.** [boat] junco *m*. ◇ *vt* jogar fora.

junket ['dʒʌŋkɪt] *n* **-1.** *(U)* [pudding] *espécie de pudim feito com leite e coalho* **-2.** ***inf pej*** [trip] viagem *f* às custas do governo.

junk food *n* ***pej*** *comida pronta e pouco saudável.*

junkie ['dʒʌŋkɪ] *n* ***drugs sl*** drogado *m*, -da *f*.

junk mail *n* ***pej*** junk mail *m*.

junk shop *n* brechó *m*, brique *m*.

Junr (*abbr of* **Junior**) Jr.

junta [***UK*** 'dʒʌntə, ***US*** 'hʊntə] *n* junta *f*.

Jupiter ['dʒu:pɪtəʳ] *n* [planet] Júpiter.

jurisdiction [ˌdʒʊərɪs'dɪkʃn] *n (U)* jurisdição *f*.

jurisprudence [ˌdʒʊərɪs'pru:dəns] *n (U)* jurisprudência *f*.

juror ['dʒʊərəʳ] *n* jurado *m*, -da *f*.

jury ['dʒʊərɪ] (*pl* **-ies**) *n* júri *m*.

jury box *n* tribunal *f* do júri.

jury service *n (U) trabalho m de jurado (num tribunal).*

just [dʒʌst] ◇ *adj* [fair] justo(ta). ◇ *adv* **-1.** [recently] agora mesmo; **he's ~ left** ele acabou de sair **-2.** [at this or that moment]**: I was ~ about to go out** eu estava quase saindo; **I'm ~ going to do it** vou fazer isso agora mesmo; **~ then there was a knock at the door** naquele momento houve uma batida na porta; **she arrived ~ as I was leaving** ela chegou no exato momento em que eu estava saindo; **why do you always arrive ~ as I'm leaving?** por que você sempre chega justamente quando estou saindo? **-3.** [only, simply] apenas, simplesmente; **in ~ a minute** *OR* **moment** *OR* **second** num minuto *OR* instante *OR* segundo; **~ a minute!** espera aí um pouquinho! **-4.** [barely, almost not] mal; **I can only ~ hear you** mal consigo ouvir você; **I only ~ caught the train** quase perdi o trem; **we have ~ enough time** quase não temos tempo **-5.** [for emphasis] simplesmente; **I ~ can't believe it!** simplesmente não consigo acreditar!; **~ look at this mess!** dá só uma olhada na bagunça! **-6.** [exactly, precisely] precisamente; **~ here** exatamente aqui **-7.** [in requests]**: could I ~ borrow your pen?** poderia me emprestar sua caneta, por favor?

◆ **just about** *adv* mais ou menos.

◆ **just as** *adv* [in comparisons]**: ~ as well as you** tão bem quanto você; **~ as bad as ever** mal como sempre.

◆ **just now** *adv* **-1.** [a short time ago] agora mesmo **-2.** [at this moment] neste momento.

justice ['dʒʌstɪs] *n* **-1.** [gen] justiça *f* **-2.** [of a cause, claim] razão *f* **-3.** [judge] juíz *m* **-4.** ***phr*: to do ~ to sthg** [to a job] fazer justiça a algo; [to a meal] apreciar devidamente; **to do ~ to sb** fazer justiça a alguém; **to do o.s. ~** desempenhar-se à altura.

Justice of the Peace (*pl* **Justices of the Peace**) *n* Juíz *m*, -za *f* de Paz.

justifiable ['dʒʌstɪfaɪəbl] *adj* justificável.

justifiable homicide *n* homicídio *m* em legítima defesa.

justifiably ['dʒʌstɪfaɪəblɪ] *adv* justificavelmente.

justification [ˌdʒʌstɪfɪ'keɪʃn] *n* **-1.** [good reason] justificativa *f* **-2.** *COMPUT*: **right-hand ~** alinhamento *m* justificado à direita.

justify ['dʒʌstɪfaɪ] (*pt* & *pp* **-ied**) *vt* **-1.** [give reasons for] justificar; **to ~ doing sthg** ter razões para fazer algo **-2.** *COMPUT & TYPO* justificar.

justly ['dʒʌstlɪ] *adv* merecidamente, imparcialmente.

justness *n (U)* justiça *f*.

jut [dʒʌt] (*pt* & *pp* **-ted**, *cont* **-ting**) *vi*: **to ~ (out)** projetar-se.

jute [dʒu:t] *n (U)* juta *f*.

juvenile ['dʒu:vənaɪl] ◇ *adj* **-1.** *JUR* juvenil **-2.** ***pej*** [childish] infantil. ◇ *n JUR* [young person] menor *mf*.

juvenile court *n* juizado *m* de menores.

juvenile delinquent *n* delinqüente *mf* juvenil.

juxtapose [ˌdʒʌkstə'pəʊz] *vt*: **to ~ sthg with sthg** justapor algo com algo.

juxtaposition [ˌdʒʌkstəpə'zɪʃn] *n (U)* justaposição *f*.

k (*pl* **k's** *OR* **ks**), **K** (*pl* **K's** *OR* **Ks**) [keɪ] *n* [letter] k, K *m*.
◆ **K** *n* **-1.** (*abbr of* **kilobyte**) K **-2.** (*abbr of* **Knight**) Cavaleiro *m* **-3.** (*abbr of* **thousand**) mil.

Kabul [ˈkɑːbʊl] *n* Cabul; **in ~** em Cabul.

kaftan [ˈkæftæn] *n* cafetã *f*.

Kalahari Desert [ˌkæləˈhɑːrɪ-] *n*: **the ~** o Deserto de Kalahari.

kale [keɪl] *n (U)* couve *f* crespa.

kaleidoscope [kəˈlaɪdəskəʊp] *n* caleidoscópio *m*.

Kampala [kæmˈpɑːlə] *n* Campala; **in ~** em Campala.

Kampuchea [ˌkæmpʊˈtʃɪə] *n* Camboja; **in ~** em Camboja.

Kampuchean ◇ *adj* cambojano(na). ◇ *n* cambojano *m*, -na *f*.

kangaroo [ˌkæŋgəˈruː] *n* canguru *m*.

Kansas [ˈkænzəs] *n* Kansas; **in ~** no Kansas.

kaolin [ˈkeɪəlɪn] *n (U)* caulim *m*.

kaput [kəˈpʊt] *adj inf* acabado(da).

karaoke [kɑːrəˈəʊkɪ] *n* karaokê *m*.

karat [ˈkærət] *n US* quilate *m*.

karate [kəˈrɑːtɪ] *n (U)* karatê *m*.

Kashmir [kæʃˈmɪə] *n* Cachemira; **in ~** na Cachemira.

Katmandu [ˌkætmænˈduː] *n* Katmandu; **in ~** em Katmandu.

kayak [ˈkaɪæk] *n* caiaque *m*.

Kazakhstan [ˌkæzækˈstɑːn] *n* Cazaquistão; **in ~** no Cazaquistão.

KB (*abbr of* **kilobyte(s)**) *n COMPUT* KB.

KBE (*abbr of* **Knight Commander of the Order of the British Empire**) *n (titular de) distinção britânica*.

KC (*abbr of* **King's Counsel**) *n título conferido a advogados de prestígio na Grã-Bretanha*.

kcal (*abbr of* **kilocalorie**) Kcal.

kebab [kɪˈbæb] *n churrasquinho picante servido com pão árabe e acompanhado de vegetais picados*, kebab *m*.

kedgeree [ˈkedʒəriː] *n (U) UK prato indiano feito com arroz, peixe e ovos*, kedgeree *m*.

keel [kiːl] *n* quilha *f*; **on an even ~** em perfeito equilíbrio.
◆ **keel over** *vi* **-1.** [ship] emborcar **-2.** [person] desmaiar.

keen [kiːn] *adj* **-1.** [enthusiastic] entusiasta; **to be ~ on sthg** gostar muito de algo, ser aficionado(da) por algo; **to be ~ on sb** gostar muito de alguém; **to be ~ to do** *OR* **on doing sthg** estar muito a fim de fazer algo; **I'm not madly ~ on going** não estou com toda essa vontade de ir **-2.** [intense] intenso(-sa) **-3.** [sharp, well-developed] apurado(da) **-4.** [wind] forte.

keenly [ˈkiːnlɪ] *adv* **-1.** [intensely] profundamente **-2.** [intently] atentamente.

keenness [ˈkiːnnɪs] *n (U)* **-1.** [enthusiasm] entusiasmo *m* **-2.** [intensity] intensidade *f* **-3.** [sharpness] perspicácia *f*.

keep [kiːp] (*pt* & *pp* **kept**) ◇ *vt* **-1.** [maintain in a particular place or state or position] manter; **to ~ sb waiting** fazer alguém esperar **-2.** [retain] ficar com; **please ~ the change** pode ficar com o troco; **they're ~ing the house in Scotland** eles estão mantendo a casa na Escócia **-3.** [continue]: **to ~ doing sthg** continuar fazendo algo; **to ~ talking** continuar falando; **to ~ going** continuar indo **-4.** [put aside, store] guardar **-5.** [prevent]: **to ~ sb/sthg from doing sthg** impedir alguém/algo de fazer algo **-6.** [detain] manter; **to ~ sb (from sthg)** privar alguém (de algo); **what kept you here?** o que te segurou aqui? **-7.** [fulfil, observe] cumprir; **to ~ a secret** guardar um segredo **-8.** [withhold news or fact of]: **to ~ sthg from sb** ocultar algo de alguém; **~ it to yourself for the moment** não conta isso para ninguém por enquanto **-9.** [diary, record, account] ter **-10.** [own - farm animals] criar; [- shop, car] ter **-11.** *phr*: **they ~ themselves to themselves** eles são muito reservados. ◇ *vi* **-1.** [remain, stay] manter-se **-2.** [continue moving] manter-se a **-3.** [last, stay fresh] conservar-se **-4.** *UK* [in health] manter-se. ◇ *n (U)* [food, board etc] sustento *m*.
◆ **for keeps** *adv* para valer.
◆ **keep at** *vt fus*: **to ~ at it** [work hard] empenhar-se.
◆ **keep back** *vt sep* conter.
◆ **keep down** *vt sep* **-1.** [stop from increasing] limitar **-2.** [food] controlar.
◆ **keep off** ◇ *vt sep* [fend off] manter afastado(da). ◇ *vt fus* [avoid] evitar; **'~ off the grass'** 'não pise na grama'.
◆ **keep on** ◇ *vi* **-1.** [continue] continuar **-2.** [talk incessantly]: **to ~ on (about sthg)** falar incessantemente (sobre algo). ◇ *vt* [continue]: **to ~ on doing sthg** [without stopping] continuar fazendo algo; [repeatedly] continuar fazendo algo sem parar.
◆ **keep on at** *vt fus UK* importunar.
◆ **keep out** ◇ *vt sep* manter-se fora. ◇ *vi*: **'~ out'** 'entrada proibida'.
◆ **keep to** ◇ *vt fus* **-1.** [observe, respect] respeitar **-2.** [not deviate from] manter-se em **-3.** [stay in] ficar em. ◇ *vt sep* [limit] limitar.
◆ **keep up** ◇ *vt sep* **-1.** [prevent from falling] segurar **-2.** [maintain, continue] manter **-3.** [prevent from going to bed] manter acordado(da). ◇ *vi* **-1.** [maintain pace, level] acompanhar; **to ~ up with sb/sthg** acompanhar alguém/algo **-2.** [remain in contact]: **to ~ up with sb** manter-se em contato com alguém.

keeper [ˈkiːpəʳ] *n* **-1.** [in zoo] zelador *m*, -ra *f*, guarda *mf* **-2.** [curator] curador *m*, -ra *f*.

keep-fit *UK* ◇ *n (U)* ginástica *f.* ◇ *comp* de ginástica.
keeping ['ki:pɪŋ] *n* **-1.** [care] cuidado *m* **-2.** [conformity, harmony]: **in/out of ~ with sthg** [rules, regulations, decision] em acordo/desacordo com algo; [clothes, furniture, style] combinando/não combinando com algo.
keepsake ['ki:pseɪk] *n* lembrança *f.*
keg [keg] *n* barrilote *m.*
kelp [kelp] *n (U)* alga *f* marinha.
ken [ken] *n*: **beyond one's ~** além do alcance de alguém.
kennel ['kenl] *n* **-1.** [shelter for dog] canil *m* **-2.** *US* = **kennels.**
◆ **kennels** *npl UK* [for boarding pets] canil *m.*
Kentucky [ken'tʌkɪ] *n* Kentucky; **in ~** em Kentucky.
Kenya ['kenjə] *n* Quênia; **in ~** no Quênia.
Kenyan ['kenjən] ◇ *adj* queniano(na). ◇ *n* queniano *m*, -na *f.*
kept [kept] *pt & pp* ▷ **keep.**
kerb [kɜ:b] *n UK* meio-fio *m.*
kerb crawler [-ˌkrɔ:ləʳ] *n UK* *pessoa que dirige o carro vagarosamente junto ao meio-fio em busca de prostitutas.*
kerbstone ['kɜ:bstəʊn] *n UK* marco *m* de pedra.
kerfuffle [kə'fʌfl] *n UK inf* escarcéu *m.*
kernel ['kɜ:nl] *n* [of nut] amêndoa *f*; **the ~ of the issue** o cerne da questão.
kerosene ['kerəsi:n] *n (U)* querosene *f.*
kestrel ['kestrəl] *n* falcão *m* europeu.
ketch *n* brigue *m.*
ketchup ['ketʃəp] *n (U)* ketchup *m.*
kettle ['ketl] *n* chaleira *f.*
kettledrum ['ketldrʌm] *n* tímpano *m.*
key [ki:] ◇ *n* **-1.** [for lock] chave *f* **- 2.** [of typewriter, computer] tecla *f* **- 3.** [explanatory list] legenda *f* **- 4.** [solution, answer]: **~ (to sthg)** chave (para algo) **- 5.** [*MUS* - of piano, organ] tom *m*; [- scale of notes] clave *f.* ◇ *adj* [main] principal; **~ position** posição-chave; **~ issue** questão-chave.
◆ **key in** *vt sep* digitar.
keyboard ['ki:bɔ:d] ◇ *n* teclado *m.* ◇ *vt* digitar.
keyboarder ['ki:bɔ:dəʳ] *n* digitador *m*, -ra *f.*
keyed up [ki:d-] *adj* excitado(da).
keyhole ['ki:həʊl] *n* buraco *m* da fechadura.
keynote ['ki:nəʊt] ◇ *n* [main point] tônica *f.* ◇ *comp*: **~ speech** conferência *f* de abertura.
keypad ['ki:pæd] *n COMPUT* teclado *m.*
keypunch ['ki:pʌntʃ] *n US* máquina *f* de perfurar cartões.
key ring *n* chaveiro *m.*
keystone ['ki:stəʊn] *n* pedra *f* angular.
keystroke ['ki:strəʊk] *n COMPUT* pressionamento *m* de tecla.
keyword *n* palavra-chave *f.*
kg (*abbr of* **kilogram**) Kg.
KGB *n* KGB *f.*
khaki ['kɑ:kɪ] ◇ *adj* cáqui *inv.* ◇ *n* **-1.** [colour] cáqui *m* **- 2.** [cloth] tecido *m* cor de cáqui.
kHz (*abbr of* **kilohertz**) *n* kHz.
kibbutz [kɪ'bʊts] (*pl* **kibbutzim** [ˌkɪbʊt'si:m], **-es**) *n* kibutz *m.*

kick [kɪk] ◇ *n* **-1.** [with foot] chute *m* **-2.** *inf* [excitement]: **to do sthg for ~s** fazer algo para se divertir; **to get a ~ from sthg** desfrutar de algo **- 3.** *inf* [of drink] efeito *m* estimulante. ◇ *vt* **- 1.** [with foot] chutar; **to ~ o.s.** *fig* morder-se de raiva **- 2.** *inf* [give up] largar. ◇ *vi* [person, baby, animal] dar pontapés.
◆ **kick about, kick around** *vi UK inf* [lie around] rodear.
◆ **kick in** *vi* fazer efeito.
◆ **kick off** *vi* **- 1.** *FTBL* dar o pontapé inicial **- 2.** *inf fig* [start] começar.
◆ **kick out** *vt sep inf* expulsar.
◆ **kick up** *vt fus inf* protestar com violência.
kickoff ['kɪkɒf] *n* pontapé *m* inicial.
kick-start *vt* dar partida em; **to give sthg a ~** dar um grande impulso a algo.
kid [kɪd] (*pt & pp* **-ded**, *cont* **-ding**) ◇ *n* **- 1.** *inf* [child, young person] criança *f*; **I've got four ~s** tenho quatro filhos **- 2.** [young goat] cabrito *m* **- 3.** [leather] pelica *f.* ◇ *comp inf* [brother, sister]: **my ~ brother** meu irmão mais novo; **my ~ sister** minha irmã mais nova. ◇ *vt inf* **- 1.** [tease] caçoar **- 2.** [delude]: **to ~ o.s.** iludir-se. ◇ *vi inf*: **to be kidding** estar brincando; **no kidding!** [in emphasis] não brinca!; [in disbelief] não acredito!
kiddie, kiddy ['kɪdɪ] (*pl* **-ies**) *n inf* guri *m*, -ria *f.*
kid gloves *npl*: **to treat** *OR* **handle sb with ~** tratar alguém com luvas de pelica.
kidnap ['kɪdnæp] (*UK pt & pp* **-ped**, *cont* **-ping**, *US pt & pp* **-ed**, *cont* **-ing**) *vt* seqüestrar.
kidnapper *UK*, **kidnaper** *US* ['kɪdnæpəʳ] *n* seqüestrador *m*, -ra *f.*
kidnapping *UK*, **kidnaping** *US* ['kɪdnæpɪŋ] *n* seqüestro *m.*
kidney ['kɪdnɪ] (*pl* **-s**) *n* rim *m.*
kidney bean *n* feijão *m* roxo.
kidney machine *n* hemodialisador *m.*
Kilimanjaro [ˌkɪlɪmən'dʒɑ:rəʊ] *n* Kilimanjaro.
kill [kɪl] ◇ *n* **- 1.** [of animal] abate *m*; **to move** *OR* **close in for the ~** dar o bote; *fig* dar o bote **- 2.** [dead animal] presa *f.* ◇ *vt* **- 1.** [gen] matar; **my feet are ~ing me** meus pés estão me matando; **to ~ o.s.** matar-se **- 2.** [murder] assassinar **- 3.** *fig* [cause to end, fail] acabar com **- 4.** [pass]: **to ~ time** matar tempo. ◇ *vi* aniquilar.
◆ **kill off** *vt sep* **- 1.** [cause death of] aniquilar **- 2.** *fig* [cause to end, fail] destruir.
killer ['kɪləʳ] *n* **- 1.** [person] assassino *m*, -na *f* **- 2.** [animal] matador *m*, -ra *f* **- 3.** [disease] doença *f* fatal.
killer whale *n* orca *f*, baleia-assassina *f.*
killing ['kɪlɪŋ] ◇ *adj inf* [very funny] de matar. ◇ *n* **- 1.** [of one person] assassinato *m* **- 2.** [of several people] matança *f* **- 3.** *inf* [profit]: **to make a ~** faturar uma grana.
killjoy ['kɪldʒɔɪ] *n* estraga-prazer *mf.*
kiln [kɪln] *n* fornalha *f.*
kilo ['ki:ləʊ] (*pl* **-s**) (*abbr of* **kilogram**) *n* quilo *m.*
kilo- [kɪlə] *prefix* quilo.
kilobyte ['kɪləbaɪt] *n* quilobyte *m.*
kilocalorie ['kɪləˌkælərɪ] *n* quilocaloria *f.*
kilogram(me) ['kɪləgræm] *n* quilograma *m.*
kilohertz ['kɪləhɜ:tz] (*pl inv*) *n* quilohertz *m.*

kilojoule ['kɪlədʒu:l] *n* quilojoule *m*.
kilometre *UK* ['kɪlə,mi:tə^r], **kilometer** *US* [kɪ'lɒmɪtə^r] *n* quilômetro *m*.
kilowatt ['kɪləwɒt] *n* quilowatt *m*.
kilt [kɪlt] *n* kilt *m*.
kimono [kɪ'məʊnəʊ] (*pl* **-s**) *n* quimono *m*.
kin [kɪn] *n* ▻ **kith**.
kind [kaɪnd] ◇ *adj* gentil, amável; **would you be so ~ as to ...?** será que você me faria a gentileza de ...? ◇ *n* espécie *f*, tipo *m*; **a ~ of** uma espécie de; **~ of** *inf* de certo modo; **I ~ of thought that ...** eu meio que achei que ...; **of a ~** [sort of] do estilo; **an agreement of a ~** um acordo do estilo; [of same kind] do mesmo tipo; **in ~** [payment] em espécie; **nothing of the ~!** de jeito nenhum!; **it's one of a ~** é um em um milhão; **they're two of a ~** os dois são muito semelhantes.
kindergarten ['kɪndə,gɑ:tn] *n* jardim-de-infância *m*.
kind-hearted [-'hɑ:tɪd] *adj* de bom coração.
kindle ['kɪndl] *vt* **-1.** [fire] pôr fogo em **-2.** *fig* [idea, feeling] inflamar.
kindling ['kɪndlɪŋ] *n (U)* [to light fire] gravetos *mpl*.
kindly ['kaɪndlɪ] (*compar* **-ier**, *superl* **-iest**) ◇ *adj* bondoso(sa), gentil. ◇ *adv* **-1.** [gen] bondosamente, gentilmente; **to look ~ on sb/sthg** olhar alguém/algo com bons olhos **-2.** [in sarcasm]: **~ leave the room!** faça o favor de sair da sala!; **will you ~ stop calling me that name!** pode fazer o favor de parar de me chamar por esse nome! **-3.** *phr*: **not to take ~ to sthg** não simpatizar com algo.
kindness ['kaɪndnɪs] *n* **-1.** *(U)* [gentleness] gentileza *f*, bondade *f* **-2.** [helpful act] generosidade *f*.
kindred ['kɪndrɪd] *adj* [similar] afim; **~ spirit** alma *f* gêmea.
kinetic [kɪ'netɪk] *adj* cinético(ca).
kinfolk(s) ['kɪnfəʊk(s)] *npl US* = **kinsfolk**.
king [kɪŋ] *n* rei *m*.
kingdom ['kɪŋdəm] *n* reino *m*.
kingfisher ['kɪŋ,fɪʃə^r] *n* martim-pescador *m*.
kingpin ['kɪŋpɪn] *n* **-1.** TECH pino-mestre *m* **-2.** *fig* [person] manda-chuva *m*.
king prawn *n* camarão *m* real.
king-size(d) [-saɪz(d)] *adj* de tamanho grande; **~ bed** cama *f* king-size.
kink [kɪŋk] *n* [in rope, hair] dobra *f*.
kinky ['kɪŋkɪ] (*compar* **-ier**, *superl* **-iest**) *adj* **-1.** *inf* [idea, behaviour] excêntrico(ca) **-2.** [sex] pervertido(da).
kinsfolk ['kɪnzfəʊk] *npl* parentes *mpl*.
kinship ['kɪnʃɪp] *n* **-1.** [relationship] parentesco *m* **-2.** [closeness] afinidade *f*.
kiosk ['ki:ɒsk] *n* **-1.** [small shop] banca *f* **-2.** *UK* [telephone box] cabine *f* telefônica.
kip [kɪp] (*pt* & *pp* **-ped**, *cont* **-ping**) *UK inf* ◇ *n* sesta *f*. ◇ *vi* sestear.
kipper ['kɪpə^r] *n* arenque *m* defumado.
Kirk [kɜ:k] *n Scot*: **the ~** *a igreja nacional escocesa*.
kirsch [kɪəʃ] *n* quirche *m*.
kiss [kɪs] ◇ *n* beijo *m*; **to give sb a ~** dar um beijo em alguém. ◇ *vt* beijar; **to ~ sb goodbye** dar um beijo de despedida em alguém. ◇ *vi* beijar-se.
kiss curl *n UK pequeno anel de cabelo que se penteia para ficar reto na testa, na nuca ou na frente da orelha*.
kiss of death *n fig*: **the ~** o beijo da morte.
kiss of life *n* [to resuscitate sb]: **to give sb the ~** fazer respiração boca-a-boca em alguém.
kissogram ['kɪsəgræm] *n* beijograma *m*, *forma de homenagear uma pessoa contratando alguém para lhe dar um beijo, ao estilo das telemensagens*.
kit [kɪt] (*pt* & *pp* **-ted**, *cont* **-ting**) *n* **-1.** [set] estojo *m* **-2.** *(U)* [clothes] equipamento *m* **-3.** [to be assembled] kit *m*, modelo *m*.
◆ **kit out** *vt sep UK* equipar.
kit bag *n* mochila *f* de viagem.
kitchen ['kɪtʃɪn] *n* cozinha *f*.
kitchenette [,kɪtʃɪ'net] *n* kitchenette *f*, copa-cozinha *f*.
kitchen garden *n* horta *f*.
kitchen roll *n* papel-toalha *m*.
kitchen sink *n* pia *f* de cozinha.
kitchen unit *n* módulo *m* de cozinha.
kitchenware ['kɪtʃɪnweə^r] *n* utensílios *mpl* para cozinha.
kite [kaɪt] *n* **-1.** [toy] pipa *f* **-2.** [bird] milhafre *m*.
Kite-mark *n UK* marca *f* de padrão de qualidade.
kith [kɪθ] *n*: **~ and kin** amigos *mpl* e parentes.
kitsch [kɪtʃ] *n (U)* kitsch *mf*.
kitten ['kɪtn] *n* gatinho *m*, -nha *f*.
kitty ['kɪtɪ] (*pl* **-ies**) *n* **-1.** [shared fund - for bills, drinks] vaquinha *f*; [- in card games] bolo *m* **-2.** [cat] gatinho *m*, -nha *f*.
kiwi ['ki:wi:] *n* **-1.** [bird] quivi *m* **-2.** *inf* [New Zealander] neozelandês *m*, -esa *f*.
kiwi fruit *n* quivi *m*.
KKK (*abbr of* **Ku Klux Klan**) *n* Ku Klux Klan *f*.
klaxon ['klæksn] *n* buzina *f* elétrica.
Kleenex® ['kli:neks] *n* lenço *m* de papel.
kleptomaniac [,kleptə'meɪnɪæk] *n* cleptomaníaco *m*, -ca *f*.
km (*abbr of* **kilometre**) km.
km/h (*abbr of* **kilometres per hour**) km/h.
knack [næk] *n* inclinação *m*, queda *f*; **to have the ~ (of doing sthg)** levar jeito (para fazer algo); **to have a ~ (for doing sthg)** ter uma queda (para fazer algo).
knacker ['nækə^r] *UK* ◇ *n* [horse slaughterer] matador *m*, -ra *f* de cavalos velhos. ◇ *vt inf* [tire, break] acabar.
knackered ['nækəd] *adj UK v inf* [tired, broken] acabado(da).
knapsack ['næpsæk] *n* mochila *f*.
knave [neɪv] *n* [playing card] valete *m*.
knead [ni:d] *vt* [dough, clay] misturar.
knee [ni:] *n* ANAT joelho *m*; **to be on one's ~s** [kneeling] ajoelhar-se; **to bring sb to their ~s** pôr alguém de joelhos.
kneecap ['ni:kæp] *n* rótula *f*.
knee-deep *adj* **-1.** [snow, water] até o joelho **-2.** [person] enterrado(da) até o joelho.
knee-high *adj* à altura dos joelhos.
kneel [ni:l] (*UK pt* & *pp* **knelt**, *US pt* & *pp* **knelt** OR **-ed**) *vi* ajoelhar-se.

◆ **kneel down** *vi* ajoelhar, ajoelhar-se.
knee-length *adj* até o joelho.
knees-up *n UK inf* festa *f* barulhenta.
knell [nel] *n* **-1.** dobre *m* dos sinos **-2.** *fig*: **to sound the death ~ for sthg** decretar a sentença de morte para algo.
knelt [nelt] *pt & pp* ▷ **kneel**.
knew [nju:] *pt* ▷ **know**.
knickers ['nɪkəz] *npl* **-1.** *UK* [underwear] calcinha *f* **-2.** *US* [knickerbockers] calções *mpl* (presos à altura dos joelhos).
knick-knack ['nɪknæk] *n* penduricalho *m*.
knife [naɪf] (*pl* **knives**) ◇ *n* faca *f*. ◇ *vt* esfaquear.
knifing *n* facada *f*.
knight [naɪt] ◇ *n* **-1.** [gen] cavaleiro *m* **-2.** [in chess] cavalo *m*. ◇ *vt* nomear cavaleiro(ra).
knighthood ['naɪthʊd] *n* título *m* da classe dos cavaleiros.
knit [nɪt] (*pt & pp* **knit** OR **-ted**, *cont* **-ting**) ◇ *adj*: **closely** OR **tightly ~** *fig* fortemente unido(da). ◇ *vt* [make with wool] tricotar. ◇ *vi* **-1.** [with wool] fazer tricô, tricotar **-2.** [join] juntar-se.
knitted ['nɪtɪd] *adj* [scarf, hat] de malha.
knitting ['nɪtɪŋ] *n (U)* **-1.** [activity] trabalho *m* de tricô **-2.** [work produced] tricô *m*.
knitting machine *n* máquina *f* de tricô.
knitting needle *n* agulha *f* de tricô.
knitting pattern *n* molde *m* de tricô.
knitwear ['nɪtweəʳ] *n (U)* roupa *f* de tricô.
knives [naɪvz] *pl* ▷ **knife**.
knob [nɒb] *n* **-1.** [on door] maçaneta *f* **-2.** [on drawer] puxador *m* **-3.** [on walking stick, furniture] nó *m* **-4.** [on TV, radio] botão *m*.
knobbly *UK* ['nɒblɪ], **knobby** *US* ['nɒbɪ] (*compar* **-ier**, *superl* **-iest**) *adj* **-1.** [gen] nodoso(sa) **-2.** [knees] ossudo(da).
knock [nɒk] ◇ *n* **-1.** [blow] pancada *f*, batida *f* **-2.** *inf* [piece of bad luck] azar *m*. ◇ *vt* **-1.** [gen] bater contra; **to ~ one's head on sthg** bater com a cabeça em algo; **to ~ a hole in the wall** abrir um buraco na parede; **to ~ a nail into sthg** pregar um prego em algo **-2.** *inf fig* [criticize] criticar. ◇ *vi* **-1.** [on door]: **to ~ at** OR **on sthg** bater em algo **-2.** [car engine] bater.
◆ **knock about, knock around** *inf* ◇ *vt sep* [beat up] tratar com violência. ◇ *vi* **-1.** *inf* [wander about] perambular **-2.** *inf* [spend time]: **to ~ about with sb** perder tempo com alguém.
◆ **knock back** *vt sep inf* **-1.** [drink] enxugar **-2.** *inf* [cost] custar a.
◆ **knock down** *vt sep* **-1.** [subj: car, driver] atropelar **-2.** [building] derrubar **-3.** [price] abater.
◆ **knock off** ◇ *vt sep* **-1.** [lower price by] abaixar **-2.** *UK inf* [steal] abafar **-3.** *v inf* [sleep with] dormir com. ◇ *vi inf* [stop working] parar de trabalhar.
◆ **knock out** *vt sep* **-1.** [make unconscious - subj: person, punch] pôr a nocaute; [- subj: drug] derrubar **-2.** [from competition] eliminar.
◆ **knock over** *vt sep* **-1.** [push over] derrubar **-2.** [in car] atropelar.
◆ **knock up** ◇ *vt sep* [produce hurriedly] preparar apressadamente. ◇ *vi* TENNIS bater bola.
knocker ['nɒkəʳ] *n* [on door] aldrava *f*.
knocking ['nɒkɪŋ] *n* **-1.** *(U)* [noise] pancadas *fpl* **-2.** *inf* [defeat] nocaute *m*; [criticism] crítica *f*.
knock-kneed [-'ni:d] *adj* de pernas tortas.
knock-on effect *n UK* efeito *m* dominó.
knockout ['nɒkaʊt] *n* **-1.** [in boxing] nocaute *m* **-2.** *inf* [sensation]: **she's a real ~** ela é de arrasar.
knockout competition *n UK* competição *f* com eliminatórias.
knock-up *n* TENNIS bate-bola *f*.
knot [nɒt] (*pt & pp* **-ted**, *cont* **-ting**) ◇ *n* **-1.** [gen] nó *m*; **to tie/untie a ~** fazer/desfazer um nó **-2.** [of people] grupo *m*. ◇ *vt* [rope, string] dar um nó em.
knotted *adj* **-1.** [tied in or with a knot] atado(da) com nós, emaranhado(da) **-2.** *phr UK*: **get ~!** *inf* te arranca!
knotty ['nɒtɪ] (*compar* **-ier**, *superl* **-iest**) *adj* [difficult] cabeludo(da).
know [nəʊ] (*pt* **knew**, *pp* **known**) ◇ *vt* **-1.** [become acquainted with] conhecer; **to get to ~ sb** conhecer alguém **-2.** [fact, information] saber; **to ~ (that)** saber que; **to get to ~ sthg** saber algo **-3.** [language, skill] ter conhecimento de; **to ~ how to do sthg** saber fazer algo **-4.** [recognize] reconhecer **-5.** [distinguish] diferenciar **-6.** [nickname, call]: **to be known as** ser conhecido(da) como. ◇ *vi* saber; **to ~ of sthg** saber de algo; **to ~ about sthg** [be aware of] saber sobre algo; [be expert in] saber de algo; **you ~** [for emphasis, to add information] você sabe; **there is no ~ing ...** é impossível saber ...; **to ~ sthg backwards** conhecer algo de cor e salteado; **not to ~ when one is well off** não saber a sorte que se tem; **to ~ better** não cair nessa. ◇ *n*: **to be in the ~** estar bem-informado(da) sobre.
know-all *n UK* sabichão *m*, -ona *f*.
know-how *n* experiência *f*, know-how *m*.
knowing ['nəʊɪŋ] *adj* [look, smile] de cumplicidade.
knowingly ['nəʊɪŋlɪ] *adv* **-1.** [look, smile] conscientemente **-2.** [act] de propósito.
know-it-all *n* = **know-all**.
knowledge ['nɒlɪdʒ] *n* conhecimento *m*; **it's common ~ that** é do senso comum que; **to my ~** que eu saiba; **to the best of my ~** até onde eu sei.
knowledgeable ['nɒlɪdʒəbl] *adj* entendido(da).
known [nəʊn] ◇ *pp* ▷ **know**. ◇ *adj* conhecido(da).
knuckle ['nʌkl] *n* **-1.** ANAT nó *m (do dedo)* **-2.** [of meat] mocotó *m*.
◆ **knuckle down** *vi*: **to ~ down to sthg/to doing sthg** dedicar-se com afinco a algo/a fazer algo.
◆ **knuckle under** *vi* dar-se por vencido(da).
knuckle-duster *n* soqueira *f* de metal.
KO (*abbr of* **knockout**) *n* K.O. *m*, nocaute *m*.
koala (bear) [kəʊ'ɑ:lə-] *n* coala *m*.
kohl *n cosmético usado no Oriente para escurecer as áreas acima e abaixo dos olhos.*
kook [ku:k] *n US inf* biruta *mf*.
kooky ['ku:kɪ] (*compar* **-ier**, *superl* **-iest**) *adj US inf* biruta.
Koran [kɒ'rɑ:n] *n*: **the ~** o Alcorão.
Korea [kə'rɪə] *n* Coréia; **in ~** na Coréia.

Korean [kə'rɪən] ◇ *adj* coreano(na). ◇ *n* **-1.** [person] coreano *m*, -na *f* **-2.** [language] coreano *m*.

kosher ['kəʊʃə^r] *adj* **-1.** [meat] kosher **-2.** *fig inf* [reputable] limpo(pa), puro(ra).

Kosovan ['kɒsəvən], **Kosovar** ['kɒsəvɑː(r)] ◇ *adj* kosovar. ◇ *n* kosovar *mf*.

Kosovar Albanian ◇ *adj* albano-kosovar. ◇ *n* albano-kosovar *mf*.

Kosovo ['kɒsəvəʊ] *n* Kosovo; **in ~** em Kosovo.

Koweit *n* = **Kuwait**; **in ~** no Kuwait.

kowtow [ˌkaʊ'taʊ] *vi*: **to ~ (to sb)** [behave humbly] humilhar-se (diante de alguém).

Krakow ['krækaʊ] *n* = **Cracow**; **in ~** em Cracow.

Kremlin ['kremlɪn] *n*: **the ~** o Kremlin.

KS *abbr of* **Kansas**.

Kt (*abbr of* **Knight**) cav.

Kuala Lumpur [ˌkwɑːlə'lʊmpə^r] *n* Cuala Lumpur; **in ~** no Cuala Lumpur.

kudos ['kjuːdɒs] *n (U)* glória *f*.

Ku Klux Klan [kuːklʌks'klæn] *n*: **the ~** a Ku Klux Klan.

kumquat ['kʌmkwɒt] *n árvore cítrica da China.*

kung fu [ˌkʌŋ'fuː] *n (U)* kung fu *m*.

Kurd [kɜːd] *n* curdo *m*, -da *f*.

Kurdish ['kɜːdɪʃ] *adj* curdo(da).

Kurdistan [kɜːdɪ'stɑːn] *n* Curdistão; **in ~** no Curdistão.

Kuwait [kjuː'weɪt] *n* **-1.** [country] Kuwait; **in ~** no Kuwait **-2.** [city] Kuwait.

Kuwaiti [kjuː'weɪtɪ] ◇ *adj* kuwaitiano(na). ◇ *n* kuwaitiano *m*, -na *f*.

kW (*abbr of* **kilowatt**) Kw.

kWh (*abbr of* **kilowatt-hour**) kWh.

KY *abbr of* **Kentucky**.

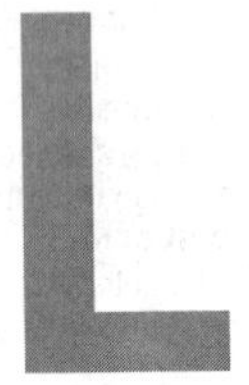

l[1] (*pl* **l's** *or* **ls**), **L** (*pl* **L's** *or* **Ls**) [el] *n* [letter] l, L *m*.
◆ **L -1.** (*abbr of* **lake**) lago *m* **-2.** (*abbr of* **large**) G **-3.** (*abbr of* **left**) esq. **-4.** (*abbr of* **learner**) aprendiz *mf*.

l[2] (*abbr of* **litre**) l.

L

Na Grã-Bretanha, a letra L, afixada na traseira de um veículo, indica que seu motorista está aprendendo a dirigir (é um *learner*, ou aprendiz) e, portanto, ainda não possui carteira de motorista.

La *abbr of* **Louisiana**.

LA ◇ *n abbr of* **Los Angeles**. ◇ *abbr of* **Louisiana**.

lab [læb] *n inf* laboratório *m*.

label ['leɪbl] (*UK pt* & *pp* **-led**, *cont* **-ling**, *US pt* & *pp* **-ed**, *cont* **-ing**) ◇ *n* **-1.** [identification - on bottle] rótulo *m*; [- on luggage, clothing] etiqueta *f* **-2.** [of record] selo *m*. ◇ *vt* **-1.** [fix label to - bottle] rotular; [- luggage, clothing] etiquetar **-2.** [describe] descrever; **to ~ sb as sthg** rotular alguém de algo.

labor *etc n US* = **labour**.

laboratory [*UK* lə'bɒrətrɪ, *US* 'læbrəˌtɔːrɪ] (*pl* **-ies**) ◇ *n* laboratório *m*. ◇ *comp* de laboratório.

Labor Day *n US* Dia *m* do Trabalho.

LABOR DAY

Nos Estados Unidos, o dia do trabalho é comemorado na primeira segunda-feira de setembro. Não há desfiles ou manifestações: a data marca apenas o último feriado prolongado do verão, e muita gente tem o dia livre. Como a maior parte das escolas retoma suas aulas na semana que se segue ao dia do trabalho, a data marca também o fim das férias escolares e o início do ano letivo.

laborious [lə'bɔːrɪəs] *adj* trabalhoso(sa).

labor union *n US* sindicato *m (de trabalhadores)*.

labour *UK*, **labor** *US* ['leɪbə^r] ◇ *n* **-1.** [work] trabalho *m*; **manual ~** trabalho manual; **to withdraw one's ~** abandonar o trabalho **-2.** [effort] esforço *m* **-3.** *(U)* [work force] mão-de-obra *f*; **parts and ~** peças e mão-de-obra **-4.** *MED* [giving birth] trabalho *m* de parto; **to go into ~** entrar em trabalho de parto. ◇ *vt* [insist on] insistir em. ◇ *vi* **-1.** [work] trabalhar **-2.** [struggle]: **to ~ at** *or* **over sthg** trabalhar em algo; **to ~ under a delusion/misapprehension** estar redondamente enganado(da).
◆ **Labour** *UK POL* ◇ *adj* trabalhista. ◇ *n UK* o Partido Trabalhista.

labour camp *n* campo *m* de trabalhos forçados.

labour costs *npl* custos *mpl* com pessoal.

laboured *UK*, **labored** *US* ['leɪbəd] *adj* **-1.** [breathing] forçado(da) **-2.** [style] elaborado(da).

labourer *UK*, **laborer** *US* ['leɪbərə^r] *n* peão *m*.

labour force *n* mão-de-obra *f*.

labour-intensive *adj* que exige muita mão-de-obra.

labour market *n* mercado *m* de trabalho.

labour of love *n* trabalho *m* por amor à arte.

labour pains *npl* dores *fpl* do parto.

Labour Party *n UK*: **the ~** o Partido Trabalhista.

labour relations *npl* relações *fpl* trabalhistas.

laboursaving *UK*, **laborsaving** *US* ['leɪbəseɪvɪŋ] *adj*: **~ device** mecanismo *m* que poupa trabalho.

Labrador ['læbrədɔː^r] *n* **-1.** [dog] labrador *m* **-2.** *GEOGR* Labrador.

laburnum *n* laburno *m*.

labyrinth ['læbərɪnθ] *n* labirinto *m*.

lace [leɪs] ◇ *n* **-1.** *(U)* [fabric] renda *f* **-2.** [shoelace] cadarço *m*. ◇ *comp* de renda. ◇ *vt* **-1.** [shoe, boot] amarrar **-2.** [drink, food] misturar álcool em.
◆ **lace up** *vt sep* amarrar.

lacemaking ['leɪsˌmeɪkɪŋ] *n (U)* fabricação *f* de renda.

laceration [ˌlæsə'reɪʃn] *n fml* & *MED* laceração *f*.

lace-up ⇔ *adj* de cordões. ⇔ *n UK* sapato *m* de amarrar.

lack [læk] ⇔ *n* falta *f*; **for** *OR* **through ~ of** por falta de; **with no ~ of** sem falta de. ⇔ *vt* sentir falta de, carecer de. ⇔ *vi*: **you're ~ing in experience** te falta experiência; **to be ~ing** estar faltando.

lackadaisical [ˌlækə'deɪzɪkl] *adj pej* desinteressado(da), apático(ca).

lackey ['lækɪ] (*pl* **-s**) *n pej* pau-mandado *m*.

lacklustre *UK*, **lackluster** *US* ['lækˌlʌstəʳ] *adj* sem brilho.

laconic [lə'kɒnɪk] *adj* lacônico(ca).

lacquer ['lækəʳ] ⇔ *n* **-1.** [for wood, metal] verniz *m* **-2.** [for hair] fixador *m*. ⇔ *vt* **-1.** [wood, metal] envernizar **-2.** [hair] aplicar fixador em.

lacrosse [lə'krɒs] *n (U) jogo canadense semelhante ao hóquei*.

lactic acid ['læktɪk-] *n* ácido *m* láctico.

lacy ['leɪsɪ] (*compar* **-ier**, *superl* **-iest**) *adj* rendado(da).

lad [læd] *n inf* **-1.** [young boy] rapaz *m* **-2.** [male friend] amigo *m*; **he went out for a drink with the ~s** ele saiu para beber com a rapazeada **-3.** *UK* [stable boy] empregado *m* de estábulo.

ladder ['lædəʳ] ⇔ *n* **-1.** [for climbing] escada *f* de mão **-2.** *UK* [in tights] defeito *m*. ⇔ *vt UK* [tights] puxar fio em. ⇔ *vi UK* [tights] puxar fio.

laden ['leɪdn] *adj* carregado(da); **~ with sthg** carregado com algo.

la-di-da [ˌlɑ:dɪ'dɑ:] *adj inf pej* afetado(da).

ladies *UK* ['leɪdɪz], **ladies room** *US n* senhoras *fpl*, damas *fpl*.

lading ['leɪdɪŋ] *n* ▻ **bill**.

ladle ['leɪdl] ⇔ *n* concha *f*. ⇔ *vt* servir com concha.

lady ['leɪdɪ] (*pl* **-ies**) ⇔ *n* **-1.** [woman] senhora *f* **-2.** [by birth or upbringing] dama *f* **-3.** *US inf* [to address woman] senhora *f*. ⇔ *comp*: **~ doctor** médica *f*.

◆ **Lady** *n* **-1.** [member of nobility] Lady *f* **-2.** *RELIG*: **Our Lady** Nossa Senhora.

ladybird *UK* ['leɪdɪbɜ:d], **ladybug** *US* ['leɪdɪbʌg] *n* joaninha *f*.

lady-in-waiting [-'weɪtɪŋ] (*pl* **ladies-in-waiting**) *n* dama *f* de companhia.

lady-killer *n inf* mulherengo *m*, -ga *f*, conquistador *m*, -ra *f*.

ladylike ['leɪdɪlaɪk] *adj* elegante, refinado(da).

Ladyship ['leɪdɪʃɪp] *n*: **her/your ~** Vossa Senhoria.

lag [læg] (*pt* & *pp* **-ged**, *cont* **-ging**) ⇔ *n* [in time] atraso *m*, demora *f*. ⇔ *vt* revestir com material isolante. ⇔ *vi* [move more slowly]: **to ~ (behind)** ficar (para trás).

lager ['lɑ:gəʳ] *n* cerveja *m* tipo Pilsen.

lager lout *n UK* beberrão *m*, -rona *f* jovem.

lagging ['lægɪŋ] *n (U)* revestimento *m*.

lagoon [lə'gu:n] *n* lagoa *f*.

Lagos ['leɪgɒs] *n* Lagos; **in ~** em Lagos.

lah-di-dah [ˌlɑ:dɪ'dɑ:] *adj* = **la-di-da**.

laid [leɪd] *pt* & *pp* ▻ **lay**.

laid-back *adj inf* descontraído(da).

lain [leɪn] *pp* ▻ **lie**.

lair [leəʳ] *n* toca *f*.

laissez-faire [ˌleɪseɪ'feəʳ] ⇔ *adj* do laissez-faire. ⇔ *n (U)* laissez-faire *m*.

laity ['leɪətɪ] *n RELIG*: **the ~** os laicos.

lake [leɪk] *n GEOGR* lago *m*.

Lake District *n*: **the ~** a Região dos Lagos.

Lake Geneva *n* o Lago de Gênova.

lakeside ['leɪksaɪd] *adj* às margens do lago.

lama (*pl* **-s**) *n* lama *m*.

lamb [læm] *n* [animal, meat] cordeiro *m*.

lambast [læm'bæst], **lambaste** [læm'beɪst] *vt* criticar severamente.

lamb chop *n* costeleta *f* de cordeiro.

lambing ['læmɪŋ] *n (U)* parição *f (de ovelhas)*.

lambskin ['læmskɪn] *n* pele *f* de cordeiro.

lambswool ['læmzwʊl] ⇔ *n (U)* lã *f* de cordeiro. ⇔ *comp* de lã de cordeiro.

lame [leɪm] *adj* **-1.** [person, horse] manco(ca) **-2.** [excuse, argument] pouco convincente.

lamé ['lɑ:meɪ] *n (U)* lamê *m*.

lame duck ⇔ *adj US fig* [president] em final de mandato. ⇔ *n* **-1.** *fig* [business] fracasso *m* **-2.** *fig* [person] inútil *mf*.

lamely ['leɪmlɪ] *adv* [unconvincingly] de forma não-convincente.

lament [lə'ment] ⇔ *n* lamento *m*. ⇔ *vt* lamentar.

lamentable ['læməntəbl] *adj* lamentável.

laminated ['læmɪneɪtɪd] *adj* laminado(da).

lamp [læmp] *n* lâmpada *f*.

lamplight ['læmplaɪt] *n* luz *f* de lâmpada.

lampoon [læm'pu:n] ⇔ *n* sátira *f*. ⇔ *vt* satirizar.

lamppost ['læmppəʊst] *n* poste *m* de iluminação.

lampshade ['læmpʃeɪd] *n* quebra-luz *m*.

lance [lɑ:ns] ⇔ *n* [spear] lança *f*. ⇔ *vt MED* lancetar.

lance corporal *n UK* ≃ cabo *m*.

lancet ['lɑ:nsɪt] *n MED* bisturí *m*, lanceta *f*.

land [lænd] ⇔ *n* **-1.** [gen] terra *f* **-2.** [property, estate] terreno *m* **-3.** [nation] país *m*. ⇔ *vt* **-1.** [plane] aterrissar **-2.** [cargo, passengers] desembarcar **-3.** [fish] recolher **-4.** *inf* [job, contract] fechar **-5.** *inf* [put, place]: **to ~ sb in trouble** pôr alguém em apuros; **to ~ sb in jail** fazer com que alguém acabe na cadeia **-6.** *inf* [encumber]: **to ~ sb with sb/sthg** incomodar alguém com alguém/algo. ⇔ *vi* **-1.** [plane, passenger] aterrissar **-2.** [fall] cair **-3.** [from ship] desembarcar.

◆ **land up** *vi inf* acabar; **to ~ up in serious debt** acabar com um monte de dívidas; **to ~ up in** *OR* **at** [place] acabar em, ir parar em.

landed gentry ['lændɪd-] *npl* proprietários *mpl* de terra.

landing ['lændɪŋ] *n* **-1.** [of stairs] patamar *m* **-2.** [of aeroplane] aterrissagem *f* **-3.** [of goods from ship] desembarque *m*.

landing card *n* cartão *m* de desembarque.

landing craft *n* navio *m* de desembarque.

landing gear *n (U)* trem *m* de aterrissagem.

landing stage *n* cais *m inv* de desembarque.

landing strip *n* pista *f* de aterrissagem.

landlady ['lændˌleɪdɪ] (*pl* **-ies**) *n* [gen] senhoria *f*; [in guesthouse, pub] proprietária *f*.

landlocked [ˈlændlɒkt] *adj* cercado(da) de terra.
landlord [ˈlændlɔːd] *n* **-1.** [in lodgings] senhorio *m* **-2.** [of pub] proprietário *m*.
landmark [ˈlændmɑːk] *n* **-1.** [prominent feature] ponto *m* de referência **-2.** *fig* [in history] marco *m* divisório.
landmine [ˈlændmaɪn] *n* mina *f* terrestre.
landowner [ˈlænd,əʊnəʳ] *n* proprietário *m*, -ria *f* de terras.
landscape [ˈlændskeɪp] ◇ *n* paisagem *f*. ◇ *vt* ajardinar.
landscape gardener *n* paisagista *mf*.
landslide [ˈlændslaɪd] ◇ *n* **-1.** [of earth, rocks] desmoronamento *m* **-2.** *POL* vitória *f* esmagadora. ◇ *comp POL* esmagador(ra).
landslip [ˈlændslɪp] *n* deslizamento *m* de terra.
lane [leɪn] *n* **-1.** [road - in country] senda *f*; [- in town, village] ruela *f* **-2.** [division of road] pista *f*, faixa *f*; **'get/keep in ~'** 'entrar/manter-se na pista' **-3.** [in swimming pool, on racetrack] raia *f* **-4.** [for shipping, aircraft] pista *f*.
langoustine *n* lagostim *m*.
language [ˈlæŋgwɪdʒ] *n* **-1.** [spoken, foreign] língua *f* **-2.** [style, mode of communication] linguagem *f*.
language laboratory *n* laboratório *m* de línguas.
languid [ˈlæŋgwɪd] *adj* lânguido(da).
languish [ˈlæŋgwɪʃ] *vi* **-1.** [suffer] sofrer **-2.** [become weak] debilitar-se.
languorous [ˈlæŋgərəs] *adj literary* langoroso(sa).
lank [læŋk] *adj* liso(sa).
lanky [ˈlæŋkɪ] (*compar* **-ier**, *superl* **-iest**) *adj* magricela.
lanolin(e) [ˈlænəlɪn] *n (U)* lanolina *f*.
lantern [ˈlæntən] *n* lanterna *f*.
Laos [laʊs] *n* Laos; **in ~** em Laos.
Laotian [ˈlaʊʃən] ◇ *adj* laosiano(na). ◇ *n* **-1.** [person] laosiano *m*, -na *f* **-2.** [language] laosiano *m*.
lap [læp] (*pt* & *pp* **-ped**, *cont* **-ping**) ◇ *n* **-1.** [knees] colo *m* **-2.** *SPORT* volta *f*. ◇ *vt* **-1.** [subj: animal] lamber **-2.** *SPORT* [runner, car] estar uma volta à frente de. ◇ *vi* [water, waves] marulhar.
◆ **lap up** *vt sep* **-1.** [drink] beber com volúpia **-2.** *fig* [compliments, lies, information] receber com impaciência.
laparoscopy [,læpəˈrɒskəpɪ] (*pl* **-ies**) *n* laparoscopia *f*.
La Paz [læˈpæz] *n* La Paz; **in ~** em La Paz.
lapdog [ˈlæpdɒg] *n* [dog] cão *m* de estimação.
lapel [ləˈpel] *n* lapela *f*.
Lapland [ˈlæplænd] *n* Lapônia; **in ~** na Lapônia.
Lapp [læp] ◇ *adj* lapão(ona). ◇ *n* **-1.** [person] lapão *m*, -ona *f* **-2.** [language] lapão *m*.
lapse [læps] ◇ *n* **-1.** [failing] lapso *m* **-2.** [in behaviour] deslize *m* **-3.** [of time] intervalo *m*. ◇ *vi* **-1.** [custom, licence] caducar **-2.** [passport] expirar **-3.** [law] prescrever **-4.** [deteriorate] decair **-5.** [subj: person]: **to ~ into** [coma] entrar em; [silence, dialect] mergulhar em; [bad habits] adquirir.
lapsed [læpst] *adj* descrente.
lap-top (computer) *n* (computador *m*) laptop *m*.
larceny [ˈlɑːsənɪ] *n (U)* furto *m*.
larch [lɑːtʃ] *n* larício *m*.
lard [lɑːd] *n (U)* toicinho *m*, banha *f (de porco)*.
larder [ˈlɑːdəʳ] *n* despensa *f*.
large [lɑːdʒ] *adj* grande.
◆ **at large** ◇ *adj* [escaped prisoner, animal] em liberdade. ◇ *adv* [as a whole] em geral.
largely [ˈlɑːdʒlɪ] *adv* em grande parte.
larger-than-life [ˈlɑːdʒəʳ-] *adj* exagerado(da).
large-scale *adj* **-1.** [wide-ranging] de grande escala **-2.** [map, diagram] em grande escala.
largesse, largess *US* [lɑːˈdʒes] *n (U)* grandeza *f*.
lark [lɑːk] *n* **-1.** [bird] cotovia *f* **-2.** *inf* [joke] brincadeira *f*; **for a ~** de brincadeira.
◆ **lark about** *vi* fazer palhaçadas.
larva [ˈlɑːvə] (*pl* **-vae** [-viː]) *n* larva *f*.
laryngitis [,lærɪnˈdʒaɪtɪs] *n (U)* laringite *f*.
larynx [ˈlærɪŋks] (*pl* **-es**) *n* laringe *f*.
lasagna, lasagne [ləˈzænjə] *n (U)* lasanha *f*.
lascivious [ləˈsɪvɪəs] *adj* lascivo(va).
laser [ˈleɪzəʳ] *n* laser *m*.
laser beam *n* raio *m* laser.
laser printer *n* impressora *f* a laser.
laser show *n* show *m* com laser.
lash [læʃ] ◇ *n* **-1.** [eyelash] cílio *m* **-2.** [part of whip] chicote *m* **-3.** [blow with whip] chicotada *f*. ◇ *vt* **-1.** [whip] chicotear **-2.** [subj: wind, rain, waves] fustigar **-3.** [tie] atar; **to ~ sthg to sthg** atar algo em algo.
◆ **lash out** *vi* **-1.** [physically]: **to ~ out (at** *OR* **against sb)** atacar alguém com extrema violência **-2.** [verbally]: **to ~ out (at** *OR* **against sb)** atacar alguém verbalmente **-3.** *UK inf* [spend money]: **to ~ out (on sthg)** esbanjar dinheiro (em algo).
lass [læs] *n* [girl] moça *f*.
lasso [læˈsuː] (*pl* **-s**, *pt* & *pp* **-ed**, *cont* **-ing**) ◇ *n* laço *m*. ◇ *vt* laçar.
last [lɑːst] ◇ *adj* **-1.** [gen] último(ma); **~ but one** penúltimo(ma); **~ but two** antepenúltimo(ma) **-2.** [with dates, time of day] último(ma), passado(da); **~ week** na semana passada, na última semana; **~ year** no ano passado **-3.** [least likely]: **you're the ~ person I expected to see** você é a última pessoa que eu esperava ver. ◇ *adv* **-1.** [in final place] em último lugar **-2.** [most recently]: **when did you ~ visit them?** quando você os visitou pela última vez?; **at ~** finalmente; **at ~!** até que enfim! ◇ *pron* o último, a última; **to leave sthg till ~** deixar algo para o fim; **the week before ~** na semana retrasada; **the day before ~** anteontem. ◇ *n* [final thing]: **the ~ I saw/heard of him** a última coisa que eu soube dele. ◇ *vi* **-1.** [gen] durar; **they only had food to ~ another week** eles só tinham comida para mais uma semana **-2.** [survive] sobreviver.
◆ **at (long) last** *adv* por fim.
last-ditch *adj* derradeiro(ra).
lasting [ˈlɑːstɪŋ] *adj* duradouro(ra).
lastly [ˈlɑːstlɪ] *adv* **-1.** [to conclude] por fim **-2.** [at the end] finalmente.
last-minute *adj* de última hora.
last name *n* sobrenome *m*.
last post *n* **-1.** [postal collection] última coleta *f* **-2.** *MIL* toque *m* de recolher.

last rites *npl* últimos sacramentos *mpl*.
last straw *n*: **it was the ~** foi a gota d'água.
Last Supper *n*: **the ~** a Última Ceia.
last word *n*: **to have the ~** ter a palavra final.
Las Vegas *n* Las Vegas; **in ~** em Las Vegas.
lat. (*abbr of* **latitude**) lat.
latch [lætʃ] *n* trinco *m*; **on the ~** fechado(da) com o trinco.
◆ **latch onto** *vt fus inf* agarrar-se a.
latchkey ['lætʃki:] (*pl* **-s**) ◇ *adj* [child] que fica sozinho(nha) em casa. ◇ *n* tranca *f (para porta exterior)*.
late [leɪt] ◇ *adj* **-1.** [delayed] atrasado(da); **to be ~ for sthg** estar atrasado(da) para algo **-2.** [later than normal] tarde **-3.** [near end of]: **in ~ December** no final de dezembro **-4.** [dead] falecido(da). ◇ *adv* [not on time] tarde; **he arrived 20 minutes ~** ele chegou 20 minutos atrasado; **~ in December** no final de dezembro; **to work ~** trabalhar até tarde.
◆ **of late** *adv* recentemente.
latecomer ['leɪt,kʌməʳ] *n* retardatário *m*, -ria *f*.
lately ['leɪtlɪ] *adv* ultimamente.
lateness ['leɪtnɪs] *n* **-1.** [of person, train] atraso *m* **-2.** [of meeting, event] hora *f* avançada.
late-night *adj* noturno(na), da noite; **~ opening** aberto(ta) até tarde da noite.
latent ['leɪtənt] *adj* latente.
later ['leɪtəʳ] ◇ *adj* **-1.** [last, final] último(ma) **-2.** [subsequent, following] posterior **-3.** [train, bus, boat] que sai mais tarde. ◇ *adv* [at a later time]: **~ (on)** mais tarde.
lateral ['lætərəl] *adj* lateral.
latest ['leɪtɪst] ◇ *adj* [most recent] último(ma). ◇ *n*: **at the ~** no mais tardar.
latex ['leɪteks] ◇ *n (U)* látex *m inv*. ◇ *comp* de látex.
lath [lɑ:θ] *n* ripa *f*, sarrafo *m*.
lathe [leɪð] *n* torno *m* mecânico.
lather ['lɑ:ðəʳ] ◇ *n* espuma *f*. ◇ *vt* ensaboar. ◇ *vi* fazer espuma.
Latin ['lætɪn] ◇ *adj* latino(na). ◇ *n* [language] latim *m*.
Latin America *n* América Latina; **in ~** na América Latina.
Latin American ◇ *adj* latino-americano(na). ◇ *n* [person] latino-americano *m*, -na *f*.
latitude ['lætɪtju:d] *n* **-1.** GEOGR latitude *f* **-2.** *fml* [freedom] liberdade *f (de expressão)*.
latrine [lə'tri:n] *n* latrina *f*.
latter ['lætəʳ] ◇ *adj* **-1.** [later] último(ma) **-2.** [second] segundo(da). ◇ *n*: **the ~** o último, a última; **we prefer the ~ house to the former** preferimos esta casa àquela.
latter-day *adj* contemporâneo(nea).
latterly ['lætəlɪ] *adv* recentemente.
lattice ['lætɪs] *n* [fence, frame] treliça *f*.
lattice window *n* janela *f* de treliça.
Latvia ['lætvɪə] *n* Letônia; **in ~** na Letônia.
Latvian ['lætvɪən] ◇ *adj* letão(ona). ◇ *n* **-1.** [person] letão *m*, -ona *f* **-2.** [language] letão *m*.
laudable ['lɔ:dəbl] *adj* louvável.
laugh [lɑ:f] ◇ *n* **-1.** [sound] riso *m*, risada *f*; **to have the last ~** rir por último **-2.** *inf* [fun, joke] piada *f*; **to do sthg for ~s** *OR* **a ~** fazer algo por prazer. ◇ *vi* rir, gargalhar.
◆ **laugh at** *vt fus* [mock] rir-se de, gozar com.
◆ **laugh off** *vt sep* [dismiss] disfarçar com um sorriso.
laughable ['lɑ:fəbl] *adj pej* [absurd] risível.
laughing gas ['lɑ:fɪŋ-] *n (U)* gás *m* hilariante.
laughingstock *n* motivo *m* de riso.
laughter ['lɑ:ftəʳ] *n (U)* risada *f*, risos *mpl*.
launch [lɔ:ntʃ] ◇ *n* **-1.** [gen] lançamento *m* **-2.** [start, initiation] início *m*. ◇ *vt* **-1.** [gen] lançar **-2.** [start, initiate] iniciar.
◆ **launch into** *vt fus* **-1.** [attack, fight] empreender **-2.** [lecture, explanation] proferir.
launching ['lɔ:ntʃɪŋ] *n* lançamento *m*.
launch(ing) pad ['lɔ:ntʃ(ɪŋ)-] *n* [for rocket, missile, satellite] plataforma *f* de lançamento.
launder ['lɔ:ndəʳ] *vt* **-1.** [clothes] lavar e passar **-2.** *inf* [money] lavar.
laund(e)rette [lɔ:n'dret], **Laundromat**® *US* ['lɔ:ndrəmæt] *n* lavanderia *f* automatizada.
laundry ['lɔ:ndrɪ] (*pl* **-ies**) *n* **-1.** *(U)* [clothes - about to be washed] roupa *f* suja; [- newly washed] roupa *f* lavada **-2.** [room, business] lavanderia *f*.
laundry basket *n* cesto *m* de roupa suja.
laureate ['lɔ:rɪət] *n* ▷ **poet laureate**.
laurel *n* louro *m*.
◆ **laurels** *npl*: **to rest on one's ~s** deitar na própria fama.
lava ['lɑ:və] *n (U)* lava *f*.
lavatory ['lævətrɪ] (*pl* **-ies**) *n* **-1.** [receptacle] privada *f* **-2.** [room] toalete *f*.
lavatory paper *n UK* papel *m* higiênico.
lavender ['lævəndəʳ] ◇ *adj* [colour] da cor da alfazema. ◇ *n* **-1.** [plant] alfazema *f*, lavanda *f* **-2.** [colour] lavanda *f*.
lavish ['lævɪʃ] ◇ *adj* **-1.** [generous] generoso(sa); **to be ~ with sthg** ser generoso(sa) com algo **-2.** [sumptuous] suntuoso(sa). ◇ *vt*: **to ~ sthg on sb/sthg** encher alguém/algo de algo.
lavishly ['lævɪʃlɪ] *adv* **-1.** [generously] generosamente **-2.** [sumptuously] suntuosamente.
law [lɔ:] ◇ *n* **-1.** [gen] lei *f*; **to break the ~** transgredir a lei; **against the ~** contra a lei; **~ and order** lei e ordem; **the ~ of the jungle** a lei da selva **-2.** [system, subject] direito *m* **-3.** *(U) inf* [police]: **the ~** a lei **-4.** *phr*: **to lay down the ~** *pej* ditar as ordens. ◇ *comp* de direito.
law-abiding [-ə,baɪdɪŋ] *adj* obediente à lei.
law-breaker *n* infrator *m*, -ra *f* da lei.
law court *n* tribunal *m* de justiça.
lawful ['lɔ:fʊl] *adj fml* lícito(ta).
lawfully ['lɔ:fʊlɪ] *adv fml* licitamente.
lawless ['lɔ:lɪs] *adj* **-1.** *fml* [illegal] ilegal **-2.** [without laws] sem lei **-3.** [person] indisciplinado(da).
Law Lords *npl UK* JUR: **the ~** ≃ o Supremo Tribunal Federal.
lawmaker ['lɔ:,meɪkəʳ] *n* legislador *m*, -ra *f*.
lawn [lɔ:n] *n* [grass] gramado *m*.
lawnmower ['lɔ:n,məʊəʳ] *n* cortador *m* de grama.
lawn party *n US* recepção *f* ao ar livre.
lawn tennis *n* tênis *m inv* de gramado.

law school *n* escola *f* de direito.
lawsuit ['lɔ:su:t] *n* ação *f* judicial.
lawyer ['lɔ:jəʳ] *n* advogado *m*, -da *f*.
lax [læks] *adj* negligente.
laxative ['læksətɪv] *n* laxante *m*.
laxity ['læksətɪ], **laxness** ['læksnɪs] *n (U)* negligência *f*.
lay [leɪ] (*pt* & *pp* **laid**) <> *pt* ▷ **lie**. <> *vt* **-1.** [in specified position] colocar **-2.** [prepare - trap, snare] armar; [- plans] traçar; **to ~ the table** pôr a mesa **-3.** [bricks] assentar; [carpet] colocar; [cable] afixar; [pipes, foundations] preparar **-4.** [egg] pôr **-5.** [blame, emphasis] aplicar. <> *adj* **-1.** *RELIG* leigo(ga) **-2.** [untrained, unqualified] desqualificado(da).
◆ **lay aside** *vt sep* **-1.** [save] poupar **-2.** [put down, abandon] abandonar.
◆ **lay before** *vt sep* [present] apresentar.
◆ **lay down** *vt sep* **-1.** [formulate] formular **-2.** [put down] depor.
◆ **lay into** *vt fus inf* [attack - physically] surrar; [- verbally] dar uma bronca em.
◆ **lay off** <> *vt sep* [make redundant] dispensar. <> *vt fus inf* **-1.** [leave alone] deixar sozinho(nha) **-2.** [stop, give up] parar de.
◆ **lay on** *vt sep UK* [provide, supply] providenciar.
◆ **lay out** *vt sep* **-1.** [arrange, spread out] dispor **-2.** [plan, design] projetar.
◆ **lay over** *vi US* pernoitar.
layabout ['leɪəbaʊt] *n UK inf* vadio *m*, -dia *f*.
lay-by (*pl* **-s**) *n UK* acostamento *m*.
lay days *npl prazo estipulado para carga e descarga de um navio.*
layer ['leɪəʳ] *n* **-1.** [of substance, material] camada *f* **-2.** *fig* [level] nível *m*.
layette [leɪ'et] *n* enxoval *m* do bebê.
layman ['leɪmən] (*pl* **-men** [-mən]) *n* leigo *m*; **in ~'s terms** em termos gerais.
lay-off *n* [redundancy] demissão *f*.
layout ['leɪaʊt] *n* [design] leiaute *m*.
layover ['leɪəʊvəʳ] *n US* parada *f (durante uma viagem)*.
laze [leɪz] *vi*: **to ~ (about** *OR* **around)** vadiar.
lazily ['leɪzɪlɪ] *adv* [without effort] preguiçosamente.
laziness ['leɪzɪnɪs] *n* [idleness] preguiça *f*.
lazy ['leɪzɪ] (*compar* **-ier**, *superl* **-iest**) *adj* **-1.** [person] preguiçoso(sa) **-2.** [action] ocioso(sa).
lazybones ['leɪzɪbəʊnz] (*pl inv*) *n inf* preguiçoso *m*, -sa *f*.
lb *abbr of* **pound**.
lbw (*abbr of* **leg before wicket**) *proteção ilegal do gol com a perna no jogo de cricket.*
l.c. (*abbr of* **lower case**) caixa-baixa *f*.
L/C (*abbr of* **letter of credit**) carta *f* de crédito.
LCD (*abbr of* **liquid crystal display**) *n* tela *f* de cristal líquido, LCD *m*.
Ld (*abbr of* **Lord**) Lorde.
L-driver (*abbr of* **learner driver**) *n UK* ≃ auto-escola *f (indicação no veículo)*.
LDS (*abbr of* **Licentiate in Dental Surgery**) *n (titular de) graduação em odontologia na Grã-Bretanha.*
LEA (*abbr of* **local education authority**) *n órgão responsável pela educação numa área da Grã-Bretanha.*
lead[1] [li:d] (*pt* & *pp* **led**) <> *n* **-1.** *(U)* [winning position] dianteira *f*; **to be in** *OR* **have the ~** estar na frente **-2.** [amount ahead] vantagem *f* **-3.** *(U)* [initiative, example] exemplo *m*; **to take the ~** [do sthg first] tomar a iniciativa **-4.** *(U)* [most important role]: **the ~** o papel principal **-5.** [clue] pista *f* **-6.** [for dog] correia *f* **-7.** [wire, cable] fio *m*. <> *adj* [most important] principal. <> *vt* **-1.** [be in front of] dirigir **-2.** [take, guide] conduzir **-3.** [head, be in charge of] chefiar, comandar **-4.** [organize] organizar; **to ~ the way** assumir a direção **-5.** [life, existence] reger **-6.** [cause, influence]: **to ~ sb to do sthg** induzir alguém a fazer algo. <> *vi* **-1.** [go] levar **-2.** [give access to]: **that door ~s to the kitchen** aquela porta dá para a cozinha **-3.** [be winning] estar na frente **-4.** [result in]: **to ~ to sthg** resultar em algo.
◆ **lead off** <> *vt fus* [subj: door, room] começar a partir de. <> *vi* **-1.** [road, corridor]: **to ~ off (from)** começar (a partir de) **-2.** [begin] começar.
◆ **lead up to** *vt fus* **-1.** [precede] conduzir a **-2.** [in conversation] levar a.
lead[2] [led] <> *n* **-1.** *(U)* [metal] chumbo *m* **-2.** [in pencil] grafite *m*. <> *comp* [made of or with lead] de chumbo.
leaded ['ledɪd] *adj* **-1.** [petrol] com chumbo **-2.** [window] com almofada de vidro.
leaden ['ledn] *adj* **-1.** *literary* [dark grey] plúmbeo(-bea) **-2.** *literary* [heavy] soturno(na) **-3.** [very dull] moroso(sa).
leader ['li:dəʳ] *n* **-1.** [gen] líder *mf* **-2.** *UK* [in newspaper] editorial *m*.
leadership ['li:dəʃɪp] *n* **-1.** [people in charge]: **the ~** a liderança **-2.** [position of leader] liderança *f*.
lead-free [led-] *adj* sem chumbo.
leading ['li:dɪŋ] *adj* **-1.** [prominent] destacado(da) **-2.** [main, principal]: **to play the ~ part** *OR* **role in sthg** *lit* & *fig* desempenhar o papel principal em algo **-3.** *SPORT* [at front] primeiro(ra).
leading article *n UK* editorial *m*.
leading lady *n* atriz *f* principal, protagonista *f*.
leading light *n* figura *f* central.
leading man *n* ator *m* principal.
leading question *n* pergunta *f* com resposta induzida.
lead pencil [led-] *n* lápis *m inv* de grafita.
lead poisoning [led-] *n* saturnismo *m*.
lead time [li:d-] *n COMM* prazo *m* de entrega.
leaf [li:f] (*pl* **leaves**) *n* **-1.** [gen] folha *f* **-2.** [of table] aba *f*.
◆ **leaf through** *vt fus* folhear.
leaflet ['li:flɪt] <> *n* folder *m*, folheto *m*. <> *vt* distribuir folhetos em.
leafy ['li:fɪ] (*compar* **-ier**, *superl* **-iest**) *adj* **-1.** [with many leaves] frondoso(sa) **-2.** [with many trees] arborizado(-da).
league [li:g] *n* liga *f*; **to be in ~ with sb** [work with] estar confabulado(da) com alguém.
league table *n* tabela *f* de classificação da liga.
leak [li:k] <> *n* **-1.** [gen] vazamento *m*; **a ~ in the roof** uma goteira **-2.** *fig* [disclosure] vazamento *m (de informações)*. <> *vt* [make known] vazar. <> *vi* **-1.** [gen] vazar; [boat, shoe]: **to be ~ing** estar com infiltração **-2.** [roof] ter goteiras.

◆ **leak out** *vi* [gen] vazar; **to ~ (out) from sthg** vazar de dentro de algo.

leakage ['li:kɪdʒ] *n* vazamento *m*.

leaky ['li:kɪ] (*compar* **-ier**, *superl* **-iest**) *adj* com furos; **a ~ roof** um teto com goteiras.

lean [li:n] (*pt* & *pp* **leant** *OR* **-ed**) ◇ *adj* **-1.** [gen] magro(gra) **-2.** *fig* [harvest, year] improdutivo(va). ◇ *vt* [support, prop]: **to ~ sthg against sthg** apoiar algo contra algo. ◇ *vi* **-1.** [bend, slope] inclinar-se **-2.** [rest]: **to ~ on/against sthg** apoiar-se em/contra algo.

◆ **lean back** *vi* [person] recostar-se.

leaning ['li:nɪŋ] *n*: **~ (towards sthg)** inclinação *f* (para algo).

leant [lent] *pt* & *pp* ▷ **lean**.

lean-to (*pl* **-s**) *n* alpendre *m*.

leap [li:p] (*pt* & *pp* **leapt** *OR* **-ed**) ◇ *n* **-1.** [jump] salto *m*, pulo *m* **-2.** [increase] pulo *m*; **in ~s and bounds** com extrema rapidez. ◇ *vi* **-1.** [jump] saltar, pular **-2.** [increase] disparar; **to ~ to the eye** saltar aos olhos.

◆ **leap at** *vt fus fig* não deixar escapar.

leapfrog ['li:pfrɒg] (*pt* & *pp* **-ged**, *cont* **-ging**) ◇ *n (U)* jogo *m* de pular carniça; **to play ~** brincar de pular carniça. ◇ *vi* **-1.** [jump]: **to ~ over sthg** saltar por cima de algo **-2.** *fig* aproveitar-se de.

leapt [lept] *pt* & *pp* ▷ **leap**.

leap year *n* ano *m* bissexto.

learn [lɜ:n] (*pt* & *pp* **-ed** *OR* **learnt**) ◇ *vt* **-1.** [gen] aprender; **to ~ (how) to do sthg** aprender a fazer algo **-2.** [hear] ouvir; **to ~ that** ficar sabendo que. ◇ *vi* **-1.** [acquire knowledge, skill] aprender **-2.** [hear]: **to ~ of** *OR* **about sthg** ficar sabendo de algo.

learned ['lɜ:nɪd] *adj* **-1.** [person] culto(ta), erudito(-ta) **-2.** [journal, paper, book] erudito(ta).

learner ['lɜ:nəʳ] *n* aprendiz *mf*.

learner (driver) *n* aprendiz *mf* de direção.

learning ['lɜ:nɪŋ] *n* **-1.** [knowledge] erudição *f* **-2.** [study] aprendizagem *f*.

learning curve *n* curva *f* de aprendizagem.

learnt [lɜ:nt] *pt* & *pp* ▷ **learn**.

lease [li:s] ◇ *n JUR* arrendamento *m*, contrato *m* de locação; **to give sb a new ~ of life** *UK*, **to give a new ~ on life to sb** *US* dar uma nova vida a alguém. ◇ *vt* [premises] arrendar, alugar; **to ~ sthg from/to sb** arrendar algo de/para alguém; [car] fazer um leasing.

leaseback ['li:sbæk] *n contrato pelo qual o comprador aluga a propriedade comprada ao ex-proprietário.*

leasehold ['li:shəʊld] ◇ *adj* arrendado(da). ◇ *adv* em arrendamento.

leaseholder ['li:s,həʊldəʳ] *n* arrendatário *m*, -ria *f*.

leash [li:ʃ] *n* [for dog] coleira *f*.

least [li:st] ◇ *adj (superl of little)* [smallest in amount, degree]: **the ~** o (a) menor; **he earns the ~ money of all** de todos ele é o que ganha menos. ◇ *pron (superl of little)* [smallest amount]: **the ~** o mínimo; **it's the ~ we'll have to spend** é o mínimo que teremos de gastar; **that's the ~ of my worries!** essa é a menor das minhas preocupações!; **it's the ~ (that) he can do** é o mínimo que ele podia fazer; **not in the ~** em absoluto, de modo algum; **to say the ~** para não dizer outra coisa. ◇ *adv* [to the smallest amount, degree] menos; **to aim for the ~ possible expenditure** desejar alcançar o menor gasto possível.

◆ **at least** *adv* **-1.** [gen] pelo menos, no mínimo **-2.** [qualifying sthg one has said] pelo menos.

◆ **least of all** *adv* muito menos.

◆ **not least** *adv fml* em especial.

leather ['leðəʳ] ◇ *n (U)* couro *m*. ◇ *comp* de couro.

◆ **leathers** *npl* [of motorbike rider] roupas *fpl* de couro.

leatherette [,leðə'ret] *n (U)* couro *m* sintético.

leave [li:v] (*pt* & *pp* **left**) ◇ *n* **-1.** [time off] licença *f*; **to be on ~** estar de licença **-2.** *fml* [permission] licença *f*, permissão *f*. ◇ *vt* **-1.** [gen] deixar; **~ me alone!** me deixa em paz!; **it ~s me cold** isso me deixa indiferente; **it ~s a lot to be desired** isso deixa muito a desejar **-2.** [depart from] sair de **-3.** [entrust]: **to ~ it to sb to do sthg** deixar que alguém faça algo; **to ~ sthg/with sb** deixar algo com alguém; **~ it with me!** deixa (isso) comigo!; **to ~ sb sthg, to ~ sthg to sb** deixar algo para alguém **-4.** [husband, wife] deixar, largar. ◇ *vi* **-1.** [gen] partir, ir embora **-2.** [end relationship] ir embora.

◆ **leave behind** *vt sep* **-1.** [abandon] abandonar **-2.** [forget] esquecer.

◆ **leave off** ◇ *vt sep* **-1.** [omit] deixar fora, não incluir **-2.** [stop] parar de; **to ~ off doing sthg** parar de fazer algo; **~ off!** *inf* corta essa! ◇ *vi* [stop] deixar; **to carry on from where one left off** continuar de onde se havia parado.

◆ **leave out** *vt sep* [omit] excluir, deixar de fora; **to feel left out** sentir-se ignorado(da).

leave of absence *n* licença *f*.

leaves [li:vz] *pl* ▷ **leaf**.

Lebanese [,lebə'ni:z] (*pl inv*) ◇ *adj* libanês(esa). ◇ *n* [person] libanês *m*, -esa *f*.

Lebanon ['lebənən] *n* Líbano; **in (the) ~** no Líbano.

lecherous ['letʃərəs] *adj* lascivo(va).

lechery ['letʃərɪ] *n (U)* lascívia *f*.

lectern ['lektən] *n* atril *m*.

lecture ['lektʃəʳ] ◇ *n* **-1.** [talk - at university] aula *f*; [- at conference] palestra *f*, conferência *f*; **to give a ~ (on sthg)** dar uma palestra (sobre algo) **-2.** [criticism, reprimand] sermão *m*. ◇ *vt* [scold] dar um sermão em. ◇ *vi* [university]: **to ~ (on/in sthg)** dar uma aula (sobre algo); [at conference] dar uma palestra (sobre algo).

lecture hall *n* [in conference centre] **-1.** sala *f* de conferências **-2.** [in university] sala *f* de aula.

lecturer ['lektʃərəʳ] *n* **-1.** [teacher] professor *m*, -ra *f* **-2.** [speaker] palestrante *mf*, conferencista *mf*.

lecture theatre *n* anfiteatro *m*.

led [led] *pt* & *pp* ▷ **lead**[1].

LED (*abbr of* **light-emitting diode**) *n* LED *m*.

ledge [ledʒ] *n* **-1.** [of window] parapeito *m* **-2.** [of mountain] saliência *f*.

ledger ['ledʒəʳ] *n* livro *m* contábil.

lee [li:] *n* [shelter]: **in the ~ of sthg** ao abrigo de algo.

leech [li:tʃ] *n* **-1.** [creature] sanguessuga *f* **-2.**

fig & *pej* [person] sanguessuga *f*.
leek [li:k] *n* alho-poró *m*.
leer [lɪəʳ] ◇ *n* olhar *m* malicioso. ◇ *vi*: **to ~ at sb** olhar maliciosamente para alguém.
Leeward Islands ['li:wəd-] *npl*: **the ~** as Ilhas de Sotavento.
leeway ['li:weɪ] *n (U)* **-1.** [room to manoeuvre] liberdade *f* de ação **-2.** [time lost]: **to make up ~** recuperar o tempo perdido.
left [left] ◇ *pt & pp* ▻ **leave**. ◇ *adj* **-1.** [remaining] sobrando; **do you have any money ~?** tem algum dinheiro sobrando?; **to be ~** sobrar; **there's no milk ~** não sobrou leite **-2.** [side, hand, foot] esquerdo(da). ◇ *adv* para a esquerda. ◇ *n (U)* [direction]: **on/to the ~** à esquerda; **keep ~** mantenha-se à esquerda.
◆ **Left** *n POL*: **the Left** a esquerda.
left-hand *adj* esquerdo(da); **~ side** lado *m* esquerdo.
left-hand drive ◇ *adj* com direção do lado esquerdo. ◇ *n* veículo *m* com direção do lado esquerdo.
left-handed [-'hændɪd] ◇ *adj* **-1.** [person] canhoto(ta) **-2.** [implement] para canhotos **-3.** *US* [compliment] com duplo sentido. ◇ *adv* com a (mão) esquerda.
left-hander [-'hændəʳ] *n* canhoto *m*, -ta *f*.
Leftist *POL* ◇ *adj* esquerdista, de esquerda. ◇ *n* esquerdista *mf*.
left luggage (office) *n UK* guarda-bagagem *m*.
leftover ['leftəʊvəʳ] *adj* restante.
◆ **leftovers** *npl* sobras *fpl*.
left wing *n POL* esquerda *f*.
◆ **left-wing** *adj POL* esquerdista, de esquerda.
left-winger *n POL* esquerdista *mf*.
lefty ['leftɪ] (*pl* **-ies**) *n* **-1.** *UK inf pej* & *POL* esquerdista *mf* **-2.** *US* [left-handed person] canhoto *m*, -ta *f*.
leg [leg] *n* **-1.** [gen] perna *f*; **to be on one's last ~s** estar nas últimas; **you don't have a ~ to stand on** você não tem em que se basear; **to pull sb's ~** pegar no pé de alguém; [of animal, bird, insect] pata *f* **-2.** [*CULIN* - of chicken] coxa *f*; [- of frog, lamb] perna *f*; [- of pork] pernil *m* **-3.** [of journey, tournament] etapa *f*.
legacy ['legəsɪ] (*pl* **-ies**) *n* **-1.** [gift of money] legado *m* **-2.** *fig* [consequence] herança *f*.
legal ['li:gl] *adj* **-1.** [concerning the law] jurídico(ca) **-2.** [lawful] legal.
legal action *n* ação *f* legal; **to take ~ against sb** iniciar uma ação legal contra alguém.
legal aid *n (U)* auxílio *m* oficial de um advogado.
legality [li:'gælətɪ] *n (U)* legalidade *f*.
legalize, -ise ['li:gəlaɪz] *vt* legalizar.
legally ['li:gəlɪ] *adv* legalmente; **~ binding** com força da lei.
legal tender *n (U)* moeda *f* corrente.
legation [lɪ'geɪʃn] *n* legação *f*.
legend ['ledʒənd] *n* **-1.** [myth] lenda *f* **-2.** *fig* [person] lenda *f*.
legendary ['ledʒəndrɪ] *adj* lendário(ria).
leggings ['legɪŋz] *npl* calças *fpl* stretch.
leggy ['legɪ] (*compar* **-ier**, *superl* **-iest**) *adj* **-1.** [person] de pernas compridas e bonitas **-2.** [plant] de longo caule.
legible ['ledʒəbl] *adj* legível.
legibly ['ledʒəblɪ] *adv* de forma legível.
legion ['li:dʒən] ◇ *adj fml*: **to be ~** ser inumerável. ◇ *n* **-1.** *MIL* legião *f* **-2.** *fig* [large number] legião *f*.
legionnaire's disease [ˌli:dʒə'neəz-] *n (U)* doença *f* do legionário, *doença muito rara semelhante à pneumonia*.
legislate ['ledʒɪsleɪt] *vi* legislar, elaborar leis; **to ~ for/against sthg** elaborar leis a favor de/contra algo.
legislation [ˌledʒɪs'leɪʃn] *n (U)* legislação *f*.
legislative ['ledʒɪslətɪv] *adj* legislativo(va).
legislator ['ledʒɪsleɪtəʳ] *n* legislador *m*, -ra *f*.
legislature ['ledʒɪsleɪtʃəʳ] *n* legislatura *f*.
legitimacy [lɪ'dʒɪtɪməsɪ] *n* legitimidade *f*.
legitimate [lɪ'dʒɪtɪmət] *adj* legítimo(ma).
legitimately [lɪ'dʒɪtɪmətlɪ] *adv* legitimamente.
legitimize, -ise [lɪ'dʒɪtəmaɪz] *vt* [make legal] legitimar.
legless ['leglɪs] *adj UK inf* [drunk] bêbado(da) como um gambá.
legroom ['legrʊm] *n (U)* espaço *m* para as pernas.
leg-warmers [-ˌwɔ:məz] *npl* polainas *fpl*.
legwork ['legwɜ:k] *n (U)*: **to do the ~** fazer o trabalho de campo.
leisure [*UK* 'leʒəʳ, *US* 'li:ʒər] *n (U)* lazer *m*; **do it at (your) ~** faça quando puder.
leisure centre *n* centro *m* de lazer.
leisurely [*UK* 'leʒəlɪ, *US* 'li:ʒərlɪ] ◇ *adj* calmo(ma). ◇ *adv* calmamente.
leisure time *n* (tempo *m* de) lazer *m*.
lemming ['lemɪŋ] *n* **-1.** [animal] lemingue *m* **-2.** *fig* [person] marionete *f*.
lemon ['lemən] *n* [fruit] limão *m*.
lemonade [ˌlemə'neɪd] *n* **-1.** *UK* [fizzy] soda *f* limonada **-2.** [made with fresh lemons] limonada *f*.
lemon curd *n (U) UK espécie de geléia ou creme feito com suco de limão, açúcar, ovos e manteiga*.
lemon juice *n* suco *m* de limão.
lemon sole *n* solha-limão *m*.
lemon squash *n UK* suco *m* de limão.
lemon squeezer [-'skwi:zəʳ] *n* espremedor *m* de limão.
lemon tea *n* chá *m* com limão.
lend [lend] (*pt* & *pp* **lent**) *vt* **-1.** [money, book] emprestar; **to ~ sb sthg, to ~ sthg to sb** emprestar algo para alguém **-2.** [support, assistance]: **to ~ sthg (to sb)** dar algo (a alguém) **-3.** [credibility, quality]: **to ~ sthg to sthg** conferir algo a algo **-4.** *phr*: **it doesn't ~ itself to that** não se presta para isso.
lender ['lendəʳ] *n* [of money] emprestador *m*, -ra *f*.
lending library ['lendɪŋ-] *n* biblioteca *f* pública.
lending rate ['lendɪŋ-] *n* taxa *f* de empréstimo.
length [leŋθ] *n* **-1.** [gen] comprimento *m*; **what ~ is it?** quanto tem de comprimento?; **it's five metres in ~** são cinco metros de comprimento; **she walked the ~ and breadth of England** ela caminhou por toda a Inglaterra **-2.** [of swimming pool] piscina *f* **-3.** [piece] pedaço *m* **-4.** *(U)* [duration] duração *f* **-5.** *phr*: **to go to great ~s to do sthg** não medir esforços para fazer algo.

◆ **at length** *adv* **-1.** [eventually] no final das contas **- 2.** [in detail] detalhadamente.

lengthen ['leŋθən] ◇ *vt* **- 1.** [skirt] alongar **- 2.** [life] prolongar. ◇ *vi* alongar-se, ficar mais longo(ga).

lengthways ['leŋθweɪz] *adv* ao comprido.

lengthy ['leŋθɪ] (*compar* **-ier**, *superl* **-iest**) *adj* longo(-ga).

leniency ['li:njənsɪ] *n (U)* leniência *f*, indulgência *f*.

lenient ['li:njənt] *adj* leniente, indulgente.

lens [lenz] *n* **- 1.** [made of glass] lente *f* **- 2.** [contact lens] lente *f* (de contato).

lent [lent] *pt & pp* ▷ **lend**.

Lent [lent] *n (U)* quaresma *f*.

lentil ['lentɪl] *n* lentilha *f*.

Leo ['li:əʊ] *n* **- 1.** [sign] leão *m* **- 2.** [person] leonino(na); **I'm** ~ sou de Leão.

leopard ['lepəd] *n* leopardo *m*.

leopardess ['lepədɪs] *n* leoparda *f*.

leotard ['li:ətɑ:d] *n* malha *f (usada por dançarinos, acrobatas)*.

leper ['lepə^r] *n* [person with leprosy] leproso *m*, -sa *f*.

leprechaun ['leprəkɔ:n] *n* leprechaun *m*, duende *m*.

leprosy ['leprəsɪ] *n (U)* lepra *f*.

lesbian ['lezbɪən] ◇ *adj* lésbico(ca). ◇ *n* lésbica *f*.

lesbianism ['lezbɪənɪzm] *n (U)* lesbianismo *m*.

lesion ['li:ʒn] *n MED* lesão *f*.

Lesotho [lə'sɑʊtəʊ] *n* Lesoto; **in** ~ no Lesoto.

less [les] (*compar of little*) ◇ *adj* [not as much] menos; ~ **... than** menos ... (do) que; ~ **and** ~ cada vez menos. ◇ *pron* [not as much] menos; ~ **than** menos (do) que; **the** ~ **you work the** ~ **you earn** quanto menos você trabalha, menos você ganha; **no** ~ **than** nada menos que. ◇ *adv* [to a smaller extent] menos; ~ **and** ~ cada vez menos. ◇ *prep* [minus] menos.

lessee [le'si:] *n fml* arrendatário *m*, -ria *f*, locatário *m*, -ria *f*.

lessen ['lesn] *vt & vi* diminuir.

lesser ['lesə^r] *adj* menor; **to a** ~ **extent** *OR* **degree** em menor grau.

lesson ['lesn] *n* **- 1.** [class] aula *f*; **to give/take** ~**s (in sthg)** dar/receber aulas (de algo) **- 2.** [example] lição *f*; **to teach sb a** ~ ensinar uma lição a alguém.

lessor [le'sɔ:^r] *n fml* arrendador *m*, -ra *f*.

lest [lest] *conj fml* para que não; **I did what she asked,** ~ **she become even angrier** fiz o que ela pediu, temendo que ela ficasse ainda mais irritada.

let [let] (*pt & pp* **let**, *cont* **-ting**) *vt* **- 1.** [allow]: **to** ~ **sb do sthg** deixar alguém fazer algo; **she** ~ **her hair grow** ela deixou o cabeço crescer; **to** ~ **go of sb/sthg, to** ~ **sb/sthg go** soltar alguém/algo; [release] soltar alguém/algo; **to** ~ **sb know sthg** informar alguém de algo, informar algo a alguém **- 2.** *(in verb forms)*: ~**'s go!** vamos!; ~**'s see** agora vejamos; ~ **them wait!** eles que esperem! **- 3.** [rent out] alugar; **'to** ~**'** 'aluga-se'.

◆ **let alone** *conj* [much less]: **he couldn't walk,** ~ **alone jump** ele não conseguia caminhar, que dirá pular.

◆ **let down** *vt sep* **- 1.** [deflate] esvaziar **- 2.** [disappoint] desapontar.

◆ **let in** *vt sep* **- 1.** [admit] deixar entrar **- 2.** [air, water] deixar entrar.

◆ **let in for** *vt sep*: **to** ~ **o.s. in for sthg** meter--se em algo.

◆ **let in on** *vt sep*: **he** ~ **me in on his secret** ele me revelou o seu segredo.

◆ **let off** *vt sep* **- 1.** [excuse, allow not to do]: **to** ~ **sb off sthg** eximir alguém de algo **- 2.** [criminal, pupil, child] deixar impune **- 3.** [bomb, explosive] detonar **- 4.** [firework] estourar.

◆ **let on** *vi* contar *(um segredo)*; **don't** ~ **on!** não conta nada!

◆ **let out** *vt sep* **- 1.** [gen] deixar sair **- 2.** [sound, cry, laugh] emitir **- 3.** [garment] alargar.

◆ **let up** *vi* **- 1.** [heat, rain] cessar **- 2.** [person] relaxar.

letdown ['letdaʊn] *n inf* decepção *f*.

lethal ['li:θl] *adj* letal.

lethargic [lə'θɑ:dʒɪk] *adj* letárgico(ca).

lethargy ['leθədʒɪ] *n (U)* letargia *f*.

Letraset® *n (U)* letraset® *f*.

let's [lets] = **let us**.

letter ['letə^r] *n* **- 1.** [written message] carta *f* **- 2.** [of alphabet] letra *f*.

◆ **letters** *npl fml* [literature] letras *fpl*.

letter bomb *n* carta-bomba *f*.

letterbox ['letəbɒks] *n UK* **- 1.** [in door] portinhola *f* para cartas **- 2.** [in street] caixa *f* de correio.

letterhead ['letəhed] *n* cabeçalho *m* em papel timbrado.

lettering ['letərɪŋ] *n (U)* [characters] letras *fpl*.

letter of credit *n* carta *f* de crédito.

letter opener *n* abridor *m* de cartas.

letter-perfect *adj US* impecável.

letter quality *n COMPUT* qualidade *f* carta.

letters patent *npl* **- 1.** *JUR* carta *f* patente **- 2.** [of inventor] patente *f*.

lettuce ['letɪs] *n* alface *f*.

letup ['letʌp] *n* pausa *f*, intervalo *m*.

leuk(a)emia [lu:'ki:mɪə] *n* leucemia *f*.

levee ['levɪ] *n US* [embankment] barragem *f*.

level ['levl] (*UK pt & pp* **-led**, *cont* **-ling**, *US pt & pp* **-ed**, *cont* **-ing**) ◇ *adj* **- 1.** [equal in height] nivelado(-da); **to be** ~ **(with sthg)** estar nivelado(da) (com algo) **- 2.** [equal in standard] em pé de igualdade **- 3.** [flat - floor, field] plano(na); [- spoon, cup] raso(sa). ◇ *adv*: **to draw** ~ **with sb** empatar com alguém, alcançar alguém. ◇ *n* **- 1.** [gen] nível *m*; **to be on a** ~ **(with sthg)** estar no mesmo nível (de algo) **- 2.** *US* [spirit level] nível *m* (de bolha) **- 3.** [storey] andar *m* **- 4.** *phr*: **to be on the** ~ *inf* ser sincero(ra). ◇ *vt* **- 1.** [make flat] nivelar, aplainar **- 2.** [demolish] derrubar **- 3.** [aim]: **to** ~ **a gun at sb/sthg** apontar uma arma para alguém/algo; **to** ~ **an accusation at** *OR* **against sb** lançar uma acusação contra *OR* sobre alguém.

◆ **level off, level out** *vi* estabilizar-se.

◆ **level with** *vt fus inf* [be honest with] ser sincero(ra) com.

level crossing *n UK* passagem *f* de nível.

level-headed [-'hedɪd] *adj* equilibrado(da), sensato(ta).

level pegging [-'pegɪŋ] *adj UK*: **to be ~** estar igualado(da).
lever [*UK* 'li:vəʳ, *US* 'levər] *n* alavanca *f*.
leverage [*UK* 'li:vərɪdʒ, *US* 'levərɪdʒ] *n (U)* **-1.** *fig* [influence] influência *f* **-2.** [force] alavancagem *f*, força *f*.
leviathan [lɪ'vaɪəθn] *n* [large body, organization] leviatã *m*, gigante *m*.
levitation [ˌlevɪ'teɪʃn] *n (U)* levitação *f*.
levity ['levətɪ] *n (U)* leviandade *f*.
levy ['levɪ] (*pt* & *pp* **-ied**) <> *n* [financial contribution, tax]: **~ (on sthg)** taxa *f* (sobre algo). <> *vt* [demand, collect] arrecadar.
lewd [lju:d] *adj* [behaviour] lascivo(va), obsceno(na).
lexical ['leksɪkl] *adj* lexical.
liability [ˌlaɪə'bɪlətɪ] (*pl* **-ies**) *n* **-1.** [hindrance] estorvo *m* **-2.** *JUR (U)* [legal responsibility]: **~ (for sthg)** responsabilidade *f* (por algo).
◆ **liabilities** *npl FIN* [debts] passivos *mpl*, obrigações *fpl*.
liable ['laɪəbl] *adj* **-1.** [likely]: **she is ~ to do something stupid** é bem provável que ela faça algo estúpido **-2.** [prone]: **to be ~ to sthg** estar propenso(sa) a algo **-3.** *JUR*: **to be ~ (for sthg)** [legally responsible] ser legalmente responsável (por algo); **to be ~ to sthg** [punishable] estar sujeito(ta) a algo.
liaise [lɪ'eɪz] *vi*: **to ~ (with)** fazer contato (com); **to ~ (between)** criar vínculos (entre).
liaison [lɪ'eɪzɒn] *n* **-1.** *(U)* [contact, cooperation]: **~ (with/between)** relação *f* (com/entre) **-2.** [affair, relationship]: **~ (with/between)** ligação *f OR* caso *m* (com/entre).
liar ['laɪəʳ] *n* mentiroso *m*, -sa *f*.
Lib -1. (*abbr of* **Liberal**) liberal **-2.** (*abbr of* **liberation**) liberação *f*.
libel ['laɪbl] (*UK pt* & *pp* **-led**, *cont* **-ling**, *US pt* & *pp* **-ed**, *cont* **-ing**) <> *n* libelo *m*. <> *vt* difamar.
libellous *UK*, **libelous** *US* ['laɪbələs] *adj* difamatório(ria).
liberal ['lɪbərəl] <> *adj* **-1.** [tolerant] liberal **-2.** [generous] generoso(sa). <> *n* liberal *mf*.
◆ **Liberal** *POL* <> *adj* liberal. <> *n* liberal *mf*.
liberal arts *npl esp US* ciências *fpl* humanas.
Liberal Democrat <> *adj* liberal democrata. <> *n* liberal democrata *mf*.
liberalize, -ise ['lɪbərəlaɪz] *vt* liberalizar.
liberal-minded [-'maɪndɪd] *adj* liberal.
Liberal Party *n*: **the ~** o Partido Liberal.
liberate ['lɪbəreɪt] *vt* libertar.
liberation [ˌlɪbə'reɪʃn] *n (U)* **-1.** [release] libertação *f* **-2.** *fig* [emancipation] libertação *f*.
liberator ['lɪbəreɪtəʳ] *n* libertador *m*, -ra *f*.
Liberia [laɪ'bɪərɪə] *n* Libéria; **in ~** na Libéria.
Liberian [laɪ'bɪərɪən] <> *adj* liberiano(na). <> *n* liberiano *m*, -na *f*.
libertine ['lɪbəti:n] *n* libertino *m*, -na *f*.
liberty ['lɪbətɪ] (*pl* **-ies**) *n* [gen] liberdade *f*; **at ~** em liberdade; **to be at ~ to do sthg** ter liberdade para fazer algo; **to take liberties (with sb)** tomar liberdades (com alguém).
libido [lɪ'bi:dəʊ] (*pl* **-s**) *n* [sexual urge] libido *f*.
Libra ['li:brə] *n* **-1.** [sign] libra *f* **-2.** [person] libriano *m*, -na *f*; **I'm ~** sou de Libra.
librarian [laɪ'breərɪən] *n* bibliotecário *m*, -ria *f*.
librarianship [laɪ'breərɪənʃɪp] *n (U)* biblioteconomia *f*.
library ['laɪbrərɪ] (*pl* **-ies**) *n* biblioteca *f*.
library book *n* livro *m* de biblioteca.
libretto [lɪ'bretəʊ] (*pl* **-s**) *n* libreto *m*.
Libya ['lɪbɪə] *n* Líbia; **in ~** na Líbia.
Libyan ['lɪbɪən] <> *adj* líbio(bia). <> *n* líbio *m*, -bia *f*.
lice [laɪs] *pl* ▷ **louse**.
licence ['laɪsəns] <> *n* **-1.** [permit - gen] licença *f*; [- for marriage] autorização *f*; [- for pilot] brevê *m* **-2.** *COMM* licença *f*; **under ~ from** com permissão de. <> *vt US* = **license**.
license ['laɪsəns] <> *vt COMM* autorizar. <> *n US* = **licence**.
licensed ['laɪsənst] *adj* **-1.** [person]: **to be ~ to do sthg** estar autorizado(da) a fazer algo **-2.** [object - car, dog] com licença; [- gun] registrado(da) **-3.** *UK* [premises] autorizado(da) a vender álcool.
licensee [ˌlaɪsən'si:] *n* licenciado *m*, -da *f*.
license plate *n US* placa *f (de automóvel)*.
licensing hours ['laɪsənsɪŋ-] *npl UK horário de funcionamento dos bares*.

LICENSING HOURS

Tradicionalmente, o horário de funcionamento dos *pubs* na Grã-Bretanha sempre esteve sujeito a regulamentação bastante estrita, vinculada à legislação sobre a venda de bebidas alcoólicas. Mas, a partir de 1988, as regras se tornaram mais flexíveis. Em vez de abrirem das 11:30 às 14:30h, e das 18 às 23:00h, os *pubs* passaram a abrir das 11 às 23h, menos aos domingos, quando funcionam das 11 às 15h e das 19 às 22:30h. Na Escócia, os horários são menos rigorosos.

licensing laws ['laɪsənsɪŋ-] *npl UK leis que controlam a venda de bebidas alcoólicas*.
licentious [laɪ'senʃəs] *adj fml* & *pej* licencioso(sa).
lichen ['laɪkən] *n* líquen *m*.
lick [lɪk] <> *n* **-1.** [act of licking] lambida *f* **-2.** *inf* [small amount]: **a ~ of paint** uma demão de tinta. <> *vt* **-1.** [with tongue] lamber; **to ~ one's lips** lamber os beiços **-2.** *fig* [subj: flames, waves] lamber **-3.** *inf* [defeat] derrotar.
licorice ['lɪkərɪs] *n* = **liquorice**.
lid [lɪd] *n* **-1.** [cover] tampa *f* **-2.** [eyelid] pálpebra *f*.
lido ['li:dəʊ] (*pl* **-s**) *n* **-1.** *UK* [swimming pool] piscina *f* pública **-2.** [beach] praia *f*.
lie [laɪ] (*pt sense 1* **lied**, *pt senses 2-7* **lay**, *pp sense 1* **lied**, *pp senses 2-7* **lain**, *cont all senses* **lying**) <> *n* mentira *f*; **to tell ~s** contar mentiras. <> *vi* **-1.** [tell untruth] mentir; **to ~ to sb** mentir para alguém **-2.** [to be lying down] estar deitado(da) **-3.** [lie down] deitar **-4.** [be situated] encontrar-se **-5.** [corpse] jazer **-6.** : **who knows what ~s ahead?** quem sabe o que nos espera? **-7.** *phr*: **to ~ low** ficar escondido(da).
◆ **lie about, lie around** *vi* **-1.** [people] andar sem fazer nada, vadiar **-2.** [things] estar jogado(da).
◆ **lie down** *vi* deitar-se; **he won't take it lying down** ele não vai ficar agüentando isso.
◆ **lie in** *vi UK* ficar na cama até tarde.

Liechtenstein ['lɪktən,staɪn] *n* Liechtenstein; **in ~** em Liechtenstein.

lie detector *n* detector *m* de mentiras.

lie-down *n UK*: **to have a ~** repousar.

lie-in *n UK*: **to have a ~** ficar na cama até tarde.

lieu [lju:, lu:] ◆ **in lieu** *adv* em troca; **in ~ of** em vez de.

Lieut. (*abbr of* **lieutenant**) Ten.

lieutenant [*UK* lef'tenənt, *US* lu:'tenənt] *n* tenente *m*.

lieutenant colonel *n* tenente-coronel *m*.

life [laɪf] (*pl* **lives**) <> *n* **-1.** [gen] vida *f*; **to breathe ~ into sthg** dar vida a algo; **to come to ~** criar vida; **that's ~!** é a vida!; **for ~** para toda a vida; **for the ~ of me** *inf* por mais que eu tente; **to lay down one's ~** entregar a vida; **to risk ~ and limb** arriscar a pele; **to scare the ~ out of sb** quase matar alguém do coração; **to take sb's/one's own ~** tirar a vida de alguém/a própria vida **-2.** *(U) inf* [life imprisonment] prisão *f* perpétua. <> *comp* vitalício(cia).

life-and-death *adj* de vida ou morte.

life annuity *n* renda *f* vitalícia.

life assurance *n* = **life insurance**.

life belt *n* cinto *m* salva-vidas.

lifeblood ['laɪfblʌd] *n (U) fig* [source of strength] força *f* vital.

lifeboat ['laɪfbəʊt] *n* **-1.** [on ship] bote *m* salva-vidas **-2.** [on shore] lancha *f* de salvamento.

lifeboatman [-mən] (*pl* **-men**) *n* salva-vidas *m inv (de barco)*.

life buoy *n* bóia *f* salva-vidas.

life cycle *n* ciclo *m* vital.

life expectancy *n* espectativa *f* de vida.

lifeguard ['laɪfgɑ:d] *n* salva-vidas *mf inv*.

life imprisonment [-ɪm'prɪznmənt] *n* prisão *f* perpétua.

life insurance *n (U)* seguro *m* de vida.

life jacket *n* colete *m* salva-vidas.

lifeless ['laɪflɪs] *adj* **-1.** [dead] sem vida, morto(ta) **-2.** [listless] apagado(da).

lifelike ['laɪflaɪk] *adj* **-1.** [statue, doll] realista **-2.** [portrait] fiel.

lifeline ['laɪflaɪn] *n* **-1.** [rope] corda *f* de segurança **-2.** *fig* [with outside] cordão *m* umbilical.

lifelong ['laɪflɒŋ] *adj* de toda a vida.

life peer *n UK nobre britânico com título não-hereditário.*

life preserver [-prɪ,zɜ:vəʳ] *n US* **-1.** [belt] cinto *m* salva-vidas **-2.** [jacket] colete *m* salva-vidas.

life raft *n* balsa *f* salva-vidas.

lifesaver ['laɪf,seɪvəʳ] *n* **-1.** [person] salva-vidas *mf inv* **-2.** *fig* [relief, help] ajuda *f*.

life sentence *n* pena *f* de prisão perpétua.

life-size(d) [-saɪz(d)] *adj* em tamanho natural.

lifespan ['laɪfspæn] *n* **-1.** [of person, animal, plant] vida *f* **-2.** [of product, machine] vida *f* útil.

lifestyle ['laɪfstaɪl] *n* estilo *m* de vida.

life-support system *n* sistema *m* de respiração artificial.

lifetime ['laɪftaɪm] *n* [length of time] vida *f*.

lift [lɪft] <> *n* **-1.** [ride] carona *f* **-2.** *UK* [elevator] elevador *m*. <> *vt* **-1.** [gen] levantar; **he ~ed the books off the shelf** ele tirou os livros da estante **-2.** [ban, embargo] revogar **-3.** [plagiarize] plagiar **-4.** *inf* [steal] levantar. <> *vi* **-1.** [lid, top] levantar **-2.** [mist, fog, clouds] dissipar-se **-3.** [heart, spirits] melhorar.

◆ **lift up** <> *vt sep* [bag, baby, books] levantar. <> *vi* [lid, top] levantar.

lift-off *n* decolagem *f*.

ligament ['lɪgəmənt] *n ANAT* ligamento *m*.

light [laɪt] (*pt* & *pp* **lit** OR **-ed**) <> *adj* **-1.** [gen] leve **-2.** [not dark] claro(ra). <> *adv*: **to travel ~** viajar com pouca bagagem. <> *n* **-1.** [gen] luz *f* **-2.** [for cigarette, pipe] fogo *m*; **to set ~ to sthg** atear fogo em algo **-3.** [perspective]: **in the ~ of** *UK*, **in ~ of** *US* à luz de; **to see sb/sthg in a different ~** ver alguém/algo de forma diferente **-4.** *literary* [in sb's eyes] brilho *m* **-5.** *phr*: **to come to ~** vir à luz; **to see the ~** [understand] ver claramente; **to throw** OR **cast** OR **shed ~ on sthg** lançar luz sobre algo; **there's a ~ at the end of the tunnel** há uma luz no fim do túnel; **to make ~ of sthg** não dar a devida importância a algo. <> *vt* **-1.** [ignite] acender **-2.** [illuminate] iluminar.

◆ **light out** *vi US inf* dar no pé.

◆ **light up** <> *vt sep* **-1.** [illuminate] iluminar **-2.** [start smoking] acender. <> *vi* **-1.** [look happy] iluminar-se **-2.** *inf* [start smoking] pôr-se a fumar.

light aircraft (*pl inv*) *n* pequeno aeroplano *m*.

light ale *n (U) UK tipo de cerveja escura e suave.*

light bulb *n* lâmpada *f*.

light cream *n US* creme *m* light.

lighted ['laɪtɪd] *adj* **-1.** [illuminated] iluminado(da) **-2.** [on fire] aceso(sa).

light-emitting diode [-ɪ'mɪtɪŋ-] *n* diodo *m* emissor de luz.

lighten ['laɪtn] <> *vt* **-1.** [make brighter] clarear **-2.** [make less heavy] aliviar. <> *vi* **-1.** [brighten] iluminar-se **-2.** [become happier, more relaxed] alegrar-se.

◆ **lighten up** *vi inf* levar na brincadeira.

lighter ['laɪtəʳ] *n* [cigarette lighter] isqueiro *m*.

light-fingered [-'fɪŋgəd] *adj inf* gatuno(na); **to be ~** ter mão leve.

light-headed [-'hedɪd] *adj* tonto(ta).

light-hearted [-'hɑ:tɪd] *adj* **-1.** [cheerful] despreocupado(da) **-2.** [amusing] alegre.

lighthouse ['laɪthaʊs, *pl* -haʊzɪz] *n* farol *m*.

light industry *n* indústria *f* leve.

lighting ['laɪtɪŋ] *n (U)* iluminação *f*.

lighting-up time *n (U)* hora *f* de acendimento da iluminação pública.

lightly ['laɪtlɪ] *adv* **-1.** [tap, knock] suavemente **-2.** [cook, grill] ligeiramente **-3.** [remark, say] levianamente.

light meter *n PHOT* fotômetro *m*.

lightning ['laɪtnɪŋ] *n (U)* raio *m*, relâmpago *m*.

lightning conductor *UK*, **lightning rod** *US* *n* pára-raios *m inv*.

lightning strike *n UK* greve-relâmpago *f*.

light opera *n* opereta *f*.

light pen *n* caneta *f* óptica.

lightship *n* navio-farol *m*.

lights-out *n (U) hora em que se apagam as luzes.*

lightweight ['laɪtweɪt] <> *adj* **-1.** [object] leve **-2.** *fig & pej* [person] de pouca expressão. <> *n* **-1.** [boxer] peso *m* leve **-2.** *fig & pej* [person] joão-ninguém *m*.
light year *n* ano-luz *m*.
likable ['laɪkəbl] *adj* simpático(ca), agradável.
like [laɪk] <> *prep* **-1.** [similar to] como; **to look ~ sb/sthg** parecer-se com alguém/algo, parecer alguém/algo; **what did it taste ~?** tinha gosto de quê?; **what did it look ~?** como era?; **what did it sound ~?** como era o barulho?; **~ this/that** assim **-2.** [typical of]: **that's just ~ him** isso é típico dele **-3.** [such as] (tal) como. <> *vt* **-1.** [enjoy, find pleasant, approve of] gostar; **to ~ doing** OR **to do sthg** gostar de fazer algo **-2.** [want, wish] querer; **to ~ to do sthg** desejar fazer algo; **to ~ sb to do sthg** desejar que alguém faça algo; **I'd ~ you to come** gostaria que você viesse. <> *adj* [similar] igual. <> *n*: **the ~ of sb/sthg** alguém/algo do estilo; **and the ~** e similares, e coisas do estilo.
◆ **likes** *npl* [things one likes] gostos *mpl*.
likeable ['laɪkəbl] *adj* = **likable**.
likelihood ['laɪklɪhʊd] *n (U)* probabilidade *f*; **in all ~** com toda certeza.
likely ['laɪklɪ] *adj* **-1.** [probable] provável; **rain is ~ later on** é provável que chova mais tarde; **to be ~ to do sthg** ser provável que algo aconteça; **he's ~ to come** é provável que ele venha; **a ~ story!** *iro* pura invenção! **-2.** [suitable] indicado(da).
like-minded [-'maɪndɪd] *adj* de mesma opinião.
liken ['laɪkn] *vt*: **to ~ sb/sthg to** comparar alguém/algo a.
likeness ['laɪknɪs] *n* semelhança *f*; **~ to sb/sthg** semelhança com alguém/algo.
likewise ['laɪkwaɪz] *adv* [similarly] da mesma maneira; **to do ~** fazer o mesmo.
liking ['laɪkɪŋ] *n*: **~ for sb/sthg** afeição *f* por alguém/algo; **to have a ~ for sb/sthg** ter afeição por alguém/algo; **to be to sb's ~** estar ao gosto de alguém; **he's too confident for my ~** ele é muito atrevido para o meu gosto.
lilac ['laɪlək] <> *adj* [colour] lilás. <> *n* **-1.** [tree] lilás *m* **-2.** *(U)* [colour] lilás *m*.
Lilo® ['laɪləʊ] (*pl* **-s**) *n UK* colchão *m* inflável.
lilt [lɪlt] *n* [in voice] melodia *f*; [in melody] cadência *f*.
lilting ['lɪltɪŋ] *adj* [voice] melodioso(sa); [melody] cadenciado(da).
lily ['lɪlɪ] (*pl* **-ies**) *n* lírio *m*.
lily of the valley (*pl* **lilies of the valley**) *n* lírio-do-vale *m*.
Lima ['li:mə] *n* Lima.
limb [lɪm] *n* **-1.** [of body] membro *m* **-2.** [of tree] ramo *m* **-3.** *phr*: **to be out on a ~** estar em apuros.
limber ['lɪmbə^r] ◆ **limber up** *vi* fazer aquecimento, aquecer.
limbo ['lɪmbəʊ] (*pl* **-s**) *n* **-1.** *(U)* [uncertain state]: **to be in ~** estar no limbo **-2.** [dance]: **the ~** *dança caribenha na qual se passa por baixo de uma barra com o corpo inclinado para trás*, danca *f* da cordinha.
lime [laɪm] *n* **-1.** [fruit] lima *f*; **~ (juice)** (suco *m* de) lima *f* **-2.** [linden tree] tília *f* **-3.** *(U)* [substance] cal *f*.
lime cordial *n* refresco *m* de lima.
lime-green *adj* de cor verde-limão.
limelight ['laɪmlaɪt] *n*: **to be in the ~** estar no/ser o centro das atenções.
limerick ['lɪmərɪk] *n poema humorístico de cinco linhas*.
limestone ['laɪmstəʊn] *n (U)* calcário *m*, pedra *f* calcária.
limey ['laɪmɪ] (*pl* **-s**) *n US inf termo pejorativo que designa um inglês*.
limit ['lɪmɪt] <> *n* limite *m*; **to be off ~s** ser/estar proibido(da); **within ~s** [to a certain extent] até certo ponto; **he's/she's the ~!** *inf* ele/ela é o cúmulo! <> *vt* limitar, restringir; **to ~ o.s. to sthg** limitar-se a algo.
limitation [ˌlɪmɪ'teɪʃn] *n* limitação *f*.
limited ['lɪmɪtɪd] *adj* [restricted] limitado(da); **to be ~ to sthg** estar limitado(da) a algo.
limited company *n* companhia *f* limitada.
limited edition *n* edição *f* limitada.
limited liability company *n* = **limited company**.
limitless ['lɪmɪtlɪs] *adj* ilimitado(da).
limo ['lɪməʊ] *n inf* limusine *f*.
limousine ['lɪməzi:n] *n* limusine *f*.
limp [lɪmp] <> *adj* **-1.** [hand, handshake] sem firmeza **-2.** [body, lettuce] murcho(cha) **-3.** [excuse] mole. <> *n* manqueira *f*. <> *vi* mancar.
limpet ['lɪmpɪt] *n* lapa *f*.
limpid *adj literary* límpido(da).
limply ['lɪmplɪ] *adv* **-1.** [lie, hang] sem firmeza **-2.** [reply] de forma vacilante.
linchpin ['lɪntʃpɪn] *n fig* [important person, thing] peça-chave *f*.
linctus ['lɪŋktəs] *n (U) UK* expectorante *m*.
line [laɪn] <> *n* **-1.** [gen] linha *f*; **washing ~** corda *f* de varal; **power ~** cabo *m* de força; **to draw the ~ at doing sthg** *fig* estabelecer limites para fazer algo **-2.** [row] fileira *f*, linha *f* **-3.** [queue] fila *f*; **to stand** OR **wait in ~** ficar OR esperar em fila; **to be in ~ for promotion** estar a caminho da promoção **-4.** [alignment] alinhamento *m*; **in ~** alinhado(da); **in ~ with** em linha com; **to step out of ~** sair da linha **-5.** [RAIL - railway track] linha *f (férrea)*; [- route] linha *f* **-6.** NAUT: **shipping ~** companhia *f* marítima **-7.** [in writing - of text] linha *f*; **to read between the ~s** ler nas entrelinhas; [- of poetry, song] verso *m* **-8.** [wrinkle] ruga *f* **-9.** TELEC [telephone connection] linha *f (telefônica)* **-10.** *inf* [short letter]: **to drop sb a ~** escrever umas linhas para alguém **-11.** [of ideas, reasoning] linha *f* de raciocínio; **along the same ~s** seguindo a mesma linha; **to be on the right ~s** estar num bom caminho **-12.** *inf* [field of activity] ramo *m* **-13.** [lineage, ancestry] linhagem *f*. <> *vt* **-1.** [form rows along] alinhar-se ao longo de; **crowds ~d the street** a multidão lotava a rua **-2.** [cover inside surface of] forrar.
◆ **lines** *npl* **-1.** SCH *castigo que consiste em escrever a mesma frase inúmeras vezes* **-2.** [actor's words] texto *m*.
◆ **on the line** *adv*: **to put sthg on the ~** pôr algo em jogo.
◆ **out of line** *adj* inaceitável.
◆ **line up** <> *vt sep* **-1.** [in rows] alinhar **-2.** *inf* [organize] arranjar, organizar. <> *vi* **-1.** [in a row]

alinhar-se **-2.** [in a queue] pôr-se na fila.
lineage ['lɪnɪɪdʒ] *n fml* linhagem *f.*
linear ['lɪnɪəʳ] *adj* linear.
lined [laɪnd] *adj* **-1.** [paper] pautado(da) **-2.** [face] enrugado(da).
line drawing *n* desenho *m* a traço.
line feed *n COMPUT* avanço *m* de linha.
linen ['lɪnɪn] *(U)* <> *n* **-1.** [cloth] linho *m* **-2.** [sheets] roupa *f* de cama **-3.** [tablecloths] toalha *f (de mesa).* <> *comp* **-1.** [suit, napkins] de linho **-2.** [cupboard, drawer]: ~ **cupboard** *armário no qual se guardam as roupas de cama e de mesa.*
linen basket *n* cesto *m* de roupa suja.
line-out *n RUGBY formação para recomeço do jogo quando a bola saiu de campo.*
line printer *n COMPUT* impressora *f* de linha.
liner ['laɪnəʳ] *n* [ship] transatlântico *m.*
linesman ['laɪnzmən] (*pl* **-men** [-mən]) *n SPORT* juiz *m* de linha.
line-up *n* **-1.** [of players, competitors] seleção *f* **-2.** *US* [identification parade] fila *f* de identificação.
linger ['lɪŋgəʳ] *vi* **-1.** [dawdle] demorar-se **-2.** [persist] persistir.
lingerie ['lænʒərɪ] *n (U)* lingerie *f.*
lingering ['lɪŋgrɪŋ] *adj* **-1.** [persistent] persistente **-2.** [slow] lento(ta) **-3.** [long] prolongado(da).
lingo ['lɪŋgəʊ] (*pl* **-es**) *n inf* idioma *f.*
linguist ['lɪŋgwɪst] *n* **-1.** [someone good at languages] pessoa *f* com facilidade para os idiomas **-2.** [student or teacher of linguistics] lingüista *mf.*
linguistic [lɪŋ'gwɪstɪk] *adj* lingüístico(ca).
◆ **linguistics** *n (U)* lingüística *f.*
liniment ['lɪnɪmənt] *n (U)* linimento *m.*
lining ['laɪnɪŋ] *n* **-1.** [of coat, curtains, box] forro *m* **-2.** [of stomach, nose] paredes *fpl* internas **-3.** *AUT* [of brakes] revestimento *m.*
link [lɪŋk] <> *n* **-1.** [of chain] elo *m* **-2.** *COMPUT* linque *m* **-3.** [connection] conexão *f*; ~ **between sb/sthg** vínculo *m OR* ligação *f* entre alguém/algo; ~ **with sb/sthg** vínculo *OR* ligação com alguém/algo. <> *vt* **-1.** [relate] ligar, relacionar; **to** ~ **sb/sthg with** *OR* **to sb/sthg** ligar alguém/algo com *OR* a alguém/algo, relacionar alguém/algo com *OR* a alguém/algo **-2.** [connect physically] enlaçar.
◆ **link up** <> *vt sep* [connect] conectar; **to** ~ **sthg up with sthg** conectar algo a algo. <> *vi* [connect]: **to** ~ **up (with sb/sthg)** conectar-se (a alguém/algo).
linkage ['lɪŋkɪdʒ] *n* [connection] conexão *f*, vínculo *m.*
linked [lɪŋkt] *adj* **-1.** [related] relacionado(da) **-2.** [connected physically] enlaçado(da); **arms** ~**ed** de braços dados.
links [lɪŋks] (*pl inv*) *n SPORT* campo *m* de golfe.
link-up *n* conexão *f.*
lino ['laɪnəʊ], **linoleum** [lɪ'nəʊljəm] *n (U)* linóleo *m.*
linseed oil ['lɪnsi:d-] *n (U)* óleo *m* de linhaça.
lint [lɪnt] *n* **-1.** [dressing] gaze *f* **-2.** *US* [fluff] fiapo *m.*
lintel ['lɪntl] *n* verga *f (de porta ou janela).*
lion ['laɪən] *n* leão *m.*
lion cub *n* filhote *m* de leão.
lioness ['laɪənes] *n* leoa *f.*
lionize, -ise ['laɪənaɪz] *vt* tratar como celebridade, endeusar.
lip [lɪp] *n* **-1.** [of mouth] lábio *m*; **to keep a stiff upper** ~ manter-se firme; **my** ~**s are sealed** eu sou um túmulo **-2.** [of container] borda *f.*
liposuction ['lɪpəʊ,sʌkʃən] *n* lipoaspiração *f.*
lip-read *vi* ler nos lábios.
lip-reading *n (U)* leitura *f* dos lábios.
lip salve [-sælv] *n UK* pomada *f* para lábios.
lip service *n*: **to pay** ~ **to sthg** concordar com algo da boca para fora.
lipstick ['lɪpstɪk] *n* batom *m.*
liquefy ['lɪkwɪfaɪ] (*pt* & *pp* **-ied**) <> *vt* liquefazer. <> *vi* liquefazer-se.
liqueur [lɪ'kjʊəʳ] *n* licor *m.*
liquid ['lɪkwɪd] <> *adj* [fluid] líquido(da). <> *n* [fluid] líquido *m.*
liquid assets *npl* ativo *m* disponível.
liquidate ['lɪkwɪdeɪt] *vt* liquidar.
liquidation [,lɪkwɪ'deɪʃn] *n (U) FIN* falência *f*; **to go into** ~ abrir falência.
liquidator ['lɪkwɪdeɪtəʳ] *n FIN* liquidante *mf.*
liquid crystal display *n* tela *f* de cristal líquido.
liquidity [lɪ'kwɪdətɪ] *n (U)* **-1.** [having money] liquidez *f* **-2.** [being liquid] condição *f* de ser líquido.
liquidize, -ise ['lɪkwɪdaɪz] *vt UK CULIN* liquidificar.
liquidizer ['lɪkwɪdaɪzəʳ] *n UK* liquidificador *m.*
liquor ['lɪkəʳ] *n US* [alcohol] álcool *m*; [spirits] bebida *f* alcoólica.
liquorice ['lɪkərɪʃ, 'lɪkərɪs] *n (U)* alcaçuz *m.*
liquor store *n US* armazém *m* de bebidas alcoólicas.
lira ['lɪərəl] *n* [Italian] lira *f.*
Lisbon ['lɪzbən] *n* Lisboa; **in** ~ em Lisboa.
lisp [lɪsp] <> *n* ceceio *m.* <> *vi* cecear.
lissom(e) ['lɪsəm] *adj literary* grácil, esbelto(ta).
list [lɪst] <> *n* lista *f.* <> *vt* [in writing, speech] listar. <> *vi NAUT* adernar.
listed building [,lɪstɪd-] *n UK* prédio *m* tombado.
listed company [,lɪstɪd-] *n UK* sociedade *f* de capital aberto.
listen ['lɪsn] *vi* **-1.** [give attention] escutar, ouvir; **to** ~ **to sb/sthg** escutar alguém/algo; **to** ~ **for sthg** estar atento(ta) a algo **-2.** [heed advice] dar atenção a; **to** ~ **to sb/sthg** escutar alguém/algo.
◆ **listen in** *vi* **-1.** *RADIO* escutar um programa numa estação; **to** ~ **in to sthg** sintonizar em algo **-2.** [eavesdrop] escutar a conversa alheia; **to** ~ **in on sthg** [conversation] prestar atenção em algo; [phone call] interceptar algo.
◆ **listen up** *vi US inf* prestar atenção.
listener ['lɪsnəʳ] *n* ouvinte *mf.*
listing ['lɪstɪŋ] *n* listagem *f.*
◆ **listings** *npl* [of events] programação *f* cultural.
listless ['lɪstlɪs] *adj* apático(ca).
list price *n* preço *m* de catálogo.
lit [lɪt] *pt* & *pp* ▷ **light**.
litany ['lɪtənɪ] (*pl* **-ies**) *n* **-1.** *RELIG* ladainha *f*, litania *f* **-2.** [series] ladainha *f.*
liter *n US* = **litre**.
literacy ['lɪtərəsɪ] *n (U)* alfabetização *f.*

literal ['lɪtərəl] *adj* literal.
literally ['lɪtərəlɪ] *adv* literalmente; **to take sthg ~** levar algo ao pé da letra.
literary ['lɪtərərɪ] *adj* literário(ria); **a ~ man** um literato.
literate ['lɪtərət] *adj* **-1.** [able to read and write] alfabetizado(da); **computer-~** que tem conhecimentos de informática **-2.** [well-read] letrado(da), culto(ta).
literature ['lɪtrətʃəʳ] *n (U)* **-1.** [novels, plays, poetry] literatura *f* **-2.** [books on a particular subject] literatura *f*, bibliografia *f* **-3.** [printed information] informações *fpl*.
lithe [laɪð] *adj* ágil.
lithium ['lɪθɪəm] *n* lítio *m*.
lithograph ['lɪθəgrɑːf] *n* litografia *f*.
lithography *n (U)* litografia *f*.
Lithuania [ˌlɪθjʊ'eɪnɪəl *n* Lituânia; **in ~** na Lituânia.
Lithuanian [ˌlɪθjʊ'eɪnjən] ◇ *adj* lituano(na). ◇ *n* **-1.** [person] lituano *m*, -na *f* **-2.** [language] lituano *m*.
litigant ['lɪtɪgənt] *n fml* litigante *mf*.
litigate ['lɪtɪgeɪt] *vi fml* litigar.
litigation [ˌlɪtɪ'geɪʃn] *n (U) fml* litígio *m*.
litmus paper ['lɪtməs-] *n* papel *m* tornassol.
litre *UK*, **liter** *US* ['liːtəʳ] *n* **-1.** [metric unit] litro *m* **-2.** [capacity of engine] cilindrada *f*.
litter ['lɪtəʳ] ◇ *n* **-1.** *(U)* [waste material] lixo *m* **-2.** [newborn animals] ninhada *f* **-3.** [for litter tray]: **(cat) ~** areia *f* química *(para fezes de gato)*. ◇ *vt*: **to be ~ed with sthg** estar coberto(ta) de algo.
litter bin *n UK* cesto *m* de lixo.
litter lout *UK*, **litterbug** *n inf pessoa que suja as vias públicas*.
litter tray *n recipiente com areia química para o gato fazer suas necessidades*.
little ['lɪtl] ◇ *adj* **-1.** [gen] pequeno(na) **-2.** [younger] menor; **my ~ brother** meu irmão mais novo **-3.** [short in time or distance] curto(ta) **-4.** [not much] pouco(ca); **she has a ~ money left** ela tem pouco dinheiro sobrando. ◇ *pron* [small amount] pouco(ca); **a ~** um pouco; **a ~ (bit)** um pouquinho. ◇ *adv* **-1.** [to a limited extent] pouco; **he's ~ more than a waiter** ele é pouco mais do que um garçom; **~ by ~** pouco a pouco **-2.** [rarely] raramente; **we go there as ~ as possible** vamos lá o mínimo possível.
little finger *n* dedo *m* mínimo, minguinho *m*.
little-known *adj* pouco conhecido(da).
liturgy ['lɪtədʒɪ] *(pl* **-ies)** *n* [form of worship] liturgia *f*.
live¹ [lɪv] ◇ *vi* **-1.** [gen] viver **-2.** [reside] morar, viver. ◇ *vt* viver; **to ~ it up** *inf* curtir a vida.
◆ **live down** *vt sep* redimir-se de.
◆ **live for** *vt fus* viver para.
◆ **live in** *vi* **-1.** [student] ser interno(na) **-2.** [servant, nanny] dormir na casa.
◆ **live off** *vt fus* **-1.** [savings] viver de **-2.** [parents, family] viver às custas de.
◆ **live on** ◇ *vt fus* **-1.** [money] viver **-2.** [food] viver de. ◇ *vi* [memory, feeling, works] perdurar.
◆ **live out** ◇ *vt fus* acabar; **she won't ~ out the month** ela não chega até o final do mês. ◇ *vi* dormir fora.
◆ **live together** *vi* [cohabit] viver juntos(tas).
◆ **live up to** *vt fus* estar à altura de.
◆ **live with** *vt fus* **-1.** [cohabit with] viver com **-2.** *inf* [accept] conviver com.
live² [laɪv] ◇ *adj* **-1.** [living] vivo(va) **-2.** [burning] aceso(sa) **-3.** [unexploded] carregado(da) **-4.** *ELEC* com eletricidade **-5.** *MUS, RADIO & TV* ao vivo. ◇ *adv* ao vivo.
live-in [lɪv-] *adj* residente.
livelihood ['laɪvlɪhʊd] *n* meio *m* de vida, sustento *m*.
liveliness ['laɪvlɪnɪs] *n* **-1.** [of person] vivacidade *f* **-2.** [of debate] ânimo *m* **-3.** [of mind] sagacidade *f*.
lively ['laɪvlɪ] *(compar* **-ier**, *superl* **-iest)** *adj* **-1.** [gen] animado(da) **-2.** [mind, curiosity, imagination] sagaz, perspicaz **-3.** [colour] vivo(va).
liven ['laɪvn] ◆ **liven up** ◇ *vt sep* animar. ◇ *vi* [person] animar-se.
liver ['lɪvəʳ] *n* fígado *m*.
Liverpudlian [ˌlɪvə'pʌdlɪən] ◇ *adj de ou relativo a Liverpool*. ◇ *n morador ou residente de Liverpool*.
liver sausage *UK*, **liverwurst** *US* ['lɪvəwɜːst] *n (U)* salsicha *f* de fígado.
livery ['lɪvərɪ] *(pl* **-ies)** *n* **-1.** [uniform] libré *f* **-2.** [of a company] marca *f* distintiva.
lives [laɪvz] *pl* ▷ **life**.
livestock ['laɪvstɒk] *n (U)* animais *mpl* de uma fazenda.
live wire [laɪv-] *n* **-1.** [wire] cabo *m* com corrente **-2.** *inf* [person] pessoa *f* dinâmica, empreendedor *m*, -ra *f*.
livid ['lɪvɪd] *adj* **-1.** *inf* [angry] furioso(sa) **-2.** [blue-grey] roxo(xa).
living ['lɪvɪŋ] ◇ *adj* vivo(va); **~ proof** prova *f* viva. ◇ *n* **-1.** [people]: **the ~** os vivos **-2.** [means of earning money]: **what do you do for a ~?** o que você faz para ganhar a vida?; **to scrape a ~** mal ganhar a vida **-3.** *(U)* [lifestyle] (estilo *m* de) vida *f*; **healthy ~** vida *f* saudável.
living conditions *npl* condições *fpl* de vida.
living expenses *npl* despesas *fpl* básicas.
living room *n* sala *f* de estar.
living standards *npl* padrão *m* de vida.
living wage *n* salário *m* básico.
lizard ['lɪzəd] *n* **-1.** [large] lagarto *m* **-2.** [small] lagartixa *f*.
llama ['lɑːməl *(pl inv* OR **-s)** *n* lhama *m*.
LLB *(abbr of* **Bachelor of Laws)** *n (titular de) graduação em direito*.
LLD *(abbr of* **Doctor of Laws)** *n (titular de) doutorado em direito*.
LMT *(abbr of* **Local Mean Time)** *n* horário *m* local.
lo [ləʊ] *excl*: **~ and behold** olha só!
load [ləʊd] ◇ *n* **-1.** [gen] carga *f*; **to take a ~ off one's mind** tirar um peso da consciência **-2.** [burden] fardo *m* **-3.** [large amount]: **~s of, a ~ of** *inf* um monte de; **a ~ of rubbish** *inf* um monte de bobagem. ◇ *vt* **-1.** [container, vehicle, person] carregar; **to ~ sb/sthg with sthg** carregar alguém/algo de algo **-2.** [gun]: **to ~ sthg (with sthg)** carregar algo (com algo) **-3.** [in camera, video recorder]: **to ~ a film** colocar filme *(na câmera)*;

to ~ **a tape** colocar fita *(na filmadora)* **-4.** *COMPUT* [program] carregar.

◆ **load up** ◇ *vt sep* carregar. ◇ *vi* [with furniture, boxes] carregar.

loaded ['ləʊdɪd] *adj* **-1.** [question, statement] com duplo sentido **-2.** [gun, camera] carregado(da) **-3.** *inf* [rich] forrado(da).

loading bay ['ləʊdɪŋ-] *n* zona *f* de carga e descarga.

loaf [ləʊf] (*pl* **loaves**) *n* [of bread] (pedaço *m* de) pão *m*.

◆ **loaf about** *vi* vagabundear.

loafer ['ləʊfəʳ] *n* **-1.** [shoe] mocassim *m* **-2.** [lazy person] vadio *m*, -dia *f*.

loam [ləʊm] *n (U)* marga *f*.

loan [ləʊn] ◇ *n* empréstimo *m*; **on** ~ por empréstimo. ◇ *vt* emprestar; **to** ~ **sthg to sb, to** ~ **sb sthg** emprestar algo a alguém.

loan account *n* conta *f* de empréstimo.

loan capital *n (U)* capital *f* de empréstimo.

loan shark *n inf pej* agiota *mf*.

loath [ləʊθ] *adj*: **to be** ~ **to do sthg** estar pouco inclinado(da) a fazer algo.

loathe [ləʊð] *vt* odiar, detestar; **to** ~ **doing sthg** odiar fazer algo.

loathing ['ləʊðɪŋ] *n (U)* ódio *m*.

loathsome ['ləʊðsəm] *adj* repugnante.

loaves [ləʊvz] *pl* ▷ **loaf**.

lob [lɒb] (*pt* & *pp* **-bed**, *cont* **-bing**) ◇ *n TENNIS* lob *m*. ◇ *vt* **-1.** [throw] lançar **-2.** [*TENNIS* - ball] rebater com um lob; [- opponent] dar um lob em.

lobby ['lɒbɪ] (*pl* **-ies**, *pt* & *pp* **-ied**) ◇ *n* **-1.** [hall] saguão *m* **-2.** [pressure group] lobby *m*, grupo *m* de pressão. ◇ *vt* pressionar.

lobbyist ['lɒbɪɪst] *n* lobista *mf*.

lobe [ləʊb] *n ANAT* lóbulo *m*.

lobelia [lə'bi:ljə] *n* lobélia *f*.

lobotomy [lə'bɒtəmɪ] (*pl* **-ies**) *n* lobotomia *f*.

lobster ['lɒbstəʳ] *n* lagosta *f*.

lobster pot *n* armadilha *f* para pegar lagostas.

local ['ləʊkl] ◇ *adj* local. ◇ *n inf* **-1.** [person]: **the** ~**s** os habitantes do lugar **-2.** *UK* [pub] pub *m* local **-3.** *US* [bus, train] municipal *m*.

local anaesthetic *n* anestesia *f* local.

local area network *n COMPUT* rede *f* local.

local authority *n UK* autoridade *f* local.

local call *n* chamada *f* local.

local colour *n (U)* cor *f* local.

local derby *n UK* clássico *m* local.

locale [ləʊ'kɑ:l] *n fml* local *m*.

local government *n (U)* governo *m* local.

locality [ləʊ'kælətɪ] (*pl* **-ies**) *n* localidade *f*.

localized, -ised ['ləʊkəlaɪzd] *adj* localizado(da).

locally ['ləʊkəlɪ] *adv* [in region] localmente ; [in neighbourhood] na região.

local time *n (U)* hora *f* local.

locate [*UK* ləʊ'keɪt, *US* 'ləʊkeɪt] ◇ *vt* localizar. ◇ *vi US* [settle] localizar-se.

location [ləʊ'keɪʃn] *n* **-1.** [place] localização *f* **-2.** *CINEMA*: **on** ~ em locação.

loc. cit. (*abbr of* **loco citato**) loc. cit.

loch [lɒk] *n Scot* lago *m*.

lock [lɒk] ◇ *n* **-1.** [of door, window, box] fechadura *f*; **under** ~ **and key** fechado(da) a sete chaves **-2.** [on canal] eclusa *f* **-3.** *AUT* [steering lock] ângulo *m* de giro **-4.** [of hair] mecha *f* **-5.** *phr*: ~**, stock and barrel** com tudo. ◇ *vt* **-1.** [fasten securely] fechar com chave **-2.** [keep safely] trancar **-3.** [immobilize] bloquear **-4.** [hold firmly]: **to be** ~**ed in an embrace** estar fortemente abraçado(da); **to be** ~**ed in combat** estar envolvido(da) em disputa. ◇ *vi* **-1.** [fasten securely] fechar com chave, chavear **-2.** [become immobilized] trancar.

◆ **locks** *npl literary* [hair] cachos *mpl*.

◆ **lock away** *vt sep* trancar a sete chaves.

◆ **lock in** *vt sep* encerrar.

◆ **lock out** *vt sep* **-1.** [accidentally] trancar do lado de fora **-2.** [deliberately] deixar na rua.

◆ **lock up** ◇ *vt sep* **-1.** [person] trancafiar **-2.** [house] trancar **-3.** [valuables] fechar com chave **-4.** [with padlock] fechar com cadeado. ◇ *vi* trancar-se.

lockable ['lɒkəbl] *adj* com fechadura.

locker ['lɒkəʳ] *n* [for clothes, luggage, books] compartimento *m* com chave.

locker room *n US* vestiário *m*.

locket ['lɒkɪt] *n* medalhão *m*.

lockjaw *n (U)* tétano *m*.

lockout ['lɒkaʊt] *n* greve *f* patronal, lockout *m*.

locksmith ['lɒksmɪθ] *n* serralheiro *m*, -ra *f*.

lock-up *n* **-1.** [prison] prisão *f*, cárcere *m* **-2.** *UK* [garage] garagem *f*.

loco ['ləʊkəʊ] (*pl* **-s**) *inf* ◇ *adj US* louco(ca). ◇ *n UK* [locomotive] locomotiva *f*.

locomotive ['ləʊkə,məʊtɪv] *n* locomotiva *f*.

locum ['ləʊkəm] (*pl* **-s**) *n* interino *m*, -na *f*.

locust ['ləʊkəst] *n* gafanhoto *m*.

lodge [lɒdʒ] ◇ *n* **-1.** [caretaker's room] portaria *f* **-2.** [of manor house] guarita *f* **-3.** [of Freemasons] loja *f* **-4.** [for hunting] região *f* de caça. ◇ *vt fml* [register] apresentar. ◇ *vi* **-1.** [stay, live]: **to** ~ **with sb** hospedar-se na casa de alguém **-2.** [become stuck] alojar-se **-3.** *fig* [in mind] gravar-se na mente.

lodger ['lɒdʒəʳ] *n* pensionista *mf (em casa de família)*.

lodging ['lɒdʒɪŋ] *n* ▷ **board**.

◆ **lodgings** *npl* alojamentos *mpl*.

loft [lɒft] *n* [attic] sótão *m*; ~ **(apartment)** *apartamento transformado na cobertura de um armazém ou de uma fábrica, em geral amplo e sem divisórias internas.*

lofty ['lɒftɪ] (*compar* **-ier**, *superl* **-iest**) *adj* **-1.** [noble] elevado(da), nobre **-2.** *pej* [haughty] arrogante **-3.** *literary* [high] elevado(da).

log [lɒg] (*pt* & *pp* **-ged**, *cont* **-ging**) ◇ *n* **-1.** [of wood] tronco *m* **-2.** [written record - of ship] diário *m* de bordo; [- of plane] diário *m* de vôo. ◇ *vt* **-1.** [information - on paper] registrar; [- in computer] registrar em log **-2.** [speed, distance, time] anotar.

◆ **log in** *vi COMPUT* entrar (no sistema), efetuar login.

◆ **log out** *vi COMPUT* sair (do sistema), efetuar logout.

loganberry ['ləʊgənbərɪ] (*pl* **-ies**) *n tipo de framboesa de maior tamanho.*

logarithm ['lɒgərɪðm] *n* logaritmo *m*.

logbook ['lɒgbʊk] *n* **-1.** [of ship] diário *m* de bordo **-2.** [of plane] diário *m* de vôo **-3.** [of car] documentação *f*.
log cabin *n* cabana *f*.
log fire *n* fogueira *f*.
loggerheads ['lɒgəhedz] *n*: **at ~ with** em desavença com.
logic ['lɒdʒɪk] *n* lógica *f*.
logical ['lɒdʒɪkl] *adj* lógico(ca).
logically ['lɒdʒɪklɪ] *adv* logicamente.
logistical [lə'dʒɪstɪkl] *adj* logístico(ca).
logistics [lə'dʒɪstɪks] ◇ *n* MIL logística *f*. ◇ *npl fig* [organization] logística *f*.
logjam ['lɒgdʒæm] *n fig* problema *f* crônico.
logo ['ləʊgəʊ] (*pl* **-s**) *n* logotipo *m*.
logrolling ['lɒgrəʊlɪŋ] *n (U) US* troca *f* de favores.
logy *adj US inf* vagaroso(sa).
loin [lɔɪn] *n* lombo *m*.
◆ **loins** *npl* ANAT quadris *mpl*; **to gird one's ~s** *fig* preparar-se para a batalha.
loincloth ['lɔɪnklɒθ] *n* tanga *f*.
loiter ['lɔɪtə^r] *vi* **-1.** [hang about] demorar-se **-2.** [dawdle] vadiar.
loll [lɒl] *vi* **-1.** [sit, lie about] recostar-se, refestelar-se **-2.** [hang down] estar pendente.
lollipop ['lɒlɪpɒp] *n* pirulito *m*.
lollipop lady *n UK* guarda *f* escolar.
lollipop man *n UK* guarda *m* escolar.
lolly ['lɒlɪ] (*pl* **-ies**) *n* **-1.** [lollipop] pirulito *m* **-2.** *UK* [ice cream] picolé *m* **-3.** *(U) UK inf* [money] grana *f*.
London ['lʌndən] *n* Londres; **in ~** em Londres.
Londoner ['lʌndənə^r] *n* londrino *m*, -na *f*.
lone [ləʊn] *adj* solitário(ria).
loneliness ['ləʊnlɪnɪs] *n (U)* solidão *f*.
lonely ['ləʊnlɪ] (*compar* **-ier**, *superl* **-iest**) *adj* **-1.** [gen] solitário(ria), só **-2.** [place] isolado(da).
lone parent *n UK* pai *m* solteiro, mãe *f* solteira.
loner ['ləʊnə^r] *n* solitário *m*, -ria *f*.
lonesome ['ləʊnsəm] *adj US inf* **-1.** [person] solitário(ria), só **-2.** [place] isolado(da).
long [lɒŋ] ◇ *adj* **-1.** [in time] longo(ga); **two days ~** de dois dias de duração; **how ~ will it take?** quanto tempo vai demorar? **-2.** [in space] comprido(da), longo(ga); **10 metres ~** com 10 metros de comprimento; **it's five hundred pages ~** tem quinhentas páginas. ◇ *adv* [for a long time] por muito tempo; **how ~ have you been waiting?** há quanto tempo você está esperando?; **as** OR **so ~ as** desde que; **before ~** agora; **for ~** muito tempo; **no ~er** não mais; **I can't wait any ~er** não posso mais esperar; **so ~!** *inf* até logo! ◇ *n*: **the ~ and the short of it is that ...** em poucas palavras, o que aconteceu é que ... ◇ *vt*: **to ~ to do sthg** ansiar por fazer algo.
◆ **as long as, so long as** *conj* [if] desde que; **as ~ as you're happy about it** desde que você esteja feliz com isso.
◆ **long for** *vt fus* ansiar por.
long. (*abbr of* **longitude**) long.
long-awaited [-ə'weɪtɪd] *adj* tão esperado(da).
long-distance *adj* de longa distância.
long-distance call *n* chamada *f* de longa distância.
long division *n (U)* divisão *f* detalhada.
long-drawn-out *adj* interminável.
long drink *n bebida resultante da mistura de álcool e refresco.*
longevity [lɒn'dʒevətɪ] *n* [of person] longevidade *f*.
long-haired *adj* **-1.** [rabbit, sheep] de pêlo comprido **-2.** [person] de cabelo comprido.
longhand ['lɒŋhænd] *n (U)* escrita *f* à mão.
long-haul *adj* de grande distância.
longing ['lɒŋɪŋ] ◇ *adj* ansioso(sa). ◇ *n* desejo *m*; **~ (for sthg)** ânsia *f* (por algo).
longingly ['lɒŋɪŋlɪ] *adv* ansiosamente.
Long Island *n* Long Island.
longitude ['lɒndʒɪtju:d] *n* GEOGR *(U)* longitude *f*.
long johns *npl* ceroulas *fpl*.
long jump *n* salto *m* em distância.
long-lasting *adj* de longa duração, duradouro(-ra).
long-life *adj* longa-vida.
long-lost *adj* perdido(da) há muito tempo.
long-playing record [-'pleɪɪŋ-] *n* LP *m*.
long-range *adj* **-1.** [missile, bomber] de longo alcance **-2.** [plan, forecast] a longo prazo.
long-running *adj* **-1.** [play] de muita duração **-2.** [dispute] que já dura muito tempo **-3.** [programme] há muito tempo no ar.
longshoreman ['lɒŋʃɔ:mən] (*pl* **-men** [-mən]) *n US* estivador *m*.
long shot *n fig* possibilidade *f* remota.
long-sighted *adj* **-1.** MED presbita **-2.** *fig* [having foresight] previdente.
long-standing *adj* de longa data.
long-suffering *adj* sofrido(da).
long term *n*: **in the ~** a longo prazo.
◆ **long-term** *adj* a longo prazo.
long vacation *n UK* UNIV férias *fpl* de verão.
long wave *n (U)* onda *f* longa.
longways ['lɒŋweɪz] *adv* ao comprido, longitudinalmente.
long-wearing *adj US* resistente, duradouro(ra).
long weekend *n* feriadão *m*.
long-winded *adj* cansativo(va).
loo [lu:] (*pl* **-s**) *n UK inf* toalete *m*.
loofa(h) ['lu:fə] *n* esponja *f* vegetal.
look [lʊk] ◇ *n* **-1.** [with eyes] olhada *f*; **to give sb a ~** dar uma olhada em alguém; **to have a ~ (for sthg)** dar uma olhada (procurando algo); **to take** OR **have a ~ (at sthg)** dar uma olhada (em algo) **-2.** [appearance] aparência *f*; **by the ~ (s) of things** pelo jeito. ◇ *vi* **-1.** [with eyes] olhar; **to ~ at sb/sthg** olhar alguém/algo **-2.** [search] procurar **-3.** [have stated appearance] parecer; **to ~ like** parecer como; **it ~s like rain** parece que vai chover; **to ~ as if** parecer como se; **you ~ as if you haven't slept** parece que você não dormiu. ◇ *vt* **-1.** [look at] olhar **-2.** [appear]: **to ~ one's age** aparentar a idade que se tem; **to ~ one's best** vestir-se elegantemente. ◇ *excl*: **~ (here)!** olha (só)!
◆ **looks** *npl* [attractiveness] aparência *f*, beleza *f*.
◆ **look after** *vt fus* [take care of] cuidar de; **to ~ after o.s.** cuidar-se.

◆ **look at** *vt fus* **-1.** [examine] examinar **-2.** [analise] analisar **-3.** [regard, consider] olhar para.
◆ **look back** *vi* [reminisce] recordar; **she's never ~ed back** ela nunca retrocedeu.
◆ **look down on** *vt fus* [condescend to] desdenhar de, depreciar.
◆ **look for** *vt fus* procurar (por).
◆ **look forward to** *vt fus* aguardar (ansiosamente).
◆ **look into** *vt fus* [examine] analisar, examinar.
◆ **look on** <> *vt fus* = **look upon**. <> *vi* [watch] observar.
◆ **look onto** *vi* [face] ter vista para, dar para.
◆ **look out** *vi* [take care] tomar cuidado; **~ out!** cuidado!
◆ **look out for** *vt fus* [try to spot] estar atento(ta) a.
◆ **look round** <> *vt fus* [visit] visitar. <> *vi* **-1.** [look at surroundings] percorrer com o olhar ao redor **-2.** [turn] virar-se.
◆ **look through** *vt fus* [report, document] examinar o conteúdo de.
◆ **look to** *vt fus* **-1.** [depend on] contar com **-2.** [think about] pensar em.
◆ **look up** <> *vt sep* **-1.** [in book] consultar **-2.** [visit] visitar. <> *vi* [improve] melhorar.
◆ **look upon** *vt fus* [consider]: **I ~ upon him as my father** eu o considerava meu pai.
◆ **look up to** *vt fus* [admire] prezar, respeitar.

look-alike *n* sósia *mf*.

look-in *n UK*: **to get a ~** [chance to participate] ter a possibilidade de participar *OR* fazer parte.

lookout ['lʊkaʊt] *n* **-1.** [place] posto *m* de observação, guarita *f* **-2.** [person] vigia *mf* **-3.** [search]: **to be on the ~ for sthg** estar à espreita de algo.

look-up table *n COMPUT* tabela *f* de consulta.

loom [lu:m] <> *n* tear *m*. <> *vi* **-1.** [rise up] erguer-se **-2.** *fig* [be imminent] aproximar-se, ser iminente; **to ~ large** crescer em tamanho.
◆ **loom up** *vi* despontar sombriamente.

looming ['lu:mɪŋ] *adj* iminente.

loony ['lu:nɪ] (*compar* **-ier**, *superl* **-iest**, *pl* **-ies**) *inf* <> *adj* lunático(ca). <> *n* lunático *m*, -ca *f*.

loop [lu:p] <> *n* **-1.** [shape] laço *m* **-2.** [contraceptive] DIU *m* **-3.** *COMPUT* loop *m*, laço *m*. <> *vt* [rope, string] enlaçar. <> *vi* [road, river] fazer uma curva acentuada.

loophole ['lu:phəʊl] *n* furo *m (na lei)*.

loo roll *n UK inf* rolo *m* de papel higiênico.

loose [lu:s] <> *adj* **-1.** [not firmly fixed] frouxo(xa) **-2.** [unattached, unpackaged - sheets of paper] avulso(sa); [- sweets, nails] solto(ta) **-3.** [not tight-fitting] folgado(da) **-4.** [free, not restrained] solto(ta) **-5.** *pej & dated* [promiscuous] promíscuo(cua) **-6.** [inexact] impreciso(sa) **-7.** [informal] informal **-8.** *US inf* [relaxed]: **to stay ~** ficar relaxado(da). <> *n (U)*: **to be on the ~** andar solto(ta).

loose change *n (U)* trocado *m*.

loose end *n* ponta *f* solta; **yet another ~ we can't explain** outra incógnita que a gente não consegue explicar; **to be at a ~** *UK*, **to be at ~s** *US* estar entediado(da), não ter o que fazer.

loose-fitting *adj* folgado(da).

loose-leaf binder *n* pasta *f* de folhas soltas.

loosely ['lu:slɪ] *adv* **-1.** [not firmly] sem apertar **-2.** [inexactly] imprecisamente.

loosen ['lu:sn] <> *vt* [make less tight] afrouxar. <> *vi* [become less tight] afrouxar.
◆ **loosen up** *vi* **-1.** [before game, race] aquecer-se **-2.** *inf* [relax] relaxar.

loot [lu:t] <> *n (U)* saque *m*. <> *vt* saquear.

looter ['lu:tə^r] *n* saqueador *m*, -ra *f*.

looting ['lu:tɪŋ] *n (U)* saque *m*.

lop [lɒp] (*pt & pp* **-ped**, *cont* **-ping**) *vt* podar.
◆ **lop off** *vt sep* cortar.

lope [ləʊp] *vi* **-1.** [animal] trotar **-2.** [person] andar a passos largos e ligeiros.

lop-sided [-'saɪdɪd] *adj* **-1.** [uneven] assimétrico(ca) **-2.** *fig* [biased] distorcido(da).

lord [lɔ:d] <> *n UK* [man of noble rank] lorde *m*. <> *vt*: **to ~ it over** humilhar.
◆ **Lord** *n* **-1.** *RELIG*: **the Lord** [God] o Senhor; **good Lord!** *UK* Deus meu! **-2.** [in titles] lorde *m* **-3.** [as form of address]: **my Lord** [bishop] Reverendíssimo *m*; [judge] Meritíssimo *m*, -ma *f*.
◆ **Lords** *npl UK POL*: **the (House of) Lords** a Câmara dos Lordes.

Lord Chancellor *n UK POL presidente da Câmara dos Lordes e responsável pela Justiça na Inglaterra e no País de Gales.*

lordly ['lɔ:dlɪ] (*compar* **-ier**, *superl* **-iest**) *adj* **-1.** [noble] nobre **-2.** *pej* [arrogant] arrogante.

Lord Mayor *n UK prefeito da cidade de Londres e outras metrópoles.*

Lordship ['lɔ:dʃɪp] *n*: **your/his ~** Vossa/Sua Senhoria.

Lord's Prayer *n*: **the ~** o Pai Nosso.

lore [lɔ:^r] *n (U)* crença *f* popular.

lorry ['lɒrɪ] (*pl* **-ies**) *n UK* caminhão *m*.

lorry driver *n UK* motorista *mf* de caminhão.

lose [lu:z] (*pt & pp* **lost**) <> *vt* **-1.** [gen] perder; **to ~ sight of sb/sthg** perder alguém/algo de vista; **to ~ one's way** [get lost] perder-se; **to ~ weight** emagrecer, perder peso; **you have nothing to ~** *inf* você não tem nada a perder **-2.** [subj: clock, watch]: **my watch ~s 5 minutes a day** meu relógio atrasa 5 minutos por dia **-3.** [elude, shake off] escapar de. <> *vi* **-1.** [fail to win] perder **-2.** [time] atrasar-se.
◆ **lose out** *vi* sair perdendo; **to ~ out on sthg** sair perdendo em algo.

loser ['lu:zə^r] *n* [gen] perdedor *m*, -ra *f*; **to be a good/bad ~** saber/não saber perder, ser um bom/mau perdedor.

losing ['lu:zɪŋ] *adj* vencido(da).

loss [lɒs] *n* **-1.** [gen] perda *f* **-2.** [failure to win] derrota *f* **-3.** *COMM* [of money] prejuízo *m*; **to make a ~** ter prejuízo; **to cut one's ~es** cortar a fonte de prejuízos **-4.** *phr*: **to be at a ~ to explain sthg** não saber como explicar algo.

loss adjuster [-ə'dʒʌstə^r] *n* perito *m*, -ta *f* na determinação de avarias.

loss leader *n COMM* artigo *m* em liquidação, chamariz *m*.

lost [lɒst] <> *pt & pp* ⊳ **lose**. <> *adj* **-1.** [gen] perdido(da); **to get ~** [lose way] perder-se; **get ~!** *inf* te some! **-2.** [wasted]: **to be ~ on sb** não surtir efeito em alguém.

lost-and-found office *n US* setor *m* de achados e perdidos.
lost cause *n* causa *f* perdida.
lost property *n (U)* achados *mpl* e perdidos.
lost property office *n UK* setor *m* de achados e perdidos.
lot [lɒt] *n* **-1.** [large amount]: **a ~ of, ~s of** muito(ta); **a ~ of people** muita gente, muitas pessoas; **~s of problems** muitos problemas; **he talks a ~** ele fala muito **-2.** *inf* [group of things]: **I bought two ~s of shares last week** comprei dois lotes de ações na semana passada; **put this ~ in my office** *inf* coloca tudo isso no meu escritório **-3.** *inf* [group of people]: **one ~ of refugees arrived yesterday** um grupo de refugiados chegou ontem; **what a mean ~ you are!** *inf* são todos uns mesquinhos! **-4.** [destiny] destino *m*, sorte *f* **-5.** [at auction] lote *m* **-6.** [entire amount]: **the ~** tudo **-7.** *US* [of land] lote *m*; [car park] estacionamento *m* **-8.** *phr*: **to draw ~s** tirar à sorte.
◆ **a lot** *adv* muito; **~ better** muito melhor.
loth [ləʊθ] *adj* = **loath**.
lotion ['ləʊʃn] *n* loção *f*.
lottery ['lɒtərɪ] (*pl* **-ies**) *n* loteria *f*.
LOTTO® ['lɒtəʊ] *n* loteria *f* nacional (britânica), ≃ loto *f*.
lotus position ['ləʊtəs-] *n* posição *f* de lótus.
loud [laʊd] ◇ *adj* **-1.** [person] barulhento(ta) **-2.** [voice, music, TV] alto(ta) **-3.** [bang] forte **-4.** [emphatic]: **to be ~ in sthg** ser enfático(ca) em algo **-5.** [garish] espalhafatoso(sa). ◇ *adv* alto; **~ and clear** alto e claro; **out ~** em voz alta.
loudhailer [,laʊd'heɪlə^r] *n UK* megafone *m*.
loudly ['laʊdlɪ] *adv* **-1.** [shout] alto **-2.** [talk] em voz alta **-3.** [garishly] de forma espalhafatosa.
loudmouth ['laʊdmaʊθ, *pl* -maʊðz] *n inf* tagarela *mf*, gasguita *mf*.
loudness ['laʊdnɪs] *n (U)* intensidade *f* do som.
loudspeaker [,laʊd'spi:kə^r] *n* alto-falante *m*.
lough *n Irish* lago *m*.
Louisiana [lu:,i:zɪ'ænəl] *n* Louisiana; **in ~** em Louisiana.
lounge [laʊndʒ] (*cont* **loungeing**) ◇ *n* **-1.** [in house] sala *f* de estar **-2.** [in airport] sala *f* de espera **-3.** *UK* [bar] = **lounge bar**. ◇ *vi* recostar-se.
◆ **lounge about, lounge around** *vi* vadiar.
lounge bar *n UK* sala *f* mais confortável *(num bar)*.
lounge lizard *n* parasita *mf* social.
lounge suit *n UK* traje *m* social, terno *m*.
louse [laʊs] (*pl sense 1* **lice**, *pl sense 2* **-s**) *n* **-1.** [insect] piolho *m* **-2.** *inf pej* [person] canalha *mf*.
◆ **louse up** *vt sep US vinf* melar.
lousy ['laʊzɪ] (*compar* **-ier**, *superl* **-iest**) *adj inf* **-1.** [poor-quality] péssimo(ma); **his performance was ~** a apresentação dele foi uma porcaria **-2.** [ill]: **to feel ~** sentir-se mal.
lout [laʊt] *n* mal-educado *m*.
louvre *UK*, **louver** *US* ['lu:və^r] *n*: **~ door** porta *f* de veneziana; **~ window** veneziana *f*.
lovable ['lʌvəbl] *adj* amável, encantador(ra).
love [lʌv] ◇ *n* **-1.** *(U)* [affection for person] amor *m*; **give her my ~** dá um abraço nela por mim; **a ~-hate relationship** uma relação de amor e ódio; **~ from** [at end of letter] um abraço, um beijo; **to be in ~** estar apaixonado(da); **to fall in ~** apaixonar-se; **to make ~** fazer amor **-2.** [liking for sthg, for activity] paixão *f*; **to have a ~ of** *OR* **for sthg** ter paixão por algo **-3.** [beloved person, thing] amor *m* **-4.** *inf* [term of address] amor *m* **-5.** *(U) TENNIS*: **30 ~** 30 a zero. ◇ *vt* **-1.** [gen] amar **-2.** [like] adorar; **to ~ to do sthg** *OR* **doing sthg** adorar fazer algo.
love affair *n* caso *m* (de amor).
lovebite ['lʌvbaɪt] *n* chupão *m*.
loveless ['lʌvlɪs] *adj* [marriage] sem amor.
love letter *n* carta *f* de amor.
love life *n* vida *f* amorosa.
lovely ['lʌvlɪ] (*compar* **-ier**, *superl* **-iest**) *adj* **-1.** [person, child - in looks] encantador(ra); [- in character] amável **-2.** [view, day, weather] adorável; [dress, surprise, holiday] maravilhoso(sa), adorável.
love-making *n (U)* relação *f* sexual.
lover ['lʌvə^r] *n* **-1.** [sexual partner] amante *mf* **-2.** [enthusiast] amante *mf*, apaixonado *m*, -da *f*.
lovesick ['lʌvsɪk] *adj* doente de amor *(não-correspondido)*.
love song *n* canção *f* de amor.
love story *n* história *f* de amor.
loving ['lʌvɪŋ] *adj* carinhoso(sa), afetuoso(sa).
lovingly ['lʌvɪŋlɪ] *adv* carinhosamente, afetuosamente.
low [ləʊ] ◇ *adj* **-1.** [gen] baixo(xa); **we are ~ on milk** estamos com pouco leite **-2.** [poor - intelligence] pouco(ca); [- opinion] pobre; [- standard, quality, esteem] baixo(xa); [- health] debilitado(da) **-3.** [not loud or high] baixo(xa) **-4.** [light] fraco(ca) **-5.** [neckline] decotado(da) **-6.** [depressed] deprimido(da) **-7.** [vulgar] baixo(xa). ◇ *adv* **-1.** [gen] baixo **-2.** [situated, built] embaixo. ◇ *n* **-1.** [low point] baixa *f* **-2.** *METEOR* área *f* de baixa pressão.
low-alcohol *adj* de baixo teor alcoólico.
lowbrow ['ləʊbraʊ] *adj* de baixo nível intelectual.
low-calorie *adj* de baixa caloria.
Low Church *n corrente evangélica da Igreja Anglicana*.
Low Countries *npl*: **the ~** os Países Baixos.
low-cut *adj* decotado(da).
low-down *adj inf*: **~ trick** truque *m* baixo.
◆ **lowdown** *n inf*: **to give sb the lowdown (on sthg)** dar os detalhes concretos (sobre algo) a alguém.
lower¹ ['laʊə^r] ◇ *adj* inferior. ◇ *vt* **-1.** [gen] baixar **-2.** [reduce] reduzir.
lower² ['laʊə^r] *vi* **-1.** [be dark] estar escuro(ra) **-2.** [frown]: **to ~ at sb** fechar a cara para alguém.
Lower Chamber [,ləʊə^r-] *n POL* ≃ Câmara *f* Baixa.
lower class [,ləʊə^r-] *n*: **the ~(es)** as classes baixas.
Lower House [,ləʊə^r-] *n POL* Câmara *f* Baixa.
lowest common denominator ['ləʊɪst-] *n*: **the ~** o menor denominador comum.
low-fat *adj* com baixo teor de gordura.
low-flying *adj* de vôo rasante.
low frequency *n* baixa freqüência *f*.
low gear *n US* primeira *f (marcha)*.

low-key *adj* discreto(ta).
Lowlands ['ləʊləndz] *npl*: **the ~** [of Scotland] as Terras Baixas *(da Escócia)*.
low-level language *n COMPUT* linguagem *f* de baixo nível.
low-loader *n* veículo *m* com baixa plataforma de carga.
lowly ['ləʊlɪ] (*compar* **-ier**, *superl* **-iest**) *adj* humilde.
low-lying *adj* [land] baixo(xa).
Low Mass *n* missa *f* baixa.
low-necked [-'nekt] *adj* decotado(da).
low-paid *adj* mal pago(ga).
low-rise *adj* baixo(xa).
low season *n* baixa estação *f*.
low tide *n* maré *f* baixa.
loyal ['lɔɪəl] *adj* leal, fiel.
loyalist ['lɔɪəlɪst] *n* leal *mf (ao governo)*.
◆ **Loyalist** *n POL* [in Northern Ireland] *protestante que acredita que a Irlanda do Norte deva continuar fazendo parte do Reino Unido*.
loyalty ['lɔɪəltɪ] (*pl* **-ies**) *n* lealdade *f*, fidelidade *f*.
loyalty card *n* cartão *f* de fidelização.
lozenge ['lɒzɪndʒ] *n* **-1.** [tablet] pastilha *f* **-2.** [shape] losango *m*.
LP (*abbr of* **long-playing record**) *n* LP *m*.
L-plate *n UK* ≃ auto-escola *f (indicação no veículo), placa que contém a letra L em vermelho fixada no veículo conduzido por pessoa que está aprendendo a dirigir*.
LPN (*abbr of* **licensed practical nurse**) *n técnico em enfermagem nos Estados Unidos*.
LPO (*abbr of* **London Philharmonic Orchestra**) *n* Orquestra *f* Filarmônica de Londres.
LRAM (*abbr of* **Licentiate of the Royal Academy of Music**) *n membro da academia britânica de música*.
LRB (*abbr of* **London Review of Books**) *n jornal britânico de resenhas literárias e humanidades*.
LSAT (*abbr of* **Law School AdmissionsTest**) *n exame de acesso às escolas de direito nos Estados Unidos*.
LSD *n* (*abbr of* **lysergic acid diethylamide**) LSD *m*.
LSE (*abbr of* **London School of Economics**) *n escola londrina de ciências políticas e econômicas*.
LSO (*abbr of* **London Symphony Orchestra**) *n* Orquestra *f* Sinfônica de Londres.
Lt. (*abbr of* **lieutenant**) Ten.
LT (*abbr of* **low tension**) *n ELEC* baixa tensão *f*.
Ltd, ltd (*abbr of* **limited**) Ltda.
lubricant ['lu:brɪkənt] *n* lubrificante *m*.
lubricate ['lu:brɪkeɪt] *vt* lubrificar.
lubrication [ˌlu:brɪ'keɪʃn] *n (U)* lubrificação *f*.
lucid ['lu:sɪd] *adj* **-1.** [easily understood] nítido(da) **-2.** [clear-headed] lúcido(da).
lucidly ['lu:sɪdlɪ] *adv* claramente, lucidamente.
luck [lʌk] *n (U)* sorte *f*; **good ~!** boa sorte!; **bad ~** [misfortune] azar *m*; **bad ~!** [said to commiserate] que azar!; **hard ~!** azar!; **to be in ~** estar com sorte; **to try one's ~ at sthg** tentar a sorte em algo; **with (any) ~** com (um pouco de) sorte.
◆ **luck out** *vi US inf* ter sorte.
luckily ['lʌkɪlɪ] *adv* afortunadamente.
luckless ['lʌklɪs] *adj* desafortunado(da).
lucky ['lʌkɪ] (*compar* **-ier**, *superl* **-iest**) *adj* **-1.** [fortunate - person] sortudo(da), com sorte; [- event] feliz **-2.** [bringing good luck] da sorte.
lucky charm *n* amuleto *m*.
lucky dip *n UK* saco *m* de surpresas.
lucrative ['lu:krətɪv] *adj* lucrativo(va).
ludicrous ['lu:dɪkrəs] *adj* **-1.** [appearance, situation] ridículo(la) **-2.** [decision, suggestion] absurdo(da).
ludo ['lu:dəʊ] *n (U) UK* ludo *m*.
lug [lʌg] (*pt* & *pp* **-ged**, *cont* **-ging**) *vt inf* arrastar, tirar com dificuldade.
luggage ['lʌgɪdʒ] *n (U) UK* bagagem *f*.
luggage rack *n UK* porta-bagagem *m*.
luggage van *n UK RAIL* vagão *m* de bagagem.
lugubrious [lu:'gu:brɪəs] *adj fml* lúgubre.
lukewarm ['lu:kwɔ:m] *adj* **-1.** [tepid] morno(na) **-2.** [unenthusiastic] desanimado(da), indiferente.
lull [lʌl] ◇ *n* **-1.** [in activity] pausa *f*; **the ~ before the storm** *fig* a bonança antes da tempestade **-2.** [in fighting] trégua *f*. ◇ *vt* **-1.** [make sleepy]: **to ~ sb to sleep** ninar alguém para dormir **-2.** [reassure]: **to ~ sb into a false sense of security** passar a alguém uma falsa sensação de segurança.
lullaby ['lʌləbaɪ] (*pl* **-ies**) *n* cantiga *f* de ninar.
lumbago [lʌm'beɪgəʊ] *n (U)* lumbago *m*.
lumber ['lʌmbəʳ] ◇ *n* **-1.** *US* [timber] madeira *f* serrada, tábua *f* **-2.** *UK* [bric-a-brac] trastes *mpl*. ◇ *vi* [large person, animal, vehicle] andar a custo.
◆ **lumber with** *vt sep UK inf* [encumber] encarregar.
lumbering ['lʌmbərɪŋ] *adj* desengoçado(da).
lumberjack ['lʌmbədʒæk] *n* lenhador *m*, -ra *f*.
lumbermill ['lʌmbəˌmɪl] *n US* serraria *f*.
lumber-room *n UK* quarto *f* para guardar tralhas.
lumberyard ['lʌmbəja:d] *n* madeireira *f*.
luminous ['lu:mɪnəs] *adj* luminoso(sa).
lump [lʌmp] ◇ *n* **-1.** [piece - of coal] pedaço *m*; [- earth, sugar] torrão *m*; [- in sauce, soup] caroço *m* **-2.** *MED* [on body] tumor *m*. ◇ *vt*: **to ~ sthg together** agrupar algo; **you'll just have to ~ it** *inf*! você vai ter de engolir isso!
lumpectomy [ˌlʌm'pektəmɪ] (*pl* **-ies**) *n cirurgia para remoção de tumor do seio*.
lump sum *n* soma *f* global.
lumpy ['lʌmpɪ] (*compar* **-ier**, *superl* **-iest**) *adj* encaroçado(da).
lunacy ['lu:nəsɪ] *n (U)* loucura *f*.
lunar ['lu:nəʳ] *adj* lunar.
lunatic ['lu:nətɪk] ◇ *adj pej* lunático(ca). ◇ *n* **-1.** *pej* [fool] idiota *mf* **-2.** [insane person] lunático *m*, -ca *f*.
lunatic asylum *n* hospício *m*, manicômio *m*.
lunatic fringe *n* minoria *f* extremista.
lunch [lʌntʃ] ◇ *n* almoço *m*; **to have ~** almoçar. ◇ *vi* almoçar.
luncheon ['lʌntʃən] *n fml* almoço *m*.
luncheonette *n US* lanchonete *f*.
luncheon meat *n (U)* fiambre *m*.
luncheon voucher *n UK* tíquete-refeição *m*.
lunch hour *n* hora *f* do almoço.
lunchtime ['lʌntʃtaɪm] *n* hora *f* do almoço.
lung [lʌŋ] *n* pulmão *m*.

lung cancer *n (U)* câncer *m* de pulmão.
lunge [lʌndʒ] *vi* arremessar-se; **to ~ at sb** investir contra alguém.
lupin *UK* ['lu:pɪn], **lupine** *US* ['lu:paɪn] *n* tremoço *m*.
lurch [lɜ:tʃ] <> *n* [movement] cambaleio *m*, solavanco *m*; **to leave sb in the ~** deixar alguém na mão. <> *vi* [in movement] cambalear, balançar.
lure [ljʊə^r] <> *n* [attraction] fascínio *m*. <> *vt* [tempt] fascinar.
lurid ['ljʊərɪd] *adj* **-1.** [brightly coloured] sensacional **-2.** [shockingly unpleasant] chocante.
lurk [lɜ:k] *vi* espreitar.
lurking ['lɜ:kɪŋ] *adj* que segue rondando.
Lusaka [lu:'sɑ:kə] *n* Lusaka; **in ~** em Lusaka.
luscious ['lʌʃəs] *adj* **-1.** [fruit] suculento(ta) **-2.** [colour] vistoso(sa).
lush [lʌʃ] <> *adj* **-1.** [healthy, thick] viçoso(sa) **-2.** *inf* [sumptuous] luxuoso(sa). <> *n* ***US inf*** [drunkard] bêbado *m*, -da *f*.
lust [lʌst] *n* **-1.** *(U)* [sexual desire] luxúria *f* **-2.** [greed]: **~ for sthg** cobiça *f* por algo.
◆ **lust after, lust for** *vt fus* **-1.** [money, power] cobiçar **-2.** [person] desejar.
luster *n US* = **lustre**.
lustful ['lʌstfʊl] *adj* luxurioso(sa).
lustre *UK*, **luster** *US* ['lʌstə^r] *n* [brightness] brilho *m*.
lusty ['lʌstɪ] (*compar* **-ier**, *superl* **-iest**) *adj* vigoroso(sa), forte.
lute [lu:t] *n* alaúde *m*.
luv [lʌv] *n UK inf* amor *m*.
Luxembourg ['lʌksəm,bɜ:g] *n* Luxemburgo; **in ~** em Luxemburgo.
luxuriant [lʌg'ʒʊərɪənt] *adj* viçoso(sa), exuberante.
luxuriate [lʌg'ʒʊərɪeɪt] *vi* deleitar-se; **to ~ in sthg** deleitar-se com algo.
luxurious [lʌg'ʒʊərɪəs] *adj* **-1.** [expensive] luxuoso(-sa) **-2.** [voluptuous] esplêndido(da).
luxury ['lʌkʃərɪ] (*pl* **-ies**) <> *n* luxo *m*. <> *comp* de luxo.
luxury goods *npl* artigos *mpl* de luxo.
LV (*abbr of* **luncheon voucher**) *n* vale-refeição *m*.
LW (*abbr of* **long wave**) *n* onda *f* longa.
lychee [,laɪ'tʃi:] *n* lichia *f*.
Lycra® ['laɪkrə] <> *n (U)* lycra® *f*. <> *comp* de lycra.
lying ['laɪɪŋ] <> *adj* [dishonest] mentiroso(sa), falso(sa). <> *n* [dishonesty] mentiras *fpl*.
lymph gland [lɪmf-] *n* glândula *f* linfática.
lynch [lɪntʃ] *vt* linchar.
lynx [lɪnks] (*pl inv* OR **-es**) *n* lince *m*.
lyre ['laɪə^r] *n* lira *f*.
lyric ['lɪrɪk] *adj* lírico(ca).
◆ **lyrics** *npl* letra *f (de música)*.
lyrical ['lɪrɪkl] *adj* **-1.** [poetic] lírico(ca) **-2.** [enthusiastic] entusiasmado(da).

m¹ (*pl* **m's** OR **ms**), **M** (*pl* **M's** OR **Ms**) [em] *n* [letter] m, M *m*.
◆ **M -1.** *UK* (*abbr of* **motorway**) rodovia *f* **-2.** (*abbr of* **medium**) M.
m² -1. (*abbr of* **metre**) m **-2.** (*abbr of* **million**) milhão *m*. **-3.** *abbr of* **mile**.
ma [mɑ:] *n inf* mamã *f*.
MA <> *n* (*abbr of* **Master of Arts**) *(titular de) diploma de mestre em ciências humanas*. <> *abbr of* **Massachusetts**.
ma'am [mæm] *n* madame *f*.
mac [mæk] (*abbr of* **mackintosh**) *n UK inf* [coat] capa *f* de chuva.
macabre [mə'kɑ:brə] *adj* macabro(bra).
Macao [mə'kaʊ] *n* Macau; **in ~** em Macau.
macaroni [,mækə'rəʊnɪ] *n (U)* macarrão *m*.
macaroni cheese *n (U)* macarrão *m* com molho de queijo.
macaroon [,mækə'ru:n] *n biscoito doce preparado com amêndoas e coco*.
mace [meɪs] *n* **-1.** [ornamental rod] maça *f* **-2.** *(U)* [spice] macis *m inv*.
Macedonia [,mæsɪ'dəʊnɪə] *n* Macedônia; **in ~** na Macedônia.
Macedonian [,mæsɪ'dəʊnɪən] <> *adj* macedônico(ca). <> *n* macedônico *m*, -ca *f*.
machete [mə'ʃetɪ] *n* machete *m*.
Machiavellian [,mækɪə'velɪən] *adj* maquiavélico(-ca).
machinations [,mækɪ'neɪʃnz] *npl* maquinações *fpl*.
machine [mə'ʃi:n] <> *n* máquina *f*. <> *vt* **-1.** SEWING costurar à maquina **-2.** TECH usinar.
machine code *n* COMPUT código *m* de máquina.
machinegun [mə'ʃi:ngʌn] (*pt* & *pp* **-ned**, *cont* **-ning**) <> *n* metralhadora *f*. <> *vt* metralhar.
machine language *n* COMPUT linguagem *f* de máquina.
machine-readable *adj* COMPUT legível por máquina.
machinery [mə'ʃi:nərɪ] *n (U)* **-1.** [machines] maquinário *m* **-2.** *fig* [system] mecanismo *m*.
machine shop *n* oficina *f* de máquinas.
machine tool *n* máquina *f* operatriz.
machine-washable *adj* lavável à máquina.

machinist [mə'ʃi:nɪst] *n* operador *m*, -ra *f* de máquina.
machismo [mə'tʃɪzməʊ] *n (U)* machismo *m*.
macho ['mætʃəʊ] *adj inf* machista.
mackerel ['mækrəl] (*pl inv* OR **-s**) *n* cavala *f*.
mackintosh ['mækɪntɒʃ] *n UK* capa *f* de chuva.
macramé [mə'krɑ:mɪ] *n (U)* macramé *m*.
macro ['mækrəʊ] *n* COMPUT macro *f*.
macrobiotic [ˌmækrəʊbaɪ'ɒtɪk] *adj* macrobiótico(-ca).
macrocosm ['mækrəʊkɒzm] *n* macrocosmo *m*.
macroeconomics ['mækrəʊˌi:kə'nɒmɪks] *n (U)* macroeconomia *f*.
mad [mæd] (*compar* **-der**, *superl* **-dest**) *adj* **-1.** [insane] louco(ca); **to go ~** enlouquecer **-2.** *pej* [foolish] maluco(ca) **-3.** [furious] doido(da); **to go ~ at sb** ficar louco(ca) com alguém **-4.** [hectic] exasperado(da); **like ~** feito louco(ca) **-5.** [very enthusiastic]: **to be ~ about sb/sthg** ser louco(ca) por alguém/algo.
Madagascan [ˌmædə'gæskən] <> *adj* malgaxe. <> *n* **-1.** [person] malgaxe *mf* **-2.** [language] malgaxe *m*.
Madagascar [ˌmædə'gæskə^r] *n* Madagascar; **in ~** em Madagascar.
madam ['mædəm] *n fml* [form of address] senhora *f*.
madcap ['mædkæp] *adj* doido(da).
madden ['mædn] *vt* enfurecer, exasperar.
maddening ['mædnɪŋ] *adj* enlouquecedor(ra).
made [meɪd] *pt & pp* ▷ **make**.
-made [məɪd] *suffix*: **French ~** feito(ta) na França.
Madeira [mə'dɪərəl] *n* **-1.** *(U)* [wine] madeira *m* **-2.** GEOGR Ilha *f* da Madeira; **in ~** na Ilha da Madeira.
made-to-measure *adj* feito(ta) sob medida.
made-up *adj* **-1.** [with make-up] maquiado(da) **-2.** [prepared] já preparado(da) **-3.** [invented] falso(sa), esfarrapado(da).
madhouse ['mædhaʊs, *pl* -haʊzɪz] *n fig inf* hospício *m*.
madly ['mædlɪ] *adv* [frantically] alucinadamente; **~ in love** loucamente apaixonado(da).
madman ['mædmən] (*pl* **-men** [-mən]) *n* louco *m*.
madness ['mædnɪs] *n (U)* loucura *f*.
Madonna [mə'dɒnə] *n* **-1.** RELIG: **the ~** a Nossa Senhora **-2.** ART madona *f*.
Madrid [mə'drɪd] *n* Madrid; **in ~** em Madrid.
madrigal ['mædrɪgl] *n* madrigal *m*.
madwoman ['mædˌwʊmən] (*pl* **-women** [-ˌwɪmɪn]) *n* louca *f*.
maestro ['maɪstrəʊ] (*pl* **-tros** OR **-tri** [-trɪ]) *n* maestro *m*.
MAFF (*abbr of* **Ministry of Agriculture, Fisheries, and Food**) *n ministério britânico da agricultura, da pesca e dos alimentos*, ≃ Ministério *m* da Agricultura.
Mafia ['mæfɪə] *n*: **the ~** a Máfia.
mag [mæg] (*abbr of* **magazine**) *n inf* revista *f*.
magazine [ˌmægə'zi:n] *n* **-1.** [periodical] revista *f* **-2.** [news programme] programa *m* de variedades **-3.** [on a gun] câmara *f*.
magenta [mə'dʒentə] <> *adj* magenta. <> *n (U)* magenta *m*.
maggot ['mægət] *n* larva *f*.
Maghreb ['mʌgreb] *n*: **the ~** o Magrebe.
magic ['mædʒɪk] <> *adj* **-1.** [gen] mágico(ca) **-2.** [referring to conjuring] de mágica. <> *n (U)* **-1.** [gen] magia *f* **-2.** [conjuring] mágica *f*.
magical ['mædʒɪkl] *adj* [using sorcery] mágico(ca).
magic carpet *n* tapete *m* mágico.
magic eye *n UK* olho *m* mágico.
magician [mə'dʒɪʃn] *n* **-1.** [conjurer] mágico *m*, -ca *f* **-2.** [wizard] mago *m*, -ga *f*.
magic wand *n* varinha *f* mágica.
magisterial [ˌmædʒɪ'stɪərɪəl] *adj* **-1.** *fml* [authoritative] dominador(ra) **-2.** JUR magistral.
magistrate ['mædʒɪstreɪt] *n* magistrado *m*, -da *f*.
magistrates' court *n UK* tribunal *m*.
Magna Carta [ˌmægnə'kɑ:tə] *n*: **the ~** a Carta Magna.
magnanimous [mæg'nænɪməs] *adj* magnânimo(-ma).
magnate ['mægneɪt] *n* magnata *mf*.
magnesium [mæg'ni:zɪəm] *n (U)* magnésio *m*.
magnet ['mægnɪt] *n* **-1.** PHYSICS ímã *m* **-2.** *fig* [attraction] atrativo *m*.
magnetic [mæg'netɪk] *adj* **-1.** PHYSICS magnético(ca) **-2.** *fig* [personality] atraente, carismático(ca).
magnetic disk *n* disco *m* magnético.
magnetic field *n* campo *m* magnético.
magnetic tape *n (U)* fita *f* magnética.
magnetism ['mægnɪtɪzm] *n (U)* magnetismo *m*.
magnification [ˌmægnɪfɪ'keɪʃn] *n (U)* **-1.** [process] ampliação *f* **-2.** [degree of enlargement] aumento *m*.
magnificence [mæg'nɪfɪsəns] *n (U)* magnificência *f*.
magnificent [mæg'nɪfɪsənt] *adj* **-1.** [clothes, splendour, building] grandioso(sa) **-2.** [idea, book, game] magnífico(ca), brilhante.
magnify ['mægnɪfaɪ] (*pt & pp* **-ied**) *vt* **-1.** [TECH - image] ampliar; [- sound] amplificar **-2.** *fig* [exaggerate] exagerar.
magnifying glass ['mægnɪfaɪɪŋ-] *n* lupa *f*, lente *f* de aumento.
magnitude ['mægnɪtju:d] *n* magnitude *f*.
magnolia [mæg'nəʊljə] *n* **-1.** [tree, flower] magnólia *f* **-2.** [colour] creme *m*.
magnum ['mægnəm] (*pl* **-s**) *n garrafa de 1,5 litro de capacidade*.
magpie ['mægpaɪ] *n* pega *f (ave)*.
maharaja(h) [ˌmɑ:hə'rɑ:dʒə] *n* marajá *m*.
mahogany [mə'hɒgənɪ] *n* mogno *m*.
maid [meɪd] *n* [servant] empregada *f* doméstica.
maiden ['meɪdn] <> *adj* [voyage, speech] de estréia, inaugural. <> *n literary* [young girl] donzela *f*; [virgin] virgem *f*.
maiden aunt *n* tia *f* solteirona.
maiden name *n* nome *m* de solteira.
maiden speech *n* POL discurso *m* inaugural.
mail [meɪl] <> *n* **-1.** [letters, parcels] correio *m*; **by ~** pelo correio **-2.** [system] correios *mpl*. <> *vt* **-1.** [send] mandar pelo correio **-2.** [put in mail box] postar.
mailbag ['meɪlbæg] *n* sacola *f* do carteiro.
mailbox ['meɪlbɒks] *n* **-1.** *US* [for letters] caixa *f* de correio **-2.** COMPUT caixa *f* de entrada.
mailing list ['meɪlɪŋ-] *n* lista *f* de endereços.

mailman ['meɪlmən] (*pl* **-men** [-mən]) *n US* carteiro *m*.
mail order *n (U)* pedido *m* por reembolso postal.
mailshot ['meɪlʃɒt] *n* mala-direta *f*.
mail train *n* trem-correio *m*, trem *m* postal.
mail truck *n US* caminhão *m* dos correios.
mail van *n* [for delivering mail - by road] carro-correio *m*; [- by rail] vagão-correio *m*.
maim [meɪm] *vt* mutilar.
main [meɪn] <> *adj* principal. <> *n* [pipe] tubulação *f*.
◆ **mains** *npl*: **the ~s** [gas, water] as tubulações; [electric] a rede elétrica.
◆ **in the main** *adv* em geral.
main course *n* prato *m* principal.
Maine [meɪn] *n* Maine; **in ~** em Maine.
mainframe (computer) ['meɪnfreɪm-] *n* computador *m* mainframe.
mainland ['meɪnlənd] <> *adj* continental. <> *n*: **the ~** o continente.
main line *n RAIL* linha-tronco *f*.
◆ **mainline** <> *adj* [train, station] de linha-tronco. <> *vt & vi* **drugs sl** injetar-se na veia.
mainly ['meɪnlɪ] *adv* principalmente.
main road *n* rodovia *f* principal.
mainsail ['meɪnseɪl] *n* vela-mestra *f*.
mainstay ['meɪnsteɪ] *n* meio *m* de subsistência.
mainstream ['meɪnstri:m] <> *adj* predominante. <> *n*: **the ~** a tendência geral.
maintain [meɪn'teɪn] *vt* **-1.** [gen] manter **-2.** [support, provide for] sustentar, manter **-3.** [look after] manter em bom estado **-4.** [assert]: **to ~ (that)** sustentar que.
maintenance ['meɪntənəns] *n (U)* **-1.** [gen] manutenção *f* **-2.** [money] pensão *f*.
maintenance order *n UK JUR* obrigação *f* de pensão alimentícia.
maisonette [ˌmeɪzə'net] *n* duplex *m inv*.
maize [meɪz] *n (U)* milho *m*.
Maj. (*abbr of* **Major**) Maj.
majestic [mə'dʒestɪk] *adj* majestoso(sa).
majestically [mə'dʒestɪklɪ] *adv* majestosamente.
majesty ['mædʒəstɪ] (*pl* **-ies**) *n* [grandeur] majestade *f*.
◆ **Majesty** *n*: **His** *OR* **Her/Your Majesty** Sua/Vossa Majestade.
major ['meɪdʒə^r] <> *adj* **-1.** [gen] principal **-2.** *MUS* maior. <> *n* [*MIL* - in army] major *m*; [- in air force] major-aviador *m*. <> *vi US UNIV*: **to ~ in sthg** especializar-se em algo.
Majorca [mə'jɔ:kə, mə'dʒɔ:kə] *n* Maiorca; **in ~** em Maiorca.
Majorcan [mə'jɔ:kən, mə'dʒɔ:kən] <> *adj* maiorquino(na). <> *n* maiorquino *m*, -na *f*.
majorette [ˌmeɪdʒə'ret] *n* baliza *f*.
major general *n* general-de-divisão *m*.
majority [mə'dʒɒrətɪ] (*pl* **-ies**) *n* maioria *f*; **in a** *OR* **the ~** na maioria; **age of ~** maioridade *f*.
majority shareholder *n* acionista *mf* majoritário, -ria.
major road *n* estrada *f* principal.
make [meɪk] (*pt & pp* **made**) *vt* **-1.** [produce, manufacture] fazer; **to be made of** ser feito de; **to ~ lunch/dinner** fazer o almoço/jantar; **made in Japan** fabricado no Japão. **-2.** [perform, do] fazer; **to ~ a mistake** cometer um erro, enganar-se; **to ~ a phone call** dar um telefonema. **-3.** [cause to be] tornar; **to ~ sthg better** melhorar algo; **to ~ sb happy** fazer alguém feliz; **to ~ sthg safer** tornar algo mais seguro. **-4.** [cause to do, force] fazer; **to ~ sb do sthg** obrigar alguém a fazer algo; **it made her laugh** isso a fez rir. **-5.** [amount to, total] ser; **that ~s $5** são 5 dólares. **-6.** [calculate]: **I ~ it seven o'clock** calculo que sejam sete horas; **I ~ it $4** segundo os meus cálculos são 4 dólares. **-7.** [profit, loss] ter. **-8.** *inf* [arrive in time for]: **we didn't ~ the 10 o'clock train** não conseguimos apanhar o trem das 10. **-9.** [friend, enemy] fazer. **-10.** [have qualities for] dar; **this would ~ a lovely bedroom** isto dava um lindo quarto. **-11.** [bed] fazer. **-12.** [in phrases]: **to ~ do** contentar-se; [damage] reparar; **to ~ it** [arrive on time] conseguir chegar a tempo; [be able to go] poder ir; [survive a crisis] recuperar-se. <> *n* [of product] marca *f*.
◆ **make out** *vt sep* [check, receipt] passar; [form] preencher; [see] distinguir; [hear] perceber, entender.
◆ **make up** *vt sep* [invent] inventar; [comprise] constituir; [difference, extra] cobrir.
◆ **make up for** *vt fus* compensar.
make-believe *n (U)* faz-de-conta *m*.
makeover ['meɪkəʊvə^r] *n* **-1.** [for person] tratamento *m* **-2.** [for company] aperfeiçoamento *m*.
maker ['meɪkə^r] *n* **-1.** [of film] produtor *m*, -ra *f* **-2.** [of product] fabricante *mf*.
makeshift ['meɪkʃɪft] *adj* **-1.** [temporary] provisório(ria) **-2.** [improvised] improvisado(da).
make-up *n (U)* **-1.** [cosmetics] maquiagem *f*; **~ bag** nécessaire *m*; **~ remover** removedor *m* de maquiagem **-2.** [person's character] caráter *m* **-3.** [composition] composição *f*.
makeweight *n* contrapeso *m*.
making ['meɪkɪŋ] *n* [of cake] fabricação *f*; [of film] produção *f*; **in the ~** em desenvolvimento; **this is history in the ~** isto passará para a história; **your problems are of your own ~** teus problemas são todos coisas da tua cabeça; **to be the ~ of sb/sthg** ser a causa do êxito de alguém/algo; **you have the ~s of a diplomat** você tem tudo para ser um diplomata.
maladjusted [ˌmælə'dʒʌstɪd] *adj* desajustado(da).
malaise [mə'leɪz] *n (U) fml* [unease] mal-estar *m*.
malaria [mə'leərɪə] *n (U)* malária *f*.
Malawi [mə'lɑ:wɪ] Maláui; **in ~** no Maláui.
Malawian [mə'lɑ:wɪən] <> *adj* malauiano(na). <> *n* malauiano *m*, -na *f*.
Malay [mə'leɪ] <> *adj* malaio(ia). <> *n* **-1.** [person] malaio *m*, -ia *f* **-2.** [language] malaio *m*.
Malaya [mə'leɪə] *n* Malásia; **in ~** na Malásia.
Malayan [mə'leɪən] <> *adj* malaio(ia). <> *n* malaio *m*, -ia *f*.
Malaysia [mə'leɪzɪə] *n* Malásia; **in ~** na Malásia.
Malaysian [mə'leɪzɪən] <> *adj* malaio(ia). <> *n* malaio *m*, -ia *f*.
malcontent *n fml* descontente *mf*.
Maldives ['mɔ:ldi:vz] *npl*: **the ~** as Maldivas; **in the ~** nas Maldivas.

male [meɪl] ◇ *adj* **-1.** [animal] macho; ~ **kangaroo** canguru *m* macho **-2.** [human] masculino(na) **-3.** [concerning men] do homem, masculino(na). ◇ *n* **-1.** [animal] macho *m* **-2.** [human] homem *m*.

male chauvinist (pig) *n pej* porco *m* chauvinista.

male nurse *n* enfermeiro *m*.

malevolent [mə'levələnt] *adj* malévolo(la).

malformed [mæl'fɔ:md] *adj* malformado(da).

malfunction [mæl'fʌŋkʃn] ◇ *n* mau funcionamento *m*. ◇ *vi* funcionar mal.

Mali ['mɑ:lɪ] *n* Mali; **in** ~ em Mali.

malice ['mælɪs] *n (U)* malícia *f*.

malicious [mə'lɪʃəs] *adj* malicioso(sa).

malign [mə'laɪn] ◇ *adj* maligno(na). ◇ *vt* difamar, falar mal de.

malignant [mə'lɪgnənt] *adj* **-1.** [full of hate] malvado(da) **-2.** *MED* maligno(na).

malinger [mə'lɪŋgə^r] *vi pej* fazer-se de doente.

malingerer [mə'lɪŋgərə^r] *n pej* doente *mf* fingido, -da.

mall [mɔ:l] *n esp US*: **(shopping)** ~ shopping *m (center)*.

mallard *n* marreco *m*.

malleable ['mælɪəbl] *adj* **-1.** [easily influenced] influenciável **-2.** [that can be shaped] maleável.

mallet ['mælɪt] *n* [hammer] marreta *f*.

malnourished [ˌmæl'nʌrɪʃt] *adj* subnutrido(da).

malnutrition [ˌmælnju:'trɪʃn] *n (U)* subnutrição *f*.

malpractice [ˌmæl'præktɪs] *n (U) JUR* falta *f* profissional.

malt [mɔ:lt] *n* **-1.** *(U)* [grain] malte *m* **-2.** [whisky] uísque *m* de malta.

Malta ['mɔ:ltə] *n* Malta; **in** ~ em Malta.

Maltese [ˌmɔ:l'ti:z] *(pl inv)* ◇ *adj* maltês(esa). ◇ *n* **-1.** [person] maltês *m*, -esa *f* **-2.** [language] maltês *m*.

maltreat [ˌmæl'tri:t] *vt* maltratar.

maltreatment [ˌmæl'tri:tmənt] *n (U)* maus-tratos *mpl*.

malt whisky *n* uísque *m* de malte.

mammal ['mæml] *n* mamífero *m*.

Mammon *n fig* riqueza *f* maléfica.

mammoth ['mæməθ] ◇ *adj* gigantesco(ca), descomunal. ◇ *n* mamute *m*.

man [mæn] *(pl* **men**, *pt &* *pp* **-ned**, *cont* **-ning**) ◇ *n* **-1.** [gen] homem *m*; **the** ~ **in the street** o homem comum; **to talk** ~ **to** ~ conversar de homem para homem; **to be** ~ **enough to do sthg** ser homem suficiente para fazer algo **-2.** [as form of address] cara *m*. ◇ *vt* **-1.** [ship, plane] tripular **-2.** [machine, switchboard, telephone] manejar.

manacles ['mænəklz] *npl* algemas *fpl*.

manage ['mænɪdʒ] ◇ *vi* **-1.** [cope] arranjar-se **-2.** [financially] virar-se. ◇ *vt* **-1.** [be responsible for, control - organization, business] dirigir, gerenciar; [- money] administrar; [- another person] representar; [- time] organizar **-2.** [succeed]: **to** ~ **to do sthg** conseguir fazer algo **-3.** [be available for]: **I can only** ~ **an hour tonight** eu só disponho de uma hora esta noite.

manageable ['mænɪdʒəbl] *adj* **-1.** [hair, inflation] controlável **-2.** [children] dominável **-3.** [task, operation] viável.

management ['mænɪdʒmənt] *n* **-1.** *(U)* [control, running] administração *f*, gestão *f* **-2.** [people in control] gerência *f*, direção *f*.

management consultant *n* assessor *m*, -ra *f* de administração.

manager ['mænɪdʒə^r] *n* **-1.** [of organization] gerente *mf*, diretor *m*, -ra *f* **-2.** [of popstar] empresário *m*, -ria *f* **-3.** *SPORT* treinador *m*, -ra *f*.

manageress [ˌmænɪdʒə'res] *n UK* gerente *f*.

managerial [ˌmænɪ'dʒɪərɪəl] *adj* gerencial.

managing director ['mænɪdʒɪŋ-] *n* diretor-gerente *m*, diretora-gerente *f*.

Managua [mə'nægwə] *n* Manágua; **in** ~ em Manágua.

Mancunian [mæŋ'kju:njən] ◇ *adj* manchesteriano(na). ◇ *n* [person] manchesteriano *m*, -na *f*.

mandarin ['mændərɪn] *n* **-1.** [fruit] tangerina *f* **-2.** [civil servant] mandarim *m*, -na *f*.

mandate ['mændeɪt] *n* **-1.** [elected right or authority] mandato *m* **-2.** [task] incumbência *f*, missão *f*.

mandatory ['mændətrɪ] *adj* obrigatório(ria).

mandolin [mændə'lɪn] *n* bandolim *m*.

mane [meɪn] *n* **-1.** [of horse] crina *f* **-2.** [of lion] juba *f*.

man-eating [-ˌi:tɪŋ] *adj* antropófago(ga).

maneuver *US* = **manoeuvre**.

manfully ['mænfʊlɪ] *adv* valentemente.

manganese *n (U)* manganês *m*.

mange [meɪndʒ] *n (U)* sarna *f*.

manger ['meɪndʒə^r] *n* manjedoura *f*.

mangetout (pea) [ˌmɑʊʒ'tu:-] *n UK* ervilha-torta *f*.

mangle ['mæŋgl] *vt* **-1.** [body, car] destroçar **-2.** *fig* [text] assassinar.

mango ['mæŋgəʊ] *(pl* **-es** *OR* **-s**) *n* manga *f*.

mangrove ['mæŋgrəʊv] *n* mangue *m*.

mangy ['meɪndʒɪ] *(compar* **-ier**, *superl* **-iest**) *adj* sarnento(ta).

manhandle ['mænˌhændl] *vt* maltratar.

manhole ['mænhəʊl] *n* poço *m* de inspeção, boca-de-lobo *m*.

manhood ['mænhʊd] *n (U)* **-1.** [age] idade *f* adulta **-2.** [virility] virilidade *f*.

man-hour *n* hora-homem *f*.

manhunt ['mænhʌnt] *n* perseguição *f (a um criminoso)*.

mania ['meɪnjə] *n* **-1.** *(U) PSYCH* mania *f* **-2.** [excessive liking]: ~ **(for sthg)** gosto *m* excessivo (por algo).

maniac ['meɪnɪæk] *n* **-1.** [madman] maníaco *m*, -ca *f* **-2.** [fanatic] fanático *m*, -ca *f*.

manic ['mænɪk] *adj* **-1.** [overexcited] doido(da) **-2.** *PSYCH* maníaco(ca).

manic-depressive ◇ *adj* maníaco-depressivo(va). ◇ *n* maníaco-depressivo *m*, -va *f*.

manicure ['mænɪˌkjʊə^r] ◇ *n* [individual treatment]: **to give sb a** ~ fazer as unhas de alguém. ◇ *vt*: **to** ~ **one's nails** fazer as unhas.

manifest ['mænɪfest] *fml* ◇ *adj* manifesto(ta). ◇ *vt* manifestar.

manifestation [ˌmænɪfes'teɪʃn] *n fml* manifestação *f*.

manifestly ['mænɪfestlɪ] *adv fml* evidentemente, claramente.

manifesto [ˌmænɪˈfestəʊ] (*pl* **-s** *OR* **-es**) *n* manifesto *m*.
manifold [ˈmænɪfəʊld] <> *adj literary* múltiplo(-pla). <> *n AUT* coletor *m*; **exhaust** ~ cano *m* de descarga.
manila *adj* de papel manilha.
Manila [məˈnɪlə] *n* Manila; **in** ~ em Manila.
manilla [məˈnɪlə] *adj* = **manila**.
manipulate [məˈnɪpjʊleɪt] *vt* **-1.** [control for personal benefit] manipular **-2.** [operate - machine, controls] operar; [- lever] acionar.
manipulation [məˌnɪpjʊˈleɪʃn] *n (U)* **-1.** [control for personal benefit] manipulação *f* **-2.** [operation - of machine, controls] operação *f*; [- of lever] acionamento *m*.
manipulative [məˈnɪpjʊlətɪv] *adj* manipulador(-ra).
Manitoba [ˌmænɪˈtəʊbə] *n* Manitoba; **in** ~ em Manitoba.
mankind [mænˈkaɪnd] *n (U)* humanidade *f*.
manly [ˈmænlɪ] (*compar* **-ier**, *superl* **-iest**) *adj* másculo(la), viril.
man-made *adj* **-1.** [problem, disaster] produzido(-da) pelo homem **-2.** [fibre, environment] artificial.
manna [ˈmænə] *n (U)* maná *m*.
manned [mænd] *adj* tripulado(da).
mannequin [ˈmænɪkɪn] *n* [dummy] manequim *m*.
manner [ˈmænəʳ] *n* **-1.** [method] maneira *f*, forma *f*; **in a** ~ **of speaking** por assim dizer **-2.** [bearing, attitude] jeito *m*, comportamento *m* **-3.** *literary* [type, sort]: **all** ~ **of** todos os tipos de.
◆ **manners** *npl* maneiras *fpl*; **to be good/bad** ~**s to do sthg** ser de boa/má educação fazer algo.
mannered [ˈmænəd] *adj fml* afetado(da).
mannerism [ˈmænərɪzm] *n* trejeito *m*.
mannish [ˈmænɪʃ] *adj* [woman] masculino(na).
manoeuvrable *UK*, **maneuverable** *US* [məˈnuːvrəbl] *adj* manobrável.
manoeuvre *UK*, **maneuver** *US* [məˈnuːvəʳ] <> *n* **-1.** [movement] manobra *f* **-2.** *fig* [clever move] manobra *f*. <> *vt* [control physically] manobrar, manejar. <> *vi* [move physically] manobrar.
◆ **manoeuvres** *npl MIL* manobras *fpl*.
manor [ˈmænəʳ] *n* [house] solar *m*.
manpower [ˈmænˌpaʊəʳ] *n (U)* mão-de-obra *f*.
manservant [ˈmænsɜːvənt] (*pl* **menservants**) *n dated* criado *m*.
mansion [ˈmænʃn] *n* mansão *f*.
man-size(d) *adj* de tamanho extragrande.
manslaughter [ˈmænˌslɔːtəʳ] *n (U)* homicídio *m* involuntário.
mantelpiece [ˈmæntlpiːs] *n* consolo *m* de lareira.
mantle [ˈmæntl] *n* **-1.** [layer, covering] camada *f* **-2.** [of leadership, high office] posição *f (de comando)*.
man-to-man *adj* de homem para homem.
manual [ˈmænjʊəl] <> *adj* manual. <> *n* [handbook] manual *m*.
manually [ˈmænjʊəlɪ] *adv* manualmente.
manual worker *n* operário *m*, -ria *f*.
manufacture [ˌmænjʊˈfæktʃəʳ] <> *n (U)* manufatura *f*, fabricação *f*. <> *vt* **-1.** [make] manufaturar, fabricar **-2.** [invent] inventar.
manufacturer [ˌmænjʊˈfæktʃərəʳ] *n* fabricante *mf*.
manufacturing [ˌmænjʊˈfæktʃərɪŋ] *n (U)* manufatura *f*, fabricação *f*.
manufacturing industries *npl* indústrias *fpl* manufatureiras.
manure [məˈnjʊəʳ] *n (U)* esterco *m*.
manuscript [ˈmænjʊskrɪpt] *n* manuscrito *m*.
Manx [mæŋks] <> *adj* manx. <> *n* [language] manx *m*.
many [ˈmenɪ] (*compar* **more**, *superl* **most**) <> *adj* [a lot of, plenty of] muitos(tas); ~ **people** muitas pessoas, muita gente; **how** ~ **...?** quantos(tas) ...?; **too** ~ **...** demais; **there are too** ~ **books for me to read** há livros demais para eu ler; **as** ~ **... as** tantos ... quantos, tantas ... quantas; **bring as** ~ **cups as you can** traga tantas xícaras quantas você puder; **so** ~ **...** tantos(tas) ...; **a good** *OR* **great** ~ **...** muitíssimos(mas) ..., um grande número de ... <> *pron* [a lot, plenty] muitos(tas); **how** ~**?** quantos(tas)?; **too** ~ muitos(tas); **as** ~ **as** tantos(-tas) quanto; **so** ~ tantos(tas); **a good** *OR* **great** ~ muitos(tas), um grande número.
Maori [ˈmaʊrɪ] <> *adj* maori. <> *n* maori *mf*.
map [mæp] (*pt* & *pp* **-ped**, *cont* **-ping**) <> *n* mapa *m*; **to put sb/sthg on the** ~ colocar alguém/algo no mapa. <> *vt* **-1.** [chart] fazer o mapa de **-2.** *COMPUT* associar.
◆ **map out** *vt sep* planejar, planificar.
maple [ˈmeɪpl] *n* bordo *m*.
maple leaf *n* folha *f* de bordo.
maple syrup *n (U)* xarope *m* de bordo.
Maputo [məˈpuːtəʊ] *n* Maputo; **in** ~ em Maputo.
mar [mɑːʳ] (*pt* & *pp* **-red**, *cont* **-ring**) *vt* prejudicar, frustrar.
Mar. (*abbr of* **March**) mar.
marathon [ˈmærəθn] <> *adj* exaustivo(va). <> *n* maratona *f*.
marathon runner *n* maratonista *mf*.
marauder [məˈrɔːdəʳ] *n* gatuno *m*, -na *f*, saqueador *m*, -ra *f*.
marauding [məˈrɔːdɪŋ] *adj* saqueador(ra).
marble [ˈmɑːbl] *n* **-1.** *(U)* [stone] mármore *m* **-2.** [for game] bolita *f* de gude.
◆ **marbles** *n (U)* [game] jogo *m* de gude.
march [mɑːtʃ] <> *n* **-1.** [gen] marcha *f* **-2.** [steady progress] avanço *m*. <> *vi* **-1.** [gen] marchar **-2.** [approach] avançar. <> *vt* conduzir, levar à força.
March [mɑːtʃ] *n* março; *see also* **September**.
marcher [ˈmɑːtʃəʳ] *n* [protester] manifestante *mf*.
marching orders [ˈmɑːtʃɪŋ-] *npl*: **to give sb his** ~ mandar alguém passear, dar cartão vermelho para alguém.
marchioness [ˈmɑːʃənes] *n* [aristocrat] marquesa *f*.
march-past *n* parada *f*.
Mardi Gras [ˌmɑːdɪˈgrɑː] *n* Terça-Feira *f* de Carnaval.
mare [meəʳ] *n* égua *f*.
marg. (*abbr of* **margarine**) *n inf* margarina *f*.
margarine [ˌmɑːdʒəˈriːn, ˌmɑːgəˈriːn] *n (U)* margarina *f*.
marge [mɑːdʒ] *n (U) inf* margarina *f*.
margin [ˈmɑːdʒɪn] *n* **-1.** [gen] margem *f* **-2.** [of desert, forest] limite *m*.

marginal ['mɑ:dʒɪnl] *adj* **-1.** [unimportant] secundário(ria) **-2.** *UK POL:* ~ **seat** *OR* **constituency** *cadeira f ganha por uma pequena maioria de votos.*
marginally ['mɑ:dʒɪnəlɪ] *adv* ligeiramente.
marigold ['mærɪgəʊld] *n* calêndula *f.*
marihuana, marijuana [ˌmærɪ'wɑ:nə] *n (U)* maconha *f.*
marina [mə'ri:nə] *n* marina *f.*
marinade [ˌmærɪ'neɪd] ◇ *n* marinada *f.* ◇ *vt & vi* = **marinate.**
marinate ['mærɪneɪt] ◇ *vt* marinar. ◇ *vi* ficar em marinada.
marine [mə'ri:n] ◇ *adj* **-1.** [underwater] marinho(-nha) **-2.** [seafaring] marítimo(ma). ◇ *n MIL* fuzileiro *m* naval.
marionette [ˌmærɪə'net] *n* marionete *f.*
marital ['mærɪtl] *adj* conjugal.
marital status *n* estado *m* civil.
maritime ['mærɪtaɪm] *adj* marítimo(ma).
Maritime Provinces, Maritimes *npl*: **the** ~ as Províncias Marítimas.
marjoram ['mɑ:dʒərəm] *n (U)* manjerona *f.*
mark [mɑ:k] ◇ *n* **-1.** [stain] mancha *f*; [scratch] marca *f* **-2.** [in exam] nota *f* **-3.** [stage, level]: **the halfway** ~ o meio caminho; **beyond the billion** ~ acima de um bilhão **-4.** [sign, indication] sinal *f* **-5.** [currency] marco *m* **-6.** *CULIN* nível *m* de temperatura **-7.** *phr*: **to make one's** ~ deixar a marca; **to be quick/slow off the** ~ reagir rapidamente/lentamente; **wide of the** ~ longe da verdade. ◇ *vt* **-1.** [gen] marcar **-2.** [exam, essay] corrigir **-3.** [commemorate] comemorar, celebrar **-4.** [stain] manchar.
◆ **mark down** *vt sep* **-1.** [*COMM* - prices] rebaixar; [- goods] baixar o preço de **-2.** [downgrade] baixar a nota de.
◆ **mark off** *vt sep* [cross off] assinalar.
◆ **mark up** *vt sep* [*COMM* - prices] aumentar; [- goods] remarcar.
marked [mɑ:kt] *adj* [noticeable] notável.
markedly ['mɑ:kɪdlɪ] *adv* [noticeably] notavelmente.
marker ['mɑ:kə[r]] *n* **-1.** [sign] indicador *m* **-2.** *SPORT* marcador *m* **-3.** [of exam] avaliador *m*, -ra *f.*
marker pen *n* caneta *f* marcadora.
market ['mɑ:kɪt] ◇ *n* [gen] mercado *m*; **on the** ~ à venda. ◇ *vt* comercializar, vender. ◇ *vi US* [shop]: **to go** ~**ing** ir às compras.
marketable ['mɑ:kɪtəbl] *adj* vendável, comercializável.
market analysis *n (U)* análise *f* de mercado.
market day *n* dia *f* da feira.
market forces *npl COMM* tendências *fpl* do mercado.
market garden *n esp UK* horta *f.*
marketing ['mɑ:kɪtɪŋ] *n (U) COMM* marketing *m.*
marketplace ['mɑ:kɪtpleɪs] *n* mercado *m.*
market price *n COMM* preço *m* de mercado.
market research *n (U)* pesquisa *f* de mercado.
market town *n* cidade *f* com feira livre.
market value *n COMM* valor *m* de mercado.
marking ['mɑ:kɪŋ] *n (U) SCH & UNIV* correção *f.*
◆ **markings** *npl* **-1.** [of flower] manchas *fpl* **-2.** [of animal] pintas *fpl* **-3.** [of road] sinais *mpl.*
marksman ['mɑ:ksmən] (*pl* **-men** [-mən]) *n* atirador *m.*
marksmanship ['mɑ:ksmənʃɪp] *n (U)* pontaria *f.*
markup ['mɑ:kʌp] *n* margem *m* de lucro.
marmalade ['mɑ:məleɪd] *n (U)* geléia *f.*
maroon [mə'ru:n] *adj* de cor castanho-avermelhado.
marooned [mə'ru:nd] *adj* abandonado(da).
marquee [mɑ:'ki:] *n* toldo *m.*
marquess ['mɑ:kwɪs] *n* = **marquis.**
marquetry *n (U)* marchetaria *f.*
marquis ['mɑ:kwɪs] *n* marquês *m.*
marriage ['mærɪdʒ] *n* casamento *m.*
marriage bureau *n UK* agência *f* matrimonial.
marriage certificate *n* certidão *m* de casamento.
marriage guidance *n (U)* orientação *f* para casais.
marriage guidance counsellor *n* terapeuta *mf* para casais.
married ['mærɪd] *adj* **-1.** [having a spouse] casado(da) **-2.** [of marriage] de casado.
marrow ['mærəʊ] *n* **-1.** *UK* [vegetable] abóbora *f* **-2.** *(U)* [in bones] medula *f.*
marry ['mærɪ] (*pt & pp* **-ied**) ◇ *vt* casar; **will you** ~ **me?** quer se casar comigo? ◇ *vi* [get married] casar-se.
Mars [mɑ:z] *n* [planet] Marte.
marsh [mɑ:ʃ] *n* pântano *m.*
marshal ['mɑ:ʃl] (*UK pt & pp* **-led**, *cont* **-ling**, *US pt & pp* **-ed**, *cont* **-ing**) ◇ *n* **-1.** *MIL* marechal *m* **-2.** [assistant] oficial *m* **-3.** *US* [law officer] oficial *mf* de justiça. ◇ *vt* **-1.** [people] dirigir, conduzir **-2.** [support, thoughts] ordenar, organizar.
marshalling yard ['mɑ:ʃlɪŋ-] *n* pátio *m* ferroviário.
marshland ['mɑ:ʃlænd] *n (U)* pantanal *m.*
marshmallow [*UK* ˌmɑ:ʃ'mæləʊ, *US* 'mɑ:rʃˌmeləʊ] *n* **-1.** [sweet] marshmallow *m* **-2.** *(U)* [substance] de marshmallow.
marshy ['mɑ:ʃɪ] (*compar* **-ier**, *superl* **-iest**) *adj* pantanoso(sa).
marsupial [mɑ:'su:pjəl] *n* marsupial *m.*
martial ['mɑ:ʃl] *adj* marcial.
martial arts [ˌmɑ:ʃl-] *npl* artes *fpl* marciais.
martial law [ˌmɑ:ʃl-] *n (U)* lei *f* marcial.
Martian ['mɑ:ʃn] ◇ *adj* marciano(na). ◇ *n* marciano *m*, -na *f.*
martin ['mɑ:tɪn] *n* martinete *m.*
martini [mɑ:'ti:nɪ] *n* [cocktail] martini *m.*
Martinique [ˌmɑ:tɪ'ni:k] *n* Martinica; **in** ~ na Martinica.
martyr ['mɑ:tə[r]] *n* mártir *mf.*
martyrdom ['mɑ:tədəm] *n (U)* martírio *m.*
martyred ['mɑ:təd] *adj* martirizado(da).
marvel ['mɑ:vl] (*UK pt & pp* **-led**, *cont* **-ling**, *US pt & pp* **-ed**, *cont* **-ing**) ◇ *n* **-1.** [gen] maravilha *f* **-2.** [surprise, miracle] milagre *m.* ◇ *vt*: **to** ~ **that** admirar-se que. ◇ *vi*: **to** ~ **(at sthg)** maravilhar-se (com algo).
marvellous *UK*, **marvelous** *US* ['mɑ:vələs] *adj* maravilhoso(sa).
Marxism ['mɑ:ksɪzm] *n (U)* marxismo *m.*

Marxist ['mɑːksɪst] ◇ *adj* marxista. ◇ *n* marxista *mf*.
Maryland ['meərɪlænd] *n* Maryland; **in** ~ em Maryland.
marzipan ['mɑːzɪpæn] *n (U)* maçapão *m*.
mascara [mæs'kɑːrə] *n (U)* rímel *m*.
mascot ['mæskət] *n* mascote *f*.
masculine ['mæskjʊlɪn] *adj* masculino(na).
masculinity [ˌmæskjʊ'lɪnətɪ] *n (U)* masculinidade *f*.
mash [mæʃ] *vt* triturar, amassar.
MASH [mæʃ] (*abbr of* **mobile army surgical hospital**) *n hospital militar de campanha norte-americano*.
mashed potatoes [mæʃt-] *npl* purê *m* de batatas.
mask [mɑːsk] ◇ *n* **-1.** [covering face] máscara *f* **-2.** *fig* [dissimulation] máscara *f*. ◇ *vt* **-1.** [cover] mascarar **-2.** [conceal] disfarçar.
masked [mɑːskt] *adj* [face, man] mascarado(da).
masking tape ['mɑːskɪŋ-] *n (U)* fita *f* adesiva.
masochism ['mæsəkɪzm] *n (U)* masoquismo *m*.
masochist ['mæsəkɪst] *n* masoquista *mf*.
masochistic [ˌmæsə'kɪstɪk] *adj* masoquista.
mason ['meɪsn] *n* **-1.** [stonemason] pedreiro *m*, -ra *f* **-2.** [Freemason] maçom *m*.
masonic [mə'sɒnɪk] *adj* maçônico(ca).
masonry ['meɪsnrɪ] *n (U)* [stones] alvenaria *f*.
masquerade [ˌmæskə'reɪd] *vi*: **to** ~ **as** fazer-se passar por; **to** ~ **under the name of ...** esconder-se sob o nome de ...
mass [mæs] ◇ *n* **-1.** GEOGR, PHYSICS massa *f* **-2.** [large amount] grande quantidade *f* **-3.** [main part, majority]: **the** ~ **of** a maioria de. ◇ *adj* em massa. ◇ *vt* concentrar. ◇ *vi* concentrar-se.
◆ **Mass** *n* RELIG missa *f*.
◆ **masses** *npl* **-1.** *inf* [lots, plenty] montes *mpl*; ~**es of sthg** montes de algo **-2.** [ordinary people]: **the** ~**es** as massas.
Massachusetts [ˌmæsə'tʃuːsɪts] *n* Massachusetts.
massacre ['mæsəkə^r] ◇ *n* massacre *m*. ◇ *vt* massacrar.
massage [*UK* 'mæsɑːʒ, *US* mə'sɑːʒ] ◇ *n* massagem *f*. ◇ *vt* massagear.
massage parlour *n* **-1.** [for massage] clínica *f* de massagem **-2.** *euphemism* [brothel] casa *f* de massagens.
masseur [mæ'sɜːr] *n* massagista *m*.
masseuse [mæ'sɜːz] *n* massagista *f*.
massive ['mæsɪv] *adj* [in size, amount] enorme; ~ **majority** maioria em massa.
massively ['mæsɪvlɪ] *adv* enormemente.
mass-market *adj* para mercados de massa.
mass media *n or npl*: **the** ~ os meios de comunicação de massas.
mass-produce *vt* produzir em série.
mass production *n (U)* produção *f* em série.
mast [mɑːst] *n* **-1.** [on boat] mastro *m* **-2.** RADIO & TV antena *f*.
mastectomy (*pl* **-ies**) *n* mastectomia *f*.
master ['mɑːstə^r] ◇ *n* **-1.** [person in charge] senhor *m*; **a** ~ **and his servants** um amo e seus servos **-2.** *fig* [of subject, situation] dono *m* **-3.** *UK* [teacher] mestre *m* **-4.** [of ship] capitão *m* **-5.** [original copy] original *m*. ◇ *adj* **-1.** [in trade] mestre **-2.** [original] original. ◇ *vt* **-1.** [gain control of] dominar, controlar **-2.** [perfect] dominar.
master bedroom *n* quarto *m* principal.
master disk *n* COMPUT disco-mestre *m*.
masterful ['mɑːstəfʊl] *adj* dominante, autoritário(ria).
master key *n* chave-mestra *f*.
masterly ['mɑːstəlɪ] *adj* magistral.
mastermind ['mɑːstəmaɪnd] ◇ *n* cabeça *mf*; **he is the** ~ **behind the plan** ele é o cabeça do plano. ◇ *vt* ser o cabeça de.
Master of Arts (*pl* **Masters of Arts**) *n* **-1.** [degree] mestrado *m* em ciências humanas, *diploma de mestre em ciências humanas* **-2.** [person] mestre *mf* em ciências humanas, *titular de diploma de mestre em ciências humanas*.
master of ceremonies (*pl* **masters of ceremonies**) *n* mestre-de-cerimônias *mf*.
Master of Science (*pl* **Masters of Science**) *n* **-1.** [degree] mestrado *m* em ciências exatas, *diploma de mestre em ciências exatas* **-2.** [person] mestre *mf* em ciências exatas, *titular de diploma de mestre em ciências exatas*.
masterpiece ['mɑːstəpiːs] *n* obra-prima *f*.
master plan *n* plano-mestre *m*.
master's degree *n* mestrado *m*.
masterstroke ['mɑːstəstrəʊk] *n* golpe *m* de mestre.
master switch *n* chave *f* geral.
masterwork ['mɑːstəwɜːk] *n* obra-prima *f*.
mastery ['mɑːstərɪ] *n (U)* domínio *m*.
mastic ['mæstɪk] *n (U)* almécega *f*.
masticate ['mæstɪkeɪt] *fml vt & vi* mastigar.
mastiff ['mæstɪf] *n* mastim *m*.
masturbate ['mæstəbeɪt] *vi* masturbar-se.
masturbation [ˌmæstə'beɪʃn] *n (U)* masturbação *f*.
mat [mæt] *n* **-1.** [on floor] tapete *m*; **door** ~ capacho *m* **-2.** [on table]: **beer** ~ porta-copos *m inv*; **table** ~ jogo *m* americano.
match [mætʃ] ◇ *n* **-1.** [game] partida *f* **-2.** [for lighting] fósforo *m* **-3.** [equal]: **to be no** ~ **for sb** não ser páreo para alguém. ◇ *vt* **-1.** [be the same as] coincidir com **-2.** [coordinate with] combinar com **-3.** [equal] equiparar-se a. ◇ *vi* [be the same] combinar.
matchbox ['mætʃbɒks] *n* caixa *f* de fósforos.
matched [mætʃt] *adj*: **to be well** ~ [well suited] combinar bem; [equal in strength] estar igualado(da); **they are well** ~ **(as a couple)** eles formam um belo casal.
matching ['mætʃɪŋ] *adj* que combina bem.
matchless ['mætʃlɪs] *adj literary* incomparável, ímpar.
matchmaker ['mætʃˌmeɪkə^r] *n* casamenteiro *m*, -ra *f*.
match play *n* GOLF *partida de golfe entre duas equipes*.
match point *n* TENNIS **-1.** *(U)* [situation] match point *m* **-2.** [score] match point *m*, ponto *m* do jogo.
matchstick ['mætʃstɪk] *n* palito *m*.

mate [meɪt] ◇ *n* **-1.** *inf* [friend] amigo *m*, -ga *f*, companheiro *m*, -ra *f* **-2.** *UK inf* [form of address] colega *mf* **-3.** [of animal] parceiro *m*, -ra *f* **-4.** *NAUT*: **(first)** ~ contramestre *m*. ◇ *vi* [animals] acasalar-se; **to** ~ **with** acasalar-se com.

material [mə'tɪərɪəl] ◇ *adj* **-1.** material **-2.** [important] substancial. ◇ *n* material *m*.
◆ **materials** *npl* materiais *mpl*.

materialism [mə'tɪərɪəlɪzm] *n (U)* [desire for possessions] materialismo *m*.

materialist [mə'tɪərɪəlɪst] *n* [person greedy for possessions] materialista *mf*.

materialistic [mə,tɪərɪə'lɪstɪk] *adj* materialista.

materialize, -ise [mə'tɪərɪəlaɪz] *vi* **-1.** [happen] concretizar-se **-2.** [appear] materializar-se.

materially [mə'tɪərɪəlɪ] *adv* **-1.** [physically] materialmente **-2.** [importantly, essentially] essencialmente.

maternal [mə'tɜ:nl] *adj* maternal.

maternity [mə'tɜ:nətɪ] *n (U)* maternidade *f*.

maternity benefit *n (U)* auxílio-maternidade *m*.

maternity dress *n* vestido *m* de gestante.

maternity hospital *n* maternidade *f (no hospital)*.

maternity leave *n* licença-maternidade *f*.

maternity ward *n* maternidade *f*.

math *n US* = **maths**.

mathematical [,mæθə'mætɪkl] *adj* matemático(-ca).

mathematician [,mæθəmə'tɪʃn] *n* matemático *m*, -ca *f*.

mathematics [,mæθə'mætɪks] *n (U)* [subject] matemática *f*.

maths *UK* [mæθs], **math** *US* [mæθ] (*abbr of* **mathematics**) *inf* ◇ *n (U)* [subject] matemática *f*. ◇ *comp* de matemática.

maths coprocessor [-,kəʊ'prəʊsesə^r] *n COMPUT* coprocessador *m* matemático.

matinée ['mætɪneɪ] *n* matinê *f*.

matinée jacket *n UK* casaquinho *m* de bebê.

mating call ['meɪtɪŋ-] *n* chamado *m* do macho *(para acasalamento)*.

mating season ['meɪtɪŋ-] *n* época *f* de acasalamento.

matriarch ['meɪtrɪɑ:k] *n* **-1.** [of a society] matriarca *f* **-2.** *literary* [of a family] matriarca *f*.

matrices ['meɪtrɪsi:z] *pl* ▷ **matrix**.

matriculate [mə'trɪkjʊleɪt] *vi UNIV* matricular-se.

matriculation [mə,trɪkjʊ'leɪʃn] *n (U) UNIV* matrícula *f*.

matrimonial [,mætrɪ'məʊnjəl] *adj* matrimonial.

matrimony ['mætrɪmənɪ] *n (U)* matrimônio *m*.

matrix ['meɪtrɪks] (*pl* **matrices** *OR* **-es**) *n* **-1.** [gen] matriz *f* **-2.** *TECH* molde *m* para fundição.

matron ['meɪtrən] *n* **-1.** *UK* [in hospital] enfermeira-chefe *f* **-2.** [in school] enfermeira *f* **-3.** *US* [in prison] superintendente *f* **-4.** [middle-aged woman] matrona *f*.

matronly ['meɪtrənlɪ] *adj euph* matronal.

matt *UK*, **matte** *US* [mæt] *adj* fosco(ca).

matted ['mætɪd] *adj* embaraçado(da).

matter ['mætə^r] ◇ *n* **-1.** [question, situation] questão *f*, assunto *m*; **a** ~ **of life and death** uma questão de vida ou morte; **the fact** *OR* **truth of the** ~ **is ...** o xis da questão é ...; **that's another** *OR* **a different** ~ isso é outra questão/coisa; **a** ~ **of opinion** uma questão de opinião; **a** ~ **of time** uma questão de tempo; **to make** ~**s worse** piorar as coisas; **and to make** ~**s worse, ...** e para piorar (ainda mais) as coisas, ...; **as a** ~ **of course** como algo natural; **as a** ~ **of principle** por uma questão de princípios; **within a** ~ **of hours** numa questão de horas **-2.** [trouble, cause of pain] problema *m*; **what's the** ~**?** qual é o problema?, o que (é que) houve?; **what's the** ~ **with it/her?** qual é o problema com isso /ela? **-3.** *(U) PHYSICS* matéria *f* **-4.** *(U)* [material] material/ *m*; **vegetable** ~ matéria vegetal. ◇ *vi* [be important] importar; **it doesn't** ~ não importa; **it doesn't** ~ **what you decide** não interessa o que você decidir.
◆ **as a matter of fact** *adv* aliás, na verdade.
◆ **for that matter** *adv* quanto a isso.
◆ **no matter** *adv*: **no** ~ **how hard I try ...** não importa quanto eu tente ...; **no** ~ **what** aconteça o que acontecer.

Matterhorn ['mætə,hɔ:n] *n*: **the** ~ a Montanha Matterhorn.

matter-of-fact *adj* sem sentimento, prosaico(-ca).

matting ['mætɪŋ] *n (U)* esteira *f*.

mattress ['mætrɪs] *n* colchão *m*.

mature [mə'tjʊə^r] ◇ *adj* **-1.** [person] maduro(ra) **-2.** [food, drink] envelhecido(da), maturado(da) **-3.** [cheese] curado(da). ◇ *vi* **-1.** [gen] amadurecer **-2.** [animal, plant] crescer **-3.** [wine, spirit] envelhecer **-4.** [cheese] curar **-5.** [insurance policy] vencer.

mature student *n UK UNIV* estudante *mf* adulto, -ta.

maturity [mə'tjʊərətɪ] *n* maturidade *f*.

maudlin ['mɔ:dlɪn] *adj* choroso(sa).

maul [mɔ:l] *vt* [attack, savage] atacar gravemente.

Mauritania [,mɒrɪ'teɪnɪə] *n* Mauritânia; **in** ~ na Mauritânia.

Mauritanian [,mɒrɪ'teɪnɪən] ◇ *adj* mauritano(-na). ◇ *n* mauritano *m*, -na *f*.

Mauritian [mə'rɪʃən] ◇ *adj* mauriciano(na). ◇ *n* mauriciano *m*, -na *f*.

Mauritius [mə'rɪʃəs] *n* Maurício; **in** ~ em Maurício.

mausoleum [,mɔ:sə'lɪəm] (*pl* **-s**) *n* mausoléu *m*.

mauve [məʊv] ◇ *adj* da cor de malva. ◇ *n (U)* malva *f*.

maverick ['mævərɪk] ◇ *adj* inconformista. ◇ *n* inconformista *mf*.

mawkish ['mɔ:kɪʃ] *adj* piegas.

max. [mæks] (*abbr of* **maximum**) máx.

maxim ['mæksɪm] (*pl* **-s**) *n* máxima *f*.

maxima ['mæksɪmə] *pl* ▷ **maximum**.

maximize, -ise ['mæksɪmaɪz] *vt* maximizar.

maximum ['mæksɪməm] (*pl* **maxima** *OR* **-s**) ◇ *adj* [highest, largest] máximo(ma). ◇ *n* [upper limit] máximo *m*.

may [meɪ] *modal vb* **-1.** poder; **you** ~ **like it** talvez você goste; **he** ~ **well have said that** ele pode muito bem ter dito aquilo; **it** ~ **rain** pode ser que chova; **be that as it** ~ seja como for; **I would like to add, if I** ~ **...** eu gostaria de acrescentar, se possível ... **-2.** *fml* [to express wish, hope]: **long ~ it last!** que dure por muito tempo!; **~ they be very happy!** que eles sejam muito felizes!; ▻ **might.**

May [meɪ] *n* maio; *see also* **September.**

Maya ['maɪə] *n*: **the ~** os Maias.

maybe ['meɪbi:] *adv* talvez.

Mayday *n* [SOS] mayday, sinal *m* de socorro.

May Day *n* Primeiro *m* de Maio.

mayfly ['meɪflaɪ] (*pl* **-flies**) *n* efeméride *f*.

mayhem ['meɪhem] *n (U)* caos *m inv*.

mayn't = **may not.**

mayonnaise [,meɪə'neɪz] *n (U)* maionese *f*.

mayor [meə^r] *n* prefeito *m*.

mayoress ['meərɪs] *n* [female mayor] prefeita *f*; [wife of mayor] esposa *f* do prefeito.

maypole ['meɪpəʊl] *n mastro erigido para o dia 1° de maio ao redor do qual se dança.*

may've *cont* = **may have.**

maze [meɪz] *n* **-1.** [system of paths] labirinto *m* **-2.** *fig* [tangle] confusão *f*.

MB <> *n* (*abbr of* **Bachelor of Medicine**) *(titular de) bacharelado em medicina.* <> **-1.** (*abbr of* **megabyte**) MB **-2.** *abbr of* **Manitoba.**

MBA (*abbr of* **Master of Business Administration**) *n* MBA *m*.

MBBS (*abbr of* **Bachelor of Medicine and Surgery**) *n (titular de) bacharelado em medicina e cirurgia.*

MBE (*abbr of* **Member of the Order of the British Empire**) *n (beneficiário da) ordem do Império Britânico.*

MC (*abbr of* **master of ceremonies**) *n* mestre-de-cerimônias *m*.

MCAT (*abbr of* **Medical College Admissions Test**) *n exame de admissão para a faculdade de medicina nos Estados Unidos.*

MCC (*abbr of* **Marylebone Cricket Club**) *n clube londrino de críquete, responsável pelas regras do jogo.*

McCarthyism [mə'kɑ:rθɪɪzəm] *n* macartismo *m*.

McCoy [mə'kɔɪ] *n (U) inf*: **the real ~** o produto genuíno.

MCP (*abbr of* **male chauvinist pig**) *n inf* machista *m*.

MD <> *n* **-1.** (*abbr of* **Doctor of Medicine**) *(titular de) doutorado em medicina* **-2.** (*abbr of* **managing director**) diretor-gerente *m*. <> *abbr of* **Maryland.**

MDT (*abbr of* **Mountain Daylight Time**) *n horário de verão na zona das Montanhas Rochosas nos Estados Unidos.*

me [mi:] *pers pron* **-1.** *(direct, indirect)* me; **she knows ~** ela me conhece; **it's ~** sou eu; **send it to ~** mande-o para mim; **tell ~** diga-me; **-2.** *(after prep)* mim; **with ~** comigo; **it's for ~** é para mim.

ME <> *n* (*abbr of* **myalgic encephalomyelitis**) EM *f*. <> *abbr of* **Maine.**

meadow ['medəʊ] *n* campina *f*.

meagre *UK*, **meager** *US* ['mi:gə^r] *adj* magro(gra), insuficiente.

meal [mi:l] *n* refeição *f*; **to go out for a ~** sair para jantar; **to make a ~ of sthg** *UK fig* & *pej* fazer algo parecer mais cansativo do que realmente é.

meals on wheels *npl UK serviço de entrega domiciliar de refeições para idosos e necessitados.*

mealtime ['mi:ltaɪm] *n* hora *f* da refeição; **at ~s** na hora das refeições.

mealy-mouthed [,mi:lɪ'maʊðd] *adj pej* evasivo(-va), fingido(da).

mean [mi:n] (*pt* & *pp* **meant**) <> *adj* **-1.** [miserly] mesquinho(nha); **to be ~ with sthg** ser avarento com algo **-2.** [unkind] grosseiro(ra); **to be ~ to sb** ser malvado(da) com alguém **-3.** [average] médio(dia) **-4.** *iro* [inferior] inferior; **she's no ~ singer** [excellent] ela é uma cantora de primeira; **it's no ~ task** não é pouca coisa. <> *n* [average] meio-termo *m*; ▻ **means.** <> *vt* **-1.** [signify, represent] significar **-2.** [have in mind, intend] querer dizer; **to ~ to do sthg** ter a intenção de fazer algo, tencionar fazer algo; **to be meant for sb/sthg** ser feito(ta) para alguém/algo; **they're not meant to be there** eles não deveriam estar lá; **it was meant as a compliment** era para ser um elogio; **to be meant to do sthg** dever fazer algo; **to ~ well** ter boa vontade **-3.** [be serious about] falar sério; **she meant every word she said** tudo o que ela disse era a sério **-4.** [entail] acarretar **-5.** *phr*: **I ~** quer dizer.

meander [mɪ'ændə^r] *vi* **-1.** [river, road] serpentear **-2.** [in walking] vagar **-3.** [in speaking] divagar.

meaning ['mi:nɪŋ] *n* **-1.** [sense] sentido *m*, significado *m* **-2.** *(U)* [purpose, importance] sentido *m*.

meaningful ['mi:nɪŋfʊl] *adj* **-1.** [expressive] significativo(va) **-2.** [deep, profound] sério(ria).

meaningless ['mi:nɪŋlɪs] *adj* **-1.** [devoid of sense] sem sentido **-2.** [futile] fútil.

meanness ['mi:nnɪs] *n (U)* **-1.** [stinginess] avareza *f* **-2.** [unkindness] maldade *f*.

means [mi:nz] (*pl inv*) <> *n* [method, way] meio *m*; **a ~ to an end** um meio para um fim; **by ~ of** por meio de. <> *npl* [money] recursos *mpl*.

◆ **by all means** *adv* claro que sim.

◆ **by no means** *adv* de modo algum.

means test *n esp UK averiguação oficial quanto à carência de renda para fins de recebimento de pensão do governo.*

meant [ment] *pt* & *pp* ▻ **mean.**

meantime ['mi:n,taɪm] *n*: **in the ~** enquanto isso.

meanwhile ['mi:n,waɪl] *adv* **-1.** [at the same time] enquanto isso **-2.** [between two events] nesse ínterim.

measles ['mi:zlz] *n*: **to catch ~** pegar sarampo.

measly ['mi:zlɪ] (*compar* **-ier**, *superl* **-iest**) *adj inf* miserável.

measurable ['meʒərəbl] *adj* [significant] considerável.

measurably ['meʒərəblɪ] *adv* consideravelmente.

measure ['meʒə^r] <> *n* **-1.** [step, action] medida *f* **-2.** *(U)* [degree, amount] grau *m*; **the film had a ~ of success** o filme até que teve sucesso; **for good ~** para se certificar **-3.** [of alcohol] dose *f* **-4.** [indication] indicação *f* **-5.** [device] régua *f*. <> *vt* [determine size of, gauge] medir. <> *vi* [be of stated size] medir.

◆ **measure up** *vi* [be good enough] estar à altura; **to ~ up to sthg** estar à altura de algo.

measured ['meʒəd] *adj literary* ponderado(da).

measurement ['meʒəmənt] *n* **-1.** [figure, amount]

medida *f* **-2.** *(U)* [act of measuring] medição *f*.

◆ **measurements** *npl* [of sb's body] medidas *fpl*.

measuring jug ['meʒərɪŋ-] *n* jarro *m* de medidas.

measuring tape ['meʒərɪŋ-] *n* fita *f* métrica.

meat [mi:t] *n (U)* carne *f*.

meatball ['mi:tbɔ:l] *n* almôndega *f*.

meat pie *n UK* torta *f* de carne.

meaty ['mi:tɪ] (*compar* **-ier**, *superl* **-iest**) *adj fig* [full of ideas] rico(ca), sólido(da).

Mecca ['mekə] *n* **-1.** GEOGR Meca **-2.** *fig* [paradise]: **a ~ for** um paraíso para.

mechanic [mɪ'kænɪk] *n* mecânico *m*, -ca *f*.

◆ **mechanics** ◇ *n (U)* [study] mecânica *f*. ◇ *npl* [way sthg works] mecânica *f*.

mechanical [mɪ'kænɪkl] *adj* mecânico(ca).

mechanical engineering *n (U)* engenharia *f* mecânica.

mechanism ['mekənɪzm] *n* mecanismo *m*.

mechanization *n* mecanização *f*.

mechanize, -ise ['mekənaɪz] ◇ *vt* mecanizar. ◇ *vi* mecanizar-se.

Med (*abbr of* **Mediterranean Sea**) *n UK inf* Mediterrâneo *m*.

MEd [,em'ed] (*abbr of* **Master of Education**) *n (titular de) mestrado em educação*.

medal ['medl] *n* medalha *f*.

medallion [mɪ'dæljən] *n* medalhão *m*.

medallist *UK*, **medalist** *US* ['medəlɪst] *n* medalhista *mf*.

meddle ['medl] *vi* meter-se; **to ~ in/with sthg** meter-se em/com algo.

meddlesome ['medlsəm] *adj* metido(da), intrometido(da).

media ['mi:djə] ◇ *pl* ▷ **medium**. ◇ *n or npl*: **the ~** a mídia.

mediaeval [,medɪ'i:vl] *adj* = **medieval**.

media event *n* evento *m* da mídia.

median ['mi:djən] ◇ *adj* MATH mediano(na). ◇ *n US* [of road] canteiro *m* divisor.

mediate ['mi:dɪeɪt] ◇ *vt* [produce by arbitration] negociar. ◇ *vi* [arbitrate]: **to ~ between** ser mediador(ra) entre.

mediation [,mi:dɪ'eɪʃn] *n (U)* [arbitration] mediação *f*.

mediator ['mi:dɪeɪtə^r] *n* mediador *m*, -ra *f*.

medic ['medɪk] *n inf* **-1.** [medical student] estudante *mf* de medicina **-2.** [doctor] médico *m*, -ca *f*.

Medicaid ['medɪkeɪd] *n (U) US* auxílio-saúde *m*.

MEDICAID/MEDICARE

Em razão da falta de um sistema nacional de saúde nos Estados Unidos, foram criados, em 1965, os programas *Medicare* e *Medicaid*, visando a oferecer assistência médica a idosos e a pessoas sem recursos. O *Medicare* destina-se aos maiores de 65 anos e é financiado pelos impostos relativos à seguridade social. Além disso, cada participante paga uma contribuição mensal, e uma pequena taxa é cobrada cada vez que se utiliza o atendimento médico. O *Medicaid* volta-se para aqueles que não dispõem de recursos econômicos, sendo financiado pelos governos federal e estadual.

medical ['medɪkl] ◇ *adj* médico(ca). ◇ *n* [checkup] exame *m* médico, check-up *m*.

medical certificate *n* [result of medical exam] atestado *m* médico.

medical insurance *n (U)* seguro-saúde *m*.

medical student *n* estudante *mf* de medicina.

Medicare ['medɪkeə^r] *n (U) US* seguro-saúde *m (para idosos)*.

medicated ['medɪkeɪtɪd] *adj* medicinal.

medication [,medɪ'keɪʃn] *n* medicação *f*.

medicinal [me'dɪsɪnl] *adj* [drink, herb, tea] medicinal.

medicine ['medsɪn] *n* **-1.** *(U)* [treatment of illness] medicina *f* **-2.** [substance] medicamento *m*, remédio *m*.

medicine man *n* curandeiro *m*.

medieval [,medɪ'i:vl] *adj* medieval.

mediocre [,mi:dɪ'əʊkə^r] *adj* medíocre.

mediocrity [,mi:dɪ'ɒkrətɪ] *n (U)* [poor quality] mediocridade *f*.

meditate ['medɪteɪt] *vi* **-1.** [reflect, ponder] refletir; **to ~ (up)on sthg** refletir sobre algo **-2.** [practise meditation] meditar.

meditation [,medɪ'teɪʃn] *n* meditação *f*.

Mediterranean [,medɪtə'reɪnjən] ◇ *n* **-1.** [sea]: **the ~ (Sea)** o (Mar) Mediterrâneo **-2.** [area around sea]: **the ~** o mediterrâneo. ◇ *adj* mediterrâneo(nea).

medium ['mi:djəm] (*pl sense 1* **-dia**, *pl sense 2* **-diums**) ◇ *adj* [middle, average] médio(dia). ◇ *n* **-1.** [way of communicating] meio *m* de comunicação **-2.** [spiritualist] médium *mf*.

medium-dry *adj* semi-seco(ca).

medium-size(d) [-saɪzd] *adj* de tamanho médio.

medium wave *n (U)* onda *f* média.

medley ['medlɪ] (*pl* **-s**) *n* **-1.** [mixture] mistura *f* **-2.** [selection of music] coletânea *f*.

meek [mi:k] *adj* dócil, meigo(ga).

meekly ['mi:klɪ] *adv* docilmente.

meet [mi:t] (*pt & pp* **met**) ◇ *n US* [meeting] encontro *m*, competição *f*. ◇ *vt* **-1.** [gen] encontrar; **she met his gaze defiantly** ela encarou o olhar dele de forma desafiadora **-2.** [by arrangement] encontrar-se com, reunir-se com **-3.** [make acquaintance of] conhecer; **I met a really interesting guy** conheci um cara muito interessante **-4.** [wait for - person] ir esperar; [- train, plane, bus, boat] esperar **-5.** [fulfil, satisfy] satisfazer, cumprir **-6.** [deal with] enfrentar **-7.** [pay] pagar em dia **-8.** [experience, come across] deparar-se com **-9.** [hit, touch] ir de encontro a. ◇ *vi* **-1.** [gen] encontrar-se; **their eyes met across the room** os olhos deles se cruzaram na sala **-2.** [committee] reunir-se **-3.** [become acquainted] conhecer-se **-4.** [hit, touch] bater-se.

◆ **meet up** *vi* [by arrangement] encontrar-se; **to ~ up with sb** encontrar-se com alguém.

◆ **meet with** *vt fus* **-1.** [encounter] experimentar **-2.** *US* [by arrangement] encontrar.

meeting ['mi:tɪŋ] *n* **-1.** [gen] reunião *f* **-2.** [coming together] encontro *m*.

meeting place *n* ponto *m* de encontro.

mega- [megə] *prefix* **-1.** [in measurements] mega **-2.** *inf* [very big] mega.

megabit *n COMPUT* megabit *m*.
megabyte ['megəbaɪt] *n COMPUT* megabyte *m*.
megahertz ['megəhɜ:ts] *n RADIO* megahertz *m*.
megalomania [ˌmegələ'meɪnjəl *n (U)* megalomania *f*.
megalomaniac [ˌmegələ'meɪnɪæk] *n* megalomaníaco *m*, -ca *f*.
megaphone ['megəfəʊn] *n* megafone *m*.
megaton ['megətʌn] *n* megaton *m*.
megawatt ['megəwɒt] *n* megawatt *m*.
melamine ['meləmi:n] *n (U)* melanina *f*.
melancholy ['melənkəlɪ] <> *adj* [sad] melancólico(ca). <> *n (U)* melancolia *f*.
mellow ['meləʊ] <> *adj* **-1.** [gen] suave **-2.** [smooth, pleasant] melodioso(sa) **-3.** [gentle, relaxed] alegre, tranqüilo(la). <> *vt*: **to be ~ed by sthg** sentir-se amadurecido(da) por algo; **to be ~ed by wine** ficar alegre por causa do vinho. <> *vi* [become more gentle or relaxed] suavizar-se, tranqüilizar-se.
melodic [mɪ'lɒdɪk] *adj MUS* melódico(ca).
melodious [mɪ'ləʊdjəs] *adj* melodioso(sa).
melodrama ['melədrɑ:məl *n* melodrama *m*.
melodramatic [ˌmelədrə'mætɪk] *adj* melodramático(ca).
melody ['melədɪ] (*pl* **-ies**) *n* [tune] melodia *f*.
melon ['melən] *n* melão *m*.
melt [melt] <> *vt* **-1.** [make liquid] derreter **-2.** *fig* [soften] amolecer. <> *vi* **-1.** [become liquid] derreter **-2.** *fig* [soften] amolecer **-3.** *fig* [disappear]: **to ~ into sthg** desaparecer em algo, fundir-se em algo; **to ~ away** dissipar-se; **his savings ~ed away** suas economias se acabaram.
◆ **melt down** *vt sep* fundir-se.
meltdown ['meltdaʊn] *n* **-1.** *(U)* [act of melting] fusão *f* **-2.** [incident] acidente *m* nuclear.
melting point ['meltɪŋ-] *n* ponto *m* de fusão.
melting pot ['meltɪŋ-] *n fig* [of cultures, races, ideas] cadinho *m* cultural.
member ['membə[r]] <> *adj* -membro. <> *n* membro *m*.
Member of Congress (*pl* **Members of Congress**) *n US* Membro *m* do Congresso.
Member of Parliament (*pl* **Members of Parliament**) *n* [in UK] Membro *m* do Parlamento.
membership ['membəʃɪp] *n* **-1.** [gen - of party, union] associação *f*; [- of club] qualidade *f* de sócio; **I have to renew my ~** tenho que renovar o meu título **-2.** [number of members] número *m* de sócios **-3.** [people themselves]: **the ~** os sócios, os membros.
membership card *n* carteira *f* de sócio.
membrane ['membreɪn] *n ANAT* membrana *f*.
memento [mɪ'mentəʊ] (*pl* **-s**) *n* lembrança *f*.
memo ['meməʊ] (*pl* **-s**) *n* [at work] memorando *m*.
memoirs ['memwɑ:z] *npl* memórias *fpl*.
memo pad *n* rascunho *m* de memorando.
memorabilia [ˌmemərə'bɪlɪə] *npl* memorabília *f*.
memorable ['memərəbl] *adj* memorável.
memorandum [ˌmemə'rændəm] (*pl* **-da, -dums**) *n fml* memorando *m*.
memorial [mɪ'mɔ:rɪəl] <> *adj* comemorativo(va). <> *n* memorial *m*.
memorize, -ise ['meməraɪz] *vt* memorizar, decorar.
memory ['memərɪ] (*pl* **-ies**) *n* **-1.** [gen] memória *f*; **in ~ of** em memória de; **to lose one's ~** perder a memória; **from ~** de memória; **within living ~** de que se tem memória **-2.** [sthg remembered] lembrança *f*.
memory card *n COMPUT* placa *f* de memória.
men [men] *pl* ▻ **man**.
menace ['menəs] <> *n* **-1.** [gen] ameaça *f* **-2.** *inf* [nuisance, pest] praga *f*. <> *vt* ameaçar.
menacing ['menəsɪŋ] *adj* ameaçador(ra).
menacingly ['menəsɪŋlɪ] *adv* de forma ameaçadora.
menagerie [mɪ'nædʒərɪ] *n* reserva *f* particular de animais selvagens.
mend [mend] <> *n (U) inf*: **to be on the ~** estar convalescendo. <> *vt* [repair] consertar; **to ~ one's ways** corrigir-se.
mending ['mendɪŋ] *n* **-1.** [repairing]: **to do the ~** consertar **-2.** [clothes] roupas *fpl* a consertar.
menfolk ['menfəʊk] *npl* homens *mpl* em geral.
menial ['mi:njəl] *adj* simplório(ria), baixo(xa).
meningitis [ˌmenɪn'dʒaɪtɪs] *n (U) MED* meningite *f*.
menopause ['menəpɔ:z] *n (U)*: **the ~** a menopausa.
menservants ['mensɜ:vənts] *pl* ▻ **manservant**.
men's room *n US*: **the ~** o banheiro dos homens.
menstrual ['menstrʊəl] *adj* menstrual.
menstruate ['menstrʊeɪt] *vi* menstruar.
menstruation [ˌmenstrʊ'eɪʃn] *n (U)* menstruação *f*.
menswear ['menzweə[r]] *n (U)* roupa *f* masculina.
mental ['mentl] *adj* mental.
mental age *n* idade *f* mental.
mental block *n*: **to have a ~ about sthg** ter um bloqueio mental sobre algo.
mental hospital *n* hospital *m* psiquiátrico.
mentality [men'tælətɪ] *n (U)* [way of thinking] mentalidade *f*.
mentally ['mentəlɪ] *adv* mentalmente.
mentally handicapped ['mentəlɪ-] *npl*: **the ~** os deficientes mentais.
◆ **mentally-handicapped** *adj* com deficiência mental.
mental note *n*: **to make a ~ to do sthg** gravar na memória para fazer algo.
menthol ['menθɒl] *n (U)* mentol *m*.
mentholated ['menθəleɪtɪd] *adj* mentolado(da).
mention ['menʃn] <> *vt* [say, talk about] mencionar; **to ~ sthg to sb** mencionar algo para alguém; **not to ~** sem falar em; **don't ~ it!** não tem de quê! <> *n* [reference] menção *f*.
mentor ['mentɔ:[r]] *n fml* mentor *m*, -ra *f*.
menu ['menju:] *n* **-1.** [in restaurant] menu *m*, cardápio *m* **-2.** *COMPUT* menu *m*.
menu-driven *adj COMPUT* orientado(da) por menu.
meow *n & vi US* = **miaow**.
MEP (*abbr of* **Member of the European Parliament**) *n membro do parlamento europeu.*
mercantile ['mɜ:kəntaɪl] *adj* mercantil.

mercenary ['mɜ:sɪnrɪ] (*pl* **-ies**) ◇ *adj* mercenário(ria). ◇ *n* [soldier] mercenário *m*.
merchandise ['mɜ:tʃəndaɪz] *n (U)* COMM mercadoria *f*.
merchant ['mɜ:tʃənt] ◇ *adj* mercantil. ◇ *n* comerciante *mf*.
merchant bank *n UK* banco *m* mercantil.
merchant navy *UK*, **merchant marine** *US n* marinha *f* mercante.
merciful ['mɜ:sɪfʊl] *adj* **-1.** [person] piedoso(sa) **-2.** [death, release] misericordioso(sa).
mercifully ['mɜ:sɪfʊlɪ] *adv* **-1.** [fortunately] graças a Deus **-2.** [with clemency] com clemência.
merciless ['mɜ:sɪlɪs] *adj* impiedoso(sa).
mercilessly ['mɜ:sɪlɪslɪ] *adv* impiedosamente.
mercurial [mɜ:'kjʊərɪəl] *adj literary* volúvel.
mercury ['mɜ:kjʊrɪ] *n (U)* mercúrio *m*.
Mercury ['mɜ:kjʊrɪ] *n* [planet] Mercúrio.
mercy ['mɜ:sɪ] (*pl* **-ies**) *n* **-1.** *(U)* [kindness, pity] piedade *f*; **at the ~ of** *fig* à mercê de **-2.** [blessing] bênção *f*.
mercy killing *n* eutanásia *f*.
mere [mɪəʳ] *adj* **-1.** [just, no more than] mero(ra); **she's a ~ child!** ela é só uma criança! **-2.** [for emphasis] simples, mero(ra) **-3.** [amount, quantity] apenas.
merely ['mɪəlɪ] *adv* **-1.** [simply, just, only] meramente, simplesmente **-2.** [of amount, quantity] apenas.
meretricious *adj fml* falacioso(sa).
merge [mɜ:dʒ] ◇ *n* COMPUT intercalamento *m*. ◇ *vt* **-1.** COMM fundir **-2.** COMPUT intercalar. ◇ *vi* **-1.** COMM fundir-se; **to ~ with sthg** unir-se com algo **-2.** [roads, lines] unir-se **-3.** [blend, melt] misturar; **to ~ into sthg** incorporar-se em algo.
merger ['mɜ:dʒəʳ] *n* COMM fusão *f*.
meridian [mə'rɪdɪən] *n* GEOGR meridiano *m*.
meringue [mə'ræŋ] *n* merengue *m*.
merino [mə'ri:nəʊ] *adj* merino(na).
merit ['merɪt] ◇ *n (U)* [value] mérito *m*. ◇ *vt* merecer.
◆ **merits** *npl* [advantages, qualities] méritos *mpl*; **to judge sthg on its ~s** julgar algo por seus méritos.
meritocracy [ˌmerɪ'tɒkrəsɪ] (*pl* **-ies**) *n* [system] meritocracia *f*.
mermaid ['mɜ:meɪd] *n* sereia *f*.
merrily ['merɪlɪ] *adv* **-1.** [gen] divertidamente **-2.** *iro* [blithely] alegremente.
merriment ['merɪmənt] *n (U) literary* [laughter] risadas *fpl*.
merry ['merɪ] (*compar* **-ier**, *superl* **-iest**) *adj* **-1.** *literary* [laugh, joke, person] alegre, divertido(da) **-2.** [fire, party] agradável; **Merry Christmas!** Feliz Natal! **-3.** *inf* [tipsy] alegre.
merry-go-round *n* carrossel *m*.
merrymaking ['merɪˌmeɪkɪŋ] *n (U) literary* pândega *f*, folia *f*.
mesh [meʃ] ◇ *n (U)* [netting] malha *f*. ◇ *vi* **-1.** [fit together] combinar **-2.** TECH encaixar.
mesmerize, -ise ['mezməraɪz] *vt*: **to be ~d by sb/sthg** ser hipnotizado(da) por alguém/algo.
mess [mes] *n* **-1.** [gen] bagunça *f*; **to be (in) a ~** estar uma bagunça, estar de pernas para o ar **-2.** [muddle, problem] confusão *f* **-3.** MIL rancho *m*.
◆ **mess about, mess around** *inf* ◇ *vt sep* embromar. ◇ *vi* **-1.** [gen] matar tempo **-2.** [tinker]: **to ~ about with sthg** mexer em algo.
◆ **mess up** *vt sep inf* **-1.** [make untidy, dirty - room, papers, objects] bagunçar; [- clothes] sujar **-2.** [spoil] estragar.
◆ **mess with** *vt fus inf* meter-se com.
message ['mesɪdʒ] *n* **-1.** [piece of information] mensagem *f* **-2.** [idea, moral] moral *m* **-3.** *phr*: **to get the ~** *inf* receber o recado.
message switching *n* COMPUT comutação *f* de mensagem.
messenger ['mesɪndʒəʳ] *n* mensageiro *m*, -ra *f*; **by ~** por mensageiro.
Messiah [mɪ'saɪə] *n*: **the ~** o Messias.
Messrs, Messrs. ['mesəz] (*abbr of* **messieurs**) Srs.
messy ['mesɪ] (*compar* **-ier**, *superl* **-iest**) *adj* **-1.** [dirty, untidy] desarrumado(da) **-2.** [person, activity] confuso(sa) **-3.** [job] sujo(ja) **-4.** *inf* [complicated, confused] complicado(da).
met [met] *pt & pp* ▷ **meet**.
Met [met] (*abbr of* **Metropolitan Opera**) *n*: **the ~** *a Ópera Metropolitana de Nova Iorque*.
metabolism [mə'tæbəlɪzm] *n* metabolismo *m*.
metal ['metl] ◇ *n* metal *m*. ◇ *adj* de metal.
metallic [mɪ'tælɪk] *adj* **-1.** [gen] metálico(ca) **-2.** TECH [of metal] metalífero(ra).
metallurgist *n* metalúrgico *m*, -ca *f*.
metallurgy [mə'tælədʒɪ] *n (U)* metalurgia *f*.
metalwork ['metəlwɜ:k] *n (U)* [craft] trabalho *m* em metal.
metalworker ['metəlˌwɜ:kəʳ] *n* metalurgista *mf*.
metamorphose [ˌmetə'mɔ:fəʊz] *vi*: **to ~ (into sthg)** metamorfosear-se (em algo).
metamorphosis [ˌmetə'mɔ:fəsɪs, ˌmetəmɔ:'fəʊsɪs] (*pl* **-phoses** [-si:z]) *n* metamorfose *f*.
metaphor ['metəfəʳ] *n* metáfora *f*.
metaphorical [ˌmetə'fɒrɪkl] *adj* metafórico(ca).
metaphysical [ˌmetə'fɪzɪkl] *adj* PHILOSOPHY metafísico(ca).
metaphysics [ˌmetə'fɪzɪks] *n (U)* metafísica *f*.
mete [mi:t] ◆ **mete out** *vt sep*: **to ~ sthg out to sb** impor algo a alguém.
meteor ['mi:tɪəʳ] *n* meteoro *m*.
meteoric [mi:tɪ'ɒrɪk] *adj fig* [rapid] meteórico(ca).
meteorite ['mi:tjəraɪt] *n* meteorito *m*.
meteorological [ˌmi:tjərə'lɒdʒɪkl] *adj* meteorológico(ca).
meteorologist [ˌmi:tjə'rɒlədʒɪst] *n* meteorologista *mf*.
meteorology [ˌmi:tjə'rɒlədʒɪ] *n (U)* meteorologia *f*.
meter ['mi:təʳ] ◇ *n* **-1.** [device] medidor *m*; **taxi ~** taxímetro *m*; **electricity ~** relógio *m* de luz; **parking ~** parquímetro *m* **-2.** *US* = **metre**. ◇ *vt* [measure] medir.
methadone ['meθədəʊn] *n (U)* metadona *f*.
methane ['mi:θeɪn] *n (U)* metano *m*.
method ['meθəd] *n* [way, system] método *m*.
methodical [mɪ'θɒdɪkl] *adj* metódico(ca).
methodically [mɪ'θɒdɪklɪ] *adv* metodicamente.
Methodist ['meθədɪst] ◇ *adj* metodista. ◇ *n* metodista *mf*.

methodology [ˌmeθəˈdɒlədʒɪ] (*pl* **-ies**) *n fml* metodologia *f*.
meths [meθs] *n UK inf* álcool *m* metilado.
methylated spirits [ˈmeθɪleɪtɪd-] *n (U)* álcool *m* metilado.
meticulous [mɪˈtɪkjʊləs] *adj* meticuloso(sa).
meticulously [mɪˈtɪkjʊləslɪ] *adv* meticulosamente.
Met Office (*abbr of* **Meteorological Office**) *n* *instituto britânico de meteorologia.*
metre *UK*, **meter** *US* [ˈmiːtəʳ] *n* **-1.** [unit of measurement] metro *m* **-2.** [in poetry] métrica *f*.
metric [ˈmetrɪk] *adj* métrico(ca).
metrication [ˌmetrɪˈkeɪʃn] *n UK* conversão *f* ao sistema métrico.
metric system *n*: **the ~** o sistema métrico.
metric ton *n* tonelada *f* métrica.
metro [ˈmetrəʊ] (*pl* **-s**) *n* metrô *m*.
metronome [ˈmetrənəʊm] *n* metrônomo *m*.
metropolis [mɪˈtrɒpəlɪs] (*pl* **-es**) *n* [large city] metrópole *f*.
metropolitan [ˌmetrəˈpɒlɪtn] *adj* [of a metropolis] metropolitano(na).
Metropolitan Police *npl*: **the ~** a Polícia de Londres.
mettle [ˈmetl] *n (U)*: **to be on one's ~** estar preparado(da) para agir da melhor forma possível; **to show** *OR* **prove one's ~** provar seu próprio valor.
mew [mjuː] *n & vi* = **miaow**.
mews [mjuːz] (*pl inv*) *n UK* estrebaria *f*.
Mexican [ˈmeksɪkn] ◇ *adj* mexicano(na). ◇ *n* mexicano *m*, -na *f*.
Mexico [ˈmeksɪkəʊ] *n* México; **in ~** no México.
Mexico City *n* Cidade *f* do México.
mezzanine [ˈmetsəniːn] *n* mezanino *m*.
MFA (*abbr of* **Master of Fine Arts**) *n (titular de) bacharelado em belas artes.*
mfr (*abbr of* **manufacturer**) fabr. *mf*.
mg (*abbr of* **milligram**) mg.
Mgr -1. (*abbr of* **Monseigneur, Monsignor**) Mons. **-2.** (*abbr of* **manager**) gerente *mf*.
MHR (*abbr of* **Member of the House of Representatives**) *n membro do congresso norte-americano,* ≃ deputado *m*, -da *f* federal.
MHz (*abbr of* **megahertz**) MHz.
MI *abbr of* **Michigan**.
MI5 (*abbr of* **Military Intelligence 5**) *n órgão do serviço secreto britânico de contra-espionagem.*
MI6 (*abbr of* **Military Intelligence 6**) *n órgão do serviço secreto britânico de espionagem.*
MIA (*abbr of* **missing in action**) *US desaparecido em combate.*
miaow *UK* [miːˈaʊ], **meow** *US* [mɪˈaʊ] ◇ *n* miado *m*, miau *m*. ◇ *vi* miar.
mice [maɪs] *pl* ▷ **mouse**.
Mich. *abbr of* **Michigan**.
Michigan [ˈmɪʃɪgən] *n* Michigan; **in ~** em Michigan.
mickey [ˈmɪkɪ] *n*: **to take the ~ out of sb** *UK inf* tirar sarro de alguém.
MICR (*abbr of* **magnetic ink character recognition**) *n* MICR *f*.
micro [ˈmaɪkrəʊ] (*pl* **-s**) *n* micro *m*.
micro- [ˈmaɪkrəʊ] *prefix* micro.
microbe [ˈmaɪkrəʊb] *n* micróbio *m*.
microbiologist [ˌmaɪkrəʊbaɪˈɒlədʒɪst] *n* microbiologista *mf*.
microbiology [ˌmaɪkrəʊbaɪˈɒlədʒɪ] *n (U)* microbiologia *f*.
microchip [ˈmaɪkrəʊtʃɪp] *n* microchip *m*.
microcircuit [ˈmaɪkrəʊˌsɜːkɪt] *n* microcircuito *m*.
microclimate *n* microclima *m*.
microcomputer [ˌmaɪkrəʊkəmˈpjuːtəʳ] *n* microcomputador *m*.
microcosm [ˈmaɪkrəkɒzm] *n* microcosmo *m*.
microfiche [ˈmaɪkrəʊfiːʃ] (*pl inv OR* **-s**) *n* microficha *f*.
microfilm [ˈmaɪkrəʊfɪlm] *n* microfilme *m*.
microlight [ˈmaɪkrəlaɪt] *n* ultraleve *m*.
micron [ˈmaɪkrɒn] *n* mícron *m*.
microorganism [ˌmaɪkrəʊˈɔːgənɪzm] *n* microorganismo *m*.
microphone [ˈmaɪkrəfəʊn] *n* microfone *m*.
microprocessor [ˈmaɪkrəʊˌprəʊsesəʳ] *n* microprocessador *m*.
micro scooter *n* patinete *m*.
microscope [ˈmaɪkrəskəʊp] *n* microscópio *m*.
microscopic [ˌmaɪkrəˈskɒpɪk] *adj* **-1.** [very small] microscópico(ca) **-2.** [detailed] minucioso(sa).
microsecond *n* microssegundo *m*.
microsurgery [ˌmaɪkrəˈsɜːdʒərɪ] *n (U)* microcirurgia *f*.
microwave (oven) *n* forno *m* de microondas.
mid- [mɪd] *prefix*: **~height** de meia altura; **in ~morning** no meio da manhã; **in ~August** em meados de agosto; **in ~winter** em pleno inverno; **she's in her ~ twenties** ela tem uns vinte e poucos anos.
midair [mɪdˈeəʳ] ◇ *adj* no ar. ◇ *n (U)*: **in ~** no ar.
midday [ˈmɪddeɪ] *n (U)* meio-dia *m*.
middle [ˈmɪdl] ◇ *adj* **-1.** [centre] do meio **-2.** [in time]: **he was in his ~ forties** ele estava nos seus quarenta e poucos anos. ◇ *n* **-1.** [centre] meio *m*, centro *m*; **in the ~ (of sthg)** no meio (de algo); **in the ~ of nowhere** no meio do nada **-2.** [in time] meio *m*; **to be in the ~ of sthg** estar no meio de algo; **to be in the ~ of doing sthg** estar fazendo algo; **in the ~ of the night** no meio da noite, em plena madrugada; **in the ~ of September** em meados de setembro **-3.** [waist] cintura *f*.
middle age *n (U)* meia-idade *f*.
middle-aged *adj* de meia-idade.
Middle Ages *npl*: **the ~** a Idade Média.
middle-class *adj* da classe média.
middle classes *npl*: **the ~** a classe média.
middle distance *n*: **in the ~** em segundo plano.
Middle East *n*: **the ~** o Oriente Médio.
Middle Eastern *adj* do Oriente Médio.
middle finger *n* dedo *m* médio.
middleman [ˈmɪdlmæn] (*pl* **-men** [-men]) *n* intermediário *m*.
middle management *n (U)* administração *f* intermediária.

middle name *n* segundo nome *m (num nome composto).*
middle-of-the-road *adj* moderado(da).
middle school *n UK escola para crianças de 9 a 13 anos.*
middleweight ['mɪdlweɪt] *n* peso *m* médio.
middling ['mɪdlɪŋ] *adj* médio(dia), regular.
Mideast *n US*: **the** ~ o Oriente Médio.
midfield [,mɪd'fi:ld] *n FTBL* meio-campo *m.*
midge [mɪdʒ] *n* mosquito-pólvora *m.*
midget ['mɪdʒɪt] *n* anão *m*, -nã *f.*
MIDI (*abbr of* **musical instrument digital interface**) *n* MIDI *f.*
midi system ['mɪdɪ-] *n* sistema *m* MIDI.
Midlands ['mɪdləndz] *npl*: **the** ~ *a região central da Inglaterra.*
midnight ['mɪdnaɪt] <> *n (U)* meia-noite *f.* <> *comp* da meia-noite.
midriff ['mɪdrɪf] *n* diafragma *m.*
midst [mɪdst] *n* [in space, time]: **in the** ~ **of** *literary* no meio de; **in our** ~ entre nós.
midstream [mɪd'stri:m] *n* **-1.** [of river]: **in** ~ no meio da corrente **-2.** *fig* [when talking]: **in** ~ no meio da conversa.
midsummer ['mɪd,sʌmə^r] *n (U)* pleno verão *m.*
Midsummer Day *n* Dia *m* de São João *(24 de junho).*
midway [,mɪd'weɪ] *adv* **-1.** [in space]: ~ **(between)** a meio caminho (entre) **-2.** [in time]: ~ **(through)** na metade (de).
midweek [*adj* mɪd'wi:k, *adv* 'mɪdwi:k] <> *adj* do meio da semana. <> *adv* no meio da semana.
Midwest [,mɪd'west] *n*: **the** ~ o Meio Oeste *(dos Estados Unidos).*
Midwestern [,mɪd'westən] *adj* do Meio-Oeste *(dos Estados Unidos).*
midwife ['mɪdwaɪf] (*pl* **-wives** [-waɪvz]) *n* parteira *f.*
midwifery ['mɪd,wɪfərɪ] *n (U)* trabalho *m* de parteira.
miffed [mɪft] *adj inf* amuado(da).
might [maɪt] <> *modal vb* **-1.** [expressing possibility]: **I think I** ~ **go to the pub tonight** acho que é possível eu ir ao bar hoje; **he** ~ **be armed** ele poderia estar armado **-2.** [expressing suggestion]: **you** ~ **have told me** você poderia ter me contado; **it** ~ **be better to wait** talvez fosse melhor esperar **-3.** *(past tense of may) fml* [asking permission]: **he asked if he** ~ **leave the room** ele me pediu permissão para sair da sala **-4.** [in polite questions, suggestions]: ~ **I ...?** podia ...? **-5.** [contradicting a point of view]: **you** ~ **well be right, but ...** é bem possível que você tenha razão, mas ... **-6.** *phr*: **I** ~ **have known** *OR* **guessed** eu deveria ter suspeitado. <> *n* **-1.** [power] poder *m* **-2.** [physical strength] força *f.*
mightn't ['maɪtənt] = **might not.**
might've ['maɪtəv] = **might have.**
mighty ['maɪtɪ] (*compar* **-ier**, *superl* **-iest**) <> *adj* **-1.** [powerful] poderoso(sa) **-2.** [very large] enorme. <> *adv US inf* muito.
migraine ['mi:greɪn, 'maɪgreɪn] *n* enxaqueca *f.*
migrant ['maɪgrənt] <> *adj* **-1.** [bird, animal] migratório(ria) **-2.** [worker] migrante. <> *n* **-1.** [bird, animal] migratório *m*, -ria *f* **-2.** [person] emigrante *mf.*
migrate [*UK* maɪ'greɪt, *US* 'maɪgreɪt] *vi* **-1.** [bird, animal] migrar **-2.** [person] emigrar.
migration [maɪ'greɪʃn] *n* **-1.** [of birds, animals] migração *f* **-2.** [of people] emigração *f.*
migratory ['maɪgrətrɪ] *adj* [bird, animal] migratório(-ria).
mike [maɪk] (*abbr of* **microphone**) *n inf* mike *m.*
mild [maɪld] <> *adj* **-1.** [food, shampoo, sedative] suave **-2.** [person, manner] sereno(na) **-3.** [weather] temperado(da) **-4.** [surprise, criticism, reproach] moderado(da) **-5.** [illness] leve. <> *n tipo de cerveja suave.*
mildew ['mɪldju:] *n* **-1.** *(U)* [gen] mofo *m* **-2.** *(U) BOT* míldio *m.*
mildly ['maɪldlɪ] *adv* **-1.** [talk, complain, criticize] moderadamente; **to put it** ~ para não dizer coisa pior **-2.** [slightly] bastante.
mild-mannered *adj* gentil, educado(da).
mildness ['maɪldnɪs] *n* **-1.** [of food, shampoo, sedative] suavidade *f* **-2.** [of person, manner] serenidade *f* **-3.** [of weather] calmaria *f* **-4.** [of criticism, reproach] moderação *f.*
mile [maɪl] *n* milha *f*; **we could see for** ~**s** conseguíamos ver quilômetros à frente; **to be** ~**s away** *fig* estar bem longe.
◆ **miles** *adv (in comparisons)* muito; **this is** ~ **better** sem dúvida alguma isto é realmente melhor.
mileage ['maɪlɪdʒ] *n* **-1.** [distance travelled] quilometragem *f* **-2.** *(U) inf* [advantage] vantagem *f.*
mileage allowance *n* pagamento *m* por quilômetros rodados.
mileometer [maɪ'lɒmɪtə^r] *n* odômetro *m.*
milestone ['maɪlstəʊn] *n* **-1.** [marker stone] marco *m* miliário **-2.** *fig* [event] marco *m.*
milieu [*UK* 'mi:ljɜ:, *US* mi:l'ju:] (*pl* **-s** *OR* **-x**) *n* meio *m* (social).
militant ['mɪlɪtənt] <> *adj* militante. <> *n* militante *mf.*
militarism ['mɪlɪtərɪzm] *n (U)* militarismo *m.*
militarist ['mɪlɪtərɪst] *n* militarista *mf.*
militarized zone, militarised zone ['mɪlɪtəraɪzd-] *n* zona *f* militarizada.
military ['mɪlɪtrɪ] <> *adj* militar. <> *n*: **the** ~ as forças armadas, os militares.
military police *npl* polícia *f* militar.
militate ['mɪlɪteɪt] *vi fml*: **to** ~ **against sthg** militar contra algo.
militia [mɪ'lɪʃə] *n* milícia *f.*
milk [mɪlk] <> *n* leite *m.* <> *vt* **-1.** [get milk from] ordenhar **-2.** *fig* [use for one's own ends] explorar.
milk chocolate <> *n (U)* chocolate *m* ao leite. <> *comp* de chocolate ao leite.
milk float *UK*, **milk truck** *US n veículo usado na entrega domiciliar do leite.*
milking ['mɪlkɪŋ] *n (U)* ordenha *f.*
milkman ['mɪlkmən] (*pl* **-men** [-mən]) *n* leiteiro *m.*
milk round *n UK* **-1.** [by milkman] entrega *f* de leite **-2.** *UNIV* [recruitment drive] recrutamento *m* de pessoal.
milk shake *n* milk-shake *m.*
milk tooth *n* dente-de-leite *m.*

milk truck *n US* = **milk float**.
milky ['mɪlkɪ] (*compar* **-ier**, *superl* **-iest**) *adj* **-1.** *UK* [with milk] com leite **-2.** [like milk] leitoso(sa) **-3.** [pale white] pálido(da).
Milky Way *n*: **the ~** a Via Láctea.
mill [mɪl] <> *n* **-1.** [flour mill] moinho *m* **-2.** [factory] fábrica *f* **-3.** [grinder] moedor *m*. <> *vt* [grain] moer.
◆ **mill about, mill around** *vi* aglomerar-se.
millennium [mɪ'lenɪəm] (*pl* **-nnia** [-nɪəl]) *n* [thousand years] milênio *m*.
miller ['mɪlə^r] *n* moleiro *m*, -ra *f*.
millet ['mɪlɪt] *n* painço *m*.
milli- ['mɪlɪ] *prefix* mili.
millibar ['mɪlɪbɑ:^r] *n* milibar *m*.
milligram(me) ['mɪlɪgræm] *n* miligrama *m*.
millilitre *UK*, **milliliter** *US* ['mɪlɪ,li:tə^r] *n* mililitro *m*.
millimetre *UK*, **millimeter** *US* ['mɪlɪ,mi:tə^r] *n* milímetro *m*.
millinery ['mɪlɪnrɪ] *n (U)* chapelaria *f (para senhoras)*.
million ['mɪljən] *n* **-1.** [1,000,000] milhão *m* **-2.** [enormous number]: **a ~**, **~s of** milhões de.
millionaire [,mɪljə'neə^r] *n* milionário *m*, -ria *f*.
millionairess [,mɪljə'neərɪs] *n* milionária *f*.
millipede ['mɪlɪpi:d] *n* embuá *m*.
millisecond ['mɪlɪ,sekənd] *n* milissegundo *m*.
millstone ['mɪlstəʊn] *n* [for grinding] pedra *f* de moinho; **a ~ round one's neck** *fig* um grande peso sobre os ombros.
millwheel ['mɪlwi:l] *n* roda *f* de azenha.
milometer [maɪ'lɒmɪtə^r] *n* = **mileometer**.
mime [maɪm] <> *n (U)* mímica *f*. <> *vt* imitar. <> *vi* fazer mímica.
mimic ['mɪmɪk] (*pt* & *pp* **-ked**, *cont* **-king**) <> *n* [person] imitador *m*, -ra *f*. <> *vt* [person, voice, gestures] imitar.
mimicry ['mɪmɪkrɪ] *n (U)* imitação *f*.
mimosa [mɪ'məʊzə] *n* mimosa *f*.
min. [mɪn] **-1.** (*abbr of* **minute**) min. **-2.** (*abbr of* **minimum**) mín.
Min. (*abbr of* **ministry**) Min.
mince [mɪns] <> *n (U) UK* carne *f* picada. <> *vt* picar; **not to ~ one's words** não ter papas na língua. <> *vi* andar com passinhos.
mincemeat ['mɪnsmi:t] *n (U)* **-1.** [fruit] *iguaria feita de sebo, frutas cristalizadas e passas* **-2.** *US* [minced meat] picadinho *m*.
mince pie *n torta com recheio de frutas secas preparada geralmente no Natal.*
mincer ['mɪnsə^r] *n* moedor *m* de carne.
mind [maɪnd] <> *n* **-1.** [gen] mente *f*; **great ~s think alike** duas cabeças pensam melhor que uma; **to broaden one's ~** ampliar os horizontes de alguém; **state of ~** estado de espírito **-2.** [thoughts] memória *f*; **to come into/cross sb's ~** passar pela cabeça de alguém; **to have sthg on one's ~** estar peocupado(da) com algo; **to take sb's ~ off sthg** fazer alguém esquecer algo; **that was a load** *OR* **weight off my ~** isso tirou um peso da minha consciência; **to put** *OR* **set sb's ~ at rest** tranqüilizar alguém **-3.** [attention]: **to concentrate the ~** concentrar a mente; **to keep one's ~ on sthg** concentrar-se em algo; **to put one's ~ to sthg** colocar empenho em algo **-4.** [opinion]: **to my ~** na minha opinião; **to change one's ~** mudar de idéia; **to keep an open ~** manter a mente aberta; **to make one's ~ up** tomar uma decisão; **to speak one's ~** dizer o que se pensa; **to be in two ~s about sthg** estar com dois corações sobre algo **-5.** [memory] memória *f*; **to bear sthg in ~** ter algo em mente; **to call sthg to ~** trazer algo à memória; **to cast one's ~ back** pensar no que já aconteceu *(no passado)*; **to slip one's ~** fugir da memória **-6.** [intention]: **to have sthg in ~** ter algo em mente; **to have a ~ to do sthg** estar pensando em fazer algo. <> *vi* **-1.** [care, worry] importar-se; **do you ~ if ...?** você se importaria se ...?; **I don't ~** eu não me importo; **never ~** [don't worry] não faz mal; [it's not important] não tem importância **-2.** [be careful]: **~ out!** *UK* cuidado! <> *vt* **-1.** [object to] importar-se em; **I don't ~ waiting** não me importo em esperar; **I wouldn't ~ a ...** eu aceitaria um ... **-2.** [bother about] preocupar-se com **-3.** [pay attention to] prestar atenção com **-4.** [take care of] tomar conta de.
◆ **mind you** *adv*: **he didn't give me a Christmas present this year - ~, he never does** ele não me deu um presente de Natal neste ano - bom, mas ele nunca dá mesmo.
mind-bending *adj inf* confuso(sa).
minder ['maɪndə^r] *n* **-1.** [of child] pessoa *f* que cuida de crianças **-2.** *UK* [bodyguard] guarda-costas *m inv*.
mindful ['maɪndfʊl] *adj*: **~ of sthg** ciente de algo.
mindless ['maɪndlɪs] *adj* **-1.** [stupid] absurdo(da), sem sentido **-2.** [not requiring thought] tedioso(sa).
mind reader *n*: **I'm not a ~!** eu não leio pensamentos!
mindset ['maɪndset] *n* mentalidade *f*.
mind's eye *n*: **in one's ~** na imaginação de alguém.
mine¹ [maɪn] <> *n* **-1.** [gen] mina *f* **-2.** [source]: **a ~ of information** uma fonte de informação. <> *vt* **-1.** [excavate] extrair **-2.** [lay mines in] minar.
mine² [maɪn] *poss pron* o meu (a minha); **a friend of mine** um amigo meu; **those shoes are mine** esses sapatos são meus; **mine are here - where are yours?** os meus estão aqui - onde estão os seus?
mine detector *n* detector *m* de minas.
minefield ['maɪnfi:ld] *n* **-1.** [area containing mines] campo *m* minado **-2.** *fig* [dangerous topic] campo *m* minado.
minelayer ['maɪn,leɪə^r] *n* lança-minas *m inv*.
miner ['maɪnə^r] *n* mineiro *m*, -ra *f*.
mineral ['mɪnərəl] <> *adj GEOL* mineral. <> *n GEOL* mineral *m*.
mineralogy [,mɪnə'rælədʒɪ] *n (U)* mineralogia *f*.
mineral water *n (U)* água *f* mineral.
minestrone [,mɪnɪ'strəʊnɪ] *n (U)* sopa *f* minestrone.
minesweeper ['maɪn,swi:pə^r] *n* caça-minas *m inv*.
mingle ['mɪŋgl] <> *vt*: **to ~ sthg with sthg** misturar algo com algo. <> *vi* **-1.** [combine] misturar-se; **to ~ with sthg** misturar-se com algo **-2.** [socially] misturar-se; **to ~ with sb** misturar-se com alguém.

mini ['mɪnɪ] *n* [skirt, dress] minissaia *f*.
miniature ['mɪnətʃəʳ] ◇ *adj* [reduced-scale] em miniatura. ◇ *n* **-1.** [painting] miniatura *f* **-2.** [of alcohol] garrafa *f* em miniatura **-3.** [small scale]: **in ~** em miniatura.
minibus ['mɪnɪbʌs] (*pl* **-es**) *n* microônibus *m inv*.
minicab ['mɪnɪkæb] *n UK* radiotáxi *m*.
minicomputer [,mɪnɪkəm'pju:təʳ] *n* minicomputador *m*.
MiniDisc® ['mɪdɪsk] *n* MiniDisc® *m*.
MiniDisc player® *n* reprodutor *m* de MiniDisc®.
minidish [m'ɪnɪdɪʃ] *n* miniparabólica *f*.
minim ['mɪnɪm] *n MUS* mínima *f*.
minima ['mɪnɪmə] *pl* ▷ **minimum**.
minimal ['mɪnɪml] *adj* mínimo(ma).
minimize, -ise ['mɪnɪ,maɪz] *vt* [reduce] minimizar.
minimum ['mɪnɪməm] (*pl* **-mums** OR **-ma**) ◇ *adj* mínimo(ma). ◇ *n* mínimo *m*.
minimum lending rate [-'lendɪŋ-] *n* taxa *f* mínima de empréstimo.
minimum wage *n* salário *m* mínimo.
mining ['maɪnɪŋ] ◇ *adj* mineiro(ra); **~ engineer** engenheiro *m*, -ra *f* de minas. ◇ *n* mineração *f*.
minion ['mɪnjən] *n hum or pej* lacaio *m*, -a *f*.
miniseries ['mɪnɪsɪərɪz] (*pl inv*) *n* minissérie *f*.
miniskirt ['mɪnɪskɜ:t] *n* minissaia *f*.
minister ['mɪnɪstəʳ] *n* **-1.** *POL*: **~ (for sthg)** ministro *m*, -tra *f* (de algo) **-2.** *RELIG* pastor *m*, -ra *f*.
◆ **minister to** *vt fus* **-1.** [person] atender **-2.** [needs] atender a.
ministerial [,mɪnɪ'stɪərɪəl] *adj POL* ministerial.
minister of state *n*: **~ (for sthg)** secretário *m*, -ria *f* de estado (para algo).
ministry ['mɪnɪstrɪ] (*pl* **-ies**) *n* **-1.** *POL* ministério *m*; **Ministry of Defence** Ministério da Defesa **-2.** *RELIG* [clergy]: **the ~** o sacerdócio.
mink [mɪŋk] (*pl inv*) *n* **-1.** *(U)* [fur] pele *f* de visom **-2.** [animal] visom *m*.
mink coat *n* casaco *m* de visom.
Minnesota [,mɪnɪ'səʊtəl *n* Minnesota; **in ~** em Minnesota.
minnow ['mɪnəʊ] *n* [fish] peixinho *m (de água doce)*.
minor ['maɪnəʳ] ◇ *adj* [gen] menor. ◇ *n* [in age] menor *mf* de idade.
Minorca [mɪ'nɔ:kə] *n* Minorca; **in ~** em Minorca.
minority [maɪ'nɒrətɪ] (*pl* **-ies**) ◇ *adj* minoritário(-ria). ◇ *n* [gen] minoria *f*; **to be in a** OR **the ~** estar em minoria, ser minoria.
minority government *n* governo *m* minoritário.
minor road *n* caminho *m* secundário.
minster ['mɪnstəʳ] *n* catedral *f*.
minstrel ['mɪnstrəl] *n* menestrel *m*.
mint [mɪnt] ◇ *n* **-1.** *(U)* [herb] hortelã *f* **-2.** [sweet] bala *f* de hortelã **-3.** [for coins]: **the Mint** a Casa da Moeda; **in ~ condition** novo(va) em folha. ◇ *vt* [coins] cunhar.
mint sauce *n (U)* molho *m* de hortelã.
minuet [,mɪnjʊ'et] *n* minueto *m*.
minus ['maɪnəs] (*pl* **-es**) ◇ *prep* **-1.** *MATH* [less]: **4 ~ 2 is 2** 4 menos 2 é 2 **-2.** [in temperatures]: **it's ~ 5 degrees** está fazendo 5 graus abaixo de zero. ◇ *adj* **-1.** *MATH* [less than zero] negativo(va) **-2.** *SCH* [in grades] menos. ◇ *n* **-1.** *MATH* sinal *m* de menos **-2.** [disadvantage] desvantagem *f*.
minuscule ['mɪnəskju:l] *adj* minúsculo(la).
minus sign *n* sinal *m* de menos.
minute¹ ['mɪnɪt] *n* [gen] minuto *m*; **at any ~** a qualquer momento; **at the last ~** no último minuto; **this ~** agora mesmo; **up to the ~** [news, design] de última hora; [technology] de ponta; **wait a ~!** espere um pouco!
◆ **minutes** *npl* [of meeting] ata *f*.
minute² [maɪ'nju:t] *adj* [tiny] mínimo(ma).
minutiae [maɪ'nju:ʃɪaɪ] *npl* minúcias *fpl*.
miracle ['mɪrəkl] *n* milagre *m*.
miraculous [mɪ'rækjʊləs] *adj* milagroso(sa).
miraculously [mɪ'rækjʊləslɪ] *adv fig* [surprisingly] milagrosamente.
mirage [mɪ'rɑ:ʒ] *n* miragem *f*.
mire [maɪəʳ] *n (U)* lamaçal *m*.
mirror ['mɪrəʳ] ◇ *n* espelho *m*. ◇ *vt* **-1.** [copy] espelhar **-2.** *literary* [reflect] refletir.
mirror image *n* imagem *f* refletida.
mirth [mɜ:θ] *n (U) literary* alegria *f*.
misadventure [,mɪsəd'ventʃəʳ] *n fml* [unfortunate accident] desventura *f*; **death by ~** *JUR* morte *f* acidental.
misanthropist [mɪs'ænθrəpɪst] *n* misantropo *m*, -pa *f*.
misapplication *n* má aplicação *f*, abuso *m*.
misapprehension ['mɪs,æprɪ'henʃn] *n* mal-entendido *m*.
misappropriate [,mɪsə'prəʊprɪeɪt] *vt* desviar.
misappropriation ['mɪsə,prəʊprɪ'eɪʃn] *n* desvio *m*.
misbehave [,mɪsbɪ'heɪv] *vi* comportar-se mal.
misbehaviour *UK*, **misbehavior** *US* [,mɪsbɪ'heɪvjəʳ] *n (U)* mau comportamento *m*, má conduta *f*.
misc (*abbr of* **miscellaneous**) variado(da).
miscalculate [,mɪs'kælkjʊleɪt] *vt & vi* calcular mal.
miscalculation [,mɪskælkjʊ'leɪʃn] *n* erro *m* de cálculo.
miscarriage [,mɪs'kærɪdʒ] *n* aborto *m* natural.
miscarriage of justice *n* erro *m* judicial.
miscarry [,mɪs'kærɪ] (*pt & pp* **-ied**) *vi* **-1.** [woman] abortar naturalmente **-2.** [plan] fracassar.
miscellaneous [,mɪsə'leɪnjəs] *adj* diverso(sa).
miscellany [*UK* mɪ'selənɪ, *US* 'mɪsəleɪnɪ] (*pl* **-ies**) *n* miscelânea *f*.
mischance [,mɪs'tʃɑ:ns] *n fml* azar *m*, infortúnio *m*; **by ~** por azar.
mischief ['mɪstʃɪf] *n (U)* **-1.** [playfulness] malícia *f* **-2.** [naughty behaviour] travessuras *fpl* **-3.** [harm] dano *m*.
mischievous ['mɪstʃɪvəs] *adj* **-1.** [playful] cheio (cheia) de malícia **-2.** [naughty] travesso(sa).
misconceived [,mɪskən'si:vd] *adj* [plan, idea] mal concebido(da).
misconception [,mɪskən'sepʃn] *n* conceito *m* falho, idéia *f* equivocada.
misconduct [,mɪs'kɒndʌkt] *n* [bad behaviour] má conduta *f*.

misconstrue [ˌmɪskən'struː] *vt fml* interpretar erroneamente.
miscount [ˌmɪs'kaʊnt] *vt & vi* contar mal.
misdeed [ˌmɪs'diːd] *n literary* delito *m*.
misdemeanour *UK*, **misdemeanor** *US* [ˌmɪsdɪ'miːnəʳ] *n JUR* contravenção *f*.
misdirected [ˌmɪsdɪ'rektɪd] *adj* **-1.** [letter] mal endereçado(da) **-2.** [misused] mal dirigido(da).
miser ['maɪzəʳ] *n* avarento *m*, -ta *f*.
miserable ['mɪzrəbl] *adj* **-1.** [unhappy] infeliz, triste **-2.** [depressing - conditions, life] miserável; [- weather, holiday, evening] horrível **-3.** [failure] lamentável.
miserably ['mɪzrəblɪ] *adv* **-1.** [unhappily] tristemente **-2.** [in depressing fashion] miseravelmente **-3.** [fail] de forma lamentável.
miserly ['maɪzəlɪ] *adj* mesquinho(nha), miserável.
misery ['mɪzərɪ] (*pl* **-ies**) *n* **-1.** [unhappiness] tristeza *f* **-2.** [poverty] miséria *f* **-3.** [gloomy person] desgraça *f*.
misfire [ˌmɪs'faɪəʳ] *vi* **-1.** [gun] não disparar **-2.** [car engine] não dar partida **-3.** [plan] fracassar.
misfit ['mɪsfɪt] *n* desajustado *m*, -da *f*.
misfortune [mɪs'fɔːtʃuːn] *n* **-1.** *(U)* [bad luck] azar *m* **-2.** [piece of bad luck] infortúnio *m*, desgraça *f*.
misgivings [mɪs'gɪvɪŋz] *npl* receio *m*, desconfiança *f*.
misguided [ˌmɪs'gaɪdɪd] *adj* **-1.** [person] desencaminhado(da) **-2.** [attempt, opinion] equivocado(da).
mishandle [ˌmɪs'hændl] *vt* **-1.** [person, animal] maltratar **-2.** [negotiations, business] administrar mal.
mishap ['mɪshæp] *n* **-1.** *(U)* [accident]: **without ~** sem incidentes **-2.** [unfortunate event] incidente *m*, percalço *m*.
mishear [ˌmɪs'hɪəʳ] (*pt* & *pp* **-heard** [-'hɜːd]) *vt & vi* ouvir mal.
mishmash ['mɪʃmæʃ] *n inf* mixórdia *f*.
misinform [ˌmɪsɪn'fɔːm] *vt* informal mal.
misinformation [ˌmɪsɪnfə'meɪʃn] *n (U)* informação *f* errada.
misinterpret [ˌmɪsɪn'tɜːprɪt] *vt* interpretar mal.
misjudge [ˌmɪs'dʒʌdʒ] *vt* **-1.** [calculate wrongly] calcular mal **-2.** [appraise wrongly] julgar mal.
misjudg(e)ment [ˌmɪs'dʒʌdʒmənt] *n* julgamento *m* errado.
mislay [ˌmɪs'leɪ] (*pt* & *pp* **-laid**) *vt* perder, extraviar.
mislead [ˌmɪs'liːd] (*pt* & *pp* **-led**) *vt* enganar.
misleading [ˌmɪs'liːdɪŋ] *adj* enganoso(sa).
misled [ˌmɪs'led] *pt* & *pp* ▻ **mislead**.
mismanage [ˌmɪs'mænɪdʒ] *vt* administrar mal.
mismanagement [ˌmɪs'mænɪdʒmənt] *n (U)* má administração *f*.
mismatch [ˌmɪs'mætʃ] *vt*: **to be ~ed** [colours] combinar mal; [in marriage] estar desencontrado(-da).
misnomer [ˌmɪs'nəʊməʳ] *n* termo *m* impróprio.
misogynist [mɪ'sɒdʒɪnɪst] *n* misógino *m*, -na *f*.
misplace [ˌmɪs'pleɪs] *vt* extraviar, perder.
misplaced [ˌmɪs'pleɪst] *adj* [trust, confidence] inapropriado(da).
misprint ['mɪsprɪnt] *n* erro *m* de impressão.
mispronounce [ˌmɪsprə'naʊns] *vt* pronunciar mal.
misquote [ˌmɪs'kwəʊt] *vt* citar erroneamente.
misread [ˌmɪs'riːd] (*pt* & *pp* **-read**) *vt* **-1.** [read wrongly] ler erroneamente **-2.** [misinterpret] interpretar mal.
misrepresent ['mɪsˌreprɪ'zent] *vt* **-1.** [person] dar uma imagem equivocada de **-2.** [facts] deturpar.
misrepresentation ['mɪsˌreprɪzen'teɪʃn] *n* **-1.** *(U)* [wrong interpretation] má interpretação *f* **-2.** [false account] deturpação *f*.
misrule [ˌmɪs'ruːl] *n* [misgovernment] mau governo *m*.
miss [mɪs] ◇ *vt* **-1.** [gen] perder **-2.** [fail to see] não ver, perder **-3.** [fail to hit] errar; **to ~ the target** não acertar o alvo **-4.** [feel absence of - person, home, family] sentir/estar com saudades de; [- things] sentir falta de **-5.** [fail to be present at] faltar a **-6.** [escape] evitar; **I just ~ed being run over** escapei de ser atropelado por pouco. ◇ *vi* [fail to hit] não acertar. ◇ *n*: **to give sthg a ~** *inf* deixar algo.
◆ **miss out** ◇ *vt sep* omitir. ◇ *vi*: **to ~ out (on sthg)** perder (algo).
Miss [mɪs] *n* senhorita *f*.
misshapen [ˌmɪs'ʃeɪpn] *adj* **-1.** [hands, fingers] deformado(da) **-2.** [object] disforme.
missile [*UK* 'mɪsaɪl, *US* 'mɪsəl] *n* **-1.** [weapon] míssil *m* **-2.** [thrown object] projétil *m*.
missile launcher [-ˌlɔːntʃəʳ] *n* lança-mísseis *m inv*.
missing ['mɪsɪŋ] *adj* **-1.** [object] perdido(da) **-2.** [person] desaparecido(da) **-3.** [not present] que falta; **who's ~?** quem está faltando?; **to go ~** desaparecer.
missing link *n*: **here was the ~ between ...** aqui está o elo que faltava entre ...
missing person *n* pessoa *f* desaparecida.
mission ['mɪʃn] *n* missão *f*.
missionary ['mɪʃənrɪ] (*pl* **-ies**) *n* missionário *m*, -ria *f*.
Mississippi [ˌmɪsɪ'sɪpɪ] *n* **-1.** [river]: **the ~ (River)** o (Rio) Mississippi **-2.** [state] Mississippi; **in ~** em Mississippi.
missive ['mɪsɪv] *n* missiva *f*.
Missouri [mɪ'zʊərɪ] *n* Missouri; **in ~** em Missouri.
misspell [ˌmɪs'spel] (*pt* & *pp* **-spelt** *OR* **-spelled**) *vt* soletrar erroneamente.
misspelling [ˌmɪs'spelɪŋ] *n* erro *m* de ortografia.
misspelt [ˌmɪs'spelt] *pt* & *pp* ▻ **misspell**.
misspend (*pt* & *pp* **-spent**) *vt* [money, talent, youth] desperdiçar.
mist [mɪst] *n* neblina *f*.
◆ **mist over, mist up** *vi* embaçar.
mistake [mɪ'steɪk] (*pt* **-took**, *pp* **-taken**) ◇ *n* erro *m*; **to make a ~** cometer um erro, equivocar-se; **by ~** por engano. ◇ *vt* **-1.** [misunderstand] entender mal **-2.** [fail to distinguish]: **to ~ sb/sthg for** confundir alguém/algo com; **there's no mistaking ...** não tem como confundir ...
mistaken [mɪ'steɪkn] ◇ *pp* ▻ **mistake**. ◇ *adj* **-1.** [person] equivocado(da), enganado(da); **to be ~ about sb/sthg** estar enganado(da) sobre alguém/algo **-2.** [belief, idea] equivocado(da).
mistaken identity *n*: **a case of ~** um caso de identificação equivocada.
mistakenly [mɪs'teɪknlɪ] *adv* equivocadamente.

mister ['mɪstəʳ] *n inf* amigo *m*.
◆ **Mister** *n* Senhor *m*.
mistime [ˌmɪs'taɪm] *vt* calcular mal o tempo de.
mistletoe ['mɪsltəʊ] *n (U)* visco *m*.
mistook [mɪ'stʊk] *pt* ⊳ **mistake**.
mistranslation [ˌmɪstræns'leɪʃn] *n* tradução *f* incorreta.
mistreat [ˌmɪs'triːt] *vt* maltratar.
mistreatment [ˌmɪs'triːtmənt] *n (U)* maus tratos *mpl*.
mistress ['mɪstrɪs] *n* **-1.** [of house, situation] dona *f* **-2.** [female lover] amante *f* **-3.** [schoolteacher] professora *f*.
mistrial ['mɪstraɪəl] *n* processo *m* nulo.
mistrust [ˌmɪs'trʌst] ◇ *n (U)* desconfiança *f*, receio *m*. ◇ *vt* desconfiar de.
mistrustful [ˌmɪs'trʌstfʊl] *adj* desconfiado(da); ~ **of sb/sthg** desconfiado(da) de alguém/algo.
misty ['mɪstɪ] (*compar* **-ier**, *superl* **-iest**) *adj* nebuloso(sa).
misunderstand [ˌmɪsʌndə'stænd] (*pt* & *pp* **-stood**) *vt* & *vi* entender mal.
misunderstanding [ˌmɪsʌndə'stændɪŋ] *n* **-1.** *(U)* [lack of understanding] equívoco *m* **-2.** [wrong interpretation] mal-entendido *m* **-3.** [disagreement] desentendimento *m*.
misunderstood [ˌmɪsʌndə'stʊd] *pt* & *pp* ⊳ **misunderstand**.
misuse [*n* ˌmɪs'juːs, *vb* ˌ*mɪs'juːz*] ◇ *n* **-1.** *(U)* [wrong use] uso *m* indevido **-2.** [abuse] abuso *m*. ◇ *vt* **-1.** [use wrongly] usar indevidamente **-2.** [abuse] abusar de.
MIT (*abbr of* **Massachusetts Institute of Technology**) *n* MIT *m*.
mite [maɪt] *n* **-1.** ZOOL ácaro *m* **-2.** *inf* [small amount]: **a** ~ um pouquinho **-3.** *inf* [small child] criancinha *f*.
miter *n US* = **mitre**.
mitigate ['mɪtɪgeɪt] *vt fml* mitigar.
mitigating ['mɪtɪgeɪtɪŋ] *adj fml*: ~ **circumstances** circunstâncias *fpl* atenuantes.
mitigation [ˌmɪtɪ'geɪʃn] *n (U) fml* mitigação *f*, atenuante *f*.
mitre *UK*, **miter** *US* ['maɪtəʳ] *n* **-1.** [hat] mitra *f* **-2.** [joint] meia-esquadria *f*.
mitt [mɪt] *n* **-1.** = **mitten** **-2.** [in baseball] luva *f*.
mitten ['mɪtn] *n* [with fingers joined] luva *f (com separação somente para o polegar)*; [with fingers cut off] mitene *f*.
mix [mɪks] ◇ *vt* misturar; **to** ~ **sthg with sthg** misturar algo com algo. ◇ *vi* misturar-se, combinar-se; **to** ~ **with sb** misturar-se com alguém. ◇ *n* **-1.** [gen] mistura *f* **-2.** COMM: **marketing** ~ mix *m* de marketing, composto *m* mercadológico.
◆ **mix up** *vt sep* **-1.** [confuse] confundir **-2.** [disorder] misturar.
mixed [mɪkst] *adj* **-1.** [of different kinds] misturado(da) **-2.** [of different sexes] misto(ta).
mixed-ability *adj UK* de vários níveis.
mixed blessing *n*: **it was a** ~ teve um lado bom e um lado ruim.
mixed doubles *n (U)* duplas *fpl* mistas.
mixed economy *n* economia *f* mista.
mixed grill *n prato grelhado com carnes e vegetais.*
mixed marriage *n* casamento *m* misto.
mixed up *adj* **-1.** [confused] confuso(sa) **-2.** [involved]: **to be** ~ **in sthg** estar envolvido(da) em algo.
mixer ['mɪksəʳ] *n* **-1.** [machine - for food] *f* batedeira; [- for drinks] misturador *m*; [- for cement] betoneira *f* **-2.** [soft drink] *bebida não-alcoólica usada para se misturar com bebidas alcoólicas.*
mixer tap *n UK* torneira *f (para o fluxo de água fria e quente)*.
mixing bowl ['mɪksɪŋ-] *n* tigela *f*.
mixture ['mɪkstʃəʳ] *n* mistura *f*.
mix-up *n inf* engano *m*, confusão *f*.
mk, MK (*abbr of* **mark**) marco *m*.
mkt (*abbr of* **market**) mercado *m*.
ml (*abbr of* **millilitre**) *n* ml.
MLitt [ˌem'lɪt] (*abbr of* **Master of Literature, Master of Letters**) *n (titular de) mestrado em literatura.*
MLR (*abbr of* **minimum lending rate**) *taxa mínima de juros praticada para empréstimos pelo Banco da Inglaterra, referência para os demais bancos.*
mm (*abbr of* **millimetre**) mm.
MMR (*abbr of* **measles, mumps, and rubella**) *n* MMR *f*, SCR *f*.
MN ◇ *n* (*abbr of* **Merchant Navy**) marinha *f* mercante. ◇ *abbr of* **Minnesota**.
mnemonic [nɪ'mɒnɪk] *n* mnemônica *f*.
MO ◇ *n* (*abbr of* **medical officer**) *médico encarregado dos serviços de saúde.* ◇ *abbr of* **Missouri**.
moan [məʊn] ◇ *n* **-1.** [of pain, sadness] gemido *m* **-2.** *inf* [complaint] resmungo *m*, queixa *f*. ◇ *vi* **-1.** [in pain, sadness] gemer **-2.** *inf* [complain] resmungar, queixar-se; **to** ~ **about sb/sthg** resmungar OR queixar-se sobre alguém/algo.
moaning ['məʊnɪŋ] *n* **-1.** [pain, sadness] gemidos *mpl* **-2.** *(U)* [complaining] reclamação *f*, queixas *fpl*.
moat [məʊt] *n* fosso *m*.
mob [mɒb] (*pt* & *pp* **-bed**, *cont* **-bing**) ◇ *n* **-1.** multidão *f* **-2.** *pej*: **the** ~ a ralé, a plebe. ◇ *vt* cercar, amontoar-se ao redor de.
mobile ['məʊbaɪl] ◇ *adj* **-1.** [able to move] móvel **-2.** *inf* [having transport] motorizado(da). ◇ *n* **-1.** [phone] (telefone) celular *m* **-2.** [decoration] móbile *m*.
mobile home *n* trailer *m*.
mobile library *n* biblioteca *f* móvel OR ambulante.
mobile phone *n* (telefone) celular *m*.
mobile shop *n* unidade *f* móvel de vendas.
mobility [mə'bɪlətɪ] *n* mobilidade *f*.
mobility allowance *n UK ajuda financeira que recebem os deficientes físicos para poderem se locomover.*
mobilization [ˌməʊbɪlaɪ'zeɪʃn] *n* mobilização *f*.
mobilize, -ise ['məʊbɪlaɪz] ◇ *vt* mobilizar. ◇ *vi* mobilizar-se.
moccasin ['mɒkəsɪn] *n* mocassim *m*.
mock [mɒk] ◇ *adj* falso(sa); **a** ~ **exam** um simulado. ◇ *vt* [deride] zombar de. ◇ *vi* zombar.

mockery ['mɒkərɪ] *n* **-1.** *(U)* [scorn] zombaria *f* **-2.** [travesty] paródia *f*; **to make a ~ of sthg** pôr algo em ridículo.
mocking ['mɒkɪŋ] *adj* zombeteiro(ra).
mockingbird ['mɒkɪŋbɜːd] *n* tordo *m* imitador.
mock-up *n* modelo *m* em tamanho natural.
mod [mɒd] *n jovem britânico dos anos 60 que vestia roupas alinhadas e gostava da música soul americana.*
MoD (*abbr of* **Ministry of Defence**) *n* ministério *m* da defesa *(britânico)*.
mod cons [ˌmɒd-] (*abbr of* **modern conveniences**) *npl UK inf*: **all ~** todas as comodidades modernas.
mode [məʊd] *n* **-1.** [gen] modo *m* **-2.** [of transport] meio *m*.
model ['mɒdl] (*UK pt* & *pp* **-led**, *cont* **-ling**, *US pt* & *pp* **-ed**, *cont* **-ing**) ◇ *adj* **-1.** [miniature] em miniatura **-2.** [exemplary] modelo. ◇ *n* [gen] modelo *m*. ◇ *vt* **-1.** [shape] moldar **-2.** [in fashion show] desfilar com **-3.** [copy]: **to ~ o.s. on sb** ter alguém como modelo, espelhar-se em alguém. ◇ *vi* [in fashion show] desfilar.
modem ['məʊdem] COMPUT *n* modem *m*.
moderate [*adj* & *n* 'mɒdərət, *vb* 'mɒdəreɪt] ◇ *adj* moderado(da). ◇ *n* POL moderado *m*, -da *f*. ◇ *vt* moderar. ◇ *vi* moderar-se.
moderately ['mɒdərətlɪ] *adv* moderadamente.
moderation [ˌmɒdə'reɪʃn] *n* moderação *f*; **in ~** com moderação.
moderator ['mɒdəreɪtə'] *n* **-1.** [of debate] moderador *m*, -ra *f* **-2.** RELIG *presidente duma assembleia protestante.*
modern ['mɒdən] *adj* moderno(na).
modern-day *adj* dos dias de hoje.
modernism ['mɒdənɪzm] *n (U)* modernismo *m*.
modernization [ˌmɒdənaɪ'zeɪʃn] *n* modernização *f*.
modernize, -ise ['mɒdənaɪz] ◇ *vt* modernizar. ◇ *vi* modernizar-se.
modern languages *npl* línguas *fpl* modernas.
modest ['mɒdɪst] *adj* modesto(ta).
modestly ['mɒdɪstlɪ] *adv* **-1.** [to small extent] ligeiramente **-2.** [not proudly] modestamente.
modesty ['mɒdɪstɪ] *n (U)* modéstia *f*.
modicum ['mɒdɪkəm] *n fml* quantia *f* módica; **a ~ of** um mínimo de.
modification [ˌmɒdɪfɪ'keɪʃn] *n* **-1.** [minor alteration] modificação *f* **-2.** *(U)* [alteration] alteração *f*, modificação *f*.
modify ['mɒdɪfaɪ] (*pt* & *pp* **-ied**) *vt* **-1.** [alter] modificar **-2.** [tone down] moderar.
modular ['mɒdjʊlə'] *adj* **-1.** [furniture] modular **-2.** [course] em módulos.
modulated ['mɒdjʊleɪtɪd] *adj* [voice] modulado(da).
modulation [ˌmɒdjʊ'leɪʃn] *n* TECH modulação *f*.
module ['mɒdjuːl] *n* módulo *m*.
Mogadishu [ˌmɒgə'dɪʃuː] *n* Mogadíscio; **in ~** em Mogadíscio.
moggy ['mɒgɪ] (*pl* **-ies**) *n UK inf* gato *m*, -ta *f*.
mogul ['məʊgl] *n* [magnate] magnata *m*.
MOH (*abbr of* **Medical Officer of Health**) *n secretário municipal de saúde na Grã-Bretanha.*
mohair ['məʊheə'] ◇ *n* mohair *m*. ◇ *comp* de mohair.
Mohammedan [mə'hæmɪdn] ◇ *adj* maometano(na). ◇ *n* maometano *m*, -na *f*.
Mohican [məʊ'hiːkən] ◇ *adj* moicano(na). ◇ *n* **-1.** [indian] moicano *m*, -na *f* **-2.** [haircut] *corte de cabelo punk em que a cabeça é raspada nas laterais.*
moist [mɔɪst] *adj* úmido(da); **~ cake** bolo *m* fofo.
moisten ['mɔɪsn] *vt* umedecer.
moisture ['mɔɪstʃə'] *n (U)* umidade *f*.
moisturize, -ise ['mɔɪstʃəraɪz] *vt* umectar.
moisturizer ['mɔɪstʃəraɪzə'] *n* (creme) hidratante *m*.
molar ['məʊlə'] *n* molar *m*.
molasses [mə'læsɪz] *n (U)* melaço *m*.
mold *etc n* & *vt US* = **mould**.
Moldavia [mɒl'deɪvɪə] *n* Moldávia; **in ~** na Moldávia.
mole [məʊl] *n* **-1.** [animal] toupeira *f* **-2.** [on skin] sinal *m* **-3.** [spy] espião *m*, -ã *f*.
molecular [mə'lekjʊlə'] *adj* molecular.
molecule ['mɒlɪkjuːl] *n* molécula *f*.
molehill ['məʊlhɪl] *n montículo de terra deixado pelas toupeiras ao cavar seus túneis.*
molest [mə'lest] *vt* **-1.** [attack sexually - child] molestar; [- person] assediar **-2.** [bother] incomodar.
molester [mə'lestə'] *n* molestador *m*, -ra *f*; **child ~** perversor *m*, -ra *f* de menores.
mollify ['mɒlɪfaɪ] (*pt* & *pp* **-ied**) *vt fml* tranqüilizar.
mollusc, mollusk *US* ['mɒləsk] *n* molusco *m*.
mollycoddle ['mɒlɪˌkɒdl] *vt inf* mimar.
Molotov cocktail ['mɒlətɒf-] *n* coquetel *m* Molotov.
molt *vt* & *vi US* = **moult**.
molten ['məʊltn] *adj* derretido(da), fundido(da).
mom [mɒm] *n US inf* mãe *f*.
moment ['məʊmənt] *n* **-1.** [gen] momento *m*; **~ of truth** hora *f* da verdade; **for one ~** por um momento; **at any ~** a qualquer momento; **at the ~** no momento; **at the last ~** no último momento; **for the ~** por enquanto **-2.** [importance] importância *f*.
momentarily ['məʊməntərɪlɪ] *adv* **-1.** [for a short time] momentaneamente **-2.** *US* [immediately] imediatamente.
momentary ['məʊməntrɪ] *adj* momentâneo(nea).
momentous [mə'mentəs] *adj* significativo(va).
momentum [mə'mentəm] *n* **-1.** PHYSICS momento *m* **-2.** *fig* [speed, force] força *f*.
momma ['mɒmə], **mommy** ['mɒmɪ] *n US* mamãe *f*, mãezinha *f*.
Mon. (*abbr of* **Monday**) seg.
Monaco ['mɒnəkəʊ] *n* Mônaco; **in ~** em Mônaco.
monarch ['mɒnək] *n* monarca *mf*.
monarchist ['mɒnəkɪst] *n* monarquista *mf*.
monarchy ['mɒnəkɪ] (*pl* **-ies**) *n* monarquia *f*; **the ~** a monarquia.
monastery ['mɒnəstrɪ] (*pl* **-ies**) *n* monastério *m*.
monastic [mə'næstɪk] *adj* monástico(ca).
Monday ['mʌndɪ] *n* segunda-feira *f*; *see also* **Saturday**.
monetarism ['mʌnɪtərɪzm] *n (U)* monetarismo *m*.

monetarist ['mʌnɪtərɪst] *n* monetarista *mf.*
monetary ['mʌnɪtrɪ] *adj* monetário(ria).
money ['mʌnɪ] *n (U)* dinheiro *m*; **to make ~** ganhar dinheiro; **to get one's ~'s worth** fazer o dinheiro OR investimento valer a pena.
moneybox ['mʌnɪbɒks] *n* cofrinho *m.*
moneyed *adj fml* abastado(da).
moneylender ['mʌnɪˌlendəʳ] *n* prestamista *mf.*
moneymaker ['mʌnɪˌmeɪkəʳ] *n* mina *f (de ouro).*
moneymaking ['mʌnɪˌmeɪkɪŋ] *adj* rentável, lucrativo(va).
money market *n* mercado *m* financeiro.
money order *n* ordem *f* de pagamento.
money-spinner [-ˌspɪnəʳ] *n esp UK inf* mina *f (de ouro).*
money supply *n* oferta *f* de moeda.
mongol ['mɒŋgəl] *dated & offensive* ◇ *adj* mongolóide. ◇ *n* mongolóide *mf.*
◆ **Mongol** *adj & n* = **Mongolian**.
Mongolia [mɒŋ'gəʊlɪəl] *n* Mongólia; **in ~** na Mongólia.
Mongolian [mɒŋ'gəʊlɪən] ◇ *adj* mongol. ◇ *n* **-1.** [person] mongol *mf* **-2.** [language] mongol *m.*
mongoose ['mɒŋgu:s] (*pl* **-s**) *n* mangusto *m.*
mongrel ['mʌŋgrəl] *n* [dog] vira-lata *m.*
monitor ['mɒnɪtəʳ] ◇ *n TECH* monitor *m.* ◇ *vt* monitorar.
monk [mʌŋk] *n* monge *m.*
monkey ['mʌŋkɪ] (*pl* **-s**) *n* [animal] macaco *m*, -ca *f.*
monkey nut *n* amendoim *m.*
monkey wrench *n* chave *f* inglesa.
monkfish (*pl inv* OR **-es**) *n* peixe-pescador *m.*
mono ['mɒnəʊ] ◇ *adj* monofônico(ca), mono *inv.* ◇ *n inf* **-1.** [sound] som *m* mono **-2.** *US* [glandular fever] mononucleose *f* infecciosa.
monochrome ['mɒnəkrəʊm] *adj* [TV, photograph] monocromo(ma).
monocle ['mɒnəkl] *n* monóculo *m.*
monogamous [mɒ'nɒgəməs] *adj* monógamo(-ma).
monogamy [mɒ'nɒgəmɪ] *n (U)* monogamia *f.*
monogrammed ['mɒnəgræmd] *adj* bordado(da) com as iniciais.
monolingual [ˌmɒnə'lɪŋgwəl] *adj* monolíngüe.
monolithic [ˌmɒnə'lɪθɪk] *adj* monolítico(ca).
monologue, monolog *US* ['mɒnəlɒg] *n* **-1.** *THEATRE* monólogo *m* **-2.** *inf* [long speech] palestra *f* longa.
mononucleosis ['mɒnəʊˌnju:klɪ'əʊsɪs] *n US* mononucleose *f.*
monoplane ['mɒnəpleɪn] *n* monoplano *m.*
monopolize, -ise [mə'nɒpəlaɪz] *vt* monopolizar.
monopoly [mə'nɒpəlɪ] (*pl* **-ies**) *n* monopólio *m*; **~ on** OR **of sthg** monopólio em OR de algo; **the Monopolies and Mergers Commission** *UK organização que investiga a possível formação de monopólio pelas empresas.*
monorail ['mɒnəreɪl] *n* monotrilho *m.*
monosodium glutamate [ˌmɒnə'səʊdjəm'glu:təmeɪt] *n (U)* glutamato *m* monossódico.
monosyllabic [ˌmɒnəsɪ'læbɪk] *adj* monossilábico(-ca).
monosyllable ['mɒnəˌsɪləbl] *n* monossílabo *m.*
monotone ['mɒnətəʊn] *n*: **he speaks in a ~** ele fala com uma voz monótona.
monotonous [mə'nɒtənəs] *adj* [voice, job, life] monótono(na).
monotonously [mə'nɒtənəslɪ] *adv* de forma monótona.
monotony [mə'nɒtənɪ] *n (U)* monotonia *f.*
monoxide [mɒ'nɒksaɪd] *n* monóxido *m.*
Monrovia [mɒn'rəʊvɪəl] *n* Monróvia; **in ~** em Monróvia.
Monsignor [ˌmɒn'si:njəʳ] *n* Monsenhor *m.*
monsoon [mɒn'su:n] *n* [rainy season] monção *f.*
monster ['mɒnstəʳ] ◇ *adj* gigantesco(ca), enorme. ◇ *n* monstro *m.*
monstrosity [mɒn'strɒsətɪ] (*pl* **-ies**) *n* monstruosidade *f.*
monstrous ['mɒnstrəs] *adj* **-1.** [appalling] espantoso(sa) **-2.** [hideous] monstruoso(sa) **-3.** [very large] gigantesco(ca).
montage ['mɒntɑ:ʒ] *n* montagem *f.*
Montana [mɒn'tænə] *n* Montana; **in ~** em Montana.
Mont Blanc [mɒnt] *n* Monte *m* Branco.
Montenegro [ˌmɒntɪ'ni:grəʊ] *n* Montenegro; **in ~** em Montenegro.
Montevideo [ˌmɒntɪvɪ'deɪəʊ] *n* Montevidéu; **in ~** em Montevidéu.
month [mʌnθ] *n* mês *m.*
monthly ['mʌnθlɪ] (*pl* **-ies**) ◇ *adj* mensal. ◇ *adv* mensalmente. ◇ *n* [publication] revista *f* mensal.
Montreal [mɒntrɪ'ɔ:l] *n* Montreal; **in ~** em Montreal.
monument ['mɒnjʊmənt] *n* monumento *m.*
monumental [ˌmɒnjʊ'mentl] *adj* **-1.** [gen] monumental **-2.** [extremely bad] descomunal.
moo [mu:] (*pl* **-s**) ◇ *n* mugido *m.* ◇ *vi* mugir.
mooch [mu:tʃ] ◆ **mooch about, mooch around** *vi inf* perambular, vaguear.
mood [mu:d] *n* [state of feelings] humor *m*; **in a (bad) ~** de mau humor; **in a good ~** de bom humor.
moody ['mu:dɪ] (*compar* **-ier**, *superl* **-iest**) *adj pej* **-1.** [changeable] temperamental, de humor variável **-2.** [bad-tempered] mal-humorado(da).
moon [mu:n] *n* lua *f*; **to be over the ~** *inf* dar pulos de alegria.
moonbeam ['mu:nbi:m] *n* raio *m* de luar.
moonlight ['mu:nlaɪt] (*pt & pp* **-ed**) ◇ *n (U)* luar *m*, luz *f* da lua. ◇ *vi inf* [have second job] *ter um trabalho extra.*
moonlighting ['mu:nlaɪtɪŋ] *n (U)* [illegal work] trabalho *m* extra, bico *m.*
moonlit ['mu:nlɪt] *adj* enluarado(da).
moonscape ['mu:nskeɪp] *n* paisagem *f* lunar.
moon shot *n viagem para a lua em espaçonave.*
moonstone *n* pedra-da-lua *f.*
moonstruck ['mu:nstrʌk] *adj inf* lunático(ca).
moony (*compar* **-ier**, *superl* **-iest**) *adj UK inf* sonhador(ra).
moor [mɔ:ʳ] ◇ *n esp UK* brejo *m vt & vi* atracar, ancorar.
Moor [mɔ:ʳ] *n* mouro *m*, -ra *f.*
moorhen *n* frango-d'água *m.*

moorings ['mɔːrɪŋz] *npl* [of boat, ship - ropes, chains] amarras *fpl*; [- place] ancoradouro *m*.
Moorish ['mɔːrɪʃ] *adj* mouro(ra), mourisco(ca).
moorland ['mɔːlənd] *n (U) esp UK* charneca *f*.
moose [muːs] (*pl inv*) *n* [North American] alce *m*.
moot [muːt] *vt* propor.
moot point *n* questão *f* controversa.
mop [mɒp] (*pt* & *pp* **-ped**, *cont* **-ping**) <> *n* **-1.** [for cleaning] esfregão *m* **-2.** *inf* [of hair] mecha *f*. <> *vt* **-1.** [floor] esfregar, passar o esfregão em **-2.** [brow, face] enxugar.
◆ **mop up** *vt sep* **-1.** [clean up] limpar *(com esfregão)* **-2.** *fig* [clear away] eliminar.
mope [məʊp] *vi pej* lastimar-se.
◆ **mope about, mope around** *vi pej* vaguear desanimado(da).
moped ['məʊped] *n* bicicleta *f* motorizada.
moral ['mɒrəl] <> *adj* moral; ~ **support** apoio *m* moral. <> *n* [lesson] moral *f*.
◆ **morals** *npl* [principles] princípios *mpl*.
morale [mə'rɑːl] *n (U)* moral *m*.
moralistic [ˌmɒrə'lɪstɪk] *adj pej* moralista.
morality [mə'rælətɪ] (*pl* **-ies**) *n* moralidade *f*.
moralize, -ise ['mɒrəlaɪz] *vi pej*: **to** ~ **(about** *OR* **on sthg)** moralizar (sobre algo).
morally ['mɒrəlɪ] *adv* moralmente.
Moral Majority *n grupo de pressão ultraconservador apoiado pelas igrejas fundamentalistas nos EUA*.
morass [mə'ræs] *n* [mass] emaranhado *m*, confusão *f*.
moratorium [ˌmɒrə'tɔːrɪəm] (*pl* **-ria** [-rɪəl]) *n* **fml** moratória *f*; ~ **on sthg** moratória em algo.
morbid ['mɔːbɪd] *adj* [unhealthy] mórbido(da).
more [mɔːr] <> *adj* **-1.** [a larger amount of] mais; **there are** ~ **tourists than usual** há mais turistas que o normal. **-2.** [additional] mais; **is there any** ~ **cake?** tem mais bolo?; **I'd like two** ~ **bottles** queria mais duas garrafas; **there's no** ~ **wine** já não tem mais vinho. <> *adv* **-1.** [in comparatives] mais; **it's** ~ **difficult than before** é mais difícil do que antes; **speak** ~ **clearly** fale de forma mais clara; **we go there** ~ **often now** agora vamos lá mais freqüüentemente. **-2.** [to a greater degree] mais; **we ought to go to the movies** ~ devíamos ir mais vezes ao cinema. **-3.** [in phrases]: **once** ~ mais uma vez; **we'd be** ~ **than happy to help** teríamos muito prazer em ajudar.
◆ **more and more** *adv, adj & pron* cada vez mais.
◆ **more or less** *adv* mais o menos.
moreover [mɔː'rəʊvəʳ] *adv fml* além disso.
morgue [mɔːg] *n* [mortuary] necrotério *m*.
MORI ['mɔːrɪ] (*abbr of* **Market & Opinion Research Institute**) *n instituto britânico de pesquisa de mercado e opinião*.
moribund ['mɒrɪbʌnd] *adj fml* moribundo(da).
Mormon ['mɔːmən] *n* mórmon *mf*.
morning ['mɔːnɪŋ] *n* **-1.** [first part of day] manhã *f*; **in the** ~ [before lunch] de *OR* pela manhã; [tomorrow morning] pela manhã **-2.** [between midnight and noon] manhã *f*.
◆ **mornings** *adv US* de manhã.
morning-after pill *n* pílula *f* do dia seguinte.
morning dress *n esp UK* [formal clothes] *paletó preto com calça listrada*.
morning sickness *n (U)* náusea *f* matinal.
Moroccan [mə'rɒkən] <> *adj* marroquino(na). <> *n* marroquino *m*, -na *f*.
Morocco [mə'rɒkəʊ] *n* Marrocos; **in** ~ em Marrocos.
moron ['mɔːrɒn] *n* **inf** [stupid person] idiota *mf*, imbecil *mf*.
moronic [mə'rɒnɪk] *adj* [stupid] idiota, imbecil.
morose [mə'rəʊs] *adj* melancólico(ca).
morphing *n* morphing *m*.
morphine ['mɔːfiːn] *n (U)* morfina *f*.
morris dancing ['mɒrɪs-] *n (U) dança folclórica inglesa em que os homens representam personagens lendários*.
Morse (code) [mɔːs-] *n (U)* código *m* Morse.
morsel ['mɔːsl] *n* pedacinho *m*.
mortal ['mɔːtl] <> *adj* mortal. <> *n* mortal *mf*.
mortality [mɔː'tælətɪ] *n (U)* mortalidade *f*.
mortality rate *n* taxa *f* de mortalidade.
mortally ['mɔːtəlɪ] *adv* **-1.** [fatally] mortalmente **-2.** [deeply] profundamente.
mortar ['mɔːtəʳ] *n* **-1.** *(U)* [cement mixture] argamassa *f* **-2.** [gun] morteiro *m* **-3.** [bowl] almofariz *m*.
mortarboard ['mɔːtəbɔːd] *n* **-1.** *CONSTR* padiola *f (para argamassa)* **-2.** *UNIV* barrete *m* de formatura.
mortgage ['mɔːgɪdʒ] <> *n* hipoteca *f*. <> *comp* hipotecário(ria). <> *vt* hipotecar.
mortgagee [ˌmɔːgɪ'dʒiː] *n* credor *m* hipotecário, credora *f* hipotecária.
mortgagor [ˌmɔːgɪ'dʒɔːʳ] *n* devedor *m* hipotecário, devedora *f* hipotecária.
mortician [mɔː'tɪʃn] *n* **US** agente *mf* funerário, -ria.
mortified ['mɔːtɪfaɪd] *adj* mortificado(da).
mortify *vt* mortificar.
mortise lock ['mɔːtɪs-] *n* fechadura *f* embutida.
mortuary ['mɔːtʃʊərɪ] (*pl* **-ies**) *n* necrotério *m*.
mosaic [mə'zeɪɪk] *n* mosaico *m*.
Moscow ['mɒskəʊ] *n* Moscou; **in** ~ em Moscou.
Moslem ['mɒzləm] *adj* & *n* = **Muslim**.
mosque [mɒsk] *n* mesquita *f*.
mosquito [mə'skiːtəʊ] (*pl* **-es** *OR* **-s**) *n* mosquito *m*.
mosquito net *n* mosquiteiro *m*.
moss [mɒs] *n (U)* musgo *m*.
mossy ['mɒsɪ] (*compar* **-ier**, *superl* **-iest**) *adj* coberto(-ta) de musgo.
most [məʊst] <> *adj (superl of many & much)* **-1.** [the majority of] a maioria de; ~ **people** a maioria das pessoas **-2.** [largest amount of]: **(the)** ~ mais; **who's got (the)** ~ **money?** quem é que tem mais dinheiro?; **what gave me (the)** ~ **satisfaction was ...** o que me deu a maior satisfação foi ... <> *pron* **-1.** [the majority] a maioria; ~ **of** a maioria de; ~ **of the time** a maior parte do tempo **-2.** [largest amount]: **(the)** ~ o máximo; **at** ~ no máximo **-3.** *phr*: **to make the** ~ **of sthg** tirar o máximo de algo. <> *adv* **-1.** [to the greatest extent]: **what I like (the)** ~ o que eu mais gosto **-2.** *fml* [very] muito; ~ **certainly** com toda a certeza **-3.** *US* [almost] quase.

mostly ['məʊstlɪ] *adv* **-1.** [in the main] principalmente **-2.** [usually] normalmente.

MOT <> *n* (*abbr of* **Ministry of Transport (test)**) *vistoria anual obrigatória realizada pelo Ministério dos Transportes britânico em carros com mais de 3 anos de fabricação.* <> *vt*: **to have one's car ~'d** realizar a vistoria no carro.

motel [məʊ'tel] *n* hotel *m* de beira de estrada.

moth [mɒθ] *n* **-1.** ZOOL mariposa *f* **-2.** [in clothes] traça *f*.

mothball ['mɒθbɔ:l] *n* (bola de) naftalina *f*.

moth-eaten *adj* roído(da) pelas traças.

mother ['mʌðə^r] <> *n* mãe *f* <> *vt pej* [spoil] mimar.

motherboard ['mʌðə,bɔ:d] *n* COMPUT placa-mãe *f*.

motherhood ['mʌðəhʊd] *n (U)* maternidade *f*.

Mothering Sunday ['mʌðərɪŋ-] *n* Dia *m* das Mães.

mother-in-law (*pl* **mothers-in-law** OR **mother-in-laws**) *n* sogra *f*.

motherland ['mʌðəlænd] *n* pátria *f*.

motherless ['mʌðəlɪs] *adj* órfão(fã) de mãe.

motherly ['mʌðəlɪ] *adj* maternal, materno(na).

Mother Nature *n* Mãe *f* Natureza.

mother-of-pearl <> *n (U)* madrepérola *f*. <> *comp* de madrepérola.

Mother's Day *n* Dia *m* das Mães.

mother ship *n* nave-mãe *f*.

mother superior *n* madre *f* superiora.

mother-to-be (*pl* **mothers-to-be**) *n* futura mãe *f*.

mother tongue *n* língua *f* materna.

motif [məʊ'ti:f] *n* motivo *m*.

motion ['məʊʃn] <> *n* **-1.** *(U)* [process of moving] movimento *m*; **to set sthg in ~** colocar algo em marcha; **to go through the ~s** [act insincerely] fingir, mostrar um falso interesse **-2.** [proposal] proposta *f*. <> *vt*: **to ~ sb to do sthg** fazer sinal para alguém fazer algo. <> *vi*: **to ~ to sb** fazer sinal *(com a mão)* para alguém.

motionless ['məʊʃənlɪs] *adj* imóvel.

motion picture *n* **US** filme *m*.

motivate ['məʊtɪveɪt] *vt* **-1.** [give cause] motivar **-2.** [give incentive] incentivar; **to ~ sb to do sthg** incentivar alguém a fazer algo.

motivated ['məʊtɪveɪtɪd] *adj* motivado(da).

motivation [,məʊtɪ'veɪʃn] *n* **-1.** [cause] razão *f* **-2.** *(U)* [sense of purpose] motivação *f*.

motive ['məʊtɪv] *n* motivo *m*, razão *f*.

motley ['mɒtlɪ] *adj pej* heterogêneo(nea).

motocross ['məʊtəkrɒs] *n (U)* motocross *m*.

motor ['məʊtə^r] <> *adj* **UK** [relating to cars - industry, accident] automobilístico(ca); [- mechanic] de automóveis. <> *n* [engine] motor *m*. <> *vi dated* viajar de automóvel.

Motorail® ['məʊtəreɪl] *n* **UK** *serviço ferroviário de transporte de automóveis.*

motorbike ['məʊtəbaɪk] *n* moto *f*.

motorboat ['məʊtəbəʊt] *n* barco *m* a motor.

motorcade ['məʊtəkeɪd] *n caravana f*.

motorcar ['məʊtəkɑ:^r] *n* **UK** *fml* automóvel *m*.

motorcycle ['məʊtə,saɪkl] *n* motocicleta *f*.

motorcyclist ['məʊtə,saɪklɪst] *n* motociclista *mf*.

motoring ['məʊtərɪŋ] <> *adj* **UK** automobilístico (ca); **~ offence** infração *f* de trânsito. <> *n (U) dated* automobilismo *m*.

motorist ['məʊtərɪst] *n* motorista *mf*.

motorize, -ise ['məʊtəraɪz] *vt* motorizar.

motor lodge *n* **US** hotel *m* em beira de estrada.

motor racing *n (U)* corrida *f* automobilística.

motor scooter *n* lambreta *f*.

motor vehicle *n* veículo *m* motorizado.

motorway ['məʊtəweɪ] <> *n* **UK** auto-estrada *f*. <> *comp* na auto-estrada.

mottled ['mɒtld] *adj* com manchas, pintado(da).

motto ['mɒtəʊ] (*pl* **-s** OR **-es**) *n* [maxim] lema *m*.

mould, mold US [məʊld] <> *n* **-1.** *(U)* BOT mofo *m* **-2.** [shape] fôrma *f*, molde *m*. <> *vt* **-1.** [influence] moldar **-2.** [shape physically] moldar, modelar.

moulding, molding US ['məʊldɪŋ] *n* [decoration] cornija *f*.

mouldy, moldy US (*compar* **-ier**, *superl* **-iest**) ['məʊldɪ] *adj* mofado(da).

moult, molt US [məʊlt] <> *vt* trocar. <> *vi* **-1.** [bird] trocar as penas **-2.** [dog] trocar o pêlo.

mound [maʊnd] *n* **-1.** [small hill] morro *m* **-2.** [untidy pile] montanha *f*.

mount [maʊnt] <> *n* **-1.** [support, frame] moldura *f* **-2.** [horse, pony] montaria *f* **-3.** [mountain] monte *m*. <> *vt* **-1.** [climb onto] montar **-2.** *fml* [climb up] subir **-3.** [organize] montar; **to ~ guard over sb/sthg** montar guarda para vigiar alguém/algo **-4.** [photograph] emoldurar **-5.** [trophy] pôr em posição de destaque **-6.** [jewel] engastar. <> *vi* **-1.** [increase] aumentar **-2.** [climb on horse] montar.

◆ **mount up** *vi* [increase] aumentar.

mountain ['maʊntɪn] *n* [gen] montanha *f*; **to make a ~ out of a molehill** fazer uma tempestade num copo d'água.

mountain bike *n* mountain bike *f*.

mountaineer [,maʊntɪ'nɪə^r] *n* montanhista *mf*, alpinista *mf*.

mountaineering [,maʊntɪ'nɪərɪŋ] *n (U)* montanhismo *m*, alpinismo *m*.

mountainous ['maʊntɪnəs] *adj* [full of mountains] montanhoso(sa).

mountain range *n* cadeia *f* de montanhas, cordilheira *f*.

mountain rescue *n (U)* resgate *m* nas montanhas.

mounted ['maʊntɪd] *adj* [on horseback] montado(-da).

Mountie ['maʊntɪ] *n* **inf** *membro da polícia montada canadense.*

mourn [mɔ:n] <> *vt* **-1.** [the loss of] lamentar **-2.** [the death of] lamentar a morte de. <> *vi*: **to ~ for sb** fazer luto por alguém.

mourner ['mɔ:nə^r] *n* enlutado *m*, -da *f*.

mournful ['mɔ:nfʊl] *adj* lamuriento(ta), desolado(da).

mourning ['mɔ:nɪŋ] *n* **-1.** [period] luto *m* **-2.** [clothes] traje *m* de luto; **in ~** em luto.

mouse [maʊs] (*pl* **mice**) *n* **-1.** [animal] camundongo *m* **-2.** COMPUT mouse *m*.

mouse mat, mouse pad *n* COMPUT mouse pad *m*.

mousetrap ['maʊstræp] *n* ratoeira *f*.

moussaka [muːˈsɑːkə] *n prato grego à base de beringela e carne moída.*
mousse [muːs] *n* **-1.** [food] musse *f* **-2.** [for hair] mousse *m.*
moustache *UK* [məˈstɑːʃ], **mustache** *US* [ˈmʌstæʃ] *n* bigode *m.*
mouth [*n* maʊθ, *vt* maʊð] ◇ *n* **-1.** *ANAT* boca *f*; **to keep one's ~ shut** *inf* ficar de boca fechada **-2.** [entrance - of cave, hole] boca *f*; [- of river] foz *f.* ◇ *vt* **-1.** [silently]: **to ~ a reply** articular uma resposta **-2.** [pompously] dizer pomposamente.
mouthful [ˈmaʊθfʊl] *n* **-1.** [amount - of food] bocado *m*; [- of water] gole *m* **-2.** *inf* [difficult word] palavra *f* difícil de ser pronunciada, palavrão *m.*
mouthorgan [ˈmaʊθˌɔːgən] *n* harmônica *f*, gaita-de-boca *f.*
mouthpiece [ˈmaʊθpiːs] *n* **-1.** [of object] bocal *m* **-2.** [spokesperson] porta-voz *mf.*
mouth-to-mouth *adj*: **~ resuscitation** respiração *f* boca-a-boca.
mouth ulcer *n* úlcera *f* bucal.
mouthwash [ˈmaʊθwɒʃ] *n* antiséptico *m* bucal.
mouth-watering [-ˌwɔːtərɪŋ] *adj* de dar água na boca.
movable [ˈmuːvəbl] *adj* móvel.
move [muːv] ◇ *n* **-1.** [movement] movimento *m*; **to be always on the ~** [travelling around] estar sempre viajando; [beginning to move] estar a caminho; **to get a ~ on** *inf* apressar-se **-2.** [change] mudança *f* **-3.** [in board game - turn to play] vez *f*; [- action] jogada *f* **-4.** [course of action] medida *f.* ◇ *vt* **-1.** [shift] mudar, mexer; **to ~ the car** tirar o carro **-2.** [change - job, office] mudar de; [- house] mudar-se de **-3.** [affect emotionally] tocar, comover **-4.** [in debate]: **to ~ that ...** sugerir que ... **-5.** *fml* [cause]: **to ~ sb to do sthg** impelir alguém a fazer algo. ◇ *vi* **-1.** [shift] mover-se, mexer-se **-2.** [act] agir **-3.** [to new house, job] mudar-se.
◆ **move about** *vi* **-1.** [fidget] remexer-se, ir de lá para cá **-2.** [travel] viajar.
◆ **move along** ◇ *vt sep* circular. ◇ *vi* continuar andando.
◆ **move around** *vi* = **move about.**
◆ **move away** *vi* **-1.** [go in opposite direction] afastar-se **-2.** [live elsewhere] ir-se embora.
◆ **move in** ◇ *vt sep* [troops] chegar. ◇ *vi* **-1.** [to new house] instalar-se **-2.** [take control, attack] preparar-se para o ataque.
◆ **move off** *vi* [train, bus, car] sair.
◆ **move on** ◇ *vt sep* fazer circular. ◇ *vi* **-1.** [after stopping] prosseguir **-2.** [in discussion] passar para outro tema.
◆ **move out** ◇ *vt sep* [troops] retirar. ◇ *vi* [from house] mudar-se.
◆ **move over** *vi* chegar mais para lá/cá.
◆ **move up** *vi* [on seat] chegar mais para lá/cá.
moveable *adj* = **movable.**
movement [ˈmuːvmənt] *n* **-1.** [gen] movimento *m* **-2.** [transportation] movimentação *f.*
movie [ˈmuːvɪ] *n esp US* filme *m.*
movie camera *n* câmara *f* cinematográfica.
moviegoer [ˈmuːvɪˌgəʊəʳ] *n US* cinéfilo *m*, -la *f.*
movie star *n US* estrela *f* de cinema.
movie theater *n US* cinema *f.*
moving [ˈmuːvɪŋ] *adj* **-1.** [touching] tocante, comovente **-2.** [not fixed] móvel.
moving staircase *n* escada *f* rolante.
mow [məʊ] (*pt* **-ed**, *pp* **-ed** *OR* **mown**) *vt* [cut - grass, lawn] cortar; [- corn, wheat] ceifar.
◆ **mow down** *vt sep* dizimar.
mower [ˈməʊəʳ] *n* [machine] ceifadeira *f.*
mown [məʊn] *pp* ▷ **mow.**
Mozambican [ˌməʊzəmˈbiːkən] ◇ *adj* moçambicano(na). ◇ *n* moçambicano *m*, -na *f.*
Mozambique [ˌməʊzəmˈbiːk] *n* Moçambique; **in ~** em Moçambique.
MP *n* **-1.** (*abbr of* **Member of Parliament**) *membro do Parlamento Britânico* **-2.** (*abbr of* **Military Police**) *polícia militar,* ≃ PE *f* **-3.** *Can* (*abbr of* **Mounted Police**) Polícia *f* Montada.
MP3 (*abbr of* **MPEG-1 Audio Layer-3**) *n COMPUT* MP3 *m.*
MPEG (*abbr of* **Moving Pictures Expert Group**) *n COMPUT* MPEG *m.*
mpg (*abbr of* **miles per gallon**) *n* milhas *fpl* por galão.
mph (*abbr of* **miles per hour**) *n* milhas *fpl* por hora.
MPhil [ˌemˈfɪl] (*abbr of* **Master of Philosophy**) *n (titular de) mestrado em filosofia.*
MPS (*abbr of* **Member of the Pharmaceutical Society**) *n membro da sociedade britânica de farmacêuticos.*
Mr [ˈmɪstəʳ] (*abbr of* **Mister**) *n* Sr.
MRC (*abbr of* **Medical Research Council**) *n organização do governo britânico de incentivo à pesquisa médica.*
MRCP (*abbr of* **Member of the Royal College of Physicians**) *n membro do colégio real de médicos britânicos.*
MRCS (*abbr of* **Member of the Royal College of Surgeons**) *n membro do colégio real de cirurgiões britânicos.*
MRCVS (*abbr of* **Member of the Royal College of Veterinary Surgeons**) *n membro do colégio real de veterinários britânicos.*
Mrs [ˈmɪsɪz] (*abbr of* **Missus**) *n* Sra.
ms. (*abbr of* **manuscript**) *n* manuscrito *m.*
Ms [mɪz] *n abreviatura usada diante do nome de mulher quando não se quer especificar seu estado civil, válida para senhora ou senhorita.*
MS ◇ *n* **-1.** (*abbr of* **manuscript**) manuscrito *m* **-2.** (*abbr of* **Master of Science**) *(titular de) mestrado em ciências* **-3.** (*abbr of* **multiple sclerosis**) esclerose *f* múltipla. ◇ *abbr of* **Mississippi.**
MSA (*abbr of* **Master of Science in Agriculture**) *n (titular de) mestrado em agronomia.*
MSB (*abbr of* **most significant bit/byte**) *n* MSB *m.*
MSc (*abbr of* **Master of Science**) *n (titular de) mestrado em ciências.*
MSC (*abbr of* **Manpower Services Commission**) *n antiga organização do governo britânico que tratava de mão-de-obra.*
MSG (*abbr of* **monosodium glutamate**) glutamato *m* monossódico.
Msgr (*abbr of* **Monsignor**) Mons.
MST (*abbr of* **Mountain Standard Time**) *n horário oficial da região das Montanhas Rochosas nos Estados Unidos.*

MSW (*abbr of* **Master of Social Work**) *n (titular de) mestrado em serviço social.*
Mt (*abbr of* **mount**) Mte.
MT ◇ *n* (*abbr of* **machine translation**) tradução *f* automática. ◇ *abbr of* **Montana**.
much [mʌtʃ] (*compar* **more**, *superl* **most**) ◇ *adj* muito(ta); **as ~ (...) as** tanto (...) quanto; **how ~ ...?** quanto ...?; **too ~ ...** demais. ◇ *pron* muito; **how ~ have you got?** quanto você tem?; **I don't think ~ of it** não me parece grande coisa; **as ~ as** tanto quanto; **how ~?** quanto?; **too ~** demais; **this isn't ~ of a party** essa festa não está grande coisa; **I'm not ~ of a cook** não sou um grande cozinheiro; **so ~ for my hard work!** tanto desgaste por meu trabalho!; **I thought as ~** já imaginava; **it's not up to ~** *inf* não é nenhuma maravilha, não é aquilo tudo. ◇ *adv* muito; **thank you very ~** muito obrigado(da); **it's ~ too cold** está frio demais; **it's ~ the same** é praticamente a mesma coisa; **'what did you think of the film?' - 'not ~'** 'o que você achou do filme?' - 'não gostei muito'; **he's not so ~ stupid as lazy** ele é muito mais preguiçoso que bobo; **too ~** demais; **without so ~ as ...** sem nem sequer ...; **~ as** (exatamente) como; **nothing ~** nada de mais.
muchness ['mʌtʃnɪs] *n*: **to be much of a ~** vir a ser a mesma coisa.
muck [mʌk] *n inf* **-1.** [dirt] sujeira *f* **-2.** [manure] esterco *m*.
◆ **muck about, muck around** *UK inf* ◇ *vt sep* fazer perder tempo. ◇ *vi* fazer cera.
◆ **muck in** *vi UK inf* trabalhar juntos(tas).
◆ **muck out** *vt sep* limpar.
◆ **muck up** *vt sep UK inf* estragar.
muckraking ['mʌkreɪkɪŋ] *n (U) fig* sensacionalismo *m*.
mucky ['mʌkɪ] (*compar* **-ier**, *superl* **-iest**) *adj inf* sujo(ja).
mucus ['mju:kəs] *n (U)* muco *m*.
mud [mʌd] *n (U)* lama *f*, barro *m*.
muddle ['mʌdl] ◇ *n* **-1.** [disorder] desordem *f*; **to be in a ~** estar em desordem **-2.** [confusion] confusão *f*; **to be in a ~** estar confuso(sa). ◇ *vt* **-1.** [put into disorder] desordenar **-2.** [confuse] confundir, misturar.
◆ **muddle along** *vi* prosseguir de forma confusa.
◆ **muddle through** *vi* conseguir de qualquer jeito.
◆ **muddle up** *vt sep* misturar.
muddle-headed [-ˌhedɪd] *adj* **-1.** [person] incapaz de pensar com clareza **-2.** [thinking] confuso(sa).
muddy ['mʌdɪ] (*compar* **-ier**, *superl* **-iest**, *pt & pp* **-ied**) ◇ *adj* **-1.** [covered with mud - floor, boots] embarrado(da); [- river] lamacento(ta) **-2.** [in colour] turvo(va). ◇ *vt fig* [issue, situation] complicar.
mudflap ['mʌdflæp] *n* pára-lama *m*.
mudflat ['mʌdflæt] *n* estirâncio *m*.
mudguard ['mʌdgɑ:d] *n* pára-lama *m*.
mud pack *n* lama *f* medicinal.
mud-slinging *n (U) fig* difamação *f*.
muesli ['mju:zlɪ] *n UK* granola *f*.
muff [mʌf] ◇ *n* [for hands] regalo *m*; [for ears] protetor *m* de orelhas *(contra o frio)*. ◇ *vt inf* perder.
muffin ['mʌfɪn] *n* **-1.** *UK* [bread roll] *pãozinho redondo e chato que se come quente com manteiga* **-2.** *US* [cake] bolinho *m* doce com frutas/chocolate.
muffle ['mʌfl] *vt* [quieten] abafar.
muffled ['mʌfld] *adj* **-1.** [sound] abafado(da) **-2.** [wrapped up warmly]: **~ (up)** agasalhado(da).
muffler ['mʌflə^r] *n US* [for car] silenciador *m*.
mug [mʌg] (*pt & pp* **-ged**, *cont* **-ging**) ◇ *n* **-1.** caneca *f* **-2.** *inf* [fool] tolo *m*, -la *f*. ◇ *vt* [attack and rob] assaltar.
mugger ['mʌgə^r] *n* assaltante *mf*.
mugging ['mʌgɪŋ] *n* assalto *m*.
muggy ['mʌgɪ] (*compar* **-ier**, *superl* **-iest**) *adj* mormacento(ta), quente e úmido(da).
mugshot ['mʌgʃɒt] *n inf fotografia tirada pela polícia de frente e de perfil quando se é fichado.*
mujaheddin [ˌmu:dʒəhe'di:n] *npl* mujaheddin *mpl*.
mulatto [mju:'lætəʊ] (*pl* **-s** OR **-es**) *n* mulato *m*, -ta *f*.
mule [mju:l] *n* **-1.** [animal] mula *f* **-2.** [slipper] tamanco *m*.
mull [mʌl] ◆ **mull over** *vt sep* refletir sobre.
mullah ['mʌlə] *n* mulá *m*.
mulled [mʌld] *adj*: **~ wine** quentão *m*.
mullet ['mʌlɪt] (*pl inv* OR **-s**) *n* tainha *f*.
mulligatawny [ˌmʌlɪgə'tɔ:nɪ] *n (U) sopa indiana feita com caril.*
mullioned *adj* de caixilhos.
multi- ['mʌltɪ] *prefix* mult(i)-.
multi-access *adj* COMPUT de multiacesso.
multicoloured *UK*, **multicolored** *US* [ˌmʌltɪ'kʌləd] *adj* multicor.
multicultural [ˌmʌltɪ'kʌltʃərəl] *adj* multicultural.
multifarious [ˌmʌltɪ'feərɪəs] *adj* variado(da).
multilateral [ˌmʌltɪ'lætərəl] *adj* multilateral.
multilingual *adj* multilíngüe.
multimedia [ˌmʌltɪ'mi:djə] *adj* multimídia.
multimillionaire ['mʌltɪˌmɪljə'neə^r] *n* multimilionário *m*, -ria *f*.
multinational [ˌmʌltɪ'næʃənl] ◇ *adj* multinacional. ◇ *n* multinacional *f*.
multiple ['mʌltɪpl] ◇ *adj* múltiplo(pla). ◇ *n* MATH múltiplo *m*.
multiple-choice *adj* de múltipla escolha.
multiple injuries *npl* lesões *fpl* múltiplas.
multiple pileup *n* acidentes *mpl* múltiplos *(de veículos)*.
multiple sclerosis [-sklɪ'rəʊsɪs] *n (U)* esclerose *f* múltipla.
multiplex cinema ['mʌltɪpleks-] *n* cinema *m* multi-salas, cinema *m* multiplex.
multiplication [ˌmʌltɪplɪ'keɪʃn] *n* multiplicação *f*.
multiplication sign *n* sinal *m* de multiplicação.
multiplication table *n* tabuada *f*.
multiplicity [ˌmʌltɪ'plɪsətɪ] *n* multiplicidade *f*.
multiply ['mʌltɪplaɪ] (*pt & pp* **-ied**) ◇ *vt* multiplicar. ◇ *vi* **-1.** MATH multiplicar **-2.** [increase] multiplicar-se.

multi-purpose *adj* multiuso.
multiracial [ˌmʌltɪ'reɪʃl] *adj* multirracial.
multiscreen cinema *n* cinema *m* multi-salas.
multi-storey *UK*, **multistory** *US* ◇ *adj* com muitos andares. ◇ *n* edifício-garagem *m*.
multitude ['mʌltɪtjuːd] *n* **-1.** [large number] multiplicidade *f* **-2.** [crowd] multidão *f*.
mum [mʌm] *UK inf* ◇ *n* [mother] mamãe *f*. ◇ *adj*: **to keep ~** não dar um pio.
mumble ['mʌmbl] *vt* & *vi* murmurar.
mumbo jumbo ['mʌmbəʊ'dʒʌmbəʊ] *n (U) pej* palavreado *m*, enrolação *f*.
mummify ['mʌmɪfaɪ] (*pt* & *pp* **-ied**) *vt* mumificar.
mummy ['mʌmɪ] (*pl* **-ies**) *n* **-1.** *UK inf* [mother] mamãe *f*, mãe *f* **-2.** [preserved body] múmia *f*.
mumps [mʌmps] *n (U)* caxumba *f*.
munch [mʌntʃ] *vt* & *vi* mascar.
mundane [mʌn'deɪn] *adj* trivial.
mung bean [mʌŋ-] *n* feijão-fradinho *m*.
municipal [mjuː'nɪsɪpl] *adj* municipal.
municipality [mjuːˌnɪsɪ'pælətɪ] (*pl* **-ies**) *n* [city, district] município *m*.
munificent [mjuː'nɪfɪsənt] *adj fml* munificente.
munitions [mjuː'nɪʃnz] *npl* munições *fpl*.
mural ['mjuːərəl] *n* (pintura *f*) mural *m*.
murder ['mɜːdə^r] ◇ *n* assassinato *m*; **to get away with ~** fazer o que bem entender sem ser punido(da). ◇ *vt* assassinar.
murderer ['mɜːdərə^r] *n* assassino *m*.
murderess ['mɜːdərɪs] *n* assassina *f*.
murderous ['mɜːdərəs] *adj* assassino(na), homicida.
murky ['mɜːkɪ] (*compar* **-ier**, *superl* **-iest**) *adj* **-1.** [gen] sombrio(bria) **-2.** [water] turvo(va).
murmur ['mɜːmə^r] ◇ *n* **-1.** [low sound] murmúrio *m* **-2.** MED [of heart] sopro *m*. *vt* & *vi* murmurar.
MusB, MusBac (*abbr of* **Bachelor of Music**) *n (titular de) bacharelado em música*.
muscle ['mʌsl] *n* **-1.** músculo *m* **-2.** *(U) fig* [power] poder *m*.
◆ **muscle in** *vi* intrometer-se.
muscleman ['mʌslmən] (*pl* **-men** [-mən]) *n* [strong man] homem *m* musculoso.
Muscovite ['mʌskəvaɪt] ◇ *adj* moscovita. ◇ *n* moscovita *mf*.
muscular ['mʌskjʊlə^r] *adj* **-1.** [of muscles] muscular **-2.** [strong] musculoso(sa).
muscular dystrophy [-'dɪstrəfɪ] *n (U)* distrofia *f* muscular.
MusD, MusDoc (*abbr of* **Doctor of Music**) *n (titular de) doutorado em música*.
muse [mjuːz] ◇ *n* [source of inspiration] musa *f*. ◇ *vi* meditar, refletir.
museum [mjuː'ziːəm] *n* museu *m*.
mush [mʌʃ] *n (U) inf* **-1.** [gunge] mingau *m* **-2.** [drivel] pieguice *f*.
mushroom ['mʌʃrʊm] ◇ *n* cogumelo *m*. ◇ *vi* [grow quickly] expandir-se rapidamente.
mushroom cloud *n* cogumelo *m* nuclear.
mushy ['mʌʃɪ] (*compar* **-ier**, *superl* **-iest**) *adj* **-1.** [very soft] mole **-2.** [over-sentimental] água-com-açúcar, sentimentalóide.
music ['mjuːzɪk] *n* **-1.** [gen] música *f* **-2.** [written set of notes] partitura *f*.
musical ['mjuːzɪkl] ◇ *adj* **-1.** [relating to music] [melodious] musical **-2.** [talented in music] com talento para música. ◇ *n* musical *m*.
musical box *UK*, **music box** *US* *n* caixinha *f* de música.
musical chairs *n (U)* dança *f* da cadeira.
musical instrument *n* instrumento *m* musical.
music box *n US* = **musical box**.
music centre *n* [machine] aparelho *m* de som.
music hall *n UK* **-1.** [theatre] sala *f* de espetáculo **-2.** *(U)* [variety entertainment] teatro *m* de variedades.
musician [mjuː'zɪʃn] *n* músico *m*, -ca *f*.
music stand *n* atril *m (para partituras)*.
musk [mʌsk] *n (U)* almíscar *m*.
musket ['mʌskɪt] *n* mosquete *m*.
muskrat ['mʌskræt] *n* rato-almiscarado *m*.
Muslim ['mʊzlɪm] ◇ *adj* muçulmano(na). ◇ *n* muçulmano *m*, -na *f*.
muslin ['mʌzlɪn] *n (U)* musselina *f*.
musquash ['mʌskwɒʃ] *n* **-1.** [animal] rato-almiscarado *m* **-2.** *(U)* [fur] pele *f* de rato-almiscarado.
muss [mʌs] *vt US*: **to ~ sthg (up)** desarrumar algo.
mussel ['mʌsl] *n* mexilhão *m*.
must [mʌst] ◇ *modal vb* **-1.** [have to] dever, ter que; **I ~ go** eu preciso ir **-2.** [intend to] ter que **-3.** [as suggestion] precisar, ter que **-4.** [to express likelihood] dever. ◇ *n (U) inf* [necessity]: **the film is a ~** você tem que ver o filme.
mustache *n US* = **moustache**.
mustard ['mʌstəd] *n (U)* mostarda *f*; **~ and cress** *UK* brotos *mpl* de mostarda e agrião.
mustard gas *n (U)* gás *m* de mostarda.
muster ['mʌstə^r] ◇ *vt* **-1.** [assemble] reunir **-2.** [summon - strength, energy] juntar; [- support] reunir. ◇ *vi* reunir-se.
◆ **muster up** *vt fus* **-1.** [courage] armar-se de **-2.** [strength] juntar **-3.** [support] reunir.
mustn't ['mʌsnt] = **must not**.
must've ['mʌstəv] = **must have**.
musty ['mʌstɪ] (*compar* **-ier**, *superl* **-iest**) *adj* **-1.** [gen] mofado(da) **-2.** [smell] com cheiro de mofo.
mutant ['mjuːtənt] ◇ *adj* mutante. ◇ *n* mutante *mf*.
mutate [mjuː'teɪt] *vi* mutar; **to ~ into sthg** mutar-se para algo.
mutation [mjuː'teɪʃn] *n* mutação *f*.
mute [mjuːt] ◇ *adj* mudo(da). ◇ *n* [person who cannot speak] mudo *m*, -da *f*. ◇ *vt* [muffle] abafar, amortecer.
muted ['mjuːtɪd] *adj* **-1.** [soft] suave **-2.** [less strong - reaction] discreto(ta); [- feelings] contido(da).
mutilate ['mjuːtɪleɪt] *vt* mutilar.
mutilation [ˌmjuːtɪ'leɪʃn] *n* mutilação *f*.
mutineer [ˌmjuːtɪ'nɪə^r] *n* amotinado *m*, -da *f*.
mutinous ['mjuːtɪnəs] *adj* [disobedient] rebelde.
mutiny ['mjuːtɪnɪ] (*pl* **-ies**, *pt* & *pp* **-ied**) ◇ *n* motim *m*. ◇ *vi* amotinar-se.
mutt [mʌt] *n inf* **-1.** [fool] tolo *m*, -la *f*, bobo *m*, -ba *f* **-2.** *US* [dog] vira-lata *m*

mutter ['mʌtəʳ] ◇ *vt* murmurar. ◇ *vi* resmungar; **to ~ to sb** sussurrar para alguém; **to ~ to o.s.** ficar resmungando.
muttering ['mʌtərɪŋ] *n* **-1.** [muttered remark] resmungo *m* **-2.** *(U)* [muttering sound] murmúrio *m.*
mutton ['mʌtn] *n (U)* (carne *f* de) carneiro *m*; **~ dressed as lamb** *UK* lobo *m* em pele de cordeiro.
mutual ['mju:tʃʊəl] *adj* **-1.** [reciprocal] mútuo(tua) **-2.** [common] comum.
mutual fund *n US* fundo *m* mútuo.
mutually ['mju:tʃjʊəlɪ] *adv* [reciprocally] mutuamente; **~ exclusive** mutuamente excludente.
Muzak® ['mju:zæk] *n (U) gravação de música suave que toca contiuamente em locais públicos.*
muzzle ['mʌzl] ◇ *n* **-1.** [dog's nose and jaws] focinho *m* **-2.** [wire guard] focinheira *f* **-3.** [of gun] boca *f.* ◇ *vt* **-1.** [put guard on] colocar focinheira em **-2.** *fig* [silence] amordaçar.
muzzy ['mʌzɪ] (*compar* **-ier**, *superl* **-iest**) *adj* [groggy] atordoado(da), confuso(sa).
MVP (*abbr of* **most valuable player**) *n nos Estados Unidos, título dado ao melhor jogador de um time.*
MW (*abbr of* **medium wave**) onda *f* média.
my [maɪ] *poss adj* meu (minha); **~ books** os meus livros; **~ name is Joe** o meu nome é Joe.
mynah bird *n* mainá *m.*
myopic [maɪ'ɒpɪk] *adj* míope.
myriad ['mɪrɪəd] *literary* ◇ *adj* incontável. ◇ *n* miríade *f.*
myrrh [mɜ:ʳ] *n (U)* mirra *f.*
myrtle ['mɜ:tl] *n* mirto *m.*
myself [maɪ'self] *pron* **-1.** *(reflexive)* me; **I hurt ~** machuquei-me **-2.** *(after prep)* mim **-3.** *(stressed)* eu mesmo (eu mesma); **I did it ~** eu mesmo o fiz.
mysterious [mɪ'stɪərɪəs] *adj* misterioso(sa); **to be ~ about sthg** andar cheio (cheia) de mistérios sobre algo.
mysteriously [mɪ'stɪərɪəslɪ] *adv* misteriosamente.
mystery ['mɪstərɪ] (*pl* **-ies**) ◇ *adj* misterioso(sa). ◇ *n* mistério *m.*
mystery story *n* história *f* de suspense.
mystery tour *n* viagem *f* surpresa, *passeio turístico de ônibus no qual as pessoas não conhecem o roteiro.*
mystic ['mɪstɪk] ◇ *adj* místico(ca). ◇ *n* místico *m*, -ca *f.*
mystical ['mɪstɪkl] *adj* [spiritual] místico(ca).
mysticism ['mɪstɪsɪzm] *n (U)* misticismo *m.*
mystified ['mɪstɪfaɪd] *adj* [puzzled] perplexo(xa), desconcertado(da).
mystifying ['mɪstɪfaɪɪŋ] *adj* [puzzling] desconcertante.
mystique [mɪ'sti:k] *n (U)* mística *f.*
myth [mɪθ] *n* mito *m.*
mythic ['mɪθɪk] *adj* [like a myth] mítico(ca).
mythical ['mɪθɪkl] *adj* **-1.** [imaginary] mítico(ca) **-2.** [untrue] falso(sa).
mythological [,mɪθə'lɒdʒɪkl] *adj* [legendary] mitológico(ca).
mythology [mɪ'θɒlədʒɪ] (*pl* **-ies**) *n* **-1.** *(U)* [collection of myths] mitologia *f* **-2.** [set of false beliefs] mito *m.*
myxomatosis [,mɪksəmə'təʊsɪs] *n (U)* mixomatose *f.*

n (*pl* **n's** *OR* **ns**), **N** (*pl* **N's** *OR* **Ns**) [en] *n* [letter] n, N *m.*
◆ **N** (*abbr of* **north**) N.
n/a, N/A -1. (*abbr of* **not applicable**) não-aplicável **-2.** (*abbr of* **not available**) n/d.
NA (*abbr of* **Narcotics Anonymous**) *n organização norte-americana de ajuda a toxicômanos.*
NAACP (*abbr of* **National Association for the Advancement of Colored People**) *n organização norte-americana de defesa dos direitos de pessoas negras.*
NAAFI ['næfɪ] (*abbr of* **Navy, Army & Air Force Institute**) *n organização governamental encarregada das provisões das forças armadas britânicas.*
nab [næb] (*pt* & *pp* **-bed**, *cont* **-bing**) *vt inf* **-1.** [arrest] pegar **-2.** [claim quickly] pegar rapidamente.
NACU (*abbr of* **National Association of Colleges and Universities**) *n associação nacional de faculdades e universidades norte-americanas.*
nadir ['neɪ,dɪəʳ] *n* **-1.** ASTRON nadir *m* **-2.** *fig* [low point] ponto *m* mais baixo.
naff [næf] *adj UK inf* **-1.** [untrendy] brega **-2.** [mediocre] medíocre **-3.** [stupid] idiota.
NAFTA (*abbr of* **North American Free Trade Agreement**) *n* NAFTA *m.*
nag [næg] (*pt* & *pp* **-ged**, *cont* **-ging**) ◇ *n inf* **-1.** [person] estorvo *m* **-2.** *UK* [horse] rocim *m.* ◇ *vt* [pester, find fault with] incomodar; **to ~ sb to do sthg/into doing sthg** incomodar alguém para fazer algo. ◇ *vi*: **to ~ (at sb)** incomodar (alguém).
nagging ['nægɪŋ] *adj* **-1.** [thought, doubt, pain] perturbador(ra), persistente **-2.** [person] briguento(ta).
nail [neɪl] ◇ *n* **-1.** [for fastening] prego *m*; **to hit the ~ on the head** acertar na mosca **-2.** [of finger, toe] unha *f.* ◇ *vt* [fasten]: **to ~ sthg to sthg** pregar algo em algo.
◆ **nail down** *vt sep* **-1.** [fasten] pregar **-2.** *fig* [person]: **to ~ sb down to a date** pressionar alguém a fixar uma data.
◆ **nail up** *vt sep* **-1.** [fasten on wall] fixar **-2.** [close with nails] pregar.
nail-biting *adj* cheio (cheia) de suspense, muito emocionante.
nail brush *n* escova *f* de unhas.

nail clippers *npl* cortador *m* de unhas.
nail file *n* lixa *f* de unha.
nail polish *n (U)* esmalte *m* de unhas.
nail scissors *npl* tesoura *f* para unhas.
nail varnish *n (U)* esmalte *m* de unhas.
nail varnish remover [-rɪ'mu:vəʳ] *n (U)* removedor *m* de esmalte.
Nairobi [naɪ'rəʊbɪ] *n* Nairóbi.
naive, naïve [naɪ'i:v] *adj* ingênuo(nua).
naivety, naïvety [naɪ'i:vtɪ] *n (U)* ingenuidade *f*.
naked ['neɪkɪd] *adj* **-1.** [nude] nu (nua), pelado(da) **-2.** [exposed] descoberto(ta); **~ truth** verdade *f* nua e crua; **~ flame** chama *f* sem proteção; **with the ~ eye** a olho nu **-3.** [obvious, blatant - emotions] óbvio(via); [- aggression] aberto(ta).
NALGO ['nælgəʊ] (*abbr of* **National and Local Government Officers' Association**) *n antigo sindicato de funcionários britânicos.*
Nam [næm] (*abbr of* **Vietnam**) *n US* Vietnam *m*.
name [neɪm] ◇ *n* nome *m*; **what's your ~?** como você se chama?; **by ~** pelo nome; **is there anyone here by the ~ of...?** há alguém aqui que se chame ...?; **in the ~ of** em nome de; **in my/his ~** em meu/seu nome; **in ~ only** só de nome; **to call sb ~s** chamar alguém de tudo; **to make a ~ for o.s.** conquistar uma boa reputação. ◇ *vt* **-1.** [christen] batizar; **to ~ sb after sb** *UK*, **to ~ sb for sb** *US* dar nome a alguém em homenagem a alguém; **to ~ sthg after sthg** *UK*, **to ~ sthg for sthg** *US* dar um nome a algo em homenagem a algo **-2.** [reveal identity of] dizer o nome de **-3.** [choose] escolher.
name-dropping *n (U) menção do nome de pessoas famosas que se conheceu, com o intuito de impressionar.*
nameless ['neɪmlɪs] *adj* **-1.** [unknown - person] anônimo(ma); [- disease] desconhecido(da) **-2.** [indescribable] indescritível.
namely ['neɪmlɪ] *adv* a saber.
nameplate ['neɪmpleɪt] *n* placa *f* de identificação *(em portas).*
namesake ['neɪmseɪk] *n* [with same name] xará *mf*.
Namibia [nɑ:'mɪbɪə] *n* Namíbia; **in ~** na Namíbia.
Namibian [nɑ:'mɪbɪən] ◇ *adj* namibiano(na). ◇ *n* namibiano *m*, -na *f*.
nan(a) [næn(a)] *n UK inf* vó *f*.
nan bread [næn-] *n (U) pão indiano sem fermento.*
nanny ['nænɪ] (*pl* **-ies**) *n* [childminder] babá *f*.
nanny goat *n* cabra *f*.
nanny state *n* estado *m* protetor.
nap [næp] (*pt* & *pp* **-ped**, *cont* **-ping**) ◇ *n* [sleep] soneca *f*, cochilo *m*; **to take** OR **have a ~** tirar uma soneca OR um cochilo. ◇ *vi* [sleep] cochilar; **to be caught napping** *inf* ser pego de surpresa.
napalm ['neɪpɑ:m] *n (U)* napalm *m*.
nape [neɪp] *n*: **~ (of the neck)** nuca *f*.
napkin ['næpkɪn] *n* [serviette] guardanapo *m*.
nappy ['næpɪ] (*pl* **-ies**) *n UK* fralda *f*.
nappy liner *n espécie de papel descartável que mantém o bebê seco quando o restante da fralda está molhada.*
narcissi [nɑ:'sɪsaɪ] *pl* ▷ **narcissus**.
narcissism ['nɑ:sɪsɪzm] *n (U)* narcisismo *m*.
narcissistic [ˌnɑ:sɪ'sɪstɪk] *adj* narcisista.
narcissus [nɑ:'sɪsəs] (*pl* **-cissuses** OR **-cissi**) *n* narciso *m*.
narcotic [nɑ:'kɒtɪk] *n* narcótico *m*.
nark [nɑ:k] *UK inf* ◇ *n* [police informer] informante *mf*, dedo-duro *mf*. ◇ *vt* irritar.
narky ['nɑ:kɪ] (*compar* **-ier**, *superl* **-iest**) *adj UK inf* enjoado(da), mal-humorado(da).
narrate [*UK* nə'reɪt, *US* 'næreɪt] *vt* narrar.
narration [*UK* nə'reɪʃn, *US* næ'reɪʃn] *n* narração *f*.
narrative ['nærətɪv] ◇ *adj* narrativo(va). ◇ *n* narrativa *f*.
narrator [*UK* nə'reɪtəʳ, *US* 'næreɪtər] *n* [speaker] narrador *m*, -ra *f*.
narrow ['nærəʊ] ◇ *adj* **-1.** [thin, not wide] estreito(ta) **-2.** [limited, restricted] limitado(da) **-3.** [marginal, close - victory, majority] apertado(da); [- escape]: **to have a ~ escape** escapar por um triz. ◇ *vt* **-1.** [eyes] apertar **-2.** [difference] diminuir, reduzir. ◇ *vi* **-1.** [road, river] estreitar-se **-2.** [eyes] estreitar-se **-3.** [difference] diminuir, reduzir.
◆ **narrow down** *vt sep* [restrict] diminuir, reduzir.
narrow-gauge *adj* RAIL de bitola estreita.
narrowly ['nærəʊlɪ] *adv* **-1.** [win, lose, miss] por muito pouco **-2.** [escape, miss] por um triz.
narrow-minded [-'maɪndɪd] *adj* de visão limitada.
NAS (*abbr of* **National Academy of Sciences**) *n organização norte-americana de incentivo à pesquisa científica.*
NASA ['næsə] (*abbr of* **National Aeronautics and Space Administration**) *n* NASA *f*.
nasal ['neɪzl] *adj* nasal.
nascent ['neɪsənt] *adj fml* nascente.
NASDAQ (*abbr of* **National Association of Securities Dealers Automated Quotations**) *n* NASDAQ *f*.
nastily ['nɑ:stɪlɪ] *adv* [unkindly] com má intenção; **to fall ~** ter uma queda feia.
nastiness ['nɑ:stɪnɪs] *n (U)* [unkindness] má intenção *f*.
nasturtium [nəs'tɜ:ʃəm] (*pl* **-s**) *n* capuchinha *f*.
nasty ['nɑ:stɪ] (*compar* **-ier**, *superl* **-iest**) *adj* **-1.** [unkind, unpleasant] mal-intencionado(da) **-2.** [disgusting, unattractive] horrível, desagradável; **cheap and ~** barato(ta) e de mau gosto **-3.** [tricky] complicado(da) **-4.** [serious - injury, disease] sério(ria); [- fall, accident] feio (feia).
Natal [nə'tæl] *n* Natal; **in ~** em Natal.
nation ['neɪʃn] *n* [country] nação *f*.
national ['næʃənl] ◇ *adj* nacional. ◇ *n* cidadão *m*, -dã *f*.
national anthem *n* hino *m* nacional.
national curriculum *n*: **the ~** *o currículo nacional do ensino na Inglaterra e no País de Gales.*
national debt *n* dívida *f* pública.
national dress *n (U)* roupas *fpl* típicas *(de um país).*
National Front *n UK* Frente *f* Nacional, *partido político minoritário de extrema direita na Grã-Bretanha.*
national grid *n UK* rede *f* elétrica.

National Guard *n US*: **the** ~ a Guarda Nacional norte-americana.
National Health Service *n (U) UK*: **the** ~ o Serviço Nacional de Saúde, *órgão britânico gestor da saúde pública.*
National Heritage Minister *n ministro da cultura, do turismo e do desporto britânico.*
National Insurance *n (U) UK* **-1.** [system] ≃ Instituto Nacional de Seguro Social **-2.** [payments] contribuição *f* para a previdência social.
nationalism ['næʃnəlɪzm] *n (U)* nacionalismo *m.*
nationalist ['næʃnəlɪst] ◇ *adj* [pro-independence] nacionalista. ◇ *n* [supporter of independence movement] nacionalista *mf.*
nationality [,næʃə'nælətɪ] (*pl* **-ies**) *n* nacionalidade *f.*
nationalization [,næʃnəlaɪ'zeɪʃn] *n* [of company, industry] nacionalização *f.*
nationalize, -ise ['næʃnəlaɪz] *vt* [company, industry] nacionalizar.
nationalized ['næʃnəlaɪzd] *adj* [company, industry] nacionalizado(da).
National Lottery *n*: **the** ~ a loteria britânica.
national park *n* parque *m* nacional.
national service *n (U) UK MIL* serviço *m* militar.
National Trust *n (U) UK*: **the** ~ *organização britânica que promove a preservação e o acesso público a edifícios de interesse histórico ou arquitetônico e a locais de beleza natural,* ≃ o Patrimônio Nacional.
nation state *n* estado *m* nação.
nationwide ['neɪʃənwaɪd] ◇ *adj* em âmbito nacional. ◇ *adv* **-1.** [travel] por todo o país **-2.** [being shown] em todo o país **-3.** [being broadcast] para todo o país.
native ['neɪtɪv] ◇ *adj* **-1.** [country, area] natal **-2.** nativo(va); ~ **language** língua *f* materna; ~ **to** nativo(va) de. ◇ *n* **-1.** [person born in area, country] natural *mf* **-2.** *offensive* [original inhabitant] nativo *m*, -va *f.*
Native American ◇ *adj* indígena norte-americano(na). ◇ *n* indígena *mf* norte-americano, -na.

NATIVE AMERICAN

Entre os séculos XVII e XIX, as tribos aborígenes que povoavam o território norte-americano viram-se obrigadas a defender suas terras dos colonos europeus, muitas vezes tendo de lutar para mantê-las. Muitos índios morreram em combate ou por contrair doenças trazidas pelos europeus para a América. Outros foram obrigados a viver em reservas, territórios destinados especialmente a eles. Ao longo do século XX, o governo dos EUA procurou conceder mais direitos aos grupos étnicos nativos, demonstrando cada vez maior interesse por sua história e cultura tradicional.

Nativity [nə'tɪvətɪ] *n*: **the** ~ a Natividade.
nativity play *n* natividade *f.*
NATO ['neɪtəʊ] (*abbr of* **North Atlantic Treaty Organization**) *n* OTAN *f.*
natter ['nætə^r] *UK inf* ◇ *n*: **to have a** ~ bater um papo, trovar fiado. ◇ *vi* papear, bater um papo.
natty ['nætɪ] (*compar* **-ier**, *superl* **-iest**) *adj* **-1.** *inf* [person] boa-pinta **-2.** [dresser, appearance] elegante, chique.
natural ['nætʃrəl] ◇ *adj* **-1.** [gen] natural; **to die of** ~ **causes** morrer de causas naturais **-2.** [inborn, instinctive] nato(ta) **-3.** [biological] biológico(ca) **-4.** : **C** ~ dó bequadro. ◇ *n* [talented person]: **to be a** ~ ter um talento natural.
natural childbirth *n (U)* parto *m* natural.
natural gas *n (U)* gás *m* natural.
natural history *n (U)* história *f* natural.
naturalist ['nætʃrəlɪst] *n* [biologist] naturalista *mf.*
naturalize, -ise ['nætʃrəlaɪz] *vt* [make citizen] naturalizar; **to be** ~**d** naturalizar-se.
naturally ['nætʃrəlɪ] *adv* **-1.** [as expected, understandably] naturalmente **-2.** [unaffectedly] com naturalidade **-3.** [instinctively] por natureza; **to come** ~ **to sb** ser inato(ta) em alguém.
naturalness ['nætʃrəlnɪs] *n (U)* naturalidade *f.*
natural resources *npl* recursos *mpl* naturais.
natural science *n* ciências *fpl* naturais.
natural wastage *n* demissão *f* voluntária.
natural yoghurt *n* iogurte *m* natural.
nature ['neɪtʃə^r] *n* natureza *f*; **by** ~ por natureza.
nature reserve *n* reserva *f* natural.
nature trail *n* trilha *f* ecológica.
naturist ['neɪtʃərɪst] *n* naturista *mf.*
naughty ['nɔːtɪ] (*compar* **-ier**, *superl* **-iest**) *adj* **-1.** [badly behaved] malcriado(da) **-2.** [rude, indecent] obsceno(na), atrevido(da).
nausea ['nɔːsjə] *n (U)* náusea *f.*
nauseam ['nɔːzɪæm] ▻ **ad nauseam**.
nauseate ['nɔːsɪeɪt] *vt* **-1.** [cause nausea in] nausear, causar náuseas em **-2.** *fig* [disgust]: **it really** ~**s me** isso (realmente) me dá nojo.
nauseating ['nɔːsɪeɪtɪŋ] *adj* **-1.** [sickening] enjoativo(va) **-2.** *fig* [disgusting] repugnante.
nauseous ['nɔːsjəs] *adj* **-1.** [sick] enjoado(da) **-2.** *fig* [revolting] repugnante.
nautical ['nɔːtɪkl] *adj* náutico(ca).
nautical mile *n* milha *f* náutica.
naval ['neɪvl] *adj* naval.
naval officer *n* oficial *mf* da marinha.
nave [neɪv] *n* nave *f (da igreja).*
navel ['neɪvl] *n* umbigo *m.*
navigable ['nævigəbl] *adj* [deep, wide] navegável.
navigate ['nævɪgeɪt] ◇ *vt* **-1.** [steer - plane] pilotar; [- ship] comandar **-2.** [travel safely across] navegar por. ◇ *vi* **-1.** [ship] comandar **-2.** [car] ser co-piloto(ta) **-3.** [plane] pilotar.
navigation [,nævɪ'geɪʃn] *n (U)* [piloting, steering - plane] pilotagem *f*; [- ship] navegação.
navigator ['nævɪgeɪtə^r] *n* **-1.** [on a ship] navegador *m*, -ra *f* **-2.** [on a plane] comandante *mf.*
navvy ['nævɪ] (*pl* **-ies**) *n UK inf* operário *m (em escavações).*
navy ['neɪvɪ] (*pl* **-ies**) ◇ *adj* [in colour] azul-marinho. ◇ *n* **-1.** [armed force] marinha *f* (de guerra) **-2.** = **navy blue**.
navy blue ◇ *adj* azul-marinho. ◇ *n* azul-marinho *m.*
Nazareth *n* Nazaré; **in** ~ em Nazaré.
Nazi ['nɑːtsɪ] (*pl* **-s**) ◇ *adj* nazista. ◇ *n* nazista *mf.*

NB -1. (*abbr of* **nota bene**) NB **-2.** *abbr of* **New Brunswick**.

NBA *n* **-1.** (*abbr of* **National Basketball Association**) NBA *f* **-2.** (*abbr of* **National Boxing Association**) *federação de boxe norte-americana.*

NBC (*abbr of* **National Broadcasting Company**) *n rede de televisão norte-americana,* NBC *f.*

NBS (*abbr of* **National Bureau of Standards**) *n organização norte-americana de normatização de unidades de medida.*

NC -1. (*abbr of* **no charge**) grátis **-2.** *abbr of* **North Carolina**.

NCC (*abbr of* **National Curriculum Council**) *n na Grã-Bretanha, órgão responsável pelo currículo escolar,* ≃ Conselho *m* Nacional de Educação.

NCCL (*abbr of* **National Council for Civil Liberties**) *n organização britânica que defende os direitos do cidadão.*

NCO (*abbr of* **non-commissioned officer**) *n* oficial *m* subalterno.

ND *abbr of* **North Dakota**.

NE -1. *abbr of* **Nebraska -2.** *abbr of* **New England -3.** (*abbr of* **northeast**) NE.

Neanderthal [nɪ'ændətɑ:l] ◇ *adj* neandertal. ◇ *n* (homem *m* de) neandertal *m.*

neap tide [ni:p-] *n* maré *f* morta OR de quadratura.

near [nɪə^r] ◇ *adj* **-1.** [in space] perto **-2.** [in time, relationship] próximo(ma); **in the ~ future** em breve; **the nearest thing to sthg** o mais próximo de algo **-3.** [almost happened] quase; **it was a ~ thing** faltou pouco. ◇ *adv* **-1.** [in space] perto; **come ~er!** chegue mais perto! **-2.** [in time] próximo(ma) **-3.** [almost] quase; **we're nowhere ~ finding a solution** não estamos nem perto de encontrar uma solução. ◇ *prep* **-1. : ~ (to)** perto de; **phone ~er the time** ligue quando chegar a hora **-2.** [on the point of]: **~ (to)** à beira de **-3.** [similar to]: **~ (to)** próximo(ma) de. ◇ *vt* aproximar-se de. ◇ *vi* aproximar-se.

nearby [nɪə'baɪ] ◇ *adj* próximo(ma). ◇ *adv* perto, nas redondezas.

Near East *n*: **the ~** o Oriente Próximo.

nearly ['nɪəlɪ] *adv* [almost] quase; **I ~ cried** quase chorei; **not ~** nem de longe; **not ~ enough** muito pouco; **you don't make ~ enough effort** você não se esforça o suficiente OR o bastante; **he doesn't study ~ enough** ele não estuda o suficiente.

near miss *n* [nearly a collision] quase-colisão *f.*

nearness ['nɪənɪs] *n* [in distance] proximidade *f.*

nearside ['nɪəsaɪd] ◇ *adj* do lado oposto ao do condutor. ◇ *n* lado *m* oposto ao do condutor.

nearsighted [ˌnɪə'saɪtɪd] *adj US* míope.

neat [ni:t] *adj* **-1.** [tidy] arrumado(da) **-2.** [skilful] hábil **-3.** [undiluted] puro(ra) **-4.** *US inf* [very good] ótimo(-ma), maravilhoso(sa).

neatly ['ni:tlɪ] *adv* **-1.** [tidily] com capricho **-2.** [skilfully] habilmente.

neatness ['ni:tnɪs] *n* **-1.** [of room] arrumação *f* **-2.** [of appearance] asseio *m* **-3.** [of handwriting] clareza *f.*

Nebraska [nɪ'bræskə] *n* Nebrasca; **in ~** em Nebrasca.

nebulous ['nebjʊləs] *adj fml* nebuloso(sa).

NEC (*abbr of* **National Exhibition Centre**) *n centro de convenções em Birmingham, Inglaterra.*

necessarily [*UK* 'nesəsrəlɪ, ˌnesə'serəlɪ] *adv* inevitavelmente, necessariamente; **not ~** não necessariamente.

necessary ['nesəsrɪ] *adj* **-1.** [required] necessário(-ria) **-2.** [inevitable] inevitável.

necessitate [nɪ'sesɪteɪt] *vt fml* necessitar de.

necessity [nɪ'sesətɪ] (*pl* **-ies**) *n* necessidade *f*; **of ~** por necessidade.

neck [nek] ◇ *n* **-1.** ANAT pescoço *m*; **to be up to one's ~ (in sthg)** estar até o pescoço (de algo); **to breathe down sb's ~** ficar na cola de alguém; **to stick one's ~ out** arriscar-se **-2.** [of shirt, dress] gola *f* **-3.** [of bottle] gargalo *m.* ◇ *vi inf* agarrar-se.
◆ **neck and neck** *adj* **-1.** [horses] cabeça a cabeça **-2.** [competitors] emparelhado(da).

neckerchief ['nekətʃɪf] (*pl* **-chiefs** OR **-chieves** [-tʃi:vz]) *n* echarpe *f.*

necklace ['neklɪs] *n* colar *m.*

neckline ['neklaɪn] *n* decote *m.*

necktie ['nektaɪ] *n US* gravata *f.*

nectar ['nektə^r] *n (U)* [from flowers] néctar *m.*

nectarine ['nektərɪn] *n* [fruit] nectarina *f.*

née [neɪ] *adj* em solteira.

need [ni:d] ◇ *n* necessidade *f*; **~ for sthg** necessidade por algo; **~ to do sthg** necessidade de fazer algo; **to be in** OR **have ~ of sthg** necessitar de algo; **to have no ~ of sthg** não precisar de algo; **if ~ be** se necessário for; **in ~** em necessidade. ◇ *vt* precisar de, necessitar de; **to ~ to do sthg** precisar fazer algo. ◇ *modal vb*: **~ we go?** precisamos ir mesmo?; **it ~ not happen** não tem que ser assim.
◆ **needs** *adv*: **if ~s must** se preciso for.

needle ['ni:dl] ◇ *n* agulha *f*; **it's like looking for a ~ in a haystack** é como procurar uma agulha em um palheiro. ◇ *vt inf* alfinetar, importunar.

needlecord ['ni:dlkɔ:d] *n (U)* veludo *m* cotelê.

needlepoint ['ni:dlpɔɪnt] *n (U)* bordado *m.*

needless ['ni:dlɪs] *adj* desnecessário(ria); **~ to say ...** desnecessário dizer que ...

needlessly ['ni:dlɪslɪ] *adv* desnecessariamente.

needlework ['ni:dlwɜ:k] *n (U)* **-1.** [work produced] bordado *m* **-2.** [activity] costura *f.*

needn't ['ni:dnt] = **need not**.

needy ['ni:dɪ] (*compar* **-ier**, *superl* **-iest**) ◇ *adj* necessitado(da), carente. ◇ *npl*: **the ~** os necessitados.

nefarious [nɪ'feərɪəs] *adj fml* execrável.

negate [nɪ'geɪt] *vt fml* [cancel out] anular, invalidar.

negation [nɪ'geɪʃn] *n fml* [cancelling out] anulação *f*, invalidação *f.*

negative ['negətɪv] ◇ *adj* negativo(va). ◇ *n* **-1.** PHOT negativo *m* **-2.** LING negação *f*; **to answer in the ~** dizer não.

neglect [nɪ'glekt] ◇ *n* **-1.** [of duty] não-cumprimento *m* **-2.** [of work, children] desleixo *m*, descuido *m*; **in a state of ~** num estado de total abandono. ◇ *vt* **-1.** [not take care of] abandonar **-2.** [not do - duty] não cumprir com; [- work] não fazer; **to ~ to do sthg** deixar de fazer algo.

neglected [nɪ'glektɪd] *adj* [child, garden] abandonado(da).
neglectful [nɪ'glektfʊl] *adj* negligente; ~ **of sb/sthg** negligente com alguém/algo.
negligee ['neglɪʒeɪ] *n* chambre *m*.
negligence ['neglɪdʒəns] *n (U)* negligência *f*.
negligent ['neglɪdʒənt] *adj* negligente.
negligently ['neglɪdʒəntlɪ] *adv* negligentemente.
negligible ['neglɪdʒəbl] *adj* insignificante.
negotiable [nɪ'gəʊʃjəbl] *adj* [which can be discussed] negociável.
negotiate [nɪ'gəʊʃɪeɪt] <> *vt* **-1.** [obtain through negotiation] negociar **-2.** [get over] transpor **-3.** [get around - obstacle] contornar; [- bend] tomar. <> *vi* negociar; **to ~ with sb for sthg** negociar algo com alguém.
negotiation [nɪˌgəʊʃɪ'eɪʃn] *n (U)* [talking, discussion] negociação *f*.
◆ **negotiations** *npl* negociações *fpl*.
negotiator [nɪ'gəʊʃɪeɪtə^r] *n* negociador *m*, -ra *f*.
neigh [neɪ] *vi* relinchar.
neighbor etc *n US* = **neighbour etc**.
neighbour *UK*, **neighbor** *US* ['neɪbə^r] *n* vizinho *m*, -nha *f*.
neighbourhood *UK*, **neighborhood** *US* ['neɪbəhʊd] *n* **-1.** [of town] vizinhança *f*; **in the ~** na vizinhança; **in the ~ of sthg** nas proximidades de algo **-2.** [approximate area]: **in the ~ of** [approximately] por volta de.
neighbourhood watch *n UK* vigilância *f* comunitária.
neighbouring *UK*, **neighboring** *US* ['neɪbərɪŋ] *adj* vizinho(nha).
neighbourly *UK*, **neighborly** *US* ['neɪbəlɪ] *adj* de boa vizinhança; **to be ~** ser um bom vizinho.
neither ['naɪðə^r, 'ni:ðə^r] <> *adj* nenhum(ma). <> *adv* nem; **~ ... nor ...** nem ... nem ...; **that's ~ here nor there** isso não importa. <> *pron* nenhum(ma) dos dois; **~ of us** nenhum de nós dois. <> *conj*: **~ do I** nem eu.
neo- ['ni:əʊ] *prefix* neo-.
neoclassical [ˌni:əʊ'klæsɪkl] *adj* neoclássico(ca).
neolithic [ˌni:əʊ'lɪθɪk] *adj* neolítico(ca).
neologism [ni:'ɒlədʒɪzm] *n* neologismo *m*.
neon ['ni:ɒn] *n (U)* neônio *m*.
neon light *n* lâmpada *f* OR luz *f* de néon.
neon sign *n* letreiro *m* de néon.
Nepal [nɪ'pɔ:l] *n* Nepal; **in ~** no Nepal.
Nepalese [ˌnepə'li:z] *(pl inv)* <> *adj* nepalês(esa). <> *n* [person] nepalês *m*, -esa *f*.
Nepali [nɪ'pɔ:lɪ] *n* [language] nepali *m*, nepalês *m*.
nephew ['nefju:] *n* sobrinho *m*.
nepotism ['nepətɪzm] *n (U)* nepotismo *m*.
Neptune ['neptju:n] *n* [planet] Netuno *m*.
nerd *n pessoa estúpida e ridícula*.
nerve [nɜ:v] *n* **-1.** ANAT nervo *m* **-2.** [courage] coragem *f*; **to lose one's ~** perder a coragem **-3.** [cheek] petulância *f*; **to have the ~ to do sthg** ter a petulância de fazer algo.
◆ **nerves** *npl* nervos *mpl*; **to get on sb's ~s** dar nos nervos de alguém.
nerve centre *n* **-1.** ANAT centro *m* nervoso **-2.** *fig* [headquarters] centro *m* nevrálgico.
nerve gas *n (U)* gás *m* asfixiante.
nerve-racking [-ˌrækɪŋ] *adj* angustiante.
nervous ['nɜ:vəs] *adj* nervoso(sa); **to be ~ of sthg/of doing sthg** ter medo de algo/de fazer algo; **to be ~ about sthg** ficar nervoso(sa) por algo.
nervous breakdown *n* crise *f* nervosa.
nervously ['nɜ:vəslɪ] *adv* nervosamente.
nervousness ['nɜ:vəsnɪs] *n* nervosismo *m*.
nervous system *n* sistema *m* nervoso.
nervous wreck *n* pilha *f* de nervos.
nervy ['nɜ:vɪ] *(compar* **-ier**, *superl* **-iest)** *adj inf* **-1.** [nervous] nervoso(sa) **-2.** *US* [cheeky] petulante *mf*.
nest [nest] <> *n* **-1.** [gen] ninho *m* **-2.** [of ants] formigueiro *m* **-3.** [of wasps] vespeiro *m* **-4.** [of tables] conjunto *m*. <> *vi* [make a nest] fazer um ninho, aninhar-se.
nest egg *n* pé-de-meia *m*.
nestle ['nesl] *vi* **-1.** [make o.s. comfortable] aconchegar-se **-2.** [be sheltered] estar abrigado(da).
nestling ['neslɪŋ] *n* [baby bird] filhote *m*.
net [net] *(pt & pp* **-ted**, *cont* **-ting)** <> *adj* **-1.** [gen] líquido(da) **-2.** [final] final. <> *n* **-1.** [gen] rede *f* **-2.** [type of fabric] malha *f*. <> *vt* **-1.** [catch] enredar **-2.** *fig* [acquire because of skill] alcançar **-3.** [bring in as profit] render.
◆ **Net** *n*: **the Net** COMPUT a Rede.
netball ['netbɔ:l] *n (U) esporte feminino semelhante ao basquete*, bola-ao-cesto *m*.
net curtains *npl* cortinas *fpl* de voile.
Netherlands ['neðələndz] *npl*: **the ~** os Países Baixos; **in the ~** nos Países Baixos.
netiquette ['netɪket] *n* COMPUT netiqueta *f*.
net profit *n* lucro *m* líquido.
net revenue *n* receita *f* líquida.
nett *adj* = **net**.
netting ['netɪŋ] *n (U)* **-1.** [of metal, plastic] tela *f* **-2.** [fabric] voile *m*.
nettle ['netl] <> *n* urtiga *f*. <> *vt* [irritate] irritar.
network ['netwɜ:k] <> *n* **-1.** [gen] rede *f* **-2.** [group of people] grupo *m*; **a ~ of contacts** uma rede de contatos. <> *vt* **-1.** RADIO & TV [broadcast] transmitir em rede **-2.** COMPUT ligar em rede. <> *vi* [give mutual aid] criar uma rede de contatos.
networking ['netwɜ:kɪŋ] *n* COMM estabelecimento *m* de uma rede de contatos.
neuralgia [njʊə'rældʒə] *n (U)* neuralgia *f*.
neurological [ˌnjʊərə'lɒdʒɪkl] *adj* neurológico (ca).
neurologist [ˌnjʊə'rɒlədʒɪst] *n* neurologista *mf*.
neurology [ˌnjʊə'rɒlədʒɪ] *n (U)* neurologia *f*.
neurosis [ˌnjʊə'rəʊsɪs] *(pl* **-ses** [-si:z]) *n* neurose *f*.
neurosurgery [ˌnjʊərəʊ'sɜ:dʒərɪ] *n (U)* neurocirurgia *f*.
neurotic [ˌnjʊə'rɒtɪk] <> *adj* [person] neurótico(ca). <> *n* neurótico *m*, -ca *f*.
neuter ['nju:tə^r] <> *adj* **-1.** GRAM neutro(tra) **-2.** [sexless] castrado(da). <> *vt* castrar.
neutral ['nju:trəl] <> *adj* **-1.** [non-allied] [pale grey-brown & ELEC] neutro(tra) **-2.** [inexpressive] indiferente **-3.** [colourless] incolor. <> *n* **-1.** *(U)* AUT ponto *m* morto **-2.** [POL - country] país *m* neutro; [- person] pessoa *f* neutra.
neutrality [nju:'trælətɪ] *n (U)* POL neutralidade *f*.

neutralize, -ise ['nju:trəlaɪz] *vt* [effects] neutralizar.
neutron ['nju:trɒn] *n* nêutron *m*.
neutron bomb *n* bomba *f* de nêutrons.
Nevada [nɪ'vɑ:dəl] *n* Nevada; **in ~** em Nevada.
never ['nevəʳ] *adv* **-1.** [at no time] nunca; **~ ever** jamais **-2.** *inf* [in surprise, disbelief] nunca; **you ~ did!** não (me diga)! **-3.** *phr*: **well I ~!** não acredito!
never-ending *adj* interminável.
never-never *n UK inf*: **on the ~** a perder de vista.
never-never land *n* país *m* das maravilhas.
nevertheless [ˌnevəðə'les] *adv* contudo, todavia.
new [nju:] *adj* novo(va); **as good as ~** como se fosse novo; **to be ~ to sthg** ser novo em algo.
◆ **news** *n (U)* **-1.** [information] notícia *f*; **the ~s** as notícias; **a piece of ~s** uma notícia; **that's ~s to me** isto é novidade para mim; **to break the ~s to sb** dar a má notícia a alguém **-2.** RADIO & TV noticiário *m*.
New Age *n* New Age *f*, Nova Era *f*.
new blood *n (U) fig* sangue *m* novo.
newborn ['nju:bɔ:n] *adj* recém-nascido(da).
New Brunswick [-'brʌnzwɪk] *n* New Brunswick.
New Caledonia [-ˌkælɪ'dəʊnjəl *n* Nova Caledônia; **in ~** em Nova Caledônia.
New Caledonian [-ˌkælɪ'dəʊnjən] ◇ *adj* neocaledônio(nia). ◇ *n* neocaledônio *m*, -nia *f*.
newcomer ['nju:ˌkʌməʳ] *n*: **~ (to sthg)** novato *m*, -ta *f* (em algo); **~ (to somewhere)** recém-chegado *m*, -da *f* (em algum lugar).
New Delhi *n* Nova Déhli; **in ~** em Nova Délhi.
New England *n* Nova Inglaterra; **in ~** na Nova Inglaterra.
newfangled [ˌnju:'fæŋgld] *adj inf pej* modernoso(-sa).
new-found *adj* recém-descoberto(ta); **~ friend** amigo *m* recente.
Newfoundland ['nju:fəndlənd] *n* Terra *f* Nova.
New Guinea *n* Nova Guiné; **in ~** na Nova Guiné.
New Hampshire [-'hæmpʃəʳ] *n* New Hampshire; **in ~** em New Hampshire.
New Hebrides *npl*: **the ~** as Novas Hébridas; **in the ~** nas Novas Hébridas.
New Jersey *n* Nova Jérsei; **in ~** em Nova Jérsei.
newly ['nju:lɪ] *adv* recém-.
newly-weds *npl* recém-casados *mpl*, -das *fpl*.
New Mexico *n* Novo México; **in ~** no Novo México.
new moon *n* lua *f* nova.
New Orleans [-'ɔ:lɪənz] *n* Nova Orleans; **in ~** em Nova Orleans.
New Quebec *n* Nova Quebec; **in ~** em Nova Quebec.
news agency *n* agência *f* de notícias.
newsagent *UK* ['nju:zeɪdʒənt], **newsdealer** *US* ['nju:zdi:lər] *n* [person] jornaleiro *m*, -ra *f*; **~'s (shop)** banca *f* de jornais.
news bulletin *n* boletim *m* de notícias.
newscast ['nju:zkɑ:st] *n* noticiário *m*, jornal *m*.
newscaster ['nju:zkɑ:stəʳ] *n* **-1.** [television] apresentador *m*, -ra *f* de jornal **-2.** [radio] locutor(ra).
news conference *n* entrevista *f* coletiva.
newsdealer *n US* = **newsagent**.
newsflash ['nju:zflæʃ] *n* plantão *m* de notícias.
newsgroup ['nju:zgru:p] *n* COMPUT grupo *m* de notícias.
newshound ['nju:zhaʊnd] *n* repórter *mf*, caçador *m*, -ra *f* de notícias.
newsletter ['nju:zˌletəʳ] *n* boletim *m* de notícias.
newsman ['nju:zmæn] (*pl* **-men** [-men]) *n* repórter *m*.
New South Wales *n* Nova Gales do Sul.
newspaper ['nju:zˌpeɪpəʳ] *n* jornal *m*.
newspaperman ['nju:zˌpeɪpəmæn] (*pl* **-men** [-men]) *n* [journalist] **-1.** jornalista *m* **-2.** [seller] jornaleiro *m*, -ra *f*.
newsprint ['nju:zprɪnt] *n (U)* papel *m* jornal.
newsreader ['nju:zˌri:dəʳ] *n* **-1.** [TV] apresentador *m*, -ra *f* de jornal **-2.** [radio] locutor(ra).
newsreel ['nju:zri:l] *n* cinejornal *m*.
newsroom ['nju:zrʊm] *n* sala *f* de redação.
news-sheet *n* folheto *m* informativo.
news-stand *n* banca *f* de revistas.
newsworthy ['nju:zˌwɜ:ðɪ] *adj* que vale a pena ser noticiado(da), de interesse jornalístico.
newt [nju:t] *n* tritão *m*.
new technology *n (U)* nova tecnologia *f*.
New Testament *n*: **the ~** o Novo Testamento.
new town *n UK* cidade *f* planejada.
new wave *n* **-1.** CINEMA nova onda *f* **-2.** [in pop music] new wave *f*.
New World *n*: **the ~** o Novo Mundo.
New Year *n* Ano *m* Novo; **Happy ~!** Feliz Ano Novo!
New Year's Day *n* dia *m* de Ano Novo, primeiro *m* do ano.
New Year's Eve *n* véspera *f* de Ano Novo.
New York [-'jɔ:k] *n* **-1.** [city] Nova Iorque; **~ (City)** (cidade *f* de) Nova Iorque **-2.** [state]: **~ (State)** (Estado *m* de) Nova Iorque.
New Yorker [-'jɔ:kəʳ] *n* nova-iorquino *m*, -na *f*.
New Zealand [-'zi:lənd] *n* Nova Zelândia; **in ~** na Nova Zelândia.
New Zealander [-'zi:ləndəʳ] *n* neozelandês(esa).
next [nekst] ◇ *adj* **-1.** [in time] próximo(ma); **~ week** semana que vem; **the ~ week** na semana que vem; **the day after ~** depois de amanhã; **the week after ~** sem ser a próxima semana, na outra **-2.** [in space - turning, page, street] próximo(ma); [- room] ao lado. ◇ *adv* **-1.** [afterwards] depois; **when are you ~ going to Brazil?** quando você irá novamente ao Brasil? **-2.** [next time] da próxima vez (que); **when we ~ meet** da próxima vez que nos encontrarmos **-3.** *(with superlatives)*: **~ best / biggest** o segundo melhor/maior. ◇ *prep US* ao lado de. ◇ *n* próximo *m*, -ma *f*.
◆ **next to** *prep* **-1.** [physically near] ao lado de, junto a **-2.** *(in comparisons)* próximo(ma) de **-3.** [almost] quase; **~ to nothing** quase nada.
next-door ◇ *adj*: **~ neighbour** vizinho *m*, -nha *f* do lado. ◇ *adv* ao lado.
next of kin *n* parente *m* mais próximo.
NF ◇ *n* (*abbr of* **National Front**) *pequeno partido político britânico de extrema direita*. ◇ *abbr of* **Newfoundland**.

NFL (*abbr of* **National Football League**) *n federação norte-americana de futebol americano.*
NG (*abbr of* **National Guard**) *n força militar existente em cada estado norte-americano,* ≃ Guarda *f* Nacional.
NGO (*abbr of* **non-governmental organization**) *n* ONG *f.*
NH *abbr of* **New Hampshire**.
NHL (*abbr of* **National Hockey League**) *n federação norte-americana de hóquei sobre o gelo.*
NHS (*abbr of* **National Health Service**) *n órgão estatal britânico de saúde pública.*
NI ◇ *n* (*abbr of* **National Insurance**) *sistema britânico de seguridade social,* ≃ INSS *m.* ◇ *abbr of* **Northern Ireland**.
Niagara [naɪ'ægrə] *n*: ~ **Falls** as cataratas do Niágara.
nib [nɪb] *n* pena *f (de caneta).*
nibble ['nɪbl] ◇ *vt* **-1.** [subj: person, caterpillar] beliscar; [subj: rodent, goat, sheep] roer **-2.** [playfully] mordiscar. ◇ *vi*: **to** ~ **at sthg** mordiscar algo.
Nicaragua [ˌnɪkə'rægjʊə] *n* Nicarágua; **in** ~ na Nicarágua.
Nicaraguan [ˌnɪkə'rægjʊən] ◇ *adj* nicaraguano(-na). ◇ *n* nicaraguano *m,* -na *f.*
nice [naɪs] *adj* **-1.** [expressing approval - dress, picture] belo(la); [- day, weather] agradável; [- car, food] bom (boa) **-2.** [kind, pleasant] gentil; **it was** ~ **of you to help** foi muita gentileza de sua parte ajudar.
nice-looking [-'lʊkɪŋ] *adj* [attractive] bonito(ta); ~ **person** pessoa *f* atraente.
nicely ['naɪslɪ] *adv* **-1.** [well, attractively, satisfactorily] bem; **that will do** ~ será o suficiente **-2.** [politely] educadamente.
nicety ['naɪsətɪ] (*pl* **-ies**) *n* [refinement] delicadeza *f.*
niche [ni:ʃ] *n* **-1.** [gen] nicho *m* **-2.** [in life] boa colocação *f.*
nick [nɪk] ◇ *n* **-1.** [cut] talha *f,* corte *m* **-2.** *UK inf* [jail]: **he did four days in the** ~ **for burglary** ele ficou quatro dias enjaulado por roubo **-3.** *inf* [condition]: **in good/bad** ~ *UK* em bom/mau estado **-4.** *phr*: **in the** ~ **of time** em cima da hora. ◇ *vt* **-1.** [cut] talhar, cortar **-2.** *UK inf* [steal] passar a mão em **-3.** *UK inf* [arrest] enjaular.
nickel ['nɪkl] *n* **-1.** *(U)* [metal] níquel *m* **-2.** *US* [coin] moeda *f* de 5 centavos.
nickname ['nɪkneɪm] ◇ *n* apelido *m.* ◇ *vt* apelidar.
Nicosia [ˌnɪkə'si:ə] *n* Nicósia.
nicotine ['nɪkəti:n] *n (U)* nicotina *f.*
niece [ni:s] *n* sobrinha *f.*
nifty ['nɪftɪ] (*compar* **-ier**, *superl* **-iest**) *adj inf* chique.
Niger ['naɪdʒə^r] *n* **-1.** [country] Níger; **in** ~ em Níger **-2.** [river]: **the (River)** ~ o (Rio) Níger.
Nigeria [naɪ'dʒɪərɪə] *n* Nigéria; **in** ~ na Nigéria.
Nigerian [naɪ'dʒɪərɪən] ◇ *adj* nigeriano(na). ◇ *n* nigeriano *m,* -na *f.*
Nigerien [naɪ'dʒɪərɪən] ◇ *adj* nigerino(na). ◇ *n* nigerino *m,* -na *f.*
niggardly ['nɪgədlɪ] *adj* **-1.** [person] mesquinho(-nha) **-2.** [amount] miserável.
niggle ['nɪgl] ◇ *n* [worry] preocupação *f.* ◇ *vt* **-1.** [worry] preocupar **-2.** [criticize] incomodar. ◇ *vi* **-1.** [worry]: **it** ~**d at me all day** isso ficou me dando volta o dia inteiro **-2.** [criticize] reclamar.
nigh [naɪ] *adv* **-1.** *literary* [near] próximo(ma) **-2.**: **well** ~ [almost] praticamente.
night [naɪt] *n* **-1.** [not day] noite *f*; **at** ~ à *OR* de noite; ~ **and day, day and** ~ noite e dia, dia e noite **-2.** *phr*: **to have an early/a late** ~ ir dormir cedo/tarde.
◆ **nights** *adv* **-1.** *US* [at night] à *OR* de noite **-2.** *UK* [night shift]: **to work** ~**s** trabalhar durante a noite.
nightcap ['naɪtkæp] *n* **-1.** [drink] *bebida que se toma antes de se ir dormir* **-2.** [hat] touca *f* de dormir.
nightclothes ['naɪtkləʊðz] *npl* roupa *f* de dormir.
nightclub ['naɪtklʌb] *n* casa *f* noturna, nightclub *m.*
nightdress ['naɪtdres] *n* camisola *f.*
nightfall ['naɪtfɔ:l] *n (U)* anoitecer *m.*
nightgown ['naɪtgaʊn] *n* camisola *f.*
nightie ['naɪtɪ] *n inf* camisola *f.*
nightingale ['naɪtɪŋgeɪl] *n* rouxinol *m.*
nightlife ['naɪtlaɪf] *n (U)* vida *f* noturna.
nightlight ['naɪtlaɪt] *n* luz *f* fraca *(que se deixa acesa à noite).*
nightly ['naɪtlɪ] ◇ *adj* noturno(na). ◇ *adv* à noite.
nightmare ['naɪtmeə^r] *n lit* & *fig* pesadelo *m*
nightmarish ['naɪtmeərɪʃ] *adj* horripilante.
night owl *n fig* notívago *m,* -ga *f,* coruja *mf.*
night porter *n* porteiro *m,* -ra *f* do turno da noite.
night safe *n caixa externo de banco para depósitos fora do horário de expediente.*
night school *n (U)* escola *f* noturna.
night shift *n* [period] turno *m* da noite.
nightshirt ['naɪtʃɜ:t] *n* camisolão *m.*
nightspot ['naɪtspɒt] *n* clube *m* noturno.
nightstick ['naɪtstɪk] *n US* cassetete *m.*
night-time *n (U)* noite *f.*
night watchman *n* guarda-noturno *m.*
nightwear *n (U)* roupa *f* de dormir.
nihilism ['naɪəlɪzm] *n (U)* [rejection of authority] niilismo *m.*
nil [nɪl] *n (U)* **-1.** [nothing] nada *m* **-2.** *UK SPORT* zero *m.*
Nile [naɪl] *n*: **the** ~ o Nilo.
nimble ['nɪmbl] *adj* ágil.
nimbly ['nɪmblɪ] *adv* agilmente.
nine [naɪn] *num* nove; *see also* **six**.
nineteen [ˌnaɪn'ti:n] *num* dezenove; *see also* **six**.
nineteenth [naɪn'ti:nθ] *num* décimo nono, décima nona; *see also* **sixth**.
ninetieth ['naɪntɪəθ] *num* nonagésimo(ma); *see also* **sixth**.
ninety ['naɪntɪ] *num* noventa; *see also* **sixty**.
ninny (*pl* **-ies**) *n inf* bobo(ba).
ninth [naɪnθ] *num* nono(na); *see also* **sixth**.
nip [nɪp] (*pt* & *pp* **-ped**, *cont* **-ping**) ◇ *n* **-1.** [pinch] beliscão *m* **-2.** [bite] mordiscada *f* **-3.** [of drink] trago *m.* ◇ *vt* **-1.** [pinch] beliscar **-2.** [bite] mordiscar. ◇ *vi UK inf* [dash] dar uma saída.
nipper ['nɪpə^r] *n UK inf* criancinha *f.*

nipple ['nɪpl] *n* **-1.** [of breast] mamilo *m* **-2.** [of baby's bottle] bico *m*.
nippy ['nɪpɪ] (*compar* **-ier**, *superl* **-iest**) *adj* **-1.** [cold] fresquinho(nha) **-2.** [quick] rápido(da).
NIREX (*abbr of* **Nuclear Industry Radioactive Waste Executive**) *n órgão britânico que regula o lixo radiativo da indústria nuclear,* ≃ CNEN *m*.
Nissen hut *n* refúgio *m* militar.
nit [nɪt] *n* **-1.** [in hair] lêndea *f* **-2.** *UK inf* [idiot] idiota *mf*.
nit-picking *inf* ◇ *adj* minucioso(sa). ◇ *n (U)* detalhismo *m*.
nitrate ['naɪtreɪt] *n* nitrato *m*.
nitric acid ['naɪtrɪk-] *n (U)* ácido *m* nítrico.
nitrogen ['naɪtrədʒən] *n (U)* nitrogênio *m*.
nitroglycerin(e) [ˌnaɪtrəʊ'glɪsəri:n] *n (U)* nitroglicerina *f*.
nitty-gritty [ˌnɪtɪ'grɪtɪ] *n inf*: **to get down to the ~** ir ao que interessa.
nitwit ['nɪtwɪt] *n inf* idiota *mf*.
NJ *abbr of* **New Jersey**.
NLF (*abbr of* **National Liberation Front**) *n* FLN *f*.
NLRB (*abbr of* **National Labor Relations Board**) *n órgão norte-americano de justiça do trabalho*.
NM *abbr of* **New Mexico**.
no [nəʊ] (*pl* **-es**) ◇ *adv* [gen] não; **~, thanks** não obrigado(da). ◇ *adj* nenhum(ma), algum(ma); **I have ~ money left** não tehno mais um tostão. ◇ *n* não *m*.
No., no. (*abbr of* **number**) no.
Noah's ark ['nəʊəz-] *n* arca *f* de Noé.
nobble ['nɒbl] *vt UK inf* **-1.** [racehorse] drogar **-2.** [bribe] subornar **-3.** [grab, catch] apanhar.
Nobel prize [nəʊ'bel-] *n* prêmio *m* Nobel.
nobility [nə'bɪlətɪ] *n* **-1.** [aristocracy]: **the ~** a nobreza **-2.** *(U)* [nobleness] nobreza *f*.
noble ['nəʊbl] ◇ *adj* **-1.** [aristocratic, distinguished] nobre **-2.** [brave] grandioso(osa). ◇ *n* nobre *mf*.
nobleman ['nəʊblmən] (*pl* **-men** [-mən]) *n* homem *m* nobre.
noblewoman ['nəʊblˌwʊmən] (*pl* **-women** [-ˌwɪmɪn]) *n* mulher *f* nobre.
nobly ['nəʊblɪ] *adv* [generously] generosamente.
nobody ['nəʊbədɪ] (*pl* **-ies**) ◇ *pron* ninguém. ◇ *n pej* [insignificant person] joão-ninguém *m*.
no-claim(s) bonus *n* bonificação *f* de seguro.
nocturnal [nɒk'tɜ:nl] *adj* noturno(na).
nod [nɒd] (*pt* & *pp* **-ded**, *cont* **-ding**) ◇ *n* inclinação *f* de cabeça. ◇ *vt* [in agreement]: **to ~ one's head** assentir com a cabeça; [as greeting] cumprimentar com a cabeça. ◇ *vi* **-1.** [in agreement] assentir com a cabeça **-2.** [to indicate sthg] indicar com a cabeça **-3.** [as greeting]: **to ~ to sb** cumprimentar alguém com a cabeça.
◆ **nod off** *vi* cabecear.
node [nəʊd] *n* **-1.** [gen] nó *m* **-2.** COMPUT nó *m*, nodo *m*.
nodule ['nɒdju:l] *n* nódulo *m*.
no-fly zone *n* zona *f* de exclusão aérea.
no-go area *n UK* zona *f* proibida.
noise [nɔɪz] *n* [sound] barulho *m*.
noiseless ['nɔɪzlɪs] *adj* silencioso(osa).
noiselessly ['nɔɪzlɪslɪ] *adv* silenciosamente.
noisily ['nɔɪzɪlɪ] *adv* ruidosamente, fazendo barulho.
noisy ['nɔɪzɪ] (*compar* **-ier**, *superl* **-iest**) *adj* barulhento(ta).
nomad ['nəʊmæd] *n* nômade *mf*.
nomadic [nə'mædɪk] *adj* nômade.
no-man's-land *n (U)* terra *f* de ninguém.
nom de plume *n* pseudônimo *m*.
nominal ['nɒmɪnl] *adj* **-1.** [in name only] apenas no nome; **a ~ Catholic** um católico só no nome; **a ~ leader** um líder de fachada **-2.** [very small] simbólico(ca).
nominally ['nɒmɪnəlɪ] *adv* [in theory] teoricamente.
nominate ['nɒmɪneɪt] *vt* **-1.** [propose]: **to ~ sb (for/as sthg)** designar alguém (para algo) **-2.** [appoint]: **to ~ sb (sthg)** nomear alguém (algo); **to ~ sb (to sthg)** nomear alguém (para algo).
nomination [ˌnɒmɪ'neɪʃn] *n* **-1.** [proposal] indicação *f* **-2.** *(U)* [appointment]: **~ (to sthg)** nomeação *f* (para algo).
nominee [ˌnɒmɪ'ni:] *n* nomeado *m*, -da *f*.
non- [nɒn] *prefix* [not] não-.
non-addictive *adj* que não provoca dependência.
non-aggression *n (U)* não-agressão *f*.
non-alcoholic *adj* não alcoólico(ca).
non-aligned *adj* não-alinhado(da).
non-believer *n* descrente *mf*.
nonchalant [*UK* 'nɒnʃələnt, *US* ˌnɒnʃə'lɑ:nt] *adj* indiferente.
nonchalantly [*UK* 'nɒnʃələntlɪ, *US* ˌnɒnʃə'lɑ:ntlɪ] *adv* com indiferença.
non-combatant *n* não-combatente *mf*.
non-commissioned officer *n* oficial *mf* subalterno, -na, funcionário *m*, -ria *f* não-comissionado, -da *f*.
non-committal *adj* evasivo(va).
non-competitive *adj* não-competitivo(va).
non compos mentis [-ˌkɒmpəs'mentɪs] *adj* fora do juízo perfeito, que não está em posse de suas faculdades mentais.
nonconformist [ˌnɒnkən'fɔ:mɪst] ◇ *adj* inconformista. ◇ *n* inconformista *mf*.
nonconformity *n (U)* inconformismo *m*.
noncontributory [ˌnɒnkən'trɪbjʊtərɪ] *adj* não-contributivo(va).
non-cooperation *n (U)* não-cooperação *f*.
nondescript [*UK* 'nɒndɪskrɪpt, *US* ˌnɒndɪ'skrɪpt] *adj* desinteressante.
non-drinker *n* abstêmio *m*, -mia *f*.
non-drip *adj* que não pinga.
non-driver *n*: **he's a ~** ele não sabe dirigir.
none [nʌn] *pron* nehum *m*, -ma *f*; **there's ~ left** não resta nada; **~ of this is your fault** nada disso foi culpa sua.
nonentity [nɒ'nentətɪ] (*pl* **-ies**) *n* nulidade *f*, zero *mf* à esquerda.
non-essential *adj* supérfluo(flua).
nonetheless [ˌnʌnðə'les] *adv* contudo, não obstante.
non-event *n* decepção *f*, fracasso *m*.
non-executive director *n diretor ou diretora não-responsável pela tomada de decisões*

em sua instituição ou empresa.
non-existent *adj* inexistente.
non-fattening *adj* que não engorda.
non-fiction *n (U)* não-ficção *f.*
non-flammable *adj* não-inflamável.
non-infectious *adj* não-infeccioso(sa).
non-inflammable *adj* não-inflamável.
non-interference, non-intervention *n (U)* não-intervenção *f.*
non-iron *adj* que não precisa passar.
non-malignant *adj* não-maligno(na).
non-member *n* não-sócio *m*, não-membro *m.*
non-negotiable *adj* não-negociável.
no-no *n inf*: **it's a ~** isso é algo que não se faz.
no-nonsense *adj* prático(ca).
non-operational *adj* inoperante.
non-participation *n (U)* não-participação *f.*
non-payment *n (U)* inadimplência *f*, não-pagamento *m.*
nonplussed, nonplused *US* [ˌnɒn'plʌst] *adj* perplexo(xa).
non-profit-making *UK*, **non-profit** *US adj* sem fins lucrativos.
non-proliferation *n (U)* não-proliferação *f.*
non-renewable *adj* **-1.** [contract, agreement] não-prorrogável **-2.** [natural resources, fossil fuels] não-renovável.
non-resident *n* **-1.** [of country] não-residente *mf* **-2.** [of hotel]: **open to ~s** aberto ao público.
non-returnable *adj* [bottle] não-retornável, sem retorno.
nonsense ['nɒnsəns] ◇ *n (U)* **-1.** [meaningless words] bobagem *f*, asneira *f* **-2.** [foolish idea] besteira *f*; **it is ~ to suggest that ...** é um absurdo sugerir que ... **-3.** [foolish behaviour] idiotice *f*; **stop this ~ at once** pára com essas criancices agora mesmo; **to make (a) ~ of sthg** ridicularizar algo. ◇ *excl* bobagem!, que nada!
nonsensical [nɒn'sensɪkl] *adj* sem sentido, absurdo(da).
non sequitur [-'sekwɪtəʳ] *n* non sequitur *m*, incoerência *f.*
non-shrink *adj* que não encolhe.
non-skid *adj* antiderrapante.
non-slip *adj* antiderrapante.
non-smoker *n* não-fumante *mf.*
non-starter *n UK inf* [plan]: **to be a ~** estar condenado(da) ao fracasso.
non-stick *adj* antiaderente.
non-stop ◇ *adj* **-1.** [gen] contínuo(nua), incessante **-2.** [flight] sem escalas. ◇ *adv* sem parar, continuamente.
non-taxable *adj* isento(ta) de impostos.
non-toxic *adj* atóxico(ca).
non-transferable *adj* não-transferível.
non-U *adj UK dated* popular, pouco refinado(da).
non-violence *n (U)* não-violência *f.*
non-voter *n* pessoa *f* que não vota.
non-voting *adj* **-1.** [person] que não vota **-2.** *FIN* [shares] sem direito a voto.
non-white ◇ *adj* que não é da raça branca. ◇ *n* pessoa *f* que não é da raça branca.
noodles ['nu:dlz] *npl* talharim *m.*
nook [nʊk] *n* [of room] canto *m*; **every ~ and cranny** todos os cantos.
noon [nu:n] ◇ *n (U)* meio-dia *m.* ◇ *comp* do meio-dia.
noonday ['nu:ndeɪ] ◇ *n* meio-dia *m.* ◇ *comp* do meio-dia.
no one *pron* = **nobody**.
noose [nu:s] *n* [lasso] nó *m* corrediço.
no-place *adv US* = **nowhere**.
nor [nɔ:ʳ] *conj* **-1.** ▷ **neither -2.** [and not] nem; **I don't smoke - ~ do I** eu não fumo - nem eu; **I don't know, ~ do I care** não sei, nem quero saber.
Nordic ['nɔ:dɪk] *adj* nórdico(ca).
norm [nɔ:m] *n* norma *f*; **the ~** o normal.
normal ['nɔ:ml] *adj* normal.
normality [nɔ:'mælɪtɪ], **normalcy** *US* ['nɔ:mlsɪ] *n (U)* normalidade *f.*
normalize, -ise ['nɔ:məlaɪz] ◇ *vt* normalizar. ◇ *vi* normalizar-se.
normally ['nɔ:məlɪ] *adv* normalmente.
Norman ◇ *adj* normando(da). ◇ *n* normando(da).
Normandy ['nɔ:məndɪ] *n* Normandia; **in ~** na Normandia.
Norse [nɔ:s] *adj* nórdico(ca).
north [nɔ:θ] ◇ *adj* norte; **North London** o norte de Londres. ◇ *adv* para o norte; **~ of** ao norte de. ◇ *n* [direction] norte *m.*
North Africa *n* África do Norte; **in ~** na África do Norte.
North America *n* América do Norte; **in ~** na América do Norte.
North American ◇ *adj* **-1.** da América do Norte **-2.** [of USA] norte-americano(na). ◇ *n* **-1.** pessoa *f* da América do Norte **-2.** [of USA] norte-americano *m*, -na *f.*
northbound ['nɔ:θbaʊnd] *adj* com direção norte.
North Carolina [-ˌkærə'laɪnə] *n* Carolina *f* do Norte; **in ~** na Carolina do Norte.
North Country *n*: **the ~** *UK a região norte da Inglaterra.*
North Dakota [-də'kəʊtə] *n* Dakota do Norte; **in ~** em Dakota do Norte.
northeast [ˌnɔ:θ'i:st] ◇ *adj* nordeste. ◇ *n* [direction] nordeste *m.* ◇ *adv* para o nordeste; **~ of** ao nordeste de.
northeasterly [ˌnɔ:θ'i:stəlɪ] *adj* **-1.** [towards northeast, in northeast] a nordeste **-2.** [from northeast] do nordeste.
northerly ['nɔ:ðəlɪ] *adj* **-1.** [towards north, in north] ao norte **-2.** [from north] do norte.
northern ['nɔ:ðən] *adj* do norte.
Northerner ['nɔ:ðənəʳ] *n pessoa que nasceu ou vive no norte.*
Northern Ireland *n* Irlanda do Norte; **in ~** na Irlanda do Norte.
Northern Lights *npl*: **the ~** a aurora boreal.
northernmost ['nɔ:ðənməʊst] *adj* mais setentrional, mais ao norte.
Northern Territory *n* Território *m* do Norte.
North Korea *n* Coréia do Norte; **in ~** na Coréia do Norte.

North Korean <> *adj* norte-coreano(na). <> *n* norte-coreano *m*, -na *f*.

North Pole *n*: **the** ~ o Pólo Norte.

North Sea <> *n*: **the** ~ o Mar do Norte. <> *comp* **-1.** [oil, oilrig] do Mar do Norte **-2.** [fishing] no Mar do Norte.

North Star *n*: **the** ~ a estrela Polar.

North Vietnam *n* Vietnã do Norte; **in** ~ no Vietnã do Norte.

North Vietnamese <> *adj* norte-vietnamita. <> *n* norte-vietnamita *mf*.

northward ['nɔ:θwəd] <> *adj* para o norte. <> *adv* = **northwards**.

northwards ['nɔ:θwədz] *adv* para o norte.

northwest [ˌnɔ:θ'west] <> *adj* **-1.** [in the northwest, facing the northwest] noroeste **-2.** [from the northwest] do noroeste. <> *n* [direction] noroeste *m*. <> *adv* para noroeste; ~ **of** a noroeste de.

northwesterly [ˌnɔ:θ'westəlɪ] *adj* **-1.** [towards northwest, in northwest] a noroeste **-2.** [from northwest] do noroeste.

Northwest Territories *npl Can*: **the** ~ os Territórios do Noroeste.

North Yemen *n* Iêmen do Norte; **in** ~ no Iêmen do Norte.

Norway ['nɔ:weɪ] *n* Noruega; **in** ~ na Noruega.

Norwegian [nɔ:'wi:dʒən] <> *adj* norueguês(esa). <> *n* **-1.** [person] norueguês *m*, -esa *f* **-2.** [language] norueguês *m*.

Nos., nos. (*abbr of* **numbers**) nos.

nose [nəʊz] *n* **-1.** ANAT nariz *m*; **under one's** ~ debaixo do nariz de alguém; **to cut one's** ~ **off to spite one's face** prejudicar-se ao tentar prejudicar outra pessoa; **to have a** ~ **for sthg** sentir o cheiro de algo; **he gets up my** ~ *inf* ele me deixa muito irritado(da); **to keep one's** ~ **out of sthg** não meter o nariz em algo; **to look down one's** ~ **at sb/sthg** *fig* olhar de cima para alguém/algo; **to pay through the** ~ pagar os olhos da cara; **to poke** OR **stick one's** ~ **into sthg** *inf* meter o nariz em algo; **to turn up one's** ~ **at sthg** torcer o nariz para algo **-2.** [of car] ponta *f*.

◆ **nose about, nose around** *vi* bisbilhotar.

nosebag ['nəʊzbæg] *n* embornal *m*.

nosebleed ['nəʊzbli:d] *n* hemorragia *f* nasal.

nosecone ['nəʊzkəʊn] *n* ogiva *f*.

nosedive ['nəʊzdaɪv] <> *n* [of plane] mergulho *m*. <> *vi* **-1.** [plane] mergulhar **-2.** *fig* [prices, popularity] despencar.

nose ring *n* argola *f* de nariz.

nose stud *n* piercing *m* de nariz.

nosey ['nəʊzɪ] *adj* = **nosy**.

nosh [nɒʃ] *n UK inf* [food] rango *m*.

nosh-up *n UK inf* comilança *f*.

nostalgia [nɒ'stældʒəl *n (U)*: ~ **(for sthg)** nostalgia *f* (de algo).

nostalgic [nɒ'stældʒɪk] *adj* nostálgico(ca).

nostril ['nɒstrəl] *n* narina *f*.

nosy ['nəʊzɪ] (*compar* **-ier**, *superl* **-iest**) *adj* curioso(sa), abelhudo(da).

not [nɒt] *adv* não; **I hope** ~ espero que não; ~ **a** nem um (uma); ~ **even a** nem mesmo um (uma); ~ **all/every** nem todos(das); ~ **always** nem sempre; **it's** ~ **every day we get sunshine** não é todo dia que tem sol; **it's** ~ **that I'm jealous, but ...** não que eu seja ciumento, mas ...; ~ **at all** em absoluto, de maneira nenhuma; [to acknowledge thanks] de nada.

notable ['nəʊtəbl] <> *adj* notável; **to be** ~ **for sthg** destacar-se por algo. <> *n fml* celebridade *f*.

notably ['nəʊtəblɪ] *adv* **-1.** [in particular] especialmente **-2.** [noticeably] claramente, obviamente.

notary ['nəʊtərɪ] (*pl* **-ies**) *n*: ~ **(public)** notário *m*, -ria *f*.

notation [nəʊ'teɪʃn] *n* notação *f*.

notch [nɒtʃ] *n* **-1.** [cut] corte *m*, entalhe *m* **-2.** *fig* [on scale] ponto *m*.

◆ **notch up** *vt fus* conseguir.

note [nəʊt] <> *n* **-1.** [gen] nota *f* **-2.** [written reminder, record] anotação *f*, nota *f*; **to take** ~ **of sthg** prestar atenção em algo; **to compare** ~**s** trocar idéias **-3.** [short letter] bilhete *m* **-4.** [tone] tom *m* **-5.** [importance]: **of** ~ digno(na) de nota. <> *vt* **-1.** [observe] notar, observar **-2.** [mention] apontar, mencionar.

◆ **notes** *npl* [in book] anotações *fpl*.

◆ **note down** *vt sep* anotar.

notebook ['nəʊtbʊk] *n* **-1.** [for writing in] caderno *m* **-2.** COMPUT notebook *m*.

noted ['nəʊtɪd] *adj* conhecido(da), destacado(da); ~ **for sthg** conhecido(da) por algo.

notepad ['nəʊtpæd] *n* bloco *m* de notas.

notepaper ['nəʊtpeɪpə^r] *n (U)* papel *m* de carta.

noteworthy ['nəʊtˌwɜ:ðɪ] (*compar* **-ier**, *superl* **-iest**) *adj* digno(na) de menção.

nothing ['nʌθɪŋ] <> *pron* nada; ~ **new/interesting** nada de novo/interessante; **she did** ~ ela não fez nada; **for** ~ [free] de graça; [in vain] para nada.

nothingness ['nʌθɪŋnɪs] *n (U)* nada *m*.

notice ['nəʊtɪs] <> *n* **-1.** *(U)* [attention] atenção *f*; **to come to one's** ~ chegar até alguém; **to escape one's** ~ passar desapercebido(da); **to take** ~ **(of sb/sthg)** dar bola (para alguém/algo); **to take no** ~ **(of sb/sthg)** não dar bola (para alguém/algo), fazer pouco caso (de alguém/algo); **he didn't take a blind bit of** ~ ele não fez nem mesmo o mais remoto caso **-2.** *(U)* [warning, announcement] aviso *m*; **at short** ~ em cima da hora; **until further** ~ até segunda ordem **-3.** *(U)* [at work]: **to be given one's** ~ receber aviso prévio; **to hand in one's** ~ apresentar pedido de demissão. <> *vt* perceber, notar; **to** ~ **sb doing sthg** ver que alguém está fazendo algo. <> *vi* perceber.

noticeable ['nəʊtɪsəbl] *adj* notável, digno(na) de nota.

noticeably ['nəʊtɪsəblɪ] *adv* notavelmente.

notice board *n* quadro *m* de avisos.

notification [ˌnəʊtɪfɪ'keɪʃn] *n (U)* notificação *f*.

notify ['nəʊtɪfaɪ] (*pt* & *pp* **-ied**) *vt*: **to** ~ **sb (of sthg)** notificar alguém (de algo).

notion ['nəʊʃn] *n* [concept, idea] noção *f*.

◆ **notions** *npl US* [haberdashery] aviamentos *mpl*.

notional ['nəʊʃənl] *adj* [hypothetical] hipotético(ca).

notoriety [ˌnəʊtə'raɪətɪ] *n (U)* notoriedade *f*.

notorious [nəʊ'tɔ:rɪəs] *adj* notório(ria); ~ **for sthg** notório(ria) por algo.

notoriously [nəʊ'tɔːrɪəslɪ] *adv* notoriamente.
notwithstanding [ˌnɒtwɪθ'stændɪŋ] *fml* ◇ *prep* não obstante. ◇ *adv* no entanto, não obstante.
nougat ['nuːgɑː] *n* nugá *m*.
nought [nɔːt] *num* zero *m*; ~**s and crosses** jogo *m* da velha.
noun [naʊn] *n* substantivo *m*.
nourish ['nʌrɪʃ] *vt* **-1.** [feed] nutrir **-2.** [entertain, foster] alimentar.
nourishing ['nʌrɪʃɪŋ] *adj* nutritivo(va).
nourishment ['nʌrɪʃmənt] *n (U)* alimento *m*.
nouveau riche ◇ *adj* de novo-rico. ◇ *n* novo-rico *m*, nova-rica *f*.
Nov. (*abbr of* **November**) nov.
Nova Scotia [ˌnəʊvə'skəʊʃəl *n* Nova Escócia; **in** ~ na Nova Escócia.
Nova Scotian [ˌnəʊvə'skəʊʃn] ◇ *adj* neoescocês(esa). ◇ *n* neoescocês *m*, -esa *f*.
novel ['nɒvl] ◇ *adj* original. ◇ *n* romance *m*.
novelist ['nɒvəlɪst] *n* romancista *mf*.
novelty ['nɒvltɪ] (*pl* **-ies**) *n* **-1.** *(U)* [quality] originalidade *f* **-2.** [unusual object, event] novidade *f* **-3.** [cheap object] bugiganga *f*.
November [nə'vembəʳ] *n* novembro *m*; *see also* **September**.
novice ['nɒvɪs] *n* **-1.** [inexperienced person] novato *m*, -ta *f*, principiante *mf* **-2.** RELIG noviço *m*, -ça *f*.
Novocaine® ['nəʊvəkeɪn] *n (U)* novocaína® *f*.
now [naʊ] ◇ *adv* **-1.** [at this time] agora; **from** ~ **on I'm in charge** de agora em diante eu estou no comando; **any day** ~ qualquer dia destes; **any time** ~ a qualquer momento; ~ **and then** OR **again** de vez em quando; **for** ~ por ora **-2.** [already, before this time] já; **they should be here by** ~ eles já deveriam ser estar aqui; **he's been away for two weeks** ~ já faz duas semanas que ele foi embora **-3.** [at a particular time in the past] então; **we were all singing** ~ estavámos todos cantando naquele momento **-4.** [to introduce statement] agora **-5.** [nowadays] atualmente; ~ **many people use computers to work** atualmente muitas pessoas usam computadores para trabalhar. ◇ *conj*: ~ **(that)** agora que.
NOW [naʊ] (*abbr of* **National Organization for Women**) *n importante organização feminista norte-americana*.
nowadays ['naʊədeɪz] *adv* hoje em dia, atualmente.
nowhere *UK* ['nəʊweəʳ], **no-place** *US adv* em nenhum lugar; **to appear out of** OR **from** ~ aparecer do nada; ~ **near** nem de longe; **to be getting** ~ indo a lugar nenhum; **this is getting us** ~ isto não está nos levando a nada.
no-win situation *n* beco *m* sem saída.
noxious ['nɒkʃəs] *adj* nocivo(va).
nozzle ['nɒzl] *n* bocal *m*, bico *m*.
NP (*abbr of* **notary public**) tabelião *m*, -liã *f*.
NS *abbr of* **Nova Scotia**.
NSC (*abbr of* **National Security Council**) *n conselho federal que coordena a defesa e a política externa norte-americanas*.
NSF ◇ *n* (*abbr of* **National Science Foundation**) *fundação norte-americana de pesquisa científica*. ◇ (*abbr of* **not sufficient funds**) sem fundos.
NSPCC (*abbr of* **National Society for the Prevention of Cruelty to Children**) *n organização britânica de prevenção a maus tratos a crianças*.
NSU (*abbr of* **non-specific urethritis**) *n* uretrite *f* não-específica.
NSW *abbr of* **New South Wales**.
NT *n* **-1.** (*abbr of* **New Testament**) NT *m* **-2.** (*abbr of* **National Trust**) *organização britânica encarregada da preservação de edifícios históricos e locais de interesse público*.
nth [enθ] *adj inf* [umpteenth] enésimo(ma).
nuance [njuː'ɑːns] *n* [of word, meaning] nuança *f*.
nub [nʌb] *n* [crux] essência *f*.
Nubian Desert *n*: **the** ~ o Deserto Núbio.
nubile [*UK* 'njuːbaɪl, *US* 'nuːbəl] *adj fml or hum* núbil.
nubuck *n* nubuck *m*, *tipo de camurça muito fina usada na fabricação de sapatos*.
nuclear ['njuːklɪəʳ] *adj* nuclear.
nuclear bomb *n* bomba *f* nuclear.
nuclear disarmament *n (U)* desarmamento *m* nuclear.
nuclear energy *n (U)* energia *f* nuclear.
nuclear family *n* família *f* nuclear.
nuclear fission *n (U)* fissão *f* nuclear.
nuclear-free zone *n* zona *f* livre de energia nuclear.
nuclear fusion *n (U)* fusão *f* nuclear.
nuclear physics *n (U)* física *f* nuclear.
nuclear power *n (U)* energia *f* nuclear.
nuclear reactor *n* reator *m* nuclear.
nuclear war *n* guerra *f* nuclear.
nuclear winter *n* inverno *m* nuclear.
nucleus ['njuːklɪəs] (*pl* **-lei** [-lɪaɪ]) *n* núcleo *m*.
nude [njuːd] ◇ *adj* nu (nua). ◇ *n* [figure, painting] nu *m*; **in the** ~ em pêlos.
nudge [nʌdʒ] ◇ *n* **-1.** [with elbow] cutucada *f* **-2.** *fig* [to encourage] empurrada *f*. ◇ *vt* **-1.** [with elbow] cutucar **-2.** *fig* [to encourage] empurrar; **to** ~ **sb's memory** puxar a memória de alguém.
nudist ['njuːdɪst] ◇ *adj* nudista. ◇ *n* nudista *mf*.
nudity ['njuːdətɪ] *n (U)* nudez *f*.
nugget ['nʌgɪt] *n* **-1.** [of gold] pepita *f* **-2.** *fig* [valuable piece] pérola *f*.
nuisance ['njuːsns] *n* **-1.** [annoying thing, situation] chatice *f* **-2.** [annoying person] chato *m*, -ta *f* de galocha; **to make a** ~ **of o.s.** amolar.
nuke [njuːk] *inf* ◇ *n* arma *f* nuclear. ◇ *vt* bombardear com armas nucleares.
null [nʌl] *adj*: ~ **and void** nulo e sem valor.
nullify ['nʌlɪfaɪ] (*pt* & *pp* **-ied**) *vt* anular.
numb [nʌm] ◇ *adj* [shoulder, hand] adormecido(-da); [person] paralisado(da); **to be** ~ **with cold** estar congelado(da) de frio. ◇ *vt* [subj: cold, anaesthetic] paralisar.
number ['nʌmbəʳ] ◇ *n* **-1.** [gen] número *m*; **a** ~ **of** vários(as); **I've told you any** ~ **of times ...** já te disse um milhão de vezes ... **-2.** [of car] placa *f* **-3.** [song] música *f*. ◇ *vt* **-1.** [amount to] chegar a **-2.** [give a number to] numerar **-3.** [include]: **to be** ~**ed among** figurar entre.

number-crunching [-ˌkrʌntʃɪŋ] *n (U) inf* cálculo *m* em grande escala.
numberless [ˈnʌmbəlɪs] *adj* inumerável.
number one ◇ *adj* [main] número um, principal. ◇ *n* **-1.** [priority] o mais importante **-2.** *inf* [oneself]: **to look after ~** cuidar de si mesmo(ma).
numberplate [ˈnʌmbəpleɪt] *n* placa *f* do carro.
Number Ten *n*: **~ (Downing Street)** *a casa número 10 de Downing Street, residência oficial do primeiro ministro britânico*; *fig* o governo britânico.
numbness [ˈnʌmnɪs] *n* **-1.** dormência *f* **-2.** *fig* [with shock, fear] paralisia *f.*
numbskull [ˈnʌmskʌl] *n* = **numskull**.
numeracy [ˈnju:mərəsɪ] *n UK* facilidade *f* com números.
numeral [ˈnju:mərəl] *n* algarismo *m.*
numerate [ˈnju:mərət] *adj UK* que sabe fazer cálculos elementares.
numerical [nju:ˈmerɪkl] *adj* numérico(ca).
numerous [ˈnju:mərəs] *adj* inúmero(ra).
numskull [ˈnʌmskʌl] *n inf* besta *mf*, imbecil *mf.*
nun [nʌn] *n* freira *f.*
nuptial [ˈnʌpʃl] *adj fml* nupcial.
nurse [nɜ:s] ◇ *n* enfermeiro *m*, -ra *f.* ◇ *vt* **-1.** MED [care for] cuidar de, atender **-2.** [harbour, foster] nutrir **-3.** [breast-feed] amamentar.
nursemaid [ˈnɜ:smeɪd] *n* babá *f.*
nursery [ˈnɜ:sərɪ] (*pl* **-ies**) ◇ *adj* pré-escolar. ◇ *n* **-1.** [for children] creche *f* **-2.** [for plants, trees] viveiro *m* **-3.** [at home] quarto *m* das crianças.
nursery nurse *n UK* ama-seca *f.*
nursery rhyme *n* cantiga *f* infantil.
nursery school *n* pré-escola *f.*
nursery slopes *npl* SKIING pista *f* para principiantes.
nursing [ˈnɜ:sɪŋ] *n* **-1.** [profession] enfermagem *f* **-2.** [care] cuidados *mpl.*
nursing auxiliary *n* auxiliar *mf* de enfermagem.
nursing home *n* **-1.** [for old people] clínica *f* de repouso **-2.** [for childbirth] maternidade *f (privada).*
nurture [ˈnɜ:tʃəʳ] *vt* **-1.** [children, plants] criar **-2.** [hope, desire, plan] alimentar.
nut [nʌt] *n* **-1.** [to eat] noz *f* **-2.** TECH porca *f*; **the ~s and bolts** *fig* [basics] o básico **-3.** *inf* [mad person] maluco *m*, -ca *f* **-4.** *inf* [enthusiast] aficionado *m*, -da *f* **-5.** *inf* [head] cuca *f.*
◆ **nuts** *inf* ◇ *adj*: **to be ~s** estar louco(ca). ◇ *excl US* maldito seja!
nutcase [ˈnʌtkeɪs] *n inf* pirado *m*, -da *f.*
nutcrackers [ˈnʌtˌkrækəz] *npl* quebra-nozes *m.*
nutmeg [ˈnʌtmeg] *n (U)* noz-moscada *f.*
nutrient [ˈnju:trɪənt] *n* nutriente *m.*
nutrition [nju:ˈtrɪʃn] *n (U)* nutrição *f.*
nutritional [nju:ˈtrɪʃənl] *adj* nutritivo(va).
nutritionist [nju:ˈtrɪʃənɪst] *n* nutricionista *mf.*
nutritious [nju:ˈtrɪʃəs] *adj* nutritivo(va).
nutshell [ˈnʌtʃel] *n* casca *f* de noz; **in a ~** em poucas palavras.
nutter [ˈnʌtəʳ] *n UK inf* louco *m*, -ca *f.*
nuzzle [ˈnʌzl] ◇ *vt* [with nose] fuçar. ◇ *vi* [nestle]: **to ~ (up) against sb/sthg** aconchegar-se em alguém/algo.
NV *abbr of* **Nevada**.
NVQ (*abbr of* **National Vocational Qualification**) *n na Inglaterra e no País de Gales, certificado de qualificação vocacional obtido pelos estudantes de 15 a 16 anos*, ≃ diploma *m* de segundo grau.
NW (*abbr of* **northwest**) NO.
NY *abbr of* **New York**.
Nyasaland *n* Nyasaland; **in ~** em Nyasaland.
NYC *abbr of* **New York City**.
nylon [ˈnaɪlɒn] ◇ *n (U)* [fabric] náilon *m.* ◇ *comp* de náilon.
◆ **nylons** *npl dated* [stockings] meias *fpl* de náilon.
nymph [nɪmf] *n* ninfa *f.*
nymphomaniac [ˌnɪmfəˈmeɪnɪæk] ◇ *adj* ninfomaníaco(ca). ◇ *n* ninfomaníaco *m*, -ca *f.*
NYRB (*abbr of* **New York Review of Books**) *n conceituada revista norte-americana com artigos de crítica literária.*
NYSE (*abbr of* **New York Stock Exchange**) *n* Bolsa *f* de Nova Iorque.
NZ *abbr of* **New Zealand**.

o (*pl* **o's** OR **os**), **O** (*pl* **O's** OR **Os**) [əʊ] *n* **-1.** [letter] o, O *m* **-2.** [zero] zero *m.*
oaf [əʊf] *n* imbecil *mf.*
oak [əʊk] ◇ *n*: **~ (tree)** carvalho *m.* ◇ *comp* de carvalho.
OAP (*abbr of* **old age pensioner**) *n UK idoso que recebe pensão do estado.*
oar [ɔ:ʳ] *n* remo *m*; **to put** OR **stick one's ~ in** *fig* meter o bedelho em.
oarlock [ˈɔ:lɒk] *n US* [rowlock] tolete *m.*
oarsman [ˈɔ:zmən] (*pl* **-men** [-mən]) *n* remador *m.*
oarswoman [ˈɔ:zˌwʊmən] (*pl* **-women** [-ˌwɪmɪn]) *n* remadora *f.*
OAS (*abbr of* **Organization of American States**) *n* OEA *f.*
oasis [əʊˈeɪsɪs] (*pl* **oases** [əʊˈeɪsi:z]) *n* **-1.** [in desert] oásis *m inv* **-2.** *fig* [pleasant place] oásis *m inv.*
oatcake [ˈəʊtkeɪk] *n* biscoito *m* de aveia.
oath [əʊθ] *n* **-1.** [promise] juramento *m*; **on** OR **under ~** sob juramento **-2.** [swearword] blasfêmia *f.*
oatmeal [ˈəʊtmi:l] ◇ *n* [food] farinha *f* de aveia. ◇ *comp* de aveia.
oats [əʊts] *npl* [grain] aveia *f.*

OAU (*abbr of* **Organization of African Unity**) *n* OUA *f*.
obdurate ['ɒbdjʊrət] *adj fml* contumaz.
OBE (*abbr of* **Order of the British Empire**) *n (beneficiário da) ordem honorífica do Império Britânico.*
obedience [ə'bi:djəns] *n (U)*: ~ **(to sb)** obediência *f* (a alguém).
obedient [ə'bi:djənt] *adj* obediente.
obediently [ə'bi:djəntlɪ] *adv* obedientemente.
obelisk ['ɒbəlɪsk] *n* [column] obelisco *m*.
obese [əʊ'bi:s] *adj* obeso(sa).
obesity [əʊ'bi:sətɪ] *n (U)* obesidade *f*.
obey [ə'beɪ] <> *vt* obedecer a. <> *vi* obedecer.
obituary [ə'bɪtʃʊərɪ] (*pl* **-ies**) *n* obituário *m*.
object [*n* 'ɒbdʒɪkt, *vb* ɒb'dʒekt] <> *n* **-1.** [gen] objeto *m* **-2.** [aim] objetivo *m* **-3.** *GRAM* objeto *m*, complemento *m*. <> *vt*: **to** ~ **(that)** objetar (que). <> *vi* objetar; **to** ~ **to sthg/to doing sthg** opor a algo/a fazer algo.
objection [əb'dʒekʃn] *n* [argument against] objeção *f*; **to have no** ~ **to sthg/to doing sthg** não ter nenhuma objeção a algo/a fazer algo.
objectionable [əb'dʒekʃənəbl] *adj* desagrádavel.
objective [əb'dʒektɪv] <> *adj* objetivo(va). <> *n* objetivo *m*.
objectively [əb'dʒektɪvlɪ] *adv* objetivamente.
objectivity [,ɒbdʒek'tɪvətɪ] *n (U)* objetividade *f*.
object lesson ['ɒbdʒɪkt-] *n*: **an** ~ **in sthg** um exemplo perfeito de algo.
objector [əb'dʒektəʳ] *n* opositor *m*, -ra *f*.
obligate ['ɒblɪgeɪt] *vt fml* obrigar; **to** ~ **sb to do sthg** obrigar alguém a fazer algo.
obligation [,ɒblɪ'geɪʃn] *n* obrigação *f*.
obligatory [ə'blɪgətrɪ] *adj* obrigatório(ria).
oblige [ə'blaɪdʒ] <> *vt* **-1.** [force]: **to** ~ **sb to do sthg** obrigar alguém a fazer algo **-2.** *fml* [do a favour to] fazer um favor a. <> *vi* fazer um favor.
obliging [ə'blaɪdʒɪŋ] *adj* prestativo(va).
oblique [ə'bli:k] <> *adj* **-1.** [indirect - look] enviesado(da); [- reference, hint, compliment] indireto(ta) **-2.** [slanting] oblíquo(qua). <> *n TYPO* barra *f*.
obliquely [ə'bli:klɪ] *adv* [indirectly] indiretamente.
obliterate [ə'blɪtəreɪt] *vt* [destroy] obliterar.
obliteration [ə,blɪtə'reɪʃn] *n (U)* [destruction] obliteração *f*.
oblivion [ə'blɪvɪən] *n (U)* **-1.** [unconsciousness] inconsciência *f* **-2.** [state of being forgotten] esquecimento *m*.
oblivious [ə'blɪvɪəs] *adj* inconsciente; **to be** ~ **to** *OR* **of sthg** não ter consciência de algo.
oblong ['ɒblɒŋ] <> *adj* oblongo(ga). <> *n* retângulo *m*.
obnoxious [əb'nɒkʃəs] *adj* repulsivo(va), repugnante.
o.b.o. (*abbr of* **or best offer**) ou a melhor oferta.
oboe ['əʊbəʊ] *n* oboé *m*.
oboist ['əʊbəʊɪst] *n* oboísta *mf*.
obscene [əb'si:n] *adj* obsceno(na).
obscenity [əb'senətɪ] (*pl* **-ies**) *n* obscenidade *f*.
obscure [əb'skjʊəʳ] <> *adj* **-1.** [not well-known] desconhecido(da) **-2.** [difficult to see/understand] obscuro(ra). <> *vt* **-1.** [make difficult to understand] obscurecer **-2.** [hide] esconder.
obscurity [əb'skjʊərətɪ] *n (U)* obscuridade *f*.
obsequious [əb'si:kwɪəs] *adj fml & pej* servil.
observable [əb'zɜ:vəbl] *adj* visível, observável.
observably [əb'zɜ:vəblɪ] *adv* visivelmente.
observance [əb'zɜ:vns] *n (U)* observância *f*, cumprimento *m*.
observant [əb'zɜ:vnt] *adj* observador(ra).
observation [,ɒbzə'veɪʃn] *n* observação *f*.
observation post *n* ponto *m* de observação.
observatory [əb'zɜ:vətrɪ] (*pl* **-ies**) *n* observatório *m*.
observe [əb'zɜ:v] *vt* observar.
observer [əb'zɜ:vəʳ] *n* **-1.** [gen] observador *m*, -ra *f* **-2.** [political commentator] analista *mf*.
obsess [əb'ses] *vt* obsedar, obcecar; **to be** ~**ed by** *OR* **with sb/sthg** estar obcecado(da) com *OR* por alguém/algo.
obsession [əb'seʃn] *n* obsessão *f*.
obsessional [əb'seʃənl] *adj* obsessivo(va).
obsessive [əb'sesɪv] *adj* obsessivo(va).
obsolescence [,ɒbsə'lesns] *n (U)* obsolescência *f*.
obsolescent [,ɒbsə'lesnt] *adj* antiquado(da).
obsolete ['ɒbsəli:t] *adj* obsoleto(ta).
obstacle ['ɒbstəkl] *n* obstáculo *m*.
obstacle race *n* corrida *f* de obstáculos.
obstetrician [,ɒbstə'trɪʃn] *n* obstetra *mf*.
obstetrics [ɒb'stetrɪks] *n (U)* obstetrícia *f*.
obstinacy ['ɒbstɪnəsɪ] *n* [stubbornness] obstinação *f*, teimosia *f*.
obstinate ['ɒbstənət] *adj* **-1.** [stubborn] obstinado(-da), teimoso(sa) **-2.** [persistent] persistente.
obstinately ['ɒbstənətlɪ] *adv* [stubbornly] obstinadamente, teimosamente.
obstreperous [əb'strepərəs] *adj fml or hum* escandaloso(sa).
obstruct [əb'strʌkt] *vt* **-1.** [road, path, traffic] obstruir, bloquear **-2.** [progress, justice] impedir.
obstruction [əb'strʌkʃn] *n* **-1.** [blockage, obstacle] obstrução *f*, obstáculo *m* **-2.** *(U)* [act of impeding] impedimento *m* **-3.** *SPORT* obstrução *f*.
obstructive [əb'strʌktɪv] *adj* obstrutivo(va).
obtain [əb'teɪn] *vt* [get] obter.
obtainable [əb'teɪnəbl] *adj* disponível.
obtrusive [əb'tru:sɪv] *adj* **-1.** [person, behaviour] inconveniente **-2.** [smell] penetrante **-3.** [colour] gritante.
obtrusively [əb'tru:sɪvlɪ] *adv* indiscretamente, inconvenientemente.
obtuse [əb'tju:s] *adj* obtuso(sa).
obverse ['ɒbvɜ:s] *n* **-1.** [front side] reverso *m* **-2.** [opposite] contrapartida *f*.
obviate ['ɒbvɪeɪt] *vt fml* evitar, prevenir.
obvious ['ɒbvɪəs] <> *adj* **-1.** [evident] óbvio(via) **-2.** [unsubtle] evidente. <> *n*: **to state the** ~ afirmar o óbvio.
obviously ['ɒbvɪəslɪ] *adv* **-1.** [of course] evidentemente, obviamente; ~ **not** claro que não **-2.** [clearly] evidentemente; **he's** ~ **lying** é óbvio que ele está mentindo.
obviousness ['ɒbvɪəsnɪs] *n (U)* obviedade *f*.
OCAS (*abbr of* **Organization of Central American**

States) *n* Organização *f* dos Estados da América Central.

occasion [ə'keɪʒn] <> *n* **-1.** [circumstance, time] ocasião *f*; **on several ~s** em várias ocasiões; **on ~ fml** de vez em quando; **special ~** ocasião especial; **to rise to the ~** mostrar-se à altura da ocasião **-2.** *fml* [reason, motive] razão *f*. <> *vt fml* [cause] ocasionar.

occasional [ə'keɪʒənl] *adj* ocasional.

occasionally [ə'keɪʒnəlɪ] *adv* de vez em quando, ocasionalmente.

occasional table *n* mesa *f* auxiliar.

occluded front *n METEOR* frente *f* oclusa.

occult [ɒ'kʌlt] <> *adj* oculto(ta). <> *n*: **the ~** o oculto.

occupancy ['ɒkjʊpənsɪ] *n (U) fml* ocupação *f*.

occupant ['ɒkjʊpənt] *n* ocupante *mf*.

occupation [ˌɒkjʊ'peɪʃn] *n* **-1.** [job] ocupação *f*, emprego *m* **-2.** [pastime] passatempo *m* **-3.** *(U) MIL* ocupação *f*.

occupational [ˌɒkju:'peɪʃənl] *adj* ocupacional.

occupational disease *n MED* doença *f* ocupacional.

occupational hazard *n* risco *m* da profissão.

occupational therapist *n* terapeuta *mf* ocupacional.

occupational therapy *n (U)* terapia *f* ocupacional.

occupied ['ɒkjʊpaɪd] *adj* ocupado(da).

occupier ['ɒkjʊpaɪə[r]] *n* ocupante *mf*.

occupy ['ɒkjʊpaɪ] (*pt* & *pp* **-ied**) *vt* **-1.** [gen] ocupar **-2.** [keep busy]: **to ~ o.s.** ocupar-se.

occur [ə'kɜ:[r]] (*pt* & *pp* **-red**, *cont* **-ring**) *vi* **-1.** [happen] ocorrer **-2.** [exist] existir **-3.** [be found] ser encontrado(da) **-4.** [come to mind]: **to ~ to sb** ocorrer a alguém.

occurrence [ə'kʌrəns] *n* **-1.** [event] acontecimento *m* **-2.** *(U)* [fact or instance of occurring] ocorrência *f*.

ocean ['əʊʃn] *n* oceano *m*.

oceangoing ['əʊʃnˌgəʊɪŋ] *adj* de grande autonomia.

Oceania [ˌəʊʃɪ'ɑ:nɪə] *n* Oceania; **in ~** na Oceania.

Oceanian [ˌəʊʃɪ'ɑ:nɪən] <> *adj* oceânico(ca). <> *n* oceânico *m*, -ca *f*.

ochre *UK*, **ocher** *US* ['əʊkə[r]] *adj* [colour] ocre.

o'clock [ə'klɒk] *adv*: **five ~** cinco horas; **it's four ~** são quatro horas; **it's one ~** é uma hora.

OCR *n* **-1.** (*abbr of* **optical character reader**) OCR *m* **-2.** (*abbr of* **optical character recognition**) OCR *f*.

Oct. (*abbr of* **October**) out.

octagon ['ɒktəgən] *n* octógono *m*.

octagonal [ɒk'tægənl] *adj* octogonal.

octane ['ɒkteɪn] *n* octano *m*.

octane number, octane rating *n* índice *m* de octana.

octave ['ɒktɪv] *n MUS* oitava *f*.

octet [ɒk'tet] *n MUS* octeto *m*.

October [ɒk'təʊbə[r]] *n* outubro *m*; *see also* **September**.

octogenarian [ˌɒktəʊdʒɪ'neərɪən] *n* octogenário *m*, -ria *f*.

octopus ['ɒktəpəs] (*pl* **-puses** *OR* **-pi** [-paɪ]) *n* polvo *m*.

OD <> *n inf* (*abbr of* **overdose**) overdose *f*. <> *vi* **-1.** *inf* (*abbr of* **overdose**) tomar uma overdose **-2.** *fig, hum* exagerar. <> *adj* (*abbr of* **overdrawn**) *no negativo, referente a conta bancária.*

odd [ɒd] *adj* **-1.** [strange] estranho(nha) **-2.** [not part of pair] sem par **-3.** [number] ímpar **-4.** [leftover] avulso(sa) **-5.** [occasional] ocasional **-6.** *inf* [approximately]: **20 ~ years** 20 e tantos anos.

◆ **odds** *npl* **-1.** [probability] probabilidades *fpl*; **the ~s are that ...** as previsões são de que ...; **against the ~s** apesar de todas as dificuldades **-2.** [bits]: **~s and ends** miudezas *fpl* **-3.** *phr*: **to be at ~s with sb/sthg** discordar de algo/alguém.

oddball ['ɒdbɔ:l] *n inf* esquisitão *m*, -tona *f*.

oddity ['ɒdɪtɪ] (*pl* **-ies**) *n* **-1.** [strange person, thing] esquisitice *f* **-2.** *(U)* [strangeness] estranheza *f*.

odd-job man *UK*, **odd-jobber** *US* *n* faz-tudo *mf*.

odd jobs *npl* biscates *mpl*.

oddly ['ɒdlɪ] *adv* [strangely] estranhamente; **~ enough, I didn't care** surpreendentemente, não me importei.

oddments ['ɒdmənts] *npl* retalhos *mpl*.

odds-on ['ɒdz-] *adj inf*: **the ~ favourite** o grande favorito.

ode [əʊd] *n* ode *f*.

odious ['əʊdjəs] *adj* odioso(sa).

odometer [əʊ'dɒmɪtə[r]] *n* [in car] velocímetro *m*.

odor *n US* = **odour**.

odorless *adj US* = **odourless**.

odour *UK*, **odor** *US* ['əʊdə[r]] *n* odor *m*.

odourless *UK*, **odorless** *US* ['əʊdəlɪs] *adj* inodoro(ra).

odyssey ['ɒdɪsɪ] (*pl* **-s**) *n literary* odisséia *f*.

OECD (*abbr of* **Organization for Economic Cooperation and Development**) *n organização que reúne um grupo de países desenvolvidos que trabalham pelo desenvolvimento do comércio e crescimento econômico*, OECD *f*.

oesophagus *UK*, **esophagus** *US* [ɪ'sɒfəgəs] *n* esôfago *m*.

oestrogen *UK*, **estrogen** *US* [i:strədʒən] *n (U)* estrogênio *m*.

of [ɒv] *prep* **-1.** [belonging to] de; **the colour ~ the car** a cor do carro. **-2.** [expressing amount] de; **a piece ~ cake** uma fatia de bolo; **a fall ~ 20%** uma queda de 20%; **lots ~ people** muita gente. **-3.** [containing, made from] de; **a glass ~ beer** um copo de cerveja; **a house ~ stone** uma casa de pedra; **it's made ~ wood** é de madeira. **-4.** [regarding, relating to, indicating cause] de; **fear ~ spiders** medo de aranhas; **he died ~ cancer** ele morreu de câncer. **-5.** [referring to time] de; **the summer ~ 1969** o verão de 1969; **the 26th ~ August** o 26 de agosto. **-6.** [with cities, countries] de; **the city ~ San Francisco** a cidade de San Francisco. **-7.** [on the part of] de; **that was very kind ~ you** foi muito amável da sua parte. **-8.** *US* [in telling the time] menos, para; **it's ten ~ four** são dez para as quatro.

off [ɒf] <> *adv* **-1.** [away]: **to drive/walk ~** ir-se embora; **to get ~** [from bus, train, etc] descer; **we're ~ to Austria next week** vamos para a Áustria na próxima semana. **-2.** [expressing removal]: **to take sthg ~** tirar algo. **-3.** [so as to stop working]: **to turn sthg ~** [TV, radio, engine] desligar algo; [tap]

fechar algo. **-4.** [expressing distance or time away]: **it's a long way ~** [in distance] é muito longe; [in time] ainda falta muito; **it's two months ~** é daqui a dois meses. **-5.** [not at work] de folga; **I'm taking a week ~** vou tirar uma semana de férias. <> *prep* **-1.** [away from]: **to get ~ sthg** descer de algo; **~ the coast** ao largo da costa; **just ~ the main road** perto da estrada principal. **-2.** [indicating removal]: **take the lid ~ the jar** tire a tampa do frasco; **we'll take $20 ~ the price** descontaremos 20 dólares do preço. **-3.** [absent from]: **to be ~ work** não estar trabalhando. **-4.** *inf* [from] a; **I bought it ~ her** eu comprei isso dela. <> *adj* **-1.** [TV, radio, light] apagado(da), desligado(da); [tap] fechado(da); [engine] desligado(da). **-2.** [cancelled] cancelado(da).

offal ['ɒfl] *n (U)* vísceras *fpl (do animal abatido).*

off-balance *adv* **-1.** [not standing firmly] sem equilíbrio **-2.** [unprepared] desprevenido(da).

offbeat ['ɒfbi:t] *adj inf* original, excêntrico(ca).

off-centre <> *adj* descentralizado(da). <> *adv* fora do centro.

off-chance *n*: **he called on the ~ of seeing her** ele ligou com a remota esperança de vê-la.

off-colour *adj* **-1.** [ill] indisposto(ta) **-2.** [rude, offensive] ofensivo(va).

offcut ['ɒfkʌt] *n* retalho *m*.

off-day *n inf* dia *m* de folga.

off duty *adv*: **when do you get ~?** quando você fica de folga?

◆ **off-duty** *adj* de folga.

offence *UK*, **offense** *US* [ə'fens] *n* **-1.** [crime] infração *f*, delito *m* **-2.** [displeasure, hurt] insulto *m*, ofensa *f*; **to take ~** ofender-se.

offend [ə'fend] <> *vt* [upset] ofender. <> *vi* **-1.** [contravene]: **to ~ against** transgredir; [decency] pecar contra **-2.** [commit a crime] cometer (um) crime.

offended [ə'fendɪd] *adj* ofendido(da).

offender [ə'fendəʳ] *n* **-1.** [criminal] transgressor *m*, -ra *f* **-2.** [culprit] infrator *m*, -ra *f*.

offending [ə'fendɪŋ] *adj* ofensor(ra).

offense [*sense 2* 'ɒfens] *n US* **-1.** = **offence -2.** *SPORT* ataque *m*.

offensive [ə'fensɪv] <> *adj* **-1.** [causing offence] ofensivo(va) **-2.** [aggressive] agressivo(va). <> *n* **-1.** *MIL* ofensiva *f* **-2.** *fig* [attack]: **to go on** *OR* **take the ~** partir para a ofensiva.

offensiveness [ə'fensɪvnɪs] *n (U)* caráter *m* ofensivo.

offer ['ɒfəʳ] <> *n* **-1.** [something offered] oferta *f*; **on ~** [available] em oferta **-2.** [bid, proposal] proposta *f*. <> *vt* **-1.** [present, give] oferecer; **to ~ sthg to sb, to ~ sb sthg** oferecer algo a alguém **-2.** [propose]: **to ~ to do sthg** oferecer-se para fazer algo. <> *vi* oferecer-se.

offering ['ɒfərɪŋ] *n* **-1.** [something offered] oferta *f* **-2.** *RELIG* [sacrifice] oferenda *f*.

off guard *adv* desprevenido(da).

off-hand <> *adj* [unfriendly] brusco(ca). <> *adv* [at this moment] de imediato.

office ['ɒfɪs] *n* **-1.** [room] escritório *m*, gabinete *m* **-2.** [building] edifício *m* de escritórios **-3.** [staff] pessoal *m* **-4.** [government department] departamento *m* **-5.** [distribution point - for tickets] bilheteria *f*; [- for information] guichê *m*; [- for enquiries] serviço *m* de informações **-6.** [position of authority] cargo *m*; **in ~** no poder; **to take ~** tomar posse.

office automation *n* automatização *f*.

office block *n* prédio *m* de escritórios.

office boy *n* contínuo *m*, bói *m*.

officeholder ['ɒfɪs,həʊldəʳ] *n* detentor *m*, -ra *f* de cargo público.

office hours *npl* horário *m* de expediente.

office junior *n UK* assistente *mf* de escritório.

Office of Fair Trading *n* ≃ Delegacia *f* de Defesa do Consumidor.

officer ['ɒfɪsəʳ] *n* **-1.** *MIL* oficial *mf* **-2.** [in organization] diretor *m*, -ra *f* **-3.** [in police force] (agente) policial *m*.

office work *n (U)* trabalho *m* de escritório.

office worker *n* funcionário *m*, -ria *f* de escritório.

official [ə'fɪʃl] <> *adj* oficial. <> *n* [public] funcionário *m*, -ria *f*; *SPORT* oficial *mf*.

officialdom [ə'fɪʃəldəm] *n (U)* burocracia *f*.

officially [ə'fɪʃəlɪ] *adv* oficialmente.

official receiver *n* síndico *m*, -ca *f* em falências.

officiate [ə'fɪʃɪeɪt] *vi* oficiar; **to ~ at sthg** celebrar algo.

officious [ə'fɪʃəs] *adj pej* intrometido(da).

offing ['ɒfɪŋ] *n*: **in the ~** num futuro próximo.

off-key *MUS* <> *adj* desafinado(da). <> *adv* de maneira desafinada.

off-licence *n UK* loja *f* de bebidas alcoólicas.

off limits *adj esp US* proibido(da).

off-line *adj COMPUT* off-line, desconectado(da).

offload [ɒf'ləʊd] *vt inf*: **to ~ sthg (onto sb)** livrar-se de algo (passando para alguém).

off-peak <> *adj* de tarifa reduzida. <> *adv* fora do horário de pico.

off-putting [-,pʊtɪŋ] *adj* desconcertante.

off sales *npl UK* venda *f* de bebidas alcoólicas.

off season *n*: **the ~** a baixa temporada.

◆ **off-season** *adj* de baixa temporada.

offset ['ɒfset] (*pt* & *pp* **offset**, *cont* **-ting**) *vt* contrabalançar.

offshoot ['ɒfʃu:t] *n* [spin-off] ramificação *f*; **to be an ~ of sthg** ser uma ramificação de algo.

offshore ['ɒfʃɔ:ʳ] <> *adj* **-1.** [in or on the sea] em alto mar **-2.** [near coast] costeiro(ra). <> *adv* **-1.** [out at sea] ao largo **-2.** [near coast] a pouca distância da costa.

offside [*adj* & *adv* ,ɒf'saɪd, *n* 'ɒfsaɪd] <> *adj* **-1.** [part of vehicle] do lado do motorista **-2.** *SPORT* impedido(da). <> *n* [of vehicle] lado *m* do motorista.

offspring ['ɒfsprɪŋ] (*pl inv*) *n* **-1.** *fml or hum* [of people] descendência *f* **-2.** [of animals] prole *f*.

offstage [,ɒf'steɪdʒ] <> *adj* dos bastidores. <> *adv* nos bastidores.

off-the-cuff <> *adj* improvisado(da). <> *adv* de improviso.

off-the-peg *adj UK* pronto(ta), confeccionado(-da).

off-the-record <> *adj* extra-oficial. <> *adv* extra-oficialmente.

off-the-wall *adj* não usual, excêntrico(ca).

off-white *adj* de cor não totalmente branca.

OFSTED (*abbr of* **Office for Standards in Education**) *n órgão britânico que inspeciona a educação.*

OFT (*abbr of* **Office of FairTrading**) *n órgão britânico que controla as transações comerciais.*

often ['ɒfn, 'ɒftn] *adv* **-1.** [many times] muitas vezes; **how ~?** quantas vezes?; **how ~ do you visit her?** com que freqüência você a visita? **-2.** [in many cases] freqüentemente.
◆ **as often as not** *adv* geralmente.
◆ **every so often** *adv* de vez em quando.
◆ **more often than not** *adv* freqüentemente.

ogle ['əʊgl] *vt pej* comer com os olhos.

ogre ['əʊgəʳ] *n* [in fairy tales] ogro *m*.

oh [əʊ] *excl* **-1.** [to introduce comment] ah!; **~ really?** é mesmo? **-2.** [expressing emotion] ah!; **~ no!** essa não!

OH *abbr of* **Ohio**.

Ohio [əʊ'haɪəʊ] *n* Ohio; **in ~** em Ohio.

ohm [əʊm] *n* ohm *m*.

OHMS (*abbr of* **On His (or Her) Majesty's Service**) *na Grã-Bretanha, expressão que indica o caráter oficial de um documento.*

oil [ɔɪl] ◇ *n* **-1.** [gen] óleo *m* **-2.** *(U)* [petroleum] petróleo *m* **-3.** *(U)* [olive oil] azeite *m*. ◇ *vt* [lubricate] lubrificar.
◆ **oils** *npl* ART tintas *fpl* a óleo.

oilcan ['ɔɪlkæn] *n* almotolia *f*.

oil change *n* troca *f* de óleo.

oilcloth ['ɔɪlklɒθ] *n (U)* oleado *m*.

oilfield ['ɔɪlfi:ld] *n* campo *m* petrolífero.

oil filter *n* filtro *m* de óleo.

oil-fired [-ˌfaɪəd] *adj* a óleo.

oil industry *n*: **the ~** a indústria petrolífera, o setor petroleiro.

oilman ['ɔɪlmən] (*pl* **-men** [-mən]) *n* **-1.** [worker] trabalhador *m* do setor petroleiro **-2.** [businessman] executivo *m* do setor petroleiro.

oil paint *n* tinta *f* a óleo.

oil painting *n* **-1.** [art] pintura *f* a óleo **-2.** [picture] quadro *m* a óleo.

oilrig ['ɔɪlrɪg] *n* plataforma *f* petrolífera.

oilskins ['ɔɪlskɪnz] *npl* capa *f* de oleado.

oil slick *n* mancha *f* de óleo.

oil tanker *n* **-1.** [ship] petroleiro *m* **-2.** [lorry] caminhão *m* -tanque.

oil well *n* poço *m* de petróleo.

oily ['ɔɪlɪ] (*compar* **-ier**, *superl* **-iest**) *adj* **-1.** [covered in oil] gorduroso(sa) **-2.** *pej* [smarmy] bajulador(ra).

ointment ['ɔɪntmənt] *n* pomada *f*.

oiro (*abbr of* **offers in the region of**) ofertas em torno de.

OK (*pl* **OKs**, *pt* & *pp* **OKed**, *cont* **OKing**), **okay** [ˌəʊ'keɪ] *inf* ◇ *adj*: **are you ~?** você está bem?; **to be ~ with** OR **by sb** estar tudo bem com alguém. ◇ *adv* [well] bem. ◇ *n*: **to give (sb) the ~** dar sinal verde (a alguém). ◇ *excl* **-1.** [asking for, expressing agreement] está bem!, tá (bem/bom)! **-2.** [fair enough] certo! **-3.** [to introduce new topic] bom! ◇ *vt* aprovar.

Oklahoma [ˌəʊklə'həʊmə] *n* Oklahoma; **in ~** em Oklahoma.

okra ['əʊkrə] *n (U)* quiabo *m*.

old [əʊld] ◇ *adj* **-1.** [aged, ancient, longstanding] velho(lha) **-2.** [referring to age]: **how ~ are you?** quantos anos você tem? **-3.** [former, ancient, out-of-date] antigo(ga); **in the ~ days** antigamente **-4.** *inf* [for emphasis]: **any ~ clothes will do** qualquer roupa serve; **any ~ how** de qualquer jeito. ◇ *npl*: **the ~** os idosos.

old age *n (U)* velhice *f*.

old age pension *n UK* pensão *f* por idade.

old age pensioner *n UK* aposentado *m*, -da *f* por idade.

Old Bailey [-'beɪlɪ] *n*: **the ~** *o prédio do Tribunal Criminal (de Londres).*

olden ['əʊldn] *adj*: **in the ~ days** antigamente.

old-fashioned [-'fæʃnd] *adj* **-1.** [outmoded] antiquado(da) **-2.** [traditional] tradicional.

old flame *n* paixão *f* antiga.

old hat *adj inf pej*: **to be ~** estar fora de moda.

old maid *n pej* [spinster] solteirona *f*.

old master *n* **-1.** [painter] grande mestre *m* **-2.** [painting] obra-prima *f*.

old people's home *n* lar *m* de idosos.

Old Testament *n*: **the ~** o Antigo Testamento.

old-time *adj* de antigamente.

old-timer *n* **-1.** [veteran] veterano *m*, -na *f* **-2.** *esp US* [old man] velho(lha).

old wives' tale *n* conto *m* da carochinha.

Old World *n*: **the ~** o Velho Mundo.

O level (*abbr of* **ordinary level**) *n UK até há pouco tempo, primeira etapa do GCE, exame prestado pelos estudantes britânicos aos 16 anos, agora substituído pelo GCSE.*

oligarchy ['ɒlɪgɑ:kɪ] (*pl* **-ies**) *n* oligarquia *f*.

olive ['ɒlɪv] ◇ *adj* da cor de oliva. ◇ *n* **-1.** [fruit] azeitona *f* **-2.** [tree]: **~ (tree)** oliveira *f*.

olive green *adj* verde-oliva.

olive oil *n (U)* azeite *m* de oliva.

Olympic [ə'lɪmpɪk] *adj* olímpico(ca).
◆ **Olympics** *npl*: **the ~s** as Olimpíadas.

Olympic Games *npl*: **the ~** os Jogos Olímpicos.

OM (*abbr of* **Order of Merit**) *n (beneficiário da) ordem do mérito britânica.*

O & M (*abbr of* **organization and method**) *n* O & M *f*.

Oman [əʊ'mɑ:n] *n* Omã; **in ~** em Omã.

OMB (*abbr of* **Office of Management and Budget**) *n órgão norte-americano que assessora o presidente em questões orçamentárias.*

ombudsman ['ɒmbʊdzmən] (*pl* **-men** [-mən]) *n* ombudsman *mf*.

omelet(te) ['ɒmlɪt] *n* omelete *f*.

omen ['əʊmen] *n* presságio *m*.

ominous ['ɒmɪnəs] *adj* **-1.** ominoso(sa) **-2.** [threatening] ameaçador(ra).

ominously ['ɒmɪnəslɪ] *adv* ominosamente.

omission [ə'mɪʃn] *n* omissão *f*.

omit [ə'mɪt] (*pt* & *pp* **-ted**, *cont* **-ting**) *vt* omitir; **to ~ to do sthg** deixar de fazer algo.

omnibus ['ɒmnɪbəs] *n* **-1.** [book] antologia *f* **-2.** *UK* RADIO & TV programa *f* de variedades.

omnipotence [ɒm'nɪpətəns] *n (U) fml* onipotência *f*.

omnipotent [ɒm'nɪpətənt] *adj fml* onipotente.

omnipresent [ˌɒmnɪ'prezənt] *adj fml* onipresente.

omniscience *n fml* onisciência *f*.

omniscient [ɒm'nɪsɪənt] *adj fml* onisciente.

omnivorous [ɒm'nɪvərəs] *adj ZOOL* onívoro(ra).

on [ɒn] ◇ *prep* **-1.** [expressing position, location] em, sobre; **it's ~ the table** está na mesa, está sobre a mesa; **put it ~ the table** ponha-o na *OR* sobre a mesa; **~ my right** à minha direita; **~ the right** à direita; **a picture ~ the wall** um quadro na parede; **the exhaust ~ the car** o cano de descarga do carro; **we stayed ~ a farm** ficamos numa fazenda. **-2.** [with forms of transportation]: **~ the plane** no avião; **to get ~ a bus** subir num ônibus. **-3.** [expressing means, method] em; **~ foot** a pé; **~ the radio** no rádio; **~ TV** na televisão; **paid ~ an hourly basis** pago por hora. **-4.** [using] a; **it runs ~ unleaded gas** funciona com gasolina sem chumbo; **to be ~ drugs** drogar-se; **to be ~ medication** estar tomando medicamentos. **-5.** [about] sobre; **a book ~ Germany** um livro sobre a Alemanha. **-6.** [expressing time]: **~ arrival** ao chegar; **~ Tuesday** na terça-feira; **~ August 25th** no dia 25 de agosto. **-7.** [with regard to] em, sobre; **a tax ~ imports** um imposto sobre as importações; **the effect ~ the country** o impacto no país. **-8.** [describing activity, state]: **~ vacation** de férias; **~ sale** à venda. **-9.** [in phrases]: **do you have any money ~ you?** *inf* você tem dinheiro?; **the drinks are ~ me** as bebidas são por minha conta. ◇ *adv* **-1.** [in place, covering]: **to put one's clothes ~** vestir-se; **to put the lid ~** tapar. **-2.** [movie, play, programme]: **the news is ~** está passando o telejornal; **what's ~ at the movies?** o que é que está passando no cinema? **-3.** [with transportation]: **to get ~** subir. **-4.** [functioning]: **to turn sthg ~** [TV, radio, light] ligar *OR* acender algo; [tap] abrir algo; [engine] pôr algo para trabalhar. **-5.** [taking place]: **how long is the festival ~?** quanto tempo dura o festival?; **the game is already ~** o jogo já começou. **-6.** [farther forward]: **to drive ~** continuar a dirigir. **-7.** [in phrases]: **I already have something ~ tonight** já tenho planos para esta noite. ◇ *adj* [TV, radio, light] ligado(da), aceso(sa); [tap] aberto(ta); [engine] funcionando.

ON *abbr of* **Ontario**.

ONC (*abbr of* **Ordinary National Certificate**) *n diploma técnico em nível secundário na Grã-Bretanha.*

once [wʌns] ◇ *adv* **-1.** [on one occasion] uma vez; **~ again** *OR* **more** [one more time] outra vez; [yet again] novamente; **~ and for all** de uma vez por todas; **~ in a while** de vez em quando; **~ or twice** uma vez ou duas; **for ~** ao menos uma vez **-2.** [previously, formerly] outrora; **~ upon a time** era uma vez. ◇ *conj* assim que, quando.

◆ **at once** *adv* **-1.** [immediately] imediatamente **-2.** [at the same time] ao mesmo tempo; **all at ~** de repente.

once-over *n inf*: **to give sb/sthg the ~** dar uma olhada rápida em alguém/algo.

oncoming ['ɒn,kʌmɪŋ] *adj* **-1.** [traffic, vehicle] em sentido contrário **-2.** [danger] iminente.

OND (*abbr of* **Ordinary National Diploma**) *n diploma técnico em nível superior na Grã-Bretanha, obtido em curso de 3 anos.*

one [wʌn] ◇ *num* um (uma); **thirty-~** trinta e um; **~ fifth** um quinto. ◇ *adj* [only] único(ca); **~ day** um dia. ◇ *pron* [referring to a particular thing or person] um *m*, uma *f*; **the green ~** o verde; **that ~** aquele *m*, aquela *f*.

one-armed bandit *n* caça-níqueis *m*.

one-liner *n* piada *f* curta.

one-man *adj* individual, solo.

one-man band *n* **-1.** [musician] homem *m* -orquestra **-2.** [business, operation] faz-tudo *m*.

one-night stand *n* **-1.** [performance] apresentação *f* única **-2.** *inf* [sexual relationship] ficada *f* de uma noite só, transa *f* passageira.

one-off *inf* ◇ *adj* único(ca). ◇ *n* **-1.** [unique event, person] único *m*, -ca *f* **-2.** [unique product] exemplar *m* único.

one-on-one *adj US* = **one-to-one**.

one-parent family *n* família *f* que possui apenas um dos pais.

one-piece *adj* de uma peça só; **a ~ swimsuit** um maiô inteiro.

onerous ['əʊnərəs] *adj* oneroso(sa), difícil.

one's *poss adj*: **to do ~ duty** fazer o seu dever; **to be on ~ own** estar sozinho(nha).

oneself [wʌn'self] *pron fml* **-1.** *(reflexive)* se **-2.** *(after prep)* si próprio(pria), si mesmo(ma).

one-sided [-'saɪdɪd] *adj* **-1.** [unequal] desigual, unilateral **-2.** [biased] parcial.

onetime ['wʌntaɪm] *adj* [former] antigo(ga).

one-to-one *UK*, **one-on-one** *US adj* **-1.** [discussion] entre dois **-2.** [tuition] individual.

one-touch dialling *UK*, **one-touch dialing** *US n* discagem *f* automática.

one-upmanship [,wʌn'ʌpmənʃɪp] *n (U) capacidade de parecer ser melhor que os outros.*

one-way *adj* **-1.** [moving in one direction] de mão única **-2.** [for outward travel only] só de ida.

ongoing ['ɒn,gəʊɪŋ] *adj* em andamento, atual.

onion ['ʌnjən] *n* cebola *f*.

online ['ɒnlaɪn] *COMPUT adj & adv* on-line.

online banking *n* serviço *m* de banco on-line.

online shopping *n* compras *fpl* on-line.

onlooker ['ɒn,lʊkə^r] *n* espectador *m*, -ra *f*.

only ['əʊnlɪ] ◇ *adj* único(ca); **an ~ child** um filho único. ◇ *adv* **-1.** [exclusively] só **-2.** [merely, just] apenas, só **-3.** [for emphasis] só; **I was ~ too willing to help** eu queria tanto ajudar; **it's ~ natural you should be upset** é bastante natural que você fique perturbado; **not ~ ... but also** não apenas ... mas também; **~ just** por pouco. ◇ *conj* só que.

o.n.o., ono (*abbr of* **or near (est) offer**) ou a oferta mais próxima.

onrush ['ɒnrʌʃ] *n* [of feeling] irrupção *f*.

on-screen *COMPUT adj & adv* na tela.

onset ['ɒnset] *n* começo *m*.

onshore ['ɒnʃɔː^r] ◇ *adj* **-1.** [on land] terrestre **-2.** [moving towards land] em direção à costa. ◇ *adv* **-1.** [on land] em terra **-2.** [towards land] para a praia.

onside [ɒn'saɪd] *adj & adv SPORT* em posição legal.

onslaught ['ɒnslɔːt] *n* investida *f*.

Ont. *abbr of* **Ontario**.

Ontario [ɒn'teərɪəʊ] *n* [province] Ontário; **in ~** em Ontário.

on-the-job *adj* no trabalho, prático(ca).

on-the-spot *adj* no ato, no local.

onto [*unstressed before consonant* 'ɒntə, *unstressed before vowel* 'ɒntʊ, *stressed* 'ɒntu:] *prep* ▷ **on.**

onus ['əʊnəs] *n* ônus *m.*

onward ['ɒnwəd] ◇ *adj* [advancing - in time] para a frente; [- in space] adiante, para a frente. ◇ *adv* = **onwards.**

onwards ['ɒnwədz] *adv* [forwards - in space] para a frente; [- in time] em diante.

onyx ['ɒnɪks] *n (U)* ônix *m.*

oodles ['u:dlz] *npl inf*: ~ **of sthg** um montão de algo.

oof *excl inf* uff!

ooh [u:] *excl inf* aah!

oops [ʊps, u:ps] *excl inf* ôpa!

ooze [u:z] ◇ *vt fig* exalar. ◇ *vi* exsudar; **to ~ from** *OR* **out of sthg** transpirar por algo; **sweat ~d from every pore** o suor transpirava-lhe por todos os poros. ◇ *n (U)* lodo *m.*

opacity [ə'pæsətɪ] *n* **-1.** [non-transparency] opacidade *f* **-2.** *fig* [obscurity] obscuridade *f.*

opal ['əʊpl] *n* [gem] opala *m.*

opaque [əʊ'peɪk] *adj* **-1.** [not transparent] opaco(ca) **-2.** *fig* [obscure] obscuro(ra).

OPEC ['əʊpek] (*abbr of* **Organization of the Petroleum Exporting Countries**) *n* OPEP *f.*

open ['əʊpn] ◇ *adj* **-1.** [gen] aberto(ta); **to be ~ to sthg** [ready to accept] ser aberto(ta) a algo; **to be ~ to sb** [opportunity, choice] estar aberto(ta) a alguém; **to lay o.s. ~ to criticism** manter-se aberto(ta) à crítica **-2.** [frank] franco(ca) **-3.** [unfastened] descobrado(da) **-4.** [not enclosed] amplo(pla) **-5.** [uncovered] descoberto(ta) **-6.** [meeting, competition, invitation] aberto(ta) a todos **-7.** [unconcealed] manifesto(ta). ◇ *n*: **in the ~** [in the fresh air] ao ar livre; **to bring sthg out into the ~** pôr algo para fora. ◇ *vt* **-1.** [gen] abrir **-2.** [inaugurate] inaugurar **-3.** [unblock] desbloquear. ◇ *vi* abrir.

◆ **open on to** *vt fus* [subj: room, door] dar para.

◆ **open out** *vi* **-1.** [bud, petals] abrir-se **-2.** [road, path, river] alargar-se **-3.** [view, valley] revelar-se.

◆ **open up** ◇ *vt* [unlock door] destrancar a porta. ◇ *vi* **-1.** [gen] abrir-se **-2.** [shop, house] abrir.

open-air *adj* ao ar livre; ~ **swimming pool** piscina descoberta.

open-and-shut *adj* evidente.

opencast ['əʊpnkɑ:st] *adj*: ~ **mining** lavra *f* a céu aberto.

open day *n dia em que uma escola, universidade etc. podem ser visitados pelo público em geral.*

open-ended [-'endɪd] *adj* sem prazo para acabar, aberto(ta).

opener ['əʊpnəʳ] *n* abridor *m.*

open-handed [-'hændɪd] *adj* generoso(sa).

openhearted [ˌəʊpn'hɑ:tɪd] *adj* de coração aberto.

open-heart surgery *n (U)* cirurgia *f* de coração aberto.

opening ['əʊpnɪŋ] ◇ *adj* [first] primeiro(ra). ◇ *n* **-1.** [beginning] lançamento *m* **-2.** [gap] abertura *f* **-3.** [opportunity] oportunidade *f*; ~ **for sthg** oportunidade para algo **-4.** [job vacancy] vaga *f.*

opening hours *npl* horário *m* de funcionamento.

opening night *n* (noite de) estréia *f.*

opening time *n UK* hora *f* de abrir.

open letter *n* carta *f* aberta.

openly ['əʊpənlɪ] *adv* abertamente.

open market *n* mercado *m* aberto.

open marriage *n* casamento *m* aberto.

open-minded [-'maɪndɪd] *adj* compreensivo(va), sem preconceitos.

open-mouthed [-'maʊðd] *adj* boquiaberto(ta); **in ~ admiration** numa admiração de deixar de boca aberta.

open-necked [-'nekt] *adj* aberto(ta) no colo.

openness ['əʊpənnɪs] *n (U)* [frankness] franqueza *f.*

open-plan *adj* sem divisórias.

open prison *n* prisão *f* de regime aberto.

open sandwich *n* sanduíche *m* aberto.

open season *n* temporada *f.*

open shop *n local de trabalho onde não é necessário pertencer a um sindicato.*

Open University *n UK*: **the ~** *universidade britânica para alunos adultos que estudam em casa, através de uma combinação de programas de rádio e televisão e ensino à distância.*

open verdict *n JUR júri m pendente.*

opera ['ɒpərə] *n* ópera *f.*

opera glasses *npl* binóculos *mpl* de teatro.

opera house *n* teatro *m* lírico.

opera singer *n* cantor *m*, -ra *f* de ópera.

operate ['ɒpəreɪt] ◇ *vt* **-1.** [cause to work] operar **-2.** *COMM* [manage] dirigir. ◇ *vi* **-1.** [function] funcionar **-2.** *COMM* dirigir **-3.** *MED* operar; **to ~ on sb/sthg** operar alguém/algo.

operatic [ˌɒpə'rætɪk] *adj* de ópera, lírico(ca).

operating room ['ɒpəreɪtɪŋ-] *n US* = **operating theatre.**

operating system ['ɒpəreɪtɪŋ-] *n COMPUT* sistema *m* operacional.

operating theatre *UK*, **operating room** *US* ['ɒpəreɪtɪŋ-] *n* sala *f* de operações.

operation [ˌɒpə'reɪʃn] *n* **-1.** [gen] operação *f* **-2.** *MIL* manobra *f* **-3.** *COMM* administração *f* **-4.** *(U)* [functioning] funcionamento *m*; **in ~** [machine, device] em funcionamento; [law, system] em vigor **-5.** *MED* operação *f*, cirurgia *f*; **to have an ~ on one's knee** ser operado(da) no joelho; **to perform a kidney transplant ~** fazer uma cirurgia de transplante renal.

operational [ˌɒpə'reɪʃənl] *adj* operacional.

operative ['ɒprətɪv] ◇ *adj* [law] em vigor; [system] vigente. ◇ *n* [in factory] operário *m*, -ria *f.*

operator ['ɒpəreɪtəʳ] *n* **-1.** *TELEC* telefonista *mf* **-2.** [technician] operador *m*, -ra *f* **-3.** *COMM* [person in charge] encarregado *m*, -da *f.*

operetta [ˌɒpə'retə] *n* opereta *f.*

ophthalmic optician [ɒf'θælmɪk-] *n* oculista *mf.*

ophthalmologist [ˌɒfθæl'mɒlədʒɪst] *n* oftalmologista *mf.*

opinion [ə'pɪnjən] *n* opinião *f*; **to be of the ~ that** ser da opinião de que; **in my ~** na minha opinião.

opinionated [əˈpɪnjəneɪtɪd] *adj pej* teimoso(sa), cabeça-dura.
opinion poll *n* pesquisa *f* de opinião.
opium [ˈəʊpjəm] *n (U)* ópio *m.*
opponent [əˈpəʊnənt] *n* adversário *m*, -ria *f.*
opportune [ˈɒpətju:n] *adj* oportuno(na).
opportunism [ˌɒpəˈtju:nɪzm] *n (U)* oportunismo *m.*
opportunist [ˌɒpəˈtju:nɪst] *n* oportunista *mf.*
opportunity [ˌɒpəˈtju:nətɪ] (*pl* **-ies**) *n* oportunidade *f*; **to get the ~ (to do sthg)** ter a oportunidade (de fazer algo); **to take the ~ to do** *OR* **of doing sthg** aproveitar a oportunidade para fazer algo.
oppose [əˈpəʊz] *vt* opor-se a.
opposed [əˈpəʊzd] *adj* oposto(ta); **to be ~ to sthg** opor-se a algo; **as ~ to** em oposição a, em vez de; **I like beer ~ wine** prefiro vinho e não cerveja.
opposing [əˈpəʊzɪŋ] *adj* oposto(ta), contrário(ria).
opposite [ˈɒpəzɪt] <> *adj* **-1.** [facing] em frente; **the ~ side (of the street/house/door)** o outro lado (da rua/casa/porta) **-2.** [very different]: **~ (to sthg)** oposto(ta) (a algo). <> *adv* (lá) em frente. <> *prep* [facing] em frente a. <> *n* [contrary] contrário *m.*
opposite number *n* número *m* equivalente.
opposite sex *n*: **the ~** o sexo oposto.
opposition [ˌɒpəˈzɪʃn] *n* **-1.** *(U)* [gen] oposição *f* **-2.** [opposing team] adversário *m*, -ria *f.*
◆ **Opposition** *n UK POL*: **the Opposition** a Oposição.
oppress [əˈpres] *vt* **-1.** [tyrannize] oprimir **-2.** [subj: anxiety, atmosphere] deprimir.
oppressed [əˈprest] <> *adj* [people, minorities] oprimido(da). <> *npl*: **the ~** os oprimidos.
oppression [əˈpreʃn] *n (U)* opressão *f.*
oppressive [əˈpresɪv] *adj* **-1.** [gen] opressivo(va) **-2.** [heat, weather] sufocante.
oppressor [əˈpresəʳ] *n* opressor *m*, -ra *f.*
opprobrium [əˈprəʊbrɪəm] *n (U) fml* opróbrio *m.*
opt [ɒpt] <> *vt*: **to ~ to do sthg** optar por *OR* preferir fazer algo. <> *vi*: **to ~ for sthg** optar por *OR* escolher algo.
◆ **opt in** *vi*: **to ~ in (to sthg)** optar por participar (de algo).
◆ **opt out** *vi*: **to ~ out (of sthg)** optar por não participar (de algo); [give up] abrir mão (de algo).
optic [ˈɒptɪk] *adj* óptico(ca).
◆ **optics** *n (U)* óptica *f.*
optical [ˈɒptɪkl] *adj* **-1.** [relating to light] óptico(ca) **-2.** [visual] visual.
optical character reader *n COMPUT* leitora *f* óptica de caracteres.
optical character recognition *n COMPUT* reconhecimento *m* óptico de caracteres.
optical fibre *n TELEC* fibra *f* óptica.
optical illusion *n* ilusão *f* de óptica.
optician [ɒpˈtɪʃn] *n* oculista *mf*; **~'s** óptica *f.*
optimism [ˈɒptɪmɪzm] *n (U)* otimismo *m.*
optimist [ˈɒptɪmɪst] *n* otimista *mf.*
optimistic [ˌɒptɪˈmɪstɪk] *adj* otimista; **to be ~ about sthg** ser/estar otimista sobre algo.
optimize, -ise [ˈɒptɪmaɪz] *vt* otimizar.
optimum [ˈɒptɪməm] *adj* ótimo(ma).
option [ˈɒpʃn] *n* [choice] opção *f*; **to have the ~ to do** *OR* **of doing sthg** ter a opção de fazer algo.
optional [ˈɒpʃənl] *adj* opcional.
opulence [ˈɒpjʊləns] *n (U)* opulência *f.*
opulent [ˈɒpjʊlənt] *adj* opulento(ta).
opus [ˈəʊpəs] (*pl* **-es** *OR* **opera**) *n MUS* opus *m.*
or [ɔ:ʳ] *conj* **-1.** [gen] ou **-2.** [after negative] nem; **he can't read ~ write** ele não sabe ler nem escrever **-3.** [otherwise] senão; **I'd better go now ~ I'll miss my plane** acho melhor eu ir logo, senão vou perder o vôo.
OR *abbr of* **Oregon**.
oracle [ˈɒrəkl] *n* [prophet] oráculo *m.*
oral [ˈɔ:rəl] <> *adj* **-1.** [spoken] oral **-2.** [relating to the mouth] bucal. <> *n* exame *m* oral.
orally [ˈɔ:rəlɪ] *adv* **-1.** [in spoken form] oralmente **-2.** [via the mouth] por via oral.
orange [ˈɒrɪndʒ] <> *adj* [colour] laranja. <> *n* **-1.** [fruit] laranja *f* **-2.** *(U)* [colour] laranja *m inv.*
orangeade [ˌɒrɪndʒˈeɪd] *n* laranjada *f.*
orange blossom *n* [flowers] flor *f* de laranjeira.
orange juice *n* suco *m* de laranja.
Orangeman [ˈɒrɪndʒmən] (*pl* **-men** [-mən]) *n UK* orangista *mf.*
orange tree *n* laranjeira *f.*
orangutang [ɔ:ˌræŋu:ˈtæŋ] *n* orangotango *m.*
oration [ɔ:ˈreɪʃn] *n fml* discurso *m.*
orator [ˈɒrətəʳ] *n* orador *m*, -ra *f.*
oratorio [ˌɒrəˈtɔ:rɪəʊ] (*pl* **-s**) *n* oratório *m.*
oratory [ˈɒrətrɪ] *n* **-1.** *(U)* [eloquence] oratória *f* **-2.** [prayer room] oratório *m.*
orb [ɔ:b] *n* **-1.** [sphere] orbe *m* **-2.** [ornamental ball] esfera *f.*
orbit [ˈɔ:bɪt] <> *n* órbita *f*; **to be in/go into ~ (around sthg)** estar/entrar em órbita (ao redor de algo); **to put sthg into ~ (around sthg)** pôr algo em órbita (ao redor de algo). <> *vt* orbitar.
orbital road *n UK estrada que circunda uma cidade.*
orchard [ˈɔ:tʃəd] *n* pomar *m.*
orchestra [ˈɔ:kɪstrə] *n* orquestra *f.*
orchestral [ɔ:ˈkestrəl] *adj* orquestral.
orchestra pit *n* fosso *m* da orquestra.
orchestrate [ˈɔ:kɪstreɪt] *vt* **-1.** *MUS* orquestrar **-2.** *fig* [organize] osquestrar.
orchestration [ˌɔ:keˈstreɪʃn] *n MUS* & *fig* orquestração *f.*
orchid [ˈɔ:kɪd] *n* orquídea *f.*
ordain [ɔ:ˈdeɪn] *vt* **-1.** *fml* [decree] ordenar, decretar **-2.** *RELIG*: **to be ~ed** ser ordenado(da).
ordeal [ɔ:ˈdi:l] *n* experiência *f* traumática, provação *f.*
order [ˈɔ:dəʳ] <> *n* **-1.** [gen] ordem *f*; **to be under ~s to do sthg** receber ordens para fazer algo; **in ~** em ordem; **in working ~** em funcionamento; **to be out of ~** [not working] estar fora de operação, não estar funcionando; [in meeting, debate] agir de forma inaceitável; [behaviour] ser improcedente; **to keep ~** manter a ordem **-2.** *COMM* [request] pedido *m*; **to place an ~ with sb for sthg** encomendar algo com alguém; **on ~** reservado(-da); **to ~** sob encomenda **-3.** *US* [portion] porção *f.* <> *vt* **-1.** [command] ordenar; **to ~ sb to do sthg** ordenar alguém a fazer algo; **to ~ that** ordenar

que **-2.** [request - drink, food, shopping item] pedir; [- taxi] chamar. <> *vi* pedir, fazer o pedido *(em restaurante)*.

◆ **orders** *npl RELIG*: **(holy) ~s** ordens *fpl* (sagradas).

◆ **in the order of** *UK*, **on the order of** *US prep* da ordem de.

◆ **in order that** *conj* a fim de que, para que.

◆ **in order to** *conj* para.

◆ **order about, order around** *vt sep*: **he's always ~ing people about** ele está sempre mandando nas pessoas.

order book *n* livro *m* de encomendas.

order form *n* formulário *m* de encomenda.

orderly ['ɔ:dəlɪ] (*pl* **-ies**) <> *adj* **-1.** [person] obediente **-2.** [room, office] ordenado(da). <> *n* [in hospital] assistente *mf*.

order number *n* número *m* do pedido.

ordinal ['ɔ:dɪnl] <> *adj* ordinal. <> *n* ordinal *m*.

ordinarily ['ɔ:dənrəlɪ] *adv* [normally] geralmente.

ordinary ['ɔ:dənrɪ] <> *adj* **-1.** [normal] comum, normal **-2.** *pej* [unexceptional] medíocre. <> *n*: **out of the ~** fora do comum.

ordinary level *n UK* nível *m* fundamental *(na escola)*.

ordinary seaman *n UK* marinheiro *m*.

ordinary shares *npl UK FIN* ações *fpl* ordinárias.

ordination [,ɔ:dɪ'neɪʃn] *n (U)* ordenação *f*.

ordnance ['ɔ:dnəns] *n* **-1.** [military supplies] arsenal *f* bélico **-2.** [artillery] artilharia *f*.

Ordnance Survey *n UK* & *Irish* *serviço oficial de topografia e cartografia*.

ore [ɔ:ʳ] *n* minério *m*.

oregano [,ɒrɪ'gɑ:nəʊ] *n (U)* orégano *m*.

Oregon ['ɒrɪgən] *n* Oregon; **in ~** no Oregon.

organ ['ɔ:gən] *n* **-1.** [gen] órgão *m* **-2.** *fig* [mouthpiece] órgão *m*.

organic [ɔ:'gænɪk] *adj* orgânico(ca).

organically [ɔ:'gænɪklɪ] *adv AGR* organicamente.

organic chemistry *n (U)* química *f* orgânica.

organism ['ɔ:gənɪzm] *n BIOL* organismo *m*.

organist ['ɔ:gənɪst] *n* organista *mf*.

organization [,ɔ:gənaɪ'zeɪʃn] *n* organização *f*.

organization chart *n* organograma *m*.

organizational [,ɔ:gənaɪ'zeɪʃnl] *adj* organizacional.

organize, -ise ['ɔ:gənaɪz] <> *vt* organizar. <> *vi* organizar-se.

organized ['ɔ:gənaɪzd] *adj* organizado(da).

organized crime *n (U)* crime *m* organizado.

organized labour *n (U)* mão-de-obra *f* sindicalizada.

organizer ['ɔ:gənaɪzəʳ] *n* [person] organizador *m*, -ra *f*.

organza [ɔ:'gænzə] *n (U)* organza *f*.

orgasm ['ɔ:gæzm] *n* orgasmo *m*.

orgy ['ɔ:dʒɪ] (*pl* **-ies**) *n* orgia *f*.

orient ['ɔ:rɪənt] *vt esp US* = **orientate**.

Orient ['ɔ:rɪənt] *n*: **the ~** o Oriente.

oriental [,ɔ:rɪ'entl] <> *adj* oriental. <> *n* [non-PC term for East-Asian] oriental *mf*.

orientate ['ɔ:rɪenteɪt] *vt*: **to be ~d towards sb/sthg** ser orientado(da) para alguém/algo; **to ~ o.s.** orientar-se.

orientation [,ɔ:rɪen'teɪʃn] *n (U)* orientação *f*.

orienteering [,ɔ:rɪən'tɪərɪŋ] *n (U)* *esporte no qual as pessoas utilizam um mapa e uma bússola para se orientar*, corrida *f* de orientação.

orifice ['ɒrɪfɪs] *n* orifício *m*.

origami [,ɒrɪ'gɑ:mɪ] *n (U)* origami *m*.

origin ['ɒrɪdʒɪn] *n* origem *f*; **country of ~** país *m* de origem.

◆ **origins** *npl* origens *fpl*.

original [ɒ'rɪdʒənl] <> *adj* original. <> *n* original *m*.

originality [ə,rɪdʒə'nælətɪ] *n (U)* originalidade *f*.

originally [ə'rɪdʒənəlɪ] *adv* [initially] originalmente.

original sin *n (U)* pecado *m* original.

originate [ə'rɪdʒəneɪt] <> *vt* originar, produzir. <> *vi*: **to ~ (in)** originar-se (em), surgir (de); **to ~ from** originar-se de.

origination *n (U)* [invention, creation] origem *f*, criação *f*.

originator [ə'rɪdʒəneɪtəʳ] *n* autor *m*, -ra *f*, inventor *m*, -ra *f*.

Orinoco [,ɒrɪ'nəʊkəʊ] *n*: **the (River) ~** o (Rio) Orinoco.

Orkney Islands ['ɔ:knɪ-], **Orkneys** ['ɔ:knɪz] *npl*: **the ~** as Ilhas Órcadas; **in the ~** nas Ilhas Órcadas.

ornament ['ɔ:nəmənt] *n* ornamento *m*.

ornamental [,ɔ:nə'mentl] *adj* ornamental.

ornamentation [,ɔ:nəmen'teɪʃn] *n (U)* ornamentação *f*.

ornate [ɔ:'neɪt] *adj* ornado(da).

ornately [ɔ:'neɪtlɪ] *adv* vistosamente, de forma requintada.

ornery ['ɔ:nərɪ] *adj US inf* genioso(sa).

ornithologist [,ɔ:nɪ'θɒlədʒɪst] *n* ornitólogo *m*, -ga *f*.

ornithology [,ɔ:nɪ'θɒlədʒɪ] *n (U)* ornitologia *f*.

orphan ['ɔ:fn] <> *n* órfão *m*, -fã *f*. <> *vt*: **to be ~ed** ficar órfão(fã).

orphanage ['ɔ:fənɪdʒ] *n* orfanato *m*.

orthodontist [,ɔ:θə'dɒntɪst] *n* ortodontista *mf*.

orthodox ['ɔ:θədɒks] *adj* ortodoxo(xa).

Orthodox Church *n*: **the ~** a Igreja Ortodoxa.

orthodoxy ['ɔ:θədɒksɪ] *n* ortodoxia *f*.

orthopaedic [,ɔ:θə'pi:dɪk] *adj* ortopédico(ca).

orthopaedics [,ɔ:θə'pi:dɪks] *n (U)* ortopedia *f*.

orthopaedist [,ɔ:θə'pi:dɪst] *n* ortopedista *mf*.

orthopedic etc [,ɔ:θə'pi:dɪk] *adj* = **orthopaedic etc**.

OS <> *n* (*abbr of* **Ordnance Survey**) *organização oficial britânica que elabora mapas detalhados da Grã-Bretanha e da Irlanda*. <> **-1.** (*abbr of* **outsize**) GGG **-2.** (*abbr of* **out of stock**) fora de estoque.

Oscar ['ɒskəʳ] *n CINEMA* Oscar *m*.

oscillate ['ɒsɪleɪt] *vi* **-1.** [from side to side] oscilar **-2.** *fig* [vacillate]: **to ~ between** oscilar entre.

oscilloscope [ɒ'sɪləskəʊp] *n* osciloscópio *m*.

OSD (*abbr of* **optical scanning device**) *n* OSD *m*.

OSHA (*abbr of* **Occupational Safety and Health**

Administration) *n órgão norte-americano responsável pela saúde e pela segurança no trabalho.*
Oslo ['ɒzləʊ] *n* Oslo; **in ~** em Oslo.
osmosis [ɒz'məʊsɪs] *n (U)* osmose *f.*
osprey ['ɒsprɪ] *(pl* **-s**) *n* gavião-pescador *m.*
Ostend [ɒs'tend] *n* Ostend; **in ~** em Ostend.
ostensible [ɒ'stensəbl] *adj* ostensivo(va).
ostensibly [ɒ'stensəblɪ] *adv* ostensivamente.
ostentation [ˌɒstən'teɪʃn] *n (U)* ostentação *f.*
ostentatious [ˌɒstən'teɪʃəs] *adj* ostentoso(sa).
osteoarthritis [ˌɒstɪəʊɑː'θraɪtɪs] *n (U)* osteoartrite *f.*
osteopath ['ɒstɪəpæθ] *n* osteopático *m*, -ca *f.*
osteopathy [ˌɒstɪ'ɒpəθɪ] *n* osteopatia *f.*
ostracize, -ise ['ɒstrəsaɪz] *vt* condenar ao ostracismo.
ostrich ['ɒstrɪtʃ] *n* avestruz *mf.*
OT *n* **-1.** (*abbr of* **Old Testament**) AT *m* **-2.** (*abbr of* **occupational therapy**) TO *f.*
OTC (*abbr of* **Officer Training Corps**) *n unidade de formação de oficiais da reserva do exército britânico.*
OTE (*abbr of* **on target earnings**) *prêmios obtidos mediante cumprimento de objetivos.*
other ['ʌðə^r] ◇ *adj* **-1.** [gen] outro(tra); **the ~ one** o outro, a outra **-2.** *phr*: **the ~ day** no outro dia; **the ~ week** na outra semana. ◇ *adv*: **~ than** a não ser; **to be none ~ than** ser nem mais nem menos que. ◇ *pron*: **the ~** o outro, a outra; **~s** outros(tras); **the ~s** os outros, as outras; **one after the ~** um atrás do outro, uma atrás da outra; **one or ~ of you must help me** um de vocês dois deve me ajudar.
◆ **something or other** *pron* uma coisa ou outra.
◆ **somehow or other** *adv* de um jeito ou de outro.
otherwise ['ʌðəwaɪz] ◇ *adv* **-1.** [apart from that] de resto, tirando isso **-2.** [differently, in a different way] de outra maneira; **deliberately or ~** intencionalmente ou não. ◇ *conj* [or else] senão, do contrário.
other world *n*: **the ~** o outro mundo.
otherworldly [ˌʌðə'wɜːldlɪ] *adj* místico(ca), espiritual.
OTT (*abbr of* **over the top**) *adj UK inf* além dos limites; **it's a bit ~** está um pouco além dos limites.
Ottawa ['ɒtəwə] *n* Ottawa; **in ~** em Ottawa.
otter ['ɒtə^r] *n* lontra *f.*
OU (*abbr of* **Open University**) *n* universidade *f* aberta.
ouch [aʊtʃ] *excl* ai!
ought [ɔːt] *aux vb* dever; **I really ~ to go** eu realmente deveria ir; **you ~ not to have done that** você não deveria ter feito isso; **she ~ to pass her exam** ela tem chance de passar no exame.
oughtn't [ɔːtnt] *cont* = **ought not.**
Ouija board® ['wiːdʒə-] *n* ≃ jogo *m* do copo.
ounce [aʊns] *n* **-1.** [unit of measurement] onça *f* **-2.** *fig* [small amount]: **an ~ of**, um pouco de.
our ['aʊə^r] *poss adj* nosso(a); **~ books** os nossos livros.
ours ['aʊəz] *poss pron* o nosso (a nossa); **a friend of ~** um amigo nosso; **those shoes are ~** estes sapatos são (os) nossos; **~ are here - where are yours?** os nossos estão aqui - onde estão os seus?
ourselves [aʊə'selvz] *pron pl* **-1.** *(reflexive)* nos **-2.** *(after prep)* nós mesmos(mas), nós próprios(prias); **we did it ~** nós mesmos OR próprios o fizemos.
oust [aʊst] *vt fml*: **to ~ sb (from sthg)** expulsar alguém (de algo).
ouster ['aʊstə^r] *n US* **-1.** [from country] expulsão *f* **-2.** [from office] destituição *f.*
out [aʊt] ◇ *adj* [light, cigarette] apagado(da); [not in fashion] fora de moda; **cargo pants are so ~** as calças cargo estão tão fora de moda. ◇ *adv* **-1.** [outside] fora; **to get/go ~ (of)** sair (de); **it's cold ~ today** está frio lá fora hoje; **he looked ~** ele olhou para fora. **-2.** [not at home, work] fora; **to be ~** não estar em casa; **to go ~** sair. **-3.** [so as to be extinguished]: **to turn sthg ~** apagar algo; **put your cigarette ~** apague o cigarro. **-4.** [expressing removal]: **to pour sthg ~** despejar algo, jogar algo fora; **to take money ~** [from cashpoint] retirar dinheiro; **to take sthg ~ (of)** tirar algo (de). **-5.** [outwards]: **to stick ~** sobressair. **-6.** [expressing distribution]: **to hand sthg ~** distribuir algo. **-7.** [in phrases]: **to get enjoyment ~ of sthg** divertir-se com algo; **stay ~ of the sun** não se exponha ao sol; **made ~ of wood** (feito) de madeira; **five ~ of ten women** cinco em cada dez mulheres; **I'm ~ of cigarettes** não tenho cigarros.
out-and-out *adj* completo(ta), absoluto(ta).
outback ['aʊtbæk] *n*: **the ~** *o interior da Austrália.*
outbid [ˌaʊt'bɪd] (*pt* & *pp* **outbid**, *cont* **-ding**) *vt*: **to ~ sb (for sthg)** sobrepujar alguém (em algo).
outboard (motor) ['aʊtbɔːd-] *n* motor *m* de popa.
outbound ['aʊtbaʊnd] *adj* **-1.** [train, flight] de ida **-2.** [traffic] de saída.
outbreak ['aʊtbreɪk] *n* **-1.** [of crime, violence] explosão *f* **-2.** [of disease] surto *m* **-3.** [of war] deflagração *f.*
outbuildings ['aʊtbɪldɪŋz] *npl* dependências *fpl.*
outburst ['aʊtbɜːst] *n* **-1.** [of emotion] manifestação *f* **-2.** [sudden occurrence] explosão *f.*
outcast ['aʊtkɑːst] *n* rejeitado *m*, -da *f.*
outclass [ˌaʊt'klɑːs] *vt* exceder, ultrapassar.
outcome ['aʊtkʌm] *n* resultado *m.*
outcrop ['aʊtkrɒp] *n* afloramento *m.*
outcry ['aʊtkraɪ] (*pl* **-ies**) *n* protestos *mpl.*
outdated [ˌaʊt'deɪtɪd] *adj* ultrapassado(da), fora de moda.
outdid [ˌaʊt'dɪd] *pt* ▷ **outdo.**
outdistance [ˌaʊt'dɪstəns] *vt* **-1.** [in race] deixar para trás **-2.** *fig* [in business, development] ultrapassar.
outdo [ˌaʊt'duː] (*pt* **-did**, *pp* **-done** [-dʌn]) *vt* ultrapassar, superar.
outdoor ['aʊtdɔː^r] *adj* ao ar livre.
outdoors [aʊt'dɔːz] *adv* ao ar livre; **let's eat ~** vamos comer fora.

outer ['aʊtəʳ] *adj* externo(na); **Outer London** a Grande Londres.

outermost ['aʊtəməʊst] *adj* mais externo(na); ~ **planet of the solar system** o planeta mais afastado do sistema solar.

outer space *n (U)* espaço *m* exterior.

outerwear *n* roupa *f* de cima.

outfit ['aʊtfɪt] *n* **-1.** [clothes] vestimenta *f*; [fancy dress] traje *m* **-2.** *inf* [organization] agrupamento *m*, grupo *m*.

outfitters ['aʊt,fɪtəz] *n UK dated* confecção *f*.

outflank [,aʊt'flæŋk] *vt* **-1.** *MIL* surpreender pela retaguarda **-2.** *fig* [in argument, business] superar.

outgoing ['aʊt,gəʊɪŋ] *adj* **-1.** [leaving] de partida **-2.** [friendly, sociable] extrovertido(da), aberto(ta).
◆ **outgoings** *npl UK* despesas *fpl*.

outgrow [,aʊt'grəʊ] (*pt* **-grew**, *pp* **-grown**) *vt* **-1.** [grow too big for]: **he has ~n his shirts** as camisas ficaram pequenas para ele **-2.** [grow too old for] ser muito grande para.

outhouse ['aʊthaʊs, *pl* -haʊzɪz] *n* dependência *f*.

outing ['aʊtɪŋ] *n* **-1.** [trip] excursão *f* **-2.** *(U)* [of homosexuals] *revelação da homossexualidade de uma pessoa famosa*.

outlandish [aʊt'lændɪʃ] *adj* estranho(nha), extravagante.

outlast [,aʊt'lɑ:st] *vt* sobreviver a, durar mais tempo que.

outlaw ['aʊtlɔ:] ◇ *n* fora-da-lei *mf*. ◇ *vt* **-1.** [make illegal] declarar ilegal **-2.** [declare an outlaw] proscrever.

outlay ['aʊtleɪ] *n* despesa *f*, desembolso *m*.

outlet ['aʊtlet] *n* **-1.** [for feelings] escape *m* **-2.** [hole, pipe] saída *f* **-3.** [shop] ponto *m* de venda **-4.** *US ELEC* tomada *f*.

outline ['aʊtlaɪn] ◇ *n* **-1.** [brief description] linhas *fpl* gerais, esboço *m*; **in ~** em linhas gerais **-2.** [silhouette] contorno *m*. ◇ *vt* **-1.** [describe briefly] resumir, esboçar **-2.** [silhouette]: **to be ~d against sthg** delinear-se contra algo.

outlive [,aʊt'lɪv] *vt* **-1.** [subj: person] viver mais que **-2.** *fig* [subj: idea, object] sobreviver.

outlook ['aʊtlʊk] *n* **-1.** [attitude, disposition] postura *f*, atitude *f* **-2.** [prospect] perspectiva *f*.

outlying ['aʊt,laɪɪŋ] *adj* distante, remoto(ta).

outmanoeuvre *UK*, **outmaneuver** *US* [,aʊtmə'nu:vəʳ] *vt* passar a perna em.

outmoded [,aʊt'məʊdɪd] *adj* antiquado(da), fora de moda.

outnumber [,aʊt'nʌmbəʳ] *vt* exceder em número.

out-of-date *adj* **-1.** [passport, season ticket] expirado(da) **-2.** [clothes, belief] antiquado(da).

out of doors *adv* ao ar livre.

out-of-the-way *adj* [isolated] remoto(ta).

outpace [,aʊt'peɪs] *vt* **-1.** [subj: person] deixar para trás **-2.** *fig* [subj: technology] deixar para trás.

outpatient ['aʊt,peɪʃnt] *n* paciente *mf* ambulatorial.

outplacement *n COMM* recolocação *f (em outra empresa)*.

outplay [,aʊt'pleɪ] *vt SPORT* superar, jogar melhor que.

outpost ['aʊtpəʊst] *n fig* [bastion] posto *m* avançado.

outpouring ['aʊt,pɔ:rɪŋ] *literary n* efusão *f*.

output ['aʊtpʊt] ◇ *n* **-1.** [production] produção *f* **-2.** [*COMPUT* - printing out] saída *f*; [- printout] cópia *f* impressa. ◇ *vt COMPUT* gerar como saída.

outrage ['aʊtreɪdʒ] ◇ *n* **-1.** *(U)* [anger, shock] indignidade *f* **-2.** [atrocity] atrocidade *f*, ultraje *m*. ◇ *vt* ultrajar.

outraged ['aʊtreɪdʒd] *adj* indignado(da).

outrageous [aʊt'reɪdʒəs] *adj* **-1.** [offensive, shocking] ultrajante **-2.** [extravagant, wild] extravagante.

outran [,aʊt'ræn] *pt* ▷ **outrun**.

outrank [,aʊt'ræŋk] *vt* exceder em hierarquia.

outrider ['aʊt,raɪdəʳ] *n* escolta *f*.

outright [*adj* 'aʊtraɪt, *adv* ,aʊt'raɪt] ◇ *adj* **-1.** [categoric, direct] claro(ra), categórico(ca) **-2.** [total, complete - disaster] completo(ta); [- victory, winner] indiscutível. ◇ *adv* **-1.** [ask] abertamente, francamente **-2.** [win, fail] indiscutivelmente, completamente **-3.** [deny] categoricamente **-4.** [be killed]: **to be killed ~** morrer no ato.

outrun [,aʊt'rʌn] (*pt* **-ran**, *pp* **-run**, *cont* **-ning**) *vt* correr mais que.

outsell [,aʊt'sel] (*pt* & *pp* **-sold**) *vt* vender mais que.

outset ['aʊtset] *n*: **at the ~** no princípio; **from the ~** desde o princípio.

outshine [,aʊt'ʃaɪn] (*pt* & *pp* **-shone** [-ʃɒn]) *vt* [do better than] eclipsar.

outside [*adv* ,aʊt'saɪd, *adj, prep* & *n* 'aʊtsaɪd] ◇ *adj* **-1.** [gen] externo(na) **-2.** [unlikely] remoto(ta). ◇ *adv* (lá) fora; **to look ~** olhar para fora; **to run ~** correr lá fora; **to go ~** ir lá para fora. ◇ *prep* **-1.** [not inside] fora de; **we live half an hour ~ London** moramos a meia hora de Londres **-2.** [beyond] além de. ◇ *n* **-1.** [exterior] exterior *m* **-2.** [limit]: **at the ~** no máximo.
◆ **outside of** *prep US* [apart from] exceto.

outside broadcast *n UK RADIO* & *TV* (transmissão *f*) externa *f*.

outside lane *n AUT* **-1.** [in UK] faixa *f* da direita **-2.** [in mainland Europe, US, Brazil etc] faixa *f* da esquerda.

outside line *n* linha *f* externa.

outsider [,aʊt'saɪdəʳ] *n* **-1.** *SPORT* azarão *m* **-2.** [from outside social group] estranho *m*, -nha *f*, desconhecido *m*, -da *f*.

outsize ['aʊtsaɪz] *adj* **-1.** [book, portion] enorme **-2.** [clothes] extra-grande.

outsized ['aʊtsaɪzd] *adj* enorme.

outskirts ['aʊtskɜ:ts] *npl*: **the ~** os arredores.

outsmart [,aʊt'smɑ:t] *vt* passar a perna em.

outsold [,aʊt'səʊld] *pt* & *pp* ▷ **outsell**.

outsource ['aʊtsɔ:s] *vt COMM* terceirizar.

outsourcing ['aʊtsɔ:sɪŋ] *n COMM* terceirização *f*.

outspoken [,aʊt'spəʊkn] *adj* franco(ca).

outspread [,aʊt'spred] *adj* estendido(da).

outstanding [,aʊt'stændɪŋ] *adj* **-1.** [excellent] destacado(da), notável **-2.** [very obvious, important] notável **-3.** [pending] pendente.

outstay [,aʊt'steɪ] *vt*: **to ~ one's welcome** abusar da hospitalidade de alguém.

outstretched [ˌaʊtˈstretʃt] *adj* estendido(da).
outstrip [ˌaʊtˈstrɪp] (*pt* & *pp* **-ped**, *cont* **-ping**) *vt* **-1.** [do better than] superar **-2.** [run faster than] ultrapassar, deixar para trás.
out-take *n* **-1.** *CINEMA* sobras *fpl* de filme **-2.** *TV* sobras *fpl* de programa.
out-tray *n* bandeja *f* de saída.
outvote [ˌaʊtˈvəʊt] *vt*: **to ~ sb** vencer alguém por receber mais votos; **the proposal was ~d by fifty to forty (votes)** a proposta foi derrotada por cinqüenta (votos) a quarenta.
outward [ˈaʊtwəd] <> *adj* **-1.** [going away] de ida **-2.** [apparent] aparente **-3.** [visible] visível. <> *adv US* = **outwards**.
outwardly [ˈaʊtwədlɪ] *adv* [apparently] aparentemente.
outwards *UK* [ˈaʊtwədz], **outward** *US adv* para fora.
outweigh [ˌaʊtˈweɪ] *vt* pesar mais que.
outwit [ˌaʊtˈwɪt] (*pt* & *pp* **-ted**, *cont* **-ting**) *vt* ser mais esperto(ta) que.
outworker [ˈaʊtˌwɜːkəʳ] *n* colaborador *m* externo, colaboradora *f* externa.
oval [ˈəʊvl] <> *adj* oval. <> *n* oval *m*.
Oval Office *n*: **the ~** o Salão Oval.
ovarian [əʊˈveərɪən] *adj* ovariano(na); **~ cancer** câncer de ovário.
ovary [ˈəʊvərɪ] (*pl* **-ies**) *n ANAT* ovário *m*.
ovation [əʊˈveɪʃn] *n* ovação *f*; **a standing ~** ovação com o público de pé.
oven [ˈʌvn] *n* [for cooking] forno *m*.
oven glove *n* luva *f* para o forno.
ovenproof [ˈʌvnpruːf] *adj* refratário(ria).
oven-ready *adj* pronto(ta) para ir ao forno.
ovenware [ˈʌvnweəʳ] *n (U)* louça *f* refratária.
over [ˈəʊvəʳ] <> *prep* **-1.** [gen] sobre; **put your coat ~ that chair** ponha o seu casaco naquela cadeira; **to rule ~ a country** governar um país **-2.** [directly above] sobre, em cima de **-3.** [on the far side of] ao outro lado de **-4.** [across the surface of] por; **she walked ~ the lawn** ela caminhou pelo gramado **-5.** [across the top or edge of] por cima de **-6.** [more than] mais de; **~ and above** bem acima de **-7.** [by means of] por **-8.** [concerning, due to] por; **it was a fight ~ a woman, I think** era uma disputa por uma mulher, acho eu **-9.** [during] durante **-10.** [recovered from] recuperado(da) (de). <> *adv* **-1.** [distance away] lá; **~ here/there** por aqui, lá **-2.** [across]: **to cross ~** cruzar; **they flew ~ to America** eles voaram para a América; **~ at mum's** na casa da minha mãe; **to ask sb ~** convidar alguém para ir lá em casa **-3.** [to the ground] para baixo **-4.** [to face a different way]: **to turn sth ~** virar algo **-5.** [more] mais **-6.** [remaining]: **that leaves £2 ~** isso nos sobra £2; **I ate the piece of cake left ~** comi o pedaçao de bolo que sobrou **-7.** *RADIO* câmbio; **~ and out!** câmbio e desligo! **-8.** [involving repetitions]: **(all) ~ again** (tudo) novamente; **~ and ~ (again)** várias e várias vezes. <> *adj* [finished] acabado(da); **the meeting was ~ by seven** a reunião acabou às sete horas. <> *n UK* [cricket] *série de seis lançamentos de um único jogador*.
◆ **all over** <> *prep* por todo(da). <> *adv* [everywhere] por todas as partes. <> *adj* [finished] acabado(da).
over- [ˈəʊvəʳ] *prefix* muito, sobre-.
overabundance [ˌəʊvərəˈbʌndəns] *n (U)* superabundância *f*.
overact [ˌəʊvərˈækt] *vi pej* [in play] exagerar na atuação.
overactive [ˌəʊvərˈæktɪv] *adj* muito ativo(va).
overall [*adj* & *n* ˈəʊvərɔːl, *adv* ˌəʊvərˈɔːl] <> *adj* [total] global, total. <> *adv* **-1.** [in total] no geral **-2.** [in general] normalmente, em geral. <> *n* **-1.** [coat] avental *m*, guarda-pó *m* **-2.** *US* [with trousers] macacão *m*.
◆ **overalls** *npl* macacão *m*.
overambitious [ˌəʊvəræmˈbɪʃəs] *adj* muito ambicioso(sa).
overanxious [ˌəʊvərˈæŋkʃəs] *adj* muito nervoso(-sa).
overarm [ˈəʊvərɑːm] <> *adj* por cima do ombro. <> *adv* por cima do ombro.
overate [ˌəʊvərˈet] *pt* ▷ **overeat**.
overawe [ˌəʊvərˈɔː] *vt* intimidar.
overbalance [ˌəʊvəˈbæləns] *vi* perder o equilíbrio.
overbearing [ˌəʊvəˈbeərɪŋ] *adj pej* arrogante.
overblown [ˌəʊvəˈbləʊn] *adj pej* exagerado(da).
overboard [ˈəʊvəbɔːd] *adv* **-1.** *NAUT*: **to fall ~** cair ao mar **-2.** *fig*: **to go ~ (about sb/sthg)** [be over-enthusiastic about] empolgar-se (com alguém/algo).
overbook [ˌəʊvəˈbʊk] *vi* ter mais reservas que lugares; **the plane was ~** deu overbook no avião.
overburden [ˌəʊvəˈbɜːdn] *vt*: **to be ~ed with sthg** estar sobrecarregado(da) de algo.
overcame [ˌəʊvəˈkeɪm] *pt* ▷ **overcome**.
overcapitalize, -ise [ˌəʊvəˈkæpɪtəlaɪz] *vi FIN* sobrecapitalizar.
overcast [ˈəʊvəkɑːst] *adj* carregado(da), nublado (da).
overcharge [ˌəʊvəˈtʃɑːdʒ] <> *vt*: **to ~ sb (for sthg)** cobrar de alguém em excesso (por algo). <> *vi*: **to ~ (for sthg)** cobrar em excesso (por algo).
overcoat [ˈəʊvəkəʊt] *n* sobretudo *m*.
overcome [ˌəʊvəˈkʌm] (*pt* **-came**, *pp* **-come**) *vt* **-1.** [control, deal with] superar, vencer **-2.** [overwhelm]: **to be ~ (by** *OR* **with sthg)** [emotion] estar tomado(da) (por algo); [smoke, fumes] estar asfixiado(da) (por algo).
overcompensate [ˌəʊvəˈkɒmpənseɪt] *vi*: **to ~ (for sthg)** compensar em excesso (por algo).
overconfident [ˌəʊvəˈkɒnfɪdənt] *adj* confiante em excesso.
overcooked *adj* cozido(da) demais.
overcrowded [ˌəʊvəˈkraʊdɪd] *adj* **-1.** [room, building] superlotado(da) **-2.** [city, country] superpovoado(da).
overcrowding [ˌəʊvəˈkraʊdɪŋ] *n* **-1.** *(U)* [of room, building] superlotação *f* **-2.** *(U)* [of city, country] superpovoamento *m*.
overdeveloped [ˌəʊvədəˈveləpt] *adj* **-1.** *PHOT submetido a longo tempo de revelação* **-2.** [exaggerated] exagerado(da).
overdo [ˌəʊvəˈduː] (*pt* **-did** [-dɪd], *pp* **-done**) *vt* **-1.** *pej*

[exaggerate] exagerar **-2.** [do too much]: **to ~ the walking** caminhar demais; **the doctor told her not to ~ it** o médico disse para ela pegar leve *OR* não exagerar **-3.** [overcook] cozinhar demais.

overdone [ˌəʊvəˈdʌn] <> *pp* ▻ **overdo.** <> *adj*: **it's ~** cozinhou demais.

overdose [*n* ˈəʊvədəʊs , *vb* əʊvəˈdəʊs] <> *n* overdose *f.* <> *vi*: **to ~ on sthg** tomar uma overdose de algo.

overdraft [ˈəʊvədrɑːft] *n* saldo *m* negativo.

overdrawn [ˌəʊvəˈdrɔːn] *adj* **-1.** [person]: **to be ~** ter saldo negativo **-2.** [account] no negativo.

overdress [ˌəʊvəˈdres] *vi* arrumar-se demais.

overdrive [ˈəʊvədraɪv] *n (U) fig*: **to go into ~** trabalhar a todo vapor.

overdue [ˌəʊvəˈdjuː] *adj* **-1.** [gen] atrasado(da); **I'm ~ for a dental checkup** já está na hora de eu fazer a revisão no dentista **-2.** [needed, awaited]: **(long) ~** (há muito) esperado(da).

overeager [ˌəʊvərˈiːgəʳ] *adj* ansioso(sa) demais.

over easy *adj US CULIN*: **eggs ~** ovos *mpl* fritos *(dos dois lados).*

overeat [ˌəʊvərˈiːt] (*pt* **-ate**, *pp* **-eaten**) *vi* comer demais, atracar-se.

overemphasize, -ise [ˌəʊvərˈemfəsaɪz] *vt* enfatizar demais.

overenthusiastic [ˈəʊvərɪnˌθjuːzɪˈæstɪk] *adj* entusiasta demais.

overestimate [ˌəʊvərˈestɪmeɪt] *vt* superestimar.

overexcited [ˌəʊvərɪkˈsaɪtɪd] *adj* sobreexaltado(-da).

overexpose [ˌəʊvərɪkˈspəʊz] *vt PHOT* superexpor.

overfeed [ˌəʊvəˈfiːd] (*pt* & *pp* **-fed** [-fed]) *vt* superalimentar.

overfill [ˌəʊvəˈfɪl] *vt* encher demais.

overflow [*vb* ˌəʊvəˈfləʊ, *n* ˈəʊvəfləʊ] <> *vi* transbordar; **to be ~ing (with sthg)** estar transbordando (de algo); **full to ~ing** entupido(da). <> *vt* transbordar. <> *n* ladrão *m.*

overgrown [ˌəʊvəˈgrəʊn] *adj* coberto(ta) de mato.

overhang [*n* ˈəʊvəhæŋ, *vb* ˌəʊvəˈhæŋ] (*pt* & *pp* **-hung**) <> *n* saliência *f.* <> *vt* sobressair-se de, projetar-se de. <> *vi* sobressair, projetar.

overhaul [*n* ˈəʊvəhɔːl, *vb* ˌəʊvəˈhɔːl] <> *n* revisão *f.* <> *vt* **-1.** [service] fazer a revisão de **-2.** [revise] revisar.

overhead [*adv* ˌəʊvəˈhed, *adj* & *n* ˈəʊvəhed] <> *adj* aéreo(rea). <> *adv* por cima, pelo alto. <> *n US* despesas *fpl* gerais, gastos *mpl* gerais.
◆ **overheads** *npl UK* despesas *fpl* gerais, gastos *mpl* gerais.

overhead projector *n* retroprojetor *m.*

overhear [ˌəʊvəˈhɪəʳ] (*pt* & *pp* **-heard** [-hɜːd]) *vt* entreouvir.

overheat [ˌəʊvəˈhiːt] <> *vt* superaquecer. <> *vi* superaquecer-se.

overhung [ˌəʊvəˈhʌŋ] *pt* & *pp* ▻ **overhang.**

overindulge [ˌəʊvərɪnˈdʌldʒ] <> *vt* ser indulgente demais com, mimar demais. <> *vi*: **to ~ (in sthg)** abusar (com algo).

overjoyed [ˌəʊvəˈdʒɔɪd] *adj*: **to be ~ (at sthg)** estar contentíssimo(ma) (com algo).

overkill [ˈəʊvəkɪl] *n (U)* exagero *m.*

overladen [ˌəʊvəˈleɪdn] <> *pp* ▻ **overload.** <> *adj* sobrecarregado(da).

overlaid [ˌəʊvəˈleɪd] *pt* & *pp* ▻ **overlay.**

overland [ˈəʊvəlænd] <> *adj* terrestre. <> *adv* por terra.

overlap [*n* ˈəʊvəlæp, *vb* ˌəʊvəˈlæp] (*pt* & *pp* **-ped**, *cont* **-ping**) <> *n* **-1.** *(U)* [similarity] coincidência *f* **-2.** [overlapping part, amount] sobreposição *f.* <> *vt* sobrepor-se a. <> *vi* **-1.** [cover each other] sobrepor-se **-2.** [be similar] coincidir; **to ~ (with sthg)** coincidir em parte (com algo).

overlay [ˌəʊvəˈleɪ] (*pt* & *pp* **-laid**) *vt*: **to be overlaid with sthg** estar revestido(da) de algo.

overleaf [ˌəʊvəˈliːf] *adv* no verso.

overload [ˌəʊvəˈləʊd] (*pp* **-loaded** *OR* **-laden**) *vt* sobrecarregar; **to be ~ed (with sthg)** estar sobrecarregado(da) de algo.

overlong [ˌəʊvəˈlɒŋ] <> *adj* muito comprido(da). <> *adv* tempo demais.

overlook [ˌəʊvəˈlʊk] *vt* **-1.** [look over] dar para **-2.** [disregard, miss] fazer vista grossa para **-3.** [excuse] desculpar.

overlord [ˈəʊvəlɔːd] *n literary* senhor *m.*

overly [ˈəʊvəlɪ] *adv* demais; **not ~** não muito.

overmanning [ˌəʊvəˈmænɪŋ] *n (U)* excesso *m* de mão-de-obra.

overnight [*adj* ˈəʊvənaɪt, *adv* ˌəʊvəˈnaɪt] <> *adj* **-1.** [stay, guest, parking] por uma noite **-2.** [clothes] para uma noite **-3.** [journey] de uma noite; **~ bag** bolsa *f* de viagem **-4.** [very sudden] da noite para o dia. <> *adv* **-1.** [for all of night] durante a noite **-2.** [very suddenly] da noite para o dia.

overpaid [ˌəʊvəˈpeɪd] <> *pt* & *pp* ▻ **overpay.** <> *adj* pago(ga) em excesso.

overpass [ˈəʊvəpɑːs] *n US* viaduto *m.*

overpay [ˌəʊvəˈpeɪ] (*pt* & *pp* **-paid**) *vt* pagar demais.

overplay [ˌəʊvəˈpleɪ] *vt* exagerar; **to ~ one's hand** exagerar *(tentando tirar mais vantagem).*

overpopulated [ˌəʊvəˈpɒpjʊleɪtɪd] *adj* superpopulado(da).

overpower [ˌəʊvəˈpaʊəʳ] *vt* **-1.** [in fight] subjugar **-2.** *fig* [overwhelm] vencer, sobrepujar.

overpowering [ˌəʊvəˈpaʊərɪŋ] *adj* **-1.** [desire, feeling] dominante **-2.** [smell] asfixiante **-3.** [heat, sensation] sufocante **-4.** [personality] opressor(ra).

overpriced [ˌəʊvəˈpraɪst] *adj* muito caro(ra).

overproduction [ˌəʊvəprəˈdʌkʃn] *n (U)* superprodução *f*, excesso *m* de produção.

overprotective [ˌəʊvəprəˈtektɪv] *adj* superprotetor(ra).

overran [ˌəʊvəˈræn] *pt* ▻ **overrun.**

overrated [ˌəʊvəˈreɪtɪd] *adj* superestimado(da).

overreach [ˌəʊvəˈriːtʃ] *vt*: **to ~ o.s.** ir longe demais, dar o passo maior que a perna.

overreact [ˌəʊvərɪˈækt] *vi*: **to ~ (to sthg)** reagir exageradamente (a algo).

override [ˌəʊvəˈraɪd] (*pt* **-rode**, *pp* **-ridden**) *vt* **-1.** [be more important than] passar por cima de, não fazer caso de **-2.** [overrule] desautorizar.

overriding [ˌəʊvəˈraɪdɪŋ] *adj* predominante.

overripe [ˌəʊvəˈraɪp] *adj* **-1.** [fruit] maduro(ra) demais **-2.** [cheese] passado(da).
overrode [ˌəʊvəˈrəʊd] *pt* ▷ **override.**
overrule [ˌəʊvəˈru:l] *vt* **-1.** [person, decision] desautorizar **-2.** [objection] negar.
overrun [ˌəʊvəˈrʌn] (*pt* **-ran**, *pp* **-run**, *cont* **-running**) ◇ *vt* **-1.** MIL [occupy] invadir **-2.** *fig* [cover, fill]: **to be ~ with sthg** estar repleto(ta) de algo. ◇ *vi* passar do tempo previsto.
oversaw [ˌəʊvəˈsɔ:] *pt* ▷ **oversee.**
overseas [*adj* ˈəʊvəsi:z, *adv* ˌəʊvəˈsi:z] ◇ *adj* **-1.** [market] exterior **-2.** [network, branches] no exterior **-3.** [sales, aid] para o exterior **-4.** [from abroad] estrangeiro(ra). ◇ *adv* **-1.** [travel, sell] para o exterior **-2.** [study, live] no exterior.
oversee [ˌəʊvəˈsi:] (*pt* **-saw**, *pp* **-seen** [-ˈsi:n]) *vt* supervisionar.
overseer [ˈəʊvəˌsi:əʳ] *n* supervisor *m*, -ra *f*.
overshadow [ˌəʊvəˈʃædəʊ] *vt* **-1.** [make darker] fazer sombra em **-2.** *fig* [outweigh, eclipse]: **to be ~ed by sb/sthg** ser eclipsado(da) por alguém/algo **-3.** *fig* [mar, cloud]: **to be ~ed by sthg** ser ofuscado(da) por algo.
overshoot [ˌəʊvəˈʃu:t] (*pt* & *pp* **-shot**) *vt* passar.
oversight [ˈəʊvəsaɪt] *n* deslize *m*, descuido *m*.
oversimplification [əʊvəˌsɪmplɪfɪˈkeɪʃn] *n* simplificação *f* excessiva.
oversimplify [ˌəʊvəˈsɪmplɪfaɪ] (*pt* & *pp* **-ied**) ◇ *vt* simplificar demais ◇ *vi* simplificar demais.
oversleep [ˌəʊvəˈsli:p] (*pt* & *pp* **-slept** [-ˈslept]) *vi* dormir demais, ficar dormindo.
overspend [ˌəʊvəˈspend] (*pt* & *pp* **-spent** [-ˈspent]) *vi* gastar além da conta.
overspill [ˈəʊvəspɪl] *n (U)* excesso *m* de população.
overstaffed [ˌəʊvəˈstɑ:ft] *adj* com excesso de funcionários.
overstate [ˌəʊvəˈsteɪt] *vt* exagerar.
overstay [ˌəʊvəˈsteɪ] *vt*: **to ~ one's welcome** abusar da hospitalidade de alguém.
overstep [ˌəʊvəˈstep] (*pt* & *pp* **-ped**, *cont* **-ping**) *vt* passar por cima de; **to ~ the mark** passar dos limites.
overstock [ˌəʊvəˈstɒk] *vt* abarrotar, entupir.
overstrike [ˈəʊvəstraɪk] (*pt* & *pp* **-struck**) COMPUT ◇ *n* sobreposição *f* de caracteres. ◇ *vt* sobrepor caracteres.
oversubscribed [ˌəʊvəsʌbˈskraɪbd] *adj* subscrito(ta) em excesso.
overt [ˈəʊvɜ:t] *adj* aberto(ta), manifesto(ta).
overtake [ˌəʊvəˈteɪk] (*pt* **-took**, *pp* **-taken** [-ˈteɪkn]) ◇ *vt* **-1.** AUT ultrapassar **-2.** [subj: disaster, misfortune] surpreender, pegar de surpresa. ◇ *vi* AUT ultrapassar.
overtaking [ˌəʊvəˈteɪkɪŋ] *n (U)* ultrapassagem *f*; **'no ~'** 'proibido ultrapassar'.
overthrow [*n* ˈəʊvəθrəʊ, *vb* ˌəʊvəˈθrəʊ] (*pt* **-threw**, *pp* **-thrown**) ◇ *n* deposição *f*, destituição *f*. ◇ *vt* **-1.** [government, president] depor, destituir **-2.** [concept, idea, standard] derrubar.
overtime [ˈəʊvətaɪm] ◇ *n* **-1.** [extra time worked] hora *f* extra **-2.** US SPORT prorrogação *f*. ◇ *adv*: **to work ~** fazer hora extra.
overtly [ˈəʊvɜ:tlɪ] *adv* abertamente, publicamente.
overtones [ˈəʊvətəʊnz] *npl* insinuações *fpl*.
overtook [ˌəʊvəˈtʊk] *pt* ▷ **overtake.**
overture [ˈəʊvəˌtjʊəʳ] *n* MUS abertura *f*.
◆ **overtures** *npl*: **to make ~s to sb** fazer uma proposta a alguém.
overturn [ˌəʊvəˈtɜ:n] ◇ *vt* **-1.** [turn over] virar **-2.** [overrule] invalidar **-3.** [overthrow] depor. ◇ *vi* **-1.** [boat] virar **-2.** [lorry, car] capotar.
overuse [ˌəʊvəˈju:z] *vt* usar demais.
overview [ˈəʊvəvju:] *n* visão *f* geral.
overweening [ˌəʊvəˈwi:nɪŋ] *adj* desmedido(da).
overweight [ˌəʊvəˈweɪt] *adj* obeso(sa), gordo(da).
overwhelm [ˌəʊvəˈwelm] *vt* **-1.** [make helpless] subjugar **-2.** MIL [gain control of] dominar, passar a controlar.
overwhelming [ˌəʊvəˈwelmɪŋ] *adj* **-1.** [feeling, quality] impressionante **-2.** [victory, defeat, majority] esmagador(ra).
overwhelmingly [ˌəʊvəˈwelmɪŋlɪ] *adv* em peso, em massa.
overwork [ˌəʊvəˈwɜ:k] ◇ *n (U)* trabalho *m* excessivo. ◇ *vt* **-1.** [give too much work to] fazer trabalhar demais **-2.** *fig* [overuse] usar demais. ◇ *vi* trabalhar demais.
overwrought [ˌəʊvəˈrɔ:t] *adj* muito nervoso(sa).
ovulate [ˈɒvjʊleɪt] *vi* ovular.
ovulation [ˌɒvjʊˈleɪʃn] *n (U)* ovulação *f*.
ow [aʊ] *excl* ai!
owe [əʊ] *vt*: **to ~ sthg to sb, to ~ sb sthg** dever algo a alguém.
owing [ˈəʊɪŋ] *adj* que se deve.
◆ **owing to** *prep* por causa de, devido a.
owl [aʊl] *n* coruja *f*.
own [əʊn] ◇ *adj* [indicating possession] próprio(pria); **my/your ~ car** meu/teu próprio carro; **he doesn't need a lift, he has his ~ car** ele não precisa de carona, tem seu próprio carro; **she has her ~ style** ela tem um estilo próprio. ◇ *pron* [indicating possession]: **my ~** o(a) meu(minha); **your ~** o(a) seu(sua); **a house of my ~** minha própria casa; **the city has a special atmosphere of its ~** a cidade tem uma atmosfera especial que lhe é própria; **on one's ~** [alone] sozinho(nha); **to get one's ~ back** dar o troco, vingar-se. ◇ *vt* possuir, ter.
◆ **own up** *vi*: **to ~ up (to sthg)** confessar (algo), admitir (algo).
own brand *n* COMM marca *f* própria.
owner [ˈəʊnəʳ] *n* proprietário *m*, -ria *f*, dono *m*, -na *f*.
owner-occupier *n esp UK* morador *m* proprietário, moradora *f* proprietária.
ownership [ˈəʊnəʃɪp] *n (U)* posse *f*, propriedade *f*.
own goal *n esp UK* **-1.** FTBL gol *m* contra; **to score an ~** marcar um gol contra **-2.** *UK fig* [foolish mistake] gol *m* contra.
ox [ɒks] (*pl* **oxen**) *n* boi *m*.
Oxbridge [ˈɒksbrɪdʒ] *n (U)* as universidades de Oxford e Cambridge.

OXBRIDGE

Oxbridge é o termo utilizado para designar conjuntamente as universidades de Oxford e Cambridge. Essas duas universidades, fundadas no século XIII, são as mais antigas e as mais respeitadas da Grã-Bretanha. Ambas se subdividem em *colleges*, muitos dos quais abrigados em belíssimos edifícios, e mantêm suas antigas tradições. Há grande rivalidade entre as duas universidades, sobretudo no que se refere ás disputas esportivas.

oxen ['ɒksn] *pl* ▷ **ox**.
OXFAM *n organização britânica de caridade para ajuda a países subdesenvolvidos.*
oxide ['ɒksaɪd] *n* óxido *m*.
oxidize, -ise ['ɒksɪdaɪz] *vi* oxidar.
oxtail soup ['ɒksteɪl-] *n (U)* rabada *f*.
ox tongue *n (U)* língua *f* de boi.
oxyacetylene [ˌɒksɪə'setɪli:n] ◇ *n (U)* oxiacetileno *m*. ◇ *comp* oxiacetilênico(ca).
oxygen ['ɒksɪdʒən] *n (U)* oxigênio *m*.
oxygenate ['ɒksɪdʒəneɪt] *vt* oxigenar.
oxygen mask *n* máscara *f* de oxigênio.
oxygen tent *n* tenda *f* de oxigênio.
oyster ['ɔɪstə^r] *n* ostra *f*.
oz. *abbr of* **ounce**.
ozone ['əʊzəʊn] *n* ozônio *m*.
ozone-friendly *adj* não-prejudicial à camada de ozônio.
ozone layer *n* camada *f* de ozônio.

p[1] (*pl* **p's** *OR* **ps**), **P** (*pl* **P's** *OR* **Ps**) [pi:] *n* [letter] p *m*.
◆ **P** **-1.** (*abbr of* **president**) Pres. **-2.** (*abbr of* **prince**) Pr.
p[2] **-1.** (*abbr of* **page**) p. **-2.** *abbr of* **penny, pence**.
P45 *n documento oficial que o empregado recebe do empregador na Grã-Bretanha ao deixar o emprego e repassa ao próximo empregador, contendo informações salariais.*
P60 *n documento oficial fornecido pelo empregador ao empregado na Grã-Bretanha com informações sobre salário recebido e impostos pagos durante aquele ano,* ≃ declaração *f* de rendimentos.
pa [pɑ:] *n inf esp US* pai *m*.
p.a. (*abbr of* **per annum**) p.a.
PA ◇ *n* **-1.** *UK* (*abbr of* **personal assistant**) assessor *m*, -ra *f* pessoal **-2.** (*abbr of* **public address system**) sistema *m* de alto-falantes **-3.** (*abbr of* **Press Association**) *agência de notícias britânica.* ◇ *abbr of* **Pennsylvania**.
PABX (*abbr of* **private automatic branch exchange**) *n* PABX *m*.
PAC *n* **-1.** (*abbr of* **political action committee**) *comitê de levantamento de fundos para causas políticas nos Estados Unidos* **-2.** (*abbr of* **Pan Africanist Congress**) Congresso *m* Pan-Africano.
pace [peɪs] ◇ *n* **-1.** *(U)* [speed, rate] ritmo *m*, andamento *m*; **at one's own ~** no próprio ritmo de alguém; **to keep ~ (with sb/sthg)** acompanhar o ritmo (de alguém/algo) **-2.** [step] passo *m*. ◇ *vt* andar por. ◇ *vi* andar de um lado para o outro.
pacemaker ['peɪsˌmeɪkə^r] *n* **-1.** *MED* marca-passo *m* **-2.** [in race] *competidor que estabelece o ritmo da corrida.*
pacesetter ['peɪsˌsetə^r] *n* *US SPORT atleta que estabelece o ritmo da corrida.*
pachyderm ['pækɪdɜ:m] *n* paquiderme *m*.
Pacific [pə'sɪfɪk] ◇ *adj* do Pacífico. ◇ *n*: **the ~ (Ocean)** o (Oceano) Pacífico.
pacification [ˌpæsɪfɪ'keɪʃn] *n (U) fml* **-1.** [of person] apaziguamento *m* **-2.** [of country, region] pacificação *f*.
Pacific Rim *n*: **the ~** a Região do Pacífico.
pacifier ['pæsɪfaɪə^r] *n US* bico *m*.
pacifism ['pæsɪfɪzm] *n (U)* pacifismo *m*.
pacifist ['pæsɪfɪst] *n* pacifista *mf*.
pacify ['pæsɪfaɪ] (*pt* & *pp* **-ied**) *vt* **-1.** [person] acalmar **-2.** [country, region] pacificar.
pack [pæk] ◇ *n* **-1.** [rucksack] mochila *f* **-2.** [bundle] pacote *m*, embrulho *m* **-3.** [of cigarettes] maço *m* **-4.** *esp US* [washing powder, tissues] caixa *f* **-5.** [of cards] baralho *m* **-6.** [of animals - dogs] matilha *f*; [- wolves] alcatéia *f*; [- of thieves] quadrilha *f* **-7.** *CYCLING, RUGBY* pelotão *m* **-8.** *phr*: **that's a ~ of lies!** é um monte de mentiras! ◇ *vt* **-1.** [bag, suitcase] fazer **-2.** [clothes, etc] colocar na mala **-3.** [put in container, parcel] embalar **-4.** [crowd into] lotar; **to be ~ed into sthg** estar socado(da) em algo. ◇ *vi* **-1.** [for journey, holiday] fazer as malas **-2.** [push tightly] apertar-se, amontoar-se.
◆ **pack in** ◇ *vt sep UK inf* [job, boyfriend, smoking] deixar; **~ it in!** [stop annoying me] pare com isso!, chega!; [shut up] boca fechada! ◇ *vi inf* pifar.
◆ **pack off** *vt sep inf* enviar, mandar.
◆ **pack up** ◇ *vt sep* arrumar. ◇ *vi* **-1.** [pack one's suitcase] fazer as malas **-2.** *inf* [finish work] cair fora (do trabalho) **-3.** *UK inf* [break down] pifar.
package ['pækɪdʒ] ◇ *n* **-1.** [gen] pacote *m* **-2.** [box] caixa *f* **-3.** *US* [of cigarettes] maço *m*, carteira *f OR m* **-4.** [set, group] pacote *m*. ◇ *vt* embalar, empacotar.
package deal *n* pacote *m* de acordo.
package holiday *n* pacote *m* de férias.
packager ['pækɪdʒə^r] *n* **-1.** [person packaging] embalador *m*, -deira *f* **-2.** *COMM* produtora *f* independente.
package tour *n* pacote *m* turístico.
packaging ['pækɪdʒɪŋ] *n (U)* embalagem *f*.
packed [pækt] *adj* **-1.** [place]: **~ (with)** lotado(da) (de) **-2.** [magazine, information pack]: **~ with** repleto(-ta) de.

packed lunch *n UK* **-1.** [for school] *f* merenda *f* **-2.** [for work] marmita *f.*
packed out *adj UK inf* apinhado(da).
packet ['pækɪt] *n* **-1.** [gen] pacote *m* **-2.** [box] caixa *f* **-3.** [of cigarettes] maço *m,* carteira *f* **-4.** *UK inf* [lot of money] bolada *f,* dinheirama *f.*
packhorse *n* cavalo *m* de carga.
pack ice *n (U)* gelo *m* flutuante.
packing ['pækɪŋ] *n (U)* **-1.** [protective material] embalagem *f* **-2.** [for journey, holiday]: **to do the ~** fazer as malas.
packing case *n* caixote *m* de embalagem.
pact [pækt] *n* pacto *m.*
pad [pæd] (*pt* & *pp* **-ded**, *cont* **-ding**) ◇ *n* **-1.** [for clothes, body]: **shoulder ~** ombreira *f*; **knee ~** joelheira *f*; **shin ~** tornozeleira *f* **-2.** [notepad] bloco *m* de anotações **-3.** [for absorbing liquid - cotton wool] chumaço *m*; [- sanitary] absorvente *m* higiênico **-4.** SPACE: **(launch) ~** plataforma *f* (de lançamento) **-5.** [of cat or dog] almofadinha *f* **-6.** *inf dated* [home] casa *f.* ◇ *vt* **-1.** [clothing, furniture] revestir, forrar **-2.** [wound] cobrir **-3.** *fig* [speech, letter, essay] alongar de forma desnecessária. ◇ *vi* andar com suavidade.
◆ **pad out** *vt sep* **-1.** [clothing, furniture] revestir, forrar **-2.** [speech, letter, essay] alongar de forma desnecessária.
padded ['pædɪd] *adj* **-1.** [jacket] revestido(da), forrado(da) **-2.** [shoulders] com ombreiras **-3.** [chair] acolchoado(da).
padded cell *n* cela *f* acolchoada.
padding ['pædɪŋ] *n (U)* **-1.** [in jacket] revestimento *m* **-2.** [in shoulders] ombreira *f* **-3.** [in chair] enchimento *m* **-4.** [in speech, essay, letter] enrolação *f.*
paddle ['pædl] ◇ *n* **-1.** [for canoe, dinghy] remo *m* **-2.** [wade]: **to have a ~** patinhar na água. ◇ *vt* remar. ◇ *vi* **-1.** [in canoe, dinghy] remar **-2.** [wade] patinhar.
paddle boat, paddle steamer *n* vapor *m* movido a rodas.
paddling pool ['pædlɪŋ-] *n* **-1.** [in park] piscina *f* infantil **-2.** [inflatable] piscina *f* inflável.
paddock ['pædək] *n* **-1.** [small field] manejo *m* **-2.** [at racecourse] paddock *m.*
paddy field ['pædɪ-] *n* arrozal *m.*
paddy wagon ['pædɪ-] *n US inf* camburão *m.*
padlock ['pædlɒk] ◇ *n* cadeado *m.* ◇ *vt* fechar com cadeado.
paederast ['pedəræst] *n* = **pederast**.
paediatric [ˌpi:dɪ'ætrɪk] *adj* = **pediatric**.
paediatrician [ˌpi:dɪə'trɪʃn] *n* = **pediatrician**.
paediatrics [ˌpi:dɪ'ætrɪks] *n* = **pediatrics**.
paedophile *UK* ['pi:dəfaɪl], **pedophile** *US n* pedófilo *m,* -la *f.*
paella [paɪ'elə] *n (U)* paelha *f.*
paeony ['pi:ənɪ] (*pl* **-ies**) *n* = **peony**.
pagan ['peɪgən] ◇ *adj* pagão(gã). ◇ *n* pagão *m,* -gã *f.*
paganism ['peɪgənɪzm] *n (U)* paganismo *m.*
page [peɪdʒ] ◇ *n* página *f.* ◇ *vt* chamar (pelo alto-falante).
page [peɪdʒ] *vt* [using pager]: **to be ~d** receber chamadas pelo pager; **to ~ sb** chamar alguém pelo pager.
pageant ['pædʒənt] *n* desfile *m,* cortejo *m* cívico.
pageantry ['pædʒəntrɪ] *n (U)* fausto *m,* pompa *f.*
page boy *n* **-1.** *UK* [at wedding] pajem *m* **-2.** [hairstyle] chanel *m.*
page break *n* COMPUT quebra *f* de página.
pager ['peɪdʒə^r] *n* pager *m.*
pagination [ˌpædʒɪ'neɪʃn] *n (U)* paginação *f.*
pagoda [pə'gəʊdə] *n* pagode *m.*
paid [peɪd] ◇ *pt* & *pp* ▷ **pay**. ◇ *adj* pago(ga); **badly/well ~** bem/mal pago(ga).
paid-up *adj UK* remido(da).
pail [peɪl] *n* balde *m.*
pain [peɪn] ◇ *n* **-1.** dor *f*; **to be in ~** sentir dor; **a ~ in the neck** *inf* uma mala-sem-alça **-2.** *(U)* [mental suffering] sofrimento *m,* pena *f* **-3.** *inf* [annoyance]: **it's such a ~!** é tão chato!; **he is a real ~!** ele é um saco! ◇ *vt fml* fazer sofrer, atormentar; **to ~ sb to do sthg** ser muito difícil para alguém fazer algo.
◆ **pains** *npl* esforços *mpl*; **to be at ~s to do sthg** empenhar-se para fazer algo; **to take ~s to do sthg** esforçar-se para fazer algo; **he got absolutely nothing for his ~s** tanto esforço e ele não conseguiu absolutamente nada.
pained [peɪnd] *adj* aflito(ta), consternado(da).
painful ['peɪnfʊl] *adj* **-1.** [sore] dolorido(da) **-2.** [causing pain] doloroso(sa) **-3.** [distressing] penoso(sa), doloroso(sa).
painfully ['peɪnfʊlɪ] *adv* **-1.** [distressingly] dolorosamente **-2.** [for emphasis] terrivelmente.
painkiller ['peɪnˌkɪlə^r] *n* analgésico *m,* calmante *m.*
painless ['peɪnlɪs] *adj* indolor, fácil.
painlessly ['peɪnlɪslɪ] *adv* **-1.** [without hurting] sem dor **-2.** [unproblematically] de forma fácil, de forma indolor.
painstaking ['peɪnzˌteɪkɪŋ] *adj* meticuloso(sa), minucioso(sa).
painstakingly ['peɪnzˌteɪkɪŋlɪ] *adv* meticulosamente, minuciosamente.
paint [peɪnt] ◇ *n* tinta *f.* ◇ *vt* **-1.** pintar; **to ~ the wall white** pintar o teto de branco **-2.** [with make-up] maquiar. ◇ *vi* pintar.
paintbox ['peɪntbɒks] *n* ART estojo *m* de tintas.
paintbrush ['peɪntbrʌʃ] *n* **-1.** [of artist] pincel *m* **-2.** [of decorator] broxa *f.*
painted ['peɪntɪd] *adj* pintado(da).
painter ['peɪntə^r] *n* pintor *m,* -ra *f.*
painting ['peɪntɪŋ] *n* **-1.** [picture] pintura *f,* quadro *m* **-2.** *(U)* ACTIVITY pintura *f.*
paint stripper *n (U)* removedor *m* (de tinta).
paintwork ['peɪntwɜ:k] *n (U)* pintura *f.*
pair [peə^r] *n* par *m*; **a ~ of idiots** uma dupla de idiotas; **a ~ of scissors** uma tesoura; **a ~ of trousers** uma calça; **a ~ of spectacles** um óculos.
◆ **pair off** ◇ *vt sep* fazer par com. ◇ *vi*: **let's ~ and meet back here later** vamos nos separar aos pares e nos encontrar aqui mais tarde.
pajamas [pə'dʒɑ:məz] *npl US* = **pyjamas**.
Pakistan [*UK* ˌpɑ:kɪ'stɑ:n, *US* ˌpækɪ'stæn] *n* Paquistão; **in ~** no Paquistão.
Pakistani [*UK* ˌpɑ:kɪ'stɑ:nɪ, *US* ˌpækɪ'stænɪ] ◇ *adj*

paquistanês(esa). <> n paquistanês, -esa f.

pal [pæl] n inf -1. [friend] camarada mf, companheiro m, -ra f -2. [as term of address]: **now wait a minute, ~, I was first!** espera um pouco, meu chapa, eu cheguei primeiro!

PAL (abbr of **phase alternate line**) n PAL f.

palace ['pælɪs] n palácio m.

palaeontology UK, **paleontology** US [,pælɪɒn'tɒlədʒɪ] n (U) paleontologia f.

palatable ['pælətəbl] adj -1. [pleasant to taste] saboroso(sa) -2. [acceptable] aceitável, admissível.

palate ['pælət] n -1. ANAT palato m -2. [sense of taste] paladar m.

palatial [pə'leɪʃl] adj palaciano(na).

palaver [pə'lɑːvəʳ] n inf -1. [talk] palavrório m -2. [fuss] bagunça f, rebuliço m.

pale [peɪl] <> adj -1. [colour] fosco(ca) -2. [light] ênue -3. [clothes] claro(ra) -4. [face, complexion] pálido(da). <> vi -1. [become pale] empalidecer -2. [become insignificant]: **to ~ into insignificance (beside sb/sthg)** perder toda importância (junto a alguém/algo).

pale ale n UK *tipo de cerveja clara.*

paleness ['peɪlnɪs] n (U) palidez f.

paleontology n US = **palaeontology**.

Palestine ['pælɪ,staɪn] n Palestina; **in ~** na Palestina.

Palestinian [,pælə'stɪnɪən] <> adj palestino(na). <> n palestino m, -na f.

palette ['pælət] n paleta f.

palette knife n espátula f.

palimony ['pælɪmənɪ] n (U) *pensão alimentícia paga à ex-amante.*

palindrome n palíndromo m.

palings ['peɪlɪŋz] npl cerca f.

pall [pɔːl] <> n -1. [of smoke] nuvem f, cortina f -2. US [coffin] caixão m. <> vi perder a graça.

pallbearer ['pɔːl,beərəʳ] n carregador m, -ra f de caixão.

pallet ['pælɪt] n palete m, plataforma f de carga.

palliative ['pælɪətɪv] n fml paliativo m.

pallid ['pælɪd] adj pálido(da).

pallor ['pæləʳ] n palor m.

palm [pɑːm] n -1. [tree] palmeira f -2. [of hand] palma f.

◆ **palm off** vt sep inf: **to ~ sthg off on sb** empurrar algo para alguém; **to ~ sb off with sthg** enganar alguém com algo; **to ~ sthg off as sthg** fazer passar algo como algo.

palmistry ['pɑːmɪstrɪ] n (U) quiromancia f.

palm oil n (U) azeite-de-dendê m.

Palm Sunday n Domingo m de Ramos.

palmtop ['pɑːmtɒp] n COMPUT palmtop m.

palm tree n palmeira f.

palomino [,pælə'miːnəʊ] (pl -s) n palomino m.

palpable ['pælpəbl] adj palpável.

palpably ['pælpəblɪ] adv obviamente.

palpitate ['pælpɪteɪt] vi palpitar.

palpitations [,pælpɪ'teɪʃənz] npl palpitações fpl.

palsy n (U) paralisia f.

paltry ['pɔːltrɪ] (compar -ier, superl -iest) adj irrisório(ria).

pampas ['pæmpəz] n: **the ~** o pampa.

pampas grass n (U) capim-dos-pampas m inv.

pamper ['pæmpəʳ] vt mimar.

pamphlet ['pæmflɪt] <> n panfleto m. <> vi panfletar.

pamphleteer [,pæmflə'tɪəʳ] n POL panfletário m, -ria f, panfletista mf.

pan [pæn] (pt & pp -ned, cont -ning) <> n -1. [for frying] fridigeira -2. [for boiling] panela f -3. US [for baking] assadeira f -4. [of scales] prato m -5. [of toilet] vaso m sanitário. <> vt inf esculachar. <> vi -1. [for gold] batear -2. CINEMA capturar uma vista panorâmica.

panacea [,pænə'sɪə] n fig: **a ~ (for sthg)** uma panacéia (para algo).

panache [pə'næʃ] n (U) bravata f, elã m.

panama n: **~ (hat)** panamá m.

Panama ['pænə,mɑː] n Panamá; **in ~** no Panamá.

Panama Canal n: **the ~** o Canal do Panamá.

Panama City n Cidade f do Panamá.

Panamanian [,pænə'meɪnɪən] <> adj panamenho(nha). <> n panamenho m, -nha f.

pan-American adj pan-americano(na).

pancake ['pæŋkeɪk] n panqueca f.

Pancake Day n UK ≃ Terça-feira f de Carnaval.

pancake roll n rolinho m primavera.

Pancake Tuesday n = **Pancake Day**.

pancreas ['pæŋkrɪəs] n pâncreas m inv.

panda ['pændə] (pl inv OR -s) n panda m.

Panda car n UK patrulha f policial.

pandemonium [,pændɪ'məʊnjəm] n (U) pandemônio m.

pander ['pændəʳ] vi: **to ~ to sb/sthg** fazer concessões a alguém/algo.

pane [peɪn] n vidraça f, vidro m de vidraça.

panel ['pænl] n -1. [group of people] equipe f -2. TECH painel m.

panel game n UK *jogo televisivo em que um grupo de pessoas deve realizar determinada tarefa.*

panelling UK, **paneling** US ['pænəlɪŋ] n (U) apainelamento m.

panellist UK, **panelist** US ['pænəlɪst] n painelista mf.

panel pin n UK prego m sem cabeça.

pang [pæŋ] n acesso m *(de fome, de culpa etc).*

panic ['pænɪk] (pt & pp -ked, cont -king) <> n (U) pânico m. <> vi entrar em pânico.

panicky ['pænɪkɪ] adj -1. [person] aterrorizado(da) -2. [feeling] aterrorizante.

panic stations n (U) inf: **it was ~** foi uma verdadeira loucura.

panic-stricken adj em pânico.

pannier ['pænɪəʳ] n -1. [on back, horse] alforje m -2. [bicycle] cesto m.

panoply ['pænəplɪ] n (U) fml panóplia f.

panorama [,pænə'rɑːmə] n panorama m.

panoramic [,pænə'ræmɪk] adj panorâmico(ca).

pansy (pl -ies) n -1. [flower] amor-perfeito m -2. inf pej [man] veado m.

pant [pænt] vi ofegar.

◆ **pants** npl -1. UK [underpants] calcinha f -2. US [trousers] calças fpl.

panther ['pænθəʳ] (pl inv OR -s) n pantera f.

panties ['pæntɪz] *npl inf* calcinha *f.*
pantihose ['pæntɪhəʊz] *npl* = **panty hose**.
panto ['pæntəʊ] (*pl* **-s**) *n UK inf* = **pantomime**.
pantomime ['pæntəmaɪm] *n UK peça de teatro para crianças realizada no Reino Unido no Natal.*
pantry ['pæntrɪ] (*pl* **-ies**) *n* despensa *f.*
panty hose ['pæntɪ-] *npl US* meia-calça *f.*
papa [*UK* pə'pɑː, *US* 'pæpə] *n* papá *m.*
papacy (*pl* **-ies**) *n* **-1.** [period] papado *m* **-2.** [office, institution]: **the ~** o papado, o pontificado.
papadum ['pæpədəm] *n* = **popadum**.
papal ['peɪpl] *adj* papal.
paparazzi [,pæpə'rætsɪ] *npl pej* paparazzi *mpl.*
papaya [pə'paɪə] *n* papaia *m.*
paper ['peɪpəʳ] <> *n* **-1.** *(U)* [material] papel *m*; **a piece of ~** uma folha de papel; **on ~** [written down] no papel; [in theory] teoricamente **-2.** [newspaper] jornal *m* **-3.** [in exam] trabalho *m* **-4.** [essay] ensaio *m* **-5.** [at conference] apostila *f,* polígrafo *m.* <> *adj* **-1.** [cup, napkin, hat] de papel **-2.** [theoretical] no papel. <> *vt* empapelar.
◆ **papers** *npl* **-1.** [identity papers] documentos *mpl* (de identidade) **-2.** [documents] documentação *f.*
◆ **paper over** *vt fus fig* encobrir, disfarçar.
paperback ['peɪpəbæk] *n*: **~ (book)** brochura *f*; **in ~** em brochura.
paper bag *n* saco *m* de papel.
paperboy ['peɪpəbɔɪ] *n* jornaleiro *m.*
paper clip *n* clipe *m.*
papergirl ['peɪpəgɜːl] *n* jornaleira *f.*
paper handkerchief *n* lenço *m* de papel.
paper knife *n* abridor *m* de cartas.
paper mill *n* fábrica *f* de papel.
paper money *n (U)* papel-moeda *m.*
paper shop *n UK* banca *f* de jornais.
paperweight ['peɪpəweɪt] *n* peso *m* para papel.
paperwork ['peɪpəwɜːk] *n (U)* papelada *f.*
papier-mâché [,pæpjeɪ'mæʃeɪ] <> *n (U)* papel *m* machê. <> *comp* de papel machê.
papist ['peɪpɪst] *n pej* papista *mf.*
paprika ['pæprɪkə] *n (U)* páprica *f.*
Papua *n* Papua.
Papuan ['pæpjʊən] <> *adj* papua. <> *n* papua *mf.*
Papua New Guinea *n* Papua Nova Guiné; **in ~** em Papua Nova Guiné.
par [pɑːʳ] *n* **-1.** [parity]: **on a ~ with sb/sthg** no mesmo nível que alguém/algo **-2.** *(U)* GOLF par *m*; **under/over ~** abaixo/acima do par **-3.** [good health]: **below** OR **under ~** indisposto(ta) **-4.** FIN valor *m* (ao par).
para ['pærə] *n UK inf* paraquedista *mf (do exército).*
parable ['pærəbl] *n* parábola *f.*
parabola [pə'ræbələ] *n* TECH parábola *f.*
paracetamol [,pærə'siːtəmɒl] *n* paracetamol *m.*
parachute ['pærəʃuːt] <> *n* pára-quedas *m inv.* <> *vi* saltar de pára-quedas.
parade [pə'reɪd] <> *n* **-1.** [procession] desfile *m* **-2.** MIL parada *f*; **on ~** em revista **-3.** *UK* [street of shops] via *f* comercial **-4.** [street, path] passeio *m* público. <> *vt* **-1.** [MIL - soldiers] fazer desfilar; [- prisoners] apresentar **-2.** [object] exibir **-3.** *fig* [flaunt] fazer alarde de, mostrar-se com. <> *vi* desfilar.
parade ground *n* praça *f* de armas.
paradigm ['pærədaɪm] *n* paradigma *m.*
paradigmatic *adj* paradigmático(ca).
paradise ['pærədaɪs] *n* paraíso *m.*
◆ **Paradise** *n* Paraíso *m.*
paradox ['pærədɒks] *n* paradoxo *m.*
paradoxical [,pærə'dɒksɪkl] *adj* paradoxal.
paradoxically [,pærə'dɒksɪklɪ] *adv* paradoxalmente.
paraffin ['pærəfɪn] *n (U)* querosene *m.*
paraffin wax *n (U)* parafina *f.*
paragliding ['pærə,glaɪdɪŋ] *n* vôo *m* de paraglider.
paragon *n* modelo *m.*
paragraph ['pærəgrɑːf] *n* parágrafo *m.*
Paraguay ['pærəgwaɪ] *n* Paraguai; **in ~** no Paraguai.
Paraguayan [,pærə'gwaɪən] <> *adj* paraguaio(ia). <> *n* paraguaio *m*, -ia *f.*
parakeet ['pærəkiːt] *n* periquito *m.*
paralegal [,pærə'liːgl] *n US secretária altamente especializada que auxilia os advogados em seu trabalho.*
parallel ['pærəlel] (*pt* & *pp* **-led**, *cont* **-ling**) <> *adj* [gen] paralelo(la); **~ to** OR **with sthg** paralelo(la) a algo. <> *n* paralelo *m*; **to have no ~** não ter precedente OR paralelo. <> *vt* igualar-se a.
parallel bars *npl* barras *fpl* paralelas.
paralyse *UK*, **paralyze** *US* ['pærəlaɪz] *vt* paralisar.
paralysed *UK*, **paralyzed** *US* ['pærəlaɪzd] *adj* MED paralisado(da).
paralysis [pə'rælɪsɪs] (*pl* **-lyses** [-lɪsiːz]) *n* **-1.** MED paralisia *f* **-2.** [of industry, traffic] imobilidade *f.*
paralytic [,pærə'lɪtɪk] <> *adj* **-1.** MED paralítico(ca) **-2.** *UK inf* [drunk] bêbado(da) feito um gambá. <> *n* paralítico *m*, -ca *f.*
paralyze *vt US* = **paralyse**.
paralyzed *adj US* = **paralysed**.
paramedic [,pærə'medɪk] *n* paramédico *m*, -ca *f.*
paramedical [,pærə'medɪkl] *adj* paramédico(ca).
parameter [pə'ræmɪtəʳ] *n* parâmetro *m.*
paramilitary [,pærə'mɪlɪtrɪ] *adj* paramilitar.
paramount ['pærəmaʊnt] *adj* vital, fundamental; **of ~ importance** de suma importância.
paranoia [,pærə'nɔɪə] *n (U)* paranóia *f.*
paranoiac [,pærə'nɔɪæk] MED <> *adj* paranóico(ca). <> *n* paranóico *m*, -ca *f.*
paranoid ['pærənɔɪd] *adj* **-1.** [person] paranóico(ca) **-2.** [disorder] paranóico(ca).
paranormal [,pærə'nɔːml] *adj* paranormal.
parapet ['pærəpɪt] *n* parapeito *m.*
paraphernalia [,pærəfə'neɪljə] *n (U)* parafernália *f.*
paraphrase ['pærəfreɪz] <> *n* paráfrase *f.* <> *vt* & *vi* parafrasear.
paraplegia *n (U)* paraplegia *f.*
paraplegic [,pærə'pliːdʒɪk] <> *adj* paraplégico(ca). <> *n* paraplégico *m*, -ca *f.*
parapsychology [,pærəsaɪ'kɒlədʒɪ] *n (U)* parapsicologia *f.*
paraquat® *n (U)* CHEM paraquat *m.*

parascending [,pærə'sendɪŋ] *n* vôo *m* de parapente.
parasite ['pærəsaɪt] *n* parasita *m*.
parasitic [,pærə'sɪtɪk] *adj* parasita.
parasol ['pærəsɒl] *n* sombrinha *f*.
paratrooper ['pærətru:pə'] *n* pára-quedista *mf* (*do exército*).
parboil ['pɑ:bɔɪl] *vt* aferventar.
parcel ['pɑ:sl] (*UK pt* & *pp* **-led**, *cont* **-ling**, *US pt* & *pp* **-ed**, *cont* **-ing**) *n* pacote *m*, encomenda *f*.
◆ **parcel up** *vt sep* empacotar.
parcel post *n* (*U*) serviço de encomenda *f* postal.
parched [pɑ:tʃt] *adj* **-1.** [grass, plain] seco(ca) **-2.** [throat, lips] ressecado(da) **-3.** *inf* [very thirsty] seco(ca).
parchment ['pɑ:tʃmənt] *n* (*U*) pergaminho *m*.
pardon ['pɑ:dn] <> *n* **-1.** *JUR* indulto *m* **-2.** (*U*) [forgiveness] perdão *m*; **I beg your ~?** [showing surprise or offence] como é?, o que foi?; [what did you say?] como?, o que você disse?; **I beg your ~!** [to apologize] perdão!, desculpe! <> *vt* **-1.** *JUR* indultar **-2.** [forgive] perdoar; **to ~ sb for sthg** perdoar alguém por algo; **~ me!** me desculpe!
pardonable ['pɑ:dnəbl] *adj* perdoável.
pare [peə'] *vt* **-1.** [apple] descascar **-2.** [fingernail] aparar, cortar.
◆ **pare down** *vt sep* **-1.** [remove layer] aparar **-2.** [reduce] reduzir.
parent ['peərənt] *n* **-1.** [mother] mãe *f* **-2.** [father] pai *m*.
◆ **parents** *npl* pais *mpl*.
parentage ['peərəntɪdʒ] *n* (*U*) ascendência *f*, origem *f*.
parental [pə'rentl] *adj* dos pais.
parent company *n* matriz *f*.
parenthesis [pə'renθɪsɪs] (*pl* **-theses** [-θɪsi:z]) *n* parêntese *m*.
parenthetical *adj* entre parênteses.
parenthood ['peərənthʊd] *n* (*U*) paternidade *f*, maternidade *f*.
parenting ['peərəntɪŋ] *n* (*U*) cuidados *mpl* dos pais.
parent-teacher association *n* associação *f* de pais e mestres.
par excellence *adj* por excelência.
pariah [pə'raɪə] *n pej* pária *mf*.
Paris ['pærɪs] *n* Paris; **in ~** em Paris.
parish ['pærɪʃ] *n* **-1.** [of church] paróquia *f* **-2.** *UK* [area of local government] distrito *m*.
parish council *n UK* conselho *m* distrital.
parishioner [pə'rɪʃənə'] *n* paroquiano *m*, -na *f*.
parish priest *n* pároco *m*.
Parisian [pə'rɪzjən] <> *adj* parisiense. <> *n* parisiense *mf*.
parity ['pærətɪ] *n* (*U*) igualdade *f*; **~ with** igualdade com; **~ between** paridade *f* de *OR* entre.
park [pɑ:k] <> *n* **-1.** [public] parque *m* **-2.** *US AUT* *posição da alavanca de carro hidramático usada para estacionar*. <> *vt* & *vi* estacionar.
parka ['pɑ:kə] *n* parca *f*.
parking ['pɑ:kɪŋ] *n* (*U*) estacionamento *m*; **I find ~ very difficult** acho muito difícil estacionar; **'no ~'** 'proibido estacionar'.
parking garage *n US* edifício-garagem *m*.
parking light *n US* luz *m* de estacionamento.
parking lot *n US* área *f* de estacionamento.
parking meter *n* parquímetro *m*.
parking place *n* vaga *f* para estacionar.
parking ticket *n* multa *f* por estacionamento proibido.
Parkinson's (disease) ['pɑ:kɪnsnz-] *n* (*U*) mal *m* de Parkinson.
park keeper *n UK* guarda *mf* de parque.
parkland ['pɑ:klænd] *n* (*U*) parque *m*.
parkway ['pɑ:kweɪ] *n US* alameda *f*.
parky ['pɑ:kɪ] (*compar* **-ier**, *superl* **-iest**) *adj UK inf* frio (fria), fresco(ca).
parlance ['pɑ:ləns] *n* (*U*): **in common/legal ~** em linguagem coloquial/legal.
parliament ['pɑ:ləmənt] *n* **-1.** [gen] parlamento *m* **-2.** [session] legislatura *f*.
parliamentarian [,pɑ:ləmen'teərɪən] *n* parlamentar *mf*.
parliamentary [,pɑ:lə'mentərɪ] *adj* parlamentar.
parlour *UK*, **parlor** *US* ['pɑ:lə'] *n* **-1.** *dated* [in house] sala *f* de visitas **-2.** [cafe]: **ice cream ~** sorveteria *f*.
parlour game *n* jogo *m* de salão.
parlous ['pɑ:ləs] *adj fml* precário(ria).
Parmesan (cheese) [,pɑ:mɪ'zæn-] *n* (*U*) queijo *m* parmesão.
parochial [pə'rəʊkjəl] *adj pej* provinciano(na).
parochial school *n US* escola *f* particular católica.
parody ['pærədɪ] (*pl* **-ies**, *pt* & *pp* **-ied**) <> *n* paródia *f*. <> *vt* parodiar.
parole [pə'rəʊl] <> *n* (*U*) liberdade *f* condicional; **on ~** em liberdade condicional. <> *vt* pôr em liberdade condicional.
paroxysm ['pærəksɪzm] *n* **-1.** [feeling] paroxismo *m* **-2.** [movement] acesso *m*.
parquet ['pɑ:keɪ] *n* (*U*) parquê *m*.
parrot ['pærət] *n* papagaio *m*.
parrot fashion *adv* como um papagaio.
parry ['pærɪ] (*pt* & *pp* **-ied**) *vt* **-1.** [blow] desviar **-2.** [question] esquivar-se de.
parsimonious [,pɑ:sɪ'məʊnjəs] *adj fml* & *pej* avarento(ta).
parsley ['pɑ:slɪ] *n* (*U*) salsa *f*.
parsnip ['pɑ:snɪp] *n* chirivia *f*.
parson ['pɑ:sn] *n* pároco *m*.
parson's nose *n UK inf* sambiquira *f*.
part [pɑ:t] <> *n* **-1.** [gen] parte *f*; **in ~** em parte; **for the most ~** em sua maioria; **~ and parcel of** parte integrante de; **that's only ~ of the story** isso é só uma parte da história; **the best** *OR* **better ~ of** a maior parte de **-2.** [component] peça *f* **-3.** [acting role] papel *m* **-4.** [involvement]: **~ in sthg** participação *f* em algo; **to take ~ in sthg** participar de algo; **to play an important ~ in sthg** ter um papel importante em algo; **to want no ~ in sthg** não querer se envolver em algo; **for my/your** etc **~** por minha/sua parte; **on my/your** etc **~** de minha/sua parte **-5.** *US* [hair parting] linha *f*. <> *adv* em parte. <> *vt* **-1.** [separate] separar **-2.** [move apart, open] abrir **-3.** [hair] repartir. <> *vi*

-1. [leave one another] separar-se **-2.** [move apart, open] abrir-se.

◆ **parts** *npl* terras *fpl*.

◆ **part with** *vt fus* desfazer-se de.

partake [pɑːˈteɪk] (*pt* **-took**, *pp* **-taken**) *vi fml*: **to ~ of** [wine] beber; [food] comer.

part exchange *n* **-1.** [deal] *negociação em que se paga parte do valor de um produto com um artigo usado* **-2.** *(U)* [system] *sistema através do qual se paga parte do valor do produto com um artigo usado*; **in ~** como parte do pagamento.

partial [ˈpɑːʃl] *adj* **-1.** [gen] parcial **-2.** [fond]: **~ to sthg** afeiçoado(da) a algo.

partiality [ˌpɑːʃɪˈælətɪ] *n* **-1.** *(U)* [bias] parcialidade *f* **-2.** [fondness]: **~ for sthg** afeição *f* a algo, predileção *f* a algo.

partially [ˈpɑːʃəlɪ] *adv* parcialmente, em parte.

partially sighted *adj* com visão parcial.

participant [pɑːˈtɪsɪpənt] *n* participante *mf*.

participate [pɑːˈtɪsɪpeɪt] *vi* participar; **to ~ in sthg** participar de algo.

participation [pɑːˌtɪsɪˈpeɪʃn] *n (U)* participação *f*.

participle [ˈpɑːtɪsɪpl] *n* particípio *m*.

particle [ˈpɑːtɪkl] *n* partícula *f*.

parti-coloured *adj* multicor, matizado(da).

particular [pəˈtɪkjʊləʳ] *adj* **-1.** [gen] especial **-2.** [fussy] exigente.

◆ **particulars** *npl* particularidades *fpl*.

◆ **in particular** *adv* em especial, em particular.

particularity (*pl* **-ies**) *n fml* particularidade *f*.

particularly [pəˈtɪkjʊləlɪ] *adv* **-1.** [in particular] especialmente **-2.** [very] muito.

parting [ˈpɑːtɪŋ] *n* **-1.** *(U)* despedida *f* **-2.** *UK* [in hair] repartição *f*.

parting shot *n* tirada *f* final; **to deliver a ~** fazer um último comentário antes de sair, dar uma tirada final.

partisan [ˌpɑːtɪˈzæn] ◇ *adj* partidário(ria). ◇ *n* guerrilheiro *m*, -ra *f*.

partition [pɑːˈtɪʃn] ◇ *n* **-1.** [wall] divisória *f* **-2.** [screen] separação *f* **-3.** [of a country] divisão *f*. ◇ *vt* **-1.** [room] separar com divisórias **-2.** [country] dividir.

partly [ˈpɑːtlɪ] *adv* em parte.

partner [ˈpɑːtnəʳ] ◇ *n* parceiro *m*, -ra *f*. ◇ *vt* ser parceiro de.

partnership [ˈpɑːtnəʃɪp] *n* parceria *f*.

partook [pɑːˈtʊk] *pt* ▷ **partake**.

partridge [ˈpɑːtrɪdʒ] (*pl inv* OR **-s**) *n* perdiz *f*.

part-time ◇ *adj* de meio período. ◇ *adv* em meio período.

part-timer *n* funcionário *m*, -ria *f* de meio período.

party [ˈpɑːtɪ] (*pl* **-ies**, *pt* & *pp* **-ied**) ◇ *n* **-1.** *POL* partido *m* **-2.** [social gathering] festa *f* **-3.** [group] grupo *m* **-4.** *JUR, COMM* [individual] parte *f* **-5.** [involved person]: **to be a ~ to sthg** ter parte em algo. ◇ *vi inf* festejar.

party line *n* **-1.** *POL* linha *f* (política) do partido **-2.** *TELEC* extensão *f* de linha telefônica.

party piece *n inf* espetáculo *m* particular.

party political broadcast *n UK* propaganda *f* política em rádio e TV.

party politics *n (U)* política *f* partidária.

party wall *n* parede-meia *f*.

parvenu [ˈpɑːvənjuː] *n pej* novo-rico *m*, nova-rica *f*.

pass [pɑːs] ◇ *n* **-1.** [gen] passe *m* **-2.** *UK* [successful result] aprovação *f*; **to get a ~** ser aprovado *m*, -da *f* em algo **-3.** [route between mountains] desfiladeiro *m* **-4.** *phr*: **to make a ~ at sb** *inf* passar-se com alguém. ◇ *vt* **-1.** [gen] passar; **to ~ sthg to sb, to ~ sb sthg** passar algo a alguém **-2.** [move past] passar por **-3.** *AUT* [overtake] ultrapassar **-4.** [exceed] passar de **-5.** [exam, test] passar em **-6.** [approve] aprovar **-7.** [express - opinion, judgment] formular; [- sentence] ditar. ◇ *vi* **-1.** [gen] passar **-2.** *AUT* [overtake] ultrapassar **-3.** *SPORT* fazer passes **-4.** [occur] ocorrer.

◆ **pass around** *vt sep* = **pass round**.

◆ **pass as** *vt fus* passar por.

◆ **pass away** *vi* falecer.

◆ **pass by** ◇ *vt sep fig* passar desapercebido (da) por. ◇ *vi* passar.

◆ **pass for** *vt fus* = **pass as**.

◆ **pass off** *vt sep*: **to pass sb/sthg off as sthg** fazer alguém/algo passar por algo.

◆ **pass on** ◇ *vt sep* **-1.** [object]: **to pass sthg on (to sb)** passar algo adiante (para alguém) **-2.** [characteristic, tradition, information] transmitir. ◇ *vi* **-1.** [move on]: **to ~ on to the next question** passar para a próxima questão **-2.** = **pass away**.

◆ **pass out** *vi* **-1.** [faint] desmaiar **-2.** *UK MIL* graduar-se.

◆ **pass over** *vt fus* passar por cima.

◆ **pass round** *vt sep* ir passando, passar.

◆ **pass to** *vt fus* passar para.

◆ **pass up** *vt sep* deixar passar.

passable [ˈpɑːsəbl] *adj* **-1.** [satisfactory] passável, aceitável **-2.** [not blocked] livre.

passably [ˈpɑːsəblɪ] *adv* aceitavelmente.

passage [ˈpæsɪdʒ] *n* **-1.** [gen] passagem *f* **-2.** *ANAT* trato *m* **-3.** [sea journey] travessia *f*.

passageway [ˈpæsɪdʒweɪ] *n* passagem *f*, corredor *m*.

passbook [ˈpɑːsbʊk] *n* caderneta *f* de conta bancária.

passé *adj pej* ultrapassado(da).

passenger [ˈpæsɪndʒəʳ] *n* passageiro *m*, -ra *f*.

passerby [ˌpɑːsəˈbaɪ] (*pl* **passersby** [ˌpɑːsəzˈbaɪ]) *n* passante *mf*, transeunte *mf*.

passing [ˈpɑːsɪŋ] ◇ *adj* passageiro(ra). ◇ *n (U)* passagem *f*.

◆ **in passing** *adv* de passagem.

passion [ˈpæʃn] *n (U)* paixão *f*; **~ for sthg** paixão por algo.

◆ **Passion** *n*: **the Passion** a Paixão de Cristo.

◆ **passions** *npl* paixões *fpl*.

passionate [ˈpæʃənət] *adj* apaixonado(da).

passionately [ˈpæʃənətlɪ] *adv* apaixonadamente.

passionfruit [ˈpæʃənfruːt] *n (U)* maracujá *m*.

passive [ˈpæsɪv] ◇ *adj* passivo(va). ◇ *n*: **the ~** a passiva.

passively [ˈpæsɪvlɪ] *adv* passivamente.

passive resistance *n (U)* resistência *f* passiva.

passive smoker *n (U)* fumante *mf* passivo, -va.

passivity [pæˈsɪvətɪ] *n (U)* passividade *f*.

passkey ['pɑ:ski:] *n* **-1.** [particular] chave *f* pessoal **-2.** [universal] chave-mestra *f*.
Passover ['pɑ:sˌəʊvəʳ] *n*: **(the)** ~ a Páscoa Judia.
passport ['pɑ:spɔ:t] *n* **-1.** [document] passaporte *m* **-2.** [means]: ~ **to sthg** passaporte para algo.
passport control *n* controle *m* de passaportes.
password ['pɑ:swɜ:d] *n* senha *f*.
past [pɑ:st] <> *adj* **-1.** [former] passado(da) **-2.** [last] último(ma); **over the ~ week** durante a última semana **-3.** [finished] terminado(da), passado(da); **our problems are now ~** nossos problemas terminaram. <> *adv* **-1.** [telling the time]: **it's ten ~ eleven** são onze e dez **-2.** [by] por; **to walk ~** passar por; **to run ~** passar correndo por; **he didn't see me as I drove ~** ele não me viu quando passei por ele de carro. <> *n* **-1.** [time]: **the ~** o passado; **in the ~** no passado **-2.** [personal history] passado *m*. <> *prep* **-1.** [telling the time]: **at five ~ nine** às nove e cinco; **it's half ~ eight** são oito e meia **-2.** [by] pela frente de **-3.** [beyond] além de; **the post office is ~ the bank** o correio é passando o banco; **to be ~ it** *inf* passar da idade disso; **I wouldn't put it ~ him** *inf* tratando-se dele eu não me surpreenderia.
pasta ['pæstə] *n (U)* massa *f*, macarrão *m*.
paste [peɪst] <> *n* **-1.** [smooth mixture] pasta *f* **-2.** *(U)* *CULIN* patê *m* **-3.** *(U)* [glue] cola *f* **-4.** *(U)* [jewellery] bijuteria *f*. <> *vt* [gen] colar.
pastel ['pæstl] <> *adj* pastel. <> *n* pastel *m*.
paste-up *n TYPO* colagem *f*.
pasteurize, -ise ['pɑ:stʃəraɪz] *vt* pasteurizar.
pastiche [pæ'sti:ʃ] *n* **-1.** [work of imitation] imitação *f* **-2.** [mixed work] pastiche *m*.
pastille ['pæstɪl] *n* pastilha *f*.
pastime ['pɑ:staɪm] *n* passatempo *m*.
pasting ['peɪstɪŋ] *n inf* surra *f*.
pastor ['pɑ:stəʳ] *n* pastor *m*.
pastoral ['pɑ:stərəl] *adj* **-1.** *RELIG* pastoral **-2.** [countryside] bucólico(ca).
past participle *n* particípio *m* passado.
pastrami [pə'strɑ:mɪ] *n (U) carne de vaca defumada e muito condimentada.*
pastry ['peɪstrɪ] *(pl* **-ies**) *n* **-1.** *(U)* [mixture] massa *f* **-2.** [cake] torta *f*.
past tense *n* passado *m*.
pasture ['pɑ:stʃəʳ] *n* pasto *m*.
pastureland ['pɑ:stʃəlænd] *n* pastagem *f*.
pasty[1] ['peɪstɪ] (*compar* **-ier**, *superl* **-iest**) *adj* pálida (da).
pasty[2] ['pæstɪ] (*pl* **-ies**) *n UK CULIN* pastelão *m* de carne.
pasty-faced ['peɪstɪ-] *adj* com rosto pálido.
pat [pæt] (*compar* **-ter**, *superl* **-test**, *pt* & *pp* **-ted**, *cont* **-ting**) <> *adj* preparado(da), ensaiado(da). <> *adv*: **to have sthg off ~** ter algo na ponta da língua. <> *n* **-1.** [light stroke] palmadinha *f* **-2.** [small portion] porção *f* pequena. <> *vt* **-1.** [surface] bater de leve em **-2.** [dog] acariciar **-3.** [back, shoulder, hand] dar uma palmadinha em.
Patagonia [ˌpætə'gəʊnɪə] *n* Patagônia; **in ~** na Patagônia.
Patagonian <> *adj* patagônio(nia). <> *n* patagônio *m*, -nia *f*.
patch [pætʃ] <> *n* **-1.** [piece of material] remendo *m* **-2.** [to cover eye] venda *f* **-3.** [small area] área *f* **-4.** [of land] pedaço *m* **-5.** [period of time] período *m* **-6.** *phr*: **not to be a ~ on sb/sthg** *inf* não se comparar nem de longe com alguém/algo. <> *vt* remendar.
◆ **patch together** *vt sep* [assemble hastily - government] formar a duras penas; [- agreement] alcançar a duras penas.
◆ **patch up** *vt sep* **-1.** [mend] consertar, remendar **-2.** *fig* [resolve] resolver.
patchwork ['pætʃwɜ:k] <> *adj* de retalhos; **a ~ quilt** uma colcha de retalhos. <> *n* **-1.** colcha *f* de retalhos **-2.** *fig* [mixed collection - of fields] mosaico *m*; [- cultures, religions] mistura *m*; *inf* [hotchpotch] salada *m*.
patchy ['pætʃɪ] (*compar* **-ier**, *superl* **-iest**) *adj* **-1.** [gen] irregular **-2.** [incomplete] incompleto(ta).
pâté ['pæteɪ] *n* patê *m*.
patent [*UK* 'peɪtənt, *US* 'pætənt] <> *adj* evidente. <> *n* patente *f*. <> *vt* patentear.
patented [*UK* 'peɪtəntɪd, *US* 'pætəntɪd] *adj* patenteado(da).
patentee [*UK* ˌpeɪtən'ti:, *US* ˌpætən'ti:] *n* detentor *m*, -ra *f* de uma patente.
patent leather *n (U)* couro *m* envernizado.
patently [*UK* 'peɪtəntlɪ, *US* 'pætəntlɪ] *adv* evidentemente.
Patent Office *n*: **the ~** o Registro de Patentes.
paternal [pə'tɜ:nl] *adj* **-1.** [love, attitude] paternal **-2.** [relation] paterno(na).
paternalistic [pəˌtɜ:nə'lɪstɪk] *adj pej* paternalista.
paternity [pə'tɜ:nətɪ] *n (U)* paternidade *f*.
paternity leave *n* licença-paternidade *f*.
paternity suit *n* ação *f* de paternidade.
path [pɑ:θ, *pl* pɑ:ðz] *n* **-1.** [track] trilha *f* **-2.** [way ahead] caminho *m*; **our ~s had crossed before** nossos caminhos já se haviam cruzado antes **-3.** [trajectory] trajetória *f* **-4.** [course of action] curso *m*.
pathetic [pə'θetɪk] *adj* **-1.** [causing pity] patético(ca) **-2.** [useless] inútil, infeliz.
pathetically [pə'θetɪklɪ] *adv* **-1.** [causing pity] pateticamente **-2.** [uselessly] inutilmente.
pathological [ˌpæθə'lɒdʒɪkl] *adj* patológico(ca).
pathologist [pə'θɒlədʒɪst] *n* patologista *mf*.
pathology [pə'θɒlədʒɪ] *n (U)* patologia *f*.
pathos ['peɪθɒs] *n (U)* patos *m*.
pathway ['pɑ:θweɪ] *n* caminho *m*.
patience ['peɪʃns] *n (U)* paciência *f*; **to try sb's ~** testar a paciência de alguém.
patient ['peɪʃnt] <> *adj* paciente. <> *n* paciente *mf*.
patiently ['peɪʃntlɪ] *adv* pacientemente.
patina ['pætɪnə] *n* pátina *f*.
patio ['pætɪəʊ] (*pl* **-s**) *n* pátio *m*.
patio doors *npl portas de vidros que dão para um pátio.*
patisserie [pə'ti:sərɪ] *n* loja *f* de bolos e tortas.
Patna rice ['pætnə-] *n (U)* arroz *m* Patna.
patois ['pætwɑ:] (*pl inv*) *n* patoá *m*.
patriarch ['peɪtrɪɑ:k] *n* patriarca *m*.
patriarchy ['peɪtrɪɑ:kɪ] (*pl* **-ies**) *n* patriarcado *m*.

patrimony [*UK* 'pætrɪmənɪ, *US* 'pætrɪməʊnɪ] *n (U) fml* patrimônio *m*.

patriot [*UK* 'pætrɪət, *US* 'peɪtrɪət] *n* patriota *mf*.

patriotic [*UK* ˌpætrɪ'ɒtɪk, *US* ˌpeɪtrɪ'ɒtɪk] *adj* patriótico(ca).

patriotism [*UK* 'pætrɪətɪzm, *US* 'peɪtrɪətɪzm] *n (U)* patriotismo *m*.

patrol [pə'trəʊl] (*pt* & *pp* **-led**, *cont* **-ling**) <> *n* patrulha *f*; **on ~** de guarda. <> *vt* patrulhar.

patrol car *n* radiopatrulha *f*.

patrolman [pə'trəʊlmən] (*pl* **-men** [-mən]) *n US* patrulheiro *m*, policial *m*.

patrol wagon *n US* camburão *m*.

patrolwoman [pə'trəʊlˌwʊmən] (*pl* **-women** [-ˌwɪmɪn]) *n US* patrulheira *f*.

patron ['peɪtrən] *n* **-1.** [gen] patrono *m*, -nesse *f* **-2.** *fml* [customer] cliente *mf*.

patronage ['pætrənɪdʒ] *n (U)* patrocínio *m*.

patronize, -ise ['pætrənaɪz] *vt* **-1.** *pej* [talk down to] tratar com condescendência **-2.** *fml* [be a customer of] ser cliente de **-3.** *fml* [back financially] patrocinar.

patronizing ['pætrənaɪzɪŋ] *adj pej* condescendente.

patron saint *n* (santo *m*) padroeiro *m*, (santa *f*) padroeira *f*.

patter ['pætəʳ] <> *n* **-1.** [sound of feet] passinhos *mpl* **-2.** *fig*: **the ~ of raindrops on the roof** o barulhinho da chuva no telhado **-3.** [talk] arenga *f*. <> *vi* **-1.** [dog] dar passinhos rápidos **-2.** [rain] tamborilar.

pattern ['pætən] <> *n* **-1.** [gen] padrão *m* **-2.** [for sewing, knitting] molde *m* **-3.** [model] modelo *m*. <> *vt*: **to be ~ed on sthg** ser baseado(ada) em algo.

patterned ['pætənd] *adj* estampado(da).

patty ['pætɪ] (*pl* **-ies**) *n* **-1.** [pasty] empanada *f* **-2.** [savoury cake] tortinha *f*.

paucity ['pɔːsətɪ] *n fml* escassez *f*.

paunch [pɔːntʃ] *n* pança *f*, barriga *f*.

paunchy ['pɔːntʃɪ] (*compar* **-ier**, *superl* **-iest**) *adj* barrigudo(da).

pauper ['pɔːpəʳ] *n* indigente *mf*.

pause [pɔːz] <> *n* **-1.** [short silence] pausa *f* **-2.** [break, rest] interrupção *f*. <> *vi* fazer uma pausa.

pave [peɪv] *vt* pavimentar; **to ~ the way for sb/sthg** preparar o terreno para alguém/algo.

paved [peɪvd] *adj* calçado(da), pavimentado(da).

pavement ['peɪvmənt] *n* **-1.** *UK* [at side of road] calçada *f* **-2.** *US* [roadway] rua *f*.

pavement artist *n UK* artista *mf* de rua.

pavilion [pə'vɪljən] *n* pavilhão *m*.

paving ['peɪvɪŋ] *n (U)* **-1.** [material] material *m* para pavimentação **-2.** [paved surface] pavimento *m*, calçamento *m*.

paving stone *n* paralelepípedo *m*.

paw [pɔː] <> *n* pata *f*. <> *vt* **-1.** [subj: animal] dar patadas em **-2.** *pej* [subj: person] apalpar.

pawn [pɔːn] <> *n* **-1.** [chesspiece] peão *m* **-2.** [unimportant person] joguete *m*, marionete *f*. <> *vt* empenhar.

pawnbroker ['pɔːnˌbrəʊkəʳ] *n* penhorista *mf*.

pawnshop ['pɔːnʃɒp] *n* casa *f* de penhores.

pay [peɪ] (*pt* & *pp* **paid**) <> *vt* **-1.** [gen] pagar; **to ~ sb/sth for sthg** pagar alguém/algo por algo; **to ~ one's way** pagar as despesas **-2.** *UK* [into bank account]: **to ~ sthg into sthg** depositar algo em algo **-3.** [be profitable to] ser rentável para; **it won't ~ you to sell just now** não vale a pena vender agora **-4.** [be advantageous to] ser proveitoso(sa) para; **it will ~ you not to say anything** é melhor você não dizer nada **-5.** [compliment, respects, attention] prestar; [visit, call] fazer. <> *vi* **-1.** [gen] pagar; **to ~ for sthg** pagar algo; **the work ~s well** o trabalho é bem remunerado; **crime doesn't ~** o crime não compensa **-2.** *fig* [suffer] pagar; **to ~ dearly for sthg** pagar caro por algo. <> *n* **-1.** [wage] paga *f* **-2.** [salary] salário *m*.

◆ **pay back** *vt sep* **-1.** [return loan of money to] devolver **-2.** [revenge o.s. on]: **to ~ sb back (for sthg)** pagar a alguém na mesma moeda (por algo).

◆ **pay off** <> *vt sep* **-1.** [repay] saldar, liquidar **-2.** [dismiss] despedir com indenização **-3.** [bribe] subornar, comprar. <> *vi* obter êxito.

◆ **pay out** <> *vt sep* **-1.** [spend] desembolsar **-2.** [let out] soltar. <> *vi* gastar.

◆ **pay up** *vi* saldar dívida.

payable ['peɪəbl] *adj* **-1.** [to be paid] a pagar **-2.** [on cheque]: **~ to sb** para crédito de alguém.

pay as you earn *n (U) UK* imposto *m* de renda retido na fonte.

pay-as-you-go *n* [for mobile phone, Internet, etc] *sistema de pagamento por tempo de uso*.

paybed ['peɪbed] *n UK* leito *m* pago *(em hospital público)*.

paycheck ['peɪtʃek] *n US* [cheque] contracheque *m*; [money] salário *m*.

pay cheque *n UK* contracheque *m*.

payday ['peɪdeɪ] *n (U)* dia *m* de pagamento.

PAYE (*abbr of* **pay as you earn**) *n (U)* imposto *m* de renda retido na fonte.

payee [peɪ'iː] *n* beneficiário *m*, -ria *f*.

pay envelope *n US* envelope *m* de pagamento.

payer ['peɪəʳ] *n* pagador *m*, -ra *f*.

paying guest ['peɪɪŋ-] *n* pensionista *mf*.

paying-in book *n UK* formulário *m* para depósitos.

payload ['peɪləʊd] *n* **-1.** [load] carga *f* útil **-2.** *MIL, AERON* carga *f*.

paymaster ['peɪˌmɑːstəʳ] *n aquele que detém o controle econômico sobre alguém*.

paymaster general *n UK responsável do governo britânico encarregado de pagar os funcionários do governo*.

payment ['peɪmənt] *n* pagamento *m*.

payoff ['peɪɒf] *n* **-1.** [result] resultado *m* **-2.** *UK* [redundancy payment] indenização *f (por demissão)*.

payola [peɪ'əʊlə] *n* [bribing] *(U) inf US* suborno *m*.

pay packet *n UK* **-1.** [envelope] envelope *m* de pagamento **-2.** [wages] pagamento *m*.

pay-per-view <> *adj* [channel] pay-per-view. <> *n* pay-per-view *m*.

pay phone, pay station *US n* telefone *m* público.

payroll ['peɪrəʊl] *n* folha *f* de pagamento.

payslip *UK* ['peɪslɪp], **paystub** *US n* contracheque *m*.
pay station *n US* = **pay phone**.
paystub ['peɪstʌb] *n US* = **payslip**.
PBS (*abbr of* **Public Broadcasting Service**) *n companhia de televisão norte-americana que produz programas de qualidade.*
PBX (*abbr of* **private branch exchange**) *n* PBX *m*.
pc <> *n* (*abbr of* **postcard**) cartão-postal *m*. <> (*abbr of* **per cent**) por cento.
p/c (*abbr of* **petty cash**).
PC <> *n* **-1.** (*abbr of* **personal computer**) PC *m* **-2.** (*abbr of* **police constable**) policial *mf*. <> *adj* (*abbr of* **politically correct**) politicamente correto.
PCB (*abbr of* **printed circuit board**) *n* placa *f* de circuito impresso.
pcm (*abbr of* **per calendar month**) por mês *(do calendário)*.
PCV (*abbr of* **passenger-carrying vehicle**) *n* veículo *m* de passageiros.
pd (*abbr of* **paid**) pg.
PD (*abbr of* **police department**) ≃ DP *f*.
PDA (*abbr of* **personal digital assistant**) *n* COMPUT PDA *m*.
PDF (*abbr of* **portable document format**) *n* COMPUT PDF *m*.
pdq (*abbr of* **pretty damn quick**) *adv* **inf** muito rápido.
PDSA (*abbr of* **People's Dispensary for Sick Animals**) *n organização britânica que oferece atendimento veterinário gratuito.*
PDT (*abbr of* **Pacific Daylight Time**) *n horário de verão na costa oeste dos Estados Unidos.*
PE (*abbr of* **physical education**) *n UK* ≃ Ed.Fis.
pea [pi:] *n* CULIN ervilha *f*.
peace [pi:s] *n (U)* **-1.** [gen] paz *f*; **to be at ~ with sb/o.s./sthg** estar em paz com alguém/consigo mesmo/com algo; **to make (one's) ~ with sb/sthg** fazer as pazes com alguém/algo **-2.** [law and order] paz *f*, ordem *f*.
peaceable ['pi:səbl] *adj* pacífico(ca).
peaceably ['pi:səblɪ] *adv* pacificamente.
Peace Corps *n organização norte-americana que colabora com os projetos dos países em desenvolvimento.*
peaceful ['pi:sfʊl] *adj* **-1.** [tranquil] tranqüilo(la) **-2.** [non-violent] pacífico(ca).
peacefully ['pi:sfʊlɪ] *adv* **-1.** [tranquilly] tranqüilamente **-2.** [without violence] pacificamente.
peacefulness ['pi:sfʊlnɪs] *n (U)* tranqüilidade *f*.
peacekeeping force ['pi:s,ki:pɪŋ-] *n* força *f* de paz.
peacemaker ['pi:s,meɪkə^r] *n* pacificador *m*, -ra *f*, conciliador *m*, -ra *f*.
peace offering *n inf* bandeira *f* branca.
peacetime ['pi:staɪm] *n (U)* tempo *m* de paz.
peach [pi:tʃ] <> *adj* da cor de pêssego. <> *n* **-1.** [fruit] pêssego *m* **-2.** [colour] cor *f* de pêssego. <> *comp* de pêssego.
Peach Melba [-'melbə] *n* pêche *m* melba, *compota de pêssego servida com sorvete de baunilha.*
peacock ['pi:kɒk] *n* pavão *m*.
peahen ['pi:hen] *n* pavoa *f*.
peak [pi:k] <> *adj* **-1.** [time] de pico **-2.** [productivity, condition] máximo(ma). <> *n* **-1.** [mountain top] pico *m* **-2.** [highest point] cume *m*, apogeu *m* **-3.** [of cap] viseira *f*. <> *vi* atingir o máximo.
peaked [pi:kt] *adj* com viseira; **~ cap** boné *m* (com viseira).
peak hour *n* hora *f* de pico.
peak period *n* período *m* de pico.
peak rate *n* tarifa *f* máxima.
peaky ['pi:kɪ] (*compar* **-ier**, *superl* **-iest**) *adj* **UK inf** acabado(da).
peal [pi:l] <> *n* **-1.** [of bells] repique *m* **-2.** [of thunder] estrondo *m*; **~ (of laughter)** gargalhada *f*. <> *vi* repicar.
peanut ['pi:nʌt] *n* amendoim *m*.
peanut butter *n (U)* manteiga *f* de amendoim.
pear [peə^r] *n* pêra *f*.
pearl [pɜ:l] *n* pérola *f*.
pearly ['pɜ:lɪ] (*compar* **-ier**, *superl* **-iest**) *adj* perolado (da).
peasant ['peznt] *n* **-1.** [in countryside] camponês *m*, -esa *f* **-2.** **pej** [ignorant person] caipira *mf*.
peasantry ['pezntrɪ] *n*: **the ~** os camponeses.
peashooter ['pi:,ʃu:tə^r] *n* sarabatana *f*.
peat [pi:t] *n (U)* turfa *f*.
peaty ['pi:tɪ] (*compar* **-ier**, *superl* **-iest**) *adj* turfoso(sa).
pebble ['pebl] *n* cascalho *m*, seixo *m*.
pebble-dash *n UK* argamassa *f* com cascalho.
pecan (nut) [pɪ'kæn-] *n* noz-pecã *f*.
pecan pie *n* torta *f* de noz-pecã.
peck [pek] <> *n* **-1.** [with beak] bicada *f* **-2.** [kiss] bicota *f*. <> *vt* **-1.** [with beak] bicar **-2.** [kiss] dar uma bicota. <> *vi* bicar.
pecking order ['pekɪŋ-] *n* hierarquia *f*.
peckish ['pekɪʃ] *adj* **UK inf** esfomeado(da).
pectin ['pektɪn] *n (U)* pectina *f*.
pectoral ['pektərəl] *adj* peitoral.
peculiar [pɪ'kju:ljə^r] *adj* **-1.** [odd] esquisito(ta) **-2.** [slightly ill] estranho(nha) **-3.** [characteristic]: **to be ~ to sb/sthg** ser característico(ca) de alguém/algo.
peculiarity [pɪ,kju:lɪ'ærətɪ] (*pl* **-ies**) *n* **-1.** [strange habit] peculiaridade *f* **-2.** [individual characteristic] singularidade *f* **-3.** [oddness] excentricidade *f*.
peculiarly [pɪ'kju:ljəlɪ] *adv* **-1.** [especially] particularmente **-2.** [oddly] estranhamente **-3.** [characteristically] tipicamente.
pecuniary [pɪ'kju:njərɪ] *adj* pecuniário(ria).
pedagogical [,pedə'gɒdʒɪkl] *adj* pedagógico(ca).
pedagogy [,pedə'gɒdʒɪ] *n (U)* pedagogia *f*.
pedal ['pedl] (*UK pt* & *pp* **-led**, *cont* **-ling**, *US pt* & *pp* **-ed**, *cont* **-ing**) <> *n* pedal *m*; **brake ~** freio *m*. <> *vi* pedalar.
pedal bin *n* lixeira *f* com pedal.
pedalo ['pedələʊ] (*pl* **-s** OR **-es**) *n UK* pedalinho *m*.
pedant ['pedənt] *n* **pej** pedante *mf*, formalista *mf*.
pedantic [pɪ'dæntɪk] *adj* **pej** pedante.
pedantry ['pedəntrɪ] *n (U)* **pej** pedantismo *m*.
peddle ['pedl] *vt* **-1.** [sell] traficar **-2.** [spread] espalhar.
peddler ['pedlə^r] *n* **-1.** [drug dealer] traficante *mf* **-2.** *US* = **pedlar**.
pederast ['pedəræst] *n* pederasta *m*.

pedestal ['pedɪstl] *n* pedestal *m*; **to put sb on a ~** colocar alguém num pedestal.
pedestrian [pɪ'destrɪən] ◇ *adj pej* enfadonho (nha). ◇ *n* pedestre *mf*.
pedestrian crossing *n UK* faixa *f* para pedestres.
pedestrianize, -ise [pɪ'destrɪənaɪz] *vt* transformar em área só para pedestres.
pedestrian precinct *UK*, **pedestrian zone** *US n* área *f* só para pedestres.
pediatric [,pi:dɪ'ætrɪk] *adj* pediátrico(ca).
pediatrician [,pi:dɪə'trɪʃn] *n* pediatra *mf*.
pediatrics [,pi:dɪ'ætrɪks] *n (U)* pediatria *f*.
pedicure ['pedɪ,kjʊə^r] *n* pedicure *mf*.
pedigree ['pedɪgri:] ◇ *adj* com pedigree. ◇ *n* **-1.** [of animal] pedigree *m* **-2.** [of person] linhagem *f*.
pedlar *UK*, **peddler** *US* ['pedlə^r] *n* vendedor *m*, -ra *f* ambulante.
pedophile ['pi:dəfaɪl] *n* = **paedophile**.
pee [pi:] *inf* ◇ *n* xixi *m*; **to have a ~** fazer xixi. ◇ *vi* fazer xixi.
peek [pi:k] *inf* ◇ *n* espiadela *f*. ◇ *vi* espiar.
peel [pi:l] ◇ *n (U)* casca *f*. ◇ *vt* & *vi* descascar.
◆ **peel off** *vt sep* **-1.** [pull off] arrancar, desgrudar **-2.** [take off] tirar.
peeler ['pi:lə^r] *n* descascador *m*.
peelings ['pi:lɪŋz] *npl* cascas *fpl*.
peep [pi:p] ◇ *n* **-1.** [look] espiada *f* **-2.** *inf* [sound] pio *m*. ◇ *vi* dar uma espiada em.
◆ **peep out** *vi* surgir.
peephole ['pi:phəʊl] *n* vigia *f (em porta)*.
peeping Tom [,pi:pɪŋ'tɒm] *n* voyeur *m*.
peep show *n* cineminha *f*, caixa que contém imagens em movimento que se pode ver através de um pequeno buraco.
peer [pɪə^r] ◇ *n* **-1.** [noble] nobre *m* **-2.** [equal] par *m*. ◇ *vi*: **to ~ at** observar; **to ~ through the clouds** observar por entre as nuvens.
peerage ['pɪərɪdʒ] *n* pariato *m*; **the ~** o pariato.
peeress ['pɪərɪs] *n* **-1.** [woman peer] nobre *f* **-2.** [wife or widow of peer] esposa *f* de nobre.
peer group *n grupo de mesma faixa etária ou classe social.*
peer pressure *n (U) pressão exercida pelo grupo da mesma faixa etária ou classe social a que se pertence.*
peeved [pi:vd] *adj inf* aborrecido(da).
peevish ['pi:vɪʃ] *adj* irritadiço(ça), mal-humorado (da).
peg [peg] (*pt* & *pp* **-ged**, *cont* **-ging**) ◇ *n* **-1.** [hook] cabide *m* **-2.** [for washing line] prendedor *m* (de roupa) **-3.** [for tent] pino *m*. ◇ *vt* [price, increase] fixar.
◆ **peg out** ◇ *vt sep* estender. ◇ *vi UK inf* esticar as canelas.
PEI *n abbr of* **Prince Edward Island**.
pejorative [pɪ'dʒɒrətɪv] *adj* pejorativo(va).
pekinese (*pl inv* OR **-s**) *n* [dog] pequinês *m*.
◆ **Pekinese, Pekingese** ◇ *adj* pequinês(esa). ◇ *n* pequinês *m*, -esa *f*.
Peking [pi:'kɪŋ] *n* Pequim; **in ~** em Pequim.
pekingese (*pl inv* OR **-s**) *n* = **pekinese**.
pelican ['pelɪkən] (*pl inv* OR **-s**) *n* pelicano *m*.
pelican crossing *n UK* faixa *f* de segurança *(com semáforo acionado pelo pedestre)*.
pellet ['pelɪt] *n* **-1.** [small ball - of paper] bolinha *f*; [- of food, mud] bolo *m* **-2.** [for gun] chumbinho *m*.
pell-mell [,pel'mel] *adv* atropeladamente.
pelmet ['pelmɪt] *n UK* bandô *m*.
Peloponnese [,peləpə'ni:z] *n*: **the ~** o Peloponeso.
pelt [pelt] ◇ *n* **-1.** [animal skin] pele *f* **-2.** [speed]: **(at) full ~** a toda velocidade. ◇ *vt*: **to ~ sb with sthg** arremessar algo em alguém. ◇ *vi* **-1.** [rain] chover a cântaros **-2.** [run very fast] correr a toda.
pelvic ['pelvɪk] *adj* pélvico(ca).
pelvis ['pelvɪs] (*pl* **-vises** OR **-ves** [-vi:z]) *n* pélvis *f inv*.
pen [pen] (*pt* & *pp* **-ned**, *cont* **-ning**) ◇ *n* **-1.** [for writing] caneta *f* **-2.** [enclosure] curral *m*. ◇ *vt* **-1.** *literary* [write] redigir, escrever **-2.** [enclose - livestock] cercar; [- people] encurralar.
penal ['pi:nl] *adj* JUR penal.
penalize, ise ['pi:nəlaɪz] *vt* **-1.** [gen] penalizar **-2.** [put at a disadvantage] prejudicar.
penal settlement *n* colônia *f* penal.
penalty ['penltɪ] (*pl* **-ies**) *n* **-1.** [punishment] penalidade *f*; **to pay the ~ (for sthg)** *fig* pagar pena (por algo) **-2.** [fine] pena *f* **-3.** SPORT pênalti *m*; **~ (kick)** pênalti.
penalty area, penalty box *n UK* SPORT área *f* de pênalti, grande área *f*.
penalty clause *n* cláusula *f* penal.
penalty goal *n* gol *m* de pênalti.
penalty kick *n* ▷ **penalty**.
penance ['penəns] *n (U)* penitência *f*.
pen-and-ink *adj* à tinta.
pence [pens] *UK pl* ▷ **penny**.
penchant [*UK* pɑɔʃɑɔ, *US* 'pentʃənt] *n*: **to have a ~ for sthg/for doing sthg** ter uma queda por algo/por fazer algo.
pencil ['pensl] (*UK pt* & *pp* **-led**, *cont* **-ling**, *US pt* & *pp* **-ed**, *cont* **-ing**) ◇ *n* lápis *m inv*; **in ~** a lápis. ◇ *vt* escrever a lápis.
◆ **pencil in** *vt sep* **-1.** [person] inscrever provisoriamente **-2.** [date] marcar provisoriamente.
pencil case *n* estojo *m* (de canetas).
pencil sharpener *n* apontador *m* de lápis.
pendant ['pendənt] *n* pendente *m*.
pending ['pendɪŋ] *fml* ◇ *adj* **-1.** [about to happen] iminente **-2.** [waiting to be dealt with] pendente. ◇ *prep* à espera de.
pending tray *n UK* bandeja *f* de assuntos pendentes.
pendulum ['pendjʊləm] (*pl* **-s**) *n* pêndulo *m*.
penetrate ['penɪtreɪt] ◇ *vt* **-1.** [get through - subj: person, object] penetrar em, adentrar-se em; [- rain] infiltrar-se em **-2.** [infiltrate - party] entrar sorrateiramente em; [- terrorist group, spy ring] infiltrar-se em. ◇ *vi inf* [be understood] cair a ficha.
penetrating ['penɪtreɪtɪŋ] *adj* **-1.** [gen] penetrante **-2.** [wind, cold] cortante.
penetration [,penɪ'treɪʃn] *n (U)* **-1.** [gen] penetração *f* **-2.** *fml* [insight] perspicácia *f*.
penfriend ['penfrend] *n* amigo *m*, -ga *f* por correspondência.
penguin ['peŋgwɪn] *n* pingüim *m*.

penicillin [,penɪ'sɪlɪn] *n (U)* penicilina *f*.
peninsula [pə'nɪnsjʊlə] (*pl* **-s**) *n* península *f*.
penis ['piːnɪs] (*pl* **penises** ['piːnɪsɪz]) *n* pênis *m inv*.
penitent ['penɪtənt] *adj fml* penitente.
penitentiary [,penɪ'tenʃərɪ] (*pl* **-ies**) *n US* penitenciária *f*.
penknife ['pennaɪf] (*pl* **-knives** [-naɪvz]) *n* canivete *m*, navalha *f*.
pen-name *n* pseudônimo *m*.
pennant ['penənt] *n* bandeirola *f*.
penniless ['penɪlɪs] *adj* sem dinheiro.
Pennines ['penaɪnz] *npl*: **the ~** as Pennines.
Pennsylvania [,pensɪl'veɪnɪə] *n* Pensilvânia.
penny ['penɪ] (*pl senses 1 & 2* **-ies**, *pl sense 3* **pence**) *n* **-1.** *UK* [coin] pêni *m* **-2.** *US* [coin] centavo *m* **-3.** *UK* [value] centavo *m* **-4.** *phr*: **a ~ for your thoughts** um centavo por seus pensamentos; **the ~ dropped** *UK inf* caiu a ficha; **to spend a ~** *UK inf* fazer xixi; **two** *OR* **ten a ~** *UK inf* a preço de banana.
penny-pinching [-,pɪntʃɪŋ] <> *adj* avarento(ta). <> *n (U)* avareza *f*.
pen pal *n inf* amigo *m*, -ga *f* por correspondência.
pension ['penʃn] *n* **-1.** *UK* [on retirement - state scheme] pensão *f*; [- private scheme] previdência *f* privada **-2.** [for disability] pensão *f* por invalidez.
◆ **pension off** *vt sep* aposentar-se.
pensionable ['penʃənəbl] *adj* com direito à aposentadoria; **~ age** idade *f* de se aposentar.
pension book *n UK carnê dado pelo governo britânico a todos os pensionistas e cujos cupons podem ser trocados semanalmente por dinheiro nas agências dos correios.*
pensioner ['penʃənə^r] *n UK*: **(old-age) ~** pensionista *mf*.
pension fund *n* fundo *m* de pensão.
pension plan, pension scheme *n* plano *m* de aposentadoria.
pensive ['pensɪv] *adj* pensativo(va).
pentagon ['pentəgən] *n* pentágono *m*.
◆ **Pentagon** *n US*: **the Pentagon** o Pentágono.

PENTAGON

O Pentágono, imenso edifício de cinco faces situado em Washington, abriga o ministério da Defesa dos EUA. De modo geral, o termo é empregado também para designar o poder militar estadunidense.

pentathlete [pen'tæθliːt] *n* pentatleta *mf*.
pentathlon [pen'tæθlən] (*pl* **-s**) *n* pentatlo *m*.
Pentecost ['pentɪkɒst] *n* Pentecostes *m inv*.
penthouse ['penthaʊs, *pl* -haʊzɪz] *n* cobertura *f*.
pent up ['pent-] *adj* contido(da), reprimido(da).
penultimate [pe'nʌltɪmət] *adj* penúltimo(ma).
penury ['penjʊrɪ] *n (U) fml* penúria *f*.
peony ['pɪənɪ] (*pl* **-ies**) *n* peônia *f*.
people ['piːpl] <> *n* [nation, race] povo *m*. <> *npl* **-1.** [gen] pessoas *fpl*; **~ say that ...** dizem que ... **-2.** [inhabitants] habitantes *mpl* **-3.** *POL*: **the ~** o povo. <> *vt*: **to be ~d by** *OR* **with** ser povoado(da) por.
people carrier *n* monovolume *m*.
pep [pep] (*pt & pp* **-ped**, *cont* **-ping**) *n inf* vigor *m*, vitalidade *f*.
◆ **pep up** *vt sep* **-1.** [person] revigorar **-2.** [party, event] animar.
PEP (*abbr of* **personal equity plan**) *n plano de poupança popular na Grã-Bretanha.*
pepper ['pepə^r] *n* **-1.** *(U)* [spice] pimenta *f*; **black / white ~** pimenta preta/branca **-2.** [vegetable] pimentão *m*; **red/green ~** pimentão vermelho/verde.
pepperbox *n US* = **pepper pot**.
peppercorn ['pepəkɔːn] *n* grão *m* de pimenta.
peppered ['pepəd] *adj* **-1.** [sprinkled]: **~ (with sthg)** salpicado(da) (de algo) **-2.** [hit repeatedly]: **~ (with sthg)** crivado(da) (de algo).
pepper mill *n* moedor *m* de pimenta.
peppermint ['pepəmɪnt] *n* **-1.** [sweet] menta *f* **-2.** *(U)* [herb] hortelã-pimenta *f*.
pepper pot *UK*, **pepperbox** *US* ['pepəbɒks] *n* pimenteira *f*.
peppery ['pepərɪ] *adj* apimentado(da).
pep talk *n inf* palavras *fpl* de ânimo *OR* incentivo.
peptic ulcer ['peptɪk-] *n* úlcera *f* péptica.
per [pɜː^r] *prep* por; **~ hour/day/kilo/person** por hora/dia/quilo/pessoa; **as ~ instructions** conforme/segundo as instruções.
per annum *adv* por ano.
p/e ratio (*abbr of* **price-earnings ratio**) *n* índice *m* de benefício.
per capita [pə'kæpɪtə] *adj, adv* per capita.
perceive [pə'siːv] *vt* **-1.** [see] distinguir **-2.** [notice, realize] perceber, ver **-3.** [conceive, consider]: **to ~ sb/sthg as** ver alguém/algo como.
per cent *adv* por cento.
percentage [pə'sentɪdʒ] *n* porcentagem *f*.
perceptible [pə'septəbl] *adj* perceptível.
perception [pə'sepʃn] *n* **-1.** *(U)* [gen] distinção *f* **-2.** *(U)* [insight, understanding] percepção *f*, perspicácia *f* **-3.** [opinion] idéia *f*.
perceptive [pə'septɪv] *adj* perspicaz.
perceptively [pə'septɪvlɪ] *adv* de modo perspicaz.
perch [pɜːtʃ] (*pl sense 3 only inv OR* **-es**) <> *n* **-1.** [for bird] poleiro *m* **-2.** [high position] posição *f* elevada **-3.** [fish] perca *f*. <> *vi*: **to ~ (on sthg)** [bird] pousar (em algo); [person] empoleirar-se (em algo).
percolate ['pɜːkəleɪt] *vi* **-1.** [brew] coar **-2.** [seep - water] infiltrar-se; [- news] vazar.
percolator ['pɜːkəleɪtə^r] *n* cafeteira *f*.
percussion [pə'kʌʃn] *n (U) MUS* percussão *f*; **the ~ (section)** a percussão.
percussionist [pə'kʌʃənɪst] *n* percussionista *mf*.
peremptory [pə'remptərɪ] *adj* peremptório(ria), categórico(ca).
perennial [pə'renjəl] <> *adj* perene. <> *n BOT* planta *f* perene.
perestroika [,perə'strɔɪkə] *n (U)* perestroika *f*.
perfect [*adj & n* 'pɜːfɪkt, *vb* pə'fekt] <> *adj* perfeito(ta); **it makes ~ sense** é perfeitamente lógico(ca). <> *n GRAMM*: **~ (tense)** o perfeito. <> *vt* aperfeiçoar.
perfect competition *n (U) ECON* concorrência *f* perfeita.
perfection [pə'fekʃn] *n* perfeição *f*; **to ~** à perfeição.
perfectionist [pə'fekʃənɪst] *n* perfeccionista *mf*.

perfectly ['pɜ:fɪktlɪ] *adv* perfeitamente; ~ **honest/ridiculous** totalmente honesto/ridículo, totalmente honesta/ridícula.
perforate ['pɜ:fəreɪt] *vt* perfurar.
perforations [,pɜ:fə'reɪʃnz] *npl* perfurações *fpl*.
perform [pə'fɔ:m] ◇ *vt* **-1.** [carry out] realizar, levar a cabo **-2.** [in front of audience - play] representar, interpretar; [- music, dance] apresentar. ◇ *vi* **-1.** [function - car, machine] funcionar; [- person, team] sair-se **-2.** [in front of audience] apresentar-se, atuar.
performance [pə'fɔ:məns] *n* **-1.** *(U)* [carrying out, doing] execução *f*, realização *f* **-2.** [show] apresentação *f* **-3.** [rendition] performance *f*, desempenho *m* **-4.** *(U)* [of car, engine] desempenho *m*, rendimento *m*.
performance art *n (U) expressão artística em que se combina diversas atividades como teatro, música, dança, escultura, fotografia etc.*
performance car *n* carro *m* de alto desempenho.
performer [pə'fɔ:mə^r] *n* performer *mf*.
performing arts [pə'fɔ:mɪŋ-] *npl*: **the** ~ as artes performáticas.
perfume ['pɜ:fju:m] *n* **-1.** [for woman] perfume *m* **-2.** [pleasant smell] aroma *f*.
perfumed [*UK* 'pɜ:fju:md, *US* pər'fju:md] *adj* perfumado(da).
perfunctory [pə'fʌŋktərɪ] *adj* superficial, feito(ta) às pressas.
perhaps [pə'hæps] *adv* talvez; ~ **you're right** talvez você esteja certo; ~ **so/not** talvez sim/não; ~ **you should go and see her?** quem sabe você vai dar uma olhada nela?
peril ['perɪl] *n (U) literary* perigo *m*; **at one's** ~ por sua conta e risco.
perilous ['perələs] *adj literary* perigoso(sa).
perilously ['perələslɪ] *adv* perigosamente.
perimeter [pə'rɪmɪtə^r] *n* perímetro *m*; ~ **fence/wall** alambrado *m*, cerca *f*.
period ['pɪərɪəd] ◇ *n* **-1.** [gen] período *m*; **free** ~ período livre **-2.** *HISTORY* era *f* **-3.** [menstruation] período *m* menstrual **-4.** *US* [full stop] ponto *m*. ◇ *comp* [dress, furniture] de época.
periodic [,pɪərɪ'ɒdɪk] *adj* periódico(ca).
periodical [,pɪərɪ'ɒdɪkl] ◇ *adj* = **periodic**. ◇ *n* periódico *m*.
periodic table *n* tabela *f* periódica.
period pains *npl* cólicas *fpl* menstruais.
period piece *n* obra *f* de época.
peripatetic [,perɪpə'tetɪk] *adj* itinerante.
peripheral [pə'rɪfərəl] ◇ *adj* **-1.** [of little importance] secundário(ria) **-2.** [at edge] periférico(ca). ◇ *n COMPUT* periférico *m*.
periphery [pə'rɪfərɪ] (*pl* **-ies**) *n* **-1.** [edge] periferia *f* **-2.** [unimportant area] margens *fpl*.
periscope ['perɪskəʊp] *n* periscópio *m*.
perish ['perɪʃ] *vi* **-1.** [die] perecer **-2.** [decay] deteriorar-se.
perishable ['perɪʃəbl] *adj* perecível.
◆ **perishables** *npl* produtos *mpl* perecíveis.
perishing ['perɪʃɪŋ] *adj UK inf* **-1.** [cold] frio (fria) de rachar; **it's** ~ está fazendo um frio de rachar **-2.** [for emphasis] danado(da).
peritonitis [,perɪtə'naɪtɪs] *n (U)* peritonite *f*.
perjure ['pɜ:dʒə^r] *vt JUR*: **to** ~ **o.s.** perjurar-se.
perjury ['pɜ:dʒərɪ] *n (U) JUR* perjúrio *m*.
perk [pɜ:k] *n inf* mordomia *m*, regalia *f*.
◆ **perk up** *vi* animar-se.
perky ['pɜ:kɪ] (*compar* **-ier**, *superl* **-iest**) *adj inf* animado(da), alegre.
perm [pɜ:m] ◇ *n* permanente *m*. ◇ *vt* fazer permanente.
permanence ['pɜ:mənəns] *n (U)* permanência *f*.
permanent ['pɜ:mənənt] ◇ *adj* **-1.** [not temporary - job] fixo(xa); [- damage, feature] permanente **-2.** [continuous, constant] permanente, constante. ◇ *n US* permanente *m*.
permanently ['pɜ:mənəntlɪ] *adv* **-1.** [forever] permanentemente **-2.** [continuously] permanentemente.
permeable ['pɜ:mjəbl] *adj* permeável.
permeate ['pɜ:mɪeɪt] *vt* permear.
permissible [pə'mɪsəbl] *adj* permissível.
permission [pə'mɪʃn] *n (U)* permissão *f*; ~ **to do sthg** permissão para fazer algo.
permissive [pə'mɪsɪv] *adj* permissivo(va), tolerante.
permissiveness [pə'mɪsɪvnɪs] *n (U)* tolerância *f*.
permit [*vb* pə'mɪt, *n* 'pɜ:mɪt] (*pt* & *pp* **-ted**, *cont* **-ting**) ◇ *n* autorização *f*. ◇ *vt* permitir; **to** ~ **sb to do sthg** permitir que alguém faça algo; **my mother won't** ~ **me to go out** minha mãe não vai me deixar sair; **to** ~ **sb sthg** permitir algo a alguém. ◇ *vi* permitir; **weather permitting** se o tempo deixar.
permutation [,pɜ:mju:'teɪʃn] *n* permutação *f*.
pernicious [pə'nɪʃəs] *adj fml* pernicioso(sa).
pernickety *UK* [pə'nɪkətɪ], **persnickety** *US adj inf* meticuloso(sa).
peroxide [pə'rɒksaɪd] *n (U)* peróxido *m*.
peroxide blonde *n* loura *f* oxigenada *OR* de farmácia.
perpendicular [,pɜ:pən'dɪkjʊlə^r] ◇ *adj* **-1.** *MATH* perpendicular; ~ **to sthg** perpendicular a algo **-2.** [upright] vertical. ◇ *n MATH* perpendicular *f*.
perpetrate ['pɜ:pɪtreɪt] *vt fml* perpetrar.
perpetration [,pɜ:pɪ'treɪʃn] *n (U) fml* perpetração *f*.
perpetrator ['pɜ:pɪtreɪtə^r] *n fml* perpetrador *m*, -ra *f*.
perpetual [pə'petʃʊəl] *adj* **-1.** *pej* [continuous] constante **-2.** [everlasting - darkness] perpétuo(tua); [- hunger] eterno(na).
perpetually [pə'petʃʊəlɪ] *adv* **-1.** *pej* [continuously] constantemente, continuamente **-2.** [forever] perpetuamente, eternamente.
perpetual motion *n (U)* moto-contínuo *m*.
perpetuate [pə'petʃʊeɪt] *vt* perpetuar.
perpetuation [pə,petʃʊ'eɪʃn] *n (U)* perpetuação *f*.
perpetuity [,pɜ:pɪ'tju:ətɪ] *n (U)*: **in** ~ *fml* para sempre.
perplex [pə'pleks] *vt* desconcertar, deixar perplexo(xa).
perplexed [pə'plekst] *adj* perplexo(xa).

perplexing [pə'pleksɪŋ] *adj* desconcertante.
perplexity [pə'pleksətɪ] *n (U)* perplexidade *f.*
perquisite ['pɜ:kwɪzɪt] *n fml* privilégios *mpl* adicionais.
per se [pɜ:'seɪ] *adv* **-1.** [as such] como tal **-2.** [in itself] em si.
persecute ['pɜ:sɪkju:t] *vt* perseguir, oprimir.
persecution [,pɜ:sɪ'kju:ʃn] *n* **-1.** [act of cruelty] perseguição *f* **-2.** [cruel treatment] opressão *f.*
persecutor ['pɜ:sɪkju:tə^r] *n* opressor *m*, -ra *f*, perseguidor *m*, -ra *f.*
perseverance [,pɜ:sɪ'vɪərəns] *n (U)* perseverança *f.*
persevere [,pɜ:sɪ'vɪə^r] *vi* **-1.** [with difficulty] perseverar; **to ~ with sthg** persistir em algo **-2.** [with determination]: **to ~ in doing sthg** insistir em fazer algo.
Persia ['pɜ:ʃə] *n* Pérsia; **in ~** na Pérsia.
Persian ['pɜ:ʃn] <> *adj* persa. <> *n* **-1.** [person] persa *mf* **-2.** [language] persa *m.*
Persian cat *n* gato *m*, -ta *f* persa.
Persian Gulf *n*: **the ~** o Golfo Pérsico.
persist [pə'sɪst] *vi* **-1.** [problem, situation, rain] persistir **-2.** [person]: **to ~ in doing sthg** insistir em fazer algo.
persistence [pə'sɪstəns] *n (U)* **-1.** [continuation] persistência *f* **-2.** [determination] obstinação *f*, determinação *f.*
persistent [pə'sɪstənt] *adj* **-1.** [constant] constante **-2.** [determined] obstinado(da) determinado(da).
persistently [pə'sɪstəntlɪ] *adv* **-1.** [constantly] constantemente **-2.** [determinedly] obstinadamente, de forma determinada.
persnickety [pə'snɪkɪtɪ] *adj* ***US*** = **pernickety**.
person ['pɜ:sn] (*pl* **people** *OR* **persons** *fml*) *n* **-1.** [man or woman] pessoa *f*; **in ~** pessoalmente, em pessoa; **in the ~ of** na pessoa de **-2.** [body]: **about one's ~** em seu corpo **-3.** *GRAMM* pessoa *f.*
persona [pə'səʊnə] (*pl* **-s** *OR* **-ae** [-i:]) *n* imagem *f.*
personable ['pɜ:snəbl] *adj* bem-apessoado(da).
personage ['pɜ:sənɪdʒ] *n fml* personalidade *f.*
personal ['pɜ:sənl] <> *adj* **-1.** [gen] pessoal **-2.** [letter, message] particular **-3.** *pej* [rude] ofensivo (va). <> *n US* [advert] nota *f* pessoal *(em jornal).*
personal account *n* conta *f* pessoal.
personal allowance *n FIN desconto m simplificado (na declaração do imposto de renda).*
personal assistant *n* assistente *mf* particular.
personal call *n* telefonema *m* particular, chamada *f* pessoal.
personal column *n* seção *f* de recados *(em jornal).*
personal computer *n* computador *m* pessoal.
personal estate *n* bens *mpl* móveis.
personal hygiene *n (U)* higiene *f* pessoal.
personality [,pɜ:sə'nælətɪ] (*pl* **-ies**) *n* personalidade *f.*
personalize, -ise ['pɜ:sənəlaɪz] *vt* **-1.** [mark with name, initials] personalizar **-2.** *pej* [issue, argument] levar para o lado pessoal.
personalized ['pɜ:sənəlaɪzd] *adj* personalizado (da).
personally ['pɜ:snəlɪ] *adv* pessoalmente; **to take sthg ~** levar algo para o lado pessoal.
personal organizer *n* agenda *f* pessoal.
personal pension plan *n* plano *m* de previdência particular.
personal pronoun *n* pronome *m* pessoal.
personal property *n (U) JUR* bens *mpl* móveis.
personal stereo *n* walkman *m.*
persona non grata [-'grɑ:tə] (*pl* **personae non gratae** [-'grɑ:ti:]) *n* persona non grata *f.*
personify [pə'sɒnɪfaɪ] (*pt* & *pp* **-ied**) *vt* personificar.
personnel [,pɜ:sə'nel] <> *n (U)* [in firm, organization] equipe *f.* <> *npl* [staff] funcionários *mpl.*
personnel department *n* departamento *m* de pessoal.
personnel officer *n* funcionário *m*, -ria *f* do departamento pessoal.
person-to-person *adj TELEC* de pessoa a pessoa.
perspective [pə'spektɪv] *n* perspectiva *f*; **to get sthg in ~** *fig* pôr algo em perspectiva.
Perspex® ['pɜ:speks] *n UK* plexiglás® *m.*
perspicacious [,pɜ:spɪ'keɪʃəs] *adj fml* perspicaz.
perspiration [,pɜ:spə'reɪʃn] *n* transpiração *f.*
perspire [pə'spaɪə^r] *vi* transpirar.
persuade [pə'sweɪd] *vt* persuadir; **to ~ sb to do sthg** persuadir alguém a fazer algo; **to ~ sb that** convencer alguém de que; **to ~ sb of sthg** convencer alguém de algo.
persuasion [pə'sweɪʒn] *n* **-1.** *(U)* [act of persuading] persuasão *f* **-2.** [belief] crença *f.*
persuasive [pə'sweɪsɪv] *adj* persuasivo(va).
persuasively [pə'sweɪsɪvlɪ] *adv* persuasivamente.
pert [pɜ:t] *adj* **-1.** [person, reply] vivo(va), atrevido(da) **-2.** [nose, bottom] gracioso(sa).
pertain [pə'teɪn] *vi fml*: **~ing to sb/sthg** relacionado(da) a alguém/algo.
pertinence ['pɜ:tɪnəns] *n (U)* pertinência *f*, relevância *f.*
pertinent ['pɜ:tɪnənt] *adj* pertinente, relevante.
perturb [pə'tɜ:b] *vt fml* perturbar.
perturbed [pə'tɜ:bd] *adj fml* perturbado(da).
Peru [pə'ru:] *n* Peru; **in ~** no Peru.
perusal [pə'ru:zl] *n* **-1.** [thorough reading] leitura *f* **-2.** [quick reading] leitura *f* rápida.
peruse [pə'ru:z] *vt* **-1.** [read thoroughly] ler com atenção **-2.** [read quickly] ler por cima.
Peruvian [pə'ru:vjən] <> *adj* peruano(na). <> *n* peruano *m*, -na *f.*
pervade [pə'veɪd] *vt* impregnar.
pervasive [pə'veɪsɪv] *adj* penetrante.
perverse [pə'vɜ:s] *adj* perverso(sa).
perversely [pə'vɜ:slɪ] *adv* perversamente.
perversion [*UK* pə'vɜ:ʃn, *US* pə'vɜ:rʒn] *n* perversão *f.*
perversity [pə'vɜ:sətɪ] *n (U)* perversidade *f.*
pervert [*n* 'pɜ:vɜ:t, *vb* pə'vɜ:t] <> *n* pervertido *m*, -da *f.* <> *vt* **-1.** [distort] distorcer **-2.** [corrupt morally] perverter.
perverted [pə'vɜ:tɪd] *adj* **-1.** [sexually deviant] pervertido(da) **-2.** [distorted] distorcido(da).
peseta [pə'seɪtə] *n* peseta *f.*

peso ['peɪsəʊ] (*pl* **-s**) *n* peso *m*.
pessary ['pesərɪ] (*pl* **-ies**) *n* pessário *m*.
pessimism ['pesɪmɪzm] *n (U)* pessimismo *m*.
pessimist ['pesɪmɪst] *n* pessimista *mf*.
pessimistic [,pesɪ'mɪstɪk] *adj* pessimista.
pest [pest] *n* [gen] praga *f*, peste *f*.
pester ['pestəʳ] *vt* importunar, incomodar.
pesticide ['pestɪsaɪd] *n* pesticida *f*.
pestle ['pesl] *n* pilão *m*.
pet [pet] (*pt* & *pp* **-ted**, *cont* **-ting**) <> *adj* [favourite] predileto(ta), preferido(da). <> *n* **-1.** [domestic animal] animal *m* de estimação **-2.** [favourite person] preferido *m*, -da *f*. <> *vt* acariciar, afagar. <> *vi* acariciar-se.
petal ['petl] *n* pétala *f*.
peter ['pi:təʳ] ◆ **peter out** *vi* **-1.** [food, interest] esgotar-se **-2.** [path] desaparecer.
pethidine ['peθɪdi:n] *n (U)* petidina *f*.
petit bourgeois [pə,ti:'bʊəʒwɑ:] (*pl* **petits bourgeois** [pə,ti:'bʊəʒwɑ:]) <> *adj* pequeno-burguês (guesa). <> *n* pequeno-burguês *m*, -guesa *f*.
petite [pə'ti:t] *adj* diminuto(ta).
petit four [,peti-] (*pl* **petits fours** [,peti-]) *n bolo pequeno ou biscoito servido com café no final da refeição.*
petition [pɪ'tɪʃn] <> *n* **-1.** [supporting campaign] abaixo-assinado *m* **-2.** *JUR* petição *f*. <> *vt* peticionar. <> *vi* **-1.** [campaign]: **to ~ for/against sthg** fazer um abaixo-assinado a favor de/contra algo **-2.** *JUR*: **to ~ for divorce** pedir o divórcio.
petitioner [pɪ'tɪʃənəʳ] *n* **-1.** *JUR* [in divorce] requerente *mf* **-2.** [on petition] peticionário *m*, -ria *f*.
pet name *n* apelido *m* carinhoso.
petrified ['petrɪfaɪd] *adj* petrificado(da).
petrify ['petrɪfaɪ] (*pt* & *pp* **-ied**) *vt* petrificar.
petrochemical [,petrəʊ'kemɪkl] *adj* petroquímico(ca).
petrodollar ['petrəʊ,dɒləʳ] *n FIN* petrodólar *m*.
petrol ['petrəl] *n (U) UK* gasolina *f*.
petrolatum *n US* vaselina *f (líquida)*.
petrol bomb *n UK* coquetel *m* molotov.
petrol can *n UK* lata *f* de gasolina.
petrol cap *n UK* tampa *f* do tanque de combustível.
petroleum [pɪ'trəʊljəm] *n (U)* petróleo *m*.
petroleum jelly *n UK* vaselina *f*.
petrol pump *n UK* bomba *f* de gasolina.
petrol pump attendant *n UK* frentista *mf*.
petrol station *n UK* posto *m* de gasolina.
petrol tank *n UK* tanque *m* de gasolina.
pet shop *n* pet shop *f*, loja *f* de produtos para animais de estimação.
petticoat ['petɪkəʊt] *n* anágua *f*.
pettiness ['petɪnɪs] *n (U)* mesquinharia *f*.
petty ['petɪ] (*compar* **-ier**, *superl* **-iest**) *adj* **-1.** [small-minded] mesquinho(nha) **-2.** [trivial] insignificante.
petty cash *n (U)* dinheiro *m* para pequenas despesas, trocado *m*.
petty officer *n* suboficial *mf*.
petulant ['petjʊlənt] *adj* petulante.
petunia [pɪ'tju:njə] *n* petúnia *f*.
pew [pju:] *n* banco *m (de igreja)*.
pewter ['pju:təʳ] *n (U)* peltre *m*.
PG (*abbr of* **parental guidance**) *para menores acompanhados.*
PGA (*abbr of* **Professional Golfers' Association**) *n associação de jogadores profissionais de golfe nos Estados Unidos.*
p & h (*abbr of* **postage and handling**) *n US valor m de postagem.*
pH (*abbr of* **potential of hydrogen**) *n CHEM* ph.
PH (*abbr of* **Purple Heart**) *n (beneficiário de) honraria concedida pelo governo norte-americano a soldados feridos em ação.*
PHA (*abbr of* **Public Housing Administration**) *n órgão norte-americano encarregado de fornecer alojamento a pessoas necessitadas.*
phallic ['fælɪk] *adj* fálico(ca); ~ **symbol** símbolo *m* fálico.
phallus ['fæləs] (*pl* **-es** *OR* **phalli** ['fælaɪ]) *n* falo *m*.
phantom ['fæntəm] <> *adj* [imaginary] ilusório(ria). <> *n* [ghost] fantasma *m*.
phantom pregnancy *n* gravidez *f* psicológica.
pharaoh ['feərəʊ] *n* faraó *m*.
Pharisee ['færɪsi:] *n* fariseu *m*.
pharmaceutical [,fɑ:mə'sju:tɪkl] *adj* farmacêutico(ca).
◆ **pharmaceuticals** *npl* produtos *mpl* farmacêuticos.
pharmacist ['fɑ:məsɪst] *n* farmacêutico *m*, -ca *f*.
pharmacology [,fɑ:mə'kɒlədʒɪ] *n (U)* farmacologia *f*.
pharmacy ['fɑ:məsɪ] (*pl* **-ies**) *n* farmácia *f*.
phase [feɪz] <> *n* fase *f*. <> *vt* dividir em etapas, escalonar.
◆ **phase in** *vt sep* introduzir gradualmente.
◆ **phase out** *vt sep* retirar gradualmente.
PhD (*abbr of* **Doctor of Philosophy**) *n (titular de) doutorado em ciências humanas.*
pheasant ['feznt] (*pl inv OR* **-s**) *n* faisão *m*.
phenobarbitone *UK* [,fi:nəʊ'bɑ:bɪtəʊn], **phenobarbitol** *US* [,fi:nəʊ'bɑ:bɪtl] *n (U)* fenobarbital *m*.
phenomena [fɪ'nɒmɪnə] *pl* ▷ **phenomenon**.
phenomenal [fɪ'nɒmɪnl] *adj* fenomenal.
phenomenon [fɪ'nɒmɪnən] (*pl* **-mena**) *n* fenômeno *m*.
phew [fju:] *excl* ufa!
phial ['faɪəl] *n* frasco *m*.
Philadelphia [,fɪlə'delfɪə] *n* Filadélfia.
philanderer [fɪ'lændərəʳ] *n* galanteador *m*, sedutor *m*.
philanthropic [,fɪlən'θrɒpɪk] *adj* filantrópico(ca).
philanthropist [fɪ'lænθrəpɪst] *n* filantropo *m*.
philately [fɪ'lætəlɪ] *n (U)* filatelia *f*.
philharmonic [,fɪlɑ:'mɒnɪk] *adj* filarmônico(ca).
Philippine ['fɪlɪpi:n] *adj* filipino(na); **the ~ Islands** as (Ilhas) Filipinas.
◆ **Philippines** *npl*: **the ~s** as Filipinas.
philistine [*UK* 'fɪlɪstaɪn, *US* 'fɪlɪsti:n] *n* filisteu *m*, -éia *f*.
Phillips® ['fɪlɪps] *comp*: ~ **screw** parafuso *m* Phillips; ~ **screwdriver** chave *f* Phillips.
philosopher [fɪ'lɒsəfəʳ] *n* filósofo *m*, -fa *f*.
philosophical [,fɪlə'sɒfɪkl] *adj* filosófico(ca).

philosophize, -ise [fɪ'lɒsəfaɪz] *vi* filosofar.
philosophy [fɪ'lɒsəfɪ] (*pl* **-ies**) *n* filosofia *f*.
phlegm [flem] *n (U)* fleuma *f*.
phlegmatic [fleg'mætɪk] *adj* fleumático(ca).
Phnom Penh [ˌnɒm'pen] *n* Phnom Penh.
phobia ['fəʊbjəl] *n* fobia *f*; **to have a ~ about sthg** ter fobia a algo.
phoenix ['fi:nɪks] *n* fênix *f*.
phone [fəʊn] ◇ *n* telefone *m*; **to be on the ~** [speaking] estar no telefone; ***UK*** [connected to network] ter telefone. ◇ *comp* telefônico(ca). ◇ *vt* telefonar, ligar para. ◇ *vi* telefonar, ligar.
◆ **phone back** *vt sep & vi* ligar de volta.
◆ **phone up** *vt sep & vi* ligar.
phone book *n* lista *f* telefônica.
phone booth *n US* cabine *f* telefônica.
phone box *n UK* cabine *f* telefônica.
phone call *n* ligação *f*, chamada *f* telefônica; **to make a ~** fazer uma ligação.
phonecard ['fəʊnkɑ:d] *n* cartão *m* telefônico.
phone-in *n RADIO, TV programa para o qual as pessoas ligam e suas perguntas ou opiniões vão para o ar.*
phone line *n* **-1.** [wire] cabo *m* telefônico **-2.** [connection] linha *f* telefônica.
phone number *n* número *m* de telefone.
phone-tapping [-ˌtæpɪŋ] *n (U)* grampo *m (no telefone).*
phonetics [fə'netɪks] *n (U)* fonética *f*.
phoney *UK*, **phony** *US* ['fəʊnɪ] (*compar* **-ier**, *superl* **-iest**, *pl* **-ies**) ◇ *adj* falso(sa). ◇ *n* farsante *mf*.
phoney war *n período entre o início da segunda guerra mundial e abril de 1940 em que houve pouca atividade militar entre a Alemanha e a Grã-Bretanha.*
phony *adj & n US* = **phoney**.
phosphate ['fɒsfeɪt] *n* fosfato *m*.
phosphorus ['fɒsfərəs] *n (U)* fósforo *m*.
photo ['fəʊtəʊ] *n* foto *f*; **to take a ~ (of sb/sthg)** tirar *OR* bater uma foto (de alguém/algo).
photo booth *n* cabine *f* de foto automática.
photocall ['fəʊtəʊkɔ:l] *n* sessão *f* de fotos.
photocopier ['fəʊtəʊˌkɒpɪə[r]] *n* fotocopiadora *f*.
photocopy ['fəʊtəʊˌkɒpɪ] (*pl* **-ies**, *pt & pp* **-ied**) ◇ *n* fotocópia *f*. ◇ *vt* fotocopiar.
photoelectric cell [ˌfəʊtəʊɪ'lektrɪk-] *n* célula *f* fotoelétrica.
photo finish *n SPORT* photo finish *f*, *decisão do vencedor de uma corrida através de fotografia.*
photofit® *n*: **~ (picture)** *retrato de alguém procurado pela polícia montado a partir de outras fotos ou feito com desenhos de diversas partes do rosto.*
photogenic [ˌfəʊtəʊ'dʒenɪk] *adj* fotogênico(ca).
photograph ['fəʊtəgrɑ:f] ◇ *n* fotografia *f*; **to take a ~ (of sb/sthg)** tirar *OR* bater uma fotografia (de alguém/algo). ◇ *vt* fotografar.
photographer [fə'tɒgrəfə[r]] *n* fotógrafo *m*, -fa *f*.
photographic [ˌfəʊtə'græfɪk] *adj* fotográfico(ca).
photographic memory *n* memória *f* fotográfica.
photography [fə'tɒgrəfɪ] *n (U)* fotografia *f*.
photojournalism [ˌfəʊtəʊ'dʒɜ:nəlɪzm] *n (U)* fotojornalismo *m*.
photon ['fəʊtɒn] *n* fóton *m*.
photo opportunity *n oportunidade, planejada ou acidental, que um político ou uma celebridade tem de ser fotografado em um contexto que o favorece.*
photosensitive [ˌfəʊtəʊ'sensɪtɪv] *adj* fotossensível.
Photostat® ['fəʊtəstæt] (*pt & pp* **-ted**, *cont* **-ting**) *n* cópia *f* fotostática.
◆ **photostat** *vt* tirar cópia fotostática.
photosynthesis [ˌfəʊtəʊ'sɪnθəsɪs] *n (U)* fotossíntese *f*.
photovoltaic cell [ˌfəʊtəʊvɒl'teɪɪk-] *n* célula *f* fotovoltaica.
phrasal verb ['freɪzl-] *n combinação de um verbo e de uma preposição ou um advérbio, que juntos possuem sentido único.*
phrase [freɪz] ◇ *n* **-1.** [part of sentence] frase *f* **-2.** [expression] expressão *f*. ◇ *vt* [express - letter] redigir; [- apology, refusal] expressar; **sorry, I've ~d that badly** desculpe, eu me expressei mal.
phrasebook ['freɪzbʊk] *n* manual *m* de conversação.
phraseology [ˌfreɪzɪ'ɒlədʒɪ] *n (U)* fraseologia *f*.
physical ['fɪzɪkl] ◇ *adj* físico(ca). ◇ *n* exame *m* médico.
physical chemistry *n (U)* físico-química *f*.
physical education *n (U) SCH* educação *f* física.
physical examination *n* exame *m* médico.
physical geography *n (U)* geografia *f* física.
physically ['fɪzɪklɪ] *adv* fisicamente.
physically handicapped ◇ *adj* portador(-ra) de deficiência física. ◇ *npl*: **the ~** os portadores de deficiência física.
physical science *n (U)* ciência *f* física.
physical training *n* treinamento *m* físico.
physician [fɪ'zɪʃn] *n* médico *m*, -ca *f*.
physicist ['fɪzɪsɪst] *n* físico *m*, -ca *f*.
physics ['fɪzɪks] *n (U)* física *f*.
physio ['fɪzɪəʊ] (*pl* **-s**) *n inf* **-1.** [physiotherapist] fisioterapeuta *mf* **-2.** [physiotherapy] fisioterapia *f*.
physiognomy [ˌfɪzɪ'ɒnəmɪ] (*pl* **-ies**) *n fml* fisionomia *f*.
physiology [ˌfɪzɪ'ɒlədʒɪ] *n* fisiologia *f*.
physiotherapist [ˌfɪzɪəʊ'θerəpɪst] *n* fisioterapeuta *mf*.
physiotherapy [ˌfɪzɪəʊ'θerəpɪ] *n (U)* fisioterapia *f*.
physique [fɪ'zi:k] *n* físico *m*.
pianist ['pɪənɪst] *n* pianista *mf*.
piano [pɪ'ænəʊ] (*pl* **-s**) *n* piano *m*; **to play the ~** tocar piano.
piano accordion *n* acordeão *m*.
Picardy ['pɪkədɪ] *n* Picardia *(região da França).*
piccalilli [ˌpɪkə'lɪlɪ] *n (U) molho quente feito com vegetais e servido com carne fria.*
piccolo ['pɪkələʊ] (*pl* **-s**) *n* flautim *m*.
pick [pɪk] ◇ *n* **-1.** [tool] picareta *f* **-2.** [selection]: **to take one's ~** escolher o que quiser **-3.** [best]: **the ~ of** o melhor de. ◇ *vt* **-1.** [select, choose] escolher; **to ~ one's way across/through sthg** atravessar algo com cuidado **-2.** [gather] colher

-3. [remove] tirar **-4.** [nose]: **to ~ one's nose** pôr o dedo no nariz **-5.** [teeth]: **to ~ one's teeth** palitar os dentes **-6.** [provoke] provocar; **to ~ a fight (with sb)** arranjar briga (com alguém) **-7.** [lock] forçar *(com instrumento ou ferramenta).* <> *vi* escolher; **to ~ and choose** ser exigente *(na escolha).*

◆ **pick at** *vt fus* [food] beliscar.

◆ **pick on** *vt fus* meter-se com.

◆ **pick out** *vt sep* **-1.** [recognize] reconhecer **-2.** [select, choose] escolher.

◆ **pick up** <> *vt sep* **-1.** [lift up] pegar, apanhar; **to ~ up the pieces** *fig* juntar os pedaços, voltar à normalidade **-2.** [collect] pegar **-3.** [acquire] adquirir; **to ~ up speed** pegar velocidade **-4.** [subj: police]: **to ~ sb up for sthg** pegar alguém por algo **-5.** *inf* [start relationship with] dar em cima de **-6.** [detect, receive] captar **-7.** [resume] retomar. <> *vi* **-1.** [improve] melhorar **-2.** [resume] retomar.

pickaxe *UK*, **pickax** *US* ['pɪkæks] *n* picareta *f.*

picker ['pɪkəʳ] *n* colheiteiro *m*, -ra *f.*

picket ['pɪkɪt] <> *n* [at place of work - person] piqueteiro *m*, -ra *f*; [- instance of picketing] piquete *m.* <> *vt* fazer piquete em.

picketing ['pɪkətɪŋ] *n (U)* piquetes *mpl.*

picket line *n* piquete *m* de grevistas.

pickings ['pɪkɪŋz] *npl*: **easy/rich ~** dinheiro *m* fácil.

pickle ['pɪkl] <> *n* **-1.** [food] picles *m inv* **-2.** *inf* [difficult situation]: **to be in a ~** estar numa enrascada. <> *vt* fazer conserva de.

pickled ['pɪkld] *adj* em conserva.

pick-me-up *n inf* estimulante *m*, tônico *m.*

pickpocket ['pɪk,pɒkɪt] *n* batedor *m*, -ra *f* de carteiras.

pick-up *n* **-1.** [of record player] pickup *f* **-2.** [truck] picape *f.*

pick-up truck *n* picape *f.*

picky ['pɪkɪ] (*compar* **-ier**, *superl* **-iest**) *adj* difícil de contentar, enjoado(da).

picnic ['pɪknɪk] (*pt* & *pp* **-ked**, *cont* **-king**) <> *n* piquenique *m.* <> *vi* fazer piquenique.

picnicker ['pɪknɪkəʳ] *n* excursionista *mf.*

Pict [pɪkt] *n*: **the ~s** os Pictos.

pictorial [pɪk'tɔ:rɪəl] *adj* ilustrado(da).

picture ['pɪktʃəʳ] <> *n* **-1.** [painting, drawing] quadro *m* **-2.** [photograph] fotografia *f* **-3.** [image] imagem *f* **-4.** [movie] filme *m* **-5.** [prospect] cenário *m* **-6.** [epitome]: **he's the ~ of misery** ele é a personificação da miséria **-7.** *phr*: **to get the ~** *inf* entender; **to put sb in the ~** colocar alguém a par; **to be in/out of the ~** estar por dentro/fora. <> *vt* **-1.** [in mind] imaginar **-2.** [in photo] fotografar **-3.** [in painting, drawing] retratar.

◆ **pictures** *npl UK*: **the ~s** o cinema.

picture book *n* livro *m* ilustrado.

picture rail *n* moldura *f* para pendurar quadros.

picturesque [,pɪktʃə'resk] *adj* pitoresco(ca).

picture window *n* janela *f* panorâmica.

piddling ['pɪdlɪŋ] *adj inf pej* irrisório(ria).

pidgin ['pɪdʒɪn] <> *n* pídgin *m.* <> *comp*: **~ English** inglês *m* macarrônico.

pie [paɪ] *n* **-1.** [sweet] torta *f* **-2.** [savoury] pastelão *m*; **~ in the sky** castelos no ar.

piece [pi:s] *n* **-1.** [gen] pedaço *m*; **to be smashed to ~s** ser esmagado(da) em pedaços; **to fall to ~s** ficar em pedaços; **to pull** *OR* **tear sb/sthg to ~s** [criticize] arrasar com alguém/algo; **to take sthg to ~s** desmontar algo; **in ~s** em pedaços; **in one ~** [intact] sem um arranhão, intacto(ta); [unharmed] são e salvo, sã e salva; **to go to ~s** *fig* vir abaixo **-2.** [of food] pedaço *f* **-3.** *(with uncountable noun)* [gen] peça *f*; **~ of paper** folha *f* de papel; **~ of luck** golpe *m* de sorte; **~ of information** informação *f* **-4.** [of journalism] artigo *m* **-5.** [coin] moeda *f.*

◆ **piece together** *vt sep* reunir.

pièce de résistance [,pjesdərezɪs'tãs] (*pl* **pièces de résistance** [,pjesdərezɪs'tãs]) *n* [main attraction] atração *m* principal.

piecemeal ['pi:smi:l] <> *adj* pouco sistemático (ca). <> *adv* aos poucos, gradualmente.

piecework ['pi:swɜ:k] *n (U)* trabalho *m* por tarefas.

pie chart *n* gráfico *m* circular.

pied-à-terre (*pl* **pieds-à-terre**) *n pequena casa ou apartamento para uso ocasional como segunda residência.*

pie-eyed *adj inf* bebum.

pie plate *n US* prato *m* para torta.

pier [pɪəʳ] *n* píer *m.*

pierce [pɪəs] *vt* **-1.** [subj: bullet, needle] furar; **to have one's ears ~d** furar as orelhas **-2.** [subj: noise, light, pain] romper.

pierced [pɪəst] *adj* furado(da).

piercing ['pɪəsɪŋ] <> *adj* **-1.** [sound, voice] agudo (da), estridente **-2.** [wind] cortante **-3.** [look, eyes] penetrante. <> *n* piercing *m.*

piety ['paɪətɪ] *n* piedade *f.*

piffle ['pɪfl] *n inf* asneira *f.*

piffling ['pɪflɪŋ] *adj inf* ridículo(la).

pig [pɪg] (*pt* & *pp* **-ged**, *cont* **-ging**) *n* **-1.** [animal] porco *m*, -ca *f* **-2.** *inf pej* [greedy eater] glutão *m*, -ona *f*; **to make a ~ of o.s.** empanturrar-se **-3.** *inf pej* [unkind person] grosseirão *m*, -rona *f.*

◆ **pig out** *vi inf* empanturrar-se.

pigeon ['pɪdʒɪn] (*pl inv OR* **-s**) *n* pomba *f.*

pigeon-chested [-,tʃestɪd] *adj* de peito para frente.

pigeonhole ['pɪdʒɪnhəʊl] <> *n* [compartment] escaninho *m.* <> *vt* [classify] classificar.

pigeon-toed [-,təʊd] *adj com pés voltados para dentro.*

piggish ['pɪgɪʃ] *adj inf* porcalhão(lhona).

piggy ['pɪgɪ] (*compar* **-ier**, *superl* **-iest**, *pl* **-ies**) <> *adj* de porco. <> *n inf* [piglet] porquinho *m*, -nha *f.*

piggyback ['pɪgɪbæk] *n*: **to give sb a ~** levar alguém na garupa.

piggybank ['pɪgɪbæŋk] *n* porquinho *m (de moedas).*

pig-headed *adj* cabeçudo(da).

piglet ['pɪglɪt] *n* leitão *m*, -toa *f*, porquinho *m*, -nha *f.*

pigment ['pɪgmənt] *n* pigmento *m.*

pigmentation [,pɪgmən'teɪʃn] *n* pigmentação *f.*

pigmy (*pl* **-ies**) *n* = **pygmy.**

pigpen *n US* = **pigsty.**

pigskin ['pɪgskɪn] <> *n (U)* couro *m* de porco. <> *comp* de couro de porco.
pigsty ['pɪgstaɪ] (*pl* **-ies**), **pigpen** *US* ['pɪgpen] *n* chiqueiro *m*.
pigswill ['pɪgswɪl] *n (U)* lavagem *f*.
pigtail ['pɪgteɪl] *n* trança *f*.
pike [paɪk] (*pl sense 1 only inv* OR **-s**) *n* **-1.** [fish] lúcio *m* **-2.** [spear] pique *m*.
pikestaff ['paɪkstɑ:f] *n*: **plain as a ~** claro como um dia de sol.
pilaster [pɪ'læstəʳ] *n* pilastra *f*.
pilchard ['pɪltʃəd] *n* sardinha *f*.
pile [paɪl] <> *n* **-1.** [heap] monte *m*; **a ~** OR **~s of sthg** *inf* um monte de algo **-2.** [neat stack] pilha *f* **-3.** [of carpet, fabric] felpa *f*. <> *vt* empilhar; **to be ~d with sthg** estar entulhado(da) de algo.
◆ **piles** *npl* MED hemorróidas *fpl*.
◆ **pile in** *vi inf* apinhar-se.
◆ **pile into** *vt fus inf* amontoar-se.
◆ **pile out** *vi inf* debandar; **to ~ out of sthg** debandar de algo.
◆ **pile up** <> *vt sep* amontoar, empilhar. <> *vi* acumular-se.
pile driver *n* bate-estaca *m*.
pile-up *n* engavetamento *m*.
pilfer ['pɪlfəʳ] <> *vt*: **to ~ sthg (from)** furtar algo (de). <> *vi*: **to ~ (from)** furtar (de), surrupiar (de).
pilgrim ['pɪlgrɪm] *n* peregrino *m*, -na *f*.

PILGRIM FATHERS

Assim é chamado o grupo de puritanos ingleses que, perseguido por suas crenças religiosas, embarcou para a América, em 1620, a bordo do navio *Mayflower*. Os *Pilgrim Fathers* fundaram a primeira colônia inglesa, onde hoje é o estado de Massachussetts. Durante o primeiro inverno que passaram no novo mundo, muitos morreram de fome. Mas, a partir do segundo ano na América, os nativos da região os ensinaram a plantar trigo e outras lavouras. Dessa forma, no outono, quando os colonos viram que tinham comida suficiente para sobreviver ao inverno, celebraram uma refeição de Ação de Graças com os nativos. Muitos anos depois, em 1863, o presidente Lincoln transformou o dia de Ação de Graças em feriado nacional, em comemoração ao sucesso daquela primeira colheita.

pilgrimage ['pɪlgrɪmɪdʒ] *n* peregrinação *f*.
pill [pɪl] *n* **-1.** MED pílula *f* **-2.** [contraceptive]: **the ~** a pílula anticoncepcional; **to be on the ~** tomar pílula (anticoncepcional).
pillage ['pɪlɪdʒ] <> *n (U)* pilhagem *f*. <> *vt* pilhar.
pillar ['pɪləʳ] *n* **-1.** ARCHIT pilar *m* **-2.** *fig* [of community, church etc] bastião *m*; **to be a ~ of strength** ser uma fortaleza; **to be a ~ of the church** ser um bastião da igreja.
pillar box *n UK* caixa *f* coletora *(do correio)*.
pillbox ['pɪlbɒks] *n* **-1.** [box for pills] caixa *f* de comprimidos **-2.** MIL casamata *f*.
pillion ['pɪljən] *n* assento *m* traseiro; **to ride ~** ir na garupa.
pillock ['pɪlək] *n UK inf* imbecil.
pillory ['pɪlərɪ] (*pl* **-ies**, *pt* & *pp* **-ied**) <> *n* [form of punishment] pelourinho *m*. <> *vt fig* [ridicule]: **to be pilloried** ser ridicularizado(da).
pillow ['pɪləʊ] *n* **-1.** [for bed] travesseiro *m* **-2.** *US* [on sofa, chair] almofada *f*.
pillowcase ['pɪləʊkeɪs], **pillowslip** ['pɪləʊslɪp] *n* fronha *f*.
pilot ['paɪlət] <> *n* piloto *m*. <> *comp* [trial] piloto; **~ project** projeto-piloto *m*. <> *vt* **-1.** [gen] pilotar **-2.** [bill] pôr em prática **-3.** [scheme] aplicar.
pilot light, pilot burner *n* [on gas appliance] piloto *m*.
pilot scheme *n* projeto-piloto *m*.
pilot study *n* estudo *m* -piloto.
pimento [pɪ'mentəʊ] (*pl inv* OR **-s**) *n* pimentão *m*.
pimp [pɪmp] *n inf* cafetão *m*.
pimple ['pɪmpl] *n* espinha *f*.
pimply ['pɪmplɪ] (*compar* **-ier**, *superl* **-iest**) *adj* espinhento(ta), cheio (cheia) de espinhas.
pin [pɪn] (*pt* & *pp* **-ned**, *cont* **-ning**) <> *n* **-1.** [for sewing] alfinete *m*; **to have ~s and needles** *fig* estar com formigamento; **to be on ~s and needles** *US* estar uma pilha **-2.** [drawing pin] percevejo *m* **-3.** [safety pin] alfinete *m* de segurança **-4.** [of plug, grenade] pino *m* **-5.** TECH pino *m*, cavilha *f* **-6.** *US* [brooch] broche *m*; [badge] bottom *m* **-7.** GOLF: **the ~** a bandeira. <> *vt* **-1.** [attach]: **to ~ sthg to** OR **on sthg** prender OR colocar algo em algo **-2.** [immobilize]: **to ~ sb against** OR **to sthg** prender alguém contra/em algo **-3.** [apportion]: **to ~ sthg on sb** botar a culpa de algo em alguém, culpar alguém de algo.
◆ **pin down** *vt sep* **-1.** [identify] determinar, identificar **-2.** [force to make a decision] obrigar a se decidir.
◆ **pin up** *vt sep* **-1.** [poster, list of results] afixar **-2.** [hem, hair] prender.
PIN [pɪn] (*abbr of* **personal identification number**) *n* senha *f*.
pinafore ['pɪnəfɔ:ʳ] *n* **-1.** [apron] avental *m* **-2.** *UK* [dress] jardineira *f*.
pinball ['pɪnbɔ:l] *n (U)* fliperama *f*.
pinball machine *n* máquina *f* de fliperama.
pincers ['pɪnsəz] *npl* **-1.** [tool] torquês *f* **-2.** [front claws] pinças *fpl*.
pinch [pɪntʃ] <> *n* **-1.** [nip] beliscão *m*; **to feel the ~** apertar o cinto **-2.** [small quantity] pitada *f*. <> *vt* **-1.** [nip] beliscar **-2.** *inf* [steal - money, clothes] passar a mão em; [- car] pegar.
◆ **at a pinch** *UK*, **in a pinch** *US adv* em último caso.
pinched [pɪntʃt] *adj* **-1.** [thin, pale] abatido(da); **~ with cold/hunger** pálido(da) de frio/fome **-2.** [short of]: **~ for sthg** escasso(sa) de algo.
pincushion ['pɪn,kʊʃn] *n* alfineteira *f*.
pine [paɪn] <> *n* **-1.** [tree] pinheiro *m* **-2.** *(U)* [wood] pinho *m*. <> *comp* [furniture] de pinho. <> *vi*: **to ~ for sb/sthg** suspirar por alguém/algo.
◆ **pine away** *vi* consumir-se (de desgosto).
pineapple ['paɪnæpl] *n* abacaxi *m*.
pine cone *n* pinha *f*.
pine needle *n* agulha *f* de pinheiro.
pine tree *n* pinheiro *m*.

pinewood ['paɪnwʊd] *n* **-1.** [forest] pinheiral *m* **-2.** *(U)* [material] madeira *f* de pinho.
ping [pɪŋ] ◇ *n* tinido *m.* ◇ *vi* retinir.
Ping-Pong® [-pɒŋ] *n (U)* ping-pong *m.*
pinhole ['pɪnhəʊl] *n* buraquinho *m.*
pinion ['pɪnjən] ◇ *n* TECH pinhão *m.* ◇ *vt* imobilizar.
pink [pɪŋk] ◇ *adj* **-1.** [in colour] cor-de-rosa **-2.** [with embarrassment] vermelho(lha); **to turn ~** ficar vermelho(lha). ◇ *n* **-1.** [colour] rosa *m* **-2.** [flower] cravina *f*, cravo *m.*
pinkie ['pɪŋkɪ] *n* **US** & **Scot** minguinho *m.*
pinking scissors, pinking shears *npl* tesoura *f* de picotar.
pink pound UK, **pink dollar** *n*: **the ~** *poder aquisitivo da comunidade gay.*
pin money *n (U) pequena quantia de dinheiro extra recebido (geralmente do marido) para despesas pessoais.*
pinnacle ['pɪnəkl] *n* **-1.** *fig* [of career, success] auge *m* **-2.** [mountain peak] topo *m* **-3.** ARCHIT [spire] pináculo *m.*
pinny ['pɪnɪ] *(pl* **-ies)** *n inf* avental *m.*
pinpoint ['pɪnpɔɪnt] *vt* **-1.** [difficulty, cause] determinar, identificar **-2.** [position, target, leak] identificar.
pinprick ['pɪnprɪk] *n* **-1.** [mark, hole] pontinho *m* **-2.** *fig* [slight irritation] chateação *f.*
pin-striped [-ˌstraɪpt] *adj* riscado(da).
pint [paɪnt] *n* **-1.** UK [unit of measurement] quartilho *m (0,568 litro)* **-2.** US [unit of measurement] pint *m (0,473 litro)* **-3.** UK [beer] cerveja *f.*
pintable *n* UK máquina *f* de fliperama.
pint-size(d) *adj inf* minúsculo(la).
pin-up *n* pin-up *f.*
pioneer [ˌpaɪə'nɪəʳ] ◇ *n* **-1.** [first settler] pioneiro *m*, -ra *f* **-2.** [innovator] pioneiro *m*, -ra *f.* ◇ *vt* lançar, ser pioneiro(na) de.
pioneering [ˌpaɪə'nɪərɪŋ] *adj* pioneiro(ra).
pious ['paɪəs] *adj* **-1.** [religious] piedoso(sa) **-2.** *pej* [sanctimonious] devoto(ta).
piously ['paɪəslɪ] *adv* **-1.** [religiously] piedosamente **-2.** *pej* [sanctimoniously] devotadamente.
pip [pɪp] *n* **-1.** [seed] semente *f* **-2.** UK [bleep] sinal *m.*
pipe [paɪp] ◇ *n* **-1.** [for gas, water] tubo *m*, cano *m* **-2.** [for smoking] cachimbo *m* **-3.** MUS flauta *f.* ◇ *vt* canalizar.
◆ **pipes** *npl* MUS [bagpipes] gaita *f* de foles.
◆ **pipe down** *vi inf* fechar a matraca.
◆ **pipe up** *vi inf*: **there was silence and then she ~d up with a suggestion** fez-se silêncio e então ela saiu com uma sugestão.
pipe cleaner *n* limpador *m* para cachimbo.
piped music [paɪpt-] *n* UK música *f* ambiente.
pipe dream *n* castelo *m* no ar, sonho *m* impossível.
pipeline ['paɪplaɪn] *n* **-1.** [for oil] oleoduto *m* **-2.** [for gas] gasoduto *m*; **to be in the ~** *fig* estar a caminho.
piper ['paɪpəʳ] *n* MUS tocador *m*, -ra *f* de gaita de foles.
piping hot ['paɪpɪŋ-] *adj* extremamente quente.
pipsqueak ['pɪpskwiːk] *n pej* coisa *f* insignificante.
piquant ['piːkənt] *adj* **-1.** [spicy] picante **-2.** [interesting] intrigante.
pique [piːk] *n (U)* ressentimento *m*; **a fit of ~** um ataque de despeito.
piracy ['paɪrəsɪ] *n* pirataria *f.*
piranha [pɪ'rɑːnə] *n* piranha *f.*
pirate ['paɪrət] ◇ *adj* [illegally copied] pirateado(da). ◇ *n* **-1.** [sailor] pirata *m* **-2.** [illegal copy] cópia *f* pirata. ◇ *vt* piratear.
pirate radio *n* UK rádio *f* pirata.
pirouette [ˌpɪrʊ'et] ◇ *n* pirueta *f.* ◇ *vi* fazer pirueta.
Pisces ['paɪsiːz] *n* **-1.** [sign] peixes *m* **-2.** [person] pisciano(na); **I'm ~** sou de Peixes.
piss [pɪs] *vulg* ◇ *n* **-1.** [urine] mijo *m*; **to take the ~ out of sb/sthg** tirar um sarro de algo/alguém **-2.** [urination]: **to have a ~** dar uma mijada. ◇ *vi* **-1.** [urinate] mijar **-2.** [rain]: **it's ~ing with rain** está chovendo canivete.
◆ **piss down** *vi* UK *vulg* [rain]: **the rain was ~ing down** chovia a cântaros.
◆ **piss off** *vulg* ◇ *vt sep* encher o saco. ◇ *vi* UK ir à merda; **~ off!** vai à merda!
pissed [pɪst] *adj vulg* **-1.** UK [drunk] mamado(da) **-2.** US [annoyed] puto(ta) da cara.
pissed off *adj vulg* de saco cheio.
pistachio [pɪ'stɑːʃɪəʊ] *(pl* **-s)** *n* pistache *m.*
piste [piːst] *n* SKIING pista *f.*
pistol ['pɪstl] *n* pistola *f.*
piston ['pɪstən] *n* pistom *m.*
pit [pɪt] *(pt* & *pp* **-ted**, *cont* **-ting)** ◇ *n* **-1.** [large hole] cova *f* **-2.** [small, shallow hole] marca *f* **-3.** [for orchestra] fosso *m* da orquestra **-4.** [mine] mina *f* **-5.** [quarry] canteiro *m* **-6.** US [of fruit] caroço *m* **-7.** *phr*: **the ~ of one's stomach** a boca do estômago. ◇ *vt*: **to be ~ted against sb** ser incitado(da) contra alguém; **to ~ one's wits against sb/sthg** medir forças contra alguém/algo.
◆ **pits** *npl* **-1.** [in motor racing]: **the ~s** o box **-2.** *inf* [awful]: **the ~s** o fim da picada.
pit bull (terrier) *n* pit bull terrier *m.*
pitch [pɪtʃ] ◇ *n* **-1.** SPORT campo *m* **-2.** MUS tom *m* **-3.** *(U)* [level, degree] grau *m* **-4.** [street vendor's place] ponto *m* **-5.** *inf* [spiel]: **sales ~** papo *m* de vendedor **-6.** [of ship, aircraft] arfagem *f* **-7.** [of slope, roof] (grau *m* de) inclinação *f* **-8.** [throw] arremesso *m* **-9.** [tar] piche *m.* ◇ *vt* **-1.** [throw] arremessar; **to be ~ed into sthg** [person] ser posto(ta) em algo da noite para o dia **-2.** [set level of - price] estabelecer um preço para; [- speech] dar um tom a **-3.** [camp, tent] armar. ◇ *vi* **-1.** [fall over] despencar; **to ~ forward** precipitar-se para frente **-2.** [ship, plane] arfar.
◆ **pitch in** *vi inf* **-1.** [start work] botar a mão na massa **-2.** [lend a hand] colaborar.
pitch-black *adj* preto(ta) como carvão.
pitched [pɪtʃt] *adj* inclinado(da).
pitched battle [ˌpɪtʃt-] *n* batalha *f* campal.
pitcher ['pɪtʃəʳ] *n* US **-1.** [jug] jarro *m* **-2.** [in baseball] lançador *m.*
pitchfork ['pɪtʃfɔːk] *n* forcado *m.*
piteous ['pɪtɪəs] *adj* lastimável, comovente.
piteously ['pɪtɪəslɪ] *adv* de forma comovente.
pitfall ['pɪtfɔːl] *n* armadilha *f*, perigo *m.*
pith [pɪθ] *n (U) parte branca da casca de uma fruta.*

pithead ['pɪthed] *n* boca *f* da mina.
pith helmet *n* chapéu *m* de palha.
pithy ['pɪθɪ] (*compar* **-ier**, *superl* **-iest**) *adj* denso(sa), contundente.
pitiable ['pɪtɪəbl] *adj* **-1.** [arousing pity] lastimoso(sa) **-2.** [arousing contempt] lamentável.
pitiful ['pɪtɪfʊl] *adj* **-1.** [arousing pity] lastimável **-2.** [arousing contempt] lastimoso(sa).
pitifully ['pɪtɪfʊlɪ] *adv* **-1.** [arousing pity] comovedoramente **-2.** [arousing contempt]: **a ~ lame excuse** uma desculpa lamentável.
pitiless ['pɪtɪlɪs] *adj* impiedoso(sa).
pit stop *n* pit stop *m*.
pitta bread ['pɪtə-] *n (U)* pão *m* sírio; *tipo de pão oval sem levedura*.
pittance ['pɪtəns] *n* miséria *f*.
pitted ['pɪtɪd] *adj* **-1.** descaroçado(da) **-2.**: **~ with sthg** marcado(da) com algo.
pitter-patter ['pɪtə,pætə^r] *n* ruído *m (de passos, de chuva)*.
pituitary [pɪ'tjuːɪtrɪ] (*pl* **-ies**) *n*: **~ (gland)** glândula *f* pituitária.
pity ['pɪtɪ] (*pt* & *pp* **-ied**) ◇ *n* **-1.** [sympathy, sorrow] compaixão *f*; **to take** OR **have ~ on sb** ficar com pena de alguém **-2.** [shame] pena *f*; **what a ~!** que pena! ◇ *vt* sentir pena de.
pitying ['pɪtɪɪŋ] *adj* compassivo(va).
pivot ['pɪvət] ◇ *n* **-1.** TECH eixo *m* **-2.** *fig* [crux] centro *m*, eixo *m*. ◇ *vi*: **to ~ (on sthg)** girar (sobre algo).
pixel ['pɪksl] *n* COMPUT píxel *m*.
pixie, pixy ['pɪksɪ] (*pl* **-ies**) *n* duende *m*.
pizza ['piːtsə] *n* pizza *f*.
pizzazz [pɪ'zæz] *n (U) inf* vitalidade *f*, energia *f*.
Pk (*abbr of* **park**) parque *m*.
pl. *abbr of* **please**.
P & L (*abbr of* **profit and loss**) *n* perdas *fpl* e lucros *mpl*.
PLA (*abbr of* **People's Liberation Army**) *n forças armadas da República Popular da China*.
placard ['plækɑːd] *n* cartaz *m*.
placate [plə'keɪt] *vt* aplacar, acalmar.
placatory [plə'keɪtərɪ] *adj* apaziguante.
place [pleɪs] ◇ *n* **-1.** [gen] lugar *m*; **~ of birth** local de nascimento; **to put sb in their ~** colocar alguém em seu lugar; **to fall into ~** fazer sentido **-2.** [suitable occasion] momento *m* **-3.** [home] casa *f*; **decimal ~** MATH casa decimal **-4.** [post, vacancy] vaga *f* **-5.** [role, function] papel *m* **-6.** [rank] posição *f* **-7.** [instance]: **why didn't you say so in the first ~?** por que você não disse isso logo?; **in the first ~ ..., and in the second ~ ...** em primeiro lugar ..., e em segundo lugar ... **-8.** *phr*: **the market takes ~ every Sunday** a feira acontece todos os domingos; **the events that took ~ that day became infamous** os acontecimentos que tiveram lugar naquele dia tornaram-se notórios; **to take the ~ of sb/sthg** tomar o lugar de alguém/algo, substituir alguém/algo. ◇ *vt* **-1.** [position, put] colocar **-2.** [lay, apportion]: **to ~ blame on sb/sthg** colocar a culpa em alguém/algo; **to ~ emphasis on sb/sthg** dar ênfase a alguém/algo; **to ~ pressure on sb/sthg** exercer pressão sobre alguém/algo; **to ~ responsibility on sb/sthg** pôr a responsabilidade em alguém/algo **-3.** [identify] identificar **-4.** [make]: **to ~ an order** COMM fazer um pedido; **to ~ a bet** fazer uma aposta **-5.** [situate] situar; **how are we ~d for money?** como estamos de dinheiro? **-6.** [in race]: **to be ~d** classificar-se.
◆ **all over the place** *adv* por todo lado.
◆ **in place** *adv* **-1.** [in proper position] no lugar **-2.** [established, set up] estabelecido(da).
◆ **in place of** *prep*: **in ~ of me** em meu lugar.
◆ **out of place** *adv* **-1.** [in wrong position] fora do lugar **-2.** [unsuitable] fora de propósito.
placebo [plə'siːbəʊ] (*pl* **-s** OR **-es**) *n* placebo *m*.
place card *n* cartão *m* de reserva *(de mesa em jantar)*.
place kick *n* tiro *m* livre *(com a bola colocada)*.
place mat *n* toalha *f* de mesa individual.
placement ['pleɪsmənt] *n* **-1.** *(U)* [positioning] disposição *f* **-2.** [work experience] estágio *m*.
placement service *n US* serviço *m* de colocação profissional.
placenta [plə'sentə] (*pl* **-s** OR **-tae** [-tiː]) *n* placenta *f*.
place setting *n* jogo *m* de mesa para uma pessoa.
placid ['plæsɪd] *adj* **-1.** [even-tempered] plácido(da) **-2.** [peaceful] sereno(na).
placidly ['plæsɪdlɪ] *adv* calmamente.
plagiarism ['pleɪdʒjərɪzm] *n (U)* plágio *m*.
plagiarist ['pleɪdʒjərɪst] *n* plagiador *m*, -ra *f*.
plagiarize, -ise ['pleɪdʒəraɪz] *vt* plagiar.
plague [pleɪg] ◇ *n* praga *f*; **to avoid sb/sthg like the ~** fugir de alguém/algo como uma praga. ◇ *vt*: **to ~ sb with sthg** importunar alguém com algo; **to be ~d by sthg** ser/estar atormentado(da) por algo.
plaice [pleɪs] (*pl inv*) *n* linguado *m*.
plaid [plæd] *n (U)* tecido *m* em xadrez da Escócia.
Plaid Cymru [,plaɪd'kʌmrɪ] *n UK* POL Plaid Cymru *(partido nacionalista galês)*.
plain [pleɪn] ◇ *adj* **-1.** [not patterned] liso(sa) **-2.** [simple, not fancy] simples; **~ yoghurt** iogurte *m* natural **-3.** [clear] claro(ra); **to make sthg ~ to sb** deixar algo claro para alguém **-4.** [blunt] direto(ta) **-5.** [absolute] absoluto(ta) **-6.** [not pretty] sem atrativos. ◇ *adv inf* [completely] claramente. ◇ *n* GEOGR planície *f*.
plain chocolate *n UK* chocolate *m* meio amargo.
plain-clothes *adj* à paisana.
plain flour *n UK* farinha *f* sem fermento.
plainly ['pleɪnlɪ] *adv* **-1.** [upset, angry] completamente **-2.** [remember, hear] claramente **-3.** [frankly] francamente, abertamente **-4.** [simply] de forma simples.
plain sailing *n (U)* caminho *m* livre.
plain-spoken *adj* franco(ca).
plaintiff ['pleɪntɪf] *n* querelante *mf*.
plaintive ['pleɪntɪv] *adj* triste, melancólico(ca).
plait [plæt] ◇ *n* trança *f*. ◇ *vt* trançar.
plan [plæn] (*pt* & *pp* **-ned**, *cont* **-ning**) ◇ *n* **-1.** [strategy] plano *m*; **to go according to ~** sair de acordo com o planejado **-2.** [outline] esboço *m* **-3.** [diagram, map - of garden, building] planta *f*; [- of inside of

a machine] esquema *m* de montagem. <> *vt* **-1.** [organize] planejar **-2.** [intend] pretender; **to ~ to do sthg** pensar em fazer algo **-3.** [design, devise] projetar. <> *vi* fazer planos; **to ~ for sthg** fazer planos para algo.

◆ **plans** *npl* planos *mpl*; **to have ~s for** ter planos para.

◆ **plan on** *vt fus*: **to ~ on doing sthg** pretender fazer algo.

◆ **plan out** *vt sep* traçar.

plane [pleɪn] <> *adj* plano(na). <> *n* **-1.** [aircraft] avião *m* **-2.** *GEOM* plano *m* **-3.** *fig* [level] patamar *m* **-4.** [tool] plaina *f* **-5.** [tree] plátano *m*. <> *vt* aplainar.

planet ['plænɪt] *n* planeta *f*.

planetarium [,plænɪ'teərɪəm] (*pl* **-riums** *OR* **-ria** [-rɪəl]) *n* planetário *m*.

planetary ['plænɪtrɪ] *adj* planetário(ria).

plane tree *n* plátano *m*.

plank [plæŋk] *n* **-1.** [piece of wood] tábua *f* **-2.** *POL* [main policy] item *m*.

plankton ['plæŋktən] *n (U)* plâncton *m*.

planned [plænd] *adj* planejado(da).

planner ['plænəʳ] *n* planejador *m*, -ra *f*; **town ~** urbanista *mf*.

planning ['plænɪŋ] *n* planejamento *m*.

planning permission *n (U)* autorização *f* para construir.

plan of action *n* plano *m* de ação.

plant [plɑ:nt] <> *n* **-1.** *BOT* planta *f* **-2.** [factory] fábrica *f*; **nuclear ~** usina *f* nuclear **-3.** *(U)* [heavy machinery] maquinários *mpl*. <> *vt* **-1.** [seed, tree] plantar; [field, garden] semear; **to ~ sthg with sthg** semear algo com algo **-2.** [blow, kiss] dar **-3.** [place - oneself] plantar-se; [- object] fincar **-4.** [offload] despachar **-5.** [spy] infiltrar **-6.** [bomb, microphone] colocar secretamente; **to ~ sthg on sb** esconder algo em alguém **-7.** [thought, idea] incutir.

◆ **plant out** *vt sep* transplantar.

plantain ['plæntɪn] *n* banana-da-terra *f*.

plantation [plæn'teɪʃn] *n* plantação *f*.

planter ['plɑ:ntəʳ] *n* **-1.** [farmer] fazendeiro *m*, -ra *f* **-2.** [container] jardineira *f*.

plant pot *n* vaso *m* para plantas.

plaque [plɑ:k] *n* placa *f*.

plasma ['plæzməl] *n (U)* plasma *m*.

plaster ['plɑ:stəʳ] <> *n* **-1.** [gen] gesso *m*; **in ~** engessado(da) **-2.** *UK* [for cut]: **(sticking) ~** esparadrapo *m*, Band-Aid® *m*. <> *vt* **-1.** [put plaster on] revestir com gesso **-2.** [cover]: **to ~ sthg with sthg** cobrir algo com algo **-3.** [make stick] fixar.

plasterboard ['plɑ:stəbɔ:d] *n (U)* chapa *f* de gesso.

plaster cast *n* molde *m* de gesso.

plastered ['plɑ:stəd] *adj inf* [drunk] de porre.

plasterer ['plɑ:stərəʳ] *n* rebocador *m*, -ra *f*.

plastering ['plɑ:stərɪŋ] *n (U)* ato *m* de rebocar.

plaster of paris *n* gesso *m* de Paris.

plastic ['plæstɪk] <> *adj* de plástico. <> *n* **-1.** [material] plástico *m* **-2.** *inf* [credit cards] cartão *m* (de crédito).

plastic bullet *n* bala *f* de borracha.

plastic explosive *n* explosivo *m* plástico.

Plasticine® *UK* ['plæstɪsi:n], **play dough** *US n (U)* plasticina *f*.

plastic money *n* cartões *mpl* de crédito.

plastic surgeon *n* cirurgião *m* plástico, cirurgiã *f* plástica.

plastic surgery *n (U)* cirurgia *f* plástica.

plastic wrap *n US* filme *m* de PVC transparente.

plate [pleɪt] <> *n* **-1.** [gen] prato *m*; **to have a lot on one's ~** ter muito com o que se preocupar; **to be handed sthg on a ~** receber algo de mão beijada **-2.** [on wall, door or surgical] placa *f* **-3.** *(U)* [gold, silver etc] baixela *f* **-4.** [photograph] chapa *f* **-5.** [in dentistry] dentadura *f* **-6.** [in baseball] base *f*. <> *vt*: **to be ~d (with sthg)** ser banhado (a algo).

Plate [pleɪt] *n*: **the River ~** o Rio da Prata.

plateau ['plætəʊ] (*pl* **-s** *OR* **-x** [-z]) *n* **-1.** *GEOGR* planalto *m* **-2.** *fig* [steady level] nível *m* estável.

plateful ['pleɪtfʊl] *n* pratada *f*.

plate-glass *adj* de vidro laminado.

platelet ['pleɪtlɪt] *n* plaqueta *f*.

plate rack *n* escorredor *m* de pratos.

platform ['plætfɔ:m] *n* **-1.** [gen] plataforma *f* **-2.** [for speaker, performer] palanque *m* **-3.** *fig* [arena] veículo *m*.

platform game *n COMPUT* jogo *m* de obstáculos.

platform ticket *n UK* bilhete *m* de plataforma.

platinum ['plætɪnəm] <> *adj* platinado(da). <> *n* platina *f*. <> *comp* de platina.

platinum blonde *n* loira *f* platinada.

platitude ['plætɪtju:d] *n* lugar-comum *m*, chavão *m*.

platonic [plə'tɒnɪk] *adj* platônico(ca).

platoon [plə'tu:n] *n* pelotão *m*.

platter ['plætəʳ] *n* travessa *f*.

platypus ['plætɪpəs] (*pl* **-es**) *n* ornitorrinco *m*.

plaudits ['plɔ:dɪts] *npl* aclamações *fpl*, aplausos *mpl*.

plausible ['plɔ:zəbl] *adj* [reason, excuse] plausível; [person] convincente.

plausibly ['plɔ:zəblɪ] *adv* plausivelmente, convincentemente.

play [pleɪ] <> *n* **-1.** *(U)* [amusement] brincadeira *f*; **children at ~** crianças brincando **-2.** [piece of drama] peça *f* **-3.** *SPORT*: **in/out of ~** em/fora de jogo **-4.** [consideration]: **to come into ~** *fig* entrar em jogo **-5.** [pun]: **~ on words** trocadilho **-6.** *TECH* folga *f*. <> *vt* **-1.** [gen] jogar; **to ~ hide-and-seek** brincar de esconde-esconde **-2.** [opposing player or team] jogar contra **-3.** [joke, trick] pregar **-4.** [perform] desempenhar, representar; **to ~ a part** *OR* **role in sthg** *fig* desempenhar um papel em algo **-5.** [*MUS* - instrument, CD] tocar; [- tune] executar **-6.** [pretend to be] fingir **-7.** *phr*: **to ~ it cool** agir com calma. <> *vi* **-1.** [amuse o.s.] brincar; **to ~ with sb/sthg** brincar com alguém/algo **-2.** *SPORT* jogar; **to ~ for sb** jogar para alguém; **to ~ against sb** jogar contra alguém **-3.** *PERFORM*: **to ~ in sthg** atuar em algo **-4.** [music] tocar **-5.** *literary* [breeze, sun, light] brincar com **-6.** *phr*: **to ~ safe** não se arriscar.

◆ **play along** *vi*: **to ~ along (with sb)** fazer o jogo (de alguém).

◆ **play at** *vt fus* fazer de conta que.

◆ **play back** *vt sep* colocar de novo.

◆ **play down** *vt sep* menosprezar.
◆ **play off** ◇ *vt sep*: **to ~ sb/sthg off against sb/sthg** colocar alguém/algo contra alguém/algo. ◇ *vi SPORT* enfrentar-se novamente *(para obter um desempate)*.
◆ **play (up)on** *vt fus* tirar proveito de.
◆ **play up** ◇ *vt sep* enfatizar. ◇ *vi* **-1.** [cause problems] dar trabalho **-2.** [misbehave] descomportar-se.
playable ['pleɪəbl] *adj* em condições de jogo.
play-act *vi* fazer fita.
playbill ['pleɪbɪl] *n* cartaz *m* de lançamento.
playboy ['pleɪbɔɪ] *n* playboy *m*.
play dough *n US* = **Plasticine®**.
player ['pleɪəʳ] *n* **-1.** [of game, sport] jogador *m*, -ra *f* **-2.** *MUS* músico *m*, -ca *f*; **guitar ~** guitarrista *mf*; **saxophone ~** saxofonista *mf* **-3.** *dated* & *THEATRE* ator *m*, atriz *f*.
playfellow ['pleɪˌfeləʊ] *n* amigo *m*, -ga *f* de infância.
playful ['pleɪfʊl] *adj* **-1.** [good-natured] divertido(da) **-2.** [frisky] brincalhão(lhona).
playfully ['pleɪfʊlɪ] *adv* divertidamente.
playgoer ['pleɪˌgəʊəʳ] *n* freqüentrador *m*, -ra *f* de teatro.
playground ['pleɪgraʊnd] *n* [at school] pátio *m* de recreio; [in park] parque *m* de diversões.
playgroup ['pleɪgruːp] *n* jardim-de-infância *m*.
playhouse ['pleɪhaʊs, *pl* -haʊzɪz] *n* **-1.** [toy house] casa *f* de brinquedo **-2.** *dated* [theatre] teatro *m*.
playing card ['pleɪɪŋ-] *n* carta *f* de baralho.
playing field ['pleɪɪŋ-] *n* quadra *f* de esportes.
playlist ['pleɪlɪst] *n UK* lista *f* de músicas *(para tocar num programa de rádio)*.
playmate ['pleɪmeɪt] *n* amigo *m*, -ga *f* de infância.
play-off *n* partida *f* de desempate.
playpen ['pleɪpen] *n* cercadinho *m* para crianças, chiqueirinho *m*.
playroom ['pleɪrʊm] *n* sala *f* de recreação.
playschool ['pleɪskuːl] *n* jardim-de-infância *m*.
plaything ['pleɪθɪŋ] *n* **-1.** [toy] brinquedo *m* **-2.** *fig* [person] joguete *m*.
playtime ['pleɪtaɪm] *n (U)* (hora *f* do) recreio *m*.
playwright ['pleɪraɪt] *n* dramaturgo *m*, -ga *f*.
plaza ['plɑːzə] *n* **-1.** [public square] praça *f* **-2.** [building complex] complexo *m*.
plc (*abbr of* **public limited company**) *UK* companhia *f* pública limitada.
plea [pliː] *n* **-1.** [appeal] apelo *m* **-2.** *JUR* contestação *f*.
plea bargaining *n (U) acordo segundo o qual o réu se declara culpado por uma acusação menor e o promotor público, em troca, o inocenta de uma acusação mais grave.*
plead [pliːd] (*pt* & *pp* **-ed** *OR* **pled**) ◇ *vt* **-1.** *JUR* defender; **to ~ insanity** alegar insanidade mental; **to ~ guilty** declarar culpado(da) **-2.** [give as excuse] alegar. ◇ *vi* **-1.** [beg] implorar; **to ~ with sb to do sthg** implorar a alguém que faça algo; **to ~ for sthg** implorar algo **-2.** *JUR* responder a uma acusação.
pleading ['pliːdɪŋ] ◇ *adj* de súplica. ◇ *n* súplica *f*.
pleasant ['pleznt] *adj* agradável.
pleasantly ['plezntlɪ] *adv* agradavelmente.
pleasantry ['plezntrɪ] (*pl* **-ies**) *n*: **to exchange pleasantries** trocar amabilidades.
please [pliːz] ◇ *adv* por favor. ◇ *vt* agradar; **to ~ o.s.** fazer o que se deseja; **~ yourself!** como queira! ◇ *vi* **-1.** [give satisfaction] agradar **-2.** [choose]: **to do as one ~s** fazer como quiser; **if you ~** se quiser.
pleased [pliːzd] *adj* contente, feliz; **to be ~ about sthg** estar satisfeito(ta) com algo; **to be ~ with sb/sthg** estar satisfeito(ta) com alguém/algo; **~ to meet you!** prazer em conhecê-lo(-la)!
pleasing ['pliːzɪŋ] *adj* agradável.
pleasingly ['pliːzɪŋlɪ] *adv* agradavelmente.
pleasurable ['pleʒərəbl] *adj* agradável.
pleasure ['pleʒəʳ] *n* **-1.** *(U)* [feeling of happiness] alegria *f*; **with ~** com (muito) prazer **-2.** [enjoyment] prazer *m*; **it's a ~** *OR* **my ~!** é um prazer!, não tem de quê!
pleat [pliːt] ◇ *n* prega *f*. ◇ *vt* fazer prega em.
pleated ['pliːtɪd] *adj* pregueado(da).
plebeian [plə'biːən] *adj pej* plebeu(béia).
plebiscite ['plebɪsaɪt] *n* plebiscito *m*.
plectrum ['plektrəm] (*pl* **-s**) *n* palheta *f*.
pled [pled] *pt* & *pp* ▷ **plead**.
pledge [pledʒ] ◇ *n* **-1.** [promise] promessa *f* **-2.** [token] símbolo *m* **-3.** [as a security] garantia *f*. ◇ *vt* **-1.** [promise to provide] prometer **-2.** [commit]: **to be ~d to sthg** estar comprometido(da) com algo; **to ~ o.s. to sthg** comprometer-se com algo **-3.** [pawn] penhorar.
plenary session ['pliːnərɪ-] *n* sessão *f* plenária.
plentiful ['plentɪfʊl] *adj* abundante.
plenty ['plentɪ] ◇ *n (U)* fartura *f*. ◇ *pron* bastante; **~ of** bastante; **~ of time** bastante tempo; **~ of reasons** inúmeras razões. ◇ *adv US* [very] muito.
plethora ['pleθərə] *n* excesso *m*.
pleurisy ['plʊərəsɪ] *n (U)* pleurisia *f*.
Plexiglas® ['pleksɪglɑːs] *n (U) US* Plexiglas® *m*.
pliable ['plaɪəbl], **pliant** ['plaɪənt] *adj* **-1.** [supple] flexível **-2.** [adaptable] dócil.
pliers ['plaɪəz] *npl* alicate *m*.
plight [plaɪt] *n* péssima situação *f*; **in a ~** em apuros.
plimsoll ['plɪmsəl] *n UK* calçados *mpl* para prática de esportes.
Plimsoll line *n* linha *f* de flutuação.
plinth [plɪnθ] *n* plinto *m*.
PLO (*abbr of* **Palestine Liberation Organization**) *n* OLP *f*.
plod [plɒd] (*pt* & *pp* **-ded**, *cont* **-ding**) *vi* **-1.** [walk slowly] arrastar-se **-2.** [work slowly] trabalhar vagarosamente.
plodder ['plɒdəʳ] *n pej* trabalhador *m* lerdo e pouco criativo.
plonk [plɒŋk] *n UK inf* vinho *m* fajuto.
◆ **plonk down** *vt sep inf* deixar cair.
plop [plɒp] (*pt* & *pp* **-ped**, *cont* **-ping**) ◇ *n* chape *m*. ◇ *vi* estatelar-se.
plot [plɒt] (*pt* & *pp* **-ted**, *cont* **-ting**) ◇ *n* **-1.** [conspiracy] compô *m*; **the ~ thickens** a coisa está se complicando **-2.** [story] enredo *m*, trama *f* **-3.** [of

land] lote *m* **-4.** ***US*** [house plan] planta *f.* <> *vt* **-1.** [conspire] tramar; **to ~ to do sthg** tramar para fazer algo **-2.** [chart] traçar **-3.** *MATH* traçar, plotar. <> *vi* conspirar; **to ~ against sb** conspirar contra alguém.

plotter ['plɒtəʳ] *n* [schemer] conspirador *m*, -ra *f.*

plough *UK*, **plow** *US* [plaʊ] <> *n* arado *m.* <> *vt* **-1.** *AGR* arar, lavrar **-2.** [invest]: **to ~ money into sthg** investir muito dinheiro em algo. <> *vi*: **to ~ into sthg** colidir contra algo.

◆ **plough on** *vi* prosseguir.

◆ **plough up** *vt sep* arar.

ploughman's ['plaʊmənz] (*pl inv*) *n UK*: **~ (lunch)** *refeição que consiste em pão, queijo, cebola e picles.*

ploughshare *UK*, **plowshare** *US* ['plaʊʃeəʳ] *n* relha *f* de arado.

plow etc *n* & *vt US* = **plough etc.**

ploy [plɔɪ] *n* estratagema *f.*

PLR (*abbr of* **Public Lending Right**) *n valor que o autor recebe na Grã-Bretanha quando um livro seu é retirado nas bibliotecas públicas.*

pls (*abbr of* **please**) por favor.

pluck [plʌk] <> *vt* **-1.** [flower, fruit] colher **-2.** [pull] apanhar; **the helicopter ~ed the survivors off the ship** o helicóptero resgatou os sobreviventes do navio **-3.** [chicken] depenar **-4.** [eyebrows] depilar **-5.** [musical instrument] dedilhar. <> *n (U) dated* [courage] garra *f.*

◆ **pluck up** *vt fus*: **to ~ up the courage to do sthg** criar coragem para fazer algo.

plucky ['plʌkɪ] (*compar* **-ier**, *superl* **-iest**) *adj dated* valente.

plug [plʌg] (*pt* & *pp* **-ged**, *cont* **-ging**) <> *n* **-1.** *ELEC* tomada *f*; [socket] plugue *m* **-2.** [for bath or sink] tampa *f*, válvula *f* **-3.** ***inf*** [in advertising] lance *m* de marketing. <> *vt* **-1.** [block] tampar **-2.** ***inf*** [advertise] fazer propaganda de.

◆ **plug in** *vt sep* ligar.

plughole ['plʌghəʊl] *n* ralo *m.*

plum [plʌm] <> *adj* **-1.** [colour] da cor de ameixa **-2.** [choice]: **a ~ job** uma jóia de emprego. <> *n* **-1.** [fruit] ameixa *m* **-2.** [colour] cor *m* de ameixa.

plumage ['plu:mɪdʒ] *n (U)* plumagem *f.*

plumb [plʌm] <> *adv* **-1.** ***UK*** [exactly] exatamente **-2.** ***US*** [completely] totalmente. <> *vt*: **to ~ the depths of sthg** atingir o auge de algo.

◆ **plumb in** *vt sep* ***UK*** instalar.

plumber ['plʌməʳ] *n* encanador *m*, -ra *f.*

plumbing ['plʌmɪŋ] *n (U)* **-1.** [fittings] encanamento *m* **-2.** [work] trabalho *m* do encanador.

plumb line *n* prumo *m.*

plume [plu:m] *n* **-1.** [on bird] pluma *f* **-2.** [on hat, helmet] penacho *m* **-3.** [column]: **a ~ of smoke** um penacho de fumaça.

plummet ['plʌmɪt] *vi* **-1.** [dive] mergulhar *(em direção ao solo)* **-2.** [decrease rapidly] despencar.

plummy ['plʌmɪ] (*compar* **-ier**, *superl* **-iest**) *adj UK inf pej* afetado(da).

plump [plʌmp] <> *adj* roliço(ça). <> *vi*: **to ~ for sthg** optar por algo.

◆ **plump up** *vt sep* afofar.

plum pudding *n* pudim *m* de passas.

plum tree *n* ameixeira *f.*

plunder ['plʌndəʳ] <> *n* **-1.** [pillaging] pilhagem *f* **-2.** [booty] saque *m.* <> *vt* saquear.

plunge [plʌndʒ] <> *n* **-1.** [rapid decrease] caída *f* **-2.** [dive] mergulho; **to take the ~** mergulhar de cabeça, dar um passo decisivo. <> *vt* **-1.** [immerse]: **to ~ sthg into sthg** mergulhar algo em algo **-2.** *fig* [thrust]: **to ~ sthg into sthg** enfiar algo em algo; **the room was ~d into darkness** a sala mergulhou na escuridão. <> *vi* **-1.** [dive, throw o.s.] mergulhar **-2.** [decrease rapidly] despencar.

plunger ['plʌndʒəʳ] *n* desentupidor *m.*

plunging ['plʌndʒɪŋ] *adj* profundo(da).

pluperfect [ˌplu:'pɜ:fɪkt] *n*: **the ~ (tense)** o (tempo) mais-que-perfeito.

plural ['plʊərəl] <> *adj* plural. <> *n* plural *m.*

pluralistic [ˌplʊərə'lɪstɪk] *adj* pluralista.

plurality [plʊ'rælətɪ] *n* **-1.** [large number]: **a ~ of** uma pluralidade de **-2.** ***US*** [majority] maioria *f.*

plus [plʌs] (*pl* **-es** *OR* **-ses**) <> *adj* mais; **thirty-five ~** trinta e cinco ou mais. <> *n* **-1.** *MATH* sinal *m* de adição, sinal *m* de mais **-2.** ***inf*** [bonus] vantagem *f.* <> *prep* mais. <> *conj* [moreover] além disso.

plus fours *npl* calças *fpl* de golfe/de caça.

plush [plʌʃ] *adj* suntuoso(sa).

plus sign *n* sinal *m* de mais.

Pluto ['plu:təʊ] *n* Plutão.

plutonium [plu:'təʊnɪəm] *n (U)* plutônio *m.*

ply [plaɪ] (*pt* & *pp* **plied**) <> *n* espessura. <> *vt* **-1.** [work at] trabalhar em **-2.** [supply, provide]: **to ~ sb with sthg** prover alguém com algo **-3.** [travel] navegar em. <> *vi* [travel] navegar em.

-ply *adj* de espessura.

plywood ['plaɪwʊd] *n (U)* compensado *m.*

p.m., pm (*abbr of* **post meridiem**): **at three ~** às três da tarde.

PM (*abbr of* **prime minister**) *n* primeiro-ministro *m*, primeira-ministra *f.*

PMS (*abbr of* **premenstrual syndrome**) *n* SPM *f.*

PMT (*abbr of* **premenstrual tension**) *n* TPM *f.*

pneumatic [nju:'mætɪk] *adj* **-1.** [air-powered] pneumático(ca) **-2.** [air-filled] de ar.

pneumatic drill *n* perfuratriz *f.*

pneumonia [nju:'məʊnjə] *n (U)* pneumonia *f.*

Po *n*: **the (River) ~** o (Rio) Pó.

PO *n* **-1.** (*abbr of* **Post Office**) correio *m* **-2.** (*abbr of* **postal order**) vale *m* postal.

poach [pəʊtʃ] <> *vt* **-1.** [hunt illegally] caçar ilegalmente **-2.** [copy] plagiar **-3.** [*CULIN* - salmon] escaldar; [- egg] escalfar. <> *vi* caçar ilegalmente.

poacher ['pəʊtʃəʳ] *n* **-1.** [person] caçador *m* furtivo, caçadora *f* furtiva **-2.** *CULIN* panela *f* para cozinhar ovos.

poaching ['pəʊtʃɪŋ] *n (U)* caça *f* ilegal.

PO Box (*abbr of* **Post Office Box**) *n* caixa *f* postal.

pocket ['pɒkɪt] <> *n* **-1.** [in clothes] bolso *m*; **to live in each other's ~s** estar sempre juntos(tas); **the deal left us £10 out of ~** o negócio nos deu um prejuízo de £10; **to pick sb's ~** roubar do bolso de alguém **-2.** [in car door etc] porta-mapas *m* **-3.** [small area] foco *m* **-4.** [of snooker, pool table] caçapa *f.* <> *adj* [pocket-sized] de bolso. <> *vt* **-1.** [place in pocket]

pôr no bolso **-2.** [steal] embolsar **-3.** [in snooker, pool] encaçapar.
pocketbook ['pɒkɪtbʊk] *n* **-1.** [notebook] livro *m* de bolso **-2.** *US* [handbag] carteira *f*.
pocketbook computer *n* computador *m* de bolso.
pocket calculator *n* calculadora *f* de bolso.
pocketful ['pɒkɪtfʊl] *n* bolso *m* cheio.
pocket-handkerchief *n* lenço *m* de bolso.
pocketknife ['pɒkɪtnaɪf] (*pl* **-knives** [-naɪvz]) *n* canivete *m*.
pocket money *n (U)* mesada *m*.
pocket-size(d) *adj* de bolso.
pockmark ['pɒkmɑ:k] *n* sinal *m* de varíola.
pod [pɒd] *n* **-1.** [of plants] vagem *f* **-2.** [of spacecraft] módulo *m*.
podgy ['pɒdʒɪ] (*compar* **-ier**, *superl* **-iest**) *adj inf* atarracado(da).
podiatrist [pə'daɪətrɪst] *n US* podiatra *mf*.
podium ['pəʊdɪəm] (*pl* **-diums** *OR* **-dia** [-dɪə]) *n* pódio *m*.
poem ['pəʊɪm] *n* poema *f*.
poet ['pəʊɪt] *n* poeta *mf*, poetisa *f*.
poetic [pəʊ'etɪk] *adj* poético(ca).
poetic justice *n (U)* justiça *f* poética.
poet laureate *n* poeta *mf* laureado, poetisa *f* laureada.
poetry ['pəʊɪtrɪ] *n (U)* **-1.** [poems] poesia *f* **-2.** *fig* [beauty] beleza *f*.
pogo stick *n* pula-pula *m*.
pogrom ['pɒgrəm] *n* massacre *m* organizado *(de um grupo étnico em particular)*.
poignancy ['pɔɪnjənsɪ] *n (U)* comoção *f*.
poignant ['pɔɪnjənt] *adj* comovente.
poinsettia [pɔɪn'setɪə] *n* poinsétia *f*.
point [pɔɪnt] <> *n* **-1.** [gen] ponto *m*; **at this ~ in time** neste momento; **~ of no return** ponto sem volta; **to have a ~** ter razão; **to make a ~** fazer uma observação; **to make one's ~** dar sua opinião; **a sore ~** questão dolorosa **-2.** [tip] ponta *f* **-3.** [essence, heart] parte *f* essencial; **to get** *OR* **come to the ~** ir ao ponto principal; **beside the ~** irrelevante; **to the ~** objetivo(va) **-4.** [feature, characteristic] característica *f* **-5.** [purpose] propósito *m*, razão *f* **-6.** [of compass] ponto *m* cardeal **-7.** *UK ELEC* ponto *m* **-8.** *US* [full stop] ponto *m* final **-9.** *phr*: **to make a ~ of doing sthg** fazer questão de fazer algo. <> *vt*: **to ~ sthg (at sb/sthg)** apontar algo (para alguém/algo); **to ~ the way (to sthg)** mostrar a direção (para algo). <> *vi* apontar; **to ~ at sb/sthg, to ~ to sb/sthg** apontar para alguém/algo.
◆ **points** *npl UK RAIL* pontos *mpl*.
◆ **up to a point** *adv* até certo ponto.
◆ **on the point of** *prep* prestes a.
◆ **point out** *vt sep* **-1.** [indicate] indicar **-2.** [call attention to] salientar.
point-blank <> *adj* **-1.** [direct] categórico(ca) **-2.** [close-range] à queima-roupa. <> *adv* **-1.** [directly] categoricamente **-2.** [at close range] à queima-roupa.
point duty *n (U) UK* serviço *m* de controle de trânsito.
pointed ['pɔɪntɪd] *adj* **-1.** [sharp] pontiagudo(da) **-2.** [meaningful] sugestivo(va).
pointedly ['pɔɪntɪdlɪ] *adv* sugestivamente.
pointer ['pɔɪntə^r] *n* **-1.** [tip, hint] dica *f* **-2.** [needle on dial] agulha *f* **-3.** [stick] indicador *m* **-4.** [dog] pointer *m* **-5.** *COMPUT* ponteiro *m*.
pointing ['pɔɪntɪŋ] *n (U)* rejuntamento *m*.
pointless ['pɔɪntlɪs] *adj* inútil.
point of order (*pl* **points of order**) *n* questão *f* de ordem.
point of sale (*pl* **points of sale**) *n COMM* ponto *m* de venda.
point of view (*pl* **points of view**) *n* ponto *m* de vista.
point-to-point *n UK corrida de cavalos que atravessa uma região, sinalizada com bandeirinhas*.
poise [pɔɪz] *n (U)* compostura *f*.
poised [pɔɪzd] *adj* **-1.** [ready] pronto(ta), preparado(da);**to be ~ to do sthg** estar pronto(ta) para fazer algo; **to be ~ for sthg** estar pronto(ta) para algo **-2.** [calm and dignified] equilibrado(da).
poison ['pɔɪzn] <> *n* veneno *m*. <> *vt* **-1.** [gen] envenenar **-2.** [pollute] poluir **-3.** *fig* [spoil, corrupt] corromper.
poisoning ['pɔɪznɪŋ] *n (U)* envenenamento *m*, intoxicação *f*.
poisonous ['pɔɪznəs] *adj* **-1.** [gas, chemical] tóxico (ca) **-2.** [snake, mushroom, plant] venenoso(sa) **-3.** *fig* [corrupting] pernicioso(sa).
poison-pen letter *n* carta *f* anônima.
poke [pəʊk] <> *n* remexida *f*. <> *vt* **-1.** [prod, jab] remexer, cutucar **-2.** [stick, thrust] enfiar em **-3.** [fire] atiçar, remexer. <> *vi* projetar-se; **his head ~d round the corner** a cabeça dele apareceu na esquina.
◆ **poke about, poke around** *vi inf* escarafunchar.
◆ **poke at** *vt fus*: **he ~d at my eye with his finger** ele cutucou meu olho com seu dedo.
poker ['pəʊkə^r] *n* **-1.** [game] pôquer *m* **-2.** [for fire] atiçador *m*.
poker-faced [-ˌfeɪst] *adj* de rosto inexpressivo.
poky ['pəʊkɪ] (*compar* **-ier**, *superl* **-iest**) *adj pej* apertado(da).
Poland ['pəʊlənd] *n* Polônia; **in ~** na Polônia.
polar ['pəʊlə^r] *adj GEOGR* polar.
polar bear *n* urso *m* polar.
polarity [pəʊ'lærətɪ] *n* polaridade *f*.
polarization [ˌpəʊlərаɪ'zeɪʃn] *n (U)* polarização *f*.
polarize, -ise ['pəʊləraɪz] *vt* polarizar.
Polaroid® ['pəʊlərɔɪd] *n* polaróide® *f*.
Polaroids® ['pəʊlərɔɪdz] *npl* [sunglasses] óculos *mpl* de sol (Polaroid).
pole [pəʊl] *n* **-1.** [gen] pólo *m*; **to be ~s apart** ser totalmente diferente(s) **-2.** [rod, post] poste *m*.
Pole [pəʊl] *n* polonês *m*, -esa *f*.
poleaxe ['pəʊlæks] *vt* nocautear.
poleaxed ['pəʊlækst] *adj* atordoado(da).
polecat ['pəʊlkæt] *n* [in Europe and Asia] furão-bravo *m*.
polemic [pə'lemɪk] *n fml* polêmica *f*.
pole position *n SPORT (U)* pole position *f*.

Pole Star *n*: the ~ a Estrela Polar.
pole vault *n*: the ~ o salto com vara.
◆ **pole-vault** *vi* saltar com vara.
pole-vaulter [-ˌvɔːltəʳ] *n* saltador(ra) com vara.
police [pəˈliːs] ◇ *npl* **-1.** [police force]: **the** ~ a polícia **-2.** [policemen, policewomen] policial *mf*. ◇ *vt* policiar.
police car *n* rádio-patrulha *f*.
police constable *n UK* policial *mf*.
police department *n US* departamento *m* de polícia, polícia *f*.
police dog *n* cão *m* policial.
police force *n* força *f* policial.
policeman [pəˈliːsmən] (*pl* **-men** [-mən]) *n* policial *m*.
police officer *n* oficial *mf* de polícia.
police record *n* ficha *f* policial; **to have a** ~ ter ficha na polícia.
police state *n* estado *m* policial.
police station *n UK* delegacia *f*.
policewoman [pəˈliːsˌwʊmən] (*pl* **-women** [-ˌwɪmɪn]) *n* policial *f*.
policy [ˈpɒləsɪ] (*pl* **-ies**) *n* **-1.** [plan, practice] política *f* **-2.** [document, agreement] apólice *f*.
policy-holder *n* segurado *m*, -da *f*.
polio [ˈpəʊlɪəʊ] *n (U)* poliomelite *f*, paralisia *f* infantil.
polish [ˈpɒlɪʃ] ◇ *n* **-1.** [cleaning material] polidor *m* **-2.** [shine] polimento *m* **-3.** *fig* [refinement] requinte *m*. ◇ *vt* **-1.** polir **-2.** *fig* [perfect]: **to ~ sthg (up)** refinar algo.
◆ **polish off** *vt sep inf* **-1.** [meal] comer/beber rapidamente **-2.** [job, book] dar um fim rápido em.
Polish [ˈpəʊlɪʃ] ◇ *adj* polonês(esa). ◇ *n* [language] polonês *m*. ◇ *npl*: **the** ~ os poloneses.
polished [ˈpɒlɪʃt] *adj* **-1.** [gen] polido(da) **-2.** [performer, performance] elegante.
polite [pəˈlaɪt] *adj* **-1.** [person, remark] educado(da), cortês(tesa) **-2.** [society] polido(da).
politely [pəˈlaɪtlɪ] *adv* educadamente.
politeness [pəˈlaɪtnɪs] *n (U)* educação *f*, cortesia *f*.
politic [ˈpɒlətɪk] *adj fml* prudente.
political [pəˈlɪtɪkl] *adj* político(ca).
political asylum *n (U)* asilo *m* político.
political football *n* debate *m* político acirrado.
political geography *n (U)* geografia *f* política.
politically [pəˈlɪtɪklɪ] *adv* politicamente.
politically correct [pəˌlɪtɪklɪ-] *adj* politicamente correto(ta).
political prisoner *n* prisioneiro *m* político, prisioneira *f* política.
political science *n (U)* ciência *f* política.
politician [ˌpɒlɪˈtɪʃn] *n* político *m*, -ca *f*.
politicize, -ise [pəˈlɪtɪsaɪz] *vt* politizar.
politics [ˈpɒlətɪks] ◇ *n* política *f*. ◇ *npl* [of a person, group] política *f*.
polka [ˈpɒlkə] *n* polca *f*; **to do the** ~ dançar a polca.
polka dot *n* bolinhas *fpl (em um padrão de tecido).*
poll [pəʊl] ◇ *n* **-1.** [election] eleição *f* **-2.** [survey] pesquisa *f*. ◇ *vt* **-1.** [people] entrevistar **-2.** [votes] receber, obter.
◆ **polls** *npl*: **to go to the ~s** ir às urnas.
pollen [ˈpɒlən] *n (U)* pólen *m*.
pollen count *n* contagem *f* de pólen.
pollinate [ˈpɒləneɪt] *vt* polinizar.
pollination [ˌpɒlɪˈneɪʃn] *n (U)* polinização *f*.
polling [ˈpəʊlɪŋ] *n (U)* votação *f*.
polling booth [ˈpəʊlɪŋ-] *n* cabine *f* de votação.
polling day [ˈpəʊlɪŋ-] *n UK* dia *f* de eleição.
polling station [ˈpəʊlɪŋ-] *n* zona *f* eleitoral.
pollster [ˈpəʊlstəʳ] *n* especialista *mf* em sondagem pública.
poll tax *n* imposto *m* per capita.
◆ **Poll Tax** *n UK imposto sobre votantes na Grã-Bretanha.*
pollutant [pəˈluːtnt] *n* poluente *m*.
pollute [pəˈluːt] *vt* poluir.
pollution [pəˈluːʃn] *n* poluição *f*.
polo [ˈpəʊləʊ] *n (U)* pólo *m*.
polo neck *n UK* **-1.** [collar] gola *f* alta **-2.** [jumper] blusão *m* de gola alta.
◆ **polo-neck** *adj UK* de gola alta.
polo shirt *n* camisa *f* pólo.
poltergeist [ˈpɒltəgaɪst] *n fantasma que move objetos e faz barulhos.*
polyanthus [ˌpɒlɪˈænθəs] (*pl* **-thuses** *OR* **-thi** [-θaɪ]) *n* primavera-dos-jardins *f*.
poly bag *n UK inf* saco *m* plástico.
polyester [ˌpɒlɪˈestəʳ] *n (U)* poliéster *m*.
polyethylene *n US* = **polythene**.
polygamist [pəˈlɪgəmɪst] *n* polígamo *m*, -ma *f*.
polygamy [pəˈlɪgəmɪ] *n (U)* poligamia *f*.
polygon [ˈpɒlɪgɒn] *n* polígono *m*.
polymer [ˈpɒlɪməʳ] *n* polímero *m*.
Polynesia [ˌpɒlɪˈniːʒəl] *n* Polinésia; **in** ~ na Polinésia; **French** ~ Polinésia Francesa.
Polynesian [ˌpɒlɪˈniːʒən] ◇ *adj* polinésio(sia). ◇ *n* **-1.** [person] polinésio *m*, -sia *f* **-2.** [language] polinésio *m*.
polyp [ˈpɒlɪp] *n* pólipo *m*.
polystyrene [ˌpɒlɪˈstaɪriːn] *n (U)* poliestireno *m*, isopor *m*.
polytechnic [ˌpɒlɪˈteknɪk] *n UK* politécnica *f*.
polythene *UK* [ˈpɒlɪθiːn], **polyethylene** *US* [ˈpɒlɪˈeθɪliːn] *n (U)* polietileno *m*.
polythene bag *n UK* saco *m* de polietileno.
polyunsaturated [ˌpɒlɪʌnˈsætʃəreɪtɪd] *adj* poliinsaturado(da).
polyurethane [ˌpɒlɪˈjʊərəθeɪn] *n (U)* poliuretano *m*.
pom [pɒm] *n Austr pej* inglês(esa).
pomander [pəˈmændəʳ] *n* sachê *m* (aromático).
pomegranate [ˈpɒmɪˌgrænɪt] *n* romã *f*.
pommel [ˈpɒml] *n* **-1.** [on saddle] maçaneta *f* **-2.** [on sword] botão *m*.
pomp [pɒmp] *n (U)* pompa *f*.
pompom [ˈpɒmpɒm] *n* pompom *m*.
pompous [ˈpɒmpəs] *adj* [pretentious - speech, style] pomposo(sa); [- person] pretensioso(sa).
ponce [pɒns] *n UK v inf pej* **-1.** [effeminate man] marica *m* **-2.** [pimp] gigolô *m*.

poncho ['pɒntʃəʊ] (*pl* -s) *n* poncho *m*.
pond [pɒnd] *n* lago *m (natural ou artificial)*; **the ~** *inf* o Atlântico.
ponder ['pɒndəʳ] <> *vt* ponderar. <> *vi* ponderar; **to ~ on** OR **over sthg** meditar sobre algo.
ponderous ['pɒndərəs] *adj* **-1.** [dull, solemn] ponderoso(sa) **-2.** [large and heavy] pesado(da) **-3.** [slow, clumsy] enfadonho(nha).
pong [pɒŋ] *UK inf* <> *n* fedor *m*. <> *vi* feder.
pontiff ['pɒntɪf] *n* pontífice *m*.
pontificate [pɒn'tɪfɪkeɪt] *vi pej* pontificar; **to ~ about** OR **on sthg** pontificar sobre algo.
pontoon [pɒn'tu:n] *n* **-1.** [bridge] barcaça *f* **-2.** *UK* [game] vinte-e-um *m*.
pony ['pəʊnɪ] (*pl* -ies) *n* pônei *m*.
ponytail ['pəʊnɪteɪl] *n* rabo-de-cavalo *m*.
pony-trekking [-ˌtrekɪŋ] *n (U)* excursão *f* em pôneis.
poodle ['pu:dl] *n* poodle *m*.
poof [pʊf] *n UK v inf offensive* veado *m*.
pooh-pooh *vt inf* fazer pouco caso de, desdenhar.
pool [pu:l] <> *n* **-1.** [natural] lago *m* **-2.** [swimming pool] piscina *f* **-3.** [of liquid, light] poça *f* **-4.** [of workers, cars, talent] grupo *m* **-5.** *(U)* SPORT bilhar *m*. <> *vt* juntar.
◆ **pools** *npl UK*: **the ~s** ≃ a loteria esportiva.
pooped [pu:pt] *adj inf* esgotado(da).
poor [pɔ:ʳ] <> *adj* pobre. <> *npl*: **the ~** os pobres.
poorhouse ['pɔ:haʊs, *pl* -haʊzɪz] *n* albergue *m (para pobres)*.
poorly ['pɔ:lɪ] <> *adj UK inf* [ill] mal. <> *adv* mal.
poor relation *n fig* primo *m* pobre.
pop [pɒp] (*pt* & *pp* **-ped**, *cont* **-ping**) <> *n* **-1.** *(U)* [music] pop *m* **-2.** *(U) inf* [fizzy drink] gasosa *f* **-3.** *esp US inf* [father] pai *m* **-4.** [noise] estouro *m*. <> *vt* **-1.** [burst] estourar **-2.** [put quickly] pôr rapidamente. <> *vi* **-1.** [burst] estourar **-2.** [spring, fly off] soltar-se **-3.** [eyes] arregalar **-4.** [go quickly] dar uma passada; **he ~ped from behind the sofa** ele apareceu de atrás do sofá.
◆ **pop in** *vi* entrar por um momento.
◆ **pop up** *vi* aparecer de repente.
popadum ['pɒpədəm] *n pão indiano frito em óleo*.
pop art *n (U)* arte *f* pop.
pop concert *n* concerto *m* pop.
popcorn ['pɒpkɔ:n] *n (U)* pipoca *f*.
pope [pəʊp] *n* papa *m*.
pop group *n* grupo *m* pop.
poplar ['pɒpləʳ] *n* choupo *m*.
poplin ['pɒplɪn] *n (U)* popeline *m*.
popper ['pɒpəʳ] *n UK* presilha *f*.
poppy ['pɒpɪ] (*pl* -ies) *n* papoula *f*.
poppycock ['pɒpɪkɒk] *n (U) inf* papo *m* furado.
Poppy Day *n UK* Dia *m* do Armistício.

POPPY DAY

O *Poppy Day* ou *Remembrance Day* é celebrado no segundo domingo de novembro. Nesse dia, os britânicos carregam uma amapola de papel na lapela, em memória de seus soldados mortos nas guerras mundiais.

Popsicle® ['pɒpsɪkl] *n US* picolé *m*.
pop singer *n* cantor *m*, -ra *f* pop.
populace ['pɒpjʊləs] *n*: **the ~** o populacho.
popular ['pɒpjʊləʳ] *adj* popular.
popularity [ˌpɒpjʊ'lærətɪ] *n (U)* popularidade *f*.
popularize, -ise ['pɒpjʊləraɪz] *vt* popularizar.
popularly ['pɒpjʊləlɪ] *adv* popularmente.
populate ['pɒpjʊleɪt] *vt* **-1.** [inhabit] povoar **-2.** [colonize] urbanizar.
populated ['pɒpjʊleɪtɪd] *adj* povoado(da).
population [ˌpɒpjʊ'leɪʃn] *n* população *f*.
population explosion *n* explosão *f* demográfica.
populist ['pɒpjʊlɪst] *n* populista *mf*.
pop-up *adj* **-1.** [toaster] com sistema de ejeção **-2.** [book] com ilustrações tridimensionais.
porcelain ['pɔ:səlɪn] *n (U)* porcelana *f*.
porch [pɔ:tʃ] *n* **-1.** [entrance] átrio *m* **-2.** *US* [veranda] alpendre *m*.
porcupine ['pɔ:kjʊpaɪn] *n* porco-espinho *m*.
pore [pɔ:ʳ] *n* poro *m*.
◆ **pore over** *vt fus* examinar minuciosamente.
pork [pɔ:k] *n (U)* carne *f* de porco.
pork chop *n* costeleta *f* de porco.
pork pie *n* pastelão *m* de porco.
porn [pɔ:n] *n (U) inf* pornô *m*; **hard ~** pornografia pesada; **soft ~** pornografia leve.
pornographic [ˌpɔ:nə'græfɪk] *adj* pornográfico (ca).
pornography [pɔ:'nɒgrəfɪ] *n (U)* pornografia *f*.
porous ['pɔ:rəs] *adj* poroso(sa).
porpoise ['pɔ:pəs] *n* porco-do-mar *m*.
porridge ['pɒrɪdʒ] *n (U)* mingau *m* com cereais.
port [pɔ:t] <> *n* **-1.** [gen] porto *m* **-2.** *(U)* NAUT bombordo *m*; **to ~** a bombordo **-3.** *(U)* [drink] vinho *m* do Porto **-4.** COMPUT porta *f*. <> *comp* **-1.** [relating to a harbour] porteiro(ra) **-2.** NAUT a bombordo.
portable ['pɔ:təbl] *adj* portável.
Portacrib® ['pɔ:təˌkrɪb] *n US* moisés *m*.
portal ['pɔ:tl] *n* **-1.** *literary* portada *f* **-2.** COMPUT portal *m*.
Port-au-Prince [ˌpɔ:təʊ'prɪns] *n* Porto-Príncipe.
portcullis [ˌpɔ:t'kʌlɪs] *n* portão *m* levadiço *(em um castelo)*.
portend [pɔ:'tend] *vt literary* prognosticar.
portent ['pɔ:tənt] *n literary* prognóstico *m*.
porter ['pɔ:təʳ] *n* **-1.** *UK* [doorman] porteiro *m*, -ra *f* **-2.** [for luggage] carregador *m*, -ra *f* **-3.** *US* [on train] cabineiro *m*, -ra *f*.
portfolio [ˌpɔ:t'fəʊljəʊ] (*pl* -s) *n* **-1.** [case] pasta *f* **-2.** [sample of work] portfólio *m* **-3.** FIN carteira *f*.
porthole ['pɔ:thəʊl] *n* vigia *mf*.
portion ['pɔ:ʃn] *n* **-1.** [part, share] porção *f* **-2.** [set amount of food] parte *f*.
portly ['pɔ:tlɪ] (*compar* **-ier**, *superl* **-iest**) *adj* corpulento(ta).
port of call *n* **-1.** NAUT porto *m* de escala **-2.** *fig* [on journey] ponto *m* de parada.
Port of Spain *n* Porto *m* de Espanha.
portrait ['pɔ:trɪt] *n* retrato *m*.

portraitist ['pɔ:trɪtɪst] *n* retratista *mf*.

portray [pɔ:'treɪ] *vt* **-1.** [in a play, film] interpretar **-2.** [describe, represent] descrever **-3.** [subj: artist] retratar.

portrayal [pɔ:'treɪəl] *n* **-1.** [in a play, film] interpretação *f* **-2.** [description, representation] descrição *f* **-3.** [painting, photograph] retrato *m*.

Portugal ['pɔ:tʃʊgl] *n* Portugal; **in ~** em Portugal.

Portuguese [,pɔ:tʃʊ'gi:z] (*pl inv*) ◇ *adj* português(guesa). ◇ *n* [language] português *m*. ◇ *npl*: **the ~** os portugueses.

POS (*abbr of* **point of sale**) *n UK* ponto *m* de venda.

pose [pəʊz] ◇ *n* **-1.** [position, stance] pose *f* **-2.** *pej* [pretence, affectation] pose *f*. ◇ *vt* **-1.** [problem, danger, threat] constituir **-2.** [question] fazer. ◇ *vi* **-1.** [model] posar **-2.** *pej* [behave affectedly] fazer-se **-3.** [pretend to be]: **to ~ as sb/sthg** fazer-se passar por alguém/algo.

poser ['pəʊzə^r] *n* **-1.** *pej* [person] fingido *m*, -da *f* **-2.** *inf* [hard question] quebra-cabeça *f*.

poseur [pəʊ'zɜ:^r] *n pej* fingido *m*, -da *f*.

posh [pɒʃ] *adj inf* **-1.** [hotel, clothes] chique **-2.** [upper-class] chique.

posit ['pɒzɪt] *vt fml* postular.

position [pə'zɪʃn] ◇ *n* **-1.** [gen] posição *f*; **in ~** em posição **-2.** [job] cargo *m* **-3.** [state, situation] posição *f*, situação *f*; **to be in a/no ~ to do sthg** estar/não estar em condições de fazer algo **-4.** [stance, opinion]: **~ on sthg** posição sobre algo. ◇ *vt* posicionar; **to ~ o.s.** posicionar-se.

positive ['pɒzətɪv] *adj* **-1.** [gen] positivo(va); **to be ~ about sthg** ser positivo(va) sobre algo; **be ~ about the exam!** seja otimista em relação à prova! **-2.** [irrefutable] irrefutável **-3.** [for emphasis]: **a ~ joy** uma ótima brincadeira; **a ~ nightmare** um pesadelo terrível.

positive discrimination *n (U)* discriminação *f* positiva.

positively ['pɒzətɪvlɪ] *adv* **-1.** [gen] positivamente **-2.** [irrefutably] irrefutavelmente **-3.** [for emphasis] definitivamente.

positive vetting *n (U) UK investigação completa a que é submetido um candidato a cargo público relacionado com a segurança nacional.*

posse ['pɒsɪ] *n* **-1.** [of sheriff] *US* destacamento *m* **-2.** *inf* [gang] bando *m* armado.

possess [pə'zes] *vt* **-1.** [gen] possuir **-2.** [subj: emotion] levar a.

possessed [pə'zest] *adj* possuído(da).

possession [pə'zeʃn] *n (U)* posse *f*; **to have sthg in one's ~, to be in ~ of sthg** estar em posse de algo.

◆ **possessions** *npl* posses *fpl*, bens *mpl*.

possessive [pə'zesɪv] ◇ *adj* **-1.** *pej* [clinging] possessivo(va) **-2.** GRAMM possessivo(va). ◇ *n* GRAMM possessivo *m*.

possessively [pə'zesɪvlɪ] *adv* possessivamente.

possessor [pə'zesə^r] *n fml* proprietário *m*, -ria *f*.

possibility [,pɒsə'bɪlətɪ] (*pl* **-ies**) *n* possibilidade *f*.

possible ['pɒsəbl] ◇ *adj* possível; **as soon as ~** o mais cedo possível; **as much as ~** o máximo possível. ◇ *n* possível *m*.

possibly ['pɒsəblɪ] *adv* **-1.** [perhaps, maybe] possivelmente **-2.** [conceivably]: **I'll do all I ~ can** vou fazer tudo que estiver ao meu alcance; **how could he ~ do that?** como ele foi capaz de fazer isso?; **I can't ~ take the money!** simplesmente não posso aceitar o dinheiro!

possum ['pɒsəm] (*pl inv* OR **-s**) *n US* gambá *m*.

post [pəʊst] ◇ *n* **-1.** [mail service]: **the ~** o correio; **by ~** pelo correio; **in the ~** no correio **-2.** *(U)* [letters etc] correio *m* **-3.** [delivery] mala *f* postal **-4.** *UK* [collection] coleta *f* **-5.** [pole] poste *m* **-6.** [position, job] posto *m* **-7.** MIL guarnição *f* **-8.** *phr*: **to pip sb at the ~** vencer alguém na última hora. ◇ *vt* **-1.** [by mail] postar, pôr no correio **-2.** [transfer] transferir **-3.** *phr*: **to keep sb ~ed** manter alguém informado(da).

post [pəʊst] *vt* COMPUT [message, query] enviar.

post- [pəʊst] *prefix* pós-.

postage ['pəʊstɪdʒ] *n (U)* franquia *f*; **~ and packing** despesas *fpl* de envio.

postage stamp *n fml* selo *m (postal)*.

postal ['pəʊstl] *adj* postal.

postal order *n* vale *m* postal.

postbag ['pəʊstbæg] *n* **-1.** *UK* [bag] sacola *f* de correio **-2.** *inf* [letters received] mala *f* de cartas.

postbox ['pəʊstbɒks] *n UK* caixa *f* de correio.

postcard ['pəʊstkɑ:d] *n* cartão *m* postal.

postcode ['pəʊstkəʊd] *n UK* código *m* (de endereçamento) postal.

post-date *vt* pós-datar.

poster ['pəʊstə^r] *n* cartaz *m*, pôster *m*.

poste restante [,pəʊst'restɑ:nt] *n (U) esp UK* posta-restante *f*.

posterior [pɒ'stɪərɪə^r] ◇ *adj* posterior. ◇ *n hum* traseiro *m*.

posterity [pɒ'sterətɪ] *n (U)* posteridade *f*.

poster paint *n* têmpera *f*.

post-free *adj esp UK* com porte pago.

postgraduate [,pəʊst'grædʒʊət] ◇ *adj* pós-graduado(da). ◇ *n* pós-graduado *m*, -da *f*.

post-haste *adv dated* de pronto.

posthumous ['pɒstjʊməs] *adj* póstumo(ma).

posthumously ['pɒstjʊməslɪ] *adv* postumamente.

post-industrial *adj* pós-industrial.

posting ['pəʊstɪŋ] *n* [assignment] nomeação *f*.

postman ['pəʊstmən] (*pl* **-men** [-mən]) *n* carteiro *m*.

postmark ['pəʊstmɑ:k] ◇ *n* carimbo *m (postal)*. ◇ *vt* carimbar.

postmaster ['pəʊst,mɑ:stə^r] *n* agente *m* de correio.

Postmaster General (*pl* **Postmasters General**) *n* diretor *m* geral dos correios.

postmistress ['pəʊst,mɪstrɪs] *n* agente *f* de correio.

postmortem [,pəʊst'mɔ:təm] ◇ *adj* post-mortem. ◇ *n* **-1.** [autopsy] autópsia *f* **-2.** *fig* [analysis] análise *f* detalhada.

postnatal [,pəʊst'neɪtl] *adj* pós-natal.

post office *n* **-1.** [organization]: **the Post Office** a Agência dos Correios **-2.** [building] correio *m*.

post office box *n* caixa *f* postal.

post-operative *adj* pós-operatório(ria).

post-paid *adj* com porte pago.
postpone [pəs'pəʊn] *vt* adiar.
postponement [ˌpəʊst'pəʊnmənt] *n* adiamento *m*.
postscript ['pəʊstskrɪpt] *n* **-1.** [to letter] pós-escrito *m* **-2.** *fig* [additional information] adendo *m*.
postulate [*n* 'pɒstjʊlət, *vb* 'pɒstjʊleɪt] *vt fml* postular.
posture ['pɒstʃəʳ] <> *n* postura *f*; ~ **on sthg** postura em relação a algo. <> *vi*: **he's always posturing** ele está sempre bancando pose.
posturing *n (U)* pose *f*, atitude *f*.
postviral syndrome [ˌpəʊst'vaɪrəl-] *n* síndrome *f* pós-virótica.
postwar [ˌpəʊst'wɔːʳ] *adj* pós-guerra.
posy ['pəʊzɪ] (*pl* **-ies**) *n* ramalhete *m*.
pot [pɒt] (*pt* & *pp* **-ted**, *cont* **-ting**) <> *n* **-1.** [for cooking] panela *f*; **to go to** ~ ir para o brejo; **the** ~ **calling the kettle black** rir-se o roto do esfarrapado **-2.** [for tea, coffee] bule *m* **-3.** [for paint, jam] frasco *m* **-4.** [flowerpot] vaso *m* **-5.** *(U) drugs sl* [cannabis] maconha *f*. <> *vt* **-1.** [plant] plantar *(em vaso)* **-2.** [billiards ball] encaçapar.
potash ['pɒtæʃ] *n (U)* potassa *f*.
potassium [pə'tæsɪəm] *n (U)* potássio *m*.
potato [pə'teɪtəʊ] (*pl* **-es**) *n* batata *f*.
potato crisps *UK*, **potato chips** *US npl* batatinhas *fpl* fritas.
potato peeler [-ˌpiːləʳ] *n* descascador *m* de batatas.
pot-bellied [-ˌbelɪd] *adj* barrigudo(da).
potboiler ['pɒtˌbɔɪləʳ] *n pej livro, quadro ou outro artigo de pouco valor artístico, produzido rapidamente com fins apenas comerciais.*
pot-bound *adj* sufocado(da) com muitas raízes.
potency ['pəʊtənsɪ] *n (U)* **-1.** [of argument] força *f* **-2.** [of drink, drug] teor *m* **-3.** [virility] potência *f*, virilidade *f*.
potent ['pəʊtənt] *adj* **-1.** [argument] forte **-2.** [drink, drug] de alto teor, poderoso(sa) **-3.** [virile] potente, viril.
potentate ['pəʊtənteɪt] *n* potentado *m*.
potential [pə'tenʃl] <> *adj* potencial, em potencial. <> *n* [of person] potencial *m*; **to have** ~ ter potencial.
potentially [pə'tenʃəlɪ] *adv* potencialmente.
pothole ['pɒthəʊl] *n* buraco *m*.
potholer ['pɒtˌhəʊləʳ] *n UK* espeleologista *mf*.
potholing ['pɒtˌhəʊlɪŋ] *n UK* espeleologia; **to go** ~ explorar cavernas.
potion ['pəʊʃn] *n* poção *f*.
potluck [ˌpɒt'lʌk] *n*: **to take** ~ [at meal] contentar-se com o que houver para comer; [in choice] arriscar *OR* tentar a sorte.
pot plant *n* planta *f* de vaso.
potpourri [ˌpəʊ'pʊərɪ] *n* pot-pourri *m*.
pot roast *n* carne *f* assada.
potshot ['pɒtˌʃɒt] *n*: **to take a** ~ **(at sthg)** atirar a esmo (em algo).
potted ['pɒtɪd] *adj* **-1.** [grown in pot] de vaso **-2.** [preserved] em conserva **-3.** *UK fig* [condensed] condensado(da).
potter ['pɒtəʳ] *n* oleiro *m*, -ra *f*.
◆ **potter about, potter around** *vi UK* ocupar-se em trabalhos pequenos.
Potteries ['pɒtərɪz] *npl*: **the** ~ os Potteries *(distrito na Inglaterra típico por sua cerâmica).*
potter's wheel *n* roda *f* de oleiro.
pottery ['pɒtərɪ] (*pl* **-ies**) *n* **-1.** [gen] cerâmica *f* **-2.** [factory] olaria *f*.
potting compost ['pɒtɪŋ-] *n (U)* adubo *m* para plantas de interiores.
potty ['pɒtɪ] (*compar* **-ier**, *superl* **-iest**, *pl* **-ies**) *UK inf* <> *adj* doido(da); **to be** ~ **about sb/sthg** ser doido(da) por alguém/algo. <> *n* [for children] penico *m*.
potty-trained [-ˌtreɪnd] *adj*: **a** ~ **child** uma criança que já sabe pedir para ir ao banheiro.
pouch [paʊtʃ] *n* bolsa *f*.
pouffe [puːf] *n UK* [seat] pufe *m*.
poultice ['pəʊltɪs] *n* cataplasma *m*.
poultry ['pəʊltrɪ] <> *n (U)* [meat] carne *f* de aves *(domésticas)*. <> *npl* [birds] aves *fpl* domésticas.
pounce [paʊns] *vi* **-1.** [subj: animal, bird]: **to** ~ **(on** *OR* **upon sthg)** agarrar (algo) **-2.** [subj: person, police]: **to** ~ **(on** *OR* **upon sb)** lançar-se (sobre alguém) **-3.** *fig* [on mistake, suggestion]: **to** ~ **(up)on sthg** precipitar-se sobre algo.
pound [paʊnd] <> *n* **-1.** *UK* [unit of money] libra *f* **-2.** *UK* [currency system]: **the** ~ a libra **-3.** [unit of weight] libra *f* **-4.** [for dogs] canil **-5.** [for cars] depósito *m (para automóveis apreendidos)*. <> *vt* **-1.** [strike loudly] esmurrar **-2.** [pulverize] pulverizar. <> *vi* **-1.** [strike loudly]: **to** ~ **on sthg** esmurrar algo **-2.** [beat, throb - heart] palpitar; [- head] latejar.
pound coin *n* moeda *f* de libra.
pounding ['paʊndɪŋ] *n* **-1.** [of drums, fists] surra *f* **-2.** [of heart] palpitação *f* **-3.** [of head] latejamento *m* **-4.** *phr*: **to get** *OR* **take a** ~ [be severely damaged] ser seriamente atingido(da); [be heavily defeated] levar uma surra.
pound sterling *n* libra *f* esterlina.
pour [pɔːʳ] <> *vt* **-1.** [cause to flow] despejar; **to** ~ **sthg into sthg** despejar algo em algo; **to** ~ **sb a drink, to** ~ **a drink for sb** servir um drinque a alguém **-2.** *fig* [invest]: **to** ~ **money into sthg** investir muito dinheiro em algo. <> *vi* **-1.** [flow quickly] fluir, correr **-2.** *fig* [rush] correr. <> *v impers* [rain hard] chover a cântaros.
◆ **pour in** *vi* vir em enxurrada.
◆ **pour out** *vt sep* **-1.** [empty] esvaziar **-2.** [serve] servir **-3.** *fig* [emotions] abrir.
pouring ['pɔːrɪŋ] *adj* [rain] torrencial.
pout [paʊt] <> *n* beiço *m*. <> *vi* fazer beiço.
poverty ['pɒvətɪ] *n (U)* **-1.** [hardship] miséria *f* **-2.** [lack]: ~ **of sthg** pobreza de algo.
poverty line *n* linha *f* da pobreza.
poverty-stricken *adj* carente, necessitado(da).
poverty trap *n UK situação na qual uma pessoa pobre não tem vantagem em arrumar emprego por perder os benefícios do governo.*
pow [paʊ] *excl inf* paf!
POW (*abbr of* **prisoner of war**) *n* prisioneiro *m*, -ra *f* de guerra.
powder ['paʊdəʳ] <> *n* [tiny particles] pó *m*; **face** ~

pó-de-arroz *m*; **gun ~** pólvora *f*; **washing ~** detergente *m*. <> *vt* [make-up] maquiar; **to ~ o.s.** maquiar-se.

powder compact *n* estojo *m (de pó-de-arroz)*.

powdered ['paʊdəd] *adj* [in powder form] em pó.

powder puff *n* esponja *f* de pó-de-arroz.

powder room *n* toalete *m*.

powdery ['paʊdərɪ] *adj* **-1.** [like powder] poeirento (ta) **-2.** [covered in powder] cheio (cheia) de pó.

power ['paʊəʳ] <> *n* **-1.** *(U)* [control, influence] poder *m*; **to be in ~** estar no poder; **to come to ~** chegar ao poder; **to have ~ over sb** ter poder sobre alguém; **to take ~** assumir o poder **-2.** [ability, capacity] força *f*; **mental ~s** poderes *mpl* mentais; **to be (with)in one's ~ to do sthg** competir a alguém fazer algo **-3.** [legal authority] autoridade *f*; **to have the ~ to do sthg** ter autoridade para fazer algo **-4.** [strength] força *f*; **the ~s that be** os poderes constituídos **-5.** *(U)* TECH energia *f* **-6.** *(U)* [electricity] luz *f*. <> *vt* alimentar.

power base *n* reduto *m (de força)*.

powerboat ['paʊəbəʊt] *n* powerboat *m*, *pequeno barco de corrida muito veloz*.

power broker *n pessoa que exerce grande influência através do controle de votos ou de indivíduos*.

power cut *n* corte *m* de energia.

power failure *n* falha *f* no sistema elétrico.

powerful ['paʊəfʊl] *adj* **-1.** [influential] poderoso(sa) **-2.** [strong] poderoso(sa), forte **-3.** [very convincing, very moving] vigoroso(sa).

powerhouse ['paʊəhaʊs, *pl* -haʊzɪz] *n fig* fonte *f* de influência.

powerless ['paʊəlɪs] *adj* fraco(ca); **to be ~ to do sthg** ser impotente para fazer algo.

power line *n* linha *f* de força.

power of attorney *n* procuração *f*.

power plant *n* central *f* elétrica.

power point *n UK* ponto *m* de força, tomada *f*.

power-sharing *n* POL divisão *f* de poder *(entre partidos políticos)*.

power station *n* estação *f* de força.

power steering *n (U)* direção *f* hidráulica.

power worker *n* eletricitário *m*, -ria *f*.

Powys ['paʊɪs] *n* Powys.

pp (*abbr of* **per procurationem**) p/.

p & p (*abbr of* **postage and packing**) *n* postagem *f* e empacotamento.

PPE (*abbr of* **philosophy, politics and economics**) *n filosofia, política e economia, famoso curso oferecido pela Universidade de Oxford*.

ppm (*abbr of* **parts per million**) ppm.

PPS <> *n* (*abbr of* **parliamentary private secretary**) *deputado britânico que assessora um ministro*. <> (*abbr of* **post postscriptum**) P.P.S.

PQ *abbr of* **Province of Quebec**.

PR <> *n* **-1.** (*abbr of* **public relations**) RP *mf* **-2.** (*abbr of* **proportional representation**) representação *f* proporcional. <> *abbr of* **Puerto Rico**.

practicable ['præktɪkəbl] *adj* praticável.

practical ['præktɪkl] <> *adj* **-1.** [gen] prático(ca) **-2.** [practicable] praticável. <> *n* prática *f*.

practicality [,præktɪ'kælətɪ] *n (U)* praticabilidade *f*.

◆ **practicalities** *npl* aspectos *mpl* práticos.

practical joke *n* peça *f*, trote *m*.

practically ['præktɪklɪ] *adv* praticamente.

practice ['præktɪs], **practise** *US n* **-1.** *(U)* [gen] prática *f*; **to be out of ~** estar destreinado(da); **the athlete is out of ~** estar fora de forma **-2.** *(U)* [implementation]: **to put sthg into ~** pôr algo em prática; **in ~** [in fact] na prática **-3.** [training session] sessão *f* de treino.

practiced *adj US* = **practised**.

practicing *adj US* = **practising**.

practise, practice *US* ['præktɪs] <> *vt* praticar. <> *vi* **-1.** [train] treinar **-2.** [professional] exercer.

practised, practiced *US* ['præktɪst] *adj* experiente, treinado(da); **to be ~ at doing sthg** ser competente ao fazer algo.

practising, practicing *US* ['præktɪsɪŋ] *adj* **-1.** [doctor, lawyer] que exerce **-2.** [Christian, Catholic] praticante **-3.** [homosexual] assumido(da).

practitioner [præk'tɪʃnəʳ] *n MED*: **a medical ~** um profissional da área médica.

pragmatic [præg'mætɪk] *adj* pragmático(ca).

pragmatism ['prægmətɪzm] *n (U)* pragmatismo *m*.

pragmatist ['prægmətɪst] *n* pragmatista *m*.

Prague [prɑːg] *n* Praga; **in ~** em Praga.

prairie ['preərɪ] *n* pradaria *f*.

praise [preɪz] <> *n* **-1.** *(U)* [commendation] elogio *m* **-2.** RELIG louvor *m*; **~ be to God!** louvado seja Deus! **-3.** *phr*: **to sing sb's ~s** tecer elogios a alguém. <> *vt* **-1.** [commend] elogiar **-2.** RELIG louvar.

praiseworthy ['preɪz,wɜːðɪ] *adj* louvável.

praline ['prɑːiːn] *n* pralina *f*.

pram [præm] *n UK* carrinho *m* de bebê.

PRAM (*abbr of* **programmable random access memory**) *n* RAM *f* programável.

prance [prɑːns] *vi* empinar-se.

prang [præŋ] *UK inf dated* <> *n* desastre *m*. <> *vt* espatifar-se.

prank [præŋk] *n* peça *f*.

prat [præt] *n UK v inf* palerma *mf*.

prattle ['prætl] *pej* <> *n* tagarelice *m*. <> *vi* tagarelar; **to ~ on about sthg** tagarelar sobre algo.

prawn [prɔːn] *n* pitu *m*.

prawn cocktail *n* coquetel *m* de pitus.

prawn cracker *n petisco de origem chinesa parecido com batatas fritas*.

pray [preɪ] *vi* RELIG rezar; **to ~ to sb** rezar para alguém; **to ~ for sthg** rezar por algo.

prayer [preəʳ] *n* **-1.** *(U)* [act of praying] prece *f* **-2.** [set of words] oração *f*; **to say one's ~s** fazer suas orações **-3.** *fig* [strong hope] pedido *m*.

◆ **prayers** *npl* [service] preces *fpl*.

prayer book *n* missal *m*.

prayer meeting *n* serviço *m* de oração.

pre- [priː] *prefix* pré-.

preach [priːtʃ] <> *vt* pregar. <> *vi* **-1.** RELIG pregar; **to ~ to sb** fazer sermões a alguém **-2.** *pej* [pontificate] dar sermões em; **to ~ at sb** dar sermões em alguém.

preacher ['priːtʃəʳ] *n* pregador *m*, -ra *f*.
preamble [priː'æmbl] *n* preâmbulo *m*.
prearranged [ˌpriːə'reɪndʒd] *adj* já combinado(-da).
precarious [prɪ'keərɪəs] *adj* precário(ria).
precariously [prɪ'keərɪəslɪ] *adv* precariamente.
precast [ˌpriː'kɑːst] *adj* pré-moldado(da).
precaution [prɪ'kɔːʃn] *n* precaução *f*; **as a ~ against sthg** como precaução contra algo.
precautionary [prɪ'kɔːʃənərɪ] *adj* de precaução.
precede [prɪ'siːd] *vt* **-1.** [gen] preceder **-2.** [walk in front of] adiantar-se.
precedence ['presɪdəns] *n*: **to take ~ over sthg** ter prioridade sobre algo; **to take ~ over sb** ter precedência sobre alguém.
precedent ['presɪdənt] *n* precedente *m*.
preceding [prɪ'siːdɪŋ] *adj* **-1.** [previous] anterior **-2.** [written before] anterior, precedente.
precept ['priːsept] *n* preceito *m*.
precinct ['priːsɪŋkt] *n* **-1.** *UK* [shopping area] zona *f* comercial **-2.** *US* [district] distrito *m*.
◆ **precincts** *npl* [around building] arredores *mpl*.
precious ['preʃəs] *adj* **-1.** [friendship, moment, time] precioso(sa), querido(da) **-2.** [jewel, object, material] precioso(sa) **-3.** *inf iro* [damned] maldito(ta); **~ little** muito pouco **-4.** [affected] afetado(da).
precious metal *n* metal *m* precioso.
precious stone *n* pedra *f* preciosa.
precipice ['presɪpɪs] *n* precipício *m*.
precipitate [*adj* prɪ'sɪpɪtət, *vb* prɪ'sɪpɪteɪt] *fml* ◇ *adj* precipitado(da). ◇ *vt* precipitar.
precipitation [prɪˌsɪpɪ'teɪʃn] *n* precipitação *f*.
precipitous [prɪ'sɪpɪtəs] *adj* **-1.** [very steep] íngreme **-2.** [hasty] precipitado(da).
précis [*UK* 'preɪsiː, *US* 'presiː] (*pl inv*) *n* resumo *m*.
precise [prɪ'saɪs] *adj* preciso(sa), exato(ta); **to be ~** [speaking exactly] para ser preciso.
precisely [prɪ'saɪslɪ] *adv* exatamente; **to describe/explain sthg ~** descrever/explicar algo com precisão.
precision [prɪ'sɪʒn] ◇ *n* (*U*) precisão *f*; **to do sthg with ~** fazer algo com precisão. ◇ *comp* de precisão.
preclude [prɪ'kluːd] *vt fml* impedir, evitar; **to ~ sb/sthg from doing sthg** impedir alguém/algo de fazer algo.
precocious [prɪ'kəʊʃəs] *adj* precoce.
precocity [prɪ'kɒsətɪ] *n* (*U*) precocidade *f*.
preconceived [ˌpriːkən'siːvd] *adj* preconcebido(-da).
preconception [ˌpriːkən'sepʃn] *n* idéia *f* preconcebida.
precondition [ˌpriːkən'dɪʃn] *n fml* precondição *f*, condição *f* prévia; **to be a ~ for** *OR* **of sthg** ser um pré-requisito para algo.
precooked [priː'kʊkt] *adj* pré-cozido(da).
precursor [ˌpriː'kɜːsəʳ] *n fml* precursor *m*, -ra *f*; **to be a ~ of** *OR* **to sthg** ser um precursor de algo.
predate [priː'deɪt] *vt* preceder, ser anterior a.
predator ['predətəʳ] *n* **-1.** [animal, bird] predador *m*, -ra *f* **-2.** *fig* [exploitative person] explorador *m*, -ra *f*.
predatory ['predətrɪ] *adj* predatório(ria).
predecease [ˌpriːdɪ'siːs] *vt fml* morrer antes de.
predecessor ['priːdɪsesəʳ] *n* **-1.** [person] predecessor *m*, -ra *f*, antecessor *m*, -ra *f* **-2.** [thing] antecessor *m*, -ra *f*.
predestination [priːˌdestɪ'neɪʃn] *n* (*U*) *RELIG* predestinação *f*.
predestine [ˌpriː'destɪn] *vt*: **to be ~d to sthg to do sthg** estar predestinado(da) a algo/a fazer algo.
predetermine [ˌpriːdɪ'tɜːmɪn] *vt* predeterminar.
predetermined [ˌpriːdɪ'tɜːmɪnd] *adj* predeterminado(da).
predicament [prɪ'dɪkəmənt] *n* aperto *m*; **to be in a ~** estar num aperto.
predicate ['predɪkət] *n GRAMM* predicado *m*.
predict [prɪ'dɪkt] *vt* prever.
predictable [prɪ'dɪktəbl] *adj* previsível.
predictably [prɪ'dɪktəblɪ] *adv* **-1.** [in an expected way] de forma previsível **-2.** [as was expected] como era de se imaginar.
prediction [prɪ'dɪkʃn] *n* **-1.** [something foretold] previsão *f*, prognóstico *m* **-2.** (*U*) [foretelling] previsão *f*.
predictor [prɪ'dɪktəʳ] *n* indicador *m*.
predigest [ˌpriːdaɪ'dʒest] *vt fig* simplificar; **~ed** mastigado (mastigada).
predilection [ˌpriːdɪ'lekʃn] *n*: **~ for sthg** predileção *f* por algo.
predispose [ˌpriːdɪs'pəʊz] *vt*: **to be ~d to sthg to do sthg** estar predisposto(ta) a algo/a fazer algo.
predisposition ['priːˌdɪspə'zɪʃn] *n*: **~ to(wards) sthg** predisposição *f* a algo; **~ to do sthg** predisposição para fazer algo.
predominance [prɪ'dɒmɪnəns] *n* **-1.** [preponderance] predominância *f*, predomínio *m* **-2.** [control] predomínio *m*.
predominant [prɪ'dɒmɪnənt] *adj* predominante.
predominantly [prɪ'dɒmɪnəntlɪ] *adv* predominantemente.
predominate [prɪ'dɒmɪneɪt] *vi* **-1.** [be greater in number] predominar **-2.** [prevail] predominar, prevalecer.
pre-eminent *adj* preeminente.
pre-empt [-'empt] *vt* antecipar-se a.
pre-emptive [-'emptɪv] *adj* preventivo(va).
pre-emptive strike *n* ataque *m* preventivo.
preen [priːn] *vt* **-1.** [subj: bird] alisar com o bico **-2.** *fig* [subj: person]: **to ~ o.s.** arrumar-se, ajeitar-se.
pre-exist *vi* preexistir.
prefab ['priːfæb] *n inf* casa *f* pré-fabricada.
prefabricate [ˌpriː'fæbrɪkeɪt] *vt* pré-fabricar.
preface ['prefɪs] ◇ *n* [in book] prefácio *m*; **~ to sthg** [to text] prefácio a algo; [to speech] preâmbulo *m*. ◇ *vt*: **to ~ sthg with sthg/by doing sthg** introduzir algo com algo/fazendo algo.
prefect ['priːfekt] *n UK* monitor *m*, -ra *f*, prefeito *m*, -ta *f* (*em escola*).
prefer [prɪ'fɜːʳ] (*pt* & *pp* **-red**, *cont* **-ring**) *vt* preferir; **to ~ sthg to sthg** preferir algo a algo; **to ~ to do sthg** preferir fazer algo.
preferable ['prefrəbl] *adj*: **to be ~ (to sthg)** ser preferível(a algo).
preferably ['prefrəblɪ] *adv* preferivelmente.

preference ['prefərəns] *n*: ~ **(for sthg)** preferência *f* (por algo); **to give sb/sthg ~, to give ~ to sb/sthg** dar preferência a alguém/algo.
preference shares *UK npl*, **preferred stock** *US n* ações *fpl* preferenciais.
preferential [,prefə'renʃl] *adj* preferencial.
preferred [prɪ'fɜ:d] *adj* preferido(da).
preferred stock *n US* = **preference shares**.
prefigure [pri:'fɪgəʳ] *vt fml* prefigurar, anunciar.
prefix ['pri:fɪks] *n GRAMM* prefixo *m*.
pregnancy ['pregnənsɪ] (*pl* **-ies**) *n* gravidez *f*.
pregnancy test *n* teste *m* de gravidez.
pregnant ['pregnənt] *adj* **-1.** [carrying unborn baby - human] grávido(da); [- animal] prenho(ha) **-2.** *fig* [significant] significativo(va).
preheated [,pri:'hi:tɪd] *adj* preaquecido(da).
prehistoric [,pri:hɪ'stɒrɪk] *adj* pré-histórico(ca).
prehistory [,pri:'hɪstərɪ] *n (U)* pré-história *f*.
pre-industrial *adj* pré-industrial.
prejudge [,pri:'dʒʌdʒ] *vt* prejulgar.
prejudice ['predʒʊdɪs] ◇ *n* **-1.** [bias] preconceito *m*; ~ **in favour of sb/sthg** tendência *f* de favorecer alguém/algo; ~ **against sb/sthg** preconceito contra alguém/algo **-2.** [harm] prejuízo *m*. ◇ *vt* **-1.** [bias] ter preconceito em relação a; **to ~ sb in favour of/against sthg** predispor alguém a favor de/contra algo **-2.** [jeopardize] prejudicar.
prejudiced ['predʒʊdɪst] *adj* preconceituoso(sa), parcial; **to be ~ in favour of sb/sthg** favorecer alguém/algo; **to be ~ against sb/sthg** ser preconceituoso(sa) em relação a alguém/algo.
prejudicial [,predʒʊ'dɪʃl] *adj* prejudicial; **to be ~ to sb/sthg** ser prejudicial para alguém/algo.
prelate ['prelɪt] *n RELIG* prelado *m*.
preliminary [prɪ'lɪmɪnərɪ] (*pl* **-ies**) *adj* preliminar.
◆ **preliminaries** *npl* **-1.** [preliminary events or stages] preliminares *fpl* **-2.** [eliminating contests] eliminatórias *fpl* **-3.** *US POL* prévias *fpl*.
prelims ['pri:lɪmz] *npl UK* [exams] exames *mpl* preliminares.
prelude ['prelju:d] *n*: ~ **to sthg** prelúdio *m* de algo.
premarital [,pri:'mærɪtl] *adj* pré-marital, antes do casamento.
premature ['premə,tjʊəʳ] *adj* prematuro(ra).
prematurely [,premə'tjʊəlɪ] *adv* prematuramente.
premeditated [,pri:'medɪteɪtɪd] *adj* premeditado (da).
premenstrual syndrome, premenstrual tension [pri:'menstrʊəl-] *n* síndrome *f* pré-menstrual.
premier ['premjəʳ] ◇ *adj* principal, primeiro(ra). ◇ *n* [prime minister] primeiro-ministro *m*, primeira-ministra *f*.
premiere ['premɪeəʳ] *n* estréia *f*.
premiership ['premɪəʃɪp] *n* [office] cargo *m* de primeiro-ministro; [term of office] mandato *m (do primeiro-ministro)*.
◆ **Premiership** *n UK FTBL*: **the ~** ≃ o Clube dos 13.
premise ['premɪs] *n* premissa *f*; **on the ~ that** com a premissa de que.
◆ **premises** *npl* [site] local *m*; **on the ~s** no local.
premium ['pri:mjəm] *n* **-1.** [gen] prêmio *m*; **at a ~** [above usual value] *a um valor superior ao nominal*; [in great demand] muito disputado(da) **-2.** *phr*: **to put** *OR* **place a high ~ on sthg** dar grande importância a algo.
premium bond *n UK obrigação emitida pelo governo que dá direito a prêmios mensais em dinheiro mediante sorteio.*
premonition [,premə'nɪʃn] *n* premonição *f*.
prenatal [,pri:'neɪtl] *adj US* pré-natal.
preoccupation [pri:,ɒkjʊ'peɪʃn] *n* preocupação *f*; ~ **with sthg** preocupação com algo.
preoccupied [pri:'ɒkjʊpaɪd] *adj* preocupado(da); **to be ~ with sthg** estar preocupado(da) com algo.
preoccupy [pri:'ɒkjʊpaɪ] (*pt* & *pp* **-ied**) *vt* preocupar.
preordain [,pri:ɔ:'deɪn] *vt* predeterminar; **to be ~ed to do sthg** estar predestinado(da) a fazer algo.
prep [prep] *n UK inf* [homework]: **to do one's ~** fazer o dever de casa.
pre-packed *adj* pré-embalado(da).
prepaid ['pri:peɪd] *adj* com porte pago.
preparation [,prepə'reɪʃn] *n* **-1.** *(U)* [act of preparing] preparação *f*; **in ~ for sthg** em preparação para algo **-2.** [prepared mixture] preparado *m*.
◆ **preparations** *npl* [plans] preparativos *mpl*; **to make ~s for sthg** fazer preparativos para algo.
preparatory [prɪ'pærətrɪ] *adj* preparatório(ria).
preparatory school *n* **-1.** [in UK] colégio pago para crianças de 7 a 13 anos **-2.** [in US] *escola particular que prepara alunos para entrar na universidade.*
prepare [prɪ'peəʳ] ◇ *vt* preparar; **to ~ to do sthg** preparar-se para fazer algo. ◇ *vi*: **to ~ for sthg** preparar-se para algo.
prepared [prɪ'peəd] *adj* [organized, done beforehand] preparado(da); **to be ~** *OR* **for sthg** *OR* **to do sthg** estar preparado(da) para algo/para fazer algo.
preponderance [prɪ'pɒndərəns] *n* predomínio *m*.
preponderantly [prɪ'pɒndərəntlɪ] *adv* predominantemente, majoritariamente.
preposition [,prepə'zɪʃn] *n* preposição *f*.
prepossessing [,pri:pə'zesɪŋ] *adj fml* atraente, agradável.
preposterous [prɪ'pɒstərəs] *adj* absurdo(da).
preppy ['prepɪ] (*pl* **-ies**) *US inf* ◇ *adj* **-1.** [male] de mauricinho **-2.** [female] de patricinha. ◇ *n* **-1.** [male] mauricinho *m* **-2.** [female] patricinha *f*.
prep school (*abbr of* **preparatory school**) *n escola particular primária para crianças de 7 a 12 anos na Grã-Bretanha.*
Pre-Raphaelite [,pri:'ræfəlaɪt] ◇ *adj* pré-rafaelita. ◇ *n* pré-rafaelita *mf*.
pre-recorded *adj* pré-gravado(da).
prerequisite [,pri:'rekwɪzɪt] *n* pré-requisito *m*; ~ **of** *OR* **for sthg** pré-requisito para algo.
prerogative [prɪ'rɒgətɪv] *n* prerrogativa *f*.
presage ['presɪdʒ] *vt fml* pressagiar.

Presbyterian [ˌprezbɪˈtɪərɪən] <> *adj* presbiteriano(na). <> *n* presbiteriano *m*, -na *f*.
presbytery [ˈprezbɪtrɪ] *n* presbitério *m*.
pre-school <> *adj* pré-escolar. <> *n* *US* pré-escola *f*.
prescient [ˈpresɪənt] *adj fml* presciente.
prescribe [prɪˈskraɪb] *vt* **-1.** *MED* prescrever **-2.** [order] ordenar, mandar.
prescription [prɪˈskrɪpʃn] *n* [*MED* - written form] receita *f* (médica); [- medicine] prescrição *f*; **on ~** com receita (médica).
prescription charge *n* *UK* *no Reino Unido, quantia fixa que se paga por quaisquer remédios receitados por um médico.*
prescriptive [prɪˈskrɪptɪv] *adj* *GRAMM* prescritivo (va).
presence [ˈprezns] *n* presença *f*; **in the ~ of sb** na presença de alguém; **to have ~** ter presença.
presence of mind *n* presença *f* de espírito.
present [*adj* & *n* ˈpreznt, *vb* prɪˈzent] <> *adj* **-1.** [gen] presente, atual **-2.** [in attendance] presente; **to be ~ at sthg** estar presente em algo. <> *n* **-1.**: **the ~** o presente; **at ~** atualmente; **for the ~** no momento **-2.** *GRAMM*: **~ (tense)** presente *m*. <> *vt* **-1.** [gen] apresentar; **to ~ sb to sb** apresentar alguém para alguém **-2.** [give] presentear; **to ~ sb with sthg**, **to ~ sthg to sb** presentar alguém com algo **-3.** [provide, pose] deparar-se com; **to ~ sb with sthg**, **to ~ sthg to sb** representar algo para alguém **-4.** [arrive, go]: **to ~ o.s.** apresentar-se.
presentable [prɪˈzentəbl] *adj* apresentável.
presentation [ˌpreznˈteɪʃn] *n* **-1.** [gen] apresentação *f* **-2.** [ceremony] cerimônia *f* **-3.** [performance] representação *f*.
presentation copy *n* cópia *f* de apresentação, exemplar *m* gratuito.
present day *n*: **the ~** o momento atual.
◆ **present-day** *adj* atual, de hoje em dia.
presenter [prɪˈzentəʳ] *n* *UK* apresentador *m*, -ra *f*.
presentiment [prɪˈzentɪmənt] *n* *fml* pressentimento *m*.
presently [ˈprezəntlɪ] *adv* **-1.** [soon] em breve, daqui a pouco **-2.** [now] atualmente.
preservation [ˌprezəˈveɪʃn] *n* *(U)* **-1.** [gen] preservação *f* **-2.** [of food] conservação *f*.
preservation order *n* *esp* *UK* ordem *f* de tombamento.
preservative [prɪˈzɜːvətɪv] *n* **-1.** [for food] conservante *m* **-2.** [for wood] revestimento *m*.
preserve [prɪˈzɜːv] <> *n* [jam] compota *f*, conserva *f*. <> *vt* **-1.** [gen] preservar **-2.** [food] conservar.
preserved [prɪˈzɜːvd] *adj* **-1.** [food] em conserva **-2.** [building] preservado(da) **-3.** [furniture, wood] conservado(da).
preset [ˌpriːˈset] (*pt* & *pp* **preset**, *cont* **-ting**) *vt* programar.
pre-shrunk *adj* pré-encolhido(da).
preside [prɪˈzaɪd] *vi* presidir; **to ~ over** *OR* **at sthg** presidir algo.
presidency [ˈprezɪdənsɪ] (*pl* **-ies**) *n* presidência *f*.
president [ˈprezɪdənt] *n* presidente *mf*.
President-elect *n* presidente *mf* eleito, -ta.
presidential [ˌprezɪˈdenʃl] *adj* presidencial.
press [pres] <> *n* **-1.** [push] pressionamento *m* **-2.** [journalism]: **the ~** a imprensa; **to get a good ~** ser elogiado(da) na/pela imprensa; **to get a bad ~** ser criticado(da) na/pela imprensa, **-3.** [printing machine] imprensa *f* **-4.** [pressing machine] prensa *f*. <> *vt* **-1.** [push firmly - switch] ligar; [- accelerator] pisar em; **to ~ sthg against sthg** prensar algo contra algo **-2.** [squeeze] espremer **-3.** [iron] passar **-4.** [press person, button] pressionar; **he didn't need much ~ and readily agreed** ele não precisava de muita pressão e concordou prontamente; **to ~ sb for sthg** pressionar alguém buscando algo; **to ~ sbto do sthg** *OR* **into doing sthg** pressionar alguém a fazer algo; **to ~ sthg (up)on sb** empurrar algo a alguém, obrigar alguém a aceitar algo **-5.** [pursue] insistir em **-6.** *JUR*: **to ~ charges (against sb)** fazer acusações (contra alguém). <> *vi* **-1.** [push hard]: **to ~ (on sthg)** apertar (algo) com força **-2.** [surge] comprimir-se; **to ~ forwards** empurrar para frente.
◆ **press on** *vi* [continue] continuar; **to ~ on with sthg** continuar com algo.
press agency *n* assessoria *f* de imprensa.
press agent *n* acessor *m*, -ra *f* de imprensa.
press baron *n* *UK* magnata *m* da imprensa.
press box *n* cabine *f* de imprensa.
press conference *n* entrevista *f* coletiva.
press corps *n* *US* equipe *f* de jornalistas.
press cutting *n* *UK* recorte *m* de jornal.
pressed [prest] *adj*: **to be ~ (for time/ money)** estar meio apertado(da) (de tempo/dinheiro).
press fastener *n* *UK* botão *m* de pressão.
press gallery *n* tribuna *f* de imprensa.
pressgang [ˈpresgæŋ] <> *n* *grupo de homens que recrutavam marinheiros à força.* <> *vt* *UK*: **to ~ sb into doing sthg** forçar alguém a fazer algo.
pressing [ˈpresɪŋ] *adj* urgente, premente.
pressman [ˈpresmæn] (*pl* **-men** [-men]) *n* *UK* jornalista *m*.
press officer *n* acessor *m*, -ra *f* de imprensa.
press release *n* press-release *m*, comunicado *m* de imprensa.
press-stud *n* *UK* botão *m* de pressão.
press-up *n* *UK* flexão *f*, apoio *m* *(como exercício)*.
pressure [ˈpreʃəʳ] <> *n* pressão *f*; **to put ~ on sb (to do sthg)** pressionar alguém (a fazer algo *OR* para que faça algo), exercer pressão sobre alguém (para fazer algo). <> *vt*: **to ~ sb to do** *OR* **into doing sthg** pressionar alguém a fazer algo.
pressure cooker *n* panela *f* de pressão.
pressure gauge *n* manômetro *m*.
pressure group *n* grupo *m* de pressão.
pressurize, -ise [ˈpreʃəraɪz] *vt* **-1.** *TECH* pressurizar **-2.** *UK* [force]: **to ~ sb to do** *OR* **into doing sthg** pressionar alguém a fazer algo.
Prestel® [ˈprestel] *n* *UK* *serviço público de videotexto oferecido pela British Telecom.*
prestige [preˈstiːʒ] <> *n* *(U)* prestígio *m*. <> *comp* de prestígio.

prestigious [pre'stɪdʒəs] *adj* prestigioso(sa).
prestressed concrete [ˌpriː'strest-] *n (U)* concreto *m* protendido.
presumably [prɪ'zjuːməblɪ] *adv* presumivelmente; **~ you've read the book** suponho que você já tenha lido o livro.
presume [prɪ'zjuːm] *vt* presumir, supor; **to be ~d dead/innocent** ser julgado(da) morto(ta)/inocente; **to ~ (that)** supor *OR* imaginar que.
presumption [prɪ'zʌmpʃn] *n* **-1.** [assumption] pressuposição *f*, suposição *f* **-2.** *(U)* [audacity] presunção *f*.
presumptuous [prɪ'zʌmptʃʊəs] *adj* presunçoso (sa).
presuppose [ˌpriːsə'pəʊz] *vt* pressupor.
pre-tax *adj* bruto(ta).
pretence, pretense *US* [prɪ'tens] *n* fingimento *m*; **under false ~s** com falsos pretextos.
pretend [prɪ'tend] ◇ *vt* **-1.** [make believe]: **to ~ to be/to do sthg** fingir ser/fazer algo; **to ~ (that)** fingir (que), fazer de conta (que) **-2.** [claim]: **to ~ to do sthg** fingir fazer algo. ◇ *vi* fingir.
pretense *n US* = **pretence**.
pretension [prɪ'tenʃn] *n* pretensão *f*; **to have ~s to sthg/to be sthg** ter pretensões de algo/de ser algo.
pretentious [prɪ'tenʃəs] *adj* pretencioso(sa).
pretentiously [prɪ'tenʃəslɪ] *adv* pretenciosamente.
pretentiousness [prɪ'tenʃəsnɪs] *n (U)* pretensão *f*, caráter *m* pretencioso.
preterite ['pretərət] *n* pretérito *m*.
pretext ['priːtekst] *n* pretexto *m*; **on** *OR* **under the ~ that** com o pretexto de que; **on** *OR* **under the ~ of doing sthg** com o pretexto de estar fazendo algo.
Pretoria [prɪ'tɔːrɪə] *n* Pretória.
prettify ['prɪtɪfaɪ] (*pt* & *pp* **-ied**) *vt* embelezar.
prettily ['prɪtɪlɪ] *adv* de uma forma encantadora.
pretty ['prɪtɪ] (*compar* **-ier**, *superl* **-iest**) ◇ *adj* bonito(ta). ◇ *adv* [quite, rather] bastante; **~ much** *OR* **well** mais ou menos.
pretzel ['pretsl] *n rosca salgada em forma de nó*, pretzel *m*.
prevail [prɪ'veɪl] *vi* **-1.** [be widespread] prevalecer, predominar **-2.** [triumph] prevalecer; **to ~ over sb/sthg** prevalecer sobre alguém/algo **-3.** [persuade]: **to ~ (up)on sb to do sthg** persuadir alguém a fazer algo *OR* para que faça algo.
prevailing [prɪ'veɪlɪŋ] *adj* predominante.
prevalence ['prevələns] *n* predomínio *m*.
prevalent ['prevələnt] *adj* predominante, prevalecente.
prevaricate [prɪ'værɪkeɪt] *vi* prevaricar.
prevent [prɪ'vent] *vt* evitar, impedir; **to ~ sb (from) doing sthg** impedir alguém de fazer algo; **to ~ sthg (from) doing sthg** evitar que algo faça algo; **they tried to ~ any pain to the animal** eles tentaram não causar nenhuma dor ao animal.
preventable [prɪ'ventəbl] *adj* evitável.
preventative [prɪ'ventətɪv] *adj* = **preventive**.
prevention [prɪ'venʃn] *n (U)* prevenção *f*; **~ is better than cure** é melhor prevenir do que remediar.
preventive [prɪ'ventɪv] *adj* preventivo(va).
preview ['priːvjuː] *n* **-1.** [early showing] pré-estréia *f* **-2.** [trailer] trailer *m*.
previous ['priːvjəs] *adj* **-1.** [earlier, prior] anterior, prévio(via); **~ convictions** antecedentes *mpl* criminais; **it was the ~ President who did it** foi o ex-presidente que fez isso **-2.** [days and dates] anterior.
previously ['priːvjəslɪ] *adv* **-1.** [formerly] anteriormente, antes **-2.** [with days and dates] antes.
prewar [ˌpriː'wɔːʳ] *adj* anterior à guerra.
pre-wash *n* pré-lavagem *f*.
prey [preɪ] *n (U)* presa *f*, vitima *f*; **to fall ~ to sb/sthg** ser vítima de alguém/algo.
◆ **prey on** *vt fus* **-1.** [live off] caçar, alimentar-se de **-2.** [trouble]: **to ~ on sb's mind** atormentar alguém.
price [praɪs] ◇ *n* **-1.** preço *m*; **at a ~** a que preço; **at any ~** a qualquer preço, a todo custo **-2.** *fig* [penalty]: **to pay the ~ for sthg** pagar o preço por algo. ◇ *vt* pôr preço em; **it was ~d highly** seu preço era muito elevado.
price-cutting *n (U)* redução *f* de preços.
price-fixing [-ˌfɪksɪŋ] *n (U)* cartel *m*.
priceless ['praɪslɪs] *adj* **-1.** [very valuable] inestimável, que não tem preço **-2.** *inf* [funny] impagável.
price list *n* lista *f* de preços.
price tag *n* **-1.** [label] etiqueta *f* de preço **-2.** [sacrifice] *fig* preço *m*.
price war *n* guerra *f* de preços.
pricey ['praɪsɪ] (*compar* **-ier**, *superl* **-iest**) *adj inf* caro(ra).
prick [prɪk] ◇ *n* **-1.** [scratch, wound] picada *f* **-2.** *vulg* [penis] cacete *m*, caralho *m* **-3.** *vulg* [stupid person] pau-no-cu *m*. ◇ *vt* **-1.** [jab, pierce] espetar **-2.** [sting] arder.
◆ **prick up** *vt fus*: **to ~ up one's ears** [subj: animal] levantar as orelhas; [subj: person] aguçar os ouvidos.
prickle ['prɪkl] ◇ *n* **-1.** [thorn] espinho *m* **-2.** [sensation] formigamento *m*, comichão *f*. ◇ *vi* formigar, comichar.
prickly ['prɪklɪ] (*compar* **-ier**, *superl* **-iest**) *adj* **-1.** [thorny] espinhoso(sa), espinhento(ta) **-2.** *fig* [touchy] suscetível.
prickly heat *n (U)* brotoeja *f*.
pride [praɪd] ◇ *n* orgulho *m*; **to swallow one's ~** engolir o orgulho; **to take ~ in sthg/in doing sthg** sentir-se orgulhoso(sa) em algo/ao fazer algo; **his new car was his ~ and joy** seu novo carro era a menina dos olhos dele; **to have ~ of place** ter lugar de honra. ◇ *vt*: **to ~ o.s. on sthg** orgulhar-se de algo.
priest [priːst] *n* **-1.** [Christian] padre *m*, sacerdote *m* **-2.** [non-Christian] homem *m* religioso.
priestess ['priːstɪs] *n* sacerdotisa *f*.
priesthood ['priːsthʊd] *n (U)* **-1.** [position, office]: **the ~** o sacerdócio **-2.** [priests collectively]: **the ~** o clero.
prig [prɪg] *n* moralista *mf*, puritano *m*, -na *f*.
prim [prɪm] (*compar* **-mer**, *superl* **-mest**) *adj* afetado

(da), empertigado(da).

primacy ['praɪməsɪ] *n (U)* primazia *f.*

prima donna [ˌpri:mə'dɒnə] *(pl* **-s**) *n* **-1.** [female singer] prima-dona *f* **-2.** *pej* [self-important person] prima-dona *f.*

primaeval [praɪ'mi:vəl] *adj* = **primeval**.

prima facie [ˌpraɪmə'feɪʃi:] *adj* à primeira vista.

primal ['praɪml] *adj* **-1.** [original] primário(ria) **-2.** [most important] principal.

primarily ['praɪmərɪlɪ] *adv* primeiramente, principalmente.

primary ['praɪmərɪ] *(pl* **-ies**) <> *adj* primário(ria). <> *n US POL* prévias *fpl.*

PRIMARIES

As *Primaries* (primárias) são as eleições norte-americanas - diretas ou indiretas, dependendo do estado - mediante as quais se selecionam os candidatos dos dois partidos nacionais, o Democrata e o Republicano, que vão concorrer às eleições presidenciais.

primary colour *n* cor *f* primária.

primary election *n US* prévias *fpl.*

primary school *n* escola *f* primária.

primary teacher *n* [in UK] professor *m* primário, professora *f* primária.

primate ['praɪmeɪt] *n* **-1.** *ZOOL* primata *m* **-2.** *RELIG* primaz *m.*

prime [praɪm] <> *adj* **-1.** [main] primeiro(ra) principal **-2.** [excellent] excelente, de primeira. <> *n* [peak] auge *m*, plenitude *f*; **in one's ~** na flor da idade. <> *vt* **-1.** [inform]: **to ~ sb about sthg** instruir alguém sobre algo **-2.** [paint] imprimar, preparar para pintura **-3.** [make ready - gun] carregar; [- machine] aprontar; [- pump] escorvar.

prime minister *n* primeiro-ministro *m*, primeira-ministra *f.*

prime mover [-'mu:vəʳ] *n fig* força *f* motora.

prime number *n* número *m* primo.

primer ['praɪməʳ] *n* **-1.** [paint] imprimadura *f* **-2.** [textbook] manual *m.*

prime time *n (U)* horário *m* nobre.

◆ **prime-time** *adj* **-1.** [TV] de maior audiência **-2.** [viewing, advertising] no horário nobre.

primeval [praɪ'mi:vl] *adj* primitivo(va).

primitive ['prɪmɪtɪv] *adj* **-1.** [not civilized, of an early type] primitivo(va) **-2.** [simple, basic] rudimentar.

primordial [praɪ'mɔ:djəl] *adj fml* primordial.

primrose ['prɪmrəʊz] *n* prímula *f.*

Primus stove® ['praɪməs-] *n* fogareiro *m.*

prince [prɪns] *n* príncipe *m*; **Prince of Wales** Príncipe de Gales.

Prince Charming *n hum* príncipe *m* encantado.

princely ['prɪnslɪ] *(compar* **-ier**, *superl* **-iest**) *adj* **-1.** [of a prince] principesco(ca) **-2.** [generous, lavish] generoso(sa).

princess [prɪn'ses] *n* princesa *f*; **Princess Royal** Princesa Real.

principal ['prɪnsəpl] <> *adj* principal. <> *n* **-1.** [of school] diretor *m*, -ra *f* **-2.** [of college] reitor *m*, -ra *f.*

principality [ˌprɪnsɪ'pælətɪ] *(pl* **-ies**) *n* principado *m.*

principally ['prɪnsəplɪ] *adv* especialmente, principalmente.

principle ['prɪnsəpl] *n* **-1.** princípio *m* **-2.** *(U)* [integrity] princípios *mpl*; **he lacks ~** ele não tem princípios; **(to do sthg) on ~** *OR* **as a matter of ~** fazer algo por (uma questão de) princípios.

◆ **in principle** *adv* em princípio.

principled ['prɪnsəpld] *adj* de princípio.

print [prɪnt] <> *n* **-1.** *(U)* [type] caracteres *mpl (de imprensa)*; **the book is still in ~** o livro ainda está disponível *(não esgotado)*; **he saw his name in ~** ele viu seu nome impresso; **to be out of ~** estar esgotado(da) **-2.** *ART* gravura *f* **-3.** [photograph] cópia *f* **-4.** [fabric] estampado *m* **-5.** [footprint] pegada *f*; [fingerprint] impressão *f* digital. <> *vt* **-1.** [produce by printing] imprimir **-2.** [publish] publicar **-3.** [on fabric] estampar **-4.** [write clearly] escrever em letra de forma. <> *vi* **-1.** [in handwriting] escrever em letra de forma **-2.** [printer] imprimir.

◆ **print out** *vt sep COMPUT* imprimir.

printed circuit ['prɪntɪd-] *n* circuito *m* impresso.

printed matter ['prɪntɪd-] *n (U)* impresso *m.*

printer ['prɪntəʳ] *n* **-1.** [person, firm] impressor *m*, -ra *f* **-2.** *COMPUT* impressora *f.*

printing ['prɪntɪŋ] *n* impressão *f.*

printing press *n* prensa *f*, máquina *f* impressora.

printout ['prɪntaʊt] *n* saída *f* de impressora, impressão *f.*

prior ['praɪəʳ] <> *adj* **-1.** [previous] prévio(via), anterior **-2.** [more important] mais importante. <> *n* [monk] prior *m.*

◆ **prior to** *prep* antes de; **~ to doing sthg** antes de fazer algo.

prioress ['praɪəres] *n* prioresa *f.*

prioritize, -ise [praɪ'ɒrɪtaɪz] *vt* priorizar, dar prioridade a.

priority [praɪ'ɒrətɪ] *(pl* **-ies**) <> *adj* prioritário (ria). <> *n* prioridade *f*; **to have** *OR* **take ~ (over sthg)** ter prioridade (sobre algo).

◆ **priorities** *npl* prioridades *fpl.*

priory ['praɪərɪ] *(pl* **-ies**) *n* convento *m (dirigido por um prior).*

prise [praɪz] *vt*: **to ~ sthg open** abrir algo com força; **to ~ sthg away** separar algo usando força.

prism ['prɪzm] *n* prisma *m.*

prison ['prɪzn] *n* prisão *f.*

prison camp *n* campo *m* de prisioneiros.

prisoner ['prɪznəʳ] *n* prisioneiro *m*, -ra *f*; **to be taken ~** ser levado prisioneiro, ser levada prisioneira.

prisoner of war *(pl* **prisoners of war**) *n* prisioneiro *m*, -ra *f* de guerra.

prissy ['prɪsɪ] *(compar* **-ier**, *superl* **-iest**) *adj* fresco(ca).

pristine ['prɪsti:n] *adj* imaculado(da).

privacy [*UK* 'prɪvəsɪ, *US* 'praɪvəsɪ] *n* privacidade *f.*

private ['praɪvɪt] <> *adj* **-1.** [confidential, not for the public] privado(da) **-2.** [not state-controlled] privado (da), particular **-3.** [personal] privado(da), pessoal **-4.** [secluded] afastado(da), retirado(da) **-5.** [reserved] reservado(da). <> *n* **-1.** [soldier] soldado *m* raso **-2.** [secrecy]: **(to do sthg) in ~** fazer algo em particular.

◆ **privates** *npl inf ANAT* partes *fpl (pudendas).*
private company *n* empresa *f* privada.
private detective *n* detetive *mf* particular.
private enterprise *n (U)* empresa *f* privada.
private eye *n* detetive *mf* particular.
private income *n UK* renda *f* pessoal.
private investigator *n* detetive *mf* particular.
private limited company *n COMM* companhia *f* privada limitada.
privately ['praɪvɪtlɪ] *adv* **-1.** [not by the state] de forma privada; ~ **owned** de propriedade privada; ~ **educated** educado(da) em escola particular **-2.** [confidentially] privadamente, em particular **-3.** [personally] no fundo.
private member's bill *n UK projeto de lei apresentado ao parlamento britânico por um deputado sem cargo no governo.*
private parts *npl inf* partes *fpl* pudendas.
private practice *n (U) UK* prática *f* privada *(de uma profissão).*
private property *n* propriedade *f* privada.
private school *n* escola *f* particular.
private sector *n (U)*: **the** ~ o setor privado.
privation [praɪ'veɪʃn] *n* privação *f.*
privatization [,praɪvɪtaɪ'zeɪʃn] *n (U)* privatização *f.*
privatize, -ise ['praɪvɪtaɪz] *vt* privatizar.
privet ['prɪvɪt] *n (U)* alfena *f.*
privilege ['prɪvɪlɪdʒ] *n* **-1.** [special advantage] privilégio *m* **-2.** [honour] privilégio *m*, honra *f.*
privileged ['prɪvɪlɪdʒd] *adj* privilegiado(da).
privy ['prɪvɪ] *adj*: **to be** ~ **to sthg** *fml* inteirar-se de algo.
Privy Council *n UK*: **the** ~ *conselho privado que aconselha o monarca em questões políticas.*
Privy Purse *n*: **the** ~ *quantia aprovada pelo parlamento britânico e destinada a cobrir os gastos do monarca.*
prize [praɪz] <> *adj* **-1.** [prizewinning] premiado(da) **-2.** [perfect] perfeito(ta) **-3.** [valued] de estimação. <> *n* prêmio *m.* <> *vt* apreciar, valorizar.
prize day *n UK* (dia *m* de) entrega *f* de prêmios.
prizefight ['praɪzfaɪt] *n* luta *f* de boxe profissional.
prize-giving [-,gɪvɪŋ] *n UK* entrega *f* de prêmios.
prize money *n* dinheiro *m* ganho em prêmio.
prizewinner ['praɪz,wɪnə^r] *n* premiado *m*, -da *f.*
pro [prəʊ] (*pl* **-s**) *n* **-1.** *inf* [professional] profissional *mf* **-2.** [advantage]: **the** ~**s and cons** os prós e os contras.
pro- [prəʊ] *prefix* pró-.
PRO *n* **-1.** (*abbr of* **public relations officer**) chefe *mf* de relações públicas **-2.** (*abbr of* **public Record Office**) *arquivo público na Grã-Bretanha.*
pro-am <> *adj* de profissionais e amadores. <> *n competição mista entre profissionais e amadores.*
probability [,prɒbə'bɪlətɪ] (*pl* **-ies**) *n* probabilidade *f*; **in all** ~ **they will win** é muito provável que eles vençam.
probable ['prɒbəbl] *adj* provável.
probably ['prɒbəblɪ] *adv* provavelmente.
probate ['prəʊbeɪt] *JUR* <> *n* legitimação *f* de testamento. <> *vt US* legitimar *(um testamento).*
probation [prə'beɪʃn] *n (U)* **-1.** [of prisoner] liberdade *f* condicional; **to put sb on** ~ colocar alguém em liberdade condicional **-2.** [trial period] período *m* de experiência; **to be on** ~ estar em período de experiência.
probationary [prə'beɪʃnrɪ] *adj* **-1.** [teacher, nurse] em período de experiência **-2.** [year] de experiência; ~ **period** período *m* de experiência.
probationer [prə'beɪʃnə^r] *n* **-1.** [employee] funcionário *m*, -ria *f* em período de experiência **-2.** [offender] pessoa *f* em liberdade condicional.
probation officer *n pessoa encarregada de vigiar detentos em liberdade condicional.*
probe [prəʊb] <> *n* **-1.** [investigation] sindicância *f*, investigação *f*; ~ **into sthg** sindicância sobre algo **-2.** *MED, TECH* sonda *f.* <> *vt* **-1.** [investigate] investigar **-2.** [prod] explorar. <> *vi*: **to** ~ **for/into sthg** investigar para encontrar algo.
probing ['prəʊbɪŋ] *adj* inquiridor(ra).
probity ['prəʊbətɪ] *n (U) fml* probidade *f.*
problem ['prɒbləm] <> *n* problema *f*; **no** ~! *inf* sem problema! <> *comp* problemático(ca).
problematic(al) [,prɒblə'mætɪk(l)] *adj* problemático(ca), difícil.
problem page *n* página *f* com perguntas dos leitores *(em revistas, jornais).*
procedural [prə'siːdʒərəl] *adj* processual.
procedure [prə'siːdʒə^r] *n* procedimento *m.*
proceed [*vb* prə'siːd, *npl* 'prəʊsiːdz] <> *vt* [do subsequently]: **to** ~ **to do sthg** passar a fazer algo. <> *vi* **-1.** [continue] prosseguir, continuar; **to** ~ **with sthg** prosseguir com algo **-2.** *fml* [go, advance] dirigir-se para.
◆ **proceeds** *npl* proventos *mpl.*
proceedings [prə'siːdɪŋz] *npl* **-1.** [series of events] ação *f* **-2.** [legal action] processo *m.*
process ['prəʊses] <> *n* processo *m*; **in the** ~ no decorrer; **to be in the** ~ **of doing sthg** estar em vias de fazer algo. <> *vt* processar.
processed cheese ['prəʊsest-] *n* queijo *m* processado.
processing ['prəʊsesɪŋ] *n* processamento *m.*
procession [prə'seʃn] *n* **-1.** [ceremony] cortejo *m* **-2.** [demonstration] passeata *f* **-3.** [continuous line] procissão *f.*
processor ['prəʊsesə^r] *n* **-1.** *COMPUT* processador *m* **-2.** *CULIN* processador *m* de alimentos.
pro-choice *adj* favorável ao direito da mulher de optar ou não pelo aborto.
proclaim [prə'kleɪm] *vt* **-1.** [declare] proclamar, declarar **-2.** [law] promulgar.
proclamation [,prɒklə'meɪʃn] *n* **-1.** proclamação *f* **-2.** [of law] promulgação *f.*
proclivity [prə'klɪvətɪ] (*pl* **-ies**) *n fml*: ~ **(to** *OR* **towards sthg)** propensão *f OR* tendência *f* (a algo).
procrastinate [prə'kræstɪneɪt] *vi* procrastinar, protelar.
procrastination [prə,kræstɪ'neɪʃn] *n (U)* procrastinação *f*, protelação *f.*
procreate ['prəʊkrɪeɪt] *vi* procriar.
procreation [,prəʊkrɪ'eɪʃn] *n (U)* procriação *f.*

procurator fiscal ['prɒkjʊreɪtə^r-] *n Scot oficial público responsável por levar as pessoas a julgamento.*
procure [prə'kjʊə^r] *vt* conseguir, obter.
procurement [prə'kjʊəmənt] *n (U)* aquisição *f.*
prod [prɒd] (*pt* & *pp* **-ded**, *cont* **-ding**) <> *n* **-1.** [push, poke] cutucão *m*, empurrão *m* **-2.** *fig* [reminder] toque *m.* <> *vt* **-1.** [push, poke] cutucar, empurrar **-2.** [remind, prompt]: **to ~ sb (into doing sthg)** dar um toque em alguém (para fazer algo *OR* para que faça algo).
prodigal ['prɒdɪgl] *adj* pródigo(ga).
prodigious [prə'dɪdʒəs] *adj* prodigioso(sa).
prodigy ['prɒdɪdʒɪ] (*pl* **-ies**) *n* prodígio *m.*
produce [*n* 'prɒdju:s, *vb* prə'dju:s] <> *n* **-1.** [goods] produtos *mpl* **-2.** [fruit and vegetables] produtos *mpl* agrícolas. <> *vt* **-1.** [gen] produzir **-2.** *BIOL* gerar **-3.** [yield - raw materials, crop] produzir; [- interest, profit] gerar **-4.** [present, show] apresentar.
producer [prə'dju:sə^r] *n* **-1.** [gen] produtor *m*, -ra *f* **-2.** [theatre] diretor *m*, -ra *f.*
product ['prɒdʌkt] *n* **-1.** [thing manufactured or grown] produto *m* **-2.** [result]: **to be a ~ of sthg** ser resultado *OR* produto de algo.
production [prə'dʌkʃn] *n* produção *f*; **to put sthg/go into ~** começar a produzir *OR* fabricar algo.
production line *n* linha *f* de produção.
production manager *n* gerente *mf* de produção.
productive [prə'dʌktɪv] *adj* produtivo(va).
productively [prə'dʌktɪvlɪ] *adv* de forma produtiva.
productivity [,prɒdʌk'tɪvətɪ] *n (U)* produtividade *f.*
productivity deal *n* acordo *m* de produtividade.
Prof. [prɒf] (*abbr of* **Professor**) *n* Prof.
profane [prə'feɪn] *adj* obsceno(na).
profanity [prə'fænətɪ] (*pl* **-ies**) *n* **-1.** [of language, behaviour] obscenidade *f*, indecência *f* **-2.** [word] blasfêmia *f.*
profess [prə'fes] *vt* **-1.** [claim] alegar; **to ~ to do/to be sthg** alegar fazer/ser algo **-2.** [declare] declarar.
professed [prə'fest] *adj* **-1.** [avowed] declarado(da) **-2.** [alleged] pretenso(sa).
profession [prə'feʃn] *n* **-1.** [career] profissão *f*; **by ~** por profissão **-2.** [body of people] categoria *f (profissional).*
professional [prə'feʃənl] <> *adj* profissional. <> *n* profissional *mf.*
professional foul *n* falta *f* intencional.
professionalism [prə'feʃnəlɪzm] *n* [high quality] profissionalismo *m.*
professionally [prə'feʃnəlɪ] *adv* profissionalmente; **to be ~ trained** receber orientação profissional.
professor [prə'fesə^r] *n* **-1.** *UK* [head of department] chefe *mf* de departamento **-2.** *US* & *Can* [teacher, lecturer] professor *m (universitário)*, professora *f (universitária).*
professorship [prə'fesəʃɪp] *n UK* cátedra *f*; *US cargo de professor universitário.*
proffer ['prɒfə^r] *vt*: **to ~ sthg (to sb)** oferecer algo (a alguém).
proficiency [prə'fɪʃənsɪ] *n (U)* proficiência *f*; **~ in sthg** proficiência em algo.
proficient [prə'fɪʃənt] *adj* proficiente, competente; **to be ~ in** *OR* **at sthg** ter competência em algo; **to be ~ in a foreign language** ter proficiência em uma língua estrangeira.
profile ['prəʊfaɪl] *n* perfil *m*; **in ~** de perfil; **to keep a low profile** *fig* não chamar a atenção.
profit ['prɒfɪt] <> *n* **-1.** [financial gain] lucro *m*; **to make a ~** ter lucro; **to sell sthg at a ~** vender algo com lucro **-2.** *(U)* [advantage] proveito *m*, benefício *m.* <> *vi*: **to ~ (from** *OR* **by sthg)** tirar proveito (de algo).
profitability [,prɒfɪtə'bɪlətɪ] *n (U)* lucratividade *f*, rentabilidade *f.*
profitable ['prɒfɪtəbl] *adj* **-1.** [making a profit] lucrativo(va), rentável **-2.** [beneficial] proveitoso (sa).
profitably ['prɒfɪtəblɪ] *adv* **-1.** [at a profit] com lucro **-2.** [usefully] de forma proveitosa.
profiteering [,prɒfɪ'tɪərɪŋ] *n (U)* especulação *f.*
profit-making <> *adj* com fins lucrativos. <> *n (U)* obtenção *f* de lucros.
profit margin *n* margem *f* de lucro.
profit sharing [-,ʃeərɪŋ] *n (U)* participação *f* nos lucros.
profligate ['prɒflɪgɪt] *adj* **-1.** [extravagant] extravagante **-2.** [immoral] libertino(na).
pro forma [-'fɔ:mə] *adj* pro forma.
profound [prə'faʊnd] *adj* profundo(da).
profoundly [prə'faʊndlɪ] *adv* **-1.** [intensely] profundamente **-2.** [wisely] com profundidade.
profuse [prə'fju:s] *adj* **-1.** [abundant] abundante **-2.** [generous, extravagant] profuso(sa).
profusely [prə'fju:slɪ] *adv* **-1.** [abundantly] abundantemente **-2.** [generously, extravagantly] profusamente.
profusion [prə'fju:ʒn] *n* profusão *f.*
progeny ['prɒdʒənɪ] (*pl* **-ies**) *n fml* progênie *f.*
progesterone [prə'dʒestərəʊn] *n (U)* progesterona *f.*
prognosis [prɒg'nəʊsɪs] (*pl* **-noses** [-'nəʊsi:z]) *n* prognóstico *m.*
prognostication [prɒg,nɒstɪ'keɪʃn] *n* prognóstico *m.*
program ['prəʊgræm] (*pt* & *pp* **-med** *OR* **-ed**, *cont* **-ming** *OR* **-ing**) <> *n* **-1.** *COMPUT* programa *m* **-2.** *US* = **programme.** <> *vt* **-1.** *COMPUT* programar **-2.** *US* = **programme.**
programer *n US* = **programmer.**
programmable [prəʊ'græməbl] *adj* programável.
programme *UK*, **program** *US* ['prəʊgræm] <> *n* programa *m.* <> *vt* programar; **to ~ sthg to do sthg** programar algo para fazer algo *OR* para que faça algo.
programmer *UK*, **programer** *US* ['prəʊgræmə^r] *n COMPUT* programador *m*, -ra *f.*
programming ['prəʊgræmɪŋ] *n COMPUT* programação *f.*
programming language *n* linguagem *f* de programação.

progress [*n* 'prəʊgres, *vb* prə'gres] <> *n* **-1.** [gen] progresso *m*; **to make ~** [improve] fazer progresso; **to make ~ in sthg** [get on] progredir em algo; **in ~** em andamento **-2.** [physical movement] avanço *m*. <> *vi* **-1.** [gen] progredir **-2.** [move forward]: **to ~ to sthg** prosseguir para algo.

progression [prə'greʃn] *n* **-1.** [advance] progressão *f* **-2.** [series] sucessão *f*.

progressive [prə'gresɪv] *adj* **-1.** [forward-looking] progressista **-2.** [gradual] progressivo(va).

progressively [prə'gresɪvlɪ] *adv* progressivamente.

progress report *n* **-1.** [on student] relatório *m* de desempenho **-2.** [on patient] boletim *m* médico **-3.** [on work, on project] relatório *m* de acompanhamento.

prohibit [prə'hɪbɪt] *vt* proibir; **to ~ sb from doing sthg** proibir alguém de fazer algo.

prohibition [,prəʊɪ'bɪʃn] *n* proibição *f*.

prohibitive [prə'hɪbətɪv] *adj* exorbitante.

project [*n* 'prɒdʒekt, *vb* prə'dʒekt] <> *n* **-1.** [plan, idea] projeto *m* **-2.** *SCH* projeto *m*, estudo *m*; **~ on sthg** projeto estudo sobre algo. <> *vt* **-1.** [gen] projetar; **to ~ sthg on to sthg** projetar algo em algo **-2.** [estimate] projetar, estimar **-3.** [present] apresentar, dar uma imagem de. <> *vi* projetar.

projectile [prə'dʒektaɪl] *n* projétil *m*.

projection [prə'dʒekʃn] *n* **-1.** [gen] projeção *f* **-2.** [protrusion] saliência *f*.

projectionist [prə'dʒekʃənɪst] *n* operador *m*, -ra *f* de projeção *(no cinema)*.

projection room *n* sala *f* de projeção.

projector [prə'dʒektəʳ] *n* projetor *m*.

proletarian [,prəʊlɪ'teərɪən] *adj* proletário(ria).

proletariat [,prəʊlɪ'teərɪət] *n* proletariado *m*.

pro-life *adj* pró-vida.

proliferate [prə'lɪfəreɪt] *vi* proliferar.

prolific [prə'lɪfɪk] *adj* prolífico(ca).

prologue, prolog *US* ['prəʊlɒg] *n* **-1.** [introduction] prólogo *m* **-2.** *fig* [preceding event]: **~ to sthg** preâmbulo *m* para algo.

prolong [prə'lɒŋ] *vt* prolongar.

prom [prɒm] *n* **-1.** *UK inf* (*abbr of* **promenade**) [at seaside] *caminho junto ao mar* **-2.** *US* [ball] *baile de gala estudantil* **-3.** *UK inf* (*abbr of* **promenade concert**): **the Proms** *concertos que acontecem no Albert Hall, em Londres, no verão.*

promenade [,prɒmə'nɑːd] *n UK* [at seaside] calçadão *m*.

promenade concert *n UK concerto sinfônico ao qual boa parte das pessoas assiste de pé.*

prominence ['prɒmɪnəns] *n (U)* **-1.** [importance] importância *f* **-2.** [conspicuousness] notoriedade *f*, proeminência *f*.

prominent ['prɒmɪnənt] *adj* **-1.** [important - person, politician] destacado(da); [- ideas, issues] proeminente **-2.** [noticeable - building, landmark] em evidência; [- cheekbones] saliente.

prominently ['prɒmɪnəntlɪ] *adv* em evidência.

promiscuity [,prɒmɪs'kjuːətɪ] *n (U)* promiscuidade *f*.

promiscuous [prɒ'mɪskjʊəs] *adj* promíscuo(cua).

promise ['prɒmɪs] <> *n* promessa *f*; **to make (sb) a ~** fazer uma promessa (a alguém); **to show ~** ser promissor(ra). <> *vt* **-1.** [pledge]: **to ~ (sb) sthg** prometer algo (a alguém); **to ~ (sb) to do sthg** prometer (a alguém) fazer algo **-2.** [indicate]: **to ~ sthg** prometer algo; **it ~s to be a wonderful day** promete ser um dia maravilhoso. <> *vi* prometer.

promising ['prɒmɪsɪŋ] *adj* promissor(ra).

promissory note ['prɒmɪsərɪ-] *n* nota *f* promissória.

promo ['prəʊməʊ] (*pl* **-s**) *n inf* filme *m* promocional.

promontory ['prɒməntrɪ] (*pl* **-ies**) *n* promontório *m*.

promote [prə'məʊt] *vt* **-1.** [foster] promover, fomentar **-2.** [push, advertise] promover **-3.** [in job]: **to ~ sb (to sthg)** promover alguém (a algo) **-4.** *SPORT*: **to be ~d to the First Division** subir para a Primeira Divisão.

promoter [prə'məʊtəʳ] *n* **-1.** [organizer] patrocinador *m*, -ra *f* **-2.** [supporter] defensor *m*, -ra *f*.

promotion [prə'məʊʃn] *n* promoção *f*; **to get** *OR* **be given ~** ser promovido(da).

prompt [prɒmpt] <> *adj* **-1.** [quick] pronto(ta), rápido(da) **-2.** [punctual] pontual. <> *adv* pontualmente. <> *n* [*THEATRE* - line] deixa *f*; [- person] ponto *m*. <> *vt* **-1.** [provoke, persuade]: **to ~ sb (to do sthg)** levar alguém (a fazer algo) **-2.** *THEATRE* dar a deixa.

prompter ['prɒmptəʳ] *n* ponto *m (no teatro)*.

promptly ['prɒmptlɪ] *adv* **-1.** [quickly] prontamente, rapidamente **-2.** [punctually] pontualmente.

promptness ['prɒmptnɪs] *n (U)* **-1.** [quickness] rapidez *f* **-2.** [punctuality] pontualidade *f*.

promulgate ['prɒmlgeɪt] *vt* **-1.** [law, decree] promulgar **-2.** [belief, idea] propagar.

prone [prəʊn] *adj* **-1.** [susceptible]: **to be ~ to sthg/to do sthg** ser propenso(sa) a algo/a fazer algo **-2.** [lying flat] (deitado(da)) de bruços.

prong [prɒŋ] *n* dente *m (de garfo)*.

pronoun ['prəʊnaʊn] *n* pronome *m*.

pronounce [prə'naʊns] <> *vt* **-1.** [say aloud] pronunciar **-2.** [declare, state] declarar. <> *vi*: **to ~ on sthg** pronunciar-se sobre algo.

pronounced [prə'naʊnst] *adj* pronunciado(da), marcado(da).

pronouncement [prə'naʊnsmənt] *n* pronunciamento *m*.

pronto ['prɒntəʊ] *adv inf* imediatamente.

pronunciation [prə,nʌnsɪ'eɪʃn] *n* pronúncia *f*.

proof [pruːf] *n* **-1.** [gen] prova *f* **-2.** [of alcohol] teor *m* alcoólico.

proofread ['pruːfriːd] (*pt* & *pp* **-read** [-red]) *vt* revisar.

proofreader ['pruːf,riːdəʳ] *n* revisor *m*, -ra *f*.

prop [prɒp] (*pt* & *pp* **-ped**, *cont* **-ping**) <> *n* **-1.** [physical support] escora *f*, estaca *f* **-2.** *fig* [supporting thing, person] apoio *m* **-3.** *RUGBY* pilar *m*. <> *vt*: **to ~ sthg against sthg** apoiar algo em *OR* contra algo.

◆ **props** *npl* [in film, play] acessórios *mpl*.

◆ **prop up** *vt sep* **-1.** [support physically] escorar, sustentar **-2.** *fig* [sustain] apoiar.

Prop. (*abbr of* **proprietor**) proprietário *m*, -ria *f*.

propaganda [,prɒpə'gændə] *n (U)* propaganda *f*.

propagate ['prɒpəgeɪt] ◇ *vt* propagar. ◇ *vi* propagar-se.
propagation [ˌprɒpə'geɪʃn] *n* **-1.** *BOT* propagação *f* **-2.** [dissemination] propagação *f*, disseminação *f*.
propane ['prəʊpeɪn] *n (U)* propano *m*.
propel [prə'pel] (*pt* & *pp* **-led**, *cont* **-ling**) *vt* **-1.** [drive forward] impulsionar **-2.** *fig* [urge] impelir.
propeller [prə'peləʳ] *n* hélice *f*.
propelling pencil [prə'pelɪŋ-] *n UK* lapiseira *f*.
propensity [prə'pensətɪ] (*pl* **-ies**) *n fml*: ~ **for** *OR* **to sthg** propensão *f* a algo; ~ **to do sthg** propensão para fazer algo.
proper ['prɒpəʳ] *adj* **-1.** [real] verdadeiro(ra) **-2.** [correct] correto(ta), exato(ta) **-3.** [decent] decente, apropriado(da) **-4.** [specifically] próprio(pria) **-5.** *UK inf* [for emphasis]: **a** ~ **idiot** um perfeito idiota.
properly ['prɒpəlɪ] *adv* **-1.** [satisfactorily] adequadamente, bem **-2.** [correctly] direito **-3.** [decently] adequadamente.
proper noun *n* nome *m* próprio.
property ['prɒpətɪ] (*pl* **-ies**) *n* **-1.** [gen] propriedade *f* **-2.** *(U)* [buildings] imóveis *mpl* **-3.** *(U)* [land] terrenos *mpl*.
property developer *n* (empresa *f*) construtora *f*.
property owner *n* proprietário *m*, -ria *f* de um imóvel.
property tax *n* imposto *m* predial e territorial.
prophecy ['prɒfɪsɪ] (*pl* **-ies**) *n* profecia *f*.
prophesy ['prɒfɪsaɪ] (*pt* & *pp* **-ied**) *vt* profetizar.
prophet ['prɒfɪt] *n* profeta *mf*.
prophetic [prə'fetɪk] *adj* profético(ca).
propitious [prə'pɪʃəs] *adj fml* propício(cia).
proponent [prə'pəʊnənt] *n* defensor *m*, -ra *f*, partidário *m*, -ria *f*.
proportion [prə'pɔːʃn] *n* **-1.** [part] parte *f* **-2.** [ratio, comparison] proporção *f*; **in** ~ **to** em proporção a; **out of all** ~ **to** totalmente fora de proporção em relação a **-3.** *(U) ART*: **in** ~ proporcional; **out of** ~ fora de proporção; **a sense of** ~ *fig* senso *m* de proporção; **to get sthg out of** ~ *fig* fazer uma tempestade em um copo d'água sobre algo.
proportional [prə'pɔːʃənl] *adj* proporcional, em proporção a; **to be** ~ **to sthg** ser proporcional a algo.
proportional representation *n (U)* representação *f* proporcional.
proportionate [prə'pɔːʃnət] *adj* proporcional; ~ **to sthg** proporcional a algo.
proposal [prə'pəʊzl] *n* proposta *f*; **marriage** ~ proposta *f (de casamento)*.
propose [prə'pəʊz] ◇ *vt* **-1.** [suggest] propor **-2.** [introduce] apresentar **-3.** [toast] brindar a **-4.** [intend]: **to** ~ **doing** *OR* **to do sthg** ter a intenção de fazer algo. ◇ *vi* [make offer of marriage] pedir em casamento; **to** ~ **to sb** pedir a mão de alguém em casamento.
proposed [prə'pəʊzd] *adj* proposto(ta).
proposition [ˌprɒpə'zɪʃn] ◇ *n* **-1.** [statement of theory] proposição *f* **-2.** [suggestion] proposta *f*; **to make sb a** ~ fazer uma proposta a alguém. ◇ *vt fml* fazer uma proposta indecorosa a.
propound [prə'paʊnd] *vt fml* expor.
proprietary [prə'praɪətrɪ] *adj fml COMM* registrado (da).
proprietor [prə'praɪətəʳ] *n* proprietário *m*, -ria *f*.
proprietorial [praˌpraɪə'tɔːrɪəl] *adj* possessivo(va).
propriety [prə'praɪətɪ] *n (U) fml* retidão *f*.
propulsion [prə'pʌlʃn] *n (U)* propulsão *f*.
pro rata [-'rɑːtə] *adj* & *adv* pro rata.
prosaic [prəʊ'zeɪɪk] *adj* prosaico(ca).
proscenium (arch) [prə'siːnjəm-] *n* proscênio *m*.
proscribe [prəʊ'skraɪb] *vt fml* proscrever.
prose [prəʊz] ◇ *n (U)* prosa *f*. ◇ *comp* em prosa.
prosecute ['prɒsɪkjuːt] ◇ *vt JUR* processar; **to be** ~**d for sthg** ser processado(da) por algo. ◇ *vi* **-1.** [bring a charge] promover ação penal **-2.** [represent in court] sustentar acusação em juizo.
prosecution [ˌprɒsɪ'kjuːʃn] *n* **-1.** [criminal charge] acusação *f* **-2.** [lawyers]: **the** ~ a acusação.
prosecutor ['prɒsɪkjuːtəʳ] *n* promotor *m*, -ra *f*.
prospect [*n* 'prɒspekt, *vb* prə'spekt] ◇ *n* **-1.** [hope] possibilidade *f* **-2.** [probability] perspectiva *f*. ◇ *vi* prospectar; **to** ~ **for sthg** prospectar algo.
◆ **prospects** *npl* [chances of success]: ~**s (for sthg)** perspectivas *fpl* (de algo).
prospecting [prə'spektɪŋ] *n (U)* prospecção *f*.
prospective [prə'spektɪv] *adj* provável, possível.
prospector [prə'spektəʳ] *n* prospector *m*, -ra *f*.
prospectus [prə'spektəs] (*pl* **-es**) *n* prospecto *m*, folheto *m* informativo.
prosper ['prɒspəʳ] *vi* prosperar.
prosperity [prɒ'sperətɪ] *n (U)* prosperidade *f*.
prosperous ['prɒspərəs] *adj* próspero(ra).
prostate (gland) ['prɒsteɪt-] *n* próstata *f*.
prosthesis [prɒs'θiːsɪs] (*pl* **-theses** ['θiːsiːz]) *n* prótese *f*.
prostitute ['prɒstɪtjuːt] *n* prostituta *f*; **male** ~ prostituto *m*.
prostitution [ˌprɒstɪ'tjuːʃn] *n (U)* prostituição *f*.
prostrate [*adj* 'prɒstreɪt, *vb* prɒ'streɪt] ◇ *adj* prostrado(da). ◇ *vt*: **to** ~ **o.s. (before sb)** prostrar-se (diante de alguém).
protagonist [prə'tægənɪst] *n* protagonista *mf*.
protect [prə'tekt] *vt* proteger; **to** ~ **sb/sthg from, to** ~ **sb/sthg against** proteger alguém/algo de/contra.
protection [prə'tekʃn] *n (U)* proteção *f*; ~ **from sb/sthg,** ~ **against sb/sthg** proteção de *OR* contra alguém/algo.
protectionism [prə'tekʃənɪzm] *n (U)* protecionismo *m*.
protectionist [prə'tekʃənɪst] *adj* protecionista.
protection money *n (U)* dinheiro *m* pago em troca de proteção.
protective [prə'tektɪv] *adj* protetor(ra); **to be/feel** ~ **towards sb** ser/sentir-se protetor(ra) em relação a alguém.
protective custody *n (U)* custódia *f* preventiva.
protectiveness [prə'tektɪvnɪs] *n (U)* sentimento *m* de proteção.
protector [prə'tektəʳ] *n* **-1.** [person] protetor *m*, -ra *f* **-2.** [on machine] dispositivo *m* de proteção.
protectorate [prə'tektərət] *n* protetorado *m*.
protégé ['prɒteʒeɪ] *n* protegido *m*.

protégée ['prɒteʒeɪ] *n* protegida *f.*
protein ['prəʊtiːn] *n (U)* proteína *f.*
protest [*n* 'prəʊtest, *vb* prə'test] ◇ *n* protesto *m.* ◇ *vt* **-1.** [state] protestar, declarar **-2.** *US* [protest against] protestar contra. ◇ *vi* [complain] protestar; **to ~ about/against sthg** protestar por/contra algo.
Protestant ['prɒtɪstənt] ◇ *adj* protestante. ◇ *n* protestante *mf.*
Protestantism ['prɒtɪstəntɪzm] *n (U)* protestantismo *m.*
protestation [ˌprɒte'steɪʃn] *n fml* **-1.** [declaration] declaração *f* **-2.** [protest] protesto *m.*
protester [prə'testəʳ] *n* manifestante *mf.*
protest march *n* marcha *f* de protesto, manifestação *f.*
protocol ['prəʊtəkɒl] *n (U)* protocolo *m.*
proton ['prəʊtɒn] *n* próton *m.*
prototype ['prəʊtətaɪp] *n* protótipo *m.*
protracted [prə'træktɪd] *adj* prolongado(da).
protractor [prə'træktəʳ] *n* transferidor *m.*
protrude [prə'truːd] *vi* salientar-se, sobressair-se; **to ~ from sthg** sobressair-se em algo.
protrusion [prə'truːʒn] *n* saliência *f.*
protuberance [prə'tjuːbərəns] *n* protuberância *f.*
proud [praʊd] *adj* **-1.** [gen] orgulhoso(sa); **to be ~ of sb/sthg** estar orgulhoso(sa) de alguém/algo; **to be ~ to do sthg** ter a honra de fazer algo **-2.** *pej* [arrogant] orgulhoso(sa), arrogante.
proudly ['praʊdlɪ] *adv* **-1.** [with satisfaction] orgulhosamente **-2.** *pej* [arrogantly] arrogantemente.
provable ['pruːvəbl] *adj* demonstrável.
prove [pruːv] (*pp* **-d** *OR* **proven**) *vt* **-1.** [show to be true] provar, demonstrar **-2.** [show o.s. to be]: **to ~ (to be) sthg** demonstrar ser algo; **to ~ o.s. to be sthg** mostrar-se algo.
proven ['pruːvn, 'prəʊvn] ◇ *pp* ▷ **prove**. ◇ *adj* comprovado(da).
Provençal [ˌprɒvɒn'sɑːl] ◇ *adj* provençal. ◇ *n* [language] provençal *m.*
Provence [prɒ'vɒns] *n* Provença; **in ~** na Provença.
proverb ['prɒvɜːb] *n* provérbio *m.*
proverbial [prə'vɜːbjəl] *adj* proverbial.
provide [prə'vaɪd] *vt* fornecer, prover; **to ~ sb with sthg** proporcionar algo a alguém; **to ~ sthg for sb** oferecer algo a alguém.
◆ **provide for** *vt fus* **-1.** [support] sustentar, manter **-2.** *fml* [make arrangements for] prever, tomar medidas para.
provided [prə'vaɪdɪd] ◆ **provided (that)** *conj* desde que, contanto que.
providence ['prɒvɪdəns] *n (U)* providência *f.*
providential [ˌprɒvɪ'denʃl] *adj fml* providencial.
provider [prə'vaɪdəʳ] *n* provedor *m*, -ra *f.*
providing [prə'vaɪdɪŋ] ◆ **providing (that)** *conj* desde que.
province ['prɒvɪns] *n* **-1.** [part of country] província *f* **-2.** [specialist subject] campo *m*, ramo *m* do conhecimento; [area of responsibility] alçada *f.*
◆ **provinces** *npl*: **the ~s** o interior.
provincial [prə'vɪnʃl] *adj* **-1.** [of a province] da província **-2.** *pej* [narrow-minded] provinciano(na).
provision [prə'vɪʒn] *n* **-1.** *(U)* [act of supplying] provisão *f* **-2.** *(U)* [arrangement] providência *f*; **to make ~ for/sthg** tomar providências para algo; **to make ~ for/sb** garantir o sustento de alguém **-3.** [in agreement, law] cláusula *f.*
◆ **provisions** *npl* [supplies] provisões *fpl.*
provisional [prə'vɪʒənl] *adj* provisório(ria).
Provisional IRA *n*: **the ~** *braço armado do Sinn Féin, Irlanda do Norte.*
provisional licence *n UK* carteira *f* provisória.
provisionally [prə'vɪʒnəlɪ] *adv* temporariamente.
proviso [prə'vaɪzəʊ] (*pl* **-s**) *n* condição *f*; **with the ~ that** com a condição de que.
provocation [ˌprɒvə'keɪʃn] *n* provocação *f.*
provocative [prə'vɒkətɪv] *adj* **-1.** [controversial] provocativo(va) **-2.** [sexy] provocante.
provocatively [prə'vɒkətɪvlɪ] *adv* **-1.** [controversially] provocativamente **-2.** [sexily] provocantemente.
provoke [prə'vəʊk] *vt* provocar.
provoking [prə'vəʊkɪŋ] *adj* provocador(ra).
provost *n* **-1.** *UK* [head of college] reitor *m*, -ra *f* **-2.** *Scot* [head of town council] prefeito *m*, -ta *f.*
prow [praʊ] *n* proa *f.*
prowess ['praʊɪs] *n (U) fml* façanha *f.*
prowl [praʊl] ◇ *n*: **on the ~** de ronda, rondando. ◇ *vt* rondar por. ◇ *vi* fazer a ronda.
prowl car *n US* carro *m* patrulha.
prowler ['praʊləʳ] *n* gatuno *m*, -na *f.*
proximity [prɒk'sɪmətɪ] *n (U) fml* proximidade *f*; **~ to sthg** proximidade a algo; **in the ~ of sthg** nas proximidades de algo.
proxy ['prɒksɪ] (*pl* **-ies**) *n*: **by ~** por procuração.
prude [pruːd] *n* pessoa *f* pudica, puritano *m*, -na *f.*
prudence ['pruːdns] *n (U) fml* prudência *f.*
prudent ['pruːdnt] *adj* prudente.
prudently ['pruːdntlɪ] *adv* prudentemente.
prudish ['pruːdɪʃ] *adj* pudico(ca).
prune [pruːn] ◇ *n* ameixa *f* seca. ◇ *vt* podar.
prurient ['prʊərɪənt] *adj fml* lascivo(va).
Prussian ['prʌʃn] ◇ *adj* prussiano(na). ◇ *n* prussiano *m*, -na *f.*
pry [praɪ] (*pt* & *pp* **pried**) *vi* bisbilhotar; **to ~ into sthg** intrometer-se em algo.
PS (*abbr of* **postscript**) *n* PS.
psalm [sɑːm] *n* salmo *m.*
pseud [sjuːd] *n UK inf* intelectualóide *mf.*
pseudo- [ˌsjuːdəʊ] *prefix* pseudo(-).
pseudonym ['sjuːdənɪm] *n* pseudônimo *m.*
psi (*abbr of* **pounds per square inch**) psi *f.*
psoriasis [sɒ'raɪəsɪs] *n (U)* psoríase *f.*
psst [pst] *excl* psiu!
PST (*abbr of* **Pacific Standard Time**) *n horário oficial da costa oeste dos Estados Unidos.*
psych [saɪk] ◆ **psych up** *vt sep inf* preparar psicologicamente; **to ~ o.s. up** preparar-se psicologicamente.
psyche ['saɪkɪ] *n* psique *f.*
psychedelic [ˌsaɪkɪ'delɪk] *adj* psicodélico(ca).
psychiatric [ˌsaɪkɪ'ætrɪk] *adj* psiquiátrico(ca).
psychiatric nurse *n* enfermeiro *m* psiquiátrico, enfermeira *f* psiquiátrica.
psychiatrist [saɪ'kaɪətrɪst] *n* psiquiatra *mf.*

psychiatry [saɪ'kaɪətrɪ] *n (U)* psiquiatria *f*.
psychic ['saɪkɪk] <> *adj* **-1.** [clairvoyant] paranormal **-2.** [mental] psíquico(ca). <> *n* paranormal *mf*, médium *mf*.
psychoanalyse, -yze *US* [ˌsaɪkəʊ'ænəlaɪz] *vt* psicanalisar.
psychoanalysis [ˌsaɪkəʊə'næləsɪs] *n (U)* psicanálise *f*.
psychoanalyst [ˌsaɪkəʊ'ænəlɪst] *n* psicanalista *mf*.
psychological [ˌsaɪkə'lɒdʒɪkl] *adj* psicológico(ca).
psychological warfare *n (U)* guerra *f* psicológica.
psychologist [saɪ'kɒlədʒɪst] *n* psicólogo *m*, -ga *f*.
psychology [saɪ'kɒlədʒɪ] *n* psicologia *f*.
psychopath ['saɪkəpæθ] *n* psicopata *mf*.
psychosis [saɪ'kəʊsɪs] (*pl* **-choses** ['kəʊsi:z]) *n* psicose *f*.
psychosomatic [ˌsaɪkəʊsə'mætɪk] *adj* psicossomático(ca).
psychotherapy [ˌsaɪkəʊ'θerəpɪ] *n (U)* psicoterapia *f*.
psychotic [saɪ'kɒtɪk] <> *adj* psicótico(ca). <> *n* psicótico *m*, -ca *f*.
pt **-1.** *abbr of* **pint** **-2.** (*abbr of* **point**) pt.
Pt. (*abbr of* **Point**) [on map] Pta.
PT (*abbr of* **physical training**) *n* treinamento *m* físico.
PTA (*abbr of* **parent-teacher association**) *n* ≃ APM *f*.
Pte. (*abbr of* **Private**) *soldado do exército britânico*.
PTO (*abbr of* **please turn over**) vide verso.
PTV *n* (*abbr of* **pay television**) televisão *f* por assinatura.
pub [pʌb] *n* pub *m*, bar *m*.

PUB

Em toda a Grã-Bretanha, o *pub* é um dos grandes centros da vida social, mas sua importância varia de acordo com a região (Inglaterra, Escócia, Irlanda ou País de Gales) e com a cidade ou povoado em que se encontra. Esses estabelecimentos, de acesso proibido a menores de 16 anos desacompanhados, eram conhecidos por seus horários rígidos de funcionamento, embora tenham se tornado mais flexíveis, de alguns anos para cá (ver *licensing hours*). Em geral, os *pubs* oferecem grande variedade de cervejas e bebidas alcoólicas. Batatinhas fritas em saquinhos eram aperitivos tradicionais nos *pubs*, mas muitos hoje servem pratos rápidos também.

pub. (*abbr of* **published**) publicado.
pub-crawl *n UK*: **to go on a ~** andar de bar em bar.
puberty ['pju:bətɪ] *n (U)* puberdade *f*.
pubescent [pju:'besnt] *adj* púbere.
pubic ['pju:bɪk] *adj* pubiano(na).
public ['pʌblɪk] <> *adj* **-1.** [gen] público(ca); **to go ~ on sthg** *inf* levar a público; **to make sthg ~** tornar algo público **-2.** *COMM*: **to go ~** abrir o capital. <> *n*: **the ~** o público; **in ~** em público.
public-address system *n* sistema *m* de auto-falantes.
publican ['pʌblɪkən] *n UK* dono *m*, -na *f* de um pub.
publication [ˌpʌblɪ'keɪʃn] *n* publicação *f*.
public company *n* sociedade *f* anônima *(com ações na Bolsa)*.
public convenience *n UK* sanitário *m* público.
public domain *n*: **in the ~** em domínio público.
public holiday *n* feriado *m* nacional.
public house *n UK fml* bar *m*, pub *m*.
publicist ['pʌblɪsɪst] *n* publicitário *m*, -ria *f*.
publicity [pʌb'lɪsɪtɪ] <> *n* publicidade *f*. <> *comp* publicitário(ria).
publicity stunt *n* golpe *f* publicitário, jogada *f* de marketing.
publicize, -ise ['pʌblɪsaɪz] *vt* divulgar.
public limited company *n* sociedade *f* anônima *(com ações na Bolsa)*.
publicly ['pʌblɪklɪ] *adv* publicamente.
public office *n* cargo *m* público.
public opinion *n (U)* opinião *f* pública.
public ownership *n (U)* bem *m* público.
public prosecutor *n* promotor *m* público, promotora *f* pública.
public relations <> *n (U)* relações *fpl* públicas. <> *npl* relações *f* públicas.
public relations officer *n* agente *mf* de relações públicas.
public school *n* **-1.** *UK* [private school] escola *f* particular **-2.** *US* & *Scot* [state school] escola *f* pública.

PUBLIC SCHOOL

Na Inglaterra e no País de Gales, a *public school* é uma escola privada tradicional. Algumas delas, como Eton e Harrow, gozam de grande fama e são muito procuradas. Considera-se que as *public schools* formam a elite da nação. Nos Estados Unidos e, por vezes, também na Escócia, o termo designa uma escola pública.

public sector *n* setor *m* público.
public servant *n* servidor *m* público, servidora *f* pública.
public service vehicle *n UK* veículo *m* do serviço público.
public-spirited *adj* com espírito cívico.
public transport *n (U)* transporte *m* público.
public utility *n* utilidade *f* pública.
public works *npl* obras *fpl* públicas.
publish ['pʌblɪʃ] <> *vt* **-1.** [gen] publicar **-2.** [make known] divulgar, tornar público(ca). <> *vi* publicar.
publisher ['pʌblɪʃə^r] *n* **-1.** [company] editora *f* **-2.** [person] editor *m*, -ra *f*.
publishing ['pʌblɪʃɪŋ] *n (U)* setor *m* editorial.
publishing company, publishing house *n* editora *f*.
pub lunch *n almoço servido em um pub*.
puce [pju:s] *adj* marrom-avermelhado(da).
puck [pʌk] *n* [ice hockey] disco *m*.
pucker ['pʌkə^r] <> *vt* franzir. <> *vi* enrugar.
pudding ['pʊdɪŋ] *n* **-1.** [food - sweet] pudim *m*; [- savoury] pastelão *m* **-2.** *(U) UK* [part of meal] sobremesa *f*.
puddle ['pʌdl] *n* poça *f*.
pudgy ['pʌdʒɪ] *adj* = **podgy**.

puerile [ˈpjʊəraɪl] *adj fml* pueril.
Puerto Rican [ˌpwɜːtəʊˈriːkən] ◇ *adj* porto-riquenho(nha). ◇ *n* porto-riquenho *m*, -nha *f*.
Puerto Rico [ˌpwɜːtəʊˈriːkəʊ] *n* Porto Rico.
puff [pʌf] ◇ *n* **-1.** [of cigarette, pipe] baforada *f* **-2.** [of air, smoke] golfada *f*. ◇ *vt* baforar. ◇ *vi* **-1.** [smoke]: **to ~ at** *OR* **on sthg** dar tragadas em algo **-2.** [pant] ofegar.
◆ **puff out** *vt sep* **-1.** [chest, cheeks] inflar **-2.** [feathers] eriçar.
◆ **puff up** *vi* **-1.** [eyes, skin] inchar **-2.** [feathers] eriçar.
puffed [pʌft] *adj* **-1.** [swollen]: **~ up** inchado(da) **-2.** *UK inf* [out of breath]: **~ (out)** ofegante.
puffed sleeve *n* manga *f* bufante.
puffin [ˈpʌfɪn] *n* papagaio-do-mar *m*.
puffiness [ˈpʌfɪnɪs] *n* inchação *f*.
puff pastry, puff paste *US n (U)* massa *f* folhada.
puffy [ˈpʌfɪ] (*compar* **-ier**, *superl* **-iest**) *adj* inchado(-da).
pug [pʌg] *n* dogue *m*.
pugnacious [pʌgˈneɪʃəs] *adj fml* belicoso(sa).
puke [pjuːk] *vi v inf* vomitar.
pull [pʊl] ◇ *n* **-1.** [tug with hand] puxão *m* **-2.** [influence] prestígio *m*. ◇ *vt* **-1.** [gen] puxar; **to ~ sthg to pieces** despedaçar algo **-2.** [curtains - open] abrir; [- close] puxar **-3.** [take out - cork, tooth] arrancar; [- gun] sacar; **she ~ed herself out of the water** ela se afastou da água **-4.** [muscle, hamstring] distender **-5.** [attract] atrair. ◇ *vi* [tug with hand] puxar.
◆ **pull ahead** *vi* ultrapassar; **to ~ ahead of sb/sthg** passar à frente de alguém/algo.
◆ **pull apart** *vt sep* desmontar.
◆ **pull at** *vt fus* puxar, dar puxões em.
◆ **pull away** *vi* **-1.** [from roadside]: **to ~ away (from)** afastar-se (da margem da estrada) **-2.** [in race]: **to ~ away (from)** disparar na frente (de).
◆ **pull back** *vi* recuar.
◆ **pull down** *vt sep* demolir.
◆ **pull in** *vi* [vehicle] encostar.
◆ **pull off** *vt sep* **-1.** [take off] tirar rapidamente **-2.** [succeed in] conseguir levar a cabo.
◆ **pull on** *vt sep* **-1.** [clothes] vestir rapidamente **-2.** [shoes] calçar rapidamente.
◆ **pull out** ◇ *vt sep* retirar. ◇ *vi* **-1.** [train] partir **-2.** [vehicle] entrar na estrada **-3.** [withdraw] retirar.
◆ **pull over** *vi* [vehicle, driver] encostar.
◆ **pull through** ◇ *vi* [patient] restabelecer-se, recuperar-se. ◇ *vt sep* [subj: doctor] ajudar na recuperação de.
◆ **pull together** ◇ *vt sep*: **to ~ o.s. together** acalmar-se. ◇ *vi* cooperar, unir forças.
◆ **pull up** ◇ *vt sep* **-1.** [raise] levantar **-2.** [move closer] aproximar **-3.** [stop]: **to ~ sb up short** deter alguém. ◇ *vi* parar, deter.
pull-down menu *n COMPUT* menu *m* suspenso.
pulley [ˈpʊlɪ] (*pl* **pulleys**) *n* roldana *f*.
pullout [ˈpʊlaʊt] *n* **-1.** [of troops] retirada *f* **-2.** [in magazine] encarte *m*.
pullover [ˈpʊlˌəʊvə[r]] *n* pulôver *m*.
pulp [pʌlp] ◇ *adj* barato(ta), de má qualidade. ◇ *n* **-1.** [soft mass] pasta *f* **-2.** [of fruit] polpa *f* **-3.** [of wood] cerne *m*. ◇ *vt* reduzir à pasta de papel.
pulpit [ˈpʊlpɪt] *n* púlpito *m*.
pulsar [ˈpʌlsɑː[r]] *n* pulsar *m*.
pulsate [pʌlˈseɪt] *vi* **-1.** [heart] pulsar, palpitar **-2.** [air, sound] vibrar; **pulsating rhythm** ritmo *m* vibrante.
pulse [pʌls] ◇ *n* **-1.** [in body] pulso *m*; **to take sb's ~** tomar o pulso de alguém **-2.** *TECH* impulso *m*. ◇ *vi* [throb - blood] pulsar; [- music, room] vibrar.
◆ **pulses** *npl* [food] grãos *mpl*.
pulverize, -ise [ˈpʌlvəraɪz] *vt* pulverizar.
puma [ˈpjuːmə] (*pl inv OR* **-s**) *n* puma *m*.
pumice (stone) [ˈpʌmɪs-] *n (U)* pedra-pomes *f*.
pummel [ˈpʌml] (*UK pt* & *pp* **-led**, *cont* **-ling**, *US pt* & *pp* **-ed**, *cont* **-ing**) *vt* esmurrar.
pump [pʌmp] ◇ *n* bomba *f*. ◇ *vt* **-1.** [convey by pumping] bombear **-2.** *inf* [invest]: **to ~ money into sthg** injetar dinheiro em algo **-3.** *inf* [interrogate] sondar. ◇ *vi* **-1.** [machine] bater **-2.** [person] arfar **-3.** [heart] palpitar.
◆ **pumps** *npl* [shoes] sapatilhas *fpl*.
pumpernickel [ˈpʌmpənɪkl] *n (U)* pão *m* de centeio.
pumpkin [ˈpʌmpkɪn] *n* abóbora *f*.
pumpkin pie *n* torta *f* de abóbora.
pun [pʌn] *n* jogo *m* de palavras.
punch [pʌntʃ] ◇ *n* **-1.** [blow] soco *m* **-2.** [tool] punção *m* **-3.** *(U)* [drink] ponche *m*. ◇ *vt* **-1.** [hit] esmurrar, soquear **-2.** [perforate - paper, ticket] picar; [- hole] perfurar.
◆ **punch in** *vi US* bater o ponto *(na entrada)*.
◆ **punch out** *vi US* bater o ponto *(na saída)*.
Punch-and-Judy show [-ˈdʒuːdɪ-] *n teatro de fantoches para crianças apresentado normalmente na praia.*
punch-bag, punching bag *US n* saco *m* de pancadas.
punch ball *n* saco *m* de pancadas.
punch bowl *n* poncheira *f*.
punch-drunk *adj* zonzo(za), grogue.
punch(ed) card [pʌntʃ(t)-] *n* cartão *m* perfurado.
punching bag *n US* = **punch-bag**.
punch line *n* frase *f* final, arremate *m (de uma história)*.
punch-up *n UK inf* briga *f*.
punchy [ˈpʌntʃɪ] (*compar* **-ier**, *superl* **-iest**) *adj inf* incisivo(va).
punctilious [pʌŋkˈtɪlɪəs] *adj fml* escrupuloso(sa), meticuloso(sa).
punctual [ˈpʌŋktʃʊəl] *adj* pontual.
punctually [ˈpʌŋktʃʊəlɪ] *adv* pontualmente.
punctuate [ˈpʌŋktʃʊeɪt] *vt* **-1.** [add punctuation to] pontuar **-2.** [interrupt]: **to be ~d by** *OR* **with sthg** ser interrompido(da) por algo.
punctuation [ˌpʌŋktʃʊˈeɪʃn] *n (U)* pontuação *f*.
punctuation mark *n* sinal *m* de pontuação.
puncture [ˈpʌŋktʃə[r]] ◇ *n* furo *m*. ◇ *vt* **-1.** [tyre, ball] furar **-2.** [lung, skin] perfurar.
pundit [ˈpʌndɪt] *n* especialista *mf*, autoridade *f (em algum assunto)*.
pungent [ˈpʌndʒənt] *adj* **-1.** [strong-smelling] forte, penetrante **-2.** *fig* [powerful] pujente.
punish [ˈpʌnɪʃ] *vt* punir; **to ~ sb for sthg/for doing**

sthg punir alguém por algo/por fazer algo.
punishable ['pʌnɪʃəbl] *adj* punível, castigável.
punishing ['pʌnɪʃɪŋ] *adj* penoso(sa).
punishment ['pʌnɪʃmənt] *n* **-1.** [gen] punição *f*, castigo *m* **-2.** [heavy use]: **to take a lot of ~** sofrer estragos.
punitive ['pju:nətɪv] *adj* punitivo(va).
Punjab [,pʌn'ʒɑ:b] *n*: **the ~** o Punjab; **in the ~** no Punjab.
Punjabi [,pʌn'ʒɑ:bɪ] ◇ *adj* punjabi. ◇ *n* **-1.** [person] punjabi *mf* **-2.** [language] punjabi *m*.
punk [pʌŋk] ◇ *adj* punk. ◇ *n* **-1.** *(U)* [music]: **~ (rock)** rock *m* punk **-2.** [person]: **~ (rocker)** roqueiro *m*, -ra *f* punk **-3.** ***US inf*** [lout] rebelde *mf*.
punnet ['pʌnɪt] *n* ***UK*** cesto *m*.
punt [pʌnt] ◇ *n* **-1.** [boat] barco *m* a remo **-2.** [Irish currency] libra *f* irlandesa. ◇ *vi* [in boat] navegar em barco a remo.
punter ['pʌntə^r] *n* **-1.** [someone who bets] apostador *m*, -ra *f* **-2.** ***UK inf*** [customer] cliente *mf*.
puny ['pju:nɪ] (*compar* **-ier**, *superl* **-iest**) *adj* **-1.** [person] raquítico(ca) **-2.** [limbs] fraco(ca) **-3.** [effort] débil.
pup [pʌp] *n* **-1.** [young dog] cachorrinho *m*, -nha *f* **-2.** [young seal, otter] filhote *m*.
pupil ['pju:pl] *n* **-1.** [student] aluno *m*, -na *f* **-2.** [follower] pupilo *m*, -la *f* **-3.** [of eye] pupila *f*.
puppet ['pʌpɪt] *n* **-1.** [string puppet] marionete *f* **-2.** [glove puppet] fantoche *m* **-3.** ***pej*** [person, country] fantoche *mf*.
puppet government *n* governo *m* de marionetes.
puppet show *n* teatro *m* de marionetes.
puppy ['pʌpɪ] (*pl* **-ies**) *n* cachorrinho *m*, -nha *f*.
puppy fat *n (U)* ***inf*** dobrinhas *fpl (do bebê)*.
purchase ['pɜ:tʃəs] ***fml*** ◇ *n* **-1.** *(U)* [act of buying] compra *f*, aquisição *f* **-2.** [thing bought] aquisição *f* **-3.** [grip] apoio *m*. ◇ *vt* comprar, adquirir.
purchase order *n* ordem *f* de compra.
purchase price *n* preço *m* de compra.
purchaser ['pɜ:tʃəsə^r] *n* comprador *m*, -ra *f*.
purchase tax *n* ***UK*** imposto *m* de compras.
purchasing power ['pɜ:tʃəsɪŋ-] *n (U)* poder *m* de compra.
purdah ['pɜ:də] *n (U)* RELIG *prática muçulmana de manter as mulheres longe do contato com os homens.*
pure [pjʊə^r] *adj* **-1.** [gen] puro(ra) **-2.** [clear] cristalino(na) **-3.** ***literary*** [chaste] puro(ra) **-4.** [for emphasis] mero(ra), puro(ra).
purebred ['pjʊəbred] *adj* puro-sangue.
puree ['pjʊəreɪ] ◇ *n* purê *m*. ◇ *vt* amassar.
purely ['pjʊəlɪ] *adv* puramente.
pureness ['pjʊənɪs] *n (U)* pureza *f*.
purgative ['pɜ:gətɪv] *n* purgante *m*.
purgatory ['pɜ:gətrɪ] *n (U)* ***hum*** [suffering] purgatório *m*.
◆ **Purgatory** *n* [place] Purgatório *m*.
purge [pɜ:dʒ] ◇ *n* POL expurgo *m*. ◇ *vt* **-1.** POL purgar **-2.** [rid]: **to ~ sthg (of sthg)** livrar algo (de algo); **to ~ o.s. (of sthg)** livrar-se (de algo).
purification [,pjʊərɪfɪ'keɪʃn] *n (U)* purificação *f*.
purifier ['pjʊərɪfaɪə^r] *n* purificador *m*.
purify ['pjʊərɪfaɪ] (*pt* & *pp* **-ied**) *vt* purificar.
purist ['pjʊərɪst] *n* purista *mf*.
puritan ['pjʊərɪtən] ◇ *adj* puritano(na). ◇ *n* puritano *m*, -na *f*.
puritanical [,pjʊərɪ'tænɪkl] *adj* ***pej*** puritano(na).
purity ['pjʊərətɪ] *n (U)* **-1.** pureza *f* **-2.** ***literary*** [chastity] pureza *f*.
purl [pɜ:l] ◇ *n* laçada *f*. ◇ *vt* dar uma laçada.
purloin [pɜ:'lɔɪn] *vt* ***fml*** surrupiar.
purple ['pɜ:pl] ◇ *adj* purpúreo(rea). ◇ *n* púrpura *f*.
purport [pə'pɔ:t] *vi* ***fml***: **to ~ to do/be sthg** pretender fazer/ser algo.
purpose ['pɜ:pəs] *n* **-1.** [objective, reason] objetivo *m*, propósito *m* **-2.** [use] propósito *m*; **to no ~** em vão **-3.** [determination] determinação *f*.
◆ **on purpose** *adv* de propósito.
purpose-built *adj* especialmente construído(da), feito(ta) sob medida.
purposeful ['pɜ:pəsfʊl] *adj* determinado(da), resoluto(ta).
purposely ['pɜ:pəslɪ] *adv* deliberadamente, intencionalmente.
purr [pɜ:^r] ◇ *n* **-1.** [of cat] ronrom *m* **-2.** [of engine] ronco *m*. ◇ *vi* **-1.** [gen] roncar **-2.** [cat] ronronar.
purse [pɜ:s] ◇ *n* **-1.** [for money] carteira *f* **-2.** ***US*** [handbag] bolsa *f*. ◇ *vt* franzir *(em desagrado)*.
purser ['pɜ:sə^r] *n* comissário *m*, -ria *f* de bordo.
purse snatcher [-,snætʃə^r] *n* ***US*** trombadinha *mf*.
purse strings *npl*: **to hold the ~** controlar os gastos, administrar o dinheiro.
pursue [pə'sju:] *vt* **-1.** [follow] perseguir **-2.** [hobby] dedicar-se a **-3.** [interest, aim] buscar, ir atrás de **-4.** [take further] aprofundar-se em.
pursuer [pə'sju:ə^r] *n* perseguidor *m*, -ra *f*.
pursuit [pə'sju:t] *n* **-1.** [gen] perseguição *f*; **in ~ of sb/sthg** de busca de alguém/algo; **to be in hot ~** perseguir de perto **-2.** [of happiness, security etc] ***fml*** busca *f* **-3.** [occupation, activity] atividade *f*.
purveyor [pə'veɪə^r] *n* ***fml*** fornecedor *m*, -ra *f*.
pus [pʌs] *n (U)* pus *m*.
push [pʊʃ] ◇ *n* **-1.** [shove] empurrão *m* **-2.** [on button, bell] pressionamento *m* **-3.** [campaign] pressão *f* **-4.** ***phr***: **to give sb the ~ *UK inf*** [end relationship] dar o fora em alguém; [dismiss] mandar alguém embora. ◇ *vt* **-1.** [press, move - door, person] empurrar; [- button] apertar **-2.** [encourage] incitar; **to ~ sb to do sthg** incitar alguém a fazer algo **-3.** [force] impelir; **to ~ sb into doing sthg** impelir alguém a fazer algo **-4.** ***inf*** [promote] promover **-5.** ***drugs sl*** [sell illegally] traficar **-6.** ***inf*** [approach]: **we were ~ing 90 miles an hour** estávamos beirando as 90 milhas por hora. ◇ *vi* **-1.** [shove] empurrar; **to ~ through** abrir caminho aos empurrões em **-2.** [on button, bell] apertar **-3.** [campaign]: **to ~ for sthg** fazer pressão por algo.
◆ **push ahead** *vi* prosseguir; **to ~ ahead with sthg** seguir em frente com algo.
◆ **push around** *vt sep* ***inf fig*** [bully] mandar.
◆ **push in** *vi* [in queue] furar.
◆ **push off** *vi* ***inf*** [go away] largar-se.
◆ **push on** *vi* [continue] seguir em frente sem parar.
◆ **push over** *vt sep* derrubar.

◆ **push through** *vt sep* [force to be accepted] conseguir que se aprove.

pushbike ['pʊʃbaɪk] *n UK* bici *f.*

push-button *adj* de botão.

pushcart ['pʊʃkɑ:t] *n* carrinho *m* de mão.

pushchair ['pʊʃtʃeəʳ] *n UK* carrinho *m* de bebê.

pushed [pʊʃt] *adj inf*: **to be ~ for sthg** andar meio curto(ta) de algo; **to be hard ~ to do sthg** estar com dificuldades para fazer algo.

pusher ['pʊʃəʳ] *n drugs sl* traficante *mf*, vendedor *m*, -ra *f* de drogas.

pushover ['pʊʃ,əʊvəʳ] *n inf* otário *m*, -ria *f.*

push-start *vt* arrancar empurrando.

push-up *n US* flexão *f.*

pushy ['pʊʃɪ] (*compar* **-ier**, *superl* **-iest**) *adj pej* agressivo(va).

puss [pʊs], **pussy (cat)** ['pʊsɪ-] *n inf* gatinho *m*, bichano *m.*

pussy willow ['pʊsɪ-] *n* salgueiro *m.*

put [pʊt] (*pt* & *pp* **put**, *cont* **-ting**) *vt* **-1.** [gen] colocar, pôr **-2.** [express] colocar, expressar; **to ~ it to sb that** expor a alguém que, colocar para alguém que **-3.** [ask] colocar, perguntar **-4.** [cause to be] colocar; **to ~ sb out of work** deixar alguém sem trabalho **-5.** [estimate]: **to ~ sthg at** avaliar algo em **-6.** [invest]: **to ~ sthg into sthg** investir algo em algo, colocar algo em algo **-7.** [apply - responsibility]: **to ~ responsiblity on sb/sthg** colocar responsabilidade em alguém/algo; **to ~ pressure on sb/sthg** pressionar alguém/algo; **to ~ tax on sthg** colocar impostos sobre algo **-8.** [write] escrever.

◆ **put across** *vt sep* expor.

◆ **put aside** *vt sep* **-1.** [place on one side] colocar de lado **-2.** [save] poupar **-3.** [disregard] deixar de lado.

◆ **put away** *vt sep* **-1.** [tidy away] colocar no lugar, organizar **-2.** *inf* [lock up] encerrar *(na prisão).*

◆ **put back** *vt sep* **-1.** [replace] repor no lugar **-2.** [postpone] adiar **-3.** [clock, watch] atrasar.

◆ **put by** *vt sep* [money] poupar.

◆ **put down** *vt sep* **-1.** [lay down] largar, pôr no chão **-2.** [quell] sufocar **-3.** *inf* [criticize] humilhar, rebaixar **-4.** [write down] apontar **-5.** *UK* [kill] sacrificar.

◆ **put down to** *vt sep* atribuir a.

◆ **put forward** *vt sep* **-1.** [propose] apresentar, propor **-2.** [advance] adiar **-3.** [clock, watch] adiantar.

◆ **put in** *vt sep* **-1.** [spend] dedicar **-2.** [submit] apresentar.

◆ **put off** *vt sep* **-1.** [postpone] adiar **-2.** [switch off - radio, light] desligar; [- brake] soltar **-3.** [cause to wait] fazer esperar **-4.** [discourage] desanimar, dissuadir **-5.** [disturb] distrair **-6.** [cause to dislike] desanimar, desestimular; **to ~ sb off sthg** desestimular alguém de algo.

◆ **put on** *vt sep* **-1.** [wear - trousers, hat] vestir; [- shoes] calçar **-2.** [arrange] montar **-3.** [gain in weight]: **to ~ on weight** engordar **-4.** [switch on - radio, light] ligar; [- brake] acionar **-5.** [play] tocar, pôr **-6.** [start cooking] colocar no fogo **-7.** [pretend] fingir **-8.** [bet] apostar **-9.** [add] acrescentar **-10.** *US inf* [tease] zombar de.

◆ **put onto** *vt sep* [tell about]: **to ~ sb onto sthg** indicar algo a alguém.

◆ **put out** *vt sep* **-1.** [place outside] colocar OR pôr para fora **-2.** [issue] tornar público(ca) **-3.** [extinguish] apagar **-4.** [switch off] desligar **-5.** [extend] espichar **-6.** *inf* [injure] deslocar **-7.** [annoy, upset]: **to be ~ out** ficar chateado(da) **-8.** [inconvenience] importunar, incomodar; **to ~ o.s. out** incomodar-se.

◆ **put over** *vt sep* = **put across.**

◆ **put through** *vt sep* TELEC transferir.

◆ **put together** *vt sep* **-1.** [assemble] montar **-2.** [combine] juntar, misturar **-3.** [organize] organizar.

◆ **put up** ◇ *vt sep* **-1.** [build] erguer **-2.** [raise and open - umbrella] abrir; [- flag] hastear **-3.** [fix to wall] afixar **-4.** [provide] pôr **-5.** [propose] indicar **-6.** [increase] aumentar **-7.** [provide accommodation for] hospedar. ◇ *vt fus* [offer, present] manifestar.

◆ **put upon** *vt fus UK*: **to be ~ upon** ser explorado(da).

◆ **put up to** *vt sep*: **to ~ sb up to sthg** induzir alguém a algo.

◆ **put up with** *vt fus* suportar, agüentar.

putative ['pju:tətɪv] *adj fml* suposto(ta).

put-down *n inf* comentário *m* maldoso.

putrefaction [,pju:trɪ'fækʃn] *n (U)* putrefação *f.*

putrefy ['pju:trɪfaɪ] (*pt* & *pp* **-ied**) *vi fml* putrefazer.

putrid ['pju:trɪd] *adj fml* putrefato(ta).

putsch [pʊtʃ] *n* golpe *m* de estado.

putt [pʌt] ◇ *n* tacada *f* leve *(no golfe).* ◇ *vt* dar uma tacada leve em. ◇ *vi* dar uma tacada leve.

putter ['pʌtəʳ] *n* taco *m* de golfe *(para tacadas leves).*

◆ **putter about, putter around** *US vi* = **potter about.**

putting green ['pʌtɪŋ-] *n* minicampo *m* sem obstáculos *(para jogar golfe).*

putty ['pʌtɪ] *n (U)* massa *f* de vidraceiro.

put-up job *n inf* embuste *m.*

put-upon *adj inf* explorado(da); **to feel ~** sentir-se usado (usa) da.

puzzle ['pʌzl] ◇ *n* **-1.** [toy, game] quebra-cabeça *m* **-2.** [mystery] enigma *m.* ◇ *vt* deixar perplexo(xa). ◇ *vi*: **to ~ over sthg** quebrar a cabeça com algo.

◆ **puzzle out** *vt sep* decifrar.

puzzled ['pʌzld] *adj* confuso(sa), perplexo(xa).

puzzling ['pʌzlɪŋ] *adj* desconcertante.

PVC (*abbr of* **polyvinyl chloride**) *n* PVC *m.*

Pvt. (*abbr of* **Private**) soldado *m* raso.

p.w. (*abbr of* **per week**) por semana.

PWR (*abbr of* **pressurized-water reactor**) *n reator de água pressurizada.*

PX (*abbr of* **post exchange**) *n loja em base militar norte-americana.*

Pygmy (*pl* **-ies**) *n* pigmeu *m*, -méia *f.*

pyjama *comp* de pijama.

pyjamas [pə'dʒɑ:məz] *npl* pijama *m.*

pylon ['paɪlən] *n* ELEC torre *f (de eletricidade).*

PYO (*abbr of* **pick your own**) *colha você mesmo, cartaz em fazendas convidando a pessoa a colher vegetais ou frutas a preços inferiores aos cobrados em supermercados.*

pyramid ['pɪrəmɪd] *n* pirâmide *f.*
pyramid selling *n (U)* vendas *fpl* em pirâmide.
pyre ['paɪəʳ] *n* pira *f.*
Pyrenean [ˌpɪrə'ni:ən] *adj* pirenaico(ca).
Pyrenees [ˌpɪrə'ni:z] *npl*: **the ~** os Pireneus.
Pyrex® ['paɪreks] <> *n (U)* pírex® *m inv.* <> *comp* de pírex.
pyromaniac [ˌpaɪrə'meɪnɪæk] *n* piromaníaco *m,* -ca *f.*
pyrotechnics [ˌpaɪrəʊ'teknɪks] <> *n (U)* [science] pirotécnica *f.* <> *npl fig* [show of brilliance] espetáculo *m* pirotécnico.
python ['paɪθn] (*pl inv* OR **-s**) *n* píton *m.*

q (*pl* **q's** OR **qs**), **Q** (*pl* **Q's** OR **Qs**) [kju:] *n* [letter] q, Q *m.*
Qatar [kæ'tɑ:ʳ] *n* Qatar; **in ~** no Qatar.
QC (*abbr of* **Queen's Counsel**) *n advogado que representa clientes nas cortes superiores britânicas.*
QED (*abbr of* **quod erat demonstrandum**) q.e.d., c.q.d.
QM (*abbr of* **quartermaster**) *n* quartelmestre *m.*
q.t., QT (*abbr of* **quiet**) *inf*: **on the ~** em segredo.
Q-tip® *n US* cotonete *m.*
qty (*abbr of* **quantity**) qtd *f.*
quack [kwæk] <> *n* **-1.** [noise] grasnido *m* **-2.** *inf pej* [doctor] curandeiro *m* charlatão, curandeira *f* charlatona. <> *vi* grasnir.
quad [kwɒd] *n* **-1.** (*abbr of* **quadruplet**) quádruplos *mpl,* -plas *fpl* **-2.** (*abbr of* **quadrangle**) *pátio cercado por edifícios, em geral em escola ou universidade.*
quadrangle ['kwɒdræŋgl] *n* **-1.** [figure] quadrângulo *m* **-2.** [courtyard] pátio *m.*
quadrant ['kwɒdrənt] *n* quadrante *m.*
quadraphonic [ˌkwɒdrə'fɒnɪk] *adj* quadrafônico (ca).
quadrilateral [ˌkwɒdrɪ'lætərəl] <> *adj* quadrilateral. <> *n* quadrilátero *m.*
quadruped ['kwɒdrʊped] *n* quadrúpede *m.*
quadruple [kwɒ'dru:pl] <> *adj* quadruplicado (da). <> *vt & vi* quadruplicar.
quadruplets ['kwɒdrʊplɪts] *npl* quadrigêmeos *mpl,* -meas *fpl.*
quads [kwɒdz] *npl inf* quadrigêmeos *mpl,* -meas *fpl.*
quaff [kwɒf] *vt dated* emborcar *(bebida alcoólica).*
quagmire ['kwægmaɪəʳ] *n* pântano *m.*
quail [kweɪl] (*pl inv* OR **-s**) <> *n* codorna *f.* <> *vi literary* amedrontar-se.
quaint [kweɪnt] *adj* pitoresco(ca), singular.
quaintness *n (U)* singularidade *f.*
quake [kweɪk] <> *n* (*abbr of* **earthquake**) *inf* terremoto *m.* <> *vi* tremer.
Quaker ['kweɪkəʳ] *n* quacre *m.*
qualification [ˌkwɒlɪfɪ'keɪʃn] *n* **-1.** [examination, certificate] qualificação *f,* título *m* **-2.** [quality, skill] qualificação *f* **-3.** [qualifying statement] restrição *f,* ressalva *f.*
qualified ['kwɒlɪfaɪd] *adj* **-1.** [trained] qualificado (da) **-2.** [able]: **to be ~ to do sthg** estar qualificado(da) para fazer algo **-3.** [limited] com ressalvas.
qualify ['kwɒlɪfaɪ] (*pt & pp* **-ied**) <> *vt* **-1.** [modify] restringir **-2.** [entitle]: **to ~ sb to do sthg** qualificar alguém para fazer algo. <> *vi* **-1.** [pass exams] habilitar-se **-2.** [be entitled]: **to ~ (for sthg)** qualificar-se(para algo) **-3.** SPORT classificar-se.
qualifying ['kwɒlɪfaɪɪŋ] *adj* **-1.** [modifying] qualificativo(va) **-2.** [entitling] qualificador(ra) **-3.** SPORT classificatório(ria); **~ round** fase *f* classificatória, eliminatórias *fpl.*
qualitative ['kwɒlɪtətɪv] *adj* qualitativo(va).
quality ['kwɒlətɪ] (*pl* **-ies**) <> *n* qualidade *f.* <> *comp* de qualidade.
quality control *n (U)* controle *m* de qualidade.
quality press *n UK*: **the ~** a imprensa não-sensacionalista OR de qualidade.
qualms [kwɑ:mz] *npl* receio *m,* escrúpulos *mpl.*
quandary ['kwɒndərɪ] (*pl* **-ies**) *n* dilema *m*; **to be in a ~ about** OR **over sthg** estar num dilema sobre algo.
quango ['kwæŋgəʊ] (*abbr of* **quasi-autonomous non-governmental organization**) (*pl* **-s**) *n UK usu pej na Grã-Bretanha, conselho administrativo não-eleito, indicado pelo governo para administrar um serviço público.*
quantifiable [kwɒntɪ'faɪəbl] *adj* quantificável.
quantify ['kwɒntɪfaɪ] (*pt & pp* **-ied**) *vt* quantificar.
quantitative ['kwɒntɪtətɪv] *adj* quantitativo(va).
quantity ['kwɒntətɪ] (*pl* **-ies**) *n* **-1.** quantidade *f*; **in ~** em quantidade **-2.** *phr*: **an unknown ~** uma incógnita.
quantity surveyor *n* calculista *mf* de obra.
quantum leap ['kwɒntəm-] *n* avanço *m* impressionante.
quantum theory ['kwɒntəm-] *n* teoria *f* quântica.
quarantine ['kwɒrənti:n] <> *n* quarentena *f*; **to be in ~** estar em OR de quarentena. <> *vt* pôr em quarentena.
quark [kwɑ:k] *n* **-1.** PHYSICS quark *m* **-2.** CULIN queijo *m* tipo quark.
quarrel ['kwɒrəl] (*UK pt & pp* **-led**, *cont* **-ling**, *US pt & pp* **-ed**, *cont* **-ing**) <> *n* discussão *f*; **to have no ~ with sb/sthg** não ter nada contra alguém/algo. <> *vi* discutir; **to ~ with sb** discutir com alguém; **to ~ with sthg** não estar de acordo sobre algo.
quarrelsome ['kwɒrəlsəm] *adj* briguento(ta).
quarry ['kwɒrɪ] (*pl* **-ies**, *pt & pp* **-ied**) <> *n* **-1.** [place] pedreira *f* **-2.** [prey] presa *f.* <> *vt* extrair.
quarry tile *n* ladrilho *m.*
quart [kwɔ:t] *n* **-1.** *UK* [unit of measurement] quarto *m* de galão *(1,14 litro)* **-2.** *US* [unit of measurement]

quarto *m* de galão *(0,95 litro)*.

quarter ['kwɔ:təʳ] *n* **-1.** [fraction] quarto *m* **-2.** [in telling time]: **it's a ~ past two** *UK*, **it's a ~ after two** *US* são duas e quinze; **it's a ~ to two** *UK*, **it's a ~ of two** *US* faltam quinze para as duas **-3.** [of year] trimestre *m* **-4.** *US* [coin] moeda *f* de 25 centavos **-5.** [four ounces] quarto *m* de libra *(113,396 gr)* **-6.** [area in town] quarteirão *m* **-7.** [direction] lugar *m*, parte *f*; **they came from all ~s of the globe** eles vieram de todos os cantos da terra.

◆ **quarters** *npl* [rooms] alojamentos *mpl*.

◆ **at close quarters** *adv* de perto.

quarterback ['kwɔ:təbæk] *n US jogador de futebol americano que lança a bola nas jogadas ofensivas.*

quarterdeck ['kwɔ:tədek] *n* tombadilho *m* superior.

quarter-final *n* quarta-de-final *f*.

quarter-hour *adj* de quinze minutos.

quarter-light *n UK* janelinha *f* para ventilação *(no automóvel)*.

quarterly ['kwɔ:təlɪ] (*pl* **-ies**) <> *adj* trimestral. <> *adv* trimestralmente. <> *n* revista *f* trimestral.

quartermaster ['kwɔ:tə,mɑ:stəʳ] *n MIL* quartel-mestre *m*.

quarter note *n US MUS* semínima *f*.

quartet [kwɔ:'tet] *n* quarteto *m*.

quarto ['kwɔ:təʊ] (*pl* **-s**) *n* in quarto *m inv*.

quartz [kwɔ:ts] *n (U)* quartzo *m*.

quartz watch *n* relógio *m* de quartzo.

quasar ['kweɪzɑ:ʳ] *n* quasar *m*.

quash [kwɒʃ] *vt* **-1.** [reject] revogar, anular **-2.** [quell] sufocar, reprimir.

quasi- ['kweɪzaɪ] *prefix* quase-.

quaver ['kweɪvəʳ] <> *n* **-1.** *MUS* colcheia *f* **-2.** [in voice] tremor *m*. <> *vi* tremer.

quavering ['kweɪvərɪŋ] *adj* trêmulo(la).

quay [ki:] *n* cais *m*.

quayside ['ki:saɪd] *n* cais *m*.

queasy ['kwi:zɪ] (*compar* **-ier**, *superl* **-iest**) *adj* enjoado(da).

Quebec [kwɪ'bek] *n* [province, city] Québec; **in ~** em Québec.

Quebecer, Quebecker [kwɪ'bekəʳ] *n* quebequense *mf*.

queen [kwi:n] *n* **-1.** [gen] rainha *f* **-2.** [playing card] dama *f*.

queen bee *n* (abelha *f*) rainha *f*.

queen mother *n*: **the ~** a rainha-mãe.

Queen's Counsel *n UK advogado inglês de alta ordem.*

Queen's English *n UK*: **the ~** *o inglês falado com perfeição na Grã-Bretanha.*

queen's evidence *n UK*: **to turn ~** *tesmunhar (um criminoso) frente a um tribunal contra outros criminosos em troca de diminuição da pena.*

queer [kwɪəʳ] <> *adj* [odd] esquisito(ta), estranho(nha). <> *n inf pej* [homosexual] veado *m*, bicha *f*.

quell [kwel] *vt* **-1.** [rebellion] sufocar, reprimir **-2.** [unease, anger] dominar, conter.

quench [kwentʃ] *vt*: **to ~ one's thirst** matar a sede.

querulous ['kwerʊləs] *adj fml* lamuriante.

query ['kwɪərɪ] (*pl* **-ies**, *pt* & *pp* **-ied**) <> *n* pergunta *f*, dúvida *f*. <> *vt* pôr em dúvida.

quest [kwest] *n literary* busca *f*; **~ for sthg** busca por algo.

question ['kwestʃn] <> *n* **-1.** [gen] questão *f* **-2.** [query] pergunta *f*; **to ask (sb) a ~** fazer uma pergunta a alguém **-3.** [doubt] dúvida *f*; **to** *OR* **call sthg into ~** por *OR* colocar algo em dúvida; **to** *OR* **bring sthg into ~** colocar algo em questão; **beyond ~** sem nenhuma dúvida; **open to ~** debatível; **without ~** sem dúvida **-4.** *phr*: **there's no ~ of ...** não há dúvida de (que) ... <> *vt* **-1.** [interrogate] interrogar **-2.** [express doubt about] questionar.

◆ **in question** *adv*: **the matter in ~** o assunto em questão.

◆ **out of the question** *adj* fora de questão.

questionable ['kwestʃənəbl] *adj* questionável.

questioner ['kwestʃənəʳ] *n* interrogador *m*, -ra *f*.

questioning ['kwestʃənɪŋ] <> *adj* de interrogação. <> *n (U)* interrogatório *m*.

question mark *n* ponto *m* de interrogação.

question master *esp UK*, **quizmaster** ['kwɪz,mɑ:stəʳ] *esp US n* apresentador *m*, -ra *f (de um show de perguntas)*.

questionnaire [,kwestʃə'neəʳ] *n* questionário *m*.

question time *n UK POL audiência no parlamento britânico na qual os ministros respondem a perguntas dos parlamentares.*

queue [kju:] *UK* <> *n* fila *f*; **to jump the ~** furar a fila. <> *vi* fazer fila; **to ~ (up) for sthg** fazer fila para algo.

queue-jump *vi UK* furar a fila.

quibble ['kwɪbl] *pej* <> *n* chorumela *f*. <> *vi* queixar-se por bobagem, lamuriar-se; **to ~ over** *OR* **about sthg** queixar-se por bobagem sobre algo.

quiche [ki:ʃ] *n* quiche *f*.

quick [kwɪk] <> *adj* rápido(da). <> *adv* depressa, rápido.

quicken ['kwɪkn] <> *vt* [make faster] apressar, acelerar. <> *vi* [get faster] acelerar(-se).

quickly ['kwɪklɪ] *adv* **-1.** [rapidly] rapidamente **-2.** [without delay] depressa, rápido.

quickness ['kwɪknɪs] *n* rapidez *f*.

quicksand ['kwɪksænd] *n* areia *f* movediça.

quicksilver ['kwɪk,sɪlvəʳ] *n (U) dated* mercúrio *m*.

quickstep ['kwɪkstep] *n*: **the ~** *dança de salão de passos rápidos.*

quick-tempered *adj* irritadiço(ça).

quick-witted [-'wɪtɪd] *adj* arguto(ta).

quid [kwɪd] (*pl inv*) *n UK inf* libra *f (esterlina)*.

quid pro quo [-'kwəʊ] (*pl* **quid pro quos**) *n* compensação *f*, troca *f*.

quiescent [kwaɪ'esnt] *adj fml* quiescente.

quiet ['kwaɪət] <> *adj* **-1.** [gen] quieto(ta); **in a ~ voice** numa voz baixa; **to keep ~ about sthg** guardar silêncio sobre algo; **be ~!** fique quieto (ta)! **-2.** [tranquil] tranqüilo(la) **-3.** [not busy] parado(da) **-4.** [discreet] suave, discreto(ta); **to have a ~**

word with sb falar discretamente com alguém **-5.** [intimate] íntimo(ma). ◇ *n (U)* tranqüilidade *f*, silêncio *m*; **on the ~** *inf* na surdina, às escondidas. ◇ *vt US* acalmar, tranqüilizar.
◆ **quiet down** ◇ *vt sep US* acalmar, tranqüilizar. ◇ *vi* acalmar-se, tranqüilizar-se.
quieten ['kwaɪətn] *vt* acalmar, tranqüilizar.
◆ **quieten down** ◇ *vt sep* acalmar, tranqüilizar. ◇ *vi* acalmar-se, tranqüilizar-se.
quietly ['kwaɪətlɪ] *adv* **-1.** [without noise] sem fazer barulho **-2.** [without excitement] tranqüilamente **-3.** [without fuss] discretamente.
quietness ['kwaɪətnɪs] *n (U)* quietude *f*, tranqüilidade *f*.
quiff [kwɪf] *n UK* topete *m*.
quill (pen) [kwɪl-] *n* pena *f (de escrever)*.
quilt [kwɪlt] *n* acolchoado *m*, edredom *m*.
quilted ['kwɪltɪd] *adj* acolchoado(da).
quince [kwɪns] *n* marmelo *m*.
quinine [kwɪ'ni:n] *n (U)* quinina *f*.
quins *UK* [kwɪnz], **quints** *US* [kwɪnts] *npl inf* quíntuplos *mpl*, -plas *fpl*.
quintessential [kwɪntə'senʃl] *adj* puro(ra); **this passage is ~ Dickens** esta passagem é Dickens puro.
quintet [kwɪn'tet] *n* quinteto *m*.
quints *npl US* = **quins**.
quintuplets [kwɪn'tju:plɪts] *npl* quíntuplos *mpl*, -plas *fpl*.
quip [kwɪp] (*pt* & *pp* **-ped**, *cont* **-ping**) ◇ *n* gracejo *m*. ◇ *vi* gracejar.
quire [kwaɪə^r] *n* mão *f* de papel.
quirk [kw3:k] *n* **-1.** [habit] mania *f*, esquisitice *f* **-2.** [strange event] estranha coincidência *f*; **by a ~ of fate** por um capricho do destino.
quirky ['kw3:kɪ] (*compar* **-ier**, *superl* **-iest**) *adj* peculiar.
quit [kwɪt] (*UK pt* & *pp* **quit** OR **-ted**, *cont* **-ting**, *US pt* & *pp* **quit**, *cont* **-ting**) ◇ *vt* **-1.** [resign from] abandonar, deixar **-2.** [stop]: **to ~ smoking** deixar de fumar. ◇ *vi* **-1.** [resign] demitir-se **-2.** [give up] desistir.
quite [kwaɪt] *adv* **-1.** [completely] completamente, totalmente **-2.** [fairly] bem; **~ a lot of people** bastante gente; **~ a few times** várias vezes **-3.** [after negative]: **I don't ~ understand** não entendo muito bem; **this room is not ~ big enough** essa sala não é tão grande quanto deveria ser **-4.** [for emphasis]: **she's ~ a singer** ela é uma cantora e tanto **-5.** [to express agreement]: **~ (so)!** exatamente!
Quito ['ki:təʊ] *n* Quito.
quits [kwɪts] *adj inf*: **to be ~ (with sb)** estar quite(com alguém); **to call it ~** ficar quite.
quitter ['kwɪtə^r] *n inf pej*: **she's not a ~** ela não é das que desistem fácil.
quiver ['kwɪvə^r] ◇ *n* **-1.** [shiver] estremecimento *m* **-2.** [for arrows] aljava *f*. ◇ *vi* estremecer.
quivering ['kwɪvərɪŋ] *adj* trêmulo(la).
quixotic [kwɪk'sɒtɪk] *adj literary* quixotesco(ca).
quiz [kwɪz] (*pl* **-zes**, *pt* & *pp* **-zed**, *cont* **-zing**) ◇ *n* **-1.** [competitions, game] jogo *m* de perguntas e respostas **-2.** *US SCH* exame *m*. ◇ *vt*: **to ~ sb (about sthg)** interrogar alguém (sobre algo).
quizmaster ['kwɪzmɑ:stə^r] *n esp US* = **question master**.
quizzical ['kwɪzɪkl] *adj* interrogativo(va).
quoits [kwɔɪts] *n (U)* jogo *m* das argolas.
Quonset hut® ['kwɒnsɪt-] *n US* barracão *m* do exército.
quorate ['kwɔ:reɪt] *adj UK* que tem quorum.
quorum ['kwɔ:rəm] *n* quórum *m*.
quota ['kwəʊtəl *n* cota *f*.
quotation [kwəʊ'teɪʃn] *n* **-1.** [citation] citação *f* **-2.** *COMM* cotação *f*.
quotation marks *npl* aspas *fpl*; **in ~** entre aspas.
quote [kwəʊt] ◇ *n* **-1.** [citation] citação *f* **-2.** *COMM* cotação *f*. ◇ *vt* **-1.** [cite] citar **-2.** *COMM* cotar; **she ~d £100** ela fixou um preço de £100. ◇ *vi* **-1.** [cite] citar; **to ~ from sthg** citar de algo **-2.** *COMM*: **to ~ for sthg** estabelecer um preço para algo.
◆ **quotes** *npl inf* aspas *fpl*; **single/double ~s** aspas simples/duplas; **in ~s** entre aspas.
quoted company ['kwəʊtɪd-] *n UK empresa f registrada em bolsa*.
quotient ['kwəʊʃnt] *n* quociente *m*.
q.v. (*abbr of* **quod vide**) veja.
qwerty keyboard ['kw3:tɪ-] *n UK* teclado *m* qwerty.

R

r (*pl* **r's** OR **rs**), **R** (*pl* **R's** OR **Rs**) [ɑ:^r] *n* [letter] r, R *m*.
◆ **R -1.** (*abbr of* **right**) dir. **-2.** (*abbr of* **River**) R. **-3.** (*abbr of* **restricted**) não recomendado(da) para menores **-4.** *US* (*abbr of* **Republican**) republicano *m*, -na *f*.
RA (*abbr of* **Royal Academy**) *n (membro da) Academia Real de Artes na Grã-Bretanha*.
RAAF (*abbr of* **Royal Australian Air Force**) *n força aérea real australiana*.
Rabat [rə'bɑ:t] *n* Rabat.
rabbi ['ræbaɪ] *n* rabino *m*.
rabbit ['ræbɪt] *n* **-1.** [animal] coelho *m*, -lha *f* **-2.** *(U)* [food] coelho *m*.
rabbit hole *n* toca *f* de coelho.
rabbit hutch *n* coelheira *f*.
rabbit warren *n* **-1.** [for rabbits] coelheira *f* **-2.** [building] labirinto *m*.
rabble ['ræbl] *n* **-1.** [disorderly crowd] povaréu *m* **-2.** [riffraff] gentalha *f*.
rabble-rousing *adj* que agita a multidão.
rabid ['ræbɪd, 'reɪbɪd] *adj* **-1.** [infected with rabies]

raivoso(sa) **-2.** *pej* [fanatical] ferrenho(nha), fanático(ca).
rabies ['reɪbi:z] *n (U)* raiva *f*.
RAC (*abbr of* **Royal Automobile Club**) *n automóvel clube britânico.*
raccoon [rə'ku:n] *n* racum *m*.
race [reɪs] <> *n* **-1.** [ethnicity] raça *f* **-2.** [competition] corrida *f*; **a ~ against time** uma corrida contra o tempo. <> *vt* competir com *(em corrida)*. <> *vi* **-1.** [compete]: **to ~ against sb** bater uma corrida com alguém **-2.** [rush] ir correndo **-3.** acelerar.
race car *n US* = **racing car**.
racecourse ['reɪskɔ:s] *n* hipódromo *m*.
race driver *n US* = **racing driver**.
racehorse ['reɪshɔ:s] *n* cavalo *m* de corrida.
race meeting *n* concurso *m* hípico.
race relations *npl* relações *fpl* inter-raciais.
race riot *n* conflito *m* racial.
racetrack ['reɪstræk] *n* autódromo *m*.
racial ['reɪʃl] *adj* racial.
racial discrimination *n (U)* discriminação *m* racial.
racialism ['reɪʃəlɪzm] *n* = **racism**.
racing ['reɪsɪŋ] *n (U) SPORT* corrida *f*.
racing car *UK*, **race car** *US n* carro *m* de corrida.
racing driver *UK*, **race driver** *US n* piloto *m* de corrida.
racism ['reɪsɪzm] *n (U)* racismo *m*.
racist ['reɪsɪst] <> *adj* racista. <> *n* racista *mf*.
rack [ræk] <> *n* **-1.** [frame - for plates] escorredor *m* de louça; [- for toast] prateleira *f*; [- for bottles] porta-garrafas *m inv* **-2.** [for luggage] porta-bagagens *m inv*. <> *vt literary*: **to be ~ed by** *OR* **with sthg** estar atormentado(da) por algo.
racket ['rækɪt] *n* **-1.** [noise] algazarra *f*, zoeira *f* **-2.** [illegal activity] golpe *m*, fraude *f* **-3.** *SPORT* raquete *f*.
racketeering [,rækə'tɪərɪŋ] *n (U) pej*: **to be indicted on ~ charges** ser acusado(da) de extorquir dinheiro.
raconteur [,rækɒn'tɜ:ʳ] *n pessoa que sabe contar piadas.*
racoon *n* = **raccoon**.
racquet ['rækɪt] *n* raquete *f*.
racy ['reɪsɪ] (*compar* **-ier**, *superl* **-iest**) *adj* vivaz.
RADA ['rɑ:də] (*abbr of* **Royal Academy of Dramatic Art**) *n academia britânica de arte dramática.*
radar ['reɪdɑ:ʳ] *n (U)* radar *m*.
radar trap *n* radar *m (usado pela polícia)*.
radial (tyre) ['reɪdjəl-] *n* pneu *m* radial.
radian ['reɪdjən] *n (U)* radiano *m*.
radiance ['reɪdjəns] *n* **-1.** [of face, smile] brilho *m* **-2.** *literary* [brilliance] brilho *m*.
radiant ['reɪdjənt] *adj* **-1.** [happy] radiante **-2.** *literary* [brilliant] brilhante **-3.** *TECH* por radiação.
radiate ['reɪdɪeɪt] <> *vt* irradiar. <> *vi* **-1.** [be emitted] irradiar **-2.** [spread from centre] sair, partir do centro.
radiation [,reɪdɪ'eɪʃn] *n* radiação *f*.
radiation sickness *n (U) doença f causada pela radiação.*
radiator ['reɪdɪeɪtəʳ] *n* **-1.** [in house] aquecedor *m* **-2.** *AUT* radiador *m*.
radiator grille *n* grade *f* do radiador.
radical ['rædɪkl] <> *adj* radical. <> *n POL* radical *mf*.
radically ['rædɪklɪ] *adv* radicalmente.
radii ['reɪdɪaɪ] *pl* ▷ **radius**.
radio ['reɪdɪəʊ] (*pl* **-s**) <> *n* **-1.** [gen] rádio *m* **-2.** [station] rádio *f*. <> *comp* de rádio. <> *vt* transmitir por rádio.
radioactive [,reɪdɪəʊ'æktɪv] *adj* radioativo(va).
radioactive waste *n (U)* lixo *m* radioativo.
radioactivity [,reɪdɪəʊæk'tɪvətɪ] *n (U)* radioatividade *f*.
radio alarm *n* rádio-relógio *m*.
radio-controlled [-kən'trəʊld] *adj* de controle remoto.
radio frequency *n* radiofreqüência *f*.
radiogram ['reɪdɪəʊ,græm] *n* radiograma *m*.
radiographer [,reɪdɪ'ɒgrəfəʳ] *n* radiologista *mf*.
radiography [,reɪdɪ'ɒgrəfɪ] *n (U)* radiografia *f*.
radiology [,reɪdɪ'ɒlədʒɪ] *n (U)* radiologia *f*.
radiotherapist [,reɪdɪəʊ'θerəpɪst] *n* radioterapeuta *mf*.
radiotherapy [,reɪdɪəʊ'θerəpɪ] *n (U)* radioterapia *f*.
radish ['rædɪʃ] *n* rabanete *m*.
radium ['reɪdɪəm] *n (U)* rádio *m*.
radius ['reɪdɪəs] (*pl* **radii**) *n* **-1.** *MATH* raio *m* **-2.** *ANAT* rádio *m*.
radon ['reɪdɒn] *n (U)* radônio *m*.
RAF [ɑ:reɪ'ef, ræf] (*abbr of* **Royal Air Force**) *n força aérea real britânica.*
raffia ['ræfɪə] *n (U)* ráfia *f*.
raffish ['ræfɪʃ] *adj que é atraente e tem estilo, apesar de não ser muito respeitável ou convencional.*
raffle ['ræfl] <> *n* rifa *f*. <> *vt* rifar.
raffle ticket *n* bilhete *m* de rifa.
raft [rɑ:ft] *n* **-1.** [of wood] jangada *f* **-2.** [of rubber, plastic] bote *m* **-3.** [large number] monte *m*; **a ~ of policies** *POL* um monte de políticas.
rafter ['rɑ:ftəʳ] *n* viga *f*.
rag [ræg] *n* **-1.** [piece of cloth] trapo *m*; **it was like a red ~ to a bull** estava pedindo pra levar **-2.** *pej* [newspaper] jornaleco *m*.
◆ **rags** *npl* [clothes] trapos *mpl*; **from ~s to riches** da pobreza à riqueza.
ragamuffin ['rægə,mʌfɪn] *n* maltrapilho *m*, -lha *f*.
rag-and-bone man *n pessoa que compra e vende roupas e móveis velhos na rua.*
ragbag ['rægbæg] *n fig* salada *f*, mixórdia *f*.
rag doll *n* boneca *f* de pano.
rage [reɪdʒ] <> *n* **-1.** [fury] fúria *f*; **to fly into a ~** ficar enraivecido(da) **-2.** *inf* [fashion]: **all the ~** a última moda. <> *vi* **-1.** [person] enfurecer-se **-2.** [storm, argument] recrudescer.
ragged ['rægɪd] *adj* **-1.** [wearing torn clothes] maltrapilho(lha) **-2.** [torn] esfarrapado(da) **-3.** [wavy] irregular **-4.** [poor-quality] pobre.
raging ['reɪdʒɪŋ] *adj* terrível.
ragout ['rægu:] *n* ragu *m*.
rag trade *n inf*: **the ~** a indústria do vestuário.
rag week *n UK semana em que as universidades britânicas organizam atividades divertidas para fins beneficentes.*

raid [reɪd] ◇ *n* **-1.** MIL [attack] incursão *f* **-2.** [forced entry - by robbers] assalto *m*; [- by police] batida *f*. ◇ *vt* **-1.** MIL [attack] atacar de surpresa **-2.** [enter by force - robbers] assaltar; [- police] fazer uma batida em.

raider [ˈreɪdəʳ] *n* **-1.** [attacker] invasor *m*, -ra *f* **-2.** [thief] ladrão *m*, -dra *f*, assaltante *mf*.

rail [reɪl] ◇ *n* **-1.** [on staircase] corrimão *m* **-2.** [on walkway] ferro *m* de proteção **-3.** [on bridge] parapeito *m* **-4.** [on ship] amurada *f* **-5.** [bar] barra *f* **-6.** [of railway line] trilho *m* **-7.** *(U)* [form of transport] trem *m*. ◇ *comp* ferroviário(a).

railcard [ˈreɪlkɑːd] *n UK* cartão *m* de desconto *(no trem)*.

railing [ˈreɪlɪŋ] *n* **-1.** [round basement] grade *f* **-2.** [on walkway] ferro *m* de proteção **-3.** [on ship] amurada *f* **-4.** [on bridge] parapeito *m*.

railway *UK* [ˈreɪlweɪ], **railroad** *US* [ˈreɪlrəʊd] *n* **-1.** [track] estrada *f* de ferro **-2.** [company] companhia *f* ferroviária **-3.** [system] sistema *m* ferroviário.

railway engine *n* locomotiva *f*.

railway line *n* **-1.** [route] linha *f* de trem **-2.** [track] via *f* férrea, trilhos *mpl*.

railwayman [ˈreɪlweɪmən] (*pl* **-men** [-mən]) *n UK* ferroviário *m*.

railway station *n* estação *f* de trem.

railway track *n* via *f* férrea, trilhos *mpl*.

rain [reɪn] ◇ *n (U)* chuva *f*. ◇ *v impers* METEOR chover. ◇ *vi* [fall like rain] cair como chuva.

◆ **rain down** *vi* chover.

◆ **rain off** *UK*, **rain out** *US vt sep*: **the match was ~ed off** o jogo foi cancelado devido ao mau tempo.

rainbow [ˈreɪnbəʊ] *n* arco-íris *m*.

rainbow trout *n* truta-arco-íris *f*.

rain check *n US*: **to take a ~ (on sthg)** deixar (algo) para outra hora OR para a próxima.

raincoat [ˈreɪnkəʊt] *n* capa *f* de chuva.

raindrop [ˈreɪndrɒp] *n* pingo *m* de chuva.

rainfall [ˈreɪnfɔːl] *n (U)* precipitação *f*.

rain forest *n* floresta *f* tropical.

rain gauge *n* pluviômetro *m*.

rainproof [ˈreɪnpruːf] *adj* impermeável.

rainstorm [ˈreɪnstɔːm] *n* pancada *f* OR temporal *m* de chuva.

rainwater [ˈreɪnˌwɔːtəʳ] *n (U)* água *f* da chuva.

rainy [ˈreɪnɪ] (*compar* **-ier**, *superl* **-iest**) *adj* chuvoso(-sa).

raise [reɪz] ◇ *n US* aumento *m*. ◇ *vt* **-1.** [gen] levantar **-2.** [lift up] levantar, erguer; **to ~ o.s.** levantar-se **-3.** [increase] aumentar; **to ~ one's voice** levantar a voz **-4.** [improve] elevar **-5.** [evoke] evocar **-6.** [child, animals] criar **-7.** [crop] cultivar **-8.** [build] erguer.

raisin [ˈreɪzn] *n* passa *f (de uva)*.

Raj [rɑːdʒ] *n*: **the ~** o Império Britânico na Índia.

rajah [ˈrɑːdʒə] *n* rajá *m*.

rake [reɪk] ◇ *n* **-1.** [implement] rastelo *m* **-2.** *dated & literary* [immoral man] devasso *m*, libertino *m*. ◇ *vt* **-1.** [smooth] rastelar **-2.** [gather] juntar com o rastelo.

◆ **rake in** *vt sep inf* faturar.

◆ **rake up** *vt sep* [past] remexer em.

rake-off *n inf* propina *f*, lucro *m* ilícito.

rakish [ˈreɪkɪʃ] *adj* **-1.** [dissolute] libertino(na) **-2.** [jaunty] charmoso(sa).

rally [ˈrælɪ] (*pl* **-ies**, *pt & pp* **-ied**) ◇ *n* **-1.** [gen] rali *m* **-2.** [meeting] comício *m*. ◇ *vt* reunir. ◇ *vi* **-1.** [come together] reunir-se **-2.** [recover] recuperar-se.

◆ **rally round** ◇ *vt fus* mobilizar. ◇ *vi* mobilizar-se.

rallying [ˈrælɪɪŋ] *n (U)* rali *m*.

rallying cry *n* grito *m* de guerra.

rallying point *n* ponto *m* de encontro.

ram [ræm] (*pt & pp* **-med**, *cont* **-ming**) ◇ *n* carneiro *m*. ◇ *vt* **-1.** [crash into] bater contra OR em **-2.** [force] enfiar **-3.** *phr*: **to ~ sthg home** deixar algo bem claro.

RAM [ræm] (*abbr of* **random-access memory**) *n* RAM *f*.

Ramadan [ˌræməˈdæn] *n (U)* ramadã *m*.

ramble [ˈræmbl] ◇ *n* passeio *m* no campo. ◇ *vi* **-1.** [walk] passear **-2.** [talk] divagar.

rambler [ˈræmbləʳ] *n* excursionista *mf*.

rambling [ˈræmblɪŋ] *adj* **-1.** [building] cheio (cheia) de voltas e curvas **-2.** [conversation, book] desconexo(xa).

RAMC (*abbr of* **Royal Army Medical Corps**) *n corpo médico das forças armadas reais britânicas*.

ramekin [ˈræmɪkɪn] *n* recipiente *f* individual *(para ir ao forno)*.

ramification [ˌræmɪfɪˈkeɪʃn] *n* ramificação *f*.

ramp [ræmp] *n* **-1.** [slope] rampa *f* **-2.** AUT [in road] viaduto *m*.

rampage [ræmˈpeɪdʒ] ◇ *n*: **to go on the ~** sair em debandada, debandar-se. ◇ *vi* sair em debandada, debandar-se.

rampant [ˈræmpənt] *adj* desenfreado(da).

ramparts [ˈræmpɑːts] *npl* muralha *f*.

ramshackle [ˈræmˌʃækl] *adj* desmantelado(da).

ran [ræn] *pt* ▷ **run**.

RAN (*abbr of* **Royal Australian Navy**) *n marinha real australiana*.

ranch [rɑːntʃ] *n* fazenda *m*, rancho *m*.

rancher [ˈrɑːntʃəʳ] *n* fazendeiro *m*, -ra *f*.

ranch house *n US* **-1.** [house on ranch] casa *f* na fazenda **-2.** [ranch-style house] casa *f* de campo.

rancid [ˈrænsɪd] *adj* rançoso(sa).

rancour *UK*, **rancor** *US* [ˈræŋkəʳ] *n (U)* rancor *m*.

random [ˈrændəm] ◇ *adj* aleatório(ria). ◇ *n*: **at ~** aleatoriamente.

random access memory *n (U)* COMPUT memória *f* de acesso aleatório, memória *f* RAM.

randomly [ˈrændəmlɪ] *adv* ao acaso.

R and R (*abbr of* **rest and recreation**) *n US termo militar norte-americano para licença*.

randy [ˈrændɪ] (*compar* **-ier**, *superl* **-iest**) *adj inf* tarado(da).

rang [ræŋ] *pt* ▷ **ring**.

range [reɪndʒ] ◇ *n* **-1.** [distance covered - of telescope, gun] alcance *m*; [- of ship, plane] autonomia *f*; **to be out of ~** estar fora de alcance; **to be within ~ of sthg** estar ao alcance de algo; **at close ~** à queima-roupa **-2.** [variety] variedade *f* **-3.** [bracket] faixa *f* **-4.** [of mountains, hills] cadeia *f* **-5.** [shooting area] linha *f* - **6.** *MUS* alcance *m.* ◇ *vt* [place in row] enfileirar. ◇ *vi* - **1.** [vary]: **to ~ from ... to ...** variar de ... a ...; **to ~ between ... and ...** oscilar entre ... e ... - **2.** [deal with, include]: **to ~ over sthg** passar por algo.

ranger ['reɪndʒəʳ] *n* guarda-florestal *mf.*

Rangoon [ræŋ'gu:n] *n* Rangum.

rank [ræŋk] ◇ *adj* - **1.** [utter, absolute - disgrace, stupidity] completo(ta); [- injustice, bad luck] total - **2.** [offensive] rançoso(sa). ◇ *n* - **1.** [in army, police] posto *m*; **the ~ and file** *MIL* soldados rasos; [of political party, organization] bases *fpl*; **to pull ~** abusar da autoridade; **to close ~s** *fig* estreitar os laços - **2.** [social class] nível *m* - **3.** [row, line] fila *f.* ◇ *vt* - **1.** [classify] classificar - **2.** *US* [outrank] ocupar posição mais alta que. ◇ *vi* classificar-se; **to ~ as/among** classificar-se como/entre.
◆ **ranks** *npl* - **1.** *MIL*: **the ~s** os soldados rasos - **2.** *fig* [members] filas *fpl.*

ranking ['ræŋkɪŋ] ◇ *n* classificação *f.* ◇ *adj* *US* [highest-ranking] do alto escalão.

rankle ['ræŋkl] *vi* causar dor; **it still ~s with me!** isso ainda me dói!

ransack ['rænsæk] *vt* - **1.** [plunder] saquear - **2.** [search] revistar.

ransom ['rænsəm] *n* resgate *m*; **to hold sb to ~** [keep prisoner] pedir resgaste por alguém; *fig* [put in impossible position] chantagear alguém.

rant [rænt] *vi* falar asneira.

ranting ['ræntɪŋ] *n* falatório *m.*

rap [ræp] (*pt* & *pp* **-ped**, *cont* **-ping**) ◇ *n* - **1.** [knock] batidinha *f* - **2.** *MUS* rap *m* - **3.** *phr*: **to take the ~** pagar o pato. ◇ *vt* [knock] dar batidinhas em. ◇ *vi* - **1.** [knock]: **to ~ on sthg** dar batidinhas em algo - **2.** *MUS* cantar rap.

rapacious [rə'peɪʃəs] *adj fml* voraz.

rapacity [rə'pæsɪtɪ] *n (U) fml* voracidade *f.*

rape [reɪp] ◇ *n* - **1.** [gen] estupro *m* - **2.** *fig* [destruction] destruição *f* - **3.** *(U)* [plant] colza *f.* ◇ *vt* estuprar.

rapeseed *n* semente *f* de colza.

rapid ['ræpɪd] *adj* rápido(da).
◆ **rapids** *npl* corredeira *f.*

rapid-fire *adj* - **1.** *MIL* de fogo cerrado - **2.** *fig* [spoken quickly] feito um atrás do outro, feita uma atrás da outra.

rapidity [rə'pɪdətɪ] *n (U)* rapidez *f.*

rapidly ['ræpɪdlɪ] *adv* rapidamente.

rapidness *n* = **rapidity**.

rapist ['reɪpɪst] *n* estuprador *m*, -ra *f.*

rapper ['ræpəʳ] *n MUS* rapper *mf.*

rapport [ræ'pɔ:ʳ] *n* afinidade *f*; **a ~ with/between** uma afinidade com/entre.

rapprochement *n* reaproximação *f.*

rapt [ræpt] *adj* absorto(ta).

rapture ['ræptʃəʳ] *n* arrebatamento *m*; **to go into ~s over sb/sthg, to go into ~s about sb/sthg** desfazer-se em elogios por alguém/algo.

rapturous ['ræptʃərəs] *adj* arrebatador(ra).

rare [reəʳ] *adj* - **1.** [gen] raro(ra) - **2.** *CULIN* [underdone] malpassado(da).

rarefied ['reərɪfaɪd] *adj* - **1.** [air, atmosphere] rarefeito(ta) - **2.** [refined] exclusivo(va).

rarely ['reəlɪ] *adv* raramente.

rareness ['reənɪs] *(U) n* - **1.** [scarcity, uncommonness] raridade *f* - **2.** [infrequency] infreqüência *f* - **3.** *CULIN* qualidade *f* de malpassado.

raring ['reərɪŋ] *adj*: **to be ~ to go** estar ansioso(sa) para começar.

rarity ['reərətɪ] (*pl* **-ies**) *n* raridade *f.*

rascal ['rɑ:skl] *n* patife *mf*, malandro *m*, -dra *f.*

rash [ræʃ] ◇ *adj* precipitado(da). ◇ *n* - **1.** *MED* erupção *f* - **2.** [spate] onda *f.*

rasher ['ræʃəʳ] *n* fatia *f* fina *(de bacon).*

rashly ['ræʃlɪ] *adv* precipitadamente.

rashness ['ræʃnɪs] *n (U)* precipitação *f.*

rasp [rɑ:sp] ◇ *n* rangido *m.* ◇ *vi* esganiçar-se.

raspberry ['rɑ:zbərɪ] (*pl* **-ies**) *n* - **1.** [fruit] framboesa *f* - **2.** [rude noise]: **to blow a ~** debochar fazendo barulho com a boca.

rasping ['rɑ:spɪŋ] *adj* áspero(ra) e estridente.

rasta ['ræstəl] *n inf* rasta *mf.*

rastafarian [ˌræstə'feərɪən] *n* rastafári *mf.*

rat [ræt] *n* - **1.** [animal] rato *m*, ratazana *f*; **to smell a ~** suspeitar que há algo errado - **2.** *pej* [person] tratante *mf.*

ratbag ['rætbæg] *n UK inf pej* canalha *mf.*

ratchet ['rætʃɪt] *n* catraca *f.*

rate [reɪt] ◇ *n* - **1.** [speed] velocidade *f*; **at this ~** nesse ritmo - **2.** [ratio, proportion - birth, death, inflation] taxa *f*; [- unemployment] índice *m* - **3.** [price] tarifa *f.* ◇ *vt* - **1.** [consider]: **to ~ sb/sthg (as)** considerar alguém/algo; **to ~ sb/sthg (among)** classificar alguém/algo (entre) - **2.** [deserve] merecer.
◆ **at any rate** *adv* pelo menos.

rateable value ['reɪtəbl-] *n UK* valor *m* tributável.

rate of exchange *n* (taxa *f* de) câmbio *m.*

ratepayer ['reɪtˌpeɪəʳ] *n UK* contribuinte *mf.*

rather ['rɑ:ðəʳ] *adv* - **1.** [slightly, a bit] um pouco - **2.** [for emphasis] bem, bastante - **3.** [expressing a preference]: **I would ~ wait** eu preferiria esperar - **4.** [more exactly]: **or ~ ...** ou melhor ... - **5.** [on the contrary]: **(but) ~ ...** (senão) pelo contrário ...
◆ **rather than** *conj* em vez de.

ratification [ˌrætɪfɪ'keɪʃn] *n (U)* ratificação *f.*

ratify ['rætɪfaɪ] (*pt* & *pp* **-ied**) *vt* ratificar.

rating ['reɪtɪŋ] *n* - **1.** [standing - high, low, popularity] índice *m*;[- opinion poll] posição *f* - **2.** *UK* [sailor] marinheiro *m*, -ra *f.*
◆ **ratings** *npl TV* índices *mpl* de audiência.

ratio ['reɪʃɪəʊ] (*pl* **-s**) *n* razão *f*, proporção *f.*

ration ['ræʃn] ◇ *n* ração *f.* ◇ *vt* [goods] racionar.
◆ **rations** *npl* ração *f.*

rational ['ræʃənl] *adj* racional.

rationale [ˌræʃə'nɑ:l] *n* lógica *f*, fundamento *m* lógico.

rationalization [ˌræʃənəlaɪ'zeɪʃn] *n* racionalização *f.*

rationalize, -ise ['ræʃənəlaɪz] *vt* racionalizar.

rationing ['ræʃənɪŋ] *n (U)* racionamento *m.*

rat race *n* competição *f* acirrada *(no mundo dos negócios).*

rattle ['rætl] ◇ *n* - **1.** [noise] barulho *m*, ruído *m* - **2.** [toy] chocalho *m.* ◇ *vt* - **1.** [make rattling noise with]

chacoalhar **-2.** [unsettle] desconcertar. <> *vi* [make rattling noise] chacoalhar.
◆ **rattle off** *vt sep* repetir de memória.
◆ **rattle on** *vi*: **to ~ on (about sthg)** tagarelar (sobre algo).
◆ **rattle through** *vt fus* tratar de encerrar.

rattlesnake ['rætlsneɪk], **rattler** *US* ['rætlə^r] *n* cascavel *f.*

ratty ['rætɪ] (*compar* **-ier**, *superl* **-iest**) *adj inf* **-1.** *UK* [in bad mood] rabugento(ta) **-2.** *US* [in bad condition] surrado(da), roto(ta).

raucous ['rɔ:kəs] *adj* **-1.** [laughter, voice] rouco(ca) e estridente **-2.** [behaviour] escandaloso(sa).

raunchy ['rɔ:ntʃɪ] (*compar* **-ier**, *superl* **-iest**) *adj* insinuante.

ravage ['rævɪdʒ] *vt* devastar.
◆ **ravages** *npl* estragos *mpl.*

rave [reɪv] <> *adj* entusiasmado(da). <> *n UK inf* [party] rave *f.* <> *vi* **-1.** [talk angrily]: **to ~ at sb** xingar alguém; **to ~ against sthg** vociferar contra algo **-2.** [talk enthusiastically]: **to ~ about sthg** falar com entusiasmo sobre algo.

raven ['reɪvn] <> *adj* totalmente negro(gra). <> *n* corvo *m.*

ravenous ['rævənəs] *adj* **-1.** [person, animal] faminto (ta) **-2.** [appetite] voraz.

raver ['reɪvə^r] *n UK inf* festeiro *m*, -ra *f.*

rave-up *n UK inf* rave *f.*

ravine [rə'vi:n] *n* ravina *f.*

raving ['reɪvɪŋ] *adj* [for emphasis] delirante; **~ lunatic** doido *m* varrido, doida *f* varrida.
◆ **ravings** *npl* delírios *mpl.*

ravioli [ˌrævɪ'əʊlɪ] *n (U)* ravióli *m.*

ravish ['rævɪʃ] *vt* **-1.** *literary* [rape] violentar **-2.** [delight] extasiar.

ravishing ['rævɪʃɪŋ] *adj* **-1.** [sight, beauty] extasiante **-2.** [person] belíssimo(ma).

raw [rɔ:] *adj* **-1.** [uncooked] cru (crua) **-2.** [untreated] bruto(ta) **-3.** [painful] em carne viva **-4.** [inexperienced] inexperiente **-5.** [cold] frio (fria).

raw deal *n*: **to get a ~** receber um tratamento injusto.

Rawlplug® ['rɔ:lplʌg] *n* bucha *f.*

raw material *n* **-1.** [natural substance] matéria-prima *f* **-2.** *(U) fig* [basis] base *f.*

ray [reɪ] *n* **-1.** [beam] raio *m* **-2.** *fig* [glimmer] resquício *m.*

rayon ['reɪɒn] *n (U)* raiom *m.*

raze [reɪz] *vt* destruir completamente, arrasar.

razor ['reɪzə^r] *n* **-1.** [electric] barbeador *m* elétrico **-2.** [disposable] barbeador *m*, aparelho *m* de barbear.

razor blade *n* lâmina *f* de barbear.

razor-sharp *adj* **-1.** [very sharp] muito afiado(da) **-2.** *fig* [very quick - person] ágil; [- mind] afiado(da), perspicaz.

razzle ['ræzl] *n UK inf*: **to go on the ~** cair na gandaia.

razzmatazz ['ræzəmətæz] *n (U) inf* auê *m.*

R & B (*abbr of* **rhythm and blues**) *n mistura de ritmos de blues e jazz precursora do rock and roll.*

RC (*abbr of* **Roman Catholic**) *adj* católico romano, católica romana.

RCA (*abbr of* **Royal College of Art**) *n escola londrina de belas artes.*

RCAF (*abbr of* **Royal Canadian Air Force**) *n força aérea real canadense.*

RCMP (*abbr of* **Royal Canadian Mounted Police**) *n polícia montada canadense.*

RCN *n* (*abbr of* **Royal Canadian Navy**) *marinha real canadense.*

Rd (*abbr of* **Road**) estrada *f.*

R & D (*abbr of* **research and development**) *n* P & D.

RDC (*abbr of* **Rural District Council**) *n câmara de vereadores de uma comunidade rural britânica.*

re [ri:] *prep* referente a.

RE *n* **-1.** (*abbr of* **religious education**) educação *f* religiosa **-2.** (*abbr of* **Royal Engineers**) *unidade de engenharia do exército britânico responsável pela construção de fortes, pontes e outras obras.*

reach [ri:tʃ] <> *n* [of arm, boxer] alcance *m*; **within (sb's) ~** [easily touched] ao alcance (de alguém); [easily travelled to] a pouca distância (de alguém); **out of** OR **beyond sb's ~** [not easily touched] fora/além do alcance de alguém; [not easily travelled to] fora/além do alcance de alguém. <> *vt* **-1.** [arrive at] chegar a, alcançar **-2.** [be able to touch] alcançar **-3.** [contact] contatar, entrar em contato com **-4.** [extend as far as] atingir **-5.** [attain, achieve] chegar a. <> *vi* **-1.** [person]: **to ~ out/across** alcançar; **to ~ down** abaixar-se **-2.** [land] alcançar, ir até.
◆ **reaches** *npl*: **the upper/lower ~es** a parte alta/baixa.

reachable ['ri:tʃəbl] *adj* **-1.** [accessible] acessível **-2.** [contactable] localizável; **he's ~ by phone** ele pode ser contatado por telefone.

react [rɪ'ækt] *vi* **-1.** [respond]: **to ~ (to sthg)** reagir (a algo) **-2.** [rebel]: **to ~ against sthg** reagir contra algo **-3.** CHEM: **to ~ with sthg** reagir com algo.

reaction [rɪ'ækʃn] *n* **-1.** reação *f* **-2.** [response]: **~ (to sthg)** reação *f* (a algo) **-3.** [rebellion]: **~ (against sthg)** reação *f* (contra algo).

reactionary [rɪ'ækʃənrɪ] <> *adj* reacionário(ria). <> *n* reacionário *m*, -ria *f.*

reactivate [rɪ'æktɪveɪt] *vt* reativar.

reactor [rɪ'æktə^r] *n* [nuclear reactor] reator *m.*

read [ri:d] (*pt* & *pp* **read** [red]) <> *n*: **to be a good ~** ser uma boa leitura. <> *vt* **-1.** [gen] ler; **to ~ sb's mind** ler os pensamentos de alguém; **to ~ events** ver os acontecimentos; **the man came to ~ the electricity meter** o funcionário veio tirar a leitura da luz; **to be well ~ in a subject** conhecer bem um assunto **-2.** [subj: sign, notice] dizer; [subj: gauge, meter, barometer] marcar **-3.** *UK* UNIV estudar. <> *vi* **-1.** [person] ler; **to ~ (to sb)** ler (para alguém); **to ~ between the lines** ler nas entrelinhas; **to ~ sb like a book** compreender alguém perfeitamente **-2.** [text]: **it ~s well/badly** isto está bem/mal escrito.
◆ **read into** *vt sep*: **I wouldn't ~ much into what he said** eu não levaria muito a sério o que ele disse; **what do you ~ into the minister's decision?** como você vê a decisão do ministro?
◆ **read out** *vt sep* ler em voz alta.
◆ **read up on** *vt fus* estudar.

readable ['ri:dəbl] *adj* **-1.** [book] interessante de se ler **-2.** COMPUT [disk] legível.

readdress [ˌriːəˈdres] *vt* reendereçar.
reader [ˈriːdəʳ] *n* leitor *m*, -ra *f*.
readership [ˈriːdəʃɪp] *n* público *m* leitor.
readily [ˈredɪlɪ] *adv* **-1.** [willingly] de boa vontade **-2.** [easily] facilmente.
readiness [ˈredɪnɪs] *n (U)* **-1.** [preparedness] prontidão *f* **-2.** [willingness]: ~ **(to do sthg)** presteza (para fazer algo).
reading [ˈriːdɪŋ] *n* **-1.** [gen] leitura *f* **-2.** [recital] recital *m* **-3.** [from gauge, meter, thermometer] marcação *f* **-4.** POL [of bill] revisão *f*.
reading lamp *n* lâmpada *f* de leitura.
reading room *n* sala *f* de leitura.
readjust [ˌriːəˈdʒʌst] ◇ *vt* reajustar. ◇ *vi*: **to ~ (to sthg)** reorganizar-se (para algo).
readmit [ˌriːədˈmɪt] *vt* readmitir.
readout [ˈriːdaʊt] *n* COMPUT exibição *f* de dados.
read-through [riːd-] *n* olhada *f* geral.
ready [ˈredɪ] (*pt* & *pp* **-ied**) ◇ *adj* **-1.** [prepared] pronto(ta); **to be ~ to do sthg** estar pronto(ta) para fazer algo; **to be ~ for sthg** estar pronto(ta) para algo; **to get ~** preparar-se; **to get sthg ~** preparar algo **-2.** [willing]: **to be ~ to do sthg** estar disposto(ta) a fazer algo **-3.** [in need of]: **to be ~ for sthg** precisar de algo **-4.** [likely]: **to be ~ to do sthg** estar prestes a fazer algo **-5.** [easily accessible] à mão. ◇ *vt* preparar.
ready cash *n (U)* dinheiro *m* em mão.
ready-made *adj* pronto(ta).
ready money *n (U)* dinheiro *m* à vista.
ready-to-wear *adj* prêt-à-porter.
reaffirm [ˌriːəˈfɜːm] *vt* reafirmar.
reafforest [ˌriːəˈfɒrɪst] *vt* reflorestar.
reafforestation [ˈriːəˌfɒrɪˈsteɪʃn] *n (U)* reflorestamento *m*.
real [ˈrɪəl] ◇ *adj* **-1.** [gen] real; **in ~ terms** em termos reais **-2.** [authentic - problem, situation] real; [- gold, jewels,] legítimo(ma); **the ~ thing** a verdade; **a ~ job** um emprego de verdade; **it's for ~** é real **-3.** [for emphasis] verdadeiro(ra). ◇ *adv* **US** bem.
real ale *n (U)* **UK** cerveja *f* artesanal.
real estate *n (U)* bens *mpl* imobiliários.
realign [ˌriːəˈlaɪn] *vt* **-1.** POL reorganizar **-2.** [brakes] realinhar.
realignment [ˌriːəˈlaɪnmənt] *n* **-1.** POL reestruturação *f* **-2.** [of wheels] realinhamento *m*.
realism [ˈrɪəlɪzm] *n (U)* **-1.** [common sense] bom senso *m* **-2.** [artistic style] realismo *m*.
realist [ˈrɪəlɪst] *n* realista *mf*.
realistic [ˌrɪəˈlɪstɪk] *adj* realista; **~ chance** chance real; **to be ~ about sthg** ser realista em relação a algo.
realistically [ˌrɪəˈlɪstɪklɪ] *adv* **-1.** [reasonably] realisticamente **-2.** [accurately] de forma realista.
reality [rɪˈælətɪ] (*pl* **-ies**) *n* [gen] realidade *f*; **in ~** [in fact] na realidade; [in real life] na vida real.
reality TV *n (U)* reality shows *mpl*.
realization [ˌrɪəlaɪˈzeɪʃn] *n (U)* **-1.** [awareness, recognition] percepção *f* **-2.** [achievement] realização *f*.
realize, -ise [ˈrɪəlaɪz] *vt* **-1.** [become aware of, understand] perceber, dar-se conta de **-2.** [achieve] concretizar **-3.** COMM atingir.
reallocate [ˌriːˈæləkeɪt] *vt* realocar.
really [ˈrɪəlɪ] ◇ *adv* **-1.** [gen] realmente **-2.** [to reduce force of negative statements] na real. ◇ *excl* **-1.** [expressing doubt]: **really?** é mesmo?, não é mesmo? **-2.** [expressing surprise, disbelief]: **really?** mesmo? **-3.** [expressing disapproval]: **really!** francamente!
realm [relm] *n* **-1.** [field] domínio *m* **-2.** [kingdom] reino *m*.
real-time *adj* COMPUT de tempo real.
realtor [ˈrɪəltər] *n* **US** corretor *m*, -ra *f* de imóveis.
ream [riːm] *n* resma *f*.
◆ **reams** *npl fig* [a lot] páginas *fpl* e páginas.
reap [riːp] *vt* colher; **you ~ what you sow** você colhe o que planta.
reappear [ˌriːəˈpɪəʳ] *vi* reaparecer.
reappearance [ˌriːəˈpɪərəns] *n* reaparecimento *m*.
reapply [ˌriːəˈplaɪ] (*pt* & *pp* **-ied**) *vi* reaplicar; **to ~ for sthg** recandidatar-se a algo.
reappraisal [ˌriːəˈpreɪzl] *n* reavaliação *f*.
reappraise [ˌriːəˈpreɪz] *vt* reavaliar.
rear [rɪəʳ] ◇ *adj* **-1.** [door, window] dos fundos **-2.** [wheel] traseiro(ra). ◇ *n* **-1.** [back - of building] fundos *mpl*; [- of vehicle] traseira *f*; **to be at the ~** estar no final; **to bring up the ~** fechar a raia **-2.** *inf* [buttocks] bunda *f*. ◇ *vt* **-1.** [children, animals, plants] criar **-2.** *fig* [lift up]: **it has ~ed its head again** ele deu as caras novamente. ◇ *vi*: **to ~ (up)** empinar, empinar-se.
rear admiral *n* contra-almirante *m*.
rearguard action [ˈrɪəgɑːd-] *n* ação *f* pela retaguarda.
rear light *n* lanterna *f* traseira.
rearm [riːˈɑːm] *vt* & *vi* rearmar.
rearmament [rɪˈɑːməmənt] *n (U)* rearmamento *m*.
rearmost [ˈrɪəməʊst] *adj* último(ma).
rearrange [ˌriːəˈreɪndʒ] *vt* **-1.** [arrange differently] reorganizar **-2.** [reschedule] reajustar.
rearrangement [ˌriːəˈreɪndʒmənt] *n* **-1.** [different arrangement] reorganização *f* **-2.** [rescheduling] reajuste *m*.
rearview mirror [ˈrɪəvjuː-] *n* espelho *m* retrovisor.
reason [ˈriːzn] ◇ *n* **-1.** [cause] razão *f*, motivo *m*; **~ for sthg** razão para algo; **by ~ of** *fml* em razão de; **for some ~** por alguma razão **-2.** *(U)* [justification]: **to have ~ to do sthg** ter razões para fazer algo **-3.** *(U)* [rationality, common sense] razão *f*; **to listen to ~** ouvir à razão; **it stands to ~** é lógico. ◇ *vt* concluir. ◇ *vi* raciocinar.
◆ **reason with** *vt fus* argumentar com.
reasonable [ˈriːznəbl] *adj* **-1.** [sensible] sensato(ta) **-2.** [acceptable] razoável **-3.** [fairly large] aceitável.
reasonably [ˈriːznəblɪ] *adv* **-1.** [quite] razoavelmente **-2.** [sensibly] sensatamente.
reasoned [ˈriːznd] *adj* racional.
reasoning [ˈriːznɪŋ] *n (U)* raciocínio *m*.
reassemble [ˌriːəˈsembl] ◇ *vt* **-1.** [machinery] remontar **-2.** [people] reagrupar. ◇ *vi* reunir-se novamente.
reassess [ˌriːəˈses] *vt* reavaliar.
reassessment [ˌriːəˈsesmənt] *n* reavaliação *f*.

reassurance [ˌri:əˈʃɔ:rəns] *n* **-1.** *(U)* [comfort] reconforto *m* **-2.** [promise] nova garantia *f.*

reassure [ˌri:əˈʃɔ:ʳ] *vt* tranqüilizar.

reassuring [ˌri:əˈʃɔ:rɪŋ] *adj* tranqüilizador(ra).

reawaken [ˌri:əˈweɪkn] *vt* redespertar.

rebate [ˈri:beɪt] *n* restituição *f.*

rebel [*n* ˈrebl, *vb* rɪˈbel] (*pt* & *pp* **-led**, *cont* **-ling**) ◇ *n* rebelde *mf.* ◇ *vi* **-1.** [revolt]: **to ~ (against sb/sthg)** rebelar-se (contra alguém/algo) **-2.** [not conform]: **to ~ (against sb/sthg)** revoltar-se (contra alguém/algo).

rebellion [rɪˈbeljən] *n* **-1.** [armed revolt] rebelião *f* **-2.** [opposition] oposição *f* **-3.** *(U)* [nonconformity] revolta *f.*

rebellious [rɪˈbeljəs] *adj* rebelde.

rebirth [ˌri:ˈbɜ:θ] *n (U)* renascimento *m.*

rebound [*n* ˈri:baʊnd, *vb* ˌrɪˈbaʊnd] ◇ *n*: **on the ~** [ball] no ricochete; [person] no impulso. ◇ *vi* **-1.** [ball] ricochetear **-2.** [harm]: **to ~ (up)on sb** recair sobre alguém.

rebuff [rɪˈbʌf] ◇ *n* recusa *f.* ◇ *vt* recusar.

rebuild [ˌri:ˈbɪld] (*pt* & *pp* **-built**) *vt* reconstruir.

rebuke [rɪˈbju:k] ◇ *n* reprimenda *f.* ◇ *vt*: **to ~ sb (for sthg)** repreender alguém (por algo).

rebut [ri:ˈbʌt] (*pt* & *pp* **-ted**, *cont* **-ting**) *vt* refutar.

rebuttal [ri:ˈbʌtl] *n* refutação *f.*

rec *n inf* **-1.** (*abbr of* **recreation ground**) *UK* playground *m* **-2.** (*abbr of* **recreation**) *US* recreação *f.*

rec. (*abbr of* **received**) recebido.

recalcitrant [rɪˈkælsɪtrənt] *adj* obstinado(da).

recall [rɪˈkɔ:l] ◇ *n* **-1.** *(U)* [memory] recordação *f* **-2.** [on faulty goods] recall *m* **-3.** [change]: **beyond ~** impossível de ser alterado(da). ◇ *vt* **-1.** [remember] relembrar-se de **-2.** [summon back - parliament] reconvocar; [- ambassador] chamar de volta.

recant [rɪˈkænt] ◇ *vt* **-1.** [faith, religion] renegar **-2.** [statement] retirar **-3.** [opinion] reconsiderar. ◇ *vi* retratar-se.

recap [ˈri:kæp] (*pt* & *pp* **-ped**, *cont* **-ping**) *inf* ◇ *n* recapitulação *f.* ◇ *vt* **-1.** [summarize] recapitular **-2.** *US* [tyre] recauchutar. ◇ *vi* [summarize] recapitular.

recapitulate [ˌri:kəˈpɪtjʊleɪt] *vt* & *vi* recapitular.

recapture [ˌri:ˈkæptʃəʳ] ◇ *n* recaptura *f.* ◇ *vt* **-1.** [prisoner, town] recapturar **-2.** [mood, feeling] resgatar.

recd, rec'd (*abbr of* **received**) recebido.

recede [ri:ˈsi:d] *vi* **-1.** [move away] afastar-se **-2.** *fig* [disappear, fade] desaparecer **-3.** [subj: hair] formar entradas.

receding [rɪˈsi:dɪŋ] *adj* **-1.** [hair]: **~ hairline** entrada *f* (no cabelo) **-2.** [chin]: **~ chin** queixo *m* retraído.

receipt [rɪˈsi:t] *n* **-1.** [piece of paper] recibo *m* **-2.** *(U)* [act of receiving] recebimento *m.*

◆ **receipts** *npl* receita *f.*

receivable [rɪˈsi:vəbl] *adj* a receber.

receive [rɪˈsi:v] ◇ *vt* **-1.** [gen] receber **-2.** [welcome] recepcionar **-3.** [greet]: **to be well/badly ~d** ser bem/mal recebido(da). ◇ *vi* [in tennis etc] receber.

receiver [rɪˈsi:vəʳ] *n* **-1.** [of telephone] fone *m* **-2.** [radio, TV set] receptor *m* **-3.** [criminal] receptador *m*, -ra *f* **-4.** FIN [official] curador *m*, -ra *f.*

receivership [rɪˈsi:vəʃɪp] *n (U)*: **to go into ~** ir para curadoria.

receiving end [rɪˈsi:vɪŋ-] *n*: **to be on the ~ (of sthg)** estar na linha de tiro (de algo).

recent [ˈri:snt] *adj* recente.

recently [ˈri:sntlɪ] *adv* recentemente; **until ~, no one knew of his existence** até pouco tempo atrás, ninguém sabia da existência dele.

receptacle [rɪˈseptəkl] *n* recipiente *m.*

reception [rɪˈsepʃn] *n* recepção *f.*

reception centre *n UK* (centro *m* de) alojamento *m.*

reception class *n* aula *f* de boas-vindas.

reception desk *n* recepção *f.*

receptionist [rɪˈsepʃənɪst] *n* recepcionista *mf.*

reception room *n* recepção *f.*

receptive [rɪˈseptɪv] *adj* receptivo(va); **to be ~ to sthg** ser receptivo(va) a algo.

receptiveness *n (U)* receptividade *f.*

recess [ˈri:ses, *UK* rɪˈses] *n* **-1.** [vacation] recesso *m*; **to be in/go into ~** estar/entrar em recesso **-2.** [alcove] reentrância *f*, vão *m* **-3.** [of mind, memory] refluxo *m* **-4.** *US* SCH recreio *m*, intervalo *m.*

recessed [ˈri:sest, *UK* rɪˈsest] *adj* embutido(da).

recession [rɪˈseʃn] *n* recessão *f.*

recessionary [rɪˈseʃənrɪ] *adj* recessivo(va).

recessive [rɪˈsesɪv] *adj* recessivo(va).

recharge [ˌri:ˈtʃɑ:dʒ] *vt* recarregar.

rechargeable [ˌri:ˈtʃɑ:dʒəbl] *adj* recarregável.

recipe [ˈresɪpɪ] *n* receita *f.*

recipient [rɪˈsɪpɪənt] ◇ *adj* recebedor(ra), receptor(ra). ◇ *n* **-1.** [of letter] destinatário(ria) **-2.** [of cheque] beneficiário(ria) **-3.** [of award] ganhador(ra).

reciprocal [rɪˈsɪprəkl] *adj* recíproco(ca).

reciprocate [rɪˈsɪprəkeɪt] ◇ *vt* retribuir a. ◇ *vi* retribuir.

recital [rɪˈsaɪtl] *n* recital *m.*

recitation [ˌresɪˈteɪʃn] *n* recitação *f.*

recite [rɪˈsaɪt] *vt* **-1.** [perform aloud] recitar **-2.** [list] enumerar.

reckless [ˈreklɪs] *adj* imprudente.

recklessness [ˈreklɪsnɪs] *n (U)* imprudência *f.*

reckon [ˈrekn] *vt* **-1.** *inf* [think] achar **-2.** [consider, judge]: **he was ~ed to be too old for the job** ele foi considerado velho demais para o trabalho **-3.** [expect]: **to ~ to do sthg** esperar fazer algo **-4.** [calculate] calcular.

◆ **reckon on** *vt fus* contar com.

◆ **reckon with** *vt fus* **-1.** [expect] esperar **-2.** [face, deal with]: **a force to be ~ed with** uma força a ser considerada.

◆ **reckon without** *vt fus* não levar em conta.

reckoning [ˈrekənɪŋ] *n* cálculo *m*; **day of ~** dia do ajuste de contas.

reclaim [rɪˈkleɪm] *vt* **-1.** [claim back] recuperar **-2.** [make fit for use] desbravar.

reclamation [ˌrekləˈmeɪʃn] *n (U)* aproveitamento *m.*

recline [rɪˈklaɪn] *vi* reclinar-se.

reclining [rɪˈklaɪnɪŋ] *adj* reclinável.

recluse [rɪˈklu:s] *n* recluso *m*, -sa *f.*

reclusive [rɪˈklu:sɪv] *adj* recluso(sa).

recognition [ˌrekəgˈnɪʃn] *n* **-1.** [identification]

reconhecimento *m*; **beyond** *OR* **out of all** ~ irreconhecível **- 2.** [acknowledgment] identificação *f*; **in** ~ **of** em reconhecimento a.

recognizable ['rekəgnaɪzəbl] *adj* reconhecível; **he was barely** ~ mal dava para reconhecê-lo.

recognize, -ise ['rekəgnaɪz] *vt* reconhecer.

recoil [*vb* rɪ'kɔɪl, *n* 'ri:kɔɪl] <> *n* coice *m*. <> *vi* recuar; **to** ~ **from/at sthg** recuar diante de algo; **she** ~**ed at his suggestion** ela recuou diante da sugestão dele.

recollect [ˌrekə'lekt] *vt* recordar-se de, lembrar-se de.

recollection [ˌrekə'lekʃn] *n* recordação *f*, lembrança *f*.

recommence [ˌri:kə'mens] *vt* & *vi* recomeçar.

recommend [ˌrekə'mend] *vt* **- 1.** [commend, speak in favour of]: **to** ~ **sb/sthg (to sb)** recomendar alguém/algo (para alguém) **- 2.** [advise] recomendar.

recommendation [ˌrekəmen'deɪʃn] *n* recomendação *f*.

recommended retail price [ˌrekə'mendɪd-] *n* preço *m* sugerido ao varejo.

recompense ['rekəmpens] <> *n*: ~ **(for sthg)** recompensa (por algo). <> *vt*: **to** ~ **sb (for sthg)** recompensar alguém (por algo).

reconcile ['rekənsaɪl] *vt* **- 1.** [beliefs, ideas] conciliar; **to** ~ **sthg with sthg** conciliar algo com algo **- 2.** [people] reconciliar; **to be** ~**d with sb** reconciliar-se com alguém **- 3.** [resign]: **to** ~ **o.s. to sthg** resignar-se a algo.

reconciliation [ˌrekənsɪlɪ'eɪʃn] *n* **- 1.** [of beliefs, ideas] conciliação *f* **- 2.** [of people] reconciliação *f*.

recondite ['rekəndaɪt] *adj* *fml* recôndito(ta).

reconditioned [ˌri:kən'dɪʃnd] *adj* recondicionado(da).

reconnaissance [rɪ'kɒnɪsəns] *n* *(U)* reconhecimento *m*.

reconnect [ˌri:kə'nekt] *vt* religar.

reconnoitre *UK*, **reconnoiter** *US* [ˌrekə'nɔɪtə^r] <> *vt* reconhecer. <> *vi* fazer um reconhecimento.

reconsider [ˌri:kən'sɪdə^r] *vt* & *vi* reconsiderar.

reconstitute [ˌri:'kɒnstɪtju:t] *vt* **- 1.** [re-form] reconstituir **- 2.** [dried food] hidratar.

reconstruct [ˌri:kən'strʌkt] *vt* reconstruir.

reconstruction [ˌri:kən'strʌkʃn] *n* **- 1.** [gen] reconstrução *f* **- 2.** [of event, crime] reconstituição *f*.

reconvene [ˌri:kən'vi:n] *vt* reunir-se novamente.

record [*n* & *adj* 'rekɔ:d, *vb* rɪ'kɔ:d] <> *adj* recorde. <> *n* **- 1.** [gen] registro *m*; **off the** ~ em off; **on** ~ [on file] em registro; [ever recorded] já registrado(da); **to go on** ~ [say publicly] ir a público **- 2.** [vinyl disc] disco *m* **- 3.** [best achievement] recorde *m* **- 4.** *phr*: **to set** *OR* **put the** ~ **straight** corrigir um mal-entendido. <> *vt* **- 1.** [write down] registrar **- 2.** [put on tape etc] gravar.

record-breaker *n* recordista *mf*.

record-breaking *adj* que quebra recordes.

recorded delivery [rɪ'kɔ:dɪd-] *n* *(U)*: **to send sthg by** ~ enviar algo como carta registrada.

recorder [rɪ'kɔ:də^r] *n* **- 1.** [machine] gravador *m* **- 2.** [musical instrument] flauta *f* doce.

record holder *n* detentor *m*, -ra *f* do recorde.

recording [rɪ'kɔ:dɪŋ] *n* gravação *f*.

recording studio *n* estúdio *m* de gravação.

record library *n* discoteca *f*.

record player *n* toca-discos *m*.

recount [*n* 'ri:kaʊnt, *vt sense 1* rɪ'kaʊnt, *sense 2* ˌri:'kaʊnt] <> *n* recontagem *f*. <> *vt* **- 1.** [narrate] relatar **- 2.** [count again] recontar.

recoup [rɪ'ku:p] *vt* recuperar.

recourse [rɪ'kɔ:s] *n* *(U)* *fml*: **to have** ~ **to sthg** recorrer a algo.

recover [rɪ'kʌvə^r] <> *vt* **- 1.** [stolen goods, money] recuperar; **to** ~ **sthg (from sb/somewhere)** recuperar algo (de alguém/algum lugar) **- 2.** [consciousness, one's breath] recobrar; **to** ~ **o.s.** recuperar-se. <> *vi* **- 1.** [from illness, accident] [finances]: **to** ~ **(from sthg)** recuperar-se (de algo) **- 2.** [from shock, setback, sb's death]: **to** ~ **(from sthg)** refazer-se (de algo).

recoverable [rɪ'kʌvrəbl] *adj* *FIN* recuperável.

recovery [rɪ'kʌvərɪ] (*pl* **-ies**) *n* **- 1.**: ~ **(from sthg)** recuperação (de algo) **- 2.** recuperação *f*.

recovery vehicle *n* *UK* guincho *m*.

recreate ['ri:krɪˌeɪt] *vt* recriar.

recreation [ˌrekrɪ'eɪʃn] *n* *(U)* recreação *f*, divertimento *m*.

recreational [ˌrekrɪ'eɪʃənl] *adj* recreativo(ta); ~ **facilities** local para recreação.

recreation room *n* **- 1.** [in public building] sala *f* de recreação **- 2.** *US* [in house] sala *f* de jogos.

recrimination [rɪˌkrɪmɪ'neɪʃn] *n* *(U)* recriminação *f*.

◆ **recriminations** *npl* recriminações *fpl*.

recrudescence [ˌri:kru:'desns] *n* *fml* recrudescimento *m*.

recruit [rɪ'kru:t] <> *n* recruta *mf*. <> *vt* recrutar; **to** ~ **sb (for sthg/to do sthg)** recrutar alguém (para algo/para fazer algo). <> *vi* [take on new staff] recrutar gente.

recruitment [rɪ'kru:tmənt] *n* *(U)* recrutamento *m*.

rectangle ['rekˌtæŋgl] *n* retângulo *m*.

rectangular [rek'tæŋgjʊlə^r] *adj* retangular.

rectification [ˌrektɪfɪ'keɪʃn] *n* *(U)* *fml* retificação *f*.

rectify ['rektɪfaɪ] (*pt* & *pp* **-ied**) *vt* *fml* retificar.

rectitude ['rektɪtju:d] *n* *(U)* *fml* retidão *f*.

rector ['rektə^r] *n* **- 1.** [priest] pároco *m* **- 2.** ***Scot*** [head - of school] diretor *m*, -ra *f*; [- of college, university] reitor *m*, -ra *f*.

rectory ['rektərɪ] (*pl* **-ies**) *n* residência *f* paroquial.

rectum ['rektəm] (*pl* **-s**) *n* reto *m*.

recuperate [rɪ'ku:pəreɪt] *vi* *fml*: **to** ~ **(from sthg)** restabelecer-se (de algo).

recuperation [rɪˌku:pə'reɪʃn] *n* *(U)* recuperação *f*, restabelecimento *m*.

recur [rɪ'kɜ:^r] (*pt* & *pp* **-red**, *cont* **-ring**) *vi* repetir-se.

recurrence [rɪ'kʌrəns] *n* *fml* recorrência *f*.

recurrent [rɪ'kʌrənt] *adj* recorrente.

recurring [rɪ'kɜ:rɪŋ] *adj* **- 1.** [often repeated] recorrente **- 2.** *MATH* periódico(ca).

recyclable [ˌri:'saɪkləbl] *adj* reciclável.

recycle [ˌri:'saɪkl] *vt* reciclar.

recycling *n* reciclagem *f*.

red [red] (*compar* **-der**, *superl* **-dest**) <> *adj* **- 1.** [gen]

vermelho(lha) **-2.** [hair] ruivo(va). <> *n (U)* [colour] vermelho *m*; **to be in the ~** *inf* estar no vermelho; **to see ~** enfurecer-se.

◆ **Red** *pej* <> *adj* [left-wing, communist] vermelho(lha). <> *n* [left-winger, communist] vermelho *m*, lha *f*.

red alert *n* **-1.** *(U)* [state of readiness]: **on ~** em alerta vermelho **-2.** [order to be ready] alerta *f* vermelho.

red blood cell *n* glóbulo *m* vermelho.

red-blooded [-'blʌdɪd] *adj hum* com aquilo roxo.

red-brick *adj UK* [building] de tijolo à vista.

◆ **redbrick** *adj UK UNIV*: **redbrick university** *universidade construída em grandes centros fora de Londres nos séculos XIX e XX.*

red card *n FTBL*: **to be shown the ~, to get a ~** receber cartão vermelho.

red carpet *n*: **to roll out the ~ for sb** estender o tapete vermelho para alguém.

◆ **red-carpet** *adj*: **to give sb the red-carpet treatment** dar tratamento VIP para alguém.

Red Crescent *n*: **the ~** o Crescente Vermelho.

Red Cross *n*: **the ~** a Cruz Vermelha.

redcurrant ['redkʌrənt] *n* **-1.** [fruit] groselha *f* **-2.** [bush] groselheira *f*.

red deer *n* veado *m*.

redden ['redn] <> *vt* [make red] avermelhar. <> *vi* [flush] ruborizar-se, ficar ruborizado(da).

redecorate [ˌri:'dekəreɪt] <> *vt* redecorar. <> *vi* redecorar a casa.

redeem [rɪ'di:m] *vt* **-1.** [save, rescue] redimir; **to ~ o.s.** redimir-se **-2.** [from pawnbroker] resgatar.

redeemer *n RELIG*: **the Redeemer** o Redentor.

redeeming [rɪ'di:mɪŋ] *adj* redentor, que redime.

redefine [ˌri:dɪ'faɪn] *vt* redefinir.

redemption [rɪ'dempʃn] *n (U) RELIG* redenção *f*, salvação *f*; **beyond** *OR* **past ~** *fig* irrecuperável.

redeploy [ˌri:dɪ'plɔɪ] *vt* remanejar.

redeployment [ˌri:dɪ'plɔɪmənt] *n (U)* remanejamento *m*.

redesign [ˌri:dɪ'zaɪn] *vt* **-1.** [replan, redraw] remodelar **-2.** [reorganize, rethink] repensar.

redevelop [ˌri:dɪ'veləp] *vt* renovar.

redevelopment [ˌri:dɪ'veləpmənt] *n (U)* renovação *f*.

red-faced [-'feɪst] *adj* **-1.** [after exercise, with heat] vermelho(lha) **-2.** [with embarrassment] corado(da).

red-haired [-'heəd] *adj* ruivo(va).

red-handed [-'hændɪd] *adj*: **to catch sb ~** pegar alguém com a mão na massa.

redhead ['redhed] *n* ruiva *f*.

red herring *n fig* pista *f* falsa.

red-hot *adj* **-1.** [extremely hot] em brasa **-2.** [very enthusiastic] apaixonado(da) **-3.** *inf* [very good] supimpa.

redid [ˌri:'dɪd] *pt* ▷ **redo**.

Red Indian <> *adj* dos peles-vermelhas. <> *n* pele-vermelha *mf*.

redirect [ˌri:dɪ'rekt] *vt* **-1.** [mail] redirecionar **-2.** [traffic, aircraft] desviar **-3.** [one's energies, money, aid] direcionar.

rediscover [ˌri:dɪs'kʌvə^r] *vt* **-1.** [re-experience] redescobrir **-2.** [make popular, famous again]: **to be ~ed** ser redescoberto(ta).

redistribute [ˌri:dɪs'trɪbju:t] *vt* redistribuir.

red-letter day *n* dia *m* memorável.

red light *n* [traffic signal] luz *f* vermelha.

red-light district *n* zona *f* do baixo meretrício.

red meat *n (U)* carne *f* vermelha.

red mullet *n* salmonete *m*.

redness ['rednɪs] *n (U)* vermelhidão *f*.

redo [ˌri:'du:] (*pt* **-did**, *pp* **-done**) *vt* **-1.** [do again] refazer **-2.** *inf* [redecorate] redecorar.

redolent ['redələnt] *adj literary* **-1.** [reminiscent]: **~ of sthg** rememorativo(va) de algo **-2.** [smelling]: **~ of sthg** com aroma de algo.

redone *pp* ▷ **redo**.

redouble [ˌri:'dʌbl] *vt*: **to ~ one's efforts (to do sthg)** redobrar os esforços (para fazer algo).

redoubtable [rɪ'daʊtəbl] *adj fml* formidável.

redraft [ˌri:'drɑ:ft] *vt* reescrever.

redraw [ˌri:'drɔ:] (*pt* **-drew**, *pp* **-drawn** [-'drɔ:n]) *vt* redesenhar.

redress [rɪ'dres] *fml* <> *n (U)* retificação *f*. <> *vt*: **to ~ the balance** compensar.

redrew [ˌri:'dru:] *pt* ▷ **redraw**.

Red Sea *n*: **the ~** o Mar Vermelho.

red setter *n* cão *m* perdigueiro.

Red Square *n* Praça *f* Vermelha.

red squirrel *n* esquilo *m* vermelho.

red tape *n (U) fig* burocracia *f*.

reduce [rɪ'dju:s] <> *vt* **-1.** [make smaller, less] reduzir; **to ~ sthg to a pulp** reduzir algo à essência **-2.** *CULIN* engrossar no fogo **-3.** [force, bring]: **to be ~d to doing sthg** ser forçado(da) a fazer algo; **to be ~d to sthg** estar reduzido(da) a algo. <> *vi US* [lose weight] emagrecer.

reduced [rɪ'dju:st] *adj* reduzido(da); **in ~ circumstances** em circunstâncias limitadas.

reduction [rɪ'dʌkʃn] *n* **-1.** [decrease]: **~ (in sthg)** redução (em algo) **-2.** [amount of decrease]: **~ (of)** redução de.

redundancy [rɪ'dʌndənsɪ] (*pl* **-ies**) *n UK* **-1.** [job loss] demissão *f* **-2.** *(U)* [jobless state] desemprego *m*.

redundancy payment *n UK* indenização *f (por demissão sem justa causa)*.

redundant [rɪ'dʌndənt] *adj* **-1.** *UK* [jobless]: **to be made ~** ficar desempregado(da) **-2.** [superfluous] supérfluo(a).

redwood ['redwʊd] *n*: **a ~ (tree)** uma sequóia.

re-echo <> *vt* [repeat] repetir. <> *vi* [echo] repercutir, ecoar.

reed [ri:d] <> *n* **-1.** [plant] junco *m* **-2.** [of musical instrument] palheta *f*. <> *comp* [made of reeds] de junco.

re-educate *vt* reabilitar.

reedy ['ri:dɪ] (*compar* **-ier**, *superl* **-iest**) *adj* [voice] estridente.

reef [ri:f] *n* recife *m*.

reek [ri:k] <> *n* fedor *m*. <> *vi*: **to ~ (of sthg)** feder (a algo).

reel [ri:l] <> *n* **-1.** [roll] rolo *m* **-2.** [on fishing rod] molinete *m*. <> *vi* **-1.** [stagger] cambalear **-2.** [head, mind] girar; **to ~ from sthg** estar confuso(sa) por (causa de) algo.

◆ **reel in** *vt sep* enrolar.

◆ **reel off** *vt sep* [list] enumerar.
re-elect *vt*: **to ~ sb (as) sthg** reeleger alguém (como algo).
re-election *n (U)* reeleição *f*.
re-emphasize *vt* reenfatizar.
re-enact *vt* reviver.
re-enter *vt* **-1.** [room, country] reentrar em **-2.** *COMPUT* [data] reinserir em.
re-entry *n* **-1.** [into room, country] reentrada *f* **-2.** *COMPUT* [of data] reinserção *f*.
re-examine *vt* **-1.** [question, case] reexaminar **-2.** [witness] reinquirir **-3.** [candidate] rever.
re-export *COMM* ◇ *n* **-1.** *(U)* [act of exporting] reexportação *f* **-2.** [goods exported] reexportações *fpl*. ◇ *vt* reexportar.
ref [ref] *n* **-1.** *inf* (*abbr of* **referee**) *SPORT* árbitro *m* **-2.** (*abbr of* **reference**) *ADMIN* ref.
refectory [rɪ'fektərɪ] (*pl* **-ies**) *n* **-1.** [in school, college] cantina *f* **-2.** [in monastery] refeitório *m*.
refer [rɪ'fɜː[r]] (*pt* & *pp* **-red**, *cont* **-ring**) *vt* **-1.** [person]: **to ~ sb to sthg** encaminhar alguém para algo **-2.** [report, case, decision]: **to ~ sthg to sb/sthg** encaminhar algo para alguém/algo.
◆ **refer to** *vt fus* **-1.** [mention, speak about] referir-se a **-2.** [apply to, concern] aplicar-se a **-3.** [consult] consultar.
referee [ˌrefə'riː] ◇ *n* **-1.** *SPORT* árbitro *m*, -tra *f* **-2.** *UK* [for job application] referência *f*. ◇ *vt* & *vi SPORT* apitar.
reference ['refrəns] *n* **-1.** [gen] referência *f* **-2.** *(U)* [act of mentioning]: **to make ~ to sb/sthg** referência a alguém/algo; **with ~ to** *fml* com referência a **-3.** [mention]: **~ (to sb/sthg)** menção a alguém /algo **-4.** *(U)* [for advice, information]: **~ (to sb/sthg)** referência a alguém/algo; **for future ~** para consulta futura **-5.** *COMM* [in letter] referências *fpl*.
reference book *n* livro *m* de consulta.
reference library *n* biblioteca *f* de consulta.
reference number *n* número *m* de referência.
referendum [ˌrefə'rendəm] (*pl* **-s** *OR* **-da** [-də]) *n POL* plebiscito *m*.
referral [rɪ'fɜːrəl] *n fml* referência *f*.
refill [*n* 'riːfɪl, *vb* ˌriː'fɪl] ◇ *n* **-1.** [for pen, lighter] carga *f* nova **-2.** *inf* [drink] dose *f* extra. ◇ *vt* [fill again - bottle, glass] encher novamente; [- petrol tank] reabastecer.
refillable [ˌriː'fɪləbl] *adj* recarregável.
refine [rɪ'faɪn] *vt* **-1.** [purify] refinar **-2.** [details, speech] aprimorar.
refined [rɪ'faɪnd] *adj* refinado(da).
refinement [rɪ'faɪnmənt] *n* **-1.** [improvement]: **~ (on sthg)** refinamento (de algo) **-2.** *(U)* [gentility] requinte *m*.
refinery [rɪ'faɪnərɪ] (*pl* **-ies**) *n* refinaria *f*.
refit [*n* 'riːfɪt, *vb* ˌriː'fɪt] (*pt* & *pp* **-ted**, *cont* **-ting**) ◇ *n* [of ship] reaparelhamento *m*. ◇ *vt* [ship] reaparelhar.
reflate [ˌriː'fleɪt] *vt ECON* reinflacionar.
reflation [ˌriː'fleɪʃn] *n (U) ECON* reflação *f*.
reflationary [riː'fleɪʃənrɪ] *adj ECON* reflacionário(-ria).
reflect [rɪ'flekt] ◇ *vt* refletir; **to be ~ed in sthg** estar refletido(da) em algo, refletir-se em algo; **to ~ that ...** refletir que ... ◇ *vi* [think, consider]: **to ~ (on** *OR* **upon sthg)** refletir (sobre algo).
reflection [rɪ'flekʃn] *n* **-1.** [gen] reflexo *m* **-2.** [comment, thought] reflexão *f*; **~ on sthg** reflexão sobre algo; **on ~** pensando bem.
reflective [rɪ'flektɪv] *adj* **-1.** [thoughtful] reflexivo(va) **-2.** [shiny] brilhante.
reflector [rɪ'flektə[r]] *n* refletor *m*.
reflex ['riːfleks] *n*: **~ (action)** (ato) reflexo *m*.
◆ **reflexes** *npl* reflexos *mpl*.
reflex camera *n* câmera *f* reflex.
reflexive [rɪ'fleksɪv] *adj GRAMM* reflexivo(va).
reflexology [ˌriːflek'sɒlədʒɪ] *n* reflexoterapia *f*.
reforest [ˌriː'fɒrɪst] *vt esp US* = **reafforest**.
reforestation [riːˌfɒrɪ'steɪʃn] *n esp US* = **reafforestation**.
reform [rɪ'fɔːm] ◇ *n* reforma *f*. ◇ *vt* **-1.** [change] reformar **-2.** [improve behaviour of] corrigir. ◇ *vi* corrigir-se.
reformat [ˌriː'fɔːmæt] (*pt* & *pp* **-ted**, *cont* **-ting**) *vt COMPUT* reformatar.
Reformation [ˌrefə'meɪʃn] *n*: **the ~** a Reforma.
reformatory [rɪ'fɔːmətrɪ] (*pl* **-ies**) *n US* reformatório *m*.
reformed [rɪ'fɔːmd] *adj* regenerado(da).
reformer [rɪ'fɔːmə[r]] *n* reformador *m*, -ra *f*.
reformist [rɪ'fɔːmɪst] ◇ *adj* reformista. ◇ *n* reformista *mf*.
refract [rɪ'frækt] ◇ *vt* refratar. ◇ *vi* refratar-se.
refrain [rɪ'freɪn] ◇ *n* refrão *m*. ◇ *vi fml*: **to ~ from doing sthg** abster-se de fazer algo.
refresh [rɪ'freʃ] *vt* refrescar; **to ~ sb's memory** refrescar a memória de alguém.
refreshed [rɪ'freʃt] *adj* revigorado(da).
refresher course [rɪ'freʃə[r]-] *n* curso *m* de aperfeiçoamento *OR* atualização.
refreshing [rɪ'freʃɪŋ] *adj* **-1.** [pleasantly different] reconfortante **-2.** [cooling, energy-giving] refrescante.
refreshments [rɪ'freʃmənts] *npl* comes *mpl* e bebes, lanche *m*.
refrigerate [rɪ'frɪdʒəreɪt] *vt* refrigerar.
refrigeration [rɪˌfrɪdʒə'reɪʃn] *n (U)* refrigeração *f*.
refrigerator [rɪ'frɪdʒəreɪtə[r]] *n* geladeira *f*, refrigerador *m*.
refuel [ˌriː'fjʊəl] (*UK pt* & *pp* **-led**, *cont* **-ling**, *US pt* & *pp* **-ed**, *cont* **-ing**) ◇ *vt* reabastecer. ◇ *vi* reabastecer-se *(de combustível)*.
refuge ['refjuːdʒ] *n* **-1.** [place of safety] refúgio *m* **-2.** *(U)* [safety]: **to seek** *OR* **take ~** [hide] procurar refúgio, refugiar-se; **to seek** *OR* **take ~ in sthg** *fig* procurar *OR* buscar refúgio em algo, refugiar-se em algo.
refugee [ˌrefjʊ'dʒiː] *n* refugiado *m*, -da *f*.
refugee camp *n* campo *m* de refugiados.
refund [*n* 'riːfʌnd, *vb* rɪ'fʌnd] ◇ *n* reembolso *m*. ◇ *vt*: **to ~ sthg to sb**, **to ~ sb sthg** reembolsar algo a alguém.
refurbish [ˌriː'fɜːbɪʃ] *vt* **-1.** [shop, office] reformar **-2.** [building] restaurar.
refurbishment [ˌriː'fɜːbɪʃmənt] *n* **-1.** [of shop, office] reforma *f* **-2.** [building] restauração *f*.
refurnish [ˌriː'fɜːnɪʃ] *vt* mobiliar novamente.

refusal [rɪ'fju:zl] *n* recusa *f*; **her ~ to accept the conditions** o fato de ela não ter aceitado as condições; **to meet with ~** ser rechaçado(da).

refuse[1] ['rɪfju:z] <> *vt* **-1.** [withhold, deny]: **to ~ sb sthg, to ~ sthg to sb** negar algo a alguém **-2.** [decline] recusar; **to ~ to do sthg** recusar-se a fazer algo, negar-se a fazer algo. <> *vi* negar-se, dizer que não.

refuse[2] ['refju:s] *n (U)* lixo *m*, refugo *m*.

refuse collection ['refju:s-] *n* coleta *f* de lixo.

refuse collector ['refju:s-] *n* lixeiro *m*, -ra *f*.

refuse dump ['refju:s-] *n* depósito *m* de lixo, lixeira *f*.

refute [rɪ'fju:t] *vt fml* refutar.

reg. (*abbr of* **registered**): **~ trademark** marca *f* registrada.

regain [rɪ'geɪn] *vt* recuperar.

regal ['ri:gl] *adj* régio(gia).

regale [rɪ'geɪl] *vt*: **to ~ sb with sthg** entreter alguém com algo.

regalia [rɪ'geɪljə] *n (U) fml* insígnias *fpl* reais.

regard [rɪ'gɑ:d] <> *n* **-1.** *(U) fml* [respect, esteem] respeito *m*, estima *f*; **~ (for sb/sthg)** respeito OR estima (por alguém/algo) **-2.** [aspect]: **in this/that ~** a este respeito. <> *vt* considerar; **to ~ o.s. intelligent** considerar-se inteligente; **to ~ sb/sthg as** considerar alguém/algo; **to ~ sb/sthg with** ver alguém/algo com; **to be highly ~ed** ser muito bem considerado(da).

◆ **regards** *npl* [in greetings] lembranças *fpl*; **with my best ~s** cordialmente.

◆ **as regards** *prep* em relação a, no que se refere a.

◆ **in regard to, with regard to** *prep* a respeito de, em relação a.

regarding [rɪ'gɑ:dɪŋ] *prep* a respeito de, em relação a.

regardless [rɪ'gɑ:dlɪs] *adv* apesar de tudo.

◆ **regardless of** *prep* independentemente de; **~ the cost** custe o que custar.

regatta [rɪ'gætə] *n* regata *f*.

regd. = **reg.**

Regency ['ri:dʒənsɪ] *adj* (com período) regencial.

regenerate [rɪ'dʒenəreɪt] <> *vt* regenerar. <> *vi* **-1.** [organs, tissue] regenerar-se **-2.** [economy] recuperar-se **-3.** [project] ser reformado(da).

regeneration [rɪˌdʒenə'reɪʃn] *n* **-1.** *(U)* [of organs, tissue] regeneração *f* **-2.** *(U)* [of economy] recuperação *f* **-3.** *(U)* [of project] reforma *f*.

regent ['ri:dʒənt] <> *adj* regente. <> *n* regente *mf*.

reggae ['regeɪ] *n (U)* reggae *m*.

regime [reɪ'ʒi:m] *n pej* regime *m*.

regiment ['redʒɪmənt] *n* MIL regimento *m*.

regimental [ˌredʒɪ'mentl] *adj* MIL do regimento, regimental.

regimented ['redʒɪmentɪd] *adj* **-1.** *pej* [workforce] estritamente controlado(da) **-2.** [in rows] ordenado(da) em fileiras.

region ['ri:dʒən] *n* **-1.** [gen] região *f* **-2.** [range]: **in the ~ of** por volta de.

regional ['ri:dʒənl] *adj* regional.

register ['redʒɪstə[r]] <> *n* registro *f*. <> *vt* **-1.** registrar **-2.** [express] expressar, mostrar. <> *vi* **-1.** [enrol]: **to ~ as/for sthg** inscrever-se como/para algo **-2.** [book in] registrar-se **-3.** *inf* [be properly understood] assimilar.

registered ['redʒɪstəd] *adj* **-1.** [officially listed] oficialmente inscrito(ta) **-2.** [letter, parcel] registrado (da).

registered nurse *n* enfermeira *f* formada.

registered post UK, **registered mail** US *n (U)*: **to send sthg by ~** enviar algo registrado (pelo correio).

registered trademark *n* marca *f* registrada.

registrar ['redʒɪstrɑ:[r]] *n* **-1.** [keeper of records] escrivão *m*, -vã *f*, oficial *mf* de registro **-2.** UNIV [administrator] secretário *m*, -ria *f* geral **-3.** UK [doctor] médico *m*, -ca *f* em estágio de especialização.

registration [ˌredʒɪ'streɪʃn] *n* **-1.** [course enrolment] matrícula *f* **-2.** [of births, marriages and deaths] registro *m* **-3.** AUT = **registration number.**

registration document *n* certificado *m* de registro de veículo.

registration number *n* AUT número *m* de licença.

registry ['redʒɪstrɪ] (*pl* **-ies**) *n* registro *m*.

registry office *n* registro *m* civil.

regress [rɪ'gres] *vi fml*: **to ~ (to sthg)** regredir (a algo).

regression [rɪ'greʃn] *n (U) fml* regressão *f*.

regressive [rɪ'gresɪv] *adj fml* regressivo(va).

regret [rɪ'gret] (*pt* & *pp* **-ted**, *cont* **-ting**) <> *n* **-1.** *(U) fml* [sorrow] pesar *m* **-2.** [sad feeling]: **to have no ~ a about sthg** não lamentar algo em absoluto. <> *vt*: **to ~ sthg/doing sthg** lamentar algo/ter feito algo; **we ~ to announce ...** lamentamos comunicar ...

regretful [rɪ'gretfʊl] *adj* **-1.** [smile look] de arrependimento **-2.** [person] arrependido(da).

regretfully [rɪ'gretfʊlɪ] *adv* pesarosamente; **~ we have to announce ...** lamentamos ter que anunciar ...

regrettable [rɪ'gretəbl] *adj fml* lamentável.

regrettably [rɪ'gretəblɪ] *adv* lamentavelmente.

regroup [ˌri:'gru:p] *vi* reagrupar-se.

regt (*abbr of* **regiment**) regto.

regular ['regjʊlə[r]] <> *adj* **-1.** [gen] regular **-2.** [frequent - occurrence] freqüente; [- customer] habitual; [- visitor] assíduo(dua) **-3.** [usual] habitual, normal **-4.** US [in size] médio(dia) **-5.** US [pleasant] amigável **-6.** US [normal] normal. <> *n* [customer, client] cliente *mf* habitual.

regular army *n* exército *m* ativo.

regularity [ˌregjʊ'lærətɪ] *n (U)* regularidade *f*.

regularly ['regjʊləlɪ] *adv* **-1.** [equally spaced] de maneira uniforme **-2.** [repeated at expected time] regularmente.

regulate ['regjʊleɪt] *vt* regular.

regulation [ˌregjʊ'leɪʃn] <> *adj* regulamentar. <> *n* **-1.** [rule] regra *f*, lei *f* **-2.** *(U)* [control] regulamento *m*, regulamentação *f*.

regurgitate [rɪ'gɜ:dʒɪteɪt] *vt* **-1.** [bring up] regurgitar **-2.** *fig* & *pej* [repeat] repetir maquinalmente.

rehabilitate [ˌri:ə'bɪlɪteɪt] *vt* **-1.** [convict, addict] reabilitar **-2.** [patient, invalid] recuperar.

rehabilitation [ˈriːəˌbɪlɪˈteɪʃn] *n* **-1.** [of convict, addict] reabilitação *f* **-2.** [of patient, invalid] recuperação *f*.

rehash [ˌriːˈhæʃ] *inf* ◇ *vt pej* retocar. ◇ *n* retoque *m*.

rehearsal [rɪˈhɜːsl] *n* ensaio *m*.

rehearse [rɪˈhɜːs] ◇ *vt* ensaiar. ◇ *vi*: **to ~ (for sthg)** ensaiar (para algo).

reheat [ˌriːˈhiːt] *vt* reaquecer, esquentar de novo.

rehouse [ˌriːˈhaʊz] *vt*: **to be ~d** ser realojado (da).

reign [reɪn] ◇ *n* reinado *m*. ◇ *vi*: **to ~ (over sb/sthg)** reinar (sobre alguém/algo).

reigning [ˈreɪnɪŋ] *adj* atual.

reimburse [ˌriːɪmˈbɜːs] *vt*: **to ~ sb (for sthg)** reembolsar alguém (por algo).

reimbursement [ˌriːɪmˈbɜːsmənt] *n (U) fml*: **~ (for sthg)** reembolso *m* (por algo).

rein [reɪn] *n fig*: **to give (a) free ~ to sb, to give sb free ~** dar carta branca a alguém; **to keep a tight ~ on sb/sthg** controlar alguém/algo com firmeza.

◆ **reins** *npl* **-1.** [for horse] rédeas *fpl* **-2.** [for child] andadeira *f*.

◆ **rein in** *vt sep* [horse] puxar as rédeas de.

reincarnation [ˌriːɪnkɑːˈneɪʃn] *n (U)* reencarnação *f*.

reindeer [ˈreɪnˌdɪəʳ] (*pl inv*) *n* rena *f*.

reinforce [ˌriːɪnˈfɔːs] *vt*: **to ~ sthg (with sthg)** reforçar algo (com algo).

reinforced concrete [ˌriːɪnˈfɔːst-] *n (U)* concreto *m* armado.

reinforcement [ˌriːɪnˈfɔːsmənt] *n* reforço *m*.

◆ **reinforcements** *npl* reforços *mpl*.

reinstate [ˌriːɪnˈsteɪt] *vt* **-1.** [person - in job] readmitir; [- in position, office] reempossar, reintegrar **-2.** [payment, idea, policy] restabelecer.

reinstatement [ˌriːɪnˈsteɪtmənt] *n* **-1.** [of person - in job] readmissão *f*; [- in position, office] reintegração *f* **-2.** [of payment, idea, policy] restabelecimento *m*.

reinterpret [ˌriːɪnˈtɜːprɪt] *vt* reinterpretar.

reintroduce [ˈriːˌɪntrəˈdjuːs] *vt* reintroduzir.

reintroduction [riːˌɪntrəˈdʌkʃn] *n (U)* reintrodução *f*.

reissue [riːˈɪʃuː] ◇ *n* reedição *f*, reimpressão *f*. ◇ *vt* reeditar, reimprimir.

reiterate [riːˈɪtəreɪt] *vt fml* reiterar.

reiteration [riːˌɪtəˈreɪʃn] *n fml* reiteração *f*.

reject [*n* ˈriːdʒekt, *vb* rɪˈdʒekt] ◇ *n* [in factory, shop] refugo *m*, rejeito *m*. ◇ *vt* **-1.** [not agree to] rejeitar, não concordar com **-2.** [dismiss, not accept] rejeitar **-3.** [for job] recusar.

rejection [rɪˈdʒekʃn] *n* **-1.** *(U)* [act of refusal] rejeição *f* **-2.** [for job] recusa *f*.

rejig [ˌriːˈdʒɪg] (*pt* & *pp* **-ged**, *cont* **-ging**) *vt UK inf* modificar *OR* alterar um pouco.

rejoice [rɪˈdʒɔɪs] *vi*: **to ~ (at *OR* in sthg)** regozijar-se *OR* alegrar-se (por algo).

rejoicing [rɪˈdʒɔɪsɪŋ] *n (U)* regozijo *m*, alegria *f*; **~ at *OR* over sthg** regozijo *m* por algo.

rejoin [rɪˈdʒɔɪn] *vt* **-1.** [group, friends] reunir-se novamente com **-2.** [regiment] reingressar em **-3.** [motorway] pegar novamente **-4.** [club, society] voltar a ser sócio(cia) de **-5.** [reply] replicar, retorquir.

rejoinder [rɪˈdʒɔɪndəʳ] *n* réplica *f*.

rejuvenate [rɪˈdʒuːvəneɪt] *vt* rejuvenescer.

rejuvenation [rɪˌdʒuːvəˈneɪʃn] *n (U)* rejuvenescimento *m*.

rekindle [ˌriːˈkɪndl] *vt fig* reacender, reavivar.

relapse [rɪˈlæps] ◇ *n* recaída *f*; **to have a ~** ter uma recaída. ◇ *vi*: **to ~ into** [coma] entrar novamente em; [drunken stupor, old ways] voltar a cair em; [crime] reincidir em.

relate [rɪˈleɪt] ◇ *vt* **-1.** [connect]: **to ~ sthg to sthg** relacionar algo a algo **-2.** [tell] contar. ◇ *vi* **-1.** [connect]: **to ~ to sthg** relacionar-se a algo **-2.** [concern]: **to ~ to sthg** referir-se a algo **-3.** [empathize]: **to ~ (to sb/sthg)** ter muito em comum (com alguém/algo).

◆ **relating to** *prep* sobre, acerca de.

related [rɪˈleɪtɪd] *adj* **-1.** [in same family] aparentado (da); **to be ~ to sb** ser aparentado(da) de alguém **-2.** [connected] relacionado(da).

relation [rɪˈleɪʃn] *n* **-1.** *(U)* [connection]: **~ (to/between)** relação *f* (com/entre); **to bear no ~ to** não ter nada a ver com; **in ~ to** [state, size] em relação a **-2.** [family member] parente *mf*, familiar *mf*.

◆ **relations** *npl* [relationship] relações *fpl*; **~ between/with** relações entre/com.

relational [rɪˈleɪʃənl] *adj COMPUT* relacional.

relationship [rɪˈleɪʃnʃɪp] *n* **-1.** [gen] relação *f* **-2.** [relations] relação *f*, relacionamento *m* **-3.** [connection] ligação *f*.

relative [ˈrelətɪv] ◇ *adj* relativo(va). ◇ *n* parente *mf*, familiar *mf*.

◆ **relative to** *prep fml* **-1.** [compared to] em comparação com **-2.** [connected with] relativo(va) a, com relação a.

relatively [ˈrelətɪvlɪ] *adv* relativamente.

relativity [ˌreləˈtɪvətɪ] *n (U)* relatividade *f*.

relax [rɪˈlæks] ◇ *vt* **-1.** [gen] relaxar **-2.** [loosen, free up] afrouxar. ◇ *vi* **-1.** [person] relaxar, descontrair-se; **~! It's OK!** relaxe! Está tudo bem! **-2.** [grip] afrouxar-se.

relaxation [ˌriːlækˈseɪʃn] *n (U)* **-1.** [rest] relaxamento *m* **-2.** [of rule, discipline, regulation] afrouxamento *m*.

relaxed [rɪˈlækst] *adj* **-1.** [person] relaxado(da), descontraído(da) **-2.** [meeting, evening, mood] descontraído(da).

relaxing [rɪˈlæksɪŋ] *adj* relaxante.

relay [ˈriːleɪ] (*pt* & *pp senses 1* & *2* **-ed**, *pt* & *pp sense 3* **relaid**) ◇ *n* **-1.** *SPORT*: **~ (race)** corrida *f* de revezamento; **in ~s** *fig* em turnos **-2.** [broadcast] retransmissão *f*. ◇ *vt* **-1.** [broadcast] retransmitir **-2.** [message, news]: **to ~ sthg (to sb)** transmitir algo (a alguém) **-3.** [cable, carpet, tiles] repor.

release [rɪˈliːs] ◇ *n* **-1.** *(U)* [from captivity] soltura *f*, libertação *f* **-2.** *(U)* [from pain, suffering] liberação *f* **-3.** [statement] comunicado *m* **-4.** *(U)* [of gas, fumes] escapamento *m*, emissão *f* **-5.** *(U)* [of film, video, CD] lançamento *m*; **on ~** *CINEMA* em exibição **-6.** [film, video, CD]: **new ~** novo lançamento. ◇ *vt* **-1.** [set free] soltar, libertar; **to ~ sb from prison/captivity** libertar *OR* soltar alguém da prisão/do cativeiro; **to ~ sb from sthg** [promise, contract] liberar alguém de algo **-2.** [make available] liberar **-3.** [control, grasp, mechanism] soltar **-4.** [let out, emit]: **heat is ~d from the liquid into the air** o calor é liberado do líquido para o ar **-5.** [film, video, CD] lançar; [statement, news story] divulgar.

relegate ['relɪgeɪt] *vt* **-1.** [demote]: **to ~ sb/sthg (to)** relegar alguém/algo (a) **-2.** *SPORT*: **to be ~d** *UK* ser rebaixado(da).

relegation [ˌrelɪ'geɪʃn] *n (U)* **-1.** [demotion]: **~ (to)** relegação *f* (a) **-2.** *SPORT*: **~ (to)** rebaixamento *m* (a).

relent [rɪ'lent] *vi* **-1.** [person] condescender **-2.** [wind, storm] abrandar-se, acalmar-se.

relentless [rɪ'lentlɪs] *adj* implacável.

relentlessly [rɪ'lentlɪslɪ] *adv* implacavelmente.

relevance ['reləvəns] *n (U)* **-1.** [connection]: **~ (to sb/sthg)** relevância *f* (a alguém/algo) **-2.** [significance]: **~ (to sb/sthg)**, **~ (for sb/sthg)** importância *f* (para alguém/algo).

relevant ['reləvənt] *adj* **-1.** [gen] relevante; **~ (to sb/sthg)** relevante (a alguém/algo) **-2.** [important]: **~ (to sb/sthg)** importante (a alguém/algo).

reliability [rɪˌlaɪə'bɪlətɪ] *n (U)* confiabilidade *f*.

reliable [rɪ'laɪəbl] *adj* **-1.** [dependable] confiável **-2.** [correct, true] seguro(ra).

reliably [rɪ'laɪəblɪ] *adv* **-1.** [dependably] de forma confiável **-2.** [correctly, truly]: **to be ~ informed that ...** saber de fonte segura que ...

reliance [rɪ'laɪəns] *n (U)*: **~ (on sb/sthg)** dependência *f* (de alguém/algo).

reliant [rɪ'laɪənt] *adj*: **~ on sb/sthg** dependente de alguém/algo.

relic ['relɪk] *n* relíquia *f*.

relief [rɪ'li:f] *n* **-1.** [comfort] alívio *m*; **she sighed with ~** ela suspirou aliviada **-2.** *(U)* [for poor, refugees] auxílio *m* **-3.** *US* [social security] subsídio *m*.

relief map *n* mapa *m* em relevo.

relief road *n UK* desvio *m*.

relieve [rɪ'li:v] *vt* **-1.** [ease, lessen] aliviar; **to ~ sb of sthg** aliviar alguém de algo **-2.** [take over from] substituir **-3.** [give help to] auxiliar.

relieved [rɪ'li:vd] *adj* aliviado(da).

religion [rɪ'lɪdʒn] *n* religião *f*.

religious [rɪ'lɪdʒəs] *adj* religioso(sa).

reline [ˌri:'laɪn] *vt* **-1.** [gen] revestir novamente **-2.** [brakes] trocar o forro de.

relinquish [rɪ'lɪŋkwɪʃ] *vt* **-1.** [power, post, claim] renunciar a **-2.** [hold] soltar.

relish ['relɪʃ] ◇ *n* **-1.** *(U)* [enjoyment]: **with (great) ~** com(grande)satisfação **-2.** [pickle] picles *mpl*. ◇ *vt* desfrutar de; **to ~ the thought** *OR* **idea** *OR* **prospect of doing sthg** desfrutar de antemão da idéia *OR* da perspectiva de fazer algo.

relive [ˌri:'lɪv] *vt* reviver.

relocate [ˌri:ləʊ'keɪt] ◇ *vt* realocar, transferir. ◇ *vi* transferir-se.

relocation [ˌrɪləʊ'keɪʃn] *n (U)* realocação *f*.

relocation expenses *npl* gastos *mpl* com transferência.

reluctance [rɪ'lʌktəns] *n (U)* relutância *f*; **with ~** com relutância.

reluctant [rɪ'lʌktənt] *adj* relutante; **to be ~ to do sthg** estar pouco disposto(ta) a fazer algo.

reluctantly [rɪ'lʌktəntlɪ] *adv* relutantemente.

rely [rɪ'laɪ] *(pt & pp* **-ied)** ◆ **rely on** *vt fus* **-1.** [count on] contar com; **to ~ on sb/sthg to do sthg** estar certo(ta) de que alguém/algo fará algo **-2.** [be dependent on]: **to ~ on sb/sthg for sthg** depender de alguém/algo para algo.

REM *(abbr of* **rapid eye movement)** *n* REM *m*.

remain [rɪ'meɪn] *vi* **-1.** [stay] permanecer, ficar; **to ~ the same** continuar sendo igual **-2.** [be left] ficar; **the problem ~** o problema continua; **to ~ to be done** ficar para ser feito(ta); **it ~s to be seen ...** isso ainda tem que ver ...
◆ **remains** *npl* **-1.** [of meal, fortune, body] restos *mpl* **-2.** [corpses] corpos *mpl* **-3.** [of ancient civilization, buildings] ruínas *fpl*.

remainder [rɪ'meɪndəʳ] *n* **-1.** [rest]: **the ~** o resto **-2.** *MATH* resto *m*; **three into ten goes three ~ one** dez (dividido) por três é igual a três e sobra um.

remaining [rɪ'meɪnɪŋ] *adj* restante; **it's my last ~ pound!** é a última libra que eu tenho!

remake [*n* 'ri:meɪk, *vb* ˌri:'meɪk] *CINEMA* ◇ *n* nova versão *f*, remake *m*. ◇ *vt* fazer uma nova versão de.

remand [rɪ'mɑ:nd] *JUR* ◇ *n*: **on ~** sob prisão preventiva. ◇ *vt* recolocar em prisão preventiva; **to be ~ed in custody** estar sob custódia.

remand centre *n UK instituição para a qual são enviadas as pessoas que aguardam julgamento.*

remark [rɪ'mɑ:k] ◇ *n* comentário *m*. ◇ *vt*: **to ~ (that)** comentar que. ◇ *vi*: **to ~ on sthg** fazer comentários sobre algo.

remarkable [rɪ'mɑ:kəbl] *adj* excepcional, extraordinário(ria).

remarkably [rɪ'mɑ:kəblɪ] *adv* excepcionalmente, extraordinariamente.

remarry [ˌri:'mærɪ] *(pt & pp* **-ied)** *vi* casar-se de novo.

remedial [rɪ'mi:djəl] *adj* **-1.** [pupil] atrasado(da) **-2.** [teacher, class] de reforço **-3.** [corrective] corretivo (va).

remedy ['remədɪ] *(pl* **-ies**, *pt & pp* **-ied)** ◇ *n* **-1.** [for ill health]: **~ (for sthg)** remédio *m* (para algo) **-2.** *fig* [solution]: **~ (for sthg)** *OR* solução *f* (para algo). ◇ *vt* remediar.

remember [rɪ'membəʳ] ◇ *vt* **-1.** lembrar-se de, lembrar; **to ~ doing sthg** lembrar-se de ter feito algo; **to ~ to do sthg** lembrar-se de fazer algo **-2.** [as greeting]: **~ me to your wife** dê lembranças minhas à sua esposa. ◇ *vi* lembrar(-se).

remembrance [rɪ'membrəns] *n (U) fml*: **in ~ of** em memória de.

Remembrance Day *n na Grã-Bretanha, dia em memória das pessoas mortas nas duas guerras mundiais.*

remind [rɪ'maɪnd] *vt* **-1.** [tell]: **to ~ sb (about sthg/to do sthg)** lembrar alguém (de algo/de fazer algo) **-2.** [be reminiscent of]: **to ~ sb of sb/sthg** fazer alguém se lembrar de alguém/algo; **she ~s me of my sister** ela me faz lembrar a minha irmã.

reminder [rɪ'maɪndəʳ] *n* **-1.** [to jog memory]: **~ of sthg/to do sthg** lembrança *f* de algo/de fazer algo **-2.** [for bill, membership, licence] lembrete *m*.

reminisce [ˌremɪˈnɪs] *vi*: **to ~ (about sthg)** rememorar(algo).
reminiscences [ˌremɪˈnɪsənsɪz] *npl* reminiscências *fpl*.
reminiscent [ˌremɪˈnɪsnt] *adj*: **~ of sb/sthg** que faz lembrar alguém/algo.
remiss [rɪˈmɪs] *adj* descuidado(da), negligente.
remission [rɪˈmɪʃn] *n* **-1.** *JUR* redução *f* de pena **-2.** *MED* remissão *f*.
remit [ˈriːmɪt] (*pt* & *pp* **-ted**, *cont* **-ting**) ◇ *n UK* alçada *f*; **that's outside my ~** isto está fora da minha alçada. ◇ *vt* remeter.
remittance [rɪˈmɪtns] *n* **-1.** [payment] remessa *f* **-2.** *COMM* [settlement of invoice] remessa *f* de valores.
remnant [ˈremnənt] *n* [of cloth] sobra *f*; [of beauty, culture] resto *m*.
remodel [ˌriːˈmɒdl] (*UK pt* & *pp* **-led**, *cont* **-ling**, *US pt* & *pp* **-ed**, *cont* **-ing**) *vt* **-1.** [change shape of] remodelar **-2.** *US* [renovate] reformar.
remold *n US* = **remould**.
remonstrate [ˈremənstreɪt] *vi fml*: **to ~ (with sb about sthg)** protestar (com alguém sobre algo).
remorse [rɪˈmɔːs] *n (U)* remorso *m*.
remorseful [rɪˈmɔːsfʊl] *adj* cheio (cheia) de remorso.
remorseless [rɪˈmɔːslɪs] *adj* **-1.** [pitiless] desapiedado(da) **-2.** [unstoppable] impiedoso(sa), implacável.
remorselessly [rɪˈmɔːslɪslɪ] *adv* **-1.** [pitilessly] de forma desapiedada **-2.** [unstoppably] impiedosamente, implacavelmente.
remote [rɪˈməʊt] *adj* **-1.** [gen] remoto(ta) **-2.** [unconnected, detached]: **~ from** distante de.
remote control *n* controle *m* remoto.
remote-controlled [-kənˈtrəʊld] *adj* operado(-da) por controle remoto.
remotely [rɪˈməʊtlɪ] *adv* remotamente.
remoteness [rɪˈməʊtnɪs] *n (U)* **-1.** [distance - in space] isolamento *f*; [- in time] distanciamento *m* **-2.** [aloofness] indiferença *m*.
remould *UK*, **remold** *US* [ˈriːməʊld] *n* pneu *m* recauchutado.
removable [rɪˈmuːvəbl] *adj* desmontável.
removal [rɪˈmuːvl] *n* **-1.** *UK* [change of house] mudança *f* **-2.** *(U)* [act of removing] remoção *f*.
removal man *n UK* encarregado *m* da mudança.
removal van *n UK* caminhão *m* de mudança.
remove [rɪˈmuːv] *vt* **-1.** [gen]: **to ~ sthg (from)** remover algo (de) **-2.** [take off garment] tirar **-3.** [from a job, post]: **to ~ sb (from)** demitir alguém (de) **-4.** [injustice, difficulty] eliminar **-5.** [problem] resolver **-6.** [suspicion] dissipar.
removed [rɪˈmuːvd] *adj*: **to be far ~ from** estar muito distante de.
remover [rɪˈmuːvəʳ] *n* removedor *m*.
remuneration [rɪˌmjuːnəˈreɪʃn] *n fml (U)* remuneração *f*.
Renaissance [rəˈneɪsəns] ◇ *n*: **the ~** o Renascimento. ◇ *comp* do Renascimento.
rename [ˌriːˈneɪm] *vt* renomear.
rend [ˈrend] (*pt* & *pp* **rent**) *vt fml* rasgar, despedaçar.
render [ˈrendəʳ] *vt* **-1.** [make, change] tornar; **to ~ sthg useless** tornar algo inútil; **to ~ sb speechless** deixar alguém boquiaberto(ta) **-2.** [give] dar, prestar; **to ~ good services** prestar bons serviços **-3.** *COMPUT* exibir.
rendering [ˈrendərɪŋ] *n* **-1.** [performance - of play] interpretação *f*; [- of song, piece of music] execução *f* **-2.** [translation] tradução *f* **-3.** *COMPUT* exibição *f*.
rendezvous [ˈrɒndɪvuː] (*pl inv*) *n* **-1.** [meeting] encontro *m* **-2.** [place] ponto *m* de encontro.
rendition [renˈdɪʃn] *n* **-1.** [of piece of music] execução *f* **-2.** [of poem] declamação *f*.
renegade [ˈrenɪgeɪd] ◇ *adj* renegado(da). ◇ *n* renegado *m*, -da *f*.
renege [rɪˈniːg] *vi fml*: **to ~ on sthg** deixar de cumprir algo.
renegotiate [ˌriːnɪˈgəʊʃɪeɪt] *vt* & *vi* renegociar.
renew [rɪˈnjuː] *vt* **-1.** [gen] renovar **-2.** [start again] reiniciar.
renewable [rɪˈnjuːəbl] *adj* renovável.
renewal [rɪˈnjuːəl] *n* renovação *f*.
rennet [ˈrenɪt] *n (U)* coalheira *f*.
renounce [rɪˈnaʊns] *vt* renunciar a.
renovate [ˈrenəveɪt] *vt* renovar, reformar.
renovation [ˌrenəˈveɪʃn] *n (U)* reforma *f*, renovação *f*.
◆ **renovations** *npl* reformas *fpl*.
renown [rɪˈnaʊn] *n (U)* renome *m*.
renowned [rɪˈnaʊnd] *adj*: **~ (for sthg)** renomado(da) (por algo).
rent [rent] ◇ *pt* & *pp* ▷ **rend**. ◇ *n* aluguel *m*. ◇ *vt* alugar.
◆ **rent out** *vt sep* alugar.
rental [ˈrentl] ◇ *adj* de aluguel. ◇ *n* [money] aluguel *m*.
rent book *n* livro *m* de registro do aluguel.
rent boy *n UK inf* garoto *m* de programa.
rented [ˈrentɪd] *adj* alugado(da).
rent-free ◇ *adj* isento(ta) de aluguel. ◇ *adv* sem pagar aluguel.
renumber [ˌriːˈnʌmbəʳ] *vt* renumerar.
renunciation [rɪˌnʌnsɪˈeɪʃn] *n (U)* renúncia *f*.
reoccurrence [ˌriːəˈkʌrəns] *n* nova ocorrência *f*, repetição *f*.
reopen [ˌriːˈəʊpn] ◇ *vt* **-1.** [open again] reabrir **-2.** [start again] recomeçar. ◇ *vi* **-1.** [open again] reabrir **-2.** [start again] recomeçar.
reorganization [ˈriːˌɔːgənaɪˈzeɪʃn] *n (U)* reorganização *f*.
reorganize, -ise [ˌriːˈɔːgənaɪz] ◇ *vt* reorganizar. ◇ *vi* reorganizar-se.
rep [rep] *n* **-1.** (*abbr of* **representative**) *inf* representante *mf* **-2.** (*abbr of* **repertory**) *apresentação de uma série de peças teatrais em seqüencia por uma mesma companhia teatral em um mesmo teatro.*
Rep. **-1.** (*abbr of* **Representative**) *US* deputado *m*, -da *f* **-2.** (*abbr of* **Republican**) republicano *m*, -na *f*.
repaid [riːˈpeɪd] *pt* & *pp* ▷ **repay**.
repaint [ˌriːˈpeɪnt] *vt* repintar.
repair [rɪˈpeəʳ] ◇ *n* **-1.** *(U)* [act of mending] reparo *m*, conserto *m*; **it's beyond ~** não tem conserto; **in good/bad ~** em bom/mau estado **-2.** [instance of mending] reparo *m*. ◇ *vt* reparar.
repair kit *n* caixa *f* de ferramentas *(de bicicleta)*.

repaper [ˌriːˈpeɪpəʳ] *vt*: **to ~ the wall** trocar o papel de parede.
reparations [ˌrepəˈreɪʃnz] *npl* indenizações *fpl*.
repartee [ˌrepɑːˈtiː] *n (U)* troca *f* de réplicas engenhosas.
repatriate [ˌriːˈpætrɪeɪt] *vt* repatriar.
repay [riːˈpeɪ] (*pt* & *pp* **repaid**) *vt* **-1.** [money] reembolsar, devolver; **to ~ sb sthg, to ~ sthg to sb** reembolsar *OR* devolver algo a alguém **-2.** [favour] retribuir; **to ~ sb for sthg** retribuir alguém por algo.
repayment [riːˈpeɪmənt] *n* **-1.** *(U)* [act of paying back] reembolso *m*, devolução *f* **-2.** [sum] pagamento *m*.
repeal [rɪˈpiːl] <> *n* revogação *f*. <> *vt* revogar.
repeat [rɪˈpiːt] <> *vt* **-1.** [gen] repetir; **to ~ o.s.** repetir-se **-2.** [broadcast] reprisar. <> *n* [broadcast] reprise *f*.
repeated [rɪˈpiːtɪd] *adj* repetido(da).
repeatedly [rɪˈpiːtɪdlɪ] *adv* repetidamente.
repel [rɪˈpel] (*pt* & *pp* **-led**, *cont* **-ling**) *vt* **-1.** [disgust] repugnar **-2.** [drive away] repelir.
repellent [rɪˈpelənt] <> *adj* repugnante. <> *n* repelente *m*.
repent [rɪˈpent] <> *vt* arrepender-se de. <> *vi*: **to ~ of sthg** arrepender-se de algo.
repentance [rɪˈpentəns] *n (U)* arrependimento *m*.
repentant [rɪˈpentənt] *adj* **-1.** [person] arrependido(da) **-2.** [smile] de arrependimento.
repercussions [ˌriːpəˈkʌʃnz] *npl* repercussões *fpl*.
repertoire [ˈrepətwɑːʳ] *n* repertório *m*.
repertory [ˈrepətrɪ] *n (U)* repertório *m*.
repertory company *n* companhia *f* teatral de repertório.
repetition [ˌrepɪˈtɪʃn] *n* repetição *f*.
repetitious [ˌrepɪˈtɪʃəs], **repetitive** [rɪˈpetɪtɪv] *adj* repetitivo(va).
rephrase [ˌriːˈfreɪz] *vt* **-1.** [question] reformular **-2.** [statement] dizer com outras palavras.
replace [rɪˈpleɪs] *vt* **-1.** [take the place of] substituir; **to ~ sthg (with sthg)** substituir *OR* trocar algo (por algo); **to ~ sb (with sb)** substituir alguém (por alguém); **if I lose your book, I'll ~ it** se eu perder o teu livro, eu te dou outro **-2.** [put back] recolocar no lugar.
replacement [rɪˈpleɪsmənt] *n* **-1.** *(U)* [act of replacing] reposição *f*, substituição *f* **-2.** [new person, object]: **~ (for sthg)** substituto *m*, -ta *f* (para algo); **~ (for sb)** suplente *mf* (para alguém).
replacement part *n* peça *f* de reposição.
replay [*n* ˈriːpleɪ, *vb* ˌriːˈpleɪ] <> *n* **-1.** [recording] replay *m* **-2.** [game] partida *f* de desempate. <> *vt* **-1.** [match, game] jogar de novo **-2.** [film, tape] reprisar.
replenish [rɪˈplenɪʃ] *vt fml*: **to ~ sthg (with sthg)** reabastecer *OR* prover novamente algo (com algo).
replete [rɪˈpliːt] *adj* **-1.** *fml* [object] cheio(a) **-2.** *fml* [person] satisfeito(ta), saciado(da).
replica [ˈreplɪkəl] *n* réplica *f*, cópia *f*.
replicate [ˈreplɪkeɪt] *vt fml* duplicar, reproduzir com exatidão.
replication [ˌreplɪˈkeɪʃn] *n fml* **-1.** *(U)* [process of copying] reprodução *f* exata **-2.** [copy] réplica *f*, cópia *f*.
reply [rɪˈplaɪ] (*pl* **-ies**, *pt* & *pp* **-ied**) <> *n* resposta *f*; **in ~ to sthg** em resposta a algo. <> *vt* responder; **to ~ that** responder que. <> *vi* responder; **to ~ to sb/sthg** responder a alguém/algo.
reply coupon *n* cupom *m* de resposta.
reply-paid *adj* pré-pago(ga), com porte pago.
report [rɪˈpɔːt] <> *n* **-1.** [description, account] relatório *m* **-2.** *PRESS* reportagem *f* **-3.** *UK SCH* boletim *m* de avaliação. <> *vt* **-1.** [news, crime] informar, comunicar **-2.** [make known]: **to ~ that** informar que; **to ~ sthg (to sb)** relatar algo (a alguém) **-3.** [complain about]: **to ~ sb (to sb)** denunciar alguém (a alguém); **to ~ sb for sthg** denunciar alguém por algo. <> *vi* **-1.** [give account] relatar; **to ~ on sthg** fazer um relatório sobre algo **-2.** *PRESS*: **to ~ on sthg** fazer uma reportagem sobre algo **-3.** [present o.s.]: **to ~ to** apresentar-se a; **to ~ for sthg** apresentar-se para algo.
◆ **report back** *vi*: **to ~ back (to sb)** dar retorno(para alguém).
reportage [ˌrepɔːˈtɑːʒ] *n* reportagem *f*.
report card *n US SCH* boletim *m*, caderneta *f* escolar.
reportedly [rɪˈpɔːtɪdlɪ] *adv* segundo se diz; **he is ~ not intending to return to this country** sabe-se que ele não pretende voltar a este país.
reported speech [rɪˈpɔːtɪd-] *n (U)* discurso *m* indireto.
reporter [rɪˈpɔːtəʳ] *n* repórter *mf*.
repose [rɪˈpəʊz] *n (U) literary* repouso *m*.
repository [rɪˈpɒzɪtrɪ] (*pl* **-ies**) *n* depósito *m*, armazém *m*.
repossess [ˌriːpəˈzes] *vt* retomar a posse de.
repossession [ˌriːpəˈzeʃn] *n (U)* reintegração *f* de posse.
repossession order *n* ordem *f* de despejo.
reprehensible [ˌreprɪˈhensəbl] *adj fml* repreensível.
represent [ˌreprɪˈzent] *vt* **-1.** [gen] representar **-2.** [describe]: **to ~ sb/sth gas** descrever *OR* representar alguém/algo como **-3.** *phr*: **to be well** *OR* **strongly ~ed** estar bem representado(da).
representation [ˌreprɪzenˈteɪʃn] *n (U)* representação *f*.
◆ **representations** *npl fml*: **to make ~s to sb** apresentar reclamações a alguém.
representative [ˌreprɪˈzentətɪv] <> *adj* representativo(va); **~ (of sb/sthg)** representativo(va) (de alguém/algo). <> *n* **-1.** [of company, organization, group] representante *mf* **-2.** *COMM*: **(sales) ~** representante *mf* (de vendas) **-3.** *US POL* deputado *m*, -da *f*.
repress [rɪˈpres] *vt* reprimir.
repressed [rɪˈprest] *adj* reprimido(da).
repression [rɪˈpreʃn] *n (U)* repressão *f*.
repressive [rɪˈpresɪv] *adj* repressivo(va).
reprieve [rɪˈpriːv] <> *n* **-1.** [of death sentence] indulto *m* **-2.** [respite] trégua *f*. <> *vt* indultar.
reprimand [ˈreprɪmɑːnd] <> *n* reprimenda *f*, repreensão *f*. <> *vt* repreender.

reprint [*n* 'ri:prɪnt, *vb* ˌri:'prɪnt] <> *n* reimpressão *f*. <> *vt* reimprimir.

reprisal [rɪ'praɪzl] *n* retaliação *f*, represália *f*.

reproach [rɪ'prəʊtʃ] <> *n* **-1.** *(U)* [disapproval] censura *f*, repreensão *f* **-2.** [words of blame] acusação *f*. <> *vt*: **to ~ sb (for** *OR* **with sthg)** censurar *OR* repreender alguém (por algo).

reproachful [rɪ'prəʊtʃfʊl] *adj* de reprovação.

reprobate ['reprəbeɪt] *n hum* réprobo *m*, -ba *f*.

reproduce [ˌri:prə'dju:s] <> *vt* reproduzir. <> *vi* reproduzir-se.

reproduction [ˌri:prə'dʌkʃn] *n* reprodução *f*.

reproductive [ˌri:prə'dʌktɪv] *adj BIOL* reprodutor (ra).

reprogram [ˌri:'prəʊgræm] (*pt* & *pp* **-ed** *OR* **-med**, *cont* **-ing** *OR* **-ming**) *vt* reprogramar.

reproof [rɪ'pru:f] *n* **-1.** [words of blame] censura *f* **-2.** *(U)* [disapproval] reprovação *f*.

reprove [rɪ'pru:f] *vt*: **to ~ sb (for sthg)** reprovar alguém (por algo).

reproving [rɪ'pru:vɪŋ] *adj* reprovador(ra), de reprovação.

reptile ['reptaɪl] *n* réptil *m*.

Repub. (*abbr of* **Republican**) *n* republicano *m*, -na *f*.

republic [rɪ'pʌblɪk] *n* república *f*.

republican [rɪ'pʌblɪkən] <> *adj* republicano(na). <> *n* republicano *m*, -na *f*.

◆ **Republican** <> *adj* **-1.** [in USA] republicano (na); **the Republican Party** o Partido Republicano **-2.** [in Northern Ireland] independentista. <> *n* **-1.** [in USA] republicano *m*, -na *f* **-2.** [in Northern Ireland] independentista *mf*.

repudiate [rɪ'pju:dɪeɪt] *vt fml* repudiar.

repudiation [rɪˌpju:dɪ'eɪʃn] *n (U) fml* repúdio *m*.

repugnant [rɪ'pʌgnənt] *adj fml* repugnante.

repulse [rɪ'pʌls] *vt* repelir.

repulsion [rɪ'pʌlʃn] *n (U)* **-1.** [disgust] repulsa *f* **-2.** *PHYSICS* repulsão *f*.

repulsive [rɪ'pʌlsɪv] *adj* repulsivo(va).

reputable ['repjʊtəbl] *adj* de boa reputação.

reputation [ˌrepjʊ'teɪʃn] *n* reputação *f*; **to have a ~ for sthg/for being sthg** ter fama de algo/de ser algo.

repute [rɪ'pju:t] *n (U) fml* **-1.** [reputation]: **of good/ill ~** de boa/má reputação **-2.** [distinction]: **of ~** de renome.

reputed [rɪ'pju:tɪd] *adj* de renome; **to be ~ to be/do sthg** ter fama de ser/fazer algo.

reputedly [rɪ'pju:tɪdlɪ] *adv* supostamente, segundo dizem.

reqd (*abbr of* **required**) requerido.

request [rɪ'kwest] <> *n*: **~ (for sthg)** solicitação *f* (de algo); **on ~** através de solicitação; **at sb's ~** por solicitação de alguém. <> *vt* solicitar, pedir; **to ~ sb to do sthg** solicitar a alguém que faça algo.

request stop *n UK* parada *f* de ônibus não-obrigatória.

requiem (mass) ['rekwɪəm-] *n* réquiem *m*.

require [rɪ'kwaɪə^r] *vt* **-1.** [need] requerer, necessitar de **-2.** [demand] exigir; **to ~ sb to do sthg** exigir que alguém faça algo; **employees are ~d to wear a uniform** exige-se que os funcionários usem uniformes.

required [rɪ'kwaɪəd] *adj* necessário(ria); **formal dress is ~d** exigem-se trajes formais.

requirement [rɪ'kwaɪəmənt] *n* **-1.** [need] necessidade *f* **-2.** [condition] requisito *m*, condição *f*.

requisite ['rekwɪzɪt] *adj fml* necessário(ria), requerido(da).

requisition [ˌrekwɪ'zɪʃn] *vt* requisitar.

reran [ˌri:'ræn] *pt* ▷ **rerun**.

reread [ˌri:'ri:d] (*pt* & *pp* **reread** [ˌri:'red]) *vt* reler.

rerecord [ˌri:rɪ'kɔ:d] *vt* regravar.

reroute [ˌri:'ru:t] *vt* redirecionar.

rerun [*n* 'ri:ˌrʌn, *vb* ri:'rʌn] (*pt* **reran**, *pp* **rerun**, *cont* **-ning**) <> *n* **-1.** [film, programme] reprise *f* **-2.** [similar situation] repetição *f*. <> *vt* **-1.** [race, competition] voltar a participar de **-2.** [film, programme] reprisar **-3.** [tape] pôr novamente.

resale price maintenance ['ri:seɪl-] *n (U) UK FIN* manutenção *f* do preço de revenda.

resat [ˌri:'sæt] *pt* & *pp* ▷ **resit**.

reschedule [*UK* ˌri:'ʃedjʊl, *US* ˌri:'skedʒʊl] *vt FIN* renegociar.

rescind [rɪ'sɪnd] *vt* [*JUR* - contract] rescindir; [- law] revogar.

rescue ['reskju:] <> *n* **-1.** [help] auxílio *f*; **to go/come to sb's ~** ir/vir em auxílio de alguém **-2.** [successful attempt] resgate *m*, salvamento *m*. <> *vt* resgatar, salvar; **to ~ sb from sb/sthg** resgatar *OR* salvar alguém de alguém/algo; **to ~ sthg from sb/sthg** salvar algo de alguém/algo.

rescue operation *n* operação *f* de resgate.

rescuer ['reskjʊə^r] *n* resgatador *m*, -ra *f*.

reseal [ˌri:'si:l] *vt* fechar novamente.

resealable [ˌri:'si:ləbl] *adj que se pode fechar novamente*.

research [ˌrɪ'sɜ:tʃ] <> *n (U)*: **~ (on** *OR* **into sthg)** pesquisa *f* (sobre algo); **~ and development** pesquisa e desenvolvimento. <> *vt* pesquisar, fazer uma pesquisa sobre. <> *vi*: **to ~ (into sthg)** fazer uma pesquisa (sobre algo).

researcher [rɪ'sɜ:tʃə^r] *n* pesquisador *m*, -ra *f*.

research work *n (U)* trabalho *m* de pesquisa.

resell [ˌri:'sel] (*pt* & *pp* **resold**) *vt* revender.

resemblance [rɪ'zembləns] *n* semelhança *f*; **~ to sb/sthg** semelhança com alguém/algo; **~ between** semelhança entre.

resemble [rɪ'zembl] *vt* assemelhar-se a, parecer-se com.

resent [rɪ'zent] *vt* ofender-se com, ressentir-se de.

resentful [rɪ'zentfʊl] *adj* ressentido(da).

resentfully [rɪ'zentfʊlɪ] *adv* com ressentimento.

resentment [rɪ'zentmənt] *n (U)* ressentimento *m*.

reservation [ˌrezə'veɪʃn] *n* **-1.** [gen] reserva *f*; **without ~** sem reserva **-2.** *US* [for Native Americans] reserva *f* (indígena).

◆ **reservations** *npl* [doubts] reservas *fpl*, dúvidas *fpl*.

reserve [rɪ'zɜ:v] <> *n* reserva *f*; **in ~** de reserva. <> *vt* **-1.** [keep for particular purpose]: **to ~ sthg for sb/sthg** reservar algo para alguém/algo **-2.** [retain]: **to ~ the right to do sthg** reservar-se o direito de fazer algo.

reserve bank *n US* banco *m* de reserva federal.
reserve currency *n* moeda *f* de reserva.
reserved [rɪ'zɜ:vd] *adj* reservado(da).
reserve price *n UK* preço *m* mínimo (de venda).
reserve team *n UK* time *m* reserva.
reservist [rɪ'zɜ:vɪst] *n* reservista *mf*.
reservoir ['rezəvwɑ:ʳ] *n* **-1.** [lake] reservatório *m* natural **-2.** [large supply] reservatório *m*.
reset [,ri:'set] (*pt* & *pp* **reset**, *cont* **-ting**) ◇ *vt* **-1.** [clock, meter, controls] reajustar **-2.** [bone] recolocar no lugar **-3.** *COMPUT* reinicializar. ◇ *vi COMPUT* reinicializar.
resettle [,ri:'setl] ◇ *vt* **-1.** [land] ocupar **-2.** [people] reassentar. ◇ *vi* [people] reassentar-se.
resettlement [,ri:'setlmənt] *n (U)* **-1.** [of land] ocupação *f* **-2.** [of people] reassentamento *m*.
reshape [,ri:'ʃeɪp] *vt* reformar, remodelar.
reshuffle [,ri:'ʃʌfl] ◇ *n POL* reorganização *f*, reforma *f*; **cabinet ~** reforma *f* do gabinete. ◇ *vt ADMIN* & *POL* reformar.
reside [rɪ'zaɪd] *vi fml* residir; **happiness does not ~ in wealth** a felicidade não reside na riqueza.
residence ['rezɪdəns] *n* **-1.** [house] residência *f* **-2.** *(U)* [fact of residing]: **to apply for ~** solicitar visto de residência; **to take up ~** *fml* estabelecer residência (em), instalar-se **-3.** *(U)* [residing at a particular time]: **to be in ~** *fml* estar presente **-4.** *(U) UNIV*: **writer in ~** escritor(ra) residente *(que atua temporariamente numa universidade)*.
residence permit *n* visto *m* de residência.
resident ['rezɪdənt] ◇ *adj* residente; **she's been ~ in france for two years** faz dois anos que ela está morando na França. ◇ *n* residente *mf*.
residential [,rezɪ'denʃl] *adj* em regime de internato.
residential area *n* zona *f* residencial.
residents' association *n* associação *f* de moradores.
residual [rɪ'zɪdjʊəl] *adj* residual.
residue ['rezɪdju:] *n CHEM* resíduo *m*.
resign [rɪ'zaɪn] ◇ *vt* **-1.** [give up - job] demitir-se de; [- post] renunciar a **-2.** [accept calmly]: **to ~ o.s. to sthg** resignar-se a algo. ◇ *vi* pedir demissão, demitir-se; **to ~ (from sthg)** pedir demissão *OR* demitir-se (de algo).
resignation [,rezɪg'neɪʃn] *n* **-1.** [from job] demissão *f* **-2.** [from post] renúncia *f* **-3.** *(U)* [calm acceptance] resignação *f*.
resigned [rɪ'zaɪnd] *adj*: **~ (to sthg)** resignado(da) (a algo).
resilience [rɪ'zɪlɪəns] *n (U)* capacidade *f* de recuperação.
resilient [rɪ'zɪlɪənt] *adj* **-1.** [rubber, metal] elástico(ca) **-2.** [person] que se recupera rapidamente, resistente.
resin ['rezɪn] *n (U)* resina *f*.
resist [rɪ'zɪst] *vt* **-1.** [gen] resistir a **-2.** [oppose] opor-se a.
resistance [rɪ'zɪstəns] *n (U)* **-1.** [to enemy, attack, infection] resistência *f*; **~ to sthg** resistência a algo **-2.** [to change, proposal, attempt] oposição *f*.
resistant [rɪ'zɪstənt] *adj* **-1.** *MED* [immune]: **~ (to sthg)** resistente (a algo) **-2.** [opposed]: **~ to sthg** que se opõe a algo.
resistor [rɪ'zɪstəʳ] *n ELEC* resistor *m*.
resit [*n* 'ri:sɪt, *vb* ,ri:'sɪt] (*pt* & *pp* **resat**, *cont* **-ting**) *UK* ◇ *n* exame *m* de recuperação. ◇ *vt* fazer de novo *(um exame)*.
resold [,ri:'səʊld] *pt* & *pp* ⊳ **resell**.
resolute ['rezəlu:t] *adj* resoluto(ta), determinado (da).
resolutely ['rezəlu:tlɪ] *adv* resolutamente, com determinação.
resolution [,rezə'lu:ʃn] *n* **-1.** [gen] resolução *f* **-2.** [vow, promise] promessa *f*.
resolve [rɪ'zɒlv] ◇ *n (U)* resolução *f*. ◇ *vt* [solve] resolver; [vow, promise]: **to ~ that** prometer que; **to ~ to do sthg** resolver fazer algo.
resonance ['rezənəns] *n (U)* ressonância *f*.
resonant ['rezənənt] *adj* ressonante.
resonate ['rezəneɪt] *vi* ressoar.
resort [rɪ'zɔ:t] *n* **-1.** [for holidays] estância *f* de férias **-2.** [solution]: **as a last ~** como último recurso; **in the last ~** em última instância.
◆ **resort to** *vt fus* apelar para.
resound [rɪ'zaʊnd] *vi* **-1.** [noise] ressoar, retumbar **-2.** [place]: **the room ~ed with laughter** as risadas ressoavam em toda a sala.
resounding [rɪ'zaʊndɪŋ] *adj* **-1.** [gen] retumbante **-2.** [extremely loud] estrondoso(sa) **-3.** [unequivocal] clamoroso(sa).
resource [rɪ'sɔ:s] *n* recurso *m*.
resourceful [rɪ'sɔ:sfʊl] *adj* versátil, habilidoso(sa).
resourcefulness [rɪ'sɔ:sfʊlnɪs] *n (U)* versatilidade *f*.
respect [rɪ'spekt] ◇ *n (U)* respeito *m*; **~ (for sb/sthg)** respeito *m OR* admiração *f* (por alguém/algo); **with ~, ...** com todo o respeito, ...; **in this ~** a este respeito; **in that ~** quanto a isso. ◇ *vt* respeitar; **to ~ sb for sthg** respeitar alguém por algo.
◆ **respects** *npl* saudações *fpl*, cumprimentos *mpl*; **to pay one's last ~s to sb** prestar uma última homenagem a alguém.
◆ **with respect to** *prep* com respeito a.
respectability [rɪ,spektə'bɪlətɪ] *n (U)* respeitabilidade *f*.
respectable [rɪ'spektəbl] *adj* respeitável.
respectably [rɪ'spektəblɪ] *adv* de forma respeitável.
respected *adj* respeitado(da).
respectful [rɪ'spektfʊl] *adj* respeitoso(sa).
respectfully [rɪ'spektfʊlɪ] *adv* respeitosamente.
respective [rɪ'spektɪv] *adj* respectivo(va).
respectively [rɪ'spektɪvlɪ] *adv* respectivamente.
respiration [,respə'reɪʃn] *n (U)* respiração *f*.
respirator ['respəreɪtəʳ] *n* **-1.** [gas mask] máscara *f* antigás **-2.** [machine] respirador *m*.
respiratory [*UK* rɪ'spɪrətrɪ, *US* 'respərətɔ:rɪ] *adj* respiratório(ria).
respire [rɪ'spaɪəʳ] *vi* respirar.
respite ['respaɪt] *n* **-1.** [pause] descanso *m* **-2.** [delay] adiamento *m*, novo prazo *m*.
resplendent [rɪ'splendənt] *adj literary* resplandescente.

respond [rɪ'spɒnd] <> *vt* responder. <> *vi*: **to ~ (to sthg)** responder (a algo); **to ~ by doing sthg** responder fazendo algo.

response [rɪ'spɒns] *n* resposta *f*; **in ~** em resposta.

responsibility [rɪˌspɒnsə'bɪlətɪ] (*pl* **-ies**) *n*: **~ (for sthg)** responsabilidade *f* (por algo); **~ (to sb)** responsabilidade *f* (diante de alguém).

responsible [rɪ'spɒnsəbl] *adj* **-1.** [gen]: **~ (for sthg)** responsável (por algo) **-2.** [answerable]: **~ to sb** que presta contas a alguém **-3.** [requiring sense] de responsabilidade.

responsibly [rɪ'spɒnsəblɪ] *adv* de forma responsável.

responsive [rɪ'spɒnsɪv] *adj* que responde muito bem; **~ (to sthg)** sensível *OR* atencioso(sa) (a algo).

respray [*n* 'ri:spreɪ, *vb* ˌri:'spreɪ] <> *n* nova pintura *f*. <> *vt* repintar.

rest [rest] <> *n* **-1.** [remainder]: **the ~** o resto; **the ~ of** o resto de **-2.** *(U)* [relaxation] descanso *m* **-3.** [break] pausa *f*, descanso *m* **-4.** [support] apoio *m* **-5.** *phr*: **to lay** *OR* **put sthg to ~** sepultar algo; **to come to ~** deter-se. <> *vt* **-1.** [relax] descansar **-2.** [support, lean]: **to ~ sthg on/against sthg** apoiar *OR* descansar algo em algo **-3.** *phr*: **~ assured (that)** fique descansado(da) que. <> *vi* **-1.** [relax, be still] descansar **-2.** [depend]: **to ~ (up)on sb/sthg** depender de alguém/algo **-3.** [duty, responsibility]: **to ~ with sb** pesar sobre alguém **-4.** [be supported]: **to ~ on/against sthg** apoiar-se em/contra algo.

rest area *n US* & *Austr* área *f* de descanso *(numa estrada)*.

restart [*n* 'ri:stɑ:t, *vb* ˌri:'stɑ:t] <> *n COMPUT* reinício *m*. <> *vt* **-1.** [vehicle, engine] ligar novamente **-2.** [work] recomeçar **-3.** *COMPUT* reiniciar. <> *vi* **-1.** [play, film] recomeçar **-2.** [vehicle] dar partida, pegar **-3.** [engine] ligar novamente.

restate [ˌri:'steɪt] *vt* reformular, expor novamente.

restaurant ['restərɒnt] *n* restaurante *m*.

restaurant car *n UK* vagão-restaurante *m*.

rest cure *n* cura *f* pelo descanso forçado.

rested ['restɪd] *adj* descansado(da).

restful ['restfʊl] *adj* tranqüilo(la), sossegado(da).

rest home *n* **-1.** [for the elderly] lar *m* de idosos **-2.** [for the sick] casa *f* de repouso.

resting place ['restɪŋ-] *n* última morada *f*.

restitution [ˌrestɪ'tju:ʃn] *n (U) fml* restituição *f*.

restive ['restɪv] *adj* inquieto(ta).

restless ['restlɪs] *adj* **-1.** [bored, dissatisfied] impaciente **-2.** [fidgety] inquieto(ta), agitado(da) **-3.** [sleepless]: **a ~ night** uma noite em claro.

restlessly ['restlɪslɪ] *adv* **-1.** [impatiently] impacientemente **-2.** [sleeplessly] sem conseguir dormir.

restock [ˌri:'stɒk] <> *vt* reabastecer. <> *vi* reabastecer-se.

restoration [ˌrestə'reɪʃn] *n (U)* restauração *f*.

restorative [rɪ'stɒrətɪv] *adj fml* revigorante.

restore [rɪ'stɔ:ʳ] *vt* **-1.** [reestablish, bring back] restabelecer; **the king was ~ed to power** o rei foi reconduzido ao poder; **I feel completely ~ed to health** sinto-me totalmente recuperado(da); **to ~ sthg to sb/sthg** devolver algo a alguém/algo **-2.** [renovate] restaurar **-3.** [give back] restituir.

restorer [rɪ'stɔ:rəʳ] *n* **-1.** [person] restaurador *m*, -ra *f* **-2.** *(U)* [substance] tônico *m*.

restrain [rɪ'streɪn] *vt* **-1.** [gen] reprimir; **to ~ o.s. from doing sthg** conter-se para não fazer algo **-2.** [overpower, bring under control] controlar.

restrained [rɪ'streɪnd] *adj* comedido(da).

restraint [rɪ'streɪnt] *n* **-1.** [rule, check] restrição *f*, limitação *f* **-2.** *(U)* [control] controle *m*.

restrict [rɪ'strɪkt] *vt* restringir, limitar; **to ~ sb to sthg** restringir alguém a algo; **to ~ sthg to sb/sthg** restringir algo a alguém/algo; **to ~ o.s. to sthg** limitar-se a algo.

restricted [rɪ'strɪktɪd] *adj* **-1.** [not public] restrito(ta) **-2.** [limited] limitado(da).

restriction [rɪ'strɪkʃn] *n* **-1.** [limitation, regulation] restrição *f*; **to place ~s on sthg** impor restrições a algo **-2.** *(U)* [impediment, hindrance] limitação *f*.

restrictive [rɪ'strɪktɪv] *adj* restritivo(va).

restrictive practices *npl* práticas *fpl* restritivas.

rest room *n US* banheiro *m*.

restructure [ˌri:'strʌktʃəʳ] *vt* reestruturar.

result [rɪ'zʌlt] <> *n* resultado *m*; **as a ~** como resultado, por conseguinte; **as a ~ of sthg** como resultado de algo. <> *vi*: **to ~ in sthg** ter algo como resultado; **to ~ from sthg** ser resultado de algo.

resultant [rɪ'zʌltənt] *adj fml* resultante.

resume [rɪ'zju:m] <> *vt* **-1.** [activity] recomeçar **-2.** *fml* [place, position] retomar. <> *vi* recomeçar, continuar.

résumé ['rezju:meɪ] *n* **-1.** [summary] resumo *m* **-2.** *US* [of career, qualifications] currículo *m*.

resumption [rɪ'zʌmpʃn] *n (U)* retomada *f*.

resurface [ˌri:'sɜ:fɪs] <> *vt* repavimentar. <> *vi* vir à tona.

resurgence [rɪ'sɜ:dʒəns] *n (U)* ressurgimento *m*.

resurrect [ˌrezə'rekt] *vt* ressuscitar.

resurrection [ˌrezə'rekʃn] *n (U)* ressurreição *f*.
◆ **Resurrection** *n RELIG*: **the Resurrection** a Ressurreição.

resuscitate [rɪ'sʌsɪteɪt] *vt* **-1.** [bring back to life] ressuscitar **-2.** [prevent from dying] reanimar.

resuscitation [rɪˌsʌsɪ'teɪʃn] *n (U)* ressuscitação *f*, reanimação *f*.

retail ['ri:teɪl] <> *n (U)* varejo *m*. <> *adv* no varejo. <> *vi*: **to ~ at** ser vendido(da) no varejo.

retailer ['ri:teɪləʳ] *n* varejista *mf*.

retail outlet *n* ponto *m* de venda.

retail price *n* preço *m* no varejo.

retail price index *n UK* índice *m* de preço ao consumidor.

retain [rɪ'teɪn] *vt* reter.

retainer [rɪ'teɪnəʳ] *n* **-1.** [fee] adiantamento *m* **-2.** [servant] criado *m*, -da *f (com muitos anos de serviço numa casa)*.

retaining wall [rɪ'teɪnɪŋ-] *n* muro *m* de arrimo.

retaliate [rɪ'tælɪeɪt] *vi* retaliar.

retaliation [rɪˌtælɪ'eɪʃn] *n* retaliação *f*.

retarded [rɪ'tɑ:dɪd] *adj* mentalmente retardado(da).

retch [retʃ] *vi* fazer força para vomitar.

retd (*abbr of* **retired**) aposentado(da).
retention [rɪ'tenʃn] *n* **-1.** [of pride, power, independence] manutenção *f* **-2.** [of heat, water] retenção *f*.
retentive [rɪ'tentɪv] *adj* retentivo(va).
rethink [*n* 'ri:θɪŋk, *vb* ˌri:'θɪŋk] (*pt* & *pp* **-thought** [-'θɔ:t]) <> *n*: **to have a ~ about sthg** ter que repensar algo; **to have a ~** dar uma repensada. <> *vt* repensar, reconsiderar. <> *vi* repensar, reconsiderar.
reticence ['retɪsəns] *n (U)* reticência *f*.
reticent ['retɪsənt] *adj* reticente.
retina ['retɪnə] (*pl* **-nas** OR **-nae** [-ni:]) *n* retina *f*.
retinue ['retɪnju:] *n* séquito *m*.
retire [rɪ'taɪə^r] *vi* **-1.** [from work] aposentar-se **-2.** *fml* [to another place] retirar-se **-3.** *fml* [to bed] recolher-se.
retired [rɪ'taɪəd] *adj* aposentado(da).
retirement [rɪ'taɪəmənt] *n* aposentadoria *f*.
retirement age *n* idade *f* de aposentadoria OR de se aposentar.
retirement pension *n* aposentadoria *f*.
retiring [rɪ'taɪərɪŋ] *adj* **-1.** [shy] retraído(da), tímido(da) **-2.** [from work] *que está a ponto de se aposentar*.
retort [rɪ'tɔ:t] <> *n* réplica *f*. <> *vt*: **to ~ (that)** retrucar (que).
retouch [ˌri:'tʌtʃ] *vt* retocar.
retrace [rɪ'treɪs] *vt*: **to ~ one's steps** refazer o mesmo caminho.
retract [rɪ'trækt] <> *vt* **-1.** [take back] retratar **-2.** [draw in] recolher. <> *vi* **-1.** [recant] retratar-se **-2.** [be drawn in] recolher-se.
retractable [rɪ'træktəbl] *adj* retrátil.
retraction [rɪ'trækʃn] *n (U)* retratação *f*.
retrain [ˌri:'treɪn] <> *vt* reabilitar. <> *vi* reabilitar-se, reciclar-se.
retraining [ˌri:'treɪnɪŋ] *n (U)* reciclagem *f*.
retread ['ri:tred] *n* pneu *m* recauchutado.
retreat [rɪ'tri:t] <> *n* **-1.** MIL [withdrawal]: **~ (from)** retirada *f* (de) **-2.** *fig* [from principle, policy, lifestyle]: **to beat a (hasty) ~** bater em retirada **-3.** [refuge] refúgio *m*. <> *vi*: **to ~ (to/from)** retirar-se (para/de).
retrenchment [ri:'trentʃmənt] *n fml* redução *f* OR corte *m* de gastos.
retrial [ˌri:'traɪəl] *n* novo julgamento *m*.
retribution [ˌretrɪ'bju:ʃn] *n (U)* castigo *m* merecido.
retrieval [rɪ'tri:vl] *n (U)* COMPUT recuperação *f*.
retrieve [rɪ'tri:v] *vt* **-1.** [get back] reaver **-2.** COMPUT recuperar **-3.** [rescue, rectify] reparar, remediar.
retriever [rɪ'tri:və^r] *n* [dog] perdigueiro *m*; [of specific breed] labrador *m*.
retroactive [ˌretrəʊ'æktɪv] *adj fml* retroativo(va).
retrograde ['retrəgreɪd] *adj fml* retrógrado(da);a **~ step** um passo para trás.
retrogressive [ˌretrə'gresɪv] *adj fml* & *pej* retrógrado(da).
retrospect ['retrəspekt] *n (U)*: **in ~** em retrospecto.
retrospective [ˌretrə'spektɪv] <> *adj* **-1.** [mood, look] retrospectivo(va) **-2.** [law, pay rise] retroativo (va). <> *n* retrospectiva *f*.
retrospectively [ˌretrə'spektɪvlɪ] *adv* **-1.** [describe, feel] retrospectivamente **-2.** [come into force, pay] de forma retroativa.
return [rɪ'tɜ:n] <> *n* **-1.** *(U)* [arrival back] volta *f*, regresso *m*; **~ (to)** regresso *m* (para); **~ to sthg** *fig* volta a algo **-2.** [giving back] devolução *f* **-3.** TENNIS rebatida *f* **-4.** *UK* [ticket] passagem *f* de ida e volta **-5.** [profit] retorno *m* **-6.** COMPUT [on keyboard] tecla *f* Return. <> *comp* [journey] de volta. <> *vt* **-1.** [gen] devolver **-2.** [reciprocate, give in exchange] retribuir **-3.** JUR dar **-4.** POL eleger. <> *vi*: **to ~ (from/to)** voltar (de/a).
◆ **returns** *npl* **-1.** COMM retorno *m*, rendimentos *mpl* **-2.** [on birthday]: **many happy ~s (of the day)!** que a data se repita por muitos e muitos anos!
◆ **in return** *adv* em troca.
◆ **in return for** *prep* em troca de.
returnable [rɪ'tɜ:nəbl] *adj* retornável.
returning officer [rɪ'tɜ:nɪŋ-] *n UK oficial existente em cada distrito eleitoral da Grã-Bretanha que organiza a eleição para o Parlamento e anuncia o resultado oficial*.
return key *n* COMPUT tecla *f* Return.
return match *n* partida *f* de volta.
return ticket *n UK* passagem *f* de ida e volta.
reunification [ˌri:ju:nɪfɪ'keɪʃn] *n (U)* reunificação *f*.
reunion [ˌri:'ju:njən] *n* reunião *f*.
Reunion [ˌri:'ju:njən] *n*: **~ (Island)** Ilha Réunion; **in ~** na Ilha Réunion.
reunite [ˌri:ju:'naɪt] *vt* reunir; **to be ~d with sb/sthg** estar reunido com alguém/algo.
reupholster [ˌri:ʌp'həʊlstə^r] *vt* estofar novamente.
reusable [ri:'ju:zəbl] *adj* reutilizável, reciclável.
reuse [*n* ˌri:'ju:s, *vb* ˌri:'ju:z] <> *n (U)* reutilização *f*. <> *vt* reutilizar.
rev [rev] (*pt* & *pp* **-ved**, *cont* **-ving**) *inf* <> *n* (*abbr of* **revolution**) rotação *f*. <> *vt*: **to ~ sthg (up)** acelerar algo. <> *vi*: **to ~ (up)** acelerar o motor.
Rev. (*abbr of* **Reverend**) Revdo.
revalue [ˌri:'vælju:] *vt* **-1.** [reassess] reavaliar **-2.** FIN [increase value of] valorizar.
revamp [ˌri:'væmp] *vt inf* **-1.** [reorganize] reformar **-2.** [redecorate] redecorar.
rev counter *n* tacómetro *m*.
reveal [rɪ'vi:l] *vt* revelar.
revealing [rɪ'vi:lɪŋ] *adj* **-1.** [clothes]: **a ~ dress** um vestido que mostra tudo **-2.** [comment] revelador(-ra), esclarecedor(ra).
reveille [*UK* rɪ'vælɪ, *US* 'revəlɪ] *n* toque *m* de alvorada.
revel ['revl] (*UK pt* & *pp* **-led**, *cont* **-ling**, *US pt* & *pp* **-ed**, *cont* **-ing**) *vi*: **to ~ in sthg** desfrutar de algo, deleitar-se com algo.
revelation [ˌrevə'leɪʃn] *n* **-1.** [surprising fact] revelação *f* **-2.** [surprising experience] surpresa *f*.
reveller *UK*, **reveler** *US* ['revələ^r] *n* farrista *mf*.
revelry ['revəlrɪ] *n (U)* farra *f*.
revenge [rɪ'vendʒ] <> *n (U)* vingança *f*; **to take ~ (on sb)** vingar-se (de alguém). <> *comp* por vingança. <> *vt* vingar; **to ~ o.s. on sb/sthg** vingar-se de alguém/algo.

revenue ['revənju:] *n* **-1.** [income] receita *f* **-2.** [from investment] rendimento *f* **-3.** *UK FIN*: **the Inland Revenue** a Receita Federal.
reverberate [rɪ'vɜ:bəreɪt] *vi* **-1.** [re-echo] ressoar, retumbar **-2.** [have repercussions] repercutir.
reverberations [rɪˌvɜ:bə'reɪʃnz] *npl* **-1.** [echoes] reverberação *f* **-2.** [repercussions] repercussões *fpl*.
revere [rɪ'vɪə^r] *vt fml* reverenciar, venerar.
reverence ['revərəns] *n (U) fml* reverência *f*.
Reverend ['revərənd] *n* reverendo *m*.
Reverend Mother *n* madre *f* superiora.
reverent ['revərənt] *adj* reverente.
reverential [ˌrevə'renʃl] *adj fml* reverencial.
reverie ['revərɪ] *n fml* devaneio *m*.
reversal [rɪ'vɜ:sl] *n* **-1.** [of trend, policy, decision] reviravolta *f* **-2.** [of roles, order, position] inversão *f* **-3.** [piece of ill luck] contratempo *m*.
reverse [rɪ'vɜ:s] ◇ *adj* reverso(sa), inverso(sa). ◇ *n* **-1.** *AUT*: **~ (gear)** marcha *f* a ré; **to be in ~** estar com a marcha a ré engatada; **to go into ~** dar ré **-2.** [opposite]: **the ~** o contrário **-3.** [back, other side - of paper] verso *m*; [- of coin] outro lado *m*. ◇ *vt* **-1.** *AUT* dar marcha a ré em **-2.** [trend, policy, decision] reverter **-3.** [roles, order, position] inverter **-4.** [turn over] virar **-5.** *UK TELEC*: **to ~ the charges** fazer uma ligação a cobrar. ◇ *vi AUT* dar marcha a ré.
reverse-charge call *n UK* chamada *f* a cobrar.
reversible [rɪ'vɜ:səbl] *adj* reversível.
reversing light [rɪ'vɜ:sɪŋ-] *n UK* luz *f* de ré.
reversion [rɪ'vɜ:ʃn] *n (U)* reversão *f*, volta *f*; **~ to sthg** reversão *OR* volta a algo.
revert [rɪ'vɜ:t] *vi*: **to ~ to sthg** voltar a algo.
review [rɪ'vju:] ◇ *n* **-1.** [examination] revisão *f*, reavaliação *f*; **to come up for ~** ser revisado(da), ser reavaliado(da); **the situation is under ~** a situação está sendo avaliada **-2.** [critique] crítica *f*, resenha *f*. ◇ *vt* **-1.** [reassess] reavaliar **-2.** [write an article on] fazer resenha *OR* crítica de **-3.** [troops] passar em revista **-4.** *US* [study] revisar.
reviewer [rɪ'vju:ə^r] *n* crítico *m*, -ca *f*.
revile [rɪ'vaɪl] *vt literary* insultar, injuriar.
revise [rɪ'vaɪz] ◇ *vt* **-1.** [reconsider] revisar **-2.** [rewrite] corrigir, alterar **-3.** *UK* [study] revisar. ◇ *vi UK*: **to ~ (for sthg)** fazer revisão (para algo).
revised [rɪ'vaɪzd] *adj* revisado(da).
revision [rɪ'vɪʒn] *n* **-1.** [alteration] alteração *f*, correção *f* **-2.** *(U)* [study] revisão *f*.
revisionist [rɪ'vɪʒnɪst] ◇ *adj* revisionista. ◇ *n* revisionista *mf*.
revisit [ˌri:'vɪzɪt] *vt* revisitar.
revitalize, -ise [ˌri:'vaɪtəlaɪz] *vt* revitalizar.
revival [rɪ'vaɪvl] *n* **-1.** *COMM* reativação *f* **-2.** [of interest, cultural activity] renovação *f* **-3.** [of play] revival *m*.
revive [rɪ'vaɪv] ◇ *vt* **-1.** [resuscitate] ressuscitar **-2.** [revitalize - plant, economy] revitalizar; [- interest, hopes] despertar **-3.** [bring back into use, being - tradition] restabelecer; [- musical, play] reviver; [- memories] trazer à baila. ◇ *vi* **-1.** [regain consciousness] voltar a si, recobrar os sentidos **-2.** [be revitalized - plant, economy] revitalizar-se; [- interest, hopes] renovar-se.
revoke [rɪ'vəʊk] *vt fml* revogar.
revolt [rɪ'vəʊlt] ◇ *n* revolta *f*, rebelião *f*. ◇ *vt* revoltar. ◇ *vi*: **to ~ (against sb/sthg)** revoltar-se *OR* rebeliar-se (contra alguém/algo).
revolting [rɪ'vəʊltɪŋ] *adj* revoltante, repugnante.
revolution [ˌrevə'lu:ʃn] *n* revolução *f*; **~ in sthg** revolução em algo.
revolutionary [revə'lu:ʃnərɪ] (*pl* **-ies**) ◇ *adj* revolucionário(ria). ◇ *n POL* revolucionário *m*, -ria *f*.
revolutionize, -ise [ˌrevə'lu:ʃənaɪz] *vt* revolucionar.
revolve [rɪ'vɒlv] *vi* girar, dar voltas; **to ~ (a)round sthg** girar em torno de algo; **to ~ (a)round sb** girar em torno de alguém.
revolver [rɪ'vɒlvə^r] *n* revólver *m*.
revolving [rɪ'vɒlvɪŋ] *adj* giratório(ria).
revolving door *n* porta *f* giratória.
revue [rɪ'vju:] *n* teatro *m* de revista.
revulsion [rɪ'vʌlʃn] *n (U)* repugnância *f*, asco *m*.
reward [rɪ'wɔ:d] ◇ *n* **-1.** [recompense] recompensa *f* **-2.** [sum of money] recompensa *f*, gratificação *f*. ◇ *vt* recompensar; **to ~ sb for/with sthg** recompensar alguém por/com algo.
rewarding [rɪ'wɔ:dɪŋ] *adj* gratificante.
rewind [ˌri:'waɪnd] (*pt* & *pp* **rewound**) *vt* rebobinar.
rewire [ˌri:'waɪə^r] *vt* trocar a fiação elétrica de.
reword [ˌri:'wɜ:d] *vt* expressar com outras palavras.
rework [ˌri:'wɜ:k] *vt* reelaborar.
rewound [ˌri:'waʊnd] *pt* & *pp* ▷ **rewind**.
rewrite [ˌri:'raɪt] (*pt* **rewrote** [ˌri:'rəʊt], *pp* **rewritten** [ˌri:'rɪtn]) *vt* reescrever.
REX (*abbr of* **real-time executive routine**) *n* [comput] *programa em tempo real*.
Reykjavik ['rekjəvɪk] *n* Reykjavik.
RFC (*abbr of* **Rugby Football Club**) *n clube de rugby britânico*.
RGN (*abbr of* **registered general nurse**) *n titular de diploma em enfermagem na Grã-Bretanha*.
r.h. (*abbr of* **right hand**) mão *f* direita.
Rh (*abbr of* **rhesus**) Rh.
rhapsody ['ræpsədɪ] (*pl* **-ies**) *n* **-1.** *MUS* rapsódia *f* **-2.** [strong approval] entusiasmo *m*.
Rheims *n* Rheims.
Rhesus ['ri:səs] *n*: **~ positive/negative** Rh *m* positivo/negativo.
rhetoric ['retərɪk] *n (U)* retórica *f*.
rhetorical question [rɪ'tɒrɪkl-] *n* pergunta *f* retórica.
rheumatic [ru:'mætɪk] *adj* reumático(ca).
rheumatism ['ru:mətɪzm] *n (U)* reumatismo *m*.
rheumatoid arthritis ['ru:mətɔɪd-] *n (U)* artrite *f* reumatóide.
Rhine [raɪn] *n*: **the ~** o Reno.
Rhineland ['raɪnlænd] *n* Renânia.
rhinestone ['raɪnstəʊn] *n* diamante *m* falso.
rhino ['raɪnəʊ] (*pl inv OR* **-s**) *n inf* rino *m*.
rhinoceros [raɪ'nɒsərəs] (*pl inv OR* **-es**) *n* rinoceronte *m*.
Rhode Island [rəʊd-] *n* Rhode Island.
Rhodes [rəʊdz] *n* Rodes.
Rhodesia [rəʊ'di:ʃə] *n* Rodésia.

Rhodesian [rəʊ'di:ʃn] ◇ *adj* rodesiano(na). ◇ *n* rodesiano *m*, -na *f*.
rhododendron [ˌrəʊdə'dendrən] *n* rododendro *m*.
Rhone *n*: **the (River)** ~ o Rio Ródano.
rhubarb ['ru:bɑ:b] *n (U)* ruibarbo *m*.
rhyme [raɪm] ◇ *n* **-1.** [word] rima *f*; **in** ~ em verso **-2.** [poem] poesia *f*, versos *mpl*. ◇ *vi* rimar; **to** ~ **with sthg** rimar com algo.
rhyming slang ['raɪmɪŋ-] *n (U)* **UK** *tipo de gíria do leste londrino que consiste em contrapor duas palavras que dão significado a uma terceira, rimando a segunda com essa terceira.*
rhythm ['rɪðm] *n* ritmo *m*.
rhythm and blues *n (U)* rhythm *m* and blues.
rhythmic(al) ['rɪðmɪk(l)] *adj* ritmado(da).
RI ◇ *n* (*abbr of* **religious instruction**) educação *f* religiosa. ◇ *abbr of* **Rhode Island**.
rib [rɪb] *n* **-1.** ANAT costela *f* **-2.** [of metal or wood] vareta *f*.
RIBA (*abbr of* **Royal Institute of British Architects**) *n instituto real dos arquitetos britânicos.*
ribald ['rɪbəld] *adj* grosseiro(ra).
ribbed [rɪbd] *adj* canelado(da).
ribbon ['rɪbən] *n* fita *f*.
rib cage *n* caixa *f* toráxica.
rice [raɪs] *n (U)* arroz *m*.
rice field *n* arrozal *m*.
rice paper *n (U)* papel *m* de palha de arroz.
rice pudding *n* arroz-doce *m*, arroz-de-leite *m*.
rich [rɪtʃ] ◇ *adj* **-1.** [gen] rico(ca); **to be** ~ **in sthg** ser rico(ca) em algo **-2.** [indigestible] pesado(da) **-3.** [vibrant] vibrante **-4.** [sumptuous, expensive] suntuoso(sa). ◇ *npl*: **the** ~ os ricos.
◆ **riches** *npl* **-1.** [natural resources] riquezas *fpl* **-2.** [wealth] riqueza *f*.
richly ['rɪtʃlɪ] *adv* [gen] ricamente; ~ **deserved** bem merecido(da).
richness ['rɪtʃnɪs] *n (U)* **-1.** [gen] riqueza *f* **-2.** [of food] peso *m*.
Richter scale ['rɪktə^r-] *n*: **the** ~ a escala Richter.
rickets ['rɪkɪts] *n (U)* raquitismo *m*.
rickety ['rɪkətɪ] *adj* instável, sem solidez.
rickshaw ['rɪkʃɔ:] *n* jinriquixá *m*.
ricochet ['rɪkəʃeɪ] (*pt* & *pp* **-ed** OR **-ted**, *cont* **-ing** OR **-ting**) ◇ *n* ricochete *m*. ◇ *vi* ricochetear; **to** ~ **off sthg** ricochetear em algo.
rid [rɪd] (*pt* **rid** OR **-ded**, *pp* **rid**, *cont* **-ding**) ◇ *adj*: **to be** ~ **of sb/sthg** estar livre de alguém/algo. ◇ *vt*: **to** ~ **sb/sthg of sthg** livrar alguém/algo de algo; **to** ~ **o.s. of sthg** livrar-se de algo; **to get** ~ **of sb/sthg** livrar-se de alguém/algo.
riddance ['rɪdəns] *n inf*: **good** ~**!** já vai tarde!, que bons ventos o levem!
ridden ['rɪdn] *pp* ▷ **ride**.
riddle ['rɪdl] *n* **-1.** [verbal puzzle] adivinhação *f* **-2.** [mystery] enigma *m*.
riddled ['rɪdld] *adj* **-1.** [holes, errors] cheio (cheia) **-2.** [bullet holes] crivado(da) **-3.** [woodworm] infestado(da).
ride [raɪd] (*pt* **rode**, *pp* **ridden**) ◇ *n* **-1.** [gen] passeio *m*; **to go for a** OR **horse/bike** ~ dar um passeio a cavalo/de bicicleta; **to go for a car** ~ dar uma volta OR um passeio de carro **-2.** *phr*: **to take sb for a** ~ *inf* [trick] levar alguém no bico. ◇ *vt* **-1.** [horse] montar em **-2.** [bicycle, motorbike] andar de **-3.** [distance] percorrer **-4.** **US** [travel in] ir de. ◇ *vi* **-1.** [on horseback] montar **-2.** [on bicycle] andar de bicicleta **-3.** [on motorbike] andar de moto **-4.** [in car, bus]: **to** ~ **in sthg** andar de algo.
◆ **ride up** *vi* subir.
rider ['raɪdə^r] *n* **-1.** [on horseback - male] jinete *m*; [- female] amazona *f* **-2.** [on bicycle] ciclista *mf* **-3.** [on motorbike] motoqueiro *m*, -ra *f*.
ridge [rɪdʒ] *n* **-1.** [on mountain] crista *f* **-2.** [on flat surface - in sand, of muscles] saliência *f*; [- in fabric] ruga *f*.
ridicule ['rɪdɪkju:l] ◇ *n (U)* zombaria *f*. ◇ *vt* ridicularizar.
ridiculous [rɪ'dɪkjʊləs] *adj* ridículo(la).
ridiculously [rɪ'dɪkjʊləslɪ] *adv* ridiculamente.
riding ['raɪdɪŋ] ◇ *n (U)* equitação *f*. ◇ *comp* de equitação.
riding crop *n* chicote *m*, rebenque *m*.
riding habit *n* traje *m* de montar.
riding school *n* escola *f* de equitação.
rife [raɪf] *adj* muito comum; **to be** ~ **with sthg** estar cheio(cheia) de algo.
riffraff ['rɪfræf] *n (U)* gentalha *f*, ralé *f*.
rifle ['raɪfl] ◇ *n* rifle *m*. ◇ *vt* roubar.
◆ **rifle through** *vt fus* vasculhar.
rifle range *n* estande *m* de tiro ao alvo.
rift [rɪft] *n* **-1.** GEOL fenda *f* **-2.** [quarrel] desavença *f*; ~ **between/in** desavença entre/em.
Rift Valley *n*: **the** ~ o Rift Valley.
rig [rɪg] (*pt* & *pp* **-ged**, *cont* **-ging**) ◇ *n* [structure - onshore] torre *f* de perfuração; [- offshore] plataforma *f* petrolífera. ◇ *vt* manipular.
◆ **rig up** *vt sep* armar, construir.
rigging ['rɪgɪŋ] *n* **-1.** [of ship] *(U)* cordame *m* **-2.** [of votes] fraude *f* em uma votação.
right [raɪt] ◇ *adj* **-1.** [gen] certo(ta), correto(ta); **to be** ~ **about sthg** estar certo(ta) sobre algo, ter razão sobre algo; **to get sthg** ~ acertar algo; **to be** ~ **to do sthg** estar certo(ta) ao fazer algo **-2.** [going well] bem **-3.** [socially desirable, appropriate] apropriado(da) **-4.** [not left] direito(ta) **-5.** **UK** *inf* [complete] perfeito(ta). ◇ *adv* **-1.** [correctly] corretamente, bem **-2.** [not left] para a direita **-3.** [emphatic use]: ~ **here** aqui mesmo; ~ **down** bem para baixo; ~ **in the middle** bem no meio **-4.** [immediately]: **I'll be** ~ **back** eu já volto; ~ **after Christmas** logo depois do Natal; ~ **now** [immediately] agora; [at this very moment] já; ~ **away** em seguida. ◇ *n* **-1.** *(U)* [moral correctness] certo *m*; **to be in the** ~ ter razão **-2.** [entitlement, claim] direito *m*; **by** ~**s** por direito; **in one's own** ~ por seus próprios méritos **-3.** [right-hand side] direita *f*; **on the** ~ à direita. ◇ *vt* **-1.** [correct] corrigir **-2.** [make upright] endireitar. ◇ *excl* certo!
◆ **Right** *n* POL: **the Right** a direita.
right angle *n* ângulo *m* reto; **at** ~**s to sthg** em ângulo reto com algo.
righteous ['raɪtʃəs] *adj* **-1.** [anger, indignation] justo(-ta) **-2.** [person] honrado(da).
righteousness ['raɪtʃəsnɪs] *n (U)* honradez *f*, retidão *f*.
rightful ['raɪtfʊl] *adj* legítimo(ma).

rightfully ['raɪtfʊlɪ] *adv* legitimamente.
right-hand *adj* direito(ta); ~ **side** o lado direito.
right-hand drive *adj* com direção do lado direito.
right-handed [-'hændɪd] *adj* destro(tra).
right-hand man *n* braço *m* direito.
rightly ['raɪtlɪ] *adv* **-1.** [gen] corretamente **-2.** [justifiably] com razão.
right-minded [-'maɪndɪd] *adj* honrado(da).
rightness *n (U)* **-1.** [soundness] correção *f* **-2.** [appropriateness] conveniência *f.*
righto ['raɪtəʊ] *excl inf* certo!
right of way *n* **-1.** AUT preferência *f* **-2.** [access] direito *m* de passagem.
rights issue *n* emissão *f* de bônus de subscrição.
right-thinking *adj* correto(ta), sensato(ta).
right wing *n*: **the** ~ a direita.
◆ **right-wing** *adj* de direita.
right-winger *n* direitista *mf.*
rigid ['rɪdʒɪd] *adj* **-1.** [gen] rígido(da) **-2.** [inflexible] inflexível.
rigidity [rɪ'dʒɪdətɪ] *n (U)* rigidez *f.*
rigidly ['rɪdʒɪdlɪ] *adv* **-1.** [fixedly] firmemente **-2.** [harshly, strictly] rigidamente.
rigmarole ['rɪgmərəʊl] *n inf pej* **-1.** [process] ritual *m* **-2.** [story] ladainha *f.*
rigor *n US* = **rigour.**
rigor mortis [-'mɔːtɪs] *n (U)* rigidez *f* cadavérica.
rigorous ['rɪgərəs] *adj* rigoroso(sa).
rigorously ['rɪgərəslɪ] *adv* rigorosamente.
rigour *UK*, **rigor** *US* ['rɪgəʳ] *n (U)* rigor *m.*
◆ **rigours** *npl* rigores *mpl.*
rig-out *n UK inf* traje *m*, beca *f.*
rile [raɪl] *vt* irritar.
rim [rɪm] *n* **-1.** [top edge of container] borda *f* **-2.** [outer edge of round object - of spectacles, glass] moldura *f*; [- of wheel] aro *m.*
rind [raɪnd] *n* casca *f.*
ring [rɪŋ] (*pt* **rang**, *pp vt senses 1 & 2 & vi* **rung**, *pt & pp vt senses 3 & 4 only* **ringed**) ◇ *n* **-1.** [telephone call]: **to give sb a** ~ dar uma ligada para alguém **-2.** [sound of bell] toque *m* **-3.** [quality, tone] tom *m*; **it has a familiar** ~ soa familiar **-4.** [circular object - for curtains, napkin] argola *f*; **napkin** ~ argola *f* para guardanapo; [- hoop] aro *m* **-5.** [piece of jewellery] anel *m* **-6.** [of people, trees] círculo *m* **-7.** [for boxing] ringue *m* **-8.** [people working together] cartel *m* **-9.** *phr*: **to run** ~**s round sb** *fig* superar alguém facilmente. ◇ *vt* **-1.** *UK* [phone] telefonar para, ligar para **-2.** [bell, doorbell] tocar **-3.** [draw a circle round] fazer um círculo ao redor de **-4.** [surround] cercar, rodear; **to be** ~**ed with sthg** estar cercado(da) de algo. ◇ *vi* **-1.** *UK* [phone] telefonar, ligar **-2.** [bell, doorbell] tocar **-3.** [to attract attention]: **to** ~ **(for sb/sthg)** chamar (por alguém/algo) **-4.** [resound]: **to** ~ **with sthg** ressoar com algo **-5.** *phr*: **to** ~ **true** soar verdadeiro(ra).
◆ **ring back** *UK* ◇ *vt sep* voltar a ligar para. ◇ *vi* voltar a ligar.
◆ **ring off** *vi UK* desligar.
◆ **ring out** *vi* **-1.** [sound] soar claramente **-2.** *UK* TELEC ligar.
◆ **ring up** *vt sep UK* ligar.
ring binder *n* fichário *m* com aros de metal.
ringer ['rɪŋəʳ] *n*: **to be a dead** ~ **for sb** ser o retrato vivo de alguém.
ring finger *n* (dedo *m*) anular *m.*
ringing ['rɪŋɪŋ] ◇ *adj* [clear, loud] alto e claro, alta e clara. ◇ *n* **-1.** *(U)* [of bell] toque *m* **-2.** *(U)* [in ears] zumbido *m.*
ringing tone *n UK* TELEC tom *m* de discagem.
ringleader ['rɪŋ,liːdəʳ] *n* cabeça *m.*
ringlet ['rɪŋlɪt] *n* anel *m* de cabelo.
ringmaster ['rɪŋ,mɑːstəʳ] *n* diretor *m*, -ra *f* de circo.
ring road *n UK* anel *m* rodoviário.
ringside ['rɪŋsaɪd] ◇ *n*: **the** ~ o ringue. ◇ *comp* de primeira fila.
ring tone *n* [for mobile phone] toque *m* musical.
ringway ['rɪŋweɪ] *n UK* anel *m* rodoviário.
ringworm ['rɪŋwɜːm] *n (U)* tinha *f.*
rink [rɪŋk] *n* rinque *m.*
rinse [rɪns] ◇ *n* enxágüe *m.* ◇ *vt* enxagüar; **to** ~ **one's mouth out** enxagüar a boca.
Rio (de Janeiro) [,riːəʊ(dədʒə'nɪərəʊ)] *n* Rio de Janeiro.
Rio Grande [,riːəʊ'grændɪ] *n*: **the** ~ o Rio Grande.
Rio Negro *n*: **the** ~ o Rio Negro.
riot ['raɪət] ◇ *n* desordem *f*; **to run** ~ descontrolar-se. ◇ *vi* amotinar-se.
rioter ['raɪətəʳ] *n* desordeiro *m*, -ra *f.*
rioting ['raɪətɪŋ] *n (U)* desordem *f.*
riotous ['raɪətəs] *adj* **-1.** [party] barulhento(ta) **-2.** [behaviour, mob] desordeiro(ra).
riot police *npl* tropa *f* de choque.
riot shield *n* escudo *m* antimotim.
rip [rɪp] (*pt & pp* **-ped**, *cont* **-ping**) ◇ *n* rasgão *m.* ◇ *vt* **-1.** [tear, shred] rasgar **-2.** [remove] arrancar. ◇ *vi* rasgar.
◆ **rip off** *vt sep inf* **-1.** [cheat] trapacear, passar a perna em **-2.** [steal] roubar.
◆ **rip up** *vt sep* rasgar, fazer em pedaços.
RIP (*abbr of* **rest in peace**) descanse em paz.
ripcord ['rɪpkɔːd] *n* corda *f* de abertura.
ripe [raɪp] *adj* maduro(ra); **to be** ~ **(for sthg)** *fig* estar pronto(ta) (para algo).
ripen ['raɪpn] *vt & vi* amadurecer.
ripeness ['raɪpnɪs] *n (U)* maturação *f.*
rip-off *n inf* **-1.** [swindle] assalto *m* **-2.** [imitation] imitação *f* barata.
ripple ['rɪpl] ◇ *n* **-1.** [in water] ondulação *f* **-2.** [of laughter, applause] onda *f.* ◇ *vt* ondular.
rip-roaring *adj inf* estrondoso(sa).
rise [raɪz] (*pt* **rose**, *pp* **risen** ['rɪzn]) ◇ *n* **-1.** *UK* [increase in amount] aumento *m*, subida *f* **-2.** *UK* [increase in salary] aumento *m* **-3.** [to power, fame] ascensão *f* **-4.** [slope] ladeira *f* **-5.** *phr*: **to give** ~ **to sthg** originar algo. ◇ *vi* **-1.** [gen] elevar-se **-2.** [sun, moon] nascer, sair **-3.** *UK* [increase] aumentar, subir **-4.** [stand up] levantar-se **-5.** *literary* [get out of bed] levantar-se **-6.** [to a challenge]: **to** ~ **to sthg** mostrar-se à altura de algo; **to** ~ **to the occasion** elevar-se à altura (de algo) **-7.** [rebel] sublevar-se **-8.** [in status] ascender; **to** ~ **to sthg** ascender a algo **-9.** [bread, soufflé] crescer.

◆ **rise above** *vt fus* superar, mostrar-se superior a.

• **riser** ['raɪzəʳ] *n*: **an early** ~ um madrugador; **a late** ~ pessoa *f* que se levanta tarde.

risible ['rɪzəbl] *adj fml* risível.

rising ['raɪzɪŋ] ◇ *adj* **-1.** [gen] em ascensão **-2.** [sloping upwards] em aclive **-3.** [tide] que sobe. ◇ *n* [rebellion] levante *m*, rebelião *f*.

rising damp *n (U)* umidade *f* proveniente do solo.

risk [rɪsk] ◇ *n* risco *m*; **to run the** ~ **of sthg/of doing sthg** correr o risco de algo/de fazer algo; **to take a** ~ arriscar-se; **it's at your own** ~ é por sua conta e risco; **at** ~ em perigo; **at the** ~ **of** sob risco de. ◇ *vt* **-1.** [put in danger] arriscar **-2.** [take the chance of]: **to** ~ **doing sthg** arriscar-se a fazer algo; **go on,** ~ **it!** vamos, arrisque-se!

risk capital *n (U)* capital *m* de risco.

risk-taking *n (U)* aceitação *f* de riscos.

risky ['rɪskɪ] (*compar* **-ier**, *superl* **-iest**) *adj* arriscado (da).

risotto [rɪ'zɒtəʊ] (*pl* **-s**) *n* risoto *m*.

risqué ['ri:skeɪ] *adj* picante.

rissole ['rɪsəʊl] *n UK* bolinho *m* de carne, rissole *m*.

rite [raɪt] *n* rito *m*.

ritual ['rɪtʃʊəl] ◇ *adj* ritual. ◇ *n* ritual *m*.

rival ['raɪvl] (*UK pt* & *pp* **-led**, *cont* **-ling**, *US pt* & *pp* **-ed**, *cont* **-ing**) ◇ *adj* **-1.** [gen] rival **-2.** [company] concorrente. ◇ *n* **-1.** [gen] rival *mf* **-2.** [company] concorrente *mf*. ◇ *vt* rivalizar OR competir com.

rivalry ['raɪvlrɪ] *n* rivalidade *f*.

river ['rɪvəʳ] *n* rio *m*.

river bank *n* margem *f* do rio.

riverbed ['rɪvəbed] *n* leito *m* do rio.

riverside ['rɪvəsaɪd] *n*: **the** ~ a margem do rio.

rivet ['rɪvɪt] ◇ *n* rebite *m*. ◇ *vt* **-1.** [fasten with rivets] rebitar **-2.** *fig* [fascinate]: **to be** ~**ed by sthg** estar fascinado(da) por algo.

riveting ['rɪvɪtɪŋ] *adj* fascinante.

Riviera [,rɪvɪ'eərə] *n*: **the French** ~ a Riviera Francesa; **the Italian** ~ a Riviera Italiana.

Riyadh ['ri:æd] *n* Riyadh.

RM (*abbr of* **Royal Marines**) *n fuzileiros navais britânicos*.

RN *n* **-1.** (*abbr of* **Royal Navy**) marinha *f* real britânica **-2.** (*abbr of* **registered nurse**) *titular de diploma de enfermagem na Grã-Bretanha*.

RNA (*abbr of* **ribonucleic acid**) *n* RNA *m*.

RNLI (*abbr of* **Royal National Lifeboat Institution**) *n organização de voluntários na Grã-Bretanha e na Irlanda que oferece resgate marítimo*.

RNZAF (*abbr of* **Royal New Zealand Air Force**) *n força aérea real neozelandesa*.

RNZN (*abbr of* **Royal New Zealand Navy**) *n marinha real neozelandesa*.

roach [rəʊtʃ] (*pl sense 1 inv* OR **-es**, *pl senses 2* & *3* **-es**) *n* **-1.** [fish] *peixe semelhante à carpa* **-2.** *drugs sl* bagana *f* de baseado **-3.** *US* [cockroach] barata *f*.

road [rəʊd] *n* **-1.** [major] estrada *f*; **by** ~ por estrada; **on the** ~ [travelling] na estrada; **on the** ~ **to** *fig* a caminho de **-2.** [minor] caminho *m* **-3.** [street] rua *f*.

road atlas *n* guia *f* rodoviário.

roadblock ['rəʊdblɒk] *n* barreira *f* policial.

road-fund licence *n UK* ≃ imposto *m* sobre veículos automotores, ≃ IPVA *m*.

road haulage *n* transportes *mpl* rodoviários.

road hog *n inf pej* dono *m*, -na *f* da estrada.

roadholding ['rəʊd,həʊldɪŋ] *n (U)* estabilidade *f (na estrada)*.

roadie ['rəʊdɪ] *n inf* roadie *mf*.

road map *n* mapa *m* rodoviário.

road rage *n* raiva *f* no trânsito.

road roller *n* rolo *m* compressor.

road safety *n (U)* segurança *f* no trânsito.

road sense *n (U)* senso *m* de direção.

roadshow ['rəʊdʃəʊ] *n programa de rádio transmitido diretamente por um disc-jóquei itinerante*.

roadside ['rəʊdsaɪd] ◇ *n*: **the** ~ a beira da estrada. ◇ *comp* de beira da estrada.

road sign *n* placa *f* de trânsito.

roadsweeper ['rəʊd,swi:pəʳ] *n* [vehicle] caminhão *m* de limpeza das ruas.

road tax *n* ≃ imposto *m* sobre veículos automotores, ≃ IPVA *m*.

road test *n* teste *m* de direção.

◆ **road-test** *vt* fazer um teste de direção com.

road transport *n (U)* transporte *m* rodoviário.

roadway ['rəʊdweɪ] *n* pista *f* (da estrada).

road works *npl* obras *fpl* na pista.

roadworthy ['rəʊd,wɜ:ðɪ] *adj* em condições de tráfego.

roam [rəʊm] ◇ *vt* vagar por. ◇ *vi* vagar.

roar [rɔ:ʳ] ◇ *vi* **-1.** [lion] rugir **-2.** [traffic, plane, engine] roncar **-3.** [person] urrar; **to** ~ **with laughter** rir às gargalhadas **-4.** [wind] bramir. ◇ *vt* bradar. ◇ *n* **-1.** [of lion] rugido *m* **-2.** [of engine] ronco *m* **-3.** [of traffic] barulho *m* **-4.** [of wind] sopro *m* **-5.** [of person] urro *m*.

roaring ['rɔ:rɪŋ] ◇ *adj* **-1.** [traffic, wind] barulhento(ta) **-2.** [fire] crepitante **-3.** [for emphasis] estrondoso(sa); **a** ~ **success** um sucesso estrondoso; **to do a** ~ **trade** vender bem. ◇ *adv* [for emphasis] completamente.

roast [rəʊst] ◇ *adj* assado(da). ◇ *n* assado *m*. ◇ *vt* **-1.** [meat, potatoes] assar **-2.** [coffee beans, nuts] torrar.

roast beef *n (U)* rosbife *m*.

roasting ['rəʊstɪŋ] *inf* ◇ *adj* muito quente; **I'm** ~**!** estou derretendo de calor! ◇ *adv*: **it's a** ~ **hot day!** hoje está um inferno de quente!

roasting tin *n* assadeira *f*.

rob [rɒb] (*pt* & *pp* **-bed**, *cont* **-bing**) *vt* roubar; **to** ~ **sb of sthg** [of money, goods] roubar algo de alguém; *fig* [of opportunity, glory] privar alguém de algo.

robber ['rɒbəʳ] *n* ladrão *m*, -dra *f*.

robbery ['rɒbərɪ] (*pl* **-ies**) *n* roubo *m*.

robe [rəʊb] *n* **-1.** [of priest] túnica *f* **-2.** [judge] toga *f* **-3.** [monarch] manto *m* **-4.** *US* [dressing gown] robe *m*.

robin ['rɒbɪn] *n* pintarroxo *m*.

robot ['rəʊbɒt] *n* robô *m*.

robotics [rəʊ'bɒtɪks] *n (U)* robótica *f*.

robust [rəʊ'bʌst] *adj* [person] **-1.** robusto(ta) **-2.** [economy] forte **-3.** [health] de ferro **-4.** [criticism, defence] vigoroso(sa).

robustly [rəʊˈbʌstlɪ] *adv* vigorosamente.
rock [rɒk] <> *n* **-1.** *(U)* [substance] rocha *f* **-2.** [boulder] rochedo *m*, penhasco *m* **-3.** *US* [pebble] pedregulho *m* **-4.** *(U)* [music] rock *m* **-5.** *(U) UK* [sweet] barra *f* de caramelo. <> *comp* [music] de rock. <> *vt* **-1.** [cause to move] balançar **-2.** [shock] abalar. <> *vi* balançar-se.
◆ **on the rocks** *adv* **-1.** [drink] com gelo, on the rocks **-2.** [marriage, relationship] que vai mal.
rock and roll *n (U)* rock and roll *m*.
rock bottom *n (U)* nível *m* baixíssimo; **to hit ~** atingir o fundo do poço.
◆ **rock-bottom** *adj* baixíssimo(ma).
rock cake *n UK bolo com frutas secas.*
rock climber *n* alpinista *mf*.
rock-climbing *n (U)* alpinismo *m*.
rocker [ˈrɒkəʳ] *n* [chair] embaladeira *f*; **to be off one's ~** *inf* ter um parafuso a menos.
rockery [ˈrɒkərɪ] (*pl* **-ies**) *n* jardim *m* de pedras.
rocket [ˈrɒkɪt] <> *n* foguete *m*. <> *vi* disparar.
rocket launcher [-ˌlɔːntʃəʳ] *n* lança-foguetes *m inv*.
rock face *n* parede *f* de pedra.
rockfall [ˈrɒkfɔːl] *n* deslizamento *m* de pedras.
rock-hard *adj* duro(ra) como pedra.
Rockies [ˈrɒkɪz] *npl*: **the ~** as Montanhas Rochosas.
rocking chair [ˈrɒkɪŋ-] *n* cadeira *f* de balanço.
rocking horse [ˈrɒkɪŋ-] *n* cavalinho *m* de balanço.
rock music *n (U)* rock *m*.
rock 'n' roll *n* = **rock and roll**.
rock pool *n piscina formada por pedras na praia.*
rock salt *n (U)* sal-gema *m*.
rock singer *n* cantor *m*, -ra *f* de rock, roqueiro *m*, -ra *f*.
rocky [ˈrɒkɪ] (*compar* **-ier**, *superl* **-iest**) *adj* **-1.** [full of rocks] rochoso(sa) **-2.** [unsteady] instável.
Rocky Mountains *npl*: **the ~** as Montanhas Rochosas.
rococo [rəˈkəʊkəʊ] *adj* rococó.
rod [rɒd] *n* **-1.** [wooden] vara *f* **-2.** [metal] barra *f*.
rode [rəʊd] *pt* ▷ **ride**.
rodent [ˈrəʊdənt] *n* roedor *m*.
rodeo [ˈrəʊdɪəʊ] (*pl* **-s**) *n* rodeio *m*.
roe [rəʊ] *n* ova *f (de peixe)*.
roe deer *n* corço *m*, -ça *f*.
rogue [rəʊg] <> *adj* **-1.** [animal] solitário e perigoso, solitária e perigosa **-2.** *fig* [person] rebelde. <> *n* **-1.** [likable rascal] malandro *m*, -dra *f* **-2.** *dated* [dishonest person] vigarista *mf*.
roguish [ˈrəʊgɪʃ] *adj* malandro(dra).
role [rəʊl] *n* **-1.** [position, function] função *f*, papel *m* **-2.** CINEMA, THEATRE papel *m*.
roll [rəʊl] <> *n* **-1.** [of material, paper, film] rolo *m* **-2.** [of banknotes] maço *m* **-3.** [of cloth] peça *f* **-4.** [of bread] pãozinho *m* **-5.** [list] lista *f* **-6.** [sound - of drum] rufar *m*; [- of thunder] estrondo *m*. <> *vt* **-1.** [turn over] rolar; **to ~ one's eyes** [in fear, despair] revirar os olhos **-2.** [make into cylinder] enrolar; **~ed into one** *fig* tudo num só. <> *vi* **-1.** [of a round object] rolar **-2.** [move] andar **-3.** [sway from side to side] balançar **-4.** [sound - drum] rufar; [- thunder] retumbar.
◆ **roll about, roll around** *vi* rolar.
◆ **roll back** *vt sep US* [prices] reduzir.
◆ **roll in** *vi inf* **-1.** [money] chegar de balde **-2.** [person] pintar.
◆ **roll over** *vi* virar-se.
◆ **roll up** <> *vt sep* **-1.** [make into cylinder] enrolar **-2.** [sleeves] arregaçar. <> *vi* **-1.** [vehicle] chegar **-2.** *inf* [person] pintar.
roll bar *n* santantônio *m*.
roll call *n* toque *m* de chamada.
rolled gold [rəʊld-] *n (U)* plaquê *m*.
roller [ˈrəʊləʳ] *n* **-1.** [cylinder] cilindro *m* **-2.** [curler] rolo *m*.
Rollerblades® [ˈrəʊləˌbleɪdz] *npl* patins *mpl* em linha.
rollerblading [ˈrəʊləˌbleɪdɪŋ] *n* patinação *f (com patins em linha)*; **to go ~** praticar patinação *(com patins em linha)*.
roller blind *n* persiana *f* de enrolar.
roller coaster *n* montanha-russa *f*.
roller skate *n* patim *m* de rodas.
◆ **roller-skate** *vi* patinar.
roller towel *n* toalha *f* de rolo.
rollicking [ˈrɒlɪkɪŋ] *adj* divertido(da).
rolling [ˈrəʊlɪŋ] *adj* **-1.** [undulating] ondulado(da) **-2.** [swaying from side to side] bamboleante **-3.** *phr*: **to be ~ in it** *inf* estar nadando em dinheiro.
rolling mill *n* laminador *m*.
rolling pin *n* rolo *m* de massa.
rolling stock *n (U)* material *m* rodante.
roll-neck *adj* com gola rulê.
roll of honour *n* lista *f* de honra.
roll-on <> *adj* de rolo, roll-on. <> *n* desodorante *m* de rolo OR roll-on.
roll-on roll-off *adj UK*: **a ~ ferry** uma balsa para veículos.
roly-poly (*pl* **-ies**) *n UK*: **~ (pudding)** rocambole *m*.
ROM [rɒm] (*abbr of* **read-only memory**) *n* ROM *f*.
romaine lettuce [rəʊˈmeɪn-] *n US* alface *f (de folha larga)*.
Roman [ˈrəʊmən] <> *adj* romano(na). <> *n* romano *m*, -na *f*.
Roman candle *n* pistolão *m*.
Roman Catholic <> *adj* católico (romano), católica (romana). <> *n* católico *m* (romano), católica *f* (romana).
romance [rəʊˈmæns] *n* **-1.** [gen] romance *m* **-2.** *(U)* [romantic quality] romantismo *m*.
Romanesque [ˌrəʊməˈnesk] *adj* românico(ca).
Romani *adj* & *n* = **Romany**.
Romania [rəˈmeɪnjəl *n* Romênia; **in ~** na Romênia.
Romanian [rəˈmeɪnjən] <> *adj* romeno(na). <> *n* **-1.** [person] romeno *m*, -na *f* **-2.** [language] romeno *m*.
Roman numerals *npl* algarismos *mpl* romanos.
romantic [rəʊˈmæntɪk] *adj* romântico(ca).
romanticism [rəʊˈmæntɪsɪzm] *n* romantismo *m*.
romanticize, -ise [rəʊˈmæntɪsaɪz] <> *vt* romantizar. <> *vi* romantizar, fantasiar.
Romany [ˈrəʊmənɪ] (*pl* **-ies**) <> *adj* cigano(na).

◇ *n* **-1.** [person] cigano *m*, -na *f* **-2.** [language] romani *m*.
Rome [rəʊm] *n* Roma.
romp [rɒmp] ◇ *n* travessura *f*. ◇ *vi* brincar ruidosamente.
rompers ['rɒmpəz] *npl*, **romper suit** ['rɒmpəʳ-] *n* macacão *m* de criança.
roof [ru:f] *n* **-1.** [covering - of vehicle] capota *f*; [- of building] telhado *m*; **not under my ~!** não na minha casa!; **under the same ~** sob o mesmo teto; **to have a ~ over one's head** ter onde morar; **to go through** *OR* **hit the ~** subir pelas paredes **-2.** [upper part - of cave] teto *m*; [- of mouth] céu *m* da boca.
roof garden *n* jardim *m* de cobertura.
roofing ['ru:fɪŋ] *n (U)* material *m* para cobertura.
roof rack *n* bagageiro *m (na capota do carro)*.
rooftop ['ru:ftɒp] *n* telhado *m*.
rook [rʊk] *n* **-1.** [bird] gralha *f* **-2.** [chess piece] torre *f*.
rookie ['rʊkɪ] *n US inf* novato *m*, -ta *f*.
room [ru:m, rʊm] *n* **-1.** [in building] sala *f* **-2.** [bedroom] quarto *m* **-3.** *(U)* [space] espaço *m*; **to make ~ for sb/sthg** abrir espaço para alguém/algo **-4.** *(U)* [opportunity, possibility] possibilidade *f*; **~ to** *OR* **for manoeuvre** espaço para manobrar.
rooming house ['ru:mɪŋ-] *n US* pensão *f*.
roommate ['ru:mmeɪt] *n* companheiro *m*, -ra *f* de quarto.
room service *n* serviço *m* de quarto.
room temperature *n* temperatura *f* ambiente.
roomy ['ru:mɪ] (*compar* **-ier**, *superl* **-iest**) *adj* espaçoso(sa), amplo(pla).
roost [ru:st] ◇ *n* poleiro *m*; **to rule the ~** cantar de galo. ◇ *vi* empoleirar-se.
rooster ['ru:stəʳ] *n* galo *m*.
root [ru:t] ◇ *adj* básico(ca), fundamental. ◇ *n* [gen] raiz *f*; **to put down ~s** [person] criar raízes; **to take ~** [plant] pegar; [idea] consolidar-se. ◇ *vi* remexer.
◆ **roots** *npl* raízes *fpl*.
◆ **root for** *vt fus esp US inf* torcer por.
◆ **root out** *vt sep* arrancar até a raiz, extirpar.
root beer *n US cerveja sem álcool feita de raízes*.
root crop *n* tubérculos *mpl*.
rooted ['ru:tɪd] *adj*: **to be ~ to the spot** ficar paralisado(da) (de medo).
rootless ['ru:tlɪs] *adj* sem raízes, desarraigado(-da).
root vegetable *n* tubérculo *m*.
rope [rəʊp] ◇ *n* corda *f*; **to know the ~s** estar por dentro do assunto. ◇ *vt* amarrar com corda.
◆ **rope in** *vt sep inf* arrastar para.
◆ **rope off** *vt sep* isolar com cordas.
rop(e)y ['rəʊpɪ] (*compar* **-ier**, *superl* **-iest**) *adj UK inf* **-1.** [poor-quality] ruim **-2.** [unwell] indisposto(ta), mal.
rosary ['rəʊzərɪ] (*pl* **-ies**) *n* rosário *m*.
rose [rəʊz] ◇ *pt* ▻ **rise**. ◇ *adj* [pink] rosa, cor-de-rosa. ◇ *n* [flower] rosa *f*; **it's not a bed of ~s** não é feito de rosas.
rosé ['rəʊzeɪ] *n (U)* vinho *m* rosé.
rosebed ['rəʊzbed] *n* canteiro *m* de rosas.
rosebud ['rəʊzbʌd] *n* botão *m* de rosa.
rose bush *n* roseira *f*.
rose-coloured *adj* cor-de-rosa.
rose hip *n* rosa-mosqueta *f*.
rosemary ['rəʊzmərɪ] *n (U)* alecrim *m*.
rose-tinted *adj*: **to look through ~ glasses** ver tudo cor-de-rosa.
rosette [rəʊ'zet] *n* roseta *f*.
rosewater ['rəʊz,wɔ:təʳ] *n (U)* água-de-rosas *f*.
rosewood ['rəʊzwʊd] *n (U)* pau-rosa *m*.
RoSPA (*abbr of* **Royal Society for the Prevention of Accidents**) *n organização britânica para prevenção de acidentes*.
roster ['rɒstəʳ] *n* lista *f*.
rostrum ['rɒstrəm] (*pl* **-trums** *OR* **-tra** [-trə]) *n* tribuna *f*, rostro *m*.
rosy ['rəʊzɪ] (*compar* **-ier**, *superl* **-iest**) *adj* **-1.** [pink] rosado(da) **-2.** [hopeful] promissor(ra).
rot [rɒt] (*pt* & *pp* **-ted**, *cont* **-ting**) ◇ *n* **-1.** [decay - of wood, food] putrefação *f*; [- in society, organization] decadência *f* **-2.** *UK dated* [nonsense] besteira *f*, bobagem *f*. ◇ *vt* [cause to decay] corroer, decompor. ◇ *vi* apodrecer.
rota ['rəʊtə] *n* lista *f* de turnos.
rotary ['rəʊtərɪ] ◇ *adj* rotatório(ria). ◇ *n US* [roundabout] rotatória *f*.
Rotary Club *n*: **the ~** o Rotary Club.
rotate [rəʊ'teɪt] ◇ *vt* **-1.** [gen] alternar **-2.** [turn] girar. ◇ *vi* **-1.** [turn] girar, dar voltas **-2.** [in sequence - jobs] alternar-se; [- crops] alternar.
rotation [rəʊ'teɪʃn] *n* **-1.** [turning movement] rotação *f* **-2.** *(U)* [sequence - of jobs] revezamento *m*, alternância *f*; [- of crops] rodízio *m*; **in ~** por turnos.
rote [rəʊt] *n (U)*: **by ~** de cor *OR* memória.
rote learning *n* decoreba *f*.
rotor ['rəʊtəʳ] *n* rotor *m*.
rotten ['rɒtn] *adj* **-1.** [decayed] podre **-2.** *inf* [poor-quality, unskilled] péssimo(ma) **-3.** *inf* [unpleasant, nasty] perverso(sa), ruim **-4.** *inf* [unenjoyable] detestável **-5.** *inf* [unwell]: **to feel ~** sentir-se péssimo(ma) **-6.** [unhappy, bad]: **to feel ~ (about sthg)** sentir-se péssimo(ma) (por algo).
rotund [rəʊ'tʌnd] *adj fml* rotundo(da).
rouble ['ru:bl] *n* rublo *m*.
rouge [ru:ʒ] *n (U)* ruge *m*.
rough [rʌf] ◇ *adj* **-1.** [not smooth - surface] áspero(ra); [- road] acidentado(da) **-2.** [violent] rude, grosseiro(ra) **-3.** [crude, basic - people, manners] rústico(ca); [- shelter, conditions, situation] precário(-ria) **-4.** [approximate - not detailed] rudimentar; [- not exact] aproximado(da) **-5.** [unpleasant, tough - life, time] duro(ra), difícil; [- area, town etc] tumultuoso(sa) **-6.** [stormy - weather] tormentoso(sa); [- crossing] movimentado(da); [- sea] agitado(da); [- wind] violento(ta); [- day] tempestuoso(sa) **-7.** [sounding harsh] áspero(ra) **-8.** [tasting harsh] azedo(da) **-9.** [tired, ill] abatido(da). ◇ *adv*: **to sleep ~** dormir na rua. ◇ *n* **-1.** *GOLF*: **the ~** o rough **-2.** [undetailed form]: **in ~** em rascunho. ◇ *vt phr*: **to ~ it** viver sem comodidades.

◆ **rough out** *vt sep* esboçar.
◆ **rough up** *vt sep* bater em, atacar.
roughage ['rʌfɪdʒ] *n* fibras *fpl.*
rough and ready *adj* rústico(ca), feito(ta) às pressas.
rough-and-tumble *n (U)* tumulto *m.*
roughcast *n (U)* reboco *m* grosso.
rough diamond *n UK fig* diamante *m* bruto.
roughen ['rʌfn] *vt* tornar áspero(ra).
rough justice *n (U)* injustiça *f.*
roughly ['rʌflɪ] *adv* **-1.** [not gently] bruscamente **-2.** [crudely] rusticamente **-3.** [approximately] aproximadamente, mais ou menos.
roughneck ['rʌfnek] *n* **-1.** [oilrig worker] *petroleiro que trabalha em campo de perfuração* **-2.** *US inf* [ruffian] casca-grossa *mf.*
roughness ['rʌfnɪs] *n (U)* **-1.** [lack of smoothness] aspereza *f* **-2.** [lack of gentleness] rudeza *f*, grosseria *f.*
roughshod ['rʌfʃɒd] *adv*: **to ride ~ over sb/sthg** tratar alguém/algo a pontapés.
roulette [ru:'let] *n (U)* roleta *f.*
round [raʊnd] ◇ *adj* **-1.** [gen] redondo(da) **-2.** [fat, curved - cheeks, hips] roliço(ça), redondo(da); [- bulge] redondo(da). ◇ *prep* **-1.** [surrounding] ao redor de **-2.** [near] em volta de; **~ here** por aqui **-3.** [all over] por todo(da) **-4.** [in circular movement, in circumference] ao redor de; **she measures 70 cm ~ the waist** ela mede *OR* tem 70 cm de cintura **-5.** [to/on the other side of]: **to drive ~ the corner** dobrar a esquina; **I live just ~ the corner** eu moro logo ali **-6.** [so as to avoid - hole, obstacle]: **to go ~ an obstacle** contornar um obstáculo; [- problem]: **to find a way ~ sthg** achar um jeito de contornar algo. ◇ *adv* **-1.** [surrounding]: **all ~** por toda a volta, por todos os lados **-2.** [near]: **~ about** [in distance] por perto; [in number, amount] aproximadamente **-3.** [all over]: **to travel ~** viajar por aí **-4.** [in circular movement]: **~ (and ~)** em círculos; **to go ~** circular; **to spin ~** girar **-5.** [in circumference]: **it's at least 3 km ~** tem no mínimo 3 km de circunferência **-6.** [to the other side or direction] ao redor; **to turn ~** virar; **to go ~** dar a volta **-7.** [on a visit]: **come ~ sometime!** apareçam uma hora dessas! ◇ *n* **-1.** [gen] rodada *f*; **a ~ of applause** uma salva de palmas **-2.** [professional visit] percurso *m* **-3.** [of ammunition] cartucho *m* **-4.** *BOXING* assalto *m* **-5.** *GOLF* partida *f.* ◇ *vt* [turn] dobrar, virar.
◆ **rounds** *npl* [professional visits] percurso *m*; **to do** *OR* **go the ~s** *fig* espalhar-se, propagar-se.
◆ **round off** *vt sep* encerrar, terminar.
◆ **round up** *vt sep* **-1.** [gather together] reunir **-2.** *MATH* arredondar.
roundabout ['raʊndəbaʊt] ◇ *adj* indireto(ta). ◇ *n UK* **-1.** [on road] rotatória *f* **-2.** [at fairground] carrossel *m* **-3.** [at playground] gira-gira *m.*
rounded ['raʊndɪd] *adj* redondo(da).
rounders ['raʊndəz] *n (U) UK* bete *m.*
Roundhead ['raʊndhed] *n HIST* *seguidor de Oliver Cromwell na guerra civil inglesa*, Cabeça *m* Redonda.
roundly ['raʊndlɪ] *adv* totalmente, terminantemente.
round-neck *adj* de gola redonda.
round-shouldered [-'ʃəʊldəd] *adj* de ombros caídos.
round-table *adj* em igualdade de condições.
round the clock *adv* durante as 24 horas do dia.
◆ **round-the-clock** *adj* contínuo(nua), 24 horas do dia.
round trip ◇ *adj US* de ida e volta. ◇ *n* viagem *f* de ida e volta.
round-up *n* resumo *m.*
rouse [raʊz] *vt* **-1.** [wake up] despertar **-2.** [impel]: **to ~ sb to do sthg** animar alguém a fazer algo; **to ~ o.s. to do sthg** animar-se a fazer algo **-3.** [excite] estimular **-4.** [give rise to] suscitar.
rousing ['raʊzɪŋ] *adj* estimulante.
rout [raʊt] ◇ *n* derrota *f* esmagadora. ◇ *vt* derrotar de forma esmagadora.
route [ru:t] ◇ *n* **-1.** [line of travel - of journey] rota *f*; [- of or person, procession] trajeto *m*, percurso *m* **-2.** [of bus, train] linha *f* **-3.** [of plane, ship] rota *f* **-4.** *fig* [to achievement] caminho *m.* ◇ *vt* **-1.** [flight, traffic] direcionar **-2.** [goods] enviar.
route map *n* mapa *m (de localização).*
route march *n* marcha *f.*
routine [ru:'ti:n] ◇ *adj* **-1.** [normal] de rotina **-2.** *pej* [humdrum, uninteresting] rotineiro(ra). ◇ *n* **-1.** *(U)* [normal pattern of activity] rotina *f* **-2.** *pej* [boring repetition] rotina *f.*
routinely [ru:'ti:nlɪ] *adv* freqüentemente.
rove [rəʊv] *literary* ◇ *vt* errar, vagar por. ◇ *vi*: **to ~ around** vagar.
roving ['rəʊvɪŋ] *adj* itinerante; **~ eyes** olhar *m* errante.
row[1] [rəʊ] ◇ *n* **-1.** [gen] fileira *f* **-2.** [succession] seqüência *f*, série *f*; **four in a ~** quatro seguidos. ◇ *vt* **-1.** [boat] remar **-2.** [person] conduzir de barco a remo. ◇ *vi* [in boat] remar.
row[2] [raʊ] ◇ *n* **-1.** [quarrel] briga *f* **-2.** *inf* [noise] alvoroço *m*, barulho *m.* ◇ *vi* [quarrel] discutir, brigar.
rowboat ['rəʊbəʊt] *n US* barco *m* a remo.
rowdiness ['raʊdɪnɪs] *n (U)* alvoroço *m*, tumulto *m.*
rowdy ['raʊdɪ] (*compar* **-ier**, *superl* **-iest**) *adj* **-1.** [person] brigão(gona) **-2.** [party, atmosphere] barulhento(ta).
rower ['rəʊə[r]] *n* remador *m*, -ra *f.*
row house [rəʊ-] *n US* casa *f* geminada.
rowing ['rəʊɪŋ] *n (U)* remo *m.*
rowing boat *n UK* barco *m* a remo.
rowing machine *n* remo *m* seco.
royal ['rɔɪəl] ◇ *adj* real. ◇ *n inf* membro *m* da família real.
Royal Air Force *n (U)*: **the ~** a Força Aérea Britânica.
royal blue *adj* azul-imperial.
royal family *n* família *f* real.
royalist ['rɔɪəlɪst] *n* monarquista *mf.*
royal jelly *n (U)* geléia *f* real.
Royal Mail *n UK*: **the ~** os Correios da Grã-Bretanha.
Royal Marines *n UK*: **the ~** os Fuzileiros Navais Britânicos.

Royal Navy *n*: the ~ a Marinha Real Britânica.
royalty ['rɔɪəltɪ] *n (U)* realeza *f*.
◆ **royalties** *npl* direitos *mpl* autorais.
RP (*abbr of* **received pronunciation**) *n pronúncia padrão do inglês.*
RPI (*abbr of* **retail price index**) *n* ≃ IPC *m*.
rpm (*abbr of* **revolutions per minute**) *npl* rpm.
RR (*abbr of* **railroad**) *US* ferrovia *f*.
RRP (*abbr of* **recommended retail price**) *n UK* preço *m* sugerido.
RSA *n* **-1.** (*abbr of* **Republic of South Africa**) República *f* da África do Sul **-2.** (*abbr of* **Royal Society of Arts**) *sociedade britânica para o fomento às artes, à indústria e ao comércio.*
RSC (*abbr of* **Royal Shakespeare Company**) *n importante companhia teatral britânica especializada em Shakespeare.*
RSI (*abbr of* **repetitive strain injury**) *n* LER *f*.
RSJ (*abbr of* **rolled steel joist**) *n* vigamento *m* folheado a aço.
RSPB (*abbr of* **Royal Society for the Protection of Birds**) *n organização britânica para a proteção de pássaros em seu habitat.*
RSPCA (*abbr of* **Royal Society for the Prevention of Cruelty to Animals**) *n sociedade britânica protetora de animais.*
RSVP (*abbr of* **répondez s'il vous plaît**) RSVP.
rub [rʌb] (*pt* & *pp* **-bed**, *cont* **-bing**) ◇ *vt* esfregar; **to ~ shoulders with** acotovelar-se com; **to ~ sthg against sthg** esfregar algo em *OR* contra algo; **to ~ sthg on sthg** [polish] esfregar algo em algo; **to ~ sthg in (to) sthg** esfregar algo em algo; **to ~ it in** *inf fig* trazer à tona; **to ~ sb up the wrong way** *UK*, **to ~ sb the wrong way** *US* ofender alguém sem intenção. ◇ *vi*: **to ~ (against** *OR* **on sthg)** roçar (em algo); **to ~ (together)** esfregar-se; **to ~ along** dar-se bem com.
◆ **rub off on** *vt fus* influir em.
◆ **rub out** *vt sep* apagar.
rubber ['rʌbə^r] ◇ *adj* de borracha. ◇ *n* **-1.** *(U)* [substance] borracha *f* **-2.** *UK* [eraser] borracha *f* **-3.** [in bridge] rubber *m* **-4.** *US inf* [condom] camisinha *f* **-5.** *US* [overshoe] galocha *f*.
rubber band *n* atilho *m*, borrachinha *f (para papel)*.
rubber boot *n US* bota *f* de borracha.
rubber dinghy *n* bote *m* de borracha.
rubberize, -ise ['rʌbəraɪz] *vt* revestir de borracha.
rubberneck ['rʌbənek] *vi US inf* [stare] olhar com curiosidade.
rubber plant *n* goma-elástica *f*.
rubber stamp *n* carimbo *m*.
◆ **rubber-stamp** *vt* aprovar sem questionar.
rubber tree *n* seringueira *f*.
rubbery ['rʌbərɪ] *adj* borrachento(ta).
rubbing ['rʌbɪŋ] *n* [of brass] calcografia *f*.
rubbish ['rʌbɪʃ] ◇ *n* **-1.** [refuse] lixo *m* **-2.** *inf fig* [worthless matter] porcaria *f* **-3.** *inf* [nonsense] besteira *f*, bobagem *f*. ◇ *vt inf* rebaixar. ◇ *excl* bobagem!
rubbish bag *n UK* saco *m* de lixo.
rubbish bin *n UK* lata *f* de lixo.
rubbish dump, rubbish tip *n UK* depósito *m* de lixo.
rubbishy ['rʌbɪʃɪ] *adj inf* porcaria.
rubble ['rʌbl] *n (U)* entulho *m*.
rubella [ru:'belə] *n (U)* rubéola *f*.
ruby ['ru:bɪ] (*pl* **-ies**) *n* rubi *m*.
RUC (*abbr of* **Royal Ulster Constabulary**) *n força policial na Irlanda do Norte.*
ruck *n* **-1.** *inf* [fight] arruaça *f* **-2.** *RUGBY* luta *f* pela posse da bola.
rucksack ['rʌksæk] *n* mochila *f*.
ructions ['rʌkʃnz] *npl inf* alvoroço *m*, tumulto *m*.
rudder ['rʌdə^r] *n* leme *m*.
ruddy ['rʌdɪ] (*compar* **-ier**, *superl* **-iest**) *adj* **-1.** [reddish] corado(da) **-2.** *UK dated* [for emphasis] maldito(ta).
rude [ru:d] *adj* **-1.** [impolite] rude, grosseiro(ra) **-2.** [dirty, naughty - joke] sujo(ja); [- word] grosseiro(ra); [- noise] violento(ta) **-3.** [unexpected] brusco(ca); **~ awakening** um despertar brusco **-4.** *literary* [primitive] rústico(ca).
rudely ['ru:dlɪ] *adv* **-1.** [gen] de forma grosseira **-2.** [unexpectedly] bruscamente, violentamente.
rudeness ['ru:dnɪs] *n (U)* grosseria *f*.
rudimentary [ˌru:dɪ'mentərɪ] *adj* rudimentar.
rudiments ['ru:dɪmənts] *npl* rudimentos *mpl*, noções *fpl* básicas.
rue [ru:] *vt* lamentar, arrepender-se de.
rueful ['ru:fʊl] *adj* arrependido(da).
ruff [rʌf] *n* gola *f* franzida.
ruffian ['rʌfjən] *n* rufião *m*, -ona *f*.
ruffle ['rʌfl] ◇ *n* rufo *m*. ◇ *vt* **-1.** [mess up - hair, fur] revolver; [- water] agitar **-2.** [upset] enervar.
rug [rʌg] *n* **-1.** [carpet] tapete *m (pequeno)* **-2.** [blanket] manta *f*.
rugby ['rʌgbɪ] *n (U)* rúgbi *m*.
Rugby League *n rúgbi profissional disputado com equipes de 13 jogadores.*
Rugby Union *n rúgbi amador disputado com equipes de 15 jogadores.*
rugged ['rʌgɪd] *adj* **-1.** [rocky, uneven] acidentado(-da) **-2.** [sturdy] potente **-3.** [roughly handsome] rústico(ca) e atraente.
ruggedness ['rʌgɪdnɪs] *n (U)* aspereza *f*.
rugger ['rʌgə^r] *n (U) UK inf* rúgbi *m*.
ruin ['ru:ɪn] ◇ *n* ruína *f*. ◇ *vt* **-1.** [spoil] arruinar, estragar **-2.** [bankrupt] arruinar.
◆ **in ruin(s)** *adv* em ruínas.
ruination [ru:ɪ'neɪʃn] *n (U)* arruinação *f*, ruína *f*.
ruinous ['ru:ɪnəs] *adj* dispendioso(sa).
rule [ru:l] ◇ *n* **-1.** [regulation - *SPORT*] regra *f*; **to bend the ~s** abrir uma exceção nas regras; [- *SCH*] norma *f* **-2.** [convention, guideline] regra *f*; **as a ~ of thumb** por experiência (própria) **-3.** [norm]: **the ~** a regra, a norma; **as a ~** via de regra **-4.** *(U)* [control] domínio *m* **-5.** [ruler] régua *f*. ◇ *vt* **-1.** [control, guide] comandar **-2.** [govern] governar **-3.** [decide]: **to ~ that** ordenar *OR* decretar que. ◇ *vi* **-1.** [give decision] deliberar **-2.** *fml* [be paramount] dominar **-3.** [govern] governar.
◆ **rule out** *vt sep* **-1.** [reject as unsuitable] descartar **-2.** [prevent, make impossible - possibility, circumstances] descartar; [- event, decision] impedir.
rulebook ['ru:lbʊk] *n*: **the ~** o regulamento.

ruled [ru:ld] *adj* pautado(da).

ruler ['ru:lə^r] *n* **-1.** [for measurement] régua *f* **-2.** [leader] soberano *m*, -na *f*.

ruling ['ru:lɪŋ] ◇ *adj* no poder, dominante. ◇ *n* sentença *f*, parecer *m*.

rum [rʌm] (*compar* **-mer**, *superl* **-mest**) ◇ *adj UK inf dated* esquisito(ta). ◇ *n (U)* rum *m*.

Rumania [ru:'meɪnjəl *n* = **Romania**.

Rumanian [ru:'meɪnjən] *adj* & *n* = **Romanian**.

rumba ['rʌmbə] *n* rumba *f*.

rumble ['rʌmbl] ◇ *n* **-1.** [noise - of thunder] estrondo *m*; [- of stomach, train] ronco *m*; [- of traffic] barulho *m* **-2.** *US inf* [fight] arruaça *f*. ◇ *vt UK inf dated* revelar, descobrir. ◇ *vi* **-1.** [thunder] trovejar **-2.** [stomach, train] roncar **-3.** [traffic] fazer barulho.

rumbustious [rʌm'bʌstʃəs] *adj UK* esfuziante, enérgico(ca).

ruminate ['ru:mɪneɪt] *vi fml*: **to ~ (about** *OR* **on sthg)** ruminar (algo).

rummage ['rʌmɪdʒ] *vi* escarafunchar.

rummage sale *n US* bazar *m* beneficente *(de artigos usados)*.

rummy ['rʌmɪ] *n (U) jogo de cartas semelhante à canastra e ao buraco*.

rumour *UK*, **rumor** *US* ['ru:mə^r] *n* rumor *m*, boato *m*.

rumoured *UK*, **rumored** *US* ['ru:məd] *adj*: **to be ~ed that** comenta-se que.

rump [rʌmp] *n* **-1.** [of animal] anca *f*, garupa *f* **-2.** *inf* [of person] nádegas *fpl*.

rumple ['rʌmpl] *vt* **-1.** [clothes] amarrotar **-2.** [hair] despentear.

rump steak *n* filé *m* de alcatra.

rumpus ['rʌmpəs] *n inf* bafafá *m*, rolo *m*.

rumpus room *n US* sala *f* de jogos.

run [rʌn] (*pt* **ran**, *pp* **run**, *cont* **-ning**) ◇ *n* **-1.** [on foot] corrida *f*; **to go for a ~** ir dar uma corrida; **to break into a ~** sair em disparada; **to take the dog for a ~** levar o cão para um passeio; **on the ~** em fuga **-2.** [in car] passeio *f*; **it's a long ~ down to Cornwall** é um longo caminho até Cornwall **-3.** [series - of luck] alternância *f*; [- of disasters, wins] série *f* **-4.** THEATRE temporada *f* **-5.** [great demand]: **~ on sthg** procura *f OR* demanda *f* por algo **-6.** [in tights] fio *m* puxado **-7.** [in cricket, baseball] ponto *m* **-8.** [sports track] pista *f* **-9.** [term, period]: **in the short/long ~** a curto/longo prazo. ◇ *vt* **-1.** [on foot] correr **-2.** [manage, control] dirigir, administrar **-3.** [machine] operar **-4.** [car] dirigir, fazer andar **-5.** [water, bath, tap] abrir **-6.** [publish] publicar **-7.** *inf* [drive] levar **-8.** [move, pass]: **to ~ sthg along/over sthg** passar algo em/sobre algo. ◇ *vi* **-1.** [gen] passar; **to be running late** estar atrasado(da) **-2.** [on foot] correr; **to ~ for it** fugir **-3.** *US* [in election]: **to ~ (for sthg)** concorrer (a algo) **-4.** [progress, develop]: **to ~ smoothly** ir bem **-5.** [machine, factory, engine] funcionar; **to ~ on** *OR* **off sthg** funcionar com algo **-6.** [liquid, river] escorrer; **to ~ dry** secar **-7.** [nose] escorrer **-8.** [tap] pingar **-9.** [colour] borrar **-10.** [continue] continuar; **to have two months to ~** o contrato ainda é válido por dois meses; **feelings are ~ning high** os ânimos estão exaltados.

◆ **run about** *vi* **-1.** [from place to place] correr (de um lugar para outro) **-2.** [associate] andar.

◆ **run across** *vt fus* encontrar-se com.

◆ **run along** *vi dated*: **~ along now!** andando!

◆ **run around** *vi* = **run about**.

◆ **run away** *vi* **-1.** [flee]: **to ~ away (from sb/sthg)** fugir (de alguém/algo) **-2.** *fig* [avoid]: **to ~ away from sthg** fugir de algo.

◆ **run away with** *vt fus*: **he lets his enthusiasm ~ away with him** ele se deixa levar pelo entusiasmo.

◆ **run down** ◇ *vt sep* **-1.** [in vehicle] atropelar **-2.** [criticize] falar mal de **-3.** [allow to decline] enfraquecer. ◇ *vi* perder força.

◆ **run in** *vt sep* [car] amaciar.

◆ **run into** *vt fus* **-1.** [encounter - problem] deparar-se com; [- person] topar com **-2.** [in vehicle] chocar-se com *OR* contra **-3.** [amount to] chegar a, atingir.

◆ **run off** ◇ *vt sep* [a copy] imprimir. ◇ *vi* [abscond, elope]: **to ~ off (with sb/sthg)** fugir (com alguém/algo).

◆ **run on** *vi* continuar.

◆ **run out** *vi* **-1.** [become used up] esgotar **-2.** [expire] vencer, caducar.

◆ **run out of** *vt fus* ficar sem; **we've ~ out of food** acabou a nossa comida.

◆ **run over** *vt sep* atropelar.

◆ **run through** *vt fus* **-1.** [spread through] permear **-2.** [practise] ensaiar, praticar **-3.** [read through] passar os olhos em.

◆ **run to** *vt fus* **-1.** [amount to] chegar a **-2.** [afford]: **my budget doesn't ~ to a new car** meu orçamento não me permite comprar um carro novo.

◆ **run up** *vt fus* contrair.

◆ **run up against** *vt fus* deparar-se com.

run-around *n inf*: **to give sb the ~** enrolar alguém.

runaway ['rʌnəweɪ] ◇ *adj* [out of control - train, inflation] descontrolado(da); [- victory] fácil. ◇ *n* fugitivo *m*, -va *f*.

rundown ['rʌndaʊn] *n* **-1.** [report] relatório *m* detalhado **-2.** [decline] desmantelamento *m* gradual.

◆ **run-down** *adj* **-1.** [dilapidated] arruinado(da), em ruínas **-2.** [tired] esgotado(da).

rung [rʌŋ] ◇ *pp* ▷ **ring**. ◇ *n* degrau *m*.

run-in *n inf* rixa *f*.

runner ['rʌnə^r] *n* **-1.** [athlete] corredor *m*, -ra *f* **-2.** [smuggler - guns] contrabandista *mf*; [- drugs] traficante *mf* **-3.** [wood or metal strip - of sledge, skate] lâmina *f*; [- of drawer] corrediça *f*.

runner bean *n UK* feijão-trepador *m*.

runner-up (*pl* **runners-up**) *n* segundo colocado *m*, segunda colocada *f*.

running ['rʌnɪŋ] ◇ *adj* **-1.** [continuous] constante **-2.** [consecutive] consecutivo(va) **-3.** [water - not stagnant] corrente; [- in pipes] encanado(da). ◇ *n* **-1.** *(U)* SPORT corrida *f*; **she loves ~ in the park** ela gosta de correr no parque **-2.** [management, control] gestão *f*, direção *f* **-3.** [of machine] funcionamento *m* **-4.** *phr*: **to make the ~** tomar as rédeas; **to be in/out ofthe ~ (for sthg)** ter/não ter

possibilidades (de algo). ◇ *comp* SPORT de corrida.
running commentary *n* comentário *m* ao vivo.
running costs *npl* despesas *fpl* de manutenção.
running mate *n* *US* candidato *m*, -ta *f* a vice-presidente.
running repairs *npl* pequenos reparos *mpl*.
runny ['rʌnɪ] (*compar* **-ier**, *superl* **-iest**) *adj* **-1.** [food - eggs] mal-passado(da); [- jam, honey] mole; [- butter, chocolate] derretido(da) **-2.** [nose] escorrendo **-3.** [eyes] lacrimejante.
run-of-the-mill *adj* corriqueiro(ra).
runt [rʌnt] *n* **-1.** [animal] filhote *m* mais fraco **-2.** *pej* [person] tampinha *mf*.
run-through *n* ensaio *m*.
run-up *n* **-1.** [preceding time] período *m* anterior **-2.** SPORT impulso *m*.
runway ['rʌnweɪ] *n* pista *f* (de pouso/decolagem).
rupture ['rʌptʃə^r] *n* **-1.** MED hérnia *f* **-2.** [of relationship] rompimento *m*.
rural ['rʊərəl] *adj* rural.
ruse [ru:z] *n* ardil *m*.
rush [rʌʃ] ◇ *n* **-1.** [hurry] pressa *f*; **there's no ~** não há pressa; **to make a ~ for sthg** disparar até algo **-2.** [demand]: **~ (for** OR **on sthg)** procura *f* excessiva (por algo); **~ to do sthg** corrida para fazer algo **-3.** [busiest period] corre-corre *m* **-4.** [surge - physical] fluxo *m*; **~ of air** corrente *m* de ar; [- mental, emotional] torrente *f*. ◇ *vt* **-1.** [hurry] apressar; **to ~ sb into sthg** apressar alguém em algo; **to ~ sb into doing sthg** apressar alguém para que faça algo **-2.** [send quickly] levar com urgência **-3.** [attack suddenly] investir repentinamente contra. ◇ *vi* **-1.** [hurry] apressar-se; **to ~ into sthg** entrar de cabeça em algo **-2.** [crowd] correr.
◆ **rushes** *npl* **-1.** BOT juncos *mpl* **-2.** CINEMA primeiras cópias *fpl*.
rushed [rʌʃt] *adj* **-1.** [person] apressado(da) **-2.** [work] feito(ta) às pressas.
rush hour *n* hora *f* do rush.
rush job *n* **-1.** [urgent job] trabalho *m* urgente **-2.** [bad work] trabalho *m* feito às pressas.
rusk [rʌsk] *n* biscoito *m* seco.
russet ['rʌsɪt] *adj* ferrugíneo(nea).
Russia ['rʌʃə] *n* Rússia; **in ~** na Russia.
Russian ['rʌʃn] ◇ *adj* russo(sa). ◇ *n* **-1.** [person] russo *m*, -sa *f* **-2.** [language] russo *m*.
Russian roulette *n (U)* roleta *f* russa.
rust [rʌst] ◇ *n (U)* ferrugem *f*. ◇ *vi* enferrujar.
rustic ['rʌstɪk] *adj* rústico(ca).
rustle ['rʌsl] ◇ *n* ruído *m*. ◇ *vt* **-1.** [paper, leaves] farfalhar **-2.** *US* [cattle] roubar. ◇ *vi* farfalhar.
rustproof ['rʌstpru:f] *adj* inoxidável.
rusty ['rʌstɪ] (*compar* **-ier**, *superl* **-iest**) *adj* enferrujado(da).
rut [rʌt] *n* **-1.** [furrow] sulco *m*; **to get into/be in a ~** tornar-se/ser escravo(va) da rotina **-2.** [animal] cio *m*.
rutabaga [,ru:tə'beɪgə] *n* *US* nabo *m* sueco.
ruthless ['ru:θlɪs] *adj* impiedoso(sa).
ruthlessly ['ru:θlɪslɪ] *adv* impiedosamente.
ruthlessness ['ru:θlɪsnɪs] *n (U)* crueldade *f*.
RV *n* **-1.** (*abbr of* **revised version**) *tradução da Bíblia para o inglês no final do século XIX* **-2.** (*abbr of* **recreational vehicle**) *US* motor-home *m*.
Rwanda [rʊ'ændə] *n* Ruanda; **in ~** em Ruanda.
Rwandan [rʊ'ændən] ◇ *adj* ruandês(esa). ◇ *n* ruandês *m*, -esa *f*.
rye [raɪ] *n (U)* centeio *m*.
rye bread *n (U)* pão *m* de centeio.
rye grass *n (U)* azevém *m*.
rye whiskey *n (U)* uísque *m* de centeio.

S

s (*pl* **ss** OR **s's**), **S** (*pl* **Ss** OR **S's**) [es] *n* [letter] s, S *m*.
◆ **S** (*abbr of* **south**) S.
SA **-1.** (*abbr of* **South Africa**) África *f* do Sul **-2.** (*abbr of* **South America**) América *f* do Sul **-3.** (*abbr of* **South Australia**) *região sul da Austrália*.
Saar *n*: **the ~** o Sarre.
Sabbath ['sæbəθ] *n*: **the ~** o sabá.
sabbatical [sə'bætɪkl] *n* período *m* sabático; **on ~** em período sabático.
saber ['seɪbə^r] *n* *US* = **sabre**.
sable *n* zibelina *f*.
sabotage ['sæbətɑ:ʒ] ◇ *n (U)* sabotagem *f*. ◇ *vt* sabotar.
saboteur [,sæbə'tɜ:^r] *n* sabotador *m*, -ra *f*.
sabre *UK*, **saber** *US* ['seɪbə^r] *n* sabre *m*.
saccharin(e) ['sækərɪn] *n (U)* sacarina *f*.
sachet ['sæʃeɪ] *n* sachê *m*.
sack [sæk] ◇ *n* **-1.** [bag] saco *m* **-2.** *UK inf* [dismissal]: **to get** OR **be given the ~** ser despedido(da). ◇ *vt* *UK inf* [dismiss] despedir, mandar embora.
sackful ['sækfʊl] *n* saca *f*.
sacking ['sækɪŋ] *n (U)* linhagem *f*.
sacrament ['sækrəmənt] *n* sacramento *m*.
sacred ['seɪkrɪd] *adj* sagrado(da).
sacrifice ['sækrɪfaɪs] ◇ *n* sacrifício *m*. ◇ *vt* sacrificar.
sacrilege ['sækrɪlɪdʒ] *n (U)* sacrilégio *m*.
sacrilegious [,sækrɪ'lɪdʒəs] *adj* sacrílego(ga).
sacrosanct ['sækrəʊsæŋkt] *adj* sacrossanto(ta).
sad [sæd] (*compar* **-der**, *superl* **-dest**) *adj* triste.
sadden ['sædn] *vt* entristecer.
saddle ['sædl] ◇ *n* **-1.** [for horse] sela *f* **-2.** [of bicycle, motorcycle] selim *m*. ◇ *vt* **-1.** [put saddle on] selar **-2.** *fig* [burden]: **to ~ sb with sthg** encarregar alguém de algo.
◆ **saddle up** ◇ *vt fus* selar. ◇ *vi* selar.
saddlebag ['sædlbæg] *n* **-1.** [for horse] alforje *m* **-2.**

[for bicycle, motorcycle] bolsa *f.*

saddler ['sædlə^r] *n* seleiro *m*, -ra *f.*

sadism ['seɪdɪzm] *n (U)* sadismo *m.*

sadist ['seɪdɪst] *n* sádico *m*, -ca *f.*

sadistic [sə'dɪstɪk] *adj* sádico(ca).

sadly ['sædlɪ] *adv* **-1.** [sorrowfully] tristemente **-2.** [regrettably] lamentavelmente.

sadness ['sædnɪs] *n* tristeza *f.*

sadomasochistic *adj* sadomasoquista.

s.a.e., sae (*abbr of* **stamped addressed envelope**) *n* *envelope-resposta com porte pago.*

safari [sə'fɑ:rɪ] *n* safári *m*; **to go on ~** fazer um safári.

safari park *n* parque-safári *m.*

safe [seɪf] <> *adj* **-1.** [not causing harm or danger] seguro(ra); **in ~ hands** em boas mãos **-2.** [not in danger] protegido(da); **to be ~ from attack** estar a salvo de ataques; **~ and sound** são e salvo, sã e salva **-3.** [not causing disagreement] pacífico(ca); **it's ~ to say that ...** pode-se dizer com segurança que ... **-4.** [not involving any risk] seguro(ra); **to be on the ~ side** por precaução **-5.** [secret] bem guardado(da). <> *n* cofre *m.*

safe-breaker *n* arrombador *m*, -ra *f* de cofre.

safe-conduct *n* **-1.** [document giving protection] salvo-conduto *m* **-2.** *(U)* [protection] salvaguarda *f.*

safe-deposit box *n* caixa-forte *f.*

safeguard ['seɪfgɑ:d] <> *n* salvaguarda *f*, proteção *f*; **~ against sthg** proteção contra algo. <> *vt*: **to ~ sb/sthg (against sthg)** proteger OR salvaguardar alguém/algo (de algo).

safe haven *n* refúgio *m.*

safe house *n* esconderijo *m.*

safe keeping *n (U)* proteção *f*, custódia *f*; **in sb's ~** aos cuidados de alguém.

safely ['seɪflɪ] *adv* **-1.** [gen] com segurança **-2.** [unharmed] ileso(sa), a salvo **-3.** [for certain]: **I can ~ say (that) ...** posso dizer seguramente que ...

safe sex *n (U)* sexo *m* seguro.

safety ['seɪftɪ] <> *n* segurança *f.* <> *comp* de segurança.

safety belt *n* cinto *m* de segurança.

safety catch *n* trava *f* de segurança.

safety curtain *n* cortina *f* corta-fogo, cortina *f* de amianto.

safety-deposit box *n* = **safe-deposit box**.

safety island *n US* ilha *f (na rua).*

safety match *n* fósforo *m* de segurança.

safety net *n* **-1.** [in circus] rede *f* de segurança **-2.** *fig* [means of protection] proteção *f.*

safety pin *n* alfinete *m* de segurança.

safety valve *n* **-1.** TECH válvula *f* de segurança **-2.** *fig* [for emotions] válvula *f* de escape.

saffron ['sæfrən] *n (U)* **-1.** [spice] açafrão *m* **-2.** [colour] amarelo-laranja *m.*

sag [sæg] (*pt* & *pp* **-ged**, *cont* **-ging**) *vi* **-1.** [sink downwards] afundar, ceder **-2.** *fig* [lessen] diminuir.

saga ['sɑ:gə] *n* **-1.** LITERATURE saga *f* **-2.** *pej* [drawn-out account] novela *f.*

sage [seɪdʒ] <> *adj* [wise] sábio(bia). <> *n* **-1.** *(U)* [herb] sálvia *f* **-2.** [wise man] sábio *m.*

saggy ['sægɪ] (*compar* **-ier**, *superl* **-iest**) *adj* [bed] afundado(da); [breasts] caído(da).

Sagittarius [,sædʒɪ'teərɪəs] *n* **-1.** [sign] Sagitário *m* **-2.** [person] sagitariano *m*, -na *f*; **I'm ~** sou de Sagitário.

Sahara [sə'hɑ:rə] *n*: **the ~ (Desert)** o (Deserto do) Saara.

Saharan [sə'hɑ:rən] *adj* saariano(na).

said [sed] *pt* & *pp* ▷ **say**.

sail [seɪl] <> *n* **-1.** [of boat] vela *f*; **to set ~** zarpar **-2.** [journey by boat]: **let's go for a ~** vamos velejar. <> *vt* **-1.** [boat] governar **-2.** [sea] cruzar. <> *vi* **-1.** [to depart] zarpar **-2.** [sport] velejar **-3.** [to travel, move - person] navegar; [- boat] singrar **-4.** *fig* [through air] voar.

◆ **sail through** *vt fus* passar fácil por.

sailboard ['seɪlbɔ:d] *n* prancha *f* de windsurfe.

sailboat *n US* = **sailing boat**.

sailcloth ['seɪlklɒθ] *n (U)* lona *f.*

sailing ['seɪlɪŋ] *n* **-1.** *(U)* SPORT navegação *f* a vela, vela *f*; **I like to go ~** eu gosto de (ir) velejar; **plain ~** sem maiores dificuldades **-2.** [trip by ship] travessia *f.*

sailing boat *UK*, **sailboat** *US* ['seɪlbəʊt] *n* barco *m* a vela.

sailing dinghy *n* dinga *f.*

sailing ship *n* veleiro *m.*

sailor ['seɪlə^r] *n* marinheiro *m*, -ra *f*; **to be a good ~** não ficar mareado(da).

saint [seɪnt] *n* **-1.** RELIG santo *m*, -ta *f* **-2.** *inf* [very good person] santo *m*, -ta *f.*

SAINT PATRICK'S DAY

Em 17 de março, comemora-se o dia de são Patrício, o patrono da Irlanda. Lá, esse dia é feriado nacional, mas a data é celebrada também em várias partes do mundo pelos irlandeses ou seus descendentes, sobretudo nos Estados Unidos. Nesse dia, a tradição manda usar um *shamrock*, uma espécie de trevo, que é o emblema nacional da Irlanda; ou vestir verde, que é a cor que representa o país.

Saint Helena *n* Santa Helena.

Saint Lawrence *n*: **the ~ (River)** o (Rio) São Lourenço.

Saint Lucia *n* Santa Lúcia.

saintly ['seɪntlɪ] (*compar* **-ier**, *superl* **-iest**) *adj* santo(-ta), santificado(da).

Saint Petersburg *n* São Petersburgo.

sake [seɪk] *n* **-1.** [benefit, advantage]: **for the ~ of** para o bem de; **for my ~** por mim **-2.** [purpose]: **for the ~ of** pelo bem de; **let us say, for the ~ of argument, that ...** digamos, só para argumentar, que ... **-3.** *phr*: **to do sthg for its own ~** fazer algo só por fazer; **for God's** OR **Heaven's ~!** pelo amor de Deus!

salad ['sæləd] *n* salada *f.*

salad bowl *n* saladeira *f.*

salad cream *n (U) UK* molho *m* para salada *(à base de maionese).*

salad dressing *n (U)* molho *m* para salada *(à base de vinagre, óleo e ervas).*

salad oil *n (U)* azeite *m* para salada.

salamander ['sælə,mændə^r] *n* salamandra *f.*

salami [sə'lɑ:mɪ] *n (U)* salame *m.*

salaried ['sælərɪd] *adj* **-1.** [employee] assalariado(da) **-2.** [job] remunerado(da).
salary ['sælərɪ] (*pl* **-ies**) *n* salário *m*.
salary scale *n* escala *f* salarial.
sale [seɪl] *n* **-1.** [gen] venda *f*; **on ~** à venda; **(up) for ~** à venda; **'for ~'** 'vende-se' **-2.** [at reduced prices] liquidação *f*, saldo *m* **-3.** [auction] leilão *m*.
◆ **sales** <> *npl* **-1.** [quantity sold] vendas *fpl* **-2.** [at reduced prices]: **the ~s** os saldos. <> *comp* de vendas.
saleroom *UK* ['seɪlrʊm], **salesroom** *US* ['seɪlzrʊm] *n* sala *f* de leilão.
sales assistant ['seɪlz-], **salesclerk** *US* ['seɪlzklɜ:rk] *n* balconista *mf*, vendedor *m*, -ra *f* *(em loja)*.
sales conference *n* conferência *f* de vendas.
sales drive *n* campanha *f* de vendas.
sales force *n* força *f* de vendas.
salesman ['seɪlzmən] (*pl* **-men** [-mən]) *n* [gen] vendedor *m*; [representative] representante *m* de vendas.
sales pitch *n* lábia *f* de vendedor.
sales rep *n inf* representante *mf* de vendas.
sales representative *n* representante *mf* de vendas.
salesroom *n US* = **saleroom**.
sales slip *n US* recibo *m*.
sales tax *n (U) imposto pago ao governo sobre mercadorias ou bens comprados.*
sales team *n* equipe *f* de vendas.
saleswoman ['seɪlz,wʊmən] (*pl* **-women** [-,wɪmɪn]) *n* [gen] vendedora *f*; [representative] representante *f* de vendas.
salient ['seɪljənt] *adj fml* evidente, notável.
saline ['seɪlaɪn] *adj* salino(na).
saliva [sə'laɪvəl] *n (U)* saliva *f*.
salivate ['sælɪveɪt] *vi* salivar.
sallow ['sæləʊ] *adj* amarelado(da).
sally ['sælɪ] (*pl* **-ies**, *pt* & *pp* **-ied**) *n* gracejo *m*, chiste *m*.
◆ **sally forth** *vi hum or literary* sair com garra e ímpeto.
salmon ['sæmən] (*pl inv* OR **-s**) *n* salmão *m*.
salmonella [,sælmə'nelə] *n (U)* salmonela *f*.
salmon pink <> *adj* rosa-salmão. <> *n* rosa-salmão *f*.
salon ['sælɒn] *n* **-1.** [hairdresser's] salão *m* **-2.** [clothes shop] butique *f*.
saloon [sə'lu:n] *n* **-1.** *UK* [car] sedã *m* **-2.** *US* [bar] bar *m* **-3.** *UK* [in pub]: **~ (bar)** *em alguns pubs e hotéis, bar finamente decorado e de preços mais altos do que os do public bar* **-4.** [on ship] salão *m*.
salopettes [,sælə'pets] *npl* calças *fpl* de ski.
salt [sɔ:lt, sɒlt] <> *n* **-1.** sal *m* **-2.** *phr*: **the ~ of the earth** o sal da terra; **to rub ~ into sb's wounds** pôr o dedo na ferida (de alguém); **to take sthg with a pinch of ~** ficar com o pé atrás em relação a algo, considerar algo com uma certa reserva. <> *comp* salgado(da). <> *vt* **-1.** [food] salgar **-2.** [roads] jogar sal em *(para derreter o gelo)*.
◆ **salt away** *vt sep inf* guardar.
SALT [sɔ:lt] (*abbr of* **Strategic Arms Limitation Talks/Treaty**) *n* SALT *m*.
salt cellar *UK*, **salt shaker** *US* [-,ʃeɪkə^r] *n* saleiro *m*.
salted ['sɔ:ltɪd] *adj* salgado(da), com sal.
saltpetre *UK*, **saltpeter** *US* [,sɔ:lt'pi:tə^r] *n (U)* salitre *m*.
salt shaker *n US* = **salt cellar**.
saltwater ['sɔ:lt,wɔ:tə^r] <> *adj* de água salgada. <> *n (U)* água *f* salgada, água *f* do mar.
salty ['sɔ:ltɪ] (*compar* **-ier**, *superl* **-iest**) *adj* salgado(da).
salubrious [sə'lu:brɪəs] *adj* salubre.
salutary ['sæljʊtrɪ] *adj* salutar.
salute [sə'lu:t] <> *n* **-1.** MIL [with hand] continência *f* **-2.** MIL [firing of guns] salva *f* **-3.** *(U)* [act of saluting] cumprimento *m* **-4.** [formal acknowledgment] saudação *f*. <> *vt* **-1.** MIL [with hand] fazer continência a **-2.** [acknowledge formally, honour] cumprimentar. <> *vi* MIL [with hand] fazer continência.
Salvadorean, Salvadorian [,sælvə'dɔ:rɪən] <> *adj* salvadorenho(nha). <> *n* salvadorenho *m*, -nha *f*.
salvage ['sælvɪdʒ] <> *n* **-1.** [rescue of ship] salvamento *m* **-2.** [property rescued] objetos *mpl* recuperados. <> *vt* **-1.** [rescue]: **to ~ sthg (from)** salvar algo (de) **-2.** *fig* [gain from failure]: **to ~ sthg (from)** preservar algo (de).
salvage vessel *n* barco *m* de salvamento.
salvation [sæl'veɪʃn] *n* salvação *f*.
Salvation Army *n*: **the ~** o Exército da Salvação.
salve [sælv] *vt*: **to do sthg to ~ one's conscience** fazer algo para aliviar a consciência.
salver ['sælvə^r] *n* salva *f*, bandeja *f*.
salvo ['sælvəʊ] (*pl* **-s** OR **-es**) *n* salva *f*.
Samaritan [sə'mærɪtn] *n*: **good ~** bom samaritano *m*.
samba ['sæmbə] *n* samba *m*.
same [seɪm] <> *adj* [gen] mesmo(ma); **at the ~ time** [simultaneously] ao mesmo tempo; [yet] mesmo assim; **one and the ~** o mesmo, a mesma. <> *adv*: **the ~** o mesmo, a mesma. <> *pron* [unchanged, identical]: **the ~** o mesmo, a mesma; **the hats they were wearing were the ~** os chapéus que eles estavam usando eram iguais; **all** OR **just the ~** [nevertheless, anyway] mesmo assim; **it's all the ~ to me** para mim dá no mesmo, para mim tanto faz; **it's not the ~** não é a mesma coisa.
sameness ['seɪmnɪs] *n* **-1.** *(U)* [lack of variety] mesmice *f* **-2.** [similarity] uniformidade *f*.
Samoa [sə'məʊə] *n* Samoa; **in ~** em Samoa; **American ~** Samoa Americana OR Oriental.
Samoan [sə'məʊən] <> *adj* samoano(na). <> *n* samoano *m*, -na *f*.
samosa [sə'məʊsə] *n espécie de pastel indiano feito de vegetais, temperos e carne.*
sample ['sɑ:mpl] <> *n* amostra *f*. <> *vt* **-1.** [taste] provar **-2.** [try out, test] experimentar **-3.** MUS amostrar.
sampler ['sɑ:mplə^r] *n* SEWING *bordado com palavras e figuras bordadas, normalmente feito como prova da habilidade de quem o confeccionou.*
sanatorium (*pl* **-riums** OR **-ria** [-rɪə]), **sanitorium** *US* (*pl* **-riums** OR **-ria** [-rɪə]) [,sænə'tɔ:rɪəm] *n* sanatório *m*.

sanctify ['sæŋktıfaı] (*pt* & *pp* **-ied**) *vt* **-1.** *RELIG* santificar **- 2.** [approve] abençoar.
sanctimonious [ˌsæŋktı'məʊnjəs] *adj pej* santarrão(rrona).
sanction ['sæŋkʃn] <> *n* sanção *f.* <> *vt* sancionar.
◆ **sanctions** *npl POL* sanções *fpl.*
sanctity ['sæŋktətı] *n (U)* santidade *f.*
sanctuary ['sæŋktʃʊərı] (*pl* **-ies**) *n* **-1.** [gen] santuário *m* **- 2.** [place of safety] abrigo *m* **- 3.** *(U)* [safety, refuge] refúgio *m.*
sanctum ['sæŋktəm] (*pl* **-s**) *n* **inf** lugar *m* sagrado, santuário *m.*
sand [sænd] <> *n (U)* areia *f.* <> *vt* lixar.
◆ **sands** *npl* [beach] areias *fpl.*
◆ **sand down** *vt sep* lixar.
sandal ['sændl] *n* sandália *f.*
sandalwood ['sændlwʊd] *n (U)* sândalo *m.*
sandbag ['sændbæg] *n* saco *m* de areia.
sandbank ['sændbæŋk] *n* banco *m* de areia.
sandblast ['sændblɑ:st] *vt limpar com jato de areia.*
sandbox *n US* = **sandpit.**
sandcastle ['sændˌkɑ:sl] *n* castelo *m* de areia.
sand dune *n* duna *f.*
sander ['sændə^r] *n* lixadeira *f.*
sandpaper ['sændˌpeıpə^r] <> *n (U)* lixa *f.* <> *vt* lixar.
sandpit *UK* ['sændpıt], **sandbox** *US* ['sændbɒks] *n* caixa *f* de areia.
sandstone ['sændstəʊn] *n (U)* arenito *m.*
sandstorm ['sændstɔ:m] *n* tempestade *f* de areia.
sand trap *n US GOLF* armadilha *f* de areia.
sandwich ['sænwıdʒ] <> *n* sanduíche *m.* <> *vt fig*: **to be ~ed between** ser prensado(da) entre.
sandwich course *n UK curso universitário que inclui um certo tempo de experiência profissional.*
sandy ['sændı] (*compar* **-ier**, *superl* **-iest**) *adj* **-1.** [made of sand] arenoso(sa) **- 2.** [sand-coloured] cor-de-areia.
sane [seın] *adj* **-1.** [not mad] são(sã) **-2.** [sensible] sensato(ta).
sang [sæŋ] *pt* ▻ **sing.**
sanguine ['sæŋgwın] *adj* esperançoso(sa), otimista.
sanitary ['sænıtrı] *adj* **-1.** [connected with health] sanitário(ria) **- 2.** [clean, hygienic] higiênico(ca).
sanitary towel, sanitary napkin *US n* absorvente *m* higiênico.
sanitation [ˌsænı'teıʃn] *n* **-1.** [in streets] saneamento *m* **- 2.** [in houses] instalações *fpl* sanitárias.
sanitation worker *n US* lixeiro *m*, -ra *f.*
sanitize, -ise ['sænıtaız] *vt* suavizar.
sanitorium *n US* = **sanatorium.**
sanity ['sænətı] *n* **-1.** [saneness] sanidade *f* **- 2.** [good sense] sensatez *f.*
sank [sæŋk] *pt* ▻ **sink.**
San Marino [ˌsænmə'ri:nəʊ] *n* San Marino; **in ~** em San Marino.
San Salvador [ˌsæn'sælvədɔ:^r] *n* São Salvador.
Sanskrit ['sænskrıt] *n* sânscrito *m.*
Santa (Claus) ['sæntə(ˌklɔ:z)] *n* Papai *m* Noel.
São Paulo [ˌsaʊ'paʊləʊ] *n* São Paulo.

sap [sæp] (*pt* & *pp* **-ped**, *cont* **-ping**) <> *n* **-1.** *(U)* [of plant] seiva *m* **- 2.** *US inf* [gullible person] bobo(ba). <> *vt* enfraquecer, consumir.
sapling ['sæplıŋ] *n* árvore *m* nova, arvorezinha *f.*
sapphire ['sæfaıə^r] *n* safira *f.*
Sarajevo [ˌsærə'jeıvəʊ] *n* Sarajevo.
sarcasm ['sɑ:kæzm] *n (U)* sarcasmo *m.*
sarcastic [sɑ:'kæstık] *adj* sarcástico(ca).
sarcophagus [sɑ:'kɒfəgəs] (*pl* **-gi** [-gaı], **-es**) *n* sarcófago *m.*
sardine [sɑ:'di:n] *n* sardinha *f.*
Sardinia [sɑ:'dınjə] *n* Sardenha; **in ~** na Sardenha.
sardonic [sɑ:'dɒnık] *adj* mordaz.
Sargasso Sea [sɑ:'gæsəʊ-] *n*: **the ~** o Mar de Sargaço.
sari ['sɑ:rı] *n* sári *m.*
sarong [sə'rɒŋ] *n* sarongue *m.*
sarsaparilla [ˌsɑ:spə'rılə] *n* salsaparrilha *f.*
sartorial [sɑ:'tɔ:rıəl] *adj fml* no vestir.
SAS (*abbr of* **Special Air Service**) *n unidade especial do exército britânico encarregada de operações de antiterrorismo e sabotagem.*
SASE (*abbr of* **self-addressed stamped envelope**) *n US envelope auto-endereçado e já selado.*
sash [sæʃ] *n* faixa *f.*
sash window *n* janela *f* de guilhotina.
Saskatchewan [ˌsæs'kætʃıwən] *n* Saskatchewan.
sassy ['sæsı] *adj US inf* descarado(da), atrevido(da).
sat [sæt] *pt* & *pp* ▻ **sit.**
Sat. (*abbr of* **Saturday**) sáb.
SAT [sæt] *n* **-1.** (*abbr of* **Standard Assessment Test**) *exames de aptidão que os estudantes da Inglaterra e do País de Gales prestam aos 7, 11 e 14 anos de idade* **- 2.** (*abbr of* **Scholastic Aptitude Test**) *exame prestado por estudantes no último ano da escola secundária nos Estados Unidos, importante ao se ingressar na universidade.*

SAT

O *Scholastic Aptitude Test* (SAT) é uma prova de conhecimentos gerais aplicada nos EUA àqueles que desejam ingressar na universidade. A prova é realizada em certas datas fixas, ao longo do ano letivo, e pode ser prestada mais de uma vez. Embora seja pré-requisito importante para o ingresso na universidade, o SAT não é o único critério de admissão. Qualificações e atividades do estudante também são levadas em consideração.

Satan ['seıtn] *n* Satã *m*, Satanás *m.*
satanic [sə'tænık] *adj* satânico(ca).
satchel ['sætʃəl] *n* pasta *f*, mochila *f* escolar.
sated ['seıtıd] *adj fml* saciado(da); **~ with sthg** saciado(da) com algo.
satellite ['sætəlaıt] <> *n* satélite *m.* <> *comp* **-1.** *TELEC* por satélite **- 2.** [dependent]: **~ city** cidade-satélite *f.*
satellite dish *n* [for TV] antena *f* parabólica.
satellite TV *n* tevê *f* via satélite.
satiate ['seıʃıeıt] *vt fml* saciar.
satin ['sætın] <> *n (U)* cetim *m.* <> *comp* **-1.** [made

of satin] de cetim **-2.** [smooth] acetinado(da).

satire ['sætaɪəʳ] *n* sátira *f*.

satirical [sə'tɪrɪkl] *adj* satírico(ca).

satirist ['sætərɪst] *n* satirista *mf*.

satirize, -ise ['sætəraɪz] *vt* satirizar.

satisfaction [ˌsætɪs'fækʃn] *n* **-1.** [gen] satisfação *f*; **to do sthg to sb's ~** fazer algo ao gosto de alguém **-2.** *(U)* [fulfilment of need] atendimento *m*, cumprimento *m*; **~ guaranteed** satisfação garantida.

satisfactory [ˌsætɪs'fæktərɪ] *adj* satisfatório(ria).

satisfied ['sætɪsfaɪd] *adj* **-1.** [happy] satisfeito(ta); **to be ~ with sthg** estar satisfeito(ta) com algo **-2.** [convinced] convencido(da); **to be ~ (that)** estar convencido(da) de que.

satisfy ['sætɪsfaɪ] (*pt* & *pp* **-ied**) *vt* **-1.** [make happy] satisfazer **-2.** [convince] convencer; **to ~ sb that** convencer alguém de que; **to ~ o.s. that** convencer-se de que **-3.** [fulfil] satisfazer, atender a.

satisfying ['sætɪsfaɪɪŋ] *adj* satisfatório(ria), agradável.

satsuma [ˌsæt'su:mə] *n tipo de tangerina proveniente do Japão.*

saturate ['sætʃəreɪt] *vt* **-1.** [drench] ensopar, empapar; **to ~ sthg with sthg** ensopar *OR* empapar algo com algo **-2.** [fill completely, swamp] inundar; **to ~ sthg with sthg** saturar algo com algo.

saturated *adj* **-1.** [drenched] ensopado(da), empapado(da) **-2.** [fat] saturado(da).

saturation [ˌsætʃə'reɪʃn] ◇ *n* **-1.** [drenching] ensopamento *m* **-2.** [complete filling] saturamento *m*. ◇ *comp* [bombing] por saturação; [TV] **~ coverage** cobertura *f* exaustiva.

saturation point *n*: **to reach ~** alcançar o ponto de saturação.

Saturday ['sætədɪ] ◇ *n* sábado *m*; **what day is it? - it's ~** que dia é hoje? - é sábado; **are you going ~?** *inf* você vai sábado?; **see you ~!** *inf* até sábado!; **on ~** no sábado; **on ~s** aos sábados; **to work ~s** trabalhar aos sábados; **last ~** sábado passado; **this ~** este sábado; **next ~** sábado da semana que vem; **every ~** todos os sábados; **every other ~** um sábado sim, outro não; **the ~ before** no sábado anterior; **the ~ before last** há dois sábados; **the ~ after next**, **~ week, a week on ~** não no próximo sábado, no outro. ◇ *comp* aos sábados; **~ morning/afternoon/night** sábado de manhã/tarde/noite; **~ evening** no fim da tarde de sábado; **a ~ job** um trabalho aos sábados.

Saturn ['sætɜ:n] *n* Saturno.

sauce [sɔ:s] *n* **-1.** *CULIN* molho *m* **-2.** *UK inf* [cheek] atrevimento *m*.

sauce boat *n* molheira *f*.

saucepan ['sɔ:spən] *n* panela *f* com um cabo.

saucer ['sɔ:səʳ] *n* pires *m inv*.

saucy ['sɔ:sɪ] (*compar* **-ier**, *superl* **-iest**) *adj inf* atrevido(da).

Saudi Arabia [ˌsaʊdɪə'reɪbjə] *n* Arábia Saudita; **in ~** na Arábia Saudita.

Saudi (Arabian) ['saʊdɪ-] ◇ *adj* árabe-saudita. ◇ *n* árabe-saudita *mf*.

sauna ['sɔ:nə] *n* sauna *f*.

saunter ['sɔ:ntəʳ] *vi* passear *(tranqüilamente)*.

sausage ['sɒsɪdʒ] *n* **-1.** *(U)* [meat] lingüiça *f* **-2.** [shaped piece of meat] salsicha *f*.

sausage roll *n UK* enroladinho *m* de salsicha.

sauté [*UK* 'səʊteɪ, *US* səʊ'teɪ] (*pt* & *pp* **sautéed** *OR* **sautéd**) ◇ *adj* sauté. ◇ *vt* fritar levemente.

savage ['sævɪdʒ] ◇ *adj* selvagem. ◇ *n* selvagem *mf*. ◇ *vt* **-1.** [attack physically] atacar ferozmente **-2.** [criticize] atacar.

savageness ['sævɪdʒnɪs], **savagery** ['sævɪdʒrɪ] *n (U)* selvageria *f*.

savanna(h) [sə'vænə] *n* savana *f*.

save [seɪv] ◇ *n SPORT* defesa *f*. ◇ *prep fml*: **~ (for)** exceto. ◇ *vt* **-1.** [gen] salvar; **to ~ sb from sthg/from doing sthg** salvar alguém de algo/de fazer algo; **to ~ sb's life** salvar a vida de alguém **-2.** [prevent waste of] economizar **-3.** [set aside] guardar **-4.** [make unnecessary] poupar; **to ~ sb/sthg from doing sthg** poupar alguém/algo de fazer algo **-5.** *SPORT* defender. ◇ *vi* economizar.

◆ **save up** *vi* economizar.

save as you earn *n UK forma de poupança em que a contribuição mensal gera renda livre de impostos.*

saveloy ['sævəlɔɪ] *n UK* salsichão *m* de porco.

saver ['seɪvəʳ] *n* **-1.** [object]: **a time/money ~** algo que economiza tempo/dinheiro **-2.** *FIN* [at bank, building society] poupador *m*, -ra *f*.

saving grace ['seɪvɪŋ-] *n* mérito *m*.

savings ['seɪvɪŋz] *npl* economias *fpl*.

savings account *n US* (caderneta *f* de) poupança *f*.

savings and loan association *n US* sociedade *f* de empréstimos imobiliários.

savings bank *n* caixa *f* econômica, banco *m* só de cadernetas de poupança.

saviour *UK*, **savior** *US* ['seɪvjəʳ] *n* salvador *m*, -ra *f*.

◆ **Saviour** *n*: **the Saviour** o Salvador.

savoir-faire [sævwɑ:'feəʳ] *n (U)* savoir-faire *m*.

savour *UK*, **savor** *US* ['seɪvəʳ] *vt* **-1.** [enjoy taste of] saborear **-2.** *fig* [enjoy greatly] saborear, aproveitar.

savoury *UK* (*pl* **-ies**), **savory** (*pl* **-ies**) *US* ['seɪvərɪ] ◇ *adj* **-1.** [not sweet] condimentado(da) **-2.** [respectable, pleasant] agradável. ◇ *n* tira-gosto *m*.

Savoy *n* Savoy.

savoy (cabbage) *n* repolho *m* crespo.

saw [sɔ:] (*UK pt* **-ed**, *pp* **sawn**, *US pt* & *pp* **-ed**) ◇ *pt* ▻ **see.** ◇ *n* serra *f*. ◇ *vt* serrar.

◆ **saw up** *vt sep* serrar.

sawdust ['sɔ:dʌst] *n (U)* serragem *f*.

sawed-off shotgun *n US* = **sawn-off shotgun**.

sawmill ['sɔ:mɪl] *n* serraria *f*.

sawn [sɔ:n] *pp UK* ▻ **saw**.

sawn-off shotgun *UK*, **sawed-off shotgun** *US* [sɔ:d-] *n* arma *f* de cano serrado.

sax [sæks] *n inf* sax *m*.

Saxon ['sæksn] ◇ *adj* saxão(xã). ◇ *n* saxão *m*, -xã *f*.

saxophone ['sæksəfəʊn] *n* saxofone *m*.

saxophonist [*UK* ˌsæks'ɒfənɪst, *US* 'sæksəfəʊnɪst] *n* saxofonista *mf*.

say [seɪ] (*pt* & *pp* **said**) ◇ *vt* **-1.** [gen] dizer; **to ~**

sthg again repetir algo; **to ~ yes** dizer que sim; **to ~ to o.s.** dizer para si mesmo(ma); **to ~ nothing of** sem mencionar; **to ~ (that)** dizer que; **he's said to be the best footballer in the world** dizem que ele é o melhor jogador do mundo **-2.** [giving information] mostrar; **the clock ~s two thirty** o relógio está marcando duas e meia **-3.** [assume, suppose] supor; **let's ~ you win** digamos que você vença **-4.** *phr*: **that goes without ~ing** nem precisa dizer isso; **I'll ~ this for him/her ...** há que se admitir *OR* dizer que ele/ela ...; **it has a lot to be said for it** tem muitos pontos em seu favor; **she didn't have much to ~ for herself** *inf* ela era uma pessoa muito reservada; **what have you got to ~ for yourself?** o que você tem a dizer para se defender?; **you don't ~!** não diga!, não é verdade! ◇ *n* [power of decision]: **to have a/no ~ (in sthg)** ter/não ter voz nem vez (em algo); **let me have my ~** deixe-me dizer o que eu penso.
◆ **that is to say** *adv* quer dizer.

SAYE (*abbr of* **save as you earn**) *n tipo de poupança na Grã-Bretanha com vantagens em relação a impostos.*

saying ['seɪɪŋ] *n* ditado *m* popular, dito *m*.

say-so *n inf* [permission] permissão *f*.

SBA (*abbr of* **Small Business Administration**) *n órgão do governo norte-americano de ajuda à pequena empresa.*

s/c (*abbr of* **self-contained**) *UK acomodação, normalmente um apartamento, que contém cozinha, banheiro e geralmente porta externa próprios.*

SC ◇ *n* (*abbr of* **supreme court**) ≃ STF *m*. ◇ *abbr of* **South Carolina**.

scab [skæb] *n* **-1.** [of wound] casca *f*, crosta *f* **-2.** *pej* [non-striker] fura-greve *mf*.

scabby ['skæbɪ] (*compar* **-ier**, *superl* **-iest**) *adj* coberto(ta) de feridas.

scabies ['skeɪbi:z] *n (U)* sarna *f*.

scaffold ['skæfəʊld] *n* **-1.** [frame] andaime *m* **-2.** [for executions] cadafalso *m*, patíbulo *m*.

scaffolding ['skæfəldɪŋ] *n (U)* andaime *m*.

scalawag *n US* = **scallywag**.

scald [skɔ:ld] ◇ *n* escaldadura *f*. ◇ *vt* escaldar.

scalding ['skɔ:ldɪŋ] *adj* escaldante.

scale [skeɪl] ◇ *n* **-1.** [gen] escala *f*; **to ~** em escala **-2.** [size, extent] tamanho *m*; **on a large ~** de grande escala **-3.** [of fish, snake] escama *f* **-4.** *US* = **scales**. ◇ *vt* **-1.** [climb] escalar **-2.** [remove scales from] escamar.
◆ **scales** *npl* balança *f*.
◆ **scale down** *vt fus* reduzir.

scale diagram *n* diagrama *m* em escala.

scale model *n* maquete *f*.

scallion ['skæljən] *n US & Irish* [spring onion] cebolinha *f* verde.

scallop ['skɒləp] ◇ *n* [shellfish] vieira *f*. ◇ *vt* [decorate edge of] guarnecer.

scallywag *UK* ['skælɪwæg], **scalawag** *US* ['skæləwæg] *n* **-1.** *inf* [child] pestinha *mf* **-2.** [adult] safado(-da).

scalp [skælp] ◇ *n* **-1.** *ANAT* couro *m* cabeludo **-2.** [removed from head] escalpo *m*. ◇ *vt* escalpelar.

scalpel ['skælpəl] *n* bisturi *m*.

scalper ['skælpəʳ] *n US* [tout] cambista *mf*.

scam [skæm] *n inf* esquema *f*, estratagema *m*.

scamp [skæmp] *n inf* pestinha *mf*, moleque *mf*.

scamper ['skæmpəʳ] *vi* fugir rapidamente.

scampi ['skæmpɪ] *n (U)* camarão-castanho *m*.

scan [skæn] (*pt & pp* **-ned**, *cont* **-ning**) ◇ *n MED & TECH* exame *m*, escaneamento *m*. ◇ *vt* **-1.** [gen] escanear **-2.** [examine carefully] examinar cuidadosamente **-3.** [glance at] correr os olhos por. ◇ *vi* **-1.** *LITERATURE* estar bem escandido(da) **-2.** *COMPUT* escanear.

scandal ['skændl] *n* escândalo *m*.

scandalize, ise ['skændəlaɪz] *vt* escandalizar.

scandalous ['skændələs] *adj* **-1.** [shocking] escandaloso(sa) **-2.** [infuriating] exasperador(ra).

Scandinavia [,skændɪ'neɪvjə] *n* Escandinávia; **in ~** na Escandinávia.

Scandinavian [,skændɪ'neɪvjən] ◇ *adj* escandinavo(va). ◇ *n* escandinavo *m*, -va *f*.

scanner ['skænəʳ] *n* escaneador *m*, scanner *m*.

scant [skænt] *adj* insuficiente, escasso(sa).

scanty ['skæntɪ] (*compar* **-ier**, *superl* **-iest**) *adj* **-1.** [dress] mínimo(ma) **-2.** [amount, resources] escasso(sa) **-3.** [meal] insuficiente.

scapegoat ['skeɪpgəʊt] *n* bode *m* expiatório.

scar [skɑ:ʳ] (*pt & pp* **-red**, *cont* **-ring**) ◇ *n* **-1.** [physical] cicatriz *f* **-2.** *fig* [mental] seqüela *f*. ◇ *vt* **-1.** [physically] deixar cicatriz em **-2.** *fig* [mentally] deixar seqüelas em.

scarce ['skeəs] *adj* escasso(sa); **to make o.s. ~** manter-se afastado(da).

scarcely ['skeəslɪ] *adv* apenas; **~ anyone/ever** quase ninguém/nunca.

scarcity ['skeəsətɪ] *n (U)* escassez *f*.

scare [skeəʳ] ◇ *n* **-1.** [sudden fright] susto *m* **-2.** [public panic] ameaça *f*; **bomb ~** ameaça de bomba. ◇ *vt* assustar.
◆ **scare away, scare off** *vt sep* afugentar.

scarecrow ['skeəkrəʊ] *n* espantalho *m*.

scared ['skeəd] *adj* **-1.** [very frightened] apavorado(da); **to be ~ stiff** *OR* **to death** estar morrendo de medo **-2.** [nervous, worried]: **to be ~ that ...** estar com medo de que ...

scaremonger *n* alarmista *mf*.

scarey ['skeərɪ] *adj* = **scary**.

scarf [skɑ:f] (*pl* **-s** *OR* **scarves**) *n* **-1.** [long - to keep warm] cachecol *m*; [- as accessory] echarpe *f* **-2.** [square] lenço *m*.

scarlet ['skɑ:lət] ◇ *adj* escarlate. ◇ *n* escarlate *m*.

scarlet fever *n (U)* escarlatina *f*.

scarper *vi UK inf* fugir.

scarves [skɑ:vz] *pl* ▷ **scarf**.

scary ['skeərɪ] (*compar* **-ier**, *superl* **-iest**) *adj inf* apavorante.

scathing ['skeɪðɪŋ] *adj* mordaz; **to be ~ about sb/sthg** fazer uma crítica mordaz a alguém/algo.

scatter ['skætəʳ] ◇ *vt* espalhar. ◇ *vi* dispersar-se.
◆ **scatter about, scatter around** *vt sep* espalhar.

scatterbrained ['skætəbreɪnd] *adj inf* desmiolado(da), avoado(da).

scattered ['skætəd] *adj* disperso(sa).

scattering ['skætərɪŋ] *n*: **a ~ of snow** uma fina camada de neve.

scatty ['skætɪ] (*compar* **-ier**, *superl* **-iest**) *adj UK inf* desmiolado(da), avoado(da).

scavenge ['skævɪndʒ] ◇ *vt* [subj: animal, bird]: **to ~ sthg** cavucar algo; *fig* [subj: person] cavucar algo. ◇ *vi* [animal, bird]: **to ~ for sthg** cavucar por algo; *fig* [person] cavucar por algo.

scavenger ['skævɪndʒə^r] *n* **-1.** [animal] *animal que se alimenta de carniça* **-2.** *fig* [person] catador *m*, -ra *f* de lixo.

SCE (*abbr of* **Scottish Certificate of Education**) *n exame de conhecimentos em três níveis prestado pelos estudantes na Escócia.*

scenario [sɪ'nɑːrɪəʊ] (*pl* **-s**) *n* cenário *m*.

scene [siːn] *n* **-1.** [gen] cena *f*; **on the ~** no local; **a change of ~** uma mudança de ares *OR* ambiente; **behind the ~s** nos bastidores **-2.** [picture of place] paisagem *f*, cenário *m* **-3.** [sight, impression] vista *f* **-4.** [area of activity] área *f* **-5.** [embarrassing fuss] cena *f*, escândalo *m* **-6.** *phr*: **to set the ~** [for person] descrever a cena; [for event] preparar o cenário.

scenery ['siːnərɪ] *n (U)* **-1.** [of countryside] paisagem *f* **-2.** *THEATRE* cenário *m*.

scenic ['siːnɪk] *adj* **-1.** [view] pitoresco(ca) **-2.** [tour] turístico(ca).

scenic route *n* rota *f* turística.

scent [sent] ◇ *n* **-1.** [smell - of flowers] perfume *m*, fragrância *f*; [- of animal] cheiro *m*, odor *m* **-2.** *fig* [track] rastro *m*, pista *f* **-3.** *(U)* [perfume] perfume *m*. ◇ *vt* **-1.** [subj: animal] farejar **-2.** *fig* [subj: person] sentir cheiro de.

scented ['sentɪd] *adj* perfumado(da).

scepter *n US* = **sceptre**.

sceptic *UK*, **skeptic** *US* ['skeptɪk] *n* céptico(ca).

sceptical *UK*, **skeptical** *US* ['skeptɪkl] *adj* céptico (ca); **to be ~ about sthg** ser céptico(ca) em relação a algo.

scepticism *UK*, **skepticism** *US* ['skeptɪsɪzml] *n (U)* ceticismo *m*.

sceptre *UK*, **scepter** *US* ['septə^r] *n* cetro *m*.

SCF (*abbr of* **Save the Children Fund**) *n organização internacional de caridade pelo bem-estar das crianças.*

schedule [*UK* 'ʃedjuːl, *US* 'skedʒʊl] ◇ *n* **-1.** [plan] plano *m*; **(according) to ~** de acordo com o planejado; **to be ahead of ~** estar adiantado(da); **to be behind ~** estar atrasado(da); **on ~** sem atraso **-2.** [written list - of prices, contents] lista *f*; [- of times] horários *mpl*. ◇ *vt*: **to ~ sthg (for)** marcar algo(para).

scheduled flight [*UK* 'ʃedjuːld-, *US* 'skedʒʊld-] *n* vôo *m* regular.

schematic [skɪ'mætɪk] *adj* esquemático(ca).

scheme [skiːm] ◇ *n* **-1.** [plan] projeto *m* **-2.** *pej* [dishonest plan] esquema *f* **-3.** [arrangement, decoration] disposição *f*; **colour ~** combinação *f* de cores **-4.** *phr*: **in the ~ of things** na ordem das coisas. ◇ *vt pej*: **to ~ to do sthg** conspirar para fazer algo. ◇ *vi pej* tramar.

scheming ['skiːmɪŋ] *adj* que faz intriga.

schism ['sɪzm, 'skɪzm] *n* cisma *m*.

schizophrenia [ˌskɪtsə'friːnjə] *n (U)* esquizofrenia *f*.

schizophrenic [ˌskɪtsə'frenɪk] ◇ *adj* esquizofrênico(ca). ◇ *n* esquizofrênico *m*, -ca *f*.

schlepp *US inf* ◇ *vt* arrastar. ◇ *vi*: **to ~ (around)** ficar de papo pro ar.

schmal(t)z [ʃmɔːlts] *n (U) inf* sentimentalismo *m*.

schmuck [ʃmʌk] *n US inf* idiota *mf*.

scholar ['skɒlə^r] *n* **-1.** [expert]: **he's a Greek ~** ele é perito em grego **-2.** *dated* [student] aluno *m*, -na *f* **-3.** [holder of scholarship] bolsista *mf*.

scholarship ['skɒləʃɪp] *n* **-1.** [grant] bolsa *f* **-2.** *(U)* [learning] erudição *f*.

scholastic [skə'læstɪk] *adj fml* educacional.

school [skuːl] *n* **-1.** [place of education] escola *f*, colégio *m* **-2.** [hours spent in school] escola *f* **-3.** *UNIV* [department] faculdade *f* **-4.** *US* [university] universidade *f* **-5.** [group of fish] cardume *m* **-6.** [of whales, dolphins] grupo *m*.

school age *n (U)* idade *f* escolar.

schoolbook ['skuːlbʊk] *n* livro *m* escolar.

schoolboy ['skuːlbɔɪ] *n* aluno *m*.

schoolchild ['skuːltʃaɪld] (*pl* **-children** [-tʃɪldrənl]) *n* aluno *m*, -na *f*.

schooldays ['skuːldeɪz] *npl* tempos *mpl* de colégio *OR* escola.

school dinner *n* refeição *f* escolar.

school district *n US autoridade local nos Estados Unidos com competência em termos de educação primária e secundária.*

school friend *n* colega *mf* (de escola).

schoolgirl ['skuːlgɜːl] *n* aluna *f*.

schooling ['skuːlɪŋ] *n (U)* educação *f*, ensino *m*.

schoolkid ['skuːlkɪd] *n inf* aluno *m*, -na *f*.

school-leaver [-ˌliːvə^r] *n UK jovem que concluiu o ensino obrigatório.*

school-leaving age [-'liːvɪŋ-] *n (U) UK idade de conclusão do ensino obrigatório.*

schoolmarm *n US* professora *f* antiquada.

schoolmaster ['skuːlˌmɑːstə^r] *n dated* mestre *m*.

schoolmistress ['skuːlˌmɪstrɪs] *n dated* mestra *f*.

school of thought *n* escola *f* de pensamento.

school report *n* boletim *m* escolar.

schoolroom ['skuːlrʊm] *n dated* classe *f*.

schoolteacher ['skuːlˌtiːtʃə^r] *n* professor *m*, -ra *f*.

school uniform *n* uniforme *m* escolar.

schoolwork ['skuːlwɜːk] *n (U)* trabalho *m* escolar.

school year *n* ano *m* letivo.

schooner ['skuːnə^r] *n* **-1.** [ship] escuna *f* **-2.** *UK* [sherry glass] caneca *f (para xerez)*.

sciatica [saɪ'ætɪkə] *en (U)* ciática *f*.

science ['saɪəns] ◇ *n* ciência *f*. ◇ *comp* **-1.** [student] de ciências **-2.** [degree] em ciências.

science fiction *n (U)* ficção *f* científica.

science park *n* complexo *m* científico *(em empresas)*.

scientific [ˌsaɪən'tɪfɪk] *adj* científico(ca).

scientist ['saɪəntɪst] *n* cientista *mf*.

sci-fi ['saɪ'faɪ] (*abbr of* **science fiction**) *n inf* ficção *f* científica.

Scilly Isles ['sɪlɪ-], **Scillies** ['sɪlɪz] *npl*: **the ~** as Ilhas Scilly; **in the ~** nas Ilhas Scilly.

scintillating ['sɪntɪleɪtɪŋ] *adj* brilhante.

scissors ['sɪzəz] *npl* tesoura *f*; **a pair of ~** uma tesoura.

sclerosis *n* ▷ **multiple sclerosis.**

scoff [skɒf] ◇ *vt UK inf* devorar, engolir. ◇ *vi* zombar; **to ~ at sb/sthg** zombar de alguém/algo.

scold [skəʊld] *vt* repreender, xingar.

scone [skɒn] *n bolinho geralmente tomado à hora do chá com manteiga ou geléia.*

scoop [sku:p] ◇ *n* **-1.** [kitchen implement - for sugar] colher *f*; [- for ice cream] pá *f* **-2.** [scoopful] concha *f*, colher *f* grande; **two ~s of ice cream** duas bolas de sorvete **-3.** [news report] furo *m*. ◇ *vt* **-1.** [with hands] tirar com as mãos **-2.** [with implement] tirar com colher.

◆ **scoop out** *vt sep* tirar com colher.

scoot [sku:t] *vi inf* correr com muita pressa.

scooter ['sku:tə^r] *n* **-1.** [toy] patinete *f* **-2.** [motorcycle] lambreta *f*.

scope [skəʊp] *n (U)* **-1.** [opportunity] possibilidades *fpl* **-2.** [range] escopo *m*.

scorch [skɔ:tʃ] ◇ *vt* **-1.** [clothes, food, skin] chamuscar **-2.** [grass, fields] queimar. ◇ *vi* **-1.** [clothes, food] chamuscar **-2.** [face, skin] queimar.

scorched earth policy [skɔ:tʃt-] *n* política *f* de terra queimada.

scorcher ['skɔ:tʃə^r] *n inf* dia *m* escaldante.

scorching ['skɔ:tʃɪŋ] *adj inf* escaldante.

score [skɔ:^r] ◇ *n* **-1.** *SPORT* placar *m* **-2.** [in test, competition] nota *f* **-3.** *dated* [twenty] vintena *f* **-4.** *MUS* partitura *f* **-5.** [subject]: **on that ~** a esse respeito. ◇ *vt* **-1.** *SPORT* marcar **-2.** [achieve] conseguir, obter **-3.** [win in an argument] ganhar **-4.** [cut] gravar, entalhar. ◇ *vi* **-1.** *SPORT* marcar **-2.** [in an argument]: **to ~ over sb** levar vantagem sobre alguém.

◆ **scores** *npl* [lots]: **~s (of sthg)** um monte (de algo).

◆ **score out** *vt sep UK* riscar.

scoreboard ['skɔ:bɔ:d] *n* placar *m*.

scorecard ['skɔ:kɑ:d] *n* cartão *m* para marcação de pontos.

score-draw *n FTBL* empate *m* com gols.

scorer ['skɔ:rə^r] *n* **-1.** [official] anotador *m*, -ra *f* de pontos **-2.** [player - football] goleador *m*, -ra *f*; [- basketball] cestinha *mf*; [- sports in general] jogador(ra) que marca mais pontos.

scorn [skɔ:n] ◇ *n (U)* desdém *m*, menosprezo *m*; **to pour ~ on sb/sthg** menosprezar alguém/algo, desdenhar de alguém/algo. ◇ *vt* **-1.** [despise] desprezar **-2.** *fml* [refuse to accept] desdenhar.

scornful ['skɔ:nfʊl] *adj* desdenhoso(osa); **to be ~ of sthg** desdenhar de algo.

Scorpio ['skɔ:pɪəʊ] (*pl* **-s**) *n* **-1.** [sign] Escorpião *m* **-2.** [person] escorpiano *m*, -na *f*; **I'm ~** sou de Escorpião.

scorpion ['skɔ:pjən] *n* escorpião *m*.

Scot [skɒt] *n* escocês *m*, -esa *f*.

scotch [skɒtʃ] *vt* **-1.** [idea] acabar com **-2.** [rumour] desmentir.

Scotch [skɒtʃ] ◇ *adj* escocês(esa). ◇ *n* [whisky] uísque *m* escocês.

Scotch egg *n UK ovo cozido coberto com lingüiça e farinha de rosca e depois frito em óleo quente.*

Scotch (tape)® *n US* fita *f* adesiva, durex® *m*.

scot-free *adj inf*: **to get off ~** sair impune.

Scotland ['skɒtlənd] *n* Escócia; **in ~** na Escócia.

Scotland Yard *n* Scotland Yard *f*.

Scots [skɒts] ◇ *adj* escocês(esa). ◇ *n (U)* [dialect] escocês *m*.

Scotsman ['skɒtsmən] (*pl* **-men** [-mən]) *n* escocês *m*.

Scotswoman ['skɒtswʊmən] (*pl* **-women** [-ˌwɪmɪn]) *n* escocesa *f*.

Scottish ['skɒtɪʃ] *adj* escocês(esa).

Scottish National Party *n*: **the ~** o Partido Nacionalista Escocês.

scoundrel ['skaʊndrəl] *n dated* canalha *mf*.

scour [skaʊə^r] *vt* **-1.** [clean] esfregar **-2.** [search] esquadrinhar.

scourer ['skaʊrə^r] *n* esponja *f* de aço, bombril® *m*.

scourge [skɜ:dʒ] *n* **-1.** [cause of suffering] flagelo *m* **-2.** [critic] tormento *m*.

Scouse *n inf* **-1.** [person] *pessoa proveniente de Liverpool* **-2.** [accent] *dialeto falado pelas pessoas provenientes de Liverpool.*

scout [skaʊt] *n MIL* batedor *m*, explorador *m*.

◆ **Scout** *n* escoteiro *m*.

◆ **scout around** *vi*: **to ~ around (for sthg)** explorar a área (em busca de algo).

scoutmaster *n* chefe *m* dos escoteiros.

scowl [skaʊl] ◇ *n* carranca *f*, cara *f* feia. ◇ *vi* franzir o cenho; **to ~ at sb** fazer cara feia para alguém.

scrabble ['skræbl] *vi* **-1.** [scramble] escalar com dificuldade; **to ~ up/down** subir/descer escalando **-2.** [scrape]: **to ~ at sthg** arranhar algo **-3.** [feel around] escarafunchar; **to ~ around for sthg** escarafunchar à procura de algo.

Scrabble® ['skræbl] *n (U)* Palavras *fpl* Cruzadas *(jogo).*

scraggy ['skrægɪ] (*compar* **-ier**, *superl* **-iest**) *adj inf* magricela.

scram [skræm] (*pt* & *pp* **-med**, *cont* **-ming**) *vi inf* chispar.

scramble ['skræmbl] ◇ *n* briga *f*. ◇ *vi* **-1.** [climb] trepar em **-2.** [move clumsily] caminhar cambaleando; **she ~d for her handbag in the crush** ela teve que brigar pela bolsa no meio do tumulto.

scrambled eggs ['skræmbld-] *npl* ovos *mpl* mexidos.

scrambler ['skræmblə^r] *n COMPUT* misturador *m*.

scrap [skræp] (*pt* & *pp* **-ped**, *cont* **-ping**) ◇ *n* **-1.** [small piece] pedaço *m*; **~ of conversation** trecho *m*; **~ of information** uma informação; **there isn't a ~ of evidence** não há prova alguma; **it won't make a ~ of difference** não fará a mínima diferença **-2.** [metal] sucata *f* **-3.** *inf* [fight, quarrel] briga *f*. ◇ *vt* abandonar.

◆ **scraps** *npl* sobras *fpl*.

scrapbook ['skræpbʊk] *n* album *m* de recortes.

scrap dealer *n* ferro-velho *m*, sucateiro *m*, -ra *f*.

scrape [skreɪp] ◇ *n* **-1.** [scraping noise] rangido *m*, arranhão *m* **-2.** *dated* [difficult situation] enrascada *f*. ◇ *vt* **-1.** [remove]: **to ~ sthg off sthg** raspar algo de algo **-2.** [peel] raspar **-3.** [rub against - car, bumper, glass] riscar; [- knee, elbow, skin] arranhar. ◇ *vi* **-1.**

[rub]: **to ~ against/on sthg** raspar contra/em algo **-2.** [save money] economizar.

◆ **scrape through** *vt fus* passar com as calças na mão.

◆ **scrape together, scrape up** *vt sep* juntar a duras penas.

scraper ['skreɪpəʳ] *n* raspador *m*.

scrap heap *n* **-1.** [of waste metal] monte *m* de sucata **-2.** *fig*: **to end up on the** [of people] **~** acabar rejeitado(da); [of ideas] acabar na lata de lixo.

scrapings ['skreɪpɪŋz] *npl* raspas *fpl*.

scrap merchant *n UK* sucateiro *m*, -ra *f*.

scrap metal *n (U)* sucata *f*, ferro-velho *m*.

scrap paper *UK*, **scratch paper** *US n (U)* papel *m* rascunho.

scrappy ['skræpɪ] (*compar* **-ier**, *superl* **-iest**) *adj pej* desconexo(xa).

scrapyard ['skræpjɑːd] *n* ferro-velho *m*.

scratch [skrætʃ] ◇ *n* **-1.** [gen] arranhão *m* **-2.** *phr*: **to do sthg from ~** fazer algo começando do nada; **to be up to ~** estar à altura. ◇ *vt* **-1.** [wound] arranhar **-2.** [surface] riscar **-3.** [rub] coçar; **to ~ o.s.** coçar-se. ◇ *vi* **-1.** [branch, knife, thorn]: **to ~ at/against sthg** roçar em algo **-2.** [person, animal] coçar-se.

scratchpad ['skrætʃpæd] *n US* bloco *m* de anotações.

scratch paper *n US* = **scrap paper**.

scratchy ['skrætʃɪ] (*compar* **-ier**, *superl* **-iest**) *adj* **-1.** [sound] arranhado(da) **-2.** [material] que pinica.

scrawl [skrɔːl] ◇ *n* rabisco *m*. ◇ *vt* rabiscar.

scrawny ['skrɔːnɪ] (*compar* **-ier**, *superl* **-iest**) *adj* esquelético(ca).

scream [skriːm] ◇ *n* **-1.** [of person] grito *m*; **~s of laughter** gargalhadas *fpl* **-2.** [of tyres, machine] guincho *m* **-3.** *inf* [funny person] pessoa *f* divertida. ◇ *vt* gritar. ◇ *vi* **-1.** [person] gritar, vociferar **-2.** [tyres, machine] guinchar.

scree [skriː] *n (U) acúmulo de pedras soltas na encosta de uma montanha*.

screech [skriːtʃ] ◇ *n* **-1.** [gen] guincho *m* **-2.** [of person] grito *m*; **a ~ of laughter** gargalhadas *fpl*. ◇ *vt* berrar, gritar. ◇ *vi* **-1.** [gen] guinchar **-2.** [person] gritar, berrar.

screen [skriːn] ◇ *n* **-1.** [viewing surface] tela *f* **-2.** *CINEMA*: **the (big) ~** a tela de cinema **-3.** [protective or dividing panel] biombo *m*. ◇ *vt* **-1.** [gen] exibir **-2.** [hide, shield] proteger; **to ~ sb/sthg (from sb/sthg)** proteger alguém/algo (de alguém/algo) **-3.** [question, examine] examinar; **to ~ sb for sthg** fazer exames em alguém em busca de algo.

◆ **screen off** *vt sep* separar com biombo.

screen door *n* porta *f* com tela.

screen dump *n COMPUT* despejo *m* de tela.

screening ['skriːnɪŋ] *n* **-1.** [in cinema] exibição *f*, projeção *f* **-2.** [on TV] exibição *f* **-3.** *(U)* [for security] triagem *f* **-4.** *(U) MED* [examination] exame *m* médico.

screenplay ['skriːnpleɪ] *n* roteiro *m*.

screen print *n* serigrafia *f*.

screen saver *n COMPUT* protetor *m* de tela.

screen test *n* teste *m* de filmagem.

screenwriter ['skriːn,raɪtəʳ] *n* roteirista *mf*.

screw [skruː] ◇ *n* parafuso *m*. ◇ *vt* **-1.** [fix with screws]: **to ~ sthg to sthg** aparafusar algo em algo **-2.** [twist] enroscar **-3.** *vulg* [have sex with] trepar com, foder. ◇ *vi* **-1.** [fix together] enroscar **-2.** *vulg* [have sex] trepar, foder.

◆ **screw up** *vt sep* **-1.** [crumple up] amassar **-2.** [contort, twist] contrair **-3.** *inf* [ruin] ferrar.

screwball ['skruːbɔːl] *n US inf* cabeça *mf* oca.

screwdriver ['skruː,draɪvəʳ] *n* chave *f* de fenda.

screwtop jar ['skruːtɒp-] *n* pote *m* com tampa de rosca.

screwy ['skruːɪ] *adj US inf* maluco(ca).

scribble ['skrɪbl] ◇ *n* rabisco *m*, garrancho *m*. ◇ *vt* & *vi* rabiscar.

scribe [skraɪb] *n fml* escriba *m*.

scrimp [skrɪmp] *vi*: **to ~ and save (to do sthg)** apertar o cinto (para fazer algo).

script [skrɪpt] *n* **-1.** [of play, film] script *m*, roteiro *m* **-2.** [system of writing] escrita *f* **-3.** [handwriting] letra *f*.

scripted ['skrɪptɪd] *adj* com roteiro.

Scriptures ['skrɪptʃəz] *npl*: **the ~** as Escrituras.

scriptwriter ['skrɪpt,raɪtəʳ] *n* roteirista *mf*.

scroll [skrəʊl] ◇ *n* rolo *m* de papel *OR* pergaminho. ◇ *vt COMPUT* rolar.

◆ **scroll down** *vi COMPUT* mover para baixo, baixar.

◆ **scroll up** *vi COMPUT* mover para cima, subir.

scroll bar *n COMPUT* barra *f* de rolagem.

scrooge [skruːdʒ] *n inf pej* avarento *m*, -ta *f*, miserável.

scrotum ['skrəʊtəm] (*pl* **-ta** [-tə], **-tums**) *n* escroto *m*.

scrounge [skraʊndʒ] *inf* ◇ *vt*: **to ~ sthg (off sb)** filar algo (de alguém). ◇ *vi* filar; **to ~ off sb** *UK* viver às custas de alguém.

scrounger ['skraʊndʒəʳ] *n inf* parasita *mf*.

scrub [skrʌb] (*pt* & *pp* **-bed**, *cont* **-bing**) ◇ *n* **-1.** [rub] esfregação *f*; **give it a good ~** dá uma boa esfregada (nisso) **-2.** *(U)* [undergrowth] moita *f*. ◇ *vt* esfregar.

scrubbing brush *UK* ['skrʌbɪŋ-], **scrub brush** *US n* escovão *m*.

scruff [skrʌf] *n ANAT*: **by the ~ of the neck** pelo cangote.

scruffy ['skrʌfɪ] (*compar* **-ier**, *superl* **-iest**) *adj* **-1.** [gen] sujo(ja) **-2.** [room, part of town] bagunçado(da).

scrum(mage) ['skrʌm(ɪdʒ)] *n RUGBY* disputa *f* de bola.

scrumptious ['skrʌmpʃəs] *adj inf* delicioso(sa).

scrumpy ['skrʌmpɪ] *n UK* cidra *f (de alto teor alcoólico)*.

scrunch [skrʌntʃ] *inf* ◇ *vt* amassar. ◇ *vi* ranger, estalar.

scrunchy ['skrʌntʃɪ] (*pl* **-ies**) *n* rabicó *m*.

scruples ['skruːplz] *npl* escrúpulos *mpl*.

scrupulous ['skruːpjʊləs] *adj* **-1.** [fair] escrupuloso(sa) **-2.** [thorough] completo(ta).

scrupulously ['skruːpjʊləslɪ] *adv* **-1.** [fairly] com escrúpulos **-2.** [thoroughly] totalmente.

scrutinize, -ise ['skruːtɪnaɪz] *vt* escrutinar.

scrutiny ['skruːtɪnɪ] *n (U)* escrutínio *m*.

scuba diving ['skuːbə-] *n (U)*: **to go ~** mergulhar com tubo de oxigênio.

scud [skʌd] (*pt* & *pp* **-ded**, *cont* **-ding**) *vi literary* deslizar rapidamente.

scuff [skʌf] *vt* **-1.** [drag] arrastar **- 2.** [damage - shoes] gastar; [- surface] riscar.

scuffle ['skʌfl] <> *n* briga *f.* <> *vi* brigar; **to ~ with sb** brigar com alguém.

scull [skʌl] <> *n* ginga *f.* <> *vi* remar.

scullery ['skʌlərɪ] (*pl* **-ies**) *n* copa *f (para lavar e guardar louça).*

sculpt [skʌlpt] *vt* esculpir.

sculptor ['skʌlptəʳ] *n* escultor *m*, -ra *f.*

sculpture ['skʌlptʃəʳ] <> *n* escultura *f.* <> *vt* esculpir.

scum [skʌm] *n* **-1.** [froth] espuma *f* **- 2.** *v inf pej* [worthless people] escória *f.*

scupper ['skʌpəʳ] *vt* **-1.** *NAUT* [sink] afundar **- 2.** *UK fig* [ruin] arruinar.

scurf [skɜ:f] *n (U)* caspa *f.*

scurrilous ['skʌrələs] *adj fml* difamatório(ria).

scurry ['skʌrɪ] (*pt* & *pp* **-ied**) *vi*: **to ~ off** escapulir-se.

scurvy ['skɜ:vɪ] *n (U)* escorbuto *m.*

scuttle ['skʌtl] <> *n* balde *m* para carvão. <> *vi* correr.

scuzzy (*compar* **-ier**, *superl* **-iest**) *adj inf* chulo(la).

scythe [saɪð] <> *n* foice *f.* <> *vt* ceifar.

SD *abbr of* **South Dakota**.

SDI (*abbr of* **Strategic Defense Initiative**) *n plano estratégico norte-americano de defesa antimíssil, conhecido também como Star Wars.*

SDLP (*abbr of* **Social Democratic and Labour Party**) *n partido político da Irlanda do Norte que defende a integração pacífica com a República da Irlanda.*

SE (*abbr of* **southeast**) SE.

sea [si:] <> *n* mar *m*; **to be at ~** [ship, sailor] estar no mar; **to be all at ~** *fig* [person] estar totalmente perdido(da); **by ~** pelo mar; **by the ~** junto ao mar; **out to ~** [away from land] para alto mar. <> *comp* **-1.** [travel, voyage] marítimo(ma) **- 2.** [animal] marinho(nha).

◆ **seas** *npl*: **the ~s** os mares.

sea air *n (U)* ar *m* do mar.

sea anemone *n* anêmona *f* do mar.

seabed ['si:bed] *n*: **the ~** o fundo do mar.

seabird ['si:bɜ:d] *n* ave *f* marinha.

seaboard ['si:bɔ:d] *n fml* litoral *m.*

sea breeze *n* brisa *f* do mar.

seafaring ['si:ˌfeərɪŋ] *adj* **-1.** [man] do mar **- 2.** [nation] de navegantes.

seafood ['si:fu:d] *n (U)* frutos *mpl* do mar.

seafront ['si:frʌnt] *n* orla *f* marítima.

seagoing ['si:ˌgəʊɪŋ] *adj* de alto-mar.

seagull ['si:gʌl] *n* gaivota *f.*

seahorse ['si:hɔ:s] *n* cavalo *m* marinho.

seal [si:l] (*pl sense 1 only inv OR* **-s**) <> *n* **-1.** [gen] selo *m*; **~ of approval** carimbo *m* de aprovação; **to put** *OR* **set the ~ on sthg** selar algo **- 2.** [animal] foca *f* **- 3.** *TECH* vedação *f.* <> *vt* **-1.** [stick down] selar **- 2.** [block up] vedar.

◆ **seal off** *vt sep* interditar.

sealable ['si:lɪbl] *adj* vedável.

sea lane *n* rota *f* marítima.

sealant ['si:lənt] *n* selador *m.*

sea level *n (U)* nível *m* do mar.

sealing wax ['si:lɪŋ-] *n (U)* lacre *m.*

sea lion (*pl inv OR* **-s**) *n* leão-marinho *m.*

sealskin ['si:lskɪn] *n (U)* pele *f* de foca.

seam [si:m] *n* **-1.** *SEWING* costura *f*; **the room was bursting at the ~s** a sala estava entupida de gente **- 2.** [of coal] veio *m.*

seaman ['si:mən] (*pl* **-men** [-mən]) *n* marinheiro *m.*

seamanship ['si:mənʃɪp] *n (U)* náutica *f.*

sea mist *n (U)* nevoeiro *m* do mar.

seamless ['si:mlɪs] *adj* **-1.** [gen] sem costuras **- 2.** *fig* [faultless] perfeito(ta).

seamstress ['semstrɪs] *n* costureira *f.*

seamy ['si:mɪ] (*compar* **-ier**, *superl* **-iest**) *adj* sórdido(-da).

séance ['seɪɒns] *n* sessão *f* espírita.

seaplane ['si:pleɪn] *n* hidroavião *m.*

seaport ['si:pɔ:t] *n* porto *m* de mar.

search [sɜ:tʃ] <> *n* **-1.** [for lost person, object] procura *f*, busca *f*; **~ for sthg** busca *OR* procura por algo; **in ~ of** a procura de, em busca de **- 2.** [of person, luggage, house] procura *f.* <> *vt* **-1.** [gen] procurar; **to ~ sthg for sthg** procurar algo em algo **- 2.** [mind, memory] vasculhar **- 3.** [frisk] revistar. <> *vi* **-1.** [look for] procurar; **to ~ for sb/sthg** procurar (por) alguém/algo **- 2.** [try to recall]: **to ~ for sthg** tentar lembrar algo.

◆ **search out** *vt sep* descobrir, encontrar.

search engine *n COMPUT* mecanismo *m* de busca.

searcher ['sɜ:tʃəʳ] *n* investigador *m*, -ra *f.*

searching ['sɜ:tʃɪŋ] *adj* **-1.** [question] perspicaz **- 2.** [examination, review] minucioso(sa) **- 3.** [look] penetrante.

searchlight ['sɜ:tʃlaɪt] *n* holofote *m.*

search party *n* equipe *f* de busca.

search warrant *n* mandado *m* de busca.

searing ['sɪərɪŋ] *adj* **-1.** [intense] intenso(sa) **- 2.** [highly critical] contundente.

sea salt *n (U)* sal *m* marinho.

seashell ['si:ʃel] *n* concha *f* (marinha).

seashore ['si:ʃɔ:ʳ] *n*: **the ~** o litoral.

seasick ['si:sɪk] *adj* mareado(da).

seaside ['si:saɪd] *n*: **the ~** a praia.

seaside resort *n* local *m* de veraneio *(na praia).*

season ['si:zn] <> *n* **-1.** [time of year] estação *f* **- 2.** [for particular activity] período *m*, época *f* **- 3.** [of holiday] temporada *f*; **out of ~** fora de temporada **- 4.** [of food]: **in ~** da estação; **out of ~** fora da estação **- 5.** [series - of films] festival *m*; [- of lectures] série *f.* <> *vt* temperar.

seasonal ['si:zənl] *adj* sazonal.

seasoned ['si:znd] *adj* experiente.

seasoning ['si:znɪŋ] *n* tempero *m.*

season ticket *n* bilhete *m* para a temporada.

season-ticket holder *n pessoa que comprou um bilhete que lhe dá direito de assistir a todos os jogos da temporada.*

seat [si:t] <> *n* **-1.** [gen] assento *m* **- 2.** [place to sit] banco *m* **- 3.** [of clothing] fundilho *m* **- 4.** *POL* [in parliament] cadeira *f.* <> *vt* **-1.** [sit down] sentar; **to ~ o.s.** sentar-se **- 2.** [subj: building, vehicle] acomodar.

seat belt *n* cinto *m* de segurança.
seated ['si:tɪd] *adj* sentado(da).
-seater ['si:tə^r] *suffix*: **a two~ car** um carro com dois lugares.
seating ['si:tɪŋ] <> *n (U)* acomodação *f*. <> *comp* de acomodação; ~ **plan** distribuição *f* dos lugares *(na mesa)*.
SEATO ['si:təʊ] (*abbr of* **South-East Asia Treaty Organization**) *n* OTSEA *f*.
sea urchin *n* ouriço-do-mar *m*.
seawall ['si:'wɔ:l] *n* quebra-mar *m*, dique *m*.
seawater ['si:ˌwɔ:tə^r] *n (U)* água *f* do mar.
seaweed ['si:wi:d] *n (U)* alga *f* marinha.
seaworthy ['si:ˌwɜ:ðɪ] *adj* em condições de navegar.
sebaceous [sɪ'beɪʃəs] *adj* sebáceo(cea).
sec. (*abbr of* **second**) *n* seg.
Sec. (*abbr of* **secretary**) secretário *m*, -ria *f*.
SEC (*abbr of* **Securities and Exchange Commission**) *n* *organismo do governo norte-americano que supervisiona as transações da bolsa.*
secateurs [ˌsekə'tɜ:z] *npl* **UK** tesoura *f* para podar.
secede [sɪ'si:d] *vi* **fml** separar-se; **to ~ from sthg** separar-se de algo.
secession [sɪ'seʃn] *n (U)* **fml** secessão *f*.
secluded [sɪ'klu:dɪd] *adj* isolado(da), afastado(da).
seclusion [sɪ'klu:ʒn] *n (U)* isolamento *m*.
second[1] ['sekənd] <> *n* **-1.** [gen] segundo *m* **-2. UK** UNIV diploma *m* com louvor **-3.** AUT: **~ (gear)** segunda *f*. <> *num* segundo(da); **what are you doing on the ~?** o que você vai fazer no dia dois (deste mês)?; **the ~ of March** dia 2 de Março; **... ~ only to Boris** ... perdendo apenas para Boris; **he is ~ to none** ele não perde para ninguém; *see also* **sixth**. <> *vt* secundar.
◆ **seconds** *npl* **-1.** COMM artigos *mpl* de segunda linha **-2.** [of food] repetição *f*.
second[2] [sɪ'kɒnd] *vt* **UK** transferir provisoriamente.
secondary ['sekəndrɪ] *adj* secundário(ria); **to be ~ to sthg** ser secundário para algo.
secondary picketing *n (U)* *piquete feito por pessoas não envolvidas na categoria reivindicante.*
secondary school *n* escola *f* secundária.
second best ['sekənd-] *adj* segundo(da) melhor; **to settle for ~** contentar-se com a segunda opção.
second-class ['sekənd-] *adj* **-1.** [gen] de segunda classe **-2.** *pej* [less important] de segunda classe **-3. UK** UNIV *tipo de grau universitário com louvor concedido por universidades britânicas.*
second cousin ['sekənd-] *n* primo *m*, -ma *f* em segundo grau.
second-degree burn ['sekənd-] *n* queimadura *f* de segundo grau.
seconder ['sekəndə^r] *n* pessoa *f* que secunda.
second floor ['sekənd-] *n* **-1. UK** [third storey] terceiro andar *m* **-2. US** [second storey] segundo andar *m*.
second-guess ['sekənd-] *vt* **-1. US** [with hindsight] julgar a posteriori **-2.** [predict] prever.
second-hand ['sekənd-] <> *adj* **-1.** [gen] de segunda mão **-2.** [shop] de objetos usados. <> *adv* **-1.** [not new] de segunda mão **-2.** *fig* [indirectly]: **to hear sthg ~** ouvir algo de terceiros.
second hand ['sekənd-] *n* ponteiro *m* dos segundos.
second-in-command ['sekənd-] *n* suplente *mf*.
secondly ['sekəndlɪ] *adv* em segundo lugar.
secondment [sɪ'kɒndmənt] *n* **UK** transferência *f* temporária.
second nature ['sekənd-] *n (U)* segunda natureza *f*.
second-rate ['sekənd-] *adj pej* de segunda categoria.
second thought ['sekənd-] *n*: **to have ~s about sthg** estar em dúvida sobre algo; **on ~s UK**, **on ~ US** pensando bem.
secrecy ['si:krəsɪ] *n (U)* sigilo *m*.
secret ['si:krɪt] <> *adj* secreto(ta); **to keep sthg ~** manter algo em segredo. <> *n* segredo *m*; **in ~** em segredo.
secret agent *n* agente *mf* secreto.
secretarial [ˌsekrə'teərɪəl] *adj* **-1.** [course] de secretário **-2.** [staff] de secretários **-3.** [training] para secretariado.
secretariat [ˌsekrə'teərɪət] *n* secretariado *m*.
secretary [**UK** 'sekrətrɪ, **US** 'sekrəˌterɪ] (*pl* **-ies**) *n* **-1.** [gen] secretário *m*, -ria *f* **-2.** POL [minister] ministro *m*, -tra *f*.
secretary-general (*pl* **secretaries-general**) *n* secretário *m*, -ria *f* geral.
Secretary of State *n* **-1. UK** [minister]: **~ (for sthg)** ministro *m* (de algo) **-2. US** [in charge of foreign affairs] secretário *m*, -ria *f* das relações exteriores.
secrete [sɪ'kri:t] *vt* **-1.** [produce] secretar **-2. fml** [hide] ocultar.
secretion [sɪ'kri:ʃn] *n* secreção *f*.
secretive ['si:krətɪv] *adj* **-1.** [person] reservado(da) **-2.** [organization] secreto(ta).
secretly ['si:krɪtlɪ] *adv* secretamente, em segredo.
secret police *n (U)* polícia *f* secreta.
secret service *n* serviço *m* secreto.
sect [sekt] *n* seita *f*.
sectarian [sek'teərɪən] *adj* sectário(ria).
section ['sekʃn] <> *n* seção *f*. <> *vt* **-1.** GEOM seccionar **-2. fml** [cut] seccionar.
sector ['sektə^r] *n* setor *m*.
secular ['sekjʊlə^r] *adj* secular.
secure [sɪ'kjʊə^r] <> *adj* **-1.** [tightly locked up] seguro(ra), protegido(da) **-2.** [fixed in place] seguro(ra), firme **-3.** [safe, not likely to change] garantido(da) **-4.** [strong, solid] firme **-5.** [free of anxiety, confident] confiante. <> *vt* **-1.** [obtain] conseguir, obter **-2.** [make safe] proteger **-3.** [fasten] fechar bem.
securely [sɪ'kjʊəlɪ] *adv* firmemente.
security [sɪ'kjʊərətɪ] (*pl* **-ies**) <> *n* **-1.** [gen] segurança *f* **-2.** *(U)* [legal protection] segurança *f*, garantia *f*; **~ of tenure** cargo *m* vitalício. <> *comp* de segurança.
◆ **securities** *npl* FIN papéis *mpl* negociáveis.
security blanket *n* *cobertor ou outro obejto de estimação com o qual a pessoa se sente protegida.*

Security Council *n*: **the ~** o Conselho de Segurança.

security forces *npl* forças *fpl* de segurança.

security guard *n* (guarda *mf* de) segurança *mf*.

security risk *n* ameaça *f* à segurança.

sedan [sɪ'dæn] *n* *US* sedã *m*.

sedan chair *n* liteira *f*.

sedate [sɪ'deɪt] ◇ *adj* calmo(ma), sossegado(da). ◇ *vt* sedar.

sedation [sɪ'deɪʃn] *n* *(U)* sedação *f*.

sedative ['sedətɪv] ◇ *adj* sedativo(va). ◇ *n* sedativo *m*.

sedentary ['sedntrɪ] *adj* sedentário(ria).

sediment ['sedɪmənt] *n* sedimento *m*.

sedition [sɪ'dɪʃn] *n* *(U)* sedição *f*.

seditious [sɪ'dɪʃəs] *adj* sedicioso(sa).

seduce [sɪ'dju:s] *vt* seduzir; **to ~ sb into doing sthg** persuadir alguém a fazer algo.

seduction [sɪ'dʌkʃn] *n* sedução *f*.

seductive [sɪ'dʌktɪv] *adj* sedutor(ra).

see [si:] (*pt* **saw**, *pp* **seen**) ◇ *vt* **-1.** [gen] ver; **we're going to ~ each other tonight** vamos nos ver hoje à noite; **~ you!** até mais!; **~ you soon/later/tomorrow!** até breve/mais tarde/amanhã! **-2.** [friend, doctor] visitar **-3.** [realize]: **to ~ (that)** perceber que **-4.** [understand] entender **-5.** [accompany] levar, acompanhar **-6.** [find out, ascertain] descobrir; **I'll ~ what I can do** verei o que posso fazer **-7.** [make sure]: **I'll ~ (that the work gets done)** vou providenciar (para que o trabalho fique pronto) **-8.** [judge, consider] ver, considerar **-9.** [subj: day, date]: **today saw ...** hoje aconteceu ... ◇ *vi* **-1.** [perceive with eyes] enxergar **-2.** [understand] entender; **I ~** entendo; **you ~, ...** veja bem, ... **-3.** [find out] ver; **to ~ if one can do sthg** ver se se pode fazer algo; **let's ~, let me ~** vamos ver, vejamos.

◆ **seeing as, seeing that** *conj inf* já que, como.

◆ **see about** *vt fus* **-1.** [organize]: **I'll ~ about getting you some work** vou dar um jeito de te arrumar algum trabalho **-2.** [think about] ver.

◆ **see off** *vt sep* **-1.** [say goodbye to] despedir-se de **-2.** *UK* [chase away] afugentar.

◆ **see through** ◇ *vt fus* [not be deceived by] não se deixar enganar por. ◇ *vt sep* [to conclusion] levar a termo.

◆ **see to** *vt fus* cuidar de.

seed [si:d] ◇ *n* **-1.** [of plant] semente *f* **-2.** *SPORT* pré-selecionado *m*, -da *f*. ◇ *vt*: **she's ~ed first in the world** ela é a número um do mundo.

◆ **seeds** *npl fig* [beginnings] semente *f*.

seedless ['si:dlɪs] *adj* sem semente/caroço.

seedling ['si:dlɪŋ] *n* muda *f*.

seedy ['si:dɪ] (*compar* **-ier**, *superl* **-iest**) *adj* **-1.** [person] maltrapilho(lha) **-2.** [room, area] usado(da).

seek [si:k] (*pt* & *pp* **sought**) *fml* ◇ *vt* procurar; **to ~ to do sthg** procurar fazer algo. ◇ *vi* **-1.** [search]: **to ~ for sthg** procurar (por) algo **-2.** [request]: **to ~ for sthg** pedir algo.

◆ **seek out** *vt sep* perseguir.

seem [si:m] ◇ *vi* parecer; **it ~s too good to be true** parece bom demais para ser verdade; **I ~ to remember that ...** parece que eu me lembro de que ...; **I can't ~ to do that** por mais que eu tente, não consigo fazer isso. ◇ *v impers*: **it ~s (that)** parece que.

seeming ['si:mɪŋ] *adj fml* aparente.

seemingly ['si:mɪŋlɪ] *adv* aparentemente.

seemly (*compar* **-ier**, *superl* **-iest**) *adj literary* decoroso(sa).

seen [si:n] *pp* ▷ **see**.

seep [si:p] *vi* infiltrar-se, penetrar.

seersucker ['sɪə,sʌkə^r] *n* *(U)* *tecido leve de algodão listado.*

seesaw ['si:sɔ:] *n* gangorra *f*.

seethe [si:ð] *vi* fervilhar; **to be seething with sthg** estar fervilhando com algo.

seething ['si:ðɪŋ] *adj* **-1.** [furious] furioso(sa) **-2.** [teeming] fervilhante.

see-through *adj* transparente.

segment ['segmənt] *n* **-1.** [of market, report, audience] segmento *m* **-2.** [of fruit] gomo *m*.

segregate ['segrɪgeɪt] *vt* segregar.

segregation [,segrɪ'geɪʃn] *n* *(U)* segregação *f*.

Seine [seɪn] *n*: **the (River) ~** o (Rio) Sena.

seismic ['saɪzmɪk] *adj* sísmico(ca).

seize [si:z] *vt* **-1.** [grab] agarrar, pegar **-2.** [win, capture] tomar **-3.** [arrest] prender, deter **-4.** [take advantage of] aproveitar.

◆ **seize (up)on** *vt fus* valer-se de.

◆ **seize up** *vi* **-1.** [body] enrijecer **-2.** [engine] emperrar.

seizure ['si:ʒə^r] *n* **-1.** *MED* ataque *m* **-2.** *(U)* [taking, capturing] tomada *f*.

seldom ['seldəm] *adv* raramente.

select [sɪ'lekt] ◇ *adj* **-1.** [carefully chosen] selecionado(da) **-2.** [exclusive] seleto(ta). ◇ *vt* selecionar.

select committee *n* comissão *f* parlamentar de inquérito.

selected [sɪ'lektɪd] *adj* escolhido(da).

selection [sɪ'lekʃn] *n* **-1.** [gen] seleção *f* **-2.** [range of goods] coleção *f*.

selective [sɪ'lektɪv] *adj* seletivo(va).

selector [sɪ'lektə^r] *n* *SPORT* selecionador *m*, -ra *f*.

self [self] (*pl* **selves**) *n*: **she's her old ~** ela volta a ser ela mesma; **the ~** o eu.

self- [self] *prefix* auto-; **~defence** *UK*, **~defense** *US* autodefesa *f*; **~accusation** auto-acusação *f*.

self-addressed envelope [-ə'drest-] *n* envelope *m* de resposta.

self-addressed stamped envelope [-ə,drest'stæmpt-] *n* *US* envelope *m* de resposta pré-pago.

self-adhesive *adj* auto-adesivo(va).

self-appointed [-ə'pɔɪntɪd] *adj pej* autodesignado(da).

self-assembly *adj* *UK* desmontável.

self-assertive *adj* seguro(ra) de si.

self-assurance *n* *(U)* autoconfiança *f*.

self-assured *adj* confiante em si mesmo(ma), seguro(ra) de si.

self-catering *adj* sem refeições incluídas.

self-centred [-'sentəd] *adj* egocêntrico(ca).

self-cleaning *adj* autolimpante.

self-coloured *adj* *UK* unicolor.

self-confessed [-kən'fest] *adj* assumido(da).

self-confidence *n* autoconfiança *f*.
self-confident *adj* **-1.** [person] seguro(ra) de si **-2.** [remark, attitude] que passa segurança.
self-conscious *adj* inibido(da).
self-contained [-kən'teɪnd] *adj* **-1.** [person] reservado(da) **-2.** [flat] independente.
self-control *n (U)* autocontrole *m*.
self-controlled *adj* controlado(da), sereno(na).
self-defence *n (U)* legítima defesa *f*; **in ~** em legítima defesa.
self-denial *n (U)* abnegação *f*.
self-destruct [-dɪs'trʌkt] ◇ *adj* autodestrutivo (va). ◇ *vi* autodestruir-se.
self-determination *n (U)* autodeterminação *f*.
self-discipline *n (U)* autodisciplina *f*.
self-doubt *n (U)* insegurança *f*.
self-drive *adj UK* alugado(da) sem motorista.
self-educated *adj* autodidata.
self-effacing [-ɪ'feɪsɪŋ] *adj* modesto(ta), humilde.
self-employed [-ɪm'plɔɪd] *adj* autônomo(ma), que trabalha por conta própria.
self-esteem *n (U)* amor-próprio *m*.
self-evident *adj* óbvio(via).
self-explanatory *adj* claro(ra), manifesto(ta).
self-expression *n (U)* expressão *f* própria.
self-focusing [-'fəʊkəsɪŋ] *adj* com foco automático.
self-government *n (U)* governo *m* autônomo.
self-help *n (U)* auto-ajuda *f*.
self-important *adj* ***pej*** presunçoso(sa), convencido(da).
self-imposed [-ɪm'pəʊzd] *adj* imposto a si mesmo, imposta a si mesma.
self-indulgent *adj* ***pej*** comodista, que se permite excessos.
self-inflicted [-ɪn'flɪktɪd] *adj* auto-infligido(da).
self-interest *n (U)* ***pej*** interesse *m* pessoal *OR* próprio.
selfish ['selfɪʃ] *adj* egoísta.
selfishness ['selfɪʃnɪs] *n (U)* egoísmo *m*.
selfless ['selflɪs] *adj* desinteressado(da).
self-locking [-'lɒkɪŋ] *adj* de fechamento automático.
self-made *adj* que se fez por si mesmo(ma).
self-opinionated *adj* ***pej*** presunçoso(sa).
self-perpetuating [-pə'petʃʊeɪtɪŋ] *adj* que se perpetua a si mesmo(ma).
self-pity *n (U)* ***pej*** autocomiseração *f*.
self-portrait *n* auto-retrato *m*.
self-possessed [-pə'zest] *adj* dono de si mesmo, dona de si mesma.
self-preservation *n* autopreservação *f*.
self-proclaimed [-prə'kleɪmd] *adj* ***pej*** autodenominado(da).
self-raising flour *UK* [-ˌreɪzɪŋ-], **self-rising flour** *US n (U)* farinha *f* com fermento.
self-regard *n (U)* **-1.** [self-esteem] amor-próprio *m* **-2.** ***pej*** [conceit] narcisismo *m*.
self-regulating [-'regjʊleɪtɪŋ] *adj* auto-regulador (ra).
self-reliant *adj* independente.
self-respect *n (U)* amor *m* próprio.
self-respecting [-rɪs'pektɪŋ] *adj* que se presta, digno(na).
self-restraint *n (U)* autocontrole *m*.
self-righteous *adj* ***pej*** hipócrita.
self-rising flour *n US* = **self-raising flour**.
self-rule *n (U)* autonomia *f (de um governo)*.
self-sacrifice *n (U)* abnegação *f*.
selfsame ['selfseɪm] *adj* mesmíssimo(míssima).
self-satisfied *adj* ***pej*** convencido(da).
self-sealing [-'si:lɪŋ] *adj* auto-adesivo(va).
self-seeking [-'si:kɪŋ] ***pej*** *adj* interesseiro(ra).
self-service ◇ *n (U)* auto-serviço *m*, self-service *m*. ◇ *comp* de auto-serviço, self-service; **a ~ shop** uma loja self-service.
self-starter *n* **-1.** *AUT* arranque *m* automático **-2.** [person] empreendedor *m*, -ra *f*.
self-styled [-'staɪld] *adj* ***pej*** pretenso(sa).
self-sufficient *adj*: **~ (in sthg)** auto-suficiente (em algo).
self-supporting [-sə'pɔ:tɪŋ] *adj* economicamente independente.
self-tanning *adj* autobronzeador(ra).
self-taught *adj* autodidata.
self-test *vi COMPUT* autotestar.
self-willed *adj* ***pej*** obstinado(da).
sell [sel] (*pt* & *pp* **sold**) ◇ *vt* **-1.** vender; **to ~ sthg to sb, to ~ sb sthg** vender algo para alguém; **to ~ sthg for** vender algo por; **to ~ o.s.** vender-se; **to ~ o.s. short** desmerecer-se **-2.** ***fig*** [make enthusiastic about]: **to ~ sthg to sb, to ~ sb sthg** vender algo para alguém; **to ~ sb an idea** vender uma idéia a alguém; **I'm not really sold on the idea** não consigo comprar essa idéia. ◇ *vi* vender; **to ~ for** *OR* **at** ser vendido(da) por *OR* a.
◆ **sell off** *vt sep* liquidar.
◆ **sell out** ◇ *vt sep*: **to be sold out** estar esgotado(da). ◇ *vi* **-1.** [shop, ticket office]: **to ~ out (of sthg)** vender todo o estoque (de algo) **-2.** [betray one's principles] vender-se.
◆ **sell up** *vi* vender tudo.
sell-by date *n UK* prazo *m* de validade.
seller ['selə^r] *n* vendedor *m*, -ra *f*.
seller's market *n* mercado *m* de demanda *OR* favorável ao vendedor.
selling ['selɪŋ] *n (U)* venda *f*.
selling price ['selɪŋ-] *n* preço *m* de venda.
Sellotape® ['seləteɪp] *n UK* fita *f* adesiva, durex® *m*.
◆ **sellotape** *vt* segurar com fita adesiva.
sell-out *n* **-1.** [performance, match] sucesso *m* de bilheteria **-2.** [of principles] traição *f*.
sell-through *n US COMM* venda *f* direta (ao consumidor).
seltzer *n US* água *f* de soda.
selves [selvz] *pl* ▷ **self**.
semantic [sɪ'mæntɪk] *adj* semântico(ca).
◆ **semantics** *n (U)* semântica *f*.
semaphore ['seməfɔ:^r] *n (U)* semáforo *m*.
semblance ['sembləns] *n fml* aparência *f*.
semen ['si:mən] *n (U)* sêmen *m*.
semester [sɪ'mestə^r] *n* semestre *m*.
semi ['semɪ] *n* **-1.** ***UK inf*** [house] casa *f* geminada **-2.** ***US*** [lorry] caminhão *m* articulado.

semi- ['semɪ] *prefix* semi-.
semi-automatic *adj* semi-automático(ca).
semicircle ['semɪˌsɜ:kl] *n* semicírculo *m*.
semicircular [ˌsemɪ'sɜ:kjʊlə^r] *adj* semicircular.
semicolon [ˌsemɪ'kəʊlən] *n* ponto-e-vírgula *m*.
semi-conscious *adj* semiconsciente.
semi-detached ◇ *adj UK* geminado(do). ◇ *n UK* casa *f* geminada.
semi-final *n* semifinal *f*.
semi-finalist *n* semifinalista *mf*.
seminal *adj* **-1.** [important] muito influente **-2.** [of semen] seminal.
seminar ['semɪnɑ:^r] *n* seminário *m*.
seminary ['semɪnərɪ] (*pl* **-ies**) *n RELIG* seminário *m*.
semiotics *n (U)* semiótica *f*.
semi-precious *adj* semiprecioso(sa).
semi-skilled *adj* semi-especializado(da).
semi-skimmed [-'skɪmd] *adj* semidesnatado(-da).
semi-trailer *n* **-1.** [trailer] reboque *m* **-2.** *US* [lorry] caminhão *m* articulado.
semolina [ˌsemə'li:nə] *n (U)* semolina *f*.
Sen. -1. (*abbr of* **senator**) Sen. **-2.** (*abbr of* **Senior**) sênior.
Senate ['senɪt] *n POL*: **the** ~ o Senado; **the United States** ~ o Senado dos Estados Unidos.

SENATE

Senado e Câmara de Representantes (*House of Representatives*) formam o poder legislativo nos EUA. Composto de 100 membros, dois senadores por estado, o Senado norte-americano tem entre suas prerrogativas a solicitação do *impeachment* do presidente da república.

senator ['senətə^r] *n* senador *m*, -ra *f*.
send [send] (*pt* & *pp* **sent**) *vt* **-1.** [letter, message, money] enviar, mandar; **to** ~ **sb sthg, to** ~ **sthg to sb** enviar *OR* mandar algo para alguém **-2.** [tell to go]: **to** ~ **sb (to)** mandar alguém (para); **to** ~ **sb for sthg** mandar alguém buscar algo **-3.** [propel] lançar **-4.** [into a specific state] deixar; **to** ~ **sb mad** deixar alguém louco(ca); **to** ~ **to sleep** dar sono em alguém; **to** ~ **sb flying** arremessar alguém longe.
◆ **send back** *vt sep* devolver; **to** ~ **sb back** fazer alguém voltar.
◆ **send down** *vt sep inf* encarcerar.
◆ **send for** *vt fus* **-1.** [person] mandar chamar **-2.** [by post] encomendar.
◆ **send in** *vt sep* **-1.** [visitor] fazer entrar **-2.** [troops, police] enviar, mandar **-3.** [submit] enviar.
◆ **send off** *vt sep* **-1.** [by post] enviar *(pelo correio)* **-2.** *SPORT* expulsar.
◆ **send off for** *vt fus* encomendar *(pelo correio)*.
◆ **send up** *vt sep inf* **-1.** *UK* [imitate] arremedar, imitar **-2.** *US* [send to prison] mandar para a prisão.
sender ['sendə^r] *n* remetente *mf*.
send-off *n* despedida *f*.
send-up *n UK inf* paródia *f*, sátira *f*.
Senegal [ˌsenɪ'gɔ:l] *n* Senegal; **in** ~ no Senegal.
Senegalese [ˌsenɪgə'li:z] ◇ *adj* senegalês(esa). ◇ *npl*: **the** ~ os senegaleses.
senile ['si:naɪl] *adj* senil.
senile dementia *n (U)* demência *f* senil.
senility [sɪ'nɪlətɪ] *n (U)* senilidade *f*.
senior ['si:njə^r] ◇ *adj* **-1.** [highest-ranking] superior(ra) **-2.** [higher-ranking]: ~ **to sb** superior a alguém **-3.** *SCH* [pupils, classes] veterano(na); ~ **year** *US último ano do ensino secundário e das universidades nos Estados Unidos.* ◇ *n* **-1.** [older person] mais velho(lha); **I'm five years his** ~ sou cinco anos mais velho do que ele **-2.** *SCH* & *UNIV* veterano *m*, -na *f*.
senior citizen *n* idoso *m*, -sa *f*.
senior high school *n US* escola *f* de ensino médio *(dos 16 aos 18 anos)*.
seniority [ˌsi:nɪ'ɒrətɪ] *n (U)* grau *m* de poder ou competência.
sensation [sen'seɪʃn] *n* sensação *f*.
sensational [sen'seɪʃənl] *adj* **-1.** [causing a stir] sensacional **-2.** *inf* [wonderful] sensacional **-3.** [sensationalist] sensacionalista.
sensationalist [sen'seɪʃnəlɪst] *adj pej* sensacionalista.
sense [sens] ◇ *n* **-1.** [gen] sentido *m*; **to make** ~ [have clear meaning] fazer sentido; [be logical] ser lógico(ca); **to make** ~ **of sthg** entender algo **-2.** [feeling, sensation - of guilt, terror, honour] sentimento *m*; [- of justice, duty, urgency] senso *m* **-3.** [natural ability]: ~ **of direction** senso *m* de direção; ~ **of style** idéia *f* de estilo **-4.** *(U)* [wisdom, reason] bom senso *m*, sabedoria *f*; **to talk** ~ falar seriamente; **there's no** ~ **in arguing/fighting** não faz sentido brigar/lutar **-5.** *phr*: **to come to one's** ~**s** [be sensible again] recobrar o juízo; [regain consciousness] recobrar os sentidos; **to be out of one's** ~**s** perder o juízo. ◇ *vt* sentir; **to** ~ **that** sentir que.
◆ **in a sense** *adv* de certo modo, em certo sentido.
senseless ['senslɪs] *adj* **-1.** [stupid] sem sentido, estúpido(da) **-2.** [unconscious] inconsciente; **to knock sb** ~ bater em alguém até ficar inconsciente.
sensibilities [ˌsensɪ'bɪlətɪz] *npl* sensibilidade *f*.
sensible ['sensəbl] *adj* **-1.** [reasonable, practical] prático(ca) **-2.** [person] sensato(ta).
sensibly ['sensəblɪ] *adv* sensatamente.
sensitive ['sensɪtɪv] *adj* **-1.** [eyes, skin]: ~ **(to sthg)** sensível (a algo) **-2.** [understanding, aware]: ~ **(to sthg)** compreensivo(va) (com algo) **-3.** [easily hurt, touchy]: ~ **(to/about sthg)** sensível *OR* suscetível (a algo) **-4.** [controversial] delicado(da) **-5.** [instrument] sensível.
sensitivity [ˌsensɪ'tɪvətɪ] *n* sensibilidade *f*.
sensor ['sensə^r] *n* sensor *m*.
sensual ['sensjʊəl] *adj* sensual.
sensuous ['sensjʊəs] *adj* sensual.
sent [sent] *pt* & *pp* ▷ **send**.
sentence ['sentəns] ◇ *n* **-1.** [group of words] frase *f*, oração *f* **-2.** *JUR* sentença *f*. ◇ *vt*: **to** ~ **sb (to sthg)** condenar alguém (a algo).
sententious [sen'tenʃəs] *adj pej* sentencioso(sa).
sentiment ['sentɪmənt] *n* **-1.** [feeling] sentimento *m* **-2.** [opinion] opinião *f* **-3.** *(U) pej* [sentimentality] sentimentalismo *m*.

sentimental [ˌsentɪ'mentl] *adj* **-1.** *pej* [over-emotional] sentimental **-2.** [emotional] sentimental.
sentimentality [ˌsentɪmen'tælətɪ] *n (U) pej* sentimentalismo *m.*
sentinel ['sentɪnl] *n* sentinela *mf.*
sentry ['sentrɪ] (*pl* **-ies**) *n* sentinela *mf.*
Seoul [səʊl] *n* Seul.
separable ['seprəbl] *adj*: ~ **(from sthg)** separável (de algo).
separate [*adj* & *n* 'seprət, *vb* 'sepəreɪt] ◇ *adj* **-1.** [not joined, apart] separado(da); ~ **from sthg** separado(da) de algo **-2.** [individual] separado(da), diferente **-3.** [distinct] distinto(ta). ◇ *vt* separar; **to ~ sb/sthg from** separar alguém/algo de; **to ~ sb/sthg into** separar alguém/algo em; **to ~ sb/sthgfrom** separar alguém/algo de. ◇ *vi* **-1.** [gen] separar-se; **to ~ into sthg** separar-se em algo **-2.** [go different ways]: **to ~ (from sb/sthg)** separar-se (de alguém/algo).
◆ **separates** *npl UK* peças *fpl* avulsas *(de roupa).*
separated ['sepəreɪtɪd] *adj* separado(da).
separately ['seprətlɪ] *adv* separadamente.
separation [ˌsepə'reɪʃn] *n* separação *f*; ~ **(from sb/sthg)** separação (de alguém/algo).
separatism *n* separatismo *m.*
separatist ['seprətɪst] *n* separatista *mf.*
sepia ['si:pjə] *adj* sépia.
Sept. (*abbr of* **September**) set.
September [sep'tembəʳ] ◇ *n* setembro; **when are you going? - ~** quando você vai? - em setembro; **one of the hottest ~s on record** um dos setembros mais quentes que já se registrou; **in ~** em setembro; **last/this/next ~** em setembro do ano passado/deste ano/do ano que vem; **by ~** até setembro; **every ~** todos os anos em setembro; **during ~** em setembro, durante o mês de setembro; **at the beginning/end of ~** no início/fim de setembro; **in the middle of ~** em meados de setembro, no meio do mês de setembro. ◇ *comp* de setembro; **~ birthday** aniversário *m* em setembro.
septet *n* septeto *m.*
septic ['septɪk] *adj* séptico(ca); **to go ~** infeccionar.
septicaemia *UK*, **septicemia** *US* [ˌseptɪ'si:mɪə] *n (U)* septicemia *f.*
septic tank *n* fossa *f* séptica.
sepulchre *UK*, **sepulcher** *US* ['sepʌlkər] *n literary* sepulcro *m.*
sequel ['si:kwəl] *n* **-1.** [book, film]: **~ to sthg** continuação *f* de algo **-2.** [consequence]: **~ to sthg** seqüela *f* de algo.
sequence ['si:kwəns] *n* **-1.** [gen] seqüência *f*; **in ~** em seqüência **-2.** [series] seqüência *f*, sucessão *f.*
sequester, sequestrate *vt* JUR confiscar, colocar sob custódia.
sequin ['si:kwɪn] *n* lantejoula *f.*
sera ['sɪərə] *pl* ▷ **serum.**
Serb *adj* & *n* = **Serbian.**
Serbia ['sɜ:bjə] *n* Sérvia; **in ~** na Sérvia.
Serbian ['sɜ:bjən], **Serb** [sɜ:b] ◇ *adj* sérvio(via). ◇ *n* **-1.** [person] sérvio *m*, -via *f* **-2.** [language] sérvio *m.*
Serbo-Croat [ˌsɜ:bəʊ'krəʊæt], **Serbo-Croatian** [ˌsɜ:bəʊkrəʊ'eɪʃn] ◇ *adj* servo-croata. ◇ *n* [language] servo-croata *m.*
serenade [ˌserə'neɪd] ◇ *n* serenata *f.* ◇ *vt* fazer uma serenata para.
serene [sɪ'ri:n] *adj* sereno(na).
serenely [sɪ'ri:nlɪ] *adv* serenamente.
serenity [sɪ'renətɪ] *n (U)* serenidade *f.*
serf [sɜ:f] *n* HIST servo *m*, -va *f.*
serge [sɜ:dʒ] *n (U)* sarja *f.*
sergeant ['sɑ:dʒənt] *n* **-1.** MIL sargento *m* **-2.** POLICE tenente *m.*
sergeant major *n* primeiro-sargento *m.*
serial ['sɪərɪəl] *n* série *f*, seriado *m.*
serialize, -ise ['sɪərɪəlaɪz] *vt* publicar em folhetim.
serial killer *n* assassino *m*, -na *f* em série, serial killer *m.*
serial number *n* número *m* de série.
series ['sɪəri:z] (*pl inv*) *n* **-1.** [sequence] série *f* **-2.** RADIO & TV série *f*, seriado *m.*
serious ['sɪərɪəs] *adj* **-1.** [gen] sério(ria); **are you ~?** fala sério? **-2.** [problem, illness] grave.
serious crime *n* crime *m* grave.
seriously ['sɪərɪəslɪ] *adv* **-1.** [earnestly] seriamente; **to take sb/sthg ~** levar alguém/algo a sério **-2.** [very badly] gravemente.
seriousness ['sɪərɪəsnɪs] *n (U)* **-1.** [of person, expression, voice] seriedade *f*; **in all ~** seriamente **-2.** [of illness, situation, loss] gravidade *f.*
sermon ['sɜ:mən] *n* **-1.** RELIG sermão *m* **-2.** *fig* & *pej* [lecture] sermão *m.*
serpent ['sɜ:pənt] *n literary* serpente *f.*
serrated [sɪ'reɪtɪd] *adj* serrilhado(da), dentado(da).
serum ['sɪərəm] (*pl* **serums** OR **sera**) *n* soro *m.*
servant ['sɜ:vənt] *n* criado *m*, -da *f*, empregado *m*, -da *f.*
serve [sɜ:v] ◇ *n* SPORT serviço *m*, saque *m.* ◇ *vt* **-1.** [gen] servir; **to ~ sthg to sb, to ~ sb sthg** servir algo a alguém **-2.** [have effect]: **to ~ to do sthg** servir para fazer algo; **to ~ a purpose** cumprir o propósito **-3.** [provide] abastecer; **which motorway ~s Birmingham** que rodovia atende à região de Birmingham? **-4.** JUR: **to ~ sb with sthg, to ~ sthg on sb** entregar algo a alguém **-5.** [complete, carry out] cumprir; **he's serving time** ele está cumprindo pena **-6.** SPORT servir, sacar **-7.** *phr*: **it ~s you right** bem feito! ◇ *vi* **-1.** [be employed - as soldier] servir o exército; [- in profession, on committee] prestar serviços **-2.** [function]: **to ~ as sthg** servir como algo **-3.** [in shop, bar etc] servir **-4.** SPORT sacar.
◆ **serve out, serve up** *vt sep* servir.
server ['sɜ:vəʳ] *n* COMPUT servidor *m.*
service ['sɜ:vɪs] ◇ *n* **-1.** [gen] serviço *m*; **in ~** em funcionamento; **out of ~** fora de serviço **-2.** *(U)* [in shop, bar etc] atendimento *m* **-3.** [mechanical check] revisão *f* **-4.** RELIG serviço *m*, culto *m* **-5.** [set of tableware] jogo *m*; **dinner ~** aparelho *m* de jantar **-6.** SPORT serviço *m*, saque *m* **-7.** [use, help]: **to be of ~ (to sb)** servir (a alguém). ◇ *vt* **-1.** [car, machine] fazer a revisão de **-2.** FIN [debt, loan] pagar os juros de.
◆ **services** *npl* **-1.** [on motorway] estação *f* de serviços **-2.** [armed forces]: **the ~s** as forças

armadas **-3.** [help] serviços *mpl*.

serviceable ['sɜ:vɪsəbl] *adj* resistente, prático(ca).

service area *n* estação *f* de serviços.

service charge *n* taxa *f* de serviço.

service industries *npl* setor *m* de prestação de serviços.

serviceman ['sɜ:vɪsmən] (*pl* **-men** [-mən]) *n* *MIL* militar *m*.

service provider *n COMPUT* provedor *m*.

service station *n* posto *m* de gasolina, posto *m* de serviços.

servicewoman ['sɜ:vɪs,wʊmən] (*pl* **-women**) *n MIL* militar *f*.

serviette [,sɜ:vɪ'et] *n* guardanapo *m*.

servile ['sɜ:vaɪl] *adj* servil.

servility [sɜ:'vɪlətɪ] *n (U)* servilismo *m*.

serving ['sɜ:vɪŋ] ◇ *adj* **-1.** [spoon, dish, fork] de servir **-2.** [member, chairman] que presta serviços. ◇ *n* [portion] porção *f*.

sesame ['sesəmɪ] *n (U)* gergelim *m*, sésamo *m*; **open ~!** abre-te, sésamo!

session ['seʃn] *n* **-1.** [gen] sessão *f*; **in ~** em sessão **-2.** *US* [school term] período *m* letivo.

set [set] (*pt* & *pp* **set**, *cont* **-ting**) ◇ *adj* **-1.** [specified, prescribed] estabelecido(da) **-2.** [fixed, rigid] fixo(xa); **~ phrase** frase *f* feita; **to be ~ in one's ways** ter costumes arraigados **-3.** [ready] pronto(ta); **~ for sthg/to do sthg** pronto(ta) para algo/para fazer algo **-4.** [determined]**: to be ~ on sthg/on doing sthg** estar empenhado(da) em algo/em fazer algo; **to be dead ~ against sthg** ser completamente contra algo. ◇ *n* **-1.** [collection, group - stamps] série *f*; [- chess, tea] jogo *m* (de); [- keys, tyres, saucepans] conjunto *m*; [- books] coleção *f* (de) **-2.** [apparatus] aparelhagem *f* **-3.** [of film, play] cenário *m* **-4.** *TENNIS* set *m*. ◇ *vt* **-1.** [put in specified position, place] pôr, colocar **-2.** [fix, insert]**: to ~ sthg in(to) sthg** fixar algo em algo **-3.** [indicating change of state or activity] pôr; **to ~ sb free** pôr alguém em liberdade; **to ~ sb's mind at rest** tranqüilizar alguém; **to ~ sthg in motion** pôr algo em movimento; **to ~ sthg right** emendar algo; **to ~ sb thinking** fazer alguém pensar; **to ~ sthg on fire** pôr fogo em algo **-4.** [lay, prepare in advance] pôr, colocar **-5.** [adjust] ajustar, botar; **she ~ the meter at zero** ela ajustou o medidor para zero **-6.** [decide on] estabelecer, fixar **-7.** [establish, create - example] dar; [- precedent] abrir; [- trend] impor; [- record] estabelecer **-8.** [assign - target, problem] determinar; [- school work] passar; [- exam, test work] aplicar **-9.** *MED* [mend] recompor **-10.** *MUS* [arrange]**: to ~ sthg to music** musicar algo **-11.** [story] passar-se; **the film is ~ in Scotland** o filme se passa na Escócia **-12.** [hair] fazer mise-en-plis. ◇ *vi* **-1.** [sun] pôr-se **-2.** [solidify - jelly] endurecer; [- glue, cement] secar.

◆ **set about** *vt fus*: **to ~ about sthg** começar algo; **to ~ about doing sthg** pôr-se a fazer algo.

◆ **set against** *vt sep* **-1.** [compare] comparar **-2.** [put in opposition] pôr contra; **the war ~ brother against brother** a guerra colocou irmão contra irmão **-3.** *FIN* compensar com; **we can ~ our expenses against tax** podemos deduzir nossos gastos do imposto de renda.

◆ **set ahead** *vt sep US* [clock] adiantar.

◆ **set apart** *vt sep* distinguir; **to ~ sb/sthg apart from** distinguir alguém/algo de.

◆ **set aside** *vt sep* **-1.** [keep, save] guardar **-2.** [not consider] deixar de lado.

◆ **set back** *vt sep* **-1.** [delay] atrasar **-2.** *inf* [cost]: **this book ~ me back £20** este livro me custou £20.

◆ **set down** *vt sep* **-1.** [write down] pôr por escrito **-2.** [put down] deixar.

◆ **set in** *vi* manifestar-se.

◆ **set off** ◇ *vt sep* **-1.** [initiate, cause] provocar **-2.** [ignite] fazer explodir. ◇ *vi* pôr-se a caminho.

◆ **set on** *vt sep* atiçar em; **he ~ the dogs on her** ele atiçou os cachorros nela.

◆ **set out** ◇ *vt sep* **-1.** [arrange, spread out] dispor **-2.** [clarify, explain] expor. ◇ *vt fus*: **to ~ out to do sthg** propor-se a fazer algo. ◇ *vi* pôr-se a caminho.

◆ **set up** ◇ *vt sep* **-1.** [gen] montar **-2.** [establish, arrange - company] montar, fundar; [- committee, organization] criar; [- interview, meeting] organizar; **to ~ o.s. up** estabelecer-se; **to ~ up house** *OR* **home** instalar-se **-3.** *inf* [make appear guilty] convencer; **to ~ sb up** armar contra alguém; **I was ~ up!** me armaram uma! ◇ *vi* estabelecer-se.

setback ['setbæk] *n* contratempo *m*.

set menu *n* cardápio *m* a preço fixo.

set piece *n ART* & *LITERATURE* *parte de um filme, romance ou música de grande efeito dramático e que normalmente não é parte essencial da história principal.*

set square *n UK* esquadro *m*.

settee [se'ti:] *n* sofá *m*.

setter ['setə^r] *n* cão *m* de caça.

setting ['setɪŋ] *n* **-1.** [surroundings] cenário *m* **-2.** [of dial, control] posição *f*.

settle ['setl] ◇ *vt* **-1.** [conclude, decide] resolver **-2.** [pay] saldar **-3.** [make comfortable] acomodar; **to ~ o.s. somewhere** acomodar-se em algum lugar **-4.** [calm] acalmar, tranqüilizar. ◇ *vi* **-1.** [go to live] instalar-se **-2.** [make o.s. comfortable] acomodar-se **-3.** [come to rest] depositar-se; **to ~ on sthg** pousar em algo.

◆ **settle down** *vi* **-1.** [give one's attention]: **to ~ down (to sthg/to doing sthg)** dedicar-se (a algo/a fazer algo) **-2.** [become stable] estabelecer-se **-3.** [make o.s. comfortable] acomodar-se; **to ~ down (for sthg)** preparar-se (para algo) **-4.** [become calm] acalmar-se.

◆ **settle for** *vt fus* conformar-se com.

◆ **settle in** *vi* **-1.** [new house] instalar-se **-2.** [in new job] adaptar-se.

◆ **settle on** *vt fus* decidir-se por.

◆ **settle up** *vi*: **to ~ up (with sb)** ajustar as contas (com alguém).

settled ['setld] *adj* estável.

settlement ['setlmənt] *n* **-1.** [agreement] acordo *m* **-2.** [village] povoado *m* **-3.** [payment] pagamento *m*.

settler ['setlə^r] *n* colonizador *m*, -ra *f*.

set-to *n inf* briga *f*.

set-up *n inf* **-1.** [system, organization] estrutura *f* **-2.** [deception to incriminate] armação *f*.

seven ['sevn] *num* sete; *see also* **six**.

seventeen [ˌsevn'tiːn] *num* dezessete; *see also* **six**.
seventeenth [ˌsevn'tiːnθ] *num* décimo sétimo, décima sétima; *see also* **sixth**.
seventh ['sevnθ] *num* sétimo(ma); *see also* **sixth**.
seventh heaven *n (U)*: **to be in ~** estar no sétimo céu.
seventieth ['sevntjəθ] *num* septuagésimo(ma); *see also* **sixth**.
seventy ['sevntɪ] *num* setenta; *see also* **sixty**.
sever ['sevə[r]] *vt* **-1.** [rope, limb] cortar **-2.** [relationship] romper.
several ['sevrəl] <> *adj* vários(rias). <> *pron* vários *mpl*, -rias *fpl*.
severance ['sevrəns] *n (U) fml* rompimento *m*.
severance pay *n (U)* indenização *m* por demissão.
severe [sɪ'vɪə[r]] *adj* **-1.** [extreme, bad - shock] forte; [- weather] ruim; [- pain] agudo(da); [- injury, illness] grave **-2.** [stern] severo(ra).
severely [sɪ'vɪəlɪ] *adv* **-1.** [extremely, badly] gravemente **-2.** [sternly] severamente.
severity [sɪ'verətɪ] *n (U)* **-1.** [seriousness] gravidade *f* **-2.** [strength] força *f* **-3.** [sternness] severidade *f*.
sew [səʊ] (*UK pp* **sewn**, *US pp* **sewed** *OR* **sewn**) *vt & vi* costurar.
◆ **sew up** *vt sep* **-1.** [join] costurar **-2.** *inf* [arrange, fix] costurar; **it's all sewn up!** está tudo muito bem costurado!
sewage ['suːɪdʒ] *n (U)* águas *fpl* residuais.
sewage farm *n* estação *f* de tratamento de esgoto.
sewage works *n* estação *f* de tratamento de esgoto.
sewer ['sʊə[r]] *n* esgoto *m*; **the city's ~ system** o sistema de esgotos da cidade.
sewerage ['sʊərɪdʒ] *n (U)* rede *f* de esgotos.
sewing ['səʊɪŋ] *n (U)* **-1.** [activity] trabalho *m* de costura **-2.** [items] costura *f*.
sewing machine *n* máquina *f* de costura.
sewn [səʊn] *pp* ▻ **sew**.
sex [seks] *n* sexo *m*; **to have ~ (with sb)** fazer sexo (com alguém).
sex appeal *n (U)* sex appeal *m*, atração *f* sexual.
sex education *n (U)* educação *f* sexual.
sexism ['seksɪzm] *n (U)* sexismo *m*.
sexist ['seksɪst] <> *adj* sexista. <> *n* sexista *mf*.
sex life *n* vida *f* sexual.
sex object *n* objeto *m* sexual.
sex shop *n* sex shop *m*.
sextet [seks'tet] *n* sexteto *m*.
sextuplet [seks'tjʊː plɪt] *n* sêxtuplo *m*.
sexual ['sekʃʊəl] *adj* sexual.
sexual assault *n* ataque *m* sexual.
sexual discrimination *n* discriminação *f* sexual.
sexual harassment *n (U)* assédio *m* sexual.
sexual intercourse *n (U)* relações *fpl* sexuais.
sexuality [ˌsekʃʊ'ælətɪ] *n (U)* sexualidade *f*.
sexually transmitted disease *n* doença *f* sexualmente transmissível.
sexy ['seksɪ] (*compar* **-ier**, *superl* **-iest**) *adj inf* sexy, sexualmente atraente.

Seychelles [seɪ'ʃelz] *npl*: **the ~** as Ilhas Seychelles; **in the ~** nas Ilhas Seychelles.
sf, SF (*abbr of* **science fiction**) *n* ficção *f* científica.
SFO (*abbr of* **Serious Fraud Office**) *n departamento de polícia britânico que investiga questões econômicas.*
SG (*abbr of* **Surgeon General**) *n autoridade responsável pela saúde pública nos Estados Unidos.*
Sgt (*abbr of* **sergeant**) Sgt.
sh [ʃ] *excl* psiu!
shabby ['ʃæbɪ] (*compar* **-ier**, *superl* **-iest**) *adj* **-1.** [in bad condition - clothes, briefcase] em mau estado; [- street] abandonado(da) **-2.** [wearing old clothes] esfarrapado(da) **-3.** [mean] mesquinho(nha).
shack [ʃæk] *n* cabana *f*.
shackle ['ʃækl] *vt* **-1.** [chain] algemar **-2.** *literary* [restrict] impedir.
◆ **shackles** *npl* **-1.** [metal restraints] algemas *pl* **-2.** *literary* [restrictions] impedimentos *mpl*.
shade [ʃeɪd] <> *n* **-1.** *(U)* [shadow] sombra *f* **-2.** [lampshade] abajur *m*, quebra-luz *m* **-3.** [colour] tonalidade *f* **-4.** [nuance] tom *m*. <> *vt* **-1.** [from light] fazer sombra em, proteger do sol; **to ~ one's eyes** proteger os olhos do sol *(usando a mão)* **-2.** [by drawing lines] sombrear. <> *vi*: **to ~ into sthg** fundir-se em algo.
◆ **shades** *npl inf* óculos *mpl* escuros.
shading ['ʃeɪdɪŋ] *n* sombreado *m*.
shadow ['ʃædəʊ] <> *n* **-1.** [dark area] sombra *f* **-2.** [under eyes] olheiras *fpl* **-3.** *phr*: **to be a ~ of one's former self** ser uma sombra do que se era; **there's not a** *OR* **the ~ of a doubt** não há sombra de dúvida. <> *adj UK POL* na sombra.
shadow cabinet *n* gabinete-sombra *m*, *gabinete do principal partido de oposição na Grã-Bretanha.*
shadowy ['ʃædəʊɪ] *adj* **-1.** [dark] escuro(ra) **-2.** [hard to see] vago(ga) **-3.** [unknown, sinister] obscuro (ra).
shady ['ʃeɪdɪ] (*compar* **-ier**, *superl* **-iest**) *adj* **-1.** [sheltered from sun] sombreado(da) **-2.** [providing shade] que dá sombra **-3.** *inf* [dishonest, sinister] suspeito(ta).
shaft [ʃɑːft] <> *n* **-1.** [vertical passage] poço *m* **-2.** [rod] haste *f* **-3.** [of light] feixe *m*. <> *vt v inf* [dupe, treat unfairly] ludibriar.
shaggy ['ʃægɪ] (*compar* **-ier**, *superl* **-iest**) *adj* **-1.** [hair, beard] desgrenhado(da) **-2.** [dog] peludo(da) **-3.** [carpet, rug] felpudo(da).
shaggy-dog story *n* piada *f* longa e boba.
shake [ʃeɪk] (*pt* **shook**, *pp* **shaken** ['ʃeɪkən]) <> *vt* **-1.** [gen] abalar **-2.** [move vigorously] sacudir; **to ~ sb's hand** apertar a mão de alguém; **to ~ hands** apertar as mãos; **to ~ one's head** [to say no] negar com a cabeça. <> *vi* tremer. <> *n* sacudida *f*.
◆ **shake down** *vt sep US inf* **-1.** [rob] chantagear **-2.** [search] revistar.
◆ **shake off** *vt sep* livrar-se de.
◆ **shake up** *vt sep* abalar.
shakedown *n US inf* **-1.** [extortion] extorsão *f* **-2.** [search] revista *f*.
shaken ['ʃeɪkn] *pp* ▻ **shake**.
shake-out *n* **-1.** *FIN* [slight recession] ligeira recessão *f* **-2.** [shake-up] reestruturação *f*.

Shakespearean [ʃeɪk'spɪərɪən] *adj* shakespeariano(na).

shake-up *n inf* reestruturação *f.*

shaky ['ʃeɪkɪ] (*compar* **-ier**, *superl* **-iest**) *adj* **-1.** [unsteady - chair, table] frágil, instável; [- hand, writing, voice] trêmulo(la); [- person] abalado(da) **-2.** [weak, uncertain] débil.

shale [ʃeɪl] *n (U)* xisto *m.*

shall [*weak form* ʃəl, *strong form* ʃæl] *aux vb* **-1.** [to express future tense]: **we ~ be in Scotland in June** estaremos na Escócia em junho; **I ~ ring next week** vou ligar semana que vem **-2.** [in questions]: **~ we have our tea now?** vamos tomar nosso chá agora?; **where ~ I put this?** onde eu coloco isto?; **~ I give her a ring, then?** ligo para ela, então?; **I'll do that, ~ I?** eu faço isso, pode ser? **-3.** [will definitely]: **we ~ overcome!** venceremos!; **you ~ go to the ball, Cinderella!** você irá ao baile, Cinderela! **-4.** [in orders]: **you ~ tell me what happened!** você deve me contar o que aconteceu!

shallot [ʃə'lɒt] *n* cebolinha *f.*

shallow ['ʃæləʊ] *adj* **-1.** [in size] raso(sa) **-2.** *pej* [superficial] superficial **-3.** [breathing] não-profundo(da).
 ◆ **shallows** *npl* baixio *m.*

sham [ʃæm] (*pt* & *pp* **-med**, *cont* **-ming**) ◇ *adj* falso(sa), fingido(da). ◇ *n* farsa *f.* ◇ *vi* fingir.

shambles ['ʃæmblz] *n* **-1.** [disorder] confusão *f* **-2.** [fiasco] fiasco *m.*

shame [ʃeɪm] ◇ *n* **-1.** *(U)* [remorse] vergonha *f* **-2.** *(U)* [dishonour]: **to bring ~ (up)on sb** trazer desonra *OR* vergonha a alguém **-3.** [pity]: **it's a ~ (that)** é uma pena *OR* lástima que; **what a ~!** que pena! ◇ *vt* **-1.** [fill with shame] envergonhar **-2.** [force by making ashamed]: **I ~d him into telling the truth** eu o forcei a dizer a verdade ao fazê-lo sentir-se envergonhado por não dizer.

shamefaced [ˌʃeɪm'feɪst] *adj* envergonhado(da).

shameful ['ʃeɪmfʊl] *adj* vergonhoso(sa).

shameless ['ʃeɪmlɪs] *adj* desavergonhado(da).

shammy ['ʃæmɪ] (*pl* **-ies**) *n inf*: **~ (leather)** camurça *f.*

shampoo [ʃæm'puː] (*pl* **-s**, *pt* & *pp* **-ed**, *cont* **-ing**) ◇ *n* **-1.** [liquid - for hair] xampu *m*; [- for carpet] detergente *m* **-2.** [act of shampooing] lavada *f* com xampu. ◇ *vt* lavar.

shamrock ['ʃæmrɒk] *n (U)* trevo *m.*

shandy ['ʃændɪ] (*pl* **-ies**) *n* shandy *m*, *bebida preparada com limonada e cerveja.*

shan't [ʃɑːnt] *cont* = **shall not**.

shanty town *n* ≃ favela *f.*

shape [ʃeɪp] ◇ *n* **-1.** [form] forma *f*; **to take ~** tomar forma **-2.** [figure, silhouette] silhueta *f* **-3.** [guise]: **in the ~ of** na forma de; **not in any ~ or form** de maneira nenhuma **-4.** [form, health]: **to be in good/bad ~** estar em boa/má forma; **to lick** *OR* **knock sb/sthg into ~** deixar alguém no ponto. ◇ *vt* **-1.** [mould physically]: **to ~ sthg (into)** dar a algo forma (de); **a birthmark ~d like a strawberry** uma marca de nascença com a forma de morango **-2.** [influence] influenciar.
 ◆ **shape up** *vi* desenvolver-se.

SHAPE [ʃeɪp] (*abbr of* **Supreme Headquarters Allied Powers Europe**) *n quartel-general das potências aliadas na Europa.*

-shaped ['ʃeɪpt] *suffix com forma de*; **star~** em forma de estrela.

shapeless ['ʃeɪplɪs] *adj* sem forma.

shapely ['ʃeɪplɪ] (*compar* **-ier**, *superl* **-iest**) *adj* bem formado(da); **~ legs** pernas *fpl* bem torneadas.

shard [ʃɑːd] *n* caco *m.*

share [ʃeəʳ] ◇ *n*: **~ (of/in sthg)** parte *f* (em/de algo); **to have/do one's ~ of sthg** ter/fazer a parte que toca a alguém de algo; **everyone must do his ~ of the work** todo mundo deve fazer a parte que lhe toca do trabalho; **to have a ~ in the profits** ter participação nos lucros. ◇ *vt* **-1.** [gen] compartilhar; **to ~ sthg (with sb)** compartilhar algo (com alguém) **-2.** [reveal] revelar; **to ~ sthg (with sb)** revelar algo (a alguém). ◇ *vi* dividir, compartilhar; **to ~ in sthg** compartilhar algo.
 ◆ **shares** *npl FIN* ações *fpl.*
 ◆ **share out** *vt sep* dividir, compartilhar.

share capital *n (U)* capital *m* acionário.

share certificate *n* cautela *f* de ações.

shareholder ['ʃeəˌhəʊldəʳ] *n* acionista *mf.*

share index *n* índice *m* de cotações.

share-out *n* compartilhamento *m*, divisão *f.*

shareware ['ʃeəˌweəʳ] *n* shareware *m.*

shark [ʃɑːk] (*pl inv OR* **-s**) *n* **-1.** [fish] tubarão *m* **-2.** *fig* [dishonest person] trapaceiro *m*, -ra *f.*

sharp [ʃɑːp] ◇ *adj* **-1.** [not blunt - teeth, pencil] apontado(da); [- needle] pontudo(da); [- knife, razor] afiado(da) **-2.** [well-defined] claro(ra), bem-definido(da) **-3.** [intelligent, keen - person, mind] inteligente, esperto(ta); [- eyesight] penetrante; [- hearing] atento(ta) **-4.** [abrupt, sudden] abrupto(ta), brusco(ca) **-5.** [angry, severe] seco(ca) **-6.** [sound, pain] agudo(da) **-7.** [cold, wind] cortante **-8.** [bitter] acre **-9.** *MUS* sustenido(da); **C ~** dó sustenido. ◇ *adv* **-1.** [punctually] pontualmente; **at eight o'clock ~** pontualmente às oito horas **-2.** [quickly, suddenly] de repente. ◇ *n MUS* sustenido *m.*

sharpen ['ʃɑːpn] ◇ *vt* **-1.** [make sharp - knife, tool] afiar; [- pencil] apontar **-2.** [heighten - sense, abilities] apurar; [- disagreements, differences] aumentar. ◇ *vi* **-1.** [become keener, quicker - senses, abilities] apurar; [- appetite, disagreements] aumentar **-2.** [become more piercing, louder] esganiçar-se.

sharp end *n UK fig*: **to be at the ~ of sthg** levar todo o peso de algo nas costas.

sharpener ['ʃɑːpnəʳ] *n* **-1.** [for pencil] apontador *m* **-2.** [for knife] amolador *m.*

sharp-eyed [-'aɪd] *adj* perspicaz.

sharply ['ʃɑːplɪ] *adv* **-1.** [distinctly] claramente **-2.** [suddenly] de repente, repentinamente **-3.** [harshly] duramente.

sharpness ['ʃɑːpnɪs] *n (U)* **-1.** [of point, edge - of pencil] ponta *f*; [- of knife, razor] fio *m* **-2.** [of outline, image] nitidez *f* **-3.** [of mind, senses, sound] agudeza *f* **-4.** [of pain] intensidade *f* **-5.** [of remarks, criticism, tone] dureza *f*, aspereza *f* **-6.** [of taste, smell] acridez *f.*

sharpshooter *n* atirador *m*, -ra *f* de primeira.

sharp-tongued *adj* de língua afiada, mordaz.

sharp-witted [-'wɪtɪd] *adj* perspicaz, sagaz.

shat [ʃæt] *pt* & *pp* ▷ **shit**.

shatter ['ʃætəʳ] ◇ *vt* **-1.** [glass, window] estilhaçar **-2.** *fig* [beliefs, hopes, dreams] destruir, arrasar; **to**

be ~ed (by sthg) ficar arrasado(da) (com algo). <> vi estilhaçar-se.
shattered ['ʃætəd] *adj* -1. [shocked, upset] arrasado(da) -2. *UK inf* [very tired] podre.
shattering ['ʃætərɪŋ] *adj* -1. [gen] arrasador(ra) -2. *UK* [very tiring] extenuante.
shatterproof ['ʃætəpru:f] *adj* que não estilhaça.
shave [ʃeɪv] <> *n*: **to have a ~** fazer a barba; **to be a close ~** *fig* ser por pouco *OR* por um triz. <> *vt* -1. [with razor - face] barbear, fazer a barba de; [- body] depilar, raspar -2. [cut pieces off] cortar. <> *vi* barbear-se, fazer a barba.
◆ **shave off** *vt sep* raspar.
shaven ['ʃeɪvn] *adj* raspado(da).
shaver ['ʃeɪvə^r] *n* barbeador *m*, aparelho *m* de barbear.
shaving brush ['ʃeɪvɪŋ-] *n* pincel *m* de barba.
shaving cream ['ʃeɪvɪŋ-] *n (U)* creme *m* de barbear.
shaving foam ['ʃeɪvɪŋ-] *n (U)* espuma *f* de barbear.
shavings ['ʃeɪvɪŋz] *npl* -1. [of wood] cavacos *mpl*, lascas *fpl* -2. [of metal] cisalha *f*.
shaving soap ['ʃeɪvɪŋ-] *n (U)* sabão *m* de barbear.
shawl [ʃɔ:l] *n* xale *m*.
she [ʃi:] <> *pers pron* ela; **~'s tall** ela é alta.
sheaf [ʃi:f] (*pl* **sheaves**) *n* -1. [of papers, letters] maço *m* -2. [of corn, grain] feixe *m*.
shear [ʃɪə^r] (*pt* **-ed**, *pp* **-ed** *OR* **shorn**) *vt* tosquiar.
◆ **shears** *npl* -1. [for garden] tesoura *f* de podar -2. [for dressmaking] tesoura *f*.
◆ **shear off** <> *vt sep* romper. <> *vi* romper-se.
sheath [ʃi:θ] (*pl* **-s**) *n* -1. [for sword, dagger] bainha *f* -2. *UK* [condom] camisinha *f*.
sheathe [ʃi:ð] *vt* -1. [sword, dagger] embainhar -2. [cable, pipe]: **~d in sthg** revestido(da) de algo.
sheath knife *n* faca *f* com bainha.
sheaves [ʃi:vz] *pl* ▻ **sheaf**.
shed [ʃed] (*pt* & *pp* **shed**, *cont* **-ding**) <> *n* galpão *m*. <> *vt* -1. [lose naturally] perder -2. [discard, get rid of] desfazer-se de; **the company decided to ~ 100 employees** a empresa decidiu despedir 100 funcionários; **after a drink she ~s any inhibition** depois de um drinque, ela deixa de lado qualquer inibição -3. [accidentally lose] perder -4. [tears, blood] derramar.
she'd [*weak form* ʃɪd, *strong form* ʃi:d] = **she had**, **she would**.
sheen [ʃi:n] *n* brilho *m*.
sheep [ʃi:p] (*pl inv*) *n* -1. [animal] ovelha *f*, -2. *fig* [person] cordeiro *m*.
sheepdog ['ʃi:pdɒg] *n* cão *m* pastor.
sheepfold *n* aprisco *m*, redil *m*.
sheepish ['ʃi:pɪʃ] *adj* encabulado(da).
sheepishly ['ʃi:pɪʃlɪ] *adv* encabuladamente.
sheepskin ['ʃi:pskɪn] *n (U)* pele *f* de carneiro.
sheepskin jacket *n* jaqueta *f* de couro *(de carneiro)*.
sheepskin rug *n* tapete *m* de pele de carneiro.
sheer [ʃɪə^r] *adj* -1. [absolute] puro(ra) -2. [very steep - cliff] escarpado(da); [- drop] vertical -3. [delicate] diáfano(na).
sheet [ʃi:t] *n* -1. [for bed] lençol *m*; **as white as a ~** branco(ca) como uma folha de papel -2. [of paper] folha *f* -3. [of glass, metal, wood] lâmina *f*.
sheet feed *n* alimentador *m* de papel.
sheet ice *n (U)* capa *f* de gelo.
sheeting ['ʃi:tɪŋ] *n (U)* chapa *f*.
sheet lightning *n (U)* relâmpago *m* irradiado entre nuvens.
sheet metal *n (U)* metal *m* em chapas.
sheet music *n (U)* partituras *fpl* soltas.
sheik(h) [ʃeɪk] *n* xeque *m*.
shelf [ʃelf] (*pl* **shelves**) *n* prateleira *f*.
shelf life *n* validade *f (de um produto)*.
shell [ʃel] <> *n* -1. [gen] casca *f* -2. [of tortoise] carapaça *f* -3. [on beach] concha *f* -4. [of building] estrutura *f* -5. [of boat] casco *m* -6. [of car] chassi *m* -7. *MIL* granada *f*. <> *vt* -1. [remove covering] descascar -2. *MIL* [fire shells at] bombardear.
◆ **shell out** *inf* <> *vt sep* desembolsar. <> *vi*: **to ~ out for sthg** desembolsar para algo.
she'll [ʃi:l] *cont* = **she will**, **she shall**.
shellfish ['ʃelfɪʃ] (*pl inv*) *n* -1. [creature] molusco *m*, crustáceo *m* -2. *(U)* [food] marisco *m*.
shelling ['ʃelɪŋ] *n (U)* bombardeio *m*.
shell shock *n (U)* trauma *f* de guerra.
shell suit *n UK conjunto de calça e jaqueta de náilon à prova d'água*.
shelter ['ʃeltə^r] <> *n* -1. [building, structure] abrigo *m*, refúgio *m* -2. *(U)* [cover, protection] abrigo *m*, proteção *f* -3. *(U)* [accommodation] abrigo *m*. <> *vt* -1. [from rain, sun, bombs]: **to be ~ed by/from sthg** estar protegido(da) por/de algo -2. [give asylum to] abrigar. <> *vi*: **to ~ from/in sthg** abrigar-se de/em algo.
sheltered ['ʃeltəd] *adj* -1. [protected] protegido(da) -2. [supervised] assistencial.
shelve [ʃelv] <> *vt* engavetar. <> *vi* inclinar-se.
shelves [ʃelvz] *pl* ▻ **shelf**.
shelving ['ʃelvɪŋ] *n (U)* prateleiras *fpl*.
shenanigans *npl inf* -1. [trickery] trapaça *f* -2. [mischief] travessura *f*.
shepherd ['ʃepəd] <> *n* pastor *m*. <> *vt fig* acompanhar.
shepherd's pie ['ʃepədz-] *n (U) gratinado de carne moída temperada com ervas e coberto com purê de batatas*.
sherbet ['ʃɜ:bət] *n* -1. *(U) UK* [sweet powder] *pó efervescente ingerido como doce* -2. *US* [sorbet] sorvete *m* de frutas.
sheriff ['ʃerɪf] *n* -1. *US* [law officer] xerife *m* -2. *Scot* [judge] juiz *m*, -íza *f*.
sherry ['ʃerɪ] (*pl* **-ies**) *n* xerez *m*.
she's [ʃi:z] = **she is**, **she has**.
Shetland ['ʃetlənd] *n*: **~**, **the ~ Islands** as Ilhas Shetland; **in ~**, **in the ~ Islands** nas Ilhas Shetland.
shh [ʃ] *excl* = **sh**.
shield [ʃi:ld] <> *n* -1. [armour] escudo *m* -2. *UK* [sports trophy] troféu *m (na forma de escudo)* -3. [protection]: **~ against sthg** proteção *f* contra algo. <> *vt*: **to ~ sb (from sthg)** proteger alguém (de algo); **to ~ o.s. (from sthg)** proteger-se (de algo).
shift [ʃɪft] <> *n* -1. [gen] turno *m* -2. [slight change]

mudança *f*. <> *vt* **-1.** [move, put elsewhere] mover, mudar de lugar **-2.** [change slightly] mudar de **-3.** *fig* [blame, responsibility]: **to ~ sthg (onto sb)** transferir algo (a alguém) **-4.** *US AUT* [gear] trocar **-5.** [stain] remover, limpar. <> *vi* **-1.** [move] mover-se **-2.** [change slightly] mudar **-3.** *US AUT* trocar de marcha **-4.** [stain] sair.

shift key *n* tecla *f* shift.

shiftless ['ʃɪftlɪs] *adj* folgado(da).

shift stick *n US* alavanca *f* de mudanças, alavanca *f* de marcha.

shifty ['ʃɪftɪ] (*compar* **-ier**, *superl* **-iest**) *adj inf* matreiro(ra).

Shiite ['ʃi:aɪt] <> *adj* xiita. <> *n* xiita *mf*.

shilling ['ʃɪlɪŋ] *n UK* xelim *m*.

shilly-shally ['ʃɪlɪ,ʃælɪ] (*pt* & *pp* **-ied**) *vi* vacilar, titubear.

shimmer ['ʃɪmə^r] <> *n* reflexo *m* trêmulo, cintilação *f*. <> *vi* cintilar, tremeluzir.

shin [ʃɪn] (*pt* & *pp* **-ned**, *cont* **-ning**) *n* canela *f (na perna)*.

◆ **shin up** *UK*, **shinny up** *US vt fus* trepar em.

shin bone *n* tíbia *f*.

shine [ʃaɪn] (*pt* & *pp* **shone**) <> *n* brilho *m*. <> *vt* **-1.** [focus] direcionar **-2.** [polish] lustrar. <> *vi* **-1.** [give out light] brilhar **-2.** [excel]: **to ~ at sthg** sobressair-
se em algo.

shingle ['ʃɪŋgl] *n (U)* cascalhos *m*, pedrinhas *fpl*.

◆ **shingles** *n MED* herpes-zoster *m*.

shining ['ʃaɪnɪŋ] *adj* brilhante.

shinny ◆ **shinny up** *vt fus US* = **shin up**.

shin pads *npl* caneleira *f*.

shiny ['ʃaɪnɪ] (*compar* **-ier**, *superl* **-iest**) *adj* brilhante.

ship [ʃɪp] (*pt* & *pp* **-ped**, *cont* **-ping**) <> *n* navio *m*, barco *m*. <> *vt* enviar por via marítima.

shipbuilder ['ʃɪp,bɪldə^r] *n* empresa *f* de construção naval.

shipbuilding ['ʃɪp,bɪldɪŋ] *n (U)* construção *f* naval.

ship canal *n* canal *m* de navegação.

shipment ['ʃɪpmənt] *n* carregamento *m*.

shipper ['ʃɪpə^r] *n* **-1.** [person] exportador(ra) **-2.** [company] empresa *f* exportadora.

shipping ['ʃɪpɪŋ] *n (U)* **-1.** [transport] envio *m*, transporte *m* **-2.** [ships] navegação *f*.

shipping agent *n* **-1.** [person] agente *m* marítimo **-2.** [company] agência *f* marítima.

shipping company *n* companhia *f* de navegação.

shipping forecast *n* previsão *f* das condições marítimas.

shipping lane *n* rota *f* marítima.

shipshape ['ʃɪpʃeɪp] *adj* em ordem.

shipwreck ['ʃɪprek] <> *n* **-1.** [destruction of ship] naufrágio *m* **-2.** [wrecked ship] navio *m* naufragado. <> *vt*: **to be ~ed** naufragar.

shipwrecked ['ʃɪprekt] *adj* naufragado(da).

shipyard ['ʃɪpjɑ:d] *n* estaleiro *m*.

shire [ʃaɪə^r] *n* condado *m*.

◆ **Shire** *n*: **the Shires** the Shires, *os condados centrais da Inglaterra*.

shire horse *n* cavalo *m* de tiro.

shirk [ʃɜ:k] *vt* escapar a.

shirker ['ʃɜ:kə^r] *n* vadio *m*, -dia *f*.

shirt [ʃɜ:t] *n* camisa *f*.

shirtsleeves ['ʃɜ:tsli:vz] *npl*: **to be in (one's) ~** estar em mangas de camisa.

shirt tail *n* fralda *f (da camisa)*.

shirty ['ʃɜ:tɪ] (*compar* **-ier**, *superl* **-iest**) *adj UK inf* estúpido(da).

shit [ʃɪt] (*pt* & *pp* **shit** *OR* **-ted** *OR* **shat**, *cont* **-ting**) *vulg* <> *n* merda *f*. <> *vi* cagar. <> *excl* merda!

shiver ['ʃɪvə^r] <> *n* tremer; **to give sb the ~s** dar arrepios a alguém. <> *vi*: **to ~ (with sthg)** tremer (de algo).

shoal [ʃəʊl] *n* cardume *m*.

shock [ʃɒk] <> *n* **-1.** [gen] choque *m* **-2.** *(U) MED*: **to be suffering from ~, to be in (a state of) ~** estar em estado de choque **-3.** [thick mass] mecha *f*. <> *vt* **-1.** [upset] chocar **-2.** [offend] ofender. <> *vi* chocar.

shock absorber [-əb,zɔ:bə^r] *n* amortecedor *m*.

shocked [ʃɒkt] *adj* **-1.** [upset] chocado(da) **-2.** [offended] chocado(da), ofendido(da).

shocking ['ʃɒkɪŋ] *adj* **-1.** [very bad] péssimo(ma) **-2.** [scandalous] escandaloso(sa) **-3.** [horrifying] chocante.

shockproof ['ʃɒkpru:f] *adj* à prova de choque.

shock tactics *npl* **-1.** *MIL* tática *f* de choque **-2.** *fig* [surprising manoeuvre] tratamento *m* de choque.

shock therapy, shock treatment *n (U) MED* terapia *f* à base de eletrochoques.

shock troops *npl* tropas *fpl* de choque.

shock wave *n* onda *f* de choque.

shod [ʃɒd] <> *pt* & *pp* ▻ **shoe**. <> *adj* calçado(da).

shoddy ['ʃɒdɪ] (*compar* **-ier**, *superl* **-iest**) *adj* **-1.** [badly done or made] de segunda qualidade **-2.** *fig* [poor, unworthy] inferior.

shoe [ʃu:] (*pt* & *pp* **-ed** *OR* **shod**, *cont* **-ing**) <> *n* **-1.** [for person] sapato *m* **-2.** [for horse] ferradura *f* **-3.** [for brake] sapata *f*. <> *vt* ferrar.

shoebrush ['ʃu:brʌʃ] *n* escova *f* para sapato.

shoe cleaner *n* [liquid] líquido *m* para limpar sapatos.

shoehorn ['ʃu:hɔ:n] *n* calçadeira *f*.

shoelace ['ʃu:leɪs] *n* cadarço *m*.

shoemaker ['ʃu:,meɪkə^r] *n* sapateiro *m*, -ra *f*.

shoe polish *n (U)* graxa *f* de sapato.

shoe repairer *n* sapateiro *m*, -ra *f*.

shoe shop *n* sapataria *f*.

shoestring ['ʃu:strɪŋ] <> *adj* restrito(ta). <> *n fig*: **on a ~** com orçamento mínimo.

shoetree ['ʃu:tri:] *n* fôrma *f* para sapato.

shone [ʃɒn] *pt* & *pp* ▻ **shine**.

shoo [ʃu:] <> *vt* enxotar. <> *excl* xô!

shook [ʃʊk] *pt* ▻ **shake**.

shoot [ʃu:t] (*pt* & *pp* **shot**) <> *vt* **-1.** [fire gun at - killing] matar a tiros, balear; [- wounding] ferir a tiros, balear; **to ~ o.s.** [kill o.s.] dar-se um tiro, atirar em si mesmo(ma) **-2.** *UK* [hunt] caçar **-3.** [arrow, question] disparar **-4.** [glance, look] relancear **-5.** *CINEMA* filmar, rodar **-6.** *US* [pool] jogar. <> *vi* **-1.** [fire gun]: **to ~ (at sb/sthg)** atirar (em alguém/algo) **-2.** *UK* [hunt] caçar **-3.** [move quickly]: **to ~ in/**

out/past entrar/sair/passar rapidamente; **to ~ ahead** sair na frente; **to ~ off** partir rapidamente **-4.** CINEMA filmar, rodar **-5.** [SPORT - football] chutar; [- basketball, netball etc] arremessar. <> *n* **-1.** *UK* [hunting expedition] caçada *f* **-2.** [new growth] brote *m*. <> *excl US inf* **-1.** [go ahead] manda! **-2.** [damn] droga!

◆ **shoot down** *vt sep* **-1.** [person] matar a tiros **-2.** [plane] derrubar **-3.** *fig* [reject] derrubar por terra.

◆ **shoot up** *vi* **-1.** [grow quickly] dar um pulo **-2.** [increase quickly] disparar **-3.** *drugs sl* [take drugs] drogar-se.

shooting ['ʃuːtɪŋ] *n* **-1.** [firing of gun] tiroteio *m* **-2.** *(U)* [hunting] caça *f*.

shooting range *n* área *f* de tiro.

shooting star *n* estrela *f* cadente.

shooting stick *n bastão que serve como assento.*

shoot-out *n* tiroteio *m*.

shop [ʃɒp] (*pt* & *pp* **-ped**, *cont* **-ping**) <> *n* **-1.** [store] loja *f*; **to talk ~** falar sobre trabalho **-2.** [workshop] oficina *f*, seminário *m*. <> *vi* comprar; **to go shopping** fazer compras.

◆ **shop around** *vi* comparar preços.

shop assistant *n UK* vendedor *m*, -ra *f* (de loja).

shop floor *n*: **the ~** o chão de fábrica, os operários.

shopkeeper ['ʃɒp,kiːpə^r] *n* lojista *mf*.

shoplifter ['ʃɒp,lɪftə^r] *n* ladrão *m*, -dra *f* de lojas.

shoplifting ['ʃɒp,lɪftɪŋ] *n (U)* roubo *m* numa loja.

shopper ['ʃɒpə^r] *n* comprador *m*, -ra *f*.

shopping ['ʃɒpɪŋ] *n* compras *fpl*; **to go ~** fazer compras.

shopping bag *n* sacola *f* de compras.

shopping basket *n UK* **-1.** [in supermarket] cesta *f* **-2.** [for online shopping] cesta *f* de compras.

shopping cart *n US* **-1.** [in supermarket] carrinho *m* **-2.** [for online shopping] carrinho *m* de compras.

shopping centre *UK*, **shopping mall** *US*, **shopping plaza** *US* [-,plɑːzəl *n* shopping (center) *m*, centro *m* comercial.

shopping list *n* lista *f* de compras.

shopping mall, shopping plaza *n US* = **shopping centre**.

shopsoiled *UK* ['ʃɒpsɔɪld], **shopworn** *US* ['ʃɒpwɔːn] *adj* deteriorado(da) por ficar exposto numa loja.

shop steward *n* representante *mf* sindical.

shopwalker *n UK* supervisor *m*, -ra *f (de loja)*.

shopwindow [,ʃɒp'wɪndəʊ] *n* vitrina *f*.

shopworn *adj US* = **shopsoiled**.

shore [ʃɔː^r] *n* **-1.** [land by water] beira *f*, margem *f*; **sea ~** litoral *m* **-2.** *(U)* [not at sea]: **on ~** em terra.

◆ **shore up** *vt sep* **-1.** [prop up] reforçar, sustentar **-2.** *fig* [sustain] sustentar.

shore leave *n (U)* licença *f* para desembarcar.

shoreline ['ʃɔːlaɪn] *n* linha *f* costeira.

shorn [ʃɔːn] <> *pp* ⊳ **shear**. <> *adj* **-1.** [grass] cortado(da) **-2.** [hair] raspado(da); **~ of** *fig* desprovido(da) de, despojado(da) de; **she was shorn of her responsibility** retiraram todo o poder dela.

short [ʃɔːt] <> *adj* **-1.** [in length, distance] curto(ta) **-2.** [in height] baixo(xa) **-3.** [in time] curto(ta), breve; **in two ~ days we'll be in Spain!** em apenas dois dias, estaremos na Espanha! **-4.** [curt]: **to be ~ (with sb)** ser seco(ca) (com alguém) **-5.** [lacking]: **money is always ~ around Christmas** o dinheiro anda sempre curto no Natal; **we're a pound ~** falta(-nos) uma libra; **she's a bit ~ on brain power** falta a ela um pouco de agilidade mental; **to be ~ of sthg** andar mal de algo; **to be ~ of breath** estar com falta de ar **-6.** [abbreviated]: **to be ~ for sthg** ser o diminutivo de algo. <> *adv* **-1.** [lacking]: **we're running ~ of food** está acabando a comida **-2.** [suddenly, abruptly]: **to cut sthg ~** interromper algo antes do fim; **to stop ~** parar de repente; **to bring** OR **pull sb up ~** fazer alguém parar de repente. <> *n* **-1.** *UK* [alcoholic drink] drinque *m (bebida forte)* **-2.** CINEMA [film] curta *f*.

◆ **shorts** *npl* **-1.** [short trousers] shorts *mpl* **-2.** *US* [underwear] cuecas *fpl*.

◆ **for short** *adv* para abreviar, para simplificar.

◆ **in short** *adv* enfim.

◆ **nothing short of** *prep*: **it was nothing ~ of madness** foi uma verdadeira loucura.

◆ **short of** *prep*: **~ of doing sthg** a não ser fazendo algo.

shortage ['ʃɔːtɪdʒ] *n* falta *f*, escassez *f*.

short back and sides *n UK* corte *m* de cabelo do exército.

shortbread ['ʃɔːtbred] *n (U)* biscoito *m* amanteigado.

short-change *vt* **-1.** [in shop, restaurant] dar mal o troco a **-2.** *fig* [reward unfairly] passar para trás.

short circuit *n* curto-circuito *m*, curto *m*.

◆ **short-circuit** <> *vt* provocar curto-circuito em. <> *vi* dar curto-circuito.

shortcomings ['ʃɔːt,kʌmɪŋz] *npl* defeitos *mpl*.

shortcrust pastry ['ʃɔːtkrʌst-] *n (U)* massa *f* podre.

short cut *n* **-1.** [quick route] atalho *m* **-2.** [quick method] método *m* rápido.

shorten ['ʃɔːtn] <> *vt* encurtar; **'Robert' can be ~ed to 'Bob'** Bob é a forma reduzida de Robert. <> *vi* encurtar.

shortening ['ʃɔːtnɪŋ] *n (U)* CULIN gordura *f* vegetal.

shortfall ['ʃɔːtfɔːl] *n* déficit *m*; **~ in** OR **of sthg** déficit em OR de algo.

shorthand ['ʃɔːthænd] *n (U)* **-1.** [writing system] taquigrafia *f*, estenografia *f* **-2.** [short form]: **~ (for sthg)** maneira *f* suave (de dizer algo).

shorthanded [,ʃɔːt'hændɪd] *adj*: **to be ~** estar com falta de pessoal.

shorthand typist *n UK* taquígrafo *m*, -fa *f*, estenógrafo *m*, -fa *f*.

short-haul *adj* de curta distância.

short list *n UK* **-1.** [for job] lista *f* de candidatos selecionados **-2.** [for prize] relação *f* dos finalistas.

◆ **short-list** *vt UK*: **to be short-listed (for sthg)** [for job] estar entre os candidatos selecionados (para algo); [for prize] estar entre os finalistas (de algo).

short-lived [-'lɪvd] *adj* fugaz, efêmero(ra).

shortly ['ʃɔːtlɪ] *adv* **-1.** [soon] em breve, logo; ~

before/after pouco antes/depois de **-2.** [curtly, abruptly] bruscamente, secamente.

shortness ['ʃɔ:tnɪs] *n (U)* **-1.** [in time] brevidade *f* **-2.** [in length] curteza *f* **-3.** [in height] baixa estatura *f* **-4.** [in distance] proximidade *f.*

short-range *adj* **-1.** [missile, weapon] de curto alcance **-2.** [forecast] a curto prazo.

short shrift [-'ʃrɪft] *n*: **to give sb ~** prestar pouca atenção a alguém.

shortsighted [,ʃɔ:t'saɪtɪd] *adj* **-1.** [myopic] míope **-2.** *fig* [lacking foresight] de visão curta.

short-staffed [-'stɑ:ft] *adj*: **to be ~** estar com falta de pessoal.

short-stay *adj*: **a ~ car park** *estacionamento para curtos períodos de tempo, geralmente 2-3 horas*; **~ accommodation** acomodação para poucos dias; **a ~ patient** *paciente hospitalizado por três dias ou menos.*

short story *n* conto *m.*

short-tempered [-'tempəd] *adj* irritadiço(ça).

short-term *adj* **-1.** [happening soon] a curto prazo **-2.** [of short duration] de curto prazo.

short time *n UK*: **to be on ~** trabalhar com jornada reduzida.

short wave *n* onda *f* curta.

shot [ʃɒt] ◇ *pt* & *pp* ▻ **shoot**. ◇ *n* **-1.** [gunshot] tiro *m*; **like a ~** [quickly] como um raio **-2.** [marksman] atirador *m*, -ra *f* **-3.** *SPORT* chute *m* **-4.** [photograph] foto *f* **-5.** *CINEMA* tomada *f* **-6.** *inf* [try, go] tentativa *f* **-7.** [injection] injeção *f* **-8.** [of alcohol] dose *f.*

shotgun ['ʃɒtgʌn] *n* espingarda *f.*

shot put *n*: **the ~** o lançamento de peso.

should [ʃʊd] *aux vb* **-1.** [indicating duty, necessity]: **we ~ leave now** deveríamos ir agora **-2.** [seeking advice, permission]: **~ I go too?** eu vou também? **-3.** [as suggestion]: **I ~ deny everything** eu negaria tudo **-4.** [indicating probability]: **she ~ be home soon** ela deve chegar em casa logo **-5.** [was or were expected to]: **they ~ have won the match** eles deveriam ter ganhado o jogo **-6.** *(as conditional)*: **I ~ like to come with you** eu gostaria de ir com você; **how ~ I know?** como é que eu poderia saber?; **~ you be interested, ...** caso você esteja interessado, ... **-7.** *(in subordinate clauses)*: **we decided that you ~ meet him** decidimos que você deveria encontrá-lo **-8.** [expressing uncertain opinion]: **I ~ think he's about 50 years old** eu diria que ele tem uns 50 anos **-9.** *(after who or what)* [expressing surprise]: **and who ~ I see but Ann!** e então quem é que eu vejo? A Ann!

shoulder ['ʃəʊldə^r] ◇ *n* **-1.** [part of body] ombro *m*; **to look over one's ~** olhar para trás; **a ~ to cry on** um ombro no qual chorar; **to rub ~s with sb** conviver com alguém *(rico e famoso)* **-2.** [part of clothing] ombreira *f* **-3.** *CULIN* [joint] quarto *m* dianteiro. ◇ *vt* **-1.** [load] carregar nos ombros **-2.** [responsibility] arcar com.

shoulder bag *n* mochila *f.*

shoulder blade *n* omoplata *f.*

shoulder-length *adj* na altura dos ombros.

shoulder pad *n* ombreira *f.*

shoulder strap *n* alça *f.*

shouldn't ['ʃʊdnt] = **should not**.

should've ['ʃʊdəv] = **should have**.

shout [ʃaʊt] ◇ *n* grito *m.* ◇ *vt* gritar. ◇ *vi* gritar; **to ~ at sb** [tell off] gritar com alguém.

◆ **shout down** *vt sep* calar com gritos.

◆ **shout out** *vt sep* gritar.

shouting ['ʃaʊtɪŋ] *n (U)* gritos *mpl*; **a lot of ~** uma gritaria.

shove [ʃʌv] *inf* ◇ *n*: **to give sb/sthg a ~** dar um empurrão em alguém/algo. ◇ *vt* empurrar; **to ~ sb in** colocar alguém para dentro aos empurrões; **to ~ sb out** tirar alguém aos empurrões.

◆ **shove off** *vi* **-1.** [in boat] afastar-se da costa **-2.** *inf* [go away] cair fora.

shovel ['ʃʌvl] (*UK pt* & *pp* **-led**, *cont* **-ling**, *US pt* & *pp* **-ed**, *cont* **-ing**) ◇ *n* pá *f.* ◇ *vt* **-1.** [with a shovel] tirar com pá **-2.** *fig* [food, meal] devorar; **they ~led down their food and left** eles engoliram a janta e saíram.

show [ʃəʊ] (*pt* **-ed**, *pp* **shown** *OR* **-ed**) ◇ *n* **-1.** [piece of entertainment - theatre] espetáculo *m*; [- TV, radio] show *m*, programa *m* **-2.** *CINEMA* sessão *f* **-3.** [exhibition] exposição *f*; **on ~** à mostra **-4.** [display] demonstração *f*; **for ~** para bonito **-5.** [pretence] demonstração *f* falsa. ◇ *vt* **-1.** [gen] mostrar; **to ~ sb sthg, to ~ sthg to sb** mostrar algo para alguém; **to ~ sb how to do sthg** mostrar a alguém como fazer algo; **to have something to ~ for sthg** ganhar alguma coisa por algo; **to have nothing to ~ for sthg** não ter ganhado nada por algo; **to ~ o.s.** apresentar-se; **it just goes to ~ (that) ...** isso só prova que ... **-2.** [reveal] mostrar, revelar; **to ~ sb sthg** demostrar algo por alguém **-3.** [escort]: **to ~ sb to sthg** levar *OR* acompanhar alguém até algo **-4.** [broadcast] apresentar, passar **-5.** [profit, loss] registrar **-6.** [work of art, produce] mostrar, exibir. ◇ *vi* **-1.** [indicate, make clear] mostrar, indicar **-2.** [be visible] aparecer; **inside he was very angry but it didn't ~** por dentro ele estava muito bravo mas não aparentava **-3.** *CINEMA* passar.

◆ **show around** *vt sep* = **show round**.

◆ **show in** *vt sep* mandar entrar.

◆ **show off** ◇ *vt sep* exibir. ◇ *vi* exibir-se.

◆ **show out** *vt sep* levar até a porta.

◆ **show round** *vt sep* mostrar *(uma cidade, um apartamento)*; **to ~ sb round town** mostrar a cidade a alguém.

◆ **show up** ◇ *vt sep*: **to ~ sb up in public** fazer alguém passar vergonha em público. ◇ *vi* **-1.** [stand out] destacar-se **-2.** [arrive] aparecer.

showbiz ['ʃəʊbɪz] *n (U) inf* showbiz *m.*

show business *n (U)* showbusiness *m*, mundo *m* dos espetáculos.

showcase ['ʃəʊkeɪs] *n* **-1.** [glass case] vitrina *f* **-2.** *fig* [advantageous setting] prato *m* cheio.

showdown ['ʃəʊdaʊn] *n*: **to have a ~ with sb** ter um acerto final de contas com alguém.

shower ['ʃaʊə^r] ◇ *n* **-1.** [gen] chuva *f* **-2.** [device] chuveiro *m* **-3.** [wash]: **to have** *OR* **take a ~** tomar uma ducha **-4.** *US* [for wedding] chá *m* de panela **-5.** [for a baby] chá *m* de fralda. ◇ *vt* **-1.** [sprinkle] jogar; **the newlyweds were ~ed with confetti** os recém-casados ganharam uma chuva de confetes **-2.** [bestow]: **to ~ sb with sthg, to ~ sthg**

(up)on sb encher alguém de algo. <> *vi* tomar banho.

shower cap *n* touca *f* de banho.

showerproof ['ʃaʊəpru:f] *adj* resistente à chuva, impermeável.

showery ['ʃaʊərɪ] *adj* chuvoso(sa).

showing ['ʃəʊɪŋ] *n* sessão *f.*

show jumping [-,dʒʌmpɪŋ] *n (U)* concurso *m* hípico de saltos.

showman ['ʃəʊmən] (*pl* **-men** [-mən]) *n* **-1.** [at fair, circus] apresentador *m* **-2.** *fig* [publicity-seeker] astro *m*, showman *m.*

showmanship ['ʃəʊmənʃɪp] *n (U)* encenação *f*; **to be pure ~** ser um verdadeiro show *OR* espetáculo.

shown [ʃəʊn] *pp* ▻ **show.**

show-off *n inf* exibido(da).

show of hands *n*: **they voted by a ~** eles votaram levantando as mãos.

showpiece ['ʃəʊpi:s] *n* atração *f* principal.

showroom ['ʃəʊrʊm] *n* salão *m* de exposição.

showy ['ʃəʊɪ] (*compar* **-ier**, *superl* **-iest**) *adj* chamativo(va).

shrank [ʃræŋk] *pt* ▻ **shrink.**

shrapnel ['ʃræpnl] *n (U)* metralha *f.*

shred [ʃred] (*pt* & *pp* **-ded**, *cont* **-ding**) <> *n* **-1.** [small piece] pedaço *m* **-2.** *fig* [scrap]: **there was not a ~ of evidence that ...** não havia a mais remota evidência de que ...; **a ~ of truth** um pingo de verdade. <> *vt* **-1.** *CULIN* picar **-2.** [paper] picar, rasgar.

shredder ['ʃredəʳ] *n* **-1.** *CULIN* [in food processor] triturador *m* **-2.** [for documents] picadora *f* de papel.

shrew [ʃru:] *n* musaranho *m.*

shrewd [ʃru:d] *adj* perspicaz, astuto(ta).

shrewdness ['ʃru:dnɪs] *n (U)* perspicácia *f*, astúcia *f.*

shriek [ʃri:k] <> *n* grito *m*; **a ~ of laughter** uma gargalhada. <> *vt* gritar. <> *vi*: **to ~ (with/in)** gritar (de); **to ~ with laughter** gargalhar.

shrill [ʃrɪl] *adj* agudo(da).

shrimp [ʃrɪmp] *n* camarão *m.*

shrine [ʃraɪn] *n* santuário *m.*

shrink [ʃrɪŋk] (*pt* **shrank**, *pp* **shrunk**) <> *vt* encolher. <> *vi* **-1.** [become smaller] encolher **-2.** *fig* [contract, diminish] diminuir **-3.** [recoil]: **to ~ away from sthg** recuar frente a algo **-4.** [be reluctant]: **to ~ from sthg/from doing sthg** fugir de algo/de fazer algo. <> *n inf* [psychoanalyst] psicanalista *mf.*

shrinkage ['ʃrɪŋkɪdʒ] *n (U)* **-1.** [loss in size] encolhimento *m* **-2.** *fig* [contraction] redução *f.*

shrink-wrap *vt* embalar com plástico termorretrátil.

shrivel ['ʃrɪvl] (*UK pt* & *pp* **-led**, *cont* **-ling**, *US pt* & *pp* **-ed**, *cont* **-ing**) <> *vt*: **to ~ (up)** secar, murchar. <> *vi*: **to ~ (up)** secar, murchar.

shroud [ʃraʊd] <> *n* mortalha *f.* <> *vt*: **to be ~ed in sthg** [darkness, fog] estar encoberto(ta) em algo; [mystery] estar envolto(ta) em algo.

Shrove Tuesday ['ʃrəʊv-] *n* terça-feira *f* de Carnaval.

shrub [ʃrʌb] *n* arbusto *m.*

shrubbery ['ʃrʌbərɪ] (*pl* **-ies**) *n* arbustos *mpl.*

shrug [ʃrʌg] (*pt* & *pp* **-ged**, *cont* **-ging**) <> *n* encolhimento *m* dos ombros; **to give a ~** dar de ombros. <> *vt* encolher. <> *vi* dar de ombros, encolher os ombros.

◆ **shrug off** *vt sep* não dar bola para.

shrunk [ʃrʌŋk] *pp* ▻ **shrink.**

shrunken ['ʃrʌŋkn] *adj* **-1.** [person] enrugado(da) **-2.** [business] reduzido(da) **-3.** [fruit] seco(ca).

shucks [ʃʌks] *excl US inf* **-1.** [it was nothing] ora bolas! **-2.** [damn] droga!

shudder ['ʃʌdəʳ] <> *n* calafrio *m.* <> *vi* **-1.** [person]: **to ~ (with sthg)** estremecer-se (de algo); **I ~ to think** me dá calafrios só de pensar **-2.** [machine, vehicle] tremer, balançar.

shuffle ['ʃʌfl] <> *n* **-1.** [of feet] arrasto *m* **-2.** [of cards] baralhamento *m*; **to give the cards a ~** embaralhar as cartas. <> *vt* **-1.** [feet] arrastar **-2.** [cards] embaralhar **-3.** [papers] mudar de lugar. <> *vi* **-1.** [walk]: **to ~ (in/out/along)** entrar/sair/andar arrastando os pés **-2.** [fidget] remexer-se nervosamente.

shun [ʃʌn] (*pt* & *pp* **-ned**, *cont* **-ning**) *vt* evitar.

shunt [ʃʌnt] *vt* **-1.** *RAIL* manobrar, trocar de via férrea **-2.** *fig* [move]: **we were ~ed from one room to another** ficaram nos mandando de uma sala para outra.

shunter *n* **-1.** [engine] locomotiva *f* de manobras **-2.** [person] guarda-chaves *mf inv.*

shush [ʃʊʃ] *excl* psit!

shut [ʃʌt] (*pt* & *pp* **shut**, *cont* **-ting**) <> *adj* fechado(da). <> *vt* & *vi* fechar; **~ your mouth** *OR* **face!** *v inf* fecha o bico *OR* a matraca.

◆ **shut away** *vt sep* **-1.** [criminal] trancafiar; **to ~ o.s. away** encerrar-se **-2.** [valuables] guardar.

◆ **shut down** <> *vt sep* & *vi* fechar.

◆ **shut in** *vt sep* trancar; **to ~ o.s. in** trancar-se em.

◆ **shut out** *vt sep* **-1.** [of building, room] não deixar entrar **-2.** [block out of mind] bloquear.

◆ **shut up** <> *vt sep* **-1.** [shop, factory] fechar **-2.** [silence] calar, fazer calar. <> *vi* **-1.** *inf* [be quiet] calar a boca **-2.** [close] fechar.

shutter ['ʃʌtəʳ] *n* **-1.** [on window] veneziana *f* **-2.** [in camera] obturador *m.*

shuttle ['ʃʌtl] <> *adj*: **~ service** [of planes] ponte *f* aérea; [of buses, train] linha *f* regular. <> *n* **-1.** [train, bus] linha *f* regular **-2.** [plane] avião *m* da ponte aérea. <> *vi* ir e vir. <> *vt* transportar.

shuttlecock ['ʃʌtlkɒk] *n* peteca *f.*

shy [ʃaɪ] (*pt* & *pp* **shied**) <> *adj* tímido(da); **to be ~ of doing sthg** não se atrever a fazer algo. <> *vi* espantar-se.

◆ **shy away from** *vt fus*: **to ~ away from sthg** fugir de algo; **to ~ away from doing sthg** negar-se a fazer algo.

shyly ['ʃaɪlɪ] *adv* timidamente.

shyness ['ʃaɪnɪs] *n (U)* timidez *f.*

Siam *n* Sião; **in ~** no Sião.

Siamese [,saɪə'mi:z] (*pl inv*) <> *adj* siamês(esa). <> *n* **-1.** [person] siamês *m*, -esa *f* **-2.** [cat] gato *m* siamês.

Siamese twins *npl* irmãos *mpl* siameses, irmãs *fpl* siamesas.

SIB (*abbr of* **Securities and Investment Board**) *n organismo britânico regulador de investimentos na bolsa.*
Siberia [saɪˈbɪərɪə] *n* Sibéria; **in** ~ na Sibéria.
Siberian [saɪˈbɪərɪən] <> *adj* siberiano(na). <> *n* siberiano *m*, -na *f*.
sibling [ˈsɪblɪŋ] *n* irmão *m*, -mã *f*.
Sicilian [sɪˈsɪljən] <> *adj* siciliano(na). <> *n* siciliano *m*, -na *f*.
Sicily [ˈsɪsɪlɪ] *n* Sicília; **in** ~ na Sicília.
sick [sɪk] *adj* **-1.** [unwell] doente **-2.** [nauseous]: **to feel** ~ sentir-se mal **-3.** [vomiting]: **to be** ~ *UK* vomitar **-4.** [fed up]: **to be** ~ **of sthg/of doing sthg** estar farto(ta) de algo/de fazer algo **-5.** [angry, disgusted]: **to make sb** ~ *fig* deixar alguém doente **-6.** [offensive] de mau gosto.
sickbay [ˈsɪkbeɪ] *n* enfermaria *f*.
sickbed [ˈsɪkbed] *n* leito *m* de doente.
sicken [ˈsɪkn] <> *vt* deixar doente. <> *vi UK*: **to be** ~**ing for sthg** estar ficando doente de algo.
sickening [ˈsɪknɪŋ] *adj* **-1.** [disgusting] repugnante **-2.** *hum* [infuriating] irritante, exasperante.
sickle [ˈsɪkl] *n* foice *f*.
sick leave *n (U)* licença *f* de saúde.
sickly [ˈsɪklɪ] (*compar* **-ier**, *superl* **-iest**) *adj* **-1.** [unhealthy] doentio(tia) **-2.** [nauseating] nauseante.
sickness [ˈsɪknɪs] *n* **-1.** *(U)* [general illness] doença *f*, enfermidade *f* **-2.** *UK (U)* [nausea, vomiting] náusea *f*, enjôo *m* **-3.** [specific illness] doença *f*.
sickness benefit *n (U)* ≃ auxílio-doença *m*.
sick pay *n (U) espécie de auxílio-doença pago pelo empregador.*
sickroom [ˈsɪkrʊm] *n* enfermaria *f*.
side [saɪd] <> *n* **-1.** [gen] lado *m*; **on every** ~, **on all** ~**s** por todos os lados; **from** ~ **to** ~ de um lado a outro; **to put sthg to** *OR* **on one** ~ pôr *OR* colocar algo de lado; **at** *OR* **by sb's** ~ ao lado de alguém; ~ **by** ~ lado a lado; **on my mother's** ~ por parte da minha mãe **-2.** [surface] lateral *f* **-3.** [of table, river] borda *f*, beira *f* **-4.** [slope] ladeira *f*, encosta *f* **-5.** [in sport] equipe *f* **-6.** [viewpoint] ponto *m* de vista; **to take sb's** ~ ficar do lado de alguém; **to be on sb's** ~ estar do lado de alguém **-7.** [aspect] aspecto *m*; **to be on the safe** ~ por via das dúvidas **-8.** *phr*: **on the large/small** ~ um pouco grande/pequeno demais; **to do sthg on the** ~ [in addition] fazer algo para ganhar um dinheiro extra; [dishonestly] fazer algo por fora *(sem que a Receita saiba)*; **to keep** *OR* **stay on the right** ~ **of sb** ficar quieto(ta) ao lado de alguém. <> *adj* lateral.
◆ **side with** *vt fus* pôr-se ao lado de.
sideboard [ˈsaɪdbɔːd] *n* armário *m*, guarda-louça *m*.
sideboards *UK* [ˈsaɪdbɔːdz], **sideburns** *US* [ˈsaɪdbɜːnz] *npl* suíças *fpl*, costeletas *fpl*.
sidecar [ˈsaɪdkɑːʳ] *n* side-car *m*.
side dish *n* acompanhamento *m*, guarnição *f*.
side effect *n* efeito *m* colateral.
sidekick [ˈsaɪdkɪk] *n inf* cupincha *mf*, comparsa *mf*.
sidelight [ˈsaɪdlaɪt] *n* luz *f* lateral.
sideline [ˈsaɪdlaɪn] *n* **-1.** [extra business] ocupação *f* secundária **-2.** *SPORT* [painted line] linha *f* lateral **-3.** [periphery]: **on the** ~**s** nas margens.
sidelong [ˈsaɪdlɒŋ] <> *adj* de lado. <> *adv*: **to look** ~ **at sb/sthg** olhar de lado para alguém/algo.
side-on <> *adj* lateral. <> *adv* de lado.
side plate *n* prato *m* para pão.
side road *n* estrada *f* secundária.
sidesaddle [ˈsaɪdˌsædl] *adv*: **to ride** ~ montar de silhão.
sideshow [ˈsaɪdʃəʊ] *n área de jogos ou de espetáculos paralelos numa feira ou num circo.*
sidestep [ˈsaɪdstep] (*pt* & *pp* **-ped**, *cont* **-ping**) *vt* **-1.** [step to one side to avoid] desviar, evitar **-2.** *fig* [problem, question] esquivar-se de.
side street *n* rua *f* secundária.
sidetrack [ˈsaɪdtræk] *vt*: **to be** ~**ed** desviar (dos objetivos).
sidewalk [ˈsaɪdwɔːk] *n US* calçada *f*.
sideways [ˈsaɪdweɪz] <> *adj* **-1.** [movement] lateral **-2.** [look] de soslaio. <> *adv* **-1.** [move] de lado **-2.** [look] de soslaio.
siding [ˈsaɪdɪŋ] *n* **-1.** *UK* [for shunting] via *f* morta **-2.** *US* [loop line] tapume *m*.
sidle [ˈsaɪdl] ◆ **sidle up** *vi*: **to** ~ **up to sb** aprochegar-se furtivamente de alguém.
SIDS (*abbr of* **sudden infant death syndrome**) *n morte súbita de recém-nascido.*
siege [siːdʒ] *n* cerco *m*.
Sierra Leone [sɪːˌeərəlɪˈəʊn] *n* Serra Leoa; **in** ~ em Serra Leoa.
Sierra Leonean [sɪːˌeərəlɪˈəʊnɪən] <> *adj* serra-leonês(esa). <> *n* serra-leonês *m*, -esa *f*.
siesta [sɪˈestə] *n* sesta *f*.
sieve [sɪv] <> *n* peneira *f*; **to have a head** *OR* **memory like a** ~ ter uma memória terrível. <> *vt* peneirar.
sift [sɪft] <> *vt* **-1.** [sieve] peneirar **-2.** *fig* [examine carefully] examinar cuidadosamente. <> *vi*: **to** ~ **through sthg** analisar algo minuciosamente.
sigh [saɪ] <> *n* suspiro *m*; **to heave a** ~ **of relief** suspirar aliviado(da). <> *vi* suspirar.
sight [saɪt] <> *n* **-1.** visão *f*; **his first** ~ **of the sea** a primeira vez que ele viu o mar; **in** ~ à vista; **out of** ~ longe de vista; **to catch** ~ **of sb/sthg** avistar alguém/algo; **to know sb by** ~ conhecer alguém de vista; **to lose** ~ **of sb/sthg** perder algo/alguém de vista; **to shoot on** ~ atirar sem aviso; **at first** ~ à primeira vista **-2.** [spectacle] espetáculo *m* **-3.** [on gun] mira *f*; **to set one's** ~**s on doing sthg** propor-se a fazer algo; **to set one's** ~ **on sthg** botar algo na cabeça **-4.** [a lot]: **a** ~ **better/worse** muito melhor/pior. <> *vt* avistar, divisar.
◆ **sights** *npl* pontos *mpl* turísticos.
sighting [ˈsaɪtɪŋ] *n*: **there have been two** ~**s of the prisoner** o prisioneiro foi visto duas vezes.
sightseeing [ˈsaɪtˌsiːɪŋ] *n (U)* turismo *m*; **to do some** ~ fazer turismo.
sightseer [ˈsaɪtˌsiːəʳ] *n* turista *mf*.
sign [saɪn] <> *n* **-1.** [gen] sinal *m* **-2.** [in music] símbolo *m* **-3.** [notice] placa *f*. <> *vt* **-1.** [document] assinar **-2.** *SPORT* [player] contratar.
◆ **sign away** *vt sep* ceder *(assinando um documento).*

◆ **sign for** *vt fus* **-1.** [sign receipt for] assinar o recibo de **- 2.** [sign contract for] assinar um contrato com.

◆ **sign in** *vi* dar entrada.

◆ **sign on** *vi* **-1.** [enrol]: **to ~ on (for sthg)** [for course] inscrever-se (em algo); *MIL* alistar-se (em algo) **- 2.** [register as unemployed] cadastrar-se para receber o seguro desemprego.

◆ **sign out** *vi* dar saída.

◆ **sign up** ◇ *vt sep* **-1.** [employee] contratar **- 2.** [soldier] recrutar. ◇ *vi* [enrol]: **to ~ up (for sthg)** [for course] inscrever-se (em algo); *MIL* alistar-se (em algo).

signal ['sɪgnl] (*UK pt & pp* **-led**, *cont* **-ling**, *US pt & pp* **-ed**, *cont* **-ing**) ◇ *n* sinal *m*. ◇ *vt* **-1.** [send signals to] enviar sinais a **- 2.** [indicate - a turn] sinalizar; [- a warning] indicar; **to ~ sb (to do sthg)** fazer sinal para alguém (fazer algo) **- 3.** *fig* marcar, anunciar. ◇ *adj fml* marcante. ◇ *vi* **-1.** *AUT* sinalizar **- 2.** [indicate]: **to ~ to sb (to do sthg)** fazer sinal para alguém (fazer algo); **he ~led to the waiter for the bill** ele fez um sinal para o garçom pedindo a conta.

signal box *UK*, **signal tower** *US n* cabina *f* de sinaleiro.

signalman ['sɪgnlmən] (*pl* **-men** [-mən]) *n* sinaleiro *m*.

signal tower *n US* = **signal box**.

signatory ['sɪgnətrɪ] (*pl* **-ies**) *n* signatário *m*, -ria *f*.

signature ['sɪgnətʃəʳ] *n* assinatura *f*.

signature tune *n* tema *m*.

signet ring ['sɪgnɪt-] *n* anel *m* com sinete.

significance [sɪg'nɪfɪkəns] *n (U)* **-1.** [importance] importância *f* **- 2.** [meaning] significado *m*.

significant [sɪg'nɪfɪkənt] *adj* significativo(va).

significantly [sɪg'nɪfɪkəntlɪ] *adv* **-1.** [improve, increase, change] significativamente **- 2.** [smile, nod, wink] sugestivamente.

signify ['sɪgnɪfaɪ] (*pt & pp* **-ied**) *vt* significar.

signing ['saɪnɪŋ] *n UK* contratação *f*.

sign language *n (U)* linguagem *f* de sinais.

signpost ['saɪnpəʊst] *n* placa *f* de sinalização.

Sikh [si:k] ◇ *adj* sique. ◇ *n* sique *mf*.

Sikhism ['si:kɪzm] *n (U)* siquismo *m*.

silage ['saɪlɪdʒ] *n (U)* silagem *f*.

silence ['saɪləns] ◇ *n* silêncio *m*; **in ~** em silêncio. ◇ *vt* silenciar, calar.

silencer ['saɪlənsəʳ] *n* **-1.** [on gun] silenciador *m* **- 2.** *AUT* silenciador *m*, silencioso *m*.

silent ['saɪlənt] *adj* **-1.** [gen] silencioso(sa) **- 2.** [taciturn] silencioso(sa), taciturno(na) **- 3.** [not revealing anything]: **to be ~ about sthg** ser discreto(ta) sobre algo **- 4.** *CINEMA & LING* mudo(da).

silently ['saɪləntlɪ] *adv* **-1.** [without speaking] em silêncio **- 2.** [noiselessly] silenciosamente.

silent partner *n US* sócio *m* comanditário, sócia *f* comanditária.

silhouette [ˌsɪlu:'et] ◇ *n* silhueta *f*. ◇ *vt*: **to be ~d against sthg** destacar-se (contra algo).

silicon ['sɪlɪkən] *n (U)* silício *m*.

silicon chip [ˌsɪlɪkən-] *n* chip *m* de silício.

silicone ['sɪlɪkəʊn] *n (U)* silicone *m*.

Silicon Valley *n* Vale do Silício.

silk [sɪlk] ◇ *n (U)* seda *f*. ◇ *comp* de seda.

silk screen printing *n (U)* serigrafia *f*.

silkworm ['sɪlkwɜ:m] *n* bicho-da-seda *m*.

silky ['sɪlkɪ] (*compar* **-ier**, *superl* **-iest**) *adj* sedoso(sa).

sill [sɪl] *n* peitoril *m*.

silliness ['sɪlɪnɪs] *n (U)* imbecilidade *f*, estupidez *f*.

silly ['sɪlɪ] (*compar* **-ier**, *superl* **-iest**) *adj* **-1.** [foolish] bobo(ba) **- 2.** [comical] bobo(ba), ridículo(la).

silo ['saɪləʊ] (*pl* **-s**) *n* silo *m*.

silt [sɪlt] *n (U)* sedimento *m*, lodo *m*.

◆ **silt up** *vi* assorear.

silver ['sɪlvəʳ] ◇ *adj* prateado(da). ◇ *n (U)* **-1.** [metal] prata *f* **- 2.** [coins] moedas *fpl* **- 3.** [silverware] prataria *f*. ◇ *comp* [made of silver] de prata.

silver-plated [-'pleɪtɪd] *adj* prateado(da).

silver screen *n inf*: **the ~** o cinema.

silversmith ['sɪlvəsmɪθ] *n* prateiro *m*, -ra *f*.

silverware ['sɪlvəweəʳ] *n* **-1.** [objects made of silver] prataria *f* **- 2.** *US* [cutlery] prataria *f*.

silver wedding *n* bodas *fpl* de prata.

silvery ['sɪlvərɪ] *adj* prateado(da).

similar ['sɪmɪləʳ] *adj* parecido(da), semelhante; **~ to sthg** parecido(da) *OR* similar a algo.

similarity [ˌsɪmɪ'lærətɪ] (*pl* **-ies**) *n*: **~ (between)** semelhança *f* (entre), similaridade *f* (entre); **~ to sthg** semelhança *f* com algo.

similarly ['sɪmɪləlɪ] *adv* igualmente, da mesma forma.

simile ['sɪmɪlɪ] *n* símile *m*.

simmer ['sɪməʳ] *vt & vi* cozinhar em fogo baixo.

◆ **simmer down** *vi inf* sossegar o facho.

simper ['sɪmpəʳ] ◇ *n* sorriso *m* bobo. ◇ *vi* sorrir de forma boba.

simpering ['sɪmpərɪŋ] *adj* **-1.** [person] que sorri com cara de bobo(ba) **- 2.** [smile] bobo(ba).

simple ['sɪmpl] *adj* **-1.** [gen] simples **- 2.** *inf* [mentally retarded] simplório(ria).

simple-minded [-'maɪndɪd] *adj* simplório(ria).

simpleton ['sɪmpltən] *n dated* basbaque *mf*.

simplicity [sɪm'plɪsətɪ] *n* simplicidade *f*.

simplification [ˌsɪmplɪfɪ'keɪʃn] *n* simplificação *f*.

simplify ['sɪmplɪfaɪ] (*pt & pp* **-ied**) *vt* simplificar.

simplistic [sɪm'plɪstɪk] *adj* simplista.

simply ['sɪmplɪ] *adv* **-1.** [gen] simplesmente; **you ~ must go and see the film** você só tem que ir ver o filme **- 2.** [in an uncomplicated way] de forma simples.

simulate ['sɪmjʊleɪt] *vt* **-1.** [feign] simular, fingir **- 2.** [produce effect, appearance of] simular.

simulation [ˌsɪmjʊ'leɪʃn] *n* **-1.** [feigning] simulação *f*, fingimento *m* **- 2.** [simulated appearance, effect] simulacro *m* **- 3.** *COMPUT* simulação *f*.

simulator ['sɪmjʊleɪtəʳ] *n* simulador *m*.

simultaneous [*UK* ˌsɪmʊl'teɪnjəs, *US* ˌsaɪməl'teɪnjəs] *adj* simultâneo(nea).

simultaneously [*UK* ˌsɪmʊl'teɪnjəslɪ, *US* ˌsaɪməl'teɪnjəslɪ] *adv* simultaneamente.

sin [sɪn] (*pt & pp* **-ned**, *cont* **-ning**) ◇ *n* pecado *m*; **to live in ~** viver em pecado. ◇ *vi*: **to ~ (against sb/sthg)** pecar (contra alguém/algo).

sin bin *n inf ICE HOCKEY* banco *m* para os suspensos do jogo.

since [sɪns] ◇ *adv*: **~ (then)** desde então; **long ~**

há muito tempo. ◇ *prep* desde. ◇ *conj* **-1.** [in time]: **it's ages ~ I saw him** faz séculos que eu não o vejo **-2.** [because] já que, como.

sincere [sɪn'sɪəʳ] *adj* sincero(ra).

sincerely [sɪn'sɪəlɪ] *adv* sinceramente; **Yours ~** [at end of letter] atenciosamente.

sincerity [sɪn'serətɪ] *n (U)* sinceridade *f.*

sine [saɪn] *n MATH* seno *m.*

sinecure ['saɪnɪˌkjʊəʳ] *n* sinecura *f.*

sinew ['sɪnju:] *n* tendão *m.*

sinewy ['sɪnju:ɪ] *adj* musculoso(sa).

sinful ['sɪnfʊl] *adj* **-1.** [guilty of sin] pecador(ra) **-2.** [wicked, immoral] pecaminoso(sa).

sing [sɪŋ] (*pt* **sang**, *pp* **sung**) ◇ *vt* cantar; **to ~ sb a song, to ~ a song to sb** cantar uma música para alguém. ◇ *vi* cantar.

Singapore [ˌsɪŋə'pɔ:ʳ] *n* Cingapura.

Singaporean [ˌsɪŋəpə'rɪən] ◇ *adj* cingapuriano(-na). ◇ *n* cingapuriano *m*, -na *f.*

singe [sɪndʒ] (*cont* **singeing**) *vt* chamuscar.

singer ['sɪŋəʳ] *n* cantor *m*, -ra *f.*

Singhalese [ˌsɪŋə'li:z] ◇ *adj* cingalês(esa). ◇ *n* **-1.** [person] cingalês *m*, -esa *f* **-2.** [language] cingalês *m.*

singing ['sɪŋɪŋ] ◇ *adj* de canto. ◇ *n* canto *m.*

singing telegram *n* telegrama *m* cantado.

single ['sɪŋgl] ◇ *adj* **-1.** [sole] único(ca); **to sweep up every ~ leaf** varrer todas as folhas, sem deixar nenhuma; **every ~ day** todo santo dia **-2.** [unmarried] solteiro(ra) **-3.** *UK* [one-way] de ida. ◇ *n* **-1.** *UK* [one-way ticket] passagem *f* de ida **-2.** *MUS* single *m.*

◆ **singles** *npl TENNIS* simples *f inv.*

◆ **single out** *vt sep*: **to ~ sb out (for sthg)** escolher alguém (para algo).

single bed *n* cama *f* de solteiro.

single-breasted [-'brestɪd] *adj* não-trespassado (da).

single cream *n (U) UK* creme *m* leve.

single-decker (bus) *n UK* ônibus *m inv* de um andar.

Single European Market *n*: **the ~** o Mercado Comum Europeu.

single file *n*: **in ~** em fila indiana.

single-handed [-'hændɪd] *adv* sem ajuda.

single-minded [-'maɪndɪd] *adj* determinado(da), resoluto(ta); **to be ~ about sthg** ter um objetivo muito claro em relação a algo.

single parent *n* pai *m* solteiro, mãe *f* solteira.

single-parent family *n* família *f* em que falta um dos pais.

single room *n* quarto *m* simples.

singles bar *n* bar *m* para solteiros.

singlet ['sɪŋglɪt] *n* camiseta *f* (sem mangas).

single ticket *n UK* passagem *f* de ida.

singsong ['sɪŋsɒŋ] *inf* ◇ *adj* monótono(na). ◇ *n UK* reunião *f* para cantar.

singular ['sɪŋgjʊləʳ] ◇ *adj* **-1.** *GRAMM* no singular **-2.** [unusual, remarkable] singular. ◇ *n* singular *m.*

singularly ['sɪŋgjʊləlɪ] *adv* notavelmente.

Sinhalese ['sɪnhəli:z] *adj* & *n* = **Singhalese.**

sinister ['sɪnɪstəʳ] *adj* sinistro(tra).

sink [sɪŋk] (*pt* **sank**, *pp* **sunk**) ◇ *n* pia *f.* ◇ *vt* **-1.** [cause to go underwater] afundar **-2.** [cause to penetrate]: **to ~ sthg into sthg** cravar algo em algo. ◇ *vi* **-1.** [gen] afundar; **to ~ without trace** sumir sem deixar vestígio **-2.** [below ground - person] afundar-se; [- sun] pôr-se **-3.** [slump]: **he sank back into his chair** ele se afundou na cadeira; **she sank to her knees** ela caiu sobre os joelhos **-4.** *fig* [heart, spirits] congelar **-5.** [fall] baixar; **her voice sank to a whisper** sua voz foi baixando até ficar um sussurro **-6.** *fig* [slip]: **to ~ into sthg** [despair, poverty] cair em algo; [depression, coma] entrar em algo.

◆ **sink in** *vi*: **it hasn't sunk in yet** ainda não caiu a ficha.

sinking ['sɪŋkɪŋ] *n* afundamento *m.*

sinking fund *n* fundo *m* de amortização.

sink unit *n* pia *f.*

sinner ['sɪnəʳ] *n* pecador *m*, -ra *f.*

Sinn Fein [ˌʃɪn'feɪn] *n* Sinn Fein *m*, *braço político do IRA.*

sinuous ['sɪnjʊəs] *adj* sinuoso(sa).

sinus ['saɪnəs] (*pl* **-es**) *n* seio *m (paranasal).*

sinusitis [ˌsaɪnəs'aɪtɪs] *n* sinusite *f.*

sip [sɪp] (*pt* & *pp* **-ped**, *cont* **-ping**) ◇ *n* gole *m.* ◇ *vt* bebericar.

siphon ['saɪfn] ◇ *n* sifão *m.* ◇ *vt* **-1.** [draw off] tirar com sifão **-2.** *fig* [transfer] desviar.

◆ **siphon off** *vt sep* **-1.** [draw off] tirar com sifão **-2.** *fig* [transfer] desviar.

sir [sɜ:ʳ] *n* **-1.** [form of address] senhor *m* **-2.** [in titles] sir *m.*

siren ['saɪərən] *n* sirene *f.*

sirloin (steak) ['sɜ:lɔɪn] *n* bife *m* de lombo de vaca.

sissy ['sɪsɪ] (*pl* **-ies**) *n inf* fresco *m.*

sister ['sɪstəʳ] ◇ *adj* **-1.** [organization] congênere **-2.** [ship] gêmeo(mea). ◇ *n* **-1.** [gen] irmã *f* **-2.** [nun] irmã *f*, freira *f* **-3.** *UK* [senior nurse] (enfermeira *f*) supervisora *f.*

sisterhood ['sɪstəhʊd] *n (U)* irmandade *f.*

sister-in-law (*pl* **sisters-in-law** *OR* **sister-in-laws**) *n* cunhada *f.*

sisterly ['sɪstəlɪ] *adj* de irmã.

sit [sɪt] (*pt* & *pp* **sat**, *cont* **-ting**) ◇ *vt* **-1.** [place] sentar **-2.** *UK* [examination] fazer. ◇ *vi* **-1.** [gen] sentar-se **-2.** [be member]: **to ~ on sthg** integrar algo, fazer parte de algo **-3.** [be in session] reunir-se **-4.** [be situated] ficar **-5.** *phr*: **to ~ tight** ficar onde se está.

◆ **sit about, sit around** *vi* ver o tempo passar.

◆ **sit back** *vi* **-1.** [relax] recostar-se, relaxar **-2.** [not act] ficar sentado(da).

◆ **sit down** ◇ *vt sep* sentar. ◇ *vi* sentar-se.

◆ **sit in on** *vt fus* estar presente (sem tomar parte).

◆ **sit out** *vt sep* **-1.** [tolerate] agüentar *(até o final)* **-2.** [not participate in] *não participar de.*

◆ **sit through** *vt fus* agüentar até o final.

◆ **sit up** *vi* **-1.** [be sitting upright] sentar-se reto(ta); [move into upright position] endireitar-se **-2.** [stay up] ficar acordado(da).

sitcom ['sɪtkɒm] *n inf* comédia *f* de situação, sitcom *f.*

sit-down <> *adj* [gen] com os participantes sentados à mesa; **a ~ strike** uma greve de braços cruzados. <> *n UK*: **to have a ~** sentar-se um pouco.

site [saɪt] <> *n* **-1.** [piece of land - archaelogy] sítio *m*; [- building] lote *m*; [- missile] campo *m*; [- camp] área *f* **-2.** [location, place] local *m* **-3.** *COMPUT* site *m*. <> *vt* localizar-se, situar-se.

sit-in *n* greve *f* branca.

sitter ['sɪtəʳ] *n* **-1.** *ART* modelo *mf* vivo, -va **-2.** [babysitter] babá *f*.

sitting ['sɪtɪŋ] *n* **-1.** [serving of meal] turno *m* para as refeições **-2.** [session] sessão *f*.

sitting duck *n inf* alvo *m* fácil, presa *f* fácil.

sitting room *n* sala *f* de estar.

sitting tenant *n UK* *inquilino que tem o direito de permanecer numa casa mesmo após sua venda.*

situate ['sɪtjʊeɪt] *vt* **-1.** [locate] situar **-2.** [put in context] contextualizar.

situated ['sɪtjʊeɪtɪd] *adj*: **to be ~** estar localizado (da), localizar-se.

situation [ˌsɪtjʊ'eɪʃn] *n* **-1.** [gen] situação *f* **-2.** [location] localização *f* **-3.** [job] emprego *m*, colocação *f*; **'Situations Vacant'** *UK* 'Empregos'.

situation comedy *n* comédia *f* de situação.

sit-up *n* abdominal *m*.

SI unit (*abbr of* **Système international d'unités unit**) *n unidade do sistema internacional de medidas, como o metro, o litro etc.*

six [sɪks] <> *num adj* **-1.** [numbering six] seis **-2.** [referring to age]: **she's ~ (years old)** ela tem seis anos (de idade). <> *num pron* seis; **I want ~** quero seis; **~ of us went** seis do nosso grupo foram; **there were ~ of us** éramos seis; **groups of ~** grupos *mpl* de seis. <> *num n* **-1.** [gen] seis; **two hundred and ~** duzentos e seis **-2.** [six o'clock] seis *(horas)*; **we arrived at ~** chegamos às seis **-3.** [six degrees]: **it's ~ below** faz seis graus abaixo de zero **-4.** [in addresses]: **~ Peyton Place** Praça Peyton, casa *OR* número 6; **we sell them in ~es** são vendidos(das) de seis em seis; **to form into ~es** formar grupos de seis; **~-nil** seis a zero.

six-shooter [-'ʃu:təʳ] *n US* revólver *m* (de seis tiros).

sixteen [sɪks'ti:n] *num* dezesseis; *see also* **six**.

sixteenth [sɪks'ti:nθ] *num* décimo sexto, décima sexta; *see also* **sixth**.

sixth [sɪksθ] <> *num adj* sexto(ta). <> *num adv* sexto. <> *num pron* sexto(ta). <> *n* **-1.** [fraction] sexto *m* **-2.** [in dates]: **the ~** o dia seis; **the ~ of September** o dia seis de setembro.

sixth form *n UK SCH* *curso opcional de dois anos no ensino secundário britânico oferecido aos alunos de 16 anos a fim de ingressarem na universidade.*

sixth form college *n UK* *escola pública na Inglaterra para adolescentes de 16 a 18 anos na qual se preparam para ingressar na universidade ou para fazer testes de formação profissional.*

sixth sense *n* sexto sentido *m*.

sixtieth ['sɪkstɪəθ] *num* sexagésimo(ma); *see also* **sixth**.

sixty ['sɪkstɪ] (*pl* **-ies**) *num* sessenta; *see also* **six**.

◆ **sixties** *npl* **-1.** [decade]: **the sixties** os anos sessenta **-2.** [in ages]: **to be in one's sixties** estar na casa dos sessenta.

size [saɪz] *n* **-1.** tamanho *m*; **an organization of that ~** uma organização daquele porte **-2.** *phr*: **to cut sb down to ~** colocar alguém em seu devido lugar.

◆ **size up** *vt sep* **-1.** [situation] avaliar **-2.** [person] julgar.

sizeable ['saɪzəbl] *adj* considerável.

-sized [saɪzd] *suffix*: **life ~ models** modelos *mpl* em tamanho natural; **medium ~ companies** empresas *fpl* de médio porte.

sizzle ['sɪzl] *vi* chiar.

SK *abbr of* **Saskatchewan**.

skate [skeɪt] (*pl sense 3 only inv OR* **-s**) <> *n* **-1.** [gen] patim *m* **-2.** [fish] raia *f*. <> *vi* **-1.** [on ice skates] patinar no gelo **-2.** [on roller skates] patinar, andar de patins.

◆ **skate over, skate round** *vt fus* evitar, fugir de.

skateboard ['skeɪtbɔ:d] *n* skate *m*.

skateboarder ['skeɪtbɔ:dəʳ] *n* skatista *mf*.

skater ['skeɪtəʳ] *n* patinador *m*, -ra *f*.

skating ['skeɪtɪŋ] *n (U)* **-1.** [on ice] patinação *f* no gelo; **to go ~** patinar no gelo **-2.** [on roller skates] patinação *f*; **to go ~** andar de patins.

skating rink *n* [for ice skating] pista *f* de patinação no gelo; [for roller skating] rinque *m*, pista *f* de patinação.

skein [skeɪn] *n* madeixa *f*.

skeletal ['skelɪtl] *adj* esquelético(ca).

skeleton ['skelɪtn] <> *adj* básico(ca), mínimo (ma). <> *n* esqueleto *m*; **to have a ~ in the cupboard** *fig* ter o rabo preso.

skeleton key *n* chave-mestra *f*.

skeleton staff *n* contingente *m* mínimo de pessoal.

skeptic etc *n US* = **sceptic etc**.

sketch [sketʃ] <> *n* **-1.** [drawing] esboço *m*, croqui *m* **-2.** [brief description] resumo *m* **-3.** [on TV, radio, stage] esquete *m*. <> *vt* **-1.** [draw] fazer um esboço de **-2.** [describe] resumir. <> *vi* fazer croquis.

◆ **sketch in, sketch out** *vt sep* dar uma rápida idéia de.

sketchbook ['sketʃbʊk] *n* caderno *m* de desenhos.

sketchpad ['sketʃpæd] *n* bloco *m* de desenhos.

sketchy ['sketʃɪ] (*compar* **-ier**, *superl* **-iest**) *adj* incompleto(ta), pouco detalhado(da).

skew [skju:] <> *n UK*: **on the ~** torcido(da). <> *vt* distorcer. <> *vi* atravessar-se.

skewer ['skjʊəʳ] <> *n* espeto *m*. <> *vt* espetar.

skew-whiff [ˌskju:'wɪf] *adj UK inf* torto(ta).

ski [ski:] (*pt* & *pp* **skied**, *cont* **skiing**) <> *n* esqui *m*. <> *comp* de esqui. <> *vi* esquiar.

ski boots *npl* botas *fpl* de esqui.

skid [skɪd] (*pt* & *pp* **-ded**, *cont* **-ding**) <> *n AUT* derrapagem *f*; **to go into a ~** derrapar. <> *vi* derrapar.

skid mark *n* marca *f* de derrapagem.

skid row [-rəʊ] *n (U) US inf*: **to be on ~** estar na rua da amargura.

skier ['ski:ə^r] *n* esquiador *m*, -ra *f*.

skiing ['ski:ɪŋ] ◇ *n (U)* esqui *m*; **to go ~** ir esquiar. ◇ *comp* **-1.** [holiday, accident] de esqui **-2.** [enthusiast] do esqui.

ski instructor *n* instrutor *m*, -ra *f* de esqui.

ski jump *n* **-1.** [slope] rampa *f* para saltos de esqui **-2.** [sporting event] salto *m* de esqui.

skilful, skillful *US* ['skɪlfʊl] *adj* hábil.

skilfully, skillfully *US* ['skɪlfʊlɪ] *adv* habilmente.

ski lift *n* teleférico *m*.

skill [skɪl] *n* **-1.** *(U)* [expertise] experiência *f*, destreza *f* **-2.** [craft, technique] habilidade *f*.

skilled [skɪld] *adj* **-1.** [skilful] habilidoso(sa); **to be ~ in** *OR* **at doing sthg** ter muito jeito para fazer algo **-2.** [trained] especializado(da), qualificado(da).

skillet ['skɪlɪt] *n US* frigideira *f*.

skillful *etc adj US* = **skilful** *etc*.

skim [skɪm] (*pt* & *pp* **-med**, *cont* **-ming**) ◇ *vt* **-1.** [remove - cream] tirar a nata de; [- fat] tirar a gordura de; [- sap] extrair **-2.** [glide over] roçar **-3.** [glance through] passar os olhos em. ◇ *vi* **-1.** **: to ~ over sthg** [bird] dar uma rasante em algo; [stone] ricochetear em algo **-2.** [read]**: to ~ through sthg** ler algo por cima.

skim(med) milk [skɪm(d)mɪlk] *n (U)* leite *m* desnatado.

skimp [skɪmp] *vi*: **to ~ on sthg** [food, material, time] restringir algo; [money] economizar em algo; [work] fazer algo correndo.

skimpy ['skɪmpɪ] (*compar* **-ier**, *superl* **-iest**) *adj* **-1.** [meal] parco(ca) **-2.** [clothes] justo(ta) **-3.** [facts] insuficiente.

skin [skɪn] (*pt* & *pp* **-ned**, *cont* **-ning**) ◇ *n* **-1.** *(U)* [gen] pele *f*; **to do sthg by the ~ of one's teeth** fazer algo por um triz; **to jump out of one's ~** *UK* perder o chão; **it makes my ~ crawl** me dá calafrios; **to save one's own ~** salvar a própria pele **-2.** [of fruit, vegetable, on paint, pudding] casca *f* **-3.** [on milk] nata *f*. ◇ *vt* **-1.** [remove skin from - fruit] descascar; [- dead animal] pelar **-2.** [graze] esfolar.

skin-deep *adj* superficial.

skin diver *n* mergulhador *m*, -ra que pratica mergulho livre *f*.

skin diving *n (U)*: **to go ~** praticar mergulho *m* livre.

skinflint ['skɪnflɪnt] *n* pão-duro *m*.

skin graft *n* enxerto *m* de pele.

skinhead ['skɪnhed] *n UK* skinhead *m*.

skinny ['skɪnɪ] (*compar* **-ier**, *superl* **-iest**) *adj inf* magricela.

skint [skɪnt] *adj UK v inf* pelado(da), sem um tostão.

skin test *n* teste *m* de pele.

skin-tight *adj* muito justo(ta).

skip [skɪp] (*pt* & *pp* **-ped**, *cont* **-ping**) ◇ *n* **-1.** [little jump] pulinho *m* **-2.** *UK* [large container] caçamba *f* *(para entulho)*. ◇ *vt* **-1.** [page] pular **-2.** [class] perder **-3.** [meal] faltar a. ◇ *vi* **-1.** [move in little jumps] ir pulando **-2.** *UK* [using rope] pular.

ski pants *npl* calças *fpl* de esqui.

ski pole *n* bastão *m* de esqui.

skipper ['skɪpə^r] *n* capitão *m*, -tã *f*.

skipping ['skɪpɪŋ] *n UK*: **to do some ~** pular corda.

skipping rope ['skɪpɪŋ-] *n UK* corda *f* de pular.

ski resort *n* estação *f* de esqui.

skirmish ['skɜ:mɪʃ] ◇ *n* **-1.** *MIL* escaramuça *f* **-2.** *fig* [disagreement] desavença *f*. ◇ *vi MIL* & *fig* ter uma escaramuça.

skirt [skɜ:t] ◇ *n* [garment] saia *f*. ◇ *vt* **-1.** [go round] contornar **-2.** [avoid dealing with] evitar.

◆ **skirt round** *vt fus* **-1.** [go round]: **to ~ round sb/sthg** desviar de alguém/algo **-2.** [avoid dealing with]: **to ~ round sthg** evitar algo.

skirting board ['skɜ:tɪŋ-] *n UK* rodapé *m*.

ski stick *n* bastão *m* de esqui.

skit [skɪt] *n*: **~ on sthg** sátira *f* *OR* paródia *f* sobre algo.

ski tow *n* ski lift *m*.

skittish ['skɪtɪʃ] *adj* **-1.** [person] esquivo(va) **-2.** [animal] arisco(ca).

skittle ['skɪtl] *n UK* pino *m* de boliche.

◆ **skittles** *n (U) UK* boliche *m*.

skive [skaɪv] *vi UK inf*: **to ~ (off)** [at school] matar aula; [at work] matar o serviço.

skivvy ['skɪvɪ] (*pl* **-ies**, *pt* & *pp* **-ied**) *UK inf* ◇ *n* serviçal *mf*. ◇ *vi*: **to ~ (for sb)** servir de empregada(da) *(para alguém)*.

skulduggery [skʌl'dʌgərɪ] *n (U)* trapaça *f*.

skulk [skʌlk] *vi* esconder-se.

skull [skʌl] *n* **-1.** *ANAT* crânio *m* **-2.** [on skeleton] caveira *f*.

skullcap ['skʌlkæp] *n* solidéu *m*.

skunk [skʌŋk] *n* gambá *m*.

sky [skaɪ] (*pl* **skies**) *n* céu *m*.

skycap *n US* carregador *m*, -ra *f* de bagagem *(no aeroporto)*.

skydiver ['skaɪˌdaɪvə^r] *n* pára-quedista *mf*.

skydiving ['skaɪˌdaɪvɪŋ] *n (U)* pára-quedismo *m*.

sky-high *inf* ◇ *adj* nas alturas. ◇ *adv*: **to blow sthg ~** [bridge, building] mandar algo para os ares; *fig* [argument, theory] mandar algo para o espaço; **to go ~** ir para as alturas.

skylark ['skaɪlɑ:k] *n* calandra *f*.

skylight ['skaɪlaɪt] *n* clarabóia *f*.

skyline ['skaɪlaɪn] *n* linha *f* do horizonte.

skyscraper ['skaɪˌskreɪpə^r] *n* arranha-céu *m*.

slab [slæb] *n* **-1.** [of concrete, stone] laje *f* **-2.** [of meat, cake] fatia *f* **-3.** [of chocolate] barra *f*.

slack [slæk] ◇ *adj* **-1.** [not tight] frouxo(xa) **-2.** [not busy] parado(da) **-3.** [not efficient] desleixado(da), negligente. ◇ *n (U)* ponta *f* solta.

◆ **slacks** *npl dated* slack *m*.

slacken ['slækn] ◇ *vt* **-1.** [make slower] reduzir **-2.** [make looser] afrouxar. ◇ *vi* **-1.** [become slower] reduzir **-2.** [become looser] afrouxar.

◆ **slacken off** *vi* **-1.** [rain, storm] abrandar **-2.** [work, trade] desacelerar.

slag [slæg] *n* **-1.** *(U)* [waste material] escombros *mpl* **-2.** *inf pej* [promiscuous woman] vagabunda *f*.

slagheap ['slæghi:p] *n* monte *m* de entulho.

slain [sleɪn] *pp* ▻ **slay**.

slalom ['slɑ:ləm] *n* corrida *f* com obstáculos *(de esqui e canoagem)*.

slam [slæm] (*pt* & *pp* **-med**, *cont* **-ming**) ◇ *vt* **-1.** [shut] bater **-2.** [place roughly]: **to ~ sthg on (to) sthg** jogar algo com violência sobre algo **-3.** *fig* [criticize] criticar. ◇ *vi* [shut] bater.

slander ['slɑ:ndəʳ] ◇ *n (U)* calúnia *f.* ◇ *vt* caluniar.
slanderous ['slɑ:ndrəs] *adj* calunioso(sa).
slang [slæŋ] ◇ *adj* popular. ◇ *n (U)* gíria *f.*
slant [slɑ:nt] ◇ *n* **-1.** [diagonal angle - of table, shelf] inclinação *f*; [- of land] declive *m*; **on** *OR* **ata ~** inclinado(da) **-2.** [point of view] perspectiva *f*, enfoque *m.* ◇ *vt* [bias] distorcer. ◇ *vi* [slope] inclinar-se.
slanting ['slɑ:ntɪŋ] *adj* inclinado(da).
slap [slæp] (*pt & pp* **-ped**, *cont* **-ping**) ◇ *n* **-1.** [on face] bofetada *f*; **a ~ in the face** [fig] uma bofetada **-2.** [on back] tapa *m.* ◇ *vt* **-1.** [smack - on face] esbofetear; [- on back] dar um tapa em **-2.** [put]: **to ~ sthg on** dar uma retocada em. ◇ *adv inf* [exactly] em cheio; **~ in the middle of the city** bem no meio da cidade.
slapdash ['slæpdæʃ], **slaphappy** ['slæp,hæpɪ] *adj* relaxado(da).
slapstick ['slæpstɪk] *n (U)* pastelão *m*; **the film is pure ~** este filme é um pastelão só.
slap-up *adj UK inf* farto(ta); **a ~ dinner** um jantar formidável.
slash [slæʃ] ◇ *n* **-1.** [long cut] rasgão *m*, corte *m* **-2.** [oblique stroke] barra *f* oblíqua; **forward ~** barra *f* (inclinada) **-3.** *UK inf* [pee]: **to have a ~** fazer xixi. ◇ *vt* **-1.** [cut - material, tyres] rasgar; [- wrists] cortar **-2.** *inf* [reduce drastically] cortar.
slat [slæt] *n* ripa *f*, sarrafo *m.*
slate [sleɪt] ◇ *n* **-1.** *(U)* [material] ardósia *f* **-2.** [on roof] telha *f* de ardósia; **to wipe the ~ clean** sacudir a poeira; **put it on the ~** põe na conta. ◇ *vt* [criticize] malhar.
slatted *adj* com ripas.
slaughter ['slɔ:təʳ] ◇ *n* **-1.** [of animals] matança *f* **-2.** [of people] chacina *f.* ◇ *vt* **-1.** [animals] matar, carnear **-2.** [people] chacinar.
slaughterhouse ['slɔ:təhaʊs, *pl* -haʊzɪz] *n* matadouro *m.*
Slav [slɑ:v] ◇ *adj* eslavo(va). ◇ *n* eslavo *m*, -va *f.*
slave [sleɪv] ◇ *n* escravo *m*, -va *f*; **to be a ~ to sthg** ser escravo(va) de algo. ◇ *vi* [work hard]: **to ~ (over sthg)** trabalhar como um escravo em algo, trabalhar como uma escrava em algo.
slaver ['sleɪvəʳ] *vi* babar.
slavery ['sleɪvərɪ] *n (U)* escravidão *f.*
slave trade *n*: **the ~** o tráfico *OR* comércio de escravos.
Slavic ◇ *adj* eslavo(va). ◇ *n* **-1.** [language] eslavo *m* **-2.** *HIST* eslavo *m*, -va *f.*
slavish ['sleɪvɪʃ] *adj pej* [unoriginal, servile] servil.
Slavonic [slə'vɒnɪk] *adj & n* = **Slavic**.
slay [sleɪ] (*pt* **slew**, *pp* **slain**) *vt literary* assassinar.
sleaze *n* sujeira *f.*
sleazy ['sli:zɪ] (*compar* **-ier**, *superl* **-iest**) *adj* sujo(ja).
sledge [sledʒ], **sled** *US* [sled] *n* trenó *m.*
sledgehammer ['sledʒ,hæməʳ] *n* marreta *f.*
sleek [sli:k] *adj* **-1.** [hair] sedoso(sa) **-2.** [fur] brilhoso(sa) **-3.** [animal, bird] lustroso(sa) **-4.** [car, plane] vistoso(sa) **-5.** [person] polido(da).
sleep [sli:p] (*pt & pp* **slept**) ◇ *n* **-1.** *(U)* [rest] sono *m*; **to go to ~** [doze off] adormecer; [go numb] ficar dormente; **to put to ~** [patient] anestesiar; [animal] sacrificar **-2.** [period of sleeping] sono *m.* ◇ *vi* dormir.
◆ **sleep around** *vi inf pej* dormir com qualquer um(ma).
◆ **sleep in** *vi* dormir até mais tarde.
◆ **sleep off** *vt sep*: **to ~ sthg off** curar algo dormindo.
◆ **sleep through** *vt fus*: **to ~ through sthg** não despertar com algo.
◆ **sleep together** *vi euphemism* dormir juntos(tas).
◆ **sleep with** *vt fus euphemism* dormir com.
sleeper ['sli:pəʳ] *n* **-1.** [person]: **to be a heavy/light ~** ter sono pesado/leve **-2.** [sleeping compartment] leito *m* **-3.** [train] trem-leito *m* **-4.** *UK* [on railway track] dormente *m.*
sleepily ['sli:pɪlɪ] *adv* sonolentamente, quase dormindo.
sleeping bag ['sli:pɪŋ-] *n* saco *m* de dormir.
sleeping car ['sli:pɪŋ-] *n* vagão-leito *m.*
sleeping partner ['sli:pɪŋ-] *n UK* sócio *m* comanditário, sócia *f* comanditária.
sleeping pill ['sli:pɪŋ-] *n* pílula *f* para dormir.
sleeping policeman ['sli:pɪŋ-] *n UK inf* quebra-molas *m inv.*
sleeping tablet ['sli:pɪŋ-] *n* comprimido *m* para dormir.
sleepless ['sli:plɪs] *adj* em claro, sem dormir.
sleeplessness ['sli:plɪsnɪs] *n (U)* falta *f* de sono, insônia *f.*
sleepwalk ['sli:pwɔ:k] *vi* sonambular.
sleepy ['sli:pɪ] (*compar* **-ier**, *superl* **-iest**) *adj* **-1.** [person] sonolento(ta) **-2.** [place] pacato(ta).
sleet [sli:t] ◇ *n (U)* granizo *m.* ◇ *v impers* chover granizo.
sleeve [sli:v] *n* **-1.** [of garment] manga *f*; **to have sthg up one's ~** ter uma carta escondida na manga **-2.** [for record] capa *f.*
sleeveless ['sli:vlɪs] *adj* sem mangas.
sleigh [sleɪ] *n* trenó *m.*
sleight of hand [,slaɪt-] *n (U)* **-1.** [skill with hands] prestidigitação *f* **-2.** *fig* [deception] artimanha *f.*
slender ['slendəʳ] *adj* **-1.** [thin - person, figure] esbelto(ta); [- legs] delgado(da) **-2.** [scarce] escasso(sa).
slept [slept] *pt & pp* ▷ **sleep**.
sleuth [slu:θ] *n inf hum* detetive *mf.*
slew [slu:] ◇ *pt* ▷ **slay**. ◇ *vi*: **the car ~ed off the road** o carro rodopiou para fora da estrada.
slice [slaɪs] ◇ *n* **-1.** [gen] fatia *f* **-2.** [of lemon] rodela *f* **-3.** [proportion] parte *f* **-4.** *SPORT* cortada *f.* ◇ *vt* **-1.** [cut into slices] fatiar **-2.** *SPORT* cortar. ◇ *vi*: **to ~ through/into sthg** cortar algo com facilidade.
◆ **slice off** *vt sep* [sever] arrancar fora.
◆ **slice up** *vt sep* [food] fatiar, cortar em fatias.
sliced bread [slaɪst-] *n (U)* pão *m* fatiado.
slick [slɪk] ◇ *adj* **-1.** [smoothly efficient - performance, teamwork] talentoso(sa); [- technique, crime] engenhoso(sa) **-2.** *pej* [glib] ardiloso(sa). ◇ *n* local *m* escorregadio.
slicker *n US* capa *f* de chuva.
slide [slaɪd] (*pt & pp* **slid** [slɪd]) ◇ *n* **-1.** *PHOT* eslaide *m* **-2.** [in playground] escorregador *m* **-3.** [for microscope] lâmina *f* **-4.** *UK* [for hair] passador *m* **-5.**

[decline] declínio *m.* ◇ *vt* [move smoothly] deslizar. ◇ *vi* **-1.** [on ice, slippery surface] escorregar **-2.** [move quietly] deslizar **-3.** [decline gradually] sucumbir a; **to let things ~** deixar que as coisas piorem.

slide projector *n* projetor *m* de eslaides.

slide rule *n* régua *f* de cálculo.

sliding door [ˌslaɪdɪŋ-] *n* porta *f* de correr.

sliding scale [ˌslaɪdɪŋ-] *n* escala *f* móvel.

slight [slaɪt] ◇ *adj* **-1.** [minor] ligeiro(ra); **not in the ~est** nem de leve; **I haven't got the ~est interest in his car** eu não tenho o menor interesse no carro dele **-2.** [slender] de aspecto frágil. ◇ *n* menosprezo *m.* ◇ *vt* [offend] menosprezar.

slightly ['slaɪtlɪ] *adv* **-1.** [to small extent] ligeiramente, levemente **-2.** [slenderly]: **~ built** magrinho(nha).

slim [slɪm] (*compar* **-mer**, *superl* **-mest**, *pt* & *pp* **-med**, *cont* **-ming**) ◇ *adj* **-1.** [person] esbelto(ta) **-2.** [object] fino(na) **-3.** [chance, possibility] remoto(ta). ◇ *vi* [lose weight] emagrecer; **I'm ~ming** estou de dieta; [diet] emagrecer.

slime [slaɪm] *n (U)* muco *m.*

slimline *adj* mais fino(na) *(que o normal).*

slimmer ['slɪmə^r] *n* pessoa *f* de dieta.

slimming ['slɪmɪŋ] ◇ *n (U)* emagrecimento *m.* ◇ *adj* **-1.** [magazine] de dieta **-2.** [product] para emagrecer.

slimness ['slɪmnɪs] *n (U)* esbelteza *f*, elegância *f.*

slimy ['slaɪmɪ] (*compar* **-ier**, *superl* **-iest**) *adj* **-1.** [covered in slime] coberto(ta) com lodo OR muco **-2.** *pej* [servile] fingido(da).

sling [slɪŋ] (*pt* & *pp* **slung**) ◇ *n* **-1.** [for injured arm] tipóia *f* **-2.** [for carrying things] linga *f.* ◇ *vt* **-1.** [hang roughly] pendurar **-2.** *inf* [throw] atirar, jogar **-3.** [hang by both ends] pendurar.

slingback ['slɪŋbæk] *n* sandália *f.*

slingshot ['slɪŋʃɒt] *n US* catapulta *f.*

slink [slɪŋk] (*pt* & *pp* **slunk**) *vi*: **to ~ (away** OR **off)** escapulir-se.

slip [slɪp] (*pt* & *pp* **-ped**, *cont* **-ping**) ◇ *n* **-1.** [mistake] deslize *m*, descuido *m*; **a ~ of the pen** um erro de ortografia; **a ~ of the tongue** um lapso verbal **-2.** [form] formulário *m* **-3.** [of paper] folha *f* **-4.** [underwear] combinação *f*, anágua *f* **-5.** *phr*: **to give sb the ~** *inf* safar-se de alguém. ◇ *vt* **-1.** [slide] enfiar, meter **-2.** [clothes]: **to ~ sthg on** vestir algo rapidamente; **~ your clothes off** tira fora essas tuas roupas **-3.** [escape] fugir; **it ~ped my mind** me esqueci. ◇ *vi* **-1.** [lose balance] escorregar **-2.** [move unexpectedly] escapulir **-3.** [move gradually] entrar em **-4.** [decline] baixar; **to let things ~** deixar escapar algo *(falando)* **-5.** [move discreetly] escapulir-se; **to ~ into/out of sthg** [clothes] vestir/tirar algo **-6.** AUT [clutch] patinar **-7.** *phr*: **to let sthg ~** dizer algo sem querer.

◆ **slip away** *vi* [leave] ir embora.

◆ **slip on** *vt sep* [clothes, shoes] enfiar.

◆ **slip up** *vi* [make a mistake] cometer um deslize.

slip-on *adj* [shoes] sem cadarço.

◆ **slip-ons** *npl* [shoes] mocassim *m.*

slippage *n (U)* deslizamento *m.*

slipped disc [ˌslɪpt-] *n* hérnia *f* de disco.

slipper ['slɪpə^r] *n* pantufa *f.*

slippery ['slɪpərɪ] *adj* **-1.** [surface, soap] escorregadio(dia) **-2.** *pej* [person] evasivo(va).

slip road *n UK* acesso *m (na estrada).*

slipshod ['slɪpʃɒd] *adj* desleixado(da).

slipstream ['slɪpstriːm] *n* rastro *m.*

slip-up *n inf* mancada *f.*

slipway ['slɪpweɪ] *n* carreira *f (para navios).*

slit [slɪt] (*pt* & *pp* **slit**, *cont* **-ting**) ◇ *n* **-1.** [opening] fenda *f* **-2.** [cut] corte *m.* ◇ *vt* **-1.** [cut open] cortar **-2.** [cut through] fender.

slither ['slɪðə^r] *vi* **-1.** [car, person] arrastar-se **-2.** [snake] rastejar.

sliver ['slɪvə^r] *n* **-1.** [gen] caco *f* **-2.** [of ice, wood] lasca *f.*

slob [slɒb] *n inf* [disgusting person - in habits] porcalhão *m*, -lhona *f*; [- in appearance] porco *m*, -ca *f.*

slobber ['slɒbə^r] *vi* babar.

slog [slɒg] (*pt* & *pp* **-ged**, *cont* **-ging**) *inf* ◇ *n* **-1.** [tiring work] chatice *f* **-2.** [tiring journey] maçada *f.* ◇ *vi* **-1.** [work]: **to ~ (away) at sthg** trabalhar sem descanso em algo **-2.** [walk, move] andar a custo.

slogan ['sləʊgən] *n* slogan *m.*

slop [slɒp] (*pt* & *pp* **-ped**, *cont* **-ping**) ◇ *vt* derramar. ◇ *vi* transbordar.

slope [sləʊp] ◇ *n* **-1.** [of roof, ground] inclinação *f* **-2.** [hill] encosta *f* **-3.** *phr*: **he's on the slippery ~ to alcoholism** ele está indo direto para o alcoolismo. ◇ *vi* inclinar-se.

sloping ['sləʊpɪŋ] *adj* inclinado(da).

sloppy ['slɒpɪ] (*compar* **-ier**, *superl* **-iest**) *adj* **-1.** [careless] desleixado(da), relaxado(da) **-2.** *inf* [sentimental] meloso(sa), piegas.

slosh [slɒʃ] ◇ *vt* **-1.** [spill] chapinhar **-2.** [pour] despejar **-3.** [apply] espalhar. ◇ *vi* **-1.** [liquid] chapinhar **-2.** [through liquid, mud] patinhar.

sloshed [slɒʃt] *adj UK inf* com a cara cheia.

slot [slɒt] (*pt* & *pp* **-ted**, *cont* **-ting**) *n* **-1.** [opening] abertura *f* **-2.** [groove] ranhura *f* **-3.** [place in schedule] espaço *m* **-4.** COMPUT slot *m.*

◆ **slot in** ◇ *vt sep* [insert] encaixar. ◇ *vi* [fit neatly] encaixar.

sloth [sləʊθ] *n* **-1.** [animal] bicho-preguiça *m* **-2.** *(U) literary* [laziness] preguiça *f.*

slot machine *n* **-1.** [vending machine] máquina *f* automática *(de bebidas, cigarros etc)* **-2.** [arcade machine] caça-níqueis *m inv.*

slot meter *n UK* medidor *m (de luz ou gás)* que funciona com moedas.

slouch [slaʊtʃ] ◇ *n* [person] incompetente *mf.* ◇ *vi* [in posture] ter má postura.

slough *vt sep* **-1.** [shed] trocar OR mudar *(de pele)* **-2.** *fig* [get rid of] livrar-se de.

Slovak ['sləʊvæk] ◇ *adj* eslavo(va). ◇ *n* **-1.** [person] eslavo *m*, -va *f* **-2.** [language] eslavo *m.*

Slovakia [slə'vækɪə] *n* Eslováquia; **in ~** na Eslováquia.

Slovakian [slə'vækɪən] ◇ *adj* eslovaco(ca). ◇ *n* eslovaco *m*, -ca *f.*

Slovenia [slə'viːnjə] *n* Eslovênia; **in ~** na Eslovênia.

Slovenian [slə'viːnjən] ◇ *adj* esloveno(na). ◇ *n* esloveno *m*, -na *f.*

slovenly ['slʌvnlɪ] *adj* **-1.** [person, work] desmazelado(da) **-2.** [appearance] desleixado(da) **-3.** [dress] desalinhado(da).

slow [sləʊ] ◇ *adj* **-1.** [not fast] lento(ta) **-2.** [clock, watch] atrasado(da) **-3.** [not busy] parado(da) **-4.** [not intelligent] lerdo(da). ◇ *adv*: **to go ~** [driver] ir devagar; [workers] fazer operação-tartaruga. ◇ *vt* retardar. ◇ *vi* ir mais devagar, desacelerar.
◆ **slow down, slow up** ◇ *vt sep* **-1.** [growth] retardar **-2.** [car] reduzir a velocidade de. ◇ *vi* **-1.** [car] reduzir a velocidade de **-2.** [walker] diminuir a marcha.

slow-acting *adj* de ação lenta.

slowcoach ['sləʊkəʊtʃ], **slowpoke** *US n inf* molenga *mf*.

slowdown ['sləʊdaʊn] *n* desaceleração *f*.

slow handclap *n aplauso lento e ritmado em sinal de protesto.*

slowly ['sləʊlɪ] *adv* devagar; **~ but surely** devagar e sempre.

slow motion *n (U)* câmera *f* lenta.
◆ **slow-motion** *adj* em câmera lenta.

slowpoke *n US* = **slowcoach**.

SLR (*abbr of* **single-lens reflex**) *n tipo de câmera fotográfica que usa uma lente única.*

sludge [slʌdʒ] *n* **-1.** [mud] lama *f* **-2.** [sediment] lodo *m*.

slug [slʌg] (*pt* & *pp* **-ged**, *cont* **-ging**) ◇ *n* **-1.** ZOOL lesma *f* **-2.** *inf* [of alcohol] trago *m* **-3.** *US inf* [bullet] bala *f (de revólver)*. ◇ *vt inf* [hit] esmurrar.

sluggish ['slʌgɪʃ] *adj* **-1.** [lethargic] vagaroso(sa) **-2.** [reaction, business] moroso(sa).

sluice [slu:s] ◇ *n* [lock] comporta *f*. ◇ *vt* [rinse]: **to ~ sthg down/out** lavar algo com muita água.

slum [slʌm] (*pt* & *pp* **-med**, *cont* **-ming**) ◇ *n* [area of poor housing] favela *f*, cortiço *m*. ◇ *vt*: **to ~ it** *inf* baixar o padrão de vida.

slumber ['slʌmbəʳ] *literary* ◇ *n (U)* sono *m*. ◇ *vi* adormecer.

slump [slʌmp] ◇ *n* **-1.** [decline]: **~ (in sthg)** queda *f* (em algo) **-2.** ECON crise *f* econômica. ◇ *vi* **-1.** [business, prices, market] cair **-2.** [person] afundar-se.

slung [slʌŋ] *pt* & *pp* ▷ **sling**.

slunk [slʌŋk] *pt* & *pp* ▷ **slink**.

slur [slɜ:ʳ] (*pt* & *pp* **-red**, *cont* **-ring**) ◇ *n* **-1.** [in voice] balbuceio *m* **-2.** [insult]: **~ (on sb/sthg)** ultraje *m* OR afronta *f* (a alguém/algo). ◇ *vt* [speech] balbuciar; **to ~ one's words** engolir as palavras.

slurp [slɜ:p] *vt* sorver fazendo barulho.

slurred [slɜ:d] *adj* ininteligível.

slurry *n (U)* purina *f*.

slush [slʌʃ] *n (U)* neve *f* meio derretida.

slush fund, slush money *US n* caixa *m* dois.

slut [slʌt] *n* **-1.** *inf* [dirty or untidy woman] mulher *f* relaxada **-2.** *v inf* [sexually immoral woman] rameira *f*.

sly [slaɪ] (*compar* **slyer** OR **slier**, *superl* **slyest** OR **sliest**) ◇ *adj* **-1.** [look, smile, grin] dissimulado(da) **-2.** [cunning] astuto(ta) **-3.** [secretive] fingido(da). ◇ *n*: **on the ~** às escondidas.

slyness ['slaɪnɪs] *n (U)* dissimulação *f*.

S & M (*abbr of* **sadism and masochism**) *n* SM *m*.

smack [smæk] ◇ *n* **-1.** [slap] palmada *f* **-2.** [impact] batida *f*. ◇ *vt* **-1.** [slap] dar uma palmada em **-2.** [put] colocar bruscamente **-3.** [make sound]: **to ~ one's lips** estalar os lábios. ◇ *vi*: **to ~ of sthg** cheirar a algo. ◇ *adv inf* [exactly]: **~ in the middle** bem no meio.

small [smɔ:l] ◇ *adj* **-1.** [gen] pequeno(na); **in a ~ way** em pequena escala **-2.** [person] baixo(xa) **-3.** [importance] pouco(ca) **-4.** [matter, alteration] de pouca importância. ◇ *n*: **the ~ of the back** a região lombar.
◆ **smalls** *npl UK inf dated* roupa *f* de baixo.

small ads [-ædz] *npl UK* classificados *mpl*.

small arms *npl* armas *fpl* portáteis OR de mão.

small change *n (U)* trocado *m*.

small fry *n (U)* peixe *m* pequeno, fichinha *f*.

smallholder ['smɔ:lˌhəʊldəʳ] *n UK* minifundiário *m*, -ria *f*.

smallholding ['smɔ:lˌhəʊldɪŋ] *n UK* minifúndio *m*.

small hours *npl* primeiras horas *fpl* da manhã.

small letters *npl*: **in ~** em minúscula.

smallness ['smɔ:lnɪs] *n* **-1.** *(U)* [of building, person] pequenez *f* **-2.** [rise, amount] escassez *f*.

smallpox ['smɔ:lpɒks] *n (U)* varíola *f*.

small print *n*: **the ~** as letras miúdas *(de um contrato)*.

small-scale *adj* em pequena escala.

small talk *n (U)*: **to make ~** conversar amenidades.

small-time *adj* de segunda; **a ~ criminal** um ladrão de galinha.

smarmy ['smɑ:mɪ] (*compar* **-ier**, *superl* **-iest**) *adj inf* adulador(ra).

smart [smɑ:t] ◇ *adj* **-1.** [elegant] elegante **-2.** [clever] inteligente **-3.** [fashionable, exclusive] chique, elegante **-4.** [rapid] rápido(da) **-5.** [impertinent] insolente. ◇ *vi* **-1.** [sting] pungir, arder **-2.** [feel anger, humiliation] ofender-se.

smart card *n* cartão *m* inteligente.

smarten ['smɑ:tn] ◆ **smarten up** *vt sep* arrumar; **to ~ o.s. up** arrumar-se.

smash [smæʃ] ◇ *n* **-1.** [sound] estilhaço *m* **-2.** *inf* [car crash] acidente *m* **-3.** *inf* [success] estouro *m* **-4.** TENNIS cortada *f*. ◇ *vt* **-1.** [break into pieces] quebrar **-2.** [hit, crash] bater em; **to ~ one's fist into sthg** dar um soco em algo **-3.** *fig* [defeat] derrotar. ◇ *vi* **-1.** [break into pieces] quebrar-se **-2.** [crash, collide]: **to ~ through/into sthg** espatifar-se contra/em algo.
◆ **smash up** *vt sep* destruir completamente.

smash-and-grab (raid) *n UK* saque *m* após arrombamento *(numa loja)*.

smashed [smæʃt] *adj inf* mamado(da) *(de bêbado)*.

smash hit *n* sucesso *m* absoluto.

smashing ['smæʃɪŋ] *adj inf* fabuloso(sa), fenomenal.

smash-up *n* choque *m* violento, desastre *m*.

smattering ['smætərɪŋ] *n* noções *fpl*; **to have a ~ of Welsh** falar meia dúzia de palavras de galês.

SME (*abbr of* **small and medium-sized enterprise**) *n* pequena e média empresa *f*.

smear [smɪəʳ] ◇ *n* **-1.** [dirty mark] mancha *f (de gordura)* **-2.** MED esfregaço *m* **-3.** [slander] calúnia *f*. ◇ *vt* **-1.** [smudge - page] manchar; [- painting] borrar **-2.** [spread]: **to ~ sthg onto sthg** espalhar algo sobre algo; **to ~ sthg with sthg** untar algo com algo **- 3.** [slander] caluniar.

smear campaign *n* campanha *f* de difamação.

smear test *n* esfregaço *m.*

smell [smel] (*pt* & *pp* **-ed** *OR* **smelt**) <> *n* **- 1.** [odour] cheiro *m*, odor *m* **- 2.** *(U)* [sense of smell] olfato *m.* <> *vt* **- 1.** [notice an odour of] sentir cheiro de **- 2.** [sniff at] cheirar **- 3.** *fig* [sense] pressentir. <> *vi* **- 1.** [have sense of smell] sentir cheiro **- 2.** [have particular smell]: **to ~ of sthg** cheirar a algo; **to ~ like sthg** cheirar como algo; **to ~ good/bad** cheirar bem/mal **- 3.** [smell unpleasantly] feder.

smelling salts *npl* sais *mpl* aromáticos.

smelly ['smelɪ] (*compar* **-ier**, *superl* **-iest**) *adj* fedorento(ta).

smelt [smelt] <> *pt* & *pp* ▷ **smell.** <> *vt TECH* fundir.

smile [smaɪl] <> *n* sorriso *m.* <> *vi* sorrir. <> *vt* sorrir; **to ~ one's thanks** sorrir em agradecimento.

smiley ['smaɪlɪ] *n COMPUT* smiley *m.*

smiling ['smaɪlɪŋ] *adj* sorridente, risonho(nha).

smirk [smɜːk] <> *n* sorriso *m* afetado. <> *vi* sorrir de forma afetada.

smith [smɪθ] *n* ferreiro *m*, -ra *f.*

smithereens [ˌsmɪðə'riːnz] *npl inf*: **to be smashed to ~** ser quebrado(da) em pedacinhos *OR* em mil pedaços.

smithy ['smɪðɪ] (*pl* **-ies**) *n* ferraria *f.*

smitten ['smɪtn] *adj inf hum*: **to be ~ (with sb/sthg)** estar apaixonado(da) (por alguém/algo).

smock [smɒk] *n* avental *m*, guarda-pó *m.*

smog [smɒg] *n (U)* bruma *f.*

smoke [sməʊk] <> *n* **- 1.** *(U)* [from burning] fumaça *f* **- 2.** [act of smoking]: **to have a ~** fumar. <> *vt* **- 1.** [cigarette, cigar] fumar **- 2.** [fish, meat, cheese] defumar. <> *vi* **- 1.** [chimney, engine, lamp] fumegar **- 2.** [person] fumar.

smoked [sməʊkt] *adj* [food] defumado(da).

smokeless fuel ['sməʊklɪs-] *n (U)* combustível *m* limpo.

smokeless zone ['sməʊklɪs-] *n área na qual se proíbe o uso de combustíveis que produzam fumaça.*

smoker ['sməʊkə^r] *n* **- 1.** [person who smokes] fumante *mf* **- 2.** *inf RAIL* [compartment] vagão *m* para fumantes.

smokescreen ['sməʊkskriːn] *n fig* cortina *f* de fumaça.

smoke shop *n US* tabacaria *f.*

smokestack *n* chaminé *f.*

smokestack industry *n US* indústria *f* pesada *OR* de base.

smoking ['sməʊkɪŋ] *n (U)*: **~ is bad for you** fumar não te faz bem; **'no ~'** 'é proibido fumar'.

smoking compartment *UK*, **smoking car** *US n* vagão *m* para fumantes.

smoky ['sməʊkɪ] (*compar* **-ier**, *superl* **-iest**) *adj* **- 1.** [full of smoke] enfumaçado(da) **- 2.** [resembling smoke - taste] com gosto de fumaça; [- colour] cinzento(ta).

smolder *vi US* = **smoulder.**

smooch [smuːtʃ] *vi inf* dar amassos.

smooth [smuːð] <> *adj* **- 1.** [surface - skin, fabric] macio(cia); [- stone] liso(sa); [- water, sea] calmo(ma) **- 2.** *CULIN* [texture] uniforme **- 3.** [flow, supply] fluido(da) **- 4.** [pace] tranqüilo(la) **- 5.** [taste, ride] suave **- 6.** [engine] macio(cia) **- 7.** *pej* [person, manner] lisonjeiro(ra) **- 8.** [trouble-free] tranqüilo(la), sem problemas. <> *vt* **- 1.** [gen] alisar; **to ~ the way** preparar o terreno **- 2.** [rub] passar.

◆ **smooth out** *vt sep* **- 1.** [gen] alisar **- 2.** *fig* [difficulties] resolver-se.

◆ **smooth over** *vt fus* resolver.

smoothly ['smuːðlɪ] *adv* **- 1.** [gen] suavemente **- 2.** [talk] calmamente, sem se alterar **- 3.** [without problems] tranqüilamente, sem problemas.

smoothness ['smuːðnɪs] *n (U)* **- 1.** [gen - skin, fabric, engine] maciez *f*; [- road, stone] lisura *f*; [- sea, water, flight] tranqüilidade *f*; [- finish] perfeição *f* **- 2.** *CULIN* [of texture] uniformidade *f* **- 3.** [of flow, supply] fluidez *f* **- 4.** [of pace] tranqüilidade *f*, calma *f.*

smooth-talking *adj* de lábia fácil.

smother ['smʌðə^r] *vt* **- 1.** [cover thickly]: **to ~ sthg in** *OR* **with sthg** cobrir algo de algo **- 2.** [suffocate] sufocar **- 3.** [extinguish] abafar **- 4.** *fig* [repress] reprimir **- 5.** [suffocate with love] mimar demais.

smoulder *UK*, **smolder** *US* ['sməʊldə^r] *vi* **- 1.** [fire] fumegar **- 2.** *fig* [feelings] arder.

SMS (*abbr of* **short message service**) *n COMPUT* SMS *m*, mensagens *fpl* curtas de texto.

smudge [smʌdʒ] <> *n* [dirty mark] borrão *m.* <> *vt* [spoil - by blurring] borrar; [- by dirtying] manchar.

smug [smʌg] (*compar* **-ger**, *superl* **-gest**) *adj pej* presunçoso(sa).

smuggle ['smʌgl] *vt* **- 1.** [across frontiers] contrabandear **- 2.** [against rules]: **to ~ sthg in/out** trazer algo escondido.

smuggler ['smʌglə^r] *n* contrabandista *mf.*

smuggling ['smʌglɪŋ] *n (U)* contrabando *m.*

smugness ['smʌgnɪs] *n (U) pej* presunção *f.*

smut [smʌt] *n* **- 1.** [of soot, dirt] sujeira *f*, fuligem *f* **- 2.** *(U) inf pej* [lewd matter] obscenidade *f.*

smutty ['smʌtɪ] (*compar* **-ier**, *superl* **-iest**) *adj inf pej* obsceno(na), indecente.

snack [snæk] <> *n* lanche *m.* <> *vi US* lanchar.

snack bar *n* lancheria *f.*

snag [snæg] (*pt* & *pp* **-ged**, *cont* **-ging**) <> *n* **- 1.** [small problem] dificuldade *f* **- 2.** [in nail, tights, fabric] ponta *f* saliente. <> *vt* enganchar. <> *vi*: **to ~ (on sthg)** enganchar-se (em algo).

snail [sneɪl] *n* caracol *m.*

snail mail *n* correio *m* tradicional.

snake [sneɪk] <> *n* cobra *f*, serpente *f.* <> *vi* serpentear.

snap [snæp] (*pt* & *pp* **-ped**, *cont* **-ping**) <> *adj* atropelado(da), repentino(na). <> *n* **- 1.** [act or sound of snapping] estalo *m* **- 2.** *inf* [photograph] foto *f* **- 3.** [card game] *jogo de cartas semelhante ao burro mecânico.* <> *vt* **- 1.** [break] partir (em dois) **- 2.** [make cracking sound with]: **to ~ sthg open/shut** abrir/fechar algo com um golpe; **to ~ one's fingers** estalar os dedos **- 3.** [speak sharply] falar bruscamente **- 4.** *inf* [photograph] bater foto. <> *vi* **- 1.** [break] partir (em dois) **- 2.** [make cracking sound] estalar; **to ~ into place** ir para o lugar com uma pancada **- 3.** [attempt to bite]: **to ~ (at sb/sthg)** tentar morder (alguém/algo) **- 4.** [speak sharply]: **to ~ (at sb)** ficar brabo(ba) (com alguém) **- 5.** *phr*: **to ~ out of it** animar-se de repente.

◆ **snap up** *vt sep* não deixar escapar.
snap fastener *n esp US* botão *m* de pressão.
snappy ['snæpɪ] (*compar* **-ier**, *superl* **-iest**) *adj inf* **-1.** [stylish] chique **-2.** [quick] rápido(da); **make it ~!** anda logo!
snapshot ['snæpʃɒt] *n* instantânea *f.*
snare [sneəʳ] ◇ *n* armadilha *f.* ◇ *vt* pegar numa armadilha.
snarl [snɑ:l] ◇ *n* rosnado *m.* ◇ *vi* **-1.** [animal] rosnar **-2.** [person] resmungar.
snarl-up *n* rolo *m*, confusão *f.*
snatch [snætʃ] ◇ *n* [fragment] trecho *m.* ◇ *vt* **-1.** [grab] agarrar **-2.** *fig* [sleep, opportunity, look] aproveitar; **to ~ some sleep** tirar um tempo para dormir. ◇ *vi* [grab]: **to ~ (at sthg)** tentar agarrar (algo).
snazzy ['snæzɪ] (*compar* **-ier**, *superl* **-iest**) *adj inf* chamativo(va).
sneak [sni:k] (*US pt* **snuck**) ◇ *n UK inf* mexeriqueiro *m*, -ra *f.* ◇ *vt* levar escondido(da); **to ~ a look at sb/sthg** espiar alguém/algo. ◇ *vi* [move quietly] esgueirar-se.
sneakers ['sni:kəz] *npl US* tênis *m inv.*
sneaking ['sni:kɪŋ] *adj* [feeling, suspicion] secreto(ta).
sneak preview *n* pré-estréia *f.*
sneaky ['sni:kɪ] (*compar* **-ier**, *superl* **-iest**) *adj inf* sorrateiro(ra).
sneer [snɪəʳ] ◇ *n* escárnio *m.* ◇ *vi* **-1.** [smile unpleasantly] sorrir com escárnio **-2.** [ridicule]: **to ~ (at sthg)** zombar (de algo).
sneeze [sni:z] ◇ *n* espirro *m.* ◇ *vi* espirrar; **it's not to be ~d at** *inf* não é de se jogar fora.
snicker ['snɪkəʳ] *vi* rir por dentro.
snide [snaɪd] *adj* sarcástico(ca).
sniff [snɪf] ◇ *n* fungada *f.* ◇ *vt* **-1.** [smell] fungar **-2.** [drug] cheirar. ◇ *vi* **-1.** [to clear nose] assoar **-2.** [to show disapproval] torcer o nariz.
◆ **sniff out** *vt sep* **-1.** [detect by sniffing] farejar **-2.** *inf* [seek out] descobrir.
sniffer dog ['snɪfəʳ-] *n* cão *m* farejador.
sniffle ['snɪfl] *vi* fungar.
snigger ['snɪgəʳ] ◇ *n* escárnio *m.* ◇ *vi* rir por dentro.
snip [snɪp] (*pt* & *pp* **-ped**, *cont* **-ping**) ◇ *n inf* [bargain] pechincha *f.* ◇ *vt* [cut] cortar *(em pedaços).*
snipe [snaɪp] *vi* **-1.** [shoot]: **to ~ (at sb/sthg)** disparar (em alguém/algo) **-2.** [criticize]: **to ~ at sb** criticar alguém.
sniper ['snaɪpəʳ] *n* franco-atirador *m*, -ra *f.*
snippet ['snɪpɪt] *n* fragmento *m.*
snivel ['snɪvl] (*UK pt* & *pp* **-led**, *cont* **-ling**, *US pt* & *pp* **-ed**, *cont* **-ing**) *vi* choramingar.
snob [snɒb] *n* esnobe *mf.*
snobbery ['snɒbərɪ] *n (U)* esnobismo *m.*
snobbish ['snɒbɪʃ], **snobby** ['snɒbɪ] (*compar* **-ier**, *superl* **-iest**) *adj* esnobe.
snog (*pt* & *pp* **-ged**, *cont* **-ging**) *vi UK inf* agarrar-se.
snooker ['snu:kəʳ] ◇ *n (U)* snooker *m.* ◇ *vt UK inf* [thwart]: **to be ~ed** estar com as mãos atadas.
snoop [snu:p] *vi inf* bisbilhotar.
snooper ['snu:pəʳ] *n inf* bisbilhoteiro *m*, -ra *f.*
snooty ['snu:tɪ] (*compar* **-ier**, *superl* **-iest**) *adj* presunçoso(sa).
snooze [snu:z] ◇ *n* cochilo *m*, soneca *f*; **to have a ~** tirar uma soneca OR um cochilo. ◇ *vi* cochilar.
snore [snɔ:ʳ] ◇ *n* ronco *m.* ◇ *vi* roncar.
snoring ['snɔ:rɪŋ] *n (U)* roncos *mpl.*
snorkel ['snɔ:kl] *n* (tubo *m*) snorkel *m.*
snorkelling *UK*, **snorkeling** *US* ['snɔ:klɪŋ] *n (U)* mergulho *m* com (tubo) snorkel.
snort [snɔ:t] ◇ *n* bufo *m.* ◇ *vi* bufar. ◇ *vt* **drugs** *sl* cheirar.
snotty ['snɒtɪ] (*compar* **-ier**, *superl* **-iest**) *adj inf* [snooty] presunçoso(sa).
snout [snaʊt] *n* focinho *m.*
snow [snəʊ] ◇ *n (U)* neve *f.* ◇ *v impers* nevar.
◆ **snow in** *vt sep*: **to be ~ed in** estar preso(sa) por causa da neve.
◆ **snow under** *vt sep*: **to be ~ed under (with sthg)** estar atolado(da) (de algo).
snowball ['snəʊbɔ:l] ◇ *n* bola *f* de neve. ◇ *vi fig* [increase rapidly] crescer como bola de neve.
snow blindness *n* ofuscação *f (da neve).*
snowboard ['snəʊbɔ:d] *n* snowboard *m.*
snowboarding ['snəʊbɔ:dɪŋ] *n* snowboard *m*; **to go ~** praticar snowboard.
snowbound ['snəʊbaʊnd] *adj* bloqueado(da) pela neve.
snow-capped [-ˌkæpt] *adj* com o pico coberto de neve.
snowdrift ['snəʊdrɪft] *n* monte *m* de neve.
snowdrop ['snəʊdrɒp] *n* campainha *f* branca.
snowfall ['snəʊfɔ:l] *n* **-1.** [fall of snow] nevada *f* **-2.** [amount of snow over time] quantidade *f* de neve.
snowflake ['snəʊfleɪk] *n* floco *m* de neve.
snowman ['snəʊmæn] (*pl* **-men** [-men]) *n* boneco *m* de neve.
snow pea *n US* ervilha *f* torta.
snowplough *UK*, **snowplow** *US* ['snəʊplaʊ] *n* [vehicle] limpa-neve *m.*
snowshoe ['snəʊʃu:] *n* raquete *f* de neve.
snowstorm ['snəʊstɔ:m] *n* nevasca *f.*
snowy ['snəʊɪ] (*compar* **-ier**, *superl* **-iest**) *adj* **-1.** [weather, day] de muita neve **-2.** [road, landscape] com muita neve.
SNP (*abbr of* **Scottish National Party**) *n partido nacional escocês que prega a independência da Grã-Bretanha.*
Snr, snr (*abbr of* **senior**) sênior.
snub [snʌb] (*pt* & *pp* **-bed**, *cont* **-bing**) ◇ *n* repulsa *f.* ◇ *vt* desprezar.
snuck [snʌk] *pt US* ▷ **sneak**.
snuff [snʌf] ◇ *n (U)* [tobacco] rapé *m.* ◇ *vt*: **to ~ it** *inf* morrer.
snuffle ['snʌfl] *vi* fungar.
snuff movie *n filme pornográfico com um assassinato como desenlace.*
snug [snʌg] (*compar* **-ger**, *superl* **-gest**) *adj* **-1.** [person, feeling] agradável **-2.** [place] confortável **-3.** [close-fitting] cômodo(da).
snuggle ['snʌgl] *vi* aconchegar-se; **to ~ down** cobrir-se *(com coberta).*
so [səʊ] ◇ *adv* **-1.** [emphasizing degree] tão; **don't be ~ stupid!** não seja tão idiota!; **it's ~ difficult (that ...)** é tão difícil (que ...); **~ much** tanto(ta); **~ many**

tantos(tas). **-2.** [referring back]: **I don't think ~** acho que não; **I'm afraid ~** receio que sim; **~ you knew already** então você já sabia; **if ~** nesse caso. **-3.** [also] também; **~ do I** eu também. **-4.** [in this way] deste modo, assim. **-5.** [expressing agreement]: **~ there is** pois é, é verdade. **-6.** [in phrases]: **or ~** mais ou menos; **~ as** para; **~ that** para. <> *conj* **-1.** [therefore] por isso; **I'm away next week ~ I won't be there** viajo na semana que vem, portanto não estarei lá. **-2.** [summarizing] então; **~ what have you been up to?** então, o que é que você tem feito? **-3.** [in phrases]: **~ what?** *inf* e daí?; **~ there!** *inf* pronto!, nada a fazer!

SO (*abbr of* **standing order**) débito *m* em conta.

soak [səʊk] <> *vt* **-1.** [leave immersed] pôr de molho **-2.** [wet thoroughly] ensopar; **to be ~ed with sthg** estar ensopado(da) de algo. <> *vi* **-1.** [become thoroughly wet]: **to leave sthg to ~, to let sthg ~** deixar algo de molho **-2.** [spread]: **to ~ into sthg** espalhar-se por algo; **to ~ through (sthg)** infiltrar-se em algo.

◆ **soak up** *vt sep* [liquid] absorver.

soaked [səʊkt] *adj* ensopado(da); **to be ~ through** ficar ensopado(da) dos pés à cabeça.

soaking ['səʊkɪŋ] *adj* ensopado(da).

so-and-so *n inf* **-1.** [to replace a name] fulano *m*, --na *f* **-2.** [annoying person] filho *m*, -lha *f* da mãe.

soap [səʊp] <> *n* **-1.** *(U)* [for washing] sabão *m* **-2.** *TV* novela *f*. <> *vt* ensaboar.

soap bubble *n* bolha *f* de sabão.

soap dish *n* saboneteira *f*.

soap flakes *npl* sabão *m* em flocos.

soap opera *n* novela *f*.

soap powder *n (U)* sabão *m* em pó.

soapsuds ['səʊpsʌdz] *npl* espuma *f* de sabão.

soapy ['səʊpɪ] (*compar* **-ier**, *superl* **-iest**) *adj* **-1.** [full of soap] ensaboado(da) **-2.** [resembling soap] de sabão.

soar [sɔːʳ] *vi* **-1.** [bird] levantar vôo **-2.** [rise into the sky] subir **-3.** [increase rapidly] aumentar rapidamente **-4.** *literary* [be impressively high] elevar-se **-5.** [rise in volume or pitch] aumentar de intensidade.

soaring ['sɔːrɪŋ] *adj* **-1.** [rapidly increasing] cada vez mais alto(ta) **-2.** [spire, tower] altíssimo(ma) **-3.** [rising in volume or pitch] cada vez mais intenso(sa).

sob [sɒb] (*pt* & *pp* **-bed**, *cont* **-bing**) <> *n* soluço *m*. <> *vt* soluçar. <> *vi* [cry] soluçar.

sobbing ['sɒbɪŋ] *n (U)* soluços *mpl*.

sober ['səʊbəʳ] *adj* **-1.** [not drunk] sóbrio(bria) **-2.** [serious] sério(ria) **-3.** [plain] simples.

◆ **sober up** *vi* ficar sóbrio(bria).

sobering ['səʊbərɪŋ] *adj* que faz refletir.

sobriety [səʊ'braɪətɪ] *n (U) fml* sobriedade *f*.

Soc. (*abbr of* **Society**) Soc.

so-called [-kɔːld] *adj* **-1.** [misleadingly named] suposto(ta) **-2.** [widely known as] chamado(da).

soccer ['sɒkəʳ] *n (U)* futebol *m*.

sociable ['səʊʃəbl] *adj* sociável.

social ['səʊʃl] *adj* social.

social climber *n pej* arrivista *mf*.

social club *n* clube *m* social.

social conscience *n* consciência *f* social.

social democracy *n (U)* social-democracia *f*.

social event *n* evento *m* social.

social fund *n na Grã-Bretanha, fundo de auxílio em casos de extrema necessidade.*

socialism ['səʊʃəlɪzm] *n (U)* socialismo *m*.

socialist ['səʊʃəlɪst] <> *adj* socialista. <> *n* socialista *mf*.

socialite ['səʊʃəlaɪt] *n* socialite *m*.

socialize, -ise ['səʊʃəlaɪz] *vi*: **to ~ (with sb)** socializar-se (com alguém).

socialized medicine *n US* saúde *f* pública.

social life *n* **-1.** [of individual] vida *f* social **-2.** *(U)* [in general] vida *f* em sociedade.

socially ['səʊʃəlɪ] *adv* **-1.** [towards society] socialmente **-2.** [outside business] fora do trabalho.

social order *n* ordem *f* social.

social science *n* ciência *f* social; **the ~s** as ciências sociais.

social security *n (U)* previdência *f* social.

social services *npl* assistência *f* social.

social studies *n* estudos *mpl* sociais.

social work *n (U)* trabalho *m* social.

social worker *n* assistente *mf* social.

society [sə'saɪətɪ] (*pl* **-ies**) *n* sociedade *f*.

socioeconomic ['səʊsɪəʊˌiːkə'nɒmɪk] *adj POL* socioeconômico(ca).

sociological [ˌsəʊsjə'lɒdʒɪkl] *adj* sociológico(ca).

sociologist [ˌsəʊsɪ'ɒlədʒɪst] *n* sociólogo *m*, -ga *f*.

sociology [ˌsəʊsɪ'ɒlədʒɪ] *n (U)* sociologia *f*.

sock [sɒk] *n* meia *f*; **to pull one's ~s up** *inf fig* empenhar-se.

socket ['sɒkɪt] *n* **-1.** *ELEC* tomada *f* **-2.** [de lâmpada] soquete *m* **-3.** [*ANAT* - of arm, hipbone] concavidade *f*; [- of eye] órbita *f*.

sod [sɒd] *n* **-1.** [of turf] torrão *m* **-2.** **v*inf*** [person] sujeito *m*.

soda ['səʊdə] *n* **-1.** [gen] soda *f* **-2.** ***US*** [fizzy drink] refrigerante *m*.

soda syphon *n garrafa d'água com sifão para servir soda.*

soda water *n (U)* soda *f*, água *f* com gás.

sodden ['sɒdn] *adj* encharcado(da).

sodium ['səʊdɪəm] *n (U)* sódio *m*.

sofa ['səʊfə] *n* sofá *m*.

sofabed *n* sofá-cama *m*.

Sofia ['səʊfjə] *n* Sofia.

soft [sɒft] *adj* **-1.** [gen] mole **-2.** [to touch] macio(cia) **-3.** [gentle] suave **-4.** [kind, caring] meigo(ga), bondoso(sa) **-5.** [not strict] flexível.

softball *n SPORT espécie de beisebol que se joga com uma bola mais macia e maior.*

soft-boiled *adj*: **~ eggs** ovos *mpl* quentes.

soft drink *n* **-1.** [fruit juice] refresco *m* **-2.** [fizzy drink] refrigerante *m*.

soft drugs *npl* drogas *fpl* leves.

soften ['sɒfn] <> *vt* **-1.** [substance] suavizar **-2.** [blow, impact, effect] amortecer **-3.** [attitude] enternecer. <> *vi* **-1.** [substance] amaciar **-2.** [attitude] amolecer **-3.** [eyes, voice, expression] suavizar.

◆ **soften up** *vt sep inf* [make amenable] amaciar.

softener ['sɒfnəʳ] *n* [for washing] amaciante *m*.

soft focus *n (U)* foco *m* enevoado; **in ~** em foco enevoado.

soft furnishings *npl UK* complementos *mpl* para decoração.
softhearted [ˌsɒft'hɑːtɪd] *adj* de bom coração.
softly ['sɒftlɪ] *adv* **-1.** [gently, without violence] com delicadeza **-2.** [quietly] suavemente **-3.** [dimly] tenuamente **-4.** [fondly] carinhosamente.
softness ['sɒftnɪs] *n (U)* **-1.** [malleability] maleabilidade *f* **-2.** [to touch] maciez *f* **-3.** [gentleness] suavidade *f* **-4.** [kindness] bondade *f*.
soft-pedal *vi inf*: **to ~ on sthg** maneirar em algo.
soft return *n COMPUT* quebra *f* de linha condicional.
soft sell *n inf sistema de venda em que não se pressiona o comprador.*
soft-spoken *adj* de voz suave.
soft toy *n* bichinho *m* de pelúcia.
software ['sɒftweəʳ] *n (U) COMPUT* software *m*.
software package *n COMPUT* pacote *m* de software.
softwood *n* [timber] madeira *f* branca.
softy ['sɒftɪ] (*pl* **-ies**) *n inf* **-1.** *pej* [weak person] fracote *mf* **-2.** [sensitive person] manteiga-derretida *mf*.
soggy ['sɒgɪ] (*compar* **-ier**, *superl* **-iest**) *adj* empapado(da), encharcado(da).
soil [sɔɪl] ◇ *n* **-1.** [earth] terra *f*, solo *m* **-2.** *fig* [territory] solo *m*. ◇ *vt* [dirty] sujar.
soiled [sɔɪld] *adj* sujo(ja).
solace ['sɒləs] *n literary* consolo *m*.
solar ['səʊləʳ] *adj* solar.
solar energy *n* energia *f* solar.
solarium [sə'leərɪəm] (*pl* **-riums** *OR* **-ria** [-rɪə]) *n* solário *m*.
solar panel *n* painel *m* solar.
solar plexus [-'pleksəs] *n* plexo *m* solar.
solar power *n* energia *f* solar.
solar system *n* sistema *f* solar.
sold [səʊld] *pt* & *pp* ▷ **sell**.
solder ['səʊldəʳ] ◇ *n (U)* solda *f*. ◇ *vt* soldar.
soldering iron ['səʊldərɪŋ-] *n* ferro *m* de soldar.
soldier ['səʊldʒəʳ] *n* soldado(da).
◆ **soldier on** *vi UK* agüentar firme.
sold out *adj* esgotado(da).
sole [səʊl] (*pl sense 2 only inv OR* **-s**) ◇ *adj* **-1.** [only] único(ca) **-2.** [exclusive] exclusivo(va). ◇ *n* **-1.** [of foot] sola *f* **-2.** [fish] linguado *m*.
solely ['səʊllɪ] *adv* [entirely] unicamente.
solemn ['sɒləm] *adj* solene.
solemnly ['sɒləmlɪ] *adv* solenemente.
sole trader *n UK COMM* comerciante *mf* individual.
solicit [sə'lɪsɪt] ◇ *vt fml* [request] solicitar. ◇ *vi* [prostitute] oferecer seus serviços.
solicitor [sə'lɪsɪtəʳ] *n UK* solicitador *m*, -ra *f*.
solicitous [sə'lɪsɪtəs] *adj* **-1.** [caring] solícito(ta) **-2.** [anxious]: **~ of** *OR* **for sthg** desejoso(sa) de algo.
solid ['sɒlɪd] ◇ *adj* **-1.** [gen] sólido(da) **-2.** [of a single substance] maciço(ça) **-3.** [reliable, respectable] coerente **-4.** [unbroken, continuous] ininterrupto(ta). ◇ *adv*: **to be packed ~** estar superlotado(da). ◇ *n* [not liquid or gas] sólido *m*.
◆ **solids** *npl* [food] sólidos *mpl*; **she can't eat ~s** ela não pode comer nada sólido.
solidarity [ˌsɒlɪ'dærətɪ] *n (U)* solidariedade *f*.
solid fuel *n* combustível *m* sólido.
solidify [sə'lɪdɪfaɪ] (*pt* & *pp* **-ied**) *vi* solidificar-se.
solidly ['sɒlɪdlɪ] *adv* **-1.** [sturdily] solidamente **-2.** [completely, definitely] inteiramente **-3.** [without interruption] ininterruptamente.
soliloquy [sə'lɪləkwɪ] (*pl* **-ies**) *n LITER* solilóquio *m*.
solitaire [ˌsɒlɪ'teəʳ] *n* **-1.** [jewel] solitário *m* **-2.** [card game] paciência *f*.
solitary ['sɒlɪtrɪ] *adj* **-1.** [gen] solitário(ria) **-2.** [single] isolado(da).
solitary confinement *n (U)* solitária *f*.
solitude ['sɒlɪtjuːd] *n (U)* solidão *f*.
solo ['səʊləʊ] (*pl* **-s**) ◇ *adj* **-1.** *MUS* solo *inv* **-2.** [attempt, flight] único(ca). ◇ *n MUS* solo *m*. ◇ *adv* **-1.** *MUS* em solo **-2.** [fly, climb] sozinho(nha).
soloist ['səʊləʊɪst] *n* solista *mf*.
Solomon Islands ['sɒləmən-] *npl*: **the ~** as Ilhas Salomão; **in the ~** nas Ilhas Salomão.
solstice ['sɒlstɪs] *n* solstício *m*.
soluble ['sɒljʊbl] *adj* **-1.** [substance] solúvel **-2.** [problem] solucionável.
solution [sə'luːʃn] *n* **-1.** [to problem, puzzle]: **~ (to sthg)** solução *f* (para algo) **-2.** [liquid] solução *f*.
solve [sɒlv] *vt* resolver.
solvency ['sɒlvənsɪ] *n (U) FIN* solvência *f*.
solvent ['sɒlvənt] ◇ *adj FIN* solvente. ◇ *n* [substance] solvente *m*.
solvent abuse [-ə'bjuːs] *n (U)* inalação *f* de cola e solventes.
Somali [sə'mɑːlɪ] ◇ *adj* somali. ◇ *n* **-1.** [person] somali *mf* **-2.** [language] somali *m*.
Somalia [sə'mɑːlɪə] *n* Somália; **in ~** na Somália.
sombre *UK*, **somber** *US* ['sɒmbəʳ] *adj* **-1.** [person, mood] lúgubre **-2.** [colour, place] sombrio(bria).
some [sʌm] ◇ *adj* **-1.** [certain, large amount of] algum (alguma); **~ meat** um pouco de carne; **~ money** um pouco de dinheiro; **I had ~ difficulty getting here** tive algumas dificuldades para chegar aqui. **-2.** [certain, large number of] alguns (algumas); **~ sweets** alguns doces; **~ people** algumas pessoas; **I've known him for ~ years** já o conheço há alguns anos. **-3.** [not all] alguns (algumas); **~ jobs are better paid than others** alguns empregos são mais bem pagos que outros. **-4.** [in imprecise statements] um (uma) ... qualquer; **~ woman phoned** telefonou uma mulher. ◇ *pron* **-1.** [certain amount] algum *m*, alguma *f*, parte *f*; **can I have ~?** posso ficar com uma parte?; **~ of the money** algum dinheiro, parte do dinheiro. **-2.** [certain number] alguns *mpl*, algumas *fpl*; **can I have ~?** posso ficar com alguns?; **~ (of them) left early** alguns (deles) foram embora cedo. ◇ *adv* [approximately] aproximadamente; **there were ~ 7,000 people there** havia umas 7.000 pessoas.
somebody ['sʌmbədɪ] *pron* alguém.
someday ['sʌmdeɪ] *adv* algum dia.
somehow ['sʌmhaʊ], **someway** *US* ['sʌmweɪ] *adv* **-1.** [by some action] de alguma maneira **-2.** [for some reason] por alguma razão; **~ I don't think he'll come** tenho a impressão de que ele não virá.
someone ['sʌmwʌn] *pron* = **somebody**.

someplace *adv US* = **somewhere**.
somersault ['sʌməsɔ:lt] ◇ *n* salto *m* mortal. ◇ *vi* dar um salto mortal.
Somerset *n* Somerset.
something ['sʌmθɪŋ] ◇ *pron* **-1.** algo, alguma coisa; **or ~** *inf* ou (qualquer) coisa parecida **-2.** *phr*: **it's really ~!** é demais! ◇ *adv* [in approximations]: **~ like** uns(umas), qualquer coisa como.
sometime ['sʌmtaɪm] *adv*: **~ in June** em junho.
sometimes ['sʌmtaɪmz] *adv* às *OR* por vezes.
someway *adv US* = **somehow**.
somewhat ['sʌmwɒt] *adv* um tanto.
somewhere *UK* ['sʌmweə^r], **someplace** *US* ['sʌmpleɪs] *adv* **-1.** [unknown place] em algum lugar, em alguma parte **-2.** [specific place] a alguma parte **-3.** [in approximations]: **~ around** *OR* **between** aproximadamente.
son [sʌn] *n* filho *m*.
sonar ['səʊnɑ:^r] *n (U)* sonar *m*.
sonata [sə'nɑ:tə] *n* sonata *f*.
song [sɒŋ] *n* **-1.** [piece of music] música *f*; **for a ~** [cheaply] por uma bagatela; **to make a ~ and dance about sthg** *inf* fazer uma tempestade num copo d'água em relação a algo **-2.** *(U)* [act of singing]: **they burst into ~** desataram a cantar **-3.** [of bird] canto *m*.
songbook ['sɒŋbʊk] *n* cancioneiro *m*.
sonic ['sɒnɪk] *adj* sônico(ca).
sonic boom *n* ruído *m* sônico.
son-in-law (*pl* **sons-in-law** *OR* **son-in-laws**) *n* genro *m*.
sonnet ['sɒnɪt] *n* soneto *m*.
sonny ['sʌnɪ] *n inf* filhinho *m*.
soon [su:n] *adv* **-1.** [in a short time] logo **-2.** [early] cedo; **how ~ can you finish it?** para quando você consegue terminar?; **as ~ as** assim que; **as ~ as possible** o quanto antes **-3.** *phr*: **I'd just as ~ ...** eu preferiria (que) ...
sooner ['su:nə^r] *adv* **-1.** [earlier] mais cedo; **no ~ did he arrive than ...** ele tinha acabado de chegar quando ...; **~ or later** mais cedo ou mais tarde; **the ~ the better** quanto mais cedo, melhor **-2.** [expressing preference]: **I'd ~ ...** preferiria ...
soot [sʊt] *n (U)* fuligem *f*.
soothe [su:ð] *vt* **-1.** [relieve] aliviar **-2.** [calm] acalmar.
soothing ['su:ðɪŋ] *adj* **-1.** [pain-relieving] analgésico(ca), calmante **-2.** [calming] tranqüilizante.
sooty ['sʊtɪ] (*compar* **-ier**, *superl* **-iest**) *adj* fuliginoso(-sa).
sop *n pej* compensação *f* de pouco valor; **~ to sb/sthg** compensação de pouco valor para alguém/algo.
SOP (*abbr of* **standard operating procedure**) *n* procedimento *m* habitual.
sophisticated [sə'fɪstɪkeɪtɪd] *adj* **-1.** [stylish] sofisticado(da) **-2.** [intelligent] inteligente **-3.** [complicated] complicado(da).
sophistication [sə,fɪstɪ'keɪʃn] *n (U)* **-1.** [stylishness] sofisticação *f* **-2.** [intelligence] inteligência *f* **-3.** [complexity] complexidade *f*.
sophomore ['sɒfəmɔ:^r] *n US estudante do segundo ano de faculdade*.
soporific [,sɒpə'rɪfɪk] *adj* soporífero(ra).
sopping ['sɒpɪŋ] *adj*: **~ (wet)** encharcado(da).
soppy ['sɒpɪ] (*compar* **-ier**, *superl* **-iest**) *adj inf pej* sentimentalóide.
soprano [sə'prɑ:nəʊ] (*pl* **-s**) *n* **-1.** [person] soprano *mf* **-2.** [voice] soprano *f*.
sorbet ['sɔ:beɪ] *n* sorbet *m*.
sorcerer ['sɔ:sərə^r] *n* feiticeiro *m*.
sorceress *n* feiticeira *f*.
sordid ['sɔ:dɪd] *adj* sórdido(da).
sore [sɔ:^r] ◇ *adj* **-1.** [painful] dolorido(da); **a ~ throat** uma dor de garganta **-2.** *US inf* [angry] zangado(da) **-3.** *literary* [dire, great] imenso(sa). ◇ *n MED* inflamação *f*.
sorely ['sɔ:lɪ] *adv literary* imensamente.
sorority [sə'rɒrətɪ] (*pl* **-ies**) *n US irmandade feminina numa universidade*.
sorrel ['sɒrəl] *n (U)* azeda-miúda *f*.
sorrow ['sɒrəʊ] *n* **-1.** *(U)* [feeling of sadness] mágoa *f* **-2.** [cause of sadness] desgosto *m*.
sorrowful ['sɒrəfʊl] *adj* magoado(da), triste.
sorry ['sɒrɪ] (*compar* **-ier**, *superl* **-iest**) ◇ *adj* **-1.** [expressing apology]: **I'm ~** desculpe; **to be ~ about sthg** lamentar algo; **to be ~ for sthg** estar arrependido(da) por algo; **to be ~ to do sthg** desculpar-se por fazer algo **-2.** [expressing disappointment]: **to be ~ (that)** lamentar que; **to be ~ about sthg** ficar sentido(da) por algo **-3.** [expressing regret]: **I'm ~ to have to say that ...** lamento ter que dizer que ...; **to be ~ to do sthg** estar triste por fazer algo **-4.** [expressing sympathy]: **to be** *OR* **feel ~ for sb** estar com/sentir pena de alguém; **to be** *OR* **feel ~ for o.s.** estar com/sentir pena de si mesmo **-5.** [expressing polite disagreement]: **I'm ~, but I think that ...** me desculpa, mas eu acho que ... **-6.** [poor, pitiable] lamentável. ◇ *excl* **-1.** [expressing apology] desculpe! **-2.** [asking for repetition] como! **-3.** [to correct o.s.]: **a boy, ~, a man** um garoto, quer dizer, um homem.
sort [sɔ:t] ◇ *n* **-1.** [gen] tipo *m*; **a ~ of** um tipo de, uma espécie de **-2.** [act of sorting out] escolha *f*. ◇ *vt* [classify, separate] classificar.
◆ **sorts** *npl*: **a lawyer of ~s** um advogado medíocre, um advogadozinho; **to be out of ~s** não se sentir bem.
◆ **sort of** *adv* [rather] mais ou menos.
◆ **sort out** *vt sep* **-1.** [into groups] classificar **-2.** [tidy up] pôr em ordem **-3.** [solve] resolver **-4.** [work out] concluir.
sortie ['sɔ:ti:] *n* [*MIL* - by troops] surtida *f*; [- by aircraft] ação *f* de reconhecimento.
sorting office ['sɔ:tɪŋ-] *n* centro *f* de triagem.
sort-out *n UK inf*: **to have a ~** dar uma geral.
SOS (*abbr of* **save our souls**) *n* SOS *f*.
so-so *inf adj, adv* mais ou menos.
soufflé ['su:fleɪ] *n* suflê *m*.
sought [sɔ:t] *pt & pp* ▷ **seek**.
sought-after *adj* solicitado(da).
soul [səʊl] *n* **-1.** [gen] alma *f* **-2.** [emotional depth] sentimento *m* **-3.** [perfect example] exemplo *m* perfeito **-4.** *(U)* [music] (música *f*) soul *m*.
soul-destroying [-dɪ,strɔɪɪŋ] *adj* [boring] massante; [discouraging] desmoralizador(ra).

soul food *n US comida tradicional dos negros do sul dos Estados Unidos.*
soulful ['səʊlfʊl] *adj* cheio (cheia) de sentimentos.
soulless ['səʊllɪs] *adj* desalmado(da).
soul mate *n* alma *f* gêmea.
soul music *n (U)* música *f* soul.
soul-searching *n (U)* exame *m* de consciência.
sound [saʊnd] <> *adj* **-1.** [healthy] sadio(dia) **-2.** [sturdy] sólido(da) **-3.** [reliable] confiável, seguro(ra) **-4.** [thorough] completo(ta). <> *adv*: **to be ~ asleep** estar num sono profundo. <> *n* **-1.** [particular noise] barulho *m* **-2.** *(U)* [in general] som *m* **-3.** *(U)* [volume] volume *m* **-4.** [impression, idea] tom *m*. <> *vt* [alarm, bell, horn] tocar. <> *vi* **-1.** [make a noise] fazer barulho; **to ~ like sthg** soar como algo **-2.** [seem] parecer; **to ~ like sthg** parecer algo.
◆ **sound out** *vt sep*: **to ~ sb out (on** OR **aboutsthg)** sondar alguém(sobre algo).
sound barrier *n* barreira *f* do som.
sound bite *n* declaração *f* mordaz *(feita por políticos no rádio ou na tevê)*.
sound card *n* COMPUT placa *f* de som.
sound effects *npl* efeitos *mpl* sonoros.
sounding board *n* **-1.** caixa *f* de ressonância **-2.** *fig* [person]: **he needs a ~, rather than thinking alone** ele precisa de alguém com quem possa trocar idéias, em vez de pensar sozinho.
sounding ['saʊndɪŋ] *n* **-1.** NAUT [measurement] prumada *f* **-2.** *fig* [investigation] sondagem *f*.
soundly ['saʊndlɪ] *adv* **-1.** [thoroughly] completamente **-2.** [deeply] profundamente.
soundness ['saʊndnɪs] *n (U)* [reliability] solidez *f*.
soundproof ['saʊndpru:f] *adj* à prova de som.
soundtrack ['saʊndtræk] *n* trilha *f* sonora.
sound wave *n* onda *f* sonora.
soup [su:p] *n* sopa *f*, caldo *m*.
◆ **soup up** *vt sep inf* [car] envenenar.
soup kitchen *n* bandejão *m* público.
soup plate *n* prato *m* fundo.
soup spoon *n* colher *f* de sopa.
sour [saʊə^r] <> *adj* **-1.** [acidic] ácido(da) **-2.** [milk] azedo(da); **to go** OR **turn sour** [milk] azedar; *fig* [be spoiled] degringolar **-3.** [ill-tempered] mal-humorado(da). <> *vt* & *vi* [person, relationship] azedar.
source [sɔ:s] *n* **-1.** [gen] fonte *f* **-2.** [cause] origem *f* **-3.** [of river] nascente *f*.
soured cream *n (U)* nata *f* azeda.
sour grapes *n (U) inf* inveja *f* pura.
sourness ['saʊənɪs] *n (U)* **-1.** [gen] azedume *m* **-2.** [acidity] acidez *f*.
south [saʊθ] <> *adj* sul. <> *adv* para o sul; **~ of** ao sul de. <> *n* **-1.** [direction] sul *m* **-2.** [region]: **the ~** o sul.
South Africa *n* África *f* do Sul; **in ~** na África do Sul; **the Republic of ~** a República da África do Sul.
South African <> *adj* sul-africano(na). <> *n* [person] sul-africano *m*, -na *f*.
South America *n* América *f* do Sul; **in ~** na América do Sul.
South American <> *adj* sul-americano(na). <> *n* [person] sul-americano *m*, -na *f*.
southbound ['saʊθbaʊnd] *adj* para o sul.
South Carolina *n* Carolina *f* do Sul.
South Dakota *n* Dakota *f* do Sul.
south-east <> *adj* sudeste. <> *adv* para o sudeste; **~ of** a sudeste de. <> *n* **-1.** [direction] sudeste *m* **-2.** [region]: **the ~** o sudeste.
South-East Asia *n* Sudeste *m* Asiático; **in ~** no Sudeste Asiático.
south-easterly *adj* **-1.** [in the south-east] sudeste **-2.** [towards the south-east] para o sudeste **-3.** [from the south-east] do sudeste.
south-eastern *adj* do sudeste.
southerly ['sʌðəlɪ] *adj* **-1.** [in the south] ao sul **-2.** [towards the south] para o sul **-3.** [from the south] do sul.
southern ['sʌðən] *adj* sulista.
Southern Africa *n* África Meridional; **in ~** na África Meridional.
Southerner ['sʌðənə^r] *n* sulista *mf*.
South Korea *n* Coréia *f* do Sul; **in ~** na Coréia do Sul.
South Korean <> *adj* sul-coreano(na). <> *n* sul-coreano *m*, -na *f*.
South Pole *n*: **the ~** o Pólo Sul.
South Vietnam *n* Vietnã *m* do Sul; **in ~** no Vietnã do Sul.
South Vietnamese <> *adj* sul-vietnamita. <> *n* sul-vietnamita *mf*.
southward ['saʊθwəd] <> *adj* sul. <> *adv* = **southwards**.
southwards ['saʊθwədz] *adv* para o sul.
south-west <> *adj* sudoeste. <> *adv* para o sudoeste; **~ of** a sudoeste de. <> *n* **-1.** [direction] sudoeste *m* **-2.** [region]: **the ~** o sudoeste.
south-westerly *adj* **-1.** [in the south-west] ao sudoeste **-2.** [towards the south-west] para o sudoeste **-3.** [from the south-west] do sudoeste.
south-western *adj* do sudoeste.
South Yemen *n* Iêmen *m* do Sul; **in ~** no Iêmen do Sul.
South Yorkshire *n* South Yorkshire.
souvenir [ˌsu:və'nɪə^r] *n* suvenir *m*, lembrança *f*.
sou'wester [saʊ'westə^r] *n* [hat] sueste *m*.
sovereign ['sɒvrɪn] <> *adj* **-1.** [state, territory] soberano(na) **-2.** [excellent] magnífico(ca). <> *n* **-1.** [ruler] soberano *m*, -na *f* **-2.** [coin] soberano *m*.
sovereignty ['sɒvrɪntɪ] *n* [supreme power] soberania *f*.
soviet *n* soviético(ca).
◆ **Soviet** <> *adj* soviético *m*, -ca *f*. <> *n* [person] soviético *m*, -ca *f*.
Soviet Union *n*: **the (former) ~** a (antiga) União Soviética; **in the ~** na União Soviética.
sow[1] [səʊ] (*pt* **-ed**, *pp* **sown** OR **-ed**) *vt* semear.
sow[2] [saʊ] *n* [pig] porca *f*.
sown [səʊn] *pp* ▻ **sow**.
sox *npl US* ▻ **bobby sox**.
soya ['sɔɪə] *n (U)* soja *f*.
soy(a) bean ['sɔɪ(ə)-] *n* grão *m* de soja.
soy sauce [sɔɪ-] *n (U)* molho *m* de soja.
sozzled ['sɒzld] *adj UK inf* pinguço(ça).
spa [spɑ:] *n* **-1.** [mineral spring] termas *fpl* **-2.** [for health care] spa *m*.
space [speɪs] <> *n* **-1.** [gen] espaço *m*; **to stare into**

~ olhar para o nada **-2.** [gap] lugar *m*, espaço *m* **-3.** [period of time] intervalo *m* **-4.** [seat, place] lugar *m*. ◇ *comp* espacial. ◇ *vt* espaçar.

◆ **space out** *vt sep* [arrange] espaçar.

space age *n*: **the ~** a era espacial.

◆ **space-age** *adj inf* da era espacial.

space bar *n* barra *f* de espaço.

space capsule *n* cápsula *f* espacial.

spacecraft ['speɪskrɑ:ft] (*pl inv*) *n* espaçonave *f*.

spaceman ['speɪsmæn] (*pl* **-men** [-men]) *n inf* [astronaut] astronauta *m*.

space probe *n* sonda *f* espacial.

spaceship ['speɪsʃɪp] *n* nave *f* espacial, astronave *f*.

space shuttle *n* ônibus *m inv* espacial.

space station *n* estação *f* espacial.

spacesuit ['speɪssu:t] *n* roupa *f* espacial.

spacewoman ['speɪs,wʊmən] (*pl* **-women** [-,wɪmɪn]) *n inf* [astronaut] astronauta *f*.

spacing ['speɪsɪŋ] *n (U)* TYPO espaçamento *m*.

spacious ['speɪʃəs] *adj* espaçoso(sa).

spade [speɪd] *n* **-1.** [tool] pá *f* **-2.** [playing card] espada *f*.

◆ **spades** *npl* espadas *fpl*; **the six of ~s** o seis de espadas.

spadework ['speɪdwɜ:k] *n (U) inf* trabalho *m* preliminar.

spaghetti [spə'getɪ] *n (U)* espaguete *m*.

Spain [speɪn] *n* Espanha *f*; **in ~** na Espanha.

spam [spæm] (*pt* & *pp* **-med**, *cont* **-ming**) COMPUT ◇ *n* spam *m*. ◇ *vt* enviar spam para.

span [spæn] (*pt* & *pp* **-ned**, *cont* **-ning**) ◇ *pt* ▷ **spin**. ◇ *n* **-1.** [in time] período *m*; **concentration ~** tempo *m* de concentração **-2.** [range] gama *f* **-3.** [of hand] palmo *m* **-4.** [of arms] braçada *f* **-5.** [of wings] envergadura *f* **-6.** [of bridge, arch] extensão *f*. ◇ *vt* **-1.** [encompass] cobrir um período de **-2.** [cross] atravessar, cruzar.

spandex *n* spandex *m*.

spangled ['spæŋgld] *adj literary*: **~ (with sthg)** adornado(da) (de algo).

Spaniard ['spænjəd] *n* espanhol *m*, -la *f*.

spaniel ['spænjəl] *n* cocker *m* spaniel.

Spanish ['spænɪʃ] ◇ *adj* espanhol(la). ◇ *n* [language] espanhol *m*. ◇ *npl*: **the ~** os espanhóis.

Spanish America *n* América Espanhola.

Spanish American ◇ *adj* **-1.** [in US] hispano(-na) **-2.** [in Latin America] hispano-americano(na). ◇ *n* **-1.** [in US] hispano *m*, -na *f* **-2.** [in Latin America] hispano-americano *m*, -na *f*.

spank [spæŋk] ◇ *n* palmada *f*. ◇ *vt* dar palmadas em.

spanner ['spænəʳ] *n* chave *f* inglesa.

spar [spɑ:ʳ] (*pt* & *pp* **-red**, *cont* **-ring**) *vi* **-1.** BOXING treinar boxe **-2.** [verbally]: **to ~ (with sb)** discutir amigavelmente (com alguém).

spare [speəʳ] ◇ *adj* **-1.** [surplus] sobressalente, de sobra; **have you got a ~ pencil?** você tem um lápis sobrando? **-2.** [free] livre. ◇ *n* [surplus object] sobressalente *mf*. ◇ *vt* **-1.** [put aside, make available] dispor de; **to have sthg to ~** [extra] ter algo de sobra **-2.** [not harm] preservar **-3.** [economize] poupar; **to ~ no expense** não poupar despesas **-4.** [save, protect from]: **to ~ sb sthg** poupar alguém de algo.

spare part *n* peça *f* sobressalente.

spare tyre *n* estepe *m*.

spare wheel *n* roda *f* sobressalente.

spare room *n* quarto *m* de hóspedes.

spare time *n (U)* tempo *m* livre.

sparing ['speərɪŋ] *adj*: **to be ~ with** OR **of sthg** ser econômico(ca) em algo.

sparingly ['speərɪŋlɪ] *adv* com moderação.

spark [spɑ:k] ◇ *n* **-1.** [from fire] fagulha *f* **-2.** [from electricity] faísca *f* **-3.** *fig* [of interest, humour *etc*] lampejo *m*. ◇ *vt* [trigger] provocar.

sparking plug ['spɑ:kɪŋ-] *n UK* = **spark plug**.

sparkle ['spɑ:kl] ◇ *n* **-1.** [gen] brilho *m* **-2.** [of person, conversation, wit] estilo *m*, brilho *m*. ◇ *vi* **-1.** [gen] brilhar **-2.** [person, conversation, wit] ser brilhante, brilhar.

sparkler ['spɑ:kləʳ] *n* [firework] estrelinha *f*.

sparkling *adj* **-1.** [mineral water] com gás, gaseificado(da) **-2.** [wit] brilhante.

sparkling wine ['spɑ:klɪŋ-] *n* vinho *m* espumante.

spark plug *n* vela *f (de ignição)*.

sparrow ['spærəʊ] *n* pardal *m*.

sparse [spɑ:s] *adj* esparso(sa).

spartan ['spɑ:tn] *adj* espartano(na).

spasm ['spæzm] *n* **-1.** MED [muscular contraction] espasmo *m* **-2.** [fit] acesso *m*.

spasmodic [spæz'mɒdɪk] *adj* [intermittent] espasmódico(ca).

spastic ['spæstɪk] MED ◇ *adj* espástico(ca). ◇ *n* espasmofílico *m*, -ca *f*.

spat [spæt] *pt* & *pp* ▷ **spit**.

spate [speɪt] *n* série *f*, sucessão *f*.

spatial ['speɪʃl] *adj* espacial; **~ awareness** noção *f* de espaço.

spatter ['spætəʳ] *vt* & *vi* respingar.

spatula ['spætjʊlə] *n* CULIN, MED espátula *f*.

spawn [spɔ:n] ◇ *n (U)* [of frogs, fish] ovas *fpl*. ◇ *vt fig* [produce] gerar. ◇ *vi* ZOOL desovar.

spay [speɪ] *vt* castrar *(fêmea)*.

speak [spi:k] (*pt* **spoke**, *pp* **spoken**) ◇ *vt* **-1.** [say] dizer **-2.** [express opinion]: **to ~ ill of sb** falar mal de alguém **-3.** [language] falar. ◇ *vi* **-1.** [say words] falar; **to ~ to** OR **with sb** falar com alguém; **to ~ to sb about sthg** falar com alguém sobre algo; **to ~ about sb/sthg** falar sobre alguém/algo; **to ~ well** OR **highly of sb** falar bem de alguém; **nobody/nothing to ~ of** ninguém/nada em especial **-2.** [make a speech] discursar; **to ~ to sb** discursar para alguém; **to ~ on sthg** falar OR discursar sobre algo **-3.** [in giving an opinion]: **generally ~ing** falando em termos gerais; **personally ~ing** pessoalmente falando; **~ing as** [in the position of] falando como; **~ing of** [on the subject of] falando sobre.

◆ **so to speak** *adv* por assim dizer.

◆ **speak for** *vt fus* [represent] falar em nome de; **it ~s for itself** isso fala por si mesmo; **~ for yourself!** fala isso por ti!

◆ **speak out** *vi* falar publicamente; **to ~ out**

against sb/sthg fazer declarações contra alguém/algo.
◆ **speak up** *vi* **-1.** [say something] falar claro; **to ~ up for sb/sthg** sair em defesa de alguém/algo **-2.** [speak louder] falar mais alto.
speaker ['spi:kəʳ] *n* **-1.** [person talking, of a language] falante *mf* **-2.** [in lecture] orador *m*, -ra *f*, conferencista *mf* **-3.** [loudspeaker] alto-falante *m* **-4.** [in stereo system] caixa *f* de som.
◆ **Speaker** *n UK* [in House of Commons] Presidente *mf* da Câmara dos Comuns.
speaking ['spi:kɪŋ] *n* discurso *m*.
speaking clock *n UK* serviço *m* de hora certa.
spear [spɪəʳ] ◇ *n* [weapon] lança *f*. ◇ *vt* lancear.
spearhead ['spɪəhed] ◇ *n* ponta-de-lança *f*. ◇ *vt* encabeçar.
spec [spek] *n UK inf*: **to buy sthg on ~** comprar algo sem garantia; **to go on ~** ir sem ter feito reserva.
special ['speʃl] ◇ *adj* especial. ◇ *n* **-1.** [on menu]: **today's ~** prato *m* do dia **-2.** [on TV] especial *m* **-3.** [train] trem *m* especial.
special agent *n* agente *mf* especial.
special constable *n UK* policial *mf* voluntário, -ria.
special correspondent *n* correspondente *mf* especial.
special delivery *n (U)* [service] entrega *f* especial.
special effects *npl* efeitos *mpl* especiais.
specialist ['speʃəlɪst] ◇ *adj* especializado(da). ◇ *n* [expert] especialista *mf*.
speciality [ˌspeʃɪ'ælətɪ] (*pl* **-ies**), **specialty** *US* ['speʃltɪ] (*pl* **-ies**) *n* especialidade *f*.
specialize, -ise ['speʃəlaɪz] *vi* especializar-se; **to ~ in sthg** especializar-se em algo.
specially ['speʃəlɪ] *adv* **-1.** [on purpose, specifically] especialmente **-2.** [really] realmente; **do you want to go? - not ~** quer ir? - na verdade não.
special offer *n* oferta *f* especial, promoção *f*.
special school *n* escola *f* especial.
specialty *n US* = **speciality**.
species ['spi:ʃi:z] (*pl inv*) *n* espécie *f*.
specific [spə'sɪfɪk] *adj* [particular, precise] específico(-ca); **~ to sb/sthg** específico(ca) de alguém/algo.
◆ **specifics** *npl* [details] detalhes *mpl* específicos.
specifically [spə'sɪfɪklɪ] *adv* especificamente.
specification [ˌspesɪfɪ'keɪʃn] *n* [plan] especificação *f*.
◆ **specifications** *npl TECH* especificações *fpl* técnicas.
specify ['spesɪfaɪ] (*pt* & *pp* **-ied**) *vt* especificar.
specimen ['spesɪmən] *n* **-1.** [example] espécime *m*, exemplar *m* **-2.** [sample] amostra *f*.
specimen copy *n* cópia *f* de amostra.
specimen signature *n* assinatura *f* reconhecida em cartório.
speck [spek] *n* **-1.** [small stain] mancha *f* pequena **-2.** [small particle] partícula *f*.
speckled ['spekld] *adj* manchado(da); **~ with sthg** pintado(da) de algo.
specs [speks] *npl inf* [glasses] óculos *m inv*.
spectacle ['spektəkl] *n* **-1.** [sight] visão *f* **-2.** [event] espetáculo *m*.
◆ **spectacles** *npl UK* [glasses] óculos *m inv*.
spectacular [spek'tækjʊləʳ] ◇ *adj* espetacular. ◇ *n* espetáculo *m*.
spectate [spek'teɪt] *vi* assistir como espectador(-ra).
spectator [spek'teɪtəʳ] *n* espectador *m*, -ra *f*.
spectator sport *n* esporte *m* de multidões.
spectre *UK*, **specter** *US* ['spektəʳ] *n* **-1.** *fml* [ghost] espectro *m* **-2.** *fig* [frightening prospect]: **the ~ of famine** o fantasma da fome.
spectrum ['spektrəm] (*pl* **-tra** [-trə]) *n* **-1.** *PHYS* espectro *m* **-2.** *fig* [range] gama *f*.
speculate ['spekjʊleɪt] ◇ *vt*: **to ~ that** especular que. ◇ *vi* especular.
speculation [ˌspekjʊ'leɪʃn] *n* especulação *f*.
speculative ['spekjʊlətɪv] *adj* especulativo(va).
speculator ['spekjʊleɪtəʳ] *n FIN* especulador *m*, -ra *f*.
sped [sped] *pt* & *pp* ▷ **speed**.
speech [spi:tʃ] *n* **-1.** [gen] fala *f* **-2.** [formal talk]: **to give** *OR* **make a ~ (on sthg)** dar *OR* fazer um discurso (sobre algo); **to give** *OR* **make a ~ (to sb)** dar *OR* fazer um discurso (para alguém) **-3.** [manner of speaking] maneira *f* de falar **-4.** *(U)* [dialect] dialeto *m*, maneira *f* de falar **-5.** *GRAMM* discurso *m*.
speech day *n UK* *dia de encerramento do ano letivo quando são proferidos discursos e os estudantes recebem prêmios.*
speech impediment *n* defeito *m* na fala.
speechless ['spi:tʃlɪs] *adj*: **to be ~ (with sthg)** ficar emudecido(da) (de algo).
speech processing *n COMPUT* processamento *m* da fala.
speech therapist *n* fonoaudiólogo *m*.
speech therapy *n (U)* fonoaudiologia *f*.
speed [spi:d] (*pt* & *pp* **-ed** *OR* **sped**) ◇ *n* **-1.** [rate, pace] velocidade *f*; **at ~** a grande velocidade **-2.** *(U)* [rapid rate] rapidez *f* **-3.** [gear] marcha *f*. ◇ *vi* **-1.** [move fast]: **to ~ (along/away/by)** ir/acelerar/passar a toda velocidade **-2.** *AUT* [go too fast] exceder a velocidade.
◆ **speed up** ◇ *vt sep* acelerar. ◇ *vi* acelerar.
speedboat ['spi:dbəʊt] *n* lancha *f*.
speed-dial button *n* [on phone, fax] tecla *m* de discagem rápida.
speeding ['spi:dɪŋ] *n (U)* excesso *m* de velocidade.
speed limit *n* limite *m* de velocidade.
speedo (*pl* **-s**) *n UK inf* velocímetro *m*.
speedometer [spɪ'dɒmɪtəʳ] *n* velocímetro *m*.
speed trap *n* **-1.** [radar] radar *m* **-2.** [camera] pardal *m*.
speedway ['spi:dweɪ] *n* **-1.** *SPORT* corrida *f* de motos **-2.** *US* [road] pista *f* de corrida.
speedy ['spi:dɪ] (*compar* **-ier**, *superl* **-iest**) *adj* rápido(da).
speleology [ˌspi:lɪ'ɒlədʒɪ] *n (U) fml* espeleologia *f*.
spell [spel] (*UK pt* & *pp* **spelt** *OR* **-ed**, *US pt* & *pp* **-ed**) ◇ *n* **-1.** [period of time] período *m* **-2.** [enchantment] feitiço *m*, encanto *m* **-3.** [magic words] palavras *fpl* mágicas. ◇ *vt* **-1.** [write] soletrar **-2.** *fig* [signify] significar. ◇ *vi* escrever corretamente.

◆ **spell out** *vt sep* **-1.** [read aloud] soletrar **-2.** [explain]: **to ~ sthg out (for** *OR* **to sb)** explicar algo em detalhes (para alguém).
spellbound ['spelbaʊnd] *adj* encantado(da).
spellcheck ['speltʃek] *vt COMPUT* passar o corretor ortográfico em.
spellchecker ['speltʃekəʳ] *n COMPUT* corretor *m* ortográfico.
spelling ['spelɪŋ] *n* ortografia *f*.
spelt [spelt] *pt & pp UK* ▷ **spell**.
spend [spend] (*pt & pp* **spent**) *vt* **-1.** [pay out] gastar; **to ~ sthg on sb/sthg** gastar algo em alguém/algo **-2.** [time, life] passar **-3.** [energy] gastar.
spender ['spendəʳ] *n* [person] esbanjador *m*, -ra *f*, gastador *m*, -ra *f*.
spending ['spendɪŋ] *n (U)* gastos *mpl*.
spending money *n (U)* dinheiro *m* para pequenos gastos pessoais.
spending power *n (U)* poder *m* aquisitivo.
spendthrift ['spendθrɪft] *n* perdulário *m*, -ria *f*.
spent [spent] ◇ *pt & pp* ▷ **spend**. ◇ *adj* [consumed, burned out - matches, ammunition] usado(da); [- force, patience, energy] esgotado(da).
sperm [spɜːm] (*pl inv OR* **-s**) *n* esperma *m*.
spermicidal cream [ˌspɜːmɪ'saɪdl-] *n* creme *m* espermicida.
sperm whale *n* baleia *f* cachalote.
spew [spjuː] ◇ *vt* [cause to flow, spread] expelir, cuspir. ◇ *vi* [flow, spread]: **to ~ (out) from sthg** lançar-se(para fora)de algo; **flames ~ed out of the volcano** o vulcão cuspia chamas.
sphere [sfɪəʳ] *n* esfera *f*.
spherical ['sferɪkl] *adj* esférico(ca).
sphincter ['sfɪŋktəʳ] *n* esfíncter *m*.
sphinx [sfɪŋks] (*pl* **-es**) *n* esfinge *f*.
spice [spaɪs] ◇ *n* tempero *m*. ◇ *vt* **-1.** *CULIN*: **to ~ sthg (with sthg)** temperar algo (com algo) **-2.** *fig* [add excitement to]: **to ~ sthg (up)** dar sabor a algo.
spick-and-span [ˌspɪkən'spæn] *adj* asseado(da).
spicy ['spaɪsɪ] (*compar* **-ier**, *superl* **-iest**) *adj* picante.
spider ['spaɪdəʳ] *n* aranha *f*.
spider's web, spiderweb *US* ['spaɪdəweb] *n* teia *f* de aranha.
spidery ['spaɪdərɪ] *adj* aranhoso(sa).
spiel [ʃpiːl] *n* lábia *f*.
spike [spaɪk] ◇ *n* **-1.** [on railings] prego *m* **-2.** [on shoe] cravo *m* **-3.** [on plant] espigão *m* **-4.** [of hair] corte *m* escovinha. ◇ *vt* reforçar com mais álcool.
◆ **spikes** *npl UK* tênis *m inv* com travas.
spiky ['spaɪkɪ] (*compar* **-ier**, *superl* **-iest**) *adj* **-1.** [branch] pontudo(da) **-2.** [plant] espinhento(ta) **-3.** [hair] eriçado(da).
spill [spɪl] (*UK pt & pp* **spilt** *OR* **-ed**, *US pt & pp* **-ed**) ◇ *vt* derramar. ◇ *vi* **-1.** [liquid] derramar; **the wine ~ed all over the carpet** o vinho esparramou por todo o carpete **-2.** [salt, sugar, etc] esparramar **-3.** [crowd]: **the fans ~ed out of stadium** os torcedores saíram em massa do estádio; **the crowd ~ed into the main square** a multidão espalhou-se pela praça principal.
spillage ['spɪlɪdʒ] *n* derramamento *m*.
spilt [spɪlt] *pt & pp UK* ▷ **spill**.
spin [spɪn] (*pt* **span** *OR* **spun**, *pp* **spun**, *cont* **-ning**) ◇ *n* **-1.** [turn] giro *m*, volta *f* **-2.** *AERON* parafuso *m* **-3.** *inf* [in car] volta *f* **-4.** *SPORT* [on ball] efeito *m*. ◇ *vt* **-1.** [cause to rotate] rodar, girar **-2.** [in spin-dryer] centrifugar **-3.** [thread, cloth, wool] fiar **-4.** *SPORT* [ball] fazer girar. ◇ *vi* **-1.** [rotate] girar, dar voltas **-2.** [feel dizzy]: **to be spinning** estar rodando **-3.** [spinner] fiar **-4.** [in spin-dryer] centrifugar.
◆ **spin out** *vt sep* **-1.** [story, explanation] prorrogar **-2.** [food, money] esticar.
spina bifida [ˌspaɪnə'bɪfɪdə] *n (U)* espinha *f* bífida.
spinach ['spɪnɪdʒ] *n (U)* espinafre *m*.
spinal column ['spaɪnl-] *n* coluna *f* vertebral.
spinal cord *n* medula *f* espinhal.
spindle ['spɪndl] *n* **-1.** [machine rod] eixo *m* **-2.** [for spinning] fuso *m*.
spindly ['spɪndlɪ] (*compar* **-ier**, *superl* **-iest**) *adj* longo e fino, longa e fina.
spin doctor *n* ***pej*** *pessoa encarregada das relações com a imprensa, geralmente para um político ou partido, e que manipula as informações a serem dadas.*
spin-dry *vt UK* centrifugar.
spin-dryer *n UK* centrifugadora *f (de roupas)*.
spine [spaɪn] *n* **-1.** *ANAT* espinha *f* dorsal **-2.** [of book] lombada *f* **-3.** [spike, prickle] espinho *m*.
spine-chilling *adj* de arrepiar, horripilante.
spineless ['spaɪnlɪs] *adj* [feeble] pobre de espírito.
spinner ['spɪnəʳ] *n* [of thread] fiandeiro *m*, -ra *f*.
spinning ['spɪnɪŋ] *n (U)* fiação *f*.
spinning top *n* pião *m*.
spin-off *n* [by-product] subproduto *m*.
spinster ['spɪnstəʳ] *n* solteirona *f*.
spiral ['spaɪərəl] (*UK pt & pp* **-led**, *cont* **-ling**, *US pt & pp* **-ed**, *cont* **-ing**) ◇ *adj* espiral. ◇ *n* **-1.** [curve] espiral *f* **-2.** [increase] escalada *f* **-3.** [decrease] queda *f*. ◇ *vi* **-1.** [move in spiral curve] mover-se em espiral **-2.** [increase rapidly] subir vertiginosamente **-3.** [decrease rapidly]: **to ~ downwards** despencar.
spiral staircase *n* escada *f* caracol.
spire [spaɪəʳ] *n* pináculo *m*.
spirit ['spɪrɪt] ◇ *n* espírito *m*; **to enter into the ~ of sthg** entrar no espírito de algo. ◇ *vt*: **to ~ sb into/out ofsthg** colocar/tirar alguém às escondidas de algo.
◆ **spirits** *npl* **-1.** [mood] astral *m*; **to be in high/low ~s** estar de alto/baixo astral **-2.** [alcohol] bebidas *fpl* destiladas.
spirited ['spɪrɪtɪd] *adj* animado(da).
spirit level *n* nível *m* de pedreiro *OR* bolha.
spiritual ['spɪrɪtʃʊəl] *adj* espiritual.
spiritualism ['spɪrɪtʃʊəlɪzm] *n (U)* espiritualismo *m*.
spiritualist ['spɪrɪtʃʊəlɪst] *n* espiritualista *mf*.
spit [spɪt] (*UK pt & pp* **spat**, *cont* **-ting**, *US pt & pp* **spit**, *cont* **-ting**) ◇ *n* **-1.** *(U)* [saliva] cuspe *m* **-2.** [skewer] espeto *m*. ◇ *vi* [from mouth] cuspir. ◇ *v impers UK* [rain lightly] chuviscar.
◆ **spit out** *vt sep* cuspir; **come on, ~ it out!** vamos, desembucha!
spite [spaɪt] ◇ *n (U)* rancor *m*; **to do sthg out of** *OR* **from ~** fazer algo por maldade. ◇ *vt* magoar.
◆ **in spite of** *prep* apesar de; **to do sthg in ~ of**

o.s. [unintentionally] fazer algo a contragosto.

spiteful ['spaɪtfʊl] *adj* maldoso(sa), mal-intencionado(da).

spitting image ['spɪtɪŋ-] *n*: **to be the ~ of sb** ser o retrato cuspido e escarrado de alguém.

spittle ['spɪtl] *n (U)* cuspe *m*.

splash [splæʃ] ◇ *n* **-1.** [sound] chape *m*, pancada *f* na água **-2.** [small quantity] respingo *m*; **a ~ of lemonade** uma esguichada de limonada **-3.** [patch] mancha *f*. ◇ *vt* **-1.** [subj: person] respingar **-2.** [subj: water] molhar **-3.** [apply haphazardly] espalhar. ◇ *vi* **-1.** [person]: **to ~ about** OR **around** patinhar **-2.** [water, liquid]: **to ~ on/against sthg** espirrar em/contra algo.

◆ **splash down** *vi* amerissar.

◆ **splash out** *inf* ◇ *vt sep*: **to ~ sthg out on sthg** gastar algo em algo. ◇ *vi*: **to ~ out (on sthg)** gastar um dinheirão (em algo).

splashdown ['splæʃdaʊn] *n* amerissagem *f*.

splash guard *n US* pára-lama *m*.

splay [spleɪ] ◇ *vt* esticar. ◇ *vi*: **to ~ (out)** esticar.

spleen [spli:n] *n* **-1.** ANAT baço *m* **-2.** *(U) fig* [anger] cólera *f*.

splendid ['splendɪd] *adj* **-1.** [very good] esplêndido(-da) **-2.** [magnificent, beautiful] esplendoroso(sa).

splendidly ['splendɪdlɪ] *adv* **-1.** [perform, write, behave] maravilhosamente **-2.** [design, dress, entertain] magnificamente, esplendidamente.

splendour *UK*, **splendor** *US* ['splendəʳ] *n* **-1.** *(U)* [beauty, magnificence] esplendor *m* **-2.** [magnificent feature] maravilha *f*.

splice [splaɪs] *vt* [join - rope] juntar, unir; [- film, tape] montar.

splint [splɪnt] *n* tala *f*.

splinter ['splɪntəʳ] ◇ *n* lasca *f*. ◇ *vt*: **to be ~ed** estar lascado(da). ◇ *vi* [glass, bone, wood] lascar.

splinter group *n* grupo *m* dissidente.

split [splɪt] (*pt* & *pp* **split**, *cont* **-ting**) ◇ *n* **-1.** [crack] racha *f*, fenda *f*; **~ (in sthg)** fenda (em algo) **-2.** [tear] rasgão *m*; **~ in sthg** rasgão em algo **-3.** [division, schism] separação *f*; **~ in sthg** racha *m* em algo; **~ between** divisão *f* entre. ◇ *vt* **-1.** [crack] rachar, partir **-2.** [tear] rasgar **-3.** [divide - group, organization] rachar; [- road] dividir-se **-4.** [share] dividir; **to ~ the difference** rachar a diferença. ◇ *vi* **-1.** [crack] rachar-se **-2.** [tear] rasgar-se **-3.** *inf* [leave] sair.

◆ **splits** *npl*: **to do the ~s** fazer espacato OR grande écart.

◆ **split off** ◇ *vt sep* [snap off]: **to ~ sthg off (from sthg)** separar algo (de algo). ◇ *vi* **-1.** [snap off]: **to ~ off (from sthg)** desprender-se (de algo) **-2.** [separate]: **to ~ off (from sb)** separar-se (de alguém).

◆ **split up** ◇ *vt sep*: **to ~ sthg up (into sthg)** dividir algo (em algo). ◇ *vi* separar-se; **to ~ up with sb** romper com alguém.

split end *n* ponta *f* dupla *(no cabelo)*.

split-level *adj* **-1.** [building, house, room] dúplex *inv* **-2.** [grill] duplo.

split peas *npl* ervilhas *fpl* secas.

split personality *n* dupla personalidade *f*.

split screen *n* **-1.** CINEMA & TV tela *f* múltipla **-2.** COMPUT divisão *f* de tela.

split second *n* fração *f* de segundo.

splitting ['splɪtɪŋ] *adj*: **~ headache** enxaqueca *f*.

splutter ['splʌtəʳ] ◇ *n* [of person] balbucio *m*. ◇ *vi* **-1.** [person] balbuciar **-2.** [car, engine] estalar **-3.** [spit] crepitar.

spoil [spɔɪl] (*pt* & *pp* **-ed** OR **spoilt**) *vt* **-1.** [ruin] estragar **-2.** [pamper] mimar; **to ~ sb** fazer um agrado a alguém; **to ~ o.s.** dar-se um capricho.

◆ **spoils** *npl* butim *m*; **~ of war** despojos *mpl* de guerra.

spoiled [spɔɪld] *adj* = **spoilt**.

spoiler ['spɔɪləʳ] *n* spoiler *m*.

spoilsport ['spɔɪlspɔ:t] *n* desmancha-prazeres *mf inv*.

spoilt [spɔɪlt] ◇ *pt* & *pp* ▷ **spoil**. ◇ *adj* **-1.** [child] mimado(da) **-2.** [food, dinner] estragado(da).

spoke [spəʊk] ◇ *pt* ▷ **speak**. ◇ *n* raio *m (da roda)*.

spoken ['spəʊkn] *pp* ▷ **speak**.

spokesman ['spəʊksmən] (*pl* **-men** [-mən]) *n* porta-voz *m*.

spokesperson ['spəʊks,pɜ:sn] (*pl* **spokespeople**) *n* porta-voz *mf*.

spokeswoman ['spəʊks,wʊmən] (*pl* **-women** [-,wɪmɪn]) *n* porta-voz *f*.

sponge [spʌndʒ] (*UK cont* **spongeing**, *US cont* **sponging**) ◇ *n* **-1.** [for cleaning, washing] esponja *f* **-2.** [cake] pão-de-ló *m*. ◇ *vt* limpar com esponja. ◇ *vi inf*: **to ~ off sb** viver às custas de alguém.

sponge bag *n UK* nécessaire *m*.

sponge cake *n* pão-de-ló *m*.

sponge pudding *n UK* *pudim de bolacha feito ao banho-maria.*

sponger ['spʌndʒəʳ] *n inf pej* parasita *mf*.

spongy ['spʌndʒɪ] (*compar* **-ier**, *superl* **-iest**) *adj* esponjoso(sa).

sponsor ['spɒnsəʳ] ◇ *n* patrocinador *m*, -ra *f*. ◇ *vt* **-1.** patrocinar **-2.** [bill, appeal, proposal] dar o respaldo a.

sponsored walk [,spɒnsəd-] *n* marcha *f* beneficente.

sponsorship ['spɒnsəʃɪp] *n (U)* patrocínio *m*.

spontaneity [,spɒntə'neɪətɪ] *n (U)* espontaneidade *f*.

spontaneous [spɒn'teɪnjəs] *adj* espontâneo(nea).

spontaneously [spɒn'teɪnjəslɪ] *adv* espontaneamente.

spoof [spu:f] *n*: **~ (of** OR **on sthg)** sátira *f* (de OR sobre algo).

spook [spu:k] *vt US* assustar.

spooky ['spu:kɪ] (*compar* **-ier**, *superl* **-iest**) *adj* **-1.** *inf* [place, house] assombrado(da) **-2.** *inf* [film] aterrorizante.

spool [spu:l] ◇ *n* **-1.** [of thread, tape, film] carretel *m* **-2.** COMPUT spool *m*. ◇ *vi* COMPUT direcionar trabalho de impressão para o spool.

spoon [spu:n] ◇ *n* **-1.** [piece of cutlery] colher *f* **-2.** [spoonful] colherada *f*. ◇ *vt*: **to ~ sthg onto/into sthg** pôr OR colocar uma colherada de algo em algo.

spoon-feed *vt* **-1.** [feed with spoon] dar de comer

com colher a **-2.** ***fig*** [give too much help to] dar mastigado *OR* de mão beijada a.

spoonful ['spu:nfʊl] (*pl* **-s** *OR* **spoonsful** ['spu:nzfʊl]) *n* colherada *f.*

sporadic [spə'rædɪk] *adj* esporádico(ca).

sport [spɔ:t] ◇ *n* **-1.** [gen] esporte *m* **-2.** ***dated*** [cheerful person] pessoa *f* amável. ◇ *vt* [wear] exibir, ostentar.

◆ **sports** ◇ *npl* ***UK*** ▷ **sports day**. ◇ *comp* esportivo(va).

sporting ['spɔ:tɪŋ] *adj* **-1.** [relating to sport] esportivo(va) **-2.** [generous, fair] nobre; **that's very ~ of you** é muita bondade sua.

sports car ['spɔ:ts-] *n* carro *m* esporte.

sports day *n* ***UK*** *dia dedicado a competições esportivas na escola.*

sports jacket ['spɔ:ts-] *n* jaqueta *f* esportiva.

sportsman ['spɔ:tsmən] (*pl* **-men** [-mən]) *n* esportista *m.*

sportsmanship ['spɔ:tsmənʃɪp] *n (U)* espírito *m* esportivo.

sports pages *npl* página *f OR* seção *f* de esportes.

sportswear ['spɔ:tsweə^r] *n (U)* roupas *fpl* esportivas.

sportswoman ['spɔ:ts,wʊmən] (*pl* **-women** [-,wɪmɪn]) *n* esportista *f.*

sporty ['spɔ:tɪ] (*compar* **-ier**, *superl* **-iest**) *adj* ***inf*** **-1.** [person] aficcionado(da) por esportes **-2.** [car, clothes] esportivo(va).

spot [spɒt] (*pt* & *pp* **-ted**, *cont* **-ting**) ◇ *n* **-1.** [mark, dot] mancha *f* **-2.** [pimple] sinal *m* **-3.** ***inf***: **a ~ of sleep** uma dormida; **a ~ of work** um pouco de trabalho; [- of milk, liquid] gole *m*; [- of rain] pingo *m*, gota *f* **-4.** [place] local *m*; **on the ~** no local; **to do sthg on the ~** fazer algo no ato **-5.** *RADIO & TV* espaço *m* **-6.** ***phr***: **to have a soft ~ for sb** ter uma leve caída por alguém; **to put sb on the ~** colocar alguém em maus lençóis. ◇ *vt* [notice] enxergar.

spot check *n* controle *m* aleatório.

spotless ['spɒtlɪs] *adj* [clean] impecável.

spotlight ['spɒtlaɪt] *n* [bright light] refletor *m*; **to be in the ~** ***fig*** ser o centro das atenções.

spot-on *adj* ***UK inf*** certeiro(ra).

spot price *n* preço *m* para entrega imediata.

spotted ['spɒtɪd] *adj* de bolinhas.

spotty ['spɒtɪ] (*compar* **-ier**, *superl* **-iest**) *adj* **-1.** ***UK*** [skin] sardento(ta) **-2.** ***US*** [patchy] de remendos, irregular.

spouse [spaʊs] *n* esposo *m*, -sa *f.*

spout [spaʊt] ◇ *n* **-1.** [of container] bico *m* **-2.** [of water - from fountain, geyser] jorro *m*; [- from whale] esguicho *m.* ◇ *vt* ***pej*** [churn out] jorrar. ◇ *vi*: **to ~ from** *OR* **out of sthg** jorrar de algo.

sprain [spreɪn] ◇ *n* torção *f*, distensão *f.* ◇ *vt* torcer, distender.

sprang [spræŋ] *pt* ▷ **spring**.

sprat [spræt] *n* espadilha *f.*

sprawl [sprɔ:l] ◇ *n (U)* expansão *f*; **urban ~** expansão *f* urbana descontrolada. ◇ *vi* **-1.** [person] estirar-se **-2.** [city, suburbs] expandir-se.

sprawling ['sprɔ:lɪŋ] *adj* [city, suburbs] de expansão descontrolada.

spray [spreɪ] ◇ *n* **-1.** *(U)* [droplets] borrifo *m* **-2.** [pressurized liquid] spray *m* **-3.** [insect] pulverizador *m* **-4.** [can, container] vaporizador *m* **-5.** [of flowers] ramo *m.* ◇ *vt* & *vi* **-1.** [treat] pulverizar **-2.** [apply] borrifar.

spray can *n* spray *m*, aerosol *m.*

spray paint *n* tinta *f* spray.

spread [spred] (*pt* & *pp* **spread**) ◇ *n* **-1.** *(U) CULIN* [paste] pasta *f* **-2.** [diffusion, growth] propagação *f* **-3.** [range] extensão *f* **-4.** *PRESS* chapado *m* **-5.** [buffet] banquete *m* **-6.** ***US*** [bedspread] colcha *f.* ◇ *vt* **-1.** [open out, unfold - map, tablecloth, rug] estender; [- arms, legs, fingers] abrir **-2.** [apply - butter, jam] untar; **to ~ sthg over sthg** untar algo com algo; [- glue] passar; **to ~ sthg over sthg** passar algo em algo **-3.** [diffuse, disseminate] espalhar **-4.** [over a period of time]: **to be ~ over ...** ter uma duração de ... **-5.** [over an area] espalhar; **the floor was ~ with straw** o chão estava coberto de palha **-6.** [distribute evenly] expandir. ◇ *vi* [gen] espalhar-se; [disease, infection] alastrar-se.

◆ **spread out** ◇ *vt sep* **-1.** [distribute]: **to be ~ out** [far apart] estar espalhado(da); [sprawling] estender-se **-2.** [open out, unfold - fingers, arms] abrir; [- map, tablecloth, rug] estender. ◇ *vi* [disperse] dispersar-se.

spread-eagled [-,i:gld] *adj* de braços e pernas abertos.

spreadsheet ['spredʃi:t] *n COMPUT* panilha *f* eletrônica.

spree [spri:] *n* farra *f.*

sprig [sprɪg] *n* broto *m*, ramo *m.*

sprightly ['spraɪtlɪ] (*compar* **-ier**, *superl* **-iest**) *adj* ativo(va).

spring [sprɪŋ] (*pt* **sprang**, *pp* **sprung**) ◇ *n* **-1.** [season] primavera *f*; **in ~** na primavera **-2.** [coil] mola *f* **-3.** [leap] pulo *m* **-4.** [water source] fonte *f.* ◇ *comp* **-1.** [rain, weather, colours] de primavera **-2.** [mattress] de mola **-3.** [water] de nascente. ◇ *vt* **-1.** [make known suddenly]: **to ~ sthg on sb** revelar subitamente algo a alguém **-2.** [develop]: **to ~ a leak** começar a fazer água. ◇ *vi* **-1.** [leap] saltar; **to ~ into action/to life** pôr-se em marcha/funcionamento **-2.** [be released] soltar-se; **to ~ shut/open** fechar/abrir rapidamente **-3.** [originate]: **to ~ from sthg** originar-se de algo.

◆ **spring up** *vi* **-1.** [get up] levantar-se **-2.** [grow in size, height] elevar-se **-3.** [appear] surgir de repente.

springboard ['sprɪŋbɔ:d] *n* ***fig*** [launch pad]: **~ for/to sthg** trampolim *m* para algo.

spring-clean ◇ *vt* fazer uma faxina geral em. ◇ *vi* fazer uma faxina geral.

spring-loaded *adj* de mola.

spring onion *n* ***UK*** cebolinha *f* verde.

spring roll *n* ***UK*** rolinho *m* primavera.

spring tide *n* maré *f* viva.

springtime ['sprɪŋtaɪm] *n (U)*: **in (the) ~** na primavera.

springy ['sprɪŋɪ] (*compar* **-ier**, *superl* **-iest**) *adj* **-1.** [carpet, mattress, ground] flexível **-2.** [rubber] elástico(ca).

sprinkle ['sprɪŋkl] *vt* **-1.** salpicar; **to ~ sthg over** *OR* **on sthg** salpicar algo sobre *OR* em algo; **to ~ sthg with sthg** regar algo com algo **-2.** [powder]

polvilhar **-3.** [liquid] borrifar.
sprinkler ['sprɪŋklə^r] *n* **-1.** [for gardens] regador *m* **-2.** [for extinguishing fires] extintor *m*.
sprinkling ['sprɪŋklɪŋ] *n* **-1.** [of water] borrifo *m* **-2.** [of sand] punhado *m* **-3.** [of people] grupo *m* pequeno **-4.** [of salt] pitada *f*.
sprint [sprɪnt] ◇ *n* SPORT [race] corrida *f* de velocidade. ◇ *vi* correr a toda (velocidade).
sprinter ['sprɪntə^r] *n* [runner] corredor *m*, -ra *f* de velocidade.
sprite *n* fada *f*.
spritzer ['sprɪtsə^r] *n* *vinho com água mineral*.
sprocket ['sprɒkɪt] *n* [wheel] roda *f* dentada.
sprout [spraʊt] ◇ *n* **-1.** CULIN: **(brussels) ~s** couve-de-bruxelas *f* **-2.** [shoot] broto *m*. ◇ *vt* **-1.** [germinate] germinar **-2.** [bud] brotar **-3.** [grow] crescer. ◇ *vi* **-1.** [germinate] germinar **-2.** [bud] brotar **-3.** [grow] crescer **-4.** [appear]: **to ~ (up)** surgir rapidamente.
spruce [spru:s] ◇ *adj* alinhado(da). ◇ *n* [tree] abeto *m*.
◆ **spruce up** *vt sep* arrumar; **to ~ o.s. up** arrumar-se.
sprung [sprʌŋ] *pp* ▷ **spring**.
spry [spraɪ] (*compar* **-ier**, *superl* **-iest**) *adj* ativo(va).
SPUC (*abbr of* **Society for the Protection of the Unborn Child**) *n organização antiaborto*.
spud [spʌd] *n inf* batata *f*.
spun [spʌn] *pt & pp* ▷ **spin**.
spunk [spʌŋk] *n (U) inf* [courage] coragem *f*.
spur [spɜ:^{r}] (*pt & pp* **-red**, *cont* **-ring**) ◇ *n* **-1.** [incentive]: **~ (to sthg)** estímulo *m* (a algo) **-2.** [on rider's boot] espora *f*. ◇ *vt* **-1.** [encourage]: **to ~ sb to do sthg** incentivar alguém a fazer algo **-2.** [horse] esporear.
◆ **on the spur of the moment** *adv* sem pensar duas vezes.
◆ **spur on** *vt sep* [encourage] estimular.
spurious ['spʊərɪəs] *adj* **-1.** [not genuine] espúrio(ria) **-2.** [based on false reasoning] falso(sa).
spurn [spɜ:n] *vt* rejeitar, desprezar.
spurt [spɜ:t] ◇ *n* **-1.** [of steam] jato *m* **-2.** [of water] jorro *m* **-3.** [of flame] labareda *f* **-4.** [of activity, energy] acesso *m* **-5.** [burst of speed] acelerada *f*; **to put on a ~** [while running, cycling] dar uma acelerada; [while working] dar um esforço. ◇ *vi* **-1.** [water]: **to ~ (out of** OR **from sthg)** jorrar (de algo); [steam] sair um jato de vapor (de algo); [flame] sair uma labareda (de algo) **-2.** [run] acelerar.
sputter ['spʌtə^r] *vi* **-1.** [engine] estalar **-2.** [stutter] gaguejar **-3.** [fire] crepitar **-4.** [oil in pan] espirrar.
spy [spaɪ] (*pl* **spies**, *pt & pp* **spied**) ◇ *n* espião *m*, -ã *f*. ◇ *vt inf* espionar. ◇ *vi* **-1.** [work as spy] espionar **-2.** [watch secretly]: **to ~ on sb** espionar alguém.
spying ['spaɪɪŋ] *n (U)* espionagem *f*.
spy satellite *n* satélite *m* espião.
Sq., sq. (*abbr of* **square**) pça.
squabble ['skwɒbl] ◇ *n* rinha *f*, discussão *f*. ◇ *vi*: **to ~ (about** OR **over sthg)** discutir (sobre algo).
squad [skwɒd] *n* **-1.** [of police] esquadrão *m* **-2.** MIL pelotão *m* **-3.** [SPORT, group of players - of club] time *m*; [- of national team] seleção *f*.
squad car *n* radiopatrulha *f*.
squadron ['skwɒdrən] *n* esquadrão *m*.
squadron leader *n UK* comandante *m* de aviação.
squalid ['skwɒlɪd] *adj* **-1.** [filthy] esquálido(da), sórdido(da) **-2.** [base, dishonest] depreciável.
squall [skwɔ:l] *n* [storm] tempestade *f*.
squalor ['skwɒlə^r] *n (U)* sordidez *f*, miséria *f*.
squander ['skwɒndə^r] *vt* desperdiçar.
square [skweə^r] ◇ *adj* **-1.** quadrado(da) **-2.** [not owing money]: **we're ~ now** estamos quites agora. ◇ *n* **-1.** [shape] quadrado *m* **-2.** [in town, city] praça *f* **-3.** *inf* [unfashionable person] quadrado *m*, -da *f* **-4.** *phr*: **to be back to ~ one** voltar ao ponto de partida. ◇ *vt* **-1.** MATH [multiply by itself] elevar ao quadrado **-2.** [balance, reconcile]: **to ~ sthg with sthg** conciliar algo com algo.
◆ **square up** *vi* **-1.** [settle up]: **to ~ up with sb** acertar-se com alguém, acertar as contas com alguém **-2.** [confront]: **to ~ up to sb/sthg** fazer frente a alguém/algo.
squared [skweəd] *adj* quadriculado(da).
square dance *n* quadrilha *f (de dança)*.
square deal *n* negócio *m* limpo.
squarely ['skweəlɪ] *adv* **-1.** [directly] exatamente **-2.** [honestly] honestamente, abertamente.
square meal *n* boa refeição *f*.
square root *n* raiz *f* quadrada.
squash [skwɒʃ] ◇ *n* **-1.** *(U)* SPORT squash *m* **-2.** *UK* [drink]: **lemon/orange ~** refresco *m* de limão/laranja **-3.** *US* [vegetable] abóbora *f*. ◇ *vt* [squeeze, flatten] esmagar.
squat [skwɒt] (*compar* **-ter**, *superl* **-test**, *pt & pp* **-ted**, *cont* **-ting**) ◇ *adj* atarracado(da). ◇ *n UK* [building] moradia *f* ilegal. ◇ *vi* **-1.** [crouch]: **to ~ (down)** agachar-se **-2.** *UK* [be a squatter] *viver num lugar ilegalmente*.
squatter ['skwɒtə^r] *n UK* [in empty building] posseiro *m*, -ra *f*.
squawk [skwɔ:k] ◇ *n* [of bird] grasnado *m*. ◇ *vi* [bird] grasnar.
squeak [skwi:k] ◇ *n* **-1.** [of animal] guincho *m* **-2.** [of door, hinge] rangido *m*. ◇ *vi* **-1.** [animal] guinchar **-2.** [floorboard, bed, hinge] ranger.
squeaky ['skwi:kɪ] (*compar* **-ier**, *superl* **-iest**) *adj* **-1.** [floorboard, bed, hinge] que range **-2.** [voice] estridente.
squeal [skwi:l] ◇ *n* **-1.** [of person, animal] grito *m* agudo **-2.** [of brakes, tyres] guincho *m*. ◇ *vi* **-1.** [person, animal] gritar **-2.** [brakes, tyres] guinchar.
squeamish ['skwi:mɪʃ] *adj* apreensivo(va).
squeeze [skwi:z] ◇ *n* **-1.** [pressure] aperto *m* **-2.** *inf* [crush of people] aperto *m*. ◇ *vt* **-1.** [press firmly] apertar **-2.** [extract, press out] espremer **-3.** [cram]: **to ~ sthg into sthg** [into place] espremer algo dentro de algo; [into time] virar-se para fazer algo em algo **-4.** *fig* [information]: **to ~ sthg out of sb** arrancar algo de alguém. ◇ *vi*: **to ~ into/through sthg** conseguir se enfiar em algo.
squeezebox *n UK* acordeão *m*.
squeezer ['skwi:zə^r] *n* espremedor *m*.
squelch [skweltʃ] *vi* chapinhar.
squib [skwɪb] *n*: **damp ~** decepção *f*.

squid [skwɪd] (*pl inv* OR **-s**) *n* lula *f*.
squiffy (*compar* **-ier**, *superl* **-iest**) *adj UK inf dated* embriagado(da).
squiggle ['skwɪgl] *n* rabisco *m*.
squint [skwɪnt] ◇ *n* MED estrabismo *m*. ◇ *vi* **-1.** MED ser estrábico(ca) **-2.** [half-close one's eyes]: **to ~ at sthg** olhar com os olhos semicerrados para algo.
squire ['skwaɪə^r] *n* [landowner] proprietário *m*, -ria *f* rural.
squirm [skwɜ:m] *vi* **-1.** [wriggle] contorcer-se **-2.** [wince]: **to ~ (with sthg)** demostrar mal-estar (com algo).
squirrel [*UK* 'skwɪrəl, *US* 'skwɜ:rəl] *n* esquilo *m*.
squirt [skwɜ:t] ◇ *vt* **-1.** [force out] esguichar **-2.** [cover with liquid]: **to ~ sb/sthg with sthg** esguichar algo em alguém/algo. ◇ *vi*: **to ~ (out of sthg)** esguichar (para fora de algo).
Sr -1. (*abbr of* **senior**) *forma utilizada após o nome de um homem para indicar que ele é pai de alguém com o mesmo nome* **-2.** (*abbr of* **sister**) irmã *f (de caridade)*.
SRC *n* **-1.** (*abbr of* **Science Research Council**) *conselho britânico de pesquisa científica* **-2.** (*abbr of* **Students' Representative Council**) *diretório acadêmico britânico*.
Sri Lanka [ˌsri:'læŋkə] *n* Sri Lanka; **in ~** em Sri Lanka.
Sri Lankan ◇ *adj* de Sri Lanka. ◇ *n* [person] *habitante de Sri Lanka*.
SS (*abbr of* **steamship**) SS.
SSA (*abbr of* **Social Security Administration**) *n organismo norte-americano de previdência social*.
SSSI (*abbr of* **Site of Special Scientific Interest**) *n área de especial interesse científico na Grã-Bretanha*.
St (*abbr of* **saint**) Sto.
ST (*abbr of* **Standard Time**) *n* hora *f* oficial.
stab [stæb] (*pt* & *pp* **-bed**, *cont* **-bing**) ◇ *n* **-1.** [with knife] punhalada *f* **-2.** *inf* [attempt]: **to have a ~ (at sthg)** ter uma experiência (em algo) **-3.** [twinge] pontada *f*. ◇ *vt* **-1.** apunhalar, esfaquear **-2.** [jab] fincar. ◇ *vi* [jab]: **to ~ at sthg** fincar em algo.
stabbing ['stæbɪŋ] ◇ *adj* lancinante. ◇ *n* punhalada *f*.
stability [stə'bɪlətɪ] *n (U)* estabilidade *f*.
stabilize, -ise ['steɪbəlaɪz] ◇ *vt* estabilizar. ◇ *vi* estabilizar-se.
stabilizer ['steɪbəlaɪzə^r] *n* [on ship, aircraft, bicycle] estabilizador *m*.
stable ['steɪbl] ◇ *adj* **-1.** [gen] estável **-2.** [solid, anchored] firme. ◇ *n* [building] estábulo *m*; [horses] cavalariça *f*.
stable lad *n* cavalariço *m*.
staccato [stə'kɑ:təʊ] ◇ *adj* staccato. ◇ *adv* em staccato.
stack [stæk] ◇ *n* **-1.** [pile] pilha *f* **-2.** *inf* [a lot, lots]: **~s** OR **a ~ of sthg** um monte de algo. ◇ *vt* **-1.** [pile up] empilhar **-2.** [fill]: **to be ~ed with sthg** estar empilhado(da) de algo.
◆ **stack up** *vi* **-1.** *inf* [add up, work out] encaixar-se **-2.** *inf* [compare]: **to ~ up against** OR **to sb/sthg** comparar-se com relação a alguém/algo.
stadium ['steɪdjəm] (*pl* **-diums** OR **-dia** [-djə]) *n* estádio *m*.
staff [stɑ:f] ◇ *n* [employees] pessoal *m*, quadro *m*. ◇ *vt*: **the shop was ~ed by women** a equipe da loja era composta de mulheres.
staffing ['stɑ:fɪŋ] *n (U)* contratação *f* de pessoal.
staff nurse *n UK* enfermeiro *m*, -ra *f* assistente.
staff room *n* sala *f* dos professores.
stag [stæg] (*pl inv* OR **-s**) *n* ZOOL veado *m*.
stage [steɪdʒ] ◇ *n* **-1.** [period, phase] etapa *f*, estágio *m* **-2.** [platform] palco *m*; **on ~** em cena; **to set the ~ for sthg** preparar o terreno para algo **-3.** [acting profession]: **the ~** o teatro. ◇ *vt* **-1.** THEATRE representar **-2.** [organize] organizar.
stagecoach ['steɪdʒkəʊtʃ] *n* diligência *f*.
stage door *n* entrada *f* de artistas.
stage fright *n (U)* medo *m* do palco.
stagehand ['steɪdʒhænd] *n* assistente *mf* de palco.
stage-manage *vt* **-1.** THEATRE dirigir **-2.** *fig* [orchestrate] orquestrar.
stage manager *n* contra-regra *mf*, diretor *m*, -ra *f* de cena.
stage name *n* nome *m* artístico.
stagflation *n* POL estagflação *f*.
stagger ['stægə^r] ◇ *vt* **-1.** [astound] abalar, chocar **-2.** [arrange at different times] escalonar. ◇ *vi* [totter] cambalear.
staggering ['stægərɪŋ] *adj* assombroso(sa).
staging ['steɪdʒɪŋ] *n* **-1.** THEATRE encenação *f* **-2.** [performing, organizing] organização *f*.
stagnant ['stægnənt] *adj* **-1.** [water, air] estancado(-da) **-2.** [business, career, economy] estagnado(da).
stagnate [stæg'neɪt] *vi* **-1.** [water, air] estancar **-2.** [business, career, economy] estagnar-se.
stagnation [stæg'neɪʃn] *n* **-1.** [of water, air] estancamento *m* **-2.** [of business, career, economy] estagnação *f*.
stag night OR **party** *n* despedida *f* de solteiro.
staid [steɪd] *adj* sério(ria), recatado(da).
stain [steɪn] ◇ *n* [mark] mancha *f*. ◇ *vt* [discolour] manchar.
stained [steɪnd] *adj* **-1.** [soiled, marked] manchado(-da) **-2.** [wood] tingido(da).
stained glass [ˌsteɪnd-] *n (U)* vitral *m*.
stained-glass window *n* janela *f* de vitral.
stainless steel [ˌsteɪnlɪs-] *n (U)* aço *m* inoxidável.
stain remover [-rɪˌmu:və^r] *n* removedor *m* de manchas.
stair [steə^r] *n* [step] degrau *m*.
◆ **stairs** *npl* [flight] escada *f*.
staircase ['steəkeɪs] *n* escadas *fpl*.
stairway ['steəweɪ] *n* escadas *fpl*, escadaria *f*.
stairwell ['steəwel] *n* vão *m* OR poço *m* das escadas.
stake [steɪk] ◇ *n* **-1.** [share]: **to have a ~ in sthg** ter interesses em algo **-2.** [wooden post] estaca *f* **-3.** [in gambling] aposta *f*. ◇ *vt* **-1.** [risk]: **to ~ sthg (on** OR **upon sthg)** arriscar algo (com algo) **-2.** [in gambling] apostar **-3.** [state]: **to ~ a claim to sthg** reivindicar algo.
◆ **stakes** *npl* **-1.** [prize] prêmio *m* **-2.** [contest] disputa *f*.
◆ **at stake** *adv*: **to be at ~** estar em jogo.

stakeout ['steɪkaʊt] *n esp* ***US*** [police surveillance] vigilância *f.*
stalactite ['stæləktaɪt] *n* estalactite *f.*
stalagmite ['stæləgmaɪt] *n* estalagmite *f.*
stale [steɪl] *adj* **-1.** [food] passado(da) **-2.** [air] viciado(da) **-3.** [bread] amanhecido(da) **-4.** [breath] velho(lha) **-5.** [athlete] esgotado(da) **-6.** [artist] sem inspiração **-7.** [idea] batido(da).
stalemate ['steɪlmeɪt] *n* **-1.** [deadlock] impasse *m* **-2.** CHESS empate *m.*
staleness ['steɪlnɪs] *n* **-1.** [person, news, idea, air] envelhecimento *m* **-2.** [of bread] dureza *f* **-3.** [of food] rancidez *f.*
stalk [stɔ:k] ◇ *n* **-1.** [of flower, plant] caule *m* **-2.** [of leaf] talo *m* **-3.** [of fruit] cabo *m.* ◇ *vt* [hunt] tocaiar. ◇ *vi* [walk] andar de forma irritada.
stall [stɔ:l] ◇ *n* **-1.** [table] estande *m*, banca *f* **-2.** [in stable] baia *f.* ◇ *vt* **-1.** AUT fazer morrer **-2.** [delay] ganhar tempo. ◇ *vi* **-1.** AUT morrer **-2.** [delay] ganhar tempo.
◆ **stalls** *npl* ***UK*** platéia *f.*
stallholder ['stɔ:l,həʊldəʳ] *n* ***UK*** dono *m*, -na *f* de banca *(no mercado).*
stallion ['stæljən] *n* garanhão *m.*
stalwart ['stɔ:lwət] ◇ *adj* [loyal] leal, fiel. ◇ *n* leal partidário *m*, -ia *f.*
stamen ['steɪmən] *n* estame *m.*
stamina ['stæmɪnəl] *n (U)* resistência *f.*
stammer ['stæməʳ] ◇ *n* gagueira *f.* ◇ *vi* gaguejar.
stamp [stæmp] ◇ *n* **-1.** [postage stamp] selo *m* **-2.** [rubber stamp] carimbo *m* **-3.** *fig* [hallmark] selo *m.* ◇ *vt* **-1.** [mark, word, sign] carimbar **-2.** [pattern] timbrar **-3.** [stomp]: **to ~ one's foot** bater com o pé no chão **-4.** [stick stamp on] selar **-5.** *fig* [with characteristic quality] estampar. ◇ *vi* **-1.** [walk] andar com passos pesados **-2.** [with one foot]: **to ~ on sthg** pisar em algo.
◆ **stamp out** *vt sep* **-1.** [fire] abafar **-2.** [opposition] sufocar **-3.** [crime, disease] erradicar.
stamp album *n* álbum *m* de selos.
stamp-collecting *n (U)* filatelia *f.*
stamp collector *n* filatelista *mf.*
stamp duty *n (U)* ***UK*** imposto *m* de selo.
stamped addressed envelope ['stæmptə,drest-] *n* ***UK*** *envelope selado e endereçado ao remetente, que o usa para enviar algo a si próprio através de outra pessoa.*
stampede [stæm'pi:d] ◇ *n* **-1.** [of animals] debandada *f* **-2.** [of people] fuga *f* em pânico. ◇ *vi* [animals] debandar.
stamp machine *n* máquina *f* de selos.
stance [stæns] *n* **-1.** [posture] atitude *f*, postura *f* **-2.** [attitude]: **~ (on sthg)** postura (sobre algo) **-3.** ***Scot*** [for bus] ponto *m.*
stand [stænd] (*pt* & *pp* **stood**) ◇ *n* **-1.** [stall] banca *f*, barraca *f* **-2.** [for umbrella, hat] cabide *m* **-3.** [for bicycle, lamp] suporte *m* **-4.** SPORT arquibancada *f* **-5.** MIL posição *f*; **to make a ~** resistir ao inimigo **-6.** [position] posição *f*; **to take a ~ on sthg** tomar uma posição em algo **-7.** ***US*** JUR depoimento *m*; **to take the ~** tomar o depoimento. ◇ *vt* **-1.** [place] colocar **-2.** [withstand] agüentar **-3.** [put up with] suportar **-4.** [treat]: **to ~ sb sthg** convidar algo para alguém **-5.** JUR: **to ~ trial** ser processado(-da). ◇ *vi* **-1.** [be on one's feet] ficar em pé **-2.** [rise to one's feet] levantar-se **-3.** [be located] estar **-4.** [be left undisturbed] repousar **-5.** [be valid] seguir de pé **-6.** [indicating current situation]: **as things ~ ...** do jeito que as coisas andam; **unemployment ~s at three million** o desemprego já atinge três milhões de pessoas **-7.** [on issue]: **where do you ~ on ...?** qual é a sua opinião sobre ...? **-8.** ***UK*** POL [be a candidate], candidatar-se (a) **-9.** [be likely]: **I ~ to win** é provável que eu ganhe **-10.** ***US*** [stop]: **'no ~ing'** proibido parar e estacionar.
◆ **stand aside** *vi* [move aside] ficar de lado.
◆ **stand back** *vi* [get out of way] afastar-se.
◆ **stand by** ◇ *vt fus* **-1.** [person] estar ao lado de **-2.** [promise, decision, offer] manter. ◇ *vi* **-1.** [in readiness]: **to ~ by (for sthg/to do sthg)** estar preparado (da) (a algo/a fazer algo) **-2.** [not intervene] ficar de lado.
◆ **stand down** *vi* [resign] retirar-se.
◆ **stand for** *vt fus* **-1.** [signify] significar, representar **-2.** [tolerate] agüentar.
◆ **stand in** *vi*: **to ~ in (for sb)** substituir (alguém).
◆ **stand out** *vi* **-1.** [be clearly visible] sobressair **-2.** [be distinctive] destacar-se.
◆ **stand up** ◇ *vt sep inf* [miss appointment with] deixar plantado(da). ◇ *vi* **-1.** [be on one's feet, upright] ficar de pé **-2.** [rise to one's feet] levantar-se **-3.** [be accepted as true] ser convincente.
◆ **stand up for** *vt fus* sair em defesa de.
◆ **stand up to** *vt fus* **-1.** [weather, heat, bad treatment] resistir a **-2.** [person, boss] peitar.
standard ['stændəd] ◇ *adj* **-1.** [gen] normal **-2.** [type, feature] comum **-3.** [size] padronizado **-4.** [text, work] -padrão; **~ practice** prática-padrão *f.* ◇ *n* **-1.** [level] nível *m* **-2.** [point of reference] padrão *m*, critério *m* **-3.** [flag] estandarte *m.*
◆ **standards** *npl* [principles] valores *mpl* morais.
standard-bearer *n* ***fig*** porta-estandarte *mf.*
standardize, -ise ['stændədaɪz] *vt* padronizar.
standard lamp *n* ***UK*** abajur *m* de pé.
standard of living (*pl* **standards of living**) *n* padrão *m* de vida.
standard time *n (U)* hora *f* oficial.
standby ['stændbaɪ] (*pl* **standbys**) ◇ *n* [substitute] reserva *f*; **to be on ~** estar a postos. ◇ *comp* stand-by.
stand-in *n* **-1.** [replacement] suplente *mf*, **-2.** [stunt person] dublê *mf.*
standing ['stændɪŋ] ◇ *adj* [permanent] permanente; **a ~ joke** uma piada manjada; **a ~ invitation** um convite em aberto. ◇ *n* **-1.** [reputation] reputação *f* **-2.** [duration] duração *f*; **friends of 20 years' ~** amigos há mais de 20 anos.
standing charge *n* taxa *f* fixa.
standing committee *n* comissão *f* permanente.
standing order *n* débito *m* automático em conta.
standing ovation *n* ovação *f* em pé.
standing room *n (U)* lugar *m* em pé.
standoffish [,stænd'ɒfɪʃ] *adj* reservado(da).
standpipe *n* tubo *m* ascendente.

standpoint ['stændpɔɪnt] *n* ponto *m* de vista.

standstill ['stændstɪl] *n*: **at a ~** [not moving] parado(da); *fig* [not active] paralisado(da); **to come to a ~** [stop moving] parar; *fig* [cease] estancar.

stand-up *adj*: **~ comedian** comediante *mf* de platéia; **~ fight** briga *f* violenta.

stank [stæŋk] *pt* ▷ **stink**.

Stanley knife® *n* estilete *m*.

stanza ['stænzə] *n* estrofe *f*.

staple ['steɪpl] ◇ *adj* [principal] básico(ca), de primeira necessidade. ◇ *n* **-1.** [for paper] grampo *m* **-2.** [principal commodity] produto *m* de primeira necessidade. ◇ *vt* grampear.

staple diet *n* dieta *f* básica.

staple gun *n* grampeador *m* industrial.

stapler ['steɪplə^r] *n* grampeador *m*.

star [stɑː^r] (*pt* & *pp* **-red**, *cont* **-ring**) ◇ *n* **-1.** [gen] estrela *f* **-2.** [asterisk] asterisco *m*. ◇ *comp* de estrela. ◇ *vt* [include as celebrity]: **the film ~s Mel Gibson** o filme é estrelado por Mel Gibson. ◇ *vi* [actor]: **to ~ (in sthg)** ser protagonista(de algo).

◆ **stars** *npl* [horoscope] horóscopo *m*.

star attraction *n* atração *f* principal.

starboard ['stɑːbəd] ◇ *adj* de estibordo. ◇ *n* *(U)* estibordo *m*; **to ~** a estibordo.

starch [stɑːtʃ] *n* **-1.** [stiffening substance] goma *f* **-2.** [in food] amido *m*.

starched [stɑːtʃt] *adj* engomado(da).

starchy ['stɑːtʃɪ] (*compar* **-ier**, *superl* **-iest**) *adj* [foods] amiláceo(cea).

stardom ['stɑːdəm] *n (U)* estrelato *m*.

stare [steə^r] ◇ *n* olhar *m* fixo. ◇ *vi*: **to ~ (at sb/sthg)** olhar fixamente (para alguém/algo).

starfish ['stɑːfɪʃ] (*pl inv* OR **-es**) *n* estrela-do-mar *f*.

stark [stɑːk] ◇ *adj* **-1.** [bare, bleak] desolado(da) **-2.** [rock] áspero(ra) **-3.** [decoration] desguarnecido(da) **-4.** [room] sem mobília **-5.** [contrast] duro(ra) **-6.** [reality] nu(a) e cru(a) **-7.** [fact] às claras. ◇ *adv*: **~ naked** em pêlo.

starlet *n pej* estrelinha *f*.

starlight ['stɑːlaɪt] *n (U)* luz *f* das estrelas.

starling ['stɑːlɪŋ] *n* estorninho *m*.

starlit ['stɑːlɪt] *adj* iluminado(da) pelas estrelas.

starry ['stɑːrɪ] (*compar* **-ier**, *superl* **-iest**) *adj* estrelado(da).

starry-eyed [-'aɪd] *adj* [naive] iludido(da).

Stars and Stripes *n*: **the ~** *a bandeira dos Estados Unidos.*

star sign *n* signo *m* (do horóscopo).

star-studded *adj*: **a ~ cast** um elenco de estrelas.

start [stɑːt] ◇ *n* **-1.** [beginning] início *m*, começo *m*; **for a ~** para começar **-2.** [jump] sobressalto *m*, susto *m* **-3.** SPORT saída *f* **-4.** [lead] vantagem *f*. ◇ *vt* **-1.** [begin] começar; **to ~ doing** OR **to do sthg** começar a fazer algo **-2.** [turn on] ligar **-3.** [set up - ger] criar, formar; [- business] montar **-4.** [initiate, instigate] iniciar. ◇ *vi* **-1.** [begin] começar; **to ~ with sb/sthg** começar com alguém/algo; **to ~ with, ...** [at first] para começar, ... **-2.** [car] pegar **-3.** [engine] pôr-se em funcionamento **-4.** [tape] ligar **-5.** [set out] sair **-6.** [jump] sobressair-se, assustar-se **-7.** *inf* [be annoying]: **don't you ~!** não começa!

◆ **start off** ◇ *vt sep* [cause to start - person] pôr-se a caminho; **this should be enough work to ~ you off** com isso já tem trabalho suficiente para começar; [- meeting] começar; [- rumour, discussion] desencadear. ◇ *vi* **-1.** [begin] começar **-2.** [set out] sair.

◆ **start on** *vt fus* [begin] começar; **she finished off the biscuits and ~ed on the cake** ela terminou com os biscoitos e partiu para o bolo.

◆ **start out** *vi* **-1.** [in life, career] começar **-2.** [set out] partir.

◆ **start up** ◇ *vt sep* **-1.** [set up - business] montar; [- shop] botar; [- women's group] criar, formar **-2.** [car, engine, machine] ligar. ◇ *vi* **-1.** [guns, music, noise] começar **-2.** [car, engine, machine] ligar **-3.** [set up business] estabelecer-se.

starter ['stɑːtə^r] *n* **-1.** *UK* [hors d'oeuvre] entrada *f*, primeiro prato *m* **-2.** AUT (motor *m* de) arranque *m* **-3.** [SPORT - official] juiz *m*, -íza *f*; [- competitor] corredor *m*, -ra *f*.

starter motor *n* (motor *m* de) arranque *m*.

starter pack *n* pacote *m* inicial.

starting block ['stɑːtɪŋ-] *n* bloco *m* de partida *(numa corrida)*.

starting point ['stɑːtɪŋ-] *n* ponto *m* de partida.

starting price *n* preço *m* de inauguração.

startle ['stɑːtl] *vt* assustar.

startling ['stɑːtlɪŋ] *adj* assustador(ra), surpreendente.

starvation [stɑː'veɪʃn] *n (U)* fome *f*, inanição *f*.

starve [stɑːv] ◇ *vt* **-1.** [deprive of food] não dar comida para **-2.** [deprive]: **to ~ sb of sthg** privar alguém de algo. ◇ *vi* **-1.** [have no food] passar fome **-2.** *inf* [be hungry]: **I'm starving to death!** estou morrendo de fome!

starving *adj* **-1.** [without food] esfomeado(da) **-2.** *inf* [hungry] faminto(ta).

star wars *n* guerra *f* nas estrelas, *programa espacial militar norte-americano.*

state [steɪt] ◇ *n* **-1.** [condition] estado *m*; **not to be in a fit ~ to do sthg** não estar em condições de fazer algo; **to be in a ~** estar com os nervos à flor da pele **-2.** [authorities]: **the ~** o Estado. ◇ *comp* de estado. ◇ *vt* [declare] afirmar, declarar; **to ~ that** afirmar que; [specify] estabelecer.

◆ **State** *n* [government]: **the State** o Estado.

◆ **States** *npl* [USA]: **the States** os Estados Unidos.

state-controlled *adj* controlado(da) pelo estado.

State Department *n US* ≃ Ministério *m* das Relações Exteriores.

state education *n UK* ensino *m* público.

stateless *adj* sem pátria.

stately ['steɪtlɪ] (*compar* **-ier**, *superl* **-iest**) *adj* [dignified] majestoso(sa).

stately home *n UK casa grande de campo aberta à visitação.*

statement ['steɪtmənt] *n* **-1.** [declaration] afirmação *f*, declaração *f* **-2.** JUR declaração *f* **-3.** [from bank] extrato *m*.

state of affairs *n* situação *f* em geral.

state of emergency *n* estado *m* de emergência.

state of mind (*pl* **states of mind**) *n* estado *m* de espírito.
state-of-the-art *adj* de vanguarda, moderno(-na).
state-owned [-'əʊnd] *adj* estatal.
state school *n* escola *f* pública.
state secret *n* segredo *m* de estado.
state's evidence *n* *US*: **to turn ~** *testemunhar a favor de um delinqüente num tribunal contra outros em troca de uma redução na pena.*
stateside ['steɪtsaɪd] ◇ *adj* dos Estados Unidos. ◇ *adv* **-1.** [travel] para os Estados Unidos **-2.** [live] nos Estados Unidos.
statesman ['steɪtsmən] (*pl* **-men** [-mən]) *n* estadista *m*, homem *m* de estado.
statesmanship ['steɪtsmənʃɪp] *n (U)* competência *f* para governar.
static ['stætɪk] ◇ *adj* [unchanging] estável. ◇ *n (U)* *ELEC* estática *f*.
static electricity *n (U)* eletricidade *f* estática.
station ['steɪʃn] ◇ *n* **-1.** [gen] estação *f*; **police ~** delegacia *f*; **fire ~** corpo *m* de bombeiros **-2.** [position] posto *m* **-3.** *fml* [rank] posição *f*. ◇ *vt* **-1.** [position] situar, colocar **-2.** *MIL* estacionar.
stationary ['steɪʃnərɪ] *adj* estacionário(ria).
stationer *n* dono *m*, -na *f* de papelaria; **~'s (shop)** papelaria *f*.
stationery ['steɪʃnərɪ] *n (U)* artigos *mpl* de escritório.
station house *n* *US* distrito *m* policial.
stationmaster ['steɪʃn,mɑ:stə^r] *n* chefe *mf* da estação.
station wagon *n* *US* perua *f (camioneta)*.
statistic [stə'tɪstɪk] *n* [number] estatística *f*.
◆ **statistics** *n (U)* [science] estatística *f*.
statistical [stə'tɪstɪkl] *adj* estatístico(ca).
statistician [,stætɪ'stɪʃn] *n* estatístico *m*, -ca *f*.
statue ['stætʃu:] *n* estátua *f*.
statuesque [,stætjʊ'esk] *adj* escultural.
statuette [,stætjʊ'et] *n* estatueta *f*.
stature ['stætʃə^r] *n (U)* **-1.** [height, size] estatura *f* **-2.** [importance] categoria *f*.
status ['steɪtəs] *n (U)* **-1.** [legal or social position] condição *f*, estado *m* **-2.** [prestige] status *m inv*.
status bar *n* *COMPUT* barra *f* de status.
status quo [-'kwəʊ] *n*: **the ~** o status quo.
status symbol *n* símbolo *m* de status.
statute ['stætju:t] *n* estatuto *m*.
statute book *n*: **the ~** o código de leis.
statutory ['stætjʊtrɪ] *adj* estatutário(ria).
staunch [stɔ:ntʃ] ◇ *adj* leal, fiel. ◇ *vt* estancar.
stave [steɪv] (*pt* & *pp* **-d** *OR* **stove**) *n* *MUS* pauta *f*.
◆ **stave off** *vt sep* afastar temporariamente.
stay [steɪ] ◇ *n* [visit] estada *f*, estadia *f*. ◇ *vi* **-1.** [remain] ficar; **to ~ put** ficar no lugar **-2.** [reside temporarily] ficar, permanecer **-3.** [continue to be] permanecer; **I don't want to ~ a teacher all my life** não quero ser professor toda a minha vida; **she ~ed awake till midnight** ficou acordada até a meia-noite **-4.** *Scot* [reside permanently] hospedar-se.
◆ **stay away** *vi*: **to ~ away from sb/somewhere** ficar longe de alguém/algum lugar.
◆ **stay in** *vi* [stay at home] ficar em casa.
◆ **stay on** *vi* ficar, permanecer.
◆ **stay out** *vi* **-1.** [not come home] ficar fora **-2.** [strikers] permanecer em greve **-3.** [not get involved]: **to ~ out of sthg** ficar fora de algo.
◆ **stay up** *vi* **-1.** [not go to bed] ficar acordado(da) **-2.** [not fall] ficar de pé.
stayer *n* *UK* **-1.** [horse] cavalo *m* resistente **-2.** [person] pessoa *f* resistente.
staying power ['steɪɪŋ-] *n (U)* resistência *f*.
St Bernard [*UK* -'bɜ:nəd, *US* -bər'nɑ:rd] *n* [dog] são-bernardo *m*.
STD *n* **-1.** (*abbr of* **subscriber trunk dialling**) *sistema de chamadas telefônicas diretas de longa distância na Grã-Bretanha* **-2.** (*abbr of* **sexually transmitted disease**) DST *f*.
stead [sted] *n*: **to stand sb in good ~** servir muito a alguém.
steadfast ['stedfɑ:st] *adj* **-1.** [supporter] fiel **-2.** [resolve] resoluto(ta) **-3.** [gaze] fixo(xa).
steadily ['stedɪlɪ] *adv* **-1.** [gradually] gradualmente **-2.** [regularly] normalmente **-3.** [calmly - look, stare] fixamente; [- say] calmamente.
steady ['stedɪ] (*compar* **-ier**, *superl* **-iest**, *pt* & *pp* **-ied**) ◇ *adj* **-1.** [gradual] gradual **-2.** [regular, constant] constante **-3.** [not shaking] firme **-4.** [calm - voice] calmo(ma); [- stare] fixo(xa) **-5.** [stable - boyfriend, girlfriend] firme; [- relationship] sério(ria); [- job] estável **-6.** [sensible] sensato(ta). ◇ *vt* **-1.** [stabilize] estabilizar; **to ~ o.s.** equilibrar-se **-2.** [calm] controlar; **to ~ o.s.** acalmar-se, controlar os nervos.
steak [steɪk] *n* **-1.** *(U)* [meat] bife *m* **-2.** [piece of meat or fish] filé *m*.
steakhouse ['steɪkhaʊs, *pl* -haʊzɪz] *n* churrascaria *f*.
steal [sti:l] (*pt* **stole**, *pp* **stolen**) ◇ *vt* roubar; **to ~ a glance at sb** lançar um olhar furtivo em alguém. ◇ *vi* **-1.** [take illegally] roubar **-2.** [move stealthily] mover-se furtivamente.
stealing ['sti:lɪŋ] *n (U)* roubo *m*.
stealth [stelθ] *n (U)*: **by ~** furtivamente, às escondidas.
stealthy ['stelθɪ] (*compar* **-ier**, *superl* **-iest**) *adj* furtivo(va).
steam [sti:m] ◇ *n (U)* vapor *m*; **to let off ~** desabafar; **to run out of ~** ficar sem forças. ◇ *comp* a vapor. ◇ *vt* *CULIN* cozinhar no vapor. ◇ *vi* **-1.** [gen] largar vapor **-2.** [train, ship] partir largando fumaça.
◆ **steam up** ◇ *vt sep* **-1.** [mist up] embaçar **-2.** *fig* [get angry]: **to get ~ed up about sthg** soltar fumaça pelas ventas por causa de algo. ◇ *vi* [window, glasses] embaçar.
steamboat ['sti:mbəʊt] *n* barco *m* a vapor.
steam engine *n* máquina *f* a vapor.
steamer ['sti:mə^r] *n* **-1.** [ship] navio *m* a vapor **-2.** *CULIN* panela *f* que cozinha no vapor.
steam iron *n* ferro *m* a vapor.
steamroller ['sti:m,rəʊlə^r] *n* rolo *m* compressor.
steam shovel *n* *US* escavadeira *f* a vapor.
steamy ['sti:mɪ] (*compar* **-ier**, *superl* **-iest**) *adj* **-1.** [full of steam] cheio (cheia) de vapor **-2.** *inf* [erotic] quente.

steel [sti:l] ◇ *n (U)* aço *m.* ◇ *comp* de aço. ◇ *vt*: **to ~ o.s. (for sthg)** encher-se de forças (para algo).

steel industry *n* indústria *f* do aço.

steel wool *n (U)* palha *f* de aço.

steelworker ['sti:l,wɜ:kəʳ] *n* operário *m* siderúrgico, operária *f* siderúrgica.

steelworks ['sti:lwɜ:ks] (*pl inv*) *n* (usina *f*) siderúrgica *f.*

steely ['sti:lɪ] (*compar* **-ier**, *superl* **-iest**) *adj* **-1.** [steel-coloured] azerado(da) **-2.** [strong, determined] inflexível, inabalável.

steep [sti:p] ◇ *adj* **-1.** [hill, road] íngreme **-2.** [increase, fall] acentuado(da) **-3.** *inf* [expensive] abusivo(va) **-4.** *inf* [unreasonable] exagerado(da). ◇ *vt* **-1.** [soak] embeber, molhar **-2.** [fruit] macerar.

steeped [sti:pt] *adj fig*: **~ in sthg** imerso(sa) em algo.

steeple ['sti:pl] *n* agulha *f (do campanário).*

steeplechase ['sti:pltʃeɪs] *n* corrida *f* de obstáculos.

steeplejack *n* consertador *m*, -ra *f* de chaminés e campanários.

steeply ['sti:plɪ] *adv* **-1.** [at steep angle] vertiginosamente **-2.** [considerably] consideravelmente.

steer ['stɪəʳ] ◇ *n* [bullock] boi *m.* ◇ *vt* conduzir, guiar. ◇ *vi* conduzir; **the car ~s well** é um carro bom de dirigir; **the bus ~ed into the hedge** o ônibus foi direto para a cerca viva; **to ~ clear (of sb/sthg)** *fig* ficar longe (de alguém/algo).

steering ['stɪərɪŋ] *n (U)* AUT direção *f.*

steering column *n* coluna *f* de direção.

steering committee *n* comitê *m* de direção.

steering lock *n* capacidade *f* de giro.

steering wheel *n* volante *m*, direção *f.*

stellar ['steləʳ] *adj* estelar.

stem [stem] (*pt* & *pp* **-med**, *cont* **-ming**) ◇ *n* **-1.** [of plant] caule *m* **-2.** [of glass] pé *m*, base *f* **-3.** [of pipe] tubo *m* **-4.** GRAMM raiz *f.* ◇ *vt* [stop - flow] conter; [- blood] estancar.

◆ **stem from** *vt fus* derivar-se de, ser o resultado de.

stench [stentʃ] *n* fedor *m.*

stencil ['stensl] (*UK pt* & *pp* **-led**, *cont* **-ling**, *US pt* & *pp* **-ed**, *cont* **-ing**) ◇ *n* [template] matriz *f.* ◇ *vt* reproduzir com matriz.

stenographer [stə'nɒgrəfəʳ] *n* estenógrafo *m*, -fa *f.*

stenography [stə'nɒgrəfɪ] *n (U)* estenografia *f.*

step [step] (*pt* & *pp* **-ped**, *cont* **-ping**) ◇ *n* **-1.** [pace] passo *m*; **in ~ with** *fig* [in touch with] em acordo com; **out of ~ with** *fig* [out of touch with] em desacordo com; **to watch one's ~** [when walking] olhar onde se pisa; *fig* [be cautious] tomar cuidado **-2.** [action] medida *f* **-3.** [stage, degree] grau *m*; **~ by ~** passo a passo **-4.** [stair, ladder] degrau *m* **-5.** *US* MUS tom *m.* ◇ *vi* **-1.** [take a single step] dar um passo; **to ~ forward** dar um passo à frente; **watch where you ~** olhe onde você pisa; **to ~ off sthg** descer de algo; **to ~ over sthg** pisar em algo **-2.** [put one's foot down]: **to ~ on sthg** pisar em algo; **~ on it!** [drive fast, hurry up] acelera!; **to ~ in sthg** meter o pé em algo.

◆ **steps** *npl* **-1.** [stairs] escadas *fpl* **-2.** *UK* [stepladder] escada *f* de mão.

◆ **step aside** *vi* **-1.** [move to one side] afastar-se, ficar de lado **-2.** [resign] renunciar.

◆ **step back** *vi* [pause to reflect] parar para pensar.

◆ **step down** *vi* [resign] renunciar.

◆ **step in** *vi* [intervene] intervir.

◆ **step up** *vt sep* [increase] aumentar.

step aerobics *n* step *m.*

stepbrother ['step,brʌðəʳ] *n* meio-irmão *m.*

stepchild ['steptʃaɪld] (*pl* **-children** [-,tʃɪldrən]) *n* enteado *m*, -da *f.*

stepdaughter ['step,dɔ:təʳ] *n* enteada *f.*

stepfather ['step,fɑ:ðəʳ] *n* padrasto *m.*

stepladder ['step,lædəʳ] *n* escada *f* de mão.

stepmother ['step,mʌðəʳ] *n* madrasta *f.*

stepping-stone ['stepɪŋ-] *n* **-1.** [in river] passadeira *f* **-2.** *fig* [way to success] trampolim *m.*

stepsister ['step,sɪstəʳ] *n* meia-irmã *f.*

stepson ['stepsʌn] *n* enteado *m.*

stereo ['sterɪəʊ] (*pl* **-s**) ◇ *adj* estéreo(rea). ◇ *n* **-1.** [stereo system] (aparelho *m* de) som *m* **-2.** *(U)* [stereo sound] estéreo *m.*

stereophonic *adj* estereofônico(ca).

stereotype ['sterɪətaɪp] ◇ *n* estereótipo *m.* ◇ *vt* estereotipar.

sterile ['steraɪl] *adj* **-1.** [germ-free] esterilizado(da) **-2.** [unable to produce offspring] estéril **-3.** *pej* [unimaginative] improdutivo(va).

sterility [ste'rɪlətɪ] *n (U)* **-1.** [gen] esterilidade *f* **-2.** *pej* [lack of imagination] improdutividade *f.*

sterilization [,sterəlaɪ'zeɪʃn] *n (U)* [gen] esterilização *f.*

sterilize, -ise ['sterəlaɪz] *vt* esterilizar.

sterilized milk ['sterəlaɪzd-] *n (U)* leite *m* esterilizado.

sterling ['stɜ:lɪŋ] ◇ *adj* **-1.** [of British money] esterlino(na) **-2.** [excellent] excelente. ◇ *n (U)* libra *f* esterlina. ◇ *comp* em libras esterlinas.

sterling silver *n (U)* prata *f* de lei.

stern [stɜ:n] ◇ *adj* severo(ra). ◇ *n* popa *f.*

sternly ['stɜ:nlɪ] *adv* [disapprovingly] em desaprovação.

steroid ['stɪərɔɪd] *n* esteróide *m.*

stethoscope ['steθəskəʊp] *n* estetoscópio *m.*

stetson ['stetsn] *n* chapéu *m* de vaqueiro.

stevedore ['sti:vədɔ:ʳ] *n US* estivador *m*, -ra *f.*

stew [stju:] ◇ *n* ensopado *m*, refogado *m.* ◇ *vt* ensopar, refogar. ◇ *vi*: **to let sb ~** *fig* deixar alguém cozinhando.

steward ['stjʊəd] *n* **-1.** *UK* [on plane] comissário *m* de bordo **-2.** *UK* [ship, train] camareiro *m* **-3.** *UK* [marshal] coordenador *m*, -ra *f (de uma corrida, um desfile etc).*

stewardess ['stjʊədɪs] *n* comissária *f* de bordo.

stewing steak *UK* ['stju:ɪŋ-], **stewbeef** *US* ['stju:bi:f] *n (U)* carne *f* para refogado.

St. Ex. (*abbr of* **stock exchange**) bolsa *f* de valores.

stg (*abbr of* **sterling**) libra *f* esterlina.

stick [stɪk] (*pt* & *pp* **stuck**) ◇ *n* **-1.** [piece of wood] graveto *m* **-2.** [of chalk] (pedaço *m* de) giz *m* **-3.** [of dynamite] (banana *f*) de dinamite **-4.** [of celery] talho *m* de aipo **-5.** [walking stick] bastão *m* **-6.** *SPORT* taco *m* **-7.** *phr:* **to get the wrong end of the ~** entender justamente o contrário. <> *vt* **-1.** [jab]: **to ~ sthg in(to) sthg** fincar *OR* espetar algo em algo; **to ~ sthg through sthg** atravessar algo com algo **-2.** [with adhesive] colar; **to ~ sthg on** *OR* **to sthg** colar algo em algo **-3.** *inf* [put] socar **-4.** *UK inf* [tolerate] agüentar; **to ~ it** conseguir agüentar. <> *vi* **-1.** [arrow, dart, spear]: **I've got a splinter stuck in my finger** há uma felpa enfiada no meu dedo **-2.** [adhere]: **to ~ (to sthg)** colar (em algo) **-3.** [become jammed] emperrar **-4.** [remain]: **to ~ in one's mind** ficar na cabeça de alguém.

◆ **sticks** *npl pej* [country]: **(out) in the ~s** lá nos cafundós, no fim do mundo.

◆ **stick around** *vi inf* ficar.

◆ **stick at** *vt fus* continuar firme em; **to ~ at it** continuar firme.

◆ **stick by** *vt fus* **-1.** [person] ficar ao lado de **-2.** [decision] manter.

◆ **stick out** <> *vt sep* **-1.** [extend] colocar para fora; **to ~ one's tongue out at sb** botar a língua (para alguém) **-2.** *inf* [endure]: **to ~ it out** agüentar. <> *vi* **-1.** [protrude] sobressair **-2.** *inf* [be noticeable] destacar-se, chamar a atenção.

◆ **stick out for** *vt fus UK* insistir até conseguir.

◆ **stick to** *vt fus* **-1.** [person, path] não abandonar **-2.** [principles, decision] ser fiel a; **if I were you, I'd ~ to French** se eu fosse tu, ficaria apenas com o francês **-3.** [promise] cumprir.

◆ **stick together** *vi* [people] manter-se unidos(-das).

◆ **stick up** <> *vt sep* **-1.** [sign, notice, postcard] fixar na parede **-2.** [with gun]: **~ 'em up!** mãos ao alto! <> *vi* sobressair; **to be ~ing up** estar espetado(da).

◆ **stick up for** *vt fus* defender.

◆ **stick with** *vt fus* **-1.** [activity, decision] manter **-2.** [person] ficar perto de.

sticker ['stɪkəʳ] *n* [piece of paper] adesivo *m*.

sticking plaster ['stɪkɪŋ-] *n* **-1.** *(U)* [bandaging material] esparadrapo *m* **-2.** [bandage] curativo *m*.

stick insect *n* bicho-pau *m*.

stick-in-the-mud *n inf* retrógrado *m*, -da *f*.

stickleback ['stɪklbæk] *n* esgana-gata *m*.

stickler ['stɪkləʳ] *n*: **~ for sthg** obsessivo(va) por algo.

stick-on *adj* adesivo(va).

stickpin *n US* alfinete *m* de gravata.

stick shift *n US* [gear lever] alavanca *f* da marcha *OR* mudança; [car] carro *m* com câmbio manual.

stick-up *n inf* assalto *m* à mão armada.

sticky ['stɪkɪ] (*compar* **-ier**, *superl* **-iest**) *adj* **-1.** [tacky] grudento(ta) **-2.** [adhesive] adesivo(va) **-3.** *inf* [awkward] chato(ta) **-4.** [humid] abafado(da).

stiff [stɪf] <> *adj* **-1.** [inflexible] duro(ra) **-2.** [difficult to move] emperrado(da) **-3.** [difficult to stir] consistente **-4.** [aching] dolorido(da); **~ neck** torcicolo *m* **-5.** [formal] formal **-6.** [severe] severo(ra) **-7.** [difficult] duro(ra) **-8.** *inf* [drink] forte **-9.** [breeze] forte. <> *adv inf* [for emphasis] muito; **to be bored ~** estar completamente entediado(da); **to be scared/frozen ~** estar morrendo de medo/de frio.

stiffen ['stɪfn] <> *vt* **-1.** [paper, fabric] endurecer **-2.** [resistance, resolve] reforçar. <> *vi* **-1.** [tense up - people] ficar tenso(sa); [- joints, muscles, back] enrijecer **-2.** [become difficult to move] emperrar **-3.** [become more severe, intense - competition] ficar mais acirrado(da); [- resistance, resolve] fortalecer-se **-4.** [breeze] ficar mais forte.

stiffener ['stɪfnəʳ] *n* [in collar] *tira fina de plástico ou cartão inserida num colar para manter os pontos compactados.*

stiffness ['stɪfnɪs] *n (U)* **-1.** [of paper, fabric] rigidez *f* **-2.** [of hinge, handle, door] emperramento *m* **-3.** [of joints, limbs, back] enrijecimento *m*, tensão *f* **-4.** [of manner, smile, welcome] formalidade *f*, frieza *f* **-5.** [of sentence, punishment] rigorosidade *f* **-6.** [of resistance, resolve] firmeza *f* **-7.** [of exam] dificuldade *f*.

stifle ['staɪfl] <> *vt* **-1.** [suffocate] sufocar **-2.** [suppress] sufocar, reprimir. <> *vi* [suffocate] sufocar.

stifling ['staɪflɪŋ] *adj* sufocante.

stigma ['stɪgmə] *n* estigma *m*.

stigmatize, -ise ['stɪgmətaɪz] *vt* estigmatizar.

stile [staɪl] *n escada para passar sobre uma cerca.*

stiletto (heel) [stɪ'letəʊ-] *n UK* salto *m* alto.

still [stɪl] <> *adv* **-1.** [in time] ainda; **do you ~ live in ...?** você ainda mora em ...? **-2.** [all the same] ainda assim **-3.** *(with comparatives)* ainda; **more interesting ~, ...** ainda mais interessante que isso, ... **-4.** [motionless] sem se mover; **sit ~!** te senta e fica quieto! <> *adj* **-1.** [not moving] parado(da) **-2.** [calm, quiet] calmo(ma), tranqüilo(la) **-3.** [not windy] sem vento **-4.** [not fizzy] sem gás. <> *n* **-1.** *PHOT* foto *f* fixa **-2.** [for making alcohol] alambique *m*.

stillborn ['stɪlbɔːn] *adj* nado-morto(ta).

still life (*pl* **-s**) *n* natureza-morta *f*.

stillness ['stɪlnɪs] *n (U)* quietude *f*.

stilted ['stɪltɪd] *adj* forçado(da).

stilts [stɪlts] *npl* **-1.** [for person] pernas *fpl* de pau **-2.** [for building] estacas *fpl*.

stimulant ['stɪmjʊlənt] *n* estimulante *m*.

stimulate ['stɪmjʊleɪt] *vt* **-1.** [gen] estimular **-2.** [physically] excitar.

stimulating ['stɪmjʊleɪtɪŋ] *adj* estimulante.

stimulation [ˌstɪmjʊ'leɪʃn] *n (U)* estímulo *m*.

stimulus ['stɪmjʊləs] (*pl* **-li** [-laɪ]) *n* estímulo *m*.

sting [stɪŋ] (*pt* & *pp* **stung**) <> *n* **-1.** [from bee] ferroada *f*; **to take the ~ out of sthg** *fig* atenuar algo **-2.** [from insect] picada *f* **-3.** [from nettle] urticária *f* **-4.** [part of bee, wasp, scorpion] ferrão *m*. <> *vt* **-1.** [subj: bee, wasp, scorpion] picar; [subj: nettle] queimar; [subj: smoke, acid] irritar **-2.** *fig* [subj: remark, criticism] ferir. <> *vi* **-1.** [bee, wasp, scorpion] picar; [nettle] queimar; [smoke, acid] irritar **-2.** [eyes, skin] arder.

stinging nettle ['stɪŋɪŋ-] *n UK* urtiga *f*.

stingy ['stɪndʒɪ] (*compar* **-ier**, *superl* **-iest**) *adj* **-1.** *inf* [person] sovina **-2.** *inf* [amount] escasso(sa).

stink [stɪŋk] (*pt* **stank** *OR* **stunk**, *pp* **stunk**) <> *n* fedor *m*. <> *vi* **-1.** [smell] feder **-2.** *inf fig* [be worthless] ser uma porcaria, não valer nada.

stink-bomb *n* bomba *f* de cheiro.

stinking ['stɪŋkɪŋ] *inf* <> *adj* **-1.** [smelly] fedorento(ta) **-2.** *fig* [for emphasis] maldito(ta). <> *adv* extremamente; **he's ~ rich** está podre de rico.

stint [stɪnt] <> *n* [period of time] período *m.* <> *vi*: **to ~ on sthg** pechinchar algo.
stipend ['staɪpend] *n* estipêndio *m.*
stipulate ['stɪpjʊleɪt] *vt* estipular.
stipulation [ˌstɪpjʊ'leɪʃn] *n* **-1.** *(U)* [stating of conditions] estipulação *f* **-2.** [condition] condição *f.*
stir [stɜːʳ] (*pt* & *pp* **-red**, *cont* **-ring**) <> *n* **-1.** [act of mixing] mexida *f* **-2.** [public excitement] agitação *f,* alvoroço *m.* <> *vt* **-1.** [mix] mexer, misturar **-2.** [move physically] mexer; **to ~ o.s.** mexer-se *(para fazer algo)* **-3.** [rouse, excite] instigar. <> *vi* **-1.** [move gently] mover-se, mexer-se **-2.** [awaken] despertar.
◆ **stir up** *vt sep* **-1.** [dust, mud] levantar **-2.** [trouble, dissent, feelings, memories] provocar.
stir-fry *vt* refogar.
stirring ['stɜːrɪŋ] <> *adj* instigante. <> *n* [feeling] indício *m.*
stirrup ['stɪrəp] *n* estribo *m.*
stitch [stɪtʃ] <> *n* **-1.** GEN ponto *m* **-2.** [pain]: **to have a ~** sentir pontadas de dor **-3.** *phr*: **to be in ~es** chorar de tanto rir. <> *vt* costurar.
stitching ['stɪtʃɪŋ] *n (U)* costura *f.*
stoat [stəʊt] *n* arminho *m.*
stock [stɒk] <> *n* **-1.** [gen] estoque *m*; **in ~** em estoque; **out of ~** esgotado(da) **-2.** [FIN - of company] capital *m*; [- of government] títulos *mpl* do governo; **~s and shares** títulos *mpl* mobiliários, ações *fpl* **-3.** *(U)* [ancestry] estirpe *f,* linhagem *f* **-4.** CULIN caldo *m* **-5.** *(U)* [livestock] rebanho *m* **-6.** [of gun] coronha *f* **-7.** *phr*: **to take ~ (of sthg)** refletir (sobre algo). <> *adj* [typical] típico(ca). <> *vt* **-1.** COMM ter em estoque **-2.** [fill] encher (de); **to be ~ed with** estar cheio (cheia) de.
◆ **stock up** *vi*: **to ~ up (on** OR **with sthg)** fazer estoque (de algo).
stockade [stɒ'keɪd] *n* paliçada *f.*
stockbroker ['stɒkˌbrəʊkəʳ] *n* corretor *m*, -ra *f* da bolsa.
stockbroking ['stɒkˌbrəʊkɪŋ] *n (U)* corretagem *f* na bolsa.
stockcar *n* stockcar *m.*
stock company *n* **US** sociedade *f* anônima de capital acionário.
stock control *n* controle *m* de estoque.
stock cube *n* **UK** caldo *m* em cubo.
stock exchange *n* bolsa *f* de valores.
stockholder ['stɒkˌhəʊldəʳ] *n* **US** acionista *mf.*
Stockholm ['stɒkhəʊm] *n* Estocolmo; **in ~** em Estocolmo.
stocking ['stɒkɪŋ] *n* meia *f.*
stock-in-trade *n* **-1.** *(U)* [usual behaviour] mote *m* **-2.** *(U)* [work] ferramenta *f* de trabalho.
stockist ['stɒkɪst] *n* **UK** varejista *mf.*
stock market *n* mercado *m* de ações.
stock phrase *n* frase *f* feita.
stockpile ['stɒkpaɪl] <> *n* estoque *m.* <> *vt* estocar, armazenar.
stockroom ['stɒkrʊm] *n* depósito *m.*
stock-still *adv* imóvel.
stocktaking ['stɒkˌteɪkɪŋ] *n (U)* inventário *m.*
stocky ['stɒkɪ] (*compar* **-ier**, *superl* **-iest**) *adj* reforçado(da), corpulento(ta).
stodgy ['stɒdʒɪ] (*compar* **-ier**, *superl* **-iest**) *adj* **-1.** [indigestible] pesado(da) **-2.** *pej* [uninteresting] enfadonho(-nha).
stoic ['stəʊɪk] <> *adj* estóico(ca). <> *n* estóico *m*, -ca *f.*
stoical ['stəʊɪkl] *adj* estóico(ca).
stoicism ['stəʊɪsɪzm] *n* estoicismo *m.*
stoke [stəʊk] *vt* [keep burning] alimentar.
stole [stəʊl] <> *pt* ▻ **steal**. <> *n* [shawl] estola *f.*
stolen ['stəʊln] *pp* ▻ **steal**.
stolid ['stɒlɪd] *adj* impassível.
stomach ['stʌmək] <> *n* **-1.** [organ] estômago *m*; **on a full/an empty stomach** com o estômago cheio/vazio **-2.** [abdomen] ventre *m.* <> *vt* [tolerate] tolerar.
stomach ache *n* dor *f* de estômago.
stomach pump *n* bomba *f* para lavagem estomacal.
stomach ulcer *n* úlcera *f* de estômago.
stomach upset [-'ʌpset] *n* indigestão *f.*
stomp [stɒmp] *vi* pisar forte.
stone [stəʊn] (*pl sense 5 only inv* OR **-s**) <> *n* **-1.** [gen] pedra *f*; **a ~'s throw from** bem perto de **-2.** [jewel] pedra *f* preciosa **-3.** [in fruit] caroço *m* **-4.** [unit of measurement] *equivalent to 6,35kg.* <> *comp* de pedra. <> *vt* apedrejar.
Stone Age *n*: **the ~** a Idade da Pedra.
stone-cold *adj* gelado(da) como pedra.
stoned [stəʊnd] *adj vinf* **-1.** [drunk] mamado(da) **-2.** [drugged] chapado(da).
stonemason ['stəʊnˌmeɪsn] *n* canteiro *m*, -ra *f.*
stonewall [ˌstəʊn'wɔːl] *vi* [avoid questions] andar com evasivas.
stoneware *n (U)* faiança *f.*
stonewashed ['stəʊnwɒʃt] *adj* estonado(da).
stonework ['stəʊnwɜːk] *n (U)* cantaria *f.*
stony ['stəʊnɪ] (*compar* **-ier**, *superl* **-iest**) *adj* **-1.** [covered with stones] pedregoso(sa) **-2.** [unfriendly] impassível, frio (fria).
stood [stʊd] *pt* & *pp* ▻ **stand**.
stooge [stuːdʒ] *n* **-1.** *inf* [manipulated person] fantoche *m* **-2.** [in comedy act] comparsa *mf.*
stool [stuːl] *n* [seat] mocho *m*, banquinho *m.*
stoop [stuːp] <> *n* **-1.** [bent back]: **to walk with a ~** caminhar encurvado(da) **-2.** **US** [of house] varanda *f.* <> *vi* **-1.** [bend forwards and down] abaixar-se **-2.** [hunch shoulders] encurvar-se **-3.** *fig* [debase o.s.]: **to ~ to sthg** rebaixar-se a algo.
stop [stɒp] (*pt* & *pp* **-ped**, *cont* **-ping**) <> *n* **-1.** [gen] parada *f* **-2.** [standstill]: **to come to a ~** dar uma parada **-3.** [end]: **to put a ~ to sthg** dar um basta em algo **-4.** [in punctuation] ponto *m* **-5.** *phr*: **to pull out all the ~s** *fig* remover todos os empecilhos **-6.** TECH trava *f,* ferrolho *m.* <> *vt* **-1.** [gen] parar; **to ~ doing sthg** parar de fazer algo **-2.** [prevent] impedir; **to ~ sb/sthg from doing sthg** impedir alguém/algo de fazer algo **-3.** [interrupt - wages] suspender; [- cheque] sustar; [- match] interromper; [- newspaper] parar **-4.** [hole, gap] tapar. <> *vi* **-1.** [gen] parar; **to ~ at nothing (to do sthg)** não parar por nada (para conseguir algo) **-2.** [stay] ficar.
◆ **stop off** *vi* dar uma parada.

◆ **stop over** *vi* passar a noite.
◆ **stop up** ◇ *vt sep* [block] entupir. ◇ *vi UK* ficar acordado(da).
stopcock ['stɒpkɒk] *n* torneira *f* de passagem.
stopgap ['stɒpgæp] *n* quebra-galho *m*.
stopover ['stɒp,əʊvəʳ] *n* parada *f*.
stoppage ['stɒpɪdʒ] *n* **-1.** [strike] paralização *f* **-2.** *UK* [deduction] dedução *f*.
stopper ['stɒpəʳ] *n* rolha *f*.
stopping *adj UK*: **~ train** *trem com parada em todas as estações.*
stop press *n* notícias *fpl* de última hora.
stop sign *n AUT* sinal *m* de parada.
stopwatch ['stɒpwɒtʃ] *n* cronômetro *m*.
storage ['stɔ:rɪdʒ] *n (U)* armazenamento *m*.
storage heater *n UK aquecedor que acumula calor à noite, quando a eletricidade é mais barata, e libera calor durante o dia.*
store [stɔ:ʳ] ◇ *n* **-1.** *esp US* [shop] loja *f* **-2.** [supply] reserva *f*, provisão *f* **-3.** [storage place] depósito *m* **-4.** *phr*: **to set great ~ by** *OR* **on sthg** dar muita importância a algo. ◇ *vt* **-1.** [gen] armazenar **-2.** [details, address, ideas] guardar.
◆ **in store** *adv* [imminent]: **who knows what the future has in ~ for us?** quem sabe o que o futuro nos reserva?
◆ **store up** *vt sep* **-1.** [objects] armazenar **-2.** [facts, information] guardar.
store card *n* cartão *m* de crédito *(de lojas)*.
store detective *n* segurança *mf* de loja.
storehouse ['stɔ:haʊs, *pl* -haʊzɪz] *n* **-1.** *esp US* [warehouse] depósito *m* **-2.** *fig* [treasury] mina *f*.
storekeeper ['stɔ:,ki:pəʳ] *n US* lojista *mf*.
storeroom ['stɔ:rʊm] *n* **-1.** [gen] almoxarifado *m* **-2.** [for food] despensa *f*.
storey *UK* (*pl* **storeys**), **story** *US* (*pl* **-ies**) ['stɔ:rɪ] *n* andar *m*.
stork [stɔ:k] *n* cegonha *f*.
storm [stɔ:m] ◇ *n* **-1.** [bad weather] temporal *m*, tempestade *f*; **a ~ in a teacup** uma tempestade num copo d'água **-2.** [violent reaction] torrente *f*. ◇ *vt* **-1.** *MIL* tomar de assalto **-2.** [say angrily] esbravejar. ◇ *vi* [go angrily]: **to ~ into/out of** entrar/sair intempestivamente.
storm cloud *n* [bringing rain] nuvem *f* de chuva.
storming *n* **-1.** [assault] assalto *m*, investida *f* **-2.** [capture] tomada *f*.
stormy ['stɔ:mɪ] (*compar* **-ier**, *superl* **-iest**) *adj* **-1.** [weather, sea] tempestuoso(sa) **-2.** *fig* [relationship, meeting] turbulento(ta).
story ['stɔ:rɪ] (*pl* **-ies**) *n* **-1.** [tale] história *f*, conto *m*; **it's the (same) old ~** é a velha história de sempre; **to cut a long ~ short, ...** para encurtar a história ... **-2.** *HIST* & *euphemism* história *f* **-3.** [article - newspaper] artigo *m*; [- TV, radio] reportagem *f* **-4.** *US* = **storey**.
storybook ['stɔ:rɪbʊk] *adj* de novela.
storyteller ['stɔ:rɪ,teləʳ] *n* **-1.** [teller of story] contador *m*, -ra *f* de histórias **-2.** *euphemism* [liar] mentiroso *m*, -sa *f*.
stout [staʊt] ◇ *adj* **-1.** [corpulent] corpulento(ta) **-2.** [strong] forte, resistente **-3.** [brave] firme, forte. ◇ *n (U)* cerveja *f* escura, stout *f*.
stoutness ['staʊtnɪs] *n (U)* [corpulence] corpulência *f*.
stove [stəʊv] ◇ *pt & pp* ▷ **stave**. ◇ *n* **-1.** [for cooking] forno *m* **-2.** [for heating] estufa *f*.
stow [stəʊ] *vt*: **to ~ sthg (away)** guardar algo.
◆ **stow away** *vi* [on ship, plane] embarcar como clandestino(na).
stowaway ['stəʊəweɪ] *n* clandestino *m*, -na *f*.
straddle ['strædl] *vt* **-1.** [subj: person] escarranchar -se em **-2.** [subj: bridge, town] atravessar, cruzar.
strafe *vt MIL* metralhar.
straggle ['strægl] *vi* **-1.** [buildings, hair, plant] espalhar -se **-2.** [person, group] ficar para trás.
straggler ['strægləʳ] *n* retardatário *m*, -ria *f*.
straggly ['stræglɪ] (*compar* **-ier**, *superl* **-iest**) *adj* emaranhado(da).
straight [streɪt] ◇ *adj* **-1.** [gen] reto(ta) **-2.** [not curly] liso(sa) **-3.** [honest, frank] direto(ta), franco(ca) **-4.** [tidy] arrumado(da) **-5.** [simple] fácil, simples **-6.** [undiluted] puro(ra) **-7.** *inf* [conventional] convencional **-8.** *gay sl* [heterosexual] heterossexual **-9.** [quits] quite **-10.** *phr*: **to get something ~** deixar uma coisa clara. ◇ *adv* **-1.** [in a straight line]: **~ ahead** bem na frente; **I couldn't see ~** não podia ver direito **-2.** [upright] reto(ta); **why won't that painting hang ~** por que aquele quadro não fica reto? **-3.** [directly, immediately] imediatamente; **I'll go ~ to bed** vou direto para a cama **-4.** [honestly, frankly] com toda a franqueza **-5.** [undiluted]: **I drink my whisky ~** tomo meu uísque puro **-6.** *phr*: **to go ~** corrigir-se. ◇ *n SPORT*: **the ~** a reta final.
◆ **straight off** *adv* no ato.
◆ **straight out** *adv* sem rodeios.
straightaway *adv* em seguida.
straighten ['streɪtn] ◇ *vt* **-1.** [tidy] arrumar, organizar **-2.** [make straight] endireitar **-3.** [make level] pôr reto(ta), endireitar. ◇ *vi* [stand or sit up]: **to ~ (up)** endireitar-se.
◆ **straighten out** *vt sep* [sort out - mess] arrumar; [- problem] resolver.
straight face *n*: **to keep a ~** ficar sério(ria).
straightforward [,streɪt'fɔ:wəd] *adj* **-1.** [easy] simples **-2.** [honest, frank - answer] direto(ta); [- person] aberto(ta), franco(ca).
strain [streɪn] ◇ *n* **-1.** [mental] tensão *f* **-2.** *MED* [of muscle, back] distenção *f* **-3.** [*TECH* - weight] peso *m*; [- pressure] pressão *f*; [- force] força *f* **-4.** [type, variety] variedade *f*. ◇ *vt* **-1.** [work hard] forçar **-2.** *MED* [injure] distender **-3.** [overtax - resources, budget] esticar; [- enthusiasm] acabar; [- patience] esgotar **-4.** [drain - vegetables] escorrer; [- tea] coar **-5.** *TECH* [rope, girder, ceiling] estirar. ◇ *vi* [try very hard]: **to ~ to do sthg** esforçar-se para fazer algo.
◆ **strains** *npl literary* [of music] acordes *mpl*.
strained [streɪnd] *adj* **-1.** [forced] forçado(da) **-2.** [tense] tenso(sa) **-3.** *MED* [sprained] distendido(da) **-4.** [culin - liquid] coado(da); [- vegetables] escorrido (da).
strainer ['streɪnəʳ] *n* coador *m*.
strait [streɪt] *n GEOGR* estreito *m*.
◆ **straits** *npl*: **in dire** *OR* **desperate ~s** em sérios apuros.
straitened ['streɪtnd] *adj fml*: **~ circumstances** dificuldades financeiras.

straitjacket ['streɪt,dʒækɪt] *n* [garment] camisa *f* de força.
straitlaced [,streɪt'leɪst] *adj pej* puritano(na).
Strait of Gibraltar *n*: **the** ~ o Estreito de Gibraltar.
Strait of Hormuz *n*: **the** ~ o Estreito de Hormuz.
strand [strænd] *n* **-1.** [of hair, cotton, wool] mecha *f*; **a** ~ **of hair** um fio de cabelo **-2.** [of story, argument, plot] linha *f*.
stranded ['strændɪd] *adj* **-1.** [person] preso(sa) **-2.** [car] atolado(da) **-3.** [boat] encalhado(da).
strange [streɪndʒ] *adj* **-1.** [unusual, unexpected] estranho(nha) **-2.** [unfamiliar] desconhecido(da), estranho(nha).
strangely ['streɪndʒlɪ] *adv* **-1.** [in an odd manner] de forma estranha **-2.** [unexpectedly, mysteriously] inesperadamente **-3.** [surprisingly]: ~ **(enough)** por mais estranho que pareça.
stranger ['streɪndʒəʳ] *n* **-1.** [unknown person] estranho *m*, -nha *f*; **to be a/no** ~ **to sthg** estar/não estar familiarizado com algo **-2.** [person from elsewhere] forasteiro *m*, -ra *f*.
strangle ['stræŋgl] *vt* **-1.** [kill - person] estrangular; [- chicken] torcer o pescoço de **-2.** *fig* [stifle] sufocar.
stranglehold ['stræŋglhəʊld] *n* **-1.** [round neck] gravata *f* **-2.** *fig* [strong influence]: ~ **(on sb/sthg)** controle *m* total (sobre alguém/algo).
strangulation [,stræŋgjʊ'leɪʃn] *n (U)* [act of killing] estrangulamento *m*.
strap [stræp] (*pt* & *pp* **-ped**, *cont* **-ping**) <> *n* **-1.** [for carrying] correia *f*, tira *f* **-2.** [for fastening] alça *f* **-3.** [of watch] pulseira *f*. <> *vt* [fasten] prender *(com correia)*.
strapless ['stræplɪs] *adj* [garment] sem alça.
strapping ['stræpɪŋ] *adj* robusto(ta).
Strasbourg ['stræzbɜːg] *n* Estrasburgo; **in** ~ em Estrasburgo.
strata ['strɑːtə] *pl* ▻ **stratum**.
stratagem ['strætədʒəm] *n* estratagema *m*.
strategic [strə'tiːdʒɪk] *adj* estratégico(ca).
strategist ['strætɪdʒɪst] *n* MIL estrategista *mf*.
strategy ['strætɪdʒɪ] (*pl* **-ies**) *n* estratégia *f*.
stratified ['strætɪfaɪd] *adj* estratificado(da).
stratosphere ['strætə,sfɪəʳ] *n*: **the** ~ a estratosfera.
stratum ['strɑːtəm] (*pl* **-ta**) *n* **-1.** GEOL estrato *m* **-2.** *fig* [of society] estrato *m* social.
straw [strɔː] <> *n* **-1.** *(U)* [dried corn] palha *f* **-2.** [for drinking] canudinho *m* **-3.** *phr*: **to clutch at** ~**s** agarrar-se a qualquer coisa em desespero; **the last** ~ a gota d'água. <> *comp* de palha.
strawberry ['strɔːbərɪ] (*pl* **-ies**) <> *n* [fruit] morango *m*. <> *comp* de morango.
straw poll *n* sondagem *f* de opinião.
stray [streɪ] <> *adj* perdido(da). <> *n* [animal] animal *m* perdido. <> *vi* **-1.** [from group] perder-se **-2.** [from path] desviar-se **-3.** [thoughts, mind]: **to** ~ **from the point** desviar-se do tema.
streak [striːk] <> *n* **-1.** [of grease] faixa *f* **-2.** [of lightning] raio *m* **-3.** [in hair] listra *f* **-4.** [in character] traço *m* **-5.** [period]: **a winning/losing** ~ período *m* em que só se ganha/perde. <> *vi* [move quickly] passar como um raio.
streaked [striːkt] *adj* [marked]: ~ **with sthg** manchado(da) de algo.
streaky ['striːkɪ] (*compar* **-ier**, *superl* **-iest**) *adj* [colour, surface] riscado(da), listrado(da).
streaky bacon *n UK* bacon *m*.
stream [striːm] <> *n* **-1.** [brook] riacho *m* **-2.** [of liquid] curso *m* **-3.** [of air] corrente *f* **-4.** [of light] raio *m*, faixa *f* **-5.** [of liquid, air, light] rio *m* **-6.** [of people, traffic] torrente *f* **-7.** [of abuse, queries, complaints, books] série *f* **-8.** *UK* SCH grupo *m*. <> *vt UK* SCH *agrupar de acordo com o rendimento escolar.* <> *vi* **-1.** [gen] jorrar **-2.** [air] fluir **-3.** [people]: **to** ~ **in/out** entrar/sair em massa **-4.** [traffic] mover-se rapidamente.
streamer ['striːməʳ] *n* [for party] serpentina *f*, flâmula *f*.
streamline ['striːmlaɪn] *vt* **-1.** [make aerodynamic] dar forma aerodinâmica a **-2.** [make efficient] racionalizar.
streamlined ['striːmlaɪnd] *adj* **-1.** [aerodynamic] aerodinâmico(ca) **-2.** [efficient] racional.
street [striːt] *n* rua *f*; **to be right up sb's** ~ *UK inf* ser exatamente o que se precisa; **to be** ~**s ahead of sb/sthg** *UK* estar muito além de alguém/algo.
streetcar ['striːtkɑːʳ] *n US* bonde *m*.
street-cred(ibility) *n (U) inf* imagem *f*, aceitação *f (entre as pessoas jovens)*.
street lamp, street light *n* lâmpada *f* de rua.
street lighting *n (U)* iluminação *f* pública.
street map *n* mapa *m (da cidade)*.
street market *n* feira *f* ao ar livre.
street plan *n* mapa *m* viário.
street value *n* preço *m* de venda (de uma droga).
streetwise ['striːtwaɪz] *adj* esperto(ta); **she's very** ~ ela se vira muito bem na rua.
strength [streŋθ] *n* **-1.** *(U)* [gen] força *f* **-2.** *(U)* [power, influence] poder *m*; **on the** ~ **of** com base em; **to go from** ~ **to** ~ ir de vento em popa **-3.** [quality, ability] ponto *m* forte **-4.** *(U)* [solidity] solidez *f* **-5.** [intensity - gen] intensidade *f*; [- of alcohol] teor *m* alcoólico; [- of drug] potência *f* **-6.** FIN [of currency] solidez *f* **-7.** *(U)* [number] número *m*; **to be at full** ~ estar com força total; **to be below** ~ não estar com força total; **in** ~ em grande número.
strengthen ['streŋθn] <> *vt* **-1.** [gen] fortalecer **-2.** [reinforce] reforçar **-3.** [intensify] intensificar **-4.** [make braver, more confident] encorajar. <> *vi* **-1.** [physically - body, muscle] fortalecer-se; [- voice] tornar-se mais forte **-2.** [intensify] intensificar-se **-3.** FIN [currency] fortalecer-se.
strenuous ['strenjʊəs] *adj* extenuante.
stress [stres] <> *n* **-1.** [emphasis]: ~ **(on sthg)** ênfase *f* (em algo) **-2.** [tension, anxiety] estresse *m*; **to be under** ~ estar estressado(da) **-3.** TECH [physical pressure]: ~ **(on sthg)** pressão *f* (sobre algo) **-4.** LING [on word, syllable] acento *m* tônico. <> *vt* **-1.** [emphasize] enfatizar, realçar **-2.** LING [word, syllable] acentuar *(na pronúncia)*.
stressed [strest] *adj* estressado(da).
stressful ['stresfʊl] *adj* estressante.
stretch [stretʃ] <> *n* **-1.** [area] extensão *f* **-2.** [period

of time] período *m* **-3.** [effort]: **by no ~ of the imagination** por mais que se queira. <> *vt* **-1.** [gen] esticar **-2.** [pull taut] estirar **-3.** [rules, meaning, truth] distorcer **-4.** [challenge] fazer render ao máximo. <> *vi* **-1.** [gen] esticar-se **-2.** [area]: **to ~ over** estender-se por; **to ~ from ... to** estender-se de ... até **-3.** [person] espreguiçar-se. <> *adj* elástico(ca).

◆ **at a stretch** *adv* sem parar.

◆ **stretch out** <> *vt sep* estender, esticar. <> *vi* esticar-se *(deitando)*.

stretcher ['stretʃəʳ] *n* maca *f*.

stretcher party *n* (equipe *f* de) padioleiros *mpl*.

stretchmarks ['stretʃmɑ:ks] *npl* estrias *fpl*.

stretchy ['stretʃɪ] (*compar* **-ier**, *superl* **-iest**) *adj* elástico(ca).

strew [stru:] (*pt* **-ed**, *pp* **strewn** [stru:n], **-ed**) *vt*: **to be strewn on** *OR* **over sthg** estar esparramado(da) em/sobre algo; **to be strewn with sthg** estar coberto(ta) de algo.

stricken ['strɪkn] *adj*: **to be ~ by** *OR* **with sthg** [grief] estar abalado(da) por algo; [doubt, horror, panic] ser tomado(da) por algo; [illness, complaint] estar atacado(da) por algo.

strict [strɪkt] *adj* **-1.** [severe] rígido(da) **-2.** [inflexible] rigoroso(sa) **-3.** [exact, precise] exato(ta), preciso(-sa).

strictly ['strɪktlɪ] *adv* **-1.** [severely] rigidamente **-2.** [rigidly, absolutely] estritamente **-3.** [precisely, exactly] exatamente, precisamente; **~ speaking** a rigor **-4.** [exclusively] exclusivamente.

strictness ['strɪktnɪs] *n (U)* **-1.** [severity] rigidez *f* **-2.** [rigidity] rigor *m*.

stride [straɪd] (*pt* **strode**, *pp* **stridden** ['strɪdn]) <> *n* passada *f*; **to take sthg in one's ~** *fig* encarar algo com tranqüilidade. <> *vi* caminhar a passos largos.

◆ **strides** *npl*: **to make (great) ~s** fazer (grandes) progressos.

strident ['straɪdnt] *adj* **-1.** [voice, sound] estridente **-2.** [demand] rigoroso(sa).

strife [straɪf] *n (U) fml* conflitos *mpl*.

strike [straɪk] (*pt* & *pp* **struck**) <> *n* **-1.** [gen] greve *f*; **to be (out) on ~** estar em greve; **to go on ~** entrar em greve **-2.** *MIL* [attack] ataque *m* **-3.** [find] descoberta *f*. <> *comp* de greve. <> *vt* **-1.** [hit - deliberately] bater, golpear; [- accidentally] atingir, pegar em **-2.** [subj: hurricane, disaster, lightning] atingir **-3.** [subj: thought] ocorrer; **to ~ sb as sthg** parecer algo a alguém **-4.** [impress]: **to be struck by** *OR* **with sthg** ficar impressionado(da) com algo **-5.** [reach, arrive at] fechar **-6.** [ignite] acender **-7.** [find] descobrir; **to ~ a balance (between)** encontrar um ponto de equilíbrio (entre); **to ~ a serious/happy note** passar uma idéia séria/alegre **-8.** [chime] bater **-9.** *phr*: **to be struck blind/dumb** ficar cego/mudo, ficar cega/muda; **to ~ fear** *OR* **terror into sb** infundir medo/terror em alguém; **to ~ (it) lucky** ter sorte; **to ~ it rich** ficar rico(ca). <> *vi* **-1.** [stop working] entrar em greve **-2.** [hit accidentally]: **to ~ against sthg** bater em algo **-3.** [happen suddenly - hurricane, disaster] ocorrer; [- lightning] cair **-4.** [attack] atacar **-5.** [chime]: **the clock struck seven** o relógio bateu sete horas.

◆ **strike back** *vi* revidar.

◆ **strike down** *vt sep* derrubar.

◆ **strike off** *vt sep*: **to be struck off** perder a licença profissional.

◆ **strike out** <> *vt sep* rasurar. <> *vi* **-1.** [head out] partir, pôr-se a caminho **-2.** [do sthg different] partir para outra.

◆ **strike up** <> *vt fus* **-1.** [friendship, conversation] travar **-2.** [music] começar a tocar. <> *vi* começar a tocar.

strikebound ['straɪkbaʊnd] *adj* paralisado(da) pela greve.

strikebreaker ['straɪk,breɪkəʳ] *n* fura-greve *mf*.

strike pay *n (U)* fundo *m* de greve.

striker ['straɪkəʳ] *n* **-1.** [person on strike] grevista *mf* **-2.** *FTBL* atacante *mf*.

striking ['straɪkɪŋ] *adj* **-1.** [noticeable, unusual] impressionante, chocante **-2.** [attractive] que chama a atenção.

striking distance *n (U)*: **within ~ (of sthg)** muito perto (de algo).

string [strɪŋ] (*pt* & *pp* **strung**) <> *n* **-1.** *(U)* [thin rope] cordão *m*, barbante *m* **-2.** [piece of thin rope] cordel *m*; **(with) no ~s attached** sem restrições; **to pull ~s** mexer os pauzinhos **-3.** [row, chain - of beads, pearls] colar *m*; [- of onions] réstia *f* **-4.** [series] série *f*, sucessão *f* **-5.** [for bow, tennis racket] corda *f*; **to be highly strung** *fig* ter o pavio curto **-6.** *COMPUT* string *m*. <> *comp* [vest, bag] de cordão.

◆ **strings** *npl MUS*: **the ~s** as cordas.

◆ **string along** *vt sep inf* dar falsas esperanças a.

◆ **string out** *vt sep*: **to be strung out** estar disperso(sa).

◆ **string together** *vt sep fig* juntar.

◆ **string up** *vt sep inf* enforcar.

string bean *n* vagem *f*.

stringed instrument ['strɪŋd-] *n* instrumento *m* de corda.

stringent ['strɪndʒənt] *adj* rigoroso(sa).

string quartet *n* quarteto *m* de cordas.

stringy (*compar* **-ier**, *superl* **-iest**) *adj* fibroso(sa).

strip [strɪp] (*pt* & *pp* **-ped**, *cont* **-ping**) <> *n* **-1.** [of fabric, paper, carpet] tira *f*; **to tear a ~ off sb, to tear sb off a ~** *UK* dar uma bronca em alguém **-2.** [of land, water, forest] faixa *f* **-3.** *UK SPORT* camiseta *f (de time)*. <> *vt* **-1.** [undress] despir; **~ped to the waist** nu (nua) até o peito **-2.** [remove layer of] descascar **-3.** [take away from]: **to ~ sb of sthg** despojar alguém de algo. <> *vi* **-1.** [undress] despir-se **-2.** [do a striptease] fazer um striptease.

◆ **strip off** <> *vt sep* tirar. <> *vi* despir-se.

strip cartoon *n UK* tira *f* em quadrinhos.

stripe [straɪp] *n* **-1.** [band of colour] lista *f*, faixa *f* **-2.** [sign of rank] galão *m*.

striped [straɪpt] *adj* listado(da).

strip lighting *n (U)* iluminação *f* fluorescente.

stripper ['strɪpəʳ] *n* **-1.** [performer of striptease] stripper *mf* **-2.** [tool, liquid] removedor *m*.

strip-search <> *n* revista *f* policial *(fazendo tirar a roupa)*. <> *vt* revistar *(fazendo tirar a roupa)*.

strip show *n* show *m* de striptease.

striptease ['strɪpti:z] *n* striptease *m*.

stripy ['straɪpɪ] (*compar* **-ier**, *superl* **-iest**) *adj* listado(-da).

strive [straɪv] (*pt* **strove**, *pp* **striven** ['strɪvn]) *vi fml*: **to ~ for sthg/to do sthg** lutar por algo/para fazer algo.

strobe (light) ['strəʊb-] *n* luz *f* estroboscópica.

strode [strəʊd] *pt* ⊳ **stride**.

stroke [strəʊk] <> *n* **-1.** MED derrame *m* cerebral **-2.** [of brush] pincelada *f* **-3.** [of pen] traço *m* **-4.** [in swimming - movement] braçada *f*; [- style] nado *m* **-5.** [movement in rowing] remada *f* **-6.** [in tennis] raquetada *f* **-7.** [in golf] tacada *f* **-8.** [of clock] batida *f* **-9.** [of bell] dobre *m* **-10.** *UK* TYPO [slash] barra *f* **-11.** [piece]: **a ~ of genius** um lance de gênio; **a ~ of luck** um golpe de sorte; **not to do a ~ of work** não levantar um dedo; **at a ~** de um golpe só. <> *vt* acariciar.

stroll [strəʊl] <> *n* passeio *m*. <> *vi* passear.

stroller ['strəʊlə^r] *n* *US* [for baby] carrinho *m* de bebê.

strong [strɒŋ] <> *adj* **-1.** [gen] forte; **I've never been ~ in mathematics** matemática nunca foi o meu forte; **~ point** ponto forte; **~ nerves** nervos *mpl* de aço **-2.** [solid, sturdy] reforçado(da) **-3.** [in number] de ... pessoas; **the crowd was 2000 ~** a multidão tinha 2000 pessoas. <> *adv*: **to be still going ~** [person, group] ser forte ainda; [machine] funcionar bem ainda.

strongarm ['strɒŋɑ:m] *adj*: **to use ~ tactics** ter pulso firme.

strongbox ['strɒŋbɒks] *n* caixa-forte *f*.

stronghold ['strɒŋhəʊld] *n fig* baluarte *m*.

strong language *n (U) euphemism* linguagem *f* pesada.

strongly ['strɒŋlɪ] *adv* **-1.** [sturdily, solidly - built] solidamente; [- protected] fortemente **-2.** [in degree or intensity] intensamente; **the kitchen smells ~ of onions** tem um cheiro forte de cebola na cozinha **-3.** [very definitely] totalmente; **to feel ~ about sthg** ter uma opinião firme sobre algo.

strong man *n* homem *m* forte.

strong-minded [-'maɪndɪd] *adj* de caráter.

strong room *n* casa-forte *f*.

strong-willed [-'wɪld] *adj* obstinado(da).

stroppy ['strɒpɪ] (*compar* **-ier**, *superl* **-iest**) *adj UK inf* emburrado(da).

strove [strəʊv] *pt* ⊳ **strive**.

struck [strʌk] *pt & pp* ⊳ **strike**.

structural ['strʌktʃərəl] *adj* estrutural.

structurally ['strʌktʃərəlɪ] *adv* estruturalmente.

structure ['stʌktʃə^r] <> *n* **-1.** [organization, arrangement] estrutura *f* **-2.** [building, construction] construção *f*. <> *vt* estruturar.

struggle ['strʌgl] <> *n* **-1.** [gen]: **~ (for sthg/to do sthg)** luta *f* (por algo/por fazer algo) **-2.** [fight] briga *f*. <> *vi* **-1.** [try hard, strive] esforçar-se; **to ~ free** lutar para ser solto(ta); **to ~ (for sthg/to do sthg)** lutar (por algo/por fazer algo) **-2.** [fight]: **to ~ (with sb)** brigar (com alguém) **-3.** [move with difficulty] mover-se com dificuldade; **he ~d to his feet** ele conseguiu se levantar a duras penas.

◆ **struggle on** *vi*: **to ~ on (with sthg)** continuar (algo)a duras penas.

struggling ['strʌglɪŋ] *adj* esforçado(da).

strum [strʌm] (*pt & pp* **-med**, *cont* **-ming**) <> *vt* dedilhar. <> *vi*: **to ~ (on sthg)** dedilhar (algo).

strung [strʌŋ] *pt & pp* ⊳ **string**.

strut [strʌt] (*pt & pp* **-ted**, *cont* **-ting**) <> *n* **-1.** CONSTR escora *f* **-2.** AERON montante *m*. <> *vi* andar empertigado(da).

strychnine ['strɪkni:n] *n (U)* estricnina *f*.

stub [stʌb] (*pt & pp* **-bed**, *cont* **-bing**) <> *n* **-1.** [of cigarette, pencil] toco *m* **-2.** [of ticket, cheque] canhoto *m*. <> *vt*: **to ~ one's toe (on)** dar uma topada com o dedo do pé (em).

◆ **stub out** *vt sep* apagar.

stubble ['stʌbl] *n (U)* **-1.** [in field] restolho *m* **-2.** [on chin] barba *f* curta.

stubborn ['stʌbən] *adj* **-1.** [person] teimoso(sa), cabeçudo(da) **-2.** [stain] persistente, difícil.

stubbornly ['stʌbənlɪ] *adv* **-1.** [wait] teimosamente **-2.** [refuse] resistentemente **-3.** [declare] resolutamente.

stubby ['stʌbɪ] (*compar* **-ier**, *superl* **-iest**) *adj* atarracado(da).

stucco ['stʌkəʊ] *n (U)* estuque *m*.

stuck [stʌk] <> *pt & pp* ⊳ **stick**. <> *adj* **-1.** [gen] preso(sa) **-2.** [window] emperrado(da) **-3.** [stumped]: **can you help with this problem? I'm ~** pode me ajudar com esse problema? (eu) empaquei.

stuck-up *adj inf pej* convencido(da), metido(da).

stud [stʌd] *n* **-1.** [metal decoration] tachão *m* **-2.** [earring] pingente *m* **-3.** *UK* [on boot, shoe] taco *m* **-4.** *(U)* [of horses] plantel *m*; **to be put out to ~** ser usado(da) para reprodução.

studded ['stʌdɪd] *adj*: **~ (with sthg)** adornado(da) (com algo); **a ~ jacket** uma jaqueta adornada; **~ with precious stones** cravejado(da) de pedras preciosas.

student ['stju:dnt] <> *n* **-1.** [at college, university] estudante *mf* **-2.** [scholar] estudioso *m*, -sa *f*. <> *comp* **-1.** [nurse, teacher] em estágio **-2.** [politics] estudantil **-3.** [lifestyle] de estudante **-4.** [disco] para estudantes.

student loan *n UK* crédito *m* educativo.

students' union *n* grêmio *m* estudantil.

stud farm *n* haras *m inv*.

studied ['stʌdɪd] *adj* **-1.** [answer] pensado(da) **-2.** [smile] estudado(da).

studio ['stju:dɪəʊ] (*pl* **-s**) *n* estúdio *m*.

studio apartment *n US* = **studio flat**.

studio audience *n* público *m* no auditório.

studio flat *UK*, **studio apartment** *US* *n* (apartamento *m*) JK *m*.

studious ['stju:djəs] *adj* estudioso(sa).

studiously ['stju:djəslɪ] *adv* cuidadosamente.

study ['stʌdɪ] (*pl* **-ies**, *pt & pp* **-ied**) <> *n* **-1.** *(U)* [gen] estudo *m* **-2.** [room] sala *f* de estudos. <> *vt* **-1.** [learn] estudar **-2.** [examine] examinar, estudar. <> *vi* estudar.

◆ **studies** *npl* estudos *mpl*.

stuff [stʌf] <> *n (U) inf* **-1.** [matter, things] coisa *f*; **to know one's ~** entender do riscado; **and all that ~** e tudo isso **-2.** [substance]: **what's that ~ in your pocket?** o que é isso aí no seu bolso? **-3.** [belongings] coisas *fpl*. <> *vt* **-1.** [push, put] enfiar **-2.** [fill, cram]: **to ~ sthg (with sthg)** encher algo (com algo) **-3.** [with food]: **to ~ o.s. (with** OR **on sthg)** *inf*

empanturrar-se (de algo) **-4.** *CULIN* rechear.
stuffed [stʌft] *adj* **-1.** [filled, crammed]: ~ **with sthg** atulhado(da) de algo **-2.** *inf* [with food] empanturrado(da) **-3.** *CULIN* recheado(da) **-4.** [animal] empalhado(da) **-5.** *phr*: **get ~!** *UK v inf* vai te catar!
stuffing ['stʌfɪŋ] *n (U)* **-1.** [filling - for furniture] estofamento *m*; [- for toys] enchimento *m* **-2.** *CULIN* recheio *m*.
stuffy ['stʌfɪ] (*compar* **-ier**, *superl* **-iest**) *adj* **-1.** [room] abafado(da) **-2.** [formal, old-fashioned] retrógrado(-da).
stumble ['stʌmbl] *vi* **-1.** [trip] tropeçar **-2.** [hesitate, make mistake] equivocar-se.
◆ **stumble across, stumble on** *vt fus* **-1.** [person] topar com **-2.** [objects] encontrar por acaso.
stumbling block ['stʌmblɪŋ-] *n* pedra *f* no caminho, obstáculo *m*.
stump [stʌmp] ◇ *n* **-1.** [of tree] toco *m* **-2.** [of limb] coto *m*. ◇ *vt* deixar perplexo(xa). ◇ *vi* caminhar com passo firme; **he ~ed up the steps** ele subiu a escada com passo firme.
◆ **stumps** *npl CRICKET* varetas *fpl* verticais.
◆ **stump up** *vt fus inf UK* desembolsar.
stun [stʌn] (*pt* & *pp* **-ned**, *cont* **-ning**) *vt* **-1.** [knock unconscious] deixar sem sentidos **-2.** [shock, surprise] atordoar.
stung [stʌŋ] *pt* & *pp* ▷ **sting**.
stun grenade *n* granada *f* de efeito moral.
stunk [stʌŋk] *pt* & *pp* ▷ **stink**.
stunned *adj* **-1.** [unconscious] inconsciente **-2.** [shocked, surprised] atordoado(da).
stunning ['stʌnɪŋ] *adj* **-1.** [very beautiful] imponente **-2.** [very shocking, surprising] espantoso(sa).
stunt [stʌnt] ◇ *n* **-1.** [for publicity] golpe *m* publicitário **-2.** *CINEMA* cena *f* arriscada, cena *f* perigosa. ◇ *vt* inibir.
stunted ['stʌntɪd] *adj* mirrado(da).
stunt man *n* dublê *m*.
stunt woman *n* dublê *f*.
stupefy ['stju:pɪfaɪ] (*pt* & *pp* **-ied**) *vt* **-1.** [tire, bore] entorpecer **-2.** [surprise] deixar estupefato(ta).
stupendous [stju:'pendəs] *adj inf* **-1.** [wonderful] estupendo(da) **-2.** [very large] enorme.
stupid ['stju:pɪd] *adj* **-1.** [foolish] estúpido(da) **-2.** *inf* [wretched, damned] idiota.
stupidity [stju:'pɪdətɪ] *n (U)* estupidez *f*.
stupidly ['stju:pɪdlɪ] *adv* estupidamente.
stupor ['stju:pə^r] *n* estupor *m*.
sturdy ['stɜ:dɪ] (*compar* **-ier**, *superl* **-iest**) *adj* **-1.** [person] forte, robusto(ta) **-2.** [furniture, platform] sólido(-da), firme.
sturgeon ['stɜ:dʒən] (*pl inv*) *n* esturjão *m*.
stutter ['stʌtə^r] ◇ *n* gagueira *f*. ◇ *vi* gaguejar.
sty [staɪ] (*pl* **sties**) *n* chiqueiro *m*.
stye [staɪ] *n* terçol *m*.
style [staɪl] ◇ *n* **-1.** [manner] estilo *m*; **in the ~ of** ao estilo de **-2.** *(U)* [smartness, elegance] classe *f* **-3.** [fashion, design] modelo *m*. ◇ *vt* pentear de acordo com a moda.
styling mousse *n (U)* mousse *f* modeladora.
stylish ['staɪlɪʃ] *adj* de estilo.
stylist ['staɪlɪst] *n* estilista *mf*.
stylized, -ised ['staɪlaɪzd] *adj* estilizado(da).
stylus ['staɪləs] (*pl* **-es**) *n* **-1.** [on record player] agulha *f* **-2.** *COMPUT* caneta *f* gráfica.
stymie ['staɪmɪ] *vt inf*: **to be ~d** estar entravado(-da).
suave [swɑ:v] *adj* afável.
sub [sʌb] *n inf* **-1.** *SPORT* (*abbr of* **substitute**) reserva *mf* **-2.** (*abbr of* **submarine**) submarino *m* **-3.** *UK* (*abbr of* **subscription**) assinatura *f* **-4.** *UK* (*abbr of* **advance payment**) adiantamento *m* **-5.** *US* [sandwich] *tipo de sanduíche*.
sub- [sʌb] *prefix* sub(-).
subcommittee ['sʌbkə,mɪtɪ] *n* subcomissão *f*.
subconscious [,sʌb'kɒnʃəs] ◇ *adj* subconsciente. ◇ *n*: **the ~** o subconsciente.
subconsciously [,sʌb'kɒnʃəslɪ] *adj* de forma subconsciente.
subcontinent [,sʌb'kɒntɪnənt] *n* subcontinente *m*.
subcontract [,sʌbkən'trækt] *vt* subcontratar.
subculture ['sʌb,kʌltʃə^r] *n* subcultura *f*.
subdivide [,sʌbdɪ'vaɪd] *vt* subdividir.
subdue [səb'dju:] *vt* **-1.** [enemy, rioters, crowds] subjugar **-2.** [feelings, passions] conter, dominar.
subdued [səb'dju:d] *adj* **-1.** [person] desanimado(-da) **-2.** [feelings] reprimido(da) **-3.** [light, sound, colour] fraco(ca).
subeditor [,sʌb'edɪtə^r] *n* copidesque *mf*.
subgroup ['sʌbgru:p] *n* subgrupo *m*.
subheading ['sʌb,hedɪŋ] *n* subtítulo *m*.
subhuman [,sʌb'hju:mən] *adj pej* subumano(na).
subject [*adj, n & prep* 'sʌbdʒekt, *vt* səb'dʒekt] ◇ *adj*: **~ (to sthg)** sujeito(ta) (a algo). ◇ *n* **-1.** [topic, person under consideration] assunto *m*, tema *m* **-2.** *GRAMM* sujeito *m* **-3.** *SCH & UNIV* cadeira *f* **-4.** [citizen] súdito *m*, -ta *f*. ◇ *vt* **-1.** [bring under strict control] sujeitar, dominar **-2.** [force to experience]: **to ~ sb to sthg** sujeitar alguém a algo.
◆ **subject to** *prep* sujeito(ta) a; **~ to the budget** dependendo do orçamento.
subjection [səb'dʒekʃn] *n* sujeição *f*, subordinação *f*.
subjective [səb'dʒektɪv] *adj* subjetivo(va).
subjectively [səb'dʒektɪvlɪ] *adv* subjetivamente.
subject matter ['sʌbdʒekt-] *n (U)* temática *f*, tema *m*.
sub judice *adj JUR* sub judice.
subjugate ['sʌbdʒʊgeɪt] *vt fml* **-1.** [gen] subjugar **-2.** [feelings, desires] dominar.
subjunctive [səb'dʒʌŋktɪv] *n GRAMM*: **~ (mood)** (modo *m*) subjuntivo *m*.
sublet [,sʌb'let] (*pt* & *pp* **sublet**, *cont* **-ting**) *vt* sublocar.
sublime [sə'blaɪm] *adj* sublime; **from the ~ to the ridiculous** do sublime ao ridículo.
sublimely [sə'blaɪmlɪ] *adv* totalmente, completamente.
subliminal [,sʌb'lɪmɪnl] *adj* subliminar.
submachine gun [,sʌbmə'ʃi:n-] *n* metralhadora *f*.
submarine [,sʌbmə'ri:n] *n* submarino *m*.
submerge [səb'mɜ:dʒ] ◇ *vt* **-1.** [flood] inundar **-2.** [plunge into liquid] submergir **-3.** *fig* [in activity]: **to ~ o.s. in sthg** mergulhar em algo. ◇ *vi* mergulhar.

submission [səb'mɪʃn] *n (U)* **-1.** [obedience, capitulation] submissão *f* **-2.** [presentation] apresentação *f*.
submissive [səb'mɪsɪv] *adj* submisso(sa).
submit [səb'mɪt] (*pt* & *pp* **-ted**, *cont* **-ting**) <> *vt* submeter. <> *vi*: **to ~ (to sb)** render-se (a alguém); **to ~ (to sthg)** submeter-se (a algo).
subnormal [ˌsʌb'nɔ:ml] *adj* subnormal.
subordinate [*adj* & *n* sə'bɔ:dɪnət, *vt* sə'bɔ:dɪneɪt] <> *adj fml*: **~ (to sthg)** subordinado(da) (a algo). <> *n* subordinado *m*, -da *f*. <> *vt fml* subordinar.
subordinate clause [sə'bɔ:dɪnət-] *n* oração *f* subordinada.
subordination [səˌbɔ:dɪ'neɪʃn] *n (U)*: **~ (of/to sthg)** subordinação *f* (de/a algo).
subpoena [sə'pi:nə] (*pt* & *pp* **-ed**) *JUR* <> *n* intimação *f (para comparecimento em juízo)*. <> *vt* intimar *(para comparecimento em juízo)*.
sub-post office *n* **UK** *pequena agência de correios local que oferece menos serviços que uma agência central.*
subroutine ['sʌbru:ˌti:n] *n COMPUT* sub-rotina *f*.
subscribe [səb'skraɪb] <> *vi* **-1.** [to magazine, newspaper]: **to ~ (to sthg)** fazer assinatura (de algo) **-2.** [to view, belief]: **to ~ to sthg** concordar com algo. <> *vt* contribuir com, doar.
subscriber [səb'skraɪbə^r] *n* **-1.** [to magazine, newspaper] assinante *mf* **-2.** [to service] usuário *m*, -ria *f* **-3.** [to charity, campaign] doador *m*, -ra *f*.
subscription [səb'skrɪpʃn] *n* **-1.** [to newspaper, magazine] assinatura *f* **-2.** [to club, organization - monthly] mensalidade *f*; [- yearly] anuidade *f*.
subsection ['sʌbˌsekʃn] *n* subseção *f*.
subsequent ['sʌbsɪkwənt] *adj* subseqüente.
subsequently ['sʌbsɪkwəntlɪ] *adv* subseqüentemente, por conseguinte.
subservient [səb'sɜ:vjənt] *adj* **-1.** [servile]: **~ (to sb)** subserviente (a alguém) **-2.** [less important]: **~ (to sthg)** subordinado(da) (a algo).
subset *n MATH* subconjunto *m*.
subside [səb'saɪd] *vi* **-1.** [storm, anger] acalmar; [pain, grief] passar **-2.** [floods] baixar; [swelling] diminuir **-3.** *CONSTR* ceder.
subsidence [səb'saɪdns, 'sʌbsɪdns] *n (U) CONSTR*: **the problems were caused by ~** os problemas foram causados pelo fato de o terreno ter cedido.
subsidiarity [səbsɪdɪ'ærɪtɪ] *n política de permitir que as próprias pessoas numa organização tomem decisões sobre questões que as afetam, em vez de deixá-las para o grupo todo.*
subsidiary [səb'sɪdjərɪ] (*pl* **-ies**) <> *adj* subsidiário(ria). <> *n*: **~ (company)** (empresa *f*) subsidiária *f*.
subsidize, -ise ['sʌbsɪdaɪz] *vt* subsidiar.
subsidy ['sʌbsɪdɪ] (*pl* **-ies**) *n* subsídio *m*.
subsist [səb'sɪst] *vi*: **to ~ (on sthg)** sobreviver (à base de algo).
subsistence [səb'sɪstəns] *n (U)* subsistência *f*.
subsistence allowance *n* **UK** diária *f*.
subsistence farming *n (U)* agricultura *f* de subsistência.
subsistence level *n* nível *m* mínimo de subsistência.
substance ['sʌbstəns] *n* **-1.** [gen] substância *f* **-2.** [essence, gist] essência *f* **-3.** *(U)* [importance] importância *f*.
substandard [ˌsʌb'stændəd] *adj* inferior.
substantial [səb'stænʃl] *adj* **-1.** [large, considerable] substancial **-2.** [solid, well-built] sólido(da).
substantially [səb'stænʃəlɪ] *adv* **-1.** [quite a lot] substancialmente, consideravelmente **-2.** [mainly] basicamente.
substantiate [səb'stænʃɪeɪt] *vt fml* fundamentar.
substantive *adj fml* pertinente, substancioso(-sa).
substitute ['sʌbstɪtju:t] <> *n* **-1.** [replacement]: **~ (for sb/sthg)** substituto *m*, -ta *f* (de alguém/algo); **to be no ~ (for sthg)** não estar à altura (de algo) **-2.** *SPORT* reserva *mf*, suplente *mf*. <> *vt*: **to ~ sb for sb** substituir alguém por alguém; **to ~ sthg for sthg** substituir algo por algo. <> *vi*: **to ~ for sb/sthg** substituir alguém/algo.
substitute teacher *n* **US** professor *m*, -ra *f* suplente.
substitution [ˌsʌbstɪ'tju:ʃn] *n* substituição *f*.
subterfuge ['sʌbtəfju:dʒ] *n* subterfúgio *m*.
subterranean [ˌsʌbtə'reɪnjən] *adj* subterrâneo(-nea).
subtitle ['sʌbˌtaɪtl] *n* subtítulo *m*.
◆ **subtitles** *npl CINEMA* legenda *f*.
subtle ['sʌtl] *adj* sutil.
subtlety ['sʌtltɪ] *n* **-1.** [gen] sutileza *f* **-2.** [delicacy, understatement] delicadeza *f*.
subtly ['sʌtlɪ] *adv* sutilmente.
subtotal ['sʌbtəʊtl] *n* subtotal *m*.
subtract [səb'trækt] *vt*: **to ~ sthg (from sthg)** subtrair algo (de algo).
subtraction [səb'trækʃn] *n* subtração *f*.
subtropical [ˌsʌb'trɒpɪkl] *adj* subtropical.
suburb ['sʌbɜ:b] *n* periferia *f*.
◆ **suburbs** *npl*: **the ~s** a periferia.
suburban [sə'bɜ:bn] *adj* **-1.** [of suburbs] da periferia **-2.** *pej* [boring] suburbano(na).
suburbia [sə'bɜ:bɪə] *n (U)* bairros *mpl* residenciais.
subversion [səb'vɜ:ʃn] *n (U)* subversão *f*.
subversive [səb'vɜ:sɪv] <> *adj* subversivo(va). <> *n* subversivo *m*, -va *f*.
subvert [səb'vɜ:t] *vt* subverter.
subway ['sʌbweɪ] *n* **-1.** **UK** [underground walkway] passagem *f* subterrânea **-2.** **US** [underground railway] metrô *m*.
sub-zero *adj* abaixo de zero.
succeed [sək'si:d] <> *vt* **-1.** [person] suceder a **-2.** [event, emotion]: **to be ~ed by sthg** ser sucedido(-da) por algo. <> *vi* **-1.** [achieve desired result]: **to ~ in sthg/in doing sthg** conseguir algo/fazer algo **-2.** [work well, come off] dar bons resultados, sair-se bem **-3.** [go far in life] triunfar.
succeeding [sək'si:dɪŋ] *adj* seguinte.
success [sək'ses] *n* sucesso *m*.
successful [sək'sesfʊl] *adj* **-1.** [attempt] bem-sucedido(da) **-2.** [film, book *etc*] de sucesso **-3.** [person] bem-sucedido(da), de sucesso.
successfully [sək'sesfʊlɪ] *adv* com sucesso.
succession [sək'seʃn] *n* **-1.** [series] sucessão *f*; **to**

follow in (quick OR close) ~ ocorrer numa (rápida) seqüência -2. *(U)* *fml* [to high position] sucessão *f*.
successive [sək'sesɪv] *adj* sucessivo(va).
successor [sək'sesə^r] *n* sucessor *m*, -ra *f*.
success story *n* história *f* de sucesso.
succinct [sək'sɪŋkt] *adj* sucinto(ta).
succinctly [sək'sɪŋktlɪ] *adv* sucintamente.
succulent ['sʌkjʊlənt] *adj* suculento(ta).
succumb [sə'kʌm] *vi*: **to ~ (to sthg)** sucumbir (a algo).
such [sʌtʃ] <> *adj* **-1.** [referring back] tal, semelhante; **I never heard ~ nonsense!** nunca ouvi tal absurdo! **-2.** [referring forward] assim; **have you got ~ a thing as a tin opener?** você teria algo como um abridor de latas?; **~ words as 'duty' and 'honour'** palavras como dever e honra **-3.** [whatever]: **I've spent ~ as I had** gastei o pouco dinheiro que eu tinha **-4.** [so great, so extreme]: **~ ... that** tal ... que; **the state of the economy is ~ that ...** tal é o estado da economia que ... <> *adv* tão; **~ nice people** essas pessoas tão gentis; **~ a lot of books** tantos livros; **~ a long time** tanto tempo. <> *pron* [referring back]: **and ~ (like)** e coisas do gênero; **this is my car, ~ as it is** este é o meu carro, embora não seja grande coisa; **help yourself to wine, ~ as there is** sirva-se de vinho, ainda que não tenha muito.
◆ **as such** *adv* propriamente dito(ta).
◆ **such and such** *adj*: **at ~ and ~ a time** de tal em tal hora.
suchlike ['sʌtʃlaɪk] <> *adj* deste tipo, do estilo. <> *pron* **-1.** [things] coisas do estilo **-2.** [people] gente desse tipo.
suck [sʌk] *vt* **-1.** [by mouth] chupar **-2.** [draw in] aspirar, sugar **-3.** *fig* [involve]: **to be ~ed into sthg** estar absorvido(da) em algo.
◆ **suck up** *vi* *inf*: **to ~ up (to sb)** puxar o saco (de alguém).
sucker ['sʌkə^r] *n* **-1.** [suction pad] ventosa *f* **-2.** *inf* [gullible person] trouxa *mf*.
suckle ['sʌkl] <> *vt* amamentar. <> *vi* amamentar.
sucrose ['su:krəʊz] *n (U)* sacarose *f*.
suction ['sʌkʃn] *n (U)* **-1.** [drawing in] sucção *f* **-2.** [adhesion] adesão *f*.
suction pump *n* bomba *f* de sucção.
Sudan [su:'dɑ:n] *n* Sudão *m*; **in (the) ~** no Sudão.
Sudanese [ˌsu:də'ni:z] <> *adj* sudanês(esa). <> *n* sudanês *m*, -esa *f*. <> *npl*: **the ~** os sudaneses.
sudden ['sʌdn] *adj* **-1.** [quick] repentino(na); **all of a ~** de repente **-2.** [unforeseen] inesperado(da).
sudden death *n* FTBL morte *f* súbita.
suddenly ['sʌdnlɪ] *adv* de repente.
suddenness ['sʌdnnɪs] *n (U)* rapidez *f* repentina OR inesperada.
suds [sʌdz] *npl* espuma *f* de sabão.
sue [su:] *vt*: **to ~ sb (for sthg)** processar alguém (por algo).
suede [sweɪd] <> *n (U)* camurça *f*. <> *comp* de camurça.
suet ['sʊɪt] *n (U)* sebo *m*.
Suez ['sʊɪz] *n* Suez.
Suez Canal *n*: **the ~** o Canal de Suez.
suffer ['sʌfə^r] <> *vt* sofrer. <> *vi* **-1.** [feel physical pain] sofrer de; **to ~ from sthg** MED sofrer de algo **-2.** [experience difficulties or loss] sair prejudicado(-da).
sufferance ['sʌfrəns] *n (U)*: **on ~** por condescendência OR tolerância.
sufferer ['sʌfrə^r] *n* paciente *mf*.
suffering ['sʌfrɪŋ] *n* sofrimento *m*.
suffice [sə'faɪs] *vi* *fml* ser suficiente, bastar.
sufficient [sə'fɪʃnt] *adj* suficiente.
sufficiently [sə'fɪʃntlɪ] *adv* suficientemente.
suffix ['sʌfɪks] *n* sufixo *m*.
suffocate ['sʌfəkeɪt] <> *vt* sufocar, asfixiar. <> *vi* sufocar-se, asfixiar-se.
suffocation [ˌsʌfə'keɪʃn] *n (U)* asfixia *f*.
suffrage ['sʌfrɪdʒ] *n (U)* sufrágio *m*.
suffuse [sə'fju:z] *vt*: **~d with sthg** banhado(da) de algo.
sugar ['ʃʊgə^r] <> *n (U)* açúcar *m*. <> *vt* adoçar.
sugar beet *n (U)* beterraba *f (açucareira)*.
sugar bowl *n* açucareiro *m*.
sugarcane ['ʃʊgəkeɪn] *n (U)* cana-de-açúcar *f*.
sugar-coated [-'kəʊtɪd] *adj* cristalizado(da).
sugared ['ʃʊgəd] *adj* adoçado(da).
sugar lump *n* torrão *m* de açúcar.
sugar refinery *n* refinaria *f* de açúcar.
sugary ['ʃʊgərɪ] *adj* **-1.** [high in sugar] açucarado(da), muito doce **-2.** *fig* & *pej* [sentimental] meloso(sa).
suggest [sə'dʒest] *vt* **-1.** [propose] sugerir, propor; **to ~ that sb do sthg** sugerir que alguém faça algo **-2.** [imply] insinuar.
suggestion [sə'dʒestʃn] *n* **-1.** [gen] sugestão *f* **-2.** *(U)* [implication] insinuação *f*.
suggestive [sə'dʒestɪv] *adj* **-1.** [implying sexual connotation] insinuante, provocante **-2.** [implying a certain conclusion]: **~ (of sthg)** indicativo(va) (de algo) **-3.** [reminiscent]: **~ of sthg** evocativo(va) de algo.
suicidal [sʊɪ'saɪdl] *adj* suicida.
suicide ['su:ɪsaɪd] *n (U)* suicídio *m*; **to commit ~** cometer suicídio, suicidar-se.
suicide attempt *n* tentativa *f* de suicídio.
suit [su:t] *n* **-1.** [of matching clothes - for man] terno *m*; [- for woman] conjunto *m* **-2.** SPORT [outfit] traje *m* **-3.** [in cards] naipe *m*; **to follow ~** seguir no mesmo naipe; *fig* seguir o exemplo **-4.** JUR processo *m*. <> *vt* **-1.** [look attractive on] cair bem **-2.** [be convenient or agreeable to] convir; **~ yourself!** como quiser! **-3.** [be appropriate to]: **that job ~s you perfectly!** este trabalho é a sua cara! <> *vi* [be convenient or agreeable]: **does that ~?** está bom para ti?
suitability [ˌsu:tə'bɪlətɪ] *n (U)* adequação *f*, conveniência *f*.
suitable ['su:təbl] *adj* adequado(da), apropriado (da); **the most ~ person** a pessoa mais indicada.
suitably ['su:təblɪ] *adv* adequadamente, apropriadamente.
suitcase ['su:tkeɪs] *n* mala *f*.
suite [swi:t] *n* **-1.** [of rooms] suíte *f* **-2.** [of furniture] conjunto *m*.
suited ['su:tɪd] *adj* **-1.** [suitable]: **~ to/for sthg** adequado(da) para algo **-2.** [compatible]: **they are well ~** eles combinam muito bem.
suitor ['su:tə^r] *n* *dated* pretendente *m*.

sulfate *n US* = **sulphate**.
sulfur *n US* = **sulphur**.
sulfuric acid *n US* = **sulphuric acid**.
sulk [sʌlk] *n*: **to go into a ~** ficar emburrado(da). ◇ *vi* emburrar-se.
sulky ['sʌlkɪ] (*compar* **-ier**, *superl* **-iest**) *adj* emburrado(da).
sullen ['sʌlən] *adj* mal-humorado(da), atacado(da).
sulphate *UK*, **sulfate** *US* ['sʌlfeɪt] *n (U)* sulfato *m*.
sulphur *UK*, **sulfur** *US* ['sʌlfəʳ] *n (U)* enxofre *m*.
sulphuric acid *UK*, **sulfuric acid** *US* [sʌl'fjʊərɪk-] *n (U)* ácido *m* sulfúrico.
sultan ['sʌltən] *n* sultão *m*.
sultana [səl'tɑːnə] *n UK* [dried grape] passa *f* branca.
sultry ['sʌltrɪ] (*compar* **-ier**, *superl* **-iest**) *adj* **-1.** [hot] abafado(da), mormacento(ta) **-2.** [sexy] quente.
sum [sʌm] (*pt* & *pp* **-med**, *cont* **-ming**) *n* soma *f*.
◆ **sum up** *vt sep* [summarize] resumir. ◇ *vi* recapitular.
Sumatra *n* Sumatra; **in ~** em Sumatra.
Sumatran *adj de ou relativo a Sumatra*. ◇ *n habitante ou natural de Sumatra*.
summarily ['sʌmərəlɪ] *adv* sumariamente.
summarize, -ise ['sʌməraɪz] *vt* resumir. ◇ *vi* resumir.
summary ['sʌmərɪ] (*pl* **-ies**) *adj fml* sumário(ria). ◇ *n* resumo *m*.
summation [sʌ'meɪʃn] *n* **-1.** [summing-up] recapitulação *f* **-2.** [total] soma *f*.
summer ['sʌməʳ] *n* verão *m*; **in ~** no verão. ◇ *comp* de verão.
summer camp *n US* colônia *f* de férias.
summer house *n* **-1.** [in garden] quiosque *m (em jardim)* **-2.** [for holidays] casa *f* de veraneio.
summer school *n* escola *f* de verão.
summertime ['sʌmətaɪm] *adj* de verão. ◇ *n*: **(the) ~** o verão.
Summer Time *n UK* horário *m* de verão.
summery ['sʌmərɪ] *adj* de verão.
summing-up [ˌsʌmɪŋ-] (*pl* **summings-up**) *n JUR* recapitulação *f*.
summit ['sʌmɪt] *n* **-1.** [mountaintop] topo *m*, cume *m* **-2.** [meeting] reunião *f* de cúpula.
summon ['sʌmən] *vt* convocar.
◆ **summon up** *vt sep* armar-se de.
summons ['sʌmənz] (*pl* **summonses**) *JUR n* intimação *f*. ◇ *vt* intimar.
sumo (wrestling) ['suːməʊ-] *n* sumô *m*.
sump [sʌmp] *n AUT* cárter *m*.
sumptuous ['sʌmptʃʊəs] *adj* suntuoso(sa).
sum total *n* soma *f* total.
sun [sʌn] (*pt* & *pp* **-ned**, *cont* **-ning**) *n*: **the ~** o sol. ◇ *vt*: **to ~ o.s.** tomar sol.
Sun. (*abbr of* **Sunday**) dom.
sunbathe ['sʌnbeɪð] *vi* tomar (banho de) sol.
sunbather ['sʌnbeɪðəʳ] *n* banhista *mf*.
sunbeam ['sʌnbiːm] *n* raio *m* de sol.
sunbed ['sʌnbed] *n* câmara *f* de bronzeamento artificial.
sunburn ['sʌnbɜːn] *n (U)* queimadura *f* de sol.
sunburned ['sʌnbɜːnd], **sunburnt** ['sʌnbɜːnt] *adj* queimado(da) de sol.
sun cream *n (U)* protetor *m* solar.
sundae ['sʌndeɪ] *n* sundae *m*.
Sunday ['sʌndɪ] *n* domingo *m*; *see also* **Saturday**.
Sunday paper *n UK* edição *f* dominical *(de um jornal)*.
Sunday school *n* catequese *f*.
sundial ['sʌndaɪəl] *n* relógio *m* de sol.
sundown ['sʌndaʊn] *n (U)* crepúsculo *m*.
sun-dried *adj* seco(ca), desidratado(da).
sundry ['sʌndrɪ] *adj fml* diversos(sas); **all and ~** todos(das) sem exceção.
◆ **sundries** *npl fml* artigos *mpl* diversos.
sunflower ['sʌnˌflaʊəʳ] *n* girassol *m*.
sung [sʌŋ] *pp* ▻ **sing**.
sunglasses ['sʌnˌglɑːsɪz] *npl* óculos *mpl* escuros *OR* de sol.
sunhat ['sʌnhæt] *n* chapéu *m* de praia.
sunk [sʌŋk] *pp* ▻ **sink**.
sunken ['sʌŋkən] *adj* **-1.** [in water] submerso(sa) **-2.** [low-level - garden] rebaixado(*f* da); [- bath] embutido(da) **-3.** [cheeks] encovado(da) **-4.** [eyes] fundo(-da).
sunlamp ['sʌnlæmp] *n* lâmpada *f* ultravioleta.
sunlight ['sʌnlaɪt] *n (U)* luz *f* do sol *OR* solar.
sunlit ['sʌnlɪt] *adj* ensolarado(da).
Sunni ['sʊnɪ] (*pl* **-s**) *adj* sunita. ◇ *n* sunita *mf*.
sunny ['sʌnɪ] (*compar* **-ier**, *superl* **-iest**) *adj* **-1.** [full of sun] ensolarado(da) **-2.** *fig* [cheerful] luminoso(sa) **-3.** *phr*: **~ side up** *US* [fried egg] com a gema para cima.
sunray lamp *n* lâmpada *f* ultravioleta.
sunrise ['sʌnraɪz] *n* **-1.** [time of day] amanhecer *m* **-2.** [event] nascer *m* do sol.
sunroof ['sʌnruːf] *n* teto *m* solar.
sunset ['sʌnset] *n* **-1.** *(U)* [time of day] anoitecer *m* **-2.** [event] pôr-do-sol *m*, crepúsculo *m*.
sunshade ['sʌnʃeɪd] *n* guarda-sol *m*.
sunshine ['sʌnʃaɪn] *n (U)* (luz *f* do) sol *m*.
sunspot ['sʌnspɒt] *n* **-1.** *ASTRON* mancha *f* solar **-2.** [holiday resort] *local ensolarado para se passar as férias*.
sunstroke ['sʌnstrəʊk] *n (U)* insolação *f*.
suntan ['sʌntæn] *n* bronzeado *m*. ◇ *comp* bronzeador(ra).
suntanned ['sʌntænd] *adj* bronzeado(da).
suntrap ['sʌntræp] *n* local *m* muito ensolarado.
sun-up *n US inf* nascer *m* do sol.
super ['suːpəʳ] *adj inf* excelente. ◇ *n* [petrol] gasolina *f* premium.
superabundance [ˌsuːpərə'bʌndəns] *n* superabundância *f*.
superannuation ['suːpəˌrænjʊ'eɪʃn] *n* **-1.** *(U)* [pension] aposentadoria *f*, pensão *f* **-2.** [contribution] contribuição *f* para a previdência.
superb [suː'pɜːb] *adj* soberbo(ba).
superbly [suː'pɜːblɪ] *adv* soberbamente.
Super Bowl *n US*: **the ~** *a final do campeonato de futebol americano*.
supercilious [ˌsuːpə'sɪlɪəs] *adj* convencido(da), arrogante.
superficial [ˌsuːpə'fɪʃl] *adj* superficial.
superfluous [suː'pɜːflʊəs] *adj* supérfluo(flua).

superglue ['su:pəglu:] *n (U)* superbonder® *f.*
superhuman [ˌsu:pə'hju:mən] *adj* sobre-humano (na).
superimpose [ˌsu:pərɪm'pəʊz] *vt*: **to ~ sthg on sthg** sobrepor algo a algo.
superintend [ˌsu:pərɪn'tend] *vt* superintender.
superintendent [ˌsu:pərɪn'tendənt] *n* **-1.** *UK* [of police] chefe *mf* de polícia **-2.** *fml* [of department] superintendente *mf.*
superior [su:'pɪərɪəʳ] *adj* **-1.** [gen] superior; **~ to sthg/sb** superior a algo/alguém **-2.** *pej* [arrogant] arrogante. <> *n* superior *m*, -ra *f.*
superiority [su:ˌpɪərɪ'ɒrətɪ] *n (U)* **-1.** [gen] superioridade *f* **-2.** *pej* [arrogance] arrogância *f.*
superlative [su:'pɜ:lətɪv] *adj* [of the highest quality] excelente. <> *n* GRAMM superlativo *m.*
superloo *n toalete público com dispositivos especiais e muitas vezes automatizado.*
superman *n* super-homem *m.*
supermarket ['su:pəˌmɑ:kɪt] *n* supermercado *m.*
supernatural [ˌsu:pə'nætʃrəl] *adj* sobrenatural. <> *n*: **the ~** o sobrenatural.
superpower ['su:pəˌpaʊəʳ] *n* superpotência *f.*
superscript *adj* sobrescrito(ta).
supersede [ˌsu:pə'si:d] *vt* suplantar.
supersonic [ˌsu:pə'sɒnɪk] *adj* supersônico(ca).
superstar ['su:pəstɑ:ʳ] *n* superstar *mf.*
superstition [ˌsu:pə'stɪʃn] *n* **-1.** *(U)* [superstitious beliefs] superstição *f* **-2.** [particular belief] crendice *f.*
superstitious [ˌsu:pə'stɪʃəs] *adj* supersticioso(sa).
superstore ['su:pəstɔ:ʳ] *n* hipermercado *m.*
superstructure ['su:pəˌstrʌktʃəʳ] *n* superestrutura *f.*
supertanker ['su:pəˌtæŋkəʳ] *n* superpetroleiro *m.*
supertax ['su:pətæks] *n* sobretaxa *f.*
supervise ['su:pəvaɪz] *vt* supervisionar.
supervision [ˌsu:pə'vɪʒn] *n (U)* supervisão *f.*
supervisor ['su:pəvaɪzəʳ] *n* supervisor *m*, -ra *f.*
supper ['sʌpəʳ] *n* **-1.** [main evening meal] jantar *m* **-2.** [snack before bedtime] lanche *m* antes de dormir.
supplant [sə'plɑ:nt] *vt fml* suplantar.
supple ['sʌpl] *adj* flexível.
supplement [*n* 'sʌplɪmənt, *vb* 'sʌplɪment] *n* **-1.** [addition] acréscimo *m* **-2.** [in book] suplemento *m*; [of newspaper] suplemento *m*, encarte *m.* <> *vt* complementar.
supplementary [ˌsʌplɪ'mentərɪ] *adj* suplementar.
supplier [sə'plaɪəʳ] *n* fornecedor *m*, -ra *f.*
supply [sə'plaɪ] (*pl* **-ies**, *pt* & *pp* **-ied**) *n* **-1.** [store, reserve] estoque *m*; **to be in short ~** estar escasso(sa) **-2.** *(U)* [network] abastecimento *m* **-3.** *(U)* ECON oferta *f.* <> *vt*: **to ~ sthg (to sb)** fornecer algo (a alguém); **if you ~ the food, I'll bring the drink** se você entrar com a comida, eu trago a bebida; **to ~ sb (with sthg)** prover alguém (com algo); **to ~ sthg with sthg** abastecer algo com algo.
◆ **supplies** *npl* **-1.** [food] provisões *fpl* **-2.** [office equipment] material *m* **-3.** MIL apetrechos *mpl.*
supply teacher *n UK* professor *m* substituto, professora *f* substituta.
support [sə'pɔ:t] *n* **-1.** [gen] apoio *m* **-2.** *(U)* [financial] ajuda *f* **-3.** *(U)* [substantiation] embasamento *m* **-4.** [object, person] suporte *m.* <> *vt* **-1.** [physically] sustentar, apoiar **-2.** [back, back up] apoiar **-3.** [financially] ajudar **-4.** [theory] fundamentar **-5.** SPORT torcer para.
supporter [sə'pɔ:təʳ] *n* **-1.** [of person, plan] partidário *m*, -ria *f* **-2.** SPORT torcedor *m*, -ra *f.*
supportive [sə'pɔ:tɪv] *adj* incentivador(ra).
suppose [sə'pəʊz] *vt* **-1.** [assume] supor; **I don't ~ ...?** [in polite requests] eu não sei se você poderia ...?; **you don't ~ ...?** [asking opinion] você não acha que ...? **-2.** [concede reluctantly] supor, achar. <> *vi* **-1.** [assume] crer; **I ~ (so)** suponho que sim; **I ~ not** suponho que não **-2.** [admit] admitir; **I ~ so/not** admito que sim/que não. <> *conj* [what if]: **~ we went out?** que tal OR e se a gente saísse?
supposed [sə'pəʊzd] *adj* **-1.** [doubtful] suposto(posta) **-2.** [intended]: **you weren't ~ to be outside** não era para você estar na rua **-3.** [reputed]: **he was ~ to be here at eight** era para ele estar aqui às oito horas; **it's ~ to be very good** dizem que é muito bom.
supposedly [sə'pəʊzɪdlɪ] *adv* supostamente.
supposing [sə'pəʊzɪŋ] *conj*: **~ we went out?** que tal OR e se a gente saísse?
supposition [ˌsʌpə'zɪʃn] *n* suposição *f.*
suppository [sə'pɒzɪtrɪ] (*pl* **-ies**) *n* supositório *m.*
suppress [sə'pres] *vt* **-1.** [uprising, revolt] reprimir **-2.** [information, report] ocultar **-3.** [emotions] conter.
suppression [sə'preʃn] *n (U)* **-1.** [of uprising, revolt] repressão *f* **-2.** [of information, report] ocultação *f* **-3.** [of emotions] dissimulação *f.*
suppressor *n* ELEC supressor *m.*
supranational *adj* supranacional.
supremacy [sʊ'preməsɪ] *n (U)* supremacia *f.*
supreme [sʊ'pri:m] *adj* **-1.** [highest in rank] supremo(ma) **-2.** [great] extraordinário(ria).
Supreme Court *n* [in US]: **the ~** a Suprema Corte.

SUPREME COURT

A Corte Suprema é a mais alta instância judiciária federal dos Estados Unidos. Seus nove membros, chamados *justices* (juízes), são nomeados pelo presidente da República em caráter vitalício. Eles cumprem o papel de aprovar ou vetar as leis estaduais e federais, e também de interpretar a Constituição.

supremely [sʊ'pri:mlɪ] *adv*: **~ important** de suma importância.
supremo [sʊ'pri:məʊ] (*pl* **-s**) *n UK inf* manda-chuva *mf.*
Supt (*abbr of* **superintendent**) superintendente *mf.*
surcharge ['sɜ:tʃɑ:dʒ] *n*: **~ (on sthg)** sobretaxa *f* (a algo). <> *vt*: **to ~ sb (on sthg)** sobretaxar alguém (em algo).
sure [ʃʊəʳ] *adj* **-1.** [reliable] confiável, seguro(ra) **-2.** [certain] certo(ta); **to be ~ about sthg** ter certeza sobre algo; **to be ~ of sthg** estar certo de algo; **to be ~ of doing sthg** ter certeza de que vai fazer algo; **the dollar is ~ to fall soon** [be certain] com (toda) certeza o dólar vai cair em breve; [remember] certificar-se de; **to make ~ (that) ...** certificar-se de que ...; **I'm ~ (that) ...** tenho certeza de que

... **-3.** [confident]: **to be ~ of o.s.** estar seguro(ra) de si mesmo(ma). <> *adv* **-1.** *inf* [yes] com certeza, claro **-2.** *US* [really] realmente.
◆ **for sure** *adv* com (toda) certeza.
◆ **sure enough** *adv* de fato.

surefire ['ʃʊəfaɪə^r] *adj inf* certeiro(ra).

surefooted [,ʃʊə'fʊtɪd] *adj* com os pés firmes.

surely ['ʃʊəlɪ] *adv* com certeza; **~ you can't be serious!** você não pode estar falando a verdade!

sure thing *excl US inf* [expressing assent] claro!

surety ['ʃʊərətɪ] *n* garantia *f*, fiança *f*.

surf [sɜ:f] *n (U)* espuma *f (das ondas do mar)*. <> *vi* surfar. <> *vi*: **to ~ the Internet** navegar na Internet.

surface ['sɜ:fɪs] *n* **-1.** superfície *f*; **on the ~** à primeira vista; **below** *OR* **beneath the ~** abaixo *OR* acima da superfície **-2.** *phr*: **to scratch the ~** encher lingüíça. <> *vi* **-1.** [from water] emergir, vir à tona **-2.** [become generally known] vir à tona **-3.** *inf hum* [appear, reappear - after sleep] acordar; [- after prolonged absence] dar o ar da graça.

surface mail *n* correio *m* terrestre *OR* marítimo.

surface-to-air *adj* terra-ar.

surfboard ['sɜ:fbɔ:d] *n* prancha *f* de surfe.

surfeit ['sɜ:fɪt] *n fml* excesso *m*.

surfer ['sɜ:fə^r] *n* surfista *mf*.

surfing ['sɜ:fɪŋ] *n (U)* surfe *m*; **to go ~** ir surfar.

surge [sɜ:dʒ] *n* **-1.** [gen] onda *f*; [of electricity] sobretensão *f* **-2.** [of water] torrente *f* **-3.** [of sales, applications] onda *f*, aumento *m*. <> *vi* **-1.** [gen] aumentar **-2.** [people, vehicles] avançar em massa **-3.** [water] subir **-4.** [emotion] intensificar-se **-5.** [interest, support] crescer.

surgeon ['sɜ:dʒən] *n* cirurgião *m*, -giã *f*.

surgery ['sɜ:dʒərɪ] (*pl* **-ies**) *n* **-1.** *(U) MED* [activity, operation] cirurgia *f* **-2.** *UK MED* [place] consultório *m* **-3.** *UK MED* [consulting period] consulta *f* **-4.** *UK POL* audiência *f*.

surgical ['sɜ:dʒɪkl] *adj* **-1.** [connected with surgery] cirúrgico(ca) **-2.** [worn as treatment] ortopédico(ca).

surgical spirit *n (U) UK* anti-séptico *m*.

Surinam *n* Suriname; **in ~** no Suriname.

surly ['sɜ:lɪ] (*compar* **-ier**, *superl* **-iest**) *adj* ríspido(da).

surmise [sɜ:'maɪz] *vt fml* presumir.

surmount [sɜ:'maʊnt] *vt* superar, vencer.

surname ['sɜ:neɪm] *n* sobrenome *m*.

surpass [sə'pɑ:s] *vt fml* ultrapassar, superar.

surplus ['sɜ:pləs] *adj* excedente; **he was ~ to requirements** ele estava além do que se precisava. <> *n* **-1.** [gen] excedente *m* **-2.** [in budget] superávit *m*.

surprise [sə'praɪz] *n* surpresa *f*; **to take sb by ~** pegar alguém de surpresa. <> *vt* surpreender.

surprised [sə'praɪzd] *adj* surpreso(*f* sa); **I wouldn't be ~ (if ...)** não me surpreenderia (se ...).

surprising [sə'praɪzɪŋ] *adj* surpreendente.

surprisingly [sə'praɪzɪŋlɪ] *adv* surpreendentemente.

surreal [sə'rɪəl] *adj* surreal.

surrealism [sə'rɪəlɪzm] *n (U)* surrealismo *m*.

surrealist [sə'rɪəlɪst] *adj* surrealista. <> *n* surrealista *mf*.

surrender [sə'rendə^r] *n* rendição *f*. <> *vt* **-1.** [weapons, passport] entregar **-2.** [liberty, right, claims] renunciar a. <> *vi* **-1.** [stop fighting]: **to ~ (to sb)** render-se (a alguém) **-2.** *fig* [give in]: **to ~ (to sthg)** sucumbir *OR* ceder (a algo).

surreptitious [,sʌrəp'tɪʃəs] *adj* clandestino(na), furtivo(va).

surrogate ['sʌrəgeɪt] *adj* suplente. <> *n* substituto *m*, -ta *f*.

surrogate mother *n* mãe *f* de aluguel.

surround [sə'raʊnd] *n* borda *f*. <> *vt* **-1.** [encircle] circundar, rodear **-2.** [trap] cercar **-3.** *fig* [be associated with] rondar.

surrounding [sə'raʊndɪŋ] *adj* **-1.** [all around] circundante **-2.** [associated] relacionado(da).
◆ **surroundings** *npl* **-1.** [physical] arredores *mpl* **-2.** [social] ambiente *m*.

surtax ['sɜ:tæks] *n (U)* sobretaxa *f*.

surveillance [sɜ:'veɪləns] *n (U)* vigilância *f*.

survey [*n* 'sɜ:veɪ, *vb* sə'veɪ] *n* **-1.** [statistical investigation] pesquisa *f*, levantamento *m* **-2.** [physical examination - of land] medição *f*; [- of building] vistoria *f*, inspeção *f*. <> *vt* **-1.** [contemplate] contemplar **-2.** [investigate statistically] fazer um levantamento de **-3.** [examine, assess - land] medir; [- building] vistoriar, inspecionar.

surveyor [sə'veɪə^r] *n* [of land] agrimensor *m*, -ra *f*; [of building] vistoriador *m*, -ra *f*.

survival [sə'vaɪvl] *n* **-1.** *(U)* [continuing to live] sobrevivência *f* **-2.** [relic] relíquia *f*.

survive [sə'vaɪv] *vt* **-1.** [live through] sobreviver a **-2.** [live longer than] sobreviver. <> *vi* **-1.** [gen] sobreviver **-2.** *inf* [cope successfully] sobreviver.
◆ **survive on** *vt fus* sustentar-se *OR* manter-se com.

survivor [sə'vaɪvə^r] *n* **-1.** [gen] sobrevivente *mf* **-2.** *fig* [fighter] lutador *m*, -ra *f*.

susceptible [sə'septəbl] *adj* **-1.** [likely to be influenced]: **~ (to sthg)** suscetível (a algo) **-2.** *MED*: **~ (to sthg)** propenso(sa) (a algo).

suspect [*adj & n* 'sʌspekt, *vb* sə'spekt] *adj* suspeito(ta). <> *n* suspeito *m*, -ta *f*. <> *vt* **-1.** suspeitar; **I ~ corruption in the system** imagino que haja corrupção no sistema **-2.** [consider guilty]: **to ~ sb (of sthg)** suspeitar de alguém (em algo).

suspend [sə'spend] *vt* **-1.** [gen] suspender **-2.** [temporarily discontinue] suspender, interromper.

suspended animation [sə'spendɪd-] *n (U)* morte *f* aparente.

suspended sentence [sə'spendɪd-] *n* condenação *f* condicional.

suspender belt [sə'spendə^r-] *n UK* cinta-liga *f*.

suspenders [sə'spendəz] *npl* **-1.** *UK* [for stockings] cintas-ligas *fpl* **-2.** *US* [for trousers] suspensórios *mpl*.

suspense [sə'spens] *n (U)* suspense *m*; **to keep sb in ~** deixar alguém em suspense.

suspension [sə'spenʃn] *n* suspensão *f*.

suspension bridge *n* ponte *f* suspensa.

suspicion [sə'spɪʃn] *n* suspeita *f*; **under ~** sob suspeita.

suspicious [sə'spɪʃəs] *adj* **-1.** [having suspicions] desconfiado(da) **-2.** [causing suspicion] suspeito(ta).

suspiciously [sə'spɪʃəslɪ] *adv* **-1.** [showing a suspicious attitude] desconfiadamente; **he asked me ~ if ...** ele me perguntou desconfiado se ... **-2.** [causing suspicion] de forma suspeita.

suss ◆ **suss out** *UK inf vt sep* sacar; **I can't suss him out at all** ainda não saquei qual é a dele.

sustain [sə'steɪn] *vt* **-1.** [gen] manter **-2.** [nourish spiritually] sustentar **-3.** [suffer] sofrer **-4.** [withstand] suportar.

sustenance ['sʌstɪnəns] *n (U) fml* subsistência *f.*

suture ['su:tʃə^r] *n* sutura *f.*

svelte [svelt] *adj* esbelto(ta).

SW -1. (*abbr of* **short wave**) OC *f* **-2.** (*abbr of* **southwest**) SO.

swab [swɒb] *n* (bucha *f* de) algodão *m.*

swagger ['swægə^r] *n* andar *m* garboso. ◇ *vi* andar com ar garboso.

Swahili [swɑ:'hi:lɪ] *adj* suaíli. ◇ *n* [language] suaíli *m.*

swallow ['swɒləʊ] *n* **-1.** [bird] andorinha *f* **-2.** [of food] bocado *m* **-3.** [of drink] gole *m.* ◇ *vt* **-1.** [gen] engolir **-2.** *fig* [hold back] engolir em seco. ◇ *vi* engolir.

swam [swæm] *pt* ▷ **swim.**

swamp [swɒmp] *n* pântano *m*, brejo *m.* ◇ *vt* **-1.** [flood] inundar **-2.** [overwhelm]: **to ~ sb/sthg (with sthg)** sobrecarregar alguém/algo (de algo).

swan [swɒn] *n* cisne *m.*

swap [swɒp] (*pt* & *pp* **-ped**, *cont* **-ping**) *n* troca *f.* ◇ *vt*: **to ~ sthg (with sb)** trocar algo com alguém; **to ~ sthg (over** OR **round)** trocar algo; **to ~ sthg for sthg** trocar algo por algo. ◇ *vi* trocar.

swap meet *n US* mercado *m* de trocas.

swarm [swɔ:m] *n* **-1.** [of bees] enxame *m* **-2.** *fig* [of people] mundaréu *m.* ◇ *vi* **-1.** [bees] enxamear **-2.** *fig* [people] apinhar-se **-3.** *fig* [place]: **to be ~ing (with)** estar fervilhando de.

swarthy ['swɔ:ðɪ] (*compar* **-ier**, *superl* **-iest**) *adj* moreno(*f* na).

swashbuckling ['swɒʃˌbʌklɪŋ] *adj* de aventura.

swastika ['swɒstɪkəl] *n* suástica *f.*

swat [swɒt] (*pt* & *pp* **-ted**, *cont* **-ting**) *vt* golpear.

swatch [swɒtʃ] *n* amostra *f.*

swathe [sweɪð] *n* vastidão *f.*

swathed [sweɪðd] *adj literary*: **~ in sthg** enrolado(-da) em algo.

swatter ['swɒtə^r] *n* mata-moscas *m inv.*

sway [sweɪ] *vt* **-1.** [cause to swing] balançar **-2.** [influence] persuadir, convencer. ◇ *vi* oscilar. ◇ *n (U) fml*: **to come under the ~ of sb/sthg** ficar sob influência de alguém/algo; **to hold ~ (over sb/sthg)** exercer influência (sobre alguém/algo).

Swazi *n* suazi *mf.*

Swaziland ['swɑ:zɪlænd] *n* Suazilândia; **in ~** na Suazilândia.

swear [sweə^r] (*pt* **swore**, *pp* **sworn**) *vt* **-1.** [gen] jurar; **to ~ to do sthg** jurar fazer algo **-2.** [pronounce]: **to ~ an oath** prestar juramento **-3.** *inf* [state emphatically] jurar. ◇ *vi* **-1.** [state emphatically] jurar **-2.** [use swearwords] praguejar.

◆ **swear by** *vt fus inf* confiar totalmente em.

◆ **swear in** *vt sep* JUR prestar juramento a.

swearword ['sweəwɜ:d] *n* blasfêmia *f*, palavrão *m.*

sweat [swet] *n* **-1.** *(U)* [perspiration] suor *m* **-2.** *(U) inf* [hard work] trabalheira *f* **-3.** *inf* [state of anxiety] suador *m*; **to be in a cold ~** suar frio. ◇ *vi* **-1.** [perspire] suar **-2.** *inf* [worry] preocupar-se com.

sweatband ['swetbænd] *n* **-1.** [for wrist] munhequeira *f* **-2.** [for head] faixa *f* para cabeça.

sweater ['swetə^r] *n* suéter *m.*

sweatshirt ['swetʃɜ:t] *n* moletom *m.*

sweatshop ['swetʃɒp] *n estabelecimento que oferece más condições de trabalho e baixos salários aos empregados.*

sweaty ['swetɪ] (*compar* **-ier**, *superl* **-iest**) *adj* **-1.** [skin, clothes] suado(*f* da) **-2.** [place] abafado(*f* da) **-3.** [activity] exaustivo(*f* va).

swede [swi:d] *n UK* rutabaga *f.*

Swede [swi:d] *n* sueco *m*, -ca *f.*

Sweden ['swi:dn] *n* Suécia; **in ~** na Suécia.

Swedish ['swi:dɪʃ] *adj* sueco(ca). ◇ *n* [language] sueco *m.* ◇ *npl*: **the ~** os suecos.

sweep [swi:p] (*pt* & *pp* **swept**) *n* **-1.** [sweeping movement] movimento *m* (circular) **-2.** [with brush] varrida *f* **-3.** [electronic examination] varredura *f* **-4.** [chimneysweep] limpador *m*, -ra *f* de chaminé. ◇ *vt* **-1.** [gen] varrer **-2.** [with eyes] examinar **-3.** [spread through] disseminar **-4.** [for bugs or bombs] vasculhar, examinar **-5.** [force] arrastar; **to ~ sb off his/her feet** abarrotar o coração dele/dela **-6.** [push with hand] afastar; **she swept the papers off her desk** ela tirou os papéis do escritório. ◇ *vi* **-1.** [wind, rain] precipitar-se **-2.** [vehicle] ir a toda velocidade **-3.** [emotion, laughter, rumour] espalhar-se; **fear swept through the crowd** o medo se espalhou pela multidão **-4.** [walk quickly] passar como um raio.

◆ **sweep aside** *vt sep* afastar.

◆ **sweep away** *vt sep* varrer do mapa.

◆ **sweep up** ◇ *vt sep* & *vi* escovar.

sweeper ['swi:pə^r] *n* FTBL líbero *m.*

sweeping ['swi:pɪŋ] *adj* **-1.** [effect] radical **-2.** [statement] muito genérico(ca) **-3.** [curve] amplo(-pla).

sweepstake ['swi:psteɪk] *n loteria que se baseia nas corridas de cavalo.*

sweet [swi:t] *adj* **-1.** [gen] doce **-2.** [smell] doce, perfumado(da) **-3.** [sound] doce, melodioso(sa) **-4.** [gentle, kind] amável; **that's very ~ of you** é muita gentileza de sua parte **-5.** [attractive] meigo(ga). ◇ *n UK* **-1.** [candy] doce *m* **-2.** [dessert] sobremesa *f.*

sweet-and-sour *adj* agridoce.

sweet corn *n (U)* milho *m* verde.

sweeten ['swi:tn] *vt* adoçar.

sweetener ['swi:tnə^r] *n* **-1.** [substance] adoçante *m* **-2.** *inf fig* [bribe] suborno *m.*

sweetheart ['swi:thɑ:t] *n* **-1.** [term of endearment] querido *m*, -da *f* **-2.** [boyfriend or girlfriend] namorado *m*, -da *f.*

sweetness ['swi:tnɪs] *n (U)* **-1.** [gen] doçura *f* **-2.** [of feelings] prazer *f* **-3.** [of smell] aroma *f* **-4.** [of sound] melodia *f.*

sweet pea *n* ervilha-de-cheiro *f.*

sweet potato *n* batata-doce *f.*

sweet shop *n UK* confeitaria *f.*

sweet-talk *vt*: **to ~ sb (into doing sthg)** levar alguém na conversa (para fazer algo).

sweet tooth *n inf*: **to have a ~** ser louco(ca) por doce.
swell [swel] (*pt* **-ed**, *pp* **swollen** *OR* **-ed**) *vi* **-1.** [become larger]: **to ~ (up)** inchar **-2.** [fill with air] inflar **-3.** [increase in number] aumentar **-4.** [become louder] intensificar-se **-5.** [with pride] encher-se. ◇ *vt* aumentar. ◇ *n* elevação *f*; **sea ~** vaivém *m* do mar. ◇ *adj US inf* genial, excelente.
swelling ['swelıŋ] *n* **-1.** *(U)* [swollenness] inchamento *m* **-2.** [swollen area] inchaço *m*.
sweltering ['sweltərıŋ] *adj* **-1.** [weather] abafado(da) **-2.** [person] sufocado(da).
swept [swept] *pt & pp* ▻ **sweep**.
swerve [swɜ:v] *vi* **-1.** [car, lorry] dar uma guinada **-2.** [person] desviar repentinamente.
swift [swıft] *adj* **-1.** [fast] veloz **-2.** [prompt, ready] rápido(da). ◇ *n* [bird] andorinhão *m* preto.
swiftly ['swıftlı] *adj* **-1.** [rapidly] velozmente **-2.** [without delay] rapidamente.
swiftness ['swıftnıs] *n (U)* rapidez *f*.
swig [swıg] (*pt & pp* **-ged**, *cont* **-ging**) *inf vt* beber a grandes goles. ◇ *n* trago *m*.
swill [swıl] *n (U)* lavagem *f*. ◇ *vt UK* enxaguar.
swim [swım] (*pt* **swam**, *pp* **swum**, *cont* **-ming**) *n* banho *m (de mar, de piscina)*; **to have a ~** nadar; **to go for a ~** ir nadar *OR* tomar banho *(de mar, de piscina)*. ◇ *vi* **-1.** [move through water] nadar; **can you ~?** você sabe nadar? **-2.** [feel dizzy] dar voltas; **my head was ~ming** minha cabeça estava girando.
swimmer ['swımə^r] *n* nadador *m*, -ra *f*.
swimming ['swımıŋ] *n* [bathing] natação *f*; **to go ~** ir nadar.
swimming baths *npl UK* piscina *f* pública coberta.
swimming cap *n* touca *f* de natação.
swimming costume *n UK* traje *m* de banho.
swimming pool *n* piscina *f*.
swimming trunks *npl* sunga *m*.
swimsuit ['swımsu:t] *n* traje *m* de banho.
swindle ['swındl] *n* logro *m*, fraude *f*. ◇ *vt* lograr; **to ~ sb out of sthg** lograr alguém em algo.
swine [swaın] *n inf pej* [person] porco *m*, -ca *f*.
swing [swıŋ] (*pt & pp* **swung**) *n* **-1.** [child's toy] balanço *m* **-2.** [change] virada *f*, mudança *f* **-3.** [swaying movement] rebolado *m* **-4.** *inf* [blow]: **to take a ~ at sb** dar um golpe em alguém **-5.** *phr*: **to be in full ~** estar a todo vapor; **to get into the ~ of sthg** entrar no ritmo de algo. ◇ *vt* **-1.** [move back and forth] balançar **-2.** [turn] virar bruscamente. ◇ *vi* **-1.** [move back and forth] balançar **-2.** [turn] girar; **to ~ open** abrir-se **-3.** [hit out]: **to ~ at sb** dar um golpe em alguém **-4.** [change] virar, mudar.
swing bridge *n* ponte *f* giratória.
swing door *n* porta *f* corrediça.
swingeing ['swındʒıŋ] *adj* severo(ra).
swinging ['swıŋıŋ] *adj inf* **-1.** [party] divertido(da), alegre **-2.** [era, lifestyle] descontraído(da).
swipe [swaıp] ◇ *n*: **to take a ~ at sb/sthg** tentar bater em algo/alguém. ◇ *vt* **-1.** *inf* [steal] roubar **-2.** [plastic card] passar. ◇ *vi*: **to ~ at sthg** tentar golpear algo.
swirl [swɜ:l] ◇ *n* **-1.** [swirling movement] rodopio *m* **-2.** [eddy] redemoinho *m*. ◇ *vt* girar como um redemoinho. ◇ *vi* girar.
swish [swıʃ] ◇ *adj inf* [posh] bacana. ◇ *n* [movement - of dress] ruge-ruge *m*; [- of tail] meneio *m*. ◇ *vt* [tail] balançar, agitar. ◇ *vi* [move] menear.
Swiss [swıs] ◇ *adj* suíço(ça). ◇ *n* [person] suíço *m*, -ça *f*. ◇ *npl*: **the ~** os suíços.
Swiss chard *n* acelga *f*.
swiss roll *n UK* rocambole *m*.
switch [swıtʃ] ◇ *n* **-1.** [control device] chave *f*, interruptor *m* **-2.** [change] mudança *f*, virada *f* **-3.** *US RAIL* desvio *m*. ◇ *vt* **-1.** [transfer] trocar; **to ~ one's attention to sthg** dirigir a atenção a algo **-2.** [swap, exchange] trocar de; **to ~ sthg round** trocar algo de lugar. ◇ *vi* [transfer] trocar; **to ~ to/from sthg** transferir para/de algo.
◆ **switch off** ◇ *vt sep* desligar. ◇ *vi inf* [person] desconcentrar-se.
◆ **switch on** *vt sep* ligar.
Switch® [swıtʃ] *n UK cartão de débito automático Switch.*
switchblade ['swıtʃbleıd] *n US* canivete *m*.
switchboard ['swıtʃbɔ:d] *n* mesa *f* telefônica.
switchboard operator *n* telefonista *mf*.
switched-on *adj inf* [person] antenado(da).
Switzerland ['swıtsələnd] *n* Suíça; **in ~** na Suíça.
swivel ['swıvl] (*UK pt & pp* **-led**, *cont* **-ling**, *US pt & pp* **-ed**, *cont* **-ing**) *vt & vi* girar.
swivel chair *n* cadeira *f* giratória.
swollen ['swəʊln] ◇ *pp* ▻ **swell**. ◇ *adj* **-1.** [ankle, arm] inchado(da) **-2.** [river] cheio (cheia).
swoon [swu:n] *vi literary or hum* desmaiar.
swoop [swu:p] ◇ *n* **-1.** [downward flight] arremetida *f*; **in one fell ~** de uma só vez **-2.** [raid] ataque -surpresa *m*. ◇ *vi* **-1.** [fly downwards] precipitar-se, mergulhar **-2.** [pounce] atacar de surpresa.
swop [swɒp] *n, vt & vi* = **swap**.
sword [sɔ:d] *n* espada *f*; **to cross ~s (with sb)** discutir (com alguém).
swordfish ['sɔ:dfıʃ] (*pl inv OR* **-es**) *n* peixe-espada *m*.
swordsman ['sɔ:dzmən] (*pl* **-men** [-mən]) *n* esgrimista *m*, espadachim *m*.
swore [swɔ:^r] *pt* ▻ **swear**.
sworn [swɔ:n] ◇ *pp* ▻ **swear**. ◇ *adj* **-1.** [committed]: **to be ~ enemies** ser inimigos declarados **-2.** *JUR* sob juramento.
swot [swɒt] (*pt & pp* **-ted**, *cont* **-ting**) *UK inf* ◇ *n pej* cê-dê-efe *mf*. ◇ *vi*: **to ~ (for sthg)** matar-se de estudar (para algo).
◆ **swot up** *inf* ◇ *vt sep* matar-se de estudar. ◇ *vi*: **to ~ up (on sthg)** matar-se de estudar (algo).
swum [swʌm] *pp* ▻ **swim**.
swung [swʌŋ] *pt & pp* ▻ **swing**.
sycamore ['sıkəmɔ:^r] *n* falso-plátano *m*.
sycophant ['sıkəfænt] *n* bajulador *m*, -ra *f*.
Sydney ['sıdnı] *n* Sydney.
syllable ['sıləbl] *n* sílaba *f*.
syllabub ['sıləbʌb] *n doce feito de creme, claras de ovos e vinho ou suco de frutas.*

syllabus ['sɪləbəs] (*pl* **-buses** OR **-bi** [-baɪ]) *n* programa *m* da disciplina.
symbol ['sɪmbl] *n* símbolo *m*.
symbolic [sɪm'bɒlɪk] *adj* simbólico(ca); **to be ~ of sthg** ser símbolo de algo.
symbolism ['sɪmbəlɪzm] *n (U)* simbolismo *m*.
symbolize, -ise ['sɪmbəlaɪz] *vt* simbolizar.
symmetrical [sɪ'metrɪkl] *adj* simétrico(ca).
symmetry ['sɪmətrɪ] *n (U)* simetria *f*.
sympathetic [ˌsɪmpə'θetɪk] *adj* **-1.** [understanding] compreensivo(va) **-2.** [willing to support] favorável; **~ to sthg** favorável a algo **-3.** [likable] simpático(-ca), agradável.
sympathize, -ise ['sɪmpəθaɪz] *vi* **-1.** [feel sorry] compadecer-se; **to ~ with sb** solidarizar-se com alguém, compadecer-se de alguém **-2.** [understand] compreender; **to ~ with sthg** compreender algo **-3.** [support]: **to ~ with sthg** apoiar algo.
sympathizer, -iser ['sɪmpəθaɪzə[r]] *n* simpatizante *mf*.
sympathy ['sɪmpəθɪ] *n* **-1.** [understanding] empatia *f*; **~ for sb** empatia por alguém **-2.** [agreement] simpatia *f*; **in ~ (with sthg)** de acordo (com algo) **-3.** [support]: **in ~** em solidariedade; **in ~ with sb** em solidariedade a alguém.
◆ **sympathies** *npl* **-1.** [approval] simpatias *fpl* **-2.** [condolences] pêsames *mpl*.
symphonic [sɪm'fɒnɪk] *adj* sinfônico(ca).
symphony ['sɪmfənɪ] (*pl* **-ies**) *n* sinfonia *f*.
symphony orchestra *n* orquestra *f* sinfônica.
symposium [sɪm'pəʊzjəm] (*pl* **-siums** OR **-sia** [-zjə]) *n fml* simpósio *m*.
symptom ['sɪmptəm] *n* sintoma *m*.
symptomatic [ˌsɪmptə'mætɪk] *adj* sintomático(ca); **to be ~ of sthg** ser um sintoma de algo.
synagogue ['sɪnəgɒg] *n* sinagoga *f*.
sync [sɪŋk] *n (U) inf*: **out of ~** fora de sincronia; **in ~** sincronizado(da).
synchronize, -ise ['sɪŋkrənaɪz] *vt, vi* sincronizar.
synchronized swimming ['sɪŋkrənaɪzd-] *n (U)* nado *m* sincronizado.
syncopated ['sɪŋkəpeɪtɪd] *adj* sincopado(da).
syncopation [ˌsɪŋkə'peɪʃn] *n (U)* síncope *f*.
syndicate [*n* 'sɪndɪkət, *vb* 'sɪndɪkeɪt] ◇ *n* sindicato *m*. ◇ *vt* PRESS distribuir em cadeia.
syndrome ['sɪndrəʊm] *n* síndrome *f*.
synergy (*pl* **-ies**) *n* sinergia *f*.
synod *n* sínodo *m*.
synonym ['sɪnənɪm] *n* sinônimo *m*; **~ for** OR **of sthg** sinônimo para OR de algo.
synonymous [sɪ'nɒnɪməs] *adj* **-1.** [having the same meaning] sinônimo(ma) **-2.** [associated]: **~ with sthg** sinônimo de algo.
synopsis [sɪ'nɒpsɪs] (*pl* **-ses** [-si:z]) *n* sinopse *f*.
syntax ['sɪntæks] *n* LING sintaxe *f*.
synthesis ['sɪnθəsɪs] (*pl* **-ses** [-si:z]) *n* síntese *f*.
synthesize, -ise ['sɪnθəsaɪz] *vt* sintetizar.
synthesizer ['sɪnθəsaɪzə[r]] *n* MUS sintetizador *m*.
synthetic [sɪn'θetɪk] *adj* **-1.** [man-made] sintético(ca) **-2.** *pej* [insincere] artificial.
syphilis ['sɪfɪlɪs] *n (U)* sífilis *f inv*.
syphon ['saɪfn] *n & vt* = **siphon**.
Syria ['sɪrɪə] *n* Síria; **in ~** na Síria.
Syrian ['sɪrɪən] ◇ *adj* sírio(ria). ◇ *n* sírio *m*, -ria *f*.
syringe [sɪ'rɪndʒ] (*cont* **syringeing** OR **syringing**) ◇ *n* seringa *f*. ◇ *vt* lavar, limpar.
syrup ['sɪrəp] *n (U)* **-1.** [sugar and water] calda *f* **-2.** *UK* [golden syrup] melado *m* **-3.** [medicine] xarope *m*.
system ['sɪstəm] *n* **-1.** [gen] sistema *m* **-2.** [network, structure - road] rede *f*; [- railway] malha *f* **-3.** *inf* [government]: **the ~** o sistema **-4.** *(U)* [methodical approach] sistemática *f* **-5.** *phr*: **to get sthg out of one's ~** *inf* parar de se preocupar com algo.
systematic [ˌsɪstə'mætɪk] *adj* sistemático(ca).
systematize, -ise ['sɪstəmətaɪz] *vt UK* sistematizar.
system disk *n* COMPUT disco *m* de sistema.
systems analyst ['sɪstəmz-] *n* COMPUT analista *mf* de sistemas.
systems engineer ['sɪstəmz-] *n* COMPUT engenheiro *m*, -ra *f* de sistemas.
system software *n* COMPUT software *m* de sistema.

t (*pl* **t's** OR **ts**), **T** (*pl* **T's** OR **Ts**) [ti:] *n* t, T *m*.
ta [tɑ:] *excl UK inf* brigado(da!); **~ very much** brigado(da)!
TA (*abbr of* **Territorial Army**) *n organização militar britânica de pessoas que não são membros regulares do exército*.
tab [tæb] *n* **-1.** [of cloth] etiqueta *f* **-2.** [of metal] lingüeta *f* **-3.** *US* [bill] conta *f*; **to pick up the ~** pagar a conta **-4.** (*abbr of* **tabulator**) [on keyboard] (tecla *f*) tab *m* **-5.** *phr*: **to keep ~s on sb** ficar de olho em alguém.
tabby ['tæbɪ] (*pl* **-ies**) *n*: **~ (cat)** gato *m* tigrado.
tabernacle ['tæbənækl] *n* tabernáculo *m*.
tab key *n* tecla *f* tab.
table ['teɪbl] ◇ *n* **-1.** [piece of furniture] mesa *f* **-2.** [diagram] tabela *f* **-3.** *phr*: **to turn the ~s on sb** inverter as posições com alguém. ◇ *vt* **-1.** *UK* [propose] apresentar **-2.** *US* [postpone] adiar.
tableau ['tæbləʊ] (*pl* **-x** ['tæbləʊz], **-s**) *n* quadro *m* vivo.
tablecloth ['teɪblklɒθ] *n* toalha *f* de mesa.
table d'hôte ['tɑ:blˌdəʊt] *n*: **the ~** o cardápio do dia.
table football *n* pebolim *m*.
table lamp *n* luminária *f*.
table licence *n licença para venda de bebidas alcoólicas apenas com a refeição*.

table linen *n (U)* roupa *f* de mesa.
table manners *npl* modos *mpl* à mesa.
table mat *n* descanço *m* para panelas.
table of contents *n* sumário *m*.
table salt *n (U)* sal *m* de mesa.
tablespoon ['teɪblspu:n] *n* **-1.** [spoon] colher *f (de sopa)* **-2.** [spoonful] colherada *f* de sopa.
tablet ['tæblɪt] *n* **-1.** [pill] comprimido *m*, pastilha *f* **-2.** [piece of stone] pedra *f* lascada **-3.** [piece of soap] barra *f*.
table tennis *n (U)* tênis *m inv* de mesa.
tableware *n (U)* utensílios *mpl* de mesa.
table wine *n (U)* vinho *m* de mesa.
tabloid ['tæblɔɪd] *n*: ~ **(newspaper)** tablóide *m*; **the ~ press** a imprensa sensacionalista.

TABLOID

Nos países anglo-saxões, o formato pequeno, ou tablóide, é característico dos jornais sensacionalistas. No Reino Unido, são publicações diárias desse tipo o *Daily Express*, o *Daily Mail*, *Daily Mirror*, *The Star* e *The Sun*. Nos Estados Unidos, esse tipo de jornal também existe, embora sua publicação seja, em geral, semanal. Os mais conhecidos são *The National Enquirer*, *The Star* e *The Globe*.

taboo [tə'bu:] (*pl* **-s**) <> *adj* tabu. <> *n* tabu *m*.
tabulate ['tæbjʊleɪt] *vt* dispor em formato de tabela.
tachograph ['tækəgrɑ:f] *n* tacógrafo *m*.
tachometer [tæ'kɒmɪtə^r] *n* tacômetro *m*.
tacit ['tæsɪt] *adj fml* tácito(ta).
taciturn ['tæsɪtɜ:n] *adj fml* taciturno(na).
tack [tæk] <> *n* **-1.** [nail] tacha *f* **-2.** NAUT rumo *m* **-3.** *fig* [course of action] tática *f*; **to change ~** mudar de tática. <> *vt* **-1.** [fasten with nail] afixar (com tachas) **-2.** [in sewing] alinhavar. <> *vi* NAUT virar.
◆ **tack on** *vt sep inf* [add as afterthought] anexar.
tackle ['tækl] <> *n* **-1.** FTBL entrada *f* **-2.** RUGBY obstrução *f* **-3.** [equipment, gear] apetrechos *mpl* **-4.** [for lifting] guincho *m*. <> *vt* **-1.** [job] lidar com **-2.** [problem] atacar **-3.** FTBL roubar a bola de **-4.** RUGBY derrubar **-5.** [attack] enfrentar **-6.** [talk to]: **to ~ sb about** OR **on sthg** pegar alguém para falar sobre algo.
tacky ['tækɪ] (*compar* **-ier**, *superl* **-iest**) *adj* **-1.** *inf* [cheap and nasty] barato(ta) **-2.** [sticky] grudento(ta), pegajoso(sa).
taco ['tækəʊ] (*pl* **-s**) *n* taco *m*.
tact [tækt] *n (U)* tato *m*.
tactful ['tæktfʊl] *adj* discreto(ta); **that wasn't very ~ of you** você não agiu com muito tato.
tactfully ['tæktfʊlɪ] *adv* discretamente.
tactic ['tæktɪk] *n* tática *f*.
◆ **tactics** *n (U)* MIL tática *f*.
tactical ['tæktɪkl] *adj* **-1.** [gen] estratégico(ca) **-2.** MIL tático(ca).
tactical voting *n (U)* UK votação *f* tática.
tactile *adj* tátil.
tactless ['tæktlɪs] *adj* indiscreto(ta); **he's so ~** falta tato nele.
tactlessly ['tæktlɪslɪ] *adv* indiscretamente.
tadpole ['tædpəʊl] *n* girino *m*.
Tadzhikistan [tɑ:ˌdʒɪkɪ'stɑ:n] *n* Tadjiquistão; **in ~** no Tadjiquistão.
taffeta ['tæfɪtə] *n (U)* tafetá *m*.
taffy ['tæfɪ] (*pl* **-ies**) *n* US puxa-puxa *m*.
tag [tæg] (*pt & pp* **-ged**, *cont* **-ging**) <> *n* **-1.** [gen] etiqueta *f* **-2.** *(U)* [game] pega-pega *f* **-3.** COMPUT tag *f*, marca *f*. <> *vt* etiquetar.
◆ **tag along** *vi inf*: **she always has to ~ along** ela sempre tem de vir junto.
Tagus *n*: **the ~** o Tejo.
Tahiti [tɑ:'hi:tɪ] *n* Taiti; **in ~** no Taiti.
Tahitian <> *adj* taitiano(na). <> *n* taitiano *m*, -na *f*.
tail [teɪl] <> *n* **-1.** [gen] rabo *m*; **with one's ~ between one's legs** [person] com o rabo entre as pernas **-2.** [of coat, shirt] fralda *f* **-3.** [of comet, plane] cauda *f* **-4.** [of car] parte *f* traseira. <> *comp* [rear] traseiro(ra). <> *vt inf* ir atrás de.
◆ **tails** <> *adv* [when tossing a coin] coroa *f*. <> *npl* [coat] fraque *m*.
◆ **tail off** *vi* diminuir.
tailback ['teɪlbæk] *n* UK fila *f (de carros)*.
tailcoat ['teɪlˌkəʊt] *n* fraque *m*.
tail end *n* final *m*, parte *f* final.
tailgate ['teɪlgeɪt] *n* tampa *f* traseira.
taillight ['teɪllaɪt] *n* luz *f* traseira.
tailor ['teɪlə^r] <> *n* alfaiate *m*. <> *vt* adaptar.
tailored ['teɪləd] *adj* [well-fitting] feito(ta) sob medida.
tailor-made *adj fig* [role, job] sob medida.
tail pipe *n* US cano *m* de descarga.
tailplane ['teɪlpleɪn] *n* leme *m (do avião)*.
tailwind ['teɪlwɪnd] *n* vento *m* de cauda.
taint [teɪnt] <> *n* mancha *f*. <> *vt* manchar.
tainted ['teɪntɪd] *adj* **-1.** [reputation] manchado(da) **-2.** US [food] estragado(da).
Taiwan [ˌtaɪ'wɑ:n] *n* Taiwan; **in ~** em Taiwan.
Taiwanese [ˌtaɪwə'ni:z] <> *adj* taiwanês(esa). <> *n* taiwanês *m*, -esa *f*.
take [teɪk] (*pt* **took**, *pp* **taken**) <> *vt* **-1.** [gen] levar **-2.** [accompany] levar, acompanhar **-3.** [capture, undergo, swallow, measure] tomar **-4.** [receive] receber; **to ~ a seat** sentar-se; **to ~ control/command** tomar o controle/comando **-5.** [rent] alugar **-6.** [object, hand, road, means of transport] pegar **-7.** [accept, take on] aceitar; **~ my word for it** acredita em mim; **what batteries does it ~?** que pilha vai aí? **-8.** [contain] suportar **-9.** [bear] agüentar **-10.** [require] precisar; **it could ~ years** pode levar anos **-11.** [holiday] tirar; **to ~ a walk** dar uma caminhada; **to ~ a bath** tomar um banho; **to ~ a photo** tirar OR bater uma foto **-12.** [pity, interest] ter; **to ~ offence** ofender-se; **I ~ the view that ...** sou da opinião de que ...; **to ~ sthg seriously/badly** levar algo a sério/a mal **-13.** [wear as a particular size - shoe] calçar; [- dress] vestir **-14.** [consider] pensar em, considerar **-15.** [assume]: **I ~ it (that) ...** presumo que ... <> *vi* [have intended effect - dye] tingir; [- fire] prender. <> *n* tomada *f*.
◆ **take aback** *vt sep* surpreender; **to be taken aback** ficar espantado(da).
◆ **take after** *vt fus* parecer-se com.
◆ **take apart** *vt sep* desmontar.
◆ **take away** *vt sep* **-1.** [remove] levar embora

-**2.** [deduct] subtrair, tirar.
◆ **take back** *vt sep* **-1.** [return] devolver **-2.** [accept] aceitar de volta **-3.** [statement, accusation] retirar.
◆ **take down** *vt sep* **-1.** [dismantle] desmontar **-2.** [write down] escrever, tomar nota de **-3.** [lower] baixar.
◆ **take in** *vt sep* **-1.** [deceive] enganar **-2.** [understand] compreender **-3.** [include] incluir **-4.** [provide accommodation for] acolher.
◆ **take off** <> *vt sep* **-1.** [remove] tirar **-2.** [have as holiday] tirar de folga; **she took the afternoon off** ela tirou a tarde de folga; **to ~ time off** tirar uma folga **-3.** *UK inf* [imitate] imitar **-4.** *inf* [go away suddenly]: **to ~ o.s. off** mandar-se (embora). <> *vi* **-1.** [gen] decolar **-2.** [go away suddenly] mandar-se (embora), ir-se embora.
◆ **take on** <> *vt sep* **-1.** [accept - work, job] aceitar; [- responsibility] assumir **-2.** [employ] admitir **-3.** [confront] desafiar. <> *vt fus* [assume, develop] adquirir.
◆ **take out** *vt sep* **-1.** [from container] tirar **-2.** [delete] suprimir, tirar **-3.** [go out with] convidar para sair **-4.** *phr*: **to ~ it** *OR* **a lot out of one** *inf* esgotar alguém.
◆ **take out on** *vt sep* descarregar em, descontar em.
◆ **take over** <> *vt sep* **-1.** [take control of] tomar o controle de, assumir **-2.** [job, role] assumir. <> *vi* **-1.** [take control] tomar o poder **-2.** [in job] assumir.
◆ **take to** *vt fus* **-1.** [feel a liking for - person] ter afeição especial por; [- activity] gostar de **-2.** [begin]: **to ~ to doing sthg** começar a fazer algo.
◆ **take up** *vt fus* **-1.** [begin - acting, singing] começar a se dedicar a; [- post, job] assumir **-2.** [continue] prosseguir **-3.** [discuss further] voltar a discutir **-4.** [use up - time] tomar; [- space] ocupar; [- effort] exigir.
◆ **take up on** *vt sep* **-1.** [an offer] aceitar **-2.** [ask to explain]: **I'd like to ~ you up on that point** gostaria que você explicassemelhor esse ponto.
◆ **take upon** *vt sep*: **to ~ it upon o.s. to do sthg** permitir-se fazer algo.

takeaway *UK* ['teɪkəˌweɪ], **takeout** *US* ['teɪkaʊt] <> *n* **-1.** [shop] *estabelecimento que vende comida para levar* **-2.** [food] comida *f* para levar. <> *comp* [food] para levar.
take-home pay *n (U)* salário *m* líquido.
taken ['teɪkn] <> *pp* ▻ **take**. <> *adj* [pleased]: **~ with sb/sthg** contente com alguém/algo.
takeoff ['teɪkɒf] *n* decolagem *f*.
takeout *n US* = **takeaway**.
takeover ['teɪkˌəʊvəʳ] *n* **-1.** [of company] aquisição *f* **-2.** [of government] tomada *f* do poder.
takeover bid *n* oferta *f* pública de compra de ações.
taker ['teɪkəʳ] *n* interessado *m*, -da *f*.
takeup ['teɪkʌp] *n* [of shares] resposta *f*.
taking *adj dated* gracioso(sa).
takings *npl* féria *f*, arrecadação *f*.
talc [tælk], **talcum (powder)** ['tælkəm-] *n (U)* talco *m*.
tale [teɪl] *n* **-1.** [fictional story] conto *m* **-2.** [anecdote] história *f*.
talent ['tælənt] *n*: **~ (for sthg)** talento *m* (para algo).
talented ['tæləntɪd] *adj* talentoso(sa).
talent scout *n* caçador *m*, -ra *f* de talentos.
talisman ['tælɪzmən] (*pl* **-s**) *n* talismã *m*.
talk [tɔ:k] <> *n* **-1.** [conversation] conversa *f* **-2.** *(U)* [gossip] boatos *mpl*, falatório *m* **-3.** [lecture] palestra *f*. <> *vi* **-1.** [gen] falar; **to ~ to sb** falar *OR* conversar com alguém; **to ~ about sb/sthg** falar sobre alguém/algo; **~ing of sb/sthg, ...** falando de alguém/algo, ..., por falar em alguém/algo, ...; **to ~ big** contar vantagem **-2.** [gossip] fofocar **-3.** [make a speech] dar palestra; **to ~ on** *OR* **about sthg** falar sobre algo. <> *vt* **-1.** [discuss] tratar de **-2.** [spout] falar.
◆ **talks** *npl* negociações *fpl*.
◆ **talk down to** *vt fus* desmerecer.
◆ **talk into** *vt sep*: **to ~ sb into sthg/into doing sthg** convencer alguém de algo/a fazer algo.
◆ **talk out of** *vt sep*: **to ~ sb out of sthg/out of doing sthg** dissuadir alguém de algo/de fazer algo.
◆ **talk over** *vt sep* discutir.

talkative ['tɔ:kətɪv] *adj* loquaz.
talker ['tɔ:kəʳ] *n* orador *m*, -ra *f*.
talking point ['tɔ:kɪŋ-] *n* tema *m* da conversa.
talking-to ['tɔ:kɪŋ-] *n inf* bronca *f*.
talk show *US* <> *n* programa *m* de entrevistas, talk-show *m*. <> *comp* de programa de entrevistas.
talk time *n (U)* [on mobile phone] tempo *m* de conversação.
tall [tɔ:l] *adj* [in height] alto(ta); **she's two metres ~** ela mede dois metros (de altura); **how ~ are you?** qual é a sua altura?
tallboy ['tɔ:lbɔɪ] *n* cômoda *f*.
tall order *n* tarefa *f* impossível.
tall story *n* história *f* fantasiosa.
tally ['tælɪ] (*pl* **-ies**, *pt* & *pp* **-ied**) <> *n* [record] conta *f*; **to keep ~ of sthg** manter registro de algo. <> *vi* [correspond] fechar.
talon ['tælən] *n* garra *f*.
tambourine [ˌtæmbəˈri:n] *n* pandeiro *m*.
tame [teɪm] <> *adj* **-1.** [animal, bird] domesticado(da) **-2.** *pej* [person] parado(da) **-3.** *pej* [unexciting] monótono(na). <> *vt* **-1.** [animal, bird] domesticar **-2.** [person] dominar.
tamely ['teɪmlɪ] *adv* docilmente.
tamer ['teɪməʳ] *n* domador *m*, -ra *f*.
Tamil ['tæmɪl] <> *adj* tâmil. <> *n* **-1.** [person] tâmil *mf* **-2.** [language] tâmil *m*.
tamper ['tæmpəʳ] ◆ **tamper with** *vt fus* **-1.** [gen] mexer em **-2.** [lock] forçar.
tampon ['tæmpɒn] *n* absorvente *m* interno.
tan [tæn] (*pt* & *pp* **-ned**, *cont* **-ning**) <> *adj* castanho(nha). <> *n* bronzeado *m*; **to get a ~** bronzear-se. <> *vi* bronzear-se.
tandem ['tændəm] *n* [bicycle] bicicleta *f* de dois lugares; **in ~** em colaboração com.
tandoori [tænˈdʊərɪ] <> *n (U)* *método indiano de assar a carne em forno de barro.* <> *comp* cozido(da) em forno de barro.

tang [tæŋ] *n* [smell] cheiro *m* forte; [taste] gosto *m* forte.
tangent ['tændʒənt] *n GEOM* tangente *f*; **to go off at a ~** *fig* sair pela tangente.
tangerine [ˌtæn'dʒəri:n] *n* tangerina *f*.
tangible ['tændʒəbl] *adj* tangível.
Tangier [tæn'dʒɪəʳ] *n* Tânger.
tangle ['tæŋgl] <> *n* **-1.** [mass] emaranhado *m* **-2.** *fig* [mess] rolo *m*; **they got into a ~** eles se meteram num rolo. <> *vt*: **to get ~d (up)** emaranhar-se. <> *vi* emaranhar-se.
◆ **tangle with** *vt fus inf* meter-se com.
tangled ['tæŋgld] *adj* **-1.** [gen] emaranhado(da) **-2.** *fig* [life, relationship] enrolado(da).
tango ['tæŋgəʊ] (*pl* **-s**, *pt* & *pp* **-ed**, *cont* **-ing**) <> *n* tango *m*. <> *vi* dançar tango.
tangy ['tæŋɪ] (*compar* **-ier**, *superl* **-iest**) *adj* forte.
tank [tæŋk] *n* tanque *m*.
tankard ['tæŋkəd] *n* canecão *m (para cerveja)*.
tanker ['tæŋkəʳ] *n* **-1.** [ship] navio-tanque *m*; **oil ~** petroleiro *m* **-2.** [truck] caminhão-tanque *m* **-3.** [train] vagão-tanque *m*.
tankful ['tæŋkfʊl] *n* tanque *m*.
tanned [tænd] *adj* bronzeado(da).
tannin ['tænɪn] *n (U)* tanino *m*.
Tannoy® ['tænɔɪ] *n* alto-falante *m*.
tantalize, -ise ['tæntəlaɪz] *vt* tentar, provocar.
tantalizing ['tæntəlaɪzɪŋ] *adj* tentador(ra).
tantamount ['tæntəmaʊnt] *adj*: **~ to sthg** equivalente a algo.
tantrum ['tæntrəm] (*pl* **-s**) *n* acesso *m* de fúria.
Tanzania [ˌtænzə'nɪə] *n* Tanzânia; **in ~** na Tanzânia.
Tanzanian [ˌtænzə'nɪən] <> *adj* tanzaniano(na). <> *n* tanzaniano *m*, -na *f*.
Taoiseach *n primeiro ministro da República da Irlanda*.
tap [tæp] (*pt* & *pp* **-ped**, *cont* **-ping**) <> *n* **-1.** [device] torneira *f* **-2.** [light blow] batida *f* leve, palmadinha *f*. <> *vt* **-1.** [knock] bater de leve; **to ~ one's fingers on sthg** tamborilar em algo **-2.** [make use of] utilizar **-3.** [listen secretly to] grampear. <> *vi* bater.
tap dance *n* sapateado *m*.
tap dancer *n* sapateador *m*, -ra *f*.
tape [teɪp] <> *n* **-1.** [gen] fita *f* **-2.** *SPORT* [at finishing line] fita *f* de chegada **-3.** [adhesive material] fita *f* adesiva. <> *vt* **-1.** [record] gravar **-2.** [fasten with adhesive tape] juntar com fita adesiva **-3.** *US* [bandage] enfaixar.
tape deck *n* deck *m*.
tape measure *n* fita *f* métrica.
taper ['teɪpəʳ] <> *n* vela *f* fina. <> *vi* estreitar-se, afilar-se.
◆ **taper off** *vi* ir diminuindo.
tape-record [-rɪˌkɔ:d] *vt* gravar.
tape recorder *n* gravador *m*.
tape recording *n* gravação *f*.
tapered ['teɪpəd] *adj* afilado(da).
tapestry ['tæpɪstrɪ] (*pl* **-ies**) *n* **-1.** [gen] tapeçaria *f* **-2.** *fig* [of life] trama *f*.
tapeworm ['teɪpwɜ:m] *n* solitária *f*.
tapioca [ˌtæpɪ'əʊkə] *n (U)* tapioca *f*.
tapir ['teɪpəʳ] (*pl inv OR* **-s**) *n* anta *f*, tapir *m*.
tappet *n* tucho *m*.
tar [tɑ:ʳ] *n (U)* alcatrão *m*.
tarantula [tə'ræntjʊlə] *n* tarântula *f*.
target ['tɑ:gɪt] <> *n* **-1.** [gen] alvo *m* **-2.** *fig* [goal] meta *f*; **to be on ~ to do sthg** fazer algo de acordo com o previsto. <> *vt* **-1.** [as object of attack] mirar **-2.** [as customer] visar.
tariff ['tærɪf] *n* **-1.** [tax] tarifa *f* **-2.** *UK* [price list] tabela *f* de preços.
Tarmac® ['tɑ:mæk] *n* alcatrão *m*.
◆ **tarmac** *n AERON*: **the tarmac** a pista.
tarnish ['tɑ:nɪʃ] <> *vt* **-1.** [make dull] embaciar **-2.** *fig* [damage] manchar. <> *vi* [become dull] embaciar.
tarnished ['tɑ:nɪʃt] *adj* **-1.** [dull] embaciado(da) **-2.** *fig* [damaged] manchado(da).
tarot ['tærəʊ] *n*: **the ~** o tarô.
tarot card *n* carta *f* de tarô.
tarpaulin [tɑ:'pɔ:lɪn] *n* **-1.** *(U)* [material] encerado *m* **-2.** [sheet] lona *f* alcatroada.
tarragon ['tærəgən] *n (U)* estragão *m*.
tart [tɑ:t] <> *adj* **-1.** [bitter-tasting] azedo(da) **-2.** [sarcastic] mordaz. <> *n* **-1.** [sweet pastry] torta *f* **-2.** *UK vinf* [prostitute] piranha *f*.
◆ **tart up** *vt sep UK inf pej* [smarten up]: **to ~ o.s. up** emperiquitar-se.
tartan ['tɑ:tn] <> *n* **-1.** [pattern] xadrez *m* **-2.** *(U)* [cloth] tartan *m*. <> *comp* de tartan.
tartar *n* tártaro *m*.
tartar(e) sauce ['tɑ:təʳ-] *n (U)* molho *m* tártaro.
tartness ['tɑ:tnɪs] *n (U)* **-1.** [of taste] acidez *f* **-2.** [of comment] mordacidade *f*.
task [tɑ:sk] *n* tarefa *f*.
task force *n* força-tarefa *f*.
taskmaster ['tɑ:skˌmɑ:stəʳ] *n* capataz *m*; **a hard ~** um tirano.
Tasmania [tæz'meɪnjə] *n* Tasmânia.
Tasmanian [tæz'meɪnjən] <> *adj* tasmaniano(na). <> *n* tasmaniano *m*, -na *f*.
tassel ['tæsl] *n* borla *f*.
taste [teɪst] <> *n* **-1.** [gen] gosto *m*; **in bad/good ~** de mau/bom gosto **-2.** *fig* [liking, preference]: **~ (for sthg)** gosto (por algo) **-3.** *fig* [experience]: **I've had a ~ of success** eu senti o gostinho do sucesso **-4.** *(U)* [sense of taste] paladar *m* **-5.** [try]: **have a ~** dá uma provada. <> *vt* **-1.** [gen] sentir o gosto de **-2.** [test, try] provar. <> *vi*: **it ~s horrible** tem um gosto horrível; **to ~ of/like sthg** ter gosto de algo.
taste bud *n* papila *f* gustativa.
tasteful ['teɪstfʊl] *adj* de bom gosto.
tastefully ['teɪstfʊlɪ] *adv* com bom gosto.
tasteless ['teɪstlɪs] *adj* **-1.** [cheap and unattractive] sem graça **-2.** [offensive] de mau gosto **-3.** [without flavour] sem gosto.
taster ['teɪstəʳ] *n* degustador *m*, -ra *f*.
tasty ['teɪstɪ] (*compar* **-ier**, *superl* **-iest**) *adj* saboroso(-sa).
tat [tæt] *n (U) UK inf pej* bugigangas *fpl*.
tattered ['tætəd] *adj* **-1.** [clothes] esfarrapado(da) **-2.** [paper] gasto(ta).
tatters ['tætəz] *npl*: **in ~** [clothes] em farrapos; *fig* [confidence, reputation] em frangalhos.

tattle-tale *n US* = **telltale**.
tattoo [tə'tu:] (*pl* **-s**) ◇ *n* **-1.** [design] tatuagem *f* **-2.** [rhythmic beating] rufar *m* de tambores **-3.** *UK* [military display] parada *f* OR desfile *m* militar. ◇ *vt* tatuar.
tattooist [tə'tu:ɪst] *n* tatuador *m*, -ra *f*.
tatty ['tætɪ] (*compar* **-ier**, *superl* **-iest**) *adj UK inf pej* **-1.** [clothes] surrado(da) **-2.** [area] enxovalhado(da).
taught [tɔ:t] *pt & pp* ▷ **teach**.
taunt [tɔ:nt] ◇ *n* insulto *m*. ◇ *vt* insultar.
Taurus ['tɔ:rəs] *n* **-1.** [sign] Touro *m* **-2.** [person] taurino(na); **I'm ~** sou de Touro.
taut [tɔ:t] *adj* retesado(da).
tauten ['tɔ:tn] ◇ *vt* retesar. ◇ *vi* retesar.
tautology [tɔ:'tɒlədʒɪ] *n* tautologia *f*.
tavern ['tævn] *n dated* taberna *f*.
tawdry ['tɔ:drɪ] (*compar* **-ier**, *superl* **-iest**) *adj pej* de mau gosto.
tawny ['tɔ:nɪ] *adj* fulvo(va).
tax [tæks] ◇ *n* imposto *m*. ◇ *vt* **-1.** [gen] tributar **-2.** [strain, test] esgotar.
taxable ['tæksəbl] *adj* tributável.
tax allowance *n* limite *m* de isenção fiscal.
taxation [tæk'seɪʃn] *n (U)* **-1.** [system] sistema *m* tributário **-2.** [amount] tributação *f*.
tax avoidance [-ə'vɔɪdəns] *n (U)* dedução *f* fiscal.
tax collector *n* cobrador *m*, -ra *f* de impostos.
tax cut *n* redução *f* tributária.
tax-deductible [-dɪ'dʌktəbl] *adj* dedutível.
tax disc *n UK disco fixado no pára-brisa do veículo para mostrar que o imposto já foi pago.*
tax evasion *n (U)* sonegação *f* de impostos.
tax-exempt *adj US* = **tax-free**.
tax exemption *n (U)* isenção *f* de impostos.
tax exile *n UK pessoa que vive no exterior para evitar o pagamento de impostos.*
tax-free *UK*, **tax-exempt** *US adj* isento(ta) de imposto.
tax haven *n* paraíso *m* fiscal.
taxi ['tæksɪ] ◇ *n* táxi *m*. ◇ *vi* taxiar.
taxicab ['tæksɪkæb] *n* táxi *m*.
taxidermist ['tæksɪdɜ:mɪst] *n* empalhador *m*, -ra *f*.
taxi driver *n* motorista *mf* de táxi, taxista *mf*.
taximeter *n* taxímetro *m*.
taxing ['tæksɪŋ] *adj* árduo(a).
tax inspector *n* inspetor *m*, -ra *f* da Receita.
taxi rank *UK*, **taxi stand** *n* ponto *m* de táxi.
taxman ['tæksmæn] (*pl* **-men** [-men]) *n* **-1.** [tax collector] coletor *m* de impostos **-2.** *inf* [tax office]: **the ~** ≃ o Leão, ≃ o Fisco.
taxpayer ['tæks,peɪəʳ] *n* contribuinte *mf*.
tax relief *n (U)* dedução *f* tributária.
tax return *n* declaração *f* de renda.
tax year *n* ano *m* fiscal.
TB (*abbr of* **tuberculosis**) *n* tuberculose *f*.
T-bone steak *n* bisteca *f* de boi.
tbs., tbsp. (*abbr of* **tablespoon(ful)**) colher *f* de sopa.
TD *n* **-1.** (*abbr of* **Treasury Department**) *departamento do tesouro norte-americano* **-2.** (*abbr of* **touchdown**) *jogada do futebol norte-americano e do rugby.*

tea [ti:] *n* **-1.** [gen] chá *m* **-2.** *UK* [afternoon meal] lanche *m* **-3.** *UK* [evening meal] chá *m*.
teabag ['ti:bæg] *n* saquinho *m* de chá.
tea ball *n US esfera metálica perfurada na qual são colocadas as folhas de chá para infusão.*
tea break *n UK* pausa *f* para o chá.
tea caddy [-,kædɪ] *n* caixa *f* para chá.
teacake ['ti:keɪk] *n UK* bolinho *m (que acompanha o chá).*
teach [ti:tʃ] (*pt & pp* **taught**) ◇ *vt* **-1.** [instruct] ensinar; **to ~ sb sthg, to ~ sthg to sb** ensinar algo a alguém; **to ~ sb to do sthg** ensinar alguém a fazer algo; **to ~ (sb) that** ensinar (a alguém) que **-2.** [give lessons in] dar aulas de **-3.** [advocate] preconizar. ◇ *vi* lecionar.
teacher ['ti:tʃəʳ] *n* professor *m*, -ra *f*.
teachers college *n US* = **teacher training college**.
teacher's pet *n pej* queridinho *m*, -nha *f* da classe.
teacher training college *UK*, **teachers college** *US n* curso *f* de licenciatura.
teaching ['ti:tʃɪŋ] *n* **-1.** *(U)* [profession, work] magistério *m* **-2.** [thing taught] ensinamento *m*.
teaching aid *n* material *m* pedagógico.
teaching hospital *n UK* hospital-escola *m*.
teaching practice *n (U)* prática *f* de ensino.
teaching staff *n* corpo *m* docente.
tea cloth *n* **-1.** [tablecloth] toalha *f* de mesa **-2.** [tea towel] pano *m* de prato.
tea cosy *UK*, **tea cozy** *US n* abafador *m (de chá).*
teacup ['ti:kʌp] *n* xícara *f* de chá.
teak [ti:k] ◇ *n (U)* teca *f*. ◇ *comp* de teca.
tealeaves *npl* borra *f* de chá.
team [ti:m] *n* **-1.** SPORT time *m* **-2.** [group] equipe *f*.
◆ **team up** *vi* montar uma equipe; **to ~ up with sb** associar-se a alguém.
team game *n* esporte *m* de equipe.
teammate ['ti:mmeɪt] *n* companheiro *m*, -ra *f* de equipe.
team spirit *n (U)* espírito *m* de equipe.
teamster ['ti:mstəʳ] *n US* caminhoneiro *m*, -ra *f*.
teamwork ['ti:mwɜ:k] *n (U)* trabalho *m* em equipe.
tea party *n* chá *m* da tarde.
teapot ['ti:pɒt] *n* bule *m* de chá.
tear¹ [tɪəʳ] *n* lágrima *f*; **in ~s** aos prantos; **to burst into ~s** debulhar-se em lágrimas.
tear² [teəʳ] (*pt* **tore**, *pp* **torn**) ◇ *vt* **-1.** [rip] rasgar; **to ~ sthg open** abrir algo rasgando; **to ~ sb/sthg to pieces** *fig* [criticize] demolir alguém/algo; **to be torn between** *fig* estar dividido(da) entre **-2.** [remove roughly] arrancar. ◇ *vi* **-1.** [rip] rasgar **-2.** *inf* [move quickly] ir a toda **-3.** *phr*: **to ~ loose** [get free] soltar-se. ◇ *n* [rip] rasgão *m*.
◆ **tear apart** *vt sep* **-1.** [rip up] destroçar **-2.** *fig* [disrupt greatly] desmantelar **-3.** [upset greatly] magoar.
◆ **tear at** *vt fus* avançar contra.
◆ **tear away** *vt sep*: **to ~ o.s. away (from sthg)** desvencilhar-se (de algo).
◆ **tear down** *vt sep* **-1.** [demolish] demolir **-2.** [remove] remover.
◆ **tear off** *vt sep* [clothes] arrancar.
◆ **tear out** *vt sep* [coupon, page] arrancar.

◆ **tear up** *vt sep* despedaçar, fazer em pedaços.
tearaway ['teərə,weɪ] *n UK inf* arruaceiro *m*, -ra *f*.
teardrop ['tɪədrɒp] *n* lágrima *f*.
tearful ['tɪəfʊl] *adj* **-1.** [person] choroso(rosa) **-2.** [event] triste.
tear gas [tɪəʳ-] *n (U)* gás *m* lacrimogêneo.
tearing ['teərɪŋ] *adj inf* apressado(da).
tear jerker *n hum* dramalhão *m*.
tearoom ['ti:rʊm] *n* salão *f* de chá.
tease [ti:z] ◇ *n inf* **-1.** [joker] gozador *m*, -ra *f* **-2.** [sexually] provocador *m*, -ra *f*. ◇ *vt*: **to ~ sb (about sthg)** gozar de alguém (sobre algo).
tea shop *n* casa *f* de chá.
teasing ['ti:zɪŋ] *adj* importuno(na).
teaspoon ['ti:spu:n] *n* colher *f* de chá.
tea strainer *n* coador *m* de chá.
teat [ti:t] *n* **-1.** [of animal] teta *f* **-2.** [of bottle] bico *m*.
teatime ['ti:taɪm] *n (U) UK* hora *f* do chá.
tea towel *n* pano *m* de prato.
tea urn *n cilindro dotado de torneira usado para preparar grandes quantidades de chá.*
technical ['teknɪkl] *adj* técnico(ca).
technical college *n UK* escola *f* técnica.
technical drawing *n (U)* desenho *m* técnico.
technicality [,teknɪ'kælətɪ] (*pl* **-ies**) *n* detalhe *m* técnico.
technically ['teknɪklɪ] *adv* tecnicamente.
technician [tek'nɪʃn] *n* **-1.** [worker] técnico *m*, -ca *f* **-2.** [artist] especialista *mf*.
Technicolor® ['teknɪ,kʌləʳ] *n (U)* tecnicolor® *m*.
technique [tek'ni:k] *n* técnica *f*.
techno ['teknəʊ] *n MUS* tecno *m*.
technocrat ['teknəʊkræt] *n* tecnocrata *mf*.
technological [,teknə'lɒdʒɪkl] *adj* tecnológico(ca).
technologist [tek'nɒlədʒɪst] *n* tecnologista *mf*, tecnólogo *m*, -ga *f*.
technology [tek'nɒlədʒɪ] (*pl* **-ies**) *n* tecnologia *f*.
teddy ['tedɪ] (*pl* **-ies**) *n*: **~ (bear)** ursinho *m* de pelúcia.
tedious ['ti:djəs] *adj* tedioso(sa).
tedium ['ti:djəm] *n fml* tédio *m*.
tee [ti:] *n GOLF* **-1.** [area] tee *m*, ponto *m* de partida **-2.** [for ball] tee *m*.
◆ **tee off** *vi GOLF* dar a tacada inicial.
teem [ti:m] *vi* **-1.** [rain] chover torrencialmente; **the rain ~ed down** caiu uma chuva torrencial **-2.** [be busy]: **to be ~ing with** estar inundado(da) de.
teen [ti:n] *adj inf* adolescente.
teenage ['ti:neɪdʒ] *adj* adolescente.
teenager ['ti:n,eɪdʒəʳ] *n* adolescente *mf*.
teens [ti:nz] *npl* adolescência *f*.
teeny (weeny) [,ti:nɪ('wi:nɪ)], **teensy (weensy)** [,ti:nzɪ('wi:nzɪ)] *adj inf* pequenininho(-nha).
tee shirt *n* camiseta *f*.
teeter ['ti:təʳ] *vi* **-1.** [wobble] balançar, oscilar **-2.** *fig* [be in danger]: **to ~ on the brink of bankruptcy** estar à beira da falência.
teeter-totter *n US* gangorra *f*.
teeth [ti:θ] *pl* ▷ **tooth**.
teethe [ti:ð] *vi* começar a ter dentes.
teething ring ['ti:ðɪŋ-] *n* mordedor *m*.
teething troubles ['ti:ðɪŋ-] *npl fig* dificuldades *fpl* iniciais.
teetotal [ti:'təʊtl] *adj* abstêmio(mia).
teetotaller *UK*, **teetotaler** *US* [ti:'təʊtləʳ] *n* abstêmio *m*, -mia *f*.
TEFL ['tefl] (*abbr of* **teaching of English as a foreign language**) *n ensino de inglês para estrangeiros.*
Teflon® ['teflɒn] ◇ *n (U)* teflon® *m*. ◇ *comp* de teflon®.
Teh(e)ran *n* Teerã.
tel. (*abbr of* **telephone**) tel. *m*.
Tel-Aviv [,telə'vi:v] *n*: **~ (-Jaffa)** Tel-Aviv(-Jafa).
tele- ['telɪ] *prefix* [over a distance] tele-.
telecast ['telɪkɑ:st] *n* programa *m* de televisão.
telecom ['telɪkɒm] *n UK*, **telecoms** ['telɪkɒmz] *npl inf* telecom.
telecommunications ['telɪkə,mju:nɪ'keɪʃnz] *npl* telecomunicações *fpl*.
telecon (*abbr of* **telephone conversation**) *n*.
telegram ['telɪgræm] *n* telegrama *m*.
telegraph ['telɪgrɑ:f] ◇ *n* telégrafo *m*. ◇ *vt* telegrafar.
telegraph pole, telegraph post *UK n* poste *m* de telégrafo.
telepathic [,telɪ'pæθɪk] *adj* telepático(ca).
telepathy [tɪ'lepəθɪ] *n (U)* telepatia *f*.
telephone ['telɪfəʊn] ◇ *n (U)* telefone *m*; **to be on the ~** *UK* [have a telephone line] ter telefone; [be talking on the telephone] estar no telefone. ◇ *vt* telefonar. ◇ *vi* telefonar.
telephone banking *n* serviço *m* de banco por telefone.
telephone book *n* lista *f* telefônica.
telephone booth *n UK* telefone *m* público.
telephone box *n UK* cabine *f* telefônica.
telephone call *n* telefonema *m*.
telephone directory *n* lista *f* telefônica.
telephone exchange *n* central *f* telefônica.
telephone kiosk *n UK* cabine *f* telefônica.
telephone line *n* linha *f* de telefone.
telephone number *n* número *m* de telefone.
telephone operator *n* telefonista *mf*.
telephone tapping *n (U)* escuta *f* telefônica.
telephonist [tɪ'lefənɪst] *n UK* telefonista *mf*.
telephoto lens [,telɪ'fəʊtəʊ-] *n* (lente *f*) teleobjetiva *f*.
teleprinter ['telɪ,prɪntəʳ], **teletypewriter** *US* [,telɪ'taɪp,raɪtəʳ] *n* teleimpressor *m*, teletipo *m*.
Teleprompter® [,telɪ'prɒmptəʳ] *n* teleprompter *m*.
telesales ['telɪseɪlz] *npl* televendas *fpl*.
telescope ['telɪskəʊp] *n* telescópio *m*.
telescopic [,telɪ'skɒpɪk] *adj* telescópico(ca).
teleshopping *n* telecompras *fpl*.
teletext ['telɪtekst] *n (U)* teletexto *m*.
telethon ['telɪθɒn] *n* teleton *m*.
teletypewriter *n US* = **teleprinter**.
televideo [telɪ'vɪdɪəʊ] *n* televisor *m* com videocassete.
televise ['telɪvaɪz] *vt* televisionar.
television ['telɪ,vɪʒn] *n* televisão *f*; **on ~** na televisão.

television licence *n UK* *taxa paga ao governo para ter acesso à televisão.*

television programme *n* programa *f* de televisão.

television set *n* (aparelho *m* de) televisão *f.*

teleworker ['telıwɜ:kəʳ] *n* teletrabalhador *m*, -ra *f.*

teleworking *n* teletrabalho *m.*

telex ['teleks] ◇ *n* telex *m.* ◇ *vt* transmitir por telex.

tell [tel] (*pt* & *pp* **told**) ◇ *vt* **-1.** [gen] contar; **to ~ sb (that)** contar a alguém que; **to ~ sb sthg, to ~ sthg to sb** contar algo a alguém; **I told you so!** eu te falei! **-2.** [instruct, judge, reveal] dizer; **do as you're told!** faça como lhe disseram!; **to ~ sb to do sthg** dizer para alguém fazer algo; **to ~ sb (that)** dizer a alguém que; **to ~ what sb is thinking** saber o que alguém está pensando; **there's no ~ing ...** nunca se sabe ... ◇ *vi* **-1.** [speak] falar **-2.** [judge] dizer **-3.** [have effect] surtir efeito.

◆ **tell apart** *vt sep* distinguir, diferenciar.

◆ **tell off** *vt sep* repreender.

teller ['teləʳ] *n* **-1.** [of votes] escrutinador *m*, -ra *f* **-2.** [in bank] caixa *mf.*

telling ['telıŋ] *adj* **-1.** [relevant] contundente **-2.** [revealing] revelador(ra).

telling-off (*pl* **tellings-off**) *n* bronca *f.*

telltale ['telteıl] ◇ *adj* revelador(ra). ◇ *n* mexeriqueiro *m*, -ra *f.*

telly ['telı] (*pl* **-ies**) *n UK inf* televisão *f*; **on ~** na televisão.

temerity [tı'merətı] *n (U) fml* temeridade *f.*

temp *UK* [temp] *inf* ◇ *n* (*abbr of* **temporary (employee)**) funcionário *m* temporário, funcionária *f* temporária. ◇ *vi* trabalhar em emprego temporário.

temp. (*abbr of* **temperature**) temp. *f.*

temper ['tempəʳ] ◇ *n* **-1.** [state of mind, mood] humor *m*; **to be in a good/bad ~** estar de bom/mau humor; **to lose one's ~** perder a cabeça; **to have a short ~** ter pavio curto **-2.** [temperament] temperamento *m.* ◇ *vt fml* controlar, conter.

temperament ['temprəmənt] *n* temperamento *m.*

temperamental [,temprə'mentl] *adj* temperamental.

temperance ['temprəns] *n (U)* **-1.** *fml* [moderation] temperança *f* **-2.** [not drinking alcohol] abstinência *f.*

temperate ['temprət] *adj* temperado(da).

temperature ['temprətʃəʳ] *n* temperatura *f*; **to have a ~** ter febre; **to take sb's ~** tirar a temperatura de alguém.

tempered ['tempəd] *adj* contido(da), comedido(-da).

tempest ['tempıst] *n literary* tempestade *f.*

tempestuous [tem'pestjʊəs] *adj* **-1.** *literary* [stormy] turbulento(ta) **-2.** *fig* [emotional] tempestuoso(sa).

tempi ['tempi:] *pl* ▷ **tempo.**

template ['templıt] *n* **-1.** [of shape, pattern] molde *m*, modelo *m* **-2.** COMPUT gabarito *m.*

temple ['templ] *n* **-1.** RELIG templo *m* **-2.** ANAT têmpora *f.*

templet *n* = **template.**

tempo ['tempəʊ] (*pl* **-pos** OR **-pi**) *n* **-1.** MUS ritmo *m*, velocidade *f* **-2.** [of an event] tempo *m.*

temporarily [,tempə'rerəlı] *adv* temporariamente.

temporary ['tempərərı] *adj* temporário(ria).

tempt [tempt] *vt* tentar; **to ~ sb to do sthg** tentar alguém a fazer algo; **to be** OR **feel ~ed to do sthg** estar/sentir-se tentado(da) a fazer algo.

temptation [temp'teıʃn] *n* tentação *f.*

tempting ['temptıŋ] *adj* tentador(ra).

ten [ten] *num* dez; *see also* **six.**

tenable ['tenəbl] *adj* **-1.** [reasonable, credible] sustentável **-2.** [job, post] seguro(ra), estável; **the post is ~ for one year** o cargo terá duração de um ano.

tenacious [tı'neıʃəs] *adj* tenaz.

tenacity [tı'næsətı] *n (U)* tenacidade *f.*

tenancy ['tenənsı] (*pl* **-ies**) *n* **-1.** [period] aluguel *m* **-2.** *(U)* [possession] locação *f.*

tenant ['tenənt] *n* **-1.** [of a house] inquilino *m*, -na *f* **-2.** [of a pub] locatário *m*, -ria *f.*

Ten Commandments *npl*: **the ~** os Dez Mandamentos.

tend [tend] *vt* **-1.** [have tendency]: **to ~ to do sthg** ter a tendência a fazer algo; **I ~ to think (that) ...** sou levado(da) a crer que ... **-2.** [look after] cuidar.

tendency ['tendənsı] (*pl* **-ies**) *n* **-1.** [gen]: **~ towards sthg/to do sthg** tendência *f* a algo/a fazer algo; **~ towards sthg** tendência *f* a algo **-2.** [leaning, habit] tendência *f.*

tender ['tendəʳ] ◇ *adj* **-1.** [caring, gentle] terno(na), meigo(ga) **-2.** [meat] macio(cia) **-3.** [sore] dolorido(-da) **-4.** [young, innocent]: **at a ~ age** em tenra idade. ◇ *n* COMM proposta *f*, oferta *f.* ◇ *vt fml* oferecer.

tenderize, -ise ['tendəraız] *vt* amaciar.

tenderly ['tendəlı] *adv* carinhosamente.

tenderness ['tendənıs] *n (U)* **-1.** [care, compassion] ternura *f*, meiguice *f* **-2.** [soreness] sensibilidade *f.*

tendon ['tendən] *n* tendão *m.*

tendril ['tendrəl] *n* gavinha *f.*

tenement ['tenəmənt] *n* cortiço *m.*

Tenerife *n* Tenerife; **in ~** em Tenerife.

tenet ['tenıt] *n fml* dogma *m.*

tenner ['tenəʳ] *n* *UK inf* **-1.** [amount]: **it cost a ~** custou dez libras **-2.** [note] nota *f* de dez libras.

Tennessee *n* Tennessee.

tennis ['tenıs] ◇ *n (U)* tênis *m.* ◇ *comp* de tênis.

tennis ball *n* bola *f* de tênis.

tennis court *n* quadra *f* de tênis.

tennis player *n* jogador *m*, -ra *f* de tênis.

tennis racket *n* raquete *f* de tênis.

tenor ['tenəʳ] ◇ *adj* de tenor. ◇ *n* **-1.** [singer] tenor *m* **-2.** *fml* [meaning, mood] teor *m.*

tenpin bowling *UK* ['tenpın-], **tenpins** *US* ['tenpınz] *n (U)* boliche *m* (com dez pinos).

tense [tens] ◇ *adj* tenso(sa). ◇ *n* GRAMM tempo *m* (verbal). ◇ *vt* tencionar, retesar. ◇ *vi* endurecer-se.

tensed up [tenst-] *adj* tenso(sa).

tension ['tenʃn] *n* tensão *f.*

◆ **tensions** *npl* conflitos *mpl.*

ten-spot *n US* nota *f* de dez dólares.

tent [tent] *n* tenda *f*, barraca *f.*

tentacle ['tentəkl] *n* tentáculo *m.*

tentative ['tentətɪv] *adj* **-1.** [unconfident, hesitant - person] indeciso(sa); [- handshake] vacilante **-2.** [temporary, not final] provisório(ria).
tentatively ['tentətɪvlɪ] *adv* **-1.** [hesitantly] hesitantemente **-2.** [not finally] provisoriamente.
tenterhooks ['tentəhʊks] *npl*: **to be on ~** estar com os nervos à flor da pele.
tenth [tenθ] *num* décimo(ma); *see also* **sixth**.
tent peg *n* estaca *f* de barraca.
tent pole *n* mastro *m* de barraca.
tenuous ['tenjʊəs] *adj* **-1.** [argument] pouco convincente **-2.** [connection] de pouca importância **-3.** [hold] tênue.
tenuously ['tenjʊəslɪ] *adv* sutilmente.
tenure ['tenjə^r] *n (U) fml* **-1.** [of property] posse *f* **-2.** [of job] estabilidade *f*.
tepee ['ti:pi:] *n* tenda *f* indígena.
tepid ['tepɪd] *adj* **-1.** [liquid] tépido(da), morno(na) **-2.** *pej* [lacking gusto] morno(na).
tequila [tɪ'ki:lə] *n* tequila *f*.
Ter. *abbr of* **terrace**.
term [tɜ:m] ◇ *n* **-1.** [word, expression] termo *m* **-2.** *SCH & UNIV* [third of school year] semestre *m* **-3.** *POL* [period in political office]: **~ (of office)** mandato *m* **-4.** [stretch of time] período *m*; **in the long/short ~** a longo/curto prazo. ◇ *vt* designar.
◆ **terms** *npl* **-1.** [of contract, agreement] termos *mpl* **-2.** [conditions]: **in international/real ~s** em termos internacionais/reais **-3.** [of relationship]: **on equal** *OR* **the same ~s** de igual para igual, em condições de igualdade; **to be on good ~s (with sb)** dar-se bem (com alguém); **are you on speaking ~s?** vocês estão se falando? **-4.** *phr*: **to come to ~s with sthg** aceitar algo.
◆ **in terms of** *prep* no que diz respeito a; **to think in ~s of doing sthg** pensar em fazer algo.
terminal ['tɜ:mɪnl] ◇ *adj* terminal. ◇ *n* terminal *m*.
terminally ['tɜ:mɪnəlɪ] *adv*: **to be ~ ill** ser um doente (em fase) terminal.
terminate ['tɜ:mɪneɪt] ◇ *vt* **-1.** [agreement, discussion] *fml* pôr fim a, encerrar **-2.** [pregnancy] interromper **-3.** [contract] rescindir. ◇ *vi* **-1.** [bus, train]: **this bus ~s in the city centre** este ônibus pára no centro na cidade **-2.** [contract] terminar.
termination [,tɜ:mɪ'neɪʃn] *n* **-1.** *(U) fml* [ending] término *m* **-2.** [abortion] interrupção *f* da gravidez.
termini ['tɜ:mɪnaɪ] *pl* ▷ **terminus**.
terminology [,tɜ:mɪ'nɒlədʒɪ] *n* terminologia *f*.
terminus ['tɜ:mɪnəs] (*pl* **-ni** *OR* **-nuses**) *n* terminal *m*.
termite ['tɜ:maɪt] *n* cupim *m*.
terrace ['terəs] *n* **-1.** *UK* [of houses] fileira *f* de casas geminadas **-2.** [patio] terraço *m* **-3.** [on hillside] terraço *m*, socalco *m*.
◆ **terraces** *npl FTBL*: **the ~s** as arquibancadas.
terraced ['terəst] *adj* escalonado(da).
terraced house *n UK* casa *f* geminada.
terracotta [,terə'kɒtə] *n (U)* terracota *f*.
terrain [te'reɪn] *n (U)* terreno *m*.
terrapin ['terəpɪn] (*pl inv OR* **-s**) *n* tartaruga *f* aquática.
terrestrial [tə'restrɪəl] *adj fml* terrestre.
terrible ['terəbl] *adj* terrível.
terribly ['terəblɪ] *adv* **-1.** [very badly] terrivelmente **-2.** [extremely] imensamente.
terrier ['terɪə^r] *n* terrier *m*.
terrific [tə'rɪfɪk] *adj* **-1.** [wonderful] fabuloso(sa), maravilhoso(so) **-2.** [enormous] enorme.
terrified ['terɪfaɪd] *adj*: **~ (of sb/sthg)** aterrorizado(da) (com alguém/algo); **to be ~ of sthg** ter horror a algo.
terrify ['terɪfaɪ] (*pt & pp* **-ied**) *vt* aterrorizar.
terrifying ['terɪfaɪɪŋ] *adj* aterrorizante.
terrine [te'ri:n] *n* terrina *f*.
territorial [,terɪ'tɔ:rɪəl] *adj* territorial.
Territorial Army *n UK*: **the ~** *o exército voluntário da Grã-Bretanha*.
territorial waters *npl* águas *fpl* territoriais.
territory ['terətrɪ] (*pl* **-ies**) *n* **-1.** [political area] território *m* **-2.** [terrain] terreno *m* **-3.** [area of knowledge] campo *m*, área *f*.
terror ['terə^r] *n* **-1.** *(U)* [fear] terror *m* **-2.** [something feared] horror *m* **-3.** *inf* [rascal] pestinha *mf*.
terrorism ['terərɪzm] *n (U)* terrorismo *m*.
terrorist ['terərɪst] *n* terrorista *mf*.
terrorize, -ise ['terəraɪz] *vt* aterrorizar.
terror-stricken *adj* em pânico, aterrorizado(-da).
terry (cloth) *n (U)* tecido *m* atoalhado.
terse [tɜ:s] *adj* seco(ca).
tersely ['tɜ:slɪ] *adv* secamente.
tertiary ['tɜ:ʃərɪ] *adj fml* terciário(ria).
tertiary education *n (U)* educação *f* de terceiro grau.
Terylene® ['terəli:n] *n (U)* tergal® *m*.
TES (*abbr of* **Times Education Supplement**) *n suplemento semanal do Times britânico direcionado à educação*.
TESL ['tesl] (*abbr of* **teaching of English as a second language**) *n ensino de inglês como segunda língua*.
TESOL (*abbr of* **teaching of English to speakers of other languages**) *n ensino de inglês para falantes de outras línguas*.
TESSA ['tesə] (*abbr of* **tax-exempt special savings account**) *n sistema de poupança britânica que tem isenção de impostos sobre o juro do capital depositado a prazo fixo*.
test [test] ◇ *n* **-1.** [trial] teste *m*; **to put sb/sthg to the ~** colocar alguém/algo à prova **-2.** [*MED*, examination of knowledge, skill] exame *m*; *SCH* prova *f*, teste *m*. ◇ *vt* **-1.** [try out] testar **-2.** [examine, check] examinar; **to ~ sb on sthg** examinar algo de alguém.
testament ['testəmənt] *n* **-1.** [gen] testamento *m* **-2.** [proof]: **~ to sthg** testemunho *m* de algo.
test ban *n* suspensão *f* de testes nucleares.
test card *n UK* mira *f*.
test case *n JUR* caso *m* precedente.
test-drive *vt* test-drive *m*.
tester ['testə^r] *n* **-1.** [person testing] provador *m*, -ra *f* **-2.** [sample] amostra *f*.
test flight *n* vôo *m* de prova.
testicles ['testɪklz] *npl* testículos *mpl*.
testify ['testɪfaɪ] (*pt & pp* **-ied**) ◇ *vt* declarar; **to ~**

that testemunhar que. <> *vi* **-1.** *JUR* declarar sob juramento **-2.** [be proof]: **to ~ to sthg** evidenciar algo.
testimonial [ˌtestɪˈməʊnjəl] *n* **-1.** [reference] carta *f* de recomendação **-2.** [tribute] homenagem *f*.
testimony [*UK* ˈtestɪmənɪ, *US* ˈtestəməʊnɪ] *n (U)* **-1.** *JUR* depoimento *m*, testemunho *m*; **to bear ~** testemunhar **-2.** [proof, demonstration]: **~ to sthg** testemunho de algo.
testing [ˈtestɪŋ] *adj* [trying, difficult] duro(ra).
testing ground *n* área *f* de testes.
test match *n UK* partida *f* internacional.
testosterone *n* testosterona *f*.
test paper *n* **-1.** *SCH* teste *m* escrito **-2.** *CHEM* papel *m* reativo.
test pattern *n US* padrão *m* de teste.
test pilot *n* piloto *m* de prova.
test tube *n* tubo *m* de ensaio, proveta *f*.
test-tube baby *n* bebê *m* de proveta.
testy [ˈtestɪ] (*compar* **-ier**, *superl* **-iest**) *adj* **-1.** [person] irritadiço(ça) **-2.** [remark, comment] agressivo(va).
tetanus [ˈtetənəs] *n (U)* tétano *m*.
tetchy [ˈtetʃɪ] (*compar* **-ier**, *superl* **-iest**) *adj* irritável, rabugento(ta).
tête-à-tête [ˌteɪtɑːˈteɪt] *n* tête-à-tête *m*.
tether [ˈteðəʳ] <> *vt* **-1.** [horse] apear **-2.** [dog] amarrar. <> *n*: **to be at the end of one's ~** estar no limite.
Texan [ˈteksnl] *n* texano *m*, -na *f*.
Texas [ˈteksəs] *n* Texas.
Tex-Mex *adj* mexicano(na) do Texas.
text [tekst] *n* texto *m*.
textbook [ˈtekstbʊk] *n* livro-texto *m*.
textile [ˈtekstaɪl] <> *n* tecido *m*. <> *comp* **-1.** [industry] têxtil **-2.** [worker] da indústria têxtil.
texting [ˈtekstɪŋ] *n inf* mensagens *fpl* de texto.
text message *n* [on mobile phone] mensagem *m* de texto.
text messaging [-ˈmesɪdʒɪŋ] *n* [on mobile phone] mensagem *f* de texto.
texture [ˈtekstʃəʳ] *n* textura *f*.
Thai [taɪ] <> *adj* tailandês(esa). <> *n* **-1.** [person] tailandês *m*, -esa *f* **-2.** [language] tailandês *m*.
Thailand [ˈtaɪlænd] *n* Tailândia; **in ~** na Tailândia.
thalidomide [θəˈlɪdəmaɪd] *n (U)* talidomida *f*.
Thames [temz] *n*: **the ~** o Tâmisa.
than [*weak form* ðən, *strong form* ðæn] <> *conj* que; **more ~ ten** mais de dez; **I'd rather stay in ~ go out** prefiro ficar em casa a sair.
thank [θæŋk] *vt*: **to ~ sb (for sthg)** agradecer alguém (por algo); **~ God** *OR* **goodness** *OR* **heavens!** graças a Deus/aos céus!
◆ **thanks** <> *npl* agradecimento *m*. <> *excl* obrigado(da)!
◆ **thanks to** *prep* graças a.
thankful [ˈθæŋkfʊl] *adj* agradecido(da); **~ for sthg** agradecido(da) por algo.
thankfully [ˈθæŋkfʊlɪ] *adv* **-1.** [with gratitude] agradecidamente **-2.** [thank goodness] graças a Deus.
thankless [ˈθæŋklɪs] *adj* ingrato(ta).
thanksgiving *n* ação *f* de graças.
◆ **Thanksgiving (Day)** *n* Dia *m* de Ação de Graças.

THANKSGIVING

Nos Estados Unidos, o dia de Ação de Graças, a quarta quinta-feira de novembro, comemora o estabelecimento dos primeiros colonos no país. O almoço em família, que geralmente marca essa data, consiste em peru com mirtilos, acompanhado de batatas, e, para terminar, torta de abóbora. No Canadá, comemoração similar acontece em 1° de outubro.

thank you *excl* obrigado(da); **~ for** obrigado(da) por.
◆ **thankyou** *n* agradecimento *m*.
that [ðæt, *weak form of pron & conj* ðət] (*pl* **those**) <> *adj* **-1.** [referring to thing, person mentioned] esse (essa); **I prefer ~ book** prefiro esse livro. **-2.** [referring to thing, person farther away] aquele (aquela); **~ book at the back** aquele livro lá atrás; **I'll have ~ one** quero aquele (ali) *OR* esse. <> *pron* **-1.** [referring to thing, person mentioned] esse *m*, essa *f*; [indefinite] isso; **what's ~?** o que é isso?; **who's ~?** [on the phone] quem fala?; [pointing] e esse, quem é?; **~'s interesting** que interessante. **-2.** [referring to thing, person farther away] aquele *m*, aquela *f*; [indefinite] aquilo; **is ~ Lucy?** [pointing] aquela é a Lucy?; **I want those at the back** quero aqueles lá atrás; **what's ~ on the roof?** o que é aquilo no telhado? **-3.** [introducing relative clause] que; **a shop ~ sells antiques** uma loja que vende antiguidades; **the movie ~ I saw** o filme que eu vi; **the room ~ I slept in** o quarto onde *OR* em que dormi. <> *adv* assim tão; **it wasn't ~ bad/good** não foi assim tão mau/bom; **it didn't cost ~ much** não custou tanto assim. <> *conj* que; **tell him ~ I'm going to be late** diga-lhe que vou chegar atrasado.
thatched [θætʃt] *adj* com telhado de palha.
Thatcherism [ˈθætʃərɪzml] *n (U)* thatcherismo *m*.
that's [ðæts] = **that is**.
thaw [θɔː] <> *vt* **-1.** [ice] derreter **-2.** [frozen food] descongelar. <> *vi* **-1.** [ice] derreter **-2.** [food] descongelar **-3.** *fig* [people, relations] tornar-se um pouco mais amistoso. <> *n* [warm spell] degelo *m*.
the [*weak form* ðə, *before vowel* ðɪ, *strong form* ðiː] *definite article* **-1.** [gen] o (a), os (as) *(pl)*; **~ book** o livro; **~ apple** a maçã; **~ girls** as meninas; **~ Wilsons** os Wilson; **to play ~ piano** tocar piano. **-2.** [with an adjective to form a noun] o (a), os (as) *(pl)*; **~ British** os britânicos; **~ young** os jovens; **~ impossible** o impossível. **-3.** [in dates]: **~ twelfth** o dia doze; **~ forties** os anos quarenta. **-4.** [in titles]: **Elizabeth ~ Second** Elizabeth Segunda.
theatre, theater *US* [ˈθɪətəʳ] *n* **-1.** [building] teatro *m* **-2.** [art, industry]: **the ~** o teatro **-3.** [in hospital] sala *f* de cirurgia **-4.** *US* [cinema] cinema *m*.
theatregoer, theatergoer *US* [ˈθɪətəˌgəʊəʳ] *n* aficionado *m*, -da *f* por teatro.
theatrical [θɪˈætrɪkl] *adj* teatral.
theft [θeft] *n* roubo *m*.
their [ðeəʳ] *adj* seu (sua), deles (delas); **~ house** a sua casa, a casa deles.

theirs [ðeəz] *pron* o/a deles (o/a delas); **a friend of ~** um amigo deles; **these books are ~** estes livros são (os) deles; **these are ours - where are ~?** estes são os nossos - onde estão os deles?
them [*weak form* ðəm, *strong form* ðem] *pron* **-1.** *(direct)* os *mpl*, as *fpl*; **I know ~** eu os conheço **-2.** *(indirect)* lhes; **send this to ~** mande-lhes isso; **tell ~** diga-lhes **-3.** *(after prep)* eles *mpl*, elas *fpl*; **Anna and Sam brought it with ~** a Anna e o Sam trouxeram-no com eles.
thematic [θɪ'mætɪk] *adj* temático(ca).
theme [θi:m] *n* **-1.** [gen] tema *m* **-2.** [signature tune] sintonia *f*.
theme park *n* parque *m* temático.
theme song *n* música-tema *f*, tema *m* musical.
theme tune *n* música-tema *f*, tema *f* musical.
themselves [ðem'selvz] *pron* **-1.** *(reflexive)* se; **they hurt ~** eles machucaram-se **-2.** *(after prep)* eles *mpl* próprios, elas *fpl* próprias, si *mpl* próprios, si *fpl* próprias; **they blame ~** eles culpam-se a si próprios; **they did it ~** fizeram-no eles mesmos OR próprios.
then [ðen] <> *adv* **-1.** [later, as a result] então; **if you help me out now, ~ I'll return the favour** se você me ajudar agora, eu te devolvo o favor; **it starts at eight - I'll see you ~** começa às oito - te vejo a essa hora **-2.** [next, afterwards] depois **-3.** [in that case] então, neste caso; **all right ~** então, tudo certo **-4.** [therefore] então, portanto **-5.** [furthermore, also] além disso. <> *adj* então.
thence [ðens] *adv fml & literary* de lá.
theologian [θɪə'ləʊdʒən] *n* teólogo *m*, -ga *f*.
theology [θɪ'ɒlədʒɪ] *n* teologia *f*.
theorem ['θɪərəm] *n* teorema *f*.
theoretical [θɪə'retɪkl] *adj* teórico(ca).
theoretically [θiə'retɪklɪ] *adv* teoricamente, em teoria.
theorist ['θɪərɪst] *n* teórico *m*, -ca *f*.
theorize, -ise ['θɪəraɪz] *vi*: **to ~ (about sthg)** teorizar (sobre algo).
theory ['θɪərɪ] (*pl* **-ies**) *n* teoria *f*; **in ~** em teoria.
therapeutic [ˌθerə'pju:tɪk] *adj* terapêutico(ca).
therapist ['θerəpɪst] *n* terapeuta *mf*.
therapy ['θerəpɪ] *n (U)* terapia *f*.
there [ðeəʳ] <> *pron* [indicating existence of sthg]: **~ is/are** há; **~'s someone at the door** tem alguém na porta <> *adv* **-1.** [in existence, available] lá, alí; **is Sam ~, please?** [when telephoning] o Sam está? **-2.** [referring to place] lá; **I'm going ~ next week** vou lá para a semana; **over ~** ali; **it's right ~ by the phone** está aí bem ao lado do telefone.
◆ **there you are** *adv* handing sthg to sb] aqui está.
thereabouts [ˌðeərə'baʊts], **thereabout** *US* [ˌðeərə'baʊt] *adv*: **or ~** ou por ali; **by 1998 or ~** mais ou menos em 1998.
thereafter [ˌðeər'ɑ:ftəʳ] *adv fml* conseqüentemente, depois disso.
thereby [ˌðeər'baɪ] *adv fml* desse modo.
therefore ['ðeəfɔ:ʳ] *adv* portanto, por isso.
therein [ˌðeər'ɪn] *adv fml* **-1.** [inside] lá dentro **-2.** [in that matter]: **~ lies the problem** aí é que está o problema.
there's [ðeəz] *cont* = **there is**.
thereupon [ˌðeərə'pɒn] *adv fml* **-1.** [as a result] em razão disso **-2.** [then] por isso.
thermal ['θɜ:ml] *adj* térmico(ca); **~ waters** águas *fpl* termais.
thermal reactor *n* reator *m* térmico.
thermal underwear *n (U)* roupa *f* térmica.
thermodynamics [ˌθɜ:məʊdaɪ'næmɪks] *n (U)* termodinâmica *f*.
thermoelectric *adj* termoelétrico(ca).
thermometer [θə'mɒmɪtəʳ] *n* termômetro *m*.
thermonuclear [ˌθɜ:məʊ'nju:klɪəʳ] *adj* termonuclear.
thermoplastic [ˌθɜ:məʊ'plæstɪk] <> *adj* termoplástico(ca). <> *n* (polímero *m*) termoplástico *m*.
Thermos (flask)® ['θɜ:məs-] *n* garrafa *f* térmica.
thermostat ['θɜ:məstæt] *n* termostato *m*.
thesaurus [θɪ'sɔ:rəs] (*pl* **-es**) *n* tesauro *m*.
these [ði:z] *pl* ▷ **this**.
thesis ['θi:sɪs] (*pl* **theses** ['θi:si:z]) *n* tese *f*.
they [ðeɪ] *pers pron pl* eles *mpl*, elas *fpl*.
they'd [ðeɪd] = **they had**, **they would**.
they'll [ðeɪl] = **they shall**, **they will**.
they're [ðeəʳ] = **they are**.
they've [ðeɪv] = **they have**.
thick [θɪk] <> *adj* **-1.** [bulky] grosso(sa); **it's 6 cm ~** tem 6 cm de grossura; **how ~ is that wall?** qual é a espessura da parede? **-2.** [dense] denso(sa) **-3.** *inf* [stupid] estúpido(da) **-4.** [viscous] espesso(sa) **-5.** [voice - with anger] enraivecido(da); [- with emotion] embargado(da); [- with drink] enrolado(da) **-6.** [full, covered]: **to be ~ with sthg** estar cheio (cheia) de algo. <> *n*: **to be in the ~ of sthg** estar no centro de algo.
◆ **thick and fast** *adv*: **questions came ~ and fast** choviam perguntas de todos os lados.
◆ **through thick and thin** *adv*: **I'll do it through ~ and thin!** vou fazer isso de qualquer maneira!
thicken ['θɪkn] <> *vt* engrossar. <> *vi* **-1.** [become denser] ficar mais denso(sa) **-2.** [become more solid] engrossar.
thicket ['θɪkɪt] *n* moita *f*.
thickly ['θɪklɪ] *adv* **-1.** [not thinly - spread] em camadas grossas; [- cut] em fatias grossas **-2.** [voice - with anger] com voz enraivecida; [- with emotion] com voz embargada; [- with drink] com voz enrolada **-3.** [densely] densamente.
thickness ['θɪknɪs] *n* **-1.** [width, depth] espessura *f* **-2.** [density - of forest, hedge] densidade *f*; [- of hair] grossura *f* **-3.** [of soup, sauce] consistência *f*.
thickset [ˌθɪk'set] *adj* robusto(ta).
thick-skinned [-'skɪnd] *adj* insensível.
thief [θi:f] (*pl* **thieves**) *n* ladrão *m*, -dra *f*.
thieve [θi:v] <> *vt* roubar. <> *vi* roubar.
thieves [θi:vz] *pl* ▷ **thief**.

thieving ['θi:vɪŋ] ◇ *adj* ladrão(dra). ◇ *n (U)* roubo *m*, furto *m*.

thigh [θaɪ] *n* coxa *f*.

thighbone ['θaɪbəʊn] *n* fêmur *m*.

thimble ['θɪmbl] *n* dedal *m*.

thin [θɪn] (*compar* **-ner**, *superl* **-nest**, *pt* & *pp* **-ned**, *cont* **-ning**) ◇ *adj* **-1.** [in width, depth] fino(na) **-2.** [skinny] magro(gra) **-3.** [watery] ralo(la), aguado(da) **-4.** [sparse - crowd, vegetation] disperso(sa); [- hair] ralo(la); **to be ~ on top** estar ficando calvo(va) **-5.** [excuse] fraco(ca). ◇ *adv*: **to be wearing ~** [becoming boring] estar perdendo o interesse; [beginning to fail] **my patience is wearing ~** está acabando a minha paciência. ◇ *vi*: **my hair is ~ning** meu cabelo está começando a cair.
◆ **thin down** *vt sep* diluir.

thin air *n (U)*: **to appear out of ~** aparecer do nada; **to disappear into ~** desaparecer sem deixar vestígio.

thing [θɪŋ] *n* **-1.** [gen] coisa *f*; **you poor ~!** coitadinho(nha); **the next ~ on the list** o próximo item da lista; **the (best) ~ to do would be ...** o melhor a fazer seria ...; **for one ~** em primeiro lugar; **(what) with one ~ and another** entre uma coisa e outra; **the ~ is ...** a questão é ..., acontece que ...; **it's just one of those ~s** *inf* é apenas uma dessas coisas que acontecem; **to have a ~ about sb/sthg** *inf* [like] gostar muito de alguém/algo; [dislike] não suportar alguém/algo; **to make a ~ (out) of sthg** *inf* fazer um alarde de algo **-2.** [anything]: **not a ~** nada; **I don't know a ~ (about)** não sei nada (sobre OR de) **-3.** *inf* [fashion]: **the ~** a última moda.
◆ **things** *npl* **-1.** [clothes, possessions] coisas *fpl* **-2.** *inf* [life] coisas *fpl*.

thingamabob ['θɪŋəmə,bɒb], **thingamajig** ['θɪŋəmədʒɪg], **thingummy(jig)** *UK* ['θɪŋəmɪ-], **thingy** *UK* ['θɪŋɪ] *n* **-1.** [thing] coisa *f* **-2.** [person] fulano(na).

think [θɪŋk] (*pt* & *pp* **thought**) ◇ *vt* **-1.** [believe]: **to ~ (that)** achar OR acreditar que; **I ~ so** acho que sim; **I don't ~ so** acho que não **-2.** [have in mind] pensar **-3.** [imagine] entender, imaginar **-4.** [remember] pensar, lembrar **-5.** [in polite requests]: **do you ~ you could help me?** você acha que pode me ajudar? ◇ *vi* **-1.** [use mind] pensar **-2.** [have stated opinion]: **what do you ~ of OR about his new film?** o que você acha do novo filme dele?; **I don't ~ much of them/it** não tenho uma opinião muito boa sobre eles/ele; **to ~ a lot of sb/sthg** ter alguém/algo em grande estima **-3.** *phr*: **to ~ better of sthg/of doing sthg** pensar melhor sobre algo/sobre fazer algo; **he ~s nothing of doing it** ele tira isso de letra; **to ~ twice** pensar duas vezes. ◇ *n inf*: **to have a ~ (about sthg)** pensar (sobre algo).
◆ **think about** *vt fus* [consider] pensar em; **I'll have to ~ about it** vou ter que pensar sobre isso.
◆ **think back** *vi*: **to ~ back (to sthg)** recordar-se (de algo).
◆ **think of** *vt fus* **-1.** [gen] pensar em; **to ~ of doing sthg** pensar em fazer algo **-2.** [remember] lembrar-se de **-3.** [show consideration for]: **it was kind of you to ~ of me** foi muito gentil de tua parte se lembrar de mim.
◆ **think out, think through** *vt sep* **-1.** [plan] elaborar **-2.** [problem] examinar.
◆ **think over** *vt sep* refletir sobre.
◆ **think up** *vt sep* imaginar, bolar.

thinker ['θɪŋkə^r] *n* pensador *m*, -ra *f*.

thinking ['θɪŋkɪŋ] ◇ *adj*: **the ~ man** o homem que pensa. ◇ *n (U)* **-1.** [opinion] opinião *f*; **to my way of ~** na minha opinião **-2.** [reflection] reflexão *f*; **I'll have to do a lot of hard ~ about your proposal** vou ter que pensar bastante sobre a tua proposta **-3.** [theory] teoria *f*.

think tank *n* assessoria *f* técnica.

thinly ['θɪnlɪ] *adv* **-1.** [in width, depth - slice] em fatias finas; [- spread] numa camada fina **-2.** [forested] escassamente **-3.** [barely] pouco.

thinner ['θɪnə^r] *n (U)* tíner *m*, solvente *m*.

thinness ['θɪnnɪs] *n* **-1.** [in width, depth] finura *f* **-2.** [slim build] magreza *f*.

thin-skinned [-'skɪnd] *adj* suscetível.

third [θɜ:d] ◇ *num* terceiro(ra). ◇ *n* **-1.** [fraction] terço *m* **-2.** *UK UNIV* ≃ nota *f* C *(num título universitário)*; *see also* **sixth**.

third-class *adj UK UNIV* ≃ nota *f* C *(num título universitário)*.

third-degree burns *npl* queimaduras *fpl* de terceiro grau.

thirdly ['θɜ:dlɪ] *adv* em terceiro lugar.

third party *n* terceiros *mpl*.

third party insurance *n* seguro *m* contra terceiros.

third-rate *adj pej* de terceira categoria.

Third World *n*: **the ~** o Terceiro Mundo.

thirst [θɜ:st] *n* sede *f*; **~ for sthg** *fig* sede de algo.

thirsty ['θɜ:stɪ] (*compar* **-ier**, *superl* **-iest**) *adj* **-1.** [parched]: **to be OR feel ~** estar com OR sentir sede **-2.** [causing thirst] que dá sede.

thirteen [,θɜ:'ti:n] *num* treze; *see also* **six**.

thirteenth [,θɜ:'ti:nθ] *num* décimo terceiro, décima terceira; *see also* **sixth**.

thirtieth ['θɜ:tɪəθ] *num* trigésimo(ma); *see also* **sixth**.

thirty ['θɜ:tɪ] (*pl* **-ies**) *num* trinta; *see also* **sixty**.

thirty-something *adj típico das pessoas que já passaram dos trinta anos e vivem confortavelmente*.

this [ðɪs] (*pl* **these**) ◇ *adj* **-1.** [referring to thing, person] este (esta); **these chocolates are delicious** estes chocolates são deliciosos; **~ morning/week** esta manhã/semana; **I prefer ~ book** prefiro este livro; **I'll take ~ one** quero este. **-2.** *inf* [used when telling a story]: **there was ~ man ...** havia um homem ... ◇ *pron* [referring to thing, person] este *m*, esta *f*; [indefinite] isto; **~ is for you** isto é para você; **what are these?** o que é isto?, o que é que são estas coisas?; **~ is David Gregory** [introducing someone] este é o David Gregory; [on telephone] aqui fala David Gregory. ◇ *adv*: **it was ~ big** era deste tamanho; **I don't remember it being ~ tiring** não me lembro de ser tão cansativo assim.

thistle ['θɪsl] *n* cardo *m*.

thither ['ðɪðəʳ] *adv* ⊳ **hither**.
tho' [ðəʊ] *conj & adv* = **though**.
thong [θɒŋ] *n* **-1.** [piece of leather] correia *f*, tira *f* de couro **-2.** [bikini] tanga *f* **-3.** *US* [sandal] sandália *f*.
thorn [θɔ:n] *n* **-1.** [prickle] espinho *m*; **to be a ~ in sb's flesh** *OR* **side** ser um tormento na vida de alguém **-2.** [bush, tree] espinheiro *m*.
thorny ['θɔ:nɪ] (*compar* **-ier**, *superl* **-iest**) *adj* **-1.** [prickly] espinhoso(sa), cheio (cheia) de espinhos **-2.** *fig* [tricky, complicated] espinhoso(sa).
thorough ['θʌrə] *adj* **-1.** [gen] completo(ta) **-2.** [meticulous] minucioso(sa).
thoroughbred ['θʌrəbred] *n* puro-sangue *m*.
thoroughfare ['θʌrəfeəʳ] *n fml* via *f* pública.
thoroughly ['θʌrəlɪ] *adv* **-1.** [fully, in detail] a fundo, exaustivamente **-2.** [completely, utterly] completamente, totalmente.
thoroughness ['θʌrənɪs] *n (U)* **-1.** [exhaustiveness] profundidade *f*, meticulosidade *f* **-2.** [meticulousness] minúcia *f*.
those [ðəʊz] *pl* ⊳ **that**.
though [ðəʊ] ◇ *conj* **-1.** [in spite of the fact that] embora **-2.** [even if] ainda que; **even ~** embora. ◇ *adv* no entanto.
thought [θɔ:t] ◇ *pt & pp* ⊳ **think**. ◇ *n* **-1.** [notion] idéia *f* **-2.** *(U)* [act of thinking] reflexão *f* **-3.** *(U)* [philosophy] pensamento *m* **-4.** [gesture] intenção *f*.
◆ **thoughts** *npl* **-1.** [reflections] opiniões *fpl*; **she keeps her ~ to herself** ela não expressa o que pensa; **to collect one's ~s** concentrar-se **-2.** [views] opiniões *fpl*, idéias *fpl*.
thoughtful ['θɔ:tfʊl] *adj* **-1.** [pensive] pensativo(va) **-2.** [considerate] atencioso(sa).
thoughtfulness ['θɔ:tfʊlnɪs] *n (U)* **-1.** [pensiveness] ar *m* pensativo **-2.** [considerateness] atenção *f*, consideração *f*.
thoughtless ['θɔ:tlɪs] *adj* indelicado(da).
thoughtlessness ['θɔ:tlɪsnɪs] *n (U)* indelicadeza *f*.
thousand ['θaʊznd] *num*: **a ~** mil; **two ~** dois mil; **~s of** milhares de.
thousandth ['θaʊzntθ] *num* **-1.** milésimo(ma) **-2.** [fraction] milésimo(ma); *see also* **sixth**.
thrash [θræʃ] *vt* **-1.** [beat, hit] surrar, dar uma surra em **-2.** *inf* [trounce] dar uma surra em.
◆ **thrash about, thrash around** *vi* debater-se; **to be ~ing about in one's sleep** ter um sono agitado.
◆ **thrash out** *vt sep* esgotar *(um assunto)*.
thrashing ['θræʃɪŋ] *n* **-1.** [beating, hitting] surra *f* **-2.** *inf* [trouncing] surra *f*.
thread [θred] ◇ *n* **-1.** [of cotton, wool] fio *m* **-2.** [of screw] rosca *f* **-3.** *fig* [theme] fio *m* da meada. ◇ *vt* **-1.** [pass thread through] enfiar **-2.** [move]: **to ~ one's way through** abrir caminho.
threadbare ['θredbeəʳ] *adj* **-1.** [clothes, carpet] surrado(da) **-2.** [argument, joke] manjado(da).
threat [θret] *n* **-1.** [warning] ameaça *f* **-2.** [menace]: **~ (to sb/sthg)** ameaça (a alguém/algo) **-3.** [risk]: **~ (of sthg)** ameaça (de algo).
threaten ['θretn] ◇ *vt* **-1.** [issue threat]: **to ~ sb (with sthg)** ameaçar alguém (com algo); **to ~ to do sthg** ameaçar fazer algo **-2.** [endanger] ameaçar. ◇ *vi* ameaçar.
threatening ['θretnɪŋ] *adj* ameaçador(ra).
three [θri:] *num* três; *see also* **six**.
three-D *adj* tridimensional.
three-day event *n concurso hípico de três dias.*
three-dimensional [-dɪ'menʃənl] *adj* tridimensional.
threefold ['θri:fəʊld] ◇ *adj* triplo(pla). ◇ *adv* três vezes; **to increase ~** triplicar.
three-legged race [-'legɪd-] *n* corrida *f* de três pernas.
three-piece *adj* de três peças.
three-ply *adj* **-1.** [wood] com três espessuras **-2.** [wool] com três fios.
three-point turn *n UK* volta *f* de três pontos.
three-quarters *npl* três quartos *mpl*.
threesome ['θri:səm] *n* trio *m*.
three-star *adj* de três estrelas.
three-wheeler [-'wi:ləʳ] *n* triciclo *m*.
thresh [θreʃ] *vt* debulhar.
threshing machine ['θreʃɪŋ-] *n* debulhadora *f*.
threshold ['θreʃhəʊld] *n* **-1.** [doorway] soleira *f* **-2.** [level] limiar *m* **-3.** *fig* [verge]: **to be on the ~ of sthg** estar no limiar de algo.
threshold agreement *n* acordo *m* para indexação salarial.
threw [θru:] *pt* ⊳ **throw**.
thrift [θrɪft] *n* **-1.** [prudent expenditure] economia *f*, poupança *f* **-2.** *US* [savings bank] = **thrift institution**.
thrift institution *n US* ≃ banco *m* de poupança.
thrift shop *n US* loja *f* beneficente.
thrifty ['θrɪftɪ] (*compar* **-ier**, *superl* **-iest**) *adj* econômico(ca).
thrill [θrɪl] ◇ *n* **-1.** [sudden feeling - of joy] vibração *f*; [- of horror] estremecimento *m* **-2.** [exciting experience] emoção *f*. ◇ *vt* emocionar, entusiasmar. ◇ *vi*: **to ~ to sthg** emocionar-se *OR* entusiasmar-se com algo.
thrilled [θrɪld] *adj*: **~ (with sthg/to do sthg)** encantado(da) (com algo/por fazer algo).
thriller ['θrɪləʳ] *n* suspense *m (enquanto obra)*.
thrilling ['θrɪlɪŋ] *adj* emocionante.
thrive [θraɪv] (*pt* **-d** *OR* **throve**, *pp* **-d**) *vi* **-1.** [person, plant] desenvolver-se **-2.** [business] prosperar.
thriving ['θraɪvɪŋ] *adj* **-1.** próspero(ra) **-2.** [plant] que se desenvolve.
throat [θrəʊt] *n* **-1.** [inside mouth] garganta *f*; **to ram** *OR* **force sthg down sb's ~** *fig* empurrar algo goela abaixo (em alguém); **to stick in sb's ~** *fig* ficar preso(sa) na garganta de alguém **-2.** [front of neck] pescoço *m*; **to be at each other's ~s** estar batendo boca; **to cut sb's ~** [kill] cortar a garganta de alguém.
throaty ['θrəʊtɪ] (*compar* **-ier**, *superl* **-iest**) *adj* rouco(ca).
throb [θrɒb] (*pt & pp* **-bed**, *cont* **-bing**) ◇ *n* **-1.** [of pulse] pulsação *f* **-2.** [of head] latejamento *m* **-3.** [of heart] palpitação *f*; [of engine, machine, drums] vibração *f*. ◇ *vi* **-1.** [beat - pulse, blood] pulsar; [- heart] palpitar; [- engine, machine] vibrar; [- music, drums] vibrar, ressoar **-2.** [be painful] latejar.
throes [θrəʊz] *npl*: **death ~** agonia *f* da morte; **to**

be in the ~ of sthg estar no meio de algo.
thrombosis [θrɒm'bəʊsɪs] (*pl* **-boses** [-si:z]) *n* trombose *f.*
throne [θrəʊn] *n* **-1.** [chair] trono *m* **-2.** [position, authority]: **the** ~ o trono.
throng [θrɒŋ] <> *n* aglomeração *f.* <> *vt* aglomerar. <> *vi* aglomerar-se.
throttle ['θrɒtl] <> *n* **-1.** [valve] válvula *f* de estrangulamento **-2.** [lever] alavanca *f (da válvula de estrangulamento)*; [pedal] afogador *m.* <> *vt* estrangular.
through [θru:] <> *adj* [finished] terminado(da); **to be** ~ **with sthg** ter terminado algo; **to be** ~ **with sb** terminar com alguém. <> *adv* **-1.** [from one end to another] até o fim; **they let us** ~ nos deixaram passar **-2.** [until] até; **I slept** ~ **till ten** dormi até as dez. <> *prep* **-1.** [from one side to another] através de; **to cut** ~ cortar algo; **to get** ~ **sthg** passar por algo **-2.** [during, throughout] durante; **to go** ~ **an experience** passar por uma experiência **-3.** [because of] por; **to happen** ~ **sthg** acontecer devido a algo **-4.** [by means of] graças a **-5.** *US* [up till and including]: **Monday** ~ **Friday** de segunda a sexta.
◆ **through and through** *adv* **-1.** [completely] dos pés à cabeça **-2.** [thoroughly]: **to know sthg** ~ **and** ~ conhecer algo de cima a baixo.
throughout [θru:'aʊt] <> *prep* **-1.** [during] durante todo(da) **-2.** [everywhere in] por todo(da). <> *adv* **-1.** [all the time] o tempo todo **-2.** [everywhere] por todo o lado.
throughput [θru:ˌpʊt] *n UK* **-1.** rendimento *m* **-2.** *COMPUT* throughput *m.*
throve [θrəʊv] *pt* ▷ **thrive.**
throw [θrəʊ] (*pt* **threw**, *pp* **thrown**) <> *vt* **-1.** [gen] atirar; **to** ~ **one's arms around sb/sthg** abraçar alguém/algo **-2.** [move suddenly]: **to** ~ **o.s.** jogar-se, atirar-se; **to** ~ **o.s. into sthg** *fig* atirar-se em algo **-3.** [rider] derrubar, desmontar **-4.** *fig* [force into]: **we were all thrown into confusion** ficamos todos muito confusos; **he was thrown into the job at short notice** largaram o trabalho nas costas dele sem avisar **-5.** [shadow, light]: **to** ~ **sthg on sthg** projetar algo em algo **-6.** [tantrum, fit]: **to** ~ **a tantrum/fit** ter um acesso de fúria/um ataque **-7.** *fig* [confuse] deixar confuso(sa). <> *n* [toss, pitch] arremesso *m*, lançamento *m.*
◆ **throw away** *vt sep* jogar fora.
◆ **throw in** *vt sep* incluir *(como brinde).*
◆ **throw out** *vt sep* **-1.** [discard] jogar fora **-2.** *fig* [reject] rejeitar **-3.** [force to leave] expulsar.
◆ **throw up** <> *vt sep* [cause to rise] jogar. <> *vi inf* [vomit] vomitar, botar para fora.
throwaway ['θrəʊəˌweɪl *adj* **-1.** [disposable] descartável **-2.** [casual] fortuito(ta), casual.
throwback ['θrəʊbæk] *n*: ~ **(to sthg)** retrocesso *m* (a algo).
throw-in *n UK FTBL* arremesso *m* lateral.
thrown [θrəʊn] *pp* ▷ **throw.**
thru [θru:] *adj, adv & prep US inf* = **through.**
thrush [θrʌʃ] *n* **-1.** [bird] tordo *m* **-2.** *MED* cândida *f.*
thrust [θrʌst] (*pt & pp* **thrust**) <> *n* **-1.** [forward movement - of knife, sword] golpe *m*; [- of army] investida *f*; [- of body] impulso *m* **-2.** *(U)* [forward force] (força *f* de) propulsão *f* **-3.** [main aspect] essência *f.* <> *vt* **-1.** [shove, jab] empurrar **-2.** [jostle]: **to** ~ **one's way** abrir caminho à força.
◆ **thrust upon** *vt sep*: **to** ~ **sthg upon sb** impor algo a alguém.
thrusting ['θrʌstɪŋ] *adj* agressivo(va).
thruway ['θru:weɪ] *n US* rodovia *f.*
thud [θʌd] (*pt & pp* **-ded**, *cont* **-ding**) <> *n* baque *m.* <> *vi* dar um baque seco.
thug [θʌg] *n* marginal *mf.*
thumb [θʌm] <> *n* [of hand] polegar *m*; **to twiddle one's** ~**s** ficar à toa. <> *vt inf* [hitch]: **to** ~ **a lift** pedir carona *(com o dedo).*
◆ **thumb through** *vt fus* folhear.
thumb index *n* índice *m* alfabético.
thumbnail ['θʌmneɪl] <> *adj* breve. <> *n* unha *f* do polegar.
thumbnail sketch *n* descrição *f* breve.
thumbs down [ˌθʌmz-] *n*: **to get** *OR* **be given the** ~ ser recebido(da) com desaprovação, não ser bem recebido(da).
thumbs up [ˌθʌmz-] *n* [go-ahead]: **to give sb/sthg the** ~ dar luz verde a alguém/algo.
thumbtack ['θʌmtæk] *n US* percevejo *m (para fixar).*
thump [θʌmp] <> *n* **-1.** [blow] soco *m* **-2.** [thud] baque *m.* <> *vt* **-1.** [punch] dar um soco em **-2.** [place heavily]: **he** ~**ed the books down on the table** ele bateu os livros na mesa com força. <> *vi* **-1.** [move heavily] caminhar pesadamente; **to** ~ **in/out** entrar/sair com passos pesados **-2.** [pound - heart] palpitar; [- head] latejar.
thunder ['θʌndə^r] <> *n (U)* **-1.** *METEOR* trovão *m* **-2.** *fig* [loud sound] estrondo *m.* <> *vt* [say angrily] vociferar, esbravejar. <> *vi* [make loud sound] fazer um estrondo. <> *v impers METEOR* trovejar.
thunderbolt ['θʌndəbəʊlt] *n* **-1.** *METEOR* raio *m* **-2.** *fig* [shock] choque *m.*
thunderclap ['θʌndəklæp] *n* trovão *m.*
thundercloud ['θʌndəklaʊd] *n* nuvem *f* de temporal.
thundering *adj* enorme, descomunal.
thunderous ['θʌndərəs] *adj* ensurdecedor(ra).
thunderstorm ['θʌndəstɔ:m] *n* temporal *m.*
thunderstruck ['θʌndəstrʌk] *adj fig* atônito(ta).
thundery ['θʌndərɪ] *adj* carregado(da).
Thur, Thurs (*abbr of* **Thursday**) qui.
Thursday ['θɜ:zdɪ] *n* quinta-feira *f*; *see also* **Saturday.**
thus [ðʌs] *adv fml* **-1.** [as a consequence] assim, por isso **-2.** [in this way] desse modo **-3.** [as follows] assim.
thwart [θwɔ:t] *vt* frustrar, impedir.
thyme [taɪm] *n (U)* tomilho *m.*
thyroid ['θaɪrɔɪd] *n* tireóide *f.*
tiara [tɪ'ɑ:rə] *n* tiara *f.*
Tiber ['taɪbə^r] *n*: **the (River)** ~ o (Rio) Tibre.
Tibet [tɪ'bet] *n* Tibete; **in** ~ no Tíbete.
Tibetan [tɪ'betn] <> *adj* tibetano(na). <> *n* **-1.** [person] tibetano *m*, -na *f* **-2.** [language] tibetano *m.*
tibia ['tɪbɪə] (*pl* **-biae** [-bɪi:], **-s**) *n* tíbia *f.*
tic [tɪk] *n* tique *m.*
tick [tɪk] <> *n* **-1.** [written mark] (sinal *m* de) visto *m* **-2.** [sound] tiquetaque *m*; **I shan't be a** ~ não vou

demorar **-3.** [insect] carrapato *m.* <> *vt* marcar *(com sinal de visto).* <> *vi* **-1.** [make ticking sound] fazer tiquetaque **-2.** *fig* [behave in a certain way]: **what makes him ~?** o que o motiva? ◆ **tick away, tick by** *vi* passar.

◆ **tick off** *vt sep* **-1.** [mark off] marcar *(com sinal de visto)* **-2.** [tell off]: **to ~ sb off (for sthg)** dar uma bronca em alguém (por algo).

◆ **tick over** *vi* funcionar em marcha lenta.

ticked [tɪkd] *adj US inf* [annoyed] incomodado(da).

ticker tape *n (U)* fita *f* de teleimpressor; **~ parade** desfile *m* com confete e serpentinas.

ticket ['tɪkɪt] *n* **-1.** [for entry, access - plane] bilhete *m*; [- bus, train] passagem *f*; [- for footbal match, concert] entrada *f*, ingresso *m* **-2.** [label on product] etiqueta *f* **-3.** [notice of traffic offence] multa *f* **-4.** *POL* chapa *f*.

ticket agency *n agência que vende entradas de teatro ou passagens de trem, avião etc.*

ticket collector *n UK* revisor *m*, -ra *f (no trem).*

ticket holder *n* portador *m*, -ra *f* do ingresso.

ticket inspector *n UK* revisor *m*, -ra *f (no trem).*

ticket machine *n* máquina *f* automática que vende ingressos.

ticket office *n* **-1.** [in theatre] bilheteria *f* **-2.** [in station] guichê *m* de venda.

ticking off ['tɪkɪŋ-] (*pl* **tickings off**) *n*: **to get a ~** levar uma bronca; **to give sb a ~** dar uma bronca em alguém.

tickle ['tɪkl] <> *vt* **-1.** [touch lightly] fazer cócegas em **-2.** *fig* [amuse] divertir. <> *vi*: **my feet are tickling** sinto cócegas nos pés.

ticklish ['tɪklɪʃ] *adj* **-1.** [sensitive to touch]: **to be ~** sentir cócegas **-2.** *fig* [delicate] delicado(da).

tick-tack-toe *n US* [game] jogo-da-velha *m*.

tidal ['taɪdl] *adj* da maré.

tidal wave *n* maremoto *m*.

tidbit *n US* = **titbit**.

tiddler ['tɪdləʳ] *n UK* [fish] peixinho *m*.

tiddly ['tɪdlɪ] (*compar* **-ier**, *superl* **-iest**) *adj inf* **-1.** [tipsy] grogue **-2.** [tiny] pequenininho(nha).

tiddlywinks ['tɪdlɪwɪŋks], **tiddledywinks** *US* ['tɪdldɪwɪŋks] *n (U)* [game] jogo *m* da pulga.

tide [taɪd] *n* **-1.** [of sea] maré *f* **-2.** *fig* [trend] tendência *f*; **the ~ of history** o curso da história **-3.** *fig* [large quantity] corrente *f*.

◆ **tide over** *vt sep* dar uma força *(por um certo tempo).*

tidemark *n* **-1.** [of sea] linha *f* da maré alta **-2.** *UK* [round bath] marca *f* do nível da água escoada.

tidily ['taɪdɪlɪ] *adv* [nearly] ordenadamente.

tidiness ['taɪdɪnɪs] *n* **-1.** [or room, desk] *(U)* ordem *f* **-2.** [of appearance] asseio *m*.

tidings ['taɪdɪŋz] *npl literary* novas *fpl*.

tidy ['taɪdɪ] (*compar* **-ier**, *superl* **-iest**, *pt* & *pp* **-ied**) <> *adj* **-1.** [gen] arrumado(da) **-2.** [in habits] asseado(da) **-3.** *inf* [sizeable] razoável. <> *vt* arrumar.

◆ **tidy away** *vt sep* pôr em ordem.

◆ **tidy up** <> *vt sep* arrumar. <> *vi*: **I'll have to ~ up before going out** [objects] vou ter que arrumar tudo antes de sair.; [hair, appearance] vou ter que me arrumar antes de sair.

tie [taɪ] (*pt* & *pp* **tied**, *cont* **tying**) <> *n* **-1.** [necktie] gravata *f* **-2.** [string, cord] nó *m*, laçada *f* **-3.** [bond, link] laço *m*, vínculo *m* **-4.** [in game, competition] empate *m* **-5.** *US RAIL* dormente *m*. <> *vt* **-1.** [attach]: **to ~ sthg (on)to sthg** amarrar algo (em algo); **to ~ sthg round sthg** amarrar algo em volta de algo; **to ~ sthg with sthg** amarrar algo com algo **-2.** [do up, fasten - shoelaces] atar, amarrar; [- knot] dar **-3.** *fig* [link]: **to be ~d to sb/sthg** estar ligado(da) a alguém/algo **-4.** *fig* [restricted]: **to be ~d to sthg** estar limitado(da) a algo. <> *vi* [draw]: **to ~ (with sb)** empatar (com alguém).

◆ **tie down** *vt sep fig* [restrict] prender; **to feel tied down by sthg** sentir-se preso(sa) a algo.

◆ **tie in with** *vt fus* concordar com, ajustar-se com.

◆ **tie up** *vt sep* **-1.** [secure with string, rope] amarrar **-2.** *fig* [restrict use of] limitar o uso de **-3.** *fig* [link]: **to be ~d up with sthg** estar ligado(da) a algo.

tiebreak(er) ['taɪbreɪk(əʳ)] *n* **-1.** *TENNIS* tie-break *m* **-2.** [extra question] desempate *m*.

tied [taɪd] *adj SPORT* empatado(da).

tied cottage *n UK casa que o agricultor aluga a um de seus trabalhadores enquanto durar o serviço.*

tied up *adj* [busy] ocupado(da).

tie-dye *vt* tie-dye.

tie-in *n* **-1.** [link]: **~ between/with sthg** ligação *f* entre/com algo **-2.** [promotional product] produto *m* promocional *(de um filme, programa de televisão).*

tiepin ['taɪpɪn] *n* alfinete *m* de gravata.

tier [tɪəʳ] *n* **-1.** [of seats, shelves] fileira *f* **-2.** [cake] camada *f*.

Tierra del Fuego *n* Terra do Fogo; **in ~** na Terra do Fogo.

tie-up *n* **-1.** [link]: **~ between/with sthg** relação *f* próxima entre/com algo **-2.** *US* [interruption - in work] suspensão *f*; [- in traffic] engarrafamento *m* rápido.

tiff [tɪf] *n* desavença *f*, briguinha *f*.

tiger ['taɪgəʳ] *n* tigre *m*.

tiger cub *n* filhote *m* de tigre.

tight [taɪt] <> *adj* **-1.** [gen] apertado(da); **a ~ fit** justo(ta) **-2.** [taut] esticado(da), teso(sa) **-3.** [close together] comprimido(da) **-4.** [painful]: **my chest feels ~** sinto uma dor forte no peito **-5.** [strict] rigoroso(sa) **-6.** [at sharp angle] cerrado(da) **-7.** *inf* [drunk] bêbado(da) **-8.** *inf* [miserly] sovina. <> *adv* **-1.** [firmly, securely] com força; **to hold ~** segurar bem; **to shut** *OR* **close sthg ~** fechar bem algo **-2.** [tautly] bem esticado(da).

◆ **tights** *npl* meia-calça *f*.

tighten ['taɪtn] <> *vt* **-1.** [knot, belt, rules] apertar **-2.** [make tauter] esticar **-3.** [strengthen]: **to ~ one's hold** *OR* **grip on sthg** agarrar *OR* segurar algo com força **-4.** [security] intensificar. <> *vi* [make tighter] apertar.

◆ **tighten up** *vt sep* **-1.** [belt, screw, rule] apertar **-2.** [control, security] intensificar.

tightfisted [ˌtaɪt'fɪstɪd] *adj inf pej* pão-duro.

tightknit [ˌtaɪt'nɪt] *adj* muito unido(da).

tight-lipped [-'lɪpt] *adj* **-1.** [with lips pressed together] de lábios cerrados **-2.** [silent] calado(da).

tightly ['taɪtlɪ] *adv* **-1.** [closely]: **the dress fitted her**

~ o vestido entrava bem apertado nela **-2.** [firmly, securely] com força; [fasten, tie] bem **-3.** [tautly] bem esticado(da).

tightness ['taɪtnɪs] *n (U)* **-1.** [gen] aperto *m* **-2.** [strictness] rigor *m* **-3.** [of schedule] pressão *f* de tempo.

tightrope ['taɪtrəʊp] *n* corda *f* bamba; **to be on** *OR* **walking a ~** estar *OR* andar na corda bamba.

tightrope walker *n* funâmbulo *m*, -la *f*.

Tigré *n* Tigre; **in ~** em Tigre.

tigress ['taɪgrɪs] *n* tigresa *f*.

Tigris *n*: **the (River) ~** o (Rio) Tigre.

tilde ['tɪldə] *n* til *m*.

tile [taɪl] *n* **-1.** [on roof] telha *f* **-2.** [on floor] piso *m* **-3.** [on wall] azulejo *m*.

tiled [taɪld] *adj* **-1.** [roof] telhado(da) **-2.** [floor] ladrilhado(da) **-3.** [wall] azulejado(da).

tiling ['taɪlɪŋ] *n (U)* **-1.** [act of tiling - roof, floor, wall] colocação *f* **-2.** [tiled surface - roof] telhas *fpl*; [- floor] piso *m*; [- wall] azulejos *mpl*.

till [tɪl] <> *prep* até; **~ now** até agora. <> *conj* até; **wait ~ I come back** espere até eu voltar *OR* que eu volte. <> *n* caixa *f* (registradora).

tiller ['tɪlə^r] *n* cana *f* do leme.

tilt [tɪlt] <> *n* inclinação *f*. <> *vt* inclinar. <> *vi* inclinar-se.

timber ['tɪmbə^r] *n* **-1.** *(U)* [wood] madeira *f (para a construção)* **-2.** [beam - of ship] viga *f* mestra; [- of house] madeiramento *m*.

timbered ['tɪmbəd] *adj* revestido(da) com madeira.

time [taɪm] <> *n* **-1.** *(U)* [general measurement, spell] tempo *m*; **to get the ~ to do sthg** ter tempo para fazer algo; **to take ~** levar tempo; **to take ~ out to do sthg** tirar tempo para fazer algo; **it's high ~ ...** já é hora de ...; **to get ~ and a half** receber o pagamento combinado mais a metade; **to have no ~ for sb/sthg** não ter tempo a perder com alguém/algo; **to make good ~** fazer uma boa média (de tempo); **to pass the ~** passar o tempo; **to play for ~** tentar ganhar tempo; **to take one's ~ (doing sthg)** dar-se seu tempo(para fazer algo); **it was a long ~ before he came** passou muito tempo antes que ele viesse; **for a ~** por um tempo **-2.** [as measured by clock, moment] hora *f*; **the ~ is three o'clock** são três horas; **what ~ is it?, what's the ~?** que horas são?, tem horas?; **in a week's/year's ~** daqui a uma semana/um mês; **to keep ~** manter a hora certa; **to lose ~** atrasar; **to tell the ~** dizer as horas; **now would be a good ~ to ask** agora seria uma boa hora para perguntar **-3.** [point in time in past] época *f*; **at that ~** naquela época **-4.** [era] era *f*; **in ancient ~s** na antiguidade; **to be ahead of one's ~** estar à frente de seu tempo; **before my ~** [before I was born] antes de eu nascer; [before I worked here] antes de eu trabalhar ali; **to be behind the ~s** estar parado(da) no tempo **-5.** [occasion] vez *f*; **at the best of ~s** até nos melhores momentos; **from ~ to ~** de vez em quando; **~ after ~, ~ and again** uma e outra vez **-6.** [experience]: **we had a good ~** nos divertimos muito; **we had a terrible ~** foi uma situação horrível; **to have a hard ~ trying to do sthg** ter dificuldade tentando fazer algo **-7.** [degree of lateness]: **in good ~** na hora certa; **ahead of ~** cedo; **on ~** na hora **-8.** *MUS* compasso *m*. <> *vt* **-1.** [schedule] marcar **-2.** [measure duration, speed of] cronometrar **-3.** [choose appropriate moment for] escolher o momento certo para.

◆ **times** <> *npl*: **four ~s as much as me** quatro vezes mais do que eu. <> *prep MATH*: **four ~s five is twenty** quatro vezes cinco é vinte.

◆ **about time** *adv*: **it's about ~** já era hora.

◆ **at a time** *adv*: **for months at a ~** por meses seguidos; **one at a ~** um (uma) por vez; **I always read several maganizes at a ~** sempre leio várias revistas ao mesmo tempo.

◆ **at (any) one time** *adv* em qualquer momento.

◆ **at times** *adv* às vezes.

◆ **at the same time** *adv* ao mesmo tempo.

◆ **for the time being** *adv* por enquanto.

◆ **in time** *adv* **-1.** [not late]: **in ~ (for sthg)** a tempo (para algo) **-2.** [eventually] com o tempo.

time-and-motion study *n estudo de métodos e técnicas para melhorar o rendimento no trabalho*.

time bomb *n* bomba-relógio *f*.

time-consuming [-kən,sju:mɪŋ] *adj* que exige muito tempo.

timed [taɪmd] *adj* **-1.** [race, test] cronometrado(da) **-2.** [opportune]: **well ~** oportuno(na); **badly ~** pouco oportuno(na).

time difference *n* diferença *f* de fuso horário.

time-honoured *adj* consagrado(da).

timekeeping ['taɪm,ki:pɪŋ] *n (U)* pontualidade *f*; **he was sacked for bad ~** foi demitido por chegar atrasado.

time lag *n* intervalo *m*.

time-lapse *adj PHOT* time-lapse.

timeless ['taɪmlɪs] *adj* eterno(na).

time limit *n* prazo *m*, limite *m* de tempo.

timely ['taɪmlɪ] (*compar* **-ier**, *superl* **-iest**) *adj* oportuno(na).

time machine *n* máquina *f* do tempo.

time off *n (U)* (tempo *m* de) folga *f*; **~ (from) sthg** folga (de algo); **I'm owed ~** me devem alguns dias de folga.

time-out (*pl* **time-outs** *OR* **times-out**) *n US SPORT* intervalo *m*.

timepiece ['taɪmpi:s] *n dated* relógio *m*.

timer ['taɪmə^r] *n* temporizador *m*.

timesaving ['taɪm,seɪvɪŋ] *adj* que economiza tempo.

time scale *n* escala *f* de tempo.

time-share *n UK* propriedade *f* comprada em sociedade.

time sheet *n* folha *f* de ponto.

time signal *n* sinal *m* horário *(emitido nas rádios)*.

time switch *n* temporizador *m (numa máquina)*.

timetable ['taɪm,teɪbl] *n* **-1.** [gen] horário *m* **-2.** [schedule] programação *f*, programa *m*.

time zone *n* fuso *m* horário.

timid ['tɪmɪd] *adj* tímido(da).

timidly ['tɪmɪdlɪ] *adv* timidamente.

timing ['taɪmɪŋ] *n (U)* **-1.** [of actor, musician, tennis player] timing *m* **-2.** [chosen moment]: **she made her comment with perfect ~** ela fez seu comentário no momento certo **-3.** *SPORT* [measuring] cronometragem *f.*

timing device *n* dispositivo *m* de retardamento *(numa bomba).*

timpani ['tɪmpənɪ] *npl* timbales *mpl*, tímpanos *mpl.*

tin [tɪn] ◇ *n* **-1.** *(U)* [metal] estanho *m*; **~plate** folha-de-fandres *f* **-2.** *UK* [for food, storage] lata *f* **-3.** [for cooking] assadeira *f.* ◇ *comp* **-1.** [tin] de estanho **-2.** [tinplate] de folha-de-flandres.

tin can *n* lata *f.*

tinder *n (U)* isca *f (para acender o fogo).*

tinfoil ['tɪnfɔɪl] *n (U)* papel *m* OR folha *f* de estanho.

tinge [tɪndʒ] *n* **-1.** [of colour] tom *m*, matiz *m* **-2.** [of feeling] rápida sensação *f*; **a ~ of guilt** uma ponta de culpa.

tinged [tɪndʒd] *adj* **-1.** [colour]: **~ with sthg** com um toque de algo **-2.** [feeling]: **~ with sthg** com uma pontinha de algo.

tingle ['tɪŋgl] *vi* formigar; **to ~ with sthg** agitar-se com algo.

tingling ['tɪŋglɪŋ] *n* formigamento *m.*

tinker ['tɪŋkəʳ] ◇ *n* **-1.** *pej* [gipsy] cigano *m*, -na *f* **-2.** [rascal] diabinho *m*, -nha *f.* ◇ *vi* atamancar; **to ~ with sthg** fuçar em algo.

tinkle ['tɪŋkl] ◇ *n* **-1.** [of bell] tilintar *m* **-2.** *UK inf* [phone call]: **to give sb a ~** bater um fio para alguém. ◇ *vi* **-1.** [bell] tilintar **-2.** [phone] tocar.

tin mine *n* mina *f* de estanho.

tinned [tɪnd] *adj UK* enlatado(da), em conserva.

tinny ['tɪnɪ] (*compar* **-ier**, *superl* **-iest**) *adj* **-1.** [sound] metálico(ca) **-2.** *inf pej* [badly made] malfeito(ta).

tin opener *n UK* abridor *m* de lata.

tinpot *adj UK pej* de araque.

tinsel ['tɪnsl] *n (U)* lantejoula *f*, ouropel *m.*

tint [tɪnt] ◇ *n* matiz *m.* ◇ *vt* **-1.** [gen] matizar **-2.** [window, glass] colorir **-3.** [hair] tingir.

tinted ['tɪntɪd] *adj* **-1.** [window, glass] colorido(da) **-2.** [hair] tingido(da).

tiny ['taɪnɪ] (*compar* **-ier**, *superl* **-iest**) *adj* minúsculo(-la), diminuto(ta).

tip [tɪp] (*pt* & *pp* **-ped**, *cont* **-ping**) ◇ *n* **-1.** [end] ponta *f*; **it's on the ~ of my tongue** está na ponta da língua **-2.** *UK* [dump]: **rubbish ~** lixão *m*, depósito *m* de lixo **-3.** [gratuity] gorjeta *f* **-4.** [piece of advice] dica *f.* ◇ *vt* **-1.** [tilt] inclinar **-2.** [spill] derramar **-3.** [give a gratuity to] dar gorjeta a. ◇ *vi* **-1.** [tilt] inclinar-se **-2.** [spill] derramar **-3.** [give a gratuity] dar gorjeta.

◆ **tip off** *vt sep* avisar, alertar.

◆ **tip over** *vt sep* & *vi* virar.

◆ **tip up** *vi* virar.

tip-off *n* informação *f (secreta).*

tipped [tɪpt] *adj* **-1.** [spear] com ponta de aço **-2.** [cigarette] com filtro **-3.** [pen]: **felt-~ pen** caneta *f* hidrográfica.

Tipp-Ex® ['tɪpeks] *n UK* ≃ errorex® corretivo *m.*

◆ **tipp-ex** *vt UK* corrigir com corretivo.

tipple ['tɪpl] *n inf* bebida *f.*

tipsy ['tɪpsɪ] (*compar* **-ier**, *superl* **-iest**) *adj inf* alto(ta) *(por ingerir bebida alcóolica)*, tocado(da).

tiptoe ['tɪptəʊ] ◇ *n*: **on ~** nas pontas dos pés. ◇ *vi* andar nas pontas dos pés.

tip-top *adj inf dated* ótimo(ma).

tirade [taɪ'reɪd] *n* descascadela *f.*

Tirana, Tiranë *n* Tirana.

tire ['taɪəʳ] ◇ *n US* = **tyre**. ◇ *vt* cansar. ◇ *vi* **-1.** [get tired] cansar-se, ficar cansado(da) **-2.** [get fed up]: **to ~ of sb/sthg** cansar-se de alguém/algo.

◆ **tire out** *vt sep* esgotar.

tired ['taɪəd] *adj* **-1.** [sleepy] cansado(da) **-2.** [fed up]: **~ of sthg/of doing sthg** cansado(da) de algo/de fazer algo.

tiredness ['taɪədnɪs] *n (U)* cansaço *m.*

tireless ['taɪəlɪs] *adj* incansável.

tiresome ['taɪəsəm] *adj* cansativo(va), enfadonho(-nha).

tiring ['taɪərɪŋ] *adj* cansativo(va).

Tirol *n* = **Tyrol**.

tissue ['tɪʃuː] *n* **-1.** [paper handkerchief] lenço *m* de papel **-2.** *(U)* *BIOL* tecido *m* **-3.** *phr*: **a ~ of lies** um emaranhado de mentiras.

tissue paper *n (U)* papel *m* de seda.

tit [tɪt] *n* **-1.** [bird] chapim *m* **-2.** *vulg* [breast] teta *f.*

titbit *UK* ['tɪtbɪt], **tidbit** *US* ['tɪdbɪt] *n* **-1.** [of food] petisco *m* **-2.** *fig* [of news]: **a ~ of gossip** uma pequena fofoca.

tit for tat [-'tæt] *n*: **it's ~** é olho por olho.

titillate ['tɪtɪleɪt] ◇ *vt* excitar. ◇ *vi* excitar-se.

titivate ['tɪtɪveɪt] *vt* arrumar, enfeitar.

title ['taɪtl] *n* título *m.*

titled ['taɪtld] *adj* com título de nobreza.

title deed *n* título *m* de propriedade.

titleholder ['taɪtlˌhəʊldəʳ] *n SPORT* campeão *m*, -peã *f.*

title page *n* página *f* de rosto.

title role *n* papel *m* principal.

titter ['tɪtəʳ] *vi* rir baixinho.

tittle-tattle ['tɪtlˌtætl] *n (U) inf pej* mexerico *m.*

titular ['tɪtjʊləʳ] *adj* honorário(ria), nominal.

T-junction *n* junção-tê *f.*

TLS (*abbr of* **Times Literary Supplement**) *n suplemento semanal do Times britânico direcionado à literatura.*

TM ◇ *n* **-1.** (*abbr of* **transcendental meditation**) meditação *f* transcendental **-2.** (*abbr of* **translation memory**) MT *f.* ◇ *abbr of* **trademark**.

TN *abbr of* **Tennessee**.

TNT (*abbr of* **trinitrotoluene**) *n* TNT *m.*

to [*unstressed before consonant* tə, *unstressed before vowel* tʊ, *stressed* tuː] ◇ *prep* **-1.** [indicating direction] para; **to go ~ Brazil** ir ao Brasil; **to go ~ school** ir para a escola. **-2.** [indicating position] a; **~ the left/right** à esquerda/direita. **-3.** [expressing indirect object] a; **to give sthg ~ sb** dar algo a alguém; **give it ~ me** dê-me isso; **to listen ~ the radio** ouvir rádio. **-4.** [indicating reaction, effect]: **~ my surprise** para surpresa minha; **it's ~ your advantage** é em seu benefício. **-5.** [until] até; **to count ~ ten** contar até dez; **we work from nine ~ five** trabalhamos das nove (até) às cinco. **-6.** [in stating opinion] para; **~ me, he's lying** para mim, ele está mentindo. **-7.** [indicating change of state]: **to turn ~ sthg** transformar-se em algo; **it could lead ~ trouble** pode vir a dar problemas. **-8.** *UK* [in expressions of time] para; **it's ten ~ three** são dez para as três; **at quarter ~ seven** às quinze para as sete. **-9.** [in ratios, rates]: **40 miles ~ the gallon** 40 milhas por galão. **-10.** [of, for]: **the answer ~ the question** a resposta à pergunta; **the key ~ the car** a chave do carro; **a letter ~ my daughter** uma carta para a minha filha. **-11.** [indicating attitude] (para) com; **to be rude ~ sb** ser grosseiro com alguém. ◇ *with infinitive* **-1.** [forming simple infinitive]: **~ walk** andar; **~ laugh** rir. **-2.** [following another verb]: **to begin ~ do sthg** começar a fazer algo; **to try ~ do sthg** tentar fazer algo. **-3.** [following an adjective]: **difficult ~ do** difícil de fazer; **pleased ~ meet you** prazer em conhecê-lo; **ready ~ go** pronto para partir. **-4.** [indicating purpose] para; **we came here ~ look at the castle** viemos para ver o castelo.

toad [təʊd] *n* sapo *m*.

toadstool ['təʊdstu:l] *n* cogumelo *m* venenoso.

toady ['təʊdɪ] (*pl* **-ies**, *pt* & *pp* **-ied**) *pej* ◇ *n* bajulador *m*, -ra *f*. ◇ *vi*: **to ~ (to sb)** puxar o saco (de alguém).

toast [təʊst] ◇ *n* **-1.** *(U)* [bread] torrada *f*, pão *m* torrado **-2.** [drink] brinde *m*; **to drink a ~ to sb/sthg** fazer um brinde a alguém/algo **-3.** [person]: **the ~ of the town** o herói da cidade. ◇ *vt* **-1.** [bread] tostar, torrar **-2.** [person] brindar a.

toasted sandwich [ˌtəʊstɪd-] *n* misto-quente *m*.

toaster ['təʊstə^r] *n* torradeira *f*.

toast rack *n* porta-torradas *m inv*.

tobacco [tə'bækəʊ] *n* tabaco *m*.

tobacconist *n* charuteiro *m*, -ra *f*, vendedor *m*, -ra *f* de fumo *OR* tabaco; **~'s (shop)** tabacaria *f*.

Tobago [tə'beɪgəʊ] *n* ▷**Trinidad and Tobago**.

toboggan [tə'bɒgən] ◇ *n* tobogã *m*. ◇ *vi* deslizar-se em tobogã.

today [tə'deɪ] ◇ *adv (U)* **-1.** [this day] hoje **-2.** [nowadays] de hoje, atual; **~'s technology** a tecnologia hoje em dia. ◇ *adv* **-1.** [this day] hoje **-2.** [nowadays] hoje (em dia).

toddle ['tɒdl] *vi* **-1.** [walk unsteadily] dar os primeiros passos **-2.** *inf* [go]: **to ~ off** *OR* **along** cair fora.

toddler ['tɒdlə^r] *n* criança *f* pequena *(que começa a andar)*.

toddy ['tɒdɪ] (*pl* **-ies**) *n* ponche *m*.

to-do (*pl* **-s**) *n* ***inf dated*** tumulto *m*, alvoroço *m*.

toe [təʊ] ◇ *n* **-1.** [of foot] dedo *m (do pé)* **-2.** [of sock] ponta *f* **-3.** [of shoe] biqueira *f*. ◇ *vt*: **to ~ the line** cumprir as normas.

toehold ['təʊhəʊld] *n* **-1.** [in rock] ponto *m* de apoio **-2.** *fig* [in market]: **to gain a ~ in** conseguir uma brecha em.

toenail ['təʊneɪl] *n* unha *f* do pé.

toffee ['tɒfɪ] *n* **-1.** [sweet] tofe *m*, caramelo *m* **-2.** *(U)* [substance] tofe *m*.

toffee apple *n* ***UK*** maçã *f* do amor.

tofu ['təʊfu:] *n (U)* tofu *m*.

toga ['təʊgə] *n* toga *f*.

together [tə'geðə^r] ◇ *adj* ***inf*** sensato(ta). ◇ *adv* juntos(tas); **to go ~** combinar.

◆ **together with** *prep* junto com.

togetherness [tə'geðənɪs] *n (U)* união *f*, camaradagem *f*.

toggle switch ['tɒgl-] *n* **-1.** *ELECTRON* chave *f* articulada **-2.** *COMPUT* comutador *m* (alternado).

Togo ['təʊgəʊ] *n* Togo; **in ~** no Togo.

Togolese ◇ *adj* togolês(esa). ◇ *n* togolês *m*, -esa *f*.

togs [tɒgz] *npl* ***inf*** traje *m*, roupa *f*.

toil [tɔɪl] ***fml*** ◇ *n* trabalho *m* duro. ◇ *vi* trabalhar duro.

◆ **toil away** *vi*: **to ~ away (at sthg)** trabalhar duro (em algo).

toilet ['tɔɪlɪt] *n* vaso *m* sanitário; **to go to the ~** ir ao banheiro.

toilet bag *n* nécessaire *m*.

toilet paper *n (U)* papel *m* higiênico.

toiletries ['tɔɪlɪtrɪz] *npl* artigos *mpl* de toalete.

toilet roll *n* **-1.** *(U)* [paper] papel *m* higiênico **-2.** [roll] rolo *m* de papel higiênico.

toilet soap *n (U)* sabonete *f*.

toilet tissue *n (U)* papel *m* higiênico.

toilet-trained [-ˌtreɪnd] *adj* que já sabe ir ao banheiro.

toilet water *n (U)* água-de-colônia *f*, colônia *f*.

to-ing and fro-ing [ˌtu:ɪŋən'frəʊɪŋ] *n (U)* idas *fpl* e vindas.

token ['təʊkn] ◇ *adj* simbólico(ca). ◇ *n* **-1.** [voucher, disc - for machines] ficha *f*; [- for books, records] vale *m*; **-2.** [symbol] símbolo *m*, mostra *f*.

◆ **by the same token** *adv* da mesma forma.

Tokyo ['təʊkjəʊ] *n* Tóquio; **in ~** em Tóquio.

told [təʊld] *pt* & *pp* ▷ **tell**.

tolerable ['tɒlərəbl] *adj* tolerável, passável.

tolerably ['tɒlərəblɪ] *adv* razoavelmente.

tolerance ['tɒlərəns] *n* tolerância *f*.

tolerant ['tɒlərənt] *adj* **-1.** [not bigoted]: **~ of sb/sthg** tolerante com alguém/algo **-2.** [resistant]: **~ to sthg** resistente a algo.

tolerate ['tɒləreɪt] *vt* **-1.** [put up with] suportar, tolerar **-2.** [permit] tolerar.

toleration [ˌtɒlə'reɪʃn] *n (U)* tolerância *f*.

toll [təʊl] ◇ *n* **-1.** [number]: **death ~** número *m* de vítimas fatais **-2.** [fee] pedágio *m* **-3.** *phr*: **to take its ~** ter suas implicações. ◇ *vt* [bell] tocar, badalar. ◇ *vi* [bell] tocar, dobrar.

tollbooth ['təʊlbu:θ] *n* cabine *f* de pedágio.

toll bridge *n* ponte *f* com pedágio.

toll-free ***US*** ◇ *adj* gratuito(ta). ◇ *adv*: **to call ~** telefonar *OR* ligar gratuitamente.

tomato [***UK*** tə'mɑ:təʊ, ***US*** tə'meɪtəʊ] (*pl* **-es**) *n* tomate *m*.

tomb [tu:m] *n* túmulo *m*, tumba *f*.

tombola [tɒm'bəʊlə] *n esp **UK*** tômbola *f*.

tomboy ['tɒmbɔɪ] *n menina que gosta de jogos e brincadeiras de meninos*.

tombstone ['tu:mstəʊn] *n* lápide *f*.

tomcat ['tɒmkæt] *n* gato *m (macho)*.

tomfoolery [tɒm'fu:lərɪ] *n (U)* tolice *f*.

tomorrow [tə'mɒrəʊ] ◇ *n* **-1.** [day after today] amanhã *m* **-2.** *fig* [future] futuro *m*. ◇ *adv* **-1.** [the day after today] amanhã; **~ week** uma semana a contar de amanhã **-2.** [in future] no futuro.

ton [tʌn] (*pl inv* OR **-s**) *n* **-1.** *UK* [imperial unit of measurement] tonelada *f* inglesa OR longa *(1016,05 kg)* **-2.** *US* [unit of measurement] tonelada *f (907,19 kg)* **-3.** [metric unit of measurement] tonelada *f* métrica **-4.** *phr*: **to weigh a ~** *inf* pesar uma tonelada; **to come down on sb like a ~ of bricks** soltar os cachorros em cima de alguém.
◆ **tons** *npl UK inf*: **~s (of)** um monte de.
tonal ['təʊnl] *adj* tonal.
tone [təʊn] *n* **-1.** [gen] tom *m* **-2.** TELEC sinal *m*; **dialling ~** linha *f* de discagem **-3.** *phr*: **to lower the ~ of sthg** baixar o nível de algo.
◆ **tone down** *vt sep* suavizar, moderar.
◆ **tone in** *vi* combinar; **to ~ in with sthg** combinar com algo.
◆ **tone up** *vt sep* pôr em forma.
tone-deaf *adj* que não tem ouvido musical.
toner ['təʊnə^r] *n* **-1.** [for photocopier, printer] toner *m* **-2.** [cosmetic] tônico *m*, tonificante *m*.
tongs [tɒŋz] *npl* **-1.** [for sugar] pinça *f* para açúcar **-2.** [for hair] pinças *fpl*.
tongue [tʌŋ] *n* **-1.** [gen] língua *f*; **to have one's ~ in one's cheek** *inf* falar brincando; **to hold one's ~** *fig* fechar o bico; **~s will wag** as pessoas vão falar a respeito **-2.** *fml* [language] língua *f* **-3.** [of shoe] lingüeta *f*.
tongue-in-cheek *adj* em tom de brincadeira.
tongue-tied [-ˌtaɪd] *adj* mudo(da) *(por timidez ou nervosismo)*.
tongue twister [-ˌtwɪstə^r] *n* trava-língua *m*.
tonic ['tɒnɪk] *n* **-1.** [gen] tônico *m* **-2.** *(U)* [tonic water] (água *f*) tônica *f* **-3.** *fig* [beneficial thing] bálsamo *m*.
tonic water *n (U)* (água *f*) tônica *f*.
tonight [tə'naɪt] ◇ *n (U)* esta noite *f*. ◇ *adv* hoje à noite, esta noite.
tonnage ['tʌnɪdʒ] *n (U)* NAUT **-1.** [weight] tonelagem *f* **-2.** [amount of cargo] tonelagem *f* (de arqueação).
tonne [tʌn] (*pl inv* OR **-s**) *n* tonelada *f* métrica.
tonsil ['tɒnsl] *n* amígdala *f*.
tonsil(l)itis [ˌtɒnsɪ'laɪtɪs] *n (U)* amigdalite *f*.
too [tu:] *adv* **-1.** [also] também **-2.** [excessively]: **~ much** demais; **~ old** velho demais; **~ many things** muitas e muitas coisas; **~ long a book** um livro longo demais; **all ~ soon** cedo demais; **only ~ ...** muito ...; **I'd be only ~ happy to help** eu adoraria ajudar **-3.** *(with negatives)*: **not ~ bad** nada mal; **I wasn't ~ impressed** não fiquei muito impressionado.
took [tʊk] *pt* ▻ **take**.
tool [tu:l] *n* **-1.** [implement] ferramenta *f*; **to down ~s** *UK* parar de trabalhar em protesto **-2.** *fig* [means] ferramenta *f*, instrumento *m*; **the ~s of one's trade** as ferramentas de trabalho de alguém.
◆ **tool around** *vi US inf* passear.
tool box *n* caixa *f* de ferramentas.
tool kit *n* jogo *m* de ferramentas.
toot [tu:t] ◇ *n* buzinada *f*. ◇ *vt* buzinar. ◇ *vi* buzinar.
tooth [tu:θ] (*pl* **teeth**) *n* dente *m*; **to be long in the ~** *UK pej* estar um pouco passado(da); **to be fed up to the back teeth with sthg** *UK inf* estar até aqui com algo; **to grit one's teeth** cerrar os dentes; **to have no teeth** *fig* [be powerless] não ter poder algum; **to lie through one's teeth** mentir até não poder mais.
toothache ['tu:θeɪk] *n (U)* dor *f* de dente.
toothbrush ['tu:θbrʌʃ] *n* escova *f* de dentes.
toothless ['tu:θlɪs] *adj* desdentado(da).
toothpaste ['tu:θpeɪst] *n (U)* pasta *f* de dentes.
toothpick ['tu:θpɪk] *n* palito *m*.
tooth powder *n (U)* pó *m* dentifrício.
tootle ['tu:tl] *vi inf* [move unhurriedly] passear.
top [tɒp] (*pt* & *pp* **-ped**, *cont* **-ping**) ◇ *adj* **-1.** [highest] de cima, superior **-2.** [most important, successful] importante; **she got the ~ mark** ela tirou a melhor nota **-3.** [maximum] máximo(ma). ◇ *n* **-1.** [gen] topo *m*, parte *f* de cima; **from ~ to bottom** de cima a baixo; **on ~** em cima; **to go over the ~** *UK* passar um pouco dos limites; **at the ~ of one's voice** a toda voz **-2.** [highest point - of list, class] primeiro(ra); [- of tree] copa *f*; [- of hill] cume *m*; [- of page] topo *m* **-3.** [lid, cap] tampa *f* **-4.** [upper side] superfície *f* **-5.** [clothing - bikini, pyjama] parte *f* de cima; [- blouse] blusa *f* **-6.** [toy] pião *m* **-7.** [highest rank - of an organization] topo *m*; [- of a league, class] primeiro(ra). ◇ *vt* **-1.** [to be first in - league, poll] liderar, estar em primeiro lugar em; [- table, chart] liderar, encabeçar **-2.** [better] superar **-3.** [exceed] passar de **-4.** [put on top of] cobrir.
◆ **on top of** *prep* **-1.** [in space] em cima de **-2.** [in addition to] além de; **on ~ of that** como se não bastasse **-3.** [in control of]: **to be ~ of sthg** ter algo sob controle **-4.** *phr*: **to get on ~ of sb** deixar alguém preocupado(da).
◆ **top up** *UK*, **top off** *US vt sep* encher novamente.
topaz ['təʊpæz] *n* topázio *m*.
top brass *n (U) inf*: **the ~** os altos cargos, os figurões.
topcoat ['tɒpkəʊt] *n* **-1.** [item of clothing] sobretudo *m* **-2.** [paint] última demão *f*.
top dog *n inf* manda-chuva *mf*.
top-flight *adj* de primeira qualidade.
top floor *n* último andar *m*.
top gear *n* marcha *f* mais rápida *(de um veículo)*.
top hat *n* cartola *f*.
top-heavy *adj* muito pesado(da) na parte de cima.
topic ['tɒpɪk] *n* tópico *m*.
topical ['tɒpɪkl] *adj* atual, da atualidade.
topknot ['tɒpnɒt] *n* coque *m*.
topless ['tɒplɪs] *adj* [barebreasted] topless; **to go ~** fazer topless.
top-level *adj* do mais alto nível.
topmost ['tɒpməʊst] *adj* mais alto(ta).
top-notch *adj inf* de primeira.
topographer *n* topógrafo *m*, -fa *f*.
topography [tə'pɒgrəfɪ] *n (U)* topografia *f*.
topped [tɒpt] *adj*: **~ by** OR **with sthg** com algo em cima.
topping ['tɒpɪŋ] *n* cobertura *f*.
topple ['tɒpl] ◇ *vt* derrubar. ◇ *vi* vir abaixo.
◆ **topple over** *vi* vir abaixo.
top-ranking [-'ræŋkɪŋ] *adj* do mais alto nível.
TOPS [tɒps] (*abbr of* **Training Opportunities Scheme**)

n programa de formação vocacional do governo britânico.
top-secret *adj* ultra-secreto(ta).
top-security *adj* de segurança máxima.
topsoil ['tɒpsɔɪl] *n (U)* solo *m* arável, camada *f* superficial do solo.
topspin *n (U)* topspin *m*.
topsy-turvy [ˌtɒpsɪ'tɜːvɪ] ◇ *adj* **-1.** [messy] de pernas para o ar **-2.** [haywire] louco(ca). ◇ *adv* [upside down] de ponta-cabeça.
top-up card *n* [for mobile phone] cartão *m* de recarga.
tor *n esp UK* [hill] colina *f* rochosa *(típica da Inglaterra)*.
torch [tɔːtʃ] *n* **-1.** *UK* [electric] lanterna *f* **-2.** [flaming stick] tocha *f*.
tore [tɔːʳ] *pt* ▷ **tear** ².
torment [*n* 'tɔːment, *vb* tɔː'ment] ◇ *n* tormento *m*. ◇ *vt* atormentar.
tormentor [tɔː'mentəʳ] *n* atormentador *m*, -ra *f*.
torn [tɔːn] *pp* ▷ **tear** ².
tornado [tɔː'neɪdəʊ] (*pl* **-es** *OR* **-s**) *n* tornado *m*.
Toronto *n* Toronto; **in ~** em Toronto.
torpedo [tɔː'piːdəʊ] (*pl* **-es**) ◇ *n* torpedo *m*. ◇ *vt* torpedear.
torpedo boat *n* torpedeiro *m*.
torpor ['tɔːpəʳ] *n (U)* torpor *m*.
torque [tɔːk] *n TECH* torque *m*.
torrent ['tɒrənt] *n* torrente *f*.
torrential [tə'renʃl] *adj* torrencial.
torrid ['tɒrɪd] *adj* tórrido(da).
torso ['tɔːsəʊ] (*pl* **-s**) *n* torso *m*.
tortoise ['tɔːtəs] *n* tartaruga *f* terrestre.
tortoiseshell ['tɔːtəʃel] ◇ *adj* [cat] escama-de-tartaruga. ◇ *n (U)* [material] tartaruga *f*. ◇ *comp* de tartaruga.
tortuous ['tɔːtʃʊəs] *adj* **-1.** [twisty] sinuoso(sa) **-2.** [over-complicated] tortuoso(sa).
torture ['tɔːtʃəʳ] ◇ *n* tortura *f*. ◇ *vt* torturar.
torturer ['tɔːtʃərəʳ] *n* torturador *m*, -ra *f*.
Tory ['tɔːrɪ] (*pl* **-ies**) ◇ *adj* tóri, do partido conservador britânico. ◇ *n* tóri *mf*, membro *m* do partido conservador britânico.
toss [tɒs] ◇ *vt* **-1.** [throw carelessly] atirar, jogar **-2.** [head] sacudir **-3.** [food] misturar **-4.** [coin] jogar *(ao ar)*; **to ~ a coin** tirar no cara ou coroa **-5.** [throw about] jogar, arremessar. ◇ *vi* **-1.** [with coin] tirar no cara ou coroa **-2.** [move about]: **to ~ and turn** rolar na cama. ◇ *n* **-1.** [of coin] arremesso *m (de moeda)* **-2.** [of head] sacudida *f*, meneio *m*.
◆ **toss up** *vi* disputar no cara ou coroa.
toss-up *n inf*: **it's a ~ whether they win or lose** impossível dizer *OR* saber se eles ganham ou perdem.
tot [tɒt] (*pt* & *pp* **-ted**, *cont* **-ting**) *n* **-1.** *inf* [small child] nenezinho *f*, -nha **-2.** [of drink] golinho *m*.
◆ **tot up** *vt sep inf* somar.
total ['təʊtl] (*UK pt* & *pp* **-led**, *cont* **-ling**, *US pt* & *pp* **-ed**, *cont* **-ing**) ◇ *adj* total. ◇ *n* total *m*; **in ~** no total. ◇ *vt* **-1.** [add up] somar **-2.** [amount to] totalizar **-3.** *US inf* [wreck] arruinar.
totalitarian [ˌtəʊtælɪ'teərɪən] *adj* totalitário(ria).
totality [təʊ'tælətɪ] *n* totalidade *f*.
totally ['təʊtəlɪ] *adv* totalmente.
tote bag [təʊt-] *n US* sacola *f* de compras.
totem pole ['təʊtəm-] *n* totem *m*.
totter ['tɒtəʳ] *vi* cambalear.
toucan ['tuːkən] *n* tucano *m*.
touch [tʌtʃ] ◇ *n* **-1.** [gen] toque *m*; **to put the finishing ~es to sthg** dar os últimos retoques a algo **-2.** [contact]: **to get in ~ (with sb)** entrar em contato (com alguém); **to keep in ~ (with sb)** manter contato (com alguém); **to lose ~ (with sb)** perder o contato (com alguém); **to be out of ~ with sthg** estar por fora de algo **-3.** [small amount]: **a ~ (of sthg)** um pouco (de algo) **-4.** *SPORT*: **in ~** na lateral **-5.** *phr*: **it was ~ and go whether we left or stayed** a gente não sabia se saía ou ficava; **to be a soft ~** [for money] não saber dizer que não *(empresta dinheiro)* **-6.** *(U)* [sense] tato *m*; **soft to the ~** suave ao toque; **the ~ of her lips** o toque de seus lábios. ◇ *vt* **-1.** [make contact with] tocar **-2.** [move emotionally] tocar, comover **-3.** [eat] comer **-4.** [drink] beber. ◇ *vi* **-1.** [make contact] tocar **-2.** [be in contact] tocar-se.
◆ **a touch** *adv* um pouco.
◆ **touch down** *vi* [plane] aterrissar.
◆ **touch on** *vt fus* tocar por cima.
◆ **touch up** *vt sep* [paintwork] retocar.
touch-and-go *adj* incerto(ta), duvidoso(sa).
touchdown ['tʌtʃdaʊn] *n* **-1.** [on land, sea] aterrissagem *f* **-2.** [in American football] touchdown *m*.
touched [tʌtʃt] *adj* **-1.** [grateful] comovido(da), emocionado(da) **-2.** *inf* [slightly mad] tantã.
touching ['tʌtʃɪŋ] *adj* tocante, comovente.
touch judge *n RUGBY* bandeirinha *m*, juiz *m*, -íza *f* de linha.
touchline ['tʌtʃlaɪn] *n SPORT* linha *f* lateral.
touchpaper ['tʌtʃˌpeɪpəʳ] *n* estopim *m*.
touch screen *n* tela *f* tátil.
touch-type *vi* **-1.** [typewriter] datilografar sem olhar para o teclado **-2.** [computer] digitar sem olhar para o teclado.
touchy ['tʌtʃɪ] (*compar* **-ier**, *superl* **-iest**) *adj* **-1.** [person] suscetível; **to be ~ about sthg** ser sensível em relação a algo **-2.** [subject, question] delicado(-da).
tough [tʌf] *adj* **-1.** [gen] duro(ra) **-2.** [person, character] forte **-3.** [material] resistente **-4.** [decision, life] difícil **-5.** [criminal, neighbourhood] da pesada **-6.** *inf* [unfortunate] difícil; **~ luck** má sorte; [as exclamation] que azar!
toughen ['tʌfn] *vt* endurecer.
toughened ['tʌfnd] *adj* temperado(da).
toughness ['tʌfnɪs] *n (U)* **-1.** [of character - strength] força *f*; [- hardness] firmeza *f* **-2.** [of material] resistência *f* **-3.** [of meat] dureza *f*.
toupee ['tuːpeɪ] *n* peruca *f*.
tour [tʊəʳ] ◇ *n* **-1.** [trip] excursão *f*, viagem *f* **-2.** [of building, town, museum] visita *f*; **guided ~** visita *f* guiada **-3.** [official journey] turnê *f*. ◇ *vt* **-1.** [visit] visitar **-2.** *SPORT* & *THEATRE* fazer uma turnê por. ◇ *vi* [go on trip] fazer uma excursão, viajar; **to ~ round somewhere** fazer uma excursão em algum lugar, viajar por algum lugar.
tourer ['tʊərəʳ] *n* [car] carro *m* de turismo.

touring ['tʊərɪŋ] <> *adj* **-1.** [exhibition] itinerante **-2.** [show, theatre group] em turnê. <> *n (U)* viagens *fpl* turísticas; **to go ~** fazer turismo.
tourism ['tʊərɪzm] *n (U)* turismo *m*.
tourist ['tʊərɪst] *n* turista *mf*.
tourist class *n (U)* classe *f* econômica *OR* turística.
tourist (information) office *n* (serviço *m* de) informações *fpl* turísticas.
touristy ['tʊərɪstɪ] *adj pej* muito turístico(ca).
tournament ['tɔːnəmənt] *n CHESS & SPORT* torneio *m*.
tourniquet ['tʊənɪkeɪ] *n* torniquete *m*.
tour operator *n* agência *f* de viagens.
tousle *vt* **-1.** [hair] despentear **-2.** [fur, feathers] desarrumar.
tout [taʊt] <> *n* cambista *mf*. <> *vt* [tickets, goods] revender *(como cambista)*. <> *vi*: **to ~ for sthg** angariar algo; **to ~ for trade** tentar obter algo; **to ~ for clients** aliciar algo; **to ~ for investment** buscar algo.
tow [təʊ] <> *n* reboque *m*; **on ~** *UK* a reboque; **with sb in ~** com alguém a reboque. <> *vt* rebocar.
towards *UK* [tə'wɔːdz], **toward** *US* [tə'wɔːd] *prep* **-1.** [in the direction of] para, em direção a **-2.** [indicating attitude] em relação a **-3.** [near in time, space] perto de **-4.** [as contribution to] para.
towaway zone ['təʊəweɪ-] *n US* zona *f* de estacionamento proibido.
towbar ['təʊbɑː] *n* engate *m* para reboque.
towel ['taʊəl] *n* toalha *f*.
towelling *UK*, **toweling** *US* ['taʊəlɪŋ] <> *n (U)* tecido *m* atoalhado. <> *comp* atoalhado(da).
towel rail *n* toalheiro *m*.
tower ['taʊə[r]] <> *n* torre *f*; **a ~ of strength** *UK* um forte apoio. <> *vi* destacar-se; **to ~ over sb** ser muito mais alto(ta) do que alguém; **to ~ over/sthg** destacar-se por cima de algo.
tower block *n UK* prédio *m* alto de escritórios.
towering ['taʊərɪŋ] *adj* [very tall] altíssimo(ma).
town [taʊn] *n* **-1.** [population centre] cidade *f* **-2.** *(U)* [centre of town, city] centro *m* (da cidade); **to go out on the ~** ir divertir-se; **to go to ~** *fig* botar para quebrar.
town centre *n* centro *m* (da cidade).
town clerk *n* secretário *m*, -ria *f* da câmara municipal.
town council *n* câmara *f* municipal.
town hall *n* **-1.** [building] prefeitura *f* **-2.** *(U) fig* [council] prefeitura *f*.
town house *n* [fashionable house] mansão *f*.
town plan *n* **-1.** [map] mapa *m* da cidade **-2.** [project, plan] projeto *m* de urbanização.
town planner *n* urbanista *mf*.
town planning *n (U)* **-1.** [study] urbanismo *m* **-2.** [practice] urbanização *f*.
townsfolk ['taʊnzfəʊk], **townspeople** ['taʊnz,piːpl] *npl*: **the ~** os habitantes *(de uma cidade)*, os cidadãos.
township ['taʊnʃɪp] *n* **-1.** [in South Africa] *zona urbana atribuída antigamente pelo governo à população negra* **-2.** [in US] ≃ município *m*.
towpath ['təʊpɑːθ, *pl* -pɑːðz] *n* caminho *m* de sirga.
towrope ['təʊrəʊp] *n* cabo *m* para reboque.
tow truck *n US* guincho *m*, reboque *m*.
toxic ['tɒksɪk] *adj* tóxico(ca).
toxin ['tɒksɪn] *n* toxina *f*.
toy [tɔɪ] *n* brinquedo *m*.
◆ **toy with** *vt fus* **-1.** [idea]: **to ~ with sthg** pensar em algo **-2.** [play]: **to ~ with sthg** brincar com algo.
toyboy *n inf* amante *m* de uma coroa.
toy shop *n* loja *f* de brinquedos.
trace [treɪs] <> *n* **-1.** [evidence, remains] vestígio *m*; **without ~** sem deixar vestígio **-2.** [small amount] vestígio *m*. <> *vt* **-1.** [find] localizar **-2.** [follow progress of] traçar **-3.** [mark outline of] traçar ; [with tracing paper] decalcar.
trace element *n CHEM* elemento-traço *m*.
tracer bullet ['treɪsə[r]-] *n* projétil *m* luminoso.
tracing ['treɪsɪŋ] *n* [on paper] decalque *m*.
tracing paper ['treɪsɪŋ-] *n (U)* papel *m* de decalque.
track [træk] <> *n* **-1.** [path] trilha *f*; **off the beaten ~** isolado(da) **-2.** *SPORT* pista *f* **-3.** *RAIL* trilho *m* **-4.** [mark, trace] pegada *f*; **to hide** *OR* **cover one's ~s** não deixar rasto; **to stop dead in one's ~s** parar atônito(ta) **-5.** [on record, tape, CD] faixa *f* **-6.** *phr*: **to keep ~ of sb/sthg** não perder alguém/algo de vista; **to lose ~ of sb/sthg** perder alguém/algo de vista; **to be on the right/wrong ~** estar no caminho certo/errado. <> *vt* [follow] seguir a pista de. <> *vi* [camera] seguir.
◆ **track down** *vt sep* localizar.
tracker dog ['trækə[r]-] *n* cão *m* de caça *OR* policial.
track event *n* prova *f* de atletismo *(na pista)*.
tracking station ['trækɪŋ-] *n* estação *f* de rastreamento.
track record *n* histórico *m (de reputação)*.
track shoes *npl* calçados *mpl* de corrida.
tracksuit ['træksuːt] *n* abrigo *m* esportivo.
tract [trækt] *n* **-1.** [pamphlet] panfleto *m* **-2.** [of land, forest] extensão *f* **-3.** *MED* trato *m*; **digestive ~** aparelho *m* digestivo.
traction ['trækʃn] *n (U)* **-1.** *PHYSICS* tração *f* **-2.** *MED* tração *f*; **to have one's leg in ~** fazer tração na perna.
traction engine *n* veículo *m* de carga pesada.
tractor ['træktə[r]] *n* trator *m*.
tractor-trailer *n US* veículo *m* articulado.
trade [treɪd] <> *n* **-1.** *(U)* [commerce] comércio *m* **-2.** [job] profissão *f*, ofício *m*; **by ~** por formação. <> *vt* [exchange] negociar; **to ~ sthg for sthg** trocar algo por algo. <> *vi* **-1.** *COMM* [do business] negociar; **to ~ with sb** negociar com alguém **-2.** *US* [shop]: **to ~ at** *OR* **with** comprar em.
◆ **trade in** *vt sep* [exchange] dar como entrada.
trade barrier *n* barreira *f* comercial.
trade deficit *n* déficit *m* comercial.
trade discount *n (U)* desconto *m* para revendedor.
trade fair *n* feira *f* industrial.
trade gap *n* déficit *m* na balança comercial.
trade-in *n objeto ou artigo que se entrega como entrada ao se comprar um novo*, base *f* de troca.

trademark ['treɪdmɑ:k] *n* **-1.** *COMM* marca *f* registrada **-2.** *fig* [characteristic] marca *f* registrada.
trade name *n COMM* razão *f* social.
trade-off *n* equilíbrio *m*.
trade price *n* preço *m* de atacado.
trader ['treɪdəʳ] *n* comerciante *mf*.
trade route *n* rota *f* de comércio.
trade secret *n* segredo *m* comercial.
tradesman ['treɪdzmən] (*pl* **-men** [-mən]) *n* [shopkeeper, trader] comerciante *m*.
tradespeople ['treɪdz,pi:pl] *npl* comerciantes *mfpl*.
trades union *n UK* = **trade union**.
Trades Union Congress *n UK*: **the ~** *a associação britânica dos sindicatos*.
trades unionist *n UK* = **trade unionist**.
trade union *n* sindicato *m*.
trade unionist *n* sindicalista *mf*.
trading ['treɪdɪŋ] *n (U)* comércio *m*.
trading estate *n UK* distrito *m* industrial.
trading stamp *n* cupom *m* promocional.
tradition [trə'dɪʃn] *n* **-1.** *(U)* [system of customs] tradição *f* **-2.** [established practice] costume *m*.
traditional [trə'dɪʃənl] *adj* tradicional.
traditionally [trə'dɪʃnəlɪ] *adv* tradicionalmente.
traffic ['træfɪk] (*pt* & *pp* **-ked**, *cont* **-king**) ◇ *n (U)* **-1.** [vehicles] tráfego *m* **-2.** [illegal trade] tráfico *m*; **~ in sthg** tráfico de algo. ◇ *vi*: **to ~ in sthg** traficar algo.
traffic circle *n US* rotatória *f*.
traffic island *n* canteiro *m* central.
traffic jam *n* congestionamento *m*.
trafficker ['træfɪkəʳ] *n* traficante *mf*; **~ in sthg** traficante de algo.
traffic lights *npl* semáforo *m*.
traffic offence *UK*, **traffic violation** *US n* infração *f* de trânsito.
traffic sign *n* sinal *m* de trânsito.
traffic violation *n US* = **traffic offence**.
traffic warden *n UK* guarda *mf* de trânsito.
tragedy ['trædʒədɪ] (*pl* **-ies**) *n* **-1.** *(U)* [ill fate, dramatic form] tragédia *f* **-2.** [terrible event, play] tragédia *f*.
tragic ['trædʒɪk] *adj* trágico(ca).
tragically ['trædʒɪklɪ] *adv* tragicamente.
trail [treɪl] ◇ *n* **-1.** [path] trilha *f*; **to blaze a ~** *fig* abrir caminho **-2.** [traces] rastro *m*; **on the ~ of sb/sthg** na pista de alguém/algo. ◇ *vt* **-1.** [drag behind, tow] arrastar **-2.** [lag behind] estar atrás de. ◇ *vi* **-1.** [drag behind] arrastar **-2.** [move slowly] andar lentamente **-3.** *SPORT* [lose] perder.
◆ **trail away, trail off** *vi* apagar-se.
trailblazing ['treɪl,bleɪzɪŋ] *adj* pioneiro(ra).
trailer ['treɪləʳ] *n* **-1.** [vehicle for luggage] reboque *m* **-2.** *esp US* [for living in] trailer *m* **-3.** *CINEMA* trailer *m*.
trailer court, trailer park *n US* camping *m (para trailers)*.
train [treɪn] ◇ *n* **-1.** *RAIL* trem *m* **-2.** [of dress] cauda *f* **-3.** [connected sequence]: **~ of thought** linha *f* de raciocínio. ◇ *vt* **-1.** [teach] treinar; **to ~ sb to do sthg** treinar alguém para fazer algo; **to ~ sb in sthg** treinar alguém em algo **-2.** [for job]: **to ~ sb as sthg** preparar *OR* formar alguém para ser algo **-3.** *SPORT* treinar; **to ~ sb for sthg** treinar alguém para algo **-4.** [plant] dirigir **-5.** [gun, camera] apontar. ◇ *vi* **-1.** [for job] preparar-se; **to ~ as sthg** estudar para algo **-2.** *SPORT* treinar; **to ~ for sthg** treinar para algo.
train driver *n* maquinista *mf*.
trained [treɪnd] *adj* **-1.** [psychologist] formado(da) **-2.** [singer] profissional **-3.** [cartographer] qualificado(-da) **-4.** [doctor] especializado(da).
trainee [treɪ'ni:] ◇ *adj* estagiário(ria). ◇ *n* estagiário *m*, -ria *f*, trainee *mf*.
trainer ['treɪnəʳ] *n* **-1.** [of animals] amestrador *m*, -ra *f* **-2.** *SPORT* treinador *m*, -ra *f*.
◆ **trainers** *npl UK* [shoes] tênis *m inv* para a prática desportiva.
training ['treɪnɪŋ] *n (U)* **-1.** [for job]: **~ in sthg** formação *f* em algo, treinamento *m* para algo **-2.** *SPORT* treinamento *m*.
training college *n UK* escola *f* profissionalizante.
training course *n* curso *m* de formação profissional.
training shoes *npl UK* tênis *m inv* para a prática desportiva.
train set *n* trenzinho *m*.
train spotter [-,spɒtəʳ] *n aficcionado por trens que vai até as estações para contar o número que trens que passam*.
train station *n US* & *Scot* estação *f* ferroviária.
traipse [treɪps] *vi* vaguear.
trait [treɪt] *n* traço *m*.
traitor ['treɪtəʳ] *n* traidor *m*, -ra *f*; **~ to sthg** traidor(ra) de algo.
trajectory [trə'dʒektərɪ] (*pl* **-ies**) *n TECH* trajetória *f*.
tram [træm], **tramcar** ['træmkɑ:ʳ] *n UK* bonde *m*.
tramcar *n UK fml* bonde *m*.
tramlines ['træmlaɪnz] *npl* **-1.** [for trams] trilhos *mpl* do bonde **-2.** *TENNIS* linha *f* lateral de duplas.
tramp [træmp] ◇ *n* vagabundo *m*, -da *f*. ◇ *vt* caminhar a pé por. ◇ *vi* andar com passos pesados.
trample ['træmpl] ◇ *vt* esmagar com os pés, pisar em. ◇ *vi* **-1.** [tread]: **to ~ on sthg** pisar em algo **-2.** *fig* [act cruelly]: **to ~ on sb** espezinhar alguém.
trampoline ['træmpəli:n] *n* trampolim *m*.
trance [trɑ:ns] *n* [hypnotic state] transe *m*; **in a ~** em transe.
tranquil ['træŋkwɪl] *adj literary* plácido(da).
tranquility *n US* = **tranquillity**.
tranquilize *vt US* = **tranquillize**.
tranquilizer *n US* = **tranquillizer**.
tranquillity *UK*, **tranquility** *US* [træŋ'kwɪlətɪ] *n (U)* tranqüilidade *f*.
tranquillize, -ise *UK*, **tranquilize** *US* ['træŋkwɪlaɪz] *vt* tranqüilizar.
tranquillizer *UK*, **tranquilizer** *US* ['træŋkwɪlaɪzəʳ] *n* tranqüilizante *m*.
transact [træn'zækt] *vt fml* fazer, levar a cabo.
transaction [træn'zækʃn] *n* transação *f*.
transatlantic [,trænzət'læntɪk] *adj* **-1.** [crossing the Atlantic] transatlântico(ca) **-2.** [on the other side of the Atlantic] de além-mar.

transceiver [træn'si:vəʳ] *n* rádio *m* transmissor-receptor.
transcend [træn'send] *vt fml* [go beyond] transcender.
transcendental meditation [ˌtrænsen'dentl-] *n (U)* meditação *f* transcedental.
transcribe [træn'skraɪb] *vt* transcrever.
transcript ['trænskrɪpt] *n* [of speech, conversation] transcrição *f*.
transept ['trænsept] *n* transepto *m*.
transfer [*n* 'trænsfɜ:ʳ, *vb* træns'fɜ:r] (*pt* & *pp* **-red**, *cont* **-ring**) <> *n* **-1.** [gen] transferência *f* **-2.** [design] decalcomania *f* **-3.** *US* [ticket] passagem *f* válida para conexão. <> *vt* transferir. <> *vi* transferir -se.
transferable [træns'fɜ:rəbl] *adj* transferível.
transference ['trænsfərəns] *n (U) fml* [act of transferring] transferência *f*.
transfer fee *n UK* SPORT (valor *m* do) passe *m*.
transfigure [træns'fɪgəʳ] *vt literary* transfigurar.
transfix [træns'fɪks] *vt* [immobilize] paralisar.
transform [træns'fɔ:m] *vt* transformar; **to ~ sb/sthg into sthg** transformar alguém/algo em algo.
transformation [ˌtrænsfə'meɪʃn] *n* transformação *f*.
transformer [træns'fɔ:məʳ] *n* ELEC transformador *m*.
transfusion [træns'fju:ʒn] *n* transfusão *f*.
transgress [træns'gres] *fml* <> *vt* transgredir. <> *vi* cometer uma transgressão.
transgression [træns'greʃn] *n fml* transgressão *f*.
transient ['trænzɪənt] <> *adj fml* [fleeting] transitório(ria). <> *n US* [person] pessoa *f* em trânsito.
transistor [træn'zɪstəʳ] *n* ELECTRON transistor *m*.
transistor radio *n dated* (rádio *m*) transistor *m*.
transit ['trænsɪt] *n*: **in ~** de passagem.
transit camp *n* acampamento *m* provisório.
transition [træn'zɪʃn] *n* **-1.** [change] transição *f* **-2.** *(U)* [act of changing] transição *f*; **~ from sthg to sthg** transição de algo para algo; **in ~** em transição.
transitional [træn'zɪʃənl] *adj* de transição.
transitive ['trænzɪtɪv] *adj* GRAMM transitivo(va).
transit lounge *n* sala *f* de trânsito.
transitory ['trænzɪtrɪ] *adj* transitório(ria).
translate [træns'leɪt] <> *vt* **-1.** [languages] traduzir **-2.** *fig* [transform]: **to ~ sthg into sthg** transformar algo em algo. <> *vi* **-1.** [words] traduzir-se; **to ~ from sthg into sthg** traduzir de algo para algo **-2.** [person] traduzir.
translation [træns'leɪʃn] *n* tradução *f*.
translator [træns'leɪtəʳ] *n* tradutor *m*, -ra *f*.
translucent [trænz'lu:snt] *adj* translúcido(da).
transmission [trænz'mɪʃn] *n* transmissão *f*.
transmit [trænz'mɪt] (*pt* & *pp* **-ted**, *cont* **-ting**) *vt* transmitir.
transmitter [trænz'mɪtəʳ] *n* ELECTRON transmissor *m*.
transparency [trans'pærənsɪ] (*pl* **-ies**) *n* transparência *f*.
transparent [træns'pærənt] *adj* **-1.** [gen] transparente **-2.** [obvious] óbvio(via).
transpire [træn'spaɪəʳ] *fml* <> *vt*: **it ~s that ...** descobre-se que ... <> *vi* [happen] acontecer, ocorrer.
transplant [*n* 'trænsplɑ:nt, *vb* træns'plɑ:nt] <> *n* transplante *m*. <> *vt* **-1.** [gen] transplantar **-2.** [population] transferir.
transport [*n* 'trænspɔ:t, *vb* træn'spɔ:t] <> *n* transporte *m*. <> *vt* [goods, people] transportar.
transportable [træn'spɔ:təbl] *adj* transportável.
transportation [ˌtrænspɔ:'teɪʃn] *n (U) esp US* = **transport**.
transport cafe ['trænspɔ:t-] *n UK* lanchonete *m* de estrada.
transporter [træn'spɔ:təʳ] *n* caminhão *m* para transporte de automóveis.
transpose [træns'pəʊz] *vt* [change round] inverter.
transsexual [træns'sekʃʊəl] *n* transexual *mf*.
transvestite [trænz'vestaɪt] *n* travesti *mf*.
trap [træp] (*pt* & *pp* **-ped**, *cont* **-ping**) <> *n* **-1.** [for animal, bird] armadilha *f* **-2.** *fig* [trick] cilada *f*. <> *vt* **-1.** [animal, bird] apanhar em armadilha **-2.** *fig* [trick] armar uma cilada **-3.** [immobilize, catch]: **to be ~ped in sthg** ficar preso(sa) em algo **-4.** [retain] guardar.
trapdoor [ˌtræp'dɔ:ʳ] *n* alçapão *m*.
trapeze [trə'pi:z] *n* trapézio *m*.
trapper ['træpəʳ] *n* caçador *m*, -ra *f* que põe armadilhas.
trappings ['træpɪŋz] *npl* pompas *fpl*.
trash [træʃ] <> *n (U)* **-1.** *US* [refuse] lixo *m* **-2.** *inf pej* [sthg of poor quality] lixo *m*, porcaria *f*. <> *vt US* **-1.** [criticize] acabar com, demolir **-2.** [damage] arrasar.
trashcan ['træʃkæn] *n US* lata *f* de lixo.
trashy ['træʃɪ] (*compar* **-ier**, *superl* **-iest**) *adj inf* imprestável.
trauma ['trɔ:mə] *n* **-1.** [distressing experience] trauma *m* **-2.** *(U)* [distress] trauma *m*.
traumatic [trɔ:'mætɪk] *adj* traumático(ca).
traumatize, -ise ['trɔ:mətaɪz] *vt* [shock] traumatizar.
travel ['trævl] (*UK pt* & *pp* **-led**, *cont* **-ling**, *US pt* & *pp* **-ed**, *cont* **-ing**) <> *n (U)* viagem *f*; **I'm keen on ~** eu adoro viajar. <> *vt* **-1.** [place] viajar por **-2.** [distance] viajar. <> *vi* **-1.** [gen] viajar **-2.** [news] voar.
◆ **travels** *npl* viagens *fpl*.
travel agency *n* agência *f* de viagens.
travel agent *n* agente *mf* de viagens; **~'s** agência *f* de viagens.
travel brochure *n* catálogo *m* de viagens.
travel card *n* passe *m*.
traveler *etc n US* = **traveller** *etc*.
travelled *UK*, **traveled** *US* ['trævld] *adj* **-1.** [person] viajado(da) **-2.** [road, route] movimentado(da).
traveller *UK*, **traveler** *US* ['trævləʳ] *n* **-1.** [gen] viajante *mf* **-2.** [sales representative] representante *mf* comercial.
traveller's cheque *n* cheque *m* de viagem, traveler's cheque *m*.
travelling *UK*, **traveling** *US* ['trævlɪŋ] *adj* **-1.** [itinerant] itinerante, ambulante **-2.** [portable, of travel] de viagem.
travelling expenses *npl* despesas *fpl* de viagem.
travelling salesman *n* caixeiro-viajante *m*.
travelogue, travelog *US* ['trævəlɒg] *n* **-1.** [talk]

conferência *f* sobre uma viagem **-2.** [film] documentário *m* sobre viagem.

travelsick ['trævəlsɪk] *adj* enjoado(da) *(pela viagem).*

traverse ['trævəs, ˌtrə'vɜːs] *vt fml* atravessar.

travesty ['trævəstɪ] (*pl* **-ies**) *n* paródia *f*.

trawl [trɔːl] ◇ *n* **-1.** [fishing net] rede *f* de arrasto **-2.** [search] busca *f*. ◇ *vt* **-1.** [fish]: **to ~ sthg (for sthg)** vasculhar algo (à procura de algo) **-2.** [search]: **to ~ sthg for sthg** conferir algo à procura de algo. ◇ *vi* **-1.** [fish]: **to ~ for sthg** pescar com rede de arrasto à procura de algo **-2.** [search]: **to ~ for sthg** procurar (por) algo.

trawler ['trɔːləʳ] *n* traineira *f*.

tray [treɪ] *n* bandeja *f*.

treacherous ['tretʃərəs] *adj* **-1.** [person] traidor(ra) **-2.** [plan, behaviour] traiçoeiro(ra) **-3.** [dangerous] perigoso(sa).

treachery ['tretʃərɪ] *n (U)* traição *f*.

treacle ['triːkl] *n (U) UK* melado *m*.

tread [tred] (*pt* **trod**, *pp* **trodden**) ◇ *n* **-1.** [on tyre] banda *f* de rodagem **-2.** [shoe] sola *f* **-3.** [sound or way of walking] passos *mpl*. ◇ *vt* [crush] esmagar com os pés; **to ~ sthg into sthg** esmagar algo em algo. ◇ *vi* **-1.** [place foot]: **to ~ on sthg** pisar em algo **-2.** [walk, progress] andar; **to ~ carefully** *fig* andar com cuidado.

treadle ['tredl] *n* pedal *m*.

treadmill ['tredmɪl] *n* **-1.** [wheel] roda *f* de moinho **-2.** *fig* [dull routine] rotina *f*.

treas. (*abbr of* **treasurer**) tesoureiro *m*, -ra *f*.

treason ['triːzn] *n (U)* traição *f*.

treasure ['treʒəʳ] ◇ *n lit* & *fig* tesouro *m*. ◇ *vt* dar valor a.

treasure hunt *n* caça *f* ao tesouro.

treasurer ['treʒərəʳ] *n* tesoureiro *m*, -ra *f*.

treasure trove *n (U) JUR* tesouro *m* escondido.

treasury ['treʒərɪ] (*pl* **-ies**) *n* [room] sala *f* do tesouro.
◆ **Treasury** *n*: **the Treasury** ≃ o Ministério da Fazenda.

treasury bill *n* letra *f* do Tesouro.

treat [triːt] ◇ *vt* **-1.** [handle, deal with] tratar; **to ~ sb/sthg as sthg, to ~ sb/sthg like sthg** tratar alguém/algo como algo **-2.** [give sthg special]: **to ~ sb (to sthg)** invitar alguém (para algo); **to ~ o.s. to sthg** presentear-se com algo **-3.** [*MED*, process] tratar. ◇ *n* **-1.** [food] delícia *f* **-2.** [gift] prazer *m*.

treatise ['triːtɪs] *n fml*: **~ (on sthg)** tratado *m* (sobre algo).

treatment ['triːtmənt] *n* tratamento *m*.

treaty ['triːtɪ] (*pl* **-ies**) *n* [written agreement] tratado *m*.

treble ['trebl] ◇ *adj* **-1.** *MUS* de soprano **-2.** [with numbers]: **my phone extension is ~ 4** meu ramal é 444. ◇ *n MUS* soprano *m*. ◇ *vt* & *vi* triplicar.

treble clef *n* clave *f* de sol.

tree [triː] *n* árvore *f*; **to be barking up the wrong ~** acusar erroneamente.

tree-lined *adj* arborizado(da).

tree surgeon *n especialista no cuidado de árvores.*

treetop ['triːtɒp] *n* copa *f* (de árvore).

tree-trunk *n* tronco *m* (de árvore).

trek [trek] (*pt* & *pp* **-ked**, *cont* **-king**) ◇ *n* expedição *f*. ◇ *vi* **-1.** [go on long journey] fazer uma expedição **-2.** *inf* [walk laboriously] caminhar com dificuldade.

trellis ['trelɪs] *n* treliça *f*.

tremble ['trembl] *vi* tremer.

tremendous [trɪ'mendəs] *adj* **-1.** [impressive, large] tremendo(da), enorme **-2.** *inf* [really good] fabuloso(sa).

tremendously [trɪ'mendəslɪ] *adv* [impressively, hugely] enormemente.

tremor ['treməʳ] *n* tremor *m*.

tremulous ['tremjʊləs] *adj literary* trêmulo(la).

trench [trentʃ] *n* **-1.** [narrow channel] vala *f* **-2.** *MIL* trincheira *f*.

trenchant ['trentʃənt] *adj fml* mordaz.

trench coat *n* capa *f* de chuva.

trench warfare *n (U)* guerra *f* de trincheiras.

trend [trend] *n* [tendency] tendência *f*.

trendsetter ['trendˌsetəʳ] *n* iniciador *m*, -ra *f* de modas.

trendy ['trendɪ] (*compar* **-ier**, *superl* **-iest**, *pl* **-ies**) *inf* ◇ *adj* **-1.** [person] moderno(na) **-2.** [clothes, music] da moda. ◇ *n* pessoa *f* moderna.

trepidation [ˌtrepɪ'deɪʃn] *n (U) fml*: **in** *OR* **with ~** com ansiedade.

trespass ['trespəs] *vi* [on sb's land] invadir; **'no ~ing'** 'entrada proibida'.

trespasser ['trespəsəʳ] *n* invasor *m*, -ra *f*; **'~s will be prosecuted'** 'os invasores serão punidos por lei'.

trestle ['tresl] *n* cavalete *m*.

trestle table *n* mesa *f* de cavalete.

trial ['traɪəl] *n* **-1.** *JUR* julgamento *m*; **to be on ~ (for sthg)** ser processado(da) (por algo) **-2.** [test, experiment] teste *m*; **on ~** em testes; **by ~ and error** por tentativa e erro **-3.** [unpleasant experience] suplício *m*; **~s and tribulations** dificuldades *fpl* e problemas.

trial basis *n*: **on a ~** como experiência.

trial period *n* período *m* de experiência.

trial run *n* ensaio *m*.

trial-size(d) *adj* em tamanho de amostra.

triangle ['traɪæŋgl] *n* **-1.** [gen] triângulo *m* **-2.** *US* [set square] esquadro *m*.

triangular [traɪ'æŋgjʊləʳ] *adj* [in triangle shape] triangular.

triathlon [traɪ'æθlɒn] (*pl* **-s**) *n* triatlo *m*.

tribal ['traɪbl] *adj* tribal.

tribe [traɪb] *n* [social group] tribo *f*.

tribulation [ˌtrɪbjʊ'leɪʃn] *n* ▷ **trial**.

tribunal [traɪ'bjuːnl] *n* tribunal *m*.

tribune ['trɪbjuːn] *n HIST* tribuno *m*.

tributary ['trɪbjʊtrɪ] (*pl* **-ies**) *n GEOGR* afluente *m*.

tribute ['trɪbjuːt] *n* **-1.** [act of respect, admiration] tributo *m*; **to be a ~ to sb/sthg** ser um tributo para alguém/algo; **to pay ~ (to sb/sthg)** prestar homenagem (a alguém/algo) **-2.** [evidence] prova *f* **-3.** *(U)* [respect, admiration] homenagem *f*; **to pay ~ (to sb/sthg)** prestar homenagem (a alguém/algo).

trice [traɪs] *n*: **in a ~** num abrir e fechar de olhos.

triceps ['traɪseps] (*pl inv OR* **-cepses**) *n* tríceps *m inv*.

trick [trɪk] ◇ *n* **-1.** [to deceive] trapaça *f*; **to play a ~ on sb** pregar uma peça em alguém **-2.** [to entertain] truque *m* **-3.** [ability, knack] hábito *m*; **to do the ~** dar resultado. ◇ *adj* **-1.** [knife] de brincadeira **-2.** [moustache] postiço(ça). ◇ *vt* enganar; **to ~ sb into sthg** enrolar alguém sobre algo; **to ~ sb into doing sthg** enrolar alguém para que faça algo.
trickery ['trɪkərɪ] *n (U)* trapaça *f*.
trickle ['trɪkl] ◇ *n* **-1.** [of liquid] fio *m* **-2.** [of people or things] pingo *m*. ◇ *vi* **-1.** [liquid] gotejar, pingar **-2.** [people, things]: **to trickle in/out** entrar/sair aos poucos.
trick or treat *n (U)* gostosuras *fpl* ou travessuras.
trick question *n* pega-ratão *m*.
tricky ['trɪkɪ] (*compar* **-ier**, *superl* **-iest**) *adj* [difficult] enrolado(da), complicado(da).
tricycle ['traɪsɪkl] *n* triciclo *m*.
trident ['traɪdnt] *n* tridente *m*.
tried [traɪd] ◇ *pt* & *pp* ▷ **try**. ◇ *adj*: **~ and tested** testado e aprovado, testada e aprovada.
trier ['traɪə^r] *n* batalhador *m*, -ra *f*.
trifle ['traɪfl] *n* **-1.** CULIN *sobremesa de biscoito feito com gelatina, creme, frutas e nata* **-2.** [unimportant thing] ninharia *f*.
◆ **a trifle** *adv fml* ligeiramente, um pouco.
◆ **trifle with** *vt fus*: **he's not a person to be ~d with** não é uma pessoa com a qual se possa brincar.
trifling ['traɪflɪŋ] *adj pej* insignificante.
trigger ['trɪgə^r] ◇ *n* [on gun] gatilho *m*. ◇ *vt* **-1.** [mechanism] acionar **-2.** [explosion, reaction] desencadear **-3.** [revolution, protest] provocar.
◆ **trigger off** *vt sep* = **trigger**.
trigger-happy *adj* provocador(ra).
trigonometry [,trɪgə'nɒmətrɪ] *n (U)* trigonometria *f*.
trilby ['trɪlbɪ] (*pl* **-ies**) *n UK* chapéu *m* de feltro.
trill [trɪl] ◇ *n* **-1.** MUS tremolo *m* **-2.** [of birds] trinado *m*. ◇ *vi* trinar.
trillions ['trɪljənz] *npl inf* milhares *mpl*; **~ of** um monte de.
trilogy ['trɪlədʒɪ] (*pl* **-ies**) *n* trilogia *f*.
trim [trɪm] (*compar* **-mer**, *superl* **-mest**, *pt* & *pp* **-med**, *cont* **-ming**) ◇ *adj* **-1.** [neat and tidy] bem cuidado(-da) **-2.** [slim] esbelto(ta). ◇ *n* **-1.** [cut - hair] corte *m*; [- hedge] poda *f* **-2.** [decoration] enfeite *m*. ◇ *vt* **-1.** [cut - hair, nails, lawn] cortar; [- hedge] podar; [- moustache] aparar **-2.** [decorate] enfeitar; **to ~ sthg with sthg** enfeitar algo com algo.
◆ **trim away, trim off** *vt sep* cortar.
trimmed [trɪmd] *adj*: **~ with sthg** enfeitado(da) com algo.
trimming *n* [on clothing] enfeite *m*.
◆ **trimmings** *npl* **-1.** CULIN guarnição *f* **-2.** [scraps] aparas *fpl*.
Trinidad and Tobago ['trɪnɪdæd-] *n* Trinidad e Tobago; **in ~** em Trinidad e Tobago.
Trinidadian ◇ *adj* trinitário(ria). ◇ *n* trinitário *m*, -ria *f*.
Trinity ['trɪnətɪ] *n* RELIG: **the ~** a Trindade.
trinket ['trɪŋkɪt] *n* adorno *m*.
trio ['tri:əʊ] (*pl* **-s**) *n* trio *m*.
trip [trɪp] (*pt* & *pp* **-ped**, *cont* **-ping**) ◇ *n* **-1.** [journey] viagem *f* **-2.** *drugs sl* [experience] viagem *f*. ◇ *vt* [make stumble] fazer tropeçar, passar uma rasteira em. ◇ *vi* [stumble]: **to ~ (over)** tropeçar (em); **to ~ over sthg** tropeçar em algo.
◆ **trip up** *vt sep* **-1.** [make stumble] fazer tropeçar **-2.** [catch out] passar uma rasteira em.
tripartite [,traɪ'pɑ:taɪt] *adj fml* [agreement, talks] tripartite.
tripe [traɪp] *n (U)* **-1.** CULIN dobradinha *f* **-2.** *inf* [nonsense] bobajada *f*.
triple ['trɪpl] ◇ *adj* triplo(pla). ◇ *vt* & *vi* triplicar.
triple jump *n*: **the ~** o salto triplo.
triplets ['trɪplɪts] *npl* trigêmeos *mpl*, -meas *fpl*.
triplicate ['trɪplɪkət] ◇ *adj fml* em triplicata. ◇ *n*: **in ~** em três vias.
tripod ['traɪpɒd] *n* tripé *m*.
Tripoli ['trɪpəlɪ] *n* Tripoli.
tripper ['trɪpə^r] *n esp UK* excursionista *mf*, turista *mf*.
tripwire ['trɪpwaɪə^r] *n* fio *m* de armadilha.
trite [traɪt] *adj pej* banal.
triumph ['traɪəmf] ◇ *n* **-1.** [success] triunfo *m* **-2.** *(U)* [satisfaction] triunfo *m*. ◇ *vi* triunfar; **to ~ over sb/sthg** triunfar sobre alguém/algo.
triumphal [traɪ'ʌmfl] *adj fml* triunfal.
triumphant [traɪ'ʌmfənt] *adj* [exultant] triunfante.
triumphantly [trɪ'ʌmfəntlɪ] *adv* triunfalmente.
triumvirate *n* HIST triunvirato *m*.
trivet *n* **-1.** [over fire] trempe *f* **-2.** [to protect table] suporte *m* para pratos.
trivia ['trɪvɪə] *n (U)* trivialidades *fpl*.
trivial ['trɪvɪəl] *adj pej* trivial.
triviality [,trɪvɪ'ælətɪ] (*pl* **-ies**) *n* **-1.** [sthg unimportant] trivialidade *f* **-2.** *(U)* [lack of importance] trivialidade *f*.
trivialize, -ise ['trɪvɪəlaɪz] *vt* banalizar.
trod [trɒd] *pt* ▷ **tread**.
trodden ['trɒdn] ◇ *pp* ▷ **tread**. ◇ *adj* pisoteado(da).
Trojan ['trəʊdʒən] ◇ *adj* HIST troiano(na). ◇ *n* **-1.** HIST troiano *m*, -na *f* **-2.** *fig* [hard worker]: **to work like a ~** trabalhar como um escravo.
troll [trəʊl] *n* [goblin] troll *m*, trasgo *m*.
trolley ['trɒlɪ] (*pl* **trolleys**) *n* **-1.** *UK* [gen] carrinho *m* **-2.** *US* [vehicle] bonde *m*.
trolleybus ['trɒlɪbʌs] *n* ônibus *m inv* elétrico.
trolley case *n* mala *f* com rodinhas.
trombone [trɒm'bəʊn] *n* trombone *m*.
troop [tru:p] ◇ *n* [band] bando *m*, grupo *m*. ◇ *vi* [march] andar em bando; **to ~ in/out** entrar/sair em bando.
◆ **troops** *npl* MIL tropas *fpl*.
trooper ['tru:pə^r] *n* **-1.** MIL soldado *m* de cavalaria **-2.** *US* [policeman] policial *mf* militar.
troopship ['tru:pʃɪp] *n* navio-transporte *m*.
trophy ['trəʊfɪ] (*pl* **-ies**) *n* SPORT troféu *m*.
tropical ['trɒpɪkl] *adj* tropical.
Tropic of Cancer ['trɒpɪk-] *n*: **the ~** o Trópico de Cancer.
Tropic of Capricorn ['trɒpɪk-] *n*: **the ~** o Trópico de Capricórnio.
tropics ['trɒpɪks] *npl*: **the ~** os trópicos.

trot [trɒt] (*pt* & *pp* **-ted**, *cont* **-ting**) <> *n* **-1.** [of horse] trote *m* **-2.** [of person] passo *m* apressado. <> *vi* **-1.** [horse] trotar **-2.** [person] andar apressadamente.
◆ **on the trot** *adv inf*: **four times on the ~** quatro vezes seguidas.
◆ **trot out** *vt sep pej*: **to ~ out the same old excuses** ficar repetindo as mesmas desculpas manjadas.

Trotskyism ['trɒtskɪɪzm] *n (U)* trotskismo *m*.

trotter ['trɒtə^r] *n* [pig's foot] pé *m* de porco.

trouble ['trʌbl] <> *n* **-1.** *(U)* [difficulty] problema *m*; **to be in ~** [having problems] estar com problemas; **to get into ~** [with sb in authority] ter conflitos; **the ~ with sb/sthg is ...** o problema com alguém/algo é ... **-2.** [bother] incômodo *m*; **to take the ~ to do sthg** dar-se ao trabalho de fazer algo; **to be asking for ~** procurar problema **-3.** *(U)* [pain, illness] problema *m* **-4.** *(U)* [fighting] confusão *f* **-5.** POL [unrest] agitação *f*. <> *vt* **-1.** [worry, upset] preocupar **-2.** [interrupt, disturb] importunar **-3.** [cause pain to] incomodar.
◆ **troubles** *npl* **-1.** [worries] problemas *mpl*, preocupações *fpl* **-2.** POL [unrest] conflitos *mpl*.

troubled ['trʌbld] *adj* **-1.** [worried, upset] preocupado(da) **-2.** [disturbed - sleep] agitado(da); [- life, place, time] tumultuado(da).

trouble-free *adj* sem problemas.

troublemaker ['trʌbl,meɪkə^r] *n* agitador *m*, -ra *f*.

troubleshooter ['trʌbl,ʃu:tə^r] *n* solucionador *m*, -ra *f* de problemas; **he's the ~ here** é ele quem resolve os problemas aqui.

troublesome ['trʌblsəm] *adj* problemático(ca).

trouble spot *n* área *f* de conflito.

trough [trɒf] *n* **-1.** [for animals] cocho *m* **-2.** [low point] baixa *f*.

trounce [traʊns] *vt inf* [team, rivals] dar uma surra em, derrubar.

troupe [tru:p] *n* trupe *f*.

trouser press ['traʊzə^r-] *n* máquina *f* de passar calças.

trousers ['traʊzəz] *npl* calças *fpl*.

trouser suit ['traʊzə^r-] *n* **UK** terninho *m*.

trousseau ['tru:səʊ] (*pl* **-x** [-z], **-s**) *n* enxoval *m*.

trout [traʊt] (*pl inv* OR **-s**) *n* truta *f*.

trove [trəʊv] ▻ **treasure trove**.

trowel ['traʊəl] *n* **-1.** [for the garden] pá *f* de jardim **-2.** [for cement, plaster] colher *f* de pedreiro.

truancy ['tru:ənsɪ] *n (U)* gazeio *m*, falta *f* às aulas.

truant ['tru:ənt] *n* [child] criança *f* que mata às aulas; **to play ~** gazear OR matar aula.

truce [tru:s] *n* trégua *f*; **~ between** trégua entre.

truck [trʌk] <> *n* **-1.** *esp* **US** [lorry] caminhão *m* **-2.** RAIL vagão *m*. <> *vt* **US** transportar de caminhão.

truck driver *n esp* **US** motorista *mf* de caminhão.

trucker ['trʌkə^r] *n* **US** caminhoneiro *m*, -ra *f*.

truck farm *n* **US** chácara *f*.

trucking ['trʌkɪŋ] *n (U)* **US** transporte *m* por caminhão.

truck stop *n* **US** restaurante *m* para caminhoneiros.

truculent ['trʌkjʊlənt] *adj* truculento(ta).

trudge [trʌdʒ] <> *n* caminhada *f* difícil. <> *vi* arrastar-se.

true [tru:] *adj* **-1.** [factual] verdadeiro(ra); **I can't believe it's ~** não acredito que seja verdade; **to come ~** tornar-se realidade **-2.** [faithful, genuine] verdadeiro(ra); [- friend] de verdade **-3.** [precise, exact] exato(ta).

true-life *adj* baseado(da) na vida real.

truffle ['trʌfl] *n* trufa *f*.

truism ['tru:ɪzm] *n* truísmo *m*.

truly ['tru:lɪ] *adv* **-1.** [in fact] verdadeiramente **-2.** [sincerely] realmente; **~, I didn't do it** com toda sinceridade eu não fiz isso **-3.** [for emphasis] realmente **-4.** *phr*: **yours ~** [at end of letter] cordialmente; **and who do you think did that? - yours ~, of course!** e quem você acha que fez isso? - euzinho em pessoa, obviamente!

trump [trʌmp] <> *n* [card] trunfo *m*. <> *vt* trunfar.

trump card *n fig* trunfo *m*.

trumped-up ['trʌmpt-] *adj pej* forjado(da).

trumpet ['trʌmpɪt] <> *n* MUS trompete *m*. <> *vi* [elephant] barrir.

trumpeter ['trʌmpɪtə^r] *n* trompetista *mf*.

truncate *vt fml* truncado(da).

truncheon ['trʌntʃən] *n* cassetete *m*.

trundle ['trʌndl] <> *vt* empurrar lentamente. <> *vi* rodar lentamente.

trunk [trʌŋk] *n* **-1.** [gen] tronco *m* **-2.** [of elephant] tromba *f* **-3.** [box] baú *m* (de viagem) **-4.** **US** [of car] porta-malas *m inv*.
◆ **trunks** *npl* [for swimming] calção *m* de banho, sunga *f*.

trunk road *n* **UK** ≃ rodovia *f* nacional.

truss [trʌs] *n* **-1.** MED funda *f* OR cinta *f* para hérnia **-2.** CONSTR viga *f*.

trust [trʌst] <> *vt* **-1.** [have confidence in] confiar em; **to ~ sb to do sthg** confiar em alguém para fazer algo; **~ you!** *iro* conto com você! **-2.** [entrust]: **to ~ sb with sthg** confiar algo a alguém **-3.** *fml* [hope]: **to ~ (that)** esperar que. <> *n* **-1.** *(U)* [faith] confiança *f*; **~ in sb/sthg** confiança em alguém/algo; **to put** OR **place one's ~ in sb/sthg** pôr OR depositar sua confiança em alguém/algo; **to take sthg on ~** tomar algo como verdade **-2.** *(U)* [responsibility] confiança *f* **-3.** FIN fideicomisso *m*; **in ~** em fideicomisso **-4.** COMM truste *m*.

trust company *n* sociedade *f* fiduciária.

trusted ['trʌstɪd] *adj* de confiança.

trustee [trʌs'ti:] *n* **-1.** FIN & JUR fideicomissário *m*, -ria *f* **-2.** [of institution] curador *m*, -ra *f*.

trusteeship [,trʌs'ti:ʃɪp] *n (U)* fideicomisso *m*.

trust fund *n* fundo *m* fiduciário.

trusting ['trʌstɪŋ] *adj* crédulo(la).

trustworthy ['trʌst,wɜ:ðɪ] *adj* (digno(na)) de confiança.

trusty ['trʌstɪ] (*compar* **-ier**, *superl* **-iest**) *adj hum* fiel.

truth [tru:θ] *n* **-1.** [gen]: **the ~** a verdade; **to tell the ~** dizer a verdade; **to tell the ~, ...** para dizer a verdade, ... **-2.** *(U)* [veracity] veracidade *f*; **in (all) ~** em verdade, na realidade.

truth drug *n* droga *f* da verdade.

truthful ['tru:θfʊl] *n* **-1.** [person] sincero(ra), verdadeiro(ra) **-2.** [story] verídico(ca).

try [traɪ] (*pt* & *pp* **-ied**, *pl* **-ies**) <> *vt* **-1.** [attempt]

tentar; **to ~ to do sthg** tentar fazer algo **-2.** [sample, test] experimentar **-3.** *JUR* levar a juízo **-4.** [tax, strain] cansar; **to ~ sb's patience** esgotar a paciência de alguém. <> *vi* tentar; **to ~ for sthg** tratar de conseguir algo. <> *n* **-1.** [attempt] tentativa *f*; **to give sthg a ~** provar algo; **to have a ~ at sthg** tentar fazer algo **-2.** *RUGBY* *ato de levar a bola até a linha de fundo do adversário e posicioná-la no solo para se marcar pontos.*
◆ **try on** *vt sep* [clothes] experimentar.
◆ **try out** *vt sep* **-1.** [car, machine] testar **-2.** [plan] pôr à prova.
trying ['traɪɪŋ] *adj* difícil, árduo(dua).
try-out *n inf*: **can I have a ~ of the car?** posso experimentar o carro?
tsar [zɑː^r] *n* czar *m*.
T-shirt *n* camiseta *f*.
tsp. (*abbr of* **teaspoon**) colher *f* de chá.
T-square *n* régua-tê *f*.
TT (*abbr of* **teetotal**) *adj* abstêmio(mia).
Tuareg *npl* [people] tuaregue *mf*.
tub [tʌb] *n* **-1.** [container - for ice cream, margarine] pote *m*; [- for water] tina *f* **-2.** *inf* [bath] banheira *f*.
tuba ['tjuːbə] *n* tuba *f*.
tubby ['tʌbɪ] (*compar* **-ier**, *superl* **-iest**) *adj inf* rolha-de-poço, gorducho(cha).
tube [tjuːb] *n* **-1.** [gen] tubo *m* **-2.** *UK* [underground train] metrô *m*; [underground system]: **the ~** o metrô; **by ~** de metrô.
tubeless ['tjuːblɪs] *adj* [tyre] sem câmara (de ar).
tuber ['tjuːbə^r] *n* tubérculo *m*.
tuberculosis [tjuːˌbɜːkjʊ'ləʊsɪs] *n (U)* tuberculose *f*.
tube station *n UK* estação *f* de metrô.
tubing ['tjuːbɪŋ] *n (U)* tubulação *f*.
tubular ['tjuːbjʊlə^r] *adj* tubular.
TUC (*abbr of* **Trades Union Congress**) *n federação dos sindicatos na Grã-Bretanha*, ≃ CUT *f*.
tuck [tʌk] <> *n SEWING* prega *f*. <> *vt* [place neatly] enfiar, meter.
◆ **tuck away** *vt sep* [store] guardar; **to be ~ed away** [hidden] estar escondido(da).
◆ **tuck in** <> *vt sep* **-1.** [child, patient in bed] ajeitar na cama **-2.** [clothes] meter para dentro. <> *vi inf* comer com apetite.
◆ **tuck up** *vt sep* enfiar, meter.
tuck shop *n UK* confeitaria *f (perto de um colégio)*.
Tudor ['tjuːdə^r] <> *adj* **-1.** *HIST* da dinastia Tudor **-2.** *ARCHIT* da era Tudor. <> *n*: **the ~s** os Tudors.
Tue., Tues. (*abbr of* **Tuesday**) ter.
Tuesday ['tjuːzdɪ] *n* terça-feira *f*; *see also* **Saturday**.
tuft [tʌft] *n* tufo *m*.
tug [tʌg] (*pt* & *pp* **-ged**, *cont* **-ging**) <> *n* **-1.** [pull] puxão *m* **-2.** [boat] rebocador *m*. <> *vt* dar um puxão em. <> *vi* dar um puxão; **to ~ at sthg** dar um puxão em algo.
tugboat ['tʌgbəʊt] *n* (barco *m*) rebocador *m*.
tug-of-love *n UK inf conflito pela custódia de uma criança.*
tug-of-war *n* cabo-de-guerra *m*.
tuition [tjuː'ɪʃn] *n (U)* ensino *m*; **private ~** aulas *fpl* particulares.
tulip ['tjuːlɪp] *n* tulipa *f*.
tulle *n (U)* tule *m*.
tumble ['tʌmbl] <> *vi* **-1.** [person] tombar **-2.** [water] jorrar **-3.** *fig* [prices] despencar. <> *n* tombo *m*.
◆ **tumble down** *vi* [building] vir abaixo.
◆ **tumble to** *vt fus UK inf* sacar, tocar-se de.
tumbledown ['tʌmbldaʊn] *adj* em ruínas.
tumble-dry *vt* secar em secadora.
tumble-dryer [-ˌdraɪə^r] *n* secadora *f* (de roupa).
tumbler ['tʌmblə^r] *n* [glass] copo *m*.
tummy ['tʌmɪ] (*pl* **-ies**) *n inf* **-1.** [outside of stomach] barriga *f* **-2.** [inside of stomach] barriga *f*.
tumour *UK*, **tumor** *US* ['tjuːmə^r] *n* tumor *m*.
tumult ['tjuːmʌlt] *n fml* tumulto *m*.
tumultuous ['tjuːmʌltjʊəs] *adj fml* [applause] efusivo(va).
tuna [*UK* 'tjuːnə, *US* 'tuːnə] (*pl inv OR* **-s**), **tuna fish** (*pl* **tuna fish**) *n* **-1.** [fish] atum *m* **-2.** *(U)* [food] atum *m*.
tundra ['tʌndrə] *n* tundra *f*.
tune [tjuːn] <> *n* [song, melody] melodia *f*; **to the ~ of** *fig* no montante de; **to change one's ~** *inf* virar a casaca. <> *vt* **-1.** *MUS* afinar **-2.** *RADIO* & *TV* sintonizar; **to ~ sthg to sthg** sintonizar algo em algo **-3.** [engine] ajustar, regular. <> *vi RADIO* & *TV*: **to ~ to sthg** sintonizar em algo.
◆ **tune in** *vi RADIO* & *TV* sintonizar-se; **to ~ in to sthg** sintonizar-se em algo.
◆ **tune up** *vi MUS* afinar *OR* consertar os instrumentos.
◆ **in tune** <> *adj MUS* afinado(da). <> *adv* **-1.** *MUS* harmonicamente **-2.** [in agreement]: **in ~ with sb/sthg** em sintonia com alguém/algo.
◆ **out of tune** <> *adj MUS* desafinado(da). <> *adv* **-1.** *MUS* desarmonicamente **-2.** [not in agreement]: **out of ~ with sb/sthg** fora de sintonia com alguém /algo.
tuneful ['tjuːnfʊl] *adj* melodioso(sa).
tuneless ['tjuːnlɪs] *adj* desarmônico(ca).
tuner ['tjuːnə^r] *n* **-1.** *RADIO* & *TV* sintonizador *m* **-2.** *MUS* afinador *m*.
tuner amplifier *n* amplificador *m* sintonizador.
tungsten ['tʌŋstən] <> *n (U)* tungstênio *m*. <> *comp* de tungstênio.
tunic ['tjuːnɪk] *n* [clothing] túnica *f*.
tuning fork ['tjuːnɪŋ-] *n* diapasão *m*.
Tunis ['tjuːnɪs] *n* Túnis.
Tunisia [tjuː'nɪzɪə] *n* Tunísia *f*; **in ~** na Tunísia.
Tunisian [tjuː'nɪzɪən] <> *adj* tunisiano(na). <> *n* [person] tunisiano *m*, -na *f*.
tunnel ['tʌnl] (*UK pt* & *pp* **-led**, *cont* **-ling**, *US pt* & *pp* **-ed**, *cont* **-ing**) <> *n* túnel *m*. <> *vi*: **to ~ through sthg** atravessar um túnel por algo.
tunnel vision *n (U)* **-1.** *MED* visão *f* em túnel **-2.** *fig* & *pej* [narrow-mindedness] visão *f* estreita.
tunny ['tʌnɪ] (*pl inv OR* **-ies**) *n* [fish] tuna *f*.
tuppence *n UK dated* (moeda *f* de) dois pennies *mpl*.
turban ['tɜːbən] *n* [man's headdress] turbante *m*.
turbid ['tɜːbɪd] *adj* túrbido(da).
turbine ['tɜːbaɪn] *n* turbina *f*.
turbo ['tɜːbəʊ] (*pl* **-s**) *n* turbo *m*.

turbocharged [ˈtɜ:bəʊtʃɑ:dʒd] *adj* com turbo; ~ car carro-turbo *m*.
turbojet [ˌtɜ:bəʊˈdʒet] *n* **-1.** [engine] turborreator *m* **-2.** [plane] turbojacto *m*.
turboprop *n* **-1.** [engine] turbopropulsor *m* **-2.** [plane] avião *m* com turbopropulsor.
turbot [ˈtɜ:bət] (*pl inv* OR **-s**) *n* linguado *m*.
turbulence [ˈtɜ:bjʊləns] *n (U)* turbulência *f*.
turbulent [ˈtɜ:bjʊlənt] *adj* turbulento(ta).
tureen [təˈri:n] *n* sopeira *f*.
turf [tɜ:f] (*pl* **-s** OR **turves**) ◇ *n* **-1.** *(U)* [grass surface] gramado *m* **-2.** [clod] turfa *f*. ◇ *vt* [with grass] gramar.
◆ **turf out** *vt sep UK inf* **-1.** [evict] chutar, dar patadas em **-2.** [throw away] jogar fora.
turf accountant *n UK fml* agenciador *m*, -ra *f* de apostas.
turgid [ˈtɜ:dʒɪd] *adj fml* [style, prose] empolado(da).
Turk [tɜ:k] *n* turco *m*, -ca *f*.
Turkestan, Turkistan [ˌtɜ:kɪˈstɑ:n] *n* Turquistão; in ~ no Turquistão.
turkey [ˈtɜ:kɪ] (*pl* **turkeys**) *n* **-1.** [bird] peru *m* **-2.** *(U)* [meat] peru *m*.
Turkey [ˈtɜ:kɪ] *n* Turquia; **in** ~ na Turquia.
Turkish [ˈtɜ:kɪʃ] ◇ *adj* turco(ca). ◇ *n* [language] turco *m*. ◇ *npl*: **the** ~ os turcos.
Turkish bath *n* banho *m* turco.
Turkish delight *n (U) doce feito de substância gelatinosa em cubos com cobertura de açúcar ou chocolate.*
Turkistan *n* = **Turkestan**.
Turkmenian *adj* turcomano(na).
Turkmenistan [ˌtɜ:kmenɪˈstɑ:n] *n* Turcomênia.
turmeric [ˈtɜ:mərɪk] *n (U)* [spice] açafrão-da-terra *m*.
turmoil [ˈtɜ:mɔɪl] *n (U)* desordem *f*.
turn [tɜ:n] ◇ *n* **-1.** [in road, river] curva *f* **-2.** [revolution, twist] volta *f* **-3.** [change] reviravolta *f*; **to take a** ~ **for the better/worse** mudar para melhor/pior **-4.** [in game]: **it's my** ~ é a minha vez **-5.** [in order] vez *f*; **in** ~ por vez; **to take (it in)** ~**s to do sthg** revezar-se para fazer algo **-6.** [end] virada *f*; **the** ~ **of the century** a virada do século **-7.** [performance] número *m*, apresentação *f* **-8.** MED ataque *m*, crise *f* **-9.** *phr*: **to do sb a good** ~ fazer uma boa ação a alguém. ◇ *vt* **-1.** [cause to rotate] girar **-2.** [move round, turn over] virar **-3.** [go round] dobrar **-4.** [direct]: **to** ~ **sthg to sb/sthg** voltar algo para alguém/algo **-5.** [change]: **to** ~ **sthg into sthg** transformar algo em algo **-6.** [make, cause to become] deixar; **to** ~ **sthg inside out** virar algo pelo avesso. ◇ *vi* **-1.** [change direction] virar, dobrar; **to** ~ **to sb/sthg** voltar-se para alguém/algo **-2.** [rotate] girar **-3.** [move round] voltar-se **-4.** [in book]: ~ **to page 102** vão até a página 102 **-5.** [for consolation]: **to** ~ **to sb/sthg** buscar consolo em alguém/algo **-6.** [become] tornar-se; **my hair's** ~**ing grey** meu cabelo está ficando branco; **to** ~ **into sthg** transformar-se em algo.
◆ **turn against** *vt fus* voltar-se contra.
◆ **turn around** *vt sep & vi* = **turn round**.
◆ **turn away** ◇ *vt sep* [refuse entry to] não deixar entrar. ◇ *vi* distanciar-se.
◆ **turn back** ◇ *vt sep* **-1.** [force to return] fazer voltar **-2.** [fold back] dobrar. ◇ *vi* [return] voltar atrás.
◆ **turn down** *vt sep* **-1.** [reject] recusar **-2.** [heating, lighting] diminuir **-3.** [sound] abaixar.
◆ **turn in** *vi inf* [go to bed] ir dormir.
◆ **turn off** ◇ *vt fus* [road, path] sair de. ◇ *vt sep* [switch off - appliance, engine] desligar; [- gas, tap] fechar. ◇ *vi* [leave road, path] dobrar.
◆ **turn on** ◇ *vt sep* **-1.** [make work - appliance, engine] ligar; [- gas, tap] abrir; [- light] acender **-2.** *inf* [excite sexually] acender. ◇ *vt fus* [attack] avançar em.
◆ **turn out** ◇ *vt sep* **-1.** [switch off] apagar **-2.** *inf* [produce] fazer; **the factory** ~**s out cars** a fábrica produz carros **-3.** [eject] expulsar **-4.** [empty] esvaziar. ◇ *vt fus*: **to** ~ **out to be** acabar sendo, vir a ser; **it** ~**s out that ...** acontece que ... ◇ *vi* **-1.** [end up] acabar, terminar **-2.** [attend]: **to** ~ **out (for sthg)** comparecer (em algo).
◆ **turn over** ◇ *vt sep* **-1.** [playing card, stone, page] virar **-2.** [consider]: **I** ~**ed his ideas over in my mind** fiquei com as idéias dele dando voltas na minha cabeça **-3.** [hand over] entregar; **to** ~ **sb/sthg over to sb** entregar alguém/algo para alguém. ◇ *vi* **-1.** [roll over] revirar-se **-2.** *UK* TV mudar de canal.
◆ **turn round** ◇ *vt sep* **-1.** [chair, picture] virar **-2.** [wheel] girar **-3.** [words, sentence] expressar de outra maneira **-4.** [quantity of work] aliviar **-5.** [company] reerguer. ◇ *vi* [person] virar-se.
◆ **turn up** ◇ *vt sep* [heat, lighting, radio, TV] aumentar. ◇ *vi inf* **-1.** [gen] aparecer **-2.** [opportunity, solution] surgir.
turnabout [ˈtɜ:nəbaʊt] *n* mudança *f* radical.
turnaround *n US* = **turnround**.
turncoat [ˈtɜ:nkəʊt] *n pej* vira-casaca *mf*.
turning [ˈtɜ:nɪŋ] *n* [side road]: **the first** ~ **to the left** a primeira (rua) à esquerda.
turning circle *n* raio *m* de viragem.
turning point *n* momento *m* decisivo.
turnip [ˈtɜ:nɪp] *n* nabo *m*.
turnout [ˈtɜ:naʊt] *n* [attendance] comparecimento *m*, número *m* de participantes.
turnover [ˈtɜ:nˌəʊvəʳ] *n (U)* **-1.** [of personnel] rotatividade *f* **-2.** FIN volume *m* de vendas.
turnpike [ˈtɜ:npaɪk] *n US* rodovia *f* com pedágio.
turnround *UK* [ˈtɜ:nraʊnd], **turnaround** *US* [ˈtɜ:nəraʊnd] *n* **-1.** COMM tempo *m* de carga e descarga *(de um barco, avião)* **-2.** [change] reviravolta *f*.
turn signal lever *n US* pisca-pisca *m*.
turnstile [ˈtɜ:nstaɪl] *n* borboleta *f (em ônibus)*.
turntable [ˈtɜ:nˌteɪbl] *n* [on record player] prato *m* (giratório).
turn-up *n UK* **-1.** [on trousers] bainha *f* **-2.** *inf* [surprise]: **a** ~ **for the books** *inf* uma surpresa total.
turpentine [ˈtɜ:pəntaɪn] *n (U)* terebentina *f*.
turps [tɜ:ps] *n UK inf* aguarrás *f inv*.
turquoise [ˈtɜ:kwɔɪz] ◇ *adj* turquesa. ◇ *n* **-1.** *(U)* [mineral, gem] turquesa *f* **-2.** [colour] turquesa *m*.
turret [ˈtʌrɪt] *n* [on castle] torre *f* pequena.
turtle [ˈtɜ:tl] (*pl inv* OR **-s**) *n* tartaruga *f*.
turtledove [ˈtɜ:tldʌv] *n* pomba-rola *f*.

turtleneck ['tɜːtlnek] *n* **-1.** [garment] blusa *f* de gola olímpica **-2.** [neck] gola *f* olímpica.
turves [tɜːvz] *UK pl* ⊳ **turf**.
tusk [tʌsk] *n* [of animal] presa *f*.
tussle ['tʌsl] ◇ *n* briga *f*. ◇ *vi* brigar; **to ~ over sthg** brigar por algo.
tut [tʌt] *excl* tsc!
tutor ['tjuːtəʳ] ◇ *n* **-1.** [private] professor *m*, -ra *f* particular **-2.** *UNIV* professor *m* universitário, professora *f* universitária. ◇ *vt*: **to ~ sb in sthg** dar aulas particulares de algo para alguém. ◇ *vi* dar aulas particulares.
tutorial [tjuː'tɔːrɪəl] ◇ *adj*: **~ group** *grupo reduzido de estudantes que assiste a uma aula*. ◇ *n* aula *f* para grupos pequenos.
tutu ['tuːtuː] *n* tutu *f*.
tux [tʌks] *n inf* smoking *m*.
tuxedo [tʌk'siːdəʊ] (*pl* **-s**) *n US* smoking *m*.
TV (*abbr of* **television**) ◇ *n* **-1.** [medium, industry, apparatus] TV *f*; **on ~** na TV. ◇ *comp* de TV.
TV dinner *n refeição completa em porção individual pronta para esquentar*.
TVP (*abbr of* **textured vegetable protein**) *n* proteína *f* vegetal.
twaddle ['twɒdl] *n inf pej* lorota *f*.
twang [twæŋ] ◇ *n* **-1.** [sound - of guitar] som *m* metálico; [- of string, elastic] som *m* vibrante **-2.** [accent] som *m* nasalado. ◇ *vt* **-1.** [guitar] vibrar **-2.** [wire, string] fazer vibrar. ◇ *vi* produzir um som vibrante.
tweak [twiːk] *vt inf* [pull] beliscar.
twee [twiː] *adj UK pej* piegas *inv*.
tweed [twiːd] ◇ *n (U)* tweed *m*. ◇ *comp* de tweed.
tweet [twiːt] *vi inf* piar.
tweezers ['twiːzəz] *npl* pinças *fpl*.
twelfth [twelfθ] *num* décimo segundo, décima segunda; *see also* **sixth**.
Twelfth Night *n* Noite *f* de Reis.
twelve [twelv] *num* doze; *see also* **six**.
twentieth ['twentɪəθ] *num* vigésimo(ma); *see also* **sixth**.
twenty ['twentɪ] (*pl* **-ies**) *num* vinte; *see also* **sixty**.
twenty-twenty vision *n (U)* visão *f* perfeita.
twerp [twɜːp] *n UK inf* imbecil *mf*.
twice [twaɪs] *adv* duas vezes; **~ a week** duas vezes por semana; **he earns ~ as much as me** ele ganha o dobro que eu.
twiddle ['twɪdl] ◇ *vt* girar (entre os dedos). ◇ *vi*: **to ~ with sthg** brincar com algo entre os dedos.
twig [twɪg] *n* graveto *m*.
twilight ['twaɪlaɪt] *n* **-1.** [in evening] crepúsculo *m* vespertino **-2.** *fig* [last stages, end] ocaso *m*.
twill [twɪl] *n (U)* sarja *f*.
twin [twɪn] ◇ *adj* **-1.** [child, sibling] gêmeo(mea) **-2.** [beds] duplo(pla) **-3.** [towns, towers] gêmeos(meas). ◇ *n* [sibling] gêmeos *mpl*, -meas *fpl*.
twin-bedded [-'bedɪd] *adj* com duas camas.
twin carburettor *n* carburador *m* duplo.
twine [twaɪn] ◇ *n (U)* barbante *m*. ◇ *vt*: **to ~ sthg round sthg** enrolar algo em algo.
twin-engined [-'endʒɪnd] *adj* bimotor.
twinge [twɪndʒ] *n* **-1.** [of pain] pontada *f* **-2.** [of guilt] remorso *m*.
twinkle ['twɪŋkl] ◇ *n* brilho *m*. ◇ *vi* **-1.** [star, light] cintilar **-2.** [eyes] brilhar.
twin room *n* quarto *m* com duas camas.
twinset *n UK conjunto de blusa e casaquinho*.
twin town *n* cidade-irmã *f*.
twin tub *n* máquina *f* de lavar e secar.
twirl [twɜːl] ◇ *vt* **-1.** [spin] girar **-2.** [twist] torcer. ◇ *vi* rodopiar.
twist [twɪst] ◇ *n* **-1.** [gen] volta *f* **-2.** [turn, twirl] giro *m*; **to give sthg a ~** girar algo **-3.** *fig* [in plot] reviravolta *f*. ◇ *vt* **-1.** [gen] retorcer **-2.** [face, frame] torcer **-3.** [head] voltar **-4.** [lid, knob, dial] girar **-5.** [words, meaning] distorcer. ◇ *vi* **-1.** [road, river] dar voltas **-2.** [body, part of body] torcer.
twisted ['twɪstɪd] *adj pej* [bizarre] deturpado(da).
twister ['twɪstəʳ] *n US* tornado *m*.
twisty ['twɪstɪ] (*compar* **-ier**, *superl* **-iest**) *adj inf* cheio (cheia) de curvas.
twit [twɪt] *n UK inf* idiota *mf*, imbecil *mf*.
twitch [twɪtʃ] ◇ *n* espasmo *m*; **nervous ~** tique *m* nervoso. ◇ *vt* [ears, nose] tremer. ◇ *vi* contrair-se.
twitter ['twɪtəʳ] *vi* **-1.** [bird] cantar, pipilar **-2.** *pej* [person] cantar vantagem.
two [tuː] *num* dois (duas); **in ~** em dois; *see also* **six**.
two-bit *adj US pej* barato(ta); **a ~ little dictator** um ditadorzinho de meia-tigela *OR* de araque.
two-dimensional *adj* **-1.** [picture] em duas dimensões, bidimensional **-2.** *pej* [report, description] simples, sem profundidade.
two-door *adj* [car] de duas portas.
twofaced [ˌtuː'feɪst] *adj pej* de duas caras.
twofold ['tuːfəʊld] ◇ *adj* duplo(pla). ◇ *adv*: **to increase ~** duplicar-se.
two-handed [-'hændɪd] *adj* **-1.** [sword] que se usa com as duas mãos **-2.** [backhand] que se dá com as duas mãos.
two-piece *adj* [suit, swimsuit] de duas peças.
two-ply *adj* de duas camadas.
two-seater [-'siːtəʳ] *n* carro *m* esporte *(com apenas dois lugares)*.
twosome ['tuːsəm] *n inf* dupla *f*.
two-stroke ◇ *adj* **-1.** [engine] de dois tempos **-2.** [oil] para motor de dois tempos. ◇ *n* motor *m* de dois tempos.
two-time *vt inf* botar chifre em.
two-tone *adj* bicolor.
two-way *adj* **-1.** [traffic] de mão dupla **-2.** [discussion, debate] de duas vias **-3.** [cooperation] mútuo(-tua) **-4.** *TELEC*: **~ radio** aparelho *m* emissor e receptor.
TX *abbr of* **Texas**.
tycoon [taɪ'kuːn] *n* magnata *mf*.
type [taɪp] ◇ *n* **-1.** [gen] tipo *m* **-2.** *(U) TYPO*: **in bold/italic ~** em negrito/itálico. ◇ *vt* & *vi* **-1.** [on typewriter] datilografar **-2.** [on computer] digitar; **to ~ sthg into sthg** inserir algo em algo.
◆ **type up** *vt sep* **-1.** [on typewriter] datilografar **-2.** [on computer] digitar.
typecast ['taɪpkɑːst] (*pt* & *pp* **typecast**) *vt* escalar sempre para o mesmo tipo de papel; **to be ~ as**

sthg ser sempre escalado(da) (para atuar) como algo.
typeface ['taɪpfeɪs] *n* TYPO tipo *m*, letra *f*.
typescript ['taɪpskrɪpt] *n* cópia *f* datilografada.
typeset ['taɪpset] (*pt* & *pp* **typeset**, *cont* **-ting**) *vt* TYPO compor.
typesetter *n* [company] tipografia *f*.
typesetting *n* composição *f* (para impressão).
typewriter ['taɪpˌraɪtəʳ] *n* máquina *f* de escrever.
typhoid (fever) ['taɪfɔɪd-] *n* (*U*) **febre** *f* tifóide.
typhoon [taɪ'fu:n] *n* tufão *m*.
typhus ['taɪfəs] *n* (*U*) tifo *m*.
typical ['tɪpɪkl] *adj* típico(ca); ~ **of sb/sthg** típico(-ca) de alguém/algo.
typically ['tɪpɪklɪ] *adv* **-1.** [usually] geralmente, normalmente **-2.** [characteristically] tipicamente.
typify ['tɪpɪfaɪ] (*pt* & *pp* **-ied**) *vt* **-1.** [be characteristic of] tipificar **-2.** [embody, symbolize] simbolizar.
typing ['taɪpɪŋ] *n* **-1.** (*U*) [on typewriter] datilografia *f* **-2.** (*U*) [on computer] digitação *f*.
typing error *n* **-1.** [on typewriter] erro *m* de datilografia **-2.** [on computer] erro *m* de digitação.
typing pool *n* **-1.** [typewriter] serviço *m* de datilografia **-2.** [computer] serviço *m* de digitação.
typist ['taɪpɪst] *n* **-1.** [on typewriter] datilógrafo *m*, -fa *f* **-2.** [on computer] digitador *m*, -ra *f*.
typo ['taɪpəʊ] *n inf* erro *m* tipográfico.
typographic(al) error [ˌtaɪpə'græfɪk(l)-] *n* erro *m* tipográfico.
typography [taɪ'pɒgrəfɪ] *n* **-1.** (*U*) [process, job] tipografia *f* **-2.** [format] composição *f* tipográfica.
tyrannical [tɪ'rænɪkl] *adj* tirânico(ca).
tyranny ['tɪrənɪ] *n* (*U*) [of person, government] tirania *f*.
tyrant ['taɪrənt] *n* tirano *m*, -na *f*.
tyre *UK*, **tire** *US* ['taɪəʳ] *n* pneu *m*.
tyre pressure *n* (*U*) pressão *f* do pneu.
Tyrol, Tirol [tɪ'rəʊl] *n*: **the** ~ o Tirol.
Tyrolean [tɪrə'li:ən], **Tyrolese** [ˌtɪrə'li:z] <> *adj* tirolês(esa). <> *n* tirolês *m*, -esa *f*.
Tyrrhenian Sea [tɪ'ri:nɪən-] *n*: **the** ~ o Mar Tirreno.
tzar [zɑ:ʳ] *n* = **tsar**.

u (*pl* **u's** OR **us**), **U** (*pl* **U's** OR **Us**) [ju:] *n* [letter] u, U *m*.
◆ **U** (*abbr of* **universal**) livre.
U (*abbr of* **universal**) *filme de censura livre.*
UAE (*abbr of* **United Arab Emirates**) *n* EAU *mpl*.
UB40 (*abbr of* **unemployment benefit form 40**) *n* *certificado de recebimento do seguro-desemprego na Grã-Bretanha.*
U-bend *n* sifão *m*.
ubiquitous [ju:'bɪkwɪtəs] *adj fml* ubíquo(qua).
u.c. (*abbr of* **upper case**) *n* caixa-alta *f*.
UCAS (*abbr of* **Universities and Colleges Admissions Service**) *n organização britânica que trata da admissão às faculdades e universidades.*
UCL (*abbr of* **University College, London**) *n uma das faculdades da Universidade de Londres.*
UDA (*abbr of* **Ulster Defence Association**) *n organização paramilitar protestante da Irlanda do Norte, favorável à permanência da Irlanda do Norte no Reino Unido.*
UDC (*abbr of* **Urban District Council**) *n câmara de vereadores britânica de comunidade urbana.*
udder ['ʌdəʳ] *n* úbere *m*.
UDI (*abbr of* **unilateral declaration of independence**) *n* **-1.** HIST *declaração unilateral de independência (na Rodésia)* **-2.** *hum*: **to declare** ~ **on sb** passar alguém para trás.
UDR (*abbr of* **Ulster Defence Regiment**) *n antigo regimento de reservistas na Irlanda do Norte, agora parte do Regimento Real Irlandês.*
UEFA [ju:'eɪfə] (*abbr of* **Union of European Football Associations**) *n* UEFA *f*.
UFC (*abbr of* **Universities Funding Council**) *n órgão britânico responsável por gerir as doações universitárias.*
UFO (*abbr of* **unidentified flying object**) *n* OVNI *m*.
Uganda [ju:'gændə] *n* Uganda; **in** ~ em Uganda.
Ugandan [ju:'gændən] <> *adj* ugandense. <> *n* [person] ugandense *mf*.
ugh [ʌg] *excl* puf!
ugliness ['ʌglɪnɪs] *n* (*U*) **-1.** [unattractiveness] feiúra *f* **-2.** *fig* [unpleasantness] repulsa *f*.
ugly ['ʌglɪ] (*compar* **-ier**, *superl* **-iest**) *adj* **-1.** [unattractive] feio (feia) **-2.** *fig* [unpleasant] desagradável.
UHF (*abbr of* **ultra-high frequency**) *n* UHF *m*.
UHT (*abbr of* **ultra-heat treated**) *adj* UHT; ~ **milk** leite *m* longa-vida.
UK (*abbr of* **United Kingdom**) *n* RU *m*.
UKAEA (*abbr of* **United Kingdom Atomic Energy Authority**) *n órgão responsável pelo controle da energia atômica no Reino Unido.*
Ukraine [ju:'kreɪn] *n*: **the** ~ a Ucrânia; **in the** ~ na Ucrânia.
Ukrainian [ju:'kreɪnjən] <> *adj* ucraniano(na). <> *n* **-1.** [person] ucraniano *m*, -na *f* **-2.** [language] ucraniano *m*.
ulcer ['ʌlsəʳ] *n* **-1.** [in stomach] úlcera *f* **-2.** [in mouth] afta *f*.
ulcerated ['ʌlsəreɪtɪd] *adj* ulcerado(da).
Ulster ['ʌlstəʳ] *n* Irlanda *f* do Norte; **in** ~ na Irlanda do Norte.
Ulster Unionist Party *n partido político norte-irlandês que defende a permanência da Irlanda do Norte como parte do Grã-Bretanha.*
ulterior [ʌl'tɪərɪəʳ] *adj*: ~ **motive** motivo *m* ulterior.
ultimata [ˌʌltɪ'meɪtə] *pl* ▷ **ultimatum**.
ultimate ['ʌltɪmət] <> *adj* **-1.** [success, objetive] final,

definitivo(va) **-2.** [failure] último(ma) **-3.** [most powerful] máximo(ma). <> *n*: **the ~ in sthg** a última palavra em algo.

ultimately [ˈʌltɪmətlɪ] *adv* **-1.** [finally, in the long term] finalmente, por fim **-2.** [fundamentally] no fundo.

ultimatum [ˌʌltɪˈmeɪtəm] (*pl* **-tums** OR **-ta**) *n* ultimato *m*.

ultra- [ˈʌltrə] *prefix* ultra-.

ultramarine [ˌʌltrəməˈriːn] *adj* ultramarino(na).

ultrasonic [ˌʌltrəˈsɒnɪk] *adj* ultra-sônico(ca).

ultrasound [ˈʌltrəsaʊnd] *n (U)* ultra-som *m*.

ultraviolet [ˌʌltrəˈvaɪələt] *adj* ultravioleta.

um [ʌm] *excl* hum!

umbilical cord [ʌmˈbɪlɪkl-] *n* cordão *m* umbilical.

umbrage [ˈʌmbrɪdʒ] *n*: **to take ~ (at sthg)** ofender-se (com algo).

umbrella [ʌmˈbrelə] <> *n* **-1.** [gen] guarda-chuva *m*; **-2.** [fixed] guarda-sol *m*. <> *adj* guarda-chuva; **~ word** palavra guarda-chuva.

UMIST (*abbr of* **University of Manchester Institute of Science and Technology**) *n instituto de ciência e tecnologia da Universidade de Manchester*, UMIST *m*.

umpire [ˈʌmpaɪəʳ] <> *n* árbitro *m*. <> *vt* & *vi* arbitrar, apitar.

umpteen [ˌʌmpˈtiːn] *num adj inf*: **~ times** um milhão de vezes.

umpteenth [ˌʌmpˈtiːnθ] *num adj inf* enésimo(ma).

UN (*abbr of* **United Nations**) *n*: **the ~** a ONU.

unabashed [ˌʌnəˈbæʃt] *adj* imperturbável.

unabated [ˌʌnəˈbeɪtɪd] *adj* incessante.

unable [ʌnˈeɪbl] *adj* incapaz; **to be ~ to do sthg** não poder fazer algo.

unabridged [ˌʌnəˈbrɪdʒd] *adj* integral.

unacceptable [ˌʌnəkˈseptəbl] *adj* inaceitável.

unaccompanied [ˌʌnəˈkʌmpənɪd] *adj* **-1.** [child] sozinho(nha) **-2.** [luggage] desacompanhado(da) **-3.** [song] sem acompanhamento.

unaccountable [ˌʌnəˈkaʊntəbl] *adj* **-1.** [inexplicable] incompreensível **-2.** [not responsible] que não é responsável; **to be ~ for sthg** não ser responsável por algo; **to be ~ to sb** não ter de dar satisfações para alguém.

unaccountably [ˌʌnəˈkaʊntəblɪ] *adv* [inexplicably] inexplicavelmente.

unaccounted [ˌʌnəˈkaʊntɪd] *adj*: **~ for** desaparecido(da).

unaccustomed [ˌʌnəˈkʌstəmd] *adj* **-1.** [unused]: **to be ~ to sthg/to doing sthg** estar desacostumado(da) a algo/a fazer algo **-2.** *fml* [not usual] inusual.

unacquainted [ˌʌnəˈkweɪntɪd] *adj*: **to be ~ with sb/sthg** não conhecer alguém/algo.

unadulterated [ˌʌnəˈdʌltəreɪtɪd] *adj* **-1.** [unspoiled] não-adulterado(da) **-2.** [absolute] puro(ra).

unadventurous [ˌʌnədˈventʃərəs] *adj* pouco aventureiro(ra).

unaffected [ˌʌnəˈfektɪd] *adj* **-1.** [unchanged] intacto(ta); **to be ~ by sthg** não ser atingido(da) por algo **-2.** [natural] natural.

unafraid [ˌʌnəˈfreɪd] *adj* destemido(da).

unaided [ˌʌnˈeɪdɪd] <> *adj* feito(ta) sem ajuda. <> *adv* sem ajuda.

unambiguous [ˌʌnæmˈbɪgjʊəs] *adj* inequívoco(-ca).

un-American [ˈʌn-] *adj* antiamericano(na).

unanimity [ˌjuːnəˈnɪmətɪ] *n (U) fml* unanimidade *f*.

unanimous [juːˈnænɪməs] *adj* unânime.

unanimously [juːˈnænɪməslɪ] *adv* unanimemente.

unannounced [ˌʌnəˈnaʊnst] <> *adj* não-anunciado(da). <> *adv* sem anunciar.

unanswered [ˌʌnˈɑːnsəd] *adj* não-respondido(da).

unappealing [ˌʌnəˈpiːlɪŋ] *adj* desagradável.

unappetizing, -ising [ˌʌnˈæpɪtaɪzɪŋ] *adj* **-1.** [food] pouco apetitoso(sa) **-2.** [sight, thought] pouco apetecível.

unappreciated [ˌʌnəˈpriːʃɪeɪtɪd] *adj* não-reconhecido(da).

unappreciative [ˌʌnəˈpriːʃɪətɪv] *adj* ingrato(ta); **to be ~ of sthg** ser incapaz de apreciar algo.

unapproachable [ˌʌnəˈprəʊtʃəbl] *adj* [person] inacessível.

unarmed [ˌʌnˈɑːmd] *adj* desarmado(da).

unarmed combat *n (U)* combate *m* sem armas.

unashamed [ˌʌnəˈʃeɪmd] *adj* descarado(da).

unassisted [ˌʌnəˈsɪstɪd] *adj* sem ajuda.

unassuming [ˌʌnəˈsjuːmɪŋ] *adj* despretensioso(-sa).

unattached [ˌʌnəˈtætʃt] *adj* **-1.** [not fastened, linked] independente; **~ to sthg** separado(da) de algo **-2.** [without partner] sem compromisso.

unattainable [ˌʌnəˈteɪnəbl] *adj* inatingível.

unattended [ˌʌnəˈtendɪd] *adj* **-1.** [luggage, children] desacompanhado(da) **-2.** [fire, shop] sem vigilância.

unattractive [ˌʌnəˈtræktɪv] *adj* **-1.** [person, building, place] sem atrativos **-2.** [idea, prospect] sem brilho.

unauthorized, -ised [ˌʌnˈɔːθəraɪzd] *adj* não-autorizado(da).

unavailable [ˌʌnəˈveɪləbl] *adj* que não está disponível.

unavoidable [ˌʌnəˈvɔɪdəbl] *adj* inevitável.

unavoidably [ˌʌnəˈvɔɪdəblɪ] *adj* inevitavelmente.

unaware [ˌʌnəˈweəʳ] *adj* desconhecedor(ra); **to be ~ of sb/sthg** não estar consciente de alguém/algo.

unawares [ˌʌnəˈweəz] *adv*: **to catch** OR **take sb ~** pegar alguém desprevenido(da).

unbalanced [ˌʌnˈbælənst] *adj* **-1.** [biased] parcial **-2.** [deranged] desequilibrado(da).

unbearable [ʌnˈbeərəbl] *adj* insuportável, insustentável.

unbearably [ʌnˈbeərəblɪ] *adv* insuportavelmente, insustentavelmente.

unbeatable [ˌʌnˈbiːtəbl] *adj* imbatível.

unbecoming [ˌʌnbɪˈkʌmɪŋ] *adj fml* [dress, colour] pouco favorecedor(ra).

unbeknown(st) [ˌʌnbɪˈnəʊn(st)] *adv*: **~ to** sem o conhecimento de.

unbelievable [ˌʌnbɪˈliːvəbl] *adj* **-1.** [amazing] incrível **-2.** [not believable] inacreditável.

unbelievably [ˌʌnbɪˈliːvəblɪ] *adv* [extremely] extremamente.

unbend [ˌʌnˈbend] (*pt* & *pp* **unbent**) *vi* [relax] relaxar.

unbending [ˌʌnˈbendɪŋ] *adj* [intransigent] resoluto(-ta).

unbent [ˌʌn'bent] *pt & pp* ▷ **unbend.**
unbia(s)sed [ˌʌn'baɪəst] *adj* imparcial.
unblemished [ˌʌn'blemɪʃt] *adj fig* irretocável.
unblock [ˌʌn'blɒk] *vt* **-1.** [drain, tunnel] desbloquear **-2.** [pipe] desentupir.
unbolt [ˌʌn'bəʊlt] *vt* [door] destrancar.
unborn [ˌʌn'bɔːn] *adj* [child] nascituro(ra).
unbreakable [ˌʌn'breɪkəbl] *adj* inquebrável.
unbridled [ˌʌn'braɪdld] *adj* desenfreado(da).
unbuckle [ˌʌn'bʌkl] *vt* desafivelar.
unbutton [ˌʌn'bʌtn] *vt* desabotoar.
uncalled-for [ˌʌn'kɔːld-] *adj* injusto(ta), desnecessário(ria).
uncanny [ʌn'kænɪ] (*compar* **-ier**, *superl* **-iest**) *adj* sinistro(tra).
uncared-for [ˌʌn'keəd-] *adj* abandonado(da).
uncaring [ˌʌn'keərɪŋ] *adj* insensível.
unceasing [ˌʌn'siːsɪŋ] *adj fml* incessante.
unceremonious ['ʌnˌserɪ'məʊnjəs] *adj* [abrupt] abrupto(ta).
unceremoniously ['ʌnˌserɪ'məʊnjəslɪ] *adj* [abruptly] abruptamente.
uncertain [ʌn'sɜːtn] *adj* **-1.** [gen] incerto(ta) **-2.** [person] indeciso(sa); **in no ~ terms** sem meias palavras.
unchain [ˌʌn'tʃeɪn] *vt* desacorrentar.
unchallenged [ˌʌn'tʃælɪndʒd] *adj* [authority, leadership, version] inquestionável.
unchanged [ˌʌn'tʃeɪndʒd] *adj* sem alterar.
unchanging [ˌʌn'tʃeɪndʒɪŋ] *adj* imutável.
uncharacteristic ['ʌnˌkærəktə'rɪstɪk] *adj* não-característico(ca).
uncharitable [ˌʌn'tʃærɪtəbl] *adj* mesquinho(nha).
uncharted [ˌʌn'tʃɑːtɪd] *adj* **-1.** [not recorded on maps] não-cartografado(da) **-2.** *fig* [unfamiliar] desconhecido(da).
unchecked [ˌʌn'tʃekt] ◇ *adj* [unrestrained] desenfreado(da). ◇ *adv* [unrestrained] sem restrições.
uncivilized, -ised [ˌʌn'sɪvɪlaɪzd] *adj* [barbaric] não-civilizado(da).
unclassified [ˌʌn'klæsɪfaɪd] *adj* **-1.** [not confidential] não-confidencial **-2.** [not categorised] não-classificado.
uncle ['ʌŋkl] *n* tio *m*.
unclean [ˌʌn'kliːn] *adj* **-1.** [dirty] sujo(ja) **-2.** RELIG impuro(ra).
unclear [ˌʌn'klɪə[r]] *adj* **-1.** [meaning, instructions] confuso(sa), pouco claro(ra) **-2.** [future] obscuro(ra) **-3.** [motives, details] confuso(sa) **-4.** [person]: **to be ~ about sthg** não ter algo claro.
unclothed [ˌʌn'kləʊðd] *adj fml* despido(da).
uncomfortable [ˌʌn'kʌmftəbl] *adj* **-1.** [giving discomfort] desconfortável **-2.** *fig* [awkward] desagradável **-3.** [person - in physical discomfort] desconfortável; [- ill at ease] incomodado(da).
uncomfortably [ˌʌn'kʌmftəblɪ] *adv* **-1.** [in physical discomfort] desconfortavelmente **-2.** *fig* [uneasily] de forma incômoda **-3.** [unpleasantly] desagradavelmente.
uncommitted [ˌʌnkə'mɪtɪd] *adj* não-comprometido(da).
uncommon [ʌn'kɒmən] *adj* **-1.** [rare] raro(ra) **-2.** *fml* [extreme] fora do comum.
uncommonly [ʌn'kɒmənlɪ] *adv fml* extraordinariamente.
uncommunicative [ˌʌnkə'mjuːnɪkətɪv] *adj* reservado(da).
uncomplicated [ˌʌn'kɒmplɪkeɪtɪd] *adj* descomplicado(da).
uncomprehending ['ʌnˌkɒmprɪ'hendɪŋ] *adj* atônito(ta).
uncompromising [ˌʌn'kɒmprəmaɪzɪŋ] *adj* resoluto(ta), inflexível.
unconcerned [ˌʌnkən'sɜːnd] *adj* [not anxious] indiferente.
unconditional [ˌʌnkən'dɪʃənl] *adj* incondicional.
uncongenial [ˌʌnkən'dʒiːnjəl] *adj fml* desagradável.
unconnected [ˌʌnkə'nektɪd] *adj* desconexo(xa).
unconquered [ˌʌn'kɒŋkəd] *adj* não-conquistado(da).
unconscious [ʌn'kɒnʃəs] ◇ *adj* **-1.** [gen] inconsciente **-2.** *fig* [unaware]: **to be ~ of sthg** não estar ciente de algo. ◇ *n* PSYCH: **the ~** o inconsciente.
unconsciously [ʌn'kɒnʃəslɪ] *adv* inconscientemente.
unconstitutional ['ʌnˌkɒnstɪ'tjuːʃənl] *adj* inconstitucional.
uncontested [ˌʌnkən'testɪd] *adj* **-1.** [gen] incontestado(da) **-2.** [election] sem oponente.
uncontrollable [ˌʌnkən'trəʊləbl] *adj* incontrolável.
uncontrolled [ˌʌnkən'trəʊld] *adj* descontrolado(da).
unconventional [ˌʌnkən'venʃənl] *adj* não-convencional.
unconvinced [ˌʌnkən'vɪnst] *adj* não-convencido(da).
unconvincing [ˌʌnkən'vɪnsɪŋ] *adj* não-convincente.
uncooked [ˌʌn'kʊkt] *adj* cru (crua).
uncooperative [ˌʌnkəʊ'ɒpərətɪv] *adj* não-disposto(ta) a ajudar.
uncork [ˌʌn'kɔːk] *vt* desarrolhar.
uncorroborated [ˌʌnkə'rɒbəreɪtɪd] *adj* não-confirmado(da).
uncouth [ʌn'kuːθ] *adj* grosseiro(ra).
uncover [ʌn'kʌvə[r]] *vt* **-1.** [saucepan] destampar **-2.** [corruption, truth] revelar, expor.
uncurl [ˌʌn'kɜːl] *vi* **-1.** [hair] alisar **-2.** [wire] esticar **-3.** [animal] desenroscar-se.
uncut [ˌʌn'kʌt] *adj* **-1.** [film] sem cortes **-2.** [jewel] bruto(ta).
undamaged [ˌʌn'dæmɪdʒd] *adj* intacto(ta).
undaunted [ˌʌn'dɔːntɪd] *adj* inabalável, destemido(da).
undecided [ˌʌndɪ'saɪdɪd] *adj* **-1.** [person] indeciso(sa) **-2.** [issue] pendente.
undemanding [ˌʌndɪ'mɑːndɪŋ] *adj* **-1.** [task] que exige pouco esforço **-2.** [person] pouco exigente.
undemonstrative [ˌʌndɪ'mɒnstrətɪv] *adj* [person] reservado(da).
undeniable [ˌʌndɪ'naɪəbl] *adj* inegável.
under ['ʌndə[r]] ◇ *prep* **-1.** [beneath, below] embaixo de; **they walked ~ the bridge** passaram por baixo da ponte **-2.** [less than] menos de **-3.** [indicating

conditions or circumstances]: ~ **the circumstances** dadas as circunstâncias; **I'm ~ the impression that ...** tenho a impressão de que ... **-4.** [undergoing]: ~ **discussion** em discussão **-5.** [directed, governed by]: **he has ten people ~ him** tem dez pessoas trabalhando sob seu comando **-6.** [according to] de acordo com **-7.** [in classification, name, title]: **he filed it ~ 'D'** arquivou na letra D; ~ **an alias** sob outro nome. <> *adv* **-1.** [beneath] embaixo; **to go ~** fracassar **-2.** [less]: **children of five years and ~** crianças de cinco anos ou menos.

under- ['ʌndəʳ] *prefix* sub-.

underachiever [,ʌndərə'tʃi:vəʳ] *n pessoa que não rende tudo o que pode.*

underage [ʌndər'eɪdʒ] *adj* **-1.** [person] menor de idade **-2.** [drinking, sex] para menor de idade.

underarm ['ʌndərɑ:m] <> *adj* **-1.** [deodorant, hair] para as axilas **-2.** *SPORT* [bowling] com a mão por baixo do ombro. <> *adv* [throw, bowl] por baixo do ombro.

underbrush ['ʌndəbrʌʃ] *n US* vegetação *f* rasteira *(numa floresta).*

undercarriage ['ʌndə,kærɪdʒ] *n* trem *m* de aterrissagem.

undercharge [,ʌndə'tʃɑ:dʒ] *vt* cobrar menos que o estipulado.

underclothes ['ʌndəkləʊðz] *npl* roupas *fpl* íntimas *OR* de baixo.

undercoat ['ʌndəkəʊt] *n* [of paint] primeira demão *f.*

undercook [,ʌndə'kʊk] *vt* não cozinhar suficientemente.

undercover ['ʌndə,kʌvəʳ] <> *adj* secreto(ta). <> *adv* na clandestinidade.

undercurrent ['ʌndə,kʌrənt] *n fig* [tendency] sentimento *m* oculto.

undercut [,ʌndə'kʌt] (*pt* & *pp* **undercut**, *cont* **-ting**) *vt* [in price] vender mais barato que.

underdeveloped [,ʌndədɪ'veləpt] *adj* subdesenvolvido(da), em desenvolvimento.

underdog ['ʌndədɒg] *n*: **the ~** os menos favorecidos.

underdone [,ʌndə'dʌn] *adj* [food] meio cru (crua).

underemployment [,ʌndərɪm'plɔɪmənt] *n (U)* subemprego *m.*

underestimate [*n* ʌndər'estɪmət, *vb* ,ʌndər'estɪmeɪt] <> *n* subestimação *f.* <> *vt* subestimar.

underexposed [,ʌndərɪk'spəʊzd] *adj PHOT* subexposto(ta).

underfinanced [,ʌndə'faɪnænst] *adj* insuficientemente financiado(da).

underfoot [,ʌndə'fʊt] *adv* debaixo dos pés; **the ground is wet ~** o chão está molhado.

undergo [,ʌndə'gəʊ] (*pt* **-went**, *pp* **-gone**) *vt* **-1.** [change, difficulties] passar por **-2.** [operation, examination] submeter-se a.

undergraduate [,ʌndə'grædʒʊət] <> *adj* de graduação. <> *n* universitário *m,* -ria *f (que ainda não colou grau).*

underground [*adj* & *n* 'ʌndəgraʊnd, *adv* ,ʌndə'graʊnd] <> *adj* **-1.** [below the ground] subterrâneo(nea) **-2.** *fig* [secret, illegal] clandestino(na). <> *adv*: **to go ~** passar à clandestinidade; **to be forced ~** ter de passar à clandestinidade. <> *n* **-1.** *UK* [transport system] metrô *m* **-2.** [activist movement] resistência *f.*

undergrowth ['ʌndəgrəʊθ] *n (U)* vegetação *f* rasteira *(numa floresta).*

underhand [,ʌndə'hænd] *adj* clandestino(na).

underinsured [,ʌndərɪn'ʃʊəd] *adj segurado(da) abaixo do valor corrente.*

underlay ['ʌndəleɪ] *n* [for carpet] forração *f.*

underline [,ʌndə'laɪn] *vt* **-1.** [draw line under] sublinhar **-2.** *fig* [stress] salientar.

underling *n* subalterno *m,* -na *f.*

underlying [,ʌndə'laɪɪŋ] *adj* subjacente.

undermanned [,ʌndə'mænd] *adj* com falta de mão-de-obra.

undermentioned [,ʌndə'menʃnd] *adj fml* abaixo mencionado(da).

undermine [,ʌndə'maɪn] *vt fig* [weaken] minar.

underneath [,ʌndə'ni:θ] <> *prep* debaixo de. <> *adv* **-1.** [beneath] por baixo **-2.** *fig* [within oneself] por dentro, no fundo. <> *adj inf* de baixo. <> *n* [underside]: **the ~** a parte de baixo; **on the ~** no fundo; **on the ~ of the box** na parte de baixo da caixa.

undernourished [,ʌndə'nʌrɪʃt] *adj* subnutrido(-da).

underpaid [*pt* & *pp* ʌndə'peɪd, *adj* 'ʌndəpeɪd] <> *pt* & *pp* ▻ **underpay**. <> *adj* mal pago(ga).

underpants ['ʌndəpænts] *npl* cueca *f.*

underpass ['ʌndəpɑ:s] *n* passagem *f* subterrânea.

underpay [,ʌndə'peɪ] (*pt* & *pp* **-paid**) *vt* pagar mal.

underpin [,ʌndə'pɪn] (*pt* & *pp* **-ned**, *cont* **-ning**) *vt fig* [back up] embasar.

underplay [,ʌndə'pleɪ] *vt* [minimize the importance of] minimizar.

underprice [,ʌndə'praɪs] *vt* cotar algo abaixo de seu valor real.

underprivileged [,ʌndə'prɪvɪlɪdʒd] *adj* [children] desamparado(da).

underproduction [,ʌndəprə'dʌkʃn] *n (U)* produção *f* insuficiente.

underrated [,ʌndə'reɪtɪd] *adj* subestimado(da).

underscore [,ʌndə'skɔ:ʳ] *vt* **-1.** [underline] sublinhar **-2.** *fig* [emphasize] salientar.

undersea ['ʌndəsi:] *adj* submarino(na).

undersecretary [,ʌndə'sekrətərɪ] (*pl* **-ies**) *n* subsecretário *m,* -ria *f.*

undersell [,ʌndə'sel] (*pt* & *pp* **-sold**) *vt* **-1.** *COMM* [sell at lower prices than] vender mais barato que **-2.** *fig* [undervalue]: **to ~ o.s.** vender-se barato.

undershirt ['ʌndəʃɜ:t] *n US* camiseta *f.*

underside ['ʌndəsaɪd] *n*: **the ~** a parte de baixo.

undersigned ['ʌndəsaɪnd] *n fml*: **the ~** o abaixo-assinado.

undersize(d) [,ʌndə'saɪz(d)] *adj* menor que o normal.

underskirt ['ʌndəskɜ:t] *n* anágua *f.*

undersold [,ʌndə'səʊld] *pt* & *pp* ▻ **undersell**.

understaffed [,ʌndə'stɑ:ft] *adj* com falta de pessoal.

understand [,ʌndə'stænd] (*pt* & *pp* **-stood**) <> *vt* **-1.** entender, compreender; **to make o.s. understood** fazer-se entender **-2.** *fml* [believe]: **to ~ that**

acreditar que. ◇ *vi* entender, compreender.
understandable [ˌʌndəˈstændəbl] *adj* compreensível.
understandably [ˌʌndəˈstændəblɪ] *adv* naturalmente; **he was ~ upset** é compreensível que ele estivesse chateado.
understanding [ˌʌndəˈstændɪŋ] ◇ *n* **-1.** [knowledge, insight] compreensão *f*, entendimento *m* **-2.** *(U)* [sympathy] compreensão *f* mútua **-3.** [interpretation, conception]: **it is my ~ that ...** tenho a impressão de que ... **-4.** [informal agreement] entendimento *m*; **on the ~ that ...** à condição de que ... ◇ *adj* [sympathetic] compreensivo(va).
understate [ˌʌndəˈsteɪt] *vt* [minimize] atenuar.
understated *adj* [elegance, clothes] sóbrio(bria).
understatement [ˌʌndəˈsteɪtmənt] *n* **-1.** [inadequate statement] atenuação *f* **-2.** *(U)* [quality of understating] atenuação *f*; **he is a master of ~** ele é o rei dos eufemismos.
understood [ˌʌndəˈstʊd] *pt & pp* ▻ **understand**.
understudy [ˈʌndəˌstʌdɪ] (*pl* **-ies**, *pt & pp* **-ied**) ◇ *n* ator *m* substituto, atriz *f* substituta. ◇ *vt*: **to ~ the role of Macbeth** substituit alguém no papel de Macbeth.
undertake [ˌʌndəˈteɪk] (*pt* **-took**, *pp* **-taken**) *vt* **-1.** [take on - responsibility, control] assumir; [- task] incumbir-se de **-2.** [promise]: **to ~ to do sthg** comprometer-se a fazer algo.
undertaker [ˈʌndəˌteɪkəʳ] *n* agente *mf* funerário, -ria; **~'s** [place] funerária *f*.
undertaking [ˌʌndəˈteɪkɪŋ] *n* **-1.** [task] incumbência *f* **-2.** [promise] promessa *f*.
undertone [ˈʌndətəʊn] *n* **-1.** [quiet voice] voz *f* baixa **-2.** [vague feeling] traço *m*; **an ~ of sadness** um traço de tristeza.
undertook [ˌʌndəˈtʊk] *pt* ▻ **undertake**.
undertow [ˈʌndətəʊ] *n* ressaca *f (no mar)*.
undervalue [ˌʌndəˈvæljuː] *vt* **-1.** [person] subestimar **-2.** [house, object] avaliar algo abaixo de seu real valor.
underwater [ˌʌndəˈwɔːtəʳ] ◇ *adj* submarino(na). ◇ *adv* debaixo d'água.
underwear [ˈʌndəweəʳ] *n (U)* roupa *f* íntima OR de baixo.
underweight [ˌʌndəˈweɪt] *adj abaixo do peso*.
underwent [ˌʌndəˈwent] *pt* ▻ **undergo**.
underwired *adj* [bra] com suporte.
underworld [ˈʌndəˌwɜːld] *n* [criminal society]: **the ~** o submundo.
underwrite [ˈʌndəraɪt] (*pt* **-wrote**, *pp* **-written**) *vt* **-1.** *fml* [guarantee] comprometer-se com **-2.** [in insurance business] subscrever.
underwriter [ˈʌndəˌraɪtəʳ] *n* segurador *m*, -ra *f*.
underwritten [ˈʌndəˌrɪtn] *pp* ▻ **underwrite**.
underwrote [ˈʌndərəʊt] *pt* ▻ **underwrite**.
undeserved [ˌʌndɪˈzɜːvd] *adj* não-merecido(da).
undesirable [ˌʌndɪˈzaɪərəbl] *adj* indesejável.
undeveloped [ˌʌndɪˈveləpt] *adj* **-1.** [country] subdesenvolvido(da), em desenvolvimento **-2.** [land, resource] não explorado(da).
undid [ˌʌnˈdɪd] *pt* ▻ **undo**.
undies [ˈʌndɪz] *npl inf* roupas *fpl* íntimas OR de baixo.
undignified [ʌnˈdɪgnɪfaɪd] *adj* indecoroso(sa), impróprio(pria).
undiluted [ˌʌndaɪˈljuːtɪd] *adj* **-1.** [quality, emotion] puro(ra) **-2.** [liquid] não-diluído(da).
undiplomatic [ˌʌndɪpləˈmætɪk] *adj* pouco diplomático(ca), indelicado(da).
undischarged [ˌʌndɪsˈtʃɑːdʒd] *adj* **-1.** [debt] pendente **-2.** [person]: **~ bankrupt** pessoa *f* falida não-reabilitada.
undisciplined [ʌnˈdɪsɪplɪnd] *adj* indisciplinado(-da).
undiscovered [ˌʌndɪˈskʌvəd] *adj* [unknown] não -descoberto(ta).
undisputed [ˌʌndɪˈspjuːtɪd] *adj* indiscutível.
undistinguished [ˌʌndɪˈstɪŋgwɪʃt] *adj* sem graça.
undivided [ˌʌndɪˈvaɪdɪd] *adj* [whole] inteiro(ra); **my ~ attention** toda a minha atenção.
undo [ˌʌnˈduː] (*pt* **-did**, *pp* **-done**) *vt* **-1.** [knot] desfazer, desatar **-2.** [buttons] desabotoar **-3.** [garment] desamarrar **-4.** [good work, efforts] anular.
undoing [ˌʌnˈduːɪŋ] *n (U) fml* ruína *f*, perdição *f*.
undone [ˌʌnˈdʌn] ◇ *pp* ▻ **undo**. ◇ *adj* **-1.** [coat] desabotoado(da) **-2.** [shoe] desamarrado(da) **-3.** *fml* [not done] por fazer.
undoubted [ʌnˈdaʊtɪd] *adj* indubitável.
undoubtedly [ʌnˈdaʊtɪdlɪ] *adv* indubitavelmente.
undreamed-of [ʌnˈdriːmdɒv], **undreamt-of** [ʌnˈdremtɒv] *adj* [unimaginable] jamais imaginado(-da).
undress [ˌʌnˈdres] ◇ *vt* despir. ◇ *vi* despir-se.
undressed [ˌʌnˈdrest] *adj* [person] despido(da); **to get ~** tirar a roupa, despir-se.
undrinkable [ˌʌnˈdrɪŋkəbl] *adj* **-1.** [dangerous to drink] não-potável **-2.** [bad-tasting] intragável.
undue [ˌʌnˈdjuː] *adj fml* desmedido(da).
undulate [ˈʌndjʊleɪt] *vi fml* ondular.
unduly [ˌʌnˈdjuːlɪ] *adv fml* demasiadamente.
undying [ʌnˈdaɪɪŋ] *adj literary* imperecível.
unearned income [ˌʌnˈɜːnd-] *n (U)* renda *f* diferida.
unearth [ˌʌnˈɜːθ] *vt* **-1.** [dig up] desenterrar **-2.** *fig* [discover] descubrir.
unearthly [ʌnˈɜːθlɪ] *adj* **-1.** [ghostly] sobrenatural **-2.** *inf* [time of day]: **at an ~ hour in the morning** num horário absurdo da manhã.
unease [ʌnˈiːz] *n (U)* inquietação *f*, apreensão *f*.
uneasy [ʌnˈiːzɪ] (*compar* **-ier**, *superl* **-iest**) *adj* **-1.** [troubled] apreensivo(va) **-2.** [embarrassed] constrangido(da); **an ~ silence** um silêncio constrangedor **-3.** [peace, truce] duvidoso(sa).
uneatable [ˌʌnˈiːtəbl] *adj* **-1.** [dangerous to eat] *que não se pode comer* **-2.** [bad-tasting] indigesto(ta).
uneaten [ˌʌnˈiːtn] *adj*: **lots of ~ food** muita comida que sobrou.
uneconomic [ˈʌnˌiːkəˈnɒmɪk] *adj* pouco rentável.
uneducated [ˌʌnˈedjʊkeɪtɪd] *adj* **-1.** [person] inculto(ta), sem instrução **-2.** [behaviour, manners, speech] em que se percebe falta de instrução.
unemotional [ˌʌnɪˈməʊʃənl] *adj* **-1.** [person] impassível **-2.** [voice, tone] frio (fria) **-3.** [statement] objetivo(va).

unemployable [ˌʌnɪm'plɔɪəbl] *adj* que dificilmente encontrará trabalho.
unemployed [ˌʌnɪm'plɔɪd] ◇ *adj* [out-of-work] desempregado(da). ◇ *npl*: **the ~** os desempregados.
unemployment [ˌʌnɪm'plɔɪmənt] *n* desemprego *m*.
unemployment benefit *UK*, **unemployment compensation** *US n (U)* ≃ seguro-desemprego *m*.
unenviable [ˌʌn'envɪəbl] *adj* nada invejável.
unequal [ˌʌn'i:kwəl] *adj* desigual.
unequalled *UK*, **unequaled** *US* [ˌʌn'i:kwəld] *adj* inigualável.
unequivocal [ˌʌnɪ'kwɪvəkl] *adj fml* inequívoco(ca).
unerring [ˌʌn'ɜ:rɪŋ] *adj* infalível.
UNESCO [ju:'neskəʊ] (*abbr of* **United Nations Educational, Scientific and Cultural Organization**) *n* UNESCO *f*.
unethical [ʌn'eθɪkl] *adj* antiético(ca).
uneven [ˌʌn'i:vn] *adj* **-1.** [surface] irregular **-2.** [road] acidentado(da) **-3.** [performance, coverage *etc*] desigual, desparelho(lha) **-4.** [competition] injusto(ta).
uneventful [ˌʌnɪ'ventfʊl] *adj* sem maiores incidentes.
unexceptional [ˌʌnɪk'sepʃənl] *adj* sem nada de mais, normal.
unexpected [ˌʌnɪk'spektɪd] *adj* inesperado(da).
unexpectedly [ˌʌnɪk'spektɪdlɪ] *adv* inesperadamente.
unexplained [ˌʌnɪk'spleɪnd] *adj* inexplicado(da).
unexploded [ˌʌnɪk'spləʊdɪd] *adj* [bomb] que não detonou.
unexpurgated [ˌʌn'ekspəgeɪtɪd] *adj* sem cortes, na íntegra.
unfailing [ʌn'feɪlɪŋ] *adj* [loyalty, support, good humour] infalível.
unfair [ˌʌn'feə^r] *adj* injusto(ta).
unfair dismissal *n (U)* demissão *f* sem justa causa.
unfairly *adv* injustamente.
unfairness [ˌʌn'feənɪs] *n* injustiça *f*.
unfaithful [ˌʌn'feɪθfʊl] *adj* [sexually] infiel.
unfamiliar [ˌʌnfə'mɪljə^r] *adj* **-1.** [not well-known] desconhecido(da) **-2.** [not acquainted]: **to be ~ with sb/sthg** desconhecer alguém/algo.
unfashionable [ˌʌn'fæʃnəbl] *adj* ultrapassado(-da).
unfasten [ˌʌn'fɑ:sn] *vt* **-1.** [garment, buttons] desabotoar **-2.** [rope] desamarrar.
unfavourable *UK*, **unfavorable** *US* [ˌʌn'feɪvrəbl] *adj* desfavorável.
unfeeling [ʌn'fi:lɪŋ] *adj* insensível.
unfinished [ˌʌn'fɪnɪʃt] *adj* inacabado(da).
unfit [ˌʌn'fɪt] *adj* **-1.** [not in good shape] fora de forma **-2.** [not suitable]: **~ (for sthg)** inadequado(da) (para algo).
unflagging [ˌʌn'flægɪŋ] *adj* **-1.** [support, enthusiasm] inesgotável **-2.** [supporter] incansável.
unflappable [ˌʌn'flæpəbl] *adj esp UK* inabalável.
unflattering [ˌʌn'flætərɪŋ] *adj* pouco favorecedor(ra).
unflinching [ʌn'flɪntʃɪŋ] *adj* impávido(da).
unfold [ʌn'fəʊld] ◇ *vt* **-1.** [open out] desdobrar **-2.** [explain] expor. ◇ *vi* [become clear] esclarecer-se.
unforeseeable [ˌʌnfɔ:'si:əbl] *adj* imprevisível.
unforeseen [ˌʌnfɔ:si:n] *adj* imprevisto(ta).
unforgettable [ˌʌnfə'getəbl] *adj* inesquecível.
unforgivable [ˌʌnfə'gɪvəbl] *adj* imperdoável.
unformatted [ˌʌn'fɔ:mætɪd] *adj COMPUT* não-formatado(da).
unfortunate [ʌn'fɔ:tʃnət] *adj* **-1.** [unlucky] azarento(ta) **-2.** [regrettable] lamentável.
unfortunately [ʌn'fɔ:tʃnətlɪ] *adv* infelizmente.
unfounded [ˌʌn'faʊndɪd] *adj* infundado(da).
unfriendly [ˌʌn'frendlɪ] (*compar* **-ier**, *superl* **-iest**) *adj* hostil.
unfulfilled [ˌʌnfʊl'fɪld] *adj* **-1.** [ambition, promise, prophecy] que não se realizou **-2.** [person] insatisfeito(ta).
unfurl [ˌʌn'fɜ:l] *vt* **-1.** [flag, sail] desfraldar **-2.** [umbrella] abrir.
unfurnished [ˌʌn'fɜ:nɪʃt] *adj* desmobiliado(da), sem móveis.
ungainly [ʌn'geɪnlɪ] *adj* desajeitado(da).
ungenerous [ˌʌn'dʒenərəs] *adj* **-1.** [mean] miserável; **a not ~ gift** um presente bastante generoso **-2.** [uncharitable] pouco generoso(sa).
ungodly [ˌʌn'gɒdlɪ] *adj* **-1.** [irreligious] ímpio(pia) **-2.** *inf* [unreasonable]: **why are you phoning me at this ~ hour?** por que você está me ligando nesta hora da madrugada?
ungrateful [ʌn'greɪtfʊl] *adj* mal-agradecido(da).
ungratefulness [ʌn'greɪtfʊlnɪs] *n (U)* ingratidão *f*.
unguarded [ˌʌn'gɑ:dɪd] *adj* **-1.** [not guarded] desprotegido(da) **-2.** [careless]: **in an ~ moment** num momento de descuido.
unhappily [ʌn'hæpɪlɪ] *adv* **-1.** [sadly] tristemente **-2.** *fml* [unfortunately] lamentavelmente.
unhappiness [ʌn'hæpɪnɪs] *n (U)* infelicidade *f*.
unhappy [ʌn'hæpɪ] (*compar* **-ier**, *superl* **-iest**) *adj* **-1.** [sad] triste **-2.** [uneasy]: **to be ~ (with** *OR* **about sthg)** estar descontente(com algo) **-3.** *fml* [unfortunate] lamentável, infeliz.
unharmed [ˌʌn'hɑ:md] *adj* ileso(sa).
UNHCR (*abbr of* **United Nations High Commission for Refugees**) *n organização internacional que faz parte da ONU responsável pela ajuda a refugiados*.
unhealthy [ʌn'helθɪ] (*compar* **-ier**, *superl* **-iest**) *adj* **-1.** [in bad health] doentio(tia) **-2.** [causing bad health] insalubre **-3.** *fig* [undesirable] prejudicial.
unheard [ˌʌn'hɜ:d] *adj*: **to be** *OR* **go ~** passar sem ser ouvido(da).
unheard-of [ʌn'hɜ:d-] *adj* **-1.** [unknown, completely absent] inaudito(ta) **-2.** [unprecedented] sem precedente.
unheeded [ˌʌn'hi:dɪd] *adj*: **to go ~** passar despercebido(da).
unhelpful [ˌʌn'helpfʊl] *adj* **-1.** [unwilling to help - person] pouco prestativo(va); [- attitude] com má vontade **-2.** [not useful] inútil.
unhindered [ʌn'hɪndəd] *adj* sem impedimentos.
unhook [ˌʌn'hʊk] *vt* **-1.** [unfasten hooks of] desenganchar **-2.** [remove from hook] desprender.
unhurt [ˌʌn'hɜ:t] *adj* ileso(sa).

unhygienic [ˌʌnhaɪˈdʒiːnɪk] *adj* anti-higiênico(ca).
uni (*abbr of* **university**) *n UK inf* universidade *f*.
UNICEF [ˈjuːnɪˌsef] (*abbr of* **United Nations Children's Fund**) *n* UNICEF *f*.
unicorn [ˈjuːnɪkɔːn] *n* unicórnio *m*.
unicycle [ˈjuːnɪsaɪkl] *n* monociclo *m*.
unidentified [ˌʌnaɪˈdentɪfaɪd] *adj* não-identificado(da).
unidentified flying object *n* objeto *m* voador não-identificado.
unification [ˌjuːnɪfɪˈkeɪʃn] *n (U)* unificação *f*.
uniform [ˈjuːnɪfɔːm] ◇ *adj* uniforme. ◇ *n* uniforme *m*.
uniformity [ˌjuːnɪˈfɔːmətɪ] *n (U)* uniformidade *f*.
uniformly [ˈjuːnɪfɔːmlɪ] *adv* uniformemente.
unify [ˈjuːnɪfaɪ] (*pt* & *pp* **-ied**) *vt* unificar.
unifying [ˈjuːnɪfaɪɪŋ] *adj* unificador(ra).
unilateral [ˌjuːnɪˈlætərəl] *adj* unilateral.
unimaginable [ˌʌnɪˈmædʒɪnəbl] *adj* inimaginável.
unimaginative [ˌʌnɪˈmædʒɪnətɪv] *adj* sem imaginação.
unimpaired [ˌʌnɪmˈpeəd] *adj* **-1.** [gen] intacto(ta) **-2.** [health] inalterado(da).
unimpeded [ˌʌnɪmˈpiːdɪd] *adj* desimpedido(da), sem obstáculos.
unimportant [ˌʌnɪmˈpɔːtənt] *adj* insignificante, sem importância.
unimpressed [ˌʌnɪmˈprest] *adj* pouco impressionado(da).
uninhabited [ˌʌnɪnˈhæbɪtɪd] *adj* desabitado(da).
uninhibited [ˌʌnɪnˈhɪbɪtɪd] *adj* desinibido(da).
uninitiated [ˌʌnɪˈnɪʃɪeɪtɪd] *npl*: **the** ~ os inexperientes.
uninjured [ˌʌnˈɪndʒəd] *adj* ileso(sa).
uninspiring [ˌʌnɪnˈspaɪərɪŋ] *adj* nada inspirador(-ra).
unintelligent [ˌʌnɪnˈtelɪdʒent] *adj* pouco inteligente.
unintentional [ˌʌnɪnˈtenʃənl] *adj* involuntário(-ria).
uninterested [ˌʌnˈɪntrəstɪd] *adj* desinteressado(-da).
uninterrupted [ˈʌnˌɪntəˈrʌptɪd] *adj* ininterrupto(-ta).
uninvited [ˌʌnɪnˈvaɪtɪd] *adj* não-convidado(da).
union [ˈjuːnjən] ◇ *n* **-1.** [trade union] sindicato *m* **-2.** [alliance] união *f*. ◇ *comp* sindical.
Unionist [ˈjuːnjənɪst] *n UK POL membro de partido político que deseja que a Irlanda do Norte continue fazendo parte do Reino Unido*, unionista *mf*.
unionize, -ise [ˈjuːnjənaɪz] *vt* sindicalizar.
unionized, -ised *adj* sindicalizado(da).
Union Jack *n*: the ~ *a bandeira do Reino Unido*.
union shop *n US empresa na qual todos os empregados devem pertencer a um sindicato*.
unique [juːˈniːk] *adj* **-1.** [unparalleled] incomparável, único(ca) **-2.** *fml* [peculiar, exclusive]: ~ **to sb/sthg** peculiar a alguém/algo.
uniquely [juːˈniːklɪ] *adv* **-1.** *fml* [exclusively] unicamente **-2.** [exceptionally] excepcionalmente.
unisex [ˈjuːnɪseks] *adj* unissex *inv*.
unison [ˈjuːnɪzn] *n (U)* [agreement] harmonia *f*; **in** ~ [simultaneously] em uníssono.
UNISON [ˈjuːnɪzn] *n sindicato gigante que reúne a maioria dos funcionários britânicos*, ≃ CUT *f*.
unit [ˈjuːnɪt] *n* **-1.** [gen] unidade *f* **-2.** [piece of furniture] módulo *m*.
unit cost *n* custo *m* unitário.
unite [juːˈnaɪt] ◇ *vt* unificar. ◇ *vi* unir-se, juntar-se.
united [juːˈnaɪtɪd] *adj* **-1.** [in harmony] unido(da); **they are ~ on this point** eles estão todos de acordo neste ponto **-2.** [unified] unificado(da).
United Arab Emirates *npl*: **the** ~ os Emirados Árabes Unidos.
united front *n*: **to present a** ~ fazer frente única.
United Kingdom *n*: **the** ~ o Reino Unido.
United Nations *n*: **the** ~ as Nações Unidas.
United States *n*: **the ~ (of America)** os Estados Unidos (da América); **in the** ~ nos Estados Unidos.
unit price *n* preço *m* unitário.
unit trust *n UK* fundo *m* de investimento.
unity [ˈjuːnətɪ] *n* **-1.** [union] união *f*, unidade *f* **-2.** [harmony] união *f*.
Univ. (*abbr of* **University**) univ.
universal [ˌjuːnɪˈvɜːsl] *adj* [belief, truth] universal.
universal joint *n* junta *f* universal.
universe [ˈjuːnɪvɜːs] *n ASTRON* universo *m*.
university [ˌjuːnɪˈvɜːsətɪ] (*pl* **-ies**) ◇ *n* universidade *f*. ◇ *comp* universitário(ria); ~ **student** estudante *m* universitário, -ria *f*.
unjust [ˌʌnˈdʒʌst] *adj* injusto(ta).
unjustifiable [ʌnˈdʒʌstɪˌfaɪəbl] *adj* injustificável.
unjustified [ʌnˈdʒʌstɪfaɪd] *adj* injustificado(da).
unkempt [ˌʌnˈkempt] *adj* [hair, beard, appearance] desajeitado(da).
unkind [ʌnˈkaɪnd] *adj* **-1.** [gen] indelicado(da) **-2.** *fig* [climate] rigoroso(sa).
unkindly [ʌnˈkaɪndlɪ] *adv* de forma indelicada.
unknown [ˌʌnˈnəʊn] ◇ *adj* desconhecido(da). ◇ *n* **-1.** [unknown thing]: **the** ~ o desconhecido **-2.** [unknown person] desconhecido *m*, -da *f*, estranho *m*, -nha *f*.
unlace [ˌʌnˈleɪs] *vt* desamarrar.
unladen [ˌʌnˈleɪdn] *adj* sem carga.
unlawful [ˌʌnˈlɔːfʊl] *adj* ilegal.
unleaded [ˌʌnˈledɪd] *adj* sem chumbo.
unleash [ˌʌnˈliːʃ] *vt literary* desencadear.
unleavened [ˌʌnˈlevnd] *adj* [bread] sem fermento.
unless [ənˈles] *conj* a menos que; ~ **I'm mistaken, ...** a não ser que eu esteja enganado, ...
unlicensed, unlicenced *US* [ˌʌnˈlaɪsənst] *adj* **-1.** [fishing, hunting] proibido(da) **-2.** [car] não-licenciado(da) **-3.** [premises, restaurant] sem licença.
unlike [ˌʌnˈlaɪk] *prep* **-1.** [different from] diferente de **-2.** [in contrast to] ao contrário de **-3.** [not typical of] atípico(ca); **it's very ~ you to complain** você não é de reclamar.
unlikely [ʌnˈlaɪklɪ] *adj* **-1.** [not probable] improvável **-2.** [bizarre] estranho(nha).
unlimited [ʌnˈlɪmɪtɪd] *adj* ilimitado(da).

unlisted [ʌn'lɪstɪd] *adj US* [phone number] fora da lista.
unlit [ˌʌn'lɪt] *adj* **-1.** [not burning] apagado(da) **-2.** [dark] sem luz.
unload [ˌʌn'ləʊd] *vt* **-1.** [gen] descarregar **-2.** *fig* [unburden]: **to ~ sthg on(to) sb** descarregar algo em alguém.
unlock [ˌʌn'lɒk] *vt* destrancar, abrir *(com chave)*.
unloved [ˌʌn'lʌvd] *adj*: **to be/feel ~** não ser/se sentir amado(da).
unluckily [ʌn'lʌkɪlɪ] *adv* infelizmente; **~ for us, ...** para nosso azar, ...
unlucky [ʌn'lʌkɪ] (*compar* **-ier**, *superl* **-iest**) *adj* **-1.** [unfortunate] infeliz **-2.** [bringing bad luck] de mau agouro.
unmanageable [ʌn'mænɪdʒəbl] *adj* **-1.** [vehicle, situation] fora de controle **-2.** [size, parcel] de difícil manuseio.
unmanly [ˌʌn'mænlɪ] (*compar* **-ier**, *superl* **-iest**) *adj* [behaviour, attitude] indigno(na) de um homem.
unmanned [ˌʌn'mænd] *adj* não-tripulado(da).
unmarked [ˌʌn'mɑːkt] *adj* **-1.** [uninjured] sem marca **-2.** [unidentified] não-identificado(da).
unmarried [ˌʌn'mærɪd] *adj* solteiro(ra).
unmask [ˌʌn'mɑːsk] *vt* desmascarar.
unmatched [ˌʌn'mætʃt] *adj* inigualável.
unmentionable [ʌn'menʃnəbl] *adj* indizível.
unmistakable [ˌʌnmɪ'steɪkəbl] *adj* inconfundível.
unmitigated [ʌn'mɪtɪgeɪtɪd] *adj* completo(ta), absoluto(ta); **he's talking ~ nonsense!** ele não está dizendo coisa com coisa!
unmoved [ˌʌn'muːvd] *adj*: **to be ~ by sthg** ser indiferente a algo.
unnamed [ˌʌn'neɪmd] *adj* [anonymous] anônimo(-ma).
unnatural [ʌn'nætʃrəl] *adj* **-1.** [unusual, strange] estranho(nha) **-2.** [affected] pouco natural.
unnecessary [ʌn'nesəsərɪ] *adj* desnecessário(ria).
unnerving [ˌʌn'nɜːvɪŋ] *adj* enervante.
unnoticed [ˌʌn'nəʊtɪst] *adj* desapercebido(da).
UNO (*abbr of* **United Nations Organization**) *n* ONU *f*.
unobserved [ˌʌnəb'zɜːvd] *adj* desapercebido(da).
unobtainable [ˌʌnəb'teɪnəbl] *adj* inacessível.
unobtrusive [ˌʌnəb'truːsɪv] *adj* discreto(ta).
unoccupied [ˌʌn'ɒkjʊpaɪd] *adj* desocupado(da).
unofficial [ˌʌnə'fɪʃl] *adj* não-oficial.
unopened [ˌʌn'əʊpənd] *adj* fechado(da).
unorthodox [ˌʌn'ɔːθədɒks] *adj* não-ortodoxo(xa).
unpack [ˌʌn'pæk] ◇ *vt* **-1.** [bag, suitcase] desfazer **-2.** [clothes, books, shopping] desembrulhar. ◇ *vi* desfazer as malas.
unpaid [ˌʌn'peɪd] *adj* não-remunerado(da).
unpalatable [ʌn'pælətəbl] *adj* **-1.** [unpleasant to taste] intragável **-2.** *fig* [difficult to accept] desagradável.
unparalleled [ʌn'pærəleld] *adj* sem paralelo.
unpatriotic ['ʌnˌpætrɪ'ɒtɪk] *adj* antipatriótico(ca).
unpick [ˌʌn'pɪk] *vt* descosturar.
unpin [ˌʌn'pɪn] (*pt* & *pp* **-ned**, *cont* **-ning**) *vt* [remove pin from] desprender.
unplanned [ˌʌn'plænd] *adj* não-planejado(da).
unpleasant [ʌn'pleznt] *adj* desagradável.
unpleasantness [ʌn'plezntnɪs] *n (U)* **-1.** [of person, experience, weather] dissabor *m* **-2.** [discord] desentendimento *m*.
unplug [ʌn'plʌg] (*pt* & *pp* **-ged**, *cont* **-ging**) *vt ELEC* desligar.
unpolished [ˌʌn'pɒlɪʃt] *adj* **-1.** [furniture, brass, shoes] não-polido(da) **-2.** [person, manner] grosseiro(ra).
unpolluted [ˌʌnpə'luːtɪd] *adj* despoluído(da).
unpopular [ˌʌn'pɒpjʊlə[r]] *adj* impopular.
unprecedented [ʌn'presɪdəntɪd] *adj* sem precedente.
unpredictable [ˌʌnprɪ'dɪktəbl] *adj* imprevisível.
unprejudiced [ˌʌn'predʒʊdɪst] *adj* imparcial.
unprepared [ˌʌnprɪ'peəd] *adj*: **to be ~ (for sthg)** não estar preparado(da) (para algo).
unprepossessing ['ʌnˌpriːpə'zesɪŋ] *adj* pouco atraente.
unpretentious [ˌʌnprɪ'tenʃəs] *adj* despretencioso(sa).
unprincipled [ʌn'prɪnsəpld] *adj* inescrupuloso(-sa).
unprintable [ˌʌn'prɪntəbl] *adj* impublicável.
unproductive [ˌʌnprə'dʌktɪv] *adj* improdutivo(-va).
unprofessional [ˌʌnprə'feʃənl] *adj* não-profissional.
unprofitable [ˌʌn'prɒfɪtəbl] *adj* [not making a profit] não-lucrativo(va).
unprompted [ˌʌn'prɒmptɪd] *adj* espontâneo(-nea).
unpronounceable [ˌʌnprə'naʊnsəbl] *adj* impronunciável.
unprotected [ˌʌnprə'tektɪd] *adj* [person, skin] desprotegido(da); **~ sex** relação *f* sexual desprotegida.
unprovoked [ˌʌnprə'vəʊkt] *adj* não-provocado(-da), espontâneo(nea).
unpublished [ˌʌn'pʌblɪʃt] *adj* inédito(ta).
unpunished [ˌʌn'pʌnɪʃt] *adj*: **to go ~** ficar impune.
unqualified [ˌʌn'kwɒlɪfaɪd] *adj* **-1.** [not qualified] desqualificado(da) **-2.** [total, complete] absoluto(ta).
unquestionable [ʌn'kwestʃənəbl] *adj* inquestionável.
unquestioning [ʌn'kwestʃənɪŋ] *adj* incondicional.
unravel [ʌn'rævl] (*UK pt* & *pp* **-led**, *cont* **-ling**, *US pt* & *pp* **-ed**, *cont* **-ing**) ◇ *vt* **-1.** [undo] desembaraçar **-2.** *fig* [solve] elucidar. ◇ *vi* [become undone] desembaraçar-se.
unreadable [ˌʌn'riːdəbl] *adj* **-1.** [gen] ilegível **-2.** [difficult, tedious to read] difícil de ler.
unreal [ˌʌn'rɪəl] *adj* [strange] irreal.
unrealistic [ˌʌnrɪə'lɪstɪk] *adj* pouco realista.
unreasonable [ʌn'riːznəbl] *adj* **-1.** [unfair, not sensible] injusto(ta) **-2.** [not justifiable] absurdo(da), irracional.
unrecognizable [ˌʌn'rekəgnaɪzəbl] *adj* irreconhecível.
unrecognized [ˌʌn'rekəgnaɪzd] *adj* **-1.** [not known, noticed] não-reconhecido(da); **to be ~** não ser reconhecido(da) **-2.** [unacknowledged] inconfesso(-sa).

unrecorded [ˌʌnrɪ'kɔ:dɪd] *adj* **-1.** [remark, fact, event] não-registrado(da) **-2.** [music, voice] desconhecido(-da).
unrefined [ˌʌnrɪ'faɪnd] *adj* **-1.** [petrol, sugar, flour] não-refinado(da) **-2.** [person, manners] impolido(da).
unrehearsed [ˌʌnrɪ'hɜ:st] *adj* improvisado(da).
unrelated [ˌʌnrɪ'leɪtɪd] *adj*: **to be ~ (to sthg)** não estar relacionado(da) (a algo).
unrelenting [ˌʌnrɪ'lentɪŋ] *adj* **-1.** [pressure] contínuo(nua) **-2.** [questions] implacável.
unreliable [ˌʌnrɪ'laɪəbl] *adj* inconfiável.
unrelieved [ˌʌnrɪ'li:vd] *adj* **-1.** [pain] que não alivia **-2.** [gloom, boredom]: **a period of ~ boredom** um período de tédio sem fim.
unremarkable [ˌʌnrɪ'mɑ:kəbl] *adj* comum.
unremitting [ˌʌnrɪ'mɪtɪŋ] *adj* incessante.
unrepeatable [ˌʌnrɪ'pi:təbl] *adj* **-1.** [not fit to be repeated] irrepetível **-2.** [exceptional] excepcional.
unrepentant [ˌʌnrɪ'pentənt] *adj* não-arrependido(da).
unrepresentative [ˌʌnreprɪ'zentətɪv] *adj* pouco representativo(va); **~ of sthg** pouco representativo de algo.
unrequited [ˌʌnrɪ'kwaɪtɪd] *adj* não-correspondido(da).
unreserved [ˌʌnrɪ'zɜ:vd] *adj* **-1.** [admiration, support, approval] integral **-2.** [seat, place] não-reservado(-da).
unresolved [ˌʌnrɪ'zɒlvd] *adj* sem solução.
unresponsive [ˌʌnrɪ'spɒnsɪv] *adj*: **to be ~ to sthg** ser indiferente a algo.
unrest [ˌʌn'rest] *n (U)* agitação *f*.
unrestrained [ˌʌnrɪ'streɪnd] *adj* desenfreado(da).
unrestricted [ˌʌnrɪ'strɪktɪd] *adj* irrestrito(ta).
unrewarding [ˌʌnrɪ'wɔ:dɪŋ] *adj* pouco compensador(ra).
unripe [ˌʌn'raɪp] *adj* verde.
unrivalled *UK*, **unrivaled** *US* [ʌn'raɪvld] *adj* incomparável.
unroll [ˌʌn'rəʊl] *vt* [unfold] desenrolar.
unruffled [ˌʌn'rʌfld] *adj* [calm] sereno(na).
unruly [ʌn'ru:lɪ] (*compar* **-ier**, *superl* **-iest**) *adj* **-1.** [wayward] indisciplinado(da) **-2.** [untidy] desarrumado(da).
unsafe [ˌʌn'seɪf] *adj* **-1.** [dangerous] perigoso(sa) **-2.** [in danger] inseguro(ra).
unsaid [ˌʌn'sed] *adj*: **to leave sthg ~** não falar algo.
unsaleable, unsalable *US* [ˌʌn'seɪləbl] *adj* invendável.
unsatisfactory ['ʌnˌsætɪs'fæktərɪ] *adj* insatisfatório(ria).
unsavoury, unsavory *US* [ˌʌn'seɪvərɪ] *adj* **-1.** [behaviour, person, habits] *(moralmente)* ofensivo(va) **-2.** [smell] repugnante.
unscathed [ˌʌn'skeɪðd] *adj* ileso(sa), são e salvo, sã e salva.
unscheduled [*UK* ˌʌn'ʃedjʊld, *US* ˌʌn'skedʒʊld] *adj* imprevisto(ta).
unscientific ['ʌnˌsaɪən'tɪfɪk] *adj* não-científico(ca).
unscrew [ˌʌn'skru:] *vt* **-1.** [lid, bottle top] desenroscar **-2.** [sign, mirror] desparafusar.
unscripted [ˌʌn'skrɪptɪd] *adj* de improviso.
unscrupulous [ʌn'skru:pjʊləs] *adj* inescrupuloso(sa).
unseat [ˌʌn'si:t] *vt* **-1.** [rider] derrubar *(da sela)* **-2.** *fig* [politician] depor.
unseeded [ˌʌn'si:dɪd] *adj* [player, team] que não é cabeça de chave.
unseemly [ʌn'si:mlɪ] (*compar* **-ier**, *superl* **-iest**) *adj* inconveniente.
unseen [ˌʌn'si:n] ◇ *adj* [not observed] despercebido(da); [not visible] escondido(da). ◇ *adv* despercebido(da).
unselfish [ˌʌn'selfɪʃ] *adj* desinteressado(da).
unselfishly [ˌʌn'selfɪʃlɪ] *adv* desinteressadamente.
unsettle [ˌʌn'setl] *vt* inquietar.
unsettled [ˌʌn'setld] *adj* **-1.** [unstable - person] inquieto(ta); [- weather] instável **-2.** [unfinished, unresolved - argument] incerto(ta); [- issue] vago(ga) **-3.** [account, bill] duvidoso(sa) **-4.** [area, region] despovoado(da).
unsettling [ˌʌn'setlɪŋ] *adj* inquietante.
unshak(e)able [ʌn'ʃeɪkəbl] *adj* inabalável.
unshaven [ˌʌn'ʃeɪvn] *adj* [face, chin] com a barba por fazer.
unsheathe [ˌʌn'ʃi:ð] *vt* desembainhar.
unsightly [ʌn'saɪtlɪ] *adj* de péssima aparência.
unskilled [ˌʌn'skɪld] *adj* [worker] não-especializado(da), incapaz; [work] não-especializado(da).
unsociable [ʌn'səʊʃəbl] *adj* [person, place] anti-social.
unsocial [ˌʌn'səʊʃl] *adj*: **to work ~ hours** trabalhar fora de hora.
unsold [ˌʌn'səʊld] *adj* não-vendido(da).
unsolicited [ˌʌnsə'lɪsɪtɪd] *adj* que não foi pedido(-da).
unsolved [ˌʌn'sɒlvd] *adj* não-solucionado(da).
unsophisticated [ˌʌnsə'fɪstɪkeɪtɪd] *adj* **-1.** [gen] simples **-2.** [person - in dress, style] pouco sofisticado(da); [- in attitudes] simples, natural.
unsound [ˌʌn'saʊnd] *adj* **-1.** [based on false ideas] equivocado(da) **-2.** [in poor condition] inseguro(ra); **to be of ~ mind** estar fora de si.
unspeakable [ʌn'spi:kəbl] *adj* terrível.
unspeakably [ʌn'spi:kəblɪ] *adv* terrivelmente.
unspecified [ˌʌn'spesɪfaɪd] *adj* indefinido(da).
unspoiled [ˌʌn'spɔɪld], **unspoilt** [ˌʌn'spɔɪlt] *adj* **-1.** [person] incólume **-2.** [place] intocado(da).
unspoken [ˌʌn'spəʊkən] *adj* **-1.** [not expressed openly] subentendido(da) **-2.** [tacit] tácito(ta).
unsporting [ˌʌn'spɔ:tɪŋ] *adj* pouco esportivo(va).
unstable [ˌʌn'steɪbl] *adj* instável.
unstated [ˌʌn'steɪtɪd] *adj* não-afirmado(da).
unsteady [ˌʌn'stedɪ] (*compar* **-ier**, *superl* **-iest**) *adj* **-1.** [person, step, voice] inseguro(ra) **-2.** [chair, ladder] pouco seguro(ra).
unstinting [ˌʌn'stɪntɪŋ] *adj* irrestrito(ta).
unstoppable [ˌʌn'stɒpəbl] *adj* inevitável.
unstrap [ˌʌn'stræp] (*pt* & *pp* **-ped**, *cont* **-ping**) *vt* desapertar.
unstructured [ˌʌn'strʌktʃəd] *adj* desorganizado(-da).
unstuck [ˌʌn'stʌk] *adj*: **to come ~** [notice, stamp,

label] descolar-se; *fig* [plan, system] degringolar; *fig* [person] dar-se mal.

unsubstantiated [ˌʌnsəb'stænʃɪeɪtɪd] *adj* **-1.** [statement, story, report] que não foi confirmado(da) **-2.** [accusation] sem provas.

unsuccessful [ˌʌnsək'sesfʊl] *adj* malsucedido(da).

unsuccessfully [ˌʌnsək'sesfʊlɪ] *adv* em vão.

unsuitable [ˌʌn'su:təbl] *adj* incoveniente; **to be ~ for sthg** ser inapropriado(da) para algo.

unsuited [ˌʌn'su:tɪd] *adj* **-1.** [not appropriate]: **to be ~ to** *OR* **for sthg** ser inadequado(da) para algo **-2.** [not compatible]: **to be ~ (to each other)** ser totalmente incompatível (um em relação ao outro).

unsung [ˌʌn'sʌŋ] *adj* [deed, hero] não-aclamado(da).

unsure [ˌʌn'ʃɔ:ʳ] *adj* **-1.** [not confident]: **to be ~ (of o.s.)** não ser seguro(ra) (de si) **-2.** [not certain]: **to be ~ (about/of sthg)** não ter certeza (sobre/de algo).

unsurpassed [ˌʌnsə'pɑ:st] *adj* incomparável.

unsuspecting [ˌʌnsə'spektɪŋ] *adj* insuspeitável.

unsweetened [ˌʌn'swi:tnd] *adj* sem açúcar.

unswerving [ʌn'swɜ:vɪŋ] *adj* resoluto(ta).

unsympathetic ['ʌnˌsɪmpə'θetɪk] *adj* [unfeeling] insensível.

untamed [ˌʌn'teɪmd] *adj* **-1.** [not domesticated] não-domesticado(da) **-2.** [not cultivated] não-cultivado(da) **-3.** [not subjugated] indômito(ta).

untangle [ˌʌn'tæŋgl] *vt* [disentangle] desemaranhar.

untapped [ˌʌn'tæpt] *adj* [unexploited] inexplorado(da).

untaxed [ˌʌn'tækst] *adj* isento(ta) de imposto.

untenable [ˌʌn'tenəbl] *adj* insustentável.

unthinkable [ʌn'θɪŋkəbl] *adj* [inconceivable] inconcebível.

unthinkingly [ʌn'θɪŋkɪŋlɪ] *adv* sem pensar.

untidy [ʌn'taɪdɪ] (*compar* **-ier**, *superl* **-iest**) *adj* **-1.** [gen] desarrumado(da) **-2.** [person, work] desleixado(da).

untie [ˌʌn'taɪ] (*cont* **untying**) *vt* [string, knot, bonds] desatar; [prisoner] soltar.

until [ən'tɪl] ◇ *prep* **-1.** [up to, till] até **-2.** *(after negative)* antes de; **I can't come ~ tomorrow** eu não posso vir antes de amanhã. ◇ *conj* **-1.** [up to, till] até; **we were told to wait ~ he arrived** pediram-nos para esperar até que ele chegasse *OR* até ele chegar **-2.** *(after negative)* antes de, até; **they never help ~ I tell them to** eles só ajudam quando eu peço; **don't sign ~ you've checked everything** não assine nada antes de ter verificado tudo.

untimely [ʌn'taɪmlɪ] *adj* **-1.** [premature] prematuro(ra) **-2.** [inopportune] inoportuno(na).

untiring [ʌn'taɪərɪŋ] *adj* incansável.

untold [ˌʌn'təʊld] *adj* [incalculable, vast] inimaginável.

untouched [ˌʌn'tʌtʃt] *adj* intocado(da).

untoward [ˌʌntə'wɔ:d] *adj* [unfortunate] inconveniente.

untrained [ˌʌn'treɪnd] *adj* destreinado(da).

untrammelled *UK*, **untrammeled** *US* [ʌn'træməld] *adj fml* irrestrito(ta); **~ by** não restrito(ta) a, livre de.

untranslatable [ˌʌntræns'leɪtəbl] *adj* intraduzível.

untreated [ˌʌn'tri:tɪd] *adj* **-1.** *MED* não-tratado(da) **-2.** [unprocessed] sem tratamento.

untried [ˌʌn'traɪd] *adj* [not tested] não-testado(da).

untroubled [ˌʌn'trʌbld] *adj* [undisturbed]: **to be ~ by sthg** ficar calmo(ma) diante de algo.

untrue [ˌʌn'tru:] *adj* **-1.** [inaccurate] falso(sa) **-2.** [unfaithful, disloyal]: **to be ~ to sb** ser infiel a alguém.

untrustworthy [ˌʌn'trʌstˌwɜ:ðɪ] *adj* indigno(na) de confiança.

untruth [ˌʌn'tru:θ] *n* inverdade *f*.

untruthful [ˌʌn'tru:θfʊl] *adj* mentiroso(sa).

untutored [ˌʌn'tju:təd] *adj* [untrained] destreinado(da).

unusable [ˌʌn'ju:zəbl] *adj* inutilizável, imprestável.

unused [*sense 1* ˌʌn'ju:zd, *sense 2* ʌn'ju:st] *adj* **-1.** [new] novo(va) **-2.** [unaccustomed]: **to be ~ to sthg/to doing sthg** não estar acostumado(da) a algo/a fazer algo.

unusual [ʌn'ju:ʒl] *adj* [rare] raro(ra).

unusually [ʌn'ju:ʒəlɪ] *adv* [exceptionally] excepcionalmente.

unvarnished [ʌn'vɑ:nɪʃt] *adj fig* [plain, straightforward] cru.

unveil [ˌʌn'veɪl] *vt* **-1.** [remove covering from] desvelar **-2.** *fig* [reveal, divulge] expor.

unwaged [ˌʌn'weɪdʒd] *adj UK* desassalariado(da).

unwanted [ˌʌn'wɒntɪd] *adj* indesejado(da).

unwarranted [ʌn'wɒrəntɪd] *adj* injustificado(da).

unwavering [ʌn'weɪvərɪŋ] *adj* firme.

unwelcome [ʌn'welkəm] *adj* **-1.** [news, experience] desagradável **-2.** [visitor] desconfortável.

unwell [ˌʌn'wel] *adj*: **to be/feel ~** estar/sentir-se indisposto(ta).

unwholesome [ˌʌn'həʊlsəm] *adj* **-1.** [food, drink] insalubre **-2.** [behaviour, thought] doentio(tia) **-3.** [appearance] doente.

unwieldy [ʌn'wi:ldɪ] (*compar* **-ier**, *superl* **-iest**) *adj* **-1.** [cumbersome] pesado(da) **-2.** *fig* [inefficient] ineficiente.

unwilling [ˌʌn'wɪlɪŋ] *adj* [reluctant] relutante; **to be ~ to do sthg** estar relutante para/em fazer algo.

unwind [ˌʌn'waɪnd] (*pt* & *pp* **-wound**) ◇ *vt* desenrolar. ◇ *vi fig* [person] relaxar.

unwise [ˌʌn'waɪz] *adj* imprudente.

unwitting [ʌn'wɪtɪŋ] *adj fml* inadvertido(da), impremeditado(da).

unwittingly [ʌn'wɪtɪŋlɪ] *adv fml* inadvertidamente.

unworkable [ˌʌn'wɜ:kəbl] *adj* impraticável.

unworldly [ˌʌn'wɜ:ldlɪ] *adj* [spiritual, ascetic] espiritual.

unworthy [ʌn'wɜ:ðɪ] (*compar* **-ier**, *superl* **-iest**) *adj* [undeserving]: **to be ~ of sb/sthg** ser indigno(na) de alguém/algo.

unwound [ˌʌn'waʊnd] *pt* & *pp* ▷ **unwind**.

unwrap [ˌʌn'ræp] (*pt* & *pp* **-ped**, *cont* **-ping**) *vt* desembrulhar.

unwritten law [ˌʌn'rɪtn-] *n* lei *f* não-escrita.

unyielding [ʌn'ji:ldɪŋ] *adj* inflexível.

unzip [ˌʌn'zɪp] (*pt* & *pp* **-ped**, *cont* **-ping**) *vt* abrir o zíper de.

unzip [ˌʌn'zɪp] *vt* descompactar.

up [ʌp] ◇ *adv* **-1.** [toward higher position, level] para cima; **to go ~** subir; **prices are going ~** os preços estão subindo; **we walked ~ to the top** subimos até o topo; **to pick sthg ~** apanhar algo. **-2.** [in higher position]: **she's ~ in her bedroom** está lá em cima no seu quarto; **~ there** ali *OR* lá em cima. **-3.** [into upright position]: **to stand ~** pôr-se em *OR* de pé; **to sit ~** [from lying position] sentar-se; [sit straight] sentar-se direito. **-4.** [northward]: **~ in Canada** no Canadá. **-5.** [in phrases]: **to walk ~ and down** andar de um lado para o outro; **to jump ~ and down** dar pulos; **~ to six weeks** até seis semanas; **~ to ten people** até dez pessoas; **are you ~ to travelling?** você está em condições de viajar?; **what are you ~ to?** o que você está tramando?; **it's ~ to you** depende de você; **~ until ten o'clock** até às dez horas. <> *prep* **-1.** [toward higher position]: **to walk ~ a hill** subir um monte; **I went ~ the stairs** subi as escadas. **-2.** [in higher position] no topo de; **~ a hill** no topo de um monte; **~ a ladder** no topo de uma escada. **-3.** [at end of]: **they live ~ the block from us** eles vivem no final da nossa rua. <> *adj* **-1.** [out of bed] levantado(da); **I got ~ at six today** levantei-me às seis hoje. **-2.** [at an end]: **time's ~** acabou-se o tempo. **-3.** [rising]: **the ~ escalator** a escada rolante ascendente. <> *n*: **~s and downs** altos e baixos *mpl*.

up-and-coming *adj* promissor(ra).

up-and-up *n*: **to be on the ~** *UK* [improving] estar para cima; *US* [honest] ser confiável.

upbeat ['ʌpbi:t] *adj* otimista.

upbraid [ʌp'breɪd] *vt fml*: **to ~ sb (for sthg/for doing sthg)** repreender alguém por algo/por fazer algo.

upbringing ['ʌp,brɪŋɪŋ] *n (U)* educação *f*.

update [,ʌp'deɪt] *vt* [bring up-to-date] atualizar.

upend [ʌp'end] *vt* [stand on end] pôr de pé; [turn upside down] virar de ponta-cabeça.

upfront [,ʌp'frʌnt] <> *adj*: **to be ~ (about sthg)** ser franco(ca) sobre algo. <> *adv* adiantado(da).

upgrade [,ʌp'greɪd] *vt* **-1.** [improve - facilities] melhorar; [- computer system] fazer um upgrade em **-2.** [promote] promover.

upheaval [ʌp'hi:vl] *n* convulsão *f*.

upheld [ʌp'held] *pt & pp* ▷ **uphold**.

uphill [,ʌp'hɪl] <> *adj* **-1.** [rising] íngreme **-2.** *fig* [difficult] árduo(dua). <> *adv* para cima.

uphold [ʌp'həʊld] (*pt & pp* **-held**) *vt* [support] apoiar.

upholster [ʌp'həʊlstə^r] *vt* estofar.

upholstery [ʌp'həʊlstərɪ] *n (U)* estofamento *m*.

upkeep ['ʌpki:p] *n (U)* manutenção *f*.

upland ['ʌplənd] *adj* no planalto.
◆ **uplands** *npl* planaltos *mpl*.

uplift [ʌp'lɪft] *vt* [cheer] extasiar.

uplifting [ʌp'lɪftɪŋ] *adj* [cheering] extasiante, edificante.

uplighter *n ELEC luminária que projeta a luz para cima*.

up-market *adj* de alta categoria.

upon [ə'pɒn] *prep fml* **-1.** [gen] sobre; **the weekend is ~ us** o final de semana já está em cima da gente; **summer is ~ us** o verão está chegando **-2.** [when] após.

upper ['ʌpə^r] <> *adj* **-1.** [gen] superior **-2.** *GEOGR* [inland] alto(ta). <> *n* [of shoe] gáspea *f*.

upper class *n*: **the ~** a alta classe.
◆ **upper-class** *adj* de alta classe.

upper-crust *adj* da alta roda.

uppercut ['ʌpəkʌt] *n* direto *m* no queixo.

upper hand *n*: **to have the ~** ter a palavra final; **to gain** *OR* **get the ~** obter o controle.

Upper House *n UK POL* Câmara *f* dos Lordes.

uppermost ['ʌpəməʊst] *adj* **-1.** [highest] mais alto(ta) **-2.** [most important]: **to be ~ in one's mind** ser o mais importante na cabeça de alguém.

Upper Volta [-'vɒltə] *n* Alto Volta; **in ~** em Alto Volta.

uppity ['ʌpətɪ] *adj inf* arrogante.

upright [*adj senses 1 & 2 & adv* ,ʌp'raɪt, *n* 'ʌpraɪt] <> *adj* **-1.** [erect] vertical **-2.** *fig* [honest] honesto(ta). <> *adv* verticalmente. <> *n* **-1.** [of door] marco *m* **-2.** [of bookshelf] pilar *m* **-3.** [of goal] poste *m*.

upright piano *n* piano *m* de armário.

uprising ['ʌp,raɪzɪŋ] *n* revolta *f* rebelião *f*.

uproar ['ʌprɔ:^r] *n* **-1.** [commotion] algazarra *f* **-2.** [protest] protesto *m*.

uproarious [ʌp'rɔ:rɪəs] *adj* [noisy] barulhento(ta).

uproot [ʌp'ru:t] *vt* **-1.** [force to leave] arrancar; **to ~ o.s.** desarraigar-se **-2.** *BOT* [tear out of ground] arrancar.

upset [ʌp'set] (*pt & pp* **upset**, *cont* **-ting**) <> *adj* **-1.** [distressed] descontrolado(da); [offended] chateado(da) **-2.** *MED*: **to have an ~ stomach** ter um estômago fraco. <> *n* **-1.** *MED*: **to have a stomach ~** ficar com dor de estômago **-2.** [surprise result] surpresa *f*. <> *vt* **-1.** [distress] deixar nervoso(sa), irritar **-2.** [mess up] atrapalhar **-3.** [overturn, knock over] virar.

upsetting [ʌp'setɪŋ] *adj* [distressing] desconcertante.

upshot ['ʌpʃɒt] *n* desfecho *m*.

upside down [,ʌpsaɪd-] <> *adj* [inverted] invertido(da), ao contrário. <> *adv* de cabeça para baixo; **to turn sthg ~** *fig* [disorder] virar algo de pernas para o ar.

upstage [,ʌp'steɪdʒ] *vt fig* roubar a cena de.

upstairs [,ʌp'steəz] <> *adj* de cima. <> *adv* **-1.** [not downstairs] em cima **-2.** [on one of the floors above] de cima. <> *n* andar *m* de cima.

upstanding [,ʌp'stændɪŋ] *adj* [honest] honrado (da).

upstart ['ʌpstɑ:t] *n* novo-rico *m*, nova-rica *f*.

upstate [,ʌp'steɪt] *US* <> *adj*: **~ New York** do interior de Nova Iorque. <> *adv* no interior.

upstream [,ʌp'stri:m] <> *adj*: **the bridge is a few miles ~ (from here)** a ponte fica poucas milhas rio acima (a partir daqui). <> *adv* correnteza acima.

upsurge ['ʌpsɜ:dʒ] *n*: **~ of/in sthg** aumento *m* de/em algo.

upswing ['ʌpswɪŋ] *n*: **~ (in sthg)** impulso *m* (em algo).

uptake ['ʌpteɪk] *n*: **to be quick/slow on the ~** ter um raciocínio rápido/lento.

uptight [ʌp'taɪt] *adj inf* nervoso(sa).

up-to-date *adj* **-1.** [machinery, methods] moderno(na) **-2.** [news, information] atualizado(da); **to keep ~ with sthg** manter-se a par de algo.

up-to-the-minute *adj* mais recente.
uptown [ˌʌp'taʊn] *US* <> *adj* da parte alta da cidade. <> *adv* na parte alta da cidade.
upturn ['ʌptɜ:n] *n*: ~ **(in sthg)** melhoria *f* (em algo).
upturned [ʌp'tɜ:nd] *adj* **-1.** [pointing upwards] virado(da) para cima; ~ **nose** nariz *m* arrebitado **-2.** [upside down] virado(da) de cabeça para baixo.
upward ['ʌpwəd] <> *adj* [movement, trend] para cima. <> *adv US* = **upwards.**
upwardly-mobile *adj* de franca ascensão.
upwards ['ʌpwədz] *adv* para cima.
◆ **upwards of** *prep* mais de.
upwind [ˌʌp'wɪnd] *adj*: **to be ~ of sb/sthg** estar fora do raio de ação de alguém/algo.
URA (*abbr of* **Urban Renewal Administration**) *n órgão norte-americano responsável pelo desenvolvimento das áreas urbanas menos favorecidas.*
Urals ['jʊərəlz] *npl*: **the** ~ os Urais; **in the** ~ nos Urais.
uranium [jʊ'reɪnjəm] *n (U)* urânio *m*.
Uranus ['jʊərənəs] *n* [planet] Urano *m*.
urban ['ɜ:bən] *adj* urbano(na).
urbane [ɜ:'beɪn] *adj* gentil.
urbanize, -ise ['ɜ:bənaɪz] *vt* urbanizar.
urban renewal *n* reurbanização *f*.
Urdu ['ʊədu:] *n (U)* urdu *m*.
urge [ɜ:dʒ] <> *n* impulso *m*; **to have an ~ to do sthg** ter um impulso de fazer algo. <> *vt* **-1.** [try to persuade]: **to ~ sb to do sthg** incitar alguém a fazer algo **-2.** [advocate] defender.
urgency ['ɜ:dʒənsɪ] *n (U)* urgência *f*.
urgent ['ɜ:dʒənt] *adj* **-1.** [pressing] urgente **-2.** [desperate] insistente.
urgently ['ɜ:dʒəntlɪ] *adv* [as soon as possible] urgentemente.
urinal [ˌjʊə'raɪnl] *n* [receptacle] urinol *m*; [room] mictório *m*.
urinary ['jʊərɪnərɪ] *adj* urinário(ria).
urinate ['jʊərɪneɪt] *vi* urinar.
urine ['jʊərɪn] *n (U)* urina *f*.
URL (*abbr of* **uniform resource locator**) *n COMPUT* URL *f*.
urn [ɜ:n] *n* **-1.** [for ashes] urna *f* funerária **-2.** [for tea, coffee] chaleira *f*.
Uruguay ['jʊərəgwaɪ] *n* Uruguai *m*; **in ~** no Uruguai.
Uruguayan [ˌjʊərə'gwaɪən] <> *adj* uruguaio(-guaia). <> *n* uruguaio *m*, -guaia *f*.
us [ʌs] *pers pron (direct)* nos; *(indirect, after prep)* nós; **they know ~** conhecem-nos; **it's ~** somos nós; **send it to ~** envie-nos isso; **tell ~** diga-nos; **we brought it with ~** trouxemo-lo conosco.
US (*abbr of* **United States**) *n*: **the** ~ os EUA; **in the** ~ nos EUA.
USA *n* **-1.** (*abbr of* **United States of America**): **the** ~ os EUA; **in the** ~ nos EUA **-2.** (*abbr of* **United States Army**) forças armadas norte-americanas.
usable ['ju:zəbl] *adj* utilizável, usável.
USAF (*abbr of* **United States Air Force**) *n força aérea norte-americana.*
usage ['ju:zɪdʒ] *n* **-1.** *(U)* [use of language] uso *m* **-2.** [meaning] sentido *m* **-3.** *(U)* [handling, treatment] uso *m*.
USB (*abbr of* **Universal Serial Bus**) *n COMPUT* USB *m*.
USB port *n COMPUT* porta *f* USB.
USCG (*abbr of* **United States Coast Guard**) *n guarda-costeira norte-americana.*
USDA (*abbr of* **United States Department of Agriculture**) *n ministério da agricultura norte-americano.*
USDI (*abbr of* **United States Department of the Interior**) *n ministério do interior norte-americano.*
use [*n & aux vb* ju:s, *vt* ju:z] <> *n* **-1.** [gen] uso *m*; **to be in ~** estar em uso; **to be out of ~** estar fora de uso; **to make ~ of sthg** fazer uso de algo; **to let sb have the ~ of sthg** deixar que alguém utilize algo **-2.** [purpose, usefulness] utilidade *f*; **to be of ~** ser útil; **to be no ~** ser inútil; **what's the ~ (of doing sthg)?** qual é a utilidade(de se fazer algo)? <> *aux vb* costumar; **I ~d to live in London** eu morava em Londres; **there ~d to be a tree here** havia uma árvore aqui. <> *vt* **-1.** [utilize] usar, utilizar **-2.** *pej* [exploit] usar.
◆ **use up** *vt sep* esgotar.
used [*sense 1* ju:zd, *sense 2* ju:st] *adj* **-1.** [object, car *etc*] usado(da) **-2.** [accustomed]: **to be ~ to sthg/to doing sthg** estar acostumado(da) a algo/a fazer algo; **to get ~ to sthg** acostumar-se a algo.
useful ['ju:sfʊl] *adj* útil; **to come in ~** mostrar-se útil.
usefulness ['ju:sfʊlnɪs] *n (U)* utilidade *f*.
useless ['ju:slɪs] *adj* **-1.** [gen] inútil **-2.** *inf* [hopeless] incorrigível.
uselessness ['ju:slɪsnɪs] *n (U)* inutilidade *f*.
user ['ju:zə[r]] *n* usuário *m*, -ria *f*.
user-friendly *adj* de fácil utilização.
USES (*abbr of* **United States Employment Service**) *n ministério do trabalho norte-americano.*
usher ['ʌʃə[r]] <> *n* **-1.** [at wedding] recepcionista *m* **-2.** [at theatre, concert] lanterninha *m*. <> *vt* conduzir.
usherette [ˌʌʃə'ret] *n* **-1.** [at wedding] recepcionista *f* **-2.** [at theatre, concert] lanterninha *f*.
USIA (*abbr of* **United States Information Agency**) *n agência de informações norte-americana.*
USM *n* **-1.** (*abbr of* **United States Mail**) *serviço de correio norte-americano* **-2.** (*abbr of* **United States Mint**) *casa da moeda norte-americana* **-3.** (*abbr of* **unlisted securities market**) *parte da bolsa de valores de Londres que negocia os papéis das empresas menores.*
USN (*abbr of* **United States Navy**) *n marinha norte-americana.*
USPHS (*abbr of* **United States Public Health Service**) *n ministério norte-americano de saúde e previdência social.*
USS (*abbr of* **United States Ship**) *navio de guerra norte-americano.*
USSR (*abbr of* **Union of Soviet Socialist Republics**) *n*: **the (former)** ~ a (ex-)URSS.
usu. (*abbr of* **usually**) usualmente.
usual ['ju:ʒəl] *adj* usual, habitual; **as ~** [as normal] como de costume; [as often happens] como sempre.
usually ['ju:ʒəlɪ] *adv* geralmente, normalmente; **more than ~** mais do que normalmente.

usurp [ju:'zɜ:p] *vt fml* usurpar.
usury ['ju:ʒʊrɪ] *n (U) fml* usura *f*.
UT *abbr of* **Utah**.
Utah ['ju:tɑ:] *n* Utah.
utensil [ju:'tensl] *n* utensílio *m*.
uterus ['ju:tərəs] (*pl* **-ri** [-raɪ], **-ruses**) *n* útero *m*.
utilitarian [ˌju:tɪlɪ'teərɪən] *adj* [functional] utilitário(ria), funcional.
utility [ju:'tɪlətɪ] (*pl* **-ies**) *n* **-1.** *(U)* [usefulness] utilidade *f* **-2.** [public service] serviço *m* público **-3.** COMPUT utilitário *m*.
utility room *n* área *f* de serviços.
utilize, -ise ['ju:təlaɪz] *vt* utilizar.
utmost ['ʌtməʊst] <> *adj* máximo(ma), supremo(ma). <> *n* **-1.** [best effort]: **to do one's ~** fazer o impossível **-2.** [maximum] máximo *m*; **to the ~** ao máximo, até não poder mais.
utopia [ju:'təʊpjə] *n* utopia *f*.
utter ['ʌtə^r] <> *adj* total, completo(ta). <> *vt* **-1.** [sound, cry] emitir **-2.** [word] proferir.
utterly ['ʌtəlɪ] *adv* totalmente, completamente.
U-turn *n* **-1.** [turning movement] retorno *m* **-2.** *fig* [complete change] guinada *f* de 180 graus.
UV (*abbr of* **ultraviolet**) U.V.
Uzbek <> *adj* usbeque. <> *n* **-1.** [person] usbeque *mf* **-2.** [language] usbeque *m*.
Uzbekistan [ʊzˌbekɪ'stɑ:n] *n* Usbequistão; **in ~** no Usbequistão.

v[1] (*pl* **v's** OR **vs**), **V** (*pl* **V's** OR **Vs**) [vi:] *n* [letter] v, V *m*.
v[2] **-1.** (*abbr of* **verse**) v **-2.** (*abbr of* **vide**) [cross-reference] vide **-3.** (*abbr of* **versus**) versus **-4.** (*abbr of* **volt**) v.
VA *abbr of* **Virginia**.
vacancy ['veɪkənsɪ] (*pl* **-ies**) *n* **-1.** [job, position] vaga *f* **-2.** [room available] quarto *m* livre; **'vacancies'** 'há vagas'; **'no vacancies'** 'lotação esgotada'.
vacant ['veɪkənt] *adj* **-1.** [gen] vago(ga) **-2.** [look, expression] distraído(da).
vacant lot *n* lote *m* disponível.
vacantly ['veɪkəntlɪ] *adv* distraidamente.
vacate [və'keɪt] *vt* **-1.** [give up, resign] deixar vago(ga) **-2.** [leave empty, stop using] desocupar.
vacation [və'keɪʃn] *n* **-1.** UNIV [period when closed] férias *fpl* **-2.** *US* [holiday] férias *fpl*.
vacationer [və'keɪʃənə^r] *n US* veranista *mf*.
vacation resort *n US* colônia *f* de férias.
vaccinate ['væksɪneɪt] *vt*: **to ~ sb (against sthg)** vacinar alguém (contra algo).
vaccination [ˌvæksɪ'neɪʃn] *n* vacinação *f*; **have you had your ~?** já tomou sua vacina?
vaccine [*UK* 'væksi:n, *US* væk'si:n] *n* vacina *f*.
vacillate ['væsəleɪt] *vi*: **to ~ (between)** oscilar (entre); **she ~d for a long time before making up her mind** ela hesitou por muito tempo antes de se decidir.
vacuum ['vækjʊəm] <> *n* **-1.** [gen] vácuo *m* **-2.** [machine]: **~ (cleaner)** aspirador *m* (de pó). <> *vt* aspirar, passar o aspirador em.
vacuum cleaner *n* aspirador *m* de pó.
vacuum-packed *adj* embalado(da) a vácuo.
vacuum pump *n* bomba *f* de vácuo.
vagabond ['vægəbɒnd] *n literary* vagabundo *m*, -da *f*.
vagaries ['veɪgərɪz] *npl fml* caprichos *mpl*.
vagina [və'dʒaɪnə] *n* vagina *f*.
vaginal *adj* vaginal.
vagrancy ['veɪgrənsɪ] *n (U)* vagabundagem *f*.
vagrant ['veɪgrənt] *n* vagabundo *m*, -da *f*.
vague [veɪg] *adj* **-1.** [imprecise] vago(ga), impreciso(-sa) **-2.** [feeling] leve **-3.** [evasive] evasivo(va) **-4.** [absent-minded] distraído(da) **-5.** [indistinct] vago(ga).
vaguely ['veɪglɪ] *adv* **-1.** [imprecisely] vagamente **-2.** [slightly, not very] levemente **-3.** [absent-mindedly] distraidamente **-4.** [indistinctly]: **I could ~ make out a ship on the horizon** mal dava para distinguir um navio no horizonte.
vain [veɪn] *adj* **-1.** *pej* [conceited] vaidoso(sa) **-2.** [futile, worthless] vão (vã).
◆ **in vain** *adv* em vão.
vainly ['veɪnlɪ] *adv* **-1.** [in vain] em vão **-2.** [conceitedly] vaidosamente.
valance ['væləns] *n* **-1.** [on bed] dossel *m* **-2.** *US* [on curtains] sanefa *f*.
vale [veɪl] *n literary* vale *m*.
valedictory [ˌvælɪ'dɪktərɪ] *adj fml* de adeus.
valentine card ['væləntaɪn-] *n* cartão *m* de dia dos namorados.
Valentine's Day ['væləntaɪnz-] *n*: **(St) ~** Dia *m* dos Namorados.
valet ['væleɪ, 'vaelɪt] *n* [manservant] camareiro *m*.
valet parking *n*: **'~'** serviço *m* de manobrista.
valet service *n* serviço *m* de lavanderia.
valiant ['væljənt] *adj* valente.
valid ['vælɪd] *adj* válido(da).
validate ['vælɪdeɪt] *vt* **-1.** [argument, claim] validar, corroborar **-2.** [document] validar, legitimar.
validity [və'lɪdətɪ] *n* validade *f*.
Valium® ['vælɪəm] *n (U)* valium® *m*.
valley ['vælɪ] (*pl* **valleys**) *n* vale *m*.
valour *UK*, **valor** *US* ['vælə^r] *n (U) fml & literary* valor *m*.
valuable ['væljʊəbl] *adj* valioso(sa).
◆ **valuables** *npl* objetos *mpl* de valor.
valuation [ˌvæljʊ'eɪʃn] *n* avaliação *f*.
value ['vælju:] <> *n* **-1.** *(U)* [gen] valor *m*; **to place a high ~ on sthg** dar muita importância a algo **-2.** [financial] valor *m*; **to be good ~** estar com o preço muito bom; **to be ~ for money** estar bem em conta; **to take sb/sthg at face ~** levar alguém/algo ao pé da letra. <> *vt* **-1.** [estimate price of] avaliar **-2.** [cherish] valorizar.

◆ **values** *npl* [morals] valores *mpl* morais, princípios *mpl*.
value added tax *n* ≃ imposto *m* sobre circulação de mercadorias e serviços.
valued ['vælju:d] *adj* estimado(da).
value judg(e)ment *n* juízo *m* de valor.
valuer ['væljʊəʳ] *n* avaliador *mf*, -ra de preços.
valve [vælv] *n* válvula *f*.
vamoose [və'mu:s] *vi* ***inf*** dar o fora.
vamp *n* vampe *f*.
vampire ['væmpaɪəʳ] *n* vampiro *m*.
van [væn] *n* **-1.** AUT caminhonete *f*, van *f* **-2.** ***UK*** RAIL vagão *m* de carga.
vandal ['vændl] *n* vândalo *m*, -la *f*.
vandalism ['vændəlɪzm] *n (U)* vandalismo *m*.
vandalize, -ise ['vændəlaɪz] *vt* destruir.
vanguard ['væŋgɑ:d] *n* vanguarda *f*; **in the ~ of sthg** na vanguarda de algo.
vanilla [və'nɪlə] ◇ *n (U)* baunilha *f*. ◇ *comp* de baunilha.
vanish ['vænɪʃ] *vi* desaparecer.
vanishing point ['vænɪʃɪŋ-] *n* ponto *m* de fuga.
vanity ['vænətɪ] *n (U)* ***pej*** vaidade *f*.
vanity unit *n* armário *m* de banheiro.
vanquish ['væŋkwɪʃ] *vt* ***literary*** vencer.
vantage point ['vɑ:ntɪdʒ,pɔɪnt] *n* **-1.** [for view] ponto *m* de observação **-2.** ***fig*** [advantageous position] posição *f* vantajosa.
vapour ***UK***, **vapor** ***US*** ['veɪpəʳ] *n (U)* vapor *m*.
vapour trail *n* risco *m* de fumaça *(de avião no céu)*.
variable ['veərɪəbl] ◇ *adj* variável. ◇ *n* **-1.** [indefinite thing] variáveis *fpl* **-2.** MATH variável *f*.
variance ['veərɪəns] *n* ***fml***: **at ~ with sthg** em desacordo com algo.
variant ['veərɪənt] ◇ *adj* [different] variante. ◇ *n* [different form, spelling] variante *f*.
variation [,veərɪ'eɪʃn] *n* **-1.** *(U)* [fact of difference] variação *f*; **~ in sthg** variação em algo **-2.** [degree of difference] variação *f*; **~ in sthg** variação em algo **-3.** [different version & MUS] variação *f*; **~ on sthg** variação em algo.
varicose veins ['værɪkəʊs-] *npl* varizes *fpl*.
varied ['veərɪd] *adj* variado(da).
variety [və'raɪətɪ] *(pl* **-ies***)* *n* **-1.** *(U)* [difference in type] variedade *f* **-2.** [selection] variedade *f* **-3.** [type] tipo *m* **-4.** *(U)* THEATRE (teatro *m* de) variedades *fpl*.
variety show *n* programa *m* de variedades.
various ['veərɪəs] *adj* **-1.** [several] vários(rias) **-2.** [different] variados(das).
varnish ['vɑ:nɪʃ] ◇ *n* **-1.** [for wood] verniz *m* **-2.** [for nails] esmalte *m*. ◇ *vt* **-1.** [wood] envernizar **-2.** [nails] pintar.
varnished ['vɑ:nɪʃt] *adj* **-1.** [wood, pottery] envernizado(da) **-2.** [nails] pintado(da).
vary ['veərɪ] *(pt & pp* **-ied***)* ◇ *vt* variar. ◇ *vi*; **to ~ in sthg** variar em algo; **to ~ with sthg** variar de acordo com algo.
varying ['veərɪɪŋ] *adj* [different] variado(da); [fluctuating] diverso(sa).
vascular ['væskjʊləʳ] *adj* vascular.
vase [***UK*** vɑ:z, ***US*** veɪz] *n* vaso *m*.
vasectomy [və'sektəmɪ] *(pl* **-ies***)* *n* **-1.** *(U)* [process] vasectomia *f* **-2.** [operation] vasectomia *f*.
Vaseline® ['væsəli:n] *n (U)* vaselina® *f*.
vast [vɑ:st] *adj* enorme, imenso(sa).
vastly ['vɑ:stlɪ] *adv* enormemente, muito.
vastness ['vɑ:stnɪs] *n (U)* [hugeness] imensidão *f*.
vat [væt] *n* tina *f*.
Vatican ['vætɪkən] *n*: **the ~** o Vaticano.
Vatican City *n* Cidade *f* do Vaticano; **in ~** na Cidade do Vaticano.
vault [vɔ:lt] ◇ *n* **-1.** [in bank] caixa-forte *f* **-2.** [in church] cripta *f* **-3.** [roof] abóbada *f* **-4.** [jump] salto *m*. ◇ *vt* saltar. ◇ *vi*: **to ~ over sthg** pular por cima de algo.
vaulted ['vɔ:ltɪd] *adj* ARCHIT abobadado(da).
vaulting horse ['vɔ:ltɪŋ-] *n* SPORT cavalo-de-pau *m (na ginástica)*.
vaunted ['vɔ:ntɪd] *adj* ***fml*** alardeado(da).
veal [vi:l] *n (U)* vitela *f*.
veer [vɪəʳ] *vi* **-1.** [vehicle, road, wind] virar **-2.** ***fig*** [conversation, mood] alternar-se.
veg [vedʒ] *n* ***UK inf*** **-1.** *(abbr of* **vegetable***)* verduras *fpl* **-2.** *(U) (abbr of* **vegetables***)* verduras *fpl*.
vegan ['vi:gən] ◇ *adj* vegan. ◇ *n* vegan *mf*.
vegetable ['vedʒtəbl] ◇ *n* **-1.** BOT vegetal *m* **-2.** [food] hortaliças *fpl*, legume *m*. ◇ *adj* **-1.** [protein] vegetal **-2.** [soup] de legumes.
vegetable garden *n* horta *f*.
vegetable oil *n (U)* óleo *m* vegetal.
vegetarian [,vedʒɪ'teərɪən] ◇ *adj* vegetariano(-na). ◇ *n* vegetariano *m*, -na *f*.
vegetarianism [,vedʒɪ'teərɪənɪzm] *n (U)* vegetarianismo *m*.
vegetate ['vedʒɪteɪt] *vi* ***pej*** vegetar.
vegetation [,vedʒɪ'teɪʃn] *n (U)* vegetação *f*.
veggie ['vedʒɪ] ***UK inf*** ◇ *adj* vegetariano(na). ◇ *n* vegetariano *m*, -na *f*.
vehement ['vi:əmənt] *adj* **-1.** [gesture, attack] violento(ta) **-2.** [person, denial] veemente.
vehemently ['vi:əməntlɪ] *adv* **-1.** [attack] violentamente **-2.** [deny, refuse] veementemente.
vehicle ['vi:əkl] *n* **-1.** [for transport] veículo *m* **-2.** ***fig*** [medium]: **a ~ for sthg** um meio para algo.
vehicular [vɪ'hɪkjʊləʳ] *adj* ***fml*** de veículos automotores.
veil [veɪl] *n* **-1.** [for face] véu *m* **-2.** ***fig*** [obscuring thing] manto *m*.
veiled [veɪld] *adj* [hidden] velado(da).
vein [veɪn] *n* **-1.** ANAT veia *f* **-2.** [of leaf] nervura *f* **-3.** [of mineral] veio *m* **-4.** [style, mood] estilo *m*; **in the same ~** no mesmo estilo.
Velcro® ['velkrəʊ] *n (U)* velcro® *m*.
vellum ['veləm] *n (U)* papel *m* velino.
velocity [vɪ'lɒsətɪ] *(pl* **-ies***)* *n* PHYSICS velocidade *f*.
velour [və'lʊəʳ] *n (U)* tecido *m* aveludado.
velvet ['velvɪt] ◇ *n (U)* veludo *m*. ◇ *comp* de veludo.
vend *vt* **-1.** ***fml*** [sell] vender **-2.** JUR vender.
vendetta [ven'detə] *n* vendeta *f*.
vending machine ['vendɪŋ-] *n* máquina *f* de venda automática.
vendor ['vendɔ:ʳ] *n* vendedor *m*, -ra *f*.

veneer [və'nɪəʳ] *n* **-1.** *(U)* [of wood] compensado *m* **-2.** *fig* [appearance] aparência *f.*
venerable ['venərəbl] *adj fml* venerável.
venerate ['venəreɪt] *vt fml & RELIG* venerar.
venereal disease [vɪ'nɪərɪəl-] *n (U)* doença *f* venérea.
Venetian [vɪ'ni:ʃn] ◇ *adj* veneziano(na). ◇ *n* veneziano *m*, -na *f.*
venetian blind *n* persiana *f.*
Venezuela [ˌvenɪz'weɪlə] *n* Venezuela; **in ~** na Venezuela.
Venezuelan [ˌvenɪz'weɪlən] ◇ *adj* venezuelano(-na). ◇ *n* venezuelano *m*, -na *f.*
vengeance ['vendʒəns] *n (U)* vingança *f*; **it started raining with a ~** começou a chover para valer.
vengeful ['vendʒfʊl] *adj literary* vingativo(va).
Venice ['venɪs] *n* Veneza; **in ~** em Veneza.
venison ['venɪzn] *n (U)* carne *f* de veado.
venom ['venəm] *n (U)* **-1.** [poison] veneno *m* **-2.** *fig* [spite, bitterness] veneno *m.*
venomous ['venəməs] *adj* venenoso(sa).
vent [vent] ◇ *n* saída *f* de ar, abertura *f* de ar; **to give ~ to sthg** dar vazão a algo. ◇ *vt* [express] descarregar; **to ~ sthg on sb/sthg** descarregar algo em alguém/algo.
ventilate ['ventɪleɪt] *vt* ventilar.
ventilation [ˌventɪ'leɪʃn] *n (U)* ventilação *f.*
ventilator ['ventɪleɪtəʳ] *n* ventilador *m.*
ventriloquist [ven'trɪləkwɪst] *n* ventríloquo *m*, -qua *f.*
venture ['ventʃəʳ] ◇ *n* empreendimento *m.* ◇ *vt* [proffer] arriscar; **to ~ to do sthg** arriscar-se a fazer algo. ◇ *vi* **-1.** [go somewhere dangerous] aventurar-se **-2.** [embark]: **to ~ into sthg** lançar-se em algo.
venture capital *n (U)* capital *m* de risco.
venturesome *adj* **-1.** [person] aventureiro(ra) **-2.** [action] arriscado(da).
venue ['venju:] *n* local *m (em que se realiza algo).*
Venus ['vi:nəs] *n* [planet] Vênus.
veracity [və'ræsətɪ] *n (U) fml* veracidade *f.*
veranda(h) [və'rændə] *n* varanda *f.*
verb [vɜ:b] *n* verbo *m.*
verbal ['vɜ:bl] *adj* verbal.
verbally ['vɜ:bəlɪ] *adv* [in spoken words] verbalmente.
verbatim [vɜ:'beɪtɪm] ◇ *adj* literal. ◇ *adv* literalmente, palavra por palavra.
verbose [vɜ:'bəʊs] *adj fml* prolixo(xa).
verdict ['vɜ:dɪkt] *n* **-1.** *JUR* veredito *m* **-2.** [opinion] parecer *m*; **~ on sthg** parecer sobre algo.
verge [vɜ:dʒ] *n* **-1.** [edge, side] acostamento *m* **-2.** [brink]: **on the ~ of sthg** à beira de algo; **on the ~ of doing sthg** a ponto de fazer algo.
◆ **verge (up)on** *vt fus* beirar.
verger ['vɜ:dʒəʳ] *n* sacristão *m.*
verification [ˌverɪfɪ'keɪʃn] *n* **-1.** [check] *(U)* verificação *f* **-2.** [confirmation] confirmação *f.*
verify ['verɪfaɪ] (*pt & pp* **-ied**) *vt* **-1.** [check] verificar **-2.** [confirm] confirmar.
veritable ['verɪtəbl] *adj fml or hum* legítimo(ma).
vermilion [və'mɪljən] ◇ *adj* vermelho-alaranjado(da). ◇ *n* vermelhão *m.*
vermin ['vɜ:mɪn] *npl* **-1.** [*ZOOL* - rodents] bichos *mpl*; [- insects] insetos *mpl* nocivos **-2.** *pej* [people] parasita *mf.*
Vermont *n* Vermonte.
vermouth ['vɜ:məθ] *n (U)* vermute *m.*
vernacular [və'nækjʊləʳ] ◇ *adj LING* vernacular. ◇ *n*: **the ~** o vernáculo.
verruca [və'ru:kə] (*pl* **-cas** *OR* **-cae** [-kaɪ]) *n* verruga *f.*
versa ▷ **vice versa**.
versatile ['vɜ:sətaɪl] *adj* **-1.** [multitalented] versátil **-2.** [multipurpose] multifuncional.
versatility [ˌvɜ:sə'tɪlətɪ] *n (U)* **-1.** [multitalented nature] versatilidade *f* **-2.** [multipurpose nature] multifuncionalidade *f.*
verse [vɜ:s] *n* **-1.** *(U)* [poetry] versos *mpl*, poesia *f* **-2.** [stanza] estrofe *m* **-3.** [in Bible] versículo *m.*
versed [vɜ:st] *adj*: **to be well ~ in sthg** ser bem versado(da) em algo.
version ['vɜ:ʃn] *n* **-1.** [gen] versão *f* **-2.** [translation] tradução *f.*
versus ['vɜ:səs] *prep* **-1.** *SPORT* contra **-2.** [as opposed to] em oposição a.
vertebra ['vɜ:tɪbrə] (*pl* **-brae** [-bri:]) *n* vértebra *f.*
vertebrate ['vɜ:tɪbreɪt] *n* vertebrado *m.*
vertical ['vɜ:tɪkl] *adj* vertical.
vertical integration *n (U) FIN* integração *f* vertical.
vertically ['vɜ:tɪklɪ] *adv* verticalmente.
vertigo ['vɜ:tɪgəʊ] *n (U)* vertigem *f.*
verve [vɜ:v] *n (U)* vivacidade *f*, entusiasmo *m.*
very ['verɪ] ◇ *adv* **-1.** [for emphasis] muito; **to like sthg ~ much** gostar muito de algo **-2.** [as euphemism]: **he's not ~ intelligent** ele não é muito inteligente. ◇ *adj* mesmíssimo(ma); **the ~ book I've been looking for** justo o livro que eu estava procurando; **the ~ thought make me bad** só de pensar eu já fico mal; **fighting for his ~ life** lutando por sua própria vida; **the ~ best** o melhor de todos; **a house of my ~ own** minha própria casa.
◆ **very well** *adv* muito bem; **you can't ~ well stop him now** é um pouco tarde para impedi-lo.
vespers ['vespəz] *n (U)* vésperas *fpl.*
vessel ['vesl] *n fml* **-1.** [boat] embarcação *f* **-2.** [container] recipiente *m*, vasilha *f.*
vest [vest] *n* **-1.** *UK* [undershirt] camiseta *f* **-2.** *US* [waistcoat] colete *m.*
vested interest ['vestɪd-] *n* capital *m* investido; **~ in sthg** capital investido em algo.
vestibule ['vestɪbju:l] *n* **-1.** *fml* [entrance hall] vestíbulo *m* **-2.** *US* [on train] vestíbulo *m.*
vestige ['vestɪdʒ] *n fml* vestígio *m.*
vestry ['vestrɪ] (*pl* **-ies**) *n* sacristia *f.*
Vesuvius [vɪ'su:vjəs] *n* Vesúvio *m.*
vet [vet] (*pt & pp* **-ted**, *cont* **-ting**) ◇ *n* **-1.** *UK* (*abbr of* **veterinary surgeon**) veterinário *m*, -ria *f* **-2.** *US* (*abbr of* **veteran**) veterano *m*, -na *f* de guerra. ◇ *vt UK* [check] submeter a uma investigação.
veteran ['vetrən] ◇ *adj* [experienced] veterano(na). ◇ *n* veterano *m*, -na *f.*
veteran car *n UK* carro *m* de época *(feito antes de 1905).*
Veterans Day *n US* Dia *m* dos Veteranos, *11 de*

novembro, dia em que os Estados Unidos comemoram o fim das duas guerras mundiais e homenageiam seus veteranos.

veterinarian [ˌvetərɪ'neərɪən] *n US* veterinário *m*, -ria *f*.

veterinary science ['vetərɪnrɪ-] *n (U)* veterinária *f*.

veterinary surgeon ['vetərɪnrɪ-] *n UK fml* veterinário *m*, -ria *f*.

veto ['vi:təʊ] (*pl* **-es**, *pt* & *pp* **-ed**, *cont* **-ing**) ◇ *n* **-1.** *(U)* [power to forbid] veto *m* **-2.** [act of forbidding] veto *m*. ◇ *vt* vetar.

vetting ['vetɪŋ] *n (U)* investigação *f (sobre o passado de uma pessoa)*.

vex [veks] *vt fml* [annoy] importunar.

vexed question [ˌvekst-] *n* pomo *m* de discórdia.

VI *abbr of* **Virgin Islands**.

via ['vaɪə] *prep* **-1.** [travelling through] via; **they flew to China ~ Karachi** eles viajaram para a China (passando) por Karachi **-2.** [by means of] através de; **~ satellite** via satélite.

viability [ˌvaɪə'bɪlətɪ] *n* viabilidade *f*.

viable ['vaɪəbl] *adj* viável.

viaduct ['vaɪədʌkt] *n* viaduto *m*.

vibrant ['vaɪbrənt] *adj* **-1.** [colour, light] forte **-2.** [person] dinâmico(ca) **-3.** [city, atmosphere] animado(da) **-4.** [sound] vibrante.

vibrate [vaɪ'breɪt] *vi* vibrar.

vibration [vaɪ'breɪʃn] *n* vibração *f*.

vicar ['vɪkə^r] *n* vigário *m*, pároco *m*.

vicarage ['vɪkərɪdʒ] *n* casa *f* paroquial.

vicarious [vɪ'keərɪəs] *adj* indireto(ta).

vice [vaɪs] *n* **-1.** *(U)* [immorality] vício *m* **-2.** [moral fault] vício *m* **-3.** [tool] torno *m* de mesa.

vice- [vaɪs] *prefix* vice-.

vice-admiral *n* vice-almirante *m*.

vice-chairman *n* vice-presidente *m*.

vice-chancellor *n UK UNIV* reitor *m*, -ra *f*.

vice-president *n* vice-presidente *mf*.

vice squad *n* delegacia *f* de costumes.

vice versa [ˌvaɪsɪ'vɜ:sə] *adv* vice-versa.

vicinity [vɪ'sɪnətɪ] *n* **-1.** [neighbourhood] proximidades *fpl*, redondezas *fpl*; **in the ~ (of)** nas proximidades OR redondezas(de) **-2.** [approximate figures]: **in the ~ of** cerca de.

vicious ['vɪʃəs] *adj* **-1.** [attack, blow] violento(ta) **-2.** [person, gossip] cruel **-3.** [dog] feroz, brabo(ba).

vicious circle *n* círculo *m* vicioso.

viciousness ['vɪʃəsnɪs] *n* **-1.** [of attack] violência *f* **-2.** [of person, gossip] crueldade *f* **-3.** [of dog] ferocidade *f*.

vicissitudes [vɪ'sɪsɪtju:dz] *npl fml* vicissitudes *fpl*.

victim ['vɪktɪm] *n* vítima *f*.

victimize, -ise ['vɪktɪmaɪz] *vt* vitimar.

victor ['vɪktə^r] *n* vencedor *m*, -ra *f*.

Victoria Cross [vɪk'tɔ:rɪə-] *n condecoração militar britânica*.

Victoria Falls [vɪk'tɔ:rɪə-] *npl*: **the ~** as Cataratas de Vitória.

Victorian [vɪk'tɔ:rɪən] *adj* **-1.** [from Victorian era] vitoriano(na) **-2.** *usu* **pej** [overstrict] vitoriano(na).

Victoriana [ˌvɪktɔ:rɪ'ɑ:nə] *n (U)* antiguidades *fpl* da era vitoriana.

victorious [vɪk'tɔ:rɪəs] *adj* [winning] vitorioso(sa).

victory ['vɪktərɪ] (*pl* **-ies**) *n* **-1.** *(U)* [act of winning] vitória *f* **-2.** [win] vitória *f*; **~ over sb/sthg** vitória sobre alguém/algo.

video ['vɪdɪəʊ] (*pl* **-s**, *pt* & *pp* **-ed**, *cont* **-ing**) ◇ *n* **-1.** *(U)* [medium] vídeo *m* **-2.** [recording, machine] vídeo *m* **-3.** [cassette] videocassete *m*. ◇ *comp* de vídeo. ◇ *vt* **-1.** [using videorecorder] gravar em vídeo **-2.** [using camera] gravar um vídeo de.

video camera *n* câmera *f* de vídeo.

video cassette *n* videocassete *m*, vídeo *m*.

videodisc *UK*, **videodisk** *US* ['vɪdɪəʊdɪsk] *n* videodisco *m*.

video game *n* video game *m*.

video machine *n* vídeo *m*.

videophone ['vɪdɪəʊfəʊn] *n* videofone *m*.

videorecorder ['vɪdɪəʊrɪˌkɔ:də^r] *n* videocassete *m*, vídeo *m*.

video recording *n* **-1.** [copy on video] cópia *f* em vídeo **-2.** *(U)* TV gravação *f* em vídeo.

video shop *n* videolocadora *f*.

videotape ['vɪdɪəʊteɪp] *n* **-1.** [cassette] videoteipe *m* **-2.** *(U)* [ribbon] fita *f*.

vie [vaɪ] (*pt* & *pp* **vied**, *cont* **vying**) *vi*: **to ~ for sthg** competir por algo; **to ~ with sb (for sthg/to do sthg)** competir com alguém (por algo/para fazer algo).

Vienna [vɪ'enə] *n* Viena.

Viennese [ˌvɪə'ni:z] ◇ *adj* vienense. ◇ *n* vienense *mf*.

Vietnam [*UK* ˌvjet'næm, *US* ˌvjet'nɑ:m] *n* Vietnã; **in ~** no Vietnã.

Vietnamese [ˌvjetnə'mi:z] ◇ *adj* vietnamita. ◇ *n* **-1.** [person] vietnamita *mf* **-2.** [language] vietnamita *m*. ◇ *npl*: **the ~** os vietnamitas.

view [vju:] ◇ *n* **-1.** [opinion] visão *f*, opinião *f*; **~ of sthg** visão de algo; **~ on sb/sthg** opinião sobre alguém/algo; **in my ~** na minha opinião; **to take the ~ that** ser da opinião de que **-2.** [vista] vista *f* **-3.** [ability to see] visão *f*; **to come into ~** aparecer. ◇ *vt* **-1.** [consider] ver **-2.** *fml* [house] visitar **-3.** [solar system] observar.

◆ **in view of** *prep* em vista de.

◆ **with a view to** *conj* com o intuito de.

viewer ['vju:ə^r] *n* **-1.** [person] telespectador *m*, -ra *f* **-2.** [apparatus] visor *m*.

viewfinder ['vju:ˌfaɪndə^r] *n* visor *m*.

viewpoint ['vju:pɔɪnt] *n* **-1.** [opinion] ponto *m* de vista **-2.** [place] mirante *m*.

vigil ['vɪdʒɪl] *n* vigília *f*.

vigilance ['vɪdʒɪləns] *n (U)* vigilância *f*.

vigilant ['vɪdʒɪlənt] *adj* vigilante.

vigilante [ˌvɪdʒɪ'læntɪ] *n* vigilante *mf*.

vigor *n US* = **vigour**.

vigorous ['vɪgərəs] *adj* **-1.** [gen] vigoroso(sa) **-2.** [attempt] enérgico(ca) **-3.** [person, animal] vivaz **-4.** [plant] viçoso(sa).

vigour *UK*, **vigor** *US* ['vɪgə^r] *n (U)* vigor *m*.

Viking ['vaɪkɪŋ] ◇ *adj* viking, viquingue. ◇ *n* viking *mf*, viquingue *mf*.

vile [vaɪl] *adj* **-1.** [person] vil **-2.** [mood] muito ruim **-3.** [act] desprezível **-4.** [food] repugnante.

vilify ['vɪlɪfaɪ] (*pt* & *pp* **-ied**) *vt fml* difamar.

villa ['vɪlə] *n* casa *f* de campo, chalé *m*.
village ['vɪlɪdʒ] *n* vilarejo *m* povoado *m*.
villager ['vɪlɪdʒə^r] *n* população *f* de um vilarejo.
villain ['vɪlən] *n* **-1.** [of film, book, play] vilão *m*, -lã *f* **-2.** *dated* [criminal] criminoso *m*, -sa *f*.
vinaigrette [ˌvɪnɪ'gret] *n (U)* molho *m* vinagrete.
vindicate ['vɪndɪkeɪt] *vt* [confirm] vindicar; [justify] justificar.
vindication [ˌvɪndɪ'keɪʃn] *n* [confirmation] vindicação *f*; [justification] justificação *f*.
vindictive [vɪn'dɪktɪv] *adj* vingativo(va).
vine [vaɪn] *n* [grapevine] videira *f*, parreira *f*.
vinegar ['vɪnɪgə^r] *n (U)* vinagre *m*.
vine leaf *n* folha *f* de parreira.
vineyard ['vɪnjəd] *n* vinhedo *m*.
vintage ['vɪntɪdʒ] ◇ *adj* **-1.** [wine] de boa safra **-2.** *fig* [classic] clássico(ca). ◇ *n* [wine] safra *f*.
vintage car *n UK* carro *m* de época *(feito entre 1919 e 1930)*.
vintage wine *n* vinho *m* de uma boa safra.
vintner *n* comerciante *mf* de vinhos.
vinyl ['vaɪnɪl] ◇ *n (U)* vinil *m*. ◇ *comp* de vinil.
viola [vɪ'əʊlə] *n* **-1.** *MUS* viola *f* **-2.** *BOT* violeta *f*.
violate ['vaɪəleɪt] *vt* **-1.** [disregard] violar **-2.** [disrupt] invadir **-3.** [break into] profanar.
violation [ˌvaɪə'leɪʃn] *n* **-1.** *(U)* [disregarding] violação *f* **-2.** [disruption] invasão *f* **-3.** [breaking into] profanação *f*.
violence ['vaɪələns] *n (U)* **-1.** [physical force] violência *f* **-2.** [of words, reaction] violência *f*.
violent ['vaɪələnt] *adj* **-1.** [gen] violento(ta) **-2.** [emotion, colour] intenso(sa).
violently ['vaɪələntlɪ] *adv* violentamente.
violet ['vaɪələt] ◇ *adj* violeta. ◇ *n* **-1.** [flower] violeta *f* **-2.** *(U)* [colour] violeta *f*.
violin [ˌvaɪə'lɪn] *n* violino *m*.
violinist [ˌvaɪə'lɪnɪst] *n* violinista *mf*.
viper ['vaɪpə^r] *n* víbora *f*.
viral ['vaɪrəl] *adj* viral, virótico(ca).
virgin ['vɜ:dʒɪn] ◇ *adj literary* **-1.** [sexually] virgem **-2.** [forest, snow, soil] virgem. ◇ *n* virgem *mf*.
Virginia [və'dʒɪnjə] *n* Virgínia.
Virginia creeper *n* videira *f* virgem.
Virgin Islands *n*: **the ~** as Ilhas Virgens; **in the ~** nas Ilhas Virgens.
virginity [və'dʒɪnətɪ] *n (U)* virgindade *f*.
Virgo ['vɜ:gəʊ] *(pl* **-s***)* *n* **-1.** [sign] Virgem *m* **-2.** [person] virginiano *m*, -na *f*; **I'm ~** sou de Virgem.
virile ['vɪraɪl] *adj* viril.
virility [vɪ'rɪlətɪ] *n (U)* virilidade *f*.
virtual ['vɜ:tʃʊəl] *adj* [certainty, necessity] virtual.
virtually ['vɜ:tʃʊəlɪ] *adv* [almost] praticamente.
virtual memory *n COMPUT* memória *f* virtual.
virtual reality *n* realidade *f* virtual.
virtue ['vɜ:tju:] *n* **-1.** *(U)* [goodness] virtude *f* **-2.** [merit, quality] virtude *f* **-3.** [benefit] vantagem *f*; **~ in sthg** vantagem em algo.
◆ **by virtue of** *prep fml* em virtude de.
virtuoso [ˌvɜ:tjʊ'əʊzəʊ] *(pl* **-sos** *OR* **-si** [-si:]*)* *n* virtuoso *m*, -sa *f*.
virtuous ['vɜ:tʃʊəs] *adj* virtuoso(sa).
virulent ['vɪrʊlənt] *adj* **-1.** *fml* [bitter and hostile] virulento(ta) **-2.** *MED* [very powerful] virulento(ta).
virus ['vaɪrəs] *n* vírus *m inv*.
visa ['vi:zəl] *n* visto *m*.
vis-à-vis [ˌvi:zɑ:'vi:] *prep fml* em relação a.
viscose ['vɪskəʊs] *n (U)* **-1.** [solution] viscose *f* **-2.** [material] viscose *f*.
viscosity [vɪ'skɒsətɪ] *n CHEM* viscosidade *f*.
viscount ['vaɪkaʊnt] *n* visconde *m*.
viscous ['vɪskəs] *adj CHEM* viscoso(sa).
vise [vaɪs] *n US* torno *m* de mesa.
visibility [ˌvɪzɪ'bɪlətɪ] *n* visibilidade *f*.
visible ['vɪzəbl] *adj* visível.
visibly ['vɪzəblɪ] *adv* [clearly] visivelmente.
vision ['vɪʒn] *n* **-1.** *(U)* [ability to see] visão *f*, vista *f* **-2.** *(U) fig* [foresight] visão *f* **-3.** [impression, dream] visão *f* **-4.** *(U) TV* imagem *f*.
visionary ['vɪʒənrɪ] *(pl* **-ies***)* ◇ *adj* [full of foresight] visionário(ria). ◇ *n* [person] visionário *m*, -ria *f*.
visit ['vɪzɪt] ◇ *n* visita *f*; **on a ~ to** numa visita a. ◇ *vt* visitar.
◆ **visit with** *vt fus US* **-1.** [talk with] conversar com **-2.** [go and see] visitar, ir ver.
visiting card ['vɪzɪtɪŋ-] *n* cartão *m* de visita.
visiting hours ['vɪzɪtɪŋ-] *npl* hora *f* de visita.
visitor ['vɪzɪtə^r] *n* **-1.** [to person] visita *mf* **-2.** [to place] visitante *mf*.
visitors' book *n* livro *m* de visitantes.
visitor's passport *n UK* passaporte *m* temporário.
visor ['vaɪzə^r] *n* [on helmet] viseira *f*.
vista ['vɪstə] *n* **-1.** [view] vista *f*, perspectiva *f* **-2.** *fig* [perspective] perspectiva *f*.
visual ['vɪʒʊəl] *adj* **-1.** [gen] visual **-2.** [examination] de vista.
visual aids *npl* recursos *mpl* visuais.
visual display unit *n* monitor *m*.
visualize, -ise ['vɪʒʊəlaɪz] *vt* visualizar; **to ~ (sb) doing sthg** imaginar (alguém) fazendo algo.
visually ['vɪʒʊəlɪ] *adv* visualmente; **~ handicapped person** pessoa *f* com problemas visuais.
vital ['vaɪtl] *adj* **-1.** [essential] vital, essencial **-2.** [full of life] cheio (cheia) de vida.
vitality [vaɪ'tælətɪ] *n (U)* vitalidade *f*.
vitally ['vaɪtəlɪ] *adv* extremamente.
vital statistics *npl inf* [of figure] medidas *fpl (do corpo de uma mulher)*.
vitamin [*UK* 'vɪtəmɪn, *US* 'vaɪtəmɪn] *n* vitamina *f*.
vitreous *adj* vítreo(trea).
vitriolic [ˌvɪtrɪ'ɒlɪk] *adj fml* acrimonioso(osa), virulento(ta).
viva ['vaɪvə] *n UNIV* = **viva voce**.
vivacious [vɪ'veɪʃəs] *adj* vivaz, animado(da).
vivacity [vɪ'væsətɪ] *n (U)* vivacidade *f*.
viva voce [ˌvaɪvə'vəʊsɪ] *n UNIV* exame *m* oral.
vivid ['vɪvɪd] *adj* **-1.** [bright] vivo(va) **-2.** [clear] vívido(-da).
vividly ['vɪvɪdlɪ] *adv* **-1.** [brightly] com cores muito vivas **-2.** [clearly] vividamente.
vivisection [ˌvɪvɪ'sekʃn] *n (U)* vivissecção *f*.
vixen ['vɪksn] *n* raposa *f* (fêmea).
viz [vɪz] *(abbr of* **videlicet***)* a saber.
VLF *(abbr of* **very low frequency***)* *n* VLF *f*.

V-neck *n* **-1.** [sweater, dress] decote *m* em V **-2.** [neck] gola *f* em V.

VOA (*abbr of* **Voice of America**) *n emissora oficial de rádio norte-americana com transmissões para todo o mundo em inglês e outras línguas.*

vocabulary [və'kæbjʊlərɪ] (*pl* **-ies**) *n* vocabulário *m*.

vocal ['vəʊkl] *adj* **-1.** [outspoken] sincero(ra) **-2.** [of the voice] vocal.
◆ **vocals** *npl* vocais *mpl*; **on ~s** no vocal.

vocal cords *npl* cordas *fpl* vocais.

vocalist ['vəʊkəlɪst] *n* vocalista *mf*.

vocation [vəʊ'keɪʃn] *n* [calling] vocação *f*.

vocational [vəʊ'keɪʃənl] *adj* vocacional.

vociferous [və'sɪfərəs] *adj fml* vociferante.

vodka ['vɒdkə] *n* vodca *f*.

vogue [vəʊg] ◇ *adj* em voga. ◇ *n* moda *f*; **~ for sthg** moda de algo; **in ~** na moda, em voga.

voice [vɔɪs] ◇ *n* **-1.** [gen] voz *f*; **to raise/lower one's ~** levantar/baixar a voz; **to keep one's ~ down** manter a voz baixa **-2.** [influence] influência *f*. ◇ *vt* [opinion, emotion] manifestar.

voice box *n* laringe *f*.

Voice of America *n* Voz *f* da América *(emissora de rádio dos Estados Unidos)*.

voice-over *n* narração *f (num comercial para tevê)*.

void [vɔɪd] ◇ *adj* **-1.** [invalid] inválido(da) ▷ **null -2.** *fml* [empty]: **~ of sthg** desprovido(da) de algo. ◇ *n literary* vazio *m*.

voile [vɔɪl] *n (U)* voile *m*.

vol. (*abbr of* **volume**) vol.

volatile [*UK* 'vɒlətaɪl, *US* 'vɒlətl] *adj* [unpredictable - situation] imprevisível; [- person] volúvel; [- market] volátil.

vol-au-vent ['vɒləʊvu:] *n petisco de massa folhada com recheio.*

volcanic [vɒl'kænɪk] *adj* [of volcanoes] vulcânico(ca).

volcano [vɒl'keɪnəʊ] (*pl* **-es** *OR* **-s**) *n* vulcão *m*.

vole [vəʊl] *n* rato-calunga *m*.

Volga ['vɒlgə] *n*: **the (River) ~** o (Rio) Volga.

volition [və'lɪʃn] *n fml*: **of one's own ~** por vontade própria.

volley ['vɒlɪ] (*pl* **volleys**) ◇ *n* **-1.** [of gunfire] rajada *f*, saraivada *f* **-2.** *fig* [rapid succession] torrente *f* **-3.** *SPORT* voleio *m*. ◇ *vt* dar de voleio em.

volleyball ['vɒlɪbɔ:l] *n (U)* voleibol *m*, vôlei *m*.

volt [vəʊlt] *n* volt *m*.

Volta ['vɒltə] *n* **-1.** [river]: **the (River) ~** o (Rio) Volta **-2.** [lake]: **Lake ~** Lago *m* Volta.

voltage ['vəʊltɪdʒ] *n* voltagem *f*.

voluble ['vɒljʊbl] *adj fml* loquaz.

volume ['vɒlju:m] *n (U)* volume *m*.

volume control *n* controle *m* de volume.

voluminous [və'lu:mɪnəs] *adj fml* **-1.** [garment] volumoso(sa) **-2.** [container] espaçoso(sa).

voluntarily [*UK* 'vɒləntrɪlɪ, *US* ˌvɒlən'terəlɪ] *adv* voluntariamente.

voluntary ['vɒləntrɪ] *adj* voluntário(ria); **~ organization** organização *f* beneficente.

voluntary liquidation *n (U)* liquidação *f* voluntária.

voluntary redundancy *n UK* demissão *f* voluntária.

voluntary work *n* trabalho *m* voluntário.

volunteer [ˌvɒlən'tɪə[r]] ◇ *n* voluntário *m*, -ria *f*. ◇ *vt* **-1.** [offer of one's free will]: **to ~ to do sthg** oferecer-se (de livre e espontânea vontade) para fazer algo **-2.** [information, advice] oferecer. ◇ *vi* **-1.** [freely offer one's services]: **to ~ (for sthg)** oferecer-se (para algo) **-2.** *MIL* alistar-se como voluntário(ria).

voluptuous [və'lʌptjʊəs] *adj* voluptuoso(sa).

vomit ['vɒmɪt] ◇ *n (U)* vômito *m*. ◇ *vi* vomitar.

voodoo *n* vodu *m*.

voracious [və'reɪʃəs] *adj* voraz.

vortex ['vɔ:teks] (*pl* **-texes** *OR* **-tices** [-tɪsi:z]) *n* **-1.** *TECH* vórtice *m* **-2.** *fig* [of events] turbilhão *m*.

vote [vəʊt] ◇ *n* **-1.** [individual decision] voto *m*; **~ for sb/sthg** voto em alguém/algo; **~ against sb/sthg** voto contra alguém/algo **-2.** [session, ballot] votação *f*; **to put sthg to the ~** levar algo à votação **-3.** [result of ballot]: **the ~** a votação **-4.** [section of voters] eleitorado *m* **-5.** [suffrage] voto *m*. ◇ *vt* **-1.** [declare, elect] eleger **-2.** [choose in ballot] votar em; **they ~ed to return to work** eles votaram pela volta ao trabalho **-3.** [suggest] votar. ◇ *vi* [express one's choice] votar; **to ~ for/against sb** votar em/contra alguém; **to ~ for/against sthg** votar a favor de/contra algo.
◆ **vote in** *vt sep* eleger.
◆ **vote out** *vt sep* derrotar (nas urnas).

vote of confidence (*pl* **votes of confidence**) *n* voto *m* de confiança.

vote of no confidence (*pl* **votes of no confidence**) *n* voto *m* de censura.

vote of thanks (*pl* **votes of thanks**) *n*: **to give a ~** fazer um discurso de agradecimento.

voter ['vəʊtə[r]] *n* votante *mf*.

voting ['vəʊtɪŋ] *n* votação *f*.

vouch [vaʊtʃ] ◆ **vouch for** *vt fus* **-1.** [take responsibility for] responsabilizar-se por **-2.** [declare belief in] dar testemunho de.

voucher ['vaʊtʃə[r]] *n* [for restaurant, purchase, petrol] vale *m*.

vow [vaʊ] ◇ *n* **-1.** juramento *m*, promessa *f* solene **-2.** *RELIG* voto *m*. ◇ *vt*: **to ~ to do sthg** jurar fazer algo; **to ~ (that)** jurar que.

vowel ['vaʊəl] *n* vogal *f*.

voyage ['vɔɪɪdʒ] *n* viagem *f*.

voyeur [vwɑ:'jɜ:[r]] *n* voyeur *m*, -euse *f*.

voyeurism [vwɑ:'jɜ:rɪzm] *n (U)* voyeurismo *m*.

VP *n* (*abbr of* **vice-president**) vice-presidente *mf*.

vs (*abbr of* **versus**) vs.

VSO (*abbr of* **Voluntary Service Overseas**) *n organização britânica de voluntários para ajuda a países em desenvolvimento.*

VSOP (*abbr of* **very special old pale**) *expressão que indica que uma bebida tem de 20 a 25 anos.*

VT *abbr of* **Vermont.**

VTOL (*abbr of* **vertical takeoff and landing**) *n decolagem e aterrissagem na vertical.*

VTR (*abbr of* **videotape recorder**) *n* vídeo *m*.

vulgar ['vʌlgə[r]] *adj* **-1.** [common] comum **-2.** [rude] vulgar, baixo(xa).

vulgarity [vʌl'gærətɪ] *n (U)* **-1.** [commonness] vulgaridade *f* **-2.** [rudeness] grosseria *f*, vulgaridade *f*.

vulnerability [ˌvʌlnərəˈbɪlətɪ] *n* vulnerabilidade *f*.

vulnerable [ˈvʌlnərəbl] *adj* **-1.** [easily hurt] vulnerável; ~ **to sthg** [to being hurt] vulnerável a algo **-2.** [easily influenced]: ~ **(to sthg)** facilmente influenciável (por algo).

vulture [ˈvʌltʃəʳ] *n* **-1.** [bird] abutre *m*, urubu *m* **-2.** *fig* [exploitative person] abutre *m*.

W

w (*pl* **w's** *OR* **ws**), **W** (*pl* **W's** *OR* **Ws**) [ˈdʌblju:] *n* w, W *m*.

◆ **W -1.** (*abbr of* **west**) O. **-2.** (*abbr of* **watt**) W *m*.

WA *abbr of* **Washington**.

wacky [ˈwækɪ] (*compar* **-ier**, *superl* **-iest**) *adj inf* excêntrico(ca), extravagante.

wad [wɒd] *n* **-1.** [of cotton wool] chumaço *m*; [of paper, bank notes, documents] pilha *f*; [of tobacco] masca *f* **-2.** [of chewing gum] pedaço *f*.

wadding [ˈwɒdɪŋ] *n* [stuffing] enchimento *m*.

waddle [ˈwɒdl] *vi* caminhar se balançando.

wade [weɪd] *vi* patinhar.

◆ **wade through** *vt fus fig*: **he was wading through the documents** ele penava muito para ler os documentos.

wadge [wɒdʒ] *n* **-1.** *UK inf* [gen] pilha *f*, porção *f* **-2.** [of cotton wool] chumaço *m*; [of papers] feixe *m*; [of pie] fatia *f*.

wading pool [ˈweɪdɪŋ-] *n US* piscina *f* para crianças.

wafer [ˈweɪfəʳ] *n* [thin biscuit] wafer *m*.

wafer-thin *adj* finíssimo(ma).

waffle [ˈwɒfl] ◇ *n* **-1.** *CULIN* waffle *m* **-2.** *(U) UK inf* [vague talk] lengalenga *f*, ladainha *f*. ◇ *vi inf* enrolar.

waft [wɑ:ft, wɒft] *vi* flutuar.

wag [wæg] (*pt* & *pp* **-ged**, *cont* **-ging**) ◇ *vt* sacudir. ◇ *vi* [tail] abanar.

wage [weɪdʒ] ◇ *n* salário *m*. ◇ *vt*: **to** ~ **war against sb/sthg** guerrear com alguém/algo.

◆ **wages** *npl* [of worker] pagamento *m*, salário *m*; **I always get my** ~**s at the end of the week** eu recebo sempre nos finais de semana.

wage claim *n* reivindicação *f* salarial.

wage differential *n* diferença *f* salarial.

wage earner [-ˌɜ:nəʳ] *n* assalariado *m*, -da *f*.

wage freeze *n* congelamento *m* de salário.

wage packet *n* **-1.** [envelope] envelope *m* de pagamento **-2.** [pay] pagamento *m*.

wager [ˈweɪdʒəʳ] *n* aposta *f*.

wage rise *n UK* aumento *m* de salário.

waggish *adj* **-1.** *inf* [remark, mood, behaviour] jocoso(sa) **-2.** *inf* [person] divertido(da).

waggle [ˈwægl] *inf vt* & *vi* balançar.

wagon [ˈwægən], **waggon** *UK n* **-1.** [horse-drawn vehicle] carroça *f* **-2.** *UK RAIL* vagão *m*.

wagtail *n* lavandisca *f*.

waif [weɪf] *n literary* criança *f* abandonada.

wail [weɪl] ◇ *n* lamento *m*, gemido *m*. ◇ *vi* **-1.** [baby] choramingar **-2.** [person] gemer **-3.** [wind, siren] soar.

wailing [ˈweɪlɪŋ] *n* **-1.** [of baby] choramingo *m* **-2.** [of person] gemido *m* **-3.** [of wind, siren] som *m*.

waist [weɪst] *n* cintura *f*.

waistband [ˈweɪstbænd] *n* cintura *f*, cós *m*.

waistcoat [ˈweɪskəʊt] *n* colete *m*.

waistline [ˈweɪstlaɪn] *n* cintura *f*.

wait [weɪt] ◇ *n* espera *f*; **to lie in** ~ **for sb** esperar alguém numa emboscada. ◇ *vi* esperar; **to** ~ **and see** esperar para ver; ~ **a minute** *OR* **second** *OR* **moment** [interrupting sb] espere um minuto/segundo/momento; [interrupting o.s.] espera (aí) um pouquinho; **(just) you** ~**!** espere que você vai ver! ◇ *vt* **-1.**: **I/he** *etc* **couldn't** ~ **to do sthg** eu/ele mal podia esperar para fazer algo **-2.** *US* [delay]: **don't** ~ **dinner for me** não precisa me esperar para jantar.

◆ **wait about, wait around** *vi* esperar, aguardar.

◆ **wait for** *vt fus* esperar; **to** ~ **for sb to do sthg** esperar que alguém faça algo.

◆ **wait on** *vt fus* [serve food to] servir; **she** ~**s on her family hand and foot** ela responde a todas as necessidades da família.

◆ **wait up** *vi* ficar acordado(da) esperando.

waiter [ˈweɪtəʳ] *n* garçom *m*.

waiting game [ˈweɪtɪŋ-] *n*: **to play a** ~ esperar o momento certo.

waiting list [ˈweɪtɪŋ-] *n* lista *f* de espera.

waiting room [ˈweɪtɪŋ-] *n* sala *f* de espera.

waitress [ˈweɪtrɪs] *n* garçonete *f*.

waive [weɪv] *vt* **-1.** *fml* [rule] não aplicar **-2.** *fml* [entrance fee] abrir mão de.

waiver [ˈweɪvəʳ] *n JUR* renúncia *f*.

wake [weɪk] (*pt* **woke** *OR* **-d**, *pp* **woken** *OR* **-d**) ◇ *n* **-1.** [of ship, boat] esteira *f*; **in one's** ~ *fig* pelo caminho; **in the** ~ **of** *fig* nas águas de **-2.** [for dead person] velório *m*. ◇ *vt* acordar. ◇ *vi* acordar -se.

◆ **wake up** ◇ *vt sep* acordar. ◇ *vi* **-1.** [wake] acordar-se **-2.** *fig* [become aware]: **to** ~ **up (to sthg)** conscientizar-se (de algo).

waken [ˈweɪkən] *fml* ◇ *vt* despertar. ◇ *vi* despertar-se.

waking hours [ˈweɪkɪŋ-] *npl* horas *fpl* de vigília.

Wales [weɪlz] *n* País de Gales; **in** ~ no País de Gales.

walk [wɔ:k] ◇ *n* **-1.** [stroll] passeio *m*, caminhada *f*; **to go for a** ~ dar um passeio **-2.** [path] caminho *m* **-3.** [gait] jeito *m* de andar. ◇ *vt* **-1.** [escort] acompanhar **-2.** [take out for exercise] levar para passear **-3.** [cover on foot] caminhar; **to** ~ **the streets** [be homeless] vagar pela rua; [in search of sthg] percorrer as ruas; [prostitute] prostituir-se. ◇ *vi* caminhar, andar.

◆ **walk away with** *vt fus inf fig* [carry off] levar.

◆ **walk in on** *vt fus* [interrupt] interromper.

◆ **walk off** *vt sep* [headache, cramp, meal] dar uma volta para aliviar.
◆ **walk off with** *vt fus inf* **-1.** [steal] levar **-2.** [win easily] levar de barbada.
◆ **walk out** *vi* **-1.** [leave suddenly] sair **-2.** [go on strike] entrar em greve branca.
◆ **walk out on** *vt fus* deixar, abandonar.

walkabout ['wɔ:kəˌbaʊt] *n* ***UK*** [by politician] caminhada *f* pelas ruas; **to go on a ~** caminhar entre as pessoas *(nas ruas)*.

walker ['wɔ:kə^r] *n* [for pleasure, sport] caminhante *mf*.

walkie-talkie [ˌwɔ:kɪ'tɔ:kɪ] *n* walkie-talkie *m*.

walk-in *adj* **-1.** [cupboard] espaçoso(sa) **-2.** ***US*** [easy] fácil.

walking ['wɔ:kɪŋ] *n* [for pleasure, sport] caminhada *f*; **to go ~** dar uma caminhada.

walking shoes *npl* sapatos *mpl* de caminhada.

walking stick *n* bengala *f*.

Walkman® ['wɔ:kmən] *n* walkman® *m*.

walk of life (*pl* **walks of life**) *n* **-1.** [job] profissão *f* **-2.** [social position] posição *f* social.

walk-on *adj* de figurante.

walkout ['wɔ:kaʊt] *n* [of members, spectators, workers] greve *f* branca.

walkover ['wɔ:kˌəʊvə^r] *n* ***UK inf*** [victory] barbada *f*, vitória *f* fácil.

walkway ['wɔ:kweɪ] *n* passadiço *m*, passagem *f*.

wall [wɔ:l] *n* **-1.** [interior] parede *f* **-2.** [exterior] muro *m*; **to come up against a brick ~** chegar a um beco sem saída; **to drive sb up the ~** deixar alguém louco **-3.** *ANAT* parede *f*.

wallaby ['wɒləbɪ] (*pl* **-ies**) *n* *marsupial australiano parecido com um pequeno canguru*.

wallchart ['wɔ:ltʃɑ:t] *n* mural *m*.

wall cupboard *n* armário *m* embutido.

walled [wɔ:ld] *adj* cercado(da) *(com muros)*.

wallet ['wɒlɪt] *n* carteira *f*.

wallflower ['wɔ:lˌflaʊə^r] *n* **-1.** [plant] aleli *m* **-2.** ***inf fig*** [person] azeite *m*.

Walloon ◇ *adj* valão(ona). ◇ *n* **-1.** [person] valão *m*, -ona *f* **-2.** [language] valão *m*.

wallop ['wɒləp] ***inf*** ◇ *n* surra *f*. ◇ *vt* [hit] surrar.

wallow ['wɒləʊ] *vi* **-1.** [in water] mergulhar **-2.** [in mud] chafurdar **-3.** [in emotion]: **to ~ in sthg** afundar-se em algo.

wall painting *n* afresco *m*, mural *m*.

wallpaper ['wɔ:lˌpeɪpə^r] ◇ *n (U)* papel *m* de parede. ◇ *vt* forrar com papel de parede.

Wall Street *n* Wall Street; **on ~** em Wall Street.

WALL STREET

A *Wall Street*, em Nova York, é o centro financeiro mais importante dos Estados Unidos. É nessa rua que se situa o edifício da Bolsa de Valores. Por extensão, o termo é utilizado para designar o mundo financeiro estadunidense.

wall-to-wall *adj*: **~ carpet** carpete *m*.

wally ['wɒlɪ] (*pl* **-ies**) *n* ***UK inf*** pateta *mf*.

walnut ['wɔ:lnʌt] *n* **-1.** [nut] noz *m* **-2.** [tree, material] nogueira *f*.

walrus ['wɔ:lrəs] (*pl inv OR* **-es**) *n* morsa *f*.

waltz [wɔ:ls] ◇ *n* valsa *f*. ◇ *vi* **-1.** [dance] dançar uma valsa **-2.** ***inf*** [walk confidently]: **to ~ in/out** entrar/sair de fininho.

wan [wɒn] (*compar* **-ner**, *superl* **-nest**) *adj* abatido(da).

wand [wɒnd] *n* varinha *f* mágica.

wander ['wɒndə^r] *vi* **-1.** [person] perambular **-2.** [mind, thoughts] divagar.

wanderer ['wɒndərə^r] *n* andarilho *m*, -lha *f*.

wandering ['wɒndərɪŋ] *adj* [itinerant] ambulante.

wanderlust ['wɒndəlʌst] *n (U)* paixão *f* por viajar.

wane [weɪn] ◇ *n*: **on the ~** em declínio. ◇ *vi* **-1.** [influence, interest] declinar **-2.** [moon] minguar.

wangle ['wæŋgl] *vt inf* arranjar, conseguir.

wanna ['wɒnə] *cont esp* ***US*** = **want a**, **want to**.

wannabe *adj inf* *que gostaria de ser igual a outra pessoa ou grupo de pessoas*.

want [wɒnt] ◇ *n* **-1.** [need] necessidade *f* **-2.** [lack] falta *f*; **for ~ of** por falta de **-3.** *(U)* [deprivation] penúria *f*; **to be in ~** passar necessidades. ◇ *vt* **-1.** [desire] querer; **to ~ to do sthg** querer fazer algo; **to ~ sb to do sthg** querer que alguém faça algo **-2.** ***inf*** [need] precisar.

want ad *n* ***US inf*** anúncio *m* (classificado).

wanted ['wɒntɪd] *adj*: **to be ~ (by the police)** ser procurado(da) (pela polícia).

wanting ['wɒntɪŋ] *adj* ***fml*** [inadequate]: **to be ~ (in sthg)** carecer (de algo); **the play is ~ in humour** está faltando humor na peça; **to be found ~** deixar a desejar.

wanton ['wɒntən] *adj* **-1.** ***fml*** [malicious] gratuito(ta), sem motivo **-2.** [immoral] libertino(na).

WAP [wæp] (*abbr of* **wireless application protocol**) *n* WAP *m*.

WAP phone *n* telefone *m* WAP.

war [wɔ:^r] (*pt* & *pp* **-red**, *cont* **-ring**) *n* guerra *f*; **at ~** em guerra; **to go to ~** entrar em guerra; **to have been in the ~s** ***UK*** estar num estado deplorável.

warble ['wɔ:bl] *vi* ***literary*** [bird] trinar, chilrear.

war crime *n* crime *m* de guerra.

war criminal *n* criminoso *m*, -sa *f* de guerra.

war cry *n* [in battle] grito *m* de guerra.

ward [wɔ:d] *n* **-1.** [in hospital] ala *f* **-2.** ***UK*** *POL* distrito *m* eleitoral **-3.** *JUR* tutelado *m*, -da *f*.
◆ **ward off** *vt fus* proteger-se de.

war dance *n* dança *f* de guerra.

warden ['wɔ:dn] *n* **-1.** [of park] guarda *mf* **-2.** ***UK*** [of youth hostel, hall of residence] diretor *m*, -ra *f* **-3.** ***US*** [prison governor] diretor *m*, -ra *f*.

warder ['wɔ:də^r] *n* [in prison] carcereiro *m*, -ra *f*.

ward of court *n* menor *mf* sob tutela judicial.

wardrobe ['wɔ:drəʊb] *n* **-1.** [piece of furniture] guarda-roupa *m*, armário *m* **-2.** [collection of clothes] guarda-roupa *m*.

wardrobe mistress *n* ***UK*** figurinista *f*.

warehouse ['weəhaʊs, *pl* -haʊzɪz] *n* armazém *m*, depósito *m*.

wares [weəz] *npl* ***literary*** mercadorias *fpl*.

warfare ['wɔ:feə^r] *n* combate *m*; **gang ~** disputa *f* entre gangues.

war game *n* **-1.** [military exercise] manobra *f OR* exercício *m* militar **-2.** [game of strategy] jogo *m* de estratégia militar.

warhead ['wɔ:hed] *n* *MIL* ogiva *f*.

warily ['weərəlɪ] *adv* com desconfiança.
warlike ['wɔ:laɪk] *adj* guerreiro(ra), belicoso(sa).
warm [wɔ:m] ◇ *adj* **-1.** [gen] quente; **I'm ~** estou com calor; **are you ~ enough?** não está com frio, certo? **-2.** [clothing, blanket] que protege do frio **-3.** [sound] cálido(da) **-4.** [person] afetuoso(sa), caloroso(sa) **-5.** [friendly - congratulations] efusivo(va); [- attitude, smile, handshake] caloroso(sa). ◇ *vt* [heat gently] aquecer.
◆ **warm over** *vt sep US* **-1.** [food] requentar **-2.** [ideas] insistir em.
◆ **warm to** *vt fus* tomar simpatia por.
◆ **warm up** ◇ *vt sep* **-1.** [heat] esquentar **-2.** [audience] esquentar. ◇ *vi* **-1.** [get warmer - gen] esquentar; [- person] esquentar-se **-2.** [prepare - for exercise] aquecer, aquecer-se; [- for performance] preparar-se.
warm-blooded [-'blʌdɪd] *adj* de sangue quente.
war memorial *n* memorial *m* de guerra.
warm front *n* frente *f* quente.
warm-hearted [-'hɑ:tɪd] *adj* afetuoso(sa).
warmly ['wɔ:mlɪ] *adv* **-1.** [in warm clothes]: **to dress ~** agasalhar-se bem **-2.** [in a friendly way] calorosamente, efusivamente.
warmness ['wɔ:mnɪs] *n (U)* [friendliness] cordialidade *f.*
warmonger ['wɔ:,mʌŋgə'] *n* belicista *mf.*
warmth [wɔ:mθ] *n (U)* **-1.** [of temperature] calor *m* **-2.** [of welcome, smile, support] cordialidade *f.*
warm-up *n* [preparation] aquecimento *m.*
warn [wɔ:n] ◇ *vt* **-1.** [advise] advertir, prevenir; **to ~ sb of** OR **about sthg** advertir alguém de/sobre algo; **to ~ sb against doing sthg** advertir alguém sobre (os riscos de) fazer algo; **to ~ sb not to do sthg** avisar a alguém para que não faça algo **-2.** [inform] avisar. ◇ *vi* [forecast]: **to ~ of sthg** alertar para a possbilidade de algo.
warning ['wɔ:nɪŋ] ◇ *adj* de advertência. ◇ *n* **-1.** [official caution] advertência *f* **-2.** [prior notice] aviso *m.*
warning light *n* luz *f* de advertência.
warning triangle *n UK* triângulo *m* luminoso *(do carro).*
warp [wɔ:p] ◇ *n* [of cloth] urdidura *f.* ◇ *vt* **-1.** [wood] empenar **-2.** [personality, mind] desvirtuar; [judgement] distorcer. ◇ *vi* [wood] empenar.
warpath ['wɔ:pɑ:θ] *n*: **to be/go on the ~** *fig* estar procurando briga.
warped [wɔ:pt] *adj* **-1.** [wood] empenado(da) **-2.** [person] corrompido(da).
warrant ['wɒrənt] ◇ *n JUR* [written order] mandado *m* (judicial). ◇ *vt fml* [justify] merecer.
warrant officer *n* **-1.** *MIL* suboficial *mf* **-2.** *NAUT* subtenente *mf.*
warranty ['wɒrəntɪ] (*pl* **-ies**) *n* garantia *f.*
warren ['wɒrən] *n* [of rabbit] toca *f.*
warring ['wɔ:rɪŋ] *adj* rival.
warrior ['wɒrɪə'] *n literary* guerreiro *m*, -ra *f.*
Warsaw ['wɔ:sɔ:] *n* Varsóvia; **in ~** em Varsóvia; **the ~ Pact** o Pacto de Varsóvia.
warship ['wɔ:ʃɪp] *n* navio *m* de guerra.
wart [wɔ:t] *n* verruga *f.*
wartime ['wɔ:taɪm] ◇ *adj* de guerra. ◇ *n (U)* tempos *mpl* de guerra; **in ~** em tempos de guerra.
war widow *n* viúva *f* de guerra.
wary ['weərɪ] (*compar* **-ier**, *superl* **-iest**) *adj* receoso (sa); **~ of sthg/of doing sthg** receoso(sa) de algo/ de fazer algo.
was [*weak form* wəz, *strong form* wɒz] *pt* ▷ **be**.
wash [wɒʃ] ◇ *n* **-1.** [act of washing] lavada *f*; **to have a ~** lavar-se; **to give sthg a ~** dar uma lavada em algo **-2.** [clothes to be washed] roupa *f* para lavar OR suja **-3.** [from boat] esteira *f.* ◇ *vt* **-1.** [clean] lavar **-2.** [subj: current, sea, rain] levar, arrastar. ◇ *vi* [clean o.s.] lavar-se.
◆ **wash away** *vt sep* levar, arrastar.
◆ **wash down** *vt sep* **-1.** [food] regar **-2.** [clean] lavar.
◆ **wash out** *vt sep* **-1.** [stain, dye] tirar lavando **-2.** [container] enxaguar.
◆ **wash up** ◇ *vt sep* **-1.** *UK* [dishes] lavar **-2.** [subj: sea, river] trazer, arrastar. ◇ *vi* **-1.** *UK* [wash the dishes] lavar os pratos **-2.** *US* [wash o.s.] lavar-se.
washable ['wɒʃəbl] *adj* lavável.
wash-and-wear *adj que não precisa ser passado.*
washbasin *UK* ['wɒʃ,beɪsn], **washbowl** *US* ['wɒʃbəʊl] *n* lavatório *m.*
washcloth ['wɒʃ,klɒθ] *n US* toalha *f* de rosto.
washed-out [wɒʃt-] *adj* **-1.** [pale] desbotado(da) **-2.** [exhausted] exausto(ta).
washed-up [wɒʃt-] *adj inf* acabado(da).
washer ['wɒʃə'] *n* **-1.** *TECH* arruela *f* **-2.** [washing machine] lavadora *f* (de roupa).
washer-dryer *n* lavadora *f* e secadora.
washing ['wɒʃɪŋ] *n (U)* **-1.** [act] lavagem *f* **-2.** [clothes] roupa *f* para lavar OR suja.
washing line *n* varal *m.*
washing machine *n* lavadora *f* (de roupa).
washing powder *n (U) UK* sabão *m* em pó.
Washington ['wɒʃɪŋtən] *n* **-1.** [state]: **~ State** Estado de Washington **-2.** [city]: **~ D.C.** Washington D.C.
washing-up *n* **-1.** *UK* [crockery, pans etc] louça *f* para lavar OR suja **-2.** [act]: **to do the ~** lavar a louça.
washing-up liquid *n UK* detergente *m.*
washout ['wɒʃaʊt] *n inf* fracasso *m*, desastre *m.*
washroom ['wɒʃrʊm] *n US* lavabo *m.*
wasn't [wɒznt] = **was not**.
wasp [wɒsp] *n* [insect] vespa *f.*
Wasp, WASP [wɒsp] (*abbr of* **White Anglo-Saxon Protestant**) *n* **inf** *nos Estados Unidos e no Canadá, pessoa branca de origem anglo-saxônica e protestante.*
waspish ['wɒspɪʃ] *adj* mordaz.
wastage ['weɪstɪdʒ] *n* desperdício *m.*
waste [weɪst] ◇ *adj* **-1.** [material, fuel] de sobra **-2.** [area of land] improdutivo(va). ◇ *n* **-1.** [misuse] desperdício *m*; **to go to ~** perder-se; **a ~ of time** uma perda de tempo **-2.** [refuse] resíduos *mpl.* ◇ *vt* [misuse] desperdiçar; **it would be ~d on me** eu não saberia aproveitar isso.
◆ **wastes** *npl literary* [wastelands] desertos *mpl.*
◆ **waste away** *vi* definhar.

wastebasket *n US* cesto *m* de lixo.
wasted *adj* [misused] perdido(da).
waste disposal unit *n* triturador *m* de lixo.
wasteful ['weɪstfʊl] *adj*: **to be very ~ to do sthg** ser muito desperdício fazer algo.
waste ground *n (U)* terra *f* improdutiva, descampados *mpl*.
wasteland ['weɪstˌlænd] *n* terreno *m* deserto.
waste paper *n (U)* papel *m* usado.
wastepaper basket [ˌweɪst'peɪpəʳ-], **wastepaper bin** [ˌweɪst'peɪpəʳ-], **wastebasket** *US* ['weɪstˌbɑ:skɪt] *n* cesto *m* para papel.
watch [wɒtʃ] ◇ *n* **-1.** [timepiece] relógio *m* **-2.** [act of guarding]: **to keep ~** ficar de guarda; **to keep ~ on sb/sthg** vigiar alguém/algo **-3.** [guard] guarda *mf*. ◇ *vt* **-1.** [look at - television, programme, match] ver; [- scene, activity] contemplar **-2.** [spy on] vigiar **-3.** [be careful about] cuidar; **~ what you're doing** presta atenção no que você está fazendo; **~ it!** *inf* cuidado! ◇ *vi* [observe] observar.
◆ **watch for** *vt fus* esperar.
◆ **watch out** *vi* **-1.** [be careful]: **to ~ out (for sthg)** ter cuidado (com algo); **~ out!** cuidado! **-2.** [keep a lookout]: **to ~ out for sthg** prestar atenção em algo.
◆ **watch over** *vt fus* [look after] cuidar de.
watchdog ['wɒtʃdɒg] *n* **-1.** [dog] cão *m* de guarda **-2.** *fig* [organization] *comissão que fiscaliza as empresas e impede que realizem ações ilegais ou irresponsáveis*.
watchful ['wɒtʃfʊl] *adj* [vigilant] atento(ta); **to keep a ~ eye on sb/sthg** estar atento(ta) a alguém/algo.
watchmaker ['wɒtʃˌmeɪkəʳ] *n* relojoeiro *m*, -ra *f*.
watchman ['wɒtʃmən] (*pl* **-men** [-mən]) *n* segurança *m*, vigia *m*.
watchword ['wɒtʃwɜ:d] *n* palavra *f* de ordem, lema *m*.
water ['wɔ:təʳ] ◇ *n* **-1.** [gen] água *f*; **to pour** *OR* **throw cold ~ on sthg** *fig* dar um banho de água fria em algo; **to tread ~** [in sea, pool] boiar mexendo as pernas; *fig* [do same thing] marcar passo; **that's ~ under the bridge** são águas passadas **-2.** [urine]: **to pass ~** tirar água do joelho. ◇ *vt* [plants, soil] regar. ◇ *vi* **-1.** [eyes] lacrimejar **-2.** [mouth]: **it makes my mouth ~** fico com água na boca.
◆ **waters** *npl* águas *fpl*.
◆ **water down** *vt sep* **-1.** [dilute] diluir **-2.** *usu* **pej** [moderate] suavizar, moderar.
water bed *n* colchão *m* d'água.
water bird *n* ave *f* aquática.
water biscuit *n* bolacha *f* de água e sal.
waterborne ['wɔ:təbɔ:n] *adj* transmitido(da) pela água.
water bottle *n* garrafa *f* d'água, cantil *m*.
water buffalo *n* búfalo-da-índia *m*.
water cannon *n* canhão *m* de água.
water chestnut *n* castanha-d'água *f*.
water closet *n dated* w.c. *m*.
watercolour ['wɔ:təˌkʌləʳ] *n* aquarela *f*.
water-cooled [-ˌku:ld] *adj* refrigerado(da) a água.
watercourse ['wɔ:təkɔ:s] *n* [river, stream] córrego *m*.
watercress ['wɔ:təkres] *n (U)* agrião *m*.
watered-down [ˌwɔ:təd-] *adj usu pej* suavizado(-da).
waterfall ['wɔ:təfɔ:l] *n* queda-d'água *f*, cachoeira *f*.
waterfront ['wɔ:təfrʌnt] *n* orla *f* marítima.
water heater *n* aquecedor *m* de água.
waterhole ['wɔ:təhəʊl] *n* cacimba *f*.
watering can ['wɔ:tərɪŋ-] *n* regador *m*.
water jump *n* valado *m* de água *(nas corridas de cavalo)*.
water level *n* nível *m* de água.
water lily *n* nenúfar *m*.
waterline ['wɔ:təlaɪn] *n NAUT* linha-d'água *f*.
waterlogged ['wɔ:təlɒgd] *adj* **-1.** [land] alagado(-da) **-2.** [vessel] inundado(da).
water main *n* adutora *f*.
watermark ['wɔ:təmɑ:k] *n* **-1.** [in paper] marca *f* d'água **-2.** [showing water level] linha-d'água *f*.
watermelon ['wɔ:təˌmelən] *n* melancia *f*.
water pipe *n* [in building] cano *m* de água.
water pistol *n* pistola *f* d'água.
water polo *n (U)* pólo *m* aquático.
waterproof ['wɔ:təpru:f] ◇ *adj* à prova d'água. ◇ *n* capa *f* impermeável; **~s** roupa *f* à prova d'água. ◇ *vt* impermeabilizar.
water rates *npl UK* tarifa *f* de água.
water-resistant *adj* resistente à água.
watershed ['wɔ:təʃed] *n* **-1.** *GEOGR* linha *f* divisória das águas **-2.** *fig* [turning point] divisor *m* de águas.
waterside ['wɔ:təsaɪd] ◇ *adj* ribeirinho(nha). ◇ *n*: **the ~** a orla.
water skiing *n (U)* esqui *m* aquático.
water softener *n* abrandador *m* de água.
water-soluble *adj* solúvel em água.
watersports *npl* esportes *mpl* aquáticos.
waterspout *n* tromba *f* d'água.
water supply *n* fornecimento *m* de água.
water table *n* (nível *m* do) lençol *m* freático.
water tank *n* caixa *f* d'água.
watertight ['wɔ:tətaɪt] *adj* **-1.** [waterproof] hermético(ca) **-2.** *fig* [faultless] infalível.
water tower *n* torre *f* d'água.
waterway ['wɔ:təweɪ] *n* via *f* navegável, canal *m*.
waterworks ['wɔ:təwɜ:ks] (*pl inv*) *n* [building] instalações *fpl* para a distribuição de água.
watery ['wɔ:tərɪ] *adj* **-1.** [food, drink] aguado(da) **-2.** [light, sun, moon] pálido(da).
watt [wɒt] *n* watt *m*.
wattage ['wɒtɪdʒ] *n* potência *f* em watts.
wave [weɪv] ◇ *n* **-1.** *GEN* onda *f* **-2.** [of people] leva *f* **-3.** [in hair] ondulação *f* **-4.** [gesture] aceno *m*. ◇ *vt* **-1.** [brandish - hand, flag] agitar; [- baton] manejar; [- stick, pistol, gun] empunhar **-2.** [gesture to] fazer sinal para **-3.** [hair] ondular. ◇ *vi* **-1.** [with hand] abanar; **to ~ at** *OR* **to sb** abanar para alguém **-2.** [flag] tremular **-3.** [tree] balançar **-4.** [hair] ondular.
◆ **wave aside** *vt sep fig* [dismiss] rejeitar.
◆ **wave down** *vt sep* fazer sinal para parar.
wave band *n* faixa *f* de onda.
wavelength ['weɪvleŋθ] *n* comprimento *m* de onda; **to be on the same ~** *fig* estar em sintonia.

waver ['weɪvəʳ] *vi* **-1.** [gen] vacilar; **to ~ in sthg** hesitar em algo **-2.** [light, temperature] oscilar **-3.** [flame] tremer.
wavy ['weɪvɪ] (*compar* **-ier**, *superl* **-iest**) *adj* **-1.** [hair] ondulado(da) **-2.** [line] sinuoso(sa).
wax [wæks] <> *n* [gen] cera *f.* <> *vt* **-1.** [floor, table] encerar ; [skis] passar cera em **-2.** [legs] depilar com cera. <> *vi* **-1.** *dated or hum* [become] tornar-se; **to ~ and wane** aumentar e diminuir **-2.** [moon] crescer.
waxen ['wæksən] *adj* [face, complexion] pálido(da).
wax paper *n US* papel *m* encerado.
waxworks ['wækswɜ:ks] (*pl inv*) *n* [museum] museu *m* de cera.
way [weɪ] <> *n* **-1.** [means, method] maneira *f*, modo *m*; **~s and means** meios *mpl*; **to get** *OR* **have one's ~** conseguir o que se quer; **to have everything one's own ~** ter o que se quer **-2.** [manner, style] jeito *m*, maneira *f*; **in the same ~** da mesma forma; **this/that ~** dessa/daquela forma; **in a ~** de certa forma *OR* maneira; **in a big/small ~** em grande/pequena escala; **to fall for sb in a big ~** apaixonar-se loucamente por alguém; **to be in a bad ~** ficar mal; **in no ~** de maneira alguma **-3.** [skill]: **to have a ~ with sb/sthg** ter jeito para lidar com alguém/algo; **to have a ~ of doing sthg** ter o costume de fazer algo **-4.** [thoroughfare, path] caminho *m*; **across** *OR* **over the ~** do outro lado da rua; **'give ~'** *UK AUT* dê passagem **-5.** [route leading to a specified place] caminho *m*; **do you know the ~ to the cathedral?** sabe como se faz para chegar na catedral?; **to lose one's ~** perder-se; **out of one's ~** [place] fora do caminho de alguém; **can you post this letter on the** *OR* **one's ~ (to the shops)** quando você for (fazer compras), pode colocar esta carta no correio?; **to be under ~** [ship] estar navegando; [project, meeting] estar em andamento; **to get under ~** [ship] zarpar; [project, meeting] estar em andamento; **to be in the ~** estar na passagem *OR* frente; **to be out of the ~** [finished] estar pronto(ta); [not blocking] **if you put your suitcase over there, it will be out of the ~** se colocar sua mala lá, ela não vai ficar atrapalhando; **to go out of one's ~ to do sthg** não poupar esforços para fazer algo; **to keep out of sb's ~** não cruzar o caminho de alguém; **keep out of the ~!** saia do caminho!; **to make one's ~** dirigir-se; **to make ~ for sb/sthg** abrir espaço para alguém/algo; **to stand in sb's ~** *fig* ficar no caminho de alguém; **to work one's ~ to** abrir caminho para chegar a **-6.** [route leading in a specified direction]: **come this ~** vem por aqui; **~ in** entrada; **~ out** saída **-7.** [side] lado *m*; **the right/wrong ~ round** do jeito certo/errado; **the right/wrong ~ up** com o lado certo/errado para cima **-8.** [distance]: **all the ~** todo o caminho; **most of the ~** quase todo o caminho; **a long ~** um longo caminho; **to go a long ~ towards doing sthg** *fig* contribuir muito no sentido de se fazer algo **-9.** *phr*: **to give ~** [under weight, pressure] ceder; **no ~!** de maneira alguma! <> *adv inf* [by far] muito; **it's ~ too big!** é enorme de grande!
◆ **ways** *npl* [customs, habits] costumes *mpl*, hábitos *mpl*.
◆ **by the way** *adv* a propósito, aliás.
◆ **by way of** *prep* **-1.** [via] passando por **-2.** [as a sort of] como forma de.
◆ **in the way of** *prep* [in the form of]: **what do you have in the of ~ red wine?** o que tem de vinho branco?
waylay [ˌweɪ'leɪ] (*pt* & *pp* **-laid**) *vt* abordar.
way of life *n* estilo *m OR* modo *m* de vida.
way-out *adj inf* arrojado(da).
wayside ['weɪsaɪd] *n* [roadside] beira *f* da estrada; **to fall by the ~** *fig* ir por água abaixo.
wayward ['weɪwəd] *adj* incorrigível.
WC (*abbr of* **water closet**) *n* WC *m.*
WCC (*abbr of* **World Council of Churches**) *n conselho mundial de igrejas.*
we [wi:] *pers pron pl* nós **~'re young** (nós) somos jovens.
weak [wi:k] *adj* **-1.** [gen] fraco(ca) **-2.** [lacking knowledge, skill]: **to be ~ on sthg** ser fraco(ca em algo).
weaken ['wi:kn] <> *vt* **-1.** [gen] enfraquecer; *FIN* [devalue] desvalorizar **-2.** [debilitate] debilitar. <> *vi* **-1.** [person - physically] debilitar-se; [- morally] desgastar-se; **no signs of ~ing** nenhum sinal de desgaste **-2.** [influence, power] diminuir **-3.** [structure] enfraquecer-se **-4.** *FIN* [dollar, mark] desvalorizar-se.
weak-kneed [-'ni:d] *adj inf pej* sem iniciativa.
weakling ['wi:klɪŋ] *n pej* fraco *m*, -ca *f (de corpo e mente).*
weakly ['wi:klɪ] *adv* fracamente.
weak-minded [-'maɪndɪd] *adj* fraco(ca) de caráter.
weakness ['wi:knɪs] *n* **-1.** *(U)* [of person - physical] fraqueza *f*; [- moral] ponto *m* fraco; **to have a ~ for sthg** ter um fraco por algo **-2.** [of government, structure, plan] debilidade *f* **-3.** *FIN* [of currency] fragilidade *f.*
weal [wi:l] *n* vergão *m.*
wealth [welθ] *n* **-1.** *(U)* [riches] riqueza *f* **-2.** [abundance]: **a ~ of sthg** uma profusão de algo.
wealth tax *n UK* imposto *m* sobre bens.
wealthy ['welθɪ] (*compar* **-ier**, *superl* **-iest**) *adj* rico(-ca).
wean [wi:n] *vt* **-1.** [from mother's milk] desmamar **-2.** [from habit]: **to ~ sb from** *OR* **off sthg** afastar alguém gradualmente de algo.
weapon ['wepən] *n* arma *f.*
weaponry ['wepənrɪ] *n (U)* armamento *m.*
wear [weəʳ] (*pt* **wore**, *pp* **worn**) <> *n* **-1.** [type of clothes] roupa *f* **-2.** [damage] desgaste *m*; **~ and tear** desgaste **-3.** [use] uso *m*; **to be the worse for ~** [tired] estar um trapo; [drunk] estar num estado deplorável. <> *vt* **-1.** [gen] usar **-2.** [clothes] vestir **-3.** [shoes] calçar **-4.** [damage - gen] danificar; [- holes] abrir. <> *vi* **-1.** [deteriorate] gastar **-2.** [last]: **to ~ well/badly** durar bastante/pouco **-3.** *phr*: **to ~ thin** ficar gasto(ta).
◆ **wear away** <> *vt sep* desgastar. <> *vi* desgastar-se.
◆ **wear down** <> *vt sep* **-1.** [reduce size of] gastar **-2.** [weaken] esgotar. <> *vi* gastar, desgastar.
◆ **wear off** *vi* passar.
◆ **wear on** *vi* transcorrer.
◆ **wear out** <> *vt sep* **-1.** [clothing, machinery]

usar até estragar **-2.** [patience, strength, reserves] esgotar **-3.** [person] ficar esgotado(da). ◇ *vi* [clothing, shoes] gastar.
wearable ['weərəbl] *adj* que se pode usar.
wearily ['wɪərɪlɪ] *adv* com cansaço.
weariness ['wɪərɪnɪs] *n (U)* exaustão *f*, cansaço *m*.
wearing ['weərɪŋ] *adj* [exhausting] fatigante.
weary ['wɪərɪ] (*compar* **-ier**, *superl* **-iest**) *adj* **-1.** [exhausted] exausto(ta) **-2.** [fed up]: **to be ~ of sthg/of doing sthg** estar farto(ta) de algo/de fazer algo.
weasel ['wi:zl] *n* doninha *f*.
weather ['weðə[r]] ◇ *n* tempo *m*; **to make heavy ~ of sthg** complicar algo desnecessariamente; **to be under the ~** estar se sentindo um pouco indisposto(ta). ◇ *vt* [survive] superar. ◇ *vi* ser resistente.
weather-beaten [-ˌbi:tn] *adj* **-1.** [stone, rocks] desgastado(da) **-2.** [face, skin] desgastado(da) pelo tempo.
weathercock ['weðəkɒk] *n* cata-vento *m (em forma de galo)*.
weathered ['weðəd] *adj* **-1.** [face] marcado(da) **-2.** [wood, building, stone] deteriorado(da).
weather forecast *n* previsão *f* do tempo.
weatherman ['weðəmæn] (*pl* **-men** [-men]) *n* meteorologista *m*.
weather map *n* mapa *m* do tempo.
weatherproof ['weðəpru:f] *adj* **-1.** [clothing] impermeável **-2.** [building] resistente às intempéries.
weather report *n* previsão *f* do tempo.
weather ship *n* navio *m* meteorológico.
weather vane [-veɪn] *n* cata-vento *m*.
weave [wi:v] (*pt* **wove**, *pp* **woven**) ◇ *n* trama *f (do tecido)*. ◇ *vt* **-1.** [using loom] tecer **-2.** [move along]: **to ~ one's way** costurar *(no trânsito)*. ◇ *vi* [move]: **to ~ in and out** ziguezaguear.
weaver ['wi:və[r]] *n* tecelão *m*, -lã *f*.
web [web] *n* **-1.** [cobweb] teia *f* **-2.** *fig* [of lies, intrigue] rede *f* **-3.** COMPUT Web *f*, Rede *f*.
webbed [webd] *adj* palmado(da).
webbing ['webɪŋ] *n (U)* [material] tira *f* de tecido resistente.
web browser *n* COMPUT navegador *m*.
webcam ['webkæm] *n* câmera *f* web, webcam *f*.
webcast ['webkɑ:st] *n* transmissão *f* ao vivo pela Internet.
web designer *n* web designer *mf*.
web-footed [-'fʊtɪd] *adj* palmípede.
web page *n* página *f* da Web.
webphone ['webfəʊn] *n* webphone *m*.
website ['websaɪt] *n* site *m* da Web.
wed [wed] (*pt* & *pp* **wed** OR **-ded**) *literary* ◇ *vt* [marry] desposar. ◇ *vi* casar.
we'd [wi:d] = **we had**, **we would**.
Wed. (*abbr of* **Wednesday**) qua.
wedded ['wedɪd] *adj* [committed]: **~ to sthg** dedicado(da) a algo.
wedding ['wedɪŋ] *n* casamento *m (cerimônia)*.
wedding anniversary *n* aniversário *m* de casamento.
wedding cake *n* bolo *m* de casamento.
wedding dress *n* vestido *m* de noiva.
wedding night *n* noite *f* de núpcias.
wedding reception *n* recepção *f* de casamento.
wedding ring *n* aliança *f*.
wedge [wedʒ] ◇ *n* **-1.** [gen] cunha *f*; **to drive a ~ between** piorar o relacionamento entre; **the thin end of the ~** a ponta do iceberg **-2.** [of cheese, cake, pie] fatia *f*, porção *f*. ◇ *vt* **-1.** [make fixed or steady] calçar com cunha **-2.** [squeeze, push] enfiar; **she sat ~d between us** ela se sentou enfiada entre nós.
wedlock ['wedlɒk] *n (U) literary* matrimônio *m*.
Wednesday ['wenzdɪ] *n* quarta-feira *f*; *see also* **Saturday**.
wee [wi:] ◇ *adj Scot* pequenino(na). ◇ *n inf* xixi *m*. ◇ *vi inf* fazer xixi.
weed [wi:d] ◇ *n* **-1.** [wild plant] erva *f* daninha **-2.** *UK inf* [feeble person] fracote *m*, -ta *f*. ◇ *vt* capinar.
◆ **weed out** *vt sep* eliminar.
weeding ['wi:dɪŋ] *n (U)* capina *f*.
weedkiller ['wi:dˌkɪlə[r]] *n* herbicida *m*.
weedy ['wi:dɪ] (*compar* **-ier**, *superl* **-iest**) *adj* **-1.** [overgrown with weeds] com muito inço **-2.** *UK inf* [feeble] fracote(ta).
week [wi:k] *n* [gen] semana *f*; **during the ~** durante a semana; **in three ~s' time** dentro de três semanas; **a ~ on Saturday** OR **Saturday ~** sem ser este sábado, no outro; **a ~ last Saturday** uma semana antes de sábado.
weekday ['wi:kdeɪ] *n* dia *m* da semana.
weekend [ˌwi:k'end] *n* fim *m* de semana; **at the ~** no fim de semana.
weekend bag *n* bolsa *f* pequena *(para sair no fim de semana)*.
weekly ['wi:klɪ] (*pl* **-ies**) ◇ *adj* semanal. ◇ *adv* semanalmente. ◇ *n* semanário *m*.
weeny *adj UK inf* pouquinho(nha); **a ~ bit** um pouquinho.
weep [wi:p] (*pt* & *pp* **wept**) ◇ *n*: **to have a ~** chorar. ◇ *vt* derramar. ◇ *vi* chorar.
weeping willow [ˌwi:pɪŋ-] *n* salgueiro-chorão *m*.
weepy [wi:pɪ] (*compar* **-ier**, *superl* **-iest**) ◇ *adj* choroso(sa), triste. ◇ *n* [sentimental film] dramalhão *m*.
weft *n* trama *f*.
weigh [weɪ] ◇ *vt* **-1.** [gen] pesar **-2.** [raise]: **to ~ anchor** levantar âncora. ◇ *vi* [have specific weight] pesar.
◆ **weigh down** *vt sep* **-1.** [physically] sobrecarregar **-2.** [mentally]: **to be ~ed down by** OR **with sthg** estar prostrado(da) por algo.
◆ **weigh (up)on** *vt fus* oprimir.
◆ **weigh out** *vt sep* pesar.
◆ **weigh up** *vt sep* [situation, pros and cons] pesar; [person, opposition] fazer uma idéia de.
weighbridge ['weɪbrɪdʒ] *n UK* balança *f* para veículos.
weighing machine ['weɪɪŋ-] *n* balança *f*.
weight [weɪt] ◇ *n* **-1.** [gen] peso *m*; **to put on** OR **gain ~** engordar; **to lose ~** perder peso; **to take the ~ off one's feet** descansar **-2.** *fig* [power, influence]: **the ~ of public opinion** a opinião pública

em peso; **to carry** ~ ter peso; **to pull one's** ~ fazer sua parte; **to throw one's** ~ **about** ficar dando ordens. <> *vt*: **to** ~ **sthg (down)** colocar lastro em algo.

weighted ['weɪtɪd] *adj*: **to be** ~ **in favour of/against sb** pesar a favor de/contra alguém; **to be** ~ **in favour of/against sthg** pesar a favor de/contra algo.

weighting ['weɪtɪŋ] *n (U) pagamento adicional por se viver numa cidade com alto custo de vida.*

weightlessness ['weɪtlɪsnɪs] *n (U)* imponderabilidade *f*, ausência *f* de peso.

weight lifter *n* levantador *m*, -ra *f* de peso, halterofilista *mf*.

weight lifting *n (U)* levantamento *m* de peso.

weight training *n (U)* levantamento *m* de peso.

weighty ['weɪtɪ] (*compar* **-ier**, *superl* **-iest**) *adj* [serious, important] de peso.

weir [wɪəʳ] *n* represa *f*.

weird [wɪəd] *adj* estranho(nha), esquisito(ta).

weirdo ['wɪədəʊ] (*pl* **-s**) *n inf* excêntrico *m*, -ca *f*.

welcome ['welkəm] <> *adj* **-1.** [gen] bem-vindo(-da); **to make sb** ~ receber alguém muito bem **-2.** [free]: **to be** ~ **to do sthg** ter toda a liberdade para fazer algo **-3.** [in reply to thanks]: **you're** ~ de nada. <> *n* acolhida *f*. <> *vt* [gen] acolher. <> *excl* bem-vindo(da)!

welcoming ['welkəmɪŋ] *adj* cordial.

weld [weld] <> *n* solda *f*. <> *vt* soldar.

welder ['weldəʳ] *n* soldador *m*, -ra *f*.

welfare ['welfeəʳ] <> *adj* de assistência social. <> *n* **-1.** [state of wellbeing] bem-estar *m* **-2.** *US* [income support] assistência *f* social *(do governo)*.

welfare state *n* estado *m* de bem-estar social.

well [wel] (*compar* **better**, *superl* **best**) <> *adj* bem; **to get** ~ ficar bem; **all is** ~ está tudo bem; **(all)** ~ **and good** tudo bem; **just as** ~ ainda bem que. <> *adv* **-1.** [gen] bem; **to go** ~ ir bem; ~ **done!** muito bem!; ~ **and truly** completamente; **to be** ~ **in with sb** *inf* ser muito amiguinho(nha) de alguém; **you're** ~ **out of it** *inf* ainda bem que você caiu fora **-2.** [definitely, certainly] certamente, definitivamente; **it was** ~ **worth it** claro que valeu a pena; **she's** ~ **over 40** ela tem muito mais de 40 **-3.** [easily, possibly] (muito) bem. <> *n* [water, oil] poço *m*. <> *excl* **-1.** [in hesitation] bem!, bom! **-2.** [to correct o.s.] bem **-3.** [to express resignation]: **oh** ~**!** enfim! **-4.** [in surprise] quem diria!, olha só!

◆ **as well** *adv* [in addition] também; **you may/might as** ~ **tell the truth** e por que você não conta a verdade?

◆ **as well as** *conj* além de.

◆ **well up** *vi* brotar.

we'll [wi:l] = **we shall, we will.**

well-adjusted *adj* [psychologically] sensato(ta).

well-advised [-əd'vaɪzd] *adj* prudente; **he/you would be** ~ **to do sthg** seria prudente que ele/você fizesse algo.

well-appointed [-ə'pɔɪntɪd] *adj* bem equipado(-da).

well-balanced *adj* **-1.** [mentally healthy] equilibrado(da) **-2.** [nutritious] balanceado(da).

well-behaved [-bɪ'heɪvd] *adj* bem-comportado(-da).

wellbeing [ˌwel'bi:ɪŋ] *n (U)* bem-estar *m*.

well-bred [-'bred] *adj* bem-educado(da).

well-built *adj* [person] robusto(ta), fornido(da).

well-chosen *adj* bem escolhido(da).

well-disposed *adj*: **to be** ~ **to(wards) sb/sthg** ser favorável a alguém/algo.

well-done *adj* [thoroughly cooked] bem passado(-da).

well-dressed [-'drest] *adj* bem vestido(da).

well-earned [-'ɜ:nd] *adj* merecido(da).

well-established *adj* **-1.** [custom, tradition] antigo(ga) **-2.** [company] de sólida reputação.

well-fed *adj* bem alimentado(da).

well-groomed [-'gru:md] *adj* bem-apresentado(da).

wellhead *n* nascente *f*.

well-heeled [-hi:ld] *adj inf* rico(ca).

wellies ['welɪz] *npl UK inf* botas *fpl* impermeáveis.

well-informed *adj*: **to be** ~ **(about/on sthg)** estar bem informado(da) (sobre algo).

wellington (boot) *n* bota *f* impermeável.

well-intentioned [-ɪn'tenʃnd] *adj* bem-intencionado(da).

well-kept *adj* **-1.** [garden, village] bem cuidado(da) **-2.** [secret] bem guardado(da).

well-known *adj* conhecido(da).

well-mannered [-'mænəd] *adj*: **to be** ~ ter boas maneiras.

well-meaning *adj* bem-intencionado(da).

well-nigh [-naɪ] *adv* quase.

well-off *adj* **-1.** [financially] rico(ca), próspero(ra) **-2.** [in a good position]: **to be** ~ **for sthg** estar bem de algo; **not to know when one is** ~ *inf* não se dar conta da própria sorte.

well-paid *adj* bem pago(ga).

well-preserved *adj fig* [person] bem conservado(da).

well-proportioned [-prə'pɔ:ʃnd] *adj* bem-proporcionado(da).

well-read [-'red] *adj* instruído(da), culto(ta).

well-rounded [-'raʊndɪd] *adj* [varied] variado(da).

well-spoken *adj*: **to be** ~ falar bem.

well-thought-of *adj* de boa reputação.

well-thought-out *adj* bem elaborado(da).

well-timed *adj* oportuno(na).

well-to-do *adj* abastado(da), de dinheiro.

well-wisher *n* simpatizante *mf*.

well-woman clinic *n UK clínica para o bem-estar da mulher.*

welly (*pl* **-ies**) (*abbr of* **wellington**) *n UK inf* botas *fpl* de borracha.

Welsh [welʃ] <> *adj* galês(esa). <> *n (U)* [language] galês *m*. <> *npl*: **the** ~ os galeses.

Welshman ['welʃmən] (*pl* **-men** [-mən]) *n* galês *m*.

Welsh rarebit [-'reəbɪt] *n torrada coberta com queijo derretido.*

Welshwoman ['welʃˌwʊmən] (*pl* **-women** [-ˌwɪmɪn]) *n* galesa *f*.

welter ['weltəʳ] *n* confusão *f*, rebuliço *m*.

welterweight ['weltəweɪt] *n* peso *m* meio-médio.

wend [wend] *vt literary*: **to ~ one's way** dirigir-se vagarosamente.
wendy house ['wendɪ-] *n UK* casa *f* de bonecas.
went [went] *pt* ▻ **go**.
wept [wept] *pt & pp* ▻ **weep**.
were [wɜː[r]] *vb* ▻ **be**.
we're [wɪə[r]] = **we are**.
weren't [wɜːnt] = **were not**.
werewolf ['wɪəwʊlf] (*pl* **-wolves** [-wʊlvz]) *n* lobisomem *m*.
west [west] ◇ *n* **-1.** [direction] oeste *m*; **the ~** o oeste **-2.** [region]: **the ~** o Oeste. ◇ *adj* oeste. ◇ *adv* para o oeste; **~ of** ao oeste de.
◆ **West** *n* POL: **the West** o Ocidente.
West Bank *n*: **the ~** a Cisjordânia; **on the ~** na Cisjordânia.
westbound ['westbaʊnd] *adj* em direção ao oeste.
West Country *n*: **the ~** o sudoeste da Inglaterra.
westerly ['westəlɪ] *adj* **-1.** [towards the west]: **in a ~ direction** para o oeste **-2.** [in the west] ocidental **-3.** [from the west] oeste.
western ['westən] ◇ *adj* **-1.** [part of country, continent] ocidental **-2.** POL [relating to the West] do Ocidente. ◇ *n* [book, film] western *m*.
Westerner ['westənə[r]] *n* **-1.** POL [inhabitant of the West] ocidental *mf* **-2.** [inhabitant of west of country] habitante *mf* do oeste.
westernize, -ise ['westənaɪz] *vt* ocidentalizar.
Western Isles *npl* Western Isles.
Western Samoa *n* Samoa Ocidental; **in ~** em Samoa Ocidental.
West German ◇ *adj* da Alemanha Ocidental. ◇ *n* [person] alemão *m*, -mã *f* ocidental.
West Germany *n*: **(former) ~** a (antiga)Alemanha Ocidental; **in ~** na Alemanha Ocidental.
West Indian ◇ *adj* antilhano(na). ◇ *n* [person] antilhano *m*, -na *f*.
West Indies [-'ɪndiːz] *npl*: **the ~** as Antilhas; **in the ~** nas Antilhas.
Westminster ['westmɪnstə[r]] *n* **-1.** [area] Westminster **-2.** *fig* [British parliament] parlamento *m* britânico.

WESTMINSTER

A *City of Westminster* é a área do centro de Londres em que se situam o palácio de Buckingham e as casas do Parlamento britânico. No coração dessa área encontra-se a famosa abadia de Westminster, de estreitos vínculos com a monarquia: é nela que se celebram as coroações e os funerais de reis e rainhas. Westminster é também termo muito utilizado para designar o Parlamento britânico.

West Virginia *n* Virgínia Ocidental.
westward ['westwəd] ◇ *adj* para o oeste. ◇ *adv* = **westwards**.
westwards ['westwədz] *adv* para o oeste.
wet [wet] (*compar* **-ter**, *superl* **-test**, *pt & pp* **wet** OR **-ted**, *cont* **-ting**) ◇ *adj* **-1.** [damp] úmido(da) **-2.** [soaked] molhado(da) **-3.** [rainy] chuvoso(sa) **-4.** [ink, concrete] fresco(ca); **'~ paint'** tinta fresca **-5.** *UK inf pej* [weak, feeble] fraco(ca). ◇ *n inf UK* POL *político conservador moderado*. ◇ *vt* **-1.** [soak] molhar **-2.** [dampen] umedecer **-3.** [bed]: **to ~ the bed** fazer xixi na cama; **to ~ o.s.** mijar-se.
wet blanket *n inf pej* desmancha-prazeres *mf inv*.
wet-look *adj* brilhante.
wetness ['wetnɪs] *n* **-1.** [dampness] umidade *f* **-2.** *UK inf pej* [feebleness] fraqueza *f*.
wet nurse *n* ama-de-leite *f*.
wet rot *n* [decay] apodrecimento *f (devido à umidade)*.
wet suit *n* roupa *f* de mergulho.
WEU (*abbr of* **Western European Union**) *n união de países da Europa Ocidental formada em 1955 para elaboração de políticas de defesa*.
we've [wiːv] = **we have**.
whack [wæk] *inf* ◇ *n* **-1.** [hit] pancada *f* **-2.** *inf* [share]: **one's ~ of the profits** a sua parte nos lucros. ◇ *vt* dar pancadas em.
whacked [wækt] *adj UK inf* [exhausted] demolido(da).
whacky *adj* = **wacky**.
whale [weɪl] *n* [animal] baleia *f*; **to have a ~ of a time** *inf* divertir-se para valer.
whaling ['weɪlɪŋ] *n (U)* caça *f* às baleias.
wham [wæm] *excl inf* bum!
wharf [wɔːf] (*pl* **-s** OR **wharves** [wɔːvz]) *n* cais *m inv*.
what [wɒt] ◇ *adj* **-1.** [in questions] que; **~ colour is it?** de que cor é?; **he asked me ~ colour it was** ele perguntou-me de que cor era. **-2.** [in exclamations] que; **~ a surprise!** mas que surpresa!; **~ a beautiful day!** mas que dia lindo! ◇ *pron* **-1.** [in questions] o que; **~ is going on?** o que é que está acontecendo?; **~ is that?** o que é isso?; **~ is that thing called?** como é que se chama aquilo?; **~ is the problem?** qual é o problema?; **she asked me ~ had happened** ela perguntou-me o que é que tinha acontecido; **she asked me ~ I had seen** ela perguntou-me o que é que eu tinha visto. **-2.** (in questions: after prep) que; **~ are they talking about?** de que é que eles estão falando?; **~ is it for?** para que é isso?; **she asked me ~ I was thinking about** ela me perguntou em que eu estava pensando. **-3.** [introducing relative clause] o que; **I didn't see ~ happened** não vi o que aconteceu; **you can't have ~ you want** você não pode ter o que quer. **-4.** [in phrases]: **~ for?** para quê?; **~ about going out for a meal?** que tal irmos comer fora? ◇ *excl* o quê!
whatever [wɒt'evə[r]] ◇ *adj* qualquer; **eat ~ food you find** come o que encontrar; **no chance ~** nem a mais remota chance; **nothing ~** absolutamente nada. ◇ *pron* **-1.** [no matter what] o que quer que; **~ they may offer** ofereçam o que oferecerem **-2.** [indicating surprise]: **~ did you say?** o que foi que você disse? **-3.** [indicating lack of precision]: **~ that is** seja lá o que for; **or ~** ou o que seja.
whatnot ['wɒtnɒt] *n inf* [something, anything]: **and ~** e coisas assim.
what's-her-name *n inf* a tal fulana.
what's-his-name *n inf* o tal fulano.
whatsit *n inf* treco *m*.
whatsoever [ˌwɒtsəʊ'evə[r]] *adj* absolutamente.
wheat [wiːt] *n* trigo *m*.
wheat germ *n (U)* germe *m* de trigo.

wheatmeal ['wi:tmi:l] *n (U)* farinha *f* de trigo integral.

wheedle ['wi:dl] *vt*: **to ~ sb into doing sthg** bajular alguém para que faça algo; **to ~ sthg out of sb** conseguir algo de alguém por bajulação.

wheel [wi:l] <> *n* **-1.** [of bicycle, car, train] roda *f* **-2.** *AUT* [steering wheel] direção *f* (do carro). <> *vt* empurrar *(algo com rodas)*. <> *vi* **-1.** [move in circle] dar voltas **-2.** [turn round]: **to ~ round** dar a volta.

wheelbarrow ['wi:l,bærəʊ] *n* carrinho *m* de mão.

wheelbase *n* distância *f* entre eixos.

wheelchair ['wi:l,tʃeə^r] *n* cadeira *f* de rodas.

wheel clamp *n grampo posto nas rodas de veículo estacionado em lugar proibido.*

◆ **wheel-clamp** *vt* grampear a roda *(de veículo mal estacionado)*.

wheeler-dealer ['wi:lə^r-] *n pej* negociante *mf* astuto, -ta.

wheelie bin *n UK* lixeira *f* com rodas.

wheeling and dealing ['wi:lɪŋ-] *n (U) pej* negócios *m* escusos.

wheeze [wi:z] <> *n* [sound of wheezing] respiração *f* ofegante. <> *vi* resfolegar.

wheezy ['wi:zɪ] (*compar* **-ier**, *superl* **-iest**) *adj* resfolegante.

whelk [welk] *n* caramujo *m*.

when *adv* & *conj* quando.

whenever [wen'evə^r] <> *conj* sempre que. <> *adv* **-1.** [indicating surprise] quando é que **-2.** [indicating lack of precision]: **or ~** ou quando quiser.

where [weə^r] *adv* & *conj* onde.

whereabouts [*adv* ,weərə'baʊts, *n* 'weərəbaʊts] <> *adv* por onde. <> *npl* paradeiro *m*.

whereas [weər'æz] *conj* enquanto que, ao passo que.

whereby [weə'baɪ] *conj fml* através do (da) qual, pelo(la) qual.

wheresoever *conj* & *adv* = **wherever**.

whereupon [,weərə'pɒn] *conj fml* depois do que.

wherever [weər'evə^r] <> *conj* **-1.** [no matter where, everywhere] em todo o lugar que **-2.** [anywhere, in whatever place] onde quer que; **sit ~ you like** senta onde quiser **-3.** [in any situation] sempre que **-4.** [indicating ignorance]: **~ that is** seja lá onde for. <> *adv* **-1.** [indicating surprise] onde é que **-2.** [indicating lack of precision] em qualquer lugar.

wherewithal ['weəwɪðɔ:l] *n fml*: **to have the ~ to do sthg** dispor dos meios necessários para fazer algo.

whet [wet] (*pt* & *pp* **-ted**, *cont* **-ting**) *vt*: **to ~ sb's appetite (for sthg)** despertar o interesse de alguém (por algo).

whether ['weðə^r] *conj* **-1.** [indicating choice, doubt] se **-2.** [no matter if]: **~ I want to or not** queira ou não queira.

whew [hwju:] *excl* uau!

whey *n (U)* soro *m* do leite.

which [wɪtʃ] <> *adj* [in questions] qual, que; **~ room do you want?** qual é o quarto que você quer?, que quatro você quer?; **~ one?** qual (deles)?; **she asked me ~ room I wanted** ela perguntou-me qual *OR* que quarto eu queria <> *pron* **-1.** [in questions] qual; **~ one is the cheapest?** qual é o mais barato?; **~ one do you prefer?** qual (é o que) você prefere?; **he asked me ~ one I preferred** ele perguntou-me qual é que eu preferia **-2.** [introducing relative clause: subject]: **I can't remember ~ was better** não me lembro qual era o melhor **-3.** [introducing relative clause: object, after prep] que; **the sofa on ~ I'm sitting** o sofá em que estou sentado **-4.** [to refer back to a clause] o que; **he's late, ~ annoys me** ele está atrasado, o que me aborrece; **he's always late, ~ I don't like** ele está sempre atrasado, coisa que eu detesto

whichever [wɪtʃ'evə^r] <> *adj* **-1.** [no matter which]: **~ route you take** por qualquer dos caminhos que você for **-2.** [the one which]: **~ colour you prefer** a cor que preferir. <> *pron* **-1.** [the one which] o (a) que, os (as) que **-2.** [no matter which one] qualquer um(ma).

whiff [wɪf] *n* **-1.** [smell] cheirinho *m* **-2.** *fig* [sign] cheiro *m*.

while [waɪl] <> *n* algum tempo *m*; **it's a long ~ since I did that** faz muito tempo que não faço isso; **for a ~** por algum tempo; **after a ~** depois de algum tempo; **to be worth one's ~** valer a pena para alguém. <> *conj* **-1.** [as long as, during the time that] enquanto **-2.** [whereas] enquanto (que), ao passo que.

◆ **while away** *vt sep* passar o tempo *(de forma agradável)*.

whilst [waɪlst] *conj* = **while**.

whim [wɪm] *n* capricho *m*.

whimper ['wɪmpə^r] <> *n* choradeira *f*. <> *vt* lamuriar-se. <> *vi* choramingar.

whimsical ['wɪmzɪkl] *adj* **-1.** [idea, story] fantasioso(sa) **-2.** [look] estranho(nha) **-3.** [remark] esquisito(ta).

whine [waɪn] <> *n* **-1.** [child] gemido *m* **-2.** [dog] ganido *m* **-3.** [siren] grito *m* **-4.** [engine] zunido *m*. <> *vi* **-1.** [child] gemer **-2.** [dog] ganir **-3.** [siren] gritar **-4.** [engine] zunir **-5.** [complain]: **to ~ (about sb/sthg)** queixar-se (de alguém/algo).

whinge [wɪndʒ] (*cont* **whingeing**) *vi UK*: **to ~ (about sb/sthg)** queixar-se (de alguém/algo).

whip [wɪp] (*pt* & *pp* **-ped**, *cont* **-ping**) <> *n* **-1.** [for hitting] chicote *m* **-2.** *UK POL membro do partido político responsável por fazer com que seus correligionários compareçam a votações importantes no parlamento.* <> *vt* **-1.** [beat with whip] chicotear **-2.** *fig* [subj: rain, wind] açoitar **-3.** [take quickly]: **to ~ sthg out/off** arrancar algo de **-4.** *CULIN* bater.

◆ **whip up** *vt sep* [provoke] incitar.

whiplash injury ['wɪplæʃ-] *n* lesão *f* por efeito chicote.

whipped cream [wɪpt-] *n* creme *m* batido.

whippet ['wɪpɪt] *n* galgo *m*.

whip-round *n UK inf*: **to have a ~** fazer uma vaquinha.

whirl [wɜ:l] <> *n* **-1.** [rotating movement] redemoinho *m*; **to be in a ~** estar totalmente confuso(sa) **-2.** *fig* [flurry, round] turbilhão *m*, agitação *f* **-3.** *phr*: **let's give it a ~** *inf* vamos tentar. <> *vt*: **to ~**

sb/sthg round rodopiar alguém/algo. ◇ *vi* **-1.** [move around] rodopiar **-2.** *fig* [be confused, excited] dar voltas.

whirlpool ['wɜːlpuːl] *n* redemoinho *m*.

whirlwind ['wɜːlwɪnd] ◇ *adj fig* vertiginoso(sa). ◇ *n* furacão *m*.

whirr [wɜː^r] ◇ *n* zumbido *m*. ◇ *vi* zumbir.

whisk [wɪsk] ◇ *n* CULIN batedeira *f*. ◇ *vt* **-1.** [put or take quickly - away]: **to ~ sb/sthg away** levar alguém/algo rapidamente; [- out]: **to ~ sthg out** tirar algo rapidamente **-2.** CULIN bater.

whisker ['wɪskə^r] *n* [of animal] bigode *m*.

◆ **whiskers** *npl* [of man] suíças *fpl*.

whiskey (*pl* **whiskeys**) *n* uísque *m* (de cevada).

whisky *UK* (*pl* **-ies**), **whiskey** *US* & *Irish* (*pl* **-s**) ['wɪskɪ] *n* uísque *m*.

whisper ['wɪspə^r] ◇ *n* sussurro *m*, cochicho *m*. ◇ *vt* sussurrar, cochichar. ◇ *vi* sussurrar, cochichar.

whispering ['wɪspərɪŋ] *n (U)* cochichos *mpl*, sussurros *mpl*.

whist [wɪst] *n (U)* uíste *m*.

whistle ['wɪsl] ◇ *n* **-1.** [gen] apito *m* **-2.** [through lips] assobio *m* **-3.** [of bird] piado *m*, pio *m* **-4.** [of kettle] chiar *m*. ◇ *vt* assobiar. ◇ *vi* **-1.** [gen] assobiar; **to ~ at sb** assobiar para alguém **-2.** [using whistle] apitar **-3.** [bird] piar **-4.** [kettle] chiar.

whistle-stop tour *n percurso rápido com várias paradas no caminho*.

whit *n*: **not a ~** nem um pouco.

Whit [wɪt] *n UK* Pentecostes *m*.

white [waɪt] ◇ *adj* **-1.** [gen] branco(ca); **to go** OR **turn ~** [hair] ficar branco(ca); [face] empalidecer **-2.** [milky] com leite. ◇ *n* **-1.** [gen] branco *m* **-2.** [person] branco *m*, -ca *f* **-3.** [of egg] clara *f*.

◆ **whites** *npl* roupas *fpl* brancas.

white blood cell *n* glóbulo *m* branco.

whiteboard ['waɪtbɔːd] *n* quadro *m* branco.

white Christmas *n* Natal *m* com neve.

white-collar *adj* de colarinho branco.

white elephant *n fig* elefante *m* branco.

white goods *npl* [household machines] eletrodomésticos *mpl*.

white-haired [-'heəd] *adj* de cabelos brancos.

Whitehall ['waɪthɔːl] *n* Whitehall.

WHITEHALL

Nessa rua de Londres encontram-se os principais órgãos da administração britânica. Por extensão, o termo é empregado também para designar o aparato administrativo britânico.

white horses *npl UK* [on sea] crista *f* da onda.

white-hot *adj* incandescente.

White House *n*: **the ~** a Casa Branca.

WHITE HOUSE

A Casa Branca é a residência oficial e o local de trabalho do presidente dos Estados Unidos da América. Ela se situa na cidade de Washington, capital do país e sede do governo federal. A Casa Branca é um símbolo tanto da presidência quanto do poder executivo estadunidense.

white knight *n pessoa ou organização que auxilia uma empresa em dificuldades*.

white lie *n* mentira *f* branca.

white light *n* luz *f* branca.

white magic *n (U)* magia *f* branca.

white meat *n (U)* carne *f* branca.

whiten ['waɪtn] ◇ *vt* **-1.** [clothes] branquear **-2.** [shoes] clarear **-3.** [wall] caiar. ◇ *vi* branquear.

whitener ['waɪtnə^r] *n* **-1.** [for clothes] alvejante *m* **-2.** [for shoes] branqueador *m*.

whiteness ['waɪtnɪs] *n (U)* brancura *f*.

white noise *n* ruído *m* branco.

whiteout ['waɪtaʊt] *n perda total de visibilidade devido à neve*, whiteout *m*.

white paper *n* POL relatório *m* oficial do governo.

white sauce *n (U)* molho *m* branco.

White Sea *n*: **the ~** o Mar Branco.

white spirit *n (U) UK* aguarrás *f inv*.

white-tie *adj* de gala.

white trash *n US pej* [people] branquelo *m*, -la *f*.

whitewash ['waɪtwɒʃ] ◇ *n* **-1.** *(U)* [paint] (água *f* de) cal *f* **-2.** *pej* [cover-up] disfarce *m*. ◇ *vt* **-1.** [paint] caiar, pintar com cal **-2.** *pej* [cover up] disfarçar.

whitewater rafting ['waɪt,wɔːtə^r-] *n* rafting *m*.

white wedding *n* casamento *m* tradicional.

whiting ['waɪtɪŋ] (*pl inv* OR **-s**) *n* merlúcio *m*.

Whit Monday *n* segunda-feira *f* de Pentecostes.

Whitsun ['wɪtsn] *n* [day] Pentecostes *m inv*.

whittle ['wɪtl] *vt*: **to ~ sthg away** OR **down** reduzir algo gradualmente.

whiz (*pt* & *pp* **-zed**, *cont* **-zing**), **whizz** [wɪz] ◇ *n inf*: **to be a ~ at sthg** ser uma fera em algo. ◇ *vi* passar zunindo.

whiz(z) kid *n inf* (menino *m*) prodígio *m*, (menina *f*) prodígia *f*.

who [huː] *pron* **-1.** *(in direct, indirect questions)* quem **-2.** *(in relative clauses)* que.

WHO (*abbr of* **World Health Organization**) *n* OMS *f*.

who'd [huːd] = **who had**, **who would**.

whodu(n)nit [,huː'dʌnɪt] *n inf* romance *m* policial.

whoever [huː'evə^r] *pron* **-1.** [gen] quem quer que; **I don't like him, ~ he is** não gosto dele, quem quer que ele seja **-2.** [indicating surprise] quem será que; **~ can that be?** quem poderá ser?

whole [həʊl] ◇ *adj* **-1.** [entire, complete] inteiro(ra) **-2.** [for emphasis]: **a ~ lot of** muitos e muitos, muitas e muitas, ; **a ~ lot bigger** muitíssimo maior. ◇ *adv* [for emphasis] totalmente. ◇ *n* **-1.** [all, entirety]: **the ~ of the summer** o verão todo **-2.** [unit, complete thing] todo *m*.

◆ **as a whole** *adv* como um todo.

◆ **on the whole** *adv* em geral.

wholefood ['həʊlfuːd] *n UK* comida *f* integral.

whole-hearted [-'hɑːtɪd] *adj* sincero(ra).

wholemeal *UK* ['həʊlmiːl], **whole wheat** *US adj* integral.

wholemeal bread *n UK* pão *m* integral.

whole note *n US* semibreve *f*.

wholesale ['həʊlseɪl] ◇ *adj* **-1.** [bulk] por atacado **-2.** *pej* [excessive - slaughter] exagerado(da); [- destruction] em massa, em grande escala; [- theft]

indiscriminado(da). <> *adv* **-1.** [in bulk] por atacado **-2.** *pej* [excessively] indiscriminadamente.
wholesaler ['həʊl,seɪləʳ] *n* atacadista *mf*.
wholesome ['həʊlsəm] *adj* saudável.
whole wheat *adj US* = **wholemeal**.
who'll [hu:l] = **who will**.
wholly ['həʊlɪ] *adv* totalmente, completamente.
whom [hu:m] *pron fml* **-1.** *(in direct, indirect questions)* quem **-2.** *(in relative clauses)* que; **to** ~ a quem.
whoop [wu:p] <> *n* grito *m*; **a** ~ **of glee** um grito de alegria. <> *vi* gritar.
whoopee [wʊ'pi:] *excl* hip hurra!
whooping cough ['hu:pɪŋ-] *n (U)* coqueluche *f*.
whoops [wʊps] *excl* opa!
whoosh [wʊʃ] *inf* <> *n* [sudden rush - of air] rajada *f*; [- of water] esguicho *m*. <> *vi* **-1.** [air] soprar forte **-2.** [water] esguichar.
whop *(pt & pp* **-ped**, *cont* **-ping**) *vt inf* [defeat] derrubar, derrotar.
whopper ['wɒpəʳ] *n inf* **-1.** [something big] exagero *m* **-2.** [lie] mentira *f* deslavada.
whopping ['wɒpɪŋ] *inf* <> *adj* tremendo(da), enorme. <> *adv*: **a** ~ **great lie** uma mentira enorme.
whore [hɔ:ʳ] *n pej* puta *f*, vagabunda *f*.
who're ['hu:əʳ] = **who are**.
whose [hu:z] <> *pron* de quem <> *adj* **-1.** *(in direct, indirect questions)* de quem; ~ **book is this?** de quem é este livro? **-2.** *(in relative clauses)* cujo(ja).
whosoever [,hu:səʊ'evəʳ] *pron literary*: ~ **it is** quem quer que seja, seja quem for.
who's who [hu:z-] *n* [book] quem é quem *m*, *livro contendo informações sobre as pessoas mais ricas e famosas do mundo*.
who've [hu:v] = **who have**.
why [waɪ] <> *adv & conj* porque; ~ **not?** porque não?; **I know** ~ **Tom isn't here** eu sei porque é que o Tom não está; **tell me** ~ (diga-me) porquê.
WI <> *n* (*abbr of* **Women's Institute**) *associação britânica de mulheres que se reúnem para atividades sociais e culturais, principalmente em áreas rurais*. <> **-1.** *abbr of* **West Indies -2.** *abbr of* **Wisconsin**.
wick [wɪk] *n* **-1.** pavio *m* **-2.** *phr*: **to get on sb's** ~ *UK inf* dar nos nervos de alguém.
wicked ['wɪkɪd] *adj* **-1.** [evil] malvado(da) **-2.** [mischievous, devilish] perverso(sa) **-3.** *inf* [very good] bárbaro(ra).
wickedness *n* **-1.** [evil] maldade *f* **-2.** [mischievousness] perversidade *f*.
wicker ['wɪkəʳ] *adj* de vime.
wickerwork ['wɪkəwɜ:k] <> *n (U)* trabalho *m* em vime. <> *comp* de vime.
wicket ['wɪkɪt] *n* CRICKET **-1.** [stumps] meta *f* **-2.** [pitch] wicket *m* **-3.** [dismissal] demissão *f* do batedor.
wicket keeper *n* guarda-meta *mf*.
wide [waɪd] <> *adj* **-1.** [gen] largo(ga); **it's 6 metres** ~ tem 6 metros de largura; **how** ~ **is the room?** qual é a largura da sala? **-2.** [eyes] arregalado(da) **-3.** [coverage, selection] amplo(pla) **-4.** [implications, issues] maior **-5.** [shot, punch, ball] desviado(da). <> *adv* **-1.** [as far as possible] amplamente; **open** ~! abra bem! **-2.** [off-target]: **to go** ~ desviar-se.
wide-angle lens *n* PHOT (objetiva *f*) grande-angular *f*.
wide-awake *adj* desperto(ta), bem acordado(-da).
wide boy *n UK inf pej* pilantra *m*.
wide-eyed [-'aɪd] *adj* **-1.** [surprised, frightened] de olhos arregalados **-2.** [innocent, gullible] ingênuo(-nua).
widely ['waɪdlɪ] *adv* **-1.** [gen] muito; ~ **known** amplamente conhecido(da) **-2.** [considerably] bastante.
widen ['waɪdn] <> *vt* **-1.** [make broader] alargar **-2.** [increase scope or variety of] ampliar **-3.** [gap, difference] aumentar. <> *vi* **-1.** [become broader] alargar **-2.** [increase in scope or variety] estender **-3.** [eyes] arregalar **-4.** [gap, difference] aumentar.
wide open *adj* **-1.** [window, door] escancarado(da) **-2.** [eyes] arregalado(da) **-3.** [spaces] extenso(sa).
wide-ranging [-'reɪndʒɪŋ] *adj* de amplo alcance.
widescreen TV ['waɪdskri:n-] *n* tv *f* widescreen.
widespread ['waɪdspred] *adj* disseminado(da), geral.
widow ['wɪdəʊ] *n* viúva *f*.
widowed ['wɪdəʊd] *adj* viúvo(va).
widower ['wɪdəʊəʳ] *n* viúvo *m*.
width [wɪdθ] *n* **-1.** [breadth] largura *f*; **in** ~ de largura **-2.** [in swimming pool] largura *f*; **she swam 20** ~**s** ela nadou 20 piscinas.
widthways ['wɪdθweɪz] *adv* na transversal, transversalmente.
wield [wi:ld] *vt* **-1.** [weapon] manejar **-2.** [power] controlar, exercer.
wife [waɪf] (*pl* **wives**) *n* esposa *f*.
wig [wɪg] *n* peruca *f*.
wiggle ['wɪgl] *inf* <> *n* **-1.** [movement] balanço *m* **-2.** [wavy line] linha *f* ondulada. <> *vt* balançar, agitar. <> *vi* balançar.
wiggly ['wɪglɪ] (*compar* **-ier**, *superl* **-iest**) *adj inf* **-1.** [wavy] ondulado(da) **-2.** [movable] solto(ta).
wigwam ['wɪgwæm] *n* tenda *f* indígena *(em forma de cone)*.
wild [waɪld] <> *adj* **-1.** [animal, land] selvagem **-2.** [person, dog, attack] violento(ta) **-3.** [plant] silvestre **-4.** [scenery, landscape] agreste **-5.** [sea] revolto(ta) **-6.** [weather] turbulento(ta) **-7.** [laughter, crowd, applause] frenético(ca); **the crowd went** ~ a multidão foi à loucura; **to run** ~ descontrolar-se **-8.** [hair] desarrumado(da) **-9.** [eyes, features] inquieto(-ta) agitado(ta) **-10.** [dream, scheme] maluco(ca) **-11.** [estimate]: **a** ~ **guess** uma vaga idéia **-12.** *inf* [very enthusiastic]: **to be** ~ **about sthg** ser louco(ca) por algo. <> *n*: **in the** ~ na natureza, em seu habitat natural.
◆ **wilds** *npl*: **the** ~**s** as regiões selvagens.
wild card *n* COMPUT **-1.** curinga *m* **-2.** [person]: **to be a** ~ ser completamente imprevisível.
wildcat ['waɪldkæt] *n* gato-mourisco *m*.
wildcat strike *n* greve-relâmpago *f*.
wildebeest ['wɪldɪbi:st] (*pl inv* OR **-s**) *n* gnu *m*.
wilderness ['wɪldənɪs] *n* **-1.** [barren land] sertão *m* **-2.** [overgrown land] matagal *m* **-3.** *fig* [unimportant place]: **in the political** ~ no ostracismo político.
wildfire ['waɪld,faɪəʳ] *n*: **to spread like** ~

espalhar-se como fogo na mata.

wild flower *n* flor *f* silvestre.

wildfowl *n* aves *fpl* silvestres.

wild-goose chase *n inf* busca *m* infrutífera.

wildlife ['waɪldlaɪf] *n (U)* fauna *f*.

wildly ['waɪldlɪ] *adv* **-1.** [enthusiastically, fanatically] freneticamente **-2.** [without reason or control] inadvertidamente **-3.** [very] extremamente **-4.** [menacingly] ameaçadoramente.

wild rice *n (U)* arroz *m* silvestre.

wild west *n inf*: **the ~** o oeste selvagem.

wiles [waɪlz] *npl* artimanhas *fpl*.

wilful *UK*, **willful** *US* ['wɪlfʊl] *adj* **-1.** [determined] que sempre apronta das suas **-2.** [deliberate] proposital, intencional.

will¹ [wɪl] ◇ *n* **-1.** [wish, desire] vontade *f*; **against my ~** contra a minha vontade **-2.** [document] testamento *m*.

will² [wɪl] *aux vb* **-1.** [expressing future tense]: **it ~ be difficult to repair** vai ser difícil de consertar; **~ you be here next Friday?** você vai estar aqui na próxima sexta?; **I ~ see you next week** vejo-lhe para a semana; **yes I ~** sim; **no I won't** não. **-2.** [expressing willingness]: **I won't do it** recuso-me a fazê-lo. **-3.** [expressing polite question]: **~ you have some more tea?** você quer mais um chá? **-4.** [in commands, requests]: **~ you please be quiet!** pode ficar calado, por favor!; **close that window, ~ you?** feche a janela, por favor.

willful *adj US* = **wilful**.

willing ['wɪlɪŋ] *adj* **-1.** [prepared] disposto(ta); **to be ~ to do sthg** estar disposto(ta) a fazer algo **-2.** [eager] prestativo(va).

willingly ['wɪlɪŋlɪ] *adv* de bom grado.

willingness ['wɪlɪŋnɪs] *n* **-1.** [preparedness] disposição *f*, boa vontade *f*; **~ to do sthg** disposição para fazer algo **-2.** [keenness] determinação *f*, ânsia *f*.

willow (tree) ['wɪləʊ-] *n* salgueiro *m*.

willowy ['wɪləʊɪ] *adj* longilíneo(nea).

willpower ['wɪl,paʊəʳ] *n (U)* força *f* de vontade.

willy ['wɪlɪ] (*pl* **-ies**) *n UK inf* piu-piu *m*.

willy-nilly [,wɪlɪ'nɪlɪ] *adv* **-1.** [at random] ao acaso **-2.** [wanting to or not] quer queria quer não.

wilt [wɪlt] *vi* **-1.** [plant] murchar **-2.** *fig* [person] definhar.

wily ['waɪlɪ] (*compar* **-ier**, *superl* **-iest**) *adj* ardiloso (sa).

wimp [wɪmp] *n inf pej* bunda-mole *mf*.

win [wɪn] (*pt* & *pp* **won**, *cont* **-ning**) ◇ *n* vitória *f*. ◇ *vt* **-1.** [gen] ganhar **-2.** [game, fight, competition] vencer. ◇ *vi* ganhar; **you/I** *etc* **can't ~** não tem jeito.

◆ **win over, win round** *vt sep* convencer.

wince [wɪns] ◇ *vi* contrair-se; **to ~ at sthg** perturbar-se com algo; **to ~ with sthg** retrair-se de algo. ◇ *n* contração *f* de dor.

winch [wɪntʃ] ◇ *n* guindaste *m*. ◇ *vt* levantar OR suspender com guindaste.

Winchester disk *n* COMPUT winchester *m*, disco *m* rígido.

wind¹ [wɪnd] ◇ *n* **-1.** METEOR vento *m* **-2.** *(U)* [breath] fôlego *m*; **to get one's second ~** *fig* recobrar o fôlego **-3.** *(U)* [in stomach] gases *mpl*; **to break ~** *euphemism* soltar gases **-4.** [in orchestra] instrumento *m* de sopro **-5.** *phr*: **to get ~ of sthg** *inf* tomar conhecimento de algo; **to sail close to the ~** andar na corda bamba; **to put the ~ up sb** *inf* fazer alguém tremer nas bases; **it really put the ~ up me** *inf* realmente tremi nas bases. ◇ *vt* **-1.** [knock breath out of] ficar sem fôlego **-2.** *UK* [baby] arrotar.

wind² [waɪnd] (*pt* & *pp* **wound**) ◇ *vt* **-1.** [string, thread] enrolar **-2.** [clock] dar corda em **-3.** *phr*: **to ~ one's way** serpentear. ◇ *vi* [river, road] serpentear.

◆ **wind back** *vt sep* [tape] rebobinar.

◆ **wind down** ◇ *vt sep* **-1.** [car window] baixar **-2.** [business] fechar aos poucos. ◇ *vi* **-1.** [clock] parar **-2.** [relax] espairecer.

◆ **wind forward** *vt sep* [tape] avançar.

◆ **wind on** *vt sep* rebobinar.

◆ **wind up** ◇ *vt sep* **-1.** [finish - meeting] encerrar; [- business] fechar, liquidar **-2.** [clock] dar corda em **-3.** [car window] levantar **-4.** *UK inf* [deliberately annoy] azucrinar **-5.** *inf* [end up]: **to ~ up doing sthg** acabar fazendo algo. ◇ *vi inf* [end up] acabar em.

windbreak ['wɪndbreɪk] *n* quebra-vento *m*.

windcheater *UK* ['wɪnd,tʃi:təʳ], **windbreaker** *US* ['wɪnd,breɪkəʳ] *n dated* japona *f*.

windchill ['wɪndtʃɪl] *n (U)* sensação *m* térmica.

winded ['wɪndɪd] *adj* sem fôlego.

windfall ['wɪndfɔ:l] *n* **-1.** [fruit] fruto *m* caído *(da árvore)* **-2.** [unexpected gift] dinheiro *m* que caiu do céu.

wind farm [wɪnd-] *n* parque *m* eólico.

winding ['waɪndɪŋ] *adj* sinuoso(sa).

wind instrument [wɪnd-] *n* instrumento *m* de sopro.

windmill ['wɪndmɪl] *n* moinho *m* de vento.

window ['wɪndəʊ] *n* **-1.** [gen] janela *f* **-2.** [of shop] vitrina *f* **-3.** [free time] tempo *m* livre.

window box *n* floreira *f* de janela.

window cleaner *n* limpador *m* de vidros.

window display *n* vitrina *f*.

window dressing *n* **-1.** [in shop] decoração *m* de vitrina **-2.** *fig* [non-essentials] fachada *f*.

window envelope *n* envelope *m* de janela.

window frame *n* caixilho *m* de janela.

window ledge *n* parapeito *m*.

windowpane *n* vidraça *f*.

window shade *n US* persiana *f*.

window-shopping *n (U)*: **to go ~** ir olhar vitrinas.

window sill *n* parapeito *m*.

windpipe ['wɪndpaɪp] *n* traquéia *f*.

windscreen *UK* ['wɪndskri:n], **windshield** *US* ['wɪndʃi:ld] *n* pára-brisa *m*.

windscreen washer *n* lavador *m* de pára-brisa.

windscreen wiper *n* limpador *m* de pára-brisa.

windshield *n US* = **windscreen**.

windsock ['wɪndsɒk] *n* biruta *f*.

windsurfer ['wɪnd,sɜ:fəʳ] *n* **-1.** [person] windsurfista

mf **-2.** [board] prancha *f* de windsurfe.
windsurfing ['wɪnd,sɜ:fɪŋ] *n (U)* windsurfe *m*; **to go ~** praticar windsurfe.
windswept ['wɪndswept] *adj* **-1.** [scenery] varrido(-da) ao vento **-2.** [person, hair] em desalinho.
wind tunnel [wɪnd-] *n* tunel *m* aerodinâmico.
wind turbine [wɪnd-] *n* turbina *f* eólica.
windy ['wɪndɪ] (*compar* **-ier**, *superl* **-iest**) *adj* **-1.** [weather, day] de muito vento; **it's ~** está ventando **-2.** [place] exposto(ta) ao vento.
wine [waɪn] *n* vinho *m*; **red/rosé/white ~** vinho tinto/rosé/branco.
wine bar *n UK* cantina *f*.
wine bottle *n* garrafa *f* de vinho.
wine box *n* garrafão *m* de vinho.
wine cellar *n* adega *f*.
wineglass ['waɪnglɑ:s] *n* copo *m* de vinho.
wine list *n* carta *f* de vinhos.
wine merchant *n UK* mercador *m*, -ra *f* de vinhos.
winepress ['waɪnpres] *n* lagar *m*.
wine rack *n* suporte *m* para vinhos.
wine tasting [-,teɪstɪŋ] *n (U)* degustação *f* de vinhos.
wine waiter *n* sommelier *m*.
wing [wɪŋ] *n* **-1.** [gen] asa *f* **-2.** [of car] flanco *m* **-3.** [of building, organization] ala *f*.
◆ **wings** *npl* THEATRE: **the ~s** os bastidores.
wing commander *n UK* tenente-coronel *m (de aviação)*.
winger ['wɪŋə^r] *n* SPORT ala *f*; **left-~** ponta-esquerda *mf*; **right-~** ponta-direita *mf*.
wing nut *n* porca *f* borboleta.
wingspan ['wɪŋspæn] *n* envergadura *f*.
wink [wɪŋk] ◇ *n* [of eye] piscada *f*; **to have forty ~s** *inf* tirar uma soneca; **not to sleep a ~**, **not to get a ~ of sleep** *inf* não pregar o olho. ◇ *vi* **-1.** [eye] piscar, pestanejar; **to ~ at sb** piscar para alguém **-2.** *literary* [lights] cintilar.
winkle ['wɪŋkl] *n* caramujo *m*.
◆ **winkle out** *vt sep* **-1.** [remove] arrancar **-2.** *fig* [extract]: **to ~ sthg out of sb** arrancar algo de alguém.
winner ['wɪnə^r] *n* **-1.** [person] vencedor *m*, -ra *f*, ganhador *m*, -ra *f* **-2.** *inf* [success] vencedor *m*, -ra *f*; **to be onto a ~** ser bem-sucedido(da).
winning ['wɪnɪŋ] *adj* **-1.** [victorious, successful] vencedor(ra), vitorioso(sa) **-2.** [pleasing] encantador(ra).
◆ **winnings** *npl* ganhos *mpl (de aposta)*.
winning post *n* meta *f*.
Winnipeg *n* Winnipeg.
winsome ['wɪnsəm] *adj literary* encantador(ra).
winter ['wɪntə^r] ◇ *n* inverno *m*; **in ~** no inverno. ◇ *comp* de inverno.
winter sports *npl* esportes *mpl* de inverno.
wintertime ['wɪntətaɪm] *n (U)* inverno *m*; **in ~** no inverno.
wint(e)ry ['wɪntrɪ] *adj* invernal, de inverno.
wipe [waɪp] ◇ *n* [clean]: **to give sthg a ~** dar uma limpada em algo. ◇ *vt* **-1.** [rub to clean] limpar, passar um pano em **-2.** [rub to dry] secar.
◆ **wipe away** *vt sep* [tears] enxugar.
◆ **wipe out** *vt sep* **-1.** [erase] limpar **-2.** [kill] aniquilar **-3.** [eradicate] erradicar.
◆ **wipe up** ◇ *vt sep* **-1.** [dirt, mess] limpar **-2.** [water] secar. ◇ *vi* limpar.
wiper ['waɪpə^r] *n* [windscreen wiper] limpador *m* de pára-brisa.
wire ['waɪə^r] ◇ *n* **-1.** *(U)* [metal] cabo *m*, fio *m* **-2.** [length of wire] fio *m* **-3.** *US* [telegram] telegrama *m*. ◇ *comp* de arame. ◇ *vt* **-1.** [fasten, connect]: **to ~ sthg to sthg** ligar algo em algo **-2.** ELEC ligar à rede elétrica; **he ~d the whole house himself** ele mesmo fez a instalação elétrica da casa **-3.** *US* [send telegram to] passar um telegrama para.
◆ **wire up** *vt sep* [house] fazer a instalação elétrica.
wire brush *n* escova *f* de aço.
wire cutters *npl* alicate *m* de arame.
wireless ['waɪəlɪs] *n dated* radiofone *m*.
wire netting *n (U)* tela *f* de arame.
wire-tapping [-,tæpɪŋ] *n (U)* escuta *f* telefônica.
wire wool *n UK* esponja *f* de aço.
wiring ['waɪərɪŋ] *n (U)* instalação *f* elétrica.
wiry ['waɪərɪ] (*compar* **-ier**, *superl* **-iest**) *adj* **-1.** [hair] eriçado(da) **-2.** [body, man] esguio(guia).
Wisconsin *n* Wisconsin.
wisdom ['wɪzdəm] *n (U)* sabedoria *f*.
wisdom tooth *n* dente *m* do juízo.
wise [waɪz] *adj* sábio(bia); **to get ~ to sthg** *inf* manjar algo; **to be no ~r** OR **none the ~r** continuar sem entender.
◆ **wise up** *vi US* compreender.
wisecrack ['waɪzkræk] *n pej* gafe *f*, mancada *f*.
wisely *adv* sabiamente.
wish [wɪʃ] ◇ *n* **-1.** [desire] desejo *m*; **~ to do sthg** desejo de fazer algo; **~ for sthg** desejo por algo **-2.** [magic request] pedido *m*. ◇ *vt* **-1.** [want]: **to ~ to do sthg** *fml* desejar fazer algo; **to ~ (that)** esperar que **-2.** [desire, request by magic]: **to ~ (that)** desejar que; **I ~ I were rich** ah, se eu fosse rico **-3.** [in greeting]: **to ~ sb sthg** desejar algo a alguém. ◇ *vi* [by magic]: **to ~ for sthg** pedir algo.
◆ **wishes** *npl*: **best ~es** cumprimentos *mpl*, parabéns *mpl*; **(with) best ~es** [at end of letter] com os cumprimentos.
◆ **wish on** *vt sep*: **to ~ sthg on sb** desejar algo para alguém.
wishbone ['wɪʃbəʊn] *n* osso *m* da sorte.
wishful thinking [,wɪʃfʊl-] *n (U)* fantasia *f*, ilusão *f*.
wishy-washy ['wɪʃɪ,wɒʃɪ] *adj inf pej* [vague] sem graça.
wisp [wɪsp] *n* **-1.** [tuft - of hair] mecha *f*, tufo *m*; [- of grass] bola *f* **-2.** [small cloud] nuvem *f*.
wispy ['wɪspɪ] (*compar* **-ier**, *superl* **-iest**) *adj* ralo(la).
wisteria *n* glicínia *f*.
wistful ['wɪstfʊl] *adj* melancólico(ca), triste.
wit [wɪt] *n* **-1.** *(U)* [humour] presença *f* de espírito, gracejo *m* **-2.** [funny person] brincalhão *m*, -na *f* **-3.** [intelligence]: **to have the ~ to do sthg** ter astúcia para fazer algo.
◆ **wits** *npl* [intelligence, mind]: **to have** OR **keep one's ~s about one** manter-se alerta; **to be scared out of one's ~s** *inf* estar morto(ta) de medo;

to be at one's ~s end estar à beira da loucura.
witch [wɪtʃ] *n* bruxa *f*.
witchcraft ['wɪtʃkrɑ:ft] *n (U)* bruxaria *f*.
witchdoctor ['wɪtʃˌdɒktəʳ] *n* curandeiro *m*, -ra *f*.
witch-hazel *n* **-1.** *(U)* [liquid] água *f* de hamamélis **-2.** [tree] hamamélis *f inv*.
witch-hunt *n pej* caça *f* às bruxas.
with [wɪð] *prep* **-1.** [in company of] com; **come ~ me/us** venha comigo/conosco; **can I go ~ you?** posso ir com você?; **we stayed ~ friends** ficamos em casa de amigos. **-2.** [in descriptions] com; **a man ~ a beard** um homem de barba; **a room ~ a bathroom** um quarto com banheiro. **-3.** [indicating means, manner] com; **I washed it ~ detergent** lavei-o com detergente; **they won ~ ease** ganharam com facilidade. **-4.** [indicating emotion] de; **to tremble ~ fear** tremer de medo. **-5.** [regarding] com; **be careful ~ that!** tenha cuidado com isso! **-6.** [indicating opposition] com; **to argue ~ sb** discutir com alguém. **-7.** [indicating covering, contents]: **to fill sthg ~ sthg** encher algo com *OR* de algo; **packed ~ people** cheio de gente; **topped ~ cream** coberto com creme.
withdraw [wɪð'drɔ:] (*pt* **-drew**, *pp* **-drawn**) ◇ *vt* **-1.** [remove] afastar; **to ~ sthg from sthg** remover algo de algo **-2.** *FIN* sacar **-3.** [troops, statement, offer] retirar. ◇ *vi* **-1.** [gen] retirar-se; **to ~ from** retirar-se de; **to ~ to** retirar-se para **-2.** [quit, give up] afastar-se; **to ~ from sthg** afastar-se de algo.
withdrawal [wɪð'drɔ:əl] *n* **-1.** *(U)* [gen] retirada *f*; **~ from sthg** afastamento *m* de algo **-2.** *(U)* [removal] remoção *f* **-3.** *(U)* [retraction] retratação *f* **-4.** *(U) MED* (síndrome *f* da) abstinência *f* **-5.** *FIN* saque *m*.
withdrawal symptoms *npl* síndrome *f* de abstinência.
withdrawn [wɪð'drɔ:n] ◇ *pp* ▻ **withdraw**. ◇ *adj* [shy, quiet] retraído(da).
withdrew [wɪð'dru:] *pt* ▻ **withdraw**.
wither ['wɪðəʳ] ◇ *vt* secar. ◇ *vi* **-1.** [dry up] murchar **-2.** [become weak] debilitar-se.
withered ['wɪðəd] *adj* **-1.** [plant] murcho(cha) **-2.** [skin] seco(ca).
withering ['wɪðərɪŋ] *adj* **-1.** [look] fulminante **-2.** [remark] mordaz.
withhold [wɪð'həʊld] (*pt* & *pp* **-held** [-'held]) *vt* reter.
within [wɪ'ðɪn] ◇ *prep* **-1.** [gen] dentro de **-2.** [less than - distance]: **~ 5 quilometers of London** a menos de 5 quilômetros de Londres; [- time] em menos de. ◇ *adv* dentro.
without [wɪð'aʊt] ◇ *prep* sem; **~ doing sthg** sem fazer algo. ◇ *adv*: **to go** *OR* **do ~ (sthg)** ficar sem (algo).
withstand [wɪð'stænd] (*pt* & *pp* **-stood** [-'stʊd]) *vt* resistir a, agüentar.
witness ['wɪtnɪs] ◇ *n* **-1.** testemunha *f*; **to be ~ to sthg** ser testemunha de algo **-2.** *(U)* [testimony]: **to bear ~ to sthg** [give testimony of] dar testemunho de algo; [be proof of] testemunhar algo. ◇ *vt* **-1.** [see] testemunhar **-2.** [countersign] assinar como testemunha.
witness box *UK*, **witness stand** *US* *n* banco *m* das testemunhas.
witter ['wɪtəʳ] *vi UK inf pej* dizer abobrinhas.
witticism ['wɪtɪsɪzm] *n* sagacidade *f*.
witty ['wɪtɪ] (*compar* **-ier**, *superl* **-iest**) *adj* espirituoso(sa).
wives [waɪvz] *pl* ▻ **wife**.
wizard ['wɪzəd] *n* **-1.** [man with magic powers] feiticeiro *m*, mago *m* **-2.** *fig* [skilled person] gênio *m*.
wizened ['wɪznd] *adj* envelhecido(da).
wk (*abbr of* **week**) semana *f*.
WO (*abbr of* **warrant officer**) *n posto militar*.
wobble ['wɒbl] *vi* **-1.** [chair] cambalear **-2.** [hands] tremer **-3.** [aeroplane] balançar.
wobbly ['wɒblɪ] (*compar* **-ier**, *superl* **-iest**) *adj* **-1.** [table, chair] *inf* bambo(ba) **-2.** [jelly] molenga.
woe [wəʊ] *n literary* lamúria *f*, infortúnio *m*.
wok [wɒk] *n* panela *f* wok.
woke [wəʊk] *pt* ▻ **wake**.
woken ['wəʊkn] *pp* ▻ **wake**.
wolf [wʊlf] (*pl* **wolves**) ◇ *n* **-1.** [animal] lobo *m* **-2.** [man] gavião *m*, paquerador *m*. ◇ *vt inf*: **to ~ sthg (down)** devorar algo.
wolf whistle *n* fiu-fiu *m (para as mulheres)*, assobio *m (para as mulheres)*.
wolves ['wʊlvz] *pl* ▻ **wolf**.
woman ['wʊmən] (*pl* **women**) ◇ *n* mulher *f*. ◇ *comp*: **a ~ doctor** uma doutora; **a ~ governor** uma governadora; **a ~ teacher** uma professora; **a ~ footballer** uma jogadora de futebol; **a ~ prime minister** uma primeira-ministra.
womanhood ['wʊmənhʊd] *n* **-1.** [adult life] maioridade *f* feminina **-2.** [all women] mulheres *fpl*.
womanizer, -iser *n pej* paquerador *m*.
womanly ['wʊmənlɪ] *adj* feminino(na).
womb [wu:m] *n* ventre *m*.
wombat ['wɒmbæt] *n* vombatídeo *m*.
women ['wɪmɪn] *pl* ▻ **woman**.
women's group *n* grupo *m* feminista.
Women's Institute *n UK*: **the ~** *organização de mulheres, especialmente da área rural, que se encontram regularmente e participam de atividades culturais e trabalho social*.
women's lib [-'lɪb] *n inf* libertação *f* da mulher.
women's liberation *n* **-1.** [aim] libertação *f* da mulher **-2.** [movement] movimento *m* pela libertação da mulher.
won [wʌn] *pt* & *pp* ▻ **win**.
wonder ['wʌndəʳ] ◇ *n* **-1.** *(U)* [amazement] espanto *m* **-2.** [cause for surprise]: **it's a ~ (that) ...** é de se admirar que ...; **no** *OR* **little** *OR* **small ~** não é de se admirar **-3.** [amazing thing, person] maravilha *f*; **to work** *OR* **do ~s** realizar milagres. ◇ *vt* **-1.** [speculate] perguntar-se; **to ~ if** *OR* **whether** perguntar -se a si próprio(pria) se **-2.** [in polite requests]: **I ~ whether you would mind shutting the window?** será que você se importaria de fechara janela? ◇ *vi* **-1.** [speculate] perguntar; **why did you ask? - oh, I just ~ed** por que você perguntou isso? - ah, foi só por perguntar; **to ~ about sthg** pensar sobre algo **-2.** *literary* [be amazed]: **to ~ at sthg** admirar-se com algo.
wonderful ['wʌndəfʊl] *adj* maravilhoso(sa).

wonderfully ['wʌndəfʊlɪ] *adv* maravilhosamente.
wonderland ['wʌndəlænd] *n* [fairyland] paraíso *m*.
wonky ['wɒŋkɪ] (*compar* **-ier**, *superl* **-iest**) *adj* ***UK inf*** [wobbly] cambaleante; [crooked] torto(ta).
wont [wəʊnt] <> *adj*: **to be ~ to do sthg** estar acostumado(da) a fazer algo. <> *n* ***dated** or **literary***: **as is one's ~** como é do feitio de alguém.
won't [wəʊnt] = **will not**.
woo [wu:] *vt* **-1.** ***literary*** [court] cortejar **-2.** ***fig*** [try to win over] persuadir.
wood [wʊd] <> *n* **-1.** *(U)* [timber] madeira *f* **-2.** [group of trees] bosque *m*, floresta *f* **-3.** GOLF bastão *m (de madeira)* **-4.** *phr*: **not to see the ~ for the trees** ***UK*** prender-se às partes e não ver o todo; **touch ~!** bata na madeira! <> *comp* de madeira.
◆ **woods** *npl* floresta *f*.
wooded ['wʊdɪd] *adj* arborizado(da).
wooden ['wʊdn] *adj* **-1.** [of wood] de madeira **-2.** ***pej*** [actor] sem expressão.
wooden spoon *n* colher *f* de pau; **to win** OR **get the ~** ***UK fig*** vir na rabeira.
woodland ['wʊdlənd] *n* floresta *f*.
woodlouse (*pl* **-lice**) *n* bicho-de-conta *m*.
woodpecker ['wʊd,pekə^r] *n* pica-pau *m*.
wood pigeon *n* pombo *m* torcaz.
woodshed ['wʊdʃed] *n* depósito *m* para madeira.
woodwind ['wʊdwɪnd] <> *adj* instrumento *m* doce *(de madeira)*. <> *n*: **the ~** os instrumentos doces.
woodwork ['wʊdwɜ:k] *n* **-1.** [wooden objects] obra *f* de madeira **-2.** [craft] carpintaria *f*.
woodworm ['wʊdwɜ:m] *n* caruncho *m*.
woof [wu:f] <> *n* uivo *m*. <> *excl* auu!
wool [wʊl] *n* **-1.** [gen] lã *f* **-2.** *phr*: **he is pulling the ~ over your eyes** ***inf*** ele está te vendendo gato por lebre.
woollen ***UK***, **woolen** ***US*** ['wʊlən] *adj* [garment] de lã.
◆ **woollens** *npl* produtos *mpl* de lã.
woolly ['wʊlɪ] (*compar* **-ier**, *superl* **-iest**, *pl* **-ies**) <> *adj* **-1.** [woollen] de lã, lanoso(sa) **-2.** ***inf*** [fuzzy, unclear] desatinado(da). <> *n* ***inf*** roupas *fpl* de lã.
woolly-headed [-'hedɪd] *adj* ***inf pej*** desatinado (desatina) da.
woozy ['wu:zɪ] (*compar* **-ier**, *superl* **-iest**) *adj* ***inf*** atordoado(da).
Worcester sauce ['wʊstə^r-] *n (U)* molho *m* inglês.
word [wɜ:d] <> *n* **-1.** [gen] palavra *f*; **~ for ~** ao pé da letra; **in other ~s** em outras palavras; **in your own ~s** em suas próprias palavras; **not in so many ~s** não com todas as palavras; **in a ~** em uma palavra; **too ... for ~s** ser extremamente ...; **by ~ of mouth** oralmente; **to put in a (good) ~ for sb** recomendar alguém; **just say the ~** é só avisar; **to have a ~ (with sb)** ter uma palavra (com alguém), falar (com alguém); **to have ~s with sb** ***inf*** bater boca com alguém; **to have the last ~** ter a última palavra; **she doesn't mince her ~s** ela não tem papas na língua; **to weigh one's ~s** medir as palavras; **I couldn't get a ~ in edgeways** eu não pude entrar na conversa; **to give sb one's ~** dar a palavra a alguém; **to be as good as one's ~**, **to be true to one's ~** cumprir bem a palavra **-2.** *(U)* [news] notícias *fpl*. <> *vt* redigir.
word game *n qualquer jogo que envolva a construção ou a seleção de palavras.*
wording ['wɜ:dɪŋ] *n (U)* palavreado *m*.
word-perfect *adj* de cor e salteado.
wordplay ['wɜ:dpleɪ] *n (U)* jogo *m* de palavras.
word processing *n (U)* processamento *m* de texto.
word processor [-'prəʊsesə^r] *n* processador *m* de texto.
wordwrap ['wɜ:dræp] *n* COMPUT marginação *f* automática.
wordy ['wɜ:dɪ] (*compar* **-ier**, *superl* **-iest**) *adj* ***pej*** floreado(da).
wore [wɔ:^r] *pt* ▷ **wear**.
work [wɜ:k] <> *n* **-1.** *(U)* [employment] emprego *m*; **temporary/casual ~** trabalho temporário; **in/out of ~** empregado/desempregado; **at ~** no trabalho **-2.** *(U)* [activity, tasks] trabalho *m*; **at ~** em atividade; **to have one's ~ cut out doing sthg** OR **to do sthg** ser extremamente difícil para alguém fazer algo **-3.** [something made, created, composed] obra *f* **-4.** *phr*: **he's a nasty piece of ~** ***inf*** ele é uma pessoa detestável. <> *vt* **-1.** [person, staff] fazer trabalhar **-2.** [machine] operar **-3.** [shape, manipulate] trabalhar em **-4.** [cultivate] cultivar **-5.** [cause to become]: **to ~ o.s. into sthg** contrair-se em algo **-6.** [make]: **to ~ one's way** [progress physically] avançar; [in career] progredir. <> *vi* **-1.** [do a job] trabalhar **-2.** [function, succeed] funcionar **-3.** [have effect]: **to ~ against sb/sthg** ir contra alguém/algo **-4.** [gradually become] tornar-se; **to ~ loose** soltar-se; **to ~ into a tangle** entrelaçar -se.
◆ **works** <> *n* [factory] usina *f*. <> *npl* **-1.** [mechanism] mecanismo *m* **-2.** [digging, building] obras *fpl* **-3.** ***inf*** [everything]: **the ~s** os aparatos.
◆ **work at** *vt fus* tentar melhorar.
◆ **work off** *vt sep* libertar-se de.
◆ **work on** *vt fus* **-1.** [concentrate on] dedicar-se a **-2.** [take as basis] basear-se em **-3.** [try to persuade] tentar persuadir.
◆ **work out** <> *vt sep* **-1.** [formulate] elaborar **-2.** [calculate] calcular. <> *vi* **-1.** [figure, total]: **to ~ out at** totalizar; **the bill ~s out at £5 a head** a conta dá 5 libras para cada um **-2.** [turn out] surtir efeito **-3.** [be successful] dar certo **-4.** [train, exercise] treinar.
◆ **work up** *vt sep* **-1.** [excite]: **to ~ o.s. up into a frenzy** excitar-se de tal forma **-2.** [generate] gerar.
workable ['wɜ:kəbl] *adj* viável.
workaday ['wɜ:kədeɪ] *adj **pej*** prosaico(ca).
workaholic [,wɜ:kə'hɒlɪk] *n* burro *m* de carga, workaholic *mf*.
workbasket *n* cesta *f* de costura.
workbench ['wɜ:kbentʃ] *n* bancada *f*.
workbook ['wɜ:kbʊk] *n* livro-texto *m*.
workday ['wɜ:kdeɪ] *n* **-1.** [day's work] dia *m* de trabalho **-2.** [not weekend] dia *m* útil.
worked up [,wɜ:kt-] *adj* exaltado(da).

worker ['wɜ:kəʳ] *n* trabalhador *m*, -ra *f*, operário *m*, -ria *f*; **an office ~** um empregado de escritório; **a hard/good ~** um ótimo/bom trabalhador.
workforce ['wɜ:kfɔ:s] *n* força *f* de trabalho.
workhouse ['wɜ:khaʊs] *n* **-1.** *UK* [poorhouse] albergue *m* **-2.** *US* [prison] casa *f* de correção.
working ['wɜ:kɪŋ] *adj* **-1.** [in operation] em operação; **to be ~** estar funcionando **-2.** [having employment - mothers, children] que trabalha; [- population] ativo(va) **-3.** [relating to work] de trabalho.
◆ **workings** *npl* **-1.** [of system, machine] operação *f* **-2.** *fig* [of mind] funcionamento *m*.
working capital *n* **-1.** [assets minus liabilities] capital *m* de giro **-2.** [assets] ativo *m* circulante **-3.** [available money] dinheiro *m* em caixa.
working class *n*: **the ~** a classe operária.
◆ **working-class** *adj* da classe operária.
working day *n* = **workday**.
working group *n* grupo *m* de trabalho.
working knowledge *n* conhecimento *m* de causa.
working man *n* trabalhador *m*.
working model *n* maquete *m*.
working order *n (U)*: **in ~** em funcionamento.
working party *n* grupo *m* de trabalho.
working week *n* semana *f* de trabalho.
work-in-progress *n* trabalho *m* em andamento.
workload ['wɜ:kləʊd] *n* carga *f* de trabalho.
workman ['wɜ:kmən] (*pl* **-men** [-mən]) *n* trabalhador *m*, operário *m*.
workmanship ['wɜ:kmənʃɪp] *n (U)* acabamento *m*.
workmate ['wɜ:kmeɪt] *n* colega *mf* de trabalho.
work of art *n* obra *f* de arte.
workout ['wɜ:kaʊt] *n* treinamento *m*.
work permit [-ˌpɜ:mɪt] *n* visto *m* de trabalho.
workplace ['wɜ:kpleɪs] *n* local *m* de trabalho.
work placement *n* colocação *f* no mercado de trabalho.
workroom ['wɜ:krʊm] *n* sala *f* de trabalho.
works council *n* comissão *f* de trabalhadores.
workshop ['wɜ:kʃɒp] *n* **-1.** [room] oficina *f* **-2.** [building] fábrica *f* **-3.** [discussion] oficina *f*, workshop *f*.
workshy ['wɜ:kʃaɪ] *adj UK* avesso(sa) ao trabalho.
workstation ['wɜ:kˌsteɪʃn] *n* COMPUT estação *f* de trabalho.
work surface *n* superfície *f* de trabalho.
worktable ['wɜ:kˌteɪbl] *n* mesa *f* de trabalho.
worktop ['wɜ:ktɒp] *n UK* superfície *f* de trabalho.
work-to-rule *n UK* paralisação *f* de trabalho extra.
world [wɜ:ld] <> *n* **-1.** [gen] mundo *m*; **to be dead to the ~** estar ferrado(da) no sono; **the best of both ~s** o melhor de dois mundos; **the ~** o mundo; **how/what/in the ~ ...?** como/o que é que ..., pelo amor de Deus?; **where/why in the ~ ...?** onde/por que diabos ...?; **the ~ over** no mundo inteiro **-2.** [great deal]: **to think the ~ of sb** ter grande afeição por alguém; **to do one the ~ of good** fazer alguém se sentir extremamente feliz; **a ~ of difference** toda uma diferença. <> *comp* mundial.
World Bank *n*: **the ~** o Banco Mundial.
world-class *adj* muito superior(ra).
World Cup FTBL <> *n*: **the ~** a Copa do Mundo. <> *comp* da Copa do Mundo.
world-famous *adj* famoso(sa) no mundo todo.
worldly ['wɜ:ldlɪ] *adj* mundano(na); **~ goods** coisas mundanas.
world music *n (U)* música *f* mundial.
world power *n* força *f* OR potência *f* mundial.
World Series *n US*: **the ~** o Campeonato Nacional de Beisebol.

WORLD SERIES

A *World Series* é a grande final do campeonato norte-americano de beisebol. Ela é disputada em até sete partidas, nas quais, ao final da temporada, se enfrentam os campeões das duas mais importantes ligas do país: a *National League* e a *American League*. O campeão será o time que primeiro obtiver quatro vitórias. Trata-se de um dos mais importantes acontecimentos esportivos anuais do país. Conforme a tradição, a primeira bola do jogo é lançada pelo presidente da República.

World Service *n serviço da BBC que transmite programas de rádio e TV em inglês e em vários idiomas para o mundo todo.*
world-weary *adj* entediado(da).
worldwide ['wɜ:ldwaɪd] <> *adj* mundial. <> *adv* no mundo inteiro.
worm [wɜ:m] <> *n* [animal - in stomach] lombriga *f*, verme *m*; [- earthwork] minhoca *f*. <> *vt*: **to ~ one's way** mover-se; **to ~ one's way into sb's confidence** engambelar alguém.
◆ **worms** *npl* vermes *mpl*.
◆ **worm out** *vt sep*: **to ~ sthg out of sb** arrancar algo de alguém.
worn [wɔ:n] <> *pp* ▷ **wear**. <> *adj* **-1.** [threadbare] surrado(da) **-2.** [tired] exausto(ta).
worn-out *adj* **-1.** [old, threadbare] usado(da), gasto(ta) **-2.** [tired] exausto(ta).
worried ['wʌrɪd] *adj* preocupado(da); **to be ~ about sb/sthg** estar preocupado(da) com alguém/algo; **to be ~ sick** estar profundamente preocupado(da).
worrier ['wʌrɪəʳ] *n*: **he's a terrible ~** ele se preocupa com tudo.
worry ['wʌrɪ] (*pl* **-ies**, *pt* & *pp* **-ied**) <> *n* **-1.** *(U)* [feeling] preocupação *f* **-2.** [problem] problema *m*. <> *vt* [cause to be troubled] preocupar. <> *vi* preocupar-se; **to ~ about sb/sthg** preocupar-se com alguém/algo; **not to ~!** nada com o que se preocupar!
worrying ['wʌrɪɪŋ] *adj* preocupante.
worse [wɜ:s] <> *adj* pior; **to get ~** piorar. <> *adv* pior; **~ off** em pior situação. <> *n* pior *m*; **for the ~** para o pior.
worsen ['wɜ:sn] *vt* & *vi* agravar, piorar.
worsening ['wɜ:snɪŋ] *adj* agravante, que piora.
worship ['wɜ:ʃɪp] (*UK pt* & *pp* **-ped**, *cont* **-ping**, *US pt*

& *pp* -**ed**, *cont* -**ing**) ◇ *vt* -**1.** RELIG adorar -**2.** [admire, adore] admirar, adorar. ◇ *n (U)* adoração *f*.

◆ **Worship** *n*: **Your/Her/His Worship** Vossa Excelência.

worshipper *UK*, **worshiper** *US* ['wɜːʃɪpəʳ] *n* -**1.** RELIG devoto *m*, -ta *f* -**2.** [admirer] admirador *m*, -ra *f*.

worst [wɜːst] ◇ *adj* & *adv* pior. ◇ *n*: **the ~** o pior; **if the ~ comes to the ~** se o pior acontecer; **to get the ~ of it** ficar com o pior.

◆ **at (the) worst** *adv* na pior das hipóteses.

worsted ['wʊstɪd] *n (U)* lã *f* penteada.

worth [wɜːθ] ◇ *prep* -**1.** [having the value of] valor *m*; **it's ~ £50** vale £50 -**2.** [deserving of]: **it's ~ going to Brazil** vale a pena ir para a Brasil; **it's ~ a visit** vale a visita; **to be ~ doing sthg** valer a pena fazer algo. ◇ *n* -**1.** [value] valor *m* -**2.** [supply] provisão *f*.

worthless ['wɜːθlɪs] *adj* -**1.** [object] sem valor -**2.** [person] inútil.

worthwhile [ˌwɜːθ'waɪl] *adj* que vale a pena.

worthy ['wɜːðɪ] (*compar* -**ier**, *superl* -**iest**) *adj* -**1.** [deserving of respect] respeitável -**2.** [deserving]: **to be ~ of sthg** ser merecedor(ra) de algo -**3.** *pej* [good but unexciting] adequado(da).

would [wʊd] *modal vb* -**1.** [in reported speech]: **she said she ~ come** ela disse que viria; **he promised he ~ help me** ele prometeu que me ajudaria -**2.** [indicating likely result]: **what ~ you do if he phoned?** o que você faria se ele ligasse?; **I doubt she ~ have noticed** duvido que ela percebesse; **if he had lost, he ~ have resigned** se tivesse perdido, ele teria renunciado -**3.** [indicating willingness]: **she ~n't go** ela não queria ir embora; **he ~ do anything for her** ele faria qualquer coisa por ela; **she ~n't give an answer even if ...** ela não teria respondido mesmo que ... -**4.** [in polite questions]: **~ you like a drink?** você gostaria de tomar um drinque?; **~ you mind closing the window?** você poderia fechar a janela, por favor?; **help me shut the door, ~ you?** me ajuda a fechar a porta, por favor? -**5.** [indicating inevitability]: **he ~ say that** não me surpreende que ele tenha dito isso; **I said yes - well, you ~** eu disse sim - bem, era o esperado -**6.** [expressing opinions]: **I ~ have thought that she'd be pleased** eu pensava que ela tivesse gostado; **I ~ prefer a blue one** eu preferia um azul -**7.** [in giving advice]: **I'd report it if I were you** no teu lugar, eu denunciaria -**8.** [describing habitual past actions]: **I ~ go for a walk every evening** eu costumava dar uma caminhada todas as tardes; **we ~ meet and he ~ say...** a gente se encontrava e ele dizia ...

would-be *adj* aspirante.

wouldn't ['wʊdnt] = **would not**.

would've ['wʊdəv] = **would have**.

wound¹ [wuːnd] ◇ *n* ferida *f*, ferimento *m*; **to lick one's ~s** recuperar-se. ◇ *vt* ferir.

wound² [waʊnd] *pt* & *pp* ▷ **wind ²**.

wounded ['wuːndɪd] ◇ *adj* ferido(da). ◇ *npl*: **the ~** os feridos.

wounding ['wuːndɪŋ] *adj* prejudicial.

wove [wəʊv] *pt* ▷ **weave**.

woven ['wəʊvn] *pp* ▷ **weave**.

wow [waʊ] *inf* ◇ *n* estouro *m*. ◇ *vt* empolgar. ◇ *excl* uau!

WP ◇ *n* -**1.** (*abbr of* **word processing**) processamento *m* de textos -**2.** (*abbr of* **word processor**) processador *m* de textos. ◇ (*abbr of* **weather permitting**) se o tempo permitir.

WPC (*abbr of* **woman police constable**) *n policial feminina britânica de posto inferior.*

wpm (*abbr of* **words per minute**) ppm.

WRAC [ræk] (*abbr of* **Women's Royal Army Corps**) *n corporação feminina do exército britânico.*

WRAF [ræf] (*abbr of* **Women's Royal Air Force**) *n corporação feminina da força aérea real britânica.*

wrangle ['ræŋgl] ◇ *n* disputa *f*, briga *f*. ◇ *vi* brigar; **to ~ with sb (over sthg)** discutir com alguém (sobre algo).

wrap [ræp] (*pt* & *pp* -**ped**, *cont* -**ping**) ◇ *vt* -**1.** [cover in paper or cloth] embrulhar; **to ~ sthg in sthg** enrolar algo em algo; **to ~ sthg (a)round sthg** enrolar algo ao redor de algo -**2.** [encircle]: **to ~ sthg (a)round sthg** enrolar algo em algo. ◇ *n* [garment] xale *m*.

◆ **wrap up** ◇ *vt sep* -**1.** [cover in paper or cloth] embrulhar -**2.** *inf* [complete] terminar. ◇ *vi* [put warm clothes on]: **~ up well** OR **warmly!** agasalhe-se bem!

wrapped up [ræpt-] *adj inf*: **to be ~ in sb/sthg** estar afundado(da) em alguém/algo.

wrapper ['ræpəʳ] *n* embalagem *f*.

wrapping ['ræpɪŋ] *n* embrulho *m*, invólucro *m*.

wrapping paper *n (U)* papel *m* de embrulho.

wrath [rɒθ] *n (U) literary* ira *f*.

wreak [riːk] *vt* causar.

wreath [riːθ] *n* coroa *f (de flores)*.

wreathe [riːð] *vt literary* envolver.

wreck [rek] ◇ *n* -**1.** [car, plane] destroços *mpl* -**2.** [ship] restos *mpl* -**3.** *inf* [person] caco *m*. ◇ *vt* -**1.** [break, destroy] destruir -**2.** NAUT [cause to run aground] naufragar -**3.** [spoil, ruin] arruinar.

wreckage ['rekɪdʒ] *n* -**1.** [of plane, car] restos *mpl* -**2.** [of building] escombros *mpl*.

wrecker ['rekəʳ] *n US* reboque *m*.

wren [ren] *n* garriça *f*.

wrench [rentʃ] ◇ *n* -**1.** [tool] chave *f* inglesa -**2.** [injury, twist] torcedura *f*, distensão *f* -**3.** [cause of sadness] tristeza *f*. ◇ *vt* -**1.** [pull violently] arrancar -**2.** [twist and injure] torcer, distender -**3.** [force away] arrebatar; **to ~ sthg away from sthg** varrer algo para longe de algo.

wrest [rest] *vt literary*: **to ~ sthg from sb** extorquir algo de alguém.

wrestle ['resl] ◇ *vt* derrubar. ◇ *vi* -**1.** [fight] lutar; **to ~ with sb** lutar com alguém -**2.** *fig* [struggle]: **to ~ with sthg** lutar contra algo.

wrestler ['resləʳ] *n* lutador *m*, -ra *f* de luta livre.

wrestling ['reslɪŋ] *n (U)* luta *f* livre.

wretch [retʃ] *n* [unhappy person] desgraçado *m*, -da *f*.

wretched ['retʃɪd] *adj* -**1.** [miserable] infeliz -**2.** *inf* [damned] maldito(ta).

wriggle ['rɪgl] ◇ *vt* mexer. ◇ *vi* -**1.** [move about] mexer-se -**2.** [twist] retorcer-se.

◆ **wriggle out of** *vt fus*: **to ~ out of sthg/of doing sthg** safar-se de algo/de fazer algo.

wring [rɪŋ] (*pt* & *pp* **wrung**) *vt* **-1.** [squeeze out water from] torcer **-2.** *literary* [hands] esfregar **-3.** [neck] virar.

◆ **wring out** *vt sep* arrancar.

wringing ['rɪŋɪŋ] *adj*: **~ (wet)** encharcado(da), ensopado(da).

wrinkle ['rɪŋkl] ◇ *n* **-1.** [on skin] ruga *f* **-2.** [in cloth] prega *f*. ◇ *vt* [screw up] enrugar. ◇ *vi* [crease] dobrar-se.

wrinkled ['rɪŋkld], **wrinkly** ['rɪŋklɪ] *adj* **-1.** [skin] enrugado(da) **-2.** [cloth] com prega.

wrist [rɪst] *n* pulso *m*.

wristband ['rɪstbænd] *n* [of watch] pulseira *f*.

wristwatch ['rɪstwɒtʃ] *n* relógio *m* de pulso.

writ [rɪt] *n* mandado *m* judicial.

write [raɪt] (*pt* **wrote**, *pp* **written**) ◇ *vt* **-1.** [gen] escrever; **to ~ sb a letter** escrever uma carta para alguém **-2.** *US* [person] escrever para **-3.** [cheque, prescription] preencher **-4.** *COMPUT* gravar. ◇ *vi* **-1.** [gen] escrever; **to ~ to sb** escrever para alguém **-2.** *COMPUT* gravar.

◆ **write back** ◇ *vt sep* escrever de volta. ◇ *vi* responder.

◆ **write down** *vt sep* anotar.

◆ **write in** *vi* [to radio or TV station, shop] responder.

◆ **write into** *vt sep* [contract] acrescentar.

◆ **write off** ◇ *vt sep* **-1.** [project] cancelar **-2.** [debt, investment] cancelar, reduzir **-3.** [person] descartar **-4.** *UK inf* [vehicle] destroçar. ◇ *vi* [for information] solicitar *(informações)*; **to ~ off to sb/sthg** solicitar informações a alguém; **to ~ off for sthg** solicitar algo.

◆ **write out** *vt sep* [list, names] escrever por extenso.

◆ **write up** *vt sep* [notes] redigir.

write-off *n* [car] perda *f* total.

write-protect *vt COMPUT* proteger contra gravação.

writer ['raɪtə^r] *n* escritor *m*, -ra *f*.

write-up *n inf* crítica *f*.

writhe [raɪð] *vi* contorcer-se.

writing ['raɪtɪŋ] *n* **-1.** [gen] escrita *f*; **I couldn't see the ~** não conseguia ler o que estava escrito; **in ~** por escrito **-2.** [handwriting] caligrafia *f*; **I can't read your ~** não consigo ler o que você escreveu.

◆ **writings** *npl* escritos *mpl*.

writing case *n UK* estojo *m* para escrever.

writing desk *n* escrivaninha *f*.

writing paper *n (U)* papel *m* de carta.

written ['rɪtn] ◇ *pp* ▷ **write**. ◇ *adj* **-1.** [not oral] escrito(ta) **-2.** [official] por escrito.

WRNS (*abbr of* **Women's Royal Naval Service**) *n corporação feminina da marinha real britânica.*

wrong [rɒŋ] ◇ *adj* **-1.** [gen] errado(da); **to be ~ to do sthg** enganar-se ao fazer algo **-2.** [morally bad] feio (feia). ◇ *adv* [incorrectly] errado; **to get sthg ~** enganar-se sobre algo; **to go ~** [make a mistake] errar; [stop functioning] funcionar mal; **don't get me ~** *inf* não me interprete mal. ◇ *n* erro *m*; **to be in the ~** estar equivocado(da). ◇ *vt literary* ofender.

wrong-foot *vt UK* **-1.** *SPORT* fintar **-2.** *fig* [surprise] surpreender.

wrongful ['rɒŋfʊl] *adj* injusto(ta).

wrongly ['rɒŋlɪ] *adv* **-1.** [unsuitably] inadequadamente **-2.** [mistakenly] erroneamente.

wrong number *n* número *m* errado.

wrote [rəʊt] *pt* ▷ **write**.

wrought iron [rɔːt-] *n (U)* ferro *m* forjado.

wrung [rʌŋ] *pt* & *pp* ▷ **wring**.

WRVS (*abbr of* **Women's Royal Voluntary Service**) *n associação de voluntárias britânicas para ajuda a necessitados em emergências.*

wry [raɪ] *adj* **-1.** [amused] entretido(da) **-2.** [displeased] desgostoso(sa).

wt. (*abbr of* **weight**) peso *m*.

WV *abbr of* **West Virginia**.

WW (*abbr of* **world war**) GM *f*.

WWF (*abbr of* **World Wildlife Fund**) *n organização internacional de proteção a plantas, animais selvagens e áreas naturais*, WWF *m*.

WY *abbr of* **Wyoming**.

Wyoming *n* Wyoming.

WYSIWYG ['wɪzɪwɪg] (*abbr of* **what you see is what you get**) *adj* WYSIWYG.

x (*pl* **x's** *OR* **xs**), **X** (*pl* **X's** *OR* **Xs**) [eks] *n* **-1.** [letter] x, X *m* **-2.** [unknown name] X *m* **-3.** [unknown quantity] x *m* **-4.** [in algebra] x *m* **-5.** [at end of letter] beijos *mpl*.

xenophobia [ˌzenə'fəʊbjə] *n (U)* xenofobia *f*.

Xerox® *n* Xerox® *f*.

◆ **xerox** *vt* xerocar.

Xmas ['eksməs] ◇ *n (U)* Natal *m*. ◇ *comp* de Natal.

X-ray ◇ *n* **-1.** [ray] raio *m* X **-2.** [picture] raio-X *m*. ◇ *vt* tirar um raio-X de, tirar uma radiografia de.

xylophone ['zaɪləfəʊn] *n* xilofone *m*.

y (*pl* **y's** *OR* **ys**), **Y** (*pl* **Y's** *OR* **Ys**) [waɪ] *n* [letter] y, Y *m*.
yacht [jɒt] *n* iate *m*.
yachting ['jɒtɪŋ] *n (U)* iatismo *m*.
yachtsman ['jɒtsmən] (*pl* **-men** [-mən]) *n* iatista *m*.
yachtswoman ['jɒts,wʊmən] (*pl* **-women** [-,wɪmɪn]) *n* iatista *f*.
yahoo [,jæ'hu:] *n* brutamontes *mf inv*.
yak [jæk] *n* iaque *m*.
Yale lock® [jeɪl-] *n* fechadura *f* cilíndrica.
yam [jæm] *n* inhame *m*.
Yangon *n* = **Rangoon**.
yank [jæŋk] *vt* arrancar.
Yank [jæŋk] *n UK inf pej* ianque *mf*.
Yankee ['jæŋkɪ] *n* **-1.** *UK inf pej* [American] ianque *mf* **-2.** *US* [northerner] *pessoa oriunda dos Estados do norte*.

YANKEE

Em sua origem, o termo *yankee* referia-se aos imigrantes holandeses que se estabeleceram sobretudo no noroeste dos Estados Unidos. Mais tarde, passou a designar qualquer pessoa proveniente dessa região. Assim, 'ianques' eram chamados os soldados nortistas, durante a Guerra de Secessão nos Estados Unidos. Nos dias atuais, sulistas ainda empregam a palavra em tom pejorativo, para referir-se aos americanos do norte do país.

yap [jæp] (*pt* & *pp* **-ped**, *cont* **-ping**) *vi* **-1.** [dog] ganir, latir **-2.** *pej* [person] tagarelar.
yard [jɑ:d] *n* **-1.** [unit of measurement] jarda *f* **-2.** [walled area] pátio *m* **-3.** [place of work] oficina *f* **-4.** *US* [attached to house] jardim *m*.
yardstick ['jɑ:dstɪk] *n* padrão *m* de medida.
yarn [jɑ:n] *n* **-1.** *(U)* [thread] fio *m* **-2.** *inf* [story] lorota *f*; **to spin sb a ~** contar lorotas para alguém.
yashmak ['jæʃmæk] *n* burca *f*.
yawn [jɔ:n] ◇ *n* **-1.** [when tired] bocejo *m* **-2.** *UK inf* [boring event] chateação *f*. ◇ *vi* **-1.** [when tired] bocejar **-2.** [gape] abrir-se.
yd *abbr of* **yard**.
yeah [jeə] *adv inf* sim; **bring us something to drink - ~, ~!** traz algo para a gente beber - tá, já trago!
year [jɪə^r] *n* ano *m*; **all (the) ~ round** durante todo o ano; **~ in ~ out** entra ano, sai ano.
◆ **years** *npl* [ages] séculos *mpl*.
yearbook ['jɪəbʊk] *n* anuário *m*.
yearling ['jɪəlɪŋ] *n* **-1.** [horse] potro *m* **-2.** [sheep, calves] filhote *m*.
yearly ['jɪəlɪ] ◇ *adj* anual. ◇ *adv* anualmente.
yearn [jɜ:n] *vi*: **to ~ for sthg/to do sthg** ansiar por algo/para fazer algo.
yearning ['jɜ:nɪŋ] *n* ânsia *f*; **~ for sb/sthg** ânsia por alguém/algo.
yeast [ji:st] *n (U)* levedura *f*.
yell [jel] ◇ *n* grito *m*. ◇ *vi* gritar. ◇ *vt* gritar.
yellow ['jeləʊ] ◇ *adj* **-1.** [in colour] amarelo(la) **-2.** *inf* [cowardly] covarde. ◇ *n* amarelo *m*. ◇ *vi* amarelar.
yellow card *n FTBL* cartão *m* amarelo.
yellow fever *n (U)* febre *f* amarela.
yellow lines *n* faixa *f* amarela.
yellowness *n (U)* amarelidão *m*.
Yellow Pages® *n UK*: **the ~** as Páginas Amarelas.
Yellow River *n*: **the ~** o Rio Amarelo.
Yellow Sea *n*: **the ~** o Mar Amarelo.
yelp [jelp] ◇ *n* latido *m*. ◇ *vi* latir.
Yemen ['jemən] *n*: **(the) ~** o Iêmen; **in (the) ~** no Iêmen.
Yemeni ['jemənɪ] ◇ *adj* iemenita. ◇ *n* iemenita *mf*.
yen [jen] (*pl sense 1 inv*) *n* **-1.** [Japanese currency] iene *m* **-2.** [longing]: **to have a ~ for sthg/to do sthg** desejar muito algo/fazer algo.
yeoman of the guard (*pl* **-men of the guard**) *n* membro *m* da guarda real.
yep *adv inf* sim.
yes [jes] ◇ *adv* sim; **~, please** sim, por favor; **to say ~ to sthg** dizer sim para algo. ◇ *n* [vote in favour] sim *m*.
yes-man *n pej* capacho *m*.
yesterday ['jestədɪ] ◇ *n* ontem *m*; **the day before yesterday** anteontem. ◇ *adv* **-1.** [day before today] ontem **-2.** [the past] passado.
yet [jet] ◇ *adv* **-1.** [gen] ainda; **not ~** ainda não **-2.** [up until now] já; **as ~** até agora **-3.** [in the future] até **-4.** [to emphasize number, frequency] mais; **~ again** mais uma vez. ◇ *conj* porém.
yeti *n* ieti *m*.
yew [ju:] *n* teixo *m*.
Y-fronts *npl UK* cueca *f* com abertura na frente.
YHA (*abbr of* **Youth Hostels Association**) *n associação britânica de albergues da juventude*.
Yiddish ['jɪdɪʃ] ◇ *adj* relativo(va) ao iídiche. ◇ *n (U)* iídiche *m*.
yield [ji:ld] ◇ *n* lucro *m*, rendimento *m*. ◇ *vt* **-1.** [produce - fruit, answer, clue] produzir; [- profits, result] gerar **-2.** [give up] ceder. ◇ *vi* **-1.** [open, give way, break] ceder **-2.** *fml* [give up, surrender] render-se; **to ~ to sb/sthg** ceder a alguém/algo.
yippee [*UK* jɪ'pi:, *US* 'jɪpɪ] *excl* iupi!
Y2K (*abbr of* **year two thousand**) *n* ano *m* 2000.
YMCA (*abbr of* **Young Men's Christian Association**) *n* ≃ ACM *f*.
yo *excl inf* oi!
yob(bo) ['jɒb(əʊ)] *n UK inf* bagunceiro *m*, -ra *f*.

yodel ['jəʊdl] (*UK pt* & *pp* **-led**, *cont* **-ling**, *US pt* & *pp* **-ed**, *cont* **-ing**) *vi* cantar à moda dos tiroleses.

yoga ['jəʊgə] *n (U)* ioga *f.*

yoghourt, yoghurt, yogurt [*UK* 'jɒgət, *US* 'jəʊgərt] *n* iogurte *m.*

yoke [jəʊk] *n* **-1.** [for oxen] junta *f* **-2.** *literary* [burden, suffering] jugo *m.*

yokel ['jəʊkl] *n pej* caipira *mf.*

yolk [jəʊk] *n* gema *f.*

yonder ['jɒndə^r] *adv literary* acolá.

Yorkshire pudding ['jɔ:kʃə^r-] *n comida preparada com farinha, ovos e leite, e servida com carne.*

you [ju:] *pron* **-1.** [subject: singular] você, tu; [subject: singular polite form] o senhor (a senhora); [subject: plural] vocês; [subject: plural polite form] os senhores (as senhoras); **do ~ speak Portuguese?** [singular] você fala português?; [polite form] (o senhor) fala português?; **~ Brazilians** vocês brasileiros. **-2.** [direct object: singular] o (a), te; [direct object: singular polite form] o senhor (a senhora); [direct object: plural] os (as), vos; [direct object: plural polite form] os (as), os senhores (as senhoras); **I saw ~** [singular] eu o vi; **can I help ~?** [polite form: singular] em que posso ajudá-lo?; [polite form: plural] em que posso ajudá-los?; **I'll see ~ later** [plural] vejo-os mais tarde. **-3.** [indirect object: singular] lhe, te; [indirect object: singular polite form] lhe; [indirect object: plural] lhes, vos; **I would like to ask ~ something** [polite form: singular] gostaria de perguntar algo a você; **didn't I tell ~ what happened?** [polite form: plural] não lhes contei o que aconteceu? **-4.** [after prep: singular] você, ti; [after prep: singular polite form] o senhor (a senhora), si; [after prep: plural] vocês; [after prep: plural polite form] os senhores (as senhoras), vós; **this is for ~** isto é para você/o senhor, etc; **with ~** [singular] com você, contigo; [singular: polite form] com o senhor (a senhora); [plural] com vocês; [plural: polite form] com os senhores (as senhoras). **-5.** [indefinite use: subject]: **the coffee ~ get in Brazil is very strong** o café que se bebe no Brasil é muito forte; **~ never know** nunca se sabe. **-6.** [indefinite use: object]: **exercise is good for ~** exercício faz bem (para a saúde).

you'd [ju:d] = **you had, you would.**

you'll [ju:l] = **you will.**

young [jʌŋ] ◇ *adj* **-1.** [person] jovem **-2.** [plant, wine, animal] novo(va). ◇ *npl* **-1.** [young people]: **the ~** a juventude **-2.** [baby animals] filhotes *mpl.*

younger *adj* mais novo(va); **Pitt the Younger** Pitt Júnior.

youngish ['jʌŋɪʃ] *adj* bem novo(va).

young man *n* moço *m*, rapaz *m.*

youngster ['jʌŋstə^r] *n* **-1.** [child] filho *m*, -lha *f* **-2.** [young person] jovem *mf.*

young woman *n* moça *f*, rapariga *f.*

your [jɔ:r] *adj* **-1.** [singular subject] o seu (a sua), o teu (a tua); [singular subject: polite form] o/a do senhor (da senhora); [plural subject] o vosso (a vossa); [plural subject: polite form] o/a dos senhores (das senhoras); **~ dog** o seu/teu/vosso cão, o cão do senhor (da senhora), o cão dos senhores (das senhoras); **~ house** a sua/tua/vossa casa, etc; **~ children** os seus/teus/vossos filhos, etc. **-2.** [indefinite subject]: **it's good for ~ health** é bom para a saúde.

you're [jɔ:^r] = **you are.**

yours [jɔ:z] *pron* [singular subject] o seu (a sua), o teu (a tua); [plural subject] o vosso (a vossa); [formal - singular subject] o/a do senhor (da senhora); [- plural subject] o/a dos senhores (das senhoras); **a friend of ~** um amigo seu/teu/vosso/do senhor/da senhora/dos senhores/das senhoras; **these shoes are ~** estes sapatos são (os) teus/seus/vossos, etc; **these are mine – where are ~?** estes são os meus – onde estão os seus/teus/vossos, etc?

yourself [jɔ:r'self] *pron* **-1.** [reflexive: singular] se, te; [reflexive: plural] se; **did you hurt ~?** [singular] você se machucou? **-2.** [after prep: singular] você mesmo(-ma), tu mesmo(ma); [after prep: plural] vocês mesmos(mas); [after prep: plural polite form] os senhores mesmos (as senhoras mesmas), vós mesmos(mas); **did you do it ~?** [singular] você fez isso sozinho?; [polite form] foi o senhor mesmo que o fez?; **did you do it yourselves?** vocês fizeram isso sozinhos?; [polite form] foram os senhores mesmos que o fizeram?

youth [ju:θ] *n* **-1.** [gen] juventude *f* **-2.** [boy, young man] mocidade *f* **-3.** *(U)* [young people] mocidade *f*, juventude *f.*

youth club *n* clube *m* da juventude.

youthful ['ju:θfʊl] *adj* juvenil.

youthfulness ['ju:θfʊlnɪs] *n (U)* juventude *f.*

youth hostel *n* albergue *m* da juventude.

youth hostelling [-'hɒstəlɪŋ] *n UK*: **to go youth hostelling** ir para albergues da juventude.

you've [ju:v] *cont* = **you have.**

yowl [jaʊl] ◇ *n* **-1.** [dog] uivo *m* **-2.** [cat] miado *m.* ◇ *vi* **-1.** [dog] uivar **-2.** [cat] miar.

yo-yo ['jəʊjəʊ] *n* ioiô *m.*

yr (*abbr of* **year**) ano *m.*

YT *n abbr of* **Yukon Territory.**

Yucatan [jʌkə'tɑ:n] *n* Yucatan.

yucca *n* iúca *f.*

yuck [jʌk] *excl inf* argh!

Yugoslav *adj* & *n* = **Yugoslavian.**

Yugoslavia [ju:gə'slɑ:vɪə] *n* Iugoslávia *f*; **in ~** na Iugoslávia.

Yugoslavian [ju:gə'slɑ:vɪən], **Yugoslav** [ju:gə'slɑ:v] ◇ *adj* iugoslavo(va). ◇ *n* iugoslavo *m*, -va *f.*

Yukon Territory *n* território *m* Yukon.

yule log *n* **-1.** [piece of wood] acha *f* de Natal **-2.** [cake] torta *f* de Natal.

yuletide ['ju:ltaɪd] *n (U) literary* época *f* de Natal.

yummy ['jʌmɪ] (*compar* **-ier**, *superl* **-iest**) *adj inf* delicioso(sa).

yuppie, yuppy ['jʌpɪ] (*pl* **-ies**) (*abbr of* **young urban professional**) *n* yuppie *mf.*

YWCA (*abbr of* **Young Women's Christian Association**) *n* ≃ ACM *f.*

Z

z (*pl* **z's** OR **zs**), **Z** (*pl* **Z's** OR **Zs**) [*UK* zed, *US* zi:] *n* [letter] z, Z *m*.
Zagreb *n* Zagreb.
Zaïre [zɑ:'ɪəʳ] *n* Zaire; **in ~** no Zaire.
Zaïrese <> *adj* zairense. <> *n* zairense *mf*.
Zambesi, Zambezi *n*: **the ~** o Zambesi.
Zambia ['zæmbɪəl] *n* Zâmbia; **in ~** no Zâmbia.
Zambian ['zæmbɪən] <> *adj* zambiano(na). <> *n* zambiano *m*, -na *f*.
zany ['zeɪnɪ] (*compar* **-ier**, *superl* **-iest**) *adj* ***inf*** bobo(ba).
Zanzibar *n* Zanzibar.
zap [zæp] (*pt* & *pp* **-ped**, *cont* **-ping**) ***inf*** <> *vt* **-1.** [kill] despachar **-2.** [in video games] destruir. <> *vi* **-1.** [rush] correr; **to ~ off to** correr para; **to ~ through sthg** passar os olhos por algo **-2.** TV zapear; **to ~ from channel to channel** ficar trocando de um canal para o outro.
zeal [zi:l] *n (U)* ***fml*** zelo *m*.
zealot ['zelət] *n* ***fml*** fanático *m*, -ca *f*.
zealous ['zeləs] *adj* ***fml*** zeloso(sa).
zebra [*UK* 'zebrə, *US* 'zi:brə] (*pl inv* OR **-s**) *n* zebra *f*.
zebra crossing *n* ***UK*** faixa *f* de segurança.
zenith [*UK* 'zenɪθ, *US* 'zi:nəθ] *n* **-1.** ASTRON zênite *m* **-2.** ***fig*** [highest point] apogeu *m*.
zeppelin ['zepəlɪn] *n* zepelim *m*.
zero [*UK* 'zɪərəʊ, *US* 'zi:rəʊ] (*pl* **-s** OR **-es**, *pt* & *pp* **-ed**, *cont* **-ing**) <> *adj* zero. <> *n* zero *m*.
◆ **zero in on** *vt fus* **-1.** [subj: weapon] fazer mira em **-2.** [subj: person] concentrar-se em.
zero-rated [-ˌreɪtɪd] *adj* ***UK*** ≃ isento(ta) de IVA.
zest [zest] *n* **-1.** [excitement] entusiasmo *m* **-2.** *(U)* [eagerness] vivacidade *f* **-3.** *(U)* [of orange, lemon] sabor *m*.
zigzag ['zɪgzæg] (*pt* & *pp* **-ged**, *cont* **-ging**) <> *n* ziguezague *m*. <> *vi* ziguezaguear.
zilch [zɪltʃ] *n* ***US inf***: **I know she'll do ~ while I'm away** nada de nada, sei que ela não vai fazer nada de nada enquanto eu estiver fora.
Zimbabwe [zɪm'bɑ:bwɪ] *n* Zimbábue; **in ~** no Zimbábue.
Zimbabwean [zɪm'bɑ:bwɪən] <> *adj* zimbabuano(na). <> *n* zimbabuano *m*, -na *f*.
Zimmer frame® ['zɪməʳ-] *n* andador *m*.
zinc [zɪŋk] *n (U)* zinco *m*.
Zionism ['zaɪənɪzm] *n* sionismo *m*.
Zionist ['zaɪənɪst] <> *adj* sionista. <> *n* sionista *mf*.
zip [zɪp] (*pt* & *pp* **-ped**, *cont* **-ping**) <> *n* ***UK*** [fastener] fecho *m* ecler, zíper *m*. <> *vt* **-1.** [clothing] fechar com zíper **-2.** COMPUT zipar, compactar.
◆ **zip up** *vt sep* fechar o zíper de.
zip [zɪp]
zip code *n* ***US*** ≃ CEP *m*.
Zip disk® *n* COMPUT disco *m* Zip®.
Zip drive® *n* COMPUT unidade *f* Zip®.
zip fastener *n* ***UK*** = **zip**.
zipper ['zɪpəʳ] *n* ***US*** = **zip**.
zippy (*compar* **-ier**, *superl* **-iest**) *adj* ***inf*** [car] possante.
zit [zɪt] *n esp* ***US inf*** mancha *f (na pele)*.
zither ['zɪðəʳ] *n* citara *f*.
zodiac ['zəʊdɪæk] *n*: **the ~** o zodíaco; **sign of the ~** signo *m* do zodíaco.
zombie ['zɒmbɪ] *n* [automaton] zumbi *m*.
zone [zəʊn] *n* [district] zona *f*.
zoo [zu:] *n* zoológico *m*.
zoological [ˌzəʊə'lɒdʒɪkl] *adj* zoológico(ca).
zoologist [zəʊ'ɒlədʒɪst] *n* zoólogo *m*, -ga *f*, zoologista *mf*.
zoology [zəʊ'ɒlədʒɪ] *n (U)* zoologia *f*.
zoom [zu:m] *vi* ***inf*** **-1.** [move quickly] arrancar-se **-2.** [rise rapidly] disparar.
◆ **zoom in** *vi*: **to ~ in (on sb/sthg)** dar um close em alguém/algo.
◆ **zoom off** *vi* ***inf*** arrancar-se.
zoom lens *n* (lentes *fpl* de) zum *m*.
zucchini [zu:'ki:nɪ] (*pl inv* OR **-s**) *n* ***US*** abobrinha *f* italiana.
Zulu ['zu:lu:] <> *adj* zulu. <> *n* zulu *mf*.
Zürich ['zjʊərɪk] *n* Zurique; **in ~** em Zurique.

PORTUGUESE VERBS
ENGLISH IRREGULAR VERBS

CONJUGAÇÃO DOS VERBOS PORTUGUESES
VERBOS IRREGULARES INGLESES

	1 ter	2 haver	3 ser
ind. presente	eu tenho, tu tens, ele tem, nós temos, vós tendes, eles têm	eu hei, tu hás, ele há, nós havemos/hemos, vós haveis/heis, eles hão	eu sou, tu és, ele é, nós somos, vós sois, eles são
ind. imperfeito	eu tinha	eu havia	eu era
ind. perfeito	eu tive	eu houve	eu fui
ind. m.-q.-p. simpl.	eu tivera	eu houvera	eu fora
ind. m.-q.-p. comp.	eu tinha tido	eu tinha havido	eu tinha sido
ind fut. do pres.	eu terei	eu haverei	eu serei
ind fut. do pret.	eu teria	eu haveria	eu seria
subj. presente	que eu tenha	que eu haja	que eu seja
subj. imperfeito	que eu tivesse	que eu houvesse	que eu fosse
subj. perfeito	que eu tenha tido	que eu tenha havido	que eu tenha sido
subj. m.-q.-perf.	que eu tivesse tido	que eu tivesse havido	que eu tivesse sido
subj. futuro	quando eu tiver	quando eu houver	quando eu for
inf. pessoal	eu ter, tu teres, ele ter, nós termos, vós terdes, eles terem	eu haver, tu haveres, ele haver, nós havermos, vós haverdes, eles haverem	eu ser, tu seres, ele ser, nós sermos, vós serdes, eles serem
imper. afirm.	tem (tu)	há (tu)	sê (tu)
imper. neg.	não tenhas	não hajas	não sejas
gerúndio	tendo	havendo	sendo
particípio	tido	havido	sido

	4 falar	5 comer	6 partir
ind. presente	eu falo, tu falas, ele fala, nós falamos, vós falais, eles falam	eu como, tu comes, ele come, nós comemos, vós comeis, eles comem	eu parto, tu partes, ele parte, nós partimos, vós partis, eles partem
ind. imperfeito	eu falava	eu comia	eu partia
ind. perfeito	eu falei	eu comi	eu parti
ind. m.-q.-p. simpl.	eu falara	eu comera	eu partira
ind. m.-q.-p. comp.	eu tinha falado	eu tinha comido	eu tinha partido
ind fut. do pres.	eu falarei	eu comerei	eu partirei
ind fut. do pret.	eu falaria	eu comeria	eu partiria
subj. presente	que eu fale	que eu coma	que eu parta
subj. imperfeito	que eu falasse	que eu comesse	que eu partisse
subj. perfeito	que eu tenha falado	que eu tenha comido	que eu tenha partido
subj. m.-q.-perf.	que eu tivesse falado	que eu tivesse comido	que eu tivesse partido
subj. futuro	quando eu falar	quando eu comer	quando eu partir
inf. pessoal	eu falar, tu falares, ele falar, nós falarmos, vós falardes, eles falarem	eu comer, tu comeres, ele comer, nós comermos, vós comerdes, eles comerem	eu partir, tu partires, ele partir, nós partirmos, vós partirdes, eles partirem
imper. afirm.	fala (tu)	come (tu)	parte (tu)
imper. neg.	não fales	não comas	não partas
gerúndio	falando	comendo	partindo
particípio	falado	comido	partido

	7 cortar-se	8 chamá-lo	9 ser amado
ind. presente	eu me corto, tu te cortas, ele se corta, nós nos cortamos, vós vos cortais, eles se cortam	eu o chamo, tu o chamas, ele o chama, nós o chamamos, vós o chamais, eles o chamam	eu sou amado, tu és amado, ele é amado, nós somos amados, vós sois amados, eles são amados
ind. imperfeito	eu me cortava	eu o chamava	eu era amado
ind. perfeito	eu me cortei	eu o chamei	eu fui amado
ind. m.-q.-p. simpl.	eu me cortara	eu o chamara	eu fora amado
ind. m.-q.-p. comp.	eu me tinha cortado	eu o tinha chamado	eu tinha sido amado
ind fut. do pres.	eu me cortarei	eu o chamarei	eu serei amado
ind fut. do pret.	eu me cortaria	eu o chamaria	eu seria amado
subj. presente	que eu me corte	que eu o chame	que eu seja amado
subj. imperfeito	que eu me cortasse	que eu o chamasse	que eu fosse amado
subj. perfeito	que eu me tenha cortado	que eu o tenha chamado	que eu tenha sido amado
subj. m.-q.-perf.	que eu me tivesse cortado	que eu o tivesse chamado	que eu tivesse sido amado
subj. futuro	quando eu me cortar	quando eu o chamar	quando eu for amado
inf. pessoal	eu me cortar, tu te cortares, ele se cortar, nós nos cortarmos, vós vos cortardes, eles se cortarem	eu o chamar, tu o chamares, ele o chamar, nós o chamarmos, vós o chamardes, eles o chamarem	eu ser amado, tu seres amado, ele ser amado, nós sermos amados, vós serdes amados, eles serem amados
imper. afirm.	corta-te (tu)	chama-o (tu)	sê amado (tu)
imper. neg.	não te cortes	não o chames	não sejas amado
gerúndio	cortando	chamando	amando
particípio	cortado	chamado	amado

	10 estar	11 dar	12 ficar
ind. presente	eu estou, tu estás, ele está, nós estamos, vós estais, eles estão	eu dou, tu dás, ele dá, nós damos, vós dais, eles dão	eu fico, tu ficas, ele fica, nós ficamos, vós ficais, eles ficam
ind. imperfeito	eu estava	eu dava	eu ficava
ind. perfeito	eu estive	eu dei	eu fiquei
ind. m.-q.-p. simpl.	eu estivera	eu dera	eu ficara
ind. m.-q.-p. comp.	eu tinha estado	eu tinha dado	eu tinha ficado
ind fut. do pres.	eu estarei	eu darei	eu ficarei
ind fut. do pret.	eu estaria	eu daria	eu ficaria
subj. presente	que eu esteja	que eu dê	que eu fique
subj. imperfeito	que eu estivesse	que eu desse	que eu ficasse
subj. perfeito	que eu tenha estado	que eu tenha dado	que eu tenha ficado
subj. m.-q.-perf.	que eu tivesse estado	que eu tivesse dado	que eu tivesse ficado
subj. futuro	quando eu estiver	quando eu der	quando eu ficar
inf. pessoal	eu estar, tu estares, ele estar, nós estarmos, vós estardes, eles estarem	eu dar, tu dares, ele dar, nós darmos, vós dardes, eles darem	eu ficar, tu ficares, ele ficar, nós ficarmos, vós ficardes, eles ficarem
imper. afirm.	está (tu)	dá (tu)	fica (tu)
imper. neg.	não estejas	não dês	não fiques
gerúndio	estando	dando	ficando
particípio	estado	dado	ficado

	13 dançar	14 pagar	15 passear
ind. presente	eu danço, tu danças, ele dança, nós dançamos, vós dançais, eles dançam	eu pago, tu pagas, ele paga, nós pagamos, vós pagais, eles pagam	eu passeio, tu passeias, ele passeia, nós passeamos, vós passeais, eles passeiam
ind. imperfeito	eu dançava	eu pagava	eu passeava
ind. perfeito	eu dancei	eu paguei	eu passeei
ind. m.-q.-p. simpl.	eu dançara	eu pagara	eu passeara
ind. m.-q.-p. comp.	eu tinha dançado	eu tinha pagado	eu tinha passeado
ind fut. do pres.	eu dançarei	eu pagarei	eu passearei
ind fut. do pret.	eu dançaria	eu pagaria	eu passearia
subj. presente	que eu dance	que eu pague	que eu passeie
subj. imperfeito	que eu dançasse	que eu pagasse	que eu passeasse
subj. perfeito	que eu tenha dançado	que eu tenha pagado	que eu tenha passeado
subj. m.-q.-perf.	que eu tivesse dançado	que eu tivesse pagado	que eu tivesse passeado
subj. futuro	quando eu dançar	quando eu pagar	quando eu passear
inf. pessoal	eu dançar, tu dançares, ele dançar, nós dançarmos, vós dançardes, eles dançarem	eu pagar, tu pagares, ele pagar, nós pagarmos, vós pagardes, eles pagarem	eu passear, tu passeares, ele passear, nós passearmos, vós passeardes, eles passearem
imper. afirm.	dança (tu)	paga (tu)	passeia (tu)
imper. neg.	não dances	não pagues	não passeies
gerúndio	dançando	pagando	passeando
particípio	dançado	pagado/pago	passeado

	16 enviar	17 odiar	18 comerciar
ind. presente	eu envio, tu envias, ele envia, nós enviamos, vós enviais, eles enviam	eu odeio, tu odeias, ele odeia, nós odiamos, vós odiais, eles odeiam	eu comerc(e)io, tu comerc(e)ias, ele comerc(e)ia, nós comerciamos, vós comerciais, eles comerc(e)iam
ind. imperfeito	eu enviava	eu odiava	eu comerciava
ind. perfeito	eu enviei	eu odiei	eu comerciei
ind. m.-q.-p. simpl.	eu enviara	eu odiara	eu comerciara
ind. m.-q.-p. comp.	eu tinha enviado	eu tinha odiado	eu tinha comerciado
ind fut. do pres.	eu enviarei	eu odiarei	eu comerciarei
ind fut. do pret.	eu enviaria	eu odiaria	eu comerciaria
subj. presente	que eu envie	que eu odeie	que eu comerc(e)ie
subj. imperfeito	que eu enviasse	que eu odiasse	que eu comerciasse
subj. perfeito	que eu tenha enviado	que eu tenha odiado	que eu tenha comerciado
subj. m.-q.-perf.	que eu tivesse enviado	que eu tivesse odiado	que eu tivesse comerciado
subj. futuro	quando eu enviar	quando eu odiar	quando eu comerciar
inf. pessoal	eu enviar, tu enviares, ele enviar, nós enviarmos, vós enviardes, eles enviarem	eu odiar, tu odiares, ele odiar, nós odiarmos, vós odiardes, eles odiarem	eu comerciar, tu comerciares, ele comerciar, nós comerciarmos, vós comerciardes, eles comerciarem
imper. afirm.	envia (tu)	odeia (tu)	comerc(e)ia (tu)
imper. neg.	não envies	não odeies	não comerc(e)ies
gerúndio	enviando	odiando	comerciando
particípio	enviado	odiado	comerciado

	19 saudar	20 doar	21 averiguar
ind. presente	eu saúdo, tu saúdas, ele saúda, nós saudamos, vós saudais, eles saúdam	eu dôo, tu doas, ele doa, nós doamos, vós doais, eles doam	eu averiguo, tu averiguas, ele averigua, nós averiguamos, vós averiguais, eles averiguam
ind. imperfeito	eu saudava	eu doava	eu averiguava
ind. perfeito	eu saudei	eu doei	eu averigüei
ind. m.-q.-p. simpl.	eu saudara	eu doara	eu averiguara
ind. m.-q.-p. comp.	eu tinha saudado	eu tinha doado	eu tinha averiguado
ind fut. do pres.	eu saudarei	eu doarei	eu averiguarei
ind fut. do pret.	eu saudaria	eu doaria	eu averiguaria
subj. presente	que eu saúde	que eu doe	que eu averigúe
subj. imperfeito	que eu saudasse	que eu doasse	que eu averiguasse
subj. perfeito	que eu tenha saudado	que eu tenha doado	que eu tenha averiguado
subj. m.-q.-perf.	que eu tivesse saudado	que eu tivesse doado	que eu tivesse averiguado
subj. futuro	quando eu saudar	quando eu doar	quando eu averiguar
inf. pessoal	eu saudar, tu saudares, ele saudar, nós saudarmos, vós saudardes, eles saudarem	eu doar, tu doares, ele doar, nós doarmos, vós doardes, eles doarem	eu averiguar, tu averiguares, ele averiguar, nós averiguarmos, vós averiguardes, eles averiguarem
imper. afirm.	saúda (tu)	doa (tu)	averigua (tu)
imper. neg.	não saúdes	não does	não averigúes
gerúndio	saudando	doando	averiguando
particípio	saudado	doado	averiguado

	22 enxaguar	23 adequar	24 relampaguear
ind. presente	eu enxáguo, tu enxáguas, ele enxágua, nós enxaguamos, vós enxaguais, eles enxáguam	nós adequamos, vós adequais	relampagueia, relampagueiam
ind. imperfeito	eu enxaguava	eu adequava	
ind. perfeito	eu enxagüei	eu adeqüei	
ind. m.-q.-p. simpl.	eu enxaguara	eu adequara	
ind. m.-q.-p. comp.	eu tinha enxaguado	eu tinha adequado	
ind fut. do pres.	eu enxaguarei	eu adequarei	
ind fut. do pret.	eu enxaguaria	eu adequaria	
subj. presente	que eu enxágüe		
subj. imperfeito	que eu enxaguasse	que eu adequasse	
subj. perfeito	que eu tenha enxaguado	que eu tenha adequado	
subj. m.-q.-perf.	que eu tivesse enxaguado	que eu tivesse adequado	
subj. futuro	quando eu enxaguar	quando eu adequar	
inf. pessoal	eu enxaguar, tu enxaguares, ele enxaguar, nós enxaguarmos, vós enxaguardes, eles enxaguarem	eu adequar, tu adequares, ele adequar, nós adequarmos, vós adequardes, eles adequarem	relampaguear
imper. afirm.	enxágua (tu)	adequai (vós)	
imper. neg.	não enxágües		
gerúndio	enxaguando	adequando	relampagueando
particípio	enxaguado	adequado	relampagueado

	25 agradecer	26 eleger	27 erguer
ind. presente	eu agradeço, tu agradeces, ele agradece, nós agradecemos, vós agradeceis, eles agradecem	eu elejo, tu eleges, ele elege, nós elegemos, vós elegeis, eles elegem	eu ergo, tu ergues, ele ergue, nós erguemos, vós ergueis, eles erguem
ind. imperfeito	eu agradecia	eu elegia	eu erguia
ind. perfeito	eu agradeci	eu elegi	eu ergui
ind. m.-q.-p. simpl.	eu agradecera	eu elegera	eu erguera
ind. m.-q.-p. comp.	en tinha agradecido	en tinha elegido	eu tinha erguido
ind fut. do pres.	eu agradecerei	eu elegerei	eu erguerei
ind fut. do pret.	eu agradeceria	eu elegeria	eu ergueria
subj. presente	que eu agradeça	que eu eleja	que eu erga
subj. imperfeito	que eu agradecesse	que eu elegesse	que eu erguesse
subj. perfeito	que eu tenha agradecido	que eu tenha elegido	que eu tenha erguido
subj. m.-q.-perf.	que eu tivesse agradecido	que eu tivesse elegido	que eu tivesse erguido
subj. futuro	quando eu agradecer	quando eu eleger	quando eu erguer
inf. pessoal	eu agradecer, tu agradeceres, ele agradecer, nós agradecermos, vós agradecerdes, eles agradecerem	eu eleger, tu elegeres, ele eleger, nós elegermos, vós elegerdes, eles elegerem	eu erguer, tu ergueres, ele erguer, nós erguermos, vós erguerdes, eles erguerem
imper. afirm.	agradece (tu)	elege (tu)	ergue (tu)
imper. neg.	não agradeças	não elejas	não ergas
gerúndio	agradecendo	elegendo	erguendo
particípio	agradecido	elegido, eleito	erguido

	28 roer	29 dizer	30 trazer
ind. presente	eu rôo, tu róis, ele rói, nós roemos, vós roeis, eles roem	eu digo, tu dizes, ele diz, nós dizemos, vós dizeis, eles dizem	eu trago, tu trazes, ele traz, nós trazemos, vós trazeis, eles trazem
ind. imperfeito	eu roía	eu dizia	eu trazia
ind. perfeito	eu roí	eu disse	eu trouxe
ind. m.-q.-p. simpl.	eu roera	eu dissera	eu trouxera
ind. m.-q.-p. comp.	eu tinha roído	eu tinha dito	eu tinha trazido
ind fut. do pres.	eu roerei	eu direi	eu trarei
ind fut. do pret.	eu roeria	eu diria	eu traria
subj. presente	que eu roa	que eu diga	que eu traga
subj. imperfeito	que eu roesse	que eu dissesse	que eu trouxesse
subj. perfeito	que eu tenha roído	que eu tenha dito	que eu tenha trazido
subj. m.-q.-perf.	que eu tivesse roído	que eu tivesse dito	que eu tivesse trazido
subj. futuro	quando eu roer	quando eu disser	quando eu trouxer
inf. pessoal	eu roer, tu roeres, ele roer, nós roermos, vós roerdes, eles roerem	eu dizer, tu dizeres, ele dizer, nós dizermos, vós dizerdes, eles dizerem	eu trazer, tu trazeres, ele trazer, nós trazermos, vós trazerdes, eles trazerem
imper. afirm.	rói (tu)	diz, dize (tu)	traz, traze (tu)
imper. neg.	não roas	não digas	não tragas
gerúndio	roendo	dizendo	trazendo
particípio	roído	dito	trazido

	31 fazer	32 aprazer	33 jazer
ind. presente	eu faço, tu fazes, ele faz, nós fazemos, vós fazeis, eles fazem	eu aprazo, tu aprazes, ele apraz, nós aprazemos, vós aprazeis, eles aprazem	eu jazo, tu jazes, ele jaz, nós jazemos, vós jazeis, eles jazem
ind. imperfeito	eu fazia	eu aprazia	eu jazia
ind. perfeito	eu fiz	eu aprouve	eu jazi
ind. m.-q.-p. simpl.	eu fizera	eu aprouvera	eu jazera
ind. m.-q.-p. comp.	eu tinha feito	eu tinha aprazido	eu tinha jazido
ind fut. do pres.	eu farei	eu aprazerei	eu jazerei
ind fut. do pret.	eu faria	eu aprazeria	eu jazeria
subj. presente	que eu faça	que eu apraza	que eu jaza
subj. imperfeito	que eu fizesse	que eu aprouvesse	que eu jazesse
subj. perfeito	que eu tenha feito	que eu tenha aprazido	que eu tenha jazido
subj. m.-q.-perf.	que eu tivesse feito	que eu tivesse aprazido	que eu tivesse jazido
subj. futuro	quando eu fizer	quando eu aprouver	quando eu jazer
inf. pessoal	eu fazer, tu fazeres, ele fazer, nós fazermos, vós fazerdes, eles fazerem	eu aprazer, tu aprazeres, ele aprazer, nós aprazermos, vós aprazerdes, eles aprazerem	eu jazer, tu jazeres, ele jazer, nós jazermos, vós jazerdes, eles jazerem
imper. afirm.	faz, faze (tu)	apraz, apraze (tu)	jaz, jaze (tu)
imper. neg.	não faças	não aprazas	não jazas
gerúndio	fazendo	aprazendo	jazendo
particípio	feito	aprazido	jazido

	34 caber	35 saber	36 poder
ind. presente	eu caibo, tu cabes, ele cabe, nós cabemos, vós cabeis, eles cabem	eu sei, tu sabes, ele sabe, nós sabemos, vós sabeis, eles sabem	eu posso, tu podes, ele pode, nós podemos, vós podeis, eles podem
ind. imperfeito	eu cabia	eu sabia	eu podia
ind. perfeito	eu coube	eu soube	eu pude
ind. m.-q.-p. simpl.	eu coubera	eu soubera	eu pudera
ind. m.-q.-p. comp.	eu tinha cabido	eu tinha sabido	eu tinha podido
ind fut. do pres.	eu caberei	eu saberei	eu poderei
ind fut. do pret.	eu caberia	eu saberia	eu poderia
subj. presente	que eu caiba	que eu saiba	que eu possa
subj. imperfeito	que eu coubesse	que eu soubesse	que eu pudesse
subj. perfeito	que eu tenha cabido	que eu tenha sabido	que eu tenha podido
subj. m.-q.-perf.	que eu tivesse cabido	que eu tivesse sabido	que eu tivesse podido
subj. futuro	quando eu couber	quando eu souber	quando eu puder
inf. pessoal	eu caber, tu caberes, ele caber, nós cabermos, vós caberdes, eles caberem	eu saber, tu saberes, ele saber, nós sabermos, vós saberdes, eles saberem	eu poder, tu poderes, ele poder, nós podermos, vós poderdes, eles poderem
imper. afirm.		sabe (tu)	
imper. neg.		não saibas	
gerúndio	cabendo	sabendo	podendo
particípio	cabido	sabido	podido

	37 crer	38 querer	39 requerer
ind. presente	eu creio, tu crês, ele crê, nós cremos, vós credes, eles crêem	eu quero, tu queres, ele quer, nós queremos, vós quereis, eles querem	eu requeiro, tu requeres, ele requer, nós requeremos, vós requereis, eles requerem
ind. imperfeito	eu cria	eu queria	eu requeria
ind. perfeito	eu cri	eu quis	eu requeri
ind. m.-q.-p. simpl.	eu crera	eu quisera	eu requerera
ind. m.-q.-p. comp.	eu tinha crido	eu tinha querido	eu tinha requerido
ind fut. do pres.	eu crerei	eu quererei	eu requererei
ind fut. do pret.	eu creria	eu quereria	eu requereria
subj. presente	que eu creia	que eu queira	que eu requeira
subj. imperfeito	que eu cresse	que eu quisesse	que eu requeresse
subj. perfeito	que eu tenha crido	que eu tenha querido	que eu tenha requerido
subj. m.-q.-perf.	que eu tivesse crido	que eu tivesse querido	que eu tivesse requerido
subj. futuro	quando eu crer	quando eu quiser	quando eu requerer
inf. pessoal	eu crer, tu creres, ele crer, nós crermos, vós crerdes, eles crerem	eu querer, tu quereres, ele querer, nós querermos, vós quererdes, eles quererem	eu requerer, tu requereres, ele requerer, nós requerermos, vós requererdes, eles requererem
imper. afirm.	crê (tu)	quer (tu)	requer (tu)
imper. neg.	não creias	não queiras	não requeiras
gerúndio	crendo	querendo	requerendo
particípio	crido	querido	requerido

	40 ver	41 prover	42 ler
ind. presente	eu vejo, tu vês, ele vê, nós vemos, vós vedes, eles vêem	eu provejo, tu provês, ele provê, nós provemos, vós provedes, eles provêem	eu leio, tu lês, ele lê, nós lemos, vós ledes, eles lêem
ind. imperfeito	eu via	eu provia	eu lia
ind. perfeito	eu vi	eu provi	eu li
ind. m.-q.-p. simpl.	eu vira	eu provera	eu lera
ind. m.-q.-p. comp.	eu tinha visto	eu tinha provido	eu tinha lido
ind fut. do pres.	eu verei	eu proverei	eu lerei
ind fut. do pret.	eu veria	eu proveria	eu leria
subj. presente	que eu veja	que eu proveja	que eu leia
subj. imperfeito	que eu visse	que eu provesse	que eu lesse
subj. perfeito	que eu tenha visto	que eu tenha provido	que eu tenha lido
subj. m.-q.-perf.	que eu tivesse visto	que eu tivesse provido	que eu tivesse lido
subj. futuro	quando eu vir	quando eu prover	quando eu ler
inf. pessoal	eu ver, tu veres, ele ver, nós vermos, vós verdes, eles verem	eu prover, tu proveres, ele prover, nós provermos, vós proverdes, eles proverem	eu ler, tu leres, ele ler, nós lermos, vós lerdes, eles lerem
imper. afirm.	vê (tu)	provê (tu)	lê (tu)
imper. neg.	não vejas	não provejas	não leias
gerúndio	vendo	provendo	lendo
particípio	visto	provido	lido

	43 valer	44 perder	45 pôr
ind. presente	eu valho, tu vales, ele vale, nós valemos, vós valeis, eles valem	eu perco, tu perdes, ele perde, nós perdemos, vós perdeis, eles perdem	eu ponho, tu pões, ele põe, nós pomos, vós pondes, eles põem
ind. imperfeito	eu valia	eu perdia	eu punha
ind. perfeito	eu vali	eu perdi	eu pus
ind. m.-q.-p. simpl.	eu valera	eu perdera	eu pusera
ind. m.-q.-p. comp.	eu tinha valido	eu tinha perdido	eu tinha posto
ind fut. do pres.	eu valerei	eu perderei	eu porei
ind fut. do pret.	eu valeria	eu perderia	eu poria
subj. presente	que eu valha	que eu perca	que eu ponha
subj. imperfeito	que eu valesse	que eu perdesse	que eu pusesse
subj. perfeito	que eu tenha valido	que eu tenha perdido	que eu tenha posto
subj. m.-q.-perf.	que eu tivesse valido	que eu tivesse perdido	que eu tivesse posto
subj. futuro	quando eu valer	quando eu perder	quando eu puser
inf. pessoal	eu valer, tu valeres, ele valer, nós valermos, vós valerdes, eles valerem	eu perder, tu perderes, ele perder, nós perdermos, vós perderdes, eles perderem	eu pôr, tu pores, ele pôr, nós pormos, vós pordes, eles porem
imper. afirm.	vale (tu)	perde (tu)	põe (tu)
imper. neg.	não valhas	não percas	não ponhas
gerúndio	valendo	perdendo	pondo
particípio	valido	perdido	posto

	46 acontecer	47 chover	48 doer
ind. presente	acontece, acontecem	chove	dói, doem
ind. imperfeito	acontecia, aconteciam	chovia	doía, doíam
ind. perfeito	aconteceu, aconteceram	choveu	doeu, doeram
ind. m.-q.-p. simpl.	acontecera, aconteceram	chovera	doera, doeram
ind. m.-q.-p. comp.	tinha acontecido	tinha chovido	tinha doído
ind. fut. do pres.	acontecerá, acontecerão	choverá	doerá, doerão
ind. fut. do pret.	aconteceria, aconteceriam	choveria	doeria, doeriam
subj. presente	que ele aconteça	chova	doa, doam
subj. imperfeito	que ele acontecesse	chovesse	doesse, doessem
subj. perfeito	que ele tenha acontecido	tenha chovido	tenha doído
subj. m.-q.-perf.	que ele tivesse acontecido	tivesse chovido	tivesse doído
subj. futuro	quando ele acontecer	quando chover	quando doer
inf. pessoal	ele acontecer, eles acontecerem	chover	doer, doerem
imper. afirm.			
imper. neg.			
gerúndio	acontecendo	chovendo	doendo
particípio	acontecido	chovido	doído

	49 prazer	50 precaver	51 reaver
ind. presente	praz, prazem	nós precavemos, vós precaveis	nós reavemos, vós reaveis
ind. imperfeito	prazia, praziam	eu precavia	eu reavia
ind. perfeito	prouve, prouveram	eu precavi	eu reouve
ind. m.-q.-p. simpl.	prouvera, prouveram	eu precavera	eu reouvera
ind. m.-q.-p. comp.	tinha prazido	eu tinha precavido	eu tinha reavido
ind fut. do pres.	prazerá, prazerão	eu precaverei	eu reaverei
ind fut. do pret.	prazeria, prazeriam	eu precaveria	eu reaveria
subj. presente	praza, prazam		
subj. imperfeito	prouvesse, prouvessem	que eu precavesse	que eu reouvesse
subj. perfeito	que ele tenha prazido	que eu tenha precavido	que eu tenha reavido
subj. m.-q.-perf.	que ele tivesse prazido	que eu tivesse precavido	que eu tivesse reavido
subj. futuro	quando ele prouver	quando eu precaver	quando eu reouver
inf. pessoal	prazer, prazerem	eu precaver, tu precaveres, ele precaver, nós precavermos, vós precaverdes, eles precaverem	eu reaver, tu reaveres, ele reaver, nós reavermos, vós reaverdes, eles reaverem
imper. afirm.	praza (você)	precavei (vós)	reavei (vós)
imper. neg.	não praza (você)		
gerúndio	prazendo	precavendo	reavendo
particípio	prazido	precavido	reavido

	52 fingir	53 distinguir	54 servir
ind. presente	eu finjo, tu finges, ele finge, nós fingimos, vós fingis, eles fingem	eu distingo, tu distingues, ele distingue, nós distinguimos, vós distinguis, eles distinguem	eu sirvo, tu serves, ele serve, nós servimos, vós servis, eles servem
ind. imperfeito	eu fingia	eu distinguia	eu servia
ind. perfeito	eu fingi	eu distingui	eu servi
ind. m.-q.-p. simpl.	eu fingira	eu distinguira	eu servira
ind. m.-q.-p. comp.	eu tinha fingido	eu tinha distinguido	eu tinha servido
ind fut. do pres.	eu fingirei	eu distinguirei	eu servirei
ind fut. do pret.	eu fingiria	eu distinguiria	eu serviria
subj. presente	que eu finja	que eu distinga	que eu sirva
subj. imperfeito	que eu fingisse	que eu distinguisse	que eu servisse
subj. perfeito	que eu tenha fingido	que eu tenha distinguido	que eu tenha servido
subj. m.-q.-perf.	que eu tivesse fingido	que eu tivesse distinguido	que eu tivesse servido
subj. futuro	quando eu fingir	quando eu distinguir	quando eu servir
inf. pessoal	eu fingir, tu fingires, ele fingir, nós fingirmos, vós fingirdes, eles fingirem	eu distinguir, tu distinguires, ele distinguir, nós distinguirmos, vós distinguirdes, eles distinguirem	eu servir, tu servires, ele servir, nós servirmos, vós servirdes, eles servirem
imper. afirm.	finge (tu)	distingue (tu)	serve (tu)
imper. neg.	não finjas	não distingas	não sirvas
gerúndio	fingindo	distinguindo	servindo
particípio	fingido	distinguido	servido

	55 seguir	56 sentir	57 ferir
ind. presente	eu sigo, tu segues, ele segue, nós seguimos, vós seguis, eles seguem	eu sinto, tu sentes, ele sente, nós sentimos, vós sentis, eles sentem	eu firo, tu feres, ele fere, nós ferimos, vós feris, eles ferem
ind. imperfeito	eu seguia	eu sentia	eu feria
ind. perfeito	eu segui	eu senti	eu feri
ind. m.-q.-p. simpl.	eu seguira	eu sentira	eu ferira
ind. m.-q.-p. comp.	eu tinha seguido	eu tinha sentido	eu tinha ferido
ind fut. do pres.	eu seguirei	eu sentirei	eu ferirei
ind fut. do pret.	eu seguiria	eu sentiria	eu feriria
subj. presente	que eu siga	que eu sinta	que eu fira
subj. imperfeito	que eu seguisse	que eu sentisse	que eu ferisse
subj. perfeito	que eu tenha seguido	que eu tenha sentido	que eu tenha ferido
subj. m.-q.-perf.	que eu tivesse seguido	que eu tivesse sentido	que eu tivesse ferido
subj. futuro	quando eu seguir	quando eu sentir	quando eu ferir
inf. pessoal	eu seguir, tu seguires, ele seguir, nós seguirmos, vós seguirdes, eles seguirem	eu sentir, tu sentires, ele sentir, nós sentirmos, vós sentirdes, eles sentirem	eu ferir, tu ferires, ele ferir, nós ferirmos, vós ferirdes, eles ferirem
imper. afirm.	segue (tu)	sente (tu)	fere (tu)
imper. neg.	não sigas	não sintas	não firas
gerúndio	seguindo	sentindo	ferindo
particípio	seguido	sentido	ferido

	58 prevenir	59 dormir	60 polir
ind. presente	eu previno, tu prevines, ele previne, nós prevenimos, vós prevenis, eles previnem	eu durmo, tu dormes, ele dorme, nós dormimos, vós dormis, eles dormem	eu pulo, tu pules, ele pule, nós polimos, vós polis, eles pulem
ind. imperfeito	eu prevenia	eu dormia	eu polia
ind. perfeito	eu preveni	eu dormi	eu poli
ind. m.-q.-p. simpl.	eu prevenira	eu dormira	eu polira
ind. m.-q.-p. comp.	eu tinha prevenido	eu tinha dormido	eu tinha polido
ind fut. do pres.	eu prevenirei	eu dormirei	eu polirei
ind fut. do pret.	eu preveniria	eu dormiria	eu poliria
subj. presente	que eu previna	que eu durma	que eu pula
subj. imperfeito	que eu prevenisse	que eu dormisse	que eu polisse
subj. perfeito	que eu tenha prevenido	que eu tenha dormido	que eu tenha polido
subj. m.-q.-perf.	que eu tivesse prevenido	que eu tivesse dormido	que eu tivesse polido
subj. futuro	quando eu prevenir	quando eu dormir	quando eu polir
inf. pessoal	eu prevenir, tu prevenires, ele prevenir, nós prevenirmos, vós prevenirdes, eles prevenirem	eu dormir, tu dormires, ele dormir, nós dormirmos, vós dormirdes, eles dormirem	eu polir, tu polires, ele polir, nós polirmos, vós polirdes, eles polirem
imper. afirm.	previne (tu)	dorme (tu)	pule (tu)
imper. neg.	não previnas	não durmas	não pulas
gerúndio	prevenindo	dormindo	polindo
particípio	prevenido	dormido	polido

	61 subir	62 fugir	63 frigir
ind. presente	eu subo, tu sobes, ele sobe, nós subimos, vós subis, eles sobem	eu fujo, tu foges, ele foge, nós fugimos, vós fugis, eles fogem	eu frijo, tu friges, ele frige, nós frigimos, vós frigis, eles frigem
ind. imperfeito	eu subia	eu fugia	eu frigia
ind. perfeito	eu subi	eu fugi	eu frigi
ind. m.-q.-p. simpl.	eu subira	eu fugira	eu frigi
ind. m.-q.-p. comp.	eu tinha subido	eu tinha fugido	eu tinha frigido
ind fut. do pres.	eu subirei	eu fugirei	eu frigirei
ind fut. do pret.	eu subiria	eu fugiria	eu frigiria
subj. presente	que eu suba	que eu fuja	que eu frija
subj. imperfeito	que eu subisse	que eu fugisse	que eu frigisse
subj. perfeito	que eu tenha subido	que eu tenha fugido	que eu tenha frigido
subj. m.-q.-perf.	que eu tivesse subido	que eu tivesse fugido	que eu tivesse frigido
subj. futuro	quando eu subir	quando eu fugir	quando eu frigir
inf. pessoal	eu subir, tu subires, ele subir, nós subirmos, vós subirdes, eles subirem	eu fugir, tu fugires, ele fugir, nós fugirmos, vós fugirdes, eles fugirem	eu frigir, tu frigires, ele frigir, nós frigirmos, vós frigirdes, eles frigirem
imper. afirm.	sobe (tu)	foge (tu)	frige (tu)
imper. neg.	não subas	não fujas	não frijas
gerúndio	subindo	fugindo	frigindo
particípio	subido	fugido	frigido, frito

	64 convergir	65 refletir	66 ir
ind. presente	eu convirjo, tu converges, ele converge, nós convergimos, vós convergis, eles convergem	eu reflito, tu refletes, ele reflete, nós refletimos, vós refletis, eles refletem	eu vou, tu vais, ele vai, nós vamos, vós ides, eles vão
ind. imperfeito	eu convergia	eu refletia	eu ia
ind. perfeito	eu convergi	eu refleti	eu fui
ind. m.-q.-p. simpl.	eu convergira	eu refletira	eu fora
ind. m.-q.-p. comp.	eu tinha convergido	eu tinha refletido	eu tinha ido
ind fut. do pres.	eu convergirei	eu refletirei	eu irei
ind fut. do pret.	eu convergiria	eu refletiria	eu iria
subj. presente	que eu convirja	que eu reflita	que eu vá
subj. imperfeito	que eu convergisse	que eu refletisse	que eu fosse
subj. perfeito	que eu tenha convergido	que eu tenha refletido	que eu tenha ido
subj. m.-q.-perf.	que eu tivesse convergido	que eu tivesse refletido	que eu tivesse ido
subj. futuro	quando eu convergir	quando eu refletir	quando eu for
inf. pessoal	eu convergir, tu convergires, ele convergir, nós convergirmos, vós convergirdes, eles convergirem	eu refletir, tu refletires, ele refletir, nós refletirmos, vós refletirdes, eles refletirem	eu ir, tu ires, ele ir, nós irmos, vós irdes, eles irem
imper. afirm.	converge (tu)	reflete (tu)	vai (tu)
imper. neg.	não convirjas	não reflitas	não vás
gerúndio	convergindo	refletindo	indo
particípio	convergido	refletido	ido

	67 vir	68 sair	69 rir
ind. presente	eu venho, tu vens, ele vem, nós vimos, vós vindes, eles vêm	eu saio, tu sais, ele sai, nós saímos, vós saís, eles saem	eu rio, tu ris, ele ri, nós rimos, vós rides, eles riem
ind. imperfeito	eu vinha	eu saía	eu ria
ind. perfeito	eu vim	eu saí	eu ri
ind. m.-q.-p. simpl.	eu viera	eu saíra	eu rira
ind. m.-q.-p. comp.	eu tinha vindo	eu tinha saído	eu tinha rido
ind fut. do pres.	eu virei	eu sairei	eu rirei
ind fut. do pret.	eu viria	eu sairia	eu riria
subj. presente	que eu venha	que eu saia	que eu ria
subj. imperfeito	que eu viesse	que eu saísse	que eu risse
subj. perfeito	que eu tenha vindo	que eu tenha saído	que eu tenha rido
subj. m.-q.-perf.	que eu tivesse vindo	que eu tivesse saído	que eu tivesse rido
subj. futuro	quando eu vier	quando eu sair	quando eu rir
inf. pessoal	eu vir, tu vires, ele vir, nós virmos, vós virdes, eles virem	eu sair, tu saires, ele sair, nós sairmos, vós sairdes, eles saírem	eu rir, tu rires, ele rir, nós rirmos, vós rirdes, eles rirem
imper. afirm.	vem (tu)	sai (tu)	ri (tu)
imper. neg.	não venhas	não saias	não rias
gerúndio	vindo	saindo	rindo
particípio	vindo	saído	rido

	70 pedir	71 ouvir	72 produzir
ind. presente	eu peço, tu pedes, ele pede, nós pedimos, vós pedis, eles pedem	eu ouço/oiço, tu ouves, ele ouve, nós ouvimos, vós ouvis, eles ouvem	eu produzo, tu produzes, ele produz, nós produzimos, vós produzis, eles produzem
ind. imperfeito	eu pedia	eu ouvia	eu produzia
ind. perfeito	eu pedi	eu ouvi	eu produzi
ind. m.-q.-p. simpl.	eu pedira	eu ouvira	eu produzira
ind. m.-q.-p. comp.	eu tinha pedido	eu tinha ouvido	eu tinha produzido
ind fut. do pres.	eu pedirei	eu ouvirei	eu produzirei
ind fut. do pret.	eu pediria	eu ouviria	eu produziria
subj. presente	que eu peça	que eu ouça	que eu produza
subj. imperfeito	que eu pedisse	que eu ouvisse	que eu produzisse
subj. perfeito	que eu tenha pedido	que eu tenha ouvido	que eu tenha produzido
subj. m.-q.-perf.	que eu tivesse pedido	que eu tivesse ouvido	que eu tivesse produzido
subj. futuro	quando eu pedir	quando eu ouvir	quando eu produzir
inf. pessoal	eu pedir, tu pedires, ele pedir, nós pedirmos, vós pedirdes, eles pedirem	eu ouvir, tu ouvires, ele ouvir, nós ouvirmos, vós ouvirdes, eles ouvirem	eu produzir, tu produzires, ele produzir, nós produzirmos, vós produzirdes, eles produzirem
imper. afirm.	pede (tu)	ouve (tu)	produz, produze (tu)
imper. neg.	não peças	não ouças	não produzas
gerúndio	pedindo	ouvindo	produzindo
particípio	pedido	ouvido	produzido

	73 construir	74 atribuir	75 argüir
ind. presente	eu construo, tu constróis, ele constrói, nós construímos, vós construís, eles constroem	eu atribuo, tu atribuis, ele atribui, nós atribuímos, vós atribuís, eles atribuem	eu arguo, tu argúis, ele argúi, nós argüimos, vós argüis, eles argúem
ind. imperfeito	eu construía	eu atribuía	eu argüia
ind. perfeito	eu construí	eu atribuí	eu argüi
ind. m.-q.-p. simpl.	eu construíra	eu atribuíra	eu argüira
ind. m.-q.-p. comp.	eu tinha construído	eu tinha atribuído	eu tinha argüido
ind fut. do pres.	eu construirei	eu atribuirei	eu argüirei
ind fut. do pret.	eu construiria	eu atribuiria	eu argüiria
subj. presente	que eu construa	que eu atribua	que eu argua
subj. imperfeito	que eu construísse	que eu atribuísse	que eu argüisse
subj. perfeito	que eu tenha construído	que eu tenha atribuído	que eu tenha argüido
subj. m.-q.-perf.	que eu tivesse construído	que eu tivesse atribuído	que eu tivesse argüido
subj. futuro	quando eu construir	quando eu atribuir	quando eu argüir
inf. pessoal	eu construir, tu construíres, ele construir, nós construirmos, vós construirdes, eles construírem	eu atribuir, tu atribuíres, ele atribuir, nós atribuirmos, vós atribuirdes, eles atribuírem	eu argüir, tu argüires, ele argüir, nós argüirmos, vós argüirdes, eles argüirem
imper. afirm.	constrói (tu)	atribui (tu)	argúi (tu)
imper. neg.	não construas	não atribuas	não arguas (tu)
gerúndio	construindo	atribuindo	argüindo
particípio	construído	atribuído	argüido

	76 reunir	77 proibir	78 emergir
ind. presente	eu reúno, tu reúnes, ele reúne, nós reunimos, vós reunis, eles reúnem	eu proíbo, tu proíbes, ele proíbe, nós proibimos, vós proibis, eles proíbem	eu emerjo, tu emerges, ele emerge, nós emergimos, vós emergis, eles emergem
ind. imperfeito	eu reunia	eu proibia	eu emergia
ind. perfeito	eu reuni	eu proibi	eu emergi
ind. m.-q.-p. simpl.	eu reunira	eu proibira	eu emergira
ind. m.-q.-p. comp.	eu tinha reunido	eu tinha proibido	eu tinha emergido
ind fut. do pres.	eu reunirei	eu proibirei	eu emergirei
ind fut. do pret.	eu reuniria	eu proibiria	eu emergiria
subj. presente	que eu reúna	que eu proíba	que eu emerja
subj. imperfeito	que eu reunisse	que eu proibisse	que eu emergisse
subj. perfeito	que eu tenha reunido	que eu tenha proibido	que eu tenha emergido
subj. m.-q.-perf.	que eu tivesse reunido	que eu tivesse proibido	que eu tivesse emergido
subj. futuro	quando eu reunir	quando eu proibir	quando eu emergir
inf. pessoal	eu reunir, tu reunires, ele reunir, nós reunirmos, vós reunirdes, eles reunirem	eu proibir, tu proibires, ele proibir, nós proibirmos, vós proibirdes, eles proibirem	eu emergir, tu emergires, ele emergir, nós emergirmos, vós emergirdes, eles emergirem
imper. afirm.	reúne (tu)	proíbe (tu)	emerge (tu)
imper. neg.	não reúnas	não proíbas	não emerjas
gerúndio	reunindo	proibindo	emergindo
particípio	reunido	proibido	emergido, emerso

	79 falir	80 remir
ind. presente	nós falimos, vós falis	nós remimos, vós remis
ind. imperfeito	eu falia	eu remia
ind. perfeito	eu fali	eu remi
ind. m.-q.-p. simpl.	eu falira	eu remira
ind. m.-q.-p. comp.	eu tinha falido	eu tinha remido
ind fut. do pres.	eu falirei	eu remirei
ind fut. do pret.	eu faliria	eu remiria
subj. presente		
subj. imperfeito	que eu falisse	que eu remisse
subj. perfeito	que eu tenha falido	que eu tenha remido
subj. m.-q.-perf.	que eu tivesse falido	que eu tivesse remido
subj. futuro	quando eu falir	quando eu remir
inf. pessoal	eu falir, tu falires, ele falir, nós falirmos, vós falirdes, eles falirem	eu remir, tu remires, ele remir, nós remirmos, vós remirdes, eles remirem
imper. afirm.	fali (vós)	remi (vos)
imper. neg.		
gerúndio	falindo	remindo
particípio	falido	remido

Infinitive	Past Tense	Past Participle
arise	arose	arisen
awake	awoke	awoken
be	was, were	been
bear	bore	born(e)
beat	beat	beaten
become	became	become
begin	began	begun
bend	bent	bent
beseech	besought	besought
bet	bet (*also* betted)	bet (*also* betted)
bid	bid (*also* bade)	bid (*also* bidden)
bind	bound	bound
bite	bit	bitten
bleed	bled	bled
blow	blew	blown
break	broke	broken
breed	bred	bred
bring	brought	brought
build	built	built
burn	burnt (*also* burned)	burnt (*also* burned)
burst	burst	burst
buy	bought	bought
can	could	-
cast	cast	cast
catch	caught	caught
choose	chose	chosen
cling	clung	clung
come	came	come
cost	cost	cost
creep	crept	crept
cut	cut	cut
deal	dealt	dealt
dig	dug	dug
do	did	done
draw	drew	drawn
dream	dreamed (*also* dreamt)	dreamed (*also* dreamt)
drink	drank	drunk
drive	drove	driven
dwell	dwelt	dwelt
eat	ate	eaten
fall	fell	fallen
feed	fed	fed
feel	felt	felt
fight	fought	fought
find	found	found
flee	fled	fled
fling	flung	flung
fly	flew	flown
forbid	forbade	forbidden
forget	forgot	forgotten
forsake	forsook	forsaken
freeze	froze	frozen
get	got	got (*US* gotten)

Infinitive	Past Tense	Past Participle
give	gave	given
go	went	gone
grind	ground	ground
grow	grew	grown
hang	hung (*also* hanged)	hung (*also* hanged)
have	had	had
hear	heard	heard
hide	hid	hidden
hit	hit	hit
hold	held	held
hurt	hurt	hurt
keep	kept	kept
kneel	knelt (*also* kneeled)	knelt (*also* kneeled)
know	knew	known
lay	laid	laid
lead	led	led
lean	leant (*also* leaned)	leant (*also* leaned)
leap	leapt (*also* leaped)	leapt (*also* leaped)
learn	learnt (*also* learned)	learnt (*also* learned)
leave	left	left
lend	lent	lent
let	let	let
lie	lay	lain
light	lit (*also* lighted)	lit (*also* lighted)
lose	lost	lost
make	made	made
may	might	-
mean	meant	meant
meet	met	met
mistake	mistook	mistaken
mow	mowed	mown (*also* mowed)
pay	paid	paid
put	put	put
quit	quit (*also* quitted)	quit (*also* quitted)
read	read	read
rend	rent	rent
rid	rid	rid
ride	rode	ridden
ring	rang	rung
rise	rose	risen
run	ran	run
saw	sawed	sawn
say	said	said
see	saw	seen
seek	sought	sought
sell	sold	sold
send	sent	sent
set	set	set
shake	shook	shaken
shall	should	-
shear	sheared	shorn (*also* sheared)
shed	shed	shed
shine	shone	shone

Infinitive	Past Tense	Past Participle
shoot	shot	shot
show	showed	shown
shrink	shrank	shrunk
shut	shut	shut
sing	sang	sung
sink	sank	sunk
sit	sat	sat
slay	slew	slain
sleep	slept	slept
slide	slid	slid
sling	slung	slung
slit	slit	slit
smell	smelt (*also* smelled)	smelt (*also* smelled)
sow	sowed	sown (*also* sowed)
speak	spoke	spoken
speed	sped (*also* speeded)	sped (*also* speeded)
spell	spelt (*also* spelled)	spelt (*also* spelled)
spend	spent	spent
spill	spilt (*also* spilled)	spilt (*also* spilled)
spin	spun	spun
spit	spat	spat
split	split	split
spoil	spoiled (*also* spoilt)	spoiled (*also* spoilt)
spread	spread	spread
spring	sprang	sprung
stand	stood	stood
steal	stole	stolen
stick	stuck	stuck
sting	stung	stung
stink	stank	stunk
stride	strode	stridden
strike	struck	struck (*also* stricken)
strive	strove	striven
swear	swore	sworn
sweep	swept	swept
swell	swelled	swollen (*also* swelled)
swim	swam	swum
swing	swung	swung
take	took	taken
teach	taught	taught
tear	tore	torn
tell	told	told
think	thought	thought
throw	threw	thrown
thrust	thrust	thrust
tread	trod	trodden
wake	woke (*also* waked)	woken (*also* waked)
wear	wore	worn
weave	wove (*also* weaved)	woven (*also* weaved)
wed	wedded	wedded
weep	wept	wept
win	won	won
wind	wound	wound
wring	wrung	wrung
write	wrote	written

Achevé d'imprimer par l'Imprimerie
Maury-Eurolivres à Manchecourt, en février 2003
N° de projet 10083480/10101282
Dépôt légal : février 2003 - N° d'imprimeur : 98976

Imprimé en France - (Printed in France)